# Labels used in the dictionary

The following labels are used with words that express a particular attitude or are appropriate in a particular situation.

**approving** expressions show that you feel approval or admiration, for example *feisty, petite*.

**disapproving** expressions show that you feel disapproval or contempt, for example *blinkered, newfangled*.

**figurative** language is used in a non-literal or metaphorical way, as in *He didn't want to cast a shadow on* (= spoil) *their happiness*.

**formal** expressions are usually only used in serious or official language and would not be appropriate in normal everyday conversation. Examples are *admonish, besmirch*.

**humorous** expressions are intended to be funny, for example *fisticuffs, ignoramus*.

**informal** expressions are used between friends or in a relaxed or unofficial situation. They are not appropriate for formal situations. Examples are *bonkers, dodgy*.

**ironic** language uses words to mean the opposite of the meaning that they seem to have, as in *You're a great help, I must say!* (= no help at all).

**literary** language is used mainly in literature and imaginative writing, for example *aflame, halcyon*.

**offensive** expressions are used by some people to address or refer to people in a way that is very insulting, especially in connection with their race, religion, sex or disabilities. You should not use these words.

**slang** is very informal language, sometimes restricted to a particular group of people, for example people of the same age or those who have the same interests or do the same job. Examples are *dosh, gnarly*.

**specialist** language is used by people who specialize in particular subject areas, for example *accretion, adipose*.

**taboo** expressions are likely to be thought by many people to be very offensive or shocking. You should not use them.

The following labels show other restrictions on the use of words.

**dialect** describes expressions that are mainly used in particular regions of the British Isles, not including Ireland, Scotland or Wales, for example *beck, nowt*.

**old-fashioned** expressions are passing out of current use, for example *beanfeast, bothersome*.

**old use** describes expressions that are no longer in current use, for example *ere, perchance*.

**saying** describes a well-known fixed or traditional phrase, such as a proverb, that is used to make a comment, give advice, etc., for example *actions speak louder than words*.

**™** shows a trademark of a manufacturing company, for example *Band-Aid, Frisbee*.

**lean** and muscle; (of meat) containing no fat. ❷ not productive; of poor quality, as *a lean harvest*; *lean years* (i. e. years during which not much is produced). —*n.* U meat without fat. **lean-ness** [liːnnis] *n.*

²**lean** [liːn] *vi. & t.* (pret. & p. p. **leaned** [liːnd] or **leant** [lent]) ❶ (P 21, 23) slope or incline; be out of the perpendicular, as *the Leaning Tower of Pisa*; *trees that lean over in the wind*. ❷ (P 23, 24) rest on or against something in order to get support, as *to lean on a table*; *to lean upon one's elbows* (i. e. bend the upper part of the body and support oneself on the elbows). *Lean on my arm.* ❸ (P 23, 24) bend the body, as *to lean forward [back]*; *to lean over a fence*; *to lean out of a window.* ❹ (P 24) (fig.) rely or depend, as *to lean on a friend's advice*; *to lean on others for support.* ❺ (P 24) tend to or be inclined to. *Do all oriental philosophies lean towards fatalism?* ❻ (P 18) cause to rest against; put into a leaning position, as *to lean a ladder against a wall*; *to lean one's elbows on the table.* —*n.* a slope, as *a tower with a slight lean.* **lean-ing** [liːniŋ] *n.* C a tendency or liking, as *to have a leaning towards pacifism.*

The Leaning Tower of Pisa

**leant** [lent] pret. & p. p. of *lean.*

**lean=to** [liːntuː] *n.* a building or shelter (usu. small) that has a roof that slopes only in one way and which rests against the wall of another building (or a wall of rock); (used attrib.) *a lean-to roof [shelter].*

**leap** [liːp] *vi. & t.* (pret. & p. p. **leapt** [lept] or **leaped** [liːpt]) ❶ (P 21, 23, 24) jump. *He leapt on his enemy with a knife in his hand. Look before you leap. He leapt at the opportunity* (fig., i. e. seized it eagerly). ❷ (P 1) jump or spring over, as *to leap a wall*; cause to jump over, as *to leap a horse over a hedge.* —*n.* a jump or spring; a sudden forward or upward movement. **a leap in the dark,** an attempt to do something, the result of which must be very doubtful. **by leaps and bounds,** with very rapid progress. **leap=frog,** *n.* a game in which one player jumps over others standing with bent backs. **leap year,** *n.* a year in which February has 29 days.

**leapt** [lept] pret. & p.p. of *leap.*

Playing leap-frog

**learn** [ləːn] *vt. & i.* (pret. & p. p. **learned** [ləːnd] or **learnt** [ləːnt]) (P 1, 2, 10, 11, 13, 15, 21) gain as knowledge; become familiar with by studying, by being taught, by practice, etc.; become aware; be informed of. *How long have you been learning English? He is learning to swim. You should learn (how) to ride a horse. Has he learnt his lessons? I was sorry to learn the sad news of his death [to learn that he died]. We have not yet learned* (i. e. been informed) *whether he arrived safely. Some boys learn slowly.*

**learn-er** [ləːnə] *n.* one who is learning; a beginner.

**learn-ed** [ləːnid] *part. adj.* having or showing much knowledge; scholarly, as *a learned man [book]*; *to look learned.* **learn-ed-ly,** *adv.*

**learn-ing** [ləːniŋ] *n.* U knowledge gained by study, as *a man of great learning.*

**learnt** [ləːnt] pret. & p. p. of *learn.*

**lease** [liːs] *n.* C a contract or agreement by which one person (the *lessor*) agrees to allow another (the *lessee*) to use land or a building for a certain period of time, usu. in return for a money payment (called *rent*); the rights given under such a contract, as *to take a house [farm, etc.] on a lease of several years*; *to take a lease of a piece of land*; *to put out land on lease. When does the lease expire* (i. e. how long does it last)? *We hold the land by [on] lease.* **a new lease of life,** a new chance of living or of being active, due to recovery of health, the removal of anxiety, etc. —*vt.* (P 1) give or take possession of (land, a

# Oxford Advanced Learner's Dictionary *of Current English*

## A S Hornby

**Tenth edition**

*Managing Editors* **Diana Lea**
**Jennifer Bradbery**

*Senior Editors* Victoria Bull
Leonie Hey

*Editors* Stacey Bateman
Kallah Pridgeon

*Phonetics Editor* Gary Leicester

# OXFORD
UNIVERSITY PRESS

Great Clarendon Street, Oxford, OX2 6DP, United Kingdom

Oxford University Press is a department of the University of Oxford. It furthers the University's objective of excellence in research, scholarship, and education by publishing worldwide. Oxford is a registered trade mark of Oxford University Press in the UK and in certain other countries

© Oxford University Press 2020

Database right Oxford University Press (maker)

First published 1948 (12 impressions)
Second edition 1963 (19 impressions)
Third edition 1974 (28 impressions)
Fourth edition 1989 (50 impressions)
Fifth edition 1995 (65 impressions)
Sixth edition 2000 (117 impressions)
Seventh edition 2005 (105 impressions)
Eighth edition 2010 (69 impressions)
Ninth edition 2015 (39 impressions)
Tenth edition 2020

**No unauthorized photocopying**

All rights reserved. No part of this publication may be reproduced, stored in a retrieval system, or transmitted, in any form or by any means, without the prior permission in writing of Oxford University Press, or as expressly permitted by law, by licence or under terms agreed with the appropriate reprographics rights organization. Enquiries concerning reproduction outside the scope of the above should be sent to the ELT Rights Department, Oxford University Press, at the address above

You must not circulate this work in any other form and you must impose this same condition on any acquirer

This dictionary includes some words which have or are asserted to have proprietary status as trademarks or otherwise. Their inclusion does not imply that they have acquired for legal purposes a non-proprietary or general significance nor any other judgement concerning their legal status. In cases where the editorial staff have some evidence that a word has proprietary status this is indicated in the entry for that word but no judgement concerning the legal status of such words is made or implied thereby

Links to third party websites are provided by Oxford in good faith and for information only. Oxford disclaims any responsibility for the materials contained in any third party website referenced in this work

ISBN: 978-0-19-479850-1 (paperback/app/online pack)
2023 2022 2021 2020
9 8 7 6 5 4 3 2 1

ISBN: 978-0-19-479851-8 (hardback/app/online pack)
2023 2022 2021 2020
9 8 7 6 5 4 3 2 1

ISBN: 978-0-19-479856-3 (paperback in pack)
ISBN: 978-0-19-479857-0 (hardback in pack)
ISBN: 978-0-19-479862-4 (app)
ISBN: 978-0-19-479873-0 (online access)

Design: Peter Burgess, Julian Littlewood

Data management: Frank Keenan, Bill Coumbe, Ian Hughson, Tim Teasdale

Typeset by Data Standards Ltd.

Printed in India by Thomson Press India Ltd.

This book is printed on paper from certified and well-managed sources

## Consultants and lexicographers

### Phonetics
Dr Michael Ashby
Dr Matthew Moreland
Isaiah Mweteri
Dr Catherine Sangster

### American English
Daniel Barron

### World English
Peter Chambers (*Canadian*)
Mallika Ghosh (*Indian*)
Prof Paul Gunashekar (*Indian*)
Franky Lau (*South-East Asian*)
Dr Amanda Laugesen (*Australian*)
Linda Roos (*South African*)
Florence Waeni (*East African*)

### Scientific and technical terms
Ron Bowater
Dr Mike Clugston
Dr Tania Young

### Oxford Writing Tutor
Dr Maggie Charles
Bruce Wade

### Oxford Speaking Tutor
Mark Hancock

### Oxford 3000™
Prof James Milton
Prof Paul Nation

### Oxford Phrasal Academic Lexicon™
Andrew Delahunty
Prof Michael McCarthy

### Senior lexicographers
Stephen Bullon
Joanna Turnbull
Sally Wehmeier

### Lexicographers
Rosalind Combley
Andrew Delahunty
Robert Duncan
Penny Hands
Alison Macaulay
Kate Mohideen
Elizabeth Potter
Miranda Steel
Alison Waters
Dr Donald Watt

# Contents

| | |
|---|---|
| inside front cover | Abbreviations, symbols and labels used in the dictionary |
| vi | Foreword |
| vii | Key to dictionary entries |
| x | The Oxford 3000™ and Oxford 5000™ |
| xi | The Oxford Phrasal Academic Lexicon™ |
| xii | Numbers |

## 1–1820 The Dictionary

| | |
|---|---|
| WT1–30 | Oxford Writing Tutor |
| ST1–10 | Oxford Speaking Tutor |
| V1–8 | Visual Vocabulary Builder |
| R1–31 | Reference Section |

### Reference Section Contents

| | |
|---|---|
| R1 | Irregular verbs |
| R4 | Verbs |
| R8 | Phrasal verbs |
| R10 | Nouns and adjectives |
| R12 | Collocation |
| R13 | Idioms |
| R14 | English across the world |
| R16 | British and American English |
| R17 | Punctuation |
| R20 | Numbers |
| R24 | Geographical names |
| R28 | Acknowledgements |
| R30 | Pronunciation and phonetic symbols |

# Foreword

With *A Learner's Dictionary of Current English*, first published by Oxford University Press in 1948, A. S. Hornby effectively invented the concept of 'a learner's dictionary'. As a teacher, he realized that what learners needed from a dictionary was quite different: simple definitions and helpful illustrations to aid understanding, but also information on how to use the language – how to pronounce words and how to combine them correctly in phrases and sentences.

Over 70 years later much has changed in the world, in the language and in English language teaching. English language learners worldwide are continually increasing in their numbers and in the diversity of their learning contexts. Traditional classroom teaching is still very strong but digital media now also have a significant role to play.

This new edition of the *Oxford Advanced Learner's Dictionary* remains true to the principles that Hornby established: the needs of the learner are paramount and have informed every policy decision and the construction of every entry. At the same time, it takes advantage of technology to offer learners additional resources to complement the print dictionary, as well as alternative modes of accessing the dictionary itself (online or app) that may better meet the needs of many learners in the digital age.

Whatever the medium, the focus is on building vocabulary and developing skills. We have revised and updated the Oxford 3000, our core vocabulary list, and added 2,000 words to the core list for advanced-level students, creating the Oxford 5000. See page x for more details about these lists. The Writing Tutor and Speaking Tutor (with interactive iWriter and iSpeaker online) offer models and tips for exam students and for everyday communication.

Skills development is also one of the purposes of the Hornby Educational Trust, founded by A. S. Hornby with the aim of advancing the teaching and learning of English as a foreign language. The Trust supports a range of activities both in the UK and around the world. Since the Trust was set up in 1961 more than 400 professionals from around the world have received Hornby Scholarships to study at a British university and learn more about the teaching of English. Below, one of them writes about his experience as a Hornby Scholar, and how he has been able to pass on the fruits of this experience to others.

Diana Lea
Managing Editor

## Being a Hornby Scholar

I graduated as a teacher of English in Argentina in 2000 and soon after graduation I decided to live in a small Patagonian city, Esquel, where I am still based. In 2008 I was honoured with a Hornby Scholarship to undertake MA studies in the UK. In my case I chose the University of Warwick as I was interested in their professional development modules. That year at Warwick was amazing, with far-reaching reverberations at personal and professional levels. Living on campus in a multicultural society provided me with opportunities to develop intercultural awareness and make friends I am still in contact with. At a professional level, the MA programme allowed me to gain confidence and knowledge in English language teacher education and academic literacy.

Looking back, my experience as a Hornby Scholar has enabled me to make an impact in three broad areas: language curriculum development, professional development opportunities and teacher identity.

Concerning language curricula, since 2008 I have co-developed official English language teaching curricula for primary, secondary and pre-service English language teacher education. What was innovative in these curricula was the introduction of content and language integrated learning (CLIL) as a language teaching approach for state schools in Argentina. In Chubut, these curricula marked the beginning of bottom-up curriculum design in language education, which seeks to democratize decision-making processes in terms of education policies.

Supported by the Ministry of Education in Chubut and APIZALS, a teacher association based in Patagonia, I started to design and implement professional development opportunities in Patagonia. Before my initiatives, professional development opportunities in Patagonia used to be mostly led by experts from Buenos Aires. However, thanks to the knowledge gained in my MA programme, I have facilitated courses on action research and ELT methods and contributed to promoting local expertise and spreading professional development opportunities. These provide context-responsive pedagogies set in southern Argentina.

Last, I founded the *Argentinian Journal of Applied Linguistics* in order to promote teacher research identity among teachers. Drawing on my experience in the UK, I encourage other teachers to become involved in activities such as presenting at conferences in Argentina and Latin America, doing classroom research and writing for publication. Language educators from less-known institutions have accepted the challenge of presenting and publishing, drawing on their classroom experiences. This has become a source of teacher motivation as teachers feel they can engage in other professional activities apart from teaching.

The experience generated thanks to the Hornby Scholarship has taught me that I do not need to be based in a big city or a large university to introduce changes in my context. I have learnt that I have to make things happen and engage others in doable context-responsive projects which aim at improving language education and making our social fabric stronger and fairer.

Dr Darío Luis Banegas
Ministerio de Educación del Chubut, Argentina
Hornby Scholar 2008–2009

# Key to dictionary entries

## Finding the word

Information in the dictionary is given in **entries**, arranged in alphabetical order of **headwords**. **Compound words** are in separate entries, also arranged alphabetically.

*headwords* —

> **book·bind·er** /ˈbʊkbaɪndə(r)/ *noun* a person whose job is fastening the pages of books together and putting covers on them ▶ **book·bind·ing** *noun* [U]
> **book·case** /ˈbʊkkeɪs/ *noun* a piece of furniture with shelves for keeping books on ⊃ VISUAL VOCAB page V36
> **ˈbook club** *noun* **1** an organization that sells books cheaply to its members **2** = BOOK GROUP

— *entry*

Some headwords can have more than one part of speech.

*Squares show where the information on each part of speech begins.*

> **blind·fold** /ˈblaɪndfəʊld/ *noun, verb, adv.*
> ■ *noun* something that is put over sb's eyes so they cannot see
> ■ *verb* ~ **sb** to cover sb's eyes with a piece of cloth or other material so that they cannot see: *The hostages were tied up and blindfolded.*
> ■ *adv.* (BrE) (*also* **blind·fold·ed** BrE, NAmE) with the eyes covered: *The reporter was taken blindfold to a secret location.* ◊ *I knew the way home blindfold* (= because it was so familiar). ◊ *I could do that blindfold* (= very easily, with no problems).

— *headword and all possible parts of speech*

There are some words in English that have the same spelling as each other but different pronunciations.

*The small **homonym number** shows that this is the first of two headwords spelled gill.*

> **gill¹** /gɪl/ *noun* [usually pl.] one of the openings on the side of a fish's head that it breathes through ⊃ VISUAL VOCAB page V14
> **IDM** **to the ˈgills** (*informal*) until completely full: *I was stuffed to the gills with chocolate cake.*
> **gill²** /dʒɪl/ *noun* a unit for measuring liquids, equal to 0.142 of a LITRE in the UK and some other countries, and 0.118 of a LITRE in the US. There are four gills in a PINT.

*Different pronunciation is given at each headword.*

There are also some words in English that have more than one possible spelling, and both spellings are acceptable. Information about these words is given at the most frequent spelling.

*The variant spelling is given in brackets.*

> **ban·is·ter** (*also* **ban·nis·ter**) /ˈbænɪstə(r)/ *noun* (BrE *also* **ban·is·ters** [pl.]) the posts and RAIL that you can hold for support when going up or down stairs: *to hold on to the banister/banisters* ⊃ picture at STAIRCASE

At the entry for the less frequent spelling a cross reference directs you to the main entry.

> **ban·nis·ter** = BANISTER

Irregular forms of verbs are treated in the same way.

Some words that are **derivatives** of other words do not have their own entry in the dictionary because they can be easily understood from the meaning of the word from which they are derived (the root word). They are given in the same entry as the root word, in a specially marked section.

> **be·lated** /bɪˈleɪtɪd/ *adj.* coming or happening late: *a belated birthday present* ▶ **be·lated·ly** *adv.*

*The blue triangle shows where the derivative section starts.*

You can find **idioms** and **phrasal verbs** in separate sections, marked with special symbols.

> **fetch** /fetʃ/ verb **1** (especially BrE) to go to where sb/sth is and bring them/it back: ~**sb/sth** to fetch help/a doctor ◊ The inhabitants have to walk a mile to fetch water. ◊ She's gone to fetch the kids from school. ◊ ~**sb sth** Could you fetch me my bag? **2** ~**sth** to be sold for a particular price **SYN** sell: The painting is expected to fetch $10000 at auction. **IDM** **fetch and ˈcarry (for sb)** to do a lot of little jobs for sb as if you were their servant
> **PHRV** **ˌfetch ˈup** (especially BrE, informal) to arrive somewhere without planning to: And then, a few years later, he somehow fetched up in Rome.

*phrasal verbs section with symbol* **PHRV** *(see pages R8–9)*

*idioms section with symbol* **IDM** *(see page R13)*

**Wordfinder notes** help you to find words that you don't know or have forgotten. They suggest entries that you can look up to find vocabulary related to the headword. For example, you will find this Wordfinder note at the entry for **home**.

> **WORDFINDER** accommodation, deed, house, lease, let, location, mortgage, squat, tenant

## Finding the meaning

Some words have very long entries. It is not usually necessary to read the whole entry from the beginning if you already know something about the general meaning that you are looking for.

> **spin** ⓘ+ **C1** /spɪn/ verb, noun
> ■ *verb* (**spin·ning**, **spun**, **spun** /spʌn/)
> • TURN ROUND QUICKLY **1** ⓘ+ **C1** [I, T] to turn round and round quickly; to make sth do this: (**+ adv./prep.**) The plane was spinning out of control. ◊ a spinning ice skater ◊ My head is spinning (= I feel as if my head is going round and I can't balance). ◊ ~**round/around** The dancers spun round and round. ◊ ~**sth (round/around)** to spin a ball/coin/wheel **2** ⓘ+ **C1** [I, T] ~**(sb) round/around** | **+ adv./prep.** to turn round quickly once; to make sb do this: He spun around to face her.
> • MAKE THREAD **3** [I, T] to make THREAD from wool, cotton, silk, etc. by TWISTING it: She sat by the window spinning. ◊ ~**sth** to spin and knit wool ◊ ~**A into B** spinning silk into thread ◊ ~**B from A** spinning thread from silk

*Shortcuts show the context or general meaning.*

*Meanings that are closely related share the same shortcut.*

## Understanding and using the word

> **abil·ity** ⓘ **A2** ⓞ /əˈbɪləti/ noun (pl. **-ies**) **1** **A2** [sing.] ~**to do sth** the fact that sb/sth is able to do sth: People with the disease may lose their ability to communicate. ◊ This program has the ability to adapt to its user. ◊ Students must demonstrate the ability to understand simple texts.

*Words printed in larger type and with a ⓘ symbol are part of the **Oxford 3000** list of important words (see page x). The **A2** tells you the CEFR level of the word. Small keys indicate which parts of the entry are most important.*

*Words from the **Oxford Phrasal Academic Lexicon** (OPAL) written and spoken word lists are marked with ⓞ (see page xi).*

> **ab·sent** ⓘ+ **C1** Ⓦ adj., verb, prep.
> ■ *adj.* /ˈæbsənt/ **1** ⓘ+ **C1** ~**(from …)** not in a place because of illness, etc.: to be absent from work **OPP** present **2** ⓘ+ **C1** ~**(from sth)** not present in sth: Love was totally absent from his childhood. **OPP** present **3** showing that you are not really looking at or thinking about what is happening around you: an absent expression ⊃ see also ABSENTLY

*Words with a ⓘ+ symbol are part of the **Oxford 5000** list of important words (see page x).*

*Words from the OPAL written word list are marked with Ⓦ (see page xi).*

> **ac·tu·al·ly** ⓘ **A2** Ⓢ /ˈæktʃuəli/ adv. **1** **A2** used in speaking to emphasize a fact or a comment, or that sth is really true: What did she actually say? ◊ It's not actually raining now. ◊ The book was never actually published.

*Words from the OPAL spoken word list are marked with Ⓢ (see page xi).*

ix

Stress marks show stress on compounds. — **ba·by 'grand** noun a small GRAND PIANO

Irregular forms of verbs, with their pronunciations. Irregular plurals of nouns are also shown. — **cling** /klɪŋ/ verb (clung, clung /klʌŋ/) **1** [I] to hold on tightly to sb/sth: **~ to sb/sth** *survivors clinging to a raft* ◇ **on to sb/sth** *She clung on to her baby.* ◇ **on** *Cling on tight!* ◇ **~ together** *They clung together, shivering with cold.* ⊃ SYNONYMS at HOLD **2** [I] to stick to sth: *a dress that clings* (= fits closely and shows the shape of your body) ◇ **~ to sth** *The wet shirt clung to his chest.* ◇ *The smell of smoke still clung to her clothes.* **3** [I] **~ (to sb)** (*usually disapproving*) to stay close to sb, especially because you need them emotionally: *After her mother's death, Sara clung to her aunt more than ever.* — prepositions, adverbs and structures that can be used with this word

examples of use in italic type

verb code (see pages R4–7)

label giving information about usage (see inside front cover)

comparatives and superlatives of adjectives — **hearty** /ˈhɑːti; *NAmE* ˈhɑːrti/ *adj., noun*
■ *adj.* (**heart·i·er, hearti·est**) **1** [*usually before noun*] showing friendly feelings for sb: *a hearty welcome* **2** (*sometimes disapproving*) loud, cheerful and full of energy: *a hearty and boisterous fellow* ◇ *a hearty voice* **3** [*only before noun*] — pronunciation, with American pronunciation where it is different (see pages R30–31).

information on use of adjectives (see page R11)

**bag** /bæɡ/ *noun, verb*
■ *noun*
• CONTAINER **1** [C] (often in compounds) a container made of cloth, leather, plastic or paper, used to carry things in, especially when shopping or travelling: *He was carrying a heavy bag of groceries.* ◇ *It was wrapped in a brown paper bag.* ◇ *Put it in a black plastic garbage bag.* ◇ *She tipped out the contents of her bag* (= HANDBAG). **2** [C] a bag or case that you take when you are travelling; a piece of LUGGAGE: *I packed my bags and left for the airport.* ◇ *Each passenger is allowed one carry-on bag.* ⊃ see also DUFFEL BAG, SPONGE BAG, TOILET BAG ⊃ VISUAL VOCAB page V20
• AMOUNT **3** [C] **~ (of sth)** the amount contained in a bag: *She ate a bag of chips.* ⊃ see also GRAB BAG, MIXED BAG, RAGBAG ⊃ VISUAL VOCAB page V47 **4 bags** [U, pl.] **~ (of sth)** (*BrE, informal*) a large amount or a large number of sth: *Get in! There's bags of room.*

word used in definition that is not in the **Oxford 3000**

common phrase in **bold type** in example (see page R12)

information on different types of noun (see pages R10–11)

fixed form of noun

## Build your vocabulary

The dictionary also contains a lot of information that will help you increase your vocabulary and use the language productively. **Language banks** and **Synonyms** notes give useful vocabulary, especially for writing, and **Express yourself** notes help you find the right words in everyday situations.

▼ EXPRESS YOURSELF
**Offering somebody something**
Particularly when you are the host, you may want to make polite offers to your guests:
• **Would you like** *a magazine to read?*
• **Can I get you** *a coffee?*
• **Can I offer you** *something to drink?*

Special symbols show synonyms and opposites. — **child·ish** /ˈtʃaɪldɪʃ/ *adj.* **1** connected with or typical of a child: *childish handwriting* **2** (*disapproving*) (of an adult) behaving in a stupid or silly way SYN immature: *Don't be so childish!* OPP mature ⊃ compare CHILDLIKE ▶ **child·ish·ly** *adv.*: *to behave childishly* **child·ish·ness** *noun* [U] — Cross references refer you to information in other parts of the dictionary, for example words that sometimes get confused with the word at this entry.

# The Oxford 3000™ and Oxford 5000™

## What is the Oxford 3000?

The **Oxford 3000** is a list of the 3,000 core words that every learner of English needs to know. The words have been carefully selected based on their frequency in the language and their relevance to learners. Every word has been assigned a level, from A1 to B2 on the CEFR, guiding learners from beginner to upper-intermediate level on the most important words to learn.

The **frequency** of the words was measured in the Oxford English Corpus (OEC). A corpus is an electronic database containing large numbers of written or spoken texts that can be searched, sorted and analysed. The OEC contains over 2 billion words from different subject areas and contexts, covering British, American and world English. Frequency is the most important criterion for deciding the importance of a word: the most frequent 2,000 words in English make up around 80 per cent of almost any English text.

The **relevance** of the words to English language learners was measured by their frequency in a specially created corpus of Secondary and Adult English courses published by Oxford University Press. This means that the list covers words that learners will come across in class and in their study texts, even if they are less frequent in a general corpus. These include, for example, words for everyday things and places (*banana*, *cafe*, *T-shirt*), words for describing feelings (*amazed*, *annoyed*, *unhappy*) and words connected with studying (*dictionary*, *exam*).

## What is the CEFR?

CEFR stands for the 'Common European Framework of Reference' for languages, which is a description of the language abilities of students at different levels of learning. The CEFR can be used to compare standards in language learning and create teaching programmes.

It grades language skills at six levels:
- A1 and A2 indicate elementary and pre-intermediate levels of ability.
- B1 and B2 indicate lower- and upper-intermediate levels.
- C1 indicates advanced level.
- C2 indicates complete proficiency in the language.

The CEFR grades language skills – what students can do in the language, for example 'can understand the main ideas of complex text on both concrete and abstract topics' (at B2). It does not grade specific grammar points or vocabulary items. However, we have aligned the words in the Oxford 3000 to the levels of the CEFR from A1 to B2 in order to guide learners of English on the most important words to learn at each level. These levels are based on the same criteria of frequency and relevance: the corpus of Secondary and Adult English courses enabled us to track the frequency of vocabulary items at each level of a course.

## What is the Oxford 5000?

The Oxford 3000 is the core word list for learners up to B2/upper-intermediate level. The **Oxford 5000** is an expanded core word list for advanced learners of English. It includes an additional 2,000 words at B2-C1 level on the CEFR, guiding advanced learners on the most useful high-level words to learn to expand their vocabulary.

## Keywords in the dictionary

The words of the **Oxford 3000** are shown in the main section of the dictionary in larger print and with a key symbol 🔑 immediately following. The CEFR level for the core sense of the word is shown after the key. If the word has more than one meaning, a small key symbol will indicate each of the meanings that belong to the Oxford 3000. The CEFR level is shown for each of these meanings: some of the secondary meanings may have a higher level than the core sense.

The words of the **Oxford 5000** are shown in the main section of the dictionary with a 'key plus' symbol 🔑+ and the CEFR level – B2 or C1 – for the core sense of the word. Again, if there is more than one meaning, there will be a key plus symbol and a CEFR level at each meaning that belongs to the Oxford 5000.

In order to make the definitions in this dictionary easy to understand, we have written them using the keywords of the Oxford 3000. Numbers and proper names are also used in definitions, as are a few language study terms, such as *alphabet*, *noun* and *tense*. When it has been necessary to use a specialist term that is not in the Oxford 3000, the word is shown in SMALL CAPITALS. Where appropriate, a GLOSS (= a short explanation of the meaning) of the specialist term is included in brackets.

The entries for all words in the Oxford 3000 have been re-edited for this edition, using the most up-to-date corpora. Many of these entries have been expanded in order to include more information about the most frequent collocations and examples of different grammatical patterns used with these words.

For more information on the Oxford 3000 and Oxford 5000, and to see the full lists, visit www.oxford3000.com.

# The Oxford Phrasal Academic Lexicon™

## What is OPAL?

The English spoken by a professor in a lecture hall is different from the English written in an academic paper – and both are different from everyday conversation between friends, or the language used in popular fiction. If you are a student of English for Academic Purposes (EAP), it is important to become familiar with the vocabulary that you will come across when attending lectures and seminars, and that you will need for writing essays and reports.

The **Oxford Phrasal Academic Lexicon**, or **OPAL** for short, is a collection of four word lists that together provide an essential guide to the most important words to know in the field of EAP. The four lists cover both written and spoken academic English, with lists of written words, spoken words, written phrases and spoken phrases.

The words and phrases in OPAL are based on two main corpora, to give learners a true picture of academic English. The written words and phrases are based on the 71-million-word Oxford Corpus of Academic English (OCAE), a corpus composed of academic texts published by Oxford University Press across these four subject areas: physical sciences, life sciences, social sciences, and arts and humanities. The spoken words and phrases are based on the British Academic Spoken English (BASE) corpus[1]. This corpus was developed at the Universities of Warwick and Reading and contains nearly 1.2 million words of spoken academic English, recorded and transcribed from lectures and seminars across the same four subject areas.

OPAL was developed using a method called 'keyword analysis'. By comparing the list of the most frequent words and phrases in each corpus with the list of the most frequent words and phrases in a contrasting reference corpus, we identified the words and phrases that are most important in an academic setting. For the written lists, we compared the OCAE with the fiction subcorpus of the Oxford English Corpus. For the spoken lists, we compared the BASE corpus with the spoken subcorpus of the British National Corpus, containing recordings of meetings and everyday conversation.

## OPAL in the dictionary and online

Words that belong to the OPAL written and spoken word lists are indicated in the dictionary by symbols next to the headword: Ⓦ indicates a word on the OPAL written word list; Ⓢ indicates a word on the OPAL spoken word list; and Ⓞ indicates a word on both the written and spoken word lists.

To see the full lists, visit www.opalwordlist.com. The written word list is divided into 12 sublists of 100 words each and the spoken word list is divided into 6 sublists of 100 words each. Sublist 1 of each list contains the most important academic words, with the next most important in Sublist 2, and so on.

It is often not the word itself that is 'academic', but the way it is used and combined with other words in an academic context. Therefore, besides the lists of single words, OPAL also includes a list of written phrases and a list of spoken phrases, which you can also find online. The phrase lists are grouped into academic functions. The written phrase list covers 15 different functions, including 'Explaining and defining' and 'Giving examples and presenting evidence'. The spoken phrase list covers 16 functions, including 'Signposting and focusing in lectures/lessons' and 'Using vague language'.

Whether you are using the print dictionary or accessing OPAL online (from which you can click through to the dictionary entries, either in the *Oxford Advanced Learner's Dictionary* online or in the *Oxford Learner's Dictionary of Academic English*), it is important to realize that learning a word involves more than just knowing its basic meaning. Some words may have specific meanings in particular contexts: for example, the word *environment* (in Sublist 1 of the written list and Sublist 2 of the spoken list) may have a slightly different meaning, depending on whether the area of study is ecology, social science or computing. The dictionary entry will guide you on all the different meanings and also how to use them in context, with examples of use, frequent collocations and patterns with grammatical structures or prepositions.

---

1 OPAL has been created with reference to the following corpora: the Oxford Corpus of Academic English (OCAE), the fiction subcorpus of the Oxford English Corpus (OEC), the spoken element of the British National Corpus (BNC) and a subset of the British Academic Spoken English (BASE) corpus, developed within the University of Warwick and for which relevant permissions have been obtained. BASE was developed at the Universities of Warwick and Reading under the directorship of Hilary Nesi and Paul Thompson. Corpus development of BASE was assisted by funding from BALEAP, EURALEX, the British Academy and the Arts and Humanities Research Council.

# Numbers

**10 000-foot view** /ˌten ˈθaʊznd fʊt ˈvjuː/ *noun* (*business*) a broad general view or description of a problem **SYN** HELICOPTER VIEW, OVERVIEW: *Let me give you the 10000-foot view.*

**101** /ˌwʌn əʊ ˈwʌn/ *adj.* (*NAmE*) **1** relating to a university course that is intended as an introduction to a subject for people who have never studied it before: *a 101 class* **2** (*informal*) relating to the basic facts in a particular field or subject: *a social media marketing 101 guide*

**1040 form** /ˌten ˈfɔːti fɔːm; *NAmE* ˈfɔːrti fɔːrm/ *noun* (in the US) an official document in which you give details of the amount of money that you have earned so that the government can calculate how much tax you have to pay

**12** /twelv/ *noun* (in the UK) a label that is given to a film to show that it can be watched legally in a cinema only by people who are at least twelve years old; a film that has this label: *Kids can watch this too—it's a 12.*

**15** /fɪfˈtiːn/ *noun* (in the UK) a label that is given to a film to show that it can be watched legally in a cinema only by people who are at least fifteen years old; a film that has this label

**18** /eɪˈtiːn/ *noun* (in the UK) a label that is given to a film to show that it can be watched legally in a cinema only by people who are at least eighteen years old; a film that has this label

**18-wheeler** /ˌeɪtiːn ˈwiːlə(r)/ *noun* (*NAmE*) a very large truck with nine wheels on each side

**2%** /ˌtuː pəˈsent; *NAmE* pərˈsent/ *noun* (*NAmE*) milk that has had the fat removed, and then some of the fat returned, so that it contains two per cent milk fat: *Shall I get skim milk or 2%?*

**20/20 vision** (also **twenty-twenty vision**) /ˌtwenti ˌtwenti ˈvɪʒn/ *noun* [U] the ability to see with the CLARITY of a normal, healthy, young adult human

**2.1** /ˌtuː ˈwʌn/ *noun* the upper level of the second highest standard of degree given by a British or an Australian university: *I got a 2.1*

**2.2** /ˌtuː ˈtuː/ *noun* the lower level of the second highest standard of degree given by a British or an Australian university

**24-hour clock** /ˌtwenti fɔːr aʊə ˈklɒk; *NAmE* ˈklɑːk/ *noun* the system of using twenty-four numbers to talk about the hours of the day, instead of dividing it into two units of twelve hours

**24/7** (also **twenty-four seven**) /ˌtwenti fɔː ˈsevən; *NAmE* fɔːr/ *adv.* (*informal*) twenty-four hours a day, seven days a week (used to mean 'all the time'): *He's on duty 24/7.*

**360-degree feedback** /ˌθriː ˌhʌndrəd ən ˌsɪksti dɪˌɡriː ˈfiːdbæk/ (also **360-degree appraisal**) *noun* [U] (*business*) information provided by all the people that an employee deals with, used as a way of deciding how well the employee does their job: *360-degree feedback assessments*

**3D** (also **three-D**) /ˌθriː ˈdiː/ *noun* [U] the quality of having, or appearing to have, length, WIDTH and depth (= three DIMENSIONS): *These glasses allow you to see the film in 3D.*

**3D printer** /ˌθriː diː ˈprɪntə(r)/ *noun* a machine that makes solid objects from a digital file by adding more and more layers of a material until the object is complete: *The car's entire body, seats and windshield are printed by a 3D printer and are made out of carbon fibre and plastic.*

**3PS** /ˌθriː piː ˈes/ = THIRD-PERSON SHOOTER GAME (= a type of video game in which the player controls the action of a character on the screen and has to attack enemies)

**401(k)** /ˌfɔːr əʊ wʌn ˈkeɪ/ *noun* (in the US) an account in which an employee can save money for their RETIREMENT without paying tax until the money is taken out: *Does your employer have a 401(k) plan?*

**404** /ˌfɔːr əʊ ˈfɔː; *NAmE* ˈfɔːr/ *noun* (*computing*) a message that appears on a computer screen that tells you that an internet address cannot be found

**411** /ˌfɔː wʌn ˈwʌn; *NAmE* ˌfɔːr/ *noun* **1** [U] the phone number of the service that you use in the US to find out a person's phone number: *Call 411.* **2 the 411** [sing.] (*NAmE, informal*) the true facts about a situation or the information you need: *He'll give us the 411 on what to expect.*

**4G** /ˌfɔː ˈdʒiː; *NAmE* ˌfɔːr/ *abbr.* FOURTH GENERATION (used to describe technology that has been developed to send data to mobile phones, etc. at higher speeds than THIRD-GENERATION devices): *a 4G phone*

**4×4** (also **four-by-four**) /ˌfɔː baɪ ˈfɔː(r); *NAmE* ˈfɔːr baɪ fɔːr/ *noun* a vehicle with FOUR-WHEEL DRIVE (= a system in which power is given to all four wheels)

**50-yard line** /ˌfɪfti ˈjɑːd laɪn; *NAmE* ˈjɑːrd/ *noun* [sing.] the line that marks the middle of the field in AMERICAN FOOTBALL: *Try to get tickets near the 50-yard line.*

**5G** /ˌfaɪv ˈdʒiː/ *abbr.* FIFTH-GENERATION (used to describe technology that has been developed to send data to mobile phones, etc. at higher speeds than FOURTH-GENERATION devices): *5G technology can achieve connection speeds 30–50 times faster than 4G.*

**5 o'clock shadow** /ˌfaɪv əˌklɒk ˈʃædəʊ; *NAmE* əˌklɑːk/ *noun* [sing.] the dark colour that appears on the CHIN and sides of a man's face when the hair has grown a little during the day since he SHAVED in the morning

**7/7** /ˌsevn ˈsevn/ *noun* (*BrE*) the abbreviation for the date 7 July, 2005, when several bomb attacks took place in London: *a survivor of the 7/7 bombings*

**800 number** /ˌeɪt ˈhʌndrəd nʌmbə(r)/ *noun* a phone number, in the US and some other countries, beginning with 800, or with some other numbers starting with 8 such as 888, which can be called free of charge. These numbers are provided by companies so that customers can phone them to order their products, etc. In the UK such free numbers begin with 0800 or 0808.

**900 number** /ˌnaɪn ˈhʌndrəd nʌmbə(r)/ *noun* (in the US) a phone number that begins with 900. A call to it is more expensive than those to ordinary numbers, and part of the charge for the call goes to the business being called. 900 numbers are used by companies who have CHATLINES, operate competitions, offer services, etc.

**9/11** /ˌnaɪn ɪˈlevn/ *noun* the abbreviation for the date September 11, 2001, when TERRORISTS flew planes into the Twin Towers in New York, the Pentagon in Washington, D.C., and a field in Pennsylvania, killing thousands of people

**911** /ˌnaɪn wʌn ˈwʌn/ the phone number used in the US to call the police, fire or AMBULANCE services in an emergency: *Call 911.*

**99** /ˌnaɪntiˈnaɪn/ *noun* (*BrE*) an ice cream in a CONE with a stick of chocolate in the top

**999** /ˌnaɪn naɪn ˈnaɪn/ the phone number used in the UK to call the police, fire or AMBULANCE services in an emergency: *Dial 999.*

# Aa

**A** /eɪ/ noun, symbol, abbr.
- **noun** (also **a**) (pl. **As, A's, a's** /eɪz/) **1** [C, U] the first letter of the English alphabet: 'Apple' begins with (an) A/'A'. **2** A [C, U] (music) the 6th note in the SCALE of C MAJOR **3** [C, U] **~(in/for sth)** a grade that a student can get for a piece of work or course of study that shows that it is excellent: She got (an) A in biology. ◊ He had **straight** A's (= nothing but A's) all through high school. **4** A [U] used to represent the first of two or more possibilities: Shall we go for plan A or plan B? **5** A [U] used to represent a person, for example in an imagined situation or to hide their identity: Assume A knows B is guilty. ⊃ see also A-FRAME, A LEVEL, A-ROAD
  **IDM** **from A to B** from one place to another: For me a car is just a means of getting from A to B. **from A to Z** including everything there is to know about sth: He knew his subject from A to Z.
- **symbol 1** used in the UK before a number to refer to a particular important road: the A34 to Newbury **2** used (but not in the US) before numbers that show standard METRIC sizes of paper: a sheet of A4 paper (= 297×210mm) ◊ A3 (= 420×297mm) ◊ A5 (= 210×148mm)
- **abbr.** (in writing) AMP

**a** ❶ **A1** /ə, strong form eɪ/ (also **an** /ən, strong form æn/) indefinite article **HELP** The form **a** is used before consonant sounds and the form **an** before vowel sounds. When saying abbreviations like 'FM' or 'UN', use **a** or **an** according to how the first letter is said. For example, **F** is a consonant, but begins with the sound /e/ and so you say: an FM radio. **U** is a vowel but begins with /j/ and so you say: a UN declaration. **1** **A1** used before countable or singular nouns referring to people or things that have not already been mentioned: a man/horse/unit ◊ an aunt/egg/hour/X-ray ◊ I can only carry two at a time. ◊ There's a visitor for you. ◊ She's a friend of my father's (= one of my father's friends). **2** **A1** used to show that sb/sth is a member of a group or profession: Their new car's a BMW. ◊ She's a Buddhist. ◊ He's a teacher. ◊ Is that a Monet (= a painting by Monet)? **3** **A1** any; every: A lion is a dangerous animal. **4** **B1** used before uncountable nouns when these have an adjective in front of them, or phrase following them: a good knowledge of French ◊ a sadness that won't go away **5** used in front of two nouns that are seen as a single unit: a knife and fork **6** used instead of *one* before some numbers: A thousand people were there. **7** used when talking about prices, quantities and rates **SYN** **per**: They cost 50p a kilo. ◊ I can type 50 words a minute. ◊ He was driving at 50 miles an hour. **8** a person like sb: She's a little Greta Thunberg. **9** used before sb's name to show that the speaker does not know the person: There's a Mrs Green to see you. **10** used before the names of days of the week to talk about one particular day: She died on a Tuesday.

**a-** /eɪ/ prefix (in nouns, adjectives and adverbs) not; without: atheist ◊ atypical ◊ asexually

**A1** /ˌeɪ ˈwʌn/ adj. (informal) very good: The car was in A1 condition.

**AA** /ˌeɪ ˈeɪ/ abbr. **1** (usually **the AA**) Automobile Association (a British organization that provides services for car owners) **2** ALCOHOLICS ANONYMOUS

**AAA** abbr. **1** /ˌtrɪpl ˈeɪ/ American Automobile Association (an American organization that provides services for car owners) **2** /ˌθri: ˈeɪz/ (in the UK) Amateur Athletic Association

**Aad·haar** /ˈɑːdhɑː(r), ˌɑːdˈhɑː(r)/ noun [U] (IndE) the system of issuing a unique, 12-DIGIT IDENTIFICATION number to every individual resident of India: an Aadhaar number/card

**A & E** /ˌeɪ ənd ˈiː/ abbr. (BrE) ACCIDENT AND EMERGENCY: Her husband rushed her to A & E. ◊ an A & E department ⊃ compare ER ⊃ **WORDFINDER NOTE** at HOSPITAL

**A & R** /ˌeɪ ən ˈɑː(r)/ abbr. artists and repertoire (the department in a record company that is responsible for finding new singers and bands and getting them to sign a contract with the company)

**aard·vark** /ˈɑːdvɑːk; NAmE ˈɑːrdvɑːrk/ noun an animal from southern Africa that has a long nose and tongue and that eats insects

**aargh** /ɑː(r)/ exclamation used to express fear, anger or some other strong emotion: Aargh—get that cat off the table!

**aback** /əˈbæk/ adv.
  **IDM** **be taken aˈback (by sb/sth)** to be shocked or surprised by sb/sth: She was completely taken aback by his anger. ⊃ see also TAKE SB ABACK at TAKE ⊃ SYNONYMS at SURPRISE

**aba·cus** /ˈæbəkəs/ noun (pl. **aba·cuses** /-kəsɪz/) a frame with small balls that slide along wires. It is used as a tool or toy for counting.

**aba·lone** /ˌæbəˈləʊni/ noun [C, U] a SHELLFISH that can be eaten and whose shell contains MOTHER-OF-PEARL

**aban·don** ❶ **B2** /əˈbændən/ verb, noun
- **verb 1** ❓ **B2** to leave sb, especially sb you are responsible for, with no intention of returning: **~sb** The baby had been abandoned by its mother. ◊ **~sb to sth** 'We have been abandoned to our fate,' said one resident. **2** ❓ **B2** to leave a thing or place, especially because it is impossible or dangerous to stay **SYN** **leave**: **~sth** Snow forced many drivers to abandon their vehicles. ◊ He gave the order to **abandon ship** (= to leave the ship because it was sinking). ◊ ◊ **~sth to sb/sth** They had to abandon their lands to the invading forces. **3** ❓ **B2** **~sth** to stop doing sth, especially before it is finished; to stop having sth: They abandoned the match because of rain. ◊ The **plans** for reform were quietly abandoned. **4** to stop supporting or helping sb; to stop believing in sth: **~sb** The country abandoned its political leaders after the war. ◊ **~sth** By 1930 he had abandoned his Marxist principles. **5** **~yourself to sth** (literary) to feel an emotion so strongly that you can feel nothing else: He abandoned himself to despair.
- **noun** [U] (formal) a way of behaving that is not sensible and shows that you do not care about the possible results of your actions or what other people think: He spent money with careless abandon. **IDM** see GAY adj.

**aban·doned** /əˈbændənd/ adj. **1** left and no longer wanted, used or needed: an abandoned car/house ◊ The child was found abandoned but unharmed. **2** (of people or their behaviour) wild; not following accepted standards

**aban·don·ment** /əˈbændənmənt/ noun [U, C] (formal) **1** the act of leaving a person, thing or place with no intention of returning **2** the act of giving up an idea or stopping an activity with no intention of returning to it: the government's abandonment of its new economic policy

**abase** /əˈbeɪs/ verb **~yourself** (formal) to act in a way that shows that you accept sb's power over you ▸ **abase·ment** noun [U]

**abashed** /əˈbæʃt/ adj. [not before noun] embarrassed and ashamed because of sth that you have done **OPP** **unabashed**

**abate** /əˈbeɪt/ verb [I, T] (formal) to become less intense or severe; to make sth less intense or severe: The storm showed no signs of abating. ◊ **~sth** Steps are to be taken to abate pollution. ▸ **abate·ment** noun [U]

**ab·at·toir** /ˈæbətwɑː(r)/ noun (BrE) = SLAUGHTERHOUSE

**abaya** /əˈbeɪjə; NAmE əˈbaɪ-/ noun a full-length piece of clothing worn over other clothes by some Muslim women

**abba** /ˈæbɑː/ (also **appa**) noun (IndE) (especially as a form of address) a father

**ab·bess** /ˈæbes/ noun a woman who is the head of an abbey of NUNS

**abbey** /ˈæbi/ noun a large church together with a group of buildings in which MONKS or NUNS live or lived in the past: Westminster Abbey ◊ a ruined abbey

**abbot** /ˈæbət/ noun a man who is the head of an abbey of MONKS

# abbreviate

**ab·bre·vi·ate** /əˈbriːvieɪt/ *verb* [usually passive] to make a word, phrase, name or text shorter, especially by leaving out letters or using only the first letter of each word **SYN** shorten: **(be) abbreviated (to sth)** *the Jet Propulsion Laboratory (usually abbreviated to JPL)* ▶ **ab·bre·vi·at·ed** *adj.*: *Where appropriate, abbreviated forms are used.*

**ab·bre·vi·ation** /əˌbriːviˈeɪʃn/ *noun* **1** [C] ~ **(of/for sth)** a short form of a word, etc: *What's the abbreviation for 'Saint'?* **2** [U] the process of abbreviating sth

**ABC** /ˌeɪ biː ˈsiː/ *noun, abbr.*
- *noun* [sing.] (BrE) (NAmE also **ABCs** [pl.], **ABC's** [pl.]) **1** all the letters of the alphabet, especially as they are learnt by children: *Do you know your ABC?* **2** the basic facts about a subject: *the ABC of gardening* **IDM** see EASY *adj.*
- *abbr.* **1** American Broadcasting Company (a large national American television company) **2** Australian Broadcasting Corporation (the Australian national public broadcasting company)

**ab·di·cate** /ˈæbdɪkeɪt/ *verb* **1** [I, T] to give up the position of being king, queen or EMPEROR: *He abdicated in favour of his son.* ◇ ~ **sth** *She was forced to abdicate the throne of Spain.* ⊃ WORDFINDER NOTE at KING **2** [T] ~ **responsibility/your responsibilities** to fail or refuse to perform a duty ▶ **ab·di·ca·tion** /ˌæbdɪˈkeɪʃn/ *noun* [U, C]

**ab·do·men** /ˈæbdəmən/ *noun* **1** the part of the body below the chest that contains the stomach, BOWELS, etc. **2** the end part of an insect's body that is attached to its THORAX ⊃ VISUAL VOCAB page V3

**ab·dom·in·al** /æbˈdɒmɪnl; NAmE -ˈdɑːm-/ *adj., noun*
- *adj.* [only before noun] (*anatomy*) relating to or connected with the abdomen: *abdominal pains*
- *noun* **abdominals** (also informal **abs**) [pl.] the muscles of the abdomen

**ab·duct** /æbˈdʌkt/ *verb* ~ **sb** to take sb away illegally, especially using force **SYN** kidnap ▶ **ab·duc·tion** /-ˈdʌkʃn/ *noun* [U, C]

**ab·duct·ee** /ˌæbdʌkˈtiː/ *noun* a person who has been abducted

**ab·duct·or** /æbˈdʌktə(r)/ *noun* **1** a person who abducts sb **2** (also **ab'ductor muscle**) (*anatomy*) a muscle that moves a body part away from the middle of the body or from another part ⊃ compare ADDUCTOR

**abed** /əˈbed/ *adv.* (old use) in bed

**Aber·do·nian** /ˌæbəˈdəʊniən; NAmE ˌæbərˈd-/ *noun* a person from Aberdeen in Scotland ▶ **Aber·do·nian** *adj.*

**ab·er·rant** /əˈberənt; ˈæbərənt/ *adj.* (formal) not usual or not socially acceptable: *aberrant behaviour*

**ab·er·ra·tion** /ˌæbəˈreɪʃn/ *noun* [C, U] (formal) a fact, an action or a way of behaving that is not usual, and that may be unacceptable

**abet** /əˈbet/ *verb* (**-tt-**) ~ **sb** to help or encourage sb to do sth wrong: *He was abetted in the deception by his wife.* **IDM** see AID *v.*

**abey·ance** /əˈbeɪəns/ *noun* [U] **IDM** in **abeyance** (formal) not being used, or being stopped for a period of time

**ABH** /ˌeɪ eɪtʃ ˈbiː/ *abbr.* (BrE, *law*) ACTUAL BODILY HARM

**abhor** /əbˈhɔː(r)/ *verb* (not used in the progressive tenses) (**-rr-**) ~ **sth** (formal) to hate sth, for example a way of behaving or thinking, especially for moral reasons **SYN** detest, loathe

**ab·hor·rence** /əbˈhɒrəns; NAmE -ˈhɔːr-/ *noun* [U, sing.] (formal) a strong feeling of hating sb/sth, especially for moral reasons

**ab·hor·rent** /əbˈhɒrənt; NAmE -ˈhɔːr-/ *adj.* ~ **(to sb)** (formal) causing a strong feeling of hate, especially for moral reasons **SYN** repugnant: *Racism is abhorrent to a civilized society.*

**abide** /əˈbaɪd/ *verb* (**abided, abided**) **HELP** In sense 2 **abode** /əˈbəʊd/ is also used for the past tense and past participle. **1** [T] **cannot/could not abide sb/sth** to dislike sb/sth so much that you hate having to be with or deal with them 

**SYN** bear, stand: *I can't abide people with no sense of humour.* ◇ *He couldn't abide the thought of being cooped up in an office.* **2** (also **bide**) [I] + *adv./prep.* (old use or formal) to stay or live in a place: *May joy and peace abide in us all.*
**PHRV** a'**bide by sth** (formal) to accept and act according to a law, an agreement, etc: *You'll have to abide by the rules of the club.* ◇ *We will abide by their decision.* ⊃ WORDFINDER NOTE at LAW

**abid·ing** /əˈbaɪdɪŋ/ *adj.* (of a feeling or belief) lasting for a long time and not changing ⊃ see also LAW-ABIDING

**abil·ity** ⓘ **A2** ⓞ /əˈbɪləti/ *noun* (pl. **-ies**) **1** 🔑 [sing.] ~ **to do sth** the fact that sb/sth is able to do sth: *People with the disease may lose their ability to communicate.* ◇ *This program has the ability to adapt to its user.* ◇ *Students must demonstrate the ability to understand written texts.* **OPP** inability **2** 🔑 **A2** [U, C] a level of skill or intelligence: *Their athletic ability is stunning.* ◇ *A woman of her ability will easily find a job.* ◇ *students of mixed abilities* ◇ *I try to do my job to the best of my ability* (= as well as I can).

**abi·ot·ic** /ˌeɪbaɪˈɒtɪk; NAmE -ˈɑːt-/ *adj.* (specialist) not involving biology or living things: *abiotic processes.*

**ab·ject** /ˈæbdʒekt/ *adj.* [usually before noun] (formal) **1** terrible and without hope: *abject poverty/misery/failure* **2** without any respect for yourself: *an abject apology* ▶ **ab·ject·ly** *adv.*

**ab·jure** /əbˈdʒʊə(r); NAmE -ˈdʒʊr/ *verb* ~ **sth** (formal) to promise publicly that you will give up or reject a belief or a way of behaving **SYN** renounce

**ablaze** /əˈbleɪz/ *adj.* [not before noun] **1** burning quickly and strongly: *The whole building was soon ablaze.* ◇ *Cars and buses were set ablaze during the riot.* **2** full of bright light or colours: *There were lights still ablaze as they drove up to the house.* ◇ ~ **with sth** *The trees were ablaze with the colours of autumn.* **3** ~ **(with sth)** full of strong emotion or excitement: *He turned to her, his eyes ablaze with anger.*

**able** ⓘ **A2** /ˈeɪbl/ *adj.*
**1** 🔑 **A2** ~ **to do sth** (used as a modal verb) to have the skill, intelligence, opportunity, etc. needed to do sth: *You must be able to speak French for this job.* ◇ *A viral illness left her barely able to walk.* ◇ *We're still able to get visas to come and go from Thailand.* ◇ *I didn't feel able to disagree with him.* **OPP** unable ⊃ note at CAN¹ **2** (**abler** /-blə(r)/, **ablest** /-blɪst/) intelligent; good at sth: *the ablest student in the class* ◇ *We aim to help the less able in society to lead an independent life.* ⊃ see also ABLY

| WORD FAMILY |
|---|
| **able** *adj.* (≠ unable) |
| **ably** *adv.* |
| **ability** *noun* (≠ inability) |
| **disabled** *adj.* |

**-able, -ible** /əbl/ *suffix* (in adjectives) **1** that can or must be: *calculable* ◇ *taxable* **2** having the quality of: *fashionable* ◇ *comfortable* ◇ *changeable* ▶ **-ability, -ibility** /əˈbɪləti/ (in nouns): *capability* ◇ *responsibility* ▶ **-ably, -ibly** /əbli/ (in adverbs): *noticeably* ◇ *incredibly*

**able-'bodied** *adj.* physically healthy, fit and strong in contrast to sb who is weak or DISABLED

**able 'seaman** *noun* a sailor of lower rank in the British NAVY

**ab·lu·tions** /əˈbluːʃnz/ *noun* [pl.] (formal or humorous) the act of washing yourself

**ably** /ˈeɪbli/ *adv.* well and with skill: *We were ably assisted by a team of volunteers.* ⊃ see also ABLE (2)

**ABM** /ˌeɪ biː ˈem/ *noun* (CanE) a machine in or outside a bank, shop, etc., from which you can get money from your bank account using a special plastic card (the abbreviation for 'automated banking machine') **SYN** cash machine

**ab·nor·mal** ⓦ /æbˈnɔːml; NAmE -ˈnɔːrml/ *adj.* different from what is usual or expected, especially in a way that worries sb or is harmful or not wanted: *abnormal levels of sugar in the blood* ◇ *They thought his behaviour was abnormal.* **OPP** normal ▶ **ab·nor·mal·ly** /-məli/ *adv.*: *abnormally high blood pressure*

---

æ **cat** | ɑː **father** | e **bed** | ɜː **fur** | ə **about** | ɪ **sit** | iː **see** | i **happy** | ɒ **got** (BrE) | ɔː **saw** | ʌ **cup** | ʊ **put** | uː **too**

**ab·nor·mal·ity** /ˌæbnɔːˈmæləti; NAmE -nɔːrˈm-/ noun [C, U] (pl. **-ies**) a feature or characteristic in a person's body or behaviour that is not usual and may be harmful or cause illness or worry; the fact of having such a feature or characteristic: *abnormalities of the heart* ◇ *congenital/fetal abnormality*

**aboard** /əˈbɔːd; NAmE əˈbɔːrd/ adv., prep. on or onto a ship, plane, bus or train SYN **on board**: *We went aboard.* ◇ *He was already aboard the plane.* ◇ *The plane crashed, killing all 157 passengers aboard.* ◇ **All aboard!** (= the bus, boat, etc. is leaving soon) ◇ *Welcome aboard!* (= used to welcome passengers or a person joining a new organization, etc.)

**abode** /əˈbəʊd/ noun, verb
- **noun** [usually sing.] (*formal or humorous*) the place where sb lives: *homeless people of no fixed abode* (= with no permanent home) ◇ *You are most welcome to my humble abode.*
- **verb** past tense, past part. of ABIDE (2)

**abol·ish** /əˈbɒlɪʃ; NAmE əˈbɑːl-/ verb ~ **sth** to officially end a law, a system or an institution: *This tax should be abolished.*

**abo·li·tion** /ˌæbəˈlɪʃn/ noun [U] the ending of a law, a system or an institution: *the abolition of slavery*

**abo·li·tion·ist** /ˌæbəˈlɪʃənɪst/ noun a person who is in favour of the abolition of sth, especially CAPITAL PUNISHMENT (= punishment by death) or (in the past) SLAVERY

**A-bomb** noun = ATOMIC BOMB

**abom·in·able** /əˈbɒmɪnəbl; NAmE əˈbɑːm-/ adj. extremely unpleasant and causing horror SYN **appalling, disgusting**: *The judge described the attack as an abominable crime.* ◇ *We were served the most abominable coffee.*
▶ **abom·in·ably** /-bli/ adv.: *She treated him abominably.*

**A,bominable 'Snowman** noun = YETI

**abom·in·ation** /əˌbɒmɪˈneɪʃn; NAmE əˌbɑːm-/ noun (*formal*) a thing that is hated and considered extremely offensive

**abo·ri·ginal** /ˌæbəˈrɪdʒənl/ adj., noun
- **adj.** **1** (usually **Aboriginal**) relating to the original people living in Australia: *the issue of Aboriginal land rights* **2** relating to the original people, animals, etc. of a place and to a period of time before Europeans arrived: *the aboriginal peoples of Canada* ◇ *aboriginal art/culture*
- **noun** (usually **Aboriginal**) a member of a race of people who were the original people living in a country, especially Australia ⊃ see also KOORI

**abo·ri·gine** /ˌæbəˈrɪdʒəni/ noun **1** a member of a race of people who were the original people living in a country **2 Aborigine** a member of the race of people who were the original people of Australia ⊃ see also KOORI

**abort** /əˈbɔːt; NAmE əˈbɔːrt/ verb **1** [T] ~ **sth** to end a PREGNANCY early in order to prevent a baby from developing and being born alive: *to abort a child/pregnancy/fetus* **2** [I] (*specialist*) to give birth to a child or young animal too early for it to survive: *The virus can cause pregnant animals to abort.* ⊃ see also MISCARRY **3** [I, T] to end or cause sth to end before it has been completed, especially because it is likely to fail: (*computing*) *If the wrong password is given the program aborts.* ◇ ~ **sth** *We had no option but to abort the mission.* ◇ *The plan was aborted at the last minute.*

**abor·tion** /əˈbɔːʃn; NAmE əˈbɔːrʃn/ noun **1** [U] the deliberate ending of a PREGNANCY at an early stage: *to support/oppose abortion* ◇ *a woman's right to abortion* ◇ *abortion laws* ◇ *I've always been anti-abortion.* **2** [C] a medical operation to end a PREGNANCY at an early stage SYN **termination**: *She decided to have an abortion.* **3** [U] (*medical*) the process of giving birth to a baby before it is fully developed and able to survive SYN **miscarriage**

**abor·tion·ist** /əˈbɔːʃənɪst; NAmE əˈbɔːrʃ-/ noun a person who performs abortions, especially illegally

**abort·ive** /əˈbɔːtɪv; NAmE əˈbɔːrtɪv/ adj. (*formal*) (of an action) not successful; failed SYN **unsuccessful**: *an abortive military coup* ◇ *abortive attempts to divert the course of the river*

**abound** /əˈbaʊnd/ verb [I] (*formal*) to exist in great numbers or quantities: *Stories about his travels abound.*

PHRV **a'bound with/in sth** to have sth in great numbers or quantities: *The lakes abound with fish.* ⊃ see also ABUNDANCE, ABUNDANT

**about** ❶ A1 /əˈbaʊt/ prep., adv., adj.
- **prep. 1** A1 on the subject of sb/sth; in connection with sb/sth: *a book about flowers* ◇ *Tell me all about it.* ◇ *What's she so angry about?* ◇ *There's something strange about him.* ◇ *I don't know what you're on about* (= talking about). ◇ *There's nothing you can do about it now.* **2** B1 used to describe the purpose or an aspect of sth: *Movies are all about making money these days.* ◇ *What was all that about?* (= what was the reason for what has just happened?) **3** busy with sth; doing sth: *Everywhere people were going about their daily business.* ◇ *And while you're about it …* (= while you're doing that) **4** (*especially BrE*) in many directions in a place; here and there: *We wandered about the town for an hour or so.* ◇ *He looked about the room.* **5** (*especially BrE*) in various parts of a place; here and there: *The papers were strewn about the room.* **6** (*especially BrE*) next to a place or person; in the area mentioned: *She's somewhere about the office.* **7** (*literary*) surrounding sb/sth: *She wore a shawl about her shoulders.*
- IDM **how/what about …?** **1** A1 used when asking for information about sb/sth: *How about Ruth? Have you heard from her?* ◇ *I'm having fish. What about you?* **2** A1 used to make a suggestion: *How about going for a walk?* ◇ (*especially NAmE*) *How about we go for a walk?* ◇ *What about a break?*
- **adv. 1** A1 a little more or less than; a little before or after SYN **approximately**: *It costs about $10.* ◇ *They waited (for) about an hour.* ◇ *He arrived (at) about ten.* **2** nearly; very close to: *I'm just about ready.* ◇ *This is about the best we can hope for.* **3** (*especially BrE*) in many directions; here and there: *The children were rushing about in the garden.* **4** (*especially BrE*) in no particular order; in various places: *Her books were lying about on the floor.* **5** (*especially BrE*) doing nothing in particular: *People were standing about in the road.* **6** (*especially BrE*) able to be found in a place: *There was nobody about.* ◇ *There's a lot of flu about.* **7** (*specialist or formal*) facing the opposite direction: *He brought the ship about.* ⊃ note at AROUND
- IDM **that's about 'all | that's about 'it** used to say that you have finished telling sb about sth and there is nothing to add: *'Anything else?' 'No, that's about it for now.'* ⊃ more at JUST adv., OUT adv.
- **adj.**
- IDM **be about to do sth** to be close to doing sth; to be going to do sth very soon: *I was just about to ask you the same thing.* **be not about to do sth** to not be willing to do sth; to not intend to do sth: *I've never done any cooking and I'm not about to start now.*

▼ LANGUAGE BANK

**about**
Saying what a text is about
- The book **is about** homeless people in the cities.
- The report **deals with** the issue of homelessness in London.
- The writer **discusses** the problems faced by homeless people.
- The article **presents an overview of** the issues surrounding homelessness.
- The novel **explores** the theme of friendship among homeless people.
- The first chapter **examines** the relationship between homelessness and drug addiction.
- The paper **considers** the question of why so many young people become homeless.

**a,bout-'turn** (*BrE*) (also **a,bout-'face** *NAmE, BrE*) noun [sing.] a complete change of opinion, plan or behaviour: *The government did an about-turn over nuclear energy.*

**above** ❶ A1 W /əˈbʌv/ prep., adv., adj.
- **prep. 1** A1 at or to a higher place or position than sth/sb: *The water came above our knees.* ◇ *We were flying above the clouds.* ◇ *the people in the apartment above mine* ◇ *A*

# above board

captain in the navy ranks above a captain in the army. ◊ They finished the year six places above their local rivals. **2** more than sth; greater in number, level or age than sb/sth: *Inflation is above 6%.* ◊ *Temperatures have been above average.* ◊ *We cannot accept children above the age of 10.* **3** of greater importance or of higher quality than sb/sth: *I rate her above most other players of her age.* **4** too good or too honest to do sth: *She's not above lying when it suits her.* ◊ *He's above suspicion* (= he is completely trusted). **5** (of a sound) louder or clearer than another sound: *I couldn't hear her above the noise of the traffic.*

**IDM** **above 'all** most important of all; especially: *Above all, keep in touch.* ⊃ **LANGUAGE BANK** at EMPHASIS **a,bove your'self** (*disapproving*) having too high an opinion of yourself ⊃ more at OVER *prep.*

- *adv.* **1** at or to a higher place: *Put it on the shelf above.* ◊ *Seen from above the cars looked tiny.* ◊ *They were acting on instructions from above* (= from sb in a higher position of authority). **2** greater in number, level or age: *increases of 5% and above* ◊ *A score of 70 or above will get you an 'A'.* ◊ *children aged 12 and above* **3** earlier in sth written or printed: *As was stated above…* ◊ *See above, page 97.*

**IDM** **(go) a,bove and be'yond (sth)** (*informal*) (to do) even more than is expected or demanded: *Our staff members will go above and beyond to ensure that our customers are satisfied.* ⊃ see also (ABOVE AND) BEYOND THE CALL OF DUTY at CALL *noun*

- *adj.* [only before noun] mentioned or printed previously in a letter, book, etc: *Please write to us at the above address.* ▶ **the above** *noun* [sing. + sing. / pl. v.]: *Please notify us if the above is not correct.* ◊ *All the above* (= people mentioned above) *have passed the exam.*

▼ **WHICH WORD?**

**above / over**
- **Above** and **over** can both be used to describe a position higher than something: *They built a new room above/over the garage.* When you are talking about movement from one side of something to the other, you can only use **over**: *They jumped over the stream.* **Over** can also mean 'covering': *He put a blanket over the sleeping child.*
- **Above** and **over** can also mean 'more than'. **Above** is used in relation to a minimum level or a fixed point: *2000 feet above sea level* ◊ *Temperatures will not rise above zero tonight.* **Over** is used with numbers, ages, money and time: *He's over 50.* ◊ *It costs over £100.* ◊ *We waited over 2 hours.*

**a,bove 'board** *adj., adv.* legal and honest; in a legal and honest way: *Don't worry; the deal was completely above board.* **ORIGIN** *If card players kept their hands above the table (the board), other players can see what they are doing.*

**a,bove-'mentioned** *adj.* [only before noun] mentioned or named earlier in the same letter, book, etc.

**abra·ca·dabra** /ˌæbrəkəˈdæbrə/ *exclamation* a word that people say when they do a magic trick, in order to make it successful

**ab·rade** /əˈbreɪd/ *verb* ~ **sth** (*specialist*) to rub the surface of sth, such as rock or skin, and damage it or make it rough

**ab·ra·sion** /əˈbreɪʒn/ *noun* (*specialist*) **1** [C] a damaged area of the skin where it has been rubbed against sth hard and rough: *He suffered cuts and abrasions to the face.* **2** [U] damage to a surface caused by rubbing sth very hard against it: *Diamonds have extreme resistance to abrasion.*

**abra·sive** /əˈbreɪsɪv/ *adj., noun*
- *adj.* **1** an abrasive substance is rough and can be used to clean a surface or to make it smooth: *abrasive kitchen cleaners* **2** (of a person or their manner) rude and unkind; acting in a way that may hurt other people's feelings ▶ **abra·sive·ly** *adv.* **abra·sive·ness** *noun* [U]
- *noun* a substance used for cleaning surfaces or for making them smooth

**abreast** /əˈbrest/ *adv.* next to sb/sth and facing the same way: *cycling two abreast* ◊ *of sth: A police car drew abreast of us and signalled us to stop.*

**IDM** **keep abreast of sth** to make sure that you know all the most recent facts about a subject: *It is almost impossible to keep abreast of all the latest developments in computing.*

**abridge** /əˈbrɪdʒ/ *verb* ~ **sth** to make a book, play, etc. shorter by leaving parts out ▶ **abridged** *adj.*: *an abridged edition/version* **OPP** **unabridged** **abridge·ment** (*also* **abridg·ment**) *noun* [U, C]

**abroad** /əˈbrɔːd/ *adv.* **1** in or to a foreign country: *to go/travel/live/study abroad* ◊ *She worked abroad for a year.* ◊ *imports of cheap food from abroad* ◊ *He was famous, both at home and abroad* (= in his own country and in other countries). ⊃ **WORDFINDER NOTE** at TOURIST **2** (*formal*) being talked about or felt by many people: *There was news abroad that a change was coming.* **3** (*old use*) outside; outdoors

**ab·ro·gate** /ˈæbrəɡeɪt/ *verb* (*formal*) **1** ~ **sth** to officially end a law, an agreement, etc. **SYN** **repeal** **2** ~ **sth** to fail to carry out a responsibility or duty: *We believe the board is abrogating its responsibilities.* ▶ **ab·ro·ga·tion** /ˌæbrəˈɡeɪʃn/ *noun* [U, sing.]

**ab·rupt** /əˈbrʌpt/ *adj.* **1** sudden and unexpected, often in an unpleasant way: *an abrupt change/halt/departure* **2** speaking or acting in a way that seems rude and unfriendly; not taking time to say more than is necessary **SYN** **brusque, curt**: *an abrupt manner* ◊ *~ with sb She was very abrupt with me in our meeting.* ▶ **ab·rupt·ly** *adv.* **ab·rupt·ness** *noun* [U]

**ABS** /ˌeɪ biː ˈes/ *abbr.* anti-lock braking system ⊃ see also ANTI-LOCK

**abs** /æbz/ *noun* [pl.] (*informal*) = ABDOMINALS

**ab·scess** /ˈæbses/ *noun* a SWOLLEN (= larger than normal) and painful area on your skin or in your body, full of a thick yellow liquid (called PUS)

**ab·scond** /əbˈskɒnd; *NAmE* -ˈskɑːnd/ *verb* **1** [I] ~ **(from sth)** to escape from a place that you are not allowed to leave without permission **2** [I] ~ **(with sth)** to leave secretly and take with you sth, especially money, that does not belong to you: *He absconded with the company funds.*

**ab·seil** /ˈæbseɪl/ (*BrE*) (*NAmE* **rap·pel**) *verb* [I] ~ **(down, off, etc. sth)** to go down a steep CLIFF or rock while attached to a rope, pushing against the slope or rock with your feet ▶ **ab·seil** (*BrE*) (*NAmE* **rap·pel**) *noun* **ab·seil·ing** (*BrE*) (*NAmE* **rap·pel·ling**) *noun* [U]

**ab·sence** /ˈæbsəns/ *noun* **1** [U, C] the fact of sb being away from a place where they are usually expected to be; the occasion or period of time when sb is away: **in sb's** ~ *The decision was made in my absence* (= while I was not there). ◊ *We did not receive any news during his long absence.* ◊ *~ from… absence from work* ◊ *repeated absences from school* ⊃ see also LEAVE *noun* **2** [U] the fact of sb/sth not existing or not being available; a lack of sth: *the absence of any women on the board of directors* ◊ **in the ~ of sth** *The case was dismissed in the absence of any definite proof.* **OPP** **presence**

**IDM** **absence makes the heart grow 'fonder** (*saying*) used to say that when you are away from sb that you love, you love them even more ⊃ more at CONSPICUOUS

**ab·sent** *adj., verb, prep.*
- *adj.* /ˈæbsənt/ **1** ~ **(from…)** not in a place because of illness, etc: *to be absent from work* **OPP** **present** **2** ~ **(from sth)** not present in sth: *Love was totally absent from his childhood.* **OPP** **present** **3** showing that you are not really looking at or thinking about what is happening around you: *an absent expression* ⊃ see also ABSENTLY
- *verb* /æbˈsent/ ~ **yourself (from sth)** (*formal*) to not go to or be in a place where you are expected to be: *He had absented himself from the office for the day.*
- *prep.* /ˈæbsənt/ (*NAmE, formal*) without: *Absent further evidence, the police had no choice but to release him without charge.*

**ab·sen·tee** /ˌæbsənˈtiː/ *noun* a person who is not at a place where they were expected to be

**absentee ballot** (NAmE) (BrE **postal vote**) noun a vote in an election that you can send when you cannot be present

**ab·sen·tee·ism** /ˌæbsənˈtiːɪzəm/ noun [U] the fact of being frequently away from work or school, especially without good reasons

**absentee landlord** noun a person who rents their property to sb, but does not live in it and rarely visits it

**ab·sen·tia** ⊃ IN ABSENTIA

**ab·sent·ly** /ˈæbsəntli/ adv. in a way that shows you are not looking at or thinking about what is happening around you: *He nodded absently, his attention absorbed by the screen.*

**absent-ˈminded** adj. tending to forget things, perhaps because you are not thinking about what is around you, but about sth else SYN **forgetful** ▶ **absent-ˈminded·ly** adv. **absent-ˈminded·ness** noun [U]

**ab·sinthe** /ˈæbsɪnθ/ noun [U, C] a very strong green alcoholic drink that tastes of ANISEED

**ab·so·lute** ⓘ B2 ⓞ /ˈæbsəluːt/ adj., noun
■ adj. 1 B2 total and complete: *a class for absolute beginners* ◊ *'You're wrong,' she said with absolute certainty.* ◊ *Clean water is an absolute necessity.* 2 B2 [only before noun] used, especially in spoken English, to give emphasis to what you are saying: *We must keep costs to an absolute minimum.* ◊ *This room is an absolute disgrace.* ◊ *They're talking absolute nonsense.* 3 definite and without any doubt: *There was no absolute proof.* ◊ *He taught us that the laws of physics were absolute.* ◊ *The story offers no clear message, no absolute truth.* 4 (of a legal decision) final: *The divorce became absolute last week.* ⊃ see also DECREE ABSOLUTE 5 not limited in any way: *absolute power/authority* ◊ *an absolute ruler/monarchy* (= one with no limit to their power) 6 existing or measured independently and not in relation to sth else: *Although prices are falling in absolute terms, energy is still expensive.* ◊ *Beauty cannot be measured by any absolute standard.* ⊃ compare RELATIVE
■ noun an idea or a principle that is believed to be true or relevant in any circumstances: *Right and wrong are, for her, moral absolutes.*

**ab·so·lute·ly** ⓘ B1 /ˈæbsəluːtli/ adv. 1 B1 used to emphasize that sth is completely true: *You're absolutely right.* ◊ *He made it absolutely clear.* ◊ *absolutely certain/sure* ◊ *absolutely necessary/essential/vital* ◊ *The place was absolutely packed.* 2 B1 **absolutely no…**, **absolutely nothing** used to emphasize sth negative: *There's absolutely nothing more the doctors can do.* 3 B1 used with adjectives or verbs that express strong feelings or extreme qualities to mean 'extremely': *absolutely delighted/thrilled* ◊ *We were absolutely devastated at the news.* ◊ *I absolutely love strawberries.* ◊ *absolutely fantastic/amazing* ◊ *He's an absolutely brilliant cook.* 4 B1 /ˌæbsəˈluːtli/ used to emphasize that you agree with sb, or to give sb permission to do sth: *'They could have told us, couldn't they?' 'Absolutely!'* ◊ *'Can we leave a little early?' 'Absolutely!'* 5 B1 **absolutely not** used to emphasize that you strongly disagree with sb, or to refuse permission: *'Was it any good?' 'No, absolutely not.'* 6 not considered in relation to other things: *White-collar crime increased both absolutely and in comparison with other categories.*

**absolute maˈjority** noun more than half of the total number of votes or winning candidates

**absolute ˈzero** noun [U] the lowest temperature that is thought to be possible

**ab·so·lu·tion** /ˌæbsəˈluːʃn/ noun [U, C] (especially in the Christian Church) a formal statement that a person is forgiven for what he or she has done wrong

**ab·so·lut·ism** /ˈæbsəluːtɪzəm/ noun [U] 1 a political system in which a leader or government has total power at all times 2 belief in a political, religious or moral principle that is thought to be true in all circumstances ▶ **ab·so·lut·ist** /-tɪst/ noun, adj.

**ab·solve** /əbˈzɒlv/ NAmE -ˈzɑːlv/ verb (formal) 1 ~ **sb (of/ from sth)** to state formally that sb is not guilty or responsible for sth: *The court absolved him of all responsibility for the accident.* 2 ~ **sb (from/of sth)** (of a priest) to give absolution to sb: *I absolve you from all your sins.*

**ab·sorb** B2 /əbˈzɔːb; NAmE -ˈzɔːrb/ verb
• LIQUID/GAS 1 B2 to take in a liquid, gas or other substance from the surface or space around: ~ **sth** *Plants absorb carbon dioxide from the air.* ◊ ~ **sth into sth** *The cream is easily absorbed into the skin.* ⊃ WORDFINDER NOTE at LIQUID
• HEAT/LIGHT/ENERGY/SOUND 2 B2 ~ **sth** to take in and keep heat, light, sound, etc. instead of reflecting it: *Black walls absorb a lot of heat during the day.*
• SHOCK/IMPACT 3 C1 ~ **sth** to reduce the effect of a physical impact or movement: *This tennis racket absorbs shock on impact.* ⊃ see also SHOCK ABSORBER
• INFORMATION 4 C1 ~ **sth** to take sth into the mind and learn or understand it SYN **take in**: *It's a lot of information to absorb all at once.*
• INTEREST SB 5 C1 ~ **sb** to interest sb very much so that they pay no attention to anything else SYN **engross**: *This work had absorbed him for several years.*
• MAKE PART OF STH LARGER 6 C1 [often passive] to make sth smaller become part of sth larger: ~ **sth** *The country simply cannot absorb this influx of refugees.* ◊ **be absorbed into sth** *The surrounding small towns have been absorbed into the city.*
• MONEY/TIME/CHANGES 7 ~ **sth** to use up a large supply of sth, especially money or time: *The new proposals would absorb $80 billion of the federal budget.* 8 ~ **sth** to deal with changes, effects, costs, etc: *The company is unable to absorb such huge losses.*

**ab·sor·bance** /əbˈzɔːbəns; NAmE -ˈzɔːrb-/ noun [U, C] (physics) the ability of a substance to absorb light

**ab·sorbed** /əbˈzɔːbd; NAmE -ˈzɔːrbd/ adj. [not usually before noun] ~ **in sth/sb** very interested in sth/sb so that you are not paying attention to anything else: *She seemed totally absorbed in her book.*

**ab·sorb·ent** /əbˈzɔːbənt; NAmE -ˈzɔːrb-/ adj. able to take in sth easily, especially liquid: *absorbent paper/materials* ▶ **ab·sorb·ency** /-bənsi/ noun [U]

**ab·sorb·ing** /əbˈzɔːbɪŋ; NAmE -ˈzɔːrb-/ adj. interesting and fun and holding your attention completely: *an absorbing book/game* ⊃ SYNONYMS at INTERESTING

**ab·sorp·tion** /əbˈzɔːpʃn; NAmE -ˈzɔːrp-/ noun [U] 1 the process of a liquid, gas or other substance being taken in: *Vitamin D is necessary to aid the absorption of calcium from food.* 2 ~ **(of sb/sth) (into sth)** the process of a smaller group, country, etc. becoming part of a larger group or country: *the absorption of immigrants into the host country* 3 ~ **(in sth)** the fact of sb being very interested in sth so that it takes all their attention: *His work suffered because of his total absorption in sport.*

**ab·stain** /əbˈsteɪn/ verb [I] 1 ~ **(from sth)** to choose not to use a vote, either in favour of or against sth: *Ten people voted in favour, five against and two abstained.* 2 ~ **(from sth)** to decide not to do or have sth, especially sth you like or enjoy, because it is bad for your health or considered morally wrong: *to abstain from alcohol/sex/drugs* 3 ~ **(from sth)** (IndE) to stay away from sth: *The workers who abstained from work yesterday have been suspended.* ⊃ see also ABSTENTION, ABSTINENCE

**ab·stain·er** /əbˈsteɪnə(r)/ noun 1 a person who chooses not to vote in favour of or against sth 2 a person who abstains from sth, especially alcohol

**ab·ste·mi·ous** /əbˈstiːmiəs/ adj. (formal) not allowing yourself to have much food or alcohol, or to do things that are fun

**ab·sten·tion** /əbˈstenʃn/ noun 1 [C, U] ~ **(from sth)** an act of choosing not to use a vote either in favour of or against sth: *The voting was 15 in favour, 3 against and 2 abstentions.* 2 [U] ~ **(from sth)** (formal) the act of not allowing yourself to have or do sth fun or sth that is considered bad ⊃ see also ABSTAIN

# abstinence

**ab·stin·ence** /ˈæbstɪnəns/ noun [U] ~ (from sth) (formal) the practice of not allowing yourself sth, especially food, alcoholic drinks or sex, for moral, religious or health reasons: *total abstinence from strong drink* ⇒ see also ABSTAIN

**ab·stin·ent** /ˈæbstɪnənt/ adj. (formal) not allowing yourself sth, especially alcoholic drinks, for moral, religious or health reasons

**ab·stract** 🔑+ B2 adj., noun, verb
- adj. /ˈæbstrækt/ **1** 🔑+ B2 based on general ideas and not on any particular real person, thing or situation: *abstract knowledge/principles* ◇ *The research shows that pre-school children are capable of thinking in abstract terms.* ⇒ compare CONCRETE **2** 🔑+ B2 existing in thought or as an idea but not having a physical reality: *We may talk of beautiful things but beauty itself is abstract.* **3** (of art) not representing people or things in a realistic way, but expressing the artist's ideas about them ⇒ compare FIGURATIVE (2), REPRESENTATIONAL ▸ **ab·stract·ly** adv.
- noun /ˈæbstrækt/ **1** an abstract work of art **2** a short piece of writing containing the main ideas in a document SYN summary
- IDM **in the ˈabstract** in a general way, without referring to a particular real person, thing or situation
- verb /æbˈstrækt/ **1** ~ sth (from sth) to remove sth from somewhere: *She abstracted the main points from the argument.* **2** ~ sth (specialist) to make a written summary of a book, etc.

**ab·stract·ed** /æbˈstræktɪd/ adj. (formal) thinking deeply about sth and not paying attention to what is around you ▸ **ab·stract·ed·ly** adv.

**abstract exˈpressionism** noun [U] a style and movement in abstract art that developed in New York in the middle of the 20th century and tries to express the feelings of the artist rather than showing a physical object ▸ **abstract exˈpressionist** noun: *abstract expressionists like Jackson Pollock* **abstract exˈpressionist** adj. [usually before noun]: *abstract expressionist art*

**ab·strac·tion** /æbˈstrækʃn/ noun **1** [C, U] (formal) a general idea not based on any particular real person, thing or situation; the quality of being abstract **2** [U] (formal) the state of thinking deeply about sth and not paying attention to what is around you **3** [U, C] the action of removing sth from sth else; the process of being removed from sth else: *water abstraction from rivers*

**ˈabstract ˈnoun** noun (grammar) a noun, for example *goodness* or *freedom*, that refers to an idea or a general quality, not to a physical object ⇒ compare COMMON NOUN, PROPER NOUN

**ab·struse** /əbˈstruːs/ adj. (formal, often disapproving) difficult to understand: *an abstruse argument*

**ab·surd** 🔑+ C1 /əbˈsɜːd; NAmE -ˈsɜːrd/ adj. **1** 🔑+ C1 extremely silly; not logical and sensible SYN ridiculous: *That uniform makes the guards look absurd.* ◇ *Of course it's not true, what an absurd idea.* **2** 🔑+ C1 **the absurd** noun [sing.] things that are or that seem to be absurd: *He has a good sense of the absurd.* ▸ **ab·surd·ity** noun [U, C] (pl. -ies): *It was only later that she could see the absurdity of the situation.* **ab·surd·ly** adv. SYN ridiculously: *The paintings were sold for absurdly high prices.*

**abun·dance** 🔑+ C1 /əˈbʌndəns/ noun [sing., U] ~ (of sth) (formal) a large quantity that is more than enough
- IDM **in abundance** in large quantities: *Fruit and vegetables grew in abundance on the island.*

**abun·dant** /əˈbʌndənt/ adj. (formal) existing in large quantities; more than enough SYN plentiful: *Fish are abundant in the lake.* ◇ *We have abundant evidence to prove his guilt.*

**abun·dant·ly** /əˈbʌndəntli/ adv. **1** ~ **clear** very clear: *She made her wishes abundantly clear.* **2** in large quantities: *Calcium is found most abundantly in milk.*

**abuse** 🔑+ C1 noun, verb
- noun /əˈbjuːs/ **1** 🔑+ C1 [U, sing.] the use of sth in a way that is wrong or harmful SYN misuse: *alcohol/drug/solvent abuse* ◇ *The system of paying cash bonuses is open to abuse* (= might be used in the wrong way). ◇ ~ **of sth** *He was arrested on charges of corruption and abuse of power.* ◇ *What she did was an abuse of her position as manager.* ⇒ see also SUBSTANCE ABUSE ⇒ WORDFINDER NOTE at DRUG **2** 🔑+ C1 [U, sing.] unfair, cruel or violent treatment of sb: *child abuse* ◇ *sexual abuse* ◇ *reported abuses by the secret police* ◇ *She suffered years of physical abuse.* ⇒ see also CHILD ABUSE, ELDER ABUSE, SELF-ABUSE **3** 🔑+ C1 [U] rude and offensive remarks, usually made when sb is very angry SYN insult: *to scream/hurl/shout abuse* ◇ *a stream/torrent of abuse*
- verb /əˈbjuːz/ **1** 🔑+ C1 ~ **sth** to make bad use of sth, or to use so much of sth that it harms your health: *to abuse alcohol/drugs* ◇ *He systematically abused his body with heroin and cocaine.* **2** 🔑+ C1 ~ **sth** to use power or knowledge unfairly or wrongly: *She abused her position as principal by giving jobs to her friends.* ◇ *He felt they had abused his trust by talking about him to the press* (= tricked him, although he had trusted them). **3** 🔑+ C1 ~ **sb/sth** to treat a person or an animal in a cruel or violent way, especially sexually: *The boy had been sexually abused.* ◇ *All the children had been physically and emotionally abused.* ◇ *abused children* **4** 🔑+ C1 ~ **sb** to make rude or offensive remarks to or about sb SYN insult: *The referee had been threatened and verbally abused.* ◇ *He claimed he had been racially abused.*
▸ **ab·user** noun: *a drug abuser* ◇ *a child abuser*

**abu·sive** /əˈbjuːsɪv/ adj. **1** (of speech or of a person) rude and offensive; criticizing rudely and unfairly: *abusive language/remarks* ◇ *He became abusive when he was drunk.* **2** (of behaviour) involving violence: *an abusive relationship* ◇ *emotionally/physically/sexually abusive* **3** involving the use of power or knowledge unfairly or wrongly: *the abusive practices of some businesses* ▸ **abu·sive·ly** adv.

**abut** /əˈbʌt/ verb [I, T] (-tt-) ~ **(on/onto) sth** (formal) (of land or a building) to be next to sth or to have one side touching the side of sth: *His land abuts onto a road.*

**abut·ment** /əˈbʌtmənt/ noun a structure built to support the ends of a bridge or an ARCH

**abys·mal** /əˈbɪzməl/ adj. extremely bad or of a very low standard SYN terrible ▸ **abys·mal·ly** /-məli/ adv.

**abyss** /əˈbɪs/ noun [usually sing.] (formal or literary) a very deep wide space or hole that seems to have no bottom: *Ahead of them was a gaping abyss.* ◇ (figurative) *an abyss of ignorance/despair/loneliness* ◇ (figurative) *The country is stepping back from the edge of an abyss.*

**AC** /ˌeɪ ˈsiː/ abbr. **1** (also **ac**, **a/c**) (especially NAmE) AIR CONDITIONING **2** ALTERNATING CURRENT ⇒ compare DIRECT CURRENT

**a/c** abbr. (in writing) **1** (especially BrE) account **2** AIR CONDITIONING

**aca·cia** /əˈkeɪʃə/ (also aˈcacia tree) noun a tree with yellow or white flowers. There are several types of acacia tree, some of which produce a sticky liquid used in making GLUE.

**aca·demia** /ˌækəˈdiːmiə/ (also formal or humorous **aca·deme** /ˈækədiːm/) noun [U] the world of learning, teaching, research, etc. at universities, and the people involved in it

**aca·dem·ic** 🔑 B1 🔑 /ˌækəˈdemɪk/ adj., noun
- adj. **1** 🔑 B1 [usually before noun] connected with education, especially studying in schools and universities: *an academic career* ◇ *academic institutions* ◇ *improving the academic achievement of all students* ◇ *We are deeply committed to safeguarding academic freedom.* **2** 🔑 B1 [usually before noun] involving a lot of reading and studying rather than practical or technical skills: *a mixture of vocational and academic courses* **3** good at subjects involving a lot of reading and studying: *She wasn't very academic and hated school.* **4** not connected to a real or practical situation and therefore not important: *It's a purely academic question.* ◇ *The whole thing's academic now—we can't win anyway.* ▸ **aca·dem·ic·al·ly** /-kli/ adv.: *You have to do well academically to get into medical school.*
- noun 🔑 B2 a person who teaches and/or does research at a university or college: *a leading/distinguished/prominent academic*

**acad·em·ician** /əˌkædəˈmɪʃn; NAmE ˌækəd-/ noun a member of an ACADEMY

**aˌcademic ˈyear** noun the period of the year during which students go to school or university

**acad·emy** /əˈkædəmi/ noun (pl. -ies) 1 a school or college for special training: *the Royal Academy of Music* ◊ *a police/military academy* 2 (usually **Academy**) a type of official organization that aims to encourage and develop art, literature, science, etc: *the Royal Academy of Arts* 3 a SECONDARY SCHOOL in Scotland 4 a private school in the US 5 a school in England that is independent of local authority control

**Aˌcademy Aˈward™** (also **Oscar**™) noun one of the awards given every year by the US Academy of Motion Picture Arts and Sciences for achievement in the making of films

**açai** /æˈsaɪiː, ˌæsɑːˈiː/ noun (pl. **açai**) a type of South American PALM tree that produces small dark fruit that can be eaten or made into juice: *açai berries*

**a capˈpella** /ˌæ kəˈpelə, ˌɑː/ adj. (of music) for singing voices alone, without musical instruments ▶ **a capˈpella** adv.

**ac·cede** /əkˈsiːd/ verb [I] (formal) 1 ~ (**to sth**) to agree to a request, proposal, etc: *He acceded to demands for his resignation.* 2 ~ (**to sth**) to achieve a high position, especially to become king or queen: *Queen Victoria acceded to the throne in 1837.* ⊃ WORDFINDER NOTE at KING 3 ~ (**to sth**) to become a member of an organization: *Croatia acceded to the EU in 2013.* ⊃ see also ACCESSION

**ac·cel·er·ate** /əkˈseləreɪt/ verb 1 [I, T] to happen faster or earlier; to make sth happen faster or earlier: *Inflation continues to accelerate.* ◊ ~ **sth** *Exposure to the sun can accelerate the ageing process.* 2 [I] (of a vehicle or person) to start to go faster: *The runners accelerated smoothly around the bend.* ◊ *The car accelerated to overtake me.* ⊃ WORDFINDER NOTE at CAR **OPP decelerate**

**ac·cel·er·ation** /əkˌseləˈreɪʃn/ noun 1 [U, sing.] ~ (**in sth**) an increase in how fast sth happens: *an acceleration in the rate of economic growth* 2 [U] the rate at which a vehicle increases speed: *a car with good acceleration* 3 [U] (physics) the rate at which the VELOCITY (= speed in a particular direction) of an object changes

**ac·cel·er·ator** /əkˈseləreɪtə(r)/ noun 1 (also ˈ**gas pedal**) the PEDAL in a car or other vehicle that you press with your foot to control the speed of the engine 2 (physics) a machine for making ELEMENTARY PARTICLES move at high speeds

**ac·cel·er·om·eter** /əkˌseləˈrɒmɪtə(r); NAmE -ˈrɑːm-/ noun (physics) an instrument for measuring ACCELERATION

**ac·cent** noun, verb
■ noun /ˈæksent, -sənt/ 1 a way of pronouncing the words of a language that shows which country, area or social class a person comes from; how well sb pronounces a particular language: *a northern/Dublin/Scottish accent* ◊ *a strong/broad accent* (= one that is easy to notice) ◊ **with an~** *She spoke English with an accent.* ◊ *The Americans had learned Korean and spoke with a good accent.* ⊃ compare DIALECT ⊃ WORDFINDER NOTE at LANGUAGE 2 the emphasis that you should give to part of a word when saying it **SYN stress**: *In 'today' the accent is on the second syllable.* 3 a mark on a letter to show that it should be pronounced in a particular way: *Canapé has an accent on the 'e'.* ⊃ see also ACUTE ACCENT, CIRCUMFLEX, GRAVE² 4 [sing.] a special importance that is given to sth **SYN emphasis**: *In all our products the accent is on quality.*
■ verb /ækˈsent/ ~ **sth** to emphasize a part of sth

**ac·cent·ed** /ˈæksentɪd/ adj. 1 spoken with a foreign accent: *He spoke heavily accented English.* 2 (specialist) spoken with particular emphasis: *accented vowels/syllables* 3 (specialist) (of a letter of the alphabet) written or printed with a special mark on it to show it should be pronounced in a particular way: *accented characters*

**ac·cen·tu·ate** /əkˈsentʃueɪt/ verb ~ **sth** to emphasize sth or make it easier to notice ▶ **ac·cen·tu·ation** /əkˌsentʃuˈeɪʃn/ noun [U]

# accepted

**ac·cept** /əkˈsept/ verb
• OFFER/INVITATION 1 [I, T] to take willingly sth that is offered; to say 'yes' to an offer, invitation, etc: *He asked me to marry him and I accepted.* ◊ ~ **sth** *Please accept our sincere apologies.* ◊ *It was pouring with rain so I accepted his offer of a lift.* ◊ **to accept an invitation/a proposal** ◊ *She's decided not to accept the job.* ◊ ~ **sth from sb** *He is charged with accepting bribes from a firm of suppliers.* ◊ ~ **sth for sth** *She said she'd accept $15 for it.* **OPP refuse¹**
• AGREE 2 [T] to agree to or approve of sth: ~ **sth** *They accepted the court's decision.* ◊ *The judge refused to accept his evidence.* ◊ ~ **sth from sb** *She won't accept advice from anyone.* ◊ ~ **sth for sth** *My article has been accepted for publication.* **OPP reject** ⊃ SYNONYMS at AGREE
• PAYMENT 3 [T] ~ **sth** to take payment in a particular form: *This machine only accepts coins.* ◊ *Credit cards are widely accepted.*
• RESPONSIBILITY 4 [T] ~ **sth** to admit that you are responsible or to blame for sth: *He accepts full responsibility for what happened.* ◊ *You have to accept the consequences of your actions.*
• DIFFICULT SITUATION 5 [T] to continue in a difficult situation without complaining, because you realize that you cannot change it: ~ **sth** *You just have to accept the fact that we're never going to be rich.* ◊ **to be willing/prepared to accept sth** ◊ ~ **sth as sth** *They accept the risks as part of the job.* ◊ ~ **that ...** *He just refused to accept that his father was no longer there.*
• WELCOME 6 [T] to make sb feel welcome and part of a group: ~ **sb** *It may take years to be completely accepted by the local community.* ◊ ~ **sb into sth** *She had never been accepted into what was essentially a man's world.* ◊ ~ **sb as sth** *He never really accepted her as his own child.* **OPP reject**
• BELIEVE 7 [T] to believe that sth is true: ~ **sth** *I don't accept his version of events.* ◊ ~ **sth as sth** *Can we accept his account as the true version?* ◊ ~ **that ...** *I accept that this will not be popular.* ◊ **it is accepted that ...** *It is generally accepted that people are motivated by success.* ◊ **sth is accepted to be, have, etc. sth** *Their workforce is widely accepted to have the best conditions in Europe.*
• ALLOW SB TO JOIN 8 [T] to allow sb to join an organization, attend an institution, use a service, etc: ~ **sb** *The college he applied to has accepted him.* ◊ ~ **sb into sth** *She was disappointed not to be accepted into the club.* ◊ ~ **sb as sth** *The landlord was willing to accept us as tenants.* ◊ ~ **sb to do sth** *She was accepted to study music.* **OPP reject**

**ac·cept·able** /əkˈseptəbl/ adj. 1 agreed or approved of by most people in a society: *Children must learn socially acceptable behaviour.* 2 that sb agrees is of a good enough standard or allowed: *For this course a pass in English at grade B is acceptable.* ◊ *Air pollution in the city had reached four times the acceptable levels.* ◊ ~ **to sb** *We want a political solution that is acceptable to all parties.* 3 not very good but good enough: *The food was acceptable, but no more.* **OPP unacceptable**
▶ **ac·cept·abil·ity** /əkˌseptəˈbɪləti/ noun [U] **ac·cept·ably** /əkˈseptəbli/ adv.

**ac·cept·ance** /əkˈseptəns/ noun 1 [U, C] the act of accepting a gift, an invitation, an offer, etc: *Please confirm your acceptance of this offer in writing.* ◊ *He made a short acceptance speech/speech of acceptance.* ◊ *Invitations have been sent out and 80 acceptances have already been received.* 2 [U] the act of agreeing with sth and approving of it: *The new laws have gained widespread acceptance.* 3 [U] ~ (**into sth**) the process of allowing sb to join sth or be a member of a group: *Your acceptance into the insurance plan is guaranteed.* ◊ *Social acceptance is important for most young people.* 4 [U] the quality of being willing to accept an unpleasant or difficult situation: *acceptance of death/suffering*

**ac·cept·ed** /əkˈseptɪd/ adj. generally believed to be correct: *What if the accepted wisdom is wrong?* ◊ *accepted norms/principles/standards*

---

s see | t tea | v van | w wet | z zoo | ʃ shoe | ʒ vision | tʃ chain | dʒ jam | θ thin | ð this | ŋ sing

# access

**ac·cess** /ˈækses/ noun, verb

- **noun** [U] **1** the opportunity or right to use sth or to see sb/sth: *High-speed internet access has become a necessity.* ◊ **~to sth/sb** *You need a password to get access to the computer system.* ◊ *access to information/services/resources* ◊ *access to healthcare/education* ◊ *Journalists were denied access to the President.* ◊ *Many divorced fathers only have access to their children at weekends* (= they are allowed by law to see them only at weekends). ⊃ compare VISITATION ⊃ **WORDFINDER NOTE** at WEB ⊃ see also MULTI-ACCESS, OPEN ACCESS, PUBLIC ACCESS, SELF-ACCESS **2** a way of entering or reaching a place: *The police gained access through a broken window.* ◊ *There is easy access by road.* ◊ **~to sth** *Disabled visitors are welcome; there is good wheelchair access to most facilities.* ⊃ compare EGRESS ⊃ see also DIRECT ACCESS, RANDOM ACCESS, REMOTE ACCESS

- **verb 1** **~sth** (*computing*) to open a computer file or use a computer system: *Most people use their phones to access the internet.* ◊ *to access a file/database* ◊ *to access information/data* ◊ **~sth via/through sth** *Their website can be accessed via the link below.* **2** **~sth** to be able to have or use sth, especially sth that you have a right to: *Being informed is the first step toward accessing better health services.* **3** [often passive] (*formal*) to reach, enter or use sth: **be accessed** (+ *adv./prep.*) *The loft can be accessed by a ladder.*

**ˈaccess course** noun (*BrE*) a course of education that prepares students without the usual qualifications, so that they can study at university or college

**ac·ces·sible** /əkˈsesəbl/ adj. **1** that can be reached, entered, used, seen, etc: *The remote desert area is accessible only by helicopter.* ◊ **~to sb** *These documents are not accessible to the public.* **2** that can be reached, entered, used, etc. by sb who has problems walking: *accessible toilets for wheelchair users* **3** easy to understand: *Her poetry is always very accessible.* ◊ **~to sb** *a programme making science more accessible to young people* **4** (of a person) easy to talk to and to get to know **OPP** **inaccessible** ▸ **ac·ces·si·bil·ity** /əkˌsesəˈbɪləti/ noun [U]

**ac·ces·sion** /əkˈseʃn/ noun **1** [U] **~(to sth)** the act of getting a position of rank or power: *the accession of Queen Victoria to the throne* ⊃ see also ACCEDE **2** [U] **~(to sth)** the act of becoming part of an international organization: *the accession of new member states to the EU* ◊ *the new accession states of the EU* **3** [C] (*specialist*) a thing that is added to a collection of objects, paintings, etc. in a library or museum

**ac·ces·sor·ize** (*BrE also* -**ise**) /əkˈsesəraɪz/ verb **~sth** to add fashionable items or extra decorations to sth, especially to your clothes

**ac·ces·sory** /əkˈsesəri/ noun, adj.

- **noun** (*pl.* -**ies**) **1** [usually pl.] an extra piece of equipment that is useful but not essential or that can be added to sth else as a decoration: *bicycle accessories* ◊ *a range of furnishings and accessories for the home* **2** [usually pl.] a thing that you can wear or carry that matches your clothes, for example a belt or a bag **3** **~(to sth)** (*law*) a person who helps sb to commit a crime or who knows about it and protects the person from the police: *He was charged with being an accessory to murder.*

- **adj.** (*specialist*) not the most important when compared to others: *the accessory muscles of respiration*

**ˈaccess provider** noun = SERVICE PROVIDER

**ˈaccess road** noun a road used for driving into or out of a particular place ⊃ compare SLIP ROAD

**ˈaccess time** noun [U, C] (*computing*) the time taken to obtain data stored on a computer

**ac·ci·dent** /ˈæksɪdənt/ noun **1** [C] an unpleasant event, especially in a vehicle, that happens unexpectedly and causes injury or damage: *a car/road/traffic accident* ◊ **in an~** *He was killed in an accident.* ◊ *One in seven accidents is caused by sleepy drivers.* ◊ *The accident happened at 3p.m.* ◊ **to have an accident** ◊ *a serious/minor accident* ◊ *a fatal accident* (= in which sb is killed) ◊ *accidents in the home* ◊ *a climbing/riding accident* ◊ *Take out accident insurance before you go on your trip.* ◊ *I didn't mean to break it—it was an accident.*

**WORDFINDER** ambulance, casualty, first aid, hospital, injure, paramedic, stretcher, victim, witness

**2** [C, U] something that happens unexpectedly and is not planned in advance: *Their early arrival was just an accident.* ◊ *It is no accident that men fill most of the top jobs in nursing.* ◊ *an accident of birth/fate/history* (= describing facts and events that are due to chance or circumstances) ⊃ **SYNONYMS** at LUCK

**IDM** **accidents will ˈhappen** people say **accidents will happen** to tell sb who has had an accident, for example breaking sth, that it does not matter and they should not worry **by accident** in a way that is not planned or organized: *We met by accident at the airport.* ◊ *Helen got into acting purely by accident.* **OPP** **deliberately, on purpose** ⊃ more at CHAPTER, WAIT v.

**ac·ci·den·tal** /ˌæksɪˈdentl/ adj. happening by chance; not planned: *a verdict of accidental death* ◊ *I didn't think our meeting was accidental—he must have known I would be there.*

**ac·ci·den·tal·ly** /ˌæksɪˈdentəli/ adv. by chance; in a way that was not planned: *As I turned around, I accidentally hit him in the face.* ◊ *The damage couldn't have been caused accidentally.*

**ˌaccident and eˈmergency** noun [U] (*abbr.* **A & E**) (*BrE*) (*NAmE* **eˈmergency room**) [C] the part of a hospital where people who need immediate treatment are taken: *The teenager was rushed to accident and emergency.* ◊ *the hospital accident and emergency department* ⊃ see also CASUALTY

**ˈaccident-prone** adj. more likely to have accidents than other people, companies, etc.

**ac·claim** /əˈkleɪm/ verb, noun

- **verb** [usually passive] to praise or welcome sb/sth publicly: **be acclaimed (as sth)** *The work was acclaimed as a masterpiece.* ◊ *a highly/widely acclaimed performance*

- **noun** [U] praise and approval for sb/sth, especially an artistic achievement: *international/popular/critical acclaim*

**ac·clam·ation** /ˌækləˈmeɪʃn/ noun **1** (*formal*) loud and enthusiastic approval or welcome **2** (*specialist*) the act of electing sb using a spoken not written vote: **by ~** *The decision was taken by acclamation.*

**ac·cli·mate** /ˈækləmeɪt/ verb (*especially NAmE*) = ACCLIMATIZE ▸ **ac·cli·ma·tion** /ˌækləˈmeɪʃn/ noun [U]

**ac·cli·ma·tize** (*BrE also* -**ise**) /əˈklaɪmətaɪz/ (*also* **ac·cli·mate** *especially in NAmE*) verb [I, T] to get used to a new place, situation or climate: **~(to sth)** *Arrive two days early in order to acclimatize.* ◊ **be/get acclimatized to sth** *We haven't got acclimatized to village life yet.* ◊ **~yourself (to sth)** *She was fine once she had acclimatized herself to the cold.* ▸ **ac·cli·ma·tiza·tion, -isa·tion** /əˌklaɪmətaɪˈzeɪʃn/; *NAmE* -təˈz-/ (*NAmE also* **ac·cli·ma·tion**) noun [U]

**ac·col·ade** /ˈækəleɪd/ noun (*formal*) praise or an award for an achievement that people admire

**ac·com·mo·date** /əˈkɒmədeɪt; *NAmE* əˈkɑːm-/ verb **1** [T] **~sb** to provide sb with a room or place to sleep, live or sit: *The hotel can accommodate up to 500 guests.* **2** [T] **~sb/sth** to provide enough space for sb/sth: *The garage can accommodate three cars.* **3** [T] **~sth** (*formal*) to consider sth such as sb's opinion or a particular fact and be influenced by it when you are deciding what to do or explaining sth: *Our proposal tries to accommodate the special needs of minority groups.* **4** [T] **~sb (with sth)** (*formal*) to help sb by doing what they want **SYN** **oblige**: *I have accommodated the press a great deal, giving numerous interviews.* **5** [I, T] **~(sth/yourself) to sth** (*formal*) to change your behaviour so that you can deal with a new situation better: *I needed to accommodate to the new schedule.*

---

| æ cat | ɑː father | e bed | ɜː fur | ə about | ɪ sit | iː see | i happy | ɒ got (*BrE*) | ɔː saw | ʌ cup | ʊ put | uː too |

**ac·com·mo·dat·ing** /əˈkɒmədeɪtɪŋ; NAmE əˈkɑːm-/ adj. ~ (to sb) (formal) willing to help and do things for other people SYN **obliging**

**ac·com·mo·da·tion** ❶ B1 /əˌkɒməˈdeɪʃn; NAmE əˌkɑːm-/ noun **1** B1 [U] (BrE) a place to live, work or stay in: *rented/temporary accommodation* ◇ *Hotel accommodation is included in the price of your holiday.* ◇ *We may have to* **provide** *alternative* **accommodation** *for you.* ◇ *First-class accommodation is available on all flights.* ⇒ WORDFINDER NOTE at HOME **2 accommodations** [pl.] (NAmE) somewhere to live or stay, often also providing food or other services: *More and more travelers are looking for bed and breakfast accommodations in private homes.* **3** [C, U] (formal) an agreement or arrangement between people or groups with different opinions that is acceptable to everyone; the process of reaching this agreement: *They were forced to reach an accommodation with the rebels.*

**ac·com·pani·ment** /əˈkʌmpənimənt/ noun **1** [C, U] ~ (to sth) music that is played to support singing or another instrument: *traditional songs with piano accompaniment* **2** [C] ~ (to/for sth) something that you eat, drink or use together with sth else: *The wine makes a good accompaniment to fish dishes.* **3** [C] ~ (to sth) (formal) something that happens or exists at the same time as another thing: *High blood pressure is a common accompaniment to this disease.* IDM **to the accompaniment of sth** **1** while a musical instrument is being played: *They performed to the accompaniment of guitars.* **2** while sth else is happening: *She made her speech to the accompaniment of loud laughter.*

**ac·com·pan·ist** /əˈkʌmpənɪst/ noun a person who plays a musical instrument, especially a piano, while sb else plays or sings the main part of the music

**ac·com·pany** ❶ B2 /əˈkʌmpəni/ verb (ac·com·pan·ies, ac·com·pany·ing, ac·com·pan·ied, ac·com·pan·ied) **1** B2 (formal) to travel or go somewhere with sb/sth: ~ **sb/sth + adv./prep.** *His wife accompanied him on the trip.* ◇ *He was accompanied by his wife.* ◇ ~ **sb/sth** *Warships will accompany the convoy.* **2** B2 to happen or appear with sth else: ~ **sth** *Shouts of protest accompanied this announcement.* ◇ **accompanied by sth** *strong winds accompanied by heavy rain* **3** ~ **sb (at/on sth)** to play a musical instrument, especially a piano, while sb else sings or plays the main tune: *The singer was accompanied at the piano by her sister.*

**ac·com·pany·ing** /əˈkʌmpəniɪŋ/ adj. [only before noun] provided with sth else: *The curator of the exhibition also wrote the accompanying catalogue.*

**ac·com·plice** /əˈkʌmplɪs; NAmE əˈkɑːm-/ noun a person who helps another to commit a crime or to do sth wrong

**ac·com·plish** B2 /əˈkʌmplɪʃ; NAmE əˈkɑːm-/ verb ~ **sth** to succeed in doing or completing sth SYN **achieve**: *The first part of the plan has been safely accomplished.* ◇ *I don't feel I've accomplished very much today.* ◇ *That's it.* **Mission accomplished** (= we have done what we aimed to do).

**ac·com·plished** /əˈkʌmplɪʃt; NAmE əˈkɑːm-/ adj. very good at a particular thing; having a lot of skills: *an accomplished artist/actor/chef* ◇ *She was an elegant and accomplished woman.*

**ac·com·plish·ment** C1 /əˈkʌmplɪʃmənt; NAmE əˈkɑːm-/ noun **1** C1 [C] an impressive thing that is done or achieved after a lot of work SYN **achievement**: *It was one of the President's greatest accomplishments.* **2** C1 [C, U] a skill or special ability: *Drawing and singing were among her many accomplishments.* ◇ *a poet of rare accomplishment* **3** C1 [U] (formal) the successful completing of sth: *Money will be crucial to the accomplishment of our objectives.*

**ac·cord** /əˈkɔːd; NAmE əˈkɔːrd/ noun, verb
■ **noun** a formal agreement between two organizations, countries, etc: *The two sides signed a* **peace accord** *last July.* ⇒ WORDFINDER NOTE at ALLY
IDM **in accord (with sth/sb)** (formal) in agreement with: *This action would not be in accord with our policy.* **of your own accord** without being asked, forced or helped: *He came back of his own accord.* ◇ *The symptoms will clear up of their own accord.* **with one accord** (BrE, formal) if people do sth **with one accord**, they do it at the same time, because they agree with each other
■ **verb** [T] (formal) to give sb/sth authority, status or a particular type of treatment: ~ **sth to sb/sth** *Our society accords great importance to the family.* ◇ ~ **sb/sth sth** *Our society accords the family great importance.*
PHRV **acˈcord with sth** to agree with or match sth: *These results accord closely with our predictions.*

**ac·cord·ance** C1 /əˈkɔːdns; NAmE əˈkɔːrd-/ noun
IDM **in accordance with sth** C1 (formal) according to a rule or the way that sb says that sth should be done: *in accordance with legal requirements*

**ac·cord·ing·ly** C1 W /əˈkɔːdɪŋli; NAmE əˈkɔːrd-/ adv. **1** C1 in a way that is appropriate to what has been done or said in a particular situation: *We have to discover his plans and act accordingly.* **2** C1 (used especially at the beginning of a sentence) for that reason SYN **therefore**: *The cost of materials rose sharply last year. Accordingly, we were forced to increase our prices.*

**ac·cord·ing to** ❶ A2 ◉ /əˈkɔːdɪŋ tə, before vowels tu; NAmE əˈkɔːrd-/ prep. **1** A2 as stated or reported by sb/sth: *According to Mick, it's a great movie.* ◇ *You've been absent six times according to our records.* ⇒ LANGUAGE BANK at ILLUSTRATE **2** B2 following, agreeing with or depending on sth: *The work was done according to her instructions.* ◇ *Everything went according to plan.* ◇ *The salary will be fixed according to qualifications and experience.* IDM see COAT n.

▼ **LANGUAGE BANK**

**according to**

Reporting someone's opinion

- Photography is, **according to** Vidal, the art form of untalented people.
- **For** Vidal, photography is the art form of untalented people.
- His **view is that** photography is not art but merely the mechanical reproduction of images.
- Smith **takes the view that** photography is both an art and a science.
- **In** Brown's **view**, photography should be treated as a legitimate art in its own right.
- James **is of the opinion that** a good painter can always be a good photographer if he or she so decides.
- Emerson **believed that** a photograph should only reflect what the human eye can see.

⇒ LANGUAGE BANK at ARGUE, OPINION

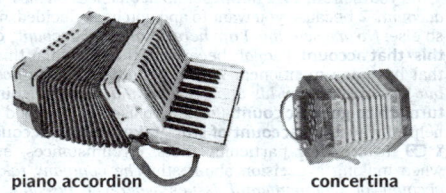

piano accordion     concertina

**ac·cor·dion** /əˈkɔːdiən; NAmE əˈkɔːrd-/ noun a musical instrument that you hold in both hands to produce sounds. You press the two ends together and pull them apart and press buttons and/or keys to produce the different notes. ⇒ see also PIANO ACCORDION

**ac·cost** /əˈkɒst; NAmE əˈkɔːst/ verb ~ **sb** (formal) to go up to sb and speak to them, especially in a way that is rude or frightening: *She was accosted in the street by a complete stranger.*

**ac·count** ❶ B1 ◉ /əˈkaʊnt/ noun, verb
■ **noun**
• **AT BANK** **1** C1 (abbr. **a/c** especially in BrE, NAmE usually **acct.**) an arrangement that sb has with a bank, etc. to keep money there, take some out, etc: *I don't have a bank*

# accountability

*account.* ◊ *I paid the money into my savings account.* ◊ *a joint account* (= one in the name of more than one person) ◊ *~ with sb/sth Do you have an account with us?* ◊ *at sth He opened an account at a bank in Germany.* ⬈ WORDFINDER NOTE at BANK ⬈ see also BANK ACCOUNT, CHECKING ACCOUNT, CURRENT ACCOUNT, DEPOSIT ACCOUNT, SAVINGS ACCOUNT
- COMPUTING **2** [B2] an arrangement that sb has with a company that allows them to use the internet, send and receive messages by email, social media, etc: *an email/a Twitter account*
- DESCRIPTION **3** [B2] a written or spoken description of sth that has happened: *an eyewitness account* (= a description given by sb who saw what happened) ◊ *~ of sth Can you give us an account of what happened?* ⬈ SYNONYMS at REPORT **4** *~ (of sth)* an explanation or a description of an idea, a theory or a process: *the Biblical account of the creation of the world*
- BUSINESS RECORDS **5** [usually pl.] a written record of money that is owed to a business and of money that has been paid by it: *to do the accounts* ◊ *the accounts department* ◊ *She works in Accounts* (= the accounts department). ⬈ see also EXPENSE ACCOUNT, PROFIT AND LOSS ACCOUNT
- WITH SHOP **6** (*BrE also* **credit account**) (*NAmE also* **charge account**) an arrangement with a shop or business to pay bills for goods or services at a later time, for example in regular amounts every month: *Put it on my account please.* ◊ *We have accounts with most of our suppliers.* ⬈ SYNONYMS at BILL ⬈ see also CHARGE ACCOUNT, CREDIT ACCOUNT
- BILL **7** (*BrE*) a bill for goods or services provided over a period: *Departing guests should settle their accounts at the office.*
- REGULAR CUSTOMER **8** (*business*) a regular customer: *The agency has lost several of its most important accounts.*

**IDM** **by/from all accounts** according to what other people say: *I've never been there, but it's a lovely place, by all accounts.* **by your own account** according to what you say yourself: *By his own account he had an unhappy childhood.* **give a good ac'count of yourself** (*BrE*) to do sth or perform well, especially in a contest: *The team gave a good account of themselves in the match.* **of no/little ac'count** (*formal*) not important **on account** if you buy sth or pay **on account**, you pay nothing or only a small amount immediately and the rest later **on sb's account** because of what you think sb wants: *Please don't change your plans on my account.* **on account of sb/sth** because of sb/sth: *She retired early on account of ill health.* ⬈ LANGUAGE BANK at BECAUSE OF **on no account | not on any account** (used to emphasize sth) not for any reason: *On no account should the house be left unlocked.* **on your own ac'count 1** for yourself: *In 2012 Smith set up in business on his own account.* **2** because you want to and you have decided, not sb else: *No one sent me. I am here on my own account.* **on this/that account** (*formal*) because of the particular thing that has been mentioned: *Weather conditions were poor, but he did not delay his departure on that account.* **put/turn sth to good ac'count** (*formal*) to use sth in a good or helpful way **take account of sth | take sth into account** [B2] to consider particular facts, circumstances, etc. when making a decision about sth: *The company takes account of environmental issues wherever possible.* ◊ *Coursework is taken into account as well as exam results.* ⬈ more at BLOW *n.*, CALL *v.*, SETTLE *v.*

■ *verb* [usually passive] (*formal*) to have the opinion that sb/sth is a particular thing: **be accounted + adj**. *In English law a person is accounted innocent until they are proved guilty.* ◊ **be accounted + noun** *The event was accounted a success.*

**IDM** **there's no accounting for 'taste** (*saying*) used to say how difficult it is to understand why sb likes sb/sth that you do not like at all: *She thinks he's wonderful—oh well, there's no accounting for taste.*

**PHRV** **ac'count for sth 1** [B2] to be the explanation or cause of sth **SYN** **explain**: *The poor weather may have accounted for the small crowd.* ◊ *Oh well, that accounts for it* (= I understand now why it happened). **2** [B2] to give

an explanation of sth **SYN** **explain**: *How do you account for the show's success?* **3** [B2] to be a particular amount or part of sth: *The Japanese market accounts for 35 per cent of the company's revenue.* ⬈ LANGUAGE BANK at PROPORTION **ac'count for sb/sth 1** to know where sb/sth is or what has happened to them, especially after an accident: *All passengers have now been accounted for.* **2** (*informal*) to defeat or destroy sb/sth: *Our anti-aircraft guns accounted for five enemy bombers.* **ac'count for sth (to sb)** to give a record of how the money in your care has been spent: *We have to account for every penny we spend on business trips.*

**ac·count·abil·ity** [+ C1] **W** /əˌkaʊntəˈbɪləti/ *noun* [U] (*formal*) the fact of being responsible for your decisions or actions and expected to explain them when you are asked: *~ (of sb) (to sb) the accountability of a company's directors to the shareholders*

**ac·count·able** [+ C1] /əˈkaʊntəbl/ *adj.* [not usually before noun] responsible for your decisions or actions and expected to explain them when you are asked: *~ to sb Politicians are ultimately accountable to the voters.* ◊ *for sth Someone must be held accountable for the killings.* ⬈ compare UNACCOUNTABLE

**ac·count·ancy** /əˈkaʊntənsi/ *noun* [U] the work or profession of an accountant

**ac·count·ant** [+ B2] /əˈkaʊntənt/ *noun* a person whose job is to keep or check financial accounts ⬈ WORDFINDER NOTE at BUSINESSMAN ⬈ see also CHARTERED ACCOUNTANT, CERTIFIED PUBLIC ACCOUNTANT

**ac'count executive** *noun* a business person, especially one working in advertising, marketing or PUBLIC RELATIONS, who is responsible for dealing with one of the company's regular customers

**ac·count·ing** /əˈkaʊntɪŋ/ *noun* [U] the process or work of keeping financial accounts: *a career in accounting* ◊ *accounting methods* ⬈ see also CREATIVE ACCOUNTING

**ac,counts 'payable** *noun* [pl.] (*business*) money that is owed by a company; the department of the company that deals with paying this money

**ac,counts re'ceivable** *noun* [pl.] (*business*) money that is owed to a company; the department of a company that deals with this money, sending out INVOICES, etc.

**ac·coutre·ments** /əˈkuːtrəmənts/ (*US also* **ac·couter·ments** /əˈkuːtəmənts/; *NAmE also* -tərm-/) *noun* [pl.] (*formal or humorous*) pieces of equipment that you need for a particular activity

**ac·credit** /əˈkredɪt/ *verb* **1** [usually passive] (*formal*) to believe that sb is responsible for doing or saying sth: **be accredited to sb** *The discovery of distillation is usually accredited to the Arabs of the 11th century.* ◊ **be accredited with sth** *The Arabs are usually accredited with the discovery of distillation.* **2** [usually passive] (*specialist*) to choose sb for an official position, especially as an AMBASSADOR: **be accredited to ...** *He was accredited to Madrid.* **3** **~sth/sb** to officially approve sth/sb as being of an accepted quality or standard: *Institutions that do not meet the standards will not be accredited for teacher training.*

**ac·cred·it·ation** /əˌkredɪˈteɪʃn/ *noun* [U] official approval given by an organization stating that sb/sth has achieved a required standard: *a letter of accreditation*

**ac·cred·it·ed** /əˈkredɪtɪd/ *adj.* [usually before noun] **1** (of a person) officially recognized as sth; with official permission to be sth: *our accredited representative* ◊ *Only accredited journalists were allowed entry.* **2** officially approved as being of an accepted quality or standard: *a fully accredited school/university/course*

**ac·cre·tion** /əˈkriːʃn/ *noun* (*specialist or formal*) **1** [C] a layer of a substance or a piece of matter that is slowly added to sth **2** [U] the process of new layers or matter being slowly added to sth

**ac·crue** /əˈkruː/ *verb* (*formal*) **1** [I] to increase over a period of time: *Interest will accrue if you keep your money in a savings account.* ◊ *~ (to sb) (from sth) economic benefits accruing to the country from tourism* **2** [T] *~ sth* to allow a sum of money or debts to grow over a period of time **SYN** **accumulate**: *The firm had accrued debts of over $6m.* ▸ **ac·crual** /-əl/ *noun* [U, C]: *the accrual of interest*

**acct.** *abbr.* (*NAmE*) (in writing) account (= an arrangement that sb has with a bank, etc. to keep money there)

**ac·cul·tur·ate** /əˈkʌltʃəreɪt/ *verb* [I, T] ~ **(sb) (to sth)** (*formal*) to learn to live successfully in a different culture; to help sb to do this ▸ **ac·cul·tur·ation** /əˌkʌltʃəˈreɪʃn/ *noun* [U]

**ac·cu·mu·late** /əˈkjuːmjəleɪt/ *verb* **1** [T] ~ **sth** to gradually get more and more of sth over a period of time SYN **amass**: *I seem to have accumulated a lot of books.* ◊ *By investing wisely she accumulated a fortune.* ⇒ SYNONYMS at COLLECT **2** [I] to gradually increase in number or quantity over a period of time SYN **build up**: *Debts began to accumulate.* ⇒ SYNONYMS at COLLECT

**ac·cu·mu·la·tion** /əˌkjuːmjəˈleɪʃn/ *noun* **1** [U] the process of gradually increasing or getting more and more of sth over a period of time: *the accumulation of wealth* **2** [C] an amount of sth that has gradually increased over a period of time: *an accumulation of toxic chemicals*

**ac·cu·mu·la·tive** /əˈkjuːmjələtɪv/ *adj.* (*formal*) growing by increasing gradually: *the accumulative effects of pollution*

**ac·cu·mu·la·tor** /əˈkjuːmjəleɪtə(r)/ *noun* **1** (*computing*) a section of a computer that is used for storing the results of what has been calculated **2** (*BrE*) (*NAmE* **storage battery**) a large battery that you can fill with electrical power (= that you can RECHARGE) **3** (*BrE*) a bet on a series of races or other events, where the money won or originally bet is placed on the next race, etc.

**ac·cur·acy** /ˈækjərəsi/ *noun* (*pl.* **-ies**) **1** [U] the state of being exact or correct; the ability to do sth with skill and without making mistakes: *They questioned the accuracy of the information in the file.* ◊ *She hits the ball with great accuracy.* OPP **inaccuracy 2** [U, C] the degree to which a measurement, CALCULATION, etc. is exact or correct: *the accuracy of radiocarbon dating* ◊ *to achieve accuracies of 50–70 per cent*

**ac·cur·ate** /ˈækjərət/ *adj.* **1** correct and true in every detail: *an accurate description/picture of sth* ◊ *Accurate measurements are essential.* ◊ *The film is not historically accurate.* **2** able to give completely correct information or to do sth in an exact way: *a highly accurate electronic compass* ◊ *My watch is not very accurate.* **3** *an accurate throw, shot, weapon, etc. hits or reaches the thing that it was aimed at*: *There were only two accurate shots on goal.* OPP **inaccurate**

**ac·cur·ate·ly** /ˈækjərətli/ *adv.* **1** in a way that is correct and true in every detail: *The article accurately reflects public opinion.* **2** in an exact way: *Quantities must be measured accurately.* **3** hitting or reaching the thing that was aimed at: *You need to hit the ball accurately.*

**ac·cursed** /əˈkɜːsɪd, əˈkɜːst; *NAmE* əˈkɜːrsɪd, əˈkɜːrst/ *adj.* (*old-fashioned*) having a CURSE (= a bad magic SPELL) on it

**ac·cus·ation** /ˌækjuˈzeɪʃn/ *noun* [C, U] a statement saying that you think a person is guilty of doing sth wrong or illegal; the fact of accusing sb: *I don't want to make an accusation until I have some proof.* ◊ *There was a hint of accusation in her voice.* ◊ **~ of sth** *accusations of corruption/cruelty/racism* ◊ **~ against sb** *No one believed her wild accusations against her husband.* ◊ **~ that …** *He denied the accusation that he had ignored the problems.*

**ac·cusa·tive** /əˈkjuːzətɪv/ *noun* (*grammar*) (in some languages) the form of a noun, a pronoun or an adjective when it is the DIRECT OBJECT of a verb, or connected with the DIRECT OBJECT: *In the sentence, 'I saw him today', the word 'him' is in the accusative.* ⇒ compare DATIVE, GENITIVE, INSTRUMENTAL (2), LOCATIVE, NOMINATIVE, VOCATIVE ▸ **ac·cusa·tive** *adj.*

**ac·cusa·tory** /əˈkjuːzətəri, ˌækjuˈzeɪtəri; *NAmE* əˈkjuːzətɔːri/ *adj.* (*formal*) suggesting that you think sb has done sth wrong

11

**ac·cuse** /əˈkjuːz/ *verb* to say that sb has done sth wrong or is guilty of sth: **~ sb of sth** *to accuse sb of murder/a crime* ◊ **~ sb of doing sth** *She accused him of lying.* ◊ *to be falsely/wrongly/unjustly accused of sth* ◊ (*formal*) *They stand accused of crimes against humanity.* ⇒ WORDFINDER NOTE at TRIAL ▸ **ac·cuser** *noun*: *He demanded the right to face his accusers at a public hearing.*

**the ac·cused** /ði əˈkjuːzd/ *ncun* (*pl.* **the ac·cused**) a person who is on trial for committing a crime: *The accused was found innocent.* ◊ *All the accused have pleaded guilty.* ⇒ compare DEFENDANT

**ac·cus·ing** /əˈkjuːzɪŋ/ *adj.* showing that you think sb has done sth wrong: *an accusing look/finger/tone* ◊ *Her accusing eyes were fixed on him.* ▸ **ac·cus·ing·ly** *adv.*

**ac·cus·tom** /əˈkʌstəm/ *verb*
PHRV **acˈcustom yourself / sb to sth** to make yourself/sb familiar with sth or become used to it: *It took him a while to accustom himself to the idea.*

**ac·cus·tomed** /əˈkʌstəmd/ *adj.* **1** (*rather formal*) familiar with sth and accepting it as normal or usual SYN **used to**: **~ to sth** *to become/get accustomed tc sth* ◊ *My eyes slowly grew accustomed to the dark.* ◊ **~ to doing sth** *She was a person accustomed to having eight hours' sleep a night.* **2** [usually before noun] (*formal*) usual SYN **habitual**: *He took his accustomed seat by the fire.* OPP **unaccustomed**

**ace** /eɪs/ *noun, adj., verb*
■ *noun* **1** a PLAYING CARD with a large single symbol on it, which has either the highest or the lowest value in a particular card game: *the ace of spades/hearts/diamonds/clubs* ⇒ WORDFINDER NOTE at CARD **2** (*informal*) a person who is very good at doing sth: *a soccer/flying ace* ◊ *an ace marksman* **3** (in tennis) a SERVE (= the first hit) that is so good that your opponent cannot reach the ball: *He served 20 aces in the match.*
IDM **an ace up your ˈsleeve** (*BrE*) (*NAmE* **an ace in the ˈhole**) (*informal*) a secret advantage, for example a piece of information or a skill, that you are ready to use if you need to **hold all the aces** to have all the advantages in a situation **play your ˈace** to use your best argument, etc. in order to get an advantage in a situation **within an ace of sth/of doing sth** (*BrE*) very close to sth: *We came within an ace of victory.*
■ *adj.* (*informal*) very good: *We had an ace time.*
■ *verb* ~ **sth** (*informal, especially NAmE*) to be successful in sth: *He aced all his tests.*

**acer** /ˈeɪsə(r)/ *noun* [C, U] a tree or plant that is often grown for its attractive leaves and bright autumn colours

**acerb·ic** /əˈsɜːbɪk; *NAmE* əˈsɜːrb-/ *adj.* (*formal*) (of a person or what they say) critical in a direct and rather cruel way: *The letter was written in her usual acerbic style.* ▸ **acerb·ity** /-bəti/ *noun* [U]

**acet·amino·phen** /əˌsiːtəˈmɪnəfen; *NAmE* (*BrE* **paracetamol**) *noun* [U, C] a drug used to reduce pain and high temperature

**acet·ate** /ˈæsɪteɪt/ *noun* **1** [U] a chemical made from ACETIC ACID, used in making plastics, etc. **2** [U] a chemical used to make FIBRES that are used to make clothes, etc. **3** [C] a clear plastic sheet that you can write or print sth on and show on a screen using an OVERHEAD PROJECTOR

**acet·ic acid** /əˌsiːtɪk ˈæsɪd/ *noun* [U] the ACID in VINEGAR that gives it its taste and smell

**acet·one** /ˈæsɪtəʊn/ *noun* [U] a clear liquid with a strong smell used for cleaning things, making paint thinner and producing various chemicals

**acetyl·ene** /əˈsetəliːn/ *noun* (*also* **eth·yne**) *noun* [U] (*symb.* $C_2H_2$) a gas that burns with a very hot bright flame, used for cutting or joining metal

**ach** /ɑːx/ *exclamation* (*ScotE*) used to express the fact that you are surprised, sorry, etc.

---

**O** Oxford Phrasal Academic Lexicon (OPAL) written and spoken word lists | **W** OPAL written word list | **S** OPAL spoken word list

**ach·cha** /ˈætʃɑː; NAmE ˈɑːtʃɑː/ exclamation (IndE, informal) **1** used to show that the speaker agrees with, accepts, understands, etc. sth: *Achcha! We'll meet at eight.* **2** used to express surprise, happiness, etc.

**ache** /eɪk/ verb, noun
- **verb** [I] **1** to feel a continuous pain that is not severe SYN **hurt**: *I'm aching all over.* ◇ *~ from sth Her eyes ached from lack of sleep.* ◇ *(figurative) It makes my heart ache (= it makes me sad)* ⇒ *to see her suffer.* ⇒ SYNONYMS at HURT **2** (formal) to have a strong desire for sb/sth or to do sth SYN **long**: *~ for sb/sth I was aching for home.* ◇ *~ to do sth He ached to see her.*
- **noun** (often in compounds) a continuous feeling of pain in a part of the body: *Mummy, I've got a tummy ache.* ◇ *Muscular aches and pains can be soothed by a relaxing massage.* ◇ *(figurative) an ache in my heart (= a continuous sad feeling)* ⇒ see also ACHY, BACKACHE, BELLYACHE *noun*, HEADACHE, HEARTACHE, STOMACH ACHE, TOOTHACHE

**achieve** ⓘ A2 ⓦ /əˈtʃiːv/ verb **1** ⓘ A2 [T] *~ sth* to succeed in reaching a particular goal, status or standard, especially by making an effort for a long time SYN **attain**: *He had finally achieved success.* ◇ *They have both achieved great results.* ◇ *She has worked hard to achieve her goal.* ◇ *to achieve an objective/aim* **2** [T] *~ sth* to succeed in doing sth or causing sth to happen SYN **accomplish**: *I haven't achieved very much today.* ◇ *All you've achieved is to upset my parents.* **3** [I] to be successful: *Their background gives them little chance of achieving at school.* ⇒ see also OVERACHIEVE, UNDERACHIEVE ▸ **achiev·able** adj.: *Profits of $20m look achievable.* ◇ *achievable goals* OPP **unachievable**

**achieve·ment** ⓘ B1 ⓦ /əˈtʃiːvmənt/ noun **1** ⓘ B1 [C] a thing that sb has done successfully, especially using their own effort and skill: *the greatest scientific achievement of the decade* ◇ *sporting/artistic/academic achievements* ◇ *It was a remarkable achievement for such a young player.* ◇ *an outstanding achievement* **2** B1 [U] the act or process of achieving sth: *the need to raise standards of academic/educational achievement* ◇ *Even a small success gives you a sense of achievement (= a feeling of pride).* **3** [C] a reward that you can earn in some video games by completing a challenge or level

**achiever** /əˈtʃiːvə(r)/ noun **1** a person who achieves a high level of success, especially in their career **2** (after an adjective) a person who achieves the particular level of success that is stated: *a low achiever*

**Achil·les heel** /əˌkɪliːz ˈhiːl/ noun [usually sing.] a weak point or fault in sb's character, which can be attacked by other people ⇒ compare ACHILLES TENDON ORIGIN Named after the Greek hero **Achilles**. When he was a small child, his mother held him below the surface of the river Styx to protect him against any injury. She held him by his heel, which therefore was not touched by the water. Achilles died after being wounded by an arrow in the heel.

**A·chilles 'tendon** (also **Achil·les** /əˈkɪliːz/) noun the TENDON that connects the muscles at the back of the lower part of the leg to the heel ⇒ compare ACHILLES HEEL

**ach·ing·ly** /ˈeɪkɪŋli/ adv. (literary) (of qualities or feelings) very great and affecting you deeply: *an achingly beautiful song*

**ach·kan** /ˈæʃkən/ noun a piece of men's clothing that reaches to the knees, with buttons down the front, worn in South Asia

**achoo** /əˈtʃuː/ exclamation = ATISHOO

**achy** /ˈeɪki/ adj. (informal) suffering from a continuous slight pain: *I feel all achy.* ◇ *an achy back*

**acid** ⓘ+ B2 /ˈæsɪd/ noun, adj.
- **noun 1** ⓘ+ B2 [U, C] (chemistry) a chemical, usually a liquid, that contains HYDROGEN and has a PH of less than seven. The HYDROGEN can be replaced by a metal to form a salt. Acids usually have a bitter sharp taste and can often burn holes in or damage things they touch. ⇒ compare ALKALI ⇒ WORDFINDER NOTE at CHEMISTRY ⇒ see also ACETIC ACID, AMINO ACID, ASCORBIC ACID, CITRIC ACID, FATTY ACID, FOLIC ACID, FORMIC ACID, HYDROCHLORIC ACID, LACTIC ACID, NITRIC ACID, NUCLEIC ACID, SULPHURIC ACID **2** [U] (slang) = LSD
- **adj. 1** ⓘ+ C1 (specialist) that contains acid or has the essential characteristics of an acid; that has a PH of less than seven: *Rye is tolerant of poor, acid soils.* ⇒ compare ALKALINE **2** ⓘ+ C1 that has a bitter sharp taste SYN **sour**: *acid fruit* ⇒ SYNONYMS at BITTER **3** (of a person's remarks) critical and unkind SYN **sarcastic, cutting**: *an acid wit*

**'acid house** noun [U] a type of electronic music with a strong steady beat, popular in the 1980s, often played at parties where some people take harmful drugs

**acid·ic** /əˈsɪdɪk/ adj. **1** having a very bitter sharp taste: *Some fruit juices are very acidic.* **2** containing ACID: *acidic soil*

**acid·ify** /əˈsɪdɪfaɪ/ verb [I, T] (acid·ifies, acid·ify·ing, acid·ified, acid·ified) ~ (sth) (specialist) to become or make sth become an ACID

**acid·ity** /əˈsɪdəti/ noun [U] the state of having a bitter sharp taste or of containing ACID

**acid 'jazz** noun [U] a type of dance music that combines jazz, FUNK, SOUL, and HIP-HOP

**acid·ly** /ˈæsɪdli/ adv. in an unpleasant or critical way: *'Thanks for nothing,' she said acidly.*

**acid 'rain** noun [U] rain that contains harmful chemicals from factory gases and that damages trees, crops and buildings

**acid 'test** (also **'litmus test**) noun [sing.] a way of deciding whether sth is successful or true: *The acid test of a good driver is whether he or she remains calm in an emergency.*

**ackee** (also **akee**) /ˈæki/ noun **1** [C] a type of tree that produces bright red fruit, originally from West Africa **2** [U] the fruit from this tree, which is poisonous to eat unless it is completely RIPE

**ac·know·ledge** ⓘ B2 ⓦ /əkˈnɒlɪdʒ; NAmE -ˈnɑːl-/ verb
- ADMIT **1** ⓘ B2 to accept that sth is true: *~ sth She refuses to acknowledge the need for reform.* ◇ *I have to acknowledge the fact that I am partly responsible.* ◇ *~ that … He does not acknowledge that he has done anything wrong.* ◇ *~ sth to be, have, etc. sth It is generally acknowledged to be true.* ⇒ SYNONYMS at ADMIT
- ACCEPT STATUS **2** ⓘ B2 to accept that sb/sth has a particular authority or status SYN **recognize**: *~ sb/sth The country acknowledged his claim to the throne.* ◇ *be acknowledged as sth He is widely acknowledged as the best player in the world.* ◇ *be acknowledged to be, have, etc. sth He is widely acknowledged to be the best player in the world.*
- REPLY TO LETTER/EMAIL **3** *~ sth* (formal) to tell sb that you have received sth that they sent to you: *All applications will be acknowledged.* ◇ *Please acknowledge receipt of this letter.*
- SMILE/WAVE **4** *~ sb/sth* (formal) to show that you have noticed sb/sth by smiling, waving, etc: *I was standing right next to her, but she didn't even acknowledge me.*
- EXPRESS THANKS **5** *~ sth* (formal) to publicly express thanks for help you have been given: *I gratefully acknowledge financial support from several local businesses.*

**ac·know·ledge·ment** (also **ac·know·ledg·ment**) /əkˈnɒlɪdʒmənt; NAmE -ˈnɑːl-/ noun **1** [sing., U] an act of accepting that sth exists or is true, or that sth is there: *This report is an acknowledgement of the size of the problem.* ◇ *She gave me a smile of acknowledgement (= showed that she had seen and recognized me).* **2** [C, U] an act or a statement expressing thanks to sb; something that is given to sb as thanks: *The flowers were a small acknowledgement of your kindness.* ◇ *I was sent a free copy in acknowledgement of my contribution.* **3** [C] a letter or an email saying that sth has been received: *I didn't receive an acknowledgement of my application.* **4** [C, usually pl.] a statement, especially at the beginning of a book, in which the writer expresses thanks to the people who have helped

**ac,knowledgement of 'country** (also **Acknowledgement of Country**) noun [sing., U] (in Australia) an act of formally recognizing the traditional Aboriginal owners of the land at an event such as a conference or festival, and in Parliament

**acme** /ˈækmi/ noun [usually sing.] (formal) the highest stage of development or the most excellent example of sth **SYN** height

**acne** /ˈækni/ noun [U] a skin condition, common among young people, that produces many PIMPLES (= spots), especially on the face and neck: *to suffer from/have acne*

**aco·lyte** /ˈækəlaɪt/ noun **1** (formal) a person who follows and helps a leader **2** (specialist) a person who helps a priest in some church ceremonies

**acorn** /ˈeɪkɔːn; NAmE -kɔːrn/ noun the small brown nut of the OAK tree, that grows in a base that is like a cup ⸰ VISUAL VOCAB page V6 **IDM** see OAK

**acous·tic** /əˈkuːstɪk/ (NAmE also **acous·tic·al** /əˈkuːstɪkl/) adj. **1** related to sound or to the sense of hearing **2** [usually before noun] (of a musical instrument or performance) designed to make natural sound, not sound AMPLIFIED (= made louder) by electrical equipment ▶ **acous·tic·al·ly** /-kli/ adv.

**acous·tics** /əˈkuːstɪks/ noun **1** [pl.] (also **acoustic** [sing.]) the shape, design, etc. of a room or theatre that make it good or bad for carrying sound: *The acoustics of the new concert hall are excellent.* **2** [U] the scientific study of sound

**ac·quaint** /əˈkweɪnt/ verb ~ **sb/yourself with sth** (formal) to make sb/yourself familiar with or aware of sth: *Please acquaint me with the facts of the case.* ◇ *You will first need to acquaint yourself with the filing system.*

**ac·quaint·ance** /əˈkweɪntəns/ noun **1** [C] a person that you know but who is not a close friend: *Claire has a wide circle of friends and acquaintances.* ⸰ WORDFINDER NOTE at FRIEND **2** [U, C] ~ **(with sb)** (formal) slight friendship: *He hoped their acquaintance would develop further.* **3** [U, C] ~**with sth** (formal) knowledge of sth: *I had little acquaintance with modern poetry.*
**IDM** **make sb's acquaintance | make the acquaintance of sb** (formal) to meet sb for the first time: *I am delighted to make your acquaintance, Mrs Baker.* ◇ *I made the acquaintance of several musicians around that time.* **of your ac'quaintance** (formal) that you know: *No one else of my acquaintance was as rich or successful.* **on first ac'quaintance** (formal) when you first meet sb: *Even on first acquaintance it was clear that he was not 'the right type'.*

**ac·quaint·ed** /əˈkweɪntɪd/ adj. [not before noun] **1** ~ **with sth** (formal) familiar with sth, having read, seen or experienced it: *The students are already acquainted with the work of Shakespeare.* ◇ *Employees should be fully acquainted with emergency procedures.* **2** not close friends with sb, but having met a few times before: *We got acquainted at the conference* (= met and started to get to know each other). ◇ ~**with sb** *I am well acquainted with her family.*

**ac·qui·esce** /ˌækwiˈes/ verb [I] ~ **(in/to sth)** (formal) to accept sth without arguing, even if you do not really agree with it: *Senior government figures must have acquiesced in the cover-up.*

**ac·qui·es·cence** /ˌækwiˈesns/ noun [U] (formal) the fact of being willing to do what sb wants and to accept their opinions, even if you are not sure that they are right: *There was general acquiescence in the UN sanctions.* ▶ **ac·qui·es·cent** /-ˈesnt/ adj.

**ac·quire** ❶ **B2** ⓞ /əˈkwaɪə(r)/ verb (formal) **1** **B2** ~ **sth** to gain sth by your own efforts, ability or behaviour: *She has acquired a good knowledge of English.* ◇ *How long will it take to acquire the necessary skills?* ◇ *I would love to apply the newly acquired skills to a job that I enjoy.* **2** **B2** ~ **sth** to obtain sth by buying or being given it: *Not all of the land acquired for the road has been paid for yet.* ◇ *Austria has pledged not to acquire nuclear weapons.*
**IDM** **an acquired 'taste** a thing that you do not like much at first but gradually learn to like: *Abstract art is an acquired taste.*

13

**across**

**ac·qui·si·tion** ❶ **C1** ⓦ /ˌækwɪˈzɪʃn/ noun **1** ❶ **C1** [U] the act of getting sth, especially knowledge, a skill, etc.: *theories of child language acquisition* **2** ❶ **C1** [C] something that sb buys to add to what they already own, usually sth valuable: *His latest acquisition is a racehorse.* **3** ❶ **C1** [C, U] (business) a company, piece of land, etc. bought by sb, especially another company; the act of buying it: *They have made acquisitions in several EU countries.* ◇ *the acquisition of shares by employees* ⸰ WORDFINDER NOTE at DEAL

**ac·quisi·tive** /əˈkwɪzətɪv/ adj. (formal, disapproving or business) wanting very much to buy or get new possessions ▶ **ac·quisi·tive·ness** noun [U]

**ac·quit** /əˈkwɪt/ verb (-tt-) **1** ~ **sb (of sth)** to decide and state officially in court that sb is not guilty of a crime: *The jury acquitted him of murder.* **OPP** convict **2** ~ **yourself well, badly, etc.** (formal) to perform or behave well, badly, etc: *He acquitted himself brilliantly in the exams.*

**ac·quit·tal** /əˈkwɪtl/ noun [C, U] an official decision in court that a person is not guilty of a crime: *The case resulted in an acquittal.* ◇ *The jury voted for acquittal.* **OPP** conviction

**acre** ❶ **C1** /ˈeɪkə(r)/ noun (in Britain and North America) a unit for measuring an area of land; 4840 square yards or about 4050 square metres: *3000 acres of parkland* ◇ *a three-acre wood* ◇ (informal) *Each house has acres of space around it* (= a lot of space).

**acre·age** /ˈeɪkərɪdʒ/ noun [U, C] an area of land measured in ACRES

**acrid** /ˈækrɪd/ adj. having a strong, bitter smell or taste that is unpleasant **SYN** pungent: *acrid smoke from burning tyres* ⸰ SYNONYMS at BITTER

**acri·mo·ni·ous** /ˌækrɪˈməʊniəs/ adj. (formal) (of an argument, etc.) angry and full of strong bitter feelings and words **SYN** bitter: *His parents went through an acrimonious divorce.* ▶ **acri·mo·ni·ous·ly** adv.

**acri·mony** /ˈækrɪməni; NAmE -məʊni/ noun [U] (formal) angry bitter feelings or words: *The dispute was settled without acrimony.*

**acro·bat** /ˈækrəbæt/ noun a person who performs difficult acts such as balancing on high ropes, especially at a CIRCUS

**acro·bat·ic** /ˌækrəˈbætɪk/ adj. involving or performing difficult acts or movements with the body: *acrobatic feats* ◇ *an acrobatic dancer* ▶ **acro·bat·ic·al·ly** /-kli/ adv.

**acro·bat·ics** /ˌækrəˈbætɪks/ noun [pl.] acrobatic acts and movements: *acrobatics on the high wire* ◇ (figurative) *vocal acrobatics* (= performing skilfully with the voice when singing)

**acro·nym** /ˈækrənɪm/ noun a word formed from the first letters of the words that make up the name of sth, for example 'AIDS' is an acronym for 'acquired immune deficiency syndrome'

**acrop·olis** /əˈkrɒpəlɪs; NAmE əˈkrɑːp-/ noun (in an ancient Greek city) a castle, or an area that is designed to resist attack, especially one on top of a hill

**across** ❶ **A1** /əˈkrɒs; NAmE əˈkrɔːs/ prep., adv.
■ prep. **1** ❶ **A1** from one side to the other side of sth: *He walked across the field.* ◇ *I drew a line across the page.* ◇ *A grin spread across her face.* ◇ *Where's the nearest bridge across the river?* **2** ❶ **A1** on the other side of sth: *There's a bank right across the street.* **3** on or over a part of the body: *He hit him across the face.* ◇ *It's too tight across the back.* **4** in every part of a place, group of people, etc. **SYN** throughout: *Her family is scattered across the country.* ◇ *This view is common across all sections of the community.* **5** (BrE) knowing a lot about sth; covering or in control of sth: *We need someone who is across all the issues.*
■ adv. **HELP** For the special uses of **across** in phrasal verbs, look at the entries for the verbs. For example **come across** is in the phrasal verb section at come. **1** ❶ **A1** from one side to the other side: *It's too wide. We can't swim across.* ◇ *The yard measures about 50 feet across.* **2** ❶ **A2** in a particular direction towards or at sb/sth: *When my name was called,*

# acrostic 14

he looked across at me. **3** A2 **across from** opposite: *There's a school just across from our house.* **4** (of an answer in a CROSSWORD) written from side to side: *I can't do 3 across.*

**ac·ros·tic** /əˈkrɒstɪk; *NAmE* əˈkrɔːs-/ *noun* a poem or other piece of writing in which particular letters in each line, usually the first letters, can be read downwards to form a word or words

**acryla·mide** /əˈkrɪləmaɪd/ *noun* [U, C] a substance used in various industrial processes. Acrylamide is also found in food that has been cooked at high temperatures, and may be a cause of cancer.

**acryl·ic** /əˈkrɪlɪk/ *adj.*, *noun*
- *adj.* made of a substance produced by chemical processes from a type of ACID: *acrylic paints/fibres ◇ an acrylic sweater*
- *noun* **1** [U] a type of FIBRE produced by chemical processes, used to make clothes, etc. **2** [C, usually pl.] a type of paint used by artists

**ACT**™ /ˌeɪ siː ˈtiː/ *abbr.* American College Test (an exam that some HIGH SCHOOL students take before they go to college)

**act** 🔑 A2 Ⓦ /ækt/ *verb*, *noun*
- *verb*
- • DO STH **1** 🔑 A2 [I] to do sth for a particular purpose or in order to deal with a situation: *~ to do sth It is vital that we act to stop the destruction of the rainforests. ◇ + adv./prep. By acting quickly doctors saved her life. ◇ He claims he acted in self-defence.*
- • BEHAVE **2** 🔑 A2 [I] to behave in a particular way: *+ adv. The man was seen acting suspiciously. ◇ Decide what your priorities are and act accordingly* (= in an appropriate way). *◇ ~ like sb/sth Stop acting like spoilt children! ◇ ~ as if/though ... She was acting as if she'd seen a ghost.* HELP In spoken English people often use **like** instead of **as if** or **as though** in this meaning, especially in *NAmE*: *She was acting like she'd seen a ghost.* This is not considered correct in written *BrE*.
- • PERFORM IN PLAY/FILM **3** 🔑 A2 [I, T] to perform a part in a play or film: *Have you ever acted? ◇ Most of the cast act well. ◇ The play was well acted. ◇ Who's acting the part of Hamlet?*
- • PRETEND **4** 🔑 B2 [I] to pretend by your behaviour to be a particular type of person: *+ noun He's been acting the devoted husband all day. ◇ + adj. I decided to act dumb. ◇ to act weird/strange/normal/stupid* ⇒ see also PLAY-ACT
- • PERFORM FUNCTION **5** 🔑 B2 [I] to perform a particular role or function: *~ as sth She acted as an adviser to the committee. ◇ Can you act as interpreter? ◇ We hope this sentence will act as a deterrent to others. ◇ ~ like sth hormones in the brain that act like natural painkillers*
- • HAVE EFFECT **6** [I] *~(on sth)* to have an effect on sth: *Alcohol acts quickly on the brain.* IDM see AGE *n.*, FOOL *n.*, OWN *v.*
- PHRV ˈact for/on behalf of sb to be employed to deal with sb's affairs for them, for example by representing them in court ˈact on/upon sth to take action as a result of advice, information, etc: *Acting on information from a member of the public, the police raided the club. ◇ Why didn't you act on her suggestion?* ˌact sth↔ˈout **1** to perform a ceremony or show how sth happened, as if performing a play: *The ritual of the party conference is acted out in the same way every year.* ◇ *The children started to act out the whole incident.* **2** to act a part in a real situation: *She acted out the role of the wronged lover.* ˌact ˈup (*informal*) **1** to behave badly: *The kids started acting up.* **2** to not work as it should: *How long has your ankle been acting up?*
- *noun*
- • STH THAT SB DOES **1** 🔑 B1 [C] a particular thing that sb does: *a terrorist/criminal act ◇ ~ of sth an act of kindness ◇ acts of terrorism/terror/violence/aggression ◇ The murder was the act of a psychopath.* ⇒ SYNONYMS at ACTION ⇒ see also BALANCING ACT, SPEECH ACT
- • LAW **2** 🔑 B1 **Act** [C] a law that has been passed by a parliament: *an Act of Congress/Parliament ◇ the Care Act 2014 ◇ to pass/repeal/amend an Act ◇ under an~ A Committee on Safety of Medicines was set up under the Act.* ⇒ WORDFINDER NOTE at PARLIAMENT
- • PRETENDING **3** [sing.] a way of behaving that is not sincere but is intended to have a particular effect on others: *Don't take her seriously—it's all an act. ◇ You could tell she was just putting on an act.*
- • IN PLAY/ENTERTAINMENT **4** [C] one of the main divisions of a play, an OPERA, etc: *a play in five acts ◇ The hero dies in Act 5, Scene 3.* ⇒ WORDFINDER NOTE at PLAY **5** [C] a performance, especially one of several short pieces of entertainment in a show: *a circus/comedy/magic act* ⇒ see also DOUBLE ACT **6** [C] a performer or group of musicians: *They were one of rock's most impressive live acts.*
- IDM ˌact of ˈGod (*law*) an event caused by natural forces beyond human control, such as a storm, a flood or an earthquake **be/get in on the act** (*informal*) to be/become involved in an activity that sb else has started, especially to get sth for yourself **do, perform, stage a disapˌpearing/ˈvanishing act** (*informal*) to go away or be impossible to find when people need or want you **get your ˈact together** (*informal*) to organize yourself and your activities in a more effective way in order to achieve sth: *He needs to get his act together if he's going to pass.* **a ˌhard/ˌtough act to ˈfollow** a person or event that is so good or successful at sth that it will be difficult for anyone/anything else coming after them to be as good or successful **in the act (of doing sth)** while you are doing sth: *He was caught in the act of stealing a car.* ⇒ more at CLEAN *v.*, READ *v.*

**act·ing** /ˈæktɪŋ/ *noun*, *adj.*
- *noun* [U] the activity or profession of performing in plays, films, etc. ⇒ see also METHOD ACTING, PLAY-ACTING
- *adj.* [only before noun] doing the work of another person for a short time SYN **temporary**: *the acting manager*

**ac·tion** 🔑 A1 Ⓞ /ˈækʃn/ *noun*, *verb*
- *noun*
- • WHAT SB DOES **1** 🔑 A1 [U] the process of doing sth in order to make sth happen or to deal with a situation: *The time has come for action if these beautiful animals are to survive. ◇ Firefighters took action immediately to stop the blaze spreading. ◇ Divers were close at hand, ready to go into action if the stunt went wrong. ◇ What is the best course of action in the circumstances? ◇ She began to explain her plan of action to the group.* ⇒ see also AFFIRMATIVE ACTION **2** 🔑 A1 [C] a thing that sb does: *Each of us must take responsibility for our own actions.* ⇒ WORDFINDER NOTE at BEHAVIOUR
- • STOPPING WORK **3** 🔑 B2 [U, C] things that workers do, especially stopping work, to protest to their employers about sth: *Workers voted in favour of strike action.* ⇒ see also DIRECT ACTION, INDUSTRIAL ACTION
- • LEGAL PROCESS **4** 🔑 B2 [C, U] a legal process to stop a person or company from doing sth, or to make them pay for a mistake, etc: *A libel action is being brought against the magazine that published the article. ◇ ~ against sb/sth He is considering taking legal action against the hospital.* ⇒ see also CLASS ACTION, LEGAL ACTION
- • IN WAR **5** 🔑 B2 [U] fighting in a battle or war: *military action ◇ in~ soldiers killed in action*
- • IN STORY/PLAY **6** [U] the events in a story, play, etc: *The action takes place in France.* ⇒ see also LIVE ACTION, LIVE-ACTION
- • EXCITING EVENTS **7** [U] exciting events: *I like films with plenty of action. ◇ New York is where the action is.*
- • EFFECT **8** [U] *~ of sth (on sth)* the effect that sth such as a chemical has on sth: *the action of sunlight on the skin*
- • OF PART OF THE BODY **9** [U, C] (*specialist*) the way a part of the body moves or functions: *a study of the action of the liver*
- • OF MACHINE **10** [sing.] the MECHANICAL parts of a piano, gun, clock, etc. or the way the parts move ⇒ see also BOLT-ACTION, DOUBLE-ACTION, PUMP-ACTION
- IDM **actions speak louder than ˈwords** (*saying*) what a person actually does means more than what they say they will do **in ˈaction** 🔑 B2 if sb/sth is **in action**, they are doing

the activity or work that is typical for them: *Just press the button to see your favourite character in action.* ◊ *I've yet to see all the players in action.* **into 'action** if you put an idea or a plan **into action**, you start making it happen or work: *The new plan for traffic control is being put into action on an experimental basis.* **out of 'action** not able to work or be used because of injury or damage: *Jon will be out of action for weeks with a broken leg.* ◊ *The photocopier is out of action today.* **a ˌpiece/ˌslice of the 'action** (*informal*) a share or role in an interesting or exciting activity, especially one that makes money: *Foreign firms will all want a piece of the action if the new airport goes ahead.* ➔ more at EVASIVE, SPRING *v.*, SWING *v.*

■ *verb* ~ **sth** to make sure that sth is done or dealt with: *Your request will be actioned.*

▼ SYNONYMS
**action**
measure • step • act • move
These are all words for a thing that sb does.
**action** a thing that sb does: *Can you explain your actions?*
**measure** an official action that is done in order to achieve a particular aim: *Tougher measures against racism are needed.*
**step** one of a series of things that you do in order to achieve sth: *This was a first step towards a united Europe.*
**act** a thing that sb does: *an act of kindness*
ACTION OR ACT?
These two words have the same meaning but are used in different patterns. An **act** is usually followed by *of* and/or used with an adjective. **Action** is not usually used with *of* but is often used with *his, her, etc: a heroic act of bravery* ◊ *a heroic action of bravery* ◊ *his heroic actions/acts during the war.* **Action** often combines with *take* but **act** does not: *We shall take whatever acts are necessary.*
**move** (used especially in the media) an action that you do or need to do to achieve sth: *They are waiting for the results of the opinion polls before deciding their next move.*
PATTERNS
• to **take** action/measures/steps
• to **make** a step/move
• a **heroic/brave/daring** action/step/act/move

**ˈac·tion·able** /ˈækʃənəbl/ *adj.* **1** giving sb a legally acceptable reason to bring a case to court **2** that can be done or acted on: *The research is aimed at getting actionable solutions.*

**ˈac·tion·er** /ˈækʃənə(r)/ *noun* (*NAmE, informal*) = ACTION MOVIE

**ˈaction figure** *noun* a DOLL representing a soldier or a character from a film, TV show, etc.

**ˈaction film** *noun* (*BrE*) = ACTION MOVIE

**ˈaction group** *noun* (often as part of a name) a group that is formed to work for social or political change: *the Child Poverty Action Group*

**ˈAction Man**™ *noun* **1** a toy in the form of a man, often a soldier **2** a strong, active man: *The illness damaged his Action Man image.*

**ˈaction movie** (*BrE also* **ˈaction film**) (*also NAmE, informal* **ˈac·tion·er**) *noun* a film that has a lot of exciting action and adventure

**ˈaction-packed** *adj.* full of exciting events and activity: *an action-packed weekend*

**ˈaction point** *noun* a suggestion for action that must be taken, especially one that is made in a meeting

**ˈaction ˈreplay** *noun* (*BrE*) **1** [C, U] = INSTANT REPLAY **2** [C] an event or a situation that repeats sth that has happened before: *It was an action replay of the problems of his first marriage.*

**ˈaction research** *noun* [U] studies done by people doing a particular job or activity, especially in education, to improve the working methods of those involved

15 **actor**

**ˈaction ˌstations** *noun* [pl.] the positions to which soldiers go to be ready for fighting

**ac·ti·vate** ᵢ+ B2 /ˈæktɪveɪt/ *verb* ~ **sth** to make sth such as a device or chemical process start working: *The burglar alarm is activated by movement.* ◊ *The gene is activated by a specific protein.* ➔ see also VOICE-ACTIVATED

**ac·ti·vation** ᵢ+ C1 /ˌæktɪˈveɪʃn/ *noun* [U] the act of making sth such as a device or chemical process start working: *The activation of several target genes results in two major effects.* ◊ *to trigger/inhibit/block the activation of sth*

**ac·tive** ᵢ A2 ○ /ˈæktɪv/ *adj., noun*
■ *adj.*
• BUSY **1** ᵢ A2 always busy doing things, especially physical activities: *Staying physically active in later years can also keep you feeling younger.* ◊ *an active lifestyle* OPP **inactive**
• TAKING PART **2** ᵢ B1 involved in sth; making a determined effort and not leaving sth to happen by itself: *They were both politically active.* ◊ *his active involvement/participation in the arts* ◊ *an active role/part in sth* ◊ *an active participant/member* ◊ ~ **in (doing) sth** *The parents were active in campaigning against cuts to the education budget.* ◊ *They took active steps to prevent the spread of the disease.*
• DOING AN ACTIVITY **3** ᵢ B1 doing sth regularly; functioning: *sexually active teenagers* ◊ *These animals are active only at night.* ◊ *The virus is still active in the blood.* ◊ *an active volcano* (= likely to ERUPT) OPP **inactive** ➔ compare DORMANT
• LIVELY **4** lively and full of ideas: *That child has a very active imagination.*
• WORKING/IN USE **5** working; in use or able to be used: *The old watermill was active until 1960.* ◊ *Ensure the website URL is an active link.*
• CHEMICAL **6** having or causing a chemical effect: *What is the active ingredient in aspirin?* OPP **inactive**
• GRAMMAR **7** connected with a verb whose subject is the person or thing that performs the action: *In 'He was driving the car', the verb is active.* ➔ compare PASSIVE ▶ **ac·tive·ly** *adv.*: *Your proposal is being actively considered.* ◊ *She was actively looking for a job.*
■ *noun* (*also* **ˌactive ˈvoice**) [sing.] the form of a verb in which the subject is the person or thing that performs the action ➔ compare PASSIVE

**ˌactive ˈservice** (*especially BrE*) (*also* **ˌactive ˈduty** *especially in NAmE*) *noun* [U] taking part in military action as a member of the armed forces, especially during a war: **on** ~ *troops on active service*

**ac·tiv·ist** ᵢ+ C1 /ˈæktɪvɪst/ *noun* a person who works to achieve political or social change, especially as a member of an organization with particular aims: *human/civil/animal rights activists* ▶ **ac·tiv·ism** /-vɪzəm/ *noun* [U] ➔ see also JUDICIAL ACTIVISM

**ac·tiv·ity** ᵢ A1 ○ /ækˈtɪvəti/ *noun* (*pl.* **-ies**) **1** ᵢ A1 [C, usually pl.] a thing that you do for interest or pleasure: *leisure/outdoor/recreational activities* ◊ *The club provides a wide variety of activities including tennis, swimming and squash.* **2** ᵢ A1 [C, usually pl.] a thing that sb does in order to achieve a particular aim: *criminal/terrorist/illegal activities* ◊ *The book contains plenty of ideas for classroom activities.* ➔ see also DISPLACEMENT ACTIVITY **3** ᵢ B1 [U] a situation in which sth is happening or a lot of things are being done: *economic activity* ◊ *The streets were noisy and full of activity.* ◊ *Muscles contract and relax during physical activity.* ➔ compare INACTIVITY

**acˈtivity tracker** *noun* = FITNESS TRACKER

**actor** ᵢ A1 /ˈæktə(r)/ *noun* **1** ᵢ A1 a person who performs on the stage, on television or in films, especially as a profession: *Both lead actors* (= the ones who play the main parts) *are outstanding.* ◊ *a Hollywood actor* ➔ see also ACTRESS, METHOD ACTOR ➔ WORDFINDER NOTE at FILM

WORDFINDER audition, body double, cameo, cast, play, role, star, stuntman, understudy

**2** a person who plays a part, pretending by their behaviour to be a particular kind of person: *I don't know if he*

*really meant the things he said—he was always a good actor.* **3** (*formal*) a participant in an action or process: *Employers are key actors within industrial relations.*

**actor-ˈmanager** *noun* an actor who is in charge of a theatre company and acts in the plays that they perform

**acˈtress** 🔑 **A1** /ˈæktrəs/ *noun* **1** **A1** a woman who performs on the stage, on television or in films, especially as a profession: *We will hold auditions to find a talented young actor or actress for the role.* **HELP** Many women now prefer to be called **actors**, although when the context is not clear, **an actor** is usually understood to refer to a man. ⊃ note at GENDER **2** a woman who plays a part, pretending by her behaviour to be a particular kind of person: *I became a very good actress and they nearly always believed me.*

**acˈtual** 🔑 **B2** **W** /ˈæktʃuəl/ *adj.* [only before noun] **1** **B2** used to emphasize sth that is real or exists in fact: *James looks younger than his wife but* **in actual fact** (= really) *he is five years older.* ◇ *The actual cost was higher than we expected.* ◇ *The actual number of unemployed is more than 15 million.* **2** **B2** used to emphasize the most important part of sth: *The rehearsal was fabulous, the actual performance even better.*

▼ **WHICH WORD?**

**actual / current / present**

- **Actual** does not mean **current** or **present**. It means 'real' or 'exact', and is often used in contrast with something that is not seen as real or exact: *I need the actual figures, not an estimate.*
- **Present** means 'existing or happening now': *How long have you been in your present job?*
- **Current** also means 'existing or happening now', but can suggest that the situation is temporary: *The factory cannot continue its current level of production.*
- **Actually** does not mean 'at the present time'. Use **currently**, **at present** or **at the moment** instead.
⊃ note at PRESENTLY

**ˌactual ˌbodily ˈharm** *noun* [U] (*abbr.* **ABH**) (*BrE, law*) the crime of causing sb minor physical injury ⊃ compare GRIEVOUS BODILY HARM

**acˈtuˈality** /ˌæktʃuˈæləti/ *noun* (*pl.* **-ies**) (*formal*) **1** [U] the state of sth existing in reality: **in ~** *The building looked as impressive in actuality as it did in photographs.* **2** [C, usually pl.] things that exist **SYN** **fact, reality**: *the grim actualities of prison life*

**acˈtuˈalˈize** (*BrE also* **-ise**) /ˈæktʃuəlaɪz/ *verb* **~ sth** (*formal*) to make sth real; to make sth happen: *He finally actualized his dream.*

**acˈtuˈalˈly** 🔑 **A2** **S** /ˈæktʃuəli/ *adv.* **1** **A2** used in speaking to emphasize a fact or a comment, or that sth is really true: *What did she actually say?* ◇ *It's not actually raining now.* ◇ *The book was never actually published.* **2** **A2** used to show a contrast between what is true and what sb believes, and to show surprise about this contrast: *It was actually kind of fun after all.* ◇ *Our turnover actually increased last year.* ◇ *I couldn't believe it had all actually happened.* **3** **A2** used to correct sb in a polite way: *We're not American, actually. We're Canadian.* ◇ *Actually, it would be much more sensible to do it later.* ◇ *They're not married, actually.* **4** **A2** used to get sb's attention, to introduce a new topic or to say sth that sb may not like, in a polite way: *Actually, I'm busy at the moment—can I call you back?* ◇ *Well, actually, I think she's done a pretty good job.* ⊃ note at ACTUAL

**acˈtuˈary** /ˈæktʃuəri; NAmE -tʃueri/ *noun* (*pl.* **-ies**) a person whose job involves calculating insurance risks and payments for insurance companies by studying how frequently accidents, fires, deaths, etc. happen ⊃ WORDFINDER NOTE at INSURANCE ▶ **acˈtuˈarˈial** /ˌæktʃuˈeəriəl; NAmE -ˈer-/ *adj.*

**acˈtuˈate** /ˈæktʃueɪt/ *verb* (*formal*) **1 ~ sth** to make a machine or device start to work **SYN** **activate** **2** [usually passive] to make sb behave in a particular way **SYN** **motivate**: **be actuated by sth** *He was actuated entirely by malice.*

**acˈuˈity** /əˈkjuːəti/ *noun* [U] (*formal*) the ability to think, see or hear clearly

**acˈuˈmen** /ˈækjəmən, əˈkjuːmən/ *noun* [U, sing.] the ability to understand and decide things quickly and well: *He had demonstrated considerable business acumen.*

**acˈuˈpresˈsure** /ˈækjupreʃə(r)/ (*also* **shiˈatsu**) *noun* [U] a form of medical treatment, originally from East Asia, in which pressure is applied to particular parts of the body using the fingers

**acˈuˈpuncˈture** /ˈækjupʌŋktʃə(r)/ *noun* [U] a Chinese method of treating pain and illness using special thin needles that are pushed into the skin in particular parts of the body ⊃ WORDFINDER NOTE at TREATMENT

**acˈuˈpuncˈturˈist** /ˈækjupʌŋktʃərɪst/ *noun* a person who is trained to perform acupuncture

**acˈute** **C1** /əˈkjuːt/ *adj.* **1** **C1** very serious or severe: *There is an acute shortage of water.* ◇ *acute pain* ◇ *the world's acute environmental problems* ◇ *Competition for jobs is acute.* **2** **C1** an acute illness is one that has quickly become severe and dangerous: *acute appendicitis* **OPP** **chronic** ⊃ WORDFINDER NOTE at HEALTH **3** describing or designed for patients suffering from an acute illness: *acute patients* ◇ *an acute ward* **4** **C1** (of the senses) very sensitive and well developed **SYN** **keen**: *Dogs have an acute sense of smell.* **5** **C1** intelligent and quick to notice and understand things: *He is an acute observer of the social scene.* ◇ *Her judgement is acute.* **6** [usually before noun] (*geometry*) (of an angle) less than 90° ⊃ compare OBTUSE (2) ▶ **acuteˈness** *noun* [U]

**aˌcute ˈaccent** *noun* the mark placed over a vowel to show how it should be pronounced, as over the *e* in *fiancé* ⊃ compare CIRCUMFLEX, GRAVE², TILDE, UMLAUT

**aˌcute ˈangle** *noun* an angle of less than 90° ⊃ picture at ANGLE ⊃ compare OBTUSE ANGLE, REFLEX ANGLE, RIGHT ANGLE

**acuteˈly** /əˈkjuːtli/ *adv.* **1 ~ aware / conscious** noticing or feeling sth very strongly: *I am acutely aware of the difficulties we face.* **2** (describing unpleasant feelings) very; very strongly: *acutely embarrassed* **3** to a severe and dangerous degree: *acutely ill* **OPP** **chronically**

**-acy** ⊃ -CY

**AD** (*also* **A.D.** *especially in US*) /ˌeɪ ˈdiː/ *abbr.* used in the Christian CALENDAR to show a particular number of years since the year when Christ was believed to have been born (from Latin 'Anno Domini'): *in (the year) AD 55* ◇ *in 55 AD* ◇ *in the fifth century AD* ⊃ compare AH, BC, BCE, CE

**ad** 🔑 **B1** /æd/ *noun* (*informal*) = ADVERTISEMENT: *The TV ads were first run last year.* ◇ *an ad for a new chocolate bar* ⊃ SYNONYMS at ADVERTISEMENT ⊃ see also BANNER AD

**adage** /ˈædɪdʒ/ *noun* a well-known phrase expressing a general truth about people or the world **SYN** **saying**

**adaˈgio** /əˈdɑːdʒiəʊ/ *noun* (*pl.* **-os**) (*music, from Italian*) a piece of music to be played slowly ▶ **adaˈgio** *adj., adv.*

**Adam** /ˈædəm/ *noun* **IDM** see KNOW *v.*

**adˈamˈant** /ˈædəmənt/ *adj.* determined not to change your mind or to be persuaded about sth: *Eva was adamant that she would not come.* ▶ **adˈamˈantˈly** *adv.*: *His family were adamantly opposed to the marriage.*

**ˌAdam's ˈapple** *noun* the part at the front of the throat that sticks out, particularly in men, and moves up and down when you SWALLOW

**adˈapt** 🔑 **B2** /əˈdæpt/ *verb* **1** **B2** [I, T] to change your behaviour in order to deal more successfully with a new situation **SYN** **adjust**: *It's amazing how soon you adapt.* ◇ *The organisms were forced to adapt in order to survive.* ◇ **~ to sth** *Some animals have a remarkable ability to adapt to changing environments.* ◇ *A large organization can be slow to adapt to change* ◇ **~ yourself to sth** *It took him a while to adapt himself to his new surroundings.* **2** **B2** [T] to change sth in order to make it suitable for a new use or situation **SYN** **modify**: **~ sth** *These styles can be adapted to suit individual tastes.* ◇ **~ sth for sth** *Most of these tools* have been specially adapted for use by disabled people. **3** [T] ~ **sth (for sth) (from sth)** to change a book or play so that it can be made into a play, film, television drama, etc: *Three of her novels have been adapted for television.*

**adapt·able** /əˈdæptəbl/ *adj.* (*approving*) able to change or be changed in order to deal successfully with new situations: *Older workers can be as adaptable and quick to learn as anyone else.* ◊ *Successful businesses are highly adaptable to economic change.* ▶ **adapt·abil·ity** /əˌdæptəˈbɪləti/ *noun* [U]

**adap·ta·tion** /ˌædæpˈteɪʃn/ (*also less frequent* **adap·tion** /əˈdæpʃn/) *noun* **1** [U, C] ~ **(to sth)** the action or process of changing sth, or of being changed, to suit a new purpose or situation: *The process of adaptation to a new school is difficult for some children.* **2** [C] a film, television drama or play that is based on a particular book or play but has been changed to suit the new medium: *a screen adaptation of Shakespeare's 'Macbeth'* **3** [U, C] ~ **(of sth) (to sth)** (*biology*) the process of change by which a species becomes better suited to its environment: *the adaptation of desert species to the hot conditions*

**adap·ter** (*also* **adap·tor**) /əˈdæptə(r)/ *noun* **1** a device for connecting pieces of electrical equipment that were not designed to fit together **2** (*BrE*) a device for connecting more than one piece of equipment to the same SOCKET (= a place in the wall where equipment is connected to the electricity supply) **3** a person who changes a book or play so that it can be made into a play, film, television drama, etc.

**adap·tive** /əˈdæptɪv/ *adj.* (*specialist*) connected with changing; able to change when necessary in order to deal with different situations: *Adaptive learning systems offer students customized learning experiences according to their needs and capabilities.*

**ˈad blocker** *noun* a piece of software that removes the advertisements from a web page when you view it

**ADC** /ˌeɪ diː ˈsiː/ *noun* AIDE-DE-CAMP

**ADD** /ˌeɪ diː ˈdiː/ *abbr.* ATTENTION DEFICIT DISORDER

**add** /æd/ *verb* **1** [T] to put sth together with sth else so as to increase the size, number, amount, etc: ~ **sth** *Next add the flour.* ◊ *The juice contains no added sugar.* ◊ *As an* **added bonus**, *the book includes many black-and-white photographs.* ◊ ~ **sth to sth** *Shall I add your name to the list?* ◊ *They are looking at ways to* **add** *further* **value** *to their products.* **2** [I, T] to put numbers or amounts together to get a total: ~ **A to B** *Add 9 to the total.* ◊ ~ **A and B together** *If you add all these amounts together you get a huge figure.* **OPP** **subtract** **3** [T] to say sth more; to make a further remark: + **speech** *'And don't be late,' she added.* ◊ ~ **sth (to sth)** *I have nothing to add to my earlier statement.* ◊ ~ **that ...** *He added that they would return a week later.* **4** [T] ~ **sth (to sth)** to give a particular quality to an event, a situation, etc: *The suite will add a touch of class to your bedroom.*

**IDM** **add ˈinsult to ˈinjury** to make a bad relationship with sb worse by offending them even more **ˈadded to this ... | ˈadd to this ...** used to introduce another fact that helps to emphasize a point you have already made: *Add to this the excellent service and you can see why it's the most popular hotel on the island.*

**PHRV** **add sth↔ˈin** to include sth with sth else: *Remember to add in the cost of drinks.* **ˈadd sth↔ˈon (to sth)** to include or attach sth extra: *A service charge of 15 per cent was added on to the bill.* ⊃ *related noun* ADD-ON **ˈadd to sth** to increase sth in size, number, amount, etc: *The bad weather only added to our difficulties.* ◊ *The findings* **add greatly to** *our understanding of this period.* ◊ *The house has been added to* (= new rooms, etc. have been built on to it) *from time to time.* **ˌadd ˈup** (*informal*) **1** (especially in negative sentences) to seem reasonable; to make sense: *His story just doesn't add up.* **2** (especially in negative sentences) (of numbers) to make a total that seems reasonable or is useful: *We can't sponsor this project. The figures simply don't add up.* **3** to increase by small amounts until there is a large total: *When you're feeding a family of six the bills soon add up.* **ˌadd ˈup | ˌadd sth↔ˈup to**

17

**addition**

calculate the total of two or more numbers or amounts: *The waiter can't add up.* ◊ *Add up all the money I owe you.* **ˌadd ˈup to sth** **1** to make a total amount of sth: *The numbers add up to exactly 100.* **2** to lead to a particular result; to show sth **SYN** **amount to sth**: *These clues don't really add up to very much* (= give us very little information).

**ad·den·dum** /əˈdendəm/ *noun* (*pl.* **ad·den·da** /-də/) (*formal*) a section of extra information that is added to sth, especially to a book

**adder** /ˈædə(r)/ *noun* a small snake, often with marks in the shape of diamonds on its back Adders are the only poisonous snakes in Britain.

**ad·dict** /ˈædɪkt/ *noun* a person who is unable to stop using or doing sth as a habit, especially sth harmful: *a heroin/drug addict* ◊ *a gambling/social media addict* ⊃ WORDFINDER NOTE at DRUG

**ad·dict·ed** /əˈdɪktɪd/ *adj.* [not before noun] ~ **(to sth)** unable to stop using or doing sth as a habit, especially sth harmful: *to become addicted to drugs/gambling/social media*

**ad·dic·tion** /əˈdɪkʃn/ *noun* [U, C] the condition of being unable to stop using or doing sth as a habit, especially sth harmful: *cocaine addiction* ◊ ~ **to sth** *He is now fighting his addiction to alcohol.*

**ad·dict·ive** /əˈdɪktɪv/ *adj.* **1** if a substance or activity is **addictive**, it makes people unable to stop using it or doing it: *Heroin is* **highly addictive**. **2** (of sb's personality or behaviour) easily becoming addicted to sth; showing this

**ˈadd-in** *noun* (*computing*) a computer program that can be added to a larger program to allow it do more things ▶ **ˈadd-in** *adj.* [only before noun]: *add-in software*

▼ **LANGUAGE BANK**

**addition**

**Adding another item**

- Bilingual children do better in IQ tests than children who speak only one language. **In addition**/**What is more**, they seem to find it easier to learn third or even fourth languages.
- Learning another language **not only** improves children's job prospects in later life, **but also** boosts their self-esteem.
- Teaching children a second language improves their job prospects in later life. **Other** benefits **include** increased self-esteem and greater tolerance of other cultures.
- **Another**/**One further**/**One additional** reason for encouraging bilingual education is that it boosts children's self-esteem.
- Studies suggest that bilingual children find it easier to learn additional languages. There is, **moreover**, increasing evidence that bilingual children perform better across a range of school subjects, not just foreign languages.
- His claim that children find bilingual education confusing is based on very little evidence. **Moreover**, the evidence he does provide is seriously flawed.
- Research has shown that first-language development is not impeded by exposure to a second language. **Furthermore**, there is no evidence to support the claim that children find bilingual education confusing.

**ad·di·tion** /əˈdɪʃn/ *noun* **1** [C] a thing that is added to sth else: ~ **to sth** *the latest addition to our range of cars* ◊ *This is a* **welcome addition** *to the literature of western art history.* **2** [U] the act of adding sth to sth else: ~ **of sth** *Pasta's basic ingredients are flour and water, sometimes* **with the addition of** *eggs or oil.* **3** (*NAmE*) (*BrE* **extension**) [C] ~ **(to sth)** a new part that is added to a building: *architects who specialize in home additions* **4** [U] the process of adding two or more numbers together to find their total: *children learning addition and subtraction* **OPP** **subtraction**

**IDM** **in addition (to sb/sth)** used when you want to mention another person or thing after sth else: *In addition to these arrangements, extra ambulances will be on duty*

# additional 18

until midnight. ◊ *There is, in addition, one further point to make.*

**ad·di·tion·al** ❶ B2 W /əˈdɪʃnəl/ *adj.* more than was first mentioned or is usual SYN **extra**: *additional resources/funds/security/funding/costs* ◊ *The government provided an additional £25 million to expand the service.* ⊃ see also EAL

**ad·di·tion·al·ly** ?+ B2 W /əˈdɪʃnəli/ *adv.* in a way that is more than was first mentioned or is usual SYN **in addition (to sb/sth)**: *Additionally, the bus service will run on Sundays, every two hours.*

**ad·di·tive** /ˈædətɪv/ *noun* a substance that is added in small amounts to sth, especially food, in order to improve it, give it colour, make it last longer, etc: *food additives* ◊ *additive-free orange juice* ◊ *chemical additives in petrol*

**ad·dled** /ˈædld/ *adj.* **1** confused; unable to think clearly: *his addled brain* **2** (*BrE, old-fashioned*) (of an egg) not fresh; bad to eat

**ˈadd-on** *noun* a thing that is added to sth else: *The company offers scuba-diving as an add-on to the basic holiday price.* ◊ *add-on software* (= added to a computer)

**ad·dress** ❶ A1 W *noun, verb*
■ *noun* /əˈdres/ *NAmE also* ˈædres/ **1** ʔ A1 [C] details of where sb lives or works and where letters, etc. can be sent: *What's your name and address?* ◊ *Is that your home address?* ◊ *Please note my change of address.* ◊ (*especially NAmE*) *Each entry must include a valid mailing address.* ◊ (*BrE usually*) *a postal address* ◊ *Police found him at an address* (= a house or flat) *in West London.* ◊ *people with no fixed address* (= with no permanent home) ⊃ see also FORWARDING ADDRESS, RETURN ADDRESS **2** ʔ A1 [C] (*computing*) a series of words and symbols that tells you where you can find sth using a computer or phone, for example on the internet: *What's your email address?* ◊ *The project has a new web address.* ⊃ see also IP ADDRESS ⊃ WORDFINDER NOTE at MESSAGE **3** [C] a formal speech that is made in front of an audience: *tonight's televised presidential address* ⊃ SYNONYMS at SPEECH **4** [U] *form/mode of~* the correct title, etc. to use when you talk to sb
■ *verb* /əˈdres/ **1** ʔ B2 (*formal*) to think about a problem or a situation and decide how you are going to deal with it: *~sth Your essay does not address the real issues.* ◊ *to address a problem/concern/question* ◊ *The policy fails to address the needs of the poor.* ◊ *~yourself to sth We must address ourselves to the problem of traffic pollution.* **2** [often passive] to write on an ENVELOPE, etc. the name and address of the person, company, etc. that you are sending it to by mail: *be addressed The letter was correctly addressed, but delivered to the wrong house.* ◊ *~sth (to sb/sth) Address your application to the General Manager.* ⊃ see also SAE, SASE **3** to make a formal speech to a group of people: *to address a meeting/conference* **4** (*formal*) to say sth directly to sb: *~sb I was surprised when he addressed me in English.* ◊ *~sth to sb Any questions should be addressed to your teacher.* **5** *~sb (as sth)* to use a particular name or title for sb when you speak or write to them: *The judge should be addressed as 'Your Honour'.*

**ad·dress·able** /əˈdresəbl/ *adj.* **1** (of a problem or situation) that can be addressed: *Let's start with the more easily addressable issues.* **2** (*computing*) (of a part of a computer system) that is identified using its own address: *addressable memory*

**adˈdress bar** *noun* a line near the top of a page on an internet BROWSER where you can type in the address of a website or where the website address is displayed

**adˈdress book** *noun* **1** a book in which you keep addresses, phone numbers, etc. **2** a computer file where you store email and internet addresses

**ad·dress·ee** /ˌædreˈsiː/ *noun* a person that a letter, etc. is addressed to

**ad·duce** /əˈdjuːs; *NAmE* əˈduːs/ *verb* [often passive] (*formal*) to provide evidence, reasons, facts, etc. in order to explain sth or to show that sth is true SYN **cite**: *be adduced Several factors have been adduced to explain the fall in the birth rate.*

**ad·duct·or** /əˈdʌktə(r)/ (*also* **adˈductor muscle**) *noun* (*anatomy*) a muscle that moves a body part towards the middle of the body or towards another part ⊃ compare ABDUCTOR

**ad·en·oids** /ˈædənɔɪdz/ *noun* [pl.] pieces of soft TISSUE at the back of the nose and throat, that are part of the body's IMMUNE SYSTEM and that can become larger than normal and cause breathing difficulties, especially in children ▶ **ad·en·oid·al** /ˌædəˈnɔɪdl/ *adj.*

**adept** /əˈdept/ *adj.* *~(at/in sth) | ~(at/in doing sth)* good at doing sth that is quite difficult SYN **skilful** ▶ **adept** /ˈædept/ *noun* **adept·ly** *adv.*

**ad·equate** ʔ+ B2 W /ˈædɪkwət/ *adj.* enough in quantity, or good enough in quality, for a particular purpose or need: *an adequate supply of hot water* ◊ *The room was small but adequate.* ◊ *There is a lack of adequate provision for disabled students.* ◊ *He didn't give an adequate answer to the question.* ◊ *~for sth The space available is not adequate for our needs.* ◊ *~to do sth training that is adequate to meet the future needs of industry* OPP **inadequate** ▶ **ad·equacy** /-kwəsi/ *noun* [U]: *The adequacy of the security arrangements has been questioned.* OPP **inadequacy**

**ad·equate·ly** ʔ+ B2 W /ˈædɪkwətli/ *adv.* in a way that is enough in quantity, or good enough in quality, for a particular purpose or need: *Are you adequately insured?* OPP **inadequately**

**ADHD** /ˌeɪ diː eɪtʃ ˈdiː/ *abbr.* ATTENTION DEFICIT HYPERACTIVITY DISORDER

**ad·here** ʔ+ C1 /ədˈhɪə(r); *NAmE* -ˈhɪr/ *verb* [I] *~(to sth)* (*formal*) to stick to sth: *Once in the bloodstream, the bacteria adhere to the surface of the red cells.*
PHRV ▶ **adˈhere to sth** ʔ+ C1 (*formal*) to behave according to a particular law, rule, set of instructions, etc.; to follow a particular set of beliefs or a fixed way of doing sth: *For ten months he adhered to a strict no-fat low-salt diet.* ◊ *She adheres to teaching methods she learned over 30 years ago.*

**ad·her·ence** /ədˈhɪərəns; *NAmE* -ˈhɪr-/ *noun* [U] (*formal*) the fact of behaving according to a particular rule, etc., or of following a particular set of beliefs, or a fixed way of doing sth: *strict adherence to the rules*

**ad·her·ent** /ədˈhɪərənt; *NAmE* -ˈhɪr-/ *noun* (*formal*) a person who supports a particular set of ideas SYN **supporter**

**ad·he·sion** /ədˈhiːʒn/ *noun* [U] (*specialist*) the ability to stick or become attached to sth

**ad·he·sive** /ədˈhiːsɪv, -ˈhiːzɪv/ *noun, adj.*
■ *noun* [C, U] a substance that you use to make things stick together
■ *adj.* that can stick to sth SYN **sticky**: *adhesive tape* ⊃ see also SELF-ADHESIVE

**ad hoc** /ˌæd ˈhɒk; *NAmE* ˈhɑːk/ *adj.* (*from Latin*) arranged or happening when necessary and not planned in advance: *an ad hoc meeting to deal with the problem* ◊ *The meetings will be held on an ad hoc basis.* ▶ **ad hoc** *adv.*

**ad hom·in·em** /ˌæd ˈhɒmɪnem; *NAmE* ˈhɑːm-/ *adj., adv.* (*from Latin, formal*) directed against a person's character rather than their argument: *an ad hominem attack*

**adieu** /əˈdjuː; *NAmE* əˈduː/ *exclamation* (*from French*) (*old use or literary*) goodbye: *I bid you adieu.*

**ad in·fin·itum** /ˌæd ɪnfɪˈnaɪtəm/ *adv.* (*from Latin*) without ever coming to an end; again and again: *You cannot stay here ad infinitum without paying rent.* ◊ *The problem would be repeated ad infinitum.*

**adi·pose** /ˈædɪpəʊs, -pəʊz/ *adj.* (*specialist*) (of body TISSUE) used for storing fat

**ad·ja·cent** ʔ+ C1 /əˈdʒeɪsnt/ *adj.* next to sth: *The planes landed on adjacent runways.* ◊ *~to sth Our farm land was adjacent to the river.*

**aˌdjacent ˈangle** *noun* (*geometry*) one of the two angles formed on the same side of a straight line when another line meets it

**ad·jec·tive** /ˈædʒɪktɪv/ *noun* (*grammar*) a word that describes a person or thing, for example *big, red* and *clever* in *a big house, red wine* and *a clever idea* ▶ **ad·jec·tival** /ˌædʒekˈtaɪvl/ *adj.*: *An adjectival phrase* **ad·jec·tival·ly** /-vəli/ *adv.*: *In 'bread knife', the word 'bread' is used adjectivally.*

**ad·join** /əˈdʒɔɪn/ *verb* [T, I] ~ **(sth)** (*formal*) to be next to or joined to sth: *A barn adjoins the farmhouse.* ▶ **ad·join·ing** *adj.* [usually before noun]: *They stayed in adjoining rooms.* ◇ *We'll have more space if we knock down the adjoining wall* (= the wall between two rooms).

**ad·journ** /əˈdʒɜːn; *NAmE* əˈdʒɜːrn/ *verb* [I, T, often passive] (*formal*) to stop a meeting or an official process, such as a trial, for a period of time: *The court adjourned for lunch.* ◇ ~**sth** *The trial has been adjourned until next week.* ▶ **ad·journ·ment** *noun* [C, U]: *The judge granted us a short adjournment.*

**PHRV** **adˈjourn to …** (*formal* or *humorous*) to go to another place, especially in order to relax

**ad·judge** /əˈdʒʌdʒ/ *verb* [usually passive] (*formal*) to make a decision about sb/sth based on the facts that are available: **be adjudged + adj.** *The company was adjudged bankrupt.* ◇ **be adjudged + noun** *The tour was judged a success.* ◇ **sth is adjudged to be, have, etc. sth** *The reforms were generally adjudged to have failed.*

**ad·ju·di·cate** /əˈdʒuːdɪkeɪt/ *verb* **1** [I, T] to make an official decision about who is right between two groups or organizations that disagree: ~**(on/upon/in sth)** *A special subcommittee adjudicates on planning applications.* ◇ ~**(sth) (between A and B)** *Their purpose is to adjudicate disputes between employers and employees.* **2** [I] to be a judge in a competition: *Who is adjudicating at this year's contest?* ▶ **ad·ju·di·ca·tion** /əˌdʒuːdɪˈkeɪʃn/ *noun* [U, C]: *The case was referred to a higher court for adjudication.* **ad·ju·di·ca·tor** /əˈdʒuːdɪkeɪtə(r)/ *noun*: *You may refer your complaint to an independent adjudicator.*

**ad·junct** /ˈædʒʌŋkt/ *noun* **1** (*grammar*) an adverb or a phrase that adds meaning to the verb in a sentence or part of a sentence: *In 'She went home yesterday' and 'He ran away in a panic', 'yesterday' and 'in a panic' are adjuncts.* **2** (*formal*) a thing that is added or attached to sth larger or more important: *The memory expansion cards are useful adjuncts to the computer.*

**ad·just** /əˈdʒʌst/ *verb* **1** [T] to change sth slightly to make it more suitable for a new set of conditions or to make it work better: ~**sth** *Watch out for sharp bends and adjust your speed accordingly.* ◇ *This button is for adjusting the volume.* ◇ ~**sth to sth** *Adjust your language to the age of your audience.* **2** [I, T] to get used to a new situation by changing the way you behave and/or think **SYN** **adapt**: *They'll be fine—they just need time to adjust.* ◇ ~ **to sth** *After a while his eyes adjusted to the dark.* ◇ ~ **to doing sth** *It took her a while to adjust to living alone.* ◇ ~ **yourself to sth** *You'll quickly adjust yourself to student life.* **3** [T] ~**sth** to move sth slightly so that it looks neater or feels more comfortable: *He smoothed his hair and adjusted his tie.* ⊃ see also **WELL ADJUSTED** **IDM** see **KINDLY** *adv.*

**ad·just·able** /əˈdʒʌstəbl/ *adj.* that can be moved to different positions or changed in shape or size: *adjustable seat belts* ◇ *The height of the bicycle seat is adjustable.*

**adjustable ˈspanner** (*BrE*) (*also* **monkey wrench** *NAmE, BrE*) (*NAmE also* **adjustable ˈwrench**) *noun* a tool with a part that can be moved to hold and turn things of different widths ⊃ compare **SPANNER, WRENCH** ⊃ picture at **SPANNER**

**ad·just·ment** /əˈdʒʌstmənt/ *noun* [C, U] **1** ~ **(to sth)** a small change made to sth in order to correct or improve it: *I've made a few adjustments to the design.* ◇ *Some adjustment of the lens may be necessary.* **2** ~ **(to sth)** a change in the way a person behaves or thinks: *She went through a period of emotional adjustment after her marriage broke up.*

**ad·ju·tant** /ˈædʒutənt/ *noun* an army officer who does office work and helps other officers

**ˌadjutant ˈgeneral** *noun* (*pl.* **adjutants general**) **1** an officer of very high rank in the British army who is responsible for organization **2 Adjutant General** the offi-

cer of very high rank in the US army who is in charge of organization

**ad-lib** /ˌæd ˈlɪb/ *verb* (**-bb-**) [I, T] to say sth in a speech or a performance that you have not prepared or practised **SYN** **improvise**: *She abandoned her script and began ad-libbing.* ◇ ~**sth** *I lost my notes and had to ad-lib the whole speech.* ▶ **ad lib** *noun*: *The speech was full of ad libs.* **ad-lib** *adj.*: *an ad-lib speech* **ad lib** *adv.*: *She delivered her lines ad lib.*

**ad·man** /ˈædmæn/ *noun* (*pl.* **-men** /-men/) (*informal*) a person who works in advertising

**ad·min** /ˈædmɪn/ *noun* [U] (*informal*) the administration of a business, organization, etc.; the department in a company that does this: *She works in admin.* ◇ *a few admin problems*

**ad·min·is·ter** /ədˈmɪnɪstə(r)/ *verb* **1** ~**sth** to manage and organize the affairs of a company, an organization, a country, etc. **SYN** **manage**: *to administer a charity/fund/school* ◇ *The pension funds are administered by commercial banks.* **2** ~**sth** to make sure that sth is done fairly and in the correct way: *to administer justice/the law* ◇ *The questionnaire was administered by trained interviewers.* **3** ~ **(sth to sb)** (*formal*) to give or to provide sth, especially in a formal way: *The teacher has the authority to administer punishment.* **4** (*formal*) to give drugs, medicine, etc. to sb: ~**sth** *Police believe his wife could not have administered the poison.* ◇ ~**sth to sb** *The dose was administered to the child intravenously.* ⊃ **WORDFINDER NOTE** at **MEDICINE** **5** ~**a kick, a punch, etc. (to sb/sth)** (*formal*) to kick or to hit sb/sth: *He administered a severe blow to his opponent's head.*

**ad·min·is·tra·tion** 🔑 **B2** /ədˌmɪnɪˈstreɪʃn/ *noun* **1** **B2** (*also informal* **admin**) [U] the activities that are done in order to plan, organize and run a business, school or other institution: *Administration costs are passed on to the customer.* ◇ *the day-to-day administration of a company* ◇ *I work in the Sales Administration department.* ⊃ see also **BUSINESS ADMINISTRATION** **2** **B2** (*often* **Administration**) [C] the government of a country, especially the US: *during/under the …~ under the Trump administration* ◇ *Successive administrations have failed to solve the country's economic problems.* **3** [U] the management of public affairs **SYN** **government**: *under …~ The inhabitants of the island voted to remain under French administration.* **4** [U] the process or act of organizing the way that sth is done: *the administration of justice* **5** [C] the people who plan, organize and run a business, an institution, etc: *university administrations* **6** [U] (*formal*) the act of giving a drug to sb: *the administration of antibiotics* **7** [U] (*BrE, AustralE, law*) a situation in which the financial affairs of a business that cannot pay its debts are managed by an independent administrator: *If it cannot find extra funds, the company will go into administration.* ⊃ compare **CHAPTER 11**

**ad·min·is·tra·tive** 🔑 **C1** /ədˈmɪnɪstrətɪv; *NAmE* -streɪt-/ *adj.* connected with organizing the work of a business or an institution: *an administrative job/assistant/error* ⊃ **WORDFINDER NOTE** at **WORK** ▶ **ad·min·is·tra·tive·ly** *adv.*

**ad·min·is·tra·tor** 🔑 **C1** /ədˈmɪnɪstreɪtə(r)/ *noun* **1** **C1** a person whose job is to manage and organize the public or business affairs of a company or an institution, or a person who works in an office dealing with records, accounts, etc: *a hospital administrator* ◇ *For an application form, please contact our administrator* **2** a person who manages a computer system and controls who can access it: *If you are unable to access the site, contact your system administrator.* **3** (*BrE, AustralE, law*) a person legally **APPOINTED** (= chosen) to manage the financial affairs of a business that cannot pay its debts

**ad·mir·able** /ˈædmərəbl/ *adj.* (*formal*) having qualities that you admire and respect **SYN** **commendable**: *Her dedication to her work was admirable.* ◇ *He made his points with admirable clarity.* ▶ **ad·mir·ably** /-bli/ *adv.*: *Joe coped admirably with a difficult situation.*

# admiral

**ad·miral** /ˈædmərəl/ noun an officer of very high rank in the NAVY: *The admiral visited the ships under his command.* ◊ *Admiral Lord Nelson* ⇨ WORDFINDER NOTE at NAVY ⇨ see also FLEET ADMIRAL, REAR ADMIRAL, VICE ADMIRAL

**Admiral of the ˈFleet** (*BrE*) (*US* ˈFleet ˈAdmiral) noun an admiral of the highest rank in the NAVY

**the Ad·mir·alty** /ði ˈædmərəlti/ noun [sing. + sing./pl. v.] (in the UK in the past) the government department controlling the NAVY

**ad·mir·ation** /ˌædməˈreɪʃn/ noun [U] a feeling of respect for and approval of sb/sth: ~ **(for sb/sth)** *I have great admiration for her as a writer.* ◊ **in ~** *to watch/gaze in admiration*

**ad·mire** 🔾 B1 /ədˈmaɪə(r)/ verb 1 B1 to respect sb for what they have done or to respect their qualities: ~**sb/sth** *I really admire your enthusiasm.* ◊ *Her work was much admired by critics.* ◊ ~**sb/sth for sth** *The school is widely admired for its excellent teaching.* ◊ ~**sb for doing sth** *I don't agree with her, but I admire her for sticking to her principles.* 2 B1 ~**sth** to look at sth and think that it is attractive and/or impressive: *He stood back to admire his handiwork.* ▶ **ad·mir·ing** *adj.*: *She was used to receiving admiring glances from men.* **ad·mir·ing·ly** *adv.*

**ad·mirer** /ədˈmaɪərə(r)/ noun 1 a person who admires sb/sth, especially a well-known person or thing: *He is a great admirer of Picasso's early paintings.* 2 a person who has a romantic or sexual interest in sb: *She never married but had many admirers.*

**ad·mis·sible** /ədˈmɪsəbl/ *adj.* that can be allowed or accepted, especially in court OPP **inadmissible** ▶ **ad·mis·si·bil·ity** /ədˌmɪsəˈbɪləti/ *noun* [U]

**ad·mis·sion** 🔾+ C1 /ədˈmɪʃn/ *noun* 1 🔾+ C1 [U, C] the act of accepting sb into an institution, organization, etc.; the right to enter a place or to join an institution or organization: *Hospital admission is not necessary in most cases.* ◊ *Hospital admissions for asthma attacks have doubled.* ◊ *the university* **admissions** *policy/office* ◊ *They tried to get into the club but were refused admission.* ◊ *She failed to* **gain admission** *to the university of her choice.* ◊ ~ **to sth** *countries applying for admission to the European Union* ◊ *Last admissions to the park are at 4 p.m.* 2 🔾+ C1 [C] a statement in which sb admits that sth is true, especially sth wrong or bad that they have done: *He is a thief by his own admission* (= he has admitted it). ◊ ~**of sth** *an admission of guilt/failure/defeat* ◊ ~**that …** *The minister's resignation was an admission that she had lied.* 3 🔾+ C1 [U] the amount of money that you pay to go into a building or to an event: *admission charges/prices* ◊ *£5 admission* ◊ *What's the admission?*

**admit** 🔾 B1 /ədˈmɪt/ *verb* (-tt-)
- ACCEPT TRUTH **1** 🔾 B1 [I, T] to agree, often unwillingly, that sth is true SYN **confess**: *It was a stupid thing to do, I admit.* ◊ + **speech** *'I'm very nervous,' she admitted reluctantly.* ◊ ~**to sth** *Don't be afraid to admit to your mistakes.* ◊ ~**to doing sth** *She admits to being strict with her children.* ◊ ~**sth** *He admitted all his mistakes.* ◊ *She stubbornly refuses to admit the truth.* ◊ *Why don't you just admit defeat* (= recognize that you cannot do sth) *and let someone else try?* ◊ ~**(that) …** *They freely admit (that) they still have a lot to learn.* ◊ *You must admit that it all sounds very strange.* ◊ *She readily admits mistakes were made.* ◊ ~**to sb that …** *I couldn't admit to my parents that I was finding the course difficult.* ◊ **be admitted that …** *It was generally admitted that the government had acted too quickly.* ◊ **be admitted to be/have sth** *The appointment is now generally admitted to have been a mistake.*
- ACCEPT BLAME **2** 🔾 B1 [I, T] to say that you have done sth wrong or illegal SYN **confess**: ~**to sth** *He refused to admit to the other charges.* ◊ ~**to doing sth** *She admitted to having stolen the car.* ◊ ~**sth** *She admitted theft.* ◊ *He refused to admit his guilt.* ◊ ~**doing sth** *She admitted having driven the car without insurance.*
- ALLOW TO ENTER/JOIN **3** [T] (*formal*) to allow sb/sth to enter a place: ~**sb/sth** *Each ticket admits one adult.* ◊ ~**sb/sth**

**to/into sth** *You will not be admitted to the theatre after the performance has started.* ◊ *The narrow windows admit little light into the room.* **4** [T] (*formal*) to allow sb to become a member of a club, a school or an organization: ~**sb** *The society admits all US citizens over 21.* ◊ ~**sb to/into sth** *Women were only admitted into the club last year.*
- TO HOSPITAL **5** [T, often passive] (*formal*) to take sb to a hospital or other institution where they can receive special care: **be admitted to sth** *Two crash victims were admitted to the local hospital.* ⇨ WORDFINDER NOTE at HOSPITAL

PHRV **adˈmit of sth** (*formal*) to show that sth is possible or likely as a solution, an explanation, etc.

▼ SYNONYMS

**admit**
acknowledge • recognize • concede • confess

These words all mean to agree, often unwillingly, that sth is true.

**admit** to agree, often unwillingly, that sth is true: *It was a stupid thing to do, I admit.*

**acknowledge** (*rather formal*) to accept that sth exists, is true or has happened: *She refuses to acknowledge the need for reform.*

**recognize** to admit or be aware that sth exists or is true: *They recognized the need to take the problem seriously.*

**concede** (*rather formal*) to admit, often unwillingly, that sth is true or logical: *He was forced to concede (that) there might be difficulties.*

ADMIT OR CONCEDE?
When sb **admits** sth, they are usually agreeing that sth that is generally considered bad or wrong is true or has happened, especially when it relates to their own actions. When sb **concedes** sth, they are usually accepting, unwillingly, that a particular fact or statement is true or logical.

**confess** (*rather formal*) to admit sth that you feel ashamed or embarrassed about; to admit, especially formally or to the police, that you have done sth wrong or illegal: *She was reluctant to confess her ignorance.* ◊ *He confessed to the murder.*

PATTERNS
- to admit/acknowledge/recognize/concede/confess **that …**
- to admit/confess **to sth**
- to admit/concede/confess sth **to sb**
- to admit/acknowledge/recognize **the truth**
- to admit/confess your **mistakes/ignorance**

**ad·mit·tance** /ədˈmɪtns/ *noun* [U] (*formal*) the right to enter or the act of entering a building, an institution, etc.: *Hundreds of people were unable to* **gain admittance** *to the hall.*

**ad·mit·ted·ly** /ədˈmɪtɪdli/ *adv.* used, especially at the beginning of a sentence, when you are accepting that sth is true: *Admittedly, it is rather expensive, but you don't need to use much.*

**ad·mix·ture** /ədˈmɪkstʃə(r)/ *noun* (*formal*) **1** [C] a mixture: *an admixture of aggression and creativity* **2** [C, U] something, especially a small amount of sth, that is mixed with sth else; the act of mixing a small amount of sth with sth else: *a French-speaking region with an admixture of German speakers*

**ad·mon·ish** /ədˈmɒnɪʃ; *NAmE* -ˈmɑːn-/ *verb* (*formal*) **1** ~**sb (for sth/for doing sth)** | + **speech** to tell sb strongly and clearly that you do not approve of sth that they have done SYN **reprove**: *She was admonished for chewing gum in class.* **2** ~**sb (to do sth)** to strongly advise sb to do sth: *A warning voice admonished him not to let this happen.*

**ad·mon·ition** /ˌædməˈnɪʃn/ (*also less frequent* **ad·mon·ish·ment** /ədˈmɒnɪʃmənt; *NAmE* -ˈmɑːn-/) *noun* [C, U] (*formal*) a warning to sb about their behaviour ▶ **ad·moni·tory** /ədˈmɒnɪtri; *NAmE* -ˈmɑːnətɔːri/ *adj.*

**ad nau·seam** /ˌæd ˈnɔːziæm/ *adv.* (*from Latin*) if a person says or does sth **ad nauseam**, they say or do it again and again so that it becomes boring or annoying: *Sports commentators repeat the same phrases ad nauseam.*

**ado** /əˈduː/ *noun*
**IDM** **without further/more ado** (*old-fashioned*) without delaying; immediately

**adobe** /əˈdəʊbi/ *noun* [U] mud that is dried in the sun, mixed with STRAW and used as a building material

**ado·les·cence** /ˌædəˈlesns/ *noun* [U, sing.] the time in a person's life when he or she develops from a child into an adult **SYN** puberty

**ado·les·cent** ?+ **C1** /ˌædəˈlesnt/ *noun* a young person who is developing from a child into an adult: *adolescents between the ages of 13 and 18 and the problems they face* ⇒ WORDFINDER NOTE at AGE ▸ **ado·les·cent** *adj.*: *adolescent boys/girls/experiences*

**adopt** **①** **B2** **W** /əˈdɒpt; NAmE əˈdɑːpt/ *verb*
• CHILD **1** ? **B2** [I, T] to take sb else's child into your family and become its legal parent(s): *a campaign to encourage childless couples to adopt* ⋄ *~ sb to adopt a child* ⋄ *She was forced to have her baby adopted.* ⇒ compare FOSTER ⇒ WORDFINDER NOTE at FAMILY
• METHOD **2** ? **B2** [T] *~ sth* to start to use a particular method or to show a particular attitude towards sb/sth: *All three teams adopted different approaches to the problem.*
• SUGGESTION **3** ? **B2** [T] *~ sth* to formally accept a suggestion or policy by voting: *to adopt a resolution* ⋄ *The council is expected to adopt the new policy at its next meeting.*
• NEW NAME/COUNTRY **4** [T] *~ sth* to choose a new name, a country, a custom, etc. and begin to use it as your own: *to adopt a name/title/language* ⋄ *Early Christians in Europe adopted many of the practices of the older, pagan religions.*
• WAY OF BEHAVING **5** [T] *~ sth* (*formal*) to use a particular manner, way of speaking, expression, etc: *He adopted an air of indifference.*
• CANDIDATE **6** [T] *~ sb (as sth)* (*BrE, politics*) to choose sb as a candidate in an election; to choose sb as your representative: *She was adopted as parliamentary candidate for Wood Green.*

**adopt·ed** /əˈdɒptɪd; NAmE əˈdɑːp-/ *adj.* **1** an **adopted** child has legally become part of a family that is not the one in which he or she was born: *Danny is their adopted son.* **2** an **adopted** country is one in which sb chooses to live although it is not the one they were born in

**adopt·ee** /ˌædɒpˈtiː; NAmE əˌdɑːp-/ *noun* a person who has been adopted

**adopt·er** /əˈdɒptə(r); NAmE əˈdɑːp-/ *noun* **1** a person who adopts a child **2** a person who starts using a new technology: *early/late adopters of social media*

**adop·tion** ?+ **C1** /əˈdɒpʃn; NAmE əˈdɑːp-/ *noun* **1** ?+ **C1** [U, C] the act of adopting a child; the fact of being adopted: *She put the baby up for adoption.* ⋄ *into sth his adoption into an American family* **2** ?+ **C1** [U] the decision to start using sth such as an idea, a plan or a name: *the adoption of new technology* **3** [U, C] (*BrE, politics*) the act of choosing sb as a candidate for an election: *his adoption as the Labour candidate*

**adop·tive** /əˈdɒptɪv; NAmE əˈdɑːp-/ *adj.* [usually before noun] (of a parent, child or family) in that relationship as a result of the parent legally adopting the child

**ador·able** /əˈdɔːrəbl/ *adj.* very attractive and easy to feel love for: *What an adorable child!* ▸ **ador·ably** /-bli/ *adv.*

**ad·or·ation** /ˌædəˈreɪʃn/ *noun* [U] a feeling of great love or WORSHIP: *He gazed at her with pure adoration.* ⋄ *The painting is called 'Adoration of the Infant Christ'.*

**adore** /əˈdɔː(r)/ *verb* (not used in the progressive tenses) **1** *~ sb* to love sb very much: *It's obvious that she adores him.* ⇒ SYNONYMS at LOVE **2** (*informal*) to like sth very much: *~ sth I simply adore his music!* ⋄ *~ doing sth She adores working with children.* ⇒ SYNONYMS at LIKE

**ador·ing** /əˈdɔːrɪŋ/ *adj.* [usually before noun] showing much love ▸ **ador·ing·ly** *adv.*

**adorn** /əˈdɔːn; NAmE əˈdɔːrn/ *verb* (*formal*) to make sth/sb look more attractive by decorating it or them with sth: *~ sth/sb Gold rings adorned his fingers.* ⋄ *~ sth/sb/yourself with sth The walls were adorned with paintings.*

21 **adultery**

▸ **adorn·ment** *noun* [U, C]: *A plain necklace was her only adornment.*

**ad·renal gland** /əˈdriːnl ɡlænd/ *noun* either of the two small organs above the KIDNEYS that produce adrenaline and other HORMONES

**adrena·line** (*also* **adrena·lin**) /əˈdrenəlɪn/ *noun* [U] a substance produced in the body when you are excited, afraid or angry. It makes the heart beat faster and increases your energy and ability to move quickly: *The excitement at the start of a race can really get the adrenaline flowing.* ⋄ *an adrenaline rush* ⇒ WORDFINDER NOTE at ADVENTURE

**adrift** /əˈdrɪft/ *adj.* [not before noun] **1** if a boat or a person in a boat is **adrift**, the boat is not tied to anything or is floating without being controlled by anyone: *The survivors were adrift in a lifeboat for six days.* ⋄ *Their boat had been set adrift.* **2** (of a person) feeling alone and without a direction or an aim in life: *young people adrift in the big city* ⋄ *Without language, human beings are* **cast adrift**. **3** no longer attached or fixed in the right position: *I nearly suffocated when the pipe on my breathing apparatus* **came adrift**. ⋄ (*figurative*) *She had been* **cut adrift** *from everything she had known.* **4** *~ (of sb/sth)* (*especially BrE*) (in sport) behind the score or position of your opponents: *The team are now just six points adrift of the leaders.*

**adroit** /əˈdrɔɪt/ *adj.* (*formal*) clever and showing skill **SYN** skilful: *an adroit negotiator* ▸ **adroit·ly** *adv.* **adroit·ness** *noun* [U]

**ADSL** /ˌeɪ diː es ˈel/ *abbr.* asymmetric digital subscriber line (a system for connecting a computer to the internet using a phone line)

**ad·sorb** /ədˈzɔːb; NAmE -ˈzɔːrb/ *verb* *~ sth* (*specialist*) if a material **adsorbs** a liquid, gas or other substance, it holds it on its surface, or on internal surfaces within the material: *The dye is adsorbed onto the fibre.*

**ADT** /ˌeɪ diː ˈtiː/ *abbr.* ATLANTIC DAYLIGHT TIME

**adu·la·tion** /ˌædjuˈleɪʃn; NAmE ˌædʒəˈl-/ *noun* [U] (*formal*) great praise, especially when it is greater than necessary ▸ **adu·la·tory** /ˌædjuˈleɪtəri; NAmE ˈædʒələtɔːri/ *adj.*

**adult** **①** **A1** **S** /ˈædʌlt, əˈdʌlt; NAmE əˈdʌlt, ˈædʌlt/ *noun, adj.*
■ *noun* **1** ? **A1** a fully grown person who is legally responsible for their actions **SYN** grown-up²: *Children must be accompanied by an adult.* ⋄ *I simply can't believe that responsible adults allowed a child to wander the streets.* **2** ? **A1** a fully grown animal: *The fish return to the river as adults in order to breed.*
■ *adj.* **1** ? **A2** fully grown or developed: *preparing young people for adult life* ⋄ *He was a healthy young adult male.* ⋄ *the adult population* **2** behaving in an intelligent and responsible way; typical of what is expected of an adult **SYN** grown-up¹: *When my parents split up, it was all very adult and open.* **3** [only before noun] (of a film, magazine, book, etc.) intended for adults only because it is about sex or shows people with no clothes on: *an adult movie* ⇒ see also ADULTHOOD

**adult edu·cation** (*also* **con·tinuing edu·cation**) *noun* [U] education for adults that is available outside the formal education system, for example at evening classes or over the internet

**adul·ter·ate** /əˈdʌltəreɪt/ *verb* [often passive] *~ sth (with sth)* to make food or drink less pure by adding another substance to it **SYN** contaminate ⇒ see also UNADULTERATED ▸ **adul·ter·ation** /əˌdʌltəˈreɪʃn/ *noun* [U]

**adul·ter·er** /əˈdʌltərə(r)/ *noun* (*formal*) a person who commits adultery

**adul·ter·ess** /əˈdʌltərəs/ *noun* (*formal*) a woman who commits adultery

**adul·tery** /əˈdʌltəri/ *noun* [U] sex between a married person and sb who is not their husband or wife: *He was accused of committing adultery.* ▸ **adul·ter·ous** /-rəs/ *adj.*: *an adulterous relationship*

# adulthood

**adult·hood** /ˈædʌlthʊd, əˈdʌlthʊd; *NAmE* əˈdʌlthʊd, ˈædʌlthʊd/ *noun* [U] the state of being an adult: *a child reaching adulthood*

**ad·um·brate** /ˈædʌmbreɪt, əˈdʌmbreɪt/ *verb* ~ **sth** (*formal*) to give a general idea or description of sth without details **SYN** outline

**ad·vance** ❶ B2 /ədˈvɑːns; *NAmE* -ˈvæns/ *noun, verb, adj.*

■ *noun*
- DEVELOPMENT **1** B2 [C, U] progress or a development in a particular activity or area of understanding: *We live in an age of rapid technological advance.* ◊ **in sth** *Recent advances in technology have made the procedure safe.* ◊ **~ on sth** *an advance on the existing techniques*
- FORWARD MOVEMENT **2** [C] ~ (**on sth**) the forward movement of a group of people, especially armed forces: *We feared that an advance on the capital would soon follow.*
- MONEY **3** [C, usually sing.] money paid for work before it has been done or money paid earlier than expected: *They offered an advance of £5000 after the signing of the contract.* ◊ **~ on sth** *She asked for an advance on her salary.*
- SEXUAL **4** advances [pl.] attempts to start a sexual relationship with sb: *He had made advances to one of his students.*
- PRICE INCREASE **5** [C] ~ (**on sth**) (*business*) an increase in the price or value of sth: *Share prices showed significant advances.*
- **IDM** **in advance (of sth) 1** ꜛ B2 before the time that is expected; before sth happens: *a week/month/year in advance* ◊ *Thanks in advance for your help.* ◊ (*formal*) *The fee is payable in advance.* ◊ (*formal*) *People were evacuated from the coastal regions in advance of the hurricane.* **2** more developed than sb/sth else: *Galileo's ideas were well in advance of the age in which he lived.*

■ *verb*
- DEVELOP **1** ꜛ B2 [I, T] if knowledge, technology, etc. advances, it develops and improves: *Technology is advancing at an incredibly rapid pace.* ◊ **~ sth** *This research has done much to advance our understanding of language learning.*
- MOVE FORWARD **2** [I] to move forward towards sb/sth, often in order to attack or threaten them or it: *The troops were finally given the order to advance.* ◊ *They had advanced 20 miles by nightfall.* ◊ *the advancing Allied troops* ◊ **~ on/towards sb/sth** *The mob advanced on us, shouting angrily.* ⇨ compare RETREAT
- HELP TO SUCCEED **3** [T] to help sth to succeed **SYN** further: *Studying for new qualifications is one way of advancing your career.* ◊ *They worked together to advance the cause of democracy.*
- MONEY **4** [T] to give sb money before the time it would usually be paid: **~ sth to sb** *We are willing to advance the money to you.* ◊ **~ sb sth** *We will advance you the money.*
- SUGGEST **5** [T] ~ **sth** (*formal*) to suggest an idea, a theory or a plan for other people to discuss: *The article advances a new theory to explain changes in the climate.* ◊ *to advance an argument/agenda*
- MAKE EARLIER **6** [T] ~ **sth** (*formal*) to change the time or date of an event so that it takes place earlier: *The date of the trial has been advanced by one week.* **OPP** postpone
- MOVE FORWARD **7** [I, T] (*formal*) to move forward to a later part of sth; to move sth forward to a later part: + *adv./prep.* *These players will now advance to the next round.* ◊ **~ sth** *This button advances the hours and the red one advances the minutes in the display.*
- INCREASE **8** [I] (*business*) (of prices, costs, etc.) to increase in price or amount: *Oil shares advanced amid economic recovery hopes.*

■ *adj.* [only before noun] **1** ꜛ B2 done or given before sth is going to happen: *Please give us advance warning of any changes.* ◊ *We need advance notice of the numbers involved.* ◊ *No advance booking is necessary on most departures.* **2 ~ party/team** a group of people who go somewhere first, before the main group

**ad·vanced** ❶ B1 /ədˈvɑːnst; *NAmE* -ˈvænst/ *adj.*
**1** ꜛ B1 having the most modern and recently developed ideas, methods, etc: *advanced technology* ◊ *It is a technologically advanced society.* ◊ *advanced industrial societies* **2** ꜛ B1 (of a course of study) at a high or difficult level: *He hopes to pursue an advanced degree in economics.* ◊ *an advanced student of English* **3** at a late stage of development: *the advanced stages of the disease* ◊ *patients with advanced lung cancer*
**IDM** **of advanced ˈyears | sb's advanced ˈage** used in polite expressions to describe sb as 'very old': *He was a man of advanced years.* ◊ (*humorous*) *Even at my advanced age I still know how to enjoy myself!*

**adˈvanced level** *noun* = A LEVEL

**Adˌvanced ˈPlacement™** *noun* [U] (*abbr.* **AP**™) an advanced course for high school students in the US by which students can gain college CREDITS before they actually go to college

**adˌvance ˈguard** (also **adˌvanced ˈguard**) *noun* [C + sing./pl. v.] a group of soldiers who go somewhere to make preparations before other soldiers arrive

**ad·vance·ment** /ədˈvɑːnsmənt; *NAmE* -ˈvæn-/ *noun* (*formal*) **1** [U, C] the process of helping sth/sb to make progress or succeed; the progress that is made: *the advancement of knowledge/education/science* **2** [U] progress in a job, social class, etc: *There are good opportunities for advancement if you have the right skills.*

**ad·van·cing** /ədˈvɑːnsɪŋ; *NAmE* -ˈvæn-/ *adj.* **~ years/age** used as a polite way of referring to the fact of time passing and of sb growing older: *She is still very active, in spite of her advancing years.*

**ad·van·tage** ❶ A2 ○ /ədˈvɑːntɪdʒ; *NAmE* -ˈvæn-/ *noun, verb*

■ *noun* [C, U] **1** ꜛ A2 a thing that helps you to be better or more successful than other people: *a distinct/significant/huge advantage* ◊ *It gives you an unfair advantage* (= sth that benefits you, but not your opponents). ◊ *She had the advantage of a good education.* ◊ *You will be at an advantage* (= have an advantage) *in the interview if you have thought about the questions in advance.* ◊ **~ over sb** *The company was able to gain a competitive advantage over its rivals by reducing costs.* **OPP** disadvantage **2** ꜛ A2 a quality of sth that makes it better or more useful: *Each of these systems has its advantages and disadvantages.* ◊ **~ of (doing) sth** *A small car has the added advantage of being cheaper to run.* ◊ **in (doing) sth** *Is there any advantage in getting there early?* ◊ **to (doing) sth** *There are many advantages to online shopping.* **OPP** disadvantage **3** [U] (in tennis) the first point scored after a score of 40–40: *Advantage Miss Stephens.*
**IDM** **be/work to your adˈvantage** to give you an advantage; to change a situation in a way that gives you an advantage: *It would be to your advantage to attend this meeting.* ◊ *Eventually, the new regulations will work to our advantage.* **take adˈvantage of sth/sb 1** ꜛ B2 to make use of sth well; to make use of an opportunity: *She took advantage of the children's absence to tidy their rooms.* ◊ *We took full advantage of the hotel facilities.* **2** ꜛ B2 to make use of sb/sth in a way that is unfair or dishonest **SYN** exploit: *He took advantage of my generosity* (= for example, by taking more than I had intended to give). **to (good/best) adˈvantage** in a way that shows the best of sb/sth: *The photograph showed him to advantage.* **turn sth to your adˈvantage** to use or change a bad situation so that it helps you

■ *verb* ~ **sb** (*formal*) to put sb in a better position than other people or than they were in before

**ad·van·taged** /ədˈvɑːntɪdʒd; *NAmE* -ˈvæn-/ *adj.* being in a good social or financial situation: *We aim to improve opportunities for the less advantaged in society.* **OPP** disadvantaged

**ad·van·ta·geous** /ˌædvənˈteɪdʒəs/ *adj.* ~ (**to sb**) good or useful in a particular situation **SYN** beneficial: *A free trade agreement would be advantageous to both countries.* **OPP** disadvantageous ▶ **ad·van·ta·geous·ly** *adv.*

**ad·vent** /ˈædvent/ *noun* **1** [sing.] **the ~ of sth/sb** the coming of an important event, person, invention, etc: *the advent of new technology* **2 Advent** [U] (in the Christian religion) the period of approximately four weeks before Christmas

**¹Advent calendar** *noun* a piece of stiff paper with a picture and 24 small doors with numbers on. Children open a door each day during Advent and find a picture or a piece of chocolate behind each one.

**ad·ven·ture** 🛈 **A2** /əd'ventʃə(r)/ *noun* **1** 🔊 **A2** [C] an unusual, exciting or dangerous experience, journey or series of events: *her adventures travelling in Africa* ◇ *adventure stories* ◇ *Four members of our staff have embarked on the adventure of a lifetime.* **2** 🔊 **A2** [U] the quality of being excited and willing to take risks, try new ideas, etc: *a sense/spirit of adventure*

**WORDFINDER** adrenaline, attempt, challenge, enthusiasm, escapade, excitement, explore, kick, thrill

**ad'venture game** *noun* a type of computer game in which you play a part in an adventure

**ad'venture 'playground** *noun* (*BrE*) an area where children can play, with large structures, ropes, etc. for climbing on

**ad·ven·turer** /əd'ventʃərə(r)/ *noun* **1** (*old-fashioned*) a person who enjoys exciting new experiences, especially going to unusual places **2** (*often disapproving*) a person who is willing to take risks or act in a dishonest way in order to gain money or power

**ad·ven·ture·some** /əd'ventʃəsəm; *NAmE* -tʃərs-/ *adj.* (*NAmE*) = ADVENTUROUS

**ad·ven·tur·ism** /əd'ventʃərɪzəm/ *noun* [U] (*disapproving*) the fact of being willing to take risks in business or politics in order to gain sth for yourself

**ad·ven·tur·ous** /əd'ventʃərəs/ *adj.* **1** (*NAmE also* **ad·ven·ture·some**) (of a person) willing to take risks and try new ideas; enjoying being in new, exciting situations: *For the more adventurous tourists, there are trips into the mountains with a local guide.* ◇ *Many teachers would like to be more adventurous and creative.* **2** including new and interesting things, methods and ideas: *The menu contained traditional favourites as well as more adventurous dishes.* **3** full of new, exciting or dangerous experiences: *an adventurous trip/lifestyle* **OPP** unadventurous ▶ **ad·ven·tur·ous·ly** *adv.*

**ad·verb** /'ædvɜːb; *NAmE* -vɜːrb/ *noun* (*grammar*) a word that adds more information about place, time, manner, cause or degree to a verb, an adjective, a phrase or another adverb: *In 'speak kindly', 'incredibly deep', 'just in time' and 'too quickly', 'kindly', 'incredibly', 'just' and 'too' are all adverbs.* ⇒ *see also* SENTENCE ADVERB ▶ **ad·ver·bial** /æd'vɜːbiəl; *NAmE* -'vɜːrb-/ *adj., noun*: *'Very quickly indeed' is an adverbial (phrase).*

**ad·ver·sar·ial** /ˌædvə'seəriəl; *NAmE* -vər'ser-/ *adj.* (*formal or specialist*) (especially of political or legal systems) involving people who are in opposition and who argue against each other: *the adversarial nature of the two-party system* ◇ *an adversarial system of justice*

**ad·ver·sary** /'ædvəsəri; *NAmE* -vərseri/ *noun* (*pl.* **-ies**) (*formal*) a person that sb is opposed to and competing with in an argument or a battle **SYN** opponent

**ad·verse** 🔊+ **C1** /'ædvɜːs, əd'vɜːs; *NAmE* əd'vɜːrs, 'ædvɜːrs/ *adj.* [usually before noun] negative and unpleasant; not likely to produce a good result: *adverse change/circumstances/weather conditions* ◇ *Lack of money will have an adverse effect on our research programme.* ◇ *They have attracted strong adverse criticism.* ◇ *This drug is known to have adverse side effects.* ▶ **ad·verse·ly** *adv.*: *Her health was adversely affected by the climate.*

**ad·ver·sity** /əd'vɜːsəti; *NAmE* -'vɜːrs-/ *noun* [U, C] (*pl.* **-ies**) (*formal*) a difficult or unpleasant situation: *courage in the face of adversity* ◇ *He overcame many personal adversities.*

**ad·vert** /'ædvɜːt; *NAmE* -vɜːrt/ *noun* (*BrE, informal*) = ADVERTISEMENT: *the adverts on television* ◇ *I fast-forwarded through the adverts.* ⇒ SYNONYMS *at* ADVERTISEMENT

**ad·ver·tise** 🛈 **A2** /'ædvətaɪz; *NAmE* -vərt-/ *verb* **1** 🔊 **A2** [I, T] to tell the public about a product or a service

in order to encourage people to buy or to use it: *If you want to attract customers you need to advertise.* ◇ *to advertise on TV/online/on social media* ◇ *~ sth* to advertise *a product/service* ◇ *~ sth as sth* *The cruise was advertised as the 'journey of a lifetime'.*

**WORDFINDER** cold-calling, leaflet, maling, mailshot, marketing, poster, product placement, prospectus, publicize

**2** 🔊 **A2** [I, T] to let people know that sth is going to happen, or that a job is available by giving details about it in a newspaper, on a notice in a public place, on the internet, etc: *~ (for sb/sth) We are currently advertising for a new sales manager.* ◇ *~ sth The best jobs are not always advertised in newspapers.* **3** [T] *~ sth* to show or tell sth about yourself to other people **SYN** publicize: *I wouldn't advertise the fact that you don't have a work permit.*

**ad·ver·tise·ment** 🛈 **A2** /əd'vɜːtɪsmənt; *NAmE* ˌædvər'taɪzmənt/ *noun* **1** 🔊 **A2** [C] (*also informal* **ad**) (*also BrE, informal* **ad·vert**) a notice, picture or film telling people about a product, job or service: *a newspaper/television advertisement* ◇ *an online advertisement* ◇ *You can place an advertisement on a classifieds website.* ◇ *~ (for sth) Television and radio refused to carry advertisements for the album.* ⇒ *see also* CLASSIFIED ADVERTISEMENT **2** [C] (*BrE also* **ad·vert**) *~ for sth* an example of sth that shows its good qualities: *Dirty streets and homelessness are no advertisement for a prosperous society.* **3** [U] the act of advertising sth and making it public

▼ SYNONYMS

**advertisement**
publicity • ad • commercial • promotion • trailer
These are all words for a notice, picture or film telling people about a product, job or service.

**advertisement** a notice, picture or film telling people about a product, job or service; an example of sth that shows its good qualities; the act of advertising sth and making it public: *They ran advertisements on TV and on social media.* ◇ *Dirty streets are no advertisement for a prosperous society.*

**publicity** [U] the business of attracting the attention of the public to sb/sth such as a company, book, film, film star or product; the things that are done to attract attention: *She works in publicity.* ◇ *There has been a lot of advance publicity for her new film.*

**ad, advert** (*informal*) a notice, picture or film telling people about a product, job or service: *We put an ad on that website.* ◇ *an ad for a new chocolate bar*

**commercial** an advertisement on television or on the radio.

**promotion** a set of advertisements for a particular product or service; activities done in order to increase the sales of a product or service: *a special promotion of local products* ◇ *She works in sales and promotion.*

**trailer** (*especially BrE*) a series of short scenes from a film or television programme, shown in advance to advertise it.

PATTERNS
- (a/an) advertisement/publicity/ad/commercial/promotion/trailer **for** sth
- a **TV/television/radio/cinema** advertisement/ad/commercial/promotion
- an **online/internet** advertisement/ad/commercial/promotion
- to **run/show** a(n) advertisement/ad/commercial/trailer

**ad·ver·tiser** /'ædvətaɪzə(r); *NAmE* -vərt-/ *noun* a person or company that advertises

**ad·ver·tis·ing** 🛈 **A2** /'ædvətaɪzɪŋ; *NAmE* -vərt-/ *noun* [U] the activity and industry of advertising things to people on television, in newspapers, on the internet, etc:

# advertorial 24

*Cigarette advertising has been banned.* ◊ **radio/TV/online advertising** ◊ *a career in advertising* ◊ *Val works for an **advertising agency*** (= a company that designs advertisements). ◊ *A good **advertising campaign** will increase our sales.*

**ad·ver·tor·ial** /ˌædvəˈtɔːriəl; NAmE -vərˈt-/ *noun* an advertisement that is designed to look like an article in the newspaper or magazine in which it appears

**ad·vice** ❶ **A1** /ədˈvaɪs/ *noun* [U] an opinion or a suggestion about what sb should do in a particular situation: *expert/practical/professional/medical advice* ◊ *We were advised to seek legal advice.* ◊ **~ on sth** *The service offers information and advice on possible careers.* ◊ *Ask your teacher's advice on how to prepare for the exam.* ◊ **~ about sth** *They give good advice to parents about managing difficult behaviour.* ◊ **~ from sb** *We were advised to seek advice from an expert.* ◊ *Let me give you **a piece of advice**.* ◊ *A **word of advice**. Don't wear that dress.* ◊ *Take my advice. Don't do it.* ◊ **on the~ of sb** *I went there on the advice of a friend.* ◊ **against the~ of sb** *She went back to work against the advice of her doctor* (= her doctor advised her not to). **HELP** Advice is uncountable. we say *a piece of advice* (not 'an advice') and *some advice* (not 'some advices').

▼ **EXPRESS YOURSELF**
**Giving somebody advice**
There are a number of tactful ways of telling people what you think they should do:
• *If I were you, I'd wait.*
• *I think you should/ought to see a doctor.*
• *Why don't you/Why not/Could you maybe ask Tom to help?*
• *If you want my advice/If you want to know what I think, I'd say it's better to tell him.*
• *I'd advise you to sell it now.*

**adˈvice column** (NAmE) (BrE also ˈ**agony column**) *noun* part of a newspaper, magazine or website in which sb gives advice to readers who have sent emails or letters about their personal problems

**adˈvice columnist** (NAmE) (BrE ˈ**agony aunt/uncle**) *noun* a person who writes in a newspaper or magazine or on a website giving advice in reply to people's emails and letters about their personal problems

**ad·vis·able** /ədˈvaɪzəbl/ *adj.* [not usually before noun] sensible and a good idea in order to achieve sth: *Early booking is advisable.* ◊ **~ to do sth** *It is advisable to book early.* **OPP inadvisable** ▶ **ad·vis·abil·ity** /ədˌvaɪzəˈbɪləti/ *noun* [U]

**ad·vise** ❶ **B1** /ədˈvaɪz/ *verb* **1** **B1** [I, T] to tell sb what you think they should do in a particular situation: **~(sb) against sth/against doing sth** *I would strongly advise against going out on your own.* ◊ **~ sb** *Her mother was away and couldn't advise her.* ◊ **~ sth** *I'd advise extreme caution.* ◊ **+ speech** *'Get there early,' she advised (them).* ◊ **~ sb to do sth** *Police are advising people to stay at home.* ◊ *Doctors advised the patient to have surgery.* ◊ **~ that…** *They advise that a passport be carried with you at all times.* ◊ (BrE also) *They advise that a passport should be carried with you at all times.* ◊ **it is advised that…** *It is strongly advised that you take out insurance.* ◊ **~ doing sth** *I'd advise buying your tickets well in advance if you want to travel in August.* ⊃ see also ILL-ADVISED, WELL ADVISED ⊃ SYNONYMS at RECOMMEND **2** ❶ **B1** [I, T] to give sb help and information on a subject that you know a lot about: **~ on/about sth/about doing sth** *We employ an expert to advise on new technology.* ◊ **~ sb on/about/on doing sth** *She advises the government on environmental issues.* ◊ **~ what, which, whether, etc…** *The pharmacist will advise which medicines are safe to take.* ◊ **~ sb what, which, whether, etc…** *Your lawyer can advise you whether to take any action.* **3** [T] (*formal*) to officially tell sb sth **SYN inform**: **~ sb of sth** *Please advise us of any change of address.* ◊ **~ sb when, where, how, etc…** *I will contact you later to advise you* 

*when to come.* ◊ **~ sb that…** *I regret to advise you that the course is now full.*

**adˈvised·ly** /ədˈvaɪzədli/ *adv.* (*formal*) if you say that you are using a word **advisedly**, you mean that you have thought carefully before choosing it ⊃ see also ILL-ADVISEDLY

**ad·vise·ment** /ədˈvaɪzmənt/ *noun* [U] (NAmE, *formal*) advice: *the University Advisement Center*
**IDM** **take sth under adˈvisement** (*formal*) to think carefully about sth before making a decision about it: *The judge has taken the matter under advisement.*

**ad·viser** (*also* **ad·visor**) /ədˈvaɪzə(r)/ *noun* a person who gives advice, especially sb who knows a lot about a particular subject: *a financial adviser* ◊ **~(to sb) (on sth)** *a special adviser to the President on education*

**ad·vis·ory** /ədˈvaɪzəri/ *adj.*, *noun*
■ *adj.* having the role of giving professional advice: *an advisory committee/body/service* ◊ *He acted in an advisory capacity only.*
■ *noun* (*pl.* -**ies**) (*especially NAmE*) an official warning that sth bad is going to happen: *a tornado advisory*

**ad·vo·cacy** /ˈædvəkəsi/ *noun* [U] **1** **~(of sth)** (*formal*) public support that sb gives to an idea, a course of action or a belief **2** support, advice and help given to people, often with special needs or aims, who are unable to speak for themselves: *an **advocacy group** for the rights of the mentally ill* **3** (*specialist*) the work of lawyers who speak about cases in court

**ad·vo·cate** ❷+ **C1** *noun*, *verb*
■ *noun* /ˈædvəkət/ **1** ❷+ **C1** (*formal*) a person who supports or speaks in favour of sb or of a public plan or action: **~ for sth/sb** *an advocate for hospital workers* ◊ **~ of sth/sb** *a staunch advocate of free speech* ⊃ see also DEVIL'S ADVOCATE **2** (*law*) a person who defends sb in court **3** (*law*) (in Scotland and South Africa) a lawyer who has the right to argue cases in higher courts ⊃ note at LAWYER
■ *verb* ❷+ **C1** /ˈædvəkeɪt/ (*formal*) to support sth publicly: **~ sth** *The group does not advocate the use of violence.* ◊ **~(sb) doing sth** *Many experts advocate rewarding your child for good behaviour.* ◊ **~ that…** *The report advocated that all buildings be fitted with smoke detectors.* ◊ (BrE also) *The report advocated that all buildings should be fitted with smoke detectors.* ⊃ SYNONYMS at RECOMMEND

**Ad·ware**™ /ˈædweə(r); NAmE -wer/ *noun* [U] a type of software that displays or downloads advertisements that are not asked for on a computer screen, smartphone, etc. when a user is online ⊃ compare MALWARE, SPYWARE

**adze** (NAmE *also* **adz**) /ædz/ *noun* a heavy tool with a sharp curved BLADE at 90 degrees to the handle, used for cutting or shaping large pieces of wood

**aegis** /ˈiːdʒɪs/ *noun*
**IDM** **under the aegis of sb/sth** (*formal*) with the protection or support of a particular organization or person

**ae·olian** (US *also* **eo·lian**) /iːˈəʊliən/ *adj.* (*specialist*) connected with or caused by the action of the wind

**aeon** (BrE) (NAmE or *specialist* **eon**) /ˈiːən; BrE also ˈiːɒn; NAmE *also* ˈiːɑːn/ *noun* **1** (*formal*) an extremely long period of time; thousands of years **2** (*geology*) a major division of time, divided before ERAS: *aeons of geological history*

**aer·ate** /ˈeəreɪt; NAmE ˈer-/ *verb* **1** **~ sth** to make it possible for air to become mixed with soil, water, etc: *Earthworms do the important job of aerating the soil.* **2** **~ sth** to add a gas, especially CARBON DIOXIDE, to a liquid under pressure: *aerated water* ▶ **aer·ation** /eəˈreɪʃn; NAmE eˈr-/ *noun* [U]

**aer·ial** /ˈeəriəl; NAmE ˈer-/ *noun*, *adj.*
■ *noun* (*especially BrE*) (*also* **an·tenna** *especially in NAmE*) a piece of equipment made of wire or long straight pieces of metal for receiving or sending radio and television signals
■ *adj.* **1** from a plane: *aerial attacks/bombardment/photography* ◊ *an aerial view of Palm Island* **2** in the air; existing above the ground: *The banyan tree has aerial roots.*

**aerie** /ˈɪəri, ˈeə-; ˈaɪə-; NAmE ˈɪri, ˈeri/ (NAmE) = EYRIE

| b **b**ad | d **d**id | f **f**all | g **g**et | h **h**at | j **y**es | k **c**at | l **l**eg | m **m**an | n **n**ow | p **p**en | r **r**ed |

**aero-** /ˈeərəʊ, eərə, eəˈrɒ/; *NAmE* erəʊ, erə, eˈrɑː/ *combining form* (in nouns, adjectives and adverbs) relating to the air or aircraft: *aerodynamic* ◊ *aerospace*

**aero·bat·ics** /ˌeərəˈbætɪks; *NAmE* ˌer-/ *noun* [U + sing./pl. v.] movements performed in an aircraft that are exciting and show skill, such as flying with the top of the aircraft facing the ground, especially in front of an audience ▶ **aero·batic** *adj.*: *an aerobatic display*

**aer·obic** /eəˈrəʊbɪk; *NAmE* eˈr-/ *adj.* **1** (*biology*) needing OXYGEN: *aerobic bacteria* **2** (of physical exercise) especially designed to improve the function of the heart and lungs OPP **anaerobic**

**aer·obics** /eəˈrəʊbɪks; *NAmE* eˈr-/ *noun* [U] physical exercises intended to make the heart and lungs stronger, often done in classes, with music: *to do aerobics*

**aero·drome** /ˈeərədrəʊm; *NAmE* ˈer-/ (*BrE*) (*US* **air·drome**) *noun* (*old-fashioned*) a small airport

**aero·dy·nam·ics** /ˌeərəʊdaɪˈnæmɪks; *NAmE* ˌer-/ *noun* **1** [pl.] the qualities of an object that affect the way it moves through the air: *Research has focused on improving the car's aerodynamics.* **2** [U] the science that deals with how objects move through air ▶ **aero·dy·nam·ic** /-mɪk/ *adj.*: *the car's aerodynamic shape* (= making it able to move faster) **aero·dy·nam·ic·al·ly** /-kli/ *adv.*

**aero·foil** /ˈeərəfɔɪl; *NAmE* ˈer-/ (*BrE*) (*NAmE* **air·foil**) *noun* the basic curved structure of an aircraft's wing that helps to lift it into the air

**aero·naut·ics** /ˌeərəˈnɔːtɪks; *NAmE* ˌer-/ *noun* [U] the science or practice of building and flying aircraft ▶ **aero·naut·ic·al** /-tɪkl/ *adj.*: *an aeronautical engineer*

**aero·plane** /ˈeərəpleɪn; *NAmE* ˈer-/ (*BrE*) (*also* **air·plane** especially in *NAmE*) (*also* **plane** *BrE*, *NAmE*) *noun* a flying vehicle with wings and one or more engines

**aero·sol** /ˈeərəsɒl; *NAmE* ˈerəsɑːl/ *noun* a liquid such as paint or HAIRSPRAY that is kept under pressure in a metal container and released as a SPRAY: *ozone-friendly aerosols* ◊ *an aerosol can/spray*

**aero·space** /ˈeərəʊspeɪs; *NAmE* ˈer-/ *noun* [U] the industry of building aircraft, vehicles and equipment to be sent into space: *jobs in aerospace and defence* ◊ *the aerospace industry*

**aero·stat** /ˈeərəstæt; *NAmE* ˈer-/ *noun* (*specialist*) an aircraft such as an AIRSHIP or HOT-AIR BALLOON that is filled with a gas

**aes·thete** (*NAmE also* **es·thete**) /ˈiːsθiːt, ˈes-/; *NAmE* ˈes-/ *noun* (*formal*) a person who has a love and understanding of art and beautiful things

**aes·thet·ic** ⓘ+ C1 (*NAmE also* **es·thet·ic**) /iːsˈθetɪk, es-/; *NAmE* es-/ *adj.*, *noun*
■ *adj.* **1** ⓘ+ C1 connected with beauty and art and the understanding of beautiful things: *the aesthetic appeal of the songs* ◊ *The benefits of conservation are both financial and aesthetic.* **2** made in an artistic way and beautiful to look at: *Their furniture was more aesthetic than functional.* ▶ **aes·thet·ic·al·ly** (*NAmE also* **es-**) /-kli/ *adv.*: *aesthetically pleasing colour combinations*
■ *noun* **1** [C] the qualities and ideas in a work of art or literature that relate to beauty and the nature of art: *The students debated the aesthetic of the poems.* **2 aesthetics** [U] the branch of philosophy that studies the principles of beauty, especially in art ▶ **aes·theti·cism** (*NAmE also* **es-**) /-tɪsɪzəm/ *noun* [U]

**aeti·ology** (*BrE*) (*NAmE* **eti·ology**) /ˌiːtiˈɒlədʒi; *NAmE* -ˈɑːl-/ *noun* (*pl.* **-ies**) (*medical*) **1** [U, C] the cause of a disease or medical condition **2** [U] the scientific study of the causes of disease

**AFAIK** *abbr.* (*informal*) as far as I know (= used in text messages, on social media, etc.)

**afar** /əˈfɑː(r)/ *adv.*
IDM **from afar** (*literary*) from a long distance away: *He loved her from afar* (= did not tell her he loved her).

**afara** /əˈfɑːrə/ *WAfrE* [əˈfɑrɑ] *noun* **1** (*also* **limba**) [C] a tall tree that grows in West Africa **2** (*also* **limba**) [U] the wood

from this tree, often used for making furniture **3** *WAfrE* [əˈfɑrɑ] [C] (*WAfrE*) a bridge, usually made of wood

**AFC** /ˌeɪ ef ˈsiː/ *abbr.* **1** (*BrE*) Association Football Club: *Leeds United AFC* **2** (*NAmE*) (in the US) the American Football Conference (one of the two groups of teams in the National Football League) **3** (*BrE*) Air Force Cross (an award given to members of the AIR FORCE, for being brave when flying rather than when fighting the enemy) **4** (*specialist*) automatic frequency control (a system that allows radios and televisions to continue to receive the same signal)

**af·fable** /ˈæfəbl/ *adj.* pleasant, friendly and easy to talk to SYN **genial** ▶ **af·fa·bil·ity** /ˌæfəˈbɪləti/ *noun* [U] **af·fably** /ˈæfəbli/ *adv.*

**af·fair** ⓘ B2 /əˈfeə(r); *NAmE* əˈfer/ *noun*
• PUBLIC/POLITICAL ACTIVITIES **1** ⓘ B2 **affairs** [pl.] events that are of public interest or political importance: *world/international affairs* ◊ *an expert on foreign affairs* (= political events in other countries) ◊ *affairs of state* ⊃ see also CURRENT AFFAIRS
• EVENT **2** ⓘ B2 [C, usually sing.] an event that people are talking about or describing in a particular way: *The newspapers exaggerated the whole affair wildly.* ◊ *She wanted the celebration to be a simple family affair.* ◊ *Many people have criticized the way the government handled the affair.*
• RELATIONSHIP **3** ⓘ B2 [C] a sexual relationship between two people, usually when one or both of them are already in a relationship with sb else: *She is having an affair with her boss.* ⊃ see also LOVE AFFAIR ⊃ WORDFINDER NOTE at LOVE
• PRIVATE BUSINESS **4** ⓘ B2 **affairs** [pl.] matters connected with a person's private business and financial situation: *She manages the family's financial affairs.* ◊ *She wanted to put her affairs in order before she died.* **5** [sing.] a thing that sb is responsible for (and that other people should not be interested in) SYN **business**: *How I spend my money is my affair.*
• OBJECT **6** [C] (with an adjective) (*old-fashioned*) an object that is unusual or difficult to describe: *Her hat was an amazing affair with feathers and a huge brim.* IDM see STATE *n.*

**af·faire** /əˈfeə(r); *NAmE* əˈfer/ *noun* (from French, *literary*) a love affair

**af·fect** ⓘ A2 ⓞ /əˈfekt/ *verb* **1** ⓘ A2 ~ **sb/sth** to produce a change in sb/sth: *How will these changes affect us?* ◊ *The article deals with issues affecting the lives of children.* ◊ *Thousands of people have been adversely affected* (= affected in a negative way) *by the decision.* **2** ⓘ A2 [often passive] ~ **sb/sth** (of a disease) to attack sb or a part of the body; to make sb become ill: *The disease is more likely to affect women than men.* ◊ *Rub the cream into the affected areas.* **3** ~ **sb** [often passive] to make sb feel very sad, sorry, etc. about sb/sth: *They were deeply affected by the news of her death.* **4** ~ **(to do) sth** (*formal*) to pretend to be feeling or thinking sth: *She affected a calmness she did not feel.* **5** ~ **sth** (*formal*, *disapproving*) to use or wear sth that is intended to impress other people SYN **put on**: *I wish he wouldn't affect that ridiculous accent.*

▼ WHICH WORD?

**affect / effect**
• **affect** *verb* = 'to have an influence on sb/sth': *Does television affect children's behaviour?* It is not a noun.
• **effect** *noun* = 'result, influence': *Does television have an effect on children's behaviour?*
• **effect** *verb* is quite rare and formal and means 'to achieve or produce': *They hope to effect a reconciliation.*

**af·fect·ation** /ˌæfekˈteɪʃn/ *noun* [C, U] behaviour or an action that is not natural or sincere and that is often intended to impress other people: *His little affectations irritated her.* ◊ *Kay has no affectation at all.* ◊ *He raised his eyebrows with an affectation of surprise* (= pretending to be surprised).

# affected

**af·fect·ed** /əˈfektɪd/ *adj.* **1** changed or influenced by sth: *Rub the ointment into the affected areas.* **2** (of a person or their behaviour) not natural or sincere: *an affected laugh/smile* OPP **unaffected** ▶ **af·fect·ed·ly** *adv.*

**af·fect·ing** /əˈfektɪŋ/ *adj.* (*formal*) making you feel very sad, sorry, etc. about sb/sth

**af·fec·tion** /əˈfekʃn/ *noun* **1** [U, sing.] the feeling of liking or loving sb/sth very much and caring about them: *Children need lots of love and affection.* ◇ *He didn't show his wife any affection.* ◇ *She was held in deep affection by all her students.* ◇ ~ **for sb/sth** *Mr Darcy's affection for his sister* ◇ *I have a great affection for New York.* **2 affections** [pl.] (*formal or literary*) a person's feelings of love: *Anne had two men trying to win her affections.*

**af·fec·tion·ate** /əˈfekʃənət/ *adj.* showing caring feelings and love for sb SYN **loving**: *He is very affectionate towards his children.* ◇ *an affectionate kiss* ▶ **af·fec·tion·ate·ly** *adv.*: *William was affectionately known as Billy.*

**af·fect·ive** /əˈfektɪv/ *adj.* (*specialist*) connected with emotions and attitudes: *affective disorders* ⇨ see also BIPOLAR DISORDER, SEASONAL AFFECTIVE DISORDER ▶ **af·fect·ive·ly** *adv.*

**af·fi·da·vit** /ˌæfəˈdeɪvɪt/ *noun* (*law*) a written statement that you swear is true, and that can be used as evidence in court

**af·fili·ate** *verb, noun*
- *verb* /əˈfɪlieɪt/ [T, usually passive] to link a group, a company or an organization very closely with another, larger one: **be affiliated (with/to sb/sth)** *The hospital is affiliated with the local university.* **2** [T, I] ~ **yourself) (with sb/sth)** to join, to be connected with, or to work for an organization: *The majority of people questioned affiliated themselves with a religious group.*
- *noun* /əˈfɪliət/ a company, an organization, etc. that is connected with or controlled by another, larger one

**af·fili·ated** /əˈfɪlieɪtɪd/ *adj.* closely connected to or controlled by a group or an organization: *All affiliated members can vote.* ◇ *a government-affiliated institute* OPP **unaffiliated**

**af·fili·ation** /əˌfɪliˈeɪʃn/ *noun* [U, C] (*formal*) **1** a person's connection with a political party, religion, etc: *He was arrested because of his political affiliation.* **2** one group or organization's official connection with another

**af·fin·ity** /əˈfɪnəti/ *noun* (*pl.* **-ies**) (*formal*) **1** [sing.] ~ **(for/with sb/sth)** | ~ **(between A and B)** a strong feeling that you understand sb/sth and like them or it SYN **rapport**: *Sam was born in the country and had a deep affinity with nature.* **2** [U, C] ~ **(with sb/sth)** | ~ **(between A and B)** a close relationship between two people or things that have similar qualities, structures or features: *There is a close affinity between Italian and Spanish.*

**afˈfinity group** *noun* (*especially NAmE*) a group of people who share the same interest or purpose

**af·firm** /əˈfɜːm; *NAmE* əˈfɜːrm/ *verb* (*formal*) to state clearly or publicly that sth is true or that you support sth strongly SYN **confirm**: ~ **sth** *Both sides affirmed their commitment to the ceasefire.* ◇ ~ **that …** *I can affirm that no one will lose their job.* ⇨ see also LIFE-AFFIRMING ▶ **af·firm·ation** /ˌæfəˈmeɪʃn; *NAmE* ˌæfərˈm-/ *noun* [U, C]: *She nodded in affirmation.*

**af·firma·tive** /əˈfɜːmətɪv; *NAmE* əˈfɜːrm-/ *adj., noun*
- *adj.* (*formal*) **1** an **affirmative** word or reply means 'yes' or expresses agreement **2** = POSITIVE (9) OPP **negative** ▶ **af·firma·tive·ly** *adv.*: *90 per cent voted affirmatively.*
- *noun* (*formal*) a word or statement that means 'yes'; an agreement or a CONFIRMATION: *She answered in the affirmative* (= said 'yes'). OPP **negative**
- *exclamation* (*especially NAmE, formal*) used to agree to a statement or request: *'Affirmative, sir'* responded the lieutenant.

**afˌfirmative ˈaction** (*especially NAmE; BrE usually* **posi·tive disˌcrimiˈnation**) *noun* [U] the practice or policy of making sure that a particular number of jobs, etc. are given to people from groups that are often treated unfairly because of their race, sex, etc. ⇨ compare REVERSE DISCRIMINATION

**affix** *verb, noun*
- *verb* /əˈfɪks/ [T, often passive, I] ~ **(sth) (to sth)** (*formal*) to stick or attach sth to sth else; to be able to be fixed to sth: *The label should be firmly affixed to the package.*
- *noun* /ˈæfɪks/ (*grammar*) a letter or group of letters added to the beginning or end of a word to change its meaning. The PREFIX *un-* in *unhappy* and the SUFFIX *-less* in *careless* are both affixes.

**af·flict** /əˈflɪkt/ *verb* [often passive] (*formal*) to affect sb/sth in an unpleasant or harmful way: ~ **sb/sth** *Severe drought has afflicted the region.* ◇ **be afflicted with sth** *About 40 per cent of the country's population is afflicted with the disease.*

**af·flic·tion** /əˈflɪkʃn/ *noun* [U, C] (*formal*) pain and difficulty or sth that causes it

**af·flu·ent** /ˈæfluənt/ *adj.* (*formal*) having a lot of money and a good standard of living SYN **prosperous, wealthy**: *affluent Western countries* ◇ *a very affluent neighbourhood* ⇨ SYNONYMS at RICH ▶ **af·flu·ence** /-əns/ *noun* [U] SYN **prosperity**

**af·ford** /əˈfɔːd; *NAmE* əˈfɔːrd/ *verb* **1** [no passive] (usually used with *can, could* or *be able to*, especially in negative sentences or questions) to have enough money to be able to buy or do sth: ~ **sth** *Can we afford a new car?* ◇ *None of them could afford £50 for a ticket.* ◇ ~ **to do sth** *We can't afford to go abroad this summer.* ◇ *She never took a taxi, even though she could afford to.* ◇ ~ **sth to do sth** *He couldn't afford the money to go on the trip.* ⇨ WORDFINDER NOTE at MONEY **2** [no passive] (usually used with *can* or *could*, especially in negative sentences and questions) if you say that you **can't afford** to do sth, you mean that you should not do it because it will cause problems for you if you do: ~ **to do sth** *We cannot afford to ignore this warning.* ◇ (*formal*) *They could ill afford to lose any more staff.* ◇ ~ **sth** *She felt she couldn't afford any more time off work.* **3** (*formal*) to provide sb with sth: ~ **sth** *The tree affords some shelter from the sun.* ◇ ~ **sb sth** *Being a college professor affords you the opportunity simply to write and do research.*

**af·ford·able** /əˈfɔːdəbl; *NAmE* əˈfɔːrd-/ *adj.* cheap enough that people can afford to pay it or buy it: *We offer quality products at affordable prices.* ◇ *There is a lack of affordable housing in the city.* OPP **unaffordable** ⇨ SYNONYMS at CHEAP ▶ **af·ford·abil·ity** /əˌfɔːdəˈbɪləti; *NAmE* əˌfɔːrd-/ *noun* [U] **af·ford·ably** /əˈfɔːdəbli; *NAmE* əˈfɔːrd-/ *adv.*: *affordably priced apartments*

**afˌfordable ˈhousing** *noun* [U] houses or flats that are available for people on low incomes to buy or rent at a low price, especially because the government has required house-building companies to offer a certain number of new properties at lower prices ⇨ compare SOCIAL HOUSING

**af·for·est·ation** /əˌfɒrɪˈsteɪʃn; *NAmE* əˌfɔːr-/ *noun* [U] (*specialist*) the process of planting areas of land with trees in order to form a forest ⇨ compare DEFORESTATION ▶ **af·for·est** /əˈfɒrɪst; *NAmE* əˈfɔːr-/ *verb* [usually passive]

**af·fray** /əˈfreɪ/ *noun* [C, usually sing., U] (*law*) a fight or violent behaviour in a public place that DISTURBS the peace

**af·front** /əˈfrʌnt/ *noun, verb*
- *noun* [usually sing.] ~ **(to sb/sth)** a remark or an action that offends sb/sth SYN **insult**
- *verb* [usually passive] (*formal*) to say or do sth that offends sb SYN **insult**: **be/feel affronted** *He hoped they would not feel affronted if they were not invited.* ◇ *an affronted expression*

**afi·cion·ado** /əˌfɪʃəˈnɑːdəʊ/ *noun* (*pl.* **-os**) a person who likes a particular sport, activity or subject very much and knows a lot about it

**afield** /əˈfiːld/ *adv.*
IDM **far/farther/further aˈfield** far away from home; to or in places that are not near: *You can hire a car if you want to explore further afield.* ◇ *Journalists came from as far afield as China.*

**aflame** /əˈfleɪm/ *adj.* [not before noun] (*literary*) **1** burning; on fire SYN **ablaze**: *The whole building was soon aflame.* **2** full of bright colours and lights SYN **ablaze**: *The woods were aflame with autumn colours.* **3** showing that you are excited or embarrassed: *eyes/cheeks aflame*

**afloat** /əˈfləʊt/ *adj.* [not before noun] **1** floating on water: *Somehow we kept the boat afloat.* **2** (of a business, etc.) having enough money to pay debts; able to survive: *They will have to borrow £10 million next year, just to **stay afloat**.*

**afoot** /əˈfʊt/ *adj.* [not before noun] being planned; happening: *There are plans afoot to increase taxation.* ◇ *Changes were afoot.*

**afore·men·tioned** /əˈfɔːmenʃənd, əˌfɔːˈmenʃənd/; *NAmE* əˈfɔːrmenʃənd, əˌfɔːrˈmenʃənd/ (*also* **afore·said** /əˈfɔːsed/; *NAmE* əˈfɔːrs-/) (*also* **said**) *adj.* [only before noun] (*formal or law*) mentioned before, in an earlier sentence: *The aforementioned person was seen acting suspiciously.*

**afore·thought** /əˈfɔːθɔːt/; *NAmE* əˈfɔːrθɔː-/ *adj.* IDM see MALICE

**a for·ti·ori** /ˌeɪ ˌfɔːtiˈɔːraɪ/; *NAmE* ˌɑː ˌfɔːrtiˈɔːri/ *adv.* (*formal or law, from Latin*) for or with an even stronger reason

**afoul** /əˈfaʊl/ *adv.* (*NAmE*)
IDM **run aˈfoul of sth** to do sth that is not allowed by a law or rule, or to do sth that people in authority think is bad: *to run afoul of the law*

**afraid** ❶ A1 /əˈfreɪd/ *adj.* [not before noun] **1** A1 feeling fear; frightened because you think that you might be hurt or suffer: *Don't be afraid.* ◇ *It's all over. There's nothing to be afraid of now.* ◇ *He had always been afraid of death.* ◇ *~ of doing sth I started to feel afraid of going out alone at night.* ◇ *~ to do sth She was afraid to open the door.* **2** A1 worried about what might happen: *~ of doing sth She was afraid of upsetting her parents.* ◇ *~ to do sth Don't be afraid to ask if you don't understand.* ◇ *~ (that …) We were afraid (that) we were going to capsize the boat.* **3** *~* **for sb/sth** worried or frightened that sth unpleasant, dangerous, etc. will happen to a particular person or thing: *I'm not afraid for me, but for the baby.* ◇ *They had already fired three people and he was afraid for his job.* ◇ *to be afraid for sb's life/safety*
IDM **I'm aˈfraid** A2 used as a polite way of telling sb sth that is unpleasant or disappointing, or that you are sorry about: *I can't help you, I'm afraid.* ◇ *I'm afraid we can't come.* ◇ *I'm afraid that it's not finished yet.* ◇ *He's no better, I'm afraid to say.* ◇ *'Is there any left?' 'I'm afraid not.'* ◇ *'Will it hurt?' 'I'm afraid so.'*

**A-frame** (*also* **A-frame ˈhouse**) *noun* **A-frame** (*especially NAmE*) a house with very steep sides that meet at the top in the shape of the letter A

**afresh** /əˈfreʃ/ *adv.* (*formal*) again, especially from the beginning or with new ideas: *It was a chance to **start afresh**.*

**Af·ri·can** /ˈæfrɪkən/ *adj., noun*
■ *adj.* of or connected with Africa
■ *noun* a person from Africa, especially a black person

**African Aˈmerican** *noun* a person from America who is a member of a race of people who have dark skin, originally from Africa ▶ **African Aˈmerican** *adj.*

**Af·ri·kaans** /ˌæfrɪˈkɑːns/ *noun* [U] a language that has developed from Dutch, spoken in South Africa

**Af·ri·kaner** /ˌæfrɪˈkɑːnə(r)/ *noun* a person from South Africa, usually of Dutch origin, whose first language is Afrikaans

**Afro** /ˈæfrəʊ/ *noun* (*pl.* **-os**) a HAIRSTYLE sometimes worn by black people and popular in the 1970s, which consists of a round mass of very curly hair

**Afro-** /ˈæfrəʊ/ *combining form* (in nouns and adjectives) African: *Afro-Asian*

**Afro·beat** /ˈæfrəʊbiːt/ *noun* [U] a type of music that combines traditional Nigerian rhythms and singing styles with jazz and FUNK

---

**27** **after**

▼ SYNONYMS

**afraid**
**frightened** • **scared** • **terrified** • **alarmed** • **paranoid**
These words all describe feeling or showing fear.

**afraid** [not before noun] feeling fear; worried that sth bad might happen: *There's nothing to be afraid of.* ◇ *Aren't you afraid (that) you'll fall?*

**frightened** feeling fear; worried that sth bad might happen: *a frightened child* ◇ *She was frightened that the glass would break.*

**scared** (*rather informal*) feeling fear; worried that sth bad might happen: *The thieves got scared and ran away.*

AFRAID, FRIGHTENED OR SCARED?
**Scared** is more informal, more common in speech, and often describes small fears. **Afraid** cannot come before a noun. It can only take the preposition *of*, not *about*. If you are **afraid/frightened/scared of sb/doing sth** or **afraid/frightened/scared to do sth** you think you are in danger of being hurt or suffering in some way. If you are **frightened/scared about sth/doing sth**, it is less a fear for your personal safety and more a worry that sth unpleasant might happen.

**terrified** very frightened: *I was terrified (that) she wouldn't come.* ◇ *She looked at him with wide, terrified eyes.*

**alarmed** afraid that sth dangerous or unpleasant might happen: *She was alarmed at the prospect of travelling alone.*

**paranoid** (*rather informal*) afraid of other people for no reason or suspecting that they are trying to harm you, when really they are not: *You're just being paranoid.*

PATTERNS
- afraid/frightened/scared **of** spiders, etc.
- frightened/scared/paranoid **about** …
- afraid/frightened/scared/terrified **that** …
- afraid/frightened/scared **to** open the door, etc.
- Don't be afraid/frightened/scared/alarmed.

**Afro-Caribˈbean** *noun* a person who comes, or whose family comes, from the Caribbean and who is a member of a group of people with dark skin who originally came from Africa ▶ **Afro-Caribˈbean** *adj.*

**aft** /ɑːft; *NAmE* æft/ *adv., adj.* (*specialist*) in, near or towards the back of a ship or an aircraft: *fore and aft of the cockpit* ◇ *the aft cabin/deck*

**after** ❶ A1 /ˈɑːftə(r); *NAmE* ˈæf-/ *prep., conj., adv., adj.*
■ *prep.* **1** A1 later than sth; following sth in time: *We'll leave after lunch.* ◇ *They arrived shortly after 5.* ◇ *Not long after that he resigned.* ◇ *Let's meet **the day after tomorrow/the week after next**.* ◇ *After winning the prize she became famous overnight.* ◇ *After an hour I went home (= when an hour had passed).* ◇ (*NAmE*) *It's ten after seven in the morning (= 7.10 a.m.).* **2** B1 next to and following sb/sth in order or importance: *Your name comes after mine in the list.* ◇ *He's the tallest, after Richard.* ◇ ***After you** (= Please go first).* ◇ ***After you** with the paper (= Can I have it next?).* **3** B1 behind sb when they have left; following sb: *Shut the door after you.* ◇ *I'm always having to clean up after the children (= clean the place after they have left it dirty and untidy).* ◇ *He ran after her with the book.* ◇ *She was left staring after him.* **4** B1 in contrast to sth: *It was pleasantly cool in the house after the sticky heat outside.* **5** B1 as a result of or because of sth that has happened: *I'll never forgive him after what he said.* **6** despite sth; although sth has happened: *I can't believe she'd do that, not after all I've done for her.* **7** *… after …* used to show that sth happens many times or continuously: *day after day of hot weather* ◇ *I've told you time after time not to do that.* ⊃ see also ONE AFTER ANOTHER/THE OTHER at ONE *number* **8** trying to find or catch sb/sth: *The police are after him.* ◇ *He's after a job at our place.* **9** about sb/sth: *She asked after you (= how you were).* **10** in the style of sb/sth; following the example of sb/sth: *a painting after Goya* ◇ *We named the*

# afterbirth 28

baby Ena after her grandmother. **11 after-** (in adjectives) happening or done later than the time or event mentioned: *after-hours drinking* (= after closing time) ◊ *an after-school club* ◊ *after-dinner mints*
**IDM** ˌafter ˈall **1** despite what has been said or expected: *So you made it after all!* **2** used when you are explaining sth, or giving a reason: *He should have paid. He suggested it, after all.* **be after doing sth** *(IrishE)* **1** to be going to do sth soon; to be intending to do sth soon **2** to have just done sth
■ *conj.* at a time later than sth; when sth has finished: *I'll call you after I've spoken to them.* ◊ *Several years after they'd split up they met again by chance in Paris.*
■ *adv.* later in time; afterwards: *That was in 1996. Soon after, I heard that he'd died.* ◊ *I could come next week, or the week after.* ◊ *And they all lived happily ever after.*
■ *adj.* [only before noun] *(old use)* following; later: *in after years*

**after·birth** /ˈɑːftəbɜːθ; *NAmE* ˈæftərbɜːrθ/ *noun* (usually **the afterbirth**) [sing.] the material that comes out of a woman or female animal's body after a baby has been born, and that was necessary to feed and protect the baby ⇒ compare PLACENTA

**after·burn·er** /ˈɑːftəbɜːnə(r); *NAmE* ˈæftərbɜːrn-/ *noun* (*specialist*) a device for increasing the power of a JET ENGINE

**after·care** /ˈɑːftəkeə(r); *NAmE* ˈæftərker/ *noun* [U] **1** care or treatment given to a person who has just left hospital, prison, etc: *aftercare services* **2** *(BrE)* support and advice offered to customers after they have bought a product or service

ˈ**after-effect** *noun* [usually pl.] the **after-effects** of a drug, an illness or an unpleasant event are the feelings that you experience later as a result of it

**after·glow** /ˈɑːftəgləʊ; *NAmE* ˈæftərgloʊ/ *noun* [usually sing.] (*literary*) **1** the light that is left in the sky after the sun has set **2** a pleasant feeling after a good experience

ˌ**after-ˈhours** *adj.* [only before noun] happening or open after the normal or legal closing time for a business: *an after-hours tour of the new facilities* ◊ *an after-hours bar*

**after·life** /ˈɑːftəlaɪf; *NAmE* ˈæftərl-/ *noun* [sing.] a life that some people believe exists after death

**after·mar·ket** /ˈɑːftəmɑːkɪt; *NAmE* ˈæftərmɑːrk-/ *noun* [sing.] (*especially NAmE*) **1** the demand for equipment and services that are related to a purchase: *the aftermarket for computer accessories* **2** *(finance)* the financial markets such as STOCK EXCHANGES where shares in companies are bought and sold, after their original issue

**after·math** /ˈɑːftəmæθ, -mɑːθ; *NAmE* ˈæftərmæθ/ *noun* [usually sing.] the situation that exists as a result of an important (and usually unpleasant) event, especially a war, an accident, etc: **in the~ of sth** *A lot of rebuilding took place in the aftermath of the war.* ◊ *the assassination of the prime minister and its immediate aftermath*

**after·noon** /ˌɑːftəˈnuːn; *NAmE* ˌæftərˈn-/ *noun* [U, C] the period of time from 12 o'clock in the middle of the day until about 6 o'clock in the evening: *this/yesterday/tomorrow afternoon* ◊ **in the~** *In the afternoon, they went shopping.* ◊ **on the~ of** *Where were you on the afternoon of May 21?* ◊ **during the~** *Heavy snow arrived during the afternoon.* ◊ *She studies art two afternoons a week.* ◊ *Georgia was enjoying afternoon tea with her grandmother.* ◊ *Come over on Sunday afternoon.* ⇒ see also GOOD AFTERNOON

**after·noons** /ˌɑːftəˈnuːnz; *NAmE* ˌæftərˈn-/ *adv.* during the afternoon every day: *Afternoons he works at home.*

**af·ters** /ˈɑːftəz; *NAmE* ˈæftərz/ *noun* [U] *(BrE, informal)* a sweet dish that you eat at the end of a meal: *fruit salad for afters* ⇒ see also DESSERT, PUDDING, SWEET *noun*

ˌ**after-ˈsales ˈservice** *noun* [U] the fact of providing help to customers after they have bought a product, usually involving doing repairs that are needed or giving advice on how to use the product

**after-shave** /ˈɑːftəʃeɪv; *NAmE* ˈæftərʃ-/ *noun* [U, C] a liquid with a pleasant smell that men sometimes put on their faces after they SHAVE

**after-shock** /ˈɑːftəʃɒk; *NAmE* ˈæftərʃɑːk/ *noun* a small earthquake that happens after a bigger one

**after-taste** /ˈɑːftəteɪst; *NAmE* ˈæftərt-/ *noun* [sing.] a taste (usually an unpleasant one) that stays in your mouth after you have eaten or drunk sth

**after-thought** /ˈɑːftəθɔːt; *NAmE* ˈæftərθ-/ *noun* [usually sing.] a thing that is thought of, said or added later, and is often not carefully planned: *They only invited Jack and Sarah as an afterthought.*

**after·wards** /ˈɑːftəwədz; *NAmE* ˈæftərwərdz/ *(especially BrE)* *(NAmE usually* **after·ward***) adv.* at a later time; after an event that has already been mentioned: *Shortly afterwards he met her again.* ◊ *He took his family to supper at a restaurant, and soon afterwards, he fell ill.*

**after·word** /ˈɑːftəwɜːd; *NAmE* ˈæftərwɜːrd/ *noun* a section at the end of a book that says sth about the main text, and may be written by a different author ⇒ compare FOREWORD

**ag** /æx, ʌx/ *exclamation* (SAfrE) used when you are reacting to sth that has been said, or when you are angry or annoyed by sth: *Ag, don't worry about it.* ◊ *Ag, no man!*

**Aga**™ /ˈɑːgə/ *noun* *(BrE)* a type of British cooker made of solid iron that is also used for heating. 'Aga saga' is a humorous name for a novel about the lives of British middle-class women, because Agas are very popular with this group.

**again** /əˈgen, əˈgeɪn/ *adv.* **1** one more time; on another occasion: *This must never happen again.* ◊ *Try again—it takes practice.* ◊ *Can we start again, please?* ◊ *Rowling again proves to be a superb storyteller.* ◊ *I've said it again and again* (= many times) *not to do that.* ◊ *I'll have to write it all over again* (= again from the beginning). ◊ *She tried over and over again* (= many times) *to get it right.* ◊ *He has yet again* (= as has happened many times before) *shown that he cannot be trusted.* ◊ **Once again** (= as had happened several times before), *the train was late.* **2** showing that sb/sth is in the same place or state that they were in originally: *We're very happy to be here together again.* ◊ *She spends two hours a day getting to work and back again.* **3** added to an amount that is already there: *The cost is about half as much again as it was two years ago.* ◊ *I'd like the same again* (= the same amount or the same thing). **4** used to show that a comment or fact is connected with what you have just said: *And again, we must think of the cost.* **5** **then/there~** used to introduce a fact or an opinion that contrasts with what you have just said: *We might buy it but then again we might not.* **6** used when you ask sb to tell you sth or repeat sth that you think they have told you already: *What was the name again?* **IDM** see NOW *adv.*, SAME *pron.*, TIME *n.*

**against** /əˈgenst, əˈgeɪnst/ *prep.* **HELP** For the special uses of **against** in phrasal verbs, look at the entries for the verbs. For example **count against sb** is in the phrasal verb section at **count**. **1** opposing or disagreeing with sb/sth: *the fight against terrorism* ◊ *We're playing against the league champions next week.* ◊ *We were rowing against the current.* ◊ *That's against the law.* ◊ *She was forced to marry against her will.* ◊ *Are you for or against the death penalty?* ◊ *She is against seeing* (= does not want to see) *him.* ◊ *I'd advise you against doing that.* **2** not to the advantage or favour of sb/sth: *The evidence is against him.* ◊ *Her age is against her.* ⇒ compare FOR **3** close to, touching or hitting sb/sth: *Put the piano there, against the wall.* ◊ *The rain beat against the windows.* **4** in order to prevent sth from happening or to reduce the damage caused by sth: *an injection against rabies* ◊ *They took precautions against fire.* ◊ *Are we insured against theft?* **5** with sth in the background, as a contrast: *His red clothes stood out clearly against the snow.* ◊ *(figurative) The love story unfolds against a background of civil war.* **6** used when you are comparing two things: *You must weigh the benefits against the cost.* ◊ *Check your receipts against the statement.* ◊

*What's the rate of exchange against the dollar?* **IDM** see AS *conj.*, STACKED

**agape** /əˈɡeɪp/ *adj.* [not before noun] (*formal*) if a person's mouth is **agape**, it is wide open, especially because they are surprised or shocked

**agar** /ˈeɪɡɑː(r)/ (*also* **agar-ˈagar**) *noun* [U] a substance like JELLY, used by scientists for growing CULTURES, and to make liquid foods thicker

**agate** /ˈæɡət/ *noun* [U, C] a hard stone with bands or areas of colour, used in jewellery

**agave** /əˈɡeɪvi, əˈɡɑːvi; *NAmE* əˈɡɑːvi/ *noun* a plant that grows in hot dry areas of North and South America, with sharp points on the leaves and tall groups of flowers

**agˈbada** /æɡˈbɑːdə/ *WAfrE* [aɡ͡bádá] *noun* (*WAfrE*) a long ROBE (= long piece of clothing) worn by men in some parts of West Africa

**age** 🗝 **A1** 🅦 /eɪdʒ/ *noun, verb*
■ *noun* **1** 🗝 **A1** [C, U] the number of years that a person has lived or a thing has existed: *You're the same age as my brother.* ◇ *ways of calculating the age of the earth* ◇ *to reach retirement age* ◇ **at the ~ of** … *He left school at the age of 18.* ◇ *He started playing the piano at an early age.* ◇ **from the ~ of** … *Children can start school from the age of four.* ◇ **between the ages of** … *children between the ages of 5 and 10* ◇ *The children range in age from 5 to 10.* ◇ **under / over the ~ of** … *Children over the age of 12 must pay full fare.* ◇ *The film is unsuitable for children below 12 years of age.* ◇ *Young people of all ages go there to meet.* ◇ **for your ~** *He was tall for his age* (= taller than you would expect, considering his age). ➪ see also LEGAL AGE, MENTAL AGE

**WORDFINDER** adolescent, elderly, generation, infant, juvenile, middle-aged, minor, teenage, young

**2** 🗝 **B1** *ages* [pl.] (*also* **an age** [sing.]) (*informal, especially BrE*) a very long time: *It'll probably take ages to find a parking space.* ◇ **for ages** *I waited for ages.* ◇ **ages ago** *Carlos left ages ago.* ◇ *It's been an age since we've seen them.* **3** 🗝 **B2** [U, C] a particular period of a person's life: *in middle / old age* ◇ *15 is an awkward age.* ➪ see also MIDDLE AGE, OLD AGE, SCHOOL AGE, THIRD AGE **4** 🗝 **B2** [C] a particular period of history: *the nuclear age* ◇ *We live in an age of globalization.* ◇ **through the ages** *a study of fashion through the ages* ➪ see also BRONZE AGE, GOLDEN AGE, IRON AGE, NEW AGE, SPACE-AGE, STONE AGE **5** 🗝 **B2** [U] the state of being old: *The jacket was showing signs of age.* ◇ **with ~** *Wine improves with age.* **6** [C] (*geology*) a length of time that is a division of an EPOCH
**IDM** **be / act your ˈage** to behave in a way that is suitable for sb of your age and not as though you were much younger **come of ˈage 1** when a person **comes of age**, they reach the age when they have an adult's legal rights and responsibilities ➪ see also COMING OF AGE **2** if sth **comes of age**, it reaches the stage of development at which people accept and value it **ˌlook your ˈage** to seem as old as you really are and not younger or older **ˌunder ˈage** not legally old enough to do a particular thing: *It is illegal to sell cigarettes to children who are under age.* ➪ see also UNDERAGE ➪ more at ADVANCED, CERTAIN *adj.*, DAY, FEEL *v.*, GRAND *adj.*, RIPE
■ *verb* (*BrE* **ˈage·ing** *or* **aging** *especially in NAmE*, **aged**, **aged**) **1** 🗝 **B1** [I] to become older: *As he aged, his memory got worse.* ◇ *The population is aging* (= more people are living longer). **2** [I, T] to look, feel or seem older; to make sb/sth look, feel or seem older: *My mother has really aged since she became ill.* ◇ **~sb** *The shock has aged her.* ◇ **~sth** *Exposure to the sun ages the skin.* **3** [I, T] to develop in taste over a period of time; to allow sth to do this **SYN** **mature**: *The cheese is left to age for at least a year.* ◇ **~sth** *The wine is aged in oak casks.*

**-age** /ɪdʒ/ *suffix* (in nouns) **1** the action or result of: *breakage* **2** a state or condition of: *bondage* **3** a set or group of: *baggage* **4** an amount of: *mileage* **5** the cost of: *postage* **6** a place where: *anchorage*

**aged** 🗝 **B1** *adj.* **1** 🗝 **B1** /eɪdʒd/ [not before noun] of the age of: *They have two children aged six and nine.* ◇ *volunteers aged between 25 and 40* **2** /ˈeɪdʒɪd/ (*formal*) very old:

*my aged aunt* ➪ **SYNONYMS** at OLD **3 the aged** /ˈeɪdʒɪd/ *noun* [pl.] very old people: *services for the sick and the aged*

**ˈage group** (*also less frequent* **ˈage bracket**) *noun* people of a similar age or within a particular range of ages: *men in the older age group* ◇ *education for the 16–18 age group* ◇ *Which age bracket are you?* (*Please tick the box*).

**age·ing** (*BrE*) (*also* **aging** *especially in NAmE*) /ˈeɪdʒɪŋ/ *noun, adj.*
■ *noun* [U] the process of growing old: *signs of ageing*
■ *adj.* [usually before noun] becoming older and usually less useful, safe, healthy, etc.: *ageing equipment* ◇ *an ageing rock star*

**age·ism** (*NAmE also* **agism**) /ˈeɪdʒɪzəm/ *noun* [U] unfair treatment of people because they are considered too old ▸ **ˈage·ist** *adj.*

**age·less** /ˈeɪdʒləs/ *adj.* (*literary*) **1** never looking old or never seeming to grow old **SYN** **timeless**: *Her beauty appeared ageless.* **2** existing forever; impossible to give an age to **SYN** **timeless**: *the ageless mystery of the universe*

**ˈage limit** *noun* the oldest or youngest age at which you are allowed to do sth: *the upper / lower age limit*

**ˈage-mate** *noun* a person of the same age or belonging to the same age group: *The toddlers participated in playgroups with age-mates.*

**agency** 🗝 **B2** /ˈeɪdʒənsi/ *noun* (*pl.* **-ies**) **1** 🗝 **B2** a business or an organization that provides a particular service especially when representing other businesses or organizations: *She works for an advertising agency.* ◇ *international aid agencies caring for refugees* ◇ **through an ~** *He managed to find a job through an agency.* ➪ see also CREDIT AGENCY, DATING AGENCY, EMPLOYMENT AGENCY, NEWS AGENCY, PRESS AGENCY, TRAVEL AGENCY **2** 🗝 **B2** a government department that provides a particular service: *the Central Intelligence Agency (CIA)* ◇ *law enforcement agencies* ◇ *Some laboratories are operated by government agencies.* ➪ see also CENTRAL INTELLIGENCE AGENCY
**IDM** **through the agency of** (*formal*) as a result of the action of sb/sth

**agenda** 🗝 **B2** 🅦 /əˈdʒendə/ *noun* **1** 🗝 **B2** a list of items to be discussed at a meeting: **on the ~** *The next item on the agenda is the publicity budget.* ➪ **WORDFINDER NOTE** at MEETING **2** 🗝 **B2** a plan of things to be done, or problems to be addressed: **on the ~** *In our company, quality is high on the agenda.* ◇ *They have been trying to get the issue onto the political agenda.* ◇ *Education is now at the top of the government's agenda* (= most important). ◇ *Newspapers have been accused of trying to set the agenda for the government* (= decide what is important). **3** the intention behind what sb says or does, that is often secret: *The artist is letting his own agenda affect what was meant to be a community project.* ➪ see also HIDDEN AGENDA

**agent** 🗝 **B1** 🅦 /ˈeɪdʒənt/ *noun* **1** 🗝 **B1** a person whose job is to act for, or manage the affairs of, other people in business, politics, etc: *Our agent in New York deals with all US sales.* ◇ *If you're going to rent out your house while you're abroad, you'll need someone to act as your agent here.* ➪ **WORDFINDER NOTE** at BUSINESSMAN, COMPANY ➪ see also ESTATE AGENT, EXTENSION AGENT, LAND AGENT, REAL ESTATE AGENT, STATION AGENT, TRAVEL AGENT **2** 🗝 **B1** a person whose job is to arrange work for an actor, musician, sports player, etc. or to find sb who will publish a writer's work: *a theatrical / literary agent* ➪ see also PRESS AGENT **3** 🗝 **B1** = SECRET AGENT: *He was arrested by federal agents.* ◇ *an enemy / undercover agent* ➪ see also DOUBLE AGENT, SPECIAL AGENT **4** (*formal*) a person or thing that has an important effect on a situation: *The charity has been an agent for social change.* **5** (*specialist*) a chemical or a substance that produces an effect or a change or is used for a particular purpose: *chemical / biological agents* ➪ see also NERVE AGENT **6** (*grammar*) the person or thing that does an action (expressed as the subject of an active verb, or in a 'by' phrase with a passive verb) ➪ compare PATIENT ➪ see also FREE AGENT

🅞 Oxford Phrasal Academic Lexicon (OPAL) written and spoken word lists | 🅦 OPAL written word list | 🅢 OPAL spoken word list

**agent general** *noun* (*pl.* **agents general**) the representative of an Australian state or Canadian PROVINCE in a foreign country

**agent provocateur** /ˌæʒɒ̃ prəˌvɒkəˈtɜː(r); *NAmE* ˌɑːʒɑ̃ prəʊˌvɑːkˈ-/ (also **provocateur**) *noun* (*pl.* **agents provocateurs** /ˌæʒɒ̃ prəˌvɒkəˈtɜː(r); *NAmE* ˌɑːʒɑ̃ prəʊˌvɑːk-/) (from French) a person who is employed to encourage people in political groups to do sth illegal so that they can be arrested

**age of consent** *noun* [sing.] the age at which sb is legally old enough to agree to have a sexual relationship

**age-old** *adj.* [usually before noun] having existed for a very long time: *an age-old custom/problem*

**age-set** *noun* (*EAfrE*) a group of boys or men of a similar age

**agglomerate** *verb, noun, adj.* (*specialist*)
- *verb* /əˈɡlɒməreɪt; *NAmE* əˈɡlɑːm-/ [I, T] to form into a mass or group; to collect things and form them into a mass or group: *These small particles agglomerate together to form larger clusters.* ◇ ~**sth** *They agglomerated many small pieces of research into a single large study.*
- *noun* /əˈɡlɒmərət; *NAmE* əˈɡlɑːm-/ a mass or collection of things: *a multimedia agglomerate* (= group of companies)
- *adj.* /əˈɡlɒmərət; *NAmE* əˈɡlɑːm-/ formed into a mass or group

**agglomeration** /əˌɡlɒməˈreɪʃn; *NAmE* əˌɡlɑːm-/ *noun* [C, U] (*specialist*) a group of things put together in no particular order or arrangement; the fact of putting things together in this way

**aggrandizement** (*BrE also* **-isement**) /əˈɡrændɪzmənt/ *noun* [U] (*formal, disapproving*) an increase in the power or importance of a person or country: *Her sole aim is personal aggrandizement.*

**aggravate** /ˈæɡrəveɪt/ *verb* **1** ~ **sth** to make an illness or a bad or unpleasant situation worse SYN **worsen**: *Pollution can aggravate asthma.* ◇ *Military intervention will only aggravate the conflict even further.* **2** ~ **sb** (*informal*) to annoy sb, especially deliberately SYN **irritate** ▸ **aggravating** *adj.* **aggravation** /ˌæɡrəˈveɪʃn/ *noun* [U, C]: *I don't need all this aggravation at work.* ◇ *The drug may cause an aggravation of the condition.*

**aggravated** /ˈæɡrəveɪtɪd/ *adj.* [only before noun] (*law*) an aggravated crime involves further unnecessary violence or unpleasant behaviour

**aggregate** *noun, adj., verb*
- *noun* /ˈæɡrɪɡət/ **1** [C] a total number or amount made up of smaller amounts that are collected together **2** [U, C] (*specialist*) sand or broken stone that is used to make CONCRETE or for building roads, etc.
  IDM **in (the) aggregate** (*formal*) added together as a total or single amount **on aggregate** (*BrE, sport*) when the scores of a number of games are added together: *They won 4–2 on aggregate.*
- *adj.* /ˈæɡrɪɡət/ [only before noun] (*economics or sport*) made up of several amounts that are added together to form a total number: *aggregate demand/investment/turnover* ◇ (*BrE*) *an aggregate win over their rivals*
- *verb* /ˈæɡrɪɡeɪt/ [usually passive] (*formal or specialist*) to put together different items, amounts, etc. into a single group or total: **be aggregated (with sth)** *The scores were aggregated with the first round totals to decide the winner.* ▸ **aggregation** /ˌæɡrɪˈɡeɪʃn/ *noun* [U, C]: *the aggregation of data*

**aggregator** /ˈæɡrɪɡeɪtə(r)/ *noun* (*computing*) an internet company that collects information about other companies' products and services and puts it on a single website: *a news aggregator*

**aggression** /əˈɡreʃn/ *noun* **1** [U] feelings of anger and hate that may result in THREATENING or violent behaviour: *The research shows that computer games may cause aggression.* **2** [U, C] a violent attack or threats by one person against another person or by one country against another country: *unprovoked military aggression*

⇨ WORDFINDER NOTE at CONFLICT ⇨ see also NON-AGGRESSION

**aggressive** /əˈɡresɪv/ *adj.* **1** angry, and behaving in a THREATENING way; ready to attack: *Seals have been known to exhibit aggressive behaviour towards swimmers.* ◇ *He became increasingly aggressive as the evening wore on.* ⇨ see also PASSIVE-AGGRESSIVE **2** (*sometimes disapproving*) determined and acting with force in order to succeed: *a very aggressive advertising campaign* ◇ ~**in (doing) sth** *We need to get more aggressive in our approach.* **3** (of a disease) developing quickly and difficult to treat: *an aggressive form of cancer* **4** (of medical treatment) using all possible treatment options in order to extend sb's life: *to undergo aggressive treatment for cancer* ▸ **aggressively** *adv.*: '*What do you want?' he demanded aggressively.* ◇ *aggressively marketed products* **aggressiveness** *noun* [U]

**aggressor** /əˈɡresə(r)/ *noun* a person, country, etc. that attacks first

**aggrieved** /əˈɡriːvd/ *adj.* **1** ~ **(at/by sth)** feeling that you have been treated unfairly **2** (*law*) suffering unfair or illegal treatment and making a complaint: *the aggrieved party* (= person) *in the case*

**aggro** /ˈæɡrəʊ/ *noun* [U] (*BrE, informal*) **1** violent aggressive behaviour: *Don't give me any aggro or I'll call the police.* **2** problems and difficulties that are annoying: *I had a lot of aggro at the bank.*

**aghast** /əˈɡɑːst; *NAmE* əˈɡæst/ *adj.* [not before noun] filled with horror and surprise when you see or hear sth SYN **horrified**: *Erica looked at him aghast.* ◇ ~ **at sth** *He stood aghast at the sight of so much blood.*

**agile** /ˈædʒaɪl; *NAmE* ˈædʒl/ *adj.* **1** able to move quickly and easily SYN **nimble 2** able to think quickly and in an intelligent way: *an agile mind/brain* **3** (*business*) used to describe a way of managing projects in which work is divided into a series of short tasks, with regular breaks to review the work and adapt the plans: *Agile methods replace high-level design with frequent redesign.* ▸ **agility** /əˈdʒɪləti/ *noun* [U]: *He had the agility of a man half his age.*

**aging** **agism** = AGEING, AGEISM

**agitate** /ˈædʒɪteɪt/ *verb* **1** [I, T] to argue strongly for sth you want, especially for changes in a law, in social conditions, etc. SYN **campaign**: ~ **(for/against sth)** *political groups agitating for social change* ◇ ~ **to do sth** *Her family are agitating to have her transferred to a prison in the UK.* **2** [T] ~ **sb** to make sb feel angry, anxious or nervous **3** [T] ~ **sth** (*specialist*) to make sth, especially a liquid, move around by mixing or shaking it

**agitated** /ˈædʒɪteɪtɪd/ *adj.* showing in your behaviour that you are anxious and nervous: *Calm down! Don't get so agitated.*

**agitation** /ˌædʒɪˈteɪʃn/ *noun* **1** [U] worry that you show by behaving in a nervous way: *Dot arrived in a state of great agitation.* **2** [U] ~ **(for/against sth)** public protest in order to achieve political change: *widespread agitation for social reform* **3** [C] (*IndE*) a public meeting or a MARCH (= an organized walk by many people) at which people show that they are protesting against or supporting sth: *The situation has provoked agitations all over the region.* ◇ *Protesters are expected to launch an agitation over the issue.* **4** [U] (*specialist*) the act of mixing or shaking a liquid

**agitator** /ˈædʒɪteɪtə(r)/ *noun* (*disapproving*) a person who tries to persuade people to take part in political protest

**agitprop** /ˈædʒɪtprɒp; *NAmE* -prɑːp/ *noun* [U] the use of art, films, music, etc. to spread political ideas

**aglow** /əˈɡləʊ/ *adj.* [not before noun] (*literary*) shining with colour, WARMTH or happiness

**AGM** /ˌeɪ dʒiː ˈem/ *noun* (*BrE*) an important meeting that the members of an organization hold once a year in order to elect officers, discuss past and future activities and examine the accounts (the abbreviation for 'annual general meeting') ⇨ WORDFINDER NOTE at CLUB

**ag·nos·tic** /æɡˈnɒstɪk; NAmE -ˈnɑːs-/ noun, adj.
- noun a person who believes that it is not possible to know whether God exists or not ⊃ compare ATHEIST
- adj. 1 (religion) holding or showing the belief that it is not possible to know whether God exists or not 2 not having a strong opinion about an activity or topic: *I'm largely agnostic on this issue as I know so little about it.* 3 (computing) (often in compounds) (used about computer HARDWARE or software) able to be used with many different types of computer systems, software or OPERATING SYSTEMS: *Now that the services are platform-agnostic, they can be accessed by far more users.* ▶ **ag·nos·ti·cism** /-stɪsɪzəm/ noun [U]

**ago** ⓘ A1 /əˈɡəʊ/ adv. used in expressions of time with the simple past tense to show how far in the past sth happened: *two weeks/months/years ago ◊ The letter came a few days ago. ◊ She was here just a minute ago. ◊ a short/long time ago ◊ How long ago did you buy it? ◊ It was on TV not (so) long ago. ◊ He stopped working some time ago (= quite a long time ago). ◊ They're getting married? It's not that long ago (= it's only a short time ago) that they met!* HELP It is not correct to use 'since' in this sentence: *It's not long ago since they met.* You can only use 'since' if you leave out *ago*: *It's not long since they met.*

**agog** /əˈɡɒɡ; NAmE əˈɡɑːɡ/ adj. [not before noun] excited and very interested to find out sth

**ag·on·ize** (BrE also **-ise**) /ˈæɡənaɪz/ verb [I] ~ **(over/about sth)** to spend a long time thinking and worrying about a difficult situation or problem: *I spent days agonizing over whether to take the job or not.*

**ag·on·ized** (BrE also **-ised**) /ˈæɡənaɪzd/ adj. suffering or expressing severe pain or worry: *agonized cries*

**ag·on·iz·ing** (BrE also **-is·ing**) /ˈæɡənaɪzɪŋ/ adj. causing great pain, worry or difficulty: *his father's agonizing death ◊ It was the most agonizing decision of his life.*

**ag·on·iz·ing·ly** (BrE also **-is·ing·ly**) /ˈæɡənaɪzɪŋli/ adv. used meaning 'extremely' to emphasize sth negative: *an agonizingly slow process*

**agony** /ˈæɡəni/ noun [U, C] (pl. **-ies**) extreme physical or mental pain: **in**~ *Jack collapsed in agony on the floor.* ◊ **in an ~ of sth** *She waited in an agony of suspense.* ◊ *It was agony not knowing where the children were. ◊ The worst agonies of the war were now beginning. ◊ Tell me now! Don't prolong the agony (= make it last longer).* IDM▶ see PILE v.

**ˈagony aunt** (BrE) (NAmE **adˈvice columnist**) noun a person who writes in a newspaper or magazine or on a website giving advice in reply to people's emails and letters about their personal problems ⊃ compare AGONY UNCLE

**ˈagony column** (BrE) (NAmE **adˈvice column**) noun part of a newspaper, magazine or website in which sb gives advice to readers who have sent emails or letters about their personal problems

**ˈagony uncle** noun (BrE) (NAmE **adˈvice columnist**) a man who writes in a newspaper or magazine or on a website giving advice in reply to people's emails and letters about their personal problems ⊃ compare AGONY AUNT

**agora** /ˈæɡərə/ noun (pl. **agorae** /-riː/ or **agoras**) in ancient Greece, an open space used for markets and public meetings

**agora·pho·bia** /ˌæɡərəˈfəʊbiə/ noun [U] (specialist) a fear of being in public places where there are many other people ⊃ compare CLAUSTROPHOBIA

**agora·pho·bic** /ˌæɡərəˈfəʊbɪk/ noun a person who suffers from agoraphobia ▶ **agora·pho·bic** adj.

**agrar·ian** /əˈɡreəriən; NAmE əˈɡrer-/ adj. [usually before noun] (specialist) connected with farming and the use of land for farming

**agree** ⓘ A1 /əˈɡriː/ verb
- SHARE OPINION 1 ⓘ A1 [I, T] to have the same opinion as sb; to say that you have the same opinion: *When he said that, I had to agree.* ◊ + **speech** *'That's true', she agreed.* ◊ ~ **(with sb) (about/on sth)** *He agreed with them about the need for change.* ◊ ~ **with sth** *Many experts agree wholeheartedly with this statement.* ◊ ~ **(that)** … *All parties agree (that)*

# agree

*urgent action is required.* ◊ *'It's terrible.' 'I couldn't agree more!'* (= I completely agree) OPP **disagree**
- APPROVE OF STH 2 ⓘ A2 [I] ~ **with (doing) sth** (used especially in negative sentences) to approve of sth because you think it is morally right: *I don't agree with hitting children as a punishment.*
- SAY YES 3 ⓘ A2 [I, T] to say 'yes'; to say that you will do what sb wants or that you will allow sth to happen: *I asked for a pay rise and she agreed.* ◊ ~ **to sth** *The government has finally agreed in principle* (= agreed in general but not in detail) *to the terms of the deal.* ◊ ~ **(that)** … *She agreed (that) I could go early.* ◊ ~ **to do sth** *He reluctantly agreed to pay for the damage.*
- DECIDE 4 ⓘ A2 [I, T] to decide with sb else to do sth or to have sth: ~ **on/upon sth** *Can we agree on a date?* ◊ ~ **sth** *They met at the agreed time.* ◊ *Can we agree a price?* ◊ ~ **to do sth** *We agreed to meet on Thursday.* ◊ ~ **what, where, etc** … *We couldn't agree what to do.* ◊ **as agreed** *They left at ten, as agreed.*
- ACCEPT 5 [T] ~ **sth** to officially accept a plan, request, etc. SYN **approve**: *The company agreed a deal worth $100 million.*
- BE THE SAME 6 [I] to be the same as sth SYN **tally**: *The figures do not agree.* ◊ ~ **with sth** *Your account of the accident does not agree with hers.* OPP **disagree**

▼ EXPRESS YOURSELF

**Agreeing**

In a discussion, people may say certain things which you want to support. (In addition, before you make a negative comment, you may want to say first that there are points that you agree with.)
- *Yes, that's true.*
- *That's right. On the other hand, there are some drawbacks to the plan …*
- *Exactly.*
- *Absolutely.*
- *Definitely.*
- *Yes, I suppose/guess so.*
- *I agree. It's definitely the best idea.*
- *I think you're right. We should listen to what they have to say.*
- *Sue is absolutely right. It's too early to make a decision now.*
- *I would go along with the idea that we should change the logo.*
- *We are in agreement on the best way to proceed, but we need to discuss the timing.* (formal)

▼ SYNONYMS

**agree**

accept • approve • go along with sb/sth • consent

These words all mean to say that you will do what sb wants or that you will allow sth to happen.

**agree** to say that you will do what sb wants or that you will allow sth to happen: *He agreed to let me go early.*

**accept** to be satisfied with sth that has been done, decided or suggested: *They accepted the court's decision.*

**approve** to officially agree to a plan, suggestion or request: *The committee unanimously approved the plan.*

**go along with sb/sth** (rather informal) to agree to sth that sb else has decided; to agree with sb else's ideas: *She just goes along with everything he suggests.*

**consent** (rather formal) to agree to sth or give your permission for sth: *She finally consented to answer our questions.*

PATTERNS
- to agree/consent **to** sth
- to agree/consent **to do** sth
- to agree to/accept/approve/go along with/consent to a **plan/proposal**
- to agree to/accept/approve a **request**

# agreeable

- **GRAMMAR** 7 [I] ~ **(with sth)** to match a word or phrase in NUMBER, GENDER or PERSON: *In 'Tom likes jazz', the singular verb 'likes' agrees with the subject 'Tom'.*

**IDM** **a**ˈ**gree to** ˈ**differ/disa**ˈ**gree** if two people **agree to differ/disagree**, they accept that they have different opinions about sth, but they decide not to discuss it any longer **PHRV** **not a**ˈ**gree with sb** (of food) to make you feel ill: *I love strawberries, but they don't agree with me.*

**agree·able** /əˈgriːəbl/ *adj.* (*formal*) **1** pleasant and easy to like: *We spent a most agreeable day together.* ◊ *He seemed extremely agreeable.* **OPP** **disagreeable 2** [not before noun] ~ **(to sth)** willing to do sth or allow sth: *Do you think they will be agreeable to our proposal?* **3** ~ **(to sb)** able to be accepted by sb: *The deal must be agreeable to both sides.*

**agree·ably** /əˈgriːəbli/ *adv.* (*formal*) in a pleasant, nice way: *an agreeably warm day* ◊ *They were agreeably surprised by the quality of the food.*

**agreed** /əˈgriːd/ *adj.* **1** [only before noun] discussed and accepted by everyone: *They all met at the agreed time and place.* **2** [not before noun] if people **are agreed** or sth **is agreed**, everyone has the same opinion about sth: ~ **(on/ about sth)** *Are we all agreed on this?* ◊ **it is ~ (that) … It was agreed (that)** *we should hold another meeting.* ◊ *It is generally agreed that more funding is needed for education.*

**agree·ment** /əˈgriːmənt/ *noun* **1** [C] an arrangement, a promise or a contract made with sb: *an international peace agreement* ◊ *The agreement* (= the document recording the agreement) *was signed during a meeting at the UN.* ◊ ~ **with sb** *They have entered into a free trade agreement with Australia.* ◊ ~ **between A and B** *An agreement was finally reached between management and employees.* ◊ ~ **to do sth** *They had an agreement never to talk about work at home.* ◊ **under an** ~ *The software is provided under a license agreement and may not be copied without permission.* **⊃** WORDFINDER NOTE at PEACE **⊃** see also GENTLEMAN'S AGREEMENT, PRENUPTIAL AGREEMENT **2** [U] the state of sharing the same opinion or feeling: *The two sides failed to reach agreement.* ◊ ~ **on sth** *There was broad agreement on what was needed.* ◊ ~ **(among sb) (that …)** *There is agreement among teachers that changes need to be made.* ◊ **in** ~ **(with sb) (on/about sth)** *My wife is in complete agreement with me on this issue.* **OPP** **disagreement 3** [U] the fact of sb approving of sth and allowing it to happen: **with/without the** ~ **of sb** *No images may be reproduced without the artist's agreement.* **4** [U] (*grammar*) (of words in a phrase) the state of having the same NUMBER, GENDER or PERSON **SYN** **concord**: **in** ~ **with sth** *In the sentence 'They live in the country', the plural form of the verb 'live' is in agreement with the plural subject 'they'.*

**agri-** **⊃** AGRO-

**agri·busi·ness** /ˈæɡrɪbɪznəs/ *noun* [U, C] (*specialist*) **1** farming conducted on a large scale on strictly commercial principles **2** the businesses involved in dealing with farm produce and the services needed in farming

**agric** /ˈæɡrɪk/ *adj.* (WAfrE) AGRICULTURAL

**agri·cul·tural** /ˌæɡrɪˈkʌltʃərəl/ *adj.* connected with the science or practice of farming: *agricultural policy/land/production/development*

**agri·cul·tur·al·ist** /ˌæɡrɪˈkʌltʃərəlɪst/ *noun* an expert in agriculture who gives advice to farmers

**agri·cul·ture** /ˈæɡrɪkʌltʃə(r)/ *noun* [U] the science or practice of farming: *The number of people employed in agriculture has fallen in the last decade.* **⊃** see also FARMING

**agro-** /ˈæɡrəʊ, ˈæɡrə; BrE also əˈɡrɒ; NAmE also əˈɡrɑː-/ (also **agri-** /ˈæɡrɪ/) combining form (in nouns, adjectives and adverbs) connected with farming: *agro-industry* ◊ *agriculture*

**agro·chem·ical** /ˌæɡrəʊˈkemɪkl/ *noun* any chemical used in farming, especially for killing insects or for making plants grow better

**agrono·mist** /əˈɡrɒnəmɪst; NAmE əˈɡrɑːn-/ *noun* a scientist who studies the relationship between crops and the environment ▸ **agron·omy** *noun* [U]

**aground** /əˈɡraʊnd/ *adv.* if a ship **runs/goes aground**, it touches the ground in shallow water and cannot move ▸ **aground** *adj.* [not before noun]

**AH** (BrE) (US **A.H.**) /ˌeɪ ˈeɪtʃ/ *abbr.* used in the Muslim CALENDAR to show a particular number of years since the year when Muhammad left Mecca in AD622 (from Latin 'Anno Hegirae'): *a Koran dated 556 AH* **⊃** compare AD, BC, BCE, CE

**ah** /ɑː/ *exclamation* used to express surprise, pleasure or sympathy, or when you disagree with sb: *Ah, there you are!* ◊ *Ah, this coffee is good.* ◊ *Ah well, better luck next time.* ◊ *Ah, but that may not be true.*

**aha** /ɑːˈhɑː/ *exclamation* used when you are expressing pleasure that you have understood sth or found sth out: *Aha! So that's where I left it!*

**ahchoo** /əˈtʃuː/ *exclamation* = ATISHOO

**ahead** /əˈhed/ *adv.* **HELP** For the special uses of **ahead** in phrasal verbs, look at the entries for the verbs. For example **press ahead (with sth)** is in the phrasal verb section at press. **1** further forward in space or time; in front: *I'll run ahead and warn them.* ◊ *The road ahead was blocked.* ◊ *We've got a lot of hard work ahead.* ◊ *This will create problems in the months ahead.* ◊ *He was looking straight ahead* (= straight forward, in front of him). **2** earlier **SYN** **in advance**: *The party was planned weeks ahead.* **3** winning; further advanced: *Our team was ahead by six points.* ◊ *You need to work hard to keep ahead.*

**a**ˈ**head of** *prep.* **1** further forward in space or time than sb/sth; in front of sb/sth: *Two boys were ahead of us.* ◊ *Ahead of us lay ten days of intensive training.* **2** earlier than sb/sth: *I finished several days ahead of the deadline.* **3** further advanced than sb/sth; in front of sb, for example in a race or competition: *She was always well ahead of the rest of the class.* ◊ *His ideas were way ahead of their time* (= very new and so not widely understood or accepted).

**ahem** /əˈhem, əˈhəm/ *exclamation* used in writing to show the sound of a short COUGH (= the noise made when air is forced from the throat) made by sb who is trying to get attention or to say sth that is difficult or embarrassing: *Ahem, can I make a suggestion?*

**ahis·tor·ic·al** /ˌeɪhɪˈstɒrɪkl; NAmE -ˈstɔːr-/ *adj.* (*formal*) not showing any knowledge of history or of what has happened before

**-aholic** /əˈhɒlɪk; NAmE əhɑːlɪk/ *suffix* (in nouns) liking sth very much and unable to stop doing or using it: *a shopaholic* ◊ *a chocaholic*

**ahoy** /əˈhɔɪ/ *exclamation* used by people in boats to attract attention: *Ahoy there!* ◊ *Ship ahoy!* (= there is a ship in sight)

**AI** *abbr.* **1** /ˌeɪ ˈaɪ/ ARTIFICIAL INTELLIGENCE: *This new technology uses AI to recognize character features in the same way a human brain does.* **2** ARTIFICIAL INSEMINATION

**aid** /eɪd/ *noun, verb*
■ *noun* **1** [U] money, food, etc. that is sent to help countries in difficult situations: *humanitarian/food/medical aid* ◊ *An extra £10 million in foreign aid has been provided for victims of the earthquake.* ◊ *aid agencies* (= organizations that provide help) ◊ *international aid workers* **⊃** see also FINANCIAL AID, GRANT AID, GRANT-IN-AID, LEGAL AID **2** [U] help that you need, especially to perform a particular task: **with the ~ of sb/sth** *She walks with the aid of a stick.* ◊ **without the ~ of sb/sth** *This job would be impossible without the aid of a computer.* ◊ (*formal*) *One of the staff saw he was in difficulty and came to his aid* (= helped him). **⊃** see also FIRST AID **3** [C] an object, a machine, etc. that you use to help you do sth: *Photos make useful teaching aids.* **⊃** see also HEARING AID, VISUAL AID

**IDM** **in aid of sth/sb** (BrE) in order to help sth/sb: *collecting money in aid of charity* **what's … in aid of?** (BrE, *informal*) used to ask why sth is happening: *What's all this crying in aid of?*

■ **verb** [I, T] (*formal*) **1** ⚡ B2 to help sb/sth to do sth, especially by making it easier SYN **assist**: **~ in (doing) sth** *The test is designed to aid in the diagnosis of various diseases.* ◊ **~ sb/sth** *The charity was established to aid hurricane victims.* ◊ *They were accused of aiding his escape.* ◊ **~ sb to do sth** *They were accused of aiding him to escape.* ◊ **~ sb/sth in (doing) sth** *They were accused of aiding him in his escape.* ◊ **~ sb with sth** *Words will be displayed around the room to aid students with spelling.* **2 ~ sth** to help or encourage sth to happen: *New drugs are now available to aid recovery.* 
IDM **aid and aˈbet** (*law*) to help sb to do sth illegal or wrong: *She stands accused of aiding and abetting the crime.*

**aide** ⚡+ C1 /eɪd/ *noun* a person who helps another person, especially a politician, in their job: *White House aides*

**aide-de-camp** /ˌeɪd də ˈkɒ̃; *NAmE* ˌeɪd də ˈkæmp/ *noun* (*pl.* **aides-de-camp** /ˌeɪd də ˈkɒ̃; *NAmE* ˌeɪd də ˈkæmp/) (*abbr.* **ADC**) an officer in the army or NAVY who helps a more senior officer

**AIDS** ⚡+ B2 (*BrE usually* **Aids**) /eɪdz/ *noun* [U] an illness that attacks the body's ability to resist infection and that usually causes death (the abbreviation for 'Acquired Immune Deficiency Syndrome'): *AIDS research/education/victims* ◊ *He developed full-blown AIDS five years after contracting HIV.*

**ai·ki·do** /aɪˈkiːdəʊ/ *noun* [U] (*from Japanese*) a Japanese system of fighting in which you hold and throw your opponent

**ail** /eɪl/ *verb* **1 ~ sth** (*formal*) to cause problems for sb/sth: *They discussed the problems ailing the steel industry.* **2 ~ sb** (*old use*) to make sb ill: *What is ailing you?*

**ail·eron** /ˈeɪlərɒn; *NAmE* -rɑːn/ *noun* (*specialist*) a part of the wing of a plane that moves up and down to control the plane's balance

**ail·ing** /ˈeɪlɪŋ/ *adj.* (*formal*) **1** ill and not improving: *She looked after her ailing father.* **2** (of a business, government, etc.) having problems and getting weaker: *measures to help the ailing economy*

**ail·ment** /ˈeɪlmənt/ *noun* an illness that is not very serious: *childhood/common/minor ailments* ⇒ SYNONYMS at DISEASE

**aim** ❶ B1 ⓞ /eɪm/ *verb, noun*
■ **verb 1** ⚡ B1 [I, T] to try or plan to achieve sth: *He has always aimed high* (= tried to achieve a lot). ◊ **~ for sth** *We should aim for a bigger share of the market.* ◊ **~ at sth** *The government is aiming at a 50% reduction in unemployment.* ◊ **~ to do sth** *The project aims to provide employment for people with learning difficulties.* ◊ *We aim to be there around six.* ◊ **~ at doing sth** *The training programme aims at raising employees' awareness about human rights.* **2** ⚡ B2 [T] **be aimed at doing sth** to have sth as an aim: *The initiative is specifically aimed at helping young people.* **3** B2 [T, usually passive] to say or do sth that is intended to influence or affect a particular person or group: **be aimed at sb** *The courses are aimed primarily at older people.* ◊ *My criticism wasn't aimed at you.* **4** ⚡ B2 [I, T] to point or direct a weapon, camera, shot, kick, etc. at sb/sth: **~ at sb/sth** *I was aiming at the tree but hit the car by mistake.* ◊ **~ for sb/sth** *Aim for the middle of the target.* ◊ **~ sth at sb/sth** *The gun was aimed at her head.* ◊ **~ sth** *I aimed my camera and got one shot.*
■ **noun 1** B1 [C] the purpose of doing sth; what sb is trying to achieve: *the stated aims of the study* ◊ *Our main aim is to provide affordable childcare.* ◊ *His sole aim in life is to enjoy himself.* ◊ *Teamwork is required in order to achieve these aims.* ◊ *She set out the company's aims and objectives in her speech.* ◊ **with the ~ of doing sth** *The organization was formed with the aim of helping local people.* ⇒ SYNONYMS at PURPOSE **2** [U, sing.] the action or skill of pointing a weapon at sb/sth: *Her aim was good and she hit the lion with her first shot.* ◊ *The gunman took aim* (= pointed his weapon) *and fired.* 
IDM **take ˈaim at sb/sth** (*NAmE*) to direct your criticism at sb/sth

**aim·less** /ˈeɪmləs/ *adj.* having no direction or plan: *My life seemed aimless.* ▶ **aim·less·ly** *adv.*: *He drifted aimlessly from one job to another.* **aim·less·ness** *noun* [U]

**ain't** /eɪnt/ *short form* (*non-standard or humorous*) **1** am not/is not/are not: *Things ain't what they used to be.* **2** has not/have not: *I ain't got no money.* ◊ *You ain't seen nothing yet.*
IDM **if it ain't ˌbroke, don't ˈfix it** (*informal*) used to say that if sth works well enough, it should not be changed

**air** ❶ A1 /eə(r); *NAmE* er/ *noun, verb*
■ **noun**
• GAS **1** ⚡ A1 [U] the mixture of gases that surrounds the earth and that we breathe: *Let's go out for some fresh air.* ◊ *a blast of hot air* ◊ *He stood outside, breathing the cold night air.* ◊ *I need to put some air in my tyres.* ◊ *air pollution* ◊ *The Act lays down a minimum standard for air quality.* ⇒ HOMOPHONES at HEIR ⇒ see also SEA AIR
• SPACE **2** ⚡ A1 [U] (*usually* **the air**) the space above the ground or that is around things: *Music filled the night air.* ◊ **in/into the ~** *Wave your hands in the air!* ◊ **through the ~** *Spicy smells wafted through the air.* ⇒ see also MID-AIR, OPEN AIR
• FOR PLANES **3** ⚡ A1 [U] the space above the earth where planes fly: *The temple was clearly visible from the air.* ◊ **by ~** *It only takes three hours by air* (= in a plane). ◊ *air travel/traffic* ◊ *air defence systems* (= weapons that defend against attacks from the air)
• IMPRESSION **4** [sing.] the particular feeling or impression that is given by sb/sth; the way sb does sth: *She looked at him with a defiant air.* ◊ **~ of sth** *The room had an air of luxury.*
• TUNE **5** [C] (*old-fashioned*) (often used in the title of a piece of music) a tune: *Bach's Air on a G string*
• BEHAVIOUR **6 airs** [pl.] (*disapproving*) a way of behaving that shows that sb thinks that they are more important, etc. than they really are: *I hate the way she puts on airs.* ⇒ see also HOT AIR
IDM **ˌairs and ˈgraces** (*BrE, disapproving*) a way of behaving that shows that sb thinks that they are more important, etc. than they really are SYN **airs** **ˌfloat/ˌwalk on ˈair** to feel very happy **in the ˈair** felt by a number of people to exist or to be happening: *There's romance in the air.* **on/off (the) ˈair** broadcasting or not broadcasting on television or radio: *We will be back on air tomorrow morning at 7.* ◊ *The programme was taken off the air over the summer.* **ˌup in the ˈair** not yet decided: *Our travel plans are still up in the air.* ⇒ more at BREATH, CASTLE, CLEAR *v.*, NOSE *n.*, PLUCK *v.*, THIN *adj.*
■ **verb**
• CLOTHES **1** [T, I] **~ (sth)** to put clothing, etc. in a place that is warm or has plenty of air so that it dries completely and smells fresh; to be left to dry somewhere: *Air the sheets well.* ◊ *Leave the towels out to air.* ⇒ HOMOPHONES at HEIR
• A ROOM **2** [T, I] **~ (sth)** (*BrE*) (*NAmE* **air (sth) ˈout**) to allow fresh air into a room or a building; to be filled with fresh air: *The rooms had all been cleaned and aired.*
• OPINIONS **3** [T] **~ sth** to express your opinions publicly SYN **voice**: *The weekly meeting enables employees to air their grievances.*
• RADIO/TV PROGRAMME **4** [T, I] **~ (sth)** to broadcast a programme on the radio or on television; to be broadcast: *The show will be aired next Tuesday night.* ◊ *The program aired last week.* ⇒ WORDFINDER NOTE at RADIO IDM see DIRTY *adj.*
PHRV **ˌair ˈout** | **ˌair sth↔ˈout** (*NAmE*) = AIR (2)

**ˈair ambulance** *noun* (*especially BrE*) an aircraft, especially a helicopter, with special equipment, used for taking sick or injured people to a hospital, especially in cases where a road vehicle cannot get through or cannot make the journey quickly enough ⇒ compare MEDEVAC

**air·bag** /ˈeəbæg; *NAmE* ˈerb-/ *noun* a safety device in a car that fills with air if there is an accident, to protect the people in the car

**air·base** /ˈeəbeɪs; *NAmE* ˈerb-/ *noun* a place where military aircraft fly from and are kept, and where some staff live

**air·bed** /ˈeəbed; *NAmE* ˈerb-/ (*BrE*) (*also* **ˈair bed** *NAmE*, **ˈair mattress** *NAmE, BrE*) *noun* a large plastic or rubber bag that can be filled with air and used as a bed

**air·borne** /ˈeəbɔːn; *NAmE* ˈerbɔːrn/ *adj.* **1** [not before noun] (of a plane or passengers) in the air: *Do not leave your seat*

# air brake 34

until the plane is airborne. **2** [only before noun] carried through the air: *airborne seeds/viruses* ⇨ compare WATERBORNE **3** [only before noun] (of soldiers) trained to jump out of aircraft onto enemy land in order to fight: *an airborne division*

**ˈair brake** *noun* a BRAKE in a vehicle that is worked by air pressure

**airˑbrush** /ˈeəbrʌʃ; *NAmE* ˈerb-/ *noun, verb*
- *noun* an artist's tool for SPRAYING paint onto a surface, that works by air pressure
- *verb* [often passive] to paint sth with an airbrush; to change a detail in a photograph with an airbrush: *be airbrushed (out) Somebody had been airbrushed out of the picture.* ⋄ *an airbrushed photograph of a model*

**Airˑbus™** /ˈeəbʌs; *NAmE* ˈerb-/ *noun* a plane designed to carry a large number of passengers

**ˌair chief ˈmarshal** *noun* an officer of very high rank in the British AIR FORCE: *Air Chief Marshal Sir Robin Hall*

**ˌair ˈcommodore** *noun* an officer of high rank in the British AIR FORCE: *Air Commodore Dawn McCafferty*

**ˈair conditioner** *noun* a machine that cools and dries air

**ˈair conditioning** (*also* **ˈair con**) *noun* [U] (*abbr.* **AC, a/c**) a system that cools and dries the air in a building or car ⇨ see also CLIMATE CONTROL ▸ **ˈair-conˑdiˑtioned** *adj.*: *air-conditioned offices*

**ˈair-cooled** *adj.* made cool by a current of air

**ˈair corridor** *noun* an area in the sky that aircraft must stay inside when they fly over a country

**ˈair cover** *noun* [U] protection that aircraft give to soldiers and military vehicles on the land or sea

**airˑcraft** 🛈 **B2** /ˈeəkrɑːft; *NAmE* ˈerkræft/ *noun* (*pl.* **airˑcraft**) any vehicle that can fly and carry goods or passengers: *fighter/transport/military aircraft* ⇨ see also ANTI-AIRCRAFT, LIGHT AIRCRAFT

**WORDFINDER** bomber, drone, fighter, helicopter, jet, jump jet, parachute, pilot, warplane

**ˈaircraft carrier** *noun* a large ship that carries aircraft that use it as a base to land on and take off from ⇨ WORDFINDER NOTE at NAVY

**airˑcraftˑman** /ˈeəkrɑːftmən; *NAmE* ˈerkræft-/, **airˑcraftˑwoman** /ˈeəkrɑːftwʊmən; *NAmE* ˈerkræft-/ *noun* (*pl.* **-men** /-mən/, **-women** /-wɪmɪn/) the lowest rank in the British AIR FORCE: *Aircraftman John Green*

**airˑcrew** /ˈeəkruː; *NAmE* ˈerk-/ *noun* [C + sing./pl. v.] the pilot and other people who fly a plane, especially in the air force

**ˈair-dash** *verb* [I] (*IndE*) to fly somewhere in a plane without much time for preparation: *He air-dashed to Delhi when he heard the news.*

**airˑdrome** /ˈeədrəʊm; *NAmE* ˈerd-/ (*US*) (*BrE* **aeroˑdrome**) *noun* (*old-fashioned*) a small airport

**airˑdrop** /ˈeədrɒp; *NAmE* ˈerdrɑːp/ *noun* the act of dropping supplies, soldiers, etc. from an aircraft by PARACHUTE: *The UN has begun making airdrops of food to refugees.* ▸ **ˈair-drop** *verb* (**-pp-**) ~ *sth*

**airˑfare** /ˈeəfeə(r); *NAmE* ˈerfer/ *noun* the money that you pay to travel by plane: *Take advantage of low-season airfares.*

**airˑfield** /ˈeəfiːld; *NAmE* ˈerf-/ *noun* an area of flat ground where military or private planes can take off and land

**airˑflow** /ˈeəfləʊ; *NAmE* ˈerf-/ *noun* [U, C] the flow of air, especially around a moving aircraft or vehicle

**airˑfoil** /ˈeəfɔɪl; *NAmE* ˈerf-/ (*NAmE*) (= **aeroˑfoil**) *noun* the basic curved structure of an aircraft's wing that helps to lift it into the air

**ˈair force** *noun* [C + sing./pl. v.] the part of a country's armed forces that fights using aircraft: *the US Air Force* ⋄ *air-force officers*

**ˌAir Force ˈOne** *noun* the name given to a special aircraft in the US AIR FORCE when the US President is using it

**airˑfreight** /ˈeəfreɪt; *NAmE* ˈerf-/ *noun* [U] goods that are transported by aircraft; the system of transporting goods by aircraft ▸ **ˈair freight** *verb* ~ *sth*

**ˈair freshener** *noun* [C, U] a substance or device for making a place smell more pleasant

**ˈair guitar** *noun* [U, C] used to refer to the actions of a person playing an imaginary electric guitar, especially while listening to rock music: *Whenever he hears this music, he starts playing air guitar.*

**airˑgun** /ˈeəɡʌn; *NAmE* ˈerɡ-/ *noun* a gun that uses air pressure to fire small metal balls (called PELLETS)

**airˑhead** /ˈeəhed; *NAmE* ˈerh-/ *noun* (*informal, disapproving*) a stupid person: *She's a total airhead!* ▸ **ˈair-headˑed** *adj.*

**ˈair hostess** *noun* (*BrE, old-fashioned*) a female FLIGHT ATTENDANT

**airˑily** /ˈeərəli; *NAmE* ˈer-/ *adv.* (*formal*) in a way that shows that you are not worried or that you are not treating sth as serious

**airˑing** /ˈeərɪŋ; *NAmE* ˈer-/ *noun* [sing.] **1** the expression or discussion of opinions in front of a group of people: *an opportunity to give your views an airing* ⋄ *The subject got a thorough airing in the British press.* **2** the act of allowing warm air to make clothes, beds, etc. fresh and dry

**ˈairing cupboard** *noun* (*BrE*) a warm cupboard in which clean sheets, clothes, etc. are put to make sure they are completely dry

**ˈair kiss** *noun* a way of saying hello or goodbye to sb by kissing them near the side of their face but not actually touching them ▸ **ˈair-kiss** *verb* [T, I] ~ (**sb/sth**)

**airˑless** /ˈeələs; *NAmE* ˈerl-/ *adj.* not having any fresh or moving air or wind, and therefore unpleasant: *a stuffy, airless room* ⋄ *The night was hot and airless.*

**airˑlift** /ˈeəlɪft; *NAmE* ˈerl-/ *noun, verb*
- *noun* an operation to take people, soldiers, food, etc. to or from an area by aircraft, especially in an emergency or when roads are closed or dangerous ⇨ compare SEALIFT
- *verb* ~ **sb/sth** to take sb/sth to or from an area by aircraft, especially in an emergency or when roads are closed and dangerous: *Two casualties were airlifted to safety.*

**airˑline** 🛈 **A2** /ˈeəlaɪn; *NAmE* ˈerl-/ *noun* [C + sing./pl. v.] a company that provides regular flights to take passengers and goods to different places: *an airline pilot/passenger* ⋄ *a low-cost/budget/no-frills/discount airline*

**airˑliner** /ˈeəlaɪnə(r); *NAmE* ˈerl-/ *noun* a large plane that carries passengers

**airˑlock** /ˈeəlɒk; *NAmE* ˈerlɑːk/ *noun* **1** a small room with a tightly closed door at each end, which you go through to reach another area at a different air pressure, for example on a SPACECRAFT or SUBMARINE **2** a bubble of air that blocks the flow of liquid in a PUMP or pipe

**airˑmail** /ˈeəmeɪl; *NAmE* ˈerm-/ *noun* [U] the system of sending letters, etc. by air: *Send it airmail/by airmail.*

**airˑman** /ˈeəmən; *NAmE* ˈerm-/, **airˑwoman** /ˈeəwʊmən; *NAmE* ˈerw-/ *noun* (*pl.* **-men** /-mən/, **-women** /-wɪmɪn/) **1** a member of the British AIR FORCE, especially one below the rank of an officer **2** a member of one of the lowest ranks in the US AIR FORCE: *Airman Brines*

**ˈair marshal** *noun* an officer of very high rank in the British AIR FORCE: *Air Marshal Sue Gray*

**ˈair mattress** (*especially NAmE*) (*also* **ˈair bed** *BrE*, **ˈair bed** *NAmE*) *noun* a large plastic or rubber bag that can be filled with air and used as a bed

**ˈAir Miles™** *noun* [pl.] points that you collect by buying plane tickets and other products, which you can then use to pay for air travel

**ˈair pistol** *noun* a small gun that uses air pressure to fire small metal balls (called PELLETS)

**airˑplane** /ˈeəpleɪn; *NAmE* ˈerp-/ *noun* (*especially NAmE*) = PLANE: **by** ~ *They arrived in Belgium by airplane.* ⋄ *an airplane crash/flight* ⋄ *a commercial/jet/military airplane*

**air·play** /ˈeəpleɪ; NAmE ˈerp-/ noun [U] time that is spent broadcasting a particular record, performer, or type of music on the radio: *The band is starting to get a lot of airplay.*

**ˈair pocket** noun **1** a closed area that becomes filled with air **2** an area of low air pressure that makes a plane suddenly drop while flying

**air·port** /ˈeəpɔːt; NAmE ˈerpɔːrt/ noun a place where planes land and take off and that has buildings for passengers to wait in: *Gatwick Airport* ◊ *waiting in the airport lounge/terminal* ◊ *Passengers were banned from taking hand luggage through airport security.*

**WORDFINDER** baggage reclaim, board, check-in, gate, immigration, lounge, passport, security, terminal

**ˈair power** noun [U] military forces involving aircraft

**ˈair pump** noun a piece of equipment for sending air into or out of sth

**ˈair quality** noun [U] the degree to which the air is clean and free from pollution

**ˈair rage** noun [U] a situation in which a passenger on a plane becomes violent or aggressive

**ˈair raid** noun an attack by a number of aircraft dropping many bombs on a place: *The family was killed in an air raid.* ◊ *an air-raid shelter/warning*

**ˈair rifle** noun a gun with a long BARREL that uses air pressure to fire small metal balls (called PELLETS)

**ˌair-sea ˈrescue** noun [C, U] the process of rescuing people from the sea using aircraft

**air·ship** /ˈeəʃɪp; NAmE ˈerʃ-/ noun a large aircraft without wings, filled with a gas that is lighter than air, and driven by engines

**ˈair show** noun a show at which people can watch aircraft flying

**air·space** /ˈeəspeɪs; NAmE ˈers-/ noun the part of the sky where planes fly, usually the part above a particular country that is legally controlled by that country: *The jet entered Chinese airspace without permission.*

**air·speed** /ˈeəspiːd; NAmE ˈers-/ noun the speed of an aircraft relative to the air through which it is moving ⊃ compare GROUND SPEED

**air·stream** /ˈeəstriːm; NAmE ˈers-/ noun a movement of air, especially a strong one

**ˈair strike** noun an attack made by aircraft

**air·strip** /ˈeəstrɪp; NAmE ˈers-/ noun (also **ˈlanding strip**) a narrow piece of cleared land that an aircraft can land on

**ˈair support** noun [U] help that aircraft give to soldiers and military vehicles on the land or sea

**ˈair terminal** noun a building at an airport that provides services for passengers travelling by plane

**air·tight** /ˈeətaɪt; NAmE ˈert-/ adj. not allowing air to get in or out: *Store the cake in an airtight container.* ◊ *(figurative) an airtight alibi* (= one that cannot be proved to be false)

**air·time** /ˈeətaɪm; NAmE ˈert-/ noun [U] **1** the amount of time that is given to a particular subject on radio or television **2** the amount of time that is paid for when you are using a mobile phone

**ˌair-to-ˈair** adj. [usually before noun] from one aircraft to another while they are both flying: *an air-to-air missile*

**ˌair-to-ˈground** adj. [usually before noun] directed or operating from an aircraft to the surface of the land: *air-to-ground weapons*

**ˌair-to-ˈsurface** adj. [usually before noun] moving or passing from a flying aircraft to the surface of the sea or land: *air-to-surface missiles*

**ˌair traffic conˈtrol** noun [U] **1** the activity of giving instructions by radio to pilots of aircraft so that they know when and where to take off or land **2** the group of people or the organization that provides an air traffic control service: *The pilot was given clearance to land by air traffic control.*

**ˌair traffic conˈtroller** noun a person whose job is to give instructions by radio to pilots of aircraft so that they know when and where to take off or land

**ˌair viceˈmarshal** noun an officer of very high rank in the British AIR FORCE: *Air Vice-Marshal Andrew Burns*

**air·waves** /ˈeəweɪvz; NAmE ˈerw-/ noun [pl.] radio waves that are used in broadcasting radio and television: *More and more TV and radio stations are crowding the airwaves.* ◊ *A well-known voice came over the airwaves.*

**air·way** /ˈeəweɪ; NAmE ˈerw-/ noun **1** (*medical*) the passage from the nose and throat to the lungs, through which you breathe **2** (often used in names of airlines) a route regularly used by planes: *British Airways*

**air·worthy** /ˈeəwɜːði; NAmE ˈerwɜːrði/ adj. (of aircraft) safe to fly ▶ **air·worthi·ness** noun [U]

**airy** /ˈeəri; NAmE ˈeri/ adj. (**air·ier, airi·est**) **1** with plenty of fresh air because there is a lot of space: *The office was light and airy.* **2** (*formal*) acting or done in a way that shows that you are not worried or that you are not treating sth as serious: *He dismissed her with an airy wave.* ⊃ see also AIRILY **3** (*formal, disapproving*) not serious or practical: *airy promises/speculation*

**ˌairy-ˈfairy** adj. (BrE, informal, disapproving) not clear or practical

**aisle** /aɪl/ noun a passage between rows of seats in a church, theatre, train, etc., or between rows of shelves in a supermarket: *an aisle seat* (= in a plane or train) ◊ *Coffee and tea are in the next aisle.* ⊃ compare GANGWAY ⊃ **WORD-FINDER NOTE at** TRAIN

**IDM** **go/walk down the ˈaisle** (*informal*) to get married ⊃ more at ROLL v., SIDE n.

**aitch** /eɪtʃ/ noun the letter H written as a word: *He spoke with a cockney accent and dropped his aitches* (= did not pronounce the letter H at the start of words).

**aiyo** /ˈaɪjəʊ/ (also **ai-aiyo** /aɪˈaɪjəʊ/) exclamation (IndE) used to show that you are surprised or upset: *Aiyo, what terrible news!* ◊ *Aiyo, that hurts!*

**ajar** /əˈdʒɑː(r)/ adj. [not before noun] (of a door) slightly open: *I'll leave the door ajar.*

**aka** /ˌeɪ keɪ ˈeɪ/ abbr. also known as: *Antonio Fratelli, aka 'Big Tony'*

**akimbo** /əˈkɪmbəʊ/ adv.

**IDM** **(with) arms aˈkimbo** with your hands on your HIPS and your ELBOWS pointing away from your body

**akin** /əˈkɪn/ adj. **~ to sth** (*formal*) similar to sth: *What he felt was more akin to pity than love.*

**-al** /əl, l/ suffix **1** (in adjectives) connected with: *magical* ◊ *verbal* ⊃ see also -ALLY **2** (in nouns) a process or state of: *survival*

**à la** /ˈɑː lɑː/ prep. (from French) in the same style as sb/sth else: *a new band that sings à la Beatles*

**ala·bas·ter** /ˈæləbɑːstə(r); NAmE -bæs-/ noun [U] a type of white stone that is often used to make statues and other objects: *an alabaster tomb* ◊ *(literary) her pale, alabaster* (= white and smooth) *skin*

**à la carte** /ˌɑː lɑː ˈkɑːt; NAmE ˈkɑːrt/ adj., adv. (from French) if food in a restaurant is **à la carte**, or if you eat **à la carte**, you choose from a list of dishes that have separate prices, rather than having a complete meal at a fixed price ⊃ **WORDFINDER NOTE at** RESTAURANT

**alac·rity** /əˈlækrəti/ noun [U] (*formal*) great happiness or enthusiasm: *They accepted the offer with alacrity.*

**Aladdin's cave** /əˌlædɪnz ˈkeɪv/ noun a place where there are many wonderful objects **ORIGIN** From a story in the *Arabian nights* in which the hero, Aladdin, finds hidden treasure, including a magic lamp, in a cave.

**alarm** /əˈlɑːm; NAmE əˈlɑːrm/ noun, verb

■ noun **1** [C, usually sing.] a loud noise or a signal that warns people of danger or of a problem: *She decided to sound the alarm* (= warn people that the situation was dangerous). ◊ *I hammered on all the doors to raise the alarm.*

## alarm call

⊃ see also FALSE ALARM **2** ?+ B1 [C] a device that warns people of a particular danger, or that a particular person is in danger: *a burglar/fire/smoke alarm* ◊ *The cat set off the alarm* (= made it start ringing). ◊ *A car alarm went off in the middle of the night* (= started ringing). ◊ *Carry a personal alarm with you.* ⊃ see also BURGLAR ALARM, FIRE ALARM, SMOKE ALARM **3** ?+ B1 [C] a ringing sound or a tune played by a clock or your phone after you have set it to play at a particular time to wake you up: *The alarm went off at 7 o'clock.* **4** ?+ B2 [U] fear and worry that sb feels when sth dangerous or unpleasant might happen: *in ~ 'What have you done?' Ellie cried in alarm.* ◊ *I felt a growing sense of alarm when he did not return that night.* ◊ *The doctor said there was no cause for alarm.* ⊃ SYNONYMS at FEAR
**IDM** **a'larm bells ring/are ringing** if you say that **alarm bells are ringing**, you mean that people are starting to feel worried and to suspect that sth is wrong
■ verb **1** ?+ B2 ~ **sb** to make sb anxious or afraid SYN **worry**: *I can only guess that they don't want to alarm the public yet.* ⊃ SYNONYMS at FRIGHTEN **2** ~ **sth** to fit sth such as a door with a device that warns people when sb is trying to enter illegally

**a'larm call** *noun* **1** a phone call that is intended to wake you up: *Could I have an alarm call at 5.30 tomorrow, please?* **2** a sound of warning made by a bird or animal

**a'larm clock** *noun* a clock that you can set to ring a bell, etc. at a particular time to wake you up: *I set the alarm clock for 7 o'clock.* ⊃ see also ALARM *noun* (3)

**alarmed** /əˈlɑːmd/ *NAmE* əˈlɑːrmd/ *adj.* **1** ~ (**at/by sth**) anxious or afraid that sth dangerous or unpleasant might happen: *She was alarmed at the prospect of travelling alone.* ⊃ SYNONYMS at AFRAID **2** [not before noun] protected by an alarm: *This door is alarmed.*

**alarm·ing** /əˈlɑːmɪŋ; *NAmE* əˈlɑːrm-/ *adj.* causing worry and fear: *an alarming increase in crime* ◊ *The rainforests are disappearing at an alarming rate.* ▶ **alarm·ing·ly** *adv.*: *Prices have risen alarmingly.*

**alarm·ist** /əˈlɑːmɪst; *NAmE* əˈlɑːrm-/ *adj.* (*disapproving*) causing unnecessary fear and worry: *A spokesperson for the food industry said the TV programme was alarmist.* ▶ **alarm·ist** *noun*

**alas** /əˈlæs/ *exclamation* (*old use* or *literary*) used to show you are sad or sorry: *For many people, alas, hunger is part of everyday life.*

**al·ba·tross** /ˈælbətrɒs; *NAmE* -trɑːs/ *noun* **1** a very large white bird with long wings that lives in the Pacific and Southern Oceans ⊃ VISUAL VOCAB page V2 **2** [usually sing.] (*formal*) a thing that causes problems or prevents you from doing sth

**al·beit** ?+ C1 /ˌɔːlˈbiːɪt/ *conj.* (*formal*) although: *He finally agreed, albeit reluctantly, to help us.*

**al·bin·ism** /ˈælbɪnɪzəm/ *noun* [U] (*specialist*) the condition of being an albino

**al·bino** /ælˈbiːnəʊ; *NAmE* -ˈbaɪn-/ *noun* (*pl.* **-os**) a person or an animal that is born with no PIGMENT (= colour) in the hair or skin, which are white, or in the eyes, which are pink ▶ **al·bino** *adj.* [only before noun]

**Al·bion** /ˈælbiən/ *noun* [U] (*literary*) an ancient name for Britain or England

**album** ⊙ B1 /ˈælbəm/ *noun* **1** ?+ B1 a book in which you keep photographs, stamps, etc: *a photo album* ◊ *an online album* (= a website where you can store and view photographs) **2** ?+ B1 a collection of pieces of music released as a single item, usually on the internet or on a CD: *They recently released their debut album.* ◊ *It's the singer's first solo album.* ⊃ compare SINGLE

**al·bu·men** /ˈælbjʊmɪn; *NAmE* ælˈbjuːmən/ *noun* [U] (*specialist*) the clear inside part of an egg that is white when cooked SYN **white** ⊃ compare YOLK

**al·chem·ist** /ˈælkəmɪst/ *noun* a person who studied alchemy

**al·chemy** /ˈælkəmi/ *noun* [U] **1** a form of chemistry studied in the Middle Ages that involved trying to discover how to change ordinary metals into gold **2** (*literary*) a mysterious power or magic that can change things

**Al·cher·inga** /ˌæltʃəˈrɪŋɡə/ (*also* **Dreamtime**) *noun* [U] according to some Australian Aboriginals, the time when the first people were created

**al·co·hol** ⊙ B1 /ˈælkəhɒl; *NAmE* -hɔːl/ *noun* [U] **1** ?+ B1 drinks such as beer, wine, etc. that can make people drunk: *He never drinks alcohol.* ◊ *alcohol abuse/use/dependence* ◊ *the dangers of excessive alcohol consumption* **2** ?+ B1 the clear liquid that is found in drinks such as beer, wine, etc. and is used in medicines, cleaning products, etc: *Wine contains about 10% alcohol.* ◊ *levels of alcohol in the blood* ◊ *He was arrested for driving under the influence of alcohol.* ◊ *He pleaded guilty to driving with excess alcohol.* ◊ *alcohol-free beer* ⊃ see also ETHYL ALCOHOL, RUBBING ALCOHOL

**al·co·hol·ic** ⊙ B1 /ˌælkəˈhɒlɪk; *NAmE* -ˈhɔːl-/ *adj.*, *noun*
■ *adj.* **1** ?+ B1 connected with or containing alcohol: *alcoholic drinks/beverages* OPP **non-alcoholic** ⊃ see also SOFT DRINK **2** caused by drinking alcohol: *The guests left in an alcoholic haze.* **3** regularly drinking too much alcohol and unable to stop easily, so that it has become an illness: *his alcoholic daughter*
■ *noun* a person who regularly drinks too much alcohol and cannot easily stop drinking, so that it has become an illness ⊃ see also LUSH *noun*

**Alco,holics A'nonymous**™ *noun* [U + sing./pl. v.] (*abbr.* **AA**) an international organization, begun in Chicago in 1935, for people who are trying to stop drinking alcohol. They have meetings to help each other.

**al·co·hol·ism** /ˈælkəhɒlɪzəm; *NAmE* -hɔːl-/ *noun* [U] the medical condition caused by drinking too much alcohol regularly

**al·co·pop** /ˈælkəʊpɒp; *NAmE* -paːp/ *noun* (*BrE*) a sweet FIZZY (= with bubbles) drink that contains alcohol

**al·cove** /ˈælkəʊv/ *noun* an area in a room that is formed by part of a wall being built further back than the rest of the wall: *The bookcase fits neatly into the alcove.*

**al dente** /ˌæl ˈdenteɪ, -ti/ *adj.* (*from Italian*) (of cooked food, especially PASTA) not too soft when bitten ▶ **al dente** *adv.*

**alder** /ˈɔːldə(r)/ *noun* a tree of the BIRCH family that grows in northern countries, usually in wet ground

**al·der·man** /ˈɔːldəmən; *NAmE* -dərm-/ *noun* (*pl.* **-men** /-mən/) **1** (in England and Wales in the past) a senior member of a town, BOROUGH or county council, below the rank of a MAYOR, chosen by other members of the council **2** (*feminine* **al·der·woman** /-wʊmən/, *pl.* **-women** /-wɪmɪn/) (in the US, Canada and Australia) an elected member of a town or city council: *Alderman Tim Evans*

**ale** /eɪl/ *noun* **1** [U, C] a type of beer without bubbles. There are several kinds of ale. ⊃ see also BROWN ALE, GINGER ALE, REAL ALE **2** [C] a glass, bottle or can of ale

**alec, aleck** /ˈælɪk/ ⊃ SMART ALEC

**ale·house** /ˈeɪlhaʊs/ *noun* (*BrE, old-fashioned*) a place where people used to drink beer

**alert** ?+ B1 /əˈlɜːt; *NAmE* əˈlɜːrt/ *verb*, *noun*, *adj.*
■ *verb* [often passive] **1** ?+ B1 to warn sb about a dangerous situation or one that requires immediate action: *~sb Neighbours quickly alerted the emergency services.* ◊ *(be) alerted by sth Alerted by a noise downstairs, he sat up and turned on the light.* **2** ?+ B1 to make sb aware of sth: *be alerted to sth They had been alerted to the possibility of further price rises.*
■ *noun* **1** ?+ B1 [sing., U] a situation in which people are watching for danger and ready to deal with it: *on the ~ (for sth) Police are warning the public to be on the alert for suspicious packages.* ◊ *on ~ More than 5000 troops have been placed on (full) alert.* **2** ?+ B1 [C] a warning of danger or of a problem: *a bomb/fire alert* ⊃ WORDFINDER NOTE at ATTACK ⊃ see also BOMB ALERT, RED ALERT
■ *adj.* **1** ?+ B1 able to think quickly; quick to notice things: *Suddenly he found himself awake and fully alert.* ◊ *Two*

alert scientists spotted the mistake. **2** ~ sth aware of sth, especially a problem or danger: *We must be alert to the possibility of danger.* ► **alert·ly** *adv.* **alert·ness** *noun* [U]

**A level** /ˈeɪ levl/ (*also* **ad·vanced level**) *noun* [C, U] a British exam taken in a particular subject, usually in the final year of school at the age of 18: *You need three A levels to get onto this university course.* ◇ *What A levels are you doing?* ◇ *I'm doing maths A level.* ◇ *two A level passes/two passes at A level* ⊃ compare GCE, GCSE, NVQ

**al·fal·fa** /ælˈfælfə/ *noun* [U] a plant with small divided leaves and purple flowers, grown as food for farm animals and as a salad vegetable

**al fresco** /æl ˈfreskəʊ/ *adj., adv.* (*from Italian*) outdoors: *an al fresco lunch party* ◇ *eating al fresco*

**algae** /ˈældʒiː, ˈælɡiː/ *noun* [U, pl.] very simple plants, such as SEAWEED, that have no real leaves, STEMS or roots, and that grow in or near water HELP The singular of **algae** is **alga** /ˈælɡə/ but this is a specialist term used only in scientific writing. ► **algal** /-ɡəl/ *adj.* [only before noun]: *algal blooms/growth*

**al·ge·bra** /ˈældʒɪbrə/ *noun* [U] a type of mathematics in which letters and symbols are used to represent quantities ⊃ WORDFINDER NOTE at MATHS ► **al·ge·bra·ic** /ˌældʒɪˈbreɪɪk/ *adj.*

**al·go·rithm** /ˈælɡərɪðəm/ *noun* (*computing*) a set of rules that must be followed when solving a particular problem: *The company uses machine-learning algorithms to recommend jobs to those looking for work.* ◇ *to apply a complex/sophisticated algorithm*

**al·haja** /ælˈhædʒə/ WAfrE [aláʤá] *noun* (WAfrE) a woman who is a Muslim and has completed a religious journey to Mecca (often used as a title) ⊃ compare ALHAJI

**al·haji** /ælˈhædʒi/ WAfrE [aláʤí] *noun* (WAfrE) a man who is a Muslim and has completed a religious journey to Mecca (often used as a title) ⊃ compare ALHAJA

**-alia** /ˈeɪliə/ *suffix* (in plural nouns) items connected with the particular area of activity or interest mentioned: *kitchenalia*

**alias** /ˈeɪliəs/ *adv., noun*
- *adv.* used when a person, especially a criminal or an actor, is known by two names: *Mick Clark, alias Sid Brown* ◇ *Hercule Poirot, alias David Suchet* (= David Suchet plays the part of Hercule Poirot) ◇ *David Suchet, alias Hercule Poirot of the famous TV series*
- *noun* **1** a false or different name, especially one that is used by a criminal: *He checked into the hotel under an alias.* **2** (*computing*) a name that can be used instead of the actual name for a file, internet address, etc.

**alibi** /ˈæləbaɪ/ *noun* **1** evidence that proves that a person was in another place at the time of a crime and so could not have committed it: *The suspects all had alibis for the day of the robbery.* **2** an excuse for sth that you have done wrong

**Alice in Wonder·land** /ˌælɪs ɪn ˈwʌndələnd; NAmE -dɑːrl-/ *noun* [U] used to describe a situation that is very strange, in which things happen that do not make any sense and are the opposite of what you would expect: *The country's economic system is pure Alice in Wonderland.* ► **Alice-in-Wonderland** *adj.* [only before noun]: *I felt I was in an Alice-in-Wonderland world.* ORIGIN From the title of a children's story by Lewis Carroll, describing adventures in a strange, imaginary land.

**alien** /ˈeɪliən/ *noun, adj.*
- *noun* **1** (NAmE also **non-ˈcitizen**) (*law or specialist*) a person who is not a citizen of the country in which they live or work: *an illegal alien* ⊃ compare RESIDENT ALIEN **2** a creature from another world: *aliens from outer space*
- *adj.* **1** ~ (to sb/sth) strange and frightening; different from what you are used to SYN **hostile**: *an alien environment* ◇ *In a world that had suddenly become alien and dangerous, she was her only security.* **2** (*often disapproving*) from another country or society; foreign: *an alien culture* **3** (*disapproving*) not usual or acceptable: *~to sb/sth The idea is alien to our religion.* ◇ *Cruelty was quite alien to him.* **4** connected with creatures from another world: *alien beings from outer space*

**alien·ate** /ˈeɪliəneɪt/ *verb* **1** ~ sb to make sb less friendly towards you: *His comments have alienated a lot of young voters.* **2** ~ sb (from sth/sb) to make sb feel that they do not belong in a particular group: *Very talented children may feel alienated from the others in their class.* ► **alien·ation** /ˌeɪliəˈneɪʃn/ *noun* [U]: *The new policy resulted in the alienation of many voters.* ◇ *Many immigrants suffer from a sense of alienation.*

**alight** /əˈlaɪt/ *adj., verb*
- *adj.* [not before noun] **1** on fire: *A cigarette set the dry grass alight.* ◇ *Her dress caught alight in the fire.* **2** (*formal*) (of faces or eyes) showing a feeling of happiness or excitement IDM see WORLD
- *verb* (*formal or literary*) **1** [I] ~ (in/on/upon sth) (of a bird or an insect) to land in or on sth after flying to it SYN **land** **2** [I] ~ (from sth) to get out of a bus, a train or other vehicle SYN **get off**: *Do not alight from a moving bus.* PHRV **aˈlight on/upon sth** to think of, find or notice sth, especially by chance: *Eventually, we alighted on the idea of seeking treatment.* ◇ *Her eyes suddenly alighted on the bundle of documents.*

**align** /əˈlaɪn/ *verb* **1** ~ sth (with sth) [I, T] to arrange sth in the correct position, or to be in the correct position, in relation to sth else, especially in a straight line: *Make sure the shelf is aligned with the top of the cupboard.* ◇ *The top and bottom line of each column on the page should align.* **2** [T] ~ sth (with/to sth) to change sth slightly so that it is in the correct relationship to sth else: *Domestic prices have been aligned with those in world markets.* PHRV **aˈlign yourself with sb/sth** to publicly support an organization, a set of opinions or a person that you agree with

**align·ment** /əˈlaɪnmənt/ *noun* [U, C] **1** arrangement in a straight line: *A bone in my spine was out of alignment.* **2** political support given to one country or group by another: *Japan's alignment with the West*

**alike** /əˈlaɪk/ *adv., adj.*
- *adv.* **1** in a very similar way: *They tried to treat all their children alike.* **2** used after you have referred to two people or groups, to mean 'both' or 'equally': *Good management benefits employers and employees alike.* IDM see GREAT *adj.*, SHARE *v.*
- *adj.* [not before noun] very similar: *My sister and I do not look alike.* ⊃ compare UNLIKE

**ali·men·tary canal** /ˌælɪmentəri kəˈnæl/ *noun* the passage in the body that carries food from the mouth to the ANUS

**ali·mony** /ˈælɪməni; NAmE -moʊni/ *noun* [U] (*especially NAmE*) the money that a court orders sb to pay regularly to their former wife, husband or partner when the marriage or CIVIL UNION is ended ⊃ compare MAINTENANCE

**ˈA-line** *adj.* (of a skirt or dress) wider at the bottom than at the top

**ali·quot** /ˈælɪkwɒt; NAmE -kwɑːt/ *noun* **1** (*specialist*) a small amount of sth that is taken from a larger amount, especially when it is taken in order to do chemical tests on it **2** (*mathematics*) a quantity that can be exactly divided into another

**ˈA-list** *adj.* [usually before noun] used to describe the group of people who are considered to be the most famous, successful or important: *He only invited A-list celebrities to his parties.* ⊃ compare B-LIST ► **ˈA-lister** *noun*: *A-lister Cameron Diaz*

**alive** /əˈlaɪv/ *adj.* [not before noun] **1** living; not dead: *Is your mother still alive?* ◇ *Doctors kept the baby alive for six weeks.* ◇ *She had to steal food just to stay alive.* ◇ *He was buried alive in the earthquake.* ◇ *The police are desperate to catch this man dead or alive.* **2** ~ (with sth) full of emotion, excitement, activity, etc: *Ed was alive with happiness.* **3** continuing to exist: *to keep a tradition alive*

# alkali

**4** ~ **with sth** full of living or moving things: *The pool was alive with goldfish.* **5** ~ **to sth** aware of sth; knowing sth exists and is important: *to be alive to the dangers/facts/possibilities* **IDM** ˌa**live and ˈkicking** very active, healthy or popular ˌa**live and ˈwell 1** (of a person) still living and not injured or harmed: *The missing student was found alive and well in Newcastle.* **2** (of an industry, area of activity, etc.) still popular or successful: *Contrary to popular belief, the tourism industry is alive and well in this part of the world.* **ˌbring sth aˈlive** to make sth interesting: *The pictures bring the book alive.* **ˌcome aˈlive 1** (of a subject or an event) to become interesting and exciting **SYN come to life**: *The game came alive in the second half.* **2** (of a place) to become busy and full of activity **SYN come to life**: *The city starts to come alive after dark.* **3** (of a person) to show interest in sth and become excited about it: *She came alive as she talked about her job.* ⇒ more at EAT

**al·kali** /ˈælkəlaɪ/ *noun* [C, U] (*chemistry*) a chemical substance that reacts with ACIDS to form a salt and gives a SOLUTION with a pH of more than seven when it is DISSOLVED (= mixed with a liquid and becoming part of it) in water ⇒ compare ACID

**al·ka·line** /ˈælkəlaɪn/ *adj.* **1** (*chemistry*) having the nature of an alkali **2** (*specialist*) containing alkali: *alkaline soil* ⇒ compare ACID

**al·ka·lin·ity** /ˌælkəˈlɪnəti/ *noun* [U] the state of being or containing an ALKALI

**al·kal·oid** /ˈælkəlɔɪd/ *noun* (*biology* or *medical*) a poisonous substance found in some plants. There are many different alkaloids and some are used as the basis for drugs.

**al·kane** /ˈælkeɪn/ *noun* (*chemistry*) any of a series of COMPOUNDS that contain CARBON and HYDROGEN: *Methane and propane are alkanes.*

**al·kene** /ˈælkiːn/ *noun* (*chemistry*) any of a series of gases that contain HYDROGEN and CARBON and that have a double BOND (= force of attraction) between two of the ATOMS of CARBON

**all** 🔑 **A1** /ɔːl/ *det., pron., adv.*
■ *det.* **1** 🔑 **A1** (used with plural nouns. The noun may have *the, this, that, my, her, his*, etc. in front of it, or a number.) the whole number of: *All horses are animals, but not all animals are horses.* ◊ *Cars were coming from all directions* (= every direction). ◊ *All the people you invited are coming.* ◊ *All my plants have died.* ◊ *All five men are hard workers.* **2** 🔑 **A1** (used with uncountable nouns. The noun may have *the, this, that, my, her, his*, etc. in front of it.) the whole amount of: *All wood tends to shrink.* ◊ *You've had all the fun and I've had all the hard work.* ◊ *All this mail must be answered.* ◊ *He has lost all his money.* **3** 🔑 **A1** used with singular nouns showing sth has been happening for a whole period of time: *He's worked hard all year.* ◊ *She was unemployed for all that time.* **4** the greatest possible: *In all honesty* (= being as honest as I can), *I can't agree.* **5** consisting or appearing to consist of one thing only: *The magazine was all advertisements.* ◊ *She was all smiles* (= smiling a lot). **6** any whatever: *He denied all knowledge of the crime.*
**IDM** ˌand ˈall ˈthat (jazz, rubbish, stuff, etc.) (*informal*) and other similar things: *I'm bored by history—dates and battles and all that stuff.* ˌnot ˈall that good, well, etc. not particularly good, well, etc: *He doesn't sing all that well.* ˌnot as ˈbad(ly), etc. as ˈall ˈthat not as much as has been suggested: *They're not as rich as all that.* ◊ *We didn't play particularly well, but we didn't do as badly as all that.* **of ˌall ˈpeople, ˈthings, etc.** (*informal*) used to express surprise because sb/sth seems the least likely person, example, etc: *I didn't think you, of all people, would become a vegetarian.* **of ˈall the …** (*informal*) used to express anger: *I've locked myself out. Of all the stupid things to do!* ⇒ more at FOR *prep.*, SIDE *n.*
■ *pron.* **1** 🔑 **A1** the whole number or amount: *All the food has gone.* ◊ *They've eaten all of it.* ◊ *They've eaten it all.* ◊ *I invited some of my colleagues but not all.* ◊ *Not all of them were invited.* ◊ *All of them enjoyed the party.* ◊ *They all*

---

enjoyed it. ◊ *His last movie was best of all.* **2** 🔑 **B1** (followed by a relative clause, often without *that*) the only thing; everything: *All I want is peace and quiet.* ◊ *It was all that I had.* ⇒ note at ALTOGETHER
**IDM** ˌall in ˈall when everything is considered: *All in all it had been a great success.* ˌall in ˈone having two or more uses, functions, etc: *It's a corkscrew and bottle-opener all in one.* ˌand ˈall **1** also; included; in addition: *She jumped into the river, clothes and all* (= with her clothes on). **2** (*informal*) as well; too: *'I'm freezing.' 'Yeah, me and all.'* **as/like ˌall ˈget out** (*NAmE, informal*) used to emphasize how extreme a quality or action is: *He's as crazy as all get out!* ◊ *We rushed like all get out.* **(not) at ˈall** 🔑 **A2** in any way; to any degree: *I didn't enjoy it at all.* **in ˈall** as a total **SYN altogether**: *There were twelve of us in all for dinner.* ◊ *That's £25.40 in all.* ˌnot at ˈall used as a polite reply to an expression of thanks: *'Thanks very much for your help.' 'Not at all, it was a pleasure.'* **your ˈall** everything you have: *They gave their all* (= fought and died) *in the war.* ⇒ more at ABOVE *prep.*, AFTER *prep.*, END *v.*, END *n.*, FOR *prep.*

■ *adv.* **1** 🔑 **A2** completely: *She was dressed all in white.* ◊ *He lives all alone.* ◊ *The coffee went all over my skirt.* **2** (*informal*) very: *She was all excited.* ◊ *Now don't get all upset about it.* **3** ~ **too …** used to show that sth is more than you would like: *I'm all too aware of the problems.* ◊ *The end of the trip came all too soon.* **4** (in sports and games) to each side: *The score was four all.*
**IDM** ˌall aˈlong all the time; from the beginning: *I realized it was in my pocket all along.* ˌall aˈround (*NAmE*) ⇒ ALL ROUND **ˌall the ˈbetter, ˈharder, ˈmore, etc.** so much better, harder, etc: *We'll have to work all the harder with two people off sick.* ˌall ˈbut almost: *The party was all but over when we arrived.* ◊ *It was all but impossible to read his writing.* **2** everything or everyone except sth/sb: *All but one of the plates were damaged.* ˌall ˈin **1** physically tired **SYN exhausted**: *At the end of the race he felt all in.* **2** (*BrE*) including everything: *The trip cost £750 all in.* ⇒ see also ALL-IN **all of sth** (*often ironic*) used to emphasize an amount, a size, etc. usually when it is very small: *It must be all of 100 metres to the car!* ˌall ˈover **1** everywhere: *We looked all over for the ring.* **2** (*informal*) what you would expect of the person mentioned: *That sounds like my sister all over.* ˌall ˈround (*BrE*) (*NAmE* ˌall aˈround) **1** in every way; in all respects: *a good performance all round* **2** for each person: *She bought drinks all round.* ˌall ˈthere (*informal*) having a healthy mind; thinking clearly: *He behaves very oddly at times—I don't think he's quite all there.* **be ˌall aˈbout sb/sth** used to say what the most important aspect of sth is: *It's all about money these days.* **be ˈall for sth/for doing sth** (*informal*) to believe strongly that sth should be done: *They're all for saving money where they can.* **be ˌall ˈover sb** (*informal, often disapproving*) to show a lot of interest in or enthusiasm for sb: *He was all over her at the party.* **be ˌall ˈthat** (*US, informal*) to be very attractive or impressive: *He thinks he's all that.* **be ˌall ˈup (with sb)** (*old-fashioned, informal*) to be the end for sb: *It looks as though it's all up with us now* (= we are ruined, have no further chances, etc.).

**all-** /ɔːl/ *combining form* (in adjectives and adverbs) **1** completely: *an all-British cast* ◊ *an all-inclusive price* **2** in the highest degree: *all-important* ◊ *all-powerful*

**ˈall-action** *adj.* [only before noun] having a lot of exciting events: *an all-action movie*

**Allah** /ˈælə; *BrE also* ˈɑːlə; *NAmE also* ˈɑːlə, ɑːˈlɑː/ *noun* the name of God among Muslims

**ˌall-Aˈmerican** *adj.* **1** having good qualities that people think are typically American: *a clean-cut all-American boy* **2** (of a sports player) chosen as one of the best players in the US

**ˌall-aˈround** (*NAmE*) (*BrE* **ˌall-ˈround**) *adj.* [only before noun] **1** including many different subjects, skills, etc. **2** (of a person) with a wide range of skills or abilities

**allay** /əˈleɪ/ *verb* ~ **sth** (*formal*) to make sth, especially a feeling, less strong: *to allay fears/concern/suspicion*

**ˌall-Caˈnadian** *adj.* **1** chosen as one of the best in, or representing the whole of, Canada, for example in sports **2** having qualities that people think are typically Canadian

**all-ˈclear** *noun usually* **the all-clear** [sing.] **1** a signal (often a sound) that shows that a place or situation is no longer dangerous **2** if a doctor gives sb **the all-clear**, they tell the person that he/she does not have any health problems **3** permission to do sth: *The ship was given the all-clear to sail.*

**all-conˈsum·ing** *adj.* (of an interest) taking up all of your time or energy: *an all-consuming love of jazz*

**ˈall-day** *adj.* [only before noun] continuing or available for the whole day: *an all-day meeting* ◊ *The cafe serves an all-day breakfast.*

**al·le·ga·tion** /ˌæləˈɡeɪʃn/ *noun* a public statement that is made without giving proof, accusing sb of doing sth that is wrong or illegal **SYN** **accusation**: *to investigate/deny/withdraw an allegation* ◊ *~ of sth Several newspapers made allegations of corruption in the city's police department.* ◊ *~ (of sth) against sb allegations of dishonesty against him* ◊ *~ about sb/sth The committee has made serious allegations about interference in its work.* ◊ *~ that ... an allegation that he had been dishonest* ⊃ **SYNONYMS** at **CLAIM**

**al·lege** /əˈledʒ/ *verb* [often passive] (*formal*) to state sth as a fact but without giving proof: *~ (that) ... The prosecution alleges (that) she was driving carelessly.* ◊ *it is alleged (that) ... It is alleged that he mistreated the prisoners.* ◊ *be alleged to be, have, etc. sth He is alleged to have mistreated the prisoners.* ◊ *~ sth This procedure should be followed in cases where dishonesty has been alleged.* ▶ **al·leged** *adj.* [only before noun] (*formal*): *the alleged attacker/victim/killer* (= that sb says is one) ◊ *the alleged attack/offence/incident* (= that sb says has happened)

**al·leged·ly** /əˈledʒɪdli/ *adv.* (*formal*) expressed as though sth is a fact but without giving any proof: *crimes allegedly committed during the war*

**al·le·giance** /əˈliːdʒəns/ *noun* [U, C] a person's continued support for a political party, religion, leader, etc: *to switch/transfer/change allegiance* ◊ *an oath/a vow/a statement of allegiance* ◊ *People of various party allegiances joined the campaign.* ◊ *~ (to sb/sth) to pledge/swear allegiance* ◊ *He affirmed his allegiance to the president.*

**al·le·gory** /ˈæləɡəri; NAmE -ɡɔːri/ *noun* [C, U] (*pl.* **-ies**) a story, play, picture, etc. in which each character or event is a symbol representing an idea or a quality, such as truth, evil, death, etc.; the use of such symbols: *a political allegory* ◊ *the poet's use of allegory* ⊃ see also **FABLE** ▶ **al·le·gor·ical** /ˌæləˈɡɒrɪkl; NAmE -ˈɡɔːr-/ *adj.*: *an allegorical figure/novel* **al·le·gor·ical·ly** /-kli/ *adv.*

**al·le·gro** /əˈleɡrəʊ/ *noun* (*pl.* **-os**) (*music, from Italian*) a piece of music to be played in a fast and lively manner ▶ **al·legro** *adj., adv.*

**al·lele** /əˈliːl/ *noun* (*biology*) one of two or more possible forms of a **GENE** that are found at the same place on a **CHROMOSOME**

**al·le·luia** /ˌælɪˈluːjə/ *noun, exclamation* = **HALLELUJAH**

**all-emˈbrac·ing** *adj.* (*formal*) including everything

**all-enˈcom·pass·ing** *adj.* (*formal*) including everything

**Allen key™** /ˈælən kiː/ (*BrE*) (*NAmE* **Allen wrench™**) *noun* a small tool used for turning an Allen screw™ ⊃ picture at **KEY**

**Allen screw™** *noun* a **SCREW** with a hole that has six sides in the top part

**al·ler·gen** /ˈælədʒən; NAmE ˈælərdʒ-/ *noun* a substance that causes an allergy

**al·ler·gic** /əˈlɜːdʒɪk; NAmE əˈlɜːrdʒ-/ *adj.* **1** *~ (to sth)* having an allergy to sth: *I like cats but unfortunately I'm allergic to them.* **2** caused by an allergy: *an allergic reaction/rash* **3** [not before noun] *~ to sth/sb* (*informal, humorous*) having a strong dislike of sth/sb: *You could see he was allergic to housework.*

**al·lergy** /ˈælədʒi; NAmE ˈælərdʒi/ *noun* (*pl.* **-ies**) a medical condition that causes you to react badly or feel ill when you eat or touch a particular substance: *He suffers from a severe nut allergy.* ◊ *Food allergies affect six to eight per cent of children.* ◊ *~ to sth I have an allergy to animal hair.*

# allocation

**al·le·vi·ate** /əˈliːvieɪt/ *verb* *~sth* to make sth less severe **SYN** **ease**: *to alleviate suffering* ◊ *A number of measures were taken to alleviate the problem.* ▶ **al·le·vi·ation** /əˌliːviˈeɪʃn/ *noun* [U]

**alley** /ˈæli/ *noun* **1** (*also* **al·ley·way** /ˈæliweɪ/) a narrow passage behind or between buildings: *a narrow/dark alley* ⊃ see also **BACK ALLEY**, **BLIND ALLEY**, **BOWLING ALLEY** **2** (*NAmE*) the area between the pair of straight lines on a tennis or **BADMINTON** court that mark the extra area that is used when four people are playing ⊃ compare **TRAMLINES** (2) ⊃ see also **BACK-ALLEY**

**IDM** **(right) up your ˈalley** (*NAmE*) (*especially BrE* **(right) up your ˈstreet**) (*informal*) very suitable for you because it is sth that you know a lot about or are very interested in

**ˈalley cat** *noun* a cat that lives on the streets

**al·li·ance** /əˈlaɪəns/ *noun* **1** an agreement between countries, political parties, etc. to work together in order to achieve sth that they all want: *to form/make an alliance* ◊ *~ with sb/sth The Social Democrats are now in alliance with the Greens.* ◊ *~ between A and B an alliance between education and business to develop the use of technology in schools* **2** a group of people, political parties, etc. who work together in order to achieve sth that they all want: *The Green Alliance was formed to campaign against environmental damage.*

**al·lied** *adj.* **1** /ˈælaɪd/ connected with countries or groups that join together to fight a war or work for a shared aim: *allied forces/troops* ◊ *~ to/with sb/sth The party is allied with the Communists.* **2** /ˈælaɪd/ (*also* **Allied**) [only before noun] connected with the countries that fought together against Germany in the First and Second World Wars: *Italy joined the war on the Allied side in 1915.* **3** /ˈælaɪd, əˈlaɪd/ (*formal*) (of two or more things) similar or existing together; connected with sth: *medicine, nursing, physiotherapy and other allied professions* ◊ *~ to/with sth In this job you will need social skills allied with technical knowledge.* ⊃ see also **ALLY**

**al·li·ga·tor** /ˈælɪɡeɪtə(r)/ *noun* a large **REPTILE** similar to a **CROCODILE**, with a long tail, hard skin and very big **JAWS**, that lives in rivers and lakes in North and South America and China

**ˈalligator clip** *noun* (*especially NAmE*) = **CROCODILE CLIP**

**all-imˈport·ant** *adj.* extremely important

**ˈall-in** *adj.* [only before noun] (*BrE*) including the cost of all parts of sth **SYN** **inclusive**: *an all-in price of £500 with no extras to pay* **IDM** see **ALL** *adv.*

**all-inˈclu·sive** *adj.* including everything or everyone: *Our trips are all-inclusive—there are no hidden costs.*

**all-inˈone** *adj.* [only before noun] able to do the work of two or more things that are usually separate: *an all-in-one shampoo and conditioner*

**al·lit·er·ation** /əˌlɪtəˈreɪʃn/ *noun* [U] (*specialist*) the use of the same letter or sound at the beginning of words that are close together, as in *sing a song of sixpence* ⊃ see also **ASSONANCE** ⊃ **WORDFINDER NOTE** at **IMAGE** ▶ **al·lit·era·tive** /əˈlɪtrətɪv; NAmE -təreɪt-/ *adj.*

**al·lium** /ˈæliəm/ *noun* (*specialist*) any plant that belongs to the same group as onions and **GARLIC**

**all-ˈnight** *adj.* [only before noun] **1** (of a place) open through the night: *an all-night cafe* **2** (of an activity) continuing through the night: *an all-night party*

**all-ˈnighter** *noun* (*informal*) a time when you stay up all night studying, working or at a party

**al·lo·cate** /ˈæləkeɪt/ *verb* to give sth officially to sb/sth for a particular purpose: *~ sth (for sth) A large sum has been allocated for buying new books for the library.* ◊ *~ sth (to sb/sth) They intend to allocate more places to mature students this year.* ◊ *More resources are being allocated to the project.* ◊ *~ sb/sth sth The project is being allocated more resources.* ◊ *~ sth to do sth Millions have been allocated to improve students' performance.*

**al·lo·ca·tion** /ˌæləˈkeɪʃn/ *noun* **1** [C] an amount of money, space, etc. that is given to sb for a

# allophone

particular purpose **2** [U] the act of giving sth to sb for a particular purpose: *the allocation of food to those who need it most*

**al·lo·phone** /ˈæləfəʊn/ *noun* **1** (*phonetics*) a sound that is slightly different from another sound, although both sounds belong to the same PHONEME and the difference does not affect meaning. For example, the /l/ at the beginning of *little* is different from the /l/ at the end. **2** (*CanE*) a person who comes to live in Canada, especially Quebec, from another country, whose first language is neither French nor English ▶ **allophone** *adj.*: *Within French-speaking Quebec, anglophone, allophone and Aboriginal minorities also exist.*

**ˌall-or-ˈnothing** *adj.* used to describe two extreme situations that are the only possible ones: *an all-or-nothing decision* (= one which could either be very good or very bad)

**al·lot** /əˈlɒt/; *NAmE* əˈlɑːt/ *verb* (-tt-) to give time, money, tasks, etc. to sb/sth as a share of what is available: ~ **sth** *I completed the test within the time allotted.* ◊ ~**sth to sb/sth** *How much money has been allotted to us?* ◊ ~**sb/sth sth** *How much money have we been allotted?* ⇨ **allocate**

**al·lot·ment** /əˈlɒtmənt/; *NAmE* əˈlɑːt-/ *noun* **1** [C] (*BrE*) a small area of land in a town that a person can rent in order to grow fruit and vegetables on it ⇨ compare COMMUNITY GARDEN **2** [C, U] (*formal*) an amount of sth that is given or allowed to have; the process of giving sth to sb: *Water allotments to farmers were cut back in the drought.* ◊ *the allotment of shares to company employees*

**ˌall-ˈout** *adj.* [only before noun] using or involving every possible effort and done in a very determined way: *all-out war* ◊ *an all-out attack on the opposition* ▶ **ˌall ˈout** *adv.*: *We're going all out to win.*

**ˌall-ˈover** *adj.* [only before noun] covering the whole of sth: *an all-over tan*

**al·low** /əˈlaʊ/ *verb*
• LET SB/STH DO STH **1** ~ **sb/sth to do sth**; to let sth happen or be done: ~**sb/sth to do sth** *His parents won't allow him to stay out late.* ◊ **be allowed to do sth** *He is not allowed to stay out late.* ◊ *Students are only allowed to use the equipment under supervision.* ◊ *This research must be allowed to continue.* ◊ ~**yourself to do sth** *He refused to allow himself to be kept quiet.* ◊ **be allowed** *Eating is not allowed in the classrooms.* ⇨ HOMOPHONES at ALOUD **2** ~**sb/yourself sth** to let sb have sth: *I'm not allowed visitors.* ◊ *I allow myself a treat now and then.* **3** [usually passive] to let sb/sth go into, through, out of, etc. a place: **(be) allowed** *No dogs allowed* (= you cannot bring them in). ◊ **be allowed + adv./prep.** *The prisoners are allowed out of their cells for two hours a day.* ◊ *They weren't allowed into the country.* ◊ *He was knocking at the door waiting to be allowed in.* ⇨ WORDFINDER NOTE at FREEDOM
• MAKE POSSIBLE **4** ~ **sth** to make sth possible: ~**sth** *A ramp allows easy access for wheelchairs.* ◊ ~**sb sth** *The system allows people the opportunity to browse a wide selection of books.* ◊ ~**sb to do sth** *The new technology allows users to choose exactly what they watch and when.* ⇨ LANGUAGE BANK at PROCESS¹
• TIME/MONEY/FOOD, ETC. **5** ~**sth (for sb/sth)** to make sure that you have enough of sth for a particular purpose: *You need to allow three metres of fabric for the dress.*
• ACCEPT/ADMIT **6** (*formal*) to accept or admit sth; to agree that sth is true or correct: ~**sth** *The judge allowed my claim.* ◊ (= in a court of law) *'Objection!' 'I'll allow it.'* ◊ ~**that ...** *He refuses to allow that such a situation could arise.* ◊ ~**sb sth** *She was very helpful when my mother was ill—I'll allow you that.* ⇨ compare DISALLOW
**IDM** **alˈlow me** used to offer help politely ⇨ more at REIN *n.*
**PHRV** **alˈlow for sb/sth** to consider or include sb/sth when calculating sth: *It will take about an hour to get there, allowing for traffic delays.* ◊ *All these factors must be allowed for.* **alˈlow of sth** (*formal*) to make sth possible: *The facts allow of only one explanation.*

**al·low·able** /əˈlaʊəbl/ *adj.* **1** that is allowed, especially by law or by a set of rules **2** (*BrE*, *specialist*) **allowable amour** of money are amounts that you do not have to pay tax on

**al·low·ance** /əˈlaʊəns/ *noun* **1** [C] an amount of money that is given to sb regularly or for a particular purpose: *an allowance of $20 a day* ◊ *a clothing/living/travel allowance* ◊ *Do you get an allowance for clothing?* ⇨ see also ATTENDANCE ALLOWANCE **2** [C] the amount of sth that is allowed in a particular situation: *a baggage allowance of 20 kilos* **3** [C] (*especially NAmE*) = POCKET MONEY **4** (*BrE*, *specialist*) an amount of money that can be earned or received before you start paying tax: *personal tax allowances*
**IDM** **make allowance(s) for sth** to consider sth, for example when you are making a decision or planning sth: *The budget made allowance for inflation.* ◊ *The plan makes no allowance for people working at different rates.* **make allowances (for sb)** to allow sb to behave in a way that you would not usually accept, because of a problem or because there is a special reason: *You have to make allowances for him because he's tired.*

**al·loy** *noun*, *verb*
■ *noun* /ˈælɔɪ/ [C, U] a metal that is formed by mixing two types of metal together, or by mixing metal with another substance: *Brass is an alloy of copper and zinc.*
■ *verb* /əˈlɔɪ/ ~**sth (with sth)** (*specialist*) to mix one metal with another, especially one of lower value

**ˌall-ˈparty** *adj.* [usually before noun] involving all political parties: *all-party support*

**ˌall-ˈpowerful** *adj.* having complete power: *the all-powerful secret police*

**ˌall-ˈpurpose** *adj.* [only before noun] having many different uses; able to be used in many situations

**ˌall-purpose ˈflour** (*NAmE*) (*BrE* ˌplain ˈflour) *noun* [U] flour that does not contain BAKING POWDER ⇨ compare SELF-RISING FLOUR

**all ˈright** (also *non-standard* or *informal* **alright**) *adj.*, *adv.*, *exclamation*
■ *adj.*, *adv.* **1** acceptable; in an acceptable manner **SYN** OK: *Is the coffee all right?* ◊ *Are you getting along all right in your new job?* ◊ *'They're off to Spain next week.' 'It's all right for some, isn't it?'* (= some people are lucky) **2** safe and well **SYN** OK: *I hope the children are all right.* ◊ *Do you feel all right?* ⇨ SYNONYMS at WELL **3** only just good enough **SYN** OK: *Your work is all right but I'm sure you could do better.* **4** that can be allowed **SYN** OK: *Are you sure it's all right for me to leave early?* **5** (*informal*) used to emphasize that there is no doubt about sth: *'Are you sure it's her?' 'Oh, it's her all right.'*
**IDM** **I'm all ˈright, Jack** (*BrE*, *informal*) used by or about sb who is happy with their own life and does not care about other people's problems **it'll be all ˌright on the ˈnight** (*saying*) used to say that a performance, an event, etc. will be successful even if the preparations for it have not gone well **you're all ˈright** (*BrE*, *informal*) used to refuse an offer or invitation, especially one that you think is unreasonable or not very good: *'Could I interest you in our special offer?' 'No, you're all right, mate.'* ⇨ more at BIT
■ *exclamation* **1** used to check that sb agrees or understands **SYN** OK: *We've got to get up early, all right?* **2** used to say that you agree **SYN** OK: *'Can you do it?' 'Oh, all right.'* **3** used when accepting thanks for help or a favour, or when sb says they are sorry **SYN** OK: *'I'm really sorry.' 'That's all right, don't worry.'* **4** used to get sb's attention **SYN** OK: *All right class, turn to page 20.* **5** (*BrE*, *informal*) used to say hello: *'All right, Bill.' 'All right.'*

**ˌall-ˈround** (*BrE*) (*NAmE* **ˌall-aˈround**) *adj.* [only before noun] **1** including many different subjects, skills, etc: *an all-round education* **2** (of a person) with a wide range of skills or abilities: *She's a good all-round player.*

**ˌall-ˈrounder** *noun* (*BrE*) a person who has many different skills and abilities

**All ˈSaints' Day** *noun* a Christian festival in honour of the SAINTS, held on 1 November

**all·spice** /ˈɔːlspaɪs/ *noun* [U] the dried BERRIES of a tree from the West Indies, used in cooking as a SPICE

**all-star** adj. [only before noun] including many famous actors, players, etc: *an all-star cast*

**all-star ˈgame** noun often **All-Star Game** (NAmE) a game played between the best players in their sport. The 'all-stars' are often divided into teams that represent different sections of a league (= a group of sports clubs) or different parts of the country.

**all-terˈrain** adj. [only before noun] suitable for use on rough ground: *The truck boasts high-quality all-terrain tyres to maximize grip off-road.*

**all-terrain ˈvehicle** noun (especially NAmE) = ATV

**all-ˈticket** adj. [usually before noun] for which tickets need to be obtained in advance: *an all-ticket match*

**all-time** adj. [only before noun] (used when you are comparing things or saying how good or bad sth is) of any time: *one of the all-time great players* ◊ *my all-time favourite song* ◊ *Unemployment reached an all-time record of 3 million.* ◊ *Profits are at an all-time high/low.* **IDM** see LOW n.

**al·lude** /əˈluːd/ verb
**PHRV** **alˈlude to sb/sth** (formal) to mention sth in an indirect way ⊃ see also ALLUSION

**al·lure** /əˈlʊə(r); NAmE əˈlʊr/ noun [U, sing.] (formal) the quality of being attractive and exciting: *sexual allure* ◊ *the allure of the big city*

**al·lur·ing** /əˈlʊərɪŋ; NAmE əˈlʊr-/ adj. attractive and exciting in a mysterious way: *an alluring smile* ▸ **alˈlur·ing·ly** adv.

**al·lu·sion** /əˈluːʒn/ noun [C, U] ~ **(to sb/sth)** (formal) something that is said or written that refers to or mentions another person or subject in an indirect way (= ALLUDES to it): *His statement was seen as an allusion to the recent drug-related killings.* ◊ *Her poetry is full of obscure literary allusion.*

**al·lu·sive** /əˈluːsɪv/ adj. (formal) containing allusions: *an allusive style of writing*

**al·lu·vial** /əˈluːviəl/ adj. [usually before noun] (geology) made of sand and earth that is left by rivers or floods

**al·lu·vium** /əˈluːviəm/ noun [U] (geology) sand and earth that is left by rivers or floods

**all-ˈweather** adj. [usually before noun] suitable for all types of weather: *an all-weather football pitch*

**all-wheel ˈdrive** noun (especially NAmE) = FOUR-WHEEL DRIVE

**ally** ⓘ+ **C1** noun, verb
■ noun /ˈælaɪ/ (pl. **-ies**) **1** ⓘ+ **C1** [C] a country that has agreed to help and support another country, especially in case of a war

| WORD FAMILY |
|---|
| **ally** verb, noun |
| **allied** adj. |
| **alliance** noun |

**WORDFINDER** accord, bilateral, cross-border, diplomat, embassy, international, rapprochement, relationship, treaty

**2** ⓘ+ **C1** [C] a person who helps and supports sb who is in a difficult situation, especially a politician: *a close ally and friend of the prime minister* ◊ *her most powerful political ally* **3** ⓘ+ **C1** **the Allies** [pl.] the group of countries including the UK and the US that fought together in the First and Second World Wars
■ verb /əˈlaɪ, ˈælaɪ/ [T, I] (**al·lies, ally·ing, al·lied, al·lied**) ~ **(yourself) with sb/sth** to give your support to another group or country: *The prince allied himself with the Scots.*

**-ally** /əli, li/ suffix (makes adverbs from adjectives that end in *-al*): *magically* ◊ *sensationally*

**alma mater** /ˌælmə ˈmɑːtə(r); BrE also -ˈmeɪt-/ (also **Alma Mater**) noun [sing.] (especially NAmE) the school, college or university that sb went to

**al·manac** (also less frequent **al·man·ack**) /ˈɔːlmənæk, ˈæl-/ noun **1** a book or digital resource that is released every year giving information for that year about a particular subject or activity **2** a book or digital resource that gives information about the sun, moon, times of the TIDES (= the rise and fall of the sea level), etc. for each day of the year

41    **aloe vera**

**al·mighty** /ɔːlˈmaɪti/ adj. **1** (in prayers and OATHS) having complete power: *Almighty God, have mercy on us.* ◊ *I swear by Almighty God…* **2** [only before noun] (informal) very great or severe: *an almighty bang/crash/roar* **3** (taboo, offensive) used in the expressions shown in the example, to express surprise or anger: *Christ/God Almighty! What the hell do you think you are doing?* **4 the Almighty** noun [sing.] God

**al·mirah** /ælˈmaɪrə/ noun (IndE) a piece of furniture for storing clothes, valuable items, etc. in, that stands on the floor

**al·mond** /ˈɑːmənd/ noun the flat pale sweet nut of the **ˈalmond tree** used in cooking and to make almond oil: *ground almonds* ◊ *blanched almonds* (= with their skins removed) ◊ *almond paste* ◊ *almond eyes* (= eyes shaped like almonds) ⊃ VISUAL VOCAB page V8

**al·most** ⓘ **A2** Ⓢ /ˈɔːlməʊst/ adv. not quite **SYN** **nearly**: *I like almost all of them.* ◊ *They'll eat almost anything.* ◊ *The castle is almost entirely surrounded by water.* ◊ *It's a mistake they almost always make.* ◊ *Her handwriting is almost impossible to read.* ◊ *The team faces almost certain defeat in today's match.* ◊ *The workforce has almost doubled in the past ten years.* ◊ *Housing has become almost as big a problem as education.* ◊ *The story seems almost too strange to be true.*

▼ WHICH WORD?

**almost / nearly / practically**
These three words have similar meanings and are used frequently with the following words:

| almost ~ | nearly ~ | practically ~ |
|---|---|---|
| certainly | (numbers) | all |
| all | all | every |
| every | always | no |
| entirely | every | nothing |
| impossible | finished | impossible |
| empty | died | anything |

● They are used in positive sentences: *She almost/nearly/practically missed her train.* They can be used before words like *all, every* and *everybody*: *Nearly all the students have bikes.* ◊ *I've got practically every CD they've made.* **Practically** is used more in spoken than in written English. **Nearly** is the most common with numbers: *There were nearly 200 people at the meeting.* They can also be used in negative sentences but it is more common to make a positive sentence with **only just**: *We only just got there in time.* (or: *We almost/nearly didn't get there in time.*)
● **Almost** and **practically** can be used before words like *any, anybody, anything*, etc: *I'll eat almost anything.* You can also use them before *no, nobody, never*, etc. but it is much more common to use **hardly** or **scarcely** with *any, anybody, ever*, etc: *She's hardly ever in* (or: *She's almost never in*).
● **Almost** can be used when you are saying that one thing is similar to another: *The boat looked almost like a toy.*
● In BrE you can use *very* and *so* before **nearly**: *He was very nearly caught.*
⊃ note at HARDLY

**alms** /ɑːmz/ noun [pl.] (old-fashioned) money, clothes and food that are given to poor people

**alms·house** /ˈɑːmzhaʊs/ noun (in the past in the UK) a house owned by a charity where poor people (usually the old) lived without paying rent

**aloe** /ˈæləʊ/ noun a tropical plant with thick leaves that have sharp points and that contain a lot of water. The juice of some types of aloe is used in medicine and COSMETICS.

**aloe vera** /ˌæləʊ ˈvɪərə; NAmE ˈvɪrə/ noun **1** [U] a substance that comes from a type of aloe, used in products such as skin creams **2** [C] the aloe that this substance comes from

Ⓞ Oxford Phrasal Academic Lexicon (OPAL) written and spoken word lists | Ⓦ OPAL written word list | Ⓢ OPAL spoken word list

# aloft

**aloft** /əˈlɒft; NAmE əˈlɔːft/ adv. (formal) high in the air

**aloha** /əˈləʊhɑː; NAmE -hɑː/ exclamation a Hawaiian word meaning 'love', used to say hello or goodbye

**alone** ⓘ A2 /əˈləʊn/ adj. [not before noun], adv. **1** without any other people: *not ~ in Tom is not alone in finding Rick hard to work with.* ◇ *be ~ with sb/sth She did not want to be alone with him.* ◇ *He lives alone.* ◇ *She was sitting all alone in the hall.* ◇ *Finally the two of us were alone together.* **2** without the help of other people or things: *It's hard bringing up children alone.* ◇ *The assassin said he had acted alone.* ⇨ see also STAND-ALONE **3** B1 lonely and unhappy or without any friends: *Carol felt all alone in the world.* ◇ *I've been so alone since you went away.* **4** used after a noun or pronoun to show that the person or thing mentioned is the only one: *You can't blame anyone else; you alone made the decision.* **5** used after a noun or pronoun to emphasize one particular thing: *The shoes alone cost £200.*
**IDM** **go it aˈlone** to do sth without help from anyone: *Andrew decided to go it alone and start his own business.* **ˌleave/let sb aˈlone** to stop annoying sb or trying to get their attention: *She's asked to be left alone but the press photographers follow her everywhere.* **ˌleave/let sth aˈlone** to stop touching, changing, or moving sth: *I've told you before—leave my things alone!* **ˌlet aˈlone** used after a statement to emphasize that because the first thing is not true or possible, the next thing cannot be true or possible either: *There isn't enough room for us, let alone any guests.* **ˌstand aˈlone 1** to be independent or not connected with other people, organizations or ideas: *These islands are too small to stand alone as independent states.* **2** to be not near other objects or buildings: *The arch once stood alone at the entrance to the castle.* ⇨ more at TIME *n*.

▼ **WHICH WORD?**

**alone / on your own / by yourself / lonely / lone**

- **Alone**, and **on your own/by yourself** (which are less formal and are the normal phrases used in spoken English), describe a person or thing that is separate from others. They do not mean that the person is unhappy: *I like being alone in the house.* ◇ *I'm going to London by myself next week.* ◇ *I want to finish this on my own* (= without anyone's help).
- **Lone/solitary/single** mean that there is only one person or thing there; **lone** and **solitary** may sometimes suggest that the speaker thinks the person involved is lonely: *a lone jogger in the park* ◇ *long, solitary walks*
- **Lonely** (NAmE also **lonesome**) means that you are alone and sad: *a lonely child* ◇ *Sam was very lonely when he first moved to New York.* It can also describe places or activities that make you feel lonely: *a lonely house*

**along** ⓘ A2 /əˈlɒŋ; NAmE əˈlɔːŋ/ prep., adv.
■ *prep.* **1** A2 from one end to or towards the other end of sth: *They walked slowly along the road.* ◇ *I looked along the shelves for the book I needed.* **2** A2 in a line that follows the side of sth: *Houses had been built along both sides of the river.* **3** A2 at a particular point on or next to sth long: *You'll find his office just along the corridor.*
■ *adv.* **HELP** For the special uses of **along** in phrasal verbs, look at the entries for the verbs. For example **get along with sb** is in the phrasal verb section at **get**. **1** A2 forward: *I was just walking along singing to myself.* ◇ *He pointed out various landmarks as we drove along.* **2** with sb: *We're going for a swim. Why don't you come along?* ◇ *I'll be along* (= I'll join you) *in a few minutes.* **3** B2 towards a better state or position: *The book's coming along nicely.*
**IDM** **aˌlong with sb/sth** B1 in addition to sb/sth; in the same way as sb/sth: *She lost her job when the factory closed, along with hundreds of others.*

**alongˈside** B2 /əˌlɒŋˈsaɪd; NAmE əˌlɔːŋˈsaɪd/ prep. **1** B2 next to or at the side of sth: *A police car pulled up alongside us.* **2** B2 together with or at the same time as sth/ sb: *Traditional beliefs still flourish alongside a modern urban lifestyle.* ▶ **aˈlongˌside** adv.: *Nick caught up with me and rode alongside.*

**aloo** (also **alu**) /ˈɑːluː; NAmE ˈɑːluː/ noun [U] (IndE) potatoes

**aloof** /əˈluːf/ adj. [not usually before noun] not friendly or interested in other people **SYN** **distant**, **remote** ▶ **aˈloofness** noun [U]
**IDM** **keep/hold (yourself) aloof** | **remain/stand aloof** to not be involved in sth; to show no interest in people: *The Emperor kept himself aloof from the people.*

**aloˈpeˌcia** /ˌæləˈpiːʃə/ noun [U] (medical) loss of hair from the head and body, often caused by illness

**aloud** /əˈlaʊd/ adv. **1** in a voice that other people can hear: *The teacher listened to the children reading aloud.* ◇ *He read the letter aloud to us.* ◇ *'What am I going to do?' she wondered aloud.* ⇨ note at LOUD **2** in a loud voice: *She cried aloud in protest.* **IDM** see THINK *v*.

▼ **HOMOPHONES**

**allowed ♦ aloud** /əˈlaʊd/

- **allowed** verb (past tense, past participle of **ALLOW**): *We aren't allowed out after 10 p.m.*
- **aloud** adv.: *The film made me laugh aloud.*

**alˈpaca** /ælˈpækə/ noun **1** [C] a South American animal that is related to the LLAMA and has long hair **2** [U] a type of soft wool or cloth made from the hair of the alpaca, used especially for making expensive clothes: *an alpaca coat*

**alpha** /ˈælfə/ noun **1** the first letter of the Greek alphabet (Α, α) **2** = ALPHA VERSION

**alˈphaˌbet** /ˈælfəbet/ noun a set of letters or symbols in a fixed order used for writing a language: *the letters of the alphabet* ◇ *the Hebrew/Cyrillic alphabet* **ORIGIN** From *alpha* and *beta*, the first two letters of the Greek alphabet ⇨ **WORDFINDER NOTE** at LANGUAGE ⇨ see also INTERNATIONAL PHONETIC ALPHABET, ROMAN ALPHABET

**alˌphaˈbetˌic** /ˌælfəˈbetɪk/ (also **alˌphaˈbetˌical**) adj. (of a written or printed character) being one of the letters of the alphabet, rather than a number or other symbol

**alˌphaˈbetˌical** /ˌælfəˈbetɪkl/ adj. **1** according to the correct order of the letters of the alphabet: *The names on the list are in alphabetical order.* ⇨ **WORDFINDER NOTE** at DICTIONARY **2** = ALPHABETIC ▶ **alˌphaˈbetˌically** /-kli/ adv.: *arranged/listed/stored alphabetically*

**alˈphaˌbetˌize** (BrE also **-ise**) /ˈælfəbətaɪz/ verb **~ sth** to arrange a list of words in alphabetical order

**ˈalphabet ˌsoup** noun [U] **1** (informal) a confusing mixture of things, especially language that contains many symbols or abbreviations **2** soup that contains PASTA in the shape of letters

**ˈalpha ˈmale** noun **1** [usually sing.] the man or male animal in a particular group who has the most power: *The alpha male was a large black wolf.* **2** a man who tends to take control in social and professional situations

**alphaˌnumerˌic** /ˌælfənjuːˈmerɪk; NAmE -nuː-/ (also **alphaˌnumerˌical** /ˌælfənjuːˈmerɪkl; NAmE -nuː-/) adj. containing both letters and numbers: *an alphanumeric code*

**ˈalpha ˈparticle** noun (physics) a PARTICLE with a positive electrical charge that is EMITTED (= sent out) by some RADIOACTIVE substances and is IDENTICAL to (= the same as) the NUCLEUS of a HELIUM ATOM

**ˈalpha ˈtest** noun (specialist) a test done by a company on a new product that they are developing, before the product is made available for BETA-TESTING by people outside the company ⇨ compare BETA TEST ▶ **ˈalpha-ˈtest** verb **~ sth**

**ˈalpha ˈversion** (also **alpha**) noun [usually sing.] a version of a product, especially computer software, that is not yet ready for the public to buy or use, and that is tested by the company that is developing it ⇨ compare BETA VERSION

**alˈpine** /ˈælpaɪn/ adj., noun
■ *adj.* existing in or connected with high mountains, especially the Alps in Central Europe
■ *noun* any plant that grows best on mountains

**al·pi·nist** /ˈælpɪnɪst/ *noun* a person who climbs high mountains as a sport, especially in the Alps ▶ **al·pi·nism** /-nɪzəm/ *noun* [U]

**al·ready** ⓘ **A2** ⓢ /ɔːlˈredi/ *adv.* **1** **A2** before now or before a particular time in the past: *'Lunch?' 'No thanks, I've already eaten.'* ◊ *We got there early but Mike had already left.* ◊ *By 2015, filming of the sequel was already under way.* ◊ *Much of what he said I knew already.* **2** **A2** used to express surprise that sth has happened so soon or so early: *Is it 10 o'clock already?* ◊ *You're not leaving already, are you?* **3** **B1** used to emphasize that a situation or problem exists: *I'm already late.* ◊ *The new company already has an excellent reputation.* ◊ *There are far too many people already. We can't take any more.* **4** (*NAmE*, *informal*) used after a word or phrase to show that you are annoyed: *Just stop already, no one feels sorry for you.* **IDM** see ENOUGH *pron.*

▼ **BRITISH/AMERICAN**

**already / just / yet**
- **Already** and **yet** are usually used with the present perfect tense, but in *NAmE* they can also be used with the simple past tense: *I already did it.* ◊ *Did you eat yet?*
- However, this is much more common in spoken than in written English and some Americans do not consider it acceptable, even in speech. The present perfect is more common in *NAmE* and almost always used in *BrE*: *I've already done it.* ◊ *Have you eaten yet?* When the context is past, however, use the past tense: *I already knew this because Mike had told me.*
- **Just** is mostly used with the perfect tenses in *BrE* and with the simple past in *NAmE*: (*BrE*) *I've just had some bad news.* ◊ (*NAmE*) *I just got some bad news.*

**al·right** /ɔːlˈraɪt/ *adj., adv., exclamation* (*informal*) = ALL RIGHT **HELP** Some people consider that this form should not be used in formal writing.

**Al·sa·tian** /ælˈseɪʃn/ *noun* (*BrE*) = GERMAN SHEPHERD

**also** ⓘ **A1** ⓢ /ˈɔːlsəʊ/ *adv.* (not used with negative verbs) in addition; too: *She's fluent in French and German. She also speaks a little Italian.* ◊ *rubella, also known as German measles* ◊ *I didn't like it that much. Also, it was much too expensive.* ◊ *Jake's father had also been a doctor* (= both Jake and his father were doctors). ◊ *She was not only intelligent but also very musical.* ➲ LANGUAGE BANK at ADDITION

▼ **WHICH WORD?**

**also / as well / too**
- **Also** is more formal than **as well** and **too**, and it usually comes before the main verb or after *be*: *I went to New York last year, and I also spent some time in Washington.* In *BrE* it is not usually used at the end of a sentence. **Too** is much more common in spoken and informal English. It is usually used at the end of a sentence: *'I'm going home now.' 'I'll come too.'.* In *BrE* **as well** is used like **too**, but in *NAmE* it sounds formal or old-fashioned.
- When you want to add a second negative point in a negative sentence, use **not …either**: *She hasn't phoned and she hasn't written either.* If you are adding a negative point to a positive one, you can use **not … as well / too**: *You can have a burger, but you can't have fries as well.*

**ˈalso-ran** *noun* a person who is not successful, especially in a competition or an election

**altar** /ˈɔːltə(r)/ *noun* a holy table in a church or TEMPLE: *the high altar* (= the most important one in a particular church)
**IDM** ▶ **at / on the altar of sth** (*formal*) because of sth that you think is worth suffering for: *He was willing to sacrifice his happiness on the altar of fame.*

**ˈaltar boy** *noun* a boy who helps the priest in church services, especially in the Roman Catholic church

**al·tar·piece** /ˈɔːltəpiːs; *NAmE* -tərp-/ *noun* a painting or other piece of art located near the ALTAR in a church

---

43 **alternatively**

**alter** ⓘ **B2** ⓦ /ˈɔːltə(r)/ *verb* **1** **B2** [I, T] to become different; to make sb/sth different: *Prices did not alter significantly during 2019.* ◊ **~ sb/sth** *His actions that day altered my perception of him.* ◊ *The landscape has been radically altered by changes in the climate.* ◊ *He has the power to fundamentally alter the course of history.* ◊ *Fame hasn't really altered her.* **2** [T] **~ sth** to make changes to a piece of clothing so that it will fit you better ▶ **al·ter·able** *adj.* (*formal*) **OPP** unalterable

**al·ter·ation** ⓦ /ˌɔːltəˈreɪʃn/ *noun* **1** [C] a change to sth that makes it different: *major/minor alterations* ◊ **~to sth** *They are making some alterations to the house.* ◊ **~in sth** *an alteration in the baby's heartbeat* **2** [U] the act of making a change to sth: *The dress will not need much alteration.*

**al·ter·ca·tion** /ˌɔːltəˈkeɪʃn; *NAmE* -tərˈk-/ *noun* [C, U] (*formal*) a noisy argument or DISAGREEMENT

**ˈalter ego** /ˌɔːltər ˈiːɡəʊ/ *noun* (*pl.* **alter egos**) (*from Latin*) **1** a person whose personality is different from your own but who shows or acts as another side of your personality: *Superman's alter ego was Clark Kent.* **2** a close friend who is very like yourself

**al·ter·nate** *adj., verb, noun*
- *adj.* /ɔːlˈtɜːnət; *NAmE* ˈɔːltərnət/ [usually before noun] **1** (of two things) happening or following one after the other regularly: *alternate layers of fruit and cream* **2** if sth happens on **alternate** days, nights, etc. it happens on one day, etc. but not on the next: *John has to work on alternate Sundays.* **3** (*especially NAmE*) = ALTERNATIVE ▶ **al·ter·nate·ly** *adv.*: *He felt alternately hot and cold.*
- *verb* /ˈɔːltəneɪt; *NAmE* -tərn-/ **1** [T] to make things or people follow one after the other in a repeated pattern: **~ A and B** *Alternate cubes of meat and slices of red pepper.* ◊ **~ A with B** *Alternate cubes of meat with slices of red pepper.* **2** [I] (of things or people) to follow one after the other in a repeated pattern: *alternating dark and pale stripes* ◊ **~with sth** *Dark stripes alternate with pale ones.* **3** [I] **~ between A and B** to keep changing from one thing to another and back again: *Her mood alternated between happiness and despair.* ▶ **al·ter·na·tion** /ˌɔːltəˈneɪʃn; *NAmE* -tərn-/ *noun* [U, C]: *the alternation of day and night*
- *noun* /ˈɔːltənət; *NAmE* -tərn-/ (*NAmE*) a person who does a job for sb who is away

**alˈternate ˈangles** *noun* [pl.] (*geometry*) equal angles formed on opposite sides of a line that crosses two PARALLEL lines, in the position of the inner angles of a Z ➲ picture at ANGLE ➲ compare CORRESPONDING ANGLES

**alˌternating ˈcurrent** *noun* [U, C] (*abbr.* **AC**) an electric current that changes its direction at regular INTERVALS many times a second ➲ compare DIRECT CURRENT

**al·ter·na·tive** ⓘ **A2** ⓦ /ɔːlˈtɜːnətɪv; *NAmE* -ˈtɜːrn-/ *noun, adj.*
- *noun* **A2** a thing that you can choose to do or have out of two or more possibilities: *The car is too expensive so we're trying to find a cheaper alternative.* ◊ *We had no alternative but to fire Gibson.* ◊ **~to sth** *Does this offer a viable alternative to the existing system?* ◊ **as an ~ to sth** *Fruit juice is provided as an alternative to alcoholic drinks.* ➲ SYNONYMS at OPTION
- *adj.* **1** **B1** (*also* **al·ter·nate** *especially in NAmE*) [only before noun] that can be used instead of sth else: *The road was closed so we had to find an alternative route.* ◊ *Can you offer an alternative explanation?* **2** **B1** [usually before noun] different from the usual or traditional way in which sth is done: *alternative therapy/treatments* ◊ *an alternative lifestyle*

**alˌternative ˈenergy** *noun* [U] electricity or power that is produced from the sun, wind, water, etc. in ways that do not use up the earth's natural resources or harm the environment

**alˌternative ˈfuel** *noun* [C, U] fuel that can be used instead of FOSSIL FUELS such as coal and oil, and instead of nuclear fuel

**al·ter·na·tive·ly** ⓦ /ɔːlˈtɜːnətɪvli; *NAmE* -ˈtɜːrn-/ *adv.* used to introduce a suggestion that is a second choice or

# alternative medicine

possibility: *The agency will make travel arrangements for you. Alternatively, you can organize your own transport.*

**al·ternative 'medicine** *noun* [C, U] any type of treatment that does not use the usual scientific methods of Western medicine, for example one using plants instead of artificial drugs ⮕ compare COMPLEMENTARY MEDICINE, CONVENTIONAL (3), TRADITIONAL MEDICINE ⮕ WORDFINDER NOTE at TREATMENT

**al·ternative 'vote** *noun* [sing.] (*BrE*) a system that allows people to choose candidates for an election in order of PREFERENCE. All first PREFERENCES are counted, and if no candidate achieves a majority, the candidate with the fewest votes is removed from the process and each vote for that candidate is transferred to each person's second PREFERENCE. This process is repeated until one candidate achieves the majority.

**al·ter·na·tor** /ˈɔːltəneɪtə(r)/; *NAmE* -tərn-/ *noun* a device, used especially in a car, that produces an ALTERNATING CURRENT

**al·though** 🔊 **A2** ⊙ (*US, informal* **altho**) /ɔːlˈðəʊ/ *conj.* **1** **A2** used for introducing a statement that makes the main statement in a sentence seem surprising **SYN** **though**: *Although the sun was shining, it wasn't very warm.* ◇ *Although small, the kitchen is well designed.* ⮕ LANGUAGE BANK at HOWEVER **2** **A2** used to mean 'but' or 'however' when you are commenting on a statement: *I felt he was wrong, although I didn't say so at the time.*

▼ **WHICH WORD?**

**although / even though / though**
- You can use these words to show contrast between two clauses or two sentences. **Though** is used more in spoken than in written English. You can use **although**, **even though** and **though** at the beginning of a sentence or clause that has a verb. Notice where the comma goes: *Although/Even though/Though everyone played well, we lost the game.* ◇ *We lost the game although/even though/though everyone played well.*
- You cannot use **even** on its own at the beginning of a sentence or clause instead of **although**, **even though** or **though**: *Even everyone played well, we lost the game.*

**al·tim·eter** /ˈæltɪmiːtə(r); *NAmE* ælˈtɪmətər/ *noun* an instrument for showing height above sea level, used especially in an aircraft

**al·ti·tude** /ˈæltɪtjuːd; *NAmE* -tuːd/ *noun* **1** [C, usually sing.] the height above sea level: **at an ~ of sth** *We are flying at an altitude of 6000 metres.* ◇ *The plane made a dive to a lower altitude.* **2** [C, usually pl., U] a place that is high above sea level: *Snow leopards live* **at high altitudes**. ◇ **at ~** *The athletes trained at altitude in Mexico City.* ⮕ WORDFINDER NOTE at MOUNTAIN

**'altitude sickness** *noun* [U] illness caused by a lack of OXYGEN, because of being very high above sea level, for example on a mountain

**Alt key** (*also* **ALT key**) /ˈɔːlt kiː/ *noun* a key on a computer keyboard that you press while pressing other keys, in order to change their function

**alto** /ˈæltəʊ/ *noun, adj.*
- *noun* (*pl.* **-os**) **1** (*also* **con·tralto**) [C] a singing voice with a lower range than that of a SOPRANO; a person with an alto voice **2** [sing.] a musical part that is written for an alto voice ⮕ compare BARITONE, BASS¹, COUNTERTENOR, TENOR
- *adj.* [only before noun] (of a musical instrument) with the second highest range of notes in its group: *an alto saxophone* ⮕ compare SOPRANO, TENOR

**al·together** **B2** /ˌɔːltəˈɡeðə(r)/ *adv.* **1** **B2** (used to emphasize sth) completely; in every way: *The train went slower and slower until it stopped altogether.* ◇ *I don't altogether agree with you.* ◇ *I am not altogether happy* (= I am very unhappy) *about the decision.* ◇ *It was an altogether different situation.* **2** **B2** used to give a total number or amount: *You owe me £68 altogether.* **3** **B2**

used to introduce a summary when you have mentioned a number of different things: *The food was good and we loved the music. Altogether it was a great evening.*

▼ **WHICH WORD?**

**altogether / all together**
- **Altogether** and **all together** do not mean the same thing. **Altogether** means 'in total' or 'completely': *We have invited fifty people altogether.* ◇ *I am not altogether convinced by this argument.*
- **All together** means 'all in one place' or 'all at once': *Can you put your books all together in this box?* ◇ *Let's sing 'Happy Birthday'. All together now!*

**alt-right** /ˌɔːlt ˈraɪt/ *noun* (in the US) people with extremely RIGHT-WING political views, who reject normal political processes and often use the internet to promote their beliefs

**al·tru·ism** /ˈæltruɪzəm/ *noun* [U] (*formal*) the fact of caring about the needs and happiness of other people and being willing to do things to help them, even if it brings no advantage to yourself ▶ **al·tru·is·tic** /ˌæltruˈɪstɪk/ *adj.*: *altruistic behaviour*

**alu** = ALOO

**alum** /ˈæləm/ *noun* [U] a substance formed from aluminium and another metal, used, for example, to prepare leather and to change the colour of things

**alu·mina** /əˈluːmɪnə/ *noun* [U] (*specialist*) a white substance found in many types of rock, especially CLAY

**alu·min·ium** **C1** /ˌæljəˈmɪniəm, ˌælə-/ (*BrE*) (*NAmE* **alu·mi·num** /əˈluːmɪnəm/) *noun* (*symb.* **Al**) a chemical element. Aluminium is a light, silvery-grey metal used for making pans, etc: *aluminium saucepans/window frames* ◇ *aluminium foil* (= for example, for wrapping food in)

**alumna** /əˈlʌmnə/ *noun* (*pl.* **alum·nae** /-niː/) (*especially NAmE, formal*) a former female student of a school, college or university

**alumni** /əˈlʌmnaɪ/ *noun* [pl.] (*especially NAmE*) the former male and female students of a school, college or university: *Harvard Alumni Association*

**alum·nus** /əˈlʌmnəs/ *noun* (*pl.* **alumni** /-naɪ/) (*especially NAmE, formal*) a former male student of a school, college or university

**al·veo·lus** /ˈælviːələs; *BrE also* ælˈvɪələs/ *noun* (*pl.* **al·veoli** /-laɪ, -liː/) (*anatomy*) one of the many small spaces in each lung where gases can pass into or out of the blood

**al·ways** 🔊 **A1** /ˈɔːlweɪz/ *adv.* **1** **A1** at all times; on every occasion: *There's almost always somebody at home in the evenings.* ◇ *Always lock your car.* ◇ *The children always seem to be hungry.* ◇ *Your ideas are always welcome.* ◇ *It's not always easy to do the right thing.* **2** **A2** for a long time; since you can remember: *Pat has always loved gardening.* ◇ *This is the way we've always done it.* ◇ *This painting is very good—Ellie always was very good at art* (= so it is not very surprising). ◇ *Did you always want to be an actor?* **3** **B2** for all future time: *I'll always love you.* **4** **B2** if you say a person is **always doing** sth, or sth is **always happening**, you mean that they do it, or it happens, very often, and that this is annoying: *She's always criticizing me.* ◇ *That phone's always ringing.* **5** **can/could always …, there's always …** used to suggest a possible course of action: *If it doesn't fit, you can always take it back.* ◇ *If he can't help, there's always John.*
**IDM** **as 'always** as usually happens or is expected **SYN** **as usual**: *As always, Polly was late for school.* ⮕ more at ONCE *adv.*

**always-'on** *adj.* [only before noun] of or connected with an internet connection that is available to use at any time: *The phone maintains an always-on internet connection.*

**Alz·heim·er's** /ˈæltshaɪməz, ˈɔːlts-; *NAmE* ˈɑːltshaɪmərz/ (*also* **'Alz·heim·er's disease**) *noun* [U] a serious disease, especially affecting older people, that prevents the brain from functioning normally and causes loss of memory, loss of ability to speak clearly, etc. ⮕ compare SENILE DEMENTIA

---

| æ cat | ɑː father | e bed | ɜː fur | ə about | ɪ sit | iː see | i happy | ɒ got (*BrE*) | ɔː saw | ʌ cup | ʊ put | uː too |

**AM** /ˌeɪ ˈem/ noun, abbr.
- **noun** a person who has been elected to represent an area of Wales in the Welsh Assembly, the parliament for Wales (the abbreviation for 'Assembly Member'): *Peter Black AM* ◊ *Labour AMs*
- **abbr.** amplitude modulation (one of the main methods of broadcasting sound by radio)

**am** /əm, strong form æm/ ⊃ BE verb

**a.m.** (*NAmE* also **A.M.**) /ˌeɪ ˈem/ abbr. between 12 o'clock at night and 12 o'clock in the day (from Latin 'ante meridiem'): *It starts at 10 a.m.* ⊃ compare P.M.

**amal·gam** /əˈmælɡəm/ noun **1** [C, usually sing.] ~ (of sth) (*formal*) a mixture or combination of things: *The film script is an amalgam of all three books.* **2** [U] (*specialist*) a mixture of MERCURY and another metal, used especially to fill holes in teeth

**amal·gam·ate** /əˈmælɡəmeɪt/ verb **1** [I, T] if two organizations **amalgamate** or **are amalgamated**, they join together to form one large organization SYN merge: *A number of colleges have amalgamated to form the new university.* ◊ *~ with/into sth The company has now amalgamated with another local firm.* ◊ *~ sth They decided to amalgamate the two schools.* ◊ *~ sth with/into sth The two companies were amalgamated into one.* **2** [T] ~ sth (into/with sth) to put two or more things together so that they form one SYN merge: *This information will be amalgamated with information obtained earlier.* ▸ **amal·gam·ation** /əˌmælɡəˈmeɪʃn/ noun [U, C]: *the amalgamation of small farms into larger units*

**amar·yl·lis** /ˌæməˈrɪlɪs/ noun [C, U] a tall white, pink or red flower that is like a TRUMPET in shape

**amasi** /ˈmɑːsi/ (*also* **maas**) noun [U] (*SAfrE*) milk that has an unpleasant taste or smell because it is not fresh

**amass** /əˈmæs/ verb ~ sth to collect sth, especially in large quantities over a period of time SYN accumulate: *He amassed a fortune from silver mining.* ⊃ SYNONYMS at COLLECT

**ama·teur** /ˈæmətə(r), -tʃə(r)/ adj., noun
- **adj. 1** [usually before noun] doing sth for pleasure or interest, not as a job: *an amateur photographer* **2** [usually before noun] done for pleasure, not as a job: *amateur athletics* **3** (*usually disapproving*) = AMATEURISH OPP professional
- **noun 1** a person who takes part in a sport or other activity for pleasure, not as a job: *The tournament is open to both amateurs and professionals.* **2** (*usually disapproving*) a person who does not have enough skill to be able to do sth well: *This work was done by a bunch of amateurs!* OPP professional ▸ **ama·teur·ism** noun [U]: *New rules on amateurism allow payment for promotional work.*

**amateur dramatics** (*BrE*) (*NAmE* **community theater**) noun [U] the activity of producing and acting in plays for the theatre, by people who do it for pleasure, not as a job

**ama·teur·ish** /ˈæmətərɪʃ, -tʃə-/ (*also* **ama·teur**) adj. (*usually disapproving*) not done or made well or with skill: *Detectives described the burglary as 'crude and amateurish'.* OPP professional

**amaze** /əˈmeɪz/ verb to surprise sb very much: *~sb Just the size of the place amazed her.* ◊ *~sb what, how, etc ... It never ceases to amaze me what some people will do for money.* ◊ *What amazes me is how long she managed to hide it from us.* ◊ *it amazes sb that ... It amazed her that he could be so calm at such a time.* ◊ *it amazes sb to see, find, learn, etc ... It amazes me to think what we have achieved this year.* ⊃ SYNONYMS at SURPRISE

**amazed** /əˈmeɪzd/ adj. very surprised: *an amazed look* ◊ *~ at sb/sth We were all amazed at the number of people who came.* ◊ *~ by sb/sth We are constantly amazed by the quality and range of the books.* ◊ *~ (that) ... I was banging so loudly I'm amazed (that) they didn't hear me.* ◊ *~ (at) how ... | ~ how ... She was amazed how little he had changed.* ◊ *~ to see, find, learn, discover We were amazed to find that no one was hurt.*

**amaze·ment** /əˈmeɪzmənt/ noun [U] a feeling of great surprise: *To my amazement, he remembered me.* ◊ *She looked at him in amazement.*

**amaz·ing** /əˈmeɪzɪŋ/ adj. **1** very surprising, especially in a way that you like or admire SYN astonishing, astounding, incredible: *an amazing feat/story/experience* ◊ *That's amazing, isn't it?* ◊ *to do sth It was truly amazing to see how much work goes into a Broadway musical.* ◊ *it is ~ how, what, etc ... It's amazing how quickly people adapt.* ◊ *it is ~ that ... I find it amazing that people can be so irresponsible.* **2** (*informal*) very impressive; excellent SYN fantastic: *He makes the most amazing cakes.* ◊ *That looks pretty amazing, doesn't it?* ▸ **amaz·ing·ly** adv.: *Amazingly, no one noticed.* ◊ *The meal was amazingly cheap.*

**Amazon** /ˈæməzən; *NAmE* -zɑːn/ noun **1** (in ancient Greek stories) a woman from a group of female WARRIORS (= soldiers) **2 amazon** (*literary*) a tall strong woman

**am·bas·sador** /æmˈbæsədə(r)/ noun **1** an official who lives in a foreign country as the senior representative there of his or her own country: *the British Ambassador to Italy/in Rome* ◊ *a former ambassador to the UN* **2** a person who represents or promotes a particular activity: *The best ambassadors for the sport are the players.* ⊃ see also BRAND AMBASSADOR, GOODWILL AMBASSADOR ▸ **am·bas·sad·or·ial** /æmˌbæsəˈdɔːriəl/ adj.

**amber** /ˈæmbə(r)/ noun [U] **1** a hard clear yellow-brown substance, formed in ancient times from the RESIN of trees, used in making jewellery or beautiful objects: *amber beads* **2** a yellow–brown colour: *The traffic lights were on amber.* ▸ **amber** adj.

**am·ber·gris** /ˈæmbəɡriːs, -ɡrɪs; *NAmE* -bərɡ-/ noun [U] a substance that is used in making some PERFUMES. It is produced naturally by a type of WHALE.

**ambi-** /ˈæmbi, æmbɪ, æmˈbɪ/ prefix (in nouns, adjectives and adverbs) referring to both of two: *ambidextrous* ◊ *ambivalent*

**ambi·dex·trous** /ˌæmbiˈdekstrəs/ adj. able to use the left hand or the right hand equally well

**am·bi·ence** (*also* **am·bi·ance**) /ˈæmbiəns/ noun [sing.] the character and atmosphere of a place: *the relaxed ambience of the city*

**am·bi·ent** /ˈæmbiənt/ adj. **1** [only before noun] (*specialist*) relating to the surrounding area; on all sides: *ambient temperature/light/conditions* **2** (*especially of music*) creating a relaxed atmosphere: *a compilation of ambient electronic music* ◊ *soft, ambient lighting*

**am·bi·gu·ity** /ˌæmbɪˈɡjuːəti/ noun (pl. **-ies**) **1** [U] the state of having more than one possible meaning: *Write clear definitions in order to avoid ambiguity.* **2** [C] a word or statement that can be understood in more than one way: *There were several inconsistencies and ambiguities in her speech.* **3** [U, C] the state of being difficult to understand or explain because of involving many different aspects: *You must understand the ambiguity of my position.*

**am·bigu·ous** /æmˈbɪɡjuəs/ adj. **1** that can be understood in more than one way; having different meanings: *an ambiguous word/term/statement* ◊ *Her account was deliberately ambiguous.* **2** not clearly stated or defined: *His role has always been ambiguous.* OPP unambiguous ▸ **am·bigu·ous·ly** adv.: *an ambiguously worded agreement*

**ambit** /ˈæmbɪt/ noun [sing.] (*formal*) the range of the authority or influence of sth: *within the ~ of sth This case falls clearly within the ambit of the 2001 Act.*

**am·bi·tion** /æmˈbɪʃn/ noun **1** [C] something that you want to do or achieve very much: *She had fulfilled her lifelong ambition.* ◊ *His burning ambition was to study medicine.* ◊ *political/artistic/career ambitions* ◊ *the country's nuclear ambitions* (= plans to develop nuclear weapons) ◊ *~ of being/doing sth She never achieved her ambition of becoming a famous writer.* **2** [U] the desire or strength of mind to be successful, rich, powerful, etc:

# ambitious

*She was driven by personal ambition.* ◊ *She was intelligent but suffered from a lack of ambition.*

**am·bi·tious** B1 /æmˈbɪʃəs/ *adj.* **1** determined to be successful, rich, powerful, etc.: *a fiercely ambitious young manager* ◊ *They were very ambitious for their children* (= they wanted them to be successful). **2** B2 needing a lot of effort, money or time to succeed: *the government's ambitious plans for social reform* **OPP** **unambiguous** ▸ **am·bi·tious·ly** *adv.*

**am·biva·lent** /æmˈbɪvələnt/ *adj.* ~ **(about/towards sb/sth)** having or showing both positive and negative feelings about sb/sth: *She seems to feel ambivalent about her new job.* ◊ *He has an ambivalent attitude towards her.* ▸ **am·biva·lence** /-ləns/ *noun* [U, sing.]: *Many people feel some ambivalence towards television and its effect on our lives.* ▸ **am·biva·lent·ly** *adv.*

**amble** /ˈæmbl/ *verb* [I] + **adv./prep.** to walk at a slow relaxed speed **SYN** **stroll**: *We ambled down to the beach.*

**am·bro·sia** /æmˈbrəʊziə; NAmE -ˈbrəʊʒə/ *noun* [U] **1** (in ancient Greek and Roman stories) the food of the gods **2** (*literary*) something that is very pleasant to eat **3** (NAmE) a sweet dish of fruit and cream, often with COCONUT, eaten at the end of a meal, often at THANKSGIVING

**am·bu·lance** B2 /ˈæmbjələns/ *noun* a vehicle with special equipment, used for taking sick or injured people to a hospital: *Call an ambulance!* ◊ *the ambulance service* ◊ *The ambulance crew rushed her to the hospital.* ⇒ see also AIR AMBULANCE ⇒ WORDFINDER NOTE at ACCIDENT

**am·bu·la·tory** /ˈæmbjələtəri; NAmE -tɔːri/ *adj.* (*formal*) **1** related to or adapted for walking: *an ambulatory corridor* **2** that is not fixed in one place and can move around easily **SYN** **mobile**: *an ambulatory care service*

**am·bush** /ˈæmbʊʃ/ *noun, verb*
■ *noun* [C, U] the act of hiding and waiting for sb and then making a surprise attack on them: *Two soldiers were killed in a terrorist ambush.* ◊ *They were lying in ambush, waiting for the aid convoy.*
■ *verb* ~ **sb/sth** to make a surprise attack on sb/sth from a hidden position: *The guerrillas ambushed them near the bridge.* ◊ (*figurative*) *She was ambushed by reporters.*

**ameba ameb·ic** (*US*) = AMOEBA, AMOEBIC

**ameli·or·ate** /əˈmiːliəreɪt/ *verb* ~ **sth** (*formal*) to make better sth that was bad or not good enough: *Steps have been taken to ameliorate the situation.* ▸ **ameli·or·ation** /əˌmiːliəˈreɪʃn/ *noun* [U]

**amen** /ɑːˈmen, eɪ-; NAmE eɪˈm-, ɑːˈm-/ (*also* **Amen**) *exclamation, noun* a word used at the end of prayers or HYMNS, meaning 'may it be so': *We ask this through our Lord, Amen.* ◊ *Amen to that* (= I certainly agree with that).

**amen·able** /əˈmiːnəbl; NAmE also əˈmen-/ *adj.* **1** (of people) easy to control; willing to be influenced by sb/sth: *They had three very amenable children.* ◊ ~ **to sth** *He seemed most amenable to my idea.* **2** ~ **to sth** (*formal*) that you can treat in a particular way: *'Hamlet' is the least amenable of all Shakespeare's plays to being summarized.*

**amend** B2 /əˈmend/ *verb* ~ **sth** to change a law, document, statement, etc. slightly in order to correct a mistake or to improve it: *He asked to see the amended version.*

**amend·ment** B2 /əˈmendmənt/ *noun* **1** B2 [C, U] a small change or improvement that is made to a document or proposed new law; the process of changing a document or proposed new law: *to introduce/propose/table an amendment* (= to suggest it) ◊ *Parliament passed the bill without further amendment.* ◊ ~ **to sth** *She made several minor amendments to her essay.* **2** **Amendment** [C] a statement of a change to the Constitution of the US: *The 19th Amendment gave women the right to vote.*

**amends** /əˈmendz/ *noun* [pl.]
**IDM** **make amends (to sb) (for sth / for doing sth)** to do sth for sb in order to show that you are sorry for sth wrong or unfair that you have done **SYN** **make up for sth** ⇒ WORDFINDER NOTE at SORRY

**amen·ity** /əˈmiːnəti; NAmE əˈmen-, əˈmiːn-/ *noun* [usually pl.] (*pl.* **-ies**) a feature or service that makes a place pleasant, comfortable or easy to live in: *The campsite is close to all local amenities.* ◊ *Many of the houses lacked even basic amenities* (= baths, showers, hot water, etc.). ⇒ WORDFINDER NOTE at CITY

**amen·or·rhoea** (*BrE*) (*NAmE* **amen·or·rhea**) /əˌmenəˈriːə; NAmE eɪˌm-/ *noun* [U] (*medical*) a condition in which an adult woman does not MENSTRUATE (= there is no flow of blood from her WOMB every month)

**Amer·asian** /ˌæməˈreɪʒn; BrE also -ˈreɪʃn/ *noun* a person with one Asian parent and one parent from the US ▸ **Amer·asian** *adj.*

**Ameri·can** /əˈmerɪkən/ *noun, adj.*
■ *noun* **1** a person from America, especially the US ⇒ see also AFRICAN AMERICAN, ANGLO-AMERICAN, ASIAN AMERICAN, CENTRAL AMERICAN, NATIVE AMERICAN **2** (*also* A̱merican ˈEnglish) the English language as spoken in the US
■ *adj.* of or connected with North or South America, especially the US: *I'm American.* ◊ *American culture/tourists* ⇒ see also ALL-AMERICAN, ASIAN-AMERICAN, CENTRAL AMERICAN, UN-AMERICAN
**IDM** **as A̱merican as apple ˈpie** used to say that sth is typical of America

▼ **MORE ABOUT …**

## America

- The continent of **America** is divided into **North America** and **South America**. The narrow region joining North and South America is **Central America**.
- **North America**, which is a geographical term, consists of the **United States of America**, **Canada** and **Mexico**. **Latin America**, a cultural term, refers to the non-English speaking countries of Central and South America, where mainly Portuguese and Spanish are spoken. Mexico is part of Latin America.
- The **United States of America** is usually shortened to the **USA**, the **US**, the **States** or simply **America**: *the US President* ◊ *Have you ever been to the States?* ◊ *She emigrated to America in 1995.* Many people from other parts of the continent dislike this use of **America** to mean just the US, but it is very common.
- **American** is usually used to talk about somebody or something from the United States of America: *Do you have an American passport?* ◊ *American football* ◊ *I'm not American, I'm Canadian.* **Latin American** and **South American** are used to refer to other parts of the continent: *Latin American dance music* ◊ *Quite a lot of South Americans study here.*

**Ameri·cana** /əˌmerɪˈkɑːnə; NAmE also -ˈkænə/ *noun* [pl.] things connected with the US that are thought to be typical of it

**A̱merican ˈcheese** *noun* [U] (*US*) a kind of orange cheese that is usually sold in thin slices wrapped in plastic

**the A̱merican ˈdream** *noun* [sing.] the belief that America offers the opportunity to everyone of a good and successful life achieved through hard work

**A̱merican ˈfootball** (*BrE*) (*NAmE* **ˈfoot·ball**) *noun* [U] a game played by two teams of 11 players, using an OVAL ball that players kick, throw, or carry. Teams try to put the ball over the other team's line.

**A̱merican ˈIndian** *noun* = NATIVE AMERICAN

**Ameri·can·ism** /əˈmerɪkənɪzəm/ *noun* **1** [C] a word, phrase or spelling that is typical of American English, used in another variety of English **2** [U] the essential quality of being American

**Ameri·can·ize** (*BrE also* **-ise**) /əˈmerɪkənaɪz/ *verb* ~ **sb/sth** to make sb/sth American in character ▸ **Ameri·can·iza·tion, -isa·tion** /əˌmerɪkənaɪˈzeɪʃn; NAmE -nəˈz-/ *noun* [U]

**the A̱merican ˈLeague** *noun* (in the US) one of the two organizations for professional baseball ⇒ see also NATIONAL LEAGUE

**A·merican ˈplan** (*NAmE*) (*BrE* **full ˈboard**) *noun* [U] a type of accommodation in a hotel, etc. that includes all meals

**Amer·in·dian** /ˌæməˈrɪndiən/ *noun* (*old-fashioned*) = NATIVE AMERICAN

**ameth·yst** /ˈæməθɪst/ *noun* [C, U] a purple SEMI-PRECIOUS stone, used in making jewellery: *an amethyst ring*

**ami·able** /ˈeɪmiəbl/ *adj.* pleasant; friendly and easy to like **SYN** agreeable: *an amiable tone of voice* ◊ *Her parents seemed very amiable.* ▶ **ami·abil·ity** /ˌeɪmiəˈbɪləti/ *noun* [U] **ami·ably** /ˈeɪmiəbli/ *adv.*: *'That's fine,' he replied amiably.*

**am·ic·able** /ˈæmɪkəbl/ *adj.* done or achieved in a polite or friendly way and without arguing: *an amicable relationship* ◊ *An amicable settlement was reached.* ▶ **am·ic·ably** /-bli/ *adv.*

**amid** /əˈmɪd/ (*also* **mid**, **amidst** /əˈmɪdst/) *prep.* (*formal*) **1** in the middle of or during sth, especially sth that causes excitement or fear: *He finished his speech amid tremendous applause.* ◊ *The firm collapsed amid allegations of fraud.* **2** surrounded by sth: *The hotel was in a beautiful position amid lemon groves.*

**amid·ships** /əˈmɪdʃɪps/ *adv.* (*specialist*) in or near the middle part of a ship

**amigo** /əˈmiːɡəʊ/ *noun* (*pl.* **-os**) (*NAmE*, from Spanish, *informal*) a friend: *the three amigos*

**amino acid** /əˌmiːnəʊ ˈæsɪd/ *noun* (*chemistry*) any of the substances that combine to form the basic structure of PROTEINS

**amir** = EMIR

**the Amish** /ði ˈɑːmɪʃ; *BrE also* ˈæm-/ *noun* [pl.] the members of a strict religious group in North America. The Amish live a simple farming life and reject some forms of modern technology. ▶ **Amish** *adj.*

**amiss** /əˈmɪs/ *adj., adv.*
■ *adj.* [not before noun] wrong; not as it should be: *She sensed something was amiss and called the police.*
■ *adv.*
**IDM** ▶ **not come / go aˈmiss** (*BrE*) to be useful or pleasant in a particular situation: *A little luck wouldn't go amiss right now!* **take sth aˈmiss** (*BrE*) to feel offended by sth, perhaps because you have misunderstood it in the wrong way: *Would she take it amiss if I offered to help?*

**amity** /ˈæməti/ *noun* [U] (*formal*) a friendly relationship between people or countries

**amma** /ˈʌmɑ/ *noun* (*IndE*) (especially as a form of address) a mother

**am·meter** /ˈæmiːtə(r)/ *noun* an instrument for measuring the strength of an electric current

**ammo** /ˈæməʊ/ *noun* [U] (*old-fashioned*, *informal*) = AMMUNITION

**am·mo·nia** /əˈməʊniə/ *noun* [U] (*symb.* NH₃) a gas with a strong smell; a clear liquid containing ammonia, used as a cleaning substance

**am·mon·ite** /ˈæmənaɪt/ *noun* a FOSSIL of a simple sea creature that no longer exists, and that was related to SNAILS

ammonite

**am·mo·nium** /əˈməʊniəm/ *noun* [U] (*chemistry*) an ION made from ammonia containing NITROGEN and HYDROGEN together with another element

**am·mu·ni·tion** /ˌæmjuˈnɪʃn/ *noun* [U]
**1** a supply of bullets, etc. to be fired from guns **2** information that can be used against another person in an argument: *The letter gave her all the ammunition she needed.*

**am·nesia** /æmˈniːziə; *NAmE* -ˈniːʒə/ *noun* [U] a medical condition in which sb partly or completely loses their memory ▶ **am·nesiac** /æmˈniːziæk; *NAmE* -ˈniːʒi-/ *noun*: *This new discovery helps amnesiacs keep their memory.*

**am·nesty** /ˈæmnəsti/ *noun* (*pl.* **-ies**) **1** [C, usually sing., U] an official statement that allows people who have been put in prison for crimes against the state to go free: *The president granted a general amnesty for all political prisoners.* **2** [C, usually sing.] a period of time during which people can admit to a crime or give up weapons or stolen items without being punished: *2000 knives have been handed in during the month-long amnesty.*

**ˌAmnesty Interˈnational** *noun* an international human rights organization that works to help people who have been put in prison for their beliefs or race and not because they have committed a crime. It also works to prevent TORTURE and CAPITAL PUNISHMENT (= punishment by death).

**am·nio·cen·tesis** /ˌæmniəʊsenˈtiːsɪs/ *noun* [U, sing.] a medical test that involves taking some liquid from a pregnant woman's WOMB in order to find out if the baby has particular illnesses or health problems

**amˌniotic ˈfluid** /ˌæmniɒtɪk ˈfluːɪd; *NAmE* -niɑːt-/ *noun* [U] the liquid that surrounds a baby inside the mother's WOMB

**amn't** /ˈæmənt/ *short form* (*ScotE*, *IrishE*, *informal*) am not

**amoeba** (*US also* **ameba**) /əˈmiːbə/ *noun* (*pl.* **amoe·bas** or **amoe·bae** /-biː/) a very small living creature that consists of only one cell

**amoeb·ic** (*US also* **ameb·ic**) /əˈmiːbɪk/ *adj.* related to or similar to an amoeba

**amok** /əˈmɒk; *NAmE* əˈmɑːk/ *adv.*
**IDM** **run amok** to suddenly become very angry or excited and start behaving violently, especially in a public place

**among** /əˈmʌŋ/ (*also* **amongst** /əˈmʌŋst/) *prep.* **1** surrounded by sb/sth; in the middle of sb/sth: *a house among the trees* ◊ *They strolled among the crowds.* ◊ *I found the letter amongst his papers.* ◊ *It's OK, you're among friends now.* **2** being included or happening in groups of things or people: *A British woman was among the survivors.* ◊ *He was among the last to leave.* ◊ *This attitude is common among the under-25s.* ◊ *'What was wrong with the job?' 'Well, the pay wasn't good, among other things.'* ◊ *Discuss it among yourselves* (= with each other) *first.* **3** used when you are dividing or choosing sth, and three or more people or things are involved: *They divided the money up among their three children.*

**amoral** /ˌeɪˈmɒrəl; *NAmE* -ˈmɔːr-/ *adj.* not following any moral rules and not caring about right and wrong ⊃ compare IMMORAL, MORAL ▶ **amor·al·ity** /ˌeɪməˈræləti/ *noun* [U]

**am·or·ous** /ˈæmərəs/ *adj.* showing sexual desire and love towards sb: *Mary rejected Tony's amorous advances.* ▶ **am·or·ous·ly** *adv.*

**amorph·ous** /əˈmɔːfəs; *NAmE* əˈmɔːrf-/ *adj.* [usually before noun] (*formal*) having no definite shape, form or structure **SYN** shapeless: *an amorphous mass of cells with no identity at all*

**amort·ize** (*BrE also* **-ise**) /əˈmɔːtaɪz; *NAmE* ˈæmərtaɪz/ *verb* ~ sth (*business*) to pay back a debt by making small regular payments over a period of time ▶ **amort·iza·tion**, **-isa·tion** /əˌmɔːtaɪˈzeɪʃn; *NAmE* ˌæmərtəˈz-/ *noun* [U, C]

**amount** /əˈmaʊnt/ *noun*, *verb*
■ *noun* [C, U] **1** (used especially with uncountable nouns) a quantity of sth: *I was amazed at the amount he could eat.* ~ **of sth** *an amount of money/information/work/time* ◊ *A certain amount of time has already been spent on the project.* ◊ *The server is designed to store huge amounts of data.* ◊ *Try to reduce the amount of energy and water you use at home.* **HELP** Amount is most often used with uncountable nouns: *an amount of cash/space/material/food* It is also sometimes used with countable nouns, especially in spoken or informal English: *You're competing with a massive amount of people.* However, some people consider that this is not correct and prefer to use **number** with countable nouns: *You're competing with a very large number of people.* **2** a sum of money: *Everyone has paid the same amount.* ◊ *You will receive a bill for the full amount.*
**IDM** ▶ **any amount of sth** a large quantity of sth: *There's been any amount of research into the subject.* **no amount of sth** used for saying that sth will have no effect: *No*

**amour** 48

amount of encouragement would make him jump into the pool.
■ verb
**PHRV** a'mount to sth **1** 🔓 **B2** to add up to sth; to make sth as a total: *His earnings are said to amount to £300000 per annum.* ◇ *They gave me some help in the beginning but it did **not amount to much*** (= they did not give me much help). **2** to be equal to or the same as sth: *Her answer amounted to a complete refusal.* ◇ *Their actions amount to a breach of contract.* ◇ *It'll cost a lot—well, take a lot of time, but it **amounts to the same thing**.* **3** (used especially in negative sentences) to develop into sth: *You'll never amount to anything.*

**amour** /əˈmʊə(r); NAmE əˈmʊr/ noun (from French, literary) a love affair, especially a secret one

**amp** /æmp/ noun **1** (also **am·pere** /ˈæmpeə(r); NAmE -pɪr, -per/) (abbr. **A**) the unit for measuring electric current: *a 13-amp fuse/plug* **2** (informal) = AMPLIFIER

**amped** /æmpt/ (also **amped up**) adj. (NAmE, informal) excited, especially because of an event: *an amped audience of hardcore fans* ◇ *I get pretty amped up before I compete.*

**am·per·sand** /ˈæmpəsænd; NAmE -pərs-/ noun the symbol &, used to mean 'and': *She works for Bond & Green.*

**am·phet·amine** /æmˈfetəmiːn, -mɪn/ noun [C, U] a drug that makes you feel excited and full of energy, used to treat certain medical conditions or taken illegally as a STIMULANT

**am·phib·ian** /æmˈfɪbiən/ noun any animal that can live both on land and in water. Amphibians have cold blood and skin without SCALES. FROGS, TOADS and NEWTS are all amphibians. ⊃ VISUAL VOCAB page V3 ⊃ compare REPTILE

**am·phibi·ous** /æmˈfɪbiəs/ adj. **1** able to live both on land and in water **2** (of military operations) involving soldiers landing at a place from the sea **3** suitable for use on land or water: *amphibious vehicles*

**amphi·theatre** (US **-er**) /ˈæmfiθɪətə(r); NAmE -θiːə-/ noun **1** a round building without a roof and with rows of seats that rise in steps around an open space. Amphitheatres were used especially in ancient Greece and Rome for public entertainments. **2** a room, hall or theatre with rows of seats that rise in steps **3** (specialist) an open space that is surrounded by high sloping land

**am·phora** /ˈæmfərə; NAmE also æmˈfɔːrə/ noun (pl. **am·phorae** /-riː/ or **am·phoras**) a tall ancient Greek or Roman container with two handles and a narrow neck

**ampi·cil·lin** /ˌæmpɪˈsɪlɪn/ noun [U] a form of PENICILLIN that is used to treat certain infections

**ample** /ˈæmpl/ adj. **1** enough or more than enough: *ample opportunity/evidence/space/proof* ◇ *There was ample time to get to the airport.* ◇ *Ample free parking is available.* ⊃ see also PLENTY adv. (1) **2** (of a person's figure) large, often in an attractive way: *an ample bosom* ▶ **amply** /-pli/ adv.: *His efforts were amply rewarded.*

**amp·li·fier** /ˈæmplɪfaɪə(r)/ (also informal **amp**) noun an electrical device or piece of equipment that makes sounds or radio signals louder: *a 25 watt amplifier*

**amp·lify** /ˈæmplɪfaɪ/ verb (**amp·li·fies**, **amp·li·fy·ing**, **amp·li·fied**, **amp·li·fied**) **1** [T] ~ sth to increase sth in strength, especially sound: *to amplify a guitar/an electric current/a signal* **2** [I, T] (formal) to add details to a story, statement, etc: *She refused to amplify further.* ◇ ~ sth *You may need to amplify this point.* ▶ **amp·li·fi·ca·tion** /ˌæmplɪfɪˈkeɪʃn/ noun [U]: *electronic amplification* ◇ *That comment needs some amplification.*

**amp·li·tude** /ˈæmplɪtjuːd; NAmE -tuːd/ noun [U, C] (physics) the greatest distance that a wave, especially a sound or radio wave, VIBRATES (= moves up and down) ⊃ WORDFINDER NOTE at PHYSICS ⊃ picture at WAVELENGTH

**amply** /ˈæmpli/ adv. ⊃ AMPLE

**am·poule** (US also **am·pule**) /ˈæmpjuːl; BrE also -puːl/ noun a small container, usually made of glass, containing a drug that will be used for an INJECTION

**am·pu·tate** /ˈæmpjuteɪt/ verb [T, I] ~ (sth) to cut off sb's arm, leg, finger or toe in a medical operation: *He had to have both legs amputated.* ◇ *They may have to amputate.* ⊃ WORDFINDER NOTE at OPERATION ▶ **am·pu·ta·tion** /ˌæmpjuˈteɪʃn/ noun [U, C]

**am·pu·tee** /ˌæmpjuˈtiː/ noun a person who has had an arm or a leg amputated

**amu·let** /ˈæmjulət/ noun a piece of jewellery that some people wear because they think it protects them from bad luck, illness, etc. ⊃ WORDFINDER NOTE at LUCK

**amuse** /əˈmjuːz/ verb **1** to make sb laugh or smile: ~ sb *My funny drawings amused the kids.* ◇ *This will amuse you.* ◇ it **amuses sb to do sth** *It amused him to think that they were probably talking about him at that very moment.* **2** to make time pass pleasantly for sb/yourself **SYN** entertain: ~ sb *She suggested several ideas to help Laura amuse the twins.* ◇ ~ **yourself** *I'm sure I'll be able to amuse myself for a few hours.*

**amused** /əˈmjuːzd/ adj. thinking that sth/sb is funny, so that you smile or laugh: *There was an amused look on the President's face.* ◇ *Janet was **not amused*** (= she was annoyed or angry). ◇ ~ **at/by sth** *We were all amused at his stories.* ◇ ~ **to see, find, learn,** etc. *He was amused to see how seriously she took the game.*
**IDM keep sb a'mused** to give sb interesting things to do, or to entertain them so that they do not become bored: *Playing with water can keep children amused for hours.*

**amuse·ment** /əˈmjuːzmənt/ noun **1** [U] the feeling that you have when you enjoy sth that is funny: *She could not hide her amusement at the way he was dancing.* ◇ **to sb's** ~ *To my amusement he couldn't get the door open.* ◇ **with** ~ *Her eyes twinkled with amusement.* **2** [C, usually pl.] a game, an activity, etc. that provides entertainment and pleasure: *traditional seaside amusements including boats, go-karts and a funfair* **3** [U] the fact of being entertained by sth: *What do you do for amusement around here?*

**a'musement arcade** (BrE) (also **ar·cade** NAmE, BrE) noun an indoor place where you can play games on machines that you usually operate with coins

**a'musement park** noun a large park that has a lot of things that you can ride and play on and many different activities to enjoy

**amus·ing** /əˈmjuːzɪŋ/ adj. funny and giving pleasure: *an amusing story/game/incident* ◇ *I didn't find the joke at all amusing.* ⊃ SYNONYMS at FUNNY ▶ **amus·ing·ly** adv.

**amyg·dala** /əˈmɪɡdələ/ noun (pl. **amyg·da·lae** /-liː/) (anatomy) either of two areas in the brain that are linked to memory, the emotions and the sense of smell

**amy·lase** /ˈæmɪleɪz; NAmE -leɪs/ noun [U] (chemistry) an ENZYME (= a substance that helps a chemical change to take place) that allows the body to change some substances into simple sugars

**an** /ən, strong form æn/ indefinite article ⊃ A

**-an, -ana** ⊃ -IAN, -IANA

**ana·bol·ic ster·oid** /ˌænəbɒlɪk ˈsterɔɪd, ˈstɪər-; NAmE ˌænəbɑːlɪk ˈsterɔɪd, ˈstɪr-/ noun an artificial HORMONE (= a chemical substance) that increases the size of the muscles. It is sometimes taken illegally by people who play sports. ⊃ see also STEROID

**an·achron·ism** /əˈnækrənɪzəm/ noun **1** [C] a person, a custom or an idea that seems old-fashioned and does not belong to the present: *The monarchy is seen by many people as an anachronism in the modern world.* **2** [C, U] something that is placed, for example in a book or play, in the wrong period of history; the fact of placing sth in the wrong period of history ▶ **ana·chron·is·tic** /əˌnækrəˈnɪstɪk/ adj.

**ana·conda** /ˌænəˈkɒndə; NAmE -ˈkɑːn-/ noun a large South American snake of the BOA family, that wraps itself tightly around other animals to kill them before eating them

**an·aemia** (BrE) (NAmE **an·emia**) /əˈniːmiə/ noun [U] a medical condition in which sb has too few red cells or too

| b **b**ad | d **d**id | f **f**all | g **g**et | h **h**at | j **y**es | k **c**at | l **l**eg | m **m**an | n **n**ow | p **p**en | r **r**ed |

little HAEMOGLOBIN in their blood, making them look pale and feel weak

**an·aemic** (BrE) (NAmE **an·emic**) /əˈniːmɪk/ adj. **1** suffering from anaemia: *She looks anaemic.* **2** weak and not having much effect SYN **feeble**: *an anaemic performance*

**an·aer·obic** /ˌænəˈrəʊbɪk/ adj. **1** (biology) not needing OXYGEN: *anaerobic bacteria* **2** (of physical exercise) not especially designed to improve the function of the heart and lungs OPP **aerobic**

**an·aes·the·sia** (US **an·es·the·sia**) /ˌænəsˈθiːziə; NAmE -ˈθiːʒə/ noun [U] **1** the use of anaesthetics during medical operations **2** (specialist) the state of being unable to feel anything, especially pain

**an·aes·the·sio·logist** (US **an·es·the·sio·logist**) /ˌænəsˌθiːziˈɒlədʒɪst; NAmE -ˈɑːl-/ noun a doctor who studies the use of anaesthetics

**an·aes·thet·ic** (US **an·es·thet·ic**) /ˌænəsˈθetɪk/ noun, adj.
■ *noun* [U, C] a drug that makes a person or an animal unable to feel anything, especially pain, either in the whole body or in a part of the body: **under ~** *How long will I be under anaesthetic?* ◊ *They gave him a* **general anaesthetic** (= one that makes you become unconscious.) ◊ *(a)* **local anaesthetic** (= one that affects only a part of the body) ⊃ WORDFINDER NOTE at OPERATION
■ *adj.* [only before noun] containing a substance that makes a person or an animal unable to feel pain in all or part of the body: *an anaesthetic drug/spray*

**an·aes·the·tist** (US **an·es·the·tist**) /əˈniːsθətɪst; NAmE -ˈes-/ noun a person who is trained to give anaesthetics to patients

**an·aes·the·tize** (BrE also **-ise**) (US **an·es·the·tize**) /əˈniːsθətaɪz; NAmE -ˈes-/ verb **~ sb** to make a person or animal unable to feel pain, etc., especially by giving them an anaesthetic before a medical operation

**ana·gram** /ˈænəɡræm/ noun a word or phrase that is made by arranging the letters of another word or phrase in a different order: *An anagram of 'Elvis' is 'lives'.*

**anal** /eɪnl/ adj. **1** relating to or located near the ANUS: *the anal region* ⊃ VISUAL VOCAB page V2 **2** (also **anal-re'tentive**) (disapproving) caring too much about small details and about how things are organized ► **anal·ly** /-nəli/ adv.

**an·al·gesia** /ˌænəlˈdʒiːziə; NAmE -ˈdʒiːʒə/ noun [U] (medical) the loss of the ability to feel pain while still conscious

**an·al·gesic** /ˌænəlˈdʒiːzɪk/ noun (medical) a substance that reduces pain SYN **painkiller**: *Aspirin is a mild analgesic.*
► **an·al·gesic** adj.: *analgesic drugs/effects*

**analo·gous** /əˈnæləɡəs/ adj. **~ (to / with sth)** (formal) similar in some way to another thing or situation and therefore able to be compared with it: *Sleep has often been thought of as being in some way analogous to death.*

**ana·logue** (especially BrE) (NAmE usually **ana·log**) /ˈænəlɒɡ; NAmE -lɔːɡ/ adj., noun
■ *adj.* (specialist) **1** (of an electronic process) using a continuously changing range of physical quantities to measure or store data: *an analogue circuit/computer/signal* **2** (of a clock or watch) showing the time using hands on a DIAL and not with a display of numbers ⊃ compare DIGITAL
■ *noun* (formal or specialist) a thing that is similar to another thing: *Scientists are attempting to compare features of extinct animals with living analogues.*

**ana·logy** /əˈnælədʒi/ noun (pl. **-ies**) **1** [C] a comparison of one thing with another thing that has similar features; a feature that is similar: **~ (between A and B)** *The teacher drew an analogy between the human heart and a pump.* ◊ **~ (with sth)** *There are no analogies with any previous legal cases.* **2** [U] the process of comparing one thing with another thing that has similar features in order to explain it: *learning by analogy*

**,anal-re'tentive** adj. (disapproving) = ANAL

**ana·lyse** (BrE) (NAmE **ana·lyze**) /ˈænəlaɪz/ verb **1** to examine the nature or structure of sth, especially by separating it into its parts, in order to understand or explain it: **~ sth** *The job involves collecting and analysing data.* ◊ *Learn to step back and critically analyse situations.* ◊ **~ sth for sth** *The water samples will be analysed for the presence of polluting chemicals.* ◊ **~ what, how, etc …** *We need to analyse what went wrong.* ⊃ SYNONYMS at EXAMINE **2 ~ sb** = PSYCHOANALYSE

**ana·lysis** /əˈnæləsɪs/ noun (pl. **ana·ly·ses** /-ləsiːz/) **1** [U, C] the detailed study or examination of sth in order to understand more about it; the result of the study: *statistical/data analysis* ◊ *a detailed analysis of the data* ◊ *to perform/conduct an analysis* ◊ *Further analysis revealed significant regional variations in the results.* ⊃ see also META-ANALYSIS **2** [U, C] a careful examination of a substance in order to find out what it consists of: **for ~** *The blood samples are sent to the laboratory for analysis.* ◊ *the results of a DNA sequence analysis* ⊃ WORDFINDER NOTE at SCIENCE **3** [U] = PSYCHOANALYSIS: *In analysis the individual resolves difficult emotional conflicts.*
IDM **in the final / last a'nalysis** used to say what is most important after everything has been discussed, or considered: *In the final analysis, it's a matter of personal choice.*

**ana·lyst** /ˈænəlɪst/ noun **1** a person whose job involves examining facts or materials in order to give an opinion on them: *a political/financial analyst* ◊ *a food/market analyst* ◊ *analysts expect/predict …* ◊ **according to an ~** *According to music industry analysts …* ⊃ see also SYSTEMS ANALYST **2** = PSYCHOANALYST

**ana·lytic** /ˌænəˈlɪtɪk/ adj. = ANALYTICAL

**ana·lyt·ic·al** /ˌænəˈlɪtɪkl/ (also **ana·lyt·ic**) adj. **1** using a logical method of thinking about sth in order to understand it, especially by looking at all the parts separately: *She has a clear analytical mind.* ◊ *an analytic approach to the problem* **2** using scientific analysis in order to find out about sth: *analytical methods of research* ► **ana·lyt·ic·al·ly** /-kli/ adv.

**ana·lyt·ics** /ˌænəˈlɪtɪks/ noun [U + sing. / pl. v.] a careful and complete analysis of data using a model, usually performed by a computer; information resulting from this analysis: *web/business analytics*

**ana·lyze** (NAmE) = ANALYSE

**anaphor** /ˈænəfə(r), -fɔː(r)/ noun (grammar) a word or phrase that refers back to an earlier word or phrase. For example, in the phrase 'My mother said she was leaving', 'she' is used as an anaphor for 'my mother'.

**anaph·ora** /əˈnæfərə/ noun [U] (grammar) the use of a word that refers to or replaces another word used earlier in a sentence, for example the use of 'does' in the sentence 'I disagree and so does John' ► **ana·phor·ic** /ˌænəˈfɒrɪk; NAmE -ˈfɔːr-/ adj.

**ana·phyl·axis** /ˌænəfɪˈlæksɪs/ noun [U] (pl. **ana·phyl·axes** /-ˈlæksiːz/) (medical) an extreme ALLERGIC reaction to sth that you eat or touch ► **ana·phyl·ac·tic** /-ˈlæktɪk/ adj.: *anaphylactic shock*

**an·arch·ism** /ˈænəkɪzəm; NAmE ˈænərk-/ noun [U] the political belief that laws and governments are not necessary; a political force or movement based on this belief

**an·arch·ist** /ˈænəkɪst; NAmE ˈænərk-/ noun a person who believes that laws and governments are not necessary ► **an·arch·is·tic** /ˌænəˈkɪstɪk; NAmE ˌænərˈk-/ adj.

**an·archy** /ˈænəki; NAmE ˈænərki/ noun [U] a situation in a country, an organization, etc. in which there is no government, order or control: *The overthrow of the military regime was followed by a period of anarchy.* ◊ *There was complete anarchy in the classroom when their usual teacher was away.* ► **an·arch·ic** /əˈnɑːkɪk; NAmE əˈnɑːrk-/ (also less frequent **an·arch·ic·al** /əˈnɑːkɪkl; NAmE əˈnɑːrk-/) adj.

**anath·ema** /əˈnæθəmə/ noun [U, C, usually sing.] (formal) a thing or an idea that you hate because it is the opposite of what you believe: *Racial prejudice is (an) anathema to me.*

**anato·mist** /əˈnætəmɪst/ noun a scientist who studies anatomy

**anat·omy** /əˈnætəmi/ noun (pl. **-ies**) **1** [U] the scientific study of the physical structure of humans, animals or plants **2** [C, U] the physical structure of a human, animal or plant: *the anatomy of the horse* ◊ *human anatomy* **3** [C]

# -ance  50

(*humorous*) a person's body: *Various parts of his anatomy were clearly visible.* **4** [C] (*formal*) an examination of what sth is like or why it happens: *an anatomy of the current recession* ▶ **ana·tom·ical** /ˌænəˈtɒmɪkl/; *NAmE* -ˈtɑːm-/ *adj.*: *anatomical diagrams* **ana·tom·ic·al·ly** /-kli/ *adv.*

**-ance, -ence** /əns, ns/ *suffix* (in nouns) the action or state of: *assistance ◇ confidence*

**an·ces·tor** ⁑+ B2 /ˈænsestə(r)/ *noun* **1** ⁑+ B2 a person in your family who lived a long time ago SYN **forebear**: *His ancestors had come to America from Ireland.* ⇨ WORDFINDER NOTE at RELATION **2** ⁑+ C1 an animal that lived in the past that a modern animal has developed from: *a reptile that was the common ancestor of lizards and turtles* **3** ⁑+ C1 an early form of a machine that later became more developed SYN **forerunner**: *The ancestor of the modern bicycle was called a penny-farthing.* ⊃ compare DESCENDANT ▶ **an·ces·tral** /ænˈsestrəl/ *adj.*: *her ancestral home* (= that had belonged to her ancestors)

**an·ces·try** /ˈænsestri/ *noun* [C, usually sing., U] (*pl.* **-ies**) the family or the race of people that you come from: *to have Scottish ancestry ◇ He was able to trace his ancestry back over 1000 years.*

**an·chor** ⁑+ C1 /ˈæŋkə(r)/ *noun, verb*
■ *noun* **1** ⁑+ C1 a heavy metal object that is attached to a rope or chain and dropped over the side of a ship or boat to keep it in one place: *to drop anchor ◇ We weighed anchor* (= pulled it out of the water). *◇ at ~ The ship lay at anchor two miles off the rocky coast.* **2** ⁑+ C1 a person or thing that gives sb a feeling of safety: *the anchor of the family* **3** ⁑+ C1 a person who presents a live radio or television programme and introduces reports by other people; an ANCHORMAN or ANCHORWOMAN: *ABC news anchor Peter Jennings*

anchor

■ *verb* **1** [I, T] ~ **(sth)** to let an anchor down from a boat or ship in order to prevent it from moving away: *We anchored off the coast of Spain.* **2** [T, often passive] to fix sth in position so that it cannot move: **be anchored (to sth)** *Make sure the table is securely anchored.* **3** [T, usually passive] to base sth on sth else: **be anchored (in/to sth)** *Her novels are anchored in everyday experience.* **4** [I, T] ~ **(sth)** (*especially NAmE*) to be the person who introduces reports or reads the news on television or radio: *She anchored the evening news for seven years.*

**an·chor·age** /ˈæŋkərɪdʒ/ *noun* **1** [C, U] a place where ships or boats can anchor **2** [U] the action of fastening sth securely in position; the fact of being securely fastened in position: *The plant needs firm anchorage.*

**an·chor·man** /ˈæŋkəmæn; *NAmE* -kərm-/, **an·chor·woman** /ˈæŋkəwʊmən; *NAmE* -kɜːrw-/ *noun* (*pl.* **-men** /-men/, **-women** /-wɪmɪn/) (*also* **an·chor**) a person who presents a live radio or television programme and introduces reports by other people

**an·chovy** /ˈæntʃəvi/; *NAmE* -tʃoʊvi/ *noun* (C, U) (*pl.* **-ies**) a small fish that is used for food, usually preserved in salt and oil, giving it a strong SALTY taste: *a pizza topped with cheese and anchovies*

**an·cient** ⁑ A2 /ˈeɪnʃənt/ *adj.* **1** ⁑ A2 belonging to a period of history that is thousands of years in the past: *ancient history/civilization ◇ ancient Greece/Egypt/Rome* OPP **modern** **2** A2 very old; having existed for a very long time: *an ancient oak tree ◇ ancient monuments/traditions/culture ◇* (*humorous*) *He's ancient—he must be at least fifty!* **3 the ancients** *noun* [pl.] the people who lived in ancient times, especially the Egyptians, Greeks and Romans ▶ **an·cient·ly** *adv.* (*formal*): *the area where the market was anciently held* (= in ancient times)

**an·cil·lary** /ænˈsɪləri/; *NAmE* ˈænsəleri/ *adj.* **1 ~ (to sth)** providing necessary support to the main work or activities of an organization SYN **auxiliary**: *ancillary staff/services/equipment ◇ ancillary workers in the health service* such as cooks and cleaners **2** in addition to sth else but not as important: *ancillary rights*

**-ancy, -ency** /ənsi, nsi/ *suffix* (in nouns) the state or quality of: *expectancy ◇ complacency*

**and** ⁑ A1 /ənd, ən, n, *strong form* ænd/ *conj.* (used to connect words or parts of sentences) **1** ⁑ A1 also; in addition to: *bread and butter ◇ a table, two chairs and a desk ◇ Sue and I left early. ◇ Do it slowly and carefully. ◇ Can he read and write? ◇ I cooked lunch. And I made a cake.* (= you are emphasizing how much you have done) HELP When **and** is used in common phrases connecting two things or people that are closely linked, the determiner is not usually repeated before the second: *a knife and fork ◇ my father and mother*, but: *a knife and a spoon ◇ my father and my uncle.* **2** ⁑ A1 then; following this: *She came in and took her coat off.* **3** ⁑ A1 **go, come, try, stay, etc.** ~ used before a verb instead of *to*, to show purpose: *Go and get me a pen please. ◇ I'll come and see you soon. ◇ We stopped and bought some bread.* HELP In this structure **try** can only be used in the infinitive or to tell somebody what to do: *Try and finish quickly.* **4** ⁑ A1 used to introduce a comment or a question: *'We talked for hours.' 'And what did you decide?'* **5** ⁑ A1 as a result: *Miss another class and you'll fail.* **6** ⁑ A1 added to SYN **plus**[1]: *5 and 5 makes 10. ◇ What's 47 and 16?* HELP When numbers (but not dates) are spoken, **and** is used between the hundreds and the figures that follow: *2264—two thousand, two hundred and sixty-four*, but: *1964—nineteen sixty-four.* **7** ⁑ A2 used between repeated words to show that sth is repeated or continuing: *He tried and tried but without success. ◇ The pain got worse and worse.* **8** used between repeated words to show that there are important differences between things or people of the same kind: *I like city life but there are cities and cities.* ⊃ see also AND/OR

**an·dante** /ænˈdænteɪ/ *noun* (*music, from Italian*) a piece of music to be played fairly slowly ▶ **an·dante** *adv., adj.*

**and/or** /ˌænd ˈɔː(r)/ *conj.* (*informal*) used when you say that two situations exist together, or as an alternative to each other: *There is no help for those with lots of luggage and/or small children.*

**an·dro·gen** /ˈændrədʒən/ *noun* (*biology*) a male sex HORMONE, for example TESTOSTERONE

**an·drogy·nous** /ænˈdrɒdʒənəs; *NAmE* -ˈdrɑːdʒ-/ *adj.* looking neither strongly male nor strongly female

**Android**™ /ˈændrɔɪd/ *noun* [U] a type of OPERATING SYSTEM, designed for mobile devices, which controls the way the device works and runs apps (= programs designed to do particular jobs): *I've downloaded dozens of apps on my Android phone.*

**an·droid** /ˈændrɔɪd/ *noun* (in science fiction) a robot in the shape of a person ⊃ compare DROID

**an·ec·dotal** /ˌænɪkˈdəʊtl/ *adj.* (of an account or evidence) possibly not true or accurate because it is based on personal accounts rather than facts or research: *anecdotal evidence* ▶ **an·ec·dot·al·ly** /-təli/ *adv.*: *This reaction has been reported anecdotally by a number of patients.*

**an·ec·dote** /ˈænɪkdəʊt/ *noun* [C, U] **1** a short, interesting or funny story about a real person or event: *amusing anecdotes about his brief career as an actor* **2** a personal account of an event: *This research is based on anecdote, not fact.*

**an·emia, an·emic** (*NAmE*) = ANAEMIA, ANAEMIC

**anem·one** /əˈneməni/ *noun* a small plant with white, red, blue or purple flowers that are like cups in shape and have dark centres ⊃ see also SEA ANEMONE

**an·es·the·sia, an·es·the·sio·logist, an·es·thet·ic, an·es·the·tist, an·es·the·tize** (*US*) = ANAESTHESIA, ANAESTHESIOLOGIST, ANAESTHETIC, ANAESTHETIST, ANAESTHETIZE

**an·eur·ysm** /ˈænjərɪzəm/ *noun* (*medical*) an area of extreme SWELLING on the wall of an ARTERY

**anew** /əˈnjuː; *NAmE* əˈnuː/ *adv.* (*formal*) if sb does sth **anew**, they do it again from the beginning or do it in a different way: *They started life anew in Canada.*

---

æ cat | ɑː father | e bed | ɜː fur | ə about | ɪ sit | iː see | i happy | ɒ got (*BrE*) | ɔː saw | ʌ cup | ʊ put | uː too

**angel** /ˈeɪndʒl/ noun **1** a spirit who is believed to be a servant of God, and is sent by God to deliver a message or perform a task. Angels are often shown dressed in white, with wings. ⊃ see also GUARDIAN ANGEL **2** a person who is very good and kind; a child who behaves well: *John is no angel, believe me* (= he does not behave well). **3** (*informal*) used when you are talking to sb and you are grateful to them: *Thanks Dad, you're an angel.* ◊ *Be an angel and make me a cup of coffee.* **4** (*also* ˌangel inˈvestor, ˈbusiness angel) a person who supports a business by investing money in it, especially sb who supports a new small business with their own money IDM see FOOL *n.*

**Angel·eno** (*also* Angel·ino) /ˌændʒəˈliːnəʊ/ noun (*pl.* -os) (*informal*) a person who lives in Los Angeles

**an·gel·ic** /ænˈdʒelɪk/ *adj.* good, kind or beautiful; like an angel: *an angelic smile* ▸ **an·gel·ic·al·ly** *adv.* /-kli/

**ˈangel inˌvestor** *noun* = ANGEL (4)

**an·gelus** /ˈændʒələs/ (*also* the Angelus) *noun* [sing.] (in the Roman Catholic Church) prayers said in the morning, at 12 o'clock in the middle of the day, and in the evening; a bell rung when it is time for these prayers

**anger** /ˈæŋɡə(r)/ *noun, verb*
▪ *noun* [U] the strong feeling that you have when sth has happened that you think is bad and unfair: *She had to find a way to express her pent-up anger.* ◊ *in ~ Jan slammed her fist on the desk in anger.* ◊ *~ at/over/about sth He was filled with anger at the way he had been treated.* ◊ *~ at/towards/against sb/sth There is widespread anger at the government following yesterday's announcement.* ◊ *a course in anger management* (= controlling your feelings of anger)
▪ *verb* [often passive] to make sb angry: *~ sb The question clearly angered him.* ◊ *be angered by/at sth She was angered by their selfishness and lack of concern.*

**an·gina** /ænˈdʒaɪnə/ (*medical* anˌgina pecˈtoris /ænˌdʒaɪnə ˈpektərɪs/) *noun* [U] severe pain in the chest caused by a low supply of blood to the heart during exercise because the ARTERIES are partly blocked

**angio·plasty** /ˈændʒiəʊplæsti/ *noun* [C, U] (*pl.* -ies) (*medical*) a medical operation to repair or open a blocked BLOOD VESSEL, especially either of the two ARTERIES that supply blood to the heart

**angle** /ˈæŋɡl/ *noun, verb*
▪ *noun* **1** the space between two lines or surfaces that join, measured in degrees: *a 45° angle* ⊃ see also ACUTE ANGLE, ADJACENT ANGLE, CORRESPONDING ANGLES, OBTUSE ANGLE, RIGHT ANGLE, WIDE-ANGLE LENS **2** a corner on the outside or inside of sth: *It's a modern building, all brick and glass and sharp angles.* **3** the direction that sth is leaning or pointing in when it does not go straight up and down or straight across from side to side: *at an~ The Tower of Pisa leans at an angle* ◊ *The plane was coming in at a steep angle.* ◊ *at an~ to sth Venus and the Earth orbit the Sun at a slight angle to each other.* **4** a position from which you look at sth: *The photo was taken from an unusual angle.* ◊ *The variety of camera angles gives her photographs interest.* **5** a particular way of presenting or thinking about a situation, problem, etc: *We need a new angle for our next advertising campaign.* ◊ *You can look at the issue from many different angles.* ◊ *The article concentrates on the human angle* (= the part that concerns people's emotions) *of the story.*
▪ *verb* **1** [T] ~sth to move or place sth so that it is not straight or not directly facing sb/sth: *He angled his chair so that he could sit and watch her.* **2** [T] ~sth to present information, a report, etc. based on a particular way of thinking or for a particular audience: *The programme is angled towards younger viewers.* **3** (*usually* go angling) [I] to catch fish with a line and a HOOK
PHRV ˈangle for sth to try to get a particular reaction or response from sb, without directly asking for what you want: *She was angling for sympathy.*

**ˈangle bracket** *noun* [usually pl.] one of a pair of marks, <>, used around words or figures to separate them from the surrounding text

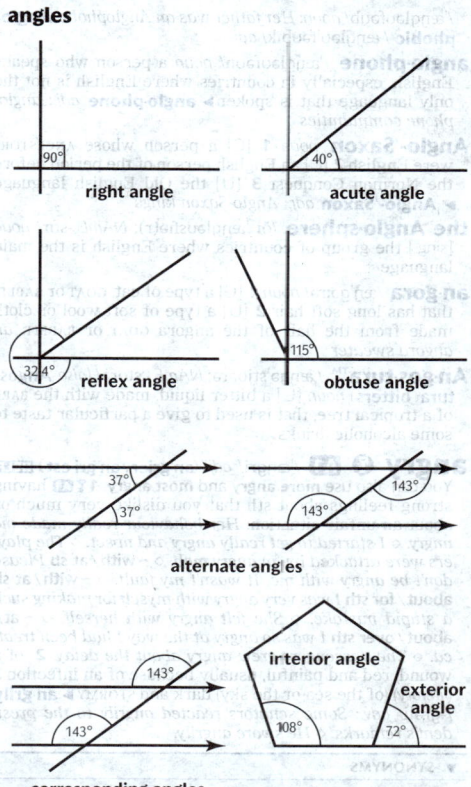

angles

right angle · acute angle · reflex angle · obtuse angle · alternate angles · interior angle · exterior angle · corresponding angles

**ang·ler** /ˈæŋɡlə(r)/ *noun* a person who catches fish (= goes angling) as a hobby ⊃ compare FISHERMAN

**An·gli·can** /ˈæŋɡlɪkən/ *noun* a member of the Church of England or of a Church connected with it in another country ▸ **An·gli·can** *adj.*: *the Anglican Church*

**An·gli·cism** /ˈæŋɡlɪsɪzəm/ *noun* a word or phrase from the English language that is used in another language: *Anglicisms used in French include 'le weekend' and 'un toast'.*

**an·gli·cize** (*BrE also* -ise) /ˈæŋɡlɪsaɪz/ *verb* ~sb/sth to make sb/sth English in character: *Gutmann anglicized his name to Goodman.*

**an·gling** /ˈæŋɡlɪŋ/ *noun* [U] the art or sport of catching fish with a FISHING ROD

**Anglo** /ˈæŋɡləʊ/ *noun* (*pl.* -os) **1** (*US*) a white person of European origin **2** (*CanE*) an ANGLOPHONE

**Anglo-** /ˈæŋɡləʊ/ *combining form* (in nouns and adjectives) English or British: *Anglo-Canadian* ◊ *Anglophile* ◊ *Anglo-Indian*

**Anglo-Aˈmerican** *noun, adj.*
▪ *noun* **1** an American whose family originally came from England or the UK **2** an American whose first language is English
▪ *adj.* **1** relating to both the UK and the US: *Anglo-American folk music* ◊ *a possible Anglo-American trade agreement* **2** originally from an English family but born or living in the US

**Anglo·phile** /ˈæŋɡləʊfaɪl/ *noun* a person who is not English or British but who likes England or the UK very much ▸ **Anglo·phile** *adj.*: *Anglophile tastes/sympathies*

**Anglo·pho·bia** /ˌæŋɡləʊˈfəʊbiə/ *noun* [U] a feeling of hate or fear of England or the UK ▸ **Anglo·phobe**

# anglophone 52

/ˈæŋɡləʊfəʊb/ noun: *Her father was an Anglophobe.* ▶ **Anglophobic** /ˌæŋɡləʊˈfəʊbɪk/ adj.

**anglo·phone** /ˈæŋɡləʊfəʊn/ noun a person who speaks English, especially in countries where English is not the only language that is spoken ▶ **anglo·phone** adj.: *anglophone communities*

**Anglo-Saxon** noun **1** [C] a person whose ANCESTORS were English **2** [C] an English person of the period before the Norman Conquest **3** [U] the Old English language ▶ **Anglo-Saxon** adj.: *Anglo-Saxon kings*

**the Anglo·sphere** /ði ˈæŋɡləʊsfɪə(r); *NAmE* -sfɪr/ noun [sing.] the group of countries where English is the main language

**an·gora** /æŋˈɡɔːrə/ noun **1** [C] a type of cat, GOAT or RABBIT that has long soft hair **2** [U] a type of soft wool or cloth made from the hair of the angora GOAT or RABBIT: *an angora sweater*

**An·gos·tura**™ /ˌæŋɡəˈstjʊərə; *NAmE* -ˈstʊrə/ (also **Angostura ˈbitters**) noun [U] a bitter liquid, made from the BARK of a tropical tree, that is used to give a particular taste to some alcoholic drinks

**angry** 🛈 **A1** /ˈæŋɡri/ adj. (**an·grier**, **an·gri·est**) HELP You can also use **more angry** and **most angry**. **1** ⓘ **A1** having strong feelings about sth that you dislike very much or about an unfair situation: *Her behaviour really made me angry.* ⋄ *I started to get really angry and upset.* ⋄ *The players were attacked by an angry mob.* ⋄ **~with/at sb** *Please don't be angry with me. It wasn't my fault.* ⋄ **~with/at sb about/for sth** *I was very angry with myself for making such a stupid mistake.* ⋄ *She felt angry with herself.* ⋄ **~at/about/over sth** *I was so angry at the way I had been treated.* ⋄ *The passengers grew angry about the delay.* **2** (of a wound) red and painful, usually because of an infection **3** (*literary*) (of the sea or the sky) dark and STORMY ▶ **an·grily** /-ɡrəli/ adv.: *Some senators reacted angrily to the president's remarks.* ⋄ *He swore angrily.*

▼ **SYNONYMS**
**angry**
mad • indignant • cross • irate
These words all describe people feeling and/or showing anger.
**angry** feeling or showing anger: *Please don't be angry with me.* ⋄ *Thousands of angry demonstrators filled the square.*
**mad** [not before noun] (*informal, especially NAmE*) angry: *He got mad and walked out.* ⋄ *She's mad at me for being late.* NOTE **Mad** is the usual word for 'angry' in informal American English. In British English, the phrase 'go mad' means 'become very angry': *Dad'll go mad when he sees what you've done.* 'Go mad' can also mean 'go crazy' or 'get very excited'.
**indignant** feeling or showing anger and surprise because you think that you or sb else has been treated unfairly: *She was very indignant at the way she had been treated.*
**cross** (*especially BrE, rather informal*) rather angry or annoyed: *I was quite cross with him for being late.* NOTE This word is often used by or to children.
**irate** very angry: *irate customers* ⋄ *an irate letter* NOTE **Irate** is not usually followed by a preposition: *She was irate with me/about it.*
**PATTERNS**
- angry/mad/indignant/cross **about/at** sth
- angry/cross **with** sb (for doing sth)
- angry/mad/indignant/cross **that** …
- to **get** angry/mad/cross
- to **make sb** angry/mad/cross

**angst** /æŋst; *NAmE also* ɑːŋst/ noun [U] (*from German*) a feeling of great worry about a situation, or about your life: *songs full of teenage angst*

**ˈangst-ridden** adj. having feelings of angst: *a generation of angst-ridden adolescents*

**ang·strom** /ˈæŋstrəm/ noun (*chemistry*, *physics*) a very small unit of length, equal to 1x10⁻¹⁰ metre, used for measuring WAVELENGTHS and the distance between ATOMS

**angsty** /ˈæŋsti; *NAmE also* ˈɑːŋ-/ adj. (*informal*) having or showing feelings of angst: *Stefan plays the role of a rebellious, angsty outsider who joins a terrorist cell.* ⋄ *angsty poetry/drama/lyrics*

**an·guish** /ˈæŋɡwɪʃ/ noun [U] (*formal*) severe physical or mental pain, difficulty or unhappiness: *He groaned in anguish.* ⋄ *Tears of anguish filled her eyes.* ▶ **an·guished** adj.: *anguished cries* ⋄ *an anguished letter from her prison cell*

**an·gu·lar** /ˈæŋɡjələ(r)/ adj. **1** (of a person) thin so that the bones can be seen clearly under the skin: *an angular face* ⋄ *a tall angular woman* **2** having angles or sharp corners: *a design of large angular shapes*

**ani·mal** 🛈 **A1** **W** /ˈænɪml/ noun, adj.
■ noun **1** ⓘ **A1** a creature that is not a bird, a fish, a REPTILE, an insect or a human: *the animals and birds of South America* ⋄ *wild/farm animals* ⋄ *domestic animals such as dogs and cats* ⋄ *the export of live animals for slaughter* ⊃ see also COMPANION ANIMAL **2** ⓘ **A1** any living thing that is not a plant or a human: *This product has not been tested on animals.* ⋄ **animal welfare/cruelty** ⋄ **the animal kingdom** ⊃ VISUAL VOCAB pages V2, V3 ⊃ see also DUMB ANIMAL **3** **A1** any living creature, including humans: *Humans are the only animals to have developed speech.* ⊃ compare VEGETABLE ⊃ see also HIGHER ANIMALS **4** a person who behaves in a cruel or unpleasant way, or who is very dirty: *The person who did this is an animal, a brute.* **5** a particular type of person, thing, organization, etc: *She's not a political animal.* ⋄ *The government that followed the election was a very different animal.* ⊃ see also PARTY ANIMAL
■ adj. [only before noun] relating to the physical needs and basic feelings of people: *animal desires/passion/instincts* ⋄ *animal magnetism* (= a quality in sb that other people find attractive, usually in a sexual way)

**ˌanimal comˈpanion** noun = COMPANION ANIMAL

**ˌanimal conˈtrol officer** noun (*NAmE, formal*) a person whose job is to catch animals that are walking freely in the streets and do not seem to have a home ⊃ compare DOGCATCHER

**ˌanimal ˈhusbandry** noun [U] (*specialist*) farming that involves keeping animals to produce food

**ˌanimal ˈrights** noun [pl.] the rights of animals to be treated well, for example by not being hunted or used for medical research: *His research work was attacked by animal rights activists.*

**an·im·ate** verb, adj.
■ verb /ˈænɪmeɪt/ **1** **~sth** to make sth more lively or full of energy: *A smile suddenly animated her face.* **2** [usually passive] **~sth** to make models, toys, images, etc. seem to move in a film, either by rapidly showing slightly different pictures of them in a series, one after another, or by using computer techniques to create moving images
■ adj. /ˈænɪmət/ (*formal*) living; having life: *animate beings* OPP inanimate

**ani·mated** /ˈænɪmeɪtɪd/ adj. **1** full of interest and energy SYN **lively**: *an animated discussion/conversation* ⋄ *Her face suddenly became animated.* **2** (of drawings, images, etc. in a film) made to look as if they are moving: *animated cartoons/graphics/models* ▶ **ani·mat·ed·ly** adv.: *People were talking animatedly.*

**ani·ma·tion** 🛈+ **B2** /ˌænɪˈmeɪʃn/ noun **1** 🛈+ **B2** [U] the process of making films, videos and computer games in which drawings, models or images of people and animals seem to move: *computer/cartoon animation* ⊃ WORDFINDER NOTE at SOFTWARE **2** 🛈+ **B2** [C] a film in which drawings, models or images of people and animals seem to move: *The electronic dictionary included some animations.* **3** [U] energy and enthusiasm in the way you look, behave or speak: *His face was drained of all colour and animation.*
⊃ see also SUSPENDED ANIMATION

**ani·ma·tor** /ˈænɪmeɪtə(r)/ noun a person who makes animated films

**anima·tron·ics** /ˌænɪməˈtrɒnɪks; NAmE -ˈtrɑːn-/ noun [U] the process of making and operating robots that look like real people or animals, used in films and other types of entertainment ► **anima·tron·ic** adj.

**anime** /ˈænɪmeɪ; NAmE also ˈɑːnɪm-/ noun [U] Japanese film and television ANIMATION, typically aimed at adults as well as children

**ani·mism** /ˈænɪmɪzəm/ noun [U] **1** the belief that plants, objects and natural things such as the weather have a living soul **2** belief in a power that organizes and controls the universe ► **ani·mist** /-nɪmɪst/ noun **ani·mis·tic** /ˌænɪˈmɪstɪk/ adj.

**ani·mos·ity** /ˌænɪˈmɒsəti; NAmE -ˈmɑːs-/ noun [U, C] (pl. -ies) a strong feeling of opposition, anger or hate SYN **hostility**: ~(toward(s) sb/sth) He felt no animosity towards his critics. ◊ ~(between A and B) personal animosities between members of the two groups

**ani·mus** /ˈænɪməs/ noun [U, sing.] ~(against sb/sth) (formal) a strong feeling of opposition, anger or hate

**anion** /ˈænaɪən/ noun (chemistry, physics) an ION with a negative electrical CHARGE ⊃ compare CATION

**anise** /ˈænɪs/ noun [U] a plant with seeds that have a strong sweet smell and taste

**ani·seed** /ˈænɪsiːd/ noun [U] the dried seeds of the anise plant, used to give a particular taste to alcoholic drinks and sweets

**ankh** /æŋk; NAmE ɑːŋk/ noun an object or design like a cross but with a LOOP instead of the top arm, sometimes worn as jewellery. The ankh was used in ancient Egypt as the symbol of life.

**ankle** 🔊 A2 /ˈæŋkl/ noun the JOINT connecting the foot to the leg; the narrow part of the leg just above the ankle joint: to *sprain/break/twist your ankle* ◊ *She suffered a serious ankle injury in training.* ◊ *to have a broken/twisted/fractured/sprained ankle* ◊ *ankle boots* (= that cover the ankle) ⊃ VISUAL VOCAB page V1

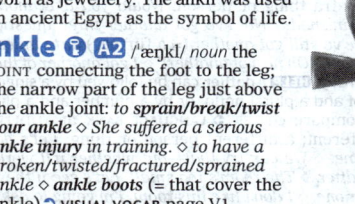
ankh

**ˈankle sock** (BrE) (US **ank·let**) noun a type of very short sock: *a girl in a blue dress and ankle socks*

**ank·let** /ˈæŋklət/ noun **1** a piece of jewellery worn around the ankle **2** (US) (BrE ˈankle sock) a type of very short sock

**anna** /ˈʌnə/ noun (IndE) **1** an older brother **2** the leader of a group of young people who go around together and sometimes cause trouble

**annals** /ˈænlz/ noun [pl.] **1** an official record of events or activities year by year; historical records: *His deeds went down in the annals of British history.* **2** used in the title of academic journals: *Annals of Science, vol. viii*

**an·neal** /əˈniːl/ verb ~sth (specialist) to heat metal or glass and allow it to cool slowly, in order to make it softer and easier to shape (= more DUCTILE)

**annex** /ˈæneks, əˈneks/ verb ~sth (formal) to take control of a country, region, etc., especially by force SYN **occupy**: *Germany annexed Austria in 1938.* ► **an·nex·ation** /ˌænekˈseɪʃn/ noun [U, C]

**an·nexe** (BrE) (also **annex** NAmE, BrE) /ˈæneks/ noun **1** a building that is added to, or is near, a larger one and that provides extra living or work space: *Our rooms were in the annexe.* **2** (formal) an extra section of a document SYN **appendix**

**an·ni·hi·late** /əˈnaɪəleɪt/ verb **1** ~sb/sth/yourself to destroy sb/sth/yourself completely: *The human race has enough weapons to annihilate itself.* **2** ~sb/sth to defeat sb/sth completely: *She annihilated her opponent, who failed to win a single game.* ► **an·ni·hi·la·tion** /əˌnaɪəˈleɪʃn/ noun [U]: *the annihilation of the whole human race*

**an·ni·ver·sary** 🔊 B2 /ˌænɪˈvɜːsəri; NAmE -ˈvɜːrs-/ noun (pl. -ies) a date that is an exact number of years after the date of an important or special event: *on the anniversary of his wife's death* ◊ *to celebrate your wedding anni-*

---

**annoying**

*versary* ◊ *the theatre's 25th anniversary celebrations* ⊃ WORDFINDER NOTE at CELEBRATE

**an·no·tate** /ˈænəteɪt/ verb ~sth to add notes to a book or text, giving explanations or comments ► **an·no·ta·tion** /ˌænəˈteɪʃn/ noun [C, U]: *It will be published with annotations and an index.* **an·no·tated** /ˈænəteɪtɪd/ adj.: *an annotated edition*

**an·nounce** 🔊 B1 /əˈnaʊns/ verb **1** 🔊 B1 to tell people sth officially, especially about a decision, plans, etc: ~sth *He officially announced his intention to resign at today's press conference.* ◊ (figurative) *A ring at the doorbell announced Jack's arrival.* ◊ ~that ... *We are pleased to announce that all five candidates were successful.* ◊ **it is announced that** ... *It was announced that new speed restrictions would be introduced.* ◊ ~**sth to sb** *The company announced its decision to the public in March.* ◊ *The government yesterday announced to the media plans to create a million new jobs.* ◊ ~sb/sth as sth *She was announced as the winner at last night's ceremony.* HELP You cannot 'announce somebody something': *They announced us their decision.* ⊃ SYNONYMS at DECLARE **2** 🔊 B1 to give information about sth in a public place, especially through a LOUDSPEAKER: ~sth *Has our flight been announced yet?* + speech *'Now boarding flight 897, destination Seattle,' the loudspeaker announced.* ◊ ~that ... *They announced that the flight would be delayed.* **3** to say sth in a loud and/or serious way: + speech *'I've given up smoking,' she announced.* ◊ ~that ... *She announced that she'd given up smoking.* ⊃ SYNONYMS at DECLARE **4** ~**yourself/sb** to tell sb your name or sb else's name when you or they arrive at a place: *Would you announce the guests as they arrive?* (= call out their names, for example at a formal party) **5** ~sth to introduce, or to give information about, a programme on the radio or television ⊃ WORDFINDER NOTE at RADIO

**an·nounce·ment** 🔊 B1 /əˈnaʊnsmənt/ noun **1** 🔊 B1 [C] a spoken or written statement that informs people about sth: *to make an announcement* ◊ *a formal/an official/a public announcement* ◊ *The campaign will run public service announcements on radio stations around the country.* ⊃ SYNONYMS at STATEMENT **2** 🔊 B1 [U] the act of publicly informing people about sth: *Announcement of the verdict was accompanied by shouts and cheers.*

**an·noun·cer** /əˈnaʊnsə(r)/ noun **1** a person who introduces, or gives information about, programmes on the radio or television ⊃ see also HOST noun, PRESENTER **2** a person who gives information about sth in a station, an airport, etc., especially through a LOUDSPEAKER **3** (NAmE) a person who broadcasts at a sports event: *a play-by-play announcer* (= who comments on a game as it is happening)

**annoy** 🔊 B1 /əˈnɔɪ/ verb **1** 🔊 B1 to make sb slightly angry SYN **irritate**: ~sb *His constant joking was beginning to annoy her.* ◊ **it annoys sb when ...** *It really annoys me when people forget to say thank you.* ◊ **it annoys sb to do sth** *It annoys me to see him getting ahead of me.* **2** ~sb to make sb uncomfortable or unable to relax SYN **bother**: *He swatted a fly that was annoying him.*

**an·noy·ance** /əˈnɔɪəns/ noun **1** [U] the feeling of being slightly angry SYN **irritation**: *He could not conceal his annoyance at being interrupted.* ◊ *Much to our annoyance, they decided not to come after all.* ◊ *She stamped her foot in annoyance.* **2** [C] something that makes you slightly angry: *The delay is now shorter but still an annoyance.*

**annoy·ed** 🔊 B1 /əˈnɔɪd/ adj. [not usually before noun] slightly angry SYN **irritated**: ~(**with sb**) (**at/about sth**) *He was beginning to get very annoyed with me about my carelessness.* ◊ *I was annoyed with myself for giving in so easily.* ◊ *I bet she was annoyed at having to write it out again.* ◊ ~that ... *I was annoyed that they hadn't turned up.* ◊ ~**to find, see**, etc. *He was annoyed to find himself going red.*

**annoy·ing** 🔊 B1 /əˈnɔɪɪŋ/ adj. making sb feel slightly angry SYN **irritating**: *This interruption is very*

---

🅞 Oxford Phrasal Academic Lexicon (OPAL) written and spoken word lists | 🅦 OPAL written word list | 🅢 OPAL spoken word list

**annoying.** ◇ *Her most annoying habit was eating with her mouth open.* ▶ **an·noy·ing·ly** *adv.*

**an·nual** /ˈænjuəl/ *adj., noun*
■ *adj.* [usually before noun] **1** happening or done once every year: *an annual meeting/event/report/conference* **2** relating to a period of one year: *an annual income/revenue/budget/fee/salary/turnover* ◇ *an average annual growth rate of 8%* ◇ *Our total annual costs have declined.* ⊃ compare BIANNUAL, SEMI-ANNUAL
■ *noun* **1** a book, especially one for children, that is published once a year, with the same title each time, but different contents **2** any plant that grows and dies within one year or season ⊃ compare BIENNIAL, PERENNIAL

**ˌannual ˈgeneral ˈmeeting** *noun* (*BrE*) = AGM

**an·nu·al·ized** (*BrE also* **-ised**) /ˈænjuəlaɪzd/ *adj.* (*specialist*) calculated for a period of a year but based on the amounts for a shorter period

**an·nu·al·ly** /ˈænjuəli/ *adv.* once a year: *The exhibition is held annually.*

**an·nu·ity** /əˈnjuːəti/; *NAmE* əˈnuː-/ *noun* (*pl.* **-ies**) **1** a fixed amount of money paid to sb each year, usually for the rest of their life **2** a type of insurance that pays a fixed amount of money to sb each year ⊃ WORDFINDER NOTE at INSURANCE

**an·nul** /əˈnʌl/ *verb* (**-ll-**) ~ **sth** to state officially that sth is not legally recognized: *Their marriage was annulled after just six months.* ▶ **an·nul·ment** *noun* [C, U]

**an·nu·lar** /ˈænjələ(r)/ *adj.* (*specialist*) having a shape like a ring

**the An·nun·ci·ation** /ðɪ əˌnʌnsiˈeɪʃn/ *noun* [sing.] (in the Christian religion) the occasion when Mary was told that she was to be the mother of Christ, celebrated on 25 March

**anode** /ˈænəʊd/ *noun* (*specialist*) the ELECTRODE in an electrical device where OXIDATION occurs; the positive electrode in an ELECTROLYTIC cell and the negative electrode in a battery ⊃ compare CATHODE

**ano·dize** (*BrE also* **-ise**) /ˈænədaɪz/ *verb* ~ **sth** to cover a metal, especially ALUMINIUM, with a layer of OXIDE in order to protect it

**ano·dyne** /ˈænədaɪn/ *adj.* (*formal*) unlikely to offend anyone or cause them to disagree; not expressing strong opinions SYN **bland**

**anoint** /əˈnɔɪnt/ *verb* ~ **sb / sth (with sth)** to put oil or water on sb's head or body as part of a religious ceremony: *The priest anointed her with oil.*

**anom·al·ous** /əˈnɒmələs/; *NAmE* əˈnɑːm-/ *adj.* (*formal*) different from what is normal or expected ▶ **anom·al·ous·ly** *adv.*

**anom·aly** /əˈnɒməli/; *NAmE* əˈnɑːm-/ *noun* [C, U] (*pl.* **-ies**) ~ **(in sth)** a thing, situation, etc. that is different from what is normal or expected: *the many anomalies in the tax system* ◇ *the apparent anomaly that those who produced the wealth, the workers, were the poorest*

**an·omie** (*also* **anomy**) /ˈænəmi/ *noun* [U] (*formal*) a lack of social or moral standards

**anon** /əˈnɒn/; *NAmE* əˈnɑːn/ *adv.* (*old-fashioned or literary*) soon: *See you anon.*

**anon.** /əˈnɒn/; *NAmE* əˈnɑːn/ *abbr.* anonymous (= used to describe a poem, piece of music, etc. when it is not known who wrote it)

**ano·nym·ity** /ˌænəˈnɪməti/ *noun* [U] **1** the state of remaining unknown to most other people: *Names of people in the book were changed to preserve anonymity.* ◇ *the anonymity of the city* (= where people do not know each other) ◇ *(especially NAmE) He agreed to give an interview on condition of anonymity* (= if his name was not mentioned). **2** the state of not having any unusual or interesting features: *the anonymity of the hotel decor*

**an·onym·ize** (*BrE also* **-ise**) /əˈnɒnɪmaɪz/; *NAmE* əˈnɑːn-/ *verb* **1** ~ **sth** (*specialist*) if you **anonymize** a test result, especially a medical test result, you remove any information that shows who it belongs to **2** ~ **sth** (*computing*) if you

**anonymize** data that is sent or received over the internet, you remove any information that identifies which particular computer that data originally came from ▶ **an·onym·iz·a·tion** /əˌnɒnɪmaɪˈzeɪʃn/; *NAmE* əˌnɑːnəməˈz-/ *noun* [U]

**an·onym·ous** /əˈnɒnɪməs/; *NAmE* əˈnɑːn-/ *adj.* **1** (of a person) with a name that is not known or that is not made public: *an anonymous donor* ◇ *The money was donated by a local businessman who wishes to remain anonymous.* **2** written, given, made, etc. by sb who does not want their name to be known or made public: *an anonymous letter* **3** without any unusual or interesting features: *long stretches of dull and anonymous countryside* ▶ **an·onym·ous·ly** *adv.*

**aˈnonymous FTP** *noun* [U] (*computing*) a system that allows anybody to download files from the internet without having to give their name

**ano·rak** /ˈænəræk/ *noun* **1** (especially *BrE*) a short coat with a HOOD that is worn as protection against rain, wind and cold **2** (*BrE, informal*) a person who spends a lot of time learning facts or collecting things that most other people think are boring

**an·or·exia** /ˌænəˈreksiə/ (*also* **an·or·exia ner·vosa** /ˌænəˌreksiə nɜːˈvəʊsə/; *NAmE* nɜːrˈv-/) *noun* [U] an emotional DISORDER, especially affecting young women, in which there is an ABNORMAL fear of being fat, causing the person to stop eating, leading to dangerous weight loss ⊃ WORDFINDER NOTE at CONDITION ⊃ compare BULIMIA

**an·or·exic** /ˌænəˈreksɪk/ *noun* a person who is suffering from anorexia ▶ **an·or·exic** *adj.*: *She's anorexic.*

**an·other** /əˈnʌðə(r)/ *det., pron.* **1** one more; an extra thing or person: *Would you like another drink?* ◇ *'Finished?' 'No, I've got another three questions to do.'* ◇ *We've still got another* (= a further) *forty miles to go.* ◇ *'It's a bill.' 'Oh no, not another!'* ◇ *I got another of those calls yesterday.* HELP **Another** can be followed by a singular noun, by **of** and a plural noun, or by a number and a plural noun. ⊃ compare OTHER ⊃ LANGUAGE BANK at ADDITION **2** different; a different person or thing: *Let's do it another time.* ◇ *We can try that—but whether it'll work is another matter.* ◇ *The room's too small. Let's see if they've got another one.* ◇ *I don't like this room. I'm going to ask for another.* **3** a person or thing of a very similar type: *She's going to be another Madonna* (= as famous as her). ◇ *There'll never be another like him.* ⊃ see also ONE ANOTHER IDM **of one kind, sort, etc. or a'nother** used when you are referring to various types of a thing, without saying exactly what you mean: *We've all got problems of one kind or another.* ⊃ more at ONE *number*

**an·swer** /ˈɑːnsə(r)/; *NAmE* ˈæn-/ *noun, verb*
■ *noun* **1** something that you say, write or do to react to a question or situation: *I rang the bell, but there was no answer.* ◇ *The short answer is no.* ◇ ~ **to sth** *I can't easily give an answer to your question.* ◇ *Have you had an answer to your letter?* ◇ **in~to sth** *As if in answer to our prayers, she offered to lend us £10000.* ◇ ~ **from sb** *You're not going to get an answer from me!* **2** ~ something that you write or say in reply to a question in a test, an exam, an exercise, etc.; the correct reply to a question in a test, etc: *the correct/right answer* ◇ *Write your answers on the sheet provided.* ◇ *Do you know the answer* (= the right one) *to question 12?* **3** a solution to a problem: *There is no easy answer.* ◇ *The answer is simple.* ◇ ~ **to sth** *This could be the answer to all our problems.* **4** ~ **to sth** a person or thing from one place that may be thought to be as good as a famous person or thing from another place: *The new theme park will be Britain's answer to Disneyland.*
IDM **ˌhave / ˌknow all the ˈanswers** (*informal, often disapproving*) to be confident that you know sth, especially when you actually do not: *He thinks he knows all the answers.* ⊃ more at NO *exclamation*
■ *verb* **1** ~ [I, T] to say, write or do sth as a reaction to a question or situation SYN **reply**: *I repeated the question, but she didn't answer.* ◇ ~ **sth** *You haven't answered my question.* ◇ *to answer a letter/an email* ◇ *to answer the phone* ◇ *to answer the door* (= to open the door when sb knocks/rings) ◇ *We are grateful to all those people who answered our call for help with fundraising.* ◇ *My prayers*

*have been answered* (= I have got what I wanted). ◇ **~ sb** *Come on, answer me! Where were you?* ◇ *He answered me with a smile.* ◇ **+ speech** *'I'd prefer to walk,' she answered.* ◇ **~ sb + speech** *'I'd prefer to walk,' she answered him.* ◇ **~(sb) that ...** *She answered that she would prefer to walk.* ◇ **~ sb sth** *Answer me this: how did they know we were here?* **2** [T] **~ sth/sb** to defend yourself against a charge or criticism: *He was summoned before the council to answer charges of treason.* **3** [T] **~ sth** *(formal)* to be suitable for sth; to match sth: *Does this answer your requirements?*
**IDM** **answer to the name of sth** (especially of a pet animal) to be called sth ⇒ more at DESCRIPTION
**PHRV** **ˌanswer ˈback** to defend yourself against criticism: *He was given the chance to answer back in a radio interview.* **ˌanswer ˈback | ˌanswer sb ˈback** to speak rudely to sb in authority, especially when they are criticizing you or telling you to do sth: *Don't answer back!* ◇ *Stop answering your mother back!* **ˈanswer for sth 1** to accept responsibility or blame for sth: *You will have to answer for your behaviour one day.* ◇ *This government has a lot to answer for* (= is responsible for a lot of bad things). **2** to promise that sb has a particular quality or can be relied on to do sth: *I can answer for her honesty.* **ˈanswer for sb** (usually in negative sentences) to say that sb else will do sth or have a particular opinion: *I agree, but I can't answer for my colleagues.* **ˈanswer to sb (for sth)** to have to explain your actions or decisions to sb: *All sales clerks answer to the store manager.*

▼ **WHICH WORD?**

**answer / reply**

**Verbs**
- **Answer** and **reply** are the most common verbs used for speaking or writing as a reaction to a question, letter, etc.
- Note that you **answer** a person, question or letter, not *answer to* them, but you **reply to** somebody or something: *I'm writing to answer your questions* ◇ *I'm writing to reply to your questions.* ◇ *I'm writing to answer to your questions.*
- **Answer** can be used with or without an object: *I haven't answered her email yet.* ◇ *I knocked on the door but nobody answered.* **Reply** is often used with the actual words spoken: *'I won't let you down,' he replied.*
- **Respond** is less common and more formal: *The directors were unwilling to respond to questions.*
- You can only **answer** a door or a phone.
⇒ see also REJOIN², RETORT, GET BACK TO SB

**Nouns**
- Note the phrases **in answer to** and **in reply to**: *I'm writing in answer to your letter.*
⇒ see also RESPONSE, REJOINDER, RETORT

**an·swer·able** /ˈɑːnsərəbl/ NAmE /ˈæn-/ adj. **1** [not before noun] **~ to sb (for sth)** having to explain your actions to sb in authority over you: *She was a free agent, answerable to no one for her behaviour.* **2** [not before noun] **~(for sth)** responsible for sth and ready to accept punishment or criticism for it: *Ministers must be made answerable for their decisions.* **3** (of a question) that can be answered

**ˈanswering machine** (BrE also **ˈan·swer·phone**) noun a machine that you connect to your phone to answer your calls and record any message left by the person calling: *I called several times, but only got the answering machine.*

**ant** /ænt/ noun a small insect that lives in highly organized groups. There are many types of ant: *an ants' nest* ◇ *an ant colony* ⇒ VISUAL VOCAB page V3 ⇒ see also ANTHILL
**IDM** **have ˈants in your pants** *(informal)* to be very excited or impatient about sth and unable to stay still

**-ant, -ent** /ənt, nt/ suffix **1** (in adjectives) that is or does sth: *significant* ◇ *different* **2** (in nouns) a person or thing that: *inhabitant* ◇ *deterrent*

**ant·acid** /æntˈæsɪd/ noun a medicine that prevents or corrects ACIDITY, especially in the stomach

**an·tag·on·ism** /ænˈtæɡənɪzəm/ noun [U, pl.] **~(to/toward(s) sb/sth) | ~(between A and B)** feelings of opposition and hate **SYN** **hostility**: *The antagonism he felt towards his old enemy was still very strong.* ◇ *the racial antagonisms in society*

**an·tag·on·ist** /ænˈtæɡənɪst/ noun *(formal)* a person who strongly opposes sb/sth **SYN** **opponent**

**an·tag·on·is·tic** /ænˌtæɡəˈnɪstɪk/ adj. **~(to/toward(s) sb/sth)** *(formal)* showing or feeling opposition **SYN** **hostile** ▶ **an·tag·on·is·tic·al·ly** /-kli/ adv.

**an·tag·on·ize** (BrE also **-ise**) /ænˈtæɡənaɪz/ verb **~ sb** to do sth to make sb angry with you: *Not wishing to antagonize her further, he said no more.*

**the Antˈarc·tic** /ði ænˈtɑːktɪk; NAmE -ˈtɑːrk-/ noun [sing.] the regions of the world around the South Pole ▶ **Antˈarc·tic** adj. [only before noun]: *Antarctic explorers* ⇒ compare ARCTIC

**the Antˌarctic ˈCircle** noun [sing] the line of LATITUDE 66° 33' South ⇒ compare ARCTIC CIRCLE

**ante** /ˈænti/ noun [sing.]
**IDM** **raise/up the ˈante** to increase the level of sth, especially demands or sums of money

**ante-** /ænti, ænti/ prefix (in nouns, adjectives and verbs) before; in front of: *anteroom* ◇ *antenatal* ◇ *antedate* ⇒ compare POST-, PRE-

**ant·eat·er** /ˈæntiːtə(r)/ noun an animal with a long nose and tongue that eats ANTS

**ante·bel·lum** /ˌæntiˈbeləm/ adj. [only before noun] *(formal)* connected with the years before a war, especially the American Civil War: *the laws of the antebellum American South*

**ante·ce·dent** /ˌæntɪˈsiːdnt/ noun, adj
■ noun **1** [C] *(formal)* a thing or an event that exists or comes before another, and may have influenced it **2** **antecedents** [pl.] *(formal)* the people in sb's family who lived a long time ago **SYN** **ancestor, forebear 3** [C] *(grammar)* a word or phrase to which the following word, especially a pronoun, refers: *In 'He grabbed the ball and threw it in the air', 'ball' is the antecedent of 'it'.*
■ adj. *(formal)* previous: *antecedent events*

**ante·cham·ber** /ˈæntɪtʃeɪmbə(r)/ noun *(formal)* = ANTEROOM

**ante·date** /ˈæntideɪt/ verb **~ sth** = PREDATE

**ante·di·lu·vian** /ˌæntidɪˈluːviən/ adj. *(formal or humorous)* very old-fashioned

**ante·lope** /ˈæntiləʊp/ noun (pl. **ante·lope** or **ante·lopes**) an African or Asian animal like a DEER that runs very fast. There are many types of antelope.

**ante·natal** /ˌæntiˈneɪtl/ (BrE) (also **pre·natal** NAmE, BrE) adj. [only before noun] relating to the medical care given to pregnant women: *antenatal care/classes/screening* ◇ *an antenatal clinic* ⇒ compare POSTNATAL ⇒ WORDFINDER NOTE at PREGNANT

**an·tenna** /ænˈtenə/ noun **1** (pl. **an·ten·nae** /-niː/) either of the two long thin parts on the heads of some insects and some animals that live in shells, used to feel and touch things with **SYN** **feeler** ⇒ VISUAL VOCAB page V3 **2** (pl. **an·ten·nas** or **an·ten·nae**) (especially NAmE) (also **aer·ial** especially in BrE) a piece of equipment made of wire or long straight pieces of metal for receiving or sending radio and television signals: *radio antennas*

**an·ter·ior** /ænˈtɪəriə(r); NAmE -ˈtɪr-/ adj. [only before noun] *(specialist)* (of a part of the body) at or near the front **OPP** **posterior**

**ante·room** /ˈæntiruːm, -rʊm/ (also formal **ante·cham·ber**) noun a room where people can wait before entering a larger room, especially in an important public building

**an·them** /ˈænθəm/ noun **1** a song that has a special importance for a country, an organization or a particular group of people, and is sung on special occasions: *The European anthem was played at the opening and closing ceremonies.* ⇒ see also NATIONAL ANTHEM **2** a short

# anthemic

religious song for a CHOIR (= a group of singers), often with an organ

**an·them·ic** /æn'θemɪk, -'θi:m-/ *adj.* (*formal*) (of a piece of music) that makes you feel happy and enthusiastic

**an·ther** /'ænθə(r)/ *noun* (*biology*) the part of a flower at the top of a STAMEN that produces POLLEN ⊃ VISUAL VOCAB page V7

**ant·hill** /'ænthɪl/ *noun* a pile of earth formed by ANTS over their NESTS

**an·tholo·gize** (*BrE also* **-ise**) /æn'θɒlədʒaɪz; *NAmE* -'θɑ:l-/ *verb* ~ **sb/sth** to include a writer or piece of writing in an anthology

**an·thol·ogy** /æn'θɒlədʒi; *NAmE* -'θɑ:l-/ *noun* (*pl.* **-ies**) a collection of poems, stories, etc. that have been written by different people and published together in a book

**an·thra·cite** /'ænθrəsaɪt/ *noun* [U] a very hard type of coal that burns slowly without producing a lot of smoke or flames

**an·thrax** /'ænθræks/ *noun* [U] a serious disease that affects sheep and cows and sometimes people, and can cause death

**an·thro·po-** /'ænθrəpəʊ, ˌænθrəpə; *BrE also* ænθrə'pɒ; *NAmE also* ænθrə'pɑ:/ *combining form* (in nouns, adjectives and adverbs) connected with humans: *anthropology*

**the An·thropo·cene** /ði 'ænθrəpəsi:n; *BrE also* æn-'θrɒp-; *NAmE also* æn'θrɑ:p-/ *noun* [sing.] the current age, viewed as the period during which human activity has had the greatest influence on climate and the environment ▶ **An·thropo·cene** *adj.* [usually before noun]: *the Anthropocene era/epoch*

**an·thro·po·cen·tric** /ˌænθrəpə'sentrɪk/ *adj.* believing that humans are more important than anything else ▶ **an·thro·po·cen·trism** /-trɪzəm/ *noun* [U]

**an·thro·poid** /'ænθrəpɔɪd/ *adj., noun* (*specialist*)
- *adj.* (of an APE) looking like a human
- *noun* any type of APE that is similar to a human

**an·thro·polo·gist** /ˌænθrə'pɒlədʒɪst; *NAmE* -'pɑ:l-/ *noun* a person who studies anthropology

**an·thro·pol·ogy** /ˌænθrə'pɒlədʒi; *NAmE* -'pɑ:l-/ *noun* [U] the study of the human race, especially of its origins, development, customs and beliefs: *Cultural anthropology covers the whole range of human activities which are learned and transmitted.* ◊ *Physical anthropology is the study of human physical variation.* ▶ **an·thro·po·logic·al** /ˌænθrəpə'lɒdʒɪkl; *NAmE* -'lɑ:dʒ-/ *adj.*

**an·thro·po·morph·ic** /ˌænθrəpə'mɔ:fɪk; *NAmE* -'mɔ:rf-/ *adj.* (of beliefs or ideas) treating gods, animals or objects as if they had human qualities ▶ **an·thro·po·morph·ism** /-fɪzəm/ *noun* [U]

**anti** /'ænti; *NAmE also* -taɪ/ *prep.* (*informal*) if sb is **anti** sb/ sth, they do not like or agree with that person or thing ⊃ compare PRO

**anti-** /ænti; *BrE also* æn'tɪ; *NAmE also* æntɪ/ *prefix* (in nouns and adjectives) **1** opposed to; against: *anti-tank weapons* ◊ *antisocial* ⊃ compare PRO- **2** the opposite of: *anti-hero* ◊ *anticlimax* **3** preventing: *antifreeze*

**anti-'aircraft** *adj.* [only before noun] designed to destroy enemy aircraft: *anti-aircraft fire/guns/missiles*

**anti·bac·ter·ial** /ˌæntibæk'tɪəriəl; *NAmE* -tɪbæk'tɪr-, -taɪb-/ *adj.* that kills bacteria: *antibacterial treatments*

**anti·biot·ic** /ˌæntibaɪ'ɒtɪk; *NAmE* -tɪbaɪ'ɑ:-, -taɪb-/ *noun* [usually pl.] a substance, for example PENICILLIN, that can destroy or prevent the growth of bacteria and cure infections: *The doctor put her on antibiotics* (= told her to take them). ▶ **anti·biot·ic** *adj.: an antibiotic drug* ◊ *effective antibiotic treatment*

**anti·body** /'æntibɒdi; *NAmE* -bɑ:di/ *noun* (*pl.* **-ies**) a substance that the body produces in the blood to fight disease, or as a reaction when certain substances are put into the body

**anti-'choice** *adj.* (*NAmE, disapproving*) against giving women the right to have an ABORTION ⊃ compare PRO-CHOICE

**Anti·christ** /'æntikraɪst; *NAmE also* -taɪk-/ (*usually* **the Antichrist**) *noun* [sing.] (in Christianity) the DEVIL; Christ's greatest enemy

**an·tici·pate** B2+ B2 /æn'tɪsɪpeɪt/ *verb* **1** B2+ B2 to expect sth: ~ **sth** *We don't anticipate any major problems.* ◊ *Our anticipated arrival time is 8.30.* ◊ *The eagerly anticipated movie will be released next month.* ◊ ~ **doing sth** *They anticipate moving to bigger premises by the end of the year.* ◊ ~ **sth doing sth** *I don't anticipate it being a problem.* ◊ ~ **that ...** *We anticipate that sales will rise next year.* ◊ **it is anticipated that ...** *It is anticipated that inflation will stabilize at 3 per cent.* ⊃ compare UNANTICIPATED **2** B2+ B2 to see what might happen in the future and take action to prepare for it: ~ **sth** *We need someone who can anticipate and respond to changes in the fashion industry.* ◊ ~ **what, how, that, etc ...** *Try and anticipate what the interviewers will ask.* **3** B2+ B2 ~ **(doing) sth** | ~ **(sth doing) sth** to think with pleasure and excitement about sth that is going to happen: *We eagerly anticipated the day we would leave school.* ◊ *The more I anticipated arriving somewhere, the more disappointed I was.* **4** ~ **sb (doing sth)** (*formal*) to do sth before it can be done by sb else SYN **forestall**: *When Scott reached the South Pole he found that Amundsen had anticipated him.* ▶ **an·tici·pa·tory** /æn'tɪsɪpətəri; *NAmE* æn'tɪsəpətɔ:ri/ *adj.* (*formal*): *a fast anticipatory movement by the goalkeeper*

**an·tici·pa·tion** /æn,tɪsɪ'peɪʃn/ *noun* [U] **1** the fact of seeing that sth might happen in the future and perhaps doing sth about it now: **in ~ of sth** *He bought extra food in anticipation of more people coming than he'd invited.* **2** a feeling of excitement about sth (usually sth good) that is going to happen: *happy/eager/excited anticipation* ◊ *The courtroom was filled with anticipation.*

**anti·cler·ic·al** /ˌænti'klerɪkl; *NAmE also* -taɪ'k-/ *adj.* opposed to priests and their influence in political life: *anticlerical movements in the seventeenth century* ▶ **anti·cler·ic·al·ism** /-kəlɪzəm/ *noun* [U]

**anti·cli·max** /ˌænti'klaɪmæks; *NAmE also* -taɪ'k-/ *noun* [C, U] a situation that is disappointing because it happens at the end of sth that was much more exciting, or because it is not as exciting as you expected: *Travelling in Europe was something of an anticlimax after the years he'd spent in Africa.* ◊ *a sense/feeling of anticlimax* ⊃ compare CLIMAX ▶ **anti·cli·mac·tic** /ˌæntiklaɪ'mæktɪk; *NAmE also* -taɪk-/ *adj.*

**anti·cline** /'æntiklaɪn/ *noun* (*geology*) an area of ground where layers of rock in the earth's surface have been folded into a curve that is higher in the middle than at the ends ⊃ compare SYNCLINE

**anti·clock·wise** /ˌænti'klɒkwaɪz; *NAmE* -ti'klɑ:k-, -taɪ'k-/ (*BrE*) (*NAmE* **coun·ter·clock·wise**) *adv., adj.* in the opposite direction to the movement of the hands of a clock: *Turn the key anticlockwise/in an anticlockwise direction.* OPP **clockwise**

**anti·coagu·lant** /ˌæntikəʊ'ægjələnt; *NAmE also* -taɪk-/ *noun* (*medical*) a substance that stops the blood from becoming thick and forming CLOTS

**anti·con·vul·sant** /ˌæntikən'vʌlsənt; *NAmE also* -taɪk-/ *noun* a drug used to prevent EPILEPTIC FITS or similar illnesses ▶ **anti·con·vul·sant** *adj.*

**antics** /'æntɪks/ *noun* [pl.] **1** behaviour that is silly and funny in a way that people usually like: *The bank staff got up to all sorts of antics to raise money for charity.* **2** behaviour which is unreasonable or dangerous

**anti·cyc·lone** /ˌænti'saɪkləʊn; *NAmE also* -taɪ's-/ *noun* an area of high air pressure that produces calm weather conditions with clear skies ⊃ compare DEPRESSION

**anti·depres·sant** /ˌæntidɪ'presnt; *NAmE also* -taɪd-/ *noun* a drug used to treat the illness DEPRESSION ▶ **anti·depres·sant** *adj.* [only before noun]: *antidepressant drugs*

**anti·dote** /'æntidəʊt/ *noun* **1** ~ **(to sth)** a substance that controls the effects of a poison or disease: *There is no known antidote to the poison.* **2** ~ **(to sth)** anything that takes away the effects of sth unpleasant: *A Mediterranean cruise was the perfect antidote to a long cold winter.*

**Antifa** /ˈæntifɑː, ˌænˈtiːfə/ *noun* [U + sing. / pl. v.] a political protest movement of people who are against FASCISM

**anti·freeze** /ˈæntifriːz/ *noun* [U] a chemical that is added to the water in the cooling system of cars and other vehicles to stop it from freezing

**anti·gen** /ˈæntɪdʒən/ *noun* (*medical*) a substance that enters the body and starts a process that can cause disease. The body then usually produces ANTIBODIES to fight the antigens.

**anti·glob·al·iza·tion** (*BrE also* **-isa·tion**) /ˌæntiˌɡləʊbəlaɪˈzeɪʃn; *NAmE* -tiˌɡloʊbələˈz-, -taɪɡ-/ *noun* [U] opposition to the increase in the power of large international companies and institutions because of the bad effects on the economies of individual countries, especially poorer ones: *antiglobalization protests at the G7 summit* ◊ *the antiglobalization movement*

**anti·grav·ity** /ˌæntiˈɡrævɪti; *NAmE also* -taɪɡ-/ *noun* [U] (*physics*) a HYPOTHETICAL (= imaginary) force that works against GRAVITY

**ˈanti-hero** *noun* the main character in a story, but one who does not have the qualities of a typical hero, and is either more like an ordinary person or morally bad ➔ WORDFINDER NOTE *at* CHARACTER

**anti·his·ta·mine** /ˌæntiˈhɪstəmiːn/ *noun* [C, U] a drug used to treat ALLERGIES, especially HAY FEVER: *antihistamine cream/injections/shots*

**ˌanti-inˈflam·ma·tory** *adj.* (of a drug) used to reduce INFLAMMATION ▶ **anti-inˈflam·ma·tory** *noun* (*pl.* **-ies**)

**ˈanti-lock** *adj.* [only before noun] **anti-lock** BRAKES stop the wheels of a vehicle locking if you have to stop suddenly, and so make the vehicle easier to control: *an anti-lock braking system or ABS*

**anti·mat·ter** /ˈæntimætə(r); *NAmE also* -taɪm-/ *noun* [U] (*physics*) matter that is made up of ANTIPARTICLES

**an·tim·ony** /ˈæntɪməni; *NAmE* -məʊni/ *noun* [U] (*symb.* **Sb**) a chemical element. Antimony is a silver-white metal that breaks easily, used especially in making ALLOYS.

**anti·oxi·dant** /ˌæntiˈɒksɪdənt; *NAmE* -tiˈɑːk-, -taɪˈɑː-/ *noun* **1** (*biology*) a substance such as vitamin C or E that removes dangerous MOLECULES, etc., such as FREE RADICALS from the body **2** (*chemistry*) a substance that helps prevent OXIDATION, especially one used to help prevent stored food products from going bad

**anti·par·ticle** /ˈæntipɑːtɪkl; *NAmE* -tipɑːrt-, -taɪp-/ *noun* (*physics*) a very small part of an ATOM that has the same mass as a normal PARTICLE but the opposite electrical CHARGE ➔ WORDFINDER NOTE *at* ATOM

**anti·pasto** /ˌæntiˈpæstəʊ; *NAmE* -ˈpɑːs-/ *noun* (*pl.* **anti·pasti** /-sti/) (in Italian cooking) a small amount of food that you eat before the main part of a meal SYN **appetizer, starter**

**an·tip·athy** /ænˈtɪpəθi/ *noun* [U, C, usually sing.] (*pl.* **-ies**) ~ (**between A and B**) | ~ (**to / toward(s) sb / sth**) (*formal*) a strong feeling of dislike SYN **hostility**: *personal/mutual antipathy* ◊ *a growing antipathy towards the idea* ▶ **anti·path·et·ic** /ˌæntɪpəˈθetɪk/ *adj.*: ~ (**to sb / sth**) antipathetic to change

**ˌanti-perˈsonnel** *adj.* [only before noun] (of weapons) designed to kill or injure people, not to destroy buildings or vehicles, etc.

**anti·per·spir·ant** /ˌæntiˈpɜːspərənt; *NAmE* -tiˈpɜːrs-, -taɪˈp-/ *noun* [U, C] a substance that people use, especially under their arms, to prevent or reduce SWEAT ➔ *see also* DEODORANT

**the An·tipo·des** /ði ænˈtɪpədiːz/ *noun* [pl.] a way of referring to Australia and New Zealand, often used in a humorous way ▶ **An·tipo·dean** /ˌæntɪpəˈdiːən/ *adj.*, *noun*

**anti·pro·ton** /ˌæntiˈprəʊtɒn; *NAmE* -ˈproʊtɑːn, -taɪp-/ *noun* (*physics*) a PARTICLE that has the same mass as a PROTON, but a negative electrical CHARGE

**anti·quar·ian** /ˌæntiˈkweəriən; *NAmE* -ˈkwer-/ *adj.*, *noun*
■ *adj.* [usually before noun] connected with the study, collection or sale of valuable old objects, especially books
■ *noun* (*also less frequent* **anti·quary** /ˈæntɪkwəri; *NAmE* -kweri/) a person who studies, collects or sells old and valuable objects

**anti·quated** /ˈæntɪkweɪtɪd/ *adj.* (*usually disapproving*) (of things or ideas) old-fashioned and no longer suitable for modern conditions SYN **outdated**

**an·tique** /ænˈtiːk/ *adj.*, *noun*
■ *adj.* [usually before noun] (of furniture, jewellery, etc.) old and often valuable: *an antique mahogany desk*
■ *noun* an object such as a piece of furniture that is old and often valuable: *Priceless antiques were destroyed in the fire.* ◊ *an antique shop* (= one that sells antiques) ◊ *an antique dealer/antiques dealer* (= a person who sells antiques)

**an·tiquity** /ænˈtɪkwəti/ *noun* (*pl.* **-ies**) **1** [U] the ancient past, especially the times of the Greeks and Romans: *The statue was brought to Rome in antiquity.* **2** [U] the state of being very old or ancient: *A number of the monuments are of considerable antiquity.* **3** [C, usually pl.] an object from ancient times: *Egyptian/Roman antiquities*

**anti·retro·viral** /ˌæntiˌretrəʊˈvaɪrəl; *NAmE also* -taɪr-/ *adj.* (*medical*) designed to stop viruses such as HIV damaging the body: *antiretroviral drugs*

**ˌanti-ˈroll bar** *noun* a metal bar that is part of a car's SUSPENSION, which stops the car from leaning too much when it goes around corners

**anti-Semitism** (*also* **anti-semˌitˈism**) /ˌæntiˈsemətɪzəm; *NAmE also* -taɪ-/ *noun* [U] hate that is felt towards Jewish people; unfair treatment of Jews ▶ **anti-Semitic** (*also* **anti-semˈitˈic**) /ˌæntisəˈmɪtɪk; *NAmE also* -taɪ-/ *adj.*: *anti-Semitic propaganda* **anti-Semite** (*also* **anti-semite**) /ˌænti ˈsiːmaɪt, ˈsem-; *NAmE* ˌænti ˈsemaɪt, ˈæntaɪ/ *noun*: *He was a notorious anti-Semite.*

**anti·sep·tic** /ˌæntiˈseptɪk/ *noun*, *adj.*
■ *noun* [C, U] a substance that helps to prevent infection in wounds by killing bacteria SYN **disinfectant**
■ *adj.* **1** able to prevent infection: *antiseptic cream/lotion/wipes* **2** very clean and free from bacteria SYN **sterile**: *Cover the burn with an antiseptic dressing.*

**anti·social** /ˌæntiˈsəʊʃl; *NAmE also* -taɪˈs-/ *adj.* **1** harmful or annoying to other people, or to society in general: *antisocial behaviour* **2** not wanting to spend time with other people: *They'll think you're being antisocial if you don't go.* ➔ *compare* SOCIABLE

**ˌanti-ˈtank** *adj.* [only before noun] (of weapons) for use against enemy tanks: *anti-tank missiles/mines*

**an·tith·esis** /ænˈtɪθəsɪs/ *noun* [usually sing.] (*pl.* **an·tith·eses** /-θəsiːz/) (*formal*) **1** the opposite of sth: *Love is the antithesis of selfishness.* ◊ *Students finishing their education at 16 is the very antithesis of what society needs.* **2** a contrast between two things: *There is an antithesis between the needs of the state and the needs of the people.* ▶ **an·ti·thet·ic·al** /ˌæntɪˈθetɪkl/ *adj.*

**anti·trust** /ˌæntiˈtrʌst; *NAmE also* -taɪt-/ *adj.* [only before noun] (of laws) preventing companies or groups of companies from controlling prices unfairly

**anti·viral** /ˌæntiˈvaɪrəl; *NAmE also* -taɪˈv-/ *adj.*, *noun*
■ *adj.* (of a drug) used to treat diseases caused by a virus
■ *noun* a drug used to treat diseases caused by a virus

**anti·virus** /ˈæntivaɪrəs; *NAmE also* -taɪv-/ *adj.* (*computing*) designed to find and destroy computer viruses: *antivirus software*

**ant·ler** /ˈæntlə(r)/ *noun* [usually pl.] one of the two HORNS that grow on the head of male DEER ➔ VISUAL VOCAB page V2

**ant·onym** /ˈæntənɪm/ *noun* (*specialist*) a word that means the opposite of another word **opposite**: *'Old' has two possible antonyms: 'young' and 'new'.* ➔ *compare* SYNONYM

**antsy** /ˈæntsi/ *adj.* (*especially NAmE, informal*) impatient; not able to keep still

**anus** /ˈeɪnəs/ *noun* (*anatomy*) the opening in a person's or animal's bottom through which solid waste leaves the body ➔ VISUAL VOCAB page V1 ➔ *see also* ANAL

# anvil

**an·vil** /ˈænvɪl/ *noun* an iron block on which a BLACKSMITH puts hot pieces of metal before shaping them with a HAMMER

**anx·iety** [B2] [W] /æŋˈzaɪəti/ *noun* (*pl.* **-ies**) **1** [U] ~ **(about / over sth)** the state of feeling nervous or worried that sth bad is going to happen: *acute/intense/deep anxiety* ◊ *Some hospital patients experience high levels of anxiety.* ⇒ see also SEPARATION ANXIETY **2** [U] (*psychology*) a mental health problem that causes sb to worry so much that it has a very negative effect on their daily life: *Some people are feeling the pressure and suffering from anxiety and depression.* **3** [C] a worry or fear about sth: *If you're worried about your health, share your anxieties with your doctor.* **4** [U] a strong feeling of wanting to do sth or of wanting sth to happen: ~ **to do sth** *the candidate's anxiety to win the vote* ◊ ~ **for sth** *the people's anxiety for the war to end*

**anx·ious** [B2] /ˈæŋkʃəs/ *adj.* **1** [B2] feeling worried or nervous: *The bus was late and Sue began to get anxious.* ◊ ~ **about sth** *I felt very anxious and depressed about the future.* ◊ ~ **for sb** *Parents are naturally anxious for their children.* ⇒ SYNONYMS at WORRIED **2** [B2] causing worry; showing worry: *The family faces another anxious wait for news.* **3** wanting sth very much: ~ **to do sth** *She was anxious to finish school and get a job.* ◊ *He was anxious not to be misunderstood.* ◊ ~ **for sth** *There are plenty of graduates anxious for work.* ◊ ~ **for sb to do sth** *I'm anxious for her to do as little as possible.* ◊ ~ **that …** *She was anxious that he should meet her father.* ▶ **anx·ious·ly** *adv.*: *to ask/look/wait anxiously* ◊ *Residents are anxiously awaiting a decision.*

**any** [A1] /ˈeni/ *det., pron., adv.*
■ *det.* **1** [A1] used with uncountable or plural nouns in negative sentences and questions, after *if* or *whether*, and after some verbs such as *prevent, ban, forbid,* etc. to refer to an amount or a number of sth, however large or small: *I didn't eat any meat.* ◊ *Are there any stamps?* ◊ *I've got hardly any money.* ◊ *You can't go out without any shoes.* ◊ *He forbids any talking in class.* ◊ *She asked if we had any questions.* **HELP** In positive sentences **some** is usually used instead of **any**: *I've got some paper if you want it.* It is also used in questions that expect a positive answer: *Would you like some milk in your tea?* **2** [A1] used with singular countable nouns to refer to one of a number of things or people, when it does not matter which one: *Take any book you like.* ◊ *Any colour will do.* ◊ *Any teacher will tell you that students learn at different rates.* ⇒ see also IN ANY CASE at CASE *noun*, IN ANY EVENT at EVENT, AT ANY RATE at RATE *noun* **3** **not just ~ sb / sth** used to show that sb/sth is special: *It isn't just any day—it's my birthday!*
■ *pron.* **1** [A1] used in negative sentences and questions and after *if* or *whether* to refer to an amount or a number, however large or small: *We need some more paint; there isn't any left.* ◊ *I need some stamps. Are there any in your bag?* ◊ *Please let me know how many people are coming, if any.* ◊ *She spent hardly any of the money.* ◊ *He returned home without any of the others.* **HELP** In positive sentences **some** is usually used instead of **any**. It is also used in questions that expect a positive reply: *I've got plenty of paper—would you like some?* **2** [A1] one or more of a number of people or things, especially when it does not matter which: *I'll take any you don't want.* ◊ *'Which colour do you want?' 'Any of them will do.'*
**IDM** **sb isn't having any (of it)** (*informal*) somebody is not interested or does not agree: *I suggested sharing the cost, but he wasn't having any of it.*
■ *adv.* **1** [A2] used to emphasize an adjective or adverb in negative sentences or questions, meaning 'at all': *He wasn't any good at French.* ◊ *I can't run any faster.* ◊ *Is your father feeling any better?* ◊ *I don't want any more.* ◊ *If you don't tell them, nobody will be **any the wiser*** (= they will not find out about it). **2** (*NAmE, informal*) used at the end of a negative sentence to mean 'at all': *That won't hurt you any.*

**any·body** [A2] /ˈenibɒdi; *NAmE* -baːdi, -bʌdi/ *pron.* = ANYONE: *Is there anybody who can help me?* ◊ *Anybody can use the pool—you don't need to be a member.* ◊ *She wasn't anybody before she got that job.* ⇒ compare EVERYBODY, NOBODY, SOMEBODY

**any·hoo** /ˈenihuː/ *adv.* (*informal, non-standard*) an informal way of saying or writing 'anyhow' (when it is used to change the subject or return to a subject), for example in conversation or an email or text to a friend: *Anyhoo, where was I? Oh yeah, Dave and his new girlfriend …* **HELP** You should not write this form in formal or standard writing.

**any·how** /ˈenihaʊ/ *adv.* **1** = ANYWAY **2** in a careless way; not arranged in an order: *She piled the papers in a heap on her desk, just anyhow.*

**any ˈmore** [A2] (*BrE*) (*also* **any·more** *NAmE, BrE*) *adv.* often used at the end of negative sentences and at the end of questions, to mean 'any longer': *She doesn't live here any more.* ◊ *Why doesn't he speak to me any more?* ◊ *Now she won't have to go out to work any more.* **HELP** Do not use 'no more' with this meaning: *She doesn't live here no more.*

**any·one** [A1] /ˈeniwʌn/ (*also* **any·body**) *pron.* **1** [A1] used instead of *someone* in negative sentences and in questions after *if/whether*, and after verbs such as *prevent, forbid, avoid,* etc: *Is anyone there?* ◊ *Does **anyone else** want to come?* ◊ *Did anyone see you?* ◊ *Hardly anyone came.* ◊ *I forbid anyone to touch that clock.* **HELP** The difference between **anyone** and **someone** is the same as the difference between **any** and **some**. Look at the notes there. **2** [A1] any person at all; it does not matter who: *Anybody can see that it's wrong.* ◊ *The exercises are so simple that almost anyone can do them.* **3** (in negative sentences) an important person: *She wasn't anyone before she got that job.*

**any·place** /ˈenipleɪs/ *adv.* (*NAmE*) = ANYWHERE

**any·thing** [A1] /ˈeniθɪŋ/ *pron.* **1** [A1] used instead of *something* in negative sentences and in questions; after *if/whether*; and after verbs such as *prevent, ban, avoid,* etc: *Would you like **anything else**?* ◊ *There's never anything worth watching on TV.* ◊ *If you remember anything at all, please let us know.* ◊ *We hope to prevent anything unpleasant from happening.* **HELP** The difference between **anything** and **something** is the same as the difference between **any** and **some**. Look at the notes there. **2** [A1] any thing at all, when it does not matter which: *I'm so hungry, I'll eat anything.* **3** any thing of importance: *Is there anything* (= any truth) *in these rumours?*
**IDM** **anything but** definitely not: *The hotel was anything but cheap.* ◊ *It wasn't cheap. Anything but.* **anything like sb / sth** (*informal*) (used in questions and negative statements) similar to sb/sth: *He isn't anything like my first boss.* **as happy, quick, etc. as anything** (*informal*) very happy, quick, etc: *I felt as pleased as anything.* **like ˈanything** (*BrE, informal*) very much: *They're always slagging me off like anything.* **not anything like as good, much, etc.** used to emphasize that sth is not as good, not enough, etc: *The book wasn't anything like as good as her first one.* **not for ˈanything** (*informal*) definitely not: *I wouldn't give it up for anything.* **or anything** (*informal*) or another thing of a similar type: *If you want to call a meeting or anything, just let me know.*

**ˈany time** (*BrE*) (*also* **any·time** *NAmE, BrE*) *adv.* at a time that is not fixed: *Call me any time.*
**IDM** **any time now | any time (now)** (*informal*) very soon: *We expect more info on this any time now.* **anytime ˈsoon** (*especially NAmE*) used in negative sentences and questions to refer to the near future: *Will she be back anytime soon?*

**any·way** [A2] /ˈeniweɪ/ (*also* **any·how**) (*also NAmE, informal* **any·ways**) *adv.* **1** [A2] used when adding sth to support an idea or argument **SYN** **besides**: *It's too expensive and anyway the colour doesn't suit you.* ◊ *We're not perfect, but it doesn't really matter anyway.* **2** [A2] despite sth; even so: *It's going to happen anyway, so we won't object to it.* ◊ *I'm afraid we can't come, but thanks for the invitation anyway.* **3** [A2] used when changing the subject of a conversation, ending the conversation or returning to a subject: *So, anyway, back to what I was saying.* ◊ *Anyway, I'd better go now—I'll see you tomorrow.* **4** [A2] used to correct or slightly change what you have said: *I think she's right. I hope so, anyway.*

**any·where** ❶ **A2** /ˈeniweə(r); NAmE -wer/ (NAmE also **any·place**) *adv., pron.*
■ *adv.* **1** **A2** used in negative sentences and in questions instead of *somewhere*: *I can't see it anywhere.* ◇ *Did you go anywhere interesting?* ◇ *Many of these animals are not found anywhere else.* ◇ *He's never been anywhere outside Britain.* **HELP** The difference between **anywhere** and **somewhere** is the same as the difference between **any** and **some**. Look at the notes there. **2** **A2** in, at or to any place, when it does not matter where: *Put the box down anywhere.* ◇ *An accident can happen anywhere.*
**IDM** **anywhere from … to …** used to indicate a range: *They cost anywhere from £100 to £500.* ⇨ more at NEAR *adv.*
■ *pron.* **A2** used in negative sentences and in questions instead of *somewhere*: *I don't have anywhere to stay.* ◇ *Do you know anywhere I can get my bike repaired?* **HELP** The difference between **anywhere** and **somewhere** is the same as the difference between **any** and **some**. Look at the notes there.

**Anzac** /ˈænzæk/ *noun* (*informal*) a person from Australia or New Zealand, especially a member of the ARMED FORCES **ORIGIN** From the first letters of 'Australian and New Zealand Army Corps' during the First World War.

**AOB** /ˌeɪ əʊ ˈbiː/ *abbr.* any other business (the things that are discussed at the end of an official meeting that are not on the rest of the agenda)

**A-OK** /ˌeɪ əʊ ˈkeɪ/ *adj.* [not before noun] (NAmE, *informal*) in good condition; in an acceptable manner: *Everything's A-OK now.* ▶ **A-OK** *adv.*: *The party went off A-OK.*

**aorta** /eɪˈɔːtə; NAmE -ˈɔːrtə/ *noun* (*anatomy*) the main ARTERY that carries blood from the heart to the rest of the body once it has passed through the LUNGS

**Ao·tea·roa** /ˌaʊteɪəˈrəʊə/ *noun* the Maori name for New Zealand, usually translated as 'the land of the long white cloud'

**apace** /əˈpeɪs/ *adv.* (*formal*) at a fast speed; quickly: *to continue/grow/proceed/develop apace*

**Apa·che** /əˈpætʃi/ *noun* (*pl.* **Apa·che** or **Apa·ches**) a member of a Native American people, many of whom live in the south-western US

**apart** ❶ **B1** /əˈpɑːt; NAmE əˈpɑːrt/ *adv.* **1** **B1** separated by a distance, of space or time: *The two houses stood 500 metres apart.* ◇ *Their birthdays are only three days apart.* ◇ (*figurative*) *The two sides in the talks are still a long way apart* (= are far from reaching an agreement). **2** **B1** not together; separate or separately: *We're living apart now.* ◇ *Over the years, Rosie and I had drifted apart.* ◇ *She keeps herself apart from other people.* ◇ *I can't tell the twins apart* (= see the difference between them). **3** **B1** into pieces: *The whole thing just came apart in my hands.* ◇ *When his wife died, his world fell apart.* ◇ *Within minutes the ship began to break apart.* **4** used to say that sb/sth is not included in what you are talking about: *Victoria apart, not one of them seems suitable for the job.* **IDM** see JOKE *v.*, POLE *n.*, RIP *v.*, WORLD

**a'part from** (*also* **a'side from** *especially in NAmE*) *prep.* **1** except for: *I've finished apart from the last question.* ⇨ LANGUAGE BANK at EXCEPT **2** in addition to; as well as: *Apart from their house in London, they also have a villa in Spain.* ◇ *It was a difficult time. Apart from everything else, we had financial problems.* ◇ *You've got to help. Apart from anything else you're my brother.*

**apart·heid** /əˈpɑːtaɪt, -teɪt; NAmE əˈpɑːrt-/ *noun* [U] the former political system in South Africa in which only white people had full political rights and other people, especially black people, were forced to live away from white people, go to separate schools, etc.

**apart·ment** ❶ **A1** /əˈpɑːtmənt; NAmE əˈpɑːrt-/ *noun* **1** **A1** (*abbr.* **apt.**) (*especially NAmE*) (*BrE usually* **flat**) a set of rooms for living in, usually on one floor of a building: *an apartment building* ◇ *I was renting a two-bedroom apartment in an old building.* ◇ *A group of developers wants to build a high-rise apartment complex.* ◇ *I lived on the ground floor of an apartment block.* ⇨ compare CONDOMINIUM **2** **A1** a set of rooms used for a holiday: *self-catering holiday apartments* **3** [*usually pl.*] (*BrE*) a room in a house, especially a large or famous house: *You can visit the whole palace except for the private apartments.*

**a'partment block** (*BrE*) (NAmE **a'partment building**) *noun* a large building with flats on each floor

**a'partment house** *noun* (*US*) a small apartment block

**apa·thet·ic** /ˌæpəˈθetɪk/ *adj.* showing no interest or enthusiasm: *The illness made her apathetic and unwilling to meet people.* ▶ **apa·thet·ic·al·ly** /-kli/ *adv.*

**ap·athy** /ˈæpəθi/ *noun* [U] the feeling of not being interested in or enthusiastic about something, or things in general: *There is widespread apathy among the electorate.*

**apato·saurus** /əˌpætəˈsɔːrəs/ (*also* **bron·to·saurus**) *noun* a very large DINOSAUR with a long neck and tail

**ape** /eɪp/ *noun, verb*
■ *noun* a large animal like a monkey, with no tail. There are different types of ape: *the great apes* (= for example, OR-ANGUTANS or CHIMPANZEES)
**IDM** **go ˈape** (*also taboo* **go ˈapeshit**) (*especially NAmE, slang*) to become extremely angry or excited
■ *verb* **1** ~ **sb/sth** (*BrE, disapproving*) to do sth in the same way as sb else, especially when it is not done very well **SYN** imitate: *For years the British film industry merely aped Hollywood.* **2** ~ **sb/sth** (*especially NAmE*) to copy the way sb else behaves or talks, in order to make fun of them **SYN** mimic: *We used to ape the teacher's southern accent.*

**aperi·tif** /əˌperəˈtiːf/ *noun* a drink, usually one containing alcohol, that people sometimes have just before a meal

**aper·ture** /ˈæpətʃə(r); NAmE ˈæpərtʃʊr/ *noun* **1** (*formal*) a small opening in sth **2** (*specialist*) an opening that allows light to reach a LENS, especially in cameras: *For flash photography, set the aperture at f.5.6.*

**ape·shit** /ˈeɪpʃɪt/ *noun* (*especially NAmE, taboo, slang*)
**IDM** **go ˈapeshit** = GO APE at APE *n.*

**apex** /ˈeɪpeks/ *noun* [*usually sing.*] (*pl.* **apexes**) the top or highest part of sth: *the apex of the roof/triangle* ◇ (*figurative*) *At 37, she'd reached the apex of her career.*

**apha·sia** /əˈfeɪziə; NAmE əˈfeɪʒə/ *noun* [U] (*medical*) the loss of the ability to understand or produce speech, because of brain damage

**aphid** /ˈeɪfɪd/ *noun* a very small insect that is harmful to plants. There are several types of aphid, including, for example, GREENFLY.

**aph·or·ism** /ˈæfərɪzəm/ *noun* (*formal*) a short phrase that says sth true or wise ▶ **aph·or·is·tic** /ˌæfəˈrɪstɪk/ *adj.*

**aph·ro·dis·iac** /ˌæfrəˈdɪziæk/ *noun* a food or drug that is said to give people a strong desire to have sex ▶ **aph·ro·dis·iac** *adj.*: *the aphrodisiac qualities of ginseng*

**api·ary** /ˈeɪpiəri; NAmE -pieri/ *noun* (*pl.* **-ies**) a place where bees are kept

**apiece** /əˈpiːs/ *adv.* (used after a noun or number) having, costing or measuring a particular amount each: *Sterling and Walcott scored a goal apiece.* ◇ *The largest stones weigh over five tonnes apiece.*

**aplenty** /əˈplenti/ *adv., adj.* [after noun] (*formal*) in large amounts, especially more than is needed

**aplomb** /əˈplɒm; NAmE əˈplɑːm/ *noun* [U] (*formal*) if sb does sth **with aplomb**, they do it in a confident and successful way, often in a difficult situation: *with considerable/great/remarkable aplomb* ◇ *He delivered the speech with his usual aplomb.*

**ap·noea** (*BrE*) (*NAmE* **ap·nea**) /ˈæpniə/ *noun* [U] (*medical*) a condition in which sb stops breathing for a short time, especially while they are sleeping

**apoca·lypse** /əˈpɒkəlɪps; NAmE əˈpɑːk-/ *noun* **1** [sing., U] the DESTRUCTION of the world: *Civilization is on the brink of apocalypse.* **2 the Apocalypse** [sing.] the end of the world, as described in the Bible **3** [sing.] a situation causing very

# apocalyptic

serious damage and destruction: *an environmental apocalypse*

**apoca·lyp·tic** /əˌpɒkəˈlɪptɪk/ *NAmE* əˌpɑːk-/ *adj.* **1** describing very serious damage and DESTRUCTION in past or future events: *an apocalyptic view of history* ◊ *apocalyptic warnings of the end of society* **2** like the end of the world: *an apocalyptic scene*

**apoc·ry·pha** /əˈpɒkrɪfə; *NAmE* əˈpɑːk-/ *noun* [pl., sing. or pl. v.] **1 Apocrypha** Christian religious texts that are related to the Bible but not officially considered to be part of it **2** writings that are not considered to be what sb claims they are

**apoc·ryph·al** /əˈpɒkrɪfl; *NAmE* əˈpɑːk-/ *adj.* (of a story) well known, but probably not true: *Most of the stories about him are apocryphal.*

**apo·gee** /ˈæpədʒiː/ *noun* [sing.] **1** (*formal*) the highest point of sth, where it is greatest or most successful **2** (*astronomy*) the point in the ORBIT of the moon, a planet or other object in space when it is furthest from the planet, for example the earth, around which it turns ⇒ compare PERIGEE ⇒ picture at ORBIT

**apol·it·ical** /ˌeɪpəˈlɪtɪkl/ *adj.* **1** (of a person) not interested in politics; not thinking politics are important **2** not connected with a political party

**apolo·get·ic** /əˌpɒləˈdʒetɪk; *NAmE* əˌpɑːl-/ *adj.* feeling or showing that you are sorry for doing sth wrong or for causing a problem: *'Sorry,' she said, with an apologetic smile.* ◊ ~ **about/for sth** *They were very apologetic about the trouble they'd caused.* ▶ **apolo·get·ic·al·ly** /-kli/ *adv.* : *'I'm sorry I'm late,' he murmured apologetically.*

**apo·lo·gia** /ˌæpəˈləʊdʒiə; *NAmE* -ˈloʊdʒiə/ *noun* ~ **(for sth)** (*formal*) a formal written defence of your own or sb else's actions or opinions: *His book was seen as an apologia for the war.*

**apolo·gist** /əˈpɒlədʒɪst; *NAmE* əˈpɑːl-/ *noun* ~ **(for sth/sb)** a person who tries to explain and defend sth/sb, especially a political system or religious ideas

**apolo·gize** 🔊 **B1** (*BrE also* -**ise**) /əˈpɒlədʒaɪz; *NAmE* əˈpɑːl-/ *verb* [I] ~ **(to sb) (for sth)** to say that you are sorry for doing sth wrong or causing a problem: *Why should I apologize?* ◊ *Go and apologize to her.* ◊ *I sincerely apologize for the enormous delay in delivery.* ⇒ WORDFINDER NOTE at SORRY ⇒ EXPRESS YOURSELF AT SORRY

**apol·ogy** 🔊+ **B2** /əˈpɒlədʒi; *NAmE* əˈpɑːl-/ *noun* (*pl.* **-ies**) **1** 🔊+ **B2** [C, U] ~ **(to sb) (for sth)** a word or statement saying you are sorry for sth that has been done wrong or that causes a problem: *to offer/make/demand/accept an apology* ◊ *You owe him an apology for what you said.* ◊ *We should like to offer our apologies for the delay to your flight today.* ◊ *We received a letter of apology.* **2** [C, usually pl.] information that you cannot go to a meeting or must leave early: *The meeting started with apologies* (= the names of people who said they could not go to the meeting). ◊ (*formal*) *She made her apologies and left early.* ⇒ WORDFINDER NOTE at MEETING **IDM** **make no aˈpology/aˈpologies for sth** if you say that you **make no apology/apologies for** sth, you mean that you do not feel that you have said or done anything wrong

**apo·plec·tic** /ˌæpəˈplektɪk/ *adj.* **1** very angry: *He was apoplectic with rage at the decision.* **2** (*old-fashioned*) connected with apoplexy: *an apoplectic attack/fit*

**apo·plexy** /ˈæpəpleksi/ *noun* [U] (*old-fashioned*) the sudden loss of the ability to feel or move, normally caused by an injury in the brain ⇒ compare STROKE (4)

**aporia** /əˈpɔːriə/ *noun* (*specialist*) a situation in which two or more parts of a theory or argument do not agree, meaning that the theory or argument cannot be true

**apos·tate** /əˈpɒsteɪt; *NAmE* əˈpɑːs-/ *noun* (*formal*) a person who has rejected their religious or political beliefs ▶ **apos·tasy** /-stəsi/ *noun* [U]

**a pos·teri·ori** /ˌeɪ pɒˌsteriˈɔːraɪ; *NAmE* ˌɑː poʊˌstɪriˈɔːri/ *adj.*, *adv.* (*from Latin, formal*) analysing sth by starting from known facts and then thinking about the possible causes of the facts, for example saying 'Look, the streets are wet so it must have been raining.' ⇒ compare A PRIORI

**apos·tle** /əˈpɒsl; *NAmE* əˈpɑːsl/ *noun* **1 Apostle** any one of the twelve men that Christ chose to tell people about him and his teachings **2** ~ **(of sth)** (*formal*) a person who strongly believes in a policy or an idea and tries to make other people believe in it: *an apostle of free enterprise*

**apos·tolic** /ˌæpəˈstɒlɪk; *NAmE* -ˈstɑːl-/ *adj.* (*specialist*) **1** connected with the Apostles or their teaching **2** connected with the Pope or Popes, who are considered to have had authority passed down to them from Christ's Apostles

**apos·tro·phe** /əˈpɒstrəfi; *NAmE* əˈpɑːs-/ *noun* **1** the mark (') used to show that one or more letters or numbers have been left out, as in *she's* for *she is* and *'63* for *1963* **2** the mark (') used before or after the letter 's' to show that sth belongs to sb, as in *Sam's watch* and *the horses' tails* **3** the mark (') used before the letter 's' to show the plural of a letter or number, as in *How many 3's are there in 9?* and *There are two m's in 'comma'.*

**apoth·ecary** /əˈpɒθəkəri; *NAmE* əˈpɑːθəkeri/ *noun* (*pl.* **-ies**) a person who made and sold medicines in the past

**apoth·eosis** /əˌpɒθiˈəʊsɪs; *NAmE* əˌpɑːθiˈoʊ-/ *noun* [usually sing.] (*pl.* **apothe·oses** /-ˈəʊsiːz/) (*formal*) **1** the highest or most perfect development of sth **2** the best time in sb's life or career **3** a formal statement that a person has become a god: *the apotheosis of a Roman emperor*

**app** 🔊 **A2** /æp/ *noun* **1** 🔊 **A2** a piece of software that you can download to a device such as a smartphone or tablet, for example to look up information or to play a game: *You first need to* **install the app** *on your device.* ◊ **to download/launch an app** ◊ **to build/develop an app** ◊ *Gaming today is all about* **mobile app** *downloads.* ◊ **app developers** ◊ *The app is available on/in the* **app store**. ⇒ see also IN-APP **2** = APPLICATION (5) ⇒ see also KILLER APP

**appa** /ˈæpə/ *noun* (*IndE*) = ABBA

**appal** (*BrE*) (*NAmE* **ap·pall**) /əˈpɔːl/ *verb* (**-ll-**) to make sb feel extremely shocked and feel very strongly that sth is bad **SYN** horrify: ~ **sb** *The brutality of the crime has appalled the public.* ◊ *The idea of sharing a room appalled her.* ◊ **it appals sb that …/to do sth** *It appalled me that they could simply ignore the problem.*

**ap·palled** /əˈpɔːld/ *adj.* feeling or showing horror at sth unpleasant or wrong **SYN** horrified: *an appalled expression/silence* ◊ *We watched appalled as the child ran in front of the car.* ◊ ~ **at sth** *They were appalled at the waste of recyclable material.*

**ap·pal·ling** /əˈpɔːlɪŋ/ *adj.* **1** (*NAmE, formal* or *BrE*) extremely bad, especially from a moral point of view **SYN** shocking: *The prisoners were living in appalling conditions.* **2** (*informal*) very bad; of very poor quality: *The bus service is appalling now.* ▶ **ap·pal·ling·ly** *adv.* : *appallingly bad/difficult* ◊ *The essay was appallingly written.*

**ap·par·at·chik** /ˌæpəˈrætʃɪk; *NAmE* ˌɑːpəˈrɑːtʃ-/ *noun* (*from Russian, disapproving* or *humorous*) an official in a large political organization: *party apparatchiks*

**ap·par·atus** 🔊+ **C1** /ˌæpəˈreɪtəs; *NAmE* -ˈræt-/ *noun* (*pl.* **ap·par·atuses**) **1** 🔊+ **C1** [U] the tools or other pieces of equipment that are needed for a particular activity or task: *a piece of laboratory apparatus* ◊ *Firefighters needed breathing apparatus to enter the burning house.* ⇒ SYNONYMS at EQUIPMENT **2** 🔊+ **C1** [C, usually sing.] the structure of a system or an organization, particularly that of a political party or a government: *the power of the state apparatus* **3** [C, usually sing.] (*specialist*) a system of organs in the body: *the sensory apparatus*

**ap·parel** /əˈpærəl/ *noun* [U] **1** (*especially NAmE*) clothing, when it is being sold in shops: *The store sells women's and children's apparel.* **2** (*old-fashioned* or *formal*) clothes, particularly those worn on a formal occasion: *lords and ladies in fine apparel*

**ap·par·ent** 🔊 **B2** 🔊 /əˈpærənt/ *adj.* **1** 🔊 **B2** [not usually before noun] easy to see or understand **SYN** obvious: *Their devotion was apparent.* ◊ *Then, for no apparent reason, the train suddenly stopped.* ◊ ~ **(from sth) (that …)** *It was apparent from her face that she was really upset.* ◊ ~ **(to sb) (that …)** *It soon became apparent to everyone that he couldn't sing.* ⇒ SYNONYMS at CLEAR ⇒ LANGUAGE BANK at

ILLUSTRATE **2** B2 [usually before noun] that seems to be real or true but may not be SYN **seeming**: *My parents were concerned at my **apparent** lack of enthusiasm for school.* ⊃ see also APPEAR

**ap·par·ent·ly** ⓘ B2 /əˈpærəntli/ *adv.* according to what you have heard or read; according to the way sth appears: *Apparently they are getting divorced soon.* ◇ *I thought she had retired, but apparently she hasn't.* ◇ *He paused, apparently lost in thought.*

**ap·par·ition** /ˌæpəˈrɪʃn/ *noun* a ghost or a ghost-like image of a person who is dead

**ˈapp drawer** (*also* **ˈapp tray**) *noun* a collection of all the apps that are installed on a device such as a smartphone or tablet

**ap·peal** ⓘ B2 /əˈpiːl/ *noun, verb*
■ *noun* **1** B2 [C, U] a deeply felt request for money, help or information that is needed immediately, especially one made by a charity or by the police: *~ (to sb) (for sth) to launch a TV appeal for donations to the charity* ◇ *~ to sb to do sth The police made an appeal to the public to remain calm.* ◇ *There was a look of silent appeal on his face.* ⊃ WORDFINDER NOTE at CHARITY **2** B2 [U] a quality that makes sb/sth attractive or interesting: *mass/wide/popular/broad/universal appeal* ◇ *The Beatles have never really lost their appeal.* ◇ *The prospect of living in a city holds little appeal for me.* ⊃ see also SEX APPEAL **3** B2 [C, U] a formal request to a court or to sb in authority for a judgement or a decision to be changed: (*BrE*) *to lodge an appeal* ◇ (*NAmE*) *to file an appeal* ◇ (*BrE*) *an appeal court/judge* ◇ (*NAmE*) *an appeals court/judge* ◇ *~against sth They have launched appeals against their convictions.* ◇ *on ~ The case was upheld on appeal.* ⊃ WORDFINDER NOTE at TRIAL ⊃ see also COURT OF APPEAL **4** [C] *~to sth* an indirect suggestion that any good, fair or reasonable person would act in a particular way: *I relied on an appeal to his finer feelings.*
■ *verb* **1** B2 [I] to make a deeply felt request, especially for sth that is needed immediately: *I am appealing* (= asking for money) *on behalf of the famine victims.* ◇ *~ (to sb) (for sth) Community leaders appealed for calm* (= urged people to remain calm). ◇ *~ for sb to do sth Police have appealed for witnesses to come forward.* ◇ *~ to sb to do sth Organizers appealed to the crowd not to panic.* **2** B2 [I] to attract or interest sb: *The prospect of a long wait in the rain did not appeal.* ◇ *~ to sb The design has to appeal to all ages and social groups.* **3** B2 [I] to make a formal request to a court or to sb in authority for a judgment or a decision to be changed: *He said he would appeal after being found guilty on four counts of murder.* ◇ *~ (to sb/sth) (against sth) The company is appealing against the ruling.* **HELP** In North American English, the form **appeal (sth) (to sb/sth)** is usually used, without a preposition: *The company has ten days to appeal the decision to the tribunal.* **4** [I] *~ (to sb)* to try to persuade sb to do sth by suggesting that it is a fair, reasonable or honest thing to do: *They needed to appeal to his sense of justice.*

**apˈpeal court** *noun* = COURT OF APPEAL

**ap·peal·ing** B2+ C1 /əˈpiːlɪŋ/ *adj.* **1** B2+ C1 attractive or interesting: *Spending the holidays in Britain wasn't a prospect that I found particularly appealing.* OPP **unappealing 2** showing that you want people to help you or to show you sympathy: *'Would you really help?' he said with an appealing look.* ▸ **ap·peal·ing·ly** *adv.*: *The dog looked up at her appealingly.*

**ap·pear** ⓘ A2 ⓞ /əˈpɪə(r); NAmE əˈpɪr/ *verb*
• BE SEEN **1** A2 [I] to start to be seen: *Three days later a rash appeared.* ◇ *+ adv./prep. A cat suddenly appeared out of nowhere.* ◇ *Smoke appeared on the horizon.*
• BEGIN TO EXIST **2** A2 [I] to begin to exist or be known or used for the first time: *Scientists are unsure when the virus first appeared.* ◇ *+ adv./prep. His work began to appear on the scene in the 1960s.*
• LOOK/SEEM **3** B1 *linking verb* (not used in the progressive tenses) to give the impression of being or doing sth SYN **seem**: *+ adj. She didn't appear at all surprised at the news.* ◇ *it appears + adj. It now appears likely that the school will be closed down.* ◇ *+ noun He appears a perfectly normal person.* ◇ *~ to do sth The couple appeared to have nothing in common.* ◇ *They appeared not to know what was happening.* ◇ *There appears to have been a mistake.* ◇ *it appears (that) … It appears that there has been a mistake.* ◇ *It would appear that this was a major problem.* ◇ *~ as if … The sunset made it appear as if the sea was made of gold.* ⊃ LANGUAGE BANK at PERHAPS
• OF BOOK, ARTICLE, PROGRAMME, ETC. **4** [I] (*+ adv./prep.*) to be published or broadcast: *His new book will be appearing in the spring.* ◇ *It was too late to prevent the story from appearing in the national newspapers.*
• IN FILM/PLAY **5** [I] (*+ adv./prep.*) to take part in a film, play, television programme, etc: *He has appeared in over 60 movies.* ◇ *She regularly appears on TV.*
• ARRIVE **6** [I] (*+ adv./prep.*) to arrive at a place: *By ten o'clock Lee still hadn't appeared.*
• BE WRITTEN/MENTIONED **7** [I] (*+ adv./prep.*) to be written or mentioned somewhere: *Your name will appear at the front of the book.*
• IN COURT **8** [I] (*+ adv./prep.*) to be present in court in order to give evidence or answer a charge: *A man will appear in court today charged with the murder.* ◇ *She appeared on six charges of theft.* ◇ *He has been asked to appear as a witness for the defence.* **9** [I] *~ for/on behalf of sb* to act as sb's lawyer in court: *James Gilbert is the lawyer appearing for the defendant.* ⊃ compare DISAPPEAR ⊃ see also APPARENT

**ap·pear·ance** ⓘ A2 /əˈpɪərəns; NAmE əˈpɪr-/ *noun*
• WAY STH LOOKS/SEEMS **1** A2 [C, U] the way that sb/sth looks on the outside; what sb/sth seems to be: *the physical/outward/external appearance of sth* ◇ *She had never been greatly concerned about her appearance.* ◇ *The dog was similar in general appearance to a spaniel.* ◇ *He gave every appearance of* (= seemed very much to be) *enjoying himself.* ◇ *Judging by appearances can be misleading.* ◇ *To all appearances* (= as far as people could tell) *he was dead.*
• SB/STH ARRIVING **2** B2 [C, usually sing.] the fact of sb/sth arriving, especially when it is not expected: *The sudden appearance of a security guard caused them to drop the money and run.* ◇ *I don't want to go to the party, but I suppose I'd better put in an appearance* (= go there for a short time). **3** B2 [C, usually sing.] the moment at which sth begins to exist or starts to be seen or used: *the early appearance of daffodils in spring* ◇ *the appearance of organic vegetables in the supermarkets*
• IN PUBLIC **4** [C] an act of appearing in public, especially as a performer, politician, etc., or in court: *The Dutch player will make his first appearance for Liverpool this Saturday.* ◇ *The show featured a guest appearance from Amy Schumer.* ◇ *The singer's first public appearance was at the age of eight.* ◇ *the defendant's appearance in court* ◇ *a court appearance*
• BEING PUBLISHED/BROADCAST **5** [C, usually sing.] an act of being published or broadcast: *the appearance of claims about the minister's private life in the press*
IDM **keep up apˈpearances** to hide the truth about a bad situation and pretend that everything is going well: *When she lost all her money she was determined to keep up appearances.*

**ap·pease** /əˈpiːz/ *verb* (*formal, usually disapproving*) **1** *~ sb* to make sb calmer or less angry by giving them what they want: *The move was widely seen as an attempt to appease critics of the regime.* **2** *~ sb/sth* to give a country what it wants in order to avoid war ▸ **ap·pease·ment** *noun* [U]: *a policy of appeasement*

**ap·pel·lant** /əˈpelənt/ *noun* (*law*) a person who APPEALS against a decision made in court

**ap·pel·late court** /əˈpelət kɔːt; NAmE kɔːrt/ *noun* (*specialist*) a court in which people can appeal against decisions made in other courts of law

**ap·pel·la·tion** /ˌæpəˈleɪʃn/ *noun* (*formal*) a name or title

**ap·pend** /əˈpend/ *verb* *~ sth (to sth)* (*formal*) to add sth to the end of a piece of writing: *Footnotes have been appended to the document.*

# appendage

**ap·pend·age** /əˈpendɪdʒ/ noun 1 (formal) a thing that is added or attached to sth larger or more important: *They treat Scotland as a mere appendage of England.* 2 (biology) part of a living thing, such as an insect, that sticks out and has a particular function

**ap·pend·ec·tomy** /ˌæpenˈdektəmi/ (BrE also **ap·pend·i·cec·tomy** /ˌæpendɪˈsektəmi/) noun [C, U] (pl. **-ies**) (medical) a medical operation to remove the appendix

**ap·pen·di·citis** /əˌpendəˈsaɪtɪs/ noun [U] a serious medical condition in which the appendix becomes painful and larger than normal

**ap·pen·dix** /əˈpendɪks/ noun (pl. **ap·pen·dixes** or **ap·pen·di·ces** /-dɪsiːz/) HELP The plural form is usually **appendixes** in sense 1 (body parts) and **appendices** in sense 2 (in a book or document). 1 a small bag of TISSUE that is attached to the large INTESTINE. In humans, the appendix has no clear function: *He had to have his appendix out* (= removed). ⇒ VISUAL VOCAB page V1 2 a section giving extra information at the end of a book or document: *Full details are given in Appendix 3.*

**ap·per·tain** /ˌæpəˈteɪn; NAmE ˌæpərˈt-/ verb
PHRV **apper'tain to sb/sth** (formal) to belong or refer to sth/sb: *rights appertaining to the property* ◇ *These figures appertain to last year's sales.*

**ap·pe·tite** ⓛ+ C1 /ˈæpɪtaɪt/ noun 1 ⓛ+ C1 [U, C, usually sing.] physical desire for food: *He suffered from headaches and loss of appetite.* ◇ *The walk gave me a good appetite.* ◇ *Don't spoil your appetite by eating between meals.* 2 ⓛ+ C1 [C] a strong desire for sth: *sexual appetites* ◇ *The preview was intended to whet your appetite* (= make you want more). ◇ **for sth** *The public have an insatiable appetite for scandal.* ◇ *There is no appetite for* (= people do not want) *massive federal investment in the US.*

**ap·pe·tizer** (BrE also **-iser**) /ˈæpɪtaɪzə(r)/ noun 1 a small amount of food or a drink that you have before a meal 2 (NAmE) (also **starter** especially in BrE) a small dish of food that is served before the main course of a meal

**ap·pe·tiz·ing** (BrE also **-is·ing**) /ˈæpɪtaɪzɪŋ/ adj. (of food, etc.) that smells or looks attractive; making you feel hungry or thirsty OPP **unappetizing**

**ap·plaud** ⓛ+ C1 /əˈplɔːd/ verb 1 ⓛ+ C1 [I, T] to show your approval of sb/sth by CLAPPING your hands (= hitting your open hands together several times) SYN **clap**: *He started to applaud and the others joined in.* ◇ **~ sb** *They rose to applaud the speaker.* ◇ *She was applauded as she came on stage.* 2 ⓛ+ C1 [T] (formal) to express praise for sb/sth because you approve of them or it: **~ sth** *We applaud her decision.* ◇ *His efforts to improve the situation are to be applauded.* ◇ **~ sb (for sth)** *I applaud her for having the courage to refuse.*

**ap·plause** /əˈplɔːz/ noun [U] the noise made by a group of people CLAPPING their hands and sometimes shouting to show their approval or pleasure: *Give her a big round of applause!* ◇ *The audience broke into rapturous applause.*

**apple** ⓞ A1 /ˈæpl/ noun a round fruit with shiny red or green skin that is fairly hard and white inside: *Peel and core the apples.* ◇ *an apple pie* ◇ *apple sauce/juice* ◇ *a garden with three apple trees* ⇒ VISUAL VOCAB page V4 ⇒ see also ADAM'S APPLE, BIG APPLE, CRAB APPLE, CUSTARD APPLE, TOFFEE APPLE
IDM **the apple doesn't fall/never falls far from the 'tree** (saying, especially NAmE) a child usually behaves in a similar way to his or her parent(s) **the ,apple of sb's 'eye** a person or thing that is loved more than any other **,apples and 'oranges** (especially NAmE) used to describe a situation in which two people or things are completely different from each other: *They really are apples and oranges.* ◇ *They are both great but you can't compare apples and oranges.* **a bad/rotten apple** one bad person who has a bad effect on others in a group ⇒ more at AMERICAN adj.

**'apple cart** noun IDM see UPSET v.

**,apple 'cider** noun [U, C] (NAmE) = CIDER (2)

**,apple 'pie** noun 1 [C, U] apples baked in a dish with PASTRY on the bottom, sides and top: *a slice of apple pie* 2 [U] (NAmE) used to represent an idea of perfect home life and comfort: *Who could argue against motherhood and apple pie?* IDM see AMERICAN adj.

**ap·pli·ance** /əˈplaɪəns/ noun a machine that is designed to do a particular thing in the home, such as preparing food, heating or cleaning: *electrical/household appliances* ◇ *They sell a wide range of domestic appliances—washing machines, dishwashers and so on.* ⇒ WORDFINDER NOTE at STORE

**ap·plic·able** ⓛ+ C1 W /əˈplɪkəbl, ˈæplɪkəbl; NAmE ˈæplɪkəbl, əˈplɪkəbl/ adj. [not usually before noun] that can be said to be true in the case of sb/sth SYN **relevant**: *Give details of children where applicable* (= if you have any). ◇ **~ to sb/sth** *Much of the form was not applicable* (= did not apply) *to me.* ▶ **ap·plic·abil·ity** /əˌplɪkəˈbɪləti, ˌæplɪ-; NAmE ˌæplɪkəˈbɪləti, əˌplɪ-/ noun [U]: *The new approach had wide applicability to all sorts of different problems.*

**ap·pli·cant** ⓛ+ B2 /ˈæplɪkənt/ noun **~ (for sth)** a person who makes a formal request for sth (= applies for it), especially for a job, a place at a college or university, etc: *There were over 500 applicants for the job.*

**ap·pli·ca·tion** ⓞ B1 W /ˌæplɪˈkeɪʃn/ noun
• FOR JOB/COURSE 1 ⓛ B1 [C, U] a formal (often written) request for sth, such as a job, permission to do sth or a place at a college or university: *a planning/patent/visa application* ◇ *We have received applications from more than 3000 students.* ◇ *You need to complete the online application form.* ◇ **for sth/to do sth** *an application for asylum/a licence* ◇ **~ to sb (for sth)** *His application to the court for bail has been refused.* ◇ **~ to sb to do sth** *They submitted an application to the council to build two houses.* ◇ **on ~ to sb** *Further information is available on application to the principal.*
• PRACTICAL USE 2 ⓛ B2 [C, U] the practical use of sth, especially a theory, discovery, etc: *The invention would have a wide range of applications in industry.* ◇ *What are the practical applications of this work?* ◇ **~ (of sth) to sth** *the application of new technology to teaching*
• OF PAINT/CREAM 3 [C, U] an act of putting or spreading sth, such as paint or medical creams, onto sth else: *It took three applications of paint to cover the graffiti.* ◇ *lotion for external application only* (= to be put on the skin, not swallowed)
• OF RULE/LAW 4 [U] an act of making a rule, etc. operate or become effective: *strict application of the law*
• COMPUTING 5 [C] (abbr. **app**) a program designed to do a particular job; a piece of software: *a database application* ⇒ WORDFINDER NOTE at SOFTWARE ⇒ see also KILLER APP
• HARD WORK 6 [U] (formal) the strength of mind to work hard at sth; great effort: *Success as a writer demands great application.*

**ap·pli·ca·tor** /ˈæplɪkeɪtə(r)/ noun a small tool that is used to put a substance onto a surface, or to put sth into an object: *Use the applicator to apply cream to the affected area.*

**ap·plied** /əˈplaɪd/ adj. [usually before noun] (especially of a subject of study) used in a practical way; not THEORETICAL: *applied mathematics* (= as used by engineers, etc.) ⇒ compare PURE

**ap,plied lin'guistics** noun [U] the scientific study of language as it relates to practical problems, in areas such as teaching and dealing with speech problems

**ap·pli·qué** /əˈpliːkeɪ; NAmE ˌæpləˈkeɪ/ noun [U] a type of NEEDLEWORK in which small pieces of cloth are SEWN or stuck in a pattern onto a larger piece ▶ **ap·pli·quéd** adj.

**apply** ⓞ A2 ⓞ /əˈplaɪ/ verb (**ap·plies, ap·ply·ing, ap·plied, ap·plied**)
• FOR JOB/COURSE 1 ⓛ A2 [I, T] to make a formal request, usually in writing, for sth such as a job, a loan, permission for sth, a place at a university, etc: *You should apply in person/by letter.* ◇ **~ for sth** *I have decided to apply for this new job.* ◇ *to apply for a visa/passport/grant/licence* ◇ *The developers applied for planning permission to build over 200 houses.* ◇ **~ to sb/sth (for sth)** *to apply to a company/*

university ◇ **~to do sth** *He has applied to join the army.*
◯ WORDFINDER NOTE at EMPLOY

> **WORDFINDER** appoint, candidate, CV, experience, interview, job description, qualification, reference, shortlist

- **BE RELEVANT 2** 🔑 **B2** [I, T] (not used in the progressive tenses) to affect or be relevant to sb/sth: *Special conditions apply if you are under 18.* ◇ **~to sb/sth** *The rules applied to employees and their behaviour at work.* ◇ *The law applied only to foreign nationals.* ◇ **~sth to sb/sth** *The word 'unexciting' could never be applied to her novels.*
- **USE 3** 🔑 **B2** [T] to use sth or make sth work in a particular situation: **~sth** *to* **apply political pressure** ◇ **~sth to sth** *The new technology was applied to farming.*
- **PAINT/CREAM 4** 🔑 **B2** [T] to put or spread sth such as paint, cream, etc. onto a surface: **~sth to sth** *Apply the cream sparingly to your face and neck.* ◇ **~sth** *She combed her hair and carefully applied her make-up.*
- **WORK HARD 5** [T] to work at sth or study sth very hard: **~yourself** *You would pass your exams if you applied yourself.* ◇ **~yourself/sth to (doing) sth** *We applied our minds to finding a solution to our problem.*
- **PRESS HARD 6** [T] to press on sth hard with your hand, foot, etc. to make sth work or have an effect on sth: **~sth** *to apply the brakes (of a vehicle)* ◇ **~sth to sth** *Pressure applied to the wound will stop the bleeding.*

**ap·point** 🔑+ **C1** /əˈpɔɪnt/ *verb* 1 🔑+ **C1** to choose sb for a job or position of responsibility: **~sb** *They have appointed a new head teacher at my son's school.* ◇ **~sb to sth** *She has recently been appointed to the committee.* ◇ **~sb (as) sth** *They appointed him (as) captain of the English team.* ◇ **~sb to do sth** *A lawyer was appointed to represent the child.*
◯ WORDFINDER NOTE at APPLY **2** [usually passive] (*formal*) to arrange or decide on a time or place for doing sth: **be appointed** *A date for the meeting is still to be appointed.* ◇ *Everyone was assembled at the **appointed time**.*

**ap·point·ee** /əˌpɔɪnˈtiː/ *noun* a person who has been chosen for a job or position of responsibility: *the new appointee to the post*

**ap·point·ment** 🛈 **B1** /əˈpɔɪntmənt/ *noun* 1 🔑 **B1** [C] a formal arrangement to meet or visit sb at a particular time, especially for a reason connected with their work: *I've got a **dental appointment** at 3 o'clock.* ◇ *to **book/make/keep an appointment*** ◇ *Viewing is **by appointment only*** (= only at a time that has been arranged in advance). ◇ **~with sb** *an appointment with my agent/doctor/specialist/consultant* ◇ **~for sth** *an appointment for a blood test* ◇ **~for sb to do sth** *She made an appointment for her son to see the doctor.* **2** [C, U] the act of choosing a person for a job or position of responsibility; the fact of being chosen for a job, etc: *They announced the **appointments** of key security officials.* ◇ **~to sth** *her recent appointment to the post* ◇ **~as sth** *his appointment as principal* **3** [C] a job or position of responsibility: *a permanent/first appointment*
◯ SYNONYMS at JOB

**ap·point·ment book** (*NAmE*) (*BrE* **diary**) *noun* a book or an app with spaces for each day of the year in which you can record things you have to do in the future

**ap·por·tion** /əˈpɔːʃn; *NAmE* əˈpɔːrʃn/ *verb* (*formal*) to divide sth among people; to give a share of sth to sb: **~sth** *The programme gives the facts but does not apportion blame.* ◇ **~sth among/between/to sb** *They apportioned the land among members of the family.* ▶ **ap·por·tion·ment** *noun* [U, C] (*formal*): *The apportionment of seats in the House of Representatives is based on the population of each state.*

**ap·po·site** /ˈæpəzɪt/ *adj.* **~(to sth)** (*formal*) very appropriate for a particular situation or in relation to sth

**ap·prais·al** /əˈpreɪzl/ *noun* [C, U] **1** a judgement of the value, performance or nature of sb/sth: *He had read many detailed critical appraisals of her work.* ◇ *She was honest in her appraisal of her team's chances.* **2** (*especially BrE*) (*also* **performance review** *BrE and NAmE*) a meeting in which an employee discusses with their manager how well they have been doing their job; the system of holding such meetings: *I have my appraisal today.* ◇ **staff/performance appraisal**

**ap·praise** /əˈpreɪz/ *verb* **1** **~sb/sth** (*formal*) to consider or examine sb/sth and form an opinion about them or it: *an **appraising glance/look*** ◇ *His eyes coolly appraised the young woman before him.* ◇ *She stepped back to appraise her workmanship.* **2** **~sth (at sth)** to officially examine a building, an object, etc. and say how much it is worth: *They appraised the painting at £200 000.* **3** **~sb** (*BrE*) to make a formal judgement about the value of a person's work, usually after a discussion with them about it: *Managers must appraise all staff.*

**ap·prais·er** /əˈpreɪzə(r)/ *noun* **1** (*NAmE*) (*BrE* **valuer**) a person whose job is to examine a building, an object, etc. and say how much it is worth **2** (*BrE*) a person who makes a formal judgement about the value of a person's work, usually after discussion with them about it

**ap·pre·ci·able** /əˈpriːʃəbl/ *adj.* large enough to be noticed or thought important **SYN** **considerable**: *The new regulations will not make an appreciable difference to most people.* ◇ *an **appreciable effect/increase/amount*** ▶ **ap·preciably** /-bli/ *adv.*: *The risk of infection is appreciably higher among children.*

**ap·pre·ci·ate** 🛈 **B1** /əˈpriːʃieɪt/ *verb* **1** 🔑 [T] (not used in the progressive tenses) **~sb/sth** to recognize the good qualities of sb/sth: *Over the years he came to appreciate the beauty and tranquillity of the river.* ◇ *His talents are not fully appreciated in that company.* ◇ *Her family doesn't appreciate her.* **2** 🔑 **B1** [T] (not usually used in the progressive tenses) to be grateful for sth that sb has done; to welcome sth: **~sth** *I'd appreciate some help.* ◇ *Your support is greatly appreciated.* ◇ *Thanks for coming. I appreciate it.* ◇ *Your kindness and generosity is much appreciated.* ◇ *I would appreciate it if you paid in cash.* ◇ **~doing sth** *I appreciate having the opportunity to discuss these important issues with you.* ◇ **~sb doing sth** *We would appreciate you letting us know of any problems.* ◯ EXPRESS YOURSELF at THANK **3** [T] (not used in the progressive tenses) to understand that sth is true **SYN** **realize**: **~sth** *What I failed to appreciate was the distance between the two cities.* ◇ **~how, what, etc ...** *I don't think you appreciate how expensive it will be.* ◇ **~that ...** *We didn't fully appreciate that he was seriously ill.* **OPP** **depreciate** **4** [I] to increase in value over a period of time: *Their investments have appreciated over the years.* ◇ **~against sth** *The euro continues to appreciate against the dollar.*

**ap·pre·ci·ation** 🔑+ **C1** /əˌpriːʃiˈeɪʃn/ *noun* **1** 🔑+ **C1** [U] pleasure that you have when you recognize and enjoy the good qualities of sb/sth: *She shows little appreciation of good music.* ◇ **in~** *The crowd murmured in appreciation.* **2** 🔑+ **C1** [U, sing.] **~of sth** a full understanding of sth, such as a situation or a problem, and of what it involves: *I had no appreciation of the problems they faced.* **3** 🔑+ **C1** [U, sing.] the feeling of being grateful for sth: **in~ of sth** *Please accept this gift in appreciation of all you've done for us.* ◇ **~for/of sth** *She never shows any appreciation for our efforts.* **4** [U, sing.] **~(in sth)** increase in value over a period of time **OPP** **depreciation 5** [C] **~(of sth)** (*formal*) a piece of writing or a speech in which the strengths and weaknesses of sb/sth, especially an artist or a work of art, are discussed and judged

**ap·pre·cia·tive** /əˈpriːʃətɪv/ *adj.* **1** **~(of sth)** feeling or showing that you are grateful for sth: *The company was very appreciative of my efforts.* **2** showing pleasure: *an **appreciative audience/smile*** ◇ *appreciative laughter/comments* ▶ **ap·pre·cia·tive·ly** *adv.*

**ap·pre·hend** /ˌæprɪˈhend/ *verb* (*formal*) **1** **~sb** (of the police) to catch sb and arrest them **2** **~sth** (*old-fashioned*) to understand or recognize sth

**ap·pre·hen·sion** /ˌæprɪˈhenʃn/ *noun* **1** [U, C] worry or fear that sth unpleasant may happen **SYN** **anxiety**: *There is growing apprehension that fighting will begin again.* ◇ *He watched the election results with some apprehension.* ◇ *childhood fears and apprehensions* **2** [U] (*formal*) the act of capturing or arresting sb, usually by the police

**ap·pre·hen·sive** /ˌæprɪˈhensɪv/ *adj.* worried or frightened that sth unpleasant may happen: *an apprehensive*

# apprentice 64

face/glance/look ◊ **~about/of sth** *I was a little apprehensive about the effects of what I had said.* ◊ *You have no reason to be apprehensive of the future.* ◊ **~that …** *She was deeply apprehensive that something might go wrong.* ▶ **ap·pre·hen·sive·ly** *adv.*

**ap·pren·tice** /əˈprentɪs/ *noun, verb*
- *noun* a young person who works for an employer for a fixed period of time in order to learn the particular skills needed in their job: *an apprentice electrician/chef* ⊃ WORDFINDER NOTE at TRAINING
- *verb* [usually passive] **~sb (to sb) (as sth)** (*old-fashioned*) to make sb an apprentice

**ap·pren·tice·ship** /əˈprentɪʃɪp/ *noun* [C, U] a period of time working as an apprentice; a job as an apprentice: *She was in the second year of her apprenticeship as a carpenter.* ◊ *He had served his apprenticeship as a plumber.*

**ap·prise** /əˈpraɪz/ *verb* **~sb of sth** (*formal*) to tell or inform sb of sth

**ap·proach** ⓘ B2 ⓞ /əˈprəʊtʃ/ *noun, verb*
- *noun*
- TO PROBLEM/TASK **1** B2 [C] a way of dealing with sb/sth; a way of doing or thinking about sth such as a problem or a task: *She took the wrong approach in her dealings with them.* ◊ *It was time to take a different approach.* ◊ **~to sth** *We need to adopt a new approach to the problem.* ◊ **~for (doing) sth** | **~for doing sth** *Will this be a successful approach for providing high-tech offices?* ⊃ WORDFINDER NOTE at BEHAVIOUR
- MOVEMENT NEARER **2** B2 [sing.] movement nearer to sb/sth in distance or time: *She hadn't heard his approach and jumped as the door opened.* ◊ *the approach of spring*
- OFFER/REQUEST **3** [C] the act of speaking to sb about sth, especially when making an offer or a request: *The club has made an approach to a local company for sponsorship.*
- PATH/ROAD **4** [C] a path, road, etc. that leads to a place: *All the approaches to the palace were guarded by troops.* ◊ *a new approach road to the port*
- OF AIRCRAFT **5** [C] the part of an aircraft's flight immediately before landing: *to begin the final approach to the runway*
- STH SIMILAR **6** [sing.] a thing that is like sth else that is mentioned: *That's the nearest approach to an apology you'll get from him.* IDM see CARROT
- *verb*
- MOVE NEAR **1** B2 [I, T] to come near to sb/sth in distance or time: *We could hear the train approaching.* ◊ *The deadline was fast approaching.* ◊ **~sb/sth** *She's approaching the end of her first year in the job.* ◊ **~(sb/sth) from …** *The men approached the creature cautiously from behind.*
- OFFER/ASK **2** B2 [T] to speak to sb about sth, especially to ask them for sth or to offer to do sth: **~sb** *We have been approached by a number of companies that are interested in our product.* ◊ *I'd like to ask his opinion but I find him difficult to approach* (= not easy to talk to in a friendly way). ◊ **~sb for sth** *She was often approached for help and advice.* ◊ **~sb about (doing) sth** *Have you approached John about organizing a concert?*
- AMOUNT/QUALITY **3** B2 [T] **~sth** to come close to sth in amount, level or quality: *Interest rates are approaching zero.* ◊ *Few writers approach his richness of language.*
- PROBLEM/TASK **4** B2 [T] **~sth** to start dealing with a problem, task, etc. in a particular way: *to approach a subject/matter/task/question* ◊ *What's the best way to approach this problem?* ◊ *The issues should be approached with caution.*

**ap·proach·able** /əˈprəʊtʃəbl/ *adj.* **1** friendly and easy to talk to; easy to understand: *Despite being a big star, she's very approachable.* ◊ *an approachable piece of music* OPP **unapproachable** **2** [not usually before noun] that can be reached by a particular route or from a particular direction: *The summit was approachable only from the south.*

**ap·pro·ba·tion** /ˌæprəˈbeɪʃn/ *noun* [U] (*formal*) approval or agreement

**ap·pro·pri·ate** ⓘ B2 ⓦ *adj., verb*
- *adj.* B2 /əˈprəʊpriət/ suitable, acceptable or correct for the particular circumstances: *an appropriate response/measure/method* ◊ *Now that the problem has been identified, appropriate action can be taken.* ◊ *Is now an appropriate time to make a speech?* ◊ *Please debit my Mastercard/Visa/American Express card (delete as appropriate)* (= cross out the options that do not apply). ◊ **~for sth** *Jeans are not appropriate for a formal party.* ◊ **~to sth** *The book was written in a style appropriate to the age of the children.* OPP **inappropriate** ▶ **ap·pro·pri·ate·ness** *noun* [U]
- *verb* /əˈprəʊprieɪt/ (*formal*) **1** **~sth** to take sth, sb's ideas, etc. for your own use, especially illegally or without permission: *He was accused of appropriating club funds.* ◊ *Some of the opposition party's policies have been appropriated by the government.* **2** **~sth (for sth)** to take or give sth, especially money for a particular purpose: *Five million dollars have been appropriated for research into the disease.* ⊃ compare MISAPPROPRIATE

**ap·pro·pri·ate·ly** B2+ ⓦ /əˈprəʊpriətli/ *adv.* in a way that is suitable, acceptable or correct for the particular circumstances: *The government has been accused of not responding appropriately to the needs of the homeless.* ◊ *The chain of volcanoes is known, appropriately enough, as the 'Ring of Fire'.*

**ap·pro·pri·ation** /əˌprəʊpriˈeɪʃn/ *noun* **1** [U, sing.] (*formal or law*) the act of taking sth that belongs to sb else, especially without permission: *dishonest appropriation of property* ⊃ compare MISAPPROPRIATION ⊃ see also CULTURAL APPROPRIATION **2** [U, sing.] (*formal*) the act of keeping or saving money for a particular purpose: *a meeting to discuss the appropriation of funds* **3** [C] (*formal*) a sum of money to be used for a particular purpose, especially by a government or company: *an appropriation of £20000 for payment of debts*

**ap·prov·al** ⓘ B2 /əˈpruːvl/ *noun* **1** B2 [U] the feeling that sb/sth is good or acceptable; a positive opinion of sb/sth: *Do the plans meet with your approval?* ◊ **in ~** *Several people nodded in approval.* ◊ *The president's approval ratings were slipping.* OPP **disapproval** **2** B2 [U, C] agreement to, or permission for sth, especially a plan or request: *The plan will be submitted to the committee for official approval.* ◊ *parliamentary/congressional/government approval* ◊ *Senior management have given their seal of approval* (= formal approval) *to the plans.* ◊ *planning approvals* ◊ **~of sth** *The government is seeking approval of its plans.* ◊ *The proposal is subject to approval by the shareholders* (= they need to agree to it). ◊ **~(for sth) (from sb)** *They required/received approval for the proposal from the shareholders.* **3** [U] if you buy goods or if goods are sold **on approval**, you can use them for a time without paying, until you decide if you want to buy them or not

**ap·prove** ⓘ B2 /əˈpruːv/ *verb* **1** B2 [I] to think that sb/sth is good, acceptable or suitable: *I told my mother I wanted to leave school but she didn't approve.* ◊ **~of sb/sth** *Do you approve of my idea?* ◊ **~of sb doing sth** *She doesn't approve of me leaving school this year.* ◊ (*formal*) **~of sb's doing sth** *She doesn't approve of my leaving school this year.* OPP **disapprove** **2** B2 [T] **~sth** to officially agree to a plan, request, etc: *The committee unanimously approved the plan.* ⊃ SYNONYMS at AGREE **3** B2 [T, often passive] to say that sth is good enough to be used or is correct: **be approved (for/as sth)** *This medicine is not approved for use in children.* ◊ **~sth** *The auditors approved the company's accounts.*

**ap·prov·ing** /əˈpruːvɪŋ/ *adj.* showing that you believe that sb/sth is good or acceptable: *He gave me an approving nod.* OPP **disapproving** ▶ **ap·prov·ing·ly** *adv.*: *She looked at him approvingly and smiled.*

**approx.** /əˈprɒks; *NAmE* əˈprɑːks/ *abbr.* (in writing) APPROXIMATE, APPROXIMATELY: *Contents: approx. 6000 beads*

**ap·proxi·mate** *adj., verb*
- *adj.* /əˈprɒksɪmət; *NAmE* əˈprɑːk-/ almost correct or accurate, but not completely so: *an approximate number/total/cost* ◊ *The cost given is only approximate.* ◊ *Use these figures as an approximate guide in your calculations.* OPP **exact**

■ **verb** /əˈprɒksɪmeɪt; NAmE əˈprɑːk-/ (*formal*) **1** [T, I] to be similar or close to sth in nature, quality, amount, etc., but not exactly the same: ~**sth** *The animals were reared in conditions which approximated the wild as closely as possible.* ◊ *The total cost will approximate £15 billion.* ◊ ~**to sth** *His story approximates to the facts that we already know.* **2** [T] ~ **sth** to calculate or estimate sth fairly accurately: *a formula for approximating the weight of a horse*

**ap·proxi·mate·ly** 🅞 🅑🅘 🅦 /əˈprɒksɪmətli; NAmE əˈprɑːk-/ *adv.* used to show that sth is almost, but not completely, accurate or correct: *The journey took approximately seven hours.* ◊ *Approximately £4 000 worth of product was stolen in the raid.*

▼ **VOCABULARY BUILDING**

**Ways of saying approximately**

- The flight takes **approximately** three hours.
- The tickets cost **about** £20 each.
- The repairs will cost $200, **give or take** a few dollars.
- How much will it cost, **more or less**?
- We are expecting thirty **or so** people to come.
- She must be 25 **or thereabouts**.
- Profits have fallen by **roughly** 15 per cent.
- You can expect to earn **round about** £40 000 a year.
- The price is **somewhere around** $800.
- She earns **somewhere in the region of** £25 000.

All these words and phrases are used in both speaking and writing; **about** is the most common and **approximately** the most formal.

**ap·proxi·ma·tion** 🅦 /əˌprɒksɪˈmeɪʃn; NAmE əˌprɑːk-/ *noun* **1** an estimate of a number or an amount that is almost correct, but not exact: *That's just an approximation, you understand.* **2** ~ **(of/to sth)** a thing that is similar to sth else, but is not exactly the same: *Our results should be a good approximation of the true state of affairs.*

'**app tray** *noun* = APP DRAWER

**ap·pur·ten·ance** /əˈpɜːtɪnəns; NAmE əˈpɜːrt-/ *noun* [usually pl.] (*formal or humorous*) a thing that forms a part of sth larger or more important

**APR** /ˌeɪ piː ˈɑː(r)/ *noun* [sing.] the amount of interest a bank charges on money that it lends, calculated for a period of a year (the abbreviation for 'annual percentage rate'): *a rate of 26.4% APR*

**après-ski** /ˌæpreɪ ˈskiː/ *noun* [U] (*from French*) social activities and entertainments that take place in hotels and restaurants after a day's skiing

**apri·cot** /ˈeɪprɪkɒt; NAmE ˈæprɪkɑːt, ˈeɪp-/ *noun* **1** [C] a round fruit with yellow or orange skin and a large hard seed inside: *dried apricots* ➔ VISUAL VOCAB page V4 **2** [U] a pale orange colour ▶ **apri·cot** *adj.*: *The room was painted apricot and white.*

**April** 🅞 🅐🅘 /ˈeɪprəl/ *noun* [U, C] (*abbr.* **Apr.**) the fourth month of the year, between March and May: **in ~** *She was born in April.* ◊ (*BrE*) *The meeting is on the fifth of April/April the fifth.* ◊ (*NAmE*) *The meeting is on April fifth.* ◊ *We went to Japan last April.* ◊ *I arrived at the end of April.* ◊ *last April's election* ◊ *April showers* (= light rain that falls in the spring) ◊ *an April wedding*

**April 'Fool** *noun* **1** a trick that is traditionally played on sb on 1 April (called **April 'Fool's Day** or **All 'Fools' Day**) **2** a person who has a trick played on them on April Fool's Day

**a pri·ori** /ˌeɪ praɪˈɔːraɪ; NAmE ˌɑː priˈɔːri/ *adj., adv.* (*from Latin, formal*) using facts or principles that are known to be true in order to decide what the likely effects or results of sth will be, for example saying 'They haven't eaten anything all day so they must be hungry.' ➔ compare A POSTERIORI

**ap·ron** /ˈeɪprən/ *noun* **1** a piece of clothing worn over the front of the body, from the chest or the WAIST down, and tied around the WAIST. Aprons are worn over other clothes to keep them clean, for example when cooking. ➔ compare PINAFORE **2** (*specialist*) an area with a hard surface at an airport, where aircraft are turned around, loaded, etc.

---

**65** | **aquifer**

**3** (*also* '**apron stage**) (*specialist*) (in a theatre) the part of the stage that is in front of the curtain

🅘🅓🅜 **(tied to) sb's apron strings** (too much under) the influence and control of sb: *The British prime minister is too apt to cling to Washington's apron strings.*

**apro·pos** /ˌæprəˈpəʊ/ (*also* **apro·pos of**) *prep.* in connection with or related to sb/sth: *Apropos (of) what you were just saying…*

**apse** /æps/ *noun* a small area in a church, often in the shape of a SEMICIRCLE and usually at the east end of the building

**apt.** *abbr.* (in writing) (*NAmE*) apartment

**apt** /æpt/ *adj.* **1** suitable or appropriate in the circumstances: *a particularly apt description/name/comment* **2** likely or tending naturally to do sth: ~**to be** … *apt to be forgetful/careless* ◊ ~**to do sth** *Babies are apt to put objects into their mouths.* **3** ~ **pupil** a person who has a natural ability to learn and understand ▶ **aptly** *adv.*: *the aptly named Grand Hotel* **apt·ness** *noun* [U]

**ap·ti·tude** /ˈæptɪtjuːd; NAmE -tuːd/ *noun* [U, C] natural ability or skill at doing sth 🅢🅨🅝 **talent**: *an aptitude test* (= one designed to show whether sb has the natural ability for a particular job or course of education) ◊ ~**for sth** *She showed a natural aptitude for the work.* ◊ ~**for doing sth** *His aptitude for dealing with children got him the job.*

**aqua** /ˈækwə; NAmE ˈɑːk-/ *noun* [U] **1** water (used especially on the labels on packages of food, drinks, medicines, etc. in order to show how much water they contain) **2** a blue-green colour

**aqua·cul·ture** /ˈækwəkʌltʃə(r); NAmE ˈɑːk-/ *noun* [U] the practice of growing plants in water or farming fish for food

**aqua·lung** (*US also* **Aqua·lung™**) /ˈækwəlʌŋ; NAmE ˈɑːk-/ *noun* a piece of breathing equipment that a DIVER wears on his/her back when swimming UNDERWATER

aqualung

**aqua·mar·ine** /ˌækwəməˈriːn; NAmE ˌɑːk-/ *noun* **1** [C, U] a pale blue-green SEMI-PRECIOUS stone **2** [U] a pale blue-green colour ▶ **aqua·mar·ine** *adj.*: *an aquamarine sea*

**aquar·ium** /əˈkweəriəm; NAmE əˈkwer-/ *noun* (*pl.* **aquar·iums** *or* **aqua·ria** /-riə/) **1** a large glass container in which fish and other water creatures and plants are kept **2** a building where people can go to see fish and other water creatures

**Aquar·ius** /əˈkweəriəs; NAmE əˈkwer-/ (*also* **the 'Water Bearer**, **the 'Water Carrier**) *noun* **1** [U] the 11th sign of the ZODIAC **2** [sing.] a person born when the sun is in this sign, that is between 21 January and 19 February ▶ **Aquar·ian** /-riən/ *noun, adj.*

**aqua·tic** /əˈkwætɪk; NAmE əˈkwɑːt-/ *adj.* [usually before noun] **1** growing or living in, on or near water: *aquatic plants/life/ecosystems* **2** connected with water: *aquatic sports*

**aquat·ics** /əˈkwætɪks; NAmE əˈkwɑːt-/ *noun* [pl.] sports that are done on or in water, for example sailing and WATERSKIING 🅢🅨🅝 **water sports**

**aqua·tint** /ˈækwətɪnt; NAmE ˈɑːk-/ *noun* [U, C] (*specialist*) a method of producing a picture using ACID on a metal plate; a picture produced using this method

**aque·duct** /ˈækwɪdʌkt/ *noun* a structure for carrying water, usually one built like a bridge across a valley or low ground

**aque·ous** /ˈeɪkwiəs/ *adj.* (*specialist*) containing water; like water

**aqueous 'humour** (*US* **aqueous 'humor**) *noun* [U] (*anatomy*) the clear liquid inside the front part of the eye ➔ compare VITREOUS HUMOUR

**aqui·fer** /ˈækwɪfə(r)/ *noun* (*geology*) a layer of rock or soil that can take in and hold water

---

🅞 Oxford Phrasal Academic Lexicon (OPAL) written and spoken word lists | 🅦 OPAL written word list | 🅢 OPAL spoken word list

# aquiline

**aquil·ine** /ˈækwɪlaɪn/ *adj.* (*formal*) a person with an **aquiline nose** or **aquiline features** has a nose that is thin and curved, similar to the BEAK of an EAGLE

**AR** /ˌeɪ ˈɑː(r)/ *noun* [U] a technology that combines computer-generated images on a screen with the real object or scene that you are looking at (the abbreviation for 'augmented reality')

**Arab** /ˈærəb/ *noun, adj.*
- *noun* **1** a person from the Middle East or North Africa, whose ANCESTORS lived in the Arabian PENINSULA **2** a type of horse originally from Arabia
- *adj.* of or connected with Arabia or Arabs: *Arab countries*

**ar·ab·esque** /ˌærəˈbesk/ *noun* **1** [C] (IN BALLET) a position in which the dancer balances on one leg with the other leg lifted and stretched out straight behind PARALLEL to the ground **2** [C, U] (in art) a type of design where lines wind around each other

**Ara·bian** /əˈreɪbiən/ *adj.* of or connected with Arabia **HELP** Arabian is used to describe places: *the Arabian peninsula*. The people are **Arabs** and the adjective to describe them is **Arab**: *Arab children*. The language is **Arabic**: *Arabic script*

**Arab·ic** /ˈærəbɪk/ *noun, adj.*
- *noun* [U] the language of the Arabs
- *adj.* of or connected with the literature and language of Arab people: *Arabic poetry*

**Arabic ˈnumeral** *noun* any of the symbols 0, 1, 2, 3, 4, etc. used for writing numbers in many countries ⊃ compare ROMAN NUMERAL

**ar·able** /ˈærəbl/ *adj.* connected with growing crops such as WHEAT: *arable farming/farms/crops* ◊ *arable land/fields* (= used or suitable for growing crops) ⊃ WORDFINDER NOTE at FARM

**arach·nid** /əˈræknɪd/ *noun* (*specialist*) any small creature of the class that includes spiders, SCORPIONS, MITES and TICKS ⊃ VISUAL VOCAB page V3 ⊃ compare INSECT

**ar·bi·ter** /ˈɑːbɪtə(r)/; *NAmE* ˈɑːrb-/ *noun* ~ (of sth) (*formal*) a person with the power or influence to make judgements and decide what will be done or accepted: *The law is the final arbiter of what is considered obscene.* ◊ *an arbiter of taste/style/fashion*

**ar·bi·trage** /ˈɑːbɪtrɑːʒ, -trɪdʒ; *NAmE* ˈɑːrbɪtrɑːʒ/ *noun* [U] (*business*) the practice of buying sth (for example, shares or foreign money) in one place and selling it in another place where the price is higher ▶ **ar·bi·tra·geur** /ˌɑːbɪˈtrɑːˈʒɜː(r); *NAmE* ˌɑːrb-/ (*also* **ar·bi·trager** /ˈɑːbɪtrɪdʒə(r); *NAmE* ˈɑːrbɪtrɑːʒər/) *noun*

**ar·bi·trary** /ˈɑːbɪtrəri, -tri; *NAmE* ˈɑːrbɪtreri/ *adj.* **1** (of an action, a decision, a rule, etc.) not seeming to be based on a reason, system or plan and sometimes seeming unfair: *The choice of players for the team seemed completely arbitrary.* ◊ *He makes unpredictable, arbitrary decisions.* **2** (*formal*) using power without limits and without considering other people: *the arbitrary powers of officials* ▶ **ar·bi·trar·ily** /ˌɑːbɪˈtreərəli, ˈɑːbɪtrəli; *NAmE* ˈɑːrbɪˈtrerəli/ *adv.*: *The leaders of the groups were chosen arbitrarily.* **ar·bi·trari·ness** /ˈɑːbɪtrərinəs, -tri-; *NAmE* ˈɑːrbɪtrerinəs/ *noun* [U]

**ar·bi·trate** /ˈɑːbɪtreɪt; *NAmE* ˈɑːrb-/ *verb* [I, T] to officially settle an argument or a DISAGREEMENT between two people or groups: *~(in/on) (sth) to arbitrate in a dispute* ◊ *~between A and B A committee was created to arbitrate between management and the unions.*

**ar·bi·tra·tion** /ˌɑːbɪˈtreɪʃn; *NAmE* ˌɑːrb-/ *noun* [U] the official process of settling an argument or a DISAGREEMENT by sb who is not involved: *Both sides in the dispute have agreed to go to arbitration.*

**ar·bi·tra·tor** /ˈɑːbɪtreɪtə(r); *NAmE* ˈɑːrb-/ *noun* a person who is chosen to settle a DISAGREEMENT

**ar·bor·eal** /ɑːˈbɔːriəl; *NAmE* ɑːrˈb-/ *adj.* (*specialist*) relating to trees; living in trees

**ar·bor·etum** /ˌɑːbəˈriːtəm; *NAmE* ˌɑːrb-/ *noun* (*pl.* **ar·bor·etums** *or* **ar·bor·eta** /-tə/) a garden where many different types of tree are grown, for people to look at or for scientific study

**ar·bor·ist** /ˈɑːbərɪst; *NAmE* ˈɑːrb-/ *noun* (*formal*) = TREE SURGEON

**ar·bour** (*US* **arbor**) /ˈɑːbə(r); *NAmE* ˈɑːrb-/ *noun* a shelter in a garden for people to sit under, made by growing climbing plants over a frame

**arc** /ɑːk; *NAmE* ɑːrk/ *noun, verb*
- *noun* **1** (*geometry*) a curved line that is part of a circle ⊃ picture at CIRCLE **2** a curved shape: *the arc of a rainbow* ◊ *The beach swept around in an arc.* **3** the basic story, of one character or the main theme in a novel, film, etc: *The vivid characters and the satisfying story arc make this a rewarding novel.* **4** (*specialist*) an electric current passing across a space between two TERMINALS ⊃ see also ARC LAMP
- *verb* (**arc·ing** /ˈɑːkɪŋ; *NAmE* ˈɑːrk-/, **arced**, **arced** /ɑːkt; *NAmE* ɑːrkt/) (*specialist*) **1** [I] to move in the shape of an arc **2** [I] to form an electric arc

**ar·cade** /ɑːˈkeɪd; *NAmE* ɑːrˈk-/ *noun* **1** a covered passage with ARCHES along the side of a row of buildings (usually a row of shops) **2** a covered passage between streets, with shops on either side **3** (*also* **ˈshopping arcade**) (*both BrE*) a large building with a number of shops in it ⊃ compare SHOPPING MALL **4** (*BrE also* **aˈmusement arcade**) a place where you can play games on machines which you use coins to operate: *arcade games*

**Ar·ca·dia** /ɑːˈkeɪdiə; *NAmE* ɑːrˈk-/ *noun* [sing.] a part of southern Greece used in poetry and stories to represent an idea of perfect country life

**Ar·ca·dian** /ɑːˈkeɪdiən; *NAmE* ɑːrˈk-/ *adj.* of or connected with Arcadia or an idea of perfect country life

**ar·ca·na** /ɑːˈkeɪnə; *NAmE* ɑːrˈk-/ *noun* **1** [pl.] things that are secret or mysterious **2** [sing.] either of the two groups of cards in a TAROT PACK, the ˌmajor arˈcana and the ˌminor arˈcana

**ar·cane** /ɑːˈkeɪn; *NAmE* ɑːrˈk-/ *adj.* (*formal*) secret and mysterious and therefore difficult to understand

**arch** /ɑːtʃ; *NAmE* ɑːrtʃ/ *noun, verb, adj.*
- *noun* **1** a curved structure that supports the weight of sth above it, such as a bridge or the upper part of a building **2** a structure with a curved top that is supported by straight sides, sometimes forming an entrance or built as a MONUMENT: *Go through the arch and follow the path.* ◊ *Marble Arch is a famous London landmark.* **3** the raised part of the foot formed by a curved section of bones ⊃ VISUAL VOCAB page V1 **4** anything that forms a curved shape at the top: *the delicate arch of her eyebrows* ⊃ see also ARCHED
- *verb* **1** [T, I] ~(sth) if you arch part of your body, or it arches, it moves and forms a curved shape: *The cat arched its back and hissed.* **2** [I] to be in a curved line or shape across or over sth: *Tall trees arched over the path.*
- *adj.* [usually before noun] (*often disapproving*) seeming pleased with yourself because you know more about a situation than other people: *an arch tone of voice* ▶ **archˈly** *adv.*: *'Guess what?' she said archly.*

**arch-** /ɑːtʃ; *NAmE* ɑːrtʃ/ *combining form* (in nouns) main; most important or most extreme: *archbishop* ◊ *arch-enemy*

**archae·olo·gist** (*NAmE also* **arche·olo·gist**) /ˌɑːkiˈɒlədʒɪst; *NAmE* ˌɑːrkiˈɑːl-/ *noun* a person who studies archaeology

**archae·ology** (*NAmE also* **arche·ology**) /ˌɑːkiˈɒlədʒi; *NAmE* ˌɑːrkiˈɑːl-/ *noun* [U] the study of cultures of the past, and of periods of history by examining the parts of buildings and objects found in the ground ⊃ see also INDUSTRIAL ARCHAEOLOGY ▶ **arch·aeo·logic·al** (*NAmE also* **arch·eo·logic·al**) /ˌɑːkiəˈlɒdʒɪkl; *NAmE* ˌɑːrkiəˈlɑːdʒ-/ *adj.*: *archaeological excavations/evidence*

**archae·op·teryx** /ˌɑːkiˈɒpterɪks; *NAmE* ˌɑːrkiˈɑːp-/ *noun* the oldest known bird, which existed about 150 million years ago

**ar·chaic** /ɑːˈkeɪɪk; *NAmE* ɑːrˈk-/ *adj.* **1** old and no longer used: *'Thou art' is an archaic form of 'you are'.* **2** very old-fashioned **SYN outdated**: *The system is archaic and unfair* *and needs changing.* **3** from a much earlier or ancient period of history: *archaic art*

**arch·a·ism** /ˈɑːkeɪɪzəm; *NAmE* ˈɑːrkiːɪzəm/ *noun* [C, U] (*specialist*) a thing that is very old or old-fashioned, especially a word or a style of language or art; the use of such a word or style

**arch·an·gel** /ˈɑːkeɪndʒl; *NAmE* ˈɑːrk-/ *noun* an ANGEL of the highest rank: *the Archangel Gabriel*

**arch·bishop** /ˌɑːtʃˈbɪʃəp; *NAmE* ˌɑːrtʃ-/ *noun* a BISHOP of the highest rank, responsible for all the churches in a large area: *the Archbishop of Canterbury* (= the head of the Church of England)

**arch·bish·op·ric** /ˌɑːtʃˈbɪʃəprɪk; *NAmE* ˌɑːrtʃ-/ *noun* **1** the position of an archbishop **2** the district for which an archbishop is responsible

**arch·deacon** /ˌɑːtʃˈdiːkən; *NAmE* ˌɑːrtʃ-/ *noun* a priest just below the rank of BISHOP, especially in the Anglican Church

**arch·dio·cese** /ˌɑːtʃˈdaɪəsɪs; *NAmE* ˌɑːrtʃ-/ *noun* a district under the care of an ARCHBISHOP

**arch·duch·ess** /ˌɑːtʃˈdʌtʃəs; *NAmE* ˌɑːrtʃ-/ *noun* (in the past) the wife of an archduke or a daughter of the EMPEROR of Austria

**arch·duke** /ˌɑːtʃˈdjuːk; *NAmE* ˌɑːrtʃˈduːk/ *noun* (in the past) a son of the EMPEROR of Austria: *Archduke Franz Ferdinand* ➾ compare GRAND DUKE

**arched** /ɑːtʃt; *NAmE* ɑːrtʃt/ *adj.* in the shape of an ARCH: *a chair with an arched back*

**arch-ˈenemy** *noun* a person's main enemy

**arche·olo·gist, arche·ology** (*NAmE*) = ARCHAEOLOGIST, ARCHAEOLOGY

**arch·er** /ˈɑːtʃə(r); *NAmE* ˈɑːrtʃ-/ *noun* a person who shoots with a BOW and ARROWS

**arch·ery** /ˈɑːtʃəri; *NAmE* ˈɑːrtʃ-/ *noun* [U] the art or sport of shooting ARROWS with a BOW

**arche·typ·al** /ˌɑːkiˈtaɪpl; *NAmE* ˌɑːrk-/ *adj.* having all the important qualities that make sb/sth a typical example of a particular kind of person or thing: *The Beatles were the archetypal pop group.*

**arche·type** /ˈɑːkitaɪp; *NAmE* ˈɑːrk-/ *noun* (*formal*) the most typical or perfect example of a particular kind of person or thing: *She is the archetype of an American movie star.*

**archi·pel·ago** /ˌɑːkɪˈpeləgəʊ; *NAmE* ˌɑːrk-/ *noun* (*pl.* **-os** or **-oes**) a group of islands and the sea surrounding them

**archi·tect** 🔊 **A2** /ˈɑːkɪtekt; *NAmE* ˈɑːrk-/ *noun, verb*
■ *noun* **1** **A2** a person whose job is designing buildings: *The house was designed by architect Louis Kahn.* ➾ see also LANDSCAPE ARCHITECT **2** a person who is responsible for planning or creating an idea, an event or a situation: *He was one of the principal architects of the revolution.* ◇ *Jones was the architect of the team's first goal.* **3** (*computing*) a person who designs or puts together a program or computer system: *a data architect*
■ *verb* (*computing*) ~ sth to design or put together a program or computer system

**archi·tec·ton·ic** /ˌɑːkɪtekˈtɒnɪk; *NAmE* ˌɑːrkɪtekˈtɑːn-/ *adj.* (*specialist*) relating to architecture or architects

**archi·tec·tural** 🔊+ **C1** /ˌɑːkɪˈtektʃərəl; *NAmE* ˌɑːrk-/ *adj.* relating to architecture and buildings: *architectural features* ▸ **archi·tec·tur·al·ly** /-rəli/ *adv.*: *The house is of little interest architecturally.*

**archi·tec·ture** 🔊 **A2** /ˈɑːkɪtektʃə(r); *NAmE* ˈɑːrk-/ *noun* **1** **A2** [U] the art and study of designing buildings: *to study architecture* **2** **A2** [U] the design or style of a building or buildings: *the architecture of the eighteenth century* ◇ *modern architecture* **3** [C, U] (*computing*) the design and structure of a computer system

**arch·ive** 🔊+ **C1** /ˈɑːkaɪv; *NAmE* ˈɑːrk-/ *noun, verb*
■ *noun* (*also* **archives** [pl.]) **1** 🔊+ **C1** a collection of historical documents or records of a government, a family, a place or an organization; the place where these records are stored: *the National Sound Archive* ◇ *archive film* ◇ *The BBC's archives are bulging with material.* **2** (*computing*) an electronic record of the data on a computer system, stored on a separate device for safety and security
■ *verb* **1** ~ sth to put or store a document or other material in an archive **2** ~ sth (*computing*) to move information that is not often needed to a different disk, tape or other computer to store it

**arch·iv·ist** /ˈɑːkɪvɪst; *NAmE* ˈɑːrk-/ *noun* a person whose job is to develop and manage an archive

**arch-ˈrival** *noun* a person's main opponent

**arch·way** /ˈɑːtʃweɪ; *NAmE* ˈɑːrtʃ-/ *noun* a passage or an entrance with an ARCH over it: *We went through a stone archway into the courtyard.*

**ˈarc lamp** (*also* **ˈarc light**) *noun* a lamp that gives very bright light that is produced by an electric ARC

**Arc·tic** /ˈɑːktɪk; *NAmE* ˈɑːrk-/ *adj., noun*
■ *adj.* **1** [only before noun] related to or happening in the regions around the North Pole: *Arctic explorers* ➾ compare ANTARCTIC **2 arctic** extremely cold: *TV pictures showed the arctic conditions.*
■ *noun* [sing.] **the Arctic** the regions of the world around the North Pole

**the ˌArctic ˈCircle** *noun* [sing.] the line of LATITUDE 66° 33′ North ➾ compare ANTARCTIC CIRCLE

**ar·dent** /ˈɑːdnt; *NAmE* ˈɑːrd-/ *adj.* [usually before noun] very enthusiastic and showing strong feelings about sth/sb **SYN** passionate: *an ardent supporter of European unity* ▸ **ar·dent·ly** *adv.*

**ar·dour** (*US* **ardor**) /ˈɑːdə(r); *NAmE* ˈɑːrd-/ *noun* [U] (*formal*) very strong feelings of enthusiasm or love **SYN** passion

**ar·du·ous** /ˈɑːdʒuəs; *NAmE* ˈɑːrdʒ-/ *adj.* involving a lot of effort and energy, especially over a period of time: *an arduous journey across the Andes* ◇ *The work was arduous.* ▸ **ar·du·ous·ly** *adv.*

**are**[1] /ə(r), *strong form* ɑː(r)/ ➾ BE *verb*

**are**[2] /ɑː(r); *BrE also* eə(r); *NAmE also* er/ *noun* a unit for measuring an area of land; 100 square metres

**area** 🔊 **A1** 🔊 /ˈeəriə; *NAmE* ˈer-/ *noun*
• **PART OF PLACE 1** 🔊 **A1** [C] part of a place, town, etc., or a region of a country or the world: *to improve access to services in rural areas* ◇ *urban/metropolitan/residential areas* ◇ *The farm and surrounding areas were flooded.* ◇ *She knows the local area very well.* ◇ ~ **around** ... *the area around San Francisco* ◇ *Large areas of the city were destroyed in the earthquake.* ◇ **over a** ... ~ *Wreckage from the plane was scattered over a wide area.* ◇ *Thousands of tourists visit the area every year.* ◇ **in the** ~ *There are lots of things to do in the area.* ◇ *John is the London area manager.* ➾ see also CATCHMENT AREA, CONSERVATION AREA, DEVELOPMENT AREA, NO-GO AREA, STAGING AREA **2** 🔊 **A1** [C] a part of a room, building or particular space that is used for a special purpose: *the hotel reception area* ◇ *a play/parking/dining area* ➾ SYNONYMS at PLACE ➾ see also REST AREA, SERVICE AREA
• **PARTICULAR PLACE 3** 🔊 **A1** [C] a particular place on an object: *The treatment targets the affected areas of the brain.* ◇ *Move the cursor to a blank area of the computer screen.*
• **SUBJECT/ACTIVITY 4** 🔊 **B1** [C] a particular subject or activity, or an aspect of it: *The course covers two main subject areas.* ◇ ~ **of sth** *The report focuses on three key areas of concern.* ◇ ~ **for sth** *We have identified several areas for improvement.* ◇ **in this** ~ *More research is needed in this area.* ◇ **in the** ~ **of sth** *to improve skills in the areas of critical thinking and problem-solving* ➾ see also GREY AREA
• **MEASUREMENT 5** 🔊 **B2** [C, U] the amount of space covered by a flat surface or piece of land, described as a measurement: *the area of a triangle* ◇ *Measure the surface area.* ◇ *The estate covers an area of 106 acres.* ◇ **in** ~ *The room is 12 square metres in area.*
• **FOOTBALL 6 the area** [sing.] (*BrE*) (in football (soccer)) = PENALTY AREA: *He shot from just outside the area.*

¹**area code** *noun* the numbers for a particular area or city, which you use when you are making a phone call from outside the local area ⇨ compare DIALLING CODE ⇨ WORDFINDER NOTE at CALL

**arena** /əˈriːnə/ *noun* **1** a place with a flat open area in the middle and seats around it where people can watch sports and entertainment: *a concert at Wembley Arena* ◇ *an indoor sports arena* ◇ *a hockey/basketball arena* **2** (*formal*) an area of activity that interests the public, especially one where there is a lot of opposition between different groups or countries: *the political/international arena*

**aren't** /ɑːnt/; *NAmE* ɑːrnt/ *short form* **1** are not **2** (in questions) am not: *Aren't I clever?*

**areola** /əˈriːələ/ *noun* (*pl.* **areo·lae** /-liː/) (*anatomy*) the round area of skin around the NIPPLE

**argon** /ˈɑːɡɒn/; *NAmE* ˈɑːrɡɑːn/ *noun* [U] (*symb.* **Ar**) a chemical element. Argon is a gas that does not react with anything and is used in electric lights.

**argot** /ˈɑːɡəʊ/; *NAmE* ˈɑːrɡət, -ɡoʊ/ *noun* [sing., U] (*from French*) words and phrases that are used by a particular group of people and not easily understood by others **SYN** jargon

**ar·gu·able** /ˈɑːɡjuəbl/; *NAmE* ˈɑːrɡju-/ *adj.* (*formal*) **1** that you can give good reasons for: *it is ~ that …* *It is arguable that giving too much detail may actually be confusing.* **2** not certain; that you do not accept without question **SYN** debatable: *it is ~ whether …* *It is arguable whether the case should ever have gone to trial* (= perhaps it should not have).

**ar·gu·ably** /ˈɑːɡjuəbli/; *NAmE* ˈɑːrɡju-/ *adv.* used (often before a comparative or superlative adjective) when you are stating an opinion that you believe you could give reasons to support: *He is arguably the best actor of his generation.*

**argue** /ˈɑːɡjuː/; *NAmE* ˈɑːrɡjuː/ *verb* **1** [I] to speak angrily to sb because you disagree with them: *My brothers are always arguing.* ◇ *~ (with sb) (about/ over sth) We're always arguing with each other about money.* ◇ *~ with sb I don't want to argue with you—just do it!* **2** [I, T] to give reasons why you think that sth is right/wrong, true/not true, etc., especially to persuade people that you are right: *~ for/against sth/doing sth They argued for the right to strike.* ◇ *~ sth She argued the case for bringing back the death penalty.* ◇ *He was too tired to argue the point* (= discuss the matter). ◇ *a well-argued article* ◇ *~ that … Critics argue that Britain is not investing enough in broadband.* ◇ *It could be argued that laws are made by and for men.* ⇨ LANGUAGE BANK at NEVERTHELESS, PERHAPS **3** [T] *~ sth* (*formal*) to show clearly that sth exists or is true: *These latest developments argue a change in government policy.* **IDM** ▸ **argue the 'toss** (*BrE, informal*) to continue to disagree about a decision, especially when it is too late to change it or it is not very important **PHRV** ▸ **argue sb 'into/'out of doing sth** to persuade sb to do/not do sth by giving them reasons: *They argued him into withdrawing his complaint.* ▸ **'argue with sth** (usually used in negative sentences) (*informal*) to disagree with a statement: *He's a really successful man—you can't argue with that.*

**ar·gu·ment** /ˈɑːɡjumənt/; *NAmE* ˈɑːrɡju-/ *noun* **1** [C, U] a conversation or discussion in which two or more people disagree, often angrily: *to win/lose an argument* ◇ *After some heated argument a decision was finally taken.* ◇ *~ (with sb) (about/over sth) We had an argument with the waiter about the bill.* ◇ *~ between A and B Jack was always the one who settled arguments between us.* **2** [C] a reason or set of reasons that sb uses to show that sth is true or correct: *a strong/convincing/compelling argument* ◇ *to advance/present an argument* ◇ *Having heard both sides of the argument, the court will make a decision.* ◇ *~ for/against sth There are strong arguments for and against euthanasia.* ◇ *~ that … The judge rejected the defence argument that the evidence was too*

▼ LANGUAGE BANK

**argue**
Verbs for reporting an opinion
- Some critics **argue** that Picasso remained a great master all his life.
- Others **maintain** that there is a significant deterioration in quality in his post-war work.
- Picasso himself **claimed** that good art is created, but great art is stolen.
- As Smith **has noted**, Picasso borrowed imagery from African art.
- As the author **points out**, Picasso borrowed imagery from African art.
- The writer **challenges the notion that** Picasso's sculpture was secondary to his painting.
- **It has been suggested that** Picasso's painting was influenced by jazz music.

⇨ LANGUAGE BANK at ABOUT, ACCORDING TO

*old to be relevant.* **3** [U] *~ (about sth)* the act of disagreeing in a conversation or discussion using a reason or set of reasons: *Let's assume for the sake of argument* (= in order to discuss the problem) *that we can't start till March.* ⇨ WORDFINDER NOTE at DEBATE

**ar·gu·men·ta·tion** /ˌɑːɡjumənˈteɪʃn/; *NAmE* ˌɑːrɡju-/ *noun* [U] logical arguments used to support a theory, an action or an idea

**ar·gu·men·ta·tive** /ˌɑːɡjuˈmentətɪv/; *NAmE* ˌɑːrɡju-/ *adj.* a person who is **argumentative** likes arguing or often starts arguing

**ar·gyle** /ɑːˈɡaɪl/; *NAmE* ˈɑːrɡaɪl/ *noun* [U] a pattern of diamond shapes on a plain background made of wool, especially on a sweater or on socks

**aria** /ˈɑːriə/ *noun* a song for one voice, especially in an OPERA or ORATORIO ⇨ WORDFINDER NOTE at OPERA

**-arian** /eəriən/; *NAmE* eriən/ *suffix* (in nouns and adjectives) believing in; practising: *humanitarian* ◇ *disciplinarian*

**arid** /ˈærɪd/ *adj.* **1** (of land or a climate) having little or no rain; very dry: *arid and semi-arid deserts* ⇨ WORDFINDER NOTE at CLIMATE **2** (*formal*) with nothing new or interesting in it: *an arid discussion* ▸ **arid·ity** /əˈrɪdəti/ *noun* [U]

**Aries** /ˈeəriːz/; *NAmE* ˈer-/ *noun* **1** [U] the first sign of the ZODIAC, the RAM **2** [sing.] a person born when the sun is in this sign, that is between 21 March and 20 April

**aright** /əˈraɪt/ *adv.* (*old-fashioned* or *literary*) correctly

**arise** /əˈraɪz/ *verb* (**arose** /əˈrəʊz/, **arisen** /əˈrɪzn/). **1** [I] (*rather formal*) (especially of a problem or a difficult situation) to happen; to start to exist **SYN** occur: *An opportunity arose to work in the United States.* ◇ *Questions naturally arise as to who was responsible.* ◇ *A serious problem can arise if the heart stops pumping effectively.* ◇ *Children should be disciplined when the need arises* (= when it is necessary). **2** [I] *~ (out of/from sth)* (*rather formal*) to happen as a result of a particular situation: *injuries arising out of a road accident* ◇ *Emotional or mental problems can arise from a physical cause.* ◇ *Are there any matters arising from the minutes of the last meeting?* **3** [I] (*formal*) to begin to exist or develop: *Several new industries arose in the town.* **4** [I] (*old use* or *literary*) to get out of bed; to stand up: *He arose at dawn.* **5** [I] *~ (against sb/sth)* (*old use*) to come together to protest about sth or to fight for sth: *The peasants arose against their masters.* **6** [I] (*literary*) (of a mountain, a tall building, etc.) to gradually start to be seen as you move towards it

**ar·is·toc·racy** /ˌærɪˈstɒkrəsi/; *NAmE* -ˈstɑːk-/ *noun* [C + sing./pl. v.] (*pl.* **-ies**) (in some countries) people born in the highest social class, who have special titles **SYN** nobility: *members of the aristocracy* ◇ *the landed aristocracy*

**ar·is·to·crat** /ˈærɪstəkræt/; *NAmE* əˈrɪstəkræt/ *noun* a member of the aristocracy ⇨ compare COMMONER

**ar·is·to·crat·ic** /ˌærɪstəˈkrætɪk/; *NAmE* əˌrɪ-/ *adj.* belonging to or typical of the ARISTOCRACY **SYN** noble: *an aristocratic name/family/lifestyle*

**Ar·is·to·tel·ian** /ˌærɪstəˈtiːliən/ adj. connected with Aristotle or his philosophy

**arith·met·ic** /əˈrɪθmətɪk/ noun [U] **1** the type of mathematics that deals with the adding, multiplying, etc. of numbers: *He's not very good at arithmetic.* **2** sums involving the adding, multiplying, etc. of numbers: *a quick bit of mental arithmetic* (= sums you do in your head, without writing anything down) ◊ *I think there's something wrong with your arithmetic.* ⇒ WORDFINDER NOTE at MATHS

**arith·met·ic·al** /ˌærɪθˈmetɪkl/ (also **arith·met·ic** /ˌærɪθˈmetɪk/) adj. relating to arithmetic: *an arithmetical calculation* ▸ **arith·met·ic·al·ly** /-kli/ adv.

**arithmetic mean** /ˌærɪθmetɪk ˈmiːn/ noun (*mathematics*) = MEAN (2)

**arithmetic progression** /ˌærɪθmetɪk prəˈɡreʃn/ (also **arithmetic ˈseries**) noun a series of numbers that decrease or increase by the same amount each time, for example 2, 4, 6, 8 ⇒ compare GEOMETRIC PROGRESSION

**the ark** /ði ˈɑːk; *NAmE* ˈɑːrk/ (also **Noah's ˈark**) noun [sing.] (in the Bible) a large boat that Noah built to save his family and two of every type of animal from the flood
**IDM** **out of the ˈark** | **sth went out with the ˈark** (*BrE, informal*) if sb says that an object or a custom is **out of the ark** or **went out with the ark**, they think that it is very old-fashioned

**arm** /ɑːm; *NAmE* ɑːrm/ noun, verb
■ noun ⇒ see also ARMS
• PART OF BODY **1** either of the two long parts that stick out from the top of the body and connect the shoulders to the hands: *He escaped with only a broken arm.* ◊ *Pearl wrapped her arms around his waist and hugged him tightly.* ◊ *He was running forward,* **waving his arms.** ◊ **by the ~** *The officer grabbed him by the arm* (= grabbed his arm). ◊ **in sb's arms** *She cradled the child in her arms.* ◊ *They fell asleep* **in each other's arms** (= holding each other). ◊ **on sb's ~** *He walked in with a tall blonde woman on his arm* (= next to him and holding his arm). ◊ **under sb's ~** *He was carrying a number of files under his arm* (= between his arm and his body). ◊ *He held the dirty rag* **at arm's length** (= as far away from his body as possible). ◊ *They walked along* **arm in arm** (= with the arm of one person linked with the arm of the other). ⇒ VISUAL VOCAB page V1
• OF CLOTHING **2** the part of a piece of clothing that covers the arm **SYN** sleeve
• OF CHAIR **3** the part of a chair, etc. on which you rest your arms
• OF A MACHINE **4** a long narrow part of an object or a machine, especially one that moves: *a robotic arm*
• OF WATER/LAND **5** a long narrow piece of water or land that is joined to a larger area: *A small bridge spans the arm of the river.*
• OF ORGANIZATION **6** [usually sing.] ~ (**of sth**) a section of a large organization that deals with one particular activity **SYN** wing: *the research arm of the company*
**IDM** **cost/pay an ˌarm and a ˈleg** (*informal*) to cost/pay a lot of money **keep sb at arm's length** to avoid having a close relationship with sb: *He keeps all his clients at arm's length.* ⇒ more at AKIMBO, BABE, BEAR *v.*, CHANCE *v.*, FOLD *v.*, LONG *adj.*, OPEN *adj.*, RIGHT *adj.*, SHOT *n.*, TWIST *v.*
■ verb **1** ~ [I, T] to provide weapons for yourself/sb in order to fight a battle or a war: *The country was arming against the enemy.* ◊ **~ yourself/sb (with sth)** *The men armed themselves with sticks and stones.* ◊ (*figurative*) *She had armed herself for the meeting with all the latest statistics.* ⇒ see also ARMED **2** [T] ~ **sth** to make a bomb, etc. ready to explode ⇒ compare DISARM ⇒ see also ARMED

**ar·mada** /ɑːˈmɑːdə; *NAmE* ɑːrˈm-/ noun a large group of armed ships sailing together: *The Spanish Armada was sent to attack England in 1588.*

**ar·ma·dillo** /ˌɑːməˈdɪləʊ; *NAmE* ˌɑːrm-/ noun (*pl.* **-os**) an American animal with a hard shell made of pieces of bone

**Ar·ma·ged·don** /ˌɑːməˈɡedn; *NAmE* ˌɑːrm-/ noun [sing., U] **1** (in the Bible) a battle between good and evil at the end of the world **2** a terrible war that could destroy the world

**ar·ma·ment** /ˈɑːməmənt; *NAmE* ˈɑːrm-/ noun **1** [C, usually pl.] weapons, especially large guns, bombs, tanks, etc: *the armaments industry* **2** [U] the process of increasing the amount of weapons an army or a country has, especially to prepare for war ⇒ compare DISARMAMENT

**arm·band** /ˈɑːmbænd; *NAmE* ˈɑːrm-/ noun **1** a cloth band worn around the arm as a sign of sth, for example that sb has an official position: *The stewards all wore armbands.* ◊ *Many people at the funeral service were wearing black armbands.* **2** either of two plastic rings that can be filled with air and worn around the arms by sb who is learning to swim ⇒ WORDFINDER NOTE at SWIMMING

**ˈarm candy** noun [U] (*informal*) an attractive person that sb takes with them to a public or social event in order to impress other people

**arm·chair** /ˈɑːmtʃeə(r); *NAmE* ˈɑːrmtʃer/ noun, adj.
■ noun a comfortable chair with sides on which you can rest your arms: *to sit in an armchair*
■ adj. [only before noun] knowing about a subject through books, television, the internet, etc., rather than by doing it for yourself: *an armchair critic/traveller*

**armed** /ɑːmd; *NAmE* ɑːrmd/ adj. **1** involving the use of weapons: *an armed robbery* ◊ *an international armed conflict* (= a war) **OPP** unarmed **2** carrying a weapon, especially a gun: *The man is armed and dangerous.* ◊ *armed guards/police* ◊ *Police were heavily armed.* ◊ **~ with a gun, etc.** *He was armed with a rifle.* **OPP** unarmed **3** ~ (**with sth**) knowing sth or carrying sth that you need in order to help you to perform a task: *He was armed with all the facts.*
**IDM** **ˌarmed to the ˈteeth** having many weapons

**the ˌarmed ˈforces** (also **the ˌarmed ˈservices**) noun [pl.] a country's army, NAVY and AIR FORCE

**arm·ful** /ˈɑːmfʊl; *NAmE* ˈɑːrm-/ noun a quantity that you can carry in one or both arms

**arm·hole** /ˈɑːmhəʊl; *NAmE* ˈɑːrm-/ noun the place in a coat, shirt, dress, etc. that your arm goes through

**ar·mis·tice** /ˈɑːmɪstɪs; *NAmE* ˈɑːrm-/ noun [sing.] a formal agreement during a war to stop fighting and discuss making peace **SYN** ceasefire ⇒ WORDFINDER NOTE at PEACE

**arm·lock** /ˈɑːmlɒk; *NAmE* ˈɑːrmlɑːk/ noun (in WRESTLING) a way of holding an opponent's arm so that they cannot move: *He had him in an armlock.*

**ar·moire** /ɑːmˈwɑː(r); *NAmE* ɑːrm-/ noun (*from French*) a cupboard with DRAWERS or shelves below, especially one that has a lot of decoration

**ar·mour** (*US* **armor**) /ˈɑːmə(r); *NAmE* ˈɑːrm-/ noun [U] **1** special metal clothing that soldiers wore in the past to protect their bodies while fighting; special clothing that soldiers or police officers wear to protect their bodies: *a suit of armour* ◊ *police officers in full body armour* **2** metal covers that protect ships and military vehicles such as tanks **3** (*specialist*) military vehicles used in war: *an attack by infantry and armour* **IDM** see CHINK *n.*, KNIGHT *n.*

**ar·moured** (*US* **ar·mored**) /ˈɑːməd; *NAmE* ˈɑːrmərd/ adj. **1** (especially of a military vehicle) protected by metal covers: *The cruiser was heavily armoured.* ◊ *an armoured car* **2** using armoured vehicles: *an armoured division*

**ˌarmoured persoˈnnel carrier** (*US* **ˌarmored persoˈnnel carrier**) noun a military vehicle used to transport soldiers

**ar·mour·er** (*US* **ar·mor·er**) /ˈɑːmərə(r); *NAmE* ˈɑːrm-/ noun a person who makes or repairs weapons and armour

**ar·moury** (*US* **ar·mory**) /ˈɑːməri; *NAmE* ˈɑːrm-/ noun (*pl.* **-ies**) **1** a place where weapons and armour are kept **SYN** arsenal **2** (in the US or Canada) a building that is the HEADQUARTERS for training people who are not professional soldiers, for example the National Guard **3** (*formal*) the things that sb has available to help them achieve sth: *Doctors have an armoury of drugs available.* **4** all the weapons and military equipment that a country has: *Britain's nuclear armoury*

**arm·pit** /ˈɑːmpɪt; *NAmE* ˈɑːrm-/ (also *NAmE, informal* **pit**) noun the part of the body under the arm where it joins the shoulder ⇒ VISUAL VOCAB page V1 ⇒ see also UNDERARM

# armrest

**IDM** **the 'armpit of sth** (*especially NAmE, informal*) the most unpleasant or ugly place in a country or region: *The city has been called the armpit of America.*

**arm·rest** /ˈɑːmrest; *NAmE* ˈɑːrm-/ *noun* the part of some types of seat, especially in planes or cars, that supports your arm

**arms** **B2** /ɑːmz; *NAmE* ɑːrmz/ *noun* [pl.] **1** **B2** (*formal*) weapons, especially as used by the army, NAVY, etc: *The UN imposed an arms embargo on the country.* ◊ *He's the world's most notorious arms dealer.* ⇨ WORDFINDER NOTE at CONFLICT ⇨ see also FIREARM, SMALL ARMS **2** ⇨ COAT OF ARMS: *the King's Arms* (= used as the name of a pub)
**IDM** **be under 'arms** (*formal*) to have weapons and be ready to fight in a war **lay down your 'arms** (*formal*) to stop fighting **take up arms (against sb)** (*formal*) to prepare to fight **(be) up in 'arms (about/over sth)** (*informal*) (of a group of people) to be very angry about sth and ready to protest strongly about it ⇨ more at BEAR *v*., CALL *n*., PRESENT *v*.

**'arms control** *noun* [U] international agreements to destroy weapons or limit the number of weapons that countries have

**'arms race** *noun* [sing.] a situation in which countries compete to get the most and best weapons

**'arm-twisting** *noun* [U] (*informal*) the use of a lot of pressure or even physical force to persuade sb to do sth

**'arm-wrestling** *noun* [U] a competition to find out which of two people is the stronger, in which they try to force each other's arm down onto a table

**army** **A2** /ˈɑːmi; *NAmE* ˈɑːrmi/ *noun* (*pl.* **-ies**) **1** **A2** [C + sing./pl. v.] a large organized group of soldiers who are trained to fight on land: *The two opposing armies faced each other across the battlefield.* ⇨ WORDFINDER NOTE at CONFLICT

**WORDFINDER** artillery, battalion, command, defend, invade, officer, regiment, tactics, weapon

**2** **A2** **the army** [sing. + sing./pl. v.] the part of a country's armed forces that fights on land: **in the ~** *Her husband is in the army.* ◊ *After leaving school, Mike went into the army.* ◊ *an army officer/chief* **3** [C + sing./pl. v.] a large number of people or things, especially when they are organized in some way or involved in a particular activity: *an army of advisers/volunteers* ◊ *An army of ants marched across the path.*

**ar·nica** /ˈɑːnɪkə; *NAmE* ˈɑːrn-/ *noun* [U] a natural medicine made from a plant, also called **arnica**, used to treat BRUISES (= marks that appear on the skin after sb has fallen, been hit, etc.)

**'A-road** *noun* (in the UK) a road that is less important than a MOTORWAY, but wider and straighter than a B-ROAD

**aroma** /əˈrəʊmə/ *noun* a pleasant smell that is easy to notice: *the aroma of fresh coffee*

**aroma·ther·apy** /əˌrəʊməˈθerəpi/ *noun* [U] the use of natural oils that smell sweet to improve physical, emotional or mental health, by rubbing them into the skin or breathing in their smell ▶ **aroma·ther·ap·ist** *noun*

**aro·mat·ic** /ˌærəˈmætɪk/ *adj.* having a pleasant smell that is easy to notice **SYN** **fragrant**: *aromatic oils/herbs*

**arose** /əˈrəʊz/ *past tense of* ARISE

**around** **A1** /əˈraʊnd/ *prep., adv.*
▪ *prep.* (*especially NAmE*) (*BrE usually* **round**) **1** **A1** surrounding sb/sth; on each side of sth: *The house is built around a central courtyard.* ◊ *He put his arms around her.* **2** **A1** on, to or from the other side of sb/sth: *Our house is just around the corner.* ◊ *The bus came around the bend.* ◊ *There must be a way around the problem.* **3** **A1** in a circle: *They walked around the lake.* **4** **A1** in or to many places in an area: *They walked around the town looking for a place to eat.* **5** to fit in with particular people, ideas, etc: *I can't arrange everything around your timetable!* **6** in connection with sb/sth **SYN** **about**: *He has issues around food and dieting.*
▪ *adv.* **HELP** For the special uses of **around** in phrasal verbs, look at the entries for the verbs. For example **come around to sth** is in the phrasal verb section at **come**. **1** **A1** approximately: *He arrived around five o'clock.* ◊ *The cost would be somewhere around £1500.* **2** **A1** on every side; surrounding sb/sth: *I could hear laughter all around.* ◊ *a yard with a fence all around* **3** **A1** (*especially NAmE*) (*BrE usually* **round**) moving in a circle: *How do you make the wheels go around?* **4** **A1** (*especially NAmE*) (*BrE usually* **round**) in a circle or curve to face another way or the opposite way: *She turned the car around and drove off.* ◊ *They looked around when he called.* ◊ *He took two steps before he turned back around.* ⇨ see also ABOUT *adv.*, ROUND *adv.* **5** **A1** (*especially NAmE*) (*BrE usually* **round**) measured in a circle: *an old tree that was at least ten feet around* **6** **A1** in or to many places: *We were all running around trying to get ready in time.* ◊ *This is our new office—Kay will show you around.* ◊ *There were papers lying around all over the floor.* **7** **A2** used to describe activities that have no real purpose: *There were several young people sitting around looking bored.* **8** **A2** present in a place; available: *She must be somewhere around here.* ◊ *The game has been around forever* (= for a long time). ◊ *I knocked but there was no one around.* **9** active and well known in a sport, profession, etc: *a new tennis champion who could be around for a long time* ◊ *She's been around as a film director since the early 2000s.*
**IDM** **have been around** to have gained knowledge and experience of the world

▼ **WHICH WORD?**

**around / round / about**
- **Around** and **round** can often be used with the same meaning in *BrE*, though **around** is more formal: *The earth goes round/around the sun.* ◊ *They live round/around the corner.* ◊ *We travelled round/around India.* ◊ *She turned round/around when I came in.* In *NAmE* only **around** can be used in these meanings.
- **Around**, **round** and **about** can also sometimes be used with the same meaning in *BrE*: *The kids were running around/round/about outside.* ◊ *I've been waiting around/round/about to see her all day.* In *NAmE* only **around** can be used in these meanings. **About** or **around** can be used in both *BrE* and *NAmE* to mean 'approximately': *We left around/about 8 o'clock.*

**a.round-the-'clock** *adj.* = ROUND-THE-CLOCK

**arouse** /əˈraʊz/ *verb* **1** ~ **sth** to make sb have a particular feeling or attitude: *to arouse sb's interest/curiosity/anger* ◊ *Her strange behaviour aroused our suspicions.* **2** ~ **sb** to make sb feel sexually excited **SYN** **excite** **3** ~ **sb** to make sb feel more active and want to start doing sth: *The whole community was aroused by the crime.* **4** ~ **sb (from sth)** (*formal*) to wake sb from sleep ⇨ see also ROUSE ▶ **arousal** /əˈraʊzl/ *noun* [U]: *emotional/sexual arousal*

**ar·peg·gio** /ɑːˈpedʒiəʊ; *NAmE* ɑːrˈp-/ *noun* (*pl.* **-os**) (*music, from Italian*) the notes of a CHORD played quickly one after the other

**arr.** *abbr.* (in writing) **1** arrives; arrival: *arr. London 06.00* ⇨ compare DEP. **2** (*music*) arranged by: *Handel, arr. Mozart*

**ar·raign** /əˈreɪn/ *verb* [usually passive] (*law*) to bring sb to court in order to formally accuse them of a crime: **be arraigned for sth** *He was arraigned for murder.* ◊ **be arraigned** *He was arraigned on a charge of murder.* ▶ **ar·raign·ment** *noun* [C, U]

**ar·range** **A2** /əˈreɪndʒ/ *verb* **1** **A2** [T, I] to plan or organize sth in advance: ~**sth** *The party was arranged quickly.* ◊ *Can I arrange an appointment for Monday?* ◊ *The meeting was provisionally arranged for 9 October.* ◊ *We met at six, as arranged.* ◊ **~ how, where, etc.** *We've still got to arrange how to get to the airport.* ◊ **~ to do sth** *Have you arranged to meet him?* ◊ **~ that ...** *I've arranged that we can borrow their car.* ◊ **~ for sth (to do sth)** *We arranged for a car to collect us from the airport.* ◊ **~ with**

**sb (about sth)** *I've arranged with the neighbours about feeding the cat while we are away.* **2** [T] ~ **sth** to put sth in a particular order; to make sth neat or attractive: *The books are arranged alphabetically by author.* ◊ *The photos are arranged in chronological order.* ◊ *She arranged the flowers in a vase.* **3** [T] ~ **sth (for sth)** to change a piece of music so that it is suitable for a particular instrument or voice: *He arranged traditional folk songs for the piano.*

**ar·ranged 'marriage** *noun* [C, U] a marriage in which the parents choose the husband or wife for their child

**ar·range·ment** /əˈreɪndʒmənt/ *noun* **1** [C, usually pl.] a plan or preparation that you make so that sth can happen: *travel arrangements* ◊ ~ **for sth** *I'll make arrangements for you to be met at the airport.* **2** [C, usually pl.] the way things are done or organized: *She's happy with her unusual living arrangements.* ◊ *new security arrangements* ◊ *There are special arrangements for people working overseas.* **3** [C, U] an agreement that you make with sb that you can both accept: *We can come to an arrangement over the price.* ◊ ~ **between A and B** *an arrangement between the school and the parents* ◊ ~ **with sb (to do sth)** *Guided tours are available by prior arrangement with the museum.* ◊ ~ **that…** *They had an arrangement that the children would spend two weeks with each parent.* **4** [C, U] a group of things that are organized or placed in a particular order or position; the act of placing things in a particular order: *plans of the possible seating arrangements* ◊ *the art of flower arrangement* **5** [C] ~ **(of sth) (for sth)** a piece of music that has been changed, for example for another instrument to play: *an arrangement of a Mozart aria for clarinet and piano*

**ar·ran·ger** /əˈreɪndʒə(r)/ *noun* **1** a person who changes a piece of music written by sb else, so that it is suitable for a particular instrument or voice **2** a person who plans or organizes things: *arrangers of care services for the elderly* ⊃ see also FLOWER ARRANGER

**ar·rant** /ˈærənt/ *adj.* [only before noun] (*old-fashioned*) used to emphasize how bad sth/sb is: *arrant nonsense*

**array** /əˈreɪ/ *noun, verb*
■ *noun* **1** [usually sing.] a group or collection of things or people, often one that is large or impressive: *a vast array of bottles of different shapes and sizes* ◊ *a dazzling array of talent* **2** (*computing*) a way of organizing and storing related data in a computer memory **3** (*specialist*) a set of numbers, signs or values arranged in rows and columns
■ *verb* [usually passive] (*formal*) **1** to arrange a group of things in an attractive way or so that they are in order: **be arrayed (+ adv./prep.)** *Jars of all shapes and sizes were arrayed on the shelves.* **2** (*specialist*) to arrange soldiers in a position from which they are ready to attack: **(be) arrayed (against sb)** (*figurative*) *the hostile forces arrayed against them*

**array·ed** /əˈreɪd/ *adj.* [not before noun] ~ **(in sth)** (*literary*) dressed in a particular way, especially in beautiful clothes: *She was arrayed in a black velvet gown.*

**ar·rears** /əˈrɪəz; *NAmE* əˈrɪrz/ *noun* [pl.] money that sb owes that they have not paid at the right time: *rent/mortgage/tax arrears*
**IDM** **be in arrears** | **get/fall into arrears** to be late in paying money that you owe: *We're two months in arrears with the rent.* **in arrears** if money or a person is paid in arrears for work, the money is paid after the work has been done

**ar·rest** /əˈrest/ *verb, noun*
■ *verb* **1** [T, often passive] if the police arrest sb, the person is taken to a POLICE STATION and kept there because the police believe they may be guilty of a crime: ~ **sb** *A man has been arrested in connection with the robbery.* ◊ *Police arrested three suspects.* ◊ ~ **sb for sth** *She was arrested for drug-related offences.* ◊ ~ **sb for doing sth** *You could get arrested for doing that.* ⊃ WORDFINDER NOTE at POLICE **2** [T] ~ **sth** (*formal*) to stop a process or a development: *They failed to arrest the company's decline.* **3** [T] ~ **sth** (*formal*) to make sb notice sth and pay attention to it: *An unusual noise arrested his attention.* **4** [I] (*medical*) if

# arroyo

sb **arrests**, their heart stops beating: *He arrested on the way to the hospital.*
■ *noun* [C, U] **1** the act of arresting sb: *The police made several arrests.* ◊ **under** ~ *She was under arrest on suspicion of murder.* ◊ *Opposition leaders were put under* **house arrest** (= not allowed to leave their houses). ⊃ see also CITIZEN'S ARREST **2** an act of sth stopping or being interrupted: *He died after suffering a* **cardiac arrest** (= when his heart suddenly stopped).

**ar·rest·ing** /əˈrestɪŋ/ *adj.* (*formal*) attracting a lot of attention; very attractive

**ar·rival** /əˈraɪvl/ *noun* **1** [U, C] an act of coming or being brought to a place: *We apologize for the late arrival of the train.* ◊ *Our estimated time of arrival is 7.15.* ◊ **on/upon** ~ *Guests receive dinner on arrival at the hotel.* ◊ *There are 120 arrivals and departures every day.* ◊ *daily arrivals of refugees* ◊ *They are eagerly awaiting the arrival of their new computer.* **OPP** **departure 2** [U] **arrivals** the part of an airport that you go through when you arrive on a plane: *I made my way through arrivals.* ⊃ compare DEPARTURES **3** [C] a person or thing that comes to a place: *The first arrivals at the concert got the best seats.* ◊ *early/late/new arrivals* ◊ *We're expecting a new arrival* (= a baby) *in the family soon.* **4** [U] the time when a new technology or idea is introduced: *the arrival of pay TV* **IDM** see DEAD *adj.*

**ar·rive** /əˈraɪv/ *verb* **1** [I] (*abbr.* **arr.**) to get to a place, especially at the end of a journey: *I'll wait until they arrive.* ◊ *I was pleased to hear you arrived home safely.* ◊ **to arrive early/late** *for a meeting* ◊ ~ **in…** *She'll arrive in New York at noon.* ◊ **at…** *The train arrived at the station 20 minutes late.* ◊ *We didn't arrive back at the hotel until very late.* ◊ *By the time I arrived on the scene, it was all over.* ◊ *Pupils may be newly arrived in Britain, with little or no English.* **2** [I] (of things) to be brought to sb: *A letter arrived for you this morning.* ◊ *Send your application to arrive by 31 October.* ◊ *We waited an hour for our lunch to arrive.* ◊ *The new product will arrive on supermarket shelves* (= be available) *early next year.* **3** [I] (of an event or a moment) to happen or come to be, especially when you have been waiting for it: *The wedding day finally arrived.* ◊ *The baby arrived* (= was born) *early.*
**IDM** **sb has arrived** (*informal*) somebody has become successful: *He knew he had arrived when he was shortlisted for the Man Booker prize.*
**PHRV** **ar'rive at sth** to decide on or find sth, especially after discussion and thought **SYN** **reach**: *to arrive at an agreement/a decision/a conclusion* ◊ *to arrive at the truth*

**ar·ro·gance** /ˈærəɡəns/ *noun* [U] the behaviour of a person when they feel that they are more important than other people, so that they are rude to them or do not consider them

**ar·ro·gant** /ˈærəɡənt/ *adj.* behaving in a proud, unpleasant way, showing little thought for other people ▸ **ar·ro·gant·ly** *adv.*

**ar·ro·gate** /ˈærəɡeɪt/ *verb* ~ **sth (to yourself)** (*formal*) to claim or take sth that you have no right to: *I do not arrogate to myself the right to decide.*

**arrow** /ˈærəʊ/ *noun* **1** a thin stick with a sharp point at one end, which is shot from a bow: *a bow and arrow* ◊ *to fire/shoot an arrow* ◊ *The road continues as straight as an arrow.* **2** a mark or sign like an arrow (→), used to show direction or position: *Follow the arrows.* ◊ *Use the arrow keys to move the cursor.*

**ar·row·head** /ˈærəʊhed/ *noun* the sharp pointed end of an ARROW

**ar·row·root** /ˈærəʊruːt/ *noun* [U] a plant whose roots can be cooked and eaten or made into a type of flour, used especially to make sauces thick; the flour itself

**ar·royo** /əˈrɔɪəʊ/ *noun* (*pl.* **-os**) (*from Spanish*) a narrow channel with steep sides cut by a river in a desert region

---
Oxford Phrasal Academic Lexicon (OPAL) written and spoken word lists | OPAL written word list | OPAL spoken word list

# arsenal

**arse** /ɑːs; *NAmE* ɑːrs/ *noun, verb*
- *noun* (*BrE*, *taboo*, *slang*) **1** (*NAmE* **ass**) the part of the body that you sit on; your bottom: *Get off your arse!* (= stop sitting around doing nothing) **2** (usually following an adjective) a stupid person ⇒ see also SMART-ARSE
- **IDM My arse!** (*BrE*, *taboo*, *slang*) used by some people to show they do not believe what sb has said **work your 'arse off** (*BrE*, *taboo*, *slang*) to work very hard ⇒ more at ASS, KISS *v*., KNOW *v*., LICK *v*., PAIN *n*.
- *verb*
- **IDM can't be 'arsed (to do sth)** (*BrE*, *taboo*, *slang*) to not want to do sth because it is too much trouble: *I was supposed to do some work this weekend but I couldn't be arsed.*
- **PHRV arse a'bout/a'round** (*BrE*, *taboo*, *slang*) to waste time by behaving in a silly way

**arse-hole** /ˈɑːshəʊl; *NAmE* ˈɑːrs-/ (*BrE*) (*NAmE* **ass-hole**) *noun* (*taboo, slang*) **1** the ANUS **2** a stupid or unpleasant person: *What an arsehole!*

**ar-senal** /ˈɑːsənl; *NAmE* ˈɑːrs-/ *noun* **1** a collection of weapons such as guns and EXPLOSIVES: *Britain's nuclear arsenal* **2** a building where military weapons and EXPLOSIVES are made or stored

**ar-senic** /ˈɑːsnɪk; *NAmE* ˈɑːrs-/ *noun* [U] (*symb.* **As**) a chemical element. Arsenic is a grey METALLOID (= has properties of both metals and other solid substances) and is very poisonous, especially in its compound forms.

**arson** /ˈɑːsn; *NAmE* ˈɑːrsn/ *noun* [U, C] the crime of deliberately setting fire to sth, especially a building: *to carry out an arson attack*

**ar-son-ist** /ˈɑːsənɪst; *NAmE* ˈɑːrs-/ *noun* a person who commits the crime of arson

**art** 🔑 **A1** /ɑːt; *NAmE* ɑːrt/ *noun, verb*
- *noun* **1** **A1** [U] the use of the imagination to express ideas or feelings, particularly in painting, drawing or sculpture: *modern/contemporary art* ◇ *an art critic/historian/lover* ◇ *Can we call television art?* ◇ *stolen works of art* ◇ *Her performance displayed great art.* ⇒ see also CLIP ART, FINE ART **2** **A1** [U] examples of objects such as paintings, drawings or sculptures: *an art gallery/exhibition* ◇ *a collection of art and antiques* ⇒ WORDFINDER NOTE at PAINTING **3** **A1** [U] the skill of creating objects such as paintings and drawings, especially when you study it: *She's good at art and design.* ◇ *He has a master's degree in fine art.* **4** **B1** **the arts** [pl.] art, music, theatre, literature, etc. when you think of them as a group: *lottery funding for the arts* ⇒ see also PERFORMING ARTS **5** [C] a type of visual or performing art: *Dance is a very theatrical art.* **6** **B1** [C, usually pl.] the subjects you can study at school or university that are not sciences, such as languages, history or literature: *an arts degree* ⇒ compare SCIENCE ⇒ see also LIBERAL ARTS **7** [C, U] an ability or a skill that you can develop with training and practice: *I've never mastered the art of making bread.* ◇ *Letter-writing is a lost art nowadays.* ◇ *Appearing confident at interviews is quite an art* (= rather difficult). **IDM** see FINE ART
- *verb* **thou art** (*old use*) used to mean 'you are', when talking to one person

**art deco** /ˌɑːt ˈdekəʊ; *NAmE* ˌɑːrt/ (*also* **Art Deco**) *noun* [U] a popular style of art in the 1920s and 1930s that has GEOMETRIC shapes with clear outlines and bright strong colours

**'art director** *noun* **1** the person who is responsible for the pictures, photos, etc. in a magazine **2** the person who is responsible for the SETS and PROPS when a film is being made

**arte-fact** (*also* **ar-ti-fact** *especially in NAmE*) /ˈɑːtɪfækt; *NAmE* ˈɑːrt-/ *noun* (*specialist*) an object that is made by a person, especially sth of historical or cultural interest

**ar-terio-scler-osis** /ɑːˌtɪəriəʊskləˈrəʊsɪs; *NAmE* ɑːrˌtɪr-/ *noun* [U] (*medical*) a condition in which the walls of the ARTERIES become thick and hard, making it difficult for blood to flow

**ar-tery** /ˈɑːtəri; *NAmE* ˈɑːrt-/ *noun* (*pl.* **-ies**) **1** any of the tubes that carry blood from the heart to other parts of the body: *blocked arteries* ⇒ compare VEIN ⇒ see also CORONARY ARTERY **2** a large and important road, river, railway line, etc. ▶ **ar-ter-ial** /ɑːˈtɪəriəl; *NAmE* ɑːrˈtɪr-/ *adj.* [only before noun]: *arterial blood/disease* ◇ *an arterial road*

**ar-te-sian** /ɑːˈtiːziən; *NAmE* ɑːrˈtiːʒn/ *adj.* [only before noun] (of a WELL or spring) in which water rises to the surface of the ground by natural pressure

**'art form** *noun* **1** [C] a particular type of artistic activity: *The short story is a difficult art form to master.* **2** [sing.] an activity that sb does very well and gives them the opportunity to show imagination: *She has elevated the dinner party into an art form.*

**art-ful** /ˈɑːtfl; *NAmE* ˈɑːrt-/ *adj.* [usually before noun] **1** (*disapproving*) clever at getting what you want, sometimes by not telling the truth **SYN** **crafty** **2** (of things or actions) designed or done in a clever way ▶ **art-ful-ly** /-fəli/ *adv.*

**'art gallery** (*also* **gal·lery**) *noun* a building where paintings and other works of art are shown to the public

**art 'history** *noun* [U] the study of the history of painting, sculpture, etc.

**'art house** *noun* a cinema that shows films that are usually made by small companies and are not usually seen by a wide audience: *an art-house cinema/theater* ◇ *art-house films/audiences*

**arth-ritic** /ɑːˈθrɪtɪk; *NAmE* ɑːrˈθ-/ *adj.* suffering from or caused by arthritis: *arthritic hands/pain*

**arth-ritis** /ɑːˈθraɪtɪs; *NAmE* ɑːrˈθ-/ *noun* [U] a disease that causes one or more JOINTS of the body to become painful and SWOLLEN (= larger than normal) ⇒ see also OSTEOARTHRITIS, RHEUMATOID ARTHRITIS

**arthro-pod** /ˈɑːθrəpɒd; *NAmE* ˈɑːrθrəpɑːd/ *noun* (*biology*) an INVERTEBRATE animal such as an insect, spider or CRAB, that has its SKELETON on the outside of its body and has JOINTS on its legs

**arthro-scopic surgery** /ˌɑːθrəˈskɒpɪk ˈsɜːdʒəri; *NAmE* ˌɑːrθrəˈskɑːpɪk ˈsɜːrdʒ-/ (*NAmE*) (*BrE* **keyhole 'surgery**) *noun* medical operations that involve only a very small cut being made in the patient's body

**Ar-thur-ian** /ɑːˈθjʊəriən; *NAmE* ɑːrˈθʊr-/ *adj.* connected with the stories about Arthur, a king of ancient Britain, his Knights of the Round Table and COURT at Camelot: *Arthurian legends*

**ar-ti-choke** /ˈɑːtɪtʃəʊk; *NAmE* ˈɑːrt-/ *noun* [C, U] **1** (*also* **globe 'arti-choke**) a round vegetable with a lot of thick green leaves. The bottom part of the leaves and the inside of the artichoke can be eaten when cooked. ⇒ VISUAL VOCAB page V5 **2** (*BrE*) = JERUSALEM ARTICHOKE

**art-icle** 🔑 **A1** 🔊 /ˈɑːtɪkl; *NAmE* ˈɑːrt-/ *noun* **1** **A1** a piece of writing about a particular subject in a newspaper or magazine, on a website, etc: *to read/write/publish an article* ◇ *~ (by sb) on/about sth* *I read an interesting article by a well-known scientist on the subject of genetics.* ◇ **according to an ~** *According to a recent newspaper article, the company is worth over $20 billion.* ⇒ see also LEADING ARTICLE ⇒ WORDFINDER NOTE at NEWSPAPER **2** (*law*) a separate item in an agreement or contract: *Article 10 of the European Convention guarantees free speech.* **3** (*formal*) a particular item or separate thing, especially one of a set **SYN** **item**: *articles of clothing* ◇ *toilet articles such as soap and shampoo* ◇ *The articles found in the car helped the police to identify the body.* **4** (*grammar*) the words *a* and *an* (**the indefinite article**) or *the* (**the definite article**).

**art-icled** /ˈɑːtɪkld; *NAmE* ˈɑːrt-/ *adj.* (*BrE*) employed by a group of lawyers, architects or ACCOUNTANTS while training to become qualified: *an articled clerk* (= sb who is training to be a SOLICITOR) ◇ *~ to sb/sth* *She was articled to a firm of solicitors.*

**article of 'faith** *noun* (*pl.* **articles of faith**) something you believe very strongly, as if it were a religious belief

**ar-ticu-late** **B2** **C1** *verb, adj.*
- *verb* /ɑːˈtɪkjuleɪt; *NAmE* ɑːrˈt-/ **1** **B2** **C1** ~ **sth (to sb)** (*formal*) to express or explain your thoughts or feelings clearly in words: *She struggled to articulate her thoughts.* **2** **B2** **C1** [I, T] to speak, pronounce or play sth in a clear way: *He was too drunk to articulate properly.* ◇ *~sth Every*

note was carefully articulated. **3** [I] ~ **(with sth)** (formal) to be related to sth so that together the two parts form a whole: *These courses are designed to articulate with university degrees.* **4** [I, T] (specialist) to be joined to sth else in this way: ~ **(with sth)** *bones that articulate with others* ◇ ~ **sth** *a robot with articulated limbs* ▶ **ar·tic·u·la·tion** /ɑːˌtɪkjuˈleɪʃn; *NAmE* ɑːrt-/ *noun* [U]: *the articulation of his theory* ◇ *The singer worked hard on the clear articulation of every note.*
- **adj.** /ɑːˈtɪkjələt; *NAmE* ɑːrˈt-/ **1** (of a person) good at expressing ideas or feelings clearly in words **2** (of speech) clearly expressed or pronounced: *All we could hear were loud sobs, but no articulate words.* **OPP** inarticulate ▶ **ar·tic·u·late·ly** *adv.*

**ar·ticu·lated** /ɑːˈtɪkjuleɪtɪd; *NAmE* ɑːrˈt-/ *adj.* (of a vehicle) with two or more sections joined together in a way that makes it easier to turn corners: *an articulated lorry/truck* ⊃ see also TRACTOR-TRAILER

**ar·ti·fact** (especially *NAmE*) = ARTEFACT

**ar·ti·fice** /ˈɑːtɪfɪs; *NAmE* ˈɑːrt-/ *noun* [U, C] (formal) the clever use of tricks to cheat sb **SYN** cunning

**ar·ti·fi·cial** 🌐 **B2** /ˌɑːtɪˈfɪʃl; *NAmE* ˌɑːrt-/ *adj.* **1** 🔊 **B2** made or produced to copy sth natural; not real: *an artificial limb/flower/sweetener/fertilizer* ◇ *artificial lighting/light* **2** 🔊 **B2** created by people; not happening naturally: *A job interview is a very artificial situation.* ◇ *the artificial barriers of race, class and gender* **3** 🔊 **B2** not what it appears to be **SYN** fake: *artificial emotion* ▶ **ar·ti·fi·ci·al·ity** /ˌɑːtɪˌfɪʃiˈæləti; *NAmE* ˌɑːrt-/ *noun* [U] **ar·ti·fi·ci·al·ly** /ˌɑːtɪˈfɪʃəli; *NAmE* ˌɑːrt-/ *adv.*: *artificially created lakes* ◇ *artificially low prices*

▼ **SYNONYMS**

### artificial
synthetic • false • man-made • fake • imitation

These words all describe things that are not real, or not naturally produced or grown.

**artificial** made or produced to copy sth natural; not real: *artificial flowers* ◇ *artificial light*

**synthetic** made by combining chemical substances rather than being produced naturally by plants or animals: *synthetic drugs* ◇ *shoes with synthetic soles*

**false** not natural: *false teeth* ◇ *a false beard*

**man-made** made by people; not natural: *man-made fibres such as nylon*

**fake** made to look like sth else; not real: *a fake-fur jacket*

**imitation** [only before noun] made to look like sth else; not real: *She would never wear imitation pearls.*

**PATTERNS**
- artificial / synthetic / man-made **fabrics / fibres / materials / products**
- artificial / synthetic / fake / imitation **fur / leather**
- artificial / synthetic / false / fake / imitation **diamonds / pearls**

ˌartificial inseminˈnation *noun* [U] (*abbr.* **AI**) the process of making a woman or female animal pregnant by an artificial method of putting male SPERM inside her, and not by sexual activity: *artificial insemination by a donor*, abbreviated to 'AID'

ˌartificial inˈtelligence *noun* [U] (*abbr.* **AI**) (*computing*) the study and development of computer systems that can copy intelligent human behaviour

**ar·til·lery** /ɑːˈtɪləri; *NAmE* ɑːrˈt-/ *noun* **1** [U] large, heavy guns which are often moved on wheels: *The town is under heavy artillery fire.* **2 the artillery** [sing.] the section of an army trained to use these guns ⊃ WORDFINDER NOTE at ARMY

**ar·ti·san** /ˌɑːtɪˈzæn; *NAmE* ˈɑːrtəzn/ *noun, adj.*
- **noun** (formal) a person who does work that needs a special skill, making things with their hands **SYN** craftsman
- **adj.** [only before noun] (also **ar·ti·san·al** /ɑːˈtɪzənl; *NAmE* ɑːrˈtiːz-/) **1** relating to an artisan, or typical of an artisan's work: *an artisan bakery* ◇ *artisanal skills* **2** (of food and

drink) made in a traditional way with high-quality ingredients: *artisan bread*

**art·ist** 🌐 **A1** /ˈɑːtɪst; *NAmE* ˈɑːrt-/ *noun* **1** 🔊 **A1** a person who creates works of art, especially paintings or drawings: *an exhibition of work by contemporary British artists* ◇ *a graphic artist* ◇ *a make-up artist* ◇ *He became a full-time artist in 1929.* **2** 🔊 **B2** (*also* **ar·tiste** /ɑːˈtiːst; *NAmE* ɑːrˈt-/) a person who is a professional singer, dancer, actor, etc: *a recording/solo artist*

**art·is·tic** 🌐 **B2** /ɑːˈtɪstɪk; *NAmE* ɑːrˈt-/ *adj.* **1** 🔊 **B2** connected with art or artists: *the artistic style of the period* ◇ *a work of great artistic merit* **2** 🔊 **B2** showing a natural skill or pleasure in art, especially being able to paint or draw well: *artistic abilities/achievements/skills/talent* ◇ *She comes from a very artistic family.* **3** 🔊 **B2** done with skill and imagination; attractive or beautiful: *an artistic arrangement of dried flowers* **IDM** see LICENCE ▶ **art·is·tic·al·ly** /-kli/ *adv.*

arˌtistic diˈrector *noun* the person in charge of deciding which plays, OPERAS, etc. a theatre company will perform, and the general artistic policy of the company ⊃ WORDFINDER NOTE at THEATRE

**art·is·try** /ˈɑːtɪstri; *NAmE* ˈɑːrt-/ *noun* [U] the skill of an artist: *He played the piece with effortless artistry.*

**art·less** /ˈɑːtləs; *NAmE* ˈɑːrt-/ *adj.* (formal) **1** simple, natural and honest: *the artless sincerity of a young child* **2** made without skill or art

**art nouˈveau** /ˌɑː nuːˈvəʊ, ˌɑː; *NAmE* ˌɑːrt, ˌɑːr/ (also **Art Nouveau**) *noun* [U] a style of art and architecture popular in Europe and the US at the end of the 19th century and beginning of the 20th century that uses complicated designs and curved patterns based on natural shapes like leaves and flowers

ˌarts and ˈcrafts *noun* [pl.] activities that need both artistic and practical skills, such as making cloth, jewellery and POTTERY

**artsy** /ˈɑːtsi; *NAmE* ˈɑːrt-/ *adj.* (*NAmE*, *informal*, *usually disapproving*) = ARTY

ˌart ˈtherapy *noun* [U] a type of PSYCHOTHERAPY in which you are encouraged to express yourself using art materials

**art·work** 🔊+ **B2** /ˈɑːtwɜːk; *NAmE* ˈɑːrtwɜːrk/ *noun* **1** 🔊+ **B2** [U] pictures and photographs prepared for books, magazines, etc. **2** 🔊+ **B2** [C, U] a work of art, especially one in a museum; works of art as a group: *a collection of artwork from tribal cultures*

**arty** /ˈɑːti; *NAmE* ˈɑːrti/ (*BrE*) (*NAmE* **artsy**) *adj.* (*informal*, *usually disapproving*) making a strong display of being very artistic or interested in the arts: *She hangs out with the arty types she met at drama school.*

**aru·gula** /əˈruːɡjulə; *NAmE* əˈruːɡələ/ (*NAmE*) (*BrE* **rocket**) *noun* [U] a plant with long green leaves that have a strong taste and are eaten raw in salads ⊃ VISUAL VOCAB page V5

**arvo** /ˈɑːvəʊ; *NAmE* ˈɑːrv-/ *noun* (*pl.* **-os**) (*AustralE*, *NZE*, *informal*) afternoon: *See you this arvo!*

**-ary** /əri, ri; *NAmE* eri, əri/ *suffix* (in adjectives and nouns) connected with: *planetary* ◇ *budgetary*

**Aryan** /ˈeəriən; *NAmE* ˈer-/ *noun* **1** a member of the group of people, who spoke an Indo-European language, that went to South Asia in around 1500 BC **2** the language of the Aryan people **3** (according to the ideas of the German Nazi party) a member of a Caucasian, not Jewish, race of people, especially one with fair hair and blue eyes ▶ **Aryan** *adj.*

**as** 🌐 **A1** /əz, *strong form* æz/ *prep., adv., conj.*
- **prep. 1** 🔊 **A1** used to describe sb/sth appearing to be sb/sth else: *They were all dressed as clowns.* ◇ *The bomb was disguised as a package.* **2** 🔊 **A1** used to describe the fact that sb/sth has a particular job or function: *She works as a courier.* ◇ *Treat me as a friend.* ◇ *I respect him as a doctor.* ◇ *You can use that glass as a vase.* ◇ *The news came as a*

# ASA

shock. ◊ She had been there often as a child (= when she was a child).
- **adv. 1** 🔑 **A2** **as … as …** used when you are comparing two people or things, or two situations: *You're as tall as your father.* ◊ *He was as white as a sheet.* ◊ *She doesn't play as well as her sister.* ◊ *I haven't known him as long as you* (= as you have known him). ◊ *He doesn't earn as much as me.* ◊ *He doesn't earn as much as I do.* ◊ *It's not as hard as I thought.* ◊ *Run as fast as you can.* ◊ *We'd like it as soon as possible.* **2** 🔑 **A2** used to say that sth happens in the same way: *As always, he said little.* ◊ *The 'h' in honest is silent, as in 'hour'.* **3 as … as …** used to emphasize an amount: *As many as 2 million people could be affected.*
- **conj. 1** 🔑 **A2** while sth else is happening: *He sat watching her as she got ready.* ◊ *As she grew older she gained in confidence.* ⊃ LANGUAGE BANK at PROCESS¹ **2** 🔑 **A2** in the way in which: *They did as I had asked.* ◊ *Leave the papers as they are.* ◊ *She lost it, just as I said she would.* **3** 🔑 **B1** used to state the reason for sth: *As you were out, I left a message.* ◊ *She may need some help as she's new.* **4** used to make a comment or to add information about what you have just said: *As you know, Julia is leaving soon.* ◊ *She's very tall, as is her mother.* **5** used to say that although sth is true, what follows is also true **SYN** **though**: *Happy as they were, there was something missing.* ◊ *Try as he might* (= however hard he tried), *he couldn't open the door.*
- **IDM** **as against sth** in contrast with sth: *They got 27 per cent of the vote as against 32 per cent at the last election.* **as and 'when** used to say that sth may happen at some time in the future, but only when sth else has happened: *We'll decide on the team as and when we qualify.* ◊ *I'll tell you more as and when* (= as soon as I can). **as for sb/sth** 🔑 **B2** used to start talking about sb/sth **SYN** **regarding**: *As for Jo, she's doing fine.* ◊ *As for food for the party, that's all being taken care of.* **as from … / as of …** used to show the time or date from which sth starts: *Our phone number is changing as from May 12.* **as if** 🔑 **B1** | **as though** 🔑 **B2** in a way that suggests sth: *He behaved as if nothing had happened.* ◊ *It sounds as though you had a good time.* ◊ *It's my birthday. As if you didn't know!* ◊ *'Don't say anything.' 'As if I would!'* (= surely you do not expect me to) **as it 'is** considering the present situation; as things are: *We were hoping to finish it by next week—as it is, it may be the week after.* ◊ *I can't help—I've got too much to do as it is* (= already). **as it 'were** used when a speaker is giving his or her own impression of a situation or expressing sth in a particular way: *Teachers must put the brakes on, as it were, when they notice students looking puzzled.* **as to sth | as regards sth** used when you are referring to sth: *As to tax, that will be deducted from your salary.* ◊ *I have a few ideas as to how we might do this.* **as you 'do** (*BrE, informal*) used as a comment on sth that you have just said: *He smiled and I smiled back. As you do.* ⊃ more at WELL *adv.*, YET *adv.*

---

▼ **WHICH WORD?**

**as / like**
You can use both **as** and **like** to say that things are similar.
- **Like** is a preposition and is used before nouns and pronouns: *He has blue eyes like me.*
- **As** is a conjunction and an adverb and is used before a clause, another adverb or a clause beginning with a preposition: *She enjoys all kinds of music, as I do.* ◊ *Repeat these five steps, as in the last exercise.*
- In informal English **like** is frequently used as a conjunction or an adverb instead of **as**: *Nobody understands him like I do.* ◊ *I don't want to upset him again like before.* It is also used instead of **as if**: *It looks like we're going to be late.* These uses of **like** are common but are not considered correct in formal written English.

You will find more help on the use of **as** and **like** in the entries for particular verbs, such as *act, behave,* etc.

---

**ASA** /ˌeɪ es 'eɪ/ *abbr.* Advertising Standards Authority (an organization in the UK that controls the standard of advertising)

**asap** /ˌeɪ es eɪ 'piː, 'eɪsæp/ *abbr.* as soon as possible

**as·bes·tos** /æs'bestɒs; *NAmE* æz'bestəs/ *noun* [U] a soft grey mineral that does not burn and can be WOVEN into material, used especially in the past in building as a protection against fire or to prevent heat loss. Asbestos is dangerous if you breathe it in.

**as·bes·tosis** /ˌæsbe'stəʊsɪs; *NAmE* ˌæzbes'toʊ-/ *noun* [U] a disease of the lungs caused by breathing in asbestos dust

**as·cend** /ə'send/ *verb* [I, T] (*formal*) to rise; to go up; to climb up: *The path started to ascend more steeply.* ◊ *The air became colder as we ascended.* ◊ *The results, ranked in ascending order* (= from the lowest to the highest) *are as follows:* ◊ **~ from sth** *Mist ascended from the valley.* ◊ **~ to sth** (*figurative*) *He ascended to the peak of sporting achievement.* ◊ **~ sth** *Her heart was thumping as she ascended the stairs.* ◊ (*figurative*) *to ascend the throne* (= become king or queen) **OPP** **descend**

**as·cend·ancy** (also **as·cend·ency**) /ə'sendənsi/ *noun* [U, sing.] (*formal*) the position of having power or influence over sb/sth: **in the ~** *The opposition party was in the ascendancy* (= gaining control). ◊ **~ over sb/sth** *The poor have a moral ascendancy over the rich.*

**as·cend·ant** (also **as·cend·ent**) /ə'sendənt/ *noun*
**IDM** **in the ascendant** (*formal*) being or becoming more powerful or popular

**as·cen·sion** /ə'senʃn/ *noun* [sing.] **1 the Ascension** (in the Christian religion) the journey of Jesus from the earth into heaven **2** (*formal*) the act of moving up or of reaching a high position: *her ascension to the throne*

**As'cension Day** *noun* (in the Christian religion) the 40th day after Easter when Christians remember when Jesus left the earth and went into heaven

**as·cent** /ə'sent/ *noun* **1** [C, usually sing.] **~ (to sth)** the act of climbing or moving up; a journey that goes up sth: *the first ascent of Mount Everest* ◊ *The cart began its gradual ascent up the hill.* ◊ *The rocket steepened its ascent.* **OPP** **descent 2** [C, usually sing.] **~ (to sth)** a path or slope that goes up sth: *At the other side of the valley was a steep ascent to the top of the hill.* **OPP** **descent 3** [U] **~ (to sth)** (*formal*) the process of moving forward to a better position or of making progress: *man's ascent to civilization*

**as·cer·tain** /ˌæsə'teɪn; *NAmE* ˌæsər't-/ *verb* (*formal*) to find out the true or correct information about sth: **~ sth** *It can be difficult to ascertain the facts.* ◊ **~ that …** *I ascertained that the driver was not badly hurt.* ◊ *it is ascertained that … It should be ascertained that the plans comply with the law.* ◊ **~ what, whether, etc …** *The police are trying to ascertain what really happened.* ◊ *Could you ascertain whether she will be coming to the meeting?* ◊ *it is ascertained what, whether, etc …* *It must be ascertained if the land is still owned by the government.* ▶ **as·cer·tain·able** *adj.* **as·cer·tain·ment** *noun* [U]

**as·cet·ic** /ə'setɪk/ *adj.* [usually before noun] not allowing yourself physical pleasures, especially for religious reasons; related to a simple and strict way of living: *The monks lived a very ascetic life.* ▶ **as·cet·ic** *noun*: *monks, hermits and ascetics* **as·ceti·cism** /-tɪsɪzəm/ *noun* [U]

**ASCII** /'æski/ *noun* [U] (*computing*) a standard code used so that data can be moved between computers that use different programs (the abbreviation for 'American Standard Code for Information Interchange')

**as·cor·bic acid** /əˌskɔːbɪk 'æsɪd; *NAmE* əˌskɔːrb-/ *noun* [U] = VITAMIN C

**ascot** /'æskɒt; *NAmE* 'æskɑːt/ *noun* (*NAmE*) = CRAVAT

**ascribe** /ə'skraɪb/ *verb*
**PHRV** **a'scribe sth to sb** to consider or state that a book, etc. was written by a particular person **SYN** **attribute**: *This play is usually ascribed to Shakespeare.* **a'scribe sth to sb/sth** (*formal*) **1** to consider that sth is caused by a particular thing or person: *He ascribed his failure to bad luck.* **2** to consider that sb/sth has or should have a particular quality **SYN** **attribute**: *We ascribe great importance to these policies.* ▶ **ascrib·able** *adj.*: **~ to sb/sth** *Their success is ascribable to the quality of their goods.* **ascrip·tion** /ə'skrɪpʃn/ *noun* [U, C]: **~ (to sb/sth)** *the ascription of meaning to objects and events*

**ASEAN** /ˈæsiæn/ abbr. Association of Southeast Asian Nations

**asep·tic** /ˌeɪˈseptɪk/ adj. (medical) free from harmful bacteria **OPP** septic

**asex·ual** /ˌeɪˈsekʃuəl/ adj. **1** (specialist) not involving sex; not having sexual organs: *asexual reproduction* **2** not having sexual qualities; not interested in sex: *the tendency to see old people as asexual* ▶ **asex·ual·ly** /-ʃəli/ adv.: *to reproduce asexually*

**ash** /æʃ/ noun **1** [U] the grey or black powder that is left after sth, especially TOBACCO, wood or coal, has burnt: *cigarette ash* ◊ *black volcanic ash* ◊ *picture at* VOLCANO **2** **ashes** [pl.] what is left after sth has been destroyed by burning: *The town was reduced to ashes in the fighting.* ◊ *the glowing ashes of the campfire* ◊ (figurative) *The party had risen, like a phoenix, from the ashes of electoral disaster.* **3** **ashes** [pl.] the powder that is left after a dead person's body has been CREMATED (= burned): *She wanted her ashes to be scattered at sea.* ◊ **WORDFINDER NOTE** *at* DIE **4** [C, U] (also **ˈash tree**) a forest tree with grey BARK ◊ **VISUAL VOCAB** *page* V6 ◊ *see also* MOUNTAIN ASH **5** [U] the hard pale wood of the ash tree **6** (specialist) the letter æ, used in Old English, and as a PHONETIC symbol to represent the vowel sound in *cat* **IDM** *see* SACKCLOTH

**ashamed** /əˈʃeɪmd/ adj. [not before noun] **1** feeling shame or feeling embarrassed about sb/sth or because of sth you have done: *~ of sth She was deeply ashamed of her behaviour at the party.* ◊ *Mental illness is nothing to be ashamed of.* ◊ *~ of sb His daughter looked such a mess that he was ashamed of her.* ◊ *~ of yourself You should be ashamed of yourself for telling such lies.* ◊ *~ that ... I feel almost ashamed that I've been so lucky.* ◊ *~ to be sth The football riots made me ashamed to be English.* ◊ **WORDFINDER NOTE** *at* SORRY **2** *~ to do sth* unwilling to do sth because of shame or fear of feeling embarrassed: *I'm ashamed to say that I lied to her.* ◊ *I cried at the end and I'm not ashamed to admit it.*

▼ WHICH WORD?

**ashamed / embarrassed**
- You feel **ashamed** when you feel guilty because of something wrong that you have deliberately done: *You should be ashamed of treating your daughter like that.* Do not use **ashamed** when you are talking about something that is not very serious or important: *I am sorry that I forgot to buy the milk.* ◊ ~~I am ashamed that I forgot to buy the milk.~~
- You feel **embarrassed** when you have made a mistake or done something stupid or feel uncomfortable in front of other people: *I was embarrassed about forgetting his name.*

**ashen** /ˈæʃn/ adj. (usually of sb's face) very pale; without colour because of illness or fear: *They listened ashen-faced to the news.* ◊ *His face was ashen and wet with sweat.*

**Ash·ken·azi** /ˌæʃkəˈnɑːzi/ noun (pl. **Ash·ken·azim** /-zɪm/) a Jew whose ANCESTORS came from central or eastern Europe ◊ *compare* SEPHARDI

**ashore** /əˈʃɔː(r)/ adv. towards, onto or on land, having come from an area of water such as the sea or a river: *to come/go ashore* ◊ *a drowned body found washed ashore on the beach* ◊ *The cruise included several days ashore.*

**ash·ram** /ˈæʃrəm/ noun a place where Hindus who wish to live away from society live together as a group; a place where other Hindus go for a short time to say prayers before returning to society

**ash·tray** /ˈæʃtreɪ/ noun a container into which people who smoke put ASH, cigarette ends, etc.

**Ash ˈWednesday** noun [U, C] the first day of Lent ◊ *see also* SHROVE TUESDAY

**Asian** /ˈeɪʒn; BrE also ˈeɪʃn/ noun, adj.
■ *noun* a person from Asia, or whose family originally came from Asia: *British Asians* **HELP** In BrE **Asian** is used especially to refer to people from India, Pakistan and Bangladesh. In NAmE it is used especially to refer to people from the Far East.
■ *adj.* of or connected with Asia: *Asian music*

**Asian Aˈmerican** noun a person from America whose family come from Asia, especially East Asia ▶ **Asian-Aˈmerican** adj.

**Asi·at·ic** /ˌeɪziˈætɪk; BrE also ˌeɪʃi-/ adj. (specialist) of or connected with Asia: *the Asiatic tropics*

**aside** /əˈsaɪd/ adv., noun
■ *adv.* **1** to one side; out of the way: *She pulled the curtain aside.* ◊ **Stand aside** *and let these people pass.* ◊ *He took me aside* (= away from a group of people) *to give me some advice.* ◊ (figurative) **Leaving aside** (= not considering at this stage) *the cost of the scheme, let us examine its benefits.* ◊ *All our protests were brushed aside* (= ignored). **2** to be used later: *We set aside some money for repairs.* **3** used after nouns to say that except for one thing, sth is true: *Money worries aside, things are going well.*
■ *noun* **1** (in the theatre) something that a character in a play says to the audience, but that the other characters on stage are not intended to hear **2** a remark, often made in a low voice, that is not intended to be heard by everyone present **3** a remark that is not directly connected with the main subject that is being discussed: *I mention it only as an aside.*

**ˈA-side** noun the side of a pop record that was considered more likely to be successful ◊ *compare* B-SIDE

**aˈside from** prep. (especially NAmE) = APART FROM: *Aside from a few scratches, I'm OK.* ◊ **LANGUAGE BANK** *at* EXCEPT

**as·in·ine** /ˈæsɪnaɪn/ adj. (formal) stupid or silly **SYN** ridiculous

**ask** /ɑːsk; NAmE æsk/ verb, noun
■ *verb*
• QUESTION **1** [I, T] to say or write sth in the form of a question, in order to get information: *How old are you—if you don't mind me/my asking?* ◊ *~ about sb/sth He asked about her family.* ◊ *~ sth Can I ask a question?* ◊ *+ speech 'Where are you going?' she asked.* ◊ *~ sb + speech 'Are you sure?' he asked her.* ◊ *~ sb sth She asked the students their names.* ◊ *I often get asked that!* ◊ *I had to ask myself some very difficult questions.* ◊ *I'd like to ask you a few questions.* ◊ *~ sb about sth The interviewer asked me about my future plans.* ◊ *~ where, what, etc... He asked where I lived.* ◊ *~ sb where, what, etc... I had to ask the teacher what to do next.* **HELP** You cannot say 'ask to sb': ~~I asked to my friend what had happened.~~
• REQUEST **2** [T] to tell sb that you would like them to do sth or that you would like sth to happen: *~ sb to do sth Anyone with information is asked to contact the police.* ◊ *Parents with young children are asked to attend this meeting.* ◊ *They were politely asked to leave the shop.* ◊ *Eric asked me to marry him.* ◊ *~ whether, what, etc... I asked whether they could change my ticket.* ◊ *~ sb whether, what, etc... She asked me if I would give her English lessons.* ◊ *~ that ...* (formal) *She asked that she be kept informed of developments.* ◊ (BrE also) *She asked that she should be kept informed.* ◊ **EXPRESS YOURSELF** *at* HELP **3** [I, T] to say that you would like sb to give you sth: *~ for sth Don't be afraid to ask for help.* ◊ *I am writing to ask for some information about courses.* ◊ *~ sth Why don't you ask his advice?* ◊ *~ sb for sth Why don't you ask him for his advice?* ◊ *~ sth of sb Can I ask a favour of you?* ◊ *~ sb sth Can I ask you a favour?* ◊ **EXPRESS YOURSELF** *at* PLEASE
• PERMISSION **4** [T] to request permission to do sth: *~ to do sth I immediately asked to speak to a supervisor.* ◊ *I asked to see the manager.* ◊ *~ if, whether, etc... I'll ask if it's all right to park here.* ◊ *~ sb if, whether, etc... She asked her boss whether she could have the day off.*
• INVITE **5** [T] to invite sb: *~ sb (+ adv./prep.) They've asked me to dinner.* ◊ *I didn't ask them in* (= to come into the house). ◊ *We must ask the neighbours round* (= to our house). ◊ *~ sb to do sth She's asked him to come to the party.* ◊ **EXPRESS YOURSELF** *at* INVITE

# askance

- **MONEY 6** [T] **~ sth (for sth)** to request a particular amount of money for sth that you are selling: *He's asking £2000 for the car.*
- **EXPECT/DEMAND 7** [T] to expect or demand sth: **~sth** *I know I'm asking a great deal.* ◊ **~sth of sb** *You're asking too much of him.* ◊ **~sth to do sth** *I know it's asking a lot to expect them to win again.* ⊃ SYNONYMS at DEMAND

**IDM** ˈask for it (*informal*) to deserve sth bad that happens to you or that sb does to you | be ˈasking for trouble | be ˈasking for it (*informal*) to behave in a way that is very likely to result in trouble ˌdon't ˈask (*informal*) if you say **don't ask** to sb, you mean that you do not want to reply to their question, because it would be difficult to explain, embarrassing, etc. ˌdon't ˈask ˈme (*informal*) if you say **don't ask me**, you mean that you do not know the answer to a question and are annoyed you have been asked for the ˈasking if you can have sth **for the asking**, it is very easy for you to get it if you ask for it: *The job is yours for the asking.* I ˈask you (*informal*) if you say **I ask you**, you are expressing shock, anger or a strong feeling of dislike about sth/sb if you ˈask ˈme (*informal*) in my personal opinion: *Their marriage was a mistake, if you ask me.*

**PHRV** ˈask after sb (*ScotE* ˈask for sb) (*BrE*) to say that you would like to know how sb is, what they are doing, etc: *He always asks after you in his letters.* ˌask aˈround to speak to a number of different people in order to try and get some information: *I don't know of any vacancies in the company but I'll ask around.* ˌask sb ˈback (*especially BrE*) to invite sb to come back to your house when you are both out together: *I hoped he wouldn't ask me back.* ˈask for sb (*ScotE*) = ASK AFTER SB ˈask for sb/sth to say that you want to speak to sb or be directed to a place: *When you arrive, ask for Jane.* ˌask sb ˈout to invite sb to go out with you, especially as a way of starting a romantic relationship: *He's too shy to ask her out.*

- *noun*

**IDM** a big, huge, tough, etc. ˈask (*informal*) a difficult thing to achieve or deal with: *Beating the world champions is certainly a big ask for the team.*

> **▼ SYNONYMS**
>
> **ask**
> enquire • demand
>
> These words all mean to say or write sth in the form of a question, in order to get information.
>
> **ask** to say or write sth in the form of a question, in order to get information: *'Where are you going?' she asked.* ◊ *She asked the students their names.* ◊ *Can I ask a question?*
>
> **enquire / inquire** (*rather formal*) to ask sb for information: *I called the station to enquire about train times.*
>
> **demand** to make a very strong request for information: *'And where have you been?' he demanded angrily.*
>
> **PATTERNS**
> - to ask / enquire about / after sb / sth
> - to ask / enquire / demand sth of sb
> - to ask / enquire / demand what / who / how, etc.
> - to ask / enquire politely
> - to ask / enquire / demand angrily

**askance** /əˈskæns; *BrE also* əˈskɑːns/ *adv.*
**IDM** look askance (at sb/sth) | look (at sb/sth) askance to look at or react to sb/sth in a critical way or in a way that shows you do not trust or believe them

**ask·ari** /əˈskɑːri/ *EAfrE* [əˈskari] *noun* (*EAfrE*) a person who is employed to guard a building, valuable things, etc.; a SECURITY GUARD

**askew** /əˈskjuː/ *adv., adj.* [not before noun] not in a straight or level position **SYN** **crooked**: *His glasses had been knocked askew by the blow.* ◊ *Her hat was slightly askew.*

ˈ**asking price** *noun* the price that sb wants to sell sth for ⊃ compare COST PRICE, PURCHASE PRICE, SELLING PRICE

**asleep** 🔑 **A2** /əˈsliːp/ *adj.* [not before noun] sleeping: *I waited while they were all fast asleep* (= sleeping deeply). ◊ *He was so exhausted that he fell asleep at his desk.* ◊ *She was still half asleep* (= not fully awake) *when she arrived at work.* **OPP** **awake**
**IDM** aˌsleep on the ˈjob | aˌsleep at the ˈwheel (*NAmE also* aˌsleep at the ˈswitch) not paying enough attention to what you need to do: *They were asleep on the job as the financial crisis deepened.*

**asp** /æsp/ *noun* **1** a small poisonous snake found in south-west Europe **2** a general name for various types of small poisonous snake found in North Africa

**as·para·gus** /əˈspærəɡəs/ *noun* [U] a plant whose young green or white STEMS are cooked and eaten as a vegetable ⊃ VISUAL VOCAB page V5

**as·par·tame** /əˈspɑːteɪm; *NAmE* ˈæspɑːrteɪm/ *noun* [U] a sweet substance used instead of sugar in drinks and food products, especially ones for people who are trying to lose weight

**as·pect** 🔑 **B2** 🅞 /ˈæspekt/ *noun* **1** 🔑 **B2** [C] a particular part or feature of a situation, an idea, a problem, etc.; a way in which it may be considered: **~ of sth** *The book aims to cover all aspects of city life.* ◊ *The exhibition will focus on various aspects of life and culture in the Middle East.* ◊ *the most important aspect of the debate* ◊ *She felt she had looked at the problem from every aspect.* **2** [sing., U] (*formal*) the appearance of a place, a situation or a person: *Events began to take on a more sinister aspect.* **3** [C, usually sing.] (*formal*) the direction in which a building, window, piece of land, etc. faces; the side of a building that faces a particular direction **SYN** **orientation** **4** [U, C] (*grammar*) the form of a verb that shows, for example, whether the action happens once or repeatedly, is completed or still continuing ⊃ see also PERFECT *adj.* (7), PROGRESSIVE *adj.* (3)

ˈ**aspect ratio** *noun* the relationship between the height and WIDTH of the image on the screen of a television, an electronic device, etc.

**aspen** /ˈæspən/ *noun* a type of POPLAR tree, with leaves that move even when there is very little wind

**Asperger's syndrome** /ˈæspɜːɡəz sɪndrəʊm; *NAmE* ˈæspɜːrɡərz/ (*also* **Asperger syndrome**, **Asperger's**) *noun* [U] a mental DISORDER related to AUTISM in which a person finds it difficult to communicate or form relationships with others

**as·per·gill·osis** /ˌæsp.ɜːdʒɪˈləʊsɪs; *NAmE* ˌæspərdʒ-/ *noun* [U] a serious condition in which parts of the body, usually the lungs, hurt because of an infection caused by FUNGI

**as·per·sions** /əˈspɜːʃnz; *NAmE* əˈspɜːrʒnz/ *noun* [pl.] (*formal*) critical or unpleasant remarks or judgements: *I wouldn't want to cast aspersions on your honesty.*

**as·phalt** /ˈæsfælt; *NAmE* -fɔːlt/ *noun* [U] a thick black sticky substance used especially for making the surface of roads

**as·phyxia** /əsˈfɪksiə/ *noun* [U] (*specialist*) the state of being unable to breathe, causing death or loss of CONSCIOUSNESS

**as·phyxi·ate** /əsˈfɪksieɪt/ *verb* **~ sb** to make sb become unconscious or die by preventing them from breathing **SYN** **suffocate** ▶ **as·phyxi·ation** /əsˌfɪksiˈeɪʃn/ *noun* [U]

**aspic** /ˈæspɪk/ *noun* [U] clear JELLY that food can be put into when it is being served cold: *in ~ chicken breast in aspic*

**as·pir·ant** /ˈæspərənt; əˈspaɪərənt/ *noun* **~ (to/for sth)** (*formal*) a person with a strong desire to achieve a position of importance or to win a competition: *aspirants to the title of world champion* ▶ **as·pir·ant** *adj.* [only before noun] = ASPIRING

**as·pir·ate** *noun, verb*
- *noun* /ˈæspərət/ (*phonetics*) a consonant pronounced with a breath that can be heard, for example the /h/ sound in *house* in English: *The word 'hour' is pronounced without an initial aspirate.*
- *verb* /ˈæspəreɪt/ **~ sth** (*phonetics*) to pronounce sth with a breath that can be heard

**as·pir·ation** 🔑 **C1** /ˌæspəˈreɪʃn/ *noun* **1** 🔑 [C, usually pl., U] a strong desire to have or do sth: *I didn't realize you had political aspirations.* ◊ **~to do sth** *He has never had any aspiration to earn a lot of money.* ◊ **~ for sth** *What changes are needed to meet women's aspirations for* *employment?* **2** [U] (*phonetics*) the action of pronouncing a word with a breath that can be heard, as in the /h/ sound in *house* in English

**as·pir·ation·al** /ˌæspəˈreɪʃənl/ *adj.* **1** wanting very much to achieve success in your career or to improve your social status and standard of living **2** an **aspirational** goal or target is very ambitious and may be more than you can achieve, but is set in order to encourage you to try harder and achieve more: *an aspirational goal of doubling sales*

**as·pire** /əˈspaɪə(r)/ *verb* [I, T] to have a strong desire to achieve or to become sth: **~(to sth)** *She aspired to a scientific career.* ◊ **~to be/do sth** *He aspired to be their next leader.*

**as·pir·in** /ˈæsprɪn, ˈæspərɪn/ *noun* (U, C] (*pl.* **as·pirin** or **as·pir·ins**) a drug used to reduce pain, high temperature and INFLAMMATION: *Do you have any aspirin?* ◊ *Take two aspirin(s) for a headache.*

**as·pir·ing** /əˈspaɪərɪŋ/ (*also less frequent* **as·pir·ant**) *adj.* [only before noun] **1** wanting to start the career or activity that is mentioned: *Aspiring musicians need hours of practice every day.* **2** wanting to be successful in life: *He came from an aspiring working-class background.*

**ass** /æs/ *noun* **1** (NAmE) (BrE **arse**) (*taboo, slang*) the part of the body that you sit on; your bottom **2** (BrE, *informal*) a stupid person **SYN** **fool**: *Don't be such an ass!* ◊ *I made an ass of myself at the meeting—standing up and then forgetting the question.* **3** (BrE, *old use*) a DONKEY
**IDM** **get your 'ass in gear** | **move your 'ass** (NAmE) (BrE **get your 'arse in gear, move your 'arse**) (*taboo, slang*) a rude way of telling sb to hurry **get your ˌass 'over/in 'here, etc.** (*taboo, NAmE, slang*) a rude way of telling sb to come here, etc. ➔ more at BLOW *v.*, BUST *v.*, COVER *v.*, KICK *v.*, KISS *v.*, PAIN *n.*

**as·sail** /əˈseɪl/ *verb* (*formal*) **1 ~ sb/sth (with sth)** to attack sb/sth violently, either physically or with words: *His attacker assailed him with fierce blows to the head.* ◊ *The proposal was assailed by the opposition party.* ◊ (*figurative*) *A vile smell assailed my nostrils.* **2** [usually passive] to worry or upset sb severely: **be assailed by sth** *to be assailed by worries/doubts/fears*

**as·sail·ant** /əˈseɪlənt/ *noun* (*formal*) a person who attacks sb, especially physically **SYN** **attacker**

**as·sas·sin** /əˈsæsɪn/ *NAmE* -sn/ *noun* a person who murders sb important or famous, for money or for political reasons

**as·sas·sin·ate** /əˈsæsɪneɪt/ *verb* [often passive] **~ sb** to murder an important or famous person, especially for political reasons: *a plot to assassinate the president* ◊ *The prime minister was assassinated by extremists.* ➔ WORDFINDER NOTE at ATTACK

**as·sas·sin·ation** /əˌsæsɪˈneɪʃn/ *noun* [C, U] the murder of an important or famous person, especially for political reasons: *The president survived a number of assassination attempts.* ◊ *the assassination of John F. Kennedy*

**as·sault** /əˈsɔːlt/ *noun, verb*
■ *noun* **1** [U, C] the crime of attacking sb physically: *Both men were charged with assault.* ◊ *sexual assaults* ◊ **~on/upon sb** *A significant number of indecent assaults on women go unreported.* ➔ see also INDECENT ASSAULT **2** [C] **~(on/upon/against sb/sth)** (by an army, etc.) the act of attacking a building, an area, etc. in order to take control of it **SYN** **attack**: *An assault on the capital was launched in the early hours of the morning.* **3** [C] **~(on/upon sth)** the act of trying to achieve sth that is difficult or dangerous: *The government has mounted a new assault on unemployment.* ◊ *Three people died during an assault on the mountain* (= while trying to climb it). **4** [C] an act of criticizing sb/sth severely **SYN** **attack**: *The suggested closures came under assault from all parties.* ◊ **~on/upon/against sb/sth** *The paper's assault on the president was totally unjustified.*
■ *verb* **1** **~sb** to attack sb violently, especially when this is a crime: *He has been charged with assaulting a police officer.* ◊ *Four women have been sexually assaulted in the area recently.* **2** **~sth** (*formal*) to affect your senses in

a way that is very unpleasant or uncomfortable: *Loud rock music assaulted our ears.*

**asˌsault and 'battery** *noun* [U] (*law*) the crime of threatening to harm sb and then attacking them physically

**asˈsault course** (BrE) (NAmE **ˈobstacle course**) *noun* an area of land with many objects that are difficult to climb, jump over or go through, which is used, especially by soldiers, for improving physical skills and strength

**assay** /əˈseɪ/ *noun* [C, U] (*specialist*) the testing of metals and chemicals for quality, often to see how pure they are ▶ **assay** *verb* **~ sth**

**as·sem·blage** /əˈsemblɪdʒ/ *noun* (*formal* or *specialist*) a collection of things; a group of people: *Tropical rainforests have the most varied assemblage of plants in the world.*

**as·sem·ble** /əˈsembl/ *verb* **1** [I, T] to come together as a group; to bring people or things together as a group: *All the students were asked to assemble in the main hall.* ◊ *She then addressed the assembled company* (= all the people there). ◊ **~sth** *to assemble evidence/data* ◊ *The manager has assembled a world-class team.* **2** [T] **~sth** to fit together all the separate parts of sth, for example a piece of furniture: *The shelves are easy to assemble.* **OPP** **disassemble** ➔ SYNONYMS at BUILD

**as·sem·bler** /əˈsemblə(r)/ *noun* **1** a person who assembles a machine or its parts **2** (*computing*) a program for changing instructions into MACHINE CODE **3** (*computing*) = ASSEMBLY LANGUAGE

**Asˌsemblies of 'God** *noun* [pl.] the largest Pentecostal Church in the US (= one that emphasizes the gifts of the Holy Spirit, such as the power to make sick people healthy again)

**as·sem·bly** /əˈsembli/ *noun* (*pl.* -**ies**) **1** (*also* **Assembly**) [C] a group of people who have been elected to meet together regularly and make decisions or laws for a particular region or country: *state/legislative/federal/local assemblies* ◊ *Power has been handed over to provincial and regional assemblies.* ◊ *The national assembly has voted to adopt the budget.* ◊ *the California Assembly* ◊ *the UN General Assembly* **2** [C, U] the meeting together of a group of people for a particular purpose; a group of people who meet together for a particular purpose: *They were fighting for freedom of speech and freedom of assembly.* ◊ *He was to address a public assembly on the issue.* ◊ *an assembly point* (= a place where people have been asked to meet) **3** [C, U] a meeting of the teachers and students in a school, usually at the start of the day, to give information, discuss school events or say prayers together: *The deputy head was taking* (= leading) *school assembly that day.* **4** [U] the process of putting together the parts of sth such as a vehicle or piece of furniture: *Putting the bookcase together should be a simple assembly job.* ◊ *a car assembly plant*

**asˈsembly language** *noun* [C, U] (*also* **as·sem·bler**) (*computing*) the language in which a program is written before it is changed into MACHINE CODE

**asˈsembly line** *noun* = PRODUCTION LINE: *workers on the assembly line* ➔ WORDFINDER NOTE at FACTORY

**as·sem·bly·man** /əˈsemblimən/ **as·sem·bly·wo·man** /əˈsembliwʊmən/ *noun* (*pl.* -**men** /-mən/ *or* -**women** /-wɪmɪn/) a person who is an elected representative in a state assembly in the US

**asˈsembly room** *noun* [usually pl.] (*especially BrE*) a public room or building in which meetings and social events are held

**as·sent** /əˈsent/ *noun, verb*
■ *noun* [U] **~(to sth)** (*formal*) official agreement to or approval of sth: *The director has given her assent to the proposals.* ◊ *He nodded (his) assent.* ◊ *There were murmurs of both assent and dissent from the crowd.* ◊ *The bill passed in Parliament has now received (the) Royal Assent* (= been approved by the king/queen).

# assert

■ **verb** [I] ~ **(to sth)** | **(+ speech)** (formal) to agree to a request, an idea or a suggestion: *Nobody would assent to the terms they proposed.*

**as·sert** /əˈsɜːt; NAmE əˈsɜːrt/ verb **1** ~ **that …** to state clearly and definitely that sth is true: ~ **that …** *She continued to assert that she was innocent.* ◇ ~ **sth** *She continued to assert her innocence.* ◇ **+ speech** '*That is wrong,*' *he asserted.* ◇ **it is asserted that …** *It is commonly asserted that older people prefer to receive care from family members.* **2** ~ **yourself** to behave in a confident and determined way so that other people pay attention to your opinions **3** ~ **sth** to make other people recognize your right or authority to do sth, by behaving in a determined and confident way: *to assert your independence/rights* ◇ *I was determined to assert my authority from the beginning.* **4** ~ **itself** to start to have an effect: *Good sense asserted itself.*

**as·ser·tion** /əˈsɜːʃn; NAmE əˈsɜːrʃn/ noun **1** [C] a statement saying that you strongly believe sth to be true **SYN claim**: *He was correct in his assertion that the minister had been lying.* ◇ *Do you have any evidence to support your assertions?* ⟹ SYNONYMS at CLAIM **2** [U, C] the act of stating, using or claiming sth strongly: *the assertion of his authority* ◇ *The demonstration was an assertion of the right to peaceful protest.*

**as·sert·ive** /əˈsɜːtɪv; NAmE əˈsɜːrt-/ adj. expressing opinions or desires strongly and with confidence, so that people take notice: *You should try and be more assertive.* ◇ *assertive behaviour* **OPP submissive** ▶ **as·sert·ive·ly** adv. **as·sert·ive·ness** noun [U]: *an assertiveness training course*

**as·sess** /əˈses/ verb **1** to make a judgement about the nature or quality of sb/sth: ~ **sb/sth** *Accurately assessing environmental impacts is very complex.* ◇ *to assess a patient's needs* ◇ ~ **sb/sth as sth** *The young men were assessed as either safe or unsafe drivers.* ◇ *I'd assess your chances as low.* ◇ ~ **whether, how, what …** *The committee assesses whether a building is worth preserving.* ◇ *We are trying to assess how well the system works.* **2** to calculate the amount or value of sth **SYN estimate**: ~ **sth** *They have assessed the amount of compensation to be paid.* ◇ ~ **sth at sth** *Damage to the building was assessed at £40 000.* ▶ **as·sess·able** adj.

**as·sess·ment** /əˈsesmənt/ noun **1** [C] an opinion or a judgement about sb/sth that has been thought about very carefully **SYN evaluation**: *a detailed assessment of the risks involved* ◇ *An adequate environmental impact assessment was not carried out on the bypass project.* ◇ *We conducted the initial assessments defining the scope of work.* ⟹ see also RISK ASSESSMENT **2** [U] the act of judging or forming an opinion about sb/sth: *Objective assessment of the severity of the problem was difficult.* **3** [U] the process of testing students and making a judgement about their knowledge, ability or progress: *written exams and other forms of assessment* ⟹ see also CONTINUOUS ASSESSMENT **4** [C] an amount that has been calculated and that must be paid: *a tax assessment*

**as'sessment centre** (*US* **as'sessment center**) noun (business) an event where people applying for a job are given a number of tests and interviews to find out what their strengths and weaknesses are; the place where this happens: *After the first interview you may be asked back for an assessment centre.*

**as·ses·sor** /əˈsesə(r)/ noun **1** an expert in a particular subject who is asked by a court or other official group to give advice **2** a person who calculates the value or cost of sth or the amount of money to be paid: *an insurance/tax assessor* **3** a person who judges how well sb has done in an exam, a competition, etc: *College lecturers acted as external assessors of the exam results.*

**asset** /ˈæset/ noun **1** a person or thing that is valuable or useful to sb/sth: *In his job, patience is an invaluable asset.* ◇ ~ **to sb/sth** *She'll be an asset to the team.* **2** [usually pl.] a thing of value, especially property, that a person or company owns, which can be used or sold to pay debts: *the net asset value of the company* ◇ *Her assets include shares in the company and a house in France.* ◇ **asset sales/management** ◇ **financial/capital assets** ⟹ compare LIABILITY ⟹ WORDFINDER NOTE at INVEST

**'asset-stripping** noun [U] (business, usually disapproving) the practice of buying a company that is in financial difficulties at a low price and then selling everything that it owns in order to make a profit

**ass·hole** /ˈæshəʊl/ (*NAmE*) (*BrE* **arse·hole**) noun (taboo, slang) **1** the ANUS **2** a stupid or unpleasant person

**as·sidu·ous** /əˈsɪdʒuəs/ adj. (formal) working very hard and taking great care that everything is done as well as it can be **SYN diligent** ▶ **as·si·du·ity** /ˌæsɪˈdjuːəti; NAmE -ˈduː-/ noun [U] **as·sidu·ous·ly** /əˈsɪdʒuəsli/ adv.

**as·sign** /əˈsaɪn/ verb **1** ~ **sth (to sb)** to give sb sth that they can use, or some work or responsibility: ~ **sth (to sb)** *The teacher assigned a different task to each of the children.* ◇ *The two large classrooms have been assigned to us.* ◇ ~ **sb sth** *We have been assigned the two large classrooms.* ◇ *The teacher assigned each of the children a different task.* **2** ~ **sb to sth/as sth** to provide a person for a particular task or position: ~ **sb (to sth/as sth)** *They've assigned their best man to the job.* ◇ ~ **sb to do sth** *British forces have been assigned to help with peacekeeping.* **3** [usually passive] to send a person to work under the authority of sb or in a particular group: **be assigned to sb/sth** *I was assigned to B platoon.* **4** ~ **sth** to say that sth has a particular value or function, or happens at a particular time or place: ~ **sth to sth** *Assign a different colour to each different type of information.* ◇ ~ **sth sth** *The painting cannot be assigned an exact date.* **5** ~ **sth to sb** (law) to say that your property or rights now belong to sb else: *The agreement assigns copyright to the publisher.*

**as·sig·na·tion** /ˌæsɪgˈneɪʃn/ noun (formal or humorous) a meeting, especially a secret one, often for sexual or romantic reasons

**as·sign·ment** /əˈsaɪnmənt/ noun **1** [C] a task or piece of work that sb is given to do, usually as part of their job or studies: *Students are required to complete all homework assignments.* ◇ *I had set myself a tough assignment.* ◇ **on an** ~ *She is in Greece on an assignment for one of the Sunday newspapers.* ◇ **on** ~ *one of our reporters on assignment in China* **2** [U] ~ **(of sb) (to sth)** the act of giving sth to sb; the act of giving sb a particular task: *his assignment to other duties in the same company*

**as·simi·late** /əˈsɪməleɪt/ verb **1** [T] ~ **sth** to fully understand an idea or some information so that you are able to use it yourself: *The committee will need time to assimilate this report.* **2** [I, T] to become, or allow sb to become, a part of a country or community rather than remaining in a separate group: ~ **(into/to sth)** *New arrivals find it hard to assimilate.* ◇ ~ **sb (into/to sth)** *Immigrants have been successfully assimilated into the community.* **3** [T, often passive] to make an idea, a person's attitude, etc. fit into sth or be acceptable: **be assimilated into/to sth** *These changes were gradually assimilated into everyday life.*

**as·simi·la·tion** /əˌsɪməˈleɪʃn/ noun [U] **1** the process of fully understanding an idea or some information so that you are able to use it yourself: *the rapid assimilation of new ideas* **2** ~ **(of sb) (into sth)** the process of becoming, or allowing sb to become, a part of a country or community rather than remaining a separate group: *his assimilation into the community*

**as·sist** /əˈsɪst/ verb, noun

■ **verb** (formal) **1** [I, T] to help sb to do sth: *Anyone willing to assist can contact this number.* ◇ ~ **in/with sth** *He assisted in the development of the business strategy.* ◇ ~ **sb** *We'll do all we can to assist you.* ◇ *They will be ably assisted by our remarkable staff.* ◇ ~ **sb in doing sth** *We will assist you in finding somewhere to live.* ◇ ~ **sb in/with sth** *The two men are assisting the police with their enquiries* (= are being questioned by the police). ◇ ~ **sb to do sth** *a course to assist adults to return to the labour market* **2** [T] ~ **sth** to help sth to happen more easily: *activities that will assist the decision-making process*

■ **noun 1** an action in ICE HOCKEY, football (soccer), etc. in which a player passes the ball in a way that helps another player on the same team to score a goal: *He had/made ten assists.* **2** an action in baseball in which a player throws the ball to another member of the team who gets an opponent out either by stepping onto the base before the runner reaches it, or by touching the runner with the ball before he or she reaches the base

**as·sist·ance** /əˈsɪstəns/ *noun* [U] (*formal*) help or support: *technical/economic/military assistance* ◇ *financial assistance for people on low incomes* ◇ *Can I be of any assistance?* ◇ *Despite his cries, no one came to his assistance.* ◇ **with the ~ of sb/sth** *He can only walk with the assistance of crutches.* ◇ **~ with sth** *She offered me practical assistance with my research.* ◇ **~ in doing sth/to do sth** *The company provides advice and assistance in finding work.*

**as·sist·ant** /əˈsɪstənt/ *noun, adj.*
■ *noun* **1** a person who helps or supports sb, usually in their job: *My assistant will now demonstrate the machine in action.* ◇ *a senior* ***research*** ***assistant*** ◇ *I work part-time as a* ***classroom*** ***assistant*** *in my local primary school.* ◇ *He was working as a special assistant to the president.* ⇒ see also GRADUATE ASSISTANT, PERSONAL ASSISTANT, PHYSICIAN'S ASSISTANT, TEACHING ASSISTANT, VOICE ASSISTANT **2** (*especially BrE*) = SALES CLERK, SHOP ASSISTANT: *an assistant in a department store* ◆ **WORDFINDER NOTE** at SHOP **3** (*BrE*) a student at university or college who spends time in a foreign country teaching his or her own language in a school
■ *adj.* [only before noun] (often in titles) (*abbr.* **Asst**) having a rank below that of a senior person and helping them in their work: *the assistant manager/director/commissioner* ◇ *She is an* ***assistant professor*** *of psychology at Ohio State University.* ◇ *Assistant Chief Constable Owen*

**as·sistant pro·ˈfessor** *noun* (in the US and Canada) a teacher at a college or university who has a rank just below the rank of an ASSOCIATE PROFESSOR

**as·sistant refe·ˈree** (*also* **referee's assistant**) *noun* (in football (soccer)) the official name for a LINESMAN (= an official who helps the REFEREE, for example in deciding whether or where a ball has passed outside the field of play)

**as·sist·ant·ship** /əˈsɪstəntʃɪp/ *noun* **1** (*BrE*) the position of being an ASSISTANT **2** (*NAmE*) a paid position for a graduate student that involves some teaching or research

**as·sisted ˈdying** *noun* [U] the act of a person ending their life with the help of a doctor, because they are suffering from a disease that has no cure

**as·sisted ˈliving** *noun* [U] accommodation for people who need help, for example with tasks like washing and dressing themselves: *assisted living apartments*

**as·sisted ˈsuicide** *noun* [U] the act of a person killing himself/herself with the help of sb such as a doctor, especially because he/she is suffering from a disease that has no cure

**as·sizes** /əˈsaɪzɪz/ *noun* [pl.] (in the past) a court of law that travelled to each county of England and Wales ► **as·size** /əˈsaɪz/ *adj.* [only before noun]: *the assize court*

**ˈass-kicking** *adj.* = KICK-ASS

**Assn.** *abbr.* (*especially NAmE*) (in writing) Association

**Assoc.** *abbr.* (in writing) Association

**Aˈssociate's degree** /əˈsəʊsiəts dɪɡriː, əˈsəʊʃi-/ *noun* (in the US) a degree given to sb who has completed two years of study at a COMMUNITY COLLEGE: *an Associate's degree in nursing*

**as·so·ci·ate** /əˈsəʊsieɪt, əˈsəʊʃi-/ *verb, adj., noun*
■ *verb* **1** [T] to make a connection between people or things in your mind: **~ sb/sth with sb/sth** *I always associate the smell of baking with my childhood.* ◇ **~ sb/sth** *You wouldn't normally associate these two writers—their styles are completely different.* **2** [I] **~ with sb** to spend time with sb, especially a person or people that sb else does not approve of **SYN mix**: *I don't like you associating with those people.* **3** [T] **~ yourself with sth** (*formal*)

to show that you support or agree with sth: *I associate myself with the prime minister's remarks* (= I agree with them). **OPP dissociate**
■ *adj.* /əˈsəʊsiət, əˈsəʊʃi-/ [only before noun] **1** (often in titles) of a lower rank; having fewer rights in a particular profession or organization: *associate membership of the European Union* ◇ *an associate member/director/editor* **2** joined to or connected with a profession or an organization: *an associate company in Japan*
■ *noun* /əˈsəʊsiət, əˈsəʊʃi-/ **1** a person that you work with, do business with or spend a lot of time with: *business associates* **2** (*also* **Associate**) an ASSOCIATE member **3 Associate** (*US*) a person who has an Associate's degree (= one that is given after completing two years of study at a junior college)

**as·so·ci·ated** /əˈsəʊsieɪtɪd, əˈsəʊʃi-/ *adj.*
**1** if one thing is **associated with** another, the two things are connected because they happen together or one thing causes the other **SYN connected**: **~ with (doing) sth** *the risks associated with taking drugs* ◇ *Salaries and associated costs have risen substantially.* **2 ~ with sth** if a person is **associated with** an organization, etc. they support it: *He no longer wished to be associated with the party's policy on education.* **3 Associated** used in the name of a business company that is made up of a number of smaller companies: *Associated Newspapers*

**asˈsociate proˈfessor** *noun* (in the US and Canada) a teacher at a college or university who has a rank just below the rank of a professor

**as·so·ci·ation** /əˌsəʊsiˈeɪʃn, əˌsəʊʃi-/ *noun* **1** [C + sing./pl. v.] (*abbr.* **Assoc.**, **Assn.** especially in *NAmE*) an official group of people who have joined together for a particular purpose **SYN organization**: *Do you belong to any professional or* ***trade*** ***associations***? ◇ *the Football Association* ◇ *a residents' association* ⇒ see also HOUSING ASSOCIATION **2** [C, U] a connection or relationship between people or organizations: **~ with sb/sth** *They have maintained a close association with a college in the US.* ◇ *his alleged association with terrorist groups* ◇ **in ~ with** *The book was published in association with* (= together with) *English Heritage.* ⇒ see also FREEDOM OF ASSOCIATION **3** [C, usually pl.] an idea or a memory that is suggested by sb/sth; a mental connection between ideas: *The seaside had all sorts of pleasant associations with childhood holidays for me.* ◇ *The cat soon made the association between human beings and food.* **4** [C, U] a connection between things where one is caused by the other: **~ between A and B** *Studies have shown strong associations between housing conditions and health.* ◇ **in ~ with sth** *cases of cancer found in association with colitis*

**Asˈsociation ˈfootball** *noun* [U] (*BrE, formal*) = FOOTBALL (1)

**as·so·cia·tive** /əˈsəʊsiətɪv, əˈsəʊʃi-; *NAmE* əˈsəʊsieɪtɪv, əˈsəʊʃi-/ *adj.* **1** relating to the association of ideas or things **2** (*mathematics*) giving the same result no matter in what order the parts of a problem are done, for example (a × b) × c = a × (b × c)

**as·son·ance** /ˈæsənəns/ *noun* [U] (*specialist*) the effect created when two syllables in words that are close together have the same vowel sound, but different consonants, or the same consonants but different vowels, for example, *sonnet* and *porridge* or *cold* and *killed* ⇒ see also ALLITERATION

**as·sort·ed** /əˈsɔːtɪd; *NAmE* əˈsɔːrt-/ *adj.* of various different sorts: *The meat is served with salad or assorted vegetables.* ◇ *The jumper comes in assorted colours.*

**as·sort·ment** /əˈsɔːtmənt; *NAmE* əˈsɔːrt-/ *noun* [usually sing.] a collection of different things or of different types of the same thing **SYN mixture**: *a wide assortment of gifts to choose from* ◇ *He was dressed in an odd assortment of clothes.*

**Asst** (*also* **Asst.** especially in *NAmE*) *abbr.* (in writing) ASSISTANT: *Asst Manager*

**as·suage** /əˈsweɪdʒ/ verb ~ sth (formal) to make an unpleasant feeling less severe

**as·sume** /əˈsjuːm; NAmE əˈsuːm/ verb
**1** to think or accept that sth is true but without having proof of it: ~ (that)… *It is reasonable to assume (that) the economy will continue to improve.* ◊ *It's probably safe to assume (that) we'll be hearing more about this story.* ◊ *Let us assume for a moment that the plan succeeds.* ◊ **it is assumed (that)**… *It is generally assumed that stress is caused by too much work.* ◊ **~ sth** *Don't always assume the worst* (= that sth bad has happened). ◊ *In this example we have assumed a unit price of $10.* ◊ **~ sb/sth to be/have sth** *I had assumed him to be a Belgian.* **2** ~ sth (formal) to take or begin to have power or responsibility: *Rebel forces have assumed control of the capital.* ◊ *The court assumed responsibility for the girl's welfare.* **3** ~ sth (formal) to begin to have a particular quality or appearance **SYN** **take on**: *This matter has assumed considerable importance.* ◊ *In the story the god assumes the form of an eagle.* **4** ~ sth (formal) to pretend to have a particular feeling or quality **SYN** **put on**: *He assumed an air of concern.*

**as·sumed** /əˈsjuːmd; NAmE əˈsuːmd/ adj. [only before noun] that you suppose to be true or to exist: *the assumed differences between the two states*

**as·sumed ˈname** noun a name that sb uses that is not their real name **SYN** **pseudonym**: *under an ~ He was living under an assumed name.*

**as·sum·ing** /əˈsjuːmɪŋ; NAmE əˈsuː-/ conj. ~ (that) used to suppose that sth is true so that you can talk about what the results might be: *Assuming (that) he's still alive, how old would he be now?* ◊ *I hope to go to college next year, always assuming I pass my exams.*

**as·sump·tion** /əˈsʌmpʃn/ noun **1** [C] a belief or feeling that sth is true or that sth will happen, although there is no proof: *an underlying/implicit assumption* ◊ *We need to challenge some of the basic assumptions of Western philosophy.* ◊ *We are working on the assumption that everyone invited will turn up.* ◊ *It was impossible to make assumptions about people's reactions.* ◊ *His actions were based on a false assumption.* **2** [C, U] ~ of sth (formal) the act of taking or beginning to have power or responsibility: *their assumption of power/control*

**as·sur·ance** /əˈʃʊərəns, əˈʃɔːr-; NAmE əˈʃʊr-/ noun
**1** [C] a statement that sth will certainly be true or will certainly happen, particularly when there has been doubt about it **SYN** **guarantee**, **promise**: *They called for assurances that the government is committed to its education policy.* ◊ *Unemployment seems to be rising, despite repeated assurances to the contrary.* **2** (also **self-ˈassurance**) [U] belief in your own abilities or strengths **SYN** **confidence**: *There was an air of easy assurance about him.* **3** [U] (BrE) a type of insurance in which money is paid out when sb dies or after an agreed period of time: *a life assurance company* ⊃ see also **QUALITY ASSURANCE**

**as·sure** /əˈʃʊə(r), əˈʃɔː(r); NAmE əˈʃʊr/ verb **1** to tell sb that sth is definitely true or is definitely going to happen, especially when they have doubts about it: ~ sb (that)… *You think I did it deliberately, but I assure you (that) I did not.* ◊ *We were assured that everything possible was being done.* ◊ *She's perfectly safe, I can assure you.* ◊ ~ sb (of sth) *We assured him of our support.* ◊ ~ sb + speech *'He'll come back,' Susan assured her.* **2** ~ sth (formal) to make yourself certain about sth: **~ yourself of sth** *He assured himself of her safety.* ◊ **~ yourself that**… *She assured herself that the letter was still in the drawer.* **3** ~ sth to make sth certain to happen **SYN** **guarantee**: ~ sth *Victory would assure a place in the finals.* ◊ **~ sb sth** *Victory would assure them a place in the finals.* **4** ~ sth (BrE) to **INSURE** sth, especially against sb's death: *What is the sum assured?*

**as·sured** /əˈʃʊəd, əˈʃɔːd; NAmE əˈʃʊrd/ adj. **1** (also **self-ˈassured**) confident in yourself and your abilities: *He spoke in a calm, assured voice.* **2** certain to happen **SYN** **guaranteed**: *Success seemed assured.* **3** ~ of sth (of a person) certain to get sth: *You are assured of a warm welcome at this hotel.* **IDM** see **REST** v.

**as·sured·ly** /əˈʃʊərədli, əˈʃɔːr-; NAmE əˈʃʊr-/ adv. (formal) certainly; definitely

**AST** /ˌeɪ es ˈtiː/ abbr. ATLANTIC STANDARD TIME

**aster** /ˈæstə(r)/ noun a garden plant that has pink, purple, blue or white flowers with many long narrow PETALS

**as·ter·isk** /ˈæstərɪsk/ noun the symbol (*) placed next to a particular word or phrase to make people notice it or to show that more information is given in another place: *I've placed an asterisk next to the tasks I want you to do first.* ▶ **as·ter·isk** verb: ~ sth *I've asterisked the tasks I want you to do first.*

**astern** /əˈstɜːn; NAmE əˈstɜːrn/ adv. (specialist) **1** in, at or towards the back part of a ship or boat **2** if a ship or boat is moving **astern**, it is moving backwards

**as·ter·oid** /ˈæstərɔɪd/ noun any one of the many small planets that go around the sun ⊃ **WORDFINDER NOTE** at UNIVERSE

**asthma** /ˈæsmə; NAmE ˈæzmə/ noun [U] a medical condition of the chest that makes breathing difficult: *a severe asthma attack*

**asth·mat·ic** /æsˈmætɪk; NAmE æzˈm-/ noun a person who suffers from asthma ▶ **asth·mat·ic** adj.: *asthmatic patients* ◊ *an asthmatic attack*

**astig·ma·tism** /əˈstɪɡmətɪzəm/ noun [U] (medical) a fault in the shape of a person's eye that prevents them from seeing clearly

**as·ton·ish** /əˈstɒnɪʃ; NAmE əˈstɑːn-/ verb to surprise sb very much **SYN** **amaze** ⊃ SYNONYMS at SURPRISE: ~ sb *The news astonished everyone.* ◊ *She astonished us by saying she was leaving.* ◊ **it astonishes sb (that)**… *It astonishes me (that) he could be so thoughtless.*

**as·ton·ished** /əˈstɒnɪʃt; NAmE əˈstɑːn-/ adj. very surprised **SYN** **amazed**: *The helicopter landed before our astonished eyes.* ◊ ~ at/by sth/sb *My parents looked astonished at my news.* ◊ ~ (that)… *She seemed astonished (that) I had never been to Paris.* ◊ ~ to find/hear/learn/see… *He was astonished to learn he'd won the competition.*

**as·ton·ish·ing** /əˈstɒnɪʃɪŋ; NAmE əˈstɑːn-/ adj. very surprising; difficult to believe **SYN** **amazing**: *She ran 100m in an astonishing 10.6 seconds.* ◊ *I find it absolutely astonishing that you didn't like it.* ▶ **as·ton·ish·ing·ly** adv.: *Jack took the news astonishingly well.* ◊ *Astonishingly, a crowd of several thousands turned out to hear him.*

**as·ton·ish·ment** /əˈstɒnɪʃmənt; NAmE əˈstɑːn-/ noun [U] a feeling of very great surprise **SYN** **amazement**: *To my utter astonishment, she remembered my name.* ◊ *He stared in astonishment at the stranger.*

**as·tound** /əˈstaʊnd/ verb ~ sb to surprise or shock sb very much **SYN** **astonish**: *His arrogance astounded her.* ◊ *She was astounded by his arrogance.* ⊃ note at SURPRISE

**as·tound·ed** /əˈstaʊndɪd/ adj. very surprised or shocked by sth, because it seems very unlikely **SYN** **astonished**: *an astounded expression* ◊ *How can you say that? I'm absolutely astounded.* ◊ ~ at/by sth *She looked astounded at the news.* ◊ ~ (that)… *The doctors were astounded (that) he survived.* ◊ ~ to find/hear/learn/see… *I was astounded to see her appear from the house.*

**as·tound·ing** /əˈstaʊndɪŋ/ adj. so surprising that it is difficult to believe **SYN** **astonishing**: *There was an astounding 20 per cent increase in sales.* ▶ **as·tound·ing·ly** adv.

**as·tral** /ˈæstrəl/ adj. [only before noun] **1** (specialist) connected with the stars: *astral navigation* **2** connected with the spiritual rather than the physical world of existence: *the astral plane*

**astray** /əˈstreɪ/ adv.
**IDM** **go aˈstray 1** to become lost; to be stolen: *Several letters went astray or were not delivered.* ◊ *We locked up our valuables so they would not go astray.* **2** to go in the wrong direction or to have the wrong result: *Fortunately the gunman's shots went astray.* ⊃ more at LEAD¹ v.

**astride** /əˈstraɪd/ prep., adv.
- **prep.** with one leg on each side of sth: *to sit astride a horse/bike/chair* ◊ *(figurative) a town astride the river*
- **adv. 1** with legs or feet wide apart **2** with one leg on each side

**astrin·gent** /əˈstrɪndʒənt/ adj., noun
- **adj. 1** (*specialist*) (of a liquid or cream) causing skin cells and other body TISSUES to become tighter **2** (*formal*) critical in a severe or clever way: *astringent writers/comments* **3** (*formal*) (of a taste or smell) slightly bitter but fresh: *the astringent taste of lemon juice* ▶ **astrin·gency** /-dʒənsi/ noun [U]
- **noun** a liquid or cream used in COSMETICS or medicine to make the skin less OILY or to stop the loss of blood from a cut

**astro-** /ˈæstrəʊ, ˈæstrə; BrE also ˈæstrɒ; NAmE also əˈstrɑː/ combining form (in nouns, adjectives and adverbs) relating to the stars or outer space: *astronaut* ◊ *astrophysics*

**astro·labe** /ˈæstrəleɪb/ noun (*astronomy*) a device used in the past for measuring the distances of stars, planets etc. and for calculating the position of a ship

**as·trol·oger** /əˈstrɒlədʒə(r); NAmE əˈstrɑːl-/ noun a person who uses astrology to tell people about their character, about what might happen to them in the future, etc.

**as·trol·ogy** /əˈstrɒlədʒi; NAmE əˈstrɑːl-/ noun [U] the study of the positions of the stars and the movements of the planets in the belief that they influence human affairs ▶ **astro·logic·al** /ˌæstrəˈlɒdʒɪkl; NAmE -ˈlɑːdʒ-/ adj.: *astrological influences*

**astro·naut** /ˈæstrənɔːt/ noun a person whose job involves travelling and working in a SPACECRAFT ⊃ WORDFINDER NOTE at SPACE

**as·tron·omer** /əˈstrɒnəmə(r); NAmE əˈstrɑːn-/ noun a scientist who studies astronomy

**astro·nom·ic·al** /ˌæstrəˈnɒmɪkl; NAmE -ˈnɑːm-/ adj. **1** connected with ASTRONOMY: *astronomical observations* **2** (*also* **astro·nom·ic**) (*informal*) (of an amount, a price, etc.) very large: *the astronomical price of land for building* ◊ *The figures are astronomical.* ▶ **astro·nom·ic·al·ly** /-kli/ adv.: *Interest rates are astronomically high.*

**astro‚nomical ˈunit** noun (abbr. **AU**) (*astronomy*) a unit of measurement equal to 149.6 million kilometres, which is the distance from the centre of the earth to the sun

**as·tron·omy** /əˈstrɒnəmi; NAmE əˈstrɑːn-/ noun [U] the scientific study of the sun, moon, stars, planets, etc. ⊃ WORDFINDER NOTE at UNIVERSE

**astro·phys·ics** /ˌæstrəʊˈfɪzɪks/ noun [U] the scientific study of the physical and chemical structure of the stars, planets, etc. ▶ **astro·physi·cist** /-zɪsɪst/ noun

**Astro·Turf™** /ˈæstrəʊtɜːf; NAmE -tɜːrf/ noun [U] an artificial surface that looks like grass, for playing sports on

**ˈA student** noun (*especially NAmE*) a student who gets or is likely to get the highest marks in his/her work or exams

**as·tute** /əˈstjuːt; NAmE əˈstuːt/ adj. very clever and quick at seeing what to do in a particular situation, especially how to get an advantage SYN **shrewd**: *an astute businessman/politician/observer* ◊ *It was an astute move to sell the shares then.* ▶ **as·tute·ly** adv. **as·tute·ness** noun [U]

**asun·der** /əˈsʌndə(r)/ adv. (*old-fashioned or literary*) into pieces; apart: *families rent/torn asunder by the revolution*

**asy·lum** ?+ C1 /əˈsaɪləm/ noun **1** ?+ C1 (*also formal* **poˈlitical aˈsylum**) [U] protection that a government gives to people who have left their own country, usually because they were in danger for political reasons: *to seek/apply for/be granted asylum* ◊ *There was a nationwide debate on whether the asylum laws should be changed.* **2** [C] (*old use*) a hospital where people who were mentally ill could be cared for, often for a long time

**aˈsylum seeker** noun a person who has been forced to leave their own country because they are in danger and who arrives in another country asking to be allowed to stay there ⊃ SYNONYMS at IMMIGRANT

**asym·met·ric** /ˌeɪsɪˈmetrɪk/ (*also* **asym·met·ric·al** /ˌeɪsɪˈmetrɪkl/) adj. **1** having two sides or parts that are not the same in size or shape: *Most people's faces are asymmetric.*

OPP **symmetrical 2** (*specialist*) not equal, for example in the way each side or part behaves: *Linguists are studying the asymmetric use of Creole by parents and children* (= parents use one language and children reply in another). ▶ **asym·met·ric·al·ly** /-kli/ adv. **asym·met·ry** /ˌeɪˈsɪmətri/ noun [C, U]

**aˌsymmetric ˈbars** noun [pl.] (*BrE*) = UNEVEN BARS

**asymp·tom·at·ic** /ˌeɪsɪmptəˈmætɪk/ adj. (*medical*) (of a person or illness) having no symptoms

**asyn·chron·ous** /eɪˈsɪŋkrənəs/ adj. (*formal*) (of two or more objects or events) not existing or happening at the same time ▶ **asyn·chron·ous·ly** adv.

**at** 🔑 A1 /ət, strong form æt/ prep. **1** ?+ A1 used to say where sth/sb is or where sth happens: *at the corner of the street* ◊ *We changed at Crewe.* ◊ *They arrived late at the airport.* ◊ *At the roundabout take the third exit.* ◊ *I'll be at home all morning.* ◊ *She's at Tom's* (= at Tom's house). ◊ *I met her at the hospital.* ◊ *How many people were there at the concert?* **2** ?+ A1 used to say where sb works or studies: *He's been at the bank longer than anyone else.* ◊ *She's at Yale* (= Yale University). **3** ?+ A1 used to say when sth happens: *We left at 2 o'clock.* ◊ *at the end of the week* ◊ *We woke at dawn.* ◊ *I didn't know at the time of writing* (= when I wrote). ◊ *At night you can see the stars.* ◊ *(BrE) What are you doing at the weekend?* **4** ?+ A1 used to state the age at which sb does sth: *She got married at 25.* ◊ *He left school at the age of 16.* **5** ?+ B1 in the direction of or towards sb/sth: *What are you looking at?* ◊ *He pointed a gun at her.* ◊ *Somebody threw paint at the prime minister.* **6** used after a verb to show that sb tries to do sth, or partly does sth, but does not succeed or complete it: *He clutched wildly at the rope as he fell.* ◊ *She nibbled at a sandwich* (= ate only small bits of it). **7** ?+ A1 used with adjectives to show how well sb does sth: *I'm good at French.* ◊ *She's hopeless at managing people.* **8** ?+ A1 used to show a rate, speed, etc.: *He was driving at 70 mph.* ◊ *The noise came at two-minute intervals* (= once every two minutes). ◊ *Prices start at $1000.* **9** ?+ A2 used to state the distance away from sth: *I held it at arm's length.* ◊ *Can you read a car number plate at fifty metres?* **10** ?+ B1 used to show the situation sb/sth is in, what sb is doing or what is happening: *The country is now at war.* ◊ *I felt at a disadvantage.* ◊ *I think Mr Harris is at lunch.* **11** ?+ B1 **~ sb's/sth's best/worst, etc.** used to say that sb/sth is as good, bad, etc. as they can be: *This was Osaka at her best.* ◊ *The garden's at its most beautiful in June.* **12** ?+ B1 used with adjectives to show the cause of sth: *They were impatient at the delay.* ◊ *She was delighted at the result.* **13** (*formal*) in response to sth: *They attended the dinner at the chairman's invitation.* **14** ?+ A1 (*NAmE*) used when giving a phone number: *You can reach me at 637-2335, extension 354.* **15** ?+ A1 /æt/ (*computing*) the symbol (@) used in email addresses
- IDM **‚at ˈthat** used when you are giving an extra piece of information: *He managed to buy a car after all—and a nice one at that.* **be ˈat it again** to be doing sth, especially sth bad: *Look at all that graffiti—those kids have been at it again.* **‚where it's ˈat** (*informal*) a place or an activity that is very popular or fashionable: *Judging by the crowds waiting to get in, this seems to be where it's at.*

**at·av·is·tic** /ˌætəˈvɪstɪk/ adj. (*formal*) related to the feelings, attitudes and behaviour of humans in ancient times that have been passed on to modern humans as a habit or INSTINCT: *an atavistic urge/instinct/fear*

**ataxia** /əˈtæksiə/ (*also* **ataxy** /əˈtæksi/) noun [U] (*medical*) the loss of full control of the body's movements ▶ **ataxic** adj.

**at-bat** /ət ˈbæt/ noun (in baseball ) an occasion when a player is trying to hit the ball with a BAT: *Who had the most at-bats last season?* ⊃ see also AT BAT at BAT noun

**ate** /et, eɪt; NAmE eɪt/ past tense of EAT

**-ate** /ət/ suffix **1** (in adjectives) full of or having the quality of: *passionate* ◊ *Italianate* **2** (in verbs) /eɪt/ to give the thing or quality mentioned to: *hyphenate* ◊ *activate* **3** (in nouns) the status or function of: *a doctorate* **4** (in nouns) a group with the status or function of: *the electorate*

# A-team

**5** /eɪt, ət/ (*chemistry*) (in nouns) a salt formed by the action of a particular ACID: *sulphate*

**ˈA-team** *noun* [usually sing.] **1** the best sports team in a school, club, etc. **2** a group of the best workers, soldiers, etc.

**atel·ier** /əˈtelieɪ; *NAmE* ˌætlˈjeɪ/ *noun* a room or building in which an artist works SYN **studio**

**athe·ism** /ˈeɪθiɪzəm/ *noun* [U] lack of belief in the existence of God or gods OPP **theism** ▸ **athe·is·tic** /ˌeɪθiˈɪstɪk/ *adj.*

**athe·ist** /ˈeɪθiɪst/ *noun* a person who does not believe that God or gods exist ⊃ compare AGNOSTIC

**ath·lete** ⓘ A2 /ˈæθliːt/ *noun* **1** A2 a person who competes in sports: *Olympic athletes* **2** (*BrE*) a person who competes in sports such as running, jumping and throwing: *He played baseball and basketball and excelled as a track athlete.* **3** a person who is good at sports and physical exercise: *She is a natural athlete.* ⊃ WORDFINDER NOTE at SPORT

**ˌathlete's ˈfoot** *noun* [U] a skin disease that affects the feet, especially between the toes

**ath·let·ic** /æθˈletɪk/ *adj.* **1** physically strong, fit and active: *an athletic figure/build* ◇ *a tall, slim athletic girl* **2** [only before noun] (*BrE*) connected with sports such as running, jumping and throwing (= athletics): *an athletic club/coach* ▸ **ath·let·ic·al·ly** /-kli/ *adv.* **ath·leti·cism** /-tɪsɪzəm/ *noun* [U]: *She moved with great athleticism about the court.*

**ath·let·ics** /æθˈletɪks/ *noun* [U] **1** (*BrE*) (*NAmE* ˌtrack and ˈfield) sports such as running and jumping that people compete in **2** (*NAmE*) any sports that people compete in: *students involved in all forms of college athletics*

**athˈletic shoe** *noun* (*NAmE*) = TENNIS SHOE

**at-home** /ˌæt ˈhəʊm/ *noun, adj.*
■ *noun* (old-fashioned) a party in sb's home: *We're having an at-home—can you come?*
■ *adj.* [only before noun] **1** done or taking place at home: *an at-home job* **2** (of a parent) staying at home rather than going out to work: *at-home dads*

**-athon** /əθɒn; *NAmE* əθɑːn/ *suffix* (in nouns) an event in which a particular activity is done for a very long time, especially one organized to raise money for charity: *a swimathon*

**-ation** ⊃ -ION

**atish·oo** /əˈtʃuː/ (*BrE*) (also **achoo**, **ah·choo** *NAmE, BrE*) *exclamation* the word for the sound people make when they SNEEZE

**-ative** /ətɪv, eɪtɪv/ *suffix* (in adjectives) doing or tending to do sth: *illustrative* ◇ *talkative* ▸ **-atively** /ətɪvli, eɪtɪvli/ *suffix* (in adverbs): *creatively*

**Atˌlantic ˈDaylight Time** *noun* [U] (*abbr.* ADT) the time used in summer in an area that includes the east of Canada, Puerto Rico and the Virgin Islands, that is three hours earlier than UTC

**Atˌlantic ˈStandard Time** *noun* [U] (*abbr.* AST) (also **Atˈlantic time**) the time used in winter in an area that includes the east of Canada, Puerto Rico and the Virgin Islands that is four hours earlier than UTC

**At·lan·tis** /ætˈlæntɪs/ *noun* [U] (in stories) an island full of beauty and wealth, that was said to have been covered by the sea and lost. There are many stories about people's attempts to find it.

**atlas** /ˈætləs/ *noun* a book of maps: *a world atlas* ◇ *a road atlas of Europe*

**ATM** /ˌeɪ tiː ˈem/ *noun* a machine in or outside a bank, shop, etc., from which you can get money from your bank account using a special plastic card (the abbreviation for 'automated teller machine' or 'automatic teller machine') SYN **cash machine**

**ˈATM card** (*US*) (*BrE* ˈcash card) *noun* a plastic card used to get money from a CASH MACHINE (= a machine in or outside a bank) ⊃ compare CREDIT CARD, DEBIT CARD

---

**at·mos·phere** ⓘ B1 /ˈætməsfɪə(r); *NAmE* -sfɪr/ *noun* **1** ⓘ B1 **the atmosphere** [sing.] the mixture of gases that surrounds the earth: *Wind power doesn't release carbon dioxide into the atmosphere.* ◇ *greenhouse gases in the earth's atmosphere* **2** ⓘ B1 [C] a mixture of gases that surrounds another planet or a star: *Saturn's atmosphere* **3** ⓘ B1 [C] the air in a room or in a small space; the air around a place: *a smoky/stuffy atmosphere* ◇ *These plants love warm, humid atmospheres.* **4** ⓘ B1 [C, sing., U] the feeling or mood that you have in a particular place or situation; a feeling between two people or in a group of people: *Before the parade, the atmosphere was electric.* ◇ *This type of lighting creates a relaxing atmosphere.* ◇ *City officials have created an atmosphere of fear.* ◇ *Use music and lighting to create a romantic atmosphere.* ◇ *There was an atmosphere of mutual trust between them.* ◇ *The old house is full of atmosphere* (= it's very interesting). IDM see HEAVY *adj.*

**at·mos·pher·ic** /ˌætməsˈferɪk; *NAmE* -ˈfɪr-, -ˈfer-/ *adj.* **1** [only before noun] related to the earth's atmosphere: *atmospheric pollution/conditions/pressure* **2** creating an exciting or emotional mood: *atmospheric music*

**at·mos·pher·ics** /ˌætməsˈferɪks; *NAmE* -ˈfɪr-, -ˈfer-/ *noun* [pl.] **1** qualities in sth that create a particular atmosphere **2** noises that sometimes interrupt a radio broadcast

**atoll** /ˈætɒl; *NAmE* ˈætɔːl/ *noun* an island made of CORAL and in the shape of a ring with a lake of SEAWATER (called a LAGOON) in the middle

**atom** /ˈætəm/ *noun* the smallest PARTICLE of a chemical element that can exist: *the splitting of the atom* ◇ *Two atoms of hydrogen combine with one atom of oxygen to form a molecule of water.* ⊃ WORDFINDER NOTE at PHYSICS

> **WORDFINDER** antiparticle, electron, ion, neutron, nucleus, particle, positron, proton, valency

**atom·ic** /əˈtɒmɪk; *NAmE* əˈtɑːm-/ *adj.* [usually before noun] **1** relating to ATOMS or an ATOM: *atomic structure* **2** relating to the energy that is produced when ATOMS are split; related to weapons that use this energy: *atomic energy/power* ◇ *the post-war atomic programme*

**aˌtomic ˈbomb** (also **ˈA-bomb**, **ˈatom bomb**) *noun* a bomb that explodes using the energy that is produced when an ATOM or ATOMS are split

**aˌtomic ˈclock** *noun* an extremely accurate clock that uses the movement of ATOMS or MOLECULES to measure time

**aˌtomic ˈenergy** (also **aˌtomic ˈpower**) *noun* [U] = NUCLEAR ENERGY

**aˌtomic ˈmass** *noun* (*chemistry*) = RELATIVE ATOMIC MASS

**aˌtomic ˈnumber** *noun* (*chemistry*) the number of PROTONS in the NUCLEUS (= centre) of an ATOM of a particular chemical element. Elements are placed in the PERIODIC TABLE according to their atomic numbers.

**aˌtomic ˈweight** *noun* (*chemistry*) = RELATIVE ATOMIC MASS

**atom·ism** /ˈætəmɪzəm/ *noun* [U] (*specialist*) the idea of understanding sth by separating it into its different parts ⊃ compare HOLISM ▸ **atom·is·tic** /ˌætəˈmɪstɪk/ *adj.*

**atom·ize** (*BrE* also **-ise**) /ˈætəmaɪz/ *verb* ~ sth to reduce sth to ATOMS or very small pieces

**atom·izer** (*BrE* also **-iser**) /ˈætəmaɪzə(r)/ *noun* a container that forces a liquid such as water or paint out as a very fine SPRAY

**atonal** /eɪˈtəʊnl/ *adj.* (of a piece of music) not written in any particular KEY OPP **tonal** ▸ **aton·al·ity** /ˌeɪtəʊˈnæləti/ *noun* [U]

**atone** /əˈtəʊn/ *verb* [I] ~ **(for sth)** (*formal*) to act in a way that shows you are sorry for doing sth wrong in the past SYN **make amends**: *to atone for a crime* ▸ **atone·ment** *noun* [U]: *to make atonement for his sins* ◇ *Yom Kippur, the Jewish day of atonement*

**atop** /əˈtɒp; *NAmE* əˈtɑːp/ (also **aˈtop of**) *prep.* (especially *NAmE*) (*old-fashioned* or *literary* in *BrE*) on top of; at the top of: *a flag high atop a pole* ◇ *a scoop of ice cream atop of a slice of apple pie*

**atopic** /eɪˈtɒpɪk; NAmE -ˈtɑːp-/ adj. (medical) relating to a form of ALLERGY where there is a reaction in a part of the body that does not have direct contact with the thing causing the ALLERGY

**-ator** /eɪtə(r)/ suffix (in nouns) a person or thing that does sth: *creator* ◇ *percolator*

**A to Z** (also **A–Z**) /ˌeɪ tə ˈzed; NAmE ˈziː/ noun [sing.] **1** (BrE) a book, app or website containing street maps of all the areas of a large city **2** a book, app or website containing all the information you need about a subject or place: *an A to Z of needlework*

**ˌat-ˈrisk** adj. [only before noun] in danger of being attacked or harmed: *Social services keep lists of at-risk children.* ⇒ see also AT RISK at RISK *noun*

**atˈrium** /ˈeɪtriəm/ noun (pl. **atria** /-triə/) **1** a large high space, usually with a glass roof, in the centre of a modern building **2** an open space in the centre of an ancient Roman VILLA (= a large house) **3** (anatomy) either of the two upper spaces in the heart that are used in the first stage of sending the blood around the body **SYN** auricle

**atrocious** /əˈtrəʊʃəs/ adj. **1** very bad or unpleasant **SYN** terrible: *She speaks French with an atrocious accent.* ◇ *Isn't the weather atrocious?* **2** very cruel and making you feel shocked: *atrocious acts of brutality* ▶ **atrociously** adv.

**atrocity** /əˈtrɒsəti; NAmE əˈtrɑːs-/ noun [C, usually pl., U] (pl. **-ies**) a cruel and violent act, especially in a war

**atrophy** /ˈætrəfi/ noun, verb
■ noun [U] (medical) the condition of losing fat, muscle, strength, etc. in a part of the body because it does not have enough blood: *(figurative, formal) The cultural life of the country will sink into atrophy unless more writers and artists emerge.*
■ verb [I] (atrophies, atrophying, atrophied, atrophied) if a part of the body atrophies, it becomes weak because it is not used or because it does not have enough blood: *patients whose muscles have atrophied* ◇ *(figurative) Memory can atrophy through lack of use.* ▶ **atrophied** adj.: *atrophied muscles* ◇ *atrophied religious values*

**atˈtach** ❶ B1 /əˈtætʃ/ verb **1** ~ sth [T] to fasten or join one thing to another: ~ sth *I attach a copy of my notes for your information.* ◇ ~ **sth to sth** *Attach the coupon to the front of your letter.* ◇ *(figurative) They have attached a number of conditions to the agreement* (= said that the conditions must be part of the agreement) ⇒ compare DETACH **2** B1 [T] to send an electronic document with an email: *I attach a copy of the spreadsheet.* **3** B2 [T] to believe that sth is important or worth thinking about: ~ **importance, significance, value, weight to sth** *I attach great importance to this research.* **4** [T] ~ **yourself to sb** to join sb for a time, sometimes when you are not welcome or have not been invited: *He attached himself to me at the party and I couldn't get rid of him.* **5** [I, T] (formal) to be connected with sb/sth; to connect sth to sth: ~ **to sb/sth** *No one is suggesting that any health risks attach to this product.* ◇ *No blame attaches to you.* ◇ **be attached to sth** *Unfortunately, there is still a stigma attached to mental illness.*

**attaché** /əˈtæʃeɪ; NAmE ˌætəˈʃeɪ/ noun a person who works at an EMBASSY, usually with a special responsibility for a particular area of activity: *a cultural attaché*

**atˈtaché case** noun a small hard flat case used for carrying business documents ⇒ compare BRIEFCASE

**atˈtached** /əˈtætʃt/ adj. **1** joined to sth: *Please complete the attached application form.* ◇ ~ **to sth** *The ball was attached to a length of thin chain.* **2** ~ **(to sb/sth)** liking sb/sth very much: *I've never seen two people so attached to each other.* ◇ *We've grown very attached to this house.* ⇒ compare UNATTACHED **3** [not before noun] ~ **to sth** working for or forming part of an organization: *The research unit is attached to the university.*

**atˈtachment** B1+ B2 /əˈtætʃmənt/ noun **1** B1+ B2 [C] (computing) a document that you send to sb using email ⇒ WORDFINDER NOTE at MESSAGE **2** B1+ C1 [U, C] the act of joining one thing to another; a thing that joins two things together: *All cars have points for the attachment of safety restraints.* ◇ ~ **of sth to sth** *They discussed the attachment of new conditions to the peace plans* ◇ ~ **to sth** *They had to check the strength of the seat attachments to the floor of the plane.* **3** B1+ C1 [C, U] ~ **(to sb)** a feeling of love for sb/sth: *a child's strong attachment to its parents* **4** [C, U] ~ **(to sth)** belief in and support for an idea or a set of values: *the popular attachment to democratic government* **5** [C] a tool that you can fix onto a machine, to make it do another job: *an electric drill with a range of different attachments* **6** [C, U] (BrE) a short time spent working with an organization such as a hospital, school or part of the armed forces: *a 4-month training attachment* ◇ **on ~ (to sth)** *She's on attachment to the local hospital.*

**atˈtack** ❶ A2 S /əˈtæk/ noun, verb
■ noun
• VIOLENCE **1** B1+ A2 [C, U] an act of using violence to try to hurt or kill sb: *Five people were killed in the attacks that took place last night.* ◇ ~ **on/upon sb/sth** *the recent series of deadly terrorist attacks on European cities* ◇ ~ **against sb** *vicious attacks against pensioners*
• IN WAR **2** B1+ A2 [C, U] an act of trying to kill or injure the enemy in war, using weapons such as guns and bombs: *a bomb/rocket/missile attack* ◇ ~ **on sb/sth** *Rebel forces launched an attack on civilian targets.* ◇ ~ **against sb/sth** *Commanders attempted to prevent an attack against the city.* ◇ **under ~ (from sb/sth)** *The patrol came under attack from all sides.* ⇒ see also COUNTER-ATTACK *noun*

WORDFINDER alert, assassinate, campaign, execute, extremist, hijack, hostage, kidnap, terrorism

• OF ILLNESS **3** B1+ B1 [C] a sudden, short period of illness, usually severe: *to suffer an asthma attack* ◇ ~ **of sth** *an attack of fever* ⇒ see also HEART ATTACK
• OF EMOTION **4** B1+ B2 [C] a sudden period of feeling an emotion such as fear: *a panic attack* ◇ ~ **of sth** *an attack of nerves* ◇ *(figurative) an attack of conscience* (= a guilty feeling about sth you have done or are planning to do)
• CRITICISM **5** B1+ B2 [C, U] strong criticism of sb/sth in speech or in writing: *He found himself the victim of an unprovoked attack by the media.* ◇ ~ **on sb/sth** *It was seen as a personal attack on the president.* ◇ **under ~ (from sb/sth) (for (sth/for doing sth))** *The school has come under attack for failing to encourage bright students.*
• IN SPORT **6** B2 [sing.] (BrE) (NAmE **offense**) the players in a team whose job is to try to score goals or points: *Germany's attack has been weakened by the loss of some key players through injury.* ⇒ compare DEFENCE **7** B1+ B2 [C, U] ~ **(on sth)** the actions that players take to try to score a goal or win the game: *a sustained attack on the Arsenal goal*
• ACTION TO STOP STH **8** [C] ~ **(on sth)** an action that you take to try to stop or change sth that you feel is bad: *to launch an all-out attack on poverty/unemployment*
• DAMAGE **9** [U, C] the action of sth such as an insect, or a disease, that causes damage to sth/sb: *The roof timbers were affected by rot and insect attack.*

■ verb
• USE VIOLENCE **1** B1+ A2 [I, T] to use violence to try to hurt or kill sb: *Most dogs will not attack unless provoked.* ◇ ~ **sb/sth** *Terrorists attacked several targets across the city.* ◇ *A woman was brutally attacked by a gang of youths.* ◇ ~ **sb with sth** *One of the men viciously attacked officers with a home-made weapon.*
• IN WAR **2** B1+ A2 [I, T] to use weapons, such as guns and bombs against an enemy in a war, etc: *Enemy forces attacked at night.* ◇ ~ **sb/sth** *There are fears that the government is planning to attack neighbouring countries.* ⇒ WORDFINDER NOTE at CONFLICT
• CRITICIZE **3** B1+ B2 [T] to criticize sb/sth severely: ~ **sb/sth** *His latest work has been bitterly attacked by the critics.* ◇ ~ **sb/sth for (doing) sth** *He was publicly attacked for his political views.*
• DAMAGE **4** B1+ B2 [T] ~ **sth** to have a harmful effect on sth: *a disease that attacks the brain* ◇ *The vines were attacked by mildew.*

❶ Oxford Phrasal Academic Lexicon (OPAL) written and spoken word lists | Ⓦ OPAL written word list | Ⓢ OPAL spoken word list

# attack dog

- **IN SPORT** **5** [I] to go forward in a game in order to try to score goals or points ⊃ compare DEFEND: *Spain attacked more in the second half and deserved a goal.*
- **DO STH WITH ENERGY 6** [T] ~ sth to deal with sth with a lot of energy: *Let's attack one problem at a time.*

**at·tack dog** *noun* **1** a dog that has been trained to attack people or other animals **2** (*disapproving*) a person who often makes strong personal attacks on other people in public: *His image has changed from statesman to attack dog.*

**at·tack·er** /əˈtækə(r)/ *noun* **1** a person who attacks sb: *She didn't really see her attacker.* **2** (*sport*) a player who tries to score in games such as football (soccer), hockey, etc.

**at·tain** /əˈteɪn/ *verb* (*formal*) **1** ~ sth to succeed in getting sth, usually after a lot of effort: *Most of our students attained five 'A' grades in their exams.* **2** ~ sth to reach a particular age, level or condition: *The cheetah can attain speeds of up to 97 kph.*

**at·tain·able** /əˈteɪnəbl/ *adj.* that you can achieve: *attainable goals/objectives/targets* ◇ *This standard is easily attainable by most students.* **OPP** unattainable

**at·tain·ment** /əˈteɪnmənt/ *noun* (*formal*) **1** [C, usually pl.] (*BrE*) something that you achieved: *a young woman of impressive educational attainments* **2** [U] success in achieving sth: *The attainment of his ambitions was still a dream.* ◇ *attainment targets* (= for example in education)

**at·tempt** /əˈtempt/ *noun, verb*

- *noun* **1** [C, U] an act of trying to do sth, especially sth difficult, often with no success: *I passed my driving test at the first attempt.* ◇ ~ to do sth *They made no attempt to escape.* ◇ **in an** ~ **to do sth** *Two factories were closed in an attempt to cut costs.* ◇ ~ at (doing) sth *The couple made an unsuccessful attempt at a compromise.* **2** [C] an act of trying to kill sb: ~ on sb's/sb's life *Someone has made an attempt on the president's life.* **3** [C] ~ (on sth) an effort to do better than sth, such as a very good performance in sport: *his attempt on the world land speed record* ⊃ **WORD-FINDER NOTE** at ADVENTURE **4** [C] ~ (at sth) a thing that you produce as a result of trying to make or achieve sth: *She picked her first attempt at a letter out of the bin.*
- *verb* to make an effort or try to do sth, especially sth difficult: ~ to do sth *I will attempt to answer all your questions.* ◇ *She never attempted to explain her behaviour to her family.* ◇ ~ sth *The prisoners attempted an escape, but failed.*

**at·tempted** /əˈtemptɪd/ *adj.* [only before noun] (of a crime, etc.) that sb has tried to do but without success: *attempted rape/murder/robbery*

**at·tend** /əˈtend/ *verb* **1** [I, T] (*rather formal*) to be present at an event: *We'd like as many people as possible to attend.* ◇ ~ sth *The meeting was attended by 90% of shareholders.* ◇ *to attend a wedding/funeral/service/ceremony* ◇ *Everyone is welcome to attend the free event.* **2** [T, I] ~ sth (*formal*) to go regularly to a place: *Our children attend the same school.* ◇ *How many people attend church every Sunday?* ◇ *Your dentist will ask you to attend for regular check-ups.* **3** [I] ~ (to sb/sth) (*formal*) to pay attention to what sb is saying or to what you are doing: *She hadn't been attending during the lesson.* **4** [T] ~ sth (*formal*) to happen at the same time as sth: *She dislikes the loss of privacy that attends TV celebrity.* **5** [T] ~ sb (*formal*) to be with sb and help them: *The president was attended by several members of his staff.*

**PHRV** ▸ at·tend to sb/sth to deal with sb/sth; to take care of sb/sth: *I have some urgent business to attend to.* ◇ *A nurse attended to his needs constantly.* ◇ (*BrE, formal*) *Are you being attended to, Sir?* (= for example, in a shop)

**at·tend·ance** /əˈtendəns/ *noun* **1** [U, C] the act of being present at a place, for example at school: *Attendance at these lectures is not compulsory.* ◇ *Teachers must keep a record of students' attendances.* **2** [C, U] the number of people present at an organized event: *high/low/falling/poor attendances* ◇ *There was an attendance of 42 at the meeting.*

**IDM** be in at'tendance (*formal*) to be present at a special event: *Several heads of state were in attendance at the funeral.* be in at'tendance (on sb) (*formal*) to be with or near sb in order to help them if necessary: *He always has at least two bodyguards in attendance.* take at'tendance (*NAmE*) to check who is present and who is not present at a place and to mark this information on a list of names ⊃ compare REGISTER (1)

**At'tendance Allowance** *noun* [U] the money that a very sick or DISABLED older person receives from the government in Britain if they need sb to care for them nearly all the time

**at·tend·ant** /əˈtendənt/ *noun, adj.*

- *noun* **1** a person whose job is to serve or help people in a public place: *a cloakroom/parking/museum attendant* ⊃ see also FLIGHT ATTENDANT **2** a person who takes care of and lives or travels with an important person or a sick or DISABLED person
- *adj.* [usually before noun] (*formal*) closely connected with sth that has just been mentioned: *attendant problems/risks/circumstances* ◇ ~ upon sth *We had all the usual problems attendant upon starting a new business.*

**at·tend·ee** /əˌtenˈdiː/ *noun* a person who attends a meeting, etc.

**at·tend·er** /əˈtendə(r)/ (*especially BrE*) (*NAmE usually* **at·tend·ee**) *noun* a person who goes to a place or an event, often on a regular basis: *She's a regular attender at evening classes.*

**at·ten·tion** /əˈtenʃn/ *noun, exclamation*

- *noun*
- **LISTENING/LOOKING CAREFULLY 1** [U] ~ (to sb/sth) the act of listening to, looking at or thinking about sth/sb carefully; interest that people show in sb/sth: *the report's attention to detail* ◇ *He turned his attention back to the road again.* ◇ *Please pay close attention* (= listen carefully) *to what I am saying.* ◇ *Don't pay any attention to what they say* (= don't think that it is important). ◇ *She tried to attract the waiter's attention.* ◇ *The event has attracted a lot of media attention.* ◇ *I tried not to draw attention to* (= make people notice) *the weak points in my argument.* ◇ *An article in the newspaper caught my attention.* ◇ *I couldn't give the programme my undivided attention.* ◇ *As the youngest child, she was always the centre of attention.* ◇ *Small children have a very short attention span.* ◇ (*formal*) *These issues should be brought to the attention of the public.* ◇ (*formal*) *It has come to my attention* (= I have been informed) *that…* ◇ (*formal*) *Can I have your attention please?* ⊃ **LANGUAGE BANK** at EMPHASIS
- **TREATMENT/ACTIONS 2** [U] special care, action or treatment: *He received urgent medical attention.* ◇ *The roof needs attention* (= needs to be repaired). ◇ **for the attention of…** (= written on the envelope of an official letter to say who should deal with it) ⊃ see also FAO **3** [C, usually pl.] things that sb does to try to please you or to show their interest in you: *She tried to escape the unwanted attentions of her former boyfriend.*
- **SOLDIERS 4** [U] the position soldiers take when they stand very straight with their feet together and their arms at their sides: *to stand at/to attention* ⊃ compare (STAND) AT EASE
- *exclamation* **1** used for asking people to listen to sth that is being announced: *Attention, please! Passengers for flight KL412 are requested to go to gate 21 immediately.* **2** used for ordering soldiers to stand to attention

**at'tention 'deficit disorder** (*also* **at'tention 'deficit hyper'activity disorder**) *noun* [U] (*abbr.* **ADD, ADHD**) a medical condition, especially in children, that makes it difficult for them to pay attention to what they are doing, to stay still for long and to learn things

**at·ten·tive** /əˈtentɪv/ *adj.* **1** listening or watching carefully and with interest: *an attentive audience* **2** helpful; making sure that people have what they need: *The hotel staff are friendly and attentive.* ◇ ~ to sb/sth *Ministers should be more attentive to the needs of families.* **OPP** inattentive
▸ **at·ten·tive·ly** *adv.* **at·ten·tive·ness** *noun* [U]

**at·ten·u·ate** /əˈtenjueɪt/ verb ~ sth (formal) to make sth weaker or less effective: *The drug attenuates the effects of the virus.* ▶ **at·tenu·ation** /əˌtenjuˈeɪʃn/ noun [U]

**at·tenu·ated** /əˈtenjueɪtɪd/ adj. (formal) **1** made weaker or less effective: *an attenuated form of the virus* **2** (of a person) very thin

**at·tenu·ator** /əˈtenjueɪtə(r)/ noun (specialist) a device consisting of a number of RESISTORS that reduce the strength of a radio sound or signal

**at·test** /əˈtest/ verb (formal) **1** [I, T] ~ (to sth) | ~ (that ...) | ~ (sth) to show or prove that sth is true SYN **bear/give witness**: *Contemporary accounts attest to his courage and determination.* **2** [T] ~ (that ...) | ~ (sth) to state that you believe that sth is true or what sb claims it is, for example in court: *to attest a will* ◊ *The signature was attested by two witnesses.*

**attic** /ˈætɪk/ noun a room or space just below the roof of a house, often used for storing things: *furniture stored in the attic* ◊ *an attic bedroom* ⇒ compare GARRET, LOFT

**at·tire** /əˈtaɪə(r)/ noun [U] (formal) clothes, especially fine or formal ones: *formal evening attire*

**at·tired** /əˈtaɪəd/; NAmE -ərd/ adj. [not before noun] (formal or literary) ~ (in sth) dressed in a particular way

**at·ti·tude** ⓘ B1 O /ˈætɪtjuːd; NAmE -tuːd/ noun **1** ? B1 [C] the way that you think and feel about sb/sth; the way that you behave towards sb/sth shows how you think and feel: *~ towards sb/sth These societies have to change their attitudes towards women.* ◊ *to have a positive/negative attitude towards sb/sth* ◊ *~ to sb/sth* ◊ *~ about/on sth social attitudes about education* ◊ *Youth is simply an attitude of mind.* ◊ *If you want to pass your exams you'd better change your attitude!* ◊ *If they can adopt that kind of attitude then the future looks very promising.* ⇒ WORDFINDER NOTE at BEHAVIOUR **2** [U] confident, sometimes aggressive behaviour that shows you do not care about other people's opinions and that you want to do things in an individual way: *You'd better get rid of that attitude and shape up, young man.* ◊ *with~ a band with attitude* **3** [C] (formal) a position of the body: **in an~of sth** *Her hands were folded in an attitude of prayer.* IDM see STRIKE v.

**¹attitude problem** noun if sb has an **attitude problem** they do not behave in a way that is acceptable to other people but do not see why they need to change their behaviour

**at·ti·tu·din·al** /ˌætɪˈtjuːdɪnl; NAmE -ˈtuː-/ adj. (formal) related to the attitudes that people have

**attn** (also **attn.** especially in NAmE) abbr. (business) (in writing) for the attention of: *Sales Dept, attn C Biggs* ⇒ see also FAO

**at·tor·ney** ?+ C1 /əˈtɜːni; NAmE əˈtɜːrni/ noun **1** ?+ C1 (especially US) a lawyer, especially one who can act for sb in court ⇒ note at LAWYER ⇒ see also DISTRICT ATTORNEY **2** a person who is given the power to act for another person in business or legal matters: *She was made her father's attorney when he became ill.* ⇒ see also POWER OF ATTORNEY **3** (SAfrE) a SOLICITOR (= a lawyer who prepares legal documents and advises on legal matters)

**at·torney ˈgeneral** noun (pl. **attorneys general** or **attorney generals**) **1** also **Attorney General** the most senior legal officer in some countries or states, for example the UK or Canada, who advises the government or head of state on legal matters **2** **the At·torney ˈGeneral** the head of the US Department of Justice and a member of the President's CABINET (= a group of senior politicians who advise the President)

**at·tract** ⓘ B1 /əˈtrækt/ verb **1** ? B1 [usually passive] if you are **attracted** by sth, it interests you and makes you want it; if you are **attracted** by sb, you like or admire them: **be attracted by sb/sth** *I had always been attracted by the idea of working abroad.* ◊ *~ sb (to sth)* **What first attracted me to her was her sense of humour.* **2** ? B1 **be attracted to sb** to have a sexual or romantic interest in sb: *I am not attracted to him at all.* **3** ? B1 to make sth come somewhere or take part in sth: *~ sb/sth (to sth)* *Officials hope to attract more tourists to the area.* ◊ *The exhib-*

85

ATV

*ition has attracted thousands of visitors.* **4** ? B1 ~ sth to make people have a particular reaction: *This proposal has attracted a lot of interest.* ◊ *His comments were bound to attract criticism.* ◊ *She tried to attract the attention of the waiter.* **5** (physics) if a MAGNET or GRAVITY **attracts** sth, it makes it move towards it OPP **repel** IDM see OPPOSITE n.

**at·tract·ant** /əˈtræktənt/ noun (specialist) a substance that attracts sth, especially an animal: *This type of trap uses no bait or other attractant.*

**at·trac·tion** ⓘ B1 /əˈtrækʃn/ noun **1** ? B1 [C] an interesting or lively place to go or thing to do: *Buckingham Palace is a major tourist attraction.* ◊ *The main attraction at Giverny is Monet's garden.* **2** ? B1 [sing., U] a feeling of liking sb, especially sexually: *She felt an immediate attraction for him.* ◊ *Sexual attraction is a large part of falling in love.* **3** ? B1 [C, U] a feature, quality or person that makes sth seem interesting and fun, and worth having or doing: *I can't see the attraction of sitting on a beach all day.* ◊ *City life holds little attraction for me.* ◊ *She is the star attraction of the show.* **4** [U] (physics) a force that pulls things towards each other: *gravitational/magnetic attraction* ⇒ compare REPULSION

**at·tract·ive** ⓘ A2 /əˈtræktɪv/ adj. **1** A2 (of a person) pleasant to look at, especially in a sexual way: *an attractive woman* ◊ *I like John but I don't find him attractive physically.* ⇒ SYNONYMS at BEAUTIFUL **2** ? A2 (of a thing or a place) pleasant: *a big house with an attractive garden* ◊ *That's one of the less attractive aspects of her personality.* **3** ? B1 having features or qualities that make sth seem interesting and worth having SYN **appealing**: *an attractive offer/proposition/option* OPP **unattractive** ▶ **at·tract·ive·ly** adv.: *The room is arranged very attractively.* ◊ *attractively priced hotel rooms* **at·tract·ive·ness** noun [U]: *the attractiveness of travelling abroad*

**at·trib·ut·able** /əˈtrɪbjətəbl/ adj. [not before noun] ~ **to sb/sth** probably caused by the thing mentioned: *Their illnesses are attributable to a poor diet.*

**at·tri·bute** ?+ C1 W verb, noun
■ verb /əˈtrɪbjuːt/ **1** ?+ C1 ~ **sth to sth** to say or believe that sth is the result of a particular thing: *She attributes her success to hard work and a little luck.* ◊ *The power failure was attributed to the recent storms and high winds.* **2** ?+ C1 ~ **sth to sb** to say or believe that sb is responsible for doing sth, especially for saying, writing or painting sth: *This play is usually attributed to Shakespeare.* **3** ?+ C1 ~ **sth (to sb/sth)** to regard a quality or feature as belonging to sb/sth: *The committee refused to attribute blame without further information.* ▶ **at·tri·bu·tion** /ˌætrɪˈbjuːʃn/ noun [U]: *The attribution of this painting to Rembrandt has never been questioned.*
■ noun ?+ C1 /ˈætrɪbjuːt/ a quality or feature of sb/sth: *Patience is one of the most important attributes in a teacher.*

**at·tribu·tive** /əˈtrɪbjətɪv/ adj. (grammar) (of adjectives or nouns) used before a noun to describe it: *In 'the blue sky' and 'a family business', 'blue' and 'family' are attributive.* ⇒ compare PREDICATIVE ▶ **at·tribu·tive·ly** adv.: *Some adjectives can only be used attributively.*

**at·tri·tion** /əˈtrɪʃn/ noun [U] (formal) **1** a process of making sb/sth, especially your enemy, weaker by repeatedly attacking them or creating problems for them: *It was a war of attrition.* **2** (especially NAmE) (BrE usually **natural ˈwastage**) the process of reducing the number of people who are employed by an organization by, for example, not replacing people who leave their jobs

**at·tuned** /əˈtjuːnd; NAmE əˈtuːnd/ adj. [not before noun] ~ **(to sb/sth)** familiar with sb/sth so that you can understand or recognize them or it and act in an appropriate way: *She wasn't yet attuned to her baby's needs.*

**ATV** /ˌeɪ tiː ˈviː/ noun (especially NAmE) a small open vehicle, usually with one seat and four wheels with very thick tyres, designed especially for use on rough ground without roads (the abbreviation for 'all-terrain vehicle') ⇒ see also QUAD BIKE

# atypical

**atyp·ical** /ˌeɪˈtɪpɪkl/ adj. not typical or usual: *atypical behaviour* **OPP** **typical**

**AU** /ˌeɪ ˈjuː/ abbr. ASTRONOMICAL UNIT

**au·ber·gine** /ˈəʊbəʒiːn; NAmE -bɜːrʒ-/ (BrE) (NAmE **egg·plant**) noun [C, U] a vegetable with shiny dark purple skin that is soft and white inside ⊃ VISUAL VOCAB page V5

**au·burn** /ˈɔːbən; NAmE -bərn/ adj. (of hair) red-brown in colour ⊃ WORDFINDER NOTE at BLONDE ▸ **au·burn** noun [U]: *the rich auburn of her hair*

**auc·tion** /ˈɔːkʃn; BrE also ˈɒk-/ noun, verb
■ noun [C, U] a public sale in which things are sold to the person who offers the most money for them: *an auction of paintings* ◇ **at ~** *A classic Rolls-Royce fetched* (= was sold for) *£25 000 at auction.* ◇ **up for ~** *The house is up for auction* (= will be sold at an auction). ◇ *an internet auction site*
■ verb [usually passive] to sell sth at an auction: **be auctioned** *The costumes from the movie are to be auctioned for charity.*
**PHRV** **auction sth↔off** to sell sth at an auction, especially sth that is no longer needed or wanted: *The army is auctioning off a lot of surplus equipment.*

**auc·tion·eer** /ˌɔːkʃəˈnɪə(r); ˌɒk-; NAmE ˌɔːkʃəˈnɪr/ noun a person whose job is to direct an auction and sell the goods

**'auction house** noun a company that sells things in AUCTIONS

**'auction room** (also **auction rooms**) noun a building in which AUCTIONS are held

**au·da·cious** /ɔːˈdeɪʃəs/ adj. (formal) willing to take risks or to do sth that shocks people **SYN** **daring**: *an audacious decision* ▸ **au·da·cious·ly** adv.

**au·da·city** /ɔːˈdæsəti/ noun [U] behaviour that is brave but likely to shock or offend people **SYN** **nerve**: *He had the audacity to say I was too fat.*

**aud·ible** /ˈɔːdəbl/ adj. that can be heard clearly: *Her voice was barely audible above the noise.* **OPP** **inaudible** ▸ **audi·bil·ity** /ˌɔːdəˈbɪləti/ noun [U] **aud·ibly** /ˈɔːdəbli/ adv.

**audi·ence** /ˈɔːdiəns/ noun **1** [C + sing./pl. v.] the group of people who have gathered to watch or listen to sth (a play, concert, sb speaking, etc.): *The audience was/were clapping for 10 minutes.* ◇ *The museum is trying to attract a wider audience.* ◇ *The debate was televised in front of a live audience.* ◇ *We encourage audience participation during our show.* ⊃ WORDFINDER NOTE at CONCERT **2** [C] a number of people or a particular group of people who watch, read, or listen to the same thing: *TV/television/cinema/movie audiences* ◇ *His book reached an even wider audience when it was made into a movie.* ◇ *The target audience for this advertisement was mainly teenagers.* **3** [C] a formal meeting with an important person: *an audience with the Pope* ⊃ SYNONYMS at INTERVIEW

**audio** /ˈɔːdiəʊ/ adj. [only before noun] connected with sound that is recorded: *audio and video recordings/files/clips* ◇ *The audio quality was poor.* ▸ **audio** noun [U]

**audio-** /ˈɔːdiəʊ; BrE also ˈɔːdiˈɒ; NAmE also ˈɔːdiˈɑː/ combining form (in nouns, adjectives and adverbs) connected with hearing or sound: *audiovisual*

**audio·book** /ˈɔːdiəʊbʊk/ noun a recording of a book, especially a novel, being read ALOUD, made available to download or on a CD ⊃ compare E-BOOK

**'audio guide** noun a small device, usually with HEADPHONES, that visitors to a museum, gallery, city, etc. can hold in their hand and use to listen to recorded information while they are walking around: *The museum provides free audio guides.*

**audi·ology** /ˌɔːdiˈɒlədʒi; NAmE -ˈɑːl-/ noun [U] the science and medicine that deals with the sense of hearing ▸ **audi·ologist** noun

**'audio tape** noun [U, C] MAGNETIC tape on which sound can be recorded

**audio-vis·ual** /ˌɔːdiəʊˈvɪʒuəl/ adj. (abbr. **AV**) using both sound and pictures: *audiovisual aids for the classroom*

**audit** /ˈɔːdɪt/ noun, verb
■ noun [C, U] **1** an official examination of business and financial records to see that they are true and correct: *an annual audit* ◇ *a tax audit* **2** an official examination of the quality or standard of sth
■ verb **1** ~ **sth** to officially examine the financial accounts of a company **2** ~ **sth** (NAmE) to attend a course at college or university but without taking any exams or receiving credit

**au·di·tion** /ɔːˈdɪʃn/ noun, verb
■ noun a short performance given by an actor, a singer, etc., so that sb can decide whether they are suitable to act in a play, sing in a concert, etc. ⊃ WORDFINDER NOTE at ACTOR
■ verb **1** [I] ~ **(for sth)** to take part in an audition: *She was auditioning for the role of Lady Macbeth.* **2** [T] ~ **sb (for sth)** to watch, listen to and judge sb at an audition: *We auditioned over 200 children for the part.*

**audit·or** /ˈɔːdɪtə(r)/ noun **1** a person who officially examines the business and financial records of a company ⊃ WORDFINDER NOTE at BUSINESSMAN **2** (NAmE) a person who attends a college course, but without having to take exams and without receiving credit

**audi·tor·ium** /ˌɔːdɪˈtɔːriəm/ noun (pl. **audi·tor·iums** or **audi·tor·ia** /-riə/) **1** the part of a theatre, concert hall, etc. in which the audience sits ⊃ WORDFINDER NOTE at THEATRE **2** (especially NAmE) a large building or room in which public meetings, concerts, etc. are held ⊃ WORDFINDER NOTE at CONCERT

**audi·tory** /ˈɔːdətri; NAmE -tɔːri/ adj. (specialist) connected with hearing: *auditory stimuli*

**'audit trail** noun the detailed record of information on paper or on a computer that can be examined to prove what happened, for example what pieces of business were done and what decisions were made

**au fait** /ˌəʊ ˈfeɪ/ adj. [not before noun] ~ **(with sth)** (from French) completely familiar with sth: *I'm new here so I'm not completely au fait with the system.*

**auger** /ˈɔːɡə(r)/ noun **1** a tool for making holes in wood, that looks like a large CORKSCREW **2** a tool like a large auger, used for making holes in the ground

**aught** /ɔːt/ pron. (old use) anything

**aug·ment** /ɔːɡˈment/ verb ~ **sth** (formal) to increase the amount, value, size, etc. of sth ▸ **aug·men·ta·tion** /ˌɔːɡmenˈteɪʃn/ noun [U, C]

**aug·mented re'ality** noun [U] (abbr. **AR**) a technology that combines computer-generated images on a screen with the real object or scene that you are looking at: *an augmented reality app/game/system*

**augur** /ˈɔːɡə(r)/ verb [I] ~ **well/badly** (formal) to be a sign that sth will be successful or not successful in the future **SYN** **bode**: *Conflicts among the various groups do not augur well for the future of the peace talks.*

**au·gury** /ˈɔːɡjəri/ noun (pl. **-ies**) (literary) a sign of what will happen in the future **SYN** **omen**

**Au·gust** /ˈɔːɡəst/ noun [U, C] (abbr. **Aug.**) the 8th month of the year, between July and September: (BrE) *August Bank Holiday* (= a public holiday on the last Monday in August in Britain) **HELP** To see how **August** is used, look at the examples at **April**.

**au·gust** /ɔːˈɡʌst/ adj. [usually before noun] (formal) impressive, making you feel respect

**auk** /ɔːk/ noun a northern bird with short narrow wings that lives in or near the sea

**auld lang syne** /ˌɔːld læŋ ˈsaɪn/ noun an old Scottish song expressing feelings of friendship, traditionally sung at midnight on New Year's Eve

**au naturel** /ˌəʊ ˌnætʃəˈrel/ adj., adv. [not before noun] (from French) in a natural way: *The fish is served au naturel, uncooked and with nothing added.*

**aunt** /ɑːnt; NAmE ænt/ noun **1** the sister of your father or mother; the wife of your uncle: *Aunt Alice* ◇ *My aunt lives in Canada.* ⊃ see also MAIDEN AUNT **2** (informal) used by children, with a first name, to address a

---

| æ cat | ɑː father | e bed | ɜː fur | ə about | ɪ sit | iː see | i happy | ɒ got (BrE) | ɔː saw | ʌ cup | ʊ put | uː too |

woman who is a friend of their parents ⇒ see also AGONY AUNT

**aun·tie** (*also* **aunty**) /ˈɑːnti; NAmE ˈæn-/ *noun* (*informal*) **1** aunt: *Auntie Mary* **2** (*IndE, SEAsianE*) used as a polite way of addressing or referring to an older woman **HELP** In this meaning, say *Lotika auntie*, not: *Auntie Lotika*. If you want to sound especially polite, you can say **auntieji** /ˈɑːntidʒi; NAmE ˈæn-/.

**Aunt Sally** /ˌɑːnt ˈsæli; NAmE ˌænt/ *noun* **1** (in some parts of the UK) a game in which people throw balls at a model of a person **2** (*BrE*) a person or thing that a lot of people criticize: *The foreign minister has become everybody's favourite Aunt Sally.*

**au pair** /ˌəʊ ˈpeə(r); NAmE ˈper/ *noun* a young person, usually a woman, who lives with a family in a foreign country in order to learn the language. An au pair helps in the house and takes care of children and receives a small wage.

**aura** /ˈɔːrə/ *noun* ~ **(of sth)** a feeling or particular quality that is very easy to notice and seems to surround a person or place: *She always has an aura of confidence.*

**aural** /ˈɔːrəl/ *adj.* (*specialist*) connected with hearing and listening: *aural and visual images* ◊ *aural comprehension tests* ▸ **aur·al·ly** /-rəli/ *adv.*

**au re·voir** /ˌəʊ rəˈvwɑː(r)/ *exclamation* (*from French*) goodbye (until we meet again)

**aur·icle** /ˈɔːrɪkl/ *noun* (*anatomy*) **1** either of the two upper spaces in the heart used to send blood around the body **SYN** atrium ⇒ compare VENTRICLE **2** the outer part of the ear

**aur·ora aus·tra·lis** /əˌrɔːrə ɒˈstreɪlɪs; NAmE ɔːˈs-/ *noun* [sing.] = SOUTHERN LIGHTS

**aur·ora bor·ealis** /əˌrɔːrə ˌbɔːriˈeɪlɪs; NAmE -ˈæl-/ *noun* [sing.] = NORTHERN LIGHTS

**aus·pices** /ˈɔːspɪsɪz/ *noun* [pl.] **IDM** **under the auspices of sb/sth** with the help, support or protection of sb/sth: *The community centre was set up under the auspices of a government initiative.*

**aus·pi·cious** /ɔːˈspɪʃəs/ *adj.* (*formal*) showing signs that sth is likely to be successful in the future **SYN** promising: *an auspicious start to the new school year* **OPP** inauspicious ▸ **aus·pi·cious·ly** *adv.*

**Aus·sie** (*also* **Oz·zie**) /ˈɒzi/ *noun* NAmE ˈɑːzi/ *noun* (*informal*) a person from Australia ▸ **Aus·sie** *adj.*

**Aussie Rules** *noun* (*informal*) = AUSTRALIAN RULES

**aus·tere** /ɒˈstɪə(r), ɔːˈs-; NAmE ɔːˈstɪr/ *adj.* **1** simple and plain; without any decorations: *her austere bedroom with its simple narrow bed* **2** (of a person) strict and serious in appearance and behaviour: *My father was a distant, austere man.* **3** allowing nothing that gives pleasure; not comfortable: *the monks' austere way of life* ▸ **aus·tere·ly** *adv.*

**aus·ter·ity** /ɒˈsterəti, ɔːˈs-; NAmE ɔːˈs-/ *noun* (*pl.* **-ies**) **1** [U] difficult economic conditions created by government policies aimed at cutting public spending: *War was followed by many years of austerity.* **2** [U] the quality of being austere: *the austerity of the monks' life* **3** [C, usually pl.] something that is part of an austere way of life: *the austerities of wartime Europe*

**aus·tral** /ˈɒstrəl, ˈɔːs-/ *NAmE* ˈɔːs-/ *adj.* (*specialist*) relating to the south

**Australia Day** /ɒˈstreɪliə deɪ; NAmE ɔːˈstreɪljə/ *noun* a national public holiday in Australia on 26 January, when people remember the founding of New South Wales on that date in 1788

**Aus·tra·lian** /ɒˈstreɪliən; NAmE ɔːˈs-/ *adj., noun*
■ *adj.* of or connected with Australia
■ *noun* a person from Australia

**Australian Rules** (*also* **Australian Rules football**) (*also informal* **Aussie Rules**) *noun* [U] an Australian game, played by two teams of 18 players, using an OVAL ball, which may be kicked, carried or hit with the hand

**Austro-** /ˈɒstrəʊ; NAmE ˈɔːstroʊ/ *combining form* (in nouns and adjectives) Austrian: *the Austro-Hungarian border*

**au·teur** /əʊˈtɜː(r); BrE *also* ɔːˈt-/ *noun* a film director who plays such an important part in making their films that they are considered to be the author **ORIGIN** From the French word *auteur*, meaning author.

**au·then·tic** /ɔːˈθentɪk/ *adj.* **1** known to be real and what sb claims it is and not a copy: *I don't know if the painting is authentic.* **OPP** inauthentic **2** true and accurate: *an authentic account of life in the desert* ◊ *the authentic voice of young black Americans* **OPP** inauthentic **3** made to be exactly the same as the original: *an authentic model of the ancient town* ▸ **au·then·tic·al·ly** /-kli/ *adv.*: *authentically flavoured Mexican dishes*

**au·then·ti·cate** /ɔːˈθentɪkeɪt/ *verb* to prove that sth is real, true or what sb claims it is: ~ **sth** *The letter has been authenticated by handwriting experts.* ◊ ~ **sth as sth** *Experts have authenticated the writing as that of Byron himself.* ▸ **au·then·ti·ca·tion** /ɔːˌθentɪˈkeɪʃn/ *noun* [U, C]

**au·then·ti·city** /ˌɔːθenˈtɪsəti/ *noun* [U] the quality of being true or what sb claims it is

**author** /ˈɔːθə(r)/ *noun, verb*
■ *noun* **1** a person who writes books or the person who wrote a particular book: *Who is your favourite author?* ◊ *He is the author of three books on art.* ◊ *best-selling author Paul Theroux* ◊ *the lead author of the report* ◊ *the author of a novel/study/article* ▸ WORDFINDER NOTE at WRITE **2** the person who creates or starts sth, especially a plan or an idea: *As the author of the proposal I cannot agree with you.*
■ *verb* ~ **sth** (*formal*) to be the author of a book, report, etc.

**author·ess** /ˈɔːθərəs/ *noun* (*old-fashioned*) a woman author

**au·thor·ial** /ɔːˈθɔːriəl/ *adj.* [usually before noun] (*specialist*) coming from or connected with the author of sth

**author·ing** /ˈɔːθərɪŋ/ *noun* [U] (*computing*) creating computer programs without using programming language, for use in MULTIMEDIA products ⇒ WORDFINDER NOTE at SOFTWARE

**au·thori·tar·ian** /ɔːˌθɒrɪˈteəriən; NAmE əˌθɔːrəˈter-/ *adj.* believing that people should obey authority and rules, even when these are unfair, and even if it means that they lose their personal freedom: *an authoritarian regime/government/state* ▸ **au·thori·tar·ian** *noun*: *Father was a strict authoritarian.* **au·thori·tar·ian·ism** *noun* [U]

**au·thori·ta·tive** /ɔːˈθɒrətətɪv; NAmE əˈθɔːrəteɪt-/ *adj.* **1** showing that you expect people to obey and respect you: *an authoritative tone of voice* **2** that you can trust and respect as true and correct: *the most authoritative book on the subject* ▸ **au·thori·ta·tive·ly** *adv.*

**au·thor·ity** /ɔːˈθɒrəti; NAmE əˈθɔːr-/ *noun* (*pl.* **-ies**)
- POWER **1** [U] the power to give orders to people: *in a position of authority* ◊ *to undermine/challenge sb's authority* ◊ ~ **over sb/sth** *She now has authority over the people who used to be her bosses.* ◊ *Nothing will be done because no one in authority* (= who has a position of power) *takes the matter seriously.* ◊ *adult authority figures such as parents and teachers* **2** [U] the power or right to do sth: *Some experts think the agency may have exceeded its authority.* ◊ ~ **to do sth** *The government has the authority to regulate the economy.*
- PERMISSION **3** [U] official permission to do sth: **without (sb's)** ~ *He took the car without authority.* ◊ **under the** ~ **of sb/sth** *We acted under the authority of the UN.*
- ORGANIZATION **4** [C, usually pl.] the people or an organization who have the power to make decisions or who have a particular area of responsibility in a country or region: *I have to report this to the authorities.* ◊ *The health authorities are investigating the problem.* ⇒ see also LOCAL AUTHORITY
- KNOWLEDGE **5** [U] the power to influence people because they respect your knowledge or official position: **with** ~ *He spoke with authority on the topic.* ◊ **to do sth** *the moral authority to run the country*
- EXPERT **6** [C] ~ **(on sth)** a person with special knowledge **SYN** specialist: *She's an authority on criminal law.*

# authorization

**IDM** **have sth on good au'thority** to be able to believe sth because you trust the person who gave you the information

**au·thor·iza·tion** (*BrE also* **-isa·tion**) /ˌɔːθəraɪˈzeɪʃn; *NAmE* -rəˈz-/ *noun* **1** [U, C] official permission or power to do sth; the act of giving permission: *You may not enter the security area without authorization.* ◊ *Who gave the authorization to release the data?* **2** [C] a document that gives sb official permission to do sth: *Can I see your authorization?*

**au·thor·ize** /ˈɔːθəraɪz/ *verb* to give official permission for sth, or for sb to do sth: ~ *sth I can authorize payments up to £5000.* ◊ ~ **sb to do sth** *I have authorized him to act for me while I am away.* ◊ *The soldiers were authorized to shoot at will.*

**au·thor·ized** (*BrE also* **-ised**) /ˈɔːθəraɪzd/ *adj.* having official permission or approval: *I bought my car from an authorized dealer.* ◊ *an authorized biography* **OPP** **unauthorized**

**author·ship** /ˈɔːθəʃɪp; *NAmE* -θərʃ-/ *noun* **1** [U] the identity of the person who wrote sth, especially a book: *The authorship of the poem is unknown.* **2** [U, C] the activity or fact of writing a book

**aut·ism** /ˈɔːtɪzəm/ *noun* [U] a mental DISORDER that starts in early childhood, in which a person finds it very difficult to communicate or form relationships with others and often shows limited or repeated patterns of thought and behaviour ⊃ **WORDFINDER NOTE** *at* CONDITION ▶ **aut·is·tic** /ɔːˈtɪstɪk/ *adj.*: *autistic behaviour/children*

**auto** /ˈɔːtəʊ/ *noun* (*pl.* **-os**) (usually before another noun) (*especially NAmE*) a car: *the auto industry*

**auto-** /ɔːtə, ɔːtəʊ; *BrE also* ɔːtə; *NAmE also* ɔːˈtɑː/ (*also* **aut-**) *combining form* (in nouns, adjectives and adverbs) **1** of or by yourself: *autobiography* **2** by itself without a person to operate it: *automatic* **3** relating to cars: *autocross*

**auto·biog·raphy** /ˌɔːtəbaɪˈɒɡrəfi; *NAmE* -ˈɑːɡ-/ *noun* [C, U] (*pl.* **-ies**) the story of a person's life, written by that person; this type of writing ⊃ compare BIOGRAPHY ▶ **auto·bio·graph·ic·al** /ˌɔːtəˌbaɪəˈɡræfɪkl/ *adj.*: *an autobiographical novel* (= one that contains many of the writer's own experiences)

**auto·clave** /ˈɔːtəʊkleɪv/ *noun* a strong closed container, used for processes that involve high temperatures or pressure

**auto·com·plete** /ˌɔːtəʊkəmˈpliːt/ *noun* [U] a piece of software that completes a word, address, etc. when you have typed the first few letters so that you do not have to type it in full ⊃ compare AUTOFILL ▶ **auto·com·plete** /ˌɔːtəʊkəmˈpliːt/ *verb* [T, I] ~ (**sth**): *When you enter the first few letters of a name from your address book, the field will autocomplete.* ◊ *The program will autocomplete your address each time you begin to type it.*

**auto·cor·rect** /ˌɔːtəʊkəˈrekt/ *noun* [U] a software feature that AUTOMATICALLY corrects mistakes in spelling or grammar or suggests how to correct them ▶ **auto·correct** /ˌɔːtəʊkəˈrekt/ *verb* [T, I] ~ (**sth**)

**au·toc·racy** /ɔːˈtɒkrəsi; *NAmE* -ˈtɑːk-/ *noun* (*pl.* **-ies**) **1** [U] a system of government of a country in which one person has complete power **2** [C] a country that is ruled by one person who has complete power

**auto·crat** /ˈɔːtəkræt/ *noun* **1** a leader who has complete power **SYN** **despot** **2** a person who expects to be obeyed by other people and does not care about their opinions or feelings ▶ **auto·crat·ic** /ˌɔːtəˈkrætɪk/ *adj.*: *an autocratic manager* **auto·crat·ic·al·ly** /-kli/ *adv.*

**Auto·cue**™ /ˈɔːtəʊkjuː/ (*BrE*) (*also* **tele·prompt·er** *NAmE*, *BrE*) *noun* a device used by people who are speaking in public, especially on television, that displays the words that they have to say

**auto·didact** /ˌɔːtəʊˈdaɪdækt/ *noun* (*formal*) a person who has taught himself or herself sth rather than having lessons ▶ **auto·didac·tic** /ˌɔːtəʊdaɪˈdæktɪk/ *adj.*

**auto·fill** /ˈɔːtəʊfɪl/ *noun* [U] a piece of software that remembers information and uses it to fill in data in an online form so that you do not have to type it again: *I often use autofill to enter delivery information for online purchases.* ⊃ compare AUTOCOMPLETE

**auto·focus** /ˈɔːtəʊfəʊkəs/ *noun* [C, U] part of a camera that ADJUSTS (= makes changes to) the FOCUS as it prepares for a picture to be taken, so that the picture will be clear

**auto·graph** /ˈɔːtəɡrɑːf; *NAmE* -ɡræf/ *noun, verb*
- *noun* a famous person's SIGNATURE (= their name written by them), especially when sb asks them to write it for them to keep: *Could I have your autograph?*
- *verb* ~ **sth** (of a famous person) to sign your name on sth for sb to keep: *The whole team has autographed a football, which will be used as a prize.*

**auto·immune** /ˌɔːtəʊɪˈmjuːn/ *adj.* [only before noun] (*medical*) an **autoimmune** disease or medical condition caused by ANTIBODIES (= substances produced in the blood to fight disease) attacking substances that are naturally present in the body

**auto·maker** /ˈɔːtəʊmeɪkə(r)/ *noun* (*NAmE*) a company that makes cars

**auto·mate** /ˈɔːtəmeɪt/ *verb* [usually passive] to use machines and computers instead of people to do a job or task: **be automated** *The entire manufacturing process has been automated.* ◊ *The factory is now **fully automated**.*

**automated 'teller machine** (*also* **automatic 'teller machine**) *noun* (*abbr.* **ATM**) = CASH MACHINE

**auto·mat·ic** /ˌɔːtəˈmætɪk/ *adj., noun*
- *adj.* **1** (of a machine, device, etc.) having controls that work without needing a person to operate them: *automatic doors* ◊ *a fully automatic driverless train* ◊ *automatic transmission* (= in a car, etc.) ◊ *an automatic rifle* (= one that continues to fire as long as the TRIGGER is pressed) **2** done or happening without thinking **SYN** **instinctive**: *Breathing is an automatic function of the body.* ◊ *My reaction was automatic.* **3** always happening as a result of a particular action or situation: *A fine for this offence is automatic.*
- *noun* **1** a gun that can fire bullets continuously as long as the TRIGGER is pressed **2** (*BrE*) a vehicle with a system of GEARS that operates without direct action from the driver ⊃ compare MANUAL (2)

**auto·mat·ic·al·ly** /ˌɔːtəˈmætɪkli/ *adv.* **1** without needing a person to operate controls: *The heating switches off automatically.* **2** without thinking **SYN** **instinctively**: *I turned left automatically without thinking.* **3** in a way that always happens as a result of a particular action or situation: *You will automatically get free dental treatment if you are under 18.*

**automatic 'pilot** (*also* **auto-pilot**) *noun* [C, U] a device in an aircraft or a ship that keeps it on a fixed course without the need for a person to control it
**IDM** **be on 'automatic 'pilot** to do sth without thinking because you have done the same thing many times before: *I got up and dressed on automatic pilot.*

**automatic trans'mission** *noun* [U, C] a system in a vehicle that changes the GEARS itself so that the driver does not have to

**automatic 'writing** *noun* [U] writing that is believed to have been done in an unconscious state or under a SUPERNATURAL influence

**auto·ma·tion** /ˌɔːtəˈmeɪʃn/ *noun* [U] the use of machines and computers to do work that was previously done by people: *Automation meant the loss of many factory jobs.*

**au·toma·ton** /ɔːˈtɒmətən; *NAmE* -ˈtɑːm-/ *noun* (*pl.* **au·toma·tons** *or* **au·tom·ata** /-tə/) **1** a person who behaves like a machine, without thinking or feeling anything **SYN** **robot** **2** a moving MECHANICAL device in the shape of a person **3** a small robot that can perform a particular range of functions

**auto·mo·bile** /ˈɔːtəməbiːl/ *noun* (*NAmE*) a car: *the automobile industry* ◊ *an automobile accident*

**auto·mo·tive** /ˌɔːtəˈməʊtɪv/ *adj.* [usually before noun] (*formal*) relating to vehicles that are driven by engines: *the automotive industry*

**au·to·nom·ic ner·vous sys·tem** /ˌɔːtənɒmɪk ˈnɜːvəs sɪstəm/ *NAmE* -nɑːmɪk ˈnɜːrv-/ *noun* (*specialist*) the part of your NERVOUS SYSTEM that controls processes that are unconscious, for example the process of your heart beating

**au·ton·o·mous** /ɔːˈtɒnəməs; *NAmE* -ˈtɑːn-/ *adj.* **1** (of a country, a region or an organization) able to govern itself or control its own affairs **SYN** **independent**: *an autonomous republic/state/province* **2** (of a person) able to do things and make decisions without help from anyone else **3** = SELF-DRIVING ▶ **au·ton·o·mous·ly** *adv.*

**au·ton·omy** ?+ **C1** /ɔːˈtɒnəmi; *NAmE* -ˈtɑːn-/ *noun* [U] (*formal*) **1** ?+ **C1** the freedom for a country, a region or an organization to govern itself independently **SYN** **independence**: *a campaign in Wales for greater autonomy* **2** ?+ **C1** the ability to act and make decisions without being controlled by anyone else: *giving individuals greater autonomy in their own lives*

**auto·pilot** /ˈɔːtəʊpaɪlət/ *noun* = AUTOMATIC PILOT

**aut·opsy** /ˈɔːtɒpsi; *NAmE* -tɑːp-/ *noun* (*pl.* **-ies**) an official examination of a dead body by a specially trained doctor in order to discover the cause of death **SYN** **post-mortem**: *an autopsy report* ◇ *to perform an autopsy*

**ˈauto racing** *noun* [U] (*NAmE*) = MOTOR RACING

**auto·rick·shaw** /ˈɔːtəʊrɪkʃɔː/ *noun* a covered motor vehicle with three wheels, a driver's seat in front and a seat for passengers at the back, used especially in some Asian countries

**auto·save** /ˈɔːtəʊseɪv/ *noun* [U] a feature in computer software that regularly saves changes to a document as you work ▶ **auto·save** *verb* [T, I] **~(sth)**

**au·tumn** ❶ **A1** /ˈɔːtəm/ (*especially BrE*) (*NAmE usually* **fall**) *noun* [U, C] the season of the year between summer and winter, when leaves change colour and the weather becomes colder: *in the ~ of sth in the autumn of 2010* ◇ *in early/late autumn* ◇ *the autumn term* (= for example at a school or college in Britain) ◇ *autumn leaves/colours* ◇ *It's been a very mild autumn this year.*

**au·tum·nal** /ɔːˈtʌmnəl/ *adj.* [usually before noun] like or connected with autumn: *autumnal colours*

**aux·il·iary** /ɔːɡˈzɪliəri/ *adj.*, *noun*
■ *adj.* **1** (of workers) giving help or support to the main group of workers **SYN** **ancillary**: *auxiliary nurses/workers/services* **2** (*specialist*) (of a piece of equipment) used if there is a problem with the main piece of equipment
■ *noun* (*pl.* **-ies**) **1** (*also* **au'xiliary 'verb**) (*grammar*) a verb such as *be*, *do* and *have* used with main verbs to show tense, etc. and to form questions and negatives **2** a worker who gives help or support to the main group of workers: *nursing auxiliaries*

**auxin** /ˈɔːksɪn/ *noun* [U] a plant HORMONE that is involved in controlling plant growth

**AV** /ˌeɪ ˈviː/ *abbr.* AUDIOVISUAL

**avail** /əˈveɪl/ *noun*, *verb*
■ *noun*
**IDM** **of little / no aˈvail** (*formal*) of little or no use: *Your ability to argue is of little avail if the facts are wrong.* **to little / no aˈvail** (*formal*) with little or no success: *The doctors tried everything to keep him alive but to no avail.*
■ *verb* **1** [T] **~ sb (sth)** | **~ sth** (*formal* or *old-fashioned*) to be helpful or useful to sb **2** [T, I] (*IndE*, *non-standard*) to make use of sth, especially an opportunity or offer: **~ sth** *To avail all these benefits, just register online.* ◇ **~ of sth** *Why not avail of our special offers?*
**PHRV** **aˈvail yourself of sth** (*formal*) to make use of sth, especially an opportunity or offer: *Guests are encouraged to avail themselves of the full range of hotel facilities.*

**avail·abil·ity** ?+ **C1** **W** /əˌveɪləˈbɪləti/ *noun* [U] **1** ?+ **C1** the fact that sth is possible to get, buy or find: *the availability of cheap flights* ◇ (*BrE*) *This offer is subject to availability.* **2** ?+ **C1** the fact that sb is free to see or talk to people: *Check her availability before you schedule the meeting.* **OPP** **unavailability**

**avail·able** ❶ **A2** **W** /əˈveɪləbl/ *adj.* **1** ?+ **A2** that you can get, buy or find: *available resources/evidence/data* ◇ *Further details are available on request.* ◇ *We'll send you a copy as soon as it becomes available.* ◇ *We have plenty of office space available.* ◇ *readily/widely/freely/publicly available* ◇ **~from sb/sth** *Tickets are currently available at reduced prices from the festival office.* ◇ **~for sth** *This data is still available for download on the company's website.* ◇ **~to sb** *When will the information be made available to the public?* **2** ? **B1** (of a person) free to see or talk to people: **~to do sth** *They'll be available to help every day next week.* ◇ **~for sth** *The director was not available for comment.* **3** (*informal*) (of a person) not currently involved in a sexual or romantic relationship

**ava·lanche** /ˈævəlɑːnʃ; *NAmE* -læntʃ/ (*NAmE also* **snow·slide**) *noun* a mass of snow, ice and rock that falls down the side of a mountain: *alpine villages destroyed in an avalanche* ◇ (*figurative*) *We received an avalanche of letters in reply to our advertisement.* ⊃ WORDFINDER NOTE at DISASTER

**avant-** /ˈævɒ̃; *NAmE* ævɑː/ *combining form* (used especially with types of popular music) in a style that is modern and very different from what has been done before: *experimental music like avant-rock* ◇ *avant-jazz* ◇ *avant-pop*

**the avant-garde** /ˌɒi ˌævɒ̃ ˈɡɑːd; *NAmE* -vɑː ˈɡɑːrd/ *noun* (from French) **1** [sing.] new and very modern ideas in art, music or literature that are sometimes surprising or shock people **2** [sing. + sing./pl. v.] a group of artists, etc. who introduce new and very modern ideas ▶ **avant-garde** *adj.*

**avar·ice** /ˈævərɪs/ *noun* [U] (*formal*) extreme desire for wealth **SYN** **greed** ▶ **avar·icious** /ˌævəˈrɪʃəs/ *adj.*

**ava·tar** /ˈævətɑː(r)/ *noun* **1** (in Hinduism and Buddhism) a god appearing in a physical form **2** a picture of a person or an animal that represents a particular computer user, on a computer screen, especially in a computer game or on SOCIAL MEDIA

**Ave.** (*NAmE also* **Av.**) *abbr.* (used in written addresses) AVENUE: *Fifth Ave.*

**avenge** /əˈvendʒ/ *verb* (*formal*) to punish or hurt sb in return for sth bad or wrong that they have done to you, your family or friends: **~sth** *He promised to avenge his father's murder.* ◇ **~yourself on sb** *She was determined to avenge herself on the man who had betrayed her.* ▶ **aven·ger** *noun*

▼ GRAMMAR POINT

**avenge / revenge**
Avenge is a verb; revenge is (usually) a noun.
• People avenge something or avenge themselves on somebody: *She vowed to avenge her brother's death.* ◇ *He later avenged himself on his wife's killers.* You take revenge on a person.
• In more formal or literary English, revenge can also be a verb. People revenge themselves on somebody or are revenged on them (with the same meaning): *He was later revenged on his wife's killers.* You cannot revenge something: *She vowed to revenge her brother's death.*

**av·enue** /ˈævənjuː; *NAmE* -nuː/ *noun* **1 Avenue** (*abbr.* **Ave., Av.**) (used in street names) a wide street in a town or city: *a hotel on Fifth Avenue* **2** a wide straight road with trees on both sides, especially one leading to a big house **3** a choice or way of making progress towards sth: *Several avenues are open to us.* ◇ *We will explore every avenue until we find an answer.*

**aver** /əˈvɜː(r)/ *verb* (**-rr-**) **~ that …** | **~ sth** | **+ speech** (*formal*) to state clearly and strongly that sth is true **SYN** **assert**, **declare**: *She averred that she had never seen the man before.*

**aver·age** ❶ **A2** ❶ /ˈævərɪdʒ/ *adj.*, *noun*, *verb*
■ *adj.* **1** ? **A2** [only before noun] calculated by adding several amounts together, finding a total, and dividing the total by the number of amounts: *The average age of participants was 52 years.* ◇ *an average rate/cost/price* ◇ *an average annual income/wage/salary* **2** ? **A2** typical or normal:

**above/below ~ sth** *children of below average intelligence* ◊ *£20 for dinner is about average.* ◊ **The average person can't afford a $60 bottle of wine every night.** **3** A2 ordinary; not special: *I was just an average sort of student.* ◊ *The quality has been pretty average* (= not very good). ▸ **aver·age·ly** *adv.*: *He was attractive and averagely intelligent.*
■ **noun** [C, U] **1** A2 the result of adding several amounts together, finding a total, and dividing the total by the number of amounts HELP The term **average** can be used for any number that expresses the central or typical value in a set of data. It is most commonly used to mean the MEAN, as defined here. However, the MEDIAN and the MODE are also types of average.: *The average of 4, 5 and 9 is 6.* ◊ **an~ of sth** *Parents spend an average of $220 a year on toys.* ◊ *Class sizes in the school are below the national average.* ◊ *We will deliver growth in the economy that is higher than the OECD average this year.* ⊃ see also BATTING AVERAGE, GRADE POINT AVERAGE **2** A2 a level that is usual: **above/below ~** *Temperatures are above average for the time of year.* ◊ **on~** *400 people a year die of this disease on average.* IDM see LAW
■ **verb 1** B1 **~ sth** [no passive] to be equal to a particular amount as an average: *Economic growth is expected to average 2% next year.* ◊ *Drivers in London can expect to average about 12 miles per hour* (= to have that as their average speed). **2** B1 **~ sth** to calculate the average of sth: *Earnings are averaged over the whole period.*
PHRV ˌaverage ˈout (at sth) to result in an average amount over a period of time or when several things are considered: *The cost should average out at about £6 per person.* ◊ *Sometimes I pay, sometimes he pays—it seems to average out* (= result in us paying the same amount). ˌaverage sth↔ˈout (at sth) to calculate the average of sth

**averse** /əˈvɜːs; *NAmE* əˈvɜːrs/ *adj.* [not before noun] **1 not ~ to (doing) sth** liking sth or wanting to do sth; not opposed to doing sth: *I mentioned it to Kate and she wasn't averse to the idea.* **2 ~ to (doing) sth** (*formal*) not liking sth or wanting to do sth; opposed to doing sth: *He was averse to any change.*

**aver·sion** /əˈvɜːʃn; *NAmE* əˈvɜːrʒn/ *noun* [C, U] a strong feeling of not liking sb/sth: *a strong aversion* ◊ **~ to sb/sth** *He had an aversion to getting up early.*

**aˈversion therapy** *noun* [U] a way of helping sb to lose a bad habit, by making the habit seem to be associated with an effect that is not pleasant

**avert** /əˈvɜːt; *NAmE* əˈvɜːrt/ *verb* (*formal*) **1 ~ sth** to prevent sth bad or dangerous from happening: *A disaster was narrowly averted.* ◊ *He did his best to avert suspicion.* **2 ~ your eyes/gaze/face (from sth)** to turn your eyes, etc. away from sth that you do not want to see: *She averted her eyes from the terrible scene in front of her.*

**avian** /ˈeɪviən/ *adj.* [usually before noun] (*specialist*) of or connected with birds

**ˌavian ˈflu** *noun* [U] (*formal*) = BIRD FLU

**avi·ary** /ˈeɪviəri; *NAmE* -vieri/ *noun* (*pl.* **-ies**) a large CAGE or building for keeping birds in, for example in a ZOO

**avi·ation** /ˌeɪviˈeɪʃn/ *noun* [U] the designing, building and flying of aircraft: *civil/military aviation* ◊ *the aviation business/industry*

**avi·ator** /ˈeɪvieɪtə(r)/ *noun* (*old-fashioned*) a person who flies an aircraft

**avid** /ˈævɪd/ *adj.* **1** [usually before noun] very enthusiastic about sth (often a hobby) SYN keen: *an avid reader/collector* ◊ *She has taken an avid interest in the project* (= she is extremely interested in it). **2 ~ for sth** wanting to get sth very much: *He was avid for more information.* ▸ **avid·ity** /əˈvɪdəti/ *noun* [U] **avid·ly** /ˈævɪdli/ *adv.*: *She reads avidly.*

**avi·on·ics** /ˌeɪviˈɒnɪks; *NAmE* -ˈɑːn-/ *noun* **1** [U] the science of ELECTRONICS when used in designing and making aircraft **2** [pl.] the electronic devices in an aircraft or a SPACECRAFT ▸ **avi·on·ic** *adj.*

**avo·cado** /ˌævəˈkɑːdəʊ/ *noun* (*pl.* **-os**) (*BrE also* ˌavo·cado ˈpear) a tropical fruit with hard, dark green skin and a soft, light green inside part that does not taste sweet and contains a large seed ⊃ VISUAL VOCAB page V4

**avo·ca·tion** /ˌævəˈkeɪʃn/ *noun* (*formal*) a hobby or other activity that you do for interest and pleasure

**avo·cet** /ˈævəset/ *noun* a bird that lives on or near water, with long legs and black and white feathers

**avoid** ⓣ A2 ⓞ /əˈvɔɪd/ *verb* **1** A2 **~ sth** to prevent sth bad from happening: *~ sth to avoid conflict/confrontation* ◊ *We must find a way to avoid similar problems in future.* ◊ *They narrowly avoided defeat.* ◊ *The name was changed to avoid confusion with another firm.* ◊ **~ doing sth** *They built a wall to avoid soil being washed away.* **2** A2 to keep away from sb/sth; to try not to do sth: **~ sb/sth** *He's been avoiding me all week.* ◊ *She kept avoiding my eyes* (= avoided looking at me). ◊ *By staying at home he manages to avoid all contact with strangers.* ◊ *Certain foods should be avoided during pregnancy.* ◊ **~ doing sth** *He tried to avoid paying his taxes and was taken to court.* **3** A2 **~ sth** to prevent yourself from hitting sth: *The car swerved to avoid a cat.*
IDM **aˌvoid sb/sth like the ˈplague** (*informal*) to try very hard not to meet sb, do sth, etc. ⊃ more at TRAP *n.*

**avoid·able** /əˈvɔɪdəbl/ *adj.* that can be prevented: *Many deaths from heart disease are actually avoidable.* OPP **unavoidable**

**avoid·ance** /əˈvɔɪdəns/ *noun* [U] **~ (of sth)** not doing sth; preventing sth from existing or happening: *A person's health improves with the avoidance of stress.* ⊃ see also TAX AVOIDANCE

**avow** /əˈvaʊ/ *verb* **~ that …** | **~ sth** | **+ speech** (*formal*) to say clearly and often publicly what your opinion is, what you think is true, etc: *An aide avowed that the president had known nothing of the deals.* ▸ **avow·al** /-əl/ *noun* (*formal*): *an avowal of love*

**avowed** /əˈvaʊd/ *adj.* [only before noun] (*formal*) that has been admitted or stated in public: *an avowed atheist* ◊ *an avowed aim/intention/objective/purpose* ▸ **avow·ed·ly** /əˈvaʊɪdli/ *adv.*

**avun·cu·lar** /əˈvʌŋkjələ(r)/ *adj.* (*formal*) behaving in a kind and friendly way towards young people, similar to the way a kind uncle treats his NIECES or NEPHEWS

**aw** /ɔː/ *exclamation* used to express DISAPPROVAL, protest or sympathy: *Aw, come on, Andy!*

**await** ⓣ+ C1 /əˈweɪt/ *verb* (*formal*) **1** ⓣ+ C1 **~ sb/sth** to wait for sb/sth: *He is in custody awaiting trial.* ◊ *Her latest novel is eagerly awaited.* **2** ⓣ+ C1 **~ sb** to be going to happen to sb: *A warm welcome awaits all our guests.*

▼ **WHICH WORD?**

**awake / awaken / wake up / waken**

- **Wake (up)** is the most common of these verbs. It can mean somebody has finished sleeping: *What time do you usually wake up?* or that somebody or something has disturbed your sleep: *The children woke me up.* ◊ *I was woken (up) by the telephone.*
- The verb **awake** is usually only used in writing and in the past tense **awoke**: *She awoke to a day of brilliant sunshine.* **Waken** and **awaken** are much more formal. **Awaken** is used especially in literature: *The Prince awakened Sleeping Beauty with a kiss.*
- **Awake** is also an adjective: *I was awake half the night worrying.* ◊ *Is the baby awake yet?* **Waking** is not used in this way.
⊃ see also ASLEEP, SLEEP *verb*

**awake** /əˈweɪk/ *adj.*, *verb*
■ *adj.* [not before noun] not asleep (especially immediately before or after sleeping): *to be half/fully awake* ◊ *to be wide awake* (= fully awake) ◊ *I was still awake when he came to bed.* ◊ *The noise was keeping everyone awake.* ◊ *I was finding it hard to stay awake.* ◊ *He lies awake at night worrying about his job.* ◊ *She was awake* (= not unconscious) *during the operation on her leg.*
■ *verb* (**awoke** /əˈwəʊk/, **awoken** /əˈwəʊkən/) (*formal*) **1** [I, T] to wake up; to make sb wake up: **~ (sb) (from/to sth)** *I awoke from a deep sleep.* ◊ **~ to do sth** *He awoke to find her gone.* ◊ **~ sb** *Her voice awoke the sleeping child.* **2** [I, T] **~ (sth)** if an emotion **awakes** or sth **awakes** an emotion,

you start to feel that emotion: *His speech is bound to awake old fears and hostilities.*
**PHRV** **a'wake to sth** to become aware of sth and its possible effects or results: *It took her some time to awake to the dangers of her situation.* ⏵ compare WAKE

**awaken** /əˈweɪkən/ *verb* (*formal*) **1** [I, T, often passive] to wake up; to make sb wake up: **~(sb) (from/to sth)** *She awakened to the sound of birds singing.* ◊ **~to do sth** *We awakened to find the others gone.* ◊ **be awakened** *He was awakened at dawn by the sound of crying.* ⏵ note at AWAKE **2** [I, T] **~(sth)** if an emotion **awakens** or sth **awakens** an emotion, you start to feel that emotion: *The dream awakened terrible memories.*
**PHRV** **a'waken (sb) to sth** to become aware or to make sb aware of sth and its possible effects or results: *I gradually awakened to the realization that our marriage was over.* ⏵ compare WAKEN

**awak·en·ing** /əˈweɪkənɪŋ/ *noun* **1** [C, usually sing.] an occasion when you realize sth or become aware of sth: *If they had expected a warm welcome, they were in for a rude awakening* (= they would soon realize that it would not be warm). **2** [C, U] the act of beginning to understand or feel sth; the act of sth starting or sb waking: *sexual awakening* ◊ *the awakening of interest in the environment*

**award** ❶ **A2** /əˈwɔːd; NAmE əˈwɔːrd/ *noun, verb*
▪ *noun* **1** **A2** [C] (often in names of particular awards) a prize such as money, etc. for sth that sb has done: *He was nominated for the best actor award.* ◊ *the UK's most prestigious literary award* ◊ *The mayor will present the awards.* ◊ **~for sth** *to win/accept an award for sth* ◊ *He received numerous awards for excellence in teaching.* ◊ *an awards ceremony* ⏵ see also ACADEMY AWARD™ **2** [C] an increase in the amount of money sb earns: *an annual pay award* **3** [C, U] an amount of money given as an official payment or grant to sb: *an award of £600000 in libel damages* **4** [U] the official decision to give sth to sb: *Satisfactory completion of the course will lead to the award of the Diploma of Social Work.*
▪ *verb* **B1** to make an official decision to give sth to sb as a payment, prize, contract, etc.: **~sth** *Knowing why and how corporations award contracts is vitally important.* ◊ **~sth to sb** *The judges awarded equal points to both finalists.* ◊ **~sb sth** *The judges awarded both finalists equal points.*

**award·ee** /əˌwɔːˈdiː; NAmE əˌwɔːrˈdiː/ *noun* a person who is awarded sth, such as a prize

**a'ward-winning** *adj.* [only before noun] having won a prize: *the award-winning TV drama*

**aware** ❶ **B1** ⓦ /əˈweə(r); NAmE əˈwer/ *adj.* **1 B1** [not before noun] knowing or realizing sth: *As you're aware, this is not a new problem.* ◊ *As far as I'm aware, nobody has done anything about it.* ◊ *acutely/painfully/keenly* (= very) *aware* ◊ **~of sth** *He was well aware of the problem.* ◊ *She slipped away without him being aware of it.* ◊ *Everybody should be made aware of the risks involved.* ◊ *We're just making the public aware of the issue.* ◊ **~that…** *Were you aware that something was wrong?* **2** (used with an adverb) interested in and knowing about sth, and thinking it is important: *Young people are very environmentally aware.* **OPP** unaware

**aware·ness** **B2** ⓦ /əˈweənəs; NAmE əˈwern-/ *noun* **1 B2** [U, sing.] knowing sth; knowing that sth exists and is important: **~of sth** *an awareness of the importance of eating a healthy diet* ◊ *There was an almost complete lack of awareness of the issues involved.* ◊ *to raise/heighten/increase public awareness of sth* ◊ *a greater/a growing/an increasing awareness of sth* ◊ *a marketing campaign to increase brand awareness* ◊ **~that…** *There seems to be a general awareness that this is not the solution.* **2** **B2** [U] interest in and concern about a particular situation or area of interest: *environmental awareness* ◊ **~about sth** *The group is trying to raise public awareness about homelessness.*

**awash** /əˈwɒʃ; NAmE əˈwɔːʃ/ *adj.* [not before noun] **1 ~ (with water)** covered with water **2 ~ with sth** having sth in large quantities: *The city is awash with drugs.*

# awfully

**away** ❶ **A1** /əˈweɪ/ *adv., adj.* **HELP** For the special uses of **away** in phrasal verbs, look at the entries for the verbs. For example **get away with sth** is in the phrasal verb section at **get**.
▪ *adv.* **1 A1** to or at a distance from sb/sth in space or time: *The beach is a mile away.* ◊ *Christmas is still months away.* ◊ **~from sb/sth** *The president was kept well away from the demonstrators.* **2 A1** to a different place or in a different direction: *Go away!* ◊ *Put your toys away.* ◊ *The bright light made her look away.* **3 A2** not present **SYN** absent: *There were ten children away yesterday.* ◊ *Sorry, he's away.* ◊ **~from sb/sth** *She was away from work for a week.* **4** used after verbs to say that sth is done continuously or with a lot of energy: *She was still writing away furiously when the bell went.* ◊ *They were soon chatting away like old friends.* **5** until disappearing completely: *The water boiled away.* ◊ *The music faded away.* **6** (*sport*) at the opponent's ground or stadium: *Chelsea are playing away this Saturday.* ⏵ compare HOME
**IDM** **away with…** (*literary*) used to say that you would like to be rid of sb/sth: *Away with all these rules and regulations!* ⏵ more at COBWEB, DANCE *v.*, FAR *adv.*, RIGHT *adv.*, STRAIGHT *adv.*
▪ *adj.* (*sport*) played or scored at the opponent's ground or stadium: *an away match/game* ◊ *an away win* ◊ *an away goal*

**a'way day** (*also* **away-day**) *noun* (*BrE, business*) a day that a group of workers spend together away from their usual place of work in order to discuss ideas or plans: *The management are having an away day to discuss strategy.*

**awe** /ɔː/ *noun, verb*
▪ *noun* [U] feelings of respect and slight fear; feelings of being very impressed by sth/sb: *awe and respect* ◊ *awe and wonder* ◊ **with~** *He speaks of her with awe.* ◊ **in~** *'It's magnificent,' she whispered in awe.*
**IDM** **be/stand in 'awe of sb/sth** to admire sb/sth and be slightly frightened of them/it: *While Diana was in awe of her grandfather, she adored her grandmother.*
▪ *verb* [usually passive] (*formal*) to fill sb with awe: **be awed (by sb/sth)** *She seemed awed by the presence of so many famous people.* ▸ **awed** *adj.*: *We watched in awed silence.*

**'awe-inspir·ing** *adj.* extremely impressive; making you admire it very much: *The building was awe-inspiring in size and design.*

**awe·some** /ˈɔːsəm/ *adj.* **1** very impressive or very difficult and perhaps rather frightening: *an awesome sight* ◊ *awesome beauty/power* ◊ *They had an awesome task ahead.* **2** (*especially NAmE, informal*) very good, great fun, etc: *I just bought this awesome new game!* ◊ *Wow! That's totally awesome!* ⏵ SYNONYMS at GREAT ▸ **awe·some·ly** *adv.*: *awesomely beautiful*

**awe·struck** /ˈɔːstrʌk/ *adj.* (*literary*) feeling very impressed by sth: *People were awestruck by the pictures the satellite sent back to Earth.*

**awful** ❶ **A2** /ˈɔːfl/ *adj., adv.*
▪ *adj.* **1 A2** (*informal*) very bad or unpleasant: *That's an awful colour.* ◊ *'They didn't even offer to pay.' 'Oh that's awful.'* ◊ *to look/feel awful* (= to look/feel ill) ◊ *There's an awful smell in here.* ◊ *The awful thing is, it was my fault.* ◊ *It sounds awful to say it, but the war was exciting.* ◊ *The weather conditions were just awful.* ⏵ note at TERRIBLE **2 A2** that shocks people very much **SYN** terrible: *the awful horrors of war* **3 B1** (*informal*) used to emphasize sth, especially that there is a large amount or too much of sth: *It's going to cost an awful lot of money.* ◊ *There's not an awful lot of room.* ◊ *I feel an awful lot better than I did yesterday.* ◊ (*BrE*) *I had an awful job persuading him to come* (= it was very difficult). ▸ **aw·ful·ness** *noun* [U]: *the sheer awfulness of the situation*
▪ *adv.* (*especially NAmE, informal, non-standard*) very; extremely: *Clint is awful smart.*

**aw·ful·ly** /ˈɔːfli/ *adv.* very; extremely **SYN** terribly: *I'm awfully sorry about that problem the other day.*

**awhile** /əˈwaɪl/ adv. (formal or literary) for a short time: *Stay awhile*. **HELP** Do not confuse the adverb **awhile** with the noun phrase **a while**: *This will take a while.* ◇ *This will take awhile*.

**awk·ward** /ˈɔːkwəd; NAmE -wərd/ adj. **1** making you feel embarrassed: *There was an awkward silence.* **2** difficult to deal with **SYN** **difficult**: *Don't ask awkward questions.* ◇ *You've put me in an awkward position.* ◇ *an awkward customer* (= a person who is difficult to deal with) ◇ *Please don't be awkward about letting him come.* **3** not convenient **SYN** **inconvenient**: *Have I come at an awkward time?* **4** difficult or dangerous because of its shape or design: *This box is very awkward for one person to carry.* **5** not moving in an easy way; not comfortable: *He tried to dance, but he was too clumsy and awkward.* ◇ *I must have slept in an awkward position—I'm aching all over.* ▶ **awk·ward·ly** adv.: *'I'm sorry,' he said awkwardly.* ◇ *She fell awkwardly and broke her ankle.* ◇ *an awkwardly shaped room* **awk·ward·ness** noun [U]: *She laughed to cover up her feeling of awkwardness.*

**awl** /ɔːl/ noun a small pointed tool used for making holes, especially in leather

**awn·ing** /ˈɔːnɪŋ/ noun a sheet of strong cloth that stretches out from above a door or window to keep off the sun or rain

**awoke** /əˈwəʊk/ past tense of AWAKE

**awoken** /əˈwəʊkən/ past part. of AWAKE

**AWOL** /ˈeɪwɒl; NAmE -wɑːl/ abbr. absent without leave (used especially in the armed forces when sb has left their group without permission): *He's gone AWOL from his base.* ◇ (humorous) *The guitarist went AWOL in the middle of the recording.*

**awry** /əˈraɪ/ adv., adj. **1** if sth **goes awry**, it does not happen in the way that was planned: *All my plans for the party had gone awry.* **2** not in the right position **SYN** **untidy**: *She rushed out, her hair awry.*

**axes**

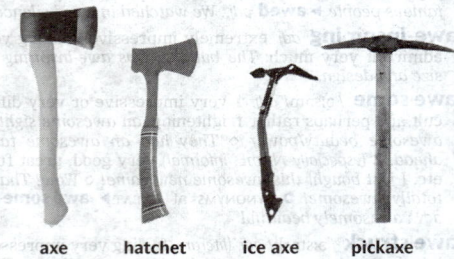

axe | hatchet | ice axe | pickaxe

**axe** /æks/ noun, verb
- noun (US usually **ax**) **1** a tool with a wooden handle and a heavy metal BLADE, used for cutting up wood, cutting down trees, etc. ⊃ see also BATTLEAXE, ICE AXE, PICKAXE **2 the axe** [sing.] (informal) (often used in newspapers) if sb gets **the axe**, they lose their job; if an institution or a project gets **the axe**, it is closed or stopped, usually because of a lack of money: *Up to 300 workers are facing the axe at a struggling Merseyside firm.* ◇ *Patients are delighted their local hospital has been saved from the axe.*
**IDM** **have an ˈaxe to grind** to have private reasons for being involved in sth or for arguing for a particular cause: *She had no axe to grind and was only acting out of concern for their safety.*
- verb (BrE) (US **ax**) [often passive] **1** (informal) (often used in newspapers) to get rid of a service, system, etc. or to reduce the money spent on it by a large amount: **be axed** *Other less profitable services are to be axed later this year.* **2** (informal) (often used in newspapers) to remove sb from their job: **be axed (from sth)** | **be axed from sth** *Jones has been axed from the team.* **3** ~ **sb** to kill sb with an axe

**axel** /ˈæksl/ noun a jump in SKATING in which you jump from the front outside edge of one SKATE, turn in the air, and land on the outside edge of your other skate

**axe·man** /ˈæksmən/ (US usually **axman**) (pl. **-men**) noun (informal) a man who attacks other people with an axe

**axial** /ˈæksiəl/ adj. (specialist) of or related to an AXIS: *an axial road*

**axiom** /ˈæksiəm/ noun (formal) a rule or principle that most people believe to be true

**axio·mat·ic** /ˌæksiəˈmætɪk/ adj. [not usually before noun] (formal) true in such an obvious way that you do not need to prove it **SYN** **self-evident**: *It is axiomatic that life is not always easy.* ▶ **axio·mat·ic·al·ly** /-kli/ adv.

**axes**

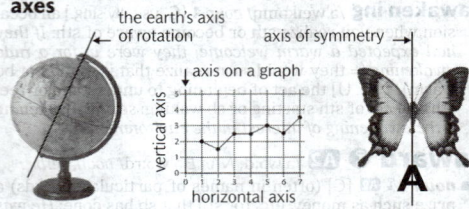

the earth's axis of rotation | axis of symmetry | axis on a graph | vertical axis | horizontal axis

**axis** /ˈæksɪs/ noun (pl. **axes** /ˈæksiːz/) **1** an imaginary line through the centre of an object, around which the object turns: *Mars takes longer to revolve on its axis than the Earth.* **2** (specialist) a fixed line against which the positions of points are measured, especially points on a GRAPH: *the vertical/horizontal axis* **3** (geometry) a line that divides a shape into two equal parts: *an axis of symmetry* ◇ *The axis of a circle is its diameter.* **4** [usually sing.] (formal) an agreement or ALLIANCE between two or more countries that forms the centre for a larger grouping of nations: *the Franco-German axis*

**axle** /ˈæksl/ noun a long straight piece of metal that connects a pair of wheels on a vehicle: *the front/rear axle*

**axman** (US) = AXEMAN

**axon** /ˈæksɒn; NAmE -sɑːn/ noun (biology) the long thin part of a nerve cell along which signals are sent to other cells ⊃ compare DENDRITE

**ayah** /ˈaɪə/ noun (IndE) **1** a woman whose job is caring for children, doing domestic work, etc. **2** a person whose job is caring for sb who is ill

**aya·tol·lah** /ˌaɪəˈtɒlə; NAmE -ˈtəʊlə/ noun a religious leader of Shiite Muslims, especially in Iran

**aye** /aɪ/ exclamation (old use or dialect) **1** yes: *'Did you see what happened?' 'Oh aye, I was there.'* **2** always; still

**ayes** /aɪz/ noun [pl.] the total number of people voting 'yes' in a formal debate, for example in a parliament: *The ayes have it* (= more people have voted for sth than against it). **OPP** **noes** ⊃ WORDFINDER NOTE at DEBATE

**Ayur·vedic medi·cine** /ˌaɪəˌveɪdɪk ˈmedsən, ˈmedsɪn; NAmE -ˌvedɪk ˈmedsən/ noun [U] (also **Ayur·veda, ayur·veda** /ˌaɪəˈveɪdə; NAmE -ərˈv-/) a type of traditional Hindu medicine that treats illnesses using a combination of foods, HERBS and breathing exercises

**aza·lea** /əˈzeɪliə/ noun a plant or bush with large flowers that may be pink, purple, white or yellow, often grown in a pot

**azi·muth** /ˈæzɪməθ/ noun (astronomy) an angle related to a distance around the earth's HORIZON, used to find out the position of a star, planet, etc.

**AZT™** /ˌeɪ zed ˈtiː; NAmE ziː/ noun [U] a drug that is used to treat AIDS

**azure** /ˈæʒə(r); BrE also ˈæzjʊə(r)/ adj. (literary) bright blue in colour like the sky ▶ **azure** noun [U]

# Bb

**B** /biː/ *noun, symbol*
- *noun* (*also* **b**) (*pl.* **Bs, B's, b's** /biːz/) **1** [C, U] the second letter of the English alphabet: *'Butter' begins with (a) B/'B'.* **2 B** [C, U] (*music*) the 7th note in the SCALE of C MAJOR **3 B** [C, U] ~ **(in/for sth)** a grade that a student can get for a piece of work or course of study that shows that it is good but not excellent: *She got (a) B in history.* **4 B** [U] used to represent the second of two or more possibilities: *Shall we go for plan A or plan B?* **5 B** [U] used to represent a person, for example in an imagined situation or to hide their identity: *Let's pretend A meets B in the park.* ⇒ see also B-ROAD **IDM** see A *n.*
- *symbol* used in the UK before a number to refer to a particular secondary road: *the B1224 to York*

**b.** *abbr.* (in writing) born: *Emily Clifton, b. 1800*

**B2B** /ˌbiː tə ˈbiː/ *abbr.* BUSINESS-TO-BUSINESS

**B2C** /ˌbiː tə ˈsiː/ *abbr.* BUSINESS-TO-CONSUMER

**BA** (*BrE*) (*NAmE usually* **B.A.**) /ˌbiː ˈeɪ/ *noun* a first university degree in an ARTS subject (the abbreviation for 'Bachelor of Arts'): *to be/have/do a BA* ◊ (*BrE*) *Darren Green BA*

**baa** /bɑː/ *noun* the sound made by a sheep or LAMB ▶ **baa** *verb* [I] (**baa·ing, baaed, baa'd**)

**baba** /ˈbɑːbɑː/ *noun* **1** a small cake, often with RUM poured over it **2** (*IndE, EAfrE*) a father (often also used as a title or form of address for any older man, showing respect) **3** (*IndE*) a holy man **4** (*IndE*) (used especially as a form of address) a small child

**bab·ble** /ˈbæbl/ *noun, verb*
- *noun* [sing.] **1** the sound of many people speaking at the same time: *a babble of voices* **2** talking that is confused or silly and is difficult to understand: *I can't listen to his constant babble.* **3** the sounds a baby makes before beginning to say actual words ⇒ see also PSYCHOBABBLE
- *verb* **1** [I, T] ~ **(away/on) (sth)** to talk quickly in a way that is difficult to understand: *They were all babbling away in a foreign language.* ◊ *I realized I was babbling like an idiot.* **2** [I] to make the sound of water flowing over rocks, like a stream: *a babbling brook*

**babby** /ˈbæbi/ *noun* (*pl.* **-ies**) (*BrE, dialect*) a baby

**babe** /beɪb/ *noun* **1** (*old use*) a baby **2** (*slang*) a word used to address a young woman, or your wife, husband or partner, usually expressing love but sometimes considered offensive if used by a man to a woman he does not know: *What're you doing tonight, babe?* **3** (*informal*) an attractive young woman
**IDM a babe in arms** (*old-fashioned*) a very small baby that cannot yet walk ⇒ more at MOUTH *n.*

**babel** /ˈbeɪbl/ *noun* [sing.] (*formal*) the sound of many voices talking at one time, especially when more than one language is being spoken **ORIGIN** From the Bible story in which God punished the people who were trying to build a tower to reach heaven (the **tower of Babel**) by making them unable to understand each others' languages.

**ba·boon** /bəˈbuːn; *NAmE* bæˈb-/ *noun* a large African or Asian monkey with a long face like a dog's

**babu** /ˈbɑːbuː/ *noun* (*IndE*) a person who works in an office

**baby** 🔵 **A1** /ˈbeɪbi/ *noun, adj., verb*
- *noun* (*pl.* **-ies**) **1** [C] a very young child or animal: *The baby's crying!* ◊ *a newborn baby* ◊ *My sister's expecting a baby* (= she is pregnant). ◊ *She had a baby last year.* ◊ *The baby was born last night.* ◊ *Mother and baby are doing well.* ◊ *a baby boy/girl* ◊ *a baby daughter/son/sister/brother* ◊ *baby food/clothes* ◊ *a baby monkey/blackbird*

**WORDFINDER** birth, dummy, feed, incubator, nappy, pram, premature, teethe

**2** (*informal*) the youngest member of a family or group: *He's the baby of the team.* **3** (*disapproving*) a person who behaves like a young child and is easily upset: *Stop crying and don't be such a baby.* **4** (*slang, especially NAmE*) a word used to address sb, especially your wife, husband or partner, in a way that expresses love but that can be offensive if used by a man to a woman he does not know

**IDM be your/sb's baby** (*informal*) to be a plan or project that sb is responsible for and cares about because they have created it **leave sb holding the baby** (*informal*) to suddenly make sb responsible for sth important that is really your responsibility: *He changed to another job and we were left holding the baby.* **throw the baby out with the bathwater** (*informal*) to lose sth that you want at the same time as you are trying to get rid of sth that you do not want ⇒ more at CANDY, SLEEP *v.*
- *adj.* [only before noun] **baby** vegetables are a very small version of particular vegetables, or are vegetables that are picked when they are very small: *baby carrots*
- *verb* (**ba·bies, baby·ing, ba·bied, ba·bied**) ~ **sb** to treat sb with too much care, as if they were a baby

**baby ˈblue** *adj.* very pale blue in colour ▶ **baby ˈblue** *noun* [U]

**baby ˈblues** *noun* [pl.] (*informal*) a depressed feeling that some women get after the birth of a baby **SYN** postnatal depression

**baby ˈboom** *noun* a period when many more babies are born than usual

**baby ˈboomer** (*NAmE also* **boom·er**) *noun* a person born during a baby boom, especially after the Second World War

**baby ˈbuggy** *noun* **1** (*BrE*) = BUGGY **2** (*NAmE, old-fashioned*) = BABY CARRIAGE

**baby ˈbump** (*also* **bump**) *noun* (*informal*) the round shape of a woman's stomach when she is pregnant

**baby ˈcarriage** (*also* **baby buggy**) (*both NAmE*) (*BrE* **pram**) *noun* a small vehicle on four wheels for a baby to go out in, pushed by a person on foot ⇒ picture at PUSHCHAIR

**ˈbaby-faced** *adj.* with a face that looks young and innocent

**baby ˈgrand** *noun* a small GRAND PIANO

**baby ˈshower** *noun* (*especially NAmE*) a party given for a woman who is going to have a baby, at which her friends give her presents for the baby

**baby·sit** /ˈbeɪbisɪt/ *verb* (**baby·sit·ting, baby·sat, baby·sat**) (*especially NAmE* **sit**) [I, T] to take care of babies or children for a short time while their parents are out: ~ **(for sb)** *She regularly babysits for us.* ◊ ~ **sb** *He's babysitting the neighbour's children.* ▶ **baby·sit·ting** *noun* [U]

**baby·sit·ter** /ˈbeɪbisɪtə(r)/ (*also* **sit·ter** *especially in NAmE*) *noun* a person who takes care of babies or children while their parents are away from home and is usually paid to do this: *I can't find a babysitter for tonight.* ⇒ see also CHILDMINDER

**baby step** *noun* [usually pl.] a small act or measure, usually at the start of a long or difficult process: *The president is taking baby steps in the direction of reform.*

**baby talk** *noun* [U] the words or sounds a baby says when it is learning to talk; the special language adults sometimes use when talking to babies

**baby tooth** (*BrE also* **milk tooth**) *noun* any of the first set of teeth in young children that drop out and are replaced by others

**baby walker** (*BrE*) (*NAmE* **walk·er**) *noun* a frame with wheels and a HARNESS that you can put a baby in so that it is supported and can walk on its own around a room

**bac·ca·laur·eate** /ˌbækəˈlɔːriət/ *noun* **1** the last SECONDARY SCHOOL exam in France and some other countries, and in some international schools: *to sit/take/pass/fail your baccalaureate* ⇒ see also INTERNATIONAL BACCALAUREATE **2** (in the US) a religious service or talk for students who have completed HIGH SCHOOL or college

**bac·carat** /ˈbækərɑː; *NAmE* ˌbækəˈrɑː/ *noun* [U] a card game in which players hold two or three cards each and

# bacchanalian

bet on whose cards will have the highest number left over when their value is divided by ten

**bac·cha·nal·ian** /ˌbækəˈneɪliən/ adj. (formal) (of a party, etc.) wild and involving large amounts of alcohol ORIGIN From the name of the Greek god **Bacchus** (also called Dionysus), the god of wine and wild enjoyment.

**baccy** /ˈbæki/ noun [U] (BrE, informal) TOBACCO

**bach** /bætʃ/ noun (NZE) a small holiday house

**bach·elor** /ˈbætʃələ(r)/ noun **1** a man who has never been married: *an eligible bachelor* (= one that many people want to marry, especially because he is rich) ◊ *a confirmed bachelor* (= a man who does not intend to marry; often used in newspapers to refer to a GAY man) ⇨ compare SPINSTER **2** (*usually* **Bachelor**) a person who has a Bachelor's degree (= a first university degree): *a Bachelor of Arts/Engineering/Science* ⇨ see also BA, BED, BSC **3** (*CanE*) = BACHELOR APARTMENT

**ˈbachelor apartment** (NAmE) (CanE also **bachelor**) noun a small apartment suitable for a person living alone

**bach·elor·ette** /ˌbætʃələˈret/ noun (NAmE) a young woman who is not married

**ˈbachelorette party** (NAmE) (BrE ˈhen party, ˈhen night) noun a party that a woman has with her female friends just before she gets married ⇨ compare BACHELOR PARTY

**bach·elor·hood** /ˈbætʃələhʊd; NAmE -lərh-/ noun [U] the time in a man's life before he is married

**ˈbachelor pad** noun (*informal*) a house or flat in which a man who is not married enjoys a lifestyle without family responsibilities

**ˈbachelor party** (NAmE) (BrE ˈstag night, ˈstag party NAmE, BrE) noun a party that a man has with his male friends just before he gets married ⇨ compare BACHELORETTE PARTY

**ba·cil·lus** /bəˈsɪləs/ noun (pl. **ba·cilli** /-laɪ/) a type of bacteria. There are several types of bacillus, some of which cause disease.

▼ WHICH WORD?

**at the back / at the rear / behind**

- **At the back** and **at the rear** have a similar meaning, but **at the rear** is used more in formal or official language: *What's that at the back of the fridge?* ◊ *Smoking is only allowed at the rear of the aircraft.* It is more usual to talk about the **back door** of a house but the **rear exit** of an aircraft or public building. If something is **behind** something else it is near to the back of it but not part of it. Compare: *Our room was at the back of the hotel* and: *There's a lovely wood just behind our hotel.*

**back** /bæk/ noun, adj., adv., verb

■ noun
- PART OF BODY **1** the part of the human body that is on the opposite side to the chest, between the neck and the tops of the legs; the part of an animal's body that CORRESPONDS to this: **on your~** *He was lying on his back on the sofa.* ◊ **with your~to sb/sth** *She was standing with her back to the camera so you can't see her face.* ◊ **behind your~** *They had their hands tied behind their backs.* ◊ *your lower/upper back* ◊ *a bad* (= painful) *back* ◊ *back pain* ◊ *A small boy rode on the elephant's back.* ⇨ see also BAREBACK, HORSEBACK noun ◊ VISUAL VOCAB page V1 **2** the row of bones in the middle of the back SYN **backbone**, **spine**: *She broke her back in a riding accident.* ◊ *He spent six months recovering from a broken back.*
- PART FURTHEST FROM FRONT **3** [usually sing.] the part or area of sth that is furthest from the front: *She was hit on the back of the head.* ◊ *He kicked the ball straight into the back of the net.* ◊ **at the~** *The house has three bedrooms at the front and two at the back.* ◊ *We could only get seats at the back* (= of a room). ◊ **in the~** (*BrE*) *There's room for three people in the back* (= of a car, etc.). ◊ **in~** (*NAmE*) *There's room for three people in back.* ◊ **around the~** *Come around the back* (= to the area behind the house) *and I'll show you the garden.* ⇨ see also HARDBACK, PAPERBACK
- OF PIECE OF PAPER **4** [usually sing.] the part of a piece of paper, etc. that is on the opposite side to the one that has information or the most important information on it: **on the~** *Take a card and write your name on the back.* ◊ **on the~of sth** *He scribbled some figures on the back of an envelope.*
- OF BOOK **5** [usually sing.] the last few pages of a book, etc: **at/in the~(of sth)** *The television guide is at the back of the paper.*
- OF CHAIR **6** the part of a chair, etc. against which you lean your back
- -BACKED **7** (in adjectives) used to describe furniture that has the type of back mentioned: *a high-backed sofa*
- IN SPORT **8** (in some sports) a player whose main role is to defend their team's goal ⇨ compare FORWARD ⇨ see also FULL BACK, HALF BACK

IDM **at/in the back of your mind** if a thought, etc. is at the back of your mind, you are aware of it but it is not what you are mainly thinking about **sb's back is turned** when sb's back is turned they are not present and not able to see what is happening **the back of beyond** (*informal*) a place that is a long way from other houses, towns, etc. **(on the) back of an envelope** used to talk about planning or calculating sth in a way that is not detailed, exact or complete **back to ˈback 1** if two people stand or sit **back to back**, they stand or sit with their backs facing or touching each other ⇨ see also BACK-TO-BACK **2** if two or more things happen **back to back**, they happen one after the other **back to ˈfront** (*BrE*) (*NAmE* **back·wards**) if you put on a piece of clothing **back to front**, you make a mistake and put the back where the front should be: *I think you've got that sweater on back to front.* ⇨ compare INSIDE OUT **be glad, etc. to see the back of sb/sth** (*informal, especially BrE*) to be happy that you will not have to deal with or see sb/sth again because you do not like them or it: *Was I pleased to see the back of her!* **behind sb's ˈback** without sb's knowledge or permission: *Have you been talking about me behind my back? ◊ They went ahead and sold it behind my back.* ⇨ compare TO SB'S FACE **be on sb's ˈback** (*informal*) to keep asking or telling sb to do sth that they do not want to do, in a way that they find annoying **break the ˈback of sth** to finish the largest or most important part of a task **get/put sb's ˈback up** (*informal*) to annoy sb: *That sort of attitude really gets my back up!* **get off sb's ˈback** (*informal*) to stop annoying sb, for example by criticizing them, or asking them to do sth: *Just get off my back, will you!* **have (got) sb's ˈback** (*NAmE, informal*) to protect and support sb: *Don't worry, I've got your back.* **have your ˈback to the ˈwall** (*informal*) to be in a difficult situation in which you are forced to do sth but are unable to make the choices that you would like **off the back of a ˈlorry** (*BrE, informal, humorous*) goods that **fell off the back of a lorry** were probably stolen. People say or accept that they came 'off the back of a lorry' to avoid saying or asking where they really came from. **off the ˈback of sth** (*informal*) immediately after sth: *They come into this game off the back of a 1-0 defeat to Chelsea.* **off/on the back of sth** as a result of an achievement or a success: *The profits growth came on the back of a 26 per cent rise in sales.* **(flat) on your back** (*informal*) in bed because you are ill: *She's been flat on her back for over a week now.* ◊ (*figurative*) *The UK market was flat on its back* (= business was very bad). **put your ˈback into sth** to use a lot of effort and energy on a particular task **turn your back** to turn so that you are facing in the opposite direction **turn your back on sb/sth 1** to move so that you are standing or sitting with your back facing sb/sth: *When on stage, try not to turn your back on the audience.* **2** to reject sb/sth that you have previously been connected with: *She turned her back on them when they needed her.* ⇨ more at COVER v., EYE n., KNOW v., PAT n., PAT v., PUSH v., ROD, SCRATCH v., SHIRT, STAB n., STAB v., STRAW, WATCH v., WATER n.

■ adj. [only before noun]
- AWAY FROM FRONT **1** located behind or at the back of sth: *We were sitting in the back row* ◊ *the back garden* (= behind the house) ◊ *a back room* (= one at the back of a

building.) ◊ *My phone's in my back pocket.* ◊ *We drove along miles of twisty **back** roads* (= away from the main roads). ⊃ compare FRONT
- **FROM PAST 2** of or from a past time: *a **back** issue of the magazine*
- **OWED 3** owed for a time in the past: ***back** pay/taxes/rent*
- **PHONETICS 4** *(phonetics)* (of a vowel) produced with the back of the tongue in a higher position than the front, for example /ɑː/ in English ⊃ compare CENTRAL, FRONT

**IDM** **on the back 'burner** *(informal)* (of an idea, a plan, etc.) left for the present time, to be done or considered later ⊃ see also BACK-BURNER ⊃ compare ON THE FRONT BURNER **(put/catch sb) on the back 'foot** (to put sb) at a disadvantage or in difficulty: *Advances in drone technology have caught lawmakers on the back foot.*

■ *adv.* **HELP** For the special uses of **back** in phrasal verbs, look at the entries for the verbs. For example **pay sb back** is in the phrasal verb section at **pay**.
- **AS BEFORE 1** A1 to or into the place, condition, situation or activity where sb/sth was before: *When is he coming **back** to work?* ◊ *Don't forget to bring it **back** when you've finished with it.* ◊ *Please give me my ball **back**.* ◊ *Could you go **back** to the beginning of the story?* ◊ *She woke up briefly and then went **back** to sleep.* ◊ *I can't wait to get **back** home.* ◊ *It takes me an hour to walk there and **back**.* ◊ *We were right **back** where we started, only this time without any money.* ◊ *It's good to have the whole family **back** together again.*
- **AWAY FROM FRONT 2** A1 away from the front or centre; behind you: *I moved **back** to let them pass.* ◊ *Sit **back** and relax.* ◊ *You've combed your hair **back**.* ◊ *He turned and looked **back**.* ◊ *She fell **back** towards the end of the race.*
  OPP forward
- **AT A PREVIOUS PLACE 3** A2 at a place previously left or mentioned: *We should have turned left five kilometres **back**.* ◊ *Back at home, her parents were worried.*
- **IN RETURN 4** A2 in return or reply: *She's a tough kid, who, when attacked, fights **back** hard.* ◊ *Could you call me **back** later, please?*
- **AT A DISTANCE 5** B1 at a distance away from sth: *The barriers kept the crowd **back**.* ◊ *Stand **back** and give me some room.*
- **IN PAST 6** B1 in or into the past; ago: *The cathedral dates **back** to 1123.* ◊ *She left **back** in November.* ◊ *That was a few years **back**.*
- **UNDER CONTROL 7** B2 under control; prevented from being expressed or coming out: *He could no longer hold **back** his tears.*
- **FASHIONABLE AGAIN 8** fashionable again: *Beards are **back**.*

**IDM** **back and 'forth** from one place to another and back again repeatedly: *ferries sailing back and forth between the islands* **back in the 'day** in the past: *My dad's always talking about how great everything was back in the day.* **back in the 'days** at a particular time in the past: *I was a fan back in the days when the band wasn't yet famous.* **back of sth** (NAmE, informal) behind sth: *the houses back of the church* ⊃ more at EARTH *n.*, SQUARE *n.*

■ *verb*
- **SUPPORT 1** B2 [T] ~ **sb/sth** to encourage sb or give them help; to give financial support to sb/sth: *Her parents backed her in her choice of career.* ◊ *The project to improve healthcare is backed (= given financial support) by the government.* **2** B2 [T] ~ **sb/sth** to support and agree with sb/sth: *Local residents are enthusiastically backing the campaign to save the library.* ◊ *Doctors have backed plans to raise the tax on cigarettes.* **3** [T, usually passive] to help prove that sth is true: **be backed by sth** *All complaints must be backed by evidence.*
- **BET MONEY 4** [T] ~ **sth** to bet money on a horse in a race, a team in a competition, etc: *I backed the winner and won fifty pounds.*
- **MUSIC 5** [T] ~ **sth** to play or sing music that supports the main singer or instrument ⊃ see also BACKING
- **MOVE BACKWARDS 6** [I, T] to move or make sth move backwards: + *adv./prep. He backed against the wall, terrified.* ◊ ~ **sth** + *adv./prep.* *If you can't drive in forwards, try backing it in.* ⊃ compare REVERSE
- **COVER BACK 7** [T] [usually passive] to cover the back of sth in order to support or protect it: **be backed with sth** *Each piece is backed with clear vinyl.*

95 **back-burner**

- **BE BEHIND 8** [T, usually passive] to be located behind sth: **be backed by sth** *The house is backed by fields.*

**IDM** **back the wrong 'horse** *(BrE)* to support sb/sth that is not successful

**PHR V** **back a'way (from sb/sth)** to move away backwards from sb/sth that is frightening or unpleasant; to avoid doing sth that is unpleasant: *He tried to back away.* ◊ *The children backed away from him in fear.* **back 'down (on/from sth)** (NAmE also **back 'off**) to take back a demand, an opinion, etc. that other people are strongly opposed to; to admit defeat: *She refused to back down on a point of principle.* **back 'off 1** to move backwards in order to get away from sb/sth frightening or unpleasant: *As the riot police approached, the crowd backed off.* **2** to stop threatening, criticizing or annoying sb: *Back off! There's no need to yell at me.* ◊ *The press have agreed to back off and leave the couple alone.* **back 'off (from sth)** to choose not to take action, in order to avoid a difficult situation: *The government backed off from a confrontation.* **back 'onto sth** (of a building) to have sth directly behind it: *Our house backs onto the river.* **back 'out (of sth)** to decide that you are no longer going to take part in sth that has been agreed: *He lost confidence and backed out of the deal at the last minute.* **back 'up | back sth↔'up** to move backwards, especially in a vehicle: *You can back up another two feet or so.* ◊ *I backed the car up to the door.* **back sb/sth↔'up 1** B2 to support sb/sth; to say that what sb says, etc. is true: *I'll back you up if they don't believe you.* ◊ *The writer doesn't back up his opinions with examples.* **2** to provide support for sb/sth: *two doctors backed up by a team of nurses* ◊ *The rebels backed up their demands with threats.* ⊃ related noun BACKUP **back sth↔'up** *(computing)* to prepare a second copy of a file, program, etc. that can be used if the main one fails or needs extra support ⊃ related noun BACKUP

**back·ache** /ˈbækeɪk/ *noun* [U, C] a continuous pain in the back: *(BrE)* *to have backache/a backache* *(NAmE)* *to have a backache*

**back-'alley** *adj.* [only before noun] happening or done secretly, often illegally: *a back-alley abortion*

**back 'alley** *noun* a narrow passage behind or between buildings

**back·beat** /ˈbækbiːt/ *noun* *(music)* a strong emphasis on one or two of the BEATS (= units of rhythm) that are not normally emphasized, used especially in jazz and rock music

**back 'bench** *noun* [usually pl.] (in the House of Commons in the UK, and in certain other parliaments) any of the seats for Members of Parliament who do not have senior positions in the government or the other parties: *He resigned as Home Secretary and returned to the back benches.* ◊ *back-bench MPs*⊃ compare FRONT BENCH

**back·bench·er** /ˌbækˈbentʃə(r)/ *noun* (in the House of Commons in the UK and in certain other parliaments) a member who sits in the rows of seats at the back, and who does not have an important position in the government or the Opposition⊃ compare FRONTBENCHER

**back·bit·ing** /ˈbækbaɪtɪŋ/ *noun* [U] unpleasant and unkind talk about sb who is not present

**back·board** /ˈbækbɔːd; NAmE -bɔːrd/ *noun* the board behind the BASKET in the game of basketball

**back·bone** /ˈbækbəʊn/ *noun* **1** [C] the row of small bones that are connected together down the middle of the back **SYN** spine ⊃ VISUAL VOCAB page V. **2** [sing.] the most important part of a system, an organization, etc. that gives it support and strength: *Agriculture forms the backbone of the rural economy.* **3** [U] the strength of character that you need to do sth difficult: *He doesn't have the backbone to face the truth.*

**'back-breaking** *adj.* (of physical work) very hard and making you tired

**back-'burner** *verb* ~ **sth** *(especially NAmE, informal)* to leave an idea or a plan for a time, to be done or considered later⊃ compare ON THE BACK BURNER

# back button

**ˈback button** *noun* a small area on a computer screen that you click on or touch to return to the previous screen or page

**ˈback catalogue** (*US also* **ˈback catalog**) *noun* all the recorded music previously produced by a musician: *The entire Beatles' back catalogue has been put online.*

**back-channel** /ˈbæktʃænl/ *noun* **1** a secret or unusual way of passing information to other people **2** (*linguistics*) a sound or sign that sb makes to show that they are listening to the person who is talking to them

**back-chat** /ˈbæktʃæt/ (*BrE*) (*NAmE* **ˈback talk**) *noun* [U] (*informal*) a way of answering that shows no respect for sb in authority

**back-cloth** /ˈbæklɒθ; *NAmE* -klɔːθ/ *noun* (*BrE*) = BACKDROP

**back-comb** /ˈbækkəʊm/ (*BrE*) (*NAmE* **tease**) *verb* ~ **sth** to COMB your hair in the opposite direction to the way it grows so that it looks thicker

**back-coun-try** /ˈbækkʌntri/ *noun* [U] (*NAmE*) an area away from roads and towns, especially in the mountains

**back-court** /ˈbækkɔːt; *NAmE* -kɔːrt/ *noun* **1** (in tennis, basketball, etc.) the area at either end of the COURT **2** (in basketball) the players who form the defence **3** (*ScotE*) an area surrounded by walls but with no roof at the back of a building

**back-crawl** /ˈbækkrɔːl/ *noun* [U, sing.] (*BrE*) = BACKSTROKE

**back-date** /ˌbækˈdeɪt/ *verb* **1** ~ **sth** to write a date on a document that is earlier than the actual date ⇨ compare POST-DATE **2** ~ **sth** (*BrE*) to make sth, especially a payment, take effect from an earlier date: *Postal workers are getting a 5.2 per cent pay rise, backdated to February.*

**back-ˈdoor** *adj.* [only before noun] using indirect or secret means in order to achieve sth

**back ˈdoor** *noun* the door at the back or side of a building **IDM** **by/through the back door** in an unfair or indirect way: *He used his friends to help him get into the civil service by the back door.*

**back-draught** (*also* **back-draft**) /ˈbækdrɑːft; *NAmE* -dræft/ *noun* **1** a current of air that flows backwards down a CHIMNEY, pipe, etc. **2** an explosion caused by more OXYGEN being supplied to a fire, for example by a door being opened

**back-drop** /ˈbækdrɒp; *NAmE* -drɑːp/ (*BrE also* **back-cloth**) *noun* **1** everything that can be seen around an event or scene: *The mountains provided a dramatic backdrop for our picnic.* **2** the general conditions in which an event takes place, which sometimes help to explain that event: *It was against this backdrop of racial tension that the civil war began.* **3** a painted piece of cloth that is hung behind the stage in a theatre as part of the SCENERY: *She was an artist who designed backdrops for movies and stage plays.* ⇨ WORDFINDER NOTE *at* STAGE

**ˈback-end** *adj.* [only before noun] **1** relating to the end of a period or process **2** (*computing*) (of a device or program) not used directly by a user, but used by a program or computer ⇨ compare FRONT-END

**ˌback ˈend** *noun* **1** (*especially BrE*) the end of a period or process: *the back end of last year* **OPP** **front end 2** (*especially BrE, informal*) a person's bottom (= the part they sit on) **SYN** **rear end 3** (*computing*) the part of a computer system that the user does not directly use and cannot easily access, usually the part that is responsible for storing and controlling data ⇨ compare FRONT END (2)

**back-er** /ˈbækə(r)/ *noun* a person or company that gives support to sb/sth, especially financial support

**back-field** /ˈbækfiːld/ *noun* [sing., U] **1** (in AMERICAN FOOTBALL) the area of play behind the line of SCRIMMAGE **2** the players who play in or around this area

**back-fill** /ˈbækfɪl/ *verb* ~ **sth** to fill a hole with the material that has been dug out of it

**back-fire** /ˌbækˈfaɪə(r)/ *verb* **1** [I] ~ (**on sb**) to have the opposite effect to the one intended, with bad or dangerous results: *Unfortunately the plan backfired.* **2** [I] (of an engine or a vehicle) to make a sudden noise like an explosion ⇨ compare MISFIRE

**back-flip** /ˈbækflɪp/ *noun* if sb does a **backflip**, they turn their body over backwards in the air and land on their feet again

**back-gam-mon** /ˈbækɡæmən/ *noun* [U] a game for two people played on a board marked with long thin TRIANGLES. Players throw DICE and move pieces around the board.

**back-ground** 🄵 **A2** 🅞 /ˈbækɡraʊnd/ *noun*
• FAMILY/EDUCATION, ETC. **1** 🅸 **A2** [C] the details of a person's family, education, experience, etc: *sb's ethnic/genetic/cultural background* ◇ *sb's family/educational background* ◇ *We come from very different backgrounds but we get on well.* ◇ **in sth** *She has a background in journalism.*
• PAST **2** 🅸 [C, usually sing., U] the circumstances or past events that help explain why sth is how it is; information about these: *background information* ◇ **~ to sth** *the historical background to the war* ◇ **against a ~ of sth** *The elections are taking place against a background of violence.* ◇ **~ on sth** *Our reporter can now provide more background on this story.*
• OF PICTURE/PHOTO **3** 🅸 **A2** [C, usually sing.] the part of a picture, photograph or view behind the main objects, people, etc: **in the~** *a photograph with trees in the background* ◇ **against the …~** *The areas of water stood out against the dark background.* ⇨ compare FOREGROUND ⇨ SYNONYMS *at* ENVIRONMENT ⇨ WORDFINDER NOTE *at* PAINTING ⇨ EXPRESS YOURSELF *at* DESCRIBE
• LESS IMPORTANT POSITION **4** 🅸 **A2** [sing.] a position in which people are not paying attention to sb/sth or not as much attention as they are paying to sth/sb else: *background music* ◇ *There was a lot of background noise (= that you could hear, but were not listening to).* ◇ **in the~** *He prefers to remain in the background and let his assistant talk to the press.* ◇ *A piano was playing gently in the background.* ⇨ compare FOREGROUND
• COLOUR UNDER STH **5** [C, usually sing.] a colour or design on which sth is painted, drawn, etc: **on a …~** *The name of the company is written in red on a white background.*
• COMPUTING **6** [sing.] used to refer to tasks or processes that the user is not actively working on at the present time: **in the~** *Programs can be left running in the background.* **IDM** *see* MERGE

**back-hand** /ˈbækhænd/ *noun* [usually sing.] (in tennis, etc.) a way of hitting the ball in some sports that is played with the back of the hand turned in the direction towards which the ball is hit: *He has a good backhand (= he can make good backhand strokes).* ◇ *a backhand volley/drive* ⇨ compare FOREHAND

**back-han-ded** /ˌbækˈhændɪd/ *adj.* having a meaning that is not directly or clearly expressed, or that is not intended **IDM** **a backhanded compliment** (*NAmE also* **ˌleft-handed ˈcompliment**) a comment that seems to express approval but could also be understood as expressing a poor opinion of sb/sth

**back-hand-er** /ˈbækhændə(r)/ *noun* (*BrE, informal*) a secret and illegal payment made to sb in exchange for a favour **SYN** **bribe**

**back-ˈheel** *verb* ~ **sth** to kick a ball using the heel: *He back-heeled the ball towards the goal.* ▸ **back-ˈheel** *noun*

**back-hoe** /ˈbækhəʊ/ *noun* a large vehicle with equipment for digging, used in building roads, etc.

**back-ing** 🅸 **C1** /ˈbækɪŋ/ *noun* **1** 🅸 **C1** [U] help and support from sb to do sth; financial support for sth **SYN** **support**: *financial backing* ◇ *The police gave the proposals their full backing.* **2** [U, C] material attached to the back of sth in order to protect it or make it stronger **3** [U, C, usually sing.] (especially in pop music) music that goes with the main singer or tune: *a backing group/singer/track*

**ˈback issue** (*BrE also* **ˈback copy**, **ˈback number**) *noun* a copy of a newspaper or magazine from a date in the past

**back-lash** /ˈbæklæʃ/ *noun* [sing.] **~ (against sth)** | **~ (from sb)** a strong negative reaction by a large number of people, for example to sth that has recently changed in society: *The government is facing an angry backlash from voters over the new tax.*

**back·less** /ˈbækləs/ *adj.* (of a dress) not covering most of the back

**back·light** /ˈbæklaɪt/ *noun, verb*
- *noun* [U] light from behind sth in a photograph or painting
- *verb* (**back-lit**, **back-lit** or **back-lighted**, **back-lighted**) ~ **sth** to shine light on sth from behind ▶ **back-lit** /-lɪt/ *adj.*: *a backlit photograph*

**back·link** /ˈbæklɪŋk/ *noun* a link on a WEB PAGE (= a document that is connected to the World Wide Web) to another website ⊃ compare HYPERLINK ▶ **back-link** *verb*

**back·list** /ˈbæklɪst/ *noun* the list of books that have been published by a company in the past and are still available

**back·log** /ˈbæklɒg; *NAmE* -lɔːg/ *noun* a quantity of work that should have been done already, but has not yet been done

**back·lot** /ˈbæklɒt; *NAmE* -lɑːt/ *noun* an outdoor area in a film studio, where pieces of SCENERY are made and some scenes are filmed

**back·most** /ˈbækməʊst/ *adj.* [usually before noun] furthest back: *the backmost teeth*

**back ˈoffice** *noun* (*business*) the part of a business company which does not deal directly with the public

**back·pack** /ˈbækpæk/ *noun, verb*
- *noun* **1** (*BrE also* **ruck-sack**) a bag that you carry on your back, made of strong material and often used by people who go climbing or walking **2** a piece of equipment that is carried on the back: *a weed-sprayer backpack*
- *verb* [I] (*usually* **go backpacking**) to travel on holiday carrying your equipment and clothes in a backpack: *They went backpacking in Spain last year.* ⊃ WORDFINDER NOTE at TOURIST ▶ **back-pack-er** *noun*

**back ˈpassage** *noun* (*BrE*) a polite way of referring to sb's RECTUM (= the part of the body where solid waste leaves the body)

**back-ˈpedal** *verb* (-ll-, *NAmE* -l-) **1** [I] ~ (**on sth**) to change an earlier statement or opinion; to not do sth that you promised to do: *The protests have forced the government to back-pedal on the new tax.* **2** [I] to PEDAL backwards on a bicycle; to walk or run backwards ⊃ WORDFINDER NOTE at CYCLING

**back·plane** /ˈbækpleɪn/ *noun* (*computing*) a CIRCUIT BOARD that other devices can be connected to

**back·rest** /ˈbækrest/ *noun* part of a seat that supports sb's back

**back ˈseat** *noun* a seat at the back of a vehicle
**IDM** **take a back seat** to allow sb else to play a more active and important role in a particular situation than you do

**back·sheesh** = BAKSHEESH

**back·side** /ˈbæksaɪd/ *noun* (*informal*) the part of the body that you sit on **SYN** **behind**, **bottom**: *Get up off your backside and do some work!* **IDM** see PAIN *n.*

**back·slap·ping** /ˈbækslæpɪŋ/ *noun* [U] loud and enthusiastic behaviour when people are praising each other for sth good they have done ▶ **back-slap-ping** *adj.* [only before noun]: *backslapping tributes*

**back·slash** /ˈbækslæʃ/ *noun* a mark (\), used in computer commands ⊃ compare FORWARD SLASH

**back·slid·ing** /ˈbækslaɪdɪŋ/ *noun* [U] the situation when sb fails to do sth that they agreed to do and returns to their former bad behaviour

**back·space** /ˈbækspeɪs/ *noun, verb*
- *noun* the key on the keyboard of a computer or other device that removes the last letter that you typed ⊃ WORD-FINDER NOTE at KEYBOARD
- *verb* [I] to use the backspace key on the keyboard of a computer or other device

**back·spin** /ˈbækspɪn/ *noun* [U] the action of making a ball turn round and round backwards when it has been hit, and go less far than it normally would

**back-stabbing** *noun* [U] the action of criticizing sb when they are not there, while pretending to be their friend at other times

**back·stage** /ˌbækˈsteɪdʒ/ *adv.* **1** in the part of a theatre where the actors and artists get ready and wait to perform: *After the show, we were allowed to go backstage to meet the cast.* **2** away from the attention of the public; in secret: *I'd like to know what really goes on backstage in government.* ▶ **back·stage** *adj.*

**back·stairs** /ˈbæksteəz; *NAmE* -sterz/ *noun, adj.*
- *noun* [pl.] stairs at the back or side of a building, sometimes used by servants
- *adj.* secret or dishonest: *backstairs deals between politicians*

**back·stop** /ˈbækstɒp; *NAmE* -stɑːp/ *noun* **1** (*sport*) a fence or screen used to stop balls from going outside the playing area: *Some of his pitches hit the backstop.* **2** (*sport*) (in ROUNDERS or baseball) the player who stands behind the person who is BATTING and catches the ball if he or she does not hit it ⊃ compare CATCHER (1) **3** something that is done or prepared in advance in order to prevent worse problems if sth goes wrong: *The country needs a financial backstop to deal with bank failures.*

**back·story** /ˈbækstɔːri/ *noun* [C, U] (*pl.* **-ies**) **1** the things that are supposed to have happened to the characters in a film, novel, etc., before the film, etc. starts: *The film spends too long establishing the characters' backstories.* **2** (*especially in journalism*) the background to a news story: *First, some backstory:…*

**back·street** /ˈbækstriːt/ *noun, adj.*
- *noun* a small quiet street, usually in a poor part of a town or city, away from main roads
- *adj.* [only before noun] acting or happening secretly, often dishonestly or illegally: *backstreet dealers ◊ backstreet abortions*

**back·stroke** /ˈbækstrəʊk/ (*BrE also* **back-crawl**) *noun* [U, sing.] a style of swimming in which you lie on your back: *Can you do (the) backstroke? ◊ He won the 100 metres backstroke* (= the race).

**back·swing** /ˈbækswɪŋ/ *noun* (*sport*) the backwards movement of your arm or arms before you hit the ball

**ˈback talk** (*NAmE*) (*BrE* **back-chat**) *noun* [U] (*informal*) a way of answering that shows no respect for sb in authority

**back-to-ˈback** *adj., noun*
- *adj.* [only before noun] **1** (of events) following one after another in a continuous series **SYN** **consecutive**: *The women's hockey team plays back-to-back games this weekend. ◊ back-to-back titles/wins/victories* ⊃ see also BACK TO BACK at BACK *noun* (2) **2** (*BrE*) (of houses) built in a row in which the houses share walls with the houses on each side and behind: *back-to-back terraced houses*
- *noun* **1** (*NAmE*) sports games that are played on CONSECUTIVE days (= with no days in between) **2** (*BrE*) a house in a row of houses that share walls with the houses on each side and behind

**back·track** /ˈbæktræk/ *verb* **1** [I] to go back along the same route that you have just come along **2** [I] to change an earlier statement, opinion or promise because of pressure from sb/sth

**back·up** /ˈbækʌp/ *noun* [U, C] **1** extra help or support that you can get if necessary: *The police had backup from the army. ◊ We can use him as a backup if one of the other players drops out. ◊ a backup power supply* **2** (*computing*) a copy of a file, etc. that can be used if the original is lost or damaged: *Always make a backup of your work. ◊ a backup copy* ⊃ see also BACK STH UP

**ˈbackup light** (*NAmE*) (*BrE* **reˈversing light**) *noun* a white light at the back of a vehicle that comes on when the vehicle moves backwards

**back·ward** /ˈbækwəd; *NAmE* -wərd/ *adj., adv.*
- *adj.* **1** [only before noun] directed or moving towards the back: *She strode past him without a backward glance.* **2** moving in a direction that means that no progress is being made **SYN** **retrograde**: *She felt that going back to*

live in her home town would be a backward step. **3** having made less progress than normal; developing slowly: *a backward part of the country, with no paved roads and no electricity* ◊ *a backward child* ◊ (*BrE, informal*) *She's not backward in coming forward* (= she's not shy). ⊃ compare FORWARD
■ *adv.* (*especially NAmE*) = BACKWARDS

**ˌbackward ˈclasses** *noun* [pl.] (in India) the people in a CASTE (= division of society) or community who are recommended by each state authority for special help in education and employment

**ˈbackward-looking** *adj.* (*disapproving*) opposed to progress or change

**back·ward·ness** /ˈbækwədnəs; *NAmE* -wərd-/ *noun* [U] the state of having made less progress than normal

**back·wards** 🔊 **B1** /ˈbækwədz; *NAmE* -wərdz/ (*also* **backward** *especially in NAmE*) *adv.* **1** 🔊 **B1** towards a place or position that is behind: *I lost my balance and fell backwards.* ◊ *He took a step backwards.* **OPP** **forward** **2** 🔊 **B1** in the opposite direction to the usual one: '*Ambulance*' *is written backwards so you can read it in the mirror.* ◊ *In the movie they take a journey backwards through time.* **3** 🔊 **B1** towards a worse state: *I felt that going to live with my parents would be a step backwards.* **OPP** **forward** **4** (*NAmE*) (*BrE* **back to ˈfront**) if you put on a piece of clothing **backwards**, you make a mistake and put the back where the front should be
**IDM** **ˌbackward(s) and ˈforward(s)** from one place or position to another and back again many times: *She rocked backwards and forwards on her chair.* **bend/lean over ˈbackwards (to do sth)** to make a great effort, especially in order to be helpful or fair: *I've bent over backwards to help him.* ⊃ more at KNOW *v.*

**ˌbackwards comˈpatible** (*also* **ˌbackward comˈpatible**) *adj.* (*computing*) able to be used with systems, machines or programs which are older

**back·wash** /ˈbækwɒʃ; *NAmE* -wɔːʃ/ *noun* [sing., U] **1** the unpleasant result of an event **2** waves caused by a boat moving through water; the movement of water back into the sea after a wave has hit the beach

**back·water** /ˈbækwɔːtə(r)/ *noun* **1** a part of a river away from the main part, where the water only moves slowly **2** (*often disapproving*) a place that is away from the places where most things happen, and is therefore not affected by events, progress, new ideas, etc.: *a sleepy/quiet/rural backwater*

**back·woods** /ˈbækwʊdz/ *noun* [pl.] a place that is away from any big towns and from the influence of modern life

**back·yard** /ˌbækˈjɑːd; *NAmE* -ˈjɑːrd/ *noun* **1** (*NAmE*) the whole area behind and belonging to a house, including an area of grass and the garden: *He grew vegetables in his backyard.* ◊ *a backyard barbecue* **2** (*BrE*) an area with a hard surface behind a house, often surrounded by a wall ⊃ see also YARD
**IDM** **in your (own) backˈyard** in or near the place where you live or work: *The residents didn't want a new factory in their backyard.* ◊ *The party leader is facing opposition in his own backyard* (= from his own members). ⊃ see also NIMBY

**bacon** /ˈbeɪkən/ *noun* [U] meat from the back or sides of a pig that has been CURED (= preserved using salt or smoke), usually served in thin slices: *a rasher of bacon* ◊ *bacon and eggs* ◊ **smoked/unsmoked bacon** ⊃ compare GAMMON, HAM, PORK **IDM** see HOME *adv.*, SAVE *v.*

**bac·teria** 🔊 **B2** /bækˈtɪəriə; *NAmE* -ˈtɪr-/ *noun* [pl.] (*sing.* **bac·ter·ium** /-riəm/) the simplest and smallest forms of life. Bacteria exist in large numbers in air, water and soil, and also in living and dead creatures and plants, and are often a cause of disease: *Neither chilling nor freezing kills all bacteria.* ⊃ WORDFINDER NOTE at DISEASE ▶ **bac·ter·ial** /-riəl/ *adj.*: *bacterial infections/growth*

**bac·teri·ology** /bækˌtɪəriˈɒlədʒi; *NAmE* -ˌtɪriˈɑːl-/ *noun* [U] the scientific study of bacteria ▶ **bac·teri·o·logic·al** /bækˌtɪəriəˈlɒdʒɪkl; *NAmE* -ˌtɪriəˈlɑːdʒ-/ *adj.* **bac·teri·olo·gist** /bækˌtɪəriˈɒlədʒɪst; *NAmE* -ˌtɪriˈɑːl-/ *noun*

▼ **VOCABULARY BUILDING**
**Bad and very bad**
Instead of saying that something is **bad** or **very bad**, try to use more precise and interesting adjectives to describe things:
• an **unpleasant**/a **foul**/a **disgusting** smell
• **appalling**/**dreadful**/**severe** weather
• an **unpleasant**/a **frightening**/a **traumatic** experience
• **poor**/**weak** eyesight
• a **terrible**/**serious**/**horrific** accident
• a **wicked**/an **evil**/an **immoral** person
• an **awkward**/an **embarrassing**/a **difficult** situation
• We were working in **difficult**/**appalling** conditions.
To refer to your health, you can say: *I feel unwell/sick/ terrible.* ◊ *I don't feel (very) well.*
In conversation, words like **terrible**, **horrible**, **awful** and **dreadful** can be used in most situations to mean 'very bad'.

**bad** 🔊 **A1** /bæd/ *adj., noun, adv.*
■ *adj.* (**worse** /wɜːs; *NAmE* wɜːrs/, **worst** /wɜːst; *NAmE* wɜːrst/)
• **UNPLEASANT 1** 🔊 **A1** unpleasant; full of problems: *I have some bad news for you, I'm afraid.* ◊ *bad weather/dreams/ habits* ◊ *I'm having a really bad day.* ◊ *It was the worst experience of her life.* ◊ *Smoking gives you bad breath.* ◊ *War is always a bad thing.* ◊ *That was just bad luck.* ◊ *Things are bad enough without our own guns shelling us.*
• **POOR QUALITY 2** 🔊 **A1** of poor quality; below an acceptable standard: *I thought it was a very bad article.* ◊ *Bad diet and lack of exercise can lead to serious health problems.* ◊ *The movie wasn't as bad as I'd expected.* ◊ *That's not a bad idea.*
• **SERIOUS 3** 🔊 **A1** serious; severe: *You're heading for a bad case of sunburn.* ◊ *The engagement was a bad mistake.* ◊ *My headache is getting worse.*
• **NOT APPROPRIATE 4** 🔊 **A1** [only before noun] not appropriate in a particular situation: *I know that this is a bad time to ask for help.* ◊ *He now realized that it had been a bad decision on his part.*
• **WICKED 5** 🔊 **A1** morally unacceptable: *The hero gets to shoot all the bad guys.* ◊ *He said I must have done something bad to deserve it.*
• **CHILDREN 6** 🔊 **A1** [usually before noun] (especially of children) not behaving well **SYN** **naughty**: *Have you been a bad boy?*
• **NOT GOOD AT STH 7** 🔊 **A1** (of a person) not able to do sth well or in an acceptable way **SYN** **poor**: *a bad teacher* ◊ *You're a bad liar!* ◊ *He's a bad loser* (= he complains when he loses a game). ◊ **~at (doing) sth** *She is so bad at keeping secrets.*
• **HARMFUL 8** 🔊 **A1** [not before noun] **~for sb/sth** harmful; causing or likely to cause damage: *Those shoes are bad for her feet.* ◊ *Weather like this is bad for business.*
• **PAINFUL 9** [usually before noun] (of parts of the body) not healthy; painful: *I've got a bad back.*
• **FOOD 10** not safe to eat because it has DECAYED (= started to be destroyed by natural processes): *Put the meat in the fridge so it doesn't go bad.*
• **TEMPER/MOOD 11 ~temper/mood** the state of feeling annoyed or angry: *It put me in a bad mood for the rest of the day.*
• **GUILTY/SORRY 12** **feel~** to feel guilty or sorry about sth: *She felt pretty bad about leaving him.* ◊ *Why should I want to make you feel bad?*
• **ILL/SICK 13** **feel/look~** to feel or look ill: *I'm afraid I'm feeling pretty bad.*
• **EXCELLENT 14** (**bad·der**, **bad·dest**) (*especially NAmE, slang*) good; excellent
**IDM** **HELP** Most idioms containing **bad** are at the entries for the nouns and verbs in the idioms, for example **be bad news (for sb/sth)** is at **news**. **ˌcan't be ˈbad** (*informal*) used to try to persuade sb to agree that sth is good: *You'll save fifty dollars, which can't be bad, can it?* **have got it ˈbad** (*informal, humorous*) to be very much in love: *You're not seeing him again tonight, are you? That's five times this week—*

you've got it bad! **not ˈbad** (*informal*) quite good; better than you expected: 'How are you?' 'Not too bad.' ◊ That wasn't bad for a first attempt. **too bad** (*informal*) **1** 🔑 B1 (*ironic*) used to say 'bad luck' or 'it's a shame' when you do not really mean it: *If sometimes they're the wrong decisions, too bad.* **2** 🔑 B1 a shame; a PITY: *Too bad every day can't be as good as this.* **3** (*old-fashioned*) annoying: *Really, it was too bad of you to be so late.*
- **noun** [U] **the bad** bad people, things, or events: *You will always have the bad as well as the good in the world.*
**IDM** **go to the ˈbad** (*old-fashioned*) to begin behaving in an IMMORAL way: *I hate to see you going to the bad.* **ˈmy bad** (*NAmE, informal*) used when you are admitting that sth is your fault or that you have made a mistake: *I'm sorry—my bad.* **take the ˈbad with the ˈgood** to accept the bad aspects of sth as well as the good ones **to the ˈbad** (*BrE*) used to say that sb now has a particular amount less money than they did before: *After the sale they were £300 to the bad.*
- **adv.** (*NAmE, informal*) badly: *She wanted it real bad.* ◊ *Are you hurt bad?*

**badam** /bʌˈdɑːm; *NAmE* ˈbɑːdɑːm/ *noun* [C] (*IndE*) an ALMOND

**bad-ass** /ˈbædæs/ *adj.* (*NAmE, informal*) **1** (of a person) tough and aggressive: *a modern, badass superhero* **2** very impressive: *the most badass moment in the movie* ▶ **bad-ass** *noun*

**ˈbad boy** *noun* (*informal*) a man who behaves badly, especially in a particular area of activity: *He used to be known as the bad boy of Hollywood.*

**ˌbad ˈbreath** *noun* [U] breath that smells unpleasant SYN halitosis: *Have I got bad breath?*

**ˌbad ˈdebt** *noun* [C, U] a debt that is unlikely to be paid

**baddy** /ˈbædi/ *noun* (*pl.* **-ies**) (*informal*) a bad or evil character in a film, book, play, etc: *As usual, the cops get the baddies in the end.* OPP goody ⊃ WORDFINDER NOTE at CHARACTER

**bade** /beɪd/ past tense of BID²

**badge** 🔑+ B2 /bædʒ/ *noun* **1** 🔑+ B2 a small piece of metal or plastic, with a design or words on it, that a person wears or carries to show that they belong to an organization, support sth, have achieved sth, have a particular rank, etc: *She wore a badge saying 'Vote for Coates'.* ◊ *All employees have to wear name badges.* ◊ *He pulled out a badge and said he was a cop.* ⊃ compare BUTTON **2** (*BrE*) (*NAmE* **patch**) a piece of material that you SEW onto clothes as part of a uniform: *the school badge* **3** a symbol of a particular quality or status: *His gun was a badge of power for him.*

**badger** /ˈbædʒə(r)/ *noun, verb*
- **noun** an animal with grey fur and wide black and white lines on its head. Badgers are NOCTURNAL (= active mostly at night) and live in holes in the ground.
- **verb** to put pressure on sb by repeatedly asking them questions or asking them to do sth SYN **pester**: ~ *sb* (**into doing sth**) *I finally badgered him into coming with us.* ◊ ~ *sb* **about sth** *Reporters constantly badger her about her private life.* ◊ ~ *sb* **to do sth** *His daughter was always badgering him to let her join the club.*

**ˌbad ˈhair day** *noun* (*informal*) a day on which everything seems to go wrong

**bad·lands** /ˈbædlændz/ *noun* [pl.] **1** large areas of land that have been farmed too much with the result that plants will not grow there **2 the Badlands** a large area of land in the western US where plants will not grow

**ˌbad ˈlanguage** *noun* [U] words that many people find offensive SYN **swear words**

**badly** 🔑 A2 /ˈbædli/ *adv.* (**worse, worst**) **1** 🔑 A2 without skill or care: *to play/sing badly* ◊ *badly designed/organized* OPP well **2** 🔑 B1 not successfully: *Things have been going badly.* ◊ *I did badly* (= was not successful) *in my exams.* OPP well **3** 🔑 B1 not in an acceptable way: *to behave/sleep badly* ◊ *badly paid/treated* ◊ *The kids took the dog's death very badly* (= they were very unhappy). OPP well **4** 🔑 B1 used to emphasize how serious a situation

or an event is: *badly damaged/injured/hurt* ◊ *The country has been badly affected by recession.* ◊ *Everything's gone badly wrong!* **5** 🔑 B1 used to emphasize how much you want, need, etc. sb/sth: *The building is* **badly in need of** *repair.* ◊ *They wanted to win so badly.* ◊ *I miss her badly.* **6** 🔑 B1 in a way that makes people get a bad opinion about sth: *The economic crisis reflects badly on the government's policies.* ◊ *She's only trying to help, so don't* **think badly of** *her.* OPP **well 7 feel ~** to feel sorry or ashamed about sth: *~* **about sth** *She felt badly about what she had done.* ◊ *~* **for sb** *I feel badly for the other guys on the team.*

**ˌbadly ˈoff** *adj.* (**worse off, worst off**) **1** not having much money SYN **poor**: *We aren't too badly off but we can't afford a house like that.* OPP **well off 2** not in a good situation: *I've got quite a big room so I'm not too badly off.* OPP **well off**
**IDM** **be badly ˈoff for sth** (*BrE*) to not have enough of sth

**bad·mash** /bʌdˈmɑːʃ/ *noun* (*IndE*) a dishonest man

**bad·min·ton** /ˈbædmɪntən/ *noun* [U] a game like tennis played by two or four people, usually indoors. Players hit a small light kind of ball, originally with feathers around it (= a SHUTTLECOCK) across a high net using a RACKET.

**ˈbad-mouth** *verb* ~ *sb* (*informal*) to say unpleasant things about sb: *No one wants to employ somebody who bad-mouths their former employer.*

**bad·ness** /ˈbædnəs/ *noun* [U] the fact of being morally bad: *There was not a hint of badness in him.*

**ˌbad-ˈtempered** *adj.* often angry; in an angry mood: *She gets very bad-tempered when she's tired.*

**bae** /beɪ/ *noun* (*US, informal*) a person's boyfriend or girlfriend: *I'm going to see my bae.* ◊ *What's wrong, bae?*

**Baˌfana Baˈfana** /bəˌfɑːnə bəˈfɑːnə/ *noun* (*SAfrE*) a popular name for the South African national men's football (soccer) team

**baf·fle** /ˈbæfl/ *verb* to confuse sb completely; to be too difficult or strange for sb to understand or explain: ~ *sb His behaviour baffles me.* ◊ **be baffled (as to) why, how, where,** *etc*… *I'm baffled as to why she hasn't called.* ◊ *I'm baffled why she hasn't called.* ▶ **baffle·ment** *noun* [U]: *His reaction was one of bafflement.*

**BAFTA** /ˈbæftə/ *abbr., noun*
- **abbr.** British Academy of Film and Television Arts
- **noun** an award presented by the British Academy of Film and Television Arts: *He won a BAFTA for the role.*

**bag** 🅘 A1 /bæg/ *noun, verb*
- **noun**
- **CONTAINER 1** 🔑 A1 [C] (often in compounds) a container made of cloth, leather, plastic or paper, used to carry things in, especially when shopping or travelling: *He was carrying a heavy bag of groceries.* ◊ *It was wrapped in a brown paper bag.* ◊ *Put it in a black plastic garbage bag.* ◊ *She tipped out the contents of her bag* (= HANDBAG). **2** 🔑 A1 [C] a bag or case that you take when you are travelling; a piece of LUGGAGE: *I packed my bags and left for the airport.* ◊ *Each passenger is allowed one carry-on bag.* ⊃ see also DUFFEL BAG, SPONGE BAG, TOILET BAG
- **AMOUNT 3** [C] ~ **(of sth)** the amount contained in a bag: *She ate a bag of chips.* ⊃ see also GRAB BAG, MIXED BAG, RAGBAG **4 bags** [U, pl.] ~ **(of sth)** (*BrE, informal*) a large amount or a large number of sth: *Get in! There's bags of room.*
- **UNDER EYES 5 bags** [pl.] dark circles or loose folds of skin under the eyes, as a result of getting old or lack of sleep
- **UNPLEASANT WOMAN 6** [C] (*informal, especially BrE*) an offensive word for an unpleasant or angry older woman ⊃ see also RATBAG, SCUMBAG, WINDBAG
- **BIRDS/ANIMALS 7** [C, usually sing.] all the birds, animals, etc. shot or caught on one occasion HELP There are many other compounds ending in **bag**. You will find them at their place in the alphabet.

# bagatelle

**IDM** ˌbag and ˈbaggage with all your possessions, especially secretly or suddenly: *He threw her out onto the street, bag and baggage.* a ˌbag of ˈbones (*informal*) a very thin person or animal be in the ˈbag (*informal*) if sth is **in the bag**, it is almost certain to be won or achieved leave sb ˈholding the ˈbag (*NAmE*, *informal*) to suddenly make sb responsible for sth important, such as finishing a difficult job, that is really your responsibility (not) sb's ˈbag (*informal*) (not) sth that you are interested in or good at: *Poetry isn't really my bag.* ⇨ more at CAT, NERVE *n.*, PACK *v.*, TRICK *n.*

■ *verb* (-gg-)
- PUT INTO BAGS 1 ~ sth (up) to put sth into bags: *The fruit is washed, sorted and bagged at the farm.*
- CATCH ANIMAL 2 ~ sth (*informal*) to catch or kill an animal
- IN SPORT 3 ~ sth (*informal*) to score a goal, point, etc: *Harkin bagged two goals in last night's win.*
- CLAIM STH 4 ~ sth (*informal*) to claim sth as yours before sb else claims it; to take sth before sb else can get it: *Sally had managed to bag the two best seats.* ◊ *Quick, bag that table over there!*
- CRITICIZE SB/STH 5 ~ sb/sth (*AustralE*, *NZE*, *informal*) to criticize sb/sth
- DECIDE NOT TO DO STH 6 ~ sth (*NAmE*, *informal*) to decide not to do sth because you think it will not be successful or because you think it will be better to do it later: *They decided to bag the trip because they were short of cash.*

**IDM** ˈbags (I) … (*BrE*, *informal*) used to claim sth as yours before sb else can claim it: *Bags I sit in the front seat!*

**baga·telle** /ˌbæɡəˈtel/ *noun* 1 [U] a game played on a board with small balls that you try to hit into holes 2 [C, usually sing.] (*literary*) a small or unimportant thing or amount: *It cost a mere bagatelle.*

**bagel** /ˈbeɪɡl/ *noun* a hard bread roll in the shape of a ring

**bag·gage** /ˈbæɡɪdʒ/ *noun* [U] 1 bags, cases, etc. that contain sb's clothes and things when they are travelling **SYN** luggage: *excess baggage* (= weighing more than the limit allowed on a plane) ◊ *baggage handlers* (= people employed to load and unload baggage at airports) ◊ (*NAmE*) *We loaded our baggage into the car.* 2 the equipment that an army carries with it: *Extensive baggage trains followed the troops.* 3 the beliefs and attitudes that sb has as a result of their past experiences: *She was carrying a lot of emotional baggage.* **IDM** see BAG *n.*

▼ **WHICH WORD?**

**baggage / luggage / bags**
- **Luggage** is the usual word in *BrE*, but **baggage** is preferred in the context of the bags and cases that passengers take on a flight. In *NAmE* **baggage** is usually used.
- In *NAmE* **luggage** is more formal than **baggage** and is often used to describe the empty bags themselves: (*NAmE*) *I need to buy some new luggage for my vacation next month.* ◊ (*BrE*) *I need to buy a new suitcase for my holiday next month.*
- Both these words are uncountable nouns: *Do you have a lot of luggage?* ◊ *Two pieces of luggage have gone missing.* ◊ *Never leave baggage unattended.*
- **Bags** are individual pieces of baggage: *You're allowed one checked bag and one carry-on.* ◊ *How many bags do you have?*

ˈbaggage carousel (*also* ˈcarousel) *noun* a moving belt from which you collect your bags at an airport

ˈbaggage reclaim (*BrE*) (*NAmE* ˈbaggage claim) *noun* [U] the place at an airport where you get your bags, cases, etc. again after you have flown ⇨ WORDFINDER NOTE at AIRPORT

**Bag·gie**™ /ˈbæɡi/ *noun* (*NAmE*) a small bag made of clear plastic that is used for storing sandwiches, etc.

**baggy** /ˈbæɡi/ *adj.* (**baggier**, **baggiest**) (of clothes) fitting loosely: *a baggy T-shirt* **OPP** tight

**bagh** /bɑːɡ/ *noun* (*IndE*) a large garden or piece of land on which fruit trees are grown

ˈbag lady *noun* (*informal*) a woman who has no home and who walks around carrying her possessions with her

ˈbag lunch *noun* (*NAmE*) a meal of sandwiches, fruit, etc. that you take to school, work, etc. in a bag ⇨ compare BOX LUNCH, PACKED LUNCH

**bag·pipes** /ˈbæɡpaɪps/ (*also* **pipes**) *noun* [pl.] (*NAmE also* **bag·pipe** [sing.]) a musical instrument played especially in Scotland. The player blows air into a bag held under the arm and then slowly forces the air out through pipes to produce a noise. ⇨ picture at PIPE ▶ **bag·pipe** *adj.*: *bagpipe music*

**ba·guette** /bæˈɡet/ *noun* 1 (*also* ˌFrench ˈloaf, ˌFrench ˈstick) a LOAF of white bread in the shape of a long thick stick 2 a small baguette or part of one that is filled with food and eaten as a sandwich: *a cheese baguette*

**bah** /bɑː/ *exclamation* used to show a sound that people make because they do not approve of sth

**Baha'i** (*also* **Bahai**) /bəˈhaɪ, bɑːˈhɑːi/ *noun* [U] a religion that teaches that all people and religions are the same, and that there should be peace

**Ba·hasa In·do·nesia** /bəˌhɑːsə ˌɪndəˈniːʒə; *BrE also* -ˈniːziə/ *noun* [U] the official language of Indonesia

**Ba·hasa Ma·lay·sia** /bəˌhɑːsə məˈleɪʒə; *BrE also* -ˈleɪziə/ *noun* [U] the official language of Malaysia

**bail**¹ 💠+ **C1** /beɪl/ *noun*, *verb*
■ *noun* 1 💠+ **C1** [U] money that sb agrees to pay if a person accused of a crime does not appear at their trial. When bail has been arranged, the accused person is allowed to go free until the trial: *Can anyone put up bail for you?* ◊ *She was released on £2000 bail.* ◊ *Bail was set at $1 million.* ◊ *The judge granted/refused bail.* ◊ **on~** *He committed another offence while he was out on bail* (= after bail had been agreed). 2 [C, usually pl.] (in CRICKET) either of the two small pieces of wood on top of each set of three wooden posts (called STUMPS)
**IDM** ˌjump/ˌskip ˈbail to fail to appear at your trial after you have paid money to be allowed to go free until the trial: *He skipped bail and went on the run for two weeks.*
■ *verb* 1 (*BrE also* **bale**) [T, usually passive] to release sb on bail: **be bailed (to do sth)** *He was bailed to appear in court on 15 March.* 2 [I] (*NAmE*, *informal*) to leave a place, especially quickly: *Sorry, I really have to bail.* 3 [T] **~ sb (up)** (*AustralE*, *NZE*, *informal*) to approach sb and talk to them, often when they do not want this
**PHRV** ˌbail ˈout (of sth) (*BrE also* ˌbale ˈout (of sth)) 1 to jump out of a plane that is going to crash 2 to escape from a situation that you no longer want to be involved in: *I'd understand if you wanted to bail out of this relationship.* ˌbail ˈout | ˌbail sth↔ˈout (*BrE also* ˌbale ˈout, ˌbale sth↔ˈout) to empty water from sth by lifting it out with your hand or a container: *He had to stop rowing to bail water out of the boat.* ◊ *The boat will sink unless we bail out.* ˌbail sb↔ˈout to pay sb's bail for them ˌbail sb↔ˈout (of sth) (*BrE also* ˌbale sb↔ˈout (of sth)) to rescue sb from a difficult situation: *The government had to bail the company out of financial difficulty.* ◊ *Ryan's late goal bailed out his team.* ⇨ SYNONYMS at SAVE

**bai·ley** /ˈbeɪli/ *noun* the open area of a castle, inside the outer wall

**bail·iff** /ˈbeɪlɪf/ *noun* 1 (*BrE*) a law officer whose job is to take the possessions and property of people who cannot pay their debts 2 (*BrE*) a person employed to manage land or a large farm for sb else 3 (*NAmE*) an official who keeps order in court, takes people to their seats, watches prisoners, etc.

**bail·out** /ˈbeɪlaʊt/ *noun* an act of giving money to a company, a foreign country, etc. that has very serious financial problems

**bairn** /beən; *NAmE* bern/ *noun* (*ScotE*, *NEngE*) a child

**bait** /beɪt/ *noun*, *verb*
■ *noun* [U, C] 1 food put on a HOOK to catch fish or in nets, TRAPS, etc. to catch animals or birds: *The fish took the bait.* ⇨ WORDFINDER NOTE at FISHING 2 a person or thing that is used to attract sb in order to catch them or make them do what you want

# balance

■ **verb 1** ~ **sth (with sth)** to place food on a HOOK, in a TRAP, etc. in order to attract or catch a wild animal or person: *He baited the trap with a piece of meat.* **2** ~ **sb** to deliberately try to make sb angry or to hurt them by making cruel remarks **3** **-baiting** (in compound nouns) the activity of attacking a wild animal with dogs: *bear-baiting*

**bait-and-ˈswitch** *noun* [C, usually sing.] a selling method where advertisements for low-priced products are used to attract customers, who are then persuaded to buy sth more expensive

**baize** /beɪz/ *noun* [U] a type of thick cloth made of wool that is usually green, used especially for covering card tables and BILLIARD, SNOOKER or POOL tables

**bake** 🔑 **B1** /beɪk/ *verb, noun*
■ **verb 1** 🔑 **B1** [T, I] to cook food in an oven without extra fat or liquid; to be cooked in this way: ~ **(sth)** *to bake bread/biscuits/cookies* ◊ *baked potatoes/apples* ◊ *the delicious smell of baking bread* ◊ *I've been baking all morning.* ◊ ~ **sth for sb** *I'm baking a birthday cake for Alex.* ◊ ~ **sb sth** *I'm baking Alex a cake.* **2** [I, T] to become hard when heated; to make sth hard by heating it: *The bricks are left in the kiln to bake.* ◊ ~ **sth (+ adj.)** *The sun had baked the ground hard.* **3** [I] (*informal*) to be or become very hot: *We sat baking in the sun.* ⟶ see also HALF-BAKED
■ **noun 1** a dish consisting of mixed ingredients that is cooked in the oven: *a pasta/vegetable bake* **2** (*NAmE*) a social event at which a specific food is cooked and eaten

**baked Alˈaska** /ˌbeɪkt əˈlæskə/ *noun* [C, U] a DESSERT made of cake and ice cream covered in MERINGUE and cooked quickly in a very hot oven

**baked ˈbeans** *noun* [pl.] **1** (*especially BrE*) small white beans cooked in a tomato sauce and usually sold in cans **2** (*NAmE*) = BOSTON BAKED BEANS

**baked ˈgoods** *noun* [pl.] (*especially NAmE*) foods like bread and cakes that are cooked in an oven

**baked poˈtato** (*BrE also* **jacket poˈtato**) *noun* a potato cooked in its skin in an oven: *a baked potato and beans*

**Bakeˈlite™** /ˈbeɪkəlaɪt; *NAmE also* -klaɪt/ *noun* [U] a type of hard plastic used in the past for electrical equipment, etc.

**baker** /ˈbeɪkə(r)/ *noun* **1** a person whose job is baking and selling bread and cakes **2** **baker's** (*pl.* **bakers**) (*BrE*) a shop that sells bread and cakes: *I'm just going to the baker's.*

**baker's ˈdozen** *noun* [sing.] (*old-fashioned*) a group of thirteen (= one more than a dozen, which is twelve) **ORIGIN** This phrase comes from bakers' old custom of adding one extra loaf to an order of a dozen.

**bakery** /ˈbeɪkəri/ *noun* (*pl.* **-ies**) (*NAmE also* **bakeˈshop**) a place where bread and cakes are made and/or sold

**ˈbake sale** *noun* (*NAmE*) an event at which cakes, etc. are baked and sold to make money, usually for a school or charity

**bakeˈshop** /ˈbeɪkʃɒp; *NAmE* -ʃɑːp/ *noun* (*NAmE*) = BAKERY

**bakeˈware** /ˈbeɪkweə(r); *NAmE* -wer/ *noun* [U] tins and other containers used for baking

**baking** /ˈbeɪkɪŋ/ *noun, adj.*
■ **noun** [U] **1** the process of cooking using dry heat in an oven: *I've always enjoyed baking.* ◊ *a baking dish/tin* **2** bread, cakes, etc. that sb has made: *Try some of Ellie's delicious home baking.*
■ **adj.** (*also* **baking ˈhot**) (*informal*) extremely hot

**ˈbaking flour** *noun* [U] (*US*) = SELF-RISING FLOUR

**ˈbaking powder** *noun* [U] a mixture of powders that are used to make cakes rise and become light as they are baked

**ˈbaking sheet** (*BrE also* **ˈbaking tray**, *NAmE also* **ˈcookie sheet**) *noun* a small sheet of metal used for baking food on

**ˈbaking soda** *noun* [U] = SODIUM BICARBONATE

**bakkie** /ˈbæki/ *SAfrE* /ˈbʌki/ *noun* (*SAfrE*) a motor vehicle with low sides and no roof at the back, used for transporting goods or people, or as a car ⟶ compare PICKUP

---

**bakˈsheesh** (*also* **backˈsheesh**) /ˌbækˈʃiːʃ/ *noun* [U] (*informal*) (in some Asian countries) a small amount of money that is given as a gift to poor people or given to sb to thank them or to persuade them to help you

**balaˈclava** /ˌbæləˈklɑːvə/ (*also* **balaclava ˈhelmet**) *noun* (*especially BrE*) a type of hat made of wool that covers most of the head, neck and face

**balaˈfon** /ˈbæləfɒn; *NAmE* -fɑːn/ *noun* a large type of XYLOPHONE (= a musical instrument with rows of wooden bars that you hit) that is used in West African music

**balaˈlaika** /ˌbæləˈlaɪkə/ *noun* a musical instrument like a guitar with a body in the shape of a TRIANGLE and two, three, or four strings, popular especially in Russia

**balance** 🔑 **B1** 🅞 /ˈbæləns/ *noun, verb*
■ **noun**
• **EQUAL AMOUNTS 1** 🔑 **B1** [U, sing.] a situation in which different things exist in equal, correct or good amounts: *This newspaper maintains a good balance in its presentation of different opinions.* ◊ *Tourists often disturb the delicate balance of nature on the island.* ◊ *His wife's death disturbed the* **balance of his mind.** ◊ ~ **between A and B** *Try to keep a balance between work and relaxation.* ◊ **in** ~ *It is important to keep the different aspects of your life in balance.* ⟶ see also WORK-LIFE BALANCE ⟶ see also IMBALANCE
• **OF BODY 2** 🔑 **B1** [U] the ability to keep steady with an equal amount of weight on each side of the body: *Athletes need a good sense of balance.* ◊ *I struggled to* **keep my balance** *on my new skates.* ◊ *She cycled round the corner,* **lost her balance** *and fell off.*
• **MONEY 3** 🔑 **B1** [C, usually sing.] the amount that is left after taking numbers or money away from a total: *to check your* **bank balance** (= to find out how much money there is in your account) ⟶ WORDFINDER NOTE at BANK **4** 🔑 **B1** [C, usually sing.] an amount of money still owed after some payment has been made: *The balance of $500 must be paid within 90 days.*
• **LARGEST PART 5 the** ~ **(of sth)** the largest part of a group or an amount; the position of advantage or attention: *The balance of opinion was that work was more important than leisure.*
• **INSTRUMENT FOR WEIGHING 6** [C] an instrument for weighing things, with a bar that is supported in the middle and has dishes hanging from each end

**IDM** **(on) the balance of ˈevidence/probaˈbility** (*formal*) (considering) the evidence on both sides of an argument, to find the most likely reason for or result of sth **(be/hang) in the ˈbalance** if the future of sth/sb, or the result of sth is/hangs **in the balance**, it is not certain: *The long-term future of the space programme hangs in the balance.* **(catch/throw sb) off ˈbalance 1** to make sb unsteady and in danger of falling: *I was thrown off balance by the sudden gust of wind.* **2** to make sb surprised and no longer calm: *The senator was clearly caught off balance by the unexpected question.* **on ˈbalance** after considering all the information: *On balance, the company has had a successful year.* ⟶ more at REDRESS *v.*, STRIKE *v.*, SWING *v.*, TIP *v.*

■ **verb**
• **KEEP STEADY 1** 🔑 **B1** [I, T] to put your body or sth else into a position where it is steady and does not fall: ~ **on sth** *How long can you balance on one leg?* ◊ ~ **sth on sth** *The television was precariously balanced on top of a pile of books.* ◊ *She balanced the cup on her knee.*
• **BE/KEEP EQUAL 2** 🔑 **B1** [T] ~ **A with/and B** to give equal importance to two things or parts of sth which are very different: *She tries to balance the needs of her children with those of her employer.* **3** 🔑 **B2** [I, T] to be equal in value, amount, etc. to sth else that has the opposite effect **SYN** **offset**: ~ **out** *The good and bad effects of any decision will usually balance out.* ◊ ~ **sth out** *This year's profits will balance out our previous losses.* ◊ **be balanced by sth** *His lack of experience was balanced by a willingness to learn.*
• **COMPARE 4** [T] ~ **A against B** to compare the relative importance of two things which are different: *The cost of obtaining legal advice needs to be balanced against its benefits.*

# balance beam

- **MONEY 5** [T] ~ **sth** to manage finances so that the money spent is equal to the money received; to show this in the accounts: *In order to* **balance the budget** *severe spending cuts had to be made.* ◊ *The law requires the council to* **balance its books** *each year.* **6** [I] (of an account) to have an equal amount of money spent and money received: *I tried to work out why the books wouldn't balance.*

**'balance beam** *noun* (*NAmE*) = BEAM

**bal·anced** /ˈbælənst/ *adj.* [usually before noun] (*approving*) keeping or showing a balance so that different things or different parts of sth exist in equal or correct amounts: *The programme presented a balanced view of the two sides of the conflict.* ◊ *a balanced diet* (= one with the quantity and variety of food needed for good health)

**balance of 'payments** *noun* [sing.] the difference between the amount a country pays for imports and the amount it receives for exports in a particular period of time

**balance of 'power** *noun* [sing.] **1** the way in which political or military strength is divided between two or more countries or groups: **the ~ between A and B** *the changing balance of power between the working and middle class* **2** the power held by a small group which can give its support to either of two larger and equally strong groups

**balance of 'trade** (*also* **'trade balance**) *noun* [sing.] the difference in value between imports and exports: *a balance-of-trade deficit* (= when a country spends more on imports than it earns from exports)

**'balance sheet** *noun* (*finance*) a written statement showing the amount of money and property that a company has and listing what has been received and paid out

**'bal·an·cing act** *noun* [usually sing.] a process in which sb tries to please two or more people or groups who want different things: *The UN must perform a delicate balancing act between the different sides in the conflict.*

**bal·cony** /ˈbælkəni/ *noun* (*pl.* **-ies**) **1** a platform that is built on the upstairs outside wall of a building, with a wall or RAIL around it. You can get out onto a balcony from an upstairs room. **2** an area of seats upstairs in a theatre ⇒ see also CIRCLE *noun*, FIRST BALCONY ⇒ **WORDFINDER NOTE** at THEATRE

**bald** /bɔːld/ *adj.* **1** having little or no hair on the head: *He started* **going bald** *in his twenties.* **2** without any of the usual hair, marks, etc. covering the skin or surface of sth: *Our dog has a bald patch on its leg.* ◊ *a bald tyre* (= a tyre whose surface has become smooth) **3** without any extra explanation or detail to help you understand or accept what is being said: *The bald fact is that we don't need you any longer.* ◊ *The letter was a bald statement of our legal position.* ⇒ see also BALDLY ▶ **bald·ness** *noun* [U] **IDM** **(as) bald as a coot** (*BrE, informal*) completely bald ⇒ more at TOP *n.*

**bald 'eagle** *noun* a North American BIRD OF PREY (= a bird that kills other creatures for food) with a white head and white tail feathers. It is used as a symbol of the US.

**bald-'faced** *adj.* (*disapproving, especially NAmE*) making no attempt to hide your dishonest behaviour **SYN** **barefaced**, **blatant**: *bald-faced lies*

**bald·ing** /ˈbɔːldɪŋ/ *adj.* starting to lose the hair on your head: *a short balding man with glasses*

**bald·ly** /ˈbɔːldli/ *adv.* in a few words with nothing extra or unnecessary: *'You're lying,' he said baldly.*

**baldy** (*also* **baldie**) /ˈbɔːldi/ *noun* (*pl.* **-ies**) (*informal, offensive*) a person who has no hair or almost no hair on their head

**bale** /beɪl/ *noun, verb*
- *noun* a large amount of a light material pressed tightly together and tied up: *bales of hay/straw/cotton/wool*
- *verb* **1** ~ **sth** to make sth into bales: *The waste paper is baled, then sent for recycling.* **2** ~ **sb (to do sth)** (*BrE*) = BAIL (1)

**PHRV** **bale 'out (of sth)** | **bale (sth) ↔ 'out** | **bale sb ↔ 'out (of sth)** (*BrE*) = BAIL OUT (OF STH), BAIL OUT, BAIL SB OUT (OF STH)

**bale·ful** /ˈbeɪlfl/ *adj.* (*literary*) **1** (of the way sb looks at sb/sth) threatening to do sth evil or to hurt sb: *a baleful glare/stare/look* ◊ *Her baleful eyes glared vindictively.* **2** having a harmful effect: *the baleful influence of the city's wealthy elite* ◊ *the baleful effects/consequences of the war* ▶ **bale·ful·ly** /-fəli/ *adv.*

**baler** /ˈbeɪlə(r)/ *noun* a machine for making paper, cotton, HAY, etc. into bales

**balk** (*especially NAmE*) = BAULK

**the Bal·kans** /ðə ˈbɔːlkənz; *BrE also* ˈbɒl-/ *noun* [pl.] a region of south-east Europe, including the countries to the south of the rivers Sava and Danube ▶ **Bal·kan** *adj.*: *the Balkan Peninsula*

**balky** /ˈbɔːlki, ˈbɒːki/ *adj.* (*NAmE*) (of a person or machine) refusing or failing to do what you want them to do

**ball** /bɔːl/ *noun, verb*
- *noun* **1** a round object used for throwing, hitting or kicking in games and sports: *a golf/tennis/bowling/soccer ball* ◊ *to* **hit/throw/kick/catch a ball** ◊ *The ball bounced off down the road.* ⇒ see also EXERCISE BALL **2** ~ **(of sth)** a round object or a thing that has been formed into a round shape: *The sun was a huge ball of fire low on the horizon.* ◊ *a ball of yarn/string* ◊ *The little girl curled into a ball in her mother's arms.* ⇒ see also DISCO BALL **3** a kick, hit or throw of the ball in some sports: *He sent over a high ball.* ⇒ see also LONG BALL **4** (in baseball) a throw by the PITCHER that is outside the STRIKE ZONE (= the area between the BATTER'S upper arms and knees) **5** ~ **of the foot/hand** the part below the big toe or the THUMB ⇒ **VISUAL VOCAB** page V1 **6** [usually pl.] (*taboo, informal*) a TESTICLE ⇒ see also BALLS *noun* **7** a large formal party with dancing

**IDM** **a ball and 'chain** a problem that prevents you from doing what you would like to do **the ball is in your/sb's 'court** it is your/sb's responsibility to take action next: *They've offered me the job, so the ball's in my court now.* **a ball of 'energy / 'fire** (*informal*) a person who is full of energy and enthusiasm **get/set/start/keep the ball 'rolling** to make sth start happening; to make sure that sth continues to happen **have a 'ball** (*informal*) to enjoy yourself a lot **have something/a lot on the 'ball** (*US, informal*) to be capable of doing a job very well; to be intelligent **(be) on the 'ball** to be aware of and understand what is happening and be able to react quickly: *The new publicity manager is really on the ball.* **pick up/take the ball and 'run with it** (*especially NAmE*) to develop an idea or plan that already exists: *It's up to the private sector to take the ball and run with it.* **play 'ball (with sb)** **1** (*NAmE*) to play with a ball: *Chris was in the park playing ball with the kids.* **2** (*informal*) to be willing to work with other people in a helpful way, especially so that sb can get what they want ⇒ more at CARRY, DROP *v.*, EYE *n.*

- *verb* **1** [I, T] to form sth or be formed into the shape of a ball: **~ (into sth)** *Her hands balled into fists.* ◊ **~ sth (into sth)** *My hands were balled into fists.* **2** [T] **~ sb** (*NAmE, taboo, slang*) (of a man) to have sex with a woman

**bal·lad** /ˈbæləd/ *noun* **1** a song or poem that tells a story: *a medieval ballad about a knight and a lady* **2** a slow song about love: *Her latest single is a ballad.*

**bal·lad·eer** /ˌbæləˈdɪə(r); *NAmE* -ˈdɪr/ *noun* a person who sings or writes BALLADS

**ball-and-'socket joint** *noun* (*anatomy*) a JOINT such as the HIP JOINT at the top of the leg, in which a piece of bone in the shape of a ball moves inside a curved hollow part

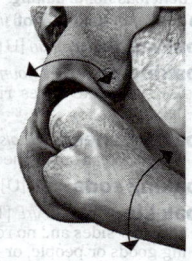
ball-and-socket joint

**bal·last** /'bæləst/ noun [U] **1** heavy material placed in a ship or HOT-AIR BALLOON to make it heavier and keep it steady **2** a layer of stones that makes a strong base on which a road, railway, etc. can be built

**ball bearing** noun a ring of small metal balls used in a machine to enable the parts to turn smoothly; one of these small metal balls

**ball·boy** /'bɔːlbɔɪ/ noun a boy who picks up the balls for the players in a tennis match ⊃ see also BALLGIRL

**ball-breaker** noun (informal) a sexually aggressive woman who destroys men's confidence
▶ **ball-breaking** adj.

**ball·cock** /'bɔːlkɒk; NAmE -kɑːk/ noun a device with a floating ball that controls the amount of water going into a container, for example the water tank of a toilet

**bal·ler·ina** /ˌbælə'riːnə/ noun a female dancer in BALLET ⊃ see also PRIMA BALLERINA

**bal·let** /'bæleɪ; NAmE bæ'leɪ/ noun **1** [U] a style of dancing that tells a dramatic story with music but no talking or singing: *She wants to be a **ballet dancer**.* ◊ *ballet shoes* ⊃ WORDFINDER NOTE at DANCE **2** [C] a story or work of art performed by a group of ballet dancers: *'Swan Lake' is one of the great classical ballets.* **3** [C + sing./pl. v.] a group of dancers who work and perform ballet together: *members of the Royal Ballet*

**bal·let·ic** /bæ'letɪk/ adj. (formal, approving) smooth and beautiful, like a movement or a dancer in ballet

**ball game** noun **1** any game played with a ball **2** (NAmE) a game of baseball: *Are you going to the ball game?*
**IDM** **a (whole) different / new ball game** (informal) a completely different kind of situation

**ball·girl** /'bɔːlɡɜːl; NAmE -ɡɜːrl/ noun a girl who picks up the balls for the players in a tennis match ⊃ see also BALLBOY

**ball·hawk** /'bɔːlhɔːk/ noun (US, informal) a player who is good at getting or catching balls, especially in AMERICAN FOOTBALL, baseball or basketball

**ball hockey** noun [U] (CanE) a version of ICE HOCKEY played on a hard surface without ice, and with a ball instead of a PUCK

**bal·listic** /bə'lɪstɪk/ adj. connected with ballistics
**IDM** **go bal'listic** (informal) to become very angry: *He went ballistic when I told him.*

**bal·listic 'missile** noun a MISSILE that is fired into the air at a particular speed and angle in order to fall in the right place

**bal·lis·tics** /bə'lɪstɪks/ noun [U] the scientific study of things that are shot or fired through the air, such as bullets and MISSILES

**bal·loon** /bə'luːn/ noun, verb
■ noun **1** a small bag made of very thin rubber that becomes larger and rounder when you fill it with air or gas. Balloons are brightly coloured and used as decorations or toys: *to blow up/burst/pop a balloon* ⊃ compare TRIAL BALLOON **2** (also **hot-air balloon**) a large balloon made of strong material that is filled with hot air or gas to make it rise in the air, usually carrying a BASKET for passengers
**IDM** **when the bal'loon goes up** (BrE, informal) when the trouble that you are expecting begins ⊃ more at LEAD²
■ verb **1** [I] ~ **(out/up)** to form a round shape: *Her skirt ballooned out in the wind.* **2** [I] to increase rapidly **3** [I] (usually **go ballooning**) to travel in a HOT-AIR BALLOON as a sport or for entertainment

**bal'loon whisk** noun a WHISK that you hold in your hand, made of thin pieces of curved wire

**bal·lot** /'bælət/ noun, verb
■ noun **1** [U, C] the system of voting in writing and usually in secret; an occasion on which a vote is held: *The chairperson is chosen by secret ballot.* ◊ *The union cannot call a strike unless it **holds a ballot** of members.* ◊ *~ **for** sth a ballot for the Conservative leadership* ◊ *~ **on/over** sth a ballot over strike action* ⊃ SYNONYMS at ELECTION **2** (BrE also **'ballot paper**) [C] the piece of paper on which sb marks who they are voting for: *What percentage of eligible voters **cast their ballots**?* **3** **the ballot** [sing.] the total number of votes in an election: *She won 58.8% of the ballot.* ⊃ see also POLL noun ⊃ WORDFINDER NOTE at UNION
■ verb **1** [T] ~ **sb (on/over sth)** to ask sb to vote in writing and secretly about sth **SYN** poll: *The union balloted its members on the proposed changes.* **2** [I] to vote secretly about sth: *~ **for** sth The workers balloted for a strike.* ◊ *~ **to do** sth Ambulance crews balloted unanimously to reject the deal.*

**'ballot box** noun **1** [C] a box in which people put their BALLOTS after voting **2 the ballot box** [sing.] the system of voting in an election: *The people make their wishes known through the ballot box.*

**'ballot paper** noun (BrE) = BALLOT (2)

**ball·park** /'bɔːlpɑːk; NAmE -pɑːrk/ noun **1** [C] (especially NAmE) a place where baseball is played **2** [sing.] an area or a range within which an amount is likely to be correct or within which sth can be measured: *The offers for the contract were all **in the same ballpark**.* ◊ *If you said five million you'd be **in the ballpark**.* ◊ *Give me a **ballpark figure** (= a number that is approximately right).*

**ball·play·er** /'bɔːlpleɪə(r)/ noun (NAmE, informal) a person who plays baseball, especially a professional: *major-league ballplayers*

**ball·point** /'bɔːlpɔɪnt/ (also **ballpoint 'pen**) noun a pen with a very small metal ball at its point, that rolls INK (= coloured liquid for writing, etc.) onto the paper ⊃ compare BIRO™

**ball·room** /'bɔːlruːm; -rʊm/ noun a very large room used for dancing on formal occasions ⊃ compare DANCE HALL ⊃ WORDFINDER NOTE at DANCE

**ballroom 'dancing** noun [U] a type of dancing done with a partner and using particular fixed steps and movements to particular types of music such as the WALTZ

**balls** /bɔːlz/ noun, verb
■ noun (taboo, slang) **1** [U] (BrE) ideas, statements or beliefs that you think are silly or not true **SYN** nonsense: *That's a load of balls!* **2** [pl.] courage: *She's got balls, I'll say that for her.* ◊ *It took a lot of balls to do that.* **3 Balls!** (BrE) exclamation used as a swear word when you are disagreeing with sth, or when you are angry about sth **HELP** Less offensive ways to express this are 'Nonsense!', 'Rubbish!' or 'Come off it!' **4** [pl.] TESTICLES
**IDM** **go 'balls out** (taboo, slang) to do sth in a very determined or extreme way, especially when it means taking risks: *The team went balls out in the final.*
■ verb
**PHRV** **balls sth↔up** (BrE, taboo, slang) to do sth very badly ⊃ related noun BALLS-UP **HELP** A more polite way of saying this is **foul sth up**, **mess sth up**, or **bungle sth**.

**'balls-up** noun (BrE, taboo, slang) something that has been done very badly: *I made a real balls-up of my exams.*

**ballsy** /'bɔːlzi/ adj. (informal, especially NAmE) very determined and showing a lot of courage: *She is one ballsy lady!*

**bally·hoo** /ˌbæli'huː; NAmE 'bælihuː/ noun [U] (informal, disapproving) unnecessary noise and excitement

**balm** /bɑːm/ noun [U, C, usually sing.] **1** (also **bal·sam**) oil with a pleasant smell that is obtained from some types of trees and plants, used in the past to help HEAL wounds (= make them better), for example **2** a liquid, cream, etc. that has a pleasant smell and is used to make wounds less painful or skin softer: *lip balm* **3** (literary) something that makes you feel calm or relaxed

**balmy** /'bɑːmi/ adj. (approving) (of the air, weather, etc.) warm and pleasant **SYN** mild: *a balmy summer evening*

**ba·lo·ney** /bə'ləʊni/ noun [U] **1** (informal, especially NAmE) ideas, statements or beliefs that you think are silly or not true; lies **SYN** nonsense: *Don't give me that baloney!* **2** [U] (NAmE) = BOLOGNA

# balsa

**bal·sa** /ˈbɔːlsə/ (also **ˈbalsa wood**) noun [U] the light wood of the tropical American **ˈbalsa tree**, used especially for making models

**bal·sam** /ˈbɔːlsəm/ noun **1** [U, C] = BALM **2** [C] any plant or tree from which BALM is obtained

**bal·sam·ic vin·egar** /ˌbɔːlˌsæmɪk ˈvɪnɪɡə(r)/ noun [U] a dark sweet Italian VINEGAR, stored in BARRELS (= round wooden containers) to give it a particular taste

**balti** /ˈbɔːlti, ˈbɒl-; NAmE ˈbɑːl-/ noun [C, U] a type of meat or vegetable dish cooked in Pakistani style, usually served in a round metal pan which gives its name to the dish

**Bal·tic** /ˈbɔːltɪk/ adj. relating to the Baltic Sea in northern Europe and the countries surrounding it: *the Baltic republics of Estonia, Latvia and Lithuania*

**bal·us·trade** /ˌbæləˈstreɪd; NAmE ˈbæləstreɪd/ noun a row of posts, joined together at the top, built along the edge of a BALCONY, bridge, etc. to prevent people from falling off, or as a decoration

**bam** /bæm/ exclamation (informal) **1** used to represent the sound of a sudden loud hit or a gun being fired: *She pointed the gun at him and—bam!* **2** used to show that sth happens very suddenly: *I saw him yesterday and—bam!—I realized I was still in love with him.*

**bam·boo** /ˌbæmˈbuː/ noun [C, U] (pl. **-oos**) a tall plant that is a member of the grass family and has hard hollow STEMS that are used for making furniture, POLES, etc: *a bamboo grove* ◊ *a bamboo chair* ◊ *bamboo shoots* (= young bamboo plants that can be eaten) ➾ VISUAL VOCAB page V7

**bam·boo·zle** /bæmˈbuːzl/ verb ~ **sb** (informal) to confuse sb, especially by tricking them

**BAME** /ˌbiː eɪ em ˈiː, beɪm/ abbr. (BrE) black, Asian and minority ethnic (used in the UK to refer to people who are not white) SYN **BME**: *Around 20% of the teachers are from BAME backgrounds.*

**ban** ❶ B1 /bæn/ verb, noun
- verb (-nn-) **1** ❶ B1 to decide or say officially that sth is not allowed SYN **prohibit**: ~ *sth The law effectively bans smoking in all public places.* ◊ *a list of **banned** substances* ◊ *~ sth from sth a campaign to ban sugary drinks from schools* **2** ❶ B1 [usually passive] to order sb not to do sth, go somewhere, etc., especially officially: **be banned from (doing) sth** *He was banned from the meeting.* ◊ *(BrE) He was banned from driving for six months.* ◊ **be banned** *The sprinter has been **banned for life** after failing a drugs test.*
- noun **1** ❶ B1 an official rule that says that sth is not allowed: *a smoking ban* ◊ *to impose/lift a ban* ◊ **~on sth** *They are calling for a **blanket ban** (= complete ban) on the use of phones while driving.* **2** an official decision that means a person is not allowed to do sth or go somewhere for a period of time: *a five-year driving ban for various offences* ◊ **~from sth** *His behaviour led to a life ban from international football.*

**banal** /bəˈnɑːl; NAmE also ˈbeɪnl/ adj. (disapproving) very ordinary and containing nothing that is interesting or important

**ban·al·ity** /bəˈnæləti/ noun [U, C] (pl. **-ies**) (disapproving) the fact of being banal; things, remarks, etc. that are banal: *the banality of modern city life* ◊ *They exchanged banalities for a couple of minutes.*

**ba·nana** ❶ A1 /bəˈnɑːnə; NAmE -ˈnænə/ noun [C, U] a long curved fruit with a thick yellow skin and that is soft inside, which grows on trees in hot countries: *a bunch of bananas* ◊ *mashed banana* ➾ VISUAL VOCAB page V4
IDM **go baˈnanas** (slang) to become angry, crazy or silly

**baˈnana belt** noun (NAmE, informal) a region where the weather is warm

**baˌnana reˈpublic** noun (disapproving, offensive) a poor country with a weak government, that depends on foreign money

**baˈnana skin** noun (BrE, informal) something that could cause sb to have problems or feel embarrassed, especially sb in a public position

**baˌnana ˈsplit** noun a cold DESSERT (= a sweet dish) made from a banana that is cut in half along its length and filled with ice cream, nuts, etc.

**band** ❶ A1 /bænd/ noun, verb
- noun
- GROUP OF MUSICIANS **1** ❶ B1 [C + sing./pl. v.] a small group of musicians who play popular music together, often with a singer or singers: *a rock/punk/jazz band* ◊ *He plays drums in a band that he formed with some friends.* ◊ *The band is/are playing a gig in Liverpool tonight.* ◊ **band members** ➾ see also BOY BAND, GIRL BAND **2** [C + sing./pl. v.] a group of musicians who play BRASS and PERCUSSION instruments: *a military band* ➾ see also BIG BAND, BRASS BAND, MARCHING BAND, ONE-MAN BAND ➾ WORDFINDER NOTE at DANCE
- GROUP OF PEOPLE **3** [C + sing./pl. v.] a group of people who do sth together or who have the same ideas, interests or achievements: *a band of outlaws/rebels* ◊ *He persuaded a small band of volunteers to help.*
- THIN PIECE OF MATERIAL/COLOUR **4** [C] a thin flat piece or circle of any material that is put around things, for example to hold them together or to make them stronger: *She always ties her hair back in a band.* ◊ *All babies in the hospital have name bands on their wrists.* ◊ *She wore a simple band of gold* (= a ring) *on her finger.* ➾ see also ARMBAND, HAIRBAND, RUBBER BAND, SWEATBAND, WAISTBAND **5** [C] a line of colour or material on sth that is different from what is around it: *a white plate with a blue band around the edge* ➾ WORDFINDER NOTE at PATTERN
- OF RADIO WAVES **6** (also **ˈwave·band**) [C] a range of radio waves: *Short-wave radio uses the 20–50-metre band.*
- RANGE **7** [C] a range of numbers, ages, prices, etc. within which people or things are counted or measured: *the 25–35 age band* ◊ *tax bands*
- verb
- WITH COLOUR/MATERIAL **1** [usually passive] to put a band of a different colour or material around sth: **be banded (+ adj.)** *Many insects are banded black and yellow.*
- PUT INTO RANGE **2** [usually passive] (BrE) to organize sth into bands of price, income, etc: **be banded** *Tax is banded according to income.*
PHRV **ˌband toˈgether** to form a group in order to achieve sth: *Local people banded together to fight the drug dealers.*

**ban·dage** /ˈbændɪdʒ/ noun, verb
- noun a long narrow piece of cloth used for tying around a part of the body that has been hurt in order to protect or support it ➾ WORDFINDER NOTE at HURT
- verb ~ **sth/sb (up)** to wrap a bandage around a part of the body in order to protect it because it is injured

**ˈBand-Aid™** noun (especially NAmE) **1** (BrE also **ˈplas·ter**, **ˈsticking plaster**) [C, U] material that can be stuck to the skin to protect a small wound or cut; a piece of this **2** (disapproving) a temporary solution to a problem that does not really solve it at all

**ban·dana** (also **ban·danna**) /bænˈdænə/ noun a piece of brightly coloured cloth worn around the neck or head

**B and B** (also **B & B, b and b, b & b**) /ˌbiː ən ˈbiː/ abbr. (informal, especially BrE) BED AND BREAKFAST

**ˈband council** noun (CanE) a local form of Aboriginal government in Canada, consisting of an elected leader and COUNCILLORS

**ban·deau** /ˈbændəʊ; NAmE bænˈdoʊ/ noun (pl. **ban·deaus** or **ban·deaux** /ˈbændəʊz; NAmE bænˈdoʊz/) **1** a narrow band worn around the head to hold the hair in place **2** a piece of women's clothing that is tied around the body to cover the breasts: *a bandeau bikini top*

**bandh** /bɑːnd/ noun (IndE) a general strike

**bandi·coot** /ˈbændikuːt/ noun **1** a small Australasian animal with a long nose and long tail, which eats mainly insects **2** (also ˌbandicoot ˈrat) an Asian RAT

**band·ing** /ˈbændɪŋ/ noun [U] (BrE) = STREAMING (1)

**ban·dit** /ˈbændɪt/ noun a member of an armed group of thieves who attack travellers

**ban·dit·ry** /ˈbændɪtri/ noun [U] (formal) acts of stealing and violence by BANDITS

**band·leader** /ˈbændliːdə(r)/ *noun* a player who is in charge of a band, especially a jazz band

**band·mas·ter** /ˈbændmɑːstə(r); NAmE -mæs-/ *noun* a person who conducts a military band or a BRASS BAND

**bando·bast** (*also* **bundo·bast, bundo·bust**) /ˈbʌndəbʌst/ *noun* [U, C, usually sing.] (*IndE*) preparation or an arrangement for dealing with sth: *The police bandobast was very effective.*

**ban·do·lier** (*also* **ban·do·leer**) /ˌbændəˈlɪə(r); NAmE -ˈlɪr/ *noun* a belt made for carrying bullets and worn over the shoulder

**bands·man** /ˈbændzmən/ *noun* (*pl.* **-men** /-mən/) a musician who plays in a military band or a BRASS band

**band·stand** /ˈbændstænd/ *noun* a covered platform outdoors, where musicians, especially a BRASS or military band, can stand and play

**band·wagon** /ˈbændwæɡən/ *noun* [usually sing.] an activity that more and more people are becoming involved in: *The World Cup bandwagon is starting to roll.* **IDM** **climb/jump on the ˈbandwagon** (*informal, disapproving*) to join others in doing sth that is becoming fashionable because you hope to become popular or successful yourself: *politicians eager to jump on the environmental bandwagon* **ORIGIN** In the US, political PARADES often included a band on a wagon. Political leaders would join them in the hope of winning popular support.

**band·width** /ˈbændwɪdθ, -wɪtθ/ *noun* [C, U] **1** a band of frequencies used for sending electronic signals **2** (*computing*) a measurement of the amount of information that a particular computer network or internet connection can send in a particular time. It is often measured in BITS per second.

**bandy** /ˈbændi/ *adj., verb, noun*
■ *adj.* (of the legs) curving, with the knees wide apart: *to be bandy-legged*
■ *verb* (**ban·dies, bandy·ing, ban·died, ban·died**) **IDM** **bandy ˈwords (with sb)** (*old-fashioned*) to argue with sb or speak rudely to them **PHRV** **bandy sth↔aˈbout/aˈround** [usually passive] if a name, a word, a story, etc., is bandied about/around, it is mentioned frequently by many people: *His name was being bandied about as a future prime minister.*
■ *noun* [U] a game similar to hockey, played on a field or on ice with a ball and large curved sticks

**bane** /beɪn/ *noun* [sing.] **the ~ of sb/sth** something that causes trouble and makes people unhappy: *The neighbours' kids are the bane of my life.*

**bane·ful** /ˈbeɪnfl/ *adj.* (*literary*) evil or causing evil

**bang** /bæŋ/ *verb, noun, adv., exclamation*
■ *verb* **1** [I, T] to hit sth in a way that makes a loud noise: **~ on sth** *She banged on the door angrily.* ◊ **~ sth (with sth)** *The baby was banging the table with his spoon.* ⊃ SYNONYMS at HIT **2** [I, T] to close sth or to be closed with a loud noise **SYN** **slam**: *A window was banging somewhere* (= opening and closing noisily). ◊ **+ adj.** *The door banged shut behind her.* ◊ **~ sth** *Don't bang the door when you go out!* ◊ **~ sth + adj.** *She banged the door shut.* **3** [T] **~ sth + adv./prep.** to put sth somewhere suddenly and violently **SYN** **slam**: *He banged the money down on the counter.* ◊ *She banged saucepans around irritably.* **4** [T] **~ sth (+ adv./prep.)** to hit sth, especially a part of the body, against sth by accident **SYN** **bump**: *She tripped and banged her knee on the desk.* **5** [T] **~ sb** (*taboo, slang*) (of a man) to have sex with a woman **IDM** see DRUM *n.*, HEAD *n.* **PHRV** **bang aˈround** (*also* **bang aˈbout** *especially in BrE*) to move around noisily: *We could hear the kids banging around upstairs.* **bang ˈinto sth/sb** to crash into or hit sth/sb by mistake: *I banged into a chair and hurt my leg.* **bang ˈon (about sth)** (*BrE, informal*) to talk a lot about sth in a boring way **SYN** **go on**: *He keeps banging on about his new job.* **bang sb↔ˈup** (*BrE, informal*) to put sb in prison **bang sth↔ˈup** (*NAmE, informal*) to damage or injure sth
■ *noun* **1** [C] a sudden loud noise: *The door swung shut with a bang.* ◊ *Suddenly there was a loud bang and a puff of smoke.* ⊃ see also BIG BANG **2** [C] a sudden painful noise on

a part of the body: *a bang on the head* **3 bangs** [pl.] (*NAmE*) (*BrE* **fringe**) the front part of sb's hair that is cut so that it hangs over their FOREHEAD **4** [U] = BHANG **5** [C] (*informal, computing*) the symbol (!)
**IDM** **ˌbang for your ˈbuck** (*especially NAmE, informal*) if you get more, better, etc. **bang for your buck**, you get better value for the money you spend or the effort you put in to sth **with a ˈbang** (*informal*) **1** very successfully: *The party went with a bang.* **2** in a way that everyone notices; with a powerful effect: *The team won their last four games, ending the season with a bang.* ⊃ more at EARTH *n.*
■ *adv.* (*informal, especially BrE*) exactly; completely: *Our computers are **bang up to date**.* ◊ *My estimate was bang on target.* ◊ *You're bang on time, as usual* ⊃ see also SLAP *adv.*
■ *exclamation* used to show the sound of sth loud, like a gun: *'Bang, bang, you're dead!' shouted the little boy.*

**ˌbanged ˈup** *adj.* (*NAmE, informal*) injured or damaged: *Two days after the accident she still looked pretty banged up.* ⊃ compare BANG SB UP, BANG STH UP

**bang·er** /ˈbæŋə(r)/ *noun* (*BrE, informal*) **1** a SAUSAGE: *bangers and mash* **2** (*NAmE* **beat·er**) an old car that is in bad condition **3** a FIREWORK that makes a loud noise when it explodes

**Bangla** /ˈbæŋɡlə/ *noun* [U] **1** the Bengali language **2** Bangladesh

**ban·gle** /ˈbæŋɡl/ *noun* a piece of jewellery in the form of a large ring of gold, silver, etc. worn loosely around the WRIST

**ˌbang-ˈup** *adj.* (*NAmE, informal*) very good

**bania** /ˈbʌnjə/ *noun* (*IndE*) **1** a person who sells things **2** (*disapproving*) a person who is interested in making money

**ban·ish** /ˈbænɪʃ/ *verb* **1** [usually passive] **~sb (from …) (to …)** to order sb to leave a place, especially a country, as a punishment **SYN** **exile**: *He was banished to Australia, where he died five years later.* ◊ *The children were banished from the dining room.* **2 ~sb/sth (from sth)** to make sb/sth go away; to get rid of sb/sth: *The sight of food banished all other thoughts from my mind.*

**ban·ish·ment** /ˈbænɪʃmənt/ *noun* [U] (*formal*) the punishment of being sent away from a place, especially from a country

**ban·is·ter** (*also* **ban·nis·ter**) /ˈbænɪstə(r)/ *noun* (*BrE also* **ban·is·ters** [pl.]) the posts and RAIL that you can hold for support when going up or down stairs: *to hold on to the banister/banisters* ⊃ picture at STAIRCASE

**banjo** /ˈbændʒəʊ/ *noun* (*pl.* **-os**) a musical instrument like a guitar, with a long neck, a round body and four or more strings

## bank ⓘ A1 /bæŋk/ *noun, verb*
■ *noun*
• **FOR MONEY 1** ⓘ A1 an organization that provides various financial services, for example keeping or lending money: *I don't have much money in the bank at the end of the month.* ◊ *I need to go to the bank* (= the local office of a bank). ◊ *a bank loan* ◊ *a bank manager* ⊃ WORDFINDER NOTE at MONEY ⊃ see also CENTRAL BANK, COMMERCIAL BANK, INVESTMENT BANK, PIGGY BANK, RESERVE BANK, SAVINGS BANK

**WORDFINDER** account, balance, credit, debit, deposit, interest, loan, statement, withdrawal

• **IN GAMBLING 2** a supply of money or things that are used as money in some games, especially those in which GAMBLING is involved
• **STH COLLECTED/STORED 3** an amount of sth that is collected; a place where sth is stored ready for use: *a bank of*

# bankable 106

*knowledge* ◊ *a blood/sperm bank* ⊃ see also DATABANK, FOOD BANK, VOTE BANK
- **FOR RECYCLING 4** a place or container where sth may be placed for recycling: *a local recycling bank* ⊃ see also BOTTLE BANK
- **OF RIVER/CANAL 5** [B1] the side of a river, CANAL, etc. and the land near it: *We strolled along the river bank.* ◊ *on the bank/banks of sth a house on the banks of the River Severn* (= on land near the river) ◊ *The river burst its banks after heavy rain.*
- **SLOPE 6** a raised area of ground that slopes at the sides, often at the edge of sth or dividing sth: *There were low banks of earth between the rice fields.* ◊ *The girls ran down the steep grassy bank.* **7** an artificial slope built at the side of a road, so that cars can drive fast around bends
- **OF CLOUD/SNOW, ETC. 8** a mass of cloud, snow, etc., especially one formed by the wind: *The sun disappeared behind a bank of clouds.*
- **OF MACHINES, ETC. 9** a row or series of similar objects, especially machines: *a bank of lights/switches/computers*

**IDM** ▸ **not break the bank** (*informal, humorous*) if you say sth **won't break the bank**, you mean that it won't cost a lot of money, or more than you can afford ⊃ more at LAUGH *v.*

■ *verb*
- **MONEY 1** [T] ~ *sth* to put money into a bank account: *She is believed to have banked* (= been paid) *£10 million in two years.* **2** [I] ~ **(with / at ...)** to have an account with a particular bank: *The family had banked with Coutts for generations.*
- **OF PLANE 3** [I] to travel with one side higher than the other when turning: *The plane banked steeply to the left.*
- **FORM PILES 4** [T] ~ *sth* (**up**) to form sth into piles: *They banked the earth* (up) *into a mound.*
- **A FIRE 5** [T] ~ *sth* (**up**) to pile coal, etc. on a fire so that the fire burns slowly for a long time: *The fire was banked up as high as if it were midwinter.*

**PHRV** ▸ **bank on sb/sth** to rely on sb/sth: *I'm banking on your help.* ◊ *'I'm sure he'll help.' 'Don't bank on it* (= it is not likely to happen).' ◊ **bank on sb/sth to do sth** *I'm banking on you to help me.* ◊ **bank on doing sth** *I was banking on getting something to eat on the train.* ▸ **bank up** to form into piles, especially because of the wind: *The snow had banked up against the wall.*

**bank·able** /ˈbæŋkəbl/ *adj.* (*informal*) likely to make money for sb: *The movie's success has made her one of the world's most bankable stars.*

**ˈbank account** *noun* an arrangement that you have with a bank that allows you to keep your money there, to pay in or take out money, etc: *to open/close a bank account*

**ˈbank balance** *noun* the amount of money that sb has in their bank account at a particular time

**ˈbank card** *noun* **1** (*also* ˈbanker's card) (*both BrE*) a plastic card provided by your bank that may be used as a DEBIT CARD or to get money from your account out of a machine **2** (*NAmE*) a credit card provided by your bank, that can also be used as a DEBIT CARD and to get money from your account out of a machine

**ˈbank draft** (*also* ˈbanker's draft) *noun* a CHEQUE (= a printed form) that can be used as a way of paying for sth by a bank to another bank or to a particular person or organization

**bank·er** /ˈbæŋkə(r)/ *noun* **1** a person who owns a bank or has an important job at a bank: *a merchant banker* **2** a person who is in charge of the money in particular games

**ˈbanker's order** *noun* (*BrE*) an instruction to your bank to pay money to sb directly from your bank account ⊃ compare STANDING ORDER

**bank ˈholiday** (*BrE*) *noun* a public holiday, for example Christmas Day, New Year's Day, etc: *Bank Holiday Monday* ◊ *a bank holiday weekend* (= a weekend followed by a Monday which is a holiday) ⊃ compare LEGAL HOLIDAY, PUBLIC HOLIDAY ⊃ see also HOLIDAY *noun*

**bank·ing** /ˈbæŋkɪŋ/ *noun* [U] the business activity of banks: *She's thinking about a career in banking.*

**ˈbank·note** /ˈbæŋknəʊt/ *noun* (*especially BrE*) = NOTE: *forged* (= illegally copied) *banknotes*

**ˈbank rate** *noun* the rate of interest charged by a bank for lending money, which is fixed by a central bank in a country

**bank·roll** /ˈbæŋkrəʊl/ *verb, noun*
■ *verb* ~ **sb/sth** (*especially NAmE, informal*) to support sb/sth by giving money **SYN** finance: *They claimed his campaign had been bankrolled with drug money.*
■ *noun* (*especially NAmE*) a supply of money: *He is the candidate with the biggest campaign bankroll.*

**bank·rupt** /ˈbæŋkrʌpt/ *adj., noun, verb*
■ *adj.* **1** without enough money to pay what you owe **SYN** insolvent: *They went bankrupt in 2009.* ◊ *The company was declared bankrupt in the High Court.* ⊃ WORDFINDER NOTE at MONEY **2** ~ **(of sth)** (*formal, disapproving*) having absolutely nothing of any value: *a government bankrupt of new ideas* ◊ *a society that is morally bankrupt*
■ *noun* (*law*) a person who has been judged by a court to be unable to pay his or her debts
■ *verb* ~ **sb** to make sb bankrupt: *The company was almost bankrupted by legal costs.*

**bank·rupt·cy** /ˈbæŋkrʌptsi/ *noun* [U, C] (*pl.* -**ies**) the state of being bankrupt **SYN** insolvency: *The company filed for bankruptcy* (= asked to be declared officially bankrupt) *in 2009.* ◊ *moral/political bankruptcy* ◊ *There could be further bankruptcies among small farmers.*

**ˈbank statement** (*also* ˈstate·ment) *noun* a printed record of all the money paid into and out of a customer's bank account within a particular period

**ban·ner** [B1+] /ˈbænə(r)/ *noun* a long piece of cloth with a message on it that is carried between two POLES or hung in a public place to show support for sth: *Protesters carried a banner reading 'Save our Wildlife'.*
**IDM** ▸ **under the banner (of sth) 1** claiming to support a particular set of ideas: *They fought the election under the banner of 'No new taxes'.* **2** as part of a particular group or organization: *Troops are in the country under the banner of the United Nations.*

**ˈbanner ad** *noun* an advertisement across the top or bottom or down the side of a page on the internet

**banner ˈheadline** *noun* a line of words printed in large letters across the front page of a newspaper

**ˈbanner year** *noun* (*NAmE*) a year in which sth is especially successful

**ban·nis·ter** = BANISTER

**banns** /bænz/ *noun* [pl.] a public statement in church that two people intend to marry each other

**ban·offi pie** (*also* ban·offee pie) /bəˈnɒfi paɪ; *NAmE* -ˌnɔːf-/ *noun* a DESSERT (= sweet dish) made with TOFFEE, bananas and cream

**ban·quet** /ˈbæŋkwɪt/ *noun* **1** a formal meal for a large number of people, usually for a special occasion, at which speeches are often made: *A state banquet was held in honour of the visiting president.* **2** a large impressive meal

**ban·quet·ing** /ˈbæŋkwɪtɪŋ/ *adj.* connected with banquets: *a banqueting hall*

**ban·quette** /bæŋˈket/ *noun* a long soft seat along a wall in a restaurant, etc.

**ban·shee** /ˈbænʃiː, bænˈʃiː/ *noun* (in Irish stories) a female spirit who makes a long sad noise as a warning to people that sb in their family is going to die soon

**ban·tam** /ˈbæntəm/ *noun* a type of small chicken

**ˈbantam·weight** /ˈbæntəmweɪt/ *noun* [U, C] a weight in BOXING and other sports, between FLYWEIGHT and FEATHERWEIGHT, in BOXING usually between 51 and 54 KILOGRAMS; a BOXER or other competitor in this class: *a bantamweight champion*

**ban·ter** /ˈbæntə(r)/ *noun, verb*
■ *noun* [U] friendly remarks and jokes: *He enjoyed exchanging banter with the customers.*
■ *verb* [I] ~ **(with sb)** to joke with sb: *He bantered with reporters and posed for photographers.*

**ban·ter·ing** /ˈbæntərɪŋ/ adj. (of a way of talking) friendly and with humour: *There was a friendly, bantering tone in his voice.*

**Bantu** /ˈbæntuː/
- adj. of or connected with a group of languages spoken in central and southern Africa, including Kiswahili, isiXhosa and isiZulu
- noun [U] a group of languages spoken in central and southern Africa, including Kiswahili, isiXhosa and isiZulu

**ban·yan** /ˈbænjən/ (also **banyan tree**) noun a South Asian tree with structures that grow down from the branches to the ground and then grow into new roots and TRUNKS

**bao·bab** /ˈbeɪəʊbæb/ noun a short thick tree, found especially in Africa and Australia, that lives for many years

**bap** /bæp/ noun (BrE) a round flat bread roll ⊃ see also BUN

**bap·tism** /ˈbæptɪzəm/ noun a Christian ceremony in which a few drops of water are poured on sb or they are covered with water, to welcome them into the Christian Church and often to name them ⊃ compare CHRISTENING
**IDM** **a ˌbaptism of ˈfire** a difficult introduction to a new job or activity

**bap·tis·mal** /bæpˈtɪzməl/ adj. [only before noun] connected with baptism: *a baptismal service/ceremony*

**Bap·tist** /ˈbæptɪst/ noun a member of a Christian Protestant Church that believes that people should be BAPTIZED when they are old enough to understand what it means and not when they are babies ▶ **Bap·tist** adj. [usually before noun]: *a Baptist church*

**bap·tize** (BrE also **-ise**) /bæpˈtaɪz; NAmE ˈbæptaɪz/ verb [usually passive] ~**sb (+ noun)** to give sb BAPTISM: *She was baptized Mary.* ◇ *I was baptized a Catholic.* ⊃ see also CHRISTEN

**Bapu** /ˈbɑːpuː/ noun (IndE) **1** (used especially as a form of address) a father **2** a name by which Mahatma Gandhi is referred to, showing love

---

▼ **VOCABULARY BUILDING**

**A bar of ...**
If you want to describe a whole unit of a particular substance, or a group of things that are normally together, for example when you buy them, there are different words to use.
- a **bar** of soap/chocolate; a candy **bar**
- a **block** of ice/stone/wood
- a **bolt**/**roll**/**length** of fabric
- an ice/a sugar **cube**
- a **loaf** of bread
- a **roll** of film/carpet
- a **slab** of marble/concrete
- a **stick** of gum
- a **bunch** of bananas/grapes
- a **bunch**/**bouquet** of flowers
- a **bundle** of sticks
- a **set**/**bunch** of keys
- a **set** of chairs/glasses/clothes/guitar strings

---

**bar** ❶ **A2** /bɑː(r)/ noun, verb, prep.
■ noun
- **FOR DRINKS/FOOD 1** **A2** [C] a place where you can buy and drink alcoholic and other drinks: *We arranged to meet in a bar called the Flamingo.* ◇ *The bar staff are very friendly.* ◇ *It's the island's only licensed bar* (= one that is allowed to sell alcoholic drinks). ◇ (BrE) *I found David in the bar of the Red Lion* (= a room in a pub where drinks are served). ⊃ see also BARROOM, LOUNGE BAR, MINIBAR, PUBLIC BAR, SALOON BAR **2** **A2** [C] (especially in compounds) a place in which a particular kind of food or drink is the main thing that is served: *a sushi bar* ◇ *The hotel has a cocktail bar on the top floor.* ⊃ see also COFFEE BAR, SALAD BAR, SNACK BAR, WINE BAR **3** **B1** [C] a long wide wooden surface where drinks, etc. are served: **at the**~ *She was sitting at the bar.* **behind the**~ *He spent the summer working behind the bar at the local pub.*
- **OF CHOCOLATE/SOAP 4** **B1** [C] a piece of sth with straight sides: *a bar of chocolate/soap* ◇ *a chocolate bar* ◇ (NAmE) *a candy bar*

---

bars

bar

sandwich bar

five-bar gate

bars on a window

bar of chocolate    bar of soap    barcode

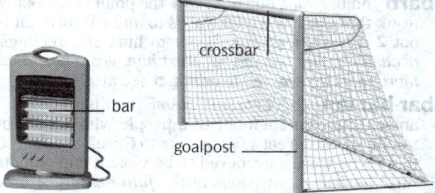
bars on an electric fire    crossbar

bar of music

- **OF METAL/WOOD 5** **B1** [C] a long straight piece of metal or wood. Bars are often used to stop sb from getting through a space: *He smashed the window with an iron bar.* ◇ *The room was small, with bars on the windows.* ◇ *a five-bar gate* (= one made with five horizontal bars of wood) ⊃ see also ROLL BAR, SPACE BAR
- **IN COMPUTING 6** a long narrow area, usually at the top or side of a computer screen, that contains links or PULL-DOWN menus or displays information about the website or program that you are using ⊃ see also ADDRESS BAR, MENU BAR, NAVIGATION BAR, SCROLL BAR, TITLE BAR
- **IN SPORTS 7 the bar** [sing.] the CROSSBAR of a goal: *His shot hit the bar.*
- **OF COLOUR/LIGHT 8** [C] a band of colour or light: *Bars of sunlight slanted down from the tall narrow windows.*
- **THAT PREVENTS STH 9** [C, usually sing.] ~ **(to sth)** a thing that stops sb from doing sth: *At that time being a woman was a bar to promotion in most professions.* ⊃ see also COLOUR BAR
- **IN MUSIC 10** (BrE) (NAmE also **meas·ure**) [C] one of the short sections of equal length that a piece of music is divided

# baraza

into, and the notes that are in it: *four beats to the bar* ◊ *the opening bars of a piece of music* ⊃ picture at MUSIC
- LAW **11 the Bar** [sing.] (*BrE*) the profession of BARRISTER (= a lawyer in a higher court): *to be called to the Bar* (= allowed to work as a qualified BARRISTER) **12 the Bar** [sing.] (*NAmE*) the profession of any kind of lawyer
- MEASUREMENT **13** a unit for measuring the pressure of the atmosphere, equal to a hundred thousand NEWTONS per square metre⊃ see also MILLIBAR
- IN ELECTRIC FIRE **14** [C] a piece of metal with wire wrapped around it that becomes red and hot when electricity is passed through it

IDM **be·hind 'bars** (*informal*) in prison: *The murderer is now safely behind bars.* **not have a 'bar of sth** (*AustralE, NZE, informal*) to have nothing to do with sth: *If he tries to sell you his car, don't have a bar of it.* **set the 'bar** to set a standard of quality or performance: *The show really sets the bar for artistic invention.* ⊃ more at LOWER¹ *v.*, RAISE *v.*

■ verb (-rr-)
- PREVENT **1** ⚹ B2 to ban or prevent sb from doing sth: **~sb from (doing) sth** *Prisoners are barred by law from voting in general elections.* ◊ **~sth** *The new law bars smoking in all public places.* ◊ **be barred to sb** *Certain activities are still barred to women.* IDM see HOLD *n.*
- CLOSE WITH BARS **2** [usually passive] to close sth with a bar or bars: **be barred** *All the doors and windows were barred.*
- BLOCK **3** **~sth** to block a road, path, etc. so that nobody can pass: *Two police officers were barring her exit.* ◊ *We found our way barred by rocks.*

■ prep. (*especially BrE*) except for sb/sth: *The students all attended, bar two who were ill.* ◊ *It's the best result we've ever had, bar none* (= none was better). IDM see SHOUTING

**bar·aza** /bəˈrɑːzə/ *EAfrE* [baˈraza] *noun* (*EAfrE*) a public meeting that is held in order to discuss important matters affecting the community

**barb** /bɑːb; *NAmE* bɑːrb/ *noun* **1** the point of an ARROW or a HOOK that is curved backwards to make it difficult to pull out **2** a remark that is meant to hurt sb's feelings: *The accusation that she did not trust him was a barb that hurt more than she wanted to admit.* ⊃ see also BARBED

**bar·bar·ian** /bɑːˈbeəriən; *NAmE* bɑːrˈber-/ *noun* **1** (in ancient times) a member of a people who did not belong to one of the great CIVILIZATIONS (Greek, Roman, Christian), who were considered to be violent and without culture: *barbarian invasions of the fifth century* **2** a person who behaves very badly and has no respect for art, education, etc.

**bar·bar·ic** /bɑːˈbærɪk; *NAmE* bɑːrˈb-/ *adj.* **1** cruel and violent and not as expected from people who are educated and respect each other: *a barbaric act/custom/ritual* ◊ *The way these animals are killed is barbaric.* **2** connected with BARBARIANS ▶ **bar·bar·ic·al·ly** /-kli/ *adv.*

**bar·bar·ism** /ˈbɑːbərɪzəm; *NAmE* -ˈbɑːrb-/ *noun* [U] **1** a state of not having any education, respect for art, etc. **2** cruel or violent behaviour: *the barbarism of war*

**bar·bar·ity** /bɑːˈbærəti; *NAmE* bɑːrˈb-/ *noun* [U, C] (*pl.* **-ies**) behaviour that deliberately causes extreme physical or mental pain or difficulty to others

**bar·bar·ous** /ˈbɑːbərəs; *NAmE* -ˈbɑːrb-/ *adj.* (*formal*) **1** extremely cruel and making you feel shocked: *the barbarous treatment of these prisoners of war* **2** showing a lack of education and good manners ▶ **bar·bar·ous·ly** *adv.*

**bar·be·cue** /ˈbɑːbɪkjuː; *NAmE* ˈbɑːrb-/ *noun, verb*
■ *noun* (*abbr.* **BBQ**) (*also informal* **bar·bie** *BrE, AustralE*) **1** a metal frame for cooking food on over an open fire outdoors: *I put another steak on the barbecue.* ◊ *a barbecue sausage* (= cooked in this way) **2** an outdoor meal or party when food is cooked in this way: *Let's have a barbecue!* ⊃ compare COOKOUT
■ *verb* [T, I] **~(sth)** to cook food on a barbecue ⊃ compare BROIL

**barbecue 'sauce** *noun* [C, U] a spicy sauce served with food that has been cooked on a barbecue

**'barbecue stopper** *noun* (*AustralE, informal*) a topic of conversation that is very interesting, often one on which people have different views: *Work-life balance is a barbecue stopper for Australians.*

**barbed** /bɑːbd; *NAmE* bɑːrbd/ *adj.* **1** (of an ARROW or a hook) having a point that is curved backwards (called a BARB) **2** (of a remark or comment) meant to hurt sb's feelings

**barbed 'wire** *noun* [U] strong wire with short sharp points on it, used especially for fences: *a barbed wire fence*

**bar·bell** /ˈbɑːbel; *NAmE* ˈbɑːrb-/ *noun* a long metal bar with weights at each end, used in the sport of WEIGHTLIFTING and for exercise⊃ picture at EXERCISE BIKE

**bar·ber** /ˈbɑːbə(r); *NAmE* ˈbɑːrb-/ *noun* **1** a person whose job is to cut men's hair and sometimes to SHAVE them **2** (*also* **barber's**) (*both BrE*) (*pl.* **bar·bers**) a shop where men can have their hair cut⊃ compare HAIRDRESSER

**bar·ber·shop** /ˈbɑːbəʃɒp; *NAmE* ˈbɑːrbərʃɑːp/ *noun* **1** (*especially NAmE*) (*also usually* **barber's**) [C] a place where a barber works **2** [U] a type of light music for four parts sung by men, without instruments: *a barbershop quartet*

**'barber's pole** *noun* a long thin straight piece of wood or metal painted with a SPIRAL of red and white that is traditionally hung outside a barber's shop

**bar·bie** /ˈbɑːbi; *NAmE* ˈbɑːrbi/ *noun* (*BrE, AustralE, informal*) = BARBECUE

**'Barbie doll**™ (*also* **Barbie**) *noun* **1** a DOLL that looks like an attractive young woman **2** (*informal, offensive*) a woman who is sexually attractive, especially one who is thought to be stupid or boring

**bar 'billiards** *noun* [U] (*BrE*) a game played on a small table, in which you try to hit balls into holes without knocking down the small wooden objects that stand in front of the holes

**bar·bit·ur·ate** /bɑːˈbɪtʃərət; *NAmE* bɑːrˈb-/ *noun* a powerful drug that makes you feel calm and relaxed or puts you to sleep. There are several types of barbiturate.

**Bar·bour**™ /ˈbɑːbə(r); *NAmE* ˈbɑːrb-/ *noun* a type of coat, usually dark green, made of special cotton with WAX on it that protects against rain and wind

**'bar chart** (*also* **'bar graph**) *noun* a diagram that uses lines or narrow RECTANGLES (= bars) of different heights (but equal WIDTHS) to show different amounts, so that they can be compared⊃ compare HISTOGRAM ⊃ picture at CHART

**bar·code** /ˈbɑːkəʊd; *NAmE* ˈbɑːrk-/ *noun* a pattern of thick and thin lines that is printed on things you buy. It contains information that a computer can read.⊃ picture at BAR

**bard** /bɑːd; *NAmE* bɑːrd/ *noun* (*literary*) a person who writes poems

**bare** ⚹ C1 /beə(r); *NAmE* ber/ *adj., verb, adv.*
■ *adj.* (**barer, bar·est**) **1** ⚹ C1 not covered by any clothes: *She likes to walk around in bare feet.* ⊃ see also BAREFOOT **2** ⚹ C1 (of trees or countryside) not covered with leaves; without plants or trees: *the bare branches of winter trees* ◊ *a bare mountainside* **3** ⚹ C1 (of surfaces and objects) not covered with or protected by anything: *bare wooden floorboards* ◊ *Bare wires were sticking out of the cable.* ◊ *The walls were bare except for a clock.* **4** ⚹ C1 (of a room, cupboard, etc.) empty: *The fridge was completely bare.* ◊ *bare shelves* ◊ **of sth** *The house was almost bare of furniture.* **5** ⚹ C1 [only before noun] just enough; the most basic or simple: *The family was short of even the bare necessities of life.* ◊ *We only had the bare essentials in the way of equipment.* ◊ *He did the bare minimum of work but still passed the exam.* ◊ *She gave me only the bare facts of the case.* ◊ *It was the barest hint of a smile.* ⊃ note at NAKED, PLAIN
▶ **bare·ness** *noun* [U]

| b bad | d did | f fall | g get | h hat | j yes | k cat | l leg | m man | n now | p pen | r red |

**IDM** **the bare ˈbones (of sth)** the basic facts: *the bare bones of the story* **lay sth ˈbare** (*formal*) to show sth that was covered or to make sth known that was secret: *Every aspect of their private lives has been laid bare.* **with your bare ˈhands** without weapons or tools: *He was capable of killing a man with his bare hands.* ⊃ more at CUPBOARD
■ **verb** ~ **sth** to remove sth that covers sth else, especially from part of the body: *She was paid several thousand dollars to bare all* (= take all her clothes off) *for the magazine.*
**IDM** **bare your ˈsoul (to sb)** to tell sb your deepest and most private feelings **bare your ˈteeth** to show your teeth in an aggressive and THREATENING way: *The dog bared its teeth and growled.*
■ **adv.** (*BrE, slang*) very: *The party on Saturday was bare good!*

▼ HOMOPHONES

**bare • bear** /beə(r); *NAmE* ber/
- **bare** *adj.*: *The room looked strangely bare without the furniture.*
- **bear** *noun*: *Staff reported finding polar bear tracks in the snow.*
- **bear** *verb*: *How can you bear this awful noise?*

**bare·back** /ˈbeəbæk; *NAmE* ˈberb-/ *adj., adv.* on a horse without a SADDLE: *a bareback rider* ◊ *riding bareback*
**bare·faced** /ˈbeəfeɪst; *NAmE* ˈberf-/ *adj.* [only before noun] (*disapproving*) showing that you do not care about offending sb or about behaving badly **SYN** **bald-faced**, **blatant**: *a barefaced lie* ◊ *barefaced cheek*
**bare·foot** /ˈbeəfʊt; *NAmE* ˈberf-/ (*also less frequent* **bare-foot·ed**) *adj., adv.* not wearing anything on your feet: *poor children going barefoot in the street*
**bare·head·ed** /ˌbeəˈhedɪd; *NAmE* ˌberˈh-/ *adj., adv.* not wearing anything to cover your head
**bare-ˈknuckle** (*also* **bare-ˈknuckled**) *adj.* [only before noun] (of a BOXER or BOXING match) without gloves
**bare·ly** ?+ **B2** /ˈbeəli; *NAmE* ˈberli/ *adv.* **1** ?+ **B2** in a way that is just possible but only with difficulty: *The music was barely audible.* ◊ *She was barely able to stand.* ◊ *We barely had time to catch the train.* **2** ?+ **C1** in a way that almost does not happen or exist: *She barely acknowledged his presence.* ◊ *There was barely any smell.* **3** ?+ **C1** just; certainly not more than (a particular amount, age, time, etc.): *Barely 50% of the population voted.* ◊ *He was barely 20 years old and already running his own company.* ◊ *They arrived barely a minute later.* **4** only a very short time before: *I had barely started speaking when he interrupted me.* ⊃ note at HARDLY
**barf** /bɑːf; *NAmE* bɑːrf/ *verb* [I] (*especially NAmE, informal*) to VOMIT ▶ **barf** *noun* [U]
**bar·fly** /ˈbɑːflaɪ; *NAmE* ˈbɑːrf-/ *noun* (*pl.* **-ies**) (*informal*) a person who spends a lot of time drinking in bars
**bar·gain** ?+ **B2** /ˈbɑːɡən; *NAmE* ˈbɑːrɡ-/ *noun, verb*
■ *noun* **1** ?+ **B2** a thing bought for less than the usual price: *I picked up a few good bargains in the sale.* ◊ *The car was a bargain at that price.* ◊ *bargain prices* **2** ?+ **B2** an agreement between two or more people or groups, to do sth for each other: *He and his partner made a bargain to tell each other everything.* ◊ *I've done what I promised and I expect you to keep your side of the bargain* (= do what you agreed in return). ◊ *Finally the two sides struck a bargain* (= reached an agreement). ◊ ~ **with sb** *I'll make a bargain with you.*
**IDM** **into the ˈbargain** (*BrE*) (*NAmE* **in the ˈbargain**) (used to emphasize an extra piece of information) also; as well: *Volunteers learn a lot and enjoy themselves into the bargain.* ⊃ more at HARD *adj.*, STRIKE *v.*
■ *verb* [I] to discuss prices, conditions, etc. with sb in order to reach an agreement that is acceptable **SYN** **negotiate**: ~(**with sb**) (**about/over/for sth**) *In the market dealers were bargaining with growers over the price of coffee.* ◊ *He said he wasn't prepared to bargain.*
**PHRV** **ˌbargain sth↔aˈway** to give sth away and not get sth of equal value in return: *They felt that their leaders had bargained away their freedom.* **ˈbargain for/on sth** (usually in negative sentences) to expect sth to happen and be prepared for it: *We hadn't bargained for this sudden change in the weather.* ◊ *When he agreed to answer a few questions, he got more than he bargained for* (= he got more questions, or more difficult ones, than he had expected). ◊ **bargain for/on doing sth** *I didn't bargain on finding them here as well.* ◊ **bargain for/on sth/sb doing sth** *I hadn't bargained on them being here.*
**ˈbargain ˈbasement** *noun* a part of a large shop, usually in the floor below street level, where goods are sold at reduced prices: *bargain-basement prices*
**ˈbargain hunter** *noun* a person who is looking for goods that are good value for money, usually because they are being sold at prices that are lower than usual ▶ **ˈbargain hunting** *noun* [U]
**bar·gain·ing** /ˈbɑːɡənɪŋ; *NAmE* ˈbɑːrɡ-/ *noun* [U] discussion of prices, conditions, etc. with the aim of reaching an agreement that is acceptable **SYN** **negotiation**: *After much hard bargaining we reached an agreement.* ◊ *wage bargaining* ◊ *Exporters are in a strong bargaining position at the moment.* ⊃ see also COLLECTIVE BARGAINING, PLEA BARGAINING
**ˈbargaining chip** (*BrE also* **ˈbargaining counter**) *noun* a fact or a thing that a person or a group of people can use to get an advantage for themselves when they are trying to reach an agreement with another group: *The release of the prisoners was used as a bargaining chip.*
**ˈbargaining power** *noun* [U] the amount of control a person or group has when trying to reach an agreement with another group in a business or political situation
**barge** /bɑːdʒ; *NAmE* bɑːrdʒ/ *noun, verb*
■ *noun* a large boat with a flat bottom, used for carrying goods and people on CANALS and RIVERS
■ *verb* [I, T] + *adv./prep.* to move in a rough and careless way, pushing people out of the way or crashing into them **SYN** **push**: *He barged past me to get to the bar.* ◊ *They barged their way through the crowds.*
**PHRV** **ˌbarge ˈin (on sb/sth)** to enter a place or join a group of people, rudely interrupting what sb else is doing or saying: *I hope you don't mind me barging in like this.* ◊ *He barged in on us while we were having a meeting.*
**bar·gee** /bɑːˈdʒiː; *NAmE* bɑːrˈdʒiː/ *noun* a person who controls or works on a BARGE
**barge-pole** /ˈbɑːdʒpəʊl; *NAmE* ˈbɑːrdʒ-/ *noun* **IDM** see TOUCH *v.*
**ˈbar graph** *noun* = BAR CHART
**ˈbar-hop** *verb* [I] (**-pp-**) (*NAmE, informal*) to drink in a series of bars in a single day or evening
**bar·is·ta** /bəˈriːstə, -ˈrɪs-/ *noun* a person who works in a COFFEE BAR
**bari·tone** /ˈbærɪtəʊn/ *noun* **1** a man's singing voice with a range between TENOR and BASS; a man with a baritone voice **2** a musical instrument that is second lowest in PITCH in its family ▶ **bari·tone** *adj.* ⊃ compare ALTO, BASS[1], TENOR
**bar·ium** /ˈbeəriəm; *NAmE* ˈber-/ *noun* [U] (*symb.* **Ba**) a chemical element. Barium is a soft silver-white metal
**ˈbarium ˈmeal** *noun* a substance containing barium that a doctor gives sb to SWALLOW before an X-RAY because it makes organs in the body easier to see
**bark** /bɑːk; *NAmE* bɑːrk/ *noun, verb*
■ *noun* [U, C] **1** the outer layer of a tree ⊃ VISUAL VOCAB page V6 **2** the short loud sound made by dogs and some other animals **3** a short loud sound made by a gun or a voice: *a bark of laughter*
**IDM** **sb's bark is worse than their bite** (*informal*) used to say that sb is not really as angry or as aggressive as they sound
■ *verb* **1** [I] ~ (**at sb/sth**) when a dog **barks**, it makes a short loud sound: *The dog suddenly started barking at us.* **2** [T] to give orders, ask questions, etc. in a loud, unfriendly way: ~ **out sth** *She barked out an order.* ◊ ~ **sth (at sb)** *He barked questions at her.* ◊ + **speech** *'Who are you?' he barked.* **3** [T]

**barker**

**~ sth** (*BrE*) to rub the skin off your knee, etc. by falling or by knocking against sth **SYN** **graze**
**IDM** **be barking up the wrong tree** (*informal*) to have the wrong idea about how to get or achieve sth: *You're barking up the wrong tree if you're expecting us to lend you any money.* ⇒more at DOG *n.*

**bark·er** /'bɑːkə(r); *NAmE* 'bɑːrk-/ *noun* a person who stands outside a place where there is entertainment and shouts to people to go in

**bark·ing 'mad** (*also* **bark·ing**) *adj.* (*BrE*, *informal*) completely crazy

**bar·ley** /'bɑːli; *NAmE* 'bɑːrli/ *noun* [U] a plant grown for its grain that is used for making food, beer and WHISKY; the grains of this plant ⇒VISUAL VOCAB page V8

**'barley sugar** *noun* [U] a hard clear sweet made from boiled sugar

**'barley water** *noun* [U, C] (*BrE*) a drink made by boiling BARLEY in water, usually with orange or lemon juice added: *lemon barley water*

**'bar line** *noun* (*music*) a straight line up and down used in written music to mark a division between BARS

**bar·maid** /'bɑːmeɪd; *NAmE* 'bɑːrm-/ (*BrE*) (*NAmE* **bar·tend·er**) *noun* a woman who works in a bar, serving drinks

**bar·man** /'bɑːmən; *NAmE* 'bɑːrm-/ *noun* (*pl.* **-men** /-mən/) (*especially BrE*) (*NAmE usually* **bar·tend·er**) a man who works in a bar, serving drinks

**bar mitz·vah** /ˌbɑː 'mɪtsvə; *NAmE* ˌbɑːr/ *noun* **1** a ceremony and celebration for a Jewish boy who has reached the age of 13, at which he accepts the religious responsibilities of an adult **2** the boy who is celebrating this occasion ⇒compare BAT MITZVAH

**barmy** /'bɑːmi; *NAmE* 'bɑːrmi/ *adj.* (*BrE*, *informal*) slightly crazy

**barn** /bɑːn; *NAmE* bɑːrn/ *noun* **1** a large farm building for storing grain or keeping animals in: *a hay barn ◇ They live in a converted barn* (= a barn that has been turned into a house). ⇒WORDFINDER NOTE at FARM **2** a large plain ugly building: *They live in a great barn of a house.* **3** (*NAmE*) a building in which buses, trucks, etc. are kept when not being used
**IDM** **close, lock, etc. the barn door after the horse has e'scaped** (*NAmE*) (*BrE* **close, lock, etc. the stable door after the horse has 'bolted**) to try to prevent or avoid loss or damage when it is already too late to do so

**bar·nacle** /'bɑːnəkl; *NAmE* 'bɑːrn-/ *noun* a small SHELLFISH that attaches itself to objects UNDERWATER, for example to rocks and the bottoms of ships

**Bar·nardo's** /bə'nɑːdəʊz; *NAmE* bər'nɑːrd-/ *noun* a British charity that helps children with social, physical and mental problems **ORIGIN** From Dr Thomas Barnardo, who opened a home for poor children without parents in London in 1870.

**'barn dance** *noun* an informal social event at which people dance traditional COUNTRY DANCES

**bar·ney** /'bɑːni; *NAmE* 'bɑːrni/ *noun* (*BrE*, *informal*) an argument

**'barn owl** *noun* a BIRD OF PREY (= a bird that kills other creatures for food) of the OWL family, that often makes its NEST in BARNS and other buildings ⇒VISUAL VOCAB page V2

**barn·storm** /'bɑːnstɔːm; *NAmE* 'bɑːrnstɔːrm/ *verb* [I, T] **~ (sth)** (*especially NAmE*) to travel quickly through an area making political speeches, or getting a lot of attention for your organization, ideas, etc: *He barnstormed across the southern states in an attempt to woo the voters.*

**barn·storm·ing** /'bɑːnstɔːmɪŋ; *NAmE* 'bɑːrnstɔːrm-/ *adj.* [only before noun] a **barnstorming** performance or show of skill in a sports game, etc. is one that people find very exciting to watch

**barn·yard** /'bɑːnjɑːd; *NAmE* 'bɑːrnjɑːrd/ *noun* an area on a farm that is surrounded by farm buildings

**bar·om·eter** /bə'rɒmɪtə(r); *NAmE* -'rɑːm-/ *noun* **1** an instrument for measuring air pressure to show when the weather will change: *The barometer is falling* (= showing that it will probably rain). **2** something that shows the changes that are happening in an economic, social or political situation: *Infant mortality is a reliable barometer of socio-economic conditions.* ▶ **baro·metric** /ˌbærə'metrɪk/ *adj.*: *barometric pressure*

**baron** /'bærən/ *noun* **1** a NOBLEMAN of the lowest rank. In the UK, barons use the title *Lord*; in other countries they use the title *Baron*. **2** a person who owns or controls a large part of a particular industry: *a press baron ◇ drug barons*

**bar·on·ess** /'bærənəs; *NAmE* ˌbærə'nes/ *noun* **1** a woman who has the same rank as a baron. In the UK, baronesses use the title *Lady* or *Baroness*: *Baroness Thatcher* **2** the wife of a baron

**bar·onet** /'bærənət/ *noun* (*abbr.* **Bart, Bt**) (in the UK) a man who has the lowest rank of honour that can be passed from a father to his son when he dies. Baronets use the title *Sir*. ⇒compare KNIGHT (2)

**bar·on·et·cy** /'bærənətsi/ *noun* (*pl.* **-ies**) the rank or position of a baronet

**bar·on·ial** /bə'rəʊniəl/ *adj.* [usually before noun] connected with or typical of a BARON: *a baronial family*

**bar·ony** /'bærəni/ *noun* (*pl.* **-ies**) **1** the rank or position of a BARON **2** an area of land that is owned and controlled by a BARON

**bar·oque** /bə'rɒk; *NAmE* -'rəʊk/ (*also* **Baroque**) *adj.* [usually before noun] used to describe European architecture, art and music of the 17th and early 18th centuries that has a grand and highly decorated style: *baroque churches/music ◇ the baroque period* ▶ **bar·oque** (*also* **Baroque**) *noun* [sing.]: *paintings representative of the baroque*

**barque** /bɑːk; *NAmE* bɑːrk/ *noun* a sailing ship with three or more MASTS (= posts that support the sails)

**bar·rack** /'bærək/ *verb* **1** [I, T] **~ (sb)** (*BrE*) to shout criticism at players in a game, speakers at a meeting, performers, etc. **2** [I, T] **~ (for) sb** (*AustralE, NZE*) to shout and encourage a person or team that you support ▶ **bar·rack·ing** *noun* [U]

**bar·racks** /'bærəks/ *noun* [C + sing./ pl. v.] (*pl.* **bar·racks**) **1** a large building or group of buildings for soldiers to live in: *an army barracks ◇ The troops were ordered back to barracks.* **2** any large ugly building or buildings ▶ **bar·rack** [only before noun]: *a barrack unit*

**bar·ra·cuda** /ˌbærə'kjuːdə; *NAmE* -'kuː-/ *noun* a large aggressive fish with sharp teeth that lives in warm seas

**bar·rage** /'bærɑːʒ; *NAmE* bə'rɑːʒ/ *noun* **1** [C, usually sing.] the continuous firing of a large number of guns in a particular direction, especially to protect soldiers while they are attacking or moving towards the enemy **2** [sing.] **~ (of sth)** a large number of sth, such as questions or comments, that are directed at sb very quickly, one after the other, often in an aggressive way: *a barrage of questions/criticisms/complaints* **3** /'bærɑːʒ; *NAmE* 'bærɪdʒ/ [C] a wall or barrier built across a river to store water, prevent a flood, etc.

**'barrage balloon** *noun* a large BALLOON that floats in the air and is held in place by cables, used in the past to make the progress of enemy aircraft more difficult

**bar·ra·mundi** /ˌbærə'mʌndi/ *noun* (*pl.* **bar·ra·mundi**) a large fish found in rivers in Australia and south-east Asia

**bar·rel** /'bærəl/ *noun, verb*
■ *noun* **1** a large round container, usually made of wood or metal, with flat ends and, usually, curved sides: *a beer/wine barrel* **2** the contents of or the amount contained in a barrel; a unit of measurement in the oil industry equal to between 120 and 159 LITRES: *They got through two barrels of beer. ◇ Oil prices fell to $9 a barrel.* **3** the part of a gun like a tube through which the bullets are fired
**IDM** **a barrel of 'laughs** (*informal, often ironic*) a lot of fun: *Life hasn't exactly been a barrel of laughs lately.* **(get/have sb) over a barrel** (*informal*) (to put/have sb) in a situation in which they must accept or do what you want: *They've got us over a barrel. Either we agree to their terms*

*or we lose the money.* ⇨ more at LOCK *n.*, SCRAPE *v.*, SHOOT *v.*
■ *verb* [I] (-ll-, *US* -l-) + *adv./prep.* (*NAmE, informal*) to move very fast in a particular direction, especially in a way that you cannot control: *He came barreling down the hill and smashed into a parked car.*

**barrel-chested** *adj.* (of a man) having a large round chest

**'barrel organ** *noun* a musical instrument that is played by turning a handle, often played in the past in the streets for money ⇨ see also ORGAN GRINDER

**bar·ren** /'bærən/ *adj.* **1** (of land or soil) not good enough for plants to grow on it: *a barren desert ◊ a barren landscape* (= one that is empty, with few plants) ⇨ **WORDFINDER NOTE** at LANDSCAPE **2** (of plants or trees) not producing fruit or seeds **SYN** **infertile 3** (*old use*) (of a woman) not able to have babies **SYN** **infertile 4** (*formal*) (of a female animal) not able to produce young animals **SYN** **infertile 5** [usually before noun] not producing anything useful or successful: *The team will come through this barren patch and start to win again.* ▸ **bar·ren·ness** /-rənnəs/ *noun* [U]

**bar·rette** /bə'ret/ (*NAmE*) (*BrE* **hair·slide, slide**) *noun* a small attractive piece of metal or plastic used by women for holding their hair in place

**bar·ri·cade** /'bærɪkeɪd; *BrE also* ˌbærɪ'keɪd/ *noun, verb*
■ *noun* a line of objects placed across a road, etc. to stop people from getting past: *The police stormed the barricades the demonstrators had put up.*
■ *verb* ~ **sth** to defend or block sth by building a barricade: *They barricaded all the doors and windows.*
**PHRV** **barricade yourself 'in/in'side (sth)** to build a barricade in front of you in order to prevent anyone from coming in: *He had barricaded himself in his room.*

**bar·rier** ❶ **B2** ⓞ /'bæriə(r)/ *noun* **1** ❡ **B2** an object like a fence that prevents people from moving forward from one place to another: *The crowd had to stand behind barriers. ◊ Concrete barriers were erected around the site.* ⇨ see also CRASH BARRIER **2** (*BrE*) a gate at a car park or railway station that controls when you may go through by being raised or lowered: *Scan your ticket at the barrier and it will automatically lift.* **3** ❡ **B2** a problem, rule or situation that prevents sb from doing sth, or that makes sth impossible: *the removal of trade barriers ◊ to overcome/break down barriers ◊ the language barrier* (= when people cannot communicate because they do not speak the same language) *◊ ~ to sth Lack of confidence is a psychological barrier to success. ◊ ~ against sth The country has removed barriers against imports.* **4** ❡ **B2** something that exists between one thing or person and another and keeps them separate: *The Yangtze River is a natural barrier to the north-east. ◊ ~ between A and B There was no real barrier between reality and fantasy in his mind. ◊ ~ against sth The cream acts as a protective barrier against sun damage.* **5** a particular amount, level or number that it is difficult to get past: *the first player whose earnings passed the $10 million barrier* ⇨ see also SOUND BARRIER

**'barrier method** *noun* a method of avoiding becoming pregnant by stopping the SPERM from reaching the egg, for example by using a CONDOM

**'barrier reef** *noun* a line of rock and CORAL in the sea, often not far from land

**bar·ring** /'bɑːrɪŋ/ *prep.* except for; unless there is/are: *Barring accidents, we should arrive on time.*

**bar·rio** /'bæriəʊ; *NAmE* 'bɑːr-/ *noun* (*from Spanish*) (*pl.* -os) **1** a district of a city in Spain or in another Spanish-speaking country **2** (*US*) a district of a city in the US where a lot of Spanish-speaking people live

**bar·ris·ter** /'bærɪstə(r)/ *noun* a lawyer in the UK who has the right to argue cases in the higher courts of law ⇨ note at LAWYER

**bar·room** /'bɑːruːm, -rʊm/ *noun* a room in which alcoholic drinks are served at a bar: *a topic much discussed in barrooms across the country ◊ a barroom brawl*

**bar·row** /'bærəʊ/ *noun* **1** (*BrE*) a small open vehicle with two wheels from which fruit, vegetables, etc. were sold in the street in the past **2** a large pile of earth built over a place where people were buried in ancient times **3** = WHEELBARROW

**'barrow boy** *noun* (*BrE*) (in the past) a man or boy who sold things from a barrow in the street

**'bar stool** *noun* a tall seat for customers at a bar to sit on

**Bart** /bɑːt; *NAmE* bɑːrt/ *abbr.* BARONET

**bar·tend·er** /'bɑːtendə(r); *NAmE* 'bɑːrt-/ *noun* (*especially NAmE*) a person who works in a bar, serving drinks ⇨ compare BARMAID, BARMAN

**bar·ter** /'bɑːtə(r); *NAmE* 'bɑːrt-/ *verb* [I, T] to exchange goods, property, services, etc. for other goods, etc. without using money: *~ (with sb) (for sth) The prisoners tried to barter with the guards for items like writing paper and books. ◊ ~ sth (for sth) The local people bartered wheat for tools.* ▸ **bar·ter** *noun* [U]: *The islanders use a system of barter instead of money.*

**basal** /'beɪsl/ *adj.* (*specialist*) forming or belonging to a bottom layer or base: *basal cells of the skin*

**bas·alt** /'bæsɔːlt; *NAmE* bə'sɔːlt/ *noun* [U] a type of dark rock that comes from VOLCANOES

**base** ❶ **B1** ⓦ /beɪs/ *noun, verb, adj.*
■ *noun*
• **LOWEST PART 1** ❡ **B1** [C, usually sing.] the lowest part of sth, especially the part or surface on which it rests or stands: *The lamp has a heavy base. ◊ the base of a column/glass ◊ at the ~ of sth a pain at the base of the spine* ⇨ **HOMOPHONES** at BASS¹ ⇨ **SYNONYMS** at BOTTOM
• **MAIN PLACE 2** ❡ **B1** [C] the main place where you live or stay or where a business operates from: *I spend a lot of time in Britain but Paris is still my base. ◊ ~ for (doing) sth The town is an ideal base for touring the area. ◊ The company has its base in New York, and branch offices all over the world.*
• **OF ARMY, ETC. 3** ❡ **B1** [C, U] a place where an army, a NAVY, etc. operates from: *a military/naval base ◊ an air base ◊ After the attack, they returned to base.* ⇨ **WORDFINDER NOTE** at NAVY
• **OF SUPPORT/INCOME/POWER 4** ❡ **B2** [C, usually sing.] the people, activity, etc. from which sb/sth gets most of their support, income, power, etc: *These policies have a broad base of support. ◊ an economy with a solid manufacturing base ◊ The singer has built a loyal fan base.* ⇨ see also CUSTOMER BASE, POWER BASE **5** (*especially NAmE*) (*BrE usually* **basic**) **~ pay/salary/wage** the pay that you get before anything extra is added: *All we got was base pay—we didn't reach profitability levels to award a bonus.*
• **ORIGINAL IDEA/SITUATION 6** [C] an idea, a fact, a situation, etc. from which sth is developed **SYN** **basis**: *She used her family's history as a base for her novel. ◊ His arguments have a sound economic base.* ⇨ **SYNONYMS** at BASIS
• **FIRST/MAIN SUBSTANCE 7** [C, usually sing.] the first or main part of a substance to which other things are added: *a drink with a rum base ◊ Put some moisturizer on as a base before putting your make-up.*
• **CHEMISTRY 8** [C] a chemical substance, for example an ALKALI, that can combine with an ACID to form a salt
• **MATHEMATICS 9** [C, usually sing.] a number on which a system of counting and expressing numbers is built up, for example 10 in the DECIMAL system and 2 in the BINARY system
• **IN BASEBALL/ROUNDERS 10** [C] one of the four positions that a player must reach in order to score points: *to reach second/third base* ⇨ see also FIRST BASE, SECOND BASE, THIRD BASE ⇨ see also DATABASE
**IDM** **off 'base** (*NAmE, informal*) completely wrong about sth: *If that's what you think, you're way off base.* ⇨ more at COVER *v.*, FIRST BASE, TOUCH *v.*
■ *verb* ❡ **B1** [usually passive] to use a particular city, town, etc. as the main place for a business, holiday, etc: **be based in …** *The organization is now based in Geneva. ◊ ~ sth/sb/ yourself in … We're going to base ourselves in Tokyo and make trips from there.* ⇨ **HOMOPHONES** at BASS¹
**PHRV** **'base sth on/upon sth** [usually passive] to use an idea, a fact, a situation, etc. as the point from which sth

# baseball

can be developed: *What are you basing this theory on?* ◊ **be based on sth** *The maps are based on satellite data.* ⊃ see also BASED
- *adj.* (**baser**, **bas·est**) (*formal*) having no moral principles or rules: *He acted from base motives.* ⊃ HOMOPHONES at BASS¹ ▶ **base·ly** *adv.*

**base·ball** ❶ A2 /ˈbeɪsbɔːl/ *noun* 1 A2 [U] a game played especially in the US by two teams of nine players, using a BAT and ball. Each player tries to hit the ball and then run around four BASES before the other team can return the ball: *a baseball bat/team/cap/fan/player/game* ◊ *to play major league baseball* ⊃ compare ROUNDERS **2** [C] the ball used in this game

**ˈbaseball cap** *noun* a cap with a long PEAK (= a curved part sticking out in front), originally worn by baseball players

**base·board** /ˈbeɪsbɔːd; *NAmE* -bɔːrd/ (*NAmE*) (*BrE* **ˈskirting board**, **skirt·ing**) *noun* [C, U] a narrow piece of wood that is fixed along the bottom of the walls in a house

**ˈbase camp** *noun* a camp where people start their journey when climbing high mountains

**based** ❶ A2 ⦿ /beɪst/ *adj.* [not before noun] 1 ⁓ **A2** **~ (on sth)** if one thing is **based** on another, it uses it or is developed from it: *The movie is based on a real-life incident.* ◊ *The report is based on figures from six different European cities.* **2** ⁓ A2 (also in compounds) if a person or business is **based** in a particular place, that is where they live or work, or where the work of the business is done: **based in …** *We're based in Chicago.* ◊ *a Chicago-based company* **3** ⁓ B1 **-based** (in compounds) containing sth as an important part or feature: *lead-based paints* ◊ *a class-based society* ◊ *the importance of evidence-based decision-making* ⊃ see also BROAD-BASED

**ˈbase form** *noun* (*grammar*) the basic form of a word to which endings can usually be added, for example *wall* is the base form of *walls* and *walled*. The base form is the form in which words in the dictionary are usually shown.

**ˈbase jumping** (*also* **BASE jumping**) *noun* [U] the sport of jumping with a PARACHUTE from a high place such as a building or a bridge ▶ **ˈbase jumper** *noun*

**base·less** /ˈbeɪsləs/ *adj.* (*formal*) not supported by good reasons or facts SYN **unfounded**: *The rumours were completely baseless.*

**base·line** /ˈbeɪslaɪn/ *noun* [usually sing.] **1** (*sport*) a line marking each end of the COURT in tennis or the edge of the area where a player can run in baseball **2** (*specialist*) a line or measurement that is used as a starting point when comparing facts: *The figures for 2014 were used as a baseline for the study.* ⊃ compare BASSLINE

**base·man** /ˈbeɪsmən/ *noun* (*pl.* **-men** /-mən/) (in baseball) a player who defends first, second or third base

**base·ment** ⁓+ B2 /ˈbeɪsmənt/ *noun* a room or rooms in a building, partly or completely below the level of the ground: *Kitchen goods are sold in the basement.* ◊ *a basement flat/apartment* ⊃ see also BARGAIN BASEMENT

**ˈbase ˌmetal** *noun* a metal, for example iron or LEAD, that is not a PRECIOUS METAL such as gold

**ˈbase rate** *noun* (*finance*) a rate of interest, set by a central bank, that banks in the UK use when calculating the amount of interest that they charge on money they lend ⊃ compare PRIME RATE

**bases 1** /ˈbeɪsɪz/ *pl.* of BASIS **2** /ˈbeɪsɪz/ *pl.* of BASE

**bash** /bæʃ/ *verb*, *noun*
- *verb* (*informal*) **1** [T, I] to hit sb/sth very hard: *~sb/sth + adv./prep. He bashed her over the head with a hammer.* ◊ **~into sb/sth** *I braked too late and bashed into the car in front.* ⊃ SYNONYMS at HIT **2** [T] **~sb/sth** to criticize sb/sth strongly: *Bashing politicians is normal practice in the press.* ◊ *a liberal-bashing administration* ⊃ see also BASHING

**PHRV** **ˌbash aˈway (on/at sth)** | **ˌbash ˈon (with sth)** (*BrE*, *informal*) to continue working hard at sth: *He sat bashing away at his essay all day.* ◊ *We'll never get finished at this rate. We'd better bash on.* **ˌbash sth↔ˈdown/ˈin** (*informal*) to destroy sth by hitting it very hard and often: *The police bashed the door down.* ◊ *I'll bash your head in if you do that again.* **ˌbash sth↔ˈout** (*informal*) to produce sth quickly and in large quantities, but not of very good quality SYN **knock out**: *She bashed out about four books a year.* **ˌbash sb ˈup** (*BrE*, *informal*) to attack sb violently
- *noun* (*informal*) **1** a hard hit: *He gave Mike a bash on the nose.* **2** a large party or celebration: *a birthday bash* IDM **have a ˈbash (at sth)** (*BrE*, *informal*) to try to do sth, especially when you are not sure if you will succeed: *I'm not sure I'll be any good but I'll have a bash.*

**bash·ful** /ˈbæʃfl/ *adj.* shy and easily embarrassed ▶ **bash·ful·ly** /-fəli/ *adv.*: *She smiled bashfully.* **bash·ful·ness** *noun* [U]

**bash·ing** /ˈbæʃɪŋ/ *noun* [U, C] (often in compounds) **1** (used especially in newspapers) very strong criticism of a person or group: *union-bashing* **2** a physical attack, or a series of attacks, on a person or group of people: *gay-bashing* (= attacking GAY people) ◊ *to give sb a bashing*

**BASIC** /ˈbeɪsɪk/ *noun* [U] a simple language, using familiar English words, for writing computer programs

**basic** ❶ B1 ⦿ /ˈbeɪsɪk/ *adj.* **1** ⁓ B1 forming the part of sth that is most necessary and from which other things develop: *basic information/facts/ideas* ◊ *the basic principles of law* ◊ *basic life skills* ◊ *~to sth Drums are basic to African music.* **2** ⁓ B1 of the simplest kind or at the simplest level: *The campsite has only basic amenities.* ◊ *My knowledge of French is pretty basic.* **3** ⁓ B1 [only before noun] necessary and important to all people: *basic human rights* ◊ *basic needs like food, shelter and security* ◊ *the cost of basic foods* **4** (*especially BrE*) (*NAmE usually* **base**) before anything extra is added: *The basic pay of the average worker has risen by 3 per cent.*

**ba·sic·al·ly** ❶ B2 Ⓢ /ˈbeɪsɪkli/ *adv.* **1** ⁓ B2 in the most important ways, without considering things that are less important SYN **essentially**: *I think we are basically saying the same thing.* ◊ *There have been some problems but basically it's a good system.* ◊ *The growth in productivity basically means companies are getting more work out of fewer people.* **2** ⁓ B2 used when you are giving your opinion or stating what is important about a situation: *Basically, there's not a lot we can do about it.* ◊ *He basically just sits there and does nothing all day.* ◊ *Well, basically I did not believe anything he told me.*

**ˌBasic ˈEnglish** *noun* [U] a set of 850 carefully chosen words of English, used for international communication

**basics** /ˈbeɪsɪks/ *noun* [pl.] **1 ~ (of sth)** the most important and necessary facts, skills, ideas, etc. from which other things develop: *the basics of computer programming* **2** the simplest and most important things that people need in a particular situation: *Some schools lack money for basics like books and pencils.* IDM **go/get back to ˈbasics** to think about the simple or most important ideas within a subject or an activity instead of new ideas or complicated details

**basil** /ˈbæzl; *NAmE* ˈbeɪzl/ *noun* [U] a plant with shiny green leaves that smell sweet and are used in cooking as a HERB ⊃ VISUAL VOCAB page V8

**ba·sil·ica** /bəˈzɪlɪkə/ *noun* a large church or hall with a curved end and two rows of columns inside

**basi·lisk** /ˈbæzɪlɪsk/ *noun* (in ancient stories) a creature like a snake, which can kill people by looking at them or breathing on them

**basin** /ˈbeɪsn/ *noun* **1** (*especially BrE*) = WASHBASIN **2** a large round bowl for holding liquids or (in British English) for preparing foods in; the amount of liquid, etc. in a basin: *a pudding basin* **3** an area of land around a large river with streams running down into it: *the Amazon Basin* **4** (*specialist*) a place where the earth's surface is lower than in other areas of the world: *the Pacific Basin* **5** a sheltered area of water providing a safe HARBOUR for boats: *a yacht basin*

**basis** ⓞ B1 ⓞ /ˈbeɪsɪs/ noun (pl. **bases** /ˈbeɪsiːz/) **1** ⚹ B2
[sing.] **on a ... ~** the way things are organized or arranged;
how often sth happens: *We are in contact on a **regular
basis**.* ◇ *to be employed on a permanent/temporary/part-
time basis* ◇ *Fatal accidents occur on our roads on a **daily
basis**.* ◇ *on a day-to-day/weekly/monthly basis* **2** ⚹ B2 [sing.]
the reason why people take a particular action: **on the ~ of
sth** *She was chosen for the job on the basis of her qualifications.* ◇ **on the ~ that ...** *Some movies have been banned on
the basis that they are too violent.* ⓢ SYNONYMS at REASON
**3** ⚹ [C, usually sing., U] the important facts, ideas or
events that support sth and that it can develop from: *The
basis of a good marriage is trust.* ◇ **~ for sth** *This article will
form the basis for our discussion.* ◇ **~ in sth** *The theory
seems to have no basis in fact.*

▼ SYNONYMS

**basis**
foundation • base
These are all words for the ideas or facts that sth is based
on.
**basis** [usually sing.] a principle, an idea or a fact that
supports sth and that it can develop from: *This article will
form the basis for our discussion.*
**foundation** [C, U] a principle, an idea or a fact that
supports sth and that it develops from: *Respect and
friendship provide a solid foundation for marriage.* ◇ *The
rumour is totally without foundation* (= is not based on any
facts).

BASIS OR FOUNDATION?
**Foundation** is often used to talk about larger or more
important things than **basis**: *He laid the foundations of
Japan's modern economy.* ◇ *These figures formed the basis of
their pay claim.*
**base** [usually sing.] an idea, a fact or a situation from
which sth is developed: *His arguments have a sound
economic base.*

PATTERNS
- a/the basis/foundation/base **for/of** sth
- a **secure/solid/sound/strong/weak** basis/foundation/
  base
- to **form** the basis/foundation/base of sth
- to **be without** basis/foundation

**bask** /bɑːsk; NAmE bæsk/ verb [I] **~ (in sth)** to enjoy sitting
or lying in the heat or light of sth, especially the sun: *We
sat basking in the warm sunshine.*
PHR V **ˈbask in sth** to enjoy the good feelings that you have
when other people praise or admire you, or when they
give you a lot of attention: *He had always basked in his
parents' attention.* ◇ *I never minded **basking in** my wife's
reflected glory* (= enjoying the praise, attention, etc. she
got).

**baskets**

shopping basket

washing basket

clothes basket /
hamper

picnic basket /
hamper

hanging basket

waste-paper
basket /
wastebasket

**bas·ket** ⚹ B2 /ˈbɑːskɪt; NAmE ˈbæs-/ noun **1** ⚹ B2 a container for holding or carrying things. Baskets are made of
long thin pieces of material that bends and TWISTS easily,
for example plastic, wire or WICKER: *a shopping basket* ◇ *a
picnic basket* ◇ *a clothes/laundry basket* (= in which dirty
clothes are put before being washed) ◇ *a wicker/wire basket* ◇ *a cat/dog basket* (= in which a cat or dog sleeps or is
carried around) ⓢ see also WASTEPAPER BASKET **2** ⚹ B2 the
amount contained in a basket: *a basket of fruit* **3** ⚹ B2 (also
**cart**, **ˈshopping cart** *both especially NAmE*) a facility on a
website that records the items that you select to buy: *Click
to drop items into your shopping basket.* **4** ⚹ B2 the net
and the metal ring it hangs from, high up at each end of a
basketball COURT; a point that is scored by throwing the
ball through this net: *to make/shoot a basket* **5** (*economics*)
a number of different goods or currencies: *the value of the
rupee against a basket of currencies* IDM see EGG n.

**bas·ket·ball** ⓞ A2 /ˈbɑːskɪtbɔːl; NAmE ˈbæs-/ noun
**1** ⚹ A2 [U] a game played by two teams of five players,
using a large ball which players try to throw into a high
net hanging from a ring: *a basketball game/coach/team/
player* **2** [C] the ball used in this game

**ˈbasket case** noun (*informal*) **1** a country or an organization whose economic situation is very bad **2** a person who
is slightly crazy and who has problems dealing with
situations

**bas·mati** /bæsˈmæti, bæzˈm-/ (also **basˌmati ˈrice**) noun [U]
a type of rice with long grains and a pleasant taste

**bas mitzvah** /ˌbæs ˈmɪtsvə/ noun = BAT MITZVAH

**Basque** /bæsk, bɑːsk/ noun, adj.
■ noun **1** [C] a person who was born in the Basque country
**2** [U] the language of the people living in the Basque country of France and Spain
■ adj. connected with the people or language of the Basque
country of France and Spain

**basque** /bæsk, bɑːsk/ noun a piece of women's underwear
that covers the body from just under the arms to the tops
of the legs

**bas-relief** /ˌbæs rɪˈliːf/ noun [U, C] (*specialist*) a form of
sculpture in which the shapes are cut so that they are
slightly raised from the background; a sculpture made in
this way

**bass**[1] ⚹ C1 /beɪs/ noun, adj. ⓢ see also BASS[2]
■ noun **1** ⚹ C1 [U] the lowest tone or part in music, for
instruments or voices: *He always plays his stereo with
the bass turned right up.* ◇ *He sings bass.* ◇ *a pounding bass
line* ⓢ compare TREBLE ⓢ see also DRUM AND BASS **2** ⚹ C1
(also **ˌbass guiˈtar**) [C] an electric guitar that plays very low
notes: *a bass player* ◇ *bass and drums* ◇ *Eilís Phillips on* (=
playing) *bass* **3** [C] a man's singing voice with a low range;
a man with a bass voice ⓢ compare ALTO, BARITONE, TENOR
**4** [sing.] a musical part that is written for a bass voice **5** [C]
= DOUBLE BASS
■ adj. [only before noun] low in tone: *a bass voice* ◇ *the bass
clef* (= the symbol in music showing that the notes following it are low) ⓢ picture at MUSIC ⓢ compare TREBLE

▼ HOMOPHONES

**base • bass** /beɪs/
- **base** noun: *Cut the stalks at their base.*
- **base** verb: *The government is to base its decision on the
  results of these trials.*
- **base** adj.: *The trolls typify all that is base and ugly in human
  nature.*
- **bass** noun: *This song is all treble and no bass.*
- **bass** adj.: *His powerful bass voice contributed much to the
  film.*

**bass**[2] /bæs/ noun [C, U] (*pl.* **bass**) a sea or FRESHWATER fish
that is used for food ⓢ see also BASS[1]

**bass drum** /ˌbeɪs ˈdrʌm/ noun a large drum that makes a
very low sound, used in ORCHESTRAS

# basset

**bas·set** /ˈbæsɪt/ (also **ˈbasset hound**) noun a dog with short legs, a long body and long ears

**bas·sinet** /ˌbæsɪˈnet/ noun (especially NAmE) a small bed for a baby, that looks like a BASKET

**bass·ist** /ˈbeɪsɪst/ noun a person who plays the BASS or the DOUBLE BASS

**bass line** (also **ˈbass line**) /ˈbeɪslaɪn/ noun the lowest part of a piece of music that accompanies the main tune: *The song has a lively melody and a funky bassline.* ⊃ compare BASE-LINE ⊃ see also MELODY (1)

**bas·soon** /bəˈsuːn/ noun a musical instrument of the WOODWIND group. It is like a large wooden tube in shape with a double REED that you blow into, and produces notes with a low sound.

**bas·soon·ist** /bəˈsuːnɪst/ noun a person who plays the bassoon

**bas·tard** /ˈbɑːstəd, ˈbæs-; NAmE ˈbæstərd/ noun **1** (taboo, slang) used to INSULT (= deliberately offend) sb, especially a man, who has been rude, unpleasant or cruel: *He's a real bastard.* ◊ *You bastard! You've made her cry.* **2** (BrE, slang) a word that some people use about or to sb, especially a man, who they feel very JEALOUS of or sorry for: *What a lucky bastard!* ◊ *You poor bastard!* **3** (BrE, slang) used about sth that causes difficulties or problems: *It's a bastard of a problem.* **4** (old-fashioned, disapproving) a person whose parents were not married to each other when he or she was born

**bas·tard·ize** (BrE also **-ise**) /ˈbɑːstədaɪz, ˈbæs-; NAmE ˈbæstərd-/ verb ~ sth (formal) to copy sth, but change parts of it so that it is not as good as the original

**baste** /beɪst/ verb **1** ~ sth to pour liquid fat or juices over meat, etc. while it is cooking **2** ~ sth to SEW pieces of cloth together with long, loose STITCHES ⊃ WORDFINDER NOTE at SEW

**ˈbasting brush** /ˈbeɪstɪŋ brʌʃ/ noun a brush used for brushing liquid fat or juices over meat, etc. while it is cooking

**bas·tion** /ˈbæstɪən; NAmE ˈbæstʃən/ noun **1** (formal) a group of people or a system that protects a way of life or a belief when it seems that it may disappear: *a bastion of male privilege* ◊ *a bastion of freedom* **2** a place that military forces are defending

**bat** /bæt/ noun, verb
- **noun 1** a piece of wood with a handle, made in various shapes and sizes, and used for hitting the ball in games such as baseball, CRICKET and TABLE TENNIS: *a baseball/cricket bat* ⊃ compare RACKET **2** an animal like a mouse with wings that flies and feeds at night (= it is NOCTURNAL). There are many types of bat. ⊃ see also FRUIT BAT, OLD BAT, VAMPIRE BAT ⊃ VISUAL VOCAB page V2 **IDM** **at ˈbat** (in baseball) trying to hit the ball with a bat ⊃ related noun AT-BAT **like a bat out of ˈhell** (old-fashioned, informal) very fast **off your own ˈbat** (BrE, informal) if you do sth off your own bat, it is your own idea and you do it without help or support from anyone else ⊃ more at BLIND adj., RIGHT adv.
- **verb** (-tt-) **1** [I, T] ~(sth) to hit a ball with a bat, especially in a game of baseball or CRICKET: *He bats very well.* ◊ *Who's batting first for the Orioles?* **2** [T] ~ sth + adv./prep. to hit sth small that is flying through the air: *He batted the wasp away.* **IDM** **bat your ˈeyes/ˈeyelashes** to open and close your eyes quickly, in a way that is supposed to be attractive **bat a ˈthousand** (NAmE, informal) to be very successful **go to ˈbat for sb** (NAmE, informal) to give sb help and support **not bat an ˈeyelid** (BrE) (NAmE **not bat an ˈeye**) (informal) to show no surprise or concern when sth unusual happens: *She didn't bat an eyelid when I told her my news.* **PHRV** **bat sth ↔ aˈround** (informal) to discuss whether an idea or a plan is good or not, before deciding what to do: *It's just an idea we've been batting around.*

**batch** /bætʃ/ noun, verb
- **noun 1** a number of people or things that are dealt with as a group: *Each summer a new batch of students tries to find work.* ◊ *We deliver the goods in batches.* **2** an amount of food, medicine, etc. produced at one time: *a batch of cookies* **3** (computing) a set of jobs that are processed together on a computer: *to process a batch job* ◊ *a batch file/program*
- **verb** [T, I] ~(sth) to put things into groups in order to deal with them: *The service will be improved by batching and sorting enquiries.*

**batch·mate** /ˈbætʃmeɪt/ noun (IndE) a person who is or was in the same year group as you at school or college

**batch ˈprocessing** noun [U] (computing) a way of running a group of programs or performing a series of tasks at the same time and as one group

**bated** /ˈbeɪtɪd/ adj.
**IDM** **with bated ˈbreath** (formal) feeling very anxious or excited: *We waited with bated breath for the winner to be announced.*

**bath** /bɑːθ; NAmE bæθ/ noun, verb
- **noun** (pl. **baths** /bɑːðz; NAmE bæðz/) **1** [C] (BrE) (also **bath·tub**, informal **tub** NAmE, BrE) a large, long container that you put water in and then get into to wash your whole body: *I'm in the bath!* ⊃ see also BIRDBATH **2** [C] an act of washing your whole body by sitting or lying in water: (BrE) *I think I'll have a bath and go to bed.* ◊ (especially NAmE) *to take a bath* ⊃ see also BUBBLE BATH **3** [C] the water in a bath ready to use: *a long soak in a hot bath* ◊ *Please run a bath for me* (= fill the bath with water). **4** **baths** [pl.] (BrE, old-fashioned) a public building where you can go to swim ⊃ see also SWIMMING BATH, SWIMMING POOL **5** [C, usually pl.] a public place where people went in the past to wash or have a bath: *Roman villas and baths* ⊃ see also TURKISH BATH **6** [C] (specialist) a container with a liquid such as water or a DYE in it, in which sth is washed or placed for a period of time. Baths are used in industrial, chemical and medical processes. ⊃ see also BLOODBATH **IDM** **take a ˈbath** (NAmE) to lose money on a business agreement
- **verb** (BrE) (NAmE **bathe**) **1** [T] ~ sb to give a bath to sb: *It's your turn to bath the baby.* **2** [I] (old-fashioned) to have a bath

> **▼ WHICH WORD?**
> **bath / bathe / swim / sunbathe**
> - When you wash yourself you can say that you **bath** (BrE) or **bathe** (NAmE), but it is much more common to say **have a bath** (BrE) or **take a bath** (NAmE).
> - You can also **bath** (BrE) or **bathe** (NAmE) another person, for example a baby.
> - You **bathe** a part of your body, especially to clean a wound.
> - When you go swimming it is old-fashioned to say that you **bathe**, and you cannot say that you **bath** or **take a bath**. It is more common to use **swim**, **go for a swim**, **have a swim** or **go swimming**: *Let's go for a quick swim in the pool.* ◊ *She goes swimming every morning before breakfast.* What you wear for this activity is usually called a **swimsuit** or **swimming trunks**.
> - When you lie in the sun in order to go brown you **sunbathe**.

**ˈbath chair** noun a special chair with wheels, used in the past for moving a person who was sick or old

**bathe** /beɪð/ verb, noun
- **verb 1** [T] ~ sth to wash sth with water, especially a part of your body: *Bathe the wound and apply a clean dressing.* **2** [T, I] ~ (sb) (NAmE) = BATH: *Have you bathed the baby yet?* ◊ *I bathe every day.* ⊃ note at BATH **3** [I] (old-fashioned) to go swimming in the sea, a river, etc. for pleasure ⊃ see also SUNBATHE **4** [T] ~ sth (in sth) (literary) to fill or cover sth with light: *The moon bathed the countryside in a silver light.*
- **noun** [sing.] (BrE, formal) an act of swimming in the sea, a river, etc: *to go for a bathe*

**bathed** /beɪðd/ adj. **1 ~ in sth** (literary) covered with light: *The castle was bathed in moonlight.* **2 ~ in sth** wet because you are covered with SWEAT or tears: *I was so nervous that I was bathed in perspiration.*

**bather** /ˈbeɪðə(r)/ noun **1** [C] (BrE) a person who is swimming in the sea, a river, etc. **2 bathers** [pl.] (AustralE) = SWIMMING COSTUME, SWIMMING TRUNKS

**bath-house** /ˈbɑːθhaʊs; NAmE ˈbæθ-/ noun **1** a public building in which there are baths, STEAM rooms, etc. **2** (NAmE) a building in which you change your clothes for swimming

**bath-ing** /ˈbeɪðɪŋ/ noun [U] (BrE) the activity of going into the sea, a river, etc. to swim: *facilities for bathing and boating* ◊ *a safe bathing beach*

**ˈbathing cap** (especially NAmE) (BrE also **ˈswimming cap**, **ˈswimming hat**) noun a soft rubber or plastic cap that fits closely over your head to keep your hair dry while you are swimming

**ˈbathing costume** noun (BrE, old-fashioned) = SWIMSUIT

**ˈbathing machine** noun a shelter with wheels that people in the past went into to put swimming clothes on. It was then pulled to the edge of the sea so they could swim from it.

**ˈbathing suit** noun (NAmE or old-fashioned) = SWIMSUIT

**ˈbath mat** noun **1** a piece of material that you put next to the bath to stand on when you get out **2** a piece of rubber that you put on the bottom of the bath so that you do not slip

**bathos** /ˈbeɪθɒs; NAmE -θɑːs/ noun [U] (formal) (in writing or speech) a sudden change, that is not always intended, from a serious subject or feeling to sth that is silly or not important

**bath-robe** /ˈbɑːθrəʊb; NAmE ˈbæθ-/ (also **robe**) noun **1** a loose piece of clothing worn before and after taking a bath **2** (NAmE) (BrE **ˈdressing gown**) a long loose piece of clothing, usually with a belt, worn indoors over night clothes, for example when you first get out of bed ⇒ picture at GOWN

**bath-room** ❶ **A1** /ˈbɑːθruːm, -rʊm; NAmE ˈbæθ-/ noun **1 A1** a room in which there is a bath, a WASHBASIN and often a toilet: *Go and wash your hands in the bathroom.* **2 A1** (NAmE) a room in which there is a toilet, a SINK and sometimes a bath or shower: *I have to go to the bathroom* (= use the toilet). ◊ *Where's the bathroom?* (= for example in a restaurant) ◊ *We were allowed to stop occasionally for bathroom breaks.* ⇒ note at TOILET

**bath-tub** /ˈbɑːθtʌb; NAmE ˈbæθ-/ (also informal **tub**) (both especially NAmE) (BrE also **bath**) noun a large, long container that you put water in and then get into to wash your whole body

**bath-water** /ˈbɑːθwɔːtə(r); NAmE ˈbæθ-/ noun [U] water in a bath IDM see BABY n.

**batik** /bəˈtiːk/ noun [U, C] a method of printing patterns on cloth using WAX (= a solid substance made from fat or oil) on the parts that will not have any colour; a piece of cloth printed in this way

**bat·man** /ˈbætmən/ noun (pl. **-men** /-mən/) (BrE) the personal servant of an officer in the armed forces

**bat mitzvah** /ˌbæt ˈmɪtsvə/ (also **bas ˈmitzvah**) noun **1** a ceremony and celebration that is held for a Jewish girl between the ages of 12 and 14 at which she accepts the religious responsibilities of an adult **2** the girl who is celebrating this occasion ⇒ compare BAR MITZVAH

**baton** /ˈbætɒn, ˈbætɒ̃; NAmE bəˈtɑːn/ noun **1** (also **truncheon**) (both especially BrE) (NAmE usually **ˈnight-stick**) a short thick stick that police officers carry as a weapon: *a baton charge* (= one made by police carrying batons, to force a crowd back) **2** a thin light stick used by the person (called a CONDUCTOR) who is in control of an ORCHESTRA, etc. **3** a short light stick that one member of a team in a RELAY race passes to the next person to run: *to pass/hand over the baton* ◊ (figurative) *The President handed over the baton* (= passed responsibility) *to his successor.* **4** a long

---

115

stick that is held and thrown in the air by a person MARCHING in front of a band, or by a MAJORETTE

**ˈbaton round** noun (BrE) a rubber or plastic bullet that is fired to control a crowd that has become violent

**bats·man** /ˈbætsmən/ noun (pl. **-men** /-mən/) (in CRICKET) the player who is hitting the ball

**bat·tal·ion** /bəˈtæliən/ noun **1** a large group of soldiers that form part of a BRIGADE ⇒ WORDFINDER NOTE at ARMY **2** (formal) a large group of people, especially an organized group with a particular purpose: *a battalion of supporters*

**bat·ten** /ˈbætn/ noun, verb
■ noun (specialist) a long narrow piece of wood that is used to keep other building materials in place on a wall or roof
■ verb
IDM **batten down the ˈhatches 1** to prepare yourself for a period of difficulty or trouble **2** (on a ship) to shut all the entrances to the lower part, especially because a storm is expected
PHRV **batten sth↔ˈdown** to fix sth securely in position with strips of wood: *He was busy battening down all the shutters and doors.* **ˈbatten on sb** (BrE, disapproving, formal) to live well by using other people's money, etc.

**bat·ter** /ˈbætə(r)/ verb, noun
■ verb [I, T, often passive] to hit sb/sth hard many times, especially in a way that causes serious damage: **~ at/on sth** *She battered at the door with her fists.* ◊ **~ against sth** *The waves battered against the ship.* ◊ **~ sb** *He had been badly battered around the head and face.* ◊ *Her killer had battered her to death.* ◊ **~ sth** *Severe winds have been battering the north coast.* ⇒ SYNONYMS at BEAT
PHRV **batter sth↔ˈdown** to hit sth hard many times until it breaks or comes down
■ noun **1** [U, C] a mixture of eggs, milk and flour used in cooking to cover food such as fish or chicken before you fry it, or to make PANCAKES **2** [U, C] (NAmE) a mixture of eggs, milk, flour, etc. used for making cakes **3** [C] (NAmE) (in baseball) the player who is hitting the ball

**bat·tered** /ˈbætəd; NAmE -tərd/ adj. **1** old, used a lot, and not in very good condition: *a battered old car* **2** attacked violently or repeatedly and injured: *battered women/children* ◊ *The child had suffered what has become known as 'battered baby syndrome'.* **3** [usually before noun] attacked and badly damaged by weapons or by bad weather: *Rockets and shells continued to hit the battered port.* **4** [usually before noun] (of food) covered in batter and fried: *battered fish*

**bat·ter·ing** /ˈbætərɪŋ/ noun [U, sing.] a violent attack that injures or damages sb/sth: *wife battering* ◊ (figurative) *The film took a battering from critics in the US.*

**ˈbattering ram** noun a long, heavy piece of wood used in war in the past for breaking down doors and walls

**bat·tery** ❶ **B1** /ˈbætri, -təri; NAmE -təri/ noun (pl. **-ies**) **1** ❶ **B1** [C] a device that is placed inside a car engine, clock, radio, etc. and that produces the electricity that makes it work: *to replace the batteries* ◊ *a rechargeable battery* ◊ *battery-powered/-operated* ◊ *a car battery* ◊ *The battery is flat* (= it is no longer producing electricity). ◊ *With our product you get longer battery life.* ⇒ WORDFINDER NOTE at ELECTRICITY **2** [U] electrical power that comes from a battery: *My phone ran out of battery, so I plugged it in to charge.* **3** [C] **~ (of sth)** a large number of things or people of the same type: *He faced a battery of questions.* ◊ *a battery of reporters* **4** [C] (specialist) a number of large guns that are used together **5** [C] (BrE) (often used as an adjective) a large number of small CAGES that are joined together and are used for keeping chickens, etc. in on a farm: *a battery hen* ◊ *battery eggs* ⇒ compare FREE-RANGE **6** [U] (law) the crime of attacking sb physically ⇒ see also ASSAULT AND BATTERY IDM see RECHARGE

**ˈbattery farm** noun (BrE) a farm where large numbers of chickens or other animals are kept in very small CAGES or crowded conditions ⇒ compare FACTORY FARM, FREE-RANGE ▸ **ˈbattery farming** noun [U]

---

s see | t tea | v van | w wet | z zoo | ʃ shoe | ʒ vision | tʃ chain | dʒ jam | θ thin | ð this | ŋ sing

**batting average** *noun* **1** (in CRICKET) the average score of a BATSMAN, which is the number of runs scored per completed INNINGS **2** (in baseball) the average score of a BATTER, which is the number of safe hits per official times AT BAT **3** (*US*) the level of success or achievement that a person or company has in an activity: *The company's batting average with new technologies has been spotty recently.*

**bat·tle** /ˈbætl/ *noun, verb*

■ *noun* **1** [C, U] a fight between armies, ships or planes, especially during a war; a violent fight between groups of people: *the Battle of Waterloo* ◊ *in~ His father had been killed in battle.* ◊ *~with sb Hundreds of protesters fought running battles with the police.* ◊ *~against sb In 1817 Bolivar won a series of battles against Spanish forces.* ◊ *~between A and B It ended in a gun battle between police and drug smugglers.* ⊃ see also PITCHED BATTLE **2** [C] a competition, an argument or a struggle between people or groups of people trying to win power or control: *~for sth a six-year battle for compensation* ◊ *~with sb (for sth) They are engaged in a legal battle with their competitors.* ◊ *a battle of wits* (= when each side uses their ability to think quickly to try to win) ◊ *a battle of wills* (= when each side is very determined to win) ◊ *~between A and B the endless battle between man and nature* ◊ *~over sth The government now faces a new battle over tax increases.* ⊃ SYNONYMS at CAMPAIGN **3** [C, usually sing.] a determined effort that sb makes to solve a difficult problem or succeed in a difficult situation: *~against sth She finally lost her long battle against cancer.* ◊ *He has fought an uphill battle against prejudice.* ◊ *~for sth Her life had become a battle for survival.* ◊ *~with sth his battle with alcoholism*

IDM **the battle lines are ˈdrawn** used to say that people or groups have shown which side they intend to support in an argument or contest that is going to begin **do ˈbattle (with sb) (over sth)** to fight or argue with sb **half the ˈbattle** the most important or difficult part of achieving sth **(fight) a ˈlosing ˈbattle** (to try to do) sth that you will probably never succeed in doing ⊃ more at FIGHT *v.*, JOIN *v.*

■ *verb* [I, T] to try very hard to achieve sth difficult or to deal with sth unpleasant or dangerous: *Both teams battled hard.* ◊ *~for sth The two leaders are battling for control of the government.* ◊ *~with/against sb/sth She's still battling with a knee injury.* ◊ *~it out The two sides will battle it out in the final next week.* ◊ *~to do sth I had to battle hard just to stay afloat.* ◊ *~sth He battled cancer for four years.*

**battle-axe** (*BrE*) (*US also* **battle-ax**) /ˈbætlæks/ *noun* **1** (*informal, disapproving*) an aggressive and unpleasant older woman **2** a heavy AXE with a long handle, used in the past as a weapon

**battle-cruiser** /ˈbætlkruːzə(r)/ *noun* a large fast ship used in war in the past, faster and lighter than a BATTLESHIP

**battle cry** *noun* **1** a shout that soldiers used to give in battle to encourage their own army or to frighten the enemy **2** a word or phrase used by a group of people who work together for a particular purpose, especially a political one

**battle-dress** /ˈbætldres/ *noun* [U] (*BrE*) the uniform that soldiers wear for training and when they go to fight

**battle·field** /ˈbætlfiːld/ *noun* **1** (*also* **battleground**) a place where a battle is being fought or has been fought **2** = BATTLEGROUND (1)

**battle·ground** /ˈbætlgraʊnd/ *noun* **1** (*also* **battlefield**) a situation in which people are opposed to each other; a subject that people feel strongly about and argue about: *Arkansas is among the key electoral battlegrounds.* ◊ *Education policy is an ideological battleground.* **2** = BATTLEFIELD (1)

**battle-hardened** *adj.* (of soldiers) having experience of war and therefore effective at fighting battles

**battle·ments** /ˈbætlmənts/ *noun* [pl.] a low wall around the top of a castle with spaces in it that people inside could shoot through

**battle-scarred** *adj.* a person or place that is **battle-scarred** has been in a war or fight and shows the signs of injury or damage

**battle·ship** /ˈbætlʃɪp/ *noun* a very large ship used in war, with big guns and heavy ARMOUR (= metal plates that cover the ship to protect it)

**batty** /ˈbæti/ *adj.* (*informal, especially BrE*) (of people or ideas) slightly crazy, in a way that causes no harm ⊃ SYNONYMS at MAD

**bau·ble** /ˈbɔːbl/ *noun* **1** a piece of jewellery that is cheap and has little artistic value **2** (*BrE*) a decoration for a Christmas tree in the shape of a ball

**baud** /bɔːd/ *noun* (*pl.* **baud** *or* **bauds**) (*computing*) a unit for measuring the speed at which electronic signals and information are sent from one computer to another

**baulk** (*BrE*) (*also* **balk** *especially in NAmE*) /bɔːk/ *verb* **1** [I] *~(at sth)* to be unwilling to do sth or become involved in sth because it is difficult, dangerous, etc: *Many parents may baulk at the idea of paying $100 for a pair of shoes.* **2** [I] *~(at sth)* (of a horse) to stop suddenly and refuse to jump a fence, etc. **3** [T, usually passive] (*formal*) to prevent sb from getting sth or doing sth: **(be) baulked of sth** *She looked like a lion baulked of its prey.*

**baux·ite** /ˈbɔːksaɪt/ *noun* [U] a soft mineral from which ALUMINIUM is obtained

**bawdy** /ˈbɔːdi/ *adj.* (**bawd·ier**, **bawd·iest**) (*old-fashioned*) (of songs, plays, etc.) loud, and dealing with sex in a way that makes people laugh

**bawl** /bɔːl/ *verb* **1** [I, T] to shout loudly, especially in an unpleasant or angry way: *~(at sb) She bawled at him in front of everyone.* ◊ *~(out) sth (at sb) He sat in his office bawling orders at his secretary.* ◊ *+ speech (+ out) 'Get in here now!' she bawled out.* **2** [I, T] (*+ speech*) to cry loudly, especially in an unpleasant and annoying way: *A child was bawling in the next room.* ◊ *He was bawling his eyes out* (= crying very loudly).

PHRV **bawl sb↔ˈout** (*informal*) to speak angrily to sb because they have done sth wrong: *The teacher bawled him out for being late.*

**bay** /beɪ/ *noun, verb, adj.*

■ *noun* **1** [C] a part of the sea, or of a large lake, partly surrounded by a wide curve of the land: *the Bay of Bengal* ◊ *Hudson Bay* ◊ *a magnificent view across the bay* **2** [C] a marked section of ground either inside or outside a building, for example for a vehicle to park in, for storing things, etc: *a parking/loading bay* ◊ *Put the equipment in No 3 bay.* ⊃ see also SICKBAY **3** [C] a curved area of a room or building that sticks out from the rest of the building **4** [C] a horse of a dark brown colour: *He was riding a big bay.* **5** [C] a deep noise, especially the noise made by dogs when hunting **6** [C] = BAY TREE **7** [U] the leaves of the BAY TREE, used in cooking as a HERB ⊃ VISUAL VOCAB page V8

IDM **at ˈbay** when an animal that is being hunted is **at bay**, it must turn and face the dogs and HUNTERS because it is impossible to escape from them **hold/keep sb/sth at ˈbay** to prevent an enemy from coming close or a problem from having a bad effect SYN ward sth off: *I'm trying to keep my creditors at bay.* ◊ *Charlotte bit her lip to hold the tears at bay.*

■ *verb* **1** [I] (of a dog or WOLF) to make a long deep sound, especially while hunting SYN howl: *a pack of baying hounds* **2** [I] *~(for sth)* (usually used in the progressive tenses) to demand sth in a loud and angry way: *The referee's decision left the crowd baying for blood* (= threatening violence towards him).

■ *adj.* (of a horse) dark brown in colour: *a bay mare*

**bay leaf** *noun* the dried leaf of the BAY TREE that is used in cooking as a HERB

**bay·onet** *noun, verb*

■ *noun* /ˈbeɪənət/ a long, sharp knife that is fastened onto the end of a RIFLE and used as a weapon in battle

■ **verb** /ˈbeɪənət, ˌbeɪəˈnet/ ~ **sb** to push a bayonet into sb in order to kill them

**bayou** /ˈbaɪuː/ noun a branch of a river in the southern US that moves very slowly and has many plants growing in it

**ˈbay tree** (also **bay**) noun a small tree with dark green leaves with a sweet smell that are used in cooking ⊃ see also BAY LEAF

**ˌbay ˈwindow** noun a large window, usually with glass on three sides, that sticks out from the outside wall of a house

**ba·zaar** /bəˈzɑː(r)/ noun **1** (in some Eastern countries) a street or an area of a town where there are many small shops **2** (in the UK, the US, etc.) a sale of goods, often items made by hand, to raise money for a charity or for people who need help

**ba·zooka** /bəˈzuːkə/ noun a long gun, like a tube in shape, which is held on the shoulder and used to fire ROCKETS at military vehicles

**BBC** /ˌbiː biː ˈsiː/ abbr. British Broadcasting Corporation (a national organization which broadcasts television and radio programmes and which is paid for by the public and not by advertising): *The news is on BBC One at 6.* ◊ *BBC Radio 4*

**the ˌBBC World ˈService** noun [sing.] a department of the BBC which broadcasts programmes, including news programmes, in English and many other languages to other countries

**BBQ** abbr. BARBECUE

**BC** (also **B.C.** especially in US) /ˌbiː ˈsiː/ abbr. before Christ (used in the Christian CALENDAR to show a particular number of years before the year when Christ is believed to have been born): *in (the year) 2000 BC* ◊ *the third century BC* ⊃ compare AD, AH, BCE, CE

**bcc** /ˌbiː siː ˈsiː/ abbr., verb
■ abbr. blind carbon copy (to) (used on emails to show that a copy is being sent to another person whose name and email address cannot be seen by the other person or people who receive it)
■ verb (**bcc's**, **bcc'ing**, **bcc'ed**, **bcc'ed**) to send a copy of an email to another person whose name and email address cannot be seen by the other people who receive it: ~ **sb (sth)** | ~ **sth (to sb)** *Send an email to the head of finance and bcc me.* ◊ *That company keeps bcc'ing promotional emails to me.* ◊ ~ **sb on sth** *He now bcc'ed his boss on every email he sent to difficult clients.*

**BCE** /ˌbiː siː ˈiː/ (also **B.C.E.** especially in US) abbr. before the Common Era (before the birth of Christ, when the Christian CALENDAR starts counting years. BCE can be used to give dates in the same way as BC): *in (the year) 2000 BCE* ◊ *the third century BCE* ⊃ compare AD, AH, BC, CE

**be** ⓘ A1 /bi, strong form biː/ verb, auxiliary verb ⊃ IRREGULAR VERBS
■ verb **1** A1 linking verb used when you are naming people or things, describing them or giving more information about them: + **noun** *Today is Monday.* ◊ *'Who is that?' 'It's my brother.'* ◊ *She's a great beauty.* ◊ *Susan is a doctor.* ◊ *He wants to be* (= become) *a pilot when he grows up.* ◊ + **adj.** *It's beautiful!* ◊ *Life is unfair.* ◊ *He is ten years old.* ◊ *'How are you?' 'I'm very well, thanks.'* ◊ *Be quick!* ◊ ~**(that)** … *The fact is (that) we don't have enough money.* ◊ ~**doing sth** *The problem is getting it all done in the time available.* ◊ ~**to do sth** *The problem is to get it all done in the time available.* **2** A1 linking verb **it is/was** used when you are describing a situation or saying what you think about it: + **adj.** *It was really hot in the sauna.* ◊ *It's strange how she never comes to see us any more.* ◊ *He thinks it's clever to make fun of people.* ◊ + **noun** *It would be a shame if you lost it.* ◊ *It's going to be a great match.* **3** A1 **there is/are** + **noun** to exist; to be present: *Is there a God?* ◊ *Once upon a time there was a princess …* ◊ *I tried phoning but there was no answer.* ◊ *There's a bank down the road.* ◊ *Was there a pool at the hotel?* **4** A1 [I] + **adv./prep.** to be located; to be in a place: *The town is three miles away.* ◊ *If you're looking for your file, it's on the table.* ◊ *Mary's upstairs.* **5** A1 [I] ~ **from** … used to say where sb was born or where their home is: *She's from Italy.* **6** A1 [I] + **adv./**

117 **be**

**prep.** to happen at a time or in a place: *The party is on Friday evening.* ◊ *The meetings are always in the main conference room.* **7** A1 [I] + **adv./prep.** to remain in a place: *She has been in her room for hours.* ◊ *They're here till Christmas.* **8** A1 [I] + **adv./prep.** to attend an event; to be present in a place: *I'll be at the party.* ◊ *He'll be here soon* (= will arrive soon). **9** A1 linking verb **it is/was** used to talk about time: + **noun** *It's two thirty.* ◊ + **adj.** *It was late at night when we finally arrived.* **10** A1 linking verb + **noun** to cost: *'How much is that dress?' 'Eighty dollars.'* **11** A1 linking verb + **noun** to be equal to: *Three and three is six.* ◊ *How much is a thousand pounds in euros?* ◊ *Let x be the sum of a and b.* ◊ *London is not England* (= do not think that all of England is like London). **12** A1 [I] (only used in the perfect tenses) + **adv./prep.** to visit or call: *I've never been to Spain.* ◊ *He had been abroad many times.* ◊ (BrE) *Has the postman been yet?* HELP In NAmE, **come** is used instead: *Has the mailman come yet?* **13** A1 linking verb + **noun** used to say what sth is made of: *Is your jacket real leather?* **14** A2 linking verb [I] used to say who sth belongs to or who it is intended for: ~ **mine, yours, etc.** *The money's not yours, it's John's.* ◊ ~ **for me, you, etc.** *This package is for you.* **15** A1 linking verb ~ **everything, nothing, etc. (to sb)** used to say how important sth is to sb: *Money isn't everything* (= it is not the only important thing). ◊ *A thousand dollars is nothing to somebody as rich as he is.*

IDM HELP Most idioms containing **be** are at the entries for the nouns and adjectives in the idioms, for example **be the death of sb is at death**. **as/that was** as sb/sth used to be called: *Jill Davis that was* (= before her marriage) ◊ *the Soviet Union, as was* **the ˌbe-all and ˈend-all (of sth)** (informal) the most important part; all that matters: *Her career is the be-all and end-all of her existence.* **(he, she, etc. has) been and ˈdone sth** (BrE, informal) used to show that you are surprised and annoyed by sth that sb has done: *Someone's been and parked in front of the entrance!* ⊃ see also GO AND DO STH **if it wasn't/weren't for …** used to say that sb/sth stopped sb/sth from happening: *If it weren't for you, I wouldn't be alive today.* **sth ˌis what it ˈis** (informal) used to show that you accept that sth negative cannot be changed: *I never imagined that our company share prices would fall so low, but it is what it is.* **ˌleave/ˌlet sb/sth ˈbe** to leave sb/sth alone without bothering them/it: *Leave her be, she obviously doesn't want to talk about it.* ◊ *Let the poor dog be* (= don't annoy it). **-to-be** (in compounds) future: *his bride-to-be* ◊ *mothers-to-be* (= pregnant women)

■ auxiliary verb **1** A1 used with a present participle to form progressive tenses: *I am studying Chinese.* ◊ *I'll be seeing him soon.* ◊ *What have you been doing this week?* ◊ *I'm always being criticized.* **2** A2 used to make QUESTION TAGS (= short questions added to the end of statements): *You're not hungry, are you?* ◊ *Ben's coming, isn't he?* ◊ *The old theatre was pulled down, wasn't it?* **3** B1 used with a past participle to form the passive: *He was killed in the war.* ◊ *Where were they made?* ◊ *The house was still being built.* ◊ *You will be told what to do.* **4** B1 used to avoid repeating the full form of a verb in the passive or a progressive tense: *Karen wasn't beaten in any of her games, but all the others were.* ◊ *'Are you coming with us?' 'No, I'm not.'* **5** ~ **to do sth** used to say what must or should be done: *I am to call them once I reach the airport.* ◊ *You are to report this to the police.* ◊ *What is to be done about this problem?* **6** ~ **to do sth** used to say what is arranged to happen: *They are to be married in June.* **7** ~ **to do sth** used to say what happened later: *He was to regret that decision for the rest of his life* (= he did regret it). **8** ~ **not, never, etc. to be done** used to say what could not or did not happen: *Anna was nowhere to be found* (= we could not find her anywhere). ◊ *He was never to see his wife again* (= although he did not know it would be so at the time, he did not see her again). ◊ *She wanted to write a successful novel, but* **it was not to be** (= it turned out never to happen). **9 if sb/it were to do sth** … | **were sb/it to do sth** … (formal) used to express a condition: *If we were to offer you more money, would you stay?* ◊ *Were we to offer you more money, would you stay?*

**be-** /bɪ/ prefix **1** (in verbs) to make or treat sb/sth as: *Don't belittle his achievements* (= say they are not important). ◊ *An older girl befriended me.* **2** (in adjectives ending in -*ed*) wearing or covered with: *heavily bejewelled fingers* ◊ *bespattered with mud* **3** (in verbs and adjectives ending in -*ed*) to cause sth to be: *The ship was becalmed* (= there was no wind so it could not move). ◊ *The rebels besieged the fort.* **4** used to turn INTRANSITIVE verbs (= without an object) into TRANSITIVE verbs (= with an object): *She is always bemoaning her lot.*

**beach** /biːtʃ/ noun, verb
■ noun an area of sand or small stones (called SHINGLE), next to the sea or a lake: **on the** ~ *tourists sunbathing on the beach* ◊ **to the** ~ *He decided to go to the beach for a swim.* ◊ *a sandy beach* ⊃ SYNONYMS at COAST ⊃ WORDFINDER NOTE at COAST
■ verb **1** [T] ~ **sth** to bring a boat out of the water and onto a beach: *He beached the boat and lifted the boy onto the shore.* **2** (also **be beached**) [I, T] (of a WHALE or similar animal) to become stuck on land and unable to get back into the water: *a beached whale*

**beach ball** noun a large, light, coloured plastic ball that people play games with on the beach

**beach buggy** (also **dune buggy**) noun a small car used for driving on sand

**beach·comb·er** /ˈbiːtʃkəʊmə(r)/ noun a person who walks along beaches collecting interesting or valuable things, either for pleasure or to sell

**beach·front** /ˈbiːtʃfrʌnt/ often **the beachfront** noun [sing.] (*especially* NAmE) the part of a town facing the beach: *beachfront hotels/apartments*

**beach·head** /ˈbiːtʃhed/ noun a strong position on a beach from which an army that has just landed prepares to go forward and attack ⊃ see also BRIDGEHEAD

**beach volleyball** noun [U] a form of VOLLEYBALL played on sand by teams of two players

**beach·wear** /ˈbiːtʃweə(r); NAmE -wer/ noun [U] (used especially in shops/stores) clothes for wearing on the beach

**bea·con** /ˈbiːkən/ noun **1** a light that is placed somewhere to guide vehicles and warn them of danger: *a navigation beacon* ◊ (*figurative*) *He was a beacon of hope for the younger generation.* ⊃ see also BELISHA BEACON **2** a radio station whose signal helps ships and aircraft to find their position **3** (in the past) a fire lit on top of a hill as a signal

**bead** /biːd/ noun **1** [C] a small piece of glass, wood, etc., with a hole through it, that can be put on a string with others of the same type and worn as jewellery, etc: *a necklace of wooden beads* ◊ *A beaded curtain separated the two rooms.* **2 beads** [pl.] a ROSARY **3** [C] a small drop of liquid: *There were beads of sweat on his forehead.*
IDM **draw/get a bead on sb/sth** (*especially* NAmE) to aim carefully at sb/sth before shooting a gun

**bead·ed** /ˈbiːdɪd/ adj. **1** decorated with beads: *a beaded dress* **2** ~ **with sth** with small drops of a liquid on it: *His face was beaded with sweat.*

**bead·ing** /ˈbiːdɪŋ/ noun [U] **1** a long narrow piece of wood, stone or plastic with a pattern on it, used for decorating walls, doors and furniture **2** beads that are SEWN together and used as a decoration on clothes

**beady** /ˈbiːdi/ adj. (of eyes) small, round and bright; watching everything closely or because you suspect that sth wrong, illegal or dishonest is involved in a situation: (*BrE*) *I should certainly keep a beady eye on his behaviour.*

**beady-eyed** adj. (*informal*) watching carefully and noticing every small detail

**bea·gle** /ˈbiːɡl/ noun a type of small dog with short legs, used in hunting

**beak** /biːk/ noun **1** the hard pointed or curved outer part of a bird's mouth SYN bill: *The gull held the fish in its beak.* ⊃ VISUAL VOCAB page V2 **2** (*humorous*) a person's nose, especially when it is large and/or pointed **3** (*BrE, old-fashioned, slang*) a person in a position of authority, especially a judge

**beaked** /biːkt/ adj. (usually in compounds) having a BEAK, or the type of BEAK mentioned: *flat-beaked*

**bea·ker** /ˈbiːkə(r)/ noun **1** (*BrE*) a cup, usually made of plastic and often without a handle, used for drinking from **2** (*BrE*) the amount contained in a beaker: *a beaker of coffee* **3** a glass cup with straight sides and a lip, used in chemistry, for example for measuring liquids

**beam** /biːm/ noun, verb
■ noun **1** a line of light, ELECTROMAGNETIC waves or PARTICLES: *narrow beams of light/sunlight* ◊ *the beam of a torch/flashlight* ◊ *a laser/electron beam* ◊ (*BrE*) *The car's headlights were on full beam* (= shining as brightly as possible and not directed downwards). ◊ (*NAmE*) *a car with its high beams on* **2** a long piece of wood, metal, etc. used to support weight, especially as part of the roof in a building: *The cottage had exposed oak beams.* **3** (*especially BrE*) (*NAmE usually* **balance beam**) a wooden bar that is used in the sport of GYMNASTICS for people to move and balance on **4** a wide and happy smile: *a beam of satisfaction* ⊃ WORDFINDER NOTE at EXPRESSION
IDM **off beam** (*informal*) not correct; wrong: *Your calculation is way off beam.*
■ verb **1** [I, T, no passive] to have a big happy smile on your face: ~ (**at sb**) *He beamed at the journalists.* ◊ ~ (**with sth**) *She was positively beaming with pleasure.* ◊ ~ **sth (at sb)** *The barman beamed a warm smile at her.* ◊ + **speech** '*I'd love to come,' she beamed* (= said with a large smile). **2** [T] ~ **sth + adv./prep.** to send radio or television signals over long distances using electronic equipment: *Live pictures of the ceremony were beamed around the world.* **3** [I] + **adv./prep.** to produce a stream of light and/or heat: *The morning sun beamed down on us.* ◊ *Light beamed through a hole in the curtain.* IDM see EAR
PHRV **beam sb 'down/'up** (in SCIENCE FICTION stories) to transport sb to or from a SPACESHIP using special electronic equipment ORIGIN From the American television series *Star Trek*.

**beamed** /biːmd/ adj. having beams of wood: *a high beamed ceiling*

**bean** /biːn/ noun, verb
■ noun **1** a seed, or POD containing seeds, of a climbing plant, eaten as a vegetable. There are several types of bean and the plants that they grow on are also called beans: *green beans* ◊ *runner beans* ◊ *beans* (= BAKED BEANS) *on toast* ⊃ VISUAL VOCAB page V5 **2** (usually in compounds) a seed from a coffee plant, or some other plants: *cocoa/coffee beans* ⊃ see also JELLY BEAN
IDM **full of 'beans/'life** (of a person) having a lot of energy **not have a 'bean** (*BrE, informal*) to have no money ⊃ more at HILL, KNOW v., SPILL v.
■ verb ~ **sb** (*NAmE, informal*) to hit sb on the head: *I got beaned by a rock someone threw.*

**bean·bag** /ˈbiːnbæɡ/ noun **1** a very large bag made of cloth and filled with small pieces of plastic, used for sitting on **2** a small bag of cloth filled with beans or small pieces of plastic and used as a ball

**bean counter** noun (*informal, disapproving*) a person who works with money, for example as an ACCOUNTANT and who wants to keep strict control of how much money a company spends

**bean curd** noun [U] = TOFU

**bean·feast** /ˈbiːnfiːst/ noun (*BrE, old-fashioned*) a party or celebration

**beanie** /ˈbiːni/ noun a small, round close-fitting hat

**bean·pole** /ˈbiːnpəʊl/ noun (*informal, usually disapproving*) a tall thin person

**bean sprouts** noun [pl.] bean seeds that are just beginning to grow, often eaten raw ⊃ VISUAL VOCAB page V5

**bean·stalk** /ˈbiːnstɔːk/ noun the tall fast-growing STEM of a bean plant

**bear** ⓘ **B2** /beə(r); NAmE ber/ verb, noun

■ verb (bore /bɔː(r)/, borne /bɔːn; NAmE bɔːrn/)
- ACCEPT/DEAL WITH **1** **B2** [T] (used especially with *can/could* in negative sentences and questions) to be able to accept and deal with sth unpleasant **SYN** stand: ~ sth *The pain was almost more than he could bear.* ◊ *She couldn't bear the thought of losing him.* ◊ **doing sth** *He can't bear being laughed at.* ◊ **to do sth** *He can't bear to be laughed at.* ◊ ~ **sb doing sth** *I can't bear you doing that.* ⊃ HOMOPHONES at BARE ⊃ SYNONYMS at HATE
- BE RESPONSIBLE FOR STH **2** **B2** [T] ~ sth (*formal*) to take responsibility for sth: *She bore the responsibility for most of the changes.* ◊ *Do parents have to bear the whole cost of tuition fees?* ◊ *In the end it's consumers who bear the burden of higher prices.*
- SUPPORT WEIGHT **3** **B2** [T] ~ sth to support the weight of sb/sth: *The ice is too thin to bear your weight.*
- SHOW **4** [T] ~ sth (*formal*) to show sth; to carry sth so that it can be seen: *The document bore his signature.* ◊ *He was badly wounded in the war and still bears the scars.* ◊ *She bears little resemblance to* (= is not much like) *her mother.* ◊ *The title of the essay bore little relation to* (= was not much connected with) *the contents.*
- NOT BE SUITABLE **5** [T] **not** ~ to not be suitable for sth: ~ sth *Her later work does not bear comparison with her earlier novels* (= because it is not nearly as good). ◊ *The plan won't bear close inspection* (= it will be found to be unacceptable when carefully examined). ◊ **doing sth** *The joke doesn't bear repeating* (= because it is not funny or may offend people). ◊ *His sufferings don't bear thinking about* (= because they are so terrible).
- NEGATIVE FEELING **6** [T] to have a feeling, especially a negative feeling: ~ **sth** *He bears no resentment towards them.* ◊ *He's borne a grudge against me ever since that day.* ◊ ~ **sb sth** *He's borne me a grudge ever since that day.* ◊ *She bore him no ill will.*
- NAME **7** [T] ~ sth (*formal*) to have a particular name: *a family that bore an ancient and honoured name*
- CARRY **8** [T] ~ **sb/sth** (*old-fashioned* or *formal*) to carry sb/sth, especially while moving: *three kings bearing gifts*
- YOURSELF **9** [T] ~ **yourself well, etc.** (*formal*) to move, behave or act in a particular way: *He bears himself* (= stands, walks, etc.) *proudly, like a soldier.* ◊ *She bore herself with dignity throughout the funeral.*
- CHILD **10** [T] (*formal*) to give birth to a child: ~ **sth** *She was not able to bear children.* ◊ ~ **sb sth** *She had borne him six sons.*
- OF TREES/PLANTS **11** [T] ~ **sth** (*formal*) to produce flowers or fruit
- TURN **12** [I] ~ **(to the) left, north, etc.** to go or turn in the direction mentioned: *When you get to the fork in the road, bear right.*
- **IDM** **bear ˈarms** (*old use*) to be a soldier; to fight **bear ˈfruit** to have a successful result **bear ˈhard, ˈheavily, seˈverely, etc. on sb** (*formal*) to be a cause of difficulty or worry to sb: *Taxation bears heavily on us all.* **be borne ˈin on sb** (*formal*, especially *BrE*) to be realized by sb, especially after a period of time: *It was gradually borne in on us that defeat was inevitable.* **bring sth to bear (on sb/sth)** (*formal*) to use energy, pressure, influence, etc. to try to achieve sth or make sb do sth: *We must bring all our energies to bear upon the task.* ◊ *Pressure was brought to bear on us to finish the work on time.* ⊃ more at BRUNT, CROSS n., GRIN v., MIND n., WITNESS n.
- **PHRV** **bear ˈdown on sb/sth** **1** (*BrE*) to move quickly towards sb/sth in a determined or frightening way **2** (especially *NAmE*) to press on sb/sth: *Bear down on it with all your strength so it doesn't move.* **ˈbear on sth** (*formal*) to relate to sth **SYN** **affect**: *These are matters that bear on the welfare of the community.* **bear sb/sth↔ˈout** (especially *BrE*) to show that sb is right or that sth is true: *The other witnesses will bear me out.* ◊ *The other witnesses will bear out what I say.* **bear ˈup (against/under sth)** to remain as cheerful as possible during a difficult time: *He's bearing up well under the strain of losing his job.* ◊ *'How are you?' 'Bearing up.'* **ˈbear with sb/sth** to be patient with sb/sth: *She's quite a lot of strain. Just bear with her.* ◊ *If you will bear with me* (= be patient and listen to me) *a little longer, I'll answer your question.*

■ noun **1** **A2** a heavy wild animal with thick fur and sharp CLAWS (= pointed ends on its feet). There are many types of bear: *a black bear* ⊃ see also GRIZZLY BEAR, POLAR BEAR, TEDDY BEAR ⊃ HOMOPHONES at BARE **2** (*finance*) a person who sells shares in a company, etc., hoping to buy them back later at a lower price ⊃ compare BULL ⊃ see also BEARISH
- **IDM** **like a bear with a sore ˈhead** in a bad mood; in an angry way

**bear·able** /ˈbeərəbl; NAmE ˈber-/ adj. a person or thing that is **bearable** can be accepted or dealt with: *She was the only thing that made life bearable.* **OPP** **unbearable**

**beard** /bɪəd; NAmE bɪrd/ noun, verb
■ noun [C, U] hair that grows on the CHIN and sides of a man's face; similar hair that grows on some animals: *He has decided to grow a beard and a moustache.* ◊ *a week's growth of beard* ◊ *a goat's beard* ⊃ compare MOUSTACHE
▶ **beard·ed** adj.: *a bearded face/man*
■ verb
- **IDM** **to beard the lion in his ˈden** to go to see an important or powerful person to tell them that you disagree with them, that you want sth, etc.

**bear·er** /ˈbeərə(r); NAmE ˈber-/ noun **1** a person whose job it is to carry sth, especially at a ceremony: *coffin bearers* ⊃ see also PALL-BEARER, STANDARD-BEARER, STRETCHER-BEARER **2** a person who brings a message, a letter, etc: *I'm sorry to be the bearer of bad news.* **3** (*formal*) a person who has sth with them or is the official owner of sth, such as a document: *A pass will allow the bearer to enter the building.* **4** a person who has knowledge of sth, such as an idea or a tradition, and makes sure that it is not forgotten, by teaching others about it

**ˈbear hug** noun an act of showing love for sb by holding them very tightly and strongly in your arms

**bear·ing** /ˈbeərɪŋ; NAmE ˈber-/ noun **1** [U, sing.] ~ **on sth** the way in which sth is related to sth or influences it: *Recent events had no bearing on our decision.* ◊ *Regular exercise has a direct bearing on fitness and health.* **2** [sing.] the way in which you stand, walk or behave: *Her whole bearing was alert.* **3** [C] ~ **(on sth)** (*specialist*) a direction measured from a fixed point using a COMPASS: *They took compass bearings on the tower.* **4** **your bearings** [pl.] knowledge of your position relative to everything that is around or near you: *to get/find/take your bearings* ◊ *She lost her bearings in the thick forest.* **5** [C] (*specialist*) a part of a machine that supports a moving part, especially one that is turning ⊃ see also BALL BEARING

**bear·ish** /ˈbeərɪʃ; NAmE ˈber-/ adj. (*finance*) showing or expecting a fall in the prices of shares: *a bearish market* ◊ *Japanese banks remain bearish.* ⊃ compare BULLISH

**ˈbear market** noun (*finance*) a period during which people are selling shares, etc. rather than buying, because they expect the prices to fall ⊃ compare BULL MARKET

**bear·skin** /ˈbeəskɪn; NAmE ˈbers-/ noun **1** the skin and fur of a bear: *a bearskin rug* **2** a tall hat of black fur worn for special ceremonies by some British soldiers

**beast** **+** **C1** /biːst/ noun **1** **C1** (*old-fashioned* or *formal*) an animal, especially one that is large or dangerous, or one that is unusual: *wild/savage/ferocious beasts* ◊ *mythical beasts* such as unicorns and dragons **2** a person who is cruel and whose behaviour shows a lack of control **SYN** **animal 3** (*informal*, *often humorous*) an unpleasant person or thing: *The maths exam was a real beast.* **4** (*informal*) a thing of a particular kind **SYN** **animal**: *His new guitar is a very expensive beast.*

**beast·ly** /ˈbiːstli/ adj. (*old-fashioned*, *BrE*, *informal*) unpleasant **SYN** **horrible, nasty** ▶ **beast·li·ness** /-nəs/ noun [U]

**beast of ˈburden** noun an animal used for heavy work such as carrying or pulling things

**beat** ⓘ **A2** /biːt/ verb, noun, adj.
■ verb (beat, beaten /ˈbiːtn/)
- IN GAME **1** **A2** [T] ~ **sb (at sth)** to defeat sb in a game or competition: *He beat me at chess.* ◊ *Their recent wins have*

# beat

*proved they're still **the ones to beat*** (= the most difficult team to beat).
- **BE BETTER 2** [T] ~ **sth** (*rather informal*) to do or be better than sb: *Nothing beats home cooking.* ◊ *You can't beat Italian shoes.* ◊ *For a break in the sun, Thailand is hard to beat.* ◊ *They want to beat the speed record* (= go faster than anyone before).
- **CONTROL 3** [T] ~ **sth** (*informal*) to get control of sth: *The government's main aim is to beat inflation.*
- **BE TOO DIFFICULT 4** [T] (*informal*) to be too difficult for sb **SYN** **defeat**: ~ **sb** *It is a problem that beats even the experts.* ◊ ~ **sb why, how, etc…** *It beats me* (= I don't know) *why he did it.* ◊ *What beats me* (= what I don't understand) *is how it was done so quickly.*
- **AVOID 5** [T] ~ **sth** (*informal*) to avoid sth: *If we go early we should beat the traffic.* ◊ *We were up and off early to beat the heat.*
- **HIT 6** [T] to hit a person hard and many times in order to hurt them: ~ **sb** *At that time children were regularly beaten for quite minor offences* (= as a punishment). ◊ ~ **sb** + **adv./prep.** *An elderly man was found beaten to death.* ◊ ~ **sb** + **adj.** *They beat him unconscious* (= hit him until he became unconscious). **7** [I, T] to hit sth hard several times: + **adv./prep.** *Somebody was beating at the door.* ◊ *Hailstones beat against the window.* ◊ ~ **sth** *Someone was beating a drum.* ◊ ~ **sth** + **adv./prep.** *She was beating dust out of the carpet* (= removing dust from the carpet by beating it).
- **OF HEART/DRUMS/WINGS 8** [I, T] to make, or cause sth to make, a regular sound or movement: *She's alive—her heart is still beating.* ◊ *We heard the drums beating.* ◊ *The bird was beating its wings* (= moving them up and down) *frantically.*
- **MIX 9** [T] to mix sth with short quick movements with a fork, etc: ~ **sth (up)** *Beat the eggs up to a frothy consistency.* ◊ ~ **A and B together** *Beat the flour and milk together.*
- **SHAPE METAL 10** [T, often passive] to change the shape of sth, especially metal, by hitting it with a HAMMER, etc: ~ **sth (out) (into sth)** *The gold is beaten out into thin strips.* ◊ *beaten silver* ◊ ~ **sth** + **adj.** *The metal had been beaten flat.*
- **MAKE PATH 11** [T] ~ **sth (through, across, along, etc. sth)** to make a path, etc. by walking somewhere or by pressing branches down and walking over them: *a well-beaten track* (= one that has been worn hard by much use) ◊ *The hunters beat a path through the undergrowth.*

**IDM** **beat about the ˈbush** (*BrE*) (*NAmE* **beat around the ˈbush**) to talk about sth for a long time without coming to the main point: *Stop beating about the bush and tell me what you want.* **beat sb at their own ˈgame** to defeat or do better than sb in an activity which they have chosen or in which they think they are strong **beat your ˈbrains out** (*informal, especially NAmE*) to think very hard about sth for a long time **beat your ˈbreast** to show that you feel sorry about sth that you have done, especially in public and in an EXAGGERATED way **beat the ˈclock** to finish a task, race, etc. before a particular time **beat it** (*slang*) (usually used in orders) to go away immediately: *This is private land, so beat it!* **beat a path to sb's ˈdoor** if a lot of people **beat a path to sb's door**, they are all interested in sth that person has to sell, or can do or tell them: *Top theatrical agents are beating a path to the teenager's door.* **beat the ˈrap** (*NAmE, slang*) to escape without being punished **beat a (hasty) reˈtreat** to go away or back quickly, especially to avoid sth unpleasant **beat ˈtime (to sth)** to mark or follow the rhythm of music, by waving a stick, TAPPING your foot (= hitting it against the floor), etc: *She beat time with her fingers.* **beat sb to the ˈpunch** (*informal*) to get or do sth before sb else can **if you can't beat them, ˈjoin them** (*saying*) if you cannot defeat sb or be as successful as they are, then it is more sensible to join them in what they are doing and perhaps get some advantage for yourself by doing so **off the ˌbeaten ˈtrack** far away from other people, houses, etc: *They live miles off the beaten track.* **a rod/stick to ˈbeat sb with** a fact, an argument, etc. that is used in order to blame or punish sb **take some ˈbeating** to be difficult to beat: *That score is going to take some beating.* ◊ *For sheer luxury, this hotel takes some beating.* ⊃ more at BLACK *adj.*, DAYLIGHTS, DEAD *adj.*, DRUM *n.*, HELL

**PHRV** **beat sth↔ˈdown** to hit a door, etc. many times until it breaks open **beat ˈdown (on sb/sth)** if the sun **beats down**, it shines with great heat **beat sb/sth ˈdown (to sth)** to persuade sb to reduce the price at which they are selling sth: *He wanted $8000 for the car but I beat him down to $6000.* ◊ *I beat down the price to $6000.* **beat ˈoff** (*NAmE, taboo, slang*) to MASTURBATE **beat sb/sth↔ˈoff** to force sb/sth back or away by fighting: *The attacker was beaten off.* ◊ *She beat off a challenge to her leadership.* **beat ˈon sb** (*NAmE*) = BEAT UP ON SB **beat sth↔ˈout 1** to produce a rhythm by hitting sth many times **2** to put a fire out by beating: *We beat the flames out.* **3** to remove sth by hitting it with a HAMMER, etc: *They can beat out the dent in the car's wing.* **beat sth ˈout of sb** to hit sb until they tell you what you want to know **ˈbeat sb out of sth** (*NAmE, informal*) to cheat sb by taking sth from them: *Her brother beat her out of $200.* **beat sb to sth/ˈ…** | **beat sb ˈto it** to get somewhere or do sth before sb else: *She beat me to the top of the hill.* ◊ *I was about to take the last cake, but he beat me to it.* **beat sb↔ˈup** to hit or kick sb hard, many times: *He was badly beaten up by a gang of thugs.* **beat ˈup on sb** (also **ˈbeat on sb**) (*NAmE*) to blame sb too much for sth: *Don't beat up on Paul, he tried his best.* **beat yourself ˈup (about/over sth)** (*NAmE also* **beat ˈup on yourself (about/over sth)**) (*informal*) to blame yourself too much for sth: *Look, there's no need to beat yourself up over this.*

■ **noun**
- **OF DRUMS/HEART/WINGS 1** [C] a single hit to sth, such as a drum, or a movement of sth, such as your heart; the sound that this makes: *several loud beats on the drum* **2** [sing.] a series of regular hits to sth, such as a drum; the sound that this makes: *the steady beat of the drums* ⊃ see also HEARTBEAT
- **RHYTHM 3** [C] the main rhythm, or a unit of rhythm, in a piece of music, a poem, etc: *This type of music has a strong beat to it.* ◊ *The piece has four beats to the bar.* ⊃ WORDFINDER NOTE at SING

▼ **SYNONYMS**

**beat**

**batter • pound • lash • hammer**

These words all mean to hit sb/sth many times, especially hard.

**beat** to hit sb/sth a lot of times, especially very hard: *Someone was beating at the door.* ◊ *A young man was found beaten to death last night.* ◊ *At that time, children were often beaten for quite minor offences* (= as a punishment).

**batter** to hit sb/sth hard a lot of times, especially in way that causes serious injury or damage: *He had been badly battered around the head and face.* ◊ *Severe winds have been battering the coast.*

**pound** to hit sb/sth hard a lot of times, especially in a way that makes a lot of noise: *Heavy rain pounded on the roof.*

**lash** to hit sb/sth with a lot of force: *The rain lashed at the window.* **NOTE** The subject of **lash** is often *rain, wind, hail, sea* or *waves*.

**hammer** to hit sb/sth hard a lot of times, in a way that is noisy or violent: *He hammered the door with his fists.*

**POUND OR HAMMER?**
- There is not much difference in meaning between these two, but to **pound** is sometimes a steadier action. To **hammer** can be more violent and it is often used figuratively.

**PATTERNS**
- to beat/batter/pound/lash/hammer sb/sth **with** sth
- to beat/batter/pound/lash/hammer **against** sth
- to beat/batter/pound/hammer **on** sth
- to beat/batter/hammer sth **down**
- the **rain/wind/sea** beats/batters/pounds/lashes (at) sth

- **OF POLICE OFFICER 4** [C, usually sing.] the area that a police officer walks around regularly and which he or she is responsible for: *on the~ More police officers out on the beat may help to cut crime.* IDM see HEART n., MARCH v., WALK v.
- ▪ *adj.* [not before noun] (*informal*) = DEAD BEAT

**beat-box** /ˈbiːtbɒks; NAmE -baːks/ *noun, verb*
- ▪ *noun* **1** [C] (*informal*) an electronic machine that produces drum sounds **2** [C] (*informal*) a radio, CD player, etc. that can be carried around and is used for playing loud music **3** (*also* **beat·boxer**) [C] a person who uses the voice to make sounds like a drum to create the beat in HIP-HOP **4** [U] music that is created using sounds made with the human voice
- ▪ *verb* [I] to copy the sound of a drum with the voice

**beat·box·ing** /ˈbiːtbɒksɪŋ; NAmE -baːk-/ *noun* [U] the use of the human voice to create the beat in HIP-HOP: *an amazing beatboxing performance*

**beaten-'up** *adj.* = BEAT-UP

**beat·er** /ˈbiːtə(r)/ *noun* **1** (often in compounds) a tool used for beating things: *a carpet beater* ◊ *an egg beater* **2** a person employed to drive birds and animals out of bushes, etc., into the open, so they can be shot for sport **3** **-beater** (in compounds) a person who hits someone: *a wife-beater* **4** (*NAmE*) (*BrE* **bang·er**) (*informal*) an old car that is in bad condition ⇒ see also WORLD-BEATER

**the ˌbeat generˈation** *noun* [sing.] a group of young people in the 1950s and early 1960s who rejected the way most people lived in society, wanted to express themselves freely, and liked modern jazz

**bea·tif·ic** /ˌbiːəˈtɪfɪk/ *adj.* (*formal*) showing great joy and peace: *a beatific smile/expression*

**be·atify** /biˈætɪfaɪ/ *verb* (**be·ati·fies**, **be·ati·fy·ing**, **be·ati·fied**, **be·ati·fied**) ~ **sb** (of the Pope) to give a dead person a special honour by stating officially that he/she is very holy ⇒ compare BLESS, CANONIZE ▶ **be·ati·fi·ca·tion** /biˌætɪfɪˈkeɪʃn/ *noun* [C, U]

**beat·ing** /ˈbiːtɪŋ/ *noun* **1** [C] an act of hitting sb hard and repeatedly, as a punishment or in a fight: *to give sb a beating* **2** [C] (*informal*) a very heavy defeat: *The team has taken a few beatings this season.* **3** [U] a series of regular hits to sth such as a drum, or movements of sth, such as your heart, the sound that this makes: *He could hear the beating of his own heart.* ◊ *the beating of drums/wings*
- IDM **ˌtake some ˈbeating** (*BrE*) to be difficult to do better than or be better than: *As a place to live, Oxford takes some beating.*

**beat·nik** /ˈbiːtnɪk/ *noun* a young person in the 1950s and early 1960s who rejected the way of life of ordinary society and showed this by behaving and dressing in a different way from most people

**ˌbeat-ˈup** (*also* **ˌbeaten-ˈup**) *adj.* [usually before noun] (*informal*) old and damaged: *a beat-up old truck*

**beau** /bəʊ/ *noun* (*pl.* **beaux** /bəʊz/ *or* **beaus**) (*old-fashioned*) a woman's male partner or friend

**beau·coup** /ˈbəʊkuː/ *det.* (*US, informal, from French*) many or a lot: *You can spend beaucoup bucks* (= a lot of money) *on software.*

**the ˈBeau·fort scale** /ðə ˈbəʊfət skeɪl; NAmE -fərt-/ *noun* [sing.] a range of numbers used for measuring how strongly the wind is blowing. The lowest number 0 means that there is no wind and the highest number 12 means that there is a hurricane (= a violent storm with very strong winds): *The storm measured 10 on the Beaufort scale.* ORIGIN From Sir Francis Beaufort, the English admiral who invented it.

**Beau·jo·lais** /ˈbəʊʒəleɪ; NAmE ˌbəʊʒəˈleɪ/ *noun* (*pl.* **Beau·jo·lais**) [C, U] a light wine, usually red, from the Beaujolais district of France

**beaut** /bjuːt/ *noun, adj., exclamation*
- ▪ *noun* (*NAmE, AustralE, NZE, informal*) an excellent or beautiful person or thing
- ▪ *adj., exclamation* (*AustralE, informal*) excellent; very good

121 **beauty**

**beaut·eous** /ˈbjuːtiəs/ *adj.* (*literary*) beautiful

**beaut·ician** /bjuːˈtɪʃn/ *noun* a person, usually a woman, whose job is to give beauty treatments to the face and body

**beau·ti·ful** 🔑 A1 /ˈbjuːtɪfl/ *adj.* **1** 🔑 A1 having beauty; giving pleasure to the senses or to the mind: *a beautiful woman/girl* ◊ *What a beautiful day!* ◊ *a beautiful face/baby/voice/garden/beach* ◊ *beautiful countryside/weather/music* ◊ *She looked stunningly beautiful that night.* **2** very good; very kind or showing great skill: *Thank you—you have done a beautiful thing.* ◊ *What beautiful timing!*

▼ SYNONYMS

**beautiful**
pretty • handsome • attractive • lovely • good-looking • gorgeous

These words all describe people who are pleasant to look at.

**beautiful** (especially of a woman or girl) very pleasant to look at: *She looked stunningly beautiful that night.*

**pretty** (especially of a girl or woman) pleasant to look at: *She's got a very pretty face.* NOTE **Pretty** s used most often to talk about girls. When it is used to talk about a woman, it usually suggests that she is like a girl, with small, delicate features.

**handsome** (of a man) pleasant to look at; (of a woman) pleasant to look at, with large strong features rather than small delicate ones: *He was described as 'tall, dark and handsome'.*

**attractive** (of a person) pleasant to look at, especially in a sexual way: *She's a very attractive woman.*

**lovely** (of a person) beautiful; very attractive: *She looked particularly lovely that night.* NOTE When you describe sb as **lovely**, you are usually showing that you also like them very much.

**good-looking** (of a person) pleasant to look at, often in a sexual way: *She arrived with a very good-looking man.*

**gorgeous** (*informal*) (of a person) extremely attractive, especially in a sexual way: *You look gorgeous!*

ATTRACTIVE OR GOOD-LOOKING?
- If you describe sb as **attractive** you often also mean that they have a pleasant personality as well as being pleasant to look at; **good-looking** just describes sb's physical appearance.

PATTERNS
- a(n) beautiful / pretty / handsome / attractive / lovely / good-looking / gorgeous **girl** / **woman**
- a(n) beautiful / handsome / attractive / good-looking / gorgeous **boy** / **man**
- a(n) beautiful / pretty / handsome / attractive / lovely / good-looking **face**

**beau·ti·ful·ly** /ˈbjuːtɪfli/ *adv.* **1** in a beautiful way: *She sings beautifully.* ◊ *a beautifully decorated house* **2** very well; in a way that pleases you: *It's all working out beautifully.*

**beaut·ify** /ˈbjuːtɪfaɪ/ *verb* (**beau·ti·fies**, **beau·ti·fy·ing**, **beau·ti·fied**, **beau·ti·fied**) ~ **sb/sth** to make sb/sth beautiful or more beautiful

**beauty** 🔑 B1 /ˈbjuːti/ *noun* (*pl.* **-ies**) **1** 🔑 B1 [U] the quality of giving pleasure to the senses or to the mind: *~ of sth the beauty of the sunset/of poetry/of his singing* ◊ *The woods were designated an area of outstanding natural beauty.* ◊ *beauty products/treatments* (= intended to make a person more beautiful) ◊ *She was a contestant in the Miss World beauty pageant.* **2** [C] a person or thing that is beautiful: *She had been a beauty in her day.* **3** [C] an excellent example of its type: *That last goal was a beauty!* **4** [C] an attractive feature SYN **advantage**: *One of the beauties of living here is that it's so peaceful.* ◊ *The project will require very little work to start up; that's the beauty of it.*

# Beauty and the Beast

**IDM** **beauty is in the eye of the ˈbeholder** (*saying*) people all have different ideas about what is beautiful **beauty is only skin-ˈdeep** (*saying*) how a person looks is less important than their character

**ˈBeauty and the ˈBeast** *noun* **1** a traditional story about a young girl who saves a large ugly creature from a magic SPELL by her love. He becomes a HANDSOME prince and they get married. **2** (*informal, humorous*) two people of whom one is much more attractive than the other

**ˈbeauty contest** *noun* (*BrE*) **1** a competition to choose the most beautiful from a group of women ⊃ compare PAGEANT **2** (*US* **ˈbeauty parade**) an occasion on which several competing companies or people try to persuade sb to use their services

**ˈbeauty mark** *noun* (*NAmE*) = BEAUTY SPOT

**ˈbeauty queen** *noun* a woman who is judged to be the most beautiful in a BEAUTY CONTEST

**ˈbeauty salon** (*also* **ˈbeauty parlour**) (*US also* **ˈbeauty shop**) *noun* a place where you can pay for treatment to your face, hair, nails, etc., which is intended to make you more beautiful

**ˈbeauty school** *noun* (*NAmE*) a place that trains people to cut hair, take care of nails, etc. as a job

**ˈbeauty sleep** *noun* [U] (*humorous*) enough sleep at night to make sure that you look and feel healthy and beautiful

**ˈbeauty spot** *noun* **1** (*BrE*) a place in the countryside which is famous because it is beautiful **2** (*NAmE also* **ˈbeauty mark**) a small dark spot on a woman's face, which used to be thought to make her more beautiful

**beaux** /bəʊz/ *pl.* of BEAU

**bea·ver** /ˈbiːvə(r)/ *noun, verb*
■ *noun* **1** [C] an animal with a wide flat tail and strong teeth. Beavers live in water and on land and can build DAMS (= barriers across rivers), made of pieces of wood and mud. The beaver is an official symbol of Canada. ⊃ VISUAL VOCAB page V2 **2** [U] the fur of the beaver, used in making hats and clothes **3** [C] (*especially NAmE, taboo, slang*) the area around a woman's sex organs
■ *verb*
**PHR V** **ˌbeaver aˈway (at sth)** (*informal*) to work very hard at sth: *He's been beavering away at the accounts all morning.*

**bebop** /ˈbiːbɒp; *NAmE* -bɑːp/ (*also* **bop**) *noun* [U] a type of jazz with complicated rhythms

**be·calmed** /bɪˈkɑːmd/ *adj.* (of a ship with a sail) unable to move because there is no wind

**be·came** /bɪˈkeɪm/ *past tense* of BECOME

**be·cause** 🔊 **A1** **S** /bɪˈkɒz; *BrE also* -ˈkəz; *NAmE also* -ˈkɔːz/ *conj.* for the reason that: *I did it because he told me to.* ◊ *Just because I don't complain, people think I'm satisfied.* ⊃ EXPRESS YOURSELF at WHY ▶ **beˈcause of** *prep.*: *They are here because of us.* ◊ *He walked slowly because of his bad leg.* ◊ *Because of his wife('s) being there, I said nothing about it.*

**béch·amel** /ˌbeɪʃəˈmel/ (*also* **béchamel ˈsauce**) *noun* [U] a thick sauce made with milk, flour and butter **SYN** **white sauce**

**beck** /bek/ *noun* (*BrE, dialect*) a small river **SYN** **stream**
**IDM** **at sb's beck and ˈcall** always ready to obey sb's orders: *Don't expect to have me at your beck and call.*

**beckon** /ˈbekən/ *verb* **1** [I, T] to give sb a signal using your finger or hand, especially to tell them to move nearer to or to follow you **SYN** **signal**: ~ *to sb (to do sth) He beckoned to the waiter to bring the bill.* ◊ ~ *sb (+ adv./prep.) He beckoned her over with a wave.* ◊ *The boss beckoned him into her office.* ◊ ~ *sb to do sth She beckoned him to come and join them.* **2** [I, T] to appear very attractive to sb: *The clear blue sea beckoned.* ◊ ~ *sb The prospect of a month without work was beckoning her.* **3** [I] to be sth that is likely to happen or will possibly happen to sb in the future: *For many kids leaving college the prospect of unemployment beckons.*

---

▼ **LANGUAGE BANK**

### because of
Explaining reasons

- The number of people with diabetes is growing, partly *because of* an increase in levels of obesity.
- The number of overweight children has increased dramatically in recent years, largely *as a result of* changes in diet and lifestyle.
- The increase in childhood obesity is largely *due to / the result of* changes in lifestyle and diet over the last twenty years.
- Many obese children are bullied at school *on account of* their weight.
- Part of the problem with treating childhood obesity *stems from* the fact that parents do not always recognize that their children are obese.
- Childhood obesity may be *caused by* genetic factors, as well as environmental ones.

⊃ LANGUAGE BANK at CAUSE, CONSEQUENTLY, THEREFORE

---

**be·come** 🔊 **A1** **S** /bɪˈkʌm/ *verb* (**be·came** /-ˈkeɪm/, **be·come**) **1** **A1** linking verb to start to be sth: + *adj. It soon became apparent that no one was going to come.* ◊ *It is becoming increasingly clear that something has gone seriously wrong.* ◊ + *noun She became queen in 1952.* ◊ *The bill will become law next year.* ◊ *Over the last five years she has become part of the family.* **2** [T, no passive] (not used in the progressive tenses) ~ *sb* (*formal*) to be suitable for sb: *Such behaviour did not become her.* **3** [T, no passive] (not used in the progressive tenses) ~ *sb* (*formal*) to look attractive on sb **SYN** **suit**: *Short hair really becomes you.*
**IDM** **what beˈcame, has beˈcome, will beˈcome of sb / sth?** used to ask about what has happened or what will happen to sb/sth: *What became of that student who used to live with you?* ◊ *I dread to think what will become of them if they lose their home.*

▼ **WHICH WORD?**

### become / get / go / turn
These verbs are used frequently with the following adjectives:

| become ~ | get ~ | go ~ | turn ~ |
|---|---|---|---|
| involved | used to | wrong | blue |
| clear | better | right | sour |
| accustomed | worse | bad | bad |
| pregnant | pregnant | white | red |
| extinct | tired | crazy | cold |
| famous | angry | bald | |
| ill | dark | blind | |

- **Become** is more formal than *get*. Both describe changes in people's emotional or physical state, or natural or social changes.
- **Go** is usually used for negative changes.
- **Go** and **turn** are both used for changes of colour.
- **Turn** is also used for changes in the weather.

---

**be·com·ing** /bɪˈkʌmɪŋ/ *adj.* (*formal*) **1** (of clothes, etc.) making the person wearing them look more attractive **SYN** **flattering** **2** suitable or appropriate for sb or their situation **SYN** **fitting**: *It was not very becoming behaviour for a teacher.* **OPP** **unbecoming**

**bec·que·rel** /ˈbekərel/ *noun* (*abbr.* **Bq**) (*physics*) a unit for measuring RADIOACTIVITY

**BEd** (*also* **B.Ed.** *especially in NAmE*) /ˌbiː ˈed/ *noun* a first university degree in education (the abbreviation for 'Bachelor of Education'): (*BrE*) *Sarah Wells BEd*

**bed** 🔊 **A1** /bed/ *noun, verb*
■ *noun*
• FURNITURE **1** **A1** [C, U] a piece of furniture for sleeping on: *a single/double bed* ◊ **on the ~** *She lay on the bed (= on top of the covers).* ◊ **in ~** *He lay in bed (= under the covers).* ◊ *I'm tired—I'm going to bed.* ◊ *I'll just put the kids to bed.* ◊ *It's time for bed (= time to go to sleep).* ◊ *He likes*

to have a mug of cocoa before bed (= before going to bed). ◊ to **get into/out of bed** ◊ **to make the bed** (= arrange the covers in a tidy way) ◊ Could you give me a bed for the night (= somewhere to sleep)? ◊ There's a shortage of hospital beds (= not enough room for patients to be admitted). ◊ He has been confined to bed with flu for the past couple of days. ⊃ see also AIRBED, CAMP BED, SOFA BED, TWIN BED, WATERBED
- **OF RIVER/LAKE/SEA 2** [C] the bottom of a river, the sea, etc: the ocean bed ◊ oyster beds (= an area in the sea where there are many OYSTERS)
- **FOR FLOWERS/VEGETABLES 3** [C] an area of ground in a garden or park for growing flowers, vegetables, etc: flower beds ◊ ~ **of sth** ornamental beds of roses ⊃ see also SEEDBED
- **BOTTOM LAYER 4** [C] ~ **of sth** a layer of sth that other things lie or rest on: grilled chicken, served on a bed of rice ◊ The blocks should be laid on a bed of concrete.
- **GEOLOGY 5** [C] a layer of CLAY, rock, etc. in the ground ⊃ see also BEDROCK
- **IDM** **(not) a bed of 'roses** (not) an easy or a pleasant situation: Their life together hasn't exactly been a bed of roses. **get out of bed on the wrong side** (BrE) (NAmE **get up on the wrong side of the bed**) to be in a bad mood for the whole day for no particular reason **go to bed with sb** (informal) to have sex with sb **in bed** used to refer to sexual activity: What's he like in bed? ◊ I caught them in bed together (= having sex). **take to your 'bed** to go to bed and stay there because you are ill **you've made your bed and you must 'lie in/on it** (saying) you must accept the results of your actions ⊃ more at DIE v., WET v.
- **verb** (-dd-) **1** ~ **sth (in sth)** to fix sth in sth so that it cannot move easily: The bricks were bedded in sand to improve drainage. ◊ Make sure that you bed the roots firmly in the soil. **2** ~ **sb** (old-fashioned) to have sex with sb
**PHRV** **bed 'down** to sleep in a place where you do not usually sleep: You have my room and I'll bed down in the living room.

**bed and 'board** noun [U] (BrE) a room to sleep in and food

**bed and 'breakfast** noun (abbr. B and B, B & B) **1** [U] (BrE) a service that provides a room to sleep in and a meal the next morning in private houses and small hotels: Do you do bed and breakfast? ◊ Bed and breakfast costs £50 a night. ⊃ compare FULL BOARD, HALF BOARD **2** [C] a place that provides this service: There were several good bed and breakfasts in the area.

**be·dazzle** /bɪˈdæzl/ verb [usually passive] to impress sb very much with intelligence, beauty, etc: **be bedazzled (by sb/sth)** He was so bedazzled by her looks that he couldn't speak. ▶ **be·dazzle·ment** noun [U]

**bed·bug** /ˈbedbʌɡ/ noun a small flat insect that lives especially in beds, where it bites people and drinks their blood

**bed·cham·ber** /ˈbedtʃeɪmbə(r)/ noun (old use) a bedroom: the royal bedchamber

**bed·clothes** /ˈbedkləʊðz/ (BrE also **bed·covers** /ˈbedkʌvəz; NAmE -vərz/) noun [pl.] the sheets and other covers that you put on a bed

**bed·cover** /ˈbedkʌvə(r)/ noun **1** = BEDSPREAD **2** (BrE) **bed·covers** = BEDCLOTHES

**bed·ding** /ˈbedɪŋ/ noun [U] **1** the sheets and covers that you put on a bed, and often also the MATTRESS and the PILLOWS **2** STRAW, etc. for animals to sleep on

**bedding plant** noun a plant that is planted out in a garden bed, usually just before it gets flowers. It usually grows and dies within one year.

**beddy-byes** /ˈbedi baɪz/ (BrE) (NAmE **beddy-bye**) noun [U] a child's word for bed, used when talking about the time sb goes to bed: Time for beddy-byes.

**be·deck** /bɪˈdek/ verb [usually passive] ~ **sth/sb (with/in sth)** (literary) to decorate sth/sb with flowers, flags, PRECIOUS STONES, etc.

**be·devil** /bɪˈdevl/ verb (-ll-, US -l-) ~ **sb/sth** (formal) to cause a lot of problems for sb/sth over a long period of time **SYN** beset: The expedition was bedevilled by bad weather.

---

123 **bee**

**bed·fel·low** /ˈbedfeləʊ/ noun a person or thing that is connected with or related to another, often in a way that you would not expect: strange/unlikely bedfellows

**bed·head** /ˈbedhed/ noun the part of the bed that is at the end, behind the head of the person sleeping on it

**bed·jacket** /ˈbeddʒækɪt/ noun a short jacket worn when sitting up in bed

**bed·lam** /ˈbedləm/ noun [U] a very noisy and confusing scene **SYN** chaos: It was bedlam at our house on the morning of the wedding.

**'bed linen** noun [U] sheets and PILLOWCASES for a bed

**Bed·ouin** /ˈbeduɪn/ noun (pl. **Bed·ou·in**) a member of an Arab people that traditionally lives in tents in the desert

**bed·pan** /ˈbedpæn/ noun a container used as a toilet by a person who is too ill to get out of bed

**bed·post** /ˈbedpəʊst/ noun one of the four supports at the corners of a bed (especially an old type of bed with a wooden or metal frame)

**be·drag·gled** /bɪˈdræɡld/ adj. made wet, dirty or untidy by rain, mud, etc: bedraggled hair/clothes

**bed·rid·den** /ˈbedrɪdn/ adj. having to stay in bed all the time because you are sick, injured or old

**bed·rock** /ˈbedrɒk; NAmE -rɑːk/ noun **1** [sing.] a strong base for sth, especially the facts or the principles on which it is based: The poor suburbs traditionally formed the bedrock of the party's support. ◊ Honesty is the bedrock of any healthy relationship. **2** [U] the solid rock in the ground below the loose soil and sand

**bed·roll** /ˈbedrəʊl/ noun (especially NAmE) a thick piece of material or a SLEEPING BAG that you can roll up for carrying and use for sleeping on or in, for example when you are camping

**bed·room** /ˈbedruːm, -rʊm/ noun, adj.
- **noun 1** a room for sleeping in: the spare/guest bedroom ◊ a hotel with 20 bedrooms ◊ This is the master bedroom (= the main bedroom of the house). **2 -bedroom** or **-bedroomed** having the number of bedrooms mentioned: a three-bedroomed house
- **adj.** [only before noun] used as a way of referring to sexual activity: the bedroom scenes in the movie

**'bedroom community** (also **'bedroom suburb**) (both NAmE) (BrE **'dormitory town**) noun a town that people live in and from where they travel to work in a bigger town or city

**bed·side** /ˈbedsaɪd/ noun [usually sing.] the area next to a bed: His mother has been at his bedside throughout his illness. ◊ a bedside lamp

**bedside 'manner** noun [sing.] the way in which a doctor or other person talks to sb who is ill

**bedside 'table** (especially BrE) (NAmE usually **night·stand**, **'night table**) noun a small table next to a bed

**bed·sit** /ˈbedsɪt/ (also **bed·sit·ter** /ˌbedˈsɪtə(r)/) (also formal **bed'sitting room**) noun (all BrE) a room that a person rents and uses for both living and sleeping in

**bed·sore** /ˈbedsɔː(r)/ noun a painful place on a person's skin, caused by lying in bed for a long time

**bed·spread** /ˈbedspred/ (also **bed·cover**) (NAmE also **spread**) noun an attractive cover put on top of all the sheets and covers on a bed

**bed·stead** /ˈbedsted/ noun the wooden or metal frame of an old-fashioned type of bed

**bed·time** /ˈbedtaɪm/ noun [U, C] the time when sb usually goes to bed: It's way past your bedtime. ◊ Will you read me a bedtime story?

**'bed-wetting** noun [U] the problem of URINATING in bed, usually by children while they are asleep

**bee** /biː/ noun **1** a black and yellow flying insect that can STING (= touch your skin and make you feel a sharp pain). Bees live in large groups and make HONEY (=

a sweet sticky substance that is good to eat): *Bees were buzzing in the clover.* ◊ *a swarm of bees* ◊ *a bee sting* ⊃ see also BEEHIVE, BEESWAX, BUMBLEBEE, HONEYBEE, KILLER BEE, QUEEN BEE **2** (*NAmE*) a meeting in a group where people combine work, competition and pleasure: *a sewing bee* ⊃ see also SPELLING BEE
**IDM** **the ˌbee's ˈknees** (*informal*) an excellent person or thing: *She thinks she's the bee's knees* (= she has a very high opinion of herself). **have a ˈbee in your bonnet (about sth)** (*informal*) to think or talk about sth all the time and to think that it is very important ⊃ more at BIRD *n.*, BUSY *adj.*

**the Beeb** /ðə ˈbiːb/ *noun* [sing.] an informal name for the BBC

**beech** /biːtʃ/ *noun* **1** [U, C] (*also* **ˈbeech tree** [C]) a tall forest tree with smooth grey BARK, shiny leaves and small nuts: *forests planted with beech* ◊ *beech hedges* ◊ *The great beeches towered up towards the sky.* ⊃ VISUAL VOCAB page V6 **2** (*also* **ˈbeech-wood**) [U] the wood of the beech tree

**beef** /biːf/ *noun, verb*
■ *noun* **1** [U] meat that comes from a cow: *roast beef* ◊ *beef and dairy cattle* ◊ *minced/ground beef* ⊃ see also CORNED BEEF **2** [C] (*informal*) a complaint: *What's his latest beef?*
■ *verb* [I] ~ **(about sb/sth)** (*informal*) to complain a lot about sb/sth
**PHRV** **ˌbeef sth↔ˈup** (*informal*) to make sth bigger, better, more interesting, etc.

**beef·bur·ger** /ˈbiːfbɜːɡə(r); *NAmE* -bɜːrɡ-/ *noun* (*BrE*) = HAMBURGER

**beef·cake** /ˈbiːfkeɪk/ *noun* [U] (*slang*) attractive men with big muscles

**beef·eater** /ˈbiːfiːtə(r)/ *noun* a guard who dresses in a traditional uniform at the Tower of London

**beef·steak** /ˈbiːfsteɪk/ *noun* [C, U] = STEAK

**beef ˈtea** *noun* [U] (*BrE*) a hot drink made by boiling beef in water. It used to be given to people who were sick.

**beef toˈmato** (*also* **beefsteak toˈmato** *especially in NAmE*) *noun* a type of large tomato

**beefy** /ˈbiːfi/ *adj.* (**beef·ier**, **beefi·est**) (*informal*) (of a person or their body) big or fat: *beefy men/arms/thighs*

**bee·hive** /ˈbiːhaɪv/ *noun* **1** [C] = HIVE **2** a HAIRSTYLE for women, with the hair piled high on top of the head

**bee·keep·er** /ˈbiːkiːpə(r)/ *noun* a person who owns and takes care of bees ▶ **bee·keep·ing** *noun* [U]

**bee·line** /ˈbiːlaɪn/ *noun*
**IDM** **make a ˈbeeline for sth/sb** (*informal*) to go straight towards sth/sb as quickly as you can

**Be·el·ze·bub** /biˈelzɪbʌb/ *noun* a name for the DEVIL

**been** /biːn, bɪn; *NAmE* bɪn/ *past part.* of BE, GO

**ˈbeen-to** *noun* (*WAfrE*) a person who returns to his or her home in Africa after studying, working, etc. in a foreign country. People are often identified as **been-tos** because they have a different ACCENT (= way of pronouncing the words of a language).

**beep** /biːp/ *noun, verb*
■ *noun* a short high sound such as that made by a car HORN or by electronic equipment
■ *verb* **1** [I] (of an electronic machine) to make a short high sound: *The microwave beeps to let you know when it has finished.* **2** [I, T] when a car HORN, etc. **beeps** or when you **beep** it, it makes a short noise: *The car behind started beeping at us.* ◊ **~sth** *He beeped his horn at the cyclist.* **3** (*NAmE*) (*BrE* **bleep**) [T] **~sb** to call sb on their beeper

**beep·er** /ˈbiːpə(r)/ *noun* (*especially NAmE*) = BLEEPER

**beer** /bɪə(r); *NAmE* bɪr/ *noun* **1** [U, C] an alcoholic drink made from MALT with HOPS added to give it taste. There are many types of beer: *a pint/can/bottle of beer* ◊ *a beer glass/bottle/can* ◊ *Are you a beer drinker?* **2** [C] a glass, bottle or can of beer: *Shall we have a beer?* ⊃ see also CRAFT BEER, GINGER BEER, KEG BEER, ROOT BEER, SMALL BEER

**ˈbeer belly** (*also* **ˈbeer gut**) *noun* (*informal*) a man's very fat stomach, caused by drinking a lot of beer over a long period

**ˈbeer cellar** *noun* **1** a room for storing beer below a pub or bar **2** a pub or bar that is underground or partly underground

**ˈbeer garden** *noun* an outdoor area at a pub or bar with tables and chairs

**ˈbeer goggles** *noun* [pl.] (*informal*) you say that sb is wearing **beer goggles** when they have drunk too much alcohol and are attracted to sb that they would not usually find attractive

**ˈbeer mat** *noun* (*BrE*) a small piece of thick card that you put under a glass, usually in a bar, etc. in order to protect the surface below

**beery** /ˈbɪəri; *NAmE* ˈbɪri/ *adj.* smelling of beer; influenced by the drinking of beer

**bees·wax** /ˈbiːzwæks/ *noun* [U] a yellow sticky substance that is produced by bees and is used especially for making CANDLES and POLISH for wood

**beet** /biːt/ *noun* [C, U] **1** a plant with a root that is used as a vegetable, especially for feeding animals or making sugar ⊃ see also SUGAR BEET **2** (*NAmE*) (*BrE* **ˈbeet·root**) a plant with a round dark red root that is cooked and eaten as a vegetable ⊃ VISUAL VOCAB page V3

**bee·tle** /ˈbiːtl/ *noun, verb*
■ *noun* an insect, often large and black, with a hard case on its back, covering its wings. There are several types of beetle. ⊃ VISUAL VOCAB page V3
■ *verb* [I] + *adv./prep.* (*BrE, informal*) to move somewhere quickly **SYN** **scurry**: *I last saw him beetling off down the road.*

**beet·root** /ˈbiːtruːt/ (*BrE*) (*NAmE* **beet**) *noun* [U, C] a plant with a round dark red root that is cooked and eaten as a vegetable ⊃ VISUAL VOCAB page V3

**be·fall** /bɪˈfɔːl/ *verb* (used only in the third person) (**be·fell** /-ˈfel/, **be·fallen** /-ˈfɔːlən/) (*literary*) (of sth unpleasant) to happen to sb: *They were unaware of the fate that was to befall them.*

**befit** /bɪˈfɪt/ *verb* (used only in the third person and in participles) (**-tt-**) **sth befits sb** (*formal*) to be suitable and good enough for sb/sth: *It was a lavish reception* **as befitted** *a visitor of her status.* ◊ *He lived in the style befitting a gentleman.*

**befog** /bɪˈfɒɡ; *NAmE* -ˈfɑːɡ/ *verb* (used only in the third person) **sth befogs sb/sth** to make sb confused: *Her brain was befogged by lack of sleep.*

**be·fore** /bɪˈfɔː(r)/ *prep., conj., adv.*
■ *prep.* **1** earlier than sb/sth: *before lunch* ◊ *the day before yesterday* ◊ *The year before last he won a gold medal, and the year before that he won a silver.* ◊ *She's lived there since before the war.* ◊ *He arrived before me.* ◊ *She became a lawyer as her father had before her.* ◊ *Leave your keys at reception before departure.* ◊ *Something ought to have been done before now.* ◊ *We'll know* **before long** (= soon). ◊ *Turn left just before* (= before you reach) *the bank.* **2** used to say that sb/sth is ahead of sb/sth in an order or arrangement: *Your name is before mine on the list.* ◊ *He puts his work before everything* (= regards it as more important than anything else). **3** (*rather formal*) used to say that sb/sth is in a position in front of sb/sth: *They knelt before the throne.* ◊ *Before you is a list of the points we have to discuss.* ⊃ compare BEHIND **4** used to say that sth is facing sb in the future: *The task before us is a daunting one.* ◊ *The whole summer lay before me.* **5** in the presence of sb who is listening, watching, etc: *He was brought before the judge.* ◊ *She said it before witnesses.* ◊ *They had the advantage of playing before their home crowd.* **6** (*formal*) used to say how sb reacts when they have to face sb/sth: *They retreated before the enemy.*
■ *conj.* **1** earlier than the time when: *Do it before you forget.* ◊ *Did she leave a message before she went?* **2** until: *It may be many years before the situation improves.* ◊

It was some time before I realized the truth. **3** ⓘ A2 used to warn or threaten sb that sth bad could happen: *Put that away before it gets broken.* **4** (*formal*) rather than: *I'd die before I apologized!*
- *adv.* ⓘ A2 at an earlier time; in the past; already: *You should have told me so before.* ◊ *It had been fine the week before* (= the previous week). ◊ *That had happened long before* (= a long time earlier). ◊ *I think we've met before.*

**be·fore·hand** /bɪˈfɔːhænd; *NAmE* -ˈfɔːrh-/ *adv.* earlier; before sth else happens or is done: *two weeks/three days/a few hours beforehand* ◊ *I wish we'd known about it beforehand.*

**be·friend** /bɪˈfrend/ *verb* [usually passive] ~ **sb** to become a friend of sb, especially sb who needs your help: *Shortly after my arrival at the school, I was befriended by an older girl.*

**be·fud·dled** /bɪˈfʌdld/ *adj.* confused and unable to think normally: *He was befuddled by drink.*

**beg** ⓘ B2 /beg/ *verb* (-gg-) **1** ⓘ B2 [I, T] to ask sb for sth especially in an anxious way because you want or need it very much: *Now you have to beg and plead.* ◊ ~ **for sth** *He wants to see them beg for mercy.* ◊ ~ **sb (for sth)** *They begged him for help.* ◊ ~ **sth** *She begged permission to leave.* ◊ ~ **sth of/from sb** *I managed to beg a lift from a passing motorist.* ◊ ~ **(sb) + speech** *'Give me one more chance,' he begged (her).* ◊ ~ **sb to do sth** *She begged him not to go.* ◊ ~ **to do sth** *He begged to be told the truth.* ◊ ~ **that …** (*formal*) *She begged that she be allowed to go.* **2** ⓘ B2 [I, T] to ask sb for money, food, etc., especially in the street: *London is full of homeless people begging in the streets.* ◊ *a begging letter* (= one that asks sb for money) ◊ ~ **for sth (from sb)** *The children were begging for food.* ◊ ~ **sth (from sb)** *We managed to beg a meal from the cafe owner.* ⮕ WORDFINDER NOTE at POOR **3** [I] if a dog **begs**, it sits on its back legs with its front legs in the air, waiting to be given sth
IDM **beg ˈleave to do sth** (*formal*) to ask sb for permission to do sth **be going ˈbegging** (*BrE, informal*) if sth **is going begging**, it is available because nobody else wants it **beg sb's ˈpardon** (*formal, especially BrE*) to ask sb to forgive you for sth you have said or done **beg the ˈquestion 1** to make sb want to ask a question that has not yet been answered: *All of which begs the question as to who will fund the project.* **2** to talk about sth as if it were definitely true, even though it might not be: *These assumptions beg the question that children learn languages more easily than adults.* **I beg to ˈdiffer** used to say politely that you do not agree with sth that has just been said **I beg your ˈpardon 1** (*formal*) used to tell sb that you are sorry for sth you have said or done: *I beg your pardon, I thought that was my coat.* **2** used to ask sb to repeat what they have just said because you did not hear: *'It's on Duke Street.' 'I beg your pardon.' 'Duke Street.'* **3** (*BrE*) used to tell sb that you are offended by what they have just said or by the way that they have said it: *'Just go away.' 'I beg your pardon!'*
PHRV **ˌbeg ˈoff** to say that you are unable to do sth that you have agreed to do: *He's always begging off at the last minute.*

**began** /bɪˈɡæn/ *past tense* of BEGIN

**beget** /bɪˈɡet/ *verb* (**be·get·ting, begot, begot** /bɪˈɡɒt; *NAmE* -ˈɡɑːt/) HELP In sense 1 **begat** /bɪˈɡæt/ is used for the past tense, and **be·got·ten** /bɪˈɡɒtn; *NAmE* -ˈɡɑːtn/ is used for the past participle. **1** (old use, for example in the Bible) ~ **sb** to become the father of a child: *Isaac begat Jacob.* **2** ~ **sth** (*formal* or *old-fashioned*) to make sth happen: *Violence begets violence.* ▸ **be·get·ter** /bɪˈɡetə(r)/ *noun*

**beg·gar** /ˈbeɡə(r)/ *noun, verb*
- *noun* **1** a person who lives by asking people for money or food **2** (*BrE, informal*) used with an adjective to describe sb in a particular way: *Aren't you dressed yet, you lazy beggar?*
IDM **ˌbeggars can't be ˈchoosers** (*saying*) people say **beggars can't be choosers** when there is no choice and sb must be satisfied with what is available ⮕ more at WISH *n.*
- *verb* ~ **sb/sth/yourself** to make sb/sth very poor: *Why should I beggar myself for you?*

IDM **beggar beˈlief/deˈscription** to be too extreme, horrible, etc. to believe/describe: *It beggars belief how things could have got this bad.*

**ˈbegging bowl** *noun* a bowl held out by sb asking for food or money: (*figurative*) *He is taking round the begging bowl on behalf of the party's campaign fund.*

**begin** ⓘ A1 ⓢ /bɪˈɡɪn/ *verb* (**be·gin·ning, began** /-ˈɡæn/, **begun** /-ˈɡʌn/) **1** ⓘ A1 [I, T] to start doing sth; to do the first part of sth: *Shall I begin?* ◊ ~ **at sth** *Let's begin at page 9.* ◊ ~ **with sth** *I'd like to begin with a simple question.* ◊ ~ **by doing sth** *She began by thanking us all for coming.* ◊ ~ **sth** *We began work on the project in May.* ◊ *I began* (= started reading) *this novel last month and I still haven't finished it.* ◊ ~ **sth with sth** *He always begins his lessons with a warm-up exercise.* ◊ ~ **sth as sth** *He began his political career as a student* (= when he was a student). ◊ ~ **to do sth** *I began to feel dizzy.* *Leaves are just beginning to appear.* ◊ *We have already begun to address the problem.* ◊ *I was beginning to think you'd never come.* ◊ ~ **doing sth** *Everyone began talking at once.* ⮕ LANGUAGE BANK at FIRST ⮕ SYNONYMS at START **2** ⓘ A1 [I] to start to happen or exist, especially from a particular time: *When does the concert begin? Work on the new bridge is due to begin in September.* ◊ *The evening began well.* **3** ⓘ A1 [I] to have sth as the first part or the point where sth starts: *Where does Europe end and Asia begin?* ◊ ~ **with sth** *Use 'an' before words beginning with a vowel.* ◊ *'I'm thinking of a country in Asia.' 'What does it begin with* (= what is the first letter)*?'* ◊ *Each chapter begins with a quotation.* ◊ ~ **at …** *The path begins at Livingstone village.* **4** ⓘ A1 [I, T] to start or make sth start for the first time: *The school began in 1920, with only ten pupils.* ◊ ~ **sth** *He began a new magazine on post-war architecture.* **5** ⓘ A1 [I] ~ **as sth** to be sth first, before becoming sth else: *He began as an actor, before starting to direct films.* ◊ *What began as a minor scuffle turned into a full-scale riot.* **6** ⓘ A2 [T] + **speech** to start speaking: *'Ladies and gentlemen,' he began, 'welcome to the Town Hall.'* **7** [T] **not ~ to do sth** to make no attempt to do sth or have no chance of doing sth: *I can't begin to thank you enough.* ◊ *He didn't even begin to understand my problem.*
IDM **to beˈgin with 1** at first: *I found it tiring to begin with but I soon got used to it.* ◊ *We'll go slowly to begin with.* **2** used to introduce the first point you want to make: *'What was it you didn't like?' 'Well, to begin with, our room was far too small.'* ⮕ more at CHARITY

▼ **WHICH WORD?**

**begin / start**
- There is not much difference in meaning between **begin** and **start**, though **start** is more common in spoken English: *What time does the concert start/begin?* ◊ *She started/began working here three months ago.* **Begin** is often used when you are describing a series of events: *The story begins on the island of Corfu.* **Start**, but not **begin**, can also mean 'to start a journey', 'to start something happening' or 'to start a machine working': *We'll need to start at 7.00.* ◊ *Who do you think started the fire?* ◊ *The car won't start.*
- You can use either an infinitive or a form with *-ing* after **begin** and **start**, with no difference in meaning: *I didn't start worrying/to worry until she was 2 hours late.*
- After the forms **beginning** and **starting**, the *-ing* form of the verb is not normally used: *It's starting/beginning to rain.* ◊ *It's starting/beginning raining.*

**be·gin·ner** /bɪˈɡɪnə(r)/ *noun* a person who is starting to learn sth and cannot do it very well yet: *She's in the beginners' class.*

**beˈginner's ˈluck** *noun* [U] good luck or unexpected success when you start to do sth new

**be·gin·ning** ⓘ A1 ⓢ /bɪˈɡɪnɪŋ/ *noun* **1** ⓘ A1 [C, usually sing.] the time when sth starts; the first part of an event, a story, etc: ~ **of sth** *We missed the beginning of the movie.* ◊ *She's been working there since the beginning of*

# begone

last summer. ◊ The birth of their first child **marked the beginning** of a new era in their married life. ◊ **at the~ of sth** We're going to Japan at the beginning of July. ◊ **from the ~** Let's start again from the beginning. ◊ I've read the whole book **from beginning to end** and still can't understand it. **HELP At the beginning (of)** is used for the time and place when something begins. **In the beginning** means 'at first' and suggests a contrast with a later situation: *at the beginning of the week/year/story/movie/game* ◊ *In the beginning, we just tried to keep everything very simple. Later on,...* **2 beginnings** [pl.] the first or early ideas, signs or stages of sth: *Did democracy have its beginnings in ancient Greece?* ◊ *The company has grown from humble beginnings.* **IDM the beginning of the ˈend** the first sign of sth ending

**be·gone** /bɪˈɡɒn; NAmE -ˈɡɔːn/ exclamation (old use) a way of telling sb to go away immediately

**be·gonia** /bɪˈɡəʊniə/ noun a plant with large shiny flowers that may be pink, red, yellow or white, grown indoors or in a garden

**begot** /bɪˈɡɒt; NAmE -ˈɡɑːt/ past tense of BEGET

**be·got·ten** /bɪˈɡɒtn; NAmE -ˈɡɑːtn/ past part. of BEGET

**be·grudge** /bɪˈɡrʌdʒ/ verb (often used in negative sentences) **1** to feel unhappy that sb has sth because you do not think that they deserve it: ~ **sb sth** *You surely don't begrudge him his happiness?* ◊ ~ **sb doing sth** *I don't begrudge her being so successful.* **2** to feel unhappy about having to do, pay or give sth: ~ **sth** *I begrudge every second I spent trying to help him.* ◊ ~ **doing sth** *They begrudge paying so much money for a second-rate service.*

**be·grudg·ing·ly** /bɪˈɡrʌdʒɪŋli/ adv. = GRUDGINGLY

**be·guile** /bɪˈɡaɪl/ verb (formal) **1** ~ **sb (into doing sth)** to trick sb into doing sth, especially by being nice to them: *She beguiled them into believing her version of events.* **2** ~ **sb** to attract or interest sb: *He was beguiled by her beauty.*

**be·guil·ing** /bɪˈɡaɪlɪŋ/ adj. (formal) attractive and interesting but sometimes mysterious or trying to trick you: *beguiling advertisements* ◊ *Her beauty was beguiling.* ▶ **be·guil·ing·ly** adv.

**begum** /ˈbeɪɡəm/ noun a title of respect used for a Muslim woman of high rank and for a married Muslim woman: *Begum Zia*

**begun** /bɪˈɡʌn/ past part. of BEGIN

**be·half** /bɪˈhɑːf; NAmE -ˈhæf/ noun **IDM in behalf of sb | in sb's behalf** (US) in order to help sb: *We collected money in behalf of the homeless.* **on behalf of sb | on sb's behalf 1** as the representative of sb or instead of them: *On behalf of the department I would like to thank you all.* ◊ *Mr Knight cannot be here, so his wife will accept the prize on his behalf.* **2** in order to help sb: *They campaigned on behalf of asylum seekers.* **3** because of sb; for sb: *Don't worry on my behalf.*

**be·have** /bɪˈheɪv/ verb **1** [I] + adv./prep. to do things in a particular way **SYN act**: *The doctor behaved very unprofessionally.* ◊ *They behaved very badly towards their guests.* ◊ *He behaved like a true gentleman.* ◊ *They behave differently when you're not around.* ◊ *He had always behaved in a friendly manner towards us.* ◊ *He behaved as if/though nothing had happened.* **HELP** In spoken English people often use **like** instead of **as if** or **as though**, especially in NAmE: *He behaved like nothing had happened.* This is not considered correct in written BrE. **2** [I, T] to do things in a way that people think is correct or polite: *Will you kids just behave!* ◊ *She doesn't know how to behave in public.* ◊ ~ **yourself** *I want you to behave yourselves while I'm away.* **OPP misbehave 3** -**behaved** (in adjectives) behaving in the way mentioned: *well-/badly behaved children* **4** [I] + adv./prep. (specialist) to naturally react, move, etc. in a particular way: *a study of how metals behave under pressure* **IDM** see OWN v.

**be·hav·iour** /bɪˈheɪvjə(r)/ noun **1** [U] the way that sb behaves, especially towards other people: *good/bad behaviour* ◊ *social/sexual/criminal behaviour* ◊ ~ **towards sb** *His behaviour towards her was becoming more and more aggressive.*

**WORDFINDER** action, approach, attitude, conform, eccentric, etiquette, habit, manner, morality

**2** [U, C] the way a person, an animal, a plant, a chemical, etc. behaves or functions in a particular situation: *studying human and animal behaviour* ◊ *the behaviour of dolphins/chromosomes* ◊ (specialist) *to study learned behaviours* ◊ *the effects of social media on attitudes and behaviours* ◊ *They encourage patients to adopt healthy behaviours.* ▶ **be·hav·iour·al** (US **be·hav·ior·al**) /-jərəl/ adj.: *children with behavioural difficulties* ◊ *behavioural science* (= the study of human behaviour) **be·hav·iour·al·ly** (US **be·hav·ior·al·ly**) /-rəli/ adv. **IDM be on your best beˈhaviour** to behave in the most polite way you can

**be·hav·iour·ism** (US **be·hav·ior·ism**) /bɪˈheɪvjərɪzəm/ noun [U] (psychology) the theory that all human behaviour is learnt by adapting to outside conditions and that learning is not influenced by thoughts and feelings ▶ **be·hav·iour·ist** (US **be·hav·ior·ist**) noun

**be·head** /bɪˈhed/ verb [usually passive] ~ **sb** to cut off sb's head, especially as a punishment **SYN decapitate**

**be·held** /bɪˈheld/ past tense, past part. of BEHOLD

**be·he·moth** /bɪˈhiːmɒθ/ noun (formal) something that is very big and powerful, especially a company or organization: *a multinational corporate behemoth*

**be·hest** /bɪˈhest/ noun [sing.] **IDM at sb's beˈhest** (old use or formal) because sb has ordered or requested it

**be·hind** /bɪˈhaɪnd/ prep., adv., noun
■ prep. **1** at or towards the back of sb/sth, and often hidden by it or them: *Who's the girl standing behind Jan?* ◊ *Stay close behind me.* ◊ *a small street behind the station* ◊ *She glanced behind her.* ◊ *Don't forget to lock the door behind you* (= when you leave). ◊ *The sun disappeared behind the clouds.* ◊ note at BACK ⊃ compare IN FRONT OF **2** making less progress than sb/sth: *He's behind the rest of the class in reading.* ◊ *We're **behind schedule** (= late).* **3** giving support to or approval of sb/sth: *She knew that, whatever she decided, her family was right behind her.* **4** responsible for starting or developing sth: *What's behind that happy smile* (= what is causing it)? ◊ *He was the man behind the plan to build a new hospital.* **5** used to say that sth is in sb's past: *The accident is behind you now, so try to forget it.* ◊ *She has ten years' useful experience behind her.*
■ adv. **1** at or towards the back of sb/sth; further back: *She rode off down the road with the dog running behind.* ◊ *The others are a long way behind.* ◊ *He was shot from behind as he ran away.* ◊ *I had fallen so far behind that it seemed pointless trying to catch up.* **2** in the place where sb/sth is or was: *I was told to **stay behind** after school* (= remain in school). ◊ *This bag was **left behind** after the class.* **3** late in paying money or completing work: ~ **(with sth)** *She's **fallen behind** with the payments.* ◊ ~ **(in sth)** *He was terribly behind in his work.*
■ noun (informal) a person's bottom. People often say 'behind' to avoid saying 'bottom'. **SYN backside**: *The dog bit him on his behind.*

**be·hind·hand** /bɪˈhaɪndhænd/ adj. [not before noun] ~ **(with/in sth)** late in doing sth or in paying money that is owed: *They were behindhand in settling their debts.*

**be·hold** /bɪˈhəʊld/ verb (**be·held, be·held** /-ˈheld/) ~ **sb/sth** (old use or literary) to look at or see sb/sth: *Her face was a joy to behold.* ◊ *They beheld a bright star shining in the sky.* **IDM see LO**

**be·holden** /bɪˈhəʊldən/ adj. ~ **to sb (for sth)** (formal) owing sth to sb because of sth that they have done for you: *She didn't like to be beholden to anyone.*

**be·hold·er** /bɪˈhəʊldə(r)/ noun **IDM** see BEAUTY

**be·hove** /bɪˈhəʊv/ (BrE) (NAmE **be·hoove** /bɪˈhuːv/) verb **IDM it behoves sb to do sth** (formal) it is right or necessary for sb to do sth: *It behoves us to study these findings carefully.*

**beige** /beɪʒ/ adj. light yellow-brown in colour ▶ **beige** noun [U]

**being** ⊙ B2 /ˈbiːɪŋ/ noun 1 B2 [U] existence: *The Irish Free State came into being in 1922.* ◇ *A new era was brought into being by the war.* ⊃ see also WELL-BEING 2 B2 [C] a living creature: *human beings* ◇ *a strange being from another planet* 3 [U] (*formal*) *your mind and all of your feelings:* I hated him with my whole being. ⊃ see also BE verb

**be·jew·elled** (*BrE*) (*US* **be·jew·eled**) /bɪˈdʒuːəld/ adj. (*literary*) decorated with PRECIOUS STONES; wearing jewellery

**be·la·bour** (*US* **be·la·bor**) /bɪˈleɪbə(r)/ verb
IDM **belabour the ˈpoint** (*formal*) to repeat an idea, argument, etc. many times to emphasize it, especially when it has already been mentioned or understood

**be·lated** /bɪˈleɪtɪd/ adj. coming or happening late: *a belated birthday present* ▶ **be·lat·ed·ly** adv.

**bel canto** /ˌbel ˈkæntəʊ/ noun [U] (*music, from Italian*) a style of OPERA or opera singing in the 19th century in which producing a beautiful tone was considered very important

**belch** /beltʃ/ verb 1 [I] to let air come up noisily from your stomach and out through your mouth SYN **burp**: *He wiped his hand across his mouth, then belched loudly.* 2 [I, T] ~ (**out/forth**) (**sth**) to send out large amounts of smoke, flames, etc.; to come out of sth in large amounts SYN **spew** ▶ **belch** noun: *He sat back and gave a loud belch.*

**be·lea·guered** /bɪˈliːɡəd/ *NAmE* -ɡərd/ adj. 1 (*formal*) experiencing a lot of criticism and difficulties: *The beleaguered party leader was forced to resign.* 2 surrounded by an enemy: *supplies for the beleaguered city*

**bel·fry** /ˈbelfri/ noun (*pl.* **-ies**) a tower in which bells hang, especially as part of a church

**Belgian endive** /ˌbeldʒən ˈendaɪv, -dɪv/ noun (*NAmE*) = ENDIVE (2)

**belie** /bɪˈlaɪ/ verb (**be·lies, be·ly·ing, be·lied, be·lied**) (*formal*) 1 ~ **sth** to give a false impression of sb/sth: *Her energy and youthful good looks belie her 65 years.* 2 ~ **sth** to show that sth cannot be true or correct: *Government claims that there is no poverty are belied by the number of homeless people on the streets.*

**be·lief** ⊙ B1 W /bɪˈliːf/ noun 1 B1 [U] ~ (**in sth/sb**) a strong feeling that sth/sb exists or is true; confidence that sth/sb is good or right: *I admire his passionate belief in what he is doing.* ◇ *belief in God/democracy* 2 B1 [sing., U] an opinion about sth; sth that you think is true: ~ **that** … *There is a general belief that things will soon get better.* ◇ **in the** ~ **that** … *She acted in the belief that she was doing good.* ◇ *Contrary to popular belief* (= in spite of what people may think), *he was not responsible for the tragedy.* 3 B1 [C, usually pl.] something that you believe, especially as part of your religion: *religious/political beliefs* ⊃ compare DISBELIEF, UNBELIEF
IDM **beyond beˈlief** (in a way that is) too great, difficult, etc. to be believed: *Dissatisfaction with the government has grown beyond belief.* ◇ *icy air that was cold beyond belief* ⊃ more at BEGGAR v., BEST n.

**be·liev·able** /bɪˈliːvəbl/ adj. that can be believed SYN **plausible**: *Her explanation certainly sounded believable.* ◇ *a play with believable characters* OPP **unbelievable**

**be·lieve** ⊙ A1 /bɪˈliːv/ verb (not used in the progressive tenses)
• FEEL CERTAIN 1 A1 [T] to feel certain that sth is true or that sb is telling you the truth: ~**sth** *I don't believe you!* ◇ *Do you really believe her?* ◇ *Believe me, she's not right for you.* ◇ ~**sth** *I believed his lies for years.* ◇ *I find that hard to believe.* ◇ *Don't believe a word of it* (= don't believe any part of what sb is saying). ◇ ~(**that**) … *People used to believe (that) the earth was flat.* ◇ *I do believe you're right* (= I think sb is true, even though it is surprising).
• THINK POSSIBLE 2 A1 [I, T] to think that sth is true or possible, although you are not completely certain: *'Where does she come from?' 'Spain, I believe.'* ◇ *'Does he still work there?' 'I believe so/not.'* ◇ ~(**that**) … *Police believe (that) the man may be armed.* ◇ **it is believed (that)** … *It is believed that the couple have left the country.* ◇ ~**sth** *Few people believe this claim.* ◇ **be believed to be, have, etc. sth** *The vases are believed to be worth over $20000 each.* ◇ **be believed + adj.** *Three sailors are missing, believed drowned.* ⊃ SYNONYMS at THINK
• HAVE OPINION 3 A1 [T] ~ (**that**) … to have the opinion that sth is right or true: *I strongly believe that competition is a good thing.* ◇ *She truly believes that love can change the world.* ⊃ LANGUAGE BANK at ACCORDING TO, OPINION
• BE SURPRISED/ANNOYED 4 A1 [T] **don't/can't ~** used to say that you are surprised or annoyed at sth: ~(**that**) … *She couldn't believe (that) it was all happening again.* ◇ ~**how, what, etc** … *I can't believe how much better I feel.*
• RELIGION 5 [I] to have a religious faith: *The god appears only to those who believe.*
IDM **beˈlieve it or ˈnot** (*informal*) used to introduce information that is true but that may surprise people: *Believe it or not, he asked me to marry him!* **beˈlieve (you) ˈme** (*informal*) used to emphasize that you strongly believe what you are saying: *You haven't heard the last of this, believe you me!* **don't you beˈlieve it!** (*informal*) used to tell sb that sth is definitely not true **I don't beˈlieve it!** (*informal*) used to say that you are surprised or annoyed about sth: *I don't believe it! What are you doing here?* **if you beˈlieve that, you'll believe ˈanything** (*informal*) used to say that you think sb is stupid if they believe that sth is true **make beˈlieve (that …)** to pretend that sth is true ⊃ related noun MAKE-BELIEVE **not believe your ˈears/ˈeyes** (*informal*) to be very surprised at sth you hear/see: *I couldn't believe my eyes when she walked in.* **ˈseeing is beˈlieving** (*saying*) used to say that sb will have to believe that sth is true when they see it, although they do not think it is true now **ˈwould you beˈlieve (it)?** (*informal*) used to show that you are surprised and annoyed about sth: *And, would you believe, he didn't even apologize!* **you/you'd better beˈlieve it!** (*informal*) used to tell sb that sth is definitely true ⊃ more at GIVE v.
PHRV **beˈlieve in sb/sth** A2 to feel certain that sb/sth exists: *Do you believe in God?* **beˈlieve in sb** A2 to feel that you can trust sb and/or that they will be successful: *They need a leader they can believe in.* ⊃ SYNONYMS at TRUST **beˈlieve in sth** A2 to think that sth is good, right or acceptable: **believe in doing sth** *I don't believe in hitting children.* **beˈlieve sth of sb** to think that sb is capable of sth: *Are you sure he was lying? I can't believe that of him.*

**be·liev·er** /bɪˈliːvə(r)/ noun a person who believes in the existence or truth of sth, especially sb who believes in a god or religious faith OPP **non-believer, unbeliever**
IDM **be a (great/firm) beˈliever in sth** to believe strongly that sth is good, important or valuable

**Be·li·sha bea·con** /bəˌliːʃə ˈbiːkən/ noun (in the UK) a post with an orange flashing light on top marking a place where cars must stop to allow people to cross the road

**be·lit·tle** /bɪˈlɪtl/ verb ~ **sb/sth** to make sb, or the things that sb does, seem unimportant: *She felt her husband constantly belittled her achievements.*

**bell** ⊙ B1 /bel/ noun 1 B1 a hollow metal object, often like a cup in shape, that makes a ringing sound when hit by a small piece of metal inside it; the sound that it makes: *A peal of church bells rang out in the distance.* ◇ *a bicycle bell* ◇ *His voice came down the line as clear as a bell.* ◇ *the bell of a trumpet* (= the part at the end like a bell in shape) ◇ *The church bells rang out.* ◇ *a bell-shaped flower* 2 B1 an electrical device which makes a ringing sound when a button on it is pushed; the sound that it makes, used as a signal or a warning: *Ring the bell to see if they're in.* ◇ *The bell's ringing!* ◇ *The bell went for the end of the lesson.* ◇ *An alarm bell went off.* ◇ (*figurative*) *Warning bells started ringing in her head as she sensed that something was wrong.* ⊃ see also DOORBELL
IDM **give sb a ˈbell** (*BrE, informal*) to call sb by phone ⊃ more at ALARM n., PULL v., RING² v., SOUND adj.

**bella·donna** /ˌbeləˈdɒnə; *NAmE* -ˈdɑːnə/ noun [U] 1 = DEADLY NIGHTSHADE 2 a poisonous drug made from DEADLY NIGHTSHADE

---

s see | t tea | v van | w wet | z zoo | ʃ shoe | ʒ vision | tʃ chain | dʒ jam | θ thin | ð this | ŋ sing

**bell-bottoms** noun [pl.] trousers with legs that become very wide below the knee

**bell-boy** /ˈbelbɔɪ/ (especially NAmE) (NAmE also **bell-hop**) noun a person whose job is to carry people's cases to their rooms in a hotel

**bell curve** noun (mathematics) a line on a GRAPH that rises to a high round curve in the middle, showing NORMAL DISTRIBUTION ⊃ picture at NORMAL DISTRIBUTION

**belle** /bel/ noun (old-fashioned) a beautiful woman; the most beautiful woman in a particular place

**bell-hop** /ˈbelhɒp; NAmE -hɑːp/ noun (NAmE) = BELLBOY

**bel·li·cose** /ˈbelɪkəʊs, -kəʊz/ adj. (formal) having or showing a desire to argue or fight SYN **aggressive**, **warlike** ▶ **bel·li·cos·ity** /ˌbelɪˈkɒsəti; NAmE -ˈkɑːs-/ noun [U]

**-bellied** /belid/ ⊃ BELLY noun

**bel·liger·ent** /bəˈlɪdʒərənt/ adj., noun
■ adj. 1 aggressive and unfriendly SYN **hostile**: a belligerent attitude 2 [only before noun] (formal) (of a country) fighting a war: the belligerent countries/states/nations ▶ **bel·liger·ence** /-rəns/ noun [U] **bel·liger·ent·ly** adv.
■ noun (formal) a country or group that is fighting a war

**bell jar** noun a tall round glass cover, used by scientists

**bel·low** /ˈbeləʊ/ verb 1 [I, T] to shout in a loud deep voice, especially because you are angry SYN **yell**: ~ (at sb) They bellowed at her to stop. ◊ ~ sth (at sb) The coach bellowed instructions from the sidelines. ◊ + speech 'Get over here!' he bellowed. ⊃ SYNONYMS at SHOUT 2 [I] when a large animal such as a BULL bellows, it makes a loud deep sound ▶ **bel·low** noun: to let out a bellow of rage/pain

**bel·lows** /ˈbeləʊz/ noun (pl. **bel·lows**) [C + sing./pl. v.] a piece of equipment for blowing air into or through sth. Bellows are used for making a fire burn better or for producing sound in some types of musical instruments: a pair of bellows (= a small bellows with two handles to be pushed together)

**bell pepper** (NAmE) (BrE **pep·per**) (also **sweet ˈpepper** BrE, NAmE) noun a hollow fruit, usually red, green or yellow, eaten as a vegetable either raw or cooked ⊃ VISUAL VOCAB page V5

**bell pull** noun a rope or handle that you pull to make a bell ring, for example to make sb in another room hear you

**bell-ringer** (also **ringer**) noun a person who rings church bells as a hobby ▶ **bell-ringing** noun [U]

**bells and ˈwhistles** noun [pl.] (computing) attractive extra features

**bell-wether** /ˈbelweðə(r)/ noun [usually sing.] something that is used as a sign of what will happen in the future: University campuses are often the bellwether of change.

**belly** /ˈbeli/ noun, verb
■ noun (pl. **-ies**) 1 the part of the body below the chest SYN **stomach**, **gut**: They crawled along on their bellies. ⊃ see also BEER BELLY, POT BELLY 2 (literary) the round or curved part of an object: the belly of a ship 3 **-bellied** (in adjectives) having the type of belly mentioned: swollen-bellied ◊ round-bellied
IDM **go belly ˈup** (informal) to fail completely: Last year the business went belly up after one of the partners resigned.
■ verb [I] (**bel·lies**, **belly·ing**, **bel·lied**, **bel·lied**) ~ (out) (especially of sails) to fill with air and become rounder

**belly·ache** /ˈbelieɪk/ noun, verb
■ noun [C, U] (informal) a pain in the stomach: I've got (a) bellyache.
■ verb [I] (informal) to complain a lot about sth in an annoying or unreasonable way

**belly button** noun (informal) = NAVEL

**belly dance** noun a dance, originally from the Middle East, in which a woman moves her belly and HIPS around ▶ **belly dancer** noun **belly dancing** noun [U]

**belly-flop** /ˈbeliflɒp; NAmE -flɑːp/ noun (informal) a bad DIVE into water, in which the front of the body hits the water flat

**belly·ful** /ˈbeliful/ noun
IDM **have had a ˈbellyful of sb/sth** (informal) to have had more than enough of sb/sth, so that you cannot deal with any more: I've had a bellyful of your moaning.

**belly laugh** noun (informal) a deep loud laugh

**be·long** /bɪˈlɒŋ; NAmE -ˈlɔːŋ/ verb (not used in the progressive tenses) 1 [I] + **adv./prep.** to be in the right or suitable place: Where do these plates belong (= where are they kept)? ◊ Are you sure these documents belong together? 2 [I] to feel comfortable and happy in a particular situation or with a particular group of people: I don't feel as if I belong here. ▶ **be·long·ing** noun [U]: to feel a sense of belonging
PHRV **be·ˈlong to sb/sth** 1 to be owned by sb/sth: Who does this watch belong to? ◊ The islands belong to Spain. ◊ a violin that once belonged to Mozart 2 an event, a competition, etc. that belongs to sb/sth is one in which they are the most successful or popular: British actors did well at the award ceremony, but the evening belonged to the Americans. **be·ˈlong to sth** 1 to be a member of a club, an organization, etc: Have you ever belonged to a political party? 2 to be part of a particular group, type or system: Lions and tigers belong to the cat family.

**be·long·ings** /bɪˈlɒŋɪŋz; NAmE -ˈlɔːŋ-/ noun [pl.] the things that you own which can be moved, for example not land or buildings SYN **possessions**: insurance of property and personal belongings ◊ She packed her few belongings in a bag and left. ⊃ SYNONYMS at THING

**be·loved** adj., noun
■ adj. 1 /bɪˈlʌvd/ [only before noun] loved very much: in memory of our dearly beloved son, John 2 /bɪˈlʌvd/ ~ **by/of sb** loved very much by sb; very popular with sb: the deep purple flowers so beloved by artists
■ noun /bɪˈlʌvɪd/ (old use or literary) a person who is loved very much by sb: It was a gift from her beloved.

**below** /bɪˈləʊ/ adv., prep.
■ adv. 1 at or to a lower level, position or place: They live on the floor below. ◊ I could still see the airport buildings far below. ◊ See below (= at the bottom of the page) for references. ◊ The passengers who felt seasick stayed below (= on a lower DECK). 2 at a lower rank: This ruling applies to the ranks of Inspector and below. 3 (of a temperature) lower than zero: The thermometer had dropped to a record 40 below (= –40 degrees).
■ prep. 1 at or to a lower level or position than sb/sth: He dived below the surface of the water. ◊ Please do not write below this line. ◊ Skirts will be worn below (= long enough to cover) the knee. 2 of a lower amount or standard than sb/sth: The temperatures remained below freezing all day. ◊ Her work was well below average for the class. 3 of a lower rank or of less importance than sb/sth: A police sergeant is below an inspector.

**belt** /belt/ noun, verb
■ noun 1 a long narrow piece of leather, cloth, etc. that you wear around the middle part of your body: to do up/fasten/tighten a belt ◊ a belt buckle ⊃ see also BLACK BELT, LIFEBELT, SEAT BELT, SUSPENDER BELT 2 a continuous band of material that moves round and is used to carry things along or to drive a machine ⊃ see also CONVEYOR BELT, FAN BELT 3 a narrow area or an area around the edge of sth that has particular characteristics: the country's corn/industrial belt ◊ We live in the commuter belt. ◊ a narrow belt of trees ⊃ see also GREEN BELT, RUST BELT 4 (informal) an act of hitting sth/sb hard: She gave the ball a terrific belt.
IDM **below the ˈbelt** (of a remark) unfair or cruel: That was distinctly below the belt! **belt and ˈbraces** (informal) taking more actions than are really necessary to make sure that sth succeeds or works as it should: a belt-and-braces policy **have sth under your ˈbelt** (informal) to have

already achieved or obtained sth: *She already has a couple of good wins under her belt.* ⇨ more at TIGHTEN
■ **verb 1** ~ **sb/sth** (*informal*) to hit sb/sth hard: *He belted the ball right out of the park.* ◊ *I'll belt you if you do that again.* **2** [I] + *adv./prep.* (*informal, BrE*) to move very fast SYN **tear¹**: *A truck came belting up behind us.* **3** [T] ~ **sth** to fasten a belt around sth: *The dress was belted at the waist.*
PHRV **belt sth⇿out** (*informal*) to sing a song or play music loudly **belt up** (*BrE*) **1** (*NAmE* **buckle 'up**) (*informal*) to fasten your SEAT BELT (= a belt worn by a passenger in a vehicle) **2** (*informal*) used to tell sb rudely to be quiet SYN **shut up**: *Just belt up, will you!*

**belt·ed** /ˈbeltɪd/ *adj.* with a belt around it: *a belted jacket*

**belt·er** /ˈbeltə(r)/ *noun* (*informal*) **1** (*especially BrE*) a very good example of sth: *His second goal was an absolute belter.* **2** a loud, powerful singer or song: *She finished the set with a real belter.*

**'belt-tightening** *noun* [U] changes that are made in order to spend less money: *We've all had to do some belt-tightening this year.* ⇨ see also TIGHTEN YOUR BELT at TIGHTEN

**belt·way** /ˈbeltweɪ/ *noun* (*US*) a RING ROAD, especially the one around Washington DC

**be·luga** /bəˈluːɡə/ (*pl.* **be·luga** or **be·lugas**) *noun* **1** [C] a type of small WHALE **2** [C] a type of large fish that lives in rivers and lakes in eastern Europe **3** (*also* **be luga 'caviar**) [U] a type of CAVIAR (= fish eggs), from a beluga

**be·moan** /bɪˈməʊn/ *verb* ~ **sth** (*formal*) to complain or say that you are not happy about sth: *They sat bemoaning the fact that no one would give them a chance.*

**be·mused** /bɪˈmjuːzd/ *adj.* showing that you are confused and unable to think clearly SYN **bewildered**: *a bemused expression/smile* ▸ **be·muse** *verb* ~ **sb be·mus·ed·ly** /-ˈmjuːzɪdli/ *adv.*

**bench** /bentʃ/ *noun* **1** [C] a long seat for two or more people, usually made of wood: *a park bench* **2 the bench** [sing.] (*law*) a judge in court or the seat where he/she sits; the position of being a judge or MAGISTRATE: *His lawyer turned to address the bench.* ◊ *She has recently been appointed to the bench.* **3** [C, usually pl.] (in the British parliament) a seat where a particular group of politicians sit: *There was cheering from the Opposition benches.* ⇨ see also BACK BENCH, FRONT BENCH **4 the bench** [sing.] (*sport*) the seats where players sit when they are not playing in the game: *the substitutes' bench* **5** [C] = WORKBENCH: *a carpenter's bench*

**bench·mark** /ˈbentʃmɑːk; *NAmE* -mɑːrk/ *noun, verb*
■ *noun* something that can be measured and used as a standard that other things can be compared with: *Tests at the age of seven provide a benchmark against which the child's progress at school can be measured.*
■ *verb* ~ **sth** (**against sth**) to judge the quality of sth in relation to that of other similar things: *Projects are assessed and benchmarked against the targets.*

**'bench press** *noun* an exercise in which you lie on a raised surface with your feet on the floor and raise a weight with both arms

**bench·warm·er** /ˈbentʃwɔːmə(r); *NAmE* -wɔːrm-/ *noun* (*NAmE, informal*) a sports player who is not chosen to play in a particular game, but is available if their team needs them SYN **substitute**

**bend** /bend/ *verb, noun*
■ *verb* (**bent, bent** /bent/) **1** [I, T] (especially of sb's body or head) to lean, or make sth lean, in a particular direction: *He bent and kissed her.* ◊ + *adv./prep. fields of poppies bending in the wind* ◊ *She suddenly bent over, clutching her stomach.* ◊ *His dark head bent over her.* ◊ *She bent forward to pick up the newspaper.* ◊ *Slowly bend from the waist and bring your head down to your knees.* ◊ ~ **sth** (+ *adv./prep.*) *He bent his head and kissed her.* ◊ *She was bent over her desk writing a letter.* **2** [T, I] if you **bend** your arm, leg, etc. or it **bends**, you move it so that it is no longer straight: ~ **sth** *Bend your knees, keeping your back straight.* ◊ *Lie flat and let your knees bend.* **3** [T] ~ **sth** to force sth that was straight into an angle or a curve: *Mark the pipe where you want to bend it.* ◊ *The knives were bent out of shape.* ◊ *He bent the wire into the shape of a square.* **4** [I, T] to change direction to form a curve or an angle; to make sth change direction in this way: *The road bent sharply to the right.* ◊ ~ **sth** *Glass and water both bend light.*
IDM **bend sb's 'ear (about sth)** (*informal*) to talk to sb a lot about sth, especially about a problem that you have **bend your 'mind/'efforts to sth** (*formal*) to think very hard about or put a lot of effort into one particular thing **bend the 'truth** to say sth that is not completely true **on bended 'knee(s)** if you ask for sth **on bended knee(s)**, you ask for it in a very anxious and/or HUMBLE way (= showing you think you are less important than the person you are asking) ⇨ more at BACKWARDS, RULE *n*.
PHRV **'bend to sth** to be forced or persuaded to do what sb wants or to accept their opinions: *The government finally bent to overwhelming public pressure.* **'bend sb to sth** (*formal*) to force or persuade sb to do what you want or to accept your opinions: *He manipulates people and tries to bend them to his will* (= make them do what he wants).
■ *noun* **1** [C] a curve or turn, especially in a road or river: *a sharp bend in the road* ⇨ WORDFINDER NOTE at RIVER ⇨ see also HAIRPIN BEND **2 the bends** [pl.] severe pain and difficulty in breathing experienced by a DIVER who comes back to the surface of the water too quickly SYN **decompression sickness**
IDM **round the bend/twist** (*NAmE* **around the bend**) (*informal*) crazy: *She's gone completely round the bend.* ◊ *The kids have been driving me round the bend today* (= annoying me very much).

**bend·er** /ˈbendə(r)/ *noun* (*slang*) a period of drinking a lot of alcohol or taking a lot of drugs: *to go on a bender*

**bendy** /ˈbendi/ *adj.* (*BrE, informal*) **1** that can be bent easily SYN **flexible 2** with many bends: *a bendy road*

**'bendy bus** *noun* (*BrE, informal*) a long bus that bends in the middle so that it can turn corners more easily

**be·neath** /bɪˈniːθ/ *prep.* (*forma.*) **1** in or to a lower position than sb/sth; under sb/sth: *They found the body buried beneath a pile of leaves.* ◊ *The boat sank beneath the waves.* **2** not good enough for sb: *He considers such jobs beneath him.* ◊ *They thought she had married beneath her* (= married a man of lower social status). ▸ **be·neath** *adv.*: *Her careful make-up hid the signs of age beneath.*

**Bene·dic·tine** /ˌbenɪˈdɪktɪn/ *noun* a member of a Christian group of MONKS or NUNS following the rules of St Benedict ▸ **Bene·dic·tine** *adj.*: *a Benedictine monastery*

**bene·dic·tion** /ˌbenɪˈdɪkʃn/ *noun* [C, U] (*formal*) a Christian prayer of BLESSING

**bene·fac·tion** /ˌbenɪˈfækʃn/ *noun* (*formal*) a gift, usually of money, that is given to a person or an organization in order to do good

**bene·fac·tor** /ˈbenɪfæktə(r)/ *noun* (*formal*) a person who gives money or other help to a person or an organization such as a school or charity

**bene·fice** /ˈbenɪfɪs/ *noun* the paid position of a Christian priest in charge of a PARISH

**be·nefi·cent** /bɪˈnefɪsnt/ *adj.* (*formal*) giving help; being kind SYN **generous** ▸ **be·nefi·cence** /-sns/ *noun* [U]

**bene·fi·cial** /ˌbenɪˈfɪʃl/ *adj.* ~ (**to sth/sb**) (*formal*) improving a situation; having a helpful or useful effect SYN **advantageous, favourable**: *A good diet is beneficial to health.* OPP **detrimental** ▸ **bene·fi·cial·ly** /-ʃəli/ *adv.*

**bene·fi·ciary** /ˌbenɪˈfɪʃəri; *NAmE* -ʃieri/ *noun* (*pl.* **-ies**) **1** ~ (**of sth**) a person who gains as a result of sth: *Who will be the main beneficiary of the cuts in income tax?* **2** ~ (**of sth**) a person who receives money or property when sb dies

# benefit

**bene·fit** 🔵 **A2** 🔘 /ˈbenɪfɪt/ *noun, verb*
- *noun* **1** 🔵 **A2** [C, U] an advantage that sth gives you; a helpful and useful effect that sth has: *Freedom of information brings great benefits.* ◊ **health/economic/tax benefits** ◊ *I've had the benefit of a good education.* ◊ *It was good to see her finally reaping the benefits* (= enjoying the results) *of all her hard work.* ◊ **of doing sth** *He couldn't see the benefit of arguing any longer.* ◊ **be of~to sb/sth** *The new regulations will be of benefit to everyone concerned.* ◊ **to sb's~** *It will be to your benefit to arrive early.* ⮕ see also COST-BENEFIT, FRINGE BENEFIT **2** 🔵 **B2** [C, usually pl., U] (*BrE*) (*also* **welfare** [U] *especially in NAmE*) money provided by the government to people who need financial help because they are unemployed, ill, etc: *You may be eligible to receive benefits.* ◊ *The number of people claiming unemployment benefit fell last month.* ◊ **on benefits** *The aim is to help people who are on benefits* (= receiving benefits) *to find jobs.* ⮕ see also CHILD BENEFIT, HOUSING BENEFIT, SICKNESS BENEFIT ⮕ WORDFINDER NOTE at POOR **3** [C, usually pl.] an advantage that you get from a company in addition to the money that you earn: *Private health insurance is offered as part of the employees' benefits package.* ⮕ see also FRINGE BENEFIT **4** [C, usually pl.] money from an insurance company: *The insurance plan will provide substantial cash benefits to your family in case of your death.* **5** [C] an event such as a performance, a dinner, etc., organized in order to raise money for a particular person or charity: *a benefit match/concert* ⮕ WORDFINDER NOTE at CHARITY
- **IDM** **for the benefit of sb | for sb's benefit** especially in order to help or be useful to sb: *I have typed out some lecture notes for the benefit of those people who were absent last week.* ◊ *Don't go to any trouble for my benefit!* **give sb the benefit of the doubt** to accept that sb has told the truth or behaved well because you cannot prove that they have not
- *verb* (-t- *or* -tt-) **1** 🔵 **B1** [T] **~sb** to be useful to sb or improve their life in some way: *We should spend the money on something that will benefit everyone.* **2** 🔵 **B1** [I] to be in a better position because of sth: **~(from sth)** *Who exactly stands to benefit from these changes?* ◊ **~by doing sth** *Most crime victims benefit greatly by talking about their experiences.*

**Bene·lux** /ˈbenɪlʌks/ *noun* [U] a name for Belgium, the Netherlands and Luxembourg, when they are thought of as a group

**be·nevo·lent** /bəˈnevələnt/ *adj.* **1** (*formal*) (especially of people in authority) kind, helpful and generous: *a benevolent smile/attitude* ◊ *belief in the existence of a benevolent god* **OPP** **malevolent** **2** used in the names of some organizations that give help and money to people in need: *the RAF Benevolent Fund* ▶ **be·nevo·lence** /-ləns/ *noun* [U] **be·nevo·lent·ly** *adv.*

**Ben·gali** /beŋˈɡɔːli; *NAmE* -ˈɡɑː-/ *noun* **1** [C] a person from Bangladesh or West Bengal in eastern India **2** [U] the language of people from Bangladesh or West Bengal in eastern India ▶ **Ben·gali** *adj.*

**be·night·ed** /bɪˈnaɪtɪd/ *adj.* (*old-fashioned*) **1** (of people) without understanding **2** (of places) without the benefits of modern life

**be·nign** /bɪˈnaɪn/ *adj.* **1** (*formal*) (of people) kind and gentle; not hurting anybody **2** not causing damage or harm: *environmentally benign cleaning products* **3** (*medical*) (of TUMOURS growing in the body) not dangerous or likely to cause death **OPP** **malignant** ▶ **be·nign·ly** *adv.*: *He smiled benignly.*

**bent** 🔵 **B2** /bent/ *adj., verb, noun*
- *adj.* **1** 🔵 **B2** not straight: *a piece of bent wire* ◊ *Do this exercise with your knees bent* (= not with your legs straight). ⮕ picture at TWISTED **2** (of a person) not able to stand up straight, usually as a result of being old or ill: *a small bent old woman* ◊ *He was bent double with laughter.* **3** (*BrE, informal*) (of a person in authority) dishonest
- **IDM** **'bent on (doing) sth** determined to do sth (usually sth bad): *She seems bent on making life difficult for me.* ◊ *to be bent on destruction/revenge* ⮕ see also HELL-BENT **get bent out of 'shape (about/over sth)** (*NAmE, informal*) to become angry, anxious or upset: *Don't get bent out of shape about it. It was just a mistake!*
- *verb* past tense, past part. of BEND
- *noun* [usually sing.] **~(for sth)** a natural skill or interest in sth: *She has a bent for mathematics.*

**ben·zene** /ˈbenziːn/ *noun* [U] a clear liquid obtained from PETROLEUM and COAL TAR, used in making plastics and many chemical products

**be·queath** /bɪˈkwiːð/ *verb* (*formal*) **1** to say in a WILL that you want sb to have your property, money, etc. after you die **SYN** **leave**: **~sth (to sb)** *He bequeathed his entire estate* (= all his money and property) *to his daughter.* ◊ **~sb sth** *He bequeathed his daughter his entire estate.* **2** **~sth (to sb) | ~sb sth** to leave the results of your work, knowledge, etc. for other people to use or deal with, especially after you have died

**be·quest** /bɪˈkwest/ *noun* (*formal*) money or property that you ask to be given to a particular person when you die: *He left a bequest to each of his grandchildren.*

**be·rate** /bɪˈreɪt/ *verb* **~sb/yourself** (*formal*) to criticize or speak angrily to sb because you do not approve of sth they have done

**be·reave** /bɪˈriːv/ *verb* **be bereaved** if sb **is bereaved**, a relative or close friend has just died: *The ceremony was an ordeal for those who had been recently bereaved.*

**be·reaved** /bɪˈriːvd/ *adj.* (*formal*) **1** having lost a relative or close friend who has recently died: *recently bereaved families* **2** **the bereaved** *noun* (*pl.* **the bereaved**) a person who is bereaved: *an organization offering counselling for the bereaved*

**be·reave·ment** /bɪˈriːvmənt/ *noun* **1** [U] the state of having lost a relative or close friend because they have died: *the pain of an emotional crisis such as divorce or bereavement* **2** [C] the death of a relative or close friend: *A family bereavement meant that he could not attend the conference.*

**be·reft** /bɪˈreft/ *adj.* [not before noun] (*formal*) **1** **~of sth** completely without sth; having lost sth: *bereft of ideas/hope* **2** (of a person) sad and lonely because you have lost sth: *He was utterly bereft when his wife died.*

**beret** /ˈbereɪ; *NAmE* bəˈreɪ/ *noun* a round flat cap made out of soft cloth

**berg** /bɜːɡ; *NAmE* bɜːrɡ/ *SAfrE* [berx] *noun* (*SAfrE*) **1** a mountain or group of mountains **2** **the Berg** [sing.] the Drakensberg, a group of tall mountains in South Africa

**ber·ga·mot** /ˈbɜːɡəmɒt; *NAmE* ˈbɜːrɡəmɑːt/ *noun* [U] **1** (*also* **'bergamot oil**) oil from the skin of a small orange **2** a type of HERB

**ber·i·ber·i** /ˌberiˈberi/ *noun* [U] a disease that affects the nerves and heart, caused by a lack of vitamin B

**berm** /bɜːm; *NAmE* bɜːrm/ *noun* (*specialist*) **1** an area of ground at the side of a road; a raised area of ground at the side of a river or CANAL **2** a narrow raised area of sand formed on a beach by the waves coming in from the sea

**Ber·muda shorts** /bəˈmjuːdə ʃɔːts; *NAmE* bərˈmjuːdə ʃɔːrts/ (*also* **Ber·mu·das** /bəˈmjuːdəz; *NAmE* bərˈm-/) *noun* [pl.] SHORTS (= short trousers) that come down to just above the knee: *a pair of Bermudas*

**the Ber·muda ˈTriangle** *noun* [sing.] an area in the Atlantic Ocean between Bermuda, Florida and Puerto Rico where a large number of ships and aircraft are believed to have disappeared in a mysterious way: *This area of town is known as the Bermuda Triangle because drinkers can disappear into the pubs and clubs and be lost to the world.*

**berry** /ˈberi/ *noun* (*pl.* **-ies**) (often in compounds) a small fruit that grows on a bush. There are several types of berry, some of which can be eaten: *Birds feed on nuts and berries in the winter.* ◊ *blackberries/raspberries* ⮕ VISUAL VOCAB pages V4, V6

▼ **HOMOPHONES**

**berry • bury** /ˈberi/
- **berry** noun: *He picked a berry from the bush.*
- **bury** verb: *Many people actually did bury treasure in the sand.*

**ber·serk** /bəˈzɜːk, -ˈsɜːk; NAmE bərˈzɜːrk, -ˈsɜːrk/ adj. [not usually before noun] (informal) **1** very angry, often in a violent way or without control: *He went berserk when he found out where I'd been.* **2** very excited: *People were going berserk with excitement.*

**berth** /bɜːθ; NAmE bɜːrθ/ noun, verb
- noun **1** a place to sleep on a ship or train, or in a CARAVAN SYN **bunk 2** a place where a ship or boat can stop and stay, usually in a HARBOUR IDM see WIDE adj.
- verb [T, I] ~ (sth) to put a ship in a berth or keep it there; to sail into a berth: *The ship is berthed at Southampton.*

**beryl** /ˈberəl/ noun [U] a clear pale green, blue or yellow SEMI-PRECIOUS stone, used in making jewellery

**beryl·lium** /bəˈrɪliəm/ noun [U] (symb. Be) a chemical element. Beryllium is a hard grey metal found mainly in the mineral BERYL.

**besan** /ˈbeɪsʌn/ noun [U] = GRAM FLOUR

**be·seech** /bɪˈsiːtʃ/ verb (be·sought, be·sought /-ˈsɔːt/ or be·seeched, be·seeched) ~ sb (to do sth) (formal) to ask sb for sth in an anxious way because you want or need it very much SYN **implore, beg**: *Let him go, I beseech you!*

**be·seech·ing** /bɪˈsiːtʃɪŋ/ adj. [only before noun] (formal) (of a look, tone of voice, etc.) showing that you want sth very much ▸ **be·seech·ing·ly** adv.

**beset** /bɪˈset/ verb [usually passive] (formal) (be·set·ting, beset, beset) to affect sb/sth in an unpleasant or harmful way: *The team was beset by injury all season.* ◇ *It's one of the most difficult problems besetting our modern way of life.*

**be·side** ?+ B2 /bɪˈsaɪd/ prep. **1** ?+ B2 next to or at the side of sb/sth: *He sat beside her all night.* ◇ *a mill beside a stream* **2** compared with sb/sth: *My painting looks childish beside yours.*
IDM ▸ **be beside the ˈpoint** to not be important or closely related to the main thing you are talking about: *Yes, I know it was an accident, but that's beside the point.* **be ˈside yourself (with sth)** unable to control yourself because of the strength of emotion you are feeling: *He was beside himself with rage when I told him what I had done.*

▼ **WHICH WORD?**

**beside / besides**
- The preposition **beside** usually means 'next to something/somebody' or 'at the side of something/somebody': *Sit here beside me.* The preposition **besides** means 'in addition to something': *What other sports do you play besides hockey?* Do not use **beside** with this meaning.
- The adverb **besides** is not usually used on its own with the same meaning as the preposition. It is mainly used to give another reason or argument for something: *I don't think I'll come on Saturday. I have a lot of work to do. Besides, I don't really like parties.* ◇ *She likes football. Besides, she likes tennis and basketball.*

**be·sides** ?+ B1 /bɪˈsaɪdz/ prep., adv.
- prep. ?+ B2 in addition to sb/sth; apart from sb/sth: *We have lots of things in common besides music.* ◇ *Besides working as a doctor, he also writes novels in his spare time.* ◇ *I've got no family besides my parents.* ➔ LANGUAGE BANK at EXCEPT
- adv. **1** ?+ B2 used for making an extra comment that adds to what you have just said: *I don't really want to go. Besides, it's too late now.* ➔ LANGUAGE BANK at ADDITION **2** ?+ B2 in addition; also: *discounts on televisions, stereos and much more besides*

131

▼ **WHICH WORD?**

**besides / apart from / except**
- The preposition **besides** means 'in addition to': *What other sports do you like besides football?* You use **except** when you mention the only thing that is not included in a statement: *I like all sports except football.* You can use **apart from** with both these meanings: *What other sports do you like apart from football?* ◇ *I like all sports apart from football.*

**be·siege** /bɪˈsiːdʒ/ verb **1** ~ sth to surround a building, city, etc. with soldiers until the people inside are forced to let you in SYN **lay siege to**: *Paris was besieged for four months and forced to surrender.* ◇ *(figurative) Fans besieged the box office to try and get tickets for the concert.* **2** [usually passive] ~ sb/sth (especially of sth unpleasant or annoying) to surround sb/sth in large numbers: *The actress was besieged by reporters at the airport.* **3** ~ sb (with sth) to send so many letters, ask so many questions, etc. that it is difficult for sb to deal with them all: *The radio station was besieged with calls from angry listeners.*

**be·smirch** /bɪˈsmɜːtʃ; NAmE -ˈsmɜːrtʃ/ verb ~ sb/sth (formal) to damage the opinion that people have of sb/sth SYN **sully**

**besom** /ˈbiːzəm/ noun a brush for sweeping floors, made from sticks tied onto a long handle

**be·sot·ted** /bɪˈsɒtɪd; NAmE -ˈsɑːt-/ adj. ~ (by/with sb/sth) loving sb/sth so much that you do not behave in a sensible way: *He is completely besotted with his new girlfriend.*

**be·sought** /bɪˈsɔːt/ past tense, past part. of BESEECH

**be·spat·ter** /bɪˈspætə(r)/ verb ~ sth (literary) to cover sth with small drops of water or other liquid, usually by accident

**be·speak** /bɪˈspiːk/ verb (be·spoke /-ˈspəʊk/, be·spoken /-ˈspəʊkən/) ~ sth (literary) to show or suggest sth: *His style of dressing bespoke great self-confidence.*

**be·spec·tacled** /bɪˈspektəkld/ adj. (formal) wearing SPECTACLES

**be·spoke** /bɪˈspəʊk/ adj. [usually before noun] (especially BrE, formal) **1** (NAmE usually **custom-ˈmade**) (of a product) made specially, according to the needs of an individual customer SYN **tailor-made**: *bespoke software* ◇ *a bespoke suit* **2** making products specially, according to the needs of an individual customer: *a bespoke tailor*

**bes·sie** /ˈbesi/ noun (BrE, informal) = BEZZIE

**best** ? A1 /best/ adj., adv., noun, verb
- adj. (superlative of **good**) **1** ? A1 of the most excellent type or quality: *That's the best movie I've ever seen!* ◇ *She was one of the best tennis players of her generation.* ◇ *Is that your best suit?* ◇ *They've been best friends* (= closest friends) *since they were children.* ◇ *the company's best-ever results* ◇ *We want the kids to have the best possible education.* **2** ? A1 giving most pleasure; happiest: *Those were the best years of my life.* **3** ? A1 most suitable or appropriate: *What's the best way to cook steak?* ◇ *He's the best man for the job.* ◇ *The best thing to do would be to apologize.* ◇ *It's best if you go now.* ◇ *I'm not in the best position to advise you.* HELP Idioms containing **best** adj. are at the entries for the nouns and verbs in the idioms, for example **on your best behaviour** is at **behaviour**.
- adv. (superlative of **well**, often used in adjectives) **1** ? A2 most; to the greatest extent: *Which one do you like best?* ◇ *Well-drained soil suits the plant best.* ◇ *her best-known poem* **2** ? A2 in the most excellent way; to the highest standard: *He works best in the mornings.* ◇ *Britain's best-dressed woman* ◇ *The beaches are beautiful, but, best of all, there are very few tourists.* **3** ? A2 in the most suitable or appropriate way: *Painting is best done in daylight.* ◇ *Do as you think best* (= what you think is the most suitable thing to do).
IDM **as best you ˈcan** not perfectly but as well as you are able: *We'll manage as best we can.* ➔ more at REMEMBER

○ Oxford Phrasal Academic Lexicon (OPAL) written and spoken word lists | Ⓦ OPAL written word list | Ⓢ OPAL spoken word list

# best-before date

■ **noun** [sing.] (usually **the best**) **1** ? A2 the most excellent thing or person: *We all want the best for our children.* ◊ *They only buy the best.* ◊ *They're all good players, but she's the best of all.* ◊ *We're **the best of friends** (= very close friends).* **2** ? A2 the highest standard that sb/sth can reach: *She always brings out the best in people.* ◊ *The town looks its best (= is most attractive) in the spring.* ◊ *Don't worry about the exam—just **do your best**.* ◊ *The roses are past their best now.* ◊ *I don't really feel **at my best** today.* **3** ? B1 something that is as close as possible to what you need or want: *Fifty pounds is the best I can offer you.* ◊ *The best we can hope for in the game is a draw.* **4** the highest standard that a particular person has reached, especially in a sport: *a lifetime best of 12.0 seconds* ⊃ *see also* PERSONAL BEST
**IDM ▸ all the 'best** (*informal*) used when you are saying goodbye to sb or ending a letter, to give sb your good wishes **at 'best** used for saying what is the best opinion you can have of sb/sth, or the best thing that can happen, when the situation is bad: *Their response to the proposal was, at best, cool.* ◊ *We can't arrive before Friday at best.* **be (all) for the 'best** used to say that although sth appears bad or unpleasant now, it will be good in the end: *I don't want you to leave, but perhaps it's for the best.* **the best of a bad 'bunch/lot** (*especially BrE, informal*) a person or thing that is a little better than the rest of a group, although none are very good **the best of 'three, 'five, etc.** (especially in games and sports) up to three, five, etc. games played to decide who wins, the winner being the person who wins most of them **the best that money can 'buy** the very best: *We make sure our clients get the best that money can buy.* **do, mean, etc. sth for the 'best** to do or say sth in order to achieve a good result or to help sb: *I just don't know what to do for the best.* ◊ *I'm sorry if my advice offended you—I meant it for the best.* **have/get the 'best of sth** to gain more advantage from sth than sb else: *I thought you had the best of that discussion.* **make the best of sth/it | make the best of things | make the best of a bad job** to accept a bad or difficult situation and do as well as you can **to the best of your 'knowledge/be'lief** as far as you know: *He never made a will, to the best of my knowledge.* **with the 'best (of them)** as well as anyone: *He'll be out there, dancing with the best of them.* ⊃ *more at* BUNCH *n.*, HOPE *v.*, LUCK *n.*, SUNDAY

■ **verb** [usually passive] (*formal*) to defeat or be more successful than sb: **be bested (by sb)** *He was determined not to be bested by his old rival.*

**'best-be,fore date** *noun* (*BrE*) a date printed on a container or package, advising you to use food or drink before this date as it will not be of such good quality after that ⊃ *compare* SELL-BY DATE

**bes·tial** /'bestiəl; *NAmE* 'bestʃəl/ *adj.* (*formal*) cruel and horrible; of or like a BEAST: *bestial acts/cruelty/noises*

**bes·ti·al·ity** /,besti'æləti; *NAmE* ,bestʃi-/ *noun* [U] **1** (*specialist*) sexual activity between a human and an animal **2** (*formal*) cruel or horrible behaviour

**bestie** /'besti/ *noun* (*informal*) a person's best friend: *It was fun hanging out with my bestie.* ◊ **be besties with sb** *Hank is besties with Sarah.*

**be·stir** /bɪ'stɜː(r)/ *verb* (-rr-) ~ **yourself** (*formal* or *humorous*) to start doing things after a period during which you have been doing nothing SYN **rouse**

**best 'man** *noun* [sing.] a male friend or relative of the BRIDEGROOM at a wedding, who helps him during the wedding ceremony ⊃ *compare* BRIDESMAID, GROOMSMAN, USHER (3) ⊃ WORDFINDER NOTE *at* WEDDING

**be·stow** /bɪ'stəʊ/ *verb* ~ **sth (on/upon sb)** (*formal*) to give sth to sb, especially to show how much they are respected: *It was a title bestowed upon him by the king.*

**best 'practice** *noun* [U, C] a way of doing sth that is seen as a very good example of how it should be done and can be copied by other companies or organizations

**be·stride** /bɪ'straɪd/ *verb* ~ **sth** (*literary*) to sit with one leg on either side of sth: *He bestrode his horse.*

**best·sell·er** /,best'selə(r)/ *noun* a product, usually a book, which is bought by large numbers of people: *the bestseller list* ▸ **best·sell·ing** *adj.*: *a bestselling novel/author*

**be·suit·ed** /bɪ'suːtɪd/ *adj.* (*formal*) wearing a suit: *besuited businessmen*

# bet ❶ B2

/bet/ *verb, noun*

■ **verb** (**bet·ting, bet, bet**) **1** ? B2 [I, T] to risk money on a race or an event by trying to predict the result: *You have to be over 16 to bet.* ◊ ~ **on/against (sb/sth doing) sth** *I wouldn't bet on them winning the next election.* ◊ ~ **sth (on sth)** *He bet $2000 on the final score of the game.* ◊ ~ **sb (sth) (that)** *She bet me £20 (that) I wouldn't do it.* ⊃ *see also* BETTING, GAMBLE *verb* ⊃ WORDFINDER NOTE *at* GAMBLING **2** ? B2 [T] (*informal*) used to say that you are almost certain that sth is true or that sth will happen: ~ **(that)** *... I bet (that) we're too late.* ◊ *I'm willing to bet (that) the analysts will be wrong.* ◊ ~ **sb (that)** *... I'll bet you (that) he knows all about it.*
**IDM ▸ bet the farm/ranch on sth** (*NAmE, informal*) to risk everything you have on an investment, a bet, etc: *The company bet the farm on the new marketing model, only to find that it wasn't successful.* **I/I'll 'bet!** (*informal*) **1** used to show that you can understand what sb is feeling, describing, etc: '*I nearly died when he told me.' 'I bet!'* **2** used to tell sb that you do not believe what they have just said: '*I'm going to tell her what I think of her.' 'Yeah, I bet!'* **I wouldn't 'bet on it | don't 'bet on it** (*informal*) used to say that you do not think that sth is very likely: '*She'll soon get used to the idea.' 'I wouldn't bet on it.'* **you 'bet!** (*informal*) used instead of 'yes' to emphasize that sb has guessed sth correctly or made a good suggestion: '*Are you nervous?' 'You bet!'* **you can bet your 'life/your bottom 'dollar (on sth/(that)) ...** (*informal*) used to say that you are certain that sth will happen: *You can bet your bottom dollar that he'll be late.*

■ **noun 1** ? B2 an arrangement to risk money, etc. on the result of a particular event; the money that you risk in this way: *to win/lose a bet* ◊ *I was tempted to place a large bet.* ◊ ~ **on sth** *We've got a bet on who's going to arrive first.* ◊ *He had a bet on the horses.* ◊ *They all put a bet on the race.* ◊ *I did it for a bet (= because sb had agreed to pay me money if I did).* ◊ '*Liverpool are bound to win.' 'Do you want a bet?' (= I disagree with you, I don't think they will.)* **2** (*informal*) an opinion about what is likely to happen or to have happened: *My bet is that they've been held up in traffic.*
**IDM ▸ all bets are 'off** used to say that if a particular event happens then your current prediction, agreement, etc. will no longer apply: *We expect shares to rise unless the economy slows down again, in which case all bets are off.* **the/your best 'bet** (*informal*) used to tell sb what is the best action for them to take to get the result they want: *If you want to get around London fast, the Underground is your best bet.* **a ,good/,safe/,sure 'bet** something that is likely to happen, to succeed or to be suitable: *Clothes are a safe bet as a present for a teenager.* ⊃ *more at* HEDGE *v.*

**beta** /'biːtə; *NAmE* 'beɪtə/ *noun* **1** the second letter of the Greek alphabet (B, β) **2** [usually sing.] = BETA VERSION

**'beta blocker** *noun* a drug used to control heart rhythm, treat severe chest pain and reduce high blood pressure

**beta-'carotene** *noun* [U] a substance found in carrots and other plants, which is needed by humans

**'beta decay** *noun* [U] (*physics*) the breaking up of an ATOM in which an ELECTRON is given off

**be·take** /bɪ'teɪk/ *verb* (**be·took** /-'tʊk/, **be·taken** /-'teɪkən/) ~ **yourself + adv./prep.** (*literary*) to go somewhere: *He betook himself to his room.*

**'beta particle** (also **'beta ray**) *noun* (*physics*) a fast-moving ELECTRON that is produced when some RADIOACTIVE substances DECAY (= start to break down)

**'beta test** *noun* a test on a new product, done by sb who does not work for the company that is developing the product ⊃ *compare* ALPHA TEST ▸ **'beta-test** *verb* ~ **sth**

**'beta version** (also **beta**) *noun* [usually sing.] a version of a product, especially computer software, that is almost ready for the public to buy or use, and that is tested by people who do not work for the company that is developing it ⇨ WORDFINDER NOTE at SOFTWARE

**betcha** /ˈbetʃə/ (*informal, non-standard*) a way of saying or writing 'I bet you' in informal speech: *Betcha didn't know that!* HELP You should not write this form unless you are copying sb's speech.
IDM **you betcha** (*informal*) used to say 'yes' when you are very enthusiastic about sth: '*Are you going to the game this weekend?*' '*You betcha!*'

**be·tel** /ˈbiːtl/ *noun* [U] the leaves of a climbing plant, also called betel, CHEWED (= bitten but not eaten) by people in Asia

**ˈbetel nut** *noun* the slightly bitter nut of a tropical Asian PALM, that is cut into small pieces, wrapped in betel leaves, and CHEWED (= bitten but not eaten)

**bête noire** /ˌbet ˈnwɑː(r)/ *noun* (*pl.* **bêtes noires** /ˌbet ˈnwɑːz; *NAmE* ˈnwɑːrz/) (*from French*) a person or thing that particularly annoys you and that you do not like

**be·tide** /bɪˈtaɪd/ *verb* IDM see WOE

**be·tray** ?+ C1 /bɪˈtreɪ/ *verb* 1 ?+ C1 to give information about sb/sth to an enemy: *~sb/sth He was offered money to betray his colleagues.* ◊ *~sb/sth for years they had been betraying state secrets to Russia.* 2 ?+ C1 *~sb/sth* to hurt sb who trusts you, especially by lying to or about them or telling their secrets to other people: *She felt betrayed when she found out the truth about him.* ◊ *She betrayed his trust over and over again.* ◊ *I have never known her to betray a confidence* (= tell other people sth that should be kept secret). ⇨ SYNONYMS at CHEAT 3 ?+ C1 *~sth* to ignore your principles or beliefs in order to achieve sth or gain an advantage for yourself: *He has been accused of betraying his former socialist ideals.* 4 ?+ C1 to tell sb or make them aware of a piece of information, a feeling, etc., usually without meaning to SYN **give away**: *~sth His voice betrayed the worry he was trying to hide.* ◊ *~yourself She was terrified of saying something that would make her betray herself* (= show her feelings or who she was).

**be·tray·al** /bɪˈtreɪəl/ *noun* [U, C] the act of betraying sb/sth or the fact of being betrayed: *a sense/a feeling/an act of betrayal* ◊ *I saw her actions as a betrayal of my trust.* ◊ *the many disappointments and betrayals in his life*

**be·troth·al** /bɪˈtrəʊðl/ *noun* **~(to sb)** (*formal* or *old-fashioned*) an agreement to marry sb SYN **engagement**

**be·trothed** /bɪˈtrəʊðd/ *adj.* (*formal* or *old-fashioned*) **1 ~(to sb)** having promised to marry sb SYN **engaged 2 sb's betrothed** *noun* [sing.] the person that sb has promised to marry

**bet·ter** ❶ A1 /ˈbetə(r)/ *adj., adv., noun, verb*
■ *adj.* (comparative of **good**) **1** ?+ A1 of a higher standard or less poor quality; not as bad as sth else: *We're hoping for better weather tomorrow.* ◊ *Her work is getting better and better.* ◊ *He is in a much better mood than usual.* ◊ *The meal couldn't have been better.* ◊ *There's nothing better than a long soak in a hot bath.* ◊ *If you can only exercise once a week, that's better than nothing* (= better than taking no exercise at all). **2** A1 more suitable or appropriate: *Can you think of a better word than 'nice'?* ◊ *It would be better for him to talk to his parents about his problems.* ◊ *You'd be better going by bus.* **3** ?+ A2 more able; showing more skill: *She's far better at science than her brother.* **4** ?+ A2 less ill or unhappy: *She's a lot better today.* ◊ *His leg was getting better.* ◊ *You'll feel all the better for a good night's sleep.* **5** ?+ A2 fully recovered after an illness; in good health again: *Don't go back to work until you are better.* ⇨ see also WELL *adj.*
IDM HELP Most idioms containing **better** are at the entries for the nouns and verbs in the idioms, for example **better luck next time** is at **luck**. **the ˌbigger, ˌsmaller, ˌfaster, ˌslower, etc. the ˈbetter** used to say that sth should be as big, small, etc. as possible: *I love giving parties, the bigger the better.* **ˌlittle/no ˈbetter (than sb/sth)** almost or just the same as; almost or just as bad as: *The path was no better than a sheep track.* **that's (much) ˈbetter 1** used to give support to sb who has been upset and is trying to become calmer: *Dry your eyes now. That's better.* **2** used to

133 **between**

praise sb who has made an effort to improve: *That's much better—you played the right notes this time.* ⇨ more at DISCRETION, HEAD *n.*, PART *n.*, PREVENTION
■ *adv.* (comparative of **well**) **1** ?+ A2 in a more excellent or pleasant way; not as badly: *She sings much better than I do.* ◊ *Sound travels better in water than in air.* ◊ *People are better educated now.* **2** ?+ A2 more; to a greater degree: *You'll like her when you know her better.* ◊ *A cup of tea? There's nothing I'd like better!* ◊ *Fit people are better able to cope with stress.* **3** ?+ B1 used to suggest that sth would be a suitable or appropriate thing to do: *The money could be better spent on more urgent cases.* ◊ *Some things are better left unsaid.* ◊ *You'd do better to tell her everything before she finds out from someone else.*
IDM HELP Most idioms containing **better** are at the entries for the nouns, adjectives and verbs in the idioms, for example **better the devil you know** is at **devil**. **be ˌbetter ˈoff** to have more money: *Families will be better off under the new law.* ◊ *Her promotion means she's $100 a week better off.* OPP **be ˌworse off (than sb/sth) be ˌbetter ˈoff (doing sth)** used to say that sb is/would be happier or more satisfied because they are/if they were in a particular position or doing a particular thing: *She's better off without him.* ◊ *The weather was so bad we'd have been better off staying at home.* **ˌbetter ˈyet** used to say that while one thing is good, another thing is even better: *You can see and, better yet, hear the effects of these changes on their website.* **had ˈbetter/ˈbest (do sth)** ?+ B2 used to tell sb what you think they should do: *You'd better go to the doctor about your cough.* ◊ *We'd better leave now or we'll miss the bus.* ◊ *You'd better not do that again.* ◊ *'I'll give you back the money tomorrow.' 'You'd better!'* (= as a threat) ◊ *If you think it is going to be easy, you'd best think again.* ⇨ note at SHOULD
■ *noun* **1** ?+ B1 [sing., U] something that is better: *the better of the two books* ◊ *I expected better of him* (= I thought he would have behaved better). **2 your betters** [pl.] (*old-fashioned*) people who are more intelligent or more important than you
IDM **for ˌbetter or (for) ˈworse** used to say that sth cannot be changed, whether the result is good or bad **get the ˈbetter of sb/sth** to defeat sb/sth or gain an advantage: *No one can get the better of her in an argument.* ◊ *She always gets the better of an argument.* ◊ *His curiosity got the better of him* (= he didn't intend to ask questions, but he wanted to know so badly that he did). **so much the ˈbetter/ˈworse** used to say that sth is even better/worse: *We don't actually need it on Tuesday, but if it arrives by then, so much the better.* ⇨ more at CHANGE *n.*, ELDER *n.*, THINK *v.*
■ *verb* **1** [often passive] *~sth* to be better or do sth better than sb/sth else: *The work he produced early in his career has never really been bettered.* **2** *~yourself* to improve your social position through education, a better job, etc: *Thousands of Victorian workers joined educational associations in an attempt to better themselves.*

**ˌbetter ˈhalf** *noun* = OTHER HALF

**bet·ter·ment** /ˈbetəmənt; *NAmE* -tərm-/ *noun* [U] (*formal*) the process of becoming or making sth/sb better SYN **improvement**

**bet·ting** /ˈbetɪŋ/ *noun* [U] the act of risking money, etc. on the unknown result of an event: *illegal betting* ⇨ see also SPREAD BETTING
IDM **what's the ˈbetting…? | the ˈbetting is that…** (*informal*) it seems likely that…: *What's the betting that he gets his own way?* ◊ *The betting is that he'll get his own way.*

**ˈbetting shop** *noun* (*BrE*) a shop where you can bet on horse races and other competitions

**bet·tor** (*also* **better**) /ˈbetə(r)/ *noun* (*NAmE*) a person who bets on a race or other sports event, especially sb who does this regularly

**be·tween** ❶ A1 ◉ /bɪˈtwiːn/ *prep., adv.*
■ *prep.* **1** ?+ A1 in or into the space separating two or more points, objects, people, etc: *Q comes between P and R in the English alphabet.* ◊ *I sat down between Jo and Diana.* ◊ *Switzerland lies between France, Germany, Austria and*

Italy. ◊ *The paper had fallen down between the desk and the wall.* ◊ (*figurative*) *My job is somewhere between a secretary and a personal assistant.* **2** ? A1 in the period of time that separates two days, years, events, etc: *It's cheaper between 6p.m. and 8a.m.* ◊ *Don't eat between meals.* ◊ *Children must attend school between the ages of 5 and 16.* ◊ *Many changes took place between the two world wars.* **3** ? A1 at some point along a scale from one amount, weight, distance, etc. to another: *It weighed between nine and ten kilos.* ◊ *The temperature remained between 25°C and 30°C all week.* **4** ? A1 (of a line) separating one place from another: *the border between Sweden and Norway* **5** ? A1 from one place to another: *We fly between Rome and Paris twice daily.* **6** ? A1 used to show a connection or relationship: *a difference/distinction/contrast between two things* ◊ *a link between unemployment and crime* ◊ *There's a lot of bad feeling between them.* ◊ *I had to choose between the two jobs.* **7** ? B1 shared by two or more people or things: *We ate a pizza between us.* ◊ *This is just **between you and me/between ourselves*** (= it is a secret). **HELP** People sometimes say 'between you and I' but this is wrong because the object pronoun **me** (or reflexive pronoun **ourselves**) is needed after the preposition **between**. **8** ? B1 by putting together the efforts or actions of two or more people or groups: *We ought to be able to manage it between us.* **9** ~ **doing sth** used to show that several activities are involved: *Between working full-time and taking care of the kids, he didn't have much time for hobbies.*
- *adv.* ? A2 (*usually* **in between**) in the space or period of time separating two or more points, objects, etc. or two dates, events, etc: *The house was near a park but there was a road in between.* ◊ *I see her most weekends but not very often in between.* **IDM** see BETWEEN

**be·twixt** /bɪˈtwɪkst/ *adv., prep.* (*literary or old use*) between
**IDM** be twixt and be tween (*old-fashioned*) in a middle position; neither one thing nor the other

**bevel** /ˈbevl/ *noun* **1** a sloping edge or surface, for example at the side of a picture frame or sheet of glass **2** a tool for making sloping edges on wood or stone

**bev·elled** (*US* **bev·eled**) /ˈbevld/ *adj.* [usually before noun] having a sloping edge or surface

**bevelled**

bevel

**bev·er·age** /ˈbevərɪdʒ/ *noun* (*formal*) any type of drink except water: *laws governing the sale of alcoholic beverages*

**bevvy** /ˈbevi/ *noun* (*pl.* **-ies**) (*BrE, informal*) an alcoholic drink, especially beer: *We went out for a few bevvies last night.*

**bevy** /ˈbevi/ *noun* [sing.] (*informal*) a large group of people or things of the same kind: *a bevy of beauties* (= beautiful young women)

**be·wail** /bɪˈweɪl/ *verb* ~ **sth** (*formal or humorous*) to express very sad feelings about sth

**be·ware** /bɪˈweə(r); NAmE -ˈwer/ *verb* [I, T] (used only in infinitives and in orders) if you tell sb to **beware**, you are warning them that sb/sth is dangerous and that they should be careful: ~ **of sb/sth** *Motorists have been warned to beware of icy roads.* ◊ ~ **(of) doing sth** *Beware of saying anything that might reveal where you live.* ◊ ~ **sb/sth** *It's a great place for swimming, but beware dangerous currents.*

**be·wigged** /bɪˈwɪgd/ *adj.* (*formal*) (of a person) wearing a WIG

**be·wil·der** /bɪˈwɪldə(r)/ *verb* [usually passive] ~ **sb** to confuse sb: *She was totally bewildered by his sudden change of mood.* ▶ **be·wil·dered** *adj.*: *He turned around, with a bewildered look on his face.*

**be·wil·der·ing** /bɪˈwɪldərɪŋ/ *adj.* making you feel confused because there are too many things to choose from or because sth is difficult to understand **SYN** **confusing**: *a bewildering array/range* ◊ *There is a bewildering variety of software available.* ▶ **be·wil·der·ing·ly** *adv.*: *All the houses looked bewilderingly similar.*

**be·wil·der·ment** /bɪˈwɪldəmənt; NAmE -dərm-/ *noun* [U] a feeling of being completely confused **SYN** **confusion**: *to look/stare in bewilderment*

**be·witch** /bɪˈwɪtʃ/ *verb* **1** [often passive] ~ **sb** to attract or impress sb so much that they cannot think in a sensible way: *He was completely bewitched by her beauty.* ◊ ~ **sb** to put a magic SPELL on sb **SYN** **enchant**

**be·witch·ing** /bɪˈwɪtʃɪŋ/ *adj.* so beautiful or interesting that you cannot think about anything else: *a bewitching girl/smile* ◊ *a bewitching performance*

**be·yond** ⓘ B2 ⓞ /biˈjɒnd; NAmE -ˈjɑːnd/ *prep., adv.*
- *prep.* **1** ? B2 on or to the further side of sth: *The road continues beyond the village up into the hills.* **2** ? B2 more than sth: *Our success was far beyond what we thought possible.* ◊ *She's got nothing beyond her state pension.* **3** ? B2 later than a particular time: *It won't go on beyond midnight.* ◊ *I know what I'll be doing for the next three weeks but I haven't thought beyond that.* **4** ? B2 used to say that sth is not possible: *The bicycle was beyond repair* (= is too badly damaged to repair). ◊ *The situation is beyond our control.* **5** ? B2 too far or too advanced for sb/sth: *The handle was just beyond my reach.* ◊ *The exercise was beyond the abilities of most of the class.*
**IDM** **be beyond sb** (*informal*) to be impossible for sb to imagine, understand or do: *It's beyond me why she wants to marry Jeff.*
- *adv.* ? B2 on the other side; further on: *Snowdon and the mountains beyond were covered in snow.* ◊ *The immediate future is clear, but it's hard to tell what lies beyond.* ◊ *the year 2025 and beyond* **IDM** see ABOVE *adv.*, BACK *n.*, DOUBT *n.*

**bez·el** /ˈbezl/ *noun* (*specialist*) a ring with a long narrow cut around the inside, used to hold sth in place, such as the cover of a watch or mobile phone

**bez·zie** (*also* **bezzy**) (*pl.* **-ies**) /ˈbezi/ (*also* **bessie**) *noun* (*BrE, informal*) a person's closest friend ▶ **bez·zie** *adj.*: *She's my bezzie pal.*

**BF** (*also* **bf**) /ˌbiː ˈef/ *abbr.* (*informal*) (especially in text messages, on SOCIAL MEDIA, etc.) boyfriend; best friend

**BFF** /ˌbiː ef ˈef/ *abbr.* (*informal*) (especially in text messages, on SOCIAL MEDIA, etc.) best friend (forever): *I'm going to my BFF's birthday party next week.*

**Bhag·wan** /bʌˈgwɑːn; NAmE ˈbɑːgwɑːn/ *noun* (*IndE*) **1** God: '*May Bhagwan bless you,*' *he said.* **2** a title for a GURU or a god in the form of a man: *Bhagwan Rajneesh*

**bhai** /baɪ/ *noun* (*IndE*) **1** a brother **2** used as a polite form of address to a man; in western India, often added to the first or last name: *Suresh Bhai* ◊ *Gandhi Bhai*

**bhaji** /ˈbɑːdʒi/ (*also* **bha·jia** /ˈbɑːdʒə/) *noun* (*pl.* **bhajis, bha·jia**) **1** [C] a spicy South Asian food consisting of vegetables fried in BATTER (= a mixture of flour and liquid) **2** [U] a South Asian dish of spicy fried vegetables

**bhang** (*also* **bang**) /bæŋ/ *noun* [U] the leaves and flower tops of the CANNABIS plant, used as a drug

**bhan·gra** /ˈbɑːŋɡrə/ *noun* [U] a type of dance music that combines traditional Punjabi music from India and Pakistan with Western pop music

**Bha·rata·na·tyam** /ˌbɑːrətəˈnɑːtjəm; NAmE ˌbɜːr-/ *noun* [U] a classical dance form from southern India

**bha·van** /ˈbʌvən; NAmE ˈbɑːv-/ *noun* (*IndE*) a building made or used for a special purpose, for example for meetings or concerts

**bhindi** /ˈbɪndi/ *noun* (*pl.* **bhindi** or **bhindis**) [C, U] (*IndE*) OKRA

**bi** /baɪ/ *adj.* (*informal*) = BISEXUAL

**bi-** /baɪ/ *combining form* (in nouns and adjectives) two; twice; double: *bilingual* ◊ *bicentenary* **HELP** **Bi-** with a period of time can mean either 'happening twice' in that period of time, or 'happening once in every two' periods.

**bi·an·nual** /baɪˈænjuəl/ *adj.* [only before noun] happening twice a year ⊃ compare ANNUAL ⊃ see also BIENNIAL *adj.*

**bias** /ˈbaɪəs/ noun, verb
- noun 1 [U, C, usually sing.] a strong feeling in favour of or against one group of people, or one side in an argument, often not based on fair judgement: *accusations of political bias in news programmes* (= that reports are unfair and show favour to one political party) ◊ *Employers must consider all candidates impartially and without bias.* ◊ *Some institutions still have a strong bias against women.* ◊ *The article examines gender bias in our schools.* ⇒ WORDFINDER NOTE at EQUAL 2 [C, usually sing.] an interest in one thing more than others; a special ability: *The course has a strong practical bias.* 3 [U, C] the fact that the results of research or an experiment are not accurate because a particular factor has not been considered when collecting the information: *If a response rate is low, the risk of bias in the findings will be greater.* 4 [U, sing.] the **bias** of a piece of cloth is an edge cut DIAGONALLY across the THREADS: *The skirt is cut on the bias.*
- verb (-s- or -ss-) 1 ~ sb/sth (against/towards/in favour of sb/sth) to unfairly influence sb's opinions or decisions SYN prejudice: *The newspapers have biased people against her.* 2 ~ sth to have an effect on the results of research or an experiment so that they do not show the real situation: *The experiment contained an error which could bias the results.*

**ˈbias-cut** adj. (of cloth or of an item of clothing) cut across the natural direction of the lines in the cloth

**biased** (also **biassed**) /ˈbaɪəst/ adj. 1 tending to show favour towards or against one group of people or one opinion for personal reasons; making unfair judgements: *biased information/sources/press reports* ◊ *a biased jury/witness* ◊ *~ against/towards/in favour of sb/sth They admit that they're biased towards the Republican Party.* OPP unbiased 2 ~ toward(s) sth/sb having a particular interest in one thing more than others: *a school biased towards music and art*

**bi·ath·lon** /baɪˈæθlən/ noun a sporting event that combines CROSS-COUNTRY skiing and RIFLE shooting ⇒ compare DECATHLON, HEPTATHLON, PENTATHLON, TRIATHLON

**bib** /bɪb/ noun 1 a piece of cloth or plastic that you fasten around a baby's neck to protect its clothes while it is eating 2 (*especially BrE*) a piece of cloth or plastic with a number or special colours on it that people wear on their chests and backs when they are taking part in a sport, so that people know who they are

**bible** /ˈbaɪbl/ noun 1 **the Bible** [sing.] the holy book of the Christian religion, consisting of the Old Testament and the New Testament 2 **the Bible** [sing.] the holy book of the Jewish religion, consisting of the Torah (or Law), the PROPHETS and the Writings 3 [C] a copy of the holy book of the Christian or Jewish religion 4 [C] a book containing important information on a subject, that you refer to very often: *the stamp-collector's bible*

**ˈBible-bashing** (also **ˈBible-thumping**) noun [U] (*informal, disapproving*) the act of teaching or talking about the Bible in public in a very enthusiastic or aggressive way ▶ **ˈBible-basher** (also **ˈBible-thumper**) noun

**the ˈBible Belt** noun [sing.] an area of the southern and middle western US where people have strong and strict Christian beliefs

**bib·lical** (also **Biblical**) /ˈbɪblɪkl/ adj. 1 connected with the Bible; in the Bible: *biblical scholarship/times/scenes* ◊ *biblical stories/passages* 2 very great; on a large scale: *a thunderstorm of biblical proportions*
IDM **know sb in the ˈbiblical sense** (*humorous*) to have had sex with sb: *He had known her—but not in the biblical sense.*

**biblio-** /ˈbɪbliəʊ, bɪbliə; BrE also bɪbliˈɒ; NAmE also bɪbliˈɑː/ combining form (in nouns, adjectives and adverbs) connected with books: *bibliophile*

**bibli·og·raphy** /ˌbɪbliˈɒɡrəfi; NAmE -ˈɑːɡ-/ noun (pl. -ies) 1 [C] a list of books or articles about a particular subject or by a particular author; the list of books, etc. that have been used by sb writing an article, etc. 2 [U] the study of the history of books and their production ▶ **bibli·og·rapher** /ˌbɪbliˈɒɡrəfə(r); NAmE -ˈɑːɡ-/ noun **bib·lio·graph·ical** /ˌbɪbliəˈɡræfɪkl/ (also **bib·lio·graph·ic** /-fɪk/) adj.

**bib·lio·phile** /ˈbɪbliəfaɪl/ noun (*formal*) a person who loves or collects books

**ˈbib overalls** noun [pl.] (*NAmE*) = OVERALLS

**bi·cam·eral** /ˌbaɪˈkæmərəl/ adj. (*specialist*) (of a parliament) having two main parts, such as the Senate and the House of Representatives in the US, and the House of Commons and the House of Lords in the UK

**bi·carb** /ˈbaɪkɑːb; NAmE -kɑːrb/ noun [U] (*informal*) = SODIUM BICARBONATE

**bi·car·bon·ate** /ˌbaɪˈkɑːbənət; NAmE -ˈkɑːrb-/ noun [U] (*chemistry*) a salt made from CARBONIC ACID containing CARBON, HYDROGEN and OXYGEN together with another element

**bi·ˈcarbonate of ˈsoda** noun [U] = SODIUM BICARBONATE

**bi·cen·ten·ary** /ˌbaɪsenˈtiːnəri; NAmE -ˈten-/ noun (pl. -ies) (*BrE*) (*especially NAmE* **bi·cen·ten·nial**) the year, or the day, when you celebrate an important event that happened exactly 200 years earlier ▶ **bi·cen·ten·ary** adj. [only before noun]: *bicentenary celebrations*

**bi·cen·ten·nial** /ˌbaɪsenˈteniəl/ noun (*especially NAmE*) = BICENTENARY ▶ **bi·cen·ten·nial** adj. [only before noun]: *bicentennial celebrations*

**bi·ceps** /ˈbaɪseps/ noun (pl. **bi·ceps**) the main muscle at the front of the top part of the arm ⇒ compare TRICEPS

**bicker** /ˈbɪkə(r)/ verb [I] ~ (about/over sth) to argue about things that are not important SYN squabble: *The children are always bickering about something or other.* ◊ *They bicker over whose fault it was.* ▶ **bicker·ing** noun [U]

**bi·coast·al** /ˌbaɪˈkəʊstl/ adj. (*NAmE*) involving people and places on both the east and west coasts of the US

**bi·cycle** /ˈbaɪsɪkl/ noun, verb
- noun (also *informal* **bike**) a road vehicle with two wheels that you ride by pushing the PEDALS with your feet: *He got on his bicycle and rode off.* ◊ *We went for a bicycle ride on Sunday.*
- verb [I] (+ adv./prep.) (*old-fashioned*) to go somewhere on a bicycle ⇒ compare BIKE, CYCLE

**ˈbicycle clip** noun one of the two bands that people wear around their ankles when they are riding a bicycle to stop their trousers getting caught in the chain

**ˈbicycle lane** noun (also *informal* **bike lane**) (both *NAmE*) (*BrE* **ˈcycle lane**) a part of a road that only bicycles are allowed to use

**bi·cyc·list** /ˈbaɪsɪklɪst/ noun (*old-fashioned* in British English, *formal* in North American English) a person who rides a bicycle ⇒ compare CYCLIST

**bid¹** /bɪd/ noun, verb ⇒ see also BID²
- noun 1 an offer by a person or a company to pay a particular amount of money for sth: *~ for sth A German firm launched a takeover bid for the company.* ◊ *At the auction* (= a public sale where things are sold to the person who offers the most), *the highest bid for the picture was £200.* ◊ *~ on sth* (*NAmE also*) *the highest bid on the picture* ◊ *Any more bids?* 2 **~ (for sth)** (*NAmE also*) | **~ (on sth)** an offer to do work or provide a service for a particular price, in competition with other companies, etc. SYN tender: *The company submitted a bid for the contract to clean the hospital.* 3 (used especially in newspapers) an effort to do sth or to obtain sth: *~ for sth a bid for power* ◊ *~ to do sth a desperate bid to escape from his attackers* 4 (in some card games) a statement of the number of points a player thinks he or she will win
- verb (**bid·ding**, **bid**, **bid**) 1 [I, T] to offer to pay a particular price for sth, especially at an AUCTION: **~ (sth) (for sth)** *I bid £2000 for the painting.* ◊ **~ (against sb) (for sth)** *We wanted to buy the chairs but another couple were bidding against us.* 2 [I] to offer to do work or provide a service for a particular price, in competition with other companies, etc. SYN tender: **~ for sth** *A French firm will be bidding for the contract.* ◊ **~ on sth** (*NAmE also*) *A French firm will be bidding on the contract.* ◊ **~ to do sth** *Which other cities are bidding to host the 2028 Olympics?* ⇒ WORDFINDER NOTE at DEAL 3 [T] **~ to do sth** (used

# bid

especially in newspapers) to try to do, get or achieve sth **SYN** **attempt**: *The team is bidding to retain its place in the league.* **4** [T, I] ~ **(sth)** (in some card games) to say how many points you expect to win: *She bid four hearts.*
**IDM** **what am I 'bid?** used by an AUCTIONEER when he or she is selling sth: *What am I bid for this vase?*

**bid²** /bɪd/ *verb* ⊃ see also BID¹ (**bid·ding, bade** /beɪd, bæd/, **bidden** /ˈbɪdn/ or **bid·ding, bid, bid**) **1** ~ **(sb) good morning, farewell, etc.** (*formal*) to say 'good morning', etc. to sb: *I bade farewell to all the friends I had made in Paris.* ◊ *I bade all my friends farewell.* **2** ~ **sb (do sth)** (*old use or literary*) to tell sb to do sth: *He bade me come closer.*

**bid·dable** /ˈbɪdəbl/ *adj.* (*especially BrE, formal*) (of people) willing to obey and to do what they are told to

**bid·der** /ˈbɪdə(r)/ *noun* **1** a person or group that offers to pay an amount of money to buy sth: *The painting went to the highest bidder* (= the person who offered the most money). **2** ~ **(for sth)** a person or group that offers to do sth or to provide sth for a particular amount of money, in competition with others: *There were six bidders for the catering contract.*

**bid·ding** /ˈbɪdɪŋ/ *noun* [U] **1** the act of offering prices, especially at an AUCTION: *There was fast bidding between private collectors and dealers.* ◊ *Several companies remained in the bidding.* **2** the act of offering to do sth or to provide sth for a particular price: *competitive bidding for the contract* **3** (in some card games) the process of stating the number of points that players think they will win **4** (*old-fashioned or formal*) what sb asks or orders you to do: *to do sb's bidding* (= to obey sb)

**biddy** /ˈbɪdi/ *noun* (*pl.* **-ies**) (*informal, disapproving*) an old woman, especially an annoying one

**bide** /baɪd/ *verb* [I] (*old use*) = ABIDE (2)
**IDM** **bide your 'time** to wait for the right time to do sth

**bidet** /ˈbiːdeɪ; *NAmE* bɪˈdeɪ/ *noun* a low bowl in the bathroom, usually with TAPS, that you fill with water and sit on to wash your bottom

**bi·di·rec·tion·al** /ˌbaɪdəˈrekʃənl, -dɑɪr-/ *adj.* (*specialist*) functioning in two directions

**bi·en·nial** /baɪˈeniəl/ *adj., noun*
■ *adj.* [usually before noun] happening once every two years: *a biennial convention* ▶ **bi·en·ni·al·ly** /-əli/ *adv.* ⊃ see also ANNUAL *adj.*, BIANNUAL
■ *noun* any plant that lives for two years, producing flowers in the second year ⊃ compare ANNUAL, PERENNIAL

**bier** /bɪə(r); *NAmE* bɪr/ *noun* a frame on which the dead body or the COFFIN is placed or carried at a FUNERAL

**biff** /bɪf/ *verb* ~ **sb** (*old-fashioned, informal*) to hit sb hard with your FIST: *He biffed me on the nose.* ▶ **biff** *noun*

**bi·focals** /ˌbaɪˈfəʊklz/ *noun* [pl.] a pair of glasses with each LENS made in two parts. The upper part is for looking at things at a distance, and the lower part is for looking at things that are close to you. ⊃ compare VARIFOCALS ▶ **bi·focal** *adj.* [only before noun]

**bi·fur·cate** /ˈbaɪfəkeɪt; *NAmE* -fərk-/ *verb* [I] (*formal*) (of roads, rivers, etc.) to divide into two separate parts ▶ **bi·fur·ca·tion** /ˌbaɪfəˈkeɪʃn; *NAmE* -fərˈk-/ *noun* [C, U]

**big** ❶ **A1** /bɪɡ/ *adj., adv., verb* ⊃ see also BIGS
■ *adj.* (**big·ger, big·gest**)
• LARGE **1** **A1** large in size, degree, amount, etc: *a big man/house/increase* ◊ *This shirt isn't big enough.* ◊ *It's the world's biggest computer company.* ◊ (*informal*) *He had this great big grin on his face.* ◊ *The festival is getting bigger every year.* ◊ *They were earning big money.*
• OLDER **2** **A2** (*informal*) older: *my big brother* ◊ *You're a big girl now.*
• IMPORTANT **3** **A2** [only before noun] (*rather informal*) important; serious: *Unemployment is a big problem in the region.* ◊ *This legislation will make a big difference.* ◊ *Housing is a big issue in London.* ◊ *She took the stage for her big moment.* ◊ *Tonight is the biggest match of his career.* ◊ (*informal*) *Do you really think we can take on the big boys*

(= compete with the most powerful people)? ⊃ see also BIG DEAL
• AMBITIOUS **4** (*informal*) (of a plan) needing a lot of effort, money or time to succeed: *They're full of big ideas.*
• POPULAR **5** (*informal*) popular with the public; successful: *Orange is the big colour this year.* ◊ ~ **in ...** *The band's very big in Japan.*
• ENTHUSIASTIC **6** (*informal*) enthusiastic about sb/sth: *I'm a big fan of hers.*
• DOING STH A LOT **7** doing sth often or to a large degree: *a big eater/drinker/spender*
• GENEROUS **8** ~ **of sb** (*usually ironic*) kind or generous: *He gave me an extra five pounds for two hours' work. I thought 'That's big of you'.* ▶ **big·ness** *noun* [U]
**IDM** **be/get too big for your 'boots** (*NAmE* also **be/get too big for your 'britches**) to be/become too proud of yourself; to behave as if you are more important than you really are **a ˌbig 'cheese** (*informal, humorous*) an important and powerful person, especially in an organization **the big enchi'lada** (*NAmE, informal, humorous*) the most important person or thing **a big fish (in a small pond)** an important person (in a small community) **a ˌbig girl's 'blouse** (*BrE, informal*) a weak man, who is not brave or confident **a big noise/shot/name** an important person **the big 'picture** (*informal*) the situation as a whole: *Right now forget the details and take a look at the big picture.* **the big 'stick** (*informal*) the use or threat of force or power: *The authorities used quiet persuasion instead of the big stick.* **the Big Three, Four, etc.** the three, four, etc. most important countries, people, companies, etc: *She works for one of the Big Six.* **give sb/get a big 'hand** to show your approval of sb by CLAPPING your hands; to be APPLAUDED in this way: *Ladies and gentlemen, let's give a big hand to our special guests tonight.* **have a ˌbig 'mouth 1** to be bad at keeping secrets **2** to talk too much, especially about your own abilities and achievements **me and my big 'mouth** (*informal*) used when you realize that you have said sth that you should not have said ⊃ more at BIG DEAL, EYE *n.*, FISH *n.*, THING, WAY *n.*
■ *adv.* (*informal*) in an impressive way: *We need to think big.*
**IDM** **go over 'big (with sb)** (*informal*) to make a good impression on sb; to be successful: *This story went over big with my kids.* **make it 'big** (*informal*) to be very successful: *He's hoping to make it big on TV.* ⊃ more at HIT *v.*
■ *verb* (**-gg-**)
**PHRV** **ˌbig sb/sth↔'up** (*BrE, slang*) to praise or recommend sb/sth strongly: *He's been bigging up the new album on his radio show.*

▼ WHICH WORD?

## big / large / great

These adjectives are frequently used with the following nouns:

| big ~ | large ~ | great ~ |
|---|---|---|
| man | numbers | success |
| house | part | majority |
| car | area | interest |
| boy | room | importance |
| dog | company | difficulty |
| smile | eyes | problem |
| problem | family | pleasure |
| surprise | volume | beauty |
| question | population | artist |
| difference | problem | surprise |

- **Large** is more formal than **big** and should be used in writing unless it is in an informal style. It is not usually used to describe people, except to avoid saying 'fat'.
- **Great** often suggests quality and not just size. Note also the phrases: *a large amount of* ◊ *a large number of* ◊ *a large quantity of* ◊ *a great deal of* ◊ *in great detail* ◊ *a person of great age.*

**big·am·ist** /ˈbɪɡəmɪst/ *noun* a person who commits the crime of bigamy

**big·amy** /ˈbɪɡəmi/ *noun* [U] the crime of marrying sb when you are still legally married to sb else ⊃ compare

**big·am·ous** /-məs/ adj.: a bigamous relationship

**the ˌBig ˈApple** noun [sing.] (informal) New York City

**the ˌBig Bad ˈWolf** noun [sing.] (informal) a dangerous and frightening enemy ORIGIN From the wolf in several children's stories and the song Who's Afraid of the Big Bad Wolf?

**ˈbig band** noun a large group of musicians playing jazz or dance music: the big-band sound

**ˌBig ˈBang** noun [sing.] (usually **the Big Bang**) the single large event, followed by a rapid EXPANSION, that most scientists suggest created the universe

**ˌbig ˈbox** (also ˌbig-box ˈstore) noun (NAmE, informal) a very large shop, built on one level and located outside a town, which sells goods at low prices: When a big-box store opens, smaller retailers often go out of business. ◇ Efforts were made to limit big-box expansion.

**ˌBig ˈBrother** noun [sing.] a leader, a person in authority or a government that tries to control people's behaviour and thoughts, but pretends to act for their benefit ORIGIN From George Orwell's novel Nineteen Eighty-Four, in which the leader of the government, **Big Brother**, had total control over the people. The slogan 'Big Brother is watching you' reminded people that he knew everything they did.

**ˌbig ˈbucks** noun [pl.] (especially NAmE, informal) a large amount of money

**ˌbig-ˈbudget** adj. [only before noun] involving spending a large amount of money: a big-budget Hollywood film OPP **low-budget**

**ˌbig ˈbusiness** noun [U] 1 large companies that have a lot of power, considered as a group: links between politics and big business 2 something that has become important because people are willing to spend a lot of money on it: Health and fitness have become big business.

**ˌbig ˈcat** noun any large wild animal of the cat family. Lions, TIGERS and LEOPARDS are all big cats.

**ˌBig ˈChief** noun (informal) the person in charge of a business or other organization

**ˌbig ˈdata** noun [U, pl.] (computing) sets of information that are too large or too complex to handle, analyse or use with standard methods: Customer intelligence is created from big data analysis, so customers benefit from more personalized experiences.

**ˌbig ˈdeal** noun 1 [C, usually sing.] something that people think is important, usually because it is exciting or it makes them worried: So what's the big deal about the movie? ◇ He makes a big deal about the recent rise in gender equality. ◇ The former champion made a big deal of the fact he has been boxing for 27 years. ◇ **for sb/sth** This leak is a big deal for people who reuse passwords on other websites. 2 [C] an important business agreement: Do these big deals make sense for shareholders? IDM **ˌbig ˈdeal!** (informal, ironic) used to say that you are not impressed by sth: So he earns more than me. Big deal! **no big ˈdeal** (informal) used to say that sth is not important or not a problem: If I don't win it's no big deal.

**ˌbig ˈdipper** noun 1 (old-fashioned, BrE) a small train at an AMUSEMENT PARK, which goes very quickly up and down a steep track and around bends ◇ see also ROLLER COASTER 2 **the Big Dipper** (NAmE) (BrE **the Plough**) [sing.] a group of seven bright stars that can only be seen from the northern half of the world

**ˈBig·foot** /ˈbɪɡfʊt/ noun (pl. **Big·feet** /-fiːt/) (also **Sas·quatch**) a large creature covered with hair like an APE, which some people believe lives in western North America

**ˌbig ˈgame** noun [U] large wild animals that people hunt for sport, for example elephants and lions

**big·gie** /ˈbɪɡi/ noun (informal) an important thing, person or event

**ˌbig ˈgovernment** noun [U] (disapproving) a type of government that has a lot of control over people's lives and the economy

**ˌbig ˈgun** noun (informal) a person who has a lot of power or influence

**ˌbig ˈhair** noun [U] (informal) hair in a style that makes a large shape around the head

**ˌbig-ˈheaded** adj. (informal, disapproving) having a very high opinion of how important and clever you are; too proud ▶ **ˈbig-head** noun

**ˌbig-ˈhearted** adj. very kind; generous

**ˌbig ˈhitter** noun (informal) = HEAVY HITTER

**bight** /baɪt/ noun a long curved part of a coast or river: the Great Australian Bight

**ˌbig ˈleague** noun (NAmE) 1 [C] a group of teams in a professional sport, especially baseball, that play at the highest level 2 **the big league** [sing.] (informal) a very successful and important group: Over the past year, the company has joined the big league.

**ˈbig-league** adj. (NAmE) 1 connected with sports teams that are in a big league 2 very important and successful

**ˌBig Man on ˈCampus** noun (abbr. **BMOC**) (NAmE, informal) a successful popular male student at a college or university

**ˌbig ˈmouth** noun (informal) a person who talks a lot, especially about him- or herself, and who cannot keep secrets ▶ **ˌbig-ˈmouthed** adj.

**big·ot** /ˈbɪɡət/ noun a person who has very strong, unreasonable beliefs or opinions about race, religion or politics and who will not listen to or accept the opinions of anyone who disagrees: a religious/racial bigot

**big·ot·ed** /ˈbɪɡətɪd/ adj. showing strong, unreasonable beliefs or opinions and refusing to change them

**big·ot·ry** /ˈbɪɡətri/ noun [U] the state of feeling, or the act of expressing, strong, unreasonable beliefs or opinions

**ˌBig ˈPharma** /ˌbɪɡ ˈfɑːmə; NAmE ˈfɑːrmə/ noun [U] (informal) = PHARMA

**bigs** /bɪɡz/ noun [pl.] (NAmE, informal) 1 **the bigs** the major league in a professional sport 2 large companies with a lot of money and influence: software bigs ◇ the internet travel bigs

**the ˌbig ˈscreen** noun [sing.] the cinema (when contrasted with television): The movie hits the big screen in July. ◇ her first big-screen success

**the ˌbig ˈsmoke** (also **the Smoke**) noun [sing.] (BrE, informal) London, or another large city

**ˌbig ˈtent** noun a group or philosophy that accepts and includes individuals and organizations that have a wide variety of opinions or styles SYN **broad church**: The movement soon became a big tent under which many campaign groups gathered.

**ˈbig-ticket** adj. [only before noun] costing a lot of money: big-ticket items

**ˌbig ˈtime** noun, adv. (informal)
■ noun **the big time** great success in a profession, especially the entertainment business: a bit-part actor who finally made/hit the big time ◇ compare SMALL-TIME
■ adv. on a large scale; to a great extent: This time they've messed up big time!

**ˌbig ˈtoe** noun the largest toe on a person's foot ◇ VISUAL VOCAB page V1

**ˌbig ˈtop** (usually **the big top**) noun the large tent in which a CIRCUS gives performances

**ˌbig ˈwheel** noun 1 (usually **the Big Wheel**) (BrE) (also **Ferris wheel** NAmE, BrE) a large VERTICAL wheel pointing towards the sky at an AMUSEMENT PARK that turns round and round, with seats hanging at its edge for people to ride in 2 (NAmE, informal) an important person in a company or an organization

**ˈbig·wig** /ˈbɪɡwɪɡ/ noun (informal) an important person: She had to entertain some boring local bigwigs.

**bijou** /ˈbiːʒuː/ adj. [only before noun] (BrE, sometimes ironic) (of a building or a garden) small but attractive and fashionable: The house was terribly small and cramped, but the agent described it as a bijou residence.

# bike

**bike** ❶ **A1** /baɪk/ noun, verb
- noun (informal) **1** ❷ **A1** a bicycle: *I used to ride my bike around the neighbourhood for hours.* ◇ *by ~ I usually go to work by bike.* ⊃ see also MOUNTAIN BIKE, PUSHBIKE, QUAD BIKE, ROAD BIKE **2** a motorcycle
- **IDM** **on your bike!** (*BrE, informal*) a rude way of telling sb to go away
- verb **1** [I] (+ *adv./prep.*) (*informal*) to go somewhere on a bicycle or motorcycle: *My dad bikes to work every day.* **2** [T] ~ sth (+ *adv./prep.*) (*informal*) to send sth to sb by motorcycle: *I'll bike the contract over to you this afternoon.*
  ▸ **bik·ing** noun [U]: *The activities on offer include sailing and mountain biking.* ⊃ compare BICYCLE, CYCLE

**'bike lane** noun (*NAmE, informal*) = BICYCLE LANE

**bik·er** /ˈbaɪkə(r)/ noun **1** a person who rides a motorcycle, often as a member of a large group **2** a person who rides a bicycle, especially a MOUNTAIN BIKE: *a mountain biker*

**bikie** /ˈbaɪki/ noun (*AustralE, NZE, informal*) a member of a group of people who ride motorcycles

**bi·kini** /bɪˈkiːni/ noun a piece of clothing in two pieces that women wear for swimming and lying in the sun

**bi'kini line** noun the area of skin around the bottom half of a BIKINI and the hair that grows there, which some women remove

**bi·lat·eral** /ˌbaɪˈlætərəl/ adj. **1** involving two groups of people or two countries: *bilateral relations/agreements/trade/talks* ◇ *Both nations have signed bilateral treaties with the United States.* ⊃ WORDFINDER NOTE at ALLY **2** (*medical*) involving both of two parts or sides of the body or brain ▸ **bi·lat·er·al·ly** /-rəli/ adv. ⊃ compare MULTILATERAL, TRILATERAL, UNILATERAL

**bil·berry** /ˈbɪlbəri/; *NAmE* -beri/ (*also* **whortle·berry** /ˈwɜːtlbəri/, -beri; *NAmE* ˈwɜːrtlbəri/) noun (pl. -**ies**) a small dark blue BERRY that grows on bushes on hills and in woods in northern Europe and can be eaten. The bush is also called a bilberry. ⊃ compare BLUEBERRY

**bilby** /ˈbɪlbi/ noun (pl. -**ies**) a small Australasian animal with a long nose, a long tail and big ears

**bile** /baɪl/ noun [U] **1** the green-brown liquid with a bitter unpleasant taste that is produced by the LIVER to help the body to deal with the fats we eat, and that can come into your mouth when you VOMIT with an empty stomach **2** (*formal*) a strong feeling of anger or hating sb/sth: *The critic's review of the play was just a paragraph of bile.*

**'bile duct** noun the tube that carries bile from the LIVER and the GALL BLADDER to the DUODENUM ⊃ VISUAL VOCAB page V1

**bilge** /bɪldʒ/ noun **1** [C] (*also* **bilges** [pl.]) the almost flat part of the bottom of a boat or a ship, inside or outside **2** (*also* **'bilge water**) [U] dirty water that collects in a ship's bilge

**bil·har·zia** /bɪlˈhɑːtsiə; *NAmE* -ˈhɑːrt-/ noun [U] a serious disease, common in parts of Africa and South America, caused by small WORMS that get into the blood

**bil·iary** /ˈbɪliəri/; *NAmE* -lieri/ adj. (*medical*) relating to BILE or to the BILE DUCT

**bi·lin·gual** /ˌbaɪˈlɪŋɡwəl/ adj. **1** able to speak two languages equally well: *She is bilingual in English and Punjabi.* **2** using two languages; written in two languages: *bilingual education/communities* ◇ *a bilingual dictionary*
  ▸ **bi·lin·gual** noun: *Welsh/English bilinguals* ⊃ compare MONOLINGUAL, MULTILINGUAL

**bili·ous** /ˈbɪliəs/ adj. **1** feeling as if you might VOMIT soon **2** (of colours, usually green or yellow) creating an unpleasant effect: *a bilious green dress* **3** (*formal*) angry; full of anger

**bili·ru·bin** /ˌbɪlɪˈruːbɪn/ noun [U] (*medical*) an orange substance produced in the LIVER

**bilk** /bɪlk/ verb ~ sb (out of sth) | ~ sth (from sb) (*informal, especially NAmE*) to cheat sb, especially by taking money from them: *a conman who bilked investors out of millions of dollars*

# bill

**bill** ❶ **A1** /bɪl/ noun, verb
- noun
- **FOR PAYMENT 1** ❷ **A1** a document that shows how much you owe sb for goods or services: *the phone/electricity/gas bill* ◇ *He is facing a huge tax bill.* ◇ *She always pays her bills on time.* ◇ *We ran up a massive hotel bill.* **2** ❷ **A1** (especially *BrE*) (*NAmE usually* **check**) a piece of paper that shows how much you have to pay for the food and drinks that you have had in a restaurant: *Let's ask for the bill.*
- **MONEY 3** ❷ **A2** (*NAmE*) (*BrE* **note**) (*also* **bank·note** especially in *BrE*) a piece of paper money: *a ten-dollar bill* ⊃ picture at MONEY
- **IN PARLIAMENT 4** ❷ **B2** a written suggestion for a new law that is presented to a country's parliament so that its members can discuss it: *Congress passed the energy bill last month.* ◇ *the Education Reform Bill* ⊃ WORDFINDER NOTE at PARLIAMENT
- **AT THEATRE, ETC. 5** a programme of entertainment at a theatre, etc: *a horror double bill* (= two horror films shown one after the other) ◇ **Topping the bill** (= the most important performer) *is violinist Joshua Bell.*
- **ADVERTISEMENT 6** a notice in a public place to advertise an event **SYN** **poster** ⊃ see also HANDBILL
- **OF BIRDS 7** the hard pointed or curved outer part of a bird's mouth **SYN** **beak** ⊃ VISUAL VOCAB page V2 **8** -**billed** (in adjectives) having the type of bill mentioned: *long-billed waders*
- **ON HAT 9** (*also* **visor**) (*both NAmE*) (*BrE* **peak**) the stiff front part of a cap that sticks out above your eyes
- **IDM** **fill/fit the 'bill** to be what is needed in a particular situation or for a particular purpose: *On paper, several of the applicants fit the bill.* ⊃ more at CLEAN *adj.*, FOOT *v.*
- verb
- **ASK FOR PAYMENT 1** ❷ **B2** ~ sb (for sth) to send sb a bill for sth: *Please bill me for the books.*
- **ADVERTISE 2** [usually passive] to advertise or describe sb/sth in a particular way: *be billed as sth He was billed as the new Tom Cruise.* **3** [usually passive] to advertise that sb/sth will do sth: *be billed to do sth She was billed to speak on 'China—Yesterday and Today'.*

▼ **SYNONYMS**

**bill**

account • invoice • check

These are all words for a record of how much you owe for goods or services you have bought or used.

**bill** a list of goods that you have bought or services that you have used, showing how much you owe; the price or cost of sth: *the gas bill*

**account** an arrangement with a shop or business to pay bills for goods or services at a later time, for example in regular amounts every month: *Put it on my account please.*

**invoice** (*rather formal*) a bill for goods or work that has been done for sb: *The builders sent an invoice for £250.*

**BILL OR INVOICE?**

You would get a **bill** in a restaurant, bar or hotel; from a company that supplies you with gas, electricity, etc; or from sb whose property you have damaged. An **invoice** is for goods supplied or work done as agreed between a customer and supplier.

**check** (*NAmE*) a piece of paper that shows how much you have to pay for the food and drinks that you have had in a restaurant: *Can I have the check, please?* **NOTE** In British English the usual word for this is **bill**.

**PATTERNS**
- the bill/invoice/check **for** sth
- to **pay/settle** a(n) bill/account/invoice/check
- to **put sth on** the/sb's bill/account/invoice/check

**bill·able** /ˈbɪləbl/ adj. (of work done by professional people) that a client or customer can be charged for

**billa·bong** /ˈbɪləbɒŋ/; *NAmE* -bɔːŋ/ noun (in Australia) a lake that is formed when a river floods

**bill·board** /ˈbɪlbɔːd; NAmE -bɔːrd/ noun (especially NAmE) (BrE also **hoard·ing**) a large board on the outside of a building or at the side of the road, used for putting advertisements on

**bil·let** /ˈbɪlɪt/ noun, verb
- noun a place, often in a private house, where soldiers live temporarily
- verb [T, usually passive] + adv./prep. to send soldiers to live somewhere for a period of time, especially in private houses during a war

**bill·fold** /ˈbɪlfəʊld/ noun (NAmE) = WALLET

**bill·hook** /ˈbɪlhʊk/ noun a tool with a long handle and a curved metal BLADE, used for cutting the small branches off trees

**bil·liards** /ˈbɪliədz; NAmE ˈbɪljərdz/ noun [U] a game for two people played with CUES (= long sticks) and three balls on a long table covered with green cloth. Players try to hit the balls against each other and into pockets at the edge of the table: *a game of billiards* ➲ compare POOL, SNOOKER
▶ **bil·liard** adj. [only before noun] *a billiard cue*

**bill·ing** /ˈbɪlɪŋ/ noun 1 [U] the position, especially an important one, that sb is advertised or described as having in a show, etc: *to have **top/star billing*** 2 [U] the act of preparing and sending bills to customers 3 [C, usually pl.] the total amount of business that a company does in a particular period of time: *billings around $7 million*

**bil·lion** ⓘ A2 /ˈbɪljən/ number 1 ⓘ A2 (abbr. bn) 1000000000; one thousand million: *Worldwide sales reached 2.5 billion.* ◊ *half a billion dollars* ◊ *They have spent billions on the problem* (= billions of dollars, etc.). HELP You say **a**, **one**, **two**, **several**, etc. **billion** without a final 's' on 'billion'. **Billions (of …)** can be used if there is no number or quantity before it. Always use a plural verb with **billion** or **billions**, except when an amount of money is mentioned: *Two billion (people) worldwide are expected to watch the game.* ◊ *Two billion (dollars) was withdrawn from the account.* There are more examples of how to use numbers at the entry for hundred. 2 A2 **a billion** or **billions (of …)** (informal) a very large amount: *Our immune systems are killing billions of germs right now.* 3 (BrE, old-fashioned) 1000000000000; one million million SYN **trillion**

**bil·lion·aire** /ˌbɪljəˈneə(r); NAmE -ˈner/ noun an extremely rich person, who has at least a thousand million pounds, dollars, etc. in money or property

**bill of ˈcosts** noun (pl. **bills of costs**) (BrE, law) a list of the charges and expenses that sb must pay to a lawyer or to sb who has won a legal case

**bill of exˈchange** noun (pl. **bills of exchange**) (business) a written order to pay a sum of money to a particular person on a particular date

**bill of ˈfare** noun (pl. **bills of fare**) (old-fashioned) a list of the food that can be ordered in a restaurant SYN **menu**

**bill of ˈrights** noun [sing.] a written statement of the basic rights of the citizens of a country

**bill of ˈsale** noun (pl. **bills of sale**) (business) an official document showing that sth has been bought

**bil·low** /ˈbɪləʊ/ noun, verb
- verb 1 [I] (of a sail, skirt, etc.) to fill with air and form a round shape: *The curtains billowed in the breeze.* 2 [I] if smoke, cloud, etc. **billows**, it rises and moves in a large mass: *A great cloud of smoke billowed out of the chimney.*
- noun [usually pl.] a moving mass or cloud of smoke, STEAM, etc. like a wave

**billy** /ˈbɪli/ noun (pl. **-ies**) (also **billy-can** /ˈbɪlikæn/) (both BrE) a metal can with a LID and a handle used for boiling water or for cooking when you are camping

**ˈbilly club** noun (NAmE) a short wooden stick used as a weapon by police officers

**ˈbilly goat** noun a male GOAT ➲ compare NANNY GOAT

**bil·tong** /ˈbɪltɒŋ; NAmE -tɔːŋ/ SAfrE /ˈbəltɒŋ/ noun [U] (SAfrE) raw dry meat that is eaten in small pieces. Biltong is preserved by being treated with salt.

139

**bindaas**

**bim·ble** /ˈbɪmbl/ verb, noun (BrE, informal)
- verb [I] + adv./prep. to walk or travel without hurrying: *We spent the morning bimbling around the market.* ◊ *I bimbled into town.*
- noun [usually sing.] a slow, relaxed walk or journey: *We were enjoying a pleasant bimble in the country.*

**bimbo** /ˈbɪmbəʊ/ noun (pl. **-os**) (informal, disapproving) a young person, usually a woman, who is sexually attractive but not very intelligent: *He's going out with an empty-headed bimbo half his age.*

**bi-month·ly** /ˌbaɪˈmʌnθli/ adj., adv. produced or happening every two months or twice each month

**bin** ⓘ A2 /bɪn/ noun, verb
- noun 1 ⓘ A2 (especially BrE) a container that you put waste in: *a rubbish bin* ◊ *Grey bins will be emptied weekly.* ➲ see also DUSTBIN, LITTER BIN, WASTE BIN, WHEELIE BIN 2 a large container, usually with a LID (= cover), for storing things in: *a bread bin* ➲ see also COMPOST BIN
- verb (-nn-) ~ sth (BrE, informal) to throw sth away: *Do you need to keep these letters or shall we bin them?*

**bin·ary** /ˈbaɪnəri; NAmE also -neri/ adj. 1 (computing, mathematics) using only 0 and 1 as a system of numbers: *the **binary system*** ◊ *binary arithmetic* ➲ compare DECIMAL, HEXADECIMAL 2 (specialist) based on only two numbers; consisting of two parts: ***binary code/numbers*** ➲ see also NON-BINARY ▶ **bin·ary** noun [U]: *The computer performs calculations in binary and converts the results to decimal.*

**ˈbin bag** noun (BrE, informal) a large plastic bag for putting rubbish in

**bind** ⓘ+ C1 /baɪnd/ verb, noun
- verb (bound, bound /baʊnd/)
• TIE WITH ROPE/CLOTH 1 ⓘ+ C1 [T] (formal) to tie sb/sth with rope, string, etc. so that they/it cannot move or are held together strongly: *~ sb/sth to sth She was bound to a chair.* ◊ *~ sb/sth together They bound his hands together.* ◊ *~ sb/sth He was left bound and gagged* (= tied up and with a piece of cloth tied over his mouth). 2 [~] ~ sth (up) (formal) to tie a long thin piece of cloth around sth: *She bound up his wounds.*
• FORM UNITED GROUP 3 ⓘ+ C1 [T] to make people, organizations, etc. feel united so that they live or work together more happily or effectively: *~ A (and B) (together) Organizations such as schools and clubs bind a community together.* ◊ *~ A to B She thought that having his child would bind him to her forever.*
• MAKE SB DO STH 4 [T, usually passive] to force sb to do sth by making them promise to do it or by making it their duty to do it: *~ sb (to sth) He had been bound to secrecy* (= made to promise not to tell people about sth). ◊ *~ sb to do sth The agreement binds her to repay the debt within six months.* ➲ see also BINDING, BOUND verb
• STICK TOGETHER 5 [I, T] to stick together or to make things stick together in a solid mass: *~ (together) Add an egg yolk to make the mixture bind.* ◊ *~ sth (together) Add an egg yolk to bind the mixture together.*
• BOOK 6 [T, usually passive] ~ sth (in sth) to fasten the pages of a book together and put them inside a cover: *two volumes bound in leather*
• SEW EDGE 7 [T, often passive] ~ sth (with sth) to SEW a piece of material to the edge of sth to decorate it or to make it stronger: *The blankets were bound with satin.* ➲ WORDFINDER NOTE at SEW IDM see HAND n.
PHRV **ˌbind sb ˈover** [usually passive] 1 (NAmE, law) to give sb BAIL while they are waiting to go to trial: *He was bound over for trial.* 2 (BrE, law) to give sb a formal warning that if they break the law again they will be punished: *She was bound over to keep the peace for a year.*
- noun [sing.] (BrE, informal) an annoying situation that is often difficult to avoid ➲ see also DOUBLE BIND
IDM **in a ˈbind** (especially NAmE) in a difficult situation that you do not know how to get out of

**bin·daas** /ˈbɪndɑːs/ adj. (IndE, informal) independent and seeming to have no worries or responsibilities: *a bindaas girl* ◊ *a bindaas attitude*

# binder

**bind·er** /ˈbaɪndə(r)/ noun **1** [C] a hard cover for holding sheets of paper, magazines, etc. together: *a ring binder* **2** [C] a person or machine that puts covers on books **3** [C, U] a substance that makes things stick or mix together in a solid form **4** [C] a machine that fastens WHEAT into bunches after it has been cut

**bindi** /ˈbɪndi/ noun an attractive mark worn in the middle of the FOREHEAD, usually by Hindu women

**bind·ing** /ˈbaɪndɪŋ/ adj., noun
- adj. ~ (on/upon sb) that must be obeyed because it is accepted in law: *a binding promise/agreement/contract* **OPP** non-binding ⊃ WORDFINDER NOTE at DOCUMENT
- noun **1** [C, U] the cover that holds the pages of a book together **2** [C, U] cloth that is fastened to the edge of sth to protect or decorate it **3** [C] a device on a ski that holds the heel and toe of your boot in place and releases the boot if you fall

**binge** /bɪndʒ/ noun, verb
- noun (informal) a short period of time when sb does too much of a particular activity, especially eating or drinking alcohol: *to go on a binge* ◊ *binge drinking* ◊ *One of the symptoms is binge eating.*
- verb [I] (binge·ing or bin·ging, binged, binged) ~ (on sth) to eat or drink too much, especially without being able to control yourself: *When she's depressed she binges on chocolate.* ⊃ WORDFINDER NOTE at EAT

**bingo** /ˈbɪŋɡəʊ/ noun, exclamation
- noun [U] a game in which each player has a card with numbers on. Numbers are called out in no particular order and the first player whose numbers are all called out, or who has a line of numbers called out, wins a prize: *to play bingo* ◊ *a bingo hall*
- exclamation (informal) used to express pleasure and/or surprise because you have found sth that you were looking for, or done sth that you were trying to do: *The computer program searches, and bingo! We've got a match.*

**ˈbingo wings** noun [pl.] (BrE, informal, humorous) long folds of loose skin and fat that hang down from the upper arms, especially of older people

**ˈbin liner** noun (BrE) a plastic bag that is placed inside a container for holding waste

**ˈbin lorry** (also ˈrubbish truck) (both BrE) (NAmE ˈgarbage truck) (also old-fashioned, BrE also dust·art) noun a vehicle for collecting rubbish from outside houses, etc.

**ˈbin·man** /ˈbɪnmæn/ noun (pl. -men /-men/) (BrE, informal) = DUSTMAN

**bin·ocu·lar** /bɪˈnɒkjələ(r)/; NAmE -ˈnɑːk-/ adj. (specialist) using two eyes to see: *binocular vision*

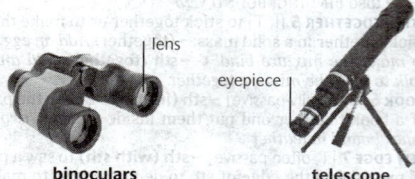

binoculars | telescope

**bin·ocu·lars** /bɪˈnɒkjələz; NAmE -ˈnɑːkjəlɚz/ (also specialist ˈfield glasses) noun [pl.] an instrument, like two small TELESCOPES fixed together, that makes objects that are far away seem nearer when you look through it: *a pair of binoculars* ◊ *We looked at the birds through binoculars.*

**bi·no·mial** /baɪˈnəʊmiəl/ noun **1** (mathematics) an expression that has two groups of numbers or letters, joined by the sign + or − ⊃ compare POLYNOMIAL **2** (linguistics) a pair of nouns joined by a word like 'and', where the order of the nouns is always the same, for example 'knife and fork' ▶ **bi·no·mial** adj.

**bint** /bɪnt/ noun (BrE, slang) an offensive way of referring to a woman: *a posh bint*

**bio-** /ˈbaɪəʊ, baɪɒ; BrE also baɪˈɒ; NAmE also baɪˈɑː/ combining form (in nouns, adjectives and adverbs) connected with living things or human life: *biodegradable* ◊ *biography*

**bio·bank** /ˈbaɪəʊbæŋk/ noun a large collection of samples of TISSUE (= a group of cells that form the different parts of humans, animals and plants) and data connected with medicine or biology, brought together for research

**bio·chem·ist** /ˌbaɪəʊˈkemɪst/ noun a scientist who studies biochemistry

**bio·chem·is·try** /ˌbaɪəʊˈkemɪstri/ noun **1** [U] the scientific study of the chemistry of living things **2** [U, C] the chemical structure and behaviour of a living thing ▶ **bio·chem·ical** /-mɪkl/ adj.

**bio·con·ver·sion** /ˌbaɪəʊkənˈvɜːʃn; NAmE -ˈvɜːrʒn/ noun [U] the process of using living ORGANISMS to change one chemical COMPOUND or form of energy into another

**bio·data** /ˈbaɪəʊdeɪtə; BrE also -dɑːtə; NAmE also -dætə/ noun **1** [U, pl.] information about a person and about what they have done in their life **2** [C] (IndE) = CURRICULUM VITAE

**bio·defence** (US bio·defense) /ˌbaɪəʊdɪˈfens/ noun [U] measures taken to protect people against an attack using BIOLOGICAL WEAPONS (= weapons of war that spread disease)

**bio·degrad·able** /ˌbaɪəʊdɪˈɡreɪdəbl/ adj. a substance or chemical that is biodegradable can be changed by the action of bacteria to a natural state that will not harm the environment **OPP** non-biodegradable

**bio·de·grade** /ˌbaɪəʊdɪˈɡreɪd/ verb [I] (of a substance or chemical) to change back, by the action of bacteria, to a natural state that will not harm the environment

**bio·diesel** /ˈbaɪəʊdiːzl/ noun [U] a type of fuel made from plant or animal material and used in DIESEL engines

**bio·di·ver·sity** /ˌbaɪəʊdaɪˈvɜːsəti; NAmE -ˈvɜːrs-/ (also less frequent ˌbio·logical diˈversity) noun [U] the existence of a large number of different kinds of animals and plants which make a balanced environment ⊃ WORDFINDER NOTE at GREEN

**bio·energy** /ˌbaɪəʊˈenədʒi; NAmE -nərdʒi/ noun [U] a type of energy produced using ORGANIC substances that can be replaced naturally, such as wood or vegetable oil: *The plant crops will be used for sustainable bioenergy.*

**bio·engin·eer·ing** /ˌbaɪəʊˌendʒɪˈnɪərɪŋ; NAmE -ˈnɪr-/ noun [U] the use of engineering methods to solve medical problems, for example the use of artificial arms and legs

**bio·etha·nol** /ˌbaɪəʊˈeθənɒl; NAmE -nɔːl, -nəʊl/ noun [U] a type of alcohol, produced from SUGAR CANE (= the plant from which sugar is made), MAIZE, etc., that is used as an alternative to petrol

**bio·eth·ics** /ˌbaɪəʊˈeθɪks/ noun [U] (specialist) the moral principles that influence research in medicine and biology

**bio·feed·back** /ˌbaɪəʊˈfiːdbæk/ noun [U] (specialist) the use of electronic equipment to record and display activity in the body that is not usually under your conscious control, for example your heart rate, so that you can learn to control that activity

**bio·fuel** /ˈbaɪəʊfjuːəl/ noun [C, U] fuel made from plant or animal sources and used in engines: *biofuels made from sugar cane and sugar beet*

**bio·gas** /ˈbaɪəʊɡæs/ noun [U] gas, especially METHANE, that is produced by dead plants and that can be burned to produce heat

**biog·raph·er** /baɪˈɒɡrəfə(r); NAmE -ˈɑːɡ-/ noun a person who writes the story of another person's life

**biog·raphy** /baɪˈɒɡrəfi; NAmE -ˈɑːɡ-/ noun [C, U] (pl. -ies) the story of a person's life written by sb else; this type of writing: *Boswell's biography of Johnson* ⊃ compare AUTOBIOGRAPHY ⊃ WORDFINDER NOTE at BOOK ▶ **bio·graph·ical** /ˌbaɪəˈɡræfɪkl/ adj.

**bio·hazard** /ˈbaɪəʊhæzəd; NAmE -zərd/ noun a risk to human health or to the environment from a BIOLOGICAL source

---

æ cat | ɑː father | e bed | ɜː fur | ə about | ɪ sit | iː see | i happy | ɒ got (BrE) | ɔː saw | ʌ cup | ʊ put | uː too

**bio·log·ic·al** /ˌbaɪəˈlɒdʒɪkl/; *NAmE* -ˈlɑːdʒ-/ *adj.* **1** connected with the science of biology: *the biological sciences* **2** connected with the processes that take place within living things: *the biological effects of radiation* ◊ *the biological control of pests* (= using living ORGANISMS to destroy them, not chemicals) **3** (of a member of a person's family) related by blood: *a child's biological parents* (= natural parents, not the people who adopted him/her) **4** (of washing powder, etc.) using ENZYMES (= chemical substances that are found in plants and animals) to get clothes, etc. clean: *biological and non-biological powders* ▶ **bio·log·ic·al·ly** /-kli/ *adv.*

**biological 'clock** *noun* (*specialist*) a natural system in living things that controls regular physical activities such as sleeping: (*figurative*) *At 35, Kate's biological clock was ticking* (= she was beginning to think that she would soon be too old to have children).

**biological di'versity** *noun* [U] = BIODIVERSITY

**biological 'warfare** *noun* [U] the use of weapons of war that spread disease **SYN** **germ warfare**

**biological 'weapon** *noun* a weapon of war that spreads disease ⊃ compare CHEMICAL WEAPON

**bi·olo·gist** /baɪˈɒlədʒɪst/; *NAmE* -ˈɑːl-/ *noun* a scientist who studies biology

**bi·ol·ogy** /baɪˈɒlədʒi/; *NAmE* -ˈɑːl-/ *noun* [U] **1** the scientific study of the life and structure of plants and animals: *a degree in biology* ⊃ compare BOTANY, ZOOLOGY

> **WORDFINDER** biotechnology, breed, cell, chromosome, DNA, gene, mutation, organism, protein

**2** the way in which the body and cells of a living thing behave: *How far is human nature determined by biology?* ◊ *the biology of marine animals*

**bio·lu·min·es·cence** /ˌbaɪəʊluːmɪˈnesns/ *noun* [U] (*biology*) the natural production of light by living creatures such as GLOW-WORMS

**bio·mass** /ˈbaɪəʊmæs/ *noun* [U, sing.] (*specialist*) **1** the total quantity or MASS (= weight) of plants and animals in a particular area or volume **2** natural materials from living or recently dead plants, trees and animals, used as fuel and in industrial production, especially in the generation of electricity: *biomass crops* ⊃ compare FOSSIL FUEL

**biome** /ˈbaɪəʊm/ *noun* (*biology*) the characteristic plants and animals that exist in a particular type of environment, for example in a forest or desert

**bio·mech·an·ics** /ˌbaɪəʊməˈkænɪks/ *noun* [U] the scientific study of the physical movement and structure of living creatures

**bio·med·ical** /ˌbaɪəʊˈmedɪkl/ *adj.* [usually before noun] relating to how biology affects medicine

**bio·metric** /ˌbaɪəʊˈmetrɪk/ *adj.* [usually before noun] using measurements of human features, such as fingers or eyes, in order to identify people

**bi·onic** /baɪˈɒnɪk/; *NAmE* -ˈɑːn-/ *adj.* having parts of the body that are electronic, and therefore able to do things that are not possible for normal humans

**bio·phys·ics** /ˌbaɪəʊˈfɪzɪks/ *noun* [U] the science that uses the laws and methods of physics to study biology

**bio·pic** /ˈbaɪəʊpɪk/ *noun* a film about the life of a particular person

**bi·opsy** /ˈbaɪɒpsi/; *NAmE* ˈbaɪɑːp-/ *noun* (*pl.* **-ies**) the process of removing and examining TISSUE from the body of sb who is ill, in order to find out more about their disease ⊃ **WORDFINDER NOTE** at EXAMINE

**bio·rhythm** /ˈbaɪəʊrɪðəm/ *noun* [usually pl.] the changing pattern of how physical processes happen in the body, which some people believe affects human behaviour

**bio·sci·ence** /ˈbaɪəʊsaɪəns/ *noun* [C, U] any of the LIFE SCIENCES (= the scientific study of humans, animals or plants)

**bio·se·cur·ity** /ˌbaɪəʊsɪˈkjʊərəti/; *NAmE* -ˈkjʊr-/ *noun* [U] the activities involved in preventing the spread of animal, human and plant diseases from one area to another

141 **birdbrain**

**bio·sphere** /ˈbaɪəʊsfɪə(r)/; *NAmE* -sfɪr/ *noun* [sing.] (*specialist*) the part of the earth's surface and atmosphere in which plants and animals can live

**bio·tech·nol·ogy** /ˌbaɪəʊtekˈnɒlədʒi/; *NAmE* -ˈnɑːl-/ (*also informal* **bio·tech** /ˈbaɪəʊtek/) *noun* [U] the use of living cells and bacteria in industrial and scientific processes ⊃ **WORDFINDER NOTE** at BIOLOGY ▶ **bio·tech·no·logic·al** /ˌbaɪəʊteknəˈlɒdʒɪkl/; *NAmE* -ˈlɑːdʒ-/ *adj.*: *biotechnological research*

**bi·ot·ic** /baɪˈɒtɪk/; *NAmE* -ˈɑːt-/ *adj.* (*biology*) of or related to living things

**bio·type** /ˈbaɪəʊtaɪp/ *noun* (*biology*) a group of living things with exactly the same combination of GENES

**bi·par·ti·san** /ˌbaɪpɑːtɪˈzæn, baɪpɑːˈtɪˈzæn/; *NAmE* ˌbaɪˈpɑːrtɪzn/ *adj.* involving two political parties: *a bipartisan policy*

**bi·par·tite** /baɪˈpɑːtaɪt/; *NAmE* -ˈpɑːrt-/ *adj.* (*specialist*) involving or made up of two separate parts

**biped** /ˈbaɪped/ *noun* (*specialist*) any creature with two feet ⊃ compare QUADRUPED

**bi·pedal** /ˌbaɪˈpiːdl/; *NAmE also* -ˈped-/ *adj.* (*specialist*) (of animals) using only two legs for walking

**bi·plane** /ˈbaɪpleɪn/ *noun* an early type of plane with two sets of wings, one above the other ⊃ compare MONOPLANE

**bi·polar** /ˌbaɪˈpəʊlə(r)/ (*also old-fashioned* **manic-de'pressive**) *adj.* (*psychology*) suffering from or connected with bipolar disorder ▶ **bi·polar** (*also old-fashioned* **manic-de'pressive**) *noun*

**bi'polar disorder** (*also* **bipolar af'fective disorder**) *noun* [U, C] (*also old-fashioned* **manic de'pression** [U]) (*psychology*) a mental illness causing sb to change suddenly from being extremely depressed to being extremely happy ⊃ **WORDFINDER NOTE** at CONDITION

**bi·racial** /ˌbaɪˈreɪʃl/ *adj.* (*especially NAmE*) = MIXED-RACE

**birch** /bɜːtʃ/; *NAmE* bɜːrtʃ/ *noun* **1** [C, U] (*also* **'birch tree** [C]) a tree with smooth BARK and thin branches that grows in northern countries ⊃ see also SILVER BIRCH **2** (*also* **birchwood** /ˈbɜːtʃwʊd/; *NAmE* ˈbɜːrtʃ-/) [U] the hard pale wood of the birch tree **3 the birch** [sing.] the practice of hitting sb with a bunch of birch sticks, as a punishment

**bird** /bɜːd/; *NAmE* bɜːrd/ *noun*, *verb*
■ *noun* **1** a creature that is covered with feathers and has two wings and two legs. Most birds can fly: *a bird's nest with two eggs in it* ◊ *a species of bird* ◊ *A small bird flew down.* ◊ *The area has a wealth of bird life.* ⊃ see also GAME BIRD, SEABIRD, SONGBIRD, WATERBIRD ⊃ **VISUAL VOCAB** page V2 **2** (*BrE, old-fashioned, slang, sometimes offensive*) a way of referring to a young woman **3** (*informal*) a person of a particular type, especially sb who is strange or unusual in some way: *a wise old bird* ◊ *She is that rare bird: a politician with a social conscience.* **IDM** **be (strictly) for the birds** (*informal*) to not be important or practical **the bird has 'flown** the wanted person has escaped **a bird in the 'hand is worth two in the 'bush** (*saying*) it is better to keep sth that you already have than to risk losing it by trying to get much more **the birds and the bees** (*humorous*) the basic facts about sex, especially as told to children **a 'bird's-eye 'view (of sth)** a view of sth from a high position looking down: *From the plane we had a bird's-eye view of Manhattan.* **birds of a 'feather (flock to'gether)** (*saying*) people of the same sort (are found together) **give sb/get the 'bird** (*informal*) **1** (*BrE*) to shout at sb to show that you do not like or approve of them; to be shouted at **2** (*NAmE*) to make a rude sign at sb with your middle finger; to have this sign made at you ⊃ more at EARLY *adj.*, KILL *v.*, LITTLE *adj.*
■ *verb* [I, T] **~ (sth)** (*NAmE, informal*) to go BIRDWATCHING

**bird·bath** /ˈbɜːdbɑːθ/; *NAmE* ˈbɜːrdbæθ/ *noun* a bowl filled with water for birds to wash in and drink from, usually in a garden

**bird·brain** /ˈbɜːdbreɪn/; *NAmE* ˈbɜːrd-/ *noun* (*especially NAmE*) a stupid person

# birdcage 142

**bird·cage** /ˈbɜːdkeɪdʒ/; *NAmE* ˈbɜːrd-/ *noun* a CAGE in which birds are kept, usually one in a house

**ˈbird dog** *noun* (*NAmE*, *informal*) **1** a dog used in hunting to bring back birds that have been shot **2** a person whose job involves searching for good players for a sports team

**bird·er** /ˈbɜːdə(r)/; *NAmE* ˈbɜːrd-/ (*informal*) = BIRDWATCHER ⊃ compare ORNITHOLOGIST

**ˈbird feeder** *noun* a container or platform in a garden in/on which people put food for birds

**ˈbird flu** (*also formal* ˌavian ˈflu) *noun* [U] a serious illness that affects birds, especially chickens, that can be spread from birds to humans and that can cause death: *Ten new cases of bird flu were reported yesterday.*

**bir·die** /ˈbɜːdi; *NAmE* ˈbɜːrdi/ *noun* **1** (*informal*) a child's word for a little bird **2** (in golf) a score of one STROKE (= hit) of the ball less than PAR (= the standard score for a hole) ⊃ compare BOGEY, EAGLE **3** (*NAmE*) = SHUTTLECOCK

**bird·ing** /ˈbɜːdɪŋ/; *NAmE* ˈbɜːrd-/ *noun* = BIRDWATCHING

**ˌbird of ˈparadise** *noun* (*pl.* birds of paradise) a bird with very bright feathers, found mainly in New Guinea

**ˌbird of ˈpassage** *noun* (*pl.* birds of passage) **1** a bird that travels regularly from one part of the world to another at different seasons of the year **2** a person who passes through a place without staying there long

**ˌbird of ˈprey** *noun* (*pl.* birds of prey) a bird that hunts and kills other creatures for food. EAGLES, HAWKS and OWLS are all birds of prey. ⊃ VISUAL VOCAB page V2

**ˈbird·seed** /ˈbɜːdsiːd; *NAmE* ˈbɜːrd-/ *noun* [U] special seeds for feeding birds

**ˈbird·song** /ˈbɜːdsɒŋ; *NAmE* ˈbɜːrdsɔːŋ/ *noun* [U] the musical sounds made by birds

**ˈbird strike** *noun* an occasion when a bird hits an aircraft

**ˈbird table** *noun* (*BrE*) a wooden platform in a garden on which people put food for birds

**bird·watch·er** /ˈbɜːdwɒtʃə(r)/; *NAmE* ˈbɜːrdwɑːtʃ-/ (*also informal* **bird·er**) *noun* a person who watches birds in their natural environment and identifies different species as a hobby ⊃ compare ORNITHOLOGIST ▶ **ˈbird·watch·ing** (*also informal* **ˈbird·ing**) *noun* [U]

**bi·retta** /bɪˈretə/ *noun* a square cap worn by Roman Catholic priests

**biri·ani**, **biri·yani** = BIRYANI

**Biro™** /ˈbaɪrəʊ/ *noun* (*pl.* -os) (*BrE*) a plastic pen with a metal ball at the top that rolls INK (= coloured liquid for writing, etc.) onto the paper ⊃ compare BALLPOINT

**birth** ⊙ A2 /bɜːθ; *NAmE* bɜːrθ/ *noun* **1** A2 [U, C] the time when a baby is born; the process of being born: *at ~ The baby weighed three kilos at birth.* ◇ *Global life expectancy at birth is about 72 years.* ◇ *John was present at the birth of both his children.* ◇ *a hospital/home birth* ◇ *from ~ Mark has been blind from birth.* ◇ *Please state your date and place of birth.* ⊃ WORDFINDER NOTE at BABY

▪ WORDFINDER breech birth, caesarean section, contraction, deliver, induce, labour, midwife, obstetrics, umbilical cord

**2** B2 [sing.] the beginning of a new situation, idea, place, etc: *the birth of a new society in South Africa* **3** [U] a person's origin or the social position of their family: *Anne was French by birth but lived most of her life in Italy.* ◇ *a woman of noble birth*

IDM **give ˈbirth (to sb/sth)** to produce a baby or young animal: *She died shortly after giving birth.* ◇ *Mary gave birth to a healthy baby girl.* ◇ (*figurative*) *It was the study of history that gave birth to the social sciences.*

**ˈbirth certificate** *noun* an official document that shows when and where a person was born

**ˈbirth control** *noun* [U] the practice of controlling the number of children a person has, using various methods of CONTRACEPTION: *a reliable method of birth control*

**birth·day** ⊙ A1 /ˈbɜːθdeɪ; *NAmE* ˈbɜːrθ-/ *noun* the day in each year which is the same date as the one on which you were born: *Happy Birthday!* ◇ *She celebrated her 21st birthday with a party for family and friends.* ◇ *a birthday card/party/present/cake* ⊃ WORDFINDER NOTE at CELEBRATE

IDM **in your ˈbirthday suit** (*humorous*) not wearing any clothes

**birth·ing** /ˈbɜːθɪŋ; *NAmE* ˈbɜːrθ-/ *noun* [U] the action or process of giving birth: *a birthing pool*

**birth·mark** /ˈbɜːθmɑːk; *NAmE* ˈbɜːrθmɑːrk/ *noun* a red or brown mark on a person's skin that has been there since they were born

**ˈbirth mother** *noun* the woman who gave birth to a child who has been adopted

**ˈbirth partner** *noun* a person whom a woman chooses to be with her when she is giving birth to a baby

**birth·place** /ˈbɜːθpleɪs; *NAmE* ˈbɜːrθ-/ *noun* **1** the house or area where a person was born, especially a famous person **2** the place where sth first happened: *Hawaii was the birthplace of surfing.*

**ˈbirth rate** *noun* the number of births every year for every 1000 people in the population of a place: *a low/high birth rate*

**birth·right** /ˈbɜːθraɪt; *NAmE* ˈbɜːrθ-/ *noun* (*formal*) a thing that sb has a right to because of the family or country they were born in, or because it is a basic right of all humans: *The property is the birthright of the eldest child.* ◇ *Education is every child's birthright.*

**birth·stone** /ˈbɜːθstəʊn; *NAmE* ˈbɜːrθ-/ *noun* a SEMI-PRECIOUS stone that is associated with the month of sb's birth or their sign of the ZODIAC

**ˈbirth weight** (*also* **birth weight**) /ˈbɜːθweɪt; *NAmE* ˈbɜːrθ-/ *noun* [U, C] the recorded weight of a baby when it is born

**biry·ani** (*also* **biri·ani**, **biri·yani**) /ˌbɪriˈɑːni/ *noun* [U, C] a South Asian dish made from rice with meat, fish or vegetables: *chicken biryani*

**bis** /bɪs/ *adv.* (*music*) (used as an instruction) again

**bis·cuit** ⊙ A2 /ˈbɪskɪt/ *noun* **1** ⊙ A2 [C] (*BrE*) a small flat dry cake for one person, usually sweet, and baked until hard: *a packet/tin of chocolate biscuits* ◇ *a selection of cheese biscuits* ⊃ compare COOKIE ▶ see also DIGESTIVE BISCUIT, DOG BISCUIT **2** [C] (*NAmE*) a soft bread roll, often eaten with GRAVY **3** [U] a pale yellow-brown colour

IDM **take the ˈbiscuit** (*BrE*) (*also* **take the ˈcake** *NAmE*, *BrE*) (*informal*) to be the most surprising, annoying, etc. thing that has happened or that sb has done: *You've done some stupid things before, but this really takes the biscuit!*

**bi·sect** /baɪˈsekt/ *verb* ~ **sth** (*specialist*) to divide sth into two equal parts

**bi·sex·ual** /ˌbaɪˈsekʃuəl/ *adj.*, *noun*

▪ *adj.* **1** (*also informal* **bi**) sexually attracted to people of more than one GENDER **2** (*biology*) having both male and female sexual organs ▶ **bi·sexu·al·ity** /ˌbaɪˌsekʃuˈæləti/ *noun* [U]

▪ *noun* a person who is bisexual ⊃ compare HETEROSEXUAL, HOMOSEXUAL

**bishop** ⊙+ C1 /ˈbɪʃəp/ *noun* **1** ⊙+ C1 a senior priest in charge of the work of the Church in a city or district: *the Bishop of Oxford* ◇ *Bishop Pritchard* ⊃ see also ARCHBISHOP **2** a piece used in the game of CHESS that is like a bishop's hat in shape and can move any number of squares in a DIAGONAL line

**bish·op·ric** /ˈbɪʃəprɪk/ *noun* **1** the position of a bishop **2** the district for which a bishop is responsible SYN diocese

**bis·muth** /ˈbɪzməθ/ *noun* [U] (*symb.* Bi) a chemical element. Bismuth is a silver-grey metal that breaks easily and is used in medicine.

**bison** /ˈbaɪsn/ *noun* (*pl.* bison) a large wild animal of the cow family that is covered with hair. There are two types of bison, the North American (*also called* BUFFALO) and the European: *a herd of bison*

**bisque** /bɪsk/ *noun* [U, C] a thick soup, especially one made from SHELLFISH: *lobster bisque* ⊃ see also CHOWDER

**bis·tro** /ˈbiːstrəʊ/ *noun* (*pl.* -os) a small informal restaurant

**bit** ❶ A2 /bɪt/ noun

- SMALL AMOUNT **1** ❜ A2 **a bit** [sing.] (used as an adverb) (*especially BrE*) rather; to some extent SYN **a little**: *These trousers are a bit tight.* ◊ *'Are you tired?' 'Yes, I am a bit.'* ◊ *It costs a bit more than I wanted to spend.* ◊ *The future looks a little bit brighter this morning.* ◊ *I can lend you fifty pounds, if you want. That should help a bit.* **2** ❜ B1 **a bit** [sing.] (*especially BrE*) a short time or distance: *Wait a bit!* ◊ *Can you move up a bit?* ◊ **for a~** *Greg thought for a bit before answering.* ◊ **in a~** *See you in a bit.* **3** ❜ B1 [C] **~ of sth** (*especially BrE*) a small amount or piece of sth: *Here are some useful bits of information.* ◊ *Let me give you a little bit of advice.* ◊ *With a bit of luck, we'll be there by 12.* ◊ *I've got a bit of shopping to do.* ◊ *bits of paper/wood/plastic*
- PART OF STH **4** ❜ B1 [C] (*especially BrE*) a part of sth larger: *The best bit of the holiday was seeing the Grand Canyon.* ◊ *I read it, but I missed out the boring bits.*
- LARGE AMOUNT **5** [sing.] **a~ (of sth)** (*especially BrE, informal*) a large amount: *'How much does he earn?' 'Quite a bit!'* ◊ *It rained a fair bit during the night.* ◊ *The new system will take a bit of getting used to* (= it will take a long time to get used to).
- COMPUTING **6** [C] the smallest unit of information used by a computer
- FOR HORSE **7** [C] a metal bar that is put in a horse's mouth so that the rider can control it
- TOOL **8** [C] a tool or part of a tool for DRILLING (= making) holes ⊃ picture at PLANE ⊃ see also DRILL *noun*
- MONEY **9** [C] (*NAmE, informal*) an amount of money equal to 12½ cents
- SEXUAL ORGANS **10 bits** [pl.] (*BrE, informal*) a person's sexual organs ⊃ see also BIT, BITE, BITTEN

IDM **be in ˈbits** (*BrE, informal*) to be very sad or worried: *Inside I'm in bits because I miss him so much.* **the (whole) … bit** (*informal, disapproving*) behaviour or ideas that are typical of a particular group, type of person or activity: *She couldn't accept the whole drug-culture bit.* **bit by ˈbit** a piece at a time; gradually: *He assembled the model aircraft bit by bit.* ◊ *Bit by bit memories of the night came back to me.* **a bit ˈmuch** (*informal*) not fair or not reasonable: *It's a bit much calling me at three in the morning.* **a bit of a …** ❜ B2 (*informal, especially BrE*) used when talking about unpleasant or negative things or ideas, to mean 'rather a …': *We may have a bit of a problem on our hands.* ◊ *The rail strike is a bit of a pain.* **a bit of all ˈright** (*BrE, slang*) a person that you think is sexually attractive **a bit of ˈrough** (*BrE, slang*) a person of a low social class who has a sexual relationship with sb of a higher class **a bit on the ˈside** (*BrE, slang*) the boyfriend or girlfriend of sb who is already married or in a steady sexual relationship with sb else **ˌbits and ˈpieces/ˈbobs** (*BrE, informal*) small objects or items of various kinds: *She stuffed all her bits and pieces into a bag and left.* **do your ˈbit** (*informal*) to do your share of a task: *We can finish this job on time if everyone does their bit.* **every bit as ˌgood, ˌbad, etc. (as sb/sth)** just as good, bad, etc.; equally good, bad, etc: *Rome is every bit as beautiful as Paris.* **ˌget the bit between your ˈteeth** (*informal*) to become very enthusiastic about sth that you have started to do so that you are unlikely to stop until you have finished **not a ˈbit | not one (little) ˈbit** not at all; not in any way: *'Are you cold?' 'Not a bit.'* ◊ *It's not a bit of use* (= there's no point in) *complaining.* ◊ *I don't like that idea one bit.* **not a ˈbit of it!** (*informal, BrE*) used for saying that sth that you had expected to happen did not happen: *You'd think she'd be tired after the journey but not a bit of it!* **not the ˈleast / ˈslightest bit** not at all: *Normally I'm not the least bit shy.* **to ˈbits 1** into small pieces: *The book fell to bits in my hands.* ◊ *She took the engine to bits, then carefully put it together again.* **2** (*informal*) very much: *I love my kids to bits.* ◊ *She was thrilled to bits when I said I'd come.* ⊃ more at BLIND *adj.*, BLOW *v.*, CHAMP *v.*

**bitch** /bɪtʃ/ *noun, verb*

- *noun* **1** [C] a female dog: *a greyhound bitch* **2** [C] (*slang, disapproving*) an offensive way of referring to a woman, especially an unpleasant one: *You stupid little bitch!* ◊ *She can be a real bitch.* **3** [sing.] (*slang*) a thing that causes problems or difficulties: *Life's a bitch.* **4** [sing.] **~ (about sb/sth)** (*informal*) a complaint about sth or a conversation in which you complain about them: *We've been having a bitch about our boss.* ⊃ see also SON OF A BITCH
- *verb* [I] **~ (about sb/sth)** (*informal*) to make unkind and critical remarks about sb/sth, especially when they are not there

**bitch·in'** (*also* **bitch·ing**) /ˈbɪtʃɪn/ *adj.* (*especially NAmE, slang*) very good

**bitchy** /ˈbɪtʃi/ *adj.* (**bitch·ier**, **bitchi·est**) (*informal*) saying unpleasant and unkind things about other people: *bitchy remarks* ▶ **bitchi·ness** *noun* [U]

**Bit·coin**™ /ˈbɪtkɔɪn/ *noun* (*abbr.* BTC) **1** [U] a system of electronic money, used for buying and selling online and without the need for a central bank **2 bitcoin** [C] a unit of the bitcoin electronic system of money

**bite** ❶ B1 /baɪt/ *verb, noun*

- *verb* (**bit** /bɪt/, **bit·ten** /ˈbɪtn/)
- USE TEETH **1** ❜ B1 [I, T] to use your teeth to cut into or through sth: *Does your dog bite?* ◊ *Come here! I won't bite!* (= you don't need to be afraid) ◊ **~ into/through sth** *She bit into a ripe juicy pear.* ◊ **~ sb/sth** *She was bitten by the family dog.* ◊ *Stop biting your nails!* ◊ **~ off sth/sth off** *He bit off a large chunk of bread/He bit a large chunk of bread off.*
- OF INSECT/SNAKE **2** ❜ B1 [I, T] to wound sb by making a small hole or mark in their skin: *Most European spiders don't bite.* ◊ **~ sb** *We were badly bitten by mosquitoes.*
- OF FISH **3** [I] if a fish **bites**, it takes food from the end of a FISHING LINE and may get caught ⊃ WORDFINDER NOTE at FISHING
- HAVE EFFECT **4** [I] to have an unpleasant effect: *The recession is beginning to bite.*

IDM **be bitten by sth** to develop a strong interest in or enthusiasm for sth: *He's been bitten by the travel bug.* **bite the ˈbullet** (*informal*) to start to deal with an unpleasant or difficult situation which cannot be avoided ORIGIN From the custom of giving soldiers a bullet to bite on during a medical operation without anaesthetic. **bite the ˈdust** (*informal*) **1** to fail, or to be defeated or destroyed: *Thousands of small businesses bite the dust every year.* **2** (*humorous*) to die **bite the hand that ˈfeeds you** to harm sb who has helped you or supported you **bite your ˈlip** to stop yourself from saying sth or from showing an emotion **bite off more than you can ˈchew** to try to do too much, or sth that is too difficult **bite your ˈtongue** to stop yourself from saying sth that might upset sb or cause an argument, although you want to speak: *I didn't believe her explanation but I bit my tongue.* ⊃ more at HAIR, HEAD *n.*, ONCE *adv.*

PHRV **ˌbite ˈback (at sb/sth)** to react angrily, especially when sb has criticized or harmed you **ˌbite ˈinto sth** to cut into the surface of sth: *The horses' hooves bit deep into the soft earth.* **ˌbite sth↔ˈback** to stop yourself from saying sth or from showing your feelings: *She bit back her anger.* ◊ *to bite back a smile/laugh/comment*

- *noun*
- USING TEETH **1** ❜ B1 [C] an act of biting: *The dog gave me a playful bite.* **2** [C, usually sing.] the way the upper and lower teeth fit together: *He has to wear a brace to correct his bite.*
- FOOD **3** ❜ B1 [C] a small piece of food that you can bite from a larger piece: *She took a couple of bites of the sandwich.* ◊ *He didn't eat a bite of his dinner* (= he ate nothing). **4 a~ (to eat)** [sing.] (*informal*) a small amount of food; a

# bite-sized

small meal: *How about a bite of lunch?* ◊ *We just have time for a bite to eat before the movie.*
- **OF INSECT / ANIMAL 5** [C] a wound made by an animal or insect: *Dog bites can get infected.* ◊ *a mosquito/snake/insect bite*
- **STRONG TASTE 6** (U) a pleasant strong taste: *Cheese will add extra bite to any pasta dish.*
- **COLD 7** [sing.] a sharp cold feeling: *There's a bite in the air tonight.*
- **POWERFUL EFFECT 8** (U) a quality that makes sth effective or powerful: *The performance had no bite to it.*
- **OF FISH 9** [C] the act of a fish biting food on a HOOK ⇒ see also FROSTBITE, LOVE BITE, SOUND BITE

**IDM** **a bite at/of the ˈcherry** (*BrE*) an opportunity to do sth: *They were eager for a second bite of the cherry.* ⇒ more at **BARK** *n.*

**ˈbite-sized** (also **ˈbite-size**) *adj.* [usually before noun] **1** small enough to put into the mouth and eat: *Cut the meat into bite-sized pieces.* **2** (*informal*) very small or short: *The exams are taken in bite-size chunks over two years.*

**bit·ing** /ˈbaɪtɪŋ/ *adj.* **1** (of a wind) very cold and unpleasant **2** (of remarks) cruel and critical: *biting sarcasm/wit* ▶ **bit·ing·ly** *adv.*

**bit·map** /ˈbɪtmæp/ *noun* (*computing*) a way in which an image is stored with a fixed number of BITS (= units of information) for each unit of the image ▶ **bit·map** *verb* (**-pp-**) ~ **sth**

**ˈbit part** *noun* a small part in a film

**ˈbit player** *noun* **1** an actor with a small part in a film **2** a person or an organization that is involved in a situation but does not have an important role and has little influence

**bit·stream** /ˈbɪtstriːm/ *noun* (*computing*) a flow of data in BINARY form

**bit·ten** /ˈbɪtn/ *past part.* of BITE

**bit·ter** /ˈbɪtə(r)/ *adj., noun*
■ *adj.* **HELP** **more bitter** and **most bitter** are the usual comparative and superlative forms, but **bitterest** can also be used. **1** (of food, etc.) having a strong, unpleasant taste; not sweet: *Black coffee leaves a bitter taste in the mouth.* ⇒ compare SWEET ⇒ **WORDFINDER NOTE** at TASTE **2** (of arguments, disagreements, etc.) very serious and unpleasant, with a lot of anger and hate involved: *a long and bitter dispute* **3** (of people) feeling angry and unhappy because you feel that you have been treated unfairly: *She is very bitter about losing her job.* **4** [usually before noun] making you feel very unhappy; caused by great unhappiness: *to weep/shed bitter tears* ◊ *Losing the match was a bitter disappointment for the team.* ◊ *I've learnt from bitter experience not to trust what he says.* **5** (of weather conditions) extremely cold and unpleasant: *bitter cold* ◊ *a bitter wind* ◊ *It's really bitter out today.* ▶ **bit·ter·ness** *noun* [U]: *The pay cut caused bitterness among the staff.* ◊ *The flowers of the hop plant add bitterness to the beer.*

**IDM** **a bitter ˈpill (for sb) (to swallow)** a fact or an event that is unpleasant and difficult to accept **to/until the bitter ˈend** continuing until you have done everything you can, or until sth is completely finished, despite difficulties and problems: *They were prepared to fight to the bitter end for their rights.*

■ *noun* **1** (*BrE*) [U, C] a type of beer with a dark colour and a strong bitter taste, that is very popular in England and Wales: *A pint of bitter, please.* ⇒ compare MILD **2 bitters** [U + sing./pl. v.] a strong bitter alcoholic liquid that is made from plants and added to other alcoholic drinks: *gin with a dash of bitters*

**ˌbitter ˈlemon** *noun* [U, C] (*BrE*) a FIZZY drink (= with bubbles) that tastes of lemon and is slightly bitter

**bit·ter·ly** /ˈbɪtəli; *NAmE* -tərli/ *adv.* **1** in a way that shows that you feel sad or angry: *She wept bitterly.* ◊ *They complained bitterly.* ◊ *The development was bitterly opposed by the local community.* **2** (describing unpleasant or sad feelings) extremely: *bitterly disappointed/ashamed* **3** ~ **cold** very cold

**bit·tern** /ˈbɪtən; *NAmE* -tərn/ *noun* a European bird of the HERON family, that lives on wet ground and has a loud call

**bitter·sweet** /ˌbɪtəˈswiːt; *NAmE* -tərˈs-/ *adj.* (*BrE*) **1** bringing pleasure mixed with the feeling of being sad: *bittersweet memories* **2** (of tastes or smells) bitter and sweet at the same time

**bitty** /ˈbɪti/ *adj.* (*BrE*, *informal*) (**bit·tier**, **bit·ti·est**) made up of many small separate parts, which do not seem to fit together well

**bitu·men** /ˈbɪtʃəmən; *NAmE* bɪˈtuːmən/ *noun* [U] **1** a black sticky substance obtained from oil, used for covering roads or roofs **2** (*AustralE*, *informal*) the surface of a road that is covered with TAR: *a kilometre and a half of bitumen*

**bi·tu·min·ous** /bɪˈtjuːmɪnəs; *NAmE* -ˈtuː-/ *adj.* containing bitumen

**bit·zer** /ˈbɪtsə(r)/ *noun* (*AustralE*, *NZE*, *informal*) **1** a thing that is made from parts that originally did not belong together **2** a dog that is a mixture of different BREEDS (= types) **SYN** mongrel

**bi·valve** /ˈbaɪvælv/ *noun* (*specialist*) any SHELLFISH with a shell in two parts, for example a MUSSEL ⇒ compare MOLLUSC

**biv·ouac** /ˈbɪvuæk/ *noun*, *verb*
■ *noun* a temporary camp or shelter, without a tent, that is made and used especially by people climbing mountains or by soldiers
■ *verb* [I] (**-ck-**) to spend the night in a bivouac

**bivvy** /ˈbɪvi/ *noun*, *verb*
■ *noun* (*pl.* **biv·vies**) a tent or temporary shelter
■ *verb* [I] (**biv·vies**, **bivvy·ing**, **biv·vied**, **biv·vied**) to sleep in a tent or temporary shelter

---

## SYNONYMS

### bitter
**pungent • sour • acrid • sharp • acid**

These words all describe a strong, unpleasant taste or smell.

**bitter** (of a taste or smell) strong and usually unpleasant; (of food or drink) having a bitter taste.

**pungent** (of a smell or taste) strong and usually unpleasant; (of food or smoke) having a pungent smell or taste: *the pungent smell of burning rubber*

**sour** (of a taste) bitter like the taste of a lemon or of fruit that is not ready to eat; (of food or drink) having a sour taste: *Too much pulp produces a sour wine.*

**acrid** (of a smell or taste) strong and unpleasant; (of smoke) having an acrid smell: *acrid smoke from burning tyres*

**sharp** (of a taste or smell) strong and slightly bitter; (of food or drink) having a sharp taste: *The cheese has a distinctively sharp taste.*

**acid** (of a taste or smell) bitter, like the taste of a lemon or of fruit that is not ready to eat; (of food or drink) having an acid taste.

**WHICH WORD?**
- A **bitter** taste is usually unpleasant, but some people enjoy the bitter taste of coffee or chocolate. No other word can describe this taste. A **sharp** or **pungent** taste is more strong than unpleasant, especially when describing cheese. **Sharp**, **sour** and **acid** all describe the taste of a lemon or a fruit that is not ready to eat. An **acrid** smell is strong and unpleasant, especially the smell of smoke or burning, but not the smell of food.

**PATTERNS**
- a(n) bitter / pungent / sour / acrid / sharp / acid **taste / flavour**
- a(n) bitter / pungent / acrid / sharp / acid **smell / odour**
- a(n) bitter / sour / sharp / acid **fruit**
- pungent / sharp **cheese**
- pungent / acrid **smoke**

**bi·week·ly** /ˌbaɪˈwiːkli/ *adj., adv.* produced or happening every two weeks or twice each week: *a biweekly newsletter* ◊ *The committee meets biweekly.*

**the biz** /ðə ˈbɪz/ *noun* [sing.] (*informal*) a particular type of business, especially one connected with entertainment: *people in the music biz*
**IDM** **be the ˈbiz** (*informal*) to be very good

**bi·zarre** /bɪˈzɑː(r)/ *adj.* very strange or unusual **SYN** **weird**: *a bizarre situation/incident/story* ◊ *bizarre behaviour* ▶ **bi·ˈzarre·ly** *adv.*: *bizarrely dressed*

**blab** /blæb/ *verb* [I, T] (**-bb-**) ~ **(to sb)** | ~ **(sth) (to sb)** (*informal*) to tell sb information that should be kept secret: *Someone must have blabbed to the police.*

**blab·ber** /ˈblæbə(r)/ *verb* [I] ~ **(on) (about sth)** (*informal*) to talk in a way that other people think is silly and annoying: *What was she blabbering on about this time?*

**blab·ber·mouth** /ˈblæbəmaʊθ; *NAmE* -bɑːrm-/ *noun* (*informal, disapproving*) a person who tells secrets because they talk too much

**black** /blæk/ *adj., noun, verb*
■ *adj.* (**black·er, black·est**)
• COLOUR **1** having the very darkest colour, like coal or the sky at night: *a shiny black car* ◊ *black storm clouds*
• WITH NO LIGHT **2** without light; completely dark: *a black night* ⊃ see also PITCH-BLACK
• PEOPLE **3** (*often* **Black**) belonging to a race of people who have dark skin; connected with black people: *The film is set in a historically black community.* ◊ *dilemmas faced by Black people* **HELP** **Black** is the word most widely used and generally accepted in Britain. In the US the currently accepted terms are **African American** or **Black American**.
• TEA/COFFEE **4** without milk: *Two black coffees, please.* ⊃ compare WHITE
• DIRTY **5** very dirty; covered with dirt: *chimneys black with smoke* ◊ *Go and wash your hands; they're absolutely black!*
• ANGRY **6** full of anger or hate: *She's been in a really black mood all day.* ◊ *Rory shot her a black look.*
• DEPRESSING **7** without hope; very depressing: *The future looks pretty black.* ◊ *It's been another black day for the north-east with the announcement of further job losses.*
• EVIL **8** (*literary*) evil or IMMORAL: *black deeds/lies*
• HUMOUR **9** dealing with unpleasant or terrible things, such as murder, in a humorous way: *'Good place to bury the bodies,' she joked with black humour.* ◊ *The play is a black comedy.* ⊃ see also BLACKLY ▶ **black·ness** *noun* [U, sing.]: *She peered out into the blackness of the night.*
**IDM** **(beat sb) black and ˈblue** (to hit sb until they are) covered with BRUISES (= blue, brown or purple marks on the body) **not as black as he/she/it is ˈpainted** not as bad as people say he/she/it is: *He's not very friendly, but he's not as black as he's painted.* ⊃ more at POT *n.*
■ *noun*
• COLOUR **1** [U] the very darkest colour, like night or coal: *the black of the night sky* ◊ *Everyone at the funeral was dressed in black.*
• PEOPLE **2** [C, usually pl.] (*offensive*) a member of a race of people who have dark skin **HELP** Using the noun **black** to refer to people with dark skin can be offensive, so it is better to use the adjective: *black people* ◊ *a black man/woman.* It is especially offensive to use the noun with the definite article ('the blacks').
**IDM** **be in the ˈblack** to have money, for example in your bank account ⊃ compare BE IN THE RED **ˌblack and ˈwhite** **1** having no colours except black, white and shades of grey (in photographs, on television, etc.): *a film made in black and white* ◊ *black-and-white photos* **(in) black and white** in a way that makes people or things seem completely bad or good, or completely right or wrong: *It's a complex issue, but he only sees it in black and white.* ◊ *This is not a black-and-white decision* (= where the difference between two choices is completely clear). **in black and white** in writing or in print: *I never thought they'd put it in black and white on the front page.*
■ *verb* **1** ~ **sth/sb** (*BrE*) to refuse to deal with goods or to do business with sb as a political protest **SYN** **boycott**: *The unions have blacked all imports from the country.* **2** ~ **sth** to make sth black **SYN** **blacken**

145

**blacken**

**PHR V** **ˌblack ˈout** to become unconscious for a short time **SYN** **faint**: *The driver had probably blacked out at the wheel.* ⊃ related noun BLACKOUT **ˌblack sth↔ˈout** **1** to make a place dark by turning off lights, covering windows, etc.: *A power failure blacked out the city last night.* ◊ *a house with blacked out windows* ⊃ related noun BLACKOUT **2** to prevent sth such as a piece of writing or a television broadcast from being read or seen: *Some lines of the document have been blacked out for security reasons.*

**the ˌblack ˈarts** *noun* [pl.] = BLACK MAGIC

**black·ball** /ˈblækbɔːl/ *verb* ~ **sb** to prevent sb from joining a club or a group by voting against them

**ˈblack belt** *noun* **1** a belt that you can earn in a sport such as JUDO or KARATE which shows that you have reached a very high standard **2** a person who has gained a black belt

**Black·Berry™** /ˈblækbəri; *NAmE* -beri/ *noun* (*pl.* **-ies**) a type of smartphone or tablet: *Check your emails via your BlackBerry.*

**black·berry** /ˈblækbəri; *NAmE* -beri/ *noun* (*pl.* **-ies**) (*BrE also* **bram·ble**) a small soft black fruit that grows on a bush with THORNS in gardens or in the countryside. The bush is also called a blackberry: *blackberry and apple pie* ⊃ VISUAL VOCAB page V4

**black·berry·ing** /ˈblækbəriɪŋ; *NAmE* -ber-/ *noun* [U] the act of picking BLACKBERRIES: *Shall we go blackberrying?*

**black·bird** /ˈblækbɜːd; *NAmE* -bɜːrd/ *noun* **1** a European bird: the male is black with a yellow BEAK and the female is brown with a brown BEAK **2** a black North American bird, larger than the European blackbird, related to the STARLING

**black·board** /ˈblækbɔːd; *NAmE* -bɔːrd/ (*also* **chalk·board** *especially in NAmE*) *noun* a large board with a smooth black or dark green surface that teachers write on with a piece of CHALK: *to write on the blackboard* ⊃ compare WHITEBOARD

**ˌblack ˈbox** *noun* **1** (*also* **ˈflight recorder**) a small machine in a plane that records all the details of each flight and is useful for finding out the cause of an accident **2** [usually sing.] (*informal*) a complicated piece of equipment, usually electronic, that you know produces particular results, but that you do not completely understand

**ˌblack ˈcab** *noun* (*BrE*) a traditional type of taxi in London and some other British cities. Its driver has a licence from the city to stop and pick up passengers in the street: *a queue of black cabs at the station*

**the ˌBlack ˈCountry** *noun* [sing.] an area in the West Midlands of England where there used to be a lot of heavy industry

**black·cur·rant** /ˌblækˈkʌrənt; *NAmE* -kɜːr-/ *noun* a small black BERRY that grows in bunches on a garden bush and can be eaten: *blackcurrant jam* ◊ *a blackcurrant bush* ⊃ VISUAL VOCAB page V4

**the ˌBlack ˈDeath** *noun* [sing.] the name used for the very serious disease that can spread very quickly, (called BUBONIC PLAGUE), which killed millions of people in Europe and Asia in the 14th century

**ˌblack ˈdiamond** *noun* **1** [C] (*BrE, informal*) a piece of coal **2** [U, C] a dark form of diamond **3** [C] (*NAmE*) a slope that is difficult to ski down: *a black diamond run*

**the ˌblack eˈconomy** (*BrE*) (*NAmE* **the ˌunderground eˈconomy**) *noun* [sing.] business activity or work that is done without the knowledge of the government or other officials so that people avoid paying tax on the money they earn

**ˌblack emˈpowerment** (*also* **ˌblack ˌecoˈnomic emˈpowerment**) *noun* [U] in southern Africa, a policy which aims to give black people the chance to earn more money, own more property, etc., and have a greater role in the economy than they did before

**black·en** /ˈblækən/ *verb* **1** [T, I] ~ **(sth)** to make sth black; to become black: *Their faces were blackened with soot.* ◊ *Smoke had blackened the walls.* **2** [T] ~ **sb's name/reputation/character** to say unpleasant things that give people a bad opinion of sb: *He accused the newspaper of trying to blacken his name.*

**Black 'English** *noun* [U] any of various forms of English spoken by black people, especially a form spoken in US cities

**black 'eye** *noun* an area of dark skin (called a BRUISE), that can form around sb's eye when they receive a hit on it

**black·face** /'blækfeɪs/ *noun* **1** [C] a type of sheep with a black face **2** [U] a dark substance used by actors to make their skin look dark

**black 'flag** *noun* **1** a black flag used in motor racing to stop a driver who has done sth wrong **2** a flag with a SKULL AND CROSSBONES on it

**Black·foot** /'blækfʊt/ *noun* (*pl.* **Black·feet** /-fiːt/ or **Black·foot**) a member of a Native American people, many of whom live in the US state of Montana and in Alberta in Canada

**Black 'Friday** *noun* [U] the day after Thanksgiving in the US, the first day of traditional Christmas shopping, when stores have special offers to attract consumers

**black 'gold** *noun* [U] (*especially NAmE, informal*) oil

**black·head** /'blækhed/ *noun* a small spot on the skin, often on the face, with a black top

**black 'hole** *noun* an area in space that nothing, not even light, can escape from, because GRAVITY (= the force that pulls objects in space towards each other) is so strong there: (*figurative*) *The company viewed the venture as a financial black hole* (= it would use a lot of the company's money with no real result).

**black 'ice** *noun* [U] ice in a thin layer on the surface of a road

**black·jack** /'blækdʒæk/ *noun* **1** (*BrE also* **pon·toon**) [U] a card game in which players try to collect cards with a total value of 21 and no more **2** [C] (*especially NAmE*) a type of CLUB used as a weapon, especially a metal pipe covered with leather

**black·leg** /'blækleg/ *noun* (*BrE, disapproving*) a person who continues to work when the people they work with are on strike; a person who is employed to work instead of those who are on strike ⇒ compare STRIKE-BREAKER ⇒ see also SCAB

**black 'light** *noun* [U] ULTRAVIOLET or INFRARED RAYS, which cannot be seen

**black·list** /'blæklɪst/ *noun, verb*
■ *noun* a list of the names of people, companies, products or countries that an organization or a government considers unacceptable and that must be avoided
■ *verb* ~ **sb/sth** to put the name of a person, a company, a product or a country on a blacklist: *She was blacklisted by all the major Hollywood studios because of her political views.*

**black 'lung** *noun* [U] (*especially NAmE*) a lung disease caused by breathing in coal dust over a long period of time

**black·ly** /'blækli/ *adv.* ~ **comic/funny/humorous/satirical** dealing with unpleasant or terrible things, such as murder, in a humorous way: *The movie takes a blackly humorous look at death.*

**black 'magic** *noun* [U] (*also* **the black 'arts** [pl.]) a type of magic which is believed to use the power of the DEVIL in order to do evil

**black·mail** /'blækmeɪl/ *noun, verb*
■ *noun* [U] **1** the crime of demanding money from a person by threatening to tell sb else a secret about them **2** the act of putting pressure on a person or a group to do sth they do not want to do, for example by making threats or by making them feel guilty: *emotional/moral blackmail*
■ *verb* to force sb to give you money or do sth for you by threatening them, for example by saying you will tell people a secret about them: ~ **sb** *She blackmailed him for years by threatening to tell the newspapers about their affair.* ◇ ~ **sb into doing sth** *The president said he wouldn't be blackmailed into agreeing to the terrorists' demands.*

**black·mail·er** /'blækmeɪlə(r)/ *noun* a person who commits blackmail

**black 'mark** *noun* (*BrE*) a note, either in writing on an official record, or in sb's mind, of sth you have done or said that makes people think badly of you: *She earned a black mark for opposing company policy.* ◇ *The public scandal was a black mark against him.*

**black 'market** *noun* [usually sing.] an illegal form of trade in which foreign money, or goods that are difficult to obtain, are bought and sold: **on the ~** *to buy or sell goods on the black market* ◇ **~ in sth** *a flourishing black market in foreign currency*

**black marke'teer** *noun* a person who sells goods on the black market

**black 'mass** *noun* a ceremony in which people WORSHIP the DEVIL

**Black 'Muslim** *noun* a member of a group of black people, especially in the US, who follow the religion of Islam and want a separate black society

**black·out** /'blækaʊt/ *noun* **1** a period when there is no light as a result of an electrical power failure ⇒ compare BROWNOUT **2** a situation when the government or the police will not allow any news or information on a particular subject to be given to the public: *a news/media blackout* **3** [usually sing.] a period of time during a war when all lights must be put out or covered at night, so that they cannot be seen by an enemy attacking by air **4** [usually pl.] (*BrE*) a piece of material that covers windows to stop light being seen from outside, or light from outside from coming into a room **5** a temporary loss of CONSCIOUSNESS, sight or memory: *She had a blackout and couldn't remember anything about the accident.*

**black 'pepper** *noun* [U] a black powder made from dried BERRIES (called PEPPERCORNS), used to give a spicy taste to food: *salt and freshly ground black pepper*

**Black 'Power** *noun* [U] a movement supporting rights and political power for black people

**black 'pudding** (*BrE*) (*NAmE* **'blood sausage**) (*also* **blood 'pudding** *BrE and NAmE*) *noun* [U, C] a type of large dark SAUSAGE made from pig's blood, fat and grain

**Black 'Rod** *noun* [U] an official who takes part in the opening ceremony of the British parliament

**black 'sheep** *noun* [usually sing.] a person who is different from the rest of their family or another group, and who is considered bad or embarrassing: *the black sheep of the family*

**black·shirt** (*also* **Black·shirt**) /'blækʃɜːt; *NAmE* -ʃɜːrt/ *noun* a member of a FASCIST organization, especially in the 1920s and 30s

**black·smith** /'blæksmɪθ/ (*also* **smith**) *noun* a person whose job is to make and repair things made of iron, especially HORSESHOES ⇒ compare FARRIER

**'black spot** *noun* (*BrE*) a place, a situation or an event that is a problem or that causes a lot of problems: *an environmental black spot* ◇ *That corner is a notorious accident black spot* (= a lot of accidents happen there).

**black·thorn** /'blækθɔːn; *NAmE* -θɔːrn/ *noun* [U] a bush with THORNS, with black branches, white flowers and purple fruit called SLOES that have a bitter, sharp taste

**black 'tie** *noun* a black BOW TIE worn with a DINNER JACKET ▸ **black 'tie** *adj.*: *The party is black tie* (= dinner jackets should be worn). ◇ *a black-tie dinner*

**black·top** /'blæktɒp; *NAmE* -tɑːp/ *noun* (*NAmE*) = TARMAC™

**black 'widow** *noun* a poisonous American spider. The female black widow often eats the male.

**blad·der** /'blædə(r)/ *noun* **1** an organ that has the shape of a bag in which liquid waste (= URINE) collects before it is passed out of the body ⇒ see also GALL BLADDER ⇒ VISUAL VOCAB page V1 **2** a bag made of rubber, leather, etc. that can be filled with air or liquid, such as the one inside a football

**blad·dered** /'blædəd; *NAmE* -dərd/ *adj.* [not before noun] (*BrE, slang*) drunk

### blades

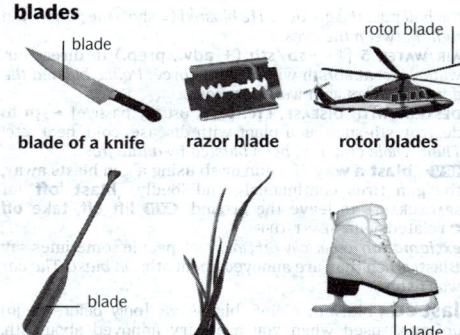

blade of a knife | razor blade | rotor blades
blade of an oar | blades of grass | blade on an ice skate

**blade** ⓘ C1 /bleɪd/ noun 1 ⓘ+ C1 the flat part of a knife, tool or machine, which has a sharp edge or edges for cutting ⇒ see also RAZOR BLADE, SWITCHBLADE 2 ⓘ+ C1 one of the flat parts that turn around in an engine or on a helicopter: *the blades of a propeller* ◊ *rotor blades on a helicopter* 3 the flat wide part of an OAR (= one of the long straight pieces of wood that are used to ROW a boat) that goes in the water 4 a single flat leaf of grass 5 the flat metal part on the bottom of an ICE SKATE ⇒ see also SHOULDER BLADE

**blad·ing** /ˈbleɪdɪŋ/ noun [U] the sport of moving on ROLLERBLADES™

**blag** /blæɡ/ verb (-gg-) ~ **sth** (*BrE, informal*) to persuade sb to give you sth, or to let you do sth, by talking to them in a clever way: *I blagged some tickets for the game.* ◊ *We blagged our way into the reception by saying that we were from the press.*

**blah** /blɑː/ noun, adj.
■ noun [U] (*informal*) people say **blah, blah, blah**, when they do not want to give the exact words that sb has said or written because they think they are not important or are boring: *They said, 'Come in, sit down, blah, blah, blah, sign here'.*
■ adj. (*NAmE, informal*) 1 not interesting: *The movie was pretty blah.* 2 not feeling well; feeling slightly unhappy

**blame** ⓘ B2 /bleɪm/ verb, noun
■ verb ⓘ B2 to think or say that sb/sth is responsible for sth bad: ~ **sb/sth for (doing) sth** *She doesn't blame anyone for her father's death.* ◊ *Why is he blaming others for his problems?* ◊ ~ **sb/sth** *It's easy to blame the media at times like this.* ◊ ~ **sth on sb/sth** *Police are blaming the accident on dangerous driving.*
IDM **be to blame (for sth)** ⓘ B2 to be responsible for sth bad: *If anyone's to blame, it's me.* ◊ *Which driver was to blame for the accident?* **don't blame ˈme** (*informal*) used to advise sb not to do sth, when you think they will do it despite your advice: *Call her if you like, but don't blame me if she's angry.* **I don't ˈblame you/her, etc. (for doing sth)** (*informal*) used to say that you think that what sb did was reasonable and the right thing to do: *'I just slammed the phone down when he said that.' 'I don't blame you!'* **only have yourself to ˈblame | have nobody/no one to blame but yourself** used to say that you think sth is sb's own fault: *If you lose your job, you'll only have yourself to blame.*
■ noun ⓘ B2 [U] ~ **(for sth)** responsibility for doing sth badly or wrongly; saying that sb is responsible for sth: *Why do I always **get the blame** for everything that goes wrong?* ◊ *to **lay/put the blame** for sth on sb* ◊ *The government will have to **take the blame** for the riots.* ◊ compare CREDIT (8)
IDM see FINGER *n*.

**blame·less** /ˈbleɪmləs/ adj. doing no wrong; free from responsibility for doing sth bad SYN innocent: *to lead a blameless life* ◊ *None of us is entirely blameless in this matter.* ▸ **blame·less·ly** adv.

**blame·worthy** /ˈbleɪmwɜːði; *NAmE* -wɜːrði/ adj. (*formal*) deserving criticism and blame; responsible for doing sth wrong

**blanch** /blɑːntʃ; *NAmE* blæntʃ/ verb 1 [I] ~ **(at sth)** (*formal*) to become pale because you are shocked or frightened 2 [T] ~ **sth** to prepare food, especially vegetables, by putting it into boiling water for a short time

**blanc·mange** /bləˈmɒnʒ; *NAmE* -ˈmɑːnʒ/ noun [C, U] (*BrE*) a cold DESSERT (= a sweet dish) that looks like JELLY that is made with milk and with fruit added to give it a sweet taste

**bland** /blænd/ adj. (**bland·er, bland·est**) 1 with little colour, excitement or interest; without anything to attract attention SYN nondescript: *bland background music* 2 not having a strong or interesting taste: *a rather bland diet of soup, bread* ⇒ WORDFINDER NOTE at TASTE 3 showing no strong emotions or excitement; not saying anything very interesting: *a bland smile* ◊ *After the meeting, a bland statement was issued.* ▸ **bland·ly** adv. **bland·ness** noun [U]

**bland·ish·ments** /ˈblændɪʃmənts/ noun [pl.] (*formal*) pleasant things that you say to sb or do for them to try to persuade them to do sth

**blank** ⓘ A2 /blæŋk/ adj., noun, verb
■ adj. 1 ⓘ A2 empty, with nothing written, printed or recorded on it: *Sign your name in the blank space below.* ◊ *a blank CD* ◊ *Write on one side of the paper and leave the other side blank.* ◊ *She turned to a blank page in her notebook.* 2 (of a wall or screen) empty; with no pictures, marks or decoration: *blank whitewashed walls* ◊ *Suddenly the screen went blank.* 3 showing no feeling, understanding or interest: *She stared at me with a blank expression on her face.* ◊ *Steve looked blank and said he had no idea what I was talking about.* ◊ *Suddenly my mind went blank* (= I could not remember anything). 4 [only before noun] (of negative things) complete and total: *a blank refusal/denial* ⇒ see also POINT-BLANK ▸ **blank·ly** adv.: *She stared blankly into space, not knowing what to say next.* **blank·ness** noun [U]
IDM **a blank ˈcanvas/ˈslate** a person or thing that has the potential to be developed or changed in many different ways
■ noun 1 ⓘ A2 [C] an empty space on a printed form or document for you to write answers, information, etc. in: *Please fill in the blanks.* ◊ *If you can't answer the question, leave a blank.* 2 [sing.] a state of not being able to remember anything: *My mind was a blank and I couldn't remember her name.* 3 [C] (also **blank ˈcartridge**) a CARTRIDGE in a gun that contains an EXPLOSIVE but no bullet: *The troops fired blanks in the air.* IDM see DRAW *v*.
■ verb 1 [T] ~ **sb** (*BrE, informal*) to ignore sb completely: *I saw her on the bus this morning, but she totally blanked me.* 2 [I] (*NAmE*) to be suddenly unable to remember or think of sth: *I knew the answer, but I totally blanked during the test.*
PHRV **blank ˈout** to suddenly become empty: *The screen blanked out.* **blank sth↔ˈout** 1 to cover sth completely so that it cannot be seen: *All the names in the letter had been blanked out.* 2 to deliberately forget sth unpleasant: *She had tried to blank out the whole experience.*

**blank ˈcall** noun (*IndE*) a phone call made by a person who does not give their name and who wants to threaten, annoy or worry sb

**blank ˈcheque** (*BrE*) (*NAmE* **blank ˈcheck**) noun 1 a CHEQUE that is signed but which does not have the amount of money to be paid written on it 2 permission or authority to do sth that is necessary in a particular situation: *The President was **given a blank check** by Congress to continue the war.*

**blan·ket** ⓘ+ B2 /ˈblæŋkɪt/ noun, adj., verb
■ noun 1 ⓘ+ B2 a large cover, often made of wool, used especially on beds to keep people warm ⇒ see also ELECTRIC BLANKET 2 ⓘ+ C1 [usually sing.] ~ **of sth** a thick layer or mass of sth: *a blanket of fog/snow/cloud* ◊ (*figurative*) *The trial was conducted under a blanket of secrecy.* ⇒ see also WET BLANKET

# blanket bath

- **adj.** [only before noun] including or affecting all possible cases, situations or people: *a blanket ban on tobacco advertising* ◊ *a blanket refusal*
- **verb** [often passive] ~ sth (*formal*) to cover sth completely with a thick layer: *The ground was soon blanketed with snow.*

**'blanket bath** *noun* (*BrE*) an act of washing the whole of sb's body when they cannot get out of bed because they are sick, injured or old

**blank 'verse** *noun* [U] (*specialist*) poetry that has a regular rhythm, usually with ten syllables and five stresses in each line, but which does not RHYME ⊃ compare FREE VERSE

**blare** /bleə(r); *NAmE* bler/ *verb, noun*
- **verb** [I, T] to make a loud unpleasant noise: *police cars with lights flashing and sirens blaring* ◊ *~ out Music blared out from the open window.* ◊ *~ sth (out) The radio was blaring (out) rock music.*
- **noun** [sing.] a loud unpleasant noise: *the blare of car horns*

**blar·ney** /'blɑːni; *NAmE* 'blɑːrni/ *noun* [U] (*informal*) talk that is friendly and humorous, but probably not true, and which may be used to persuade or trick you ORIGIN From **Blarney**, a castle in Ireland where there is a stone which is said to have magic powers: anyone who kisses the 'Blarney Stone' is given the gift of speaking persuasively ('the gift of the gab').

**blasé** /'blɑːzeɪ; *NAmE* blɑː'zeɪ/ *adj.* ~(about sth) not impressed, excited or worried about sth, because you have seen or experienced it many times before

**blas·pheme** /blæs'fiːm/ *verb* [I, T] ~sb/sth) to speak about God or the holy things of a particular religion in an offensive way; to swear using the names of God or holy things ▶ **blas·phemer** *noun*

**blas·phemy** /'blæsfəmi/ *noun* [U, C] (*pl.* -ies) behaviour or language that is offensive or shows a lack of respect for God or religion ▶ **blas·phem·ous** /-məs/ *adj.: Many people found the film blasphemous.* **blas·phem·ous·ly** *adv.*

**blast** ℞+ C1 /blɑːst; *NAmE* blæst/ *noun, verb, exclamation*
- **noun**
  - **EXPLOSION 1** ℞+ C1 [C] an explosion or a powerful movement of air caused by an explosion: *a bomb blast* ◊ *27 schoolchildren were injured in the blast.*
  - **OF AIR 2** ℞+ C1 [C] a sudden strong movement of air: *A blast of hot air hit us as we stepped off the plane.* ◊ *the wind's icy blasts*
  - **LOUD NOISE 3** ℞+ C1 [C] a sudden loud noise, especially one made by a musical instrument that you blow, or by a WHISTLE or a car HORN: *three short blasts on the ship's siren*
  - **CRITICISM 4** [C] (used especially in newspapers) strong criticism: *Blast for prison governors in judge's report.*
  - **FUN 5** [sing.] (*informal*) a very happy experience that is a lot of fun: *The party was a blast.* ◊ *We had a blast at the party.*
  - **EMAIL 6** [C] (*NAmE, informal*) a piece of advertising or information that is sent to a large number of people at the same time by email
  - IDM **a ,blast from the 'past** (*informal*) a person or thing from your past that you see, hear, meet, etc. again in the present **(at) full 'blast** with the greatest possible volume or power: *She had the car stereo on at full blast.*
- **verb**
  - **EXPLODE 1** ℞+ C1 [T, I] ~(sth) (+ adv./prep.) to violently destroy or break sth into pieces, using EXPLOSIVES: *They blasted a huge crater in the runway.* ◊ *They had to blast a tunnel through the mountain.* ◊ *All the windows were blasted inwards with the force of the explosion.* ◊ *The jumbo jet was blasted out of the sky.* ◊ *Danger! Blasting in Progress!*
  - **MAKE LOUD NOISE 2** ℞+ C1 [I, T] to make a loud unpleasant noise, especially music: *~(out) Music suddenly blasted out from the speakers.* ◊ *~sth (out) The radio blasted out rock music at full volume.*
  - **CRITICIZE 3** [T] ~sb/sth (for sth/for doing sth) (*informal*) to criticize sb/sth severely: *The movie was blasted by all the critics.*
  - **HIT/KICK/SHOOT 4** [T] ~sb/sth (+ adv./prep.) (*informal*) to hit, kick or shoot sb/sth with a lot of force: *He blasted the ball past the goalie.* ◊ *He blasted (= shot) the policeman right between the eyes.*
  - **AIR/WATER 5** [T] ~sb/sth (+ adv./prep.) to direct air, water, etc. at sb/sth with a lot of force: *Police blasted the demonstrators with water cannons.*
  - **DESTROY WITH DISEASE, ETC. 6** [T, usually passive] ~sth to destroy sth such as a plant with disease, cold, heat, etc: *Their whole crop had been blasted by a late frost.*
  - PHRV **,blast a'way** if a gun or sb using a gun **blasts away**, the gun fires continuously and loudly **,blast 'off** (of SPACECRAFT) to leave the ground SYN **lift off, take off** ⊃ related noun BLAST-OFF
- **exclamation** (*especially in BrE, informal*) people sometimes say **Blast!** when they are annoyed about sth: *Oh blast! The car won't start.*

**'blast·ed** /'blɑːstɪd; *NAmE* 'blæs-/ *adj.* [only before noun] (*informal*) used when you are very annoyed about sth: *Make your own blasted coffee!*

**'blast furnace** *noun* a large structure like an oven in which iron ORE (= rock containing iron) is reacted with LIMESTONE and CARBON at high temperatures to form iron

**'blast-off** *noun* [U] the moment when a SPACECRAFT leaves the ground

**bla·tant** /'bleɪtnt/ *adj.* (*disapproving*) (of actions that are considered bad) done in an obvious and open way without caring if people are shocked SYN **flagrant**: *a blatant attempt to buy votes* ◊ *It was a blatant lie.* ▶ **bla·tant·ly** *adv.: a blatantly unfair decision* ◊ *He just blatantly lied about it.*

**blather** /'blæðə(r)/ (*also* **blether** *especially in ScotE*) *verb* [I] ~(on) (about sth) (*informal*) to talk continuously about things that are silly or unimportant ▶ **blather** (*also* **blether** *especially in ScotE*) *noun* [U]

**blax·ploit·ation** /ˌblæksplɔɪ'teɪʃn/ *noun* [U] the use of black people in films, especially in a way which shows them in fixed ways that are different from real life

**blaze** /bleɪz/ *verb, noun*
- **verb 1** [I] to burn brightly and strongly: *A huge fire was blazing in the fireplace.* ◊ *Within minutes the whole building was blazing.* ◊ *He rushed back into the blazing house.* **2** [I] to shine brightly: *The sun blazed down from a clear blue sky.* ◊ *The garden blazed with colour.* **3** [I] ~(with sth) (*formal*) if sb's eyes **blaze**, they look extremely angry: *Her eyes were blazing with fury.* **4** (*also* **blazon**) [T, usually passive] ~(across/all over sth) to make news or information widely known by telling people about it in a way they are sure to notice: *The story was blazed all over the daily papers.* **5** [I] ~(away) if a gun or sb using a gun **blazes**, the gun fires continuously: *In the distance machine guns were blazing.*
  - IDM **blaze a 'trail** to be the first to do or to discover sth that others follow: *The department is blazing a trail in the field of laser surgery.* ⊃ compare TRAILBLAZER ⊃ more at GUN *n.*
  - PHRV **,blaze 'up 1** to suddenly start burning very strongly **2** to suddenly become very angry
- **noun 1** [C] (used especially in newspapers) a very large fire, especially a dangerous one: *Five people died in the blaze.* **2** [sing.] strong bright flames in a fire: *Dry wood makes a good blaze.* **3** [sing.] **a ~ of sth** a very bright show of lights or colour; a show of sth that is impressive or likely to attract attention: *The gardens are a blaze of colour.* ◊ *a blaze of lights in the city centre* ◊ *the bright blaze of the sun* ◊ *a blaze of glory* ◊ *They got married in a blaze of publicity.* **4** [sing.] **(a) ~ of sth** a sudden show of very strong feeling: *a blaze of anger/passion/hate* **5** [C, usually sing.] a white mark on an animal's face
  - IDM **like blazes** (*old-fashioned, informal*) very hard; very fast **what/where/who the 'blazes ...?** (*old-fashioned, informal*) used to emphasize that you are annoyed and surprised, to avoid using the word 'hell': *What the blazes have you done?*

**blazer** /'bleɪzə(r)/ *noun* a jacket, not worn with matching trousers, often showing the colours or BADGE of a club, school, team, etc.

**blaz·ing** /'bleɪzɪŋ/ *adj.* [only before noun] **1** (*also* **blazing 'hot**) extremely hot: *blazing heat* ◊ *a blazing hot day*

**2** extremely angry or full of strong emotion: *She had a blazing row with Eddie and stormed out of the house.*

**blazon** /ˈbleɪzn/ *verb* [usually passive] **1** ~ **sth (on/across/over sth)** = EMBLAZON: *He had the word 'Cool' blazoned across his chest.* **2** = BLAZE (4)

**bleach** /bliːtʃ/ *verb, noun*
- *verb* [I, T] to become white or pale by a chemical process or by the effect of light from the sun; to make sth white or pale in this way: *bones of animals bleaching in the sun* ◇ ~ **sth** *His hair was bleached by the sun.* ◇ *bleached cotton/paper* ◇ ~ **sth + adj.** *She bleached her hair blonde.*
- *noun* [U, C] a chemical that is used to make sth become white or pale and as a DISINFECTANT (= to prevent infection from spreading)

**bleach·ers** /ˈbliːtʃəz; *NAmE* -tʃərz/ *noun* [pl.] (*NAmE*) rows of seats at a sports ground that are cheaper and not covered by a roof ▶ **bleach·er** *adj.* [only before noun]: *bleacher seats*

**bleak** /bliːk/ *adj.* (**bleak·er, bleak·est**) **1** (of a situation) not giving any reason to have hope or expect anything good: *a bleak outlook/prospect* ◇ *The future looks bleak for the fishing industry.* ◇ *The medical prognosis was bleak.* **2** (of the weather) cold and unpleasant: *a bleak winter's day* **3** (of a place) exposed, empty, or with no pleasant features: *a bleak landscape/hillside/moor* ◇ *bleak concrete housing* ▶ **bleak·ly** *adv.*: *'There seems no hope,' she said bleakly.* ◇ *bleakly lit corridors* **bleak·ness** *noun* [U]

**blear·ily** /ˈblɪərəli; *NAmE* ˈblɪr-/ *adv.* with bleary eyes; in a tired way: *'I was asleep,' she explained blearily.*

**bleary** /ˈblɪəri; *NAmE* ˈblɪri/ *adj.* (of eyes) not able to see clearly, especially because you are tired: *She had bleary red eyes from lack of sleep.*

**ˌbleary-ˈeyed** *adj.* with bleary eyes and seeming tired: *He appeared at breakfast bleary-eyed and with a hangover.*

**bleat** /bliːt/ *verb* **1** [I] to make the sound that sheep and GOATS make **2** [I, T] ~ **(on) (about sth)** | ~ **that ...** | + **speech** to speak in a weak or complaining voice: *'But I've only just got here,' he bleated feebly.* ▶ **bleat** *noun*: *The lamb gave a faint bleat.* **bleat·ing** *noun* [U, C]: *the distant bleating of sheep*

**bleed** 🔑 /bliːd/ *verb* (**bled, bled** /bled/) **1** ~ **(sth)** [I] to lose blood, especially from a wound or an injury: *My finger's bleeding.* ◇ *She slowly bled to death.* ◇ *He was bleeding from a gash on his head.* ➔ WORDFINDER NOTE at HURT **2** [T] ~ **sb** (in the past) to take blood from sb as a way of treating disease **3** [T] ~ **sb (for sth)** (*informal*) to force sb to pay a lot of money over a period of time: *The company seems intent on bleeding us for every penny we have.* **4** [T] ~ **sth** to remove air or liquid from sth so that it works correctly **5** [I] ~ **(into sth)** to spread from one area of sth to another area: *Keep the paint fairly dry so that the colours don't bleed into each other.*
IDM **bleed sb ˈdry** (*disapproving*) to take away all sb's money: *The big corporations are bleeding some of these small countries dry.* ➔ more at HEART *n.*

**bleed·er** /ˈbliːdə(r)/ *noun* (*BrE, old-fashioned, informal*) a rude way of referring to a person

**bleed·ing** /ˈbliːdɪŋ/ *adj., noun*
- *adj.* [only before noun] (*BrE, taboo, slang*) = BLOODY¹
- *noun* [U] the process of losing blood from the body: *Press firmly on the wound to stop the bleeding.*

**ˌbleeding ˈedge** *noun* [sing.] **the ~ (of sth)** (*computing*) technology that is so advanced that there may be problems when you use it: *They were working at the bleeding edge of chip design.* ➔ compare CUTTING EDGE

**ˌbleeding ˈheart** *noun* (*disapproving*) a person who is too kind towards people that other people think do not deserve this treatment: *a bleeding-heart liberal*

**bleep** /bliːp/ *noun, verb*
- *noun* a short high sound made by a piece of electronic equipment
- *verb* **1** [I] to make a short high electronic sound: *The microwave will bleep when your meal is ready.* **2** (*BrE*) (*NAmE* **beep**) [T] ~ **sb** to call sb on their bleeper: *Please bleep the doctor on duty immediately.* **3** [T] ~ **sth (out)** to broadcast a short high electronic sound in place of a SWEAR WORD on a television or radio show, so that people will not be offended

**bleep·er** /ˈbliːpə(r)/ (*BrE*) (also **beep·er** especially in *NAmE*) *noun* a small electronic device that you carry around with you and that lets you know when sb is trying to contact you, by making a sound SYN **pager**

**blem·ish** /ˈblemɪʃ/ *noun, verb*
- *noun* a mark on the skin or on an object that makes it look less beautiful or perfect: *make-up to cover blemishes* ◇ (*figurative*) *His reputation is without a blemish.*
- *verb* [usually passive] ~ **sth** (*formal*) to make sth less beautiful or perfect

**blench** /blentʃ/ *verb* [I] (*BrE, formal*) to react to sth in a way that shows you are frightened

**blend** 🔑 /blend/ *verb, noun*
- *verb* **1** 🔑 [T] to mix two or more substances together: ~ **A with B** *Blend the flour with the milk to make a smooth paste.* ◇ ~ **A and B (together)** *Blend together the eggs, sugar and flour.* ➔ SYNONYMS at MIX **2** 🔑 [I] to form a mixture with sth: ~ **with sth** *Oil does not blend with water.* ◇ ~ **(together)** *Oil and water do not blend.* **3** 🔑 [I, T] to combine with sth in an attractive or effective way; to combine sth in this way: ~ **(sth) (together)** *The old and new buildings blend together perfectly.* ◇ ~ **sth (and/with sth)** *Their music blends traditional and modern styles.* **4** 🔑 [T, usually passive] ~ **sth** to produce sth by mixing different types together: *blended whisky/tea* ➔ see WOODWORK
PHRV **ˌblend ˈin (with sth/sb)** if sth **blends in**, it matches or is similar to everything that is around or near it: *Choose curtains that blend in with your decor.* ◇ *The thieves soon blended in with the crowd and got away.* **ˌblend sth↔ˈin** (in cooking) to add another substance and mix it in with the others: *Beat the butter and sugar; then blend in the egg.* **ˈblend into sth** to look so similar to the background that it is difficult for you to see it separately: *He blended into the crowd.*
- *noun* **1** 🔑 a mixture of different types of the same thing: *a blend of tea* **2** 🔑 [usually sing.] a pleasant or useful combination of different things: *a blend of youth and experience*

**ˌblended ˈfamily** *noun* (*especially NAmE*) a family that consists of two people and their children from their own relationship and from previous ones

**ˌblended ˈlearning** *noun* [U] a way of studying a subject that combines being taught in class with the use of different technologies, including learning over the internet: *Blended learning is a cost-effective way of delivering training.*

**blend·er** /ˈblendə(r)/ (*BrE also* **li·quid·izer**) *noun* an electric machine for mixing soft food or liquid

**bless** 🔑 /bles/ *verb, exclamation*
- *verb* (**blessed, blessed** /blest/) **1** 🔑 ~ **sb/sth** to ask God to protect sb/sth: *They brought the children to Jesus and he blessed them.* ◇ *God bless you!* **2** 🔑 ~ **sth** to make sth holy by saying a prayer over it: *The priest blessed the bread and wine.* **3** ~ **sb/sth** (*formal*) to call God holy; to praise God: *We bless your holy name, O Lord.* **4** ~ **sb/sth** (*old-fashioned, informal*) used to express surprise: *Bless my soul! Here comes Bill!* ◇ *'Where's Joe?' 'I'm blessed if I know!'* (= I don't know)
IDM **be ˈblessed with sth/sb** to have sth good such as ability, great happiness, etc: *She's blessed with excellent health.* ◇ *We're blessed with five lovely grandchildren.* **ˈbless you** said to sb after they have SNEEZED **ˈbless you, her, him, etc.** (*informal*) used to show that you are pleased with sb, especially because of sth they have done: *Sarah, bless her, had made a cup of tea.* ➔ more at GOD
- *exclamation* (*BrE, sometimes humorous*) used to show warm feelings for sb because of sth they have done: *'He bought us all a present.' 'Oh, bless!'*

**blessed** /ˈblesɪd/ *adj.* **1 Blessed** holy: *the Blessed Virgin Mary* **2** (in religious language) lucky: *Blessed are the poor.* **3** [only before noun] giving you a sense of peace or a feeling of freedom from worry or pain: *a moment of blessed*

# blesser

calm **4** [only before noun] (*old-fashioned, informal*) used to express mild anger: *I can't see a blessed thing without my glasses.* ▶ **bless·ed·ly** *adv.*: *The kitchen was warm and blessedly familiar.* **bless·ed·ness** *noun* [U]

**bless·er** /'blesə(r)/ *noun* (*SAfrE*) a rich older man who gives presents and money to a younger woman in return for company and sex **SYN** **sugar daddy**

**bless·ing** ?+ **C1** /'blesɪŋ/ *noun* **1** ?+ **C1** [usually sing.] God's help and protection, or a prayer asking for this: *to pray for God's blessing* ◊ *The bishop said the blessing.* **2** ?+ **C1** [usually sing.] approval of or permission for sth: *The government gave its blessing to the new plans.* ◊ *He went with his parents' blessing.* **3** ?+ **C1** something that is good or helpful: *Lack of traffic is one of the blessings of country life.* ◊ *It's a blessing that nobody was in the house at the time.* ◆ see also MIXED BLESSING

**IDM** **a blessing in dis'guise** something that seems to be a problem at first, but that has good results in the end ◆ more at COUNT *v.*

**blether** /'bleðə(r)/ *verb, noun* (*especially ScotE*) = BLATHER

**blew** /bluː/ *past tense* of BLOW ◆ HOMOPHONES at BLUE

**blight** /blaɪt/ *verb, noun*
- *verb* ~ **sth** to have a bad effect on sth, especially by causing a lot of problems: *His career has been blighted by injuries.* ◊ *an area blighted by unemployment*
- *noun* **1** [U, C] any disease that kills plants, especially crops: *potato blight* ◆ WORDFINDER NOTE at CROP **2** [sing., U] ~ **(on sb/sth)** something that has a bad effect on a situation, a person's life or the environment: *His death cast a blight on the whole of that year.* ◊ *urban blight* (= areas in a city that are ugly or not cared for well)

**blight·er** /'blaɪtə(r)/ *noun* (*BrE, old-fashioned, informal*) a way of referring to a person (usually a man) that you either find unpleasant or that you feel some sympathy for

**Blighty** /'blaɪti/ *noun* [U] (*BrE*) a name for Britain or England, used especially by soldiers in the First and Second World Wars, and now sometimes used in a humorous way

**bli·mey** /'blaɪmi/ *exclamation* (*BrE, informal*) used to express surprise or anger: *Blimey, it's hot today.*

**blimp** /blɪmp/ *noun* (*especially NAmE*) a small AIRSHIP (= an aircraft without wings)

**blin** /blɪn/ *noun sing.* of BLINI

**blind** **⓵** **B2** /blaɪnd/ *adj., verb, noun, adv.*
- *adj.* (**blind·er, blind·est**) **1** ?̂ **B2** not able to see: *Doctors think he will go blind.* ◊ *blind and partially sighted people* ◊ *One of her parents is blind.* ◊ *She has been legally blind since birth.* ◊ *The accident left her blind in one eye.* **2 the blind** *noun* [pl.] people who are blind: *recorded books for the blind* ◊ *guide dogs for the blind* **3** ~ **(to sth)** not noticing or realizing sth: *She is blind to her husband's faults.* ◊ *I must have been blind not to realize the danger we were in.* **4** [usually before noun] (of strong feelings) seeming to be unreasonable, and accepted without question; seeming to be out of control: *blind faith/obedience* ◊ *It was a moment of blind panic.* **5** [usually before noun] (of a situation or an event) that cannot be controlled by reason: *blind chance* ◊ *the blind force of nature* **6** that a driver in a car cannot see, or cannot see around: *a blind driveway* ◊ *a blind bend/corner* **7 -blind** that does not make a difference between people on the basis of the quality mentioned, or favour one group over another: *In a piece of gender-blind casting, Hamlet is played by British actress Maxine Peake.* ◆ see also COLOUR-BLIND (2) ▶ **blind·ness** *noun* [U]: *total/temporary/partial blindness* ◆ see also BLINDLY
**IDM** **(as) blind as a 'bat** (*humorous*) not able to see well **the blind leading the 'blind** a situation in which people with almost no experience or knowledge give advice to others who also have no experience or knowledge **not a blind bit/the blindest bit of…** (*BrE, informal*) not any: *He didn't take a blind bit of notice of me* (= he ignored me). ◊ *It won't make the blindest bit of difference* (= it will make no difference at all). **turn a blind 'eye (to sth)** to pretend not to notice sth bad that is happening, so you do not have to do anything about it ◆ more at LOVE *n.*
- *verb* **1** ~ **sb** to permanently destroy sb's ability to see: *She was blinded in the explosion.* **2** ~ **sb/sth** to make it difficult for sb to see for a short time: *When she went outside she was temporarily blinded by the sun.* **3** ~ **sb (to sth)** to make sb no longer able to think clearly or behave in a sensible way: *His sense of loyalty blinded him to the truth.*
**IDM** **blind sb with science** to confuse sb by using technical or complicated language that they do not understand ◆ more at EFF
- *noun* **1** (*NAmE also* **shade**, **'window shade**) [C] material that covers a window, often consisting of a roll of cloth that is fixed at the top of the window and can be pulled up and down ◆ see also VENETIAN BLIND **2** [sing.] something people say or do to hide the truth about sth in order to trick other people
- *adv.* (in connection with flying) without being able to see; using instruments only
**IDM** **blind 'drunk** extremely drunk ◆ more at ROB, SWEAR

▼ **WHICH WORD?**

**blind / blindly**
- There are two adverbs that come from the adjective **blind**. **Blindly** means 'not being able to see what you are doing' or 'not thinking about something'. The adverb **blind** is mainly used in the context of flying and means 'without being able to see', 'using instruments only'.

**blind 'alley** *noun* a way of doing sth that seems useful at first, but does not produce useful results, like following a path that suddenly stops

**blind 'date** *noun* a meeting between two people who have not met each other before. The meeting is sometimes organized by their friends because they want them to develop a romantic relationship.

**blind·er** /'blaɪndə(r)/ *noun* **1** [C, usually sing.] (*BrE, informal*) something which is excellent, especially in sport: *a blinder of a game* ◊ *Warren played a blinder in the opening match.* **2 blinders** [pl.] (*NAmE*) = BLINKERS

**blind·fold** /'blaɪndfəʊld/ *noun, verb, adv.*
- *noun* something that is put over sb's eyes so they cannot see
- *verb* ~ **sb** to cover sb's eyes with a piece of cloth or other material so that they cannot see: *The hostages were tied up and blindfolded.*
- *adv.* (*BrE*) (*also* **blind·fold·ed** *BrE, NAmE*) with the eyes covered: *The reporter was taken blindfold to a secret location.* ◊ *I knew the way home blindfold* (= because it was so familiar). ◊ *I could do that blindfold* (= very easily, with no problems).

**blind·ing** /'blaɪndɪŋ/ *adj.* [usually before noun] **1** very bright; so strong that you cannot see: *a blinding flash of light* ◊ (*figurative*) *a blinding* (= very bad) *headache* **2** (*BrE, informal*) very good or a lot of fun

**blind·ing·ly** /'blaɪndɪŋli/ *adv.* very; extremely: *The reason is blindingly obvious.* ◊ *The latest computers can work at a blindingly fast speed.*

**blind·ly** /'blaɪndli/ *adv.* **1** without being able to see what you are doing: *She groped blindly for the light switch in the dark room.* **2** without thinking about what you are doing: *He wanted to decide for himself instead of blindly following his parents' advice.* ◆ note at BLIND

**blind man's 'buff** (*NAmE also* **blind man's 'bluff**) *noun* [U] a children's game in which a player whose eyes are covered with a piece of cloth tries to catch and identify the other players

**blind·side** /'blaɪndsaɪd/ *verb* (*NAmE*) **1** ~ **sb** to attack sb from the direction where they cannot see you coming **2** [usually passive] to give sb an unpleasant surprise: *be blindsided (by sth) Just when it seemed life was going well, she was blindsided by a devastating illness.*

**'blind side** *noun* a direction in which sb cannot see very much, especially approaching danger

**'blind spot** *noun* **1** an area that sb cannot see, especially an area of the road when they are driving a car **2** if sb has a **blind spot** about sth, they ignore it or they are unwilling or unable to understand it **3** the part of the RETINA in the eye that is not sensitive to light **4** an area where a radio signal cannot be received

**blind ˈtest** *noun* a way of deciding which product out of a number of competing products is the best or most popular, or how a new product compares with others. People are asked to try the different products and to say which ones they prefer, but they are not told the names of the products.

**blind ˈtrust** *noun* a type of TRUST that takes care of sb's investments, without the person knowing how their money is being invested. It is used by politicians, for example, so that their private business does not influence their political decisions.

**bling** /blɪŋ/ (*also* **bling-bling**) *noun* [U] (*informal*) expensive shiny jewellery and bright fashionable clothes worn in order to attract attention to yourself ▶ **bling** (*also* **bling-bling**) *adj.*: *women with big hair and bling jewellery* ◊ *bling culture/lifestyles*

**blini** /ˈblɪni, ˈbliːni/ (*also* **blinis**) *noun* [pl.] (*sing.* **blin** /blɪn/) small Russian PANCAKES (= thin flat round cakes), served with SOUR CREAM

**blink** /blɪŋk/ *verb, noun*
■ *verb* **1** [I, T] **~ (sth)** when you **blink** or **blink your eyes** or **your eyes blink**, you shut and open your eyes quickly: *He blinked in the bright sunlight.* ◊ *I'll be back before you can blink* (= very quickly). ◊ *When I told him the news he didn't even blink* (= showed no surprise at all). ⊃ compare WINK **2** [I] to shine with an unsteady light; to flash on and off: *Suddenly a warning light blinked.*
**PHRV** **ˌblink sth↔aˈway/ˈback** to try to control tears or clear your eyes by blinking: *She bravely blinked back her tears.*
■ *noun* [usually sing.] the act of shutting and opening your eyes very quickly
**IDM** **in the ˌblink of an ˈeye** very quickly; in a short time **on the ˈblink** (*informal*) (of a machine) no longer working correctly

**blink·er** /ˈblɪŋkə(r)/ *noun* **1** [C] (*informal*) = INDICATOR (3), TURN SIGNAL **2 blinkers** (*NAmE also* **blind·ers**) [pl.] pieces of leather that are placed at the side of a horse's eyes to stop it from looking to the side: (*figurative*) *We need to have a fresh look at the plan, without blinkers* (= we need to consider every aspect of it).

**blink·ered** /ˈblɪŋkəd; *NAmE* -kərd/ *adj.* (*disapproving*) not aware of every aspect of a situation; not willing to accept different ideas about sth **SYN** **narrow-minded**: *a blinkered policy/attitude/approach*

**blink·ing** /ˈblɪŋkɪŋ/ *adj., adv.* (*BrE, old-fashioned, informal*) a mild swear word that some people use when they are annoyed, to avoid saying 'bloody': *Shut the blinking door!*

**blip** /blɪp/ *noun* **1** a change in a process or situation, usually when it gets worse for a short time before it gets better; a temporary blip **2** a short high sound made by an electronic device **3** a small flashing point of light on a RADAR screen, representing an object

**bliss** /blɪs/ *noun, verb*
■ *noun* [U] extreme happiness: *married/wedded/domestic bliss* ◊ *My idea of bliss is a month in the Bahamas.* ◊ *Swimming on a hot day is sheer bliss.* **IDM** see IGNORANCE
■ *verb*
**PHRV** **ˌbliss ˈout** (*also* **be ˌblissed ˈout**) to reach a state of perfect happiness, when you are not aware of anything else

**bliss·ful** /ˈblɪsfl/ *adj.* extremely happy; showing happiness: *We spent three blissful weeks away from work.* ◊ *a blissful smile* ⊃ SYNONYMS at HAPPY ▶ **bliss·ful·ly** /-fəli/ *adv.*: *blissfully happy* ◊ *blissfully ignorant/unaware*
**IDM** **blissful ˈignorance** the state of not knowing about sth and so being unable to worry about it: *We preferred to remain in blissful ignorance of what was going on.*

**ˈB-list** *adj.* [usually before noun] used to describe the group of people who are considered to be fairly famous, successful or important, but not as much as the A-LIST people: *a TV chat show full of B-list celebrities*

**blis·ter** /ˈblɪstə(r)/ *noun, verb*
■ *noun* **1** a SWELLING (= an area that is larger and rounder than normal) on the surface of the skin that is filled with liquid and is caused, for example, by rubbing or burning ⊃ see also FEVER BLISTER **2** a similar SWELLING, filled with air or liquid, on metal, painted wood or another surface
■ *verb* **1** [I, T] to form blisters; to make sth form blisters: *His skin was beginning to blister.* ◊ **~sth** *Her face had been blistered by the sun.* **2** [I, T] **~ (sth)** when a surface **blisters** or sth **blisters** it, it becomes covered with round areas that are filled with air or liquid and break open **3** [T] **~sb** (*NAmE*) to criticize sb strongly ▶ **blis·tered** *adj.*: *cracked and blistered skin* ◊ *blistered paintwork*

**blis·ter·ing** /ˈblɪstərɪŋ/ *adj.* [usually before noun] **1** (describing actions in sport) done very fast or with great energy: *The runners set off at a blistering pace.* **2** extremely hot in a way that is uncomfortable **SYN** **baking**: *a blistering July day* ◊ *blistering heat* **3** very critical: *a blistering attack* ▶ **blis·ter·ing·ly** *adv.*

**ˈblister pack** (*also* **ˈbubble pack**) *noun* a pack in which small goods, such as tablets, are sold, with each individual item in its own separate plastic or FOIL section on a piece of card

**blithe** /blaɪð/ *adj.* [usually before noun] **1** (*disapproving*) showing you do not care or are not anxious about what you are doing: *He drove with blithe disregard for the rules of the road.* **2** (*literary*) happy; not anxious: *a blithe and carefree girl* ▶ **blithe·ly** *adv.*: *He was blithely unaware of the trouble he'd caused.* ◊ *'It'll be easy,' she said blithely.*

**blith·er·ing** /ˈblɪðərɪŋ/ *adj.* [only before noun] (*BrE, old-fashioned, informal*) complete: *He was a blithering idiot.*

**BLitt** (*NAmE* **B.Litt**) /ˌbiː ˈlɪt/ *noun* a university degree in an ARTS subject that may be a first or second degree (the abbreviation for 'Bachelor of Letters' or 'Bachelor of Literature')

**blitz** /blɪts/ *noun, verb*
■ *noun* **1** [C, usually sing.] a sudden attack: *Five shops were damaged in a firebomb blitz.* **2 the Blitz** [sing.] the German air attacks on the United Kingdom in 1940–1 **3** [C, usually sing.] (*informal*) a sudden organized effort to deal with sth or achieve sth: **~ on sth** *a blitz on passengers who avoid paying fares* ◊ *I've had a blitz on the house* (= cleaned it very thoroughly). ◊ *an advertising/a media blitz* (= a lot of information about sth on television, in newspapers, etc.)
■ *verb* **1** [T] **~ sth** to attack or damage a city by dropping a large number of bombs on it in a short time **2** [T, I] **~ (sth)** (of food) to mix or cut into smaller pieces using an electric mixing machine: *Blitz the strawberries to a purée in a food processor.* ◊ *Blitz until smooth and creamy.*

**blitz·krieg** /ˈblɪtskriːɡ/ *noun* (*from German*) a sudden military attack intended to win a quick victory

**bliz·zard** /ˈblɪzəd; *NAmE* -zərd/ *noun* **1** a SNOWSTORM with very strong winds: *blizzard conditions* ◊ *a raging/howling blizzard* ⊃ WORDFINDER NOTE at SNOW **2** a large quantity of things that may seem to be attacking you: *a blizzard of documents*

**bloat** /bləʊt/ *verb* [T, I] **~ sth** to SWELL (= become bigger or rounder) or make sth SWELL, especially in an unpleasant way: *Her features had been bloated by years of drinking.*

**bloat·ed** /ˈbləʊtɪd/ *adj.* **1** full of liquid or gas and therefore bigger than normal, in a way that is unpleasant: *a bloated body floating in the canal* ◊ (*figurative*) *a bloated organization* (= with too many people in it) **2** full of food and feeling uncomfortable: *I felt bloated after the huge meal they'd served.*

**bloat·er** /ˈbləʊtə(r)/ *noun* (*BrE*) a HERRING (a type of fish) that has been left in salt water and then smoked

**blob** /blɒb; *NAmE* blɑːb/ *noun* a small amount or drop of sth, especially a liquid; a small area of colour: *a blob of ink* ◊ *a pink blob*

**bloc** /blɒk; *NAmE* blɑːk/ *noun* a group of countries that work closely together because they have similar political interests ⊃ see also EN BLOC

# block

## block ⓘ B1 /blɒk; NAmE blɑːk/ noun, verb

■ **noun**
- **SOLID MATERIAL 1** ⚑ B1 [C] a large piece of a solid material that is square or RECTANGULAR in shape and usually has flat sides: *The houses are made of concrete blocks with tin roofs.* ◇ **~ of sth** *a block of ice/wood/stone* ◇ see also BREEZE BLOCK, BUILDING BLOCK, CHOPPING BLOCK (1), CINDER BLOCK
- **BUILDING 2** ⚑ B1 [C] (*BrE*) a tall building that contains flats or offices; buildings that form part of a school, hospital, etc. which are used for a particular purpose: *a block of flats* ◇ *a tower block* ◇ *an office block* ◇ *She lives in a modern apartment block.* ◇ *the university's science block* ⮕ SYNONYMS at BUILDING
- **STREETS 3** ⚑ B1 [C] (*NAmE*) the length of one side of a piece of land or group of buildings, from the place where one street crosses it to the next: *His apartment is three blocks away from the police station.* **4** [C] a group of buildings with streets on all sides: **around the ~** *She took the dog for a walk around the block.* ◇ (*NAmE*) *The downtown area covers four city blocks.*
- **AREA OF LAND 5** [C] (*especially NAmE*) a large area of land **6** [C] (*AustralE*) an area of land for building a house on
- **AMOUNT 7** [C] a quantity of sth or an amount of time that is considered as a single unit: *a block of shares* ◇ *a block of text in a document* ◇ (*BrE*) *The theatre gives discounts for block bookings* (= a large number of tickets bought at the same time). ◇ *The three-hour class is divided into four blocks of 45 minutes each.*
- **THAT STOPS PROGRESS 8** [C, usually sing.] **~ (to sth)** something that makes movement or progress difficult or impossible SYN **obstacle**: *Lack of training acts as a block to progress in a career.* ◇ *I suddenly had a mental block and couldn't remember his name.*
  ◇ see also ROADBLOCK, STUMBLING BLOCK, WRITER'S BLOCK
- **IN SPORT 9** [C] a movement that stops another player from going forward **10 the blocks** [pl.] = STARTING BLOCKS
- **FOR PUNISHMENT 11 the block** [sing.] (in the past) the piece of wood on which a person's head was cut off as a punishment

**IDM** **go on the ˈblock** to be sold, especially at an AUCTION (= a sale in which items are sold to the person who offers the most money) **have been around the ˈblock (a few times)** (*informal*) to have a lot of experience **put/lay your head/neck on the block** to risk losing your job, damaging your reputation, etc. by doing or saying sth ⮕ more at CHIP *n.*, KNOCK *v.*, NEW

■ **verb 1** ⚑ B1 **~ sth** to stop sth from moving or flowing through a pipe, a passage, a road, etc. by putting sth in it or across it: *After today's heavy snow, many roads are still blocked.* ◇ *a blocked sink* **2** ⚑ B1 **~ the/sb's way, exit, view, etc.** to stop sb from going somewhere or seeing sth by standing in front of them or in their way: *One of the guards moved to block her path.* ◇ *An ugly new building blocked the view from the window.* **3 ~ sth** to prevent sth from happening, developing or making progress: *The proposed merger has been blocked by the government.* ◇ *Firewalls can block unauthorized access to a computer.* **4 ~ sth** to stop a ball, hit, etc. from reaching somewhere by moving in front of it: *His shot was blocked by the goalie.* **5 ~ sth** to stop a mobile/cell phone from being used, for example after it has been stolen **6 ~ sb** to prevent someone from contacting you on social media

**PHR V** **ˌblock sb/sth ↔ ˈin** to prevent a car from being able to be driven away by parking too close to it **ˌblock sth ↔ ˈin** to draw or paint sth roughly, without showing any detail: *I have blocked in the shapes of the larger buildings.* **ˌblock sth ↔ ˈoff** to close a road or an opening by placing a barrier at one end or in front of it **ˌblock sth ↔ ˈout 1** to stop light or noise from coming in: *Black clouds blocked out the sun.* **2** to stop yourself from thinking about or remembering sth unpleasant: *Over the years she had tried to block out that part of her life.* **ˌblock sth ↔ ˈup** to completely fill a hole or an opening and so prevent anything from passing through it: *One door had been blocked up.* ◇ *My nose is blocked up.*

**blockˈade** /blɒˈkeɪd; NAmE blɑːˈk-/ noun, verb
■ **noun 1** the action of surrounding or closing a place, especially a port, in order to stop people or goods from coming in or out: *a naval blockade* ◇ **to impose/lift a blockade** ◇ *an economic blockade* (= stopping goods from entering or leaving a country) **2** a barrier that stops people or vehicles from entering or leaving a place: *The police set up blockades on highways leading out of the city.*
■ **verb ~ sth** to surround a place, especially a port, in order to stop people or goods from coming in or out

**blockˈage** /ˈblɒkɪdʒ; NAmE ˈblɑːk-/ noun **1** a thing that blocks flow or movement, for example of a liquid in a narrow place SYN **obstruction**: *a blockage in an artery/a pipe/a drain* **2** the state of being blocked: *to cause/clear the blockage*

**ˌblock and ˈtackle** noun [sing.] a piece of equipment for lifting heavy objects, which works by a system of ropes and PULLEYS (= small wheels around which the ropes are stretched)

**ˈblockˌbuster** /ˈblɒkbʌstə(r); NAmE ˈblɑːk-/ noun (*informal*) something very successful, especially a very successful book or film: *a Hollywood blockbuster* ⮕ WORDFINDER NOTE at BOOK
▶ **ˈblockˌbusting** *adj.*: *a blockbusting performance*

**ˌblock ˈcapitals** (*also* **ˌblock ˈletters**) noun [pl.] separate capital letters: *Please fill out the form in block capitals.*

**ˈblockhead** /ˈblɒkhed; NAmE ˈblɑːk-/ noun (*informal*) a very stupid person

**ˈblockhouse** /ˈblɒkhaʊs; NAmE ˈblɑːk-/ noun **1** a strong CONCRETE shelter used by soldiers, for example during a battle **2** (*NAmE*) a house made of LOGS (= thick pieces of wood)

**ˈblock party** noun (*NAmE*) a party for everyone who lives on a block or in a neighbourhood, usually held on a city street that has been closed to traffic ⮕ compare STREET PARTY

**ˌblock ˈvote** noun a voting system in which each vote who votes represents a number of people

## blog ⓘ A1 /blɒɡ; NAmE blɑːɡ/ noun, verb
■ **noun** ⚑ A1 (*also less frequent* **web·log**) a website where an individual person, or people representing an organization, write regularly about recent events or topics that interest them, usually with photos and links to other websites that they find interesting: *This is a link to the museum's blog.* ◇ **in ~** *You can read about my trip in my blog.* ◇ **~ about sth** *He writes a blog about living with diabetes.* ⮕ WORDFINDER NOTE at WEB
■ **verb** [I, T] (**-gg-**) to keep a blog; to write sth in a blog: *I will be blogging from the convention all week.* ◇ *Here are some reactions to the story I blogged this morning.* ▶ **ˈblogger** noun **ˈblogging** noun [U] **ˈbloggy** *adj.* (*informal*): *The article is quite bloggy, with lots of opinions rather than facts.*

**ˈblogˌgable** /ˈblɒɡəbl; NAmE ˈblɑːɡ-/ *adj.* interesting enough to be a topic for a blog: *The film gave me a whole range of bloggable ideas.*

**ˈblogoˌsphere** /ˈblɒɡəsfɪə(r); NAmE ˈblɑːɡəsfɪr/ noun (*usually* **the blogosphere**) [sing.] (*informal*) all the personal websites that exist on the internet, viewed as a network of people communicating with each other: *It's one of the top stories in the blogosphere.* ◇ *the growing influence of the political blogosphere*

**ˈblog post** noun a piece of writing that forms part of a blog: *I wrote a series of blog posts about my trip to Vietnam.*

**ˈblogroll** /ˈblɒɡrəʊl; NAmE ˈblɑːɡ-/ noun (*computing*) a list on a website of links to other websites that the website owner thinks are useful or interesting

**bloke** /bləʊk/ noun (*BrE, informal*) a man: *He seemed like a nice bloke.*

**bloke·ish** (also **blok·ish**) /ˈbləʊkɪʃ/ adj. (BrE, informal) behaving in a way that is supposed to be typical of men, especially men enjoying themselves in a group

**blonde** ⓘ A1 /blɒnd; NAmE blɑːnd/ adj., noun
■ adj. (also **blond**) HELP In British English it is usual to spell this word **blonde** when writing about a woman or girl and **blond** when writing about a man or boy, although the spelling **blonde** is sometimes used for men and boys too. In American English the spelling **blond** is often preferred for either sex. **Blonde** may be used to describe a woman's hair, but it is sometimes considered offensive to refer to a woman as 'a blonde' because hair colour should not define what a person is like. **1** ⓘ A1 (of hair) pale gold in colour: *She had long blonde hair.* **2** ⓘ A1 (of a person) having blonde hair: *a small, blond boy*

WORDFINDER auburn, dark, fair, ginger, grey, jet black, mousy, redhead, sandy

■ noun (sometimes offensive) a woman with hair that is pale gold in colour: *Is she a natural blonde (= Is her hair naturally blonde)?* ⊃ compare BRUNETTE, REDHEAD

**blood** ⓘ A2 /blʌd/ noun, verb
■ noun **1** ⓘ A2 [U] the red liquid that flows through the bodies of humans and animals: *He lost a lot of blood in the accident.* ◇ *His hands were covered in blood.* ◇ *to give blood* (= to have blood taken from you so that it can be used in the medical treatment of other people) ◇ *He was a hot-headed warrior, always too quick to shed blood* (= attack and injure or kill sb) ◇ *to draw blood* (= to wound a person so that they lose blood) ◇ *a blood cell/sample* ◇ *to improve blood flow to the heart* **2 -blooded** (in adjectives) having the type of blood mentioned: *cold-blooded reptiles* ⊃ see also BLUE-BLOODED, HOT-BLOODED, RED-BLOODED **3** [U] (formal) family origins: *She is of noble blood.* **4** [C] (BrE, old-fashioned) a rich and fashionable man
IDM **bad ˈblood (between A and B)** (old-fashioned) feelings of hate or strong dislike **be ˈafter/ˈout for sb's ˈblood** (informal, often humorous) to be angry with sb and want to hurt or punish them **be/run in your ˈblood** to be a natural part of your character and of the character of other members of your family **blood is thicker than ˈwater** (saying) family relationships are stronger than any others **sb's ˈblood is up** (BrE) somebody is very angry and ready to argue or fight **blood, sweat and ˈtears** very hard work; a lot of effort **have sb's ˈblood on your hands** to be responsible for sb's death: *a dictator with the blood of thousands on his hands* **like getting blood out of/from a ˈstone** almost impossible to obtain: *Getting an apology from him was like getting blood from a stone.* **make sb's ˈblood boil** to make sb extremely angry **make sb's ˈblood run ˈcold** to make sb very frightened or fill them with horror **new/fresh ˈblood** new members or employees, especially young ones, with new ideas or ways of doing things ⊃ more at COLD adj., FLESH n., FREEZE v., SPILL v., SPIT v., STIR v., SWEAT v.
■ verb ~ sb (BrE) to give sb their first experience of an activity

ˈ**blood bank** noun a place where blood is kept for use in hospitals, etc.

ˈ**blood-bath** /ˈblʌdbɑːθ; NAmE -bæθ/ noun [sing.] a situation in which many people are killed violently SYN massacre

ˈ**blood brother** noun a man who has promised to treat another man as his brother, usually in a ceremony in which their blood is mixed together

ˈ**blood clot** (also **clot**) noun a thick, almost solid mass that is formed when blood dries or becomes thicker: *a blood clot on the brain*

ˈ**blood count** noun the number of red and white cells in sb's blood; a medical test to count these

ˈ**blood-curdling** adj. (of a sound or a story) filling you with horror; extremely frightening: *a blood-curdling scream/story*

ˈ**blood diamond** noun = CONFLICT DIAMOND

ˈ**blood donor** noun a person who gives some of his or her blood to be used in the medical treatment of other people

ˈ**blood drive** noun (NAmE) an organized event where people can give some of their blood for use in hospitals, etc.

ˈ**blood group** (also ˈ**blood type** especially in NAmE) noun any of the different types that human blood is separated into for medical purposes: (BrE) *What blood group are you?* ◇ (NAmE) *What blood type do you have?* ◇ *blood group/type O*

ˈ**blood heat** noun [U] the normal temperature of a human body

ˈ**blood-hound** /ˈblʌdhaʊnd/ noun a large dog with a very good sense of smell, used to follow or look for people

**blood·ied** /ˈblʌdid/ adj. covered in blood: *his bruised and bloodied nose*

**blood·less** /ˈblʌdləs/ adj. **1** without any killing: *a bloodless coup/revolution* **2** (of a person or a part of the body) very pale: *bloodless lips* **3** seeming to have no human emotion SYN **cold, unemotional**

**blood·let·ting** /ˈblʌdletɪŋ/ noun [U] **1** (formal) the killing or wounding of people SYN **bloodshed 2** a medical treatment used in the past in which some of a patient's blood was removed

**blood·line** /ˈblʌdlaɪn/ noun (specialist) the set of ANCESTORS of a person or an animal

**blood·lust** /ˈblʌdlʌst/ noun [U] a strong desire to kill or be violent

ˈ**blood money** noun [U] (disapproving) **1** money paid to a person who is hired to murder sb **2** money paid to the family of a murdered person

ˈ**blood orange** noun a type of orange that is red inside

ˈ**blood poisoning** noun an illness in which harmful bacteria get into the blood

ˈ**blood pressure** noun [U] the pressure of blood as it travels around the body: *to have high/low blood pressure* ◇ *to take* (= measure) *sb's blood pressure*

ˈ**blood-red** adj. bright red in colour, like fresh blood

ˈ**blood relation** (also ˈ**blood relative**) noun a person related to sb by birth rather than by marriage

ˈ**blood sausage** (NAmE) (BrE **black ˈpudding**) noun [U, C] a type of large dark SAUSAGE made from pig's blood, fat and grain

**blood·shed** /ˈblʌdʃed/ noun [U] the killing or wounding of people, usually during fighting or a war: *The two sides called a truce to avoid further bloodshed.*

**blood·shot** /ˈblʌdʃɒt; NAmE -ʃɑːt/ adj. (of eyes) with the part that is usually white full of red lines because of lack of sleep, etc.

ˈ**blood sport** noun [usually pl.] a sport in which animals or birds are killed

ˈ**blood·stain** /ˈblʌdsteɪn/ noun a mark or spot of blood on sth ▸ **blood-stained** adj.: *a bloodstained shirt*

ˈ**blood·stock** /ˈblʌdstɒk; NAmE -stɑːk/ noun [U] horses of one type, produced especially for racing

**blood·stream** /ˈblʌdstriːm/ noun [sing.] the blood flowing through the body: *They injected the drug directly into her bloodstream.*

**blood·suck·er** /ˈblʌdsʌkə(r)/ noun **1** an animal or insect that bites people or animals and drinks their blood **2** (informal, disapproving) a person who takes advantage of other people in order to gain financial benefit ▸ **blood·suck·ing** adj. [only before noun]: *bloodsucking insects* ◇ (disapproving) *bloodsucking lawyers*

ˈ**blood sugar** noun [U] the amount of GLUCOSE in your blood

ˈ**blood test** noun an examination of a small amount of your blood by doctors in order to make judgements about your medical condition

# bloodthirsty 154

**blood·thirsty** /ˈblʌdθɜːsti; *NAmE* -θɜːrs-/ *adj.* **1** wanting to kill or wound; enjoying seeing or hearing about killing and violence **2** (of a book, film, etc.) describing or showing killing and violence

**ˈblood transfusion** (*also* **transfusion**) *noun* [C, U] the process of putting new blood into the body of a person or an animal: *He was given a blood transfusion.*

**ˈblood type** *noun* (*especially NAmE*) = BLOOD GROUP

**ˈblood vessel** *noun* any of the tubes through which blood flows through the body ⊃ see also ARTERY, CAPILLARY, VEIN

**bloody¹** /ˈblʌdi/ *adj.* [only before noun], *adv.* (*BrE*, *taboo*, *slang*) ⊃ see also BLOODY² a swear word that many people find offensive that is used to emphasize a comment or an angry statement: *Don't be such a bloody fool.* ◊ *That was a bloody good meal!* ◊ *What bloody awful weather!* ◊ *She did bloody well to win that race.* ◊ *He doesn't bloody care about anybody else.* ◊ *'Will you apologize?' 'Not bloody likely!'* (= Certainly not!)
**IDM** **ˌbloody ˈwell** used to emphasize an angry statement or an order: *You can bloody well keep your job—I don't want it!*

**bloody²** /ˈblʌdi/ *adj.* ⊃ see also BLOODY¹ (**blood·ier**, **bloodi·est**) **1** involving a lot of violence and killing: *a bloody battle* ◊ *The terrorists have halted their bloody campaign of violence.* **2** covered with blood; BLEEDING: *to give sb a bloody nose* (= in a fight) ▶ **blood·ily** /-dɪli/ *adv.*

**Bloody Mary** /ˌblʌdi ˈmeəri; *NAmE* ˈmeri/ *noun* (*pl.* **Bloody Marys**) an alcoholic drink made by mixing VODKA with tomato juice

**ˌbloody-ˈminded** *adj.* (*informal*) behaving in a way that makes things difficult for other people; refusing to be helpful ▶ **ˌbloody-ˈminded·ness** *noun* [U]

**bloom** /bluːm/ *noun*, *verb*
■ *noun* **1** (*formal or specialist*) [C] a flower (usually one on a plant that people admire for its flowers): *the exotic blooms of the orchid* **2** [sing., U] a healthy fresh appearance: *the bloom in her cheeks*
**IDM** **in (full) ˈbloom** (of trees, plants, gardens, etc.) with the flowers fully open
■ *verb* **1** [I] to produce flowers **SYN** *flower*: *Most roses will begin to bloom from late May.* **2** [I] to become healthy, happy or confident **SYN** *blossom*: *The children had bloomed during their stay on the farm.*

**bloom·er** /ˈbluːmə(r)/ *noun* (*BrE*, *old-fashioned*, *informal*) a mistake

**bloom·ers** /ˈbluːməz; *NAmE* -mərz/ *noun* [pl.] **1** (*informal*) an old-fashioned piece of women's underwear like long loose UNDERPANTS **2** short loose trousers that fit tightly at the knee, worn in the past by women for games, riding bicycles, etc: *a pair of bloomers*

**bloom·ing** /ˈbluːmɪŋ; ˈblʊm-/ *adj.* [only before noun], *adv.* (*BrE*, *informal*) a mild swear word, used to emphasize a comment or a statement, especially an angry one: *What blooming awful weather!*

**bloop** /bluːp/ *verb* [I] (*NAmE*, *informal*) to make a mistake

**bloop·er** /ˈbluːpə(r)/ *noun* (*especially NAmE*) an embarrassing mistake that you make in public

**blos·som** /ˈblɒsəm; *NAmE* ˈblɑːs-/ *noun*, *verb*
■ *noun* [C, U] a flower or a mass of flowers, especially on a fruit tree or bush: *cherry/orange/apple blossom* ◊ *The trees are in blossom.* ⊃ VISUAL VOCAB page V6
■ *verb* **1** [I] (of a tree or bush) to produce blossom **2** [I] to become more healthy, confident or successful: *She has visibly blossomed over the last few months.* ◊ **~ into sth** *Their friendship blossomed into love.*

**blot** /blɒt; *NAmE* blɑːt/ *verb*, *noun*
■ *verb* (**-tt-**) **1** **~ sth (up)** to remove liquid from a surface by pressing soft paper or cloth on it **2** **~ sth** to make a spot or spots of INK (= coloured liquid in a pen) fall on paper
**IDM** **ˌblot your ˈcopybook** (*old-fashioned*, *informal*) to do sth to damage the opinion that other people have of you
**PHRV** **ˌblot sth↔ˈout** **1** to cover or hide sth completely: *Clouds blotted out the sun.* **2** to deliberately try to forget an unpleasant memory or thought: *He tried to blot out the image of Helen's sad face.*
■ *noun* **1** a spot or dirty mark on sth, made by INK (= coloured liquid in a pen), etc. ⊃ SYNONYMS at MARK **2** **~ (on sth)** something that damages the opinion that other people have of you, or your happiness: *Her involvement in the fraud has left a serious blot on her character.*
**IDM** **a ˌblot on the ˈlandscape** an object, especially an ugly building, that makes a place less beautiful

**blotch** /blɒtʃ; *NAmE* blɑːtʃ/ *noun* a mark, usually not regular in shape, on skin, plants, material, etc: *He had come out in* (= become covered in) *dark red blotches.*

**blotchy** /ˈblɒtʃi; *NAmE* ˈblɑːtʃi/ (*also* **blotched**) *adj.* covered in blotches: *her blotchy and swollen face*

**blot·ter** /ˈblɒtə(r); *NAmE* ˈblɑːt-/ *noun* **1** a large piece of blotting paper in a cover with a stiff back which is kept on a desk **2** (*NAmE*) the record of arrests in a police district

**ˈblotting paper** *noun* [U] soft thick paper used for drying INK (= coloured liquid in a pen) after you have written sth on a piece of paper

**blouse** /blaʊz; *NAmE* blaʊs/ *noun* a piece of clothing like a shirt, worn by women **IDM** see BIG *adj.*

**blou·son** /ˈbluːzɒn; *NAmE* ˈblaʊsɑːn/ *noun* a short loose jacket that is gathered together at the middle part of the body

**blo·vi·ate** /ˈbləʊvieɪt/ *verb* [I] (*NAmE*, *informal*, *disapproving*) to talk or write in a way that shows that you think you know a lot and have sth important to say, when in fact you do not know much and have nothing important to say

**blow** 🔑 **A2** /bləʊ/ *verb*, *noun*, *exclamation*
■ *verb* (**blew** /bluː/, **blown** /bləʊn/) **HELP** In sense 14 **blowed** is used for the past participle.
• FROM MOUTH **1** 🔑 **A2** [I, T] to send out air from the mouth: **+ adv./prep.** *You're not blowing hard enough!* ◊ *The policeman asked me to blow into the breathalyser.* ◊ **~ sth + adv./prep.** *He drew on his cigarette and blew out a stream of smoke.*
• OF WIND **2** 🔑 **A2** [I, T] when the wind or a current of air **blows**, it is moving; when **it blows**, the wind is blowing: **+ adv./prep.** *A cold wind blew from the east.* ◊ *It was blowing hard.* ◊ *It was blowing a gale* (= there was a strong wind). ⊃ HOMOPHONES at BLUE
• MOVE WITH WIND/BREATH **3** 🔑 **B1** [I, T] to be moved by the wind, sb's breath, etc.; to move sth in this way: **+ adv./prep.** *My hat blew off.* ◊ **+ adj.** *The door blew open.* ◊ **~ sb/sth + adv./prep.** *I was almost blown over by the wind.* ◊ *She blew the dust off the book.* ◊ *The ship was blown onto the rocks.* ◊ **~ sth + adj.** *The wind blew the door shut.*
• WHISTLE/INSTRUMENT **4** 🔑 **B1** [T, I] if you **blow** a WHISTLE, musical instrument, etc. or if a whistle, etc. **blows**, you produce a sound by blowing into the whistle, etc: *the sound of trumpets blowing* ◊ **~ sth** *The referee blew his whistle.*
• YOUR NOSE **5** 🔑 **B1** [T] **~ your nose** to clear your nose by blowing strongly through it into a TISSUE or HANDKERCHIEF: *She grabbed a tissue and loudly blew her nose.*
• A KISS **6** [T] **~ (sb) a kiss** to kiss your hand and then pretend to blow the kiss towards sb
• SHAPE STH **7** [T] **~ sth** to make or shape sth by blowing: *to blow smoke rings* ◊ *to blow bubbles* (= for example, by blowing onto a thin layer of water mixed with soap) ◊ *to blow glass* (= to send a current of air into melted glass to shape it)
• ELECTRICITY **8** [I, T] **~ (sth)** if a FUSE **blows** or you **blow** a FUSE, the electricity stops flowing suddenly because the FUSE (= a thin wire) has melted because the current was too strong
• TYRE **9** [I, T] to break open or apart, especially because of pressure from inside; to make a tyre break in this way: *The car spun out of control when a tyre blew.* ◊ *The truck blew a tyre and lurched off the road.*
• WITH EXPLOSIVES **10** [T] **~ sth** to break sth open with EXPLOSIVES: *The safe had been blown by the thieves.*
• SECRET **11** [T] **~ sth** (*informal*) to make known sth that was secret: *One mistake could blow your cover* (= make your real name, job, intentions, etc. known).

- **MONEY 12** [T] **~ sth (on sth)** (*informal*) to spend or waste a lot of money on sth: *He inherited over a million dollars and blew it all on drink and gambling.*
- **OPPORTUNITY 13** [T] **~ sth** (*informal*) to waste an opportunity: *She blew her chances by arriving late for the interview.* ◇ *You had your chance and you blew it.*
- **EXCLAMATION 14** [T] **~ sb/sth** (*BrE*, *informal*) used to show that you are annoyed, surprised or do not care about sth: *Blow it! We've missed the bus.* ◇ *Well, blow me down! I never thought I'd see you again.* ◇ *I'm blowed if I'm going to* (= I certainly will not) *let him treat you like that.* ◇ *Let's take a taxi and blow* (= never mind) *the expense.*
- **LEAVE SUDDENLY 15** [T, I] **~(sth)** (*NAmE*, *informal*) to leave a place suddenly: *Let's blow this joint.*

**IDM** ˌblow your/sb's ˈbrains out to kill yourself/sb by shooting yourself/them in the head ˌblow ˈchunks (*NAmE*, *slang*) to VOMIT ˌblow a ˈfuse to get very angry ˌblow the ˈgaff (on sb/sth) (*BrE*, *informal*) to tell sth secret, especially by mistake ˌblow hot and ˈcold (about sth) (*informal*) to change your opinion about sth often ˌblow sb/sth out of the ˈwater (*informal*) **1** to destroy sb/sth completely **2** to show that sb/sth is not good by being very much better than it/them: *I like my old phone, but this new model blows it out of the water.* ˌblow ˈsmoke (up sb's ˈass) (*NAmE*, *taboo*, *slang*) to try to trick sb or lie to sb, particularly by saying sth is better than it really is ˌblow sb/sth to ˈbits/ˈpieces to use bombs or other weapons to destroy sb/sth completely: *The plane was blown to pieces when the bomb exploded.* ˌblow your ˈmind (*informal*) to produce a very strong feeling of pleasure or shock: *Wait till you hear this. It'll blow your mind.* ⊃ see also MIND-BLOWING ˌblow your own ˈtrumpet (*especially BrE*) (*NAmE usually* ˌblow/toot your own ˈhorn) (*informal*) to praise your own abilities and achievements **SYN** boast **ORIGIN** This phrase refers to the custom of announcing important guests by blowing a horn. ˌblow your ˈtop (*NAmE also* ˌblow your ˈstack) (*informal*) to get very angry ˌblow up in sb's ˈface if a plan, etc. blows up in your face, it goes badly wrong in a way that causes you damage or makes you feel embarrassed ˌblow the ˈwhistle on sb/sth (*informal*) to tell sb in authority about sth wrong or illegal that sb is doing ⊃ see also WHISTLE-BLOWER ⊃ more at COBWEB, ILL *adj.*, KINGDOM, LARK *n.*, LID, PUFF *v.*, SOCK *n.*, STEAM *n.*, WAY *n.*

**PHRV** ˌblow sth↔aˈpart **1** to completely destroy sth in an explosion **2** to show that an idea is completely false: *What we discovered blew apart all our preconceptions about this fascinating species.* ˌblow sb↔aˈway (*especially NAmE, informal*) **1** to kill sb by shooting them **2** to impress sb a lot or to make them very happy **3** to defeat sb easily; to be much better than others of the same type: *This new phone blows away the competition.* ˌblow ˈin | ˌblow ˈinto sth (*informal*) to arrive or enter a place suddenly: *Look who's just blown in!* ◇ *A storm blew in around 4 a.m.* ˌblow ˈoff (*BrE*, *informal*) a rude way of saying 'WIND' (= release gas through your bottom) ˌblow sb↔ˈoff (*NAmE*) to deliberately not meet sb when you said you would; to end a romantic relationship with sb ˌblow sth↔ˈoff (*NAmE*) to deliberately not do sth that you said you would: *He looks for any excuse he can to blow off work.* ˌblow ˈout **1** if a flame, etc. blows out, it is put out by the wind, etc: *Somebody opened the door and the candle blew out.* **2** if an oil or gas WELL blows out, it sends out gas suddenly and with force ⊃ related noun BLOWOUT ˌblow itself ˈout when a storm blows itself out, it finally loses its force ˌblow sb↔ˈout (*NAmE, informal*) to defeat sb easily ˌblow sth↔ˈout to put out a flame, etc. by blowing ˌblow ˈover to go away without having a serious effect: *The storm blew over in the night.* ◇ *The scandal will soon blow over.* ˌblow ˈup **1** to explode; to be destroyed by an explosion: *The bomb blew up.* ◇ *A police officer was killed when his car blew up.* ⊃ SYNONYMS at EXPLODE **2** to start suddenly and with force: *A storm was blowing up.* ◇ *A crisis has blown up over the President's latest speech.* ˌblow sth↔ˈup **1** to destroy sth by an explosion: *The police station was blown up by terrorists.* ⊃ SYNONYMS at EXPLODE **2** to fill sth with air or gas so that it becomes fairly hard: *The tyres on my bike need blowing up.* **3** to make a photograph bigger **SYN** enlarge ⊃ related noun BLOW-UP **4** to make sth seem more important, better, worse, etc. than it really is: *The whole affair was blown up out of all proportion.* ˌblow ˈup (at sb) (*informal*) to get angry with sb **SYN** lose your temper: *I'm sorry I blew up at you.* ⊃ related noun BLOW-UP

- **noun 1** [C+B2] a hard hit with the hand, a weapon, etc: *She received a severe blow on the head.* ◇ *He was knocked out by a single blow to the head.* ◇ *The two men were exchanging blows.* ◇ *He landed a blow on Bill's nose.* **2** [C+B2] **~(to sb/sth)** a sudden event that hurts or damages sb/sth, causing the people affected to be sad or disappointed: *Losing his job came as a terrible blow to him.* ◇ *It was a shattering blow to her pride.* ⊃ see also BODY BLOW **3** the action of blowing: *Give your nose a good blow* (= clear it completely).

**IDM** a ˌblow-by-ˌblow acˈcount, deˈscription, etc. (of sth) (*informal*) a description of an event that gives you all the details in the order in which they happen ˌcome to ˈblows (over sth) to start fighting because of sth ˌsoften/ˌcushion the ˈblow to make sth that is unpleasant seem less unpleasant and easier to accept ⊃ more at DEAL *v.*, STRIKE *v.*

- **exclamation** (*BrE, old-fashioned*) used to show that you are annoyed about sth: *Blow! I completely forgot it.*

**blow·back** /ˈbləʊbæk/ *noun* [U, C] **1** (*specialist*) a process in which gases expand or travel in a direction that is opposite to the usual one: *blowback gas* ◇ *Blowback may be caused by a defective mechanism.* **2** *especially NAmE* the results of a political action or situation that are not what was intended or wanted: *The policy has led to blowback.* ◇ *The war created a ferocious blowback*

**blow-dry** *verb* **~ sth** to dry hair with a HAIRDRYER and shape it into a particular style ▶ **ˈblow-dry** *noun*: *a cut and blow-dry*

**blow·er** /ˈbləʊə(r)/ *noun* **1** [C] a device that produces a current of air: *a hot-air blower* **2** **the blower** [sing.] (*BrE, old-fashioned, informal*) the phone ⊃ see also WHISTLE-BLOWER

**blow·fly** /ˈbləʊflaɪ/ *noun* (*pl.* **blow·flies**) a large fly that lays its eggs on meat and other food

**blow·hard** /ˈbləʊhɑːd; *NAmE* -hɑːrd/ *noun* (*NAmE, informal, disapproving*) a person who talks too proudly about sth they own or sth they have done

**blow·hole** /ˈbləʊhəʊl/ *noun* **1** a hole in the top of a WHALE's head through which it breathes ⊃ VISUAL VOCAB page V2 **2** a hole in a large area of ice, through which SEALS, etc. breathe

**blowie** /ˈbləʊi/ *noun* (*AustralE, NZE, informal*) a BLOWFLY

**ˈblow-in** *noun* (*AustralE, informal*) a person who has recently arrived somewhere

**ˈblow job** *noun* (*taboo, slang*) the act of touching a man's PENIS with the tongue and lips to give sexual pleasure **SYN** fellatio

**ˈblow-lamp** /ˈbləʊlæmp/ *noun* (*BrE*) = BLOWTORCH

**blown** /bləʊn/ *past part.* of BLOW

**blow·out** /ˈbləʊaʊt/ *noun* **1** an occasion when a tyre suddenly BURSTS (= explodes) on a vehicle while it is moving **SYN** puncture: *to have a blowout* **2** [*usually sing.*] (*informal*) a large meal at which people eat too much: *a four-course blowout* **3** (*NAmE*) a large party or social occasion: *We're going to have a huge blowout for Valentine's Day.* **4** (*NAmE, informal*) an easy victory: *The game was a blowout, 8–1.* **5** a sudden escape of oil or gas from an OIL WELL

**blow·pipe** /ˈbləʊpaɪp/ *noun* **1** a weapon consisting of a long tube through which an ARROW is blown **2** a long tube for blowing glass into a particular shape

**blowsy** (*also* **blowzy**) /ˈblaʊzi/ *adj.* (*BrE, informal, disapproving*) a woman who is blowsy is big and fat and looks untidy

**blow·torch** /ˈbləʊtɔːtʃ; *NAmE* -tɔːrtʃ/ (*NAmE also* **torch**) (*BrE also* **blow·lamp**) *noun* a tool for directing a very hot flame onto part of a surface, for example to remove paint

**ˈblow-up** *noun* **1** an ENLARGEMENT of a photograph, picture or design: *Can you do me a blow-up of his face?* **2** (*NAmE*) an occasion when sb suddenly becomes angry

# BLT                                                                 156

**BLT** /ˌbiː el ˈtiː/ *noun* a sandwich filled with BACON, LETTUCE and tomato: *I'll have a BLT with extra mayonnaise.*

**blub** /blʌb/ *verb* (**-bb-**) [I] (*BrE, informal*) to cry

**blub·ber** /ˈblʌbə(r)/ *noun, verb*
- *noun* [U] the fat of WHALES and other sea animals
- *verb* [I, T] (**+ speech**) (*informal, disapproving*) to cry noisily: *There he sat, blubbering like a baby.*

**bludge** /blʌdʒ/ *verb, noun* (*AustralE, NZE, informal*)
- *verb* **1** [I] to not do any work and live from what other people give you **2** [T] **~ sth** to ask sb for sth especially because you cannot or do not want to pay for it yourself **SYN** **cadge, scrounge**: *The girls bludged smokes.*
- *noun* an easy job

**bludg·eon** /ˈblʌdʒən/ *verb* **1** **~ sb** to hit sb several times with a heavy object **2** **~ sb (into sth/into doing sth)** to force sb to do sth, especially by arguing with them: *They tried to bludgeon me into joining their protest.*

**bludger** /ˈblʌdʒə(r)/ *noun* (*AustralE, NZE, informal*) **1** a lazy person **2** a person who asks other people for sth because they cannot or do not want to pay for it **SYN** **scrounger**

**blue** ⓘ **A1** /bluː/ *adj., noun*
- *adj.* (**bluer, blu·est**) **1** **A1** having the colour of a clear sky or the sea on a clear day: *piercing blue eyes* ◇ *The sun shone brilliantly in the clear blue sky.* **2** (of a person or part of the body) looking slightly blue in colour because the person is cold or cannot breathe easily: *His lips were turning blue.* ◇ **~ with sth** *Her hands were blue with cold.* **3** (*informal*) sad **SYN** **depressed**: *He'd been feeling blue all week.* **4** films, jokes or stories that are **blue** are about sex: *a blue movie* **5** (*politics*) (of an area in the US) having more people who vote for the DEMOCRATIC candidate than the REPUBLICAN one: *blue states/counties* **OPP** **red** ⇒ see also TRUE-BLUE ▸ **blue-ness** *noun* [U, sing.]: *the blueness of the water*
**IDM** **do sth till you are blue in the ˈface** (*informal*) to try to do sth as hard and as long as you possibly can but without success: *You can argue till you're blue in the face, but you won't change my mind.* ⇒ more at BLACK *adj.*, DEVIL, ONCE *adv.*, SCREAM *v.*
- *noun* ⇒ see also BLUES **1** **A1** [C, U] the colour of a clear sky or the sea on a clear day: *bright/dark/light/pale/deep blue* ◇ *The room was decorated in vibrant blues and yellows.* ◇ *She was dressed in blue.* ◇ *The walls are a light shade of blue.* ⇒ see also NAVY BLUE **2** [C] (*BrE*) a person who has played a particular sport for Oxford or Cambridge University; a title given to them **3** [C] (*AustralE, NZE, informal*) a mistake **4** [C] (*AustralE, NZE, informal*) a name for a person with red hair **5** [C] (*AustralE, NZE, informal*) a fight
**IDM** **out of the ˈblue** unexpectedly; without warning: *The decision came out of the blue.* ⇒ more at BOLT *n.*, BOY *n.*

▼ **HOMOPHONES**
blew • blue /bluː/
- **blew** *verb* (*past tense of* BLOW): *The wind blew the door shut.*
- **blue** *adj.*: *Both candidates wore blue jeans.*
- **blue** *noun*: *They chose an intense blue for the walls.*

**ˌblue ˈbaby** *noun* a baby whose skin is slightly blue at birth because there is sth wrong with its heart

**blue·bell** /ˈbluːbel/ *noun* **1** a garden or wild flower with a short STEM and small blue or white flowers that have the shape of bells ⇒ VISUAL VOCAB page V7 **2** (*ScotE*)

**blue·berry** /ˈbluːbəri; NAmE -beri/ *noun* (*pl.* **-ies**) a dark blue BERRY that grows on bushes in North America and can be eaten ⇒ compare BILBERRY ⇒ VISUAL VOCAB page V4

**blue·bird** /ˈbluːbɜːd; NAmE -bɜːrd/ *noun* a small North American bird with blue feathers on its back or head

**ˌblue-ˈblooded** *adj.* from a royal or NOBLE family ▸ **ˌblue ˈblood** *noun* [U]

**ˈblue book** *noun* **1** (*US*) a book with a blue cover used by students for writing the answers to examination questions in **2** (*NAmE*) a book that lists the prices that people should expect to pay for used cars

**blue·bot·tle** /ˈbluːbɒtl; NAmE -bɑːtl/ *noun* a large fly with a blue body

**ˌblue ˈcheese** *noun* [U, C] cheese with lines of blue MOULD in it

**ˌblue-ˈchip** *adj.* [only before noun] (*finance*) a **blue-chip** investment is thought to be safe and likely to make a profit: *blue-chip companies*

**ˌblue-ˈcollar** *adj.* [only before noun] connected with people who do physical work in industry: *blue-collar workers/voters/votes* ⇒ compare WHITE-COLLAR

**ˌblue ˈcrane** *noun* a type of CRANE (= a large bird with long legs and a long neck) that has blue-grey feathers. It is the national bird of South Africa.

**ˌblue-eyed ˈboy** *noun* [usually sing.] (*BrE, informal, often disapproving*) a person treated with special favour by sb: *He's the manager's blue-eyed boy.*

**blue·fish** /ˈbluːfɪʃ/ *noun* (*pl.* **blue·fish**) a blue-coloured sea fish that is caught for sport and food

**ˌblue ˈflag** *noun* **1** (*BrE*) a blue flag used in motor racing to show that a driver who is much further ahead is trying to pass **2** an award given to beaches in Europe that are clean and safe

**blue·grass** /ˈbluːɡrɑːs; NAmE -ɡræs/ *noun* [U] a type of traditional American country music played on guitars and BANJOS

**ˌblue ˈhelmet** *noun* a member of a United Nations force that is trying to prevent war or violence in a place

**blue·jay** /ˈbluːdʒeɪ/ *noun* a large North American bird with blue feathers on its back and a row of feathers (called a CREST) standing up on its head

**ˈblue jeans** *noun* [pl.] (*especially NAmE*) trousers made of blue DENIM

**ˈblue law** *noun* [usually pl.] (in the US) a law that bans business and certain other activities, such as sports, on Sundays

**ˌblue-on-ˈblue** *adj.* [only before noun] (*BrE*) in a war, used to describe an accident or attack in which people are hit by a bomb or weapon that is fired by their own side ⇒ compare FRIENDLY FIRE

**blue·print** /ˈbluːprɪnt/ *noun* **1** a PHOTOGRAPHIC print of a plan for a building or a machine, with white lines on a blue background **2** **~ (for sth)** a plan which shows what can be achieved and how it can be achieved: *a blueprint for the privatization of healthcare* **3** (*specialist*) the pattern in every living cell, which decides how the plant, animal or person will develop and what it will look like: *DNA carries the genetic blueprint which tells any organism how to build itself.*

**ˌblue ˈriband** /ˌbluː ˈrɪbənd/ (*BrE*) (*also* **ˌblue ˈribbon** *NAmE, BrE*) *noun* an honour (sometimes in the form of a blue RIBBON) given to the winner of the first prize in a competition: *a blue-riband event* (= a very important one)

**blues** /bluːz/ *noun* **1** (*often* **the blues**) [U] a type of slow sad music with strong rhythms, developed by African American musicians in the southern US: *a blues band/singer* **2** [C] (*pl.* **blues**) a blues song **3** **the blues** [pl.] (*informal*) sad feelings: *the Monday morning blues* ⇒ see also BABY BLUES

**ˌblue-ˈsky** *adj.* [only before noun] involving new and interesting ideas for things which are not yet possible or practical: *The government has been doing some blue-sky thinking on how to improve school standards.*

**blue·stock·ing** /ˈbluːstɒkɪŋ; NAmE -stɑːk-/ *noun* (*old-fashioned, sometimes disapproving*) a well-educated woman who is more interested in ideas and studying than in traditionally FEMININE things

**bluesy** /ˈbluːzi/ adj. having the slow strong rhythms and sad mood of blues music: *a bluesy sound/voice*

**blue tit** noun a small European bird of the TIT family, with a blue head, wings and tail, and yellow parts below

**Blue·tooth™** /ˈbluːtuːθ/ noun [U] a radio technology that makes it possible for mobile phones, computers and other electronic devices to be linked over short distances, without needing to be connected by wires: *Bluetooth-enabled devices*

**blue ˈwhale** noun a type of WHALE that is the largest known living animal

**bluff** /blʌf/ verb, noun, adj.
- **verb** [I, T] ~ (sth) to try to make sb believe that you will do sth that you do not really intend to do, or that you know sth that you do not really know: *I don't think he'll shoot—I think he's just bluffing.*
- **IDM** **bluff it ˈout** to get out of a difficult situation by continuing to tell lies, especially when people suspect you are not being honest
- **PHR V** **bluff sb into doing sth** to make sb do sth by tricking them, especially by pretending you have more experience, knowledge, etc. than you really have **bluff your way ˈin/ˈout/ˈthrough | bluff your way ˈinto/ˈout of/ˈthrough sth** to succeed in dealing with a difficult situation by making other people believe sth which is not true: *She successfully bluffed her way through the interview.*
- **noun** [U, C] an attempt to trick sb by making them believe that you will do sth when you really have no intention of doing it, or that you know sth when you do not, in fact, know it: *It was just a game of bluff.* ◊ *He said he would resign if he didn't get more money, but it was only a bluff.* ⇒ see also DOUBLE BLUFF **2** [C] a steep CLIFF or slope, especially by the sea or a river **IDM** SEE CALL v.
- **adj.** (of people or their manner) very direct and cheerful, with good intentions, although not always very polite: *Beneath his bluff exterior he was a sensitive man.*

**blu·ish** /ˈbluːɪʃ/ adj. fairly blue in colour: *a bluish-green carpet*

**blun·der** /ˈblʌndə(r)/ noun, verb
- **noun** a stupid or careless mistake: *to make a terrible blunder* ◊ *a series of political blunders*
- **verb** [I] to make a stupid or careless mistake: *The government had blundered in its handling of the affair.*
- **PHR V** **blunder aˈbout, aˈround, etc.** to move around in a way that is not smooth or steady, knocking into things, as if you cannot see where you are going **blunder ˈinto sth 1** to knock into sth because you move carelessly or are not able to see **2** to find yourself in a difficult or unpleasant situation by accident **blunder ˈon** to continue doing sth in a careless or stupid way

**blun·der·buss** /ˈblʌndəbʌs; NAmE -dərb-/ noun an old type of gun with a wide end

**blunt** /blʌnt/ adj., verb
- **adj.** (**blunt·er**, **blunt·est**) **1** without a sharp edge or point: *a blunt knife* ◊ *This pencil's blunt!* ◊ *The police said he had been hit with a blunt instrument.* **OPP** sharp **2** (of a person or remark) very direct; saying exactly what you think without trying to be polite: *She has a reputation for blunt speaking.* ◊ *To be blunt, your work is appalling.* ⇒ SYNONYMS at HONEST ▶ **blunt·ness** noun [U]
- **verb 1** ~ sth to make sth weaker or less effective: *Age hadn't blunted his passion for adventure.* **2** ~ sth to make a point or an edge less sharp

**blunt·ly** /ˈblʌntli/ adv. in a very direct way, without trying to be polite or kind: *To put it bluntly, I want a divorce.* ◊ *'Is she dead?' he asked bluntly.*

**blur** /blɜː(r)/ noun, verb
- **noun** [usually sing.] **1** a shape that you cannot see clearly, often because it is moving too fast: *His arm was a rapid blur of movement as he struck.* ◊ *Everything is a blur when I take my glasses off.* **2** something that you cannot remember clearly: *The events of that day were just a blur.*
- **verb** (**-rr-**) **1** [I, T] if the shape or outline of sth **blurs**, or if sth **blurs** it, it becomes less clear and sharp: *The writing blurred and danced before his eyes.* ◊ ~ sth *The mist blurred the edges of the buildings.* **2** [T, I] ~ (sth) if sth **blurs** your eyes or vision, or your eyes or vision **blur**, you cannot see things clearly: *Tears blurred her eyes.* **3** [I, T] to become or make it become difficult to recognize a clear difference between things: *The differences between art and life seem to have blurred.* ◊ ~ sth *She tends to blur the distinction between her friends and her colleagues.*

**Blu-ray** /ˈbluː reɪ/ noun [U] technology that uses a blue LASER (= a very strong line of light) to record and play large amounts of high quality data on a type of DVD: *These high definition movies are all out on Blu-ray.*

**ˈBlu-ray Disc™** noun (abbr. **BD**, **BD-ROM** /ˌbiː diː ˈrɒm; NAmE ˈrɑːm/) a type of DVD on which large amounts of data can be stored, used especially to play high quality video

**blurb** /blɜːb; NAmE blɜːrb/ noun a short description of a book, a new product, etc., written by the people who have produced it, that is intended to attract your attention and make you want to buy it

**blurred** /blɜːd; NAmE blɜːrd/ adj. **1** not clear; without a clear outline or shape: *She suffered from dizziness and blurred vision.* ◊ *a blurred image/picture* **2** difficult to remember clearly: *blurred memories* **3** difficult to recognize, so differences are not clear: *blurred distinctions/boundaries*

**blurry** /ˈblɜːri/ adj. (informal) without a clear outline; not clear: *blurry, distorted photographs* ◊ (figurative) *a blurry policy*

**blurt** /blɜːt; NAmE blɜːrt/ verb ~ sth (**out**) | ~ that … | ~ what, how, etc … | + speech to say sth suddenly and without thinking carefully enough: *She blurted it out before I could stop her.* ⇒ SYNONYMS at CALL

**blush** /blʌʃ/ verb, noun
- **verb 1** [I] to become red in the face because you are embarrassed or ashamed **SYN** go red: ~ (**with sth**) (**at sth**) *to blush with embarrassment/shame* ◊ *She blushed furiously at the memory of the conversation.* ◊ + adj./noun *He blushed scarlet at the thought.* **2** [T] ~ **to do sth** to be ashamed or embarrassed about sth: *I blush to admit it, but I quite like her music.*
- **noun 1** [C] the red colour that spreads over your face when you are embarrassed or ashamed: *She felt a warm blush rise to her cheeks.* ◊ *He turned away to hide his blushes.* **2** [U, C] (NAmE) = BLUSHER **IDM** SEE SPARE v.

**blush·er** /ˈblʌʃə(r)/ (NAmE also **blush**) noun [U, C] a coloured cream or powder that some people put on their CHEEKS (= on their faces below the eyes) to give them more colour ⇒ WORDFINDER NOTE at MAKE-UP

**blus·ter** /ˈblʌstə(r)/ verb **1** [T, I] ~ (**sth**) | + speech to talk in an aggressive or THREATENING way, but with little effect: *'I don't know what you're talking about,' he blustered.* ◊ *a blustering bully* **2** [I] (of the wind) to blow violently ▶ **blus·ter** noun [U]: *I wasn't frightened by what he said—it was all bluster.*

**blus·tery** /ˈblʌstəri/ adj. (of weather) with strong winds: *blustery winds/conditions* ◊ *The day was cold and blustery.*

**Blu-tack™** /ˈbluː tæk/ noun [U] a blue sticky material used to attach paper to walls

**Blvd.** abbr. (used in written addresses) BOULEVARD

**BME** /ˌbiː em ˈiː/ abbr. (BrE) black and minority ethnic (used in the UK to refer to people who are not white) **SYN** BAME: *The research was based on focus groups of BME mothers of children under five.*

**BMI** /ˌbiː em ˈaɪ/ abbr. BODY MASS INDEX

**BMOC** /ˌbiː em əʊ ˈsiː/ abbr. (US) BIG MAN ON CAMPUS

**ˈB-movie** (also **ˈB-picture**) noun a film that is made cheaply and is not considered to be of high quality: *a B-movie actress*

**BMus** (NAmE **B.Mus**) /ˌbiː em ˈmʌz/ noun a university degree in music that is usually a first degree (the abbreviation for 'Bachelor of Music')

**BMX** /ˌbiː em ˈeks/ noun **1** [C] a strong bicycle which can be used for riding on rough ground **2** (also **BMXing**) [U] the sport of racing BMX bicycles on rough ground

**bn** *abbr.* (*BrE*) (in writing) BILLION

**BO** /ˌbiː ˈəʊ/ *noun* [U] an unpleasant smell from a person's body, especially of SWEAT (the abbreviation for 'body odour'): *She's got BO.*

**boa** /ˈbəʊə/ *noun* **1** = BOA CONSTRICTOR **2** = FEATHER BOA

**boa con‧stric‧tor** /ˌbəʊə kənˈstrɪktə(r)/ (*also* **boa**) *noun* a large South American snake that kills animals for food by winding its long body tightly around them

**boar** /bɔː(r)/ *noun* (*pl.* **boar** *or* **boars**) **1** (*also* **wild 'boar**) a wild pig **2** a male pig that has not been CASTRATED ⇨ compare HOG, SOW²

**board** 🔑 A2 /bɔːd/ *noun*, *verb*
▪ *noun*
- PIECE OF WOOD, ETC. **1** A2 [C, U] a long thin piece of strong hard material, especially wood, used, for example, for making floors, building walls and roofs and making boats: *He had ripped up the carpet, leaving only the bare boards.* ⇨ see also CHIPBOARD, FLOORBOARD, HARDBOARD, SKIRTING BOARD **2** A2 [C] (especially in compounds) a piece of wood, or other strong material, that is used for a special purpose: *a whiteboard* ◊ *I'll write it up on the board.* ◊ (*BrE*) *a noticeboard* ◊ (*NAmE*) *a bulletin board* ◊ *The exam results went up on the board.* ◊ *a diving board* ◊ *She jumped off the top board.* ◊ *a chessboard* ◊ *He removed the figure from the board.*
- IN SPORTS **3** [C] (especially in compounds) the piece of equipment on which sb stands in various water sports and in SNOWBOARDING and SKATEBOARDING
- GROUP OF PEOPLE **4** B2 [C + *sing.* / *pl. v.*] a group of people who have power to make decisions and control a company or other organization: *The board is/are unhappy about falling sales.* ◊ *members of the board* ◊ **on the ~** *She has a seat on the board of directors.* ◊ *a board member/meeting* ◊ (*NAmE*) *the Board of Education* (= a group of elected officials who are in charge of all the public schools in a particular area) ⇨ see also SCHOOL BOARD
- ORGANIZATION **5** [C] used in the name of some organizations: *the Welsh Tourist Board* (= responsible for giving tourist information)
- MEALS **6** [U] the meals that are provided when you stay in a hotel, GUEST HOUSE, etc.; what you pay for the meals: *He pays £90 a week board and lodging.* ⇨ see also BED AND BOARD, FULL BOARD, HALF BOARD
- EXAMS **7 boards** [*pl.*] (*old-fashioned*, *US*) exams that you take when you apply to go to college in the US
- IN THEATRE **8 the boards** [*pl.*] (*old-fashioned*, *informal*) the stage in a theatre: *His play is on the boards on Broadway.* ◊ *She's treading the boards* (= working as an actress).
- ICE HOCKEY **9 the boards** [*pl.*] (*NAmE*) the low wooden wall surrounding the area where a game of ICE HOCKEY is played: *The puck went wide, hitting the boards.* HELP There are many other compounds ending in **board**. You will find them at their place in the alphabet. ⇨ see also ABOVE BOARD, MORTAR BOARD
IDM **a‧cross the 'board** involving everyone or everything in a company, an industry, etc: *The industry needs more investment across the board.* ◊ *an across-the-board wage increase* **go by the 'board** (of plans or principles) to be rejected or ignored; to be no longer possible: *All her efforts to be polite went by the board and she started to shout.* **on 'board 1** B2 on or in a ship, an aircraft or a train SYN **aboard**: *Have the passengers gone on board yet?* **2** giving your support to an idea or a project: *We must get more sponsors on board.* ◊ *You need to bring the whole staff on board.* **take sth on 'board** to accept and understand an idea or a suggestion: *I told her what I thought, but she didn't take my advice on board.* ⇨ more at SWEEP *v.*
▪ *verb*
- GET ON PLANE/SHIP, ETC. **1** B1 [I, T] (*formal*) to get on a ship, train, plane, bus, etc: *Passengers are waiting to board.* ◊ *~ sth He tried to board a plane at Nice airport.* ◊ **to board a bus/train/ship/flight** ⇨ see also ONBOARD **2** B1 [I] **be boarding** when a plane or ship **is boarding**, it is ready for passengers to get on: *Flight BA193 for Paris is now boarding at Gate 37.* ⇨ WORDFINDER NOTE at AIRPORT
- LIVE SOMEWHERE **3** [I] **~ at … / with sb** to live and take meals in sb's home, in return for payment: *She always had one or two students boarding with her.* **4** [I] to live at a school during the school year
PHRV **board sb 'out** (*BrE*) to arrange for sb to live somewhere away from their place of work, school, etc. in return for payment **board sth⇔'up** to cover a window, door, etc. with wooden boards

▼ **HOMOPHONES**

**board** • **bored** /bɔːd/ *NAmE* bɔːrd/
- **board** *noun*: *The rules were written on the board.*
- **board** *verb*: *They are waiting to board a plane for New York.*
- **bored** *adj.*: *The others began to look bored.*

**board‧er** /ˈbɔːdə(r)/ *NAmE* ˈbɔːrd-/ *noun* (*especially BrE*) **1** a child who lives at school and goes home for the holidays: *boarders and day pupils* **2** a person who pays money to live in a room in sb else's house SYN **lodger**

**'board game** *noun* any game played on a board, often using DICE and small pieces that are moved around

**board‧ing** /ˈbɔːdɪŋ/ *NAmE* ˈbɔːrd-/ *noun* [U] **1** long pieces of wood that are put together to make a wall, etc. **2** the arrangement by which school students live at their school, going home during the holidays: *boarding fees*

**'boarding card** (*BrE*) (*also* **'boarding pass** *NAmE*, *BrE*) *noun* a card that you show before you get on a plane or boat

**'boarding house** *noun* a private house where people can pay for accommodation and meals

**'boarding kennel** *noun* [*usually pl.*] a place where people can leave their dogs to be taken care of when they go on holiday ⇨ see also KENNEL (2)

**'boarding school** *noun* a school where children can live during the school year ⇨ compare DAY SCHOOL

**board‧room** /ˈbɔːdruːm, -rʊm/ *NAmE* ˈbɔːrd-/ *noun* a room in which the meetings of the board of a company (= the group of people who control it) are held: *a boardroom row*

**board‧sail‧ing** /ˈbɔːdseɪlɪŋ/ *NAmE* ˈbɔːrd-/ *noun* [U] = WINDSURFING

**board‧walk** /ˈbɔːdwɔːk/ *NAmE* ˈbɔːrd-/ *noun* (*especially NAmE*) a path made of wooden boards, especially on a beach or near water

**boast** 🔑+ C1 /bəʊst/ *verb*, *noun*
▪ *verb* **1** 🔑+ C1 [I, T] to talk in a way that shows you are too proud of sth that you have or can do: *I don't want to boast, but I can actually speak six languages.* ◊ **~ about sth** *She is always boasting about how wonderful her children are.* ◊ **~ of sth** *He openly boasted of his skill as a burglar.* ◊ **~ that …** *Sam boasted that she could beat anyone at poker.* ◊ **+ speech** *'I won!' she boasted.* **2** 🔑+ C1 [T] (not used in the progressive tenses) **~ sth** to have sth that is impressive: *The hotel also boasts two swimming pools and a golf course.*
▪ *noun* **~ (that …)** (*often disapproving*) something that a person talks about in a very proud way, often to seem more important or clever: *Despite his boasts that his children were brilliant, neither of them went to college.* ◊ *It was her proud boast that she had never missed a day's work because of illness.*

**boast‧ful** /ˈbəʊstfl/ *adj.* (*disapproving*) talking about yourself in a very proud way: *I tried to emphasize my good points without sounding boastful.*

**boat** 🔑 A1 /bəʊt/ *noun* **1** A1 a vehicle (smaller than a ship) that travels on water, moved by OARS, sails or a motor: *a rowing/sailing boat* ◊ *a fishing boat* ◊ *You can take a boat trip along the coast.* ◊ *A boat carrying more than 60 people capsized and sank.* ⇨ see also CANAL BOAT, LIFEBOAT, MOTORBOAT, POWERBOAT, SPEEDBOAT, STEAMBOAT **2** A1 any ship: *'How are you going to France?' 'We're going by boat'* (= by FERRY). ◊ *The island is just a short boat ride from the mainland.*

**IDM** **be in the same ˈboat** to be in the same difficult situation ⇒ more at BURN v., FLOAT v., MISS v., PUSH v., ROCK v.

**boat·er** /ˈbəʊtə(r)/ noun a hard STRAW hat with a flat top

**boat·hook** /ˈbəʊthʊk/ noun a long POLE with a HOOK at one end, used for pulling or pushing boats

**boat·house** /ˈbəʊthaʊs/ noun a building next to a river or lake for keeping a boat in

**boat·ing** /ˈbəʊtɪŋ/ noun [U] the activity of using a small boat for pleasure: *to go boating* ◊ *Local activities include walking, boating and golf.*

**boat·load** /ˈbəʊtləʊd/ noun **1** as many goods or passengers as a ship or boat can carry: *a boatload of bananas* **2** (*informal*) a large number of people or things; a large amount of sth: *We made boatloads of food for the party.*

**boat·man** /ˈbəʊtmən/ noun (*pl.* **-men** /-mən/) a man who earns money from small boats, either by carrying passengers or goods on them, or by renting them out

**ˈboat people** noun [pl.] people who escape from their own country in small boats to try to find safety in another country

**boat·swain** = BOSUN

**boat·yard** /ˈbəʊtjɑːd; *NAmE* -jɑːrd/ noun a place where boats are built, repaired or kept

**Bob** /bɒb; *NAmE* bɑːb/ noun
**IDM** **ˈBob's your ˈuncle** (*BrE, informal*) used to say how easy and quick it is to do a particular task: *Press here and Bob's your uncle! It's disappeared.*

**bob** /bɒb; *NAmE* bɑːb/ verb, noun
■ verb (**-bb-**) **1** [I, T] to move or make sth move quickly up and down, especially in water: ~ **up and down** *Tiny boats bobbed up and down in the harbour.* ◊ ~ **sth (up and down)** *She bobbed her head nervously.* **2** [T] ~ **sth** to cut sb's hair so that it is the same length all the way around
**PHRV** ˌbob ˈup to come to the surface suddenly: *The dark head of a seal bobbed up a few yards away.*
■ noun **1** a quick movement down and up of your head and body: *a bob of the head* **2** a style of a woman's hair in which it is cut the same length all the way around: *She wears her hair in a bob.* **3** (*pl.* **bob**) (*informal*) an old British coin, the SHILLING, worth 12 old pence: *That'll cost a few bob* (= a lot of money). **4** = BOBSLEIGH **IDM** see BIT

**bobbed** /bɒbd; *NAmE* bɑːbd/ adj. (of hair) cut so that it hangs loosely to the level of the CHIN all around the back and sides

**bob·ber** /ˈbɒbə(r); *NAmE* ˈbɑːb-/ noun **1** a floating object used in fishing to hold the HOOK at the right depth **2** (*BrE*) a person who rides on a BOBSLEIGH

**bob·bin** /ˈbɒbɪn; *NAmE* ˈbɑːb-/ noun a small device on which you wind THREAD, used, for example, in a SEWING machine

**bob·ble** /ˈbɒbl; *NAmE* ˈbɑːbl/ noun, verb
■ noun **1** (*BrE*) a small, soft ball, usually made of wool, that is used especially for decorating clothes **SYN** **pom-pom**: *a bobble hat* (= a woolly hat with a bobble on top) **2** a piece of ELASTIC with a small ball or other decoration on it, used to tie hair back
■ verb (*informal*) **1** [I] + *adv. / prep.* to move along the ground with small BOUNCES: *The ball somehow bobbled into the net.* **2** [T] ~ **sth** (*NAmE*) to drop a ball or to fail to stop it: *She tried to catch the ball but bobbled it.* **3** [I] (*BrE, informal*) (of a piece of clothing, especially one made of wool) to become covered in very small balls of FIBRE

**ˈbobble hat** noun (*BrE*) a close-fitting hat made of wool with a ball of wool on the top

**bobby** /ˈbɒbi; *NAmE* ˈbɑːbi/ noun (*pl.* **-ies**) (*BrE, old-fashioned, informal*) a police officer **ORIGIN** Named after Sir Robert Peel, the politician who created London's police force in the 19th century. **Bobby** is a familiar form of 'Robert'.

**ˈbobby pin** noun (*NAmE*) (*BrE* **hair-grip, grip**) noun a small thin piece of metal or plastic folded in the middle, used by women for holding their hair in place ⇒ compare HAIRPIN

**ˈbobby socks** noun [pl.] short white socks worn with a dress or skirt, especially by girls and young women in the US in the 1940s and 50s

**bob·cat** /ˈbɒbkæt; *NAmE* ˈbɑːb-/ noun a North American wild cat

**bobs** /bɒbz; *NAmE* bɑːbz/ noun [pl.] **IDM** see BIT

**bob·sleigh** /ˈbɒbsleɪ; *NAmE* ˈbɑːb-/ (*BrE*) (*NAmE* **bob·sled** /ˈbɒbsled; *NAmE* ˈbɑːb-/) (also **bob**) noun a racing SLEDGE (= a vehicle for two or more people that slides over snow)

**bob·tail** /ˈbɒbteɪl; *NAmE* ˈbɑːb-/ noun **1** a dog, cat or horse with a tail that has been cut short **2** a tail that has been cut short

**bod** /bɒd; *NAmE* bɑːd/ noun (*informal*) **1** (*BrE*) a person: *She's a bit of an odd bod* (= rather strange). **2** a person's body: *He's got a great bod.*

**boda-boda** (*also* **boda boda**) /ˌbəʊdəˈbəʊdə/ *EAfrE* [ˈbodaˌboda] noun (*EAfrE*) (in some countries) a type of motorcycle or bicycle with a space for a passenger or for carrying goods, often used as a taxi: *boys on bodabodas riding on Kampala's streets*

**bo·da·cious** /bəʊˈdeɪʃəs/ adj. (*especially NAmE, informal*) **1** excellent; extremely good **2** willing to take risks or to do sth that shocks people **SYN** **audacious**

**bode** /bəʊd/ verb
**IDM** **bode ˈwell / ˈill (for sb / sth)** (*formal*) to be a good/bad sign for sb/sth **SYN** **augur**: *These figures do not bode well for the company's future.*

**bo·dega** /bəʊˈdeɪɡə/ noun (*from Spanish*) (in the US) a small store selling food, wine and household goods, especially in a neighbourhood where most people speak Spanish: *Try your local deli, bodega or convenience store.*

**bodge** /bɒdʒ; *NAmE* bɑːdʒ/ verb ~ **sth (up / together)** (*BrE, informal*) to make or repair sth in a way that is not as good as it should be

**Bodhi·sat·tva** /ˌbɒdɪˈsætvə; *NAmE* ˌbəʊd-/ noun (in Mahayana Buddhism) a person who is able to reach NIRVANA (= a state of peace and happiness) but who delays doing this because of the suffering of other humans

**bodh·rán** /ˈbaʊrɑːn; ˈbɔːr-/ noun (*IrishE*) a shallow Irish drum that you hold on its side in your hand and play with a short wooden stick

**bod·ice** /ˈbɒdɪs; *NAmE* ˈbɑːd-/ noun the top part of a woman's dress, above the middle part of the body

**ˈbodice-ripper** noun (*informal*) a romantic novel or film with a lot of sex in it, which is set in the past

**bod·ily** /ˈbɒdɪli; *NAmE* ˈbɑːd-/ adj., adv.
■ adj. [only before noun] connected with the human body: *bodily functions/changes/needs* ◊ *bodily fluids* ◊ *bodily harm* (= physical injury)
■ adv. **1** by moving the whole of sb's body; by force: *The force of the blast hurled us bodily to the ground.* ◊ *He lifted her bodily into the air.* **2** in one piece; completely: *The monument was moved bodily to a new site.*

## body

**body** ⓘ **A1** **S** /ˈbɒdi; *NAmE* ˈbɑːdi/ noun (*pl.* **-ies**)
• **OF PERSON / ANIMAL 1** ⓘ **A1** [C] the whole physical structure of a human or an animal: *the human body* ◊ *a male/female/naked body* ◊ *His whole body was trembling.* ◊ *body fat/weight/temperature/size* ⇒ VISUAL VOCAB page V1 **2** ⓘ **A1** [C] the main part of a body not including the head, or not including the head, arms and legs: *She had injuries to her head and body.* ◊ *He has a large body, but thin legs.* **3** ⓘ **A1** [C] the body of a dead person or animal: *a dead body* ◊ *A man's body was found floating in the river.*
• **MAIN PART 4** [sing.] **the ~ of sth** the main part of sth, especially a building, a vehicle or a book, an article, etc: *the body of a plane* (= the central part where the seats are) ◊ *the main body of the text*
• **GROUP OF PEOPLE 5** ⓘ **B2** [C + *sing. / pl. v.*] a group of people who work or act together, often for an official purpose, or who are connected in some other way: *a regulatory/an*

# body armour

advisory body ◊ The **governing body** of the school is/are concerned about discipline. ◊ recognized **professional bodies** such as the Law Association ◊ An **independent body** has been set up to investigate the affair. ◊ **~ of sb** A large body of people will be affected by the tax cuts. ◊ **in a~** The protesters marched in a body (= all together) to the White House. ⊃ see also STUDENT BODY
- **LARGE AMOUNT 6** [C] **~ of sth** a large amount or collection of sth: *a vast body of evidence/information/research* ◊ *large bodies of water* (= lakes or seas) ◊ *There is a powerful body of opinion against the ruling.*
- **OBJECT 7** [C] (*formal*) an object: *heavenly bodies* (= stars, planets, etc.) ◊ *an operation to remove a foreign body* (= sth that would not usually be there) *from a wound*
- **OF DRINK/HAIR 8** [U] the full strong taste of alcoholic drinks or the thick healthy quality of sb's hair: *a wine with plenty of body* ◊ *Regular use of conditioner is supposed to give your hair more body.*
- **-BODIED 9** (in adjectives) having the type of body mentioned: *full-bodied red wines* ◊ *soft-bodied insects* ⊃ see also ABLE-BODIED
- **CLOTHING 10** [C] (*BrE*) (*NAmE* **body-suit**) a piece of clothing which fits tightly over a woman's upper body and bottom, usually fastening between the legs

IDM **body and 'soul** with all your energy: *She committed herself body and soul to fighting for the cause.* **keep body and 'soul together** to stay alive with just enough of the food, clothing, etc. that you need SYN **survive**: *They barely have enough money to keep body and soul together.* ⊃ more at BONE *n.*, DEAD *adj.*, SELL *v.*

▼ **VOCABULARY BUILDING**

**Actions expressing emotions**

Often parts of the body are closely linked to particular verbs. The combination of the verb and part of the body expresses an emotion or attitude.

| action | part of body | you are ... |
|---|---|---|
| bite | lips | nervous |
| clench | fist | angry, aggressive |
| click | fingers | trying to remember sth |
| click | tongue | annoyed |
| drum/tap | fingers | impatient |
| hang | head | ashamed |
| lick | lips | anticipating sth good, nervous |
| nod | head | agreeing |
| purse | lips | disapproving |
| raise | eyebrows | enquiring, surprised |
| scratch | head | puzzled |
| shake | head | disagreeing |
| shrug | shoulders | doubtful, indifferent |
| stamp | foot | angry |
| wrinkle | nose | feeling dislike or distaste |
| wrinkle | forehead | puzzled |

For example: *She bit her lip nervously.* ◊ *He scratched his head and looked thoughtful.* ◊ *I wrinkled my nose in disgust.* ◊ *She raised questioning eyebrows.*

**body armour** (*US* **body armor**) *noun* [U] clothing worn by the police, etc. to protect themselves

**body bag** *noun* a bag for carrying a dead body in, for example in a war

**body blow** *noun* something which has damaging effects on sb/sth, creating problems or causing sb to be very disappointed

**body·board** /ˈbɒdibɔːd; *NAmE* ˈbɑːdibɔːrd/ *noun* a short light type of SURFBOARD that you ride lying on your front ▶ **body·board·ing** *noun* [U]

**body·build·ing** /ˈbɒdibɪldɪŋ; *NAmE* ˈbɑːd-/ *noun* [U] the activity of doing regular exercises in order to make your muscles bigger and stronger ▶ **body·build·er** *noun*

**body check** *noun* (IN ICE HOCKEY) an attempt to prevent a player's movement by blocking them with your shoulder or HIP

**body clock** *noun* a natural system that makes your body need sleep, food, etc. at particular times of the day

**body count** *noun* the total number of people killed in a battle or an accident: *The body count in this war grows weekly.*

**body double** *noun* a person who takes part in a film in place of an actor when the scene involves wearing no clothes, or using special or dangerous skills ⊃ WORDFINDER NOTE at ACTOR

**body·guard** /ˈbɒdigɑːd; *NAmE* ˈbɑːdigɑːrd/ *noun* [C + sing./pl. v.] a person or a group of people who are employed to protect sb: *The President's bodyguard is/are armed.*

**body image** *noun* [U, C] a person's mental picture of how good or bad their physical appearance is, especially when compared with how they think they should look

**body language** *noun* [U] the process of communicating what you are feeling or thinking by the way you place and move your body rather than by words

**body mass index** *noun* (*abbr.* **BMI**) a measure of whether sb weighs too much or too little, calculated by dividing their weight in KILOGRAMS by their height in metres squared

**body odour** (*US* **body odor**) *noun* [U] (*abbr.* **BO**) an unpleasant smell from a person's body, especially of SWEAT

**body piercing** (*also* **pier·cing**) *noun* [C] **1** [U] the making of holes in parts of the body in order to wear a ring, etc. as a decoration: *tattooing and body piercing* **2** [C] a hole made in a part of the body so that a ring, etc. can be worn: *She had a nose stud and multiple ear piercings.*

**the body 'politic** *noun* [sing.] (*formal*) all the people of a particular nation considered as an organized political group

**body-popping** *noun* [U] a way of dancing in which you make stiff movements like a robot

**body scanner** *noun* an electronic machine, used at an airport, a prison, etc., that produces a picture of a person's body through their clothes on a screen so that illegal drugs or weapons can be found

**body search** *noun* a search of a person's body, for example by the police or by a customs official, for drugs, weapons, etc.

**body shop** *noun* **1** the part of a car factory where the main bodies of the cars are made **2** a place where repairs are made to the main bodies of cars

**body·snatch·er** /ˈbɒdisnætʃə(r); *NAmE* ˈbɑːd-/ *noun* a person who stole bodies from GRAVEYARDS in the past, especially to sell for medical experiments

**body stocking** *noun* a piece of clothing that fits closely over the whole body from the neck to the ankles, often including the arms, worn for example by dancers

**body·suit** /ˈbɒdisuːt; *NAmE* ˈbɑːd-/ **1** (*NAmE*) (*BrE* **body**) *noun* a piece of clothing which fits tightly over a woman's upper body and bottom, usually fastening between the legs **2** a piece of clothing that fits closely over the body, including the arms and legs, worn by men and women for sports

**body swerve** *noun* a sudden movement that you make to the side when running to avoid crashing into sb/sth

**body warmer** *noun* (*BrE*) a thick warm jacket without arms that you wear outdoors

**body·work** /ˈbɒdiwɜːk; *NAmE* ˈbɑːdiwɜːrk/ *noun* [U] the main outside structure of a vehicle, usually made of painted metal

**Boer** /bɔː(r)/ *SAfrE* /buːr/ *noun* **1** a South African whose family originally came from the Netherlands: *the Boer War* (= the war between the Boers and the British, 1899–1902) ⊃ see also AFRIKANER **2 boer** (*SAfrE*) a farmer **3 boer** (*SAfrE*, *disapproving*) used to refer to a member of the police or the army, especially in the past

**boere·wors** /ˈbuːrəvɔːs, ˈbuər-; *NAmE* ˈbuːrəvɔːrs, ˈbur-/ *SAfrE* [ˈbuːrəvɔrs] *noun* [U] (*SAfrE*) a spicy SAUSAGE that is

prepared in a long piece and sold usually wound into a COIL (= a series of circles)

**bof·fin** /ˈbɒfɪn/ NAmE ˈbɑːf-/ noun (BrE, informal) a scientist, especially one doing research

**bog** /bɒɡ/ NAmE bɑːɡ/ noun, verb
■ noun 1 [C, U] (an area of) wet soft ground, formed of DECAYED (= destroyed by natural processes) plants: *a peat bog* ⊃ see also BOGGY 2 [C] (BrE, slang) a toilet: *Have you got any bog roll* (= toilet paper)?
■ verb (-gg-)
PHRV **bog sth/sb ˈdown (in sth)** [usually passive] 1 to make sth sink into mud or wet ground: *The tank became bogged down in mud.* 2 to prevent sb from making progress in an activity: *We mustn't get bogged down in details.*
ˌbog ˈoff (BrE, taboo, slang) only used in orders, to tell sb to go away: *Bog off, I'm trying to sleep!*

**bo·gan** /ˈbəʊɡən/ noun (AustralE, NZE, informal, disapproving) a rude or socially unacceptable person

**bo·gey** /ˈbəʊɡi/ noun 1 (also **bogy**) a thing that causes fear, often without reason 2 (also **bogy**) (both BrE) (NAmE **booger**) (informal) a piece of dried MUCUS from inside your nose 3 (also **bogy**) = BOGEYMAN 4 (in golf) a score of one STROKE (= hit of the ball) over PAR (= the standard score for a hole) ⊃ compare BIRDIE, EAGLE

**bo·gey·man** (also **bogy-man**) /ˈbəʊɡimæn/ noun (also **bogey, bogy**) (NAmE also **boo·gey·man**) (pl. **-men** /-men/) an imaginary evil spirit that is used to frighten children: *The bogeyman's coming!*

**bog·gle** /ˈbɒɡl/ NAmE ˈbɑːɡl/ verb [I] ~ **(at sth)** (informal) to be slow to do or accept sth because you are surprised or shocked by it: *Even I boggle at the idea of spending so much money.*
IDM **sth boggles the ˈmind** (also **the mind ˈboggles**) (informal) if sth **boggles the mind** or **the mind boggles** at it, it is so unusual that people find it hard to imagine or accept: *The vastness of space really boggles the mind.* ⋄ *'He says he's married to his cats!' 'The mind boggles!'* ⊃ compare MIND-BOGGLING

**boggy** /ˈbɒɡi/ NAmE ˈbɑːɡi/ adj. (**bog·gier, bog·gi·est**) (of land) soft and wet, like a BOG: *boggy ground*

**bogie** /ˈbəʊɡi/ noun 1 (especially BrE) a frame with four or six wheels that forms part of a railway carriage. The main body of the carriage usually rests on two bogies, one at each end. 2 (IndE) a railway carriage

**BOGOF** /ˈbɒɡɒf/ NAmE ˈbɑːɡɑːf/ abbr. (BrE, informal) buy one, get one free (a type of special offer used in shops): *BOGOF offers and bargains*

**bog-ˈstandard** adj. (BrE, informal) ordinary; with no special features SYN average

**bogus** /ˈbəʊɡəs/ adj. pretending to be real or true SYN false: *a bogus doctor/contract* ⋄ *bogus claims of injury by workers*

**bogy, bogy·man** = BOGEY, BOGEYMAN

**bo·he·mian** /bəʊˈhiːmiən/ noun a person, often sb who is involved with the arts, who lives in a very informal way without following accepted rules of behaviour ▶ **bo·he·mian** adj.: *a bohemian existence/lifestyle*

**boho** /ˈbəʊhəʊ/ (also ˌboho ˈchic) noun [U] a style of women's fashion that was popular at the beginning of the 21st century. It included loose tops, long skirts, wide belts and boots.

**boil** ❶ A2 /bɔɪl/ verb, noun
■ verb 1 B1 [I, T] when a liquid **boils** or when you **boil** it, it is heated to the point where it forms bubbles and turns to STEAM or VAPOUR: *The water was bubbling and boiling away.* ⋄ *sth Boil plenty of salted water, then add the spaghetti.* 2 A2 [I, T] when a KETTLE, pan, etc. **boils** or when you **boil** a KETTLE, etc., it is heated until the water inside it **boils**: (BrE) *The kettle's boiling.* ⋄ *sth I'll boil the kettle and make some tea.* ⋄ + adj. *She left the gas on by mistake and the pan boiled dry* (= the water boiled until there was none left). 3 A2 [I, T] to cook or wash sth in boiling water; to be cooked or washed in boiling water: *She put some potatoes on to boil.* ⋄ *sth boiled carrots/cabbage/potatoes* ⋄ *to boil an egg for sb* ⋄ *sb sth to boil sb an egg* 4 [I] ~ **(with sth)** if

# bold

you **boil** with anger, etc. or anger, etc. **boils** inside you, you are very angry: *He was boiling with rage.* IDM see BLOOD n., WATCH v.
PHRV **ˌboil ˈdown | ˌboil sth↔ˈdown** to be reduced or to reduce sth by boiling **ˌboil sth ˈdown (to sth)** to make sth, especially information, shorter by leaving out the parts that are not important: *The original speech I had written got boiled down to about ten minutes.* **ˌboil ˈdown to sth** (not used in the progressive tenses) (of a situation, problem, etc.) to have sth as a main or basic part: *In the end, what it all boils down to is money, or the lack of it.* ⋄ *The argument/question/issue boils down to this:…* **ˌboil ˈover 1** (of liquid) to boil and flow over the side of a pan, etc. **2** (informal) to become very angry **3** (of a situation, an emotion, etc.) to change into sth more dangerous or violent SYN **explode**: *Racial tension finally boiled over in the inner city riots.* **ˌboil ˈup** if a situation or an emotion boils up, it becomes dangerous, makes you worried, etc: *I could feel anger boiling up inside me.* **ˌboil sth↔ˈup** to heat a liquid or some food until it boils
■ noun 1 [sing.] a period of boiling; the point at which liquid boils: (BrE) *Bring the soup to the boil, then allow it to simmer for five minutes.* ⋄ (NAmE) *Bring the soup to a boil.* 2 [C] a painful SWELLING (= an area that is larger and rounder than normal) under the skin which is full of a thick yellow liquid (called PUS)
IDM **off the ˈboil** (BrE) less good than before: *The second series of the show really went off the boil.* **on the ˈboil** very active: *We have several projects all on the boil at once.*

**ˌboiled ˈsweet** noun [C] (BrE) (NAmE ˌhard ˈcandy) [C, U]) a hard sweet made from boiled sugar, often tasting of fruit

**boil·er** /ˈbɔɪlə(r)/ (also **fur·nace** especially in NAmE) noun a container in which water is heated to provide hot water and heating in a building or to produce STEAM in an engine

**boiler·maker** /ˈbɔɪləmeɪkə(r); NAmE -lərm-/ noun 1 a person or company that makes BOILERS 2 (NAmE) a person who makes and repairs metal objects for industry 3 (NAmE) a drink of WHISKY followed immediately by a glass of beer

**boiler·plate** /ˈbɔɪləpleɪt; NAmE -lərp-/ noun [C, U] (NAmE) a standard form of words that can be used as a model for writing parts of a business document, legal agreement, etc.

**ˈboiler room** noun 1 a room in a building or ship containing the boiler 2 (NAmE) a room or office used by people using phones to sell sth, especially shares, in an aggressive or a dishonest way

**ˈboiler suit** noun (especially BrE) (NAmE usually **cov·er·alls**) a piece of clothing like trousers and a jacket in one piece, worn for doing dirty work ⊃ compare OVERALLS

**boil·ing** /ˈbɔɪlɪŋ/ (also ˌboiling ˈhot) adj. very hot SYN baking: *You must be boiling in that sweater!* ⋄ *a boiling hot day* OPP **freezing**

**ˈboiling point** noun [U, C] 1 the temperature at which a liquid starts to boil 2 the point at which a person becomes very angry, or a situation is likely to become violent: *Racial tension has reached boiling point.*

**bois·ter·ous** /ˈbɔɪstərəs/ adj. (of people, animals or behaviour) noisy and full of life and energy: *It was a challenge, keeping ten boisterous seven-year-olds amused.* ▶ **bois·ter·ous·ly** adv.

**bok choy** /ˌbɒk ˈtʃɔɪ; NAmE ˌbɑːk/ (NAmE) (BrE **pak choi**) noun [U] a type of CHINESE CABBAGE with long dark green leaves and thick white STEMS

**bold** B1+ B2 /bəʊld/ adj., noun
■ adj. 1 (**bold·er, bold·est**) B1+ B2 (of people or behaviour) brave and confident; not afraid to say what you feel or to take risks: *It was a bold move on their part to open a business in France.* ⋄ *The wine made him bold enough to approach her.* 2 B1+ B2 (of printed words or letters) in a thick, dark TYPE: *Highlight the important words in bold type.* ⋄ *bold lettering* 3 (of shape, colour, lines, etc.) that can be easily seen; having a strong clear appearance: *the*

Ⓞ Oxford Phrasal Academic Lexicon (OPAL) written and spoken word lists | Ⓦ OPAL written word list | Ⓢ OPAL spoken word list

# bole

bold outline of a mountain against the sky ◊ She paints with bold strokes of the brush. ▶ **bold·ly** adv. **bold·ness** noun [U]
**IDM** **be/make so bold (as to do sth)** (formal) used especially when politely asking a question or making a suggestion which you hope will not offend anyone (although it may criticize them slightly): If I may be so bold as to suggest that he made a mistake in his calculations… **(as) bold as brass** (informal) without showing any respect, shame or fear
■ noun (also **bold·face** /ˈbəʊldfeɪs/) [U] (specialist) thick, dark TYPE used for printing words or letters: Headwords are printed **in bold**.

**bole** /bəʊl/ noun the main STEM of a tree **SYN** trunk

**bol·ero** /bəˈleərəʊ; NAmE -ˈler-/ noun (pl. **-os**) **1** a traditional Spanish dance; a piece of music for this dance **2** /ˈbɒləraʊ, ˈbɒləraʊ; NAmE ˈbɑːləraʊ/ a women's short jacket that is not fastened at the front

**bol·etus** /bəˈliːtəs/ (also **bol·ete** /bəˈliːt/) noun [C, U] a MUSHROOM with small round holes under the top part. Some types of boletus can be eaten.

**boll** /bəʊl/ noun the part of the cotton plant that contains the seeds

**bol·lard** /ˈbɒlɑːd; NAmE ˈbɑːlərd/ noun **1** (BrE) a short thick post that is used to stop vehicles from going on to a road or part of a road **2** a short thick post on a ship, or on land close to water, to which a ship's rope may be tied

**bol·lock·ing** /ˈbɒləkɪŋ; NAmE ˈbɑːl-/ noun (BrE, taboo, slang) an occasion when sb tells you that they are very angry with you, often by shouting at you: to give sb a bollocking ◊ to get a bollocking **HELP** There are more polite ways to express this, for example **to give sb/to get a rocket**, or **to tear a strip off sb**.

**bol·locks** /ˈbɒləks; NAmE ˈbɑːl-/ noun (BrE, taboo, slang) **1** [U] ideas, statements or beliefs that you think are silly or not true **SYN** nonsense: You're talking a load of bollocks! **2** [pl.] a man's TESTICLES **3** Bollocks! exclamation used as a swear word when sb is disagreeing with sth, or when they are angry about sth: Bollocks! He never said that!

**boll weevil** noun an insect that damages cotton plants

**Bol·ly·wood** /ˈbɒliwʊd; NAmE ˈbɑːli-/ noun [U] (informal) used to refer to the Hindi film industry, which is mainly based in the Indian city of Mumbai (in the past called Bombay)

**bol·ogna** /bəˈləʊnjə; BrE also -ˈlɒn-/ noun [U] (NAmE) a type of SAUSAGE that is put in sandwiches, made of a mixture of meats

**bolo tie** /ˈbəʊləʊ taɪ/ noun (NAmE) a string worn around the neck and fastened with an attractive CLASP or bar

**Bol·shevik** /ˈbɒlʃɪvɪk; NAmE ˈbəʊl-/ noun a member of the group in Russia that took control after the 1917 Revolution ▶ **Bol·shevik** adj. **Bol·shevism** /-vɪzəm/ noun [U]

**bol·shie** (also **bol·shy**) /ˈbɒlʃi; NAmE ˈbəʊl-/ adj. (BrE, informal, disapproving) (of a person) creating difficulties or arguments deliberately, and refusing to be helpful

**bol·ster** /ˈbəʊlstə(r)/ verb, noun
■ verb to improve sth or make it stronger: **~ sth** to bolster sb's confidence/courage/morale ◊ **~ sth up** Falling interest rates may help to bolster up the economy.
■ noun a long thick PILLOW that is placed across the top of a bed under the other PILLOWS

**bolt** /bəʊlt/ noun, verb, adv.
■ noun **1** a long, narrow piece of metal that you slide across the inside of a door or window in order to lock it **2** a piece of metal like a thick nail without a point which is used with a circle of metal (= a NUT) to fasten things together: nuts and bolts **3** **~ of lightning** a sudden flash of LIGHTNING in the sky, appearing as a line **4** a short heavy ARROW shot from a CROSSBOW **5** a long piece of cloth wound in a roll around a piece of CARDBOARD
**IDM** **a bolt from the blue** an event or a piece of news which is sudden and unexpected; a complete surprise: Her dismissal came as a bolt from the blue. **make a ˈbolt for**

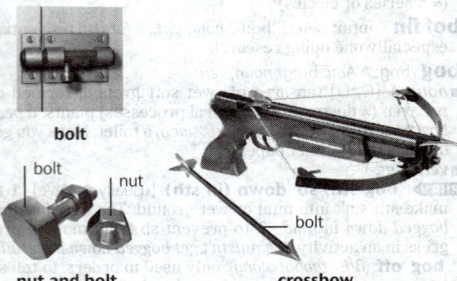

**bolts**

nut and bolt

crossbow

sth | **make a ˈbolt for it** to run away very fast, in order to escape ⇨ more at NUT n., SHOOT v.
■ verb **1** [T, I] **~ (sth)** to fasten sth such as a door or window by sliding a bolt across; to be able to be fastened in this way: Don't forget to bolt the door. ◊ The gate bolts on the inside. **2** [T] to fasten things together with a bolt: **~ A to B** The vice is bolted to the workbench. ◊ **~ A and B together** The various parts of the car are then bolted together. **3** [I] if an animal, especially a horse, **bolts**, it suddenly runs away because it is frightened **4** [I] **(+ adv./prep.)** (of a person) to run away, especially in order to escape: When he saw the police arrive, he bolted down an alley. **5** [T] **~ sth (down)** to eat sth very quickly: Don't bolt your food! **6** (NAmE) [T, I] **~ (sth)** to stop supporting a particular group or political party: Many Democrats bolted the party to vote Republican. **7** [I] (of a plant, especially a vegetable) to grow too quickly and start producing seeds and so become less good to eat **IDM** see STABLE n.
■ adv.
**IDM** **sit/stand bolt ˈupright** to sit or stand with your back straight

**ˈbolt-action** adj. (of a gun) having a back part that is opened by turning a BOLT and sliding it back

**ˈbolt-hole** /ˈbəʊlthəʊl/ noun (BrE) a place that you can escape to, for example when you are in a difficult situation

**ˈbolt-on** adj. [only before noun] able to be easily added to a machine, etc. to make it able to do sth new

**bolus** /ˈbəʊləs/ noun **1** (medical) a single amount of a drug that is given at one time **SYN** dose **2** (specialist) a small round mass of a substance, especially food that has been CHEWED to make it soft before it is SWALLOWED

**boma** /ˈbəʊmə/ EAfrE /ˈbɒmə/ noun (EAfrE, SAfrE) (in wild country) an area surrounded by a fence, often made of sticks, used to protect animals or people

**bomb** 🔊 **B1** /bɒm; NAmE bɑːm/ noun, verb
■ noun **1** **B1** [C] a weapon designed to explode at a particular time or when it is dropped or thrown: a **bomb goes off/explodes** ◊ Hundreds of **bombs** were dropped on the city. ◊ a roadside bomb (= one that is designed to blow up vehicles) ◊ a **bomb attack/blast** ⇨ see also ATOMIC BOMB, DIRTY BOMB, PIPE BOMB **2** **the bomb** [sing.] nuclear weapons (ATOMIC or HYDROGEN bombs): countries that have the bomb **3** **a bomb** [sing.] (BrE, informal) a lot of money: That dress must have cost a bomb! **4** **a bomb** [sing.] (NAmE, informal) a complete failure: The musical was a complete bomb on Broadway. **5** [C] (NAmE) (in AMERICAN FOOTBALL) a long forward throw of the ball **6** [C] (NAmE) a container in which a liquid such as paint or insect poison is kept under pressure and released as a SPRAY or as FOAM: a bug bomb (= used for killing insects)
**IDM** **be the ˈbomb** (NAmE) to be very good; to be the best: Check out the new website. It's the bomb! **go down a ˈbomb | go (like) a ˈbomb** (BrE) to be very successful: Our performance went down a bomb. ◊ The party was really going like a bomb. **go like a ˈbomb** (BrE) (of a vehicle) to go very fast
■ verb **1** **B1** [T] **~ sth/sb** to attack sth/sb by leaving a bomb in a place or by dropping bombs from a plane: Warplanes bombed targets in and around the capital. ◊ The city was

heavily bombed in the war. **2** [I] + **adv./prep.** (BrE, informal) to move very fast, especially in a vehicle, in a particular direction: *They were bombing down the road at about 80 miles an hour.* **3** [T, I] ~ **(sth)** (NAmE, informal) to fail a test or an exam very badly: *The exam was impossible! I definitely bombed it.* **4** [I] (informal) (of a play, show, etc.) to fail very badly: *His latest musical bombed and lost thousands of dollars.*
**PHRV** **be ˌbombed ˈout 1** if you are **bombed out**, your home is destroyed by bombs: ~ **(of sth)** *a programme of house-building for those who were bombed out of their homes* **2** if a building is **bombed out**, it has been destroyed by bombs

**ˈbomb alert** *noun* (BrE) = BOMB SCARE

**bom·bard** /bɒmˈbɑːd; NAmE bɑːmˈbɑːrd/ *verb* **1** ~ **sb/sth (with sth)** to attack a place by firing large guns at it or dropping bombs on it continuously **2** ~ **sb/sth (with sth)** to attack sb with a lot of questions, criticisms, etc. or by giving them too much information: *We have been bombarded with letters of complaint.* ▶ **bom·bard·ment** *noun* [U, C]: *The city came under heavy bombardment.*

**bom·bard·ier** /ˌbɒmbəˈdɪə(r); NAmE ˌbɑːmbərˈdɪr/ *noun* **1** the person on a military plane in the US AIR FORCE who is responsible for aiming and dropping bombs **2** a member of a low rank in the Royal Artillery (= a part of the British army that uses large guns)

**bom·bast** /ˈbɒmbæst; NAmE ˈbɑːm-/ *noun* [U] (formal) words which sound important but have little meaning, used to impress people ▶ **bom·bas·tic** /bɒmˈbæstɪk; NAmE bɑːm-/ *adj.*: *a bombastic speaker*

**ˈbomb bay** *noun* a part of an aircraft in which bombs are held and from which they can be dropped

**ˈbomb disposal** *noun* [U] the job of removing or exploding bombs in order to make an area safe: *a bomb disposal expert/squad/team*

**bombed** /bɒmd; NAmE bɑːmd/ *adj.* [not before noun] (informal) extremely drunk

**bomb·er** /ˈbɒmə(r); NAmE ˈbɑːm-/ *noun* **1** a plane that carries and drops bombs ⇒ WORDFINDER NOTE at AIRCRAFT **2** a person who puts a bomb somewhere illegally

**ˈbomber jacket** *noun* a short jacket that fits tightly around the middle part of the body and fastens with a ZIP

**bomb·ing** /ˈbɒmɪŋ; NAmE ˈbɑːm-/ *noun* [C, U] an occasion when a bomb is dropped or let off somewhere; the act of doing this: *recent bombings in major cities ◊ enemy bombing*

**bom·bora** /bɒmˈbɔːrə; NAmE bɑːm-/ *noun* (AustralE) **1** a wave which forms over an UNDERWATER rock, sometimes producing a dangerous area of water **2** an area of rock UNDERWATER

**bomb·proof** /ˈbɒmpruːf; NAmE ˈbɑːm-/ *adj.* strong enough to give protection against an attack by a bomb

**ˈbomb scare** (*also* **ˈbomb threat** *especially in NAmE*) (BrE *also* **ˈbomb alert**) *noun* an occasion when sb says that they have put a bomb somewhere and everyone has to leave the area

**bomb·shell** /ˈbɒmʃel; NAmE ˈbɑːm-/ *noun* [usually sing.] (informal) **1** an event or a piece of news which is unexpected and usually unpleasant: *The news of his death came as a bombshell. ◊ She dropped a bombshell at the meeting and announced that she was leaving.* **2 a ˌblond(e) ˈbombshell** a very attractive woman with blonde hair

**ˈbomb site** *noun* an area where all the buildings have been destroyed by bombs: *The kids used to play on an old bomb site.*

**bona fide** /ˌbəʊnə ˈfaɪdi/ *adj.* [usually before noun] (from Latin) real, legal or true; not false: *a bona fide reason ◊ Is it a bona fide, reputable organization?*

**bona fides** /ˌbəʊnə ˈfaɪdiːz/ *noun* [pl.] (from Latin) evidence that sb is who they say that they are; evidence that sb/sth is honest

**bon·anza** /bəˈnænzə/ *noun* [sing.] **1** a situation in which people can make a lot of money or be very successful: *a cash bonanza for investors ◊ a bonanza year for the com-* *puter industry* **2** a situation where there is a large amount of sth pleasant: *the usual bonanza of sport in the summer*

**bon·bon** /ˈbɒnbɒn; NAmE ˈbɑːnbɑːn/ *noun* a sweet, especially one with a soft centre

**bonce** /bɒns; NAmE bɑːns/ *noun* (BrE, informal) a person's head

**bond** ⓘ **B2** /bɒnd; NAmE bɑːnd/ *noun, verb*
■ *noun*
• STRONG CONNECTION **1** ⓘ **B2** [C] something that forms a connection between people or groups, such as a feeling of friendship or shared ideas and experiences: ~ **between A and B** *A bond of friendship had been forged between them. ◊ The agreement strengthened the bonds between the two countries. ◊ the special bond between mother and child ◊* ~ **with sb** *The students formed strong bonds with each other.* ⇒ WORDFINDER NOTE at FRIEND
• MONEY **2** [C] an agreement by a government or a company to pay you interest on the money you have lent; a document containing this agreement ⇒ see also JUNK BOND ⇒ WORDFINDER NOTE at INVEST **3** [C] (especially NAmE, law) a sum of money that is paid as BAIL: *He was released on $5000 bond.* **4** [C] (*also* **ˈmortgage bond**) (SAfrE) a legal agreement by which a bank lends you money to buy a house, etc. which you pay back over many years; the sum of money that is lent: *to pay off a bond ◊ We had to take out a second bond on the property. ◊ bond rates* (= of interest)
• ROPES/CHAINS **5 bonds** [pl.] (formal) the ropes or chains keeping sb prisoner; anything that stops you from being free to do what you want: *to release sb from their bonds ◊ the bonds of oppression/injustice*
• LEGAL AGREEMENT **6** [C] (formal) a legal written agreement or promise: *We entered into a solemn bond.*
• JOIN **7** [C] the way in which two things are joined together: *a firm bond between the two surfaces*
• CHEMISTRY **8** [C] the way in which ATOMS are held together in a chemical COMPOUND **IDM** see WORD *n.*
■ *verb*
• JOIN TOGETHER **1** [T, I] to join two things strongly together; to join strongly to sth else: ~ **sth** *This new glue bonds a variety of surfaces in seconds. ◊* ~ **(A) to B** *It cannot be used to bond wood to metal. ◊* ~ **(A and B) together** *The atoms bond together to form a molecule.*
• DEVELOP RELATIONSHIP **2** [I, T] ~ **(with sb)** to develop or create a relationship of trust with sb: *Mothers who are depressed sometimes fail to bond with their children.*

**bond·age** /ˈbɒndɪdʒ; NAmE ˈbɑːn-/ *noun* [U] **1** (old-fashioned or formal) the state of being a slave or prisoner **SYN** slavery: (figurative) *women's liberation from the bondage of domestic life* **2** the practice of being tied with ropes, chains, etc. in order to gain sexual pleasure

**ˌbonded ˈlabour** (US **ˌbonded ˈlabor**) *noun* [U] forced work for an employer for a fixed time without being paid, often as a way of paying a debt: *Many of the immigrants are used as bonded labour.* ▶ **ˌbonded ˈlabourer** (US **ˌbonded ˈlaborer**) *noun*

**ˌbonded ˈwarehouse** *noun* a government building where imported goods are stored until tax has been paid on them

**bond·ing** /ˈbɒndɪŋ; NAmE ˈbɑːn-/ *noun* **1** the process of forming a special relationship with sb or with a group of people: *mother-child bonding* ⇒ see also MALE BONDING **2** (chemistry) the process of ATOMS joining together: *hydrogen bonding*

**bone** ⓘ **A2** /bəʊn/ *noun, verb*
■ *noun* **1** ⓘ **A2** [C] any of the hard parts that form the SKELETON of the body of a human or an animal: *He survived the accident with no broken bones. ◊ This fish has a lot of bones in it.* **2** [U] the hard substance that bones are made of: *knives with bone handles* **3** **-boned** (in adjectives) having bones of the type mentioned: *fine-boned*
**IDM** **a bone of conˈtention** a subject that causes people to disagree **ˌclose to the ˈbone** (informal) (of a remark, joke, story, etc.) so honest or clearly expressed that it is likely

# bone china

to cause offence to some people **cut, pare, etc. sth to the 'bone** to reduce sth, such as costs, as much as you possibly can **have a 'bone to pick with sb** (*informal*) to be angry with sb about sth and want to discuss it with them **make no bones about (doing) sth** (*informal*) to be honest and open about sth; to not hesitate to do sth: *She made no bones about telling him exactly what she thought of him.* **not have a … bone in your body** (*informal*) to have none of the quality mentioned: *She was honest and hard-working, and didn't have an unkind bone in her body.* **throw sb a 'bone** to give sb a small part of what they want as a way of showing that you want to help them, without offering them the main thing they want **to the 'bone** affecting you very strongly: *His threats chilled her to the bone.* ⇒ more at BAG n., BARE adj., DOG n., FEEL v., FINGER n., FLESH n., SKIN n.
- **verb** ~ **sth** to take the bones out of fish or meat
- PHRV **bone 'up on sth** (*informal*) to try to learn about sth or to remind yourself of what you already know about it: *She had boned up on the city's history before the visit.*

**bone 'china** *noun* [U] very thin CHINA made of CLAY mixed with CRUSHED bone (= that has been broken and pressed into a powder); cups, plates, etc. made of this

**bone 'dry** *adj.* [not usually before noun] completely dry

**bone·head** /ˈbəʊnhed/ *noun* (*informal*) a stupid person

**bone·less** /ˈbəʊnləs/ *adj.* (of meat or fish) without any bones: *boneless chicken breasts*

**'bone marrow** (*also* **mar·row**) *noun* [U] a soft substance that fills the hollow parts of bones: *a bone marrow transplant*

**bone·meal** /ˈbəʊnmiːl/ *noun* [U] a substance made from CRUSHED animal bones, used to make soil richer

**boner** /ˈbəʊnə(r)/ *noun* (*NAmE, informal*) **1** (*taboo*) an ERECTION of the PENIS **2** an embarrassing mistake

**bon·fire** /ˈbɒnfaɪə(r)/ *NAmE* ˈbɑːn-/ *noun* a large outdoor fire for burning waste or as part of a celebration

**'Bonfire Night** (*also* **Guy 'Fawkes night**) *noun* [U, C] the night of 5 November, when there is a tradition in the UK that people light BONFIRES and have FIREWORKS to celebrate the failure of the plan in 1605 to destroy the parliament buildings with EXPLOSIVES

**bong** /bɒŋ/ *NAmE* bɑːŋ/ *noun* **1** the sound made by a large bell: *the bongs of Big Ben* **2** a long pipe for smoking CANNABIS and other drugs, which passes the smoke through a container of water

**bongo** /ˈbɒŋɡəʊ; *NAmE* ˈbɑːŋ-/ (*pl.* **-os**) (*also* **'bongo drum**) *noun* a small drum, usually one of a pair, that you play with your fingers

**bon·homie** /ˈbɒnəmi; *NAmE* ˌbɑːnəˈmiː/ *noun* [U] (*from French, formal*) a feeling of cheerful friendship

**bonk** /bɒŋk; *NAmE* bɑːŋk/ *noun, verb*
- **noun** (*BrE, informal*) **1** [sing.] an act of having sex with sb **2** [C] the act of hitting sb on the head or of hitting your head on sth
- **verb** (*BrE, informal*) **1** [T, I] ~ **(sb)** to have sex with sb: *He's been bonking one of his students.* **2** [T] ~ **sth** to hit sb lightly on the head or to hit yourself by mistake: *I bonked my head on the doorway.*

**bonk·ers** /ˈbɒŋkəz; *NAmE* ˈbɑːŋkərz/ *adj.* [not before noun] (*informal*) completely crazy and silly: *I'll go bonkers if I have to wait any longer.* IDM see RAVING adj.

**bon mot** /ˌbɒn ˈməʊ; *NAmE* ˌbɑːn ˈmoʊ/ *noun* (*pl.* **bons mots** /ˌbɒn ˈməʊ; *NAmE* ˌbɑːn ˈmoʊ/) (*from French, formal*) a funny and clever remark

**bon·net** /ˈbɒnɪt; *NAmE* ˈbɑːn-/ *noun* **1** a hat tied with strings under the CHIN, worn by babies and, especially in the past, by women **2** (*BrE*) (*NAmE* **hood**) the metal part over the front of a vehicle, usually covering the engine IDM see BEE

**bonny** (*also* **bonnie**) /ˈbɒni; *NAmE* ˈbɑːni/ *adj.* (**bon·nier**, **bon·ni·est**) (*dialect, especially ScotE*) very pretty; attractive: *a bonny baby/lass*

**bon·sai** /ˈbɒnsaɪ; *NAmE* ˈbɑːn-/ *noun* (*pl.* **bon·sai**) **1** [C] a small tree that is grown in a pot and prevented from reaching its normal size **2** [U] the Japanese art of growing bonsai

**bon·sella** /bɒnˈselə; *NAmE* bɑːn-/ *noun* (*SAfrE, informal*) something that you receive as a present or reward, especially money

**bonus** /ˈbəʊnəs/ *noun* (*pl.* **-es**) **1** an extra amount of money that is added to a payment, especially to sb's wages or salary as a reward: *a £100 Christmas bonus* ◇ *productivity bonuses* ⇒ WORDFINDER NOTE at PAY ⇒ see also NO-CLAIMS BONUS **2** [usually sing.] anything pleasant that is extra and more or better than you were expecting: *Being able to walk to work is an added bonus of the new job.*

**bon vivant** /ˌbɒn viːˈvɒ̃; *NAmE* ˌbɑːn viːˈvɑːnt/ (*also* **bon viveur** /ˌbɒn viːˈvɜː(r); *NAmE* ˌbɑːn viːˈvɜːr/) *noun* (*from French*) a person who enjoys going out with friends and eating good food, drinking good wine, etc. HELP The plural forms can be **bon vivants** or **bons vivants**; **bon viveurs** or **bons viveurs** but the pronunciation is the same as the singular.

**bon voyage** /ˌbɒn vɔɪˈɑːʒ; *NAmE* ˌbɑːn/ *exclamation* (*from French*) said to sb who is leaving on a journey, to wish them a good journey

**bony** /ˈbəʊni/ *adj.* (**boni·er**, **boni·est**) **1** (of a person or part of the body) very thin so that the bones can be seen under the skin **2** (of fish) full of small bones **3** consisting of or like bone

**boo** /buː/ *exclamation, noun, verb*
- **exclamation, noun 1** a sound that people make to show that they do not like an actor, speaker, etc: '*Boo!*' *they shouted,* '*Get off!*' ◇ *The speech was greeted with loud boos from the audience.* **2** people shout **Boo!** when they want to surprise or frighten sb IDM see SAY v.
- **verb** [I, T] to show that you do not like a person, performance, idea, etc. by shouting '*boo*': *The audience booed as she started her speech.* ◇ ~ **sb** *He was booed off the stage.*

**boob** /buːb/ *noun, verb*
- **noun 1** (*slang*) a woman's breast **2** (*BrE, informal*) a stupid mistake: *I made a bit of a boob deleting that file.* **3** (*NAmE*) a stupid person
- **verb** [I] (*informal*) to make a stupid mistake

**'boo-boo** *noun* **1** (*informal*) a stupid mistake: *I think I've made a boo-boo.* **2** (*NAmE*) a child's word for a small cut or injury

**'boob tube** *noun* (*informal*) **1** (*BrE*) (*NAmE* **'tube top**) a piece of women's clothing that is made of cloth that stretches and covers the chest **2** (*NAmE, disapproving*) the television

**booby** /ˈbuːbi/ *noun* (*pl.* **-ies**) **1** (*informal*) a stupid person: *Don't be such a booby!* **2** [usually pl.] (*informal*) a word for a woman's breast, used especially by children **3** a large tropical bird with brightly coloured feet that lives near the sea

**'booby prize** *noun* a prize that is given as a joke to the person who is last in a competition ⇒ compare WOODEN SPOON

**'booby trap** *noun* **1** a hidden bomb that explodes when the object that it is connected to is touched **2** a hidden device that is meant as a joke to surprise sb, for example an object placed above a door so that it will fall on the first person who opens the door

**'booby-trap** *verb* (**-pp-**) ~ **sth** to place a booby trap in or on sth

**boo·ger** /ˈbʊɡə(r); *BrE also* ˈbuːɡ-/ (*NAmE*) (*BrE* **bogey**, **bogy**) *noun* (*informal*) a piece of dried MUCUS from inside your nose

**boo·gey·man** /ˈbuːɡimæn; *NAmE* ˈbʊɡ-/ *noun* (*NAmE*) = BOGEYMAN

**boo·gie** /ˈbuːgi; NAmE ˈbugi/ noun, verb
- **noun** (also **boogie-woogie** /ˌbuːgi ˈwuːgi; NAmE ˌbugi ˈwugi/) [U] a type of blues music played on the piano, with a fast strong rhythm
- **verb** [I] (informal) to dance to fast pop music

**ˈboogie board** noun a small board used for riding on waves in a lying position

**boo·hoo** /ˌbuːˈhuː/ exclamation used in written English to show the sound of sb crying

**book** ⓘ A1 /bʊk/ noun, verb
- **noun**
  - PRINTED WORK **1** A1 [C] a set of printed pages that are fastened inside a cover so that you can turn them and read them: *a pile of books* ◇ *hardback/paperback books* **2** A1 [C] a written work published in printed or electronic form: *to read/write/publish a book* ◇ *reference/children's/library books* ◇ *~ by sb a new book by J. K. Rowling* ◇ *~ about/on sth a book about wildlife* ⊃ WORDFINDER NOTE at WRITE

  WORDFINDER biography, blockbuster, character, editor, narrator, novel, plot, publish, title

  - FOR WRITING IN **3** A1 [C] (especially in compounds) a set of sheets of paper that are fastened together inside a cover and used for writing in: *an exercise book* ◇ *a notebook* ⊃ see also ADDRESS BOOK, COLOURING BOOK
  - OF STAMPS/TICKETS/MATCHES, ETC. **4** [C] a set of things that are fastened together like a book: *a book of stamps/tickets/matches* ◇ *a chequebook*
  - ACCOUNTS **5** the **books** [pl.] the written records of the financial affairs of a business: *to do the books* (= to check the accounts)
  - SECTION OF BIBLE, ETC. **6** [C] a section of a large written work: *the books of the Bible*
  - FOR BETTING **7** [C] (BrE) a record of bets made on whether sth will happen, sb will win a race, etc.

  IDM ▶ **be in sb's good/bad ˈbooks** (informal) used to say that sb is pleased/annoyed with you: *I'm in her good books at the moment because I cleared up the kitchen.* **bring sb to ˈbook (for sth)** (especially BrE, formal) to punish sb for doing sth wrong and make them explain their behaviour **by the ˈbook** following rules and instructions in a very strict way: *She always does everything by the book.* **have your head/nose in a ˈbook** to be reading: *She always has her nose in a book.* **in my ˈbook** (informal) used when you are giving your opinion: *That's cheating in my book.* **(be) on sb's ˈbooks** (to be) on an organization's list, for example of people who are available for a particular type of work: *We have very few nurses on our books at the moment.* ◇ *Most of the houses on our books are in the north of the city.* **throw the ˈbook at sb** (informal) to punish sb who has committed an offence as severely as possible ⊃ more at CLOSE¹ v., CLOSED, COOK v., HISTORY, JUDGE v., LEAF n., OPEN adj., READ v., SUIT v., TRICK n.

- **verb 1** A2 [I, T] to arrange to have or use sth on a particular date in the future; to buy a ticket to sth in advance: *Book early to avoid disappointment.* ◇ *~ sth She booked a flight to Chicago.* ◇ *The performance is booked up* (= there are no more tickets available). ◇ *I'm sorry—we're fully booked.* ◇ (BrE) *I'd like to book a table for two for 8 o'clock tonight.* HELP In American English **book** is not used if you do not have to pay in advance; instead use **make a reservation**: *I'd like to make a reservation for 8 o'clock tonight.* ⊃ compare RESERVE ⊃ WORDFINDER NOTE at HOTEL **2** A2 [T] to arrange for sb to have a seat on a plane, etc.: *~ sb + adv./prep. I've booked you on the 10 o'clock flight.* ◇ *~ sb (+ adv./prep.) I've booked you a room at the Park Hotel.* ⊃ see also DOUBLE-BOOK **3** [T] *~ sb/sth (for sth)* to arrange for a singer, etc. to perform on a particular date: *We've booked a band for the wedding reception.* **4** [T] *~ sb (for sth)* (informal) to write down sb's name and address because they have committed a crime or an offence: *He was booked for possession of cocaine.* **5** [T] *~ sb* (BrE) (of a REFEREE) to write down in an official book the name of a player who has broken the rules of the game

  PHRV **ˌbook ˈin/ˈinto sth** (BrE) to arrive at a hotel, etc. and arrange to stay there: *I got in at ten and booked straight into a hotel.* **ˌbook sb ˈin/ˈinto sth** to arrange for sb to have a room at a hotel, etc.

**book·able** /ˈbʊkəbl/ adj. **1** tickets, etc. that are **bookable** can be ordered in advance **2** (BrE) if an offence in football (soccer) is **bookable**, the name of the player responsible can be written down in a book by the REFEREE as a punishment **3** (NAmE) if a crime is a **bookable** offence, the person responsible can be arrested

**book·bind·er** /ˈbʊkbaɪndə(r)/ noun a person whose job is fastening the pages of books together and putting covers on them ▶ **ˈbook·bind·ing** noun [U]

**book·case** /ˈbʊkkeɪs/ noun a piece of furniture with shelves for keeping books on

**ˈbook club** noun **1** an organization that sells books cheaply to its members **2** = BOOK GROUP

**book·end** /ˈbʊkend/ noun [usually pl.] one of a pair of objects used to keep a row of books standing up

**ˈbook group** (also **ˈbook club**, **ˈreading group**) noun a group of people who meet together regularly to discuss a book they have all read

**bookie** /ˈbʊki/ noun (informal) = BOOKMAKER

**book·ing** ⓘ B2 /ˈbʊkɪŋ/ noun **1** ⓘ B2 [C, U] (especially BrE) an arrangement that you make in advance to buy a ticket to travel somewhere, go to the theatre, etc.: *a booking form/hall/clerk* ◇ *Can I make a booking for Friday?* ◇ *Early booking is recommended.* ◇ *No advance booking is necessary.* ◇ *We can't take any more bookings.* ⊃ compare RESERVATION **2** [C] an arrangement for sb to perform at a theatre, in a concert, etc. **3** [C] (BrE) (in football (soccer)) an act of the REFEREE writing a player's name in a book, as a punishment because an offence has been committed

**ˈbooking office** noun (BrE) a place where you can buy tickets, at a train or bus station or at a theatre

**book·ish** /ˈbʊkɪʃ/ adj. (often disapproving) interested in reading and studying, rather than in more active or practical things

**book·keep·er** /ˈbʊkkiːpə(r)/ noun a person whose job is to keep an accurate record of the accounts of a business ▶ **ˈbook·keep·ing** noun [U]

**ˈbook learning** noun [U] knowledge from books or study rather than from experience

**book·let** /ˈbʊklət/ noun a small thin book with a paper cover that contains information about a particular subject

**book·maker** /ˈbʊkmeɪkə(r)/ (also informal **bookie**) (also BrE, formal **ˈturf accountant**) noun a person whose job is to take bets on the result of horse races, etc. and pay out money to people who win ▶ **ˈbook·mak·ing** noun [U]

**book·mark** /ˈbʊkmɑːk; NAmE -mɑːrk/ noun **1** a long narrow piece of paper, etc. that you put between the pages of a book when you finish reading so that you can easily find the place again **2** (computing) a record of the address of a file, a page on the internet, etc. that enables you to find it quickly ⊃ compare FAVOURITE (3) ⊃ WORDFINDER NOTE at WEBSITE ▶ **ˈbook·mark** verb: *~ sth Do you want to bookmark this site?*

**book·mobile** /ˈbʊkməbiːl/ (NAmE) (BrE **ˌmobile ˈlibrary**) noun a van that contains a library and travels from place to place so that people in different places can borrow books

**book·sel·ler** /ˈbʊksɛlə(r)/ noun a person whose job is selling books

**book·shelf** /ˈbʊkʃɛlf/ noun (pl. **book·shelves** /-ʃɛlvz/) a shelf that you keep books on

**book·shop** /ˈbʊkʃɒp; NAmE -ʃɑːp/ (especially BrE) (NAmE usually **book·store** /ˈbʊkstɔː(r)/) noun a shop that sells books

**ˈbook-smart** adj. (NAmE, becoming old-fashioned, often disapproving) having a lot of academic knowledge learned from books and studying, but not necessarily knowing much about people and living in the real world: *He's book-smart but he's got no common sense.* ⊃ compare STREET-SMART

# bookstall 166

**book·stall** /ˈbʊkstɔːl/ (*especially BrE*) (*NAmE usually* **news-stand**) *noun* a small shop that is open at the front, where you can buy books, newspapers or magazines, for example at a station or an airport

**ˈbook token** *noun* (*BrE*) a card, usually given as a gift, that you can exchange for books of a particular value

**book·worm** /ˈbʊkwɜːm; *NAmE* -wɜːrm/ *noun* a person who likes reading very much

**Bool·ean** /ˈbuːliən/ *adj.* (*mathematics, computing*) connected with a system, used especially in COMPUTING and ELEC-TRONICS, that uses only the numbers 1 (to show sth is true) and 0 (to show sth is false)

**Boolean ˈoperator** *noun* (*computing*) a symbol or word such as 'or' or 'and', used in computer programs and searches to show what is or is not included

**boom** ⁊+ C1 /buːm/ *noun, verb*
■ *noun*
- **IN BUSINESS/ECONOMY 1** ⁊+ C1 a sudden increase in trade and economic activity; a period of wealth and success: *Living standards improved rapidly during the post-war boom.* ◇ **~ in sth** *a boom in car sales* ◇ *a boom year* (*for trade, exports, etc.*) ◇ *a property/housing boom* ◇ *a chaotic period of boom and bust* ⊃ WORDFINDER NOTE at TREND ⊃ compare SLUMP ⊃ see also BABY BOOM
- **POPULAR PERIOD 2** ⁊+ C1 [usually sing.] a period when sth such as a sport or a type of music suddenly becomes very popular and successful: *The only way to satisfy the golf boom was to build more courses.*
- **ON BOAT 3** a long POLE that the bottom of a sail is attached to and that you move to change the position of the sail
- **SOUND 4** [usually sing.] a loud deep sound: *the distant boom of the guns* ⊃ see also SONIC BOOM
- **IN RIVER/HARBOUR 5** a floating barrier that is placed across a river or the entrance to a HARBOUR to prevent ships or other objects from coming in or going out
- **FOR MICROPHONE 6** a long POLE that carries a MICROPHONE or other equipment
■ *verb*
- **MAKE LOUD SOUND 1** [I] to make a loud deep sound: *Outside, thunder boomed and crashed.* **2** [T, I] to say sth in a loud deep voice: **+ speech** *'Get out of my sight!' he boomed.* ◇ **~(out)** *A voice boomed out from the darkness.* ◇ *He had a booming voice.*
- **OF BUSINESS/ECONOMY 3** [I] to have a period of rapid growth; to become bigger, more successful, etc: *By the 1980s, the computer industry was booming.* ◇ *Business is booming!*

**boom·burb** /ˈbuːmbɜːb; *NAmE* -bɜːrb/ *noun* (*NAmE*) an area of a city that is outside the centre and that is quickly becoming larger as many people move there

**boom·er** /ˈbuːmə(r)/ *noun* **1** (*NAmE*) = BABY BOOMER **2** a large male KANGAROO

**boom·er·ang** /ˈbuːməræŋ/ *noun, verb*
■ *noun* a curved flat piece of wood that you throw and that can fly in a circle and come back to you. Boomerangs were first used by Australian Aborigines as weapons when they were hunting.

**boomerang**

■ *verb* [I] if a plan **boomerangs** on sb, it hurts them instead of the person it was intended to hurt SYN backfire

**ˈboomerang kid** (*also* **ˈboomerang child**) *noun* (*informal*) an adult child who returns home to live with his or her parents after being away for some time

**ˈboom town** *noun* a town that has become rich and successful because trade and industry has developed there

**boon** /buːn/ *noun* ~ (**to/for sb**) something that is very helpful and makes life easier for you: *The new software will prove a boon to internet users.*

**ˈboon comˈpanion** *noun* (*literary*) a very good friend

**boon·docks** /ˈbuːndɒks; *NAmE* -dɑːks/ (*also* **boon·ies**) *noun* [pl.] (*NAmE, informal, disapproving*) an area far away from cities or towns

**boon·dog·gle** /ˈbuːndɒɡl; *NAmE* -dɑːɡl/ *noun* (*NAmE, informal*) a piece of work that is unnecessary and that wastes time and/or money

**boor** /bʊə(r), bɔː(r); *NAmE* bʊr/ *noun* (*old-fashioned*) a rude unpleasant person

**boor·ish** /ˈbʊərɪʃ, ˈbɔːr-; *NAmE* ˈbʊr-/ *adj.* (of people and their behaviour) very unpleasant and rude

**boost** ⁊+ B2 /buːst/ *verb, noun*
■ *verb* **1** ⁊+ B2 **~sth** to make sth increase, or become better or more successful: *to boost exports/profits* ◇ *The movie helped boost her screen career.* ◇ **to boost sb's confidence/morale** ◇ *Getting that job did a lot to boost his ego* (= make him feel more confident). **2** **~sth** (*NAmE, informal, becoming old-fashioned*) to steal sth
■ *noun* [usually sing.] **1** ⁊+ B2 something that helps or encourages sb/sth: *a great/tremendous/welcome boost* ◇ *The tax cuts will give a much needed boost to the economy.* ◇ *Winning the competition was a wonderful boost for her morale.* **2** ⁊+ B2 an increase in sth: *a boost in car sales* **3** an increase in power in an engine or a piece of electrical equipment **4** (*especially NAmE*) an act of pushing sb up from behind: *He gave her a boost over the fence.*

**boost·er** /ˈbuːstə(r)/ *noun* **1** (*also* **booster rocket**) a ROCKET that gives a SPACECRAFT extra power when it leaves the earth, or that makes a MISSILE go further **2** a device that gives extra power to a piece of electrical equipment **3** an extra small amount of a VACCINE that is given to increase the effect of one given earlier, for example to protect you from a disease for longer: *a tetanus booster* **4** a thing that helps, encourages or improves sb/sth: *a morale/confidence booster* **5** (*especially NAmE*) a person who gives their support to sb/sth, especially in politics: *a meeting of Republican boosters*

**ˈbooster seat** *noun* a seat that you put on a car seat, or on a chair at a table, so that a small child can sit higher

**boot** 🔊 A1 /buːt/ *noun, verb*
■ *noun* **1** ⁊ A1 a strong shoe that covers the foot and ankle and often the lower part of the leg: (*BrE*) *walking boots* ◇ (*NAmE*) *hiking boots* ◇ *a pair of black leather boots* ⊃ see also COWBOY BOOT, FOOTBALL BOOT, WELLINGTON **2** (*BrE*) (*NAmE* **trunk**) the space at the back of a car that you put bags, cases, etc. in: *I'll put the luggage in the boot.* ⊃ see also CAR BOOT SALE **3** [usually sing.] (*informal*) a quick hard kick: *He gave the ball a tremendous boot.* **4** (*NAmE*) = DEN-VER BOOT
IDM **be given the ˈboot** | **get the ˈboot** (*informal*) to be told that you must leave your job or that a relationship you are having with sb is over · **the ˈboot is on the other ˈfoot** (*BrE*) (*NAmE* **the ˈshoe is on the other ˈfoot**) used to say that a situation has changed so that sb now has power or authority over the person who used to have power or authority over them · **put/stick the ˈboot in** (*BrE, informal*) **1** to kick sb very hard, especially when they are on the ground **2** to attack sb by criticizing them when they are in a difficult situation · **to ˈboot** (*old-fashioned or humorous*) used to add a comment to sth that has just been said: *He was a vegetarian, and a fussy one to boot.* ⊃ more at BIG *adj.*, FILL *v.*, LICK *v.*, SHAKE *v.*, TOUGH *adj.*
■ *verb* **1** [T] **~sth + adv./prep.** to kick sb/sth hard with your foot: *He booted the ball clear of the goal.* **2** [I, T] **~(sth) (up)** (*computing*) to prepare a computer for use by loading its OPERATING SYSTEM; to be prepared in this way **3** [T] **be/get booted** (*NAmE, informal*) if you or your car is **booted**, a piece of equipment is fixed to the car's wheel so that you cannot drive it away, usually because the car is illegally parked ⊃ see also CLAMP *verb*
PHRV **ˌboot sb**↔**ˈout (of sth)** (*informal*) to force sb to leave a place or job SYN throw out

**ˈboot camp** *noun* **1** a training camp for new members of the armed forces, where they have to work hard **2** a type of prison for young criminals where there is strict discipline **3** a short course of very hard physical training: *I joined a boot camp to get fit.* ◇ (*figurative*) *You can cram for the exam at a one-week boot camp.*

**bootee** (also **bootie**) /ˈbuːtiː; BrE also buːˈtiː/ noun **1** a baby's sock, worn instead of shoes: *a pair of bootees* **2** a woman's short boot

**booth** /buːð; NAmE buːθ/ noun **1** a small place with walls or sides where you can do sth privately, for example make a phone call or vote: *a phone booth* ◇ *a polling/voting booth* ◇ *an information/a ticket booth* ⊃ see also PHOTO BOOTH, TOLLBOOTH **2** a small tent or temporary structure at a market, an exhibition or a FAIRGROUND, where you can buy things, get information or watch sth **3** a place to sit in a restaurant which consists of two long seats with a table between them **4** (NAmE) a place in a sports ground, theatre, etc. where the people who introduce or describe an event for radio or television sit: *the broadcast booth* ⊃ compare COMMENTARY BOX

ˈ**booth capturing** noun [U] (*IndE*) a practice carried out by members of a political party during an election, that involves staying in a POLLING BOOTH for long periods of time, stopping people entering who are registered to vote, and voting in their place in order to give the party an unfair advantage

**bootie** = BOOTEE

**boot·lace** /ˈbuːtleɪs/ noun [usually pl.] a long thin piece of leather or string used to fasten boots or shoes

**boot·leg** /ˈbuːtleg/ adj., verb
■ adj. [only before noun] made and sold illegally: *a bootleg CD* (= for example, one recorded illegally at a concert) ⊃ see also PIRATE ▶ **boot·leg** noun: *a bootleg of the concert*
■ verb (-gg-) ~ sth to make or sell goods, especially alcohol, illegally ▶ **boot·leg·ger** noun **boot·leg·ging** noun [U]

**boot·lick·er** /ˈbuːtlɪkə(r)/ noun (*informal, disapproving*) a person who is too friendly to sb in authority and is always ready to do what they want ▶ **boot·lick·ing** noun [U]

ˈ**boot sale** noun (BrE) = CAR BOOT SALE

**boot·strap** /ˈbuːtstræp/ noun, verb
■ noun **1** (often used in compounds) an approach to creating sth that uses the minimum amount of resources possible: *In classic bootstrap fashion, Fred invested his personal savings and convinced friends to work for him for free.* **2** (on a computer) the process of loading a program, usually an operating system, by first loading a smaller program **3** a piece of cloth or leather at the back of a boot that is used to help you pull it on
IDM **pull/drag yourself up by your (own)** ˈ**bootstraps** (*informal*) to improve your situation yourself, without help from other people
■ verb [T, I] (-pp-) **1** ~ (sth) to create sth using the minimum amount of resources possible: *We have bootstrapped the business using our own funds so far.* **2** ~ (sth) (on a computer) to load a program, usually an operating system, by first loading a smaller program

**booty** /ˈbuːti/ (*pl.* **-ies**) noun **1** [U] valuable things that are stolen, especially by soldiers in a time of war SYN **loot 2** [U] (*informal*) valuable things that sb wins, buys or obtains: *When we got home from our day's shopping, we laid all our booty out on the floor.* **3** [C] (*especially NAmE, informal*) the part of the body that you sit on SYN **buttocks**: *to shake your booty* (= to dance with great energy)

**boo·ty·li·cious** /ˌbuːtiˈlɪʃəs/ adj. (*especially NAmE, informal*) sexually attractive

ˈ**boo word** noun (BrE, informal) a word or an expression for sth that people dislike or think is bad: *Elitism has become a boo word in education.*

**booze** /buːz/ noun, verb
■ noun [U] (*informal*) alcoholic drink
■ verb [I] (usually used in the progressive tenses) (*informal*) to drink alcohol, especially in large quantities: *He's out boozing with his mates.*

**boozer** /ˈbuːzə(r)/ noun (*informal*) **1** (BrE) a pub **2** a person who drinks a lot of alcohol

**boozy** /ˈbuːzi/ adj. (*informal*) liking to drink a lot of alcohol; involving a lot of alcoholic drink: *one of my boozy friends* ◇ *a boozy lunch*

**bop** /bɒp; NAmE bɑːp/ noun, verb
■ noun **1** [C] (BrE, informal) a dance to pop music; a social event at which people dance to pop music **2** [U] = BEBOP
■ verb (-pp-) (*informal*) **1** [I] (BrE) to dance to pop music **2** [T] ~ sb to hit sb lightly

**bor·age** /ˈbɒrɪdʒ; NAmE ˈbɔːr-/ noun [U] a Mediterranean plant with blue flowers that are like stars in shape, and leaves covered with small hairs. Borage leaves are eaten raw as a salad vegetable.

**borax** /ˈbɔːræks/ noun [U] a white mineral, usually in powder form, used in making glass and as an ANTISEPTIC (= a substance that helps to prevent infection in wounds)

**bor·dello** /bɔːˈdeləʊ; NAmE bɔːrˈd-/ noun (*pl.* **-os**) (*especially NAmE*) = BROTHEL

**bor·der** 🅞 🅱🅑 /ˈbɔːdə(r); NAmE ˈbɔːrd-/ noun, verb
■ noun **1** 🅑 🅱🅑 the line that divides two countries or areas; the land near this line: *in the US, near the Canadian border* ◇ *to cross the border* ◇ ~ **between A and B** *a national park on the border between Kenya and Tanzania* ◇ (*figurative*) *It is difficult to define the border between love and friendship.* ◇ ~ **with sth** *Denmark's border with Germany* ◇ **across/over the** ~ *They fled across the border.* ◇ **on the** ~ *The incident happened on Nevada's northern border.* ◇ *border crossings* ◇ *border patrols/security/guards* ⊃ WORDFINDER NOTE at TOURIST **2** a long narrow piece around the edge of sth such as a picture or a piece of cloth: *a pillowcase with a lace border* ⊃ picture at EDGE **3** (in a garden) a long narrow area of soil which is planted with flowers, along the edge of the grass
■ verb **1** 🅑 🅱🅒 ~ sth (of a country or an area) to share a border with another country or area: *the countries bordering the Baltic* **2** ~ sth to form a line along or around the edge of

▼ SYNONYMS

**border**
boundary • frontier

These are all words for a line that marks the edge of sth and separates it from other areas or things.

**border** the line that separates two countries or areas; the land near this line: *a national park on the border between Kenya and Tanzania*

**boundary** a line that marks the edges of an area of land and separates it from other areas: *The fence marked the boundary between my property and hers.*

**frontier** (BrE) the line that separates two countries or areas; the land near this line: *The river formed the frontier between the land of the Saxons and that of the Danes.*

**WHICH WORD?**
The point where you cross from one country to another is usually called the **border**. In British English it can also be called the **frontier**, but this is often in a context of wildness, danger and uncertainty: *The rebels control the frontier and the surrounding area.* The line on a map that shows the border of a country can be called the **boundary** but 'boundary' is not used when you cross from one country to another: *After the war the national boundaries were redrawn.* ◇ T̶h̶o̶u̶s̶a̶n̶d̶s̶ ̶o̶f̶ ̶i̶m̶m̶i̶g̶r̶a̶n̶t̶s̶ ̶c̶r̶o̶s̶s̶ ̶t̶h̶e̶ ̶b̶o̶u̶n̶d̶a̶r̶y̶ ̶e̶v̶e̶r̶y̶ ̶d̶a̶y̶. **Boundary** can also be a physical line between two places, for example between property belonging to two different people, marked by a fence or wall: *the boundary fence/wall between the properties*

**PATTERNS**
- **across/along/on/over a**/the border/boundary/frontier
- **at the** boundary/frontier
- **the** border/boundary/frontier **with a** place
- **the northern/southern/eastern/western** border/boundary/frontier
- **a national/common/disputed** border/boundary/frontier

---

Oxford Phrasal Academic Lexicon (OPAL) written and spoken word lists | Ⓦ OPAL written word list | Ⓢ OPAL spoken word list

*sth: Meadows bordered the path to the woods.* ◊ *The large garden is bordered by a stream.* **PHRV** ˈborder on sth **1** to come very close to being sth, especially a strong or unpleasant emotion or quality: *She felt an anxiety bordering on hysteria.* **2** to be next to sth: *areas bordering on the Black Sea*

**ˈBorder ˈcollie** noun a medium-sized black and white dog, often used as a SHEEPDOG

**bor·der·land** /ˈbɔːdəlænd; NAmE ˈbɔːrdərl-/ noun **1** [C] an area of land close to a border between two countries **2** [sing.] an area between two qualities, ideas or subjects that has features of both but is not clearly one or the other: *the murky borderland between history and myth*

**bor·der·line** /ˈbɔːdəlaɪn; NAmE ˈbɔːrdərl-/ adj., noun
■ *adj.* not clearly belonging to a particular condition or group; not clearly acceptable: *In borderline cases teachers will take the final decision, based on the student's previous work.* ◊ *a borderline pass/fail in an exam*
■ *noun* the division between two qualities or conditions: *This biography sometimes crosses the borderline between fact and fiction.*

**bore** /bɔː(r)/ verb, noun
■ *verb* **1** [T] to make sb feel bored, especially by talking too much: ~ **sb** *I'm not boring you, am I?* ◊ **sb with sth** *Has he been boring you with his stories about his trip?* **2** [I, T] to make a long deep hole with a tool or by digging: ~ **into/through sth** *The drill is strong enough to bore through solid rock.* ◊ ~ **sth (in/through sth)** *to bore a hole in sth* **3** [I] ~ **into sb/sth** (of eyes) to stare in a way that makes sb feel uncomfortable: *His blue eyes seemed to bore into her.* **4** *past tense of* BEAR
■ *noun* **1** [C] a person who is very boring, usually because they talk too much **2** [sing.] a situation or thing that is boring or that annoys you: *It's such a bore having to stay late this evening.* **3** [C] (*also* gauge *especially in NAmE*) the hollow inside of a tube, such as a pipe or a gun; the measurement from one side of the hole to the other: *a tube with a wide/narrow bore* ◊ *a twelve-bore shotgun* **4** [C] a strong, high wave that rushes along a river from the sea at particular times of the year **5** [C] (*also* bore·hole) a deep hole made in the ground, especially to find water or oil

**bor·eal** /ˈbɔːriəl/ adj. [only before noun] (*specialist*) describing or relating to the climate zone south of the Arctic: *the boreal forests of northern Canada*

**bored 🔑 A1** /bɔːd; NAmE bɔːrd/ adj. feeling tired and impatient because you have lost interest in sth/sb or because you have nothing to do: *There was a bored expression on her face.* ◊ ~ **with/of sb/sth** | ~ **with/of doing sth** *The children quickly got bored with staying indoors.*
◆ HOMOPHONES *at* BOARD
**IDM** bored ˈstiff/ˈsilly | bored to ˈdeath/ˈtears | bored out of your ˈmind (*informal*) extremely bored ⊃ *more at* WITLESS

**bore·dom** /ˈbɔːdəm; NAmE ˈbɔːrd-/ noun [U] the state of feeling bored; the fact of being very boring: *I started to eat too much out of sheer boredom.* ◊ *Television helps to relieve the boredom of the long winter evenings.*

**bore·hole** /ˈbɔːhəʊl; NAmE ˈbɔːrh-/ noun = BORE

**bore·well** /ˈbɔːwel; NAmE ˈbɔːrw-/ noun (*IndE*) a pipe that is put into a hole that has been BORED in the ground, and used with a PUMP in order to get water from under the ground

**bor·ing 🔑 A1** /ˈbɔːrɪŋ/ adj. not interesting; making you feel tired and impatient: *a boring man* ◊ *a boring job/book/evening* ▸ **bor·ing·ly** adv.: *boringly normal*

**born 🔑 A1** /bɔːn; NAmE bɔːrn/ verb, adj.
■ *verb* be born (used only in the passive, without by) **1 🔑** (*abbr.* **b.**) to come out of your mother's body at the beginning of your life: *I was born in 1976.* ◊ ~ **into sth** *She was born into a very musical family.* ◊ ~ **of/to sb** *He was born of/to German parents.* ◊ ~ **with sth** *She was born with a rare heart condition.* ◊ + *adj.* *Her brother was born blind* (= was blind when he was born). ◊ + *noun* *John Wayne was born Marion Michael Morrison* (= that was his name at birth). **2** (of an idea, an organization, a feeling, etc.) to start to exist: *the city where the protest movement was born* ◊ ~ **(out) of sth** *She acted with a courage born (out) of desperation.* **3** -born (in compounds) born in the order, way, place, etc. mentioned: *firstborn* ◊ *nobly born* ◊ *French-born* ⊃ *see also* NEWBORN
**IDM** be ˈborn to ˈbe/ˈdo sth to have sth as your DESTINY (= what is certain to happen to you) from birth: *He was born to be a great composer.* born and ˈbred born and having grown up in a particular place with a particular background and education: *He was born and bred in Boston.* ◊ *I'm a Londoner, born and bred.* born with a silver ˈspoon in your mouth (*saying*) having rich parents in all my born ˈdays (*old-fashioned, informal*) used when you are very surprised at sth you have never heard or seen before: *I've never heard such nonsense in all my born days.* not be born ˈyesterday (*informal*) used to say that you are not stupid enough to believe what sb is telling you: *Oh yeah? I wasn't born yesterday, you know.* there's one born every ˈminute (*saying*) used to say that sb is very stupid ⊃ *more at* KNOW v., MANNER, WAY n.
■ *adj.* [only before noun] having a natural ability or skill for a particular activity or job: *a born athlete/writer/leader* ◊ *a born loser* (= a person who always loses or is unsuccessful)

**born-aˈgain** adj. [usually before noun] having come to have a strong belief in a particular religion (especially EVANGELICAL Christianity) or idea, and wanting other people to have the same belief: *a born-again Christian* ◊ *a born-again vegetarian*

**borne** /bɔːn; NAmE bɔːrn/ **1** *past part.* of BEAR **2** -borne (in adjectives) carried by: *waterborne diseases*

**boron** /ˈbɔːrɒn; NAmE -rɑːn/ noun [U] (*symb.* **B**) a chemical element. Boron is a solid substance used in making steel ALLOYS and parts for nuclear REACTORS.

**bor·ough** /ˈbʌrə; NAmE ˈbɜːroʊ/ noun a town or part of a city that has its own local government: *the London borough of Westminster* ◊ *The Bronx is one of the five boroughs of New York.* ◊ *a borough council*

**bor·row 🔑 A2** /ˈbɒrəʊ; NAmE ˈbɔːr-/ verb **1 🔑 A2** [T] to take and use sth that belongs to sb else, and return it to them at a later time: ~ **sth** *Can I borrow your umbrella?* ◊ ~ **sth from sb/sth** *Members can borrow up to ten books from the library at any one time.* ◊ ~ **sth off sb** (*BrE, informal*) *I borrowed the tools I needed off my brother.* ⊃ compare LEND **2 🔑 A2** [T, I] to take money from a person or bank and agree to pay it back to them at a later time: ~ **sth** *How much did you have to borrow to pay for this?* ◊ ~ **sth from sb/sth** *She borrowed £2000 from her parents.* ◊ ~ **from sb/sth** *I don't like to borrow from friends.* ◊ ~ **sth off sb** (*informal*) *I had to borrow the money off a friend.* ⊃ compare LEND **3** [I, T] to take words, ideas, etc. from another language, person, etc. and use them as your own: ~ **(from sb/sth)** *The*

---

**▼ SYNONYMS**

**boring**
dull • tedious

These words all describe a subject, activity, person or place that is not interesting or exciting.

**boring** not interesting; making you feel tired and impatient: *He's such a boring man!* ◊ *She found her job very boring.*

**dull** not interesting or exciting: *Life in a small town could be deadly dull.*

**tedious** lasting or taking too long and not interesting, so that you feel bored and impatient: *The journey soon became tedious.*

**PATTERNS**
- to be boring / dull / tedious for sb
- boring / dull / tedious subjects / books
- boring / dull / tedious jobs / work / games
- a boring / dull place / man / woman / person
- deadly boring / dull

*author borrows heavily from Henry James.* ◊ ~ **sth (from sb/sth)** *Some musical terms are borrowed from Italian.* **IDM** be (living) on borrowed 'time 1 to still be alive after the time when you were expected to die 2 to be doing sth that other people are likely to soon stop you from doing

▼ **WHICH WORD?**
**borrow / lend**
• These two words are often confused. You **borrow** something from someone else, while they **lend** it to you: *Can I borrow your pen?* ◊ *Can I borrow a pen from you?* ◊ *Here, I'll lend you my pen.*

**bor·row·er** /ˈbɒrəʊə(r); NAmE ˈbɔːr-/ *noun* a person or an organization that borrows money, especially from a bank ⊃ compare LENDER

**bor·row·ing** /ˈbɒrəʊɪŋ; NAmE ˈbɔːr-/ *noun* **1** [C, U] the money that a company, an organization or a person borrows; the act of borrowing money: *an attempt to reduce bank borrowings* ◊ *High interest rates help to keep borrowing down.* **2** [C] a word, a phrase or an idea that sb has taken from another person's work or from another language and used in their own

**borscht** /bɔːʃt; NAmE bɔːrʃt/ (*BrE also* **borsch** /bɔːʃ; NAmE bɔːrʃ/) *noun* [U] a Russian or Polish soup made from BEETROOT (= a dark red root vegetable)

**bor·stal** /ˈbɔːstl; NAmE ˈbɔːrstl/ *noun* [C, U] (in the UK in the past) a type of prison for young criminals ⊃ see also YOUTH CUSTODY

**bor·zoi** /ˈbɔːzɔɪ; NAmE ˈbɔːrzɔɪ/ *noun* a large Russian dog with soft white hair

**bos·ber·aad** /ˈbɒsbərɑːt; NAmE ˈbɔːs-/ *SAfrE* [ˈbɔsbəraːt] *noun* (*SAfrE*) a meeting of business leaders, politicians, etc. at a place that is a long way from a town, in order to discuss important matters

**bosom** /ˈbʊzəm/ *noun* **1** [C] a woman's chest or breasts: *her ample bosom* ◊ *She pressed him to her bosom.* **2** [C] the part of a piece of clothing that covers a woman's bosom: *a rose pinned to her bosom* **3 the ~ of sth** [sing.] a situation in which you are with people who love and protect you: *to live in the bosom of your family*

**bosom 'friend** (*NAmE also* **bosom 'buddy**) *noun* a very close friend

**boss** ❶ **A2** /bɒs; NAmE bɔːs/ *noun, verb, adj.*
■ *noun* **1 A2** a person who is in charge of other people at work and tells them what to do: *I'll ask my boss if I can have the day off.* ◊ *I like being my own boss* (= working for myself and making my own decisions). ◊ *Who's the boss* (= who's in control) *in this house?* **2** (*informal*) a person who is in charge of a large organization: *the new boss at IBM* ◊ *Hospital bosses protested at the decision.* **IDM** see SHOW *v.*
■ *verb* ~ **sb (about/around)** to tell sb what to do in an aggressive and/or annoying way: *I'm sick of you bossing me around!*
■ *adj.* (*especially NAmE, slang*) very good

**bossa nova** /ˌbɒsə ˈnəʊvə; NAmE ˌbɔːs-/ *noun* [U, C] a style of Brazilian popular music, popular in the 1960s

**bossy** /ˈbɒsi; NAmE ˈbɔːsi/ *adj.* (*disapproving*) (**boss·ier, bossi·est**) always telling people what to do ▶ **boss·ily** /-səli/ *adv.* **bossi·ness** /-sinəs/ *noun* [U]

**Boston baked beans** /ˌbɒstən beɪkt ˈbiːnz; NAmE ˌbɔːs-/ (*also* **baked 'beans**) *noun* [pl.] (*NAmE*) small white beans baked with PORK (= meat from a pig) and brown sugar or MOLASSES (= a dark, sweet, thick liquid obtained from sugar)

**bo·sun** (*also* **bo'sun, boat·swain**) /ˈbəʊsn/ *noun* an officer on a ship whose job is to take care of the equipment and the people who work on the ship

**bot** /bɒt; NAmE bɑːt/ *noun* (*computing*) **1** a computer program that runs AUTOMATED tasks over the internet ⊃ see also CHATBOT **2** (especially in science fiction) a robot

**bo·tan·ic·al** /bəˈtænɪkl/ *adj.* connected with the science of botany

bo,tanical 'garden (*also* **botanic garden** /bəˌtænɪk ˈɡɑːdn; NAmE ˈɡɑːrdn/) *noun* [*usually pl.*] a park where plants, trees and flowers are grown for scientific study

**bot·an·ist** /ˈbɒtənɪst; NAmE ˈbɑːt-/ *noun* a scientist who studies botany

**bot·any** /ˈbɒtəni; NAmE ˈbɑːt-/ *noun* [U] the scientific study of plants and their structure ⊃ compare BIOLOGY, ZOOLOGY

**botch** /bɒtʃ; NAmE bɑːtʃ/ *verb, noun.*
■ *verb* ~ **sth (up)** (*informal*) to do sth badly: *He completely botched up the interview.* ◊ *The work they did on the house was a botched job.*
■ *noun* (*also* **'botch-up**) (*BrE, informal*) a piece of work or a job that has been done badly: *I've made a real botch of the decorating.*

**both** ❶ **A1** /bəʊθ/ *det., pron.* **1 A1** used with plural nouns to mean 'the two' or 'the one as well as the other': *Both women were French.* ◊ *Both the women were French.* ◊ *Both of the women were French.* ◊ *I talked to the women. Both of them were French/They were both French.* ◊ *I liked them both.* ◊ *We were both tired.* ◊ *Both of us were tired.* ◊ *We have both seen the movie.* ◊ *I have two sisters. Both of them live in London/They both live in London.* ◊ *Both (my) sisters live in London.* **2 A1 both … and …** not only … but also …: *Both his mother and his father will be there.* ◊ *For this job you will need a good knowledge of both Italian and Spanish.* ⊃ LANGUAGE BANK *at* SIMILARLY

**bother** ❶ **B1** /ˈbɒðə(r); NAmE ˈbɑːð-/ *verb, noun, exclamation*
■ *verb* **1 B1** [I, T] (often used in negative sentences and questions) to spend time and/or energy doing sth: *'Shall I wait?' 'No, don't bother'.* ◊ *I don't know why I bother! Nobody ever listens!* ◊ ~ **with/about sth** *It's not worth bothering with* (= using) *an umbrella—the car's just outside.* ◊ *I don't know why you bother with that crowd* (= why you spend time with them). ◊ ~ **to do sth** *He didn't even bother to let me know he was coming.* ◊ ~ **doing sth** *Why bother asking if you're not really interested?* **2** **B1** [T] to annoy, worry or upset sb; to cause sb trouble or pain: ~ **sb** *The thing that bothers me is …* ◊ *That sprained ankle is still bothering her* (= hurting). ◊ *'I'm sorry he was so rude to you.' 'It doesn't bother me.'* ◊ ~ **sb with sth** *I don't want to bother her with my problems at the moment.* ◊ ~ **sb that … ** *Does it bother you that she earns more than you?* ◊ **it bothers sb to do sth** *It bothers me to think of her alone in that big house.* **3 B1** [T] to interrupt sb; to talk to sb when they do not want to talk to you: ~ **sb** *Stop bothering me when I'm working.* ◊ *Let me know if he bothers you again.* ◊ *Sorry to bother you, but there's a call for you on line two.*
**IDM** **be bothered (about sb/sth)** (*especially BrE, informal*) to think that sb/sth is important: *I'm not bothered about what he thinks.* ◊ *'Where shall we eat?' 'I'm not bothered.'* (= I don't mind where we go.) **can't be bothered (to do sth)** used to say that you do not want to spend time and/or energy doing sth: *I should really do some work this weekend but I can't be bothered.* ◊ *All this has happened because you couldn't be bothered to give me the message.* **not bother yourself/your head with/about sth** (*especially BrE*) to not spend time/effort on sth, because it is not important or you are not interested in it ⊃ more *at* HOT *adj.*
■ *noun* **1** [U] trouble or difficulty: *You seem to have got yourself into a spot of bother.* ◊ *I don't want to put you to any bother* (= cause you any trouble). ◊ *Don't go to the bother of tidying up on my account* (= don't make the effort to do it). ◊ *'Thanks for your help!' 'It was no bother.'* ◊ *Call them and save yourself the bother of going round.* **2 a bother** [sing.] an annoying situation, thing or person **SYN** *nuisance*: *I hope I haven't been a bother.*
■ *exclamation* (*BrE, informal*) used to express the fact that you are annoyed about sth/sb: *Bother! I've left my wallet at home.* ◊ *Oh, bother him! He's never around when you need him.*

**both·er·some** /ˈbɒðəsəm; NAmE ˈbɑːðərs-/ *adj.* (*old-fashioned*) causing trouble or difficulty **SYN** *annoying*

**bothy** /ˈbɒθi/ *NAmE* /ˈbɔːθi/ *noun* (*pl.* **-ies**) a small building in Scotland for farm workers to live in or for people to shelter in

**bot·net** /ˈbɒtnet/ *NAmE* /ˈbɑːt-/ *noun* (*computing*) a group of computers that are controlled by MALWARE (= software such as a virus that the users do not know about or want): *The internet has been flooded with botnets, unnoticed by the public.*

**Bo·tox**™ /ˈbəʊtɒks/ *NAmE* -tɑːks/ *noun* [U] a substance that makes muscles relax. It is sometimes INJECTED into the skin around sb's eyes to remove lines and make the skin look younger. ▶ **Bo·tox** *verb* ~ **sb/sth** [usually passive]: *Do you think she's been Botoxed?*

**bot·tle** ❶ A1 /ˈbɒtl/ *NAmE* /ˈbɑːtl/ *noun*, *verb*
■ *noun* **1** [C] a glass or plastic container, usually round with straight sides and a narrow neck, used especially for storing liquids: *a wine/beer/milk/water bottle* ◊ *Put the top back on the bottle.* **2** [C] (*also* **bot·tle·ful** /ˈbɒtlfʊl/ *NAmE* /ˈbɑːt-/) the amount contained in a bottle: *He drank a whole bottle of wine.* **3 the bottle** [sing.] (*informal*) alcoholic drink: *After his wife died, he really hit the bottle* (= started drinking heavily). **4** [C, usually sing.] a bottle used to give milk to a baby; the milk from such a bottle (used instead of mother's milk): *It's time for her bottle.* **5** [U] (*BrE, informal*) courage or confidence, for example to do sth that is dangerous or unpleasant SYN **nerve**: *It took a lot of bottle to do that.* IDM see GENIE

■ *verb* **1** ~ **sth** to put a liquid into a bottle: *The wines are bottled after three years.* **2** ~ **sth** to put fruit or vegetables into glass containers in order to preserve them ▶ **bot·tled** *adj.*: *bottled beer/water/pickles* ◊ *bottled gas* (= sold in metal containers for use in heating and cooking)
IDM **bottle it** (*BrE, informal*) to not do sth, or not finish sth, because you are frightened
PHRV **bottle ˈout (of sth/doing sth)** (*BrE, informal*) to not do sth that you had intended to do because you are too frightened **bottle sth↔ˈup** to not allow other people to see that you are unhappy, angry, etc., especially when this happens over a long period of time: *Try not to bottle up your emotions.*

**ˈbottle bank** *noun* (*BrE*) a large container in a public place where people can leave their empty bottles so that the glass can be used again (= recycled); a public place with several of these containers

**bottle ˈblonde** (*also* **bottle ˈblond**) *adj.* (*disapproving*) (of hair) artificially made to look blonde ▶ **bottle ˈblonde** *noun*: *She's a bottle blonde.*

**ˈbottle-feed** *verb* [T, I] ~ **(sb)** to feed a baby with artificial milk from a bottle ⊃ compare BREASTFEED

**ˈbottle-ˈgreen** *adj.* (*especially BrE*) dark green in colour: *a bottle-green coat* ▶ **bottle ˈgreen** *noun* [U]

**bottle·neck** /ˈbɒtlnek/ *NAmE* /ˈbɑːt-/ *noun* **1** a narrow or busy section of road where the traffic often gets slower and stops **2** anything that delays development or progress, particularly in business or industry ⊃ compare LOGJAM

**ˈbottle opener** *noun* a small tool for opening bottles with metal tops, for example beer bottles

**ˈbottle party** *noun* (*BrE*) a party to which the people who have been invited are asked to bring a bottle, usually of wine

**ˈbottle store** (*also* **ˈbottle shop**) *noun* (*AustralE, NZE, SAfrE*) a shop that sells a variety of alcoholic drinks in bottles, cans, etc. to take away ⊃ compare OFF-LICENCE

**bot·tom** ❶ A2 /ˈbɒtəm/ *NAmE* /ˈbɑːt-/ *noun, adj., verb*
■ *noun*
• LOWEST PART **1** A2 [C, usually sing.] the lowest part of sth: *the bottom of the screen/stairs/hill* ◊ **at the ~ of sth** *Footnotes are given at the bottom of each page.* ◊ **at the ~** *The book I want is right at the bottom* (= of the pile). OPP **top**
• **2** A2 [C, usually sing.] the part of sth that faces downwards and is not usually seen: **on the ~ of sth** *The ingredients are listed on the bottom of the box.*
• OF CONTAINER **3** A2 [C, usually sing.] the lowest surface on the inside of a container: **at the ~ of sth** *I found some coins at the bottom of my bag.*
• OF LAKE/SEA/POOL **4** A2 [sing.] the ground below the water in a lake, the sea, a swimming pool, etc.: **on the ~ (of sth)** *He dived in and hit his head on the bottom.*
• LOWEST POSITION **5** B1 [sing.] the lowest position in a class, on a list, etc.; a person, team, etc. that is in this position: *When the list came out, my name was near the bottom.* ◊ *I was always bottom of the class in math.* ◊ **at the ~ of sth** *a battle between the teams at the bottom of the league* ◊ **at the ~** *You have to be prepared to start at the bottom and work your way up.* OPP **top**
• PART OF BODY **6** B1 [C] (*especially BrE*) the part of the body that you sit on: *We sat on our bottoms on the damp grass.* SYN **backside, behind**
• CLOTHING **7** [C, usually pl.] the lower part of a set of clothes that consists of two pieces: *a pair of pyjama/tracksuit bottoms* ◊ *a bikini bottom* ⊃ compare TOP
• END OF STH **8** [sing.] (*especially BrE*) the part of sth that is furthest from you, your house, etc.: **at the ~ of sth** *There was a stream at the bottom of the garden.*
• OF SHIP **9** [C] the lower part of a ship that is below the surface of the water SYN **hull**
• -BOTTOMED **10** (in adjectives) having the type of bottom mentioned: *a flat-bottomed boat*
IDM **at bottom** used to say what sb/sth is really like: *Their offer to help was at bottom self-centred.* **be/lie at the bottom of sth** to be the original cause of sth, especially sth unpleasant **the bottom drops/falls out (of sth)** people stop buying or using the products of a particular industry: *The bottom has fallen out of the travel market.* **bottoms ˈup!** (*informal*) used to express good wishes when drinking alcohol, or to tell sb to finish their drink **get to the bottom of sth** to find out the real cause of sth, especially sth unpleasant ⊃ more at HEAP *n.*, HEART *n.*, PILE *n.*, RACE *n.*, SCRAPE *v.*, TOP *n.*, TOUCH *v.*

■ *adj.* **1** A2 [only before noun] in the lowest, last or furthest place or position: *your bottom lip* ◊ *the bottom line/row/edge* ◊ *on the bottom left/right of the page* ◊ *in the bottom corner of the screen* ◊ *on the bottom shelf* ◊ *Their house is at the **bottom end** of Bury Road* (= the end furthest from where you enter the road).: *to go up a hill in bottom gear* ◊ *She was sitting on the bottom step.* **2** A2 the lowest or last position in a scale or competition: *the bottom end of the*

---

▼ **SYNONYMS**

**bottom**
base • foundation • foot

These are all words for the lowest part of sth.

**bottom** [usually sing.] the lowest part of sth: *Footnotes are given at the bottom of each page.* ◊ *I waited for them at the bottom of the hill.*

**base** [usually sing.] the lowest part of sth, especially the part or surface on which it rests or stands: *The lamp has a heavy base.*

**foundation** [usually pl.] a layer of stone, concrete, etc. that forms the solid underground base of a building: *to lay the foundations of the new school*

**foot** [sing.] the lowest part of sth: *At the foot of the stairs she turned to face him.*

BOTTOM OR FOOT?
• **Foot** is used to talk about a limited number of things: it is used most often with *tree, hill/mountain, steps/stairs* and *page*. **Bottom** can be used to talk about a much wider range of things, including those mentioned above for **foot**. **Foot** is generally used in more literary contexts.

PATTERNS
• **at/near/towards** the bottom/base/foot of sth
• **on** the bottom/base of sth
• (a) **firm/solid/strong** base/foundation(s)

---

æ cat | ɑː father | e bed | ɜː fur | ə about | ɪ sit | iː see | i happy | ɒ got (*BrE*) | ɔː saw | ʌ cup | ʊ put | uː too

*price range* ◊ *We came bottom with 12 points.* **IDM** see BET *v.*
■ *verb*
**PHR V** **ˌbottom ˈout** (of prices, a bad situation, etc.) to stop getting worse: *The recession is finally beginning to show signs of bottoming out.*

**ˈbottom feeder** *noun* **1** (*NAmE, informal*) a person who earns money by taking advantage of bad things that happen to other people or by using things that other people throw away **2** a fish that feeds at the bottom of a river, lake or the sea

**botˑtomˑless** /ˈbɒtəmləs; *NAmE* ˈbɑːt-/ *adj.* (*formal*) very deep; seeming to have no bottom or limit
**IDM** **a bottomless ˈpit (of sth)** a thing or situation which seems to have no limits or seems never to end: *There isn't a bottomless pit of money for public spending.* ◊ *the bottomless pit of his sorrow*

**ˌbottom ˈline** *noun* **1 the bottom line** [*sing.*] the most important thing that you have to consider or accept; the essential point in a discussion, etc: *The bottom line is that we have to make a decision today.* **2** (*business*) [C] the amount of money that is a profit or a loss after everything has been calculated: *The bottom line for 2014 was a pre-tax profit of £85 million.* ⊃ compare TOP LINE

**ˌbottom-ˈup** *adj.* (of a plan, project, etc.) starting with details and then later moving on to more general principles: *a bottom-up approach to tackling the problem* ⊃ compare TOP-DOWN

**botuˑlin** /ˈbɒtʃəlɪn; *NAmE* ˈbɑːtʃ-/ *noun* [U] the poisonous substance in the bacteria that cause BOTULISM

**botuˑlism** /ˈbɒtʃəlɪzəm; *NAmE* ˈbɑːtʃ-/ *noun* [U] a serious illness caused by bacteria in badly preserved food

**bouˑdoir** /ˈbuːdwɑː(r)/ *noun* (*old-fashioned*) a woman's small private room or bedroom

**boufˑfant** /ˈbuːfɒ̃; *NAmE* buːˈfɑːnt/ *adj.* (of a person's hair) in a style that raises it up and back from the head in a high round shape

**bouˑgainˑvilˑlea** (*also* **bouˑgainˑvilˑlaea**) /ˌbuːɡənˈvɪliə/ *noun* a tropical climbing plant with red, purple, white or pink flowers

**bough** /baʊ/ *noun* (*formal* or *literary*) a large branch of a tree

**bought** /bɔːt/ *past tense, past part.* of BUY

**bouilˑlaˑbaisse** /ˌbuːjəbeɪs; *NAmE* ˌbuːjəˈbeɪs/ *noun* [U] (*from French*) a spicy fish soup from the south of France

**bouilˑlon** /ˈbuːjɒn, ˈbuːjɒ̃; *NAmE* ˈbuːjɑːn/ *noun* [U, C] (*from French*) a liquid made by boiling meat or vegetables in water, used for making clear soups or sauces

**boulˑder** /ˈbəʊldə(r)/ *noun* a very large rock which has been shaped by water or the weather

**boulˑderˑing** /ˈbəʊldərɪŋ/ *noun* [U] the sport or activity of climbing on large rocks

**boule** (*also* **boules**) /buːl/ *noun* [U] a French game in which players take turns to roll metal balls as near as possible to a small ball

**bouleˑvard** /ˈbuːləvɑːd; *NAmE* ˈbʊləvɑːrd/ *noun* **1** a wide city street, often with trees on either side **2** (*abbr.* **Blvd.**) (*NAmE*) a wide main road (often used in the name of streets): *Sunset Boulevard*

**bounce** /baʊns/ *verb, noun*
■ *verb*
• **MOVE OFF SURFACE 1** [I, T] if sth **bounces** or you **bounce** it, it moves quickly away from a surface it has just hit or you make it do this: *The ball bounced twice before he could reach it.* ◊ **~off sth** *Short sound waves bounce off even small objects.* ◊ *The light bounced off the river and dazzled her.* ◊ **~ sth (against/on/off sth)** *She bounced the ball against the wall.*
• **MOVE UP AND DOWN 2** [T] **~ (up and down) (on sth)** (of a person) to jump up and down on sth: *She bounced up and down excitedly on the bed.* **3** [T] **~sb (up and down) (on sth)** to move a child up and down while he or she is sitting on your knee in order to entertain him or her **4** [I, T] **~(sth) (up and down)** to move up and down; to move sth up and down: *Her hair bounced as she walked.*
• **5** [I] **+ adv./prep.** to move up and down in a particular direction: *The bus bounced down the hill.*
• **MOVE WITH ENERGY 6** [I] **+ adv./prep.** (of a person) to move somewhere in a lively and cheerful way: *He bounced across the room to greet them.*
• **CHEQUE 7** [I, T] **~(sth)** (*informal*) if a CHEQUE **bounces**, or a bank **bounces** it, the bank refuses to accept it because there is not enough money in the bank account to pay it
• **IDEAS 8** [T] **~ideas (off sb)/(around)** to tell sb your ideas in order to find out what they think about them: *He bounced ideas off colleagues everywhere he went.*
• **COMPUTING 9** [I, T] **~(sth) (back)** if an email **bounces** or the system **bounces** it, it returns to the person who sent it because the system cannot deliver it
• **MAKE SB LEAVE 10** [T] **~sb (from sth)** (*especially NAmE, informal*) to force sb to leave a job, team, place, etc: *He was soon bounced from the post.*
**IDM** **be ˈbouncing off the walls** (*informal*) to be so full of energy or so excited that you cannot keep still
**PHR V** **ˌbounce ˈback** to become healthy, successful or confident again after being ill or having difficulties **SYN** recover: *He's had a lot of problems, but he always seems to bounce back pretty quickly.* **ˌbounce ˈback (from sth)** (*business*) (of prices, shares, etc.) to return to their previous high level or value after a period of difficulty: *The airline's shares have bounced back from two days of heavy losses.* **ˌbounce sb ˈinto sth** (*BrE*) to make sb do sth without giving them enough time to think about it
■ *noun*
• **MOVEMENT 1** [C] the action of bouncing: *one bounce of the ball* ◊ (*NAmE*) *a bounce* (= increase) *in popularity* **2** [U] the ability to bounce or to make sth bounce: *There's not much bounce left in these balls.* ◊ *Players complained about the uneven bounce of the tennis court.*
• **ENERGY 3** [U, C] the energy that a person has: *All her old bounce was back.* ◊ *There was a bounce to his step.*
• **OF HAIR 4** [U] the quality in a person's hair that shows that it is in good condition and means that it does not lie flat: *thin fine hair, lacking in bounce*
**IDM** **on the ˈbounce** (*BrE, informal*) one after the other, without anything else coming between: *We've won six matches on the bounce.*

**ˈbounce house** (*also* **bouncer**) (*both NAmE*) (*also* **bouncy castle** *especially in BrE*) *noun* a plastic castle or other shape that is filled with air and that children can jump and play on

**bounˑcer** /ˈbaʊnsə(r)/ *noun* **1** a person employed to stand at the entrance to a club, pub, etc. to stop people who are not wanted from going in, and to throw out people who are causing trouble inside **2** (in CRICKET) a ball thrown very fast that rises high after it hits the ground **3** (*NAmE*) = BOUNCE HOUSE

**ˈbounce rate** *noun* (*specialist*) the number of people who visit a particular website but only view one page, expressed as a percentage of all the people who visit the site

**bounˑcing** /ˈbaʊnsɪŋ/ *adj.* **~(with sth)** healthy and full of energy: *a bouncing baby boy*

**bouncy** /ˈbaʊnsi/ *adj.* (**bounˑcier**, **bounˑciˑest**) **1** that bounces well or that has the ability to make sth bounce: *a very bouncy ball* ◊ *his bouncy blond curls* **2** lively and full of energy

**ˌbouncy ˈcastle** (*especially in BrE*) (*NAmE usually* **bounce house**, **bouncer**) *noun* a plastic castle or other shape that is filled with air and that children can jump and play on

**bound** /baʊnd/ *adj., verb, noun* ⊃ see also BIND *verb*
■ *adj.* [not before noun] **1** **~ to do/be sth** certain or likely to happen, or to do or be sth: *There are bound to be changes when the new system is introduced.* ◊ *It's bound to be sunny again tomorrow.* ◊ *You've done so much work—you're bound to pass the exam.* ◊ *It was bound to happen sooner or later* (= we should have expected it). ◊ *You're bound to be nervous the first time* (= it's easy to understand). ⊃ SYNONYMS at CERTAIN **2** forced to do sth by law, duty or a particular situation: **~by sth** *We are not*

# boundary 172

bound by the decision. ◊ You are bound by the contract to pay before the end of the month. **~ (by sth) to do sth**: (formal) I am **bound to say** I disagree with you on this point. **3** (in compounds) prevented from going somewhere or from working normally by the conditions mentioned: *Strike-bound travellers face long delays.* ◊ *fogbound airports* **4** (also in compounds) travelling, or ready to travel, in a particular direction or to a particular place: *homeward bound* (= going home) ◊ *Paris-bound* ◊ *northbound/southbound/eastbound/westbound* ◊ **for …** *a plane bound for Dublin* ◊ *college-bound high school students*
- **IDM** **be bound 'up in sth** very busy with sth; very interested or involved in sth: *He's too bound up in his work to have much time for his children.* **be bound to'gether by/in sth** to be closely connected: *communities bound together by customs and traditions* **bound and de'termined** (NAmE) very determined to do sth **bound 'up with sth** closely connected with sth: *From that moment my life became inextricably bound up with hers.* **I'll be bound** (old-fashioned, BrE, informal) I feel sure ⇒ more at HONOUR n.
- **verb 1** [I] + adv./prep. to run with long steps, especially in an enthusiastic way: *The dogs bounded ahead.* **2** [T, usually passive] (formal) to form the edge or limit of an area: **be bounded by sth** *The field was bounded on the left by a wood.*
- **noun** (formal) a high or long jump ⇒ see also BOUNDS
  **IDM** see LEAP n.

**bound·ary** /ˈbaʊndri/ noun (pl. **-ies**) **1** a real or imagined line that marks the limits or edges of sth and separates it from other things or places; a dividing line: *national boundaries* ◊ (BrE) *county boundaries* ◊ *boundary changes/disputes* ◊ *The fence marks the boundary between my property and hers.* ◊ *Scientists continue to push back the boundaries of human knowledge.* ◊ *the boundary between acceptable and unacceptable behaviour* ⇒ SYNONYMS at BORDER **2** (in CRICKET) a hit of the ball that crosses the boundary of the playing area and scores extra points **IDM** see PUSH v.

**bound·en** /ˈbaʊndən/ adj.
**IDM** **a/your bounden 'duty** (old-fashioned, formal) something that you feel you must do; a responsibility which cannot be ignored

**bound·er** /ˈbaʊndə(r)/ noun (old-fashioned, informal) a man who behaves badly and cannot be trusted

**bound·less** /ˈbaʊndləs/ adj. without limits; seeming to have no end **SYN** infinite

**bounds** /baʊndz/ noun [pl.] the accepted or furthest limits of sth: *beyond/outside/within the bounds of decency* ◊ *Public spending must be kept within reasonable bounds.* ◊ *It was not beyond the bounds of possibility that they would meet again one day.* ◊ *His enthusiasm knew no bounds* (= was very great).
- **IDM** **out of 'bounds 1** (in some sports) outside the area of play which is allowed: *His shot went out of bounds.* **2** (NAmE) not reasonable or acceptable: *His demands were out of bounds.* **out of 'bounds (to/for sb)** (especially BrE) if a place is **out of bounds**, you are not allowed to go there ⇒ see also OFF-LIMITS ⇒ more at LEAP n.

**boun·teous** /ˈbaʊntiəs/ adj. (formal or literary) giving very generously

**boun·ti·ful** /ˈbaʊntɪfl/ adj. (formal or literary) **1** in large quantities; large: *a bountiful supply of food* **2** giving generously **SYN** generous: *belief in a bountiful god*

**bounty** /ˈbaʊnti/ noun (pl. **-ies**) **1** [U, C] (literary) generous actions; sth provided in large quantities **2** [C] money given as a reward: *a bounty hunter* (= sb who catches criminals or kills people for a reward)

**bou·quet** /buˈkeɪ/ noun **1** [C] a bunch of flowers arranged in an attractive way so that it can be carried in a ceremony or presented as a gift: *The little girl presented the princess with a large bouquet of flowers.* **2** [C, U] the pleasant smell of a type of food or drink, especially of wine

**bour·bon** /ˈbɜːbən; NAmE ˈbɜːrb-/ noun **1** [U, C] a type of American WHISKY made with CORN (MAIZE) and RYE **2** [C] a glass of bourbon

**bour·geois** /ˈbʊəʒwɑː, ˌbʊəˈʒwɑː; NAmE bʊrˈʒwɑː, ˈbʊrʒwɑː/ adj. **1** belonging to the middle class: *a traditional bourgeois family* ⇒ see also PETIT BOURGEOIS **2** (disapproving) interested mainly in possessions and social status and supporting traditional values: *bourgeois attitudes/tastes* ◊ *They've become very bourgeois since they got married.* **3** (politics) supporting the interests of CAPITALISM: *bourgeois ideology* ▸ **bour·geois** noun (pl. **bour·geois**)

**the bour·geoi·sie** /ðə ˌbʊəʒwɑːˈziː; NAmE ˌbʊrʒ-/ noun [sing. + sing./pl. v.] **1** the middle classes in society: *the rise of the bourgeoisie in the nineteenth century* **2** (politics) the CAPITALIST class: *the proletariat and the bourgeoisie*

**bourse** /bʊəs; NAmE bʊrs/ noun (from French) a STOCK EXCHANGE, especially the one in Paris

**bout** /baʊt/ noun **1** a short period of great activity; a short period during which there is a lot of a particular thing, usually sth unpleasant: *a drinking bout* ◊ **~ of sth/of doing sth** *the latest bout of inflation* **2 ~(of sth)** an attack or period of illness: *a severe bout of flu/coughing* ◊ *He suffered occasional bouts of depression.* ◊ **~(with sth)** (NAmE) *a bout with the flu* **3** a BOXING or WRESTLING match

**bou·tique** /buːˈtiːk/ noun, adj.
- **noun** a small shop that sells fashionable clothes or expensive gifts
- **adj.** [only before noun] (of a business) small and offering products or services of a high quality to a small number of customers: *a boutique hotel that offers an escape from the outside world* ◊ *a boutique investment bank*

**bou·ton·nière** /ˌbuːtɒnˈjeə(r); NAmE -tnˈɪr, -ˈjer/ (NAmE, from French) (BrE **but·ton·hole**) noun a flower that is worn in the BUTTONHOLE of a coat or jacket

**bo·vine** /ˈbəʊvaɪn/ adj. [usually before noun] **1** (specialist) connected with cows: *bovine diseases* **2** (disapproving) (of a person) stupid and slow

**bows**

bow — bow of a boat — take a bow

**bow¹** /baʊ/ verb, noun ⇒ see also BOW²
- **verb 1** [I] to move your head or the top half of your body forwards and downwards as a sign of respect or to say hello or goodbye: **~(to/before sb/sth)** *He bowed low to the assembled crowd.* ◊ **~down (to/before sb/sth)** *The people all bowed down before the emperor.* **2** [T] **~ your head** to move your head forwards and downwards: *She bowed her head in shame.* ◊ *They stood in silence with their heads bowed.* **3** [I, T] to bend or make sth bend: **(+ adv./prep.)** *The pines bowed in the wind.* ◊ **~sth (+ adv./prep.)** *Their backs were bowed under the weight of their packs.*
- **IDM** **bow and 'scrape** (disapproving) to be too polite to an important person in order to gain their approval
- **PHRV** **bow 'down to sb/sth** (disapproving) to allow sb/sth to tell you what to do **bow 'out (of sth)** to stop taking part in an activity, especially one in which you have been successful in the past: *She has finally decided it's time to bow out of international tennis.* **'bow to sth** to agree unwillingly to do sth because other people want you to: *They finally bowed to pressure from the public.* ◊ *She bowed to the inevitable* (= accepted a situation in which she had no choice) *and resigned.*
- **noun 1** the act of bending your head or the upper part of your body forward in order to say hello or goodbye to sb or to show respect **2** (also **bows** [pl.]) the front part of a boat or ship ⇒ compare STERN
- **IDM** **take a/your 'bow** (of a performer) to bow to the audience as they are APPLAUDING you ⇒ more at SHOT n.

# bows 173 box

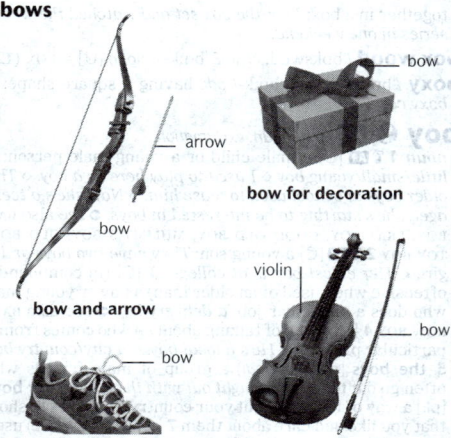

bow
bow for decoration
arrow
bow
bow and arrow
violin
bow
bow
shoelaces tied in a bow
violin bow

**bow²** /bəʊ/ noun, verb ⊃ see also BOW¹

■ noun 1 a weapon used for shooting ARROWS, consisting of a long curved piece of wood or metal with a tight string joining its ends: *He was armed with a bow and arrow.* 2 a KNOT with two LOOPS and two loose ends which is used for decoration on clothes, in hair, etc. or for tying shoes: *to tie your shoelaces in a bow* ◊ *Her hair was tied back in a neat bow.* ⊃ picture at KNOT 3 a long thin piece of wood with thin string stretched along it, used for playing musical instruments such as the VIOLIN **IDM** see STRING *n.*

■ verb [I, T] ~ (sth) to use a bow to play a musical instrument that has strings

**bowd·ler·ize** (*BrE also* **-ise**) /ˈbaʊdləraɪz/ verb ~ sth (*usually disapproving*) to remove the parts of a book, play, etc. that you think are likely to shock or offend people **ORIGIN** Named after Dr Thomas **Bowdler**, who in 1818 produced a version of Shakespeare from which he had taken out all the material which he considered not suitable for family use.

**bowel** /ˈbaʊəl/ noun 1 [C, usually pl.] the tube along which food passes after it has been through the stomach, especially the end where waste is collected before it is passed out of the body: (*medical*) *to empty/move/open your bowels* (= to pass solid waste out of the body) ◊ *bowel cancer/ cancer of the bowel* 2 **the bowels of sth** [pl.] (*literary*) the part that is deepest inside sth: *A rumble came from the bowels of the earth* (= deep underground).

**ˈbowel movement** (*also* **movement**) *noun* (*medical*) an act of emptying waste material from the bowels; the waste material that is emptied

**bower** /ˈbaʊə(r)/ noun (*literary*) a pleasant place in the shade under trees or climbing plants in a wood or garden

**bower·bird** /ˈbaʊəbɜːd; *NAmE* -ɜːrbɜːrd/ noun a bird found in Australia, the male of which decorates a place with shells, feathers, etc. to attract females

**bowl** ❶ 🄰🄰 /bəʊl/ noun, verb

■ noun
• CONTAINER 1 ❓ 🄰🄰 [C] (especially in compounds) a deep round dish with a wide open top, used especially for holding food or liquid: *a salad/fruit/sugar bowl* ◊ *a washing-up bowl* ⊃ see also BEGGING BOWL, GOLDFISH BOWL, MIXING BOWL
• AMOUNT 2 ❓ 🄰🄰 [C] (*also* **bowl·ful** /ˈbəʊlfʊl/) the amount contained in a bowl: *a bowl of soup*
• SHAPE 3 [C] the part of some objects that is like a bowl in shape: *the bowl of a spoon* ◊ *a toilet/lavatory bowl*
• THEATRE 4 [C] (*especially NAmE*) (in names) a large round theatre without a roof, used for concerts, etc. outdoors: *the Hollywood Bowl*
• BALL 5 [C] a heavy wooden ball that is used in the games of bowls and BOWLING

• GAME 6 **bowls** [U] (*NAmE also* **lawn bowling**) a game played on an area of very smooth grass, in which players take turns to roll bowls as near as possible to a small ball
• FOOTBALL GAME 7 [C] (*NAmE*) (in names) a game of AMERICAN FOOTBALL played after the main season between the best teams: *the Super Bowl*

■ verb
• ROLL BALL 1 [I, T] ~ (sth) to roll a ball in the games of bowls and BOWLING
• IN CRICKET 2 [I, T] ~ (sth) to throw a ball to the BATSMAN (= the person who hits the ball) ⊃ SYNONYMS at THROW 3 [T] ~ sb (out) to make the BATSMAN have to leave the field by throwing a ball that hits the WICKET
• MOVE QUICKLY 4 [I] + adv./prep. to move quickly in a particular direction, especially in a vehicle: *Soon we were bowling along the country roads.*
**PHR V** **ˌbowl sb ˈover 1** to run into sb and knock them down **2** to surprise or impress sb a lot

**bow legs** /ˌbəʊ ˈlegz/ noun [pl.] legs that bend out in a curve at the knees ▶ **bow-legged** /-legɪd/ adj.

**bowl·er** /ˈbəʊlə(r)/ noun 1 (in CRICKET) a player who throws the ball towards the BATSMAN 2 (*also* **bowler ˈhat**) (*both especially BrE*) (*NAmE usually* **derby**) a hard black hat with a curved BRIM and round top, worn, for example, in the past by men in business in Britain

**bowl·ing** /ˈbəʊlɪŋ/ noun [U] 1 a game in which players roll heavy balls (called bowls) along a special track towards a group of PINS (= objects that are like bottles in shape) and try to knock over as many of them as possible ⊃ compare BOWLS 2 (in CRICKET) the action of the bowler in throwing the ball towards the BATSMAN: *a brilliant display of fast bowling*

**ˈbowling alley** noun a building or part of a building where people can go bowling

**ˈbowling green** noun an area of grass that has been cut short on which the game of bowls is played

**bow·man** /ˈbəʊmən/ noun (*pl.* **-men** /-mən/) (*old-fashioned*) = ARCHER

**bow·ser** /ˈbaʊzə(r)/ noun (*especially BrE*) a container, often on wheels, used for holding liquids such as water or fuel, often because the normal supply is not available

**bow·string** /ˈbəʊstrɪŋ/ noun the string on a BOW which is pulled back to shoot ARROWS

**bow tie** /ˌbəʊ ˈtaɪ/ noun a man's tie that is tied in the shape of a BOW and that does not hang down

**box** ❶ 🄰🄰 /bɒks; *NAmE* bɑːks/ noun, verb

■ noun
• CONTAINER 1 ❓ 🄰🄰 [C] (especially in compounds) a container made of wood, thick card, metal, etc. with a flat stiff base and sides and often a LID (= cover), used especially for holding solid things: *cardboard boxes* ◊ *in a ~ She kept all the letters in a box.* ◊ *a money box* ◊ *a toolbox* ◊ *a matchbox* 2 🄰🄰 [C] ~ (of sth) a box and its contents; the things a box contains: *a box of chocolates/cereal/tissues* ◊ *People buy low-fat cookies and then eat the whole box.* ⊃ see also JUICE BOX
• SHAPE 3 ❓ 🄰🄰 [C] a square or RECTANGLE on a page or computer screen for people to put information in or containing extra information: (*BrE*) **to tick a box** ◊ (*NAmE*) **to check a box** ◊ *Type your query in the search box.* ◊ *There are over 300 special note boxes in the dictionary.* ⊃ see also DIALOG BOX
• IN THEATRE/COURT 4 [C] a small area in a theatre, court or sports stadium, separated off from where other people sit: *a box at the opera* ◊ *the jury box* ⊃ see also COMMENTARY BOX, WITNESS BOX
• SHELTER 5 [C] a small shelter used for a particular purpose: *a sentry/signal box* ◊ (*BrE, old-fashioned*) *a telephone box* ◊ *I called him from the phone box on the corner.*

---

**O** Oxford Phrasal Academic Lexicon (OPAL) written and spoken word lists | **W** OPAL written word list | **S** OPAL spoken word list

# boxcar

- **TELEVISION** 6 **the box** [sing.] (*especially BrE, old-fashioned, informal*) the television
- **ON ROAD** 7 [C] (*BrE*) = BOX JUNCTION: *Only traffic turning right may enter the box.*
- **IN SPORT** 8 [C] an area on a sports field that is marked by lines and used for a particular purpose: (*BrE*) *He was fouled in the box* (= the penalty box).
- **FOR MAIL** 9 [C] = BOX NUMBER ⇒ see also PO BOX
- **PROTECTION** 10 [C] (*BrE*) a piece of plastic that a man wears over his sex organs to protect them while he is playing a sport, especially CRICKET ⇒ compare CUP (10)
- **TREE/WOOD** 11 [C, U] a small EVERGREEN tree or bush with thick dark leaves, used especially for garden HEDGES 12 (*also* **box·wood**) [U] the hard wood of the box tree

**IDM** **give sb a box on the ˈears** (*old-fashioned*) to hit sb with your hand on the side of their head as a punishment ⇒ more at THINK *v.*, TICK *v.*, TRICK *n.*

■ *verb*
- **FIGHT** 1 [I, T] ~ **(sb)** to fight sb in the sport of BOXING
- **PUT IN CONTAINER** 2 [T] ~ **sth (up)** to put sth in a box

**IDM** **box ˈclever** (*BrE, informal*) to act in a clever way to get what you want, sometimes tricking sb **box sbˈs ˈears** (*old-fashioned*) to hit sb with your hand on the side of their head as a punishment

**PHRV** **ˌbox sb/sth ˈin** 1 to prevent sb/sth from being able to move by surrounding them with people, vehicles, etc: *Someone had parked behind us and boxed us in.* 2 [usually passive] (of a situation) to prevent sb from doing what they want by creating unnecessary problems: *She felt boxed in by all their petty rules.*

**box·car** /ˈbɒkskɑː(r); NAmE ˈbɑːk-/ *noun* (*especially NAmE*) a closed coach on a train, with a sliding door, used for carrying goods

**boxed** /bɒkst; NAmE bɑːkst/ *adj.* put and/or sold in a box: *a boxed set of original recordings*

**boxer** /ˈbɒksə(r); NAmE ˈbɑːk-/ *noun* 1 a person who boxes, especially as a job: *a professional/amateur/heavyweight boxer* 2 a large dog with smooth hair, a short flat nose and a tail that has often been cut very short

**ˈboxer shorts** (*also* **boxers**) (*NAmE also* **shorts**) *noun* [pl.] men's UNDERPANTS similar to the SHORTS worn by boxers: *a pair of boxer shorts*

**box·ful** /ˈbɒksfʊl; NAmE ˈbɑːks-/ *noun* a full box (of sth)

**box·ing** /ˈbɒksɪŋ; NAmE ˈbɑːk-/ *noun* [U] a sport in which two people fight each other with their hands, while wearing very large thick gloves (called **ˈboxing gloves**): *a boxing champion/match* ◊ *heavyweight boxing*

**ˈBoxing Day** *noun* [U, C] (*BrE*) the first day after Christmas Day. Boxing Day is an official holiday in the UK and some other countries.

**ˈbox junction** (*also* **box**) *noun* (*BrE*) a place where two roads cross or join, marked with a pattern of yellow lines to show that vehicles must not stop in that area

**ˈbox lunch** *noun* (*NAmE*) a meal of sandwiches, fruit, etc. that you take to school, work, etc. in a box ⇒ compare BAG LUNCH, PACKED LUNCH

**ˈbox number** (*also* **box**) *noun* a number used as an address, especially one given in newspaper advertisements to which replies can be sent

**ˈbox office** *noun* the place at a theatre, cinema, etc. where the tickets are sold: *The movie has been a huge box-office success* (= many people have been to see it). ⇒ WORDFINDER NOTE at THEATRE

**ˈbox room** *noun* (*BrE*) a small room in a house for storing things in

**ˈbox score** *noun* (*NAmE*) the results of a baseball game or other sporting event shown in the form of rows and columns which include details of each player's performance

**ˈbox seat** *noun*

**IDM** **in the ˈbox seat** (*AustralE, NZE, informal*) in a position in which you have an advantage

**ˈbox set** (*also* **ˈboxed set**) *noun* a set of connected items, especially recordings of TV series or films on DVD, sold together in a box: *I got the box set and watched the whole series in one weekend.*

**box·wood** /ˈbɒkswʊd; NAmE ˈbɑːks-/ *noun* [U] = BOX (12)

**boxy** /ˈbɒksi; NAmE ˈbɑːk-/ *adj.* having a square shape: *a boxy car*

**boy** 🔑 **A1** /bɔɪ/ *noun, exclamation*

■ *noun* 1 **A1** [C] a male child or a young male person: *a little/small/young boy* ◊ *I used to play here as a boy.* ◊ *The older boys at school used to tease him.* ◊ *Now she's a teenager, she's starting to be interested in boys.* ⇒ see also BAD BOY, FRAT BOY, GOOD OLD BOY, MUMMY'S BOY, OLD BOY, TOY BOY 2 **A1** [C] a young son: *They have two boys and a girl.* ◊ *Her eldest boy is at college.* 3 [C] (in compounds; offensive when used of an older man) a boy or young man who does a particular job: *a delivery boy* ⇒ see also BARROW BOY 4 [C] a way of talking about sb who comes from a particular place, etc: *He's a local boy.* ◊ *a city/country boy* 5 **the boys** [pl.] (*informal*) a group of male friends who often go out together: *a night out with the boys* 6 **our boys** [pl.] a way of talking about your country's soldiers to show that you like and care about them 7 [C] (*NAmE, taboo*) used as an offensive way of addressing a black man, especially in the past

**IDM** **the boys in ˈblue** (*informal*) the police **ˌboys will be ˈboys** (*saying*) you should not be surprised when boys or men behave in a noisy or rough way as this is part of typical male behaviour ⇒ more at JOB, MAN *n.*, WORK *n.*

■ *exclamation* (*informal, especially NAmE*) used to express feelings of surprise, pleasure, pain, etc: *Boy, it sure is hot!* ◊ *Oh boy! That's great!*

**ˈboy band** *noun* a group of attractive young men who sing pop music and dance, and who are especially popular with young people

**boy·cott** /ˈbɔɪkɒt; NAmE -kɑːt/ *verb, noun*
■ *verb* ~ **sth** to refuse to buy, use or take part in sth as a way of protesting: *We are asking people to boycott goods from companies that use child labour.*
■ *noun* an act of boycotting sb/sth: ~ **(of sth)** *a trade boycott of British goods* ◊ ~ **(on sth)** *a boycott on the use of tropical wood*

**boy·friend** 🔑 **A1** /ˈbɔɪfrend/ *noun* a man or boy that sb has a romantic or sexual relationship with: *She's got a new boyfriend.*

**boy·hood** /ˈbɔɪhʊd/ *noun* [U] (*becoming old-fashioned*) the time in a man's life when he is a boy: *boyhood days/memories/friends*

**boy·ish** /ˈbɔɪɪʃ/ *adj.* (*approving*) looking or behaving like a boy, in a way that is attractive: *boyish charm/enthusiasm* ◊ *her slim boyish figure* ▶ **ˈboy·ish·ly** *adv.*

**boyo** /ˈbɔɪəʊ/ *noun* (*WelshE, informal*) used for addressing a boy or a man

**ˈboy ˌracer** *noun* (*BrE, informal, disapproving*) a man, especially a young man, who drives his car too fast and without care

**Boy ˈScout** *noun* (*US or old-fashioned*) a boy who is a member of the SCOUTS

**ˈboy toy** *noun* (*NAmE, informal*) 1 (*BrE* **ˈtoy boy**) (*humorous*) a man in a sexual relationship who is much younger than his partner 2 (*disapproving*) a young woman who is happy to be considered only for her sexual attraction and not for her character or intelligence

**ˌboy ˈwonder** *noun* (*informal, humorous*) a boy or young man who is extremely good at sth

**bozo** /ˈbəʊzəʊ/ *noun* (*pl.* **-os**) (*especially NAmE, informal*) a stupid person

**BPhil** (*NAmE* **B.Phil**) /ˌbiː ˈfɪl/ (*NAmE also* **B.Ph.**) *noun* a university degree in philosophy that is usually a second degree (the abbreviation for 'Bachelor of Philosophy')

**bpi** *abbr.* (*computing*) bits per inch (a measure of the amount of data that can fit onto a tape or disk)

**B-picture** *noun* = B-MOVIE

**bps** *abbr.* (*computing*) bits per second (a measure of the speed at which data is sent or received)

**Bq** *abbr.* (in writing) = BECQUEREL

**Br.** *abbr.* (in writing) British

**bra** /brɑː/ *noun* (*also formal* **brassière**) a piece of women's underwear worn to cover and support the breasts

**braai** /braɪ/ *noun, verb* (*SAfrE*)
- *noun* **1** (*also* **braai-vleis**) a social event at which food is cooked outdoors over an open fire: *We're having a braai at our place next Saturday.* ◇ *A bring-and-braai* (= everyone brings their own meat) **2** the surface or piece of equipment where the fire is made
- *verb* [T, I] (**braais, braai·ing, braaied, braaied**) ~ (**sth**) to cook food over an open fire, especially as part of a social event ⊃ compare BARBECUE

**braai·vleis** /ˈbraɪfleɪs/ *noun* (*SAfrE*) **1** [C] = BRAAI **2** [U] meat that is cooked over an open fire

**brace** /breɪs/ *noun, verb*
- *noun* **1** [C] a device that holds things together or holds and supports things in position: *a neck brace* (= worn to support the neck after an injury) **2** [C] (*NAmE* **braces** [pl.]) a metal device that people, especially children, wear inside the mouth to help their teeth grow straight **3 braces** (*BrE*) (*NAmE* **sus·pend·ers**) [pl.] long narrow pieces of cloth, leather, etc. for holding trousers up. They are fastened to the top of the trousers at the front and back and passed over the shoulders: *a pair of braces* **4** (*NAmE*) (*BrE* **cal·li·per**) [C, usually pl.] a metal support for weak or injured legs **5** [C] either of the two marks, { }, used to show that the words, etc. between them are connected ⊃ compare BRACKET **6** [C] (*pl.* **brace**) a pair of birds or animals that have been killed in hunting IDM see BELT *n.*
- *verb* **1** ~ **sb/yourself (for sth)** | ~ **sb/yourself (to do sth)** to prepare sb/yourself for sth difficult or unpleasant that is going to happen: *UN troops are braced for more violence.* ◇ *They are bracing themselves for a long legal battle.* **2** ~ **sth/yourself (against sth)** to press your body or part of your body strongly against sth in order to stop yourself from falling: *They braced themselves against the wind.* **3** ~ **sth** to contract the muscles in your body or part of your body before doing sth that is physically difficult: *He stood with his legs and shoulders braced, ready to lift the weights.* **4** ~ **sth** (*specialist*) to make sth stronger or more solid by supporting it with sth: *The roof was braced by lengths of timber.*

**brace·let** /ˈbreɪslət/ *noun* a piece of jewellery worn around the WRIST or arm

**bra·chio·pod** /ˈbrækiəpɒd; *NAmE* -pɑːd/ *noun* (*biology*) a SHELLFISH that has two joined shells and uses small TENTACLES (= long thin parts) to find food

**brac·ing** /ˈbreɪsɪŋ/ *adj.* (especially of weather) making you feel full of energy because it is cold: *bracing sea air*

**bracken** /ˈbrækən/ *noun* [U] a wild plant with large leaves that grows thickly on hills and in woods and turns brown in the autumn

**bracket** /ˈbrækɪt/ *noun, verb*
- *noun* **1** (*also* ˈ**round bracket**) (*both BrE*) (*also* **par·en·thesis** *NAmE or formal*) [usually pl.] either of a pair of marks, ( ), placed around extra information in a piece of writing or part of a problem in mathematics: *Publication dates are given in brackets after each title.* ◇ *Add the numbers in brackets first.* ⊃ see also ANGLE BRACKET ⊃ compare BRACE **2** (*NAmE*) (*especially BrE* ˈ**square bracket**) [usually pl.] either of a pair of marks, [ ], placed at the beginning and end of extra information in a text, especially comments made by an editor **3 price, age, income, etc.** ~ prices, etc. within a particular range: *people in the lower income bracket* ◇ *Most of the houses are out of our price bracket.* ◇ *the 30–34 age bracket* (= people aged between 30 and 34) **4** a piece of wood, metal or plastic fixed to the wall to support a shelf, lamp, etc.
- *verb* **1** ~ **sth** to put words, information, etc. between brackets **2** ~ **A and B (together)** | ~ **A (together) with B** [often passive] to consider people or things to be similar or con-

nected in some way: *It is unfair to bracket together those who cannot work with those who will not.*

**brack·ish** /ˈbrækɪʃ/ *adj.* (of water) containing salt and tasting of it in an unpleasant way: *brackish lakes/lagoons/marshes*

**brad** /bræd/ *noun* a small thin nail with a small head and a flat tip

**brae** /breɪ/ *noun* (*ScotE*) (often in place names) a steep slope or hill

**brag** /bræg/ *verb, noun*
- *verb* [I, T] (-**gg**-) ~ **(to sb) (about/of sth)** | ~ **that …** | + speech (*disapproving*) to talk too proudly about sth you own or sth you have done SYN **boast**: *He bragged to his friends about the crime.*
- *noun* [U] a card game which is a simple form of POKER

**brag·ga·docio** /ˌbrægəˈdəʊtʃiəʊ/ *noun* (*from Italian, literary*) behaviour that seems too proud or confident

**brag·gart** /ˈbrægət; *NAmE* -gərt/ *noun* (*old-fashioned*) a person who brags

ˈ**bragging rights** *noun* [pl.] (*informal*) if you say that a person, a team, an organization, etc. has bragging rights, you mean that they have achieved a good result or are better or more successful than their competitors or opponents at that time

**Brah·man** /ˈbrɑːmən/ *noun* (*also* **Brah·min**) *noun* a Hindu who belongs to the CASTE (= division of society) that is considered the highest, originally that of priests

**Brah·min** /ˈbrɑːmɪn/ *noun* **1** = BRAHMAN **2** (*NAmE*) a person who is rich and has a lot of influence in society, especially sb from New England whose family belongs to the highest social class: *a Boston Brahmin*

**braid** /breɪd/ *noun, verb*
- *noun* **1** [U] thin coloured rope that is used to decorate furniture and military uniforms: *The general's uniform was trimmed with gold braid.* **2** (*especially NAmE*) (*BrE usually* **plait**) [C] a long piece of sth, especially hair, that is divided into three parts and TWISTED together: *She wears her hair in braids.*
- *verb* ~ **sth** (*especially NAmE*) (*BrE usually* **plait**) to TWIST three or more long pieces of hair, rope, etc. together to make one long piece: *She'd braided her hair.*

**Braille** /breɪl/ (*also* **braille**) *noun* [U] a system of printing for blind people in which the letters of the alphabet and the numbers are printed as raised DOTS (= small round marks) that can be read by touching them

**brain** 🄾 A2 /breɪn/ *noun, verb*
- *noun*
- **IN HEAD 1** 🄾 A2 [C] the organ inside the head that controls movement, thought, memory and feeling: *The human brain is a complex organ.* ◇ *brain damage* ◇ *brain cells/tissue* ◇ *a brain tumour/haemorrhage/injury* ⊃ VISUAL VOCAB page V1
- **FOOD 2 brains** [pl.] the brain of an animal, eaten as food: *sheep's brains*
- **INTELLIGENCE 3** [U, C, usually pl.] the ability to learn quickly and think about things in a logical and intelligent way: *It doesn't take much brain to work out that both stories can't be true.* ◇ *Teachers spotted that he had a good brain at an early age.* ◇ *You need brains as well as brawn* (= intelligence as well as strength) *to do this job.* ⊃ see also NO-BRAINER
- **INTELLIGENT PERSON 4** [C, usually pl.] (*informal*) an intelligent person: *one of the best scientific brains in the country* **5 the brains** [sing.] the most intelligent person in a particular group; the person who is responsible for thinking of and organizing sth: *He's always been the brains of the family.* ◇ ~ **behind sth** *The band's drummer is the brains behind their latest venture.*

IDM **have sth on the brain** (*informal*) to think about sth all the time, especially in a way that is annoying: *He's got football on the brain.* ⊃ more at BEAT *v.*, BLOW *v.*, PICK *v.*, RACK *v.*

# brainbox

- **verb** ~ sb/sth/yourself (*informal*) to kill a person or an animal by hitting them very hard on the head: *I nearly brained myself on that low beam.*

**brain·box** /ˈbreɪnbɒks; *NAmE* -bɑːks/ *noun* (*BrE, informal*) a person who is very intelligent

**brain·child** /ˈbreɪntʃaɪld/ *noun* [sing.] an idea or invention of one person or a small group of people

**ˈbrain damage** *noun* [U] permanent damage to the brain caused by illness or an accident ▶ **ˈbrain-damaged** *adj.*

**ˈbrain-dead** *adj.* **1** suffering from serious damage to the brain and needing machines to stay alive **2** (*humorous*) very stupid and boring; not intelligent

**ˈbrain death** *noun* [U] very serious damage to the brain that cannot be cured. A person who is suffering from brain death needs machines to keep them alive, even though their heart is still beating.

**ˈbrain drain** *noun* [sing.] (*informal*) the movement of highly SKILLED and qualified people to a country where they can work in better conditions and earn more money

**brain·iac** /ˈbreɪniæk/ *noun* (*NAmE, informal*) a very intelligent person ORIGIN From the name of a character in the *Superman* stories.

**brain·less** /ˈbreɪnləs/ *adj.* stupid; not able to think or talk in an intelligent way

**brain·power** /ˈbreɪnpaʊə(r)/ *noun* [U] the ability to think; intelligence

**brain·stem** /ˈbreɪnstem/ *noun* (*anatomy*) the central part of the brain, which continues downwards to form the SPINAL CORD

**brain·storm** /ˈbreɪnstɔːm; *NAmE* -stɔːrm/ *noun* [sing.] **1** (*BrE*) a sudden failure to think clearly which causes unusual behaviour: *She had a brainstorm in the exam and didn't answer a single question.* **2** (*NAmE*) = BRAINWAVE

**brain·storm·ing** /ˈbreɪnstɔːmɪŋ; *NAmE* -stɔːrm-/ *noun* [U] a way of making a group of people all think about sth at the same time, often in order to solve a problem or to create good ideas: *a brainstorming session* ⊃ WORDFINDER NOTE at MEETING ▶ **brain·storm** *verb* [T, I]: **~(sth)** *Brainstorm as many ideas as possible.*

**ˈbrain surgery** *noun* [U] IDM **it's not ˈbrain surgery** (*informal*) used to emphasize that sth is easy to do or understand SYN **rocket science**: *Look, this isn't brain surgery we're doing here.*

**ˈbrain-teaser** *noun* a problem that is difficult but fun to solve

**brain·wash** /ˈbreɪnwɒʃ; *NAmE* -wɔːʃ/ *verb* to force sb to accept your ideas or beliefs, for example by repeating the same thing many times or by preventing the person from thinking clearly: **~ sb** *The group is accused of brainwashing its young members.* ◇ **~ sb into doing sth** *Women have been brainwashed into thinking that they must go out to work in order to fulfil themselves.* ▶ **brain·wash·ing** *noun* [U]: *the victims of brainwashing and torture*

**brain·wave** /ˈbreɪnweɪv/ *noun* **1** (*NAmE also* **brain·storm**) a sudden good idea: *I've had a brainwave!* **2** an electrical signal in the brain

**brainy** /ˈbreɪni/ *adj.* (**brain·ier, braini·est**) (*informal*) very intelligent

**braise** /breɪz/ *verb* **~ sth** to cook meat or vegetables very slowly with a little liquid in a closed container: *braising steak* (= that is suitable for braising)

**brak** /bræk/ *adj.* (*SAfrE*) (of water or soil) containing salt or ALKALI

**brake** /breɪk/ *noun, verb*
- **noun 1** a device for slowing or stopping a vehicle: *to put/slam on the brakes* ◇ *the brake pedal* ⊃ *see also* AIR BRAKE, DISC BRAKE, FOOTBRAKE, HANDBRAKE **2 ~ (on sth)** a thing that stops sth or makes it difficult: *High interest rates are a brake on the economy.* IDM *see* JAM *v.*
- **verb** [I, T] to go slower or make a vehicle go slower using the brake: *The car braked and swerved.* ◇ *The truck braked to a halt.* ◇ *You don't need to brake at every bend.* ◇ *She had*

*to brake hard to avoid running into the car in front.* ◇ **~sth** *He braked the car and pulled in to the side of the road.*
⊃ WORDFINDER NOTE at CAR

▼ HOMOPHONES

**brake • break** /breɪk/
- **brake** *noun*: *The parking brake comes on by itself.*
- **brake** *verb*: *There wasn't even time for the driver to brake.*
- **break** *verb*: *Break the biscuits into small pieces.*
- **break** *noun*: *They left the office for a tea break.*

**ˈbrake fluid** *noun* [U] liquid used in brakes to make the different parts move smoothly

**ˈbrake light** (*NAmE also* **ˈstop light**) *noun* a red light on the back of a vehicle that comes on when the brakes are used

**ˈbrake pad** *noun* a thin block that presses onto the disc in a DISC BRAKE in a vehicle, in order to stop the vehicle

**bram·ble** /ˈbræmbl/ *noun* **1** (*especially BrE*) a wild bush with THORNS on which BLACKBERRIES grow **2** (*BrE*) = BLACKBERRY

**bran** /bræn/ *noun* [U] the outer layer of grain which is left when the grain is made into flour

**branch** ❶ B1 /brɑːntʃ; *NAmE* bræntʃ/ *noun, verb*
- **noun**
  - **• OF TREE 1** B1 a part of a tree that grows out from the main STEM and on which leaves, flowers and fruit grow ⊃ VISUAL VOCAB page V6 ⊃ *see also* OLIVE BRANCH
  - **• OF COMPANY 2** B1 a local office or shop belonging to a large company or organization: *The bank has branches all over the country.* ◇ *Our New York branch is dealing with the matter.*
  - **• OF GOVERNMENT 3** B1 a part of a government or other large organization that deals with one particular aspect of its work SYN **department**: *the anti-terrorist branch* ⊃ *see also* EXECUTIVE BRANCH, JUDICIAL BRANCH, LEGISLATIVE BRANCH
  - **• OF KNOWLEDGE 4** B1 a division of an area of knowledge or a group of languages: *the branch of computer science known as 'artificial intelligence'*
  - **• OF RIVER/ROAD 5** a smaller or less important part of a river, road, railway, etc. that leads away from the main part: *a branch of the Rhine* ◇ *a branch line* (= a small line off a main railway line, often in country areas)
  - **• OF FAMILY 6** a group of members of a family who all have the same ANCESTORS: *My uncle's branch of the family emigrated to Canada.* ⊃ WORDFINDER NOTE at RELATION IDM *see* ROOT *n.*
- **verb** [I] to divide into two or more parts, especially smaller or less important parts: *The accident happened where the road branches.*
  PHRV **ˌbranch ˈoff 1** (of a road or river) to be joined to another road or river but lead in a different direction: *Just after the lake, the path branches off to the right.* **2** (of a person) to leave a road or path and travel in a different direction **ˌbranch ˈout (into sth)** to start to do an activity that you have not done before, especially in your work or business SYN **diversify**: *The company branched out into selling insurance.* ◇ *I decided to branch out on my own.*

**brand** ❶ B1 /brænd/ *noun, verb*
- **noun 1** B1 a type of product, service, etc. made or offered by a particular company under a particular name: *a well-known brand of toothpaste* ◇ (*BrE*) *You pay less for the supermarket's own brand.* ◇ (*NAmE*) *You pay less for the store brand.* ◇ *luxury/premium brands* ◇ *brand loyalty* (= when customers continue buying the same brand) ◇ *brand awareness/recognition* ⊃ *see* OWN-BRAND **2** a particular type or kind of sth: *an unorthodox brand of humour* **3** a mark made with a piece of hot metal, especially on farm animals to show who owns them
- **verb** [often passive] **1** B1 to apply a brand name, image or identity to sth: **~ sth (with sth)** *Stadiums are branded with corporate logos.* ◇ **~ sth (as) sth** *Their products are branded as organic.* ◇ **~ itself (as) sth** *The city is trying to brand itself a world-class capital.* **2 ~ sb/sth (as) sth** to describe sb/sth as being sth bad or unpleasant, especially unfairly: *They were branded as liars and cheats.* ◇ *The newspapers*

branded her a hypocrite. **3** ~ **sth (with sth)** to mark an animal with a BRAND to show who owns it

**'brand ambassador** *noun* a famous person who is paid to promote the products or services of a particular company

**brand·ed** /'brændɪd/ *adj.* [only before noun] (of a product) made by a well-known company and having that company's name on it: *branded drugs/goods/products* **OPP** unbranded

**brand·ing** /'brændɪŋ/ *noun* [U] the activity of giving a particular name and image to goods and services so that people will be attracted to them and want to buy them

**bran·dish** /'brændɪʃ/ *verb* ~ **sth** to hold or wave sth, especially a weapon, in an aggressive or excited way

**'brand name** (also **'trade name**) *noun* the name given to a product by the company that produces it

**brand 'new** *adj.* completely new: *a brand new computer* ◇ *She bought her car brand new.*

**brandy** /'brændi/ *noun (pl.* **-ies)** **1** [U, C] a strong alcoholic drink made from wine **2** [C] a glass of brandy

**brash** /bræʃ/ *adj.* (*disapproving*) **1** confident in an aggressive way: *Beneath his brash exterior, he's still a little boy inside.* **2** (of things and places) too bright or too noisy in a way that is not attractive ▶ **brash·ly** *adv.* **brash·ness** *noun* [U]

**brass** /brɑːs; *NAmE* bræs/ *noun*
- METAL **1** [U] a bright yellow metal made by mixing COPPER and ZINC; objects made of brass: *solid brass fittings/door handles* ◇ *a brass plate* (= a sign outside a building giving the name and profession of the person who works there) ◇ *to clean/polish the brass*
- MUSICAL INSTRUMENTS **2** [U + sing./pl. v.] the musical instruments made of metal, such as TRUMPETS or FRENCH HORNS, that form a band or section of an ORCHESTRA; the people who play them: *music for piano, strings and brass* ⊃ compare PERCUSSION, STRINGS, WIND INSTRUMENT, WOODWIND
- FOR A HORSE **3** [C] (*BrE*) a decorated piece of brass used as an attractive object, especially a round flat piece attached to a horse's HARNESS
- IN CHURCH **4** [C] (*especially BrE*) a flat piece of brass with words or a picture on it, fixed to the floor or wall of a church in memory of sb who has died
- IMPORTANT PEOPLE **5** (*especially NAmE*) (also informal **top 'brass**) [U + sing./pl. v.] the people who are in the most important positions in a company, an organization, etc.
- MONEY **6** [U] (*BrE, old-fashioned, informal*) money ⊃ see also BRASSY

**IDM** **brass 'monkeys** | **brass 'monkey weather** (*BrE, slang*) if you say that it is **brass monkeys** or **brass monkey weather**, you mean that it is very cold weather **brass 'neck** (*BrE, informal*) a combination of confidence and lack of respect: *I didn't think she would have the brass neck to do that.* **the brass 'ring** (*NAmE, informal*) the opportunity to be successful; success that you have worked hard to get: *The girls' outdoor track team has grabbed the brass ring seven times.* **ORIGIN** From the custom of giving a free ride to any child who grabbed one of the rings hanging around the side of a merry-go-round at a fairground. **(get down to) brass 'tacks** (*informal*) (to start to consider) the basic facts or practical details of sth ⊃ more at BOLD *adj.*, MUCK *n.*

**'brass band** *noun* [C + sing./pl. v.] a group of musicians who play brass instruments

**brassed 'off** *adj.* (*BrE, slang*) annoyed **SYN** **fed up**

**bras·serie** /'bræsəri; *NAmE* ˌbræsəˈriː/ *noun* a type of restaurant, often one in a French style that is not very expensive

**bras·sica** /'bræsɪkə/ *noun* a plant of a type that includes CABBAGE, RAPE and MUSTARD

**brass·ière** /'bræzɪə(r); *NAmE* brəˈzɪr/ *noun* (*formal*) = BRA (1)

**brass 'knuckles** *noun* [pl.] (*NAmE*) = KNUCKLEDUSTER

**brassy** /'brɑːsi; *NAmE* 'bræsi/ *adj.* **1** (*sometimes disapproving*) (of music) loud and unpleasant **2** (*informal, disapproving*) (of

---

177 **brazier**

a woman) dressing in a way that makes her sexual attraction obvious, but without style: *the brassy blonde behind the bar* **3** like BRASS in colour; too yellow and bright **4** (*NAmE, informal*) saying what you think, without caring about other people

**brat** /bræt/ *noun* (*informal, disapproving*) a person, especially a child, who behaves badly: *a spoiled/spoilt brat* ▶ **bratty** /'bræti/ *adj.*: *a bratty kid*

**bra·vado** /brəˈvɑːdəʊ/ *noun* [U] a confident way of behaving that is intended to impress people, sometimes as a way of hiding a lack of confidence: *an act of sheer bravado*

**brave** **0** **B1** /breɪv/ *adj., verb, noun*

■ *adj.* (**braver, bravest**) **1** **B1** (of a person) willing to do things that are difficult, dangerous or painful; not afraid **SYN** courageous: *brave men and women* ◇ *Be brave!* ◇ *I wasn't brave enough to tell her what I thought of her.* **2** **B1** (of an action) requiring or showing courage: *a brave decision* ◇ *She died after a brave fight against cancer.* ◇ *He felt homesick, but made a brave attempt to appear cheerful.* **3** ~ **new** (*sometimes ironic*) new in an impressive way: *a vision of a brave new Britain* ▶ **brave·ly** *adv.* **bravery** *noun* [U] **SYN** courage: *an award for outstanding bravery* ◇ *acts of skill and bravery*

**IDM** **(a) brave new 'world** a situation or society that changes in a way that is meant to improve people's lives but is often a source of extra problems: *the brave new world of technology* **put on a brave face** | **put a brave 'face on sth** to pretend that you feel confident and happy when you do not

■ *verb* ~ **sb/sth** to have to deal with sth difficult or unpleasant in order to achieve sth: *He did not feel up to braving the journalists at the airport.* ◇ *Over a thousand people braved the elements* (= went outside in spite of the bad weather) *to attend the march.*

■ *noun* **1 the brave** [pl.] people who are brave: *America, the land of the free and the home of the brave* **2** [C] (*old-fashioned*) a Native American WARRIOR

**bravo** /ˌbrɑːˈvəʊ/ *exclamation* (*becoming old-fashioned*) people say **Bravo!** at the end of sth they have enjoyed, such as a play at the theatre

**bra·vura** /brəˈvjʊərə; *NAmE* -ˈvjʊrə/ *noun* [U] (*formal*) great skill and enthusiasm in doing sth artistic: *a bravura performance*

**brawl** /brɔːl/ *noun, verb*
■ *noun* a noisy and violent fight involving a group of people, usually in a public place: *a drunken brawl* ⊃ SYNONYMS at FIGHT
■ *verb* [I] to take part in a noisy and violent fight, usually in a public place: *They were arrested for brawling in the street.* ▶ **brawl·er** /'brɔːlə(r)/ *noun*

**brawn** /brɔːn/ *noun* [U] physical strength: *In this job you need brains as well as brawn.*

**brawny** /'brɔːni/ *adj.* (*informal*) having strong muscles **SYN** burly: *He was a great brawny brute of a man.*

**bray** /breɪ/ *verb* **1** [I] when a DONKEY **brays**, it makes a loud unpleasant sound **2** [I] (of a person) to talk or laugh in a loud unpleasant voice: *He brayed with laughter.* ◇ *a braying voice* ▶ **bray** *noun*

**bra·zen** /'breɪzn/ *adj., verb*
■ *adj.* **1** (*disapproving*) open and without shame, usually about sth that shocks people **SYN** shameless: *She had become brazen about the whole affair.* ◇ *his brazen admission that he was cheating* **2** made of, or the colour of, BRASS ▶ **brazen·ly** *adv.*: *She had brazenly admitted allowing him back into the house.* **brazen·ness** /-znnəs/ *noun* [U]
■ *verb*
**IDM** **brazen it 'out** to behave as if you are not ashamed or embarrassed about sth even though you should be: *Now that everyone knew the truth, the only thing to do was to brazen it out.*

**bra·zier** /'breɪziə(r); *NAmE* 'breɪʒər/ *noun* a large metal container that holds a fire and is used to keep people warm when they are outside

# brazil 178

**bra·zil** /brəˈzɪl/ (*also* **braˈzil nut**) *noun* the curved nut of a large South American tree. It has a hard shell with three sides. ⊃ VISUAL VOCAB page V8

**Bra·zil·ian** /brəˈzɪliən/ *adj., noun*
- *adj.* from or connected with Brazil
- *noun* a person from Brazil

**BRB** /ˌbiː ɑː ˈbiː; *NAmE* ɑːr/ *abbr.* (*informal*) (especially in emails, messages sent using an INSTANT MESSAGING service, etc.) be right back (when you have to leave your computer, etc. for a short time)

**breach** /briːtʃ/ *noun, verb*
- *noun* (*formal*) **1** [C, U] ~ of sth a failure to do sth that must be done by law: *a breach of contract/copyright/warranty* ◇ *They are in breach of Article 119.* ◇ (*a*) *breach of the peace* (= the crime of behaving in a noisy or violent way in public) **2** [C, U] ~ of sth an action that breaks an agreement to behave in a particular way: *a breach of confidence/trust* ◇ *a breach of security* (= when sth that is normally protected is no longer secure) **3** [C] a break in a relationship between people or countries: *a breach in Franco-German relations* **4** [C] an opening that is created during a military attack or by strong winds or seas: *They escaped through a breach in the wire fence.* IDM see STEP *v.*
- *verb* (*formal*) **1** ~ sth to not keep to an agreement or not keep a promise SYN break: *The government is accused of breaching the terms of the treaty.* **2** ~ sth to make a hole in a wall, fence, etc. so that sb/sth can go through it: *The dam had been breached.*

**bread** /bred/ *noun* [U] **1** a type of food made from flour, water and usually YEAST mixed together and baked: *a loaf/slice/piece of bread* ◇ *white/brown/wholemeal bread* ◇ *the smell of freshly baked bread* ◇ *a plate of bread and butter* ⊃ see also FRENCH BREAD, GARLIC BREAD, GINGERBREAD **2** (*old-fashioned, slang*) money
IDM **take the bread out of sb's ˈmouth** to take away sb's job so that they are no longer able to earn enough money to live ⊃ more at DAILY *adj.*, HALF *det.*, KNOW *v.*, SLICED BREAD

**bread and ˈbutter** *noun* [U] **1** slices of bread that have been spread with butter: *a piece of bread and butter* **2** (*informal*) a person or company's main source of income

**bread-and-ˈbutter** *adj.* [only before noun] basic; very important: *Employment and taxation are the bread-and-butter issues of politics.*

**bread-and-butter ˈpudding** *noun* [U, C] a DESSERT (= sweet dish) consisting of layers of bread with butter on, cooked with dried fruit in a mixture of eggs and milk

**bread·bas·ket** /ˈbredbɑːskɪt; *NAmE* -bæs-/ *noun* [sing.] the part of a country or region that produces large amounts of food, especially grain, for the rest of the country or region

**bread·board** /ˈbredbɔːd; *NAmE* -bɔːrd/ *noun* a flat board used for cutting bread on

**bread·crumbs** /ˈbredkrʌmz/ *noun* [pl.] **1** very small pieces of bread that can be used in cooking **2** (*also* **breadcrumb trail** [C]) a series of links displayed at the top of a web page, indicating the path to that page

**bread·ed** /ˈbredɪd/ *adj.* covered in breadcrumbs

**bread·fruit** /ˈbredfruːt/ *noun* [C, U] (*pl.* **breadfruit**) a large tropical fruit with a thick skin, that tastes and feels like bread when it is cooked. It grows on a tree which is called a **breadfruit tree**.

**bread·line** /ˈbredlaɪn/ *noun* **1** [sing.] the lowest level of income on which it is possible to live: *Many people without jobs are living on the breadline* (= are very poor). **2** [C] (*NAmE*) (in the past) a line of people waiting to receive free food

**bread ˈroll** *noun* = ROLL (1)

**bread·stick** /ˈbredstɪk/ *noun* **1** a long thin piece of bread, which is dry like a biscuit **2** a piece of fresh bread, baked in the shape of a small stick

**breadth** /bredθ/ *noun* [U, C] **1** the distance or measurement from one side to the other; how broad or wide sth is SYN **width**: *She estimated the breadth of the lake to be 500 metres.* ⊃ compare LENGTH **2** a wide range (of knowledge, interests, etc.): *He was surprised at her breadth of reading.* ◇ *The curriculum needs breadth and balance.* ◇ *a new political leader whose breadth of vision* (= willingness to accept new ideas) *can persuade others to change* IDM see LENGTH

**bread·win·ner** /ˈbredwɪnə(r)/ *noun* a person who supports their family with the money they earn

**break** /breɪk/ *verb, noun*
- *verb* (**broke** /brəʊk/, **broken** /ˈbrəʊkən/)
- • IN PIECES **1** [I, T] to be damaged and separated into two or more parts, as a result of force; to damage sth in this way: *All the windows broke with the force of the blast.* ◇ ~ in/into sth *She dropped the plate and it broke into pieces.* ◇ ~ sth *to break a cup/window* ◇ *She fell off a ladder and broke her arm.* ◇ ~ sth in/into sth *He broke the chocolate in two.* ⊃ HOMOPHONES at BRAKE
- • STOP WORKING **2** [I, T] to stop working as a result of being damaged; to damage sth and stop it from working: *My watch has broken.* ◇ ~ sth *I think I've broken the washing machine.*
- • SKIN **3** [T] ~ **the skin** to cut the surface of the skin and make it BLEED: *The dog bit me but didn't break the skin.*
- • LAW/PROMISE **4** [T] ~ sth to do sth that is against the law; to not keep a promise, etc: *to break the law/rules* ◇ *to break a promise* ◇ *to break an agreement/a contract/your word* ◇ *He was breaking the speed limit* (= travelling faster than the law allows).
- • STOP FOR SHORT TIME **5** [I, T] to stop doing sth for a while, especially when it is time to eat or have a drink: ~ **for sth** *Let's break for lunch.* ◇ ~ sth *Their sleep was broken by noise from the street.* ◇ (*especially BrE*) *We broke our journey in Oxford* (= stopped in Oxford on the way to the place we were going to).
- • END STH **6** [T] ~ sth to interrupt sth so that it ends suddenly: *She broke the silence by coughing.* ◇ *A tree broke his fall* (= stopped him as he was falling). ◇ *The phone rang and broke my train of thought.* **7** [T] ~ sth to make sth end by using force or strong action: *an attempt to break the year-long siege* ◇ *Management has not succeeded in breaking the strike.* **8** [T] ~ sth to end a connection with sth or a relationship with sb: *He broke all ties with his parents.*
- • ESCAPE **9** [I] ~ **free (from sb/sth)** (of a person or an object) to manage to get away from or out of a position in which they have been caught: *He finally managed to break free from his attacker.*
- • DESTROY, BE DESTROYED **10** [T, I] ~ (sb/sth) to destroy sth or make sb/sth weaker; to become weak or be destroyed: *to break sb's morale/resistance/resolve/spirit* ◇ *The government was determined to break the power of the trade unions.* ◇ *The scandal broke him* (= ruined his reputation and destroyed his confidence). ◇ *She broke under questioning* (= was no longer able to bear it) *and confessed to everything.*
- • IN TENNIS **11** [T] ~ **sb's serve** to win a game in which it is your opponent's turn to SERVE (= hit the ball across the net first)
- • MAKE SB FEEL BAD **12** [T] ~ sb to make sb feel so sad, lonely, etc. that they cannot live a normal life: *The death of his wife broke him completely.*
- • OF WEATHER **13** [I] to change suddenly, usually after a period when it has been fine
- • OF CLOUDS **14** [I] to show an opening: *The clouds broke and the sun came out.*
- • SURFACE **15** ~ **the surface** to come up through the surface of water in the sea, a pool, etc: *When his head broke the surface he took in deep gulps of air.*
- • OF DAY/DAWN/STORM **16** [I] when the day or DAWN or a storm **breaks**, it begins: *Dawn was breaking when they finally left.* ⊃ see also DAYBREAK
- • OF NEWS **17** [I] if a piece of news **breaks**, it becomes known: *There was a public outcry when the scandal broke.* ◇ *breaking news* (= news that is arriving about events that have just happened) **18** [T] ~ **it/the news to sb** to be the

**break**

first to tell sb some bad news: *Who's going to break it to her?* ◊ *I'm sorry to be the one to break the news to you.*
- **OF VOICE 19** [I] if sb's voice **breaks**, it changes its tone because of emotion: *Her voice broke as she told us the dreadful news.* **20** [I] when a boy's voice **breaks**, it becomes permanently deeper at about the age of 13 or 14
- **A RECORD 21** [T] ~ **a record** to do sth better, faster, etc. than anyone has ever done it before: *She had broken the world 100 metres record.* ◊ *The movie broke all box-office records.*
- **OF WAVES 22** [I] when waves **break**, they rise and are DISSOLVED into FOAM, usually near land: *the sound of waves breaking on the beach* ◊ *The sea was breaking over the wrecked ship.*
- **STH SECRET 23** [T] ~ **a code/cipher** to find the meaning of sth secret: *to break a code*
- **MONEY 24** [T] ~ **sth** (*especially NAmE*) to change a BANKNOTE for coins: *Can you break a twenty-dollar bill?* **HELP** Idioms containing **break** are at the entries for the nouns and adjectives in the idioms, for example **break sb's heart** is at **heart**.

**PHR V** **break aˈway (from sb/sth) 1** to escape suddenly from sb who is holding you or keeping you prisoner: *The prisoner broke away from his guards.* **2** to leave a political party, state, etc., especially to form a new one: *The people of the province wished to break away and form a new state.* ⇨ related noun BREAKAWAY **3** to move away from a crowd or group, especially in a race: *She broke away from the pack and opened up a two-second lead.*
ˌbreak ˈdown **1** (of a machine or vehicle) to stop working because of a fault: *The telephone system has broken down.* ◊ *We (= the car) broke down on the freeway.* ⇨ related noun BREAKDOWN **2** to fail: *Negotiations between the two sides have broken down.* ⇨ related noun BREAKDOWN **3** to become very bad: *Her health broke down under the pressure of work.* ⇨ see also NERVOUS BREAKDOWN **4** to lose control of your feelings and start crying: *He broke down and wept when he heard the news.* **5** to divide into parts to be analysed: *Expenditure on the project breaks down as follows: wages $10m, plant $4m, raw materials $5m.* ⇨ related noun BREAKDOWN ⇨ **LANGUAGE BANK** at ILLUSTRATE ˌbreak sth↔ˈdown **1** to make sth fall down, open, etc. by hitting it hard: *Firefighters had to break the door down to reach the people trapped inside.* **2** to destroy sth or make it disappear, especially a particular feeling or attitude that sb has: *to break down resistance/opposition* ◊ *to break down sb's reserve/shyness* ◊ *Attempts must be made to break down the barriers of fear and hostility which divide the two communities.* **3** to divide sth into parts in order to analyse it or make it easier to do: *Break your expenditure down into bills, food and other.* ◊ *Each lesson is broken down into several units.* ⇨ related noun BREAKDOWN **4** to make a substance separate into parts or change into a different form in a chemical process: *Sugar and starch are broken down in the stomach.* ⇨ related noun BREAKDOWN
ˈbreak for sth to suddenly run towards sth when you are trying to escape: *She had to hold him back as he tried to break for the door.*
ˌbreak ˈin to enter a building by force: *Burglars had broken in while we were away.* ⇨ related noun BREAK-IN
ˌbreak sb/sth ˈin **1** to train sb/sth in sth new that they must do: *to break in new recruits* ◊ *The young horse was not yet broken in (= trained to carry a rider).* **2** to wear sth, especially new shoes, until they become comfortable
ˌbreak ˈin (on sth) to interrupt sth: *She longed to break in on their conversation but didn't want to appear rude.* ◊ + *speech* '*I didn't do it!' she broke in.*
ˌbreak ˈinto sth **1** to enter a building by force; to open a car, etc. by force: *We had our car broken into last week.* ⇨ related noun BREAK-IN **2** to begin laughing, singing, etc. suddenly: *As the president's car drew up, the crowd broke into loud applause.* **3** to suddenly start running; to start running faster than before: *He broke into a run when he saw the police.* ◊ *Her horse broke into a trot.* **4** (*BrE*) to use a BANKNOTE of high value to buy sth that costs less: *I had to break into a £20 note to pay the bus fare.* **5** to open and use sth that has been kept for an emergency: *They had to break into the emergency food supplies.* **6** to be successful when you get involved in sth: *The company is having difficulty breaking into new markets.*
ˌbreak ˈoff **1** to become separated from sth as a result of force: *The back section of the plane had broken off.* **2** to stop speaking or stop doing sth for a time: *He broke off in the middle of a sentence.* ˌbreak sth↔ˈoff **1** to separate sth, using force: *She broke off a piece of chocolate and gave it to me.* **2** to end sth suddenly: *Britain threatened to break off diplomatic relations.* ◊ *They've broken off their engagement.*
ˌbreak ˈout (of war, fighting or other unpleasant events) to start suddenly: *They had escaped to America shortly before war broke out in 1939.* ◊ *Fighting had broken out between rival groups of fans.* ◊ *Fire broke out during the night.* ⇨ related noun OUTBREAK ˌbreak ˈout (of sth) to escape from a place or situation: *Several prisoners broke out of the jail.* ◊ *She needed to break out of her daily routine and do something exciting.* ⇨ related noun BREAKOUT
ˌbreak ˈout in sth to suddenly be affected by an unpleasant feeling or problem on your skin: *Her face broke out in a rash.* ◊ *He broke out in a cold sweat (= for example, through fear).*
ˌbreak ˈthrough to make new and important discoveries: *Scientists think they are beginning to break through in the fight against cancer.* ⇨ related noun BREAKTHROUGH ˌbreak ˈthrough | ˌbreak ˈthrough sth **1** to make a way through sth using force: *Demonstrators broke through the police cordon.* **2** (of the sun or moon) to appear from behind clouds: *The sun broke through at last in the afternoon.* ˌbreak ˈthrough sth to succeed in dealing with an attitude that sb has and the difficulties it creates **SYN** overcome: *He had finally managed to break through her reserve.*
ˌbreak ˈup **1** to separate into smaller pieces: *The ship broke up on the rocks.* **2** to come to an end: *Their marriage has broken up.* ⇨ related noun BREAK-UP **3** to go away in different directions: *The meeting broke up at eleven o'clock.* **4** (*especially BrE*) to begin the holidays when school closes at the end of a term: *When do you break up for Christmas?* **5** (*BrE*) to become very weak: *He was breaking up under the strain.* **6** (*NAmE*) to laugh very hard: *Woody Allen makes me just break up.* **7** when a person who is talking on a mobile phone **breaks up**, you can no longer hear them clearly because the signal has been interrupted ˌbreak sb↔ˈup (*especially NAmE*) to make sb feel upset: *The thought of hurting her just breaks me up.* ˌbreak sth↔ˈup **1** to make sth separate into smaller pieces; to divide sth into smaller parts: *The ship was broken up for scrap metal.* ◊ *Sentences can be broken up into clauses.* **2** to end a relationship, a company, etc: *They decided to break up the partnership.* ⇨ related noun BREAK-UP **3** to make people leave sth or stop doing sth, especially by using force: *Police were called in to break up the fight.* ˌbreak ˈup (with sb) to end a relationship with sb: *She's just broken up with her boyfriend.* ⇨ related noun BREAK-UP
ˈbreak with sth to end a connection with sth: *to break with tradition/old habits/the past*

---

▼ **VOCABULARY BUILDING**

### Words that mean 'break'

| | |
|---|---|
| burst | *The balloon hit a tree and burst* |
| crack | *The ice started to crack.* |
| crumble | *Crumble the cheese into a bowl.* |
| cut | *Now cut the wire in two.* |
| fracture | *He fell and fractured his hip.* |
| shatter | *The vase hit the floor and shattered.* |
| smash | *Vandals had smashed two windows.* |
| snap | *I snapped the pencil in half.* |
| split | *The bag had split open on the way home.* |
| tear | *She tore the letter into pieces.* |

All these verbs, except **cut**, can be used with or without an object.

---

**O** Oxford Phrasal Academic Lexicon (OPAL) written and spoken word lists | **W** OPAL written word list | **S** OPAL spoken word list

# breakable

## noun

- **SHORT STOP** **1** [C] a short period of time when you stop what you are doing and rest, eat, etc: *She was on her lunch break.* ◊ *a coffee/tea break* ◊ *Let's take a break.* ◊ *~ for sth a break for lunch* ◊ *She worked all day without a break.*
  ⊃ HOMOPHONES at BRAKE ⊃ SYNONYMS at REST **2** (*also* **break time**) (*both BrE*) (*NAmE* **recess**) [U] a period of time between lessons at school: *Come and see me at break.* **3** [C] a period of time when sth stops before starting again: *Employees can take a career break of up to one year.* ◊ *~ in sth a break in my daily routine* ◊ *~ from (doing) sth I need a break from caring for the children.* ◊ *the summer/ winter break*⊃ see also SPRING BREAK **4** [C] (*also* **commercial break**) [C] a short period of time when a television or radio show stops for advertisements: *More news after the break.*
- **HOLIDAY/VACATION** **5** [C] a short holiday: *We had a weekend break in New York.* ◊ *a well-earned break*⊃ WORD-FINDER NOTE at HOLIDAY
- **CHANGE IN SITUATION** **6** [sing.] the moment when a situation or a relationship that has existed for a time changes, ends or is interrupted: *I wanted to leave but was nervous about making the break.* ◊ *~ with sb/sth He needed to make a complete break with the past.* ◊ *a break with tradition* (= a change from what is accepted, in sth such as art, behaviour, etc.) ◊ *~ in sth a break in the weather* (= a change from one type of weather to a different one) ◊ *~ from sth This event represents a real break from tradition.*
- **OPENING/SPACE** **7** [C] *~ (in sth)* a space or an opening between two or more things: *We could see the moon through a break in the clouds.*
- **OPPORTUNITY** **8** [C] (*informal*) an opportunity to do sth, usually to get sth that you want or to achieve success: *I got my lucky break when I won a 'Young Journalist of the Year' competition.* ◊ *We've had a few bad breaks* (= pieces of bad luck) *along the way.*
- **OF BONE** **9** [C] a place where sth, especially a bone in your body, has broken: *The X-ray showed there was no break in his leg.*
- **IN TENNIS** **10** (*also* **break of 'serve**) [C] a win in a game in which your opponent is SERVING: *It was her second break in the set.*⊃ see also BREAK POINT (2)
- **IN BILLIARDS/SNOOKER** **11** [C] a series of successful shots by one player; the number of points scored in a series of successful shots: *He's put together a magnificent break.* ◊ *a 147 break* (= the highest possible break in SNOOKER)

IDM **break of 'day/'dawn** (*literary*) the moment in the early hours of the morning when it begins to get light **give me a 'break!** (*informal*) used when sb wants sb else to stop doing or saying sth that is annoying, or to stop saying sth that is not true **give sb a 'break** (*informal*) to give sb a chance; to not judge sb too severely: *Give the lad a break— it's only his second day on the job.* **make a 'break for sth/ for it** to run towards sth in order to try and escape: *He suddenly leapt up and made a break for the door.* ◊ *They decided to make a break for it* (= to try and escape) *that night.* ⊃ more at CLEAN *adj.*

**break·able** /ˈbreɪkəbl/ *adj.* likely to break; easily broken

**break·age** /ˈbreɪkɪdʒ/ *noun* **1** [C, usually pl.] an object that has been broken: *The last time we moved house there were very few breakages.* **2** [U, C] the act of breaking sth: *Wrap it up carefully to protect against breakage.*

**break·away** /ˈbreɪkəweɪ/ *adj., noun*
- *adj.* [only before noun] (of a political group, an organization, or a part of a country) having separated from a larger group or country: *a breakaway faction/ group/section* ◊ *a breakaway republic*
- *noun* [sing.] **1** an occasion when members of a political party or an organization leave it in order to form a new party, etc. **2** a change from an accepted style: *a breakaway from his earlier singing style*

**break·beat** /ˈbreɪkbiːt/ *noun* **1** [C] a series of drum BEATS (= hits) that are repeated to form the rhythm of a piece of dance music **2** [U] dance music, for example HIP-HOP, that uses breakbeats

---

**180**

**break·bone fever** /ˈbreɪkbəʊn ˈfiːvə(r)/ *noun* [U] = DENGUE

**break·dan·cing** /ˈbreɪkdɑːnsɪŋ; *NAmE* -dæn-/ *noun* [U] a style of dancing with ACROBATIC movements, often performed in the street ▶ **break·dance** *verb* [I] **break·dan·cer** *noun*

**break·down** /ˈbreɪkdaʊn/ *noun* **1** [C] an occasion when a vehicle or machine stops working: *a breakdown on the motorway* ◊ *a breakdown recovery service* **2** [C, U] a failure of a relationship, discussion or system: *the breakdown of a marriage* ◊ *marriage breakdown* ◊ *a breakdown in communications* ◊ *The breakdown of the negotiations was not unexpected.* ◊ *the breakdown of law and order* **3** [C, usually sing.] detailed information that you get by studying a set of figures: *First, let's look at a breakdown of the costs.* **4** [U] (*specialist*) the process of a substance breaking into the parts of which it is made: *the breakdown of proteins in the digestive system* **5** [C] = NERVOUS BREAKDOWN: *She's still recovering from her breakdown.*

**ˈbreakdown lane** (*US*) (*BrE* **hard ˈshoulder**) *noun* a narrow piece of ground with a hard surface next to a major road such as a MOTORWAY or INTERSTATE where vehicles can stop in an emergency

**ˈbreakdown truck** (*BrE*) (*also* **ˈtow truck** *NAmE, BrE*) *noun* a truck that is used for taking cars away to be repaired when they have had a breakdown

**break·er** /ˈbreɪkə(r)/ *noun* a large wave covered with white bubbles that is moving towards land ⊃ see also CIRCUIT BREAKER, ICEBREAKER, LAWBREAKER, RECORD-BREAKER, STRIKE-BREAKER, TIEBREAKER

**ˈbreak-even** *noun* [U] (*business*) a time when a company or piece of business earns just enough money to pay for its costs: *The company expects to reach break-even next year.* ⊃ see also EVEN *adj.*

**break·fast** /ˈbrekfəst/ *noun, verb*
- *noun* [C, U] the first meal of the day: *They were having breakfast when I arrived.* ◊ *She doesn't eat much breakfast.* ◊ (*especially BrE*) *a cooked breakfast* ◊ *for ~ Do you want bacon and eggs for breakfast?* ◊ *a bowl of* **breakfast cereal** ⊃ see also BED AND BREAKFAST, CONTINENTAL BREAKFAST, ENGLISH BREAKFAST, WEDDING BREAKFAST IDM see DOG *n.*
- *verb* [I] *~ (on sth)* (*formal*) to eat breakfast

**ˈbreak-in** *noun* an entry into a building using force, usually to steal sth

**ˈbreaking and ˈentering** *noun* [U] (*NAmE or old-fashioned*) the crime of entering a building illegally and using force

**ˈbreaking point** (*also* **ˈbreak point**) *noun* [U] the time when problems become so great that a person, an organization or a system can no longer deal with them: *to be at/ to reach breaking point* ◊ *to be stretched to breaking point*

**break·neck** /ˈbreɪknek/ *adj.* [only before noun] very fast and dangerous: *to drive, etc. at breakneck speed*

**break·out** /ˈbreɪkaʊt/ *noun, adj.*
- *noun* an escape from prison, usually by a group of prisoners: *a mass breakout from a top security prison*
- *adj.* [only before noun] **1** (*NAmE, informal*) suddenly extremely popular and successful; establishing sb's reputation: *a breakout hit/movie* **2** taking place separately from the main meeting with a smaller number of people: *a breakout session before the plenary* ◊ *a breakout group on ethical issues* ⊃ WORDFINDER NOTE at MEETING

**ˈbreak point** *noun* **1** **ˈbreak point** (*specialist*) the point where sth, especially a computer program, is interrupted **2** **ˈbreak ˈpoint** (*especially in tennis*) a point that the person who is SERVING must win in order not to lose a game **3** = BREAKING POINT

**break·through** /ˈbreɪkθruː/ *noun, adj.*
- *noun* an important development that may lead to an agreement or achievement: *to make/achieve a breakthrough* ◊ *a significant breakthrough in negotiations* ◊ *a major breakthrough in cancer research*

■ **adj.** [only before noun] in which a performer or type of product is successful for the first time, when it is likely to be even more successful in the future: *It was a breakthrough album for the band.* ◇ *breakthrough technology/products*

**'break time** *noun* [U] (*BrE*) = BREAK

**'break-up** *noun* **1** [C, usually sing., U] the ending of a relationship or an association: *a marital break-up* **2** [C] the division of a large organization or country into smaller parts

**break·water** /ˈbreɪkwɔːtə(r)/ *noun* a wall built out into the sea to protect the SHORE or HARBOUR from the force of the waves

**bream** /briːm/ *noun* (*pl.* **bream**) a FRESHWATER or sea fish that is used for food

**breast** 🔑 **B2** /brest/ *noun*, *verb*
■ *noun*
• PART OF BODY **1** 🔑 **B2** [C] either of the two round soft parts at the front of a woman's body that produce milk when she has had a baby: *She put the baby to her breast.* ◇ *breast cancer* ◇ *breast milk* **2** [C] the similar, smaller part on a man's body, which does not produce milk **3** [C] (*literary*) the top part of the front of your body, below your neck **SYN** **chest**: *He cradled the child against his breast.*
• CLOTHING **4** [C] the part of a piece of clothing that covers your chest: *A row of medals was pinned to the breast of his coat.*
• OF BIRD **5** [C] the front part of a bird's body: *breast feathers* ◇ *The robin has a red breast.*
• MEAT **6** [C, U] meat from the front part of the body of a bird or an animal: *chicken/turkey breasts* ◇ *breast of lamb*
• -BREASTED **7** (in adjectives) having the type of chest or breasts mentioned: *a small-breasted/full-breasted woman* ◇ *bare-breasted* ◇ *the yellow-breasted male of the species* ⊃ see also DOUBLE-BREASTED, SINGLE-BREASTED
• HEART **8** [C] (*literary*) the part of the body where the feelings and emotions are thought to be: *a troubled breast*
**IDM** see BEAT *v.*, CLEAN *adj.*
■ *verb* (*formal*) **1** ~ **sth** to reach the top of a hill, etc: *As they breasted the ridge, they saw the valley and lake before them.* **2** ~ **sth** to push through sth, touching it with your chest: *He strode into the ocean, breasting the waves.*

**breast·bone** /ˈbrestbəʊn/ *noun* the long flat bone in the chest that the seven top pairs of RIBS are connected to **SYN** **sternum** ⊃ VISUAL VOCAB page V1

**breast·feed** /ˈbrestfiːd/ *verb* [I, T] (**breast·fed, breast·fed** /-fed/) ~ (**sb**) when a woman **breastfeeds**, she feeds her baby with milk from her breasts ⊃ compare BOTTLE-FEED, NURSE

**breast·plate** /ˈbrestpleɪt/ *noun* a piece of ARMOUR worn by soldiers in the past to protect the upper front part of the body

**'breast pocket** *noun* a pocket on a shirt, or on the outside or inside of the part of a jacket that covers the chest

**'breast pump** *noun* a device for getting milk from a woman's breasts, so that her baby can be fed later from a bottle

**breast·stroke** /ˈbreststrəʊk/ *noun* [U, sing.] a style of swimming that you do on your front, moving your arms and legs away from your body and then back towards it in a circle

**breath** 🔑 **B1** /breθ/ *noun* **1** 🔑 **B1** [U] the air that you take into your lungs and send out again: *His breath smelt of garlic.* ◇ *bad breath* (= that smells bad) ◇ *She was very short of breath* (= had difficulty breathing). ◇ *Patients develop a cough and shortness of breath.* **2** 🔑 **B1** [C] an amount of air that enters the lungs at one time: *to take a deep breath* ◇ *He recited the whole poem in one breath.* **3** [sing.] ~ **of sth** (*formal*) a small amount of sth; slight evidence of sth: *a breath of suspicion/scandal* **4** [sing.] **a~of air/wind** (*literary*) a slight movement of air
**IDM** **a breath of (fresh) 'air** clean air breathed in after being indoors or in a dirty atmosphere: *We'll get a breath of fresh air at lunchtime.* **a breath of fresh 'air** a person, 

thing or place that is new and different and therefore interesting and exciting **the breath of 'life to/for sb** (*literary*) an essential part of a person's existence **get your 'breath (again/back)** (*BrE*) (*also* **catch your 'breath** *NAmE, BrE*) to breathe normally again after running or doing exercise that makes you tired **hold your 'breath 1** to stop breathing for a short time: *Hold your breath and count to ten.* **2** to be nervous while you are waiting for sth that you are anxious about: *He held his breath while the results were read out.* **3** (*informal*) people say **don't hold your breath!** to emphasize that sth will take a long time or may not happen: *She said she'd do it this week, but don't hold your breath!* **in the same 'breath** immediately after saying sth that suggests the opposite intention or meaning: *He praised my work and in the same breath told me I would have to leave.* **his/her last/dying 'breath** the last moment of a person's life **out of 'breath** having difficulty breathing after exercise: *We were out of breath after only five minutes.* **say sth, speak, mutter, etc. under your 'breath** to say sth quietly so that people cannot hear: *'Rubbish!' she muttered under her breath.* **take sb's 'breath away** to be very surprising or beautiful: *My first view of the island from the air took my breath away.* ⊃ more at BATED, CATCH *v.*, DRAW *v.*, SAVE *v.*, WASTE *v.*

**breath·able** /ˈbriːðəbl/ *adj.* (*specialist*) (of material used in making clothes) allowing air to pass through: *Breathable, waterproof clothing is essential for most outdoor sports.*

**breath·alyse** (*BrE*) (*NAmE* **breath·alyze**) /ˈbreθəlaɪz/ *verb* [usually passive] ~ **sb** to check how much alcohol a driver has drunk by making him or her breathe into a breathalyser: *Both drivers were breathalysed at the scene of the accident.*

**breath·alyser** (*BrE*) (*NAmE* **Breath·alyzer**™) /ˈbreθəlaɪzə(r)/ *noun* a device used by the police to measure the amount of alcohol in a driver's breath

**breathe** 🔑 **B1** /briːð/ *verb*
• AIR/BREATH **1** 🔑 **B1** [I, T] to take air into your lungs and send it out again through your nose or mouth: *He breathed deeply before speaking again.* ◇ *The air was so cold we could hardly breathe.* ◇ *She was beginning to breathe more easily.* ◇ ~ **sth** *Most people don't realize that they are breathing polluted air.* **2** [T] ~ **sth** (+ *adv./prep.*) to send air, smoke or a particular smell out of your mouth: *He came up close, breathing alcohol fumes all over me.*
• SAY QUIETLY **3** [T] ~ **sth** | + **speech** (*literary*) to say sth quietly: *'I'm over here,' she breathed.*
• OF WINE **4** [I] if you allow wine to **breathe**, you open the bottle and let air get in before you drink it
• OF CLOTH/SKIN **5** [I] if cloth, leather, skin, etc. can **breathe**, air can move around or through it: *Cotton clothing allows your skin to breathe.*
• FEELING/QUALITY **6** [T] ~ **sth** (*formal*) to be full of a particular feeling or quality: *Her performance breathed wit and charm.*
**IDM** **breathe (easily/freely) again** to feel calm again after sth unpleasant or frightening has ended **breathe down sb's 'neck** (*informal*) to watch closely what sb is doing in a way that makes them feel anxious and/or annoyed **breathe your 'last** (*literary*) to die **breathe (new) 'life into sth** to improve sth by introducing new ideas and making people more interested in it ⊃ more at EASY *adv.*, LIVE[1]
**PHRV** **breathe 'in** to take air into your lungs through your nose or mouth **SYN** **inhale** **breathe sth↔'in** to take air, smoke, etc. into your lungs through your nose or mouth: *His illness is a result of breathing in paint fumes over many years.* **breathe 'out** to send air out of your lungs through your nose or mouth **SYN** **exhale** **breathe sth↔'out** to send air, smoke, etc. out of your lungs through your nose or mouth: *Humans take in oxygen and breathe out carbon dioxide.*

**breather** /ˈbriːðə(r)/ *noun* (*informal*) a short break for rest or to relax: *to take/have a breather* ◇ *Tell me when you need a breather.* ◇ *a five-minute breather*

**breath·ing** 🔊 **B1** /ˈbriːðɪŋ/ noun [U] the action of taking air into the lungs and sending it out again: *Her breathing became steady and she fell asleep.* ◊ *Deep breathing exercises will help you relax.* ◊ *Heavy* (= loud) *breathing was all I could hear.*

**ˈbreathing space** (also **ˈbreathing room** especially in NAmE)) noun [C, U] a short rest in the middle of a period of mental or physical effort ⊃ SYNONYMS at REST

**breath·less** /ˈbreθləs/ adj. **1** having difficulty in breathing; making it difficult for sb to breathe: *He arrived breathless at the top of the stairs.* ◊ *They maintained a breathless* (= very fast) *pace for half an hour.* **2** (formal) experiencing, or making sb experience, a strong emotional reaction: *the breathless excitement of seeing each other again* ◊ **~ with sth** *breathless with terror* **3** (formal) with no air or wind: *the breathless heat of a summer afternoon*
▶ **breath·less·ly** adv. **breath·less·ness** noun [U]

**breath·tak·ing** /ˈbreθteɪkɪŋ/ adj. **1** very exciting or impressive (usually in a pleasant way): *a breathtaking view of the mountains* ◊ *The scene was one of breathtaking beauty.* **2** very surprising: *He spoke with breathtaking arrogance.* ▶ **breath·tak·ing·ly** adv.: *a breathtakingly expensive diamond*

**ˈbreath test** noun a test used by the police to show the amount of alcohol in a driver's breath

**breathy** /ˈbreθi/ adj. speaking or singing with a sound of breathing that can be heard clearly

**bred** /bred/ past tense, past part. of BREED

**breech** /briːtʃ/ noun the part of a gun at the back where the bullets are loaded

**ˈbreech birth** (also **ˌbreech deˈlivery**) noun a birth in which the baby's bottom or feet come out of the mother first ⊃ WORDFINDER NOTE at BIRTH

**breeches** /ˈbrɪtʃɪz/ noun [pl.] short trousers fastened just below the knee: *a pair of breeches* ◊ *riding breeches*

**breed** 🔊+ **C1** /briːd/ verb, noun
■ verb (**bred**, **bred** /bred/) **1** 🔊+ **C1** [I] (of animals) to have sex and produce young: *Many animals breed only at certain times of the year.* ⊃ see also INTERBREED **2** 🔊+ **C1** [T, I] to keep animals or plants in order to produce young ones for a particular purpose: **~ sth (for/as sth)** *The rabbits are bred for their long coats.* ⊃ see also CROSS-BREED noun, THOROUGHBRED **3** [T] **~ sth** to be the cause of sth: *Nothing breeds success like success.* **4** [T, usually passive] **~ sth into sb** to educate sb in a particular way as they are growing up: *Fear of failure was bred into him at an early age.* ⊃ see also WELL BRED
IDM **ˌbreed like ˈrabbits** (informal) to have a lot of babies in a short space of time ⊃ more at BORN v., FAMILIARITY
■ noun **1** 🔊+ **C1** a particular type of animal that has been developed by people in a certain way, especially a type of dog, cat or farm animal: *Labradors and other large breeds of dog* ◊ *a breed of cattle/sheep* ◊ *a farm that keeps rare breeds* ⊃ WORDFINDER NOTE at BIOLOGY

WORDFINDER class, classification, genus, hybrid, kingdom, order, phylum, species, taxonomy

**2** [usually sing.] a type of person: *He represents a new breed of politician.* ◊ *Players as skilful as this are a rare breed.*

**breed·er** /ˈbriːdə(r)/ noun a person who breeds animals (= keeps animals in order to produce young): *a dog/horse/cattle, etc. breeder*

**breed·ing** /ˈbriːdɪŋ/ noun [U] **1** the keeping of animals in order to breed (= produce young) from them: *the breeding of horses* **2** the producing of young animals, plants, etc: *the breeding season* **3** the family or social background that is thought to result in good manners: *a sign of good breeding*

**ˈbreeding ground** noun **1** [usually pl.] a place where wild animals go to produce their young **2** **~ (for sth)** [usually sing.] a place where sth, especially sth bad, is able to develop: *This area of the city has become a breeding ground for violent crime.*

---

**breeze** /briːz/ noun, verb
■ noun **1** [C] a light wind: *a sea breeze* ◊ *The flowers were gently swaying in the breeze.* ◊ *A light breeze was blowing.* ⊃ WORDFINDER NOTE at WIND¹ **2** [sing.] (informal) a thing that is easy to do: *It was a breeze.* IDM see SHOOT v.
■ verb [I] **+ adv./prep.** (informal) to move in a cheerful and confident way in a particular direction: *She just breezed in and asked me to help.*
PHRV **ˌbreeze ˈthrough sth** (informal) to do sth successfully and easily: *He breezed through the tests.*

**ˈbreeze block** (BrE) (NAmE **ˈcinder block**) noun a light building block, made of sand, coal ASHES and CEMENT

**breeze·way** /ˈbriːzweɪ/ noun (NAmE) an outside passage with a roof and open sides between two separate parts of a building

**breezy** /ˈbriːzi/ adj. (**breez·ier**, **breezi·est**) **1** with the wind blowing quite strongly: *It was a bright, breezy day.* ◊ *the breezy east coast* **2** having or showing a cheerful and relaxed manner: *You're very bright and breezy today!*
▶ **breez·ily** /-zɪli/ adv.: *'Hi folks,' he said breezily.* **breezi·ness** /-zɪnəs/ noun [U]

**breth·ren** /ˈbreðrən/ noun [pl.] (old-fashioned) **1** used to talk to people in church or to talk about the members of a male religious group: *Let us pray, brethren.* **2** people who are part of the same society as yourself: *We should do all we can to help our less fortunate brethren.*

**Bre·ton** /ˈbretən/ noun, adj.
■ noun **1** [U] the Celtic language of Brittany in north-west France **2** [C] a person who was born in Brittany or who lives in Brittany
■ adj. connected with Brittany or its language or culture

**brev·ity** /ˈbrevəti/ noun [U] (formal) **1** the quality of using few words when speaking or writing SYN **conciseness**: *The report is a masterpiece of brevity.* **2** the fact of lasting a short time: *the brevity of human life* ⊃ see also BRIEF noun

**brew** /bruː/ verb, noun
■ verb **1** [T, I] **~ sth** to make beer: *This beer is brewed in the Czech Republic.* **2** [T] **~ sth** to make a hot drink of tea or coffee: *freshly brewed coffee* **3** [I] (especially BrE) (of tea or coffee) to be mixed with hot water and become ready to drink: *Always let tea brew for a few minutes.* **4** [I] **~ (up)** (usually used in the progressive tenses) if sth unpleasant **is brewing** or **brewing up**, it seems likely to happen soon
PHRV **ˌbrew ˈup** | **ˌbrew sth ˈup** (BrE, informal) to make a hot drink, especially tea: *Whose turn is it to brew up?*
■ noun **1** [C, U] a type of beer, especially one made in a particular place: *I thought I'd try the local brew.* ◊ *home brew* (= beer made at home) **2** [C, usually sing.] (BrE, informal) an amount of tea made at one time: *I'll make a fresh brew.* ◊ *Let's have a brew.* **3** [C, usually sing.] a mixture of different ideas, events, etc: *The movie is a potent brew of adventure, sex and comedy.* ◊ *His music is a heady brew* (= a powerful mixture) *of heavy metal and punk.*
IDM **a ˌwitch's/an ˌevil ˈbrew** (BrE, informal) an unpleasant drink that is a mixture of different things

**brew·er** /ˈbruːə(r)/ noun a person or company that makes beer

**brew·ery** /ˈbruːəri/ noun (pl. **-ies**) a factory where beer is made; a company that makes beer

**brew·house** /ˈbruːhaʊs/ noun a factory where beer is made SYN **brewery**

**Brexit** /ˈbreksɪt, ˈbreɡzɪt/ noun [U] used to refer to the departure of the United Kingdom from the European Union

**Brexit·eer** /ˌbreksɪˈtɪə(r); NAmE -ˈtɪr/ (also **Brexit·er** /ˈbreksɪtə(r)/) noun a person supporting Brexit (= the departure of the United Kingdom from the European Union)

**briar** (also **brier**) /ˈbraɪə(r)/ noun **1** a wild bush with THORNS, especially a wild ROSE bush **2** a bush with a hard root that is used for making TOBACCO pipes; a tobacco pipe made from this root

**bribe** /braɪb/ *noun, verb*

■ *noun* a sum of money or sth valuable that you give or offer to sb to persuade them to help you, especially by doing sth dishonest: *It was alleged that he had taken bribes while in office.* ◊ *She had been offered a $50000 bribe to drop the charges.*

■ *verb* to give sb money or sth valuable in order to persuade them to help you, especially by doing sth dishonest: *~sb (with sth) They bribed the guards with cigarettes.* ◊ *~sb into doing sth She was bribed into handing over secret information.* ◊ *~sb to do sth She bribed him to sign the certificate.* ◊ *~your way … He managed to bribe his way onto the ship.*

**brib·ery** /ˈbraɪbəri/ *noun* [U] the giving or taking of bribes: *She was arrested on bribery charges.* ◊ *allegations of bribery and corruption*

**BRIC** /brɪk/ *abbr.* Brazil, Russia, India, China (used to refer to these countries as a group in the context of how fast their economies are growing): *All four BRIC countries appeared among the top ten smartphone markets.*

**bric-a-brac** /ˈbrɪk ə bræk/ *noun* [U] ORNAMENTS and other small attractive objects of little value: *market stalls selling cheap bric-a-brac*

**brick** ⓘ+ B2 /brɪk/ *noun, verb*

■ *noun* 1 ⓘ+ B2 [C, U] baked CLAY used for building walls, houses and other buildings; an individual block of this: *The school is built of brick.* ◊ *a pile of bricks* ◊ *a brick wall* ⊃ see also RED-BRICK 2 [C] a plastic or wooden block, used as a toy for young children to build things with 3 [C, usually sing.] (*BrE, old-fashioned, informal*) a friend that you can rely on when you need help

ⓘⒹⓜ **be up against a brick ˈwall** to be unable to make any progress because there is a difficulty that stops you **make bricks without ˈstraw** (*BrE*) to try to work without the necessary material, money, information, etc. ⊃ more at CAT, DROP *v.*, HEAD *n.*, TON

■ *verb*

ⓟⒽⓡⓥ **brick sth↔ˈin/ˈup** to fill an opening in a wall with bricks: *The windows had been bricked up.*

**brick·bat** /ˈbrɪkbæt/ *noun* [usually pl.] an offensive remark criticizing sb, made in public

**brick·lay·er** /ˈbrɪkleɪə(r)/ (*also BrE, informal* **brickie** /ˈbrɪki/) *noun* a person whose job is to build walls, etc. with bricks
▸ **brick·lay·ing** *noun* [U]

**bricks and ˈmortar** *noun* 1 [U, pl.] buildings, when you are thinking of them in connection with how much they cost to build or how much they are worth; housing, when it is considered as an investment: *People invested in bricks and mortar.* 2 [C] a business that operates from a shop or a building that customers visit, rather than only online: *They translated a bricks and mortar to the Web.* ◊ **bricks-and-mortar businesses** ◊ (*NAmE also*) **brick-and-mortar businesses**

**brick·work** /ˈbrɪkwɜːk; *NAmE* -wɜːrk/ *noun* 1 [U] the bricks in a wall, building, etc: *Plaster had fallen away in places, exposing the brickwork.* 2 **brick·works** [C] (*pl.* **brick·works**) (*BrE*) a place where bricks are made

**bri·dal** /ˈbraɪdl/ *adj.* [only before noun] connected with a bride or a wedding: *a bridal gown* ◊ *the bridal party* (= the bride and the bridegroom and the people helping them at their wedding, sometimes used to refer only to the bride and those helping her) ◊ *a bridal suite* (= a set of rooms in a hotel for a couple who have just got married) ◊ (*NAmE*) *a bridal shower* (= a party for a woman who will get married soon)

**bride** ⓘ B1 /braɪd/ *noun* a woman on her wedding day, or just before or just after it: *a toast to the bride and groom* ◊ *The bride wore an elegant gown of ivory satin.*
⊃ WORDFINDER NOTE at WEDDING

**bride·groom** /ˈbraɪdɡruːm/ (*also* **groom**) *noun* a man on his wedding day, or just before or just after it

**brides·maid** /ˈbraɪdzmeɪd/ *noun* a young woman or girl who helps a bride before and during the marriage ceremony ⊃ compare BEST MAN, PAGEBOY

---

183

**bridges**

bridge over a river

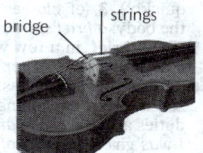

bridge of the nose

bridge of a pair of glasses

bridge of a violin

**bridge** ⓘ A2 /brɪdʒ/ *noun, verb*

■ *noun*
• OVER ROAD/RIVER 1 ⓘ A2 [C] a structure that is built over a road, railway, river, etc. so that people, vehicles, etc. can cross from one side to the other: *We crossed the bridge over the River Windrush.* ⊃ see also SUSPENSION BRIDGE, SWING BRIDGE
• CONNECTION 2 [C] a thing that provides a connection or contact between two different things: *Cultural exchanges are a way of building bridges between countries.*
• OF SHIP 3 [C, usually sing.] (*usually* **the bridge**) the part of a ship where the captain and other officers stand when they are controlling the ship
• CARD GAME 4 [U] a card game for two pairs of players who have to predict how many cards they will win. They score points if they succeed in winning that number of cards and lose points if they fail.
• OF NOSE 5 **the ~ of sb's nose** [sing.] the hard part at the top of the nose, between the eyes
• OF GLASSES 6 [C] the part of a pair of glasses that rests on your nose
• OF GUITAR/VIOLIN 7 [C] a small piece of wood on a guitar, VIOLIN, etc. over which the strings are stretched
• FALSE TEETH 8 [C] a false tooth or false teeth, held permanently in place by being fastened to natural teeth on either side ⓘⒹⓜ see BURN *v.*, CROSS *v.*, WATER *n.*

■ *verb*
• BUILD/FORM BRIDGE ~**sth** to build or form a bridge over sth: *The valley was originally bridged by the Romans.* ◊ *A plank of wood bridged the stream.*
ⓘⒹⓜ **bridge the ˈgap/ˈgulf/diˈvide (between A and B)** to reduce or get rid of the differences that exist between two things or groups of people

**ˈbridge-building** *noun* [U] activities intended to make relations between two groups, countries, etc. friendlier

**bridge·head** /ˈbrɪdʒhed/ *noun* 1 a strong position that an army has captured in enemy land, from which it can go forward or attack the enemy 2 [usually sing.] a good position from which to make progress

**ˈbridging loan** (*BrE*) (*NAmE* **ˈbridge loan**) *noun* an amount of money that a bank lends you for a short time, especially so that you can buy a new house while you are waiting to sell your old one

**bri·dle** /ˈbraɪdl/ *noun, verb*

■ *noun* a set of leather bands, attached to REINS, which is put around a horse's head and used for controlling it ⊃ WORDFINDER NOTE at HORSE

■ *verb* 1 [T] ~**sth** to put a bridle on a horse 2 [I] ~**(at sth)** (*literary*) to show that you are annoyed and/or offended at sth, especially by moving your head up and backwards in a proud way: *She bridled at the suggestion that she was lying.*

**bridle path** (BrE also **bridle-way**) /ˈbraɪdlweɪ/ noun a rough path that is suitable for people riding horses or walking, but not for cars

**Brie** /briː/ noun [U, C] a type of soft French cheese

**brief** ⓘ B2 /briːf/ adj., noun, verb
- **adj.** (**brief·er**, **brief·est**) **1** B2 lasting only a short time; short: *a brief visit/meeting/conversation* ◇ *Mozart's life was brief.* ◇ *He said nothing during the brief court appearance.* **2** B2 using few words: *a brief description/summary/overview* ◇ *Please be brief* (= say what you want to say quickly). **3** (of clothes) short and not covering much of the body: *a brief skirt* ⇒ see also BREVITY, BRIEFLY
  - IDM **in brief** in a few words, without details: *In brief, the meeting was a disaster.* ◇ *Now the rest of the news in brief.*
- **noun** ⇒ see also BRIEFS **1** (BrE) the instructions that a person is given explaining what their job is and what their duties are: *It wasn't part of his brief to speak to the press.* ◇ *I was given the brief of reorganizing the department.* ◇ **to stick to your brief** (= to only do what you are asked to do) ◇ **to prepare/produce a brief for sb 2** (BrE, law) a legal case that is given to a lawyer to argue in court; a piece of work for a BARRISTER **3** (NAmE, law) a written summary of the facts that support one side of a legal case that will be presented to a court **4** (BrE, informal) a SOLICITOR or a defence lawyer: *I want to see my brief.* **5** (especially NAmE) = BRIEFING (2): *Officials are pushing for this target to be included in the next presidential brief.*
  - IDM **hold no brief for sb/sth** (formal) to not support or be in favour of sb/sth: *I hold no brief for either side in this war.*
- **verb 1** to give sb information about sth so that they are prepared to deal with it: **~sb** *I expect to be kept fully briefed at all times.* ◇ **~sb on/about sth** *The officer briefed her on what to expect.* ⇒ compare DEBRIEF **2** **~sb (to do sth)** (BrE, law) to give a lawyer, especially a BARRISTER, the main facts of a legal case so that it can be argued in court

**brief·case** /ˈbriːfkeɪs/ noun a flat case used for carrying papers and documents ⇒ compare ATTACHÉ CASE

**brief·ing** /ˈbriːfɪŋ/ noun **1** [C] a meeting in which people are given instructions or information: *a press briefing* ⇒ compare DEBRIEFING **2** (also **brief** especially in NAmE) [C, U] the detailed instructions or information that are given at such a meeting: *Captain Trent gave his men a full briefing.* ◇ *a briefing session/paper*

**brief·ly** B1 B2 ⓢ /ˈbriːfli/ adv. **1** B2 for a short time: *He had spoken to Emma only briefly.* **2** B2 in few words: *Briefly, the argument is as follows…* ◇ *Let me tell you briefly what happened.*

**briefs** /briːfs/ noun [pl.] men's UNDERPANTS or women's KNICKERS: *a pair of briefs*

**brier** = BRIAR

**brig** /brɪɡ/ noun **1** a ship with two MASTS (= posts that support the sails) and square sails **2** (NAmE) a prison, especially one on a WARSHIP

**Brig.** abbr. (in writing) BRIGADIER

**bri·gade** /brɪˈɡeɪd/ noun **1** a large group of soldiers that forms a unit of an army **2** [usually sing.] (often disapproving) used, always with a word or phrase in front of it, to describe a group of people who share the same opinions or are similar in some other way: *the anti-smoking brigade* ⇒ see also FIRE BRIGADE IDM see HEAVY adj.

**briga·dier** /ˌbrɪɡəˈdɪə(r)/ NAmE -ˈdɪr/ noun (abbr. **Brig.**) an officer of high rank in the British army: *Brigadier Michael Swift*

**brigadier ˈgeneral** noun an officer of high rank in the US army, AIR FORCE or MARINES

**brig·and** /ˈbrɪɡənd/ noun (old-fashioned) a member of a group of criminals that steals from people, especially one that attacks travellers SYN **bandit**

**bright** ⓘ A2 /braɪt/ adj., adv., noun
- **adj.** (**bright·er**, **bright·est**) **1** A2 full of light; shining strongly: *bright light/sunshine* ◇ *a bright room* ◇ *Her eyes were bright with tears.* ◇ *a bright morning* (= with the sun shining) **2** A2 (of a colour) strong and easy to see: *I like bright colours.* ◇ *a bright yellow dress* ◇ *Jack's face turned bright red.* **3** B1 giving reason to believe that good things will happen; likely to be successful: *This young musician has a bright future.* ◇ *Prospects for the coming year look bright.* ◇ *a bright start to the week* **4** B2 intelligent; quick to learn: *the brightest pupil in the class* ◇ *Do you have any bright ideas* (= clever ideas)? ⇒ SYNONYMS at INTELLIGENT **5** cheerful and lively: *His eyes were bright and excited.* ◇ *She gave me a bright smile.* ◇ *Why are you so bright and cheerful today?* ◇ *His face was bright with excitement.*
  - ▶ **bright·ly** adv.: *a brightly lit room* ◇ *'Hi!' she called brightly.* **bright·ness** noun [U]
  - IDM **bright and ˈearly** very early in the morning: *You're up bright and early today!* **(as) bright as a ˈbutton** (BrE, informal) intelligent and quick to understand **the bright ˈlights** the excitement of city life: *Although he grew up in the country, he's always had a taste for the bright lights.* **a bright ˈspark** (BrE, informal, often ironic) a lively and intelligent person, especially sb young: *Some bright spark* (= stupid person) *left the tap running all night.* **a/the ˈbright spot** a good or pleasant part of sth that is unpleasant or bad in all other ways: *The win last week was the only bright spot in their last ten games.* **look on the ˈbright side** to be cheerful or positive about a bad situation, for example by thinking only of the advantages and not the disadvantages
- **adv.** (**bright·er**, **bright·est**) (literary) (usually with the verbs *burn* and *shine*) brightly: *The stars were shining bright.*
- **noun brights** [pl.] (NAmE) the HEADLIGHTS on a vehicle set to a position in which they are shining as brightly as possible and not directed downwards

▼ SYNONYMS

**bright**
brilliant • vivid • vibrant
These words all describe things that are shining or full of light or colours that are strong and easy to see.
**bright** full of light; shining strongly; (of colours) strong and easy to see: *a bright yellow dress*
**brilliant** very bright: *The sky was a brilliant blue.*
**vivid** (approving) (of colours) bright and strong: *His eyes were a vivid green.*
**vibrant** (approving) (of colours) bright and strong: *The room was decorated in vibrant blues and greens.*
VIVID OR VIBRANT?
- These two words are very similar, but **vivid** emphasizes how bright a colour is, while **vibrant** suggests a more lively and exciting colour or combination of colours.
PATTERNS
- bright/brilliant/vivid/vibrant **colours**
- bright/brilliant **light/sunlight/sunshine/eyes**

**bright·en** /ˈbraɪtn/ verb **1** [I, T] to become or make sth lighter or brighter in colour: *In the distance, the sky was beginning to brighten.* **~sth** *a shampoo to brighten and condition your hair* **2** [I, T] to become, feel or look happier; to make sb look happier: *Her eyes brightened.* ◇ **~up** *He brightened up at their words of encouragement.* ◇ **~sth (up)** *A smile brightened her face.* **3** [T, I] **~(sth) (up)** to become or make sth become more pleasant; to bring hope: *A personal letter will usually brighten up a person's day.* **4** [T] **~sth (up)** to make sth look more brightly coloured and attractive: *Fresh flowers will brighten up any room in the house.* **5** [I] **~(up)** (of the weather) to improve and become brighter: *According to the forecast, it should brighten up later.*

**bright-ˈeyed** (also **bright-eyed and ˈbushy-ˌtailed** informal) adj. (of a person) full of interest and enthusiasm

**bright young ˈthing** noun an enthusiastic and intelligent young person who wants to be successful in their career ORIGIN From the name used in the 1920s for rich young people whose behaviour was considered shocking.

**brill** /brɪl/ adj. (BrE, informal) very good

**bril·liant** ⓘ A2 /ˈbrɪliənt/ adj. **1** A2 extremely clever or impressive: *What a brilliant idea!* ◇ *a brilliant performance/invention* **2** (BrE, informal) very good;

excellent: 'How was it?' 'Brilliant!' ◊ Thanks. You've been brilliant (= very helpful). ⊃ SYNONYMS at GREAT **3** A2 very intelligent or showing a lot of skill: *a brilliant young scientist* ◊ *She has one of the most brilliant minds in the country.* ⊃ SYNONYMS at INTELLIGENT **4** very successful: *a brilliant career* ◊ *The play was a brilliant success.* **5** (of light or colours) very bright: *brilliant sunshine* ◊ *brilliant blue eyes* ⊃ SYNONYMS at BRIGHT ▶ **bril·liance** /-əns/ *noun* [U] **bril·liant·ly** *adv.*: *The plan worked brilliantly.* ◊ *It was brilliantly sunny.*

**brim** /brɪm/ *noun, verb*

■ *noun* **1** the top edge of a cup, bowl, glass, etc: *two wine glasses, filled to the brim* **2** the flat edge around the bottom of a hat that sticks out **3 -brimmed** (in adjectives) having the type of brim mentioned: *a wide-brimmed hat*

■ *verb* [I] (**-mm-**) to be full of sth; to fill sth: *Tears brimmed in her eyes.* ◊ ~ **with sth** *Her eyes brimmed with tears.* ◊ *The team were brimming with confidence before the game.*

PHRV ˌbrim ˈover (with sth) (of a cup, container, etc.) to be so full of a liquid that it flows over the edge SYN **overflow**: (*figurative*) *Her heart was brimming over with happiness.*

**brim·ful** /ˈbrɪmfʊl/ *adj.* ~ **of sth** completely full of sth: *She's certainly brimful of energy.* ◊ *a jug brimful of cream*

**brim·stone** /ˈbrɪmstəʊn/ *noun* (*old use*) the chemical element SULPHUR

**brin·dle** /ˈbrɪndl/ (*also* **brin·dled** /ˈbrɪndld/) *adj.* (of dogs, cats and cows) brown with bands or marks of another colour

**brine** /braɪn/ *noun* [U] water that contains a lot of salt, used especially for preserving food ⊃ see also BRINY

**bring** ⓞ A1 /brɪŋ/ *verb* ~ **sb/sth** (**brought, brought** /brɔːt/)

• COME WITH SB/STH **1** A1 to come to a place with sb/sth: ~ **sb/sth** (**with you**) *Don't forget to bring your books with you.* ◊ *Can we bring the children?* ◊ ~ **sb/sth to sb** *She brought her boyfriend to the party.* ◊ ~ **sth for sb** *Bring a present for Helen.* ◊ ~ **sb sth** *Bring Helen a present.*

• GIVE/PROVIDE **2** A2 to give or provide sb/sth with sth: ~ **sb/sth sth** *They brought us some good news.* ◊ ~ **sth to sb/sth** *The team's new manager brings ten years' experience to the job.*

• CAUSE **3** A2 to cause sth: ~ **sth** *The revolution brought many changes.* ◊ ~ **sth to sth** *The news brought tears to his eyes* (= made him cry). ◊ ~ **sth with it** *Retirement often brings with it a massive drop in income.* **4** B1 to cause sb/sth to be in a particular condition or place: ~ **sb/sth to sth** *to bring a meeting to an end* ◊ *to bring an end to the conflict* ◊ *Bring the water to the boil.* ◊ *The issue was only brought to my attention this morning.* ◊ ~ **sb/sth into sth** *His travels brought him into contact with many famous artists.* ◊ ~ **sb/sth + adv./prep.** *Hello Simon! What brings you here?* **5** B1 ~ **sb/sth to sth** used to move a speech or piece of writing on from one point to the next: *This brings me to the second point I'd like to make:…*

• MAKE SB/STH MOVE **6** to make sb/sth move in a particular direction or way: ~ **sb/sth + adv./prep.** *The judge brought his hammer down on the table.* ◊ ~ **sb/sth running** *Her cries brought the neighbours running* (= made them run to her).

• LEGAL ACTION **7** to start legal action against sb/sth; to make sb/sth answer a case in court: ~ **sth against sb** *to bring charges/legal action/proceedings against sb* ◊ ~ **sth** *The decision comes in a case brought by the residents of a small town in Alabama.*

• FORCE YOURSELF **8** ~ **yourself to do sth** to force yourself to do sth: *She could not bring herself to tell him the news.*

IDM HELP Idioms containing **bring** are at the entries for the nouns and adjectives in the idioms, for example **bring sb/sth to heel** is at **heel**. ˌbring it ˈon! (*also* ˌbring ˈit!) (*informal*) used to express confidence about a challenge: *We've trained hard and we're ready. Bring it on!*

PHRV ˌbring sth↔aˈbout to make sth happen SYN **cause**: *What brought about the change in his attitude?* ⊃ LANGUAGE BANK at CAUSE

ˌbring sb aˈround (NAmE) = BRING SB ROUND | ˌbring sth aˈround to sth (NAmE) = BRING STH ROUND TO STH
ˌbring sb/sth↔ˈback to return sb/sth: *Please bring back all library books by the end of the week.* ◊ *He brought me back* (= gave me a ride home) *in his car.* ˌbring sth↔ˈback **1** to make sb remember sth or think about it again: *The photographs brought back many pleasant memories.* **2** to make sth that existed before be introduced again SYN **reintroduce**: *Most people are against bringing back the death penalty.* ˌbring sb sth↔ˈback | ˌbring sth↔ˈback (for sb) to return with sth for sb: *What did you bring the kids back from Italy?* ◊ *I brought a T-shirt back for Mark.*
ˌbring sb/sth beˈfore sb (*formal*) to present sb/sth for discussion or judgement: *The matter will be brought before the committee.* ◊ *He was brought before the court and found guilty.*
ˌbring sb↔ˈdown **1** to make sb lose power or be defeated: *The scandal may bring down the government.* **2** (in sports) to make sb fall over: *He was brought down in the penalty area.* ˌbring sth↔ˈdown **1** to reduce sth: *We aim to bring down prices on all our computers.* **2** to land an aircraft: *The pilot managed to bring the plane down in a field.* **3** to make an aircraft fall out of the sky: *Twelve enemy fighters had been brought down.* **4** to make an animal or a bird fall down or fall out of the sky by killing or wounding it: *He brought down the bear with a single shot.*
ˌbring sb/sth↔ˈforth (*old use or formal*) to give birth to sb; to produce sth: *She brought forth a son.* ◊ *trees bringing forth fruit*
ˌbring sth↔ˈforward **1** to move sth to an earlier date or time: *The meeting has been brought forward from 10 May to 3 May.* **2** to suggest sth for discussion: *Please bring the matter forward at the next meeting.* **3** to move a total sum from the bottom of one page or column of numbers to the top of the next: *A credit balance of $50 was brought forward from his September account.*
ˌbring sb/sth↔ˈin **1** to ask sb to do a particular job or to be involved in sth: *Local residents were angry at not being brought in on* (= asked for their opinion about) *the new housing proposal.* ◊ **bring sb in to do sth** *Experts were brought in to advise the government.* **2** (of the police) to bring sb to a police station in order to ask them questions or arrest them: *Two men were brought in for questioning.*
ˌbring sb/sth↔ˈin **1** to introduce a new law: *They want to bring in a bill to limit arms exports.* **2** to attract sb/sth to a place or business: *We need to bring in a lot more new business.* **3** to give a decision in court: *The jury brought in a verdict of guilty.* ˌbring sb ˈin on sth | ˌbring ˈin sth to make or earn a particular amount of money: *His freelance work brings him in about $20000 a year.* ◊ *How much does she bring in now?*
ˌbring sth↔ˈoff to succeed in doing sth difficult SYN **pull sth off**: *It was a difficult task but we brought it off.* ◊ *The goalie brought off a superb save.*
ˌbring sb↔ˈon to help sb develop or improve while they are learning to do sth ˌbring sth↔ˈon **1** to make sth develop, usually sth unpleasant SYN **cause**: *He was suffering from stress brought on by overwork.* **2** to make crops, fruit, etc. grow well ˌbring sth on yourˈself/sb to be responsible for sth unpleasant that happens to you/sb: *I have no sympathy—you brought it all on yourself.*
ˌbring sb↔ˈout (*BrE*) to make people go on strike ˌbring sb ˈout of himself, herself, etc. to help sb to feel more confident: *She's a shy girl who needs friends to bring her out of herself.* ˌbring sth↔ˈout **1** to make sth appear: *A crisis brings out the best in her.* **2** to make sth easy to see or understand: *That dress really brings out the colour of your eyes.* **3** to produce sth; to publish sth: *The band have just brought out their second album.* ˌbring sb ˈout in sth to make sb's skin be covered in spots, etc: *The heat brought him out in a rash.*
ˌbring sb ˈround (*BrE*) (*NAmE* ˌbring sb aˈround) (*also* ˌbring sb ˈto*)* to make sb who is unconscious become conscious again ˌbring sb ˈround (to …) (*BrE*) (*NAmE* ˌbring sb aˈround) to bring sb to sb's house: *Bring the family round one evening. We'd love to meet them.* ˌbring sb

# bring-and-buy sale 186

**ˌround (to sth)** (BrE) (NAmE **ˌbring sb aˈround**) to persuade sb to agree to sth: *He didn't like the plan at first, but we managed to bring him round.* **ˌbring sth ˈround to sth** (BrE) (NAmE **ˌbring sth aˈround to sth**) to direct a conversation to a particular subject **ˌbring sb ˈto** = BRING SB ROUND **ˌbring A and B toˈgether** to help two people or groups to end a DISAGREEMENT: *The loss of their son brought the two of them together.* **ˌbring sb↔ˈup** 1 ? B2 [often passive] to care for a child, teaching him or her how to behave, etc. SYN **raise**: *She brought up five children.* ◊ *He was brought up by his aunt.* ◊ *a well/badly brought up child* ◊ **ˌbring sb up to do sth** *They were brought up to* (= taught as children to) *respect authority.* ◊ *~ (as) sth I was brought up (as) a Catholic.* ➔ related noun UPBRINGING 2 (*law*) to make sb appear for trial: *He was brought up on a charge of drunken driving.* **ˌbring sth↔ˈup** 1 to mention a subject or start to talk about it SYN **raise**: *Bring it up at the meeting.* 2 to VOMIT: *to bring up your lunch* 3 to make sth appear on a computer screen: *Click with the right mouse button to bring up a new menu.* **ˌbring sb ˈup against sth** to force sb to know about sth and have to deal with it: *Working in the slums brought her up against the realities of poverty.*

**ˌbring-and-ˈbuy sale** *noun* (BrE) a sale, usually for charity, at which people bring things for sale and buy those brought by others

**brin·jal** /ˈbrɪndʒl/ *noun* [C, U] (IndE, SAfrE) an AUBERGINE (= a vegetable with shiny dark purple skin that is soft and white inside)

**brink** /brɪŋk/ *noun* [sing.] 1 **the ~ (of sth)** if you are on the **brink** of sth, you are almost in a very new, dangerous or exciting situation: *on the brink of collapse/war/death/disaster* ◊ *Scientists are on the brink of making a major new discovery.* ◊ *He's pulled the company back from the brink* (= he has saved it from disaster). 2 (*literary*) the extreme edge of land, for example at the top of a CLIFF or by a river: *the brink of the precipice* IDM see TEETER

**brink·man·ship** /ˈbrɪŋkmənʃɪp/ (NAmE also **brinks·man·ship** /ˈbrɪŋksmənʃɪp/) *noun* [U] the activity, especially in politics, of getting into a situation that could be very dangerous in order to frighten people and make them do what you want

**briny** /ˈbraɪni/ *adj.* (of water) containing a lot of salt SYN **salty** ➔ see also BRINE

**brio** /ˈbriːəʊ/ *noun* [U] (*formal*) enthusiasm and individual style

**bri·oche** /ˈbriːɒʃ; NAmE briˈəʊʃ/ *noun* [C, U] a type of sweet bread made from flour, eggs and butter, usually in the shape of a small bread roll

**bri·quette** /brɪˈket/ *noun* a small hard block made from coal dust and used as fuel

**brisk** /brɪsk/ *adj.* (**brisk·er, brisk·est**) 1 quick; busy: *a brisk walk* ◊ *to set off at a brisk pace* ◊ *Ice-cream vendors were doing a brisk trade* (= selling a lot of ice cream). 2 (of a person, their voice or manner) practical and confident; showing a desire to get things done quickly: *His tone became brisk and businesslike.* 3 (of wind and the weather) cold but pleasantly fresh: *a brisk wind/breeze* ▶ **brisk·ly** *adv.* **brisk·ness** *noun* [U]

**bris·ket** /ˈbrɪskɪt/ *noun* meat that comes from the chest of an animal, especially a cow

**bris·tle** /ˈbrɪsl/ *noun, verb*
■ *noun* 1 a short stiff hair: *the bristles on his chin* 2 one of the short stiff hairs or wires in a brush
■ *verb* 1 [I] **~ (with sth) (at sth)** to suddenly become very annoyed or offended at what sb says or does: *His lies made her bristle with rage.* 2 [I] (of an animal's fur) to stand up on the back and neck because the animal is frightened or angry
PHRV **ˈbristle with sth** to contain a large number of sth: *The whole subject bristles with problems.*

**brist·ly** /ˈbrɪsli/ *adj.* like or full of bristles; rough: *a bristly chin/moustache*

**Brit** /brɪt/ *noun* (*informal*) a British person ➔ note at BRITISH

**Brit·ain** /ˈbrɪtn/ *noun* [sing.] the island containing England, Scotland and Wales ➔ see also GREAT BRITAIN, UNITED KINGDOM

**Bri·tan·nia** /brɪˈtæniə/ *noun* [sing.] a figure of a woman used as a symbol of Britain. She is usually shown sitting down wearing a HELMET and holding a SHIELD and a TRIDENT (= a long weapon with three points).

**Bri·tan·nic** /brɪˈtænɪk/ *adj.* (*old-fashioned, formal*) (used mainly in names or titles) relating to Britain or the British Empire: *Her Britannic Majesty* (= the Queen)

**britches** /ˈbrɪtʃɪz/ *noun* (*especially NAmE*) = BREECHES IDM = BE/GET TOO BIG FOR YOUR BOOTS at BIG *adj.*

**Brit·ish** /ˈbrɪtɪʃ/ *adj.* 1 (*abbr.* **Br.**) connected with the United Kingdom of Great Britain and Northern Ireland or the people who live there: *the British Government* ◊ *He was born in France but his parents are British.* ◊ *British-based/British-born/British-made* 2 **the British** *noun* [pl.] the people of Great Britain or the United Kingdom ▶ **Brit·ish·ness** *noun* [U]

▼ MORE ABOUT ...

**the British**
- There is no singular noun which is commonly used to refer to a person from Britain. Instead the adjective **British** is used: *She's British.* ◊ *The British have a very odd sense of humour.* The adjective **English** refers only to people from England, not the rest of the United Kingdom.
- The noun **Briton** is used mainly in newspapers: *The survivors of the avalanche included 12 Britons.* It also describes the early inhabitants of Britain: *the ancient Britons.* **Brit** is informal. **Britisher** is now very old-fashioned.

➔ note at SCOTTISH

**the ˌBritish ˈCouncil** *noun* [sing.] an organization that represents British culture in other countries and develops closer cultural relations with them

**ˌBritish ˈEnglish** *noun* [U] the English language as spoken in the UK and certain other countries

**Brit·ish·er** /ˈbrɪtɪʃə(r)/ *noun* (NAmE, *old-fashioned, informal*) a person from Britain

**ˌBritish ˌoverseas ˈterritory** *noun* (BrE) an area that is not part of the United Kingdom but in which the British government is responsible for defence and relations with other countries

**ˌBritish ˈSummer Time** *noun* [U] (*abbr.* **BST**) the time used in the UK in summer that is one hour ahead of UTC

**Briton** /ˈbrɪtn/ *noun* (*formal*) a person from Britain: *the ancient Britons* ◊ *the first Briton to climb Everest without oxygen* ➔ note at BRITISH

**brit·tle** /ˈbrɪtl/ *adj.* 1 hard but easily broken: *brittle bones/nails* 2 a **brittle** mood or state of mind is one that appears to be happy or strong but is actually nervous and easily damaged: *a brittle temperament* 3 (of a sound) hard and sharp in an unpleasant way: *a brittle laugh* ▶ **brittle·ness** *noun* [U]

**ˌbrittle ˈbone disease** *noun* [U] (*medical*) 1 a rare disease in which sb's bones break extremely easily 2 = OSTEOPOROSIS

**bro** /brəʊ/ *noun* (*pl.* **bros** /brəʊz/) (*informal*) 1 a brother 2 (*especially NAmE*) a friendly way of addressing a male person: *Thanks, bro!*

**broach** /brəʊtʃ/ *verb* **~ sth (to/with sb)** to begin talking about a subject that is difficult to discuss, especially because it is embarrassing or because people disagree about it: *She was dreading having to broach the subject of money to her father.*

**ˈB-road** *noun* (in the UK) a road that is less important than an A-ROAD and usually joins small towns and villages

## broad

**broad** ⓘ B2 ○ /brɔːd/ *adj., noun*

**WORD FAMILY**
broad *adj.*
broadly *adv.*
broaden *verb*
breadth *noun*

■ *adj.* (broad·er, broad·est)
- **WIDE 1** B2 wide: *a broad street/avenue/river* ◇ *broad shoulders* ◇ *He is tall, broad and muscular.* ◇ *a broad smile/grin* (= one in which your mouth is stretched very wide because you are very pleased) **OPP narrow 2** used after a measurement of distance to show how wide sth is: *two metres broad and one metre high*
- **WIDE RANGE 3** B2 including a great variety of people or things: *a broad range of products* ◇ *a broad spectrum of interests* ◇ *There is broad support for the government's policies.* ◇ *She took a broad view of the duties of being a teacher* (= she believed her duties included a wide range of things). **OPP narrow**
- **GENERAL 4** B2 [only before noun] general; not detailed: *the broad outline of a proposal* ◇ *The negotiators were in broad agreement on the main issues.* ◇ *She's a feminist, in the broadest sense of the word.* ◇ *In broad terms, the paper argues that each country should develop its own policy.*
- **LAND/WATER 5** B2 covering a wide area: *a broad expanse of water*
- **ACCENT 6** if sb has a **broad** ACCENT (= a way of pronouncing the words of a language), you can hear very easily which area they come from **SYN strong**
- **HINT 7** if sb gives a **broad** hint, they make it very clear what they are thinking or what they want
- **HUMOUR 8** (*NAmE*) dealing with sex in a way that makes people laugh: *The movie mixes broad humor with romance.* ⊃ note at **WIDE**

**IDM a broad 'church** (*BrE*) an organization that accepts a wide range of opinions **SYN big tent (in) broad 'daylight** (in) the clear light of day, when it is easy to see: *The robbery occurred in broad daylight, in a crowded street.* **it's as broad as it's 'long** (*BrE, informal*) it makes no real difference which of two possible choices you make ⊃ more at **PAINT** *v.*

■ *noun* (*NAmE, old-fashioned, slang*) an offensive way of referring to a woman

**broad·band** B+ C1 /'brɔːdbænd/ *noun* [U] **1** B+ C1 a way of connecting to the internet that allows you to receive information, including pictures, etc., very quickly and that is always active (so that the user does not have to connect each time): *plans to provide rural areas with fast broadband* **2** (*specialist*) signals that use a wide range of frequencies ⊃ compare **NARROWBAND**

**broad-'based** (*also* **broadly 'based**) *adj.* based on a wide variety of people, things or ideas; not limited

**broad 'bean** (*BrE*) (*NAmE usually* **fava bean**) *noun* a type of round, pale green bean. Several broad beans grow together inside a fat POD.

**broad-'brush** *adj.* [only before noun] dealing with a subject or problem in a general way rather than considering details: *a broad-brush approach*

**broad·cast** ⓘ B2 /'brɔːdkɑːst/ *NAmE* -kæst/ *verb, noun*

■ *verb* (broad·cast, broad·cast) **1** B2 [T, I] **~(sth)** to send out programmes on television or radio: *The concert will be broadcast live* (= at the same time as it takes place) *tomorrow evening.* ◇ *They began broadcasting in 1922.* **2** [T] **~ sth** to tell a lot of people about sth: *I don't like to broadcast the fact that my father owns the company.*

■ *noun* B2 a radio or television programme: (*BrE*) *a party political broadcast* (= for example, before an election) ◇ *We watched a live broadcast of the speech* (= one shown at the same time as the speech was made).

**broad·cast·er** B+ B2 /'brɔːdkɑːstə(r)/ *NAmE* -kæs-/ *noun* **1** B+ B2 a person whose job is presenting or talking on television or radio programmes **2** B+ B2 a company that sends out television or radio programmes

**broad·cast·ing** /'brɔːdkɑːstɪŋ/ *NAmE* -kæs-/ *noun* [U] the business of making and sending out radio and television programmes: *to work in broadcasting* ◇ *the British Broadcasting Corporation* (= the BBC)

## broil

**broad·en** /'brɔːdn/ *verb* **1** [I] to become wider: *Her smile broadened.* **2** [T, I] **~(sth)** to affect or make sth affect more people or things: *a promise to broaden access to higher education* ◇ *The party needs to broaden its appeal to voters.* **3** [T] **~ sth** to increase your experience, knowledge, etc: *Few would disagree that travel broadens the mind* (= helps you to understand other people's customs, etc.). ◇ *Spending a year working in the city helped to broaden his horizons.*

**PHRV broaden 'out** (of a road, river, etc.) to become wider **SYN widen**

**'broad jump** *noun often* **the broad jump** [sing.] (*NAmE*) = **LONG JUMP**

**broad-leaved** /'brɔːdliːvd/ (*also less frequent* **broad-leaf** /'brɔːdliːf/) *adj.* (*specialist*) (of plants) having broad flat leaves

**broad·ly** B+ B2 Ⓦ /'brɔːdli/ *adv.* **1** B+ B2 generally, without considering details: *Broadly speaking, I agree with you.* ◇ **broadly similar/comparable/equivalent/consistent 2** if you smile **broadly**, you smile with your mouth stretched very wide because you are very pleased or are enjoying sth very much

**broad-'minded** *adj.* willing to listen to other people's opinions and accept behaviour that is different from your own **SYN tolerant OPP narrow-minded**
▸ **broad-'minded·ness** *noun* [U]

**broad·ness** /'brɔːdnəs/ *noun* [U] the quality of being broad

**broad-scale** /'brɔːdskeɪl/ *adj.* on a large scale: *The broad-scale cutting down of trees is damaging the environment.*

**broad·sheet** /'brɔːdʃiːt/ *noun* **1** a newspaper printed on a large size of paper, generally considered more serious than smaller newspapers ⊃ compare **TABLOID 2** a large piece of paper printed on one side only with information or an advertisement

**broad·side** /'brɔːdsaɪd/ *noun, adv., verb*

■ *noun* an aggressive attack in words, whether written or spoken: *The prime minister fired a broadside at his critics.*
■ *adv.* with one side facing sth **SYN sideways**: *The car skidded and crashed broadside into another car.* ◇ (*BrE*) *The boat swung broadside on to the current of the river.*
■ *verb* **~ sth** (*NAmE*) to crash into the side of sth: *The driver ran a stop light and broadsided the truck.*

**broad-'spectrum** *adj.* [only before noun] (*specialist*) (of a drug or chemical) effective against a large variety of bacteria, insects, etc.

**broad·sword** /'brɔːdsɔːd/ *NAmE* -sɔːrd/ *noun* a large SWORD with a broad flat BLADE (= metal cutting edge)

**Broad·way** /'brɔːdweɪ/ *noun* [U] a street in New York City where there are many theatres, sometimes used to refer to the US theatre industry in general: *a Broadway musical* ◇ *The play opened on Broadway in 2013.* ⊃ see also **OFF-BROADWAY**

**bro·cade** /brə'keɪd/ *NAmE* broʊ'k-/ *noun* [U, C] a type of thick heavy cloth with a raised pattern made especially from gold or silver silk THREAD

**broc·coli** /'brɒkəli/ *NAmE* 'brɑːk-/ *noun* [U] a vegetable with a thick green STEM and several dark green or purple flower heads ⊃ **VISUAL VOCAB** page V5

**bro·chure** /'brəʊʃə(r)/ *NAmE* broʊ'ʃʊr/ *noun* a small magazine or book containing pictures and information about sth or advertising sth: *a travel brochure*

**broer** /'bruː(r)/ *SAfrE* /bruːr/ *noun* (*SAfrE, informal*) **1** a brother **2** (used of a boy or man) a friend **3** a friendly form of address that is used by one boy or man to another: *How's it going, my broer?*

**brogue** /brəʊg/ *noun* **1** [usually pl.] a strong shoe which usually has a pattern in the leather: *a pair of brogues* **2** [usually sing.] the ACCENT (= the way of pronouncing the words of a language) that sb has when they are speaking, especially the ACCENT of Irish or Scottish speakers of English

**broil** /brɔɪl/ *verb* **1** [T] **~ sth** (*NAmE*) to cook meat or fish under direct heat or over heat on metal bars: *broiled*

# broiler

chicken ⊃ compare BARBECUE, GRILL **2** [I, T] ~(sb) to become or make sb become very hot: *They lay broiling in the sun.*

**broil·er** /ˈbrɔɪlə(r)/ *noun* **1** (*also* **broiler chicken**) (*especially NAmE*) a young chicken suitable for broiling or ROASTING **2** (*NAmE*) the part inside the oven of a cooker that directs heat downwards to cook food that is placed under it ⊃ compare GRILL

**broke** /brəʊk/ *adj., verb*
- *adj.* [not before noun] (*informal*) having no money: *I'm always broke by the end of the month.* ◊ *During the recession thousands of small businesses went broke* (= had to stop doing business). ◊ *flat/stony broke* (= completely broke)
  **IDM** **go for ˈbroke** (*informal*) to risk everything in one determined effort to do sth ⊃ more at AIN'T
- *verb past tense of* BREAK

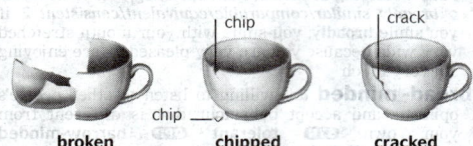

chip — crack
broken — chipped — cracked

**broken** ❶ **A2** /ˈbrəʊkən/ *adj., verb*
- *adj.*
- **DAMAGED 1** **A2** that has been damaged or injured; no longer whole or working correctly: *a broken window/plate* ◊ *a broken leg/arm/bone* ◊ *pieces of broken glass* ◊ *How did this dish get broken?* ◊ *The TV's broken.* ⊃ see also BROKEN HEART
- **PROMISE/AGREEMENT 2** **B1** [usually before noun] not kept: *Voters are disillusioned with the government's broken promises.*
- **RELATIONSHIP 3** **B1** [usually before noun] ended or destroyed: *a broken marriage/engagement* ⊃ see also BROKEN HOME
- **NOT CONTINUOUS 4** **B2** [usually before noun] not continuous; interrupted or DISTURBED: *a night of broken sleep* ◊ *a single broken white line across the road*
- **PERSON 5** [only before noun] made weak and tired by illness or difficulties: *He was a broken man after the failure of his business.*
- **LANGUAGE 6** [only before noun] (of a language that is not your own) spoken slowly and with a lot of mistakes; not FLUENT: *to speak in broken English*
- **GROUND 7** having a rough surface: *an area of broken, rocky ground*
  **IDM** **like a ˌbroken ˈrecord** (*BrE also* **like a ˌstuck ˈrecord**) in a way that keeps repeating a statement or opinion in an annoying way
- *verb past part. of* BREAK

**broken-ˈdown** *adj.* [usually before noun] in a very bad condition; not working correctly; very tired and sick: *a broken-down old car/horse*

**ˌbroken ˈheart** *noun* a very sad feeling, especially when sb you love has died or left you: *No one ever died of a broken heart.* ▶ **ˌbroken-ˈhearted** *adj.*: *He was broken-hearted when his wife died.* ⊃ compare HEARTBROKEN

**ˌbroken ˈhome** *noun* a family in which the parents are divorced or separated: *She comes from a broken home.*

**broken·ly** /ˈbrəʊkənli/ *adv.* (*formal*) (of sb's manner of speaking) in phrases that are very short or not complete, with a lot of breaks; not FLUENTLY

**broker** /ˈbrəʊkə(r)/ *noun, verb*
- *noun* **1** a person who buys and sells things for other people: *an insurance broker* **2** = STOCKBROKER **3** ~ **(between A and B)** a person who arranges the details of an agreement between two groups or countries that disagree or oppose each other ⊃ see also HONEST BROKER, PAWNBROKER, POWER BROKER

- *verb* ~**sth** to arrange the details of an agreement, especially between different countries: *a peace plan brokered by the UN* **WORDFINDER NOTE** at DEAL

**broker·age** /ˈbrəʊkərɪdʒ/ *noun* [U] **1** the business of being a broker: *a brokerage firm/house* **2** an amount of money charged by a broker for work that he/she does

**ˈbroker-dealer** *noun* (*finance*) a person who works on the Stock Exchange buying shares from and selling shares to brokers and the public

**brolly** /ˈbrɒli; *NAmE* ˈbrɑːli/ *noun* (*pl.* **-ies**) (*BrE, informal*) = UMBRELLA

**bro·mance** /ˈbrəʊmæns/ *noun* (*informal*) a very close friendship between two men **ORIGIN** From **brother** and **romance**.

**brom·ide** /ˈbrəʊmaɪd/ *noun* [C, U] a chemical which contains BROMINE, used, especially in the past, to make people feel calm

**brom·ine** /ˈbrəʊmiːn/ *noun* [U] (*symb.* **Br**) a chemical element. Bromine is a dark red poisonous liquid and has a very strong unpleasant smell. It is mainly found in the form of salts in SEAWATER.

**bronc** /brɒŋk; *NAmE* brɑːŋk/ *noun* (*NAmE, informal*) = BRONCO

**bron·chial** /ˈbrɒŋkiəl; *NAmE* ˈbrɑːŋ-/ *adj.* [usually before noun] (*medical*) of or affecting the two main branches of the WINDPIPE (called **ˈbronchial tubes**) leading to the lungs: *bronchial pneumonia* ⊃ VISUAL VOCAB page V1

**bron·chitis** /brɒŋˈkaɪtɪs; *NAmE* brɑːŋ-/ *noun* [U] an illness that affects the bronchial tubes leading to the lungs: *He was suffering from chronic bronchitis.* ▶ **bron·chit·ic** /-ˈkɪtɪk/ *adj.*: *a bronchitic cough*

**bron·chus** /ˈbrɒŋkəs; *NAmE* ˈbrɑːŋ-/ *noun* (*pl.* **bron·chi** /-kaɪ/) (*anatomy*) any one of the system of tubes which make up the main branches of the WINDPIPE through which air passes in and out of the lungs

**bronco** /ˈbrɒŋkəʊ; *NAmE* ˈbrɑːŋ-/ *noun* (*pl.* **-os**) (*NAmE, informal* **bronc**) a wild horse of the western US: *a bucking bronco in the rodeo*

**bron·to·saurus** /ˌbrɒntəˈsɔːrəs; *NAmE* ˌbrɑːn-/ *noun* = APATOSAURUS

**Bronx cheer** /ˌbrɒŋks ˈtʃɪə(r); *NAmE* ˌbrɑːŋks ˈtʃɪr/ *noun* (*NAmE, informal*) = RASPBERRY (2)

**bronze** /brɒnz; *NAmE* brɑːnz/ *noun, adj.*
- *noun* **1** [U] a dark red-brown metal made by mixing COPPER and tin: *a bronze statue* ◊ *a figure cast in bronze* **2** [U] a dark red-brown colour, like bronze **3** [C] a work of art made of bronze, for example a statue **4** [C, U] = BRONZE MEDAL
- *adj.* dark red-brown in colour: *bronze skin*

**the ˌBronze ˈAge** *noun* [sing.] the period in history between the Stone Age and the Iron Age when people used tools and weapons made of bronze

**bronzed** /brɒnzd; *NAmE* brɑːnzd/ *adj.* having skin that has been turned brown in an attractive way by the sun **SYN** **tanned**

**ˌbronze ˈmedal** (*also* **bronze**) *noun* [C, U] a MEDAL given as third prize in a competition or race: *an Olympic bronze medal winner* ◊ *She won (a) bronze at the Olympics.* ⊃ compare GOLD MEDAL, SILVER MEDAL ▶ **ˌbronze ˈmedallist** (*BrE*) (*NAmE* **ˌbronze ˈmedalist**) *noun*: *She's an Olympic bronze medallist.*

**brooch** /brəʊtʃ; *NAmE also* bruːtʃ/ *noun* (*especially BrE*) (*NAmE usually* **pin**) *noun* a piece of jewellery with a pin on the back of it, that can be fastened to your clothes

**brood** /bruːd/ *verb, noun*
- *verb* **1** [I] ~ **(over / on / about sth)** to think a lot about sth that makes you annoyed, anxious or upset: *You're not still brooding over what he said, are you?* **2** [I, T] ~ **(sth)** if a bird **broods**, or **broods** its eggs, it sits on the eggs in order to HATCH them (= make the young come out of them)
- *noun* [C + sing. / pl. v.] **1** all the young birds or creatures that a mother produces at one time **SYN** **clutch 2** (*humorous*) a large family of children

---

| æ cat | ɑː father | e bed | ɜː fur | ə about | ɪ sit | iː see | i happy | ɒ got (*BrE*) | ɔː saw | ʌ cup | ʊ put | uː too |

**brood·ing** /ˈbruːdɪŋ/ adj. (literary) sad and mysterious or THREATENING: *dark, brooding eyes* ◊ *a brooding silence* ◊ *Ireland's brooding landscape*

**broody** /ˈbruːdi/ adj. **1** (of a woman) wanting very much to have a baby: *I reached the age of 27 and suddenly started to feel broody.* **2** (of a female bird) wanting to lay eggs and sit on them: *a broody hen* **3** quiet and thinking about sth because you are unhappy or disappointed ▶ **brood·i·ness** noun [U]

**brook** /brʊk/ noun, verb
■ noun a small river
■ verb **not brook sth / not brook sb doing sth / brook no ...** (formal) to not allow sth: *The tone in his voice brooked no argument.*

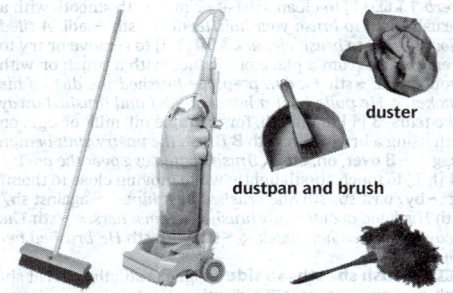
duster
dustpan and brush
broom    vacuum cleaner    feather duster

**broom** /bruːm/ noun **1** [C] a brush on the end of a long handle, used for sweeping floors **2** [U] a wild bush with small yellow flowers IDM see NEW

**ˈbroom cupboard** (BrE) (NAmE **ˈbroom closet**) noun **1** a large built-in cupboard used for keeping cleaning equipment, etc. in **2** (often humorous) a very small room: *I couldn't afford more than a broom cupboard to set up office in.*

**broom·stick** /ˈbruːmstɪk/ noun a broom with a long handle and small thin sticks at the end, or the handle of a broom. In stories WITCHES (= women with evil magic powers) ride through the air on broomsticks.

**Bros** /BrE sometimes brps/ (also **Bros.** especially in NAmE) abbr. (used in the name of a company) Brothers: *Warner Bros.*

**broth** /brɒθ; NAmE brɔːθ/ noun [U, C] thick soup made by boiling meat or fish and vegetables in water: *chicken broth* IDM see COOK n.

**brothel** /ˈbrɒθl; NAmE ˈbrɑːθl/ (also **bor·dello** especially in NAmE) noun a house where people pay to have sex with PROSTITUTES

**brother** ⓘ A1 /ˈbrʌðə(r)/ noun, exclamation
■ noun
• IN FAMILY **1** A1 a boy or man who has the same mother and father as another person: *We're brothers.* ◊ *an older/younger brother* ◊ *a twin brother* ◊ *Does she have any brothers and sisters?* ◊ *Edward was the youngest of the Kennedy brothers.* ◊ *He was like a brother to me* (= very close). ◊ *My son really wanted a little brother.* ⊃ see also HALF-BROTHER, STEPBROTHER
• OTHER MEN **2** (pl. brothers or old-fashioned brethren) used for talking to or talking about other male members of an organization or other men who have the same ideas, purpose, etc. as yourself: *We must work together, brothers!* ◊ *He was greatly respected by his brother officers.* ◊ *We must support our weaker brethren.*
• IN RELIGIOUS GROUP **3** (also **Brother**) (pl. brethren or brothers) a male member of a religious group, especially a MONK: *Brother Luke* ◊ *The Brethren meet regularly for prayer.*
• FORM OF ADDRESS **4** (NAmE, informal) used by black people as a form of address for a black man
• AT COLLEGE/UNIVERSITY **5** (in the US) a member of a FRATERNITY (= a club for a group of male students at a college or university)

■ exclamation (especially NAmE, old-fashioned) used to express the fact that you are annoyed or surprised: *Oh brother!*

**brother·hood** /ˈbrʌðəhʊd; NAmE -ðərh-/ noun **1** [U] friendship and understanding between people: *to live in peace and brotherhood* **2** [C + sing./pl. v.] an organization formed for a particular purpose, especially a religious society or political organization **3** [U] the relationship of brothers: *the ties of brotherhood*

**brother-in-law** (pl. **brothers-in-law**) noun the brother of your husband or wife; your sister's or brother's husband; the husband of your husband's or wife's sister or brother ⊃ compare SISTER-IN-LAW

**brother·ly** /ˈbrʌðəli; NAmE -ðərli/ adj. [usually before noun] being kind and showing feelings of love in a way that you would expect a brother to behave: *brotherly love/advice* ◊ *He gave her a brotherly kiss on the cheek.*

**brought** /brɔːt/ past tense, past part. of BRING IDM see LOW adj.

**brou·haha** /ˈbruːhɑːhɑː/ noun [U, sing.] (old-fashioned, informal) noisy excitement or complaints about sth

**brow** /braʊ/ noun **1** (literary) the part of the face above the eyes and below the hair SYN **forehead**: *The nurse mopped his fevered brow.* ◊ *Her brow furrowed in concentration.* **2** [usually pl.] = EYEBROW: *One dark brow rose in surprise.* **3** [usually sing.] the top part of a hill: *The path disappeared over the brow of the hill.* ⊃ see also HIGHBROW, LOWBROW, MIDDLEBROW IDM see KNIT v.

**brow·beat** /ˈbraʊbiːt/ verb (**brow·beat**, **brow·beat·en** /-biːtn/) ~ **sb (into doing sth)** to frighten or threaten sb in order to make them do sth SYN **intimidate**: *They were browbeaten into accepting the offer.*

**brown** ⓘ A1 /braʊn/ adj., noun, verb
■ adj. (**brown·er**, **brown·est**) **1** A1 having the colour of earth or coffee: *brown eyes/hair* ◊ *brown bread/sugar/rice* ◊ *dark brown shoe polish* ◊ *a package wrapped in brown paper* **2** A1 having skin that is naturally brown or has been made brown by the sun: (BrE) *I don't go brown very easily.* ◊ *After the summer in Spain, the children were brown as berries.*
IDM **in a brown ˈstudy** (old-fashioned, BrE) thinking deeply so that you do not notice what is happening around you
■ noun A1 [U, C] the colour of earth or coffee: *leaves of various shades of brown* ◊ *Brown doesn't* (= brown clothes do not) *suit you.*
■ verb [I, T] to become brown; to make sth brown: *Heat the butter until it browns.* ◊ *The grass was browning in patches.* ◊ ~ **sth** *Brown the onions before adding the meat.*
IDM **browned ˈoff (with sb/sth)** (BrE, informal) bored, unhappy or annoyed SYN **fed up**: *By now the passengers were getting browned off with the delay.*

**brown ˈale** noun (BrE) **1** [U, C] a type of mild sweet dark beer sold in bottles **2** [C] a bottle or glass of brown ale

**brown-bag** verb (-gg-) ~ **it** (NAmE, informal) to bring your lunch with you to work or school, usually in a brown paper bag: *My kids have been brown-bagging it this week.*

**brown ˈdwarf** noun (astronomy) an object in space that is between a large planet and a small star in size, and produces heat

**brown·field** /ˈbraʊnfiːld/ adj. [only before noun] used to describe an area of land in a city that was used by industry or for offices in the past and that may now be cleared for new building development: *a brownfield site* ⊃ compare GREENFIELD

**Brownian motion** /ˌbraʊniən ˈməʊʃn; NAmE ˈmoʊʃn/ noun [U] (physics) the movement without any regular pattern made by very small pieces of matter in a liquid or gas

**brownie** /ˈbraʊni/ noun **1** [C] a thick soft flat cake made with chocolate and sometimes nuts and served in small squares: *a fudge brownie* **2 the Brownies** [pl.] a branch of the SCOUT ASSOCIATION for girls between the ages of 7 and 10 or 11: *to join the Brownies* **3** [C] **Brownie** (BrE also

# brownie point

**'Brownie Guide**) a member of the Brownies ⊃ compare CUB, GUIDE, SCOUT

**'brownie point** noun [usually pl.] (informal) if sb does sth to earn **brownie points**, they do it to make sb in authority have a good opinion of them

**brown·ish** /'braʊnɪʃ/ (also less frequent **browny** /'braʊni/) adj. fairly brown in colour: *You can't see in this light, but my new coat is a sort of brownish colour.*

**'brown-nose** verb [I, T] (informal, disapproving) ~ **(sb)** to treat sb in authority with special respect in order to make them approve of you or treat you better: *She spends her time brown-nosing those in power.*

**'brown-out** /'braʊnaʊt/ noun (especially NAmE) a period of time when the amount of electrical power that is supplied to an area is reduced ⊃ compare BLACKOUT (1)

**,brown 'rat** (also **,common 'rat, ,Norway 'rat**) noun a common type of RAT

**,brown 'rice** noun [U] rice that is light brown because it has not had all of its outside part removed

**,brown 'sauce** noun [U] **1** (BrE) a sauce made with VINEGAR and SPICES, sold in bottles **2** (NAmE) a sauce made with fat and flour, cooked until it becomes brown

**'brown·stone** /'braʊnstəʊn/ noun (NAmE) a house built of, or with a front made of, a type of red-brown stone, which is also called brownstone: *New York brownstones*

**,brown 'sugar** noun [U] sugar that has a brown colour and has only been partly REFINED

**browse** /braʊz/ verb **1** [I, T] to look at a lot of things in a shop rather than looking for one particular thing: *You are welcome to come in and browse.* ◊ ~ **sth** *She browsed the shelves for something interesting to read.* **2** [I, T] to look through a book, newspaper, website, etc. without reading everything: *I spent the whole evening just browsing on the internet.* ◊ *to browse through the catalogue* ◊ ~ **sth** *I browsed the website for information about the event but didn't find anything useful.* ⊃ WORDFINDER NOTE at WEB **3** [I] ~ **(on sth)** (of cows, GOATS, etc.) to eat leaves, etc. that are growing high up ▶ **browse** noun [sing.]: *The gift shop is well worth a browse.*

**browser** 🔑 C1 /'braʊzə(r)/ noun **1** 🔑 C1 (also **web browser**) a computer program that lets you look at or read documents on the World Wide Web **2** a person who looks through books, magazines, etc. or at things for sale, but may not seriously intend to buy anything

**brrr** /bɜːr/ exclamation a sound that people make to show that they are very cold: *Brrr, it's freezing here.*

**bru·cel·losis** /ˌbruːsəˈləʊsɪs/ noun [U] a disease caused by bacteria that affects cows and that can cause a high temperature in humans

**bruise** /bruːz/ noun, verb
- noun **1** a blue, brown or purple mark that appears on the skin after sb has fallen, been hit, etc: *to be covered in bruises* ◊ *cuts and bruises* ⊃ SYNONYMS at INJURE **2** a mark on a fruit or vegetable where it is damaged
- verb **1** [I, T] to develop a bruise, or make a bruise or bruises appear on the skin of sb/sth: *Strawberries bruise easily.* ◊ ~ **sth** *She had slipped and badly bruised her face.* ⊃ SYNONYMS at INJURE ⊃ WORDFINDER NOTE at HURT **2** [T, usually passive] to affect sb badly and make them feel unhappy and less confident: **be bruised (by sth)** *They had been badly bruised by the defeat.* ▶ **bruised** adj.: *He suffered badly bruised ribs in the crash.* ◊ *bruised fruit* ◊ *a bruised ego* **bruis·ing** noun [U]: *She suffered severe bruising, but no bones were broken.* ◊ *internal bruising* ⊃ see also BRUISING

**bruiser** /'bruːzə(r)/ noun (informal) a large strong aggressive man

**bruis·ing** /'bruːzɪŋ/ adj. difficult and unpleasant, making you feel tired or weak: *a bruising meeting/experience*

**Brum·mie** /'brʌmi/ noun (BrE, informal) a person from the city of Birmingham in England ▶ **Brum·mie** adj.: *a Brummie accent*

**brunch** /brʌntʃ/ noun [C, U] a meal that you eat in the late morning as a combination of breakfast and lunch

**bru·nette** /bruːˈnet/ noun (sometimes offensive) a white-skinned woman with dark brown hair ⊃ compare BLONDE, REDHEAD

**brunt** /brʌnt/ noun
- IDM **bear, take, etc. the 'brunt of sth** to receive the main force of sth unpleasant: *Schools will bear the brunt of cuts in government spending.*

**brus·chetta** /bruːˈsketə/ noun [U] (from Italian) an Italian dish consisting of pieces of warm bread covered with oil and small pieces of raw tomato: *a first course of bruschetta*

**brush** 🔑 A2 /brʌʃ/ verb, noun
- verb **1** 🔑 A2 [T] to clean, POLISH or make sth smooth with a brush: ~ **sth** *to brush your hair/teeth* ◊ ~ **sth** + adj. *A tiled floor is easy to brush clean.* **2** 🔑 B1 [T, I] to remove or try to remove sth from a place or surface with a brush or with your hand: ~ **sth** + adv./prep. *He brushed the dirt off his jacket.* ◊ *He pulled out a handkerchief and* **brushed away the tears.** **3** [T] to put sth, for example oil, milk or egg, on sth using a brush: ~ **A with B** *Brush the pastry with beaten egg.* ◊ ~ **B over, on, etc. A** *Brush beaten egg over the pastry.* **4** [I, T] to touch sb/sth lightly while moving close to them/it: ~ **by/past sb/sth** *She brushed past him.* ◊ ~ **against sb/sth** *His hand accidentally brushed against hers.* ◊ ~ **sth** *The leaves brushed her cheek.* ◊ ~ **sth with sth** *He brushed her lips with his.*
- PHR V **brush sb/sth↔a'side** to ignore sb/sth; to treat sb/sth as unimportant SYN **dismiss**: *He brushed aside my fears.* **brush sb/yourself 'down** (BrE) = BRUSH SB/YOURSELF OFF **brush sth↔'down** to clean sth by brushing it: *to brush a coat/horse down* **brush 'off** to be removed by brushing: *Mud brushes off easily when it is dry.* **brush sb↔'off** to rudely ignore sb or refuse to listen to them: *She brushed him off impatiently.* ⊃ related noun BRUSH-OFF **brush sb/yourself 'off** (BrE) **brush sb/yourself 'down**) to make sb/yourself tidy, especially after you have fallen, by brushing your clothes, etc. with your hands **brush sth↔'up** | **brush 'up on sth** to quickly improve a skill, especially when you have not used it for a time: *I must brush up on my Spanish before I go to Seville.*
- noun **1** 🔑 A2 [C] an object made of short stiff hairs (called BRISTLES) or wires set in a block of wood or plastic, usually attached to a handle. Brushes are used for many different jobs, such as cleaning, painting and tidying your hair: *a paintbrush* ◊ *a hairbrush* ◊ *a toothbrush* ◊ *brush strokes* (= the marks left by a brush when painting) ◊ *a dustpan and brush* ◊ *Apply the paint with a fine brush.* ◊ picture at BROOM ⊃ see also SCRUBBING BRUSH **2** [sing.] an act of brushing: *to give your teeth a good brush* **3** [sing.] a light touch made in passing sth/sb: *the brush of his lips on her cheek* **4** [C] ~ **with sb/sth** a short unfriendly meeting with sb; an occasion when you nearly experience sth unpleasant: *She had a nasty brush with her boss this morning.* ◊ *In his job he's had frequent brushes with death.* ◊ *a brush with the law* **5** [U] land covered by small trees or bushes: *a brush fire* **6** [C] the tail of a FOX IDM see DAFT, PAINT v., TAR v.

**'brush-off** noun [sing.] (informal) rude or unfriendly behaviour that shows that a person is not interested in sb: *Paul asked Tara out to dinner but she* **gave him the brush-off.**

**brush·wood** /'brʌʃwʊd/ noun [U] small broken or dead branches of trees, often used to make fires

**brush·work** /'brʌʃwɜːk; NAmE -wɜːrk/ noun [U] the particular way in which an artist uses a brush to paint

**brusque** /bruːsk, brʊsk; NAmE brʌsk/ adj. using very few words and sounding rude SYN **abrupt, curt**: *The doctor spoke in a brusque tone.* ▶ **brusque·ly** adv.: *'What's your name?' he asked brusquely.* **brusque·ness** noun [U]

**'Brus·sels sprout** /ˌbrʌslz ˈspraʊt/ (also **Brussel sprout, sprout**) noun a small round green vegetable like a very small CABBAGE ⊃ VISUAL VOCAB page V5

**bru·tal** 🔑 C1 /'bruːtl/ adj. **1** 🔑 C1 violent and cruel: *a brutal attack/murder/rape/killing* **2** 🔑 C1 direct and clear about sth unpleasant; not thinking of people's feelings: *With brutal honesty she told him she did not love him.*

▶ **bru·tal·ity** /bruːˈtæləti/ noun [U, C] (pl. **-ies**): police brutality ◇ the brutalities of war **bru·tal·ly** /ˈbruːtəli/ adv.: He was brutally assaulted. ◇ Let me be brutally frank about this.

**bru·tal·ism** /ˈbruːtəlɪzəm/ noun [U] (architecture, sometimes disapproving) a style of architecture used especially in the 1950s and 60s that uses large CONCRETE blocks, steel, etc., and is sometimes considered ugly and unpleasant ▶ **bru·tal·ist** /-lɪst/ adj., noun

**bru·tal·ize** (BrE also **-ise**) /ˈbruːtəlaɪz/ verb **1** [usually passive] to make sb unable to feel normal human emotions such as PITY (= sympathy for people who are suffering): **be brutalized (by sth)** soldiers brutalized by war **2** ~ **sb** to treat sb in a cruel or violent way

**brute** /bruːt/ noun, adj.
- *noun* **1** (sometimes humorous) a man who treats people in an unkind, cruel way: His father was a drunken brute. ◇ You've forgotten my birthday again, you brute! **2** an animal, as opposed to a human being **3** ~ **(of sth)** a thing which is difficult and unpleasant
- *adj.* [only before noun] **1** involving physical strength only and not thought or intelligence: *brute force/strength* **2** basic and unpleasant: *the brute facts of inequality* **3** unable to think or reason, like an animal: *brute beasts/animals*

**bru·tish** /ˈbruːtɪʃ/ adj. unkind and violent and not showing thought or intelligence ▶ **bru·tish·ness** noun [U]

**BS** (NAmE also **B.S.**) /ˌbiː ˈes/ noun, abbr.
- *noun* **1** (NAmE) = BSC **2** (BrE) a university degree in medicine (the abbreviation for 'Bachelor of Surgery') **3** (especially NAmE, taboo, slang) BULLSHIT: That guy's full of BS.
- *abbr.* British Standard (used on labels, etc. showing a number given by the British Standards Institution which controls the quality of products): *produced to BS4353*

**BSc** /ˌbiː es ˈsiː/ (BrE) (NAmE **B.S., BS**) noun a first university degree in science (the abbreviation for 'Bachelor of Science'): (BrE) *to have/do a BSc in Zoology* ◇ (BrE) *Jill Ayres BSc*

**BSE** /ˌbiː es ˈiː/ (also informal **mad ˈcow disease**) noun [U] a brain disease of cows that causes death (the abbreviation for 'bovine spongiform encephalopathy')

**BSI** /ˌbiː es ˈaɪ/ abbr. the British Standards Institution (the organization that decides the standard sizes for goods produced in the UK, and tests the safety of electrical goods, children's toys, etc.)

**ˈB-side** noun the side of a pop record that was considered less likely to be successful ⊃ compare A-SIDE

**BST** /ˌbiː es ˈtiː/ abbr. BRITISH SUMMER TIME

**BTEC** /ˈbiːtek/ noun used to refer to any of a large group of British qualifications that can be taken in many different subjects at several levels (the abbreviation for 'Business and Technology Education Council'): *a BTEC Higher National Diploma in Public Service Studies*

**Btu** (also **BTU**) /ˌbiː tiː ˈjuː/ abbr. British thermal unit (the amount of heat needed to raise one pound of water by one degree FAHRENHEIT, equal to 1.055 x 10³ JOULES) **HELP** The Btu is used as a unit of energy in the US and Canada but not (despite its name) in the UK.

**BTW** abbr. used in writing to mean 'by the way'

**bub·ble** 🔊 **B1** /ˈbʌbl/ noun, verb
- *noun* **1** 🔊 **B1** a ball of air or gas in a liquid, or a ball of air inside a solid substance such as glass: *champagne bubbles* ◇ *a bubble of oxygen* ◇ *He blew bubbles into the water through a straw.* ⊃ picture at FROTH ⊃ see also SPEECH BUBBLE **2** 🔊 **B1** a round ball of liquid, containing air, produced by soap and water: *The children like to have bubbles in their bath.* ⊃ picture at FROTH **3** a small amount of a feeling that sb wants to express: *a bubble of laughter/hope/enthusiasm* **4** a good or lucky situation that is unlikely to last long: *Economists warned of a stock-market bubble.* **IDM ˈthe bubble ˈbursts** there is a sudden end to a good or lucky situation: *When the bubble finally burst, hundreds of people lost their jobs.* ⊃ more at BURST v.
- *verb* **1** [I] to form bubbles: *The water in the pan was beginning to bubble.* ◇ ~ **up** *Add the white wine and let it bubble up.* **2** [I] (+ adv./prep.) to make a bubbling sound: *I could hear the soup bubbling away.* ◇ *A stream came bubbling*

---

**191**     **buck**

*between the stones.* **3** [I] **~ (over) with sth** to be full of a particular feeling: *She was bubbling over with excitement.* **4** [I] **+ adv./prep.** (of a feeling) to be felt strongly by a person; to be present in a situation: *Laughter bubbled up inside him.* ◇ *the anger that bubbled beneath the surface* **PHRV** **ˌbubble ˈunder** (especially BrE) (NAmE usually **ˌbubble under the ˈradar**) (informal) to be likely to be very successful or popular soon: *Here are two new songs that are bubbling under.*

**ˈbubble bath** noun **1** [U] a liquid soap that smells pleasant and makes a lot of bubbles when it is added to bath water **2** [C] a bath with bubble bath in the water

**ˈbubble·gum** /ˈbʌblɡʌm/ noun, adj.
- *noun* [U] a type of CHEWING GUM that can be blown into bubbles
- *adj.* [only before noun] simple in style, not serious, and liked mainly by young people: *This album is pure bubble-gum pop.*

**ˈbubble pack** noun = BLISTER PACK

**ˈbubble ˈtea** noun [U, C] a drink from East Asia made from cold tea mixed with milk, FLAVOURINGS, etc., which also contains small sweet balls that look like bubbles and are made from TAPIOCA

**ˈbubble wrap** (NAmE **BubbleWrap™**) noun [U] a sheet of plastic which has lots of small raised parts filled with air, used for protecting things that are being carried or sent by post

**bub·bly** /ˈbʌbli/ adj. noun
- *adj.* (**bub·blier, bub·bli·est**) **1** full of bubbles **2** (informal) (of a person) always cheerful, friendly and enthusiastic
- *noun* [U] (informal) CHAMPAGNE (= a French SPARKLING white wine that is drunk on special occasions)

**bu·bon·ic plague** /bjuːˌbɒnɪk ˈpleɪɡ; NAmE -ˌbɑːn-/ (also **the ˈplague**) noun [U] a disease spread by RATS that causes a high temperature, SWELLINGS (= areas that are larger and rounder than usual) on the body and usually death

**buc·can·eer** /ˌbʌkəˈnɪə(r); NAmE -ˈnɪr/ noun **1** (in the past) a sailor who attacked ships at sea and stole from them **SYN** pirate **2** (especially in business) a person who achieves success in a way that shows skill but that is not always honest

**buc·can·eer·ing** /ˌbʌkəˈnɪərɪŋ; NAmE -ˈnɪr-/ adj. enjoying taking risks, especially in business: *Virgin's buccaneering founder, Richard Branson*

**buck** 🔊 **+ C1** /bʌk/ noun, verb
- *noun* **1** 🔊 **+ C1** [C] (informal) a US, Australian or New Zealand dollar; a South African RAND; an Indian RUPEE: *They cost ten bucks.* ◇ *We're talking big bucks* (= a lot of money) *here.* **2** [C] a male DEER, HARE or RABBIT (also called a **ˈbuck ˈrabbit**) ⊃ compare DOE, HART, STAG **3** [C] (pl. **buck**) (SAfrE) a DEER, whether male or female: *a herd of buck* **4** [C] (old use, informal) a young man **5 the buck** [sing.] used in some expressions to refer to the responsibility or blame for sth: *It was my decision. The buck stops here* (= nobody else can be blamed). ◇ *I was tempted to pass the buck* (= make sb else responsible). **ORIGIN** From *buck*, an object which in a poker game is placed in front of the player whose turn it is to deal. **IDM ˌmake a fast/quick ˈbuck** (informal, often disapproving) to earn money quickly and easily ⊃ more at BANG n., MILLION
- *verb* **1** [I] (of a horse) to jump with the two back feet or all four feet off the ground **2** [I] to move up and down suddenly or in a way that lacks control: *The boat bucked and heaved beneath them.* **3** [T] **~ sth** (informal) to resist or oppose sth: *One or two companies have managed to buck the trend of the recession.* ◇ *He admired her willingness to buck the system* (= oppose authority or rules). **IDM ˌbuck your iˈdeas up** (BrE, informal) to start behaving in a more acceptable way, so that work gets done better, etc. **PHRV ˌbuck ˈup** (informal) **1** (often in orders) to become more cheerful **SYN** cheer up: *Buck up, kid! It's not the*

---

🟦 Oxford Phrasal Academic Lexicon (OPAL) written and spoken word lists  |  **W** OPAL written word list  |  **S** OPAL spoken word list

# bucket

*end of the game.* **2 buck up!** (*old-fashioned*) used to tell sb to hurry **SYN** hurry | **buck sb 'up** (*BrE*, *informal*) to make sb more cheerful **SYN** cheer up: *The good news bucked us all up.*

**buck·et** /ˈbʌkɪt/ *noun, verb*
- *noun* **1** [C] an open container with a handle, used for carrying or holding liquids, sand, etc. **SYN** pail: *a plastic bucket* ◊ (*BrE*) *They were playing on the beach with their buckets and spades.* ⊃ picture at MOP **2** [C] a large container that is part of a CRANE or DIGGER and is used for lifting things **3** (*also* **bucket·ful** /ˈbʌkɪtfʊl/) [C] the amount contained in a bucket: *two buckets/bucketfuls of water* ◊ **by the bucket/bucketful** *They used to drink tea by the bucketful* (= in large quantities). **4** buckets [pl.] (*informal*) a large amount: *To succeed in show business, you need buckets of confidence.* ◊ *We wept buckets.* ◊ *He was sweating buckets by the end of the race.* ◊ *The rain was coming down in buckets* (= it was raining very heavily). **IDM** see DROP *n.*, KICK *v.*
- *verb*
**PHRV** ˈbucket down (*BrE, informal*) to rain heavily **SYN** pour: *It's bucketing down.*

**ˈbucket list** *noun* a list of things that you want to do before you die: *Travelling to India has been on my bucket list for years.*

**ˈbucket seat** *noun* a seat with a curved back for one person, especially in a car

**buck·eye** /ˈbʌkaɪ/ *noun* **1** a North American tree that has bright red or white flowers and produces nuts **2** an orange and brown BUTTERFLY with large spots on its wings that look like eyes **3** Buckeye (*US, informal*) a person from the US state of Ohio

**Buck·ing·ham Pal·ace** /ˌbʌkɪŋəm ˈpæləs/ *noun* **1** the official home of the British royal family in London **2** the British royal family or the people who advise them: *Buckingham Palace refused to comment.*

**buckle** /ˈbʌkl/ *verb, noun*
- *verb* **1** [T, I] to fasten sth or be fastened with a buckle: *~ sth She buckled her belt.* ◊ *~ sth on/up He buckled on his sword.* ◊ *These shoes buckle at the side.* **2** [I, T] to become bent, damaged or broken under a weight or force; to bend, damage or break sth in this way: **~ (under sth)** *The steel frames began to buckle under the strain.* ◊ (*figurative*) *A weaker man would have buckled under the pressure.* ◊ *~ sth The crash buckled the front of my car.* **3** [I] when your knees or legs **buckle** or when you **buckle** at the knees, your knees become weak and you start to fall
**PHRV** ˌbuckle ˈdown (to sth) (*informal*) to start to do sth seriously: *I'd better buckle down to those reports.* | ˌbuckle ˈup (*NAmE*) (*BrE* ˌbelt ˈup) (*informal*) to fasten your SEAT BELT (= a belt worn by a passenger in a vehicle)
- *noun* a piece of metal or plastic used for joining the ends of a belt or for fastening a part of a bag, shoe, etc.

**ˌbuck ˈnaked** *adj.* (*NAmE, informal*) (of a person) not wearing any clothes at all

**Buck's ˈFizz** (*BrE*) (*NAmE* mi·mosa) *noun* [U, C] an alcoholic drink made by mixing SPARKLING white wine (= with bubbles) with orange juice

**buck·shot** /ˈbʌkʃɒt; *NAmE* -ʃɑːt/ *noun* [U] balls of LEAD that are fired from a SHOTGUN

**buck·skin** /ˈbʌkskɪn/ *noun* [U] soft leather made from the skin of DEER or GOATS, used for making gloves, bags, etc.

**ˌbuck ˈteeth** *noun* [pl.] top teeth that stick forward ▸ **ˌbuck-ˈtoothed** *adj.*

**buck·wheat** /ˈbʌkwiːt/ *noun* [U] small dark seed that is grown as food for animals and for making flour

**bu·col·ic** /bjuːˈkɒlɪk; *NAmE* -ˈkɑːl-/ *adj.* (*literary*) connected with the countryside or country life

**bud** /bʌd/ *noun, verb*
- *noun* **1** a small closed part that grows on a plant and from which a flower, leaf or STEM develops; a flower or leaf that is not fully open: *the first buds appearing in spring* ◊ **in ~** *The tree is in bud already.* ⊃ VISUAL VOCAB pages V6, V7

**2** (*NAmE, informal*) = BUDDY: *Listen, bud, enough of the wisecracks, OK?* ⊃ see also COTTON BUD, ROSEBUD, TASTE BUD
**IDM** see NIP *v.*
- *verb* [I] to produce buds: *The tree is already budding.*

**Bud·dha** /ˈbʊdə; *NAmE* ˈbuːdə, ˈbʊdə/ *noun* **1** (*also* **the Buddha**) [sing.] a title given to Siddhartha Gautama, the person on whose teachings the Buddhist religion is based **2** [C] a statue or picture of the Buddha **3** [C] a person who has achieved ENLIGHTENMENT (= spiritual knowledge) in Buddhism

**Bud·dhism** /ˈbʊdɪzəm; *NAmE* ˈbuːd-, ˈbʊd-/ *noun* [U] an Asian religion based on the teaching of Siddhartha Gautama (or Buddha) ▸ **Bud·dhist** /-dɪst/ *noun*: *a devout Buddhist* **Bud·dhist** *adj.* [usually before noun]: *a Buddhist monk/temple*

**bud·ding** /ˈbʌdɪŋ/ *adj.* [only before noun] beginning to develop or become successful: *a budding artist/writer* ◊ *our budding romance*

**bud·dleia** /ˈbʌdliə/ *noun* [C, U] a bush with purple or white flowers that grow in groups

**buddy** /ˈbʌdi/ *noun, verb*
- *noun* (*pl.* -ies) **1** (*NAmE also* **bud**) (*informal*) a friend: *an old college buddy of mine* ⊃ WORDFINDER NOTE at FRIEND **2** (*also* **bud**) (*both NAmE, informal*) used to speak to a man you do not know: *'Where to, buddy?' the driver asked.* **3** (*especially NAmE*) a partner who does an activity with you so that you can help each other: *The school uses a buddy system to pair newcomers with older students.*
- *verb* (**bud·dies**, **buddy·ing**, **bud·died**, **bud·died**)
**PHRV** ˌbuddy ˈup (with sb) (*especially NAmE*) (*BrE also* ˌpal ˈup (with sb)) (*informal*) to become friendly with sb: *You and your neighbour might want to buddy up to make the trip more enjoyable.* | ˌbuddy ˈup to sb (*especially NAmE, disapproving*) to become friendly with sb in order to get an advantage for yourself: *He's always trying to buddy up to the boss.*

**ˈbuddy movie** *noun* (*informal*) a film in which there is a close friendship between two people

**budge** /bʌdʒ/ *verb* (usually used in negative sentences) (*rather informal*) **1** [I, T] to move slightly; to make sth/sb move slightly: *She pushed at the door but it wouldn't budge.* ◊ *The dog refused to budge.* ◊ *~ sth I heaved with all my might but still couldn't budge it.* **2** [I, T, often passive] to change your opinion about sth; to make sb change their opinion: *~ (on sth) He won't budge an inch on the issue.* ◊ **be budged** *He was not to be budged on the issue.*
**PHRV** ˌbudge ˈup (*BrE, informal*) to move, so that there is room for other people **SYN** move over: *Budge up a bit!*

**budg·eri·gar** /ˈbʌdʒərɪɡɑː(r)/ *noun* (*also informal* **budgie**) a small bird of the PARROT family, often kept in a CAGE as a pet

**budget** /ˈbʌdʒɪt/ *noun, verb, adj.*
- *noun* **1** [C, U] the money that is available to a person or an organization and a plan of how it will be spent over a period of time: *an annual budget of £10 million* ◊ *a balanced budget* (= one where the amount spent matches the amount available) ◊ *Many families struggle to balance the household budget.* ◊ *to cut/slash a budget* ◊ *the education/defence budget* (= the amount of money that can be spent on this) ◊ *a big-budget movie* ◊ **on a ~** *We decorated the house on a tight budget* (= without much money to spend). ◊ **on/within ~** *The work was finished on time and within budget* (= did not cost more money than was planned). ◊ **over ~** *They went over budget* (= spent too much money). ◊ **under/below ~** *The project came in under budget.* ◊ *budget cuts* **2** (*BrE also* Budget) [C, usually sing.] an official statement by the government of a country's income from taxes, etc. and how it will be spent: *tax cuts in this year's budget* ◊ *a budget deficit* (= when the government spends more money than it earns)
- *verb* [I, T] to be careful about the amount of money you spend; to plan to spend an amount of money for a particular purpose: *If we budget carefully we'll be able to afford the trip.* ◊ **~ for sth** *I've budgeted for two new members of staff.* ◊ **~ sth (for sth)** *Ten million euros has been budgeted for the project.* ◊ **~ sth (at sth)** *The project has been*

budgeted at ten million euros. ⇨ SYNONYMS at SAVE
▶ **budget·ing** noun [U]
■ *adj.* [only before noun] (used in advertising, etc.) low in price: *a budget flight/hotel* ⇨ SYNONYMS at CHEAP

**budget·ary** /ˈbʌdʒɪtəri; *NAmE* -teri/ *adj.* connected with a budget: *budgetary control/policies/reform* ⇨ SYNONYMS at ECONOMIC

**budgie** /ˈbʌdʒi/ *noun* (*informal*) = BUDGERIGAR

**buff** /bʌf/ *noun, adj., verb*
■ *noun* **1** [C] (used in compounds) a person who is very interested in a particular subject or activity and knows a lot about it: *a film/movie/history buff* **2** [U] a pale yellow-brown colour SYN **beige** ⇨ see also BLIND MAN'S BUFF
IDM **in the ˈbuff** (*informal*) wearing no clothes SYN **naked**
■ *adj.* **1** pale yellow-brown in colour SYN **beige**: *a buff envelope* **2** (*informal*) physically fit and attractive, with big muscles
■ *verb* ~ **sth** (**up**) to POLISH sth with a soft cloth
PHRV **ˌbuff ˈup** | **ˌbuff yourˈself ˈup** (*informal*) to make yourself more attractive, especially by exercising in order to make your muscles bigger: *He buffed up to take the role of the commando captain.* **ˌbuff sb/sth ˈup** (*informal*) to work on sb/sth to make them/it seem more attractive or impressive: *The team will have to buff up their tarnished image.*

**buf·falo** /ˈbʌfələʊ/ *noun* (*pl.* **buf·falo** or **buf·faloes**) **1** a large animal of the cow family that has wide, curved HORNS. There are two types of buffalo, the African and the Asian. ⇨ see also WATER BUFFALO **2** a North American BISON (= a large wild animal of the cow family that is covered with hair)

**ˈBuffalo wings** *noun* [pl.] (*NAmE*) chicken wings cooked in a spicy sauce

**buf·fer** /ˈbʌfə(r)/ *noun, verb*
■ *noun* **1** a thing or person that reduces a shock or protects sb/sth against difficulties: ~ **against sth** *Support from family and friends acts as a buffer against stress.* ◇ ~ **between A and B** *She often had to act as a buffer between father and son.* ◇ *a buffer state* (= a small country between two powerful states that helps keep peace between them) ◇ *a buffer zone* (= an area of land between two opposing armies or countries) **2** (*BrE*) one of two round metal devices on the front or end of a train, or at the end of a railway track, that reduce the shock if the train hits sth **3** (*computing*) an area in a computer's memory where data can be stored for a short time **4** (*also* **old ˈbuffer**) (*BrE*, *old-fashioned*) a silly old man IDM see HIT *v.*
■ *verb* **1** ~ **sth** to reduce the harmful effects of sth: *to buffer the effects of stress on health* **2** ~ **sb/yourself** (**against sth**) to protect sb/yourself from sth: *They tried to buffer themselves against problems and uncertainties.* **3** ~ **sth** (*computing*) (of a computer) to hold data for a short time before using it

**buf·fet¹** /ˈbʌfeɪ, ˈbʊf-; *NAmE* bəˈfeɪ/ *noun* ⇨ see also BUFFET² **1** a meal at which people serve themselves from a table and then stand or sit somewhere else to eat: *a buffet lunch/supper* ◇ *Dinner will be a cold buffet, not a sit-down meal.* **2** a place, for example in a train or bus station, where you can buy food and drinks to eat or drink there, or to take away ⇨ WORDFINDER NOTE at TRAIN **3** (*BrE*) = BUFFET CAR **4** (*especially NAmE*) = SIDEBOARD

**buf·fet²** /ˈbʌfɪt/ *verb* [often passive] ⇨ see also BUFFET¹
~ **sb/sth** to knock or push sb/sth roughly from side to side: *to be buffeted by the wind* ◇ (*figurative, formal*) *The nation had been buffeted by a wave of strikes.* ⇨ WORDFINDER NOTE at WIND¹ ▶ **buf·fet·ing** *noun* [U, C, usually sing.]

**ˈbuffet car** /ˈbʌfeɪ kɑː(r), ˈbʊf-; *NAmE* bəˈfeɪ kɑːr/ (*also* **buffet**) *noun* (*BrE*) the part of a train where you can buy sth to eat and drink

**buf·foon** /bəˈfuːn/ *noun* (*old-fashioned*) a person who does silly things that make people laugh ▶ **buf·foon·ery** /-ˈfuːnəri/ *noun* [U]

**bug** /bʌɡ/ *noun, verb*
■ *noun* **1** [C] (*especially NAmE*) any small insect **2** [C] (*informal*) an illness that is usually fairly mild but spreads easily from person to person: *a flu bug* ◇ *There's a stomach bug going round* (= people are catching it from each other). ◇ *I picked up a bug in the office.* ⇨ SYNONYMS at DISEASE **3** (*usually* **the … bug**) [sing.] (*informal*) an enthusiastic interest in sth such as a sport or a hobby: *the travel bug* ◇ *She was never interested in fitness before but now she's been bitten by the bug.* **4** [C] a fault in a machine, especially in a computer system or program: *The software is full of bugs.* **5** [C] (*informal*) a small hidden device for listening to other people's conversations
■ *verb* (**-gg-**) **1** ~ **sth** to put a special device (= a bug) somewhere in order to listen secretly to other people's conversations: *They bugged her hotel room.* ◇ *They were bugging his telephone conversations.* ◇ *a bugging device* **2** ~ **sb** (*informal*) to annoy sb: *Stop bugging me!* ◇ *It's something that's been bugging me a lot recently.*
IDM **ˌbug the ˈhell/ˈcrap/ˈshit out of sb** (*taboo, slang*) to annoy sb very much: *The song just bugs the hell out of me.*
PHRV **ˌbug ˈoff!** (*NAmE, informal*) a rude way of telling sb to go away **ˌbug ˈout** (*informal*) **1** (*NAmE, AustralE*) to leave a place or situation, especially because it is becoming dangerous: *We should bug out now before it's too late.* **2** (*NAmE*) to become too frightened to do sth: *Susan started to bug out when she heard a noise in the bushes.* **ˌbug ˈout (of sth)** (*NAmE, informal*) (especially of sb's eyes) to be wide open and stick out: *Their eyes were bugging out of their heads when they saw it.*

**bug·a·boo** /ˈbʌɡəbuː/ *noun* (*NAmE, informal*) a thing that people are afraid of

**bug·bear** /ˈbʌɡbeə(r); *NAmE* -ber/ *noun* (*especially BrE*) a thing that annoys people and that they worry about: *Inflation is the government's main bugbear*

**ˈbug-eyed** *adj.* (*informal*) having eyes that stick out: *a bug-eyed monster*

**bug·ger** /ˈbʌɡə(r)/ *noun, verb*
■ *noun* (*BrE, taboo, slang*) **1** an offensive word used to show anger or dislike for sb, especially a man: *Come here, you little bugger!* ◇ *You stupid bugger! You could have run me over!* **2** used to refer to a person, especially a man, that you like or feel sympathy for: *Poor bugger! His wife left him last week.* ◇ *He's a tough old bugger.* **3** [usually sing.] a thing that is difficult or causes problems: *This door's a bugger to open.* ◇ *Question 6 is a real bugger.* IDM see SILLY *adj.*
■ *verb* **1** [I, T] (*BrE, taboo, slang*) used as a swear word when sb is annoyed about sth or to show that they do not care about sth at all: *Bugger! I've left my keys at home.* ◇ ~ **sth** *Bugger it! I've burnt the toast.* ◇ *Oh, bugger the cost! Let's get it anyway.* **2** [T] ~ **sth** (*BrE, taboo, slang*) to break sth or damage it so badly that it cannot be repaired: *I think I've buggered the computer.* **3** [T] ~ **sb** (*taboo or law*) to have ANAL sex with sb
IDM **ˌbugger ˈme** (*BrE, taboo, slang*) used to express surprise: *Bugger me! Did you see that?*
PHRV **ˌbugger aˈbout/aˈround** (*BrE, taboo, slang*) to waste time by behaving in a silly way or with no clear purpose: *Stop buggering about and get back to work.* HELP A more polite, informal way of saying this is **mess about** *BrE* or **mess around** *BrE and NAmE*. **ˌbugger sb aˈbout/aˈround** (*BrE, taboo, slang*) to treat sb in a way that is deliberately not helpful to them or wastes their time: *I'm sick of being buggered about by the company.* HELP A more polite, informal way of saying this is **mess sb about/around**. **ˌbugger ˈoff** (*BrE, taboo, slang*) (often used in orders) to go away: *Bugger off and leave me alone.* ◇ *Where is everyone? They've all buggered off.* **ˌbugger sth⇌ˈup** (*BrE, taboo, slang*) to do sth badly or fail at sth: *I buggered up the exam.* ◇ *Sorry for buggering up your plans.* HELP A more polite, informal way of saying this is **foul sth up**, **mess sth up** or **bungle sth**.

**ˌbugger ˈall** *noun* [U] (*BrE, taboo, slang*) nothing at all; none at all: *There's bugger all on TV tonight.* ◇ *Well, she was bugger all help* (= no help at all).

**bug·gered** /ˈbʌɡəd; *NAmE* -ɡərd/ *adj.* [not before noun] (*BrE, taboo, slang*) **1** very tired **2** broken, or damaged too badly to repair: *Oh no, the TV's buggered.*

**buggy**

**IDM** **I'll be buggered** (*BrE*, *taboo*, *slang*) used to express great surprise: *Well, I'll be buggered! Look who's here.* **I'm 'buggered if …** (*BrE*, *taboo*, *slang*) used to say that you do not know sth or to refuse to do sth: *'What's this meeting all about?' 'I'm buggered if I know.'* ◊ *Well I'm buggered if I'm going to help her after what she said to me.*

**bug·gery** /ˈbʌɡəri/ *noun* [U] (*BrE*, *taboo*, *slang* or *law*) ANAL SEX

**bug·gy** /ˈbʌɡi/ *noun*, *adj.*
- *noun* (*pl.* **-ies**) **1** (*BrE*) a small car, often without a roof or doors, used for a particular purpose: *a garden/golf buggy* ⊃ compare GOLF CART ⊃ see also BEACH BUGGY **2** (*BrE also* **'baby buggy**, **pushchair**) (*NAmE also* **strol·ler**) a type of light folding chair on wheels in which a baby or small child is pushed along **3** a light CARRIAGE for one or two people, pulled by one horse
- *adj.* (**bug·gier**, **bug·gi·est**) (*informal*) **1** (of a computer system or program) full of BUGS so it does not work correctly: *The software is buggy and slow.* **2** full of BUGS (= insects): *The summers are hot and humid and buggy.* **3** (*NAmE*) crazy: *With this app, kids go buggy over math.* **4** (*NAmE*) (of eyes) sticking out, especially in a way that looks crazy: *I do not believe in little alien dudes with buggy eyes.* ◊ *My eyes went buggy just looking at them.* ⊃ compare BUG-EYED

**bugle** /ˈbjuːɡl/ *noun* a musical instrument like a small TRUMPET, used in the army for giving signals

**bu·gler** /ˈbjuːɡlə(r)/ *noun* a person who plays the bugle

**bui·bui** /ˌbuːiˈbuːi/ *EAfrE* [buiˈbui] *noun* (*EAfrE*) an item of clothing worn by some Muslim women, consisting of a long black dress and a piece of black cloth that covers the head showing only the face or eyes

**build** 🔑 **A1** /bɪld/ *verb*, *noun*
- *verb* (**built**, **built** /bɪlt/) **1** 🔑 **A1** [T, I] to make sth, especially a building, by putting parts together: **~(sth)** *They have permission to build 200 new homes.* ◊ *We build computer systems for large companies.* ◊ *They're going to build on the site of the old power station.* ◊ **be built from/in/of/out of sth** *The houses are built out of local stone.* ◊ **~sth for sb** *They had a house built for them.* ◊ **~sb sth** *David built us a shed in the back yard.* **2** 🔑 **A2** [T] **~sth** to create or develop sth: *They are trying to build long-term relationships.* ◊ *to build a community/society* ◊ *We focused on building the business one customer at a time.* **3** [I] (of a feeling) to become gradually stronger: *The tension and excitement built gradually all day.* **IDM** see CASTLE, ROME
- **PHRV** **build sth aˈround sth** [usually passive] to create sth, using sth else as a basis: *The story is built around a group of high school dropouts.* **build sth↔ˈin** | **build sth ˈinto sth** [often passive] **1** to make sth a permanent part of a larger structure: *We're having new wardrobes built in.* ◊ *Manufacturers are building new security features into their products.* ◊ *The pipes were built into the concrete.* **2** to make sth a permanent part of a system, plan, etc: *A certain amount of flexibility is built into the system.* ⊃ see also BUILT-IN **ˈbuild on sth** to use sth as a basis for further progress: *This study builds on earlier work.* **ˈbuild sth on sth** [usually passive] to base sth on sth: *an argument built on sound logic* **build sth↔ˈon** | **build sth ˈonto sth** to add sth (for example, an extra room) to an existing structure by building: *They've built an extension on.* ◊ *The new wing was built onto the hospital last year.* **build ˈup (to sth)** to become greater, more powerful or larger in number: *All the pressure built up and he was off work for weeks with stress.* ◊ *The music builds up to a rousing climax.* ⊃ related noun BUILD-UP (1) **build ˈup to sth** | **build yourself ˈup to sth** to prepare for a particular moment or event: *Build yourself up to peak performance on the day of the exam.* ⊃ related noun BUILD-UP (2) **build sb/sth ˈup** [usually passive] to give a very positive and enthusiastic description of sb/sth, often making them seem better than they really are: *The play was built up to be a masterpiece but I found it very disappointing.* ⊃ related noun BUILD-UP (3) **build sb/yourself↔ˈup** to make sb/yourself healthier or stronger: *You need more protein to build you up.* **build sth↔ˈup 1** to create or develop sth: *She's built up a very successful business.* ◊ *These finds help us build up a picture of life in the Middle Ages.* ◊ *I am anxious not to build up false hopes* (= to encourage people to hope for too much). **2** to make sth higher or stronger than it was before
- *noun* **1** [U, C, usually *sing.*] the shape and size of the human body: *a man of average build* **2** [*sing.*] the process of building or constructing sth: *We are just completing the build of our new house.* ⊃ see also NEW BUILD **3** [C] a version of a piece of software that is created, especially one of a series of versions created before the final version is released **4** [*sing.*] the form or style in which sth is constructed, especially a vehicle: *a car with superb build quality*

▼ SYNONYMS

**build**
construct • assemble • erect • put sth up

These words all mean to make sth, especially by putting different parts together.

**build** to make sth, especially a building, by putting parts together: *a house built of stone* ◊ *They're going to build on the site of the old power station.*

**construct** [often passive] (*rather formal*) to build sth such as a road, building or machine

**assemble** (*rather formal*) to fit together all the separate parts of sth such as a piece of furniture or a machine: *The cupboard is easy to assemble.*

**erect** (*formal*) to build sth; to put sth in position and make it stand upright: *Police had to erect barriers to keep crowds back.*

**put sth up** to build sth or place sth somewhere: *They're putting up new hotels in order to boost tourism in the area.*

PATTERNS
- to build/construct/erect/put up a **house/wall**
- to build/construct/erect/put up some **shelves**
- to build/construct/erect/put up a **barrier/fence/shelter**
- to build/construct/assemble a(n) **engine/machine**
- to build/construct a **road/railway/tunnel**
- to erect/put up a **tent/statue/monument**

**build·er** /ˈbɪldə(r)/ *noun* **1** a person or company whose job is to build or repair houses or other buildings **2** (usually in compounds) a person or thing that builds, creates or develops sth: *a shipbuilder* ◊ *a confidence builder* ⊃ see also BODYBUILDER

**'builders' merchant** *noun* a person or shop that supplies materials to the building trade

**build·ing** 🔑 **A1** /ˈbɪldɪŋ/ *noun* **1** 🔑 **A1** [C] a structure such as a house or school that has a roof and walls: *a tall/high-rise/ten-storey building* ◊ *an apartment/office building* ◊ *the restoration of historic buildings* ◊ *to design/construct/erect a building* ⊃ see also LISTED BUILDING **2** 🔑 **B1** [U] the process and work of building: *the building of the school* ◊ *There's building work going on next door.* ◊ *the building trade* ◊ *building materials* ⊃ see also TEAM BUILDING

**'building block** *noun* **1** [C] a piece of wood or plastic used as a toy for children to build things with **2 building blocks** [*pl.*] parts that are joined together in order to make a large thing exist: *Single words are the building blocks of language.*

**'building site** (especially *BrE*) (also **conˈstruction site** *BrE and NAmE*) *noun* an area of land where sth is being built

**'building society** *noun* (*BrE*) (*US* **savings and ˈloan association**) an organization like a bank that lends money to people who want to buy a house. People also save money with a building society.

**'build-up** *noun* **1** [*sing.*, U] an increase in the amount of sth over a period of time: *a steady build-up of traffic in the evenings* **2** [C, usually *sing.*] **~(to sth)** the time before an important event, when people are preparing for it: *the build-up to the president's visit* **3** [C, usually *sing.*] a very positive and enthusiastic description of sth that is going to

▼ SYNONYMS

## building
property • premises • complex • structure • block

These are all words for a structure such as a house, office block or factory that has a roof and four walls.

**building** a structure such as a house, an office block or a factory that has a roof and four walls.

**property** a building or buildings and the surrounding land; land and buildings: *We have a buyer who would like to view the property.* ◊ *The price of property has risen enormously.* **NOTE** This word is often used when talking about buying/selling houses or other buildings and land.

**premises** [pl.] the building or buildings and surrounding land that a business owns or uses: *The company is looking for larger premises.*

**complex** a group of buildings of a similar type together in one place: *a leisure complex*

**structure** a thing that is made of several parts, especially a building: *The pier is a wooden structure.*

**block** (BrE) a tall building that contains flats or offices; a building that forms part of a school, hospital, etc. and is used for a particular purpose: *a block of flats* ◊ *the school's science block*

PATTERNS
- a(n) **commercial/industrial/residential** building/property/premises/complex/block
- an **apartment** building/complex/block
- a/the **school** building/complex/premises
- to **build** a property/complex/structure/block
- to **put up** a building/property/structure/block
- to **demolish/pull down** a building/property/complex/structure/block

---

happen, that is intended to make people excited about it: *The media have given the show a huge build-up.*

**built** /bɪlt/ *combining form* (after adverbs and in compound adjectives) made in the particular way that is mentioned: *a newly built station* ◊ *American-built cars* ⊃ see also PURPOSE-BUILT, WELL BUILT

**built-'in** *adj.* [only before noun] **1** included as part of sth and not separate from it: (BrE) *Both bedrooms have **built-in** wardrobes.* ◊ *The device has a built-in microphone and speakers.* ⊃ compare INBUILT **2** = INBUILT (1)

**built-'up** *adj.* [usually before noun] (*especially BrE*) (of an area of land) covered in buildings, roads, etc: *to reduce the speed limit in built-up areas*

**bulb** /bʌlb/ *noun* **1** = LIGHT BULB: *a halogen bulb* ◊ *a room lit by bare bulbs* (= with no decorative cover) ⊃ picture at SPOTLIGHT **2** the round underground part of some plants, like an onion in shape, that grows into a new plant every year ⊃ VISUAL VOCAB page V7 **3** an object that is like a bulb in shape, for example the end of a THERMOMETER

**bulb·ous** /ˈbʌlbəs/ *adj.* having the shape of a bulb; round and fat in an ugly way: *a bulbous red nose*

**bul·gar** (*also* **bul·gur**) /ˈbʌlɡə(r)/ (*also* **bulgar wheat**) *noun* [U] a type of food consisting of grains of WHEAT that are boiled then dried

**bulge** /bʌldʒ/ *verb, noun*
■ *verb* **1** [I] ~ **(with sth)** (usually used in the progressive tenses) to be completely full (of sth): *Her pockets were bulging with presents.* ◊ *a bulging briefcase* **2** [I] to stick out from sth in a round shape: *His eyes bulged.* **IDM** see SEAM
■ *noun* **1** a round or curved shape that sticks out from sth: *the bulge of a gun in his pocket* **2** (*informal*) fat on the body that sticks out in a round shape: *That skirt's too tight. It shows all your bulges.* **3** a sudden temporary increase in the amount of sth: *After the war there was a bulge in the birth rate.*

**bul·ging** /ˈbʌldʒɪŋ/ *adj.* that sticks out from sth in a round shape: *bulging eyes*

**bu·limia** /buˈlɪmiə, -ˈliːm-/ (*also* **bulimia nervosa** /buˌlɪmiə nɜːˈvəʊsə, -ˈliːm-; NAmE nɜːrˈv-/) *noun* [U] an emotional DIS-

---

195 **bulletin board**

ORDER in which a person repeatedly eats too much and then forces him- or herself to VOMIT ⊃ compare ANOREXIA ▶ **bu·lim·ic** /buˈlɪmɪk, -ˈliːm-/ *adj., noun*

**bulk** /bʌlk/ *noun, verb*
■ *noun* **1** [sing.] **the ~ (of sth)** the main part of sth; most of sth: *The bulk of the population lives in cities.* **2** [U] the (large) size or quantity of sth: *Despite its bulk and weight, the car is extremely fast.* ◊ *a **bulk order** (= one for a large number of similar items)* ◊ ***bulk buying** (= buying in large amounts, often at a reduced price)* ◊ *in ~ It's cheaper to buy in bulk.* **3** [sing.] the weight or shape of sb/sth large: *She heaved her bulk out of the chair.*
■ *verb* **IDM** **bulk 'large** (BrE, formal) to be the most important part of sth
**PHRV** **bulk sth↔'out/'up** to make sth bigger, thicker or heavier

**bulk·head** /ˈbʌlkhed/ *noun* (*specialist*) a wall that divides a ship or an aircraft into separate parts

**bulky** /ˈbʌlki/ *adj.* (**bulk·ier, bulki·est**) **1** (of a thing) large and difficult to move or carry: *Bulky items will be collected separately.* **2** (of a person) tall and heavy: *The bulky figure of Inspector Jones appeared at the door.*

**bull** /bʊl/ *noun* **1** [C] the male of any animal in the cow family: *a bull neck* (= a short thick neck like a bull's) ⊃ compare BULLOCK, COW, OX, STEER **2** [C] the male of the elephant, WHALE and some other large animals: *a bull elephant* ⊃ compare COW **3** [C] (*finance*) a person who buys shares in a company, hoping to sell them soon afterwards at a higher price ⊃ compare BEAR **4** [C] an official order or statement from the POPE (= the head of the Roman Catholic Church): *a papal bull* **5** [U] (*informal*) ideas, statements or beliefs that you think are silly or not true: *That's a load of bull!* **6** [C] = BULLSEYE ⊃ see also COCK AND BULL STORY **IDM** **a bull in a 'china shop** a person who is careless, or who moves or acts in a rough way, in a place or situation where skill and care are needed **take the bull by the 'horns** to face a difficult or dangerous situation directly and with courage ⊃ more at SHOOT *v.*, WAVE *v.*

**bull·dog** /ˈbʊldɒɡ; NAmE -dɔːɡ/ *noun* a short strong dog with a large head, a short flat nose and a short thick neck

**'Bulldog clip**™ *noun* (BrE) a metal device for holding papers together

**bull·doze** /ˈbʊldəʊz/ *verb* **1** [T, often passive] to destroy buildings, trees, etc. with a bulldozer: *be bulldozed The trees are being bulldozed to make way for a new superstore.* **2** [I, T] to force your way somewhere; to force sth somewhere: + *adv./prep. Sterling bulldozed through to score.* ◊ ~ *sth* + *adv./prep. They bulldozed the tax through Parliament.* ◊ *He bulldozed his way to victory.* **3** [T] ~ **sb (into doing sth)** to force sb to do sth **SYN** railroad: *They bulldozed him into selling.*

**bull·dozer** /ˈbʊldəʊzə(r)/ *noun* a powerful vehicle with a broad steel BLADE (= cutting edge) in front, used for moving earth or knocking down buildings

**bul·let** /ˈbʊlɪt/ *noun* a small metal object that is fired from a gun: *bullet wounds* ◊ *There were **bullet holes** in the door.* ◊ *He was killed by a bullet in the head.* ⊃ see also MAGIC BULLET, PLASTIC BULLET, RUBBER BULLET, SILVER BULLET **IDM** see BITE *v.*, DODGE *v.*

**bul·let·ed** /ˈbʊlɪtɪd/ *adj.* a bulleted list has a bullet point before each item on the list; a bulleted item has a bullet point before it

**bul·letin** /ˈbʊlətɪn/ *noun* **1** a short news report on the radio or television ⊃ WORDFINDER NOTE at RADIO **2** an official statement about sth important: *a bulletin on the president's health* **3** a printed report that gives news about an organization or a group

**'bulletin board** *noun* **1** (NAmE) (BrE **'notice·board**) (*also* **board** BrE, NAmE) a board for putting notices on

**bullet point** 196

**2** (*computing*) a place on a computer network where any user can write or read messages

**'bullet point** *noun* an item in a list in a document, that is printed with a square, diamond or circle in front of it in order to show that it is important. The square, etc. is also called a bullet point.

**bul·let-proof** /'bʊlɪtpruːf/ *adj.* that can stop bullets from passing through it: *a bulletproof vest*

**'bullet train** *noun* (*informal*) a Japanese train that carries passengers at high speeds

**bull·fight** /'bʊlfaɪt/ *noun* a traditional public entertainment, popular especially in Spain, in which BULLS are fought and usually killed ▶ **bull·fight·er** *noun* **bull·fight·ing** *noun* [U] ⇒ see also MATADOR

**bull·frog** /'bʊlfrɒg/; *NAmE* -frɑːg/ *noun* a large American frog with a loud CROAK

**bull·horn** /'bʊlhɔːn/; *NAmE* -hɔːrn/ *noun* (*NAmE*) = MEGAPHONE

**bul·lion** /'bʊliən/ *noun* [U] gold or silver in large amounts or in the form of bars: *gold bullion*

**bull·ish** /'bʊlɪʃ/ *adj.* **1** feeling confident and positive about the future: *in a bullish mood* **2** (*finance*) causing, or connected with, an increase in the price of shares: *a bullish market* ⇒ compare BEARISH

**'bull market** *noun* (*finance*) a period during which share prices are rising and people are buying shares ⇒ compare BEAR MARKET

**bul·lock** /'bʊlək/ *noun* a young BULL (= a male cow) that has been CASTRATED (= had part of its sex organs removed) ⇒ compare OX, STEER

**bull·pen** /'bʊlpen/ *noun* (*NAmE*) **1** the part of a baseball field where players practise PITCHING (= throwing) before the game **2** extra PITCHERS (= players who throw the ball) in a baseball team who are used, if necessary, to replace the usual pitchers: *The team's bullpen is solid this year.* **3** a type of large office which is OPEN-PLAN (= it does not have walls dividing the office area) **4** a room where prisoners wait before they go into the court for their trial

**bull·ring** /'bʊlrɪŋ/ *noun* the large round area, like an outdoor theatre, where BULLFIGHTS take place

**'bull·rush** = BULRUSH

**bulls·eye** /'bʊlzaɪ/ (*also* **bull**) *noun* [usually sing.] the centre of the target that you shoot or throw at in shooting, ARCHERY or DARTS; a shot or throw that hits this: *He scored a bullseye.*

**bull·shit** /'bʊlʃɪt/ *noun, verb*
- *noun* [U] (*taboo, slang*) (*abbr. especially NAmE* **BS**) ideas, statements or beliefs that you think are silly or not true **SYN** **nonsense**: *That's just bullshit.*
- *verb* [I, T] (*taboo, slang*) (**-tt-**) to say things that are not true, especially in order to trick sb: *She's just bullshitting.* ◊ *~ sb Don't try to bullshit me!* ▶ **bull·shit·ter** *noun*

**bull 'terrier** *noun* a strong dog with short hair, a thick neck and a long nose ⇒ see also PIT BULL TERRIER

**bully** /'bʊli/ *noun, verb, exclamation*
- *noun* (*pl.* **-ies**) a person who uses their strength or power to frighten or hurt weaker people: *the school bully*
- *verb* (**bul·lies, bully·ing, bul·lied, bul·lied**) to frighten or hurt a weaker person; to use your strength or power to make sb do sth: *~ sb My son is being bullied at school.* ◊ *~ sb into sth/into doing sth I won't be bullied into signing anything.* ▶ **bully·ing** *noun* [U]: *Bullying is a problem in many schools.* ◊ *He refused to give in to bullying and threats.* ◊ *bullying behaviour/tactics*
- *exclamation* **IDM** **bully for you, etc.** (*informal*) used to show that you do not think that what sb has said or done is very impressive: *He's got a job in New York? Well, bully for him!*

**'bully boy** *noun* (*BrE, informal*) an aggressive violent man: *The group have frequently used bully-boy tactics.*

**'bully pulpit** *noun* [sing.] (*NAmE*) a position of authority that gives sb the opportunity to speak in public about an issue

**bul·rush** (*also* **bull-rush**) /'bʊlrʌʃ/ *noun* a tall plant with long narrow leaves and a long brown head of flowers, that grows in or near water ⇒ VISUAL VOCAB page V7

**bul·wark** /'bʊlwək; *NAmE* -wɜːrk/ *noun* **1** [usually sing.] **~ (against sth)** (*formal*) a person or thing that protects or defends sth: *a bulwark against extremism* **2** [C] a wall built as a defence **3** [usually pl.] the part of a ship's side that is above the level of the DECK

**bum** /bʌm/ *noun, verb, adj.*
- *noun* (*informal*) **1** (*BrE*) the part of the body that you sit on **SYN** **backside, behind, bottom** **2** (*especially NAmE*) a person who has no home or job and who asks other people for money or food: *a beach bum* (= sb who spends all their time on the beach, without having a job) **3** a lazy person who does nothing for other people or for society: *He's nothing but a no-good bum!*
  **IDM** **bums on 'seats** (*BrE, informal*) used to refer to the number of people who attend a show, talk, etc., especially when emphasizing the need or desire to attract a large number: *They're not bothered about attracting the right audience—they just want bums on seats.* **give sb/get the bum's 'rush** (*informal, especially NAmE*) to force sb/be forced to leave a place quickly: *He was soon given the bum's rush from the club.*
- *verb* (**-mm-**) **1 ~ sth (off sb)** (*informal*) to get sth from sb by asking **SYN** **cadge**: *Can I bum a cigarette off you?* **2 ~ sb (out)** (*NAmE, informal*) to make sb feel upset or disappointed
  **PHRV** **bum a'round** (*BrE also* **bum a'bout**) (*informal*) to travel around or spend your time with no particular plans: *He bummed around the world for a year.*
- *adj.* [only before noun] (*informal*) of bad quality; wrong or not worth anything: *He didn't play one bum note.* ◊ *a bum deal* (= a situation where you do not get what you deserve or have paid for)

**'bum-bag** /'bʌmbæg/ (*BrE*) (*NAmE* **'fanny pack**) *noun* (*informal*) a small bag attached to a belt and worn around the middle part of the body, to keep money, etc. in

**bum·ble** /'bʌmbl/ *verb* [I] **+ adv./prep.** to act or move in a way that is not smooth or steady or showing clear thought: *I could hear him bumbling around in the kitchen.*

**bumble·bee** /'bʌmblbiː/ *noun* a large bee covered with small hairs that makes a loud noise as it flies ⇒ VISUAL VOCAB page V3

**bum·bling** /'bʌmblɪŋ/ *adj.* [only before noun] behaving in a confused way, often making careless mistakes

**bum·mer** /'bʌmə(r)/ *noun* **a bummer** [sing.] (*informal*) a disappointing or unpleasant situation: *It's a real bummer that she can't come.*

**bump** /bʌmp/ *verb, noun*
- *verb* **1** [I] to hit sb/sth by accident: *~ into sb/sth In the dark I bumped into a chair.* ◊ *~ against sb/sth The car bumped against the kerb.* ⇒ SYNONYMS at HIT **2** [T] **~ sth (against/on sth)** to hit sth, especially a part of your body, against or on sth: *Be careful not to bump your head on the beam when you stand up.* **3** [I, T] to move across a rough surface: **+ adv./prep.** *The jeep bumped along the dirt track.* ◊ *~ sth + adv./prep. The car bumped its way slowly down the drive.* **4** [T] **~ sb + adv./prep.** to move sb from one group or position to another; to remove sb from a group: *The airline apologized and bumped us up to first class.* ◊ *If you are bumped off an airline because of overbooking, you are entitled to compensation.* ◊ *The coach told him he had been bumped from the crew.*
  **PHRV** **bump 'into sb** (*informal*) to meet sb by chance **bump sb↔'off** (*informal*) to murder sb **bump sth↔'up** (*informal*) to increase or raise sth **bump 'up against sth** to experience a problem or factor that you did not expect: *We kept bumping up against inflexible regulations.*
- *noun* **1** [C] the action or sound of sth hitting a hard surface: *We could hear loud bumps from upstairs where the children were playing.* ◊ **with a ~** *He fell to the ground with a bump.* **2** [C] a SWELLING (= an area that is larger and

rounder than normal) on the body, often caused when you have been hit SYN **lump**: *She was covered in bumps and bruises.* ◊ *How did you get that bump on your forehead?* **3** (*informal*) = BABY BUMP **4** [C] a part of a flat surface that is not even, but raised above the rest of it: *a bump in the road* ➔ see also BUMPY **5** [C] a slight accident in which your vehicle hits sth **6 the bumps** [pl.] (*BrE*) (on a child's birthday) the act of lifting the child in the air and then putting them down on the ground, once for every year of their age: *We gave her the bumps.* IDM see EARTH *n.*, THING

**bump·er** /'bʌmpə(r)/ *noun*, *adj.*
- *noun* a bar fixed to the front and back of a car, etc. to reduce the effect if it hits anything: *a bumper sticker* (= a sign that people stick on the bumper of their cars with a message on it) ◊ *The cars were bumper to bumper on the road to the coast* (= so close that their bumpers were nearly touching).
- *adj.* [only before noun] (*approving*) unusually large; producing an unusually large amount of sth: *a bumper issue* (= of a magazine, etc.) ◊ *a bumper crop/harvest/season/year*

'**bumper car** (*especially NAmE*) (*BrE also* **dodgem**, '**dodgem car**) *noun* one of the small electric cars that you drive in DODGEM ➔ picture at DODGEM

**bump·kin** /'bʌmpkɪn/ *noun* = COUNTRY BUMPKIN

**bump·tious** /'bʌmpʃəs/ *adj.* (*disapproving*) showing that you think that you are very important; often giving your opinions in a loud, confident and annoying way

**bumpy** /'bʌmpi/ *adj.* (**bump·i·er**, **bumpi·est**) **1** (of a surface) not even; with a lot of BUMPS: *a bumpy road/track* ◊ *bumpy ground* **2** (of a journey) uncomfortable with a lot of sudden unpleasant movements caused by the road surface, weather conditions, etc.: *a bumpy ride/flight*
IDM **have/give sb a bumpy 'ride** to have a difficult time; to make a situation difficult for sb

**bun** /bʌn/ *noun* **1** [C] a small round sweet cake: *an iced bun* ➔ see also HOT CROSS BUN **2** [C] a small round flat bread roll: *a hamburger bun* ➔ compare ROLL **3** [C] long hair that has been TWISTED into a round shape and is worn on top or at the back of the head: *She wore her hair in a bun.* **4 buns** [pl.] (*slang, especially NAmE*) the two sides of a person's bottom
IDM **have a 'bun in the oven** (*informal, humorous*) to be pregnant

**bunch** ❶ B2 /bʌntʃ/ *noun*, *verb*
- *noun* **1** ❷ B2 [C] ~ (of sth) a number of things of the same type which are growing or fastened together: *a bunch of bananas, grapes, etc.* ◊ *a bunch of keys* ◊ *She picked me a bunch of flowers.* ➔ VISUAL VOCAB page V4 **2** [*sing.*] **a ~ (of sth)** (*informal, especially NAmE*) a large amount of sth; a large number of things or people: *I have a whole bunch of stuff to do this morning.* **3** [*sing.*] (*informal*) a group of people: *The people that I work with are a great bunch.* ◊ *~ of sb They're a great bunch of people/guys/kids.* **4 bunches** [pl.] (*BrE*) long hair that is divided in two and tied at each side of the head: *She wore her hair in bunches.*
IDM **the best/pick of the 'bunch** the best out of a group of people or things ➔ more at BEST *n.*, PANTIES
- *verb* [I, T] to become tight or to form tight folds; to make sth do this: *His muscles bunched under his shirt.* ◊ **~ (sth) up** *Her skirt had bunched up round her waist.* ◊ **~ sth** *His forehead was bunched in a frown.*
PHRV **bunch 'up/to'gether** | **bunch sb/sth 'up/to'gether** to move closer and form into a group; to make people or things do this: *The sheep bunched together as soon as they saw the dog.*

**bun·dle** /'bʌndl/ *noun*, *verb*
- *noun* **1** [C] a number of things tied or wrapped together; sth that is wrapped up: *a bundle of rags/papers/firewood* ◊ *She held her little bundle* (= her baby) *tightly in her arms.* **2** [C] a number of things that belong, or are sold together: *a bundle of ideas* ◊ *a bundle of graphics packages for your PC* **3** [*sing.*] **a ~ of laughs, fun, etc.** (*informal*) a person or thing that makes you laugh: *He wasn't exactly a bundle of laughs* (= a happy person to be with) *last night.* ➔ see also BUNDLE OF JOY **4 a bundle** [*sing.*] (*informal*) a large amount of money: *That car must have cost a bundle.*

IDM **not go a bundle on sb/sth** (*BrE, informal*) to not like sb/sth very much ➔ more at DROP *v.*, NERVE *n.*
- *verb* **1** [T] **~ sb + adv./prep.** to push or send sb somewhere quickly and not carefully: *They bundled her into the back of a car.* ◊ *He was bundled off to boarding school.* **2** [I] **+ adv./prep.** to move somewhere quickly in a group: *We bundled out onto the street.* **3** [T] **~ sth (with sth)** to supply extra equipment, especially software when selling a new computer, at no extra cost: *A further nine applications are bundled with the system.*
PHRV **bundle sth↔'up** | **bundle sth↔to'gether** to make or tie sth into a bundle: *He bundled up the dirty clothes and stuffed them into the bag.* ◊ *The papers were all bundled together, ready to be thrown out.* **bundle sb 'up (in sth)** to put warm clothes or thick material on sb: *I bundled her up in a blanket and gave her a hot drink.*

**bundle of 'joy** *noun* (*informal, humorous, sometimes ironic*) a baby son or daughter: *Here are the latest pictures of our little bundle of joy.*

**bundo·bast** (*also* **bundo·bust**) (*IndE*) = BANDOBAST

**bung** /bʌŋ/ *verb*, *noun*, *adj.*
- *verb* **~ sth + adv./prep.** (*BrE, informal*) to put or throw sth somewhere, carelessly and quickly: *Bung this in the bin, can you?*
PHRV **bung sth 'up (with sth)** [usually passive] to block sth: *My nose is all bunged up.* ◊ *The drains are bunged up with dead leaves.*
- *noun* **1** a round piece of wood, rubber, etc. used for closing the hole in a container such as a BARREL or JAR **2** (*BrE, informal*) an amount of money that is given to sb to persuade them to do sth illegal
- *adj.* (*AustralE, NZE, informal*) broken

**bun·ga·low** /'bʌŋɡələʊ/ *noun* **1** (*BrE*) a house built all on one level, without stairs ➔ compare RANCH HOUSE **2** (in some Asian countries) a large house, sometimes on more than one level, that is not joined to another house on either side

**bun·gee** /'bʌndʒi/ *noun* **1** a long rope that can stretch, which people tie to their feet when they do bungee jumping **2** (*also* '**bungee cord**) a thick ELASTIC rope with a HOOK at each end that can be used to hold packages together, keep things in position, etc.

'**bungee jump·ing** *noun* [U] a sport in which a person jumps from a high place, such as a BRIDGE or a CLIFF, with a bungee tied to their feet: *to go bungee jumping* ▶ '**bungee jump** *noun*: *to do a bungee jump*

**bun·gle** /'bʌŋɡl/ *verb*, *noun*
- *verb* [T, I] **~ (sth)** to do sth badly or without skill; to fail at sth SYN **botch**: *They bungled the job.* ◊ *a bungled robbery/raid/attempt* ▶ **bun·gler** /-ɡlə(r)/ *noun* **bun·gling** /-ɡlɪŋ/ *adj.* [only before noun]: *bungling incompetence*
- *noun* [usually *sing.*] something that is done badly and that causes problems: *Their pay was late because of a computer bungle.*

**bun·ion** /'bʌnjən/ *noun* a painful SWELLING (= an area that is larger and rounder than normal) on the foot, usually on the big toe

**bunk** /bʌŋk/ *noun*, *verb*
- *noun* **1** [C] a narrow bed that is fixed to a wall, especially on a ship or train **2** [C] (*also* '**bunk bed**) one of two beds that are fixed together, one above the other, especially for children **3** [U] (*old-fashioned, informal*) ideas, statements or beliefs that you think are silly or not true SYN **bunkum**, nonsense
- *verb*
PHRV **bunk 'off** | **bunk off 'school/'work** (*BrE, informal*) to stay away from school or work when you should be there; to leave school or work early SYN **skive, play truant**

**bun·ker** /'bʌŋkə(r)/ *noun*, *verb*
- *noun* **1** a strongly built shelter for soldiers or guns, usually underground: *a concrete/underground/secret bunker* **2** a container for storing coal, especially on a ship or outside a

**house:** *a coal bunker* **3** (*also especially NAmE* **'sand trap, trap**) a small area filled with sand on a GOLF COURSE
- *verb* **be bunkered** (in golf) to have hit your ball into a bunker (and therefore to be in a difficult position)

**bunk·house** /ˈbʌŋkhaʊs/ *noun* a building for workers to sleep in

**bun·kum** /ˈbʌŋkəm/ *noun* [U] (*old-fashioned, informal*) ideas, statements or beliefs that you think are silly or not true SYN **bunk**, **nonsense**

**bunny** /ˈbʌni/ *noun* (*pl.* **-ies**) (*also* **'bunny rabbit**) **1** a child's word for a RABBIT **2** a person who enjoys a particular activity or who is in a particular mood: *gym/beach/snow bunnies* ◇ *an angry bunny* IDM see HAPPY

**Bun·sen burn·er** /ˌbʌnsn ˈbɜːnə(r); *NAmE* ˈbɜːrn-/ *noun* an instrument used in scientific work that produces a hot gas flame

**bunt** /bʌnt/ *verb* [T, I] **~ (sth)** (*NAmE*) (in baseball) to deliberately hit the ball only a short distance ▸ **bunt** *noun*

**bunt·ing** /ˈbʌntɪŋ/ *noun* **1** [U] coloured flags or paper used for decorating streets and buildings in celebrations **2** [C] a small bird related to the FINCH and SPARROW families. There are several types of bunting: *a corn/reed/snow bunting*

**bun·yip** /ˈbʌnjɪp/ *noun* (*AustralE*) (in stories) a MONSTER that lives in or near water

**buoy** /bɔɪ; *NAmE* ˈbuːi, bɔɪ/ *noun, verb*
- *noun* an object which floats on the sea or a river to mark the places where it is dangerous and where it is safe for boats to go ⇒ see also LIFEBUOY
- *verb* [usually passive] **1 ~ sb (up)** to make sb feel cheerful or confident: *Buoyed by their win yesterday the team feel confident of further success.* **2 ~ sb / sth (up)** to keep sb/sth floating on water **3 ~ (sth) (up)** to keep prices at a high or acceptable level

**buoy·ant** /ˈbɔɪənt; *NAmE also* ˈbuːjənt/ *adj.* **1** (of prices, business activity, etc.) tending to increase or stay at a high level, usually showing financial success: *a buoyant economy/market* ◇ *buoyant sales/prices* ◇ *a buoyant demand for homes* **2** cheerful and feeling sure that things will be successful: *They were all in buoyant mood.* **3** floating, able to float or able to keep things floating: *The boat bobbed like a cork on the waves: light and buoyant.* ◇ *Salt water is more buoyant than fresh water.* ▸ **buoy·ancy** /ˈbɔɪənsi; *NAmE also* ˈbuːjən-/ *noun* [U]: *the buoyancy of the market* ◇ *a mood of buoyancy* ◇ *a buoyancy aid* (= sth to help you float)

**bur·ble** /ˈbɜːbl; *NAmE* ˈbɜːrbl/ *verb* **1** [I, T] **~ (on) (about sth)** | **+ speech** (*disapproving*) to speak in a confused or silly way that is difficult to hear or understand: *What's he burbling about?* **2** [I] to make the gentle sound of a stream flowing over stones

**burbs** /bɜːbz; *NAmE* bɜːrbz/ *noun* **the burbs** [pl.] (*NAmE, informal*) = SUBURBS

**bur·den** /ˈbɜːdn; *NAmE* ˈbɜːrdn/ *noun, verb*
- *noun* **1** a duty, responsibility, etc. that causes worry, difficulty or hard work: *to bear/carry/ease/reduce/share the burden* ◇ **the ~ (of sth)** *The main burden of caring for old people falls on the state.* ◇ **~ on sb** *the heavy tax burden on working people* ◇ **a ~ to sb** *I don't want to become a burden to my children when I'm old.* **2** (*formal*) a heavy load that is difficult to carry ⇒ see also BEAST OF BURDEN
- *verb* **1 ~ sb / yourself (with sth)** to give sb a duty, responsibility, etc. that causes worry, difficulty or hard work: *They have burdened themselves with a high mortgage.* ◇ *I don't want to burden you with my worries.* ◇ *to be burdened by high taxation* OPP **unburden 2 be burdened with sth** to be carrying sth heavy: *She got off the bus, burdened with two heavy suitcases.*

**the ˌburden of ˈproof** *noun* [sing.] (*law*) the task or responsibility of proving that sth is true

**bur·den·some** /ˈbɜːdnsəm; *NAmE* ˈbɜːrd-/ *adj.* (*formal*) causing worry, difficulty or hard work SYN **onerous**

**bur·dock** /ˈbɜːdɒk; *NAmE* ˈbɜːrdɑːk/ *noun* [U] a plant with flowers that become PRICKLY and stick to passing animals

**bur·eau** /ˈbjʊərəʊ; *NAmE* ˈbjʊr-/ *noun* (*pl.* **bur·eaux** /-rəʊz/ *or* **bur·eaus**) **1** (*BrE*) a desk with DRAWERS and usually a top that opens down to make a table to write on **2** (*NAmE*) = CHEST OF DRAWERS **3** an office or organization that provides information on a particular subject: *an employment bureau* **4** (in the US) a government department or part of a government department: *the Federal Bureau of Investigation*

**bur·eau·cracy** /bjʊəˈrɒkrəsi; *NAmE* bjʊˈrɑːk-/ *noun* (*pl.* **-ies**) **1** [U] (*often disapproving*) the system of official rules and ways of doing things that a government or an organization has, especially when these seem to be too complicated: *unnecessary/excessive bureaucracy* **2** [U, C] a system of government in which there are a large number of state officials who are not elected; a country with such a system: *the power of the state bureaucracy* ◇ *living in a modern bureaucracy*

**bur·eau·crat** /ˈbjʊərəkræt; *NAmE* ˈbjʊr-/ *noun* (*often disapproving*) an official working in an organization or a government department, especially one who follows the rules of the department too strictly

**bur·eau·crat·ic** /ˌbjʊərəˈkrætɪk; *NAmE* ˌbjʊr-/ *adj.* (*often disapproving*) connected with a bureaucracy or bureaucrats and involving complicated official rules which may seem unnecessary: *bureaucratic power/control/procedures/organizations* ◇ *The report revealed a great deal of bureaucratic inefficiency.* ▸ **bur·eau·crat·ic·al·ly** /-kli/ *adv.*

**bur·eau de change** /ˌbjʊərəʊ də ˈʃɑːnʒ; *NAmE* ˌbjʊr-/ *noun* (*pl.* **bur·eaux de change** /ˌbjʊərəʊ də ˈʃɑːnʒ; *NAmE* ˌbjʊr-/) (*from French*) an office at a hotel, in an airport, etc., where you can exchange money from one country for that from another

**bur·ette** (*US also* **buret**) /bjʊəˈret; *NAmE* bjʊˈr-/ *noun* a glass tube with measurements on it and a TAP at one end, used, for example, in chemical experiments for measuring out amounts of a liquid

**burg** /bɜːg; *NAmE* bɜːrg/ *noun* (*NAmE, informal*) a town or city

**bur·geon** /ˈbɜːdʒən; *NAmE* ˈbɜːrdʒ-/ *verb* [I] (*formal*) to begin to grow or develop rapidly ▸ **bur·geon·ing** *adj.*: *a burgeoning population* ◇ *burgeoning demand*

**bur·ger** /ˈbɜːgə(r); *NAmE* ˈbɜːrg-/ *noun* **1** = HAMBURGER **2 -burger** (in compounds) fish, vegetables, nuts, etc. cut into small pieces and made into flat round shapes like HAMBURGERS: *a spicy beanburger* ⇒ see also CHEESEBURGER, VEGGIE BURGER

**burgh** /ˈbʌrə; *NAmE* ˈbɜːrəʊ/ *noun* (*old-fashioned or ScotE*) a town or part of a city that has its own local government

**bur·gher** /ˈbɜːgə(r); *NAmE* ˈbɜːrg-/ *noun* (*old use or humorous*) a citizen of a particular town

**burg·lar** /ˈbɜːglə(r); *NAmE* ˈbɜːrg-/ *noun* a person who enters a building illegally in order to steal things

**ˈburglar alarm** *noun* an electronic device, often fixed to a wall, that rings a loud bell if sb tries to enter a building by force

**burg·lary** /ˈbɜːgləri; *NAmE* ˈbɜːrg-/ *noun* [U, C] (*pl.* **-ies**) the crime of entering a building illegally and stealing things from it SYN **housebreaking**: *The youth was charged with three counts of burglary.* ◇ *a rise in the number of burglaries committed in the area* ⇒ compare ROBBERY, THEFT

**bur·gle** /ˈbɜːgl; *NAmE* ˈbɜːrgl/ (*BrE*) (*NAmE* **burg·lar·ize** /ˈbɜːgləraɪz; *NAmE* ˈbɜːrg-/) *verb* **~ sb/sth** to enter a building illegally, usually using force, and steal from it: *We were burgled while we were away* (= our house was burgled). ◇ *The house next door was burgled.*

**bur·gundy** /ˈbɜːgəndi; *NAmE* ˈbɜːrg-/ *noun* **1** **Burgundy** [U, C] (*pl.* **-ies**) a red or white wine from the Burgundy area of eastern France **2** [U] a dark red colour ▸ **bur·gundy** *adj.*: *a burgundy leather briefcase*

**bur·ial** /ˈberiəl/ *noun* [U, C] the act or ceremony of burying a dead body: *a burial place/mound/site* ◇ *Her body was sent home for burial.* ◇ *His family insisted he should be given a proper burial.*

**burial ground** noun a place where dead bodies are buried, especially an ancient place

**burka** (also **burkha**, **burqa**) /ˈbʊəkə, ˈbɜːkə; NAmE ˈbɜːrkə/ noun a long, loose piece of clothing that covers the whole body, including the head and face, worn in public by some Muslim women

**bur·lap** /ˈbɜːlæp; NAmE ˈbɜːrl-/ noun [U] (NAmE) = HESSIAN

**bur·lesque** /bɜːˈlesk; NAmE bɜːrˈl-/ noun **1** [C] a performance or piece of writing which tries to make sth look silly by representing it in a humorous way **SYN** **parody**: *a burlesque of literary life* **2** [U] a type of entertainment involving humorous acts, singing, dancing, etc. and often including STRIPTEASE ▶ **bur·lesque** *adj.* [usually before noun]

**burly** /ˈbɜːli; NAmE ˈbɜːrli/ *adj.* (**bur·lier**, **bur·li·est**) (of a man or a man's body) big, strong and heavy **SYN** **brawny**

**burn 0** **A2** /bɜːn; NAmE bɜːrn/ *verb, noun*
■ *verb* (**burnt, burnt** /bɜːnt; NAmE bɜːrnt/ or **burned, burned** /bɜːnd; NAmE bɜːrnd/)
* FIRE **1** **A2** [I] to produce flames and heat: *A welcoming fire was burning in the fireplace.* ◇ *Fires were burning all over the city.* **2** **A2** [I] (used especially in the progressive tenses) to be on fire: *By nightfall the whole city was burning.* ◇ *The girl ran from the burning building.* ◇ *Two children were rescued from the burning car.* **3** **A2** [T, I] to destroy, damage, injure or kill sb/sth by fire; to be destroyed, etc. by fire: *The house burned to the ground.* ◇ *Ten people burned to death in the hotel fire.* ◇ *~ sb/sth* to burn waste paper/dead leaves ◇ *All his belongings were burnt in the fire.* ◇ *The house was burnt to the ground* (= completely destroyed). ◇ *Joan of Arc was burned at the stake.* ◇ ~**(sb/sth) alive**: *His greatest fear is of being burnt alive.*
* FUEL **4** **A2** [T, I] if you **burn** a fuel, or a fuel **burns**, it produces heat, light or energy: *Which fuel burns most efficiently?* ◇ *~ sth* a furnace that burns gas/oil/coke ◇ *(figurative) Some people burn calories* (= use food to produce energy) *faster than others.*
* FOOD **5** **A2** [I, T] if food **burns**, or if you **burn** it, it is damaged by too much heat: *I can smell something burning in the kitchen.* ◇ *~ sth* Sorry—I burnt the toast.
* SUN/HEAT **6** **A2** [I, T] to be damaged or injured by the sun, heat, ACID, etc.; to damage or injure sb/sth in this way: *My skin burns easily* (= in the sun). ◇ *~ sb* I got badly burned by the sun yesterday. ◇ *~ sth* I burnt my tongue trying to eat a hot meat pie. ◇ *~ yourself* I burned myself on the stove.
* OF PART OF BODY **7** [I] if part of your body **burns** or is **burning**, it feels very hot and painful: *Your forehead's burning. Have you got a fever?* ◇ *Her cheeks burned with embarrassment.* ⊃ SYNONYMS at HURT
* OF A LIGHT **8** [I] to produce light: *Lights were burning upstairs, but no one answered the door.*
* FEEL EMOTION/DESIRE **9** [I, T] (*literary*) to feel or show a strong emotion or desire: *~ with sth* to be burning with rage/ambition/love ◇ *~ to do sth* He was burning to go climbing again.
* GO FAST **10** [I] + *adv./prep.* (*informal*) to move very fast in a particular direction: *The car was burning down the road.*
* MAKE ANGRY **11** [T] *~ sb* (NAmE, *informal*) to make sb very angry: *So you did it just to burn me?*
* CD, DVD **12** [T, I] *~ (sth) (to sth)* to put information onto a CD or DVD
* SPEND MONEY **13** [T, I] (*business*, *informal*) to spend money: *~ sth* The project burns £2 million a year in contractor costs. ◇ *~ through sth* The state has already burned through its cash reserves. ⊃ see also BURN RATE

**IDM** **burn your ˈbridges** (BrE also **burn your ˈboats**) to do sth that makes it impossible to return to the previous situation later: *Think carefully before you resign—you don't want to burn your bridges.* **burn the candle at both ˈends** to become very tired by trying to do too many things and going to bed late and getting up early **burn your ˈfingers** | **get your ˈfingers burnt** to suffer as a result of doing sth without realizing the possible bad results, especially in business: *He got his fingers badly burnt dabbling in the stock market.* **burn a ˈhole in your pocket** if money **burns a hole in your pocket**, you want to spend it as soon as you have it **burn the midnight ˈoil** to study or work until late at night **burn ˈrubber** (*informal*) to drive very fast **burn (sth) to a ˈcinder / ˈcrisp** to become completely burnt, especially because it has been cooked for too long ⊃ more at CRASH *v.*, EAR, MONEY

**PHR V** **ˌburn aˈway** | **ˌburn sth↔aˈway** to disappear as a result of burning; to make sth do this: *Half the candle had burnt away.* ◇ *The clothing on his back got burnt away in the fire.* **ˌburn ˈdown** if a fire **burns down**, it becomes weaker and has smaller flames **ˌburn ˈdown** | **ˌburn sth↔ˈdown** to be destroyed, or to destroy sth, by fire: *The house burned down in 1895.* **ˌburn sth↔ˈoff** **1** to remove sth by burning: *Burn off the old paint before repainting the door.* **2** to use energy by doing exercise: *This workout helps you to burn off fat and tone muscles.* **ˌburn ˈout** | **ˌburn itself ˈout** (of a fire) to stop burning because there is nothing more to burn: *The fire had burnt (itself) out before the fire engines arrived.* **ˌburn ˈout** | **ˌburn sth↔ˈout** to stop working or to make sth stop working because it gets too hot or is used too much: *The clutch has burnt out.* **ˌburn ˈout** | **ˌburn yourself/sb ˈout** to become extremely tired or sick by working too hard over a period of time; to make sb do this: *If he doesn't stop working so hard, he'll burn himself out.* ◇ *By the age of 25 she was completely burned out and retired from the sport.* ⊃ related noun BURNOUT ⊃ see also BURN-OUT (2) **ˌburn sth ˈout** [usually passive] to destroy sth completely by fire so that only the outer frame remains: *The hotel was completely burnt out.* ⊃ see also BURNT-OUT (1) **ˌburn ˈup** **1** to be destroyed by heat: *The spacecraft burned up as it entered the earth's atmosphere.* **2** (usually used in the progressive tenses) (*informal*) to have a high temperature: *You're burning up—have you seen a doctor?* **3** (of a fire) to burn more strongly and with larger flames **ˌburn sb ˈup** (NAmE, *informal*) to make sb very angry: *The way he treats me really burns me up.* **ˌburn sth↔ˈup** **1** to get rid of or destroy sth by burning: *The fire burned up 1500 acres of farmland.* **2** to use CALORIES or energy by doing exercise: *Which burns up more calories—swimming or cycling?*

■ *noun*
* INJURY **1** **B2** [C] an injury or a mark caused by fire, heat or ACID: *to have minor/severe/third-degree burns* ◇ *She suffered serious burns but is expected to survive.* ◇ *~ to sth* He is recovering from burns to his face and hands. ◇ *~ on sth* cigarette burns on the furniture
* IN MUSCLES **2 the burn** [sing.] the feeling that you get in your muscles when you have done a lot of exercise
* RIVER **3** [C] (*ScotE*) a small river **SYN** **stream** **IDM** see SLOW *adj.*

> ● SYNONYMS
>
> **burn**
> char • scald • scorch • singe
> These words all mean to damage, injure, destroy or kill sb/sth with heat or fire.
>
> **burn** to damage, injure, destroy or kill sb/sth with fire, heat or acid; to be damaged, etc. by fire, heat or acid: *She burned all his letters.* ◇ *The house burned down in 1995.*
>
> **char** [usually passive] to make sth black by burning it; to become black by burning: *The bodies had been charred beyond recognition.*
>
> **scald** to burn part of your body with very hot liquid or steam.
>
> **scorch** to burn and slightly damage a surface by making it too hot: *I scorched my dress when I was ironing it.*
>
> **singe** to burn the surface of sth slightly, usually by mistake; to be burnt in this way: *He singed his hair as he tried to light his cigarette.*
>
> SCORCH OR SINGE?
> • Things are **scorched** by heat or fire. Things can only be **singed** by fire or a flame.
>
> PATTERNS
> • to burn/scald yourself/your hand
> • to burn/scorch/singe your hair/clothes
> • burnt-out/charred/scorched remains/ruins/buildings

**burn·er** /ˈbɜːnə(r); NAmE ˈbɜːrn-/ noun **1** the part of a cooker, etc. that produces a flame **2** a large, solid metal piece of equipment for burning wood or coal, used for heating a room: *a wood burner* ⊃ see also BUNSEN BURNER IDM see BACK *adj.*, FRONT *adj.*

**burn·ing** /ˈbɜːnɪŋ; NAmE ˈbɜːrn-/ *adj., adv.*
■ *adj.* [only before noun] **1** (of feelings, etc.) very strong; extreme: *a burning desire to win* ◊ *He's always had a burning ambition to start his own business.* **2 a ~ issue / question** a very important problem that requires immediate attention **3** (of pain, etc.) very strong and giving a feeling of burning ⊃ SYNONYMS at PAINFUL **4** very hot; looking and feeling very hot: *the burning sun* ◊ *her burning face* **5 ~ eyes** (*literary*) eyes that seem to be staring at you very hard
■ *adv.* **burning hot** very hot

**burn·ish** /ˈbɜːnɪʃ; NAmE ˈbɜːrn-/ *verb* **~ sth** (*formal*) to POLISH metal until it is smooth and shiny ▸ **bur·nished** *adj.* [usually before noun]: *burnished gold/copper*

**burn-out** /ˈbɜːnaʊt; NAmE ˈbɜːrn-/ *noun* [C, U] **1** the state of being extremely tired or ill, either physically or mentally, because you have worked too hard **2** the point at which a ROCKET has used all of its fuel and has no more power

**ˈburn rate** *noun* (*business*) the rate at which the money available for a project or new company is spent: *The company's burn rate is only $15 000 a month.*

**Burns Night** /ˈbɜːnz naɪt; NAmE ˈbɜːrnz/ *noun* [U, C] the evening of 25 January when Scottish people celebrate the birthday of the Scottish poet, Robert Burns, with traditional Scottish music, WHISKY and dishes such as HAGGIS

**burnt** /bɜːnt; NAmE bɜːrnt/ *adj.* damaged or injured by burning: *burnt toast* ◊ *Your hand looks badly burnt.*

**ˌburnt ˈoffering** *noun* **1** something (usually an animal) that is burnt in a religious ceremony as a gift offered to a god **2** (*BrE, humorous*) food that has been badly burnt by accident

**ˌburnt-ˈout** (also ˌburned-ˈout) *adj.* **1** destroyed or badly damaged by fire: *a burnt-out car* **2** feeling as if you have done sth for too long and need to have a rest: *I'm feeling burnt-out at work—I need a holiday.*

**burp** /bɜːp; NAmE bɜːrp/ *verb* (*informal*) **1** [I] to let out air from the stomach through the mouth, making a noise SYN belch **2** [T] **~ sb** to make a baby bring up air from the stomach, especially by rubbing or PATTING its back ▸ **burp** *noun*

**burqa** /ˈbɜːkə/ = BURKA

**burr** /bɜː(r)/ *noun* **1** [usually sing.] a strong pronunciation of the 'r' sound, typical of some ACCENTS of (= ways of pronouncing) English; an ACCENT with this type of pronunciation: *She speaks with a soft West Country burr.* **2** [usually sing.] the soft regular noise made by parts of a machine moving quickly SYN whir **3** [C] the seed container of some plants that sticks to clothes or fur

**bur·rito** /bʊˈriːtəʊ/ *noun* (*pl.* -os) (*from Spanish*) a Mexican dish consisting of a TORTILLA filled with meat or beans

**burro** /ˈbʊrəʊ; NAmE ˈbɜːr-/ *noun* (*pl.* -os) (NAmE, *from Spanish*) a small DONKEY

**bur·row** /ˈbʌrəʊ; NAmE ˈbɜːr-/ *verb, noun*
■ *verb* **1** [I, T] to make a hole or a tunnel in the ground by digging SYN dig: **(+ adv./prep.)** *Earthworms burrow deep into the soil.* ◊ **~ sth + adv./prep.** *The rodent burrowed its way into the sand.* **2** [I, T] to press yourself close to sb or under sth: **+ adv./prep.** *He burrowed down beneath the blankets.* ◊ **~ sth + adv./prep.** *She burrowed her face into his chest.* **3** [I] **+ adv./prep.** to search for sth under or among things: *She burrowed in the drawer for a pair of socks.* ◊ *He was afraid that they would burrow into his past.*
■ *noun* a hole or tunnel in the ground made by animals such as RABBITS for them to live in

**bursa** /ˈbɜːsə; NAmE ˈbɜːrsə/ *noun* (*pl.* bur·sae /-siː/ or bursas) (*anatomy*) a part inside the body like a bag, which is filled with liquid, especially around a JOINT so that it can work smoothly

**bur·sar** /ˈbɜːsə(r); NAmE ˈbɜːrs-/ *noun* (especially *BrE*) a person whose job is to manage the financial affairs of a school or college

**bur·sary** /ˈbɜːsəri; NAmE ˈbɜːrs-/ *noun* (*pl.* -ies) (especially *BrE*) an amount of money that is given to sb so that they can study, usually at a college or university SYN grant, scholarship

**bur·sitis** /bɜːˈsaɪtɪs; NAmE bɜːrˈs-/ *noun* [U] (*medical*) a condition in which a bursa becomes SWOLLEN (= larger and rounder than normal) and painful

**burst** ?+ C1 /bɜːst; NAmE bɜːrst/ *verb, noun*
■ *verb* (**burst, burst**) **1** ?+ C1 [I, T] to break open or apart, especially because of pressure from inside; to make sth break in this way: *That balloon will burst if you blow it up any more.* ◊ *The dam burst under the weight of water.* ◊ *Shells were bursting (= exploding) all around us.* ◊ (*figurative*) *He felt he would burst with anger and shame.* ◊ **~ sth** *Don't burst that balloon!* ◊ *The river burst its banks and flooded nearby towns.* ◊ *a burst pipe* ⊃ SYNONYMS at EXPLODE **2** ?+ C1 [I] **+ adv./prep.** to go or move somewhere suddenly with great force; to come from somewhere suddenly: *He burst into the room without knocking.* ◊ *The sun burst through the clouds.* ◊ *The words burst from her in an angry rush.* **3** ?+ C1 **be bursting (with sth)** to be very full of sth; to be very full and almost breaking open: *The roads are bursting with cars.* ◊ **to be bursting with ideas/enthusiasm/pride** ◊ *The hall was filled to bursting point.* ◊ *The hall was full to bursting.* ◊ (*informal*) *I'm bursting (for a pee)!* (= I need to use the toilet right now).
IDM **be bursting to do sth** to want to do sth so much that you can hardly stop yourself: *She was bursting to tell him the good news.* **ˌburst sb's ˈbubble** to bring an end to sb's hopes, happiness, etc. **ˌburst ˈopen** | **ˌburst sth ˈopen** to open suddenly or violently; to make sth open in this way: *The door burst open.* ◊ *Firefighters burst the door open and rescued them.* ⊃ more at BUBBLE *n.*, SEAM
PHRV **ˌburst ˈin on sb/sth** to interrupt sb/sth by entering a place suddenly and noisily: *He burst in on the meeting.* **ˈburst into sth** to start producing sth suddenly and with great force: *The aircraft crashed and burst into flames* (= suddenly began to burn). ◊ *She burst into tears* (= suddenly began to cry). **ˈburst on/onto sth** to appear somewhere suddenly in a way that attracts a lot of attention: *A major new talent has burst onto the literary scene.* **ˌburst ˈout 1** to speak suddenly, loudly and with strong feeling: **+ speech** *'For heavens' sake!' he burst out.* ⊃ related noun OUTBURST ⊃ SYNONYMS at CALL **2** to begin doing sth suddenly: **burst out doing sth** *Karen burst out laughing.*
■ *noun* **1** a short period of a particular activity or strong emotion that often starts suddenly: *a sudden burst of activity/energy/laughter* ◊ **in bursts** *I tend to work in bursts.* ◊ *Her breath was coming in short bursts.* ◊ *spontaneous bursts of applause* **2** an occasion when sth bursts; the hole left where sth has burst: *a burst in a water pipe* **3** a short series of shots from a gun: *frequent bursts of machine-gun fire*

**bury** 🔊 B1 /ˈberi/ *verb* (**bur·ies, bury·ing, bur·ied, bur·ied**)
• DEAD PERSON **1** 🔊 B1 to place a dead body in the ground: **~ sb/sth (+ adv./prep.)** *They killed her and buried her body.* ◊ (*figurative*) *Their ambitions were finally dead and buried.* **2 ~ sb** (*old-fashioned*) to lose sb by death: *She's 85 and has buried three husbands.*
• HIDE IN GROUND **3** 🔊 B1 to hide sth in the ground: **~ sth** *buried treasure* ◊ **~ sth + adv./prep.** *The dog had buried its bone in the garden.* ⊃ HOMOPHONES at BERRY
• COVER **4** 🔊 B2 [often passive] to cover sb/sth with soil, rocks, leaves, etc.: **~ sb/sth (+ adv./prep.)** *The house was buried under ten feet of snow.* ◊ **~ sth + adj.** *The miners were buried alive when the tunnel collapsed.* **5** 🔊 **~ sth (+ adv./prep.)** to cover sth so that it cannot be seen: *Your letter got buried under a pile of papers.* ◊ *He buried his face in his hands and wept.*
• HIDE FEELING **6 ~ sth** to ignore or hide a feeling, a mistake, etc: *She had learnt to bury her feelings.*

- **PUT DEEPLY INTO STH 7** ~ **sth (in sth)** to put sth deeply into sth else: *He walked slowly, his hands buried in his pockets.* ◊ *She always has her head buried in a book.*
- **IDM** **bury the ˈhatchet | bury your ˈdifferences** to stop not being friendly and become friends again **bury the ˈlede/ˈlead** (*US*) to give the most important point of a news story near the end instead of at the beginning ⊃ more at HEAD *n*.
- **PHR V** **ˈbury yourself in sth 1** to give all your attention to sth: *Since she left, he's buried himself in his work.* **2** to go to or be in a place where you will not meet many people: *She buried herself in the country to write a book.*

**bus** 🟦 **A1** /bʌs/ *noun, verb*
- *noun* (*pl.* **buses**, *US also* **busses**) **1** 🟦 **A1** a large road vehicle that carries passengers, especially one that travels along a fixed route and stops regularly to let people get on and off: **by** ~ *Shall we walk or go by bus?* ◊ *a school bus* ◊ *He was seriously injured when the band's tour bus crashed.* ◊ *a bus company/driver* ⊃ compare COACH ⊃ see also MINIBUS, TROLLEYBUS **2** (*computing*) a set of wires that carries information from one part of a computer system to another
- **IDM** **throw sb under the ˈbus** (*especially NAmE, informal*) to make sb else suffer in order to save yourself or gain an advantage for yourself: *Plenty of my co-workers are satisfied to throw everyone else under the bus as long as they keep their wages.*
- *verb* (**-s-** *or* **-ss-**) **1** ~ **sb (from/to …)** to transport sb by bus: *We were bussed from the airport to our hotel.* **2** ~ **sb** (in the US) to transport young people by bus to another area so that students of different races can be educated together **3** ~ **sth** (*NAmE*) to take the dirty plates, etc. off the tables in a restaurant, as a job

**bus·boy** /ˈbʌsbɔɪ/ *noun* (*NAmE*) a person who works in a restaurant and whose job is to clear the dirty dishes, etc.

**bush** 🟦 **B2** /bʊʃ/ *noun* **1** 🟦 **B2** [C] a plant that grows thickly with several hard STEMS coming up from the root: *a rose/holly bush* ◊ **in the bushes** *She was hiding in the bushes at the side of the lane.* ⊃ compare TREE **2** [C] a thing that looks like a bush, especially an area of thick hair or fur **3** (*often* **the bush**) [U] an area of wild land that has not been cleared, especially in Africa and Australia; in New Zealand an area where the forest has not been cleared **IDM** see BEAT *v.*, BIRD *n.*

**bushel** /ˈbʊʃl/ *noun* **1** [C] a unit for measuring grain and fruit (equal in volume to 8 GALLONS) **2** **bushels** [pl.] ~ **(of sth)** (*NAmE, informal*) a large amount of sth **IDM** see HIDE *v.*

**ˈbush fire** *noun* a fire in a large area of rough open ground, especially one that spreads quickly

**bu·shido** /ˈbʊʃiːdəʊ, bʊˈʃiːdəʊ/ *noun* [U] (*from Japanese*) the system of honour and morals of the Japanese SAMURAI

**Bush·man** /ˈbʊʃmən/ *noun* (*pl.* **-men** /-mən/) **1** a member of one of the races of people from southern Africa who live and hunt in the African BUSH **2** **bushman** a person who lives, works or travels in the Australian BUSH

**bush·meat** /ˈbʊʃmiːt/ *noun* [U] the meat of African wild animals used as food

**bush·ran·ger** /ˈbʊʃreɪndʒə(r)/ *noun* (*AustralE, NZE*) (in the past) an OUTLAW (= a person who has done sth illegal and is hiding to avoid being caught) who lives in the bush (= areas of wild land far away from large towns)

**bush·whack** /ˈbʊʃwæk/ *verb* **1** (*NAmE, AustralE, NZE*) [I] to live or travel in wild country **2** (*NAmE, AustralE, NZE*) [I] + *adv./prep.* to cut your way through bushes, plants, etc. in wild country: *We had to bushwhack through undergrowth.* **3** (*NAmE*) [T] ~ **sb** to attack sb very suddenly from a hidden position **SYN** ambush **4** (*NAmE*) [I] to fight as a GUERRILLA ▶ **bush·whack·er** *noun* **bush·whack·ing** *noun* [U]

**bushy** /ˈbʊʃi/ *adj.* (**bush·ier**, **bushi·est**) **1** (of hair or fur) growing thickly: *a bushy beard/tail* ◊ *bushy eyebrows* **2** (of plants) growing thickly, with a lot of leaves

**bushy-ˈtailed** *adj.* ⊃ BRIGHT-EYED

**busily** /ˈbɪzɪli/ ⊃ BUSY *adj.*

---

201 **business administration**

**busi·ness** 🟦 **A1** /ˈbɪznəs/ *noun*
- **TRADE 1** 🟦 **A1** [U, sing.] the activity of making, buying, selling or supplying goods or services for money **SYN** **commerce, trade**: *It's been a pleasure to do business with you.* ◊ **in** ~ *She has set up in business as a hairdresser.* ◊ *When he left school, he* **went into business** *with his brother.* ◊ *the music/entertainment/movie business* ◊ *Retail is a tough business.* ◊ **in the …** ~ *She works in the software business.* ◊ *We need to concentrate on our* **core business** (= the main thing that our business does). ◊ *business owners/leaders* ◊ *a business partner* ◊ *a business community* ⊃ **WORDFINDER NOTE** at TRADE ⊃ see also AGRIBUSINESS, BIG BUSINESS, E-BUSINESS, SHOW BUSINESS
- **WORK 2** 🟦 **A1** [U] work that is part of your job: *Is the trip to Rome for business or pleasure?* ◊ *a business trip/meeting/lunch* ◊ **on** ~ *He's away on business.* **3** 🟦 **A2** [U] the amount of work done by a company, etc.; the rate or quality of this work: *Business is booming.* ◊ *Business was bad.* ◊ *How's business?* ◊ *Uncertainty is bad for business.*
- **COMPANY 4** 🟦 **A1** [C] a commercial organization such as a company, shop or factory: *a small/family business* ◊ *We try to support local businesses.* ◊ *a successful/profitable business* ◊ *a retail/an online business* ◊ *to* **run/start a business** ◊ *to* **grow/expand/build a business** ⊃ **WORDFINDER NOTE** at COMPANY
- **RESPONSIBILITY 5** 🟦 **B1** [U] something that a particular person or organization is responsible for: *It is the business of the police to protect the community.* ◊ *I shall* **make it my business** *to find out who is responsible.* ◊ *My private life is* **none of your business** (= not sth that you need to know about).
- **IMPORTANT MATTERS 6** 🟦 **B2** [U] important matters that need to be dealt with or discussed: *He has some* **unfinished business** *to deal with.* ◊ *the main business of the meeting*
- **EVENT 7** [sing.] (usually with an adjective) a matter, an event or a situation: *That plane crash was a terrible business.* ◊ *I found the whole business very depressing.* ◊ *The business of the missing tickets hasn't been sorted out.*
- **BEING A CUSTOMER 8** (*especially NAmE*) (*also BrE, formal* **custom**) [U] the fact of a person or people buying goods or services at a shop or business: *We're grateful for your business.*
- **IDM** **any other ˈbusiness** the things that are discussed at the end of an official meeting that do not appear on the agenda: *I think we've finished item four. Now is there any other business?* ⊃ see also AOB **be in ˈbusiness** (*informal*) to have everything that you need in order to be able to start sth immediately: *All we need is a car and we'll be in business.* **be in the business of doing sth** to regard a particular activity as an essential part of what you do: *Restaurant owners everywhere are in the business of building relationships.* **be the ˈbusiness** (*informal*) to be very good **business as ˈusual** a way of saying that things will continue as normal despite a difficult situation **business is ˈbusiness** a way of saying that financial and commercial matters are the important things to consider and you should not be influenced by friendship, etc. **get down to ˈbusiness** to start dealing with the matter that needs to be dealt with, or doing the work that needs to be done **go about your ˈbusiness** to do the things that you normally do: *streets filled with people going about their daily business* **have no business doing sth | have no business to do sth** to have no right to do sth: *You have no business being here.* **like ˈnobody's business** (*BrE, informal*) very much, very fast, very well, etc: *I've been working like nobody's business to get it finished in time.* **not be in the business of doing sth** not to be intending to do sth (which it would be surprising for you to do): *I'm not in the business of getting other people to do my work for me.* **out of ˈbusiness** having stopped operating as a business because there is no more money or work available: *The new regulations will* **put** *many small businesses* **out of business.** ◊ *Some travel companies will probably* **go out of business** *this summer.* ⊃ more at MEAN *v.*, MIND *v.*, PLY *v.*

**ˈbusiness administration** *noun* [U] the study of how to manage a business: *a master's degree in business administration* (= *an MBA*)

# business angel

**business angel** noun = ANGEL (4)

**business card** (also **card**) noun a small card printed with sb's name and details of their job and company ⊃ compare VISITING CARD

**business casual** noun [U] a style of dressing in which people who work in business wear clothes that are suitable for their profession but less formal than traditional business clothes

**business class** (BrE also **club class**) noun [U] the part of a plane where passengers have a high level of comfort and service, designed for people travelling on business, and less expensive than first class ► **business class** (BrE also **club class**) adv.: *I always fly business class.*

**the business end** noun [sing.] 1 (also **the pointy end**) (informal) the end of a tool or weapon that performs its main function: *You don't want to find yourself on the business end of a machete.* 2 the essential or basic part of a process or an operation: *The rigs are the business end of the oil industry.*

**business hours** noun [pl.] the hours in a day that a shop or company is open

**busi·ness·like** /ˈbɪznəslaɪk/ adj. (of a person) working in an efficient and organized way and not wasting time or thinking about personal things: *She adopted a brisk businesslike tone.*

**busi·ness·man** ❶ 🅰️2️⃣ /ˈbɪznəsmæn, -mən/,
**busi·ness·woman** /ˈbɪznəswʊmən/ noun (pl. **-men** /-men, -mən/, **-women** /-wɪmɪn/) 1 ❓ 🅰️2️⃣ a person who works in business, especially at a high level

> **WORDFINDER** accountant, agent, auditor, CEO, chairman, consultant, entrepreneur, executive, manager

2 ❓ 🅱️1️⃣ a person who shows skill in business and financial matters: *I should have got a better price for the car, but I'm not much of a businessman.* ⊃ note at GENDER

**business model** noun a plan for running a business, identifying where the money will come from, who the customers are, how they will be reached, etc: *Many companies in Asia follow this business model.*

**business park** noun an area of land that is specially designed for offices and small factories

**business person** noun a person who works in business, especially at a high level

**business rates** noun [pl.] = RATES

**business school** noun a part of a college or university that teaches business, often to graduates (= people who already have a first degree)

**business studies** noun [U + sing./pl. v.] the study of subjects connected with money and managing a business: *a degree in business studies*

**business-to-business** adj. [usually before noun] (abbr. **B2B**) done between one business and another rather than between a business and its ordinary customers

**business-to-consumer** (also **business-to-customer**) adj. [usually before noun] (abbr. **B2C**) used to describe the selling of products, services or information to consumers over the internet: *Business-to-consumer e-commerce on the internet gives consumers round-the-clock access to worldwide providers.* ⊃ compare BUSINESS-TO-BUSINESS

**bus·ing** (NAmE) = BUSSING

**busk** /bʌsk/ verb [I] to perform music in a public place and ask for money from people passing by ► **busk·er** noun **busk·ing** noun [U]

**bus lane** noun a part of a road that only buses are allowed to use

**bus·load** /ˈbʌsləʊd/ noun (especially NAmE) a large group of people on a bus

**bus·man's holi·day** /ˌbʌsmənz ˈhɒlədeɪ, -di; NAmE ˈhɑːlədeɪ/ noun [sing.] a holiday that is spent doing the same thing that you do at work

**bus pass** noun 1 a ticket that allows you to travel on any bus within a particular area for a fixed period of time 2 a ticket that allows people from particular groups (for example, students or old people) to travel free or at a reduced cost: (BrE, humorous) *I'm not old enough for my bus pass yet!*

**bus shelter** noun a structure with a roof where people can stand while they are waiting for a bus

**buss·ing** (NAmE also **bus·ing**) /ˈbʌsɪŋ/ noun [U] (in the US) a system of transporting young people by bus to another area so that students of different races can be educated together

**bus stand** noun (IndE) = BUS STATION

**bus station** noun the place in a town or city where buses leave and arrive, especially to and from other towns

**bus stop** noun a place at the side of a road that is marked with a sign, where buses stop

**bust** /bʌst/ verb, noun, adj.

- verb (**bust, bust** or **bust·ed, bust·ed**) (informal) 1 ~ sth to break sth: *I bust my camera.* ◊ *The lights are busted.* ◊ *Come on, or I'll bust the door down!* 2 ~ sb/sth (for sth) (of the police) to suddenly enter a place and search it or arrest sb: *He's been busted for drugs.* 3 ~ sb (especially NAmE) to make sb lower in military rank as a punishment SYN demote
  
  **IDM** **bust a gut (doing sth/to do sth)** (NAmE also **bust your butt/chops/hump**, NAmE, taboo, slang **bust your ass**) (informal) to make a great effort to do sth **bust (out) some moves/a move** (informal) to dance: *I'm the sort of guy who loves to bust out some moves at a party.* **... or bust** (informal) used to say that you will try very hard to get somewhere or achieve sth: *For him it's the Olympics or bust.*
  
  **PHRV** **bust up** (informal) (of a couple, friends, partners, etc.) to have an argument and separate SYN **break up (with sb)**: *They bust up after five years of marriage.* ⊃ related noun BUST-UP **bust sth↔up** (informal) to make a relationship, meeting, etc. end in a way that is not gentle SYN **break sth up**: *It was his drinking that bust up his marriage.*

- noun 1 a stone or metal model of a person's head, shoulders and chest 2 (used especially when talking about clothes or measurements) a woman's breasts or the measurement around the breasts and back: *What is your bust measurement, Madam?* 3 a period of economic difficulty in which people and businesses struggle to survive: *a boom and bust cycle* 4 (informal) an unexpected visit made by the police in order to arrest people for doing sth illegal: *a drug bust* 5 (NAmE) a thing that is not good: *As a show it was a bust.*

- adj. [not usually before noun] (informal) 1 (BrE) broken: *My watch is bust.* 2 (of a person or business) failed because of a lack of money SYN **bankrupt**: *We're bust!* ◊ *We lost our money when the travel company went bust.*

**bus·tard** /ˈbʌstəd; NAmE -stərd/ noun a large European bird that can run fast

**busted** /ˈbʌstɪd/ adj. [not before noun] (NAmE, informal) caught in the act of doing sth wrong and likely to be punished: *You are so busted!*

**bus·tee** /ˈbʌstiː; NAmE bəˈstiː/ noun (IndE) an area in or near a town that is very poor and where the houses, often made of pieces of wood, metal and CARDBOARD, are in bad condition

**bus·ter** /ˈbʌstə(r)/ noun 1 (NAmE, informal) used to speak to a man you do not like: *Get lost, buster!* 2 (usually in compounds; often used in newspapers) a person or thing that stops or gets rid of sth: *crime-busters*

**bus·tier** /ˈbʌstieɪ/ noun a woman's tight top which does not cover the arms or shoulders

**bus·tle** /ˈbʌsl/ verb, noun

- verb [I, T] to move around in a busy way or to hurry sb in a particular direction: **+ adv./prep.** *She bustled around in the kitchen.* ◊ **~ sb + adv./prep.** *The nurse bustled us out of the room.*

■ **noun 1** [U] busy and noisy activity: *the hustle and bustle of city life* **2** [C] a frame that was worn under a skirt by women in the past in order to hold the skirt out at the back

**bust·ling** /ˈbʌslɪŋ/ *adj.* full of people moving about in a busy way: *a bustling city* ◊ ~ **with sth** *The market was bustling with life.*

**ˈbust-up** *noun* (*especially* BrE, *informal*) **1** an angry argument **SYN** row²: *Sue and Tony had a bust-up and aren't speaking to each other.* **2** the end of a relationship **SYN** break-up: *the final bust-up of their marriage*

**busty** /ˈbʌsti/ *adj.* (*informal*) (of a woman) having large breasts

**bus·way** /ˈbʌsweɪ/ *noun* (BrE) a road or section of a road that can only be used by buses, especially one with special tracks for guiding the buses

**busy** ❶ A1 /ˈbɪzi/ *adj., verb*

■ *adj.* (**busier, busi·est**)
- DOING STH **1** ❔ A1 having a lot to do; perhaps not free to do sth else because you are working on sth: *Are you busy tonight?* ◊ *I'm afraid the doctor is busy at the moment. Can he call you back?* ◊ *The principal is a very busy woman.* ◊ *I'll be too busy to come to the meeting.* ◊ *She was always too busy to listen.* ◊ *I've got enough work to keep you busy.* **2** ❔ A1 giving all your attention and effort to a particular activity: ~ **doing sth** *James is busy practising for the school concert.* ◊ ~ **with sth/sb** *Kate's busy with her homework.*
- PERIOD OF TIME **3** ❔ A1 full of work and activity: *I have a very busy schedule.* ◊ *This is one of the busiest times of the year for the department.* ◊ *Things are getting really busy now.*
- PLACE **4** ❔ A2 full of people, activity, vehicles, etc: *a busy road/street* ◊ *The place gets very busy at lunchtimes.*
- PHONE LINE **5** ❔ B1 (*especially* NAmE) being used **SYN** engaged: *The line is busy—I'll try again later.* ◊ *the busy signal*
- PATTERN/DESIGN **6** too full of small details ▶ **busily** /-zɪli/ *adv.*: *He was busily engaged repairing his bike.*

IDM **as busy as a ˈbee** very busy **keep (yourself) ˈbusy** to find enough things to do: *Since she retired she's kept herself very busy.*

■ *verb* (**busies, busy·ing, busied, busied**) to fill your time doing an activity or a task: ~ **yourself (with sth)** *She busied herself with the preparations for the party.* ◊ ~ **yourself (in/with) doing sth** *While we talked, Bill busied himself fixing lunch.*

**busy·body** /ˈbɪzibɒdi; NAmE -bɑːdi/ *noun* (*pl.* **-ies**) (*disapproving*) a person who is too interested in what other people are doing: *He's an interfering old busybody!*

**but** ❶ A1 /bət, *strong form* bʌt/ *conj., prep., adv., noun*

■ *conj.* **1** ❔ A1 used to introduce a word or phrase that contrasts with what was said before: *I got it wrong. It wasn't the red one but the blue one.* ◊ *His mother won't be there, but his father might.* ◊ *It isn't that he lied exactly, but he does tend to exaggerate.* **2** ❔ A1 however; despite this: *I'd asked everybody but only two people came.* ◊ *By the end of the day we were tired but happy.* ⊃ LANGUAGE BANK at NEVERTHELESS **3** ❔ A1 used when you are saying sorry about sth: *I'm sorry but I can't stay any longer.* **4** ❔ A1 used to introduce a statement that shows that you are surprised or annoyed, or that you disagree: *But that's not possible!* ◊ *'Here's the money I owe you.' 'But that's not right—it was only £10.'* **5** except: *I had no choice but to sign the contract.* **6** used before repeating a word in order to emphasize it: *Nothing, but nothing would make him change his mind.* **7** (*literary*) used to emphasize that sth is always true: *She never passed her old home but she thought of the happy years she had spent there* (= she always thought of them).

IDM **but for 1** if it were not for: *He would have played but for a knee injury.* **2** except for: *The square was empty but for a couple of cabs.* **but then (again) 1** however; on the other hand: *He might agree. But then again he might have a completely different opinion.* **2** used before a statement that explains or gives a reason for what has just been said: *She speaks very good Italian. But then she did live in Rome for a year* (= so it's not surprising). **you cannot/could not but ...** (*formal*) used to show that everything else is impos-

---

203 **butter**

sible except the thing that you are saying: *What could he do but forgive her?* (= that was the only thing possible)

■ *prep.* ❔ B2 except; apart from: *We've had nothing but trouble with this car.* ◊ *The problem is anything but easy.* ◊ *Who but Rosa could think of something like that?* ◊ *Everyone was there but him.* ◊ *I came last but one in the race* (= I wasn't last but next to last). ◊ *Take the first turning but one* (= not the first one but the one after it).

■ *adv.* only: *I don't think we'll manage it. Still, we can but try.* ◊ *There were a lot of famous people there: Lady Gaga and Hugh Jackman, to name but two.*

■ *noun* [usually pl.] /bʌt/ a reason that sb gives for not doing sth or not agreeing: *'Let us have no buts,' he said firmly. 'You are coming.'* ◊ *With so many ifs and buts, it is easier to wait and see.*

**bu·tane** /ˈbjuːteɪn/ *noun* [U] a gas produced from PETROLEUM, used in liquid form as a fuel for cooking etc.

**butch** /bʊtʃ/ *adj.* (*informal*) **1** (of a woman) behaving or dressing like a man ⊃ compare FEMME **2** (of a man) big, and often behaving in an aggressive way

**butch·er** /ˈbʊtʃə(r)/ *noun, verb*

■ *noun* **1** a person whose job is cutting up and selling meat in a shop or killing animals for this purpose **2 butcher's** (*pl.* **butchers**) a shop that sells meat: *He owns the butcher's in the main street.* **3** a person who kills people in a cruel and violent way

IDM **have/take a ˈbutcher's** (BrE, *slang*) to have a look at sth ORIGIN From rhyming slang, in which **butcher's hook** stands for 'look'.

■ *verb* **1** ~ **sb** to kill people in a very cruel and violent way **2** ~ **sth** to kill animals and cut them up for use as meat **3** ~ **sth** (*especially* NAmE) to make sth less good or successful by doing it very badly: *The script was good, but those guys butchered it.*

**butch·ery** /ˈbʊtʃəri/ *noun* [U] **1** cruel, violent and unnecessary killing **2** the work of preparing meat to be sold

**but·ler** /ˈbʌtlə(r)/ *noun* the main male servant in a large house

**butt** /bʌt/ *verb, noun*

■ *verb* **1** ~ **sb/sth** to hit or push sb/sth hard with your head **2** ~ **sb/sth** if an animal butts sb/sth, it hits them or it hard with its HORNS and head

PHRV **butt ˈin (on sb/sth) 1** to interrupt a conversation rudely: *How can I explain if you keep butting in?* ◊ + **speech** *'Is that normal?' Josie butted in.* **2** (*informal*) to become involved in a situation that should not really involve you **SYN** interfere: *I didn't ask you to butt in on my private business.* **butt ˈout** (*especially* NAmE, *informal*) used to tell sb rudely to go away or to stop INTERFERING in sth: *Butt out, Neil! This is none of your business.*

■ *noun* **1** the thick end of a weapon or tool: *a rifle butt* **2** the part of a cigarette or CIGAR that is left after it has been smoked **3** (BrE) a large round container for storing or collecting liquids: *a water butt* **4** (*especially* NAmE, *informal*) the part of the body that you sit on **SYN** buttocks: *Get off your butt and do some work!* ◊ *Get your butt over here!* (= Come here!) **5** the act of hitting sb with your head: *a butt from his head* ⊃ see also HEADBUTT

IDM **be the butt of sth** to be the person or thing that other people often joke about or criticize **SYN** target: *She was the butt of some very unkind jokes.* ⊃ more at BUST v., PAIN n.

**butte** /bjuːt/ *noun* (*especially* NAmE) a hill that is flat on top and is separate from other high ground

**but·ter** ❶ A1 /ˈbʌtə(r)/ *noun, verb*

■ *noun* ❔ A1 [U] a soft yellow food made from cream, used in cooking and for spreading on bread: *a pat/knob/tablespoon of butter* ⊃ see also BREAD AND BUTTER, PEANUT BUTTER

IDM **butter wouldn't melt (in sb's ˈmouth)** (*informal*) used to say that sb seems to be innocent, kind, etc. when they are not really ⊃ more at KNIFE n.

■ *verb* ~ **sth** to spread butter on sth: *She buttered four thick slices of bread.* IDM see KNOW v.

# buttercream

**PHR V** **ˌbutter sb↔ˈup** (*informal*) to say nice things to sb so that they will help you or give you sth

**but·ter·cream** /ˈbʌtəkriːm; *NAmE* -tərk-/ *noun* [U] a soft mixture of butter and sugar, used inside and on top of cakes

**but·ter·cup** /ˈbʌtəkʌp; *NAmE* -tərk-/ *noun* a wild plant with small shiny yellow flowers that are like cups in shape ⇨ VISUAL VOCAB page V7

**but·ter·fat** /ˈbʌtəfæt; *NAmE* -tərf-/ *noun* [U] the natural fat contained in milk and milk products

**but·ter·fin·gers** /ˈbʌtəfɪŋɡəz; *NAmE* -tərfɪŋɡərz/ *noun* [sing.] (*informal*) a person who often drops things

**but·ter·fly** /ˈbʌtəflaɪ; *NAmE* -tərf-/ *noun* (*pl.* **-ies**) **1** [C] a flying insect with a long thin body and four large, usually brightly coloured, wings: *butterflies and moths* ◇ *She's like a butterfly. She flits in and out of people's lives.* ⇨ VISUAL VOCAB page V3 **2** [U] a swimming STROKE in which you swim on your front and lift both arms forward at the same time while your legs move up and down together: *She was third in the 200m butterfly* (= a swimming race). **IDM** **have ˈbutterflies (in your stomach)** (*informal*) to have a nervous feeling in your stomach before doing sth

**ˈbutter knife** *noun* a knife that has a flat metal edge with a round end, used for spreading butter on bread

**but·ter·milk** /ˈbʌtəmɪlk; *NAmE* -tərm-/ *noun* [U] the liquid that remains when butter is made from cream, used in cooking or as a drink

**but·ter·nut** /ˈbʌtənʌt; *NAmE* -tərn-/ *noun* a North American tree grown as a decoration and for its wood

**ˌbutternut ˈsquash** *noun* [C, U] a long vegetable that grows on the ground, has a hard yellow skin and is orange inside and fatter at one end than the other ⇨ VISUAL VOCAB page V3

**but·ter·scotch** /ˈbʌtəskɒtʃ; *NAmE* -tərskɑːtʃ/ *noun* [U] **1** a type of hard pale brown sweet made by boiling butter and brown sugar together **2** (*especially NAmE*) a sweet sauce made with butterscotch, used for pouring on ice cream, etc.

**but·tery** /ˈbʌtəri/ *adj.* like, containing or covered with butter

**but·tock** /ˈbʌtək/ *noun* [usually pl.] either of the two round soft parts at the top of a person's legs: *He fell down hard on his right buttock and slid along the path.* ⇨ VISUAL VOCAB page V1

## buttons

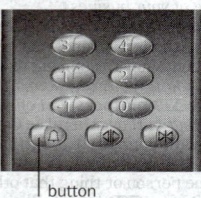

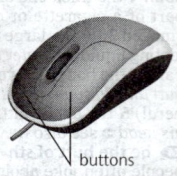

buttons on a keypad     buttons on a mouse

**but·ton** /ˈbʌtn/ *noun, verb*

■ *noun* **1** a small round piece of metal, plastic, etc. that is SEWN onto a piece of clothing and used for fastening two parts together: (*BrE*) *to do up/undo your buttons* ◇ (*NAmE*) *to button/unbutton your buttons* ◇ *to sew on a button* ◇ *One of the buttons on his jacket was missing.* **2** a small part of a machine that you press to make it work: *Adam pressed a button and waited for the lift.* ◇ *She pushed a button on the control panel.* ◇ *I hit the play button on the remote.* ◇ *The windows slide down at the touch of a button.* ⇨ see also PUSH-BUTTON **3** a small area on a computer screen that you click on to make it do sth: *Click on the back button to go back to the previous screen.* **4** (*especially NAmE*) a

BADGE, especially one with a message printed on it ⇨ see also BELLY BUTTON **IDM** **on the ˈbutton** (*informal*, *especially NAmE*) **1** at exactly the right time or at the exact time mentioned: *We arrived at 4 o'clock on the button.* **2** exactly right: *You're on the button there!* **ˌpush all the (right) ˈbuttons** (also **ˌpress all the (right) ˈbuttons** *especially in BrE*) (*informal*) to do exactly the right things to please sb: *a new satirical comedy show that pushes all the right buttons* **ˌpush sb's ˈbuttons** (also **ˌpress sb's ˈbuttons** *especially in BrE*) (*informal*) to make sb react in either a positive or a negative way: *I've known him for years, but I still don't know what pushes his buttons.* ⇨ more at BRIGHT *adj.*

■ *verb* **1** [T] to fasten sth with buttons; to fasten the buttons on a piece of clothing sb is wearing: **~ sth (up)** *She hurriedly buttoned (up) her blouse.* ◇ **~ sb into sth** *She buttoned the child into his coat.* **2** [I] **~ (up)** to be fastened with buttons: *The dress buttons (up) at the back.* **IDM** **ˈbutton it!** (*BrE, informal*) used to tell sb rudely to be quiet

**ˈbutton-down** *adj.* a button-down COLLAR, shirt, etc. has the ends of the COLLAR fastened to the shirt with buttons

**ˌbuttoned-ˈup** *adj.* (*especially BrE, informal*) not expressing your emotions openly

**but·ton·hole** /ˈbʌtnhəʊl/ *noun, verb*

■ *noun* **1** a hole on a piece of clothing for a button to be put through **2** (*BrE*) (*NAmE* **bou·ton·nière**) a flower that is worn in the buttonhole of a coat or jacket

■ *verb* **~ sb** (*informal*) to make sb stop and listen to you, especially when they do not want to

**ˌbutton ˈmushroom** *noun* a small young MUSHROOM used in cooking

**but·tress** /ˈbʌtrəs/ *noun, verb*

■ *noun* a structure made of stone or BRICK that supports a wall

■ *verb* **~ sb/sth** (*formal*) to support or give strength to sb/sth: *The sharp increase in crime seems to buttress the argument for more police officers on the street.*

**butty** /ˈbʌti/ *noun* (*pl.* **-ies**) **1** (*BrE, informal*) a sandwich: *a jam butty* **2** (*WelshE, informal*) a friend; a person that you work with

**buxom** /ˈbʌksəm/ *adj.* (of a woman) large in an attractive way, and with large breasts

**buy** /baɪ/ *verb, noun*

■ *verb* (**bought, bought** /bɔːt/)
• WITH MONEY **1** [T, I] to obtain sth by paying money for it: **~ (sth)** *Where did you buy that dress?* ◇ *If you're thinking of getting a new car, now is a good time to buy.* ◇ **~ sth from sb/sth** *I bought it from a friend for £10.* ◇ **~ sth off sb/sth** (*informal*) *She bought it off eBay for $50.* ◇ **~ sb sth** *He bought me a new coat.* ◇ **~ sth for sb** *He bought a new coat for me.* ◇ **~ sth + adv./prep.** *I bought my car second-hand.* ◇ **+ adv./prep.** *It's generally cheaper if you buy online.* **OPP** sell ⇨ HOMOPHONES at BYE ⇨ WORDFINDER NOTE at SHOP

> **WORDFINDER** discount, loyalty card, purchase, receipt, reduction, refund, short-change, store card, voucher

**2** [T] **~ sth** (of money) to be enough to pay for sth: *He gave his children the best education that money can buy.* ◇ *Five pounds doesn't buy much nowadays.* **3** [T] **~ sb** to persuade sb to do sth dishonest in return for money **SYN** bribe: *He can't be bought* (= he's too honest to accept money in this way).
• OBTAIN **4** [T, usually passive] **~ sth** to obtain sth by losing sth else of great value: *Her fame was bought at the expense of her marriage.*
• BELIEVE **5** [T] **~ sth** (*informal*) to believe that sth is true, especially sth that is not very likely: *You could say you were ill but I don't think they'd buy it* (= accept the explanation).
**IDM** **(have) ˈbought it** (*informal*) to have been killed, especially in an accident or a war **buy the ˈfarm** (*NAmE, informal*) to die **buy ˈtime** to do sth in order to delay an event, a decision, etc. ⇨ more at BEST *n.*, PIG *n.*, PUP

**buy sth↔'in** (*BrE*) to buy sth in large quantities **buy 'into sth 1** to buy shares in a company, especially in order to gain some control over it **2** (*informal*) to believe sth, especially an idea that many other people believe in: *She had never bought into the idea that to be attractive you have to be thin.* ⊃ related noun BUY-IN **buy sb↔'off** to pay sb money, especially dishonestly, to prevent them from doing sth you do not want them to do **buy sb↔'out 1** to pay sb for their share in a business, usually in order to get total control of it for yourself ⊃ related noun BUYOUT **2** to pay money so that sb can leave an organization, especially the army, before the end of an agreed period **buy sth↔'up** to buy all or as much as possible of sth: *Developers are buying up all the land on the island.*

■ *noun*
- STH BOUGHT **1 a good, better,** etc. ~ a thing that is worth the money that you pay for it: *That jacket was a really good buy.* ◊ *Best buys this week are carrots and cabbages.* **2** something that is bought or that is for sale; the act of buying sth: *Computer games are a popular buy this Christmas.*

**buyer** /'baɪə(r)/ *noun* **1** a person who buys sth, especially sth expensive: *Have you found a buyer for your house?* **OPP** **seller, vendor** ⊃ compare PURCHASER **2** a person whose job is to choose goods that will be sold in a large shop: *She was a fashion buyer for a department store.* **IDM** **a buyer's 'market** a situation in which there is a lot of a particular item for sale, so that prices are low and people buying have a choice

**buyer's re'morse** *noun* [U] (*NAmE*) the disappointed feeling sb has after they have bought sth when they think they have made a mistake

**'buy-in** *noun* [U] (*business*) the fact of accepting a policy or change because you agree with it: *If you want to make major changes you need buy-in from everyone in the organization.* ◊ *You need to win people's buy-in.* ⊃ see also BUY INTO STH at BUY

**'buy-out** /'baɪaʊt/ *noun* a situation in which a person or group gains control of a company by buying all or most of its shares: *a management buyout*

**'buy-to-'let** *adj.* [only before noun] (*BrE*) describing or connected with a house or flat that sb buys in order to rent it out to sb else, not to live in it themselves: *buy-to-let properties/investors/mortgages*

**buzz** /bʌz/ *verb, noun*
■ *verb* **1** [I] (of a bee) to make a continuous low sound: *Bees buzzed lazily among the flowers.* **2** [I] to make a sound like a bee buzzing: *The doorbell buzzed loudly.* ◊ *My ears were buzzing* (= were filled with a continuous sound). **3** [I] to be full of excitement, activity, etc: *New York buzzes from dawn to dusk.* ◊ *My head was still buzzing after the day's events.* ◊ ~ **with sth** *The place was buzzing with journalists.* **4** [I, T] ~ **(sth) (for sb/sth)** to call sb to come by pressing a BUZZER: *The doctor buzzed for the next patient to come in.* **5** [T] ~ **sb/sth** (*informal*) to fly very close to sb/sth, especially as a warning or threat
**PHRV** **buzz a'round** (*BrE* also **buzz a'bout**) to move around quickly, especially because you are very busy: *I've been buzzing around town all day sorting out my trip.* **buzz 'off** (*informal*) used to tell sb rudely to go away: *Just buzz off and let me get on with my work.*
■ *noun* **1** [C, usually sing.] (*also* **buzz·ing** [U, sing.]) a continuous sound like the one that a bee, a BUZZER or other electronic device makes: *the buzz of bees* ◊ *The buzz of the Entryphone interrupted our conversation.* ◊ *hums and buzzes from the amplifier* **2** [sing.] the sound of people talking, especially in an excited way: *The buzz of conversation suddenly stopped when she came into the room.* **3** [sing., U] (*informal*) a strong feeling of pleasure, excitement or achievement: *a buzz of excitement/expectation* ◊ *She gets a buzz out of her work.* ◊ *Flying gives me a real buzz.* ◊ *The marketing campaign created extraordinary buzz.* **4 the buzz** [sing.] (*informal*) news that people tell each other that may or may not be true **SYN** **rumour**
**IDM** **give sb a 'buzz** (*informal*) to phone sb: *I'll give you a buzz on Monday, OK?*

205 **by**

**buz·zard** /'bʌzəd; *NAmE* -zərd/ *noun* **1** (*BrE*) a large European BIRD OF PREY (= a bird that kills other creatures for food) of the HAWK family **2** (*NAmE*) a large American bird like a VULTURE that eats animals that are already dead

**'buzz cut** *noun* a style of cutting the hair in which all the hair is cut very short, close to the skin of the head

**buzz·er** /'bʌzə(r)/ *noun* an electrical device that produces a buzzing sound as a signal
**IDM** **at the 'buzzer** (*NAmE*) at the end of a game or period of play: *He missed a three-point attempt at the buzzer.*

**'buzz saw** *noun* (*NAmE*) = CIRCULAR SAW

**buzz·word** /'bʌzwɜːd; *NAmE* -wɜːrd/ (*also* **'buzz phrase**) *noun* a word or phrase, especially one connected with a particular subject, that has become fashionable and popular and is used a lot in newspapers etc.

**b/w** *abbr.* black and white (in writing)

**bwana** /'bwɑːnə/ *EAfrE* ['bwanə] *noun* a word used in parts of East Africa to address a man who has authority over you, for example your employer

**by** 🔊 **A1** /baɪ/ *prep., adv.*
■ *prep.* **1** 🔊 **A1** used for showing how or in what way sth is done: *The house is heated by gas.* ◊ *May I pay by credit card?* ◊ *I will contact you by letter.* ◊ ~ **to travel by boat/bus/car/plane** ◊ *to travel by air/land/sea* ◊ *Switch it on by pressing this button.* **2** 🔊 **A1** near sb/sth; at the side of sb/sth; next to sb/sth: *a house by the river* ◊ *The telephone is by the window.* ◊ *Come and sit by me.* **3** 🔊 **A1** used, usually after a passive verb, to show who or what does, creates or causes sth: *He was knocked down by a bus.* ◊ *a play by Ibsen* ◊ *Who's that book by?* ◊ *I was frightened by the noise.* ⊃ HOMOPHONES at BYE **4** 🔊 **A1** not later than the time mentioned; before: *Can you finish the work by five o'clock?* ◊ *I'll have it done by tomorrow.* ◊ *By this time next week we'll be in New York.* ◊ *He ought to have arrived by now/by this time.* ◊ *By the time (that) this letter reaches you I will have left the country.* **5** 🔊 **A2** used before particular nouns without *the*, to say that sth happens as a result of sth: *They met by chance.* ◊ *I did it by mistake.* ◊ *The coroner's verdict was 'death by misadventure'.* **6** 🔊 **A2** used to show the degree or amount of sth: *The bullet missed him by two inches.* ◊ *House prices went up by 10%.* ◊ *It would be better by far* (= much better) *to…* **7** 🔊 **A2** during sth; in a particular situation: *to travel by day/night* ◊ *We had to work by candlelight.* **8** 🔊 **A2** from what sth shows or says; according to sth: *By my watch it is two o'clock.* ◊ *I could tell by the look on her face that something terrible had happened.* ◊ *By law, you are a child until you are 18.* **9** 🔊 **B1** past sb/sth: *He walked by me without speaking* **10** 🔊 **B1** used to show the part of sb/sth that sb touches, holds, etc: *I took him by the hand.* ◊ *She seized her by the hair.* ◊ *Pick it up by the handle!* **11** 🔊 **B2** used with *the* to show the period or quantity used for buying, selling or measuring sth: *We rented the car by the day.* ◊ *They're paid by the hour.* ◊ *We only sell it by the metre.* **12** 🔊 **B2** used to state the rate at which sth happens: *They're improving by the day.* ◊ *We'll do it bit by bit.* ◊ *It was getting worse by the minute* (= very fast). ◊ *The children came in two by two* (= in groups of two). **13** 🔊 **B2** used to show the measurements of sth: *The room measures fifteen feet by twenty feet.* **14** 🔊 **B2** used when multiplying or dividing: *6 multiplied by 2 equals 12.* ◊ *6 divided by 2 equals 3.* **15** used for giving more information about where sb comes from, what sb does, etc: *He's German by birth.* ◊ *They're both doctors by profession.* **16** used when swearing to mean 'in the name of': *I swear by Almighty God…*
**IDM** **by the 'by/'bye** (*informal*) = BY THE WAY at WAY *n.*
■ *adv.* **1** 🔊 **B1** past: *Just drive by. Don't stop.* ◊ *He hurried by without speaking to me.* ◊ *Excuse me, I can't get by.* ◊ *Time goes by so quickly.* ⊃ HOMOPHONES at BYE **2** used to say that sth is saved so that it can be used in the future: *I've put some money by for college fees.* **3** in order to visit sb for a short time: *I'll come by this evening and pick up the books.*
**IDM** **by and 'by** (*old-fashioned*) before long; soon: *By and by she met an old man with a beard.* **by and 'large** used when you are saying something that is generally, but not

**by-**

completely, true: *By and large, I enjoyed my time at school.* ⊃ LANGUAGE BANK at GENERALLY

**by-** (also **bye-**) /baɪ/ prefix (in nouns) **1** less important: *a by-product* **2** near: *a bystander*

**by·catch** /ˈbaɪkætʃ; *NAmE* also -ketʃ/ *noun* [U] fish that are caught by ships by accident when other types of fish are being caught: *Thousands of small fish are thrown back into the sea as bycatch.*

**bye** 🔊 A1 /baɪ/ *exclamation, noun*
- *exclamation* 🔊 A1 (*informal*) (also **bye-ˈbye**, **ˈbye-bye**) goodbye: *Bye! See you next week.* ◇ *She waved bye-bye and got into the car.* ◇ *Bye for now Dad!*
- *noun* (*sport*) a situation in which a player or team does not have an opponent in one part of the competition and continues to the next part as if they had won **IDM** see WAY *n.*

▼ **HOMOPHONES**

**buy · by · bye** /baɪ/
- **buy** *verb*: *Some people buy all their groceries online.*
- **by** *prep.*: *I think he was motivated by his mother.*
- **by** *adv.*: *Don't let the opportunity pass you by.*
- **bye** *exclamation*: *Bye! See you later.*

**ˈbye-law** = BY-LAW

**ˈby-election** *noun* (*BrE*) an election of a new Member of Parliament to replace sb who has died or left parliament ⊃ compare GENERAL ELECTION

**by·gone** /ˈbaɪɡɒn; *NAmE* -ɡɔːn/ *adj.* [only before noun] happening or existing a long time ago: *a bygone age/era*

**by·gones** /ˈbaɪɡɒnz; *NAmE* -ɡɔːnz/ *noun* [pl.]
**IDM** ˌlet ˈbygones be ˈbygones to decide to forget about arguments that happened in the past

**ˈby-law** (also **ˈbye-law**) *noun* **1** (*BrE*) a law that is made by a local authority and that applies only to that area **2** (*NAmE*) a law or rule of a club or company

**by·line** /ˈbaɪlaɪn/ *noun* a line at the beginning or end of a piece of writing in a newspaper or magazine that gives the writer's name

**BYO** /ˌbiː waɪ ˈəʊ/ (also **BYOB** /ˌbiː waɪ əʊ ˈbiː/) *abbr.* (used in invitations to parties, notices in restaurants, etc.) bring your own (bottle/beer)

**by·pass** /ˈbaɪpɑːs; *NAmE* -pæs/ *noun, verb*
- *noun* **1** (*especially BrE*) a road that passes around a town or city rather than through the centre ⊃ WORDFINDER NOTE at ROAD **2** a medical operation in which blood is directed along a different route so that it does not flow through a part that is damaged or blocked, especially to improve blood flow to the heart; the new route that the blood takes: *heart bypass surgery* ◇ *a triple bypass operation* ⊃ compare GASTRIC BYPASS
- *verb* **1** ~ sth to go around or avoid a place: *A new road now bypasses the town.* **2** ~ sth/sb to ignore a rule, an official system or sb in authority, especially in order to get sth done quickly

**ˈby-product** *noun* **1** a substance that is produced during the process of making or destroying sth else: *When burnt, plastic produces dangerous by-products.* **2** a thing that happens, often unexpectedly, as the result of sth else: *One of the by-products of unemployment is an increase in crime.*

**byre** /ˈbaɪə(r)/ *noun* (*BrE, old-fashioned*) a farm building in which cows are kept **SYN** cowshed

**by·stand·er** /ˈbaɪstændə(r)/ *noun* a person who sees sth that is happening but is not involved **SYN** onlooker: *innocent bystanders at the scene of the accident* ⊃ SYNONYMS at WITNESS

**byte** /baɪt/ *noun* a unit of information stored in a computer, equal to 8 BITS. A computer's memory is measured in bytes.

**byway** /ˈbaɪweɪ/ *noun* **1** [C] a small road that is not used very much **2** **byways** [pl.] the less important areas of a subject

**by·word** /ˈbaɪwɜːd; *NAmE* -wɜːrd/ *noun* [usually sing.] **1 a ~ for sth** a person or thing that is a well-known or typical example of a particular quality: *The name Chanel became a byword for elegance.* **2** (*especially NAmE*) a word or phrase that is well known or often used

**By·zan·tine** /baɪˈzæntaɪn, bɪ-; *NAmE* ˈbɪzəntiːn/ *adj.* (*usually before noun*) **1** connected with Byzantium or the Eastern Roman Empire **2** used to describe architecture of the 5th to the 15th centuries in the Byzantine Empire, especially churches with high central DOMES and MOSAICS **3** (also **byzantine**) (*formal*) (of an idea, a system, etc.) complicated, secret and difficult to change: *an organization of byzantine complexity*

# Cc

**C** /siː/ noun, abbr., symbol
- **noun** (also **c**) [C, U] (pl. **Cs**, **C's**, **c's** /siːz/) **1** the third letter of the English alphabet: *'Cat' begins with (a) C/'C'.* **2 C** (*music*) the first note in the SCALE of C MAJOR ⇒ see also MIDDLE C **3 C ~ (in/for sth)** a grade that a student can get for a piece of work or course of study that shows that it is acceptable but not good or excellent: *She got (a) C/"C" in physics.*
- **abbr. 1 C.** CAPE: *C. Horn* (= for example, on a map) **2** CELSIUS, CENTIGRADE: *Water freezes at 0°C.* **3** (also **©**) (NAmE also **C.**) COPYRIGHT: *© Oxford University Press 2020* ⇒ see also C OF E, C & W
- **symbol 1** (also **c**) the number 100 in ROMAN NUMERALS **2** the symbol for the chemical element CARBON

**c** /siː/ (*BrE*) (also **c.** *NAmE, BrE*) abbr. **1** (in writing) CENT(S) **2** (also **C**) (in writing) century: *in the 19th c* ◊ (*NAmE*) *a C19th church* ⇒ see also CENT. **3** (also **ca**) (especially before dates) about; approximately (from Latin *circa*): *c1890* **4 c.** (*NAmE*) (in cooking) cup: *add 2c. flour*

**cab** /kæb/ noun **1** a taxi: *I'll call you a cab.* ◊ *Let's take a cab.* ⇒ see also BLACK CAB **2** the place where the driver sits in a bus, train or lorry

**cabal** /kəˈbæl; *NAmE* also -ˈbɑːl/ noun (*formal, usually disapproving*) a small group of people who are involved in secret plans to get political power

**Ca·bala** = KABBALAH

**ca·bana** /kəˈbɑːnə; *NAmE* -ˈbænə/ noun (*NAmE, from Spanish*) a small, simple building or shelter at a beach or swimming pool

**caba·ret** /ˈkæbəreɪ; *NAmE* ˌkæbəˈreɪ/ noun **1** [C, U] entertainment with singing and dancing that is performed in restaurants or clubs in the evenings: *a cabaret act/singer/band* **2** [C] a restaurant or club where cabaret entertainment is performed

**cab·bage** /ˈkæbɪdʒ/ noun **1** [U, C] a round vegetable with large green, purplish-red or white leaves that can be eaten raw or cooked: *Do you like cabbage?* ◊ *two cabbages* ◊ *white/red cabbage* ⇒ see also CHINESE CABBAGE, PAK CHOI ⇒ VISUAL VOCAB page V5 **2** [C] (*BrE, offensive*) a person who is physically alive but not capable of much mental or physical activity, for example because of an accident or illness SYN **vegetable**

**cabby** (also **cab·bie**) /ˈkæbi/ noun (pl. **-ies**) (*informal*) a person who drives a taxi as his or her job

**cabin** ⓘ+ B2 /ˈkæbɪn/ noun **1** ⓘ+ B2 a small room on a ship in which you live or sleep: *I lay in my cabin feeling miserably seasick.* **2** ⓘ+ B2 one of the areas for passengers to sit in a plane: *the first-class cabin* **3** a small house or shelter, usually made of wood: *a log cabin*

**cabin boy** noun (especially in the past) a boy or young man employed to work as a servant on a ship

**cabin crew** noun [C + sing./pl. v.] the people whose job is to take care of passengers on a plane ⇒ WORDFINDER NOTE at PLANE

**cabin cruiser** noun = CRUISER

**cab·inet** ⓘ+ C1 /ˈkæbɪnət/ noun **1** ⓘ+ C1 (usually **the Cabinet**) [C + sing./pl. v.] a group of senior members of a government that is responsible for advising and deciding on government policy: *a cabinet meeting* ◊ (*BrE*) *a cabinet minister* ◊ (*BrE*) *the shadow Cabinet* (= the most important members of the opposition party) ⇒ WORDFINDER NOTE at GOVERNMENT **2** ⓘ+ C1 [C] a piece of furniture with doors, DRAWERS and/or shelves, that is used for storing or showing things: *kitchen cabinets* ◊ *a medicine cabinet* ◊ *The china was displayed in a glass cabinet.* ⇒ see also FILING CABINET

**cab·inet-maker** /ˈkæbɪnətmeɪkə(r)/ noun a person who makes fine wooden furniture, especially as a job

**the ˈCabinet Office** noun [sing.] (in the UK) a government department that is responsible for the work of the CABINET and the CIVIL SERVICE

**cab·in·etry** /ˈkæbɪnətri/ noun [U] (*NAmE*) cabinets (= cupboards, especially fitted in a kitchen)

---

**cable** ⓘ B2 /ˈkeɪbl/ noun, verb
- **noun 1** ⓘ B2 [C, U] a set of wires covered in plastic or rubber, that carries electricity, phone signals, etc.: *fibre-optic cable* ◊ *a power cable* **2** [U, C] thick strong metal rope used on ships, for supporting bridges, etc. ⇒ picture at CABLE CAR **3** [U] = CABLE TELEVISION: *We can receive up to 500 cable channels.* **4** [C] (*old-fashioned*) a message sent by electrical signals and printed out
- **verb** [T, I] **~ (sb)** (*old-fashioned*) to send sb a CABLE

**ˈcable car** noun **1** a vehicle that hangs from and is pulled by a moving cable and that carries passengers up and down a mountain **2** (*especially NAmE*) a vehicle that runs on tracks and is pulled by a moving cable

cable car

**ˈcable television** (also **cable**, **ˈcable TV**) noun [U] a system of broadcasting television programmes along wires rather than by radio waves

**cab·ling** /ˈkeɪblɪŋ/ noun [U] all the cables that are required for particular equipment or a particular system

**ca·boo·dle** /kəˈbuːdl/ noun
IDM **the whole (kit and) caˈboodle** (*informal*) everything: *I had new clothes, a new hairstyle—the whole caboodle.*

**ca·boose** /kəˈbuːs/ noun (*NAmE*) the part at the back of a train where the person who is in charge of the train rides

**cab·ri·olet** /ˈkæbriəʊleɪ/ noun a car with a roof that can be folded down or removed SYN **convertible** ⇒ compare SOFT-TOP

**ca·cao** /kəˈkaʊ/ noun [U] a tropical tree with seeds that are used to make chocolate and COCOA; the seeds from this tree

**cache** /kæʃ/ noun, verb
- **noun 1** a hidden store of things such as weapons: *an arms cache* **2** (*computing*) a part of a computer's memory that stores copies of data that is often needed while a program is running. This data can be accessed very quickly.
- **verb 1 ~ sth** to store things in a secret place, especially weapons **2 ~ sth** (*computing*) to store data in a cache: *This page is cached.*

**cachet** /ˈkæʃeɪ; *NAmE* kæˈʃeɪ/ noun [U, sing.] (*formal*) if sth has **cachet**, it has a special quality that people admire and approve of SYN **prestige**: *No other brand name has quite the same cachet.*

**cack** /kæk/ noun [U] (*BrE, slang*) solid waste matter that is passed from the body through the BOWELS

**cack-ˈhanded** adj. (*BrE, informal, disapproving*) a **cack-handed** person often drops or breaks things or does things badly SYN **clumsy**

**cackle** /ˈkækl/ verb, noun
- **verb 1** [I] (of a chicken) to make a loud unpleasant noise **2** [I, T] (**+ speech**) to laugh in a loud unpleasant way: *They all cackled with delight.*
- **noun 1** the loud noise that a chicken makes **2** a loud unpleasant laugh

**cac·oph·ony** /kəˈkɒfəni; *NAmE* -ˈkɑːf-/ noun [U, sing.] (*formal*) a mixture of loud unpleasant sounds ▶ **cac·oph·on·ous** /-nəs/ adj.

**cac·tus** /ˈkæktəs/ noun (pl. **cac·tuses** or **cacti** /-taɪ/) a plant that grows in hot dry regions, especially one with thick STEMS covered in SPINES but without leaves. There are many different types of cactus. ⇒ VISUAL VOCAB page V7

**CAD** /kæd; ˌsiː eɪ ˈdiː/ noun [U] the use of computers to design machines, buildings, vehicles, etc. (the abbreviation for 'computer-aided design')

---

| ʌ actual | aɪ my | aʊ now | eɪ say | əʊ go | ɔɪ boy | ɪə near | eə hair | ʊə pure |

# cad

**cad** /kæd/ noun (*old-fashioned*) a man who behaves in a dishonest or unfair way

**ca·da·ver** /kəˈdævə(r)/ noun (*specialist*) a dead human body ⓢⓨⓝ **corpse**

**ca·da·ver·ous** /kəˈdævərəs/ adj. (*literary*) (of a person) extremely pale, thin and unhealthy looking ill

**cad·die** (also **caddy**) /ˈkædi/ noun, verb
- noun (*pl.* **-ies**) (in golf) a person who helps a player during a game by carrying his or her CLUBS and equipment, and by giving advice
- verb [I] (**cad·dies, caddy·ing, cad·died, cad·died**) to act as a caddie in the game of golf

**cad·dis** /ˈkædɪs/ (also **caddis fly**) noun a small insect. The young forms, called **caddis worms**, are often used for catching fish.

**caddy** = CADDIE

**ca·dence** /ˈkeɪdns/ noun **1** (*formal*) the rise and fall of the voice in speaking: *He delivered his words in slow, measured cadences.* **2** the end of a musical phrase

**ca·denza** /kəˈdenzə/ noun **1** (*music, from Italian*) a short passage, usually near the end of a piece of classical music, that is played or sung by the SOLOIST alone, and intended to show the performer's skill **2** (*SAfrE*) if sb has a **cadenza**, they react suddenly and angrily to sth, especially in a way that seems unreasonable or humorous

**cadet** /kəˈdet/ noun a young person who is training to become an officer in the police or armed forces

**cadge** /kædʒ/ verb [T, I] ~ (**sth**) (**from / off sb**) (*BrE, informal*) to ask sb for food, money, etc. especially because you cannot or do not want to pay for sth yourself: *I managed to cadge some money off my dad.* ▶ **cadger** noun

**Cad·il·lac™** /ˈkædɪlæk/ noun **1** a large and expensive US make of car **2** the ~ **of sth** (*NAmE*) something that is thought of as an example of the highest quality of a type of thing: *This is the Cadillac of watches.*

**cad·mium** /ˈkædmiəm/ noun [U] (*symb.* **Cd**) a chemical element. Cadmium is a soft poisonous blue-white metal that is used in batteries and nuclear REACTORS.

**cadre** /ˈkɑːdə(r); *NAmE* ˈkɑːdreɪ/ noun (*formal*) **1** [C + sing. / pl. v.] a small group of people who are specially chosen and trained for a particular purpose **2** [C] a member of this kind of group

**CAE** /ˌsiː eɪ ˈiː/ noun [U] a British test, now called 'C1 Advanced', that measures a person's ability to speak and write English as a foreign language at an advanced level (the abbreviation for 'Certificate in Advanced English')

**cae·cum** (*BrE*) (*NAmE* **cecum**) /ˈsiːkəm/ noun (*pl.* **cae·ca, ceca** /-kə/) a small bag that is part of the INTESTINE, between the small and the large intestine

**cae·sar·ean** (also **cae·sar·ian**) (both *BrE*) (*US* **ce·sar·ean**) /sɪˈzeəriən; *NAmE* -ˈzer-/ noun [C, U] a caesarean section: *an emergency caesarean* ◊ *She had to have a caesarean.* ⇒ WORDFINDER NOTE at BIRTH ▶ **cae·sar·ean** (also **cae·sar·ian**) (both *BrE*) (*US* **ce·sar·ean**) adj.: *a caesarean birth/delivery*

**cae·sarean ˈsection** (also **cae·sarian ˈsection**) (both *BrE*) (*US* **ce·sarean ˈsection**) (also **ˈC-section** especially in *NAmE*) noun [C, U] a medical operation in which an opening is cut in a woman's body in order to take out a baby: *The baby was born by caesarean section.* ⇒ WORDFINDER NOTE at BIRTH

**Caesar salad** /ˌsiːzə ˈsæləd; *NAmE* -zər/ noun [U, C] a salad of LETTUCE and CROUTONS served with a mixture of oil, lemon juice, egg, etc.

**cae·sium** (*BrE*) (*NAmE* **ces·ium**) /ˈsiːziəm/ noun [U] (*symb.* **Cs**) a chemical element. Caesium is a soft silver-white metal that reacts strongly in water, used in PHOTOELECTRIC CELLS.

**caes·ura** /sɪˈzjʊərə; *NAmE* -ˈzjʊrə/ noun (*specialist*) a break near the middle of a line of poetry

**cafe** 🅞 🄐🄵 (also **café**) /ˈkæfeɪ; *NAmE* kæˈfeɪ/ noun **1** 🄐🄵 a place where you can buy drinks and simple meals. Alcohol is not usually served in British or American cafes: *There are small shops and pavement cafes around every corner.* ◊ **at/in a ~** *They were having lunch at a cafe near the station.* ⇒ see also CYBERCAFE ⇒ compare RESTAURANT **2** (*SAfrE*) a small shop that sells sweets, newspapers, food, etc. and usually stays open later than other shops

**cafe·teria** /ˌkæfəˈtɪəriə; *NAmE* -ˈtɪr-/ noun a restaurant where you choose and pay for your meal before you carry it to a table. Cafeterias are often found in factories, colleges, hospitals, etc: *Consumer groups were urging school cafeterias to serve healthier food.*

**cafe·tière** /ˌkæfəˈtjeə(r); *NAmE* -ˈtjer/ (*BrE*) (*NAmE* **French ˈpress™**) noun a special glass container for making coffee with a metal FILTER that you push down

**caff** /kæf/ noun (*BrE, informal*) a cafe serving simple, basic food: *a transport caff*

**caf·fein·ated** /ˈkæfɪneɪtɪd/ adj. (of coffee or tea) containing caffeine ⇒ compare DECAFFEINATED

**caf·feine** /ˈkæfiːn; *NAmE* kæˈfiːn/ noun [U] a drug found in coffee and tea that makes you feel more active ⇒ see also DECAFFEINATED

**caffè latte** /ˌkæfeɪ ˈlɑːteɪ; *BrE* also -ˈlæt-/ noun = LATTE

**caf·tan** = KAFTAN

**cage** /keɪdʒ/ noun, verb
- noun a structure made of metal bars or wire in which animals or birds are kept: *a birdcage* ◊ *I don't like seeing animals in cages.* ⇒ see also RIBCAGE ⓘⒹⓜ see RATTLE *v.*
- verb [usually passive] ~ **sth** (**up**) to put or keep an animal in a cage: *The dogs are caged* (*up*) *at night.* ▶ **caged** adj.: *He paced the room like a caged animal.*

**cagey** /ˈkeɪdʒi/ adj. (**cagi·er, cagi·est**) ~ (**about sth**) (*informal*) not wanting to give sb information ⓢⓨⓝ **evasive, secretive**: *Tony is very cagey about his family.* ▶ **cagi·ly** /-dʒɪli/ adv.

**ca·goule** (also **ka·goul**) /kəˈguːl/ noun (*BrE*) a long light jacket with a HOOD, worn to give protection from wind and rain

**ca·hoots** /kəˈhuːts/ noun
ⒾⒹⓜ **be in cahoots** (**with sb**) (*informal*) to be planning or doing sth dishonest with sb else

**cai·man** (also **cay·man**) /ˈkeɪmən/ noun (*pl.* **-mans**) a North and South American REPTILE similar to an ALLIGATOR

**cairn** /keən; *NAmE* kern/ noun a pile of stones used to mark a path on a mountain or a place where sb is buried

**ca·jole** /kəˈdʒəʊl/ verb [T, I] to make sb do sth by talking to them and being very nice to them ⓢⓨⓝ **coax**: ~ **sb** (**into sth / into doing sth**) *He cajoled me into agreeing to do the work.* ◊ (+ *speech*) *'Please say yes,' she cajoled.* ◊ *Her voice was soft and cajoling.*

**Cajun** /ˈkeɪdʒən/ noun, adj.
- noun **1** [C] a person of French origin from Louisiana who speaks an old form of French, also called Cajun **2** [U] a type of music originally played by Cajuns, that is a mixture of BLUES and FOLK MUSIC
- adj. connected with the Cajuns, their language, music or spicy cooking: *Cajun chicken/cuisine*

**cake** 🅞 🄐🄵 /keɪk/ noun, verb
- noun **1** 🅟 [C, U] a sweet food made from a mixture of flour, eggs, butter, sugar, etc. that is baked in an oven. Cakes are made in various shapes and sizes and are often decorated, for example with cream or ICING: *a piece/slice of cake* ◊ *to make/bake a cake* ◊ *a chocolate cake* ◊ *a birthday cake* ◊ (*BrE*) *a cake tin* (= for cooking a cake in) ◊ (*NAmE*) *a cake pan* ⇒ see also CHRISTMAS CAKE, FRUIT CAKE, SPONGE CAKE, WEDDING CAKE **2** [C] a food mixture that is cooked in a round, flat shape: *potato cakes* ⇒ see also FISHCAKE
ⒾⒹⓜ **have your cake and ˈeat it** (*BrE*) (also **have your cake and eat it ˈtoo** *NAmE, BrE*) to have the advantages of sth without its disadvantages; to have both things that are available **a slice / share of the ˈcake** (*BrE*) (*BrE and NAmE* **a piece / slice / share of the ˈpie**) a share of the available money or benefits that you believe you have a right to

**take the 'cake** (*especially NAmE*) (*BrE also* **take the 'biscuit**) (*informal*) to be the most surprising, annoying, etc. thing that has happened or that sb has done ⊃ more at HOT *adj.*, ICING, PIECE *n.*
■ *verb* **1** [T, usually passive] to cover sth with a thick layer of sth soft that becomes hard when it dries: **be caked (in/ with sth)** *Her shoes were caked with mud.* **2** [I] if a substance **cakes**, it becomes hard when it dries ▸ **caked** *adj.*: *caked blood*

**cake·walk** /ˈkeɪkwɔːk/ *noun* [sing.] (*informal*) something that is extremely easy to do

**CAL** /kæl/ *abbr.* computer assisted learning ⊃ compare CALL

**cala·bash** /ˈkæləbæʃ/ *noun* **1** a container made from the hard outside layer of a fruit or vegetable; the fruit or vegetable from which a calabash is made ⊃ see also GOURD **2** (*also* **'calabash tree**) a tropical tree that produces a large round fruit with very hard skin, also called calabash

**cala·brese** /ˌkæləˈbriːs, ˌkæləˈbriːsɪ/ *noun* a type of BROCCOLI (= a vegetable with a thick green STEM and green or purple flower heads)

**ca·lam·itous** /kəˈlæmɪtəs/ *adj.* (*formal*) causing great damage to people's lives, property, etc. **SYN** **disastrous**: *The bridge collapsed in the storm, with calamitous results.*

**ca·lam·ity** /kəˈlæməti/ *noun* [C, U] (*pl.* **-ies**) an event that causes great damage to people's lives, property, etc. **SYN** **disaster**: *The country suffered a series of calamities during the 1980s.* ◇ *His financial help saved the magazine from total calamity.*

**cal·cify** /ˈkælsɪfaɪ/ *verb* [I, T] (**cal·ci·fies, cal·ci·fy·ing, cal·ci·fied, cal·ci·fied**) ~ **(sth)** (*specialist*) to become hard when CALCIUM salts are added; to make sth hard by adding CALCIUM salts ▸ **cal·ci·fi·ca·tion** /ˌkælsɪfɪˈkeɪʃn/ *noun* [U]

**cal·cite** /ˈkælsaɪt/ *noun* [U] (*chemistry*) a white or clear mineral consisting of CALCIUM CARBONATE. It forms a major part of rocks such as LIMESTONE, MARBLE and CHALK.

**cal·cium** /ˈkælsiəm/ *noun* [U] (*symb.* **Ca**) a chemical element. Calcium is a soft silver-white metal that is found in bones, teeth and CHALK.

**calcium 'carbonate** *noun* [U] (*symb.* $CaCO_3$) (*chemistry*) a white solid substance that exists naturally as CHALK, LIMESTONE and MARBLE

**cal·cul·able** /ˈkælkjələbl/ *adj.* that can be calculated: *a calculable risk* ⊃ compare INCALCULABLE

**cal·cu·late** 🔑 B2 /ˈkælkjuleɪt/ *verb* **1** 🔑 B2 to use numbers to find a total number, amount, distance, etc. **SYN** **work out**: ~ *sth An independent valuer will calculate the value of your property.* ◇ *That figure was calculated using the standard equation.* ◇ ~ **how much, what, etc.** *You'll need to calculate how much time the assignment will take.* ◇ **it is calculated that ...** *It has been calculated that at least 47 000 jobs were lost last year.* **2** to guess sth or form an opinion by using all the information available **SYN** **estimate**: ~ **that ...** *Conservationists calculate that hundreds of species could be lost in this area.* ◇ ~ **how much, what, etc.** *It is impossible to calculate what influence he had on her life.*

**cal·cu·lated** /ˈkælkjuleɪtɪd/ *adj.* [usually before noun] carefully planned to get what you want: *He took **a calculated risk** (= a risk that you decide is worth taking even though you know it might have bad results).* ◇ *It was either a ridiculous mistake or a calculated insult.*
**IDM** **be calculated to do sth** to be intended to do sth; to be likely to do sth: *Her latest play is calculated to shock.* ◇ *This sort of life is not calculated to appeal to a young man of 20.*

**cal·cu·lat·ing** /ˈkælkjuleɪtɪŋ/ *adj.* (*disapproving*) good at planning things so that you have an advantage, without caring about other people: *a cold and calculating killer* ◇ *I never realized you could be so calculating.*

**cal·cu·la·tion** 🔑+ C1 /ˌkælkjuˈleɪʃn/ *noun* **1** 🔑+ C1 [C, U] the act or process of using numbers to find out an amount: *Cathy did a rough calculation.* ◇ *By my calculation(s), we made a profit of £20 000 last year.* ◇ *Our guess was confirmed by calculation.* **2** 🔑+ C1 [C, U] the process of using your judgement to decide what the results would be of doing sth: *Decisions are shaped by political calculations.* **3** [U] (*disapproving*) careful planning for yourself without caring about other people: *an act of cold calculation*

**cal·cu·la·tor** /ˈkælkjuleɪtə(r)/ *noun* a small electronic device or piece of software for calculating with numbers: *a pocket calculator* ◇ *I used the calculator app on my phone.*

**cal·cu·lus** /ˈkælkjələs/ *noun* [U] the type of mathematics that deals with rates of change, for example in the slope of a curve or the speed of a falling object ⊃ WORDFINDER NOTE at MATHS

**cal·dera** /kælˈdeərə; *NAmE* -ˈderə/ *noun* (*specialist*) a very large hole in the top of a VOLCANO, usually caused by an ERUPTION

**cal·dron** (*US*) = CAULDRON

**Cale·do·nian** /ˌkælɪˈdəʊniən/ *adj.* connected with Scotland

**cal·en·dar** /ˈkælɪndə(r)/ *noun* **1** a page or series of pages showing the days, weeks and months of a particular year, especially one that you hang on a wall: *a calendar for 2020/ a 2020 calendar* ⊃ see also ADVENT CALENDAR **2** (*especially NAmE*) a record of what you have to do each day; the book or piece of software in which you record this: *I think I'm free on that day—let me check my calendar.* **3** [usually sing.] a list of important events or dates of a particular type during the year: *This is one of the biggest weeks in the racing calendar.* ◇ *The group has a busy social calendar.* **4** a system by which time is divided into fixed periods, showing the beginning and end of a year: *the Islamic calendar* ⊃ see also GREGORIAN CALENDAR, JULIAN CALENDAR

**ˌcalendar 'month** *noun* (*specialist*) **1** one of the twelve months of the year ⊃ compare LUNAR MONTH **2** a period of time from a particular date in one month to the same date in the next one

**ˌcalendar 'year** *noun* (*specialist*) the period of time from 1 January to 31 December in the same year

**calf** /kɑːf; *NAmE* kæf/ *noun* (*pl.* **calves** /kɑːvz; *NAmE* kævz/) **1** [C] the back part of the leg between the ankle and the knee: *I've torn a calf muscle.* ⊃ VISUAL VOCAB page V1 **2** [C] a young cow **3** [C] a young animal of some other type such as a young elephant or WHALE **4** [U] = CALFSKIN
**IDM** **in/with 'calf** (of a cow) pregnant

**calf·skin** /ˈkɑːfskɪn; *NAmE* ˈkæf-/ (*also* **calf**) *noun* [U] soft thin leather made from the skin of calves, used especially for making shoes and clothing

**cali·brate** /ˈkælɪbreɪt/ *verb* ~ **sth** (*specialist*) to mark units of measurement on an instrument such as a THERMOMETER so that it can be used for measuring sth accurately

**cali·bra·tion** /ˌkælɪˈbreɪʃn/ *noun* (*specialist*) **1** [U] the act of calibrating sth: *a calibration error* **2** [C] the units of measurement marked on a THERMOMETER or other instrument

**cali·bre** (*US* **cali·ber**) /ˈkælɪbə(r)/ *noun* **1** [U] the quality of sth, especially a person's ability **SYN** **standard**: *He was impressed by the high calibre of applicants for the job.* ◇ *The firm needs more people of your calibre.* **2** [C] the measurement from one side of the inside of a tube or gun to the other; the measurement from one side of a bullet to the other

**cal·ico** /ˈkælɪkəʊ/ *noun* [U] **1** (*especially BrE*) a type of heavy cotton cloth that is usually plain white **2** (*especially NAmE*) a type of rough cotton cloth that has a pattern printed on it

**ˈcalico cat** *noun* (*NAmE*) = TORTOISESHELL (2)

**cali·per** (*BrE also* **cal·li·per**) /ˈkælɪpə(r)/ **1 calipers** [pl.] an instrument with two long thin parts joined at one end, used for measuring the DIAMETER of tubes and round objects (= the distance across them): *a pair of calipers* **2** (*BrE*) (*NAmE* **brace**) [C, usually pl.] a metal support for weak or injured legs

calipers

# caliph

**ca·liph** /ˈkeɪlɪf/ *noun* a title used by Muslim rulers, especially in the past

**ca·liph·ate** /ˈkælɪfeɪt, ˈkeɪl-/ *NAmE* ˈkeɪl-/ *noun* **1** the position of a caliph **2** an area of land that is ruled over by a caliph

**cal·is·then·ics** (*NAmE*) = CALLISTHENICS

**CALL** /kɔːl/ *abbr.* computer assisted language learning ⊃ compare CAL

**call** ⓘ A1 Ⓢ /kɔːl/ *verb, noun*

■ **verb**

• GIVE NAME **1** A1 [T, often passive] to give sb/sth a particular name; to use a particular name or title when you are talking to sb: ~ sb/sth + noun *They decided to call the baby Mark.* ◊ *His name's Hiroshi but everyone calls him Hiro.* ◊ **be called** + noun *I don't know anyone called Scott.* ◊ *I've forgotten what the firm he works for is called.* ◊ **to be sometimes/commonly/often called** sth ◊ ~ sb/sth **after** sb/sth *They called their first daughter after her grandmother.* ◊ ~ sb/sth **by** sth *We call each other by our first names here.* ⊃ see also SO-CALLED

• PHONE **2** A1 [I, T] to phone sb: *I'll call again later.* ◊ *I got a message to call home immediately.* ◊ ~ (sb/sth) **to do sth** *I called the office to tell them I'd be late.* ◊ ~ sb/sth *My brother called me from Spain last night.* ◊ *Call 0800 33344 for a free copy.* ⊃ see also COLD-CALL **3** A1 [T] to ask sb/sth to come quickly to a particular place by phoning: ~ sb/sth *Someone called the police.* ◊ *to call an ambulance/a doctor* ◊ ~ sth **for** sb *I'll call a taxi for you.* ◊ ~ sb I'll call you a taxi. ◊ ~ sb/sth **to** sth *Fire crews were called to the building at 9 p.m.* ◊ note at PHONE

• DESCRIBE **4** B1 [T] to describe sb/sth in a particular way; to consider sb/sth to be sth: ~ sb/sth + noun *I wouldn't call German an easy language.* ◊ *Are you calling me a liar?* ◊ *She now calls Southern California home* (= she lives there). ◊ ~ sb/sth + adj. *Would you call it blue or green?* ⊃ SYNONYMS at REGARD **5** B1 [T] ~ **yourself** + noun to claim that you are a particular type of person, especially when other people question whether this is true: *Call yourself a friend? So why won't you help me, then?* ◊ *She's no right to call herself a feminist.*

• SHOUT **6** B1 [I, T] to shout or say sth loudly to attract sb's attention: *I thought I heard somebody calling.* ◊ ~ (**out**) **to** sb (**for** sth) *She called out to her father for help.* ◊ ~ (**out**) **to** sb **to do** sth *Someone called to him to wait.* ◊ ~ sth *Did somebody call my name?* ◊ ~ **out** (sth) *People in the audience called out requests.* ◊ ~ + speech *'See you later!' he called.* **7** B1 [T, I] to ask sb to come by shouting or speaking loudly: ~ sb + adv./prep. *Will you call the kids in for lunch?* ◊ ~ (sb) *He heard me call him and came to the door.* ◊ *Did you call?*

• ORDER SB TO COME **8** B1 [T, often passive] (*formal*) to order sb to come to a place: **be called** + adv./prep. *Several candidates were called for a second interview.* ◊ *The ambassador was called back to London by the prime minister.* ◊ **be called to do** sth *You may be called to give evidence.* ◊ ~ sb *The defence says it plans to call four witnesses.*

• MEETING/STRIKE, ETC. **9** B1 [T] to order sth to happen; to announce that sth will happen: ~ sth *to call a meeting/strike* ◊ ~ sth **for** ... *The prime minister has called an election for 8 June.*

• VISIT **10** [I] (*especially BrE*) to make a short visit to a person or place: *I'll call round and see you on my way home.* ◊ ~ **on** sb *Let's call on John.* ◊ ~ **to do** sth *He was out when I called to see him.*

• OF BIRD/ANIMAL **11** [I] to make the noise that is typical for it

• PREDICT **12** to predict what the result of sth will be: ~ sth *It's a very open game that is very hard to call.* ◊ ~ **it for** sb *Most media pundits called it for the Conservatives.*

• IN GAMES **13** [T, I] ~ (sth) to say which side of a coin you think will face upwards after it is thrown: *to call heads/tails*

IDM **call sb's ˈbluff** to tell sb to do what they are threatening to do, because you believe that they will not be cruel or brave enough to do it **call sth into ˈplay** (*formal*) to make

use of sth: *Chess is a game that calls into play all your powers of concentration.* **call sth into ˈquestion** to doubt sth or make others doubt sth SYN **question**: *His honesty has never been called into question.* **call it a ˈday** (*informal*) to decide or agree to stop doing sth: *After forty years in politics I think it's time for me to call it a day* (= to retire). **call it ˈquits** (*informal*) **1** to agree to end a contest, argument, etc. because both sides seem equal **2** to decide to stop doing sth **call sb ˈnames** to use offensive words about sb **call the ˈshots/ˈtune** (*informal*) to be the person who controls a situation **call a spade a ˈspade** to say exactly what you think without trying to hide your opinion **call ˈtime (on sth)** (*BrE*) to say or decide that it is time for sth to finish **call sb to acˈcount (for/over sth)** to make sb explain a mistake, etc. because they are responsible for it **call sb/sth to ˈorder** to ask people in a meeting to be quiet so that the meeting can start or continue ⊃ more at CARPET *n.*, MIND *n.*, ORDER *n.*, PAY *v.*, POT *n.*, WHAT

PHRV **ˌcall ˈat ...** (*BrE*) (of a train, etc.) to stop at a place for a short time: *This train calls at Didcot and Reading.* **ˌcall sb aˈway** to ask sb to stop what they are doing and to go somewhere else: *She was called away from the meeting to take an urgent phone call.* **ˌcall ˈback | ˌcall sb ˈback** to phone sb again or to phone sb who phoned you earlier: *She said she'd call back.* ◊ *I'm waiting for someone to call me back with a price.* **ˌcall for sb** (*especially BrE*) to collect sb in order to go somewhere: *I'll call for you at 7 o'clock.* **ˌcall for sth 1** B2 to need sth: *The situation calls for prompt action.* ◊ *'I've been promoted.' 'This calls for a celebration!'* ⊃ see also UNCALLED FOR **2** B2 to publicly ask for sth to happen: *They called for the immediate release of the hostages.* ◊ *The opposition have called for him to resign.* **ˌcall sth↔ˈforth** (*formal*) to produce a particular reaction: *His speech called forth an angry response.* **ˌcall ˈin** to phone a place, especially the place where you work: *Several people have called in sick today.* **ˌcall sb↔ˈin** to ask for the services of sb: *to call in a doctor/the police* **ˌcall sth↔ˈin** to order or ask for the return of sth: *Cars with serious faults have been called in by the manufacturers.* **ˌcall sb/sth↔ˈoff** to order a dog or a person to stop attacking, searching, etc. **ˌcall sth↔ˈoff** to cancel sth; to decide that sth will not happen: *to call off a deal/trip/strike* ◊ *They have called off their engagement* (= decided not to get married). ◊ *The game was called off because of bad weather.* **ˈcall on/upon sb** (*formal*) **1** to ask or demand that sb do sth: *She called on the government to hold a vote.* **2** to formally invite or ask sb to speak, etc: *I now call upon the chairman to address the meeting.* **ˌcall sb ˈout 1** to ask sb to come, especially to an emergency: *to call out an engineer/a plumber/the troops* **2** to order or advise workers to stop work as a protest ⊃ related noun CALL-OUT **ˌcall sb ˈout (on/for sth)** (*also* **ˌcall sb on sth**) (*NAmE*) to criticize sb, especially publicly: *Dan called her out on a couple of contradictions in her story.* **ˌcall sb↔ˈup 1** (*especially NAmE*) to make a phone call to sb **2** to make sb do their training in the army, etc. or fight in a war SYN **conscript, draft 3** to give sb the opportunity to play in a sports team, especially for their country ⊃ related noun CALL-UP **ˌcall sth↔ˈup 1** to bring sth back to your mind SYN **recall**: *The smell of the sea called up memories of her childhood.* **2** to use sth that is stored or kept available: *I called his address up on the computer.* ◊ *She called up her last reserves of strength.*

■ **noun**

• ON PHONE **1** A1 [C] (*also* **ˈphone call**, *formal* **ˈtelephone call**) the act of speaking to sb on the phone: *to get/receive a call from sb* ◊ *to give sb/make a call* ◊ *I'll take* (= answer) *the call upstairs.* ◊ *I left a message but he didn't return my call.* ◊ *a local/long-distance call* ⊃ note at PHONE ⊃ see also ALARM CALL, BLANK CALL, COLD CALL, CONFERENCE CALL, COURTESY CALL, NUISANCE CALL, WAKE-UP CALL

**WORDFINDER** area code, dial, engaged, hold, line, message, phone, ring, tone, voicemail

• SHOUT **2** B2 ~ (**for** sth) a shout or loud sound made to attract attention: *a call for help*

• OF BIRD/ANIMAL **3** [C] a loud sound made by a bird or an animal: *the distinctive call of the cuckoo*

- **REQUEST/DEMAND 4** ⚫ **B2** [C] a request, an order or a demand for sb to do sth or to go somewhere: **~ for sth** *calls for national unity* ◊ *This is the last call for passengers travelling on British Airways flight 199 to Rome.* ◊ **~ for sb to do sth** *calls for the minister to resign* ◊ **~ to sth** (*formal*) *The book is a call to action.* ⊃ see also CLARION CALL, CURTAIN CALL, ROLL CALL **5** [U] **no ~ for sth | no ~ (for sb) to do sth** no demand for sth; no reason for sb's behaviour: *There isn't a lot of call for small specialist shops nowadays.* **6** [C] **~ on sb/sth** a demand or pressure placed on sb/sth: *She is a busy woman with many calls on her time.*
- **VISIT 7** [C] a short visit to sb's house: *I'm afraid this isn't a social call.* ◊ **~ on sb** (*old-fashioned*) **to pay a call** on an old friend ⊃ see also COURTESY CALL, PORT OF CALL
- **OF A PLACE 8** [sing.] **~ (of sth)** (*literary*) a strong feeling of attraction that a particular place has for you: *the call of the sea/your homeland*
- **TO A PARTICULAR JOB 9** [sing.] **~ (to sth)** a strong feeling that you want to do sth, especially a particular job: *the call to the priesthood*
- **DECISION 10** [C] (*informal*) a decision: *It's your call!* ◊ *a good/bad call* ◊ *That's a tough call.* ⊃ see also JUDGEMENT CALL
- **IN TENNIS 11** [C] a decision made by the UMPIRE: *There was a disputed call in the second set.*
- **IN CARD GAMES 12** [C] a player's BID or turn to BID

**IDM** **(above and) beyond the call of 'duty** to a higher standard or level than is required for a job or task: *She went above and beyond the call of duty in her efforts to save his life.* **the call of 'nature** (*humorous*) the need to go to the toilet **a call to 'arms** a strong request to fight in the army; a strong request to defend sth or get ready for a fight about sth **have first 'call (on sb/sth)** to be the most important person or thing competing for sb's time, money, etc. and to be dealt with or paid for before other people or things: *The children always have first call on her time.* **(be) on 'call** (of a doctor, police officer, etc.) available for work if necessary, especially in an emergency: *I'll be on call the night of the party.* ⊃ see also ON-CALL ⊃ more at BECK, CLOSE² *adj.*

▼ **SYNONYMS**

**call**
cry out • exclaim • blurt • burst out

These words all mean to shout or say sth loudly or suddenly.

**call** to shout or say sth loudly to attract sb's attention: *I thought I heard someone calling.*

**cry out (sth)** to shout sth loudly, especially when you need help or are in trouble: *She cried out for help.* ◊ *I cried out his name.*

**exclaim** to say sth suddenly and loudly, especially because of a strong emotion: *'It isn't fair!' he exclaimed angrily.*

**blurt** to say sth suddenly and without thinking carefully enough: *He blurted out the answer without thinking.*

**burst out** to say sth suddenly and loudly, especially with a lot of emotion: *'He's a bully!' the little boy burst out.*

PATTERNS
- to call/cry out/exclaim/blurt out (sth) **to** sb
- to call/cry out **for** sth
- to cry out/exclaim **in/with** sth
- to call/cry out/exclaim/blurt out/burst out **suddenly**
- to call/cry out/exclaim/burst out **loudly**

**'call·back** /ˈkɔːlbæk/ *noun* **1** [C] a phone call that you make to sb who has just called you **2 Callback™** [U, C] = RING-BACK **3** [U, C] (*computing*) a process by which the user of a computer or phone system proves their identity by contacting a computer, which then contacts them **4** [C] (*especially NAmE*) an occasion when you are asked to return somewhere, for example for a second interview when you are trying to get a job

**'call box** *noun* (*BrE*) = PHONE BOX

**'call centre** (*BrE*) (*US* **'call center**) *noun* an office in which a large number of people work using phones, for example arranging insurance for people, or taking customers' orders and answering questions: *to work in a call centre* ◊ *call-centre employees/staff*

**call·er** /ˈkɔːlə(r)/ *noun* **1** a person who is making a phone call: *The caller hung up.* ◊ *an anonymous caller* **2** a person who goes to a house or a building **3** a person who shouts out the steps for people performing a SQUARE DANCE or COUNTRY DANCE

**'caller I'D** *noun* [U] a system that uses a device on your phone to identify and display the phone number of the person who is calling you

**'call girl** *noun* a PROSTITUTE who makes her arrangements by phone

**cal·lig·ra·phy** /kəˈlɪɡrəfi/ *noun* [U] beautiful HANDWRITING that you do with a special pen or brush; the art of producing this ▶ **cal·lig·raph·er** *noun*

**'call-in** (*NAmE*) (*BrE* **'phone-in**) *noun* a radio or television programme in which people can phone and make comments or ask questions about a particular subject

**call·ing** /ˈkɔːlɪŋ/ *noun* **1** a strong desire or feeling of duty to do a particular job, especially one in which you help other people **SYN vocation**: *He realized that his calling was to preach the gospel.* **2** (*formal*) a profession or career: *My father considered engineering one of the highest possible callings.*

**'calling bell** *noun* (*IndE*) = DOORBELL

**'calling card** *noun* **1** (*NAmE*) (*BrE* **'visiting card**) (*also* **card** *BrE, NAmE*) (especially in the past) a small card with your name on it that you leave with sb after, or instead of, a formal visit **2** (*figurative*) a sign, such as an action or a piece of work, that identifies sb or shows what they can do: *Bright, bold colours and shapes are his calling card.* **3** (*NAmE*) = PHONECARD

**cal·li·per** (*BrE*) = CALIPER

**cal·lis·then·ics** (*BrE*) (*NAmE* **cal·is·then·ics**) /ˌkælɪsˈθenɪks/ *noun* [U + sing./pl. v.] physical exercises intended to develop a strong and attractive body

**cal·lous** /ˈkæləs/ *adj.* not caring about other people's feelings, pain or problems **SYN cruel, unfeeling**: *a callous killer/attitude/act* ◊ *a callous disregard for the feelings of others* ▶ **cal·lous·ly** *adv.*

**cal·loused** (*also* **cal·lused**) /ˈkæləst/ *adj.* (of the skin) made rough and hard, usually by hard work: *calloused hands*

**cal·lous·ness** /ˈkæləsnəs/ *noun* [U] **~ (toward(s) sb)** behaviour that shows no care for other people's feelings, pain or problems **SYN cruelty**: *callousness towards the poor*

**'call-out** *noun* an occasion when sb is called to do repairs, rescue sb, etc: *a call-out charge* ◊ *ambulance call-outs*

**cal·low** /ˈkæləʊ/ *adj.* (*formal, disapproving*) young and without experience **SYN inexperienced**: *a callow youth*

**'call sign** *noun* the letters and numbers used in radio communication to identify the person who is sending a message

**'call-up** *noun* **1** [U, C, usually sing.] (*BrE*) an order to join the armed forces **SYN conscription, draft**: *Because of his occupation, he was not liable for call-up.* ◊ *to receive your call-up papers* **2** [C] **~ (to sth)** the opportunity to play in a sports team, especially for your country: *His recent form has earned him a call-up to the England squad.*

**cal·lus** /ˈkæləs/ *noun* an area of thick hard skin on a hand or foot, usually caused by rubbing

**cal·lused** = CALLOUSED

**'call waiting** *noun* [U] a phone service that tells you if sb is trying to call you when you are using the phone

**calm** 🔊 **B1** /kɑːm/ *adj., verb, noun*

■ *adj.* (**calm·er**, **calm·est**) 🔊 **B1** not excited, nervous or upset: *He always stays calm under pressure.* ◊ *Try to remain calm.* ◊ *Her voice was surprisingly calm.* ◊ *The city is calm again* (= free from trouble and fighting) *after yesterday's riots.* **2** 🔊 **B1** (of the sea) without large waves: *The*

# Calor gas

*sea was flat calm* (= with no waves at all). **3** (of the weather) without wind: *a calm, cloudless day* ⇨ WORDFINDER NOTE at WIND¹ ▶ **calm·ly** *adv.*: '*I'll call the doctor,'* he said calmly. **calm·ness** *noun* [U]: *He was calmness personified.*
■ *verb* ~ **sb/sth/yourself** to make sb/sth become quiet and more relaxed, especially after strong emotion or excitement: *Have some tea; it'll calm your nerves.* ◇ *I breathed in slowly, trying to calm myself.* ⇨ see also TRAFFIC CALMING
**PHRV** **,calm 'down** | **calm sb/sth/yourself↔'down** to become or make sb/sth/yourself become calm: *Look, calm down! We'll find her.* ◇ *We waited inside until things calmed down.* ◇ *He took a few deep breaths to calm himself down.*
■ *noun* [C, U] **1** a quiet and peaceful time or situation: *The police appealed for calm.* ◇ *The bombings ended a period of relative calm.* **2** a time when there is no wind: *They landed in a flat calm.* **3** a quiet and relaxed manner: *Her previous calm gave way to terror.*
**IDM** **the calm before the storm** a calm time immediately before an expected period of violent activity or argument

▼ WHICH WORD?

**calm / calmness**

• The noun **calm** is usually used to talk about a peaceful time or situation: *There was a short period of uneasy calm after the riot.* It can also be used to describe a person's manner: *She spoke with icy calm.* **Calmness** is usually used to talk about a person: *We admired his calmness under pressure.*

**Calor gas™** /'kælə gæs; *NAmE* -lər/ (*BrE*) (*US* **cooking gas**) *noun* [U] a type of gas stored as a liquid under pressure in metal containers and used for heating and cooking in places where there is no gas supply

**cal·orie** /'kæləri/ *noun* **1** a unit for measuring how much energy food will produce: *A fried egg contains about 100 calories—about the same as you would burn off if you ran a mile.* ◇ *No sugar for me, thanks—I'm counting my calories.* ◇ *a low-calorie drink/diet* ⇨ WORDFINDER NOTE at EAT **2** (*specialist*) a unit for measuring a quantity of heat; the amount of heat needed to raise the temperature of a GRAM of water by one degree Celsius

**cal·or·if·ic** /,kælə'rɪfɪk/ *adj.* [usually before noun] **1** (*specialist*) relating to the amount of energy contained in food or fuel: *the calorific value of food* (= the quantity of heat or energy produced by a particular amount of food) **2** (of food and drink) containing a lot of calories and likely to make you fat: *calorific chocolate cake*

**cal·or·im·eter** /,kælə'rɪmɪtə(r)/ *noun* (*specialist*) a device that measures the amount of heat in a chemical reaction

**cal·umny** /'kæləmni/ *noun* (*pl.* **-ies**) (*formal*) **1** [C] a false statement about a person that is made to damage their reputation **2** [U] the act of making such a statement **SYN** slander

**Cal·va·dos** /'kælvədɒs; *NAmE* ,kælvə'dəʊs/ *noun* [U, C] a French strong alcoholic drink made by DISTILLING apple juice

**calve** /kɑːv; *NAmE* kæv/ *verb* [I] (of a cow) to give birth to a CALF

**calves** /kɑːvz; *NAmE* kævz/ *pl.* of CALF

**Cal·vin·ist** /'kælvɪnɪst/ (*also* **Cal·vin·is·tic**) *adj.* **1** connected with a Church that follows the teachings of the French Protestant, John Calvin **2** having very strict moral attitudes ▶ **Cal·vin·ism** /-nɪzəm/ *noun* [U] **Cal·vin·ist** /-nɪst/ *noun*

**ca·lypso** /kə'lɪpsəʊ/ *noun* [C, U] (*pl.* **-os**) a Caribbean song about a subject of current interest; this type of music

**calyx** /'keɪlɪks/ *noun* (*pl.* **ca·lyxes** or **ca·ly·ces** /-lɪsiːz/) (*specialist*) the ring of small green leaves (called SEPALS) that protect a flower before it opens

**CAM** /kæm/ *abbr.* computer-aided manufacturing (the use of computers to make products in factories)

**cam** /kæm/ *noun* **1** a part on a wheel that sticks out and changes the CIRCULAR movement of the wheel into up-and-down or backwards and-forwards movement **2** (especially in compounds) (*informal*) a camera: *a video/digital/traffic cam* ⇨ see also DASHCAM, WEBCAM

**cama·rad·erie** /,kæmə'rɑːdəri; *NAmE* -kɑːm-/ *noun* [U] a feeling of friendship and trust among people who work or spend a lot of time together: *the wartime spirit of camaraderie*

**cam·ber** /'kæmbə(r)/ *noun* a slight curve that goes downwards from the middle of a road to each side

**cam·cord·er** /'kæmkɔːdə(r); *NAmE* -kɔːrd-/ *noun* a video camera that records pictures and sound and that can be carried around

**came** /keɪm/ *past tense* of COME

**camel** /'kæml/ *noun* **1** [C] an animal with a long neck and one or two HUMPS on its back, used in desert countries for riding on or for carrying goods ⇨ compare DROMEDARY **2** [U] = CAMEL HAIR: *a camel coat* **IDM** see STRAW

**'camel hair** *noun* [U] (*also* **camel**) a type of thick soft pale brown cloth made from camel's hair or a mixture of camel's hair and wool, used especially for making coats: *a camel-hair coat*

**cam·el·lia** /kə'miːliə/ *noun* a bush with shiny leaves and white, red or pink flowers that look like ROSES and are also called camellias

**Cam·em·bert** /'kæməmbeə(r); *NAmE* -ber/ *noun* [U, C] a type of soft French cheese with a strong taste

**cameo** /'kæmiəʊ/ *noun* (*pl.* **-os**) **1** a small part in a film or play for a famous actor: *a cameo role/appearance* ⇨ WORDFINDER NOTE at ACTOR **2** a short piece of writing that gives a good description of sb/sth **3** a piece of jewellery that consists of a raised design, often of a head, on a background of a different colour: *a cameo brooch/ring*

**cam·era** /'kæmrə/ *noun* a piece of equipment for taking photographs, moving pictures or television pictures. It can be a separate item or part of another device: *Just point the camera and press the button.* ◇ *The camera has captured the drama of the event.* ◇ *a TV/video camera* ◇ *a camera crew*
**IDM** **in 'camera** (*law*) in a judge's private room, without the press or the public being present: *The trial was held in camera.* **off 'camera** without a camera recording what is happening: *The incident occurred off camera.* **on 'camera** while a camera is recording what is happening: *Are you prepared to tell your story on camera?*

**cam·era·man** /'kæmrəmæn/, **came·ra·woman** /'kæmrəwʊmən/ *noun* (*pl.* **-men** /-men/, **-women** /-wɪmɪn/) a person whose job is operating a camera for making films or television programmes ⇨ note at GENDER

**camera obscura** /,kæmrə əb'skjʊərə; *NAmE* -'skjʊrə/ *noun* an early form of camera consisting of a dark box with a tiny hole or LENS in the front and a small screen inside, on which the image appears

**'camera operator** *noun* (*also* **'camera person** *pl.* **'camera people**) a person whose job is operating a camera for making films or television programmes

**cam·era·work** /'kæmrəwɜːk; *NAmE* -wɜːrk/ *noun* [U] the style in which sb takes photographs or uses a film camera

**cami·sole** /'kæmɪsəʊl/ *noun* a short piece of women's underwear that is worn on the top half of the body and is held up with narrow pieces of material over the shoulders

**camo·mile** (*especially BrE*) (*also* **chamo·mile** *especially in NAmE*) /'kæməmaɪl/ *noun* [U] a plant with a sweet smell and small white and yellow flowers. Its dried leaves and flowers are used to make tea, medicine, etc: *camomile tea*

**cam·ou·flage** /'kæməflɑːʒ/ *noun*, *verb*
■ *noun* **1** [U] a way of hiding soldiers and military equipment, using paint, leaves or nets, so that they look like part of what is around or near them: *a camouflage jacket* (= covered with green and brown marks and worn by soldiers) ◇ *troops dressed in camouflage* **2** [U, sing.] the way in which an animal's colour or shape matches what is around or near it and makes it difficult to see: *The*

*whiteness of polar bears and arctic foxes provides camouflage.* **3** [U, sing.] *behaviour that is deliberately meant to hide the truth:* Her angry words were camouflage for the way she felt.
- **verb** ~ sth/yourself (with sth) to hide sb/sth/yourself by making them/it/yourself look like the things around, or like sth else: *The soldiers camouflaged themselves with leaves.* ◇ *Her size was camouflaged by the long loose dress she wore.* ⇨ SYNONYMS at HIDE

## camp ❶ A2 /kæmp/ noun, verb, adj.

- **noun**
- IN TENTS **1** A2 [U] a place where people live temporarily in tents or temporary buildings: *Let's return to camp.* ◇ *to pitch/set up camp* (= put up tents) ◇ *to break/strike camp* (= take down tents) ⇨ see also BASE CAMP, HOLIDAY CAMP, SQUATTER CAMP, TRAINING CAMP
- HOLIDAY/VACATION **2** A2 (also **'summer camp**) [C, U] (especially in North America) a place where children go in the summer and take part in sports and other activities: *a tennis/soccer/music camp* ◇ **at~** *He spent two weeks at camp this summer.* ⇨ see also FAT CAMP
- PRISON, ETC. **3** A2 [C] (used in compounds) a place where people are kept in temporary buildings or tents, especially by a government and often for long periods: *a refugee camp* ◇ *a detention/an internment camp* ◇ *a camp guard* ⇨ see also BOOT CAMP (2), CONCENTRATION CAMP, LABOUR CAMP, PRISON CAMP, TRANSIT CAMP
- ARMY **4** [C, U] a place where soldiers live while they are training or fighting: *an army camp* ⇨ see also BOOT CAMP (1)
- GROUP OF PEOPLE **5** [C] a group of people who have the same ideas about sth and oppose people with other ideas: *the socialist camp* ◇ *We were in opposing camps.* **6** [C] one of the sides in a competition and the people connected with it: *There was an air of confidence in the England camp.* **IDM** see FOOT n.

- **verb**
- LIVE IN TENT **1** A2 [I] to put up a tent and live in it for a short time: *I camped overnight in a field.* **2** A2 [I] **go camping** to stay in a tent, especially while you are on holiday: *They go camping in France every year.* ⇨ WORDFINDER NOTE at HOLIDAY
- STAY FOR SHORT TIME **3** [I] ~ (out) to live in sb's house for a short time, especially when you do not have a bed there: *I'm camping out at a friend's apartment at the moment.* **4** [I] (of a character in a video game) to stay in one place in order to keep attacking enemies and gain an advantage
- **PHR V** **camp 'out** to live outside for a short time: *Dozens of reporters camped out on her doorstep.* **camp it 'up** (*informal*) to behave in a very EXAGGERATED manner, especially to attract attention to yourself or to make people laugh

- (especially BrE) (also **campy** especially in NAmE) **adj. 1** (of a man or his manner) deliberately behaving in a way that some people think is typical of a GAY man **SYN effeminate**: *He's so camp, isn't he?* **2** EXAGGERATED in style, especially in a deliberately humorous way: *The movie is a camp celebration of the fashion industry.*

## cam·paign ❶ B1 /kæmˈpeɪn/ noun, verb

- **noun 1** B1 a series of planned activities that are intended to achieve a particular social, commercial or political aim: *an advertising/a marketing campaign* ◇ *an election campaign* ◇ **~ for sth** *the campaign for parliamentary reform* ◇ **~ against sth** *a campaign against ageism in the workplace* ◇ **~ to do sth** *Today police launched a campaign to reduce road accidents.* ◇ *to mount/begin/start a campaign* ◇ *to wage/run/lead/spearhead a campaign* ◇ *the governor's campaign manager* ⇨ see also DEFIANCE CAMPAIGN, WHISPERING CAMPAIGN **2** a series of attacks and battles that are intended to achieve a particular military aim during a war: *a bombing campaign* ⇨ WORDFINDER NOTE at ATTACK
- **verb** B1 [I, T] to take part in or lead a campaign, for example to achieve social or political change, or in order to win an election: *The party campaigned vigorously in the north of the country.* ◇ **~ for/against sb/sth** *We have actively campaigned against whaling for the last 15 years.* ◇ **~ to do sth** *They are campaigning to save the area from building development.* ▶ **cam·paign·ing** *noun* [U]

### ▼ SYNONYMS
**campaign**
battle • struggle • drive • war • fight

These are all words for an effort made to achieve or prevent sth.

**campaign** a series of planned activities that are intended to achieve a particular social, commercial or political aim: *the campaign for parliamentary reform* ◇ *an advertising campaign*

**battle** a competition or argument between people or groups of people trying to win power or control: *She finally won the legal battle for compensation.* ◇ *the endless battle between man and nature*

**struggle** a competition or argument between people or groups of people trying to win power or control: *the struggle for independence* ◇ *the struggle between good and evil*

**BATTLE OR STRUGGLE?**
A **struggle** is always about things that seem absolutely necessary, such as life and death or freedom. A **battle** can also be about things that are not absolutely necessary, just desirable, or about the pleasure of winning: *the battle/struggle between good and evil* ◇ *a legal struggle for compensation* ◇ *a struggle of wills/wits*.

**drive** an organized effort by a group of people to achieve sth: *the drive for greater efficiency* ◇ *a drive to reduce energy consumption*

**CAMPAIGN OR DRIVE?**
A **campaign** is usually aimed at getting other people to do sth; a **drive** may be an attempt by people to get themselves to do sth: *From today, we're going on an economy drive* (= we must spend less). A **campaign** may be larger, more formal and more organized than a **drive**.

**war** [sing.] an effort over a long period of time to get rid of or stop sth bad: *the war against crime*

**fight** [sing.] the work of trying to stop or prevent sth bad or achieve sth good; an act of competing, especially in a sport: *Workers won their fight to stop compulsory redundancies.*

**WAR OR FIGHT?**
- A **war** is about stopping things, like drugs and crime, that everyone agrees are bad. A **fight** can be about achieving justice for yourself.

**PATTERNS**
- a campaign/battle/struggle/drive/war/fight **against** sth
- a campaign/battle/struggle/drive/fight **for** sth
- a one-man/one-woman/personal campaign/battle/struggle/war
- a **bitter** campaign/battle/struggle/drive/war/fight
- to **launch/embark on** a campaign/battle/drive
- to **lead/continue** the campaign/battle/struggle/drive/fight
- to **win/lose** a battle/struggle/war/fight

**cam·paign·er** /kæmˈpeɪnə(r)/ *noun* a person who leads or takes part in a campaign, especially one for social or political change: *a leading human rights campaigner* ◇ **~on sth** *a campaigner on environmental issues* ◇ **~for/against sth** *an active campaigner for animal rights* ◇ *an old/veteran/seasoned campaigner* (= a person with a lot of experience of a particular activity) ◇ (*especially NAmE*) *Clinton campaigners* (= people working for Clinton in a campaign)

**cam·pa·nile** /ˌkæmpəˈniːli/ *noun* a tower that contains a bell, especially one that is not part of another building

**'camp bed** (*BrE*) (*NAmE* **cot**) *noun* a light narrow bed that you can fold up and carry easily

**camp·er** /ˈkæmpə(r)/ *noun* **1** a person who spends a holiday living in a tent or at a holiday camp **2** (also **'camper van**) (*both BrE*) (*NAmE* **RV**, **recreˌational 'vehicle**) (also **'motor·home** *NAmE*, *BrE*) a large vehicle designed for people to live and sleep in when they are travelling **3** (*NAmE*) (*BrE* **caraˌvan**) a road vehicle without an engine

# campfire

that is pulled by a car, designed for people to live and sleep in, especially when they are on holiday [IDM] see HAPPY

**camp·fire** /'kæmpfaɪə(r)/ noun an outdoor fire made by people who are sleeping outside or living in a tent

**,camp 'follower** noun **1** a person who supports a particular group or political party but is not a member of it **2** (in the past) a person who was not a soldier but followed an army from place to place to sell goods or services

**camp·ground** /'kæmpgraʊnd/ (NAmE) (BrE **camp·site**, **'camping site**) noun a place where people on holiday can put up their tents, park their CARAVAN, etc., often with toilets, water, etc.

**cam·phor** /'kæmfə(r)/ noun [U] a white substance with a strong smell, used in medicine, for making plastics and to keep insects away from clothes

**camp·ing** [A2] /'kæmpɪŋ/ noun [U] living in a tent, etc. on holiday: *Do you go camping?* ◇ *a camping trip* ◇ *No overnight camping is allowed in city parks.*

**camp·site** /'kæmpsaɪt/ noun **1** (also **'camping site**) (both BrE) (NAmE **'camp·ground**) a place where people on holiday can put up their tents, park their CARAVAN, etc., often with toilets, water, etc. **2** (NAmE) (BrE **pitch**) a place in a campground where you can put up one tent or park one CAMPER, etc.

**cam·pus** [B1] /'kæmpəs/ noun the buildings of a university or college and the land around them: *university/college campuses* ◇ **on** ~ *She lives on campus* (= within the main university area).

**campy** /'kæmpi/ adj. (**camp·i·er**, **camp·i·est**) (especially NAmE) = CAMP

**cam·shaft** /'kæmʃɑːft; NAmE -ʃæft/ noun a long straight piece of metal with a CAM on it joining parts of a machine, especially in a vehicle

**can¹** [A1] [S] /kən, strong form kæn/ modal verb ⇒ see also CAN² (negative **can·not** /'kænɒt; NAmE -nɑːt/, short form **can't** /kɑːnt; NAmE kænt/, pt **could** /kʊd/, strong form kud/, negative **could not**, short form **couldn't** /'kʊdnt/) **1** [A1] used to say that it is possible for sb/sth to do sth, or for sth to happen: *I can run fast.* ◇ *Can you call back tomorrow?* ◇ *He couldn't answer the question.* ◇ *The stadium can be emptied in four minutes.* ◇ *I can't promise anything, but I'll do what I can.* ◇ *Please let us know if you cannot attend the meeting.* **2** [A1] used to say that sb knows how to do sth: *She can speak Spanish.* ◇ *Can he cook?* ◇ *I could drive a car before I left school.* **3** [A1] used with the verbs 'feel', 'hear', 'see', 'smell', 'taste': *She could feel a lump in her breast.* ◇ *I can hear music.* **4** [A2] used to show that sb is allowed to do sth: *You can take the car, if you want.* ◇ *We can't wear jeans at work.* **5** [A2] used to ask permission to do sth: *Can I read your newspaper?* ◇ *Can I take you home?* **6** [A2] used to ask sb to help you: *Can you help me with this box?* ◇ *Can you feed the cat, please?* **7** [A2] used to make suggestions: *We can eat in a restaurant, if you like.* ◇ *I can take the car if necessary.* **8** [B1] used in the negative for saying that you are sure sth is not true: *That can't be Mary—she's in New York.* ◇ *He can't have slept through all that noise.* **9** [B1] used to express doubt or surprise: *What can they be doing?* ◇ *Can he be serious?* ◇ *Where can she have put it?* **10** used to say what sb/sth is often like: *He can be very tactless sometimes.* ◇ *It can be quite cold here in winter.* **11** (informal) used to say that sb must do sth, usually when you are angry: *You can shut up or get out!* ⇒ note at MODAL
[IDM] **as happy, simple, sweet, etc. as can be** as happy, etc. as possible **can't be doing with sb/sth** | **can't be doing with sb doing sth** (informal) used to say that you do not like sth and are unwilling to accept it: *I can't be doing with people who complain all the time.* **no can 'do** (informal) used to say that you are not able or willing to do sth: *Sorry, no can do. I just don't have the time.*

▼ **GRAMMAR POINT**

**can / could / be able to / manage**

- **Can** is used to say that somebody knows how to do something: *Can you play the piano?* It is also used with verbs of seeing, noticing, etc: *I can hear someone calling.*
- **Can** is also used with passive infinitives to talk about what it is possible to do: *The podcast can be downloaded here.*
- **Can** or **be able to** are used to say that something is possible or that somebody has the opportunity to do something: *Can you/are you able to come on Saturday?*
- You use **be able to** to form the future and perfect tenses and the infinitive: *You'll be able to get a taxi outside the station.* ◇ *I haven't been able to get much work done today.* ◇ *She'd love to be able to play the piano.*
- **Could** is used to talk about what someone was generally able to do in the past: *Our daughter could walk when she was nine months old.*
- You use **was/were able to** or **manage** (but not **could**) when you are saying that something was possible on a particular occasion in the past: *I was able to/managed to find some useful books in the library.* ◇ *I could find some useful books in the library.* In negative sentences, **could not** can also be used: *We weren't able to/didn't manage to/couldn't get there in time.* **Could** is also used with this meaning with verbs of seeing, noticing, understanding, etc: *I could see there was something wrong.*
- **Could have** is used when you are saying that it was possible for somebody to do something in the past but they did not try: *I could have won the game but decided to let her win.*

▼ **WHICH WORD?**

**can / may**

- **Can** and **cannot** (or **can't**) are the most common words used for asking for, giving or refusing permission: *Can I borrow your calculator?* ◇ *You can come with us if you want to.* ◇ *You can't park your car there.*
- **May** (negative **may not**) is used as a polite and fairly formal way to ask for or give permission: *May I borrow your newspaper?* ◇ *You may come if you wish.* It is often used in official signs and rules: *Visitors may use the swimming pool between 7 a.m. and 7 p.m.* ◇ *Students may not use the college car park.* The form **mayn't** is hardly ever used in modern English.

**can²** [A2] [W] /kæn/ noun, verb ⇒ see also CAN¹
■ noun **1** [A2] (BrE also **tin**) [C] a metal container in which food and drink is sold: ~ **of** sth *a can of beans/beer/soda* ◇ *a beer can* [HELP] In NAmE **can** is the usual word used for both food and drink. In BrE **can** is always used for drink, but **tin** or **can** can be used for food and other substances such as paint or varnish. **2** [A2] [C] the amount contained in a can: ~ **of** sth *We drank a can of Coke each.* **3** [C] a metal or plastic container for holding or carrying liquids: *an oil can* ⇒ see also WATERING CAN **4** [C] a metal container in which liquids are kept under pressure and let out in a fine SPRAY when you press a button on the top: *a can of hairspray* ⇒ see also SPRAY CAN **5 the can** [sing.] (NAmE, slang) prison **6 the can** [sing.] (NAmE, slang) the toilet ⇒ see also GARBAGE CAN, TRASH CAN
[IDM] **be in the 'can** (informal) (especially of filmed or recorded material) to be completed and ready for use **a can of 'worms** (informal) if you open up **a can of worms**, you start doing sth that will cause a lot of problems and be very difficult ⇒ more at CARRY
■ verb (**-nn-**) **1** ~ **sth** (especially NAmE) to preserve food by putting it in a can **2** ~ **sb** (NAmE, informal) to dismiss sb from their job [SYN] **fire**, **sack**

**Canada Day** /'kænədə deɪ/ noun (in Canada) a national holiday held on 1 July to celebrate the original joining together of PROVINCES to form Canada in 1867

**Canada 'goose** noun a common North American GOOSE with a black head and neck

**Can·a·dian** /kəˈneɪdiən/ *adj., noun*
■ *adj.* from or connected with Canada
■ *noun* a person from Canada

**canal** ʔ+ B2 /kəˈnæl/ *noun* 1 ʔ+ B2 a long straight passage dug in the ground and filled with water for boats and ships to travel along; a smaller passage used for carrying water to fields, crops, etc: *the Panama/Suez Canal* ◇ *an irrigation canal* 2 a tube inside the body through which liquid, food or air can pass ⊃ see also ALIMENTARY CANAL, ROOT CANAL

**ca·nal boat** *noun* a long narrow boat used on canals

**can·al·ize** (*BrE also* **-ise**) /ˈkænəlaɪz/ *verb* 1 ~ *sth* (*specialist*) to make a river wider, deeper or straighter; to make a river into a canal 2 ~ *sth* (*formal*) to control an emotion, activity, etc. so that it is aimed at a particular purpose SYN channel ▶ **can·al·iza·tion, -isa·tion** /ˌkænəlaɪˈzeɪʃn; *NAmE* -ləˈz-/ *noun* [U]

**can·apé** /ˈkænəpeɪ; *NAmE* ˌkænəˈpeɪ/ *noun* [usually pl.] a small biscuit or piece of bread with cheese, meat, fish, etc. on it, usually served with drinks at a party

**can·ard** /ˈkænɑːd, kəˈnɑːd; *NAmE* ˈkænɑːrd/ *noun* (*formal*) a false report or piece of news

**can·ary** /kəˈneəri; *NAmE* -ˈneri/ *noun* (*pl.* **-ies**) a small yellow bird with a beautiful song, often kept in a CAGE as a pet
IDM **a ca·nary in a/the ˈcoal mine** something that gives you an early warning of danger ⊃ more at CAT

**can·asta** /kəˈnæstə/ *noun* [U] a card game played with two packs of cards, in which players try to collect sets of cards

**can·can** /ˈkænkæn/ *noun* (*often* **the cancan**) [sing.] a fast dance in which a line of women kick their legs high in the air

**can·cel** ʔ B2 /ˈkænsl/ *verb* (-**ll**-, *US* -**l**-) 1 [T] ~ *sth* to decide that sth that has been arranged will not now take place: *All flights have been cancelled because of bad weather.* ◇ *The prime minister has abruptly cancelled a trip to Washington.* ⊃ compare POSTPONE 2 ʔ B2 [T, I] to say that you no longer want to continue with an agreement, especially one that has been legally arranged: *No charge will be made if you cancel within 10 days.* ◇ ~ *sth* *to cancel a contract/policy/subscription* ◇ *Is it too late to cancel my order?* ◇ *The US has agreed to cancel debts (= say that they no longer need to be paid) totalling $10 million.* 3 [T] ~ *sth* to mark a ticket or stamp so that it cannot be used again
PHRV **ˌcancel ˈout**, **ˌcancel sth↔ˈout** if two or more things **cancel out** or one **cancels out** the other, they are equally important but have an opposite effect on a situation so that the situation does not change: *Recent losses have cancelled out any profits made at the start of the year.* ◇ *The advantages and disadvantages would appear to cancel each other out.*

**can·cel·la·tion** (*US* **can·cel·ation**) /ˌkænsəˈleɪʃn/ *noun* 1 [U, C] a decision to stop sth that has already been arranged from happening; a statement that sth will not happen: *We need at least 24 hours' notice of cancellation.* ◇ *a cancellation fee* ◇ *Heavy seas can cause cancellation of ferry services.* ◇ *Cancellations must be made in writing.* 2 [C] something that has been cancelled: *Are there any cancellations for this evening's performance? (= tickets that have been returned)* 3 [U] the fact of ending an agreement, especially one that has been legally arranged: *the cancellation of the contract*

**Can·cer** /ˈkænsə(r)/ *noun* 1 [U] the fourth sign of the ZODIAC, the CRAB 2 [sing.] a person born when the sun is in this sign, that is between 22 June and 22 July, approximately ▶ **Can·cer·ian** /kænˈsɪəriən; *NAmE* -ˈsɪr-/ *noun, adj.*

**can·cer** ʔ B2 /ˈkænsə(r)/ *noun* 1 ʔ B2 [U, C] a serious disease in which GROWTHS of cells, also called cancers, form in the body and kill normal body cells. The disease often causes death: *breast/lung cancer* ◇ *Most skin cancers are completely curable.* ◇ ~ *of sth cancer of the colon/cervix* ◇ *The cancer has spread to his stomach.* ◇ *Smokers face an increased risk of developing lung cancer.* ◇ *cancer patients/survivors* ◇ *cancer research* 2 [C] (*literary*) an evil or dangerous thing that spreads quickly: *Violence is a cancer in our society.* ▶ **can·cer·ous** /-sərəs/ *adj.:* *to become cancerous* ◇ *cancerous cells/growths/tumours*

**can·dela** /kænˈdiːlə, -ˈdelə/ *noun* (*physics*) (*abbr.* **cd**) a unit for measuring the amount of light that shines in a particular direction

**can·de·la·bra** /ˌkændəˈlɑːbrə/ (*also less frequent* **can·de·la·brum** /ˌkændəˈlɑːbrəm/) *noun* (*pl.* **can·de·la·bra, can·de·la·bras**, *US also* **can·de·la·brums**) an object with several branches for holding CANDLES or lights

**candelabra** — wick — candle

**can·did** /ˈkændɪd/ *adj.* 1 saying what you think openly and honestly; not hiding your thoughts: *a candid statement/interview* ◇ *I felt she was being less than candid with me.* ⊃ see also CANDOUR 2 a **candid** photograph is one that is taken without the person in it knowing that they are being photographed ▶ **can·did·ly** *adv.*

**can·dida** /ˈkændɪdə/ *noun* [U] (*medical*) the FUNGUS that can cause an infection of THRUSH

**can·di·dacy** /ˈkændɪdəsi/ *noun* [C, U] (*pl.* **-ies**) (*also* **can·di·da·ture** *especially in BrE*) the fact of being a candidate in an election: *to announce/declare/withdraw your candidacy for the post*

**can·di·date** ʔ B1 /ˈkændɪdət, -deɪt/ *noun* 1 B1 a person who is trying to be elected or is applying for a job: *a presidential candidate* ◇ ~ **for sth** *one of the leading candidates for the presidency* ◇ *He is the best candidate for the job.* ◇ (*BrE*) *She stood as a candidate in the local elections.* ◇ *The party is fielding more candidates than ever before.* ◇ *to nominate/select a candidate* ◇ *to endorse a candidate (= say you support them)* ⊃ WORDFINDER NOTE at APPLY 2 ʔ B1 (*BrE*) a person taking an exam: ~ **for sth** *a candidate for the degree of MPhil* ⊃ WORDFINDER NOTE at EXAM 3 ~ (**for sth**) a person or group that is considered suitable for sth or that is likely to get sth or to be sth: *Our team is a prime candidate for relegation this year.* ◇ *Your father is an obvious candidate for a heart attack.*

**can·di·da·ture** /ˈkændɪdətʃə(r)/ *noun* [U, C] (*especially BrE*) = CANDIDACY

**can·did·ly** *adv.* ⊃ CANDID

**can·died** /ˈkændid/ *adj.* [only before noun] (of fruit or other food) preserved by boiling in sugar; cooked in sugar: *candied fruit*

**can·dle** ʔ+ B2 /ˈkændl/ *noun* a round stick of WAX with a piece of string (called a WICK) through the middle that is lit to give light as it burns: *The room was lit by candles.* ⊃ picture at CANDELABRA
IDM **cannot hold a ˈcandle to sb/sth** is not as good as sb or sth else: *His singing can't hold a candle to Bocelli's.* ⊃ more at BURN *v.*, WORTH *adj.*

**candle·light** /ˈkændllaɪt/ *noun* [U] the light that a candle produces: *to read by candlelight*

**candle·lit** /ˈkændllɪt/ *adj.* [only before noun] lit by candles: *a romantic candlelit dinner*

**candle·stick** /ˈkændlstɪk/ *noun* an object for holding a candle

**can-ˈdo** *adj.* [only before noun] (*informal*) willing to try new things and expecting that they will be successful: *a can-do attitude/spirit*

**cand·our** (*US* **can·dor**) /ˈkændə(r)/ *noun* [U] the quality of saying what you think openly and honestly SYN frankness: *'I don't trust him,' he said in a rare moment of candour.* ⊃ see also CANDID

**C & W** *abbr.* COUNTRY AND WESTERN

**candy** /ˈkændi/ *noun* [U, C] (*pl.* **-ies**) (*NAmE*) sweet food made of sugar and/or chocolate, eaten between meals; a

# candy apple

piece of this SYN **sweet**: *a box of candy ◊ a candy store ◊ a candy bar ◊ Who wants the last piece of candy? ◊ She had enough candies in her pocket for all the children.* ⊃ see also ARM CANDY, EYE CANDY, HARD CANDY
IDM **be like taking ˌcandy from a ˈbaby** (*informal*) used to emphasize how easy it is to do sth

**ˈcandy apple** (*NAmE*) (*BrE* **ˈtoffee apple**) *noun* an apple covered with a thin layer of hard toffee and fixed on a stick

**ˈcandy cane** *noun* (*especially NAmE*) a stick of hard candy with a curved end

**ˈcandy-floss** /ˈkændiflɒs; *NAmE* -flɑːs/ (*BrE*) (*NAmE* **ˌcotton ˈcandy**) *noun* [U] a type of sweet in the form of a mass of sticky THREADS made from melted sugar and served on a stick, especially at FAIRGROUNDS

**cane** /keɪn/ *noun, verb*
- *noun* **1** [C] the hard hollow STEM of some plants, for example BAMBOO or sugar⊃ see also CANDY CANE, SUGAR CANE **2** [U] these STEMS used as a material for making furniture, etc: *a cane chair* **3** [C] a piece of cane or a thin stick, used as a support for plants **4** [C] a piece of cane or a thin stick, used to help sb to walk⊃ see also WALKING STICK **5** [C] a piece of cane or a thin stick, used in the past in some schools for beating children as a punishment: *to get the cane* (= be punished with a cane)
- *verb* ~ **sb** to hit sb with a cane as a punishment ▶ **ˈcan·ing** *noun* [U, C]: *the abolition of caning in schools*

**ˈcane rat** *noun* a type of large RODENT found in wild areas of Africa, which can be used for food⊃ see also CUTTING GRASS

**ˈcane sugar** *noun* [U] sugar obtained from the juice of SUGAR CANE

**ca·nine** /ˈkeɪnaɪn/ *adj., noun*
- *adj.* connected with dogs
- *noun* **1** (*also* **ˈcanine tooth**) one of the four pointed teeth in the front of a human's or animal's mouth⊃ compare INCISOR, MOLAR, PREMOLAR, WISDOM TOOTH **2** (*formal*) a dog

**can·is·ter** /ˈkænɪstə(r)/ *noun* **1** a container with a LID (= cover) for holding tea, coffee, etc. **2** a strong metal container containing gas or a chemical substance, especially one that explodes or BURSTS (= breaks open) when it is fired from a gun or thrown: *tear-gas canisters* **3** a flat, round metal container used for storing film: *a film canister*

**can·ker** /ˈkæŋkə(r)/ *noun* **1** [U] a disease that destroys the wood of plants and trees **2** [C] a damaged area in a plant or tree caused by disease or injury **3** [C] a disease that causes painful areas in the ears of animals, especially dogs and cats **4** [C] (*literary*) an evil or dangerous influence that spreads and affects people's behaviour

**can·na·bis** /ˈkænəbɪs/ *noun* [U] a drug made from the dried leaves and flowers or RESIN of the HEMP plant, which is smoked or eaten and which gives the user a feeling of being relaxed. Use of the drug is illegal in many countries.

**canned** /kænd/ *adj.* **1** (*BrE also* **tinned**) (of food) preserved in a can: *canned food/soup* **2** ~ **laughter/music** the sound of people laughing or music that has been previously recorded and is used in television and radio programmes

**can·nel·loni** /ˌkænəˈləʊni; *NAmE* -ˈloʊni/ *noun* [U] (*from Italian*) large tubes of PASTA that are served filled with meat, vegetables or cheese

**can·nery** /ˈkænəri/ *noun* (*pl.* **-ies**) a factory where food is put into cans

**can·ni·bal** /ˈkænɪbl/ *noun* **1** a person who eats other people: *a tribe of cannibals* **2** an animal that eats other animals of the same kind ▶ **ˈcan·ni·bal·ism** /-bəlɪzəm/ *noun* [U]: *to practise cannibalism* **ˌcan·ni·balˈis·tic** /ˌkænɪbəˈlɪstɪk/ *adj.*

**can·ni·bal·ize** (*BrE also* **-ise**) /ˈkænɪbəlaɪz/ *verb* **1** ~ **sth** (*business*) (of a company) to reduce the sales of one of its products by introducing a similar new product **2** ~ **sth** to take the parts of a machine, vehicle, etc. and use them to repair or build another **3** (of an animal) to eat an animal of its own kind ▶ **ˌcan·ni·bal·iˈza·tion, -isaˈtion** /ˌkænɪbəl-aɪˈzeɪʃn; *NAmE* -ləˈ-/ *noun* [U]

**can·non** /ˈkænən/ *noun, verb*
- *noun* (*pl.* **can·non** *or* **can·nons**) **1** an old type of large, heavy gun, usually on wheels, that fires solid metal or stone balls⊃ see also LOOSE CANNON, WATER CANNON **2** a gun that fires many shots from an aircraft or TANK: *a burst of cannon fire*
- *verb* [I] + *adv./prep.* to hit sb/sth with a lot of force while you are moving: *He ran around the corner, cannoning into a group of kids.*

**can·non·ade** /ˌkænəˈneɪd/ *noun* a continuous firing of large guns

**can·non·ball** /ˈkænənbɔːl/ *noun* a large metal or stone ball that is fired from a CANNON

**ˈcannon fodder** *noun* [U] soldiers who are thought of not as people whose lives are important, but as material to be used up in war

**can·not** ❶ A1 /ˈkænɒt; *NAmE* -nɑːt/ the negative of can; can not: *I cannot believe the price of the tickets!* HELP In informal English we use **can't**.

**can·nula** /ˈkænjələ/ *noun* (*pl.* **can·nulae** /-liː/ *or* **can·nulas**) (*medical*) a thin tube that is put into a VEIN or other part of the body, for example to give sb medicine

**canny** /ˈkæni/ *adj.* intelligent, careful and showing good judgement, especially in business or politics: *a canny politician ◊ a canny move* ▶ **ˈcan·nily** /-nɪli/ *adv.*

**canoe** /kəˈnuː/ *noun, verb*
- *noun* a light narrow boat that you move along in the water with a PADDLE⊃ see also KAYAK
- *verb* [I] (*often* **go canoeing**) (**ca·noe·ing, ca·noed, ca·noed**) to travel in a canoe: *Last summer we went canoeing on the River Wye. ◊ She dreamed of canoeing down the Amazon.*

**ca·noe·ing** /kəˈnuːɪŋ/ *noun* [U] the sport of travelling in or racing a CANOE: *to go canoeing ◊ Canoeing is an Olympic sport.*

**ca·noe·ist** /kəˈnuːɪst/ *noun* a person travelling in a canoe

**can·ola** (*CanE* **Can·ola**™) /kəˈnəʊlə/ *noun* [U] a variety of RAPESEED that was developed in Canada and is grown widely in North America and is used to make cooking oil, also called **canola**

**canon** /ˈkænən/ *noun* **1** a Christian priest with special duties in a CATHEDRAL **2** (*formal*) a generally accepted rule, standard or principle by which sth is judged: *the canons of good taste* **3** a list of the books or other works that are generally accepted as the real work of a particular writer or as being important: *the Shakespeare canon ◊ 'Wuthering Heights' is a central book in the canon of English literature.* **4** a piece of music in which singers or instruments take it in turns to repeat the MELODY (= tune)

**ca·non·ical** /kəˈnɒnɪkl; *NAmE* -ˈnɑːn-/ (*also* **ca·non·ic**) *adj.* **1** included in a list of holy books that are accepted as what they are claimed to be **2** according to the law of the Christian Church **3** accepted as belonging to the group of writers or works of literature that must be highly respected **4** accepted as being true, correct and established **5** (*specialist*) in the simplest accepted form in mathematics

**can·on·ize** (*BrE also* **-ise**) /ˈkænənaɪz/ *verb* [usually passive] ~ **sb** (of the POPE) to state officially that sb is now a SAINT ⊃ compare BEATIFY ▶ **ˌcan·on·iˈza·tion, -isaˈtion** /ˌkænən-aɪˈzeɪʃn; *NAmE* -nəˈz-/ *noun* [C, U]

**ˌcanon ˈlaw** *noun* [U] the law of the Christian church

**ca·noo·dle** /kəˈnuːdl/ *verb* [I] (*old-fashioned, informal*) (of two people) to kiss and touch each other in a sexual way

**ˈcan opener** (*especially NAmE*) (*BrE also* **ˈtin opener**) *noun* a kitchen UTENSIL (= a tool) for opening cans of food

**can·opy** /ˈkænəpi/ *noun* (*pl.* **-ies**) **1** a cover that is fixed or hangs above a bed, seat, etc. as a shelter or decoration **2** a layer of sth that spreads over an area like a roof, especially branches of trees in a forest: *The canopy of a rainforest is about 10 metres thick.* **3** (*especially NAmE*) a roof that is supported on posts and is sometimes also attached at one side to a building: *a new steel entrance canopy for the* building ◇ *a fabric canopy to provide shade in the backyard* **4** a cover for the COCKPIT of an aircraft

**canst** /kænst/ *verb* **thou canst** (*old use*) used to mean 'you can', when talking to one person

**cant** /kænt/ *noun, verb*
■ *noun* [U] statements, especially about moral or religious issues, that are not sincere and that you cannot trust SYN **hypocrisy**
■ *verb* [I, T] **~ (sth)** (*formal*) to be in a sloping position; to put sth into a sloping position

**can't** /kɑːnt; *NAmE* kænt/ short form **cannot**

**Cantab** /ˈkæntæb/ *abbr.* (used after degree titles) of Cambridge University: *James Cox MA (Cantab)*

**can·ta·loupe** /ˈkæntəluːp; *NAmE* -loʊp/ *noun* a MELON (= a type of fruit) with a green skin that is orange inside

**can·tan·ker·ous** /kænˈtæŋkərəs/ *adj.* often angry; always complaining: *a cantankerous old man*

**can·ta·ta** /kænˈtɑːtə/ *noun* a short musical work, often on a religious subject, sung by SOLO singers, often with a CHOIR and ORCHESTRA ⊃ compare MOTET, ORATORIO

**can·teen** /kænˈtiːn/ *noun* **1** (*especially BrE*) a place where food and drink are served in a factory, a school, etc. **2** a small container used by soldiers, travellers, etc. for carrying water or other liquid **3 ~ of cutlery** (*BrE*) a box containing a set of knives, forks and spoons

**can·ter** /ˈkæntə(r)/ *noun, verb*
■ *noun* [usually sing.] a movement of a horse at a speed that is fairly fast but not very fast; a ride on a horse moving at this speed: *She set off at a canter.*
■ *verb* [I, T] **1 ~ (sth)** (of a horse or rider) to move at a canter; to make a horse move at a canter: *We cantered along the beach.* ⊃ compare GALLOP, TROT **2 ~ home/to victory/to a win** (*especially BrE*) (in sport) to win easily

**can·ti·cle** /ˈkæntɪkl/ *noun* a religious song with words taken from the Bible

**can·ti·lever** /ˈkæntɪliːvə(r)/ *noun* a long piece of metal or wood that sticks out from a wall to support the end of a bridge or other structure: *a cantilever bridge*

**can·tina** /kænˈtiːnə/ *noun* (*from Spanish*) a Mexican-style bar, especially in the south-western US

**canto** /ˈkæntəʊ/ *noun* (*pl.* **-os**) one of the sections of a long poem ⊃ see also BEL CANTO

**can·ton** /ˈkæntɒn; *NAmE* -tən, -tɑːn/ *noun* one of the official regions that some countries, such as Switzerland, are divided into

**Can·ton·ese** /ˌkæntəˈniːz/ *noun, adj.*
■ *noun* **1** (*also* **Yue**) [U] a form of Chinese spoken mainly in southern China, including Hong Kong **2** [C] (*pl.* **Cantonese**) a person whose first language is Cantonese
■ *adj.* of or relating to people who speak Cantonese, or their language or culture: *Cantonese cooking*

**can·ton·ment** /kænˈtuːnmənt; *NAmE* -ˈtɑːn-/ *noun* a military camp, especially a permanent British military camp in India in the past

**can·tor** /ˈkæntɔː(r)/ *noun* the person who leads the singing in a SYNAGOGUE or in a church CHOIR

**Ca·nuck** /kəˈnʌk/ *noun* (*NAmE, informal*) a person from Canada, especially sb whose first language is French. In the US this term is sometimes offensive.

**can·vas** /ˈkænvəs/ *noun* **1** [U] a strong rough material used for making tents, sails, etc. and by artists for painting on **2** [C] a piece of canvas used for painting on; a painting done on a piece of canvas, using oil paints: *a sale of the artist's early canvases* ⊃ WORDFINDER NOTE at PAINTING
IDM **under 'canvas** in a tent ⊃ more at BLANK *adj.*

**can·vass** /ˈkænvəs/ *verb* **1** [I, T] to ask people to support a particular person, political party, etc., either by going around an area and talking to people or by phoning them: **~ (for sth)** *He spent the whole month canvassing for votes.* ◇ **~ sb (for sth)** *Party workers are busy canvassing local residents.* **2** [T] to ask people about sth in order to find

217

# capability

out what they think about it: **~ sth** *He has been canvassing opinion on the issue.* ◇ **~ sb (for sth)** *People are being canvassed for their views on the proposed new road.* **3** [T] **~ support** to try and get support from a group of people SYN **drum up 4** [T] **~ sth** to discuss an idea carefully and completely: *The proposal is currently being canvassed.*
▶ **can·vass** *noun*: *to carry out a canvass* **can·vass·er** *noun*

**can·yon** /ˈkænjən/ *noun* a deep valley with steep sides of rock SYN **gorge**

**cap** ⓘ B1 /kæp/ *noun, verb*
■ *noun*
• HAT **1** ⓘ B1 a type of soft flat hat with a PEAK (= a hard curved part sticking out in front). Caps are worn especially by men and boys, often as part of a uniform: *to wear a cap.* ⊃ see also BASEBALL CAP, CLOTH CAP **2** (usually in compounds) a soft hat that fits closely and is worn for a particular purpose: *a shower cap* ⊃ see also BATHING CAP, SWIMMING CAP **3** a soft hat with a square flat top worn by some university teachers and students at special ceremonies ⊃ compare MORTAR BOARD
• IN SPORT **4** (*BrE*) a cap given to sb who is chosen to play for a school, country, etc.; a player chosen to play for their country, etc: *He won his first cap (= was first chosen to play) for England against France.* ◇ *There are three new caps in the side.*
• ON PEN/BOTTLE **5** a cover or top for a pen, bottle, etc: *a lens cap* ⊃ see also HUBCAP ⊃ SYNONYMS at LID
• ON TOOTH **6** an artificial cover for a damaged tooth SYN **crown**
• ON MOUNTAIN/WAVE **7** the top of a mountain or a wave: *Purple mist sat below the snowy mountain caps.*
• LIMIT ON MONEY **8** an upper limit on an amount of money that can be spent or borrowed by a particular institution or in a particular situation: *The government has placed a cap on local council spending.* ⊃ see also RATE CAP
• IN TOY GUNS **9** a small paper container with EXPLOSIVE powder inside it, used especially in toy guns
• FOR WOMAN **10** (*BrE*) = DIAPHRAGM (2) ⊃ see also DUNCE'S CAP, ICE CAP, THINKING CAP
IDM **go cap in ˈhand (to sb)** (*especially BrE*) (*NAmE usually* **go hat in ˈhand**) to ask sb for sth, especially money, in a very polite way that makes you seem less important **if the cap fits (, wear it)** (*BrE*) (*NAmE* **if the shoe fits (, wear it)**) (*informal*) if you feel that a remark applies to you, you should accept it and take it as a warning or criticism: *I didn't actually say that you were lazy, but if the cap fits…* ⊃ more at FEATHER *n.*
■ *verb* (**-pp-**)
• COVER TOP **1** [usually passive] to cover the top or end of sth with sth: **capped (with sth)** *mountains capped with snow* ◇ *snow-capped mountains*
• LIMIT MONEY **2** [often passive] (*especially BrE*) to limit the amount that can be charged for sth or spent on sth: **be capped (by sb/sth)** *Council expenditure could be capped by the government.*
• BEAT **3 ~ sth** (*especially BrE*) to say or do sth that is funnier, more impressive, etc. than sth that has been said or done before: *What an amazing story. Can anyone cap that?*
• TOOTH **4** [usually passive] to put an artificial layer on a tooth to protect it or make it look more attractive SYN **crown**: **have sth/be capped** *He's had his front teeth capped.*
• IN SPORT **5** [usually passive] (*BrE*) to choose sb to play in their country's national team for a particular sport: **be capped** *He has been capped more than 30 times for Wales.*
IDM **to cap/top it ˈall** (*informal*) used to introduce the final piece of information that is worse than the other bad things that you have just mentioned

**cap·abil·ity** ⓘ C1 Ⓦ /ˌkeɪpəˈbɪləti/ *noun* [C, U] (*pl.* **-ies**)
**1** ⓘ C1 the ability or qualities necessary to do sth: *Age affects the range of a person's capabilities.* ◇ **~ to do sth** *She has the capability to become a very fine actor.* ◇ **~ of doing sth** *Animals in the zoo have lost the capability of catching food for themselves.* ◇ **~ for doing sth** *his capability for making sensible decisions* ◇ **beyond/within the capabilities of sth/sb** *beyond/within the capabilities of current*

**cap·able** ⓘ B2 ⓦ /ˈkeɪpəbl/ adj. 1 B2 having the ability or qualities necessary for doing sth: **~ of sth** *You are capable of better work than this.* ◊ **~ of doing sth** *He's quite capable of lying to get out of trouble.* ◊ *I'm perfectly capable of doing it myself, thank you.* 2 B2 having the ability to do things well SYN **skilled, competent**: *She's a very capable teacher.* ◊ *I'll leave the organization in your capable hands.* OPP **incapable** ▸ **cap·ably** /-bli/ adv.

**cap·acious** /kəˈpeɪʃəs/ adj. (formal) having a lot of space to put things in SYN **roomy**: *capacious pockets*

**cap·aci·tance** /kəˈpæsɪtəns/ noun [U] (physics) **1** the ability of a system to store an electrical charge **2** a comparison between change in electrical charge and change in electrical POTENTIAL

**cap·aci·tor** /kəˈpæsɪtə(r)/ noun (physics) a device used to store an electrical charge

**cap·acity** ⓘ B2 ⓞ /kəˈpæsəti/ noun (pl. **-ies**)
• OF CONTAINER **1** ⓘ B2 [U, C, usually sing.] the number of things or people that a container or space can hold: *a fuel tank with a maximum capacity of 50 litres* ◊ *The theatre has a seating capacity of 2 000.* ◊ **to ~** *The hall was filled to capacity* (= was completely full). ◊ *They played to a capacity crowd* (= one that filled all the space or seats).
• ABILITY **2** ⓘ B2 [C, usually sing., U] the ability to understand or to do sth: *mental/intellectual capacity* ◊ **~ for sth** *She has an enormous capacity for hard work.* ◊ **~ for doing sth** *Limited resources are restricting our capacity for developing new products.* ◊ **~ to do sth** *your capacity to enjoy life is beyond/within sb's ~* *The mountain walk is well within the capacity of most fit people.*
• ROLE **3** [C, usually sing.] the official position or function that sb has SYN **role**: **in a …~** *We are simply involved in an advisory capacity on the project.* ◊ **in your~ as sth** *She was acting in her capacity as manager.*
• OF FACTORY/MACHINE **4** [sing., U] the quantity that a factory, machine, etc. can produce: *Spare oil production capacity will probably remain low.* ◊ **at~** *The factory is working at (full) capacity.* ⊃ WORDFINDER NOTE at FACTORY
• OF ENGINE **5** [C, U] the size or power of a piece of equipment, especially the engine of a vehicle: *an engine with a capacity of 1 600 cc*

**cape** /keɪp/ noun **1** a loose outer piece of clothing that has no SLEEVES (= parts covering the arms), fastens at the neck and hangs from the shoulders, like a CLOAK but shorter: *a bullfighter's cape* **2** (abbr. **C.**) (often in place names) a piece of high land that sticks out into the sea: *Cape Horn*

**caped** /keɪpt/ adj. wearing a cape

**caper** /ˈkeɪpə(r)/ noun, verb
■ noun **1** [usually pl.] the small green flower BUD of a Mediterranean bush, preserved in VINEGAR and used in preparing sauces and other dishes **2** (informal) an activity, especially one that is illegal or dangerous: *A call to the police should put an end to their little caper.* **3** a humorous film that contains a lot of action: *a British spy caper* **4** a short jumping or dancing movement: *He cut a little celebratory caper* (= jumped or danced a few steps) *in the middle of the road.*
■ verb [I] (+ adv. / prep.) (formal) to run or jump around in a happy and excited way

**ca·pil·lary** /kəˈpɪləri; NAmE ˈkæpəleri/ noun (pl. **-ies**) (anatomy) any of the smallest tubes in the body that carry blood ⊃ VISUAL VOCAB page V1

**ca·pillary action** noun [U] (specialist) the force that makes a liquid move up a narrow tube

**cap·ital** ⓘ A1 /ˈkæpɪtl/ noun, adj.
■ noun
• CITY **1** ⓘ A1 (also **capital 'city**) [C] the most important town or city of a country or region, where the government operates from: *Cairo is the capital of Egypt.* ◊ *the provincial/state capital* ◊ (figurative) *Paris, the fashion capital of the world*
• LETTER **2** ⓘ A1 (also **capital 'letter**) [C] a letter of the form and size that is used at the beginning of a sentence or a name (= A,B,C rather than a,b,c): *Use block capitals* (= separate capital letters). ◊ **in capitals** *Please write in capitals.*
• MONEY **3** ⓘ B2 [U] wealth or property that is owned by a business or a person and can be invested or used to start a business: *share/investment/equity capital* ◊ *He had various ideas on how to raise capital for the project.* ◊ *capital investment* (= money invested in a business) ◊ *capital expenditure/spending* (= money that an organization spends on buildings, equipment, etc.) ⊃ see also VENTURE CAPITAL, WORKING CAPITAL **4** [sing.] an amount of money that is invested or is used to start a business: *to set up a business with a starting capital of £100 000* **5** [U] (specialist) people who use their money to start businesses, considered as a group: *capital and labour* ⊃ WORDFINDER NOTE at INVEST
• RESOURCES **6** [U] (in compounds) a valuable resource of a particular kind: *intellectual/cultural capital* ⊃ see also HUMAN CAPITAL, POLITICAL CAPITAL, SOCIAL CAPITAL
• ARCHITECTURE **7** the top part of a column
IDM **make capital (out) of sth** to use a situation for your own advantage: *The opposition parties are making political capital out of the government's problems.*
■ adj.
• LETTER **1** ⓘ A1 [only before noun] (of letters of the alphabet) having the form and size used at the beginning of a sentence or a name: *English is written with a capital 'E'.* ⊃ compare LOWER CASE
• PUNISHMENT **2** [only before noun] involving punishment by death: *a capital offence*
• EXCELLENT **3** (old-fashioned) excellent
IDM **with a capital A, B, etc.** used to emphasize that a word has a stronger meaning than usual in a particular situation: *He was romantic with a capital R.*

**capital 'gain** noun [usually pl.] (economics) a profit that you make from selling sth, especially property: *to pay capital gains tax*

**capital 'goods** noun [pl.] (business) goods such as factory machines that are used for producing other goods ⊃ compare CONSUMER GOODS

**capital-in'tensive** adj. (of a business, an industry, etc.) needing large amounts of money in order to operate well ⊃ compare LABOUR-INTENSIVE

**cap·it·al·ism** ⓘ+ C1 /ˈkæpɪtəlɪzəm/ noun [U] an economic system in which a country's businesses and industry are controlled and run for profit by private owners rather than by the government ⊃ compare SOCIALISM

WORDFINDER communism, democracy, dictatorship, fascism, imperialism, liberal, radical, socialism

**cap·it·al·ist** ⓘ+ C1 /ˈkæpɪtəlɪst/ adj., noun
■ adj. ⓘ+ C1 (also less frequent **cap·it·al·is·tic**) based on the principles of capitalism: *a capitalist society/system/economy*
■ noun **1** a person who supports capitalism **2** a person who owns or controls a lot of wealth and uses it to produce more wealth

**cap·it·al·ize** (BrE also **-ise**) /ˈkæpɪtəlaɪz/ verb **1** **~ sth** to write or print a letter of the alphabet as a capital; to begin a word with a capital letter **2** **~ sth** (business) to sell possessions in order to change them into money **3** [usually passive] **~ sth** (business) to provide a company, etc. with the money it needs to function ▸ **cap·it·al·iza·tion, -isa·tion** /ˌkæpɪtəlaɪˈzeɪʃn; NAmE -ləˈz-/ noun [U, sing.] ⊃ see also MARKET CAPITALIZATION
PHRV **'capitalize on/upon sth** to gain a further advantage for yourself from a situation SYN **take advantage of**: *The team failed to capitalize on their early lead.*

**capital 'letter** noun = CAPITAL

**capital 'market** noun (economics) the part of a financial system that is concerned with raising money by dealing in STOCKS (= shares that sb has bought in a business) and

BONDS (= agreements to pay sb interest on money they have lent)

**capital punishment** noun [U] punishment by death

**capital sum** noun a single payment of money that is made to sb, for example by an insurance company

**capi·ta·tion** /ˌkæpɪˈteɪʃn/ noun [C, U] (specialist) a tax or payment of an equal amount for each person; the system of payments of this kind: *a capitation fee for each pupil*

**cap·itol** /ˈkæpɪtl/ noun **1** (usually **the Capitol**) [sing.] the building in Washington DC where the US Congress (= the national parliament) meets to work on new laws **2** [usually sing.] a building in each US state where politicians meet to work on new laws: *the California state capitol*

**Capitol Hill** (also informal **the Hill**) noun [sing.] used to refer to the US Capitol and the activities that take place there

**ca·pitu·late** /kəˈpɪtʃuleɪt/ verb **1** [I] ~ (to sb/sth) to agree to do sth that you have been refusing to do for a long time SYN **give in (to sb/sth)** SYN **yield**: *They were finally forced to capitulate to the terrorists' demands.* **2** [I] ~ (to sb/sth) to stop resisting an enemy and accept that you are defeated SYN **surrender**: *The town capitulated after a three-week siege.* ▶ **ca·pitu·la·tion** /kəˌpɪtʃuˈleɪʃn/ noun [C, U]

**capo·eira** /ˌkæpəʊˈeərə; NAmE ˌkɑːpəʊˈerə/ noun [U] a Brazilian system of movements which is similar to dance and MARTIAL ARTS

**capon** /ˈkeɪpɒn, -pən; NAmE -pɑːn/ noun a male chicken that has been CASTRATED (= had part of its sex organs removed) and made fat for eating

**cap·pella** /kəˈpelə/ ⊃ A CAPPELLA

**cap·puc·cino** /ˌkæpəˈtʃiːnəʊ/ noun (pl. **-os**) **1** [U] a type of coffee made with hot FROTHY milk and sometimes with chocolate powder on the top **2** [C] a cup of cappuccino

**ca·price** /kəˈpriːs/ noun (formal) **1** [C] a sudden change in attitude or behaviour for no obvious reason SYN **whim** **2** [U] the fact of tending to change your mind suddenly or behave unexpectedly

**ca·pri·cious** /kəˈprɪʃəs/ adj. (formal) **1** showing sudden changes in attitude or behaviour SYN **unpredictable** **2** changing suddenly and quickly SYN **changeable**: *a capricious climate* ▶ **ca·pri·cious·ly** adv. **ca·pri·cious·ness** noun [U]

**Cap·ri·corn** /ˈkæprɪkɔːn; NAmE -kɔːrn/ noun **1** [U] the tenth sign of the ZODIAC, the Goat **2** [C] a person born when the sun is in this sign, that is, between 21 December and 20 January, approximately

**ca·pri pants** /kəˈpriː pænts/ (also **ca·pris**) noun [pl.] a type of trousers for women ending between the knee and the foot

**caps** /kæps/ noun [pl.] (specialist) capital letters: *a title printed in bold caps*

**cap·sicum** /ˈkæpsɪkəm/ noun (specialist) a type of plant that has hollow fruits. Some types of these are eaten as vegetables, either raw or cooked, for example SWEET PEPPERS or CHILLIES.

**cap·size** /kæpˈsaɪz; NAmE ˈkæpsaɪz/ verb [I, T] ~ (sth) if a boat **capsizes** or sth **capsizes** it, it turns over in the water

**cap·stan** /ˈkæpstən/ noun a thick CYLINDER that winds up a rope, used for lifting heavy objects such as an ANCHOR on a ship

**cap·stone** /ˈkæpstəʊn/ noun **1** a stone placed at the top of a building or wall **2** (especially NAmE) the best and final thing that sb achieves, thought of as making their career or life complete

**cap·sule** /ˈkæpsjuːl; NAmE -sl, -suːl/ noun **1** a small container that has a measured amount of a medicine inside and that DISSOLVES (= becomes part of a liquid) when you SWALLOW it (= make it go down your throat into your stomach) ⊃ WORDFINDER NOTE at MEDICINE **2** a small plastic container with a substance or liquid inside **3** = SPACE CAPSULE **4** (specialist) a shell or container for seeds or eggs in some plants and animals ⊃ see also TIME CAPSULE

**Capt.** abbr. captain

---

**cap·tain** ⓘ B1 /ˈkæptɪn/ noun, verb
■ noun **1** B1 the person in charge of a ship or commercial aircraft: *Captain Cook* ◊ *The captain gave the order to abandon ship.* **2** B1 an officer of fairly high rank in the NAVY, the army and the US AIR FORCE: *Captain Lance Price* ⊃ see also GROUP CAPTAIN ⊃ WORDFINDER NOTE at NAVY **3** B1 the leader of a group of people, especially a sports team: *She's a former captain of the English national team.* ◊ *He has just been made team captain.* **4** an officer of high rank in a US police or fire department
■ verb ~ sth to be a captain of a sports team or a ship

**cap·tain·cy** /ˈkæptənsi/ noun [C, usually sing., U] (pl. **-ies**) the position of captain of a team; the period during which sb is captain

**captain of industry** noun (pl. **captains of industry**) used in the media to describe a person who manages a large business company

**cap·tcha** (also **CAPTCHA**) /ˈkæptʃə/ noun [C, U] a computer program that is designed to recognize the difference between human users and machines, often showing letters or numbers with their shape changed slightly: *The captcha can only be solved by humans.* ORIGIN An acronym from Completely Automated Public Turing test to tell Computers and Humans Apart.

**cap·tion** /ˈkæpʃn/ noun, verb
■ noun words that are printed below a picture, cartoon, etc. that explain or describe it
■ verb [usually passive] ~ sth to write a caption for a picture, photograph, etc.

**cap·tiv·ate** /ˈkæptɪveɪt/ verb [often passive] to keep sb's attention by being interesting, attractive, etc. SYN **enchant**: **be captivated (by sth)** *The children were captivated by her stories.*

**cap·tiv·at·ing** /ˈkæptɪveɪtɪŋ/ adj. taking all your attention; very attractive and interesting SYN **enchanting**: *He found her captivating.*

**cap·tive** /ˈkæptɪv/ adj., noun
■ adj. **1** kept as a prisoner or in a space that you cannot get out of; unable to escape: *captive animals* ◊ *They were taken captive by masked gunmen.* ◊ *captive breeding* (= the breeding of wild animals in zoos, etc.) **2** [only before noun] not free to leave a particular place or to choose what you want to do: *A salesman loves to have a captive audience* (= listening because they have no choice).
■ noun a person who is kept as a prisoner, especially in a war

**cap·tiv·ity** /kæpˈtɪvəti/ noun [U] the state of being kept as a prisoner or in a space that you cannot escape from: **in ~** *He was held in captivity for three years.* ◊ *The bird had escaped from captivity.*

**cap·tor** /ˈkæptə(r)/ noun (formal) a person who captures a person or an animal and keeps them as a prisoner

**cap·ture** ⓘ B2 /ˈkæptʃə(r)/ verb, noun
■ verb
• CATCH **1** B2 ~ sb/sth to catch a person or an animal and keep them as a prisoner or shut them in a space that they cannot escape from: *Allied troops captured over 300 enemy soldiers.* ◊ *The animals are captured in nets and sold to local zoos.*
• TAKE CONTROL **2** B2 ~ sth to take control of a place, building, etc. using force: *The city was captured in 1941.* **3** B2 ~ sth to succeed in getting control or possession of sth that other people are also trying to get: *The company has captured 90 per cent of the market.*
• MAKE SB INTERESTED **4** B2 to make sb interested in sth: *The project has captured the imagination of the local public.* ◊ *His story captured the attention of Hollywood.*
• FEELING/ATMOSPHERE **5** B2 ~ sth to succeed in accurately expressing a feeling, an atmosphere, etc. in a picture, piece of writing, film, etc. SYN **catch**: *Her photos capture the essence of her subjects.* ◊ *The song captures the spirit of those times.*
• FILM/RECORD/PAINT **6** to photograph, film, record, paint, etc. sb/sth: ~ sth *The photographer's camera captures*

# capybara 220

*images* of extreme beauty. ◊ **~ sb/sth on sth** *The attack was captured on film by security cameras.*
- **SB'S HEART** 7 **~ sb's heart** to make sb love you
- **COMPUTING** 8 **~ sth** to put sth into a computer in a form it can use

■ *noun* 1 [B2] [U] the act of capturing sb/sth or of being captured: *He evaded capture for three days.* 2 [U] the act of taking control of a place, building, etc. using force: *the capture of enemy territory* 3 [U, C] the act or process of recording sth, especially using computers: *motion/image/video capture* ◊ *I have provided a series of screen captures* (= images of what was on a screen) *below.* ⇨ see also CARBON CAPTURE AND STORAGE, DATA CAPTURE

**capy·bara** /ˌkæpiˈbɑːrə/ *noun* (*pl.* **capy·bara** or **capy·baras**) an animal like a very large RABBIT with thick legs and small ears, which lives near water in South America

**car** [A1] /kɑː(r)/ *noun* 1 [A1] (*also formal* **'motor car** *especially in BrE*) (*also NAmE, formal* **auto·mo·bile**) a road vehicle with an engine and four wheels that can carry a small number of passengers: *Paula got into the car and drove off.* ◊ **by ~** *How did you come?' 'By car.'* ◊ **in a/the ~** *Are you going in the car?* ◊ *Where can I park the car?* ◊ *a car accident/crash* ◊ *I can't find my car keys.* ⇨ see also COMPANY CAR, IN-CAR, RACE CAR, SPORTS CAR, SQUAD CAR, STOCK CAR

> **WORDFINDER** accelerate, brake, commute, licence, motorist, road, road tax, traffic

2 (*also* **rail-car** *both NAmE*) a separate section of a train: *Several cars went off the rails.* 3 (*in compounds*) a car on a train of a particular type: *a sleeping/dining car*

**ca·rafe** /kəˈræf/ *noun* a glass container with a wide neck in which wine or water is served at meals; the amount contained in a carafe

**cara·mel** /ˈkærəmel; NAmE -ml; ˈkɑːrml/ *noun* 1 [U, C] a type of hard, sticky sweet made from butter, sugar and milk; a small piece of this 2 [U] burnt sugar used for adding colour and taste to food ⇨ see also CRÈME CARAMEL 3 [U] a light brown colour

**cara·mel·ize** (*BrE also* **-ise**) /ˈkærəməlaɪz; NAmE also ˈkɑːrm-/ *verb* 1 [I] (of sugar) to turn into caramel 2 [T] **~ sth** to cook sth, especially fruit, with sugar so that it is covered with caramel

**cara·pace** /ˈkærəpeɪs/ *noun* (*specialist*) the hard shell on the back of some animals such as CRABS, which protects them

**carat** /ˈkærət/ *noun* (*abbr.* **ct**) 1 a unit for measuring the weight of diamonds and other PRECIOUS STONES, equal to 200 MILLIGRAMS 2 (*especially BrE*) (*NAmE usually* **karat**) a unit for measuring how pure gold is. The purest gold is 24 carats: *an 18-carat gold ring*

**cara·van** /ˈkærəvæn/ *noun* 1 (*BrE*) (*NAmE* **camp·er**) a road vehicle without an engine that is pulled by a car, designed for people to live and sleep in, especially when they are on holiday: *a caravan site/park* 2 (*BrE*) a covered vehicle that is pulled by a horse and used for living in: *a Gypsy caravan* 3 a group of people with vehicles or animals who are travelling together, especially across the desert

**cara·van·ning** /ˈkærəvænɪŋ/ *noun* [U] (*BrE*) the activity of spending a holiday in a caravan

**cara·way** /ˈkærəweɪ/ *noun* [U] the dried seeds of a plant of the PARSLEY family, used in cooking: *caraway seeds*

**carb** /kɑːb; NAmE kɑːrb/ *noun* (*informal*) = CARBOHYDRATE ⇨ see also LOW-CARB

**car·bine** /ˈkɑːbaɪn; NAmE ˈkɑːrb-/ *noun* a short light RIFLE

**carbo·hy·drate** /ˌkɑːbəʊˈhaɪdreɪt; NAmE ˌkɑːrbə-/ *noun* 1 (*also informal* **carb**) [C, U] a substance such as sugar or STARCH that consists of CARBON, HYDROGEN and OXYGEN. Carbohydrates in food provide the body with energy and heat. 2 **carbohydrates** (*also informal* **carbs**) [*pl.*] foods such as bread, potatoes and rice that contain a lot of carbohydrate

**car·bol·ic** /kɑːˈbɒlɪk; NAmE kɑːrˈbɑːl-/ (*also* **carˌbolic ˈacid**) *noun* [U] a chemical that kills bacteria, used as an ANTISEPTIC and as a DISINFECTANT (= to prevent infection from spreading): *carbolic soap*

**ˈcar bomb** *noun* a bomb hidden inside or under a car

**car·bon** [B2+] /ˈkɑːbən; NAmE ˈkɑːrb-/ *noun* 1 [B2+] [U] (*symb.* **C**) a chemical element. Carbon is found in all living things, existing in a pure state as diamond and GRAPHITE: *carbon fibre* 2 [B2+] [U] used when referring to the gas CARBON DIOXIDE in terms of the effect it has on the earth's climate in causing GLOBAL WARMING: *carbon emissions/levels/taxes* ◊ (*BrE*) *How do we move to a low-carbon economy?* ⇨ see also ZERO-CARBON 3 [C] = CARBON COPY 4 [C] a piece of CARBON PAPER

**car·bon·ate** /ˈkɑːbənət; NAmE ˈkɑːrb-/ *noun* (*chemistry*) a salt that contains CARBON and OXYGEN together with another chemical ⇨ see also CALCIUM CARBONATE, SODIUM CARBONATE

**car·bon·ated** /ˈkɑːbəneɪtɪd; NAmE ˈkɑːrb-/ *adj.* (*specialist*) (of a drink) containing small bubbles of CARBON DIOXIDE **SYN** fizzy

**ˌcarbon ˈcapture and ˈstorage** (*also* **ˌcarbon ˈcapture and seˈquestration**) *noun* [U] the process of collecting CARBON DIOXIDE produced by burning coal, oil, etc. and other industrial processes, and storing it so that it does not affect the atmosphere ⇨ see also CARBON SEQUESTRATION

**ˌcarbon ˈcopy** (*also* **car·bon**) *noun* 1 a copy of a document, letter, etc. made with CARBON PAPER ⇨ see also **cc** *abbr.* 2 a person or thing that is very similar to sb/sth else: *She is a carbon copy of her sister.*

**ˈcarbon credit** *noun* 1 a key element in the system of national and international CARBON TRADING. A country or organization has the right to produce a particular amount of CARBON DIOXIDE and other gases that cause GLOBAL WARMING, which is expressed in terms of **carbon credits**, which may be traded between countries or organizations: *The sale of carbon credits can finance renewable energy projects.* 2 a CARBON OFFSET, which a person or company may choose to buy as a way of reducing the level of CARBON DIOXIDE for which they are responsible: *Wind energy companies sell carbon credits to consumers.*

**ˈcarbon cycle** *noun* [*usually sing.*] the processes by which carbon is changed from one form to another within the environment, for example in plants and when wood or oil is burned

**ˌcarbon ˈdating** (*also formal* **ˌradiocarbon ˈdating**) *noun* [U] a method of calculating the age of very old objects by measuring the amounts of different forms of carbon in them

**ˌcarbon ˈdebt** *noun* the difference between the effects of the CARBON FOOTPRINT of a country, group, person, etc. and anything that has been agreed or done to reduce these effects: *A massive carbon debt will be created when the forests are harvested.*

**ˌcarbon diˈoxide** *noun* [U] (*symb.* **CO$_2$**) a gas breathed out by people and animals from the lungs or produced by burning CARBON

**ˌcarbon ˈfootprint** *noun* a measure of the amount of carbon dioxide that is produced by the activities of a person or company: *Flying is the biggest contribution to my carbon footprint.*

**carˌbonic ˈacid** /kɑːˈbɒnɪk ˈæsɪd; NAmE kɑːrˈbɑːn-/ *noun* [U] (*chemistry*) a very weak ACID that is formed when carbon dioxide is DISSOLVED in water

**car·bon·ifer·ous** /ˌkɑːbəˈnɪfərəs; NAmE ˌkɑːrb-/ *adj.* (*geology*) 1 producing or containing coal 2 **Carboniferous** of the period in the earth's history when layers of coal were formed underground

**car·bon·ize** (*BrE also* **-ise**) /ˈkɑːbənaɪz; NAmE ˈkɑːrb-/ *verb* 1 [I, T] **~ (sth)** to become CARBON; to make sth become carbon 2 [T] **~ sth** to cover sth with CARBON

▶ **car·bon·iza·tion**, **-isa·tion** /ˌkɑːbənaɪˈzeɪʃn; NAmE ˌkɑːrbənəˈz-/ noun [U]

**carbon monoxide** /ˌkɑːbən məˈnɒksaɪd; NAmE ˌkɑːrbən məˈnɑːk-/ noun [U] (symb. **CO**) a poisonous gas formed when CARBON burns partly but not completely. It is produced when petrol is burned in car engines.

**ˌcarbon-ˈneu·tral** adj. in which the amount of CARBON DIOXIDE produced has been reduced to nothing or is balanced by actions that protect the environment SYN **zero-carbon**: *All of these fuels are renewable and carbon-neutral*.

**ˈcarbon ˈoffset** noun [C, U] a way for a company or person to reduce the level of CARBON DIOXIDE for which they are responsible by paying money to a company that works to reduce the total amount produced in the world, for example by planting trees: *carbon offset initiatives for air travellers* ⇒ compare CARBON CREDIT

**ˈcarbon paper** noun [U] thin paper with a dark substance on one side, that is used between two sheets of paper for making copies of written or typed documents

**ˌcarbon ˌseque'stration** noun [U] the process of storing CARBON DIOXIDE that has been collected and removed from the atmosphere, in solid or liquid form ⇒ see also CARBON CAPTURE AND STORAGE

**ˈcarbon trading** (also eˈmissions trading) noun [U] a system that gives countries and organizations the right to produce a particular amount of CARBON DIOXIDE and other gases that cause GLOBAL WARMING, and allows them to sell this right

**ˌcar ˈboot sale** (also **ˈboot sale**, **ˌcar ˈboot**) noun (BrE) an outdoor sale where people sell things that they no longer want, using tables or the backs of their cars to put the goods on

**car·bun·cle** /ˈkɑːbʌŋkl; NAmE ˈkɑːrb-/ noun **1** a large painful SWELLING (= an area that is larger and rounder than normal) under the skin **2** a bright red JEWEL, usually cut into a round shape

**car·bur·et·tor** (BrE) (NAmE **car·bur·etor**) /ˌkɑːbəˈretə(r); NAmE ˈkɑːrbəreɪtər/ noun the part of an engine, for example in a car, where petrol and air are mixed together

**car·cass** (BrE also, less frequent **car·case**) /ˈkɑːkəs; NAmE ˈkɑːrk-/ noun the dead body of an animal, especially of a large one or of one that is ready for cutting up as meat

**car·cino·gen** /kɑːˈsɪnədʒən; NAmE kɑːr's-/ noun a substance that can cause cancer

**car·cino·gen·ic** /ˌkɑːsɪnəˈdʒenɪk; NAmE ˌkɑːrs-/ adj. likely to cause cancer

**car·cin·oma** /ˌkɑːsɪˈnəʊmə; NAmE ˌkɑːrs-/ noun (medical) a cancer that affects the top layer of the skin or the LINING of the body's internal organs

**ˈcar crash** noun **1** an accident in which a car hits sth, for example another vehicle, usually causing damage and often killing or injuring the passengers **2** (informal) a very unsuccessful event or situation that people often find interesting: *Her life is turning into a car crash.* ◇ *The whole industry is a car crash—even major investment won't save it now.* ◇ *car-crash television* ⇒ compare TRAIN WRECK

**card** ❶ A1 /kɑːd; NAmE kɑːrd/ noun, verb
■ **noun**
• **PAPER 1** A1 [U, C] (BrE) thick, stiff paper; a piece of this for writing on: *a piece of card* ◇ *Each person wrote their question on a card.*
• **WITH A MESSAGE 2** A1 [C] a piece of stiff paper that is folded in the middle and has a picture on the front of it, used for sending sb a message with your good wishes, an invitation, etc.: *a birthday/get-well/good luck card* ⇒ see also CHRISTMAS CARD, E-CARD, GREETINGS CARD **3** [C] = POSTCARD: *Did you get my card from Italy?*
• **WITH INFORMATION 4** A1 [C] a small piece of stiff paper or plastic with information on it, especially information about sb's identity: *a membership card* ◇ *an appointment card* ⇒ see also CUE CARD, GREEN CARD, ID CARD, IDENTITY CARD, INDEX CARD, LOYALTY CARD, RED CARD, REPORT CARD, YELLOW CARD **5** A1 [C] = BUSINESS CARD: *Here's my card if you need to contact me again.* **6** [C] = VISITING CARD
• **FOR MONEY 7** A1 [C] a small piece of plastic, especially one given by a bank or shop, used for buying things or obtaining money: *I put the meal on (= paid for it using) my card.* ⇒ see also ATM CARD, BANK CARD, CASH CARD, CHARGE CARD, CHIP CARD, CREDIT CARD, DEBIT CARD, GIFT CARD, GOLD CARD™, PHONECARD, SMART CARD, SWIPE CARD
• **IN GAMES 8** A2 [C] = PLAYING CARD: (BrE) *a pack of cards* ◇ (especially NAmE) *a deck of cards* ◇ *Each player in turn must play a card.* ⇒ see also FACE CARD, TRUMP CARD, WILD CARD

**WORDFINDER** ace, cut, deal, gambling, hand, jack, shuffle, suit, trump

**9** A2 **cards** [pl.] a game or games in which PLAYING CARDS are used: *Who wants to play cards?* ◇ *Let's have a game of cards.* ◇ *She won £20 at cards.*
• **COMPUTING 10** [C] a small device containing an electronic CIRCUIT that is part of a computer or added to it, enabling it to perform particular functions: *a printed circuit card* ◇ *a graphics/sound/video card* ⇒ see also SD CARD, SIM CARD
• **PERSON 11** [C] (old-fashioned, informal) an unusual or funny person
• **HORSE RACES 12** [C] a list of all the races at a particular RACE MEETING (= a series of horse races)
• **FOR WOOL/COTTON 13** [C] (specialist) a machine or tool used for cleaning and COMBING wool or cotton before it is SPUN
IDM **sb's best/strongest/winning ˈcard** something that gives sb an advantage over other people in a particular situation **have a card up your ˈsleeve** to have an idea, a plan, etc. that will give you an advantage in a particular situation and that you keep secret until it is needed **hold all the ˈcards** (informal) to be able to control a particular situation because you have an advantage over other people **hold/keep/play your cards close to your ˈchest** to keep your ideas, plans, etc. secret **lay/put your cards on the ˈtable** to tell sb honestly what your plans, ideas, etc. are **on the ˈcards** (BrE) (NAmE **in the ˈcards**) (informal) likely to happen: *The merger has been on the cards for some time now.* **play the ... ˈcard** to mention a particular subject, idea or quality in order to gain an advantage: *He accused his opponent of playing the immigration card during the campaign.* ⇒ see also RACE CARD **play your ˈcards right** to deal successfully with a particular situation so that you achieve some advantage of sth that you want ⇒ more at SHOW v., STACKED

■ **verb 1** ~ sth (specialist) to clean wool using a wire instrument **2** ~ sb (NAmE, informal) to ask a person to show their identity card, especially as a means of checking how old they are, for example if they want to buy alcohol

**car·da·mom** /ˈkɑːdəməm; NAmE ˈkɑːrd-/ noun [U] the dried seeds of a south-east Asian plant, used in cooking as a SPICE ⇒ VISUAL VOCAB page VE

**card·board** /ˈkɑːdbɔːd; NAmE ˈkɑːrdbɔːrd/ noun, adj.
■ **noun** [U] stiff material like very thick paper, often used for making boxes: *a cardboard box* ◇ *a piece of cardboard*
■ **adj.** [only before noun] not seeming real; artificial: *a novel with superficial cardboard characters*

**ˈcard-carrying** adj. [only before noun] known to be an official and usually active member of a political organization: *a card-carrying member of the Conservative party*

**ˈcard catalog** (NAmE) (BrE **ˈcard index**, **index**) noun a box of cards with information on them, arranged in alphabetical order

**ˈcard game** noun a game in which PLAYING CARDS are used

**card·hold·er** /ˈkɑːdhəʊldə(r); NAmE ˈkɑːrd-/ noun a person who has a credit card from a bank, a LOYALTY CARD from a shop, etc.

**car·diac** /ˈkɑːdiæk; NAmE ˈkɑːrd-/ adj. [only before noun] (medical) connected with the heart or heart disease: *cardiac disease/failure/surgery* ◇ *to suffer cardiac arrest (= an occasion when a person's heart stops temporarily or permanently)*

# cardigan

**car·di·gan** /ˈkɑːdɪɡən; NAmE ˈkɑːrd-/ (NAmE also **cardigan sweater**) *noun* a jacket made of wool like a sweater but fastened with buttons down the front

**car·di·nal** /ˈkɑːdɪnl; NAmE ˈkɑːrd-/ *noun, adj.*
- *noun* **1** a priest of the highest rank in the Roman Catholic Church. Cardinals elect and advise the POPE: *Cardinal Newman* **2** (*also* **cardinal 'number**) a number, such as 1, 2 and 3 (or one, two and three), used to show quantity rather than order ⇒ compare ORDINAL **3** A North American bird. The male cardinal is bright red.
- *adj.* [only before noun] (*formal*) most important; having other things based on it: *Respect for life is a cardinal principle of English law.*

**cardinal 'sin** *noun* **1** (*sometimes humorous*) an action that is a serious mistake or that other people think is bad: *He committed the cardinal sin of criticizing his teammates.* **2** a serious SIN in the Christian Church

**'card index** (*also* **index**) (*both BrE*) (NAmE **'card catalog**) *noun* a box of cards with information on them, arranged in alphabetical order

**car·dio** /ˈkɑːdiəʊ; NAmE ˈkɑːrd-/ *noun* [U] (*informal*) exercises to make your heart work harder that you do to keep yourself fit: *Cardio is the answer if you want to lose weight.* ◊ *cardio exercise/workouts* ⇒ see also CARDIOVASCULAR

**cardio-** /ˈkɑːdiəʊ, kɑːdiə, kɑːdiˈɒ; NAmE ˈkɑːrdiəʊ, ˈkɑːrdiə, ˌkɑːrdiˈɑː/ *combining form* (in nouns, adjectives and adverbs) relating to the heart: *cardiogram*

**car·di·olo·gist** /ˌkɑːdiˈɒlədʒɪst; NAmE ˌkɑːrdiˈɑːl-/ *noun* a doctor who studies and treats heart diseases ⇒ WORDFINDER NOTE at SPECIALIST ▶ **car·di·ology** /-dʒi/ *noun* [U]

**car·dio·pul·mon·ary re·sus·ci·ta·tion** /ˌkɑːdiəʊ ˌpʌlmənəri rɪˌsʌsɪˈteɪʃn; NAmE ˌkɑːrdioʊˌpʌlmənər-/ *noun* [U] = CPR

**car·dio·vas·cu·lar** /ˌkɑːdiəʊˈvæskjələ(r); NAmE ˌkɑːrd-/ *adj.* (*medical*) relating to the heart and the BLOOD VESSELS (= the tubes that carry blood around the body)

**'card reader** *noun* **1** an electronic device that reads data stored on a credit card, a card that shows that sb is a member of an organization, etc: *a credit card reader* **2** an electronic device that you can attach to or that is part of a computer, printer, etc. and that reads or transfers data from a memory device

**'card table** *noun* a small table for playing card games on, especially one that you can fold

**care** ⓘ A2 ⓞ /keə(r); NAmE ker/ *noun, verb*
- *noun* **1** ⓘ [U] the process of caring for sb/sth and providing what they need for their health or protection: *medical/patient care* ◊ *How much do men share housework and the care of the children?* ◊ *~ for sb/sth to provide care for the elderly* ◊ *skin/hair care products* ⇒ see also CHILDCARE, COMMUNITY CARE, CRITICAL CARE, DAY CARE, DUTY OF CARE, HEALTHCARE, INTENSIVE CARE, MANAGED CARE, PRIMARY CARE **2** [U] (*BrE*) the fact of providing a home in an institution run by the local authority or with another family for children who cannot live with their parents: *in~ Most children in care live with foster carers.* ◊ *The two girls were taken into care after their parents were killed.* **3** ⓘ B1 [U] attention or thought that you give to sth that you are doing so that you will do it well and avoid mistakes or damage: *Great care is needed when choosing a used car.* ◊ *with~ She chose her words with care.* ◊ *Fragile—handle with care* (= written on a container holding sth that is easily broken or damaged) **4** [C, usually pl., U] (*formal*) a feeling of worry; something that causes problems or worries: *I felt free from the cares of the day as soon as I left the building.* ◊ *Sam looked as if he didn't have a care in the world.*
  IDM **'care of sb** (NAmE also **in 'care of sb**) (*abbr.* **c/o**) used when writing to sb at another person's address: *Write to him care of his lawyer.* **in the 'care of sb/in sb's 'care** being cared for by sb: *The child was left in the care of friends.* **take 'care** (*informal*) used when saying goodbye: *Bye! Take care!* **take care (that ... /to do sth)** to be careful: *Take care (that) you don't drink too much!* ◊ *Care should be taken to close the lid securely.* **take care of sb/sth/yourself 1** ⓘ A2 to care for sb/sth/yourself; to be careful about sth: *Who's taking care of the children while you're away?* ◊ *She takes great care of her clothes.* ◊ *He's old enough to take care of himself.* **2** ⓘ A2 to be responsible for or to deal with a situation or task: *Don't worry about the travel arrangements. They're all being taken care of.* ◊ *Celia takes care of the marketing side of things.* **under the care of sb** receiving medical care from sb: *He's under the care of Dr Parks.*

- *verb* (not used in the progressive tenses) **1** ⓘ A2 [I, T] to feel that sth is important and worth worrying about: *I don't care* (= I will not be upset) *if I never see him again!* ◊ *He threatened to fire me, as if I cared!* ◊ *~about sth She cares deeply about environmental issues.* ◊ *~what, whether, etc ... I don't care what he thinks.* ◊ *~that ... She doesn't seem to care that he's been married four times before.* **2** ⓘ A2 [I] *~* **(about sb)** to like or love sb and worry about what happens to them: *He genuinely cares about his employees.* **3** [T] **~to do sth** to make the effort to do sth: *I've done this job more times than I care to remember.*
  IDM **be past 'caring** (*informal*) used to say that a person is no longer worried about or interested in sb/sth: *I'm past caring what he does.* **couldn't care 'less** (NAmE also **could care 'less**) (*informal*) used to say, often rudely, that you do not think that sb/sth is important or worth worrying about: *Quite honestly, I couldn't care less what they do.* **for all you, I, they, etc. care** (*informal*) used to say that a person is not worried about or interested in what happens to sb/sth: *I could be dead for all he cares!* **who 'cares?** | **what do I, you, etc. care?** (*informal*) used to say, often rudely, that you do not think that sth is important or interesting: *Who cares what she thinks?* **Would you care for sth?** | **Would you care to do sth?** (*formal*) used to ask sb

▼ SYNONYMS

**care**

**caution • prudence**

These are all words for attention or thought that you give to sth in order to avoid mistakes or accidents.

**care** attention or thought that you give to sth that you are doing so that you will do it well and avoid mistakes or damage: *She chose her words with care.*

**caution** care that you take in order to avoid danger or mistakes; not taking any risks: *The utmost caution must be exercised when handling explosives.*

**prudence** (*rather formal*) a sensible and careful attitude when you make judgements and decisions; behaviour that avoids unnecessary risks: *As a matter of prudence, keep a record of all your financial transactions.* NOTE **Prudence** is used particularly in financial contexts.

PATTERNS
- to do sth **with** care/caution/prudence
- **great/extreme** care/caution/prudence
- to **use/exercise** care/caution/prudence
- to **proceed** with care/caution

▼ WHICH WORD?

**take care of / look after / care for**
- You can **take care of** or, especially in *BrE*, **look after** someone who is very young, very old, or sick, or something that needs to be kept in good condition: *We've asked my mother to take care of/look after the kids while we're away.* ◊ *You can borrow my camera if you promise to take care of/look after it.*
- In more formal language you can also **care for** someone: *She does some voluntary work, caring for the elderly*, but **care for** is more commonly used to mean 'like': *I don't really care for spicy food.*

WORD FAMILY
**care** *noun, verb*
**careful** *adj.* (≠ careless)
**carefully** *adv.* (≠ carelessly)
**caring** *adj.* (≠ uncaring)

politely if they would like sth or would like to do sth, or if they would be willing to do sth: *Would you care for another drink?* ◊ *If you'd care to follow me, I'll show you where his office is.* ⊃ note at WANT ⊃ more at DAMN *n.*, FIG, HOOT *n.*, TUPPENCE

**PHR V** **'care for sb** **1** **B1** to look after sb who is sick, very old, very young, etc. **SYN** take care of: *She moved back home to care for her elderly parents.* ⊃ see also UNCARED FOR **2** to love or like sb very much: *He cared for her more than she realized.* ⊃ SYNONYMS at LOVE **not 'care for sb/ sth** (*formal*) to not like sb/sth: *He didn't much care for her friends.*

**'care assistant** *noun* (*BrE*) = CARE WORKER

**car·een** /kəˈriːn/ *verb* [I] + *adv.*/*prep.* (*especially NAmE*) (of a person or vehicle) to move forward very quickly especially in a way that is dangerous or shows a loss of control **SYN** hurtle

**car·eer** ❶ **A1** /kəˈrɪə(r); *NAmE* -ˈrɪr/ *noun*, *verb*
■ *noun* **1** **A1** the series of jobs that a person has in a particular area of work, usually involving more responsibility as time passes: *a teaching career* ◊ **~ in sth** *She plans to pursue a career in medicine.* ◊ *He had a successful career in television journalism.* ◊ **~ as sth** *He enjoyed a long and distinguished career as a historian.* ◊ *That will be a good career move* (= something that will help your career). ◊ *a career soldier/diplomat* (= a professional one) ◊ (*BrE*) *a careers adviser/officer* (= a person whose job is to give people advice and information about jobs) ⊃ SYNONYMS at WORK **2** **A1** the period of time that you spend in your life working or doing a particular thing: *She started her career as an English teacher.* ◊ *He is playing the best tennis of his career.* ◊ *My school career was not very impressive.*
■ *verb* [I] + *adv.*/*prep.* (of a person or vehicle) to move forward very quickly, especially in a way that shows a loss of control **SYN** hurtle: *The vehicle careered across the road and hit a cyclist.*

**ca'reer break** *noun* a period of time when you do not do your usual job, for example because you have children to care for

**car·eer·ist** /kəˈrɪərɪst; *NAmE* -ˈrɪr-/ *noun* (*often disapproving*) a person whose career is more important to them than anything else: *He was accused of being a cynical careerist.* ▶ **car·eer·ism** *noun* [U]

**ca'reer woman** *noun* (*sometimes disapproving*) a woman whose career is more important to her than getting married and having children

**care·free** /ˈkeəfriː; *NAmE* ˈkerf-/ *adj.* having no worries or responsibilities: *He looked happy and carefree.* ◊ *a carefree attitude/life*

**care·ful** ❶ **A2** /ˈkeəfl; *NAmE* ˈkerfl/ *adj.* **1** **A2** [not before noun] giving attention or thought to what you are doing so that you avoid hurting yourself, damaging sth or doing sth wrong: *Be careful!* ◊ **~ to do sth** *He was careful to keep out of sight.* ◊ **~ not to do sth** *Be careful not to wake the baby.* ◊ **~ when/what/how, etc.** *You must be careful when handling chemicals.* ◊ **~ of/with sth** *Please be careful with my glasses* (= Don't break them). ◊ **~ about (doing) sth** *As a young actor, you have to be extremely careful about the roles you accept.* ◊ **~ (that) …** *Be careful you don't bump your head.* ⊃ EXPRESS YOURSELF at WARN **2** **A2** giving a lot of attention to details: *After careful consideration we have decided to offer you the job.* ◊ *A successful party requires careful planning.* ◊ *He praised the careful attention to detail shown by the report's authors.* **OPP** careless ▶ **care·ful·ness** *noun* [U]
**IDM** **careful with money** not spending money on things that are unimportant **you can't be too 'careful** used to warn sb that they should take care to avoid danger or problems: *Don't stay out in the sun for too long—you can't be too careful.*

**care·ful·ly** ❶ **A2** /ˈkeəfəli; *NAmE* ˈkerf-/ *adv.* **1** **A2** with a lot of attention or thought, so that you avoid hurting yourself, damaging sth or doing sth wrong: *Drive carefully.* ◊ *She put the glass down carefully.* ◊ *Please listen carefully.* ◊ *The prime minister's words were carefully chosen.* **2** **A2** with a lot of attention to detail: *I urge the council to*

*look carefully at this proposal.* ◊ *a carefully crafted essay* **OPP** **carelessly** **IDM** see TREAD *v.*

**care·giver** /ˈkeəɡɪvə(r); *NAmE* ˈkerɡ-/ (*NAmE*) (*BrE* carer) *noun* a person who takes care of a sick or old person at home

**'care home** *noun* (*BrE*) a place where people live and are cared for when they cannot live at home or look after themselves: *a care home for the elderly* ⊃ WORDFINDER NOTE at OLD

**care in the com'munity** *noun* [U] = COMMUNITY CARE

**'care label** *noun* a label attached to the inside of a piece of clothing, giving instructions about how it should be washed and ironed

**care·less** ❶ **B1** /ˈkeələs; *NAmE* ˈkerl-/ *adj.* **1** **B1** not giving enough attention and thought to what you are doing, so that you make mistakes: *careless driving* ◊ **it is ~ (of sb) (to do sth)** *It was careless of me to leave the door open.* ◊ **~ with sth** *He's very careless with money.* **OPP** careful **2** **B1** resulting from a lack of attention and thought: *a careless mistake/error* **3** **~ of sth** (*formal*) not at all worried about sth: *He seemed careless of his own safety.* **4** not showing interest or effort **SYN** casual: *She gave a careless shrug.* ◊ *a careless laugh/smile* ▶ **care·less·ly** *adv.*: *Someone had carelessly left a window open.* ◊ *She threw her coat carelessly onto the chair.* ◊ *'I don't mind,' he said carelessly.* **care·less·ness** *noun* [U]: *a moment of carelessness*

**care·line** /ˈkeəlaɪn; *NAmE* ˈkerl-/ *noun* a phone service that you can call to get advice or information, for example on a company's products, or on a medical condition, etc: *Call our customer careline for advice.*

**carer** /ˈkeərə(r); *NAmE* ˈker-/ (*BrE*) (*NAmE* **care·giver**) *noun* a person, either a member of the family or sb who is paid, who takes care of a sick or old person at home

**ca·ress** /kəˈres/ *verb*, *noun*
■ *verb* **~ sb/sth** to touch sb/sth gently, especially in a sexual way or in a way that shows love: *His fingers gently caressed her cheek.*
■ *noun* a gentle touch or kiss to show you love sb

**care·taker** /ˈkeəteɪkə(r); *NAmE* ˈkert-/ *noun*, *adj.*
■ *noun* **1** (*BrE*) (*NAmE*, *ScotE* **jani·tor**) (*NAmE* also **cus·to·dian**) a person whose job is to take care of a building such as a school or a block of flats or an apartment building **2** (*especially NAmE*) a person who takes care of a house or land while the owner is away: (*figurative*) *They believe they are caretakers of the land for future generations.* **3** (*especially NAmE*) a person such as a teacher, parent, nurse, etc., who takes care of other people
■ *adj.* [only before noun] in charge for a short time, until a new leader or government is chosen: *a caretaker manager/government*

**'care worker** (also **'care assistant**) *noun* (*BrE*) a person whose job is to help and take care of people who are mentally ill, sick or DISABLED, especially those who live in special homes or hospitals

**care·worn** /ˈkeəwɔːn; *NAmE* ˈkerwɔːrn/ *adj.* looking tired because you have a lot of worries

**cargo** ❷+ **C1** /ˈkɑːɡəʊ; *NAmE* ˈkɑːrɡ-/ *noun* (C, U) (*pl.* **-oes**, *NAmE also* **-os**) the goods carried in a ship, an aircraft or a motor vehicle: *The tanker began to spill its cargo of oil.* ◊ *a cargo ship*

**'cargo pants** (also **car·goes**) (*BrE* also **com·bats**, **'combat trousers**, **'combat pants**) *noun* [pl.] loose trousers that have pockets in various places, for example on the side of the leg above the knee

**Carib·bean** /ˌkærɪˈbiːən; kəˈrɪbiən/ *noun*, *adj.*
■ *noun* **the Caribbean** the region consisting of the Caribbean Sea and its islands, including the West Indies, and the coasts that surround it
■ *adj.* connected with the Caribbean

**cari·bou** /ˈkærɪbuː/ *noun* (*pl.* **cari·bou**) a North American REINDEER

**caricature** 224

**car·i·ca·ture** /ˈkærɪkətʊə(r); NAmE -tʃər, -tʃʊr/ noun, verb
- **noun 1** [C] a funny drawing or description of sb that EXAGGERATES some of their features **2** [C] a description of a person or thing that makes them seem silly by EXAGGERATING some of their characteristics, or only showing some of their characteristics: *He had unfairly presented a caricature of my views.* **3** [U] the art of drawing or writing caricatures ⊃ WORDFINDER NOTE at COMEDY ▸ **car·i·ca·tur·ist** noun
- **verb** [often passive] to produce a caricature of sb; to describe or present sb as a type of person you would laugh at or not respect: **be caricatured (as sth)** *She was unfairly caricatured as a dumb blonde.*

**car·ies** /ˈkeəriːz; NAmE ˈker-/ noun [U] (*medical*) DECAY (= damage from natural causes or lack of care) in teeth or bones: *dental caries*

**car·il·lon** /kəˈrɪljən; NAmE ˈkærəlɑːn/ noun **1** a set of bells on which tunes can be played, sometimes using a keyboard **2** a tune played on bells

**car·ing** /ˈkeərɪŋ; NAmE ˈker-/ adj. [usually before noun] kind, helpful and showing that you care about other people: *He's a very caring person.* ◊ *Children need a caring environment.* ◊ *a caring profession* (= a job that involves looking after or helping other people)

**car·jack·ing** /ˈkɑːdʒækɪŋ; NAmE ˈkɑːrdʒ-/ noun [U, C] the crime of forcing the driver of a car to take you somewhere or give you their car, using threats and violence ⊃ compare HIJACKING ▸ **car·jack** verb ~ **sth car·jack·er** noun

**car·load** /ˈkɑːləʊd; NAmE ˈkɑːrl-/ noun the number of people or amount of things that a car is carrying or is able to carry

**car·mine** /ˈkɑːmaɪn; NAmE ˈkɑːrm-/ adj. (*formal*) dark red in colour ▸ **car·mine** noun [U]

**carn·age** /ˈkɑːnɪdʒ; NAmE ˈkɑːrn-/ noun [U] the violent killing of a large number of people **SYN slaughter**: *a scene of carnage*

**car·nal** /ˈkɑːnl; NAmE ˈkɑːrnl/ adj. [usually before noun] (*formal* or *law*) connected with the body or with sex: *carnal desires/appetites* ▸ **car·nal·ly** /-nəli/ adv.

**carnal ˈknowledge** noun [U] (*old-fashioned* or *law*) = SEXUAL INTERCOURSE

**car·na·tion** /kɑːˈneɪʃn; NAmE kɑːrˈn-/ noun a white, pink, red or yellow flower, often worn as a decoration on formal occasions: *He was wearing a carnation in his buttonhole.* ⊃ VISUAL VOCAB page V7

**car·ni·val** /ˈkɑːnɪvl; NAmE ˈkɑːrn-/ noun **1** [C, U] a public festival, usually one that happens at a regular time each year, that involves music and dancing in the streets, for which people wear brightly coloured clothes: *There is a local carnival every year.* ◊ *the carnival in Rio* ◊ *a carnival atmosphere* **2** [C] (*NAmE*) = FAIR **3** [C] an outdoor public event or celebration involving entertainment, games, food and drink, etc., often organized by a town or village: *The children are getting ready for the village carnival.* ⊃ compare FETE (1) **4** [sing.] ~ **of sth** (*formal*) an exciting or brightly coloured mixture of things: *this summer's carnival of sport*

**car·ni·vore** /ˈkɑːnɪvɔː(r); NAmE ˈkɑːrn-/ noun any animal that eats meat ⊃ compare HERBIVORE, INSECTIVORE, OMNIVORE ▸ **car·ni·vor·ous** /kɑːˈnɪvərəs; NAmE kɑːrˈn-/ adj.: *a carnivorous diet* ⊃ compare OMNIVOROUS

**carob** /ˈkærəb/ (*also* **ˈcarob tree**) noun a southern European tree with dark brown fruit that can be made into a powder that tastes like chocolate

**carol** /ˈkærəl/ noun, verb
- **noun** (*also* **ˈChristmas ˈcarol**) a Christian religious song sung at Christmas
- **verb** [I, T] (**-ll-**, *US* **-l-**) ~ **(sth)** | + **speech** to sing sth in a cheerful way

**ˈcarol singing** noun [U] the singing of Christmas carols especially in a church or outdoors, often to collect money for charity ▸ **ˈcarol singer** noun

**carom** /ˈkærəm/ verb [I] (*especially NAmE*) to hit a surface and come off it fast at a different angle

**car·ot·ene** /ˈkærətiːn/ noun [U] a red or orange substance found in carrots and other plants ⊃ see also BETA-CAROTENE

**ca·rot·id ˈar·tery** /kəˌrɒtɪd ˈɑːtəri; NAmE -ˌrɑːtɪd ˈɑːrt-/ noun (*anatomy*) either of the two large ARTERIES in the neck that carry blood to the head

**ca·rouse** /kəˈraʊz/ verb [I] (*literary*) to spend time drinking alcohol, laughing and enjoying yourself in a noisy way with other people

**car·ou·sel** /ˌkærəˈsel/ noun **1** (*especially NAmE*) = MERRY-GO-ROUND (1) ⊃ picture at MERRY-GO-ROUND **2** = BAGGAGE CAROUSEL

**carp** /kɑːp; NAmE kɑːrp/ noun, verb
- **noun** [C, U] (*pl.* **carp**) a large FRESHWATER fish that is used for food ⊃ see also KOI
- **verb** [I] ~ **(on) (at sb) (about sb/sth)** to keep complaining about sb/sth in an annoying way

**car·pal** /ˈkɑːpl; NAmE ˈkɑːrpl/ noun (*anatomy*) any of the eight small bones that form the WRIST (= part between the hand and the arm) ⊃ VISUAL VOCAB page V1

**carpal ˈtunnel syndrome** noun [U] (*medical*) a painful condition of the hand and fingers caused by pressure on a nerve because of repeated movements over a long period

**ˈcar park** noun (*BrE*) an area or a building where people can leave their cars ⊃ see also GARAGE noun, MULTI-STOREY CAR PARK ⊃ compare PARKING LOT

**carpe diem** /ˌkɑːpeɪ ˈdiːem; NAmE ˌkɑːrp-/ exclamation (*from Latin*) an expression used when you want to say that sb should not wait, but should take an opportunity as soon as it appears

**car·pel** /ˈkɑːpl; NAmE ˈkɑːrpl/ noun (*biology*) the part of a plant in which seeds are produced ⊃ VISUAL VOCAB page V7

**car·pen·ter** /ˈkɑːpəntə(r); NAmE ˈkɑːrp-/ noun a person whose job is making and repairing wooden objects and structures ⊃ compare JOINER

**car·pen·try** /ˈkɑːpəntri; NAmE ˈkɑːrp-/ noun [U] **1** the work of a carpenter **2** things made by a carpenter

**car·pet** /ˈkɑːpɪt; NAmE ˈkɑːrp-/ noun, verb
- **noun 1** [C, U] a piece of thick WOVEN material made of wool, etc., used to cover the floor of a room or stairs; the material used for carpets: *to lay a carpet* ◊ *a bedroom carpet* ◊ (*BrE*) *We have fitted carpets* (= carpets from wall to wall) *in our house.* ◊ *a roll of carpet* ⊃ see also CARPETING, MAGIC CARPET, PERSIAN CARPET, RED CARPET, RUG **2** [C] ~ **(of sth)** (*literary*) a thick layer of sth on the ground: *a carpet of snow*
- **IDM** (**be/get called) on the ˈcarpet** (*informal*, *especially NAmE*) called to see sb in authority because you have done sth wrong: *I got called on the carpet for being late.* ⊃ more at SWEEP v.
- **verb** [usually passive] **1** to cover the floor of a room with a carpet: **be carpeted (in/with sth)** *The hall was carpeted in blue.* **2** (*literary*) to cover sth with a thick layer of sth: **be carpeted (with/in sth)** *The forest floor was carpeted with wild flowers.* **3** (*informal*, *BrE*) to speak angrily to sb because they have done sth wrong **SYN reprimand**: *be carpeted Senior officials were carpeted for leaking information to the press.*

**ˈcarpet-bag·ger** /ˈkɑːpɪtbæɡə(r); NAmE ˈkɑːrp-/ noun **1** (*disapproving*) a politician who tries to be elected in an area where he or she is not known and is therefore not welcome **2** a person from the northern states of the US who went to the South after the Civil War in order to make money or get political power

**ˈcarpet-bomb** verb **1** ~ **sth** to drop a large number of bombs onto every part of an area **2** ~ **sb** (*business*) to send an advertisement to a very large number of people, especially by email ▸ **ˈcarpet-bombing** noun [U]

**car·pet·ing** /ˈkɑːpɪtɪŋ; NAmE ˈkɑːrp-/ noun **1** [U] carpets in general or the material used for carpets: *new offices with wall-to-wall carpeting* ◊ (*NAmE*) *We need new carpeting (= a* new carpet) *in the living room.* **2** [C] (*BrE*, *informal*) an act of speaking angrily to sb because they have done sth wrong

**car·pool** /ˈkɑːpuːl; *NAmE* ˈkɑːrp-/ *verb*
- *noun* (*especially NAmE*) a group of car owners who take turns to drive everyone in the group to work, so that only one car is used at a time
- *verb* [I] (*especially NAmE*) if a group of people **carpool**, they travel to work together in one car and divide the cost between them

**car·port** /ˈkɑːpɔːt; *NAmE* ˈkɑːrpɔːrt/ *noun* a shelter for a car, usually built next to a house and consisting of a roof supported by posts

**car·rel** /ˈkærəl/ *noun* a small area with a desk, separated from other desks by a dividing wall or screen, where one person can work in a library

**car·riage** 🔊+ **C1** /ˈkærɪdʒ/ *noun* **1** 🔊+ **C1** (*also* **coach**) (*both BrE*) (*NAmE* **car**) [C] a separate section of a train for carrying passengers: *a railway carriage* ⇒ **WORDFINDER NOTE** at TRAIN **2** 🔊+ **C1** [C] a road vehicle, usually with four wheels, that is pulled by one or more horses and was used in the past to carry people: *a horse-drawn carriage* **3** (*BrE*) (*also* **hand·ling** *NAmE*, *BrE*) [U] (*formal*) the act or cost of transporting goods from one place to another: *£16.95 including VAT and carriage* **4** [C] a moving part of a machine that supports or moves another part, for example on a TYPEWRITER: *a carriage return* (= the act of starting a new line when typing) ⇒ see also BABY CARRIAGE, GUN CARRIAGE, HACKNEY CARRIAGE, UNDERCARRIAGE

**ˈcarriage house** (*US*) (*BrE* **ˈmews house**) *noun* a house in a row of houses that were STABLES (= buildings used to keep horses in) in the past

**car·riage·way** /ˈkærɪdʒweɪ/ *noun* (*BrE*) **1** one of the two sides of a MOTORWAY or other large road, used by traffic moving in the same direction: *the eastbound carriageway of the M50* ⇒ see also DUAL CARRIAGEWAY **2** the part of a road intended for vehicles, not people walking, etc. ⇒ WORDFINDER NOTE at ROAD

**car·rier** /ˈkæriə(r)/ *noun* **1** a company that carries goods or passengers from one place to another, especially by air **2** a military vehicle or ship that carries soldiers or equipment from one place to another ⇒ see also AIRCRAFT CARRIER, ARMOURED PERSONNEL CARRIER, PERSONNEL CARRIER **3** a person or animal that passes a disease to other people or animals but does not suffer from it **4** a metal frame that is fixed to a bicycle and used for carrying bags **5** a person or thing that carries sth: *Aquarius, the Water Carrier* ◊ *a baby carrier* (= for carrying a baby on your back or in front of you) ⇒ see also MAIL CARRIER, PEOPLE CARRIER **6** (*BrE*) = CARRIER BAG **7** a company that provides a phone or internet service: *a telecoms carrier*

**ˈcarrier bag** (*also* **car·rier**) (*both BrE*) (*NAmE* **ˈshopping bag**) *noun* a paper or plastic bag for carrying shopping

**ˈcarrier pigeon** *noun* a PIGEON (= a type of bird) that has been trained to carry messages

**car·rion** /ˈkæriən/ *noun* [U] the DECAYING (= becoming destroyed by natural processes) bodies of dead animals: *crows feeding on carrion* ⇒ VISUAL VOCAB page V2

**car·rot** 🔊 **A1** /ˈkærət/ *noun* **1** 🔊 **A1** [U, C] a long pointed orange root vegetable: *grated carrot* ◊ *a slice of carrot cake* ⇒ VISUAL VOCAB page V5 **2** [C] a reward promised to sb in order to persuade them to do sth **SYN** **incentive**: *They are holding out a carrot of $120 million in economic aid.*
**IDM** **the carrot and (the) stick (approach)** if you use the **carrot and stick approach**, you persuade sb to try harder by offering them a reward if they do, or a punishment if they do not

**carry** 🔊 **A1** /ˈkæri/ *verb* (**car·ries**, **carry·ing**, **car·ried**, **car·ried**)
- **TAKE WITH YOU 1** 🔊 **A1** [T] to support the weight of sb/sth and take them or it from place to place; to take sb/sth from one place to another: *~sb/sth He was carrying a large bag.* ◊ *The plane was carrying 122 passengers and five*

225 **carry**

crew. ◊ *~sb/sth + adv./prep. She carried her baby in her arms.* **2** 🔊 **A1** [T] to have sth with you and take it wherever you go: *~sth to carry a weapon/knife* ◊ *Police in many countries carry guns.* ◊ *~sth + adv./prep. I never carry much money on me.*
- OF PIPES/WIRES **3** 🔊 **B1** [T] to contain and direct the flow of water, electricity, etc.: *~sth a pipeline carrying oil* ◊ *~sth + adv./prep. The veins carry blood to the heart.* ◊ *Canals were built to carry water from the Snake River to Milner Dam in 1905.*
- DISEASE **4** [T] *~sth* if a person, an insect, etc. **carries** a disease, they have already caught it and might spread it to others although they might not become ill themselves: *Ticks can carry a nasty disease which affects humans.*
- REMEMBER **5** [T] *~sth in your head/mind* to be able to remember sth
- SUPPORT WEIGHT **6** [T] *~sth* to support the weight of sth: *A road bridge has to carry a lot of traffic.*
- RESPONSIBILITY **7** [T] *~sth* to accept responsibility for sth; to suffer the results of sth: *He is carrying the department* (= it is only working because of his efforts). ◊ *Their group was targeted to carry the burden of job losses.* ◊ *She carries a full load of classes while also serving as department head.*
- HAVE AS QUALITY/FEATURE **8** [T] *~sth* to have sth as a quality or feature: *Her speech carried the ring of authority.* ◊ *Each bike carries a ten-year guarantee.* **9** [T] *~sth* to have sth as a result: *Crimes of violence carry heavy penalties.* ◊ *Being a combat sport, karate carries with it the risk of injury.*
- OF THROW/KICK **10** [I] + *noun* + *adv./prep.* if sth that is thrown, kicked, etc. **carries** a particular distance, it travels that distance before stopping: *The fullback's kick carried 50 metres into the crowd.*
- OF SOUND **11** [I] (+ *adv./prep.*) if a sound **carries**, it can be heard a long distance away
- TAKE TO PLACE/POSITION **12** [T] *~sth/sb to/into sth* to take sth/sb to a particular point or in a particular direction: *The war was carried into enemy territory.* ◊ *Her abilities carried her to the top of her profession.*
- APPROVAL/SUPPORT **13** [T, usually passive] *~sth* to approve of sth by more people voting for it than against it: *The resolution was carried by 340 votes to 210.* **14** [T] to win the support or sympathy of sb; to persuade people to accept your argument: *~sb His moving speech was enough to carry the audience.* ◊ *~sth She nodded in agreement, and he saw he had carried his point.*
- HAVE LABEL/MESSAGE **15** [T] *~sth* to have a particular label attached; to give a particular message or piece of information: *Cigarettes carry a health warning.* ◊ *All the marketing carries a consistent message of quality and reliability.*
- NEWS STORY **16** [T] *~sth* if a newspaper, broadcast, etc. **carries** a particular story, it publishes or broadcasts it
- ITEM IN STORE **17** [T] *~sth* if a shop **carries** a particular item, it has it for sale: *We carry a range of educational software.*
- BABY **18** [T] *be carrying sb* to be pregnant with sb: *She was carrying twins.*
- YOURSELF **19** [T] *~yourself + adv./prep.* to hold or move your head or body in a particular way: *to carry yourself well*
- ADDING NUMBERS **20** [T] *~sth* to add a number to the next column on the left when adding up numbers, for example when the numbers add up to more than ten ⇒ see also CONCEALED CARRY, OPEN CARRY

**IDM** **be/get carried aˈway** to get very excited or lose control of your feelings: *I got carried away and started shouting at the television.* **carry all/everything beˈfore you** to be completely successful **carry the ˈball** (*US*, *informal*) to take responsibility for getting sth done: *My co-worker was sick, so I had to carry the ball.* **carry the ˈcan (for sth/sb)** (*BrE*, *informal*) to accept the blame for sth, especially when it is not your fault **carry a torch for sb** to be in love with sb, especially sb who does not love you in return **carry ˈweight (with sb)** to have influence with sb: *My views don't carry much weight with the boss.* ⇒ more at DAY, FAR *adv.*, FAST *adv.*, FETCH

# carrycot

**PHRV** **carry sb ˈback (to sth)** to make sb remember a time in the past: *The smell of the sea carried her back to her childhood.* **carry sth↔ˈforward/ˈover** to move a total amount from one column or page to the next **carry sth↔ˈoff 1** to win sth: *He carried off most of the prizes.* **2** to succeed in doing sth that most people would find difficult: *She's had her hair cut really short, but she can carry it off.* **carry ˈon 1** (especially *BrE*) to continue moving: *Carry on until you get to the junction, then turn left.* **2** (*informal*) to argue or complain noisily: *He was shouting and carrying on.* ⇨ related noun CARRY-ON **carry ˈon (with sth)** | **carry sth↔ˈon** to continue doing sth: *Carry on with your work while I'm away.* ◇ *After he left I just tried to carry on as normal* (= do the things I usually do). ◇ *Carry on the good work!* ◇ **carry on doing sth** *He carried on peeling the potatoes.* **carry ˈon (with sb)** (*old-fashioned*) to have a sexual relationship with sb when you should not: *His wife found out he'd been carrying on with another woman.* **carry sth↔ˈout 1** to do sth that you have said you will do or have been asked to do: *to carry out a promise/a threat/a plan/an order* **2** to do and complete a task: *to carry out an inquiry/an investigation/a survey* ◇ *Extensive tests have been carried out on the patient.* **carry ˈover** to continue to exist in a different situation: *Attitudes learned at home carry over into the playground.* **carry sth↔ˈover 1** to keep sth from one situation and use it or deal with it in a different situation **2** to delay sth until a later time: *The match had to be carried over until Sunday.* **3** = CARRY STH FORWARD **carry sb ˈthrough** | **carry sb ˈthrough sth** to help sb to survive a difficult period: *His determination carried him through the ordeal.* **carry sth ˈthrough** to complete sth successfully: *It's a difficult job but she's the person to carry it through.* **carry ˈthrough (on/with sth)** (especially *NAmE*) to do what you have said you will do: *He has proved he can carry through on his promises.*

**carry·cot** /ˈkærɪkɒt; *NAmE* -kɑːt/ *noun* (*BrE*) a small bed for a baby, with handles at the sides so you can carry it ⇨ picture at PUSHCHAIR

**ˈcarry-on** *noun* **1** (especially *NAmE*) a small bag or case that you carry onto a plane with you: *Only one carry-on is allowed.* ◇ *carry-on baggage* **2** [usually sing.] (*BrE*, *informal*) a display of excitement, anger or silly behaviour over sth unimportant: *What a carry-on!*

**ˈcarry-out** *noun* (*US*, *ScotE*) = TAKEAWAY: *Let's get a carry-out.* ◇ *carry-out coffees*

**ˈcarry-over** *noun* **1** [usually sing.] something that remains or results from a situation in the past: *His neatness is a carry-over from his army days.* **2** an amount of money that has not been used and so can be used later: *The £20 million included a £7 million carry-over from last year's underspend.*

**ˈcar seat** *noun* **1** a special safety seat for a child that can be fitted into a car ⇨ compare CHILD SEAT **2** a seat in a car

**car·sick** /ˈkɑːsɪk; *NAmE* ˈkɑːrs-/ *adj.* [not usually before noun] feeling sick because you are travelling in a car: *Do you get carsick?* ▸ **car·sick·ness** *noun* [U]

**cart** /kɑːt; *NAmE* kɑːrt/ *noun*, *verb*
■ *noun* **1** a vehicle with two or four wheels that is pulled by a horse and used for carrying loads: *a horse and cart* ⇨ see also GOLF CART **2** (also **hand-cart**) a light vehicle with wheels that you pull or push by hand **3** (*NAmE*) (*BrE* **trol·ley**) a small vehicle with wheels that can be pushed or pulled along and is used for carrying things: *a baggage cart* ◇ *a serving cart* **4** (especially *NAmE*) = SHOPPING CART: *Add to cart.*
**IDM** **put the ˌcart before the ˈhorse** to put or do things in the wrong order
■ *verb* **1** ~ sth (+ *adv./prep.*) to carry sth in a cart or other vehicle: *The rubbish is then carted away for recycling.* **2** ~ sth + *adv./prep.* (*informal*) to carry sth that is large or heavy or difficult to carry: *We had to cart our luggage up six flights of stairs.* **3** ~ sb + *adv./prep.* (*informal*) to take sb somewhere, especially with difficulty: *The demonstrators were carted off to the local police station.* **IDM** see UPSET *v.*

**carte blanche** /ˌkɑːt ˈblɑːnʃ; *NAmE* ˌkɑːrt ˈblɑːnʃ/ *noun* **~ (to do sth)** (from French) the complete freedom or authority to do whatever you like

**car·tel** /kɑːˈtel; *NAmE* kɑːrˈt-/ *noun* [C + sing./pl. v.] a group of separate companies that agree to increase profits by fixing prices and not competing with each other

**Car·te·sian** /kɑːˈtiːziən; *NAmE* kɑːrˈtiːʒn/ *adj.* connected with the French PHILOSOPHER Descartes and his ideas about philosophy and mathematics

**car·til·age** /ˈkɑːtɪlɪdʒ; *NAmE* ˈkɑːrt-/ *noun* [U, C] the strong white TISSUE that is important in supporting and connecting parts of the body, and especially in JOINTS to prevent the bones rubbing against each other ⇨ VISUAL VOCAB page V1

**car·ti·la·gin·ous** /ˌkɑːtɪˈlædʒɪnəs; *NAmE* ˌkɑːrt-/ *adj.* (*anatomy*) made of cartilage

**cart·load** /ˈkɑːtləʊd; *NAmE* ˈkɑːrtloʊd/ *noun* **1** the amount of sth that fills a CART **2** [usually pl.] (*informal*) a large amount of sth

**car·tog·raph·er** /kɑːˈtɒɡrəfə(r); *NAmE* kɑːrˈtɑːɡ-/ *noun* a person who draws or makes maps

**car·tog·raphy** /kɑːˈtɒɡrəfi; *NAmE* kɑːrˈtɑːɡ-/ *noun* [U] the art or process of drawing or making maps ▸ **carto·graph·ic** /ˌkɑːtəˈɡræfɪk; *NAmE* ˌkɑːrt-/ *adj.*

**car·ton** /ˈkɑːtn; *NAmE* ˈkɑːrtn/ *noun* **1** a light box or pot made of thick card or plastic for holding goods, especially food or liquid; the contents of a carton: *a milk carton/a carton of milk* **2** (*NAmE*) a large container in which goods are packed in smaller containers: *a carton of cigarettes*

**car·toon** /kɑːˈtuːn; *NAmE* kɑːrˈt-/ *noun* **1** a humorous drawing in a newspaper or magazine, especially one about politics or events in the news: *a political/satirical cartoon* ⇨ EXPRESS YOURSELF at DESCRIBE **2** (also **ˈcomic strip**, *BrE* **strip carˈtoon**) a series of drawings inside boxes that tell a story and are often printed in newspapers **3** (also **aniˌmated carˈtoon**) a film or TV show made by photographing a series of gradually changing drawings or models, so that they look as if they are moving: *a Walt Disney cartoon* ◇ *a cartoon character* **HELP** A **cartoon** is really made using the old technique of photographing drawings or models; a film made with modern computer techniques (**CGI**) is usually called an **animation**, not a **cartoon**. However, some people might use the word **cartoon** for both kinds of film. **4** (*specialist*) a drawing made by an artist as a preparation for a painting

**car·toon·ish** /kɑːˈtuːnɪʃ; *NAmE* kɑːrˈt-/ *adj.* very silly or EXAGGERATED, often in a way that is not appropriate: *Her cartoonish make-up made her look ridiculous.*

**car·toon·ist** /kɑːˈtuːnɪst; *NAmE* kɑːrˈt-/ *noun* a person who draws cartoons

**car·touche** /kɑːˈtuːʃ; *NAmE* kɑːrˈt-/ *noun* an OBLONG or OVAL shape which contains a set of ancient Egyptian HIEROGLYPHS, often representing the name and title of a king or queen

**cart·ridge** /ˈkɑːtrɪdʒ; *NAmE* ˈkɑːrt-/ *noun* **1** (*NAmE* also **shell**) a tube or case containing EXPLOSIVE and a bullet or SHOT, for shooting from a gun **2** a case containing sth that is used in a machine, for example INK for a printer, film for a camera, etc. Cartridges are put into the machine and can be removed and replaced when they are finished or empty. **3** a thin tube containing INK (= coloured liquid for writing) which you put inside a pen

**cart·wheel** /ˈkɑːtwiːl; *NAmE* ˈkɑːrt-/ *noun* **1** a fast physical movement in which you turn in a circle to the side by putting your hands on the ground and bringing your legs, one at a time, over your head: *to do/turn cartwheels* **2** the wheel of a CART ▸ **cart·wheel** *verb* [I]

**carve** /kɑːv; *NAmE* kɑːrv/ *verb* **1** [T, I] to make objects, patterns, etc. by cutting away material from a piece of wood or stone, or another hard material: ~ sth *a carved doorway* ◇ ~ sth **from/out of sth** *The statue was carved out of a single piece of stone.* ◇ ~ sth **into/in sth** *The wood had been carved into the shape of a flower.* ◇ ~ **in sth** *She carves in both stone and wood.* **2** [T] ~ sth (on sth) to write sth on a surface by cutting into it:

*They carved their initials on the desk.* **3** [T, I] to cut a large piece of cooked meat into smaller pieces for eating: **~(sth) | ~(sb) sth** *Who's going to carve the turkey?* **4** [T, no passive] to work hard in order to have a successful career, reputation, etc: **~sth (out)** *He succeeded in carving out a career in the media.* ◇ **~sth (out) for yourself** *She has carved a place for herself in the fashion world.* **IDM** see STONE *n.*
**PHR V** **carve sth ↔ 'up** (*disapproving*) to divide a company, an area of land, etc. into smaller parts in order to share it between people

**car·very** /ˈkɑːvəri; *NAmE* ˈkɑːrv-/ *noun* (*pl.* **-ies**) (*BrE*) a restaurant that serves ROAST MEAT

**'carve-up** *noun* [sing.] (*BrE, informal, disapproving*) the dividing of sth such as a company or a country into separate parts

**carv·ing** /ˈkɑːvɪŋ; *NAmE* ˈkɑːrv-/ *noun* **1** [C, U] an object or a pattern made by cutting away material from a piece of wood or stone, or another hard material **2** [U] the art of making objects in this way

**'carving knife** *noun* a large sharp knife for cutting cooked meat

**'car wash** *noun* a place with special equipment, where you can pay to have your car washed

**Casa·nova** /ˌkæsəˈnəʊvə, ˌkæzə-/ *noun* a man who has sex with a lot of women **ORIGIN** From Giovanni Jacopo Casanova, an Italian man in the eighteenth century who was famous for having sex with many women.

**cas·bah** = KASBAH

**cas·cade** /kæˈskeɪd/ *noun, verb*
■ *noun* **1** a small WATERFALL, especially one of several falling down a steep slope with rocks **2** a large amount of water falling or pouring down: *a cascade of rainwater* **3** (*formal*) a large amount of sth hanging down: *Her hair tumbled in a cascade down her back.* **4** (*formal*) a large number of things falling or coming quickly at the same time: *He crashed to the ground in a cascade of oil cans.* **5** (*formal*) a number of things happening, in which each one leads to another
■ *verb* **1** [I] + **adv./prep.** to flow downwards in large amounts: *Water cascaded down the mountainside.* **2** [I] + **adv./prep.** (*formal*) to fall or hang in large amounts: *Blonde hair cascaded over her shoulders.* **3** [T, I] **~sth (to sb)** | **~to sb** to pass information, knowledge, etc. to a person or group so that they can pass it on to others; to be passed on in this way

**case** ⓘ **A2** ⓞ /keɪs/ *noun, verb*
■ *noun*
• SITUATION **1** **A2** [C] a particular situation or a situation of a particular type: *In some cases people have had to wait several weeks for an appointment.* ◇ **in cases of sth** *The company only dismisses its employees in cases of gross misconduct.* ◇ **in the ~ of sth** *In the case of banks, the law can limit activities.* ◇ **a ~ of sth** *It's a classic case* (= a very typical case) *of bad planning.* ⊃ see also WORST-CASE ⊃ SYNONYMS at EXAMPLE, SITUATION **2** **B1** **the case** [sing.] the true situation: **be the ~** *If that is the case* (= if the situation described is true), *we need more staff.* ◇ **it's the ~ that …** *It is simply not the case that prison conditions are improving.* **3** **B1** [C, usually sing.] a situation that relates to a particular person or thing: **in sb's ~** *I cannot make an exception in your case* (= for you and not for others). ◇ **in this ~** *Don't underestimate the power of the pen, or in this case, the power of the keyboard.* ◇ *Every application will be decided on a case-by-case basis* (= each one will be considered separately). ⊃ SYNONYMS at EXAMPLE
• POLICE INVESTIGATION **4** **B1** [C] a matter that is being officially investigated, especially by the police: *a murder case* ◇ *a case of theft* ◇ *Four officers are investigating the case.* ⊃ see also COLD CASE
• IN COURT **5** **B1** [C] a question to be decided in court: *a court case* ◇ *a criminal/civil case* ◇ *The case will be heard next week.* ◇ *to win/lose a case* ⊃ see also TEST CASE
• ARGUMENTS **6** **B2** [C, usually sing.] a set of facts or arguments that support one side in a trial, a discussion, etc: *Our lawyer didn't think we had a case* (= had enough good arguments to win in a court of law). ◇ **~for sth** *the case for the defence/prosecution* ◇ **~against sb/sth** *The case against her was very weak.* ◇ **~for doing sth** *The report*

227 **casework**

*makes out a strong case* (= gives good arguments) *for spending more money on hospitals.* ◇ **~that …** *They try to make the case that this war is necessary.*
• CONTAINER **7** **A2** [C] (often in compounds) a container or cover used to protect or store things; a container with its contents or the amount that it contains: *a jewellery case* ◇ *The museum was full of stuffed animals in glass cases.* ◇ **~of sth** *a case* (= 12 bottles) *of champagne* ⊃ see also ATTACHÉ CASE, JEWEL CASE, PENCIL CASE ⊃ picture at CLOCK **8** [C] = SUITCASE: *Let me carry your case for you.*
• OF DISEASE **9** **B1** [C] **~(of sth)** the fact of sb having a disease or an injury; a person suffering from a disease or an injury: *a severe case of food poisoning* ◇ *Over 130 000 cases of cholera were reported in 2016.* ◇ *The most serious cases were treated at the scene of the accident.*
• PERSON **10** [C] a person who needs, or is thought to need, special treatment or attention: *He's a hopeless case.* ⊃ see also BASKET CASE
• GRAMMAR **11** [C, U] the form of a noun, an adjective or a pronoun in some languages, that shows its relationship to another word: *the nominative/accusative/genitive case* ◇ *Latin nouns have case, number and gender.* ⊃ WORDFINDER NOTE at GRAMMAR ⊃ see also LOWER CASE, UPPER CASE
**IDM** **as the 'case may be** used to say that one of two or more possibilities is true, but which one is true depends on the circumstances: *There may be an announcement about this tomorrow—or not, as the case may be.* **be on sb's 'case** (*informal*) to criticize sb all the time: *She's always on my case about cleaning my room.* **be on the 'case** to be dealing with a particular matter, especially a criminal investigation: *We have two agents on the case.* **a case in 'point** a clear example of the problem, situation, etc. that is being discussed ⊃ LANGUAGE BANK at E.G. **get off my 'case** (*informal*) used to tell sb to stop criticizing you **in 'any case** whatever happens or may have happened: *There's no point complaining now—we're leaving tomorrow in any case.* **(just) in 'case ( …)** **B1** because of the possibility of sth happening: *You'd better take the keys in case I'm out.* ◇ *You probably won't need to call—but take my number, just in case.* ◇ *In case* (= if it is true) *you're wondering why Jo's here—let me explain …* **in case of sth** (often on official notices) if sth happens: *In case of fire, ring the alarm bell.* **in 'that case** if that happens or has happened; if that is the situation: *'I've made up my mind.' 'In that case, there's no point discussing it.'* ⊃ more at DOG *n.*, REST *v.*
■ *verb*
**IDM** **case the 'joint** (*informal*) to look carefully around a building so that you can plan how to steal things from it at a later time

**case·book** /ˈkeɪsbʊk/ *noun* a written record kept by doctors, lawyers, etc. of cases they have dealt with

**cased** /keɪst/ *adj.* **~in sth** completely covered with a particular material: *The towers are made of steel cased in granite.* ⊃ see also CASING

**'case history** *noun* a record of a person's background, past illnesses, etc. that a doctor or SOCIAL WORKER studies

**'case law** *noun* [U] (*law*) law based on decisions made by judges in earlier cases ⊃ compare COMMON LAW, STATUTE LAW ⊃ see also TEST CASE

**case·load** /ˈkeɪsləʊd/ *noun* all the people that a doctor, SOCIAL WORKER, etc. is responsible for at one time: *a heavy caseload* (= a large number of people)

**case·ment** /ˈkeɪsmənt/ (*also* **casement 'window**) *noun* a window that opens on HINGES like a door

**case-'sensitive** *adj.* (*computing*) a program which is **case-sensitive** recognizes the difference between capital letters and small letters

**'case study** *noun* a detailed account of the development of a person, a group of people or a situation over a period of time

**case·work** /ˈkeɪswɜːk; *NAmE* -wɜːrk/ *noun* [U] SOCIAL WORK (= work done to help people in the community with special

ⓞ Oxford Phrasal Academic Lexicon (OPAL) written and spoken word lists | Ⓦ OPAL written word list | Ⓢ OPAL spoken word list

# caseworker

needs) involving the study of a particular person's family and background

**case·work·er** /ˈkeɪswɜːkə(r); NAmE -wɜːrk-/ noun (especially NAmE) a SOCIAL WORKER who helps a particular person or family in the community with special needs

**cash** ⓘ A2 /kæʃ/ noun, verb
- **noun** [U] **1** A2 money in the form of coins or notes: *How much cash do you have on you?* ◊ *Customers are offered a 10% discount if they pay cash.* ◊ **in~** *Payments can be made by card or in cash.* ◊ *The thieves stole £500 in cash.* ⊃ picture at MONEY ⊃ see also COLD CASH, HARD CASH, PETTY CASH ⊃ SYNONYMS at MONEY **2** ⓘ B1 (informal) money in any form: *The museum needs to find ways of raising cash.* ◊ *I'm short of cash right now.* ◊ *I'm constantly strapped for cash* (= without enough money).
  - IDM **cash down** (BrE) (also **cash up front** NAmE, BrE) with immediate payment of cash: *to pay for sth cash down* **cash in hand** (BrE, informal) if you pay for goods and services **cash in hand**, you pay in cash, especially so that the person being paid can avoid paying tax on the amount **cash on delivery** (abbr. COD) a system of paying for goods when they are delivered
- **verb** ~ **a cheque** to exchange a CHEQUE for the amount of money that it is worth
  - PHRV **cash in (on sth)** (disapproving) to gain an advantage for yourself from a situation, especially in a way that other people think is wrong: *The film studio is being accused of cashing in on the singer's death.* **cash sth↔in** to exchange sth, such as an insurance policy, for money before the date on which it would normally end **cash up** (BrE) (NAmE **cash out**) to add up the amount of money that has been received in a shop, club, etc., especially at the end of the day

**cash and carry** noun [C, U] a large WHOLESALE shop that sells goods in large quantities at low prices to customers from other businesses who pay in cash and take the goods away themselves; the system of buying and selling goods in this way

**cash·back** (BrE) (US **cash-back**) /ˈkæʃbæk/ noun **1** [U] if you ask for **cashback** when you are paying for goods in a shop with a DEBIT CARD (= a plastic card that takes money directly from your bank account), you get a sum of money in cash, which is added to your bill **2** [U, C] a sum of money that is offered to people who buy particular products or services: *There's £200 cashback on this computer if you buy before 31 January.*

**cash bar** noun a bar at a wedding, party, etc., at which the guests have to pay for their own drinks rather than getting them free

**cash box** noun a box with a lock for keeping money in, usually made of metal

**cash card** noun (BrE) (US **ATM card**) a plastic card used to get money from a CASH MACHINE (= a machine in or outside a bank) ⊃ compare CREDIT CARD, DEBIT CARD

**cash cow** noun (business) the part of a business that always makes a profit and that provides money for the rest of the business

**cash crop** noun a crop grown for selling, rather than for use by the person who grows it ⊃ compare SUBSISTENCE

**cash desk** noun (BrE) the place in a shop where you pay for goods that you have bought

**cash dispenser** noun (BrE) = CASH MACHINE

**cashed up** adj. (especially AustralE, informal) having a lot of money available to spend: *Mark was cashed up that night, so he got the drinks.* ◊ *support from cashed-up investors*

**cash·ew** /ˈkæʃuː, kæˈʃuː/ (also **cashew nut**) noun the small curved nut of the tropical American **cashew tree**, used in cooking and often eaten salted with alcoholic drinks ⊃ VISUAL VOCAB page V8

**cash flow** noun [C, U] the movement of money into and out of a business as goods are bought and sold: *a healthy cash flow* (= having enough money to make payments when necessary) ◊ *cash flow problems*

**cash·ier** /kæˈʃɪə(r); NAmE -ˈʃɪr/ noun, verb
- **noun** a person whose job is to receive and pay out money in a bank, shop, hotel, etc.
- **verb** [usually passive] ~ **sb** to make sb leave the army, NAVY, etc. because they have done sth wrong

**cash·less** /ˈkæʃləs/ adj. done or working without using cash: *We are moving towards the cashless society.*

**cash machine** (BrE also **cash dispenser**, **cash point**™) /ˈkæʃpɔɪnt/ (also **ATM** NAmE, BrE) (also **ABM** CanE) noun a machine in or outside a bank, shop, etc., from which you can get money from your bank account using a special plastic card

**cash·mere** /ˈkæʃmɪə(r), ˈkæʒmɪə(r); NAmE ˈkæʒmɪr, ˈkæʃm-/ noun [U] fine, soft wool made from the long hair of a type of GOAT, used especially for making expensive clothes

**cash register** (BrE also **till**) (NAmE also **register**) noun a machine used in shops, restaurants, etc. for keeping money in, and that shows and records the amount of money received for each thing that is sold

**cash-rich** adj. having a lot of money available to spend: *The target market for this personal shopping service is cash-rich, time-poor professionals.* ⊃ compare TIME-POOR

**cash-starved** adj. [only before noun] without enough money, usually because another organization, such as the government, has failed to provide it: *cash-starved public services*

**cash-strapped** adj. [only before noun] without enough money: *cash-strapped governments/shoppers*

**cash transfer** noun [C, U] = MONEY TRANSFER

**cas·ing** /ˈkeɪsɪŋ/ noun a layer of material that protects sth

**ca·sino** ⓘ C1 /kəˈsiːnəʊ/ noun (pl. -os) a public building or room where people play GAMBLING games for money ⊃ WORDFINDER NOTE at GAMBLING

**cask** /kɑːsk; NAmE kæsk/ noun a small wooden BARREL used for storing liquids, especially alcoholic drinks; the amount contained in a cask: *a wine cask/a cask of wine*

**cas·ket** /ˈkɑːskɪt; NAmE ˈkæs-/ noun **1** a small decorated box for holding jewellery or other valuable things, especially in the past **2** (NAmE) (BrE **coffin** especially in BrE) a box in which a dead body is buried or CREMATED

**Cas·san·dra** /kəˈsændrə/ noun a person who predicts that sth bad will happen, especially a person who is not believed ORIGIN From the name of a princess in ancient Greek stories to whom Apollo gave the ability to predict the future. After she tricked him, he stopped people believing her.

**cas·sava** /kəˈsɑːvə/ (also **man·ioc**) noun [U] **1** a tropical plant with many branches and long roots that you can eat **2** the roots of this plant, which can be boiled, fried, ROASTED or made into flour

**cas·ser·ole** /ˈkæsərəʊl/ noun **1** [C, U] a hot dish made with meat, vegetables, etc. that are cooked slowly in liquid in an oven: *a chicken casserole* ◊ *Is there any casserole left?* **2** [C] (also **casserole dish**) a container with a LID (= cover) used for cooking meat, etc. in liquid in an oven ▶ **cas·ser·ole** verb ~ **sth**

**cas·sette** /kəˈset/ noun **1** a small flat plastic case containing tape for playing or recording music or sound: *a video cassette* (= for recording sound and pictures) ◊ *a cassette tape* ◊ *a cassette recorder/player* **2** a plastic case containing film that can be put into a camera

**cas·sock** /ˈkæsək/ noun a long piece of clothing, usually black or red, worn by some Christian priests and other people with special duties in a church

**cas·sou·let** /ˈkæsuleɪ; NAmE ˌkæsuˈleɪ/ noun [U] (from French) a dish consisting of meat and beans cooked slowly in liquid

**cas·so·wary** /ˈkæsəweəri; NAmE -weri/ noun (pl. **-ies**) a very large bird related to the EMU, that does not fly. It is found mainly in New Guinea.

**cast** ⓘ B2 /kɑːst; NAmE kæst/ verb, noun

■ **verb** (**cast, cast**)
- **A LOOK/GLANCE/SMILE** **1** ⓘ [T] to look, smile, etc. in a particular direction: ~ sth + adv./prep. *She cast a welcoming smile in his direction.*
- **LIGHT/A SHADOW** **2** ⓘ B2 [T] to make light, a shadow, etc. appear in a particular place: ~ sth *Someone was standing in the dark shadow cast by the light.* ◊ ~ sth + adv./prep. *The moon had cast a silvery light on the huts.*
- **DOUBT** **3** ⓘ B2 [T] to say, do or suggest sth that makes people doubt sth or think that sb is less honest, good, etc.: ~ sth (on/upon sth) *This latest evidence casts serious doubt on his version of events.* ◊ ~ sth over sth *The sad news cast a shadow over the proceedings* (= made people feel unhappy).
- **VOTE** **4** [T] ~ a/your vote/ballot (for sb/sth) to vote for sb/sth
- **ACTORS** **5** [T] to choose actors to play the different parts in a film, play, etc.; to choose an actor to play a particular role: ~ sth *The play is being cast in both the US and Britain.* ◊ ~ sb (as sb) *He has cast her as an ambitious lawyer in his latest movie.*
- **DESCRIBE** **6** [T] to describe or present sb/yourself in a particular way: ~ sb/yourself as sth *He cast himself as the innocent victim of a hate campaign.* ◊ ~ sb/yourself in sth *The press were quick to cast her in the role of the 'other woman'.*
- **FISHING LINE** **7** [I, T] ~ (sth) to throw one end of a FISHING LINE into a river, etc.
- **THROW** **8** [T] ~ sb/sth (*literary*) to throw sb/sth somewhere, especially using force: *The priceless treasures had been cast into the Nile.* ◊ *They cast anchor at nightfall.*
- **SKIN** **9** [T] ~ sth when a snake **casts** its skin, the skin comes off as part of a natural process SYN **shed**
- **SHOE** **10** [T] ~ sth if a horse **casts** a shoe, the shoe comes off by accident
- **SHAPE METAL** **11** [T] ~ sth (in sth) to shape hot liquid metal, etc. by pouring it into a hollow container (called a MOULD): *a statue cast in bronze* ◊ (*figurative*) *an artist cast in the mould of* (= very similar to) *Miró*.

IDM **cast your mind back (to sth)** to make yourself think about sth that happened in the past: *I want you to cast your minds back to the first time you met.* **cast your net wide** to consider a lot of different people, activities, possibilities, etc. when you are looking for sth **cast a 'spell (on sb/sth)** to use words that are thought to be magic and have the power to change or influence sb/sth ⊃ more at CAUTION *n.*, DIE *n.*, EYE *n.*, LIGHT *n.*, LOT *n.*
PHR V **cast a'bout/a'round for sth** to try hard to think of or find sth, especially when this is difficult: *She cast around desperately for a safe topic of conversation.* **cast sb/sth↔a'side** (*formal*) to get rid of sb/sth because you no longer want or need them SYN **discard** **be ˌcast a'way** to be left somewhere after a SHIPWRECK ⊃ related noun CASTAWAY **be ˌcast 'down (by sth)** (*literary*) to be sad or unhappy about sth ⊃ see also DOWNCAST **cast 'off; ˌcast sth↔'off 1** to UNTIE the ropes that are holding a boat in a fixed position, in order to sail away **2** (in knitting) to remove STITCHES from the needles in a way that forms an edge that will not become loose **ˌcast sth↔'off** (*formal*) to get rid of sth because you no longer want or need it: *The town is still trying to cast off its dull image.* **cast 'on; ˌcast sth↔'on** (in knitting) to put the first row of STITCHES on a needle **ˌcast sb/sth↔'out** (*literary*) to get rid of sb/sth, especially by using force: *He claimed to have the power to cast out demons.* ⊃ related noun OUTCAST

■ **noun**
- **ACTORS** **1** ⓘ B2 [C + sing./pl. v.] all the people who act in a play or film: *an all-star cast* (= including many well-known actors) ◊ *the supporting cast* (= not the main actors, but the others) ◊ *The whole cast performs/perform brilliantly.* ◊ *Bonus features include interviews with the cast and crew.* ◊ *a play with a large cast of characters* ◊ *None of the other cast members makes much of an impression.* ⊃ WORDFINDER NOTE at ACTOR
- **IN SHAPING METAL** **2** [C] an object that is made by pouring hot liquid metal, etc. into a MOULD (= a container with a particular shape) **3** [C] a container with a particular shape used to make an object SYN **mould**
- **APPEARANCE** **4** [sing.] (*formal*) the way that a person or thing is or appears: *He has an unusual cast of mind.* ◊ *I disliked the arrogant cast to her mouth.*
- **THROW** **5** [C] an act of throwing sth, especially a fishing line
- **ON ARM/LEG** **6** [C] = PLASTER CAST: *in a ~* *Her leg's in a cast.* ⊃ see also OPENCAST

**cas·ta·nets** /ˌkæstəˈnets/ *noun* [pl.] a musical instrument that consists of two small round pieces of wood that you hold in the hand and hit together with the fingers to make a noise. Castanets are used especially by Spanish dancers.

**cast·away** /ˈkɑːstəweɪ; NAmE ˈkæs-/ *noun* a person whose ship has sunk (= who has been SHIPWRECKED) and who has had to swim to a lonely place, usually an island

**caste** /kɑːst; NAmE kæst/ *noun* **1** [C] any of the four main divisions of Hindu society, originally those made according to functions in society: *the caste system* ◊ *high-caste Brahmins* ⊃ see also SCHEDULED CASTE **2** [C] a social class, especially one whose members do not allow others to join it: *the ruling caste* **3** [U] the system of dividing society into classes based on differences in family origin, rank or wealth ⊃ see also HALF-CASTE

**cas·ter** (NAmE) = CASTOR

**ˈcaster sugar** (*also* **ˈcastor sugar**) *noun* [U] (BrE) white sugar in the form of very fine grains, used in cooking ⊃ compare GRANULATED SUGAR

**cas·ti·gate** /ˈkæstɪɡeɪt/ *verb* ~ sb/sth/yourself (for sth) (*formal*) to criticize sb/sth/yourself severely: *He castigated himself for being so stupid.* ▸ **cas·ti·ga·tion** /ˌkæstɪˈɡeɪʃn/ *noun* [U]

**cast·ing** /ˈkɑːstɪŋ; NAmE ˈkæs-/ *noun* **1** [U] the process of choosing actors for a play or film ⊃ see also CENTRAL CASTING **2** [C] an object made by pouring hot liquid metal, etc. into a MOULD (= a container with a particular shape)

**ˈcasting couch** *noun* used to refer to a process in which actors are chosen for a film, etc. if they have sex with the person in charge of choosing the actors

**ˈcasting ˈvote** *noun* [usually sing.] the vote given by the person in charge of an official meeting to decide an issue when votes on each side are equal

**ˌcast 'iron** *noun* [U] a hard type of iron that does not bend easily and is shaped by pouring the hot liquid metal into a MOULD (= a container with a particular shape)

**ˌcast-'iron** *adj.* **1** made of cast iron: *a cast-iron bridge* **2** (BrE) very strong or certain; that cannot be broken or fail: *a cast-iron guarantee/promise* ◊ *a cast-iron excuse/ alibi* ⊃ compare IRONCLAD

**cas·tle** ⓘ A2 /ˈkɑːsl; NAmE ˈkæsl/ *noun* **1** ⓘ A2 a large strong building with thick, high walls and towers, built in the past by kings or queens, or other important people, to defend themselves against attack: *Windsor Castle* ◊ *in/at the ~* *They were invited to a banquet in the castle.* ⊃ see also BOUNCY CASTLE, SANDCASTLE **2** (*also* **rook**) (in CHESS) any of the four pieces placed in the corner squares of the board at the start of the game, usually made to look like a castle
IDM **(build) castles in the 'air** (to have) plans or dreams that are not likely to happen or come true ⊃ more at MAN *n.*

**ˈcast-off** (*especially BrE*) (*also* **ˈhand-me-down** *BrE and NAmE*) *noun* [usually pl.] a piece of clothing that the original owner no longer wants to wear ▸ **ˈcast-off** (*also* **ˈhand-me-down**) *adj.*: *a cast-off overcoat*

**cas·tor** (BrE) (NAmE **cas·ter**) /ˈkɑːstə(r); NAmE ˈkæs-/ *noun* one of the small wheels fixed to the bottom of a piece of furniture so that it can be moved easily

**ˈcastor oil** *noun* [U] a thick yellow oil obtained from a tropical plant and used in the past as a type of medicine, usually as a LAXATIVE

**ˈcastor sugar** = CASTER SUGAR

**cas·trate** /kæˈstreɪt; NAmE ˈkæstreɪt/ verb ~ sth/sb to remove the TESTICLES of a male animal or person ▶ **cas·tra·tion** /kæˈstreɪʃn/ noun [U, C]

**cas·ual** /ˈkæʒuəl/ adj., noun
■ adj.
- NOT FORMAL **1** not formal: *casual clothes* (= comfortable clothes that you choose to wear in your free time) ◊ *family parties and other casual occasions*
- WITHOUT CARE/ATTENTION **2** [usually before noun] not showing much care or thought; seeming not to be worried; not wanting to show that sth is important to you: *a casual manner* ◊ *It was just a casual remark—I wasn't really serious.* ◊ *He tried to sound casual, but I knew he was worried.* ◊ *They have a casual attitude towards safety* (= they don't care enough). **3** [usually before noun] without paying attention to detail: *a casual glance* ◊ *It's obvious even to the casual observer.*
- WORK **4** [usually before noun] not permanent; not done, or doing sth regularly: *casual workers/labour* ◊ *Students sometimes do casual work in the tourist trade.* ◊ *They are employed on a casual basis* (= they do not have a permanent job with the company).
- RELATIONSHIP **5** [usually before noun] without deep feelings: *a casual acquaintance* ◊ *a casual friendship* ◊ *to have casual sex* (= to have sex without having a steady relationship with that partner)
- BY CHANCE **6** [only before noun] happening by chance; doing sth by chance: *a casual encounter/meeting* ◊ *a casual passer-by* ◊ *The exhibition is interesting to both the enthusiast and the casual visitor.* ◊ *The disease is not spread by casual contact.* ▶ **cas·ual·ly** /-əli/ adv.: *'What did he say about me?' she asked as casually as she could.* ◊ *They chatted casually on the phone.* ◊ *dressed casually in jeans and T-shirt* **cas·ual·ness** noun [U]: *He was sure that the casualness of the gesture was deliberate.*
■ noun
- CLOTHES **1** casuals BrE [pl.] informal clothes or shoes: *dressed in casuals* ⊃ see also BUSINESS CASUAL
- WORKER **2** [C] a casual worker (= one who does not work permanently for a company)

**casu·al·iza·tion** /ˌkæʒuəlaɪˈzeɪʃn; NAmE -ləˈz-/ noun [U] the practice of employing temporary staff for short periods instead of permanent staff, in order to save costs

**casu·alty** /ˈkæʒuəlti/ noun (pl. -ies) **1** [C] a person who is killed or injured in war or in an accident: *road casualties* ◊ *Both sides had suffered heavy casualties* (= many people had been killed). ⊃ WORDFINDER NOTE at CONFLICT **2** [C] a person who suffers or a thing that is destroyed when sth else takes place SYN victim: *She became a casualty of the reduction in part-time work* (= she lost her job). ◊ *Small shops have been a casualty of the recession.* **3** [U] (also **ˈcasualty department**, **ˌaccident and eˈmergency**) (all BrE) (NAmE eˈmergency room) the part of a hospital where people who need immediate treatment are taken: *The victims were rushed to casualty.*
⊃ WORDFINDER NOTE at ACCIDENT

**casu·istry** /ˈkæzjuɪstri/ noun [U] (formal, disapproving) a way of solving moral or legal problems by using clever arguments that may be false

**casus belli** /ˌkeɪsəs ˈbelaɪ, ˌkɑːsʊs ˈbeliː/ noun (pl. **casus belli**) (formal) an act or situation that is used to justify a war

**cat** /kæt/ noun **1** a small animal with soft fur that people often keep as a pet. Cats catch and kill birds and mice: *a tin of cat food* ⊃ see also CALICO CAT, KITTEN, PERSIAN CAT, PUSSYCAT, SIAMESE CAT, TOMCAT **2** a wild animal of the cat family: *the big cats* (= lions, TIGERS, etc.). ⊃ see also FAT CAT, FRAIDY CAT, WILDCAT noun
IDM **be the cat's ˈwhiskers/pyˈjamas** (old-fashioned, informal) to be the best thing, person, idea, etc: *He thinks he's the cat's whiskers* (= he has a high opinion of himself). **let the ˈcat out of the bag** to tell a secret carelessly or by mistake: *I wanted it to be a surprise, but my sister let the cat out of the bag.* **like a ˌcat on a hot tin ˈroof** (BrE also **like a ˌcat on hot ˈbricks**) very nervous: *She was like a cat on a hot tin roof before her driving test.* **like a ˌcat that's got the ˈcream** (BrE) (US **like the ˌcat that got/ate/swallowed the canˈary**) very pleased with yourself SYN smug **look like sth the ˌcat brought/dragged ˈin** (informal) (of a person) to look dirty and untidy **not have/stand a cat in ˈhell's chance (of doing sth)** (informal) to have no chance at all **play (a game of) ˌcat and ˈmouse with sb** | **play a ˌcat-and-ˈmouse game with sb** to play a cruel game with sb in your power by changing your behaviour very often, so that they become nervous and do not know what to expect **put/set the cat among the ˈpigeons** (BrE) to say or do sth that is likely to cause trouble **when the cat's aˈway, the mice will ˈplay** (saying) people enjoy themselves more and behave with greater freedom when the person in charge of them is not there ⊃ more at CURIOSITY, HERD v., RAIN v., ROOM n., WAY n.

**ca·tab·ol·ism** /kəˈtæbəlɪzəm/ noun [U] (biology) the process by which chemical structures are broken down and energy is released

**cata·clysm** /ˈkætəklɪzəm/ noun (formal) a sudden disaster or a violent event that causes change, for example a flood or a war ▶ **cata·clys·mic** /ˌkætəˈklɪzmɪk/ adj. [usually before noun]

**cata·combs** /ˈkætəkuːmz; NAmE -koʊmz/ noun [pl.] a series of underground tunnels used for burying dead people, especially in ancient times

**Cata·lan** /ˈkætəlæn/ noun, adj.
■ noun **1** [U] a language spoken in Catalonia, Andorra, the Balearic Islands and parts of southern France **2** [C] a person who was born in or who lives in Catalonia
■ adj. connected with Catalonia, its people, its language or its culture

**cata·lepsy** /ˈkætəlepsi/ noun [U] (medical) a condition in which sb's body becomes stiff and they become unconscious for a short time ▶ **cata·lep·tic** /ˌkætəˈleptɪk/ adj. [only before noun]

**cata·logue** (US also **cata·log**) /ˈkætəlɒg; NAmE -lɔːg/ noun, verb
■ noun **1** a complete list of items, for example of things that people can look at or buy: *a mail-order catalogue* (= a book showing goods for sale to be sent to people's homes) ◊ *to consult the library catalogue* ◊ *An illustrated catalogue accompanies the exhibition.* ◊ *an on-line catalogue* ⊃ see also BACK CATALOGUE **2** a long series of things that happen (usually bad things): *a catalogue of disasters/errors/misfortunes*
■ verb **1** ~ sth to arrange a list of things in order in a catalogue; to record sth in a catalogue **2** ~ sth to give a list of things connected with a particular person, event, etc: *Interviews with the refugees catalogue a history of discrimination and violence.*

**cata·lyse** (BrE) (NAmE **cata·lyze**) /ˈkætəlaɪz/ verb ~ sth (chemistry) to make a chemical reaction happen faster ▶ **cata·lysis** /kəˈtæləsɪs/ noun [U]: *the catalysis of organic reactions*

**cata·lyst** /ˈkætəlɪst/ noun **1** (chemistry) a substance that makes a chemical reaction happen faster without being changed itself ⊃ WORDFINDER NOTE at CHEMISTRY **2** ~ (for sth) a person or thing that causes a change: *I see my role as being a catalyst for change.*

**cata·lytic** /ˌkætəˈlɪtɪk/ adj. [only before noun] (chemistry) causing a chemical reaction to happen faster: *catalytic processes*

**ˌcatalytic conˈverter** noun a device used in the EXHAUST system of vehicles to reduce the damage caused to the environment

**cata·ma·ran** /ˌkætəməˈræn/ noun a fast sailing boat with two HULLS ⊃ compare TRIMARAN

**cata·pult** /ˈkætəpʌlt/ noun, verb
■ noun **1** (BrE) (NAmE **sling-shot**) a stick that has the shape of a Y with a rubber band attached to it, used by children for shooting

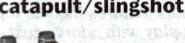
catapult/slingshot

stones **2** a weapon used in the past to throw heavy stones **3** a machine used for sending planes up into the air from a ship
- **verb** [T, I] to throw sb/sth suddenly and violently through the air; to be thrown suddenly and violently through the air: ~ **(sb/sth) + adv./prep.** *She was catapulted out of the car as it hit the wall.* ◊ *(figurative) The movie catapulted him to international stardom.*

**cat·ar·act** /ˈkætərækt/ *noun* **1** a medical condition that affects the LENS of the eye so that you gradually lose your sight **2** (*literary*) a large, steep WATERFALL

**ca·tarrh** /kəˈtɑː(r)/ *noun* [U] thick liquid (called PHLEGM) that you have in your nose and throat because, for example, you have a cold

**ca·tas·trophe** /kəˈtæstrəfi/ *noun* **1** a sudden event that causes many people to suffer SYN **disaster**: *Early warnings of rising water levels prevented another major catastrophe.* **2** an event that causes one person or a group of people to suffer, or that makes difficulties: *The attempt to expand the business was a catastrophe for the firm.* ◊ *We've had a few catastrophes with the food for the party.* ▶ **cata·stroph·ic** /ˌkætəˈstrɒfɪk; *NAmE* -ˈstrɑːf-/ *adj.* SYN **disastrous**: *catastrophic effects/losses/results* ◊ *(US) a catastrophic illness* (= one that costs a very large amount to treat) **cata·stroph·ic·al·ly** /-kli/ *adv.*

**cata·to·nia** /ˌkætəˈtəʊniə/ *noun* [U] (*medical*) a condition resulting from a mental illness, especially SCHIZOPHRENIA, in which a person does not move for long periods

**cata·ton·ic** /ˌkætəˈtɒnɪk; *NAmE* -ˈtɑːn-/ *adj.* (*medical*) not able to move or show any reaction to things because of illness, shock, etc.

**ˈcat burglar** *noun* a thief who climbs up the outside of a building in order to enter it and steal sth

**cat·call** /ˈkætkɔːl/ *noun* [usually pl.] a noise or shout expressing anger at or criticism of sb who is speaking or performing in public

**catch** 🅞 🄰🄰 /kætʃ; *NAmE also* ketʃ/ *verb, noun*
- **verb** (**caught, caught** /kɔːt/)
- **HOLD 1** 🅠 [T, I] ~ **(sth/sb)** to stop and hold a moving object or person, especially in your hands: *She managed to catch the keys as they fell.* ◊ *I caught him when he fell.* ◊ *The dog caught the stick in its mouth.* ◊ '*Throw me over that towel, will you?' 'OK. Catch!'* **2** 🅰🄰 [T] ~ **sth** to hold a liquid when it falls: *The roof was leaking and I had to use a bucket to catch the drips.* **3** [T] ~ **sb/sth (+ adv./prep.)** to take hold of sb/sth: *He caught hold of her arm as she tried to push past him.* ◊ *He caught her up in his arms.* ◊ *She caught the bar with both hands as she fell.*
- **BUS/TRAIN/PLANE 4** 🅰🄰 [T] ~ **sth** to be in time for a bus, train, plane, etc. and get on it: *to catch a bus/train/flight* ◊ *We caught the 12.15 from Oxford.*
- **CAPTURE 5** 🅠 [T] ~ **sb/sth** to capture a person or an animal that tries or would try to escape: *The murderer was never caught.* ◊ *Our cat is hopeless at catching mice.* ◊ *How many fish did you catch?*
- **ILLNESS 6** 🅱🄱 [T] to get an illness: ~ **sth** *to catch measles* ◊ ~ **sth from sb** *I think I must have caught this cold from you.*
- **INTEREST 7** 🅱🄱 [T] ~ **sb's attention, imagination, interest, etc.** if sth **catches** your attention, etc., you notice it and feel interested in it: *A sign on the wall caught my attention.*
- **NOTICE 8** 🅱🄱 [T] ~ **sth** to notice sth only for a moment: *She caught sight of a car in the distance.* ◊ *He caught a glimpse of himself in the mirror.* ◊ *I caught a look of surprise on her face.* ◊ *He caught a whiff of her perfume.*
- **HEAR/UNDERSTAND 9** 🅱🄱 [T] ~ **sth** to hear or understand sth: *Sorry, I didn't quite catch what you said.*
- **SB DOING STH 10** 🅱🄱 [T] to find or discover sb doing sth, especially sth wrong: ~ **sb doing sth** *I caught him smoking in the bathroom.* ◊ *You wouldn't catch me working* (= I would never work) *on a Sunday!* ~ **yourself doing sth** *She caught herself wondering whether she had made a mistake.* ◊ ~ **sb + adv./prep.** *He was caught with bomb-making equipment in his home.* ◊ *Mark walked in and caught them at it* (= in the act of doing sth wrong) ◊ *thieves caught in the act* ◊ *You've caught me at a bad time* (= at a time when I am busy).

- **BE IN TIME 11** [T] ~ **sb/sth** to be in time to do sth, talk to sb, etc.: *I caught him just as he was leaving the building.* ◊ *I was hoping to catch you at home* (= to see you at home when you were there). ◊ *The illness can be treated provided it's caught* (= discovered) *early enough.* ◊ (*BrE*) *to catch the post* (= post letters before the box is emptied) ◊ (*BrE, informal*) *Bye for now! I'll catch you later* (= speak to you again later).
- **SEE/HEAR 12** [T] ~ **sth** (*informal, especially NAmE*) to see or hear sth; to attend sth: *Let's eat now and maybe we could catch a movie later.* ⊃ SYNONYMS AT SEE
- **HAPPEN UNEXPECTEDLY 13** [T] ~ **sb** to happen unexpectedly and put sb in a difficult situation: *His arrival caught me by surprise.* ◊ *She got caught in a thunderstorm.*
- **BECOME STUCK 14** [I, T] to become stuck in or on sth; to make sth become stuck: ~ **(in/on sth)** *Her dress caught on a nail.* ◊ ~ **sth (in/on sth)** *He caught his thumb in the door.*
- **HIT 15** [T] to hit sb/sth: ~ **sb/sth + adv./prep.** *The stone caught him on the side of the head.* ◊ ~ **sb a blow + adv./prep.** *She caught him a blow on the chin.*
- **BURN 16** [T, I] ~ **(fire)** to begin to burn: *The wooden rafters caught fire.* ◊ *These logs are wet: they won't catch.*
- **LIGHT 17** [T] ~ **sth** if sth **catches** the light or the light **catches** it, the light shines on it and makes it shine too: *The knife gleamed as it caught the light.*
- **THE SUN 18** [T] ~ **the sun** (*informal*) if you **catch the sun**, you become red or brown because of spending time in the sun
- **SHOW ACCURATELY 19** [T] ~ **sth** to show or describe sth accurately SYN **capture**: *The artist has caught her smile perfectly.* ◊ *Cameras caught Jessica headed to a photo shoot downtown.*
- **IN CRICKET 20** [T] ~ **sb** to make a player unable to continue BATTING by catching the ball they have hit before it touches the ground

**IDM** **be/get caught in the ˈmiddle** to be involved in an argument or fight between two other people or groups **catch your ˈbreath 1** to stop breathing for a moment because of fear, shock, etc. **2** to start to be able to breathe normally again after running or doing exercise that makes you tired **catch your ˈdeath (of ˈcold)** (*old-fashioned, informal*) to catch a very bad cold **catch sb's ˈeye** to attract sb's attention: *Can you catch the waiter's eye?* **ˌcatch ˈit** (*BrE*) (*NAmE* **catch ˈhell, get ˈit**) (*informal*) to be punished or spoken to angrily about sth: *If your dad finds out you'll really catch it!* **catch sb ˈnapping** to get an advantage over sb by doing sth when they are not expecting it and not ready for it **catch sb on the ˈhop** (*informal*) to surprise sb by doing sth when they are not expecting it and not ready for it **catch sb red-ˈhanded** to catch sb in the act of doing sth wrong or committing a crime **catch sb with their ˈpants down** (*BrE also* **catch sb with their ˈtrousers down**) (*informal*) to arrive or do sth when sb is not expecting it and not ready, especially when they are in an embarrassing situation ⊃ *more at* BACK *adj.*, BALANCE *n.*, CLEFT *adj.*, EARLY *adj.*, FANCY *n.*, RAW *n.*, ROCK *n.*, SHORT *adv.*

**PHRV** **ˈcatch at sth** to touch sth or get hold of sth, especially as it goes past: *Twigs caught at her hair as she pushed through the bushes.* **ˌcatch ˈon** to become popular or fashionable: *He invented a new game, but it never really caught on.* **ˌcatch ˈon (to sth)** (*informal*) to understand sth: *He is very quick to catch on to things.* **ˌcatch sb ˈout 1** to surprise sb and put them in a difficult position: *Many investors were caught out by the fall in share prices.* **2** to show that sb does not know much or is doing sth wrong: *They tried to catch her out with a difficult question.* **ˌcatch ˈup on sth 1** to spend extra time doing sth because you have not done it earlier: *I have a lot of work to catch up on.* **2** (*also* **ˌcatch ˈup**) to find out about things that have happened: *We spent the evening catching up (on each other's news).* **be/get ˌcaught ˈup in sth** to become involved in sth, especially when you do not want to be: *Innocent passers-by got caught up in the riots.* **ˌcatch ˈup (with sb)** (*BrE also* **ˌcatch sb ˈup**) **1** to reach sb who is ahead of you by going faster: *Go on ahead. I'll catch up with you.* ◊ *I'll catch you up.* **2** to reach the same level or standard as sb who was better or more advanced: *After missing a term through* *illness,* he had to work hard to **catch up** with the others. **ˌcatch ˈup with sb 1** to finally start to cause problems for sb after they have managed to avoid this for some time: *She was terrified that one day her past problems would* **catch up** *with her.* **2** if the police or authorities **catch up with** sb, they find and punish them after some time: *The law caught up with him years later when he had moved to Spain.*

■ **noun**
- **OF BALL 1** [C] an act of catching sth, for example a ball: *to make a catch*
- **AMOUNT CAUGHT 2** [C] the total amount of things that are caught: *a huge catch of fish*
- **FASTENING 3** [C] a device used for fastening sth: *a catch on the door* ◊ *I can't open the catch on this bracelet.* ⊃ see also SAFETY CATCH
- **DIFFICULTY 4** [C, usually sing.] (*informal*) a hidden difficulty or disadvantage: *All that money for two hours' work— what's the catch?*
- **CHILD'S GAME 5** [U] a child's game in which two people throw a ball to each other
- **PERSON 6** [sing.] (*old-fashioned*) a person that other people see as a good person to marry, employ, etc.

IDM **(a) catch-22 | a catch-22 situation** (*informal*) a difficult situation from which there is no escape because you need to do one thing before doing a second, but you need to do the second thing before you can do the first: *I can't get a job because I haven't got anywhere to live but I can't afford a place to live until I get a job—it's a catch-22 situation.*

**ˈcatch-all** *noun* **1** (*especially NAmE*) a thing for holding many small objects **2** a group or description that includes different things and that does not state clearly what is included or not ▸ **ˈcatch-all** *adj.* [only before noun]: *a catch-all phrase/term*

**catch·er** /ˈkætʃə(r); NAmE also ˈketʃ-/ *noun* **1** (in baseball) the player who stands behind the BATTER and catches the ball if he or she does not hit it **2** (usually in compounds) a person or thing that catches sth: *a rat catcher*

**catch·ing** /ˈkætʃɪŋ; NAmE also ˈketʃ-/ *adj.* [not before noun] **1** (of a disease) easily caught by one person from another SYN **infectious 2** (of an emotion or a mood) passing quickly from one person to another SYN **infectious**: *Try to be as enthusiastic as possible (enthusiasm is catching)!* ⊃ see also EYE-CATCHING

**catch·ment area** /ˈkætʃmənt eəriə; NAmE er-; ˈketʃ-/ *noun* **1** the area from which a school takes its students, a hospital its patients, etc. **2** (*also* **catch·ment**) (*specialist*) the area from which rain flows into a particular river or lake

**catch·phrase** /ˈkætʃfreɪz; NAmE also ˈketʃ-/ *noun* a popular phrase that is connected with the actor, politician or other well-known person who used it and made it famous

**ˈcatch-up** *noun* **1** [U] the act of trying to reach the same level or standard as sb who is ahead of you: *It was a month of catch-up for them.* **2** [C, usually sing.] an occasion when two or more people meet to discuss what has happened since the last time they met: *We must get together for a catch-up.* ◊ *I have a catch-up meeting with my manager at two.* **3** [U] a service that allows you to watch television programmes on a computer or a special television after the time when they were originally broadcast: *catch-up TV*

IDM **play ˈcatch-up** to try to equal sb that you are competing against in a sport or game or in business: *After our bad start to the season we were always playing catch-up.*

**catch·word** /ˈkætʃwɜːd; NAmE -wɜːrd, ˈketʃ-/ *noun* a word or phrase that is used to express a particular idea, especially in order to get people's attention: *In education, 'quality' is the catchword.*

**catchy** /ˈkætʃi; NAmE also ˈketʃi/ *adj.* (*informal*) (**catch·ier**, **catchi·est**) (of music or the words of an advertisement) pleasant and easily remembered: *a catchy tune/slogan*

**ˈcat door** (*NAmE*) (*BrE* **ˈcat flap**) *noun* a hole cut in the bottom of the door to a house, covered by a piece of plastic that moves freely, so a pet cat can go in and out

**cat·ech·ism** /ˈkætəkɪzəm/ *noun* [usually sing.] a set of questions and answers that are used for teaching people about the beliefs of the Christian religion

**cat·egor·ic·al** /ˌkætəˈɡɒrɪkl; NAmE -ˈɡɔːr-/ *adj.* [usually before noun] (*formal*) expressed clearly and in a way that shows that you are very sure about what you are saying: *to make a categorical statement* ◊ *to give a categorical assurance* ▸ **cat·egor·ic·al·ly** /-kli/ *adv.*: *He categorically rejected our offer.*

**cat·egor·ize** W (*BrE also* **-ise**) /ˈkætəɡəraɪz/ *verb* to put people or things into groups according to what type they are SYN **classify**: **~ sb/sth** *Participants were categorized according to age.* ◊ **~ sb/sth as sth** *His latest work cannot be categorized as either a novel or an autobiography.* ▸ **cat·egor·iza·tion**, **-isa·tion** /ˌkætəɡəraɪˈzeɪʃn; NAmE -rəˈz-/ *noun* [U, C]

**cat·egory** /ˈkætəɡəri; NAmE -ɡɔːri/ *noun* (*pl.* **-ies**) a group of people or things with particular features in common SYN **class**: *Students over 25 fall into a different category.* ◊ *The results can be divided into three broad categories.*

**cater** /ˈkeɪtə(r)/ *verb* [I, T] to provide food and drinks for a social event: (*BrE*) **~ for sb/sth** *Most of our work now involves catering for weddings.* ◊ (*BrE and NAmE*) **~ sth** *Who will be catering the wedding?*

PHRV **ˈcater for sb/sth** to provide the things that a particular person or situation needs or wants: *The class caters for all ability ranges.* **ˈcater to sb/sth** to provide the things that a particular type of person wants, especially things that you do not approve of: *They only publish novels which cater to the mass market.*

**cater·er** /ˈkeɪtərə(r)/ *noun* a person or company whose job is to provide food and drinks at a business meeting or for a special occasion such as a wedding

**cater·ing** /ˈkeɪtərɪŋ/ *noun* [U] the work of providing food and drinks for meetings or social events: *Who did the catering for your son's wedding?* ⊃ see also SELF-CATERING

**cat·er·pil·lar** /ˈkætəpɪlə(r); NAmE -tərp-/ *noun* a small creature like a WORM with legs that develops into a BUTTERFLY or MOTH (= flying insects with large, sometimes brightly coloured, wings). Caterpillars eat the leaves of plants. ⊃ VISUAL VOCAB page V3

**cat·er·waul** /ˈkætəwɔːl; NAmE -tərw-/ *verb* [I] to make the loud unpleasant noise that is typical of a cat

**cat·fight** /ˈkætfaɪt/ *noun* (*informal*) a fight between women

**cat·fish** /ˈkætfɪʃ/ *noun, verb*
■ *noun* (*pl.* **cat·fish**) **1** a large fish with long stiff hairs, like a cat's WHISKERS, around its mouth. There are several types of catfish, most of which are FRESHWATER fish. **2** (*US, informal*) a person who pretends to be sb else, usually sb who does not really exist, on SOCIAL MEDIA in order to trick sb into having a relationship online
■ *verb* **1** [I] to fish for catfish: *go catfishing I used to go catfishing with my dad.* **2** [T, usually passive] (*US, informal*) to pretend to be sb else on SOCIAL MEDIA in order to trick sb into having a relationship online: **be/get catfished** *My cousin got catfished by a guy she met online.*

**ˈcat flap** (*BrE*) (*NAmE* **ˈcat door**) *noun* a hole cut in the bottom of the door to a house, covered by a piece of hard plastic that moves freely, so a pet cat can go in and out

**cat·gut** /ˈkætɡʌt/ (*also* **gut**) *noun* [U] thin, strong string made from animals' INTESTINES and used in making musical instruments

**cath·ar·sis** /kəˈθɑːsɪs; NAmE -ˈθɑːr-/ *noun* [U, C] (*pl.* **cath·arses** /kəˈθɑːsiːz; NAmE -ˈθɑːr-/) (*specialist*) the process of releasing strong feelings, for example through plays or other artistic activities, as a way of providing relief from anger, mental pain, etc. ▸ **cath·ar·tic** /kəˈθɑːtɪk; NAmE -ˈθɑːrt-/ *adj.*: *It was a cathartic experience.*

**cath·edral** /kəˈθiːdrəl/ *noun* the main church of a district, under the care of a BISHOP (= a priest of high rank): *St Paul's Cathedral* ◊ (*BrE*) *a cathedral city*

**Cath·er·ine wheel** /ˈkæθrɪn wiːl/ (especially BrE) (NAmE usually **pin·wheel**) noun a round flat FIREWORK that turns around in circles when lit

**cath·eter** /ˈkæθətə(r)/ noun a thin tube that is put into the body in order to remove liquid such as URINE

**cath·ode** /ˈkæθəʊd/ noun (specialist) the ELECTRODE in an electrical device where REDUCTION occurs; the negative ELECTROLYTIC cell and the positive electrode in a battery ⇒ compare ANODE

**ˌcathode ˈray tube** noun a VACUUM tube that was used in the past inside a television or computer screen, etc., and from which a stream of ELECTRONS produced images on the screen

**Cath·olic** /ˈkæθlɪk/ noun = ROMAN CATHOLIC: They're Catholics. ▸ **Cath·oli·cism** /kəˈθɒlɪsɪzəm/; NAmE -ˈθɑːl-/ noun [U] = ROMAN CATHOLICISM

**cath·olic** /ˈkæθlɪk/ adj. **1** **Catholic** = ROMAN CATHOLIC: Are they Catholic or Protestant? ◊ a Catholic church **2** (often **Catholic**) (specialist) connected with all Christians or the whole Christian Church **3** (formal) including many or most things: to have catholic tastes (= to like many different things)

**cat·ion** /ˈkætaɪən/ noun (chemistry, physics) an ION with a positive electrical CHARGE ⇒ compare ANION

**cat·kin** /ˈkætkɪn/ noun a long thin hanging bunch, or short standing group, of soft flowers on the branches of trees such as the WILLOW ⇒ VISUAL VOCAB page V6

**cat·mint** /ˈkætmɪnt/ (also **cat·nip** /ˈkætnɪp/) noun [U] a plant that has white flowers with purple spots, leaves covered with small hairs and a smell that is attractive to cats

**cat·nap** /ˈkætnæp/ noun a short sleep ▸ **cat·nap** verb (-pp-) [I]

**cat-o'-nine-tails** /ˌkæt ə ˈnaɪn teɪlz/ noun [sing.] a WHIP made of nine strings with KNOTS in them, that was used to punish prisoners in the past

**CAT scan** /ˈkæt skæn/ (also **CT scan**) noun a medical examination that uses a computer to produce an image of the inside of sb's body from X-RAY or ULTRASOUND pictures

**ˌcat's ˈcradle** noun **1** [U] a game in which you wrap string around the fingers of both hands to make different patterns **2** [C] a pattern made with string in a game of cat's cradle

cat's cradle

**Cats-eye™** /ˈkætsaɪ/ noun (BrE) one of a line of small objects that are fixed into a road and that reflect a car's lights in order to guide traffic at night

**cat·suit** /ˈkætsuːt/ noun a piece of women's clothing that fits closely and covers the body and legs

**cat·sup** (US) /ˈkætsʌp/ noun [U] = KETCHUP

**cat·tery** /ˈkætəri/ noun (pl. -ies) a place where people can pay to leave their cats to be cared for while they are away

**cat·tle** ⒵⁺ Ⓒ¹ /ˈkætl/ noun [pl.] cows and BULLS that are kept as farm animals for their milk or meat: a herd of cattle ◊ twenty head of cattle (= twenty cows) ◊ dairy/beef cattle ⇒ see also HIGHLAND CATTLE

**cat·tle duff·ing** /ˈkætl dʌfɪŋ/ noun (AustralE) the stealing of cows

**ˈcattle grid** (BrE) (NAmE **ˈcattle guard**) noun metal bars that are placed over a hole that has been made in the road. Cars can pass over the metal bars but animals such as sheep and cows cannot.

**catty** /ˈkæti/ adj. (informal) (**cat·tier**, **cat·ti·est**) (of a woman) saying unkind things about other people SYN bitchy, spiteful: a catty comment ▸ **cat·ti·ness** noun [U]

**cat·walk** /ˈkætwɔːk/ noun **1** (also **run·way** especially in NAmE) the long stage that models walk on during a fashion show **2** a narrow platform for people to walk on, for example along the outside of a building or a bridge

233

**cause**

**Cau·ca·sian** /kɔːˈkeɪʒn/ noun a member of any of the races of people who have pale skin ▸ **Cau·ca·sian** adj.

**cau·cus** /ˈkɔːkəs/ noun, verb
▪ noun (especially NAmE) **1** a meeting of the members or leaders of a political party to choose candidates or to decide policy; the members or leaders of a political party as a group ⇒ WORDFINDER NOTE at CONGRESS **2** a group of people with similar interests, often within a larger organization or political party: the Congressional Black Caucus
▪ verb [I] (NAmE) to meet in a caucus or other group to discuss sth

**caught** /kɔːt/ past tense, past part. of CATCH ⇒ see also LINE-CAUGHT

**caul·dron** (US also **cal·dron**) /ˈkɔːldrən/ noun a large deep pot for boiling liquids or cooking food over a fire: a witch's cauldron ◊ (figurative) The stadium was a seething cauldron of emotion.

**cauli·flower** /ˈkɒliflaʊə(r)/; NAmE ˈkɑːl-/ noun [U, C] a vegetable with green leaves around a large hard white head of flowers: Do you like cauliflower? ◊ two cauliflowers ⇒ VISUAL VOCAB page V5

**ˌcauliflower ˈcheese** (BrE) (NAmE **ˌcauliflower with ˈcheese**) noun [U] a hot dish of cauliflower cooked and served in a cheese sauce

**caulk** /kɔːk/ verb ~ sth to fill the holes in sth, especially a ship, with a substance that keeps out water

**causal** Ⓦ /ˈkɔːzl/ adj. **1** (formal) connected with the relationship between two things, where one causes the other to happen: the causal relationship between poverty and disease **2** ~ **conjunction/connective** (grammar) a word such as because that introduces a statement about the cause of sth ▸ **caus·al·ly** /-zəli/ adv.: Are the two factors causally connected?

**caus·al·ity** /kɔːˈzæləti/ (also **caus·ation**) noun [U] (formal) the relationship between sth that happens and the reason for it happening; the principle that nothing can happen without a cause

**caus·ation** Ⓦ /kɔːˈzeɪʃn/ noun [U] (formal) **1** the process of one event causing or producing another event **2** = CAUSALITY

**causa·tive** /ˈkɔːzətɪv/ adj. **1** (formal) acting as the cause of sth: Smoking is a causative factor in several major diseases. **2** (grammar) a **ˈcausative verb** expresses a cause, for example blacken, which means 'to cause to become black'

▼ **LANGUAGE BANK**

**cause**

X causes Y

• Childhood obesity can **cause**/**lead to** long-term health problems.
• Changes in lifestyle and diet over the last twenty years have **caused**/**led to**/**resulted in** a sharp increase in childhood obesity.
• Several factors, including changes in diet and lifestyle, **have contributed to** the increase in childhood obesity.
• Research suggests that fast food and soft drinks directly **contribute to** childhood obesity.
• Genetics, lifestyle and diet **are** all important **factors** in cases of childhood obesity.
• Even small changes in lifestyle and diet can **bring about** significant weight loss.
⇒ LANGUAGE BANK at BECAUSE OF, CONSEQUENTLY, THEREFORE

**cause** ⒷⒶ² /kɔːz/ noun, verb
▪ noun **1** Ⓐ² [C] ~ (of sth) the person or thing that makes sth happen: Unemployment is a major cause of poverty. ◊ Drinking and driving is one of the most common causes of traffic accidents. ◊ It was impossible to determine the cause of death. ◊ There was discussion about the fire and its likely cause. **2** Ⓐ² [U] a reason for having particular feelings or behaving in a particular way: ~ (for sth) There

---

Ⓞ Oxford Phrasal Academic Lexicon (OPAL) written and spoken word lists | Ⓦ OPAL written word list | Ⓢ OPAL spoken word list

# ¹cause 234

is no **cause** for concern. ◊ *The food was excellent—I had no cause for complaint.* ◊ **with/without ~** *to be absent without good cause* (= a good reason) ⊃ see also PROBABLE CAUSE **3** ⚹ B2 [C] an organization or idea that people support or fight for: *Animal welfare campaigners raised £70 000 for their cause last year.* ◊ *a good/worthy cause* (= an organization that does good work, such as a charity) ◊ *She has long championed the cause of civil liberties.* ⊃ see also LOST CAUSE **4** [C] (*law*) a case that goes to court

**IDM** **be for/in a good ˈcause** worth doing, because it is helping other people **in the cause of sth** in order to support or defend sth: *He gave his life in the cause of freedom.* ⊃ more at COMMON *adj*.

■ *verb* ⚹ A2 to make sth happen, especially sth bad or unpleasant; to make sb do sth: **~ sth** *Do they know what caused the fire?* ◊ *deaths caused by dangerous driving* ◊ **~ sth for sb/sth** *The drought is causing problems for many farmers.* ◊ **~ sth to sth/sb** *The earthquake caused widespread damage to property.* ◊ **~ sb sth** *The project is still causing him a lot of problems.* ◊ **~ sth/sb to do sth** *The poor harvest caused prices to rise sharply.*

**ˈcause** *conj*. = COS¹

**cause célèbre** /ˌkɔːz seˈlebrə/ *noun* (*from French*) (*pl*. **causes célèbres** /ˌkɔːz seˈlebrə/) an issue that attracts a lot of attention and is supported by a lot of people

**cause·way** /ˈkɔːzweɪ/ *noun* a raised road or path across water or wet ground

**caus·tic** /ˈkɔːstɪk/ *adj*. **1** (of a chemical substance) able to destroy or DISSOLVE (= remove or destroy by a chemical process) other substances **SYN** corrosive **2** critical in a bitter or SARCASTIC way **SYN** scathing: *caustic comments/wit* ▶ **caus·tic·al·ly** /-kli/ *adv*.

**caustic ˈsoda** *noun* [U] a chemical used in making paper and soap

**caut·er·ize** (*BrE also* -ise) /ˈkɔːtəraɪz/ *verb* **~ sth** (*medical*) to burn a wound, using a chemical or heat, in order to stop the loss of blood or to prevent infection

**cau·tion** ⚹ C1 /ˈkɔːʃn/ *noun, verb*
■ *noun* **1** ⚹ C1 [U] care that you take in order to avoid danger or mistakes; the fact of not taking any risks: *extreme/great caution* ◊ **with ~** *Statistics should be treated with caution.* ⊃ SYNONYMS at CARE **2** [C] (*BrE*) a warning that is given by the police to sb who has committed a crime that is not too serious: *As a first offender, she got off with a caution.* **3** [U, C] (*formal*) a warning or a piece of advice about a possible danger or risk: *a word/note of caution* ◊ *Some cautions must be mentioned—for example good tools are essential to the job well.*
**IDM** **throw/cast caution to the ˈwind(s)** to stop caring about how dangerous sth might be; to start taking risks
■ *verb* **1** [I, T] to warn sb about the possible dangers or problems of sth: **~ against (doing) sth** *I would caution against getting too involved.* ◊ **~ sb against/about (doing) sth** *She cautioned him against making a hasty decision.* ◊ **~ (sb) that …** *The government cautioned that pay increases could lead to job losses.* ◊ **~ sb to do sth** *Employees were cautioned to be careful about what they said to people outside the company.* ◊ **~ (sb) + speech** *'I'd take care if I were you,' she cautioned (him).* **2** [T] **~ sb** (*BrE, law*) to warn sb officially that anything they say may be used as evidence against them in court: *Suspects must be cautioned before any questions are asked.* **3** [T, usually passive] (*BrE, law*) to warn sb officially that they will be punished if they do sth wrong or illegal again: **be cautioned (for sth)** *She wasn't sent to the juvenile court; instead she was cautioned.*

**cau·tion·ary** /ˈkɔːʃənəri; *NAmE* -neri/ *adj*. giving advice or a warning: *a cautionary tale about the problems of buying a computer* ◊ *In her conclusion, the author sounds a cautionary note.*

**cau·tious** ⚹ C1 /ˈkɔːʃəs/ *adj*. being careful about what you say or do, especially to avoid danger or mistakes; not taking any risks: *The government has been cautious in its response to the report.* ◊ *They've taken a very cautious approach.* ◊ *They expressed cautious optimism about a solution to the crisis.* ◊ **~ about sb/sth** | **~ about doing sth** *He was very cautious about committing himself to anything.* ▶ **cau·tious·ly** *adv*.: *She looked cautiously around and then walked away from the house.* ◊ *I'm cautiously optimistic.* **cau·tious·ness** *noun* [U]

▼ **WHICH WORD?**

**cautious / careful**
- A **cautious** person is nervous that something may be dangerous or unwise, so they only do it very slowly or after a lot of thought. (opposite = **rash**)
- A **careful** person is not nervous but does take extra care to make sure that everything is correct or nothing goes wrong. (opposite = **careless**)
- Notice also:
*Be careful/Take care when you drive on icy roads.*
*Caution/Warning—thin ice.*

**cava** /ˈkɑːvə/ *noun* [U, C] a type of SPARKLING white wine (= with bubbles) from Spain

**cav·al·cade** /ˌkævlˈkeɪd, ˈkævlkeɪd/ *noun* a line of people on horses or in vehicles forming part of a ceremony

**Cava·lier** /ˌkævəˈlɪə(r); *NAmE* -ˈlɪr/ *noun* a supporter of the king in the English Civil War (1642–49) ⊃ compare ROUNDHEAD

**cava·lier** /ˌkævəˈlɪə(r); *NAmE* -ˈlɪr/ *adj*. [usually before noun] not caring enough about sth important or about the feelings of other people: *The government takes a cavalier attitude to the problems of prison overcrowding.* ▶ **cava·lier·ly** *adv*.

**cav·alry** /ˈkævlri/ *noun* (*usually* **the cavalry**) [sing. + sing./pl. v.] (in the past) the part of the army that fought on horses; the part of the modern army that uses ARMOURED vehicles

**cave** ⚹ B2 /keɪv/ *noun, verb*
■ *noun* ⚹ B2 a large hole in the side of a hill or CLIFF or under the ground: *the mouth* (= the entrance) *of the cave* ◊ *a cave-dweller* (= a person who lives in a cave) ⊃ see also ALADDIN'S CAVE
■ *verb*
**PHRV** **cave ˈin (on sb/sth)** (of a roof, wall, etc.) to fall down and towards the centre: *The ceiling suddenly caved in on top of them.* ⊃ related noun CAVE-IN **cave ˈin (to sth)** to finally do what sb wants after you have been strongly opposing them: *The president is unlikely to cave in to demands for a public inquiry.* ⊃ see also CAVING

**cav·eat** /ˈkæviæt/ *noun* (*from Latin, formal*) a warning that particular things need to be considered before sth can be done

**cav·eat emp·tor** /ˌkæviæt ˈemptɔː(r)/ *noun* (*from Latin*) the principle that a person who buys sth is responsible for finding any faults in the thing they buy

**ˈcave-in** *noun* **1** the fact of sth suddenly collapsing: *The cave-in at the mine was caused by a sudden rush of water.* **2** the act of finally doing what sb wants after you have been opposing them ⊃ see also CAVE IN (TO STH) at CAVE

**cave·man** /ˈkeɪvmæn/ *noun* (*pl*. -men /-men/) **1** a person who lived in a CAVE thousands of years ago **2** (*informal*) a man who behaves in an aggressive way

**ˈcave painting** *noun* [C, U] a PREHISTORIC painting on the walls of a CAVE, often showing animals and hunting scenes

**caver** /ˈkeɪvə(r)/ (*BrE also* **pot-holer**) (*NAmE also* **spe·lunk·er**) *noun* a person who goes into CAVES under the ground as a sport or hobby ⊃ compare SPELEOLOGIST

**cav·ern** /ˈkævən; *NAmE* -vərn/ *noun* a CAVE, especially a large one

**cav·ern·ous** /ˈkævənəs; *NAmE* -vərn-/ *adj*. (*formal*) (of a room or space) very large and often empty and/or dark; like a CAVE

**cav·iar** (*also* **cavi·are**) /ˈkæviɑː(r)/ *noun* [U] the eggs of some types of fish, especially the STURGEON, that are preserved using salt and eaten as a very special and expensive type of food

**cavil** /ˈkævl/ *verb* [I] (-ll-, *US* -l-) **~ (at sth)** (*formal*) to make unnecessary complaints about sth **SYN** quibble

**cav·ing** /ˈkeɪvɪŋ/ (BrE also **pot·hol·ing**) (NAmE also **spe·lunk·ing**) noun [U] the sport or activity of going into CAVES under the ground: *He had always wanted to go caving.*

**cav·ity** /ˈkævəti/ noun (pl. **-ies**) (formal or specialist) **1** a hole or empty space inside sth solid: *the abdominal cavity* **2** a hole in a tooth ⇒ WORDFINDER NOTE at DENTIST

**ˌcavity ˈwall** noun a wall consisting of two walls with a space between them, designed to prevent heat from escaping: *cavity wall insulation*

**ca·vort** /kəˈvɔːt; NAmE -ˈvɔːrt/ verb [I] **+ adv./prep.** to jump or move around in a noisy, excited and often sexual way: *The photos showed her cavorting on the beach with her new lover.*

**caw** /kɔː/ noun the loud, unpleasant sound that is made by birds such as CROWS and ROOKS ▶ **caw** verb [I]

**cay·enne** /keɪˈen; NAmE kaɪ-/ (also **cayenne ˈpepper**) noun [U] a type of red pepper used in cooking to give a hot, spicy taste to food

**cay·man** /ˈkeɪmən/ = CAIMAN

**CB** /ˌsiː ˈbiː/ noun [U] a range of waves on a radio which people can talk to each other over short distances, especially when driving (the abbreviation for 'Citizens' Band'): *A truck driver used his CB radio to call for help.*

**CBE** /ˌsiː biː ˈiː/ noun an award given in the UK to some people for a special achievement; a person who has received this award (the abbreviation for 'Commander (of the Order) of the British Empire'): *He was made a CBE in 2019.* ⋄ *Shami Chakrabarti CBE*

**CBI** /ˌsiː biː ˈaɪ/ abbr. Confederation of British Industry (an important organization to which businesses and industries belong)

**CBS** /ˌsiː biː ˈes/ abbr. Columbia Broadcasting System (an American recording and broadcasting company that produces records, television programmes, etc.)

**CBSA** /ˌsiː biː es ˈeɪ/ abbr. Canadian Border Services Agency (the department of the Canadian government that deals with people coming into the country and with taxes on goods that are bought and sold)

**CBT** /ˌsiː biː ˈtiː/ noun [U] a type of PSYCHOTHERAPY in which you are encouraged to change negative ways of thinking about yourself and the world in order to change behaviour patterns or treat conditions such as DEPRESSION (the abbreviation for 'cognitive behavioural therapy')

**cc** /ˌsiː ˈsiː/ abbr., verb
■ abbr. **1** carbon copy (to) (used on business letters and emails to show that a copy is being sent to another person): *to Luke Peters, cc Janet Gold* **2** cubic centimetre(s): *an 850cc engine*
■ verb (**cc's, cc'ing, cc'd, cc'd** /-ˈsiːd/) **~ sth (to sb) | ~ sb (on sth)** to send sb a copy of a letter or email message that you are sending to sb else: *Her message was sent to the company president and cc'd to us.*

**CCTV** /ˌsiː siː tiː ˈviː/ abbr. CLOSED-CIRCUIT TELEVISION

**CCU** /ˌsiː siː ˈjuː/ noun **1** part of a hospital that provides INTENSIVE CARE (the abbreviation for 'critical care unit') **2** part of a hospital that provides care for people with heart conditions (the abbreviation for 'coronary care unit' or 'cardiac care unit')

**CD** 🔊 **A1** /ˌsiː ˈdiː/ noun a small disc on which sound or information is recorded. CDs can be played or read on various types of machines, including **CD players** and computers. (the abbreviation for 'compact disc'): *on ~ His albums are available on CD and online.*

**Cdr** (also **Cdr.** especially in US) abbr. (in writing) COMMANDER: *Cdr (John) Stone*

**Cdre** abbr. (in writing) = COMMODORE

**CD-ROM** /ˌsiː diː ˈrɒm; NAmE ˈrɑːm/ noun [C, U] a type of CD used with a computer on which information, sound and pictures can only be read and not written by the computer (the abbreviation for 'compact disc read-only memory'): *The software package contains 5 CD-ROMs.* ⋄ *on ~ The encyclopedia is available on CD-ROM.* ⋄ *a CD-ROM drive* (= in a computer) ⇒ compare ROM

**CD-RW** /ˌsiː diː ɑː ˈdʌbljuː; NAmE ɑːr/ noun [C, U] a CD on which information, sound and pictures can be recorded and removed more than once (the abbreviation for 'compact disc rewritable')

**CDT** /ˌsiː diː ˈtiː/ abbr. CENTRAL DAYLIGHT TIME

**CE** /ˌsiː ˈiː/ abbr. **1** (in Britain) Church of England **2** (also **C.E.** especially in US) Common Era (the period since the birth of Christ when the Christian CALENDAR starts counting years). CE can be used to give dates in the same way as AD. ⇒ compare AD, BC, BCE

**cease** 🔊+ **C1** /siːs/ verb [I, T] (formal) to stop happening or existing; to stop sth from happening or existing: *Welfare payments cease as soon as an individual starts a job.* ⋄ **~ to do sth** *You never cease to amaze me!* ⋄ **~ sth** *They voted to cease strike action immediately.* ⋄ *He ordered his men to cease fire* (= stop shooting). ⋄ **~ doing sth** *The company ceased trading in June.* ⇒ see also CESSATION **IDM** see WONDER n.

**cease·fire** /ˈsiːsfaɪə(r)/ noun a time when enemies agree to stop fighting, usually while a way is found to end the fighting permanently **SYN** truce: *a call for an immediate ceasefire* ⋄ *Observers have reported serious violations of the ceasefire.* ⇒ WORDFINDER NOTE at PEACE

**cease·less** /ˈsiːsləs/ adj. (formal) not stopping; seeming to have no end **SYN** constant, interminable ▶ **cease·less·ly** adv.

**cecum** /ˈsiːkəm/ (NAmE) (BrE **cae·cum**) noun (pl. **ceca** /-kə/) a small bag that is part of the INTESTINE, between the small and the large intestine

**cedar** /ˈsiːdə(r)/ noun **1** (also **ˈcedar tree**) [C] a tall EVERGREEN tree with wide spreading branches **2** (also **cedar·wood** /ˈsiːdəwʊd; NAmE -dərw-/) [U] the hard red wood of the cedar, which has a sweet smell

**cede** /siːd/ verb **~ sth (to sb)** (formal) to give sb control of sth or give them power, a right, etc. especially unwillingly: *Cuba was ceded by Spain to the US in 1898.* ⇒ see also CESSION

**ce·dilla** /sɪˈdɪlə/ noun the mark placed under the letter *c* in French, Portuguese, etc. to show that it is pronounced like an *s* rather than a *k*, as in *français*; a similar mark under *s* in Turkish and some other languages

**CEFR** /ˌsiː iː ef ˈɑː(r)/ abbr. Common European Framework of Reference for languages (a description of the language abilities of students at different levels of learning that can be used to help different countries to compare standards and create teaching programmes): *The course is suitable for students at CEFR level B1.*

**cei·lidh** /ˈkeɪli/ noun a social occasion with music and dancing, especially in Scotland and Ireland

**ceil·ing** 🔊 **B1** /ˈsiːlɪŋ/ noun **1** 🔊 the top inside surface of a room: *a large room with a high ceiling* ⋄ *The walls and ceiling were painted white.* **2** the highest limit or amount of sth: *price ceilings* ⇒ compare FLOOR ⇒ see also DEBT CEILING **3** (specialist) the greatest height at which a particular aircraft is able to fly ⇒ see also GLASS CEILING

**celeb** /səˈleb/ noun (informal) a celebrity

**cele·brant** /ˈselɪbrənt/ noun **1** a priest who leads a church service, especially the COMMUNION service; a person who attends a service **2** (NAmE) a person who is celebrating sth, for example at a party

**cele·brate** 🔊 **A2** /ˈselɪbreɪt/ verb **1** 🔊 **A2** [I, T] to show that a day or an event is important by doing sth special on it: *Jake's passed his exams. We're going out to celebrate.* ⋄ **~ sth** *to celebrate a birthday* ⋄ *We celebrated our 25th wedding anniversary in Florence.* ⋄ **~ (sth) with sb/sth** *He made the trip home to celebrate Christmas with his family.*

**WORDFINDER** anniversary, birthday, commemorate, festivity, jubilee, occasion, parade, party, reception

**2** [T] **~ sth** to perform a religious ceremony, especially the Christian COMMUNION service **3** [T] **~ sb/sth** (formal)

# celebrated

to praise sb/sth: *a movie celebrating the life and work of Nelson Mandela*

**cele·brated** /ˈselɪbreɪtɪd/ *adj.* famous for having good qualities: *a celebrated painter* ◊ **~ for sth** *She was celebrated for her wit and charm.*

**cele·bra·tion** 🔊 **B1** /ˌselɪˈbreɪʃn/ *noun* **1** 🔊 **B1** [C] a special event that people organize in order to celebrate sth: *The occasion was the 40th anniversary celebrations of the orchestra.* **2** 🔊 **B1** [U, C] the act of celebrating sth: *Her triumph was a cause for celebration.* ◊ **~ of sth** *The service was a celebration of his life* (= praised what he had done in his life). ◊ **in ~ of sth** *a party in celebration of their fiftieth wedding anniversary*

**cele·bra·tory** /ˌseləˈbreɪtəri; NAmE ˈseləbrətɔːri/ *adj.* celebrating sth or marking a special occasion: *a celebratory drink/dinner*

**ce·leb·rity** 🔊 **A2** /səˈlebrəti/ *noun* (*pl.* **-ies**) **1** 🔊 **A2** (*also informal* **celeb**, *informal* **sleb**) [C] a famous person: *a celebrity chef* **2** [U] the state of being famous **SYN** **fame**: *Does he find his new celebrity intruding on his private life?*

**cel·eri·ac** /səˈleriæk/ *noun* [U] a large white root vegetable that is a type of CELERY and that is eaten raw or cooked

**cel·ery** /ˈseləri/ *noun* [U] a vegetable with long light-green STEMS that are often eaten raw: *(BrE) a stick of celery* ◊ *(NAmE) a stalk of celery* ➪ **VISUAL VOCAB** page V5

**cel·esta** /səˈlestə/ (*also* **ce·leste** /səˈlest/) *noun* a small musical instrument with a keyboard, that produces a sound like bells

**ce·les·tial** /səˈlestiəl; NAmE -ˈlestʃl/ *adj.* [usually before noun] (*formal* or *literary*) of the sky or of heaven: *celestial bodies* (= the sun, moon, stars, etc.) ◊ *celestial light/music* ➪ compare TERRESTRIAL

**cel·iac** (NAmE) = COELIAC

**celi·bate** /ˈselɪbət/ *adj.*, *noun*
- *adj.* **1** not married and not having sex, especially for religious reasons: *celibate priests* **2** not having sex: *I've been celibate for the past six months.* ▶ **celi·bacy** /-bəsi/ *noun* [U]: *a vow of celibacy*
- *noun* (*formal*) a person who has chosen not to marry; a person who never has sex

**cell** 🔊 **B2** /sel/ *noun* **1** 🔊 **B2** the smallest unit of living matter that can exist on its own. All plants and animals are made up of cells: *red and white blood cells* ◊ *the nucleus of a cell* see also STEM CELL ➪ **WORDFINDER NOTE** at BIOLOGY **2** 🔊 **B2** a room for one or more prisoners in a prison or police station: **in a ~** *He spent a night in a prison cell.* ➪ see also PADDED CELL ➪ **WORDFINDER NOTE** at PRISON **3** a small room without much furniture in which a MONK or NUN lives **4** each of the small sections that together form a larger structure, for example a HONEYCOMB **5** a device for producing an electric current, for example by the action of chemicals or light: *a photoelectric cell* **6** a small group of people who work as part of a larger political organization, especially secretly: *a terrorist cell* **7** one of the small squares in a SPREADSHEET computer program in which you enter a single piece of data **8** (*especially NAmE*, *informal*) = CELL PHONE: *Call me on my cell.*

▼ **HOMOPHONES**

**cell • sell** /sel/
- **cell** *noun*: *Genes for human skin exist in every human cell.*
- **sell** *verb*: *He suggests she sell her house and go to Brazil with him.*

**cel·lar** /ˈselə(r)/ *noun* **1** an underground room often used for storing things: *a coal cellar* ➪ see also BEER CELLAR **2** = WINE CELLAR ➪ see also SALT CELLAR

**cell·ist** /ˈtʃelɪst/ *noun* a person who plays the CELLO

**cell·mate** /ˈselmeɪt/ *noun* a prisoner with whom another prisoner shares a cell

**cello** /ˈtʃeləʊ/ (*also formal* **vio·lon·cello**) *noun* (*pl.* **-os**) a musical instrument with strings, like a large VIOLIN in shape. The player sits down and holds the cello between his or her knees.

**Cel·lo·phane**™ /ˈseləfeɪn/ *noun* [U] a thin clear plastic material used for wrapping things

**ˈcell phone** (*also* **cellular ˈphone**, *informal* **cell**) (*especially NAmE*) (*BrE usually* **mobile ˈphone**, **mo·bile**) *noun* a phone that does not have wires and works by radio, and that you can carry with you and use anywhere: *cell phone users* ◊ *I talked to her on my cell phone.* ◊ *The use of cellular phones is not permitted on most aircraft.*

**cel·lu·lar** /ˈseljələ(r)/ *adj.* **1** connected with or consisting of the cells of plants or animals: *cellular structure/processes* **2** connected with a phone system that works by radio instead of wires: *a cellular network* ◊ *cellular radio* **3** (*BrE*) (of cloth) loosely WOVEN to make it feel warmer: *cellular blankets*

**cel·lu·lite** /ˈseljulaɪt/ *noun* [U] a type of fat that some people get below their skin, which stops the surface of the skin looking smooth

**cel·lu·loid** /ˈseljulɔɪd/ *noun* [U] **1** a thin clear plastic material made in sheets, used in the past for cinema film **2** (*old-fashioned*) used as a way of referring to films

**cel·lu·lose** /ˈseljuləʊs/ *noun* [U] **1** a natural substance that forms the cell walls of all plants and trees and is used in making plastics, paper, etc. **2** any COMPOUND of cellulose used in making paint, LACQUER, etc.

**Cel·sius** /ˈselsiəs/ (*also* **centi·grade**) *adj.* (*abbr.* **C**) of or using a scale of temperature in which water freezes at 0° and boils at 100°: *It will be a mild night, around nine degrees Celsius.* ◊ *the Celsius Scale* ▶ **Cel·sius** *noun* [U]: *temperatures in Celsius and Fahrenheit*

**Celt** /kelt/ *noun* **1** a member of a race of people from western Europe who settled in ancient Britain before the Romans came **2** a person whose ANCESTORS were Celts, especially one from Ireland, Wales, Scotland, Cornwall or Brittany

**Cel·tic** /ˈkeltɪk/ *adj.* connected with the CELTS or their language: *Celtic history*

**ˌCeltic ˈcross** *noun* a cross that is taller than it is wide, with a circle round the centre

**ce·ment** /sɪˈment/ *noun*, *verb*
- *noun* [U] **1** a grey powder made by burning CLAY and LIME that sets hard when it is mixed with water. Cement is used in building to stick stones and BRICKS together and to make very hard surfaces. ➪ **WORDFINDER NOTE** at CONSTRUCTION **2** the hard substance that is formed when cement becomes dry and hard: *a floor of cement* ◊ *a cement floor* ➪ see also CONCRETE *noun*, MORTAR *noun* **3** a soft substance that becomes hard when dry and is used for sticking things together or filling in holes: *dental cement* (= for filling holes in teeth) **4** (*formal*) something that joins people together in a common interest: *values that are the cement of society*
- *verb* **1** [often passive] **~ A and B (together)** to join two things together using cement, GLUE (= a sticky substance), etc. **2** **~ sth** to make a relationship, an agreement, etc. stronger **SYN** **strengthen**: *The president's visit was intended to cement the alliance between the two countries.*

**cemen·ta·tion** /ˌsiːmenˈteɪʃn/ *noun* [U] **1** (*chemistry*) the process of changing a metal by heating it together with a powder **2** (*geology*) the process of grains of sand, etc. sticking together to form SEDIMENTARY rocks

**ˈcement mixer** (*also* **ˈconcrete mixer**) *noun* a machine with a drum that holds sand, water and cement and turns to mix them together

**cem·etery** 🔊 **C1** /ˈsemətri; NAmE -teri/ *noun* (*pl.* **-ies**) an area of land used for burying dead people, especially one that is not next to a church ➪ compare CHURCHYARD, GRAVEYARD ➪ **WORDFINDER NOTE** at DIE

**ceno·taph** /ˈsenətɑːf; NAmE -tæf/ *noun* a MONUMENT built in memory of soldiers killed in war who are buried somewhere else

---

æ cat | ɑː father | e bed | ɜː fur | ə about | ɪ sit | iː see | i happy | ɒ got (*BrE*) | ɔː saw | ʌ cup | ʊ put | uː too

**cen·ser** /ˈsensə(r)/ noun a container for holding and burning INCENSE (= a substance that produces a pleasant smell), used especially during religious ceremonies

**cen·sor** /ˈsensə(r)/ noun, verb
- noun a person whose job is to examine books, films, etc. and remove parts that are considered to be offensive or a political threat
- verb [often passive] to remove the parts of a book, film, etc. that are considered to be offensive or a political threat: **be censored** *The news reports had been heavily censored.*

**cen·sori·ous** /senˈsɔːriəs/ adj. (formal) tending to criticize people or things a lot SYN **critical**

**cen·sor·ship** /ˈsensəʃɪp/ NAmE -sərʃ-/ noun [U] the act or policy of censoring books, etc: *press censorship* ◊ *The decree imposed strict censorship of the media.* ⇒ WORDFINDER NOTE at JOURNALIST

**cen·sure** /ˈsenʃə(r)/ noun, verb
- noun [U] (formal) strong criticism: *a vote of censure on the government's foreign policy*
- verb [often passive] (formal) to criticize sb severely, and often publicly, because of sth they have done SYN **rebuke**: **be censured (for sth/for doing sth)** *He was censured for leaking information to the press.*

**cen·sus** /ˈsensəs/ noun (pl. **cen·suses**) the process of officially counting sth, especially a country's population, and recording various facts

**cent** ❶ A1 /sent/ noun (abbr. **c**, **ct**) a coin and unit of money worth 1% of the main unit of money in many countries, for example of the US dollar or of the euro: *A one-minute phone call to the UK cost 10 cents.* ⇒ see also PER CENT noun ⇒ HOMOPHONES at SCENT
- IDM ▶ **put in your two ˈcents' worth** (NAmE) **put in your two ˈpennyworth, put in your two ˈpenn'orth** (informal) to give your opinion about sth, even if other people do not want to hear it

**cent.** abbr. century: *in the 20th cent.*

**cen·taur** /ˈsentɔː(r)/ noun (in ancient Greek stories) a creature with a man's head, arms and upper body on a horse's body and legs

**cen·ten·ar·ian** /ˌsentɪˈneəriən; NAmE -ˈner-/ noun a person who is 100 years old or more

**cen·ten·ary** /senˈtiːnəri; NAmE -ˈten-/ (pl. **-ies**) (especially BrE) (NAmE usually **cen·ten·nial**) noun the 100th anniversary of an event: *The club will celebrate its centenary next year.* ◊ *the centenary year* ⇒ see also BICENTENARY, TERCENTENARY

**cen·ten·nial** /senˈteniəl/ (especially NAmE) (BrE usually **cen·ten·ary**) noun the 100th anniversary of an event: *The year 1889 was the centennial of the inauguration of George Washington.* ⇒ see also BICENTENNIAL

**cen·ter** (US) = CENTRE

**cen·tered**, **cen·ter·fold**, **cen·ter·piece** (US) = CENTRED, CENTREFOLD, CENTREPIECE

**centi-** /ˈsenti/ combining form (in nouns) 1 hundred: *centipede* 2 (often used in units of measurement) one hundredth: *centimetre*

**centi·grade** /ˈsentɪɡreɪd/ adj. = CELSIUS: *a temperature of 40 degrees centigrade* ▶ **centi·grade** noun [U]: *temperatures in centigrade and Fahrenheit*

**centi·gram** (also **centi·gramme**) /ˈsentɪɡræm/ noun a unit for measuring weight. There are 100 centigrams in a GRAM.

**centi·litre** (US **centi·liter**) /ˈsentɪliːtə(r)/ noun (abbr. **cl**) a unit for measuring liquids. There are 100 centilitres in a LITRE.

**centi·metre** (US **centi·meter**) /ˈsentɪmiːtə(r)/ noun (abbr. **cm**) a unit for measuring length. There are 100 centimetres in a metre.

**centi·pede** /ˈsentɪpiːd/ noun a small creature like an insect, with a long thin body and many legs

**cen·tral** ❶ B1 ◐ /ˈsentrəl/ adj. 1 ʀ B1 in the centre of an area or object: *central London* ◊ *Central America/Europe/Asia* ◊ *the central area of the brain* 2 ʀ B1 easily reached from many areas: *The flat is very central—just five minutes from Princes Street.* ◊ *a central location* 3 ʀ B1 most important: *The central issue is that of widespread racism.* ◊ *She has been a central figure in the campaign.* ◊ *Prevention also plays a central role in traditional medicine.* ◊ **~to sth** *Reducing inflation is central to (= is an important part of) the government's economic policy.* ⇒ SYNONYMS at MAIN 4 ʀ B1 having power or control over other parts: *the central committee (= of a political party)* ◊ *The organization has a central office in York.* 5 (phonetics) (of a vowel) produced with the centre of the tongue in a higher position than the front or the back, for example /ɜː/ in *bird* ⇒ compare BACK, FRONT ▶ **cen·tral·ity** /senˈtræləti/ noun [U] (formal): *the centrality of the family as a social institution* **cen·tral·ly** /ˈsentrəli/ adv.: *The hotel is centrally located for all major attractions.* ◊ *a centrally planned economy* ◊ *Is the house centrally heated (= does it have central heating)?*

**Central Aˈmerica** /ˌsentrəl əˈmerɪkə/ noun [U] the part of North America that consists of Guatemala, Belize, Honduras, El Salvador, Nicaragua, Costa Rica and Panama ▶ **ˌCentral Aˈmerican** adj., noun

**ˌcentral ˈbank** noun a national bank that does business with the government and other banks, and issues the country's coins and paper money

**ˌcentral ˈcasting** noun [U] a company or a department that supplies actors, usually for small, STEREOTYPICAL film roles: (figurative) *He looked like an absent-minded professor straight out of central casting.*

**ˌCentral ˈDaylight Time** noun [U] (abbr. **CDT**) the time used in summer in the central US and Canada, which is five hours earlier than UTC

**ˌCentral Euroˌpean ˈSummer Time** noun [U] (abbr. **CEST**) the time used in summer in central and part of western Europe, which is two hours later than UTC

**ˌCentral Euroˌpean ˈTime** noun [U] (abbr. **CET**) the time used in winter in central and part of western Europe, which is one hour later than UTC

**ˌcentral ˈgovernment** noun [U, C] the government of a whole country, rather than LOCAL GOVERNMENT (= government of a town or local area)

**ˌcentral ˈheating** noun [U] a system for heating a building from one source that then sends the hot water or hot air around the building through pipes

**the ˌCentral Inˈtelligence Agency** noun [sing.] = CIA

**cen·tral·ism** /ˈsentrəlɪzəm/ noun [U] a way of organizing sth, such as government or education, that involves one central group of people controlling the whole system ▶ **cen·tral·ist** adj.: *centralist control of schools*

**cen·tral·ize** ⓦ (BrE also **-ise**) /ˈsentrəlaɪz/ verb ~**sth** to give the control of a country or an organization to a group of people in one particular place: *a highly centralized system of government* ▶ **cen·tral·iza·tion**, **-isa·tion** /ˌsentrəlaɪˈzeɪʃn; NAmE -ləˈz-/ noun [U]: *the centralization of political power*

**ˌcentral ˈlocking** noun [U] a system for locking a car in which all the doors can be locked or opened at the same time

**ˌcentral ˈnervous system** noun (anatomy) the part of the system of nerves in the body that consists of the brain and the SPINAL CORD ⇒ see also NERVOUS SYSTEM

**ˌcentral ˈprocessing unit** noun (computing) (abbr. **CPU**) the part of a computer that controls all the other parts of the system

**ˌcentral reserˈvation** (BrE) (NAmE **ˈme·dian**, **ˈmedian strip**) noun a narrow piece of land that separates the two sides of a major road such as a MOTORWAY or INTERSTATE

**ˌCentral ˈStandard Time** noun [U] (abbr. **CST**) the time used in winter in the central US and Canada, which is six hours earlier than UTC

# Central time 238

**Central time** noun [U] the time at the line of LONGITUDE 90°W, which is the standard time in the central US and Canada

**centre** ⓘ A1 ⊙ (US **cen·ter**) /ˈsentə(r)/ noun, verb
■ noun
• MIDDLE **1** A1 [C] the middle point or part of sth: *the centre of a circle* ◇ **in the ~ (of sth)** *a table in the centre of the room* ◇ **at the ~ of sth** *at the centre of the universe* ⊃ picture at CIRCLE
• TOWN/CITY **2** A1 [C] (*especially BrE*) (*NAmE usually* **downtown** [usually sing.]) **(in the) ~** the main part of a town or city where there are a lot of shops and offices: *We both work in the city centre.* ◇ *the centre of town* ◇ *a town-centre car park* ⊃ see also TOWN CENTRE **3** B1 [C] a place or an area where a lot of people live; a place where a lot of business or cultural activity takes place: *major urban/industrial centres* ◇ **~ of sth** *a centre of population* ◇ *Small towns in South India serve as economic and cultural centres for the surrounding villages.*
• BUILDING **4** A2 [C] a building or place used for a particular purpose or activity: *a shopping/community/health/fitness centre* ◇ *the Centre for Policy Studies* ⊃ see also CONTROL CENTRE, DATA CENTRE, FULFILMENT CENTRE
• OF EXCELLENCE **5** [C] **~ of excellence** a place where a particular kind of work is done extremely well
• OF ATTENTION **6** [C, usually sing.] the point towards which people direct their attention: *Children like to be the centre of attention.* ◇ **at the ~ of sth** *The prime minister is at the centre of a political row over leaked Cabinet documents.*
• IN POLITICS **7** (*usually* **the centre**) [sing.] a MODERATE (= middle) political position or party, between the extremes of LEFT-WING and RIGHT-WING parties: *a party of the centre*
• IN SPORT **8** [C] (in some team sports) a player or position in the middle of the pitch, court, etc. IDM see FRONT n., LEFT adv.
■ verb **1** B1 [I, T] to be the person or thing around which most activity takes place; to make sb/sth the central person or thing: **~(sth) on/upon sb/sth** *The debate centred on an important practical question.* ◇ **~(sth) around/round sb/sth** *Leisure activities were largely centred around the family.* **2 be centred in …** [I] to take place mainly in or around the place mentioned: *Most of the fighting was centred in the north of the capital.* **3** [T] **~sth (+ adv./prep.)** to move sth so that it is in the centre of sth else: *This button will centre the image on the page.*

**ˌcentre ˈback** (US ˌcenter ˈback) (*also* ˌcentre ˈhalf, US ˌcenter ˈhalf) noun (in football (soccer) and some other sports) a player or position in the middle of the back line of players

**cen·tred** (US **cen·tered**) /ˈsentəd; NAmE -tərd/ adj. **1 -centred** (in adjectives) having the mentioned as the most important feature or centre of attention: *a child-centred approach to teaching* ⊃ see also SELF-CENTRED **2** (*especially NAmE*) calm, sensible and emotionally in control: *My family helps to keep me centred.*

**ˌcentre ˈfield** (US ˌcenter ˈfield) noun [U] (in baseball) the central part of the outer area of a baseball field, where one player (called the **centre fielder**) stands to catch balls that are hit in that area; the position of this player: *Davis will play center field and bat ninth.* ⊃ compare MIDFIELD

**ˈcentre·fold** (US **ˈcen·ter·fold**) /ˈsentəfəʊld; NAmE -tərf-/ noun **1** a large picture, often of a young woman with few or no clothes on, folded to form the middle pages of a magazine **2** a person whose picture is the centrefold of a magazine

**ˌcentre ˈforward** (US ˌcenter ˈforward) noun (in football (soccer) and some other sports) a player or position in the middle of the front line of players

**ˌcentre ˈhalf** (US ˌcenter ˈhalf) noun = CENTRE BACK

**ˌcentre-ˈleft** (US ˌcenter-ˈleft) (*also* ˌleft-of-ˈcentre, US ˌleft-of-ˈcenter /ˌleft əv ˈsentə(r)/) adj. (*politics*) having views that are between the centre and the left in politics: *a centre-left coalition government* ▶ ˌcentre-ˈleft (US ˌcenter-ˈleft) noun [sing.]: *Most of the centre-left will give their support.*

**ˌcentre of ˈgravity** (US ˌcenter of ˈgravity) noun (*pl.* **centres/centers of gravity**) the point in an object at which its weight is considered to act: at this point, the object is evenly balanced

**ˈcentre·piece** (US **ˈcen·ter·piece**) /ˈsentəpiːs; NAmE -tərp-/ noun **1** [sing.] the most important item: *This treaty is the centrepiece of the government's foreign policy.* **2** a decoration for the centre of a table

**ˌcentre-ˈright** (US ˌcenter-ˈright) (*also* ˌright-of-ˈcentre, US ˌright-of-ˈcenter /ˌraɪt əv ˈsentə(r)/) adj. (*politics*) having views that are between the centre and the right in politics: *Europe's centre-right parties* ▶ ˌcentre-ˈright (US ˌcenter-ˈright) noun [sing.]: *a politician of the centre-right*

**ˌcentre ˈspread** (US ˌcenter ˈspread) noun the two facing middle pages of a newspaper or magazine

**ˌcentre ˈstage** (US ˌcenter ˈstage) noun [U] an important position where sb/sth can easily get people's attention: *Education is taking centre stage in the government's plans.* ◇ *This region continues to occupy centre stage in world affairs.* ▶ ˌcentre ˈstage (US ˌcenter ˈstage) adv.: *The minister said, 'We are putting full employment centre stage.'*

**-centric** /ˈsentrɪk/ suffix **1** having a particular centre: *geocentric* **2** (*often disapproving*) based on a particular way of thinking: *Eurocentric* ◇ *ethnocentric*

**cen·tri·fu·gal** /ˌsentrɪˈfjuːgl, senˈtrɪfjəgl; NAmE senˈtrɪfjəgl/ adj. (*specialist*) moving or tending to move away from a centre

**cenˌtrifugal ˈforce** (*also* cenˈtrifugal force) noun (*physics*) a force that appears to cause an object moving in a circle to fly away from the centre and off its CIRCULAR path

**cen·tri·fuge** /ˈsentrɪfjuːdʒ/ noun a machine with a part that turns around very quickly to separate substances, for example liquids from solids, by forcing the heavier substance to the outer edge

**cen·tri·pet·al** /ˌsentrɪˈpiːtl, senˈtrɪpɪtl; NAmE senˈtrɪpɪtl/ adj. (*specialist*) moving or tending to move towards a centre

**cen·trist** /ˈsentrɪst/ noun a person with political views that are not extreme SYN moderate ▶ **cen·trist** adj.

**cen·tur·ion** /senˈtʃʊəriən; NAmE -ˈtʃʊr-/ noun (in ancient Rome) an army officer who commanded 100 soldiers

**cen·tury** ⓘ A1 Ⓦ /ˈsentʃəri/ noun (*pl.* **-ies**) **1** A1 a period of 100 years: *A century ago, Valparaiso was the country's main port.* ◇ **for centuries** *They have lived there for centuries.* ◇ **over/through the centuries** *Their techniques have evolved over the centuries.* **2** A1 (*abbr.* **c, cent.**) any of the periods of 100 years before or after the birth of Christ: *the twentieth century* (= AD 1901–2000 or 1900–1999) ◇ *during the second half of the fifteenth century* **3** (in CRICKET) a score of 100 RUNS by one player IDM see TURN n.

**CEO** /ˌsiː iː ˈəʊ/ noun (*pl.* **CEOs**) the person with the highest rank in a business company (the abbreviation for 'chief executive officer') ⊃ WORDFINDER NOTE at BUSINESSMAN

**ceph·al·ic** /sɪˈfælɪk; BrE also keˈf-/ adj. (*anatomy*) in or related to the head

**ceph·alo·pod** /ˈsefələpɒd, ˈkeː-; NAmE ˈsefələpɑːd/ noun (*biology*) a type of MOLLUSC with a combined head and body and large eyes. Cephalopods have arms and/or TENTACLES (= long thin parts like arms), which may have SUCKERS (= round parts that enable them to stick to a surface) on them. OCTOPUS and SQUID are cephalopods. ⊃ VISUAL VOCAB page V3

**cer·am·ic** /səˈræmɪk/ noun **1** [C, usually pl.] a pot or other object made of CLAY that has been made permanently hard by heat: *an exhibition of ceramics by Picasso* **2** **ceramics** [U] the art of making and decorating ceramics ▶ **cer·am·ic** adj.: *ceramic tiles*

**cer·eal** /ˈsɪəriəl; NAmE ˈsɪr-/ noun **1** [C] one of various types of grass that produce grains that can be eaten or are used to make flour or bread. WHEAT, BARLEY and RYE are all cereals: *cereal crops* ⊃ WORDFINDER NOTE at CROP ⊃ VISUAL VOCAB page V8 **2** [U] the grain produced by cereal crops **3** [C,

Oxford 3000 | Oxford 5000 | A1 A2 B1 B2 C1 CEFR level | PHRV phrasal verb(s) | IDM idiom(s)

U] food made from the grain of cereals, often eaten for breakfast with milk: *breakfast cereals* ◊ *a bowl of cereal* ⊃ HOMOPHONES at SERIAL

**ce·re·bel·lum** /ˌserəˈbeləm/ *noun* (*pl.* **ce·re·bel·lums** or **cere·bella** /-lə/) (*anatomy*) the part of the brain at the back of the head that controls the activity of the muscles

**cere·bral** /səˈriːbrəl, ˈserəbrəl/ *adj.* **1** relating to the brain: *a cerebral haemorrhage* **2** (*formal*) relating to the mind rather than the feelings SYN **intellectual**: *His poetry is very cerebral.*

**cerebral ˈhemisphere** *noun* = HEMISPHERE (2)

**cerebral ˈpalsy** *noun* [U] a medical condition usually caused by brain damage before or at birth that causes the loss of control of movement in the arms and legs

**cere·brum** /səˈriːbrəm, ˈserəbrəm/ *noun* (*pl.* **ce·re·bra** /-brə/) (*anatomy*) the front part of the brain, responsible for thoughts, emotions and personality

**cere·mo·nial** /ˌserɪˈməʊniəl/ *adj., noun*
- *adj.* relating to or used in a ceremony: *ceremonial occasions* ◊ *a ceremonial sword* ▶ **cere·mo·ni·al·ly** /-niəli/ *adv.*
- *noun* [U, C] the system of rules and traditions that states how things should be done at a ceremony or formal occasion: *The visit was conducted with all due ceremonial.*

**cere·mo·ni·ous** /ˌserəˈməʊniəs/ *adj.* (*formal*) behaving or performed in an extremely formal way OPP **unceremonious** ▶ **cere·mo·ni·ous·ly** *adv.*

**cere·mony** ⓘ B1 /ˈserəməni; *NAmE* -məʊni/ *noun* (*pl.* **-ies**) **1** ⓘ B1 [C] a public or religious occasion that includes a series of formal or traditional actions: *More than 1000 people attended the ceremony.* ◊ *an awards/opening ceremony* ◊ *a wedding/marriage/graduation ceremony* ⊃ WORDFINDER NOTE at WEDDING **2** [U] formal behaviour; traditional actions and words used on particular formal occasions
- IDM **stand on ˈceremony** to behave formally: *Please don't stand on ceremony* (= Please be natural and relaxed) *with me.* **without ˈceremony** in a very rough or informal way: *He found himself pushed without ceremony out of the house and the door slammed in his face.* ⊃ see also MASTER OF CEREMONIES

**cer·ise** /səˈriːz, -ˈriːs/ *adj.* between pink and red in colour ▶ **cer·ise** *noun* [U]

**cer·ium** /ˈsɪəriəm; *NAmE* ˈsɪr-/ *noun* [U] (*symb.* Ce) a chemical element. Cerium is a silver-white metal used in the production of glass and CERAMICS.

**cert** /sɜːt; *NAmE* sɜːrt/ *noun* (*BrE, informal*) a thing that is sure to happen or be successful SYN **certainty**: *That horse is a dead cert for* (= is sure to win) *the next race.*

**cert.** *abbr.* **1** CERTIFICATE **2** CERTIFIED

**cer·tain** ⓘ A2 ⓞ /ˈsɜːtn; *NAmE* ˈsɜːrtn/ *adj., pron.*
- *adj.* **1** A2 strongly believing sth; having no doubts: *I think it was him, but I can't be certain.* ◊ *~(that)... She wasn't certain (that) he had seen her.* ◊ **about/of sth** *Are you absolutely certain about this?* ◊ **~who/where, etc...** *I'm not certain who was there.* **2** A2 that you can rely on to happen or to be true: *The climbers face certain death if the rescue today is unsuccessful.* ◊ **it is ~ (that)...** *It is certain that they will agree.* ◊ **~ to do sth** *She looks certain to win an Oscar.* ◊ *One thing is certain—it will be exciting.* ◊ **~ of sth/of doing sth** *If you want to be certain of getting a ticket, book now.* ⊃ SYNONYMS at SURE **3** A2 used to mention a particular thing, person or group without giving any more details about it or them: *For certain personal reasons I shall not be able to attend.* ◊ *This car appeals to a certain type of driver.* ◊ *They refused to release their hostages unless certain conditions were met.* **4** B1 slight; easy to notice, but difficult to describe: *That's true, to a certain extent.* ◊ *I felt there was a certain coldness in her manner.* **5** (*formal*) used with a person's name to show that the speaker does not know the person: *It was a certain Dr Davis who performed the operation.*
- IDM **for ˈcertain** without doubt: *I can't say for certain when we'll arrive.* **make certain (that...)** to find out whether sth is definitely true: *I think there's a bus at 8 but you'd better make certain.* **make certain of sth/of doing**

239

# certificate

**sth** to do sth in order to be sure that sth else will happen: *You'll have to leave soon to make certain of getting there on time.* **of a certain ˈage** if you talk about a person being **of a certain age**, you mean that they are no longer young but not yet old: *The show appeals to an audience of a certain age.*
- *pron.* **certain of...** (*formal*) used for talking about some members of a group of people or things without giving their names: *Certain of those present were unwilling to discuss the matter further.*

▼ SYNONYMS

**certain**
bound • sure • definite • guaranteed
These are all words describing sth that will definitely happen or is definitely true.
**certain** that you can rely on to happen or be true: *It's certain that they will agree.* ◊ *They are certain to agree.*
**bound** [not before noun] certain to happen, or to do or be sth. NOTE **Bound** is only used in the phrase *bound to do/be*, etc.: *You've done so much work—you're bound to pass the exam.* ◊ *There are bound to be changes when the new system is introduced.*
**sure** certain to happen or be true; that can be trusted or relied on: *She's sure to be picked for the team.* ◊ *It's sure to rain.*
**definite** (*rather informal*) certain to happen; that is not going to change: *Is it definite that he's leaving?*
**guaranteed** certain to have a particular result: *That kind of behaviour is guaranteed to make him angry.*
PATTERNS
- certain/sure **of** sth
- certain/bound/sure/guaranteed **to do** sth
- certain/definite **that...**
- I couldn't say for certain/sure/definite.

▼ EXPRESS YOURSELF

**Expressing certainty or uncertainty**
When you are stating what has happened or is going to happen, you can say how certain or uncertain you are about what you are saying:
- *I'm sure/100% certain/absolutely positive I left my keys on the table.*
- *There's no doubt in my mind that this is the best option.*
- *Without a doubt,/No question, this is where it was.*
- *I'm not (at all) sure what time they arrive, to be honest.*
- *I rather doubt they'll call back.* (*BrE*)

**cer·tain·ly** ⓘ A2 /ˈsɜːtnli; *NAmE* ˈsɜːrt-/ *adv.* **1** B1 without doubt SYN **definitely**: *Without treatment, she will almost certainly die.* ◊ *Certainly, the early years are crucial to a child's development.* ◊ *I'm certainly never going there again.* ⊃ note at SURELY ⊃ LANGUAGE BANK at NEVERTHELESS **2** A2 (used in answer to questions) of course: '*May I see your passport, Mr Scott?' 'Certainly.'* ◊ '*Do you think all this money will change your life?' 'Certainly not.'*

**cer·tainty** B2 ⓦ /ˈsɜːtnti; *NAmE* ˈsɜːrt-/ *noun* (*pl.* **-ies**) **1** B2 [U] the state of being certain: *There is no certainty that the president's removal would end the civil war.* ◊ *I can't say with any certainty where I'll be next week.* **2** C1 [C] a thing that is certain: *political/moral certainties* ◊ *Her return to the team now seems a certainty.*

**cer·ti·fi·able** /ˈsɜːtɪfaɪəbl; *NAmE* ˈsɜːrt-/ *adj.* **1** a person who is **certifiable** can or should be officially stated to be INSANE: (*informal*) *He's certifiable* (= he's crazy). **2** that can or should be officially recorded: *Eighty patients met the criteria for certifiable disability.* **3** (*especially NAmE*) good enough to be officially accepted or recommended ▶ **cer·ti·fi·ably** *adv.*: *certifiably insane*

**cer·tifi·cate** B2 /ˈsɜːtɪfɪkət; *NAmE* ˈsɜːrt-/ *noun, verb*
- *noun* /səˈtɪfɪkət; *NAmE* sərˈt-/ (*abbr.* **cert.**) **1** B2 an official document that may be used to prove that the facts it states

# certificated

are true: *a birth/marriage/death certificate* ◇ **~ of sth** *a certificate of motor insurance* ⊃ see also GIFT CERTIFICATE **2** [+ B2] an official document proving that you have completed a course of study or passed an exam; a qualification obtained after a course of study or an exam: *a Postgraduate Certificate in Education* (= a British qualification for teachers) ◇ **~ of sth** *A certificate of completion will be issued to all who complete the course.* ⊃ WORDFINDER NOTE at DOCUMENT

- **verb** /sə'tɪfɪkeɪt; NAmE sər't-/ **~ sb (to do sth)** (BrE) to give sb an official document proving that they have successfully completed a training course, especially for a particular profession

**cer·ti·fi·cated** /sə'tɪfɪkeɪtɪd; NAmE sər't-/ *adj.* having the certificate that shows that the necessary training for a particular job has been done

**cer·ti·fi·ca·tion** /ˌsɜːtɪfɪ'keɪʃn; NAmE ˌsɜːrt-/ *noun* [U] (*specialist*) **1** the act of CERTIFYING sth: *the medical certification of the cause of death* **2** the process of giving certificates for a course of education: *the certification of the exam modules*

ˌcertified 'mail (NAmE) (BrE reˌcorded deˈlivery) *noun* [U] a method of sending a letter or package in which the person sending it gets an official note to say it has been posted and the person receiving it must sign a form when it is delivered ⊃ compare REGISTERED MAIL

ˌcertified ˌpublic acˈcountant (NAmE) (BrE ˌchartered acˈcountant) *noun* a fully trained and qualified ACCOUNTANT

**cer·tify** /'sɜːtɪfaɪ; NAmE 'sɜːrt-/ *verb* (**cer·ti·fies, cer·ti·fy·ing, cer·ti·fied, cer·ti·fied**) **1** (*formal*) to state officially, especially in writing, that sth is true: **~(that)** ... *He handed her a piece of paper certifying (that) she was in good health.* ◇ *This* (= this document) *is to certify that* ... ◇ **~ sb/sth + adj.** *He was certified dead on arrival.* ◇ **~ sb/sth (as) sth** *The accounts were certified (as) correct by the finance department.* ◇ **~ sb/sth to be/do sth** *The plants must be certified to be virus free.* **2** [usually passive] **~ sb (as sth)** to give sb an official document proving that they are qualified to work in a particular profession **3** [usually passive] (*law*) to officially state that sb is mentally ill, so that they can be given medical treatment: **be certified (+ adj.)** *Patients must be certified before they can be admitted to the hospital.*

**cer·ti·tude** /'sɜːtɪtjuːd; NAmE 'sɜːrtɪtuːd/ *noun* [U, C] (*formal*) a feeling of being certain; a thing about which you are certain: *'You will like Rome,' he said, with absolute certitude.* ◇ *the collapse of moral certitudes*

**cer·ul·ean** /sɪ'ruːliən/ *adj.* (*literary*) deep blue in colour

**cer·vical** /'sɜːvɪkl, sə'vaɪkl; NAmE 'sɜːrvɪkl/ *adj.* [only before noun] (*anatomy*) **1** relating to the cervix: *cervical cancer* **2** relating to the neck: *the cervical spine*

ˌcervical ˈsmear *noun* (BrE) = SMEAR TEST

**cer·vix** /'sɜːvɪks; NAmE 'sɜːrv-/ *noun* (*pl.* **cer·vi·ces** /-vɪsiːz/ or **cer·vi·xes** /-vɪksɪz/) (*anatomy*) the narrow passage at the opening of the WOMB of a woman or female animal

**ce·sar·ean, ce·sar·ian** (US) = CAESAREAN

**ce·sium** (NAmE) (BrE **cae·sium**) /'siːziəm/ *noun* (*symb.* **Cs**) [U] a chemical element. Cesium is a soft silver-white metal that reacts strongly in water, used in PHOTOELECTRIC CELLS.

**ces·sa·tion** /se'seɪʃn/ *noun* [U, C] (*formal*) the stopping of sth; a break in sth: *Mexico called for an immediate cessation of hostilities.*

**ces·sion** /'seʃn/ *noun* [U, C] (*formal*) the act of giving up land or rights, especially to another country after a war ⊃ see also CEDE

**cess·pit** /'sespɪt/ (*also* **cess-pool** /'sespuːl/) *noun* **1** a covered hole or container in the ground for collecting waste from a building, especially from the toilets **2** a place where bad or dishonest people gather: *a cesspit of corruption*

**CET** /ˌsiː iː 'tiː/ *abbr.* CENTRAL EUROPEAN TIME

**cet·acean** /sɪ'teɪʃn/ *adj., noun* (*biology*)
- **adj.** (*also* **cet·aceous** /sɪ'teɪʃəs/) connected with the group of creatures that includes WHALES and DOLPHINS
- **noun** a WHALE, DOLPHIN, or other sea creature that belongs to the same group ⊃ VISUAL VOCAB page V2

**ce·vi·che** /se'viːtʃeɪ; NAmE *also* -tʃi/ *noun* a dish, originally from South America, made with raw fish that has been left for several hours in a mixture of LIME or lemon juice, oil and SPICES

**cf.** *abbr.* (in writing) compare

**CFC** /ˌsiː ef 'siː/ *noun* [C, U] a type of gas previously used especially in AEROSOLS (= types of container that release liquid in very small drops). CFCs are harmful to the earth's OZONE LAYER and are generally no longer used in these products. (the abbreviation for 'chlorofluorocarbon')

**CFL** /ˌsiː ef 'el/ *abbr.* Canadian Football League (the organization of professional AMERICAN FOOTBALL teams in Canada)

**CFO** /ˌsiː ef 'əʊ/ *noun* (*pl.* **CFOs**) the person in a company who has the most authority over the finances (the abbreviation for 'chief financial officer')

**CGI** /ˌsiː dʒiː 'aɪ/ *abbr.* computer-generated imagery: *The movie combines CGI animation with live-action location shots.*

**ch.** *abbr.* (in writing) chapter

**chaat** /tʃɑːt/ *noun* [U] a South Asian dish consisting of fruit or vegetables with SPICES

**cha-cha** /'tʃɑː tʃɑː/ (*also* **cha-cha-cha**) *noun* a South American dance with small fast steps: *to dance/do the cha-cha*

**cha·cha** /'tʃɑːtʃɑː/ *noun* (*IndE*) **1** an uncle who is the brother of your father **2** a male cousin of your father

**cha-ching** /tʃə 'tʃɪŋ/ *exclamation* (NAmE, *informal*) = KA-CHING

**chad** /tʃæd/ *noun* the small piece that is removed when a hole is made in a piece of card, etc.

**cha·dor** /'tʃɑːdɔː(r)/ *noun* a large piece of cloth that covers a woman's head and upper body so that only the face can be seen, worn by some Muslim women

**chafe** /tʃeɪf/ *verb* **1** [I, T] if skin **chafes**, or if sth **chafes** it, it becomes painful because the thing is rubbing against it: *Her wrists chafed where the rope had been.* ◇ **~ sth** *The collar was far too tight and chafed her neck.* **2** [I] **~ (at/ under sth)** (*formal*) to feel annoyed and impatient about sth, especially because it limits what you can do: *He soon chafed at the restrictions of his situation.*

**chaff** /tʃɑːf; BrE *also* tʃæf/ *noun, verb*
- **noun** [U] **1** the outer layer of the seeds of grain such as WHEAT, which is separated from the grain before it is eaten **2** STRAW (= dried STEMS of WHEAT) and HAY (= dried grass) cut up as food for cows IDM see WHEAT
- **verb** **~ sb** (*old-fashioned* or *formal*) to make jokes about sb in a friendly way SYN tease

**chaf·finch** /'tʃæfɪntʃ/ *noun* a small European bird of the FINCH family

**cha·grin** /'ʃægrɪn; NAmE ʃə'grɪn/ *noun* [U] (*formal*) a feeling of being disappointed or annoyed ▸ **cha·grined** *adj.*

**chai** /tʃaɪ/ *noun* [U] a type of Indian tea, made especially by boiling tea leaves with milk, sugar and SPICES

**chain** ⓘ B1 ⓞ /tʃeɪn/ *noun, verb*
- **noun**
- • METAL RINGS **1** [?] B1 [C, U] a series of connected metal rings, used for pulling or fastening things; a length of chain used for a particular purpose: *She wore a heavy gold chain around her neck.* ◇ *The mayor wore his chain of office.* ◇ *a bicycle chain* ◇ **in chains** *The prisoners were kept in chains* (= with chains around their arms and legs, to prevent them from escaping). ◇ **on a~** *They kept the dog on a chain all day long.*
- • CONNECTED THINGS **2** [?] B1 [C] a series of connected things or people: *mountain/island chains* ◇ *Volunteers formed a human chain* (= line of people) *to rescue precious items from the burning house.* ◇ **~ of sb/sth** *to set in motion a chain of events* ◇ *a chain of command* (= a system in an

organization by which instructions are passed from one person to another) ⊃ see also DAISY CHAIN, FOOD CHAIN, SUPPLY CHAIN
- **OF SHOPS/HOTELS** 3 ? B1 [C] a group of shops or hotels owned by the same company: *a supermarket/hotel/retail chain*
- **RESTRICTION** 4 [C, usually pl.] (*formal* or *literary*) a thing that limits sb's freedom or ability to do sth: *the chains of fear/misery*
- **IN HOUSE BUYING** 5 [C, usually sing.] (*BrE*) a situation in which a number of people selling and buying houses must each complete the sale of their house before buying from the next person IDM see BALL *n.*, LINK *n.*, WEAK

■ *verb* ? B2 [often passive] to fasten sth with a chain; to fasten sb/sth to another person or thing with a chain, so that they do not escape or get stolen: *~sb/sth The doors were always locked and chained.* ◇ *~sb/sth up The dog was chained up for the night.* ◇ *~sb/sth to sb/sth She chained her bicycle to the gate.* ◇ (*figurative*) *I've been chained to my desk all week* (= because there was so much work).

**'chain gang** *noun* a group of prisoners held together with chains and forced to work

**'chain letter** *noun* an email or letter sent to several people asking them to send the email or copies of the letter to more people

**,chain-link 'fence** *noun* a fence made of wire in a diamond pattern

**'chain mail** (*also* **mail**) *noun* [U] ARMOUR (= clothing to protect the body when fighting) made of small metal rings linked together

**chain re'action** *noun* 1 (*chemistry, physics*) a chemical or nuclear change that forms products that themselves cause more changes and new products 2 a series of events, each of which causes the next: *It set off a chain reaction in the international money markets.*

**chain·saw** /ˈtʃeɪnsɔː/ *noun* a tool made of a chain with sharp teeth set in it that is driven by a motor and used for cutting wood

**'chain-smoke** *verb* [I, T] ~(**sth**) to smoke cigarettes continuously, lighting the next one from the one you have just smoked ▶ **'chain-smoker** *noun*

**'chain store** *noun* a shop that is one of a series of similar shops owned by the same company

**chair** ❶ A1 /tʃeə(r); NAmE tʃer/ *noun, verb*
■ *noun* 1 ? A1 [C] a piece of furniture for one person to sit on, with a back, a seat and four legs: *a table and chairs* ◇ *on a~ Sit on your chair!* ◇ *in a~ an old man asleep in a chair* (= an ARMCHAIR) ⊃ see also ARMCHAIR *noun*, BATH CHAIR, DECKCHAIR, DIRECTOR'S CHAIR, EASY CHAIR, ELECTRIC CHAIR, HIGH CHAIR, LAWN CHAIR, LOUNGE CHAIR, MUSICAL CHAIRS, ROCKING CHAIR, WHEELCHAIR 2 ? B2 **the chair** [C, usually sing.] the position of being in charge of a meeting or committee; the person who holds this position: **in the~** *Who is in the chair today?* ◇ *~of sth He was elected chair of the city council.* ⊃ WORDFINDER NOTE at CLUB 3 [C] the position of being in charge of a department in a university; a special position as a university professor: *He holds the chair of philosophy at Oxford.* 4 **the chair** (*US, informal*) [sing.] = ELECTRIC CHAIR
■ *verb* ~**sth** to act as the chairman or chairwoman of a meeting, discussion, etc: *to chair a committee* ◇ *Who's chairing the meeting?* ⊃ WORDFINDER NOTE at DEBATE

**chair·lift** /ˈtʃeəlɪft; NAmE ˈtʃerl-/ *noun* a series of chairs hanging from a moving cable, for carrying people up and down a mountain

**chair·man** ❶ B2 /ˈtʃeəmən; NAmE ˈtʃerm-/ *noun* (*pl.* **-men** /-mən/) 1 ? B2 the person in charge of a meeting, who tells people when they can speak, etc: *Sir Herbert took it upon himself to act as chairman.* 2 ? B2 the person in charge of a committee, a company, etc: *the vice/deputy chairman* ◇ *the chairman of the committee/board/party/club* ⊃ WORDFINDER NOTE at BUSINESSMAN ⊃ note at GENDER

**chair·man·ship** /ˈtʃeəmənʃɪp; NAmE ˈtʃerm-/ *noun* 1 [C] the position of a chairman or chairwoman: *the chairman-*

241

**challenge**

*ship of the committee* 2 [U] the state of being a chairman or chairwoman: *under her skilful chairmanship*

**chair·per·son** /ˈtʃeəpɜːsn; NAmE ˈtʃerpɜːrsn/ *noun* (*pl.* **-per·sons**) a chairman or chairwoman ⊃ see also CHAIR *noun*

**chair·woman** /ˈtʃeəwʊmən; NAmE ˈtʃerw-/ *noun* (*pl.* **-women** /-wɪmɪn/) a woman in charge of a meeting, a committee or an organization ⊃ note at GENDER

**chaise** /ʃeɪz/ *noun* a CARRIAGE pulled by a horse or horses, used in the past

**chaise longue** /ˌʃeɪz ˈlɒŋ; NAmE ˈlɔːŋ/ *noun* (*pl.* **chaises longues** /ˌʃeɪz ˈlɒŋ; NAmE ˈlɔːŋ/) (*from French*) 1 a long low seat with a back and one arm, on which the person sitting can stretch out their legs 2 (*also* **lounge chair**, *informal* **chaise lounge**) (*NAmE*) a long chair with a back that can be straight for sitting on or be made flat for lying on

**chakra** /ˈtʃʌkrə; ˈtʃɑːk-/ *noun* (in YOGA) each of the main centres of spiritual power in the human body

**cha·let** /ˈʃæleɪ; NAmE ʃæˈleɪ/ *noun* 1 a wooden house with a roof that slopes steeply down over the sides, usually built in mountain areas, especially in Switzerland 2 (*BrE*) a small house or HUT, especially one used by people on holiday at the sea

**chal·ice** /ˈtʃælɪs/ *noun* a large cup for holding wine, especially one from which wine is drunk in the Christian COMMUNION service IDM see POISON *v.*

**chalk** /tʃɔːk/ *noun, verb*
■ *noun* 1 [U] a type of soft white stone: *the chalk cliffs of southern England* 2 [U, C] a substance similar to chalk made into white or coloured sticks for writing or drawing: *a piece/stick of chalk* ◇ *drawing diagrams with chalk on the blackboard* ◇ *a box of coloured chalks*
IDM **chalk and cheese** (*BrE*) if two people or things are like **chalk and cheese** or as different as **chalk and cheese**, they are completely different from each other ⊃ more at LONG *adj.*
■ *verb* ~**sth (up) (on sth)** to write or draw sth with chalk: *She chalked (up) the day's menu on the board.*
PHRV **,chalk 'up sth** (*informal*) to achieve or record a success, points in a game, etc: *The team chalked up their tenth win this season.* **,chalk sth 'up to sth** (*informal*) to consider that sth is caused by sth: *We can chalk that win up to a lot of luck.* IDM see EXPERIENCE *n.*

**chalk·board** /ˈtʃɔːkbɔːd; NAmE -bɔːrd/ *noun* (*especially NAmE*) = BLACKBOARD

**chalky** /ˈtʃɔːki/ *adj.* containing chalk or like chalk

**chal·lan** /ˈtʃʌlən/ *noun, verb* (*IndE*)
■ *noun* 1 a document in which an official claim is made by the police that sb has committed a crime or a traffic offence: *The police filed a challan against the four accused in the case.* ◇ *He was issued a challan for the traffic offence and agreed to pay a fine.* 2 an official form or document relating to a payment, such as a receipt or an INVOICE: *You need to show a copy of the fee payment challan before you can take the exam.*
■ *verb* ~**sb** (of the police) to accuse sb formally of an illegal act, especially a traffic offence: *The traffic policeman challaned him for not wearing a helmet.*

**chal·lenge** ❶ B1 ⓦ /ˈtʃælɪndʒ/ *noun, verb*
■ *noun* 1 ? B1 a new or difficult task that tests sb's ability and skill: *a tough/major/significant challenge* ◇ *The role will be the biggest challenge of his acting career.* ◇ *to face a challenge* (= to have to deal with one) ◇ *~of sth/of doing sth Countries need to work together to address the challenge of climate change.* ◇ *~to sb/sth Digital piracy continues to pose huge challenges to the industry.* ⊃ WORDFINDER NOTE at ADVENTURE 2 ? B2 an invitation or a suggestion to sb that they should enter a competition, fight, etc: *to accept/take on a challenge* ◇ *to mount a challenge* 3 ? B2 a statement or an action that shows that sb refuses to accept sth and questions whether it is right, legal, etc: *Their legal challenge was unsuccessful.* ◇ *~to sth It was a direct challenge to the president's authority.*

# challenged

**verb 1** B2 to question whether a statement or an action is right, legal, etc.; to refuse to accept sth SYN dispute: ~ sth *His legal team immediately sought to challenge the decision.* ◇ *She does not like anyone challenging her authority.* ◇ ~ **sb (on sth)** *She challenged him on his old-fashioned views.* ⊃ LANGUAGE BANK at ARGUE **2** B2 to invite sb to enter a competition, fight, etc.; to suggest strongly that sb should do sth (especially when you think that they might be unwilling to do it): ~ **sb to sth** *Mike challenged me to a game of chess.* ◇ ~ **sb to do sth** *The opposition leader challenged the prime minister to call an election.* **3** B2 [I, T] ~ **(sb) (for sth)** to enter into a competition against sb to achieve sth or take sth from them: *He challenged her for the role of leader.* **4** B2 ~ **sb/yourself** to test sb's/your ability and skills, especially in an interesting way: *The job doesn't really challenge her.* **5** ~ **sb** to order sb to stop and say who they are or what they are doing: *We were challenged by police at the border.*

**chal·lenged** /ˈtʃælɪndʒd/ *adj.* (used with an adverb) a way of referring to sb who has a DISABILITY of some sort: *a competition for physically challenged athletes* ◇ (*humorous*) *I'm financially challenged at the moment* (= I have no money). HELP *Challenged* was intended to be a polite way of referring to sb with a DISABILITY but it soon came to be used in a humorous way and is now no longer considered very polite.

**chal·len·ger** /ˈtʃælɪndʒə(r)/ *noun* ~ **(for sth)** a person who competes with sb else in sport or in politics for an important position that the other person already holds: *the official challenger for the world championship title*

**chal·len·ging** B2 /ˈtʃælɪndʒɪŋ/ *adj.* **1** B2 difficult in an interesting way that tests your ability: *challenging work/questions/problems* ◇ *a challenging and rewarding career as a teacher* ⊃ SYNONYMS at DIFFICULT **2** C1 done in a way that invites people to disagree or argue with you, or shows that you disagree with them: *She gave him a challenging look. 'Are you really sure?' she demanded.* ◇ *Dealing with challenging behaviour in school is never easy.*

**cham·ber** C1 /ˈtʃeɪmbə(r)/ *noun* **1** C1 [C] a hall in a public building that is used for formal meetings: *The members left the council chamber.* ◇ *the Senate/House chamber* ⊃ see also CHAMBER OF COMMERCE **2** C1 (*also Chamber*) [C + sing./pl. v.] one of the parts of a parliament: *the Lower/Upper Chamber* (= in Britain, the House of Commons/House of Lords) ◇ *the Chamber of Deputies in the Italian parliament* ◇ *Under Senate rules, the chamber must vote on the bill by this Friday.* ⊃ see also SECOND CHAMBER ⊃ WORDFINDER NOTE at PARLIAMENT **3** [C] (in compounds) a room used for the particular purpose that is mentioned: *a burial chamber* ⊃ see also GAS CHAMBER **4** [C] a space in the body, in a plant or in a machine that is separated from the rest: *the chambers of the heart* ◇ *the rocket's combustion chamber* ◇ *the chamber of a gun* (= the part that holds the bullets) **5** [C] A space under the ground that is almost completely closed on all sides: *They found themselves in a vast underground chamber.* ⊃ see also ECHO CHAMBER **6** [C] (*old use*) a bedroom or private room

**cham·ber·lain** /ˈtʃeɪmbəlɪn/ *noun* -bərl-/ an official who managed the home and servants of a king, queen or important family in the past

**cham·ber·maid** /ˈtʃeɪmbəmeɪd/ *noun* -bərm-/ a woman whose job is to clean bedrooms, usually in a hotel

**'chamber music** *noun* [U] classical music written for a small group of instruments

**Chamber of 'Commerce** *noun* (*pl.* **Chambers of Commerce**) a group of local business people who work together to help business and trade in a particular town

**chamber of 'horrors** *noun* [sing.] a place displaying objects used to kill people in a cruel and painful way or scenes showing how they died, which people visit for entertainment

**'chamber orchestra** *noun* a small group of musicians who play classical music together

**'chamber pot** *noun* a round container that people in the past had in the bedroom and used as a toilet at night ⊃ compare POTTY

**cha·meleon** /kəˈmiːliən/ *noun* **1** a small LIZARD (= a type of REPTILE) that can change colour according to what is around or near it **2** (*often disapproving*) a person who changes their behaviour or opinions according to the situation

**cham·ois** *noun* (*pl.* **cham·ois**) **1** /ˈʃæmwɑː/ [C] an animal like a small DEER, that lives in the mountains of Europe and Asia **2** /ˈʃæmi/ (*also* **sham·my**) (*BrE also* **'chamois leather**, **'shammy leather**) [U, C] a type of soft leather, made from the skin of GOATS, sheep, etc., a piece of this, used especially for cleaning windows **3** /ˈʃæmi/ [U] (*NAmE*) a type of soft thick cotton cloth, used especially for making shirts

**chamo·mile** (*especially NAmE*) (*also* **camo·mile** *especially in BrE*) /ˈkæməmaɪl/ *noun* [U] a plant with a sweet smell and small white and yellow flowers. Its dried leaves and flowers are used to make tea, medicine, etc: *chamomile tea*

**champ** /tʃæmp/ *verb, noun*
■ *verb* [I, T] ~ **(sth)** (especially of horses) to bite or eat sth noisily
IDM **champing at the 'bit** (*informal*) impatient to do or start doing sth
■ *noun* an informal way of referring to a champion, often used in newspapers: *Scottish champs celebrate victory!*

**cham·pagne** /ʃæmˈpeɪn/ *noun* [U, C] a French SPARKLING white wine (= one with bubbles) that is drunk on special occasions: *a glass of champagne* ⊃ compare CAVA, PROSECCO™

**cham·pers** /ˈʃæmpəz; *NAmE* -pərz/ *noun* [U] (*BrE, informal*) = CHAMPAGNE

**cham·pion** B1 /ˈtʃæmpiən/ *noun, verb*
■ *noun* **1** B1 a person, team, etc. that has won a competition, especially in a sport: *the world/European/national/Olympic champion* ◇ *the defending champion* (= the person who was champion the last time and is trying to be champion again) ◇ ~ **of sth** *the heavyweight champion of the world* ⊃ WORDFINDER NOTE at SPORT **2** ~ **(of sth)** a person who fights for, or speaks in support of, a group of people or a belief: *She was a champion of the poor all her life.*
■ *verb* ~ **sth** to fight for or speak in support of a group of people or a belief: *He has always championed the cause of gay rights.*

**cham·pion·ship** B2 /ˈtʃæmpiənʃɪp/ *noun* **1** B2 (*also* **cham·pion·ships** [pl.]) a competition to find the best player or team in a particular sport: *the National Basketball Association Championship* ◇ *He won a silver medal at the European Championships.* **2** B2 the position of being a champion: *They've held the championship for the past two years.* **3** **the Championship** the football (soccer) league in England and Wales that has the second best teams in it, after the PREMIER LEAGUE

**chance** A2 /tʃɑːns; *NAmE* tʃæns/ *noun, verb, adj.*
■ *noun* **1** A2 [C, U] a possibility of sth happening, especially sth that you want: ~ **of doing sth** *She only has a slim chance of passing the exam.* ◇ ~ **that…** *There's a good chance that he'll be back in time.* ◇ ~ **of sb/sth doing sth** *What chance is there of anybody being found alive?* ◇ *There is little chance of that happening.* ◇ ~ **of sth** *The operation has a fifty-fifty chance of success.* ◇ *The Met Office said there was an 80 per cent chance of severe weather.* ◇ ~ **at sth** *Now they've met the love of his life, he finally has a chance at real happiness.* ◇ **with a** ~ *They are the one team with a chance of beating us.* ◇ *an outside chance* (= a very small one) **2** A2 [C] a suitable time or situation when you have the opportunity to do sth: *It was the chance she had been waiting for.* ◇ *Jeff deceived me once already—I won't give him a second chance.* ◇ *This is your big chance* (= opportunity for success). ◇ ~ **of sth** *We won't get another chance of a holiday this year.* ◇ ~ **to do sth** *Please give me a chance to explain.* ◇ *You'll have the chance to ask questions at the end.* ◇ ~ **for sb to do sth** *There will be a chance for parents to look around the school.* **3** A2 [C] an unpleasant

or dangerous possibility: *When installing electrical equipment don't take any chances. A mistake could kill.* **4** [U] the way that some things happen without any cause that you can see or understand: *I met her by chance* (= without planning to) *at the airport.* ◊ *Chess is not a game of chance.* ◊ *It was pure chance that we were both there.* ◊ *We'll plan everything very carefully and leave nothing to chance.* ⊃ SYNONYMS at LUCK

**IDM** **as ˌchance would ˈhave it** happening in a way that was lucky, although it was not planned: *As chance would have it, John was going to London too, so I went with him.* **be ˌin with a ˈchance (of doing sth)** (*BrE, informal*) to have the possibility of succeeding or achieving sth: '*Do you think we'll win?*' '*I think we're in with a chance.*' ◊ *He's in with a good chance of passing the exam.* **by ˌany ˈchance** used especially in questions, to ask whether sth is true, possible, etc: *Are you in love with him, by any chance?* **the ˌchances ˈare (that) …** (*informal*) it is likely that …: *The chances are you won't have to pay.* **ˌchance would be a ˈfine thing** (*BrE, informal*) people say **chance would be a fine thing** to show that they would like to do or have the thing that sb has mentioned, but that they do not think that it is very likely **give sb/sth half a ˈchance** to give sb/sth some opportunity to do sth: *That dog will give you a nasty bite, given half a chance.* **ˈno chance** (*informal*) there is no possibility: '*Do you think he'll do it?*' '*No chance.*' **on the ˈoff chance (of doing sth/that …)** because of the possibility of sth happening, although it is unlikely: *I didn't think you'd be at home but I just called by on the off chance.* **stand a ˈchance (of doing sth)** to have the possibility of succeeding or achieving sth: *The driver didn't stand a chance of stopping in time.* **take a ˈchance (on sth)** to decide to do sth, knowing that it might be the wrong choice: *We took a chance on the weather and planned to have the party outside.* **take your ˈchances** to take a risk or to use the opportunities that you have and hope that things will happen in the way that you want: *He took his chances and jumped into the water.* ⊃ more at CAT, DOG *n.*, EVEN *adj.*, EYE *n.*, FAT *adj.*, FIGHTING, SNOWBALL *n.*, SPORTING

▪ **verb** **1** [T] (*informal*) to risk sth, although you know the result may not be successful: *~ sth She was chancing her luck driving without a licence.* ◊ '*Take an umbrella.*' '*No, I'll chance it*' (= take the risk that it may rain). ◊ **~ doing sth** *I stayed hidden; I couldn't chance coming out.* **2** linking verb (*formal*) to happen or to do sth by chance: **~ to do sth** *If I do chance to find out where she is, I'll inform you immediately.* ◊ *They chanced to be staying at the same hotel.* ◊ **it chanced (that) …** *It chanced (that) they were staying at the same hotel.*

**IDM** **ˌchance your ˈarm** (*BrE, informal*) to take a risk although you will probably fail
**PHRV** **ˈchance on/upon sb/sth** (*formal*) to find or meet sb/sth unexpectedly or by chance: *One day he chanced upon Emma's diary and began reading it.*

▪ **adj.** [only before noun] not planned **SYN** **unplanned**: *a chance meeting/encounter*

**chan·cel** /ˈtʃɑːnsl; *NAmE* ˈtʃæn-/ *noun* the part of a church near the ALTAR, where the priests and the CHOIR (= singers) sit during services

**chan·cel·lery** /ˈtʃɑːnsələri; *NAmE* ˈtʃæn-/ *noun* (*pl.* **-ies**) **1** [C, usually sing.] the place where a chancellor has his or her office **2** [sing. + sing./pl. v.] the staff in the department of a chancellor

**chan·cel·lor** /ˈtʃɑːnsələ(r); *NAmE* ˈtʃæn-/ (*also* **Chancellor**) *noun* (often used in a title) **1** the head of government in Germany or Austria: *Chancellor Merkel* **2** = CHANCELLOR OF THE EXCHEQUER (in the UK): *MPs waited for the chancellor's announcement.* **3** the official head of a university in Britain. Chancellor is an HONORARY title. ⊃ compare VICE CHANCELLOR **4** the head of some American universities **5** used in the titles of some senior state officials in Britain: *the Lord Chancellor* (= a senior law official)

**Chancellor of the Exˈchequer** (*also* **Chan·cel·lor**) *noun* (in the UK) the government minister who is responsible for financial affairs

# change

**can·cer** /ˈtʃɑːnsə(r); *NAmE* ˈtʃæn-/ *noun* (*BrE, informal*) a person who is always looking for opportunities to gain an advantage, even when they do not deserve to do so

**chan·cery** /ˈtʃɑːnsəri; *NAmE* ˈtʃæn-/ *noun* [sing.] **1** **Chancery** (*law*) a division of the High Court in the UK **2** (*especially BrE*) an office where public records are kept **3** (*also* **ˈchancery court**) a court in the US that decides legal cases based on the principle of EQUITY **4** the offices where the official representative of a country works, in another country

**chancy** /ˈtʃɑːnsi; *NAmE* ˈtʃæn-/ *adj.* (*informal*) involving risks and UNCERTAINTY **SYN** **risky**

**chan·de·lier** /ˌʃændəˈlɪə(r); *NAmE* -ˈlɪr/ *noun* a large round frame hanging from the ceiling, with branches that hold lights or CANDLES. Some chandeliers are decorated with many small pieces of glass.

**chand·ler** /ˈtʃɑːndlə(r); *NAmE* ˈtʃænd-/ (*also* **ˈship's chandler**) *noun* a person or shop that sells equipment for ships and boats

## change /tʃeɪndʒ/ verb, noun

▪ **verb**
- **BECOME/MAKE DIFFERENT 1** [I] to become different: *Rick hasn't changed. He looks exactly the same as he did at school.* ◊ *changing attitudes towards education* ◊ *Things have changed dramatically since then.* ⊃ see also UNCHANGING **2** [T] **~ sb/sth** to make sb/sth different: *Fame hasn't really changed him.* ◊ *That experience changed my life.* **3** [I, T] to pass from one state or form into another; to make sb/sth pass from one state or form into another: *Wait for the traffic lights to change.* ◊ **~ from A to/into B** *The lights changed from red to green.* ◊ **~ to/into sth** *The lights changed to green.* ◊ **~ sb/sth (from A) to/into B** *With a wave of her magic wand, she changed the frog into a handsome prince.* **4** [T] **~ sth** to stop having one state, position or direction and start having another: *Leaves change colour in autumn.* ◊ *The wind has changed direction.* ◊ *Our ship changed course.*
- **REPLACE 5** [T] to replace one thing, person, service, etc. with sth new or different: **~ sb/ sth** *I want to change my doctor.* ◊ *I didn't change my name when I got married.* ◊ *That back tyre needs changing.* ◊ *We change our car every two years.* ◊ **~ A for B** *We changed the car for a bigger one.* ◊ **~ A to B** *She changed her name to his.*
- **EXCHANGE 6** [T] (used with a plural object) to exchange positions, places, etc. with sb else, so that you have what they have, and they have what you have: **~ sth** *At half-time the teams change ends.* ◊ *We asked the waiter if we could change tables.* ◊ **~ sth with sb** *Can I change seats with you?*
- **MONEY 7** [T] to exchange money into the money of another country: **~ sth** *I need to change some euros.* ◊ **~ A into B** *to change dollars into yen* **8** [T] to exchange money for the same amount in different coins or notes: **~ sth** *Can you change a £20 note?* ◊ **~ A for/into B** *to change a dollar bill for four quarters*
- **GOODS 9** [T] (*BrE*) to exchange sth that you have bought for sth else, especially because there is sth wrong with it; to give a customer a new item because there is sth wrong with the one they have bought: **~ A for B** *This shirt I bought's too small—I'll have to change it for a bigger one.* ◊ **~ sth** *If you bring the dress back with the receipt, you can change it.*
- **BUS/TRAIN/PLANE 10** [I, T] to go from one bus, train, etc. to another in order to continue a journey: *Where do I have to change?* ◊ *Change at Reading (for London).* ◊ **~ sth** *I stopped in Moscow only to change planes.*
- **CLOTHES 11** [I, T] to put on different or clean clothes: *I went into the bedroom to change.* ◊ **~ into sth** *She changed into her swimsuit.* ◊ **~ out of sth** *You need to change out of those wet things.* **~ sth:** (*especially NAmE*) *I didn't have time to change clothes before the party.* ◊ (*especially BrE*) *I didn't have time to get changed before the party* (= to put different clothes on).
- **BABY 12** [T] **~ sb/sth** to put clean clothes or a clean NAPPY on a baby: *She can't even change a nappy.* ◊ *The baby needs*

# changeable

*changing.* ◊ *There are baby changing facilities in all our stores.* • **BED 13** [T] ~ **sth** to put clean sheets, etc. on a bed: *to change the sheets* ◊ *Could you help me change the bed?*

**IDM** **change ˈhands** to pass to a different owner: *The house has changed hands several times.* **ˌchange ˈhorses in midˈstream** to change to a different or new activity while you are in the middle of sth else; to change from supporting one person or thing to another **change your/sb's ˈmind** to change a decision or an opinion: *Nothing will make me change my mind.* **change your ˈtune** (*informal*) to express a different opinion or behave in a different way when your situation changes: *Wait until it happens to him—he'll soon change his tune.* **change your ˈways** to start to live or behave in a different way from before: *Your father is unlikely to change his ways now.* ⇨ more at CHOP *v.*, LEOPARD, PLACE *n.*

**PHRV** **ˌchange sth↔aˈround** (*BrE also* **ˌchange sth↔ˈround**) to move things or people into different positions: *You've changed all the furniture around.* **ˌchange ˈback (to sth)** to return to a previous situation, etc. **ˌchange ˈback (into sth)** to take off your clothes and put on what you were wearing earlier: *She changed back into her work clothes.* **ˌchange sth ˈback (into sth)** to exchange an amount of money into the currency that it was in before: *You can change back unused dollars in pounds at the bank.* **ˌchange ˈback into sb/sth**, **ˌchange sb/sth ˈback into sb/sth** to return to a previous form; to make sb/sth return to a previous form: *The witch changed him back into a frog.* **ˌchange ˈdown (from sth) (into/to sth)** (*BrE*) to start using a lower GEAR when you are driving a car, etc: *Change down into second.* **ˌchange ˈover (from sth) (to sth)** to change from one system or position to another: *The farm has changed over to organic methods.* ⇨ related noun CHANGEOVER **ˌchange sth↔ˈround** (*BrE*) = CHANGE STH AROUND **ˌchange ˈup (from sth) (into sth)** (*BrE*) to start using a higher GEAR when driving a car, etc: *Change up into fifth.* **ˌchange sth ˈup** (*informal*) to do sth in a different way: *The team needs to change things up and engage a new player.*

■ **noun**

• **DIFFERENCE 1** [C, U] the act or result of sth becoming different: ~ **in** *a change in the weather* ◊ *I need to make some major changes in my life.* ◊ *a change in policy/law* ◊ ~ **to sth** *significant changes to the tax system* ◊ *social/political/economic change* ⇨ see also CLIMATE CHANGE, SEA CHANGE, SEX CHANGE, STEP CHANGE
• **REPLACING STH 2** [C] the process of replacing sth with sth new or different; a thing that is used to replace sth: ~ **of sth** *a change of address* ◊ *a change of government* (*BrE*) *Let's get away for the weekend. A change of scene* (= time in a different place) *will do you good.* ◊ ~ **from A to B** *a change from agriculture to industry* ◊ *There will be a crew change when we land at Dubai.* ⇨ see also BUREAU DE CHANGE, REGIME CHANGE
• **STH NEW AND INTERESTING 3** [sing.] the fact of a situation, a place or an experience being different from what is usual and therefore likely to be interesting, fun, etc: **for a~** *Let's stay in for a change.* ◊ *You can just listen for a change?* ◊ *It makes a change to read some good news for once.* ◊ **a~from sth** *The manual work made a welcome change from his previous job.*
• **MONEY 4** [U] the money that you get back when you have paid for sth giving more money than the amount it costs: *Don't forget your change!* ◊ *That's 40p change.* ◊ *The ticket machine gives change.* **5** [U] coins rather than paper money: *Do you have any change for the machine?* ◊ **in~** *I have two dollars in change* (= coins that together are worth two dollars). ◊ *I didn't have any small change* (= coins of low value) *to leave as a tip.* ◊ *He puts his loose change in a money box for the children.* ◊ **~for sth** *Could you give me change for a ten pound note* (= coins or notes that are worth that amount)? ⇨ see also BUREAU DE CHANGE, CHUMP CHANGE ⇨ SYNONYMS at MONEY
• **OF CLOTHES 6** ~ **of clothes, etc.** [C] an extra set of clothes, etc: *She packed a change of clothes for the weekend.* ◊ *I keep a change of shoes in the car.*
• **OF BUS/TRAIN/PLANE 7** [C] an occasion when you go from one bus, train or plane to another during a journey: *The journey involved three changes.*
• **IN A WOMAN'S LIFE 8 the ˈchange (of ˌlife)** [sing.] (*informal*) = MENOPAUSE

**IDM** **a ˌchange for the ˈbetter/ˈworse** a person, thing, situation, etc. that is better/worse than the previous or present one **a ˌchange of ˈheart** if you have a change of heart, your attitude towards sth changes, usually making you feel more friendly, helpful, etc. **a ˌchange of ˈmind** an act of changing what you think about a situation, etc. **ˌget no ˈchange out of sb** (*BrE*, *informal*) to get no help or information from sb ⇨ more at RING² *v.*, WIND¹ *n.*

**change·able** /ˈtʃeɪndʒəbl/ *adj.* likely to change; often changing SYN **unpredictable**: *The weather is very changeable at this time of year.* ⇨ compare UNCHANGEABLE ▶ **change·abil·ity** /ˌtʃeɪndʒəˈbɪləti/ *noun* [U]

**changed** /tʃeɪndʒd/ *adj.* [only before noun] (of people or situations) very different from what they were before: *She's a changed woman since she got that job.* ◊ *This will not be possible in the changed economic climate.* **OPP** **unchanged**

**change·less** /ˈtʃeɪndʒləs/ *adj.* (*formal*) never changing

**change·ling** /ˈtʃeɪndʒlɪŋ/ *noun* (*literary*) a child who is believed to have been secretly left in exchange for another, especially (in stories) by FAIRIES

**the ˌchange of ˈlife** *noun* [sing.] (*informal*) = MENOPAUSE

**change·over** /ˈtʃeɪndʒəʊvə(r)/ *noun* a change from one system, or method of working to another SYN **switch**: *the changeover from a manual to a computerized system* ◊ *a changeover period*

**ˈchange purse** *noun* (*NAmE*) a small bag made of leather, plastic, etc. for carrying coins ⇨ compare PURSE

**chan·ger** /ˈtʃeɪndʒə(r)/ *noun* (often in compounds) **1** a person or thing that changes sth, usually in order to improve it: *The whole experience was a life changer for me.* ⇨ see also GAME CHANGER **2** a piece of equipment that holds several discs, etc. and is able to switch between them: *The car comes with white leather seats and a 6-CD changer.*

**ˈchanging room** *noun* (*especially BrE*) a room for changing clothes in, especially before playing sports ⇨ compare LOCKER ROOM ⇨ see also FITTING ROOM

## chan·nel /ˈtʃænl/ *noun*, *verb*

■ **noun**

• **ON TELEVISION/RADIO 1** [C] a television station: *a television/TV channel* ◊ *cable/digital/satellite channels* ◊ *a news channel* ◊ *to change/switch channels* ◊ **on a~** *What's on Channel 4 tonight?* ⇨ see also PAY CHANNEL **2** [C] a band of radio waves used for making television or radio broadcasts: *radio channels*
• **FOR COMMUNICATING 3** [C] (*also* **channels** [pl.]) a method or system that people use to get information, to communicate, or to send sth somewhere: *Complaints must be made through the proper channels.* ◊ *The newsletter is a useful channel of communication between teacher and students.* ◊ *The company has worldwide distribution channels.* **4** [C] a means by which data is communicated and exchanged between elements of a computer system or other system: *an audio channel*
• **FOR IDEAS/FEELINGS 5** [C] a way of expressing ideas and feelings: *The campaign provided a channel for protest against the war.* ◊ *Music is a great channel for releasing your emotions.*
• **WATER 6** [C] a passage that water can flow along, especially in the ground, on the bottom of a river, etc: *drainage channels in the rice fields* **7** [C] a deep passage of water in a river or near the coast that can be used as route for ships **8** [C] a passage of water that connects two areas of water, especially two seas: *the Bristol Channel* **9 the Channel** [sing.] the area of sea between England and France, also known as **the English Channel**: *the Channel Tunnel* ◊ *cross-Channel ferries* ◊ **across the~** *news from across the Channel* (= from France)

■ **verb** (-ll-, *US* -l-)
- IDEAS/FEELINGS **1** ~ **sth (into sth)** to direct money, feelings, ideas, etc. towards a particular thing or purpose: *He channels his aggression into sport.*
- MONEY/HELP **2** ~ **sth (through sth)** to send money, help, etc. using a particular route: *Money for the project will be channelled through local government.*
- WATER/LIGHT **3** ~ **sth** to carry or send water, light, etc. through a passage: *A sensor channels the light signal along an optical fibre.*
- SPIRIT/CHARACTER **4** ~ **sb** to act as a MEDIUM (= a person who claims to be able to communicate with the spirits of dead people) for sb: *He believed that he could channel an ancestor from two hundred years ago.* **5** ~ **sb** to behave in the manner of sb else, as though that person has given you the idea or desire to act in that way: *When he sang, he would channel Nat King Cole.*

**'channel-hop** *verb* (-pp-) (*also* **'channel-surf**) [I] to repeatedly switch from one television channel to another

**the 'Channel Islands** *noun* [pl.] a group of islands near the north-western coast of France that belong to the UK but have their own parliaments and laws

**chant** /tʃɑːnt; *NAmE* tʃænt/ *noun, verb*
■ *noun* **1** [C] words or phrases that a group of people shout or sing again and again: *The crowd broke into chants of 'Out! Out!'* ◊ *football chants* **2** [C, U] a religious song or prayer or a way of singing, using only a few notes that are repeated many times: *a Buddhist chant* ⊃ see also GREGORIAN CHANT
■ *verb* **1** [I, T] to sing or shout the same words or phrases many times: *A group of protesters, chanting and carrying placards, waited outside.* ◊ ~ **sth** *The crowd chanted their hero's name.* ◊ *'Resign! Resign!' they chanted.* **2** [I, T] ~ **(sth)** to sing or say a religious song or prayer using only a few notes that are repeated many times ▸ **chant·ing** *noun* [U]: *The chanting rose in volume.*

**chan·ter·elle** /ˌʃɑːntəˈrel/; *NAmE* ˌʃæn-/ *noun* a yellow MUSHROOM that grows in woods, has a hollow part in the centre and can be eaten

**chant·euse** /ʃɑːnˈtɜːz; *NAmE* -ˈtuːz/ *noun* (*from French*) a female singer of popular songs, especially in a NIGHTCLUB

**chan·tey** (*also* **chanty**) /ˈʃænti/ (*both US*) (*BrE* **shanty**, **'sea shanty**) *noun* (*pl.* **-eys** *or* **-ies**) a song that sailors traditionally used to sing while pulling ropes, etc.

**chan·try** /ˈtʃɑːntri; *NAmE* ˈtʃæn-/ *noun* (*pl.* **-ies**) (*also* **'chantry 'chapel**) a small church or part of a church paid for by sb, so that priests could say prayers for them there after their death

**Cha·nu·kah** = HANUKKAH

**chaos** /ˈkeɪɒs; *NAmE* ˈkeɪɑːs/ *noun* [U] a complete lack of order: *economic/political/domestic chaos* ◊ *Heavy snow has caused total chaos on the roads.* ◊ **in** ~ *The house was in chaos after the party.*

**'chaos theory** *noun* [U] (*mathematics*) the study of a group of connected things that are very sensitive so that small changes in conditions affect them very much

**cha·ot·ic** /keɪˈɒtɪk; *NAmE* -ˈɑːt-/ *adj.* without any order; in a completely confused state: *The traffic in the city is chaotic in the rush hour.* ◊ *She had a chaotic personal life with a series of broken relationships.* ▸ **cha·ot·ic·al·ly** /-kli/ *adv.*

**chap** /tʃæp/ *noun, verb*
■ *noun* (*BrE, informal, old-fashioned*) used to talk about a man in a friendly way: *He isn't such a bad chap really.*
■ *verb* [I] (of the skin or lips) to become rough, dry and painful, especially because of wind or cold weather: *His skin is very dry and chaps easily.*

**chap.** *abbr.* (in writing) chapter

**chap·ar·ral** /ˌʃæpəˈræl/ *noun* [U] (*NAmE*) an area of dry land that is covered with small bushes

**cha·patti** (*also* **cha·pati**) /tʃəˈpæti, -ˈpɑːti/ *noun* a type of flat round South Asian bread

**chapel** /ˈtʃæpl/ *noun* **1** [C] a small building or room where Christians go to pray, attend religious services, etc. in a school, prison, large private house, etc: *a college chapel* **2** [C] a separate part of a church or CATHEDRAL, with its own ALTAR, used for some services and private prayer **3** [C, U] the word for a church used in some Christian DENOMINATIONS, for example by Nonconformists in the UK: *a Methodist chapel* ◊ *a Mormon chapel* ◊ *She always went to chapel on Sundays.* **4** [C] a small building or room used for FUNERAL services, especially at a CEMETERY or CREMATORIUM

**chapel of 'rest** *noun* (*BrE*) a room at an UNDERTAKER's where dead bodies are kept before the FUNERAL

**chap·er·one** (*also* **chap·eron**) /ˈʃæpərəʊn/, *noun, verb*
■ *noun* **1** (in the past) an older woman who, on social occasions, took care of a young woman who was not married **2** a person who takes care of children in public, especially when they are working, for example as actors **3** (*NAmE*) a person, such as a parent or a teacher, who goes with a group of young people on a trip or to a dance to encourage good behaviour
■ *verb* ~ **sb** to act as a chaperone for sb, especially a woman

**chap·kan** /ˈtʃæpkən/ *noun* a long coat worn by men, especially in northern India and Pakistan

**chap·lain** /ˈtʃæplɪn/ *noun* a priest or other Christian minister who is responsible for the religious needs of people in a prison, hospital, etc. or in the armed forces ⊃ compare PADRE, PRIEST

**chap·lain·cy** /ˈtʃæplɪnsi/ *noun* (*pl.* **-ies**) the position or work of a chaplain; the place where a chaplain works

**chap·pal** /ˈtʃæpəl/ *noun* (*IndE*) a type of light comfortable open shoe that usually has a piece of leather that goes between the big toe and the toe next to it, or leather bands that go over the foot

**chapped** /tʃæpt/ *adj.* (of the skin or lips) rough, dry and painful, especially because of wind or cold weather

**cha·prasi** /tʃəˈprɑːsi/ *noun* (*IndE*) an office worker who does tasks such as delivering messages

**chaps** /tʃæps/ *noun* [pl.] large pieces of leather worn as protection over trousers by COWBOYS, etc. when riding a horse: *a pair of chaps*

**chap·ter** **B1** /ˈtʃæptə(r)/ *noun* **1 B1** (*abbr.* **ch.**, **chap.**) [C] a separate section of a book, usually with a number or title: *to read/write a chapter* ◊ **in a** ~ *in the previous/next/first/last chapter* ◊ **of sth** *the final chapter of her autobiography* **2** [C] a period of time in a person's life or in history: *a difficult chapter in our country's history* **3** [C + sing./pl. v.] all the priests of a CATHEDRAL or members of a religious community: *a meeting of the dean and chapter* **4** [C] (*especially NAmE*) a local branch of a society, club, etc: *the local chapter of the Rotary club*
**IDM** **chapter and 'verse** the exact details of sth, especially the exact place where particular information may be found: *I can't give chapter and verse, but that's the rough outline of our legal position.* **a ˌchapter of 'accidents** (*BrE*) a series of unpleasant events caused by bad luck

**Chapter 11** /ˌtʃæptər ɪˈlevn/ *noun* [U] (*law*) in the US, a section of the law dealing with BANKRUPTCY (= being unable to pay debts), that allows companies to stop paying their debts in the normal way while they try to find a solution to their financial problems: *The company has filed for Chapter 11 bankruptcy protection.* ⊃ compare ADMINISTRATION

**Chapter '7** *noun* [U] (*law*) in the US, a section of the law dealing with BANKRUPTCY (= being unable to pay debts), that allows a court to take property belonging to a company or person, which is then sold to pay their debts ⊃ compare LIQUIDATION

**'chapter house** *noun* a building where all the priests of a CATHEDRAL or members of a religious community meet

**char** /tʃɑː(r)/ *verb* [I, T] (**-rr-**) ~ **(sth)** to become black by burning; to make sth black by burning it ⊃ see also CHARRED ⊃ SYNONYMS at BURN

**char·ac·ter** **A2** /ˈkærəktə(r)/ *noun*
- IN BOOK/PLAY/MOVIE **1 A2** [C] a person or an animal in a book, play or film: *the main character in the film* ◊ *a major/*

# characterful

*minor character in the book* ◊ *Who plays the main character?* ◊ *cartoon characters* ⮕ **WORDFINDER NOTE** at BOOK

**WORDFINDER** anti-hero, baddy, goody, hero, love interest, narrator, protagonist, trait, villain

**2** ~ **actor / part / role**, etc. a particular type of person in a play, film or TV show
- **QUALITIES / FEATURES 3** [B1] [C, usually sing.] all the qualities and features that make a person different from others: *to have a strong/weak character* ◊ *character traits* ◊ *character defects* ◊ *The book gives a fascinating insight into Mrs Obama's character.* **4** [B1] [U] (*approving*) strong personal qualities such as the ability to deal with difficult or dangerous situations: *Everyone admires her strength of character and determination.* ◊ *He showed great character returning to the sport after his accident.* ◊ *Adventure camps are considered to be character-building* (= meant to improve sb's strong qualities). **5** [B1] [C, usually sing., U] the way that sth is; a particular quality or feature that a thing, an event or a place has **SYN** **nature**: *The character of the neighbourhood hasn't changed at all.* ◊ *the delicate character of the light in the evening* ◊ **in ~** *buildings that are very simple in character* **6** [B1] [U] (*usually approving*) the interesting or unusual quality that a place or a person has: *The modern hotels here have no real character.* ◊ *a face with a lot of character*
- **STRANGE / INTERESTING PERSON 7** [C] (*informal*) (used with an adjective) a person, particularly an unpleasant or strange one: *There were some really strange characters hanging around the bar.* **8** [C] (*informal*) an interesting or unusual person: *She's a character!*
- **REPUTATION 9** [C, U] (*formal*) the opinion that people have of you, particularly of whether you can be trusted or relied on: *She was a victim of character assassination* (= an unfair attack on the good opinion people had of her). ◊ *a slur/attack on his character* ◊ *My teacher agreed to be a character witness for me in court.* ◊ *a character reference* (= a letter that a person who knows you well writes to an employer to tell them about your good qualities)
- **SYMBOL / LETTER 10** [C] a letter, sign, mark or symbol used in writing, in printing or on computers: *Chinese characters* ◊ *a line 30 characters long* ◊ *The URL contained non-standard characters like question marks.* ⮕ picture at IDEOGRAM

**IDM** **in ˈcharacter** | **out of ˈcharacter** typical/not typical of a person's character: *Her behaviour last night was completely out of character.* **in ˈcharacter (with sth)** in the same style as sth: *The new wing of the museum was not really in character with the rest of the building.*

**char·ac·ter·ful** /ˈkærəktəfl; *NAmE* -tərfl/ *adj.* very interesting and unusual

# char·ac·ter·is·tic [B2] /ˌkærəktəˈrɪstɪk/ *noun, adj.*

- **noun** [B2] a typical feature or quality that sth/sb has: *There were few similarities in the brothers' physical characteristics.* ◊ *All human languages share some common characteristics.* ◊ **of sth/sb** *The need to communicate is a key characteristic of human society.* ◊ *a defining characteristic of contemporary American culture*
- **adj.** [B2] very typical of sth or of sb's character: ~ **of sth/ sb** *Community support of families is characteristic of many societies.* **OPP** **uncharacteristic** ▶ **char·ac·ter·is·tic·al·ly** /-kli/ *adv.*: *Characteristically, Helen paid for everyone.*

**char·ac·ter·iza·tion** Ⓦ (*BrE also* **-isa·tion**) /ˌkærəktəraɪˈzeɪʃn; *NAmE* -rəˈz-/ *noun* [U, C] **1** the way that a writer makes characters in a book or play seem real **2** (*formal*) the way in which sb/sth is described or defined **SYN** **portrayal**: *This is an unfair characterization of the prime minister.*

**char·ac·ter·ize** [C1] Ⓦ (*BrE also* **-ise**) /ˈkærəktəraɪz/ *verb* (*formal*) **1** [C1] ~ **sb/sth** to be typical of a person, place or thing: *the rolling hills that characterize this part of England* ◊ *The city is characterized by tall modern buildings in steel and glass.* **2** [C1] ~ **sb/sth (as sth)** to describe or show the qualities of sb/sth in a particular way: *activities that are characterized as 'male' or 'female' work*

**char·ac·ter·less** /ˈkærəktələs; *NAmE* -tərl-/ *adj.* having no interesting qualities

**ˈcharacter recognition** *noun* [U] the ability of a computer to read numbers or letters that are printed or written by hand ⮕ see also OPTICAL CHARACTER RECOGNITION

**cha·rade** /ʃəˈrɑːd; *NAmE* -ˈreɪd/ *noun* **1** [C] a situation in which people pretend that sth is true when it clearly is not **SYN** **pretence**: *Their whole marriage had been a charade —they had never loved each other.* ◊ ~ **of (doing) sth** *We had to go through this whole charade of holding auditions for the part.* **2 charades** [U] a game in which one player acts out the syllables of a word or title and the other players try to guess what it is: *Let's play charades.*

**char·coal** /ˈtʃɑːkəʊl; *NAmE* ˈtʃɑːrk-/ *noun* [U] **1** a black substance made by burning wood slowly in an oven with little air. Charcoal is used as a fuel or for drawing: *charcoal-grilled steaks* ◊ *a charcoal drawing* **2** (*also* **charcoal ˈgrey**) a very dark grey colour

**chard** /tʃɑːd; *NAmE* tʃɑːrd/ (*also* **Swiss ˈchard**) *noun* [U] a vegetable with large green leaves and thick white, yellow or red stems

# charge Ⓘ [B1] /tʃɑːdʒ; *NAmE* tʃɑːrdʒ/ *noun, verb*

■ *noun*
- **MONEY 1** [B1] [C, U] the amount of money that sb asks for goods and services: *admission charges* ◊ ~ **for sth** *We have to make a small charge for refreshments.* ◊ *Delivery is free of charge.* ⮕ see also CONGESTION CHARGE, COVER CHARGE, REVERSE-CHARGE, SERVICE CHARGE ⮕ SYNONYMS at RATE **2** [C] (*NAmE, informal*) a CHARGE ACCOUNT: *Would you like to put that on your charge?* ◊ *'Are you paying cash?' 'No, it'll be a charge.'*
- **RESPONSIBILITY 3** [B1] [U] a position of having control over sb/sth; responsibility for sb/sth: *She has charge of the day-to-day running of the business.* ◊ *He took charge of the farm after his father's death.* ◊ **in ~ of sb / sth** *They left the au pair in charge of the children for a week.* ◊ **in sb's ~** *I'm leaving the school in your charge.* **4** [C] (*formal or humorous*) a person that you have responsibility for and care for
- **OF CRIME / STH WRONG 5** [B2] [C, U] an official claim made by the police that sb has committed a crime: *criminal charges* ◊ *a murder/an assault charge* ◊ ~ **of sth** *He will be sent back to England to face a charge of* (= to be on trial for) *armed robbery.* ◊ *Both men deny the charges.* ◊ ~ **against sb / sth** *They decided to drop the charges against the newspaper and settle out of court.* ◊ **without ~** *After being questioned by the police, she was released without charge.* **6** [B2] [C] a statement accusing sb of doing sth wrong or bad **SYN** **allegation**: *She rejected the charge that the story was untrue.* ◊ *Be careful you don't leave yourself open to charges of political bias.*
- **ELECTRICITY 7** [C, U] the amount of electricity that is put into a battery or carried by a substance: *a positive/negative charge* **8** [U] the act of putting electricity into a battery; the electricity in a battery: **on ~** *He put his phone on charge.* ◊ *My laptop had run out of charge.* ⮕ **WORDFINDER NOTE** at ELECTRICITY
- **RUSH / ATTACK 9** [C] a sudden rush or violent attack, for example by soldiers, wild animals or players in some sports: *He led the charge down the field.*
- **EXPLOSIVE 10** [C] the amount of EXPLOSIVE needed to fire a gun or make an explosion ⮕ see also DEPTH CHARGE
- **STRONG FEELING 11** [sing.] the power to cause strong feelings: *the emotional charge of the piano piece*
- **TASK 12** [sing.] (*formal*) a task or duty: *His charge was to obtain specific information.*

**IDM** **bring / press / lay / prefer ˈcharges against sb** (*law*) to accuse sb formally of a crime so that there can be a trial in court **get a ˈcharge out of sth** (*NAmE*) to get a strong feeling of excitement or pleasure from sth ⮕ more at LEAD¹ *v.*

■ *verb*
- **MONEY 1** [B1] [T, I] to ask an amount of money for goods or a service: *The fees charged by some companies are excessive.* ◊ ~ **sth for sth** *What did they charge for the repairs?* ◊

The restaurant charges £40 for the set menu. ◇ **~sb for sth** We won't charge you for delivery. ◇ **~sb sth** He only charged me half price. ◇ **~sth at sth** Calls are charged at 36p per minute. ◇ **~for sth** Do you think museums should charge for admission? ◇ **to do sth** The bank doesn't charge to stop a payment. ◇ **~sb to do sth** They charge you to change money into euros. **2** ⓘ B2 [T] to record the cost of sth as an amount that sb has to pay: **~sth to sth** They charge the calls to their credit-card account. ◇ (NAmE) **~sth** Don't worry. I'll charge it (= pay by credit card).
- WITH ELECTRICITY **3** ⓘ B1 [T, I] to pass electricity through sth so that it is stored there; to take in electricity so that it is stored and ready for use: **~(sth)** I need to charge my phone. ◇ Let the batteries charge fully before using. ◇ **~sth up** The shaver can be charged up and used when travelling.
- WITH CRIME/STH WRONG **4** ⓘ B2 [T] to accuse sb formally of a crime so that there can be a trial in court: **~sb** Several people were arrested but nobody was charged. ◇ **be charged with (doing) sth** He was charged with murder. ⊃ WORDFINDER NOTE at POLICE **5** [T] **~sb (with sth/with doing sth)** (formal) to accuse sb publicly of doing sth wrong or bad: Opposition MPs charged the minister with neglecting her duty. **6 ~ that …** to make a claim or statement that sth will happen or be the case: Opponents charged that cutting costs would reduce spending.
- RUSH/ATTACK **7** [I, T] to rush forward and attack sb/sth: The bull put its head down and charged. ◇ **~(at) sb/sth** We charged at the enemy. **8** [I] **+ adv./prep.** to rush in a particular direction: The children charged down the stairs. ◇ He came charging into my room and demanded to know what was going on.
- WITH RESPONSIBILITY/TASK **9** [T] (usually passive) (formal) to give sb a responsibility or task: **be charged with sth** The committee has been charged with the development of sport in the region. ◇ **be charged with doing sth** The governing body is charged with managing the school within its budget.
- WITH STRONG FEELING **10** [T] (usually passive) (literary) to fill sb with an emotion: **be charged (with sth)** The room was charged with hatred.
- GLASS **11** [T] **~sth** (BrE, formal) to fill a glass: Please charge your glasses and drink a toast to the bride and groom!
- GUN **12** [T] **~sth** (old use) to load a gun

**charge·able** /ˈtʃɑːdʒəbl; NAmE ˈtʃɑːrdʒ-/ adj. **1 ~(to sb/sth)** (of a sum of money) that must be paid by sb: Any expenses you may incur will be chargeable to the company. **2** (of income or other money that you earn) that you must pay tax on: chargeable earnings/income

ˈcharge account (also informal **charge**) noun (NAmE) an arrangement with a shop or business to pay for goods and services at a later time, for example in regular amounts every month SYN **account**

ˈcharge capping noun [U] (BrE) the act of setting a limit on the amount of money that the local government of an area can charge people in order to pay for public services

ˈcharge card noun a type of credit card on which the whole amount owed must be paid each month ⊃ see also CREDIT CARD

**charged** /tʃɑːdʒd; NAmE tʃɑːrdʒd/ adj. **1** full of or causing strong feelings or opinions: a highly charged atmosphere ◇ a politically charged issue ◇ **~with sth** The dialogue is charged with menace. **2** with an electric charge: positively charged ions

**chargé d'affaires** /ˌʃɑːʒeɪ dæˈfeə(r); NAmE ʃɑːrˈʒeɪ dæˈfer/ noun (pl. **chargés d'affaires** /ˌʃɑːʒeɪ dæˈfeə(r); NAmE ʃɑːrʒeɪ dæˈfer/) (from French) **1** an official who takes the place of an AMBASSADOR in a foreign country when he or she is away **2** an official below the rank of AMBASSADOR who acts as the senior representative of his or her country in a foreign country where there is no AMBASSADOR

ˈcharge nurse noun (BrE) a nurse, especially a man, who is in charge of a hospital WARD

**char·ger** /ˈtʃɑːdʒə(r); NAmE ˈtʃɑːrdʒ-/ noun **1** a piece of equipment for loading a battery with electricity: a phone charger **2** (old use) a horse that a soldier rode in battle in the past

ˈcharge sheet noun a record kept in a police station of the names of people that the police have charged with a crime

ˈcharge-sheet /ˈtʃɑːdʒiːt; NAmE ˈtʃɑːrdʒ-/ verb **~sb (for sth)** (IndE) to accuse sb formally of committing an offence and to ask for an official reply or defence

**char·grill** /ˈtʃɑːɡrɪl; NAmE ˈtʃɑːrɡ-/ verb [usually passive] **~sth** to cook meat, fish or vegetables over a very high heat so that the outside is slightly burnt

**char·iot** /ˈtʃæriət/ noun an open vehicle with two wheels, pulled by horses, used in ancient times in battle and for racing

**char·iot·eer** /ˌtʃæriəˈtɪə(r); NAmE -ˈtɪr/ noun the driver of a chariot

**cha·risma** /kəˈrɪzmə/ noun [U] the powerful personal quality that some people have to attract and impress other people: The President has great personal charisma. ◇ a lack of charisma

**char·is·mat·ic** /ˌkærɪzˈmætɪk/ adj., noun
- adj. **1** having charisma: a charismatic leader **2** (of a Christian religious group) believing in special gifts from God; holding very enthusiastic religious services ► **cha·ris·mat·ic·al·ly** /-kli/ adv.
- noun (often **Charismatic**) a charismatic Christian

**char·it·able** /ˈtʃærətəbl/ adj. **1** connected with a charity or charities: a **charitable institution/foundation/trust** ◇ a **charitable donation/gift** ◇ (BrE) to have **charitable status** (= to be an official charity) **2** helping people who are poor or in need: His later years were devoted largely to charitable work. **3** kind in your attitude to other people, especially when you are judging them: Let's be charitable and assume she just made a mistake. OPP **uncharitable** ► **char·it·ably** /-bli/ adv.: Try to think about him a little more charitably.

**char·ity** ⓘ A2 /ˈtʃærəti/ noun (pl. **-ies**) **1** ⓘ A2 [C] an organization for helping people in need: a registered charity ◇ the UK's largest children's charity ⊃ WORDFINDER NOTE at POOR **2** ⓘ A2 [U] organizations for helping people in need, considered as a group; the money, food, help, etc. that they give: Most of the runners in the London Marathon are raising money for charity. ◇ A portion of the proceeds was donated to charity. ◇ Do you give much to charity? ◇ a charity event (= organized to get money for charity)

**WORDFINDER** appeal, benefit, charity, collection, donation, fundraiser, handout, telethon, volunteer, welfare

**3** [U] (formal) kind behaviour and sympathy towards other people, especially when you are judging them: Her article showed no charity towards her former friends. IDM **charity begins at ˈhome** (saying) you should help and care for your own family, etc. before you start helping other people

ˈcharity shop (BrE) (NAmE ˈthrift shop/store) noun a shop that sells clothes and other goods given by people to raise money for a charity

**char·la·tan** /ˈʃɑːlətən; NAmE ˈʃɑːrl-/ noun a person who claims to have knowledge or skills that they do not really have

**charles·ton** /ˈtʃɑːlstən; NAmE ˈtʃɑːrl-/ noun (usually **the charleston**) [sing.] a fast dance that was popular in the 1920s

**char·lie** /ˈtʃɑːli; NAmE ˈtʃɑːrli/ noun (BrE, old-fashioned, informal) a silly person: You must have felt a proper charlie!

**charm** ⓘ+ C1 /tʃɑːm; NAmE tʃɑːrm/ noun, verb
- noun **1** ⓘ+ C1 [U] the power of pleasing or attracting people: a man of great charm ◇ The hotel is full of charm and character. **2** [C] a feature or quality that is pleasant or attractive: her physical charms (= her beauty) **3** [C] a small object worn on a chain or BRACELET that is believed to bring good luck: a lucky charm ◇ a charm bracelet ⊃ WORDFINDER NOTE at LUCK **4** [C] an act or words believed to have magic power SYN **spell**

# charmed circle

**IDM** **work like a ˈcharm** to be immediately and completely successful ⇒ more at THIRD ordinal number
▪ *verb* **1** [T, I] to please or attract sb in order to make them like you or do what you want: *~(sb) He was charmed by her beauty and wit.* ◇ *Her words had lost their power to charm.* ◇ *~sb into (doing) sth He charmed his mother into letting him have his own way.* **2** [T] *~sb/sth* to control or protect sb/sth using magic, or as if using magic: *He has led a charmed life* (= he has been lucky even in dangerous or difficult situations).
**PHRV** **ˌcharm sth ˈout of sb** to obtain sth such as information, money, etc. from sb by using charm

**ˌcharmed ˈcircle** *noun* [sing.] a group of people who have special influence

**charm·er** /ˈtʃɑːmə(r); NAmE ˈtʃɑːrm-/ *noun* a person who acts in a way that makes them attractive to other people, sometimes using this to influence others ⇒ see also SNAKE CHARMER

**charm·ing** ₊ B2 /ˈtʃɑːmɪŋ; NAmE ˈtʃɑːrm-/ *adj.* **1** ₊ B2 very pleasant or attractive: *The cottage is tiny, but it's charming.* ◇ *She's a charming person.* **2** ₊ C1 (*ironic*, *informal*) used to show that you have a low opinion of sb's behaviour: *They left me to tidy it all up myself. Charming, wasn't it?* ▸ **charm·ing·ly** *adv.*

**charm·less** /ˈtʃɑːmləs; NAmE ˈtʃɑːrm-/ *adj.* (*formal*) not at all pleasant or interesting: *a charmless industrial town*

**ˈcharm offensive** *noun* a situation in which a person, for example a politician, is especially friendly and pleasant in order to get other people to like them and to support their opinions

**ˈcharm school** *noun* (*old-fashioned* or *humorous*) a school where young people are taught to behave in a polite way

**char·nel house** /ˈtʃɑːnl haʊs; NAmE ˈtʃɑːrn-/ *noun* a place used in the past for keeping dead human bodies or bones

**char·poy** /ˈtʃɑːpɔɪ; NAmE ˈtʃɑːrp-/ *noun* (*IndE*) a light wooden or metal frame, usually with many ropes stretched and tied across it, that you can sleep on

**charred** /tʃɑːd; NAmE tʃɑːrd/ *adj.* [usually before noun] burnt and black: *the charred remains of a burnt-out car*

**charts**

bar chart    flow chart    pie chart

**chart** ❶ A1 /tʃɑːt; NAmE tʃɑːrt/ *noun, verb*
▪ *noun* **1** ₊ A1 [C] a diagram, lists of figures, etc. that shows information: *Some shares have lost two-thirds of their value since being issued* (**see chart**). ◇ *~of sb/sth The charts of 138 patients with chronic heart failure were reviewed.* ⇒ LANGUAGE BANK at ILLUSTRATE ⇒ see also BAR CHART, FLIP CHART, FLOW CHART, PIE CHART **2** [C] a detailed map of the sea: *a naval chart* **3** **the charts** [pl.] (*especially BrE*) a list, produced each week, of the songs or albums that have sold the most copies or been downloaded or listened to via STREAMING the most frequently: *The album went straight into the charts at number 1.* ◇ *to top the charts* (= to be the song or album that has sold more copies than all the others)
**IDM** **off the ˈcharts** (*informal*, *especially NAmE*) extremely high in level: *World demand for the product is off the charts.*
▪ *verb* **1** ₊ B2 *~sth* to record or follow the progress or development of sb/sth: *The exhibition charts the history of the palace.* **2** *~sth* to plan a course of action: *She had carefully charted her route to the top of her profession.* **3** *~sth* to make a map of an area **SYN** *map*: *Cook charted the coast of New Zealand in 1768.*

**char·ter** ₊ C1 /ˈtʃɑːtə(r); NAmE ˈtʃɑːrt-/ *noun, verb*
▪ *noun* **1** ₊ C1 [C] a written statement describing the rights that a particular group of people should have: *the European Social Charter of workers' rights* **2** ₊ C1 [C] a written statement of the principles and aims of an organization **SYN** *constitution*: *the United Nations Charter* **3** ₊ C1 [C] an official document stating that a government or political leader allows a new organization, town or university to be established and gives it particular rights: *The Royal College received its charter as a university in 1967.* **4** [sing.] *~(for sth)* (*BrE*) a law or policy that seems likely to help people do sth bad: *The new law will be a charter for unscrupulous financial advisers.* ◇ *a blackmailer's charter* **5** [U] the hiring of a plane, boat, etc: *a yacht available for charter*
▪ *verb* **1** *~sth* to hire a plane, boat, etc. for your own use: *They flew to Athens and then chartered a boat to the island.* ⇒ WORDFINDER NOTE at PLANE **2** [usually passive] *~sth* to state officially that a new organization, town or university has been established and has special rights

**char·tered** /ˈtʃɑːtəd; NAmE ˈtʃɑːrtərd/ *adj.* [only before noun] **1** (*BrE*) qualified according to the rules of a professional organization that has a royal charter: *a chartered accountant/surveyor/engineer* **2** (of an aircraft, a ship or a boat) hired for a particular purpose: *a chartered plane*

**ˌchartered acˈcountant** (*BrE*) (*US* **ˌcertified ˌpublic acˈcountant**) *noun* a fully trained and qualified ACCOUNTANT

**ˈcharter flight** *noun* a flight in an aircraft in which all the seats are paid for by a travel company and then sold to their customers ⇒ compare SCHEDULED FLIGHT

**ˌcharter ˈmember** (also **ˌfounding ˈmember**) (*both NAmE*) (*BrE* **ˈfounder ˌmember**) *noun* one of the first members of a society, an organization, etc., especially one who helped start it

**char·treuse** /ʃɑːˈtrɜːz; NAmE ʃɑːrˈtruːz/ *noun* **1** [U, C] a green or yellow LIQUEUR **2** [U] a pale yellow or pale green colour

**ˈchart-topping** *adj.* [only before noun] (of a song, singer, band, etc.) having reached the highest position in the music CHARTS: *his latest chart-topping hit* ▸ **ˈchart-topper** *noun*

**chary** /ˈtʃeəri; NAmE ˈtʃeri/ *adj.* *~of sth/of doing sth* not willing to risk doing sth; fearing possible problems if you do sth **SYN** *wary*

**chase** ₊ B2 /tʃeɪs/ *verb, noun*
▪ *verb*
• **RUN/DRIVE AFTER 1** ₊ B2 [T, I] to run, drive, etc. after sb/sth in order to catch them or it: *~sb/sth My dog likes chasing rabbits.* ◇ *The kids chased each other around the kitchen table.* ◇ *~after sb/sth He chased after the burglar but couldn't catch him.* ⇒ WORDFINDER NOTE at HUNT **2** ₊ B2 [T] *~sb/sth + adv./prep.* to force sb/sth to run away: *Chase the cat out—we don't want her in the kitchen.*
• **MONEY/WORK/SUCCESS 3** ₊ C1 [T] *~sth* to try to obtain or achieve sth, for example money, work or success: *Too many people are chasing too few jobs nowadays.* ◇ *The team is chasing its first win in five games.*
• **MAN/WOMAN 4** ₊ C1 [I, T] (*informal*) to try to persuade sb to have a sexual relationship with you: *~after sb Kevin's been chasing after Joan for months.* ◇ *~sb Girls are always chasing him.*
• **REMIND SB 5** ₊ C1 [T] *~sb* (*informal*) to persuade sb to do sth that they should have done already: *I need to chase him about organizing the meeting.*
• **RUSH 6** [I] *+ adv./prep.* (*informal*) to rush or hurry somewhere: *I've been chasing around town all morning looking for a present for Sharon.*
• **METAL 7** [T] *~sth* (*specialist*) to cut patterns or designs on metal: *chased silver*
**IDM** **chase your (own) ˈtail** (*informal*) to be very busy but in fact achieve very little
**PHRV** **ˌchase sb↔ˈup** to contact sb in order to remind them to do sth that they should have done already: *We need to chase up all members who have not yet paid.* **ˌchase sth↔ˈup** (*BrE*) (*NAmE* **ˌchase sth↔ˈdown**) to find sth that is needed; to deal with sth that has been forgotten: *My job was to chase up late replies.*
▪ *noun*
• **RUNNING/DRIVING AFTER 1** ₊ B2 [C] (often used with *the*) an act of running or driving after sb/sth in order to catch them or it: *The thieves were caught by police after a short*

*chase.* ◊ *a high-speed car chase* ◊ *We lost him in the narrow streets and had to* **give up the chase** (= stop chasing him). ◊ *to* **take up the chase** (= start chasing sb)
- **FOR SUCCESS/MONEY/WORK 2** [sing.] a process of trying hard to get sth: *Three teams are involved in the chase for the championship.*
- **IN SPORT 3 the chase** [sing.] hunting animals as a sport **4** [C] = STEEPLECHASE ⇒ see also WILD GOOSE CHASE
**IDM** **cut to the 'chase** (*informal*) to stop wasting time and start talking about the most important thing: *Right, let's cut to the chase. How much is it going to cost?* **give 'chase** to run after sb/sth in order to catch them: *We gave chase along the footpath.*

**chaser** /ˈtʃeɪsə(r)/ *noun* **1** a drink that you have after another of a different kind, for example a stronger alcoholic drink after a weak one: *a beer with a whisky chaser* **2** a horse for STEEPLECHASE racing (= in which horses must jump over a series of fences)

**Chas·id·ic** /xæˈsɪdɪk; *NAmE* xɑːˈsiːd-/ (*also* **Has·id·ic, Has·sid·ic**) *adj.* connected with Chasidism (= a form of the Jewish religion that has very strict beliefs)

**Chas·id·ism** /ˈxæsɪdɪzəm; *NAmE* ˈxɑːsɪd-/ *noun* [U] = HASIDISM

**chasm** /ˈkæzəm/ *noun* **1** [C] (*literary*) a deep opening or break in the ground **2** [sing.] ~ **(between A and B)** (*formal*) a very big difference between two people or groups, for example because they have different attitudes **SYN** **gulf**

**chas·sis** /ˈʃæsi/ *noun* (*pl.* **chas·sis** /-siːz/) the frame that a vehicle is built on

**chaste** /tʃeɪst/ *adj.* **1** (*old-fashioned*) not having sex with anyone; only having sex with the person that you are married to: *to remain chaste* **2** (*formal*) not expressing sexual feelings: *a chaste kiss on the cheek* **3** (*formal*) simple and plain in style; not decorated: *the cool, chaste interior of the hall* ▶ **chaste·ly** *adv.*: *He kissed her chastely on the cheek.*

**chas·ten** /ˈtʃeɪsn/ *verb* [often passive] ~ **sb** (*formal*) to make sb feel sorry for sth they have done: *He felt suitably chastened and apologized.*

**chastening** /ˈtʃeɪsnɪŋ/ *adj.* making sb feel sorry for sth they have done: *It was a chastening experience.* ◊ *She gave them a chastening lecture.* ◊ *The party suffered a chastening defeat in the elections.* ◊ *It is chastening to remember that this happened only 20 years ago.*

**chas·tise** /tʃæˈstaɪz/ *verb* **1** ~ **sb (for sth/for doing sth)** (*formal*) to criticize sb for doing sth wrong: *He chastised the team for their lack of commitment.* **2** ~ **sb** (*old-fashioned*) to punish sb physically **SYN** **beat** ▶ **chas·tise·ment** /tʃæˈstaɪzmənt, ˈtʃæstɪzmənt/ *noun* [U]

**chas·tity** /ˈtʃæstəti/ *noun* [U] the state of not having sex with anyone or only having sex with the person you are married to; being CHASTE: *vows of chastity* (= those taken by some priests)

**'chastity belt** *noun* a device worn by some women in the past to prevent them from being able to have sex

**chat** ❶ **A2** /tʃæt/ *verb, noun*
- ■ *verb* (**-tt-**) **1** [I] ~ **(to/with sb)** to talk in a friendly, informal way to sb: *My kids spend hours chatting on the phone to their friends.* ◊ ~ **away (to/with sb)** *Within minutes of being introduced they were chatting away like old friends.* ◊ ~ **about sth/sb** *What were you chatting about?* **2 A2** [I] to exchange messages with sb on the internet, when you can see and reply to messages immediately and have a written conversation: ~ **(to/with sb)** *I've been chatting on-line with my best friend.* ◊ ~ **about sth/sb** *I use social media to chat about stuff as well.* ⇒ WORDFINDER NOTE at WEB
**PHRV** **chat sb**↔**'up** (*BrE*, *informal*) to talk in a friendly way to sb who you are sexually attracted to, perhaps hoping to start a relationship with them: *She went straight over and tried to chat him up.*
- ■ *noun* **1 A2** [C] ~ **(with sb) (about sth)** a friendly informal conversation: *I had a long chat with her.* ◊ *He always enjoyed a chat about the old days.* ⇒ SYNONYMS at DISCUSSION **2 A2** [U] talking, especially informal conversation: *After a few more minutes of chat, she left.* ⇒ SYNONYMS at DISCUSSION ⇒ see also CHIT-CHAT **3** [U, C] communication between people on the internet in which they see

and reply to messages immediately and have a written conversation: *Fans are invited to an online chat.* ◊ ~ **with sb** *You can take part in a live chat with the movie's director this afternoon.* ◊ ~ **about sb/sth** *There was much chat about it on internet message boards.*

**chat·bot** /ˈtʃætbɒt; *NAmE* -bɑːt/ *noun* a computer program that can hold a conversation with a person, usually over the internet ⇒ compare VOICE ASSISTANT

**cha·teau** (*also* **châ·teau**) /ˈʃætəʊ; *NAmE* ʃæˈtoʊ/ *noun* (*pl.* **cha·teaux, châ·teaux** /ˈʃætəʊz; *NAmE* ʃæˈtoʊz/ *or* **cha·teaus, châ·teaus**) (*from French*) a castle or large country house in France

**'chat room** *noun* an area on the internet where people can communicate with each other, usually about one particular topic

**'chat show** (*BrE*) (*also* **'talk show** *NAmE, BrE*) *noun* a television or radio programme in which famous people are asked questions and talk in an informal way about their work and opinions on various topics: *a chat-show host* ⇒ WORDFINDER NOTE at PROGRAMME

**chat·tel** /ˈtʃætl/ *noun* [C, U] (*law or old-fashioned*) something that belongs to you

**chat·ter** /ˈtʃætə(r)/ *verb, noun*
- ■ *verb* **1** [I] ~ **(away/on) (to sb) (about sth)** to talk quickly and continuously, especially about things that are not important: *They chattered away happily for a while.* ◊ *The children chattered to each other excitedly about the next day's events.* **2** [I] (of teeth) to knock together continuously because you are cold or frightened **3** [I] (of birds or monkeys) to make a series of short high sounds
**IDM** **the 'chattering classes** (*BrE*, *usually disapproving*) the people in society who like to give their opinions on political or social issues
- ■ *noun* [U] **1** continuous rapid talk about things that are not important: *Jane's constant chatter was beginning to annoy him.* ◊ *idle chatter* **2** a series of quick short high sounds that some animals make: *the chatter of monkeys* **3** a series of short sounds made by things knocking together: *the chatter of teeth*

**chat·ter·box** /ˈtʃætəbɒks; *NAmE* -tərbɑːks/ *noun* (*informal*) a person who talks a lot, especially a child

**chatty** /ˈtʃæti/ *adj.* (**chat·tier, chat·ti·est**) (*informal*) **1** talking a lot in a friendly way: *You're very chatty today, Alice.* **2** having a friendly informal style: *a chatty letter*

**'chat-up** *noun* [C, U] (*BrE*, *informal*) an occasion when a person is talking to sb in a way that shows they are interested in them sexually: *Is that your best chat-up line?*

**chauf·feur** /ˈʃəʊfə(r); *NAmE* ʃoʊˈfɜːr/ *noun, verb*
- ■ *noun* a person whose job is to drive a car, especially for sb rich or important
- ■ *verb* ~ **sb** to drive sb in a car, usually as your job: *He was chauffeured to all his meetings.* ◊ *a chauffeured limousine*

**chau·vin·ism** /ˈʃəʊvɪnɪzəm; *NAmE* ʃoʊ-/ *noun* [U] (*disapproving*) **1** an aggressive and unreasonable belief that your own country is better than all others **2** = MALE CHAUVINISM

**chau·vin·ist** /ˈʃəʊvɪnɪst; *NAmE* ʃoʊ-/ *noun* (*disapproving*) **1** = MALE CHAUVINIST **2** a person who has an aggressive and unreasonable belief that their own country is better than all others ▶ **chau·vin·is·tic** /ˌʃəʊvɪˈnɪstɪk; *NAmE* ˌʃoʊ-/ (*also less frequent* **chau·vin·ist**) *adj.* **chau·vin·is·tic·al·ly** /-kli/ *adv.*

**chav** /tʃæv/ *noun* (*BrE, disapproving, slang*) a young person from the WORKING CLASS, usually without a high level of education, who typically behaves in a loud and annoying way and wears designer clothes

**chawl** /tʃɔːl/ *noun* (*IndE, SEAsianE*) (in South Asia) a large building divided into many separate apartments, offering cheap, basic accommodation to LABOURERS

**ChB** /ˌsiː ˈeɪtʃ ˈbiː/ *abbr.* (*BrE*) Bachelor of Surgery

**cheap** ❶ **A1** /tʃiːp/ *adj., adv.*
- ■ *adj.* (**cheap·er, cheap·est**)
- **LOW PRICE 1 A1** costing little money or less money than you expected **SYN** **inexpensive**: *cheap imports/flights* ◊

# cheapen 250

Their cheap prices have helped them pick up new customers. ◇ Electricity is relatively cheap in Ireland. ◇ A falling dollar will boost the economy by making exports cheaper. ◇ immigrant workers, used as a source of **cheap labour** (= workers who are paid very little, especially unfairly) ⊃ see also DIRT CHEAP **OPP** expensive **2** **A1** charging low prices: *a cheap restaurant/hotel* ◇ (BrE) *We found a cheap and cheerful cafe* (= one that is simple and charges low prices but is pleasant). **OPP** expensive
- POOR QUALITY **3** **B2** (*disapproving*) low in price and quality: *cheap perfume/jewellery/shoes* ◇ *cheap plastic toys that break within seconds* ◇ (BrE) *a cheap and nasty bottle of wine*
- UNKIND **4** unpleasant or unkind and rather obvious: *I was tired of his cheap jokes at my expense.*
- LOW STATUS **5** (*disapproving*) having a low status and therefore not deserving respect: *He's just a cheap crook.* ◇ *His treatment of her made her feel cheap* (= ashamed, because she had lost her respect for herself).
- NOT GENEROUS **6** (NAmE) (BrE **mean**) (*informal, disapproving*) not liking to spend money: *Don't be so cheap!* ▶ **cheapness** *noun* [U]

**IDM** **cheap at the ˈprice** (*also* **cheap at ˈtwice the price**) (BrE *also*, *humorous* **cheap at ˈhalf the price**) so good or useful that the cost does not seem too much **on the ˈcheap** (*usually disapproving*) spending less money than you usually need to do sth: *a guide to decorating your house on the cheap* ⊃ more at LIFE

■ *adv.* **B1** (*comparative* **cheap·er**, no superlative) (*informal*) for a low price: *I got this dress cheap in a sale.* ◇ *You can buy it cheaper elsewhere.*

**IDM** **be going ˈcheap** to be offered for sale at a lower price than usual **sth does not come ˈcheap** something is expensive: *Violins like this don't come cheap.*

▼ SYNONYMS

### cheap
competitive • budget • affordable • reasonable • inexpensive

These words all describe a product or service that costs little money or less money than you expected.

**cheap** costing little money or less money than you expected; charging low prices. **NOTE** Cheap can also be used in a disapproving way to suggest that sth is of poor quality as well as low in price: *a bottle of cheap perfume*.

**competitive** (of prices, goods or services) as cheap as or cheaper than those offered by other companies; able to offer goods or services at competitive prices.

**budget** [only before noun] (used especially in advertising) cheap because it offers only a basic level of service.

**affordable** cheap enough for most people to afford.

**reasonable** (of prices) not too expensive.

**inexpensive** (*rather formal*) cheap. **NOTE** Inexpensive is often used to mean that sth is good value for its price. It is sometimes used instead of cheap, because cheap can suggest that sth is of poor quality.

PATTERNS
- cheap/competitive/budget/affordable/reasonable prices/fares/rates
- cheap/competitive/budget/affordable/inexpensive products/services

**cheap·en** /ˈtʃiːpən/ *verb* **1** ~ sb/yourself to make people lose respect for sb or for yourself **SYN** **degrade**: *She never cheapened herself by lowering her standards.* **2** ~ sth to make sth lower in price: *to cheapen the cost of raw materials* **3** ~ sth to make sth appear to have less value: *The movie was accused of cheapening human life.*

**cheap·ly** /ˈtʃiːpli/ *adv.* without spending or costing much money: *I'm sure I could buy this more cheaply somewhere else.* ◇ *a cheaply made movie*

**cheapo** /ˈtʃiːpəʊ/ (*also* **cheapie** /ˈtʃiːpi/) *adj.* [only before noun] (*informal, disapproving*) cheap and often of poor quality: *a cheapie horror flick*

**cheap·skate** /ˈtʃiːpskeɪt/ *noun* (*informal, disapproving*) a person who does not like to spend money

### cheat ⓘ **B1** /tʃiːt/ *verb, noun*

■ *verb* **1** **B1** [T] to trick sb or make them believe sth that is not true: ~sb/sth *She is accused of attempting to cheat the taxman.* ◇ *Many people feel cheated by the election process.* ◇ ~sb out of sth *He cheated investors out of billions of dollars.* **2** **B1** ~ (at sth) to act in a dishonest way in order to gain an advantage, especially in a game, a competition, an exam, etc: *He cheats at cards.* ◇ *You're not allowed to look at the answers—that's cheating.* ◇ *Anyone caught cheating will be automatically disqualified from the examination.* **3** [I] ~ (on sb) (of sb who is married or who has a regular sexual partner) to have a secret sexual relationship with sb else

**IDM** **cheat ˈdeath** (often used in newspapers) to survive in a situation where you could have died

▼ SYNONYMS

### cheat
fool • deceive • betray • take in • trick • con

These words all mean to make sb believe sth that is not true, especially in order to get what you want.

**cheat** to make sb believe sth that is not true, in order to get money or sth else from them: *She is accused of attempting to cheat the taxman.* ◇ *He cheated his way into the job.* **NOTE** Cheat also means to act in a dishonest way in order to gain an advantage, especially in a game, competition or exam: *You're not allowed to look at the answers—that's cheating.*

**fool** to make sb believe sth that is not true, especially in order to laugh at them or to get what you want: *Just don't be fooled into investing any money with them.*

**deceive** to make sb believe sth that is not true, especially sb who trusts you, in order to get what you want: *She deceived him into handing over all his savings.*

**betray** to hurt sb who trusts you, especially by lying to or about them or telling their secrets to other people: *She felt betrayed when she found out the truth about him.*

**take sb in** [often passive] to make sb believe sth that is not true, usually in order to get what you want: *I was taken in by her story.*

**trick** to make sb believe sth that is not true, in a clever way, in order to get what you want.

**con** (*informal*) to make sb believe sth that is not true, especially in order to get money from them or get them to do sth for you: *They had been conned out of £100 000.*

WHICH WORD?
- Many of these words involve making sb believe sth that is not true, but some of them are more disapproving than others. Deceive is probably the worst because people typically deceive friends, relations and others who know and trust them. People may *feel cheated/betrayed* by sb in authority who they trusted to look after their interests. If sb **takes you in**, they may do it by acting a part and using words and charm effectively. If sb **cheats/fools/tricks/cons** you, they may get sth from you and make you feel stupid. However, sb might **fool** you just as a joke; and to **trick** sb is sometimes seen as a clever thing to do, if the person being tricked is seen as a bad person who deserves it.

PATTERNS
- to cheat/fool/trick/con sb **out of** sth
- to cheat/fool/deceive/betray/trick/con sb **into doing sth**
- to feel cheated/fooled/deceived/betrayed/tricked/conned
- to fool/deceive yourself
- to cheat/trick/con your way into sth

 Oxford 3000 | Oxford 5000 | **A1 A2 B1 B2 C1** CEFR level | **PHRV** phrasal verb(s) | **IDM** idiom(s)

PHRV ˈcheat sb of sth | ˌcheat sb ˈout of sth to prevent sb from having sth, especially in a way that is not honest or fair: *They cheated him out of his share of the profits.*
▪ **noun** (*especially BrE*) **1** 🔑 B1 (*also* **cheat‑er** *especially in NAmE*) [C] a person who cheats, especially in a game: *You little cheat!* **2** [sing.] something that seems unfair or dishonest, for example a way of doing sth with less effort than it usually needs: *It's really a cheat, but you can use ready‑made pastry if you want.* **3** [C] (*computing*) a program you can use to move immediately to the next stage of a computer game without needing to play the game: *There's a cheat you can use to get to the next level.*

**ˈcheat sheet** *noun* (*informal*) a set of notes to help you remember important information, especially one taken secretly into an exam room SYN **crib sheet**

## check ❶ A1 /tʃek/ *verb, noun, exclamation*

▪ **verb**
- **EXAMINE 1** 🔑 A1 [T] to examine sth to see if it is correct, safe or acceptable: ~ **sth** *She gave me the minutes of the meeting to read and check.* ◇ *The cars were checked to see whether the faults had been spotted.* ◇ ~ **sth for sth** *Check the container for cracks or leaks.* ◇ ~ **sth against sth** *I'll need to check these figures against last year's.*
- **MAKE SURE 2** 🔑 A1 [I, T] to look at sth or ask sb to find out if sth/sb is present, correct or true or if sth is how you think it is: *We'll check back in a couple of hours.* ◇ ~ **sth (for sth)** *Hang on—I just need to check my email.* ◇ ~ **(that)** … *Go and check (that) I've locked the windows.* ◇ ~ **(with sb) what/whether, etc** … *You'd better check with Jane what time she's expecting us tonight.* ◇ see also CROSS‑CHECK, DOUBLE‑CHECK
- **MAKE MARK 3** 🔑 A2 [T] ~ **sth** (*especially NAmE*) (*BrE usually* **tick**) to put a mark (✔) next to an item on a list, an answer, etc: *Check the box next to the right answer.*
- **CONTROL 4** [T] ~ **sth** to control sth; to stop sth from increasing or getting worse: *The government is determined to check the growth of public spending.* **5** [T] to stop yourself from saying or doing sth or from showing a particular emotion: ~ **sth** *to check your anger/laughter/tears* ◇ ~ **yourself** *She wanted to tell him the whole truth but she checked herself—it wasn't the right moment.*
- **COATS/BAGS/CASES 6** [T] ~ **sth** (*NAmE*) to leave coats, bags, etc. in an official place (called a CHECKROOM) while you are visiting a club, restaurant, etc: *Do you want to check your coats?* **7** [T] ~ **sth** (*NAmE*) (*also* **check sth in** *BrE, NAmE*) to leave bags or cases with an official so that they can be put on a plane or train

PHRV ˌcheck ˈin (at …) 🔑 A2 to go to a desk in a hotel, an airport, etc. and tell an official there that you have arrived: *Please check in at least an hour before departure.* ◇ *We've checked in at the hotel.* ◇ related noun CHECK‑IN ˌcheck sth↔ˈin 🔑 A2 to leave bags or cases with an official to be put on a plane or train: *We checked in our luggage and went through to the departure lounge.* ◇ related noun CHECK‑IN ˌcheck ˈinto … to arrive at a hotel or private hospital to begin your stay there: *He checked into a top London clinic yesterday for an operation on his knee.* ˌcheck sb/sth↔ˈoff (*especially NAmE*) (*BrE usually* **tick sb/sth ˈoff**) to put a mark (✔) next to a name or an item on a list to show that sth has been dealt with: *Check the names off as the guests arrive.* ˌcheck ˈon sb/sth to make sure that there is nothing wrong with sb/sth: *I'll just go and check on the children.* ˌcheck ˈout to be found to be true or acceptable after being examined: *The local police found her story didn't check out.* ˌcheck ˈout (of …) 🔑 A2 to pay your bill and leave a hotel, etc: *Guests should check out of their rooms by noon.* ◇ related noun CHECKOUT (2) ˌcheck sb/sth↔ˈout **1** 🔑 B1 to find out if sth is correct, or if sb is acceptable: *The police are checking out his alibi.* ◇ *We'll have to check him out before we employ him.* **2** (*informal*) to look at or examine a person or thing that seems interesting or attractive: *Check out the prices at our new store!* ◇ *Hey, check out that car!* ˌcheck sth↔ˈout to borrow sth from an official place, for example a book from a library: *The book has been checked out in your name.* ˌcheck ˈover/ˈthrough↔sth to examine sth carefully to make sure that it is correct or acceptable: *Check over your work for mistakes.* ˌcheck ˈup on sb to make sure that sb is doing what they should be doing: *My parents are always checking up on me.* ˌcheck ˈup on sth to find out if sth is true or correct: *I need to check up on a few things before I can decide.*

▪ **noun**
- **EXAMINATION 1** 🔑 A2 [C] an act of making sure that sth is safe, correct or in good condition by examining it: *Could you give the tyres a check?* ◇ *I'll just have a quick check to see if the letter's arrived yet.* ◇ ~ **of sth** *She had a thorough check of the room, but nothing had been taken.* ◇ ~ **for sth** *a check for spelling mistakes* ◇ ~ **on sth** *It is vital to keep a check on your speed* (= look at it regularly in order to control it). ◇ *A spokesperson said the company made regular checks with the police and the council.* ◇ see also CROSS‑CHECK, DOUBLE‑CHECK, REALITY CHECK, SPOT CHECK
- **INVESTIGATION 2** 🔑 B2 [C] an investigation to find out more information about sb/sth: *The agency insisted all the necessary background checks had been carried out.* ◇ ~ **on sb/sth** *The police ran a check on the registration number of the car.*
- **MARK 3** 🔑 A2 (*also* ˈ**check mark**) (*both especially NAmE*) (*BrE usually* **tick**) [C] a mark (✔) put next to a sum or an item on a list, usually to show that it has been checked or done or is correct: *The teacher put a check next to his name.* ◇ compare CROSS, X
- **MONEY 4** 🔑 A2 [C] (*NAmE*) = BILL: *Can I have the check, please?* ◇ SYNONYMS at BILL **5** [C] (*US*) = CHEQUE
- **CONTROL 6** [C] ~ **(on/to sth)** (*formal*) something that delays the progress of sth else or stops it from getting worse: *A cold spring will provide a natural check on the number of insects.* ◇ see also BODY CHECK **7** ˈ**checks** [pl.] (*formal*) rules that are designed to control the amount of power, especially political power, that one person or group has ◇ see also CHECKS AND BALANCES

▼ **SYNONYMS**

**check**
examine • inspect • go over sth

These words all mean to look closely to make sure that everything is correct, in good condition, or acceptable.

**check** to look at sth closely to make sure that everything is correct, in good condition, safe or acceptable: *Check your work before handing it in.*

**examine** to look at sb/sth closely to see if there is anything wrong or to find the cause of a problem: *The goods were examined for damage on arrival.*

**inspect** to look at sb/sth closely to make sure that everything is acceptable; to officially visit a school, factory, etc. in order to check that rules are being obeyed and that standards are acceptable: *Make sure you inspect the goods before signing for them.* ◇ *The Tourist Board inspects all recommended hotels at least once a year.*

**CHECK, EXAMINE OR INSPECT?**

All these words can be used when you are looking for possible problems, but of these three words only **check** is used for mistakes: Examine/Inspect your work before handing it in. Only **examine** is used when looking for the cause of a problem: The doctor checked/inspected her but could find nothing wrong. **Examine** is used more often about a professional person: *The surveyor examined the walls for signs of damp.* **Inspect** is used more often about an official: *Public health officials were called in to inspect the restaurant.*

**go over sth** to check sth carefully for mistakes, damage or anything dangerous: *Go over your work for spelling mistakes before you hand it in.*

**PATTERNS**
- to check/examine/inspect/go over (sth) **for** sth
- to check/examine/inspect/go over sth **to see if/whether** …
- to check/examine/inspect/go over sth **carefully/thoroughly**

# checkbook

- **PATTERN 8** [C, U] a pattern of squares, usually of two colours: *Do you prefer checks or stripes?* ◊ *a check shirt/suit* ◊ *a yellow and red check skirt* ⇒ see also CHECKED ⇒ WORDFINDER NOTE at PATTERN
- **FOR COATS/BAGS 9** [C] (*NAmE*) **coat ~** a place in a club, restaurant, etc. where you can leave your coat or bag ⇒ see also COAT CHECK **10** [C] (*NAmE*) a ticket that you get when you leave your coat, bag, etc. in, for example, a restaurant or theatre
- **IN GAME 11** [U] (in CHESS) a position in which a player's king (= the most important piece) being directly attacked by the other player's pieces: *There, you're in check.* ⇒ see also CHECKMATE

**IDM** **hold/keep sth in 'check** to keep sth under control so that it does not spread or get worse ⇒ more at RAIN CHECK
- **exclamation** used to show that you agree with sb or that sth on a list has been dealt with: *'Do you have your tickets?' 'Check.' 'Passport?' 'Check.'*

**check·book** /'tʃekbʊk/ *noun* (*US*) = CHEQUEBOOK

**check·box** /'tʃekbɒks; *NAmE* -bɑːks/ (*BrE also* **tick-box**) *noun* a small square on a computer screen that you click on with the mouse to choose whether a particular function is switched on or off

**'check card** *noun* (*US*) = DEBIT CARD

**checked** /tʃekt/ *adj.* having a pattern of squares, usually of two colours: *checked material* ⇒ see also CHECK *verb*

**check·er** /'tʃekə(r)/ *noun* ⇒ see also CHECKERS **1** (*especially US*) a person who works at the CHECKOUT in a supermarket **2** (in compounds) a computer program that you use to check sth, for example the spelling and grammar of sth you have written: *a spelling/grammar/virus checker* **3** a person who checks things: *a quality control checker*

**check·er·board** /'tʃekəbɔːd; *NAmE* -kərbɔːrd/ (*NAmE*) (*BrE* **draught·board**) *noun* a board with black and white squares, used for playing CHECKERS

**check·ered** *adj.* (*especially NAmE*) = CHEQUERED

**check·ers** /'tʃekəz; *NAmE* -kərz/ (*NAmE*) (*BrE* **draughts**) *noun* [U] a game for two players using 24 round pieces on a board marked with black and white squares

**'check-in** *noun* **1** [C, U] the place where you go to at an airport to leave your bags, cases, etc. and show your ticket **2** [U] the act of confirming your intention to take a particular flight and giving your personal details either at an airport or using a computer: *Do you know your check-in time?* ◊ (*BrE*) *the check-in desk* ◊ (*NAmE*) *the check-in counter* **3** [C, U] the time when you arrive at a hotel at the start of your stay: *We can arrange an early check-in.* **OPP** **checkout** ⇒ WORDFINDER NOTE at AIRPORT

**'checking account** (*US*) (*BrE* **'current account**) (*CanE* **'chequing account**) *noun* a type of bank account that you can take money out of at any time, and that provides you with a DEBIT CARD and (sometimes) a CHEQUEBOOK ⇒ compare DEPOSIT ACCOUNT

**check·list** /'tʃeklɪst/ *noun* a list of the things that you must remember to do, to take with you or to find out

**check·mate** /'tʃekmeɪt, ˌtʃekˈmeɪt/ (*also* **mate**) *noun* [U, sing.] **1** (in CHESS) a position in which one player cannot prevent their king (= the most important piece) being captured and therefore loses the game ⇒ see also CHECK *noun* ⇒ compare STALEMATE **2** a situation in which sb has been completely defeated ▶ **check·mate** (*also* **mate**) *verb*: *~ sb/sth His king had been checkmated.* ◊ *She hoped the plan would checkmate her opponents.*

**check·out** /'tʃekaʊt/ *noun* **1** [C] the place where you pay for the things that you are buying in a supermarket: *a checkout assistant/operator* ⇒ see also SELF-CHECKOUT **2** [U] the time when you leave a hotel at the end of your stay: *At checkout, your bill will be printed for you.* **OPP** **check-in 3** [U] part of the process of online shopping in which the customer enters delivery information and pays for the item: *Proceed to checkout.*

**'check-point** /'tʃekpɔɪnt/ *noun* a place, especially on a border between two countries, where people have to stop so their vehicles and documents can be checked

**'check-room** /'tʃekruːm, -rʊm/ *noun* (*NAmE*) = CLOAKROOM

**checks and 'balances** *noun* [pl.] **1** influences in an organization or political system that help to keep it fair and stop a small group from keeping all the power **2** (in the US) the principle of government by which the president, Congress and the Supreme Court each have some control over the others ⇒ WORDFINDER NOTE at GOVERNMENT ⇒ compare SEPARATION OF POWERS

**check·sum** /'tʃeksʌm/ *noun* (*computing*) the total of the numbers in a piece of digital data, used to check that the data is correct

**'check-up** *noun* an examination of sb/sth, especially a medical one to make sure that you are healthy: *to go for/to have a check-up* ◊ *a medical/dental/routine/thorough check-up* ⇒ WORDFINDER NOTE at DENTIST

**Ched·dar** /'tʃedə(r)/ (*also* **Cheddar 'cheese**) (*both BrE*) (*NAmE* **cheddar**, **cheddar 'cheese**) *noun* [U] a type of hard yellow cheese

**cheek** /tʃiːk/ *noun, verb*
- **noun 1** [C] either side of the face below the eyes: *chubby/rosy/pink cheeks* ◊ *He kissed her on both cheeks.* ◊ *Couples were dancing cheek to cheek.* **2 -cheeked** (in adjectives) having the type of cheeks mentioned: *chubby-cheeked/rosy-cheeked/hollow-cheeked* **3** [C] (*informal*) either of the BUTTOCKS **4** [U, sing.] (*BrE*) talk or behaviour that people think is annoying, rude or not showing enough respect **SYN** **nerve**: *What a cheek!* ◊ *He had the cheek to ask his ex-girlfriend to babysit for them.* ◊ *I think they've got a cheek making you pay to park the car.*
**IDM** **cheek by 'jowl (with sb/sth)** very close to sb/sth **turn the other 'cheek** to make a deliberate decision to remain calm and not to act in an aggressive way when sb has hurt you or made you angry ⇒ more at TONGUE *n.*
- **verb ~ sb** (*BrE, informal*) to speak to sb in a rude way that shows a lack of respect

**cheek·bone** /'tʃiːkbəʊn/ *noun* the bone below the eye ⇒ VISUAL VOCAB page V1

**cheeky** /'tʃiːki/ *adj.* (**cheek·ier**, **cheeki·est**) (*informal*) rude in a funny or annoying way: *You cheeky monkey!* ◊ *a cheeky grin* ◊ *You're getting far too cheeky!* ⇒ SYNONYMS at RUDE ▶ **cheek·ily** /-kɪli/ *adv.* **cheeki·ness** /-kinəs/ *noun* [U]

**cheep** /tʃiːp/ *verb* [I] (of young birds) to make short high sounds ▶ **cheep** *noun*

**cheer** /tʃɪə(r); *NAmE* tʃɪr/ *verb, noun*
- **verb 1** [I, T] to shout loudly, in order to show support or praise for sb, or to encourage them: *We all cheered as the team came on to the field.* ◊ *Cheering crowds greeted their arrival.* ◊ *~ sb The crowd cheered the president as he drove slowly by.* ⇒ SYNONYMS at SHOUT **OPP** **boo 2** [T] [usually passive] to encourage sb or to give them hope or comfort: **be cheered (by sth)** *She was cheered by the news from home.* ▶ **cheer·ing** *noun* [U]: *He came on stage amid clapping and cheering.* **cheer·ing** *adj.*: *The results of the test were very cheering.*
**PHRV** **cheer sb↔'on** to give shouts in order to encourage sb in a race, competition, etc. **cheer 'up** | **cheer sb/sth↔'up** to become more cheerful; to make sb/sth more cheerful: *Oh, come on—cheer up!* ◊ *Give Mary a call; she needs cheering up.* ◊ *Bright curtains can cheer up a dull room.*
- **noun** ⇒ see also CHEERS **1** [C] a shout of joy, support or praise: *A great cheer went up from the crowd.* ◊ *cheers of encouragement.* ◊ **Three cheers for the winners!** (= used when you are asking a group of people to cheer three times, in order to CONGRATULATE sb, etc.) **OPP** **boo 2** [C] (*NAmE*) a special song or cheer used by CHEERLEADERS **3** [U] (*formal or literary*) an atmosphere of happiness

**cheer·ful** /'tʃɪəfl; *NAmE* 'tʃɪrfl/ *adj.* **1** happy, and showing it by the way that you behave: *You're not your usual cheerful self today.* ◊ *a cheerful smile/voice/face/disposition* ◊ *to look/seem/sound cheerful* **2** giving you a feeling of happiness: *a bright, cheerful restaurant*

◊ walls painted in cheerful (= light and bright) colours ◊ He was whistling a cheerful tune. ▶ **cheer·ful·ly** /-fəli/ adv.: to **laugh/nod/whistle cheerfully** ◊ I could cheerfully have killed him when he said that (= I would have liked to). ◊ She cheerfully admitted that she had no experience at all (= she wasn't afraid to do so). **cheer·ful·ness** noun [U]

**cheerio** /ˌtʃɪəriˈəʊ; NAmE ˌtʃɪr-/ exclamation (BrE, informal) goodbye: Cheerio! I'll see you later.

**cheer·lead·er** /ˈtʃɪəliːdə(r); NAmE ˈtʃɪrl-/ noun **1** (especially in the US) one of the members of a group of young people (usually women) wearing special uniforms, who encourage the crowd to CHEER for their team at a sports event **2** a person who supports a particular politician, idea, or way of doing sth ▶ **cheer·lead·ing** noun [U]: a **cheerleading squad/team** ◊ the president's continued cheerleading for the 'strong dollar'

**cheer·less** /ˈtʃɪələs; NAmE ˈtʃɪrl-/ adj. (formal) (of a place, etc.) not being warm or brightly coloured so it makes you feel depressed SYN **gloomy**: a dark and cheerless room

**cheers** /tʃɪəz; NAmE tʃɪrz/ exclamation **1** a word that people say to each other as they lift up their glasses to drink **2** (BrE, informal) thank you: 'Have another biscuit.' 'Cheers.' **3** (BrE, informal) goodbye: Cheers then. See you later.

**cheery** /ˈtʃɪəri; NAmE ˈtʃɪri/ adj. (**cheer·ier**, **cheeri·est**) (informal) (of a person or their behaviour) happy and cheerful: a **cheery remark/smile/wave** ◊ He left with a cheery 'See you again soon'. ▶ **cheer·ily** /-rəli/ adv.

**cheese** 🔑 **A1** /tʃiːz/ noun **1** 🔑 **A1** [U, C] a type of food made from milk that can be either soft or hard and is usually white or yellow in colour; a particular type of this food: Cheddar cheese ◊ (BrE) goat's cheese (= made from the milk of a GOAT) ◊ a **cheese sandwich** ◊ a piece/slice/block of cheese ◊ I had cheese on toast (= TOASTED bread covered in melted cheese) for lunch. ◊ a selection of French cheeses ⊃ see also AMERICAN CHEESE, BLUE CHEESE, CAULIFLOWER CHEESE, COTTAGE CHEESE, CREAM CHEESE, FETA CHEESE, GOAT CHEESE, MACARONI CHEESE, SWISS CHEESE **2 cheese!** what you ask sb to say before you take their photograph IDM see BIG adj., CHALK n., HARD adj.

**cheese·board** /ˈtʃiːzbɔːd; NAmE -bɔːrd/ noun **1** a board that is used to cut cheese on **2** a variety of cheeses that are served at the end of a meal

**cheese·bur·ger** /ˈtʃiːzbɜːgə(r); NAmE -bɜːrg-/ noun a HAMBURGER with a slice of cheese on top of the meat

**cheese·cake** /ˈtʃiːzkeɪk/ noun [C, U] a cold DESSERT (= a sweet dish) made from a soft mixture of CREAM CHEESE, sugar, eggs, etc. on a base of cake or biscuits broken into small pieces, sometimes with fruit on top: a strawberry cheesecake ◊ Is there any cheesecake left?

**cheese·cloth** /ˈtʃiːzklɒθ; NAmE -klɔːθ/ noun [U] a type of loose cotton cloth used especially for making shirts

**cheesy** /ˈtʃiːzi/ adj. (**chees·ier**, **cheesi·est**) **1** (informal) not very good or original, and without style, in a way that is embarrassing but funny: a cheesy horror movie **2** (informal) too emotional or romantic, in a way that is embarrassing: a cheesy love song **3** (of a smile) done in an EXAGGERATED and probably not sincere way: She had a **cheesy grin** on her face. **4** smelling or tasting of cheese

**chee·tah** /ˈtʃiːtə/ noun a wild animal of the cat family that has black spots and that runs very fast

**chef** 🔑 **A2** /ʃef/ noun a person whose job is to cook, especially the most senior person in a restaurant, hotel, etc.: a new book by celebrity chef Jamie Oliver ⊃ see also PASTRY CHEF

**chem·ical** 🔑 **B1** /ˈkemɪkl/ adj., noun
■ adj. **1** 🔑 connected with chemistry: changes in the **chemical composition** of the atmosphere **2** 🔑 **B1** produced by or using processes that involve changes to ATOMS or MOLECULES: **chemical reactions/compounds 3** 🔑 **B1** using or connected with chemicals: a **chemical plant** (= a factory producing chemicals) ◊ **chemical agents** (= substances) ▶ **chem·ic·al·ly** /-kli/ adv.: The raw sewage is chemically treated.

■ noun 🔑 **B1** a substance obtained by or used in a chemical process: **toxic chemicals** ◊ Toy manufacturers have been banned from using the chemicals.

**chemical element** noun = ELEMENT (3)

**chemical engineering** noun [U] the study of the design and use of machines in industrial chemical processes ▶ **chemical engineer** noun

**chemical warfare** noun [U] the use of poisonous gases and chemicals as weapons in a war

**chemical weapon** noun a weapon that uses poisonous gases and chemicals to kill and injure people ⊃ compare BIOLOGICAL WEAPON

**chemise** /ʃəˈmiːz/ noun a piece of women's underwear or a NIGHTDRESS

**chem·ist** /ˈkemɪst/ noun **1** (also **dispensing chemist**) (both BrE, NAmE **drug·gist**) a person whose job is to prepare and sell medicines, and who works in a shop ⊃ compare PHARMACIST **2 chemist's** (pl. **chem·ists**) (BrE) a shop that sells medicines and usually also soap, MAKE-UP, etc: You can obtain the product from all good chemists. ◊ Take this prescription to the chemist's. ◊ I'll get it at the chemist's. ◊ a chemist's/chemist shop ⊃ see also DRUGSTORE ⊃ compare PHARMACY **3** a scientist who studies chemistry: a research chemist

**chem·is·try** 🔑 **A2** /ˈkemɪstri/ noun [U] **1** 🔑 **A2** the scientific study of the structure of substances, how they react when combined or in contact with one another, and how they behave under different conditions: a degree in chemistry ◊ the university's chemistry department ◊ inorganic/organic chemistry ⊃ see also BIOCHEMISTRY

**WORDFINDER** acid, catalyst, compound, formula, molecule, pH, react, solution, valency

**2** (specialist) the chemical structure and behaviour of a particular substance: the chemistry of copper ◊ The patient's blood chemistry was monitored regularly. **3** the relationship between two people, usually a strong sexual attraction: sexual chemistry ◊ The chemistry just wasn't right.

**chemo** /ˈkiːməʊ/ noun [U] (informal) = CHEMOTHERAPY

**chemo·recep·tor** /ˈkiːməʊrɪseptə(r)/ noun (biology) a cell or sense organ that is sensitive to chemical STIMULI, making a response possible

**chemo·ther·apy** /ˌkiːməʊˈθerəpi/ (also informal **chemo**) noun [U] the treatment of disease, especially cancer, with the use of chemical substances ⊃ compare RADIATION, RADIOTHERAPY ⊃ WORDFINDER NOTE at CURE

**che·nille** /ʃəˈniːl/ noun [U] a type of thick, soft THREAD; cloth made from this: a chenille sweater

**cheque** (BrE) (US **check**) /tʃek/ noun a printed form that you can write on and sign as a way of paying for sth instead of using money: to **write a cheque** ◊ to **make a cheque out to sb** ◊ to **cash a cheque** (= to get or give money for a cheque) ◊ ~ **for …** a cheque for £50 ◊ **by** ~ to pay by cheque ◊ We no longer accept payment by cheque. ⊃ see also BLANK CHEQUE, PAY CHEQUE, THIRTEENTH CHEQUE

**cheque·book** (BrE) (US **check·book**) /ˈtʃekbʊk/ noun a book of printed cheques

**che·quered** (BrE) (also **check·ered** especially in NAmE) /ˈtʃekəd; NAmE -kərd/ adj. **1 ~ past/history/career** a person's past, etc. that contains both successful and not successful periods **2** having a pattern of squares of different colours

**the chequered flag** (BrE) (also **the check·ered flag** NAmE, BrE) noun a flag with black and white squares that is waved when a driver has finished a motor race

**chequing account** noun (CanE) = CURRENT ACCOUNT

**cher·ish** /ˈtʃerɪʃ/ verb (formal) **1 ~ sb/sth** to love sb/sth very much and want to protect them or it: Children need to be cherished. ◊ her **most cherished possession 2 ~ sth** to

# Cherokee

keep an idea, a hope or a pleasant feeling in your mind for a long time: *Cherish the memory of those days in Paris.*

**Chero·kee** /ˈtʃerəki/ *noun* (*pl.* **Chero·kee** or **Chero·kees**) a member of a Native American people, many of whom now live in the US states of Oklahoma and North Carolina

**che·root** /ʃəˈruːt/ *noun* a type of CIGAR with two open ends

**cherry** /ˈtʃeri/ *noun, adj.*
- *noun* (*pl.* **-ies**) **1** [C] a small soft round fruit with shiny red or black skin and a large seed inside ⇨ VISUAL VOCAB page V4 **2** (*also* **ˈcherry tree**) [C] a tree on which cherries grow, or a similar tree, grown for its flowers: *cherry blossom* ◇ *a winter-flowering cherry* **3** (*also* **ˈcherry-wood** /ˈtʃeri-wʊd/) [U] the wood of the cherry tree **4** (*also* **ˌcherry ˈred**) [U] a bright red colour
  IDM see BITE *n.*
- *adj.* (*also* **ˌcherry ˈred**) bright red in colour: *cherry lips*

**ˈcherry-pick** *verb* [T, I] ~ (**sb/sth**) to choose the best people or things from a group and leave those that are not so good

**ˈcherry picker** *noun* a type of tall CRANE that lifts people up so that they can work in very high places

**ˈcherry-picking** *noun* [U] the act of choosing the best people or things from a group and leaving those that are not so good: *There can be no cherry-picking of statistics that happen to support your case.*

**ˌcherry toˈmato** *noun* a type of very small tomato

**cherub** /ˈtʃerəb/ *noun* **1** (*pl.* **cher·ubs** or **cher·ubim** /-əbɪm/) (in art) a type of ANGEL, shown as a small, fat, usually male child with wings ⇨ compare SERAPH **2** (*pl.* **cher·ubs**) (*informal*) a pretty child; a child who behaves well ▸ **cher·ub·ic** /tʃəˈruːbɪk/ *adj.* (*formal*): *a cherubic face* (= looking round and innocent, like a small child's)

**cher·vil** /ˈtʃɜːvɪl; *NAmE* ˈtʃɜːrv-/ *noun* [U] a plant with leaves that are used in cooking as a HERB

**chess** /tʃes/ *noun* [U] a game for two people played on a board marked with black and white squares on which each playing piece (representing a king, queen, castle, etc.) is moved according to special rules. The aim is to put the other player's king in a position from which it cannot escape (= to CHECKMATE it): *Alex plays chess as a hobby.*

**chess·board** /ˈtʃesbɔːd; *NAmE* -bɔːrd/ *noun* a board with 64 black and white squares that chess is played on

**chess·man** /ˈtʃesmæn/ *noun* (*pl.* **-men** /-men/) any of the 32 pieces used in the game of chess

**chest** ❶ **B1** /tʃest/ *noun* **1** **B1** the top part of the front of the body, between the neck and the stomach: *chest pains* ◇ *She gasped for breath, her chest heaving.* ◇ *She folded her arms across her chest* ◇ *a chest infection* ◇ **in the ~** *symptoms such as wheezing or a tightness in the chest* ⇨ VISUAL VOCAB page V1 **2 -chested** (in adjectives) having the type of chest mentioned: *flat-chested* ◇ *broad-chested* **3** a large strong box, usually made of wood, used for storing things in and/or moving them from one place to another: *a medicine chest* ◇ *a treasure chest* ⇨ see also ICE CHEST, WAR CHEST
IDM ˌget sth ˈoff your ˈchest to talk about sth that has been worrying you for a long time so that you feel less anxious ⇨ more at CARD *n.*

**ches·ter·field** /ˈtʃestəfiːld; *NAmE* -tərf-/ *noun* **1** a type of SOFA that has arms and a back that are all the same height **2** (*CanE*) any type of SOFA

**chest·nut** /ˈtʃesnʌt/ *noun, adj.*
- *noun* **1** (*also* **ˈchestnut tree**) [C] a large tree with spreading branches that produces smooth brown nuts inside cases that are covered with SPIKES. There are several types of chestnut tree. ⇨ see also HORSE CHESTNUT **2** [C] a smooth brown nut of a chestnut tree, some types of which can be eaten: *roast chestnuts* ⇨ VISUAL VOCAB page V8 ⇨ see also WATER CHESTNUT ⇨ compare CONKER **3** [U] a deep red-brown colour **4** [C] a horse of a red-brown colour **5** old

**chestnut** [C] (*informal*) an old joke or story that has been told so many times that it is no longer funny or interesting
- *adj.* red-brown in colour

**ˌchest of ˈdrawers** *noun* (*pl.* **chests of drawers**) (*NAmE also* **bur·eau, dresser**) a piece of furniture with DRAWERS (= parts like boxes built into it with handles on the front for pulling them out) for keeping clothes in

**chesty** /ˈtʃesti/ *adj.* (*informal, especially BrE*) suffering from or showing signs of chest disease

**chev·ron** /ˈʃevrən; *BrE also* -rɒn; *NAmE also* -rɑːn/ *noun* **1** a line or pattern in the shape of a V **2** a piece of cloth in the shape of a V that soldiers and police officers wear on their uniforms to show their rank

**chew** /tʃuː/ *verb, noun*
- *verb* **1** [I, T] to bite food into small pieces in your mouth with your teeth to make it easier to SWALLOW: ~ (**at/on/through sth**) *After the operation you may find it difficult to chew and swallow.* ◇ *~ sth (up) teeth designed for chewing meat* ◇ *He is always chewing gum.* **2** [I, T] to bite sth continuously, for example because you are nervous or to taste it: ~ **on/at sth** *Rosa chewed on her lip and stared at the floor.* ◇ *The dog was chewing on a bone.* ◇ *~ sth* to chew your nails ⇨ HOMOPHONES at CHOOSE
IDM ˌchew the ˈfat (*informal*) to have a long friendly talk with sb about sth ⇨ more at BITE *v.*
PHRV ˌchew sb ˈout (*NAmE, informal*) to tell sb angrily that you do not approve of their actions: *He got chewed out by the boss for lying.* ˌchew sth↔ˈover to think about or discuss sth slowly and carefully
- *noun* **1** an act of chewing sth **2** a type of sweet that you chew **3** a piece of TOBACCO that you chew

**ˈchewing gum** (*also* **gum**) *noun* [U] a sweet that you chew (= bite many times) but do not eat

**chewy** /ˈtʃuːi/ *adj.* (**chew·ier, chewi·est**) (of food) needing to be chewed a lot before it can be eaten ⇨ WORDFINDER NOTE at CRISP

**Chey·enne** /ʃaɪˈæn, -ˈen/ *noun* (*pl.* **Chey·enne** or **Chey·ennes**) a member of a Native American people, many of whom now live in the US states of Oklahoma and Montana

**chez** /ʃeɪ/ *prep.* (*from French*) at the home of: *I spent a pleasant evening chez the Stewarts.*

**chi** /kaɪ/ *noun* the 22nd letter of the Greek alphabet (X, χ)

**chiaro·scuro** /kiˌɑːrəˈskʊərəʊ; *NAmE* -ˈskʊr-/ *noun* [U] (*art*) the way light and shade are shown; the contrast between light and shade

**chic** /ʃiːk/ *adj.* very fashionable and attractive SYN stylish: *She is always so chic, so elegant.* ◇ *a chic new restaurant* ▸ **chic** *noun* [U]: *a perfectly dressed woman with an air of chic that was unmistakably French*

**chi·ca** /ˈtʃiːkə/ *noun* (*US, from Spanish, informal*) a girl or young woman

**Chi·cana** /tʃɪˈkɑːnə; *BrE also* ʃɪ-/ *noun* (*especially US, from Spanish*) a girl or woman living in the US whose family came from Mexico ⇨ compare CHICANO, HISPANIC, LATINA

**chi·cane** /ʃɪˈkeɪn/ *noun* (*BrE*) a sharp double bend, either on a track where cars race or on an ordinary road, to stop vehicles from going too fast

**chi·can·ery** /ʃɪˈkeɪnəri/ *noun* [U] (*formal*) the use of complicated plans and clever talk in order to trick people

**Chi·cano** /tʃɪˈkɑːnəʊ; *BrE also* ʃɪ-/ *noun* (*pl.* **-os**) (*especially US, from Spanish*) a person living in the US whose family came from Mexico ⇨ compare CHICANA, HISPANIC, LATINO

**chi·chi** /ˈʃiːʃiː/ *adj.* used to describe a style of decoration that contains too many details and lacks taste

**chick** /tʃɪk/ *noun* **1** a baby bird, especially a baby chicken **2** (*old-fashioned, sometimes offensive*) a way of referring to a young woman

**chicka·dee** /ˈtʃɪkədiː, ˌtʃɪkəˈdiː/ *noun* a small North American bird of the TIT family. There are many types of chickadee.

---

| æ cat | ɑː father | e bed | ɜː fur | ə about | ɪ sit | iː see | i happy | ɒ got (*BrE*) | ɔː saw | ʌ cup | ʊ put | uː too |

**chick·en** /ˈtʃɪkɪn/ noun, verb, adj.
- **noun 1** [C] a large bird that is often kept for its eggs or meat: *They keep chickens in the back yard.* ◊ *free-range chickens* ⊃ compare COCK, HEN ⊃ see also SPRING CHICKEN ⊃ VISUAL VOCAB page V2 **2** [U] meat from a chicken: *fried chicken* ◊ *roast/grilled chicken* ◊ *chicken breasts/wings* ◊ *chicken nuggets* ◊ *chicken soup* **3** [C] a person who is not brave or is afraid to do sth
- **IDM** **a chicken-and-egg situation, problem, etc.** a situation in which it is difficult to tell which one of two things was the cause of the other **play ˈchicken** to play a game in which people do sth dangerous for as long as they can to show how brave they are. The person who stops first has lost the game. ⊃ more at COUNT v., HEADLESS, HOME adv.
- **verb**
- **PHR V** **ˌchicken ˈout (of sth/of doing sth)** (*informal*) to decide not to do sth because you are afraid
- **adj.** [not before noun] (*informal*) not brave; afraid to do sth **SYN** cowardly

**ˈchicken feed** noun [U] (*informal*) an amount of money that is not large enough to be important

**chick·en·pox** /ˈtʃɪkɪnpɒks; *NAmE* -pɑːks/ noun [U] a disease, especially of children, that causes a high temperature and many spots on the skin: *to catch/get/have chickenpox*

**chick·en·shit** /ˈtʃɪkɪnʃɪt/ noun, adj.
- **noun** [U] (*NAmE*, *taboo*, *slang*) ideas, statements or beliefs that you think are silly or not true **SYN** nonsense
- **adj.** (*NAmE*, *taboo*, *slang*) (of a person) not brave **SYN** cowardly

**ˈchicken wire** noun [U] thin wire made into sheets like nets with a pattern of shapes with six sides

**ˈchick flick** noun (*informal*) a film that is intended especially for women

**ˈchick lit** noun [U] (*informal*) novels that are intended especially for women, often with a young, single woman as the main character

**chick·pea** /ˈtʃɪkpiː/ noun (*especially BrE*) (*NAmE usually* **gar·banzo**, **garˈbanzo bean**) a hard round seed, like a light brown PEA, that is cooked and eaten as a vegetable ⊃ VISUAL VOCAB page V5

**ˈchickpea flour** noun = GRAM FLOUR

**chick·weed** /ˈtʃɪkwiːd/ noun [U] a small plant with white flowers that often grows as a WEED over a wide area

**chi·co** /ˈtʃiːkəʊ/ noun (*pl.* **-os**) (*US, from Spanish, informal*) a boy or young man

**chic·ory** /ˈtʃɪkəri/ noun (*NAmE* **en·dive**, **Belgian endive**) [C, U] **1** (*BrE*) a small pale green plant with bitter leaves that are eaten raw or cooked as a vegetable. The root can be dried and used with or instead of coffee. **2** (*also* **curly ˈendive**, **fri·sée**) (*all NAmE*) (*BrE* **en·dive**) a plant with green curly leaves that are eaten raw as a vegetable

**chide** /tʃaɪd/ verb (*formal*) to criticize or blame sb because they have done sth wrong **SYN** rebuke: *~ sb/yourself (for sth/for doing sth) She chided herself for being so impatient with the children.* ◊ *~ (sb) + speech 'Isn't that a bit selfish?' he chided.*

**chief** /tʃiːf/ adj., noun
- **adj. 1** [only before noun] most important: *the chief cause/problem/reason* ◊ *He became the chief architect of the Treaty of Paris.* ◊ *~ among sb/sth Chief among his challenges is the impact that current reforms could have on small businesses.* ⊃ SYNONYMS at MAIN **2** (*often* **Chief**) [only before noun] highest in rank: *the chief economist at the World Bank* ◊ *She is Chief Medical Officer for England.* **3** **-in-ˈchief** (in nouns) of the highest rank: *commander-in-chief* ◊ *the editor-in-chief of the magazine* ⊃ see also CHIEFLY
- **noun 1** a person with a high rank or the highest rank in a company or an organization: *army/police chiefs* ◊ *~ of sb/sth He served as chief of police between 2002 and 2009.* ⊃ see also BIG CHIEF, FIRE CHIEF **2** (*often as a title*) a leader of a people or community: *Chief Buthelezi* ◊ *Chief Crazy Horse*

**chief ˈconstable** noun (in the UK) a senior police officer who is in charge of the police force in a particular area: *Chief Constable Brian Turner*

**chief·dom** /ˈtʃiːfdəm/ noun an area controlled by a chief: *The area was divided into independent chiefdoms.*

**chief eˈxecutive** noun **1** the person with the highest rank in a company or an organization ⊃ compare EXECUTIVE DIRECTOR **2 Chief Executive** the president of the US

**chief eˈxecutive ˈofficer** noun (*abbr.* CEO) the person in a company who has the most power and authority

**chief fiˈnancial ˈofficer** noun (*abbr.* CFO) the person in a company who has the most authority over the finances

**chief inˈspector** noun (in the UK) a police officer above the rank of an INSPECTOR

**chief ˈjustice** (*also* **Chief Justice**) noun the most important judge in the highest court in a country, especially the US Supreme Court

**chief·ly** /ˈtʃiːfli/ adv. not completely, but as a most important part **SYN** primarily, mainly: *We are chiefly concerned with improving educational standards.* ◊ *He's travelled widely, chiefly in Africa and Asia.*

**chief of ˈstaff** noun (*pl.* **chiefs of staff**) **1** an officer of very high rank, responsible for advising the person who commands each of the armed forces ⊃ see also JOINT CHIEFS OF STAFF **2** (*especially NAmE*) a person who advises the head of an organization and who manages the other employees

**chief ˈoperating officer** (*also* **chief opeˈrations officer**) noun = COO

**chief superinˈtendent** noun (in the UK) a police officer above the rank of SUPERINTENDENT

**chief·tain** /ˈtʃiːftən/ noun **1** the leader of a people or a CLAN **2** (*informal*) a powerful member of an organization

**chief techˈnology officer** noun = CTO

**chif·fon** /ˈʃɪfɒn; *NAmE* ʃɪˈfɑːn/ noun [U] a type of fine cloth that you can see through, made from silk or NYLON, used especially for making clothes

**chig·ger** /ˈtʃɪɡə(r); *BrE also* ˈdʒɪ-/ (*also* **jig·ger**) noun a small FLEA that lives in tropical regions and lays eggs under a person's or an animal's skin, causing painful areas on the skin

**chi·gnon** /ˈʃiːnjɒn; *NAmE* -njɑːn/ noun (*from French*) a style for women's hair in which the hair is pulled back and TWISTED into a smooth KNOT at the back

**chi·hua·hua** /tʃɪˈwɑːwə/ noun a very small dog with smooth hair

**chi·kun·gun·ya** /ˌtʃɪkʊŋˈɡʊnjə/ noun [U] a disease similar to DENGUE caused by a virus, found in East Africa and parts of Asia and carried by MOSQUITOES

**chil·blain** /ˈtʃɪlbleɪn/ noun [usually pl.] a painful red SWELLING (= an area that is larger and rounder than normal) on the hands or feet that is caused by cold or bad CIRCULATION of the blood

**child** /tʃaɪld/ noun (*pl.* **chil·dren** /ˈtʃɪldrən/) **1** a young human who is not yet an adult: *a child of 3/a 3-year-old child* ◊ *men, women and children* ◊ *an unborn child* ◊ *The film is not suitable for young children.* ◊ *I lived in London as a child.* ◊ *a child star* ⊃ WORDFINDER NOTE at BABY ⊃ see also BRAINCHILD, POSTER CHILD, SCHOOLCHILD, STREET CHILD **2** a son or daughter of any age: *They have three grown-up children.* ◊ *They can't have children.* ⊃ see also GODCHILD, GRANDCHILD, LOVE CHILD, ONLY CHILD, STEPCHILD ⊃ compare KID **3** a person who is strongly influenced by the ideas and attitudes of a particular time or person: *a child of the 90s* **4** (*disapproving*) an adult who behaves like a child and is not MATURE or responsible
- **IDM** **be ˈchild's play** (*informal*) to be very easy to do, so not even a child would find it difficult **be with ˈchild** (*old-fashioned*) to be pregnant

**ˈchild abuse** noun [U] the crime of harming a child in a physical, sexual or emotional way: *victims of child abuse*

# childbearing 256

**child·bear·ing** /ˈtʃaɪldbeərɪŋ; NAmE -ber-/ noun [U] the process of giving birth to children: *women of childbearing age*

**child ˈbenefit** noun [U] (in the UK) money that the government regularly pays to parents of children up to a particular age

**child·birth** /ˈtʃaɪldbɜːθ; NAmE -bɜːrθ/ noun [U] the process of giving birth to a baby: *pregnancy and childbirth* ◊ *in ~ His wife died in childbirth.*

**child·care** /ˈtʃaɪldkeə(r); NAmE -ker/ noun [U] the care of children, especially while parents are at work: *childcare facilities for working parents*

**child·hood** 🔑 B1 /ˈtʃaɪldhʊd/ noun [U, C] the period of sb's life when they are a child: *He spent his childhood in India.* ◊ *She had a happy childhood.* ◊ *the problem of childhood obesity* ◊ *childhood memories/experiences* ◊ *in/during (sb's) ~ in early childhood*
▶ IDM **a/sb's second ˈchildhood** a time in the life of an adult person when they behave like a child again

**child·ish** /ˈtʃaɪldɪʃ/ adj. **1** connected with or typical of a child: *childish handwriting* **2** (*disapproving*) (of an adult) behaving in a stupid or silly way SYN immature: *Don't be so childish!* OPP mature ⇒ compare CHILDLIKE ▶ **child·ish·ly** adv.: *to behave childishly* **child·ish·ness** noun [U]

**child·less** /ˈtʃaɪldləs/ adj. having no children: *a childless couple/marriage*

**child·like** /ˈtʃaɪldlaɪk/ adj. (*usually approving*) having the qualities that children usually have, especially INNOCENCE: *childlike enthusiasm/simplicity/delight* ⇒ compare CHILDISH

**child·mind·er** /ˈtʃaɪldmaɪndə(r)/ noun (BrE) a person who is paid to care for children while their parents are at work. A childminder usually does this in his or her own home. ⇒ see also BABYSITTER

**child·proof** /ˈtʃaɪldpruːf/ adj. designed so that young children cannot open, use, or damage it: *childproof containers for medicines*

**ˈchild restraint** noun a belt, or small seat with a belt, that is used in a car to control and protect a child

**ˈchild seat** noun a special safety seat for a child, fitted into a car or onto a bicycle ⇒ compare CAR SEAT

**ˈchild support** (BrE also **ˌchild ˈmaintenance**) noun [U] money that a parent must pay regularly to help support their child, when the child is no longer living with that parent

**chili** (NAmE) **1** [C, U] = CHILLI **2** [U] = CHILLI CON CARNE

**chill** /tʃɪl/ noun, verb, adj.
▪ noun **1** [sing.] a feeling of being cold: *There's a chill in the air this morning.* ◊ *A small fire was burning to take the chill off the room.* ⇒ see also WIND CHILL **2** [C] an illness caused by being cold and wet, causing a high temperature and SHIVERING (= shaking of the body) **3** [sing.] a feeling of fear: *a chill of fear/apprehension* ◊ *His words sent a chill down her spine.*
▪ verb **1** [T, usually passive] to make sb very cold: **be chilled (by sth)** *They were chilled by the icy wind.* ◊ *Let's go home, I'm chilled to the bone* (= very cold). **2** [I, T, often passive] when food or a drink **chills** or when sb **chills** it, it is made very cold but it does not freeze: *Let the pudding chill for an hour until set.* ◊ **(be) chilled** *This wine is best served chilled.* ◊ *chilled foods* (= for example in a supermarket) **3** [T] *~sb/sth* (*literary*) to frighten sb: *His words chilled her.* ◊ *What he saw chilled his blood/chilled him to the bone.* **4** [I] (*informal*) = CHILL OUT: *We went home and chilled in front of the TV.* ◊ *Just chill, Mum—everything's going to be OK.*
▶ PHRV **ˌchill ˈout** (*informal*) to spend time relaxing; to relax and stop feeling angry or nervous about sth: *They sometimes meet up to chill out and watch a movie.* ◊ *Sit down and chill out!*
▪ adj. (*formal*) (especially of weather and the wind) cold, in an unpleasant way: *the chill grey dawn* ◊ *a chill wind*

**chill·ax** /tʃɪˈlæks/ verb [I] (*slang*) to relax and stop feeling angry or nervous about sth: *Chillax, dude—I'm on your team.*

**ˌchilled-ˈout** (*also* **chilled**) adj. (*informal*) very relaxed: *a chilled-out atmosphere* ◊ *He felt totally chilled.*

**chill·er** /ˈtʃɪlə(r)/ noun **1** a machine for cooling sth or keeping sth cold, especially a fridge or cold CABINET: *a chiller cabinet full of fizzy drinks* **2** (*also* **spine-chiller**) a book, film, etc. that is frightening in an exciting way: *Sandra Bullock stars in this tense sci-fi chiller.*

**ˈchill factor** noun the extent to which the wind makes the air feel colder; a number which represents this

**chilli** (BrE) (NAmE **chili**) /ˈtʃɪli/ noun (*pl.* **chil·lies**, NAmE **chil·ies**) **1** (*also* **ˈchilli pepper**) [C, U] the small green or red fruit of a type of pepper plant that is used in cooking to give a hot taste to food, often dried or made into powder, also called chilli or **ˈchilli powder** ⇒ VISUAL VOCAB page V5 **2** [U] a hot spicy Mexican dish made with beans, chillies and often meat

**ˌchilli con ˈcarne** /ˌtʃɪli kɒn ˈkɑːni; NAmE kɑːn ˈkɑːrni/ (*especially BrE*) (BrE *also* **chilli**) (NAmE *also* **chili**) noun [U] a hot spicy Mexican dish made with meat, beans and CHILLIES

**chill·ing** /ˈtʃɪlɪŋ/ adj. frightening, usually because it is connected with sth violent or cruel: *a chilling story* ◊ *The film evokes chilling reminders of the war.* ⇒ see also SPINE-CHILLING

**chilly** /ˈtʃɪli/ adj. (**chill·ier**, **chilli·est**) **1** (especially of the weather or a place, but also of people) too cold to be comfortable: *It's chilly today.* ◊ *I was feeling chilly.* ⇒ SYNONYMS at COLD **2** not friendly: *The visitors got a chilly reception.*
▶ **chil·li·ness** noun [U]

**chime** /tʃaɪm/ verb, noun
▪ verb [I, T] (of a bell or a clock) to ring; to show the time by making a ringing sound: *I heard the clock chime.* ◊ *Eight o'clock had already chimed.* ◊ *~sth The clock chimed midday.*
▶ PHRV **ˌchime ˈin (with sth)** to join or interrupt a conversation: *He kept chiming in with his own opinions.* ◊ *+ speech 'And me!' she chimed in.* **ˌchime (in) with sth** (of plans, ideas, etc.) to agree with sth; to be similar to sth: *His opinions chimed in with the mood of the nation.*
▪ noun a ringing sound, typically one that is made by a bell: *door chimes* ⇒ see also WIND CHIMES

**chi·mera** (*also* **chi·maera**) /kaɪˈmɪərə; NAmE -ˈmɪrə/ noun **1** (in ancient Greek stories) a creature with a LION's head, a GOAT's body and a snake's tail that can breathe out fire **2** (*formal*) an impossible idea or hope **3** (*biology*) an ORGANISM (= a living thing) that contains a mixture of GENETICALLY different TISSUES

**chim·ney** /ˈtʃɪmni/ noun **1** a structure through which smoke or STEAM is carried up away from a fire, etc. and through the roof of a building; the part of this that is above the roof: *He threw a bit of paper onto the fire and it flew up the chimney.* ◊ *the factory chimneys of an industrial landscape* **2** (*specialist*) a narrow opening in an area of rock that a person can climb up

**ˈchimney pot** noun (*BrE*) a short wide pipe that is placed on top of a chimney

**ˈchimney stack** noun (*BrE*) **1** the part of the chimney that is above the roof of a building **2** (NAmE **smoke·stack**) a very tall chimney, especially one in a factory

**ˈchimney sweep** (*also* **sweep**) noun a person whose job is to clean the inside of CHIMNEYS

**chim·pan·zee** /ˌtʃɪmpænˈziː/ (*also informal* **chimp**) noun a small intelligent African APE (= an animal like a large monkey without a tail) ⇒ VISUAL VOCAB page V2

**chin** /tʃɪn/ noun the part of the face below the mouth and above the neck ⇒ see also DOUBLE CHIN
▶ IDM **(keep your) ˈchin up** (*informal*) used to tell sb to try to stay cheerful even though they are in a difficult or unpleasant situation: *Chin up! Only two exams left.* **ˌtake sth on the ˈchin** (*informal*) **1** to accept a difficult or unpleasant situation without complaining, trying to make

**china** /ˈtʃaɪnə/ noun [U] **1** white CLAY that is baked and used for making cups, plates, etc: *a china vase* ⇒ see also BONE CHINA **2** cups, plates, etc. that are made of china: *She got out the best china.* **IDM** see BULL

**China·town** /ˈtʃaɪnətaʊn/ noun [U, C] the area of a city where many people of Chinese origin live and there are Chinese shops and restaurants

**chin·chil·la** /tʃɪnˈtʃɪlə/ noun **1** [C] an animal like a RABBIT with soft silver-grey fur. Chinchillas are often kept on farms for their fur. **2** [U] the skin and fur of the chinchilla, used for making expensive coats, etc.

**Chin·ese** /ˌtʃaɪˈniːz/ adj., noun
■ *adj.* from or connected with China
■ *noun* (pl. **Chin·ese**) **1** [C] a person from China, or whose family was originally from China **2** [U] the language of China

**Chinese ˈcabbage** noun [U] (BrE also **Chinese ˈleaves** [pl.], **Chinese ˈleaf** [U]) a type of vegetable that is eaten cooked or in salads. There are two types of Chinese cabbage, one with long light-green leaves and thick white STEMS that is similar to LETTUCE and one with darker green leaves and thicker white STEMS. The first type is usually called 'Chinese leaves' in British English and the second type is called 'pak choi'(BrE) or 'bok choy'(NAmE).

**Chinese ˈchequers** (BrE) (NAmE **Chinese ˈcheckers**) noun [U] a game for two to six players who try to move the playing pieces from one corner to the opposite corner of the board, which is like a star in shape

**Chinese ˈlantern** noun **1** a lamp that is inside a paper case, with a handle to carry it **2** a plant with white flowers and round orange fruits inside a material like paper

**Chinese ˈwhispers** noun [U] (BrE) the situation when information is passed from one person to another and gets slightly changed each time

**chink** /tʃɪŋk/ noun, verb
■ *noun* **1** a narrow opening in sth, especially one that lets light through: *a chink in the curtains* **2** ~ **of light** a small area of light shining through a narrow opening **3** [usually sing.] the light ringing sound that is made when glass objects or coins touch: *the chink of glasses*
**IDM** **a chink in sb's ˈarmour** a weak point in sb's argument, character, etc., that can be used in an attack
■ *verb* [I, T] when glasses, coins or other glass or metal objects **chink** or when you **chink** them, they make a light ringing sound **SYN** **clink**: *the sound of bottles chinking* ◊ *~ sth We chinked glasses and drank to each other's health.*

**chin·less** /ˈtʃɪnləs/ adj. (of a man) having a very small CHIN (= part of the face below the mouth) (often thought of as a sign of a weak character)
**IDM** **a chinless ˈwonder** (BrE, humorous, disapproving) a young, upper-class man who is weak and stupid

**chi·nois·erie** /ʃɪnˈwɑːzəri; NAmE ʃiːnwɑːzəˈriː/ noun [U] (art) the use of Chinese images, designs and techniques in Western art, furniture and architecture

**chi·nook** /tʃɪˈnuːk, ʃɪ-/ noun **1** (also **chiˌnook ˈwind**) a warm, dry wind that blows down the east side of the Rocky Mountains at the end of winter **2** (also **chiˌnook ˈsalmon**) a large N Pacific SALMON that is eaten as food

**chinos** /ˈtʃiːnəʊz/ noun [pl.] informal trousers made from strong cotton: *a pair of chinos*

**chintz** /tʃɪnts/ noun [U, C] a type of shiny cotton cloth with a printed design, especially of flowers, used for making curtains, covering furniture, etc.

**chintzy** /ˈtʃɪntsi/ adj. **1** covered in or decorated with chintz **2** (NAmE, informal) cheap and not attractive **3** (NAmE, humorous) not willing to spend money **SYN** **cheap, stingy**

**ˈchin-up** noun (especially NAmE) = PULL-UP

**chip** ❶ **A2** /tʃɪp/ noun, verb
■ *noun* **1** ❷ **A2** (BrE) (also **French fry, fry** NAmE, BrE) [usually pl.] a long thin piece of potato fried in oil or fat: *He was eating a burger and chips.* ⇒ see also FISH AND CHIPS **2** **A2** (also **poˌtato ˈchip**) (both BrE **crisp, poˌtato ˈcrisp**) a thin round slice of potato that is fried until hard then dried and eaten cold. Chips are sold in bags and are made to taste of many different foods: *a bag of chips* **3** = TORTILLA CHIP ⇒ see also CORN CHIP **4 B1** = MICROCHIP: *computer/graphics/memory chips* ⇒ see also SILICON CHIP **5** the place from which a small piece of wood, glass, etc. has broken from an object: *This mug has a chip in it.* ⇒ picture at BROKEN ⇒ see also PAINT CHIP **6** a small piece of wood, glass, etc. that has broken or been broken off an object: *chips of wood* ◊ *chocolate chip cookies* (= biscuits containing small pieces of chocolate) ⇒ picture at BROKEN ⇒ see also PAINT CHIP **7** a small flat piece of plastic used to represent a particular amount of money in some types of GAMBLING: *a poker chip* ⇒ see also BARGAINING CHIP ⇒ WORDFINDER NOTE at GAMBLING **8** (also **ˈchip shot**) (in golf, football (soccer), etc.) an act of hitting or kicking a ball high in the air so that it lands within a short distance ⇒ see also BLUE-CHIP
**IDM** **a chip off the old ˈblock** (informal) a person who is very similar to their mother or father in the way that they look or behave **have a ˈchip on your shoulder (about sth)** (informal) to be sensitive about sth that happened in the past and become easily offended if it is mentioned because you think that you were treated unfairly **have had your ˈchips** (BrE, informal) to be in a situation in which you are certain to be defeated or killed **when the chips are ˈdown** (informal) used to refer to a difficult situation in which you are forced to decide what is important to you: *I'm not sure what I'll do when the chips are down.*
■ *verb* (-pp-) **1** [T, I] ~**(sth)** to damage sth by breaking a small piece off it; to become damaged in this way: *a badly chipped saucer* ◊ *She chipped one of her front teeth.* ◊ *These plates chip easily.* ⇒ picture at BROKEN **2** [T] ~**sth + adv./prep.** to cut or break small pieces off sth with a tool: *Chip away the damaged area.* ◊ *The fossils had been chipped out of the rock.* **3** [T, I] ~**(sth)** (especially in golf and football (soccer)) to hit or kick the ball so that it goes high in the air and then lands within a short distance **4** [T] ~**potatoes** (BrE) to cut potatoes into long thin pieces in order to fry them in deep oil **5** [T] ~**sth** to put a MICROCHIP under the skin of a dog or other animal so that it can be identified if it is lost or stolen
**PHRV** **chip aˈway at sth** to keep breaking small pieces off sth: *He was chipping away at the stone.* ◊ *(figurative) They chipped away at the power of the government* (= gradually made it weaker). **chip ˈin (with sth)** (informal) **1** to join in or interrupt a conversation; to add sth to a conversation or discussion: *Pete and Anne chipped in with suggestions.* ◊ + *speech 'That's different,' she chipped in.* **2** (also **chip ˈin sth**) to give some money so that a group of people can buy sth together **SYN** **contribute**: *If everyone chips in we'll be able to buy her a really nice present.* ◊ *We each chipped in (with) £5.* **chip ˈoff** | **chip sth↔ˈoff** to damage sth by breaking a small piece off it; to be damaged in this way: *He chipped off a piece of his tooth.* ◊ *The paint had chipped off.*

**chip and ˈPIN** (also **chip and pin**) noun [U] a system of paying for sth with a credit card or DEBIT CARD in which the card has information stored on it in the form of a MICROCHIP and you prove your identity by typing a number (your PIN) rather than by signing your name: *Chip and PIN is designed to combat credit card fraud.*

**chip·board** /ˈtʃɪpbɔːd; NAmE -bɔːrd/ noun [U] a type of board that is used for building, made of small pieces of wood that are pressed together and stuck with GLUE

**ˈchip card** noun (especially NAmE) a plastic card on which information is stored in the form of a MICROCHIP

**chip·munk** /ˈtʃɪpmʌŋk/ noun a small North American animal of the SQUIRREL family, with light and dark marks on its back

**chip·per** /ˈtʃɪpə(r)/ adj., noun
■ *adj.* (informal) cheerful and lively
■ *noun* **1** a machine that cuts wood into very small pieces **2** a device that cuts potatoes into chips **3** (ScotE, IrishE, informal) a chip shop

**chip·pings** /ˈtʃɪpɪŋz/ noun [pl.] (BrE) small pieces of stone or wood

**chippy** /ˈtʃɪpi/ noun, adj.
- noun (also **chip·pie**) (pl. **-ies**) (BrE, informal) **1** = CHIP SHOP **2** = CARPENTER
- adj. (informal) (of a person) getting annoyed or offended easily

**'chip shop** (also informal **chip·py, chip·pie**) noun (in the UK) a shop that cooks and sells fish and chips and other fried food for people to take home and eat

**'chip shot** noun = CHIP (8)

**chir·opo·dist** /kɪˈrɒpədɪst; NAmE -ˈrɑːp-/ (especially BrE) (NAmE usually **po·dia·trist**) noun a person whose job is the care and treatment of people's feet

**chir·opody** /kɪˈrɒpədi; NAmE -ˈrɑːp-/ (especially BrE) (NAmE usually **po·dia·try**) noun [U] the work of a chiropodist

**chiro·prac·tic** /ˌkaɪrəʊˈpræktɪk/ noun [U] the medical profession that involves treating some diseases and physical problems by pressing and moving the bones in a person's SPINE or JOINTS; the work of a chiropractor

**chiro·prac·tor** /ˈkaɪrəʊpræktə(r)/ noun a person whose job involves treating some diseases and physical problems by pressing and moving the bones in a person's SPINE or JOINTS ⊃ compare OSTEOPATH ⊃ WORDFINDER NOTE at TREATMENT

**chirp** /tʃɜːp; NAmE tʃɜːrp/ (also **chir·rup**) verb **1** [I] (of small birds and some insects) to make short high sounds **2** [I, T] to speak in a lively and cheerful way: + speech 'I like comics!' she chirped. ▸ **chirp** (also **chir·rup**) noun

**chirpy** /ˈtʃɜːpi; NAmE ˈtʃɜːrpi/ adj. (informal) lively and cheerful; in a good mood ▸ **chirp·ily** /-pɪli/ adv. **chirpi·ness** noun [U]

**chir·rup** /ˈtʃɪrəp/ verb, noun = CHIRP

**chisel** /ˈtʃɪzl/ noun, verb
- noun a tool with a sharp, flat edge at the end, used for shaping wood, stone or metal ⊃ picture at SCREWDRIVER
- verb (-ll-, US -l-) [T, I] **~(sth) (+ adv./prep.)** to cut or shape wood or stone with a chisel: *A name was chiselled into the stone.* ◇ *She was chiselling some marble.* ▸ **chisel·ler** (US **chisel·er**) /ˈtʃɪzlə(r)/ noun

**chis·elled** (US **chis·eled**) /ˈtʃɪzld/ adj. (of a person's face) having clear, strong features

**chi-square test** /ˌkaɪ ˈskweə test; NAmE ˈskwer/ noun (statistics) a method that is used to find out how well a set of data fits the results that were expected according to a theory

**chit** /tʃɪt/ noun **1** a short written note, signed by sb, showing an amount of money that is owed, or giving sb permission to do sth **2** (old-fashioned, disapproving) a young woman or girl, especially one who is thought to have no respect for older people

**'chit-chat** noun [U] (informal) conversation about things that are not important SYN **chat**

**chiv·al·rous** /ˈʃɪvlrəs/ adj. (of men) polite, kind and behaving with honour, especially towards women SYN **gallant** ▸ **chiv·al·rous·ly** adv.

**chiv·alry** /ˈʃɪvlri/ noun [U] **1** polite and kind behaviour that shows a sense of honour, especially by men towards women **2** (in the Middle Ages) the religious and moral system of behaviour that the perfect KNIGHT was expected to follow

**chives** /tʃaɪvz/ noun [pl.] the long, thin leaves of a plant with purple flowers. Chives taste like onions and are used to give extra taste to food. ⊃ VISUAL VOCAB page V8 ▸ **chive** adj. [only before noun]: *a chive and garlic dressing*

**chivvy** /ˈtʃɪvi/ verb (**chiv·vies, chivvy·ing, chiv·vied, chiv·vied**) to try and make sb hurry or do sth quickly, especially when they do not want to do it: **~sb into (doing) sth** *He chivvied them into the car.* ◇ **~sb along** *If you don't chivvy the others along, we'll never get there on time.*

---

chippings | 258

**chla·mydia** /kləˈmɪdiə/ noun [U] (medical) a disease caused by bacteria that is caught by having sex with a person who already has the disease

**chlor·ide** /ˈklɔːraɪd/ noun [U, C] (chemistry) a COMPOUND of CHLORINE and another chemical element ⊃ see also SODIUM CHLORIDE

**chlor·in·ate** /ˈklɔːrɪneɪt/ verb **~sth** to put chlorine in sth, especially water ▸ **chlor·in·ation** /ˌklɔːrɪˈneɪʃn/ noun [U]: *a chlorination plant*

**chlor·ine** /ˈklɔːriːn/ noun [U] (symb. **Cl**) a chemical element. Chlorine is a poisonous green gas with a strong smell. It is often used in swimming pools to keep the water clean.

**chloro·fluoro·car·bon** /ˌklɔːrəʊˈflʊərəʊkɑːbən; NAmE -ˈflʊrəʊkɑːrb-/ noun (chemistry) a CFC; a COMPOUND containing CARBON, FLUORINE and CHLORINE that is harmful to the OZONE LAYER

**chloro·form** /ˈklɒrəfɔːm; NAmE ˈklɔːrəfɔːrm/ noun [U] (symb. **CHCl₃**) a clear liquid used in the past in medicine, etc. to make people unconscious, for example before an operation

**chloro·phyll** /ˈklɒrəfɪl; NAmE ˈklɔːr-/ noun [U] the green substance in plants that takes in light from the sun to help them grow ⊃ see also PHOTOSYNTHESIS

**chloro·plast** /ˈklɒrəplæst; NAmE ˈklɔːrəplæst/ noun (biology) the structure in plant cells that contains CHLOROPHYLL and in which PHOTOSYNTHESIS takes place

**choc** /tʃɒk; NAmE tʃɑːk/ noun (BrE, informal) a chocolate: *a box of chocs*

**choca·hol·ic** = CHOCOHOLIC

**choccy** /ˈtʃɒki; NAmE ˈtʃɑːki/ noun [U, C] (pl. **-ies**) (BrE, informal) chocolate; a sweet made of chocolate: *a box of choccies*

**chock-a-block** /ˌtʃɒk ə ˈblɒk; NAmE ˌtʃɑːk ə ˈblɑːk/ (especially BrE) (BrE also **chocka** /ˈtʃɒkə; NAmE ˈtʃɑːkə/) adj. [not before noun] **~(with sth/sb)** (informal) very full of things or people pressed close together: *The shelves were chock-a-block with ornaments.* ◇ *It was chock-a-block in town today* (= full of people).

**chock-full** /ˌtʃɒk ˈfʊl; NAmE ˌtʃɑːk/ adj. [not before noun] **~(of sth/sb)** (informal) completely full

**choco·hol·ic** (also **choca·hol·ic**) /ˌtʃɒkəˈhɒlɪk; NAmE ˌtʃɑːkəˈhɑːl-/ noun (informal) a person who likes chocolate very much and eats a lot of it

**choc·olate** ❶ 🅰1 /ˈtʃɒklət; NAmE ˈtʃɑːk-/ noun
**1** 🅰1 [U] a hard brown sweet food made from COCOA beans, used in cooking to add taste to cakes, etc. or eaten as a sweet: *a chocolate bar* ◇ *chocolate chip cookies* ◇ *a chocolate cake* ⊃ see also DARK CHOCOLATE, MILK CHOCOLATE, PLAIN CHOCOLATE, WHITE CHOCOLATE **2** 🅰1 [C] a sweet that is made of or covered with chocolate: *a box of chocolates* **3** [U, C] (BrE) = HOT CHOCOLATE: *a mug of drinking chocolate* ⊃ compare COCOA **4** [U] a dark brown colour

**'chocolate-box** adj. [only before noun] (BrE) (especially of places) very pretty, but in a way that does not seem real: *a chocolate-box village*

**choice** ❶ 🅰2 👁 /tʃɔɪs/ noun, adj.
- noun **1** ❶ 🅰2 [C] an act of choosing between two or more possibilities; something that you can choose: *We are faced with a difficult choice.* ◇ **between A and B** *women forced to* **make a choice** *between family and career* ◇ *We aim to help students make more informed career choices.* ◇ *I am sure you have made the* **right choice.** ◇ *There is a wide range of choices open to you.* **2** ❶ 🅰2 [U, sing.] the right to choose; the possibility of choosing: *If I had the choice, I would stop working tomorrow.* ◇ *He had no choice but to leave* (= this was the only thing he could do). ◇ *She's going to do it. She doesn't have* **much choice**, *really, does she?* ◇ *This government is committed to extending parental choice in education.* ⊃ see also ANTI-CHOICE, PRO-CHOICE **3** ❶ 🅰2 [C] a person or thing that is chosen: *This colour wasn't my* **first choice.** ◇ **~for sth** *She's the obvious choice for the job.* ◇ *Hawaii remains a popular choice for winter vacation travel.* ◇ **~as sth** *She wouldn't be my choice as manager.* ◇

**~of sth** *I don't like his choice of friends* (= the people he chooses as his friends). **4** A2 [sing., U] the number or range of different things from which to choose: *The menu has a good choice of desserts.* ◊ *There wasn't **much choice** of colour.* ◊ *I can't decide. There's too much choice.* ⇒ see also HOBSON'S CHOICE, MULTIPLE-CHOICE

IDM **by ˈchoice** because you have chosen: *I wouldn't go there by choice.* **of ˈchoice (for sb/sth)** (used after a noun) that is chosen by a particular group of people or for a particular purpose: *It's the software of choice for business use.* **of your ˈchoice** that you choose yourself: *First prize will be a meal for two at the restaurant of your choice.* ⇒ more at PAY v., SPOILT

■ *adj.* (**choicer, choicest**) [only before noun] **1** (especially of food) of very good quality **2** (*NAmE*) (of meat) of very good, but not the highest, quality **3** ~ **words, phrases, etc.** (*humorous*) rude language that is used deliberately to have an effect: *She summed up the situation in a few choice phrases.* ◊ *He used some pretty choice language.*

▼ SYNONYMS

**choice**
favourite • preference • selection • pick

These are all words for a person or thing that is chosen, or that is liked more than others.
**choice** a person or thing that is chosen: *She's the obvious choice for the job.*
**favourite/favorite** a person or thing that you like more than the others of the same type: *Which one's your favourite?*
**preference** a thing that is liked better or best: *Tastes and preferences vary from individual to individual.*

FAVOURITE OR PREFERENCE?
Your **favourites** are the things you like best, and that you have, do, listen to, etc. often; your **preferences** are the things that you would rather have or do if you can choose.
**selection** a number of people or things that have been chosen from a larger group: *A selection of reader's comments are published below.*
**pick** (*rather informal*) a person or thing that is chosen: *She was his pick for best actress.*

PATTERNS
• sb's choice/favourite/pick **for** sth
• sb's choice/selection/pick **as** sth
• an **obvious** choice/favourite/selection
• a(n) **excellent/good/popular/fine** choice/selection

**choir** ⁅+⁆ B2 /ˈkwaɪə(r)/ *noun* **1** ⁅+⁆ B2 [C + sing./pl. v.] a group of people who sing together, for example in church services or public performances: *She sings in the school choir.* ◊ *a male voice choir* **2** [C] the part of a church where the choir sits during services IDM see PREACH

**choir·boy** /ˈkwaɪəbɔɪ; *NAmE* -bɔːr-/, **choir·girl** /ˈkwaɪəɡɜːl; *NAmE* -ɡɜːrl/ *noun* a boy or girl who sings in the choir of a church ⇒ see also CHORISTER

**choir·mas·ter** /ˈkwaɪəmɑːstə(r); *NAmE* -ərmæs-/ *noun* a person who trains a CHOIR to sing

**choke** /tʃəʊk/ *verb, noun*
■ *verb* **1** [I, T] to be unable to breathe because the passage to your lungs is blocked or you cannot get enough air; to make sb unable to breathe: *She almost choked to death in the thick fumes.* ◊ ~ **on sth** *He was choking on a piece of toast.* ◊ ~ **sb** *Very small toys can choke a baby.* **2** [T] ~ **sb** to make sb stop breathing by pressing their throat, especially with your fingers SYN **strangle**: *He may have been choked or poisoned.* **3** [I, T] to be unable to speak normally especially because of strong emotion; to make sb feel too emotional to speak normally: ~ **(with sth)** *His voice was choking with rage.* ◊ ~ **sth** *Despair choked her words.* ◊ *'I can't bear it,' he said in a choked voice.* ⇒ see also CHOKED **4** [T, usually passive] to block or fill a passage, space, etc. so that movement is difficult: **be choked with sth** *The pond was choked with rotten leaves.* ◊ **be choked up with sth** *The roads are choked up with traffic.* **5** [I] (*informal*) to fail at sth,

259 **chooser**

for example because you are nervous: *We were the only team not to choke at the big moment.*
PHR V ˌchoke sth↔ˈback to try hard to prevent your feelings from showing: *to choke back tears/anger/sobs* ˌchoke sth↔ˈdown to SWALLOW sth with difficulty ˌchoke sth↔ˈoff **1** to prevent or limit sth: *High prices have choked off demand.* **2** to interrupt sth; to stop sth: *Her screams were suddenly choked off.* ˌchoke ˈout | ˌchoke out sth to say sth with great difficulty because you feel a strong emotion: *He choked out a reply.* ◊ + speech *'I hate you!' she choked out.* ˌchoke ˈup to find it difficult to speak, because of the strong emotion that you are feeling: *She choked up when she began to talk about her mother.*

■ *noun* **1** a device that controls the amount of air flowing into the engine of a vehicle **2** an act or the sound of choking

**choked** /tʃəʊkt/ *adj.* [not before noun] ~ **up (about sth)** | ~ **(about sth)** (*informal*) upset or angry about sth, so that you find it difficult to speak

**choker** /ˈtʃəʊkə(r)/ *noun* a piece of jewellery or narrow band of cloth worn closely around the neck

**chola** /ˈtʃəʊlə/ *noun* (*from Spanish*) a woman from Latin America who has both Spanish and Native American ANCESTORS ⇒ compare CHOLO

**chol·era** /ˈkɒlərə; *NAmE* ˈkɑːl-/ *noun* [U] a serious disease caught from bacteria in water that causes severe DIARRHOEA and VOMITING and often causes death

**chol·er·ic** /ˈkɒlərɪk; *NAmE* ˈkɑːl-/ *adj.* (*formal*) easily made angry SYN **bad-tempered**

**chol·es·terol** /kəˈlestərɒl; *NAmE* -rɔːl/ *noun* [U] a FATTY substance found in most TISSUES of the body. Too much cholesterol in the blood is linked to a higher risk of heart disease.

**cholo** /ˈtʃəʊləʊ/ *noun* (*pl.* **-os**) a person from Latin America who has both Spanish and Native American ANCESTORS ⇒ compare CHOLA

**chomp** /tʃɒmp; *NAmE* tʃɑːmp/ *verb* [I, T] to eat or bite food noisily SYN **munch**: ~ **(away) (on/through sth)** *She was chomping away on a bagel.* ◊ ~ **sth** *I don't like the way he chomps his food.*

**choo-choo** /ˈtʃuː tʃuː/ *noun* (*pl.* **choo-choos**) a child's word for a train

**chook** /tʃʊk/ *noun* (*AustralE, NZE, informal*) **1** a chicken **2** an offensive word for an older woman

▼ HOMOPHONES

**chews** • **choose** /tʃuːz/
• **chews** *verb* (third person of CHEW): *She chews her lip thoughtfully before replying.*
• **choose** *verb*: *The magazine will choose six young designers.*

**choose** ⓘ A1 Ⓢ /tʃuːz/ *verb* (**chose** /tʃəʊz/, **chosen** /ˈtʃəʊzn/) **1** ⁅+⁆ A1 [I, T] to decide which thing or person you want out of the ones that are available: *You choose—I can't decide.* ◊ ~ **between A and/or B** *She had to choose between staying in the UK or going home.* ◊ ~ **sth** *Sarah chose her words carefully.* ◊ *It depends which career path you choose.* ◊ ~ **A from B** *We have to choose a new manager from a shortlist of five candidates.* ◊ *There are plenty of restaurants to choose from.* ◊ ~ **sth as/for sth** *He chose banking as a career.* ◊ *We chose Phil McSweeney as/for chairperson.* ◊ ~ **whether, what, etc . . .** *You'll have to choose whether to buy it or not.* ◊ ~ **to do sth** *We chose to go by train.* ◊ ~ **sb to be/do sth** *We chose Phil McSweeney to be chairperson.* **2** ⁅+⁆ A1 [I, T] to prefer or decide to do sth: *Employees can retire at 60 if they choose.* ◊ ~ **to do sth** *Many people choose not to marry.* ⇒ see also CHOICE
IDM **there is nothing/not much/little to choose between A and B** there is very little difference between two or more things or people ⇒ more at PICK v.

**chooser** /ˈtʃuːzə(r)/ *noun* IDM see BEGGAR n.

# choosy

## SYNONYMS

**choose**

select • pick • decide • opt • go for

These words all mean to decide which thing or person you want out of the ones that are available.

**choose** to decide which thing or person you want out of the ones that are available: *You choose—I can't decide.*

**select** [often passive] to choose sb/sth, usually carefully, from a group of people or things: *He was selected for the team.* ◊ *a randomly selected sample of 23 schools*

**pick** (*rather informal*) to choose sb/sth from a group of people or things: *She picked the best cake for herself.*

CHOOSE, SELECT OR PICK?

**Choose** is the most general of these words and the only one that can be used without an object. When you **select** sth, you choose it carefully, unless you actually say that it is *selected randomly/at random*. **Pick** is a more informal word and often a less careful action, used especially when the choice being made is not very important.

**decide** to choose between two or more possibilities: *We're still trying to decide on a venue.*

**opt** to choose to take or not to take a particular course of action: *After graduating she opted for a career in music.* ◊ *After a lot of thought, I opted against buying a motorbike.*

**go for sth** (*rather informal*) to choose sth: *I think I'll go for the fruit salad.*

PATTERNS
- to choose/decide **between** A **and/or** B
- to choose/select/pick A **from** B
- to opt/go **for** sth
- to choose/decide/opt **to do** sth
- to choose/select/pick sb/sth **carefully/at random**
- **randomly** chosen/selected/picked

**choosy** /ˈtʃuːzi/ *adj.* (**choos·ier, choosi·est**) (*informal*) careful in choosing; difficult to please SYN **fussy, picky**: *I'm very choosy about my clothes.*

**chop** ⁀+ B2 /tʃɒp/ NAmE /tʃɑːp/ *verb, noun*

■ *verb* (-pp-) **1** ⁀+ B2 to cut sth into pieces with a sharp tool such as a knife: *~ sth He was chopping logs for firewood.* ◊ *Add the finely chopped onions.* ◊ *~ sth (up) (into sth) Chop the carrots up into small pieces.* ◊ (*figurative*) *The country was chopped up into small administrative areas.* **2** [usually passive] (*informal*) to suddenly stop providing or allowing sth; to suddenly reduce sth by a large amount SYN **cut**: **be chopped** *Their training courses are to be chopped.* ◊ **be chopped from sth to sth** *The share price was chopped from 50 pence to 20 pence.* **3** *~ sb/sth* to hit sb/sth downwards with a quick, short movement

IDM **chop and change** (*BrE, informal*) to keep changing your mind or what you are doing

PHRV **'chop (away) at sth** to aim blows at sth with a heavy sharp tool such as an AXE **chop sth↔'down** to make sth, such as a tree, fall by cutting it at the base with a sharp tool **chop sth↔'off (sth)** to remove sth by cutting it with a sharp tool: *He chopped a branch off the tree.* ◊ (*informal*) *Anne Boleyn had her head chopped off.*

■ *noun* **1** [C] a thick slice of meat with a bone attached to it, especially from a pig or sheep: *a pork/lamb chop* **2** [C, usually sing.] an act of cutting sth in a quick movement downwards using an AXE or a knife **3** [C] an act of hitting sb/sth with the side of your hand in a quick movement downwards: *a karate chop* **4 chops** [pl.] (*informal*) the part of a person's or an animal's face around the mouth: *The dog sat licking its chops.* **5 chops** [pl.] the technical skill of an actor or a jazz or rock musician: *He has the acting chops to carry a major film.*

IDM **be for the 'chop** (*BrE, informal*) **1** (of a person) to be likely to be dismissed from a job: *Who's next for the chop?* **2** (of a plan, project, etc.) to be likely to be stopped or ended **get/be given the 'chop** (*BrE, informal*) **1** (of a person) to be dismissed from a job: *The whole department has been given the chop.* **2** (of a plan, project, etc.) to be stopped or ended: *Three more schemes have got the chop.* **not much 'chop** (*AustralE, NZE, informal*) not very good or useful ⊃ more at BUST *v.*

**chop-'chop** *exclamation* (*informal*) hurry up!: *Chop-chop! We haven't got all day!* ORIGIN From pidgin English based on a Chinese word for 'quick'.

**chop·per** /ˈtʃɒpə(r)/ NAmE /ˈtʃɑːp-/ *noun* **1** [C] (*informal*) a helicopter **2** [C] a large heavy knife or small AXE **3** [C] a type of motorcycle with a very long piece of metal connecting the front wheel to the HANDLEBARS **4 choppers** [pl.] (*informal*) teeth

**'chopping block** *noun* a thick wooden board or block for cutting food or wood on ⊃ compare CHOPPING BOARD

**'chopping board** (*BrE*) (*NAmE* **cutting board**) *noun* a board made of wood or plastic used for cutting meat or vegetables on ⊃ compare CHOPPING BLOCK (1)

**choppy** /ˈtʃɒpi/ NAmE /ˈtʃɑːpi/ *adj.* (**chop·pier, chop·pi·est**) **1** (of the sea, etc.) with a lot of small waves; not calm: *choppy waters* **2** (*NAmE, disapproving*) (of a style of writing) containing a lot of short sentences and changing topics too often

**chop·stick** /ˈtʃɒpstɪk/ NAmE /ˈtʃɑːp-/ *noun* [usually pl.] either of a pair of thin sticks that are used for eating with, especially in some Asian countries ⊃ picture at STICK

**chop suey** /ˌtʃɒp ˈsuːi/ NAmE /ˌtʃɑːp/ *noun* [U] a Chinese-style dish of small pieces of meat fried with vegetables and served with rice

**choral** /ˈkɔːrəl/ *adj.* connected with, written for or sung by a CHOIR (= a group of singers): *choral music*

**chor·ale** /kɒˈrɑːl; NAmE kəˈræl, -ˈrɑːl/ *noun* **1** a piece of church music sung by a group of singers **2** (*especially NAmE*) a group of singers; a CHOIR

**chord** /kɔːd; NAmE kɔːrd/ *noun* **1** (*music*) three or more notes played together **2** (*mathematics*) a straight line that joins two points on a curve ⊃ picture at CIRCLE

IDM **strike/touch a 'chord (with sb)** to say or do sth that makes people feel sympathy or enthusiasm: *The speaker had obviously struck a chord with his audience.*

**chore** /tʃɔː(r)/ *noun* **1** a task that you do regularly: *doing the household/domestic chores* **2** [usually sing.] an unpleasant or boring task: *Shopping's a real chore for me.*

**cho·rea** /kəˈriːə/ *noun* [U] (*medical*) a condition in which parts of the body make quick sudden movements and the person affected cannot control this

**choreo·graph** /ˈkɒriəɡrɑːf/ NAmE /ˈkɔːriəɡræf/ *verb* *~ sth* to design and arrange the steps and movements for dancers in a BALLET or a show ⊃ WORDFINDER NOTE at DANCE

**chore·og·raphy** /ˌkɒriˈɒɡrəfi/ NAmE /ˌkɔːriˈɑːɡ-/ *noun* [U] the art of designing and arranging the steps and movements in dances, especially in BALLET; the steps and movements in a particular ballet or show ▶ **chore·og·raph·er** /ˌkɒriˈɒɡrəfə(r); NAmE ˌkɔːriˈɑːɡ-/ *noun* **choreo·graph·ic** /ˌkɒriəˈɡræfɪk; NAmE ˌkɔːri-/ *adj.*

**chor·is·ter** /ˈkɒrɪstə(r); NAmE ˈkɔːr-/ *noun* a person who sings in the CHOIR of a church

**chor·izo** /tʃəˈriːzəʊ/ *noun* [U, C] (*pl.* **-os**) (*from Spanish*) a spicy Spanish or Latin American SAUSAGE

**chor·tle** /ˈtʃɔːtl; NAmE ˈtʃɔːrtl/ *verb* [I, T] to laugh loudly with pleasure: *Gill chortled with delight.* ▶ **chor·tle** *noun*

**chorus** /ˈkɔːrəs/ *noun, verb*

■ *noun* **1** [C] part of a song that is sung after each VERSE SYN **refrain**: *Everyone joined in the chorus.* **2** [C] a piece of music, usually part of a larger work, that is written for a CHOIR (= a group of singers): *the Hallelujah Chorus* **3** [C + sing./pl. v.] (often in names) a large group of singers SYN **choir**: *the Bath Festival Chorus* **4** [C + sing./pl. v.] a group of performers who sing and dance in a musical show: *the chorus line* (= a line of singers and dancers performing together) ⊃ WORDFINDER NOTE at OPERA **5 a ~ of sth** [sing.] the sound of a lot of people expressing approval or DISAPPROVAL at the same time: *a chorus of praise/complaint* ◊ *a chorus of voices calling for her resignation* ⊃ see also

DAWN CHORUS **6** [sing. + sing./pl. v.] (in ancient Greek drama) a group of performers who comment together on the events of the play **7** [sing.] (especially in sixteenth-century drama) an actor who speaks the opening and closing words of the play
- **IDM** **in chorus** all together **SYN** **in unison**: *'Thank you,'* *they said in chorus.*
- **verb** ~ **sth** to sing or say sth all together: *'Hello, Paul,' they chorused.*

**'chorus girl** *noun* a girl or young woman who is a member of the chorus in a musical show, etc.

**chose** /tʃəʊz/ *past tense* of CHOOSE

**chosen** /'tʃəʊzn/ *verb, adj.*
- **verb** *past part.* of CHOOSE
- **adj.** [only before noun] selected as the best or most suitable: *Music is his chosen vocation.* ◇ *Tickets to the concert were reserved for the chosen few* (= only a few people were selected to attend).

**chough** /tʃʌf/ *noun* a bird of the CROW family, with blue-black feathers, red legs and a red BEAK

**choux pastry** /ˌʃuː ˈpeɪstri/ *noun* [U] a type of very light PASTRY made with eggs, used to make ECLAIRS and PROFITEROLES

**chow** /tʃaʊ/ *noun* **1** [U] (*slang*) food **2** (*also* **'chow chow**) [C] a dog with long thick hair, a curly tail and a blue-black tongue, originally from China

**chow·der** /'tʃaʊdə(r)/ *noun* [U] a thick soup made with fish and vegetables: *clam chowder* ◑ see also BISQUE

**chowk** /tʃaʊk/ *noun* (*IndE*) an open area with a market at a place where two roads meet in a city: *Chandni Chowk*

**chow mein** /ˌtʃaʊ ˈmeɪn/ *noun* [U] a Chinese-style dish of fried NOODLES served with small pieces of meat and vegetables: *chicken chow mein*

**Chris·sake** /'kraɪseɪk/ (*also* **Chris·sakes** /'kraɪseɪks/) *noun* [U] (*taboo, informal*)
- **IDM** **for 'Chrissake** a swear word that many people find offensive, used to show that you are angry, annoyed or surprised: *For Chrissake, listen!*

**Christ** /kraɪst/ (*also* **Jesus, Jesus 'Christ**) *noun, exclamation*
- **noun** the man that Christians believe is the son of God and on whose teachings the Christian religion is based
- **exclamation** (*taboo, informal*) a swear word that many people find offensive, used to show that you are angry, annoyed or surprised: *Christ! Look at the time—I'm late!*

**chris·ten** /'krɪsn/ *verb* **1** to give a name to a baby at his or her baptism to welcome him or her into the Christian Church: ~ **sb + noun** *The child was christened Mary.* ◇ ~ **sb** *Did you have your children christened?* **2** ~ **sb / sth** (+ noun) to give a name to sb/sth: *This area has been christened 'Britain's last wilderness'.* ◇ *They christened the boat 'Oceania'.* **3** ~ **sth** (*informal*) to use sth for the first time

**Chris·ten·dom** /'krɪsndəm/ *noun* [sing.] (*old-fashioned*) all the Christian people and countries of the world

**chris·ten·ing** /'krɪsnɪŋ/ *noun* a Christian ceremony in which a baby is officially named and welcomed into the Christian Church ◑ compare BAPTISM

**Chris·tian** /'krɪstʃən/ *adj., noun*
- **adj.** **1** based on or believing the teachings of Jesus Christ: *the Christian Church/faith/religion* ◇ *She had a Christian upbringing.* ◇ *a Christian country* **2** connected with Christians: *the Christian sector of the city* **3** (*also* **christian**) showing the qualities that are thought of as typical of a Christian; good and kind
- **noun** a person who believes in the teachings of Jesus Christ or has been BAPTIZED in a Christian church: *Only 10% of the population are now practising Christians.*

**the 'Christian era** *noun* [sing.] the period of time that begins with the birth of Christ

**Chris·tian·ity** /ˌkrɪstiˈænəti/ *noun* [U] the religion that is based on the teachings of Jesus Christ and the belief that he was the son of God

**'Christian name** *noun* (in Western countries) a name given to sb when they are born or when they are CHRISTENED; a personal name, not a family name: *We're all on Christian-name terms here.* ◑ compare FIRST NAME

# chromosome

**Christian 'Science** *noun* [U] the beliefs of a religious group called **the Church of Christ, 'Scientist**, which include the belief that the physical world is not real and that you can cure illness by prayer ▸ **Christian 'Scientist** *noun*

**Christ·mas** /'krɪsməs/ *noun* [U, C] **1** (*also* **Christmas 'Day**) 25 December, the day when Christians celebrate the birth of Christ: *Christmas dinner/presents* ◑ see also BOXING DAY **2** (*also* **Christ·mas·time**) the period that includes Christmas Day and the days close to it: *the Christmas holidays/vacation* ◇ *Are you spending Christmas with your family?* ◇ *Happy Christmas!* ◇ *Merry Christmas and a Happy New Year!* ◑ see also WHITE CHRISTMAS

**'Christmas box** *noun* (*BrE, old-fashioned*) a small gift, usually of money, given at Christmas to sb who provides a service during the year, for example a POSTMAN

**'Christmas cake** *noun* [C, U] a fruit cake covered with MARZIPAN and ICING, traditionally eaten in the UK and some other countries at Christmas

**'Christmas card** *noun* a card with a picture on it that you send to friends and relatives at Christmas with your good wishes

**'Christmas 'carol** *noun* = CAROL

**'Christmas 'cracker** *noun* = CRACKER

**'Christmas 'Eve** *noun* [U, C] the day before Christmas Day, 24 December; the evening of this day

**'Christmas 'pudding** *noun* [C, U] a hot PUDDING (= a sweet dish) like a dark fruit cake, traditionally eaten in the UK at Christmas

**'Christmas 'stocking** (*also* **stocking**) *noun* a long sock that children leave out when they go to bed on Christmas Eve so that it can be filled with presents

**Christ·massy** /'krɪsməsi/ *adj.* (*informal*) typical of Christmas: *We put up the decorations and the tree and started to feel Christmassy at last.*

**Christ·mas·time** /'krɪsməstaɪm/ *noun* [U, C] = CHRISTMAS (2)

**'Christmas tree** *noun* an EVERGREEN tree, or an artificial tree that looks similar, that people cover with decorations and coloured lights and have in their homes or outside at Christmas

**chroma** /'krəʊmə/ *noun* [U] (*specialist*) the degree to which a colour is pure or strong, or the fact that it is pure or strong

**chro·mat·ic** /krəˈmætɪk/ *adj.* (*music*) of the **chro'matic 'scale**, a series of musical notes that rise and fall in SEMITONES ◑ compare DIATONIC

**chro·ma·tog·raphy** /ˌkrəʊməˈtɒɡrəfi; *NAmE* -'tɑːɡ-/ *noun* [U] (*chemistry*) the process of separating a mixture by passing it through a material through which some parts of the mixture travel further than others ▸ **chro·ma·to·graph·ic** /ˌkrəʊˌmætəˈɡræfɪk/ *adj.*

**chrome** /krəʊm/ *noun* [U] a hard shiny metal used especially as a layer that protects another metal; chromium or an ALLOY of chromium and other metals

**chrome 'steel** (*also* **chromium 'steel**) *noun* [U] a hard steel containing CHROMIUM that is used for making tools

**chro·mium** /'krəʊmiəm/ *noun* [U] (*symb.* **Cr**) a chemical element. Chromium is a hard grey metal that shines brightly when POLISHED (= made smooth and shiny by being rubbed) and is often used to cover other metals in order to prevent them from RUSTING: *chromium-plated steel*

**chromium 'steel** *noun* [U] = CHROME STEEL

**chromo·some** /'krəʊməsəʊm/ *noun* (*biology*) one of the very small structures like thin strings in the NUCLEI (= central parts) of animal and plant cells. Chromosomes carry the GENES. ◑ see also SEX CHROMOSOME, X CHROMOSOME, Y CHROMOSOME ◑ WORDFINDER NOTE at BIOLOGY ▸ **chromo·somal** /ˌkrəʊməˈsəʊml/ *adj.*: *chromosomal abnormalities*

# chronic

**chron·ic** /ˈkrɒnɪk/ *NAmE* /ˈkrɑːn-/ *adj.* **1** (of a disease) lasting for a long time; difficult to cure: *chronic bronchitis/arthritis/asthma* **OPP** **acute** **2** (of a person) having had a disease for a long time: *a chronic alcoholic/depressive* **3** (of a problem) lasting a long time; difficult to solve: *the country's chronic unemployment problem ◊ a chronic shortage of housing in rural areas* **4** (*BrE*, *informal*) very bad: *The film was just chronic.* ▸ **chron·ic·al·ly** /-kli/ *adv.*: *a hospital for the chronically ill*

**chronic fa'tigue syndrome** (*BrE also* **ME**, **my·al·gic en·ceph·alo·my·eli·tis**) *noun* [U] an illness that makes people feel extremely weak and tired and that can last a long time

**chron·icle** /ˈkrɒnɪkl/ *NAmE* /ˈkrɑːn-/ *noun*, *verb*
■ *noun* a written record of events in the order in which they happened: *the Anglo-Saxon Chronicle ◊ Her latest novel is a chronicle of life in a Devon village.*
■ *verb* ~ *sth* (*formal*) to record events in the order in which they happened: *Her achievements are chronicled in a new biography out this week.* ▸ **chron·ic·ler** /ˈkrɒnɪklə(r)/ *NAmE* /ˈkrɑːn-/ *noun*

**chrono-** /ˈkrɒnəʊ, krɒnə, krəˈnɒ/ *NAmE* /ˈkrɑːnəʊ, krɑːnə, krəˈnɑː/ *combining form* (in nouns, adjectives and adverbs) connected with time: *chronological*

**chrono·graph** /ˈkrɒnəɡrɑːf/ *NAmE* /ˈkrɑːnəɡræf/ *noun* **1** a device for recording time extremely accurately **2** a **STOPWATCH**

**chrono·logic·al** /ˌkrɒnəˈlɒdʒɪkl/ *NAmE* /ˌkrɑːnəˈlɑːdʒ-/ *adj.* (of a number of events) arranged in the order in which they happened: *The facts should be presented in chronological order.* ▸ **chrono·logic·al·ly** /-kli/ *adv.*

**chrono·logical 'age** *noun* [U, sing.] (*formal*) the number of years a person has lived as opposed to their level of physical, mental or emotional development ⇨ compare **MENTAL AGE**

**chron·ology** /krəˈnɒlədʒi/ *NAmE* /-ˈnɑːl-/ *noun* (*pl.* **-ies**) [U, C] the order in which a series of events happened; a list of these events in order: *Historians seem to have confused the chronology of these events. ◊ a chronology of Mozart's life*

**chron·om·eter** /krəˈnɒmɪtə(r)/ *NAmE* /-ˈnɑːm-/ *noun* a very accurate clock, especially one used at sea

**chrys·alis** /ˈkrɪsəlɪs/ *noun* (*also* **chrys·alid** /ˈkrɪsəlɪd/) the form of an insect, especially a **BUTTERFLY** or **MOTH**, while it is changing into an adult inside a hard case, also called a *chrysalis* ⇨ **VISUAL VOCAB** page V3 ⇨ compare **PUPA**

**chrys·an·the·mum** /krɪˈzænθəməm/ *noun* a large, brightly coloured garden flower that is like a ball in shape and is made up of many long narrow **PETALS** ⇨ **VISUAL VOCAB** page V7

**chub** /tʃʌb/ *noun* (*pl.* **chub**) a **FRESHWATER** fish with a thick body

**chub·by** /ˈtʃʌbi/ *adj.* (**chub·bier**, **chub·bi·est**) slightly fat in a way that people usually find attractive: *chubby cheeks/fingers/hands* ▸ **chub·bi·ness** *noun* [U]

**chuck** /tʃʌk/ *verb*, *noun*
■ *verb* **1** (*especially BrE*, *informal*) to throw sth carelessly or without much thought: *~ sth* (**+ adv./prep.**) *He chucked the paper in a drawer. ◊ ~ sb sth Chuck me the newspaper, would you?* ⇨ **SYNONYMS** at **THROW** **2** (*informal*) to give up or stop doing sth: *~ sth You haven't chucked your job! ◊ ~ sth in/up I'm going to chuck it all in (= give up my job) and go abroad.* **3** *~ sb* (*BrE*, *informal*) to leave your boyfriend or girlfriend and stop having a relationship with him or her: *Has he chucked her?* **4** *~ sth* (*informal*) to throw sth away: *That's no good—just chuck it.*
 **IDM** **chuck sb under the 'chin** (*old-fashioned*) to touch sb gently under the **CHIN** (= part of the face below the mouth) in a friendly way **it's 'chucking it down** (*BrE*, *informal*) it's raining heavily
 **PHRV** **chuck sth↔a'way** | **chuck sth↔'out** (*informal*) to throw sth away: *Those old clothes can be chucked out.* | **chuck sth 'off (sth)** | **chuck sb 'out (of sth)** (*informal*) to force sb to leave a place or a job: *They got chucked off the bus. ◊ You can't just chuck him out.*
■ *noun* **1** [C] a part of a tool such as a **DRILL** that can be moved to hold sth tightly ⇨ picture at **PLANE** **2** [*sing.*] (*NEngE*, *informal*) a friendly way of addressing sb: *What's up with you, chuck?* **3** (*also* **chuck 'steak**) [U] meat from the shoulder of a cow

**chuckle** /ˈtʃʌkl/ *verb* [I] *~ (at/about sth)* to laugh quietly: *She chuckled at the memory.* ▸ **chuckle** *noun*: *She gave a chuckle of delight.*

**chuffed** /tʃʌft/ *adj.* [not before noun] *~ (about sth)* (*BrE*, *informal*) very pleased

**chuff·ing** /ˈtʃʌfɪŋ/ *adj.* (*NEngE*, *slang*) a mild swear word that some people use when they are annoyed, to avoid saying 'fucking': *The whole chuffing world's gone mad.*

**chug** /tʃʌɡ/ *verb*, *noun*
■ *verb* (**-gg-**) **1** [I] (**+ adv./prep.**) to move making the sound of an engine running slowly: *The boat chugged down the river.* **2** [T] *~ sth* (*NAmE*, *informal*) to drink all of sth quickly without stopping
■ *noun* the sound made by a chugging engine

**chum** /tʃʌm/ *noun* (*old-fashioned*, *informal*) a friend: *an old school chum*

**chum·my** /ˈtʃʌmi/ *adj.* (*old-fashioned*, *informal*) very friendly ▸ **chum·mi·ness** *noun* [U]

**chump** /tʃʌmp/ *noun* (*old-fashioned*, *informal*) a stupid person: *Don't be such a chump!*

**'chump change** *noun* [U] (*NAmE*, *informal*) a small amount of money that is of little value: *For all my hard work, all I got was chump change.*

**chunk** /tʃʌŋk/ *noun* **1** a thick, solid piece that has been cut or broken off sth: *a chunk of cheese/masonry* **2** (*informal*) a fairly large amount of sth: *I've already written a fair chunk of the article.* **3** (*linguistics*) a phrase or group of words that can be learnt as a unit by sb who is learning a language. Examples of chunks are 'Can I have the bill, please?' and 'Pleased to meet you'. **IDM** see **BLOW** *v.*

**chunky** /ˈtʃʌŋki/ *adj.* (**chunki·er**, **chunki·est**) **1** thick and heavy: *a chunky gold bracelet ◊* (*BrE*) *a chunky sweater* **2** having a short strong body: *a squat chunky man* **3** (of food) containing thick pieces: *chunky marmalade*

**chun·ter** /ˈtʃʌntə(r)/ *verb* [I] *~ (on) (about sth)* (*BrE*, *informal*) to talk or complain about sth in a way that other people think is boring or annoying **SYN** **witter**

**church** /tʃɜːtʃ/ *NAmE* /tʃɜːrtʃ/ *noun* **1** [C] a building where Christians go to attend services, pray, etc: *The procession moved into the church. ◊ England has some beautiful parish churches. ◊ a church tower/spire ◊ church services* ⇨ see also **COMMUNITY CHURCH** **2** [U] a service or services in a church: *How often do you go to church?* ◊ **at ~** (*BrE*) *They're at church (= attending a church service).* ◊ **in ~** (*NAmE*) *They're in church. ◊* (*BrE and NAmE*) *Lots of people still get married in church. ◊ Church is at 9 o'clock.* ⇨ note at **SCHOOL** **3** **Church** [C] a particular group of Christians: *the Anglican Church ◊ the Catholic Church ◊ the Free Churches ◊ Linda joined the local Methodist church.* ⇨ see also **DENOMINATION**, **EPISCOPAL**, **FREE CHURCH**, **LUTHERAN**, **ORTHODOX**, **REFORMED CHURCH** **4** **(the) Church** [*sing.*] the ministers of the Christian religion; the institution of the Christian religion: *The Church has a duty to condemn violence. ◊ the conflict between Church and State ◊ to go into the Church (= to become a Christian minister)* **IDM** see **BROAD** *adj.*

**church·goer** /ˈtʃɜːtʃɡəʊə(r)/ *NAmE* /ˈtʃɜːrtʃ-/ *noun* a person who goes to church services regularly ▸ **church·going** *noun* [U]

**church·man** /ˈtʃɜːtʃmən/ *NAmE* /ˈtʃɜːrtʃ-/ *noun* (*pl.* **-men** /-mən/) (*formal*) a member of the Christian **CLERGY** or of a Church ⇨ compare **CLERGYMAN**, **CLERGYWOMAN**

**the Church of England** /ðə ˌtʃɜːtʃ əv ˈɪŋɡlənd/ *NAmE* /ˌtʃɜːrtʃ/ *noun* (*abbr.* **CE**, **C of E**) [*sing.*] the official Church in England, whose leader is the Queen or King

**the Church of Scotland** /ðə ˌtʃɜːt ʃ əv ˈskɒtlənd; NAmE ˌtʃɜːrtʃ əv ˈskɑːt-/ noun [sing.] the official (Presbyterian) Church in Scotland

**church·war·den** /ˈtʃɜːtʃwɔːdn; NAmE ˈtʃɜːrtʃwɔːrdn/ noun (in the Anglican Church) a person who is chosen by the members of a church to take care of church property and money

**churchy** /ˈtʃɜːtʃi; NAmE ˈtʃɜːrtʃi/ adj. (**church·ier**, **churchi·est**) (*disapproving*) (of a person) religious in a way that involves going to church, PRAYING, etc. a lot, but often not accepting other people's views

**church·yard** /ˈtʃɜːtʃjɑːd; NAmE ˈtʃɜːrtʃjɑːrd/ noun an area of land around a church, often used for burying people in ⊃ compare CEMETERY, GRAVEYARD

**churi·dar** /ˈtʃʊrɪdɑː(r)/ noun tight trousers worn by many people from South Asia with a KAMEEZ or KURTA

**churl** /tʃɜːl; NAmE tʃɜːrl/ noun (*old-fashioned*) a rude unpleasant person

**churl·ish** /ˈtʃɜːlɪʃ; NAmE ˈtʃɜːrl-/ adj. (*formal*) rude or very unpleasant: *It would be churlish to refuse such a generous offer.* ▸ **churl·ish·ly** adv. **churl·ish·ness** noun [U]

**churn** /tʃɜːn; NAmE tʃɜːrn/ verb, noun
■ *verb* **1** [I, T] if water, mud, etc. **churns**, or if sth **churns (up)**, it moves or is moved around violently: *~(up) The water churned beneath the huge ship.* ◊ *~sth (up) Vast crowds watched the field into a sea of mud.* **2** [I, T] *~(sth)* if your stomach **churns** or if sth **churns** your stomach, you feel a strong, unpleasant feeling of worry or fear: *My stomach churned as the names were read out.* **3** [T, I] *~(sb) (up)* to make sb feel upset or emotionally confused: *It churns me up inside to think what might have happened.* **4** [T] *~sth* to turn and mix milk in a special container in order to make butter
**PHRV** **churn sth↔ˈout** (*informal*, *often disapproving*) to produce sth quickly and in large amounts
■ *noun* **1** a machine in which milk or cream is shaken to make butter **2** (*BrE*) a large metal container in which milk was carried from a farm in the past **3** (*business*) = CHURN RATE

**ˈchurn rate** (*also* **churn**) noun (*business*) the number of people who stop using a product and change to another or who leave the company they work for and go to another

**chute** /ʃuːt/ noun **1** a tube or passage down which people or things can slide: *a water chute (= at a swimming pool)* ◊ *a laundry/rubbish/garbage chute (= from the upper floors of a high building)* **2** (*informal*) = PARACHUTE

▼ HOMOPHONES

chute ◆ shoot /ʃuːt/
• **chute** *noun*: *The laundry chute leads down to the washer-dryer area in the basement.*
• **shoot** *verb*: *The recruits are learning to shoot at targets.*
• **shoot** *noun*: *She posed for the cameras as though for a fashion shoot.*

**ˌChutes and ˈLadders**™ noun [U] (*US*) a children's game played on a special board with pictures of chutes and LADDERS on it. Players move their pieces up the ladders to go forward and down the chutes to go back. ⊃ compare SNAKES AND LADDERS

**chut·ney** /ˈtʃʌtni/ noun [U] a cold thick sauce made from fruit, sugar, SPICES and VINEGAR, eaten with cold meat, cheese, etc.

**chutz·pah** /ˈxʊtspə, ˈhʊt-/ noun [U] (*often approving*) behaviour, or a person's attitude, that offends or shocks people but is so confident that they may feel forced to admire it **SYN** nerve

**Ci** *abbr.* CURIE

**CIA** /ˌsiː aɪ ˈeɪ/ *abbr.* the Central Intelligence Agency (a department of the US government that collects information about other countries, often secretly)

**cia·batta** /tʃəˈbætə, -ˈbɑːtə/ noun [U, C] (*from Italian*) a type of Italian bread made in a long flat shape; a sandwich made with this type of bread

**ciao** /tʃaʊ/ *exclamation* (*from Italian*, *informal*) goodbye

**ci·cada** /sɪˈkɑːdə; NAmE -ˈkeɪdə/ noun a large insect with TRANSPARENT wings, common in hot countries. The male makes a continuous high sound after dark by making two MEMBRANES (= pieces of thin skin) on its body VIBRATE (= move very fast).

**CID** /ˌsiː aɪ ˈdiː/ *abbr.* Criminal Investigation Department (the department of the British police force that is responsible for solving crimes)

**-cide** /saɪd/ *combining form* (in nouns) **1** the act of killing: *suicide* ◊ *genocide* **2** a person or thing that kills: *insecticide* ▸ **-cidal** /saɪdl/ (in adjectives) *homicidal*

**cider** /ˈsaɪdə(r)/ noun **1** (*especially ErE*) (*NAmE usually* **ˌhard ˈcider**) [U, C] an alcoholic drink made from the juice of apples: *dry/sweet cider* ◊ *cider apples* ◊ *a cider press (= for squeezing the juice from apples)* **2** (*also* **ˌapple ˈcider**) [U, C] (*both NAmE*) a drink made from the juice of apples that does not contain alcohol **3** [C] a glass of cider ⊃ compare PERRY

**cigar** /sɪˈɡɑː(r)/ noun a roll of dried TOBACCO leaves that people smoke, like a cigarette but bigger and without paper around it: *cigar smoke* **IDM** see CLOSE² *adj.*

**cig·ar·ette** ❶ A2 /ˌsɪɡəˈret; NAmE ˈsɪɡəret/ noun a thin tube of paper filled with TOBACCO, for smoking: *to smoke/have a cigarette* ◊ *a decrease in cigarette smoking* ⊃ see also E-CIGARETTE, ELECTRONIC CIGARETTE

**ciga·ˈrette end** (*BrE*) (*also* **ˌcigaˈrette butt** *NAmE*, *BrE*) noun the part of a cigarette that is left when sb has finished smoking it

**cigaˈrette holder** noun a narrow tube for holding a cigarette in while you are smoking

**cigaˈrette lighter** noun = LIGHTER

**cigaˈrette paper** noun a thin piece of paper in which people roll TOBACCO to make their own cigarettes

**cig·ar·illo** /ˌsɪɡəˈrɪləʊ/ noun (*pl.* **-os**) a small CIGAR

**ciggy** /ˈsɪɡi/ noun (*pl.* **-ies**) (*BrE, informal*) a cigarette

**ci·lan·tro** /sɪˈlæntrəʊ; NAmE -ˈlɑːn-/ noun [U] (*NAmE*) the leaves of the CORIANDER plant, used in cooking as a HERB ⊃ VISUAL VOCAB page V8

**ˈciliary muscle** /ˈsɪliəri mʌsl; NAmE -lier-/ noun (*anatomy*) a muscle in the eye that controls how much the LENS curves

**C.-in-C.** /ˌsiː ɪn ˈsiː/ *abbr.* COMMANDER-IN-CHIEF

**cinch** /sɪntʃ/ noun, verb
■ *noun* [sing.] (*informal*) **1** something that is very easy **SYN** doddle: *The first question is a cinch.* **2** (*especially NAmE*) a thing that is certain to happen; a person who is certain to do sth: *He's a cinch to win the race.*
■ *verb* **1** *~sth* (*especially NAmE*) to fasten sth tightly around the middle part of your body; to be fastened around the middle part of sb's body **2** *~sth* (*NAmE*) to fasten a GIRTH around a horse **3** *~sth* (*NAmE, informal*) to make sth certain

**cin·der** /ˈsɪndə(r)/ noun [usually pl.] a small piece of ASH or partly burnt coal, wood, etc. that is no longer burning but may still be hot: *a cinder track (= a track for runners made with finely crushed cinders)* **IDM** see BURN *v.*

**ˈcinder block** (*NAmE*) (*BrE* **ˈbreeze block**) noun a light building block, made of sand, coal ASHES and CEMENT

**Cin·der·ella** /ˌsɪndəˈrelə/ noun [usually sing.] a person or thing that has been ignored and deserves to receive more attention: *For years radio has been the Cinderella of the media world.* **ORIGIN** From the European fairy tale about a beautiful girl, **Cinderella**, who was treated in a cruel way by her two ugly sisters. She had to do all the work and received no reward or thanks until she met and married Prince Charming.

**cine** /ˈsɪni/ adj. [only before noun] (*BrE*) connected with films and the film industry: *a cine camera/film/photographer*

**cine·aste** (*also* **cine·ast**) /ˈsɪniæst/ noun (*from French*) a person who knows a lot about films and is very enthusiastic about them

# cinema

**cin·ema** ⓘ A1 /ˈsɪnəmə; BrE also -mɑː/ noun 1 ⓘ A1 (especially BrE) (NAmE usually **movie theater**, **theater**, **movie house**) [C] a building in which films are shown: *in a ~* *The film has just opened in cinemas across the UK.* ⇨ see also HOME CINEMA 2 ⓘ A1 **the cinema** [sing.] (BrE) (NAmE **the movies**) when you go to **the cinema** or to **the movies**, you go to a cinema to see a film: *I used to go to the cinema every week.* 3 ⓘ B2 [U, sing.] (especially BrE) (NAmE usually **the movies**) films as an art or an industry: *one of the great successes of British cinema* ⇨ WORDFINDER NOTE at FILM

**cin·ema·goer** /ˈsɪnəməɡəʊə(r)/ noun (BrE) = FILMGOER

**cine·mat·ic** /ˌsɪnəˈmætɪk/ adj. (specialist) connected with films and how they are made: *cinematic effects/techniques*

**cine·ma·tog·raphy** /ˌsɪnəməˈtɒɡrəfi; NAmE -ˈtɑːɡ-/ noun [U] (specialist) the art or process of making films, especially the photography and CAMERAWORK ▶ **cine·ma·tog·raph·er** /ˌsɪnəməˈtɒɡrəfə(r); NAmE -ˈtɑːɡ-/ noun **cine·ma·tog·raph·ic** /ˌsɪnəmætəˈɡræfɪk/ adj.

**cine·phile** /ˈsɪnɪfaɪl/ noun a person who is very interested in films

**cinna·bar** /ˈsɪnəbɑː(r)/ noun [U] **1** a bright red mineral that is sometimes used to give colour to things **2** the bright red colour of cinnabar

**cin·na·mon** /ˈsɪnəmən/ noun [U] the inner BARK of a southeast Asian tree, used in cooking as a SPICE, especially in sweet foods ⇨ VISUAL VOCAB page V8

**ci·pher** (also **cy·pher**) /ˈsaɪfə(r)/ noun **1** [U, C] a secret way of writing, especially one in which a set of letters or symbols is used to represent others SYN **code**: *a message in cipher* ⇨ see also DECIPHER **2** [C] (formal, disapproving) a person or thing of no importance **3** [C] (BrE) the first letters of sb's name combined in a design and used to mark things

**circa** /ˈsɜːkə; NAmE ˈsɜːrkə/ prep. (from Latin) (abbr. **c**) (used with dates) about: *born circa 150 BC*

**cir·ca·dian** /sɜːˈkeɪdiən; NAmE sɜːrˈk-/ adj. [only before noun] (specialist) connected with the changes in the bodies of people or animals over each period of 24 hours

## circles

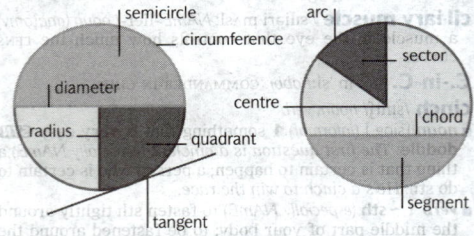

**cir·cle** ⓘ A2 /ˈsɜːkl; NAmE ˈsɜːrkl/ noun, verb
▪ **noun 1** ⓘ A2 a completely round flat shape: *the centre/circumference/radius/diameter of a circle* ⇨ picture at CONIC SECTION ⇨ see also SEMICIRCLE **2** ⓘ A2 the line that forms the edge of a circle: *Draw a circle.* ◇ *in a ~ She walked the horse round in a circle.* ⇨ see also ANTARCTIC CIRCLE, ARCTIC CIRCLE, TURNING CIRCLE **3** ⓘ A2 a thing or a group of people or things that is like a circle in shape: *~of sb/sth a circle of trees/chairs* ◇ *in a ~ The children stood in a circle.* ⇨ see also CORN CIRCLE, CROP CIRCLE, STONE CIRCLE **4** (also **bal·cony**) an upper floor of a theatre or cinema where the seats are arranged in curved rows: *We had seats in the circle.* ⇨ see also DRESS CIRCLE ⇨ WORDFINDER NOTE at THEATRE **5** a group of people who are connected because they have the same interests, jobs, etc: *the family circle* ◇ *She's well known in theatrical circles.* ◇ *a large circle of friends* ⇨ see also CHARMED CIRCLE, INNER CIRCLE, VICIOUS CIRCLE, VIRTUOUS CIRCLE
IDM **come, turn, etc. full ˈcircle** to return to the situation in which you started, after a series of events or experiences **go round in ˈcircles** to work hard at sth or discuss sth without making any progress **run round in ˈcircles** (informal) to be busy doing sth without achieving anything important or making progress ⇨ more at SQUARE *v*.
▪ **verb 1** ⓘ A2 [T] to draw a circle around sth: *~sth (in sth) Luke circled a date on the kitchen calendar.* **2** [I, T] to move in a circle, especially in the air: *~(around) (above/over sb/sth) Seagulls circled around above his head.* ◇ *~sb/sth The plane circled the airport to burn up excess fuel.*
IDM **circle the ˈwagons** (NAmE) to join together with people who have the same ideas and beliefs as you, and avoid contact with those who do not, who may threaten or attack you: *When your way of life is threatened, you have to circle the wagons and defend yourself.* ORIGIN From the practice of arranging a WAGON TRAIN in a circle to defend against attack.

**circ·let** /ˈsɜːklət; NAmE ˈsɜːrk-/ noun a round band made of PRECIOUS METAL, flowers, etc., worn around the head for decoration

**cir·cuit** ⓘ B2 /ˈsɜːkɪt; NAmE ˈsɜːrk-/ noun **1** ⓘ B2 a line, route or journey around a place: *The race ended with eight laps of a city centre circuit.* ◇ *The earth takes a year to make a circuit of* (= go around) *the sun.* **2** ⓘ B2 the complete path of wires and equipment along which an electric current flows: *an electrical circuit* ◇ *a circuit diagram* (= one showing all the connections in the different parts of the circuit) ⇨ see also CLOSED-CIRCUIT TELEVISION, INTEGRATED CIRCUIT, LOGIC CIRCUIT, PRINTED CIRCUIT, SHORT CIRCUIT **3** (in sport) a series of games or matches in which the same players regularly take part: *the women's tennis circuit* **4** a track for cars or motorcycles to race around **5** a series of places or events of a particular kind at which the same people appear or take part: *the lecture/cabaret circuit* **6** a regular journey made by a judge to hear court cases in each of the courts of law in a particular area: *a circuit court/judge*

**ˈcircuit board** noun a board that holds electrical circuits inside a piece of electrical equipment

**ˈcircuit breaker** noun a device that will stop an electric current if it becomes dangerous

**cir·cu·it·ous** /səˈkjuːɪtəs; NAmE sərˈk-/ adj. (formal) (of a route or journey) long and not direct SYN **roundabout** ▶ **cir·cu·it·ous·ly** adv.

**cir·cuit·ry** /ˈsɜːkɪtri; NAmE ˈsɜːrk-/ noun [U] a system of electrical CIRCUITS or the equipment that forms this

**ˈcircuit training** noun [U] a type of training in sport in which different exercises are each done for a short time

**cir·cu·lar** /ˈsɜːkjələ(r); NAmE ˈsɜːrk-/ adj., noun
▪ **adj. 1** having the shape of a circle; round: *a circular building* **2** moving around in a circle: *a circular tour of the city* **3** (of an argument or a theory) using an idea or a statement to prove sth that is then used to prove the idea or statement at the beginning **4** (of a letter) sent to a large number of people ▶ **cir·cu·lar·ity** /ˌsɜːkjəˈlærəti; NAmE ˌsɜːrk-/ noun [U]: *There is a dangerous circularity about this argument.*
▪ **noun** a letter, notice or advertisement that is sent to a large number of people at the same time

**circular ˈsaw** (NAmE also **ˈbuzz saw**) noun a SAW in the form of a metal disc that turns quickly, driven by a motor, and is used for cutting wood, etc.

**cir·cu·late** ⓘ C1 /ˈsɜːkjəleɪt; NAmE ˈsɜːrk-/ verb **1** ⓘ C1 [I, T] when a liquid, gas or air **circulates** or **is circulated**, it moves continuously around a place or system: *The condition prevents the blood from circulating freely.* ◇ *~sth Cooled air is circulated throughout the building.* **2** ⓘ C1 *~(sth)* [I, T] if a story, an idea, information, etc. **circulates** or if you **circulate** it, it spreads or it is passed from one person to another: *Rumours began to circulate about his financial problems.* **3** [T] *~sth (to sb)* to send goods or information to all the people in a group: *The document will be circulated to all members.* **4** [I] to move around a group, especially at a party, talking to different people

**cir·cu·la·tion** ⓘ C1 /ˌsɜːkjəˈleɪʃn; NAmE ˌsɜːrk-/ noun **1** ⓘ C1 [U] the movement of blood around the body: *Regular exercise will improve blood circulation.* ◇ *to have good/bad circulation* **2** ⓘ C1 [U] the passing or spreading of sth from one person or place to another: *the circulation of money/information/ideas* ◇ *in ~ A number of forged tickets* are in circulation. ◊ The coins were **taken out of circulation**. ◊ Copies of the magazine were **withdrawn from circulation**. **3** [C, usually sing.] the usual number of copies of a newspaper or magazine that are sold each day, week, etc: *a daily circulation of more than one million* **4** [U, C] the movement of sth (for example air, water, gas, etc.) around an area or inside a system or machine **5** [U] the fact that sb takes part in social activities at a particular time: **in ~** *Anne has been ill but now she's back in circulation.* ◊ **out of ~** *I was out of circulation for months after the baby was born.*

**cir·cu·la·tory** /ˌsɜːkjəˈleɪtəri; NAmE ˈsɜːrkjələtɔːri/ *adj.* relating to the movement of blood around the body

**cir·cum·cise** /ˈsɜːkəmsaɪz; NAmE ˈsɜːrk-/ *verb* **1 ~ sb** to remove the FORESKIN of a boy or man for religious or medical reasons **2 ~ sb** to cut off part of the sex organs of a girl or woman for non-medical reasons (a traditional practice in some cultures but illegal in many countries) ⊃ compare FGM

**cir·cum·ci·sion** /ˌsɜːkəmˈsɪʒn; NAmE ˌsɜːrk-/ *noun* [U, C] the act of circumcising sb; the religious ceremony when sb, especially a baby, is circumcised

**cir·cum·fer·ence** /səˈkʌmfərəns; NAmE sərˈk-/ *noun* [C, U] a line that goes around a circle or any other curved shape; the length of this line: *the circumference of the earth* ◊ **in ~** *The earth is almost 25000 miles in circumference.* ⊃ picture at CIRCLE ⊃ compare PERIMETER

**cir·cum·flex** /ˈsɜːkəmfleks; NAmE ˈsɜːrk-/ (also **circumflex accent**) *noun* the mark placed over a vowel in some languages to show how it should be pronounced, as over the *o* in *rôle* ⊃ compare ACUTE ACCENT, GRAVE², TILDE, UMLAUT

**cir·cum·lo·cu·tion** /ˌsɜːkəmləˈkjuːʃn; NAmE ˌsɜːrk-/ *noun* [U, C] (*formal*) the use of more words than are necessary, instead of speaking or writing in a clear, direct way

**cir·cum·navi·gate** /ˌsɜːkəmˈnævɪɡeɪt; NAmE ˌsɜːrk-/ *verb* **~ sth** (*formal*) to sail all the way around sth, especially all the way around the world ▶ **cir·cum·navi·ga·tion** /ˌsɜːkəmˌnævɪˈɡeɪʃn; NAmE ˌsɜːrk-/ *noun* [U]

**cir·cum·scribe** /ˈsɜːkəmskraɪb; NAmE ˈsɜːrk-/ *verb* **1** [often passive] (*formal*) to limit sb/sth's freedom, rights, power, etc. **SYN** **restrict**: **be circumscribed (by sth)** *The power of the monarchy was circumscribed by the new law.* **2 ~ sth** (*specialist*) to draw a circle around another shape ▶ **cir·cum·scrip·tion** /ˌsɜːkəmˈskrɪpʃn; NAmE ˌsɜːrk-/ *noun* [U]

**cir·cum·spect** /ˈsɜːkəmspekt; NAmE ˈsɜːrk-/ *adj.* (*formal*) thinking very carefully about sth before doing it, because there may be risks involved **SYN** **cautious** ▶ **cir·cum·spec·tion** /ˌsɜːkəmˈspekʃn; NAmE ˌsɜːrk-/ *noun* [U] **cir·cum·spect·ly** /ˈsɜːkəmspektli; NAmE ˈsɜːrk-/ *adv.*

**cir·cum·stance** /ˈsɜːkəmstəns, -staːns, -stæns; NAmE ˈsɜːrkəmstæns/ *noun* **1** [C, usually pl.] the conditions and facts that are connected with and affect a situation, an event or an action: *Police said there were no suspicious circumstances surrounding the boy's death.* ◊ **under … circumstances** *Under normal circumstances, your white blood cells are able to fight infections.* ◊ **in … circumstances** *The company reserves the right to cancel this agreement in certain circumstances.* ◊ *In exceptional circumstances, detainees could be denied access to a lawyer.* ◊ *Due to unforeseen circumstances, we have had to reschedule the concert.* ◊ *Britain is fortunately not facing the same set of circumstances.* ◊ *The court will take into account all the circumstances of the case.* ⊃ SYNONYMS at SITUATION **2** **circumstances** [pl.] the conditions of a person's life, especially the money they have: *We want to work towards improving the often difficult circumstances in which people find themselves.* ◊ *The particular circumstances of each individual claimant must be considered.* **3** [U] (*formal*) situations and events that affect and influence your life and that are not in your control: *a victim of circumstance* (= a person who has suffered because of a situation that they cannot control) ◊ *He had to leave the country through force of circumstance* (= events made it necessary).
**IDM** **in/under the circumstances** used before or after a statement to show that you have thought about the conditions that affect a situation before making a decision or a statement: *Under the circumstances, it seemed better not to tell him about the accident.* ◊ *She did the job very well in the circumstances.* **in/under no circumstances** used to emphasize that sth should never happen or be allowed: *Under no circumstances should you lend Paul any money.* ◊ *Don't open the door, in any circumstances.* ⊃ more at POMP, REDUCE

**cir·cum·stan·tial** /ˌsɜːkəmˈstænʃl; NAmE ˌsɜːrk-/ *adj.* **1** (*law*) containing information and details that strongly suggest that sth is true but do not prove it: *circumstantial evidence* ◊ *The case against him was largely circumstantial.* **2** (*formal*) connected with particular circumstances: *Their problems were circumstantial rather than personal.*

**cir·cum·vent** /ˌsɜːkəmˈvent; NAmE ˌsɜːrk-/ *verb* (*formal*) **1 ~ sth** to find a way of avoiding a difficulty or a rule: *They found a way of circumventing the law.* **2 ~ sth** to go or travel around sth that is blocking your way ▶ **cir·cum·ven·tion** /-ˈvenʃn/ *noun* [U]

**cir·cus** /ˈsɜːkəs; NAmE ˈsɜːrk-/ *noun* **1** [C] a group of people, sometimes with trained animals, who perform acts with skill in a show that travels around to different places **2 the circus** [sing.] a show performed by people who are members of a circus, usually in a large tent called the BIG TOP: *We took the children to the circus.* **3** [sing.] (*informal, disapproving*) a group of people or an event that attracts a lot of attention: *A media circus surrounded the royal couple wherever they went.* ◊ *the American electoral circus* **4** [C] (*BrE*) (used in some place names) a round open area in a town where several streets meet: *Piccadilly Circus* **5** [C] (in ancient Rome) a place like a big round outdoor theatre for public games, races, etc.

**cir·rho·sis** /səˈrəʊsɪs/ *noun* [U] a serious disease of the LIVER, caused especially by drinking too much alcohol

**cir·rus** /ˈsɪrəs/ *noun* [U] (*specialist*) a type of light cloud that forms high in the sky

**cissy** (*BrE*) = SISSY

**cis·tern** /ˈsɪstən; NAmE -stərn/ *noun* a container in which water is stored in a building, especially one in the roof or connected to a toilet

**cita·del** /ˈsɪtədəl, -del/ *noun* (in the past) a castle on high ground in or near a city where people could go when the city was being attacked: (*figurative*) *citadels of private economic power*

**cit·ation** /saɪˈteɪʃn/ *noun* (*formal*) **1** [C] words or lines taken from a book or a speech **SYN** **quotation 2** [C] an official statement about sth special that sb has done, especially about acts of courage in a war: *a citation for bravery* **3** [U] an act of citing or being cited: *Space does not permit the citation of the examples.* **4** [C] (*NAmE*) = SUMMONS: *The judge issued a contempt citation against the woman for violating a previous court order.*

**cite** /saɪt/ *verb* (*formal*) **1** to mention sth as a reason or an example, or in order to support what you are saying: **~ sth** *She cited examples of companies the city has helped relocate or expand.* ◊ **~ sth as sth** *He cited his heavy workload as the reason for his breakdown.* ⊃ SYNONYMS at MENTION **2** **~ sb/sth (in sth)** to speak or write the exact words from a book, an author, etc. **SYN** **quote**: *He cites no primary sources for his claims.* **3 ~ sb (for sth)** (*law*) to order sb to appear in court; to name sb officially in a legal case: *She was cited in the divorce proceedings.* **4 ~ sb (for sth)** to mention sb officially or publicly because they deserve special praise: *He was cited for bravery.*

**citi·zen** /ˈsɪtɪzn/ *noun* **1** a person who has the legal right to belong to a particular country: *The defeat of the president did not change the lives of ordinary citizens for the better.* ◊ *an economic slowdown that has left millions of our fellow citizens unemployed* ⊃ compare SUBJECT (6) ⊃ see also NON-CITIZEN **2** a person who lives in a particular place: *When you're old, people treat you like a second-class citizen.* ◊ **~ of sth** *the decent, law-abiding* *citizens* of this city ⊃ see also SENIOR CITIZEN ⊃ compare SUBJECT

**citizen 'journalism** *noun* [U] reports and pictures of events recorded by ordinary people and shown especially on the internet: *citizen journalism websites* ▶ **citizen 'journalist** *noun*

**cit·i·zen·ry** /ˈsɪtɪzənri/ *noun* [sing. + sing./pl. v.] (*formal*) (less *formal* in *NAmE*) all the citizens of a particular town, country, etc.

**citizen's ar'rest** *noun* an arrest made by a member of the public, not by the police

**cit·i·zen·ship** /ˈsɪtɪzənʃɪp/ *noun* [U] **1** the legal right to belong to a particular country: *French citizenship* ◇ *You can apply for citizenship after five years' residency.* **2** the state of being a citizen and accepting the responsibilities of it: *an education that prepares young people for citizenship*

**cit·ric** /ˈsɪtrɪk/ *adj.* relating to fruit such as lemons, oranges and LIMES: *a citric flavour*

**cit·ric acid** /ˌsɪtrɪk ˈæsɪd/ *noun* [U] a weak ACID found in the juice of lemons and other fruits with a bitter, sharp taste

**cit·ron** /ˈsɪtrən/ *noun* [C, U] a yellow fruit like a large lemon

**cit·ron·ella** /ˌsɪtrəˈnelə/ *noun* [U] a type of grass from which an oil used in PERFUMES and soap is obtained

**cit·rus** /ˈsɪtrəs/ *noun* [U] fruit belonging to the group of fruit that includes oranges, lemons, LIMES and GRAPEFRUIT: *citrus fruit/trees/growers* ◇ *fabric in bright citrus shades* (= orange, yellow or green) ⊃ VISUAL VOCAB page V4

**city** /ˈsɪti/ *noun* (*pl. -ies*) **1** [C] a large and important town: *the city centre* ◇ *a major city* ◇ *the country's capital city* ◇ *in a ~* *We live in a big city.* ◇ *the ~ of …* *a map of the city of Boston* ⊃ see also EDGE CITY, GARDEN CITY, INNER CITY, SISTER CITY

> **WORDFINDER** amenity, ghetto, high-rise, metropolitan, population, slum, suburb, urban

**2** [C] (*BrE*) a town that has been given special rights by a king or queen, usually one that has a CATHEDRAL: *the city of York* **3** [C] (*NAmE*) a town that has been given special rights by the state government **4** [sing. + sing./pl. v.] all the people who live in a city: *The city turned out to welcome the victorious team home.* **5 the City (of London)** [sing.] (*BrE*) the UK's financial and business centre, in the oldest part of London; the people who work there: *a City stockbroker* ◇ *What is the City's reaction to the cut in interest rates?* **6** [U] (*informal*) used after other nouns to say that a place is full of a particular thing: *It's not exactly fun city here is it?* IDM see FREEDOM

**'city desk** *noun* **1** (*BrE*) the department of a newspaper that deals with financial news **2** (*NAmE*) the department of a newspaper that deals with local news

**'city editor** *noun* **1** (*BrE*) a journalist who is responsible for financial news in a newspaper or magazine **2** (*NAmE*) a journalist who is responsible for local news in a newspaper or magazine

**'city father** *noun* [usually pl.] a person with experience of governing a city

**'city 'hall** *noun* [C, U] (*NAmE*) the local government of a city and the offices it uses

**'city 'planner** *noun* (*NAmE*) = PLANNER (1)

**'city 'planning** *noun* [U] (*NAmE*) = TOWN PLANNING

**city·scape** /ˈsɪtiskeɪp/ *noun* the appearance of a city or urban area, especially in a picture; a picture of a city

**'city 'slicker** *noun* (*informal, often disapproving*) a person who behaves in a way that is typical of people who live in big cities

**'city 'state** *noun* (especially in the past) an independent state consisting of a city and the area around it (for example, Athens in ancient times)

**city·wide** /ˌsɪtiˈwaɪd/ *adj., adv.* over or in all parts of a city: *a citywide smoking ban* ◇ *Candidates will campaign citywide.*

**civet** /ˈsɪvɪt/ *noun* **1** [C] a wild animal like a cat, found in central Africa and Asia **2** [U] a substance with a strong smell, obtained from a civet, and used in making PERFUME

**civic** /ˈsɪvɪk/ *adj.* (usually before noun) **1** officially connected with a town or city: *civic buildings/leaders* **2** connected with the people who live in a town or city: *a sense of civic pride* (= pride that people feel for their town or city) ◇ *civic duties/responsibilities*

**civic 'centre** *noun* **1** (*BrE*) the area where the public buildings are, in a town **2 civic center** (*NAmE*) a large building where public entertainments and meetings are held: *Atlanta Civic Center*

**civ·ics** /ˈsɪvɪks/ *noun* [U] (*especially NAmE*) the school subject that studies the way government works and deals with the rights and duties that you have as a citizen and a member of a particular society

**civil** /ˈsɪvl/ *adj.* **1** [only before noun] connected with the people who live in a country: *civil unrest* (= that is caused by groups of people within a country) ⊃ see also CIVIL WAR **2** [only before noun] connected with the state rather than with religion or with the armed forces: *the recognition of civil unions for same-sex couples* **3** [only before noun] involving personal legal matters and not criminal law: *a civil court* ⊃ compare CRIMINAL ⊃ see also CIVIL LAW **4** polite in a formal way but possibly not friendly OPP uncivil ▶ **civ·il·ly** /-vəli/ *adv.*: *She greeted him civilly but with no sign of affection.*

**civil de'fence** (*US* **civil de'fense**) *noun* [U] the organization and training of ordinary people to protect themselves from attack during a war or, in the US, from natural disasters such as hurricanes

**civil diso'bedience** *noun* [U] action taken by a large group of people in which they refuse to obey particular laws or pay taxes, usually as a form of peaceful political protest ⊃ WORDFINDER NOTE at PROTEST

**civil engi'neering** *noun* [U] the design, building and repair of roads, bridges, CANALS, etc.; the study of this as a subject ▶ **civil engi'neer** *noun*

**ci·vil·ian** /səˈvɪliən/ *noun, adj.*
■ *noun* a person who is not a member of the armed forces or the police: *Hundreds of innocent civilians have died in the air strikes.*
■ *adj.* [usually before noun] connected with people who are not members of the armed forces or the police: *He left the army and returned to civilian life.* ◇ *The bombs resulted in large numbers of civilian casualties.* ◇ *He condemned the attacks on civilian targets.* ⊃ compare MILITARY

**ci·vil·ity** /səˈvɪləti/ *noun* (*formal*) **1** [U] polite behaviour: *Staff members are trained to treat customers with civility at all times.* **2 civilities** [pl.] remarks that are said only in order to be polite

**civ·il·iza·tion** (*BrE also* **-isa·tion**) /ˌsɪvəlaɪˈzeɪʃn; *NAmE* -ləˈz-/ *noun* **1** [U] a state of human society that is very developed and organized: *the technology of modern civilization* ◇ *The Victorians regarded the railways as bringing progress and civilization.* **2** [U, C] a society, its culture and its way of life during a particular period of time or in a particular part of the world: *the civilizations of ancient Greece and Rome* ◇ *diseases that are common in Western civilization* **3** [U] all the people in the world and the societies they live in, considered as a whole: *Environmental damage threatens the whole of civilization.* **4** [U] (*often humorous*) a place that offers you the comfortable way of life of a modern society: *It's good to be back in civilization after two weeks in a tent!*

**civ·il·ize** (*BrE also* **-ise**) /ˈsɪvəlaɪz/ *verb* **~ sb/sth** to educate and improve a person or a society; to make sb's behaviour or manners better: *The girls in a class tend to have a civilizing influence on the boys.*

**civ·il·ized** (*BrE also* **-ised**) /ˈsɪvəlaɪzd/ *adj.* **1** well organized socially with a very developed culture and way of life: *the civilized world* ◇ *rising crime in our so-called civilized* societies ◊ civilized peoples **2** having laws and customs that are fair and morally acceptable: *No civilized country should allow such terrible injustices.* **3** having or showing polite and reasonable behaviour: *We couldn't even have a civilized conversation any more.* **4** typical of a comfortable and pleasant way of life: *Breakfast on the terrace—how civilized!* **OPP** uncivilized

**civil ˈlaw** *noun* [U] law that deals with the rights of private citizens rather than with crime ⇒ compare CRIMINAL LAW

**civil ˈliberty** *noun* [C, usually pl., U] the right of people to be free to say or do what they want while respecting others and staying within the law

**civil ˈmarriage** *noun* a marriage with no religious ceremony

**civil ˈparish** *noun* = PARISH (2)

**civil ˈpartnership** (*BrE*) (*NAmE* **civil ˈunion**) *noun* (in some countries) a legal relationship between two people, usually of the same sex, with the same legal status as marriage ▸ **civil ˈpartner** *noun*

**civil ˈrights** *noun* [pl.] the rights that every person in a society has, for example to be treated equally, to be able to vote, work, etc. whatever their sex, race or religion: *the civil rights movement* ⇒ WORDFINDER NOTE at SOCIETY

**the civil ˈrights movement** *noun* [sing.] (in the US) the campaign in the 1950s and 1960s to change the laws so that African Americans have the same rights as others

**civil ˈservant** *noun* a person who works in the civil service

**the civil ˈservice** *noun* [sing.] the government departments in a country and the people who work for them, except the armed forces, judges and elected politicians

**civil ˈunion** *noun* (*NAmE*) = CIVIL PARTNERSHIP

**civil ˈwar** *noun* **1** [C, U] a war between groups of people in the same country: *the Spanish Civil War* ◊ *30 years of bitter civil war* **2 the Civil War** the war fought in the US between the northern and the southern states in the years 1861 to 1865

**civ·vies** /ˈsɪviz/ *noun* [pl.] (*slang*) (used by people in the armed forces) ordinary clothes, not military uniform

**CJD** /ˌsiː dʒeɪ ˈdiː/ *abbr.* CREUTZFELDT-JAKOB DISEASE

**cl** *abbr.* (*pl.* **cl** or **cls**) CENTILITRE: *75cl*

**clack** /klæk/ *verb* [I] if two hard objects **clack**, they make a short loud sound when they hit each other: *Her heels clacked on the marble floor.* ▸ **clack** *noun* [sing.]: *the clack of high heels on the floor* ◊ *the clack of her knitting needles*

**clad** /klæd/ *adj.* (*formal* or *humorous*) **1** ~ (in sth) (often used after an adverb or in compounds) wearing a particular type of clothing **SYN** dressed: *She was clad in blue velvet.* ◊ *warmly/scantily clad* ◊ *leather-clad motorcyclists* **2 -clad** (in compounds) covered in a particular thing: *snow-clad hills*

**clad·ding** /ˈklædɪŋ/ *noun* [U] a layer of a hard material, used as protection

**claim** 🟦 B1 🔵 /kleɪm/ *verb, noun*

■ *verb*
• SAY STH IS TRUE/YOU HAVE DONE STH **1** B1 [T] to say that sth is true although it has not been proved and other people may not believe it: ~**(that)** … *He claims (that) he was not given a fair hearing.* ◊ ~**to be/do sth** *I don't claim to be an expert.* ◊ ~**sb/sth to be/do sth** *She's not the saint that many have claimed her to be.* ◊ ~**sth** *Scientists are claiming a major breakthrough in the fight against cancer.* ◊ **it is claimed that** … *It was claimed that some doctors were working 80 hours a week.* ◊ **+ speech** *'I did not tell any lies,' she claimed.* ⇒ LANGUAGE BANK at ARGUE **2** 🔵 [T] ~**sth** to state that you have done, gained or achieved sth: *He claimed victory in the presidential elections before all the results were in.* ◊ *Nobody has claimed responsibility for the bombing.*
• MONEY **3** B1 [T, I] to ask for money from the government or a company because you have a right to it: ~**sth** *He's not entitled to claim housing benefit.* ◊ ~**sth from sth** *You could have claimed the cost of the hotel room from your insur-*

267

**claimant**

*ance.* ◊ ~**(on sth) (for sth)** *You can claim on your insurance for that coat you left on the train.*
• DEMAND LEGAL RIGHT **4** 🟦 B1 [T] ~**sth** to demand or ask for sth because you believe it is your legal right to own or to have it: *A lot of lost property is never claimed.* ◊ *He claimed political asylum.*
• ATTENTION/THOUGHT **5** [T] ~**sth** to get or take sb's attention: *A most unwelcome event claimed his attention.*
• GAIN/WIN **6** [T] ~**sth** to gain, win or achieve sth: *She has finally claimed a place on the team.*
• CAUSE DEATH **7** [T] ~**sth** (of a disaster, an accident, etc.) to cause sb's death: *The car crash claimed three lives.*
**PHR V** **ˌclaim sth↔ˈback** to ask or demand to have sth returned because you have a right to it: *You can claim back the tax on your purchases.*

■ *noun*
• SAYING STH IS TRUE **1** 🟦 B1 [C] a statement that sth is true although it has not been proved and other people may not agree with or believe it: ~**about sb/sth** *The company had made false claims about its products.* ◊ ~**of sth** *to reject/dismiss/deny claims of discrimination* ◊ ~**that** … *The singer has denied the magazine's claim that she is leaving the band.*
• FOR MONEY **2** 🟦 B2 [C] a request for a sum of money that you believe you have a right to, especially from a company, the government, etc: *You can make a claim on your insurance policy.* ◊ ~**for sth** *to put in a claim for an allowance* ◊ *a claim for £2000* ◊ *a 3 per cent pay claim* ◊ *Complete a claim form (= an official document which you must use in order to request money from an organization).*
• LEGAL RIGHT **3** 🟦 B2 [C, U] a right that sb believes they have to sth, especially property, land, etc: *nineteenth-century land claims* ◊ ~**on sth** *They had no claim on the land.* ◊ ~**to sth** *She has more claim to the campaign's success than anybody (= she is responsible for it).*
**IDM** **ˌclaim to ˈfame** (*often humorous*) one thing that makes a person or place important or interesting: *His main claim to fame is that he went to school with the prime minister.* **have a ˈclaim on sb/sth** to have the right to demand time, attention, etc. from sb **ˌlay ˈclaim to sth** to state that you have a right to own sth **ˌmake no ˈclaim** used when you are saying that you cannot do sth: *I make no claim to understand modern art.* ⇒ more at STAKE *v.*

▼ SYNONYMS

### claim
allegation • assertion

These are all words for a statement that sth is true, although it has not been proved.

**claim** a statement that sth is true, although it has not been proved.

**allegation** (*rather formal*) a public statement that is made without giving proof, accusing sb of doing sth that is wrong or illegal.

**assertion** (*rather formal*) a statement of sth that you strongly believe to be true, although it has not been proved.

**CLAIM OR ASSERTION?**
- When the point in doubt is a matter of opinion, not fact, use **assertion**: *She made sweeping claims about the role of women in society.* When you are talking about a matter of fact, you can use either word; an **assertion** may be slightly stronger than a **claim** and it is a more formal word.

**PATTERNS**
- a(n) claim/allegation/assertion **that** …
- a(n) claim/allegation/assertion **about/of** sth
- **false/unfounded/conflicting** claims/allegations/assertions
- to **make/deny** a(n) claim/allegation/assertion
- to **withdraw** a(n) claim/allegation

**claim·ant** /ˈkleɪmənt/ *noun* **1** a person who claims sth because they believe they have a right to it **2** a person

# clairvoyance

who is receiving money from the state because they are unemployed, etc.

**clair·voy·ance** /kleəˈvɔɪəns; NAmE klerˈv-/ noun [U] the power that some people claim to have to be able to see future events or to communicate with people who are dead or far away ▶ **clair·voy·ant** /-ənt/ noun: *to consult a clairvoyant* **clair·voy·ant** adj.

**clam** /klæm/ noun, verb
■ noun a SHELLFISH that can be eaten. It has a shell in two parts that can open and close: *clam chowder/soup* ⊃picture at SHELLFISH
■ verb (-mm-)
PHRV ˌclam ˈup (on sb) (informal) to refuse to speak, especially when sb asks you about sth

**clam·ber** /ˈklæmbə(r)/ verb [I] + adv./prep. to climb or move with difficulty or a lot of effort, using your hands and feet SYN **scramble**: *The children clambered up the steep bank.*

**clammy** /ˈklæmi/ adj. (**clam·mier**, **clam·mi·est**) slightly wet in an unpleasant way: *His skin felt cold and clammy.* ◊ *clammy hands*

**clam·our** (US **clamor**) /ˈklæmə(r)/ verb, noun
■ verb 1 [I, T] (formal) to demand sth loudly: ~ (for sth) *People began to clamour for his resignation.* ◊ ~ **to do sth** *Everyone was clamouring to know how much they would get.* ◊ + speech *'Play with us!' the children clamoured.* 2 [I] (of many people) to shout loudly, especially in a confused way
■ noun (formal) 1 [sing.] a loud noise, especially one that is made by a lot of people or animals: *the clamour of the market* 2 [U, C] ~ **(for sth)** a demand for sth made by a lot of people: *The clamour for her resignation grew louder.*
▶ **clam·or·ous** /-mərəs/ adj.

**clamp** /klæmp/ verb, noun
■ verb 1 [T] to hold sth tightly, or fasten two things together, with a clamp: ~ **A to B** *Clamp one end of the plank to the edge of the table.* ◊ ~ **A and B (together)** *Clamp the two halves together until the glue dries.* 2 [T, I] to hold or fasten sth very tightly so that it does not move; to be held tightly: ~ **sth + adv./prep.** *He had a cigar clamped between his teeth.* ◊ *She clamped a pair of headphones over her ears.* ◊ + adv./prep. *Her lips clamped tightly together.* ◊ ~ **(sth) + adj.** *He clamped his mouth shut.* 3 [T, usually passive] (BrE) to fix a clamp to a car's wheel so that the car cannot be driven away: *be clamped Her car had been clamped.*
⊃ WORDFINDER NOTE at TRAFFIC
PHRV ˌclamp ˈdown (on sb/sth) to take strict action in order to prevent sth, especially crime: *a campaign by police to clamp down on street crime* ⊃ related noun CLAMPDOWN ˈclamp sth on sb (especially NAmE) to force sb to accept sth such as a law: *The army clamped a curfew on the city.*
■ noun 1 a tool for holding things tightly together, usually by means of a SCREW 2 (also ˈwheel clamp) (both BrE) (US ˌDenver ˈboot, boot) a device that is attached to the wheel of a car that has been parked illegally, so that it cannot be driven away

**clamp·down** /ˈklæmpdaʊn/ noun [usually sing.] sudden action that is taken in order to stop an illegal activity: *a clampdown on drinking and driving*

**clam·shell** /ˈklæmʃel/ adj. [only before noun] having a cover or other part that opens and shuts like the shell of a CLAM: *a clamshell phone* ▶ **clamˈshell** noun

**clan** /klæn/ noun [C + sing./pl. v.] 1 a group of families who are related to each other, especially in Scotland: *the MacLeod clan* ◊ *clan warfare* 2 (informal, sometimes humorous) a very large family, or a group of people who are connected because of a particular thing: *one of a growing clan of stars who have left Hollywood*

**clan·des·tine** /klænˈdestɪn, ˈklændəstaɪn/ adj. (formal) done secretly or kept secret: *a clandestine meeting/relationship*

**clang** /klæŋ/ verb [I, T] to make a loud ringing sound like that of metal being hit; to cause sth to make this sound SYN **clank**: *Bells were clanging in the tower.* ◊ + adj. *The gates clanged shut.* ◊ ~ **sth + adv./prep.** *The trams clanged their way along the streets.* ◊ *He clanged a spoon against a glass.* ▶ **clang** (also ˈclang·ing) noun [usually sing.]

**clang·er** /ˈklæŋə(r)/ noun (BrE, informal) an obvious and embarrassing mistake: *Mentioning her ex-husband was a bit of a clanger.* ◊ *He was always dropping clangers* (= making embarrassing mistakes or remarks).

**clank** /klæŋk/ verb [I, T] to make a loud sound like pieces of metal hitting each other; to cause sth to make this sound: *clanking chains* ◊ + adj. *I heard a door clank shut.* ◊ ~ **sth** *The guard clanked his heavy ring of keys.* ▶ **clank** (also **clank·ing**) noun [usually sing.]

**clan·nish** /ˈklænɪʃ/ adj. (often disapproving) (of members of a group) not showing interest in people who are not in the group

**clans·man** /ˈklænzmən/ noun (pl. **-men** /-mən/) a member of a CLAN

**clap** /klæp/ verb, noun
■ verb (**-pp-**) 1 [I, T] to hit your open hands together several times to show that you approve of or have enjoyed sth: *The audience cheered and clapped.* ◊ ~ **sb/sth** *Everyone clapped us when we went up to get our prize.* 2 [I, T] to hit your open hands together: *Everyone clapped in time to the music.* ◊ ~ **your hands** *She clapped her hands in delight.* ◊ *He clapped his hands for silence.* 3 [T] ~ **sb on the back/shoulder** to lightly hit sb with your open hand, usually in a friendly way 4 [T] ~ **sth/sb + adv./prep.** to put sth/sb somewhere quickly and suddenly: *'Oh dear!' she cried, clapping a hand over her mouth.* ◊ *to clap sb in irons/jail/prison* ▶ **clap·ping** noun [U]: *I could hear the sound of clapping from the other room.* IDM see EYE n.
■ noun 1 [sing.] an act of clapping the hands; the sound this makes: *Give him a clap!* (= to praise sb at the end of a performance) 2 [C] a sudden loud noise: *a clap of thunder* 3 (also **the clap**) [U] (informal) a disease of the sexual organs, caught by having sex with a person who already has the disease SYN **gonorrhoea**

**clap·board** /ˈklæpbɔːd; NAmE ˈklæbərd/ noun [U] (especially NAmE) = WEATHERBOARD

ˌclapped ˈout adj. (BrE, informal) (of a car or machine) old and in bad condition: *The van's totally clapped out.* ◊ *a clapped-out old Mini*

**clap·per** /ˈklæpə(r)/ noun the piece of metal inside a bell that hits the sides and makes the bell ring
IDM like the ˈclappers (BrE, informal) extremely fast: *to run/ride/drive like the clappers*

**clap·per·board** /ˈklæpəbɔːd; NAmE -pərbɔːrd/ noun a device that is used when making films. It consists of two connected boards that are put together at the start of a scene, and its purpose is to help to match the pictures with the sound.

**clap·trap** /ˈklæptræp/ noun [U] (informal) stupid talk that has no value

**claret** /ˈklærət/ noun 1 [U, C] a dry red wine, especially from the Bordeaux area of France 2 [U] a dark red colour

**clar·ify** /ˈklærəfaɪ/ verb (**clari·fies**, **clari·fy·ing**, **clarified**, **clari·fied**) 1 to make sth clearer or easier to understand: ~ **sth** *to clarify a situation/problem/issue* ◊ *I hope this clarifies my position.* ◊ ~ **what/how, etc…** *She asked him to clarify what he meant.* ⊃ LANGUAGE BANK at DEFINE 2 ~ **sth** to make sth, especially butter, pure by heating it: *clarified butter* ▶ **clari·fi·ca·tion** /ˌklærəfɪˈkeɪʃn/ noun [U, C]: *I am seeking clarification of the regulations.*

**clari·net** /ˌklærəˈnet/ noun a musical instrument of the WOODWIND group. It is like a pipe in shape and has a REED and a MOUTHPIECE at the top that you blow into.

**clari·net·tist** (NAmE **clari·net·ist**) /ˌklærəˈnetɪst/ noun a person who plays the clarinet

**clar·ion call** /ˈklæriən kɔːl/ noun [sing.] (formal) a clear message or request for people to do sth

**clar·ity** /ˈklærəti/ noun [U] 1 the quality of being expressed clearly: *a lack of clarity in the law* 2 the ability to think about or understand sth clearly: *clarity* of thought/purpose/vision 3 [C] if a picture, substance or sound has clarity, you can see or hear it very clearly, or see through it easily: *the clarity of the sound on the recording*

**clash** /klæʃ/ *noun, verb*
■ *noun*
- FIGHT 1 [C] ~ (with sb) | ~ (between A and B) a short fight between two groups of people: *Clashes broke out between police and demonstrators.* ⇨ SYNONYMS at FIGHT
- ARGUMENT 2 [C] ~ (with sb) (over sth) | ~ (between A and B) (over sth) an argument between two people or groups of people who have different beliefs and ideas SYN **conflict**: *a head-on clash between the two leaders over education policy*
- DIFFERENCE 3 [C] the difference that exists between two things that are opposed to each other SYN **conflict**: *a clash of interests/opinions/cultures ◇ a personality clash with the boss*
- OF TWO EVENTS 4 [C] a situation in which two events happen at the same time so that you cannot go to or see them both: *a clash in the timetable/schedule*
- LOUD NOISE 5 [C] [usually sing.] a loud noise made by two metal objects being hit together: *a clash of cymbals/swords*
- IN SPORT 6 (used in newspapers, about sports) an occasion when two teams or players compete against each other: *Bayern's clash with Roma in the Champions League*
- OF COLOURS 7 the situation when two colours, designs, etc. look ugly when they are put together
■ *verb*
- FIGHT/COMPETE 1 [I] ~ (with sb) to come together and fight or compete in a contest: *The two sets of supporters clashed outside the stadium.* ◇ *The two teams clash in tomorrow's final.*
- ARGUE 2 [I] ~ (with sb) (over / on sth) to argue or disagree seriously with sb about sth, and to show this in public: *The leaders and members clashed on the issue.* ◇ *The leaders clashed with party members on the issue.*
- BE DIFFERENT 3 [I] ~ (with sth) (of beliefs, ideas or personalities) to be very different and opposed to each other: *His left-wing views clashed with his father's politics.* ◇ *His views and his father's clashed.* ◇ *They have clashing personalities.*
- OF TWO EVENTS 4 [I] ~ (with sth) (of events) to happen at the same time so that you cannot go to or see them both: *Unfortunately your party clashes with a wedding I'm going to.* ◇ *There are two good movies on TV tonight, but they clash.*
- OF COLOURS 5 [I] ~ (with sth) (of colours, patterns or styles) to look ugly when put together: *The wallpaper clashes with the bracelet.* ◇ *The wallpaper and the carpet clash.*
- MAKE LOUD NOISE 6 [I, T] to hit together and make a loud ringing noise; to make two metal objects do this: ~ **(together)** *The long blades clashed together.* ◇ ~ **sth (together)** *She clashed the cymbals.*

**clasp** /klɑːsp; *NAmE* klæsp/ *verb, noun*
■ *verb* 1 ~ sth to hold sth tightly in your hand: *He leaned forward, his hands clasped tightly together.* ◇ *They clasped hands* (= held each other's hands). ◇ *I stood there, clasping the door handle.* ⇨ SYNONYMS at HOLD 2 ~ sb/sth (+ adv./prep.) to hold sb/sth tightly with your arms around them: *She clasped the children in her arms.* ◇ *He clasped her to him.* 3 ~ sth (+ adv./prep.) to fasten sth with a clasp: *She clasped the bracelet around her wrist.*
■ *noun* 1 [C] a device that fastens sth, such as a bag or the ends of a belt or a piece of jewellery: *the clasp of a necklace/handbag* 2 [sing.] a tight hold with your hand or in your arms: *He took her hand in his firm warm clasp.*

**class** /klɑːs; *NAmE* klæs/ *noun, verb, adj.*
■ *noun*
- IN EDUCATION 1 [C + sing./pl. v.] a group of students who are taught together: **in the/your**~ *We were in the same class at school.* ◇ *She is the youngest in her class.* ◇ *He came top of the class.* ◇ *The whole class was/were told to stay behind after school.* 2 [C, U] an occasion when a group of students meets to be taught SYN **lesson**: *I have a history class at 9 o'clock.* ◇ *I was late for (a) class.* ◇ *See me after class.* ◇ **in~** *She works hard in class* (= during the class). 3 [C] (*also* **classes** [pl.]) a series of classes on a particular subject SYN **course**: *Are you still doing your French evening class?* ◇ ~ **in sth** *I've been taking classes in pottery.* 4 [C + sing./pl. v.] (*especially NAmE*) a group of students who finish their studies at school, college or university in a particular year: *the class of 2020*
- IN SOCIETY 5 [C + sing./pl. v.] one of the groups of people in a society that are thought of as being at the same social or economic level: *the working/middle/upper class* ◇ *The party tries to appeal to all classes of society.* ◇ *the professional classes* ⇨ see also MIDDLE CLASS, UPPER CLASS, WORKING CLASS 6 [U] the way that people are divided into different social and economic groups: *differences of class, race or gender* ◇ *the class system* ◇ *a society in which class is more important than ability* ⇨ WORDFINDER NOTE at SOCIETY
- IN TRAIN/PLANE 7 [C] (especially in compounds) each of several different levels of comfort that are available to travellers in a plane, etc: *He always travels business class.* ◇ *The first-class compartment is situated at the front of the train.* ⇨ see also BUSINESS CLASS, CLUB CLASS, FIRST CLASS *noun*, SECOND CLASS, THIRD CLASS, TOURIST CLASS
- GROUP OF PEOPLE/ANIMALS 8 [C] a group of people, animals or things that have similar characteristics or qualities: *It was good accommodation for a hotel of this class.* ◇ *different classes of drugs* ◇ *Dickens was* **in a different class** *from* (= was much better than) *most of his contemporaries.* ◇ *As a jazz singer she's* **in a class of her own** (= better than most others). ⇨ see also FIRST-CLASS, HIGH-CLASS, LOW-CLASS, SECOND-CLASS, TOP-CLASS, WORD CLASS, WORLD-CLASS 9 [C] one of the different groups in a competition: *He came first in his class at every event.*
- SKILL/STYLE 10 [U] an attractive quality or a high level of skill that is impressive: *She has class all right—she looks like a model.* ◇ *There's a real touch of class about this team.*
- OF UNIVERSITY DEGREE 11 [C] (especially in compounds) one of the levels of achievement in a British university degree exam: *a first-/second-/third-class degree*
- BIOLOGY 12 [C] a group into which animals, plants, etc. that have similar characteristics are divided, below a PHYLUM ⇨ compare FAMILY, GENUS, SPECIES ⇨ WORDFINDER NOTE at BREED ⇨ VISUAL VOCAB page V3 IDM see CHATTER *v.*
■ *verb* [often passive] to think or decide that sb/sth is a particular type of person or thing SYN **classify**: **be classed as sth** *Immigrant workers were classed as aliens.*
■ *adj.* [only before noun] (*informal*) very good: *a class player/performer* ◇ *She's a real class act.*

**class 'action** *noun* a type of LAWSUIT that is started by a group of people who have the same problem

**class A 'drug** *noun* any of various illegal drugs that are on a list of the strongest, most harmful drugs. There is a heavy punishment for anyone caught with these drugs or selling them. Class A drugs include HEROIN, COCAINE and LSD.

**class-'conscious** *adj.* very aware of belonging to a particular social class and of the differences between social classes ▶ **class-'conscious·ness** *noun* [U]

**clas·sic** /ˈklæsɪk/ *adj., noun*
■ *adj.* [usually before noun] 1 accepted or deserving to be accepted as one of the best or most important of its kind: *a classic film/story/car/game* ◇ *I grew up listening to classic rock.* ⇨ WORDFINDER NOTE at WRITE 2 (*also less frequent* **clas·sic·al**) with all the features you would expect to find; very typical: *a classic example of poor communication* ◇ *This was a classic case of what not to do.* ◇ *She displayed the classic symptoms of depression.* 3 attractive, but simple and traditional in style or design; not affected by changes in fashion: *a classic grey suit* ◇ *classic design* 4 (*informal*) people say **That's classic!** when they find sth very funny, when they think sb has been very stupid or when sth annoying, but not surprising, happens: *She's not going to help? Oh, that's classic!*

# classical

■ **noun** 1 ? B2 [C] a book, film or song which is well known and considered to be of very high quality, setting standards for other books, etc: *The film is now a cult classic.* ◇ *The song became an instant classic.* 2 ? B2 [C] a thing that is an excellent example of its kind: *That match was a classic.* 3 a piece of clothing, a vehicle or other item that is admired for its beautiful style or design that is not affected by changes in fashion: *Classics don't lose their style.* 4 **Classics** [U] the study of ancient Greek and Roman culture, especially their languages and literature: *a degree in Classics*

▼ **WHICH WORD?**

**classic / classical**
These adjectives are frequently used with the following nouns:

| classic ~ | classical ~ |
|---|---|
| example | music |
| case | ballet |
| novel | architecture |
| work | scholar |
| car | period |

- **Classic** describes something that is accepted as being of very high quality and one of the best of its kind: *a classic movie/work*. It is also used to describe a typical example of something: *a classic example/mistake*, or something attractive but simple and traditional: *classic design*.
- **Classical** describes a form of traditional Western music and other things that are traditional in style: *a classical composer* ◇ *a classical theory*. It is also used to talk about things that are connected with the culture of Ancient Greece and Rome: *a classical scholar* ◇ *classical mythology*.

**clas·si·cal** ❶ A2 ○ /ˈklæsɪkl/ *adj.* [usually before noun] 1 ? A2 relating to classical music: *a classical composer/musician/pianist* ◇ *a classical concert* 2 widely accepted and used for a long time; traditional in style or idea: *the classical economics of Smith and Ricardo* ◇ *the classical theory of unemployment* ◇ **classical and modern ballet/dance** 3 connected with or influenced by the culture of ancient Greece and Rome: *classical studies* ◇ *a classical scholar* (= an expert in Latin and Greek) 4 = CLASSIC: *These are classical examples of food allergy.* 5 (of a language) ancient in its form and no longer used in a spoken form: *classical Arabic* 6 simple and attractive: *the classical elegance of the design* ▶ **clas·sic·al·ly** /-kli/ *adv.*: *Her face is classically beautiful.* ◇ *a classically trained singer*

**classical ˈmusic** *noun* [U] music written in a Western musical tradition, usually using an established form (for example a SYMPHONY). Classical music is generally considered to be serious and to have a lasting value: *He plays classical music, as well as pop and jazz.*

**ˈclassic ˌcar** *noun* an old car of a type which is no longer made but is still admired for its style and interest: *classic car lovers* ⇒ compare VINTAGE (2)

**clas·si·cism** /ˈklæsɪsɪzəm/ *noun* 1 a style of art and literature that is simple and beautiful and is based on the styles of ancient Greece and Rome. Classicism was popular in Europe in the eighteenth century. 2 a style or form that has simple, natural qualities and attractive combinations of parts

**clas·si·cist** /ˈklæsɪsɪst/ *noun* 1 a person who studies ancient Greek or Latin 2 a person who follows classicism in art or literature

**clas·si·fi·able** /ˈklæsɪfaɪəbl/ *adj.* that you can or should CLASSIFY: *The information was not easily classifiable.* ◇ *top-secret or classifiable information*

**clas·si·fi·ca·tion** ? C1 ⓦ /ˌklæsɪfɪˈkeɪʃn/ *noun* 1 ? C1 [U] the act or process of putting people or things into a group or class (= of CLASSIFYING them): *a style of music that defies classification* (= is like no other) 2 ? C1 [C] a group, class, division, etc. into which sb or sth is put 3 [U] (*biology*) the act of putting animals, plants, etc. into groups, classes or divisions according to their characteristics ⇒ WORDFINDER NOTE at BREED 4 [C] (*specialist*) a system of arranging books, tapes, magazines, etc. in a library into groups according to their subject

**clas·si·fied** /ˈklæsɪfaɪd/ *adj.* [usually before noun] 1 (of information) officially secret and available only to particular people: *classified information/documents/material* OPP **unclassified** 2 with information arranged in groups according to subjects: *a classified catalogue* 3 **classifieds** *noun* [pl.] = CLASSIFIED ADVERTISEMENTS

**ˌclassified adˈvertisement** (*also* classified ˈad, ˈclassified) (*BrE also* ˈsmall ad) (*NAmE also* ˈwant ad) *noun* [usually pl.] a small advertisement in a newspaper or on a website, put in a section according to its subject, that is placed by a person or small company who wants to buy or sell sth, find or offer a job, etc.

**clas·si·fier** /ˈklæsɪfaɪə(r)/ *noun* (*grammar*) an AFFIX or word that shows that a word belongs to a group of words with similar meanings. For example the prefix 'un' is a classifier that shows the word is negative.

**clas·sify** ? + B2 ⓦ /ˈklæsɪfaɪ/ *verb* (**clas·si·fies, clas·si·fy·ing, clas·si·fied, clas·si·fied**) 1 ? B2 ~ **sth** (+ *adv./prep.*) to arrange sth in groups according to features that they have in common: *The books in the library are classified according to subject.* ◇ *Patients are classified into three categories.* 2 ? B2 ~ **sb/sth as sth** to decide which type or group sb/sth belongs to: *Only eleven of these accidents were classified as major.* 3 [usually passive] ~ **sth** to state that information is officially secret: *The government insists on keeping certain documents classified.*

**class·less** /ˈklɑːsləs; *NAmE* ˈklæs-/ *adj.* 1 (*approving*) with no divisions into social classes: *Will Britain ever become a classless society?* 2 not clearly belonging to a particular social class: *a classless accent* ▶ **ˈclass·less·ness** *noun* [U]

**class·mate** /ˈklɑːsmeɪt; *NAmE* ˈklæs-/ *noun* a person who is or was in the same class as you at school or college

**class·room** ❶ A1 /ˈklɑːsruːm, -rʊm; *NAmE* ˈklæs-/ *noun* a room where a class of children or students is taught: *classroom activities* ◇ *the use of computers in the classroom* ⇒ see also FLIPPED CLASSROOM

**ˈclass ˌstruggle** *noun* (*also* ˌclass ˈwar) [U, sing.] (*also* ˌclass ˈwarfare [U]) (*politics*) opposition between the different social classes in society, especially that described in Marxist theory

**classy** /ˈklɑːsi; *NAmE* ˈklæsi/ *adj.* (**class·ier, classi·est**) (*informal*) of high quality; expensive and/or fashionable: *a classy player* ◇ *a classy hotel/restaurant*

**clat·ter** /ˈklætə(r)/ *verb* 1 [I] if hard objects **clatter**, they knock together and make a loud noise: *He dropped the knife and it clattered on the stone floor.* ◇ *Her cup clattered in the saucer.* 2 [I] + *adv./prep.* to move making a loud noise like hard objects knocking together: *The cart clattered over the cobbles.* ◇ *She heard him clattering around downstairs.* ▶ **clat·ter** (*also* **clat·ter·ing**) *noun* [sing.]: *the clatter of horses' hoofs*

**clause** ❶ B1 /klɔːz/ *noun* 1 ? B1 (*grammar*) a group of words that includes a subject and a verb, and forms a sentence or part of a sentence: *in a ~ There are languages that require the subject to come before the object in a clause.* ⇒ see also COORDINATE CLAUSE, FINAL CLAUSE, MAIN CLAUSE, SUBORDINATE CLAUSE 2 ? B2 an item in a legal document that says that a particular thing must or must not be done: *a confidentiality clause* ⇒ see also ESCAPE CLAUSE ⇒ WORDFINDER NOTE at DOCUMENT

**claus·tro·pho·bia** /ˌklɔːstrəˈfəʊbiə, ˌklɒs-; *NAmE* ˌklɔːs-/ *noun* [U] an extreme fear of being shut in a small place; the unpleasant feeling that a person gets in a situation that limits them: *to suffer from claustrophobia* ◇ *She felt she had to escape from the claustrophobia of family life.* ⇒ compare AGORAPHOBIA

**claus·tro·pho·bic** /ˌklɔːstrəˈfəʊbɪk, ˌklɒs-; *NAmE* ˌklɔːs-/ *adj.* giving you claustrophobia; suffering from claustrophobia: *the claustrophobic atmosphere of the room* ◊ *to feel claustrophobic* ▶ **claus·tro·pho·bic** *noun*

**clav·i·cle** /ˈklævɪkl/ *noun* (*anatomy*) a COLLARBONE ⇒ VISUAL VOCAB page V1

**claw** /klɔː/ *noun, verb*
■ *noun* **1** one of the sharp curved nails on the end of an animal's or a bird's foot ⇒ VISUAL VOCAB page V2 **2** a long, sharp curved part of the body of some types of SHELLFISH, used for catching and holding things: *the claws of a crab* ⇒ picture at SHELLFISH ⇒ VISUAL VOCAB page V3 **3** part of a tool or machine, like a claw, used for holding, pulling or lifting things ⇒ see also CLAW HAMMER
**IDM** **get your claws into sb** (*informal*) **1** (*disapproving*) if a woman **gets her claws** into a man, she tries hard to make him marry her or to have a relationship with her **2** to criticize sb severely: *Wait until the media gets its claws into her.* ⇒ more at RED *adj.*
■ *verb* [I, T] to SCRATCH or tear sb/sth with claws or with your nails: **~ at sb/sth** *The cat was clawing at the leg of the chair.* ◊ **~ sb/sth** *She had clawed Stephen across the face.* ◊ (*figurative*) *His hands clawed the air.*
**IDM** **claw your way back, into sth, out of sth, to sth, etc.** to gradually achieve sth or move somewhere by being determined and using a lot of effort: *She clawed her way to the top of her profession.* ◊ *Slowly, he clawed his way out from under the collapsed building.*
**PHR V** **claw sth↔ˈback 1** to get sth back that you have lost, usually by using a lot of effort **2** (of a government) to get back money that has been paid to people, usually by taxing them ⇒ related noun CLAWBACK

**claw·back** /ˈklɔːbæk/ *noun* [C, U] (*BrE, business*) the act of getting money back from people it has been paid to; the money that is paid back

ˈ**claw hammer** *noun* a HAMMER with one split, curved side that is used for pulling out nails

**clay** /kleɪ/ *noun* [U] a type of heavy, sticky earth that becomes hard when it is baked and is used to make things such as pots and BRICKS ⇒ SYNONYMS at SOIL **IDM** see FOOT *n.*

ˈ**clay court** *noun* a tennis COURT that has a surface made of clay

**clayey** /ˈkleɪi/ *adj.* containing clay; like clay: *clayey soil*

**clay ˈpigeon shooting** (*BrE*) (*NAmE* ˈ**skeet shooting**) *noun* a sport in which a disc of baked clay (called a ˈ**clay** ˈ**pigeon**) is thrown by a machine into the air for people to shoot at

**clean** ❶ 🔑 **A1** /kliːn/ *adj., verb, adv., noun*
■ *adj.* (**clean·er, clean·est**)
• NOT DIRTY **1** 🔑 **A1** not dirty: *Are your hands clean?* ◊ *She wiped all the surfaces clean.* ◊ (*BrE*) *It is your responsibility to keep the room clean and tidy.* ◊ (*NAmE*) *Keep your room neat and clean.* ◊ *I can't find a clean shirt* (= one I haven't worn since it was washed). ⇒ see also SQUEAKY CLEAN **2** **A1** having a clean appearance and living in clean conditions: *Cats are very clean animals.*
• NOT HARMFUL **3** 🔑 **A1** free from harmful or unpleasant substances: *clean water/air* ◊ *clean energy* ◊ *cleaner cars* (= not producing so many harmful substances)
• PAPER **4** [usually before noun] with nothing written on it: *a clean sheet of paper*
• NOT OFFENSIVE **5** not offensive or referring to sex; not doing anything that is considered bad or wrong: *The entertainment was good clean fun for the whole family.* ◊ *Keep the jokes clean please!* ◊ *The sport has a very clean image.*
• NOT ILLEGAL **6** not showing or having any record of doing sth that is against the law: *a clean driving licence/driver's license* ◊ *a clean police record* **7** [not usually before noun] (*informal*) not owning or carrying anything illegal such as drugs or weapons: *The police searched her but she was clean.* **8** [not usually before noun] (*informal*) not having taken drugs or alcohol: *He's been clean for three weeks.*
• FAIR **9** played or done in a fair way and within the rules: *It was a tough but clean game.*
• SMOOTH/SIMPLE **10** having a smooth edge, surface or shape; simple and regular: *A sharp knife makes a clean cut.* ◊ *a modern design with clean lines and a bright appearance*
• ACCURATE **11** done with skill and in an accurate way: *The plane made a clean take-off.*
• DOCUMENT/SOFTWARE **12** with no changes or mistakes in it: *Make a clean copy of your work.* ◊ *I do my utmost to produce clean copy, but occasionally a mistake slips in.* ◊ *It backs up data frequently, keeping a clean copy of your work.*
• TASTE/SMELL **13** tasting, smelling or looking pleasant and fresh: *The wine has a clean taste and a lovely golden colour.* ⇒ compare UNCLEAN
**IDM** **a clean bill of ˈhealth** a report that says sb is healthy or that sth is in good condition **a clean ˈbreak 1** a complete end to any connection with a person, an organization, a way of life, etc: *She wanted to make a clean break with the past.* **2** a break in a bone in one place **a clean ˈsheet/ˈslate** a record of your work or behaviour that does not show any mistakes or bad things that you have done: *No government operates with a completely clean sheet.* ◊ *They kept a clean sheet in the match* (= no goals were scored against them). **(make) a clean sweep (of sth) 1** to remove all the people or things from an organization that are thought to be unnecessary or need changing **2** to win all the prizes or parts of a game or competition; to win an election completely: *China made a clean sweep of the medals in the gymnastics events.* ◊ *The opinion poll suggests a clean sweep for the Democrats.* **come clean (with sb) (about sth)** to admit and explain sth that you have kept as a secret: *Isn't it time the government came clean about their plans for education?* **make a clean ˈbreast of sth** to tell the truth about sth so that you no longer feel guilty ⇒ more at NOSE *n.*, WIPE *v.*

▼ SYNONYMS

**clean**
wash • rinse • cleanse • dry-clean
These words all mean to remove dirt from sth, especially by using water and/or soap.

**clean** to remove dirt or dust from sth, especially by using water or chemicals: *The villa is cleaned twice a week.* ◊ *Have you cleaned your teeth?* ◊ *This coat is filthy. I'll have it cleaned* (= dry-cleaned).
**wash** to remove dirt from sth using water and usually soap: *He quickly washed his hands and face.* ◊ *These jeans need washing.*
**rinse** to remove dirt, etc. from sth using clean water only, not soap; to remove the soap from sth with clean water after washing it: *Make sure you rinse all the soap out.*
**cleanse** to clean your skin or a wound.
**dry-clean** to clean clothes using chemicals instead of water.

PATTERNS
• to clean/wash/rinse/cleanse sth **in/with** sth
• to clean/wash/rinse sth **from** sth
• to clean/wash/cleanse a **wound**
• to clean/wash the **car/floor**
• to wash/rinse your **hair**
• to **have** sth cleaned/washed/dry-cleaned

■ *verb* **1** 🔑 **A1** [T, I] to remove the dirt or dust from sth: *I spent all day cooking and cleaning.* ◊ **~ sth** *to clean the windows/bath/floor/house* ◊ *His mother told him to clean his room.* ◊ *to clean a wound* ◊ *Have you cleaned your teeth?* ⇒ see also DRY-CLEAN, SPRING-CLEAN **2** [I] to become clean: *This oven cleans easily* (= is easy to clean). **3** [T] **~ sth** = DRY-CLEAN: *This coat is filthy. I'll have it cleaned.* **4** [T] **~ sth** to remove the inside parts of a fish, chicken, etc. before you cook it
**IDM** **clean ˈhouse** (*NAmE*) **1** to remove people or things that are not necessary or wanted: *The new manager said he wanted to clean house.* **2** to make your house clean **clean up your ˈact** (*informal*) to start behaving in a moral or responsible way: *He cleaned up his act and came off drugs.*

# clean and jerk

**PHR V** **clean sth↔'down** to clean sth carefully and completely: *All the equipment should be cleaned down regularly.* ◊ **'clean sth off/from sth** | **clean sth↔'off** to remove sth from sth by brushing, rubbing, etc.: *I cleaned the mud off my shoes.* ◊ **clean sth↔'out** to clean the inside of sth carefully and completely: *I must clean the fish tank out.* ◊ **clean sb 'out** (*informal*) to use all of sb's money: *Paying for all those drinks has cleaned me out.* ◊ **clean sb/sth 'out** (*informal*) to steal everything from a person or place: *The burglars totally cleaned her out.* ◊ **clean 'up** (*informal*) to win or make a lot of money: *This film should clean up at the box offices.* ◊ **clean (yourself) 'up** (*informal*) to make yourself clean, usually by washing: *I need to change and clean up.* ◊ *Go and clean yourself up.* ◊ *You'd better get cleaned up.* ⊃ related noun CLEAN-UP ◊ **clean 'up** ⚑ **B1** | **clean sth↔'up** ⚑ **B1** to remove dirt, etc. from somewhere: *He always expected other people to clean up after him* (= when he had made the place dirty or untidy): *Who's going to clean up this mess?* ◊ *to clean up beaches after an oil spillage* ⊃ related noun CLEAN-UP ◊ **clean sth↔'up** to remove crime and IMMORAL behaviour from a place or an activity: *The new mayor is determined to clean up the city.* ◊ *Soccer needs to clean up its image.* ⊃ related noun CLEAN-UP

- **adv.** (*informal*) used to emphasize that an action takes place completely: *The thief got clean away.* ◊ *I clean forgot about calling him.*
- **noun** [sing.] the act or process of cleaning sth: *The house needed a good clean.*

**clean and 'jerk** *noun* [sing.] an exercise in WEIGHTLIFTING in which a bar with weights is lifted to the shoulder, and then raised above the head

**clean-'cut** *adj.* (especially of a young man) looking neat and clean and therefore socially acceptable: *Simon's clean-cut good looks*

**clean-er** /'kli:nə(r)/ *noun* **1** a person whose job is to clean other people's houses or offices, etc: *an office cleaner* ⊃ see also WINDOW CLEANER **2** (usually in compounds) a machine or substance that is used for cleaning: *a vacuum cleaner* ◊ *a bottle of kitchen cleaner* ⊃ see also PIPE CLEANER **3** **cleaner's** (*pl.* **cleaners**) (*also* **dry-'cleaner's**) a shop where clothes, curtains, etc. are cleaned, especially with chemicals: *Can you pick up my suit from the cleaner's?* **IDM** **take sb to the 'cleaners** (*informal*) **1** to steal all of sb's money, etc., or to get it using a trick **2** to defeat sb completely: *Our team got taken to the cleaners.*

**clean-ing** /'kli:nɪŋ/ *noun* [U] the work of making the inside of a house, etc. clean: *They pay someone to do the cleaning.* ⊃ see also DRY-CLEANING ⊃ see also SPRING CLEANING

**'cleaning lady** (*also* **'cleaning woman**) *noun* a woman whose job is to clean the rooms and furniture in an office, a house, etc.

**clean-'limbed** *adj.* (of a person) thin and with a good shape: *a clean-limbed model*

**clean-li-ness** /'klenlinəs/ *noun* [U] the state of being clean or the habit of keeping things clean: *Some people are obsessive about cleanliness.*

**clean-'living** *adj.* (of a person) living a healthy life, by not drinking alcohol, not having sex with a lot of different people, etc.

**clean-ly** /'kli:nli/ *adv.* **1** easily and smoothly in one movement: *The boat moved cleanly through the water.* **2** in a clean way: *fuel that burns cleanly*

**cleanse** /klenz/ *verb* **1** [T, I] **~ (sth)** to clean your skin or a wound: *a cleansing cream* ◊ *The wound was then cleansed and dressed.* ⊃ SYNONYMS at CLEAN **2** [T] **~ sb (of/from sth)** (*literary*) to take away sb's guilty feelings or SIN ⊃ see also ETHNIC CLEANSING

**cleans-er** /'klenzə(r)/ *noun* **1** a liquid or cream for cleaning your face, especially for removing MAKE-UP ⊃ WORD-FINDER NOTE at MAKE-UP **2** a substance that contains chemicals and is used for cleaning things

**clean-'shaven** *adj.* a man who is **clean-shaven** does not have a BEARD or MOUSTACHE (= hair that has been allowed to grow on the face)

**'clean-up** *noun* [usually sing.] the process of removing dirt, pollution, or things that are considered bad or offensive from a place: *the clean-up of the river* ◊ *a clean-up campaign*

**clear** ⚫ **A2** ⚪ /klɪə(r)/;
NAmE klɪr/ *adj., verb, adv., noun*

WORD FAMILY
**clear** *adj.* (≠ unclear)
**clearly** *adv.*
**clarity** *noun*
**clarify** *verb*

- **adj.** (**clear-er**, **clear-est**)
- **EASY TO UNDERSTAND 1** ⚑ **A2** easy to understand and not confusing: *She gave me clear and precise directions.* ◊ *Are these instructions clear enough?* ◊ *You'll do as you're told—is that clear?* ◊ **~ about sth** *She was quite clear about her reasons for leaving.* ◊ *This behaviour must stop—do I make myself clear* (= express myself clearly so there is no doubt about what I mean)? ◊ *I hope I made it clear to him that he was no longer welcome here.*
- **WITHOUT DOUBT 2** ⚑ **A2** obvious and leaving no doubt at all: *This is a clear case of fraud.* ◊ *She won the election by a clear majority.* ◊ *His height gives him a clear advantage.* ◊ *He left no clear indication of his wishes.* ◊ *They made their intentions abundantly clear.* ◊ **it is~to sb (that) ...** *It was quite clear to me that she was lying.* ◊ **~ what, how, whether, etc ...** *It is not clear what they want us to do.* ⊃ LANGUAGE BANK at EVIDENCE, IMPERSONAL **3** ⚑ **A2** not confused; having no doubt: **~ about sth** *Are you clear about the arrangements for tomorrow?* ◊ **~ on sth** *My memory is not clear on that point.* ◊ **~ what, how, whether, etc ...** *I'm still not clear what the job involves.* ◊ *We need a clear understanding of the problems involved.* ⊃ SYNONYMS at SURE ⊃ EXPRESS YOURSELF at EXPLAIN
- **MIND 4** ⚑ **A2** thinking in a sensible and logical way, especially in a difficult situation: *a clear thinker* ◊ *You'll need to keep a clear head for your interview.*

▼ **SYNONYMS**

**clear**
obvious • apparent • evident • plain

These words all describe sth that is easy to see or understand.

**clear** easy to see or understand and leaving no doubts:
*It was quite clear to me that she was lying.*

**obvious** easy to see or understand: *It's obvious from what he said that something is wrong.*

**apparent** [not usually before noun] (*rather formal*) easy to see or understand: *It was apparent from her face that she was really upset.*

**evident** (*rather formal*) easy to see or understand: *The orchestra played with evident enjoyment.*

**plain** easy to see or understand: *He made it very plain that he wanted us to leave.*

WHICH WORD?

- These words all have almost exactly the same meaning. There are slight differences in register and patterns of use. If you *make sth clear/plain*, you do so deliberately because you want people to understand sth; if you *make sth obvious*, you usually do it without meaning to: *I hope I make myself obvious.* ◊ *Try not to make it so clear/plain.* In the expressions *clear majority*, *for obvious reasons*, *for no apparent reason* and *plain to see*, none of the other words can be used instead. You can have *a clear/ an obvious/ a plain case of sth* but not: *an evident case of sth.*

PATTERNS

- clear / obvious / apparent / evident / plain **to sb/sth**
- clear / obvious / apparent / evident / plain **that/what/ who/how/where/why ...**
- **to seem / become / make sth** clear / obvious / apparent / evident / plain
- **perfectly / quite / very** clear / obvious / apparent / evident / plain

- **EASY TO SEE/HEAR** 5 [A2] easy to see or hear: *The photo wasn't very clear.* ◊ *The voice on the phone was clear and strong.* ◊ *She was in Australia but I could hear her voice as* **clear as a bell**.
- **EASY TO SEE THROUGH** 6 [A2] that you can see through; TRANSPARENT: *The water was so clear we could see the bottom of the lake.* ◊ *clear glass* ◊ *a clear colourless liquid*
- **SKY/WEATHER** 7 [A2] without cloud or MIST: *a clear blue sky* ◊ *On a clear day you can see France.*
- **SKIN** 8 without spots or marks: *clear skin* ◊ *a clear complexion*
- **EYES** 9 bright and lively: *Her clear blue eyes sparkled.*
- **NOT BLOCKED** 10 ~ (of sth) free from things that are blocking the way or covering the surface of sth: *The road was clear and I ran over.* ◊ *All exits must be kept clear of baggage.* ◊ *You won't get a clear view of the stage from here.* ◊ *I always leave a clear desk at the end of the day.*
- **CONSCIENCE** 11 if you have a **clear** CONSCIENCE or your CONSCIENCE is **clear**, you do not feel guilty
- **FREE FROM STH BAD** 12 ~ **of** sth free from sth that is unpleasant: *They were still not clear of all suspicion.* ◊ *We are finally clear of debt.*
- **NOT TOUCHING/NEAR** 13 [not before noun] ~ **(of sb/sth)** not touching sth; a distance away from sth: *The plane climbed until it was clear of the clouds.* ◊ *Make sure you park your car clear of the entrance.*
- **PERIOD OF TIME** 14 [only before noun] whole or complete: *Allow three clear days for the letter to arrive.*
- **SUM OF MONEY** 15 [only before noun] that remains when taxes, costs, etc. have been taken away **SYN** **net**: *They had made a clear profit of £2000.*
- **PHONETICS** 16 (of a speech sound) produced with the central part of the tongue close to the top of the mouth. In many ACCENTS of (= ways of pronouncing) English, clear /l/ is used before a vowel, as in *leave*. **OPP** **dark**

**IDM** **be clear/smooth 'sailing** (*NAmE*) = BE PLAIN SAILING at PLAIN *adj.* **(as) clear as 'day** easy to see or understand **(as) clear as 'mud** (*informal, humorous*) not clear at all; not easy to understand: *Oh well, that's all as clear as mud, then.* **clear blue 'water (between A and B)** a complete difference or division between two people or groups: *They failed to put clear blue water between themselves and their competitors.* ⊃ more at COAST *n.*, HEAD *n.*, LOUD *adv.*, WAY *n.*

■ *verb*

- **REMOVE STH/SB** 1 [T] to remove things that are not wanted or needed from sth: ~ **sth** *The settlers cleared the land and planted crops.* ◊ *It's your turn to* **clear the table** (= to take away the dirty plates, etc. after a meal). ◊ *They started* **clearing a path** *through the dense jungle.* ◊ *The work of* **clearing the debris** *is in its final stages.* ◊ ~ **A of B** *I cleared my desk of papers.* ◊ ~ **B from/off A** *Clear all those papers off the desk.* ⊃ see also CLEAR AWAY 2 [B1] [T] ~ **sth** to make people leave a place: *Security officials tried to clear the area, fearing more bomb attacks.*
- **NOT BE BLOCKED** 3 [B2] [I] to move freely again; to no longer be blocked: *The traffic took a long time to clear after the accident.* ◊ *The boy's lungs cleared and he began to breathe more easily.*
- **OF SMOKE, ETC.** 4 [B2] [I] ~ **(away)** when smoke, FOG, etc. **clears**, it disappears so that it is easier to see things: *The mist will clear by mid-morning.*
- **OF SKY/WEATHER** 5 [B2] [I] when the sky or the weather **clears**, it becomes brighter and free of cloud or rain: *The next day the weather cleared.* ◊ *The sky cleared after the storm.* ◊ *The rain is clearing slowly.*
- **OF LIQUID** 6 [I] when a liquid **clears**, it becomes TRANSPARENT and you can see through it: *The muddy water slowly cleared.*
- **YOUR HEAD/MIND** 7 [I, T] if your head or mind **clears**, or you **clear** it, you become free of thoughts that worry or confuse you or the effects of alcohol, a hit on the head, etc. and you are able to think clearly: *As her mind cleared, she remembered what had happened.* ◊ ~ **sth** *I went for a walk to clear my head.*
- **OF FACE/EXPRESSION** 8 [I] if your face or expression **clears**, you stop looking angry or worried
- **PROVE SB INNOCENT** 9 [T] ~ **sb (of sth)** to prove that sb is innocent: *She was cleared of all charges against her.* ◊ *Throughout his years in prison, he fought to* **clear his name**.

# clearance

- **GIVE OFFICIAL PERMISSION** 10 [T] to give or get official approval for sth to be done: ~ **sth** *His appointment had been cleared by the board.* ◊ ~ **sth with sb/sth** *I'll have to clear it with the manager.* 11 [T] ~ **sth** to give official permission for a person, a ship, a plane or goods to leave or enter a place: *The plane had been cleared for take-off.* ◊ *to clear goods through customs* 12 [T] ~ **sb** to decide officially, after finding out information about sb, that they can be given special work or allowed to see secret papers: *She hasn't been cleared by security.*
- **MONEY** 13 [I, T] ~ **(sth)** if a payment that is made into your bank account **clears**, or a bank **clears** it, the money is available for you to use: *Cheques usually take three working days to clear.* 14 [T] ~ **sth** to gain or earn a sum of money as profit: *She cleared £1000 on the deal.* 15 [T] ~ **sth** if you **clear** a debt or a loan, you pay all the money back
- **GET OVER/PAST** 16 [T] ~ **sth** to jump over or get past sth without touching it: *The horse cleared the fence easily.* ◊ *The car only just cleared* (= avoided hitting) *the gatepost.*
- **IN SPORT** 17 [T, I] ~ **(sth)** (in football (soccer) and some other sports) if you **clear** a ball, or a ball **clears**, it is kicked or hit away from the area near your own goal

**IDM** **clear the 'air** 1 to improve a difficult or TENSE situation by talking about worries, doubts, etc: *This meeting will be an opportunity to clear the air and start the healing process.* 2 to make the air less dirty or less HUMID (= warm and wet): *Storms were supposed to clear the air.* **clear the 'decks** (*informal*) to prepare for an activity, event, etc. by removing anything that is not essential to it **clear your 'throat** to COUGH (= to force out air noisily through your throat) so that you can speak clearly **clear the way (for sth/for sth to happen)** to remove things that are stopping the progress or movement of sth: *The ruling could clear the way for extradition proceedings.* ⊃ more at COBWEB

**PHR V** **clear a'way** | **clear sth↔a'way** to remove sth because it is not wanted or needed, or in order to leave a clear space: *He cleared away and made coffee.* ◊ *It's time your toys were cleared away.* **clear 'off** (*informal*) to go or run away: *He cleared off when he heard the police siren.* ◊ *You've no right to be here. Clear off!* **clear 'out (of …)** (*informal*) to leave a place quickly: *He cleared out with all the money and left her with the kids.* **clear 'out** | **clear sth↔'out** to make sth empty and clean by removing things or throwing things away: *to clear out a drawer/room* ◊ *We cleared out all our old clothes.* ◊ *I found the letters when I was clearing out after my father died.* ⊃ related noun CLEAR-OUT **clear 'up** 1 (of the weather) to become fine or bright: *I hope it clears up this afternoon.* 2 (of an illness, infection, etc.) to disappear: *Has your rash cleared up yet?* **clear 'up** | **clear sth↔'up** to make sth clean and neat: *It's time to clear up.* ◊ *I'm fed up with clearing up after you!* ◊ *Clear up your own mess!* **clear sth↔'up** to solve or explain sth: *to clear up a mystery/misunderstanding* ◊ *I hope this explanation clears up any confusion.*

■ *adv.*

- **NOT NEAR/TOUCHING** 1 ~ **(of sth/sb)** away from sth/sb; not near or touching sth/sb: *Stand clear of the train doors.* ◊ *He injured his arm as he jumped clear of the car.* ◊ *By lap two Walker was two metres clear of the rest of the runners.*
- **ALL THE WAY** 2 (*especially NAmE*) all the way to sth that is far away: *She could see clear down the highway into the town.*

**IDM** **keep/stay/steer clear (of sb/sth)** to avoid a person or thing because they may cause problems

■ *noun*

**IDM** **in the 'clear** (*informal*) no longer in danger or thought to be guilty of sth: *It seems that the original suspect is in the clear.*

**clear·ance** /ˈklɪərəns; *NAmE* ˈklɪr-/ *noun* 1 [C, U] the process of removing things that are not wanted: *forest clearances* ◊ *slum clearance* (= the process of removing houses that are in very bad condition in an area of a town) ◊ *a* **clearance sale** (= in a shop, when goods are sold cheaply to get rid of them quickly) 2 [U, C] the amount of space or distance that is needed between two objects so that they

# clear-cut

do not touch each other: *There is not much clearance for vehicles passing under this bridge.* ◊ *a clearance of one metre* **3** [U, C] official permission that is given to sb before they can work somewhere, have particular information, or do sth they want to do: *I'm waiting for clearance from headquarters.* ◊ *All employees at the submarine base require security clearance.* **4** [U] official permission for a person, vehicle or goods to enter or leave an airport or a country: *The pilot was waiting for clearance for take-off.* **5** [U, C] the process of a payment into a bank account being confirmed by the bank, so the money is available for you to use **6** [C] a **clearance** in football (soccer) and some other sports is when a player kicks or hits the ball away from the goal of his or her own team

**,clear-'cut** *adj.* definite and easy to see or identify: *There is no clear-cut answer to this question.*

**,clear-'headed** *adj.* able to think in a clear and sensible way, especially in a difficult situation

**clear·ing** /ˈklɪərɪŋ; *NAmE* ˈklɪr-/ *noun* **1** [C] an open space in a forest where there are no trees SYN **glade 2** [U] (in the UK) the system used by universities to find students for the places on their courses that have not been filled, just before the beginning of the academic year: *She got into university through clearing.* ◊ *You can apply for a place through the clearing system.* ◊ *The university has a limited number of clearing places this year.*

**'clearing bank** *noun* (in the UK) a bank that uses a clearing house when dealing with other banks

**'clearing house** *noun* **1** a central office that banks use in order to pay each other money and exchange CHEQUES, etc. **2** an organization that collects and exchanges information for other people or organizations

**clear·ly** /ˈklɪəli; *NAmE* ˈklɪrli/ *adv.* **1** in a way that is easy to see or hear: *Please speak clearly after the tone.* ◊ *The church was clearly visible from my bedroom window.* **2** in a way that is sensible and easy to understand: *She explained everything very clearly.* ◊ *These results clearly show that the government's actions are unpopular.* **3** used to emphasize that what you are saying is obvious and true SYN **obviously**: *Clearly, this will cost a lot more than we realized.*

**clear·ness** /ˈklɪənəs; *NAmE* ˈklɪrn-/ *noun* [U] (much less frequent than *clarity*) the state of being clear

**'clear-out** *noun* [usually sing.] (*informal*, *especially BrE*) a process of getting rid of things or people that you no longer want: *have a clear-out*

**,clear-'sighted** *adj.* understanding or thinking clearly; able to make good decisions and judgements

**'clear-up** *noun* (*BrE*) the process of removing rubbish and tidying things: *a massive clear-up operation*

**cleat** /kliːt/ *noun* **1** [C] a small wooden or metal bar fastened to sth, on which ropes may be fastened by winding **2** [C] a piece of rubber on the bottom of a shoe, etc. to stop it from slipping **3 cleats** [pl.] (*NAmE*) shoes with cleats, often worn for playing sports ⊃ compare FOOTBALL BOOT, SPIKE, STUD (3)

**cleav·age** /ˈkliːvɪdʒ/ *noun* **1** [C, U] the space between a woman's breasts that can be seen above a dress that does not completely cover them **2** [C] (*formal*) a difference or division between people or groups

**cleave** /kliːv/ *verb* (**cleaved**, **cleaved**) HELP Less commonly, **cleft** /kleft/ and **clove** /kləʊv/ are used for the past tense, and **cleft** and **cloven** /ˈkləʊvn/ for the past participle. **1** [T] ~ **sth** (*old-fashioned* or *literary*) to split or cut sth in two using sth sharp and heavy: *She cleaved his skull (in two) with an axe.* ◊ (*figurative*) *His skin was cleft with deep lines.* **2** [I, T] (*old-fashioned* or *literary*) to move quickly through sth: ~ **through sth** *a ship cleaving through the water* ◊ ~ **sth** *The huge boat cleaved the darkness.* **3** [I] ~ **to sth / sb** (*literary*) to stick close to sth/sb: *Her tongue clove to the roof of her mouth.* **4** (**cleaved**, **cleaved**) [I] ~ **to sth** (*formal*) to continue to believe in or support sth: *to cleave to a belief/idea* IDM see CLEFT *adj.*

**cleav·er** /ˈkliːvə(r)/ *noun* a heavy knife with a broad metal BLADE, used for cutting large pieces of meat

**clef** /klef/ *noun* (*music*) a symbol at the beginning of a line of printed music (called a STAVE or STAFF) that shows the PITCH of the notes on it: *the treble/bass clef* ⊃ picture at MUSIC

**cleft** /kleft/ *noun, verb, adj.*
■ *noun* a natural opening or line, for example in the ground or in rock, or in a person's CHIN (= part of the face below the mouth): *a cleft in the rocks*
■ *verb* past tense, past part. of CLEAVE
■ *adj.*
IDM **be (caught) in a cleft 'stick** to be in a difficult situation when any action you take will have bad results

**,cleft 'lip** *noun* a condition in which sb is born with their upper lip split

**,cleft 'palate** *noun* a condition in which sb is born with the roof of their mouth split, making them unable to speak clearly

**clem·a·tis** /ˈklemətɪs, kləˈmeɪtɪs/ *noun* [C, U] a climbing plant with white, purple or pink flowers

**clem·ency** /ˈklemənsi/ *noun* [U] (*formal*) kind treatment of sb when they are being punished; a lack of desire to punish sb so severely SYN **mercy**: *a plea for clemency*

**clem·ent** /ˈklemənt/ *adj.* (*formal*) **1** (especially of weather) mild and pleasant OPP **inclement 2** being kind and showing MERCY to sb who is being punished

**clem·en·tine** /ˈkleməntiːn/ *noun* a fruit like a small orange

**clench** /klentʃ/ *verb* **1** [T, I] when you **clench** your hands, teeth, etc., or when they **clench**, you press them together tightly, usually showing that you are angry, determined or upset: ~ **(sth)** *He clenched his fists in anger.* ◊ *Through clenched teeth he told him to leave.* ◊ *His fists clenched slowly until his knuckles were white.* **2** [T, often passive] to hold sth tightly: **be clenched between/in sth** *Her pen was clenched between her teeth.* ◊ ~ **sth** *He clenched the steering wheel tightly.*

**clere·story** /ˈklɪəstɔːri; *NAmE* ˈklɪrs-/ *noun* (*pl.* **-ies**) (*architecture*) the upper part of a wall in a large church, with a row of windows in it, above the level of the lower roofs

**clergy** /ˈklɜːdʒi; *NAmE* ˈklɜːrdʒi/ (*often* **the clergy**) *noun* [pl.] the priests or ministers of a religion, especially of the Christian Church: *All the local clergy were asked to attend the ceremony.* ◊ *The new proposals affect both clergy and laity.* ⊃ compare LAITY

**clergy·man** /ˈklɜːdʒimən; *NAmE* ˈklɜːrdʒ-/ *noun* (*pl.* **-men** /-mən/) a male priest, minister or religious leader, especially in the Christian Church ⊃ compare CHURCHMAN

**clergy·woman** /ˈklɜːdʒiwʊmən; *NAmE* ˈklɜːrdʒ-/ *noun* (*pl.* **-women** /-wɪmɪn/) a female priest or minister in the Christian Church

**cler·ic** /ˈklerɪk/ *noun* **1** a religious leader, especially a Muslim one: *Muslim clerics* **2** (*old-fashioned* or *formal*) a member of the Christian clergy

**cler·ic·al** /ˈklerɪkl/ *adj.* **1** connected with office work: *clerical workers/staff/assistants* ◊ *a clerical error* (= one made in copying or calculating sth) **2** connected with the CLERGY (= priests): *a clerical collar* (= one that fastens at the back, worn by some priests)

**clerk** /klɑːk; *NAmE* klɜːrk/ *noun, verb*
■ *noun* **1** (*NAmE*) = SALES CLERK: *The clerk at the counter gave me too little change.* **2** (*also* **desk clerk**) (*both NAmE*) a person whose job is dealing with people arriving at or leaving a hotel SYN **receptionist**: *The hotel clerk greeted us warmly.* **3** a person whose job is to keep the records or accounts and do other routine duties in an office, shop, etc: *an office clerk* **4** an official in charge of the records of a council, court, etc: *the Town Clerk* ◊ *the Clerk of the Court* ⊃ see also CLERK OF WORKS, COUNTY CLERK, PARISH CLERK
■ *verb* [I] (*NAmE*) to work as a clerk: *a clerking job*

**clerk of works** noun (BrE) a person whose job is to be in charge of repairs to buildings or of building works, for an organization or institution

## clever ⓘ A2 /ˈklevə(r)/ adj. (clev·er·er, clev·er·est)
**HELP** You can also use **more clever** and **most clever**. **1** ? A2 (especially BrE) quick at learning and understanding things **SYN** intelligent: *a clever child* ◊ *Clever girl!* ◊ *He's too clever by half, if you ask me* (= it annoys me or makes me suspicious). ⊃ SYNONYMS at INTELLIGENT **2** ? B1 (especially BrE) showing skill: *~ at (doing) sth She's clever at getting what she wants.* ◊ *~ with sth He's clever with his hands.* **3** ? B1 showing intelligence or skill, for example in the design of an object, in an idea or sb's actions: *a clever trick* ◊ *What a clever idea!* ◊ *That wasn't very clever* (= what you just didn't sensible), *was it?* ◊ *it is ~ (of sb) to do sth It was clever of him to have spotted the mistake.* **4** (BrE, informal, disapproving) quick with words in a way that annoys people or does not show respect: *Don't you get clever with me!* ▸ **clev·er·ly** adv. **clev·er·ness** noun [U] **IDM** see BOX v.

## cli·ché (also cliche) /ˈkliːʃeɪ; NAmE kliːˈʃeɪ/ noun (disapproving) **1** [C] a phrase or an idea that has been used so often that it no longer has much meaning and is not interesting: *She trotted out the old cliché that 'a trouble shared is a trouble halved.'* **2** [U] the use of clichés in writing or speaking ▸ **cli·chéd** adj.: *a clichéd view of upper-class life*

## click ⓘ B1 /klɪk/ verb, noun
▪ verb **1** ? B1 [T, I] to choose a particular function or item on a computer screen, etc., by pressing one of the buttons on a mouse or TOUCHPAD: *Click here to add your opinion to the survey.* ◊ *~ sth Click the OK button to start.* ◊ *on sth I clicked on the link to the next page of the website.* ⊃ see also DOUBLE-CLICK, POINT-AND-CLICK, RIGHT-CLICK ⊃ WORDFINDER NOTE at KEYBOARD **2** [I, T] to make or cause sth to make a short sharp sound: **(+ adv./prep.)** *The cameras clicked away.* ◊ **+ adj.** *The bolt clicked into place.* ◊ *~ sth He clicked his fingers at the waiter.* ◊ *Polly clicked her tongue in annoyance.* **3** [I] (informal) to suddenly become clear or understood: *Suddenly it clicked—we'd been talking about different people.* ◊ *It all clicked into place.* **4** [I] (informal) to become friends with sb at once; to become popular with sb: *We met at a party and clicked immediately.* ◊ *~ with sb He's never really clicked with his students.* **5** [I] (informal) to work well together: *The team don't seem to have clicked yet.*
**PHRV** ˌclick ˈthrough (to sth) to visit a website by clicking on an electronic link or advertisement on another web page
▪ noun **1** ? B1 the act of pressing the button on a computer mouse or TOUCHPAD: *a mouse click* ◊ *~ on sth a double click on the filename* ◊ *at the ~ of sth A vast amount of information now available at the click of a mouse.* **2** a short sharp sound: *The door closed with a click.* **3** (phonetics) a speech sound made by pressing the tongue against the top of the mouth or the part of the mouth behind the upper front teeth, then releasing it quickly, causing air to be taken in. Clicks are found especially in southern African languages: *click languages* **4** (NAmE, informal) = KLICK

**click·able** /ˈklɪkəbl/ adj. (computing) if text or an image is clickable, you can click on it with the mouse or TOUCHPAD in order to make sth happen

**click·bait** /ˈklɪkbeɪt/ noun [U] (informal, disapproving) material put on the internet in order to attract attention and encourage visitors to click on a link to a particular web page: *clickbait headlines*

**click·er** /ˈklɪkə(r)/ noun (NAmE, informal) a device that allows you to operate a television, etc. from a distance **SYN** remote control

**ˈclick-through** noun **1** [C, U] the action of following a link on a web page to another website, especially a commercial one: *The number of click-throughs to the site has increased in recent weeks.* ◊ *Unfortunately, the advert is still achieving a low click-through rate.* **2** [C] a link on a web page to another website, especially a commercial one: *The click-throughs on the site to other companies aren't always very useful.*

## cli·ent ⓘ B1 /ˈklaɪənt/ noun **1** ? B1 a person who uses the services or advice of a professional person or organization: *a lawyer with many famous clients* ◊ *potential/prospective clients* ◊ *to act on behalf of a client* ◊ *We will advise the client on the best way to solve the problem.* **2** (computing) a computer that is linked to a SERVER

**cli·en·tele** /ˌkliːənˈtel; NAmE ˌklaɪən-/ noun [sing. + sing./pl. v.] all the customers or clients of a shop, restaurant, organization, etc.: *an international clientele*

**ˌclient-ˈserver** adj. [only before noun] (computing) (of a computer system) in which a central SERVER provides data to a number of computers connected together in a network ⊃ see also PEER-TO-PEER

**ˈclient state** noun a country that depends on a larger and more powerful country for support and protection

## cliff ? +B2 /klɪf/ noun a high area of rock with a very steep side, often at the edge of the sea or ocean: *the cliff edge/top* ◊ *the chalk cliffs of southern England* ◊ *a castle perched high on the cliffs above the river* ⊃ WORDFINDER NOTE at COAST
**IDM** ˌfall off a ˈcliff (informal) to decrease quickly and suddenly in quantity or quality: *Sales fell off a cliff in the first quarter of the year.*

**cliff·hang·er** /ˈklɪfhæŋə(r)/ noun a situation in a story, film, competition, etc. that is very exciting because you cannot guess what will happen next, or you do not find out immediately what happens next: *The first part of the serial ended with a real cliffhanger.* ▸ **cliff·hang·ing** adj.

**cliff·top** /ˈklɪftɒp; NAmE -tɑːp/ noun the area of land at the top of a cliff

**cli·mac·tic** /klaɪˈmæktɪk/ adj. (formal) (of an event or a point in time) very exciting, most important

## cli·mate ⓘ A2 Ⓦ /ˈklaɪmət/ noun **1** ? A2 [C, U] the regular pattern of weather conditions of a particular place: *a tropical/warm/mild/temperate/cold climate* ◊ *the harsh climate of the Arctic regions* ⊃ see also CONTINENTAL CLIMATE ⊃ WORDFINDER NOTE at EARTH

**WORDFINDER** arid, continental climate, equatorial, frigid, harsh, humidity, rainfall, tropical, zone

**2** ? A2 [C] an area with particular weather conditions: *They wanted to move to a warmer climate.* **3** ? B2 [C] a general attitude or feeling; an atmosphere or a situation that exists in a particular place: *the present political/economic climate* ◊ *the current climate of opinion* (= what people generally are thinking about a particular issue) ◊ *a climate of fear/suspicion/uncertainty* ◊ *There is no money for children's centres in the current climate.* ◊ *We need to create a climate in which business can prosper.*

**ˈclimate change** noun [U] changes in the earth's weather, including changes in temperature, wind patterns and RAINFALL, especially the increase in the temperature of the earth's atmosphere that is caused by the increase of particular gases, especially CARBON DIOXIDE: *the threat of global climate change* ⊃ compare GLOBAL WARMING

**ˈclimate control** noun [U] a system that cools and dries the air in a building or car and maintains a steady temperature ⊃ compare AIR CONDITIONING ▸ **ˈclimate-controlled** adj.: *a climate-controlled environment*

**cli·mat·ic** /klaɪˈmætɪk/ adj. [only before noun] connected with the climate of a particular area: *climatic changes/conditions* ▸ **cli·mat·ic·al·ly** /-kli/ adv.

**cli·ma·tol·ogy** /ˌklaɪməˈtɒlədʒi; NAmE -ˈtɑːl-/ noun [U] the scientific study of climate ▸ **cli·ma·to·logic·al** /ˌklaɪmətə-ˈlɒdʒɪkl; NAmE -ˈlɑːdʒ-/ adj. **cli·ma·tolo·gist** /ˌklaɪmə-ˈtɒlədʒɪst; NAmE -ˈtɑːl-/ noun

## cli·max /ˈklaɪmæks/ noun, verb
▪ noun **1** the most exciting or important event or point in time: *to come to/reach a climax* ◊ *the climax of his political career* **2** the most exciting part of a play, piece of music,

# climb

etc. that usually happens near the end **3** the highest point of sexual pleasure SYN **orgasm** ⇨ compare ANTICLIMAX
- **verb 1** [I, T] to come to or form the best, most exciting, or most important point in sth: **~ with/in sth** *The festival will climax on Sunday with a gala concert.* **~ sth**: *(especially NAmE) The sensational verdict climaxed a six-month trial.* **2** [I] to have an ORGASM

**climb** 🔊 A1 /klaɪm/ *verb, noun*
- **verb**
- GO UP **1** 🔊 A1 [T, I] to go up sth towards the top: **~ (up) sth** *to climb a mountain/tree* ◊ *She climbed up the stairs.* ◊ **~ (up)** *As they climbed higher, the air became cooler.* ◊ *You can climb to the top of the tower and take in the view.* **2** 🔊 A2 **go climbing** to go up mountains or climb rocks as a hobby or sport: *He likes to go climbing most weekends.*
- GO THROUGH/DOWN/OVER **3** 🔊 A2 [I] **~ + adv./prep.** to move somewhere, especially with difficulty or effort, using hands as well as feet: *I climbed through the window.* ◊ *She opened the passenger door and climbed in.* ◊ *The boys climbed over the wall.* ◊ *Sue climbed into bed.*
- INCREASE **4** 🔊 B2 [I] (of temperature, a country's money, etc.) to increase in value or amount: *The paper's circulation continues to climb.* ◊ **~ + adv./prep.** *Interest rates climbed to 8 per cent.*
- IMPROVE POSITION/STATUS **5** [I, T] to move to a higher position in a chart, table, society or organization: **~ to sth** *The team has now climbed to fourth in the league.* ◊ **~ sth** *The song also climbed the charts in North America.* ◊ *(figurative) to climb the corporate/career ladder* IDM see BANDWAGON
- AIRCRAFT/SUN, ETC. **6** [I] to go higher in the sky: *The plane climbed to 33 000 feet.*
- SLOPE UP **7** [I] to slope upwards: *From here the path climbs steeply to the summit.*
- OF PLANTS **8** [I] to grow up a wall or frame: *a climbing rose* PHRV **ˌclimb ˈdown (over sth)** to admit that you have made a mistake or that you were wrong ⇨ related noun CLIMBDOWN
- **noun**
- MOUNTAIN/STEPS **1** 🔊 B1 an act of climbing up a mountain, rock or large number of steps; a period of time spent climbing: *an exhausting climb* ◊ *It's an hour's climb to the summit.* **2** a mountain or rock which people climb up for sport: *Titan's Wall is the mountain's hardest rock climb.*
- INCREASE **3** [usually sing.] an increase in value or amount: *the dollar's climb against the euro*
- TO A HIGHER POSITION OR STATUS **4** [usually sing.] progress to a higher status, standard or position: *a rapid climb to stardom* ◊ *the long slow climb out of the recession*

**climb-down** /ˈklaɪmdaʊn/ *noun* (BrE) an act of admitting that you were wrong, or of changing your position in an argument: *The chancellor was forced into a humiliating climbdown on his economic policies.*

**climb·er** /ˈklaɪmə(r)/ *noun* **1** a person who climbs (especially mountains) or an animal that climbs: *climbers and hill walkers* ◊ *Monkeys are efficient climbers.* **2** a climbing plant ⇨ see also SOCIAL CLIMBER

**climb·ing** /ˈklaɪmɪŋ/ *noun* [U] the sport or activity of climbing rocks or mountains: *to go climbing* ◊ *a climbing accident* ⇨ see also ROCK CLIMBING

**ˈclimbing frame** (BrE) (NAmE **ˈjungle gym**) *noun* a structure made of metal bars joined together for children to climb and play on ⇨ picture at FRAME

**ˈclimbing wall** *noun* a wall with parts to hold onto, usually inside a building, for people to practise climbing on

**clime** /klaɪm/ *noun* [usually pl.] (*literary or humorous*) a country with a particular kind of climate: *I'm heading for sunnier climes next month.*

**clinch** /klɪntʃ/ *verb, noun*
- **verb** (*informal*) **1** **~ sth** to succeed in achieving or winning sth: *to clinch an argument/a deal/a victory* **2** to provide the answer to sth; to settle sth that was not certain: **~ sth** *These findings clinched the matter.* ◊ **~ it** *'I'll pay your airfare.' 'OK, that clinches it—I'll come with you.'* ◊ *a clinching argument*
- **noun 1** (*informal*) a position in which two people hold each other tightly and with passion SYN **embrace 2** a position in a fight in which two opponents hold each other tightly

**clinch·er** /ˈklɪntʃə(r)/ *noun* [usually sing.] (*informal*) a fact, a remark or an event that settles an argument, a decision or a competition

**cline** /klaɪn/ *noun* a series of similar items in which each is almost the same as the ones next to it, but the last is very different from the first SYN **continuum**

**cling** 🔊 C1 /klɪŋ/ *verb* (**clung, clung** /klʌŋ/) **1** 🔊 C1 [I] to hold on tightly to sb/sth: **~ to sb/sth** *survivors clinging to a raft* ◊ **~ on to sb/sth** *She clung on to her baby.* ◊ **~ on** *Cling on tight!* ◊ **~ together** *They clung together, shivering with cold.* ⇨ SYNONYMS at HOLD **2** 🔊 C1 [I] to stick to sth: *a dress that clings* (= fits closely and shows the shape of your body) ◊ **~ to sth** *The wet shirt clung to his chest.* ◊ *The smell of smoke still clung to her clothes.* **3** 🔊 C1+ C1 [I] **~ (to sb)** (*usually disapproving*) to stay close to sb, especially because you need them emotionally: *After her mother's death, Sara clung to her aunt more than ever.*
PHRV **ˈcling to sth | ˌcling ˈon to sth** to be unwilling to lose sth or stop doing sth: *Throughout the trial she had clung to the belief that he was innocent.* ◊ *He had one last hope to cling on to.* ◊ *She managed to cling on to life for another couple of years.*

**ˈcling film** (BrE) (NAmE **ˈplastic wrap**, **Saran Wrap**™) *noun* [U] a thin clear plastic material that sticks to a surface and to itself, used especially for wrapping food

**cling·ing** /ˈklɪŋɪŋ/ (*also* **clingy** /ˈklɪŋi/) *adj.* **1** (of clothes or material) sticking to the body and showing its shape: *a clinging dress* **2** (*usually disapproving*) needing another person too much: *a clinging child*

**clin·ic** 🔊 C1+ B2 /ˈklɪnɪk/ *noun* **1** 🔊 C1+ C1 a building or part of a hospital where people can go for special medical treatment or advice: *the local family planning clinic* **2** 🔊 B2 (*especially BrE*) a period of time during which doctors give special medical treatment or advice: *The antenatal clinic is on Wednesdays.* **3** 🔊 B2 (*especially BrE*) a private hospital or one that treats health problems of a particular kind: *He is being treated at the London clinic.* ◊ *a rehabilitation clinic for alcoholics* **4** 🔊 B2 (NAmE) a building shared by a group of doctors who work together **5** an occasion in a hospital when medical students learn by watching a specialist examine and treat patients **6** an occasion at which a professional person, especially a SPORTSMAN or SPORTSWOMAN gives advice and training: *a coaching clinic for young tennis players*

**clin·ic·al** 🔊 C1+ C1 /ˈklɪnɪkl/ *adj.* **1** 🔊 C1+ C1 [only before noun] relating to the examination and treatment of patients and their illnesses: *clinical research* (= done on patients, not just considering theory) ◊ *clinical training* (= the part of a doctor's training done in a hospital) ◊ *clinical trials of a drug* **2** (*disapproving*) cold and calm and without feeling or sympathy: *He watched her suffering with clinical detachment.* **3** (*disapproving*) very plain; without decoration ▶ **clin·ic·al·ly** /-kli/ *adv.*: *clinically dead* (= judged to be dead from the condition of the body) ◊ *clinically depressed*

**clin·ician** /klɪˈnɪʃn/ *noun* a doctor, psychologist, etc. who has direct contact with patients

**clink** /klɪŋk/ *verb, noun*
- **verb** [I, T] to make or cause sth to make a sharp ringing sound, like that of glasses being hit against each other SYN **chink**: *clinking coins* ◊ **~ sth** *They clinked glasses and drank to each other's health.*
- **noun** [sing.] **1** (*also* **clink·ing**) a sharp ringing sound like the sound made by glasses being hit against each other **2** (*old-fashioned, slang*) prison

**clink·er** /ˈklɪŋkə(r)/ *noun* **1** [U, C] the hard rough substance left after coal has burnt at a high temperature; a piece of this substance **2** [sing.] (NAmE) a wrong musical note: *The singer hit a clinker.*

**clip** 🔊 C1+ B2 /klɪp/ *noun, verb*
- **noun 1** 🔊 C1+ B2 [C] a short part of a film that is shown separately: *Here is a clip from her latest movie.* **2** 🔊 C1+ C1 [C] (often in compounds) a small metal or plastic object used

for holding things together or in place: *a hair clip* ◊ *toe clips on a bicycle* ⊃ see also ALLIGATOR CLIP, BICYCLE CLIP, BULLDOG CLIP™, CROCODILE CLIP, PAPER CLIP **3** [C] a piece of jewellery that fastens to your clothes: *a diamond clip* **4** [sing.] the act of cutting sth to make it shorter: *He gave the hedge a clip.* **5** [C] (*BrE, informal*) a quick hit with your hand: *She gave him a clip round the ear for being cheeky.* **6** [C] a set of bullets in a metal container that is placed in or attached to a gun for firing
**IDM** **at a fast, good, steady, etc. ˈclip** (*especially NAmE*) quickly
■ *verb* (**-pp-**) **1** [T, I] to fasten sth to sth else with a clip; to be fastened with a clip: *~sth + adv./prep. He clipped the microphone (on) to his collar.* ◊ *Clip the pages together.* ◊ *+ adv./prep. Do those earrings clip on?* **2** [T] to cut sth with SCISSORS or SHEARS, in order to make it shorter or neater; to remove sth from somewhere by cutting it off: *~sth ◊ to clip a hedge* ◊ *~sth from sth/off (sth) He clipped off a length of wire.* **3** [T] to hit the edge or side of sth: *~sth The car clipped the kerb as it turned.* ◊ *~sth + adv./prep. She clipped the ball into the net.* **4** [T] *~sth (out of/from sth)* to cut sth out of sth else using SCISSORS: *to clip a coupon (out of the paper)*
**IDM** **clip sb's ˈwings** to limit a person's freedom or power **PHRV** **ˌclip sth ˈoff sth** (*informal*) to reduce the time that it takes to do sth by a particular length of time: *She clipped two seconds off her previous best time.*

**ˈclip art** *noun* [U] (*computing*) pictures and symbols that are stored in computer programs or on websites for computer users to copy and add to their own documents

**clip·board** /ˈklɪpbɔːd; *NAmE* -bɔːrd/ *noun* **1** a small board with a clip at the top for holding papers, used by sb who wants to write while standing or moving around **2** (*computing*) a place in a computer's memory where information from a computer file is stored for a time until it is added to another file

**clip-clop** /ˈklɪp klɒp; *NAmE* klɑːp/ *noun* a sound like the sound of a horse's HOOFS on a hard surface

**ˈclip-on** *adj.* [only before noun] fastened to sth with a CLIP: *clip-on earrings*

**clipped** /klɪpt/ *adj.* (of a person's way of speaking) clear and fast but not very friendly: *his clipped military tones*

**clip·per** /ˈklɪpə(r)/ *noun* **1 clippers** [pl.] a tool for cutting small pieces off things: *a pair of hedge clippers* ⊃ see also NAIL CLIPPERS **2** a fast sailing ship, used in the past

**clip·ping** /ˈklɪpɪŋ/ *noun* **1** [usually pl.] a piece cut off sth: *hedge/nail clippings* **2** (*especially NAmE*) (*also* **press clipping** *BrE, NAmE*) (*BrE also* **cutting, press cutting**) an article or a story that you cut from a newspaper or magazine and keep

**clique** /kliːk/ *noun* [C + sing./pl. v.] (*often disapproving*) a small group of people who spend their time together and do not allow others to join them

**cli·quey** /ˈkliːki/ (*also* **cliquish** /ˈkliːkɪʃ/) *adj.* (*disapproving*) tending to form a clique; controlled by cliques: *He found the school very cliquey and elitist.*

**clit·oris** /ˈklɪtərɪs/ *noun* the small sensitive organ just above the opening of a woman's VAGINA that becomes larger when she is sexually excited ▶ **clit·or·al** /-rəl/ *adj.* [only before noun]

**Cllr** *abbr.* (*BrE*) (used before names in writing) COUNCILLOR: *Cllr Michael Booth*

**cloak** /kləʊk/ *noun, verb*
■ *noun* **1** [C] a type of coat that has no arms, fastens at the neck and hangs loosely from the shoulders, worn especially in the past **2** [sing.] (*literary*) a thing that hides or covers sb/sth: *They left under the cloak of darkness.*
■ *verb* [often passive] (*literary*) to cover or hide sth: **be cloaked (in sth)** *The hills were cloaked in thick mist.* ◊ *The meeting was cloaked in mystery.* ▶ **cloaked** *adj.*: *a tall cloaked figure* (= a person wearing a cloak)

**ˌcloak-and-ˈdagger** *adj.* [only before noun] **cloak-and-dagger** activities are secret and mysterious, sometimes in a way that people think is unnecessary or silly

# clock

**cloak·room** /ˈkləʊkruːm, -rʊm/ *noun* **1** (*especially BrE*) (*NAmE usually* **check-room**, **coat check**, **coat·room**) a room in a public building where people can leave coats, bags, etc. for a time **2** (*BrE*) a room that contains a toilet or toilets ⊃ note at TOILET

**clob·ber** /ˈklɒbə(r); *NAmE* ˈklɑːb-/ *verb, noun*
■ *verb* (*informal*) **1** *~sb* to hit sb very hard **2** [often passive] to affect sb badly or to punish them, especially by making them lose money: **be/get clobbered (with sth)** *The paper got clobbered with libel damages of half a million pounds.* **3** [usually passive] to defeat sb completely: **be/get clobbered** *We got clobbered in the game on Saturday.*
■ *noun* [U] (*BrE, informal*) a person's clothes or equipment **SYN** **stuff**

**cloche** /klɒʃ; *NAmE* kləʊʃ/ *noun* **1** a glass or plastic cover placed over young plants to protect them from cold weather **2** (*also* **cloche ˈhat**) a woman's hat that is like a bell in shape and fits close to the head, worn especially in the 1920s

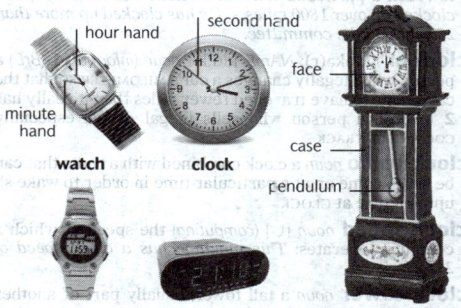

digital watch    clock radio    grandfather clock

**clock** /klɒk; *NAmE* klɑːk/ *noun, verb*
■ *noun* **1** [C] an instrument for measuring and showing time, in a room, on the wall of a building or on a computer screen (not worn or carried like a watch): *The clock struck twelve/midnight.* ◊ *The clock is fast/slow* (= showing a time later/earlier than the true time). ◊ *The clock has stopped.* ◊ **by a~** *It was ten past six by the kitchen clock.* ◊ *the clock face* (= the front part of a clock with the numbers on) ◊ *The hands of the clock crept slowly around.* ◊ *The sound of a clock ticking somewhere in the house kept him awake.* ⊃ see also ALARM CLOCK, AROUND-THE-CLOCK, ATOMIC CLOCK, BIOLOGICAL CLOCK, BODY CLOCK, CUCKOO CLOCK, GRANDFATHER CLOCK, O'CLOCK, TIME CLOCK **2 the clock** [sing.] (*informal*) = MILOMETER: **on the ~** *a used car with 20000 miles on the clock*
**IDM** **against the ˈclock** if you do sth **against the clock**, you do it fast in order to finish before a particular time **around/round the ˈclock** all day and all night without stopping: *Staff have been working around the clock to resolve the problems.* **the clock is ticking (down)** used to say that there's not much time left before sth happens: *The clock is ticking down to midnight on New Year's Eve.* **the clocks go forward/back** the time changes officially, for example at the beginning and end of summer **put/turn the ˈclock back 1** to return to a situation that existed in the past; to remember a past age: *I wish we could turn the clock back two years and give the marriage another chance.* **2** (*disapproving*) to return to old-fashioned methods or ideas: *The new censorship law will turn the clock back 50 years.* **put the clocks forward/back** (*BrE*) (*NAmE* **set/move the clocks ahead/back**) to change the time shown by clocks, usually by one hour, when the time changes officially, for example at the beginning and end of summer **run down/out the ˈclock** if a sports team tries to **run down/out the clock** at the end of a game, it stops trying to score and just tries to keep hold of the ball to stop the other team from scoring ⊃ compare TIME-WASTING ⊃ more at BEAT *v.*, RACE *n.*, STOP *v.*, WATCH *v.*

■ **verb 1** ~ **sth** to reach a particular time or speed: *He clocked 10.09 seconds in the 100 metres final.* **2** to measure the speed at which sb/sth is travelling: ~ **sb doing sth** *The police clocked her doing over 100 miles an hour.* ◇ ~ **sb/sth (at sth)** *Wind gusts at 80 mph were clocked at Rapid City.* **3** ~ **sb** | ~ **that …** | ~ **what/where, etc …** (*BrE, informal*) to notice or recognize sb: *I clocked her in the driving mirror.* **4** ~ **sb** (*informal*) to hit sb, especially on the head: *He said it again, so I clocked him on the nose!* **5** ~ **sth** (*BrE, informal*) to illegally reduce the number of miles shown on a vehicle's MILOMETER (= instrument that measures the number of miles it has travelled) in order to make the vehicle appear to have travelled fewer miles than it really has
**PHR V** ˌclock ˈin (*informal*) to reach a figure, number, amount of time, etc: *The film clocked in at nearly two hours.* ˌclock ˈin/ˈon (*BrE*) (*NAmE* ˌpunch ˈin) to record the time at which you arrive at work, especially by putting a card into a machine ˌclock ˈout/ˈoff (*BrE*) (*NAmE* ˌpunch ˈout) to record the time at which you leave work, especially by putting a card into a machine ˌclock ˈup sth to reach a particular amount or number: *On the trip we clocked up over 1 800 miles.* ◇ *He has clocked up more than 25 years on the committee.*

**clock·er** /ˈklɒkə(r)/ *NAmE* /ˈklɑːk-/ *noun* (*informal*) **1** (*BrE*) a person who illegally changes a car's MILOMETER so that the car seems to have travelled fewer miles than it really has **2** (*NAmE*) a person who sells illegal drugs, especially COCAINE or CRACK

**clock ˈradio** *noun* a clock combined with a radio that can be set to come on at a particular time in order to wake sb up ⊃ picture at CLOCK

**ˈclock speed** *noun* [U] (*computing*) the speed at which a computer operates: *This machine has a clock speed of 2.6GHz.*

**ˈclock tower** *noun* a tall tower, usually part of another building, with a clock at the top

**ˈclock-watcher** *noun* (*disapproving*) a worker who is always checking the time to make sure that they do not work longer than they need to

**clock·wise** /ˈklɒkwaɪz/ *NAmE* /ˈklɑːk-/ *adv., adj.* moving around in the same direction as the hands of a clock: *Turn the key clockwise.* ◇ *a clockwise direction* **OPP** **anticlockwise, counterclockwise**

**clock·work** /ˈklɒkwɜːk/ *NAmE* /ˈklɑːkwɜːrk/ *noun* [U] parts of a machine consisting of wheels and SPRINGS: *clockwork toys* (= toys that are wound up with a key)
**IDM** ˌgo/run like ˈclockwork to happen according to plan; to happen without difficulties or problems ⊃ more at REGULAR *adj.*

**clod** /klɒd/ *NAmE* klɑːd/ *noun* **1** [usually pl.] a small piece of earth or mud **2** (*old-fashioned, informal*) a stupid person

**clog** /klɒɡ/ *NAmE* klɑːɡ/ *verb, noun*
■ *verb* [T, often passive, I] (**-gg-**) to block sth or to become blocked: ~ **sth (up) (with sth)** *The narrow streets were clogged with traffic.* ◇ *Tears clogged his throat.* ◇ ~ **(up) (with sth)** *Within a few years the pipes began to clog up.* **OPP** **unclog**
■ *noun* a shoe that is completely made of wood or one that has a thick wooden SOLE and a leather top **IDM** see POP *v.*

**clois·ter** /ˈklɔɪstə(r)/ *noun* **1** [C, usually pl.] a covered passage with ARCHES around a square garden, usually forming part of a CATHEDRAL, CONVENT or MONASTERY **2** [sing.] life in a CONVENT or MONASTERY

**clois·tered** /ˈklɔɪstəd/ *NAmE* -stərd/ *adj.* (*formal*) protected from the problems and dangers of normal life: *a cloistered life* ◇ *the cloistered world of the university*

**clone** /kləʊn/ *noun, verb*
■ *noun* **1** (*biology*) a plant or an animal that is produced naturally or artificially from the cells of another plant or animal and is therefore exactly the same as it **2** (*sometimes disapproving*) a person or thing that seems to be an exact copy of another

■ *verb* **1** ~ **sth** to produce an exact copy of an animal or a plant from its cells: *A team from the UK were the first to successfully clone an animal.* ◇ *Dolly, the cloned sheep* **2** ~ **sth** to illegally make an electronic copy of stored information from a person's credit card or mobile phone so that you can make payments or phone calls but the owner of the card or phone receives the bill

**close¹** ❶ **A1** /kləʊz/ *verb, noun* ⊃ see also CLOSE²
■ *verb*
• WINDOW/DOOR, ETC. **1** ❷ **A1** [T, I] ~ **(sth)** to put sth into a position so that it covers an opening; to get into this position **SYN** **shut**: *He closed the door firmly.* ◇ *Would anyone mind if I closed the window?* ◇ *It's dark now—let's close the curtains.* ◇ *I closed my eyes against the bright light.* ◇ *The doors open and close automatically.* **OPP** **open**
• BOOK/UMBRELLA, ETC. **2** **A1** [T] ~ **sth** to move the parts of sth together so that it is no longer open **SYN** **shut**: *to close a book/an umbrella* ◇ *He ate greedily, without closing his mouth.* **OPP** **open**
• SHOP/STORE/BUSINESS, ETC. **3** **A1** [T, often passive, I] to make the work of a shop, etc. stop for a period of time; to not be open for people to use: **be closed** *The school was closed because of the heavy snow.* ◇ **be closed for sth** *The museum has been closed for renovation.* ◇ **be closed to sb/sth** *The road was closed to traffic for two days.* ◇ ~ **(for sth)** *What time does the bank close?* ◇ *We close for lunch between twelve and two.* **OPP** **open 4 A1** [T, I] (*also* ˌ**close ˈdown**, ˌ**close sth ˈdown**) if a company, shop, etc. closes, or if you close it, it stops operating as a business: *The hospital closed at the end of last year.* ◇ *The play closed after just three nights.* ◇ ~ **sth** *The club was closed by the police.* **OPP** **open**
• END **5** **B1** [I, T] to end or make sth end: *The meeting will close at 10.00 p.m.* ◇ *The offer closes at the end of the week.* ◇ *I will close with a few words about future events.* ◇ ~ **sth** *to close a meeting/debate* ◇ *to close a case/an investigation* ◇ *to close an account* (= to stop keeping money in a bank account) ◇ *The subject is now closed* (= we will not discuss it again). **OPP** **open** ⊃ EXPRESS YOURSELF *at* FINISH **6** [T] ~ **sth** to arrange and settle a business deal: *Right now we are trying to close the deal with our sponsors.* **7** [T] ~ **sth** to put an end to a mistake in sth that causes a security risk or gives sb an unfair advantage: *to close a security hole* ◇ *Congressional leaders have agreed to close a loophole that gave small businesses a big tax break for buying SUVs.*
• COMPUTERS **8** [T] ~ **sth** (*computing*) to stop using a computer program or file and put it away: *Once I got a few apps closed, it started working again.*
• FINANCE **9** [I] ~ **(at sth)** to be worth a particular amount at the end of the day's business: *Shares in the company closed at 265p.* ◇ *closing prices*
• DISTANCE/DIFFERENCE **10** [T, I] ~ **(sth)** to make the distance or difference between two people or things smaller; to become closer or narrower: *These measures are aimed at closing the gap between rich and poor.* ◇ *The gap between the two top teams is closing all the time.*
• COVER AND HOLD **11** [T, I] ~ **(sth) about/around/over sb/sth** to cover sb/sth and hold them/it, or to make sth do this: *She closed her hand over his.* ◇ *Her hand closed over his.*
**IDM** ˌ**close the ˈbook on sth** to stop doing sth because you no longer believe you will be successful or will find a solution: *The police have closed the book on the case* (= they have stopped trying to solve it). ˌ**close its ˈdoors** | ˌ**close ˈshop** (of a business, etc.) to stop trading: *The factory closed its doors for the last time in 2009.* ˌ**close your ˈmind to sth** to refuse to think about sth as a possibility ˌ**close ˈranks 1** if a group of people **close ranks**, they work closely together to defend themselves, especially when they are being criticized: *It's not unusual for the police to close ranks when one of their officers is being investigated.* **2** if soldiers **close ranks**, they move closer together in order to defend themselves ⊃ more at DOOR, EAR, EYE *n.*
**PHR V** ˌ**close ˈdown** (*BrE*) if a radio or television station **closes down**, it stops broadcasting at the end of the day ⊃ related noun CLOSE-DOWN ˌ**close ˈdown** | ˌ**close sth ˈdown** = CLOSE¹: *All the steelworks around here were closed down in the 1980s.* ⊃ related noun CLOSE-DOWN **OPP** **open up** ˌ**close ˈin 1** when the days **close**

in, they become gradually shorter during the autumn **2** if the weather **closes in**, it gets worse **3** when the night **closes in**, it gets darker: *They huddled around the fire as the night closed in.* ˌclose ˈin (on sb/sth) to move nearer to sb/sth, especially in order to attack them: *The lions closed in on their prey.* ˌclose sth↔ˈoff to separate sth from other parts so that people cannot use it: *The entrance to the train station was closed off following the explosion.* ˌclose sth↔ˈout **1** to finish or settle sth: *The band closes the album out with an instrumental track.* ◇ *A rock concert closed out the festivities.* **2** (*NAmE*) to sell goods very cheaply in order to get rid of them quickly ⮕ related noun CLOSEOUT ˌclose ˈover sb/sth to surround and cover sb/sth: *The water closed over his head.* ˌclose ˈup **1** when a wound **closes up**, it gets better as the skin, etc. joins together and goes back to normal **2** to hide your thoughts or emotions: *She closed up when I asked about her family.* ˌclose ˈup | ˌclose sth↔ˈup **1** to shut and lock sth such as a shop or a building, especially for a short period of time: *Why don't we close up and go out for lunch?* ◇ *Can the last one out close up the office?* **OPP** open up **2** to come closer together; to bring people or things closer together: *Traffic was heavy and cars were closing up behind each other.* **3** to become narrower and less open: *Every time he tried to speak, his throat closed up with fear.* **OPP** open up

■ **noun** [sing.] (*formal*) **1** ᵍ B2 the end of a period of time or an activity: *at the close of the seventeenth century* ◇ *His life was drawing to a close.* ◇ *Can we bring this meeting to a close?* ◇ *This chapter of her life had come to a close.* **2** the fact of sth shutting, especially a door: *The door swung to a close.*

▼ **WHICH WORD?**

**close / shut**
You can **close** and **shut** doors, windows, your eyes, mouth, etc.
• **Shut** can suggest more noise and is often found in phrases such as *slammed shut, banged shut, snapped shut.*
• **Shut** is also usually used for containers such as boxes, suitcases, etc.
• To talk about the time when shops, offices, etc. are not open, use **close** or **shut**: *What time do the banks close/shut?* ◇ *A strike has shut the factory.* You can also use **closed** or **shut** (*NAmE* usually **closed**): *The store is closed/shut today.* Especially in *NAmE*, **shut** can sound less polite.
• **Closed** is used in front of a noun, but **shut** is not: *a closed window.*
• We usually use **closed** about roads, airports, etc: *The road is closed because of the snow.*
• **Close** is also used in formal English to talk about ending a meeting or conversation.

**close²** ᵍ A2 /kləʊs/ *adj., adv., noun* ⮕ see also CLOSE¹
■ **adj. (closer, closest)**
• NEAR **1** ᵍ A2 [not usually before noun] near in space or time: *I had no idea the beach was so close.* ◇ *~ to sb/sth Our new house is close to the school.* ◇ *The children are close to each other in age.* ◇ *She is looking for a job closer to home.* ◇ *~ together The tables were too close together.* ◇ *Their birthdays are very close together.* ◇ *This is the closest we can get to the beach by car.* ◇ *We all have to work in close proximity* (= near each other). ⮕ note at NEAR
• RELATIONSHIP **2** ᵍ B1 knowing sb very well and liking them very much: *Jo is a very close friend.* ◇ *~ to sb She is very close to her father.* ◇ *She and her father are very close.* ◇ *We're a very close family.* **3** ᵍ B1 near in family relationship: *close relatives, such as your mother and father, and brothers and sisters* **OPP** distant **4** ᵍ B1 very involved in the work or activities of sb else, usually seeing and talking to them regularly: *She has kept in close contact with the victims' families.* ◇ *They have forged a close working relationship.* ◇ *a retired army general with close ties to the military* ◇ *Even their closest allies were shocked by the move.*
• CAREFUL **5** ᵍ B2 [only before noun] careful and complete: *Take a close look at this photograph.* ◇ *close inspection/*

279 close

*scrutiny/examination* ◇ *Pay close attention to what I am telling you.*
• ALMOST/LIKELY **6** ᵍ B2 [not before noun] almost in a particular state; likely to do sth soon: *~ to sth The airline is close to collapse.* ◇ *He was close to tears.* ◇ *The species is dangerously close to extinction.* ◇ *~ to doing sth We are close to signing the agreement.*
• SIMILAR **7** ᵍ B2 very similar to sth else or to an amount: *There's a close resemblance between them* (= they look very similar). ◇ *~ to sth This movie is about as close to perfect as you could wish for.* ◇ *Their chances of winning are close to zero.* ◇ *It was the closest thing to a home she had ever known.*
• COMPETITION/ELECTION, ETC. **8** ᵍ B2 won by only a small amount or distance: *a close match/contest/election* ◇ *It was pretty close but we lost.* ◇ *Our team came a close second* (= nearly won). ◇ *No one expected such a close finish.* ◇ *The game was closer than the score suggests.* ◇ *The result is going to be too close to call* (= either side may win).
• ALMOST BAD RESULT **9** used to describe sth, usually a dangerous or unpleasant situation, that nearly happens: *Phew! That was close—that car nearly hit us.* ◇ *We caught the bus in the end but it was close* (= we nearly missed it).
• WITHOUT SPACE **10** with little or no space in between: *over 1000 pages of close print* ◇ *The soldiers advanced in close formation.*
• CUT SHORT **11** cut very short, near to the skin: *a close haircut/shave*
• GUARDED **12** [only before noun] carefully guarded: *The donor's identity is a close secret.* ◇ *She was kept under close arrest.*
• WEATHER/ROOM **13** warm in an uncomfortable way because there does not seem to be enough fresh air **SYN** stuffy
• PRIVATE **14** [not before noun] *~ (about sth)* not willing to give personal information about yourself: *He was close about his past.*
• MEAN **15** [not before noun] *~ (with sth)* (*BrE*) not liking to spend money: *She's always been very close with her money.*
• PHONETICS **16** (*also* high) (of a vowel) produced with part of the tongue in the highest possible position without limiting the flow of air ⮕ compare OPEN (21) ▶ ˈclose·ness *noun* [U]
**IDM** at/from ˌclose ˈquarters very near: *fighting at close quarters* at/from ˌclose ˈrange from only a short distance away: *The president was shot at close range.* ⮕ see also CLOSE-RANGE ˌclose, but no ci'gar (*informal*) used to tell sb that their attempt or guess was almost but not quite successful a ˌclose ˈcall/ˈshave (*informal*) a situation in which you only just manage to avoid an accident, etc. a ˌclose ˈthing a situation in which success or failure is equally possible: *We got him out in the end, but it was a close thing.* ˌclose to ˈhome **1** if a remark or topic of discussion is **close to home**, it is accurate or connected with you in a way that makes you uncomfortable or embarrassed: *Her remarks about me were embarrassingly close to home.* **2** that involves sb directly: *The next year tragedy struck much closer to home.* keep a ˌclose ˈeye/ˈwatch on sb/sth to watch sb/sth carefully: *Over the next few months we will keep a close eye on sales.* too ˌclose for ˈcomfort so near that it is uncomfortable or dangerous: *When she leaves the stage, the fans can get a little too close for comfort.* up ˌclose and ˈpersonal physically very close to sb; getting to know them well *Get up close and personal with the koalas at the San Diego Zoo.* ⮕ more at HAND *n.*, HEART *n.*

■ **adv.** ᵍ B1 (**closer, closest**) near; not far away: *+ adv./prep. They sat close together.* ◇ *A second police car followed close behind.* ◇ *to come/move/get close* ◇ *The days were growing colder as winter drew closer.* ◇ *Stay close to me!* ◇ *She held Tom close and pressed her cheek to his.*
**IDM** ˌclose at ˈhand near; in a place where sb/sth can be reached easily: *There are good cafes and a restaurant close at hand.* ˌclose ˈby (sb/sth) at a short distance (from sb/sth): *Our friends live close by.* ◇ *The route passes close by the town.* ˌclose ˈon | ˌclose ˈto almost; nearly: *She is close*

on 60. ◇ **It is close on midnight.** ◇ **a profit close to £200 million a close-run 'thing** a situation in which sb only just wins or loses, for example in a competition or an election **close 'to | close 'up | up 'close** in a position very near to sth: *The picture looks very different when you see it close to.* **close up to sb/sth** very near in space to sb/sth: *She snuggled close up to him.* **come close (to sth/to doing sth)** to almost reach or do sth: *He'd come close to death.* ◇ *We didn't win but we came close.* **run sb/sth 'close** (*BrE*) to be nearly as good, fast, successful, etc. as sb/sth else: *Germany ran Argentina very close in the final.* ⇒ more at CARD *n.*, MARK *n.*, SAIL *v.*
■ *noun* **1** (*BrE*) (especially in street names) a street that is closed at one end: *Brookside Close* **2** the grounds and buildings that surround and belong to a CATHEDRAL

**close-cropped** /ˌkləʊs 'krɒpt; *NAmE* 'krɑːpt/ *adj.* (of hair, grass, etc.) cut very short

**closed** 🌐 ⓘ **A2** /kləʊzd/ *adj.* **1** **A2** shut: *Keep the door closed.* **2** **A2** [not before noun] shut, especially of a shop or public building that is not open for a period of time: *The museum is closed on Mondays.* ◇ **to sb/sth** *This road is closed to traffic.* **3** not willing to accept outside influences or new ideas: *a closed society* ◇ *He has a closed mind.* **4** [usually before noun] limited to a particular group of people; not open to everyone: *a closed membership* **OPP open** ⇒ note at CLOSE¹
**IDM behind closed 'doors** without the public being allowed to attend or know what is happening; in private **a closed 'book (to sb)** a subject or person that you know nothing about ⇒ more at EYE *n.*

ˌclosed-ˌcircuit 'television *noun* [U] (*abbr.* **CCTV**) a television system that works within a limited area, for example a public building, especially to protect it from crime

**close-down** /'kləʊz daʊn/ *noun* [U, sing.] **1** the act of stopping work, especially permanently, in an office, a factory, etc. **2** (*BrE*) (especially in the past) the end of broadcasting on a television or radio station until the next day

ˌclosed 'season *noun* [sing.] = CLOSE SEASON

ˌclosed 'shop *noun* a factory, business, etc. in which employees must all be members of a particular trade union ⇒ WORDFINDER NOTE at UNION

**close-fitting** /ˌkləʊs 'fɪtɪŋ/ *adj.* (of clothes) fitting tightly, showing the shape of the body

ˌclose 'harmony /ˌkləʊs 'hɑːməni; *NAmE* 'hɑːrm-/ *noun* [U] (*music*) a style of singing in HARMONY in which the different notes are close together

**close-knit** /ˌkləʊs 'nɪt/ (*also less frequent* ˌclosely 'knit) *adj.* (of a group of people) having strong relationships with each other and taking a close, friendly interest in each other's activities and problems: *the close-knit community of a small village*

**close·ly** ⓘ **B2** Ⓢ /'kləʊsli/ *adv.* **1** **B2** near in space or time: *He walked into the room, closely followed by the rest of the family.* ◇ *closely spaced rows of seats* **2** **B2** near in family relationship: *The two species are closely related.* **3** **B2** having a strong connection: *to be closely linked/associated/related* ◇ *The two events are closely connected.* ◇ *The country's economy remains closely tied to oil.* **4** **B2** in a way that shows you are very involved in the work or activities of sb else, usually seeing and talking to them regularly: *The organization works closely with customers in nearly 100 countries.* ◇ *The Royal Navy was closely involved in the early development of wireless technology.* ◇ *They collaborated closely together for the next four years* **5** **B2** carefully: *I sat and watched everyone very closely.* ◇ *The government has looked closely at the arguments for and against a change in the law.* ◇ *We will be closely monitoring the situation.* ◇ *a closely guarded secret* **6** **B2** in a way that is very similar to sb/sth else: *She closely resembled her mother at the same age.* ◇ *It was an exciting game between two closely matched teams.* **7** **~contested/fought** won or likely to be won by only a small amount or distance: *a closely contested election* **8** with little or no

space in between: *over 1000 closely printed pages* **9 —shaved/shaven/cut** (of hair) cut very short, near the skin: *He had a closely shaved head and a small, neat beard.*

**close-out** /'kləʊzaʊt/ *noun* (*NAmE*) an occasion when goods are sold cheaply in order to get rid of them quickly

**close-range** /ˌkləʊs 'reɪndʒ/ *adj.* [only before noun] at or from a short distance: *The close-range shot was blocked by the goalkeeper.*

**close-run** /ˌkləʊs 'rʌn/ *adj.* [usually before noun] (of a race or competition) won by a very small amount or distance: *The election was a close-run thing.*

ˌclose 'season /ˌkləʊz 'siːzn/ *noun* [sing.] (*BrE*) **1** (*also* ˌclosed 'season *NAmE*, *BrE*) the time of year when it is illegal to kill particular kinds of animal, bird and fish because they are producing young **OPP open season 2** (*NAmE* ˌoff 'season) (*sport*) a time of year when teams do not play games in a particular sport

**close-set** /ˌkləʊs 'set/ *adj.* very close together: *close-set eyes*

**closet** /'klɒzɪt; *NAmE* 'klɑːz-/ *noun, adj., verb*
■ *noun* (especially *NAmE*) a small room or a space in a wall with a door that reaches the floor, used for storing things: *a walk-in closet* ⇒ compare CUPBOARD, WARDROBE ⇒ see also WATER CLOSET
**IDM come out of the 'closet** to admit sth openly that you kept secret before, especially the fact that you are GAY **(be, remain, stay, etc.) in the 'closet** to keep sth secret, especially the fact that you are GAY: *The country's harsh policies forced him to stay in the closet.* ⇒ see also COME OUT at COME *verb* (9) ⇒ more at SKELETON
■ *adj.* [only before noun] used to describe people who want to keep some fact about themselves secret: *closet gays* ◇ *I suspect he's a closet fascist.*
■ *verb* **~sb/yourself + adv./prep.** to put sb in a room away from other people, especially so that they can talk privately with sb, or so that they cannot be alone: *He was closeted with the president for much of the day.* ◇ *She had closeted herself away in her room.*

**close-up** /'kləʊs ʌp/ *noun* [C, U] a photograph, or picture in a film, taken very close to sb/sth so that it shows a lot of detail: *a close-up of a human eye* ◇ *It was strange to see her own face in close-up on the screen.* ◇ *close-up pictures of the planet*

**clos·ing** /'kləʊzɪŋ/ *adj.*, *noun*
■ *adj.* [only before noun] coming at the end of a speech, a period of time or an activity: *his closing remarks* ◇ *the closing stages of the game* **OPP opening**
■ *noun* [U] the act of shutting sth such as a factory, hospital, school, etc. permanently: *the closing of the local school* ⇒ compare OPENING ⇒ see also EARLY CLOSING

ˈclosing date *noun* the last date by which sth must be done, such as applying for a job or entering a competition ⇒ WORDFINDER NOTE at COMPETITION

ˈclosing time *noun* [C, U] the time when a pub, shop, bar, etc. ends business for the day and people have to leave

**clos·ure** ⓘ+ **C1** /'kləʊʒə(r)/ *noun* **1** ⓘ+ **C1** [C, U] the situation when a factory, school, hospital, etc. shuts permanently: *factory closures* ◇ *The hospital has been threatened with closure.* **2** ⓘ+ **C1** [C, U] the temporary closing of a road or bridge: *road closures* **3** [U] the feeling that a difficult or unpleasant experience has come to an end or been dealt with in an acceptable way: *The conviction of their son's murderer helped to give them a sense of closure.*

**clot** /klɒt; *NAmE* klɑːt/ *noun, verb*
■ *noun* **1** = BLOOD CLOT: *They removed a clot from his brain.* **2** (*old-fashioned*, *BrE*, *informal*) a stupid person
■ *verb* [I, T] **(-tt-) ~(sth)** when blood or cream **clots** or when sth **clots** it, it forms thick, almost solid masses or **clots**: *a drug that stops blood from clotting during operations* ◇ *the blood clotting agent, Factor 8*

**cloth** ⓘ **B1** /klɒθ; *NAmE* klɔːθ/ *noun* (*pl.* **cloths** /klɒθs; *NAmE* klɔːðz/) **1** ⓘ **B1** [U] material made by WEAVING or KNITTING cotton, wool, silk, etc: *woollen/cotton/linen cloth* ◇ *a piece of cloth* ◇ *bandages made from strips of cloth* ⇒ see also OXFORD CLOTH ⇒ SYNONYMS at FABRIC **2** ⓘ+ **B1** [C] (often in compounds) a piece of cloth, often used for a special purpose, especially cleaning things or covering a table: *Wipe the surface with a damp cloth.* ◊ *a clean/wet cloth* ⸫ see also DISHCLOTH, DROP CLOTH, FLOORCLOTH, J-CLOTH™, TABLECLOTH, TEA CLOTH **3 the cloth** [sing.] (*literary*) used to refer to Christian priests as a group: *a man of the cloth* **IDM** see COAT *n*.

**cloth 'cap** (*also* **flat cap**) *noun* (*BrE*) a soft cap, normally made of wool, traditionally a symbol of working men: *The party has shed its cloth cap image* (= it is not just a working-class party any more).

**clothe** /kləʊð/ *verb* **1** ~ **sb/yourself/sth (in sth)** (*formal*) to dress sb/yourself: *They clothe their children in the latest fashions.* ◊ (*figurative*) *Climbing plants clothed the courtyard walls.* **2** ~ **sb** to provide clothes for sb to wear: *the costs of feeding and clothing a family*

**clothed** /kləʊðd/ *adj.* [not usually before noun] ~ **(in sth)** dressed in a particular way: *a man clothed in black* ◊ *She jumped fully clothed into the water.* ◊ (*figurative*) *The valley was clothed in trees and shrubs.*

**clothes** 🅘 🄐 /kləʊðz, kləʊz/ *noun* [pl.] the things that you wear, such as trousers, dresses and jackets: *They were dressed in designer clothes* (= clothes designed by famous fashion designers). ◊ *to put on/take off your clothes* ◊ *clean/dirty clothes* ◊ *She was wearing casual clothes.* ◊ *a clothes shop* ⸫ see also PLAIN CLOTHES, STREET CLOTHES **IDM** see EMPEROR

▼ SYNONYMS

**clothes**
clothing • garment • dress • wear • gear

These are all words for the things that you wear, such as shirts, jackets, dresses and trousers.

**clothes** [pl.] the things that you wear, such as shirts, jackets, dresses and trousers.

**clothing** [U] (*rather formal*) clothes, especially a particular type of clothes: *warm clothing*

CLOTHES OR CLOTHING?
**Clothing** is more formal than **clothes** and is used especially to mean 'a particular type of clothes'. There is no singular form of **clothes** or **clothing**: *a piece/an item/an article of clothing* is used to talk about one thing that you wear such as a dress or shirt.

**garment** (*formal*) a piece of clothing: *He was wearing a strange shapeless garment.* **NOTE** **Garment** should only be used in formal or literary contexts; in everyday contexts use *a piece of clothing*.

**dress** [U] clothes, especially when worn in a particular style or for a particular occasion: *We were allowed to wear casual dress on Fridays.*

**wear** [U] (usually in compounds) clothes for a particular purpose or occasion, especially when they are being sold in shops: *the children's wear department*

**gear** [U] (*informal*) clothes: *Her friends were all wearing the latest designer gear.*

PATTERNS
- **casual** clothes/clothing/dress/wear/gear
- **evening/formal** clothes/dress/wear
- **designer/sports** clothes/clothing/garments/wear/gear
- **children's/men's/women's** clothes/clothing/garments/wear
- to **have on/be in/wear** …clothes/garments/dress/gear

**'clothes hanger** *noun* = HANGER

**'clothes horse** *noun* **1** (*BrE*) a wooden or plastic folding frame that you put clothes on to dry after you have washed them **2** (*disapproving*) a person, especially a woman, who is too interested in fashionable clothes

**'clothes line** (*also* **line**) (*BrE also* **'washing line**) *noun* a piece of thin rope or wire, attached to posts, that you hang clothes on to dry outside after you have washed them

**'clothes peg** (*BrE*) (*NAmE* **clothes-pin**/'kləʊðzpɪn, 'kləʊz-/) *noun* = PEG ⸫ picture at PEG

**clo·thier** /'kləʊðiə(r)/ *noun* (*formal*) a person or company that makes or sells clothes or cloth

**cloth·ing** 🅘 🄐 /'kləʊðɪŋ/ *noun* [U] clothes, especially a particular type of clothes: *protective clothing* ◊ *a man wearing dark clothing* ◊ *an item of clothing* ⸫SYNONYMS at CLOTHES **IDM** see WOLF *n*.

**clot·ted 'cream** *noun* [U] a very thick type of cream made by slowly heating milk, made and eaten especially in the UK: *scones and jam with clotted cream*

**'clotting factor** *noun* [C, U] (*biology*) any of the substances in the blood that help it to CLOT (= become thicker and form almost solid masses)

**cloud** 🅘 🄐 /klaʊd/ *noun*, *verb*

■ *noun* **1** 🄐 [C, U] a grey or white mass that floats in the sky, made of very small drops of water: *Dark clouds were gathering in the west.* ◊ *The cloud cover is quite dense today.* ⸫ see also STORM CLOUD, THUNDERCLOUD **2** 🄑 [C] ~ **(of sth)** a large mass of sth in the air, for example dust or smoke, or a number of insects flying all together: *They watched the car disappearing in a cloud of dust.* ⸫see also MUSHROOM CLOUD **3** [C] something that makes you feel sad or anxious: *Her father's illness cast a cloud over her wedding day.* ◊ *The only dark cloud on the horizon was that they might have to move house.* ◊ *He still has a cloud of suspicion hanging over him.* **4 the cloud** [sing.] a network of SERVERS (= computers that control or supply information to other computers) on which data and software can be stored or managed and to which users have access over the internet: *Key company documents are now stored in the cloud, so you no longer need to save them to your computer's hard drive.*

**IDM** **every cloud has a silver 'lining** (*saying*) every sad or difficult situation has a positive side **on cloud 'nine** (*old-fashioned, informal*) extremely happy **under a 'cloud** if sb is **under a cloud**, other people think that they have done sth wrong and do not trust them: *She left the company under a cloud.* ⸫more at HEAD *n*.

■ *verb* **1** [T] ~ **sth** if sth **clouds** your judgement, memory, etc., it makes it difficult for you to understand or remember sth clearly: *Doubts were beginning to cloud my mind.* ◊ *His judgement was clouded by jealousy.* **2** [I, T] (*formal*) (of sb's face) to show that you feel sad, afraid, angry, etc.; to make sb look sad, afraid, angry, etc.: ~ **(over)** *Her face clouded over with anger.* ◊ ~ **sth** *Suspicion clouded his face.* **3** [T] ~ **the issue/picture** to make sth you are discussing or considering less clear, especially by introducing subjects that are not connected with it **4** [I] ~ **(over)** (of the sky) to fill with clouds: *It was beginning to cloud over.* **5** [T] ~ **sth** to make sth less pleasant: *His last years were clouded by financial worries.* **6** [I, T] if glass, water, etc. **clouds**, or if sth **clouds** it, it becomes less easy to see through: ~ **(with sth)** *Her eyes clouded with tears.* ◊ ~ **sth** *Steam had clouded the mirror.*

**cloud·burst** /'klaʊdbɜːst; *NAmE* -bɜːrst/ *noun* a sudden very heavy fall of rain

**'cloud computing** *noun* [U] a way of using computers in which data and software are stored or managed on a network of SERVERS (= computers that control or supply information to other computers), to which users have access over the internet

**cloud 'cuckoo land** (*BrE*) (*NAmE* **la-la land**) *noun* [U] (*informal, disapproving*) if you say that sb is living in **cloud cuckoo land**, you mean that they do not understand what a situation is really like, but think it is much better than it is

**'cloud forest** *noun* [C, U] a forest in tropical or SUBTROPICAL parts of the world that usually has thick cloud at the level of the tops of the trees ⸫compare RAINFOREST

**cloud·less** /'klaʊdləs/ *adj.* clear; with no clouds: *a cloudless sky*

**cloudy** /'klaʊdi/ *adj.* ( **cloud·ier**, **cloudi·est**) **1** (of the sky or the weather) covered with clouds; with a lot of clouds

# clout

**OPP** **clear**: *a grey, cloudy day* **2** (of liquids) not clear or easy to see through ▶ **cloudi·ness** *noun* [U]

**clout** /klaʊt/ *noun*, *verb*
■ *noun* **1** [U] power and influence: *political/financial clout* ◊ *I knew his opinion carried a lot of clout with them.* **2** [C, usually sing.] (*especially BrE*, *informal*) a hard hit with the hand or a hard object
■ *verb* ~ **sb** (*especially BrE*, *informal*) to hit sb hard, especially with your hand

**clove** /kləʊv/ *noun*, *verb*
■ *noun* **1** [C, U] the dried flower of a tropical tree, used in cooking as a SPICE, especially in sweet foods. Cloves look like small nails. ⊃ VISUAL VOCAB page V8 **2** [C] **a garlic ~** | **~ of garlic** one of the small separate sections of a BULB (= the round underground part) of GARLIC ⊃ VISUAL VOCAB page V5
■ *verb* past tense of CLEAVE

**cloven 'hoof** *noun* the foot of an animal such as a cow, sheep, or a GOAT, that is divided into two parts

**clo·ver** /ˈkləʊvə(r)/ *noun* [U] a small wild plant that usually has three leaves on each STEM and purple, pink or white flowers that are like balls in shape: *a four-leaf clover* (= one with four leaves instead of three, thought to bring good luck)
**IDM** **be/live in clover** (*informal*) to have enough money to be able to live a very comfortable life

**clover·leaf** /ˈkləʊvəliːf/ *NAmE* -vərl-/ *noun* (*NAmE*) a place where a number of main roads meet at different levels, with curved sections that form the pattern of a four-leaf clover

**clown** /klaʊn/ *noun*, *verb*
■ *noun* **1** an entertainer who wears funny clothes and a large red nose and does silly things to make people laugh: (*figurative*) *Robert was always the class clown* (= he did silly things to make the other students laugh). **2** (*informal*, *disapproving*) a person that you think is bad because they act in a stupid way: *What do those clowns in the government think they are doing?*
■ *verb* [I] ~ **(around)** (*often disapproving*) to behave in a silly way, especially in order to make other people laugh

**clown·fish** /ˈklaʊnfɪʃ/ *noun* a type of brightly coloured SALTWATER fish that lives with SEA ANEMONES and is protected from their STINGS

**clown·ish** /ˈklaʊnɪʃ/ *adj.* like a clown; silly

**cloy** /klɔɪ/ *verb* [I] (of sth pleasant or sweet) to start to become slightly unpleasant or annoying, because there is too much of it: *After a while, the rich sauce begins to cloy.*

**cloy·ing** /ˈklɔɪɪŋ/ *adj.* (*formal*) **1** (of food, a smell, etc.) so sweet that it is unpleasant **2** using emotion in a very obvious way, so that the result is unpleasant: *the cloying sentimentality of her novels* ▶ **cloy·ing·ly** *adv.*

**club** 🔑 **A1** /klʌb/ *noun*, *verb*
■ *noun*
• FOR ACTIVITY/SPORT **1** 🔑 **A1** [C + sing./pl. v.] (especially in compounds) an organization for people who share an interest or do a sport or activity together: *a golf/tennis/chess/film club* ◊ *to join a club* ◊ *They belong to the same golf club.* ◊ *Grandad is a member of the bowling club.* ⊃ see also FAN CLUB, GLEE CLUB, YOUTH CLUB

| WORDFINDER AGM, the chair, hobby, member, newsletter, secretary, society, subscription, treasurer |
|---|

**2** 🔑 **A2** [C] the building or rooms that a particular club uses: *We had lunch at the golf club.* ◊ *the club bar* ⊃ see also COUNTRY CLUB, HEALTH CLUB **3** 🔑 **A2** [C + sing./pl. v.] (*BrE*) a professional sports organization that includes the players, managers, owners and members: *a football/rugby/soccer club*
• MUSIC/DANCING **4** 🔑 **A2** [C] a place where people, especially young people, go and listen to music, dance, watch comedy, etc: *a jazz club* ◊ *the club scene in Newcastle* ⊃ see also CLUBBING, NIGHTCLUB, STRIP CLUB

• SOCIAL **5** [C + sing./pl. v.] (especially in the UK) an organization and a place where people can meet together socially or stay: *He's a member of several London clubs.*
• SELLING GOODS/SERVICES **6** [C] a business that offers items or services cheaply to its members: *Car club members can hire cars at special discount rates.* ⊃ see also BOOK CLUB
• WEAPON **7** [C] a heavy stick with one end thicker than the other, that is used as a weapon ⊃ see also BILLY CLUB
• IN GOLF **8** [C] = GOLF CLUB
• IN CARD GAMES **9** **clubs** [pl., U] one of the four SUITS (= sets) in a PACK of cards. The clubs have a black design with shapes like three black leaves on a short STEM: *the five/queen/ace of clubs* **10** [C] one card from the SUIT called clubs: *I played a club.*
**IDM** **be in the club** (*BrE*, *informal*) to be pregnant ⊃ more at JOIN *v.*
■ *verb* (-bb-) **1** [T] ~ **sb/sth** to hit a person or an animal with a heavy stick or similar object: *The victim was **clubbed to death** with a baseball bat.* **2** [I] **go clubbing** (*informal*) to spend time dancing and drinking in NIGHTCLUBS
**PHRV** **club to'gether** (*BrE*) if two or more people **club together**, they each give an amount of money and the total is used to pay for sth: *We clubbed together to buy them a new television.*

**club·bing** /ˈklʌbɪŋ/ *noun* the activity of going to NIGHTCLUBS regularly: *They go clubbing most weekends.* ▶ **club·ber** *noun*: *The venue was packed with 3000 clubbers.*

**'club car** *noun* (*NAmE*) a coach on a train with comfortable chairs and tables, where you can buy sth to eat or drink

**'club class** *noun* [U] (*BrE*) = BUSINESS CLASS

**'club 'foot** *noun* [C, U] a foot that has been DEFORMED (= badly bent) since birth ▶ **club-'footed** *adj.*

**club·house** /ˈklʌbhaʊs/ *noun* the building used by a club, especially a sports club

**club·land** /ˈklʌblænd/ *noun* [U] (*BrE*) popular NIGHTCLUBS in general and the people who go to them; an area of a town where there are a lot of NIGHTCLUBS: *modern clubland* ◊ *London's clubland*

**club 'sandwich** *noun* a sandwich consisting of three slices of bread with two layers of food between them

**cluck** /klʌk/ *verb*, *noun*
■ *verb* **1** [I] when a chicken **clucks**, it makes a series of short low sounds **2** [I] to make a short low sound with your tongue to show that you feel sorry for sb or that you think sth is bad: *The teacher clucked sympathetically at the child's story.*
■ *noun* the short low sounds that a chicken makes: (*figurative*) *a cluck of impatience/annoyance*

**clue** 🔑 **B1** /kluː/ *noun*, *verb*
■ *noun* **1** 🔑 **B1** an object, a piece of evidence or some information that helps the police solve a crime: **~ (about sth)** *They are searching for clues about the kidnapping.* ◊ **~ (as) to sth** *The police think the CCTV recording may offer clues to the identity of the killer.* **2** 🔑 **B1** a fact or a piece of evidence that helps you discover the answer to a problem: **~ (about sth)** *This data may provide clues about the current economic situation.* ◊ **~ (as) to sth** *Diet may hold the clue to the causes of migraine.* **3** 🔑 **B1** some words or a piece of information that helps you find the answers to a CROSSWORD, a game or a question: *'You'll never guess who I saw today!' 'Give me a clue.'*
**IDM** **not have a 'clue** (*informal*) **1** to know nothing about sth or about how to do sth: *I don't have a clue where she lives.* **2** (*disapproving*) to be very stupid: *Don't ask him to do it—he doesn't have a clue!*
■ *verb*
**PHRV** **clue sb 'in (on sth)** (*informal*) to give sb the most recent information about sth: *He's just clued me in on the latest developments.*

**clued-'up** (*BrE*) (*NAmE* **clued-'in**) *adj.* **~ (on sth)** (*informal*) knowing a lot about sth; having a lot of information about sth

**clue·less** /ˈkluːləs/ *adj.* (*informal*, *disapproving*) very stupid; not able to understand or to do sth: *He's completely clueless about computers.*

**clump** /klʌmp/ noun, verb
- **noun 1** a small group of things or people very close together, especially trees or plants; a bunch of sth such as grass or hair: *a clump of trees/bushes* **2** the sound made by sb putting their feet down very heavily
- **verb 1** [I] + **adv./prep.** (*especially BrE*) to put your feet down noisily and heavily as you walk: *The children clumped down the stairs.* **2** [I, T] **~(together) | ~A and B (together)** to come together to form a tight group; to be brought together to form a tight group: *Galaxies tend to clump together in clusters.*

**clumpy** /ˈklʌmpi/ adj. (of shoes and boots) big, thick and heavy

**clumsy** /ˈklʌmzi/ adj. (**clum·sier**, **clum·si·est**) **1** (of people and animals) moving or doing things in a way that is not smooth or steady or careful: *I spilt your coffee. Sorry—that was clumsy of me.* ◇ *His clumsy fingers couldn't untie the knot.* **2** (of actions and statements) done without skill or in a way that offends people: *She made a clumsy attempt to apologize.* **3** (of objects) difficult to move or use easily; not well designed **4** (of processes) too complicated to understand or use easily: *The complaints procedure is clumsy and time-consuming.* ▸ **clum·si·ly** /-zɪli/ adv. **clum·si·ness** noun [U]

**clung** /klʌŋ/ past tense, past part. of CLING

**clunk** /klʌŋk/ noun a sound that is not loud or clear made by two heavy objects hitting each other ▸ **clunk** verb [I]

**clunk·er** /ˈklʌŋkə(r)/ noun (*NAmE*, *informal*) **1** an old car in bad condition **2** a serious mistake

**clunky** /ˈklʌŋki/ adj. (*informal*) **1** (of shoes) solid, heavy and old-fashioned: *clunky leather shoes* **2** (of technology) old-fashioned; not well designed: *The device has clunky controls.* **3** (of writing, especially for a film) of poor quality; that does not seem realistic: *The movie is ruined by wooden acting and clunky dialogue.*

**clus·ter** 🔑+ **C1** /ˈklʌstə(r)/ noun, verb
- **noun 1** 🔑+ **C1** a group of things of the same type that grow or appear close together: *a cluster of stars* ◇ *The plant bears its flowers in clusters.* ◇ *a leukaemia cluster* (= an area where there are more cases of the disease than you would expect) **2** 🔑+ **C1** a group of people, animals or things close together: *a cluster of spectators* ◇ *a little cluster of houses* **3** (*phonetics*) a group of consonants that come together in a word or phrase, for example /str/ at the beginning of string: *a consonant cluster* ⊃ WORDFINDER NOTE at PRONUNCIATION
- **verb** [I] to come together in a small group or groups: **~together** *The children clustered together in the corner of the room.* ◇ **~around/round/at sb/sth** *The doctors clustered anxiously around his bed.*

**ˈcluster bomb** noun a type of bomb that throws out smaller bombs when it explodes

**clutch** /klʌtʃ/ verb, noun
- **verb 1** [T, I] to hold sb/sth tightly **SYN** grip: **~sb/sth (+ adv./prep.)** *He clutched the child to him.* ◇ *She stood there, the flowers still clutched in her hand.* ◇ **+ adv./prep.** *I clutched on to the chair for support.* ⊃ SYNONYMS at HOLD **2** [T, I] to take hold of sth suddenly, because you are afraid or in pain: **~sth** *He gasped and clutched his stomach.* **~at sb/sth**: (*figurative*) *Fear clutched at her heart.* **IDM** see STRAW ⊃ SYNONYMS at HOLD
- **PHRV** ˈ**clutch at sth/sb** to try to quickly get hold of sth/sb **SYN** grab: *The child clutched at his mother's skirt.*
- **noun 1** [C] the PEDAL in a car or other vehicle that you press with your foot so that you can change GEAR: *Put your foot on the clutch.* **2** [C] a device in a machine that connects and DISCONNECTS working parts, especially the engine and the GEARS: *The car needs a new clutch.* **3 a ~ of sth** [sing.] a group of people, animals or things: *He's won a whole clutch of awards.* **4 clutches** [pl.] (*informal*) power or control: *He managed to escape from their clutches.* ◇ **in your clutches** *Now that she had him in her clutches, she wasn't going to let go.* **5** [C, usually sing.] a tight hold on sb/sth **SYN** grip (*figurative*): *She felt the sudden clutch of fear.* **6** [C] a group of eggs that a bird lays at one time; the young birds that come out of a group of eggs at the same time **7** [C] = CLUTCH BAG

---

283     **coaching**

**ˈclutch bag** (*also* **clutch**) noun a small, flat bag that women carry in their hands, especially on formal occasions

**clut·ter** /ˈklʌtə(r)/ verb, noun
- **verb ~sth (up) (with sth/sb)** to fill a place or area with too many things, so that it is untidy: *Don't clutter the page with too many diagrams.* ◇ *Too many graphics can clutter the screen.* ◇ *I don't want all these files cluttering up my desk.*
- **noun** [U, sing.] (*disapproving*) a lot of things in an untidy state, especially things that are not necessary or are not being used; a lack of order **SYN** mess: *There's always so much clutter on your desk!* ◇ *Try to get rid of screen clutter.* ◇ *There was a clutter of bottles and tubes on the shelf.*

**clut·tered** /ˈklʌtəd/ NAmE -tərd/ adj. **~(up) (with sb/sth)** covered with, or full of, a lot of things or people, in a way that is untidy: *a cluttered room/desk* ◇ (*figurative*) *a cluttered mind* **OPP** uncluttered

**cm** abbr. (pl. **cm** or **cms**) CENTIMETRE

**CMS** /ˌsiː em ˈes/ noun a piece of software that is used to organize, manage or change the content of a website (the abbreviation for 'content management system'): *The CMS enables employees to add and edit web pages without the support of a web developer.*

**CND** /ˌsiː en ˈdiː/ abbr. Campaign for Nuclear Disarmament (a British organization whose aim is to persuade countries to get rid of their nuclear weapons)

**CNN** /ˌsiː en ˈen/ abbr. Cable News Network (an American broadcasting company that sends television programmes all over the world)

**CO** /ˌsiː ˈəʊ/ abbr. Commanding Officer (an officer who commands a group of soldiers, sailors, etc.)

**Co.** abbr. **1** /kəʊ/ (*business*) company: *Pitt, Briggs & Co.* **2** (in writing) county **3** /kəʊ/ **and co.** (*informal*) and other members of a group of people: *Were Jane and co. at the party?*

**co-** /kəʊ/ prefix (used in adjectives, adverbs, nouns and verbs) together with: *co-produced* ◇ *cooperatively* ◇ *co-author* ◇ *coexist*

**c/o** abbr. (used on letters to a person staying at sb else's house) care of: *Mr P Brown, c/o Ms M Jones*

**coach** 🔑 **A2** /kəʊtʃ/ noun, verb
- **noun 1** 🔑 **A2** [C] a person who trains a person or team in sport: *the head/assistant coach* ◇ *a basketball/football coach* **2** [C] a person who gives private lessons to sb, often to prepare them for an exam: *a maths coach* **3** [C] = LIFE COACH **4** 🔑 **A2** [C] (*BrE*) a comfortable bus for carrying passengers over long distances: *to take/get a coach* ◇ **by ~** *Travel is by coach overnight to Berlin.* ◇ **on a ~** *Four passengers on the coach were seriously injured in the crash.* ◇ *a coach tour/journey/trip* **5** [C] (*BrE*) = CARRIAGE: *a railway coach* **6** [C] a large closed vehicle with four wheels, pulled by horses, used in the past for carrying passengers ⊃ see also STAGECOACH **7** [U] (*NAmE*) the cheapest seats in a plane: *to fly coach* ◇ *coach fares/passengers/seats* **IDM** see DRIVE v.
- **verb 1** 🔑 **B1** to train sb to play a sport, to do a job better, or to improve a skill: **~sb** *He has coached the team for five years.* ◇ **~sb in/for sth** *Her father coached her for the Olympics.* ◇ **~sth** *He coaches basketball and soccer.* **2 ~sb (in/for sth)** (*especially BrE*) to give a student extra teaching in a particular subject especially so that they will pass an exam **3** to give sb special instructions for what they should do or say in a particular situation: **~sb (in/on sth)** *They believed the witnesses had been coached on what to say.* ◇ **~sb to do sth** *The president's advisers coached him to adopt a more serious tone.*

**ˈcoach house** noun a building where CARRIAGES pulled by horses are or were kept

**coach·ing** /ˈkəʊtʃɪŋ/ noun [U] **1** the process of training sb to play a sport, to do a job better or to improve a skill: *a coaching session* ⊃ see also LIFE COACHING **2** (*especially BrE*) the process of giving a student extra teaching in a particular subject ⊃ WORDFINDER NOTE at TRAINING

**coaching inn** *noun* in the past, an INN along a route used by coaches, at which the horses pulling the coaches could be changed

**coach-load** /ˈkəʊtʃləʊd/ *noun* (*BrE*) a group of people travelling together in a coach: *by the ~ Tourists were arriving by the coachload.*

**coach-man** /ˈkəʊtʃmən/ *noun* (*pl.* **-men** /-mən/) (in the past) a man who drove a COACH pulled by horses

**co-agu-late** /kəʊˈæɡjuleɪt/ *verb* [I, T] **~ (sth)** if a liquid **coagulates** or sth **coagulates** it, it becomes thick and partly solid SYN **congeal**: *Blood began to coagulate around the edges of the wound.* ▶ **co-agu-la-tion** /kəʊˌæɡjuˈleɪʃn/ *noun* [U]

**coal** 🔊 **B1** /kəʊl/ *noun* **1** 🔊 **B1** [U] a hard black mineral that is found below the ground and burnt to produce heat: *I put more coal on the fire.* ◊ *a lump of coal* ◊ *coal mining* ◊ *a coal fire* ◊ *the coal industry* **2** [C] a piece of coal, especially one that is burning: *A hot coal fell out of the fire and burnt the carpet.* IDM *see* HAUL *v.*

**coal-black** *adj.* very dark in colour: *coal-black eyes*

**co-alesce** /ˌkəʊəˈles/ *verb* [I] **~ (into sth)** (*formal*) to come together to form one larger group, substance, etc. SYN **amalgamate**: *The puddles had coalesced into a small stream.* ▶ **co-ales-cence** /-ˈlesns/ *noun* [U]

**coal-face** /ˈkəʊlfeɪs/ (*also* **face**) *noun* the place deep inside a mine where the coal is cut out of the rock
IDM **at the ˈcoalface** (*BrE*) where the real work is done, not just where people talk about it: *Many of the best ideas come from doctors at the coalface.*

**coal-field** /ˈkəʊlfiːld/ *noun* a large area where there is a lot of coal under the ground

**ˌcoal-ˈfired** *adj.* using coal as fuel: *a coal-fired power station*

**ˈcoal gas** *noun* [U] a mixture of gases produced from coal, that can be used for electricity and heating

**co-ali-tion** 🔊+ **C1** /ˌkəʊəˈlɪʃn/ *noun* [C + sing./pl. v., U] **1** 🔊+ **C1** a government formed by two or more political parties working together: *to form a coalition* ◊ *a two-party coalition* ◊ *a coalition government* ◊ **(in) ~ (with sb)** *The two parties governed in coalition for four years.* ◊ *They didn't rule out coalition with the Social Democrats.* ◊ **~ between A and B** *a coalition between the Socialists and Communists* ⊃ WORDFINDER NOTE *at* PARLIAMENT **2** 🔊+ **C1** a group formed by people from several different groups, especially political ones, agreeing to work together for a particular purpose: *a coalition of environmental and consumer groups*

**ˈcoal mine** (*also* **pit**) *noun* a place underground where coal is dug IDM *see* CANARY

**ˈcoal miner** (*also* **miner**) *noun* a person whose job is digging coal in a coal mine

**ˈcoal tar** *noun* [U] a thick black sticky substance produced when gas is made from coal

**coarse** /kɔːs/; *NAmE* kɔːrs/ *adj.* (**coars-er**, **coars-est**) **1** (of skin or cloth) rough: *coarse hands/linen* OPP **smooth**, **soft 2** consisting of relatively large pieces: *coarse sand/salt/hair* OPP **fine 3** rude and offensive, especially about sex SYN **vulgar**: *coarse manners/laughter* ▶ **coarse-ly** *adv.*: *coarsely chopped onions* (= cut into large pieces) ◊ *He laughed coarsely at her.* **coarse-ness** *noun* [U]

▼ **HOMOPHONES**

**coarse** • **course** /kɔːs/; *NAmE* kɔːrs/

• **coarse** *adj.*: *He wore a coarse woollen cloak.*
• **course** *noun*: *She did a course in economics.*

**ˌcoarse ˈfish** *noun* (*pl.* **coarse fish**) (*BrE*) any fish, except SALMON and TROUT, that lives in rivers and lakes rather than in the sea

**ˌcoarse ˈfishing** *noun* [U] (*BrE*) the sport of catching coarse fish: *to go coarse fishing*

**coars-en** /ˈkɔːsn/; *NAmE* ˈkɔːrsn/ *verb* **1** [I, T] to become or make sth become thicker and/or rougher: *Her hair gradually coarsened as she grew older.* ◊ *~ sth His features had been coarsened by the weather.* **2** [T, I] **~ (sb)** to become or make sb become less polite and often offensive in the way they behave: *The six long years in prison had coarsened him.*

**coast** 🔊 **A2** /kəʊst/ *noun, verb*

■ *noun* 🔊 **A2** [C, U] the land next to or near to the sea or ocean: **~ of sth** *They plan to swim around the coast of Ireland.* ◊ *the southern/northern/eastern/western coast of Spain* ◊ **on the ~** *a town on the south/east coast of England* ◊ **off the ~** *islands off the north/west coast of Scotland* ◊ **along the ~** *We walked along the coast for five miles.* ◊ **from ~ to ~** *He cycled 2 500 miles across Australia from coast to coast.* ◊ *the Atlantic coast* ⊃ WORDFINDER NOTE *at* SEA

WORDFINDER beach, cliff, dune, headland, inlet, promontory, sea, shore, tide

IDM **the ˌcoast is ˈclear** (*informal*) there is no danger of being seen or caught: *As soon as the coast was clear, he climbed in through the window.*

■ *verb* **1** [I] **(+ adv./prep.)** (of a motor vehicle or a bicycle) to move, especially down a hill, without using any power: *The car coasted along until it stopped.* ◊ *She took her feet off the pedals and coasted downhill.* **2** [I] **(+ adv./prep.)** (of

▼ **SYNONYMS**

**coast**
beach • seaside • shore • coastline • sand • seashore

These are all words for the land beside or near to the sea, a river or a lake.

**coast** the land next to or near to the sea or ocean: *a town on the south coast of Georgia* ◊ *The coast road is closed due to bad weather.* NOTE It is nearly always **the coast**, except when it is uncountable: *That's a pretty stretch of coast.*

**beach** an area of sand, or small stones, next to the sea or a lake: *She took the kids to the beach for the day.* ◊ *sandy beaches*

**seaside** (especially *BrE*) an area that is by the sea, especially one where people go for a day or a holiday: *a trip to the seaside* NOTE It is always **the seaside**, except when it is used before a noun: *a seaside resort.* **The seaside** is British English; in American English **seaside** is only used before a noun. Instead of *go to the seaside* you can say *go to the ocean/beach/shore.*

**shore** (especially *NAmE*) an area that is by the ocean or a lake, especially one where people go for a day or a vacation: *Let's go to the shore.* ◊ *The reef runs along the island's north shore.*

**coastline** the land along a coast, especially when you are thinking of its shape or appearance: *California's rugged coastline*

**sand** a large area of sand on a beach: *We went for a walk along the sand.* ◊ *a resort with miles of golden sands*

**the seashore** the land along the edge of the sea or ocean, usually where there is sand and rocks: *He liked to look for shells on the seashore.*

**BEACH OR SEASHORE?**

• **Beach** is usually used to talk about a sandy area next to the sea where people lie in the sun or play, for example when they are on holiday. **Seashore** is used more to talk about the area by the sea in terms of things such as waves, sea shells, rocks, etc, especially where people walk for pleasure.

**PATTERNS**

• **along** the coast/beach/shore/coastline/seashore
• **on** the coast/beach/shore/coastline/sands/seashore
• **at** the coast/beach/seaside/shore/seashore
• **by** the coast/seaside/shore/seashore
• **a(n) rocky/unspoiled** coast/beach/shore/coastline
• **to go to** the coast/beach/seaside/shore/seashore

a vehicle) to move quickly and smoothly, without using much power: *The plane coasted down the runway.* **3** [I] **~ (through/to sth)** to be successful at sth without having to try hard: *He coasted through his final exams.* **4** [I] **~ (along)** (*disapproving*) to put very little effort into sth: *You're just coasting—it's time to work hard now.* **5** [I] (of a ship) to stay close to land while sailing around the coast

**coast·al** ◆+ **C1** /ˈkəʊstl/ *adj.* [usually before noun] of or near a coast: *coastal waters/resorts/scenery* ◇ *a coastal path* (= one that follows the line of the coast) ⇒ compare INLAND

**coast·er** /ˈkəʊstə(r)/ *noun* **1** a small flat object that you put under a glass to protect the top of a table **2** a ship that sails from port to port along a coast ⇒ see also ROLLER COASTER

**coast·guard** /ˈkəʊstɡɑːd; *NAmE* -ɡɑːrd/ *noun* **1** (*usually* **the coastguard**) [sing.] an official organization (in the US a branch of the armed forces) whose job is to watch the sea near a coast in order to help ships and people in trouble, and to stop people from breaking the law: *The coastguard was alerted.* ◇ *They radioed Dover Coastguard.* ◇ *a coastguard station* **2** [C] (*especially BrE*) (*US usually* **coast·guards·man** /ˈkəʊstɡɑːdzmən; *NAmE* -ɡɑːrdz-/ *pl.* **-men** /-mən/) a member of this organization

**coast·line** /ˈkəʊstlaɪn/ *noun* the land along a coast, especially when you are thinking of its shape or appearance: *a rugged/rocky/beautiful coastline* ◇ *to protect the coastline from the oil spillage* ⇒ SYNONYMS at COAST

**coat** ❶ **A1** /kəʊt/ *noun, verb*
■ *noun* **1** 🔑 **A1** a piece of outdoor clothing that is worn over other clothes to keep warm or dry. Coats have SLEEVES (= parts covering the arms) and may be long or short: *to wear a coat* ◇ *to put on/take off your coat* ◇ *a fur coat* ⇒ see also DUFFEL COAT, GREATCOAT, HOUSECOAT, OVERCOAT, PEA COAT, PETTICOAT, RAINCOAT, SPORT COAT, TRENCH COAT **2** (*NAmE*) (*old-fashioned in BrE*) a jacket that is worn as part of a suit ⇒ see also FROCK COAT, MORNING COAT, TAIL-COAT, WAISTCOAT **3** 🔑 **B2** the fur, hair or wool that covers an animal's body: *a dog with a smooth/shaggy coat* ⇒ VISUAL VOCAB page V2 **4** a layer of paint or some other substance that covers a surface: *to give the walls a second coat of paint* ⇒ see also TOPCOAT, UNDERCOAT
**IDM** **cut your ˈcoat acˌcording to your ˈcloth** (*saying*) to do only what you have enough money to do and no more
■ *verb* [often passive] **~ sth (with/in sth)** to cover sth with a layer of a substance: *cookies thickly coated with chocolate* ◇ *A film of dust coated the table.* ⇒ see also SUGAR-COATED

ˈ**coat check** *noun* (*NAmE*) = CLOAKROOM

ˈ**coat hanger** *noun* = HANGER

**coat·ing** /ˈkəʊtɪŋ/ *noun* a thin layer of a substance covering a surface: *a thin coating of chocolate* ◇ *a disk with a magnetic coating*

ˌ**coat of ˈarms** *noun* (*pl.* **coats of arms**) (*also* **arms**) a design or a SHIELD that is a special symbol of a family, city or other organization: *the royal coat of arms*

**coat·room** /ˈkəʊtruːm, -rʊm/ *noun* (*NAmE*) = CLOAKROOM (1)

ˈ**coat stand** *noun* a tall stand for hanging coats and hats on

ˈ**coat-tails** *noun* [pl.]
**IDM** **on sb's ˈcoat-tails** using the success and influence of another person to help yourself become successful: *She got where she is today on her brother's coat-tails.*

**co-ˈauthor** *noun* a person who writes a book or an article with sb else ▶ **co-ˈauthor** *verb* **~ sth** **co-ˈauthorˌship** *noun* [U]

**coax** /kəʊks/ *verb* to persuade sb to do sth by talking to them in a kind and gentle way **SYN** cajole: **~ sb/sth (into doing sth)** *She coaxed the horse into coming a little closer.* ◇ **~ sb/sth (into/out of sth)** *He was coaxed out of retirement to help the failing company.* ◇ **~ sb/sth (+ adv./prep.)** (*figurative*) *She had to coax the car along.* ◇ **~ (sb/sth) + speech** *'Nearly there,' she coaxed.*

**PHRV** **ˌcoax sth ˈout of/ˈfrom sb** to gently persuade sb to do sth or give you sth: *The director coaxed a brilliant performance out of the cast.*

**coax·ing** /ˈkəʊksɪŋ/ *noun* [U] gentle attempts to persuade sb to do sth or to get a machine to start: *No amount of coaxing will make me change my mind.* ▶ **coax·ing** *adj.* **coax·ing·ly** *adv.*

**COB** /ˌsiː əʊ ˈbiː/ *abbr.* close of business (the time when business ends for the day): *We need to come to a decision by COB tomorrow.*

**cob** /kɒb; *NAmE* kɑːb/ *noun* **1** = CORNCOB: *corn on the cob* ⇒ VISUAL VOCAB page V5 **2** a strong horse with short legs **3** (*BrE*) a round LOAF of bread: *a crusty cob*

**co·balt** /ˈkəʊbɔːlt; *NAmE* -bɑːlt/ *noun* [U] **1** (*symb.* **Co**) a chemical element. Cobalt is a hard silver-white metal, often mixed with other metals and used to give a deep blue-green colour to glass. **2** (*also* ˌ**cobalt ˈblue**) a deep blue-green colour

**cob·ber** /ˈkɒbə(r)/ *noun* (*AustralE, NZE, informal*) (used especially by a man addressing another man) a friend

**cob·ble** /ˈkɒbl; *NAmE* ˈkɑːbl/ *verb* **~ sth** (*old-fashioned*) to make or repair shoes
**PHRV** **ˌcobble sth ˈtoˈgether** to produce sth quickly and without great care or effort, so that it can be used but is not perfect: *The essay was cobbled together from some old notes.*

**cob·bled** /ˈkɒbld; *NAmE* ˈkɑːb-/ *adj.* (of streets and roads) having a surface that is made of COBBLES

**cob·bler** /ˈkɒblə(r); *NAmE* ˈkɑːb-/ *noun* **1** [C] a type of fruit or meat PIE with a thick cake or PASTRY layer on top: *peach cobbler* **2** [C] a person who repairs shoes ⇒ compare SHOE-MAKER **3** [U] **cobblers** (*BrE, informal*) ideas, statements or beliefs that you think are silly or not true **SYN** nonsense: *He said it was all a load of cobblers.*

**cob·bles** /ˈkɒblz; *NAmE* ˈkɑːb-/ (*also* **cobble-stones**) *noun* [pl.] small round stones used to make the surfaces of roads, especially in the past

**cobble·stone** /ˈkɒblstəʊn; *NAmE* ˈkɑːb-/ *noun* [usually pl.] a small round stone, used with many others to cover road surfaces, especially in the past ⇒ compare COBBLES ▶ **cobble·stone** *adj.* [only before noun]

**COBOL** /ˈkəʊbɒl; *NAmE* -bɑːl/ *noun* [U] an early computer language used in business programs

**cobra** /ˈkəʊbrə/ *noun* a poisonous snake that can spread the skin at the back of its neck to make itself look bigger. Cobras live in Asia and Africa. ⇒ VISUAL VOCAB page V3

**cob·web** /ˈkɒbweb; *NAmE* ˈkɑːb-/ *noun* a fine net of THREADS made by a spider to catch insects; a single thread of this net (usually used when it is old and covered with dirt): *Thick cobwebs hung in the dusty corners.* ◇ *He brushed a cobweb out of his hair.* ⇒ see also SPIDER'S WEB, WEB ▶ **cob·webbed** /-webd/ *adj.* *cobwebbed corners*
**IDM** **blow/clear the ˈcobwebs away** to help sb have a fresh, lively state of mind again: *A brisk walk should blow the cobwebs away.*

**coca** /ˈkəʊkə/ *noun* [U] a tropical bush whose leaves are used to make the drug COCAINE

**Coca-Cola™** /ˌkəʊkə ˈkəʊlə/ (*also informal* **Coke™**) *noun* **1** [U, C] a popular type of COLA drink **2** [C] a glass, bottle or can of Coca-Cola

**co·caine** /kəʊˈkeɪn/ *noun* (*also informal* **coke**) *noun* [U] a powerful drug that some people take illegally for pleasure and can become ADDICTED to. Doctors sometimes use it as an ANAESTHETIC.

**coc·cyx** /ˈkɒksɪks; *NAmE* ˈkɑːk-/ *noun* (*pl.* **coc·cyxes** *or* **coc·cy·ges** /ˈkɒksɪdʒiːz; *NAmE* ˈkɑːk-/) (*anatomy*) the small bone at the bottom of the SPINE **SYN** tailbone ⇒ VISUAL VOCAB page V1

**coch·lea** /ˈkɒkliə; *NAmE* ˈkəʊk-, ˈkɑːk-/ *noun* (*pl.* **coch·leae** /-kliiː/) (*anatomy*) a small curved tube inside the ear that contains a small part that sends nerve signals to the brain when sounds cause it to VIBRATE

# cock

**cock** /kɒk; NAmE kɑːk/ noun, verb
- noun 1 (BrE) (also **roost·er** NAmE, BrE) [C] an adult male chicken: *The cock crowed.* ⇒ compare HEN 2 [C] (especially in compounds) a male of any other bird: *a cock pheasant* ⇒ see also PEACOCK 3 [C] (*taboo, slang*) a PENIS 4 [C] = STOPCOCK ⇒ see also BALLCOCK 5 [sing.] (BrE, old-fashioned, slang) used as a friendly form of address between men
- verb 1 ~ sth to raise a part of your body so that it is pointing upwards or at an angle: *The dog cocked its leg by every tree on our route* (= in order to URINATE). ◊ *He cocked an inquisitive eyebrow at her.* ◊ *She cocked her head to one side and looked at me.* ◊ *The dog stood listening, its ears cocked.* 2 ~ **a gun/pistol/rifle** to raise the HAMMER on a gun so that it is ready to fire
- IDM **cock an ear/eye at sth/sb** to look at or listen to sth/sb carefully and with a lot of attention **cock a snook at sb/sth** (BrE) to say or do sth that clearly shows you do not respect sb/sth: *to cock a snook at authority*
- PHRV **cock sth↔up** (BrE, slang) to do sth badly, often by making a careless or stupid mistake SYN **bungle**: *I really cocked that exam up!* ◊ *She cocked up all the arrangements for the party.* ⇒ related noun COCK-UP

**cock-a-doodle-doo** /ˌkɒk ə ˌduːdl ˈduː; NAmE ˌkɑːk/ noun the word for the sound that a ROOSTER (= an adult male chicken) makes

**cock-a-hoop** adj. [not usually before noun] ~ **(about/at/over sth)** (*informal*) very pleased and excited, especially about achieving sth

**cock·ama·mie** (also **cock·ama·my**) /ˈkɒkəmeɪmi; NAmE ˈkɑːk-/ adj. (NAmE, informal) (of an idea, a story, etc.) silly; not to be believed

**cock and bull story** noun a story that is unlikely to be true but is used as an explanation or excuse

**cocka·tiel** /ˌkɒkəˈtiːl; NAmE/ noun an Australian PARROT with a grey body and a yellow and orange face

**cocka·too** /ˌkɒkəˈtuː; NAmE ˈkɑːkətuː/ noun (pl. -oos) an Australian bird of the PARROT family, with a large row of feathers (called a CREST) standing up on its head

**cock·cha·fer** /ˈkɒktʃeɪfə(r); NAmE ˈkɑːk-/ (also **May bug**) noun a large brown insect that flies and makes a loud noise in early evening in summer

**cocked hat** noun IDM see KNOCK v.

**cock·er** /ˈkɒkə(r); NAmE ˈkɑːk-/ (also **cocker spaniel**) noun a small SPANIEL (= type of dog) with soft hair

**cock·erel** /ˈkɒkərəl; NAmE/ noun a young male chicken

**cock·eyed** /ˈkɒkaɪd; NAmE ˈkɑːk-/ adj. (*informal*) 1 not level or straight SYN **crooked**: *Doesn't that picture look cockeyed to you?* 2 not practical; not likely to succeed: *a cock-eyed scheme to make people use less water*

**cock·fight** /ˈkɒkfaɪt; NAmE ˈkɑːk-/ noun a fight between two adult male chickens, watched as a sport and illegal in many countries ▸ **cock·fight·ing** noun [U]

**cockle** /ˈkɒkl; NAmE ˈkɑːkl/ noun a small SHELLFISH that can be eaten IDM see WARM v.

**cockle-shell** /ˈkɒklʃel; NAmE ˈkɑːkl-/ noun 1 the shell of a cockle 2 a small light boat

**cock·ney** /ˈkɒkni; NAmE ˈkɑːk-/ noun 1 [C] a person from the East End of London 2 [U] the way of speaking that is typical of cockneys: *a cockney accent*

**cock·pit** /ˈkɒkpɪt; NAmE ˈkɑːk-/ noun the area in a plane, boat or racing car where the pilot or driver sits

**cock·roach** /ˈkɒkrəʊtʃ; NAmE ˈkɑːk-/ (also NAmE, informal **roach**) noun a large brown insect with wings, that lives in houses, especially where there is dirt

**cock·sucker** /ˈkɒksʌkə(r); NAmE ˈkɑːk-/ noun (taboo, slang) an offensive word used to show a great lack of respect for sb, usually a man

**cock·sure** /ˌkɒkˈʃʊə(r), -ˈʃɔː(r); NAmE ˌkɑːkˈʃʊr/ adj. (old-fashioned, informal) confident in a way that is annoying to other people and that they might find offensive

**cock·tail** /ˈkɒkteɪl; NAmE ˈkɑːk-/ noun 1 [C] a drink usually made from a mixture of one or more SPIRITS (= strong alcoholic drinks) and fruit juice. It can also be made without alcohol: *a cocktail bar/cabinet/lounge/shaker* 2 [C, U] a dish of small pieces of food, usually served cold: *a prawn/shrimp cocktail* ◊ *fruit cocktail* 3 [C] a mixture of different substances or elements, often ones that do not mix together well: *a lethal cocktail of drugs* ⇒ see also MOLOTOV COCKTAIL

**cocktail dress** noun a dress that is suitable for formal social occasions

**cocktail party** noun a formal social occasion, usually in the early evening, when people drink cocktails or other alcoholic drinks

**cocktail stick** noun (BrE) a small, sharp piece of wood on which small pieces of food are placed, for guests to eat at parties

**cock-teaser** (also **cock-tease**, **prick-teaser**, **prick-tease**) noun (taboo, slang) an offensive word used to describe a woman who makes a man think she will have sex with him when she will not

**cock-up** noun (BrE, informal) a mistake that causes sth to be a failure; sth that has not been successful because it was badly organized: *There's been a bit of a cock-up over the travel arrangements.*

**cocky** /ˈkɒki; NAmE ˈkɑːki/ adj. (**cock·ier**, **cocki·est**) (*informal*) too confident about yourself in a way that annoys other people ▸ **cocki·ness** noun [U]

**cocoa** /ˈkəʊkəʊ; NAmE/ noun 1 [U] dark brown powder made from the seeds (called **cocoa beans**) of a tropical tree 2 [U] a hot drink made by mixing cocoa powder with milk and/or water and usually sugar: *a mug of cocoa* 3 [C] a cup of cocoa ⇒ compare CHOCOLATE, DRINKING CHOCOLATE

**cocoa butter** noun [U] fat that is obtained from cocoa beans and is used in making chocolate and COSMETICS

**co·co·nut** /ˈkəʊkənʌt; NAmE/ noun 1 [C] the large nut of a tropical tree called a **coconut palm**. It grows inside a hard shell and contains a soft white substance that can be eaten and juice that can be drunk. ⇒ VISUAL VOCAB page V4 2 [U] the soft white substance inside a coconut, used in cooking, making soap, etc: *desiccated coconut* ◊ *coconut biscuits/cookies* ◊ *coconut oil*

**coconut butter** noun (NAmE) a solid substance inside coconuts that is used to make soap, CANDLES, etc.

**co·coon** /kəˈkuːn; NAmE/ noun, verb
- noun 1 a cover or case of silk THREADS that some insects make to protect themselves before they become adults 2 a layer of something soft that wraps all around a person or thing and forms a protection: (figurative) *the cocoon of a caring family*
- verb [usually passive] 1 [T] to protect sb/sth by surrounding them or it completely with sth: **(be) cocooned (in sth)** *We were warm and safe, cocooned in our sleeping bags.* 2 [I] (NAmE) to spend more of your free time at home and less time going out and doing things with other people

**coco·yam** /ˈkəʊkəʊjæm; NAmE/ noun [C, U] (WAfrE) a plant whose roots can be cooked and eaten or made into flour: *roasted cocoyam* ⇒ see also FUFU

**COD** /ˌsiː əʊ ˈdiː/ abbr. cash on delivery or (in American English) collect on delivery (payment for goods will be made when the goods are delivered)

**cod** /kɒd; NAmE kɑːd/ noun, adj.
- noun [C, U] (pl. cod) (also **cod·fish**) a large sea fish that is white inside and used for food: *fishing for cod* ◊ *cod fillets*
- adj. [only before noun] (BrE, informal) not real or what sb claims it is: *a cod American accent* ◊ *cod psychology*

**coda** /ˈkəʊdə; NAmE/ noun the final passage of a piece of music: (figurative) *The final two months were a miserable coda to the President's first period in office.*

**cod·dle** /ˈkɒdl; NAmE ˈkɑːdl/ verb 1 ~ **sb** (often disapproving) to treat sb with too much care and attention ⇒ compare MOLLYCODDLE 2 ~ **sth** to cook eggs in water slightly below boiling point

# coffee

**code** /kəʊd/ noun, verb
- **noun 1** [C, U] (often in compounds) a system of words, letters, numbers or symbols that represent a message or record information secretly or in a shorter form: *to break/crack a code* (= to understand and read the message) ◇ *in~ It's written in code.* ◇ *In the event of the machine not operating correctly, an error code will appear.* ◇ *Tap your code number into the machine.* ⇒ see also AREA CODE, BARCODE, COLOUR CODE, GENETIC CODE, MORSE CODE, POSTCODE, SORT CODE, QR CODE™, ZIP CODE **2** [C] (*BrE*) = DIALLING CODE: *There are three codes for London.* **3** [U] (*computing*) a system of computer programming instructions: *to write computer code* ◇ *malicious code that will infect your computer* ◇ *You only need to add a few lines of code.* ⇒ see also MACHINE CODE, SOURCE CODE ⇒ WORD-FINDER NOTE at PROGRAM **4** [C] a set of moral principles or rules of behaviour that are generally accepted by society or a social group: *The school enforces a strict code of conduct.* ◇ *a code of ethics* ◇ *She lives by her own moral code.* **5** [C] a system of laws or written rules that state how people in an institution or a country should behave: *the penal code* ⇒ see also DRESS CODE, HIGHWAY CODE
- **verb 1** [T] ~ sth to write or print words, letters, numbers, etc. on sth so that you know what it is, what group it belongs to, etc: *Each order is coded separately.* **2** [T] ~ sth to put a message into code so that it can only be understood by a few people **3** [T, I] ~ (sth) (*computing*) to write a computer program by putting one system of numbers, words and symbols into another system ⇒ see also HARD-CODE ⇒ compare ENCODE (2)

**coded** /ˈkəʊdɪd/ adj. **1** [only before noun] a **coded** message or **coded** information is written or sent using a special system of words, letters, numbers, etc. that can only be understood by a few other people or by a computer: *a coded warning of a bomb at the airport* ⇒ see also COLOUR-CODED **2** expressed in an indirect way: *There was coded criticism of the government from some party members.*

**co·deine** /ˈkəʊdiːn/ noun [U] a drug used to reduce pain

**'code name** noun a name used for a person or thing in order to keep the real name secret ▸ **code-named** adj. [not before noun]: *a drug investigation, code-named Snoopy*

**code of 'practice** noun (pl. **codes of practice**) a set of standards that members of a particular profession agree to follow in their work

**co·depend·ency** /ˌkəʊdɪˈpendənsi/ noun [U] (*psychology*) a situation in which two people have a close relationship in which they rely too much on each other emotionally, especially when one person is caring for the other one ▸ **co-depend·ent** adj., noun

**'code-sharing** noun [U] (*specialist*) an agreement between two or more airlines to carry each other's passengers and use their own set of letters and numbers for flights provided by another airline

**'code word** noun ~ (for sth) a word or phrase with a secret meaning that is used instead of the usual name for sth: *They were asked to bring 'cigars' to the meeting, a code word for guns.*

**codex** /ˈkəʊdeks/ noun (pl. **co·di·ces** /ˈkəʊdɪsiːz/; *BrE* also ˈkɒd-/; *NAmE* also ˈkɑːd-/ or **codexes**) **1** an ancient text in the form of a book **2** an official list of medicines or chemicals

**cod·fish** /ˈkɒdfɪʃ/; *NAmE* ˈkɑːd-/ (pl. **cod·fish**) = COD

**cod·ger** /ˈkɒdʒə(r)/; *NAmE* ˈkɑːdʒ-/ noun *old ~* (*informal*) an informal way of referring to an old man that shows that you do not respect him

**co·di·cil** /ˈkəʊdɪsɪl/; *NAmE* ˈkɑːdəsl/ noun (*law*) an instruction that is added later to a WILL, usually to change a part of it

**co·dify** /ˈkəʊdɪfaɪ/; *NAmE* ˈkɑːd-/ verb (**co·di·fies**, **co·di·fy·ing**, **co·di·fied**, **co·di·fied**) ~ sth (*specialist*) to arrange laws, rules, etc. into a system ▸ **co·difi·ca·tion** /ˌkəʊdɪfɪˈkeɪʃn/; *NAmE* ˌkɑːd-/ noun [U]

**'cod liver 'oil** noun [U] a thick yellow oil from the LIVER of COD (= a type of fish), containing a lot of vitamins A and D and often given as a medicine

**cod·piece** /ˈkɒdpiːs/; *NAmE* ˈkɑːd-/ noun a piece of cloth, usually decorated, attached to a man's lower garment and covering his GENITALS, worn in Europe in the fifteenth and sixteenth centuries

**co-driver** noun **1** a person who shares the job of driving a vehicle with another **2** (in RALLY driving) a person who sits next to the driver to give directions

**cods·wal·lop** /ˈkɒdzwɒləp/; *NAmE* ˈkɑːdzwɑːl-/ noun [U] (*BrE, old-fashioned, informal*) statements or beliefs that you think are silly or not true **SYN** nonsense: *I've never heard such a load of old codswallop in my life.*

**coed** /ˌkəʊˈed/ noun (*NAmE, old-fashioned*) a female student at a co-educational school or college

**co-edu'cation·al** (also *informal* **coed**) adj. (of a school or an educational system) where girls and boys are taught together ▸ **co-edu'cation** noun [U]

**co·ef·fi·cient** /ˌkəʊɪˈfɪʃnt/ noun **1** (*mathematics*) a number that is placed before another quantity and that multiplies it, for example 3 in the quantity 3x **2** (*physics*) a number that measures a particular property (= characteristic) of a substance: *the coefficient of friction*

**coela·canth** /ˈsiːləkænθ/ noun a large fish found mainly in the seas near Madagascar. It was thought to be EXTINCT until one was discovered in 1938.

**coel·iac** (*BrE*) (*NAmE* **cel·iac**) /ˈsiːliæk/ adj., noun
- **adj.** having or connected with COELIAC DISEASE, a condition in which food containing GLUTEN causes sb to become ill: *coeliac children/patients*
- **noun** a person who suffers from COELIAC DISEASE, a condition in which food containing GLUTEN causes them to become ill

**'coeliac disease** (*BrE*) (*NAmE* **celiac disease**) noun [U] a disease in which sb cannot DIGEST some types of food (= break them down in their body) because their body is very sensitive to GLUTEN (= a substance that is found in flour, especially WHEAT flour)

**co·erce** /kəʊˈɜːs/; *NAmE* -ˈɜːrs/ verb (*formal*) to force sb to do sth by using threats: ~ sb into (doing) sth *They were coerced into negotiating a settlement.* ◇ ~ sb to do sth *They tried to coerce him to sign away his rights.*

**co·er·cion** /kəʊˈɜːʃn/; *NAmE* -ˈɜːrʒn/ noun [U] (*formal*) the action of making sb do sth that they do not want to do, using force or threatening to use force: *He claimed he had only acted under coercion.*

**co·er·cive** /kəʊˈɜːsɪv/; *NAmE* -ˈɜːrs-/ adj. (*formal*) using force or the threat of force: *coercive measures/powers*

**co·eval** /ˌkəʊˈiːvl/ adj. ~ (with sth) (*formal*) (of two or more things) being the same age or having the same date of origin: *The industry is coeval with the construction of the first railways.*

**co·ex·ist** /ˌkəʊɪɡˈzɪst/ verb [I] ~(with sb/sth) (*formal*) to exist together in the same place or at the same time, especially in a peaceful way: *The illness frequently coexists with other chronic diseases.* ◇ *English speakers now coexist peacefully with their Spanish-speaking neighbours.* ◇ *Different traditions coexist successfully side by side.*

**co·ex·ist·ence** /ˌkəʊɪɡˈzɪstəns/ noun [U] the state of being together in the same place at the same time: *to live in uneasy/peaceful coexistence within one nation*

**C of E** /ˌsiː əv ˈiː/ abbr. Church of England ⇒ see also CE

**cof·fee** /ˈkɒfi/; *NAmE* ˈkɔːfi/ noun **1** [U, C] the ROASTED seeds (called **'coffee beans**) of a tropical bush; a powder made from them: *ground/real/instant coffee* ◇ *decaffeinated coffee* ◇ *a jar of coffee* ◇ *a blend of Brazilian and Colombian coffees* **2** [U] a hot drink made from coffee powder and boiling water. It may be drunk with milk and/or sugar added: *to drink/sip coffee* ◇ *Do you want to have coffee with me sometime?* ◇ *black/white coffee* (= without/with milk) ◇ *a cup of coffee* ◇ *a coffee cup/mug* ⇒ see also IRISH COFFEE, TURKISH COFFEE **3** [C] a cup of coffee: *Do you want to*

## coffee bar

*go and get a coffee?* **4** [U] the colour of coffee mixed with milk; light brown **IDM** see **WAKE** v.

**'coffee bar** *noun* **1** (*BrE*) (*also* **'coffee shop** *NAmE, BrE*) a place, sometimes in a store, train station, etc., where you can buy coffee, tea, other drinks without alcohol and sometimes simple meals **2** (*NAmE*) a small restaurant that sells special sorts of coffee and cakes

**'coffee break** *noun* a short period of rest when you stop working and drink coffee: *to have a coffee break*

**'coffee cake** *noun* (*NAmE*) a small cake with melted sugar on top that people eat with coffee

**'coffee house** *noun* **1** a restaurant serving coffee, etc., especially one of a type popular in Britain in the eighteenth century or one in a city in Central Europe: *the coffee houses of Vienna* **2** (*NAmE*) a restaurant serving coffee, etc. where people go to listen to music, poetry, etc.

**'coffee machine** *noun* **1** = COFFEE MAKER **2** a machine that you put coins in to get a cup of coffee

**'coffee maker** (*also* **'coffee machine**) *noun* a small machine for making cups of coffee

**'coffee morning** *noun* (*BrE*) a social event held in the morning, often at a person's house, where money is usually given to help a charity

**'coffee shop** *noun* a small restaurant, often in a store, hotel, etc., where coffee, tea, other drinks without alcohol and simple food are served

**'coffee table** *noun* a small low table for putting magazines, cups, etc. on, usually in front of a SOFA

**'coffee-table book** *noun* a large expensive book containing many pictures or photographs that is designed for people to look through rather than to read carefully

**cof·fer** /ˈkɒfə(r); *NAmE* ˈkɔːf-/ *noun* **1** [C] a large strong box, used in the past for storing money or valuable objects **2** (*also* **coffers** [pl.]) a way of referring to the money that a government, an organization, etc. has available to spend: *The nation's coffers are empty.*

**cof·fin** /ˈkɒfɪn; *NAmE* ˈkɔːf-/ (*especially BrE*) (*NAmE usually* **cas·ket**) *noun* a box in which a dead body is buried or CREMATED ⇨ WORDFINDER NOTE at DIE **IDM** see **NAIL** *n.*

**cog** /kɒɡ; *NAmE* kɑːɡ/ *noun* **1** one of a series of teeth on the edge of a wheel that fit between the teeth on the next wheel and cause it to move ⇨ picture at COGWHEEL **2** = COGWHEEL
**IDM** a ˌcog in the maˈchine/ˈwheel (*informal*) a person who is a small part of a large organization

**co·gent** /ˈkəʊdʒənt/ *adj.* (*formal*) strongly and clearly expressed in a way that influences what people believe **SYN** convincing: *She put forward some cogent reasons for abandoning the plan.* ▶ **co·gency** /-dʒənsi/ *noun* [U] **co·gent·ly** *adv.*

**cogi·tate** /ˈkɒdʒɪteɪt/ *NAmE* ˈkɑːdʒ-/ *verb* [I] ~ (about/on sth) (*formal*) to think carefully about sth ▶ **cogi·ta·tion** /ˌkɒdʒɪˈteɪʃn/ *NAmE* ˌkɑːdʒ-/ *noun* [U, C]

**co·gnac** /ˈkɒnjæk; *NAmE* ˈkoʊn-/ *noun* **1** [U, C] a type of fine BRANDY made in western France **2** [C] a glass of cognac

**cog·nate** /ˈkɒɡneɪt; *NAmE* ˈkɑːɡ-/ *adj., noun*
■ *adj.* **1** (*linguistics*) having the same origin as another word or language: *'Haus' in German is cognate with 'house' in English.* ◊ *German and Dutch are cognate languages.* **2** (*formal*) related in some way and therefore similar: *a cognate development*
■ *noun* (*linguistics*) a word that has the same origin as another: *'Haus' and 'house' are cognates.*

**cog·ni·tion** /kɒɡˈnɪʃn; *NAmE* kɑːɡ-/ *noun* [U] (*psychology*) the process by which knowledge and understanding is developed in the mind

**cog·ni·tive** /ˈkɒɡnətɪv; *NAmE* ˈkɑːɡ-/ *adj.* [usually before noun] connected with mental processes of understanding: *a child's cognitive development* ◊ *cognitive psychology*

ˌcognitive beˈhavioural ˈtherapy (*US* ˌcognitive beˈhavioral ˈtherapy) *noun* [U] = CBT

ˌcognitive ˈdissonance *noun* [U] (*psychology*) the state of having thoughts that are not consistent, especially relating to beliefs, behaviour and attitudes

**cog·ni·zance** (*BrE also* **-isance**) /ˈkɒɡnɪzəns; *NAmE* ˈkɑːɡ-/ *noun* [U] (*formal*) knowledge or understanding of sth ▶ **cog·ni·zant, -isant** /-zənt/ *adj.* [not before noun]: *cognizant of the importance of the case*
**IDM** ˌtake ˈcognizance of sth (*law*) to understand or consider sth; to take notice of sth

**co·gnos·centi** /ˌkɒnjəˈʃenti; *NAmE* ˌkɑːn-/ *noun* [pl.] **the cognoscenti** (*from Italian, formal*) people with a lot of knowledge about a particular subject

**cog·wheel** /ˈkɒɡwiːl; *NAmE* ˈkɑːɡ-/ (*also* **cog**) *noun* a wheel with a series of teeth on the edge that fit between the teeth on the next wheel and cause it to move

**co·habit** /kəʊˈhæbɪt/ *verb* [I] ~ (with sb) (*formal*) (usually of a man and a woman) to live together and have a sexual relationship without being married ▶ **co·hab·it·ation** /ˌkəʊhæbɪˈteɪʃn/ *noun* [U]

**co·here** /kəʊˈhɪə(r); *NAmE* -ˈhɪr/ *verb* (*formal*) **1** [I] ~ (with sth) (of different ideas, arguments, sentences, etc.) to have a clear logical connection so that together they make a whole: *This view does not cohere with their other beliefs.* **2** [I] (of people) to work closely together: *It can be difficult to get a group of people to cohere.*

**co·her·ence** /kəʊˈhɪərəns; *NAmE* -ˈhɪr-/ *noun* [U, sing.] (*formal*) the situation in which all the parts of sth fit together well: *The points you make are fine, but the whole essay lacks coherence.* **OPP** incoherence

**co·her·ent** /kəʊˈhɪərənt; *NAmE* -ˈhɪr-/ *adj.* **1** (of ideas, thoughts, arguments, etc.) logical and well organized; easy to understand and clear: *a coherent narrative/account/explanation* ◊ *a coherent policy for the transport system* **2** (of a person) able to talk and express yourself clearly: *She only became coherent again two hours after the attack.* **OPP** incoherent ▶ **co·her·ent·ly** *adv.*

**co·he·sion** /kəʊˈhiːʒn/ *noun* [U] **1** (*formal*) the act or state of keeping together **SYN** unity: *the cohesion of the nuclear family* ◊ *social/political/economic cohesion* **2** (*physics, chemistry*) the force causing MOLECULES of the same substance to stick together

**co·he·sive** /kəʊˈhiːsɪv/ *adj.* (*formal*) **1** forming a united whole: *a cohesive group* **2** causing people or things to become united: *the cohesive power of shared suffering* ◊ *well-structured sentences illustrating the use of cohesive markers such as 'nevertheless' and 'however'* ▶ **co·he·sive·ness** *noun* [U]

**co·hort** /ˈkəʊhɔːt; *NAmE* -hɔːrt/ *noun* [C + sing./pl. v.] **1** (*specialist*) a group of people who share a common feature or aspect of behaviour: *the 1999 birth cohort* (= all those born in 1999) **2** (*disapproving*) a member of a group of people who support another person: *Robinson and his cohorts were soon ejected from the hall.*

**coif·fure** /kwɑːˈfjʊə(r); *NAmE* -ˈfjʊr/ *noun* (*from French, formal or humorous*) the way in which a person's hair is arranged **SYN** hairstyle

**coil** /kɔɪl/ *verb, noun*
■ *verb* [I, T] to wind sth into a series of circles; to make sth do this: *~ up The snake coiled up, ready to strike.* ◊ *~ round, around, etc. sth Mist coiled around the tops of the hills.* ◊ *~ sth (+ adv./prep.) to coil a rope into a loop* ◊ *Her hair was coiled on top of her head.* ◊ *a coiled spring* ⇨ picture at KNOT
■ *noun* **1** a series of circles formed by winding up a length of rope, wire, etc: *a coil of wire* **2** one circle of rope, wire, etc. in a series: *Shake the rope and let the coils unwind.* ◊ *a snake's coils* **3** a length of wire, wound into circles, that can carry electricity **4** = IUD

**coin** /kɔɪn/ noun, verb
- **noun 1** [C] a small flat piece of metal used as money: *gold coins* ⇨ picture at MONEY **2** [U] money made of metal: *notes and coin* IDM SEE SIDE n., TWO
- **verb 1** ~ sth to invent a new word or phrase that other people then begin to use: *The term 'cardboard city' was coined to describe communities of homeless people living in cardboard boxes.* **2** ~ sth to make coins out of metal
  IDM **be 'coining it (in) | be coining 'money** (BrE, informal) to earn a lot of money quickly or easily SYN **rake in** to **coin a 'phrase 1** used to introduce a well-known expression that you have changed slightly in order to be funny **2** used to show that you are aware that you are using an expression that is not new: *Oh well, no news is good news, to coin a phrase.*

**coin·age** /ˈkɔɪnɪdʒ/ noun **1** [U] the coins used in a particular place or at a particular time; coins of a particular type: *Roman coinage ◇ gold/silver/bronze coinage* **2** [U] the system of money used in a particular country: *decimal coinage* **3** [C, U] a word or phrase that has been invented recently; the process of inventing a word or phrase: *new coinages*

**co·in·cide** /ˌkəʊɪnˈsaɪd/ verb **1** [I] (of two or more events) to take place at the same time: *It's a pity our trips to New York don't coincide.* ◇ ~ **with sth** *The strike was timed to coincide with the party conference.* **2** [I] (formal) (of ideas, opinions, etc.) to be the same or very similar: *The interests of employers and employees do not always coincide.* ◇ ~ **with sth** *Her story coincided exactly with her brother's.* **3** [I] (formal) (of objects or places) to meet; to share the same space: *At this point the two paths coincide briefly.* ◇ ~ **with sth** *The present position of the house coincides with that of an earlier dwelling.*

**co·in·ci·dence** /kəʊˈɪnsɪdəns/ noun **1** [C, U] the fact of two things happening at the same time by chance, in a surprising way: *a strange/an extraordinary/a remarkable coincidence* ◇ *What a coincidence! I wasn't expecting to see you here.* ◇ *It's not a coincidence that none of the directors are women* (= it did not happen by chance). ◇ *By (sheer) coincidence, I met the person we'd been discussing the next day.* ⇨ SYNONYMS at LUCK ⇨ WORDFINDER

▼ SYNONYMS
**cold**
cool • freezing • chilly • lukewarm • tepid
These words all describe sb/sth that has a low temperature.

**cold** having a temperature that is lower than usual or lower than the human body: (of food or drink) not heated; cooled after being cooked: *I'm cold. Turn the heating up. ◇ Outside it was bitterly cold. ◇ a cold wind ◇ hot and cold water ◇ It's cold chicken for lunch.*

**cool** (often approving) fairly cold, especially in a pleasant way: *a long cool drink ◇ We found a cool place to sit.*

**freezing** extremely cold; having a temperature below 0° Celsius: *It's absolutely freezing outside. ◇ I'm freezing!*

**chilly** (rather informal) too cold to be comfortable: *Bring a coat. It might turn chilly later.*

**lukewarm** (often disapproving) slightly warm, sometimes in an unpleasant way: *Her coffee was now lukewarm.*

**tepid** (often disapproving) slightly warm, sometimes in an unpleasant way: *a jug of tepid water*

LUKEWARM OR TEPID?
- There is really no difference in meaning or use between these words.

PATTERNS
- to feel/get cold/cool/chilly
- cold/cool/freezing/chilly air/weather
- a cold/cool/freezing/chilly wind
- cold/cool/freezing/lukewarm/tepid water
- a cold/cool/lukewarm/tepid shower/bath
- cold/lukewarm/tepid tea/coffee/food
- a cold/cool drink
- It's cold/chilly/freezing outside.

---

NOTE at LUCK **2** [sing.] (formal) the fact of things being present at the same time: *the coincidence of inflation and unemployment* **3** [sing.] (formal) the fact of two or more opinions, etc. being the same: *a coincidence of interests between the two partners*

**co·in·ci·dent** /kəʊˈɪnsɪdənt/ adj. ~ **(with sth)** (formal) happening in the same place or at the same time

**co·in·ci·dent·al** /kəʊˌɪnsɪˈdentl/ adj. [not usually before noun] happening by chance; not planned: *I suppose your presence here today is not entirely coincidental.* ◇ *It's purely coincidental that we both chose to call our daughters Emma.* ▶ **co·in·ci·dent·al·ly** /-təli/ adv.: *Coincidentally, they had both studied in Paris.*

**coir** /ˈkɔɪə(r)/ noun [U] stiff FIBRES (= strings) from the HUSK (= outer layer) of COCONUTS, used for making ropes, for covering floors, etc.

**co·itus** /ˈkɔɪtəs, ˈkəʊɪ-; NAmE ˈkəʊɪ-/ noun [U] (medical or formal) SEXUAL INTERCOURSE (= the physical activity of sex)

**Coke™** /kəʊk/ noun [C, U] (informal) = COCA-COLA™: *Can I have a Diet Coke?*

**coke** /kəʊk/ noun [U] **1** (informal) = COCAINE **2** a black substance that is produced from coal and burnt to provide heat

**Col.** abbr. (in writing) COLONEL: *Col. Stewart*

**col** /kɒl; NAmE kɑːl/ noun (specialist) a low point between two higher points in a mountain range, typically providing a PASS (= road or way) through the mountains

**col.** abbr. (in writing) COLUMN

**cola** /ˈkəʊlə/ noun **1** [U, C] a sweet brown, FIZZY drink (= with bubbles) that does not contain alcohol. Its taste comes from the seeds of a West African tree (the '**cola tree**) and other substances. **2** [C] a glass, can or bottle of cola ⇨ see also COCA-COLA™, COKE™

**col·an·der** /ˈkʌləndə(r); NAmE ˈkɑːl-/ noun a metal or plastic bowl with a lot of small holes in it, used for DRAINING water from vegetables, etc. after washing or cooking

'**cola nut** (also **kola nut** /ˈkəʊlə nʌt/) noun the seed of the cola tree, which can be CHEWED (= bitten many times but not eaten) or made into a drink

**cold** /kəʊld/ adj., noun, adv.
- **adj.** (cold·er, cold·est)
- • LOW TEMPERATURE **1** having a lower than usual temperature; having a temperature lower than the human body: *I'm cold. Turn the heating up.* ◇ *to feel cold* ◇ *cold weather/temperatures/air* ◇ *a cold day/night/winter/wind* ◇ *a cold room/house* ◇ *Hot and cold water in every room* ◇ *I was thoroughly cold and wet now.* ◇ *It's freezing cold. Hurry up—your dinner's getting cold* ◇ *a bitterly cold morning* ⇨ see also ICE-COLD, STONE COLD
- • FOOD/DRINK **2** not heated; cooled after being cooked: *a cold drink* ◇ *Hot and cold food is available in the cafeteria.* ◇ *Serve hot or cold.* ⇨ see also COLD CUTS
- • NOT FRIENDLY **3** (of a person) without emotion; not friendly: *to give sb a cold look/stare* ◇ *Her manner was cold and distant.* ◇ *He was staring at her with cold eyes.*
- • LIGHT/COLOURS **4** seeming to lack any warm feeling, in an unpleasant way: *clear cold light* ◇ *cold grey skies*
- • ROUTE **5** not easy to find: *The police followed the robbers to the airport but then the trail went cold.*
- • IN GAMES **6** used in children's games to say that the person playing is not close to finding a person or thing, or to guessing the correct answer
- • UNCONSCIOUS **7** out ~ [not before noun] (informal) unconscious: *He was knocked out cold in the second round.*
- • FACTS **8** the ~ facts/truth facts with nothing added to make them more interesting or pleasant ⇨ see also COLDLY, COLDNESS
  IDM ▶ **a cold 'fish** a person who seems unfriendly and without strong emotions **get/have cold 'feet** (informal) to suddenly become nervous about doing sth that you had planned to do: *He was going to ask her but he got cold feet and said nothing.* **give sb the cold 'shoulder** (informal) to treat sb in a way that is not friendly ⇨ see also COLD-

# cold-blooded

SHOULDER **in cold ˈblood** acting in a way that is deliberately cruel: *to kill sb in cold blood* **in the cold light of day** when you have had time to think calmly about sth; in the morning when things are clearer: *These things always look different in the cold light of day.* **leave sb ˈcold** to fail to affect or interest sb: *Most modern art leaves me cold.* **pour/throw cold ˈwater on sth** to give reasons for not being in favour of sth; to criticize sth ⊃ more at BLOOD *n.*, BLOW *v.*, HOT *adj.*

■ *noun*
• ILLNESS **1** [C] (*also less frequent the* **common ˈcold** [sing.]) a common illness that affects the nose and/or throat, making you COUGH, SNEEZE, etc: *I've got a cold.* ◇ *to have a cold* ◇ *a bad/heavy/slight/nasty cold* ◇ *to catch (a) cold*
• LOW TEMPERATURE **2** [U] a lack of heat or warm air; a low temperature, especially in the atmosphere: *He shivered with cold.* ◇ **in the~** *Don't stand outside in the cold.* ◇ *She doesn't seem to feel the cold.*
IDM **come in from the ˈcold** to become accepted or included in a group, etc. after a period of being outside it **leave sb out in the ˈcold** to not include sb in a group or an activity ⊃ more at CATCH *v.*
■ *adv.* **1** (*NAmE*) suddenly and completely: *His final request stopped her cold.* **2** without preparing: *I can't just walk in there cold and give a speech.*

**cold-ˈblooded** *adj.* **1** (of people and their actions) showing no feelings or sympathy for other people: *a cold-blooded killer* **2** (*biology*) (of animals, for example fish or snakes) having a body temperature that depends on the temperature of the surrounding air or water ⊃ compare WARM-BLOODED ▶ **cold-ˈblooded·ly** *adv.*

**cold-ˈcall** *verb* ~sb to phone sb that you do not know, in order to sell them sth ▶ **ˈcold call** *noun*

**cold-ˈcalling** *noun* [U] the practice of phoning sb that you do not know, in order to sell them sth ⊃ WORDFINDER NOTE at ADVERTISE

**ˈcold case** *noun* a crime that has not been solved and remains open to investigation if new evidence is found

**ˌcold ˈcash** (*NAmE*) (*BrE* **ˌhard ˈcash**) *noun* [U] money, especially in the form of coins and notes, that you can spend

**ˌcold ˈcomfort** *noun* [U] the fact that sth that would normally be good does not make you happy because the whole situation is bad: *A small drop in the inflation rate was cold comfort for the millions without a job.*

**ˈcold cream** *noun* [U] a thick white cream that people use for cleaning their face or making their skin soft

**ˈcold cuts** *noun* [pl.] (*especially NAmE*) slices of cooked meat that are served cold

**ˈcold frame** (*also* **frame**) *noun* a small wooden or metal frame covered with glass that you grow seeds or small plants in to protect them from cold weather ⊃ picture at FRAME

**ˌcold ˈfusion** *noun* [U] (*physics*) NUCLEAR FUSION that takes place at or near room temperature

**cold-ˈhearted** *adj.* not showing any love or sympathy for other people; unkind ⊃ compare WARM-HEARTED

**cold·ly** /ˈkəʊldli/ *adv.* without any emotion or warm feelings; in a way that is unfriendly

**cold·ness** /ˈkəʊldnəs/ *noun* [U] **1** the lack of warm feelings; unfriendly behaviour: *She was hurt by the coldness in his voice.* **2** the state of being cold: *the icy coldness of the water* OPP warmth

**cold-ˈshoulder** *verb* ~sb to treat sb in an unfriendly way ⊃ see also GIVE SB THE COLD SHOULDER at COLD *adj.*

**ˈcold snap** *noun* (*informal*) a sudden short period of very cold weather

**ˈcold sore** (*NAmE also* **ˈfever blister**) *noun* a small painful spot on the lips or inside the mouth that is caused by a virus

**ˌcold ˈstorage** *noun* [U] a place where food, etc. can be kept fresh or frozen until it is needed; the storing of sth in such a place: (*figurative*) *I've had to put my plans into cold storage* (= I've decided not to carry them out immediately but to keep them for later).

**ˈcold store** *noun* a room where food, etc. can be kept at a low temperature in order to keep it in good condition

**ˌcold ˈsweat** *noun* [usually sing.] a state when you have SWEAT on your face or body but still feel cold, usually because you are very frightened or anxious: *to break out into a cold sweat* ◇ *I woke up in a cold sweat about the interview.*

**ˌcold ˈturkey** *noun* [U] the unpleasant state that drug ADDICTS experience when they suddenly stop taking a drug; a way of treating drug ADDICTS that makes them experience this state ▶ **ˌcold ˈturkey** *adv.*: *I quit smoking cold turkey.*

**ˌcold ˈwar** *noun* [sing., U] (*often* **Cold War**) a relationship between two countries who are not friendly but are not actually fighting each other, usually used about the situation between the US and the Soviet Union after the Second World War

**cole·slaw** /ˈkəʊlslɔː/ (*also* **slaw** *especially in NAmE*) *noun* [U] pieces of raw CABBAGE, carrot, onion, etc., mixed with MAYONNAISE and eaten with meat or salads

**coley** /ˈkəʊli/ *noun* [C, U] (*pl.* **coley** *or* **coleys**) a N Atlantic fish that is used for food

**colic** /ˈkɒlɪk; *NAmE* ˈkɑːl-/ *noun* [U] severe pain in the stomach and BOWELS, suffered especially by babies ▶ **col·icky** /-ɪki/ *adj.*

**col·i·seum** (*also* **Coliseum**) /ˌkɒləˈsiːəm; *NAmE* ˌkɑːl-/ *noun* (*NAmE*) a large building used for sports events, entertainment, exhibitions, etc

**col·itis** /kəˈlaɪtɪs/ *noun* [U] (*medical*) a disease that causes pain and SWELLING (= the condition of being larger than normal) in the COLON (= part of the BOWELS)

**col·lab·or·ate** /kəˈlæbəreɪt/ *verb* **1** [I] to work together with sb in order to produce or achieve sth: *Researchers around the world are collaborating to develop a new vaccine.* ◇ ~(with sb) (on sth) *We have collaborated on many projects over the years.* ◇ ~(with sb) (in sth/in doing sth) *She agreed to collaborate with him in writing her biography.* **2** [I] ~(with sb) (*disapproving*) to help the enemy who has taken control of your country during a war

**col·lab·or·ation** /kəˌlæbəˈreɪʃn/ *noun* **1** [U, C] the act of working with another person or group of people to create or produce sth: *It was a collaboration that produced extremely useful results.* ◇ ~ (in) ~(with sb) (on sth) *The government worked in close collaboration with teachers on the new curriculum.* ◇ ~ between A and B *collaboration between the teachers and the government* **2** [C] ~(with sb/sth) | ~(between A and B) a piece of work produced by two or more people or groups of people working together: *This mission was a collaboration between the National Space Agency of Japan and NASA.* **3** [U] ~(with sb/sth) (*disapproving*) the act of helping the enemy during a war when they have taken control of your country: *his wartime collaboration with the Nazis*

**col·lab·ora·tive** /kəˈlæbərətɪv; *NAmE* -reɪt-/ *adj.* [only before noun] (*formal*) involving, or done by, several people or groups of people working together: *collaborative projects/studies/research* ◇ *a collaborative effort/venture* ▶ **col·lab·ora·tive·ly** *adv.*

**col·lab·or·ator** /kəˈlæbəreɪtə(r)/ *noun* **1** a person who works with another person to create or produce sth such as a book **2** (*disapproving*) a person who helps the enemy in a war, when they have taken control of the person's country

**col·lage** /ˈkɒlɑːʒ; *NAmE* kəˈlɑːʒ/ *noun* **1** [C] a picture made by sticking pieces of coloured paper, cloth or photographs onto a surface, or by putting images together on a computer: *a photo collage* **2** [U] the art of making collages:

---

æ cat | ɑː father | e bed | ɜː fur | ə about | ɪ sit | iː see | i happy | ɒ got (*BrE*) | ɔː saw | ʌ cup | ʊ put | uː too

*collage techniques* **3** [C] a collection of things, which may be similar or different: *an interesting collage of 1960s songs*

**col·lagen** /ˈkɒlədʒən; *NAmE* ˈkɑːl-/ *noun* [U] a PROTEIN found in skin and bone, sometimes INJECTED into the body, especially the face, to improve its appearance: *collagen injections*

## col·lapse ❶ B2 /kəˈlæps/ *verb*, *noun*

■ *verb*
- OF BUILDING **1** ? B2 [I] to fall down or fall in suddenly, often after breaking apart SYN **give way**: *The roof collapsed under the weight of snow.*
- OF SICK PERSON **2** ? B2 [I] to fall down (and usually become unconscious), especially because you are very ill: *She collapsed and was rushed to hospital.* ◊ *~ + adv./prep. The man collapsed in a heap on the floor.*
- RELAX **3** [I] (*informal*) to sit or lie down and relax, especially after working hard: *When I get home I like to collapse on the sofa and listen to music.*
- FAIL **4** [I] to fail suddenly or completely SYN **break down**: *Talks between management and unions have collapsed.* ◊ *All opposition to the plan has collapsed.*
- OF PRICES/CURRENCIES **5** [I] to decrease suddenly in amount or value: *Share prices collapsed after news of poor trading figures.*
- FOLD **6** [I, T] *~ (sth)* to fold sth into a shape that uses less space; to be able to be folded in this way SYN **fold**: *The table collapses for easy storage.*
- MEDICAL **7** [I, T] *~ (sth)* if a lung or BLOOD VESSEL **collapses** or **is collapsed**, it falls in and becomes flat and empty
  ▶ **col·lapsed** *adj.*: *collapsed buildings* ◊ *a collapsed investment bank* ◊ *a collapsed lung*

■ *noun*
- FAILURE **1** ? B2 [C, usually sing., U] a sudden failure of sth, such as an institution, a business or a course of action: *the collapse of the Soviet Union* ◊ *The peace talks were on the verge of collapse.*
- OF BUILDING **2** [U] the action of a building suddenly falling: *The walls were strengthened to protect them from collapse.*
- ILLNESS **3** [U, C, usually sing.] a medical condition when a person suddenly becomes very ill, or when sb falls because they are ill or weak: *a state of mental/nervous collapse* ◊ *She was taken to hospital after her collapse at work.*
- OF PRICES/CURRENCIES **4** [C, usually sing.] a sudden fall in value: *Shares suffered a fresh collapse today.* ◊ *the collapse of share prices/the dollar/the market* ◊ **in sth** *the collapse in the price of oil*

**col·laps·ible** /kəˈlæpsəbl/ *adj.* that can be folded flat or made into a smaller shape that uses less space: *a collapsible chair/boat/bicycle*

**col·lar** /ˈkɒlə(r); *NAmE* ˈkɑːl-/ *noun*, *verb*

■ *noun* **1** the part around the neck of a shirt, jacket or coat that usually folds down: *a coat with a fur collar* ◊ *I turned up my collar against the wind* (= to keep warm). ◊ *He always wears a collar and tie for work.* ⇒ see also BLUE-COLLAR, DOG COLLAR, WHITE-COLLAR **2** a band of leather or plastic put around the neck of an animal, especially a dog: *a collar and lead/leash* **3** (*specialist*) a band made of a strong material that is put round sth, such as a pipe or a machine, to make it stronger or to join two parts together
  IDM see HOT *adj.*

■ *verb* (*informal*) **1** *~ sb* to capture sb and hold them tightly so that they cannot escape from you: *Police collared the culprit as he was leaving the premises.* **2** *~ sb* to stop sb in order to talk to them: *I was collared in the street by a woman doing a survey.*

**col·lar·bone** /ˈkɒləbəʊn; *NAmE* ˈkɑːlərb-/ *noun* either of the two bones that go from the base of the neck to the shoulders SYN **clavicle** ⇒ VISUAL VOCAB page V1

**col·lard greens** /ˈkɒləd griːnz; *NAmE* ˈkɑːlərd/ (*also* **col·lards**) *noun* [pl.] (*NAmE*) a dark green vegetable with broad flat leaves that grows in the southern US and is eaten cooked

**col·lar·less** /ˈkɒlələs; *NAmE* ˈkɑːlərl-/ *adj.* with no collar: *a collarless shirt*

---

291　　　　　　　　　　　　　　　　　　　　**collect**

**col·late** /kəˈleɪt/ *verb* **1** *~ sth* to collect information together from different sources in order to examine and compare it: *to collate data/information/figures* **2** *~ sth* to collect pieces of paper or the pages of a book, etc. and arrange them in the correct order ▶ **col·la·tion** /-ˈleɪʃn/ *noun* [U]: *the collation of information*

**col·lat·eral** /kəˈlætərəl/ *noun*, *adj.*
- *noun* [U] (*finance*) property or sth valuable that you promise to give to sb if you cannot pay back money that you borrow
- *adj.* (*formal*) connected with sth else, but in addition to it and less important: *collateral benefits* ◊ *The government denied that there had been any collateral damage* (= injury to ordinary people or buildings) *during the bombing raid.*

## col·league ❶ A2 /ˈkɒliːɡ; *NAmE* ˈkɑːl-/ *noun* a person that you work with, especially in a profession or a business: *work/senior/male colleagues* ◊ *We were friends and colleagues for more than 20 years.* ◊ *some of his former colleagues on the council*

▼ **SYNONYMS**

### collect
gather • accumulate • amass

These words all mean to get more of sth over a period of time, or to increase in quantity over a period of time.

**collect** to bring things or information together from different people or places; to gradually increase in amount in a place: *We've been collecting data from various sources.* ◊ *Dirt had collected in the corners of the room.* NOTE People sometimes **collect** things of a particular type as a hobby: *to collect stamps.*

**gather** to bring things together that have been spread around; to collect information from different sources: *I waited while he gathered up his papers.* ◊ *Detectives have spent months gathering evidence.*

**COLLECT OR GATHER?**

Both **collect** and **gather** can be used in the same way to talk about bringing together data, information or evidence. When talking about things, **gather** is used with words like *things*, *belongings* or *papers* when the things are spread around within a short distance. **Collect** is used for getting examples of sth from different people or places that are physically separated.

**accumulate** (*rather formal*) to gradually get more and more of sth over a period of time; to gradually increase in number or quantity over a period of time: *I seem to have accumulated a lot of books.* ◊ *Debts began to accumulate.*

**amass** (*rather formal*) to collect sth in large quantities, especially money, debts or information: *He amassed a fortune from silver mining.*

**PATTERNS**
- to collect/gather/accumulate/amass **data/evidence/information**
- to accumulate/amass **a fortune/debts**
- **dirt/dust/debris** collects/accumulates
- to **gradually/slowly** collect/gather/accumulate (sth)

## col·lect ❶ A2 /kəˈlekt/ *verb*, *adj.*, *adv.*

■ *verb*
- BRING TOGETHER **1** ? B2 [T] to bring things together from different people or places SYN **gather**: *~ sth to collect data/evidence/information* ◊ *We're collecting signatures for a petition.* ◊ *~ sth from sb/sth Samples were collected from over 200 patients.*
- AS HOBBY **2** ? A2 [T] *~ sth* to buy or find things of a particular type and keep them as a hobby: *to collect stamps/postcards/coins* ⇒ see also STAMP COLLECTING
- INCREASE IN AMOUNT **3** ? B1 [I, T] to gradually increase in amount in a place; to gradually obtain more and more of sth in a place SYN **accumulate**: *~ + adv./prep. Dirt had collected in the corners of the room.* ◊ *~ sth We seem to have collected an enormous number of boxes* (= without intending to).

# collectable

- **TAKE AWAY 4** [B1] [T] to go somewhere in order to take sb/sth away: *~ sth What day do they collect the rubbish/garbage?* ◇ *~ sth from ... On arrival, collect your keys from reception.* ◇ (*BrE*) *~ sb (from ...) Someone will be at the airport to collect you.*
- **MONEY 5** [B1] [I, T] to ask people to give you money for a particular purpose: *~ for sth We're collecting for local charities.* ◇ *~ sth (for sth) Volunteers have been going door to door, collecting money.* **6** [T] *~ sth* to obtain the money, etc. that sb owes, for example by going to their house to get it: *to collect rent/debts/tax*
- **RECEIVE/WIN 7** [T, I] *~ (sth)* to receive sth; to win sth: *She collected £25 000 in compensation.* ◇ *to collect a prize/a medal*
- **OF PEOPLE 8** [I] to come together in one place to form a larger group [SYN] **gather**: *A crowd began to collect in front of the embassy.*

[IDM] **collect yourself/your thoughts 1** to try to control your emotions and become calm: *I'm fine—I just need a minute to collect myself.* **2** to prepare yourself mentally for sth: *She paused to collect her thoughts before entering the interview room.* ⇒ more at **DUST** *n*.

[PHRV] **col·lect sth↔up** to bring together things that are no longer being used: *Would somebody collect up all the dirty glasses?*

■ *adj.* (*NAmE*) (of a phone call) paid for by the person who receives the call: *to make a collect call* ⇒ see also **REVERSE** *adj.* ▸ **col·lect** *adv.*: *to call sb collect*

**col·lect·able** (also **col·lect·ible**) /kəˈlektəbl/ *adj.* worth collecting because it is beautiful or may become valuable
▸ **col·lect·able** (also **col·lect·ible**) *noun* [usually pl.]

**col·lect·ed** /kəˈlektɪd/ *adj.* **1** [not before noun] very calm and in control of yourself: *She always stays cool, calm and collected in a crisis.* **2** *~ works, papers, poems, etc.* all the books, etc. written by one author, published in one book or in a set

**col·lec·tion** ❶ [B1] /kəˈlekʃn/ *noun*
- **GROUP OF OBJECTS/PEOPLE 1** [B1] [C] a group of objects, often of the same sort, that have been collected: *an art collection* ◇ *~ of sth an extensive collection of war photographs* **2** [C] a group of objects or people: *There was a collection of books and shoes on the floor.* ◇ *There is always a strange collection of runners in the London Marathon.*
- **TAKING AWAY/BRINGING TOGETHER 3** [B1] [C, U] an act of taking sth away from a place; an act of bringing things together into one place: *The first stage in research is data collection.* ◇ *waste/rubbish/garbage/refuse collection* ◇ *The last collection from this postbox is at 5.15.* ◇ *Your suit will be ready for collection on Tuesday.* ⇒ compare **PICKUP**
- **POEMS/STORIES/MUSIC 4** [C] a group of poems, stories or pieces of music published together as one book, etc: *a collection of stories by women writers*
- **MONEY 5** [C] an act of collecting money to help a charity or during a church service; the money collected: *a house-to-house collection for Cancer Research* ◇ *The total collection last week amounted to £250.* ◇ *a collection box/bucket* (= for people to put money in) ◇ *the church collection plate* ▸ **WORDFINDER NOTE** at **CHARITY**
- **NEW CLOTHES 6** [C] a range of new clothes or items for the home that are designed, made and offered for sale, often for a particular season: *Armani's stunning new autumn collection*

**col·lect·ive** [B2+] [C1] /kəˈlektɪv/ *adj., noun*

■ *adj.* [usually before noun] **1** [B2+] [C1] done or shared by all members of a group of people; involving a whole group or society: *collective leadership/decision-making/responsibility* ◇ *collective memory* (= things that a group of people or a community know or remember, that are often passed from generation to children) **2** used to refer to all members of a group: *The collective name for mast, boom and sails on a boat is the 'rig'.* ▸ **col·lect·ive·ly** *adv.*: *the collectively agreed rate* ◇ *We have had a successful year, both collectively and individually.* ◇ *rain, snow and hail, collectively known as 'precipitation'* (= as a group)

■ *noun* a group of people who own a business or a farm and run it together; the business that they run: *an independent collective making films for television*

**col·lective ˈbargaining** *noun* [U] discussions between a trade union and an employer about the pay and working conditions of the union members ⇒ **WORDFINDER NOTE** at **UNION**

**col·lective ˈfarm** *noun* a large farm, or a group of farms, owned by the state and run by a group of people

**col·lective ˈnoun** *noun* (*grammar*) a singular noun, such as *committee* or *team*, that refers to a group of people, animals or things and, in British English, can be used with either a singular or a plural verb. In American English it must be used with a singular verb.

**col·lective unˈconscious** *noun* [sing.] (*psychology*) the part of the unconscious mind that is thought to be shared with other humans because it is passed from generation to generation

**col·lect·iv·ism** /kəˈlektɪvɪzəm/ *noun* [U] the political system in which all farms, businesses and industries are owned by the state or by all the people ▸ **col·lect·iv·ist** /-vɪst/ *adj.*

**col·lect·iv·ize** (*BrE also* **-ise**) /kəˈlektɪvaɪz/ *verb* [often passive] *~ sth* to join several private farms, industries, etc. together so that they are controlled by the community or by the state ▸ **col·lect·iv·iza·tion, -isa·tion** /kəˌlektɪvaɪˈzeɪʃn; *NAmE* -vəˈz-/ *noun* [U]

**col·lect·or** ❶ [B2] /kəˈlektə(r)/ *noun* **1** [B2] (especially in compounds) a person who collects things, either as a hobby or as a job: *a stamp collector* ◇ *ticket/tax/debt collectors* **2** the leader of a district in some South Asian countries

**col·lect·or·ate** /kəˈlektərət/ *noun* **1** (in some South Asian countries) the area under the authority of a collector **2** the office in which a collector is based

**colˈlector's item** *noun* a thing that is valued because it is very old or rare, or because it has some special interest

**col·leen** /kɒˈliːn; *NAmE* kɑːˈl-/ *noun* **1** (*IrishE*) a girl or young woman **2** (*old-fashioned* or *humorous*) a girl or young woman from Ireland

**col·lege** ❶ [A1] /ˈkɒlɪdʒ; *NAmE* ˈkɑːl-/ *noun* **1** [A1] [C, U] (often in names) (in the UK) a place where students go to study or to receive training after they have left school: *a secretarial college* ◇ *the Royal College of Art* ◇ *a college course/student* ◇ *She wanted to go to college to become a nurse.* ◇ *at~ She's at college.* ⇒ see also **COMMUNITY COLLEGE** (1), **SIXTH-FORM COLLEGE, TECHNICAL COLLEGE, TERTIARY COLLEGE** ⇒ **WORDFINDER NOTE** at **TRAINING 2** [A1] [C, U] (often in names) (in the US) a university where students can study for a degree after they have left school: *She was the first in her family to attend college.* ◇ *He's hoping to go to college next year.* ◇ *I graduated from college with an English degree.* ◇ *in~ He got interested in politics when he was in college.* ◇ *at~ She's away at college in California.* ◇ *a college campus/degree/education* ◇ *a college student/graduate/professor* ⇒ see also **COMMUNITY COLLEGE** (2), **JUNIOR COLLEGE 3** [C, U] (*CanE*) a place where you can study for higher or more specialist qualifications after you finish high school **4** [C, U] one of the separate institutions that some British universities, such as Oxford and Cambridge, are divided into: *King's College, Cambridge* ◇ *a tour of Oxford colleges* ◇ *Most students live in college.* **5** (in the US) one of the main divisions of some large universities: *The history department is part of the College of Arts and Sciences.* **6** [C + sing./pl. v.] the teachers and/or students of a college **7** [C] (especially in names, in Britain and some other countries) a **SECONDARY SCHOOL**, especially one where you must pay: *Eton College* **8** [C] (usually in names) an organized group of professional people with special interests, duties or powers: *the Royal College of Physicians* ◇ *the American College of Cardiology* ⇒ see also **ELECTORAL COLLEGE**

## BRITISH/AMERICAN
### college / university

- In both *BrE* and *NAmE* a **college** is a place where you can go to study after you leave secondary school. In Britain you can go to a **college** to study or to receive training in a particular skill. In the US you can study for your first degree at a **college**. A **university** offers more advanced degrees in addition to first degrees.
- In *NAmE* **college** is often used to mean a **university**, especially when talking about people who are studying for their first degree. The is not used when you are talking about someone studying there: *My son has gone away to college.* ◇ *'Where did you go to college?'* ◇ *'Ohio State University.'*
- In *BrE* you can say: *My daughter is at university*. In *NAmE* you cannot use **university** in this way. You use it with **a** or **the** to mean a particular university: *I didn't want to go to a large university.*

**col·le·gi·ate** /kəˈliːdʒiət/ *adj.* **1** relating to a college or its students: *collegiate life* **2** (*BrE*) divided into a number of colleges: *a collegiate university*

**col legiate ˈinstitute** *noun* (in some parts of Canada) a public high school

**col·lide** /kəˈlaɪd/ *verb* **1** [I] if two people, vehicles, etc. **collide**, they crash into each other; if a person, vehicle, etc. **collides** with another, or with sth that is not moving, they crash into it: *The car and the van collided head-on in thick fog.* ◇ **~ with/sb** *The car collided head-on with the van.* ◇ *As he fell, his head collided with the table.* ⊃ SYNONYMS at CRASH **2** [I] **~ (with sb) (over sth)** (*formal*) (of people, their opinions, etc.) to disagree strongly: *They regularly collide over policy decisions.* ⊃ see also COLLISION

**col·lider** /kəˈlaɪdə(r)/ *noun* (*physics*) a machine for making two streams of PARTICLES move at high speed and crash into each other

**col·lie** /ˈkɒli; *NAmE* ˈkɑːli/ *noun* a dog of which there are several types. One type has a long pointed nose and long thick hair and is popular as a pet. A smaller type of collie with shorter hair is often trained to help control sheep on a farm. ⊃ see also BORDER COLLIE

**col·lier** /ˈkɒliə(r)/ *noun; NAmE* ˈkɑːl-/ *noun* **1** (*especially BrE, old-fashioned*) = COAL MINER **2** a ship that carries coal

**col·liery** /ˈkɒliəri; *NAmE* ˈkɑːl-/ *noun* (*pl.* -**ies**) a coal mine with its buildings and equipment

**col·li·sion** ʔ+ C1 /kəˈlɪʒn/ *noun* [C, U] **1** ʔ+ C1 an accident in which two vehicles or people crash into each other: *~ between A and B a collision between two trains* ◇ *~ with sb/sth Stewart was injured in a collision with another player.* ◇ *a head-on collision* (= between two vehicles that are moving towards each other) ◇ *a mid-air collision* (= between two aircraft while they are flying) ◇ **in ~ with sb/sth** *His car was in collision with a motorbike.* **2** (*formal*) a strong DISAGREEMENT between two people or between ideas, opinions, etc. that are opposed to each other; the meeting of two things that are very different: **~ between A and B** *a collision between two opposing points of view* ◇ *~ of A and B In his work we see the collision of two different traditions.*
**IDM** **be on a colˈlision course (with sb/sth)** **1** to be in a situation that is almost certain to cause an argument: *I was on a collision course with my boss over the sales figures.* **2** to be moving in a direction in which it is likely that you will crash into sb/sth: *A giant iceberg was on a collision course with the ship.*

**col·lo·cate** /ˈkɒləkeɪt; *NAmE* ˈkɑːl-/ *verb* [I] **~ (with sth)** (*linguistics*) (of words) to be often used together in a language: *'Bitter' collocates with 'tears' but 'sour' does not.* ◇ *'Bitter' and 'tears' collocate.* ▶ **col·lo·cate** /-kət/ *noun*: *'Bitter' and 'tears' are collocates.*

**col·lo·ca·tion** /ˌkɒləˈkeɪʃn; *NAmE* ˌkɑːl-/ *noun* (*linguistics*) **1** [C] a combination of words in a language that happens very often and more frequently than would happen by chance: *'Resounding success' and 'crying shame' are English collocations.* **2** [U] the fact of two or more words often being used together, in a way that happens more frequently than would happen by chance: *Advanced students need to be aware of the importance of collocation.*

**col·lo·quial** /kəˈləʊkwiəl/ *adj.* (of words and language) used in conversation but not in formal speech or writing **SYN** *informal* ▶ **col·lo·qui·al·ly** /-kwiəli/ *adv.*

**col·lo·qui·al·ism** /kəˈləʊkwiəlɪzəm/ *noun* a word or phrase that is used in conversation but not in formal speech or writing

**col·lo·quium** /kəˈləʊkwiəm/ *noun* (*pl.* **col·lo·quia** /-kwiə/) a formal academic SEMINAR or conference

**col·lo·quy** /ˈkɒləkwi; *NAmE* ˈkɑːl-/ *noun* (*pl.* -**ies**) (*formal*) a conversation

**col·lude** /kəˈluːd/ *verb* [I] (*formal, disapproving*) to work together secretly or illegally in order to trick other people: **~ (with sb) (in sth/in doing sth)** *Several people had colluded in the murder.* ◇ **~ (with sb) (to do sth)** *They colluded with terrorists to overthrow the government.*

**col·lu·sion** /kəˈluːʒn/ *noun* [U] (*formal, disapproving*) secret agreement especially in order to do sth dishonest or to trick people: **in ~ with sb** *The police were corrupt and were operating in collusion with the drug dealers.* ◇ **~ (between A and B)** *There was collusion between the two witnesses* (= they gave the same false evidence). ▶ **col·lu·sive** /-ˈluːsɪv/ *adj.*

**colo·bus** /ˈkɒləbəs; *NAmE* ˈkɑːl-/ (*also* **colobus monkey**) *noun* a small African monkey that has a long tail and that eats leaves

**co·logne** /kəˈləʊn/ (*also* **eau de cologne**) *noun* [U] a type of light PERFUME

**colon** /ˈkəʊlən; *BrE also* -lɒn/ *noun* **1** the mark (:) used to introduce a list, a summary, an explanation, etc. or before reporting what sb has said ⊃ compare SEMICOLON **2** (*anatomy*) the main part of the large INTESTINE (= part of the BOWELS) ⊃ VISUAL VOCAB page V1

**col·onel** /ˈkɜːnl; *NAmE* ˈkɜːrnl/ *noun* (*abbr.* **Col.**) an officer of high rank in the army, the MARINES, or the US AIR FORCE: *Colonel Jim Edge* ⊃ HOMOPHONES at KERNEL

**co·lo·nial** ʔ+ C1 /kəˈləʊniəl/ *adj. noun*
■ *adj.* **1** ʔ+ C1 connected with or belonging to a country that controls another country: *a colonial power* ◇ *Tunisia achieved independence from French colonial rule in 1956.* ◇ *Western colonial attitudes* ⊃ see also COLONY **2** (*often* **Colonial**) typical of or connected with the US at the time when it was still a British COLONY: *life in colonial times*
■ *noun* a person who lives in a COLONY and who comes from the country that controls it: *British colonials in India*

**co·lo·ni·al·ism** /kəˈləʊniəlɪzəm/ *noun* [U] the practice by which a powerful country controls another country or other countries: *European colonialism* ▶ **co·lo·ni·al·ist** *adj., noun*: *colonialist laws*

**co·lo·nic** /kəˈlɒnɪk; *NAmE* -ˈlɑː-/ *adj.* (*anatomy*) relating to the COLON (= part of the BOWELS): *colonic irrigation* (= the process of washing out the COLON with water)

**col·on·ist** /ˈkɒlənɪst; *NAmE* ˈkɑːl-/ *noun* a person who settles in an area that has become a COLONY

**col·on·ize** (*BrE also* -**ise**) /ˈkɒlənaɪz; *NAmE* ˈkɑːl-/ *verb* **1 ~ sth** to take control of an area or a country that is not your own, especially using force, and send people from your own country to live there: *The area was colonized by the Vikings.* ⊃ WORDFINDER NOTE at EXPLORE **2 ~ sth** (*biology*) (of animals or plants) to live or grow in large numbers in a particular area: *The slopes are colonized by flowering plants.* ◇ *Bats had colonized the ruins.* ▶ **col·on·iz·a·tion**, -**isa·tion** /ˌkɒlənaɪˈzeɪʃn; *NAmE* ˌkɑːlənəˈz-/ *noun* [U]: *the colonization of the 'New World'* ◇ *plant colonization* **col·on·izer**, -**iser** /ˈkɒlənaɪzə(r); *NAmE* ˈkɑːl-/ *noun*

**col·on·nade** /ˌkɒləˈneɪd; *NAmE* ˌkɑːl-/ *noun* a row of stone columns with equal spaces between them, usually supporting a roof ▶ **col·on·nad·ed** *adj.*

**col·ony** ʔ+ B2 /ˈkɒləni; *NAmE* ˈkɑːl-/ *noun* (*pl.* -**ies**) **1** ʔ+ B2 [C] a country or an area that is governed by people from another, more powerful country: *former British colonies* **2** [sing. + sing./pl. v.] a group of people who go to live

# color

permanently in a colony **3** [C + sing./pl. v.] a group of people from the same place or with the same work or interests who live in a particular city or country or who live together: *the American colony in Paris* ◇ *an artists' colony* **4** [C] (*IndE*) a small town set up by an employer or an organization for its workers **5** [C + sing./pl. v.] (*biology*) a group of plants or animals that live together or grow in the same place: *a colony of ants* ◇ *a bird colony*

**col·or** (*US*) = COLOUR **HELP** You will find most words formed with **color** at the spelling **colour**.

**col·or·ant** (*US*) = COLOURANT

**col·or·ation** (*BrE also* **col·our·ation**) /ˌkʌləˈreɪʃn/ *noun* [U] (*specialist*) the natural colours and patterns on a plant or an animal

**col·ora·tura** /ˌkɒlərəˈtʊərə; *NAmE* ˌkʌlərəˈtʊrə/ *noun* [U] (*music, from Italian*) complicated passages for a singer, for example in OPERA: *a coloratura soprano* (= one who often sings coloratura passages) ⊃ WORDFINDER NOTE at OPERA

**'color bar** (*US*) = COLOUR BAR

**'color-blind** (*US*) = COLOUR-BLIND

**'color code** (*US*) = COLOUR CODE

**col·ored** (*US*) = COLOURED

**color·fast** /ˈkʌləfɑːst; *NAmE* -læfæst/ (*US*) = COLOUR FAST

**col·or·ful** (*US*) = COLOURFUL

**col·or·ing** (*US*) = COLOURING

**col·or·ist, col·or·istic** (*US*) = COLOURIST, COLOURISTIC

**col·or·ize** (*BrE also* **col·our·ize**) /ˈkʌləraɪz/ *verb* ~ *sth* (*specialist*) to add colour to a black and white film, using a computer process

**col·or·less** (*US*) = COLOURLESS

**'color line** (*also* **'color bar**) (*both US*) (*BrE* **'colour bar**) *noun* [*usually sing.*] a social system that does not allow black people the same rights as white people

**'color scheme** (*US*) = COLOUR SCHEME

**'color separation** (*US*) = COLOUR SEPARATION

**col·or·way** (*US*) = COLOURWAY

**col·os·sal** /kəˈlɒsl; *NAmE* -ˈlɑːsl/ *adj.* extremely large: *a colossal statue* ◇ *The singer earns a colossal amount of money.*

**col·os·sus** /kəˈlɒsəs; *NAmE* -ˈlɑː-/ *noun* **1** [sing.] (*formal*) a person or thing that is extremely important or large in size **2** [C] (*pl.* **co·lossi** /kəˈlɒsaɪ; *NAmE* -ˈlɑː-/) an extremely large statue

**col·os·tomy** /kəˈlɒstəmi; *NAmE* -ˈlɑː-/ *noun* (*pl.* **-ies**) (*medical*) an operation in which part of a person's COLON (= the lower part of the BOWELS) is removed and an opening is made in the ABDOMEN through which the person can get rid of waste matter from the body; an opening formed in this way: *a colostomy bag*

**col·os·trum** /kəˈlɒstrəm; *NAmE* -ˈlɑː-/ *noun* [U] the first milk produced by a new mother, which has a lot of ANTIBODIES that help the baby to resist disease

**col·our** ⓘ 🅐🅛 (*US* **color**) /ˈkʌlə(r)/ *noun, verb*

■ *noun*
- RED, GREEN, ETC. **1** 🅐🅛 [C, U] the appearance that things have that results from the way in which they reflect light. Red, orange and green are colours: *What's your favourite colour?* ◇ *bright/vibrant/bold colours* ◇ *available in 12 different colours* ◇ *skin/hair colour* ◇ *in ~ red/green/blue, etc. in colour* ◇ *The stage lights changed colour from red to blue.* ⊃ see also COMPLEMENTARY COLOUR, PRIMARY COLOUR **2** 🅐🅛 [U] (usually before another noun) the use of all the colours, not only black and white: *the introduction of colour television in the UK in 1967* ◇ *colour photographs* ◇ *a colour printer* ◇ *a full-colour brochure* ◇ *in ~ Do you dream in colour?* ⊃ see also FULL-COLOUR
- OF SKIN **3** 🅐🅑 [U, C] the colour of a person's skin, when it shows the race they belong to: *discrimination on the grounds of race, colour or religion* ◇ *of ~ (especially NAmE) a person/man/woman of colour* (= who is not white)
- OF FACE **4** [U] a red or pink colour in sb's face, especially when it shows that they look healthy or that they are embarrassed: *The fresh air brought colour to their cheeks.* ◇ *Colour flooded her face when she thought of what had happened.* ◇ *His face was drained of colour* (= he looked pale and ill).
- SUBSTANCE **5** [C, U] a substance that is used to give colour to sth: *a semi-permanent hair colour that lasts six to eight washes* ⊃ see also OIL COLOUR at OIL PAINT, WATERCOLOUR
- INTERESTING DETAILS **6** [U] interesting and exciting details or qualities: *The old town is full of colour and attractions.* ◇ *Her acting added warmth and colour to the production.* ◇ *to add/give/lend colour to sth* (= make it brighter, more interesting, etc.) ⊃ see also LOCAL COLOUR
- OF TEAM/COUNTRY, ETC. **7 colours** [pl.] the particular colours that are used on clothes, flags, etc. to represent a team, school, political party or country: *Red and white are the team colours.* ◇ *Spain's national colours* ◇ (*figurative*) *There are people of different political colours on the committee.* **8 colours** [pl.] (*especially BrE*) a flag, BADGE, etc. that represents a team, country, ship, etc: *Most buildings had a flagpole with the national colours flying.* ◇ *sailing under the French colours* **IDM** see FLYING *adj.*, NAIL *v.*, TRUE *adj.* ⊃ see also OFF COLOUR

■ *verb*
- PUT COLOUR ON STH **1** [I, T] to put colour on sth using paint, coloured pencils, etc: *The children love to draw and colour.* ◇ *~ sth How long have you been colouring* (= DYEING) *your hair?* ◇ *~ sth + adj. He drew a monster and coloured it green.*
- OF FACE **2** [I] ~ (at sth) (of a person or their face) to become red because the person is embarrassed **SYN** blush: *She coloured at his remarks.*
- AFFECT **3** [T] ~ *sth* to affect sth, especially in a negative way: *This incident coloured her whole life.* ◇ *Don't let your judgement be coloured by personal feelings.*
**PHR V** **colour sth↔in** to put colour inside a particular area, shape, etc. using coloured pencils, CRAYONS, etc: *I'll draw a tree and you can colour it in.*

---

▼ **SYNONYMS**

**colour**
shade • hue • tint • tinge

These words all describe the appearance of things, resulting from the way in which they reflect light.

**colour** the appearance that things have, resulting from the way in which they reflect light. Red, green and blue are colours: *What's your favourite colour?* ◇ *bright/dark/light colours*

**shade** a particular form of a colour, especially when describing how light or dark it is. Sky blue is a shade of blue: *Her eyes were a delicate shade of green.*

**hue** (*literary or technical*) a colour or a particular shade of a colour: *His face took on an unhealthy, whitish hue.*

**tint** a shade or small amount of a particular colour; a faint colour covering a surface: *leaves with red and gold autumn tints*

**tinge** a small amount of a colour: *There was a pink tinge to the sky.*

TINT OR TINGE?
- You can say: *a reddish tint/tinge* or: *a tinge of red* but not: *a tint of red*. **Tint** is often used in the plural, but **tinge** is almost always singular.

PATTERNS
- a **warm/rich** colour/shade/hue/tint
- a **bright/vivid/vibrant/dark/deep** colour/shade/hue
- a **pale/pastel/soft/subtle/delicate** colour/shade/hue
- a **light/strong/neutral/natural** colour/shade

---

**col·our·ant** (*US* **col·or·ant**) /ˈkʌlərənt/ *noun* a substance that is used to put colour in sth, especially a person's hair

**col·our·ation** (*BrE*) = COLORATION

**'colour bar** (*US* **'color bar, 'color line**) *noun* [*usually sing.*] a social system that does not allow black people the same rights as white people

**colour-blind** (US **color-blind**) adj. **1** unable to see the difference between some colours, especially red and green; unable to see colours at all (although this is rare in humans) **2** treating people with different coloured skin in exactly the same way ▶ **colour blindness** (US **color blindness**) noun [U]

**colour code** (US **color code**) noun a system of marking things with different colours so that you can easily identify them ▶ **colour-coded** (US **color-coded**) adj.: The files have labels that are colour-coded according to subject.

**col·oured** ❶ [B1] (US **col·ored**) /ˈkʌləd/; NAmE -lərd/ adj., noun
■ adj. **1** [B1] (often in compounds) having a particular colour or different colours: brightly coloured balloons ◊ He uses ink and coloured pencils in his drawings. ◊ coloured lights/glass ⊃ see also LIGHT-COLOURED, MULTICOLOURED, ROSE-COLOURED **2** (old-fashioned or offensive) (of a person) from a race that does not have white skin **3** Coloured (in South Africa) having parents who are of different races
■ noun **1** (old-fashioned or offensive) a person who does not have white skin **2** Coloured (in South Africa) a person whose parents are of different races

**colour fast** (US **color-fast**) adj. cloth that is **colour fast** will not lose colour when it is washed

**col·our·ful** ❓ [B2] (US **col·or·ful**) /ˈkʌlfl/; NAmE -lərfl/ adj. **1** ❓ [B2] full of bright colours or having a lot of different colours: colourful shop windows ◊ The male birds are more colourful than the females. **2** ❓ [C1] interesting or exciting; full of variety, sometimes in a way that shocks people: a colourful history/past/career ◊ one of the book's most colourful characters ▶ **col·our·ful·ly** (US **col·or·ful·ly**) /-fəli/ adv.: The street was colourfully decorated with flags and bunting. ◊ The tragic tale is told well and colourfully.

**col·our·ing** (US **col·or·ing**) /ˈkʌlərɪŋ/ noun **1** [U, C] a substance that is used to give a particular colour to food: red food colouring **2** [U] the colour of a person's skin, eyes and hair: Blue suited her fair colouring. **3** [U] the colours that exist in sth, especially a plant or an animal: insects with vivid yellow and black colouring

**colouring book** (US **coloring book**) noun a book of pictures drawn with a black outline so that they can be coloured in, used especially by children

**col·our·ist** (US **col·or·ist**) /ˈkʌlərɪst/ noun a person who uses colour, especially an artist or a HAIRDRESSER

**col·our·istic** (US **col·or·istic**) /ˌkʌləˈrɪstɪk/ adj. (specialist) showing or relating to a special use of colour: colouristic effects

**col·our·ize** (BrE) = COLORIZE

**col·our·less** (US **col·or·less**) /ˈkʌləles/; NAmE -lərl-/ adj. **1** without colour or very pale: a colourless liquid like water ◊ colourless lips **2** not interesting SYN **dull**: a colourless personality

**colour scheme** (US **color scheme**) noun the way in which colours are arranged, especially in the furniture and decoration of a room

**colour separation** (US **color separation**) noun (specialist) **1** [C] one of four images of sth made using only the colours CYAN, MAGENTA, yellow or black. The four images containing these colours are then used together to print an image in full colour. **2** [U] the process that is used to do this

**col·our·way** (US **col·or·way**) /ˈkʌlweɪ/; NAmE -lərw-/ noun a colour or combination of colours that a piece of clothing, etc. is available in: The designs are available in two colourways: red/grey or blue/grey.

**colt** /kəʊlt/ noun **1** a young male horse, especially one less than 4 years old ⊃ compare FILLY, STALLION **2** (BrE) a member of a sports team consisting of young players **3** Colt™ a type of small gun

**Col·um·bus Day** /kəˈlʌmbəs deɪ/ noun [U, C] a national holiday in the US on the second Monday in October when people celebrate the arrival of Christopher Columbus in America in 1492

295 **combatant**

**col·umn** ❶ [A2] ❓ /ˈkɒləm/; NAmE ˈkɑːl-/ noun **1** ❓ [A2] (abbr. **col.**) one of the straight sections from top to bottom into which text on a page or screen is divided: a dictionary with two columns per page ◊ ~ **of sth** a column of text ◊ **in a** ~ Click on the name of your account in the left-hand column. ◊ Their divorce filled a lot of column inches in the national papers (= got a lot of attention). **2** ❓ [A2] a series of numbers or words arranged one under the other down a page: ~ **of sth** to add up a column of figures ⊃ compare ROW[1] (3) **3** ❓ [A2] a part of a newspaper, magazine or website that appears regularly and deals with a particular subject or is written by a particular writer: She writes a monthly column for a leading national newspaper. ◊ a newspaper/weekly column ⊃ see also ADVICE COLUMN, AGONY COLUMN, GOSSIP COLUMN, PERSONAL COLUMN **4** a tall, solid post, usually round and made of stone, that supports or decorates a building or stands alone as a MONUMENT: The temple is supported by marble columns. ◊ Nelson's Column in London **5** a thing that is like a column in shape: a column of smoke (= smoke rising straight up) ⊃ see also SPINAL COLUMN, STEERING COLUMN **6** a long, moving line of people or vehicles: a long column of troops and tanks ⊃ see also FIFTH COLUMN

**col·um·nist** ❓ [C1] /ˈkɒləmnɪst/; NAmE ˈkɑːl-/ noun a journalist who writes regular articles for a newspaper or magazine: a newspaper columnist ⊃ see also ADVICE COLUMNIST, FIFTH COLUMNIST, GOSSIP COLUMNIST ⊃ WORDFINDER NOTE at NEWSPAPER

**com** /kɒm/; NAmE kɑːm/ abbr. (computing) (used in internet addresses) commercial organization: The internet address of Oxford University Press is www.oup.com. ⊃ see also DOT-COM

**coma** /ˈkəʊmə/ noun a deep unconscious state, usually lasting a long time and caused by serious illness or injury: to go into/be in a coma

**Com·an·che** /kəˈmæntʃi/ noun (pl. **Com·an·che** or **Com·an·ches**) a member of a Native American people, many of whom live in the US state of Oklahoma

**co·ma·tose** /ˈkəʊmətəʊs/ adj. **1** (medical) deeply unconscious; in a coma **2** (humorous) extremely tired and having no energy; sleeping deeply

**comb** /kəʊm/ noun, verb
■ noun **1** [C] a flat piece of plastic or metal with a row of thin teeth along one side, used for making your hair neat; a smaller version of this worn by women in their hair to hold it in place or as a decoration **2** [C, usually sing.] the act of using a comb on your hair: Your hair needs a good comb. **3** [C, U] = HONEYCOMB **4** [C] the soft red part on the top of the head of a male chicken IDM see FINE-TOOTH COMB
■ verb **1** [T] ~ **sth** to pull a comb through your hair in order to make it neat: Don't forget to comb your hair! ◊ Her hair was neatly combed back. **2** [T, I] to search sth carefully in order to find sb/sth SYN **scour**: ~ **sth** I combed the shops looking for something to wear. ◊ ~ **sth for sb/sth** The police combed the area for clues. ◊ ~ **through sth (for sb/sth)** They combed through the files for evidence of fraud. **3** [T] ~ **sth** (specialist) to make wool, cotton, etc. clean and straight using a special comb so that it can be used to make cloth
**PHRV** **comb sth↔out** to pull a comb through hair in order to make it neat or smooth, without any KNOTS

**com·bat** ❓ [C1] /ˈkɒmbæt/; NAmE ˈkɑːm-/ noun, verb
■ noun ❓ [C1] [U, C] fighting or a fight, especially during a time of war: **in** ~ He was killed in combat. ◊ armed/ unarmed combat (= with/without weapons) ◊ combat troops ◊ combat boots ◊ Knightly combats were only a very small part of medieval warfare. ⊃ see also SINGLE COMBAT
■ verb (-t- or -tt-) [T] ~ **sth** to stop sth unpleasant or harmful from happening or from getting worse: measures to combat crime/inflation/unemployment/disease **2** ~ **sb** (formal) to fight against an enemy

**com·bat·ant** /ˈkɒmbətənt/; NAmE kəmˈbætnt/ noun a person or group involved in fighting in a war or battle ⊃ compare NON-COMBATANT

**com·bat·ive** /ˈkɒmbətɪv; NAmE kəmˈbætɪv/ adj. ready and willing to fight or argue: *in a combative mood/spirit*

**com·bats** /ˈkɒmbæts; NAmE ˈkɑːm-/ (also **combat trousers**) noun [pl.] (BrE) = CARGO PANTS

**combi** /ˈkɒmbi; NAmE ˈkɑːm-/ = KOMBI

**com·bin·ation** ⓘ B2 ⓞ /ˌkɒmbɪˈneɪʃn; NAmE ˌkɑːm-/ noun **1** B2 [C] two or more things joined or mixed together to form a single unit: **~ of sth** *The tragedy was due to a combination of factors.* ◇ *They recommend reducing expenditure, increasing taxes, or a combination of the two.* ◇ *Technology and good management. That's a winning combination* (= one that will certainly be successful). **2** B2 [U] the act of joining or mixing together two or more things to form a single unit: **in~ with sb/sth** *The firm is working on a new product in combination with several overseas partners.* ◇ **in~** *These paints can be used individually or in combination.* **3** [C] a series of numbers or letters used to open a combination lock: *I can't remember the combination.* **4 combinations** (BrE) [pl.] a piece of underwear covering the body and legs, worn in the past

**combi·nation lock** noun a type of lock that can only be opened by using a particular series of numbers or letters

**com·bine** ⓘ B1 ⓞ verb, noun
■ verb /kəmˈbaɪn/ **1** B1 [I, T] to come together to form a single thing or group; to join two or more things or groups together to form a single one: **~ to do sth** *Hydrogen and oxygen combine to form water.* ◇ **~ with sth (to do sth)** *Hydrogen combines with oxygen to form water.* ◇ **~ sth** *a style that combines elements of tap, ballet and modern dance* ◇ *I like to travel and make films, and I'm now able to combine the two.* ◇ **~ A with B** *Combine the eggs with a little flour.* ◇ **~ A and B (together)** *Combine the eggs and the flour.* **2** B1 [T] to have two or more different features or characteristics; to put two or more different things, features or qualities together: **~ sth** *We are still looking for someone who combines all the necessary qualities.* ◇ **~ A and/with B** *The hotel combines comfort with convenience.* ◇ *This model combines a printer and scanner.* ◇ *They have successfully combined the old with the new in this room.* ◇ *a kitchen and dining room combined* **3** B1 [T] **~ A and/with B** to do two or more things at the same time: *The trip will combine business with pleasure.* ◇ *She has successfully combined a career and bringing up a family.* **4** [I, T] to come together in order to work or act together; to put two things or groups together so that they work or act together: **~ against sb/sth** *They combined against a common enemy.* ◇ **~ sth (with sth)** *You should try to combine exercise with a healthy diet.* IDM see FORCE n.
■ noun /ˈkɒmbaɪn/ NAmE /ˈkɑːm-/ **1** (BrE also **combine ˈharvester**) a large farm machine that both cuts a crop and also separates the grains from the rest of the plant **2** a group of people or organizations acting together in business

**com·bined** /kəmˈbaɪnd/ adj. (of two or more things) put, added or joined together: *The German team scored a combined total of 652 points.* ◇ *the combined effects of the two drugs* ◇ *It took the combined efforts of both the press and the public to bring about a change in the law.*

**com·bining form** noun (grammar) a part of a word that can combine with another word or another combining form to make a new word, for example *techno-* and *-phobe* in *technophobe*

**combo** /ˈkɒmbəʊ; NAmE ˈkɑːm-/ noun (pl. -os) (informal) **1** a number of different things combined together, especially different types of food: *I'll have the steak and chicken combo platter.* **2** a small band that plays jazz or dance music

**com·bust** /kəmˈbʌst/ verb [I, T] **~ (sth)** to start to burn; to start to burn sth

**com·bust·ible** /kəmˈbʌstəbl/ adj. able to begin burning easily SYN **flammable**: *combustible material/gases*

**com·bus·tion** /kəmˈbʌstʃən/ noun [U] **1** the process of burning ⬄ see also SPONTANEOUS COMBUSTION **2** (specialist) a chemical process in which substances combine with the OXYGEN in the air to produce heat and light

**comˈbustion chamber** noun a space in which combustion takes place, for example in an engine

**come** ⓘ A1 /kʌm/ verb, prep., exclamation, noun
■ verb (came /keɪm/, come)
• TO A PLACE **1** A1 [I] to move to or towards a person or place: **+ adv./prep.** *He left and said he was never coming back.* ◇ *She comes to work by bus.* ◇ *My son is coming home soon.* ◇ *Come here!* ◇ *Come and see us soon!* ◇ *Here comes Jo!* (= Jo is coming) ◇ *There's a storm coming.* ◇ **~ to do sth** *They're coming to stay for a week.* HELP In spoken English **come** can be used with **and** plus another verb, instead of with **to** and the infinitive, to show purpose or to tell sb what to do: *When did she last come and see you?* ◇ *Come and have your dinner.* The **and** is sometimes left out, especially in NAmE: *Come have your dinner.* **2** A1 [I] to arrive at or reach a place: **~ to …** *They continued until they came to a river.* ◇ *She came to work wearing a very smart suit.* ◇ *They came as far as the gate.* ◇ *Your breakfast is coming soon.* ◇ *Have any letters come for me?* ◇ *Help came at last.* **3** A1 [I] to come somewhere in order to do sth or get sth: **~ for sth** *I've come for my book.* ◇ **~ about sth** *I've come about my book.* ◇ **~ to do sth** *I've come to get my book.* ◇ **~ doing sth** *He came looking for me.* **4** A1 [I] to move or travel, especially with sb else, to a particular place or in order to be present at an event: *I've only come for an hour.* ◇ *Thanks for coming* (= to my house, party, etc.). ◇ **~ to do sth** *Ten thousand people came to hear him speak.* ◇ **(to) sth) (with sb)** *Are you coming to the club with us tonight?* ◇ **~ doing sth** *Why don't you come skating tonight?*
• TRAVEL **5** A1 [I] **+ noun** to travel a particular distance: *We've come 50 miles this morning.* ◇ (figurative) *The company has come a long way* (= made lot of progress) *in the last 5 years.*
• RUNNING/HURRYING ETC. **6** A2 [I] **~ doing sth (+ adv./prep.)** to move in a particular way or while doing sth else: *A car came flying round the corner.*
• HAPPEN **7** A2 [I] to happen: *The agreement came after several hours of negotiations.* ◇ *Spring came late this year.* ◇ *The time has come* (= now is the moment) *to act.* ◇ **~ as sth** *His resignation came as no surprise.* ◇ *More details of the event are coming soon.* **8** [T] **~ to do sth** used in questions to talk about how or why sth happened: *How did he come to break his leg?* ◇ *How do you come to be so late?*
• TO A POSITION/STATE **9** A2 [I] **+ adv./prep.** (not used in the progressive tenses) to have a particular position: *That comes a long way down my list of priorities.* ◇ *She came second* (= received the second highest score) *in the exam.* ◇ *His family comes first* (= is the most important thing in his life). **10** [I] **~ to/into sth** used in many expressions to show that sth has reached a particular state: *At last winter came to an end.* ◇ *He came to power in 2019.* ◇ *to come to an agreement/a decision* ◇ *our understanding of how the universe came into existence* **11** B1 [I] (not used in the progressive tenses) (of goods, products, etc.) to be available or to exist in a particular way: **~ in sth** *This dress comes in black and red.* ◇ **~ with sth** *The DVD comes with several bonus features.* **+ adj.** (informal): *New cars don't come cheap* (= they are expensive). **12** B2 [I, T] to become: **+ adj.** *The handle came loose.* ◇ *The buttons had come undone.* ◇ *Everything will come right in the end.* ◇ **~ to do sth** *This design came to be known as the Oriental style.* **13** [T] **~ to do sth** to reach a point where you realize, understand or believe sth: *In time she came to love him.* ◇ *She had come to see the problem in a new light.* ◇ *I've come to expect this kind of behaviour from him.*
• SEX **14** [I] (informal) to have an ORGASM
IDM HELP Most idioms containing **come** are at the entries for the nouns or adjectives in the idioms, for example **come a cropper** is at **cropper**. **be as clever, stupid, etc. as they ˈcome** (informal) to be very clever, stupid, etc. **come aˈgain?** (informal) used to ask sb to repeat sth: '*She's an entomologist.*' '*Come again?*' '*An entomologist—she studies insects.*' **come and ˈgo 1** to arrive and leave; to move freely: *They had a party next door—we heard people coming and going all night.* **2** to be present for a short time and then go away: *The pain in my leg comes and goes.* **come**

**ˈeasily, ˈnaturally, etc. to sb** (of an activity, a skill, etc.) to be easy, natural, etc. for sb to do: *Acting comes naturally to her.* **come the ...** (*informal*) to play the part of a particular type of person; to behave in a particular way: *Don't come the innocent with me.* **come to ˈnothing | not ˈcome to ˈanything** to be unsuccessful; to have no successful result: *How sad that all his hard work should come to nothing.* ◇ *Her plans didn't come to anything.* **come to ˈthat | if it comes to ˈthat** (*informal, especially BrE*) used to introduce sth extra that is connected with what has just been said: *I don't really trust him—nor his wife, come to that.* **come ˈwhat ˈmay** despite any problems or difficulties you may have: *He promised to support her come what may.* **how ˈcome ( ...)?** (*informal*) used to say you do not understand how sth can happen and would like an explanation: *'I think you owe me some money.' 'How come?'* ◇ *If she spent five years in Paris, how come her French is so bad?* **not ˈcome to much** to not be important or successful ˈcome (used after a noun) in the future: *They may well regret the decision in years to come.* ◇ *This will be a problem for some time to come* (= for a period of time in the future). **when it comes to (doing) sth** ? when it is a question of sth: *When it comes to getting things done, he's useless.* **where sb is ˈcoming from** (*informal*) somebody's ideas, beliefs, personality, etc. that makes them say what they have said: *I see where you're coming from* (= I understand what you mean).

**PHRV** **come aˈbout (that ...)** to happen: *Can you tell me how the accident came about?*
**come aˈcross** (*also* **come ˈover**) **1** to be understood: *He spoke for a long time but his meaning didn't really come across.* **2** to make a particular impression: *She comes across well in interviews.* ◇ *He came over as a sympathetic person.* **come aˈcross sb/sth** ? [no passive] to meet or find sb/sth by chance: *I came across children sleeping under bridges.* ◇ *She came across some old photographs in a drawer.* **come aˈcross (with sth)** [no passive] to provide or supply sth when you need it: *I hoped she'd come across with some more information.*
**come ˈafter sb** [no passive] to run after or follow sb
**come aˈlong 1** to arrive; to appear: *When the right opportunity comes along, she'll take it.* **2** to go somewhere with sb: *I'm glad you came along.* **3** (*informal*) to improve or develop in the way that you want **SYN** **progress**: *Your French has come along a lot recently.* **4** used in orders to tell sb to hurry, or to try harder: *Come along! We're late.* ◇ *Come along! It's easy!*
**come aˈpart** to break into pieces: *The book just came apart in my hands.* ◇ (*figurative*) *My whole life had come apart at the seams.*
**come aˈround** (*also* **come ˈround** *especially in BrE*) **1** (*also* **come ˈto**) to become conscious again: *Your mother hasn't yet come around from the anaesthetic.* **2** (of a date or a regular event) to happen again: *My birthday seems to come around more quickly every year.* **come aˈround (to ...)** (*also* **come ˈround (to ...)** *especially in BrE*) to come to a place, especially sb's house, to visit for a short time: *Do come around and see us some time.* **come aˈround (to sth)** (*also* **come ˈround (to sth)** *especially in BrE*) to change your mood or your opinion: *He'll never come around to my way of thinking.*
**come ˈat sb** [no passive] to move towards sb as though you are going to attack them: *She came at me with a knife.* ◇ (*figurative*) *The noise came at us from all sides.* **come ˈat sth** to think about a problem, question, etc. in a particular way **SYN** **approach**: *We're getting nowhere—let's come at it from another angle.*
**come aˈway (from sth)** to become separated from sth: *The plaster had started to come away from the wall.* **come aˈway with sth** [no passive] to leave a place with a particular feeling or impression: *We came away with the impression that all was not well with their marriage.*
**come ˈback** ? to return: *You came back* (= came home) *very late last night.* ◇ *The colour was coming back to her cheeks.* ◇ (*figurative*) *United came back from being two goals down to win 3–2.* ⇒ **SYNONYMS** at **RETURN** **come ˈback (at sb) (with sth)** to reply to sb angrily or with force: *She came back at the speaker with some sharp questions.* ⇒ related noun **COMEBACK** (3) **come ˈback (to sb)** to return to sb's memory: *It's all coming back to me now.* ◇ *Once you've been in France a few days, your French will soon come back.* **come ˈback ˈin** to become popular or successful again: *Long hair for men seems to be coming back in.* ⇒ related noun **COMEBACK** (2) **come ˈback to sth** [no passive] to return to a subject, an idea, etc: *Let's come back to the point at issue.* ◇ *It all comes back to a question of money.*
**come beˈfore sb/sth** [no passive] (*formal*) to be presented to sb/sth for discussion or a decision: *The case comes before the court next week.*
**come beˈtween sb and sb** [no passive] to damage a relationship between two people: *I'd hate anything to come between us.*
**come ˈby (sth)** (*NAmE*) to make a short visit to a place, in order to see sb: *She came by the house.* **come ˈby sth 1** to manage to get sth: *Jobs are hard to come by these days.* **2** to receive sth: *How did you come by that scratch on your cheek?*
**come ˈdown 1** to break and fall to the ground: *The ceiling came down with a terrific crash.* **2** (of rain, snow, etc.) to fall: *The rain came down in torrents.* **3** (of an aircraft) to land or fall from the sky: *We were forced to come down in a field.* **4** if a price, a temperature, a rate, etc. **comes down**, it gets lower: *The price of gas is coming down.* ◇ *Gas is coming down in price.* **5** to decide and say publicly that you support or oppose sb/sth: *The committee came down in support of his application.* **6** to reach as far down as a particular point: *Her hair comes down to her waist.* **7** (*informal*) to become less excited or happy, especially after taking drugs **come ˈdown (from ...)** (*BrE, formal*) to leave a university, especially Oxford or Cambridge, at the end of a term or after finishing your studies **OPP** **come ˈup (to ...)** **come ˈdown (from ...) (to ...)** to come from one place to another, usually from the north of a country to the south, or from a larger place to a smaller one **come ˈdown on sb** [no passive] (*informal*) to criticize sb severely or punish sb: *Don't come down too hard on her.* ◇ *The courts are coming down heavily on young offenders.* **come ˈdown (to sb)** to have come from a long time in the past: *The name has come down from the last century.* **come ˈdown to sth** [no passive] to depend on a single important point: *What it comes down to is either I get more money or I leave.* **come ˈdown with sth** [no passive] to get an illness that is not very serious: *I think I'm coming down with flu.*
**come ˈfor sb 1** to arrive in order to arrest sb: *Brad was at home when the police came for him.* **2** to move towards sb to attack them: *The guy was coming for me with a knife.*
**come ˈforward** to offer your help, services, etc: *Several people came forward with information.* ◇ *Police have asked witnesses of the accident to come forward.*
**come ˈfrom ...** ? (not used in the progressive tenses) to have as your place of birth or the place where you live: *She comes from London.* ◇ *Where do you come from?* **come ˈfrom sth 1** to start in a particular place or be produced from a particular thing: *Much of our butter comes from New Zealand.* ◇ *This wool comes from goats, not sheep.* ◇ *This poem comes from his new book.* ◇ *Where does her attitude come from?* ◇ *Where's that smell coming from?* ◇ *He comes from a family of actors.* ◇ *'She doesn't try hard enough.' 'That's rich, coming from you* (= you do not try hard either).' **2** = **COME OF/FROM STH** **come from beˈhind** (in sport) to win when it was not expected because you seemed to be losing
**come ˈin 1** to enter a room or building: *Come in!* (= used when sb knocks at a door) **2** when the **TIDE** **comes in**, it moves towards the land **OPP** **go out 3** to finish a race in a particular position: *My horse came in last.* **4** to become fashionable: *Long hair for men came in in the sixties.* **OPP** **go out 5** to become available: *We're still waiting for copies of the book to come in.* **6** to have a part in sth: *I understand the plan perfectly, but I can't see where I come in.* **7** to arrive somewhere; to be received: *The train is coming in now.* ◇ *News is coming in of a serious plane crash in France.* ◇ *She has over a thousand pounds a month coming in from her investments.* **8** to take part in a discussion:

*Would you like to come in at this point, Susan?* **9** (of a law or rule) to be introduced; to begin to be used **come 'in for sth** [no passive] to receive sth, especially sth unpleasant: *The government's economic policies have come in for a lot of criticism.* **come 'in (on sth)** to become involved in sth: *If you want to come in on the deal, you need to decide now.*

**come 'into sth** [no passive] **1** to be left money by sb who has died: *She came into a fortune when her uncle died.* **2** to be important in a particular situation: *I've worked very hard to pass this exam—luck doesn't come into it.*

**'come of/from sth** to be the result of sth: *I made a few enquiries, but nothing came of it in the end.* ◊ **come of/from doing sth** *That comes of eating too much!*

**come 'off** **1** to be able to be removed: *Does this hood come off?* ◊ *That mark won't come off.* **2** (*informal*) to take place; to happen: *Did the trip to Rome ever come off?* **3** (*informal*) (of a plan, etc.) to be successful; to have the intended effect or result: *They had wanted it to be a surprise but the plan didn't come off.* **4 come off well, badly, etc.** (especially *BrE, informal*) to be successful/not successful in a fight, contest, etc: *I thought they came off very well in the debate.* **come 'off (sth)** to fall from sth: *to come off your bicycle/horse* **2** to become separated from sth: *When I tried to lift the jug, the handle came off in my hand.* ◊ *A button had come off my coat.* **come 'off it** (*informal*) used to disagree with sb rudely: *Come off it! We don't have a chance.* **come 'off sth** [no passive] to stop taking medicine, a drug, alcohol, etc: *I've tried to get him to come off the tranquillizers.*

**come 'on** **1** ⚡ 🅰🅩 used in orders to tell sb to hurry or to try harder: *Come on! We don't have much time.* ◊ *Come on! Try once more.* **2** (of an actor) to walk onto the stage **3** (of a player) to join a team during a game: *Wilson came on for Kane ten minutes before the end of the game.* **4** (*informal*) to improve or develop in the way you want: *The project is coming on fine.* **5** used to show that you know what sb has said is not correct: *Oh, come on—you know that isn't true!* **6** (usually used in the progressive tenses) (of an illness or a mood) to begin: *I can feel a cold coming on.* ◊ *I think there's rain coming on.* ◊ **come on to do sth** *It came on to rain.* **7** (of a TV programme, etc.) to start: *What time does the news come on?* **8** to begin to operate: *Set the oven to come on at six.* ◊ *When does the heating come on?* **'come on/upon sb/sth** [no passive] (*formal*) to meet or find sb/sth by chance **come 'on to sb** (*informal*) to behave in a way that shows sb that you want to have a sexual relationship with them ⇒ related noun COME-ON **come 'on to sth** [no passive] to start talking about a subject: *I'd like to come on to that question later.*

**come 'out** **1** when the sun, moon or stars **come out**, they appear: *The rain stopped and the sun came out.* **2** (of flowers) to open: *The daffodils came out early this year.* **3** to be produced or published: *When is her new novel coming out?* **4** (of news, the truth, etc.) to become known: *The full story came out at the trial.* ◊ **it comes out that...** *It came out that he'd been telling lies.* **5** to be shown clearly: *Her best qualities come out in a crisis.* **6** when words **come out**, they are spoken: *I tried to say 'I love you,' but the words wouldn't come out.* **7** to say publicly whether you agree or disagree with sth: *He came out against the plan.* ◊ *In her speech, the senator came out in favour of a change in the law.* **8** (*BrE*) to stop work and go on strike **9** to no longer hide the fact that you are GAY **10** if a photograph taken on film **comes out**, it is a clear picture when it is developed and printed: *In the 1950s photographs often didn't come out at all.* **11** (of a young UPPER-CLASS girl in the past) to be formally introduced into society **come 'out (of sth)** **1** (of an object) to be removed from a place where it is fixed: *This nail won't come out.* **2** (of dirt, a mark, etc.) to be removed from sth by washing or cleaning: *These ink stains won't come out of my dress.* ◊ *Will the colour come out* (= become faint or disappear) *if I wash it?* **come 'out at sth** [no passive] to add up to a particular cost or sum: *The total bill comes out at £500.* **come 'out in sth** [no passive] (of a person) to become covered in spots, etc. on the skin: *Hot weather makes her come out*

*in a rash.* **come 'out of yourself** to relax and become more confident and friendly with other people: *It was when she started drama classes that she really came out of herself.* **come 'out of sth** [no passive] to develop from sth: *The book came out of his experiences in India.* ◊ *Rock music came out of the blues.* **come 'out with sth** [no passive] to say sth, especially sth surprising or rude: *He came out with a stream of abuse.* ◊ *She sometimes comes out with the most extraordinary remarks.*

**come 'over** **1** (*BrE, informal*) to suddenly feel sth: + **adj**. *to come over funny/dizzy/faint* ◊ *I come over all shy whenever I see her.* **2** = COME ACROSS **come 'over (to ...)** to come to a place, especially sb's house, in order to visit for a short time **come 'over (to ...) (from ...)** to travel from one place to another, usually over a long distance: *Why don't you come over to England in the summer?* ◊ *Her grandparents came over from Ireland during the famine.* **come 'over (to sth)** to change from one side, opinion, etc. to another **come 'over sb** [no passive] to affect sb: *A fit of dizziness came over her.* ◊ *I can't think what came over me* (= I do not know what caused me to behave in that way).

**come 'round (to sth)** (especially *BrE*) = COME AROUND **come 'through** (of news or a message) to arrive by phone, radio, etc. or through an official organization: *A message is just coming through.* **come 'through (sth)** to get better after a serious illness or to avoid serious injury **SYN** survive: *With such a weak heart she was lucky to come through the operation.* **come 'through (with sth)** to successfully do or complete sth that you have promised to do: *We were worried she wouldn't be able to handle it, but she came through in the end.* ◊ *The bank finally came through with the money.*

**come 'to** = COME AROUND **come to your'self** (*old-fashioned*) to return to your normal state **'come to sb** [no passive] (of an idea) to enter your mind: *The idea came to me in the bath.* ◊ **come to sb that ...** *It suddenly came to her that she had been wrong all along.* **'come to sth** [no passive] **1** to add up to sth: *The bill came to $30.* ◊ *I never expected those few items to come to so much.* **2** to reach a particular situation, especially a bad one: *The doctors will operate if necessary—but it may not come to that.* ◊ *Who'd have thought things would come to this* (= become so bad)?

**come to'gether** if two or more different people or things **come together**, they form a united group: *Three colleges have come together to create a new university.* ◊ *Bits and pieces of things he'd read and heard were coming together, and he began to understand.*

**'come under sth** [no passive] **1** to be included in a particular group: *What heading does this come under?* **2** to be a person that others are attacking or criticizing: *The head teacher came under a lot of criticism from the parents.* **3** to be controlled or influenced by sth: *All her students came under her spell.*

**come 'up** **1** (of plants) to appear above the soil: *The daffodils are just beginning to come up.* **2** (of the sun) to rise: *We watched the sun come up.* **3** to happen: *I'm afraid something urgent has come up.* ◊ *We'll let you know if any vacancies come up.* **4** to be mentioned or discussed: *The subject came up in conversation.* ◊ *The question is bound to come up at the meeting.* **5** (usually used in the progressive tenses) to be going to happen, arrive or be ready soon: *Her birthday is coming up soon.* ◊ (*informal*) *'Is lunch ready?' 'Coming up!'* **6** to be dealt with by a court: *Her divorce case comes up next month.* **7** if your number, name, ticket, etc. **comes up** in a game in which you bet money, it is chosen and you win sth **come 'up (to ...)** (*BrE, formal*) to arrive at a university, especially Oxford or Cambridge, at the beginning of a term or in order to begin your studies **OPP** come down (from ...) **come 'up (to ...) (from ...)** to come from one place to another, especially from the south of a country to the north or from a smaller place to a larger one: *Why don't you come up to Scotland for a few days?* **come 'up (to sb)** to move towards sb, in order to talk to them: *He came up to me and asked me the way to the station.* **come 'up against sb/sth** [no passive] to be faced with or opposed by sb/sth: *We expect to come up against a lot of opposition to the plan.* **come 'up for sth** [no passive] **1** to be considered for a job, an important position, etc: *She comes up for re-election next year.* **2** to be reaching the time when sth must be done: *His contract is coming up for renewal.* **,come 'up to sth** [no passive] **1** to reach as far as a particular point: *The water came up to my neck.* **2** to reach an acceptable level or standard: *His performance didn't really come up to his usual high standard.* ◊ *Their trip to France didn't come up to expectations.* **,come 'up with sth** [B1] [no passive] to find or produce an answer, a sum of money, etc: *She came up with a new idea for increasing sales.* ◊ *How soon can you come up with the money?*

- **'come upon sb/sth** = COME ON/UPON SB/STH
- **prep.** *(old-fashioned, informal)* when the time mentioned comes: *They would have been married forty years come this June.*
- **exclamation** *(old-fashioned)* used when encouraging sb to be sensible or reasonable, or when making a slight criticism: *Oh come now, things aren't as bad as all that.* ◊ *Come, come, Miss Jones, you know perfectly well what I mean.*
- **noun** [U] *(slang)* SEMEN

**come·back** /ˈkʌmbæk/ *noun* **1** [usually sing.] if a person in public life makes a **comeback**, they start doing sth again that they had stopped doing, or they become popular again: *an ageing pop star trying to stage a comeback* **2** if a thing makes a **comeback**, it becomes popular and fashionable or successful again **3** *(informal)* a quick reply to a critical remark **SYN** retort **4** a way of holding sb responsible for sth wrong that has been done to you: *You agreed to the contract, so now you have no comeback.*

**com·edian** /kəˈmiːdiən/ *noun* a person whose job is to make people laugh by telling jokes or funny stories: *a stand-up comedian*

**com·edic** /kəˈmiːdɪk/ *adj.* connected with comedy **SYN** comic: *Many comedic moments feel directed, not spontaneous.*

**com·edi·enne** /kəˌmiːdiˈen/ *noun* *(old-fashioned)* a woman whose job is to make people laugh by telling jokes or funny stories

**come·down** /ˈkʌmdaʊn/ *noun* [usually sing.] *(informal)* a situation in which a person is not as important as before, or does not get as much respect from other people

**com·edy** ❶ A2 /ˈkɒmədi/; *NAmE* /ˈkɑːm-/ *noun* (pl. -ies) **1** A2 [C, U] a play, film or TV show that is intended to be funny, usually with a happy ending; plays, films and TV shows of this type: *a romantic comedy* ◊ *a black comedy* (= a play or film that deals with unpleasant or terrible things in a humorous way) ◊ *He moved to Los Angeles to write comedy.* ◊ *a comedy series/show* ⇒ compare TRAGEDY ⇒ see also BLACK *adj.* (9), MUSICAL COMEDY, SITUATION COMEDY ⇒ WORDFINDER NOTE at DRAMA

> **WORDFINDER** caricature, funny, joke, parody, pun, sketch, slapstick, spoof, take-off

**2** B1 [U] professional entertainment with jokes, short acts, etc. that is intended to be funny: *The show combines theatre with the best of stand-up and sketch comedy.* ⇒ see also STAND-UP *adj.* (1) **3** B2 [U] a humorous aspect of sth **SYN** humour: *He didn't appreciate the comedy of the situation.*

**,comedy of 'manners** *noun* a funny play, film or book that shows the silly behaviour of a particular group of people

**come-'hither** *adj.* [only before noun] (of sb's expression) appearing to be trying to attract sb sexually: *a come-hither look*

**come·ly** /ˈkʌmli/ *adj.* *(literary)* (especially of a woman) pleasant to look at **SYN** attractive

**'come-on** *noun* [usually sing.] *(informal)* an object or action that is intended to attract sb or to persuade them to do sth: *She was definitely giving him the come-on* (= trying to attract him sexually).

**comer** /ˈkʌmə(r)/ *noun* **1** **,all 'comers** [pl.] anyone who wants to take part in an activity or a competition: *The event is open to all comers.* **2** (usually with an adjective) a person who arrives somewhere: *Early comers can enjoy the festival warm-up act.* ⇒ see also LATECOMER, NEW-

299

COMER **3** *(NAmE, informal)* a person who is likely to be successful

**comet** /ˈkɒmɪt; *NAmE* ˈkɑːm-/ *noun* a mass of ice and dust that moves around the sun and looks like a bright star with a tail ⇒ WORDFINDER NOTE at UNIVERSE

**come·up·pance** /ˌkʌmˈʌpəns/ *noun* [sing.] *(informal)* a punishment for sth bad that you have done, that other people feel you really deserve: *I was glad to see that the bad guy got his comeuppance at the end of the movie.*

**com·fort** ❶ B2 /ˈkʌmfət; *NAmE* -fərt/ *noun, verb*

> **WORD FAMILY**
> comfort *noun, verb*
> comfortable *adj.*
> (≠ uncomfortable)
> comfortably *adv.*
> (≠ uncomfortably)
> comforting *adj.*

- **noun 1** ❶ B2 [U] the state of being physically relaxed and free from pain; the state of having a pleasant life, with everything that you need: *The hotel offers a high standard of comfort and service.* ◊ **in ~** *They had enough money to live in comfort in their old age.* ◊ **in the ~ of sth** *Watch the latest movies in the comfort of your own home.* ◊ **for ~** *I dress for comfort rather than elegance.* ◊ *He's beginning to find a comfort level with his teammates now.* **2** ❶ B2 [U] a feeling of not suffering or worrying so much; a feeling of being less unhappy **SYN** consolation: *I tried to offer a few words of comfort.* ◊ **to take comfort from sb's words** *We know that they will find comfort in the knowledge that he died doing the job he loved* ◊ **to sb** *If it's any comfort to you, I'm in the same situation.* **3** ❶ B2 [sing.] a person or thing that helps you when you are suffering, worried or unhappy: **~ (to sb)** *The children have been a great comfort to me through all of this.* ◊ **it is a ~ (to sb) to do sth** *It's a comfort to know that she is safe.* ◊ **it is a ~ (to sb) that ...** *In some ways it's a comfort that they died together.* ⇒ see also COLD COMFORT **4** ❶ B2 [C, usually pl.] a thing that makes your life easier or more comfortable: *material comforts* (= money and possessions) ◊ *She desperately missed her home comforts while camping.* ⇒ see also CREATURE COMFORTS **IDM** see CLOSE[2] *adj.*
- **verb** ❶ to make sb who is worried or unhappy feel better by being kind and showing sympathy to them: **~ sb** *The victim's widow was today being comforted by family and friends.* ◊ **~ yourself with sth** *She comforted herself with the thought that it would soon be spring.* ◊ **be comforted to do sth** *He was comforted to know that most people in the class knew even less than he.* ◊ **it comforts sb to do sth** *It comforted her to feel his arms around her.*

**com·fort·able** ❶ A2 /ˈkʌmftəbl; ˈkʌmfət-; *NAmE* also ˈkʌmfərt-/ *adj.*
- **CLOTHES/FURNITURE 1** ❶ A2 (of clothes, furniture, etc.) making you feel physically relaxed; pleasant to wear, sit on, etc: *It's such a comfortable bed.* ◊ *These new shoes are not very comfortable.* ◊ *clothes that are comfortable to wear* **OPP** uncomfortable
- **PHYSICALLY RELAXED 2** ❶ A2 feeling physically relaxed in a pleasant way; warm enough, without pain, etc: *Are you comfortable? Please make yourself comfortable while I get some coffee.* ◊ *The patient is comfortable* (= not in pain) *after his operation.* ◊ *This bed is lumpy—I just can't seem to get comfortable.* **OPP** uncomfortable
- **CONFIDENT 3** ❶ B1 confident about sth and not worried or afraid: **~ with sth/sb** *He's more comfortable with computers than with people.* ◊ **~ about (doing) sth** *I didn't feel comfortable about accepting the money.* **OPP** uncomfortable
- **HAVING MONEY 4** having enough money to buy what you want without worrying about the cost: *They're not millionaires, but they're certainly very comfortable.* ⇒ SYNONYMS at RICH
- **VICTORY 5** quite large; allowing you to win easily: *The party won with a comfortable majority.* ◊ *a comfortable 2-0 win*

**com·fort·ably** /ˈkʌmftəbli; *BrE* also ˈkʌmfət-; *NAmE* also ˈkʌmfərt-/ *adv.* **1** in a comfortable way: *All the rooms were comfortably furnished.* ◊ *If you're all sitting comfortably,*

then I'll begin. **2** with no problem **SYN easily**: *He can comfortably afford the extra expense.* ◊ *They are comfortably ahead in the opinion polls.*
**IDM** ˌcomfortably ˈoff having enough money to buy what you want without worrying too much about the cost

ˈcomfort blanket *noun* (*BrE*) = SECURITY BLANKET (1): *You can't use food as a comfort blanket.*

ˈcom·fort·er /ˈkʌmfətə(r); *NAmE* -fərt-/ *noun* **1** a person or thing that makes you feel calmer or less worried **2** (*NAmE*) a type of thick cover for a bed ⇨ compare QUILT **3** (*NAmE*) = DUVET

ˈcomfort food *noun* [U, C] food that makes you feel better, often because it contains a lot of sugar, or because it reminds you of home: *Chocolate is a great comfort food.*

ˈcom·fort·ing /ˈkʌmfətɪŋ; *NAmE* -fərt-/ *adj.* making you feel calmer and less worried or unhappy: *her comforting words* ◊ *It's comforting to know that you'll be there.* ▸ ˈcom·fort·ing·ly *adv.*

ˈcom·fort·less /ˈkʌmfətləs; *NAmE* -fərt-/ *adj.* (*formal*) without anything to make a place more comfortable

ˈcomfort zone *noun* **1** (*sometimes disapproving*) a place or situation in which you feel safe or comfortable, especially when you choose to stay in this situation instead of trying to work harder or achieve more: *Stepping outside your comfort zone and trying new things can be a great experience.* **2** (*approving*) (especially in sport) a state in which you feel confident and are performing at your best: *I knew if I could find my comfort zone I would be difficult to beat.*

ˈcom·frey /ˈkʌmfri/ *noun* [U, C] a plant with large leaves covered with small hairs and small flowers that are like bells in shape

ˈcomfy /ˈkʌmfi/ *adj.* (**com·fier**, **com·fi·est**) (*informal*) comfortable: *a comfy armchair/bed* **HELP** **more comfy** is also common as a comparative.

ˈcom·ic /ˈkɒmɪk; *NAmE* ˈkɑːm-/ *adj., noun*
■ *adj.* **1** humorous and making you laugh: *a comic monologue/story* ◊ *The play is both comic and tragic.* ◊ *She can always be relied on to provide comic relief* (= sth to make you laugh) *at a boring party.* ◊ *He wore a red nose and novelty glasses for comic effect.* ⇨ SYNONYMS at FUNNY **2** [only before noun] connected with comedy (= entertainment that is funny and that makes people laugh): *a comic opera* ◊ *a comic actor* ⇨ WORDFINDER NOTE at STORY
■ *noun* **1** (*NAmE also* ˈcomic book) a magazine, usually for children, that tells stories through pictures **2** the ˈcomics [pl.] (*NAmE*) the section of a newspaper that contains COMIC STRIPS **3** a person who makes people laugh by telling jokes or funny stories **SYN** comedian

ˈcom·ic·al /ˈkɒmɪkl; *NAmE* ˈkɑːm-/ *adj.* funny, especially because it is strange or silly ▸ ˈcom·ic·al·ly /-kli/ *adv.*

ˈcomic strip (*also* ˈcar·toon) (*BrE also* ˈstrip carˈtoon) (*NAmE also* ˈstrip) *noun* a series of drawings inside boxes that tell a story and are often published in newspapers

ˈcom·ing /ˈkʌmɪŋ/ *noun, adj.*
■ *noun* [sing.] **the ~ of sth/sb** the time when sth new begins or sb arrives: *With the coming of modern technology, many jobs were lost.*
**IDM** ˌcomings and ˈgoings (*informal*) the movement of people arriving at and leaving a particular place: *It's hard to keep track of the children's comings and goings.*
■ *adj.* [only before noun] happening soon; next: *in the coming months* ◊ *This coming Sunday is her birthday.*

ˌcoming of ˈage *noun* [sing.] the time when a person reaches the age at which they have an adult's legal rights and responsibilities

ˈcom·ity /ˈkɒməti; *NAmE* ˈkɑːm-/ *noun* (*pl.* -ies) (*NAmE, formal*) an association of nations or organizations that brings benefits to each one: *the comity of nations*

ˈcomma /ˈkɒmə; *NAmE* ˈkɑːmə/ *noun* the mark (,) used to separate the items in a list or to show where there is a slight break in a sentence ⇨ see also INVERTED COMMAS

ˈcom·mand /kəˈmɑːnd; *NAmE* -ˈmænd/ *noun, verb*
■ *noun*
• ORDER **1** [C] an order given to a person or an animal: *Begin when I give the command.* ◊ *You must obey the captain's commands.* ◊ *~ to do sth He issued the command to retreat.* ⇨ WORDFINDER NOTE at ARMY
• FOR COMPUTER **2** [C] an instruction given to a computer: *The computer executes commands successively in the order they arrive.*

**WORDFINDER** connect, desktop, drag, enter, insert, refresh, scroll, select, toggle

• CONTROL **3** [U] control and authority over a situation or a group of people: **under sb's ~** *He has 1 200 men under his command.* ◊ *~ of sb/sth He has command of 1 200 men.* ◊ *The police arrived and took command of the situation.* ◊ *In 1939 he assumed command of all French naval forces.* ◊ **in ~** *Who is in command here?* ◊ **in ~ of sth/yourself** *For the first time in years, she felt in command of her life.* ⇨ see also HIGH COMMAND, SECOND IN COMMAND
• IN ARMY **4** Command [C] a part of an army, AIR FORCE, etc. that is organized and controlled separately; a group of officers who give orders: *Bomber Command*
• KNOWLEDGE **5** [U, sing.] **~ (of sth)** your knowledge of sth; your ability to use or do sth, especially a language: *Applicants will be expected to have (a) good command of English.*
**IDM** at your comˈmand if you have a skill or an amount of sth at your command, you are able to use it well and completely be at sb's comˈmand (*formal*) to be ready to obey sb: *I'm at your command—what would you like me to do?* ⇨ more at WISH *n.*
■ *verb*
• ORDER **1** (*of sb in a position of authority*) to tell sb to do sth **SYN** order: *~ sb to do sth He commanded his men to retreat.* ◊ *~ sth She requested the release of the prisoners.* ◊ *~ (sb) + speech* 'Come here!' he commanded (them). ◊ *~ that …* (*formal*) *The commission intervened and commanded that work on the building cease.*
• IN ARMY **2** *~ sb/sth* to be in charge of a group of people in the army, NAVY, etc: *In March 1942 he was appointed to command US naval forces in Europe* ◊ *The troops were commanded by General Haig.*
• DESERVE AND GET **3** [no passive] (*not used in the progressive tenses*) *~ sth* to deserve and get sth because of the special qualities you have: *to command sympathy/support* ◊ *She was able to command the respect of the class.* ◊ *The headlines commanded her attention.* ◊ *As a top lawyer, he can expect to command a six-figure salary.*
• VIEW **4** [no passive] (*not used in the progressive tenses*) *~ sth* (*formal*) to be in a position from where you can see or control sth: *The hotel commands a fine view of the valley.*
• CONTROL **5** (*not used in the progressive tenses*) *~ sth* (*formal*) to have control of sth; to have sth available for use: *The party was no longer able to command a majority in Parliament.* ◊ *the power and finances commanded by the police*

ˈcom·mand·ant /ˈkɒmədænt; *NAmE* ˈkɑːm-/ *noun* the officer in charge of a particular military group or institution

ˈcomˌmand eˈconomy *noun* = PLANNED ECONOMY

ˈcom·man·deer /ˌkɒmənˈdɪə(r); *NAmE* ˌkɑːmənˈdɪr/ *verb* *~ sth* to take control of a building, a vehicle, etc. for military purposes during a war, or by force for your own use **SYN** requisition

ˈcom·mand·er /kəˈmɑːndə(r); *NAmE* -ˈmænd-/ *noun* **1** a person who is in charge of sth, especially an officer in charge of a particular group of soldiers or a military operation: *military/allied/field/flight commanders* ◊ *the commander of the expedition* **2** (*abbr.* **Cdr**) an officer of fairly high rank in the British or American NAVY **3** (*abbr.* **Cdr**) (in England) a London police officer of high rank

comˌmander-in-ˈchief (*abbr.* **C.-in-C.**) *noun* (*pl.* comˌmanders-in-chief) the officer who commands all the armed forces of a country or all its forces in a particular area

**com·mand·ing** /kəˈmɑːndɪŋ; *NAmE* -ˈmæn-/ *adj.* **1** [only before noun] in a position of authority that allows you to give formal orders: *Who is your commanding officer?* **2** [usually before noun] if you are in a **commanding position** or have a **commanding lead**, you are likely to win a race or competition **3** [usually before noun] powerful and making people admire and obey you: *a commanding figure/presence/voice* **4** [only before noun] if a building is in a **commanding position** or has a **commanding view**, you can see the area around very well from it: *The castle occupies a commanding position on a hill.*

**com·mand·ment** /kəˈmɑːndmənt; *NAmE* -ˈmænd-/ *noun* a law given by God, especially any of the **Ten Commandments** given to the Jews in the Bible

**comˈmand module** *noun* the part of a SPACECRAFT that remains after the rest has separated from it, where the controls and the people that operate them are located

**com·man·do** /kəˈmɑːndəʊ; *NAmE* -ˈmæn-/ *noun* (*pl.* **-os**) a soldier or a group of soldiers who are trained to make quick attacks in enemy areas

**comˈmand perˈformance** *noun* [usually sing.] a special performance, for example at a theatre, that is given for a head of state

**comˈmand post** *noun* the place from which a military unit or other official operation is commanded: *Police have set up a command post outside the building.*

**com·mem·or·ate** /kəˈmeməreɪt/ *verb* **~ sth/sb** to remind people of an important event or person from the past with a special action or object; to exist to remind people of a person or an event from the past: *A series of movies will be shown to commemorate the thirtieth anniversary of his death.* ◇ *A plaque commemorates the battle.* ⊃ WORDFINDER NOTE at CELEBRATE

**com·mem·or·ation** /kəˌmeməˈreɪʃn/ *noun* [U, C] an action, or a ceremony, etc. that makes people remember and show respect for an important person or event in the past: *a commemoration service* ◇ **in ~ of sb/sth** *a statue in commemoration of a national hero*

**com·mem·ora·tive** /kəˈmemərətɪv; *NAmE* -reɪt-/ *adj.* intended to help people remember and respect an important person or event in the past: *commemorative stamps*

**com·mence** /kəˈmens/ *verb* [I, T] (*formal*) to begin to happen; to begin sth: *The meeting is scheduled to commence at noon.* ◇ *I will be on leave during the week commencing 15 February.* ◇ **~ with sth** *The day commenced with a welcome from the principal.* ◇ **~ sth** *She commenced her medical career in 1956.* ◇ **~ doing sth** *We commence building next week.* ◇ **~ to do sth** *Operators commenced to build pipelines in 1862.* ⊃ SYNONYMS at START

**com·mence·ment** /kəˈmensmənt/ *noun* [U, C, usually sing.] **1** (*formal*) beginning: *the commencement of the financial year* **2** (*NAmE*) a ceremony at which students receive their academic degrees or DIPLOMAS SYN **graduation**

**com·mend** /kəˈmend/ *verb* **1** **~ sb/sth (for sth/for doing sth)** | **~ sb/sth (on sth/on doing sth)** to praise sb/sth, especially publicly: *She was commended on her handling of the situation.* ◇ *His designs were highly commended by the judges* (= they did not get a prize but they were especially praised). **2** **~ sb/sth (to sb)** (*formal*) to recommend sb/sth to sb: *She is an excellent worker and I commend her to you without reservation.* ◇ *The movie has little to commend it* (= it has few good qualities). **3** **~ itself to sb** (*formal*) if sth **commends** itself to sb, they approve of it: *His outspoken behaviour did not commend itself to his colleagues.* **4** **~ sb/sth to sb** (*formal*) to give sb/sth to sb in order to be taken care of: *We commend her soul to God.*

**com·mend·able** /kəˈmendəbl/ *adj.* (*formal*) deserving praise and approval: *commendable honesty* ▶ **com·mend·ably** /-bli/ *adv.*

**com·men·da·tion** /ˌkɒmenˈdeɪʃn/; *NAmE* ˌkɑːm-/ *noun* **1** [U] (*formal*) praise; approval **2** [C] **~ (for sth)** an award or official statement giving public praise for sb/sth: *a commendation for bravery*

**com·men·sal** /kəˈmensl/ *adj.* (*biology*) living on another animal or plant and getting food from the situation, but doing no harm: *commensal organisms* ▶ **com·men·sal·ism** /-səlɪzəm/ *noun* [U]

**com·men·sur·ate** /kəˈmenʃərət/ *adj.* **~ (with sth)** (*formal*) matching sth in size, importance, quality, etc: *Salary will be commensurate with experience.* OPP **incommensurate** ▶ **com·men·sur·ate·ly** *adv.*

**com·ment** 🛈 A2 /ˈkɒment; *NAmE* ˈkɑːm-/ *noun*, *verb*
■ *noun* **1** B1 A2 [C, U] something that you say or write that gives an opinion on or explains sb/sth: ~ **on sth** *She made helpful comments on my work.* ◇ **~ about sth** *Have you any comment to make about the cause of the disaster?* ◇ **without ~** *He handed me the document without comment.* ◇ *You have to register to post a comment.* ◇ *Keep up to date with all the latest news and comment.* ◇ *You can post a question in the comments section below.* ⊃ SYNONYMS at STATEMENT **2** [sing., U] criticism that shows the faults of sth: *The results are a clear comment on government education policy.* ◇ *There was a lot of comment about his behaviour.* IDM **ˌno ˈcomment** (said in reply to a question, usually from a journalist) I have nothing to say about that: *'Will you resign, sir?' 'No comment!'*
■ *verb* B1 [I, T] to express an opinion about sth: *He refused to comment until after the trial.* ◇ *She said she was unable to comment further.* ◇ **~ on/upon sth** *to comment on a case/report* ◇ **~ about sth** *She declined to comment about the current situation in the party.*

▼ **SYNONYMS**

**comment**
note • remark • observe
These words all mean to say or write a fact or opinion.

**comment** to express an opinion or give facts about sth: *He refused to comment until after the trial.*

**note** (*rather formal*) to mention sth because it is important or interesting: *He noted in passing that the company's record on safety issues was not good.*

**remark** to say or write what you have noticed about a situation: *Critics remarked that the play was not original.*

**observe** (*formal*) to say or write what you have noticed about a situation: *She observed that it was getting late.*

COMMENT, REMARK OR OBSERVE?
• If you **comment on** sth you say sth about it; if you **remark on** sth or **observe** sth, you say sth about it that you have noticed: there is often not much difference between the three. However, while you can *refuse to comment* (without *on*), you cannot 'refuse to remark' or 'refuse to observe' (without *on*): *He refused to remark/observe until after the trial.*

PATTERNS
• to comment/note/remark/observe **that** …
• to comment **on**/note/remark/observe **how** …
• to comment/remark **on** sth
• to comment/remark/observe **to** sb
• '*It's long,*' he commented/noted/remarked/observed.

**com·men·tary** B1+ C1 /ˈkɒməntri; *NAmE* ˈkɑːmənteri/ *noun* (*pl.* **-ies**) **1** B1+ C1 [C, U] **~ (on sth)** a spoken description of an event that is given while it is happening, especially on the radio or television: *a sports commentary* ◇ *Our reporters will give a running commentary* (= a continuous one) *on the election results as they are announced.* ◇ *He kept up a running commentary on everyone who came in or went out.* **2** B1+ C1 [C] **~ (on sth)** a written explanation or discussion of sth such as a book or a play: *a critical commentary on the final speech of the play* **3** B1+ C1 [C, U] **~ (on sth)** a criticism or discussion of sth: *The petty quarrels were a sad commentary on the state of the government.* ◇ *political commentary*

**ˈcommentary box** *noun* (*BrE*) a place in a sports ground where the people who describe what is happening in a sports event for radio or television sit ⊃ compare BOOTH (4)

## commentate

**com·men·tate** /ˈkɒmənteɪt; NAmE ˈkɑːm-/ verb [I] ~ (on sth) to give a spoken description of an event as it happens, especially on television or radio: *Who will be commentating on the game?*

**com·men·ta·tor** ?+ B1 /ˈkɒmənteɪtə(r); NAmE ˈkɑːm-/ noun 1 ?+ B1 ~ (on sth) a person who describes an event while it is happening, especially on television or radio: *a television/sports commentator* 2 ?+ B1 ~ (on sth) a person who is an expert on a particular subject and talks or writes about it on television or radio, in a newspaper or on SOCIAL MEDIA: *a political commentator*

**com·merce** ?+ B1 /ˈkɒmɜːs; NAmE ˈkɑːmɜːrs/ noun [U] trade, especially between countries; the buying and selling of goods and services: *leaders of industry and commerce* ⊃ WORDFINDER NOTE at TRADE ⊃ see also CHAMBER OF COMMERCE, E-COMMERCE, M-COMMERCE

**com·mer·cial** ⓘ B1 ⓦ /kəˈmɜːʃl; NAmE -ˈmɜːrʃl/ *adj., noun*
■ *adj.* 1 B1 [usually before noun] connected with the buying and selling of goods and services: *residential and commercial properties* ◊ *commercial activities* ◊ *the commercial heart of the city* ◊ *a commercial vehicle* (= one that is used for carrying goods or passengers who pay) ⊃ SYNONYMS at ECONOMIC 2 B1 [only before noun] making or intended to make a profit: *The movie was not a commercial success* (= did not make money). ◊ *Risks arise when state-owned enterprises begin operating as commercial entities.* ◊ *policies to attract new industrial or commercial enterprises* ◊ *The data cannot be used for commercial purposes.* ⊃ SYNONYMS at SUCCESSFUL 3 (*disapproving*) more interested in profit and being popular than in quality: *Their more recent music is far too commercial.* 4 (of television or radio) paid for by the money charged for broadcasting advertisements: *a commercial radio station/TV channel* ▶ **com·mer·cial·ly** /-ʃəli/ *adv.*: *commercially produced/grown/developed* ◊ *The product is not yet commercially available.* ◊ *His invention was not commercially successful.*
■ *noun* ? B1 an advertisement on television, on the radio or on a website: *a TV/television commercial* ◊ **in a** ~ *actors in commercials* ◊ ~ **for sth** *He did a number of commercials for major brands.* ⊃ SYNONYMS at ADVERTISEMENT

**comˌmercial ˈbank** *noun* a bank that offers services to the general public and to businesses ⊃ compare INVESTMENT BANK

**comˌmercial ˈbreak** *noun* = BREAK (4)

**com·mer·cial·ism** /kəˈmɜːʃəlɪzəm; NAmE -ˈmɜːrʃ-/ *noun* [U] (*disapproving*) the fact of being more interested in making money than in the value or quality of things

**com·mer·cial·ize** (*BrE also* -**ise**) /kəˈmɜːʃəlaɪz; NAmE -ˈmɜːrʃ-/ *verb* [often passive] (*often disapproving*) to use sth to try to make a profit, especially in a way that other people do not approve of: **be/become commercialized** *Their music has become very commercialized in recent years.* ▶ **com·mer·cial·iza·tion**, **-isa·tion** /kəˌmɜːʃəlaɪˈzeɪʃn; NAmE -ˌmɜːrʃələˈz-/ *noun* [U]

**com·mie** /ˈkɒmi; NAmE ˈkɑːmi/ *noun* (*especially NAmE, informal, disapproving*) an offensive way of referring to sb that you think has ideas similar to those of COMMUNISTS or SOCIALISTS, or who is a member of a COMMUNIST or SOCIALIST party

**com·min·gle** /kəˈmɪŋɡl/ *verb* [I, T] (*formal or specialist*) to mix two or more things together or to be mixed, especially when it is impossible for the things to be separated afterwards: ~ (**with sth**) *The fluid must be prevented from commingling with other fluids.*: ~**sth** (**with sth**) (*finance*) *Campaign funds must not be commingled with other money.*

**com·mis·er·ate** /kəˈmɪzəreɪt/ *verb* [I, T] ~ (**with sb**) (**on/about/for/over sth**) | + **speech** to show sb sympathy when they are upset or disappointed about sth: *She commiserated with the losers on their defeat.*

**com·mis·er·ation** /kəˌmɪzəˈreɪʃn/ *noun* [U, C] (*formal*) an expression of sympathy for sb who has had sth unpleasant happen to them, especially not winning a competition: *I offered him my commiseration.* ◊ *Commiserations to the losing team!*

**com·mis·sar** /ˌkɒmɪˈsɑː(r); NAmE ˌkɑːm-/ *noun* an officer of the Communist Party, especially in the past in the Soviet Union

**com·mis·sary** /ˈkɒmɪsəri; NAmE ˈkɑːmɪseri/ *noun (pl.* -**ies**) (*NAmE*) 1 a shop that sells food, etc. in a military base, a prison, etc. 2 a restaurant for people working in a large organization, especially a film studio

**com·mis·sion** ⓘ B2 /kəˈmɪʃn/ *noun, verb*
■ *noun*
• OFFICIAL GROUP 1 B2 (*often* **Commission**) [C] an official group of people who have been given responsibility to control sth, or to find out about sth, usually for the government: *The commission is expected to report its findings next month.* ◊ (*BrE*) *The government has set up a commission of inquiry into the disturbances at the prison.* ◊ **on a** ~ *the British representative on the commission* ◊ ~ **on sth** *She was also a member of the commission on religious education.* ⊃ see also EUROPEAN COMMISSION, HIGH COMMISSION, ROYAL COMMISSION
• MONEY 2 B2 [U, C] an amount of money that is paid to sb for selling goods and that increases with the amount of goods that are sold: ~ **on sth** *You get a 10 per cent commission on everything you sell.* ◊ *He earned £2000 in commission last month.* ◊ **on** ~ *In this job you work on commission* (= are paid according to the amount you sell). ⊃ WORDFINDER NOTE at PAY 3 ? B2 [U, sing.] an amount of money that is charged by a bank, etc. for providing a particular service: *1 per cent commission is charged for exchanging foreign currency.* ◊ ~ **on sth** *The bank charges a high commission on these transactions.*
• FOR ART/MUSIC, ETC. 4 B2 [C] a formal request to sb to design or make a piece of work such as a building or a painting; the fact of making such a request: *Eventually she agreed to accept the commission.* ◊ ~ **to do sth** *He received a commission to design the new parliament building.*
• IN ARMED FORCES 5 [C] the position of an officer in the armed forces, typically with the rank of LIEUTENANT or higher ⊃ see also COMMISSIONED OFFICER, NON-COMMISSIONED OFFICER
• OF CRIME 6 [U] (*formal*) the act of doing sth wrong or illegal: *the commission of a crime*
IDM **in/out of comˈmission** available/not available to be used: *Several of the airline's planes are temporarily out of commission and undergoing safety checks.*
■ *verb*
• PIECE OF ART/MUSIC, ETC. 1 B2 to officially ask sb to write, make or create sth or to do a task for you: ~ **sb to do sth** *She has been commissioned to write a new national anthem.* ◊ ~ **sth** *to commission a study/report* ◊ *a specially commissioned piece of music* ◊ ~ **sth from sb** *The king commissioned portraits from foreign artists.*
• IN ARMED FORCES 2 [usually passive] to choose sb as an officer in one of the armed forces: **be commissioned** *She was commissioned in 2014.* ◊ **be commissioned (as) sth** *He has just been commissioned (as a) pilot officer.*

**comˌmissioned ˈofficer** *noun* an officer in the armed forces who holds a COMMISSION (typically with the rank of LIEUTENANT or higher) ⊃ compare NON-COMMISSIONED OFFICER

**com·mis·sion·er** ?+ C1 /kəˈmɪʃənə(r)/ *noun* 1 ?+ C1 (*usually* **Commissioner**) a member of a COMMISSION (= an official group of people who are responsible for controlling sth or finding out about sth): *the Church Commissioners* (= the group of people responsible for controlling the financial affairs of the Church of England) ◊ *European Commissioners* 2 (*also* **poˈlice commissioner** *especially in NAmE*) the head of a particular police force in some countries 3 the head of a government department in some countries: *the agriculture/health, etc. commissioner* ◊ *Commissioner Rhodes was unavailable for comment.* ⊃ see also HIGH COMMISSIONER 4 (*in the US*) an official chosen by a sports association to control it: *the baseball commissioner*

**com·mit** ⓘ B1 ⓦ /kəˈmɪt/ *verb* (-**tt**-)
• CRIME 1 ? B1 [T] ~ **sth** to do sth wrong or illegal: *to commit a crime/an offence* ◊ *to commit murder/fraud/adultery* ◊ *to*

**commit an act** of violence/terrorism ◇ appalling crimes committed against innocent children
- **SUICIDE** 2 ⓘ B1 [T] **~ suicide** to kill yourself deliberately
- **PROMISE/SAY DEFINITELY** 3 ⓘ B1 [T, often passive] to promise sincerely that you will definitely do sth, keep to an agreement or arrangement, etc: **~ sb/yourself** *They want to see the text of the proposed treaty before fully committing themselves.* ◇ **~ sb/yourself to (doing) sth** *Borrowers should think carefully before committing themselves to taking out a loan.* ◇ **~ sb/yourself to do sth** *Both sides committed themselves to settle the dispute peacefully.* 4 [T] **~ yourself (to sth)** to give an opinion or make a decision openly so that it is then difficult to change it: *You don't have to commit yourself now—just think about it.* ⊃ see also NON-COMMITTAL
- **STAY WITH** 5 [I] **~ (to sb/sth)** to stay with and completely support one person, organization, etc. or give all your time and effort to your work, an activity, etc: *Why are so many men scared to commit?* (= say they will stay with one person) ⊃ see also COMMITTED
- **MONEY/TIME** 6 [T] **~ sth** to spend money or time on sth/sb: *The council has committed large amounts of money to housing projects.*
- **TO HOSPITAL/PRISON** 7 [T, often passive] **~ sb to sth** to order sb to be sent to a hospital, prison, etc: *She was committed to a psychiatric hospital.*
- **SB FOR TRIAL** 8 [T] **~ sb** to send sb for trial in court
- **STH TO MEMORY** 9 [T] **~ sth to memory** to learn sth well enough to remember it exactly: *She committed the instructions to memory.*
- **STH TO PAPER/WRITING** 10 [T] **~ sth to paper/writing** to write sth down

**com·mit·ment** ⓘ B2 Ⓦ /kəˈmɪtmənt/ *noun*
1 ⓘ B2 [C, U] a promise to do sth or to behave in a particular way; a promise to support sb/sth; the fact of committing yourself: *I'm not ready to make a long-term commitment.* ◇ **~ to sb/sth** *The company has shown a commitment to diversity over the years.* ◇ *We're looking for a firm commitment from both sides.* ◇ **~ to do/doing sth** *This project demonstrates our commitment to improving the quality of the city's green spaces.* ◇ **commitments under sth** *Australia is determined to meet its commitments under the agreement.* 2 ⓘ B2 [U] the desire to work hard and give your energy and time to a job or an activity: *He has demonstrated exceptional commitment and dedication.* ◇ **~ to sth** *commitment to education/democracy/social justice* 3 ⓘ B2 [C, usually pl.] a thing that you have promised or agreed to do, or that you have to do: *He's busy for the next month with filming commitments.* ◇ *work/family commitments* 4 [C, U] a promise to pay for sth, especially regularly; a promise to use resources in order to achieve sth: *Taking on a mortgage is a huge financial commitment.* ◇ **~ (of sth) (to sth)** *the commitment of resources to education* ◇ *Achieving success at this level requires a commitment of time and energy.*

**com·mit·tal** /kəˈmɪtl/ *noun* [U] (*specialist*) the official process of sending sb to prison or to a mental hospital: *He was released on bail pending committal proceedings.*

**com·mit·ted** /kəˈmɪtɪd/ *adj.* (*approving*) willing to work hard and give your time and energy to sth; believing strongly in sth: *a committed member of the team* ◇ *They are committed socialists.* ◇ **~ to (doing) sth** *The president is personally committed to this legislation.* **OPP uncommitted**

**com·mit·tee** ⓘ B2 /kəˈmɪti/ *noun* [C + sing./pl. v.] a group of people who are chosen, usually by a larger group, to make decisions or to deal with a particular subject: *an executive/advisory/organizing committee* ◇ *The committee has/have decided to close the restaurant.* ◇ **to appoint/establish/form a committee** ◇ **to chair/head a committee** ◇ **on a~** *She's on the planning committee.* ◇ **in~** *The bill was still in committee* (= being considered by a committee) *in early December.* ◇ **~ on sth** *the US House of Representatives' committee on foreign affairs* ◇ *a committee member/chairman* ⊃ see also CONFERENCE COMMITTEE, POLITICAL ACTION COMMITTEE, SELECT COMMITTEE, SELEC-

303

TION COMMITTEE, STEERING COMMITTEE ⊃ WORDFINDER NOTE at MEETING

**com·mode** /kəˈməʊd; *NAmE* -ˈmoʊd/ *noun* 1 a piece of furniture that looks like a chair but has a toilet under the seat 2 a piece of furniture, especially an old or ANTIQUE one, with DRAWERS used for storing things in

**com·mod·ify** /kəˈmɒdɪfaɪ; *NAmE* -ˈmɑːd-/ (*also* **commoditize**, *BrE also* **-ise** /kəˈmɒdətaɪz; *NAmE* -ˈmɑːd-/) *verb* (**com·mod·ifies**, **com·mod·ify·ing**, **com·mod·ified**, **com·mod·ified**) **~ sth** to turn sth into or treat sth as a product that can be bought and sold: *Christmas has been grossly commodified over the years.* ▶ **com·modi·fi·ca·tion** /kəˌmɒdɪfɪˈkeɪʃn; *NAmE* -ˌmɑːd-/ (*also* **com·mod·it·iza·tion**, *BrE also* **-isa·tion** /kəˌmɒdɪtaɪˈzeɪʃn; *NAmE* -ˌmɑːdɪtəˈz-/) *noun* [U]

**com·mod·ious** /kəˈməʊdiəs/ *adj.* (*formal*) having a lot of space

**com·mod·ity** ⓘ+ C1 /kəˈmɒdəti; *NAmE* -ˈmɑːd-/ *noun* (*pl. -ies*) 1 ⓘ+ C1 (*economics*) a product or a raw material that can be bought and sold: *rice, flour and other basic commodities* ◇ *a drop in commodity prices* ◇ *Crude oil is the world's most important commodity.* ⊃ SYNONYMS at PRODUCT 2 ⓘ+ C1 (*formal*) a thing that is useful or has a useful quality: *Water is a precious commodity that is often taken for granted in the West.*

**com·mo·dore** /ˈkɒmədɔː(r); *NAmE* ˈkɑːm-/ *noun* (*abbr.* **Cdre**) an officer of high rank in the NAVY: *Commodore John Barry*

**com·mon** ⓘ A1 Ⓞ /ˈkɒmən; *NAmE* ˈkɑːm-/ *adj., noun*

- *adj.* (**com·mon·er**, **com·mon·est**) **HELP** **more common** and **most common** are more frequent 1 ⓘ A1 happening often; existing in large numbers or in many places: *a common problem/occurrence/practice* ◇ *a common feature/theme* ◇ *the most common type of injury* ◇ *Jackson is a common English name.* ◇ *a common spelling mistake* ◇ **~ in sb/sth** *The disease is very common in young horses.* **OPP uncommon** 2 ⓘ B1 [usually before noun] shared by or belonging to two or more people or by the people in a group: *They share a common interest in photography.* ◇ *to have a common ancestor/enemy* ◇ *the need to cooperate to achieve a common goal* ◇ *This decision was taken for the common good* (= the advantage of everyone). ◇ **~ to sb/sth** *basic features that are common to all human languages* 3 ⓘ B1 [only before noun] ordinary; not unusual or special: *Shakespeare's work was popular among the common people in his day.* ◇ *In most people's eyes she was nothing more than a common criminal.* ◇ *It's only common decency to let her know what's happening* (= people would expect it). 4 (of an animal or plant) found or living in quite large numbers; not rare: *the common garden frog* 5 (*BrE, disapproving*) typical of sb from a low social class and not having good manners: *She thought he was very common and uneducated.*
**IDM** **common or 'garden** (*BrE*) (*NAmE* **garden-variety**) (*informal*) ordinary; with no special features the **common 'touch** the ability of a powerful or famous person to talk to and understand ordinary people **make common 'cause with sb** (*formal*) to be united with sb about sth that you both agree on, believe in or wish to achieve ⊃ more at KNOWLEDGE

- *noun* 1 [C] an area of open land in a town or village that anyone may use: *We went for a walk on the common.* ◇ *Wimbledon Common* 2 **commons** [sing.] (*US*) a large room where students can eat in a school, college, etc: *The commons is next to the gym.* ⊃ see also COMMONS
**IDM** **have sth in common (with sb)** (of people) to have the same interests, ideas, etc. as sb else: *Tim and I have nothing in common./I have nothing in common with Tim.* **have sth in common (with sth)** (of things, places, etc.) to have the same features, characteristics, etc: *The two cultures have a lot in common.* **in common** (*specialist*) by everyone in a group: *They hold the property as tenants in common.* **in common with sb/sth** (*formal*) in the same way as sb/sth: *Britain, in common with many other industrialized*

**the common cold**

*countries*, has experienced major changes over the last 100 years.

**the ˌcommon ˈcold** *noun* [sing.] = COLD (1)

**Common ˈCore** *noun* [U, sing.] (*also* **Common Core ˈStandards** [pl.]) (in the US) a set of standards for teaching and testing English and mathematics in schools between KINDERGARTEN and twelfth grade

**common deˈnominator** *noun* **1** (*mathematics*) a number that can be divided exactly by all the numbers below the line in a set of FRACTIONS ⇨ *compare* DENOMINATOR **2** an idea, attitude or experience that is shared by all the members of a group ⇨ *see also* LOWEST COMMON DENOMINATOR

**com·mon·er** /ˈkɒmənə(r); NAmE ˈkɑːm-/ *noun* a person who does not come from a royal or NOBLE family ⇨ *compare* ARISTOCRAT

**Common ˈEra** *noun* [sing.] (*abbr*. CE) the period since the birth of Christ when the Christian CALENDAR starts counting years: *1890 CE*

**ˌcommon ˈground** *noun* [U] opinions, interests and aims that you share with sb, although you may not agree with them about other things: *Despite our disagreements, we have been able to find some common ground.*

**ˈcommon land** *noun* [U] (*BrE*) land that belongs to or may be used by the local community

**ˌcommon ˈlaw** *noun* [U] (in some countries) the part of the law that has been developed from customs and from decisions made by judges, not created by Parliament ⇨ *compare* CASE LAW, STATUTE LAW

**ˌcommon-law ˈhusband, ˌcommon-law ˈwife** *noun* a man/woman that a person has lived with for a long time and who is recognized (in some countries though not the UK) as a husband/wife, without a formal marriage ceremony

**com·mon·ly** 🛈 B2 Ⓦ /ˈkɒmənli; NAmE ˈkɑːm-/ *adv.* usually; very often; by most people: *Christopher is commonly known as Kit.* ◇ *This is one of the most commonly used methods.* ◇ *These fats are commonly found in processed foods.*

**ˌcommon ˈmarket** *noun* **1** [C, usually sing.] a group of countries that have agreed on low taxes on goods traded between countries in the group, and higher fixed taxes on goods imported from countries outside the group **2 the Common Market** [sing.] a former name of the European Union

**ˌcommon ˈnoun** *noun* (*grammar*) a word such as *table, cat* or *sea*, that refers to an object or a thing but is not the name of a particular person, place or thing ⇨ *compare* ABSTRACT NOUN, PROPER NOUN

**com·mon·place** /ˈkɒmənpleɪs; NAmE ˈkɑːm-/ *adj., noun*
- *adj.* done very often, or existing in many places, and therefore not unusual: *This technology is now commonplace in schools.*
- *noun* (*formal*) **1** [usually sing.] an event, etc. that happens very often and is not unusual **2** a remark, etc. that is not new or interesting

**ˌcommon ˈrat** *noun* = BROWN RAT

**ˈcommon room** *noun* **1** (*especially BrE*) a room used by the teachers or students of a school, college, etc. when they are not teaching or studying **2** (*especially NAmE*) a room shared by people who live together in a house or apartment, such as a living room

**the Com·mons** /ðə ˈkɒmənz; NAmE ˈkɑːm-/ *noun* [pl.] = HOUSE OF COMMONS ⇨ *compare* THE LORDS

**ˌcommon ˈsense** *noun* [U] the ability to think about things in a practical way and make sensible decisions: *For goodness' sake, just use your common sense!* ◇ *a common-sense approach to a problem*

**com·mon·wealth** /ˈkɒmənwelθ; NAmE ˈkɑːm-/ *noun* [sing.] **1 the Commonwealth** an organization consisting of the United Kingdom and other countries, including most of the countries that used to be part of the British Empire: *a member of the Commonwealth* ◇ *Commonwealth countries* **2** (*usually* **the Commonwealth**) used in the official names of, and to refer to, some states of the US (Kentucky, Massachusetts, Pennsylvania and Virginia): *the Commonwealth of Virginia* ◇ *The city and the Commonwealth have lost a great leader.* **3** (*NAmE*) an independent country that is strongly connected to the US: *Puerto Rico remains a US commonwealth, not a state.* **4** (*usually* **Commonwealth**) used in the names of some groups of countries or states that have chosen to be politically linked with each other: *the Commonwealth of Independent States (CIS)*

**com·mo·tion** /kəˈməʊʃn; NAmE -ˈmoʊ-/ *noun* [C, usually sing., U] sudden noisy and confused activity or excitement: *I heard a commotion and went to see what was happening.* ◇ *The crowd waiting outside was causing a commotion.* ◇ *What's all the commotion about?*

**comms** /kɒmz; NAmE kɑːmz/ *noun* [pl.] (*informal*) communications: *You'll need to get radio comms set up.*

**com·mu·nal** /kəˈmjuːnl; BrE also ˈkɒmjənl/ *adj.* **1** shared by, or for the use of, a number of people, especially people who live together SYN shared: *a communal kitchen/garden, etc.* ◇ *As a student he tried communal living for a few years.* **2** involving different groups of people in a community: *communal violence between religious groups* ▸ **com·mu·nal·ly** /-nəli/ *adv.*: *The property was owned communally.*

**com·mu·nal·ism** /kəˈmjuːnəlɪzəm; BrE also ˈkɒmjənəlɪzəm/ *noun* **1** the fact of living together and sharing possessions and responsibilities **2** (*IndE*) a strong sense of belonging to a particular community, especially a religious community, that can lead to extreme behaviour or violence towards others

**com·mune** *noun, verb*
- *noun* /ˈkɒmjuːn; NAmE ˈkɑːm-/ [C + sing./pl. v.] **1** a group of people who live together and share responsibilities, possessions, etc: *a 1970s hippy commune* **2** the smallest division of local government in France and some other countries
- *verb* /kəˈmjuːn/
**PHRV** **comˈmune with sb/sth** (*formal*) to share your emotions and feelings with sb/sth without speaking: *He spent much of his time communing with nature.*

**com·mu·nic·able** /kəˈmjuːnɪkəbl/ *adj.* (*formal*) that sb can pass on to other people or communicate to sb else: *communicable diseases*

**com·mu·ni·cant** /kəˈmjuːnɪkənt/ *noun* a person who receives COMMUNION in a Christian church service

**com·mu·ni·cate** 🛈 A2 Ⓦ /kəˈmjuːnɪkeɪt/ *verb*
- **EXCHANGE INFORMATION 1** 🛈 A2 [I, T] to share or exchange information, news, ideas, feelings, etc: *We only communicate by email.* ◇ *They communicated in sign language.* ◇ *Candidates must be able to communicate effectively.* ◇ *~ with sb/sth Dolphins use sound to communicate with each other.* ◇ *~ sth In times of uncertainty, a leader must be able to communicate a message of hope.* ◇ *~ sth to sb He was eager to communicate his ideas to the group.* ◇ *Her nervousness was communicating itself to the children.* ◇ *~ how/what, etc… They failed to communicate what was happening and why.* ⇨ SYNONYMS *at* TALK
- **IN A RELATIONSHIP 2** 🛈 A2 [I] to have a good relationship because you are able to understand and talk about your own and other people's thoughts, feelings, etc: *His inability to communicate has damaged their relationship beyond repair.* ◇ *~ with sb The novel is about a family who can't communicate with each other.*
- **DISEASE 3** [T, usually passive] *~ sth* to pass a disease from one person, animal, etc. to another: *The disease is communicated through dirty drinking water.*
- **OF TWO ROOMS 4** [I] if two rooms **communicate**, they are next to each other and you can get from one to the other: *a communicating door* (= one that connects two rooms)

**com·mu·ni·ca·tion** 🛈 B1 Ⓞ /kəˌmjuːnɪˈkeɪʃn/ *noun* **1** 🛈 B1 [U] the activity or process of expressing ideas and feelings or of giving people information: *~ between A and B Good communication between team* *leaders and members is essential.* ◊ *~with sb attempts to improve communication with customers* ◊ **communication channels** ◊ *helping students develop their communication skills* ◊ *non-verbal communication* ◊ **in ~** *We are in regular communication by email.* **2** [U] (*also* **communications** [pl.]) methods of sending information, especially phones, radio, computers, etc. or roads and railways: *communications technology* ◊ *wireless/electronic/satellite communication* ◊ *to intercept/disrupt/monitor communications* ⇒ see also COMMS **3** [C] (*formal*) a message, letter or phone call: *a communication from the leader of the party*

**com·mu·ni·ca·tive** /kəˈmjuːnɪkətɪv; *NAmE* -keɪt-/ *adj.* **1** willing to talk and give information to other people: *I don't find him very communicative.* OPP **uncommunicative 2** connected with the ability to communicate in a language, especially a foreign language: *communicative skills*

**com·mu·ni·ca·tor** /kəˈmjuːnɪkeɪtə(r)/ *noun* a person who communicates sth to others: *an effective/skilled/successful communicator* ◊ *a poor communicator* ⇒ SYNONYMS at SPEAKER

**com·mu·nion** /kəˈmjuːniən/ *noun* **1** (*also* **Com·mu·nion, Holy Com·mu·nion**) [U] a ceremony in the Christian Church during which people eat bread and drink wine in memory of the last meal that Christ had with his DISCIPLES: *to go to Communion* (= attend church for this celebration) ◊ *to take/receive communion* (= receive the bread and wine) ⇒ see also EUCHARIST, MASS **2** [U] **~ (with sb/sth)** (*formal*) the state of sharing or exchanging thoughts and feelings; the feeling of being part of sth: *poets living in communion with nature* **3** [C] (*specialist*) a group of people with the same religious beliefs: *the Anglican communion*

**com·mu·ni·qué** /kəˈmjuːnɪkeɪ; *NAmE* kəˌmjuːnəˈkeɪ/ *noun* an official statement or report, especially to newspapers

**com·mun·ism** /ˈkɒmjənɪzəm; *NAmE* ˈkɑːm-/ *noun* **1** a political movement that believes in an economic system in which the state controls the means of producing everything for the people. It aims to create a society in which everyone is treated equally. ⇒ WORDFINDER NOTE at CAPITALISM **2** *often* **Communism** the system of government by a ruling Communist Party, such as in the former Soviet Union

**com·mun·ist** /ˈkɒmjənɪst; *NAmE* ˈkɑːm-/ *adj., noun*
■ *adj.* **1** connected with communism: *communist ideology* **2** **Communist** governed by or belonging to a Communist party: *a Communist country/government/leader*
■ *noun* **1** a person who believes in or supports communism **2** **Communist** a member of a Communist Party

**the ˈCommunist Party** *noun* a political party that supports COMMUNISM or rules in a COMMUNIST country

**com·mu·nity** /kəˈmjuːnəti/ *noun* (*pl.* -ies) **1** [C, usually sing.] all the people who live in a particular area, country, etc. when talked about as a group: *The local community supported us from the start.* ◊ *the international community* (= the countries of the world as a group) ◊ *It is hoped that the campaign will encourage members of the community to get active.* ◊ **community groups/leaders** ◊ **in/within the ~** *health workers based in the community* (= working with people in a local area) ◊ *the wider/entire/whole community* ⇒ see also RETIREMENT COMMUNITY **2** [C + sing./pl. v.] a group of people who share the same religion, race, job, etc: *the business/scientific community* ◊ *the Muslim/Jewish/Christian community* ◊ *the gay community* **3** [U] the feeling of sharing things and belonging to a group in the place where you live: *There is a strong sense of community here.* ◊ **community spirit 4** [C] (*biology*) a group of plants and animals growing or living in the same place or environment

**comˈmunity ˈcare** (*also* **care in the comˈmunity**) *noun* [U] (in the UK) long-term medical and other care that is given within the community and allows people to live at home rather than in a hospital

**comˈmunity ˈcentre** (*BrE*) (*NAmE* **comˈmunity center**) *noun* a place where people from the same area can meet for social events or sports or to take classes

**comˈmunity ˈchurch** *noun* (*NAmE*) a church for a particular area or group of people, especially one that welcomes people from different Christian DENOMINATIONS (= branches of Christianity)

**comˈmunity ˈcollege** *noun* **1** (*also* **comˈmunity ˈschool**) (in Britain) a secondary school where adults from the local community can attend classes in the evening **2** (in the US) a college that is mainly for students from the local community and that offers programmes that are two years long, including programmes in practical skills

**comˈmunity ˈgarden** *noun* (*NAmE*) a large area of land where people can grow flowers, vegetables, etc. ⇒ compare ALLOTMENT (1)

**comˈmunity ˈorder** *noun* (*BrE, law*) (in the UK) a decision, made in court, to give a punishment that involves helping people in the community having treatment for an ADDICTION, etc. instead of going to prison: *He was sentenced to a community order that involved psychological counselling.*

**comˈmunity ˈorganizer** (*BrE also* **-iser**) *noun* (*especially NAmE*) a person whose job is to manage and organize work done for and by people who live in a particular area

**comˈmunity ˈproperty** *noun* [U] (*NAmE, law*) property that is considered to belong equally to a married couple

**comˈmunity ˈsentence** *noun* (*BrE, law*) (in the UK) a punishment, given by a court, that involves helping people in the community, having treatment for an ADDICTION, etc. instead of going to prison: *She was given a two-year community sentence for the assault on her neighbour.*

**comˈmunity ˈservice** *noun* [U] work helping people in the local community that sb does without being paid, either because they want to, or because they have been ordered to by a court as a punishment

**comˈmunity ˈtheater** *noun* (*NAmE*) **1** (*BrE* **amateur dramatics**) [U] the activity of producing and acting in plays by people who do it for pleasure and not as a job **2** [C] a small theatre where these plays are performed

**com·mut·able** /kəˈmjuːtəbl/ *adj.* **1** (of a place or a distance) close enough or short enough to make travelling to work every day a possibility **2** (*law*) a **commutable** punishment can be made less severe **3** (*formal*) able to be changed

**com·mu·ta·tion** /ˌkɒmjuˈteɪʃn; *NAmE* ˌkɑːm-/ *noun* [C, U] **1** (*law*) the act of making a punishment less severe: *a commutation of the death sentence to life imprisonment* **2** (*finance*) the act of replacing one method of payment with another; a payment that is replaced with another

**com·mu·ta·tive** /kəˈmjuːtətɪv/ *adj.* (*mathematics*) (of a calculation) giving the same result whatever the order in which the quantities are shown

**com·mute** /kəˈmjuːt/ *verb, noun*
■ *verb* **1** [I, T] to travel regularly by bus, train, car, etc. between your place of work and your home: **~(from A) (to B)** *She commutes from Oxford to London every day.* ◊ **~ between A and B** *He spent that year commuting between New York and Chicago.* ◊ *I live within commuting distance of Dublin.* ◊ **~sth** *People are prepared to commute long distances if they are desperate for work.* ⇒ WORDFINDER NOTE at CAR **2** [T] **~sth (to sth)** (*law*) to replace one punishment with another that is less severe **3** [T] **~sth (for/into/to sth)** (*finance*) to exchange one form of payment, for sth else
■ *noun* the journey that a person makes when they commute to work: *a two-hour commute into downtown Washington* ◊ *I have only a short commute to work.*

**com·muter** /kəˈmjuːtə(r)/ *noun* a person who travels into a city to work each day, usually from quite far away: (*BrE*) *the commuter belt* (= the area around a city where people live and from which they travel to work in the city)

**comp** /kɒmp; *NAmE* kɑːmp/ *noun* (*informal*) **1** [C] (*BrE*) = COMPREHENSIVE: *Her children go to the local comp.* **2** [C] (*BrE*) = COMPETITION **3** [C] (*NAmE*) a COMPLIMENTARY ticket, meal, etc. (= one that you do not have to pay for)

## compact

**4** [U] (*NAmE*) = COMPENSATION: *comp time* (= time off work given for working extra hours)

**com·pact** *adj., noun, verb*
- **adj.** /kəmˈpækt; *BrE also* ˈkɒmpækt; *NAmE also* ˈkɑːm-/ **1** (*usually approving*) smaller than is usual for things of the same kind: *a compact camera* ◊ *The device is small and compact and weighs only 2.2lb.* **2** using or filling only a small amount of space: *The kitchen was compact but well equipped.* **3** closely packed together: *a compact mass of earth* **4** (of a person or an animal) small and strong: *He had a compact and muscular body.* ▶ **comˈpact·ly** *adv.* **comˈpact·ness** *noun* [U]
- **noun** /ˈkɒmpækt; *NAmE* ˈkɑːm-/ **1** (*NAmE*) a small car ⊃ compare SUBCOMPACT **2** a small flat box with a mirror, containing powder that women use on their faces **3** (*formal*) a formal agreement between two or more people or countries
- **verb** /kəmˈpækt/ [usually passive] ~ **sth** to press sth tightly together: *a layer of compacted snow*

**ˌcompact ˈdisc** *noun* = CD

**com·pact·or** /kəmˈpæktə(r); *NAmE also* ˈkɑːmpæktər/ *noun* a machine that presses rubbish together

**com·padre** /kəmˈpɑːdreɪ/ *noun* (*NAmE, informal, from Spanish*) a friend or sb with whom you spend a lot of time

**com·pan·ion** /kəmˈpænjən/ *noun* **1** a person or an animal that travels with you or spends a lot of time with you: *travelling companions* ◊ (*figurative*) *Fear was the hostages' constant companion.* **2** a person who shares your experiences, especially when these are particularly pleasant or unpleasant: *She was a charming dinner companion.* ◊ *His younger brother is not much of a companion for him.* ◊ *They're drinking companions* (= they go out drinking together). ◊ *We became companions in misfortune.* ⊃ see also BOON COMPANION ⊃ WORDFINDER NOTE at FRIEND **3** a person, usually a woman, employed to live with and help sb, especially sb old or ill **4** one of a pair of things that go together or can be used together: *A companion volume is soon to be published.* **5** used in book titles to describe a book giving useful facts and information on a particular subject: *A Companion to French Literature*

**com·pan·ion·able** /kəmˈpænjənəbl/ *adj.* friendly ▶ **com·pan·ion·ably** /-bli/ *adv.*

**comˈpanion animal** (*also* **animal companion**) *noun* (*rather formal*) an animal that you have at home for pleasure, rather than one that is kept for work or food; a pet

**com·pan·ion·ship** /kəmˈpænjənʃɪp/ *noun* [U] the pleasant feeling that you have when you have a friendly relationship with sb and are not alone: *They meet at the club for companionship and advice.* ◊ *She had only her cat for companionship.*

**com·pany** /ˈkʌmpəni/ *noun* (*pl.* -ies)
- BUSINESS **1** [C + sing./pl. v.] (*abbr.* **Co.**) (often in names) a business organization that makes money by producing or selling goods or services: *insurance/oil/tech/technology/pharmaceutical companies* ◊ *the world's largest software company* ◊ *She runs her own TV production company.* ◊ *Smoking in the workplace is against company policy.* ◊ *a company pension* ⊃ see also FINANCE COMPANY, HOLDING COMPANY, JOINT-STOCK COMPANY, LIMITED COMPANY, PRIVATE COMPANY, PUBLIC COMPANY, STOCK COMPANY

  WORDFINDER agent, business, competitor, customer, director, employ, franchise, manager, shareholder

- THEATRE/DANCE **2** (often in names) [C + sing./pl. v.] a group of people who work or perform together: *a theatre/dance, etc. company* ◊ *the Royal Shakespeare Company*
- BEING WITH SB **3** [U] the fact of being with sb else and not alone: *sb's ~ I enjoy Jo's company* (= I enjoy being with her). ◊ **in the ~ of sb** *a pleasant evening in the company of friends* ◊ *She enjoys her own company* (= being by herself) *when she is travelling.* ◊ *The children are very good company* (= pleasant to be with) *at this age.* ◊ **for ~** *He's coming with me for company.*
- GUESTS **4** [U] (*formal*) guests in your house: *I didn't realize you had company.*
- GROUP OF PEOPLE **5** [U] (*formal*) a group of people together: *She told the assembled company what had happened.* ◊ **in ~** *It is bad manners to whisper in company* (= in a group of people).
- SOLDIERS **6** [C + sing./pl. v.] a group of soldiers that is part of a BATTALION

IDM **the ˈcompany sb keeps** the people that sb spends time with: *Judging by the company he kept, Mark must have been a wealthy man.* **get into/keep bad ˈcompany** to be friends with people that others think are bad **in ˈcompany with sb/sth** (*formal*) together with or at the same time as sb/sth: *She arrived in company with the ship's captain.* ◊ *The US dollar went through a difficult time, in company with the oil market.* **in good ˈcompany** if you say that sb is **in good company**, you mean that they should not worry about a mistake, etc. because sb else, especially sb more important, has done the same thing **keep sb ˈcompany** to stay with sb so that they are not alone: *I'll keep you company while you're waiting.* **two's ˈcompany (, three's a ˈcrowd)** (*saying*) used to suggest that it is better to be in a group of only two people than have a third person with you as well ⊃ more at PART *v.*, PRESENT *adj.*

**ˈcompany car** *noun* a car that is provided by the company that you work for

**com·par·able** /ˈkɒmpərəbl; *NAmE* ˈkɑːm-/ *adj.* similar to sb/sth else and able to be compared: *A comparable house in the south of the city would cost twice as much.* ◊ **~ to/with sb/sth** *The situation in the US is not directly comparable to that in the UK.* ◊ *Inflation is now at a rate comparable with that in other European countries.* ◊ **~ in sth** *The two machines are comparable in size.* ▶ **com·par·abil·ity** /ˌkɒmpərəˈbɪləti; *NAmE* ˌkɑːm-/ *noun* [U]: *Each group will have the same set of questions, in order to ensure comparability.*

**com·para·tive** /kəmˈpærətɪv/ *adj., noun*
- **adj. 1** measured or judged by how similar or different it is to sth else SYN **relative**: *Then he was living in comparative comfort* (= compared with others or with his own life at a previous time). ◊ *The company is a comparative newcomer to the software market* (= other companies have been in business much longer). **2** connected with studying things to find out how similar or different they are: *a comparative study of the educational systems of two countries* ◊ *comparative linguistics* **3** (*grammar*) relating to adjectives or adverbs that express more in amount, degree or quality, for example *better, worse, slower* and *more difficult* ⊃ compare SUPERLATIVE
- **noun** (*grammar*) the form of an adjective or adverb that expresses more in amount, degree or quality: '*Better*' is the comparative of '*good*' and '*more difficult*' is the comparative of '*difficult*'. ⊃ compare SUPERLATIVE

**com·para·tive·ly** /kəmˈpærətɪvli/ *adv.* as compared to sth/sb else SYN **relatively**: *The unit is comparatively easy to install and cheap to operate.* ◊ *He died comparatively young* (= at a younger age than most people die). ◊ *comparatively few/low/rare/recent*

**com·pare** /kəmˈpeə(r); *NAmE* -ˈper/ *verb, noun*
- **verb 1** (*abbr.* **cf., cp.**) [T] to examine people or things to see how they are similar and how they are different: **~ A and B** *It is interesting to compare their situation and ours.* ◊ *We compared the two reports carefully.* ◊ *Compare and contrast the characters of Jack and Ralph.* ◊ **~ A with/to B** *We compared the results of our study with those of other studies.* ◊ *My own problems seem insignificant compared with other people's.* ◊ *I've had some difficulties, but they were nothing compared to yours* (= they were not nearly as bad as yours). ⊃ LANGUAGE BANK at CONTRAST, ILLUSTRATE **2** [I] **~ with/to sb/sth** to be similar to sb/sth else, either better or worse: *This school compares with the best in the country* (= it is as good as them). ◊ *This house doesn't compare with our previous one* (= it is not as good). ◊ *Their prices compare favourably to those of their competitors.*

**3** [T] ~ **A to B** to show or state that sb/sth is similar to sb/sth else: *The critics compared his work to that of Martin Amis.*
**IDM** **compare ˈnotes (with sb)** if two or more people **compare notes**, they each say what they think about the same event, situation, etc. **you can't compare apples and ˈoranges** (*NAmE*) it is impossible to say that one thing is better than another if the two are completely different: *They are both great but you can't compare apples and oranges.*
■ *noun*
**IDM** **beyond / without comˈpare** (*literary*) better than anything else of the same kind

**com·pari·son** /kəmˈpærɪsn/ *noun* **1** [U] the process of comparing two or more people or things: *~ with sb/sth Comparison with other oil-producing countries is extremely interesting.* ◊ *The education system bears/stands no comparison with* (= is not as good as) *that in many Asian countries.* ◊ *for~ I enclose the two plans for comparison.* **2** [C] an occasion when two or more people or things are compared: *~ of A and B a comparison of the rail systems in Britain and France* ◊ *~ of A with B a comparison of men's salaries with those of women* ◊ *~ between A and B comparisons between Britain and the rest of Europe* ◊ *~ of A to B a comparison of the brain to a computer* (= showing what is similar) ◊ *~ with sb/sth It is difficult to make a comparison with her previous book—they are completely different.* ◊ *You can draw comparisons with the situation in Ireland* (= say how the two situations are similar). ◊ *There is no published information that would allow a direct comparison with other regions or countries.* ⊃ **LANGUAGE BANK** at SIMILARLY
**IDM** **by comˈparison** used especially at the beginning of a sentence when the next thing that is mentioned is compared with sth in the previous sentence: *By comparison, expenditure on education increased last year.* **by / in comˈparison (with sb/sth)** when compared with sb/sth: *The second half of the game was dull by comparison with the first.* ◊ *The tallest buildings in London are small in comparison with New York's skyscrapers.* **there's no comˈparison** used to emphasize the difference between two people or things that are being compared: *In terms of price there's no comparison* (= one thing is much more expensive than the other). ⊃ more at **PALE** *v.*

**comˈparison shopping** *noun* [U] (*especially NAmE*) the activity of comparing prices for similar items in different shops and websites, in order to pay the least amount of money for sth: *Be prepared to do some comparison shopping before you decide which TV to buy.* ▸ **comˈparison-shop** *verb* [I, T] **~ (sth)**

**comˈparison site** (*also* **comˈparison website**) *noun* a website that consumers use to compare the prices and features of goods and services from different companies

**com·part·ment** /kəmˈpɑːtmənt; *NAmE* -ˈpɑːrt-/ *noun* **1** one of the separate sections that sth such as a piece of furniture or equipment has for keeping things in: *The desk has a secret compartment.* ◊ *There is a handy storage compartment beneath the oven.* ⊃ see also **GLOVE COMPARTMENT** **2** one of the separate sections that a coach on a train is divided into

**com·part·men·tal·ize** (*BrE also* **-ise**) /ˌkɒmpɑːtˈmentəlaɪz; *NAmE* kəmˌpɑːrt-/ *verb* **~ sth (into sth)** to divide sth into separate sections, especially so that one thing does not affect the other: *Life today is rigidly compartmentalized into work and leisure.* ▸ **com·part·men·tal·iza·tion** (*BrE also* **-isa·tion**) /ˌkɒmpɑːtˌmentəlaɪˈzeɪʃn; *NAmE* kəmˌpɑːrtˌmentələˈz-/ *noun* [U]

**com·pass** /ˈkʌmpəs/ *noun* **1** (*also* **magˈnetic ˈcompass**) [C] an instrument for finding direction, with a needle that always points to the north: *a map and compass* ◊ *the points of the compass* (= N, S, E, W, etc.) ◊ *see also* **MORAL COMPASS** ⊃ **WORDFINDER NOTE** at **MAP** **2** [C] (*also* **compasses** [pl.]) an instrument with two long thin parts joined together at the top, used for drawing circles and measuring distances on a map: *a pair of compasses* **3** [sing.] (*formal*) a range or an extent, especially of what can be achieved in a particu-

307                                                                                           **compensate**

**compasses**

lar situation: *the compass of a singer's voice* (= the range from the lowest to the highest note that he or she can sing)

**com·pas·sion** /kəmˈpæʃn/ *noun* [U] **~ (for sb)** a strong feeling of sympathy for people or animals who are suffering and a desire to help them: *to feel/show compassion*

**com·pas·sion·ate** /kəmˈpæʃənət/ *adj.* feeling or showing sympathy for people or animals who are suffering: *He was allowed to go home on compassionate grounds* (= because he was suffering). ▸ **com·pas·sion·ate·ly** *adv.*

**comˌpassionate ˈleave** *noun* [U] time that you are allowed to be away from work because sb in your family is ill or has died

**com·pati·bil·ity** /kəmˌpætəˈbɪləti/ *noun* [U] **1** **~ (with sb/sth)** | **~ (between A and B)** the ability of people or things to live or exist together without problems **2** the ability of machines, especially computers, and computer programs to be used together

**com·pat·ible** /kəmˈpætəbl/ *adj.* **1** **~ (with sth)** (of machines, especially computers, or software) able to be used together: *The new system will be compatible with existing equipment.* **2** **~ (with sth)** (of ideas, methods or things) able to exist or be used together without causing problems: *Are measures to protect the environment compatible with economic growth?* ◊ *compatible blood groups* **3** **~ (with sb)** if two people are **compatible**, they can have a good relationship because they have similar ideas, interests, etc. **OPP** **incompatible** ▸ **com·pat·ibly** /-bli/ *adv.*

**com·pat·riot** /kəmˈpætriət; *NAmE* -ˈpeɪt-/ *noun* a person who was born in, or is a citizen of, the same country as sb else **SYN** **countryman**: *He played against one of his compatriots in the semi-final.*

**com·pel** /kəmˈpel/ *verb* (**-ll-**) (*formal*) **1** to force sb to do sth; to make sth necessary: *~ sb to do sth The law can compel fathers to make regular payments for their children.* ◊ *I feel compelled to write and tell you how much I enjoyed your book.* ◊ *~ sth Last year ill health compelled his retirement.* **2** *~ sth* (not used in the progressive tenses) to cause a particular reaction: *He spoke with an authority that compelled the attention of the whole crowd.* ⊃ see also **COMPULSION**

**com·pel·ling** /kəmˈpelɪŋ/ *adj.* **1** that makes you pay attention to it because it is so interesting and exciting: *Her latest book makes compelling reading.* ⊃ **SYNONYMS** at **INTERESTING** **2** so strong that you cannot resist it: *a compelling need/desire* **3** that makes you think it is true: *There is no compelling reason to believe him.* ◊ *compelling evidence* ▸ **com·pel·ling·ly** *adv.*: *compellingly attractive*

**com·pen·dious** /kəmˈpendiəs/ *adj.* (*formal*) containing all the necessary facts about sth: *a compendious description*

**com·pen·dium** /kəmˈpendiəm/ *noun* (*pl.* **com·pen·dia** /-diə/ *or* **com·pen·diums**) a collection of facts, drawings and photographs on a particular subject, especially in a book

**com·pen·sate** /ˈkɒmpenseɪt; *NAmE* ˈkɑːm-/ *verb* **1** [I] **~ (for sth)** to provide sth good to balance or reduce the bad effects of damage, loss, etc. **SYN** **make up for**: *Nothing can compensate for the loss of a loved one.* **2** [I] **~ (for sth)** to act in order to balance or correct sth wrong or not normal SYN **make up for**: *In the second experiment, the temperature was raised to compensate for this bias.* **3** [T] ~ **sb (for sth)** to pay sb money because they have suffered some damage, loss, injury, etc: *Her lawyers say she should be compensated for the suffering she had been caused.* ▶ **com·pen·sa·tory** /ˌkɒmpenˈseɪtəri; *NAmE* kəmˈpensətɔːri/ *adj.*: *He received a compensatory payment of $20000.*

**com·pen·sa·tion** /ˌkɒmpenˈseɪʃn; *NAmE* ˌkɑːm-/ *noun* **1** [U, C] ~ **(for sth)** something, especially money, that sb gives you because they have hurt you, or damaged sth that you own; the act of giving this to sb: *to claim/award/receive compensation* ◊ *to pay compensation for injuries at work* ◊ **in** ~ *to receive £10000 in compensation* ⇒ see also WORKERS' COMPENSATION **2** [U] (*especially NAmE*) money that an employee receives for doing their job: *Send your CV and current compensation to Executive Search Consultant.* **3** [C, usually pl., U] ~ **(for sth)** a thing or things that make a bad situation better: *I wish I were young again, but getting older has its compensations.*

**com·père** /ˈkɒmpeə(r); *NAmE* ˈkɑːmper/ *noun, verb*
■ *noun* (*BrE*) a person who introduces the people who perform in a television programme, a show in a theatre, etc. SYN **emcee**: *to act as (a) compère*
■ *verb* [T, I] ~ **(sth)** (*BrE*) to act as a compère for a show

**com·pete** /kəmˈpiːt/ *verb* **1** [I] to take part in a contest or game: ~ **in sth** *He's hoping to compete in the London marathon.* ◊ ~ **against sb** *They are competing against teams of full-time professional players.* ⇒ WORDFINDER NOTE at SPORT **2** [I] to try to be more successful or better than sb else who is trying to do the same as you: *They simply cannot compete in the international market.* ◊ ~ **for sth** *Several companies are competing for the contract.* ◊ *Young children will usually compete for their mother's attention.* ◊ ~ **against/with sb/sth** *Small independent bookshops find it difficult to compete with the online stores.* ◊ ~ **on sth** *We can't compete with them on price.* ◊ ~ **to do sth** *There are too many magazines competing to attract readers.*

**com·pe·tence** /ˈkɒmpɪtəns; *NAmE* ˈkɑːm-/ *noun* **1** (*also less frequent* **com·pe·ten·cy**) [U, C] ~ **(in sth)** | ~ **(in doing sth)** the ability to do sth well: *to gain a high level of competence in English* ◊ *professional/technical competence* OPP **incompetence 2** [U] (*law*) the power that a court, an organization or a person has to deal with sth: *The judge has to act within the competence of the court.* ◊ *outside sb's area of competence* **3** [C] (*also less frequent* **com·pe·ten·cy**) (*specialist*) a skill that you need in a particular job or for a particular task: *The syllabus lists the knowledge and competences required at this level.*

**com·pe·tency** /ˈkɒmpɪtənsi; *NAmE* ˈkɑːm-/ *noun* (*pl.* **-ies**) = COMPETENCE

**com·pe·tent** /ˈkɒmpɪtənt; *NAmE* ˈkɑːm-/ *adj.* **1** having enough skill or knowledge to do sth well or to the necessary standard: *He's very competent in his work.* ◊ ~ **to do sth** *Make sure the firm is competent to carry out the work.* ◊ **at sth** *She is highly competent at her job.* OPP **incompetent 2** of a good standard but not very good: *Ron was a competent player—more than that, he was good!* **3** having the power to decide sth: *The case was referred to a competent authority.* ▶ **com·pe·tent·ly** *adv.*: *to perform competently*

**com·pet·ing** /kəmˈpiːtɪŋ/ *adj.* [only before noun] **1** (of different ideas, interests, explanations, etc.) unable to exist or be true at the same time: *There were several competing accounts of what actually happened that night.* **2** (of different products, services or businesses) each trying to get the attention of possible customers and be more successful than others: *competing brands of diet soda* **3** used to describe the different teams or players in a competition: *Five competing teams will vie for the trophy.*

**com·pe·ti·tion** /ˌkɒmpəˈtɪʃn; *NAmE* ˌkɑːm-/ *noun* **1** [C] an event in which people compete with each other to find out who is the best at sth: *a design/an art/a talent competition* ◊ *to enter/win a competition* ◊ **in a** ~ *He won fourth place in the competition.*

**WORDFINDER** closing date, disqualify, judge, prize, round, runner-up, submit, tiebreaker, winner

**2** [U] a situation in which people or organizations compete with each other for sth that not everyone can have: *stiff/fierce/intense/tough competition* ◊ ~ **between A and B** *competition between two similar products* ◊ ~ **for sth/to do sth** *competition for resources/jobs/food, etc.* ◊ ~ **from sb/sth** *The firm is facing stiff competition from its online rivals.* ◊ **in** ~ **with sb/sth (for sth/to do sth)** *We are in competition with four other companies for the contract.* **3 the competition** [sing. + sing./pl. v.] the people who are competing against sb: *We'll be able to assess the competition at the conference.*

**com·peti·tive** /kəmˈpetətɪv/ *adj.* **1** used to describe a situation in which people or organizations compete against each other: *competitive games/sports* ◊ *Graduates have to fight for jobs in an increasingly competitive market.* ◊ *The company has succeeded in a highly competitive industry.* **2** (of a person) trying very hard to be better than others: *You have to be highly competitive to do well in sport these days.* OPP **uncompetitive 3** as good as or better than others: *a shop selling clothes at competitive prices* (= as low as any other shop) ◊ *to gain a competitive advantage over rival companies* ◊ ~ **with sb/sth** *We need to work harder to remain competitive with other companies.* ⇒ SYNONYMS at CHEAP
▶ **com·peti·tive·ly** *adv.*: *competitively priced goods*
**com·peti·tive·ness** *noun* [U]: *the competitiveness of British industry*

**com·peti·tor** /kəmˈpetɪtə(r)/ *noun* **1** a person who takes part in a competition: *Over 200 competitors entered the race.* ◊ ~ **for sth** *There are six remaining competitors for the grand prize of $50000.* **2** a person or an organization that competes against others, especially in business: *The company is outperforming its main competitors in the US market.* ◊ ~ **to sth** *They are set to become formidable competitors to American companies.* ◊ ~ **for sth** *Japan was not a major competitor for scarce resources such as oil.* ⇒ WORDFINDER NOTE at COMPANY

**com·pil·ation** /ˌkɒmpɪˈleɪʃn; *NAmE* ˌkɑːm-/ *noun* **1** [C] a collection of items, especially pieces of music or writing, taken from different places and put together: *Her latest album is a compilation of all her best singles.* ◊ *a compilation album* **2** [U] the process of compiling sth: *the compilation of a dictionary*

**com·pile** /kəmˈpaɪl/ *verb* **1** ~ **sth** to produce a book, list, report, etc. by bringing together different items, articles, songs, etc.; to collect information in order to produce a book, list, etc: *We are trying to compile a list of suitable people for the job.* ◊ *The album was compiled from live recordings from last year's tour.* ◊ *The figures were compiled from a survey of 2000 schoolchildren.* **2** ~ **sth** (*computing*) to translate instructions from one computer language into another so that a particular computer can understand them

**com·piler** /kəmˈpaɪlə(r)/ *noun* **1** a person who compiles sth **2** (*computing*) a program that translates instructions from one computer language into another for a computer to understand

**com·pla·cency** /kəmˈpleɪsnsi/ *noun* [U] (*usually disapproving*) a feeling of being satisfied with yourself or with a situation, so that you do not think any change is necessary; the state of being complacent: *Despite signs of an improvement in the economy, there is no room for complacency.*

**com·pla·cent** /kəmˈpleɪsnt/ *adj.* (*usually disapproving*) too satisfied with yourself or with a situation, so that you do not feel that any change is necessary; showing or feeling complacency: *a dangerously complacent attitude to the increase in unemployment* ◊ ~ **about sb/sth** *We must not become complacent about progress.* ▶ **com·pla·cent·ly** *adv.*

**com·plain** 🔑 **A2** /kəmˈpleɪn/ *verb* [I, T] to say that you are annoyed, unhappy or not satisfied about sb/sth: *She never complains, but she's obviously exhausted.* ◇ *(informal)* '*How are you?*' '*Oh, **I can't complain** (= I'm all right).*' ◇ **~ (to sb) (about sth)** *I'm going to complain to the manager about this.* ◇ **~ of sth** *The defendant complained of intimidation during the investigation.* ◇ **~ (that)** … *He complained bitterly that he had been unfairly treated.* ◇ **+ speech** '*It's not fair,*' *she complained.*
**PHR V** **comˈplain of sth** to say that you feel ill or are suffering from a pain: *She left early, complaining of a headache.*

> **▼ SYNONYMS**
> **complain**
> protest • object • grumble • moan • whine
> These words all mean to say that you are annoyed, unhappy or not satisfied about sb/sth.
> **complain** to say that you are annoyed, unhappy or not satisfied about sb/sth: *I'm going to complain to the manager about this.*
> **protest** to say or do sth to show that you disagree with sth or think it is bad, especially publicly; to give sth as a reason for protesting: *Students took to the streets to **protest against** the decision.*
> **object** to say that you disagree with sth or think it is bad; to give sth as a reason for objecting: *If nobody objects, we'll postpone the meeting till next week.* ◇ *He objected that the police had arrested him without sufficient evidence.*
> **grumble** (*rather informal, disapproving*) to complain about sb/sth, especially sth that is not really very serious: *They kept grumbling that they were cold.*
> **moan** (*BrE, rather informal, disapproving*) to complain about sb/sth in an annoying way: *What are you moaning about now?*
> **whine** (*rather informal, disapproving*) to complain in an annoying, crying voice: *Stop whining!* ◇ '*I want to go home,*' *whined Toby.* **NOTE** **Whine** is often used to talk about the way that young children complain.
> **PATTERNS**
> • to complain / protest / grumble / moan / whine **about** sth
> • to complain / protest / grumble / moan **at** sth
> • to complain / protest / object / grumble / moan / whine **to** sb
> • to complain / protest / object / grumble / moan / whine **that** …

**com·plain·ant** /kəmˈpleɪnənt/ *noun* (*law*) = PLAINTIFF
**com·plaint** 🔑 **B1** /kəmˈpleɪnt/ *noun* **1** 🔑 **B1** [C] a reason for not being satisfied; a statement that sb makes saying that they are not satisfied: *a formal complaint* ◇ **~ about sb/sth** *I'd like to **make a complaint** about the noise.* ◇ *(formal)* to **file/lodge** (= make) *a complaint* ◇ **~ against sb/sth** *I believe you have a **complaint against** one of our nurses.* ◇ **~ to sb** *They said their complaints to the police were often not acted on.* ◇ **~ from/by sb** *Council bosses said they would respond to complaints from residents.* ◇ **~ (that** …**)** *a complaint that he had been unfairly treated* **2** 🔑 **B1** [U] the act of complaining: *I can see no grounds for complaint.* ◇ *a letter of complaint* ◇ **without ~** *Workers were expected to accept pay cuts without complaint.* **3** [C] an illness, especially one that is not serious, and often one that affects a particular part of the body: *a skin complaint*

**com·ple·ment** 🔑+ **C1** *verb, noun*
■ *verb* 🔑+ **C1** /ˈkɒmplɪment; NAmE ˈkɑːm-/ **~ sth** to add to sth in a way that improves it or makes it more attractive: *The excellent menu is complemented by a good wine list.* ◇ *The team needs players who **complement each other**.* ⊃ note at COMPLIMENT
■ *noun* /ˈkɒmplɪmənt; NAmE ˈkɑːm-/ **1 ~ (to sth)** a thing that adds new qualities to sth in a way that improves it or makes it more attractive: *This vegetable's natural sweetness is a perfect complement to salty or rich foods.* **2** the complete number or quantity needed or allowed: *We've taken our full complement of trainees this year.* **3** (*grammar*) a word or phrase, especially an adjective or a noun, that is used after linking verbs such as *be* and *become*, and describes the subject of the verb. In some descriptions of grammar it is used to refer to any word or phrase that is GOVERNED by a verb and usually comes after the verb in a sentence: *In the sentences 'I'm angry' and 'He became a politician', 'angry' and 'politician' are complements.*

**com·ple·men·tary** /ˌkɒmplɪˈmentri NAmE ˌkɑːm-/ *adj.* **~ (to sth)** two people or things that are **complementary** are different but together form a useful or attractive combination of skills, qualities or physical features: *The school's approach must be complementary to that of the parents.* ⊃ note at COMPLIMENT

ˌcomplementary ˈcolour (*US* ˌcomplementary ˈcolor) *noun* (*specialist*) **1** a colour that, when mixed with another colour, gives black or white **2** a colour that gives the greatest contrast when combined with a particular colour: *The designer has chosen the complementary colours blue and orange.*

ˌcomplementary ˈmedicine *noun* [U] medical treatment that is not part of the usual scientific treatment used in Western countries, for example ACUPUNCTURE ⊃ compare ALTERNATIVE MEDICINE, CONVENTIONAL (3) ⊃ WORD-FINDER NOTE at TREATMENT

**com·ple·men·ta·tion** /ˌkɒmplɪmenˈteɪʃn; NAmE ˌkɑːm-/ *noun* [U] **1** the fact of COMPLEMENTING sth **2** (*grammar*) the COMPLEMENTS of a verb in a clause

**com·plete** 🔑 **A1** /kəmˈpliːt/ *adj., verb*
■ *adj.* **1** 🔑 **A1** including all the parts, etc. that are necessary; whole: *a complete list/sequence/picture/profile* ◇ *I've collected the complete set.* ◇ *The **complete works** of Tolstoy* ◇ *You've made my life complete.* ◇ *A Chinese New Year celebration would not be complete without fireworks.* **OPP** incomplete **2** 🔑 **A2** [not before noun] finished: *The job is almost complete.* ◇ *Construction of the new airport is scheduled to be complete by late September.* **OPP** incomplete **3** 🔑 **B1** [usually before noun] used when you are emphasizing sth, to mean 'to the greatest degree possible' **SYN** total: *We were in complete agreement* ◇ *a complete stranger* ◇ *The council's response shows a complete lack of understanding of the situation.* ◇ *It came as a complete surprise.* ◇ *I felt a complete idiot.* ◇ *You are talking complete and utter rubbish.* **4 ~ with sth** [not before noun] including sth as an extra part or feature: *The furniture comes complete with tools and instructions for assembly.*
▶ **com·plete·ness** *noun* [U]: *the accuracy and completeness of the information* ◇ *For the sake of completeness, all names are given in full.*
■ *verb* **1** 🔑 **A1 ~ sth** to finish making or doing sth: *to complete a course/project* ◇ *to complete a task/mission* ◇ *to complete your education/training* ◇ *She's just completed a master's degree in Law.* ◇ *The work should be completed by December.* ◇ *She recently completed the London Marathon in April.* **2** 🔑 **A1 ~ sth** to write all the information you are asked for on a form **SYN** fill in/out: *2000 shoppers completed our questionnaire.* ◇ *Has the form been correctly completed?* **3** 🔑 **A2 ~ sth** to make sth whole or perfect: *I only need one more card to complete the set.*

## completely

**com·plete·ly** /kəmˈpliːtli/ adv. (used to emphasize another word or phrase) in every way possible; in every part SYN **totally**: *completely different* ◊ *I've completely forgotten her name.* ◊ *The technique is completely new.* ◊ *The waiter completely ignored my request.* ◊ *I agree completely with what you say.*

**com·ple·tion** /kəmˈpliːʃn/ noun 1 [U] the act or process of finishing sth; the state of being finished and complete: *the completion of the new hospital building* ◊ *Satisfactory completion of the course does not ensure you a job.* ◊ *The project is due for completion in the spring.* ◊ *The road is nearing completion* (= it is nearly finished). ◊ *the date of completion/the completion date* 2 [U, C] (*BrE*) the formal act of completing the sale of property, for example the sale of a house

**com·plex** adj., noun
■ adj. /ˈkɒmpleks; NAmE kəmˈpleks, ˈkɑːmpleks/ 1 made of many different things or parts that are connected; difficult to understand SYN **complicated**: *a complex problem/issue/process/system* ◊ *complex machinery* ◊ *We live in an increasingly complex world.* ◊ *a highly complex situation* 2 (*grammar*) (of a word or sentence) containing one main part (= the ROOT of a word or MAIN CLAUSE of a sentence) and one or more other parts (called AFFIXES or SUBORDINATE CLAUSES) ⇒ compare COMPOUND
■ noun /ˈkɒmpleks; NAmE kɑːm-/ 1 a group of buildings of a similar type together in one place: *a sports/leisure/shopping complex* ◊ *an industrial complex* (= a site with many factories) ◊ (*especially NAmE*) *an apartment complex* ◊ (*especially NAmE*) *a housing complex* ⇒ SYNONYMS at BUILDING 2 a group of things that are connected: *This is just one of a whole complex of issues.* 3 (especially in compounds) a mental state that is not normal: *to suffer from a guilt complex* ⇒ see also INFERIORITY COMPLEX, OEDIPUS COMPLEX, SUPERIORITY COMPLEX 4 if sb has a **complex** about sth, they are worried about it in way that is not normal

**com·plex·ion** /kəmˈplekʃn/ noun 1 the natural colour and condition of the skin on a person's face: *a pale/bad complexion* 2 [usually sing.] the general character of sth: *a move that changed the political complexion of the country* IDM **put a new/different com'plexion on sth** to change the way that a situation appears

**com·plex·ity** /kəmˈpleksəti/ noun 1 [U] the state of being formed of many parts; the state of being difficult to understand: *the increasing complexity of modern telecommunication systems* ◊ *I was astonished by the size and complexity of the problem.* 2 **complexities** [pl.] the features of a problem or situation that are difficult to understand: *the complexities of the system*

**com·pli·ance** /kəmˈplaɪəns/ noun [U] 1 the practice of obeying rules or requests made by people in authority: *~(with sth) procedures that must be followed to ensure full compliance with the law* ◊ *in~with sth Safety measures were carried out in compliance with paragraph 6 of the building regulations.* OPP **non-compliance** ⇒ see also COMPLY 2 *~with sb/sth* (*disapproving*) the quality of being too willing to agree with sb or do what they want: *He was appalled by his parents' unquestioning compliance with the regime.*

**com·pli·ant** /kəmˈplaɪənt/ adj. 1 (*usually disapproving*) too willing to agree with other people or to obey rules: *By then, Henry seemed less compliant with his wife's wishes than he had six months before.* ◊ *We should not be producing compliant students who do not dare to criticize.* 2 in agreement with a set of rules: *This site is HTML compliant.* ⇒ see also COMPLY

**com·pli·cate** /ˈkɒmplɪkeɪt; NAmE ˈkɑːm-/ verb *~sth* to make sth more difficult to do, understand or deal with: *I do not wish to complicate the task more than is necessary.* ◊ *To complicate matters further, there will be no transport available till 8 o'clock.* ◊ *The issue is complicated by the fact that a vital document is missing.*

**com·pli·cated** /ˈkɒmplɪkeɪtɪd; NAmE ˈkɑːm-/ adj. made of many different things or parts that are connected; difficult to understand SYN **complex**: *a complicated issue/process/system* ◊ *The instructions look very complicated.* ◊ *It's all very complicated—but I'll try and explain.* ◊ *Things get complicated when the hero becomes the target of a stalker.*

**com·pli·ca·tion** /ˌkɒmplɪˈkeɪʃn; NAmE ˌkɑːm-/ noun 1 [C, U] a thing that makes a situation more complicated or difficult: *The bad weather added a further complication to our journey.* 2 [C, usually pl.] (*medical*) a new problem or illness that makes treatment of a previous one more complicated or difficult: *She developed complications after the surgery.*

**com·pli·cit** /kəmˈplɪsɪt/ adj. *~(in/with sb/sth)* involved with other people in sth wrong or illegal: *Several officers were complicit in the cover-up.*

**com·pli·city** /kəmˈplɪsəti/ noun [U] *~(in sth)* (*formal*) the act of taking part with another person in a crime SYN **collusion**: *to be guilty of complicity in the murder* ◊ *evident complicity between the two brothers*

**com·pli·ment** noun, verb
■ noun /ˈkɒmplɪmənt; NAmE ˈkɑːm-/ 1 [C] a comment that expresses praise or approval of sb: *to pay sb a compliment* (= to praise them for sth) ◊ *'You understand the problem because you're so much older.' 'I'll take that as a compliment!'* ◊ *It's a great compliment to be asked to do the job.* ◊ *to return the compliment* (= to treat sb in the same way as they have treated you) 2 **compliments** [pl.] (*formal*) polite words or good wishes, especially when used to express praise and approval: *My compliments to the chef!* ◊ (*BrE*) *Compliments of the season!* (= for Christmas or the New Year) ◊ *Please accept these flowers with the compliments of* (= as a gift from) *the manager.* IDM see BACKHANDED
■ verb /ˈkɒmplɪment; NAmE ˈkɑːm-/ *~sb (on sth)* to tell sb that you like or admire sth they have done, their appearance, etc.: *She complimented him on his excellent German.*

▼ **WHICH WORD?**

**compliment / complement**

- These words have similar spellings but completely different meanings. If you **compliment** someone, you say something very nice to them: *She complimented me on my English.* If one thing **complements** another, the two things work or look better because they are together: *The different flavours complement each other perfectly.*
- The adjectives are also often confused. **Complimentary**: *She made some very complimentary remarks about my English.* It can also mean 'free': *There was a complimentary basket of fruit in our room.* **Complementary**: *The team members have different but complementary skills.*

**com·pli·men·tary** /ˌkɒmplɪˈmentri; NAmE ˌkɑːm-/ adj. 1 given free: *complimentary tickets for the show* 2 *~(about sth)* expressing approval, praise, etc.: *a complimentary remark* ◊ *She was extremely complimentary about his work.* OPP **uncomplimentary** ⇒ note at COMPLIMENT

**com·ply** /kəmˈplaɪ/ verb [I] (**com·plies, com·ply·ing, com·plied, com·plied**) *~(with sth)* to obey a rule, an order, etc.; to meet particular standards: *They refused to comply with the UN resolution.* ◊ *All furniture must comply with the fire safety regulations.* ⇒ see also COMPLIANCE

**compo** /ˈkɒmpəʊ; NAmE ˈkɑːm-/ noun [U] (*AustralE, NZE, informal*) money that is paid to a worker if he/she gets injured at work SYN **compensation**

**com·pon·ent** /kəmˈpəʊnənt/ noun one of several parts of which sth is made: *~of sth Key components of the government's plan are…* ◊ *an essential/important component of sth* ◊ *~for sth Individual components for the car can be very expensive.* ◊ *~in sth Trust is a vital component in any relationship.* ▶ **com·pon·ent** adj. [only before noun]: *Break the problem down into its component parts.*

**com·port** /kəmˈpɔːt; NAmE -ˈpɔːrt/ verb *~yourself + adv./prep.* (*formal*) to behave in a particular way: *She always comports herself with great dignity.*

**com·port·ment** /kəmˈpɔːtmənt; *NAmE* -ˈpɔːrt-/ *noun* [U] (*formal*) the way in which sb/sth behaves: *She won admiration for her comportment during the trial.*

**com·pose** /kəmˈpəʊz/ *verb* **1** [T, I] ~ (sth) to write music: *Mozart composed his last opera shortly before he died.* **2** [T] ~ **a letter/speech/poem** to write a letter, etc. usually with a lot of care and thought: *She composed a letter of protest.* ⇨ WORDFINDER NOTE at MESSAGE **3** [T] (not used in the progressive tenses) ~ sth (*formal*) to combine together to form a whole **SYN make up**: *Ten people compose the committee.* ⇨ see also COMPOSED **4** [T, no passive] (*formal*) to manage to control your feelings or expression: ~ **yourself** *Emma frowned, making an effort to compose herself.* ◇ ~ **sth** *I was so confused that I could hardly compose my thoughts.* ⇨ see also COMPOSURE

**com·posed** /kəmˈpəʊzd/ *adj.* **1 be composed of sth** (*formal*) to be made or formed from several parts, things or people: *The committee is composed mainly of lawyers.* ⇨ SYNONYMS at CONSIST **2** [not usually before noun] calm and in control of your feelings: *She seemed outwardly composed.*

**com·poser** /kəmˈpəʊzə(r)/ *noun* a person who writes music, especially classical music

**com·pos·ite** /ˈkɒmpəzɪt; *NAmE* kəmˈpɑːzət/ *adj., noun*
- *adj.* [only before noun] made of different parts or materials: *a composite picture* (= one made from several pictures)
- *noun* **1** [C] something made by putting together different parts or materials: *The document was a composite of information from various sources.* **2** [U, C] a mixture of different materials used for building, making objects, etc: *The balls are now made of plastic composite instead of leather.* **3** (*also* **com'posite sketch**) (*both especially NAmE*) (*BrE usually* **iden·ti·kit**) [C] a picture of a person who is wanted by the police, made by putting together photographs of different features of faces from information that is given by sb who has seen the person

**com·pos·ition** /ˌkɒmpəˈzɪʃn; *NAmE* ˌkɑːm-/ *noun* **1** [U] the different parts that sth is made of; the way in which the different parts are organized: *the chemical composition of the soil* ◇ *the composition of the board of directors* ⇨ SYNONYMS at STRUCTURE **2** [C] a short text that is written as a school exercise; a short essay **3** [C] (*formal*) a piece of music or art, or a poem: *one of Beethoven's finest compositions* **4** [U] the act of composing sth, especially a piece of music; the art of writing music: *pieces performed in the order of their composition* ◇ *to study composition* **5** [U] (*art*) the arrangement of people or objects in a painting or photograph

**com·positor** /kəmˈpɒzɪtə(r); *NAmE* -ˈpɑːz-/ *noun* a person who arranges text on a page before printing

**com·pos men·tis** /ˌkɒmpəs ˈmentɪs; *NAmE* ˌkɑːm-/ *adj.* [not before noun] (*from Latin, formal or humorous*) having full control of your mind

**com·post** /ˈkɒmpɒst; *NAmE* ˈkɑːmpoʊst/ *noun, verb*
- *noun* [U, C] a mixture of DECAYED (= destroyed by natural processes) plants, food, etc. that can be added to soil to help plants grow: **potting compost** (= a mixture of soil and compost that you can buy to grow new plants in)
- *verb* **1** ~ **sth** to make sth into compost **2** ~ **sth** to put compost on or in sth

**com·post·able** /kəmˈpɒstəbl; *NAmE* -ˈpoʊs-/ *adj.* that can be made into compost: *compostable waste*

**ˈcompost bin** *noun* a container in the garden where leaves, plants, etc. are put to make compost

**ˈcompost heap** (*especially BrE*) (*NAmE usually* **ˈcompost pile**) *noun* a place in the garden where leaves, plants, etc. are piled, to make compost

**com·pos·ure** /kəmˈpəʊʒə(r)/ *noun* [U] the state of being calm and in control of your feelings or behaviour: *to keep/lose/recover/regain your composure*

**com·pote** /ˈkɒmpɒt; *NAmE* ˈkɑːmpoʊt/ *noun* [C, U] a cold DESSERT (= a sweet dish) made of fruit that has been cooked slowly with sugar

311

# compress

**com·pound** *noun, adj., verb*
- *noun* /ˈkɒmpaʊnd; *NAmE* ˈkɑːm-/ **1** a thing consisting of two or more separate things combined together **2** (*chemistry*) a substance formed by a chemical reaction of two or more elements in fixed amounts relative to each other: *Common salt is a compound of sodium and chlorine.* ⇨ compare ELEMENT, MIXTURE ⇨ WORDFINDER NOTE at CHEMISTRY **3** (*grammar*) a noun, an adjective or a verb made of two or more words or parts of words, written as one or more words, or joined by a hyphen. *Travel agent, dark-haired* and *bathroom* are all compounds. **4** an area surrounded by a fence or wall in which a factory or other group of buildings stands: *a prison compound*
- *adj.* /ˈkɒmpaʊnd; *NAmE* ˈkɑːm-/ [only before noun] (*specialist*) formed of two or more parts: *a compound adjective, such as fair-skinned* ◇ *A compound sentence contains two or more clauses.*
- *verb* /kəmˈpaʊnd/ **1** ~ **sth** to make sth bad become even worse by causing further damage or problems: *The problems were compounded by severe food shortages.* **2 be compounded of/from sth** (*formal*) to be formed from sth: *The DNA molecule is compounded from many smaller molecules.* **3** [often passive] (*formal or specialist*) to mix sth together: **(be) compounded with sth** *liquid soaps compounded with disinfectant* **4** ~ **sth** (*finance*) to pay or charge interest on an amount of money that includes any interest already earned or charged

**ˌcompound ˈeye** *noun* (*biology*) an eye like that of most insects, made up of several parts that work separately

**ˌcompound ˈfracture** *noun* an injury in which a bone in the body is broken and part of the bone comes through the skin ⇨ compare SIMPLE FRACTURE

**ˌcompound ˈinterest** *noun* [U] interest that is paid both on the original amount of money saved and on the interest that has been added to it ⇨ compare SIMPLE INTEREST

**com·pre·hend** /ˌkɒmprɪˈhend; *NAmE* ˌkɑːm-/ *verb* (*formal*) [I, T] (often used in negative sentences) to understand sth fully: *He stood staring at the dead body, unable to comprehend.* ◇ ~ **sth** *The infinite distances of space are too great for the human mind to comprehend.* ◇ ~ **how/why, etc** ... *She could not comprehend how someone would risk people's lives in that way.* ◇ ~ **that** ... *He simply could not comprehend that she could be guilty.* ⇨ SYNONYMS at UNDERSTAND

**com·pre·hens·ible** /ˌkɒmprɪˈhensəbl; *NAmE* ˌkɑːm-/ *adj.* ~ **(to sb)** (*formal*) that can be understood by sb: *easily/readily comprehensible to the average reader* **OPP incomprehensible** ▶ **com·pre·hens·ib·ility** /ˌkɒmprɪˌhensəˈbɪləti; *NAmE* ˌkɑːm-/ *noun* [U]

**com·pre·hen·sion** /ˌkɒmprɪˈhenʃn; *NAmE* ˌkɑːm-/ *noun* **1** [U] the ability to understand: *speech and comprehension* ◇ **beyond** ~ *His behaviour was completely beyond comprehension* (= impossible to understand). ◇ *She had no comprehension of what was involved.* **2** [U, C] an exercise that trains students to understand a language: *listening comprehension* ◇ *a reading comprehension*

**com·pre·hens·ive** /ˌkɒmprɪˈhensɪv; *NAmE* ˌkɑːm-/ *adj., noun*
- *adj.* **1** including all, or almost all, the items, details, facts, information, etc., that may be involved **SYN complete, full**: *a comprehensive list of addresses* ◇ *a comprehensive study* ◇ *comprehensive insurance* (= covering all risks) **2** (*BrE*) (*of education*) designed for students of all abilities in the same school **3** (*of a victory or defeat*) gained or lost by a large amount ▶ **com·pre·hens·ive·ness** *noun* [U]
- *noun* (*also* **ˌcompreˈhensive school**) (*also informal* **comp**) (in the UK) a SECONDARY SCHOOL for young people of all levels of ability

**com·pre·hens·ive·ly** /ˌkɒmprɪˈhensɪvli; *NAmE* ˌkɑːm-/ *adv.* completely; in a careful and detailed way: *They were comprehensively beaten in the final.*

**com·press** *verb, noun*
- *verb* /kəmˈpres/ **1** [T, I] to press things together or press sth into a smaller space; to be pressed in this way: ~ **sth (into sth)** *compressed air/gas* ◇ ~ **(into sth)** *Her lips*

**compressor**

compressed into a thin line. **2** [T] ~ **sth (into sth)** to reduce sth and fit it into a smaller space or amount of time ⟨SYN⟩ **condense**: *The main arguments were compressed into one chapter.* **3** [T] ~ **sth** (*computing*) to make computer files, etc. smaller so that they use less space on a disk, etc. ⟨OPP⟩ **decompress** ▶ **com·pres·sion** /-ˈpreʃn/ *noun* [U]: *the compression of air* ◇ *data compression*
- *noun* /ˈkɒmpres; *NAmE* ˈkɑːm-/ a cloth that is pressed onto a part of the body to stop the loss of blood, reduce pain, etc.

**com·pres·sor** /kəmˈpresə(r)/ *noun* a machine that compresses air or other gases

**com·prise** 🔑+ B2 Ⓦ /kəmˈpraɪz/ *verb* (not used in the progressive tenses) (*formal*) **1** 🔑+ B2 (*also* **be comprised of**) to have sb/sth as parts or members ⟨SYN⟩ **consist of**: ~ **sth** *The collection comprises 327 paintings.* ◇ **be comprised of sb/sth** *The committee is comprised of representatives from both the public and private sectors.* ⟨HELP⟩ The main meaning of **comprise** is 'have sb/sth as parts or members'. You can use it in two forms: as **comprise** with an object: *The country comprises 20 states.* Or you can use it in the passive form **be comprised of sb/sth**, which has the same meaning: *The country is comprised of twenty states.* Sometimes you may see the active form 'comprise of' but this is considered incorrect: *The property comprises of bedroom, bathroom and kitchen.* **2** 🔑+ B2 ~ **sth** to be the parts or members that form sth ⟨SYN⟩ **make up**: *Older people comprise a large proportion of those living in poverty.*
➔ SYNONYMS at CONSIST ➔ LANGUAGE BANK at PROPORTION

**com·prom·ise** 🔑+ C1 /ˈkɒmprəmaɪz; *NAmE* ˈkɑːm-/ *noun, verb*
- *noun* **1** 🔑+ C1 [C] an agreement made between two people or groups in which each side gives up some of the things they want so that both sides are happy at the end: *After lengthy talks the two sides finally reached a compromise.* ◇ *In any relationship, you have to make compromises.* ◇ *a compromise solution/agreement/candidate* **2** 🔑+ C1 [C] ~ **(between A and B)** a solution to a problem in which two or more things cannot exist together as they are, in which each thing is reduced or changed slightly so that they can exist together: *This model represents the best compromise between price and quality.* **3** 🔑+ C1 [U] the act of reaching a compromise: *Compromise is an inevitable part of life.* ◇ *There is no prospect of compromise in sight.*
- *verb* **1** 🔑+ C1 [I] to give up some of your demands in order to reach an agreement after disagreeing with sb: *Neither side is prepared to compromise.* ◇ ~ **(with sb) (on sth)** *After much argument, the judges finally compromised on* (= agreed to give the prize to) *the 18-year old pianist.* ◇ *They were unwilling to compromise with the terrorists.* **2** 🔑+ C1 [T, I] to do sth that is against your principles or does not reach standards that you have set: ~ **sth** *I refuse to compromise my principles.* ◇ **(on sth)** *We are not prepared to compromise on safety standards.* **3** 🔑+ C1 [T] ~ **sb/sth/yourself** to cause sb/sth/yourself to be in danger or to be suspected of sth, especially by acting in a way that is not very sensible: *She had already compromised herself by accepting his invitation.* ◇ *Defeat at this stage would compromise their chances* (= reduce their chances) *of reaching the finals of the competition.* **4** [T] ~ **sth** to cause sth to be in danger of attack or of working less well: *Users perform tasks every day that can compromise the security of their computers.*

**com·prom·is·ing** /ˈkɒmprəmaɪzɪŋ; *NAmE* ˈkɑːm-/ *adj.* if sth is **compromising**, it shows or tells people sth that you want to keep secret, because it is wrong or embarrassing: *compromising photos* ◇ *They were discovered together in a compromising situation.*

**comp·trol·ler** /kənˈtrəʊlə(r)/ *noun* = CONTROLLER (3)

**com·pul·sion** /kəmˈpʌlʃn/ *noun* **1** [U, C] (*formal*) strong pressure that makes sb do sth that they do not want to do: ~ **(to do sth)** *You are under no compulsion to pay immediately.* ◇ **(on sb) to do sth** *There are no compulsions on students to attend classes.* **2** [C] ~ **(to do sth)** a strong desire to do sth, especially sth that is wrong, silly or dangerous ⟨SYN⟩ **urge**: *He felt a great compulsion to tell her everything.* ➔ see also COMPEL

**com·pul·sive** /kəmˈpʌlsɪv/ *adj.* **1** (of behaviour) that is difficult to stop or control: *compulsive eating/spending/gambling* **2** (of people) not being able to control their behaviour: *a compulsive drinker/gambler/liar* **3** that makes you pay attention to it because it is so interesting and exciting: *The programme made compulsive viewing.* ▶ **com·pul·sive·ly** *adv.*: *She watched him compulsively.* ◇ *a compulsively readable book*

**com·pul·sory** 🔑+ B2 /kəmˈpʌlsəri/ *adj.* that must be done because of a law or a rule ⟨SYN⟩ **mandatory**: *English is a compulsory subject at this level.* ◇ *compulsory education/schooling* ◇ *compulsory redundancies* ◇ **it is ~ (for sb/sth) to do sth** *It is compulsory for all motorcyclists to wear helmets.* ⟨OPP⟩ **voluntary** ▶ **com·pul·sor·ily** /-rəli/ *adv.*: *Over 600 workers were made compulsorily redundant.*

**com·pulsory ˈpurchase** *noun* [U, C] (*BrE*) an occasion when sb is officially ordered to sell land or property to the government or other authority: *a compulsory purchase order*

**com·punc·tion** /kəmˈpʌŋkʃn/ *noun* (*formal*) [U] (*also* [C] in *NAmE*) (usually used in negative sentences) a guilty feeling about doing sth: *He had lied to her without compunction.* ◇ ~ **about doing sth** *She felt no compunction about leaving her job.* ◇ (*NAmE*) *She has no compunctions about rejecting the plan.*

**com·pu·ta·tion** /ˌkɒmpjuˈteɪʃn; *NAmE* ˌkɑːm-/ *noun* [C, U] (*formal*) an act or the process of calculating sth: *All the statistical computations were performed by the new software system.* ◇ *an error in the computation*

**com·pu·ta·tion·al** /ˌkɒmpjuˈteɪʃənl; *NAmE* ˌkɑːm-/ *adj.* [usually before noun] using or connected with computers: *computational methods* ◇ *a computational approach*

**com·pute** 🔑+ C1 /kəmˈpjuːt/ *verb* **1** 🔑+ C1 ~ **sth** (*formal*) to calculate sth: *The losses were computed at £5 million.* **2** [I] (in negative sentences) (*informal*) to make sense: *That just doesn't compute.* ▶ **com·put·able** /-ˈpjuːtəbl/ *adj.*

**com·puter** 🔑 A1 /kəmˈpjuːtə(r)/ *noun* an electronic machine that can store, organize and find information, do processes with numbers and other data, and control other machines: *a home computer* ◇ *by ~ The whole process is run and monitored by computer.* ◇ *on a ~ He spends all day playing on his computer.* ◇ *a computer system/program/network* ◇ *computer software/graphics/hardware* ◇ *a computer screen* ➔ see also DESKTOP COMPUTER, MAINFRAME, PERSONAL COMPUTER, SUPERCOMPUTER

⟨WORDFINDER⟩ display, drive, keyboard, memory, platform, program, reboot, router, screen

**comˈputer game** *noun* a game played on a computer

**com·ˈputer·ize** (*BrE also* **-ise**) /kəmˈpjuːtəraɪz/ *verb* **1** ~ **sth** to provide a computer or computers to do the work of sth: *The factory has been fully computerized.* **2** ~ **sth** to store information on a computer: *computerized databases* ◇ *The firm has computerized its records.* ▶ **com·pu·ter·iza·tion**, **-isa·tion** /kəmˌpjuːtəraɪˈzeɪʃn; *NAmE* -rəˈz-/ *noun* [U]

**com·puter-ˈliterate** *adj.* able to use computers well ▶ **comˌputer ˈliteracy** *noun* [U]

**comˌputer ˈscience** *noun* [U] the study of computers and how they can be used: *a degree in computer science* ▶ **comˌputer ˈscientist** *noun*

**com·put·ing** /kəmˈpjuːtɪŋ/ *noun* [U] the fact of using computers: *to work in computing* ◇ *to study computing* ◇ *educational/network/scientific computing* ◇ *computing power/devices/services/skills/systems* ➔ see also CLOUD COMPUTING

**com·rade** /ˈkɒmreɪd; *NAmE* ˈkɑːmræd/ *noun* **1** a person who is a member of the same COMMUNIST or SOCIALIST political party as the person speaking **2** (*also* **comrade-in-ˈarms**) (*old-fashioned*) a friend or other person that you work with, especially as soldiers during a war: *They were old army comrades.* ➔ WORDFINDER NOTE at FRIEND ▶ **com·rade·ly** *adj.* **com·rade·ship** *noun* [U] (*formal*): *There was a sense of comradeship between them.*

**con** /kɒn; NAmE kɑːn/ noun, verb
- **noun** (*informal*) **1** [sing.] a trick; an act of cheating sb: *The so-called bargain was just a big con!* ◊ (*BrE*) *a con trick* ◊ (*NAmE*) *a con game* ◊ *He's a real con artist* (= a person who regularly cheats others). ⊃ compare CONFIDENCE TRICK ⊃ see also CONMAN, MOD CON **2** [C] = CONVICT IDM see PRO *n*.
- **verb** (*informal*) (**-nn-**) to trick sb, especially in order to get money from them or persuade them to do sth for you: ~ **sb (into doing sth)** *I was conned into buying a useless car.* ◊ ~ **sb (out of sth)** *They had been conned out of £100000.* ◊ ~ **your way into sth** *He conned his way into the job using false references.* ⊃ SYNONYMS at CHEAT

**Con.** abbr. (in British politics) conservative

**con·cat·en·ation** /kɒnˌkætəˈneɪʃn/ noun (*formal*) a series of things or events that are linked together: *a strange concatenation of events*

**con·cave** /ˈkɒnkeɪv; NAmE kɑːn-/ *adj.* (of an outline or a surface) curving in: *a concave lens/mirror* OPP **convex** ⊃ picture at CONVEX

**con·cav·ity** /kɒnˈkævəti; NAmE kɑːn-/ noun (*pl.* **-ies**) (*specialist*) **1** [U] the quality of being concave **2** [C] a shape or place that curves in

**con·ceal** /kənˈsiːl/ verb (*formal*) to hide sb/sth: ~ **sb/sth** *The paintings were concealed beneath a thick layer of plaster.* ◊ *Tim could barely conceal his disappointment.* ◊ *She sat down to conceal the fact that she was trembling.* ◊ ~ **sb/sth from sb/sth** *For a long time his death was concealed from her.* ⊃ SYNONYMS at HIDE ⊃ see also ILL-CONCEALED

**con·cealed 'carry** noun [U] (*NAmE*) the practice of carrying a gun that is hidden from view ⊃ compare OPEN CARRY ⊃ see also CARRY (2)

**con·ceal·er** /kənˈsiːlə(r)/ noun [U, C] a skin-coloured cream or powder used to cover spots or marks on the skin or dark circles under the eyes

**con·ceal·ment** /kənˈsiːlmənt/ noun [U] (*formal*) the act of hiding sth; the state of being hidden: *the concealment of crime* ◊ *Many animals rely on concealment for protection.*

**con·cede** /kənˈsiːd/ verb **1** [T] to admit that sth is true, logical, etc. after first denying it or resisting it: + **speech** *'Not bad,' she conceded grudgingly.* ◊ ~ **(that) …** *He was forced to concede (that) there might be difficulties.* ◊ ~ **sth** *I had to concede the logic of this.* ◊ ~ **sth to sb** *He reluctantly conceded the point to me.* ◊ ~ **sb sth** *He reluctantly conceded me the point.* ◊ **it is conceded that … ** *It must be conceded that different judges have different approaches to these cases.* ⊃ SYNONYMS at ADMIT **2** [I, T] ~ **(defeat)** to admit that you have lost a game, an election, etc: *After losing this decisive battle, the general was forced to concede.* ◊ *Injury forced Hicks to concede defeat.* **3** [T] to give sth away, especially unwillingly; to allow sb to have sth: ~ **sth (to sb)** *The president was obliged to concede power to the army.* ◊ *England conceded a goal immediately after half-time.* ◊ ~ **sb sth** *Women were only conceded full voting rights in the 1950s.* ⊃ see also CONCESSION

▼ **EXPRESS YOURSELF**
**Conceding a point**
When you want to show that the other person has convinced you with their argument, at least partially, you can concede:
- *Yes, I suppose you're right.* (especially BrE)
- *Yes, I guess you're right.* (especially NAmE)
- *Yes, I see what you mean.*
- *OK, I take/see your point about the expense, but I still think it's worth it.*
- *Well, I guess you've got a point there.*
- *OK, that's a good point.*
- *No, possibly/I guess not.*
- *I suppose not.* (BrE)
- *Well, yes, OK. I hadn't really appreciated/understood that before.*
- *Well, I can't/won't argue with that.*
- *That's true. We'll need to take that into consideration.*

**con·ceit** /kənˈsiːt/ noun **1** [U] (*disapproving*) the fact of being too proud of yourself and what you do **2** [C] (*formal*) an artistic effect or device, especially one that is very clever or tries to be very clever but does not succeed: *The ill-advised conceit of the guardian angel dooms the film from the start.* **3** [C] (*specialist*) a clever expression in writing or speech that involves a comparison between two things SYN **metaphor**: *The idea of the wind singing is a romantic conceit.*

**con·ceit·ed** /kənˈsiːtɪd/ *adj.* (*disapproving*) being too proud of yourself and what you do: *a very conceited person* ◊ *It's very conceited of you to assume that your work is always the best.* ▸ **con·ceit·ed·ly** *adv.*

**con·ceiv·able** /kənˈsiːvəbl/ *adj.* that you can imagine or believe SYN **possible**: *It is conceivable that I'll see her tomorrow.* ◊ *a beautiful city with buildings of every conceivable age and style* OPP **inconceivable** ▸ **con·ceiv·ably** /-bli/ *adv.*: *The disease could conceivably be transferred to humans.*

**con·ceive** /kənˈsiːv/ verb **1** [T] ~ **sth** (*formal*) to form an idea, a plan, etc. in your mind: *He conceived the idea of transforming the old power station into an arts centre.* ◊ *The dam project was originally conceived in 1977.* **2** [T] (often used in negative sentences) (*formal*) to imagine sth: ~ **of sb/sth (as sth)** *God is often conceived of as male.* ◊ ~ **(that) …** *I cannot conceive* (= I do not believe) *(that) he would wish to harm us.* ◊ ~ **what/how, etc …** *I cannot conceive what it must be like.* **3** [I, T] when a woman **conceives** or **conceives a child**, she becomes pregnant: *She is unable to conceive.* ◊ ~ **sb** *Their first child was conceived on their wedding night.* ⊃ see also CONCEPTION

| WORD FAMILY |
|---|
| **conceive** verb |
| **conceivable** adj. |
| (≠ inconceivable) |
| **conceivably** adv. |
| **concept** noun |
| **conception** noun |
| **conceptual** adj. |

**con·cen·trate** /ˈkɒnsntreɪt; NAmE ˈkɑːn-/ verb, noun
- **verb 1** [I, T] to give all your attention to sth and not think about anything else: *I can't concentrate with all that noise going on.* ◊ ~ **on (doing) sth** *I struggled to concentrate on my job because I was worried about my son.* ◊ ~ **sth** *Nothing concentrates the mind better than the knowledge that you could die tomorrow* (= it makes you think very clearly). ◊ ~ **sth on (doing) sth** *I decided to concentrate all my efforts on finding somewhere to live.* **2** [T] ~ **sth + adv./prep.** to bring sth together in one place: *Power is largely concentrated in the hands of a small elite.* ◊ *We need to concentrate resources on the most run-down areas.* ◊ *Fighting was concentrated around the towns to the north.* **3** [T] ~ **sth** (*specialist*) to increase the strength of a substance by reducing its volume, for example by boiling it SYN **reduce** PHRV **'concentrate on sth** to spend more time doing one particular thing than others: *In this lecture I shall concentrate on the early years of Charles's reign.*
- **noun** [C, U] a substance that is made stronger because water or other substances have been removed: *mineral concentrates found at the bottom of rivers* ◊ *jams made with fruit juice concentrate*

**con·cen·trated** /ˈkɒnsntreɪtɪd; NAmE ˈkɑːn-/ *adj.* **1** showing that you are determined to do sth: *He made a concentrated effort to finish the work on time.* **2** (of a substance) made stronger because water or other substances have been removed: *concentrated orange juice* ◊ *a concentrated solution of salt in water* **3** if sth exists or happens in a **concentrated** way, there is a lot of it in one place or at one time: *concentrated gunfire*

**con·cen·tra·tion** /ˌkɒnsnˈtreɪʃn; NAmE ˌkɑːn-/ noun **1** [U] the ability to direct all your effort and attention on one thing, without thinking of other things: *This book requires a great deal of concentration.* ◊ *Tiredness affects your powers of concentration.* ◊ *He has a poor concentration span* (= cannot concentrate for long). **2** [U] ~ **(on sth)** the process of people directing effort and

# concentration camp

attention on a particular thing: *a need for greater concentration on environmental issues* **3** [C] **~ (of sth)** a lot of sth in one place: *a concentration of industry in the north of the country* **4** [C, U] the amount of a substance in a liquid or in another substance: *glucose concentrations in the blood*

**concen'tration camp** *noun* a type of prison, often consisting of a number of buildings inside a fence, where political prisoners, etc. are kept in extremely bad conditions: *a Nazi concentration camp*

**con·cen·tric** /kənˈsentrɪk/ *adj.* (*geometry*) (of circles) having the same centre: *concentric rings*

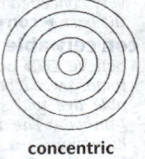

concentric circles

**con·cept** B2 /ˈkɒnsept; *NAmE* ˈkɑːn-/ *noun* **1** B2 an idea or a principle that is connected with sth ABSTRACT: **~ of sth** *the concept of social class* ◇ *basic/fundamental/key/core concepts* ◇ **~ that …** *the concept that everyone should have equality of opportunity* ◇ **the ~ behind sth** *the concepts behind an artist's work* ➔ see also HIGH-CONCEPT **2** an idea for sth new: *a novel/innovative concept* ◇ **~ in sth** *an exciting new concept in city living* ◇ *a design concept for a new school* ➔ see also PROOF OF CONCEPT

**'concept album** *noun* an album of pop music with the songs all on the same theme

**con·cep·tion** C1 /kənˈsepʃn/ *noun* **1** C1 [C, U] **~ (of sth) | ~ (that …)** an understanding or a belief of what sth/sb is or what sth/sb should be: *Marx's conception of social justice* ◇ *He has no conception of how difficult life is if you're unemployed.* **2** C1 [U] the process of forming an idea or a plan: *The plan was brilliant in its conception but failed because of lack of money.* **3** [U, C] the process of an egg being FERTILIZED inside a woman's body so that she becomes pregnant: *the moment of conception* ➔ WORDFINDER NOTE at PREGNANT ➔ see also CONCEIVE

**con·cep·tual** /kənˈseptʃuəl/ *adj.* (*formal*) related to or based on ideas: *a conceptual framework within which children's needs are assessed* ◇ *a conceptual model* ▶ **con·cep·tu·al·ly** /-əli/ *adv.*: *conceptually similar/distinct*

**con ceptual 'art** (*also* **conceptualism**) *noun* [U] art in which the idea which the work of art represents is considered to be the most important thing about it

**con·cep·tual·ism** /kənˈseptʃuəlɪzəm/ *noun* [U] **1** (*philosophy*) the theory that general qualities such as 'beauty' and 'red' exist only as ideas in the mind **2** (*art*) = CONCEPTUAL ART ▶ **con·cep·tual·ist** *noun*

**con·cep·tu·al·ize** (*BrE also* **-ise**) /kənˈseptʃuəlaɪz/ *verb* [T, I] (*formal*) **~ sth as sth | ~ (sth)** to form an idea of sth in your mind

**con·cern** B2 /kənˈsɜːn; *NAmE* -ˈsɜːrn/ *verb, noun*

■ *verb*

- **AFFECT/INVOLVE** **1** B2 **~ sb/sth** to affect sb/sth; to involve sb/sth: *Don't interfere in what doesn't concern you.* ◇ *To whom it may concern …* (= used for example, at the beginning of a public notice or of a job reference about sb's character and ability) ◇ *Please pay attention because this information concerns all of you.*
- **BE ABOUT** **2** B2 **~ sth** (*also* **be concerned with sth**) to be about sth: *The story concerns the prince's efforts to rescue Pamina.* ◇ *The book is primarily concerned with Soviet-American relations during the Cold War.* ◇ *My question concerns the way he handles the evidence.* ◇ **~ itself with sth** *This chapter concerns itself with the historical background.*
- **WORRY SB** **3** B2 **~ sb** to worry sb: *What concerns me is our lack of preparation for the change.* ◇ *it concerns sb that …* *It concerns me that you no longer seem to care.* ➔ see also CONCERNED
- **TAKE AN INTEREST** **4** **~ yourself with/about sth** to take an interest in sth: *He didn't concern himself with the details.*

■ *noun*

- **WORRY** **1** B2 [U, C] a feeling of worry, especially one that is shared by many people: **~ about sth/sb** *Villagers expressed concern about the level of traffic.* ◇ **~ over sth/sb** *The report raises serious concerns over safety at the plant.* ◇ **~ for sth/sb** *She hasn't been seen for four days and there is concern for her safety.* ◇ *to raise/voice concerns* ◇ *We are trying to address the concerns of residents.* ◇ **~ that …** *There is widespread concern that new houses will be built on protected land.* ◇ *security/safety concerns* ◇ *The president's health was giving serious cause for concern.* ➔ compare UNCONCERN
- **DESIRE TO PROTECT** **2** [U] **~ for (sb/sth)** a desire to protect and help sb/sth: *parents' concern for their children* ◇ *deep/genuine/real concern*
- **STH IMPORTANT** **3** B2 [C] something that is important to a person, an organization, etc: *Our main concern is to ensure the safety of the children.* ◇ *a big/major concern*
- **RESPONSIBILITY** **4** [C, usually sing.] (*formal*) something that is your responsibility or that you have a right to know about: *This matter is their concern.* ◇ *How much money I make is none of your concern.*
- **COMPANY** **5** [C] a company or business SYN **firm**: *a major publishing concern* IDM see GOING *adj.*

**con·cerned** B2 /kənˈsɜːnd; *NAmE* -ˈsɜːrnd/ *adj.* **1** B2 worried and feeling concern about sth/sb: *Concerned citizens can have a huge impact.* ◇ **~ about sth/sb** *The president is deeply concerned about this issue.* ◇ **~ for sth/sb** *He didn't seem in the least concerned for her safety.* ◇ **~ (that) …** *She was concerned that she might miss the turning and get lost.* ◇ **~ over/at/by sth** *Local residents are concerned over the impact of the project.* ➔ SYNONYMS at WORRIED **2** B2 [not before noun] affected by sth; involved in sth: *The loss was a tragedy for all concerned.* ◇ *Where our children's education is concerned, no compromise is acceptable.* ◇ *The individuals concerned have some explaining to do.* ◇ **be ~ in sth** *Everyone who was directly concerned in* (= had some responsibility for) *the incident has now resigned.* **3** B2 [not before noun] **~ with sth** interested in sth; dealing with sth: *The public is increasingly concerned with how food is produced.* **4 be concerned to do sth** (*formal*) to think it is important to do sth: *She was concerned to write about situations that everybody could identify with.* OPP **unconcerned** ➔ LANGUAGE BANK at ABOUT IDM see FAR *adv.*

**con·cern·ing** /kənˈsɜːnɪŋ; *NAmE* -ˈsɜːrn-/ *prep., adj.*

■ *prep.* (*formal*) about sth; involving sth/sb: *He asked several questions concerning the future of the company.* ◇ *All cases concerning children are dealt with in a special children's court.*

■ *adj.* causing worry: *This pattern of behaviour is extremely concerning.*

**con·cert** A1 /ˈkɒnsət; *NAmE* ˈkɑːnsərt/ *noun* a public performance of music: *to attend/go to a concert* ◇ *The orchestra gave a concert in Miami in January.* ◇ *a classical/rock/pop concert* ◇ **in ~** *They're in concert at Wembley arena.* ◇ **at a ~** *They also performed at a concert in Rome last month.* ◇ *a concert hall* ◇ *a concert pianist/tour/series* ➔ see also PROMENADE CONCERT

WORDFINDER audience, auditorium, interval, microphone, perform, programme, soloist, support, venue

IDM **in concert with sb/sth** (*formal*) working together with sb/sth

**con·cer·tante** /ˌkɒntʃəˈtænteɪ; *NAmE* ˌkɑːntʃərˈtɑːn-/ *adj.* [only before noun] (*music, from Italian*) related to a piece of music that contains an important part for a SOLO singer or player and that is similar to a CONCERTO in character

**'concert band** *noun* a large group of people who play wind instruments together, and who perform in a concert hall ➔ compare MILITARY BAND

**con·cert·ed** /kənˈsɜːtɪd; *NAmE* -ˈsɜːrt-/ *adj.* [only before noun] **1** done together by more than one person, government, country, etc: *a concerted approach/attack/campaign* **2** done in a planned and determined way: *She has begun to make a concerted effort to find a job.*

**con·cert·goer** /ˈkɒnsətɡəʊə(r); NAmE ˈkɑːnsərt-/ noun a person who regularly goes to concerts, especially of classical music

**ˌconcert ˈgrand** noun a piano of the largest size, used especially for concerts

**con·cer·tina** /ˌkɒnsəˈtiːnə; NAmE ˌkɑːnsərt-/ noun, verb
■ noun a musical instrument like a small ACCORDION that you hold in both hands. You press the ends together and pull them apart to produce sounds. ⊃ picture at ACCORDION
■ verb [I] (BrE) (**con·cer·tina·ing**, **con·cer·tinaed**, **con·cer·tinaed**) to fold up like a concertina: *The truck crashed into the tree and concertinaed.*

**con·cert·mas·ter** /ˈkɒnsətmɑːstə(r); NAmE ˈkɑːnsərtmæs-/ (*especially NAmE*) (*BrE usually* **lead·er**) noun the most important VIOLIN player in an ORCHESTRA

**con·certo** /kənˈtʃeətəʊ; NAmE -ˈtʃert-/ noun (pl. -os) a piece of music for one or more SOLO instruments playing with an ORCHESTRA: *a piano concerto* ◇ *~ for sth a concerto for flute and harp*

**con·ces·sion** ʔ+ C1 /kənˈseʃn/ noun **1** ʔ+ C1 [C, U] something that you allow or do, or allow sb to have, in order to end an argument or to make a situation less difficult: *The firm will be forced to* **make concessions** *if it wants to avoid a strike.* ◇ *to win a concession from sb* ◇ *a major/an important concession* ◇ *She made no concession to his age; she expected him to work as hard as she did.* ⊃ see also CONCEDE **2** ʔ+ C1 [U] *~(of sth) (to sb/sth)* the act of giving sth or allowing sth; the act of CONCEDING: *the concession of university status to some colleges* ◇ *Clinton's* **concession speech** *(= when she admitted that she had lost the election)* **3** [C, usually pl.] (*BrE*) a reduction in an amount of money that has to be paid; a ticket that is sold at a reduced price to a particular group of people: *tax concessions* ◇ *Tickets are £3; there is a £1 concession for students.* ◇ *Adults £2.50, concessions £2; family £5* **4** [C] a right or an advantage that is given to a group of people, an organization, etc., especially by a government or an employer: *The Bolivian government has granted logging concessions covering 22 million hectares.* **5** [C] the right to sell sth in a particular place; the place where you sell it, sometimes an area that is part of a larger building or store: *the burger concessions at the stadium* (*especially US*) *They went to the* **concession stand** *to get a hot dog.*

**con·ces·sion·aire** /kənˌseʃəˈneə(r); NAmE -ˈner/ noun (*especially BrE*) a person or a business that has been given a concession to sell sth

**con·ces·sion·ary** /kənˈseʃənəri; NAmE -neri/ adj. [usually before noun] (*BrE*) costing less money for people in particular situations; given as a CONCESSION: *concessionary rates/fares/travel*

**con·ces·sive** /kənˈsesɪv/ adj. (*grammar*) (of a preposition or conjunction) used at the beginning of a clause to say that the action of the main clause is in fact true or possible, despite the situation. 'Despite' and 'although' are concessive words.

**conch** /kɒntʃ; NAmE kɑːntʃ/ noun the shell of a sea creature that is also called a conch

**conc·ierge** /ˈkɒnsieəʒ; NAmE kəʊnˈsjerʒ/ noun (*from French*) **1** a person, especially in France, who takes care of a building containing flats and checks people entering and leaving the building **2** a person in a hotel whose job is to help guests by giving them information, arranging theatre tickets, etc.

**con·cili·ate** /kənˈsɪlieɪt/ verb *~sb* (*formal*) to make sb less angry or more friendly, especially by being kind and pleasant or by giving them sth SYN **pacify** ▶ **con·cili·ation** /kənˌsɪliˈeɪʃn/ noun [U]: *A conciliation service helps to settle disputes between employers and workers.*

**con·cili·ator** /kənˈsɪlieɪtə(r)/ noun (*formal*) a person or an organization that helps to end an argument between people or groups

**con·cili·atory** /kənˈsɪliətəri; NAmE -tɔːri/ adj. (*formal*) having the intention or effect of making angry people calm: *a conciliatory approach/attitude/gesture/move*

315 **conclusion**

**con·cise** /kənˈsaɪs/ adj. **1** giving only the information that is necessary and important, using few words: *a concise summary* ◇ *clear concise instructions* **2** [only before noun] (of a book) shorter than the original book, on which it was based: *a concise dictionary* ▶ **con·cise·ly** adv. **con·cise·ness** (*also less frequent* **con·ci·sion** /-ˈsɪʒn/) noun [U]

**con·clave** /ˈkɒŋkleɪv; NAmE ˈkɑːnkleɪv/ noun (*formal*) a meeting to discuss sth in private; the people at this meeting

**con·clude** ❶ B1 ◯ /kənˈkluːd/ verb **1** ʔ B1 [T] (not used in the progressive tenses) to decide or believe sth as a result of what you have heard or seen: *~sth (from sth) What do you conclude from that?* ◇ *~(that)… The report concluded (that) the cheapest option was to close the laboratory.* ◇ *~from sth that… He concluded from their remarks that they were not in favour of the plan.* ◇ *it is concluded that… It was concluded that the level of change necessary would be low.* ◇ *+ speech 'So it should be safe to continue,' he concluded.* ⊃ LANGUAGE BANK at CONCLUSION **2** ʔ B1 [I, T] (*formal*) to come to an end; to bring sth to an end: *This was how the negotiations finally concluded.* ◇ *Let me make just a few concluding remarks.* ◇ *~with sth The programme concluded with Stravinsky's 'Rite of Spring'.* ◇ *~by doing sth He concluded by wishing everyone a safe trip home.* ◇ *~sth The commission concluded its investigation last month.* ◇ *~sth with sth She concluded her speech with a quotation from Shakespeare.* ◇ *~+ speech 'Anyway, she should be back soon,' he concluded.* **3** [T] *~sth (with sb)* (*formal*) to arrange and settle an agreement with sb formally and finally: *They concluded a treaty with Turkey.* ◇ *A trade agreement was concluded between the two countries.*

**con·clu·sion** ❶ B1 ◯ /kənˈkluːʒn/ noun **1** ʔ B1 [C] something that you decide when you have thought about all the information connected with the situation: *We can safely* **draw some conclusions** *from our discussion.* ◇ *He* **arrived at a different conclusion**. ◇ *~(that)… I've* **come to the conclusion** *that he's not the right person for the job.* ◇ *New evidence might* **lead to the conclusion** *that we are wrong.* ◇ *~about/on sb/sth It is too soon to* **reach any conclusions** *about voting trends.* **2** ʔ B1 [C, usually sing.] the end of sth such as a speech or a piece of writing: *The conclusion of the book was disappointing.* ◇ *If we took this argument to its* **logical conclusion**… ◇ *~to sth The film is a fitting conclusion to the series.* ◇ *in~ In conclusion* (= finally), *I would like to thank…* **3** [U] the formal and final arrangement of sth official SYN **completion**: *the successful conclusion of a trade treaty* ⊃ EXPRESS YOURSELF at FINISH

▼ LANGUAGE BANK

**conclusion**

Summing up an argument

● *In conclusion*, the study has provided useful insights into the issues relating to people's perception of crime.
● *On the basis of this study*, **it can be concluded that** the introduction of new street lighting did not reduce reported crime.
● *To sum up*, no evidence can be found to support the view that improved street lighting reduces reported crime.
● The available evidence clearly **leads to the conclusion that** the media do have an influence on the public perception of crime.
● The **main conclusion to be drawn from** this study is that public perception of crime is significantly influenced by crime news reporting.
● *This study has shown that* people's fear of crime is out of all proportion to the crime itself.
● Fear of crime is out of all proportion to the actual level of crime, and the reasons for this **can be summarized as follows**. First…
● *Overall /In general*, women are more likely than men to feel insecure walking alone after dark.

⊃ LANGUAGE BANK at EMPHASIS, FIRST, GENERALLY

**conclusive** 316

**IDM** **jump/leap to con'clusions** | **jump/leap to the con'clusion that ...** to make a decision about sb/sth too quickly, before you know or have thought about all the facts: *There I go again—jumping to conclusions.* ⇨ more at FOREGONE

**con·clu·sive** /kənˈkluːsɪv/ *adj.* proving sth in a way that is certain and allows no doubt: *conclusive evidence/proof/results* **OPP** **inconclusive** ▶ **con·clu·sive·ly** *adv.*: *to prove sth conclusively*

**con·coct** /kənˈkɒkt; *NAmE* -ˈkɑːkt/ *verb* **1** ~ **sth** to make sth, especially food or drink, by mixing different things: *The soup was concocted from up to a dozen different kinds of fish.* **2** ~ **sth** to invent a story, an excuse, etc. or create a plan, especially for a dishonest purpose **SYN** **cook up**, **make up**: *She concocted some elaborate story to explain her absence.*

**con·coc·tion** /kənˈkɒkʃn; *NAmE* -ˈkɑːk-/ *noun* a strange or unusual mixture of things, especially drinks or medicines: *a concoction of cream and rum*

**con·comi·tant** /kənˈkɒmɪtənt; *NAmE* -ˈkɑːm-/ *adj., noun*
- *adj.* (*formal*) happening at the same time as sth else, especially because one thing is related to or causes the other
- *noun* (*formal*) a thing that happens at the same time as sth else

**con·cord** /ˈkɒŋkɔːd; *NAmE* ˈkɑːnkɔːrd/ *noun* [U] **1** ~ (with sb) (*formal*) peace and agreement **SYN** **harmony**: *living in concord with neighbouring states* **OPP** **discord** **2** ~ (with sth) (*grammar*) (of words in a phrase) the fact of having the same NUMBER, GENDER or PERSON **SYN** **agreement**

**con·cord·ance** /kənˈkɔːdəns; *NAmE* -ˈkɔːrd-/ *noun* **1** [C] an alphabetical list of the words used in a book, etc. showing where and how often they are used: *a Bible concordance* **2** [C] a list produced by a computer that shows all the examples of an individual word in a book, etc. **3** [U] (*specialist*) the state of being similar to sth or consistent with it: *There is reasonable concordance between the two sets of results.*

**con·cord·ant** /kənˈkɔːdənt; *NAmE* -ˈkɔːrd-/ *adj.* ~ (with sth) (*formal*) in agreement with sth **SYN** **consistent**: *The findings are concordant with similar studies in other countries.* **OPP** **discordant**

**con·cor·dat** /kənˈkɔːdæt; *NAmE* kənˈkɔːrdæt/ *noun* an agreement, especially between the Roman Catholic Church and the state

**con·course** /ˈkɒŋkɔːs; *NAmE* ˈkɑːnkɔːrs/ *noun* a large, open part of a public building, especially an airport or a train station: *the station concourse*

**con·crete** /ˈkɒŋkriːt; *NAmE* ˈkɑːnk-/ *adj., noun, verb*
- *adj.* **1** made of concrete: *a concrete floor* **2** /ˈkɒŋkriːt; *NAmE* kɑːnˈkriːt/ based on facts, not on ideas or guesses: *concrete evidence/proposals/proof* ◊ *'It's only a suspicion,' she said, 'nothing concrete.'* ◊ *It is easier to think in concrete terms rather than in the abstract.* ⇨ compare ABSTRACT **3** /ˈkɒŋkriːt; *NAmE* kɑːnˈkriːt/ a concrete object is one that you can see and feel ▶ **con·crete·ly** /-li/ *adv.*
- *noun* [U] building material that is made by mixing together CEMENT, sand, small stones and water: *a slab of concrete* ⇨ see also REINFORCED CONCRETE
- *verb* ~ **sth** (**over**) to cover sth with concrete: *The garden had been concreted over.*

**concrete 'jungle** *noun* [*usually sing.*] a way of describing a city or an area that is unpleasant because it has many large modern buildings and few trees or parks

**'concrete mixer** *noun* = CEMENT MIXER

**'concrete 'poetry** *noun* [U] poetry in which the meaning or effect is communicated partly by using patterns of words or letters that you can see on the page

**con·cu·bine** /ˈkɒŋkjubaɪn; *NAmE* ˈkɑːŋk-/ *noun* (especially in some societies in the past) a woman who lives with a man, often in addition to his wife or wives, but who is less important than they are

**con·cur** /kənˈkɜː(r)/ *verb* [I, T] (**-rr-**) ~ (**with sb**) (**in sth**) | ~ (**with sth**) | ~ (**that ...**) | (+ **speech**) (*formal*) to agree: *Historians have concurred with each other in this view.* ◊ *The coroner concurred with this assessment.*

**con·cur·rence** /kənˈkʌrəns; *NAmE* -ˈkɜːr-/ *noun* (*formal*) **1** [U, *sing.*] agreement: *The doctor may seek the concurrence of a relative before carrying out the procedure.* **2** [*sing.*] an example of two or more things happening at the same time: *an unfortunate concurrence of events*

**con·cur·rent** /kənˈkʌrənt; *NAmE* -ˈkɜːr-/ *adj.* ~ (**with sth**) existing or happening at the same time: *He was imprisoned for two concurrent terms of 30 months and 18 months.* ▶ **con·cur·rent·ly** *adv.*: *The prison sentences will run concurrently.*

**con·cuss** /kənˈkʌs/ *verb* ~ **sb** to hit sb on the head, making them become unconscious or confused for a short time ▶ **con·cussed** *adj.*: *She was concussed after the fall.*

**con·cus·sion** /kənˈkʌʃn/ *noun* [U, C] a temporary loss of CONSCIOUSNESS caused by a hard hit on the head; the effects of a severe hit on the head, such as not being able to think clearly and temporary loss of physical and mental abilities: *He was taken to hospital with concussion.* ◊ *She suffered a mild concussion.*

**con·demn** /kənˈdem/ *verb*
- SAY STH IS BAD **1** to say very strongly that you think sth is bad, usually for moral reasons: ~ **sb**/**sth** *The government issued a statement condemning the killings.* ◊ ~ **sb**/**sth for**/**as sth** *The editor of the newspaper was condemned as lacking integrity.*
- SB TO PUNISHMENT **2** [*usually passive*] to say what sb's punishment will be **SYN** **sentence**: **be condemned** (**to sth**) *He was condemned to death for murder and later hanged.* ◊ **be condemned to do sth** *She was condemned to hang for killing her husband.*
- SB TO DIFFICULT SITUATION **3** [*usually passive*] to force sb to accept a difficult or unpleasant situation **SYN** **doom**: **be condemned to sth** *He was condemned to a life of hardship.* ◊ **be condemned to do sth** *They were condemned to spend every holiday on a rainy campsite.*
- STH DANGEROUS **4** [*usually passive*] to say officially that sth is not safe enough to be used: **be condemned** (**as sth**) *The meat was condemned as unfit to eat.* ◊ *a condemned building*
- SHOW GUILT **5** ~ **sb** to show or suggest that sb is guilty of sth: *She is condemned out of her own mouth* (= her own words show that she is guilty).

**con·dem·na·tion** /ˌkɒndemˈneɪʃn; *NAmE* ˌkɑːn-/ *noun* [U, C] ~ (**of sb**/**sth**) an expression of very strong DISAPPROVAL: *There was widespread condemnation of the invasion.*

**con'demned 'cell** *noun* (*BrE*) a prison cell where a person who is going to be punished by death is kept

**con·den·sa·tion** /ˌkɒndenˈseɪʃn; *NAmE* ˌkɑːn-/ *noun* **1** [U] drops of water that form on a cold surface when warm water VAPOUR becomes cool **2** [U] the process of a gas changing to a liquid **3** [C, *usually sing.*, U] (*formal*) the process of making a book, etc. shorter by taking out anything that is not necessary

**con·dense** /kənˈdens/ *verb* **1** [I, T] to change from a gas into a liquid; to make a gas change into a liquid: ~ (**into sth**) *Steam condenses into water when it cools.* ◊ ~ **sth** (**into sth**) *The steam was condensed rapidly by injecting cold water into the cylinder.* ⇨ WORDFINDER NOTE at LIQUID **2** [I, T] ~ (**sth**) if a liquid condenses or you condense it, it becomes thicker and stronger because it has lost some of its water **SYN** **reduce**: *Condense the soup by boiling it for several minutes.* **3** [T] ~ **sth** (**into sth**) to put sth such as a piece of writing into fewer words; to put a lot of information into a small space: *The article was condensed into just two pages.* ◊ *The author has condensed a great deal of material into just 100 pages.*

**con·densed 'milk** *noun* [U] a type of thick sweet milk that is sold in cans

**con·dens·er** /kənˈdensə(r)/ noun 1 a device that cools gas in order to change it into a liquid 2 a device that receives or stores electricity, especially in a car engine

**con·des·cend** /ˌkɒndɪˈsend; NAmE ˌkɑːn-/ verb 1 [T] ~ **to do sth** (often disapproving) to do sth that you think it is below your social or professional position to do **SYN deign**: *We had to wait almost an hour before he condescended to see us.* 2 [I] ~ **to sb** to behave towards sb as though you are more important and more intelligent than they are: *When giving a talk, be careful not to condescend to your audience.* ▶ **con·des·cen·sion** /-ˈsenʃn/ noun [U]: *Her smile was a mixture of pity and condescension.*

**con·des·cend·ing** /ˌkɒndɪˈsendɪŋ; NAmE ˌkɑːn-/ adj. behaving as though you are more important and more intelligent than other people: *He has a condescending attitude towards women.* ▶ **con·des·cend·ing·ly** adv.

**con·di·ment** /ˈkɒndɪmənt; NAmE ˈkɑːn-/ noun [usually pl.] a substance such as salt, pepper or a sauce that is added to food to give it extra taste

**con·di·tion** 🅞 🅐🅰 🅞 /kənˈdɪʃn/ noun, verb
■ noun
• STATE OF STH **1** 🅐🅰 [U, sing.] the state that sth is in: *in …~ to be in pristine/excellent/perfect condition* ◇ *the ~ of sth The condition of the roads is poor.*
• MEDICAL **2** 🅐🅰 [U, sing.] the state of sb's health or how fit they are: *He is overweight and out of condition* (= not physically fit). ◇ *in (a)…~ The motorcyclist was in a critical condition* (= at risk of dying) *in hospital last night.* ◇ *You are in no condition* (= too ill/sick, etc.) *to go anywhere.* **3** 🅑🅱 [C] an illness or a medical problem that you have for a long time because it is not possible to cure it: *a medical/health condition* ◇ *He suffers from a serious heart condition.* ➲ WORDFINDER NOTE at HEALTH ➲ SYNONYMS at DISEASE

**WORDFINDER** anorexia, autism, bipolar disorder, dementia, depression, paranoia, psychosis, schizophrenia

• CIRCUMSTANCES **4** 🅑🅱 **conditions** [pl.] the circumstances or situation in which people live, work or do things: *working/living conditions* ◇ *economic/market conditions* ◇ *under …~ They were working under appalling conditions.* ◇ *~ for sb to improve conditions for workers* ➲ SYNONYMS at SITUATION **5** 🅑🅱 **conditions** [pl.] the physical situation that affects how sth happens: *in …~ The plants grow best in cool, damp conditions.* ◇ *adverse weather conditions* ◇ *dry/wet/harsh, etc. conditions* ◇ *under …~ Studies show that the drug may be harmful under certain conditions.*
• RULE **6** 🅑🅱 [C] a rule or decision that you must agree to, sometimes forming part of a contract or an official agreement: *Read the terms and conditions carefully before you sign.* ◇ *The offer is subject to certain conditions.* ◇ *on (the) ~ that … They agreed to lend us the car on condition that* (= only if) *we returned it before the weekend.* ◇ *They will give us the money on one condition—that we pay it back within six months.* ◇ *under the ~ that …* (especially NAmE) *They agreed under the condition that the matter be dealt with promptly.* ◇ *Congress can impose strict conditions on the bank.* ◇ *to satisfy/meet/fulfill a condition*
• NECESSARY SITUATION **7** 🅑🅱 [C] a situation that must exist in order for sth else to happen: *~ for sth a necessary condition for economic growth* ◇ *as a ~ of (doing) sth Applicants must agree to teach for three years as a condition of admission to the program.*
• STATE OF GROUP **8** [sing.] (formal) the state of a particular group of people because of their situation in life, their problems, etc: *He spoke angrily about the condition of the urban poor.* ◇ *Work is basic to the human condition* (= the fact of being alive).
**IDM** **on ˈno condition** (US also **under ˈno condition**) (formal) not in any situation; never: *You must on no condition tell them what happened.* ➲ more at MINT *n.*
■ verb **1** [usually passive] to train sb/sth to behave in a particular way or to become used to a particular situation: **be conditioned to sth** *Patients can become conditioned to particular forms of treatment.* ◇ **be conditioned to do sth** *The rats had been conditioned to ring a bell when they wanted food.* ◇ *the difference between inborn and conditioned reflexes* (= reactions that are learned/not natural) **2** [usually passive] to have an important effect on sb/sth; to influence the way that sth happens: **be conditioned (by sth)** *Gender roles are often conditioned by cultural factors.* **3** ~ **sth** to keep sth such as your hair or skin healthy: *a shampoo that cleans and conditions hair* ◇ *a polish for conditioning leather*

▼ **WHICH WORD?**

**condition / state**
The following adjectives are frequently used with these nouns:

| ~condition | ~state |
|---|---|
| good | present |
| excellent | current |
| physical | mental |
| poor | no |
| human | emotional |
| perfect | physical |
| no | natural |
| better | original |

• **State** is a more general word than **condition** and is used for the condition that something is in at a particular time. It can be used without an adjective: *the present state of medical knowledge* ◇ *We're worried about his mental state.* ◇ *What a state this room is in* (= very bad).
• **Condition** is used with an adjective and refers especially to the appearance, quality or working order of somebody or something: *The car is in excellent condition.*

**con·di·tion·al** 🅦 /kənˈdɪʃənl/ adj., noun
■ adj. **1** ~ **(on/upon sth)** depending on sth: *conditional approval/acceptance* ◇ *Payment is conditional upon delivery of the goods* (= if the goods are not delivered, the money will not be paid) ◇ *He was found guilty and given a conditional discharge* (= allowed to go free on particular conditions). ◇ *a conditional offer* (= that depends on particular conditions being met) **OPP unconditional 2** [only before noun] (grammar) expressing sth that must happen or be true if another thing is to happen or be true: *a conditional sentence/clause* ▶ **con·di·tion·al·ly** /-nəli/ adv.: *The offer was made conditionally.*
■ noun (grammar) **1** [C] a sentence or clause that begins with *if* or *unless* and expresses a condition **2 the conditional** [sing.] the form of a verb that expresses a conditional action, for example *should* in *If I should die …: the present/past/perfect conditional* ◇ *the first/second/third conditional*

**con·di·tion·er** /kənˈdɪʃənə(r)/ noun [C, U] **1** a liquid or cream used to improve the condition of hair after washing: *shampoo and conditioner* **2** a liquid, used after washing clothes, that makes them softer: *fabric conditioner*

**con·di·tion·ing** /kənˈdɪʃənɪŋ/ noun [U] the training or experience that an animal or a person has that makes them behave in a particular way in a particular situation: *Is personality the result of conditioning from parents and society, or are we born with it?* ➲ see also AIR CONDITIONING

**condo** /ˈkɒndəʊ; NAmE ˈkɑːn-/ noun (pl. **-os**) (NAmE, informal) = CONDOMINIUM

**con·dol·ence** /kənˈdəʊləns/ noun [C, usually pl., U] sympathy that you feel for sb when a person in their family or that they know well has died; an expression of this sympathy: *to give/offer/express your condolences* ◇ *Our condolences go to his wife and family.* ◇ *a letter of condolence*

**con·dom** /ˈkɒndɒm; NAmE ˈkɑːndəm/ noun **1** (BrE also **sheath**) (also NAmE, formal or specialist **prophy·lac·tic**) a thin rubber tube that a man wears over his PENIS during sex to stop a woman from becoming pregnant or to protect against disease **2 female concom** a thin rubber device that a woman wears inside her VAGINA during sex to prevent herself from becoming pregnant

**con·do·min·ium** /ˌkɒndəˈmɪniəm; NAmE ˌkɑːn-/ (also informal **condo**) noun (especially NAmE) an apartment building or group of houses in which each apartment/house is

# condone 318

owned by the person living in it but the shared areas are owned by everyone together; an apartment/a house in such a building or group of houses

**con·done** /kənˈdəʊn/ *verb* ~ sth | ~ (sb) doing sth to accept behaviour that is morally wrong or to treat it as if it were not serious: *Terrorism can never be condoned.*

**con·dor** /ˈkɒndɔː(r); NAmE ˈkɑːn-/ *noun* a large bird of the VULTURE family that lives mainly in South America

**con·du·cive** /kənˈdjuːsɪv; NAmE -ˈduː-/ *adj.* ~ to sth making it easy, possible or likely for sth to happen: *Chairs in rows are not as conducive to discussion as chairs arranged in a circle.*

**con·duct** 🔵 B2 Ⓦ *verb, noun*

▪ *verb* /kənˈdʌkt/ **1** 🔵 B2 [T] ~ sth (*formal*) to organize and/or do a particular activity: *to conduct an experiment/inquiry/investigation/interview* ◊ *to conduct a survey/poll/study/review* ◊ *to conduct a test/trial* ◊ *to conduct research/business* ◊ *Police conducted a thorough search of the building.* **2** 🔵 B2 [T, I] ~(sth) to direct a group of people who are singing or playing music: *a concert by the London Philharmonic Orchestra, conducted by Marin Alsop* ◊ *He conducted a programme of Sibelius and Tchaikovsky.* **3** [T] ~sb/sth + adv./prep. (*formal*) to lead or guide sb through or around a place: *a conducted tour of Athens* (= one with a guide, giving information about it) ◊ *The guide conducted us around the ruins of the ancient city.* **4** [T] ~ yourself + adv./prep. (*formal*) to behave in a particular way: *He conducted himself far better than expected.* **5** [T] ~ sth (*specialist*) (of a substance) to allow heat or electricity to pass along or through it: *Copper conducts electricity well.*
⊃ WORDFINDER NOTE at ELECTRICITY

▪ *noun* /ˈkɒndʌkt; NAmE ˈkɑːn-/ [U] (*formal*) **1** 🔵 B2 a person's behaviour in a particular place or in a particular situation: *The sport has a strict code of conduct.* ◊ *Any allegation of criminal conduct has to be taken seriously.* **2** ~ of sth the way in which a business or an activity is organized and managed: *There was growing criticism of the government's conduct of the war.* ⊃ see also SAFE CONDUCT

**con·duct·ance** /kənˈdʌktəns/ *noun* [U] (*physics*) the degree to which an object allows electricity or heat to pass through it

**con·duc·tion** /kənˈdʌkʃn/ *noun* [U] (*physics*) the process by which heat or electricity passes through a material

**con·duct·ive** /kənˈdʌktɪv/ *adj.* (*physics*) able to CONDUCT electricity, heat, etc. ▶ **con·duct·iv·ity** /ˌkɒndʌkˈtɪvəti; NAmE ˌkɑːn-/ *noun* [U]

**con·duct·or** /kənˈdʌktə(r)/ *noun* **1** a person who stands in front of an ORCHESTRA, a group of singers etc., and directs their performance, especially sb who does this as a profession **2** (*BrE also* **guard**) a person who is in charge of a train and travels with it, but does not drive it **3** (*BrE*) a person whose job is to collect money from passengers on a bus or train or check their tickets: *a bus conductor* **4** (*physics*) a substance that allows electricity or heat to pass along it or through it: *Wood is a poor conductor.*
⊃ see also LIGHTNING CONDUCTOR

**con·duit** /ˈkɒndjuɪt; NAmE ˈkɑːnduː-/ *noun* **1** (*specialist*) a pipe, channel or tube through which liquid, gas or electrical wire can pass **2** (*formal*) a person, an organization or a country that is used to pass things or information to other people or places: *The organization had acted as a conduit for money from the arms industry.*

**cone** /kəʊn/ *noun* **1** a solid or hollow object with a round flat base and sides that slope up to a point ⊃ picture at SOLID ⊃ see also CONIC *noun*, CONICAL **2** a solid or hollow object that is like a cone in shape: *a paper cone full of popcorn* ◊ *the cone of a volcano* ⊃ see also NOSE CONE **3** (*also* **traffic cone**) a plastic object shaped like a cone and often red and white, or yellow in colour, used on roads to show where vehicles are not allowed to go, for example while repairs are being done ⊃ WORDFINDER NOTE at TRAFFIC **4** (*also old-fashioned* **cornet**) a piece of thin dry biscuit like a cone in shape that you can put ice cream in to eat it: *an ice cream cone* **5** the hard dry fruit of a PINE or FIR tree: *a pine/fir cone* ⊃ VISUAL VOCAB page V6

**con·fab** /ˈkɒnfæb; NAmE ˈkɑːn-/ *noun* (*informal*) **1** an informal private discussion or conversation **2** (*NAmE*) a meeting or conference of the members of a profession or group: *the annual movie confab in Cannes*

**con·fabu·la·tion** /kənˌfæbjəˈleɪʃn/ *noun* [C, U] (*formal*) **1** a story that sb has invented in their mind; the act of inventing a story in your mind **2** a conversation; the activity of having a conversation

**con·fec·tion** /kənˈfekʃn/ *noun* **1** (*formal*) a cake or other sweet food that looks very attractive **2** a thing such as a building or piece of clothing, that is made in a way that is complicated or shows skill

**con·fec·tion·er** /kənˈfekʃənə(r)/ *noun* a person or a business that makes or sells cakes and sweets

**conˈfectioner's ˈsugar** (*also* **powdered ˈsugar**) (*both US*) (*BrE* **ˈicing sugar**) *noun* [U] sugar in the form of a fine white powder that is mixed with water to make icing

**con·fec·tion·ery** /kənˈfekʃənəri; NAmE -neri/ *noun* [U] sweets, chocolate, etc.

**con·fed·er·acy** /kənˈfedərəsi/ *noun* **1** [C] a union of states, groups of people or political parties with the same aim **2** **the Confederacy** [*sing.*] = CONFEDERATE STATES

**con·fed·er·ate** /kənˈfedərət/ *noun, adj.*

▪ *noun* **1** a person who helps sb, especially to do sth illegal or secret SYN **accomplice** **2** **Confederate** a person who supported the Confederate States in the American Civil War

▪ *adj.* **1** belonging to a confederacy **2** **Confederate** connected with the Confederate States: *the Confederate flag*

**the Conˌfederate ˈStates** *noun* [*pl.*] (*also* **the Confederacy**) the eleven southern states of the US that left the United States in 1860–1, starting the American Civil War

**con·fed·er·ation** /kənˌfedəˈreɪʃn/ *noun* **1** an organization consisting of countries, businesses, etc. that have joined together in order to help each other: *the Confederation of British Industry* **2** **Confederation** (in Canada) the joining together of PROVINCES and TERRITORIES forming Canada, which began 1 July, 1867

**con·fer** 🔵 C1 /kənˈfɜː(r)/ *verb* (-rr-) (*formal*) **1** 🔵 C1 [I] ~ (with sb) (on/about sth) to discuss sth with sb, in order to exchange opinions or get advice: *He wanted to confer with his colleagues before reaching a decision.* **2** 🔵 C1 [T] ~ sth (on/upon sb) to give sb an award, a university degree or a particular honour or right: *An honorary degree was conferred on him by Oxford University in 2019.*

**con·fer·ence** 🔵 A2 /ˈkɒnfərəns; NAmE ˈkɑːn-/ *noun* **1** 🔵 A2 a large official meeting, usually lasting for a few days, at which people with the same work or interests come together to discuss their views: *The hotel is used for exhibitions, conferences and social events.* ◊ *to host/organize a conference* ◊ *The conference will be held in Glasgow.* ◊ *delegates to the Labour Party's annual conference* ◊ *We met at an international conference.* ◊ ~ on sth *She is attending a three-day conference on AIDS education.* ◊ *a conference room/centre*

> WORDFINDER delegate, exhibition, name tag, plenary, register, speaker, talk, venue, workshop

**2** 🔵 A2 a meeting at which people have formal discussions: *They agreed to convene a peace conference by mid-November.* ◊ **in ~ (with sb)** *He was in conference with his lawyers all day.* ◊ *Ministers from all four countries involved will meet at the conference table this week.* ⊃ see also NEWS CONFERENCE, PRESS CONFERENCE **3** (*especially NAmE*) a group of sports teams that play against each other in a league: *Southeast Conference football champions*

**ˈconference call** *noun* a phone call in which three or more people take part

**ˈcon·fer·ence comˌmit·tee** *noun* a temporary committee formed by members of the US Congress (the House of Representatives and the Senate) to agree the final version of a bill, after different versions have been drafted

**con·fer·en·cing** /ˈkɒnfərənsɪŋ; *NAmE* ˈkɑːn-/ *noun* the activity of organizing or taking part in meetings, especially when people are in different places and use phones, computers, or video to communicate: *web conferencing* ⊃ see also VIDEOCONFERENCING

**con·fer·ment** /kənˈfɜːmənt; *NAmE* -ˈfɜːrm-/ *noun* [U, C] (*formal*) the act of giving sb an award, a university degree or a particular honour or right

**con·fess** ⚡+ B2 /kənˈfes/ *verb* 1 ⚡+ B2 [I, T] to admit, especially formally or to the police, that you have done sth wrong or illegal: *After hours of questioning, the suspect confessed.* ◇ **~to (doing) sth** *She confessed to the murder.* ◇ **~(to sb) (that)** … *He confessed that he had stolen the money.* ◇ **~your crime, error,** etc. *We persuaded her to confess her crime.* 2 ⚡+ B2 [I, T] to admit sth that you feel ashamed or embarrassed about: **~sth** *She was reluctant to confess her ignorance.* ◇ **~to (doing) sth** *I must confess to knowing nothing about golf.* ◇ **~(that)** … *I confess (that) I know nothing about golf.* ◇ **+ speech** *'I know nothing about it,'* he confessed. ◇ **~yourself + adj.**: (*formal*) *I confess myself bewildered by their explanation.* ⊃ see also SELF-CONFESSED ⊃ SYNONYMS at ADMIT 3 [I, T] **~(sth) (to sb)** (especially in the Roman Catholic Church) to tell God or a priest about the bad things you have done so that you can say that you are sorry and be forgiven 4 [T] **~sb** (of a priest) to hear sb confess their SINS (= the bad things they have done)

**con·fes·sion** ⚡+ C1 /kənˈfeʃn/ *noun* 1 ⚡+ C1 [C, U] a statement that a person makes, admitting that they are guilty of a crime; the act of making such a statement: *After hours of questioning by police, she made a full confession.* 2 ⚡+ C1 [C, U] a statement admitting sth that you are ashamed or embarrassed about; the act of making such a statement: SYN *admission*: *I've a confession to make—I lied about my age.* 3 [U, C] (especially in the Roman Catholic Church) a private statement to a priest about the bad things that you have done; an occasion when you make such a statement: *to hear sb's confession* ◇ *to go to confession* 4 [C] (*formal*) a statement of your religious beliefs, principles, etc: *a confession of faith*

**con·fes·sion·al** /kənˈfeʃənl/ *noun* a private place in a church where a priest listens to people making confessions

**con·fes·sor** /kənˈfesə(r)/ *noun* a Roman Catholic priest who listens to sb's CONFESSION

**con·fetti** /kənˈfeti/ *noun* [U] small pieces of coloured paper that people often throw at weddings over people who have just been married, or (in the US) at other special events

**con·fi·dant** (*feminine* **con·fi·dante**) /ˈkɒnfɪdænt, ˌkɒnfɪˈdɑːnt; *NAmE* /ˈkɑːnfɪdænt/ *noun* a person that you trust and who you talk to about private or secret things: *a close/trusted confidant of the president*

**con·fide** /kənˈfaɪd/ *verb* to tell sb secrets and personal information that you do not want other people to know: **~sth (to sb)** *She confided all her secrets to her best friend.* ◇ **~(to sb) that** … *He confided to me that he had applied for another job.* ◇ **+ speech** *'It was a lie,'* he confided.
PHRV ▶ **con·fide in sb** to tell sb secrets and personal information because you feel you can trust them: *It is important to have someone you can confide in.*

**con·fi·dence** ❶ B2 /ˈkɒnfɪdəns; *NAmE* ˈkɑːn-/ *noun*
• BELIEF IN OTHERS 1 ⚡ B2 [U] the feeling that you can trust, believe in and be sure about the abilities or good qualities of sb/sth: *The president's actions hardly inspire confidence.* ◇ **~in sb/sth** *The players all have confidence in their manager.* ◇ *a lack of confidence in the government* ◇ *Our aim is to increase public confidence in the democratic process.* ◇ *The new contracts have undermined the confidence of employees.* ⊃ see also CONSUMER CONFIDENCE, VOTE OF CONFIDENCE, VOTE OF NO CONFIDENCE
• BELIEF IN YOURSELF 2 ⚡ B2 [U] a belief in your own ability to do things and be successful: *People often lose confidence when they are criticized.* ◇ *He gained confidence when he went to college.* ◇ *While girls lack confidence, boys often overestimate their abilities.* ◇ **with~** *She answered my questions with confidence.* ◇ **~in sth/yourself** *I didn't have any confidence in myself at school.* ◇ **~to do sth** *The training programmes have given workers the confidence to take on more responsibility.* ⊃ see also SELF-CONFIDENCE
• FEELING CERTAIN 3 ⚡ B2 [U] the feeling that you are certain about sth: *He said he wished that he shared her confidence.* ◇ **with~** *They could not say with confidence that he would be able to walk again after the accident.* ◇ **~that** … *She expressed her confidence that they would win.*
• TRUST 4 [U] a feeling of trust that sb will keep information private: *It took a long time to gain her confidence* (= make her feel she could trust me). ◇ **in ~** *Eva told me about their relationship in confidence.* ◇ *This is in the strictest confidence.*
• A SECRET 5 [C] (*formal*) a secret that you tell sb: *The girls exchanged confidences.* ◇ *I could never forgive Mike for betraying a confidence.*
IDM **be in sb's confidence** to be trusted with sb's secrets: *He is said to be very much in the president's confidence.* **take sb into your confidence** to tell sb secrets and personal information about yourself *She took me into her confidence and told me about the problems she was facing.*

**ˈconfidence trick** (*BrE*) (*NAmE* **ˈconfidence game**) *noun* (*formal*) an act of cheating or tricking sb by persuading them to believe sth that is not true: *They were the innocent victims of an elaborate confidence trick.* ⊃ compare CON (1)

**ˈconfidence trickster** *noun* (*BrE, formal*) a person who tricks others into giving him or her money, etc.

**con·fi·dent** ❶ B1 /ˈkɒnfɪdənt; *NAmE* ˈkɑːn-/ *adj.*
1 ⚡ B1 feeling sure about your own ability to do things and be successful: *She was in a relaxed, confident mood.* ◇ **~about (doing) sth** *The teacher wants the children to feel confident about asking questions when they don't understand.* ◇ **~in sth** *He'd learned to be confident in his ability to handle anything life threw at him.* ⊃ see also SELF-CONFIDENT 2 ⚡ B1 feeling certain that sth will happen in the way that you want or expect: **~of (doing) sth** *The team feels confident of winning.* ◇ **~about sth** *We are confident about the future.* ◇ **~(that)** … *I'm confident that you will get the job.* ◇ *She was quietly confident that everything would go as planned.* ⊃ SYNONYMS at SURE ▶ **con·fi·dent·ly** *adv.*

**con·fi·den·tial** /ˌkɒnfɪˈdenʃl; *NAmE* ˌkɑːn-/ *adj.* 1 meant to be kept secret and not told to or shared with other people: *confidential information/documents* ◇ *Your medical records are strictly confidential* (= completely secret). 2 (of a way of speaking) showing that what you are saying is private or secret: *He spoke in a confidential tone, his voice low.* 3 [only before noun] (*formal*) trusted with private or secret information: *a confidential secretary* ▶ **con·fi·den·tial·ly** /-ʃəli/ *adv.*: *She told me confidentially that she is going to retire early.*

**con·fi·den·ti·al·ity** /ˌkɒnfɪˌdenʃiˈæləti; *NAmE* ˌkɑːn-/ *noun* [U] a situation in which you expect sb to keep information secret: *They signed a confidentiality agreement.* ◇ *All letters will be treated with complete confidentiality.* ◇ *She declined to give customers' names, citing client confidentiality.*

**con·fid·ing** /kənˈfaɪdɪŋ/ *adj.* [usually before noun] showing trust; showing that you want to tell sb a secret: *a confiding relationship* ▶ **con·fid·ing·ly** *adv.*

**con·fig·ur·ation** ⚡+ C1 /kənˌfɪɡəˈreɪʃn; *NAmE* -ˌfɪɡjə-/ *noun* 1 ⚡+ C1 (*formal or specialist*) an arrangement of the parts of sth or a group of things; the form or shape that this arrangement produces 2 (*computing*) the equipment and programs that form a computer system and the way that these are set up to run

**con·fig·ure** /kənˈfɪɡə(r); *NAmE* -ˈfɪɡjər/ *verb* [usually passive] **~sth** (*specialist*) to arrange sth in a particular way, especially computer equipment; to make equipment or software work in the way that the user prefers ⊃ WORDFINDER NOTE at SOFTWARE

**con·fine** ⚡+ C1 /kənˈfaɪn/ *verb* 1 ⚡+ C1 [often passive] to keep sb/sth inside the limits of a particular activity,

**confined**

subject, area, etc. **SYN** **restrict**: *be confined to (doing) sth The work will not be confined to the Glasgow area.* ◇ *~ yourself to (doing) sth I will confine myself to looking at the period from 1900 to 1916.* **2** [usually passive] to keep a person or an animal in a small or closed space: **be confined (in sth)** *Keep the dog confined in a suitable travelling cage.* ◇ *Here the river is confined in a narrow channel.* ◇ *The soldiers concerned were confined to barracks* (= had to stay in the BARRACKS, as a punishment). **3 be confined to bed, a wheelchair, etc.** to have to stay in bed, in a WHEELCHAIR, etc: *She was confined to bed with the flu.* ◇ *He was confined to a wheelchair after the accident.*

**con·fined** /kənˈfaɪnd/ *adj.* [usually before noun] (of a space or an area) small and surrounded by walls or sides: *It is cruel to keep animals in confined spaces.*

**con·fine·ment** /kənˈfaɪnmənt/ *noun* **1** [U] the state of being forced to stay in a closed space, prison, etc.; the act of putting sb there: *her confinement to a wheelchair* ◇ *years of confinement as a political prisoner* ⇒ see also HOME CONFINEMENT, SOLITARY CONFINEMENT **2** [U, C] (*formal or old-fashioned*) the time when a woman gives birth to a baby: *the expected date of confinement* ◇ *a hospital/home confinement*

**con·fines** /ˈkɒnfaɪnz; *NAmE* ˈkɑːn-/ *noun* [pl.] (*formal*) limits or borders: *It is beyond the confines of human knowledge.* ◇ *the confines of family life*

**con·firm** /kənˈfɜːm; *NAmE* -ˈfɜːrm/ *verb* **1** to state or show that sth is definitely true or correct, especially by providing evidence: *~ sth His guilty expression confirmed my suspicions.* ◇ *Rumours of job losses were later confirmed.* ◇ *She said she could not confirm or deny the allegations.* ◇ *~ (that) ... Police sources confirmed that ten people had been arrested at the march.* ◇ *~ what/when, etc … Can you confirm what happened?* ◇ **it is confirmed that ...** *It has been confirmed that an official complaint was made to the council.* **2** to make a position, an agreement, etc. more definite or official; to establish sb/sth clearly: *~ sth Please write to confirm your reservation* (= say that it is definite). ◇ *(that) ... Has everyone confirmed (that) they're coming?* ◇ **it is confirmed that ...** *It has been confirmed that the meeting will take place next week.* ◇ *~ sb as sth He was confirmed as captain for the rest of the season.* ◇ *~ sb in sth I'm very happy to confirm you in your post.* **3** *~ sth* | *~ sb in sth* to make sb feel or believe sth even more strongly: *The walk in the mountains confirmed his fear of heights.* **4** [usually passive] to perform the Christian or Jewish ceremony of confirmation: **be confirmed** *She was baptized when she was a month old and confirmed when she was thirteen.*

**con·firm·ation** /ˌkɒnfəˈmeɪʃn; *NAmE* ˌkɑːnfərˈm-/ *noun* [U, C] **1** a statement, letter, etc. that shows that sth is true, correct or definite: *I'm still waiting for confirmation of the test results.* **2** a ceremony at which a person becomes a full member of the Christian Church **3** a Jewish ceremony similar to a BAR MITZVAH or BAT MITZVAH but usually for young people over the age of 16

**con·firmed** /kənˈfɜːmd; *NAmE* -ˈfɜːrmd/ *adj.* [only before noun] having a particular habit or way of life and not likely to change: *a confirmed bachelor* (= a man who is not likely to get married, sometimes used in newspapers to refer to a GAY man)

**con·fis·cate** /ˈkɒnfɪskeɪt; *NAmE* ˈkɑːn-/ *verb* *~ sth* to officially take sth away from sb, especially as a punishment: *Their land was confiscated after the war.* ◇ *The teacher threatened to confiscate their phones if they kept using them in class.* ▶ **con·fis·ca·tion** /ˌkɒnfɪˈskeɪʃn; *NAmE* ˌkɑːn-/ *noun* [U, C]

**con·fla·gra·tion** /ˌkɒnfləˈɡreɪʃn; *NAmE* ˌkɑːn-/ *noun* (*formal*) a very large fire that destroys a lot of land or buildings

**con·flate** /kənˈfleɪt/ *verb* *~ A and/with B* (*formal*) to put two or more things together to make one new thing ▶ **con·fla·tion** /-ˈfleɪʃn/ *noun* [U, C]

**con·flict** *noun, verb*
▪ *noun* /ˈkɒnflɪkt; *NAmE* ˈkɑːn-/ [C, U] **1** a situation in which people, groups or countries disagree strongly or are involved in a serious argument: *The violence was the result of political and ethnic conflicts.* ◇ *~ between A and B* (**over sth**) *a conflict between two cultures* ◇ *~ with sb The prime minister wants to avoid conflict with the unions.* ◇ *~ over sth The government has done nothing to resolve the conflict over nurses' pay.* ◇ *in ~ with sb (over sth) She found herself in conflict with her parents over her future career.* ◇ *John often comes into conflict with his boss.* **2** a violent situation or period of fighting between two countries: *armed/military conflict* ◇ *~ with sb This isolated state faces the risk of another violent conflict with its neighbour.* ◇ *~ over sth They are engaged in a bloody conflict over the disputed territory.* ◇ *~ between A and B (over sth) A conflict between the two countries could easily spread across the whole region.*

> **WORDFINDER** aggression, arms, army, attack, casualty, defend, hostile, territory, war

**3** a situation in which there are ideas, opinions, feelings or wishes that are opposed to each other; a situation in which it is difficult to choose: *Her diary was a record of her inner conflict.* ◇ *~ between A and B The story tells of a classic conflict between love and duty.* ◇ *in ~ with sth Many of these ideas appear to be in conflict with each other.* ◇ *~ of sth He faced a conflict of loyalties.*

**IDM** **conflict of ˈinterest(s)** a situation in which sb has two jobs, aims, roles, etc. and cannot treat both of them equally and fairly at the same time: *There was a conflict of interest between his business dealings and his political activities.*

▪ *verb* /kənˈflɪkt/ [I] if two ideas, beliefs, stories, etc. **conflict**, it is not possible for them to exist together or for them both to be true **SYN** **clash**: *There are several major areas where their interests conflict.* ◇ *~ with sth These results conflict with earlier findings.*

**ˈconflict diamond** (*also* **ˈblood diamond**) *noun* a diamond that has not been shaped by cutting and that is sold illegally to provide money for an armed conflict: *The organization is trying to combat trade in conflict diamonds in the war zone.*

**con·flict·ed** /kənˈflɪktɪd/ *adj.* confused about what to do or choose because you have strong but very different feelings

**con·flict·ing** /kənˈflɪktɪŋ/ *adj.* (of two ideas, stories, feelings, etc.) unable to exist together or both be true **SYN** **contradictory**: *There were conflicting reports about the number of people injured.* ◇ *conflicting results/accounts/claims* ◇ *conflicting views/opinions/interests*

**con·flu·ence** /ˈkɒnfluəns; *NAmE* ˈkɑːn-/ *noun* [usually sing.] **1** (*specialist*) the place where two rivers flow together and become one **2** (*formal*) the fact of two or more things becoming one: *a confluence of social factors*

**con·form** /kənˈfɔːm; *NAmE* -ˈfɔːrm/ *verb* **1** [I] to behave and think in the same way as most other people in a group or society: *There is considerable pressure on teenagers to conform.* ◇ *~ to sth He refused to conform to the local customs.* ⇒ WORDFINDER NOTE at BEHAVIOUR **2** [I] *~ to/with sth* to obey a rule, law, etc. **SYN** **comply**: *The building does not conform with safety regulations.* **3** [I] *~ to/with sth* to agree with or match sth: *It did not conform to the usual stereotype of an industrial city.*

**con·form·able** /kənˈfɔːməbl; *NAmE* -ˈfɔːrm-/ *adj.* (*formal*) **1** *~ (to/with sth)* similar in form or nature to sth; in agreement with sth **SYN** **consistent**: *What happens in cases where common law is not conformable to the constitution?* **2** *~ (to sth)* (of a person) willing to obey rules and behave and think in the same way as other people ▶ **con·form·abil·ity** /kənˌfɔːməˈbɪləti; *NAmE* -ˌfɔːrm-/ *noun* [U]

**con·form·ance** /kənˈfɔːməns; *NAmE* -ˈfɔːrm-/ *noun* [U] *~ (to/with sth)* (*formal*) the fact of following the rules or standards of sth: *You need to ensure conformance to strict quality guidelines.* **SYN** **conformity**

**con·form·ation** /ˌkɒnfɔː'meɪʃn; NAmE ˌkɑːnfɔːr'm-/ noun [U, C] (formal) the way in which sth is formed; the structure of sth, especially an animal

**con·form·ist** /kən'fɔːmɪst; NAmE -'fɔːrm-/ noun (often disapproving) a person who behaves and thinks in the same way as most other people and who does not want to be different ⇒ see also NONCONFORMIST ▶ **con·form·ist** adj. ⇒ see also NONCONFORMIST

**con·form·ity** /kən'fɔːməti; NAmE -'fɔːrm-/ noun [U] (in) ~ (to/with sth) (formal) behaviour or actions that follow the accepted rules of society
**IDM** **in con'formity with sth** following the rules of sth; CONFORMING to sth: *regulations that are in conformity with European law*

**con·found** /kən'faʊnd/ verb (formal) **1** ~ sb to confuse and surprise sb **SYN** baffle: *The sudden rise in share prices has confounded economists.* **2** ~ sb/sth to prove sb/sth wrong: *to confound expectations* ◊ *She confounded her critics and proved she could do the job.* **3** ~ sb (old-fashioned) to defeat an enemy

**con·found·ed** /kən'faʊndɪd/ adj. [only before noun] (old-fashioned) used when describing sth to show that you are annoyed

**con·fra·ter·nity** /ˌkɒnfrə'tɜːnəti; NAmE ˌkɑːnfrə'tɜːrn-/ noun (pl. **-ies**) (formal) a group of people who join together especially for a religious purpose or to help other people

**con·front** ♪+ **C1** /kən'frʌnt/ verb **1** ♪+ **C1** ~ sb/sth (of problems or a difficult situation) to appear and need to be dealt with by sb: *the economic problems confronting the country* ◊ *The government found itself confronted by massive opposition.* **2** ♪+ **C1** ~ sth to deal with a problem or difficult situation **SYN** face up to: *She knew that she had to confront her fears.* **3** ♪+ **C1** ~ sb to face sb so that they cannot avoid seeing and hearing you, especially in an unfriendly or dangerous situation: *This was the first time he had confronted an armed robber.* **4** ♪+ **C1** ~ sb with sb/sth to make sb face or deal with an unpleasant or difficult person or situation: *He confronted her with a choice between her career or their relationship.* **5** be confronted by/with sth to have sth in front of you that you have to deal with or react to: *Most people when confronted with a horse will pat it.*

**con·fron·ta·tion** ♪+ **C1** /ˌkɒnfrʌn'teɪʃn; NAmE ˌkɑːnfrən-/ noun [U, C] a situation in which there is anger between people or groups who disagree because they have different opinions: ~(with sb) *She wanted to avoid another confrontation with her father.* ◊ ~ **between A and B** *confrontation between employers and unions*

**con·fron·ta·tion·al** /ˌkɒnfrʌn'teɪʃənl; NAmE ˌkɑːnfrən-/ adj. tending to deal with people in an aggressive way that is likely to cause arguments, rather than discussing things with them: *Why do they take such a confrontational approach towards Europe?* ◊ *a confrontational style of management*

**Con·fu·cian** /kən'fjuːʃən/ adj. [usually before noun] based on or believing the teachings of the Chinese PHILOSOPHER Confucius ▶ **Con·fu·cian** noun **Con·fu·cian·ism** noun [U]

**con·fus·able** /kən'fjuːzəbl/ adj. if two things are **confusable**, it is easy to confuse them: *'Historic' and 'historical' are easily confusable.* ◊ *The various types of owl are easily confusable with one another.* ▶ **con·fus·able** noun: *confusables such as 'principle' and 'principal'*

**con·fuse** 🔑 **B1** /kən'fjuːz/ verb **1** ♪ **B1** to make sb unable to think clearly or understand sth: ~**sb** *These two sets of statistics are guaranteed to confuse the public.* ◊ ~**sb with sth** *They confused me with conflicting accounts of what happened.* **2** ♪ **B2** to think wrongly that sb/sth is sb/sth else **SYN** mix up: ~**A and B** *People often confuse me and my twin sister.* ◊ ~**A with B** *Be careful not to confuse quantity with quality.* **3** ♪ **B2** ~**sth** to make a subject more difficult to understand: *His comments only served to confuse the issue further.*

**con·fused** 🔑 **B1** /kən'fjuːzd/ adj. **1** ♪ **B1** unable to think clearly or to understand what is happening or what sb is saying: *I'm confused—say all that again.* ◊ *a confused look/expression* ◊ ~**about sth** *teenagers who are confused about their sexuality* ◊ ~**by sth** *She seemed confused by the question.* **2** ♪ **B2** not clear or easy to understand: *The children gave a confused account of what had happened.* ▶ **con·fused·ly** /-'fjuːzədli/ adv.

**con·fus·ing** 🔑 **B2** /kən'fjuːzɪŋ/ adj. difficult to understand; not clear: *The instructions on the box are very confusing.* ◊ *a confusing situation/experience* ◊ ~**for/to sb** *The new signs will be very confusing for tourists.* ◊ ~**to do** *The site is somewhat confusing to navigate.* ▶ **con·fus·ing·ly** adv.

**con·fu·sion** ♪+ **B2** /kən'fjuːʒn/ noun **1** ♪+ **B2** [U, C] a state of not being certain about what is happening, what you should do, what sth means, etc: *The announcement caused a lot of confusion.* ◊ ~**about/over sth** *There is some confusion about what the correct procedure should be.* ◊ **as to sth** *a confusion as to what to do next* **2** ♪+ **B2** [U, C] the fact of making a mistake about who sb is or what sth is: *To avoid confusion, please write the children's names clearly on all their school clothes.* ◊ ~**between A and B** *confusion between letters of the alphabet like 'o' or 'a'* **3** ♪+ **B2** [U] a situation in which you feel embarrassed because you do not understand sth and are not sure what to do: **in~** *He looked at me in confusion and did not answer the question.* **4** ♪+ **B2** [U] a confused situation in which people do not know what action to take: *Fighting had broken out and all was chaos and confusion.* ◊ *Her unexpected arrival threw us into total confusion.*

**con·fute** /kən'fjuːt/ verb ~**sb/sth** (formal) to prove a person or an argument to be wrong

**conga** /'kɒŋgə; NAmE 'kɑːŋ-/ noun **1** a fast dance in which the dancers follow a leader in a long winding line, with each person holding on to the person in front; a piece of music for this dance **2** (also **'conga drum**) a tall narrow drum that you play with your hands

**con·geal** /kən'dʒiːl/ verb [I] (of blood, fat, etc.) to become thick or solid: *The cold remains of supper had congealed on the plate.* ◊ (figurative) *The bitterness and tears had congealed into hatred.* ▶ **con·gealed** adj.: *congealed blood*

**con·gen·ial** /kən'dʒiːniəl/ adj. (formal) **1** (of a person) pleasant to spend time with because their interests and character are similar to your own: *a congenial colleague* **2** ~**(to sb)** (of a place, job, etc.) pleasant because it suits your character: *a congenial working environment* **3** ~**(to sth)** (formal) suitable for sth: *a situation that was congenial to the expression of nationalist opinions*

**con·geni·tal** /kən'dʒenɪtl/ adj. **1** (of a disease or medical condition) existing since or before birth: *congenital abnormalities* **2** [only before noun] existing as part of a person's character and not likely to change: *a congenital inability to tell the truth* **3** [only before noun] (of a person) born with a particular illness: (figurative) *a congenital liar* (= one who will not change) ▶ **con·geni·tal·ly** /-təli/ adv.

**con·ger** /'kɒŋgə(r); NAmE 'kɑːŋ-/ (also **'conger eel**) noun a large EEL that lives in the sea

**con·gest·ed** /kən'dʒestɪd/ adj. **1** ~**(with sth)** crowded; full of traffic: *congested city streets* ◊ *Many of Europe's airports are heavily congested.* **2** (medical) (of a part of the body) blocked with blood or MUCUS

**con·ges·tion** /kən'dʒestʃən/ noun [U] **1** the state of being crowded and full of traffic: *traffic congestion and pollution* **2** (medical) the state of part of the body being blocked with blood or MUCUS: *congestion of the lungs* ◊ *medicine to relieve nasal congestion*

**con'gestion charge** noun (BrE) an amount of money that people have to pay for driving their cars into the centre of some cities as a way of stopping the city centre from becoming too full of traffic ▶ **con'gestion charging** noun [U]

**con·glom·er·ate** /kən'glɒmərət; NAmE -'glɑːm-/ noun **1** [C] (business) a large company formed by joining together different firms: *a media conglomerate* **2** [sing.]

# conglomeration

(*formal*) a number of things or parts that are put together to form a whole **3** [U] (*geology*) a type of rock made of small stones held together by dried CLAY

**con·glom·er·ation** /kənˌglɒməˈreɪʃn; *NAmE* -ˌglɑːm-/ *noun* **1** [C, usually sing.] **a ~ (of sth)** (*formal*) a mixture of different things that are found all together: *a conglomeration of buildings of different sizes and styles* **2** [U] the process of forming a conglomerate; the state of being a conglomerate: *We are in an age of massive media conglomeration.*

**con·grats** /kənˈgræts/ *noun* [pl.] (*informal*) = CONGRATULATIONS

**con·gratu·late** /kənˈgrætʃəleɪt/ *verb* **1** ~ **sb (on sth)** to tell sb that you are pleased about their success or achievements: *I congratulated them all on their results.* ◊ *The authors are to be congratulated on producing such a clear and authoritative work.* **2** ~ **yourself (on sth)** to feel pleased and proud because you have achieved sth or been successful at sth: *You can congratulate yourself on having done an excellent job.*

▼ EXPRESS YOURSELF

**Congratulating somebody on an achievement or a family event**

When someone tells you some good news about their family, or what they have done, you can congratulate them:
- *Congratulations on your engagement! I hope you'll be very happy.*
- *Well done for passing your driving test.* (*BrE*)
- *Good job on passing your exams.* (*NAmE*)
- *I hear you did very well in your exams/you've got a new job/you've had a baby*—**congratulations!** (*BrE*)
- *Jo tells me you're getting married*—**congratulations!**

Responses:
- *Thank you very much.*
- *Oh, thanks!*

**con·gratu·la·tion** /kənˌgrætʃəˈleɪʃn/ *noun* **1 congratulations** [pl.] a message congratulating sb (= saying that you are happy about their good luck or success): *to offer/send your congratulations to sb* **2 Congratulations!** used when you want to congratulate sb: *'We're getting married.' 'Congratulations!'* ◊ *Congratulations on your exam results!* **3** [U] the act of congratulating sb: *a letter of congratulation*

**con·gratu·la·tory** /kənˈgrætʃələtɔːri; *NAmE* kənˈgrætʃələtɔːri/ *adj.* expressing feelings of pleasure about sb's success or good luck: *a congratulatory message* ⊃ see also SELF-CONGRATULATORY

**con·gre·gant** /ˈkɒŋgrɪgənt; *NAmE* ˈkɑːŋ-/ *noun* (*especially NAmE*) a member of a church or SYNAGOGUE ⊃ see also CONGREGATION

**con·gre·gate** /ˈkɒŋgrɪgeɪt; *NAmE* ˈkɑːŋ-/ *verb* [I] to come together in a group: *Young people often congregate in the main square in the evenings.*

**con·gre·ga·tion** /ˌkɒŋgrɪˈgeɪʃn; *NAmE* ˌkɑːŋ-/ *noun* [C + sing./pl. v.] **1** a group of people who are gathered together in a church for a religious service, not including the priest or CHOIR: *The congregation stood to sing the hymn.* **2** a group of people who regularly attend a particular church: *members of local congregations* ▶ **con·gre·ga·tion·al** /-ʃənəl/ *adj.*

**Con·gre·ga·tion·al·ism** /ˌkɒŋgrɪˈgeɪʃənəlɪzəm; *NAmE* ˌkɑːŋ-/ *noun* [U] a type of Christianity in which the congregation of each church is responsible for its own affairs ▶ **Con·gre·ga·tion·al** /-nəl/ *adj.* **Con·gre·ga·tion·al·ist** *noun*

**con·gress** /ˈkɒŋgres; *NAmE* ˈkɑːŋgrəs/ *noun* **1** [C] a large formal meeting or series of meetings where representatives from different groups discuss ideas, make decisions, etc: *an international congress of trades unions* **2** [C + sing./pl. v.] **Congress** (in the US and some other countries) the name of the group of people who are elected to make laws, in the US consisting of the Senate and the HOUSE OF REP-RESENTATIVES: *Congress will vote on the proposals tomorrow.*

**WORDFINDER** caucus, electoral college, House of Representatives, nomination, president, primary, running mate, senate, swing state

**3** [C + sing./pl. v.] (often used in names) a political organization or society: *the African National Congress*

**con·gres·sion·al** (*also* **Con·gres·sion·al**) /kənˈgreʃnl/ *adj.* [only before noun] related to or belonging to a congress or the Congress in the US: *a congressional committee/bill* ◊ *the midterm Congressional elections*

**con·gressional ˈdistrict** *noun* (*NAmE*) an area within a state that elects a member of the US House of Representatives

**con·gress·man** /ˈkɒŋgrəsmən; *NAmE* ˈkɑːŋ-/, **con·gress·woman** /ˈkɒŋgrəswʊmən; *NAmE* ˈkɑːŋ-/ *noun* (often **Congressman**, **Congresswoman**) (*pl.* -**men** /-mən/, -**women** /-wɪmɪn/) (*also* **con·gress·person**, **Con·gress·person** /ˈkɒŋgrəspɜːsn; *NAmE* ˈkɑːŋgrəspɜːrsn/) a member of Congress in the US, especially the House of Representatives

**con·gru·ent** /ˈkɒŋgruənt; *NAmE* ˈkɑːŋ-/ *adj.* **1** (*geometry*) having the same size and shape: *congruent triangles* **2 ~ (with sth)** (*formal*) in agreement with sth; similar to sth and not in conflict with it SYN compatible ▶ **con·gru·ence** /-əns/ *noun* [U]

**conic** /ˈkɒnɪk; *NAmE* ˈkɑːn-/ *adj., noun* (*geometry*)
■ *adj.* of or related to a CONE
■ *noun* = CONIC SECTION

**con·ic·al** /ˈkɒnɪkl; *NAmE* ˈkɑːn-/ *adj.* having the shape of a CONE

**conic sections**

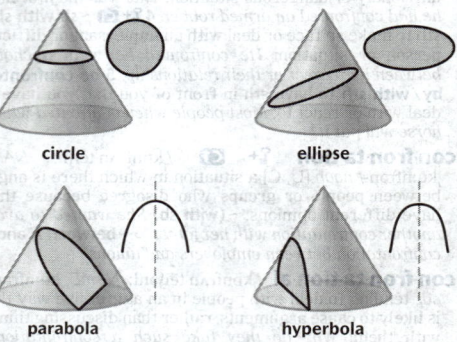

circle    ellipse

parabola    hyperbola

**conic ˈsection** (*also* **conic**) *noun* (*geometry*) a shape formed when a flat surface meets a CONE with a round base

**con·ifer** /ˈkɒnɪfə(r); *NAmE* ˈkɑːn-/ *noun* any tree that produces hard dry fruit called CONES. Most conifers are EVERGREEN (= have leaves that stay on the tree all year). ▶ **con·ifer·ous** /kəˈnɪfərəs/ *adj.*: *coniferous trees/forests*

**con·jec·ture** /kənˈdʒektʃə(r)/ *noun, verb*
■ *noun* (*formal*) **1** [C] an opinion or idea that is not based on definite knowledge and is formed by guessing SYN guess: *The truth of his conjecture was confirmed by the newspaper report.* **2** [U] the act of forming an opinion or idea that is not based on definite knowledge: *What was going through the killer's mind is a matter for conjecture.* ⊃ see also GUESSWORK ▶ **con·jec·tural** /-tʃərəl/ *adj.*
■ *verb* [I, T] (*formal*) to form an opinion about sth even though you do not have much information on it SYN guess: ~ **(about sth)** *We can only conjecture about what was in the killer's mind.* ◊ ~ **what/how, etc…** *We can only conjecture what was in the killer's mind.* ◊ ~ **that…** *He conjectured that the population might double in ten years.* ◊ ~ **sth** *She conjectured the existence of a completely new species.* ◊ **be conjectured to be/have/do sth** *The remains are conjectured to be thousands of years old.*

**con·join** /kənˈdʒɔɪn/ verb [I, T] ~(sth) (formal) to join together; to join two or more things together

**con·joined ˈtwin** noun one of two people who are born with their bodies joined together in some way, sometimes sharing the same organs

**con·joint** /kənˈdʒɔɪnt/ adj. [usually before noun] (formal) combining all or both the people or things involved ▶ **con·joint·ly** adv.

**con·ju·gal** /ˈkɒndʒəgl/ NAmE /ˈkɑːn-/ adj. [only before noun] (formal) connected with marriage and the sexual relationship between a married couple: conjugal love

**ˌconjugal ˈrights** noun [pl.] the rights that each partner has in a marriage, especially the right to have sex with their partner

**con·ju·gate** /ˈkɒndʒəgeɪt/ NAmE /ˈkɑːn-/ verb (grammar) **1** [T] ~sth to give the different forms of a verb, as they vary according to NUMBER, PERSON, tense, etc. **2** [I] (of a verb) to have different forms, showing NUMBER, PERSON, tense, etc: How does this verb conjugate? ⊃ compare DECLINE ⊃ WORDFINDER NOTE at GRAMMAR

**con·ju·ga·tion** /ˌkɒndʒuˈgeɪʃn; NAmE ˌkɑːn-/ noun (grammar) **1** [C, U] the way in which a verb conjugates: a verb with an irregular conjugation **2** [C] a group of verbs that conjugate in the same way: Latin verbs of the second conjugation

**con·junc·tion** /kənˈdʒʌŋkʃn/ noun **1** [C] (grammar) a word that joins words, phrases or sentences, for example 'and', 'but', 'or' or 'because' ⊃ see also COORDINATING CONJUNCTION, SUBORDINATING CONJUNCTION **2** [C] (formal) a combination of events, etc., that causes a particular result: The conjunction of low inflation and low unemployment came as a very pleasant surprise. **3** [C, U] (astronomy) the fact of stars, planets, etc. passing close together, as seen from the earth
**IDM** **in conˈjunction with sb/sth** (formal) together with sb/sth: The police are working in conjunction with tax officers on the investigation. ◊ The software can be used in conjunction with any other application.

**con·junc·tiv·itis** /kənˌdʒʌŋktɪˈvaɪtɪs/ noun [U] an eye disease that causes part of the eye to become red and painful

**con·jure** /ˈkʌndʒə(r)/ NAmE /ˈkɑːn-/ verb [I, T] to do clever tricks such as making things seem to appear or disappear as if by magic: Her grandfather taught her to conjure. ◊ ~sth + adv./prep. He could conjure coins from behind people's ears. **IDM** see NAME n.
**PHRV** **ˈconjure sth from/out of sth** to create sth or make sth appear in a surprising or unexpected way: He conjured a delicious meal out of a few leftovers. **ˈconjure sth↔up 1** to make sth appear as a picture in your mind SYN evoke: That smell always conjures up memories of holidays in France. **2** to make sb/sth appear by using special magic words

**con·jur·ing** /ˈkʌndʒərɪŋ/ NAmE /ˈkɑːn-/ noun [U] entertainment in the form of magic tricks, especially ones that seem to make things appear or disappear: a conjuring trick

**con·juror** (also **con·jurer**) /ˈkʌndʒərə(r)/ NAmE /ˈkɑːn-/ noun a person who performs conjuring tricks

**conk** /kɒŋk; NAmE kɑːŋk/ verb, noun
■ verb ~sb (especially NAmE, informal) to hit sb hard on their head
**PHRV** **ˌconk ˈout** (informal) **1** (of a machine, etc.) to stop working: The car conked out halfway up the hill. **2** (of a person) to go to sleep
■ noun (BrE, informal) a person's nose

**conk·er** /ˈkɒŋkə(r)/ NAmE /ˈkɑːŋ-/ noun (BrE, informal) **1** [C] the smooth shiny brown nut of the HORSE CHESTNUT tree SYN **horse chestnut** ⊃ compare CHESTNUT ⊃ VISUAL VOCAB page V6 **2 conkers** [U] a children's game played with conkers on strings, in which two players take turns to try to hit and break each other's conker

**con·man** /ˈkɒnmæn/ NAmE /ˈkɑːn-/ noun (pl. **-men** /-men/) (informal) a man who tricks others into giving him money, etc.

---

323

**connection**

**con·nect** 🅞 A2 🅦 /kəˈnekt/ verb
• JOIN **1** A2 [T, I] to join together two or more things; to be joined together: ~A and B The towns are connected by train and bus services. ◊ ~(A to/with B) The island is connected to the mainland by a bridge. ◊ The rooms on this floor connect. ◊ a connecting door (= one that connects two rooms)
• ELECTRICITY/GAS/WATER **2** A2 [T] to join sth to the main supply of electricity, gas, water, etc. or to another piece of equipment: ~sth We're waiting for the broadband to be connected. ◊ ~sth to sth First connec: the printer to the computer. OPP **disconnect** ⊃ WORDFINDER NOTE at ELECTRICITY
• INTERNET **3** B1 [I, T] to join a computer or a mobile device to the internet or to a computer network: The device can be hooked up to a mobile phone to connect wirelessly. ◊ ~to sth Click 'Continue' to connect to the internet. ◊ ~sth (to sth) Simply connect your device to the camera's Wi-Fi signal. OPP **disconnect** ⊃ WORDFINDER NOTE at COMMAND
• LINK **4** B1 [T] to notice or make a link between people, things, events, etc. SYN **associate**: ~A and B I was surprised to hear them mentioned together: I had never connected them before. ◊ ~A with/to B There was nothing to connect him with the crime.
• OF TRAIN/BUS/PLANE **5** [I] ~(with sth) to arrive just before another one leaves so that passengers can change from one to the other: His flight to Amsterdam connects with an afternoon flight to New York. ◊ There's a connecting flight at noon.
• PHONE LINES **6** [T] ~sb (to sb/sth) to put sb in contact by phone SYN **put through**: After a long wait I was connected to customer services. OPP **disconnect**
• FORM RELATIONSHIP **7** [I] ~(with sb) to form a good relationship with sb so that you like and understand each other: They met a couple of times but they didn't really connect.
• HIT **8** [I] ~(with sb/sth) (informal) to hit sb/sth: The blow connected and she felt a surge of pain.
**PHRV** **conˌnect sth↔ˈup (to sth)** | **conˌnect ˈup (to sth)** to join sth to a supply of electricity, gas, etc. or to another piece of equipment; to be joined in this way: She connected up the two computers. OPP **disconnect**

**con·nect·ed** 🅞 A2 /kəˈnektɪd/ adj. (of two or more things or people) having a link between them: The two issues are closely connected. ◊ market prices and other connected matters ◊ ~with sb/sth The fall in retail sales is directly connected with the decline in employment. ◊ ~to sb/sth Many computer files connected to the case have been erased. ◊ ~by sth They are connected by marriage. OPP **unconnected** ⊃ see also WELL CONNECTED

**con·nect·ed·ness** /kəˈnektɪdnəs/ noun [U] ~(to/with sb/sth) a feeling that you have a link with sb/sth or are part of a group: the benefits of helping students feel a sense of connectedness to their school

**con·nec·tion** 🅞 B1 🅦 /kəˈnekʃn/ noun (BrE also, old-fashioned **con·nex·ion**)
• LINK **1** B1 [C] something that connects two facts, ideas, etc. SYN **link**: ~between A and B Scientists have established a connection between cholesterol levels and heart disease. ◊ ~with sth a direct/close/strong connection with sth ◊ His resignation must have some connection with the recent scandal. ◊ ~to sth Consumers are more likely to buy something from a person or shop they feel a personal connection to. ◊ How did you make the connection (= realize that there was a connection between two facts that did not seem to be related)?
• BEING CONNECTED **2** B1 [U, C] the act of connecting or the state of being connected: a broadband/wireless/Wi-Fi/network connection ◊ I'm having problems with my internet connection. ◊ ~to sth Connection to the gas supply is delayed for three days.
• IN ELECTRICAL SYSTEM **3** B1 [C] a point, especially in an electrical system, where two parts connect: A faulty connection caused the machine to stop.
• TRAIN/BUS/PLANE **4** [C] a train, bus or plane at a station or an airport that a passenger can take soon after getting off

---

🅞 Oxford Phrasal Academic Lexicon (OPAL) written and spoken word lists | 🅦 OPAL written word list | 🅢 OPAL spoken word list

**connective**

another in order to continue their journey: **~ to** ... *We arrived in good time for the connection to Paris.* ⇒ WORDFINDER NOTE at TRAIN **5** [C, usually pl.] a means of travelling to another place: *There are good bus and train connections between the resort and major cities.*
- PERSON/ORGANIZATION **6** [C, usually pl.] a person or an organization that you know and that can help or advise you in your social or professional life SYN **contact**: *One of my business connections gave them my name.*
- DISTANT RELATIVES **7 connections** [pl.] people who are your relatives, but not members of your close family: *She is British but also has German connections.*
IDM **in connection with sb/sth** for reasons connected with sb/sth: *A man has been arrested in connection with the murder of the teenager.* ◊ *I am writing to you in connection with your recent job application.* **in this/that connection** (*formal*) for reasons connected with sth recently mentioned

**con·nect·ive** /kəˈnektɪv/ *adj., noun*
■ *adj.* (*medical or formal*) that connects things: *connective tissue*
■ *noun* (*grammar*) a word that connects two parts of a sentence: *Don't overuse a causal connective like 'because'.*

**con·nec·tiv·ity** /ˌkɒnekˈtɪvəti/ *noun* [U] (*specialist*) **1** (*computing*) the ability of systems, platforms and applications to be connected to each other: *wireless/broadband/Bluetooth connectivity* ◊ **~ to sth** *high-speed connectivity to the internet* ◊ **between A and B** *connectivity between devices* **2** the state of being connected; the degree to which two things are connected: **~ (to sth)** *There is a need to improve road, rail and air connectivity to the rest of the country.*

**con·nec·tor** /kəˈnektə(r)/ *noun* a thing that links two or more things together: *a cable connector*

**con·ning tower** /ˈkɒnɪŋ taʊə(r)/; *NAmE* ˈkɑːn-/ *noun* a raised structure on a SUBMARINE containing the PERISCOPE

**con·niv·ance** /kəˈnaɪvəns/ *noun* [U] (*disapproving*) help in doing sth wrong; the failure to stop sth wrong from happening: *The crime was committed with the connivance of a police officer.*

**con·nive** /kəˈnaɪv/ *verb* (*formal, disapproving*) **1** [I] **~ at/in sth** to seem to allow sth wrong to happen: *She knew that if she said nothing she would be conniving in an injustice.* **2** [I] **~ (with sb) (to do sth)** to work together with sb to do sth wrong or illegal SYN **conspire**: *The government was accused of having connived with the security forces to permit murder.*

**con·niv·ing** /kəˈnaɪvɪŋ/ *adj.* (*disapproving*) behaving in a way that secretly hurts others or deliberately fails to prevent others from being hurt

**con·nois·seur** /ˌkɒnəˈsɜː(r)/; *NAmE* ˌkɑːn-, -ˈsʊr/ *noun* an expert on matters involving the judgement of beauty, quality or skill in art, food or music: *a connoisseur of Italian painting* ◊ *a wine connoisseur*

**con·no·ta·tion** /ˌkɒnəˈteɪʃn/; *NAmE* ˌkɑːn-/ *noun* [C, U] an idea suggested by a word in addition to its main meaning: *The word 'professional' has connotations of skill and excellence.* ◊ *negative connotations* ⇒ compare DENOTATION ⇒ WORDFINDER NOTE at WORD

**con·note** /kəˈnəʊt/ *verb* **~ sth** (*formal*) (of a word) to suggest a feeling, an idea, etc. as well as the main meaning ⇒ compare DENOTE

**con·quer** /ˈkɒŋkə(r)/; *NAmE* ˈkɑːŋ-/ *verb* **1** **~ sb/sth** to take control of a country or city and its people by force: *The Normans conquered England in 1066.* ◊ *conquered peoples/races/territories* **2** **~ sb/sth** to defeat sb, especially in a competition, race, etc: *The world champion conquered yet another challenger last night.* **3** **~ sth** to succeed in dealing with or controlling sth: *The only way to conquer a fear is to face it.* ◊ *Mount Everest was conquered* (= successfully climbed) *in 1953.* **4** **~ sth** to become very popular or successful in a place: *The band is now setting out to conquer the world.*

**con·quer·or** /ˈkɒŋkərə(r)/; *NAmE* ˈkɑːŋ-/ *noun* a person who conquers: *William the Conqueror* (= King William I of England)

**con·quest** /ˈkɒŋkwest/; *NAmE* ˈkɑːŋ-/ *noun* **1** [C, U] the act of taking control of a country, city, etc. by force: *the Norman Conquest* (= of England in 1066) **2** [C] an area of land taken by force: *the Spanish conquests in South America* **3** [C] (*usually humorous*) a person that sb has persuaded to love them or to have sex with them: *I'm just one of his many conquests.* **4** [U] the act of gaining control over sth that is difficult or dangerous: *the conquest of inflation*

**con·quis·ta·dor** /kɒnˈkwɪstədɔː(r)/; *NAmE* kɑːŋˈkiːs-/ *noun* (*pl.* **con·quis·ta·dores** /kɒnˌkwɪstəˈdɔːreɪz/; *NAmE* kɑːŋˌkiːs-/ or **con·quis·ta·dors**) (*from Spanish*) one of the Spanish people who took control of Mexico and Peru by force in the sixteenth century

**con·san·guin·ity** /ˌkɒnsæŋˈɡwɪnəti/; *NAmE* ˌkɑːn-/ *noun* [U] (*formal*) relationship by birth in the same family

**con·science** /ˈkɒnʃəns/; *NAmE* ˈkɑːn-/ *noun* **1** [C, U] the part of your mind that tells you whether your actions are right or wrong: *to have a **clear/guilty conscience*** (= to feel that you have done right/wrong) ◊ *This is a **matter of individual conscience*** (= everyone must make their own judgement about it). ◊ *He won't let it trouble his conscience.* ⇒ see also SOCIAL CONSCIENCE **2** [U, C] a guilty feeling about sth you have done or failed to do: *She was seized by a sudden pang of conscience.* ◊ *I have a terrible conscience about it.* **3** [U] the fact of behaving in a way that you feel is right even though this may cause problems: *freedom of conscience* (= the freedom to do what you believe to be right) ◊ *Emilia is the voice of conscience in the play.* ⇒ see also PRISONER OF CONSCIENCE
IDM **in (all/good) conscience** (*formal*) believing your actions to be fair SYN **honestly**: *We cannot in all conscience refuse to help.* **on your ˈconscience** making you feel guilty for doing or failing to do sth: *I'll write and apologize. I've had it on my conscience for weeks.* ⇒ more at PRICK *v.*

**ˈconscience-stricken** *adj.* feeling guilty about sth you have done or failed to do

**con·sci·en·tious** /ˌkɒnʃiˈenʃəs/; *NAmE* ˌkɑːn-/ *adj.* taking care to do things carefully and correctly: *a conscientious student/teacher/worker* ▶ **con·sci·en·tious·ly** *adv.*: *She performed all her duties conscientiously.* **con·sci·en·tious·ness** *noun* [U]

**conscientious obˈjector** *noun* a person who refuses to serve in the armed forces for moral reasons ⇒ compare DRAFT DODGER, PACIFIST

**con·scien·tize** (*BrE also* **-ise**) /ˈkɒnʃəntaɪz/; *NAmE* ˈkɑːn-/ *verb* **~ sb/yourself** (*SAfrE*) to make sb/yourself aware of important social or political issues: *People need to be conscientized about their rights.*

**con·scious** /ˈkɒnʃəs/; *NAmE* ˈkɑːn-/ *adj.* **1** [not before noun] aware of sth; noticing sth: **~ of sth** *She's very conscious of the problems involved.* ◊ **~ of doing sth** *He became acutely conscious of having failed his parents.* ◊ **~ that** ... *I was vaguely conscious that I was being watched.* OPP **unconscious** ⇒ see also SELF-CONSCIOUS **2** able to use your senses and mental powers to understand what is happening: *A patient who is not fully conscious should never be left alone.* OPP **unconscious** **3** (of actions, feelings, etc.) deliberate; done in a careful way: *to make a conscious decision* ◊ *I made a conscious effort to get there on time.* OPP **unconscious** ⇒ compare SUBCONSCIOUS **4** being particularly interested in sth: *the band's socially conscious lyrics* ◊ *They have become increasingly health-conscious.* ⇒ see also CLASS-CONSCIOUS, FASHION-CONSCIOUS **5** (of the mind or a thought) directly under the control of the person concerned: *When you go to sleep, it is only the conscious mind that shuts down.* ▶ **con·scious·ly** *adv.*: *Consciously or unconsciously, you made a choice.*

**con·scious·ness** /ˈkɒnʃəsnəs/; *NAmE* ˈkɑːn-/ *noun* [U] **1** the state of being able to use your senses and mental powers to understand what is happening: *I can't remember any more—I must have lost consciousness.* ◊ *She did not regain consciousness and died the next day.*

**2** (C1) the state of being aware of sth SYN **awareness**: *his consciousness of the challenge facing him* ◊ **class-consciousness** (= consciousness of different classes in society) ⇒ see also SELF-CONSCIOUSNESS **3** (C1) the ideas and opinions of a person or group: *her newly developed political consciousness* ⇒ see also STREAM OF CONSCIOUSNESS

**ˈconsciousness-raising** *noun* [U] the process of making people aware of important social and political issues

**conˈscript** *verb, noun*
- *verb* /kənˈskrɪpt/ (*especially BrE*) (*NAmE usually* **draft**) [usually passive] to order sb by law to join the armed forces SYN **call up**: **be conscripted (into sth)** *He was conscripted into the army in 1939.*
- *noun* /ˈkɒnskrɪpt; NAmE ˈkɑːn-/ (*especially BrE*) (*US usually* **draftee**) a person who has been conscripted to join the armed forces: *young army conscripts* ◊ *conscript soldiers/armies* ⇒ compare VOLUNTEER

**conˈscription** /kənˈskrɪpʃn/ *noun* [U] (*especially BrE*) (*US usually* **the draft**) ~ **(of sb) (into sth)** the practice of ordering people by law to join the armed forces SYN **call-up**

**ˈconsecrate** /ˈkɒnsɪkreɪt; NAmE ˈkɑːn-/ *verb* **1** ~ **sth** to state officially in a religious ceremony that sth is holy and can be used for religious purposes: *The church was consecrated in 1853.* ◊ *consecrated ground* **2** ~ **sth** (in Christian belief) to make bread and wine into the body and blood of Christ **3** ~ **sb (as) (sth)** to state officially in a religious ceremony that sb is now a priest, etc: *He was consecrated (as) bishop last year.* **4** ~ **sth/sb/yourself to sth** (*formal*) to give sth/sb/yourself to a special purpose, especially a religious one ▸ **conseˈcration** /ˌkɒnsɪˈkreɪʃn; NAmE ˌkɑːn-/ *noun* [C, U]: *the consecration of a church/bishop*

**conˈsecutive** (C1) /kənˈsekjətɪv/ *adj.* [usually before noun] following one after another in a continuous series: *She was absent for nine consecutive days.* ◊ *He is beginning his fourth consecutive term of office.* ▸ **conˈsecutively** *adv.*

**conˈsensual** /kənˈsenʃuəl/ *adj.* (*formal*) **1** that people in general agree with: *a consensual approach* **2** (of an activity) which the people taking part have agreed to: *consensual sex*

**conˈsensus** (C1) W /kənˈsensəs/ *noun* [sing., U] an opinion that all members of a group agree with: ~ **(about/on sth)** *She is skilled at achieving consensus on sensitive issues.* ◊ *There is a growing consensus of opinion on this issue.* ◊ *an attempt to reach a consensus* ◊ ~ **(among sb) (about/on sth)** *There is a general consensus among teachers about the need for greater security in schools.* ◊ ~ **that…** *There seems to be a consensus that the plan should be rejected.* ◊ **by** ~ *They have always been governed by consensus.*

**conˈsent** (C1) W /kənˈsent/ *noun, verb*
- *noun* **1** (C1) [U] permission to do sth, especially given by sb in authority: *The written consent of a parent is required.* ◊ ~ **to sth** *Children under 16 cannot give consent to medical treatment.* ◊ **to refuse/withhold your consent** ◊ **without (sb's)** ~ *He is charged with taking a car without the owner's consent.* ⇒ see also AGE OF CONSENT **2** (C1) [U] agreement about sth: *She was chosen as leader by common consent* (= everyone agreed to the choice). ◊ *By mutual consent they didn't go out* (= they both agreed not to). **3** [C] an official document giving permission for sth
- *verb* (C1) [I] (*rather formal*) to agree to sth or give your permission for sth: *When she told them what she intended, they readily consented.* ◊ ~ **to sth** *He reluctantly consented to the proposal.* ◊ ~ **to do sth** *She finally consented to answer our questions.* ⇒ SYNONYMS at AGREE

**conˌsenting ˈadult** *noun* a person who is considered old enough, by law, to decide whether they should agree to have sex; a person who has agreed to have sex

**ˈconsequence** B1 /ˈkɒnsɪkwəns; NAmE ˈkɑːnsəkwens/ *noun* **1** [C, usually pl.] a result of sth that has happened, especially an unpleasant result: *Remember that actions have consequences.* ◊ *They must be prepared to accept the consequences of their actions.* ◊ ~ **for sb/sth** *This decision could have serious consequences for the* industry. ◊ **as a** ~ **(of sth)** *Two hundred people lost their jobs as a direct consequence of the merger.* ◊ **with … consequences** *He drove too fast, with tragic consequences.* ⇒ SYNONYMS at RESULT ⇒ LANGUAGE BANK at CONSEQUENTLY **2** [U] (*formal*) importance: *Don't worry. It's of no consequence.*

**IDM** **in ˈconsequence (of sth)** (*formal*) as a result of sth: *The child was born deformed in consequence of an injury to the mother.*

**ˈconsequent** /ˈkɒnsɪkwənt; NAmE ˈkɑːnsɪkwent/ *adj.* (*formal*) happening as a result of sth SYN **resultant**: *the lowering of taxes and the consequent increase in spending* ◊ ~ **on/upon sth** *the responsibilities consequent upon the arrival of a new child*

**conseˈquential** /ˌkɒnsɪˈkwenʃl; NAmE ˌkɑːn-/ *adj.* (*formal*) **1** happening as a result or an effect of sth SYN **resultant**: *retirement and the consequential reduction in income* **2** important; that will have important results: *The report discusses a number of consequential matters that are yet to be decided.* OPP **inconsequential** ▸ **conseˈquentially** /-ʃəli/ *adv.*

**ˈconsequently** (B2) W /ˈkɒnsɪkwəntli; NAmE ˈkɑːnsɪkwent-/ *adv.* as a result; therefore: *This poses a threat to agriculture and the food chain, and consequently to human health.*

▼ **LANGUAGE BANK**

**consequently**
Describing the effect of something
- **One consequence** of changes in diet over recent years has been a dramatic increase in cases of childhood obesity.
- Many parents today do not have time to cook healthy meals for their children. **Consequently**/**As a consequence**, many children grow up eating too much junk food.
- Many children spend their free time online instead of playing outside. **As a result**, more and more of them are becoming overweight.
- Last year junk food was banned in schools. **The effect of this** has been to create a black market in the playground, with pupils bringing sweets from home to sell to other pupils.
⇒ LANGUAGE BANK at BECAUSE OF, CAUSE, THEREFORE

**conˈservancy** /kənˈsɜːvənsi; NAmE -ˈsɜːrv-/ *noun* **1** Conservancy [sing. + sing./pl. v.] a group of officials who control the use of a port, a river, an area of land, etc: *the Thames Conservancy* ◊ *Texas Nature Conservancy* **2** [U] (*formal*) the protection of the natural environment SYN **conservation**: *nature conservancy*

**conserˈvation** (B2) W /ˌkɒnsəˈveɪʃn; NAmE ˌkɑːnsər'v-/ *noun* [U] **1** (B2) the protection of the natural environment SYN **conservancy**: *to be interested in wildlife conservation* ⇒ WORDFINDER NOTE at GREEN **2** (C1) the official protection of buildings and objects that have historical or artistic importance: *the conservation of ancient monuments/manuscripts/our cultural heritage* **3** (C1) the act of preventing sth from being lost, wasted, damaged or destroyed: *to encourage the conservation of water/fuel* ◊ *energy conservation* ⇒ see also CONSERVE *verb*

**ˌconserˈvation area** *noun* (in the UK) an area where the natural environment or the buildings are protected by law from being damaged or changed

**conserˈvationist** /ˌkɒnsəˈveɪʃənɪst; NAmE ˌkɑːnsərˈv-/ *noun* a person who takes an active part in the protection of the environment: *a meeting of local conservationists*

**conˈservatism** /kənˈsɜːvətɪzəm; NAmE -ˈsɜːrv-/ *noun* [U] **1** the wish to resist great or sudden change: *the innate conservatism of older people* **2** (*also* **Conservatism**) the political belief that society should change as little as possible: *an examination of the political theories of conservatism and liberalism* **3** (*usually* **Conservatism**) the principles of the Conservative Party in British politics

# conservative

**con·ser·va·tive** ⓘ B2 W /kənˈsɜːvətɪv/ NAmE -ˈsɜːrv-/ adj., noun

▪ **adj. 1** B2 opposed to great or sudden social change; showing that you prefer traditional styles and values: *the conservative views of his parents* ◊ *The southern state's inhabitants tend to be socially conservative.* ◊ *Her style of dress was never conservative.* ◊ *~in sth They were deeply conservative in their outlook.* **2** (*usually* **Conservative**) connected with the British Conservative Party: *Conservative members/supporters* **3** (of an estimate) lower than what is probably the real amount or number: *At a conservative estimate, he'll be earning £50 000.* ▸ **con·ser·va·tive·ly** *adv.*

▪ **noun 1** B2 a conservative person: *social/religious conservatives* **2** (*usually* **Conservative**) (*abbr.* **Con.**) a member or supporter of the British Conservative Party

**the Conˈservative Party** *noun* [sing. + sing. / pl. v.] one of the main British political parties, on the political right, which especially believes in FREE ENTERPRISE and that industry should be privately owned

**con·ser·va·toire** /kənˈsɜːvətwɑː(r)/ NAmE -ˈsɜːrv-/ (NAmE **con·ser·va·tory**) *noun* a school or college at which people are trained in music and theatre

**con·ser·va·tor** /kənˈsɜːvətə(r)/ NAmE -ˈsɜːrv-/ *noun* a person who is responsible for repairing and preserving works of art, buildings and other things of cultural interest

**con·ser·va·tory** /kənˈsɜːvətri/ NAmE -ˈsɜːrvətɔːri/ *noun* (*pl. -ies*) **1** a room (or sometimes a building) with glass walls and a glass roof. Conservatories are used for sitting in to enjoy the sun, and to protect plants from cold weather. **2** (NAmE) (BrE **con·ser·va·toire**) a school or college at which people are trained in music and theatre

**con·serve** ⓒ+ C1 W *verb, noun*

▪ **verb** /kənˈsɜːv/ NAmE -ˈsɜːrv-/ **1** ⓒ+ C1 ~sth to protect sth and prevent it from being changed or destroyed: *new laws to conserve wildlife in the area* ⊃ *see also* CONSERVATION **2** ⓒ+ C1 ~sth to use as little of sth as possible so that it lasts a long time: *Help to conserve energy by insulating your home.*

▪ **noun** /ˈkɒnsɜːv/ NAmE ˈkɑːnsɜːrv/ [C, U] jam containing large or whole pieces of fruit

**con·sider** ⓘ A2 ⓞ /kənˈsɪdə(r)/ *verb* **1** ⓒ A2 [I, T] to think about sth carefully, especially in order to make a decision: *I'd like some time to consider.* ◊ *~sth She is considering her options.* ◊ *He was seriously considering an appeal.* ◊ *a carefully considered response* ◊ *~doing sth Have you considered starting your own business?* ◊ *~how/what, etc… We need to consider how the law might be reformed.* ◊ *~sb/sth for sth We are considering her for the job of designer.* ⊃ **LANGUAGE BANK** *at* **ABOUT 2** ⓒ B1 [T] to think of sb/sth in a particular way: *~sb/sth + noun I consider her a friend.* ◊ *The award is considered a great honour.* ◊ *~sb/sth to be, have, etc. sth She is widely considered to be the greatest player ever.* ◊ *~yourself + noun He considers himself an expert on the subject.* ◊ *~sb/sth + adj. They will take any steps they consider necessary.* ◊ *~(that) … She considers that it is too early to form a definite conclusion.* ◊ *it is considered that … It is considered that the proposed development would create much-needed jobs.* ⊃ **SYNONYMS** *at* **REGARD 3** ⓒ B1 [T] ~sb/sth to think about sth, especially the feelings of other people, and be influenced by it when making a decision, etc: *You should consider other people before you act.* **4** [T] ~sb/sth (*formal*) to look carefully at sb/sth: *He stood there, considering the painting.*

**IDM all things conˈsidered** thinking carefully about all the facts, especially the problems or difficulties, of a situation: *She's had a lot of problems since her husband died but she seems quite cheerful, all things considered.* **your conˌsidered oˈpinion** your opinion that is the result of careful thought

**con·sid·er·able** ⓒ+ B2 W /kənˈsɪdərəbl/ *adj.* (*rather formal*) great in amount, size, importance, etc. SYN signifi-

cant: *The project wasted a considerable amount of time and money.* ◊ *Damage to the building was considerable.*

**con·sid·er·ably** ⓒ+ B2 W /kənˈsɪdərəbli/ *adv.* (*rather formal*) much; a lot SYN significantly: *The need for sleep varies considerably from person to person.* ◊ *Pollution levels have considerably reduced in this time.* ◊ *Prices are considerably higher than they were a year ago.*

**con·sid·er·ate** /kənˈsɪdərət/ *adj.* always thinking of other people's wishes and feelings; careful not to hurt or upset others SYN thoughtful: *She is always polite and considerate towards her employees.* ◊ *It was very considerate of him to wait.* OPP inconsiderate ▸ **con·sid·er·ate·ly** *adv.*

**con·sid·er·ation** ⓘ B2 W /kənˌsɪdəˈreɪʃn/ *noun* **1** ⓒ B2 [U, C] (*formal*) the act of thinking carefully about sth: *An employer is legally bound to give due consideration to the request.* ◊ *Careful consideration should be given to issues of health and safety.* ◊ *After a few moments' consideration, he began to speak.* ◊ *a consideration of the legal issues involved* ◊ **under~** *The proposals are currently under consideration (= being discussed).* ◊ **for (sb's)~** *I enclose the report for your consideration.* **2** ⓒ B2 [C] something that must be thought about when you are planning or deciding sth: *The government's decision was obviously motivated by political considerations.* ◊ *Time is another important consideration.* **3** ⓒ B2 [U] the quality of being sensitive towards others and thinking about their wishes and feelings: *~for sb/sth They showed no consideration whatsoever for my feelings.* ◊ **out of~for sb/sth** *Journalists stayed away from the funeral out of consideration for the bereaved family.* **4** [C] (*formal*) a reward or payment for a service

**IDM in consideration of sth** (*formal*) as payment for sth: *a small sum in consideration of your services* **take sth into consideration** to think about and include a particular thing or fact when you are forming an opinion or making a decision: *The candidates' experience and qualifications will be taken into consideration when the decision is made.* ◊ *Taking everything into consideration, the event was a great success.* ⊃ *more at* **MATURE** *adj.*

**con·sid·er·ing** /kənˈsɪdərɪŋ/ *prep., conj., adv.* used to show that you are thinking about a particular fact, and are influenced by it, when you make a statement about sth: *She's very active, considering her age.* ◊ *Considering he's only just started, he knows quite a lot about it.* ◊ (*informal*) *You've done very well, considering (= in the difficult circumstances).*

**con·sign** /kənˈsaɪn/ *verb* (*formal*) **1** ~sb/sth to sth to put sb/sth somewhere in order to get rid of them/it: *I consigned her letter to the wastebasket.* ◊ *What I didn't want was to see my mother consigned to an old people's home.* **2** ~sb/sth to sth to put sb/sth in an unpleasant situation: *The decision to close the factory has consigned 6000 people to the scrapheap.* ◊ *A car accident consigned him to a wheelchair for the rest of his life.* **3** ~sth to sb to give or send sth to sb

**con·sign·ment** /kənˈsaɪnmənt/ *noun* **1** [C] a quantity of goods that are sent or delivered somewhere: *a consignment of medicines* **2** [U] the act of sending or delivering sb/sth

**conˈsignment shop** (*also* **conˈsignment store**) *noun* (NAmE) a shop where people take their old clothes, etc. to be sold to sb else. The consignment shop keeps part of the money after an item is sold and gives the other part to the person who brought it in.

**con·sist** ⓘ B1 W /kənˈsɪst/ *verb* (not used in the progressive tenses)

PHRV **conˈsist in sth** (*formal*) to have sth as the main or only part or feature: *The beauty of the city consists in its magnificent buildings.* ◊ **consist in doing sth** *True education does not consist in simply being taught facts.* **conˈsist of sb/sth** ⓒ B1 to be formed from the people or things mentioned: *The committee consists of ten members.* ◊ *Their diet consisted largely of vegetables.* ◊ *to consist mainly/mostly of sb/sth* ◊ **consist of doing sth** *The fieldwork consisted of counting the number of species in each section of the shoreline.*

## ▼ SYNONYMS

**consist of sb/sth**
comprise • be composed of sb/sth

These words all mean to be formed from the things or people mentioned.

**consist of sb/sth** to be formed from the people, things or activities mentioned: *Their diet consists largely of vegetables.* **NOTE** **Consist of sb/sth** is the only one of these words that can be used for activities with the *-ing* form of a verb: *My work at that time just consisted of typing letters.*

**comprise** (*rather formal*) to be formed from the things or people mentioned: *The collection comprises 327 paintings.* **NOTE** You can also say **be comprised of sb/sth**: *The collection is comprised of 327 paintings.* It is not correct to say 'comprises of', even though you may say this form being used: The apartment comprises of kitchen, living room, bedroom and bathroom.

**be composed of sb/sth** (*rather formal*) to be formed from the things or people mentioned: *Around 15 per cent of our diet is composed of protein.*

---

**con·sist·ency** ?+ C1 W /kənˈsɪstənsi/ *noun* (*pl.* **-ies**) **1** ?+ C1 [U] (*approving*) the quality of always behaving in the same way or of having the same opinions, standard, etc.; the quality of being consistent: *She has played with great consistency all season.* ◊ *We need to ensure the consistency of service to our customers.* **OPP** **inconsistency** **2** ?+ [C, U] the **consistency** of a mixture or a liquid substance is how thick, smooth, etc. it is: *Beat the ingredients together to a creamy consistency.* ◊ *The cement should have the consistency of wet sand.*

**con·sist·ent** ⓘ B2 W /kənˈsɪstənt/ *adj.* **1** ? B2 (*approving*) always behaving in the same way, or having the same opinions, etc: *a consistent approach to the problem* ◊ *a consistent pattern of behaviour* ◊ *He has been Milan's most consistent player* (= who plays well most often) *this season.* ◊ **~ (in doing) sth** *She's not very consistent in the way she treats her children.* **2** ? B2 happening in the same way and continuing for a period of time: *the party's consistent failure to come up with any new policies* ◊ *a pattern of consistent growth in the economy* **3** **~ with sth** in agreement with sth; not CONTRADICTING sth: *The results are entirely consistent with our earlier research.* ◊ *injuries consistent with a fall from an upper storey* (= similar to those such a fall would have caused) **4** (of an argument or a set of ideas) having different parts that all agree with each other: *a well-thought-out and consistent argument* **OPP** **inconsistent**

**con·sist·ent·ly** ?+ B2 W /kənˈsɪstəntli/ *adv.* **1** ?+ B2 (*approving*) always the same: *Her work has been of a consistently high standard.* **OPP** **inconsistently** **2** ?+ B2 in a way that does not change and continues for a period of time: *We have argued consistently for a change in the law.* ◊ *European policymakers have consistently failed to respond to economic shocks.* **3** ?+ B2 in a way that has different parts that all agree with each other: *Studies have not consistently demonstrated any benefit.* **OPP** **inconsistently**

**con·sola·tion** /ˌkɒnsəˈleɪʃn; *NAmE* ˌkɑːn-/ *noun* [U, C] a thing or person that makes you feel better when you are unhappy or disappointed **SYN** **comfort**: *a few words of consolation* ◊ *If it's any consolation, she didn't get the job, either.* ◊ *The children were a great consolation to him when his wife died.*

**ˌconso·lation ˈprize** *noun* a small prize given to sb who has not won a competition

**con·sola·tory** /kənˈsɒlətəri; *NAmE* -ˈsəʊlətɔːri, -ˈsɑːl-/ *adj.* (*formal*) intended to make sb who is unhappy or disappointed feel better

**con·sole**[1] /kənˈsəʊl/ *verb* to give comfort or sympathy to sb who is unhappy or disappointed **SYN** **comfort**: **~ sb/ yourself** *Nothing could console him when his wife died.* ◊ *She put a consoling arm around his shoulders.* ◊ **~ sb/yourself with sth** *Console yourself with the thought that you did your best.* ◊ **~ sb/yourself that…** *I didn't like lying but I* 

---

*consoled myself that it was for a good cause.* ◊ **~ sb + speech** *'Never mind,' Anne consoled her.*

**con·sole**[2] /ˈkɒnsəʊl; *NAmE* ˈkɑːn-/ *noun* **1** a flat surface that contains all the controls and switches for a machine, a piece of electronic equipment, etc. **2** (*also* **ˈgames console**) a small electronic device for playing video games

**con·soli·date** ?+ C1 /kənˈsɒlɪdeɪt; *NAmE* -ˈsɑːl-/ *verb* **1** ?+ C1 [T, I] **~ (sth)** to make a position of power or success stronger so that it is more likely to continue: *With this new movie he has **consolidated** his position as the country's leading director.* ◊ *Italy consolidated their lead with a second goal.* **2** [T, I] **~ (sth)** (*specialist*) to join things together into one; to be joined into one: *All the debts have been consolidated.* ◊ *consolidated accounts* ◊ *The two companies consolidated for greater efficiency.* ▶ **con·soli·dation** /kənˌsɒlɪˈdeɪʃn; *NAmE* -ˌsɑːl-/ *noun* [U]: *the consolidation of power* ◊ *the consolidation of Japan's banking industry*

**con·sommé** /kənˈsɒmeɪ; *NAmE* ˌkɑːnsəˈmeɪ/ *noun* [U] a clear soup made with the juices from meat

**con·son·ance** /ˈkɒnsənəns; *NAmE* ˈkɑːn-/ *noun* **1** [U] **~ (with sth)** (*formal*) agreement: *a policy that is popular because of its consonance with traditional party doctrine* **2** [U, C] (*music*) a combination of musical notes that sound pleasant together **OPP** **dissonance**

**con·son·ant** /ˈkɒnsənənt; *NAmE* ˈkɑːn-/ *noun, adj.*
■ *noun* **1** (*phonetics*) a speech sound made by completely or partly stopping the flow of air through the mouth or nose **2** a letter of the alphabet that represents a consonant sound, for example 'b', 'c', 'd', 'f', etc. ⊃ compare VOWEL ⊃ **WORDFINDER NOTE** at PRONUNCIATION
■ *adj.* **~ with sth** (*formal*) agreeing with or being the same as sth else

**con·sort** *noun, verb*
■ *noun* /ˈkɒnsɔːt; *NAmE* ˈkɑːnsɔːrt/ **1** the husband or wife of a king, queen, leader, etc: *the Prince Consort* (= the queen's husband) **2** a group of old-fashioned musical instruments, or a group of musicians who play music from several centuries ago
■ *verb* /kənˈsɔːt; *NAmE* -ˈsɔːrt/ [I] **~ with sb** (*formal*) to spend time with sb that other people do not approve of: *He is known to have consorted with prostitutes.*

**con·sor·tium** /kənˈsɔːtiəm; *NAmE* -ˈsɔːrʃi-, -ˈsɔːrti-/ *noun* (*pl.* **con·sor·tiums** *or* **con·sor·tia** /kənˈsɔːtiə, -ˈsɔːʃə; *NAmE* kənˈsɔːrtiə, -ˈsɔːrʃə/) a group of people, countries, companies, etc. who are working together on a particular project: *the Anglo-French consortium that built the Channel Tunnel*

**con·spicu·ous** /kənˈspɪkjuəs/ *adj.* easy to see or notice; likely to attract attention: *Mary's red hair always made her conspicuous at school.* ◊ *I felt very conspicuous in my new car.* ◊ *The advertisements were all posted in a conspicuous place.* ◊ *The event was a conspicuous success* (= a very great one). **OPP** **inconspicuous** ▶ **con·spicu·ous·ly** *adv.*: *Women were conspicuously absent from the planning committee* (= not present on it, when they should have been). **con·spicu·ous·ness** *noun* [U]
**IDM** **conˌspicuous by your ˈabsence** not present in a situation or place, when it is obvious that you should be there: *When it came to cleaning up afterwards, Anne was conspicuous by her absence.*

**conˌspicuous conˈsumption** *noun* [U] the buying of expensive goods in order to impress people and show them how rich you are

**con·spir·acy** ?+ B2 /kənˈspɪrəsi/ *noun* [C, U] (*pl.* **-ies**) a secret plan by a group of people to do sth harmful or illegal: **~ (to do sth)** *a conspiracy to overthrow the government* ◊ *They were charged with conspiracy to murder.* ◊ **~ against sb/sth** *conspiracies against the president* ◊ *a conspiracy of silence* (= an agreement not to talk publicly about sth that should be made public) ◊ *a conspiracy theory* (= the belief that a secret conspiracy is responsible for a particular event)

**con·spir·ator** /kənˈspɪrətə(r)/ noun a person who is involved in a conspiracy

**con·spira·tor·ial** /kənˌspɪrəˈtɔːriəl/ adj. **1** connected with, or making you think of, a conspiracy **2** (of a person's behaviour) suggesting that a secret is being shared: *'I know you understand,' he said and gave a conspiratorial wink.* ▸ **con·spira·tori·al·ly** /-əli/ adv.

**con·spire** /kənˈspaɪə(r)/ verb (formal) **1** [I] to secretly plan with other people to do sth illegal or harmful: *~(with sb) (against sb) They were accused of conspiring against the king.* ◇ *~(together) (to do sth) They deny conspiring together to smuggle drugs.* ◇ *~(with sb) (to do sth) She admitted conspiring with her lover to murder her husband.* **2** [I] (of events) to seem to work together to make sth bad happen: *~against sb/sth Circumstances had conspired against them.* ◇ *~to do sth Everything conspired to make her life a misery.*

**con·stable** /ˈkʌnstəbl/ NAmE /ˈkɑːn-/ noun **1** (BrE) (used especially when talking to a police officer) = POLICE CONSTABLE: *Have you finished your report, Constable?* ⟹ see also CHIEF CONSTABLE, SPECIAL CONSTABLE **2** (in the US) an official with some of the powers of a police officer, typically in a small town

**con·stabu·lary** /kənˈstæbjələri/ NAmE -leri/ noun [C + sing./pl. v.] (pl. -ies) (in the UK) the police force of a particular area or town

**con·stancy** /ˈkɒnstənsi/ NAmE /ˈkɑːn-/ noun [U] (formal) **1** the quality of staying the same and not changing **2** (approving) the quality of being FAITHFUL SYN **fidelity**: *He admired her courage and constancy.*

**con·stant** 🅘 B2 W /ˈkɒnstənt/ NAmE /ˈkɑːn-/ adj., noun

■ adj. **1** B2 [usually before noun] happening all the time or repeatedly: *There were constant interruptions.* ◇ *a constant stream of visitors all day* ◇ *The ruined buildings serve as a constant reminder of the war.* **2** B2 that does not change: *travelling at a constant speed of 50 mph* ◇ *Crime levels remain constant.* ◇ *Ross was his most constant and loyal friend.*
■ noun (specialist) a number or quantity that does not vary OPP **variable**

**con·stant·ly** 🅘 B2 /ˈkɒnstəntli/ NAmE /ˈkɑːn-/ adv. all the time; repeatedly: *Fashion is constantly changing.* ◇ *I am constantly reminded how fortunate I am.* ◇ *Heat the sauce, stirring constantly.*

**con·stel·la·tion** /ˌkɒnstəˈleɪʃn/ NAmE /ˌkɑːn-/ noun **1** a group of stars that forms a shape in the sky and has a name ⟹ WORDFINDER NOTE at UNIVERSE **2** (formal) a group of related ideas, things or people: *a constellation of Hollywood talent*

**con·ster·na·tion** /ˌkɒnstəˈneɪʃn/ NAmE /ˌkɑːnstərˈn-/ noun [U] (formal) a worried, sad feeling after you have received an unpleasant surprise SYN **dismay**: *The announcement of her retirement caused consternation among tennis fans.*

**con·sti·pated** /ˈkɒnstɪpeɪtɪd/ NAmE /ˈkɑːn-/ adj. unable to get rid of waste material from the BOWELS easily

**con·sti·pa·tion** /ˌkɒnstɪˈpeɪʃn/ NAmE /ˌkɑːn-/ noun [U] the condition of being unable to get rid of waste material from the BOWELS easily (= being constipated)

**con·stitu·ency** ⁺ C1 /kənˈstɪtʃuənsi/ (pl. -ies) noun **1** ⁺ C1 (especially BrE) [C] a district that elects its own representative to parliament: *Unemployment is high in her constituency.* ◇ *He owns a house in his Darlington constituency.* ⟹ WORDFINDER NOTE at DEMOCRACY **2** [C + sing./pl. v.] the people who live in and vote in a particular district: *constituency opinion* **3** [C + sing./pl. v.] a particular group of people in society who are likely to support a person, an idea or a product

**con·stitu·ent** /kənˈstɪtʃuənt/ noun, adj.
■ noun **1** a person who lives in and can vote in a constituency: *She has the full support of her constituents.* **2** one of the parts of sth that combine to form the whole

■ adj. [only before noun] (formal) forming or helping to make a whole: *to break something up into its constituent parts/elements*

**con·stituent as·sembly** noun [C + sing./pl. v.] a group of elected representatives with the power to make or change a country's CONSTITUTION

**con·sti·tute** ⁺ C1 W /ˈkɒnstɪtjuːt/ NAmE /ˈkɑːnstɪtuːt/ verb (formal) **1** ⁺ C1 linking verb + noun (not used in the progressive tenses) to be considered to be sth: *Does such an activity constitute a criminal offence?* ◇ *The increase in racial tension constitutes a threat to our society.* **2** ⁺ C1 linking verb + noun (not used in the progressive tenses) to be the parts that together form sth SYN **make up**: *Female workers constitute the majority of the labour force.* **3** [T, usually passive] to form a group legally or officially SYN **establish, set up**: *be constituted (by sb/sth) The committee was constituted in 1974 by an Act of Parliament.*

**con·sti·tu·tion** ⁺ C1 /ˌkɒnstɪˈtjuːʃn/ NAmE /ˌkɑːnstɪˈtuː-/ noun **1** ⁺ C1 [C] the system of laws and basic principles that a state, a country or an organization is governed by: *your right to vote under the constitution* ◇ *According to the constitution …* ◇ *to propose a new amendment to the Constitution* ◇ *the South African Constitution* ⟹ WORDFINDER NOTE at GOVERNMENT **2** [C] the condition of a person's body and how healthy it is: *to have a healthy/strong/weak constitution* **3** [U, C] (formal) the way sth is formed or organized SYN **structure**: *the genetic constitution of cells* **4** [U] (formal) the act of forming sth SYN **establishment**: *He recommended the constitution of a review committee.*

**con·sti·tu·tion·al** ⁺ C1 /ˌkɒnstɪˈtjuːʃənl/ NAmE /ˌkɑːnstɪˈtuː-/ adj. **1** ⁺ C1 [only before noun] connected with the constitution of a country or an organization: *constitutional government/reform* ◇ *a constitutional amendment* **2** ⁺ C1 allowed or limited by the constitution of a country or an organization: *They can't pass this law. It's not constitutional.* ◇ *constitutional rights* ◇ *a constitutional monarchy* (= a country with a king or queen whose power is controlled by a set of laws and basic principles) OPP **unconstitutional** **3** [usually before noun] related to the body's ability to stay healthy, be strong and fight illness: *constitutional remedies* ▸ **con·sti·tu·tion·al·ly** /-nəli/ adv.: *constitutionally guaranteed rights* ◇ *He was much weakened constitutionally by the disease.*

**Consti,tutional 'Court** noun [sing.] (in South Africa) the highest court dealing with cases related to the constitution

**con·sti·tu·tion·al·ism** /ˌkɒnstɪˈtjuːʃənəlɪzəm/ NAmE /ˌkɑːnstɪˈtuː-/ noun [U] a belief in constitutional government

**con·sti·tu·tion·al·ity** /ˌkɒnstɪˌtjuːʃəˈnæləti/ NAmE /ˌkɑːnstɪˌtuː-/ noun [U] (specialist) the fact that sth is acceptable according to a CONSTITUTION: *They questioned the constitutionality of the law.*

**con·sti·tu·tive** /kənˈstɪtjutɪv, ˈkɒnstɪtjuːtɪv/ NAmE /ˈkɑːnstɪtuː-/ adj. (formal) **1** ~ (of sth) forming a part, often an essential part, of sth: *Memory is constitutive of identity.* **2** having the power to establish or give organized existence to sth

**con·strain** W /kənˈstreɪn/ verb (formal) **1** [usually passive] to force sb to do sth or behave in a particular way: *be/feel constrained to do sth The evidence was so compelling that he felt constrained to accept it.* **2** [often passive] to limit sb/sth: *be constrained (by sth) Research has been constrained by a lack of funds.* ◇ *be/feel constrained from doing sth She felt constrained from continuing by the threat of losing her job.* ⟹ see also UNCONSTRAINED

**con·strained** /kənˈstreɪnd/ adj. (formal) not natural; forced or with too much control: *constrained emotions*

**con·straint** ⁺ C1 W /kənˈstreɪnt/ noun **1** ⁺ C1 [C] a thing that limits sth, or limits your freedom to do sth SYN **restriction**: *constraints of time/money/space* ◇ *financial/economic/legal/political constraints* ◇ *~on sth This decision will impose serious constraints on all schools.* ⟹ SYNONYMS at LIMIT **2** ⁺ C1 [U] strict control over the way that you behave or are allowed to behave: *At last we could relax and talk without constraint.*

**con·strict** /kənˈstrɪkt/ verb **1** [I, T] to become tighter or narrower; to make sth tighter or narrower: *Her throat constricted and she swallowed hard.* ◊ *~ sth a drug that constricts the blood vessels* **2** *~ sb* to limit what sb is able to do: *Film-makers of the time were constricted by the censors.* ◊ *constricting rules and regulations* ▶ **con·strict·ed** *adj.*: *Her throat felt dry and constricted.* ◊ *a constricted vision of the world* **con·stric·tion** /-ˈstrɪkʃn/ *noun* [U, C]: *a feeling of constriction in the chest* ◊ *political constrictions*

**con·struct** 🅞 🅱🅲 ⓞ *verb, noun*
- *verb* /kənˈstrʌkt/ **1** 🅲 🅱🅲 [often passive] to build or make sth such as a road, building or machine: *~ sth The building was constructed in 1993.* ◊ *~ sth from / out of / of sth They constructed a shelter out of fallen branches.* ⮕ SYNONYMS at BUILD **2** 🅱🅲 *~ sth* to form sth by putting different things together 🆂🆈🅽 **put together**: *You must learn how to construct a logical argument.* ◊ *to construct a theory* ◊ *a well-constructed novel* **3** *~ sth (geometry)* to draw a line or shape according to the rules of mathematics: *to construct a triangle*
- *noun* /ˈkɒnstrʌkt/; *NAmE* ˈkɑːn-/ (*formal*) **1** an idea or a belief that is based on various pieces of evidence that have not always been proved to be true: *a contrast between lived reality and the construct held in the mind* **2** (*linguistics*) a group of words that form a phrase **3** a thing that is built or made

**con·struc·tion** 🅞 🅱🅲 🅦 /kənˈstrʌkʃn/ *noun*
- OF ROADS / BUILDINGS **1** 🅲 🅱🅲 [U] the process or method of building or making sth, especially roads, buildings, bridges, etc: *Construction began this year and will take approximately 18 months.* ◊ *the costs of road construction and maintenance* ◊ *Work has begun on the construction of the new airport.* ◊ *under ~ Our new offices are still under construction* (= being built). ◊ *the construction industry* ◊ *construction work / workers*

> **WORDFINDER** cement, foundation, girder, joist, masonry, plaster, rubble, scaffolding, site

**2** [U] the people and activities involved in making buildings: *50000 more jobs will go from construction in the next five years.* **3** 🅱🅲 [U, sing.] the way that sth has been built or made: *The bridges are similar in construction.* ◊ *ships of steel construction* ⮕ SYNONYMS at STRUCTURE
- BUILDING / STRUCTURE **4** [C] (*formal*) a thing that has been built or made: *The summer house was a simple wooden construction.*
- GRAMMAR **5** [C] the way in which words are used together and arranged to form a sentence, phrase, etc: *grammatical constructions*
- OF THEORY, ETC. **6** [U, C] the creating of sth from ideas, opinions and knowledge: *the construction of a new theory*
- MEANING **7** [C] (*formal*) the way in which words, actions, statements, etc. are understood by sb 🆂🆈🅽 **interpretation**: *What construction do you put on this letter* (= what do you think it means)?

**con·struc·tion·al** /kənˈstrʌkʃənl/ *adj.* connected with the making or building of things

**conˈstruction paper** *noun* [U] (*NAmE*) thick coloured paper that people cut out to make designs, models, etc.

**conˈstruction site** (also **ˈbuilding site** especially in *BrE*) *noun* an area of land where sth is being built

**con·struct·ive** 🅦 /kənˈstrʌktɪv/ *adj.* having a useful and helpful effect rather than being negative or with no purpose: *constructive criticism / suggestions / advice* ◊ *His work involved helping hyperactive children to use their energy in a constructive way.* ◊ *The government is encouraging all parties to play a constructive role in the reform process.* ⮕ compare DESTRUCTIVE ▶ **con·struct·ive·ly** *adv.*

**conˌstructive disˈmissal** *noun* [U] (*BrE, law*) a situation in which you are forced to leave your job because it is changed in a way that makes it impossible for you to continue doing it

**con·struct·or** /kənˈstrʌktə(r)/ *noun* a person or company that builds things, especially cars or aircraft

---

329 **consume**

**con·strue** /kənˈstruː/ *verb* [usually passive] (*formal*) to understand the meaning of a word, a sentence or an action in a particular way 🆂🆈🅽 **interpret**: **be construed** *He considered how the remark was to be construed.* ◊ **be construed as sth** *Her words could hardly be construed as an apology.*

**con·sul** /ˈkɒnsl; *NAmE* ˈkɑːn-/ *noun* a government official who is the representative of his or her country in a foreign city: *the British consul in Miami* ⮕ compare AMBASSADOR ▶ **con·su·lar** /ˈkɒnsjələ(r); *NAmE* ˈkɑːnsə-/ *adj.*: *consular officials*

**con·sul·ate** /ˈkɒnsjələt; *NAmE* ˈkɑːnsə-/ *noun* the building where a consul works ⮕ compare EMBASSY

**con·sult** 🅲+ 🅱🅲 /kənˈsʌlt/ *verb* **1** 🅲+ 🅱🅲 [T, I] to go to sb for information or advice: *~ sb If the pain continues, consult your doctor.* ◊ *~ sb about sth Have you consulted your lawyer about this?* ◊ *a consulting engineer* (= one who has expert knowledge and gives advice) ◊ (*NAmE*) *~ with sb (about / on sth) Consult with your physician about possible treatments.* **2** 🅲+ 🅱🅲 [T, I] to discuss sth with sb to get their permission for sth, or to help you make a decision: *~ sb You shouldn't have done it without consulting me.* ◊ *~ sb about / on sth I expect to be consulted about major issues.* ◊ *~ (with sb) (about / on sth) I need to consult with my colleagues on the proposals.* ◊ *We consulted quite widely before deciding what to do.* ⮕ SYNONYMS at TALK **3** 🅲+ 🅱🅲 [T] *~ sth* to look in or at sth to get information 🆂🆈🅽 **refer to**: *He consulted the manual.*

**con·sult·ancy** /kənˈsʌltənsi/ *noun.* (*pl.* **-ies**) **1** [C] a company that gives expert advice on a particular subject to other companies or organizations: *a management / design / computer, etc. consultancy* **2** [U] expert advice that a company or person is paid to provide on a particular subject: *consultancy fees*

**con·sult·ant** 🅲+ 🅱🅲 /kənˈsʌltənt/ *noun* **1** 🅲+ 🅱🅲 a person who knows a lot about a particular subject and is employed to give advice about it to other people: *a technology / design consultant* ◊ *~ on sth the president's consultant on economic affairs* ◊ *~ to sb / sth He was happy to act as a consultant to the company.* ⮕ see also MANAGEMENT CONSULTANT ⮕ WORDFINDER NOTE at BUSINESSMAN **2** (*BrE*) a hospital doctor of the highest rank who is a specialist in a particular area of medicine: *a consultant in obstetrics* ◊ *a consultant surgeon* ⮕ compare REGISTRAR ⮕ WORDFINDER NOTE at HOSPITAL

**con·sult·ation** 🅲+ 🅲🅸 /ˌkɒnslˈteɪʃn; *NAmE* ˌkɑːnsl-/ *noun* **1** 🅲+ 🅲🅸 [U] the act of discussing sth with sb or with a group of people before making a decision about it: *a consultation document / paper / period / process* ◊ *~ with sb / sth The decision was taken after close consultation with local residents.* ◊ *in ~ with sb / sth acting in consultation with all the departments involved* ⮕ SYNONYMS at DISCUSSION **2** 🅲+ 🅲🅸 [C] a formal meeting to discuss sth: *extensive consultations between the two countries* ⮕ SYNONYMS at DISCUSSION **3** 🅲+ 🅲🅸 [C] a meeting with an expert, especially a doctor, to get advice or treatment ⮕ SYNONYMS at INTERVIEW **4** 🅲+ 🅲🅸 [U] the act of looking for information in a book, etc: *There is a large collection of texts available for consultation on-screen.*

**con·sulta·tive** /kənˈsʌltətɪv/ *adj.* giving advice or making suggestions 🆂🆈🅽 **advisory**: *a consultative committee / body / document*

**conˈsulting room** *noun* a room where a doctor talks to and examines patients

**con·sum·able** /kənˈsjuːməbl; *NAmE* -ˈsuː-/ *adj., noun* (*business*)
- *adj.* intended to be bought, used and then replaced: *consumable electronic goods*
- *noun* **con·sum·ables** [pl.] goods that are intended to be used fairly quickly and then replaced: *computer consumables such as printer cartridges*

**con·sume** 🅞 🅱🅱 🅦 /kənˈsjuːm; *NAmE* -ˈsuːm/ *verb* **1** 🅲 🅱🅱 *~ sth* to use sth, especially fuel, energy or time: *The electricity industry consumes large amounts of fossil fuels.*

---

ⓞ Oxford Phrasal Academic Lexicon (OPAL) written and spoken word lists | 🅦 OPAL written word list | 🆂 OPAL spoken word list

**consumer** 330

**2** 〖B1〗 ~ sth (*formal*) to eat or drink sth: *Before he died, he had* **consumed** *a large quantity of alcohol.* ◇ *Red meat should be consumed in moderation.* **3** [often passive] (*formal*) to fill sb with a strong feeling: **be consumed with sth** *Carolyn was consumed with guilt.* ◇ **~ sb** *Rage consumed him.* **4** ~ sth (*formal*) (of fire) to completely destroy sth: *The hotel was quickly consumed by fire.* ⊃ see also ALL-CONSUMING, CONSUMING, CONSUMPTION, TIME-CONSUMING

**con·sum·er** 〖B1〗 /kənˈsjuːmə(r)/; *NAmE* -ˈsuː-/ *noun* a person who buys goods or uses services: *consumer spending/demand* ◇ *a consumer society* (= one where buying and selling is considered to be very important) ◇ *a consumer watchdog* (= sb whose job is to protect consumers' rights) ◇ *This tool may be considered too expensive for the average consumer.* ⊃ compare PRODUCER

**con·sumer ˈconfidence** *noun* [U] (*economics*) a measure of the degree of confidence people have in the economy as a whole and in their own financial situation. *If consumer confidence is high, people spend more and the economy grows; the opposite is true if consumer confidence is low: Lower interest rates would boost consumer confidence.*

**con·sumer ˈcredit** *noun* [U] money that is lent to individual customers to buy goods and services, rather than to businesses

**con·sumer ˈdurables** (*BrE*) (*NAmE* **durable ˈgoods, durables**) *noun* [pl.] (*business*) goods that are expected to last for a long time after they have been bought, such as cars, televisions, etc.

**con·sumer eˈlecˈtronics** *noun* [pl.] electronic devices such as televisions, computers and smartphones bought by individual customers rather than by businesses

**con·sumer ˈgoods** *noun* [pl.] goods such as food, clothing, etc. bought by individual customers ⊃ compare CAPITAL GOODS

**con·sumer ˈgroup** *noun* an organization that makes sure the goods and services people buy or use are safe and that consumers are treated fairly

**con·sumer·ism** /kənˈsjuːmərɪzəm; *NAmE* -ˈsuː-/ *noun* [U] (*sometimes disapproving*) the buying and using of goods and services; the belief that it is good for a society or an individual person to buy and use a large quantity of goods and services: *She was appalled by the greed and rampant consumerism she saw in modern society.* ▶ **con·sum·er·ist** *adj.*: *consumerist values*

**con·sumer ˈprice index** (*BrE also* **con·sumer ˈprices index**) *noun* [sing.] (*abbr.* **CPI**) a list of the prices of some ordinary goods and services, which shows how much these prices change each month ⊃ see also RETAIL PRICE INDEX

**con·sum·ing** /kənˈsjuːmɪŋ; *NAmE* -ˈsuː-/ *adj.* [only before noun] (of a feeling, an interest, etc.) so strong or important that it takes up all your time and energy: *Basketball is his consuming passion.* ⊃ see also ALL-CONSUMING, TIME-CONSUMING

**con·sum·mate¹** /kənˈsʌmət, ˈkɒnsəmət; *NAmE* ˈkɑːnsə-/ *adj.* [usually before noun] (*formal*) showing great skill; perfect: *She was a consummate performer.* ◇ *He played the shot with consummate skill.* ◇ (*disapproving*) *a consummate liar* ▶ **con·sum·mate·ly** *adv.*

**con·sum·mate²** /ˈkɒnsəmeɪt; *NAmE* ˈkɑːn-/ *verb* (*formal*) **1** ~ sth to make a marriage or a relationship complete by having sex: *The marriage lasted only a week and was never consummated.* **2** ~ sth to make sth complete or perfect

**con·sum·ma·tion** /ˌkɒnsəˈmeɪʃn; *NAmE* ˌkɑːn-/ *noun* [C, U] **1** the act of making a marriage or relationship complete by having sex **2** the fact of making sth complete or perfect: *The paintings are the consummation of his life's work.*

**con·sump·tion** 〖B2〗 /kənˈsʌmpʃn/ *noun* [U] **1** 〖B2〗 the act of using energy, food or materials; the amount used: *the production of fuel for domestic consumption* (= to be used in the country where it is produced) ◇ *Gas and oil consumption always increases in cold weather.* ◇ *The meat was declared unfit for human consumption.* ◇ *He was advised to reduce his alcohol consumption.* ◇ **~ of sth** *Doctors say that children need to increase their consumption of fruit and vegetables.* ◇ (*figurative*) *Her speech to party members was not intended for public consumption* (= to be heard by the public). ⊃ see also CONSUME **2** 〖C1〗 the act of buying and using products: *Consumption rather than saving has become the central feature of contemporary societies.* ⊃ see also CONSPICUOUS CONSUMPTION, CONSUME **3** (*old-fashioned*) a serious disease of the lungs 〖SYN〗 tuberculosis

**con·sump·tive** /kənˈsʌmptɪv/ *noun* (*old-fashioned*) a person who suffers from consumption (= a disease of the lungs) ▶ **con·sump·tive** *adj.*

**cont.** (*also* **contd**) *abbr.* continued: *cont. on p.74*

**con·tact** 〖B1〗 /ˈkɒntækt; *NAmE* ˈkɑːn-/ *noun*, *verb*

■ *noun*
- ACT OF COMMUNICATING **1** 〖B1〗 [U] the act of communicating with sb, especially regularly: *~ with sb I don't have much contact with my uncle.* ◇ *She's lost contact with* (= no longer sees or writes to) *her son.* ◇ *I finally made contact with* (= succeeded in speaking to or meeting) *her in Paris.* ◇ *~ between A and B There is little contact between the two organizations.* ◇ *in ~ (with sb) The Foreign Office is currently in close contact with the Indian authorities.* ◇ *Have you kept in contact with any of your friends from college* (= do you still see them or speak or write to them)? ◇ *The organization put me in contact with other people in a similar position* (= gave me their addresses or phone numbers). ◇ *two people avoiding eye contact* (= avoiding looking directly at each other) ◇ *I'll give you my contact details* (= phone number, email address, etc.) ◇ *The society's website provides contact information.*
- MEETING SB/STH **2** 〖B1〗 [U] the state of meeting sb or having to deal with sth: *~ with sb/sth She always avoided contact with the press.* ◇ *in ~ with sb/sth He'd prefer a job where he doesn't have to be in direct contact with the public.* ◇ *In her job she often comes into contact with* (= meets) *lawyers.*
- RELATIONSHIP **3** 〖B1〗 [C, usually pl.] *~ (with sb)* an occasion on which you meet or communicate with sb; a relationship with sb: *We have good contacts with the local community.* ◇ *The company has maintained trade contacts with India.*
- PERSON **4** 〖B1〗 [C] a person that you know, especially sb who can be helpful to you in your work: *social/personal contacts* ◇ *I've made some useful contacts in journalism.* ◇ *He has a contact at the White House.*
- TOUCHING SB/STH **5** 〖B2〗 [U] the state of touching sth: *a fear of physical contact* ◇ *in ~ with sth His fingers were briefly in contact with the ball.* ◇ *This substance should not come into contact with food.* ◇ *on ~ (with sth) This pesticide kills insects on contact* (= as soon as it touches them).
- ELECTRICAL **6** [C] an electrical connection: *The switches close the contacts and complete the circuit.*
- FOR EYES **7** [usually pl.] (*informal*) = CONTACT LENS
- MEDICAL **8** [C] a person who has recently been near to sb with a CONTAGIOUS disease and so might have caught the infection from them 〖IDM〗 see POINT *n.*

■ *verb* 〖B1〗 *~ sb* to communicate with sb, for example by phone, letter or email: *I've been trying to contact you all day.* ◇ *Witnesses to the accident are asked to contact the police.* ◇ *~ sb/sth on sth* (*BrE*) *He can be contacted on 01865…* ◇ *~ sb/sth at sth* (*NAmE*) *He can be contacted at 212…* ▶ **con·tact·able** *adj.*: *I'll be contactable on this number:…*

**ˈcontact lens** (*also informal* **con·tact, lens**) *noun* [usually pl.] a small round piece of thin plastic that you put on your eye to help you see better: *to wear contact lenses*

**con·tact·less** /ˈkɒntæktləs; *NAmE* ˈkɑːn-/ *adj.* relating to the technology that allows a SMART CARD (= a small plastic card used to store information electronically), mobile phone, etc. to contact an electronic device that it is not connected to, usually in order to make a payment: *contactless cards* ◇ *a contactless payment*

**ˈcontact sport** *noun* a sport in which players have physical contact with each other

**con·ta·gion** /kənˈteɪdʒən/ noun **1** [U] the spread of a disease by close contact between people: *There is no risk of contagion.* **2** [C] (*old use*) a disease that can be spread by close contact between people **3** [U, C] (*formal*) something bad that spreads quickly by being passed from person to person ⊃ compare INFECTION

**con·ta·gious** /kənˈteɪdʒəs/ adj. **1** a **contagious** disease spreads by close contact between people: *Scarlet fever is highly contagious.* ◇ (*figurative*) *His enthusiasm was contagious* (= spread quickly to other people). ◇ *a contagious laugh* **2** [not usually before noun] if a person is **contagious**, they have a disease that can be spread by close contact with other people ⊃ compare INFECTIOUS ▶ **con·ta·gious·ly** adv.

**con·tain** ⊕ A2 ⊙ /kənˈteɪn/ verb (not used in the progressive tenses) **1** A2 ~ sth if sth **contains** sth else, it has that thing inside it or as part of it: *This drink doesn't contain any alcohol.* ◇ *The documents contain sensitive information.* ◇ *His account contained an element of truth.* ◇ *to contain an amount/a number/a level of sth* ◇ *a brown envelope containing dollar bills* ◇ *The fish were found to contain traces of mercury.* ◇ *The bottle contains* (= can hold) *two litres.* ◇ **contained in/within sth** *The stories contained within these pages are highly enjoyable.* **2** to keep your feelings under control SYN **restrain**: ~ sth *She was unable to contain her excitement.* ◇ ~ yourself *I was so furious I just couldn't contain myself* (= I had to express my feelings). **3** ~ sth to prevent sth harmful from spreading or getting worse: *to contain an epidemic* ◇ *Government forces have failed to contain the rebellion.*

**con·tain·er** ⊕ B1 /kənˈteɪnə(r)/ noun **1** B1 a box, bottle, etc. in which sth can be stored or transported: *a plastic container* ◇ *in a* ~ *Food will last longer if kept in an airtight container.* **2** a large metal or wooden box of a standard size in which goods are packed so that they can easily be lifted onto a ship, train, etc. to be transported: *a shipping container* ◇ *a container ship* (= one designed to transport such containers) **3** a box or pot made of wood, CLAY, plastic, etc. for growing plants in: *Planting bulbs in containers is a great alternative if you don't have a garden.* ⊃ compare FLOWERPOT

**con·tain·er·ized** (*also* **-ised**) /kənˈteɪnəraɪzd/ adj. packed and transported in CONTAINERS: *containerized cargo* ▶ **con·tain·er·iza·tion**, **-isa·tion** /kənˌteɪnəraɪˈzeɪʃn; NAmE -rəˈz-/ noun [U]

**con·tain·ment** /kənˈteɪnmənt/ noun [U] (*formal*) **1** the act of keeping sth under control so that it cannot spread in a harmful way: *the containment of the epidemic* **2** the act of keeping another country's power within limits so that it does not become too powerful: *a policy of containment*

**con·tam·in·ant** /kənˈtæmɪnənt/ noun (*specialist*) a substance that makes sth IMPURE: *Filters do not remove all contaminants from water.*

**con·tam·in·ate** /kənˈtæmɪneɪt/ verb **1** ~ sth (**with sth**) to make a substance or place dirty or no longer pure by adding a substance that is dangerous or carries disease SYN **adulterate**: *The drinking water has become contaminated with lead.* ◇ *contaminated blood/food/soil* **2** ~ sth (*formal*) to influence people's ideas or attitudes in a bad way: *They were accused of contaminating the minds of our young people.* ⊃ see also UNCONTAMINATED ▶ **con·tam·in·ation** /kənˌtæmɪˈneɪʃn/ noun [U]: *radioactive contamination* ⊃ see also CROSS-CONTAMINATION

**contd** abbr. = CONT.

**con·tem·plate** ⟨+⟩ C1 /ˈkɒntəmpleɪt; NAmE ˈkɑːn-/ verb (*rather formal*) **1** ⟨+⟩ C1 [T] to think about whether you should do sth, or how you should do sth SYN **consider**, **think about/of**: ~ sth *You're too young to be contemplating retirement.* ◇ ~ **doing sth** *I have never contemplated living abroad.* ◇ ~ **how/what, etc…** *He continued while she contemplated how to answer.* **2** ⟨+⟩ C1 [T] to think carefully about and accept the possibility of sth happening: ~ sth *The thought of war is too awful to contemplate.* ◇ ~ **how/what, etc…** *I can't contemplate what it would be like to be alone.* ◇ ~ **that…** *She contemplated that things might get even worse.* **3** ⟨+⟩ C1 [T, I] ~(**sth**) (*formal*) to think deeply about sth for a long time: *to contemplate your future* ◇ *She lay in bed, contemplating.* **4** ⟨+⟩ C1 [~] ~ **sb/sth** (*formal*) to look at sb/sth in a careful way for a long time SYN **stare at**: *She contemplated him in silence.*

**con·tem·pla·tion** /ˌkɒntəmˈpleɪʃn; NAmE ˌkɑːn-/ noun [U] (*formal*) **1** the act of thinking deeply about sth: *He sat there deep in contemplation.* ◇ *a few moments of quiet contemplation* ◇ *a life of prayer and contemplation* **2** the act of looking at sth in a calm and careful way: *She turned from her contemplation of the photograph.* IDM **in contemˈplation** (*formal*) being considered: *By 1613 even more desperate measures were in contemplation.*

**con·tem·pla·tive** /kənˈtemplətɪv; BrE also ˈkɒntəmpleɪtɪv; NAmE also ˈkɑːn-/ adj. (*formal*) **1** thinking quietly and seriously about sth: *She was in contemplative mood.* **2** spending time thinking deeply about religious matters: *the contemplative life* (= life in a religious community)

**con·tem·por·an·eous** /kənˌtempəˈreɪniəs/ adj. ~ (**with sb/sth**) (*formal*) happening or existing at the same time SYN **contemporary**: *How do we know that the signature is contemporaneous with the document?* ◇ *contemporaneous events/accounts* ▶ **con·tem·por·an·eous·ly** adv.

**con·tem·por·ary** ⊕ B2 ⊙ /kənˈtemprəri; NAmE -pəreri/ adj., noun
▪ adj. **1** ⟨+⟩ B2 belonging to the same time: *We have no contemporary account of the battle* (= written near the time that it happened). ◇ ~ **with sb/sth** *He was contemporary with the dramatist Congreve.* **2** B2 belonging to the present time SYN **modern**: *contemporary society/culture* ◇ *contemporary art/music/dance* ◇ *The film paints a depressing picture of life in contemporary Britain.*
▪ noun (*pl.* -ies) a person who lives or lived at the same time as sb else, especially sb who is about the same age: *She and I were contemporaries at college.* ◇ *He was a contemporary of Freud and may have known him.*

**con·tempt** ⟨+⟩ C1 /kənˈtempt/ noun [U, sing.] **1** ⟨+⟩ C1 the feeling that sb/sth is without value and deserves no respect at all: **with** ~ *She looked at him with contempt.* ◇ *I shall treat that suggestion with the contempt it deserves.* ◇ **beneath** ~ *His treatment of his children is beneath contempt* (= so bad that it is not even worth feeling contempt for). ◇ **in** ~ *Politicians seem to be generally held in contempt by ordinary people.* ◇ ~ **for sb/sth** *They had shown a contempt for the values she thought important.* **2** ~ **for sth** a lack of worry or fear about rules, danger, etc: *The firefighters showed a contempt for their own safety.* ◇ *His remarks betray a staggering contempt for the truth* (= are completely false). **3** = CONTEMPT OF COURT: *He could be jailed for two years for contempt.* ◇ **in** ~ *She was held in contempt for refusing to testify.* IDM see FAMILIARITY

**con·tempt·ible** /kənˈtemptəbl/ adj. (*formal*) not deserving any respect at all SYN **despicable**: *contemptible behaviour*

**conˈtempt of ˈcourt** (*also* **conˈtempt**) noun [U] the crime of refusing to obey an order made by a court; not showing respect for a court or judge: *Any person who disregards this order will be in contempt of court.*

**con·temp·tu·ous** /kənˈtemptʃuəs/ adj. feeling or showing that you have no respect for sb/sth SYN **scornful**: *She gave him a contemptuous look.* ◇ ~ **of sb/sth** *He was contemptuous of everything I did.* ▶ **con·temp·tu·ous·ly** adv.: *to laugh contemptuously*

**con·tend** ⟨+⟩ C1 /kənˈtend/ verb **1** ⟨+⟩ C1 [T] ~ **that**… (*formal*) to say that sth is true, especially in an argument SYN **maintain**: *I would contend that the minister's thinking is flawed on this point.* **2** ⟨+⟩ C1 [ ] ~ (**for sth**) to compete against sb in order to gain sth: *Three armed groups were contending for power.* PHRV **conˈtend with sth/sb** to have to deal with a problem or with a difficult situation or person: *Nurses often have to contend with violent or drunken patients.*

**con·tend·er** ⟨+⟩ C1 /kənˈtendə(r)/ noun a person or team with a chance of winning a competition: ~ (**for sth**)

**content**

*a contender for a gold medal in the Olympics* ◇ **a leading/serious/strong contender** *for the party leadership* ◇ **~ to do sth** *Germany last night emerged as a contender to stage next year's event.*

**con·tent¹** ⓘ B1 ⊙ /ˈkɒntent; NAmE ˈkɑːn-/ *noun* ⇒ see also CONTENT² **1** B1 **contents** [pl.] the things that are contained in sth: *He tipped the contents of the bag onto the table.* ◇ *Fire has caused severe damage to the contents of the building.* ◇ *She hadn't read the letter and so was unaware of its contents.* ◇ *She picked up the glass and drank the contents.* **2** B1 **contents** [pl.] the different sections that are contained in a book: *a table of contents* (= the list at the front of a book) ◇ *a contents page* **3** B1 [U] the subject matter of a book, speech, programme, etc: *Her poetry has a good deal of political content.* ◇ *Your tone of voice is as important as the content of what you have to say.* ◇ *The content of the course depends on what the students would like to study.* **4** B1 [sing.] (following a noun) the amount of a substance that is contained in sth else: *food with a high fat content* ◇ *water/moisture/protein/DNA content* ◇ *the alcohol content of a drink* **5** [U] (*computing*) the information or other material contained on a website or other digital media: *digital/video/online content* ◇ *We plan to spend more on creating content for the website.* ◇ *delivering premium content to users* ◇ *a method of sharing content over the internet* ◇ *to stream/access/consume/view content* ◇ *content management*

**con·tent²** C1 /kənˈtent/ *adj., verb, noun* ⇒ see also CONTENT¹
■ *adj.* [not before noun] **1** C1 happy and satisfied with what you have: *He seemed more content, less bitter.* ◇ **~ with sth** *Not content with stealing my boyfriend* (= not thinking that this was enough), *she has turned all my friends against me.* ◇ *He had to be content with third place.* ⇒ SYNONYMS at HAPPY **2** C1 **~ to do sth** willing to do sth: *I was content to wait.* ⇒ compare CONTENTED
■ *verb* **1** **~ yourself with sth** to accept and be satisfied with sth and not try to have or do sth better: *Martina contented herself with a bowl of soup.* **2** **~ sb** (*formal*) to make sb feel happy or satisfied: *My apology seemed to content him.*
■ *noun* = CONTENTMENT IDM see HEART *n.*

**con·tent·ed** /kənˈtentɪd/ *adj.* [usually before noun] showing or feeling happiness or pleasure, especially because your life is good: *a contented smile* ◇ *He was a contented man.* ⇒ compare CONTENT² OPP **discontented** ⇒ SYNONYMS at HAPPY ▶ **con·tent·ed·ly** *adv.*: *She smiled contentedly.*

**con·ten·tion** C1 /kənˈtenʃn/ *noun* (*formal*) **1** C1 [U] anger between people who disagree SYN **dispute**: *One area of contention is the availability of nursery care.* ◇ *a point of contention* **2** C1 [C] **~ (that …)** a belief or an opinion that you express, especially in an argument: *It is our client's contention that the fire was an accident.* ◇ *I would reject that contention.*
IDM **in conˈtention (for sth)** with a chance of winning sth: *Only three teams are now in contention for the title.* **out of conˈtention (for sth)** without a chance of winning sth ⇒ more at BONE *n.*

**con·ten·tious** /kənˈtenʃəs/ *adj.* (*formal*) **1** likely to cause people to disagree: *a contentious issue/topic/subject* ◇ *Both views are highly contentious.* **2** liking to argue; involving a lot of arguing: *a contentious meeting*

**con·tent·ment** /kənˈtentmənt/ (*also less frequent* **con·tent**) *noun* [U] a feeling of being happy or satisfied: *He has found contentment at last.* ◇ *a sigh of contentment* ⇒ compare DISCONTENT ⇒ SYNONYMS at SATISFACTION

**ˈcontent provider** *noun* an organization that supplies information that can be used on a website

**con·test** ⓘ B2 *noun, verb*
■ *noun* /ˈkɒntest; NAmE ˈkɑːn-/ **1** B2 a competition in which people try to win sth: *to hold a singing/talent contest* ◇ *to enter/win a contest* ◇ **~ between A and B** *It was a close contest between two evenly matched crews.* ◇ **~ with sb** *He said he had enjoyed the contest with his rival for the title.* ⇒ see also BEAUTY CONTEST **2** B2 a struggle to gain control or power: *the leadership/presidential contest* ◇ **~ for sth** *a contest for the leadership of the party* ⇒ WORD-FINDER NOTE at DEMOCRACY
IDM **be ˌno ˈcontest** used to say that one side in a competition is so much stronger or better than the other that it is sure to win easily
■ *verb* /kənˈtest/ **1** **~ sth** to take part in a competition, election, etc. and try to win it: *Three candidates contested the leadership.* ◇ *The party has decided not to contest this election.* ◇ *a hotly/fiercely/keenly contested game* (= one in which the players try very hard to win and the scores are close) **2** **~ sth** to formally oppose a decision or statement because you think it is wrong: *to contest a will* (= try to show that it was not correctly made in law) ◇ *The divorce was not contested.*

**con·test·ant** /kənˈtestənt/ *noun* a person who takes part in a contest or competition: *Please welcome our next contestant.*

**con·text** ⓘ A2 ⊙ /ˈkɒntekst; NAmE ˈkɑːn-/ *noun* [C, U] **1** A2 the situation in which sth happens and that helps you to understand it: *to examine the wider/broader context of the war* ◇ *the historical/cultural/social context* ◇ *in a ~ This kind of propaganda is used in many different contexts.* ◇ **in/within the ~ of sth** *This speech needs to be set in the context of Britain in the 1960s.* ◇ **in ~** *His decision can only be understood in context.* **2** A2 the words that come just before and after a word, phrase or statement and help you to understand its meaning: *You should be able to guess the meaning of the word from the context.* ◇ **out of ~** *This quotation has been taken out of context* (= repeated without referring to the rest of the text). ◇ **in ~** *You need to look at the words in context.*

**con·text·ual** /kənˈtekstʃuəl/ *adj.* (*formal*) connected with a particular context: *contextual information* ◇ *contextual clues to the meaning* ▶ **con·text·ual·ly** /-əli/ *adv.*

**con·text·ual·ize** (*BrE also* **-ise**) /kənˈtekstʃuəlaɪz/ *verb* **~ sth** (*formal*) to consider sth in relation to the situation in which it happens or exists ▶ **con·text·ual·iza·tion, -isa·tion** /kənˌtekstʃuəlaɪˈzeɪʃn; NAmE -ləˈz-/ *noun* [U]

**con·tigu·ous** /kənˈtɪɡjuəs/ *adj.* (*formal* or *specialist*) touching or next to sth: *The countries are contiguous.* ◇ **~ with/to sth** *The bruising was not contiguous to the wound.* ▶ **con·ti·gu·ity** /ˌkɒntɪˈɡjuːəti; NAmE ˌkɑːn-/ *noun* [U]

**con·tin·ence** /ˈkɒntɪnəns; NAmE ˈkɑːn-/ *noun* [U] **1** (*formal*) the control of your feelings, especially your desire to have sex **2** the ability to control the BLADDER and BOWELS OPP **incontinence** ▶ **con·tin·ent** /-tɪnənt/ *adj.* OPP **incontinent**

**con·tin·ent** ⓘ A2 /ˈkɒntɪnənt; NAmE ˈkɑːn-/ *noun* **1** A2 [C] one of the large land masses of the earth such as Europe, Asia or Africa: *the continent of Africa* ◇ *across a ~ They trekked 1 500 miles across the Australian continent in 1931.* ◇ **on a ~** *the strongest earthquake ever recorded on the North American continent* **2** **the Continent** [sing.] (*BrE, old-fashioned*) the main part of the continent of Europe, not including Britain or Ireland

**con·tin·en·tal** /ˌkɒntɪˈnentl; NAmE ˌkɑːn-/ *adj., noun*
■ *adj.* **1** (*also* **Continental**) [only before noun] (*BrE*) of or in the continent of Europe, not including Britain and Ireland: *a popular continental holiday resort* ◇ *Britain's continental neighbours* **2** (*BrE*) following the customs of countries in western and southern Europe: *a continental lifestyle* ◇ *The shutters and the balconies make the street look almost continental.* **3** [only before noun] connected with the main part of the North American continent: *Prices are often higher in Hawaii than in the continental United States.* **4** forming part of, or typical of, any of the seven main land masses of the earth: *continental Antarctica/Asia/Europe* ◇ *to study continental geography*
■ *noun* (*BrE, old-fashioned, often disapproving*) a person who lives in the continent of Europe: *The continentals have never understood our preference for warm beer.*

**conti·nental ˈbreakfast** *noun* a light breakfast, usually consisting of coffee and bread rolls with butter and jam ⇒ compare ENGLISH BREAKFAST

**conti·nental ˈclimate** *noun* a fairly dry pattern of weather with very hot summers and very cold winters, that is typical of the central regions of the US, Canada and Russia, for example ⊃ WORDFINDER NOTE at CLIMATE

**,continental 'drift** noun [U] (geology) the slow movement of the continents towards and away from each other during the history of the earth ⊃ see also PLATE TECTONICS

**,continental 'shelf** noun [usually sing.] (geology) the area of land on the edge of a continent that slopes into the ocean

**con·tin·gency** /kənˈtɪndʒənsi/ noun [C, U] (pl. **-ies**) **1** an event that may or may not happen; the fact that events are not certain SYN **possibility**: *We must consider all possible contingencies.* ◇ *to make contingency plans* (= plans for what to do if a particular event happens or does not happen) ◇ *a contingency fund* (= to pay for sth that might happen in the future) ◇ *The contingency of life is part of the human condition.* **2** a sum of money that you keep for additional payments: *What's the contingency for legal fees?*

**conˈtingency fee** noun (in the US) an amount of money that is paid to a lawyer only if the person he or she is advising wins in court

**con·tin·gent** /kənˈtɪndʒənt/ noun, adj.
■ noun [C + sing./pl. v.] **1** a group of people at a meeting or an event who have sth in common, especially the place they come from, that is not shared by other people at the event: *The largest contingent was from the United States.* ◇ *A strong contingent of local residents were there to block the proposal.* **2** a group of soldiers that are part of a larger force: *the French contingent in the UN peacekeeping force*
■ adj. **1** ~ (**on/upon sth**) (formal) depending on sth that may or may not happen: *All payments are contingent upon satisfactory completion dates.* **2** ~ **worker/work/job** (business) a person, or work done by a person, who does not have a permanent contract with a company: *the spread of contingent work throughout the economy* ▶ **con·tin·gent·ly** adv.

**con·tin·ual** /kənˈtɪnjuəl/ adj. [only before noun] **1** repeated many times in a way that is annoying: *continual complaints/interruptions* **2** continuing without being interrupted SYN **continuous**: *He was in a continual process of rewriting his material.* ◇ *We lived in continual fear of being discovered.* ◇ *Her daughter was a continual source of delight to her.* ⊃ note at CONTINUOUS

**con·tinu·al·ly** /kənˈtɪnjuəli/ adv. **1** in a way that is repeated many times so that it is annoying: *They argue continually about money.* **2** in a way that continues without a break SYN **continuously**: *the need to adapt to new and continually changing circumstances* ◇ *New products are continually being developed.*

**con·tinu·ance** /kənˈtɪnjuəns/ noun **1** [U] (formal) the state of continuing to exist or function: *We can no longer support the President's continuance in office.* **2** [C] (NAmE, law) a decision that a court case should be heard later: *The judge refused his motion for a continuance.*

**con·tinu·ation** /kənˌtɪnjuˈeɪʃn/ noun **1** [U, sing.] an act or the state of continuing: *They are anxious to ensure the continuation of the economic reform programme.* ◇ *~ in sth This year saw a continuation in the upward trend in sales.* **2** [C] something that continues or follows sth else: *Her new book is a continuation of her autobiography.* **3** [C] something that is joined on to sth else and forms a part of it: *There are plans to build a continuation of the bypass next year.*

**con·tinue** /kənˈtɪnjuː/ verb **1** [I, T] to keep existing or happening without stopping: *If the current trend continues, that number will increase 165 per cent by 2050.* ◇ **+ adv./prep.** *The exhibition continues until 25 July.* ◇ *Fighting continued for four years.* ◇ *The tradition continues to this day.* ◇ **+ adj.** *The violence continues unabated.* ◇ ~ **to do sth** *The economy is continuing to grow.* ◇ *Costs continued to rise.* ◇ ~ **doing sth** *The rain continued falling all afternoon.* **2** [T, I] to keep doing sth without stopping: ~ **doing sth** *She wanted to continue working until she was 60.* ◇ ~ **to do sth** *We will continue to work closely with our international partners on this.* ◇ ~ **sth** *to continue a tradition/trend* ◇ *She moved to New York to continue her studies.* ◇ *He continued his work in secret.* ◇ ~ **(with sth)**

# continuous assessment

*Are you going to continue with the project?* **3** [I] (**+ adv./prep.**) to go or move further in the same direction: *The path continued over rough, rocky ground.* ◇ *He continued on his way.* **4** [I] to remain in a particular job or condition: *She will continue in her present job until a replacement can be found.* ◇ ~ **as sth** *I want you to continue as project manager.* **5** [I, T] to start or start sth again after stopping for a time SYN **resume**: *The story continues in our next issue.* ◇ ~ **sth** *They had to continue their journey on foot.* **6** [I, T] to start speaking again after stopping: *Please continue—I didn't mean to interrupt.* ◇ ~ **sth** *She simply turned her back to me and continued her phone conversation.* ◇ **+ speech** *'In fact,' he continued, 'I'd like to congratulate you.'*

**con·tinued** /kənˈtɪnjuːd/ (also **con·tinu·ing** /kənˈtɪnjuːɪŋ/) adj. [only before noun] existing in the same state without change or a break: *We are grateful for your continued/continuing support.* ◇ *continued interest* ◇ *continuing involvement*

**conˌtinuing eduˈcation** noun [U] = ADULT EDUCATION

**con·tinu·ity** /ˌkɒntɪˈnjuːəti; NAmE ˌkɑːntɪˈnuː-/ noun (pl. **-ies**) **1** [U] the fact of not stopping or not changing: *to ensure/provide/maintain continuity of fuel supplies* OPP **discontinuity** **2** [U, C] a logical connection between the parts of sth, or between two things: *The novel fails to achieve narrative continuity.* ◇ *There are obvious continuities between diet and health.* OPP **discontinuity** **3** [U] (specialist) the organization of a film or television programme, especially making sure that people's clothes, objects, etc. are the same from one scene to the next

**con·tinuo** /kənˈtɪnjuəʊ/ noun [U] (from Italian, music) a musical part played with another instrument, in which a line of low notes is shown with figures to represent the higher notes to be played above them: *a trio for two violins and continuo*

**con·tinu·ous** /kənˈtɪnjuəs/ adj. **1** happening or existing for a period of time without being interrupted: *The organization aims to create a culture of continuous improvement.* ◇ *The rain has been almost continuous for weeks.* **2** spreading in a line or over an area without any spaces: *a continuous flow of traffic* ◇ *a continuous stream of lava from the volcano* **3** (informal) repeated many times SYN **continual**: *For four days the town suffered continuous attacks.* HELP **Continual** is much more frequent in this meaning. **4** (grammar) = PROGRESSIVE: *the continuous tenses* ▶ **con·tinu·ous·ly** adv.: *He has lived and worked in France almost continuously since 1990.*

▼ **WHICH WORD?**

**continuous / continual**

These adjectives are frequently used with the following nouns:

| continuous ~ | continual ~ |
|---|---|
| process | change |
| employment | problems |
| flow | updating |
| line | questions |
| speech | pain |
| supply | fear |

- **Continuous** and **continuously** describe something that continues without stopping.
- **Continual** and **continually** usually describe an action that is repeated again and again.
- The difference between these two words is now disappearing. In particular, **continual/continually** can also mean the same as **continuous/continuously**: *Life was a continual struggle for them.* ◇ *The technology is continually improving.* However, **continuous** and **continuously** are much more frequent in this sense.

**conˌtinuous asˈsessment** noun [U] (BrE) a system of giving a student a final mark based on work done during a course of study rather than on one exam

**con·tinuum** /kənˈtɪnjuəm/ noun (pl. **con·tinua** /-njuə/) a series of similar items in which each is almost the same as the ones next to it but the last is very different from the first SYN **cline**: *It is impossible to say at what point along the continuum a dialect becomes a separate language.*

**con·tort** /kənˈtɔːt; NAmE -ˈtɔːrt/ verb [I, T] to become TWISTED or make sth TWISTED out of its natural or normal shape: *His face contorted with anger.* ◇ ~ **sth** *Her mouth was contorted in a snarl.* ▶ **con·tort·ed** adj.: *contorted limbs/bodies* ◇ *(figurative) It was a contorted version of the truth.*

**con·tor·tion** /kənˈtɔːʃn; NAmE -ˈtɔːrʃn/ noun **1** [C, U] a movement that TWISTS the face or body out of its natural shape; the state of being TWISTED in this way: *His facial contortions amused the audience of schoolchildren.* ◇ *Their bodies had suffered contortion as a result of malnutrition.* **2** [C] a complicated series of actions or thought process: *We had to go through all the usual contortions to get a ticket.* ◇ *intellectual/mental/logical contortions*

**con·tor·tion·ist** /kənˈtɔːʃənɪst; NAmE -ˈtɔːrʃ-/ noun a performer who does contortions of their body to entertain others

**con·tour** /ˈkɒntʊə(r); NAmE ˈkɑːntʊr/ noun **1** the outer edges of sth; the outline of its shape or form: *The road follows the natural contours of the coastline.* ◇ *She traced the contours of his face with her finger.* **2** (also **contour line**) a line on a map that joins points that are the same height above sea level: *a contour map* (= a map that includes these lines)

**con·toured** /ˈkɒntʊəd; NAmE ˈkɑːntʊrd/ adj. **1** with a specially designed outline that makes sth attractive or comfortable: *It is smoothly contoured to look like a racing car.* **2** having or showing contours: *contoured hills/maps*

**contra-** /ˈkɒntrə; NAmE ˈkɑːntrə/ combining form **1** (in nouns, verbs and adjectives) against; opposite: *contraflow* ◇ *contradict* **2** (in nouns) (music) having a PITCH an OCTAVE below: *a contrabassoon*

**con·tra·band** /ˈkɒntrəbænd; NAmE ˈkɑːn-/ noun [U] goods that are illegally taken into or out of a country: *contraband goods* ◇ *to smuggle contraband*

**con·tra·cep·tion** /ˌkɒntrəˈsepʃn; NAmE ˌkɑːn-/ noun [U] the practice of using artificial methods to avoid becoming pregnant when having sex; the methods of doing this SYN **birth control**: *to give advice about contraception*

**con·tra·cep·tive** /ˌkɒntrəˈseptɪv; NAmE ˌkɑːn-/ noun a drug, device or practice used to avoid becoming pregnant when having sex: *oral contraceptives* ▶ **con·tra·cep·tive** adj. [only before noun]: *a contraceptive pill* ◇ *contraceptive advice/precautions/methods*

**con·tract** ⓘ B2 noun, verb
■ **noun** /ˈkɒntrækt; NAmE ˈkɑːn-/ **1** ⓘ B2 an official written agreement: *a contract of employment* ◇ *a research/modelling/recording contract* ◇ *a lucrative government contract* ◇ ~ **with sb** *to enter into/negotiate/sign a contract with the supplier* ◇ ~ **between A and B** *These clauses form part of the contract between buyer and seller.* ◇ **for sth** *a contract for the supply of vehicles* ◇ **to do sth** *to win/be awarded a contract to build a new school* ◇ *to renew/extend/terminate/cancel a contract* ◇ **on a** ~ *I was on a three-year contract that expired last week.* ◇ **under** ~ **to/with sb/sth** *She is under contract to* (= has a contract to work for) *a major American computer firm.* ◇ **out of** ~ *The phone costs several hundred dollars more out of contract* (= without a contract with a phone company). ◇ *a contract worker* (= one employed on a contract for a fixed period of time) ◇ *Under the terms of the contract the job should have been finished yesterday.* ◇ *They were sued for breach of contract* (= not doing what they agreed to do in a contract). ◇ *see also* SOCIAL CONTRACT ◯ WORDFINDER NOTE *at* DEAL **2** ~ **(on sb)** (informal) an agreement to kill sb for money: *to take out a contract on sb*
■ **verb** /kənˈtrækt/ **1** ⓘ B2 [I, T] to become less or smaller; to make sth become less or smaller: *Glass contracts as it cools.* ◇ *The economy will contract by 2 per cent this year.* ◇ *The heart muscles contract to expel the blood.* ◇ ~ **sth** *The exercise consists of stretching and contracting the leg muscles.* ◇ ~ **sth to sth** '*I will*' *and* '*I shall*' *are usually contracted to* '*I'll*' (= made shorter). OPP **expand 2** [T] ~ **sth** (formal or medical) to get an illness: *to contract a virus/a disease/measles* **3** /ˈkɒntrækt; NAmE ˈkɑːn-/ [T] to make a legal agreement with sb for them to work for you or provide you with a service: ~ **sb to do sth** *The player is contracted to play until August.* ◇ ~ **sb (to sth)** *Several computer engineers have been contracted to the finance department.* **4** /ˈkɒntrækt; NAmE ˈkɑːn-/ [I] ~ **to do sth** to make a legal agreement to work for sb or provide them with a service: *She has contracted to work 20 hours a week.* **5** /ˈkɒntrækt; NAmE ˈkɑːn-/ [T] ~ **a marriage / an alliance (with sb)** (formal) to formally agree to marry sb / form an ALLIANCE with sb
PHRV **contract ˈin (to sth)** (BrE) to formally agree that you will take part in sth **ˌcontract ˈout (of sth)** (BrE) to formally agree that you will not take part in sth: *Many employees contracted out of the pension plan.* **ˌcontract sth↔ˈout (to sb)** to arrange for work to be done by another company rather than your own

**con·tract·ile** /kənˈtræktaɪl/ adj. (biology) (of living TISSUE, organs, etc.) able to contract or, of an opening or tube, become narrower

**con·trac·tion** /kənˈtrækʃn/ noun **1** [U] the process of becoming smaller: *the expansion and contraction of the metal* ◇ *The sudden contraction of the markets left them with a lot of unwanted stock.* OPP **expansion 2** [C, U] a sudden and painful contracting of muscles, especially the muscles around a woman's WOMB, that happens when she is giving birth to a child: *The contractions started coming every five minutes.* ◇ *Neurons control the contraction of muscles.* ◯ WORDFINDER NOTE *at* BIRTH **3** [C] (linguistics) a short form of a word: '*He's*' *may be a contraction of* '*he is*' *or* '*he has*'.

**con·tract·or** ⓘ+ C1 /kənˈtræktə(r), ˈkɒntræktə(r); NAmE ˈkɑːntræktər/ noun a person or company that has a contract to do work or provide goods or services for another company: *a building/roofing/electrical contractor* ◇ *a defence/security/military/civilian contractor* ◇ *a private/an independent contractor* ◇ *to employ an outside contractor* ◯ *see also* SUBCONTRACTOR

**con·tract·ual** /kənˈtræktʃuəl/ adj. connected with the conditions of a legal written agreement; agreed in a contract ▶ **con·tract·ual·ly** /-əli/ adv.

**con·tra·dict** ⓘ /ˌkɒntrəˈdɪkt; NAmE ˌkɑːn-/ verb **1** to say that sth that sb else has said is wrong, and that the opposite is true: ~ **sth** *All evening her husband contradicted everything she said.* ◇ ~ **sb/yourself** *You've just contradicted yourself* (= said the opposite of what you said before). ◇ ~ **(sb) + speech** '*No, it's not,*' *she contradicted (him).* **2** ~ **sth** | ~ **each other** (of statements or pieces of evidence) to be so different from each other that one of them must be wrong: *The two stories contradict each other.* ◯ LANGUAGE BANK *at* EVIDENCE

**con·tra·dic·tion** ⓘ+ C1 /ˌkɒntrəˈdɪkʃn; NAmE ˌkɑːn-/ noun **1** ⓘ+ C1 [C, U] a lack of agreement between facts, opinions, actions, etc.: ~ **(between A and B)** *There is a contradiction between the two sets of figures.* ◇ *How can we resolve this apparent contradiction?* ◇ **in** ~ **to sth** *His public speeches are in direct contradiction to his personal lifestyle.* **2** ⓘ+ C1 [U, C] the act of saying that sth that sb else has said is wrong or not true; an example of this: *I think I can say, without fear of contradiction, that* … ◇ ~ **of sth** *Now you say you both left at ten—that's a contradiction of your last statement.*
IDM **a ˌcontradiction in ˈterms** a statement containing two words that contradict each other's meaning: *A* '*nomad settlement*' *is a contradiction in terms.*

**con·tra·dict·ory** /ˌkɒntrəˈdɪktəri; NAmE ˌkɑːn-/ adj. containing or showing a lack of agreement between statements, facts, opinions or actions SYN **conflicting**: *We are faced with two apparently contradictory statements.* ◇ *The advice I received was often contradictory.* ◯ *see also* SELF-CONTRADICTORY

**con·tra·dis·tinc·tion** /ˌkɒntrədɪˈstɪŋkʃn; NAmE ˌkɑːn-/ noun
[IDM] **in contradistinction to sth/sb** (*formal*) in contrast with sth/sb

**con·tra·flow** /ˈkɒntrəfləʊ; NAmE ˈkɑːn-/ noun (*BrE*) a system that is used when one half of a large road is closed for repairs, and the traffic going in both directions has to use the other half: *A contraflow system is in operation on this section of the motorway.* ⇒ **WORDFINDER NOTE** at TRAFFIC

**con·trail** /ˈkɒntreɪl; NAmE ˈkɑːn-/ noun (*especially NAmE*) the white line that is left in the sky by a plane [SYN] **vapour trail**

**con·tra·indi·cate** /ˌkɒntrəˈɪndɪkeɪt; NAmE ˌkɑːn-/ verb [usually passive] (*medical*) if a drug or treatment is **contraindicated**, there is a medical reason why it should not be used in a particular situation: *be contraindicated This drug is contraindicated in patients with asthma.*

**con·tra·indi·ca·tion** /ˌkɒntrəˌɪndɪˈkeɪʃn; NAmE ˌkɑːn-/ noun (*medical*) a medical reason for not giving sb a particular drug or medical treatment

**con·tralto** /kənˈtræltəʊ/ noun (*pl.* **-os**) = ALTO

**con·trap·tion** /kənˈtræpʃn/ noun a machine or piece of equipment that looks strange or complicated and possibly does not work well: *She showed us a strange contraption that looked like a satellite dish.*

**con·tra·pun·tal** /ˌkɒntrəˈpʌntl; NAmE ˌkɑːn-/ adj. (*music*) having two or more tunes played together to form a whole ⇒ see also COUNTERPOINT

**con·trary¹** ?+ [C1] /ˈkɒntrəri; NAmE ˈkɑːntreri/ adj., noun ⇒ see also CONTRARY²
■ *adj.* **1** ?+ [C1] **~ to sth** different from sth; against sth: *Contrary to popular belief, many cats dislike milk.* ◊ *The government has decided that the publication of the report would be 'contrary to the public interest'.* **2** ?+ [C1] [only before noun] completely different in nature or direction [SYN] **opposite**: *contrary advice/opinions/arguments* ◊ *The contrary view is that prison provides an excellent education—in crime.*
■ *noun* ?+ [C1] **the contrary** [sing.] the opposite fact, event or situation: *In the end the contrary was proved true: he was innocent and she was guilty.*
[IDM] **on the ˈcontrary** used to introduce a statement that says the opposite of the last one: *'It must have been terrible.' 'On the contrary, I enjoyed every minute.'* **quite the ˈcontrary** used to emphasize that the opposite of what has been said is true: *I don't find him funny at all. Quite the contrary.* **to the ˈcontrary** showing or proving the opposite: *Show me some evidence to the contrary* (= proving that sth is not true). ◊ *I will expect to see you on Sunday unless I hear anything to the contrary* (= that you are not coming).

**con·trary²** /kənˈtreəri; NAmE -ˈtreri/ adj. (*formal, disapproving*) (usually of children) behaving badly; choosing to do or say the opposite of what is expected: *She was such a contrary child—it was impossible to please her.* ⇒ see also CONTRARY¹ ▶ **con·trar·ily** /kənˈtreərɪli; NAmE -ˈtrer-/ adv. **con·trari·ness** noun [U]

## con·trast ❶ [B1] ❺ noun, verb
■ *noun* /ˈkɒntrɑːst; NAmE ˈkɑːntræst/ **1** ? [B1] [C, U] a difference between two or more people or things that you can see clearly when they are compared or put close together; the fact of comparing two or more things in order to show the differences between them: *The two cities make an interesting contrast.* ◊ **~ between A and B** *There is an obvious contrast between the cultures of East and West.* ◊ **in ~** *In contrast, the south suffered very little hurricane damage.* ◊ **in ~ to sb/sth** *The situation when we arrived was in marked contrast to the news reports.* ◊ *The poverty of her childhood stands in total contrast to her life in Hollywood.* ◊ **~ with sb/sth** *to show a sharp/stark/striking contrast with sth* ◊ **~ in sth** *A wool jacket complements the silk trousers and provides an interesting contrast in texture.* ◊ **by ~** *When you look at their new system, ours seems very old-fashioned by contrast.* ◊ **~ of A and B** *Careful contrast of the two plans shows some important differences.* **2** [C, usually sing.] **~ (to sb/sth)** a person or thing that is clearly different from sb/sth else: *The work you did today is quite a contrast to* (=

very much better/worse than) *what you did last week.* **3** [U] differences in colour or in light and dark, used in photographs and paintings to create a special effect: *The artist's use of contrast is masterly.* **4** [U] the amount of difference between light and dark in a photograph or the picture on a television screen: *Use this button to adjust the contrast.*
■ *verb* /kənˈtrɑːst; NAmE -ˈtræst/ **1** ? [B1] [T] to compare two things in order to show the differences between them: **~ A and B** *The poem contrasts youth and age.* ◊ **Compare and contrast the two novels** (= discuss how they are similar and how they are different). ◊ **~ A with B** *It is interesting to contrast the British legal system with the American one.* **2** ? [B1] [I] to show a clear difference when close together or when compared: **A contrasts with B** *Her actions contrasted sharply with her promises.* ◊ **A and B~** *Her actions and her promises contrasted sharply.*

▼ **LANGUAGE BANK**

### contrast
Highlighting differences

- This survey **highlights a number of differences in** the way that teenage boys and girls in the UK spend their free time.
- **One of the main differences between** the girls **and** the boys who took part in the research was the way in which they use the internet.
- **Unlike** the girls, who use the internet mainly to keep in touch with friends, the boys questioned in this survey tend to use the internet for playing computer games.
- The girls **differ from** the boys **in that** they tend to spend more time keeping in touch with friends on the phone or on social networking websites.
- **Compared to** the boys, the girls spend much more time chatting to friends on the phone.
- On average the girls spend four hours a week chatting to friends on the phone. **In contrast** very few of the boys spend more than five minutes a day talking to their friends in this way.
- The boys prefer competitive sports and computer games, **whereas/while** the girls seem to enjoy more cooperative activities, such as shopping with friends.
- When the girls go shopping, they mainly buy clothes and cosmetics. The boys, **on the other hand**, tend to purchase computer games or gadgets.

⇒ LANGUAGE BANK at GENERALLY, ILLUSTRATE, PROPORTION, SIMILARLY, SURPRISING

**con·trast·ing** /kənˈtrɑːstɪŋ; NAmE -ˈtræs-/ adj. [usually before noun] very different in style, colour or attitude: *bright, contrasting colours* ◊ *The book explores contrasting views of the poet's early work.*

**con·trast·ive** /kənˈtrɑːstɪv; NAmE -ˈtræs-/ adj. (*formal or linguistics*) showing the differences between things, especially between languages: *a contrastive analysis of British and Australian English*

**con·tra·vene** /ˌkɒntrəˈviːn; NAmE ˌkɑːn-/ verb **~ sth** (*formal*) to do sth that is not allowed by a law or rule [SYN] **infringe**: *The company was found guilty of contravening safety regulations.* ▶ **con·tra·ven·tion** /-ˈvenʃn/ noun [U, C] [SYN] **infringement**: *These actions are in contravention of European law.*

**con·tre·temps** /ˈkɒntrətɒ̃; NAmE ˈkɑːntrətɑː/ noun (*pl.* **con·tre·temps**) (from French, *formal or humorous*) an unpleasant event or an embarrassing occasion when people disagree

## con·trib·ute ❶ [B2] ❼ /kənˈtrɪbjuːt; BrE also ˈkɒntrɪbjuːt/ verb **1** ? [B2] [I, T] to give sth, especially money or goods, to help achieve or provide sth: *Do you wish to contribute?* ◊ **~ to/towards sth** *Would you like to contribute to our collection?* ◊ *to contribute to your pension* ◊ **~ sth** *Check with your financial planner to make sure that you are contributing the correct amounts.* ◊ **~ sth to/towards sth** *We contributed £5000 to the earthquake fund.* **2** ? [B2] [I] to be one of the causes of sth: *Human error may have been*

# contribution

*a contributing factor.* ◊ **~ to sth** *It is well known that UV radiation* **contributes to** *the development of skin cancer.* ◊ *Several* **factors** *may be* **contributing to** *the fall in the number of applicants.* ⊃ LANGUAGE BANK *at* CAUSE **3** [I, T] to increase, improve or add to sth: **~ to sth** *Immigrants have contributed to British culture in many ways.* ◊ *Parental involvement* **contributes** *significantly to children's learning.* ◊ **~ sth to sth** *This book* **contributes** *little to our understanding of the subject.* **4** [I, T] to write things for a newspaper, book, website, etc. or a radio or television programme; to speak during a meeting or conversation, especially to give your opinion: *The blog now has about 20 people contributing regularly.* ◊ **~ to sth** *We hope everyone will contribute to the discussion.* ◊ **~ sth** *He contributed a piece on Canadian law.* ◊ **~ sth to sth** *She contributed a number of articles to the magazine.*

**con·tri·bu·tion** /ˌkɒntrɪˈbjuːʃn/; *NAmE* /ˌkɑːn-/ *noun* **1** [C] a gift or payment that is made to a person or an organization in order to help pay for sth SYN donation: *We rely entirely on* **voluntary contributions.** ◊ **campaign contributions** ◊ **~ to sth** *to make a substantial* **contribution** *to charity* ◊ **~ towards (doing) sth** *valuable* **contributions** *towards the upkeep of the cathedral* ◊ **~ from / by sb / sth** *Financial* **contributions** *from individuals paid for office and printing expenses.* **2** [C] a sum of money that you pay regularly to your employer or the government in order to pay for benefits such as health insurance, a pension, etc: **pension contributions** ◊ **~ to sth** *monthly* **contributions** *to the pension plan* ⊃ *see also* DEFINED CONTRIBUTION ⊃ SYNONYMS *at* PAYMENT **3** [C, usually sing.] an action or a service that helps to cause or increase sth, usually (but not necessarily) sth good or valuable: **~ to sth** *He made a very positive* **contribution** *to the success of the project.* ◊ *a significant* **contribution** *to scientific knowledge* ◊ *the car's* **contribution** *to the greenhouse effect* ◊ **~ towards (doing) sth** *She was honoured posthumously for her* **contribution** *towards the war effort.* ◊ **~ of sb / sth (to sth)** *She says the US needs to do more to recognize the* **contributions** *of women and minorities to society.* **4** [C] an item that forms part of a book, magazine, website broadcast, discussion, etc: *All* **contributions** *for the May issue must be received by Friday.* ◊ **~ to sth** *an important* **contribution** *to the debate* ◊ **~ from / by sb** *There are no* **contributions** *by scholars based in North America.* **5** [U] **~ (to sth)** the act of giving sth, especially money, to help a person or an organization: *The institute is totally funded by* **voluntary contribution.**

**con·tribu·tor** /kənˈtrɪbjətə(r)/ *noun* **1** **~ (to sth)** a person who writes articles for a magazine, book or website, or who talks on a radio or television programme or at a meeting: *I am a* **contributor** *to several blogs.* **2** **~ (to sth)** a person or thing that provides money or goods to help pay for or support sth: *Older people are important* **contributors** *to the economy.* **3** **~ (to sth)** something that helps to cause sth: *Sulphur dioxide is a pollutant and a major* **contributor** *to acid rain.*

**con·tribu·tory** /kənˈtrɪbjətəri/; *NAmE* -tɔːri/ *adj.* [usually before noun] **1** helping to cause sth: *Alcohol is a* **contributory** *factor in 10 per cent of all road accidents.* **2** involving payments from the people who will benefit: *a* **contributory** *pension scheme/plan* (= paid for by both employers and employees) OPP **non-contributory**

**con·trite** /kənˈtraɪt/; *BrE also* /ˈkɒntraɪt/ *adj. (formal)* very sorry for sth bad that you have done ▶ **con·trite·ly** *adv.* **con·tri·tion** /kənˈtrɪʃn/ *noun* [U]: *a look of contrition*

**con·triv·ance** /kənˈtraɪvəns/ *noun (formal)* **1** [C, U] *(usually disapproving)* something that sb has done or written that does not seem natural; the fact of seeming artificial: *The film is spoilt by unrealistic* **contrivances** *of plot.* ◊ *The story is told with a complete absence of* **contrivance.** **2** [C] a clever or complicated device or tool made for a particular purpose **3** [C, U] a clever plan or trick; the act of using a clever plan or trick: *an ingenious* **contrivance** *to get her to sign the document without reading it*

**con·trive** /kənˈtraɪv/ *verb (formal)* **1** **~ to do sth** to manage to do sth despite difficulties: *She* **contrived** *to spend a couple of hours with him every Sunday evening.* **2** **~ sth** to succeed in making sth happen despite difficulties: *I decided to* **contrive** *a meeting between the two of them.* **3** **~ sth** to think of or make sth, for example a plan or a machine, in a clever way: *They* **contrived** *a plan to defraud the company.*

**con·trived** /kənˈtraɪvd/ *adj. (disapproving)* planned in advance and not natural or what sb claims it is; written or arranged in a way that is not natural or realistic: *a* **contrived** *situation* ◊ *The book's happy ending seemed* **contrived.**

**con·trol** /kənˈtrəʊl/ *noun, verb*
■ *noun*
- POWER **1** [U] the power to make decisions about how a country, an area, an organization, etc. is run: **~ of sb / sth** *The party expects to* **gain control** *of the council in the next election.* ◊ *Militants have* **taken control** *of the town.* ◊ *The Democrats have* **lost control** *of Congress.* ◊ **in the ~ of sb / sth** *The city is in the control of enemy forces.* ◊ **under …~** *The area remains under international control.* **2** [U] the ability to make sb/sth do what you want: **~ over sb / sth** *The teacher had* **no control** *over the children.* ◊ **~ of sth** *She struggled to* **keep control** *of her voice.* ◊ *He got so angry he* **lost control** (= shouted and said or did things he would not normally do). ◊ **to maintain/keep control** ◊ **beyond / outside sb's ~** *Owing to circumstances beyond our control, the flight to Rome has been cancelled.* ◊ **under ~** *The situation is* **under control.** ⊃ *see also* SELF-CONTROL
- LIMITING / MANAGING **3** [U, C] (often in compounds) the act of limiting or managing sth; a method of doing this: *traffic control* ◊ **controls on sth** *tight* **controls** *on government spending* ◊ *Price* **controls** *on food were ended.* ◊ **~ of sth** *exciting advances in the* **control** *of malaria* ◊ *It was an exercise in* **damage control** (= trying to prevent further damage). ◊ *a* **pest control** *officer* ⊃ *see also* BIRTH CONTROL, CLIMATE CONTROL, GUN CONTROL, PARENTAL CONTROL, QUALITY CONTROL ⊃ SYNONYMS *at* LIMIT
- IN MACHINE **4** [C, usually pl.] the switches and buttons, etc. that you use to operate a machine or a vehicle: *the* **controls** *of an aircraft* ◊ *the* **control panel** ◊ *the* **volume control** *of a TV* ◊ **at the controls** *The co-pilot was at the* **controls** *when the plane landed.* ⊃ *see also* CRUISE CONTROL, DUAL CONTROLS, REMOTE CONTROL
- IN EXPERIMENT **5** [C] *(specialist)* a person, thing or group used as a standard of comparison for checking the results of a scientific experiment; an experiment whose result is known, used for checking working methods: *One group was treated with the new drug, and the* **control group** *was given a sugar pill.*
- PLACE **6** [sing.] a place where orders are given or where checks are made; the people who work in this place: *We went through* **passport control** *and into the departure lounge.* ⊃ *see also* AIR TRAFFIC CONTROL, GROUND CONTROL, MISSION CONTROL
- ON COMPUTER **7** [U] (*also* **con·trol key** [sing.]) (on a computer keyboard) a key that you press when you want to perform a particular operation ⊃ WORDFINDER NOTE *at* KEYBOARD

IDM **be in control (of sth)** **1** to direct or manage an organization, an area or a situation: *He's reached retiring age, but he's still firmly in control.* ◊ *There has been some violence after the match, but the police are now in control of the situation.* **2** to be able to organize your life well and keep calm: *In spite of all her family problems, she's really in control.* **be / get / run / etc. out of control** to be or become impossible to manage or to control: *The children are completely out of control since their father left.* ◊ *A truck ran out of control on the hill.* **be under control** to be being dealt with successfully: *Don't worry—everything's under control!* **bring / get / keep sth under control** to succeed in dealing with sth so that it does not cause any damage or hurt anyone: *It took two hours to bring the fire under control.* ◊ *Please keep your dog under control!*

■ *verb* (-ll-)
- HAVE POWER **1** **~ sb / sth** to have power over a person, company, country, etc. so that you are able to decide what

they must do or how it is run: *By the age of 21 he controlled the company.* ◊ *The whole territory is now controlled by the army.* ◊ *Can't you control your children?*
- **LIMIT/MANAGE** 2 **A2** to limit sth or make it happen in a particular way: ~ **sth** *It is essential for businesses to control costs.* ◊ *~ what/how, etc ... Parents should control what their kids watch on television.* 3 **A2** to stop sth from spreading or getting worse: ~ **sth** *Firefighters are still trying to control the blaze.* ◊ *~ sth with sth Most of the symptoms can be controlled with medication.*
- **MACHINE** 4 **A2** to make sth such as a machine or system work in the way that you want it to: ~ **sth** *This knob controls the volume.* ◊ *~ sth with/via/from sth lighting that you can control with your smartphone*
- **STAY CALM** 5 **A2** to manage to make yourself remain calm, even though you are upset or angry: ~ **yourself** *I was so angry I couldn't control myself.* ◊ *~ sth He was finding it difficult to control his feelings.*

**con·trol centre** (*US* **control center**) *noun* a place from which an organization or system is managed, or in which devices and controls are kept

**con'trol freak** *noun* (*informal, disapproving*) a person who always wants to be in control of their own and others' lives, and to organize how things are done

**con·trol·lable** /kənˈtrəʊləbl/ *adj.* that can be controlled

**con·trolled** /kənˈtrəʊld/ *adj.* **1** done or arranged in a very careful way: *a controlled explosion* ◊ *a controlled environment* **2** limited, or managed by law or by rules: *controlled airspace* **3** **-controlled** (in compounds) managed by a particular group, or in a particular way: *a British-controlled company* ◊ *computer-controlled systems* **4** remaining calm and not getting angry or upset: *She remained quiet and controlled.* ⊃ compare UNCONTROLLED

**con'trolled e'conomy** *noun* (*economics*) a type of economic system in which a government controls its country's industries and decides what goods should be produced and in what amounts

**con'trolled 'substance** *noun* (*specialist*) an illegal drug: *to be arrested for possession of a controlled substance*

**con·trol·ler** /kənˈtrəʊlə(r)/ *noun* **1** a person who manages or directs sth, especially a large organization or part of an organization ⊃ see also AIR TRAFFIC CONTROLLER **2** (*specialist*) a device that controls or REGULATES a machine or part of a machine: *a temperature controller* **3** (*also* **comp·trol·ler**) a person who is in charge of the financial accounts of a business company

**con'trolling 'interest** *noun* [usually sing.] (*business*) the fact of owning enough shares in a company to be able to make decisions about what the company should do

**con'trol room** *noun* a room that is a centre for the operation of a factory, a service or a particular event: *a nuclear power plant's control room*

**con'trol tower** *noun* a building at an airport from which the movements of aircraft are controlled

**con·tro·ver·sial** **B2** /ˌkɒntrəˈvɜːʃl; *NAmE* ˌkɑːntrəˈvɜːrʃl/ *adj.* causing a lot of angry public discussion and DISAGREEMENT: *a highly controversial topic* ◊ *a controversial plan to build a new road* ◊ *Winston Churchill and Richard Nixon were both controversial figures.* **OPP** **non-controversial, uncontroversial** ▶ **con·tro·ver·sial·ly** /-ʃəli/ *adv.*

**con·tro·versy** **B2** /ˈkɒntrəvɜːsi, kənˈtrɒvəsi; *NAmE* ˈkɑːntrəvɜːrsi/ *noun* [U, C] (*pl.* **-ies**) ~ **(over/about/surrounding sb/sth)** public discussion and argument about sth that many people strongly disagree about, think is bad, or are shocked by: *to arouse/cause controversy* ◊ *a bitter controversy over/about the site of the new airport* ◊ *the controversy surrounding his latest movie* ◊ *The President resigned amid considerable controversy.*

**con·tro·vert** /ˌkɒntrəˈvɜːt; *NAmE* ˈkɑːntrəvɜːrt/ *verb* ~ **sth** (*formal*) to say or prove that sth is not true **SYN** **refute** ⊃ see also INCONTROVERTIBLE

**con·tu·sion** /kənˈtjuːʒn; *NAmE* -ˈtuː-/ *noun* [C, U] (*medical*) an injury to part of the body that does not break the skin **SYN** **bruise**

---

**con·un·drum** /kəˈnʌndrəm/ *noun* **1** a confusing problem or question that is very difficult to solve **2** a question, usually involving a trick with words, that you ask for fun **SYN** **riddle**

**con·ur·ba·tion** /ˌkɒnɜːˈbeɪʃn; *NAmE* ˌkɑːnɜːrˈb-/ *noun* (*formal*) a large area where towns have grown and joined together, often around a city

**con·va·lesce** /ˌkɒnvəˈles; *NAmE* ˌkɑːn-/ *verb* [I] (*formal*) to spend time getting your health and strength back after an illness **SYN** **recuperate**: *She is convalescing at home after her operation.*

**con·va·les·cence** /ˌkɒnvəˈlesns; *NAmE* ˌkɑːn-/ *noun* [sing., U] a period of time when you get well again after an illness or a medical operation; the process of getting well: *You need four to six weeks' convalescence.*

**con·va·les·cent** /ˌkɒnvəˈlesnt; *NAmE* ˌkɑːn-/ *adj.* connected with convalescence; in the process of convalescence: *a convalescent home* (= a type of hospital where people go to get well after an illness) ◊ *a convalescent child* ▶ **con·va·les·cent** *noun*: *I treated him as a convalescent, not as a sick man.*

**con·vec·tion** /kənˈvekʃn/ *noun* [U] (*specialist*) the process in which heat moves through a gas or a liquid as the hotter part rises and the cooler, heavier part sinks

**con·vect·or** /kənˈvektə(r)/ (*also* **con'vector heater**) *noun* a device for heating the air in a room using convection

**con·vene** /kənˈviːn/ *verb* (*formal*) **1** [T] ~ **sth** to arrange for people to come together for a formal meeting: *to convene a meeting* ◊ *A Board of Inquiry was convened immediately after the accident.* **2** [I] to come together for a formal meeting: *The committee will convene at 11.30 next Thursday.* ⊃ WORDFINDER NOTE at MEETING

**con·vener** (*also* **con·venor**) /kənˈviːnə(r)/ *noun* **1** a person who arranges meetings of groups or committees **2** (*BrE*) a senior official of a trade union at a factory or other place of work

**con·veni·ence** **B2** /kənˈviːniəns/ *noun* **1** **B2** [U] the quality of being useful, easy or suitable for sb: *We have provided seats for the convenience of our customers.* ◊ *For (the sake of) convenience, the two groups have been treated as one in this report.* ◊ *In this resort you can enjoy all the comfort and convenience of modern tourism.* ⊃ compare INCONVENIENCE ⊃ see also FLAG OF CONVENIENCE, MARRIAGE OF CONVENIENCE **2** **B1** [C] something that is useful and can make things easier or quicker to do, or more comfortable: *It was a great convenience to have the school so near.* ◊ *The house had all the modern conveniences* (= central heating, etc.) *that were unusual at that time.* ⊃ see also PUBLIC CONVENIENCE
**IDM** **at sb's con'venience** (*formal*) at a time or a place that is suitable for sb: *Can you telephone me at your convenience to arrange a meeting?* ⊃ more at EARLY *adj.*

**con'venience food** *noun* [C, U] food that you buy frozen or in a box or can and that you can prepare and cook very quickly and easily

**con'venience store** *noun* a small local shop that sells food, newspapers, etc. and has long opening hours

**con·veni·ent** **B1** /kənˈviːniənt/ *adj.* **1** **B1** useful, easy or quick to do; not causing problems: *A bicycle is often more convenient than a car in towns.* ◊ *I can't see him now—it isn't convenient.* ◊ *I'll call back at a more convenient time.* ◊ *Flying is the most convenient way to travel in such a large country as China.* ◊ (*disapproving*) *He used his wife's birthday as a convenient excuse for not going to the meeting.* ◊ **~ for sb** *When would be most convenient for a visit?* ◊ **it is ~ (for sb) to do sth** *It's much more convenient for me to drive there.* **2** **B1** near to a particular place; easy to get to: *The office is just five minutes from the station, so it's very convenient.* ◊ **for sth** (*BrE*) *The house is very convenient for several schools.* ◊ **~ to sth** (*NAmE*) *The hotel is convenient to downtown.* **OPP** **inconvenient** ▶ **con·veni·ent·ly** *adv.*: *The report can be conveniently divided into three main sections.* ◊ *The hotel is conveniently situated*

**convenor** 338

close to the beach. ◇ She conveniently forgot to mention that her husband would be at the party, too (= because it suited her not to say).

**con·ven·or** = CONVENER

**con·vent** /ˈkɒnvənt; NAmE ˈkɑːnvent, -vənt/ noun **1** a building in which a Christian community of NUNS (= members of a female religious community) live together **2** (also ˈconvent school) a school run by NUNS

**con·ven·tion** /kənˈvenʃn/ noun **1** [C, U] the way in which sth is done that most people in a society expect and consider to be polite or the right way to do it: social conventions ◇ She is a young woman who enjoys flouting conventions. ◇ **by ~** By convention the deputy leader was always a woman. ⇒ WORDFINDER NOTE at SOCIETY **2** [C] a large meeting of the members of a profession, a political party, etc. SYN conference: to hold a convention ◇ the Democratic Party Convention (= to elect a candidate for president) **3** [C] an official agreement between countries or leaders: the Geneva convention ◇ the United Nations convention on the rights of the child **4** [C, U] a traditional method or style in literature, art or the theatre: the conventions of Greek tragedy

**con·ven·tion·al** /kənˈvenʃənl/ adj. **1** (often disapproving) tending to follow what is done or considered acceptable by society in general; normal and ordinary, and perhaps not very interesting: conventional behaviour/morality ◇ She's very conventional in her views. OPP unconventional **2** [usually before noun] following what is traditional or the way sth has been done for a long time: conventional methods/approaches ◇ It's not a hotel, in the conventional sense, but rather a whole village turned into a hotel. ◇ You can use a microwave or cook it in a conventional oven. OPP unconventional **3** [usually before noun] (of medical treatment) using the usual scientific methods of Western medicine such as artificial drugs and operations: conventional medicine ◇ Conventional treatments for this condition have been only partially successful. ⇒ compare ALTERNATIVE MEDICINE, COMPLEMENTARY MEDICINE **4** [usually before noun] (especially of weapons) not nuclear: conventional forces/weapons ◇ a conventional power station (= using oil or coal as fuel, rather than nuclear power) ▶ **con·ven·tion·al·ity** /kənˌvenʃəˈnæləti/ noun [U] **con·ven·tion·al·ly** /kənˈvenʃənəli/ adv.: conventionally dressed ◇ conventionally grown food (= grown according to conventional methods) IDM see WISDOM

**con·ven·tion·eer** /kənˌvenʃəˈnɪə(r); NAmE -ˈnɪr/ noun (NAmE) a person who is attending a convention (= large meeting)

**con·verge** /kənˈvɜːdʒ; NAmE -ˈvɜːrdʒ/ verb **1** [I] **~ (on …)** (of people or vehicles) to move towards a place from different directions and meet: Thousands of supporters converged on London for the rally. **2** [I] (of two or more lines, paths, etc.) to move towards each other and meet at a point: There was a signpost where the two paths converged. **3** [I] if ideas, policies, aims, etc. converge, they become very similar or the same OPP diverge ▶ **con·ver·gent** /kənˈvɜːdʒənt; NAmE -ˈvɜːrdʒ-/ adj.: convergent lines/opinions **con·ver·gence** /-dʒəns/ noun [U]

**con·ver·sant** /kənˈvɜːsnt; NAmE -ˈvɜːrs-/ adj. **~ with sth** (formal) knowing about sth; familiar with sth: You need to become fully conversant with the company's procedures.

**con·ver·sa·tion** /ˌkɒnvəˈseɪʃn; NAmE ˌkɑːnvərˈs-/ noun [C, U] an informal talk involving a small group of people or only two; the activity of talking in this way: a phone conversation ◇ The main topic of conversation was the likely outcome of the election. ◇ I tried to make conversation (= to speak in order to appear polite). ◇ **~ with sb** I had a long conversation with her the other day. ◇ (BrE) to get **into** conversation with sb ◇ (NAmE) to get into a conversation with sb ◇ **~ about sth** We had to listen to endless conversations about high prices and food shortages. ◇ **in ~** Don was deep in conversation with the girl on his right. ⇒ SYNONYMS at DISCUSSION ⇒ EXPRESS YOURSELF at OPEN

**con·ver·sa·tion·al** /ˌkɒnvəˈseɪʃnəl; NAmE ˌkɑːnvərˈs-/ adj. **1** not formal; as used in conversation SYN colloquial: a casual and conversational tone ◇ I learnt conversational Spanish at evening classes. **2** [only before noun] connected with conversation: Men have a more direct conversational style. ▶ **con·ver·sa·tion·al·ly** /-nəli/ adv.: 'Have you been here long?' he asked conversationally.

**con·ver·sa·tion·al·ist** /ˌkɒnvəˈseɪʃənəlɪst; NAmE ˌkɑːnvərˈs-/ noun a person who is good at talking to others, especially in an informal way

**ˌconverˈsation piece** noun **1** an object that is talked about a lot because it is unusual **2** (art) a type of painting in which a group of people are shown in the countryside or in a home

**ˌconverˈsation stopper** noun (informal) a remark that is unexpected or that shocks people so that they do not know how to reply to it

**con·verse¹** /kənˈvɜːs; NAmE -ˈvɜːrs/ verb [I] **~ (with sb)** (formal) to have a conversation with sb

**con·verse²** /ˈkɒnvɜːs; NAmE ˈkɑːnvɜːrs/ noun the converse [sing.] (formal) the opposite of a fact or statement: Building new roads increases traffic and the converse is equally true: reducing the number and size of roads means less traffic. ▶ **con·verse** adj.: the converse effect

**con·verse·ly** /ˈkɒnvɜːsli; NAmE ˈkɑːnvɜːrs-/ adv. (formal) in a way that is the opposite of sth: You can add the fluid to the powder, or, conversely, the powder to the fluid.

**con·ver·sion** /kənˈvɜːʃn; NAmE -ˈvɜːrʒn/ noun **1** [U, C] **~ (from sth) (into/to sth)** the act or process of changing sth from one form, use or system to another: the conversion of farm buildings into family homes ◇ No conversion from analogue to digital data is needed. ◇ a metric conversion table (= showing how to change METRIC amounts into or out of another system) ◇ a firm which specializes in house conversions (= turning large houses into several smaller flats) **2** [U, C] **~ (from sth) (to sth)** the process or experience of changing sb's or your own religion or beliefs: the conversion of the Anglo-Saxons by Christian missionaries ◇ his conversion from Judaism to Christianity **3** [C] (in rugby and AMERICAN FOOTBALL) a way of scoring extra points after scoring a TRY or a TOUCHDOWN **4** [C] **barn/loft ~** a building or room that has been changed so that it can be used for a different purpose, especially for living in

**conˈversion van** (also **ˈvan conversion**) noun (US) a vehicle in which the back part behind the driver has been arranged as a living space

**con·vert** verb, noun
■ verb /kənˈvɜːt; NAmE -ˈvɜːrt/ **1** [T, I] to change or make sth change from one form, purpose, system, etc. to another: **~ sth** They took just nine months to convert the building. ◇ You need to ensure that you've converted the data properly. ◇ **~ sth into/to sth** The hotel is going to be converted into a nursing home. ◇ What rate will I get if I convert my dollars into euros? ◇ **~ (from sth) (to sth)** We've converted from oil to gas central heating. **2** [I] **~ into/to sth** to be able to be changed from one form, purpose, or system to another: a sofa that converts into a bed ◇ In fruits, starch converts into sugar. **3** [I, T] to change your religion or beliefs; to make sb change their religion or beliefs: **~ (from sth) (to sth)** He converted from Christianity to Islam. ◇ **~ sb (from sth) (to sth)** She was soon converted to the socialist cause. **4** [I, T] to change an opinion, a habit, etc.: **~ (from sth) (to sth)** I've converted to organic food. ◇ **~ sb (from sth) (to sth)** I didn't use to like opera but my husband has converted me. **5** [T] **~ sth** (in rugby and AMERICAN FOOTBALL) to score extra points after a TRY or a TOUCHDOWN IDM see PREACH
■ noun /ˈkɒnvɜːt; NAmE ˈkɑːnvɜːrt/ **~ (from sth) (to sth)** a person who has changed their religion, beliefs or opinions: a convert to Islam ◇ converts from other faiths ◇ a convert to the cause

**con·vert·er** (also **con·ver·tor**) /kənˈvɜːtə(r); NAmE -ˈvɜːrt-/ noun **1** a person or thing that converts something: a catalytic converter **2** (physics) a device for changing ALTERNATING CURRENT into DIRECT CURRENT or the other way around

æ cat | ɑː father | e bed | ɜː fur | ə about | ɪ sit | iː see | i happy | ɒ got (BrE) | ɔː saw | ʌ cup | ʊ put | uː too

**3** (*physics*) a device for changing a radio signal from one frequency to another

**con·vert·ible** /kənˈvɜːtəbl; *NAmE* -ˈvɜːrt-/ *adj., noun*
- *adj.* that can be changed to a different form or use: *a convertible sofa* (= one that can be used as a bed) ◊ *convertible currencies* (= ones that can be exchanged for those of other countries) ◊ **~ into/to sth** *The bonds are convertible into ordinary shares.* ▸ **con·vert·ibil·ity** /kənˌvɜːtəˈbɪləti; *NAmE* -ˌvɜːrt-/ *noun* [U]
- *noun* a car with a roof that can be folded down or taken off

**con·vex** /ˈkɒnveks; *NAmE* ˈkɑːn-/ *adj.* (of an outline or a surface) curving out: *a convex lens/mirror* **OPP** **concave** ▸ **con·vex·ity** /kɒnˈveksəti; *NAmE* kɑːn-/ *noun* [U]

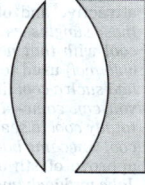
convex   concave

**con·vey** /kənˈveɪ/ *verb* **1** to make ideas, feelings, etc. known to sb **SYN** **communicate**: **~ sth** *Colours like red convey a sense of energy and strength.* ◊ **~ sth to sb** (*formal*) *Please convey my apologies to your wife.* ◊ **~ how, what, etc…** *He tried desperately to convey how urgent the situation was.* ◊ **~ that…** *She did not wish to convey that they were all at fault.* **2** **~ sb/sth (from …) (to …)** (*formal*) to take, carry or transport sb/sth from one place to another: *Pipes convey hot water from the boiler to the radiators.*

**con·vey·ance** /kənˈveɪəns/ *noun* **1** [U] (*formal*) the process of taking sb/sth from one place to another: *the conveyance of goods by rail* **2** [C] (*formal*) a vehicle: *horse-drawn conveyances* **3** [C] (*law*) a legal document that moves property from one owner to another

**con·vey·an·cer** /kənˈveɪənsə(r)/ *noun* a lawyer who is an expert in conveyancing

**con·vey·an·cing** /kənˈveɪənsɪŋ/ *noun* [U] (*law*) the branch of law that involves preparing the documents needed for moving property from one owner to another

**con·vey·or** /kənˈveɪə(r)/ *noun* **1** = **CONVEYOR BELT** **2** (*also* **con·vey·er**) (*formal*) a person or thing that carries sth or makes sth known: *Words are conveyors of meaning.*

**con'veyor belt** (*also* **con·vey·or**) *noun* a continuous moving band used for transporting goods from one part of a building to another, for example products in a factory or bags, cases, etc. in an airport: *a baggage conveyor belt*

**con·vict** *verb, noun*
- *verb* /kənˈvɪkt/ [often passive] to decide and state officially in court that sb is guilty of a crime: **be convicted (of sth)** *He was convicted of fraud.* ◊ *a convicted murderer* **OPP** **acquit**
- *noun* /ˈkɒnvɪkt; *NAmE* ˈkɑːn-/ (*also informal* **con**) a person who has been found guilty of a crime and sent to prison: *an escaped convict*

**con·vic·tion** /kənˈvɪkʃn/ *noun* **1** [C, U] the act of finding sb guilty of a crime in court; the fact of having been found guilty: *He plans to appeal against his conviction.* ◊ **on~** *She has six previous convictions for theft.* ◊ *a sentence of not more than five years' imprisonment* **OPP** **acquittal** **2** [C, U] a strong opinion or belief: *strong political/moral convictions* ◊ *She was motivated by deep religious conviction.* ◊ **~ that…** *a conviction that all would be well in the end* **3** [U] the quality of showing that you believe strongly in what you are saying: *'Not true!' she said with conviction.* ◊ *He said he agreed but his voice lacked conviction.* ◊ *The leader's speech in defence of the policy didn't carry much conviction.* **IDM** see **COURAGE**

**con·vince** /kənˈvɪns/ *verb* **1** to make sb/yourself believe that sth is true: **~ sb/yourself** *Are the prime minister's assurances enough to convince the public?* ◊ *to try/manage/fail to convince sb/yourself* ◊ **~ sb/yourself of sth** *You'll need to convince them of your enthusiasm for the job.* ◊ **~ sb/yourself (that)…** *I'd convinced myself (that) I was right.* **2** **~ sb to do sth** to persuade sb to do sth: *I've been trying to convince him to see a doctor.* ⇒ note at **PERSUADE**

**con·vinced** /kənˈvɪnst/ *adj.* **1** [not before noun] completely sure about sth: *Sam nodded but he didn't look convinced.* ◊ **~ of sth** *I am convinced of her innocence.* ◊ **~ by sb/sth** *I'm not entirely convinced by this argument.* ◊ **~ (that)…** *She became convinced that something was wrong.* **OPP** **unconvinced** ⇒ **SYNONYMS** at **SURE** **2** [only before noun] believing strongly in a particular religion or set of political ideas: *a convinced Christian*

**con·vin·cing** /kənˈvɪnsɪŋ/ *adj.* that makes sb believe that sth is true: *a convincing argument/explanation/case* ◊ *She sounded very convincing to me* (= I believed what she said). ◊ *a convincing victory/win* (= an easy one) **OPP** **unconvincing** ▸ **con·vin·cing·ly** *adv.*: *Her case was convincingly argued.* ◊ *They won convincingly.*

**con·viv·ial** /kənˈvɪviəl/ *adj.* cheerful and friendly in atmosphere or character **SYN** **sociable**: *a convivial evening/atmosphere* ◊ *convivial company* ▸ **con·vivi·al·ity** /kənˌvɪviˈæləti/ *noun* [U]

**con·vo·ca·tion** /ˌkɒnvəˈkeɪʃn; *NAmE* ˌkɑːn-/ *noun* (*formal*) **1** [C] a large formal meeting, especially of Church officials or members of a university **2** [U] the act of calling together a convocation **3** [C] (*NAmE*) a ceremony held in a university or college when students receive their degrees

**con·vo·luted** /ˈkɒnvəluːtɪd; *NAmE* ˈkɑːn-/ *adj.* **1** extremely complicated and difficult to follow: *a convoluted argument/explanation* ◊ *a book with a convoluted plot* **2** (*formal*) having many **TWISTS** or curves: *a convoluted coastline*

**con·vo·lu·tion** /ˌkɒnvəˈluːʃn; *NAmE* ˌkɑːn-/ *noun* [usually pl.] (*formal*) **1** a thing that is very complicated and difficult to follow: *the bizarre convolutions of the story* **2** a **TWIST** or curve, especially one of many: *the convolutions of the brain*

**con·voy** /ˈkɒnvɔɪ; *NAmE* ˈkɑːn-/ *noun* a group of vehicles or ships travelling together, especially when soldiers or other vehicles travel with them for protection: *a convoy of trucks/lorries/freighters* ◊ *A United Nations aid convoy loaded with food and medicine finally got through to the besieged town.*
**IDM** **in ˈconvoy** (of travelling vehicles) as a group; together: *We drove in convoy because I didn't know the route.*

**con·vulse** /kənˈvʌls/ *verb* **1** [T, I] **~ (sb) (with sth)** (*rather formal*) to cause a sudden shaking movement in sb's body; to make this movement: *A violent shiver convulsed him.* ◊ *His whole body convulsed.* **2** [T] **be convulsed with laughter, anger, etc.** to be laughing so much, so angry, etc. that you cannot control your movements

**con·vul·sion** /kənˈvʌlʃn/ *noun* [usually pl.] (*rather formal*) **1** a sudden shaking movement of the body that cannot be controlled **SYN** **fit**: *The child went into convulsions.* ◊ **in convulsions** *He fell to the ground in convulsions.* **2** a sudden important change that happens to a country or an organization **SYN** **upheaval**

**con·vul·sive** /kənˈvʌlsɪv/ *adj.* (of movements or actions) sudden and impossible to control: *a convulsive movement/attack/fit* ◊ *Her breath came in convulsive gasps.* ▸ **con·vul·sive·ly** *adv.*: *weeping convulsively*

**COO** /ˌsiː əʊ ˈəʊ/ *abbr.* Chief Operating Officer or Chief Operations Officer (the person who manages the day-to-day activities or work of a company or other institution)

**coo** /kuː/ *verb, exclamation*
- *verb* (**coo·ing, cooed, cooed**) **1** [I] when a **DOVE** or a **PIGEON** coos, it makes a soft low sound **2** [I, T] **(+ speech)** to say sth in a soft quiet voice, especially to sb you love ▸ **coo** *noun*
- *exclamation* (*BrE, old-fashioned, informal*) used to show that you are surprised: *Coo, look at him!*

**co-ocˈcur** *verb* [I] to occur together or at the same time: *The words 'heavy' and 'rain' co-occur frequently.* ▸ **co-ocˈcurrence** *noun* [U]

**cook** /kʊk/ *verb, noun*
- *verb* **1** [I, T] to prepare food by heating it, for example by boiling, baking or frying it: *Where did you learn to cook?*

# cookbook 340

◇ **~ sth** *to cook a meal* ◇ *to cook food/dinner* ◇ *What's the best way to cook trout?* ◇ (*especially BrE*) *I always have a cooked breakfast* (= consisting of cooked food) ◇ **~ sth for sb** *He cooked lunch for me.* ◇ **~ sb sth** *He cooked me lunch.* **2** [A2] [I] (of food) to be prepared by boiling, baking, frying, etc: *While the pasta is cooking, prepare the sauce.* **3** [I] **be cooking** (*informal*) to be planned secretly: *Everyone is being very secretive—there's something cooking.*
**IDM** **be cooking with ˈgas** (*informal*) to be doing sth very well and successfully **ˌcook the ˈbooks** (*informal*) to change facts or figures dishonestly or illegally: *His accountant had been cooking the books for years.* **ˌcook sb's ˈgoose** (*informal*) to destroy sb's chances of success
**PHRV** **ˌcook sth→ˈup 1** (*informal*) to invent sth, especially in order to trick sb **SYN** **concoct**: *to cook up a story* **2** to prepare a meal or a particular dish: *The friends cooked up a delicious Indian meal.*
■ *noun* [A2] a person who cooks food or whose job is cooking: *John is a very good cook* (= he cooks well). ◇ *She was employed as a cook in a hotel.* ⇒ compare CHEF
**IDM** **too many cooks spoil the ˈbroth** (*saying*) if too many people are involved in doing sth, it will not be done well

**cook·book** /ˈkʊkbʊk/ (*BrE also* **ˈcookery book**) *noun* a book that gives instructions on cooking and how to cook individual dishes

**cook·er** [A2] /ˈkʊkə(r)/ (*BrE*) (*NAmE* **range**) (*also* **stove** *NAmE, BrE*) *noun* a large piece of equipment for cooking food, containing an oven and gas or electric rings on top: *a gas cooker* ◇ *an electric cooker* ⇒ see also PRESSURE COOKER, SLOW COOKER, SOLAR COOKER

**cook·ery** /ˈkʊkəri/ *noun* [U] (*especially BrE*) the art or activity of preparing and cooking food: *a cookery course* ◇ *Italian cookery*

**ˈcookery book** *noun* (*BrE*) = COOKBOOK

**cookie** /ˈkʊki/ *noun* (*pl.* **-ies**) **1** (*especially NAmE*) a small flat sweet cake for one person, usually baked until hard and dry: *chocolate chip cookies* ◇ *a cookie jar* ⇒ compare BISCUIT, CRACKER ⇒ see also FORTUNE COOKIE **2 smart/tough ~** (*informal*) a smart/tough person **3** (*computing*) a computer file with information in it that is sent to the central SERVER each time a particular person uses a network or the internet: *Learn about our cookie policy.* ⇒ WORDFINDER NOTE at WEBSITE **IDM** see WAY *n.*

**ˈcookie cutter** *noun* (*especially NAmE*) an object used for cutting biscuits in a particular shape

**ˈcookie-cutter** *adj.* [only before noun] (*especially NAmE, disapproving*) having no special characteristics; not original in any way: *Handmade goods appeal to those who are tired of cookie-cutter products.*

**ˈcookie jar** *noun* (*NAmE*) a container for biscuits
**IDM** **get caught/found with your hand in the ˈcookie jar** (*informal*) to be discovered when doing sth that is illegal or dishonest

**ˈcookie sheet** (*NAmE*) (*BrE* **ˈbaking sheet**, **ˈbaking tray**) *noun* a small sheet of metal used for baking food on

**cook·ing** [A1] /ˈkʊkɪŋ/ *noun, adj.*
■ *noun* [U] **1** [A1] the process of preparing food by heating it: *My husband does all the cooking.* ◇ *We always use olive oil for cooking.* **2** food that has been prepared in a particular way: *The restaurant offers traditional home cooking* (= food similar to that cooked at home). ◇ *They serve good French cooking.*
■ *adj.* suitable for cooking: *cooking oil* ◇ *cooking sherry*

**ˈcooking gas** (*US*) (*BrE* **Calor gas™**) *noun* [U] a type of gas stored as a liquid under pressure in metal containers and used for heating and cooking in places where there is no gas supply

**cook·out** /ˈkʊkaʊt/ *noun* (*NAmE*) a meal or party when food is cooked over an open fire outdoors, for example at a beach ⇒ compare BARBECUE

**cook·ware** /ˈkʊkweə(r)/ *NAmE* -wer/ *noun* [U] pots and containers used in cooking ⇒ WORDFINDER NOTE at STORE

**cool** [A1] /kuːl/ *adj., verb, noun*
■ *adj.* (**ˈcool·er**, **ˈcool·est**)
• **FAIRLY COLD 1** [A1] fairly cold; not hot or warm: *cool air/water* ◇ *a cool breeze/drink/climate* ◇ *Cooler weather is forecast for the weekend.* ◇ *Let's sit in the shade and keep cool.* ◇ *Store lemons in a cool dry place.* ⇒ SYNONYMS at COLD
• **CLOTHES 2** helping you keep cool: *Wear light, cool clothing but try to avoid shorts.*
• **COLOURS 3** making you feel pleasantly cool: *a room painted in cool greens and blues*
• **APPROVING 4** [A1] (*informal*) used to show that you admire or approve of sb/sth because they are/it is fashionable, attractive and often different: *Doesn't she look cool in those sunglasses?* ◇ *He's a really cool guy.* ◇ *You look pretty cool with that new haircut.* ⇒ SYNONYMS at GREAT **5** [A1] (*informal*) used to describe sth that you like or enjoy: *We had such a cool time with Ed and his friends.* ◇ *I really hope you can come—it'd be so cool!* ◇ **it is ~ to do sth** *It was totally cool to see him in real life.* ◇ **it is ~ (that) ...** *It's really cool you came back!* **6** [A1] (*informal*) used to show that you approve of sth or agree to a suggestion: *We're meeting Jake for lunch and we can go on the yacht in the afternoon.* 'Cool!' ◇ *Can you come at 10.30 tomorrow?* 'That's cool.' ◇ **~ with sth** *I was surprised that she got the job, but I'm cool with it* (= it's not a problem for me). ◇ **~ about sth** *She's completely cool about what happened.*
• **CALM 7** [B2] calm; not excited, angry or emotional: *Keep cool!* ◇ *She tried to remain cool, calm and collected* (= calm). ◇ *He has a cool head* (= he stays calm in an emergency).
• **NOT FRIENDLY/ENTHUSIASTIC 8** [B2] not friendly, interested or enthusiastic: *They gave the prime minister a cool reception.* ◇ **~ about sth** *She was decidedly cool about the proposal.* ◇ **~ towards sb/sth** *He has been cool towards me ever since we had that argument.*
• **CONFIDENT 9** (*informal*) calm and confident in a way that lacks respect for other people, but makes people admire you even if they don't approve: *She just took his keys and walked out with them, cool as you please.*
• **MONEY 10** [only before noun] (*informal*) used about a sum of money to emphasize how large it is: *The car cost a cool thirty thousand.* ⇒ see also COOLLY, COOLNESS
**IDM** **(as) ˌcool as a ˈcucumber** very calm and showing control, especially in a difficult situation **ˌplay it ˈcool** (*informal*) to deal with a situation in a calm way and not show what you are really feeling **ˌtoo ˌcool for ˈschool** (*informal*) very fashionable: *The assistants look like they're too cool for school.* ⇒ more at LONG *adj.*
■ *verb*
• **BECOME COLDER 1** [B1] [I, T] to become cool or cooler; to make sb/sth become cool or cooler: *Glass contracts as it cools.* ◇ **~ sth** *The cylinder is cooled by a jet of water.*
• **BECOME CALMER 2** [B2] [I] to become calmer, less excited or less enthusiastic: *I think we should wait until tempers have cooled.* ◇ *Relations between them have definitely cooled* (= they are not as friendly with each other as they were).
**IDM** **ˈcool it!** (*informal*) used to tell sb to be calmer and less excited or angry **ˌcool your ˈheels** (*informal*) to have to wait for sb/sth
**PHRV** **ˌcool ˈdown/ˈoff 1** to become cool or cooler: *We cooled off with a swim in the lake.* **2** to become calm, less excited or less enthusiastic: *I think you should wait until she's cooled down a little.* **3** (*business*) to slow down or decrease: *Growth in the market has started to cool down.* **ˌcool sb↔ˈdown/ˈoff 1** to make sb feel cooler: *Drink plenty of cold water to cool yourself down.* **2** to make sb calm, less excited or less enthusiastic: *A few hours in a police cell should cool him off.* **ˌcool sth↔ˈdown/ˈoff 1** to make sth cool or cooler **2** (*business*) to make sth slower or less strong: *Demand is still too strong to cool down the property market.* **ˌcool ˈout** (*informal*) to relax and become calm after a period of activity or stress **SYN** **chill out**: *It's a wonderful place to cool out with a glass of beer.*
■ *noun* **the cool** [sing.] **1** cool air or a cool place: *the cool of the evening.* **2** [U] (*informal*) the quality of being fashionable, attractive or impressive: *all the cool of high fashion*
**IDM** **keep your ˈcool** (*informal*) to remain calm in a difficult situation **lose your ˈcool** (*informal*) to become angry or excited

**coola·bah** noun = COOLIBAH

**cool·ant** /'ku:lənt/ noun [C, U] a liquid that is used for cooling an engine, a nuclear REACTOR, etc.

**'cool bag** noun (BrE) a bag that keeps food or drinks cold and that can be used for a PICNIC ⊃ compare COOL BOX, COOLER, ICE CHEST

**'cool box** (BrE) (NAmE **'ice chest**) noun a box with thick sides that you put ice in to keep things cold, especially food and drinks ⊃ compare COOL BAG, COOLER (1)

**cool·drink** /'ku:ldrɪŋk/ noun (SAfrE) = SOFT DRINK

**cool·er** /'ku:lə(r)/ noun **1** a machine that cools things, especially drinks: *the office water cooler* ⊃ see also WATER COOLER **2** (especially NAmE) a container that keeps things cold, especially drinks: *They took a cooler full of drinks to the beach.* ⊃ compare COOL BAG, COOL BOX ⊃ see also WINE COOLER (2) **3** (NAmE) a drink with ice and usually wine in it ⊃ see also WINE COOLER (1)

**cool-'headed** adj. calm; not showing excitement or nerves: *a cool-headed assessment of the situation*

**coo·li·bah** (also **coola·bah**) /'ku:lɪbɑː/ noun an Australian tree that produces a strong hard wood

**coolie** /'ku:li/ noun (old-fashioned, taboo) an offensive word for a worker in Eastern countries with no special skills or training

**cooling-'off period** noun **1** a period of time during which two sides that disagree try to reach an agreement before taking further action, for example by going on strike **2** a period of time after sb has agreed to buy sth, such as an insurance plan, during which they can change their mind

**'cooling tower** noun a large high round building used in industry for cooling water before it is used again

**cool·ly** /'ku:lli/ adv. **1** in a way that is not friendly or enthusiastic: *'We're just good friends,' she said coolly.* ◇ *He received my suggestion coolly.* **2** in a calm way

**cool·ness** /'ku:lnəs/ noun [U] **1** the quality of being fairly cold: *the delicious coolness of the water* **2** the quality of being attractive and fashionable: *The band's frontman just exudes coolness.* **3** the ability to stay calm, and not get excited, angry or emotional: *I admire her coolness under pressure.* **4** a lack of friendly feeling: *I noticed a certain coolness between them.*

**coon** /ku:n/ noun (taboo, slang) a very offensive word for a black person

**'co-op** noun (informal) a COOPERATIVE shop, society or business: *a housing co-op*

**coop** /ku:p/ noun, verb
■ noun a CAGE for chickens, etc. IDM see FLY v.
■ verb
PHRV ▶ **,coop sb/sth 'up** [usually passive] to keep a person or an animal inside a building or in a small space

**coop·er** /'ku:pə(r)/ noun a person who makes BARRELS

**co·oper·ate** + C1 (BrE also **co-operate**) /kəʊ'ɒpəreɪt/ NAmE -'ɑːp-/ verb **1** + C1 [I] ~ (with sb) (in/on sth) to work together with sb else in order to achieve sth: *The two groups agreed to cooperate with each other.* ◇ *They had cooperated closely in the planning of the project.* **2** + C1 [I] ~ (with sb) to be helpful by doing what sb asks you to do: *Their captors told them they would be killed unless they cooperated.* ◇ *The company has agreed to cooperate with the employment survey.*

**co·oper·ation** + (BrE also **co-operation**) /kəʊˌɒpəˈreɪʃn/ NAmE -ˌɑːp-/ noun [U] **1** the fact of doing sth together or of working together towards a shared aim: *They offered their cooperation on the project.* ◇ **in ~ with sb** *a report produced by the government in cooperation with the chemical industry* ◇ **between A and B** *We would like to see closer cooperation between parents and schools.* ◇ **with sb** *We should like to thank you for your cooperation with us.* **2** ~ (with sb) (in doing sth) a desire to be helpful and do as you are asked: *We would be grateful for your cooperation in clearing the hall as quickly as possible.* ⊃ compare NONCOOPERATION

---

# coot

**341**

**co·opera·tive** + C1 W (BrE also **co-operative**) /kəʊˈɒpərətɪv; NAmE -'ɑːp-/ adj., noun
■ adj. **1** + C1 [usually before noun] involving doing sth together or working together with others towards a shared aim: *Cooperative activity is essential to effective community work.* ◇ *The documentary was a cooperative effort by film-makers from five countries.* **2** + C1 helpful by doing what you are asked to do: *Employees will generally be more cooperative if their views are taken seriously.* OPP **uncooperative 3** + C1 [usually before noun] (business) owned and run by the people involved, with the profits shared by them: *a cooperative farm* ◇ *The cooperative movement started in Britain in the nineteenth century.*
▶ **co·opera·tive·ly** (BrE also **co-operatively**) adv.
■ noun a cooperative business or other organization: *agricultural cooperatives in India* ◇ *The factory is now a workers' cooperative.*

**co-'opt** verb **1** ~ sb (onto/into sth) to make sb a member of a group, committee, etc. by the agreement of all the other members: *She was co-opted onto the board.* **2** ~ sb/sth (disapproving) to change sb/sth to a different role from the usual or original one; to take sb's idea and use it for your own purposes: *Politicians have been trying to co-opt the movement without embracing its values.*

**co·ord·in·ate** + C1 W (BrE also **co-ordinate**) verb, noun
■ verb /kəʊˈɔːdɪneɪt; NAmE -'ɔːrd-/ **1** + C1 [T] to organize the different parts of an activity and the people involved in it so that it works well: **~ sth** *They appointed a new manager to coordinate the work of the team.* ◇ *We need to develop a coordinated approach to the problem.* ◇ **~ sth with sth** *We try to coordinate our activities with those of other groups.* **2** [T] **~ sth** to make the different parts of your body work well together: *the part of the brain that coordinates body movements* ⊃ see also UNCOORDINATED **3** [I, T] **~ (sth) (with sth)** (rather formal) if you **coordinate** clothes, furniture, etc. or if they **coordinate**, they look nice together: *This shade coordinates with a wide range of other colours.*
■ noun /kəʊˈɔːdɪnət; NAmE -'ɔːrd-/ **1** [C] either of two numbers or letters used to fix the position of a point on a map or GRAPH: *the x, y coordinates of any point on a line* **2** **coordinates** [pl.] (used in shops, etc.) pieces of clothing that can be worn together because, for example, the colours look good together

**co'ordinate clause** /kəʊˌɔːdɪnət 'klɔːz; NAmE -ˌɔːrd-/ noun (grammar) each of two or more parts of a sentence, often joined by *and*, *or*, *but*, etc., that make separate statements that each have equal importance ⊃ compare SUBORDINATE CLAUSE

**Co,ordinated Uni,versal 'Time** noun [U] = UTC

**co,ord·in·ating con'junc·tion** noun (grammar) a word such as *or*, *and* or *but*, that connects clauses or sentences of equal importance ⊃ compare SUBORDINATING CONJUNCTION

**co·ord·in·ation** + C1 W (BrE also **co-ordination**) /kəʊˌɔːdɪˈneɪʃn; NAmE -ˌɔːrd-/ noun [U] **1** + C1 the act of making parts of sth, groups of people, etc. work together in an efficient and organized way: *The aim was to improve the coordination of services.* ◇ **~ between A and B** *a need for greater coordination between departments* ◇ **in ~ with sb/sth** *a pamphlet produced by the government in coordination with* (= working together with) *the Sports Council* ◇ *advice on colour coordination* (= choosing colours that look nice together, for example in clothes or furniture) **2** the ability to control your movements well: *You need good hand-eye coordination to play ball games.*

**co·ord·in·ator** + C1 (BrE also **co-ordinator**) /kəʊˈɔːdɪneɪtə(r); NAmE -'ɔːrd-/ (BrE also **co-ordinator**) noun a person who organizes the different parts of an activity and the people involved in it so that it works well: *The campaign needs an effective coordinator.*

**coot** /ku:t/ noun **1** a black bird with a white FOREHEAD and BEAK that lives on or near water **2** old ~ (NAmE, informal) a stupid person IDM see BALD

---

◉ Oxford Phrasal Academic Lexicon (OPAL) written and spoken word lists | W OPAL written word list | S OPAL spoken word list

# cop

**cop** /kɒp; NAmE kɑːp/ noun, verb
- **noun** (informal) a police officer: *Somebody call the cops!* ◊ *children playing cops and robbers* ◊ *a TV cop show*
- IDM **not much 'cop** (BrE, slang) not very good: *He's not much cop as a singer.* ⊃ more at FAIR adj.
- **verb** (-pp-) (informal) 1 ~ sth to receive or suffer sth unpleasant: *He copped all the hassle after the accident.* 2 ~ sth to notice sth: *Cop a load of this!* (= Listen to this) IDM **cop a 'plea** (NAmE, informal) to admit in court to being guilty of a small crime in the hope of receiving less severe punishment than for a more serious crime ⊃ compare PLEA BARGAINING 'cop it (BrE, slang) 1 to be punished 2 to be killed PHRV cop 'off (with sb) (BrE, slang) to start a sexual or romantic experience with sb: *Who did he cop off with at the party?* 'cop out (of sth) (informal) to avoid or stop doing sth that you should do because you are afraid, lazy, etc: *You're not going to cop out at the last minute, are you?* ⊃ related noun COP-OUT

**cope** /kəʊp/ verb, noun
- **verb** [I] to deal successfully with sth difficult SYN **manage**: *I got to the stage where I wasn't coping any more.* ◊ ~ with sth *He wasn't able to cope with the stresses and strains of the job.* ◊ *Desert plants are adapted to cope with extreme heat.*
- **noun** a long loose piece of clothing worn by priests on special occasions

**copier** /'kɒpiə(r); NAmE 'kɑːp-/ noun (especially NAmE) = PHOTOCOPIER

**'co-pilot** noun a second pilot who helps the main pilot in an aircraft

**coping** /'kəʊpɪŋ/ adj. [only before noun] that enables sb to deal with sth difficult: *a coping strategy/mechanism*

**'coping saw** noun a SAW with a very narrow BLADE (= metal cutting edge) and a frame that has the shape of a D, used for cutting curves in wood ⊃ picture at SAW

**copious** /'kəʊpiəs/ adj. in large amounts SYN **abundant**: *copious* (= large) *amounts of water* ◊ *I took copious notes.* ◊ *She supports her theory with copious evidence.* ▶ **copiously** adv.: *bleeding copiously*

**'cop-out** noun [usually sing.] (informal, disapproving) a way of avoiding doing sth that you should do, or an excuse for not doing it: *Not turning up was just a cop-out.*

**copper** /'kɒpə(r); NAmE 'kɑːp-/ noun 1 [U] (symb. **Cu**) a chemical element. Copper is a soft red-brown metal used for making electric wires, pipes and coins: *a copper mine* ◊ *copper pipes* ◊ *copper-coloured hair* 2 **coppers** [pl.] (BrE) brown coins that do not have much value: *I only paid a few coppers for it.* 3 [C] (BrE, informal) a police officer

**copperhead** /'kɒpəhed; NAmE 'kɑːpərh-/ noun one of several types of poisonous snake that are brown in colour

**copperplate** /'kɒpəpleɪt; NAmE 'kɑːpərp-/ noun [U] a neat, old-fashioned way of writing with sloping letters joined together

**coppery** /'kɒpəri; NAmE 'kɑːp-/ adj. similar to or having the colour of COPPER: *coppery hair*

**coppice** /'kɒpɪs; NAmE 'kɑːp-/ verb, noun
- **verb** [T, I] ~ (sth) (specialist) to cut back young trees in order to make them grow faster
- **noun** a wood where the young trees are regularly cut back in order to make them grow faster and to provide wood for fires or building

**copra** /'kɒprə; NAmE 'kɑːp-/ noun [U] the dried white inner part of COCONUTS, from which oil is obtained

**copse** /kɒps; NAmE kɑːps/ noun a small area of trees growing together

**'cop shop** noun (BrE, informal) a police station

**copter** /'kɒptə(r); NAmE 'kɑːp-/ noun (informal) a helicopter

**copula** /'kɒpjələ; NAmE 'kɑːp-/ noun (grammar) = LINKING VERB

**copulate** /'kɒpjuleɪt; NAmE 'kɑːp-/ verb [I] ~ (with sb/sth) (specialist) to have sex ▶ **copulation** /ˌkɒpju'leɪʃn; NAmE ˌkɑːp-/ noun [U]

**copy** /'kɒpi; NAmE 'kɑːpi/ noun, verb
- **noun** (pl. -ies) 1 [C] a thing that is made to be the same as sth else, especially a document or a work of art: *The thieves replaced the original painting with a copy.* ◊ ~ of sth *a copy of a letter/report/document* ◊ *to have/get/obtain/receive a copy of sth* ◊ *He made careful copies of all the documents he found in the library.* ⊃ see also CARBON COPY, FAIR COPY, HARD COPY 2 [C] a single example of a book, newspaper, etc. of which many have been made: *The book sold 20000 copies within two weeks.* ◊ *to have/get/obtain/buy/order a copy* ◊ ~ of sth *a copy of a book* ◊ *a copy of 'The Times'* 3 [U] written material that is to be published in a newspaper, magazine, etc.; news or information that can be used in a newspaper article or advertisement: *The subeditors prepare the reporters' copy for the paper and write the headlines.* ◊ *This will make great copy for the advertisement.* 4 [C] = PHOTOCOPY: *Could I have ten copies of this page, please?* 5 [C] (IndE) a book used by students for writing exercises, etc. in
- **verb** (**copies, copying, copied, copied**) 1 [T] to make sth that is exactly like sth else: ~ sth *He taught himself by copying paintings in the Louvre.* ◊ ~ sth from sth *They copied the designs from those on Greek vases.* ⊃ WORDFINDER NOTE at FILE 2 [T] to write sth exactly as it is written somewhere else: ~ sth *The monks spent their days copying manuscripts.* ◊ ~ sth (from sth) (into/onto sth) *She copied the phone number into her address book.* ◊ ~ sth down/out *I copied out several poems.* 3 [T] (computing) to create an IDENTICAL (= similar in every detail) version of data, a program, etc. so that you can use it again somewhere else: ~ sth *The software has been illegally copied.* ◊ ~ sth to sth *You can copy the data to your new laptop in the usual way.* ◊ ~ sth (from sth) (into/onto sth) *Use the clipboard to copy and paste information from websites.* 4 [T] ~ sb/sth to behave or do sth in the same way as sb else SYN **imitate**: *She copies everything her sister does.* ◊ *Their tactics have been copied by other terrorist organizations.* 5 [I, T] to cheat in an exam, school work, etc. by writing what sb else has written and pretending it is your own work: ~ (from/off sb) *She was caught copying off another student.* ◊ ~ sth *Copying other students' work is not acceptable.* 6 [T] ~ sth = PHOTOCOPY PHRV copy sb 'in (on sth) to send sb a copy of a letter, an email message, etc. that you are sending to sb else: *Can you copy me in on your report?*

**copybook** /'kɒpibʊk; NAmE 'kɑːp-/ noun, adj.
- **noun** a book, used in the past by children in school, containing examples of writing which school students had to copy IDM see BLOT v.
- **adj.** [only before noun] (BrE) done exactly how it should be done: *It was a copybook operation by the police.*

**copycat** /'kɒpikæt; NAmE 'kɑːp-/ noun, adj.
- **noun** (informal, disapproving) used especially by children about and to a person who copies what sb else does because they have no ideas of their own
- **adj.** [only before noun] (of crimes or other actions) similar to and seen as copying an earlier well-known crime or action

**'copy editor** noun a person whose job is to correct and prepare a text for printing ▶ **'copy-edit** verb [T, I]

**copyist** /'kɒpiɪst; NAmE 'kɑːp-/ noun a person who makes copies of written documents or works of art

**copyright** /'kɒpiraɪt; NAmE 'kɑːp-/ noun, adj., verb
- **noun** [U, C] if a person or an organization holds the **copyright** on a piece of writing, music, etc., they are the only people who have the legal right to publish, broadcast, perform it, etc., and other people must ask their permission to use it or any part of it: *Copyright expires seventy years after the death of the author.* ◊ *They were sued for breach/infringement of copyright.* ◊ ~ in/on sth *Who owns the copyright on this song?*
- **adj.** (abbr. **C**) protected by copyright; not allowed to be copied without permission: *copyright material*
- **verb** ~ sth to get the copyright for sth

**copy·writer** /ˈkɒpiraɪtə(r); NAmE ˈkɑːp-/ noun a person whose job is to write the words for advertising material

**co·quette** /kɒˈket; NAmE koʊˈk-/ noun (literary, often disapproving) a woman who behaves in a way that is intended to attract men SYN **flirt** ▸ **co·quet·tish** /-ˈketɪʃ/ adj.: a coquettish smile **co·quet·tish·ly** adv.

**cor** /kɔː(r)/ (also **cor ˈblimey**) exclamation (BrE, old-fashioned, informal) used when you are surprised, pleased or impressed by sth: Cor! Look at that!

**cor·acle** /ˈkɒrəkl; NAmE ˈkɔːr-/ noun a small round boat with a wooden frame, used especially in Wales and Ireland

**coral** /ˈkɒrəl; NAmE ˈkɔːr-/ noun, adj.
■ noun 1 [U] a hard substance that is red, pink or white in colour, and that forms on the bottom of the sea from the bones of very small creatures. Coral is often used in jewellery: *coral reefs/islands* ◊ *a coral necklace* 2 [C] a creature that produces coral
■ adj. pink or red in colour, like coral: *coral lipstick*

**cor ang·lais** /ˌkɔːr ɒŋˈɡleɪ; NAmE ɔːn-/ noun (pl. **cors anglais** /ˌkɔːr ɒŋˈɡleɪ; NAmE ɔːn-/) (especially BrE) (also **English ˈhorn** especially in NAmE) a musical instrument of the WOODWIND group, like an OBOE but larger and playing lower notes

**cor·bel** /ˈkɔːbl; NAmE ˈkɔːrbl/ noun (architecture) a piece of stone or wood that sticks out from a wall to support sth, for example an ARCH

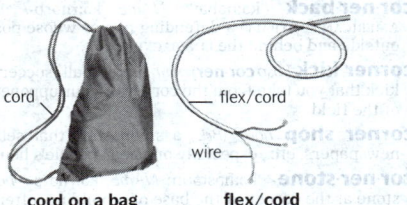
cord on a bag    flex/cord

**cord** /kɔːd; NAmE kɔːrd/ noun 1 [U, C] strong thick string or thin rope; a piece of this: *a piece/length of cord* ◊ *picture cord* (= used for hanging pictures) ◊ *a silk bag tied with a gold cord* 2 (especially NAmE) (BrE also **flex**) [C, U] a piece of wire that is covered with plastic, used for carrying electricity to a piece of equipment: *an electrical cord* ◊ *telephone cord* ⇒ see also CORDLESS 3 [C] (often in compounds) a part of the body that is like a piece of cord: *The baby was still attached to its mother by the cord.* ⇒ see also SPINAL CORD, UMBILICAL CORD, VOCAL CORDS 4 [U] = CORDUROY: *a cord jacket* 5 **cords** (also old-fashioned **cor·du·roys**) [pl.] trousers made of CORDUROY: *a pair of cords*

**cord·ed** /ˈkɔːdɪd; NAmE ˈkɔːrd-/ adj. 1 (of cloth) having raised lines SYN **ribbed** 2 (of a muscle) TENSE and standing out so that it looks like a piece of cord 3 that has a cord attached: *a corded phone* OPP **cordless**

**cor·dial** /ˈkɔːdiəl; NAmE ˈkɔːrdʒəl/ adj., noun
■ adj. (formal) pleasant and friendly: *a cordial atmosphere/meeting/relationship* ▸ **cor·di·al·ity** /ˌkɔːdiˈæləti; NAmE ˌkɔːrdʒi-/ noun [U]: *I was greeted with a show of cordiality.*
■ noun 1 (BrE) [U, C] a sweet drink that does not contain alcohol, made from fruit juice. It is drunk with water added: *blackcurrant cordial* 2 [U, C] (NAmE) = LIQUEUR 3 [C] a glass of cordial

**cor·di·ally** /ˈkɔːdiəli; NAmE ˈkɔːrdʒə-/ adv. (formal) 1 in a pleasant and friendly manner: *You are cordially invited to a celebration for Mr Michael Brown on his retirement.* 2 (used with verbs showing dislike) very much: *They cordially detest each other.*

**cord·ite** /ˈkɔːdaɪt; NAmE ˈkɔːrd-/ noun [U] an EXPLOSIVE used in bullets, bombs, etc.

**cord·less** /ˈkɔːdləs; NAmE ˈkɔːrd-/ adj. (of a phone or an electrical tool) not connected to its power supply by wires: *a cordless phone/drill* OPP **corded**

**cor·don** /ˈkɔːdn; NAmE ˈkɔːrdn/ noun, verb
■ noun a line or ring of police officers, soldiers, etc. guarding sth or stopping people from entering or leaving a place: *Demonstrators broke through the police cordon.* ⇒ WORDFINDER NOTE at POLICE
■ verb
PHRV **ˌcordon sth↔ˈoff** to stop people from getting into an area by surrounding it with police, soldiers, etc: *Police cordoned off the area until the bomb was made safe.*

**ˌcor·don ˈbleu** /ˌkɔːdɒ̃ ˈblɜː; NAmE ˌkɔːrdɒn ˈblɜː/ adj. [usually before noun] (from French) of the highest standard of skill in cooking: *a cordon bleu chef* ◊ *cordon bleu cuisine*

**cor·du·roy** /ˈkɔːdərɔɪ; NAmE ˈkɔːrd-/ noun 1 (also **cord**) [U] a type of strong soft cotton cloth with a pattern of raised straight lines on it, used for making clothes: *a corduroy jacket* 2 **cor·du·roys** [pl.] (old-fashioned) = CORDS

**core** 🔑 B2 W /kɔː(r)/ noun, adj., verb
■ noun 1 🔑 B2 the most important or central part of sth: *the core of the argument* ◊ *Dutch paintings form the core of the collection.* ◊ **at the~of sth** *Concern for the environment is at the core of our policies.* ⇒ see also COMMON CORE 2 the central part of an object: *the earth's core* ◊ *the core of a nuclear reactor* 3 the hard central part of a fruit such as an apple, that contains the seeds: *an apple core* ⇒ VISUAL VOCAB page V4 4 the muscles of the lower back and stomach area which help you to maintain good balance, etc. 5 a small group of people who take part in a particular activity: *He gathered a small core of advisers around him.* ⇒ see also HARD CORE, SOFT-CORE
IDM **to the ˈcore** so that the whole of a thing or a person is affected: *She was shaken to the core by the news.* ◊ *He's a politician to the core* (= in all his attitudes and actions).
■ adj. 1 🔑 most important; main or essential: *core subjects* (= subjects that all the students have to study) *such as English and mathematics* ◊ *the core curriculum* ◊ *We need to concentrate on our core business.* ◊ **~to sth** *The use of new technology is core to our strategy.* 2 B2 used to describe the most important or central beliefs, etc. of a person or group: *core beliefs/principles* ◊ *The party is losing touch with its core values.* 3 used to describe the most important members of a group: *The team is built around a core group of players.*
■ verb ~ sth to take out the core of a fruit

**corgi** /ˈkɔːɡi; NAmE ˈkɔːrɡi/ noun (pl. **corgis**) a small dog with short legs and a pointed nose

**cori·an·der** /ˌkɒriˈændə(r); NAmE ˌkɔːr-/ noun [U] a plant whose leaves are used in cooking as a HERB and whose seeds are used in cooking as a SPICE ⇒ compare CILANTRO ⇒ VISUAL VOCAB page V8

**Cor·inth·ian** /kəˈrɪnθiən/ adj. [usually before noun] (architecture) used to describe a style of architecture in ancient Greece that has thin columns with decorations of leaves at the top: *Corinthian columns/capitals*

**cork** /kɔːk; NAmE kɔːrk/ noun, verb
■ noun 1 [U] a light, soft material that is the thick BARK of a type of Mediterranean OAK tree: *a cork mat* ◊ *cork tiles* 2 [C] a small round object made of cork or plastic, that is used for closing bottles, especially wine bottles ⇒ SYNONYMS at LID
■ verb ~ sth to close a bottle with a cork OPP **uncork**

**corked** /kɔːkt; NAmE kɔːrkt/ adj (of wine) with a bad taste because the cork has DECAYED (= become destroyed by natural processes)

**cork·er** /ˈkɔːkə(r); NAmE ˈkɔːrk-/ noun [usually sing.] (BrE, old-fashioned, informal) a person or thing that is extremely good, beautiful or funny

**cork·screw** /ˈkɔːkskruː; NAmE ˈkɔːrk-/ noun, verb
■ noun a tool for pulling CORKS from bottles. Most corkscrews have a handle and a long TWISTED piece of metal for pushing into the cork.
■ verb [I] (+ adv./prep) to move in a particular direction while turning in circles

**corm** /kɔːm; NAmE kɔːrm/ noun the small round underground part of some plants, from which the new plant grows every year

# cormorant 344

**cor·mor·ant** /ˈkɔːmərənt; *NAmE* ˈkɔːrm-/ *noun* a large black bird with a long neck that lives near the sea or other areas of water

**corn** /kɔːn; *NAmE* kɔːrn/ *noun* **1** (*BrE*) [U] any plant that is grown for its grain, such as WHEAT, the grain of these plants: *a field of corn* ⋄ *ears/sheaves of corn* ⊃ see also SEED CORN **2** (*NAmE*) (*BrE* **maize**) [U] a tall plant grown for its large yellow grains that are used for making flour or eaten as a vegetable; the grains of this plant: *The major crops are wheat, barley and corn.* ⊃ VISUAL VOCAB page V5 ⊃ see also CORNCOB, CORN ON THE COB **3** (*BrE* **sweet·corn**) [U] the yellow seeds of a type of corn (MAIZE) plant, also called **corn**, which grow on thick STEMS and are cooked and eaten as a vegetable: *fresh corn and arugula salad* **4** [C] a small area of hard skin on the foot, especially the toe, that is sometimes painful

**ˌcorn ˈbeef** *noun* [U] = CORNED BEEF

**the ˈCorn Belt** *noun* the US states of the Midwest where CORN (MAIZE) is an important crop

**corn·bread** /ˈkɔːnbred; *NAmE* ˈkɔːrn-/ *noun* (*NAmE*) a kind of flat bread made with CORN (MAIZE) flour

**ˈcorn chip** *noun* [usually pl.] (*NAmE*) a thin hard piece of food made from CORN (MAIZE) that has been made into a flour and fried

**ˈcorn circle** *noun* = CROP CIRCLE

**corn·cob** /ˈkɔːnkɒb; *NAmE* ˈkɔːrnkɑːb/ (especially *BrE*) (also **cob** *NAmE*, *BrE*) *noun* the long hard part of the MAIZE plant that the rows of yellow grains grow on

**cor·nea** /ˈkɔːniə; *NAmE* ˈkɔːrn-/ *noun* (*anatomy*) the clear layer that covers and protects the outer part of the eye ▶ **cor·neal** /-əl/ *adj.* [only before noun]: *a corneal transplant*

**corned beef** /ˌkɔːnd ˈbiːf; *NAmE* ˈkɔːrnd/ (also **ˌcorn ˈbeef**) *noun* [U] beef that has been cooked and preserved using salt, often sold in tins

**cor·ner** ❶ ⒶⒶ /ˈkɔːnə(r); *NAmE* ˈkɔːrn-/ *noun, verb*

■ *noun*

• OF BUILDING/OBJECT/SHAPE **1** ⒶⒶ a part of sth where two or more sides, lines or edges join: *the four corners of a square* ⋄ *Write your address in the top right-hand corner of the letter.* ⋄ *the left/right corner* ⋄ *A smile lifted the corner of his mouth.* ⋄ **in the~of sth** *a speck of dirt in the corner of her eye* ⋄ *He scored with a shot into the bottom corner of the goal.*
• -CORNERED **2** (in adjectives) with the number of corners mentioned; involving the number of groups mentioned: *a three-cornered hat* ⋄ *a three-cornered fight*
• OF ROOM/BOX **3** ❶ ⒶⒶ the place inside a room or a box where two sides join; the area around this place: *A large desk occupies another corner of the room.* ⋄ **in the~(of sth)** *They made straight for the table in the corner.* ⋄ *a corner table/seat/cupboard*
• OF ROADS **4** ⒶⒶ a place where two streets join: *The wind hit him as he turned the corner.* ⋄ **on the~(of sth)** *There was a group of youths standing on the street corner.* ⋄ **at the ~(of sth)** *Turn right at the corner of Sunset and Crescent Heights Boulevards.* ⋄ **around/round the~(from sth)** *The bus stop is around the corner, I think.* **5** ⒶⒶ a sharp bend in a road: *The car was taking the corners too fast.*
• AREA/REGION **6** a region or an area of a place (sometimes used for one that is far away or difficult to reach): *She lives in a quiet corner of rural Yorkshire.* ⋄ *Students come here from the four corners of the world.* ⋄ *He knew every corner of the old town.*
• DIFFICULT SITUATION **7** [usually sing.] a difficult situation: *to back/drive/force sb into a corner* ⋄ *They had got her in a corner, and there wasn't much she could do about it.* ⋄ *He was used to talking his way out of tight corners.*
• IN SPORT **8** (in sports such as football (soccer) and hockey) a free kick or hit that you take from the corner of your opponent's end of the field: *to take a corner* ⋄ *The referee awarded a corner.* ⊃ see also CORNER KICK **9** (IN BOXING and WRESTLING) any of the four corners of a RING; the supporters who help in the corner

IDM **(just) around/round the ˈcorner** very near: *Her house is just around the corner.* ⋄ (*figurative*) *There were good times around the corner* (= they would soon come). **be in sb's ˈcorner** | **have sb in your ˈcorner** to support and encourage sb; to have sb who supports and encourages you **cut ˈcorners** (*disapproving*) to do sth in the easiest, cheapest or quickest way, often by ignoring rules or leaving sth out **cut the ˈcorner** (also **cut off the ˈcorner** especially in *BrE*) to go across the corner of an area and not around the sides of it, because it is quicker **see sth out of the corner of your ˈeye** to see sth by accident or not very clearly because you see it from the side of your eye and are not looking straight at it: *Out of the corner of her eye, she saw him coming closer.* **turn the ˈcorner** to pass a very important point in an illness or a difficult situation and begin to improve ⊃ more at FIGHT *v.*, SPOT *n.*

■ *verb*
• TRAP SB **1** [T, often passive] **~sb/sth** to get a person or an animal into a place or situation from which they cannot escape: *The man was finally cornered by police in a garage.* ⋄ *If cornered, the snake will defend itself.* **2** [T] **~sb** to go towards sb in a determined way, because you want to speak to them: *I found myself cornered by her on the stairs.*
• THE MARKET **3** [T] **~the market (in sth)** to get control of the trade in a particular type of goods: *They've cornered the market in silver.*
• OF VEHICLE/DRIVER **4** [I] to go around a corner: *The car corners well* (= it is easy to go around corners in it).

**cor·ner·back** /ˈkɔːnəbæk; *NAmE* ˈkɔːrnərb-/ *noun* (in AMERICAN FOOTBALL) a defending player whose position is outside and behind the LINEBACKERS

**ˈcorner kick** (also **corˈner**) *noun* (in football (soccer)) a free kick that you take from the corner of your opponent's end of the field

**ˈcorner shop** *noun* (*BrE*) a small shop that sells food, newspapers, etc., especially one near people's houses

**cor·ner·stone** /ˈkɔːnəstəʊn; *NAmE* ˈkɔːrnərs-/ *noun* **1** a stone at the corner of the base of a building, often laid in a special ceremony **2** the most important part of sth that the rest depends on: *This study is the cornerstone of the whole research programme.*

**cor·net** /ˈkɔːnɪt; *NAmE* ˈkɔːrn-/ *noun* **1** a BRASS musical instrument like a small TRUMPET **2** (*BrE*, *old-fashioned*) = CONE (4): *an ice-cream cornet*

**ˈcorn exchange** *noun* (*BrE*) a building where grain used to be bought and sold

**corn·field** /ˈkɔːnfiːld; *NAmE* ˈkɔːrn-/ *noun* a field in which CORN is grown

**corn·flakes** /ˈkɔːnfleɪks; *NAmE* ˈkɔːrn-/ *noun* [pl.] a breakfast food made from small dry yellow pieces of MAIZE, usually eaten with milk and sugar

**corn·flour** /ˈkɔːnflaʊə(r); *NAmE* ˈkɔːrn-/ (*BrE*) (*NAmE* **corn·starch**) *noun* [U] fine white flour made from MAIZE, used especially for making sauces thicker

**corn·flower** /ˈkɔːnflaʊə(r); *NAmE* ˈkɔːrn-/ *noun* a small wild plant with blue flowers

**cor·nice** /ˈkɔːnɪs; *NAmE* ˈkɔːrn-/ *noun* (*architecture*) a border around the top of the walls in a room or on the outside walls of a building

**Corn·ish** /ˈkɔːnɪʃ; *NAmE* ˈkɔːrn-/ *noun, adj.*
■ *noun* [U] the Celtic language that was spoken in Cornwall in England. Nobody now uses Cornish as a first language.
■ *adj.* connected with Cornwall, or its people, language or culture

**ˌCornish ˈpasty** *noun* (*BrE*) a small PIE in the shape of a half circle, containing meat and vegetables

**corn·meal** /ˈkɔːnmiːl; *NAmE* ˈkɔːrn-/ *noun* [U] flour made from MAIZE

**ˌcorn on the ˈcob** *noun* [U] MAIZE that is cooked with all the grains still attached to the inner part and eaten as a vegetable ⊃ VISUAL VOCAB page V5

**corn·rows** /ˈkɔːnrəʊz; *NAmE* ˈkɔːrn-/ *noun* [pl.] a HAIRSTYLE worn especially by black women, in which the hair is put into lines of PLAITS along the head

---

æ cat | ɑː father | e bed | ɜː fur | ə about | ɪ sit | iː see | i happy | ɒ got (*BrE*) | ɔː saw | ʌ cup | ʊ put | uː too

**corn‑starch** /ˈkɔːnstɑːtʃ/ *NAmE* ˈkɔːrnstɑːrtʃ/ (*NAmE*) (*BrE* **corn flour**) *noun* [U] fine white flour made from CORN (MAIZE), used especially for making sauces thicker

**ˈcorn syrup** *noun* [U] a thick sweet liquid made from MAIZE and used in cooking

**cor‑nu‑co‑pia** /ˌkɔːnjuˈkəʊpiə/ *NAmE* ˌkɔːrnəˈk-/ *noun* **1** an object like an animal's HORN in shape, shown in art as full of fruit and flowers **2** (*formal*) something that is or contains a large supply of good things: *The book is a cornucopia of good ideas.*

**corny** /ˈkɔːni/ *NAmE* ˈkɔːrni/ *adj.* (**corn‑ier**, **corni‑est**) (*informal*) not original; used too often to be interesting or to sound sincere: *a corny joke/song* ◊ *I know it sounds corny, but it really was love at first sight!*

**cor‑olla** /kəˈrɒlə/ *NAmE* -ˈroʊlə, -ˈrɑːlə/ *noun* (*biology*) the ring of PETALS around the central part of a flower

**cor‑ol‑lary** /kəˈrɒləri/ *NAmE* ˈkɔːrəleri/ *noun* (*pl.* **-ies**) **~ (of/to sth)** (*formal* or *specialist*) a situation, an argument or a fact that is the natural and direct result of another one

**cor‑ona** /kəˈrəʊnə/ *noun* (*pl.* **co·ro·nae** /-niː/) (*astronomy*) (*also informal* **halo**) a ring of light seen around the sun or moon, especially during an ECLIPSE

**cor‑on‑ary** /ˈkɒrənri/ *NAmE* ˈkɔːrəneri/ *adj.* (*medical*) relating to the heart, particularly the ARTERIES that take blood to the heart: *coronary (heart) disease* ◊ *a coronary patient* (= sb suffering from coronary disease)

**ˌcoronary ˈartery** *noun* (*anatomy*) either of the two ARTERIES that supply blood to the heart

**ˌcoronary throm‑ˈbosis** (*also informal* **cor‑on·ary**) *noun* [C, U] (*medical*) a blocking of the flow of blood by a blood CLOT in an ARTERY supplying blood to the heart ⊃ compare HEART ATTACK

**cor‑on‑ation** /ˌkɒrəˈneɪʃn/ *NAmE* ˌkɔːr-/ *noun* a ceremony at which a CROWN (= an object in the shape of a circle, usually made of gold and precious stones) is formally placed on the head of a new king or queen and they officially become king or queen

**cor‑on‑er** /ˈkɒrənə(r)/ *NAmE* ˈkɔːr-/ *noun* an official whose job is to discover the cause of any sudden, violent or SUSPICIOUS death by holding an INQUEST

**cor‑onet** /ˈkɒrənet/ *NAmE* ˌkɔːrəˈnet/ *noun* **1** a small CROWN worn on the head on formal occasions by princes, princesses, lords, etc. **2** a round decoration for the head, especially one made of flowers

**Corp.** *abbr.* CORPORATION

**cor‑pora** /ˈkɔːpərə/ *NAmE* ˈkɔːrp-/ *pl.* of CORPUS

**cor‑poral** /ˈkɔːpərəl/ *NAmE* ˈkɔːrp-/ *noun* (*abbr.* **Cpl**) a member of one of the lower ranks in the army, the MARINES or the British AIR FORCE: *Corporal Smith* ⊃ see also LANCE CORPORAL

**ˌcorporal ˈpunishment** *noun* [U] the physical punishment of people, especially by hitting them

**cor‑por‑ate** ⓘ B2 /ˈkɔːpərət/ *NAmE* ˈkɔːrp-/ *adj.* [only before noun] **1** ⓘ B2 connected with a large business company: *corporate finance/profits/tax* ◊ *corporate executives/clients/sponsors* ◊ *corporate identity* (= the image of a company, which all its members share) ◊ *corporate hospitality* (= when companies entertain customers to help develop good business relationships) **2** (*specialist*) forming a CORPORATION (= an organization or group of organizations that is recognized by law as a single unit): *The BBC is a corporate organization.* ◊ *The law applies both to individuals and to corporate bodies.* **3** involving or shared by all the members of a group ▶ **cor‑por·ate·ly** *adv.*: *The apartment block is corporately owned.* ◊ *corporately sponsored events*

**ˌcorporate ˈraider** *noun* (*business*) a person or company that regularly buys large numbers of shares in other companies against their wishes, either to control the company or to sell the shares again for a large profit

**ˌcorporate reˈsponsiˈbility** *noun* [U] the idea that a large company has a duty to treat people fairly and to play a positive part in society

**ˌcorporate ˈwelfare** *noun* [U] (especially *NAmE*, *disapproving*) government support of private business, for example by special payments or tax deals

**cor‑por‑ation** ⓘ+ B2 /ˌkɔːpəˈreɪʃn/ *NAmE* ˌkɔːrp-/ *noun* **1** ⓘ+ B2 (*abbr.* **Corp.**) a large business company: *multinational corporations* ◊ *the Chrysler corporation* **2** an organization or a group of organizations that is recognized by law as a single unit: *urban development corporations* **3** (*BrE*) a group of people elected to govern a large town or city and provide public services

**ˌcorpoˈration tax** *noun* [U] (*BrE*) a tax that companies pay on their profits

**cor‑por‑at‑ism** /ˈkɔːpərətɪzəm/ *NAmE* ˈkɔːrp-/ *noun* [U] the control of a country, etc. by large groups, especially businesses

**cor‑por‑at‑or** /ˈkɔːpəreɪtə(r)/ *NAmE* ˈkɔːrp-/ *noun* (*IndE*) an elected member of the government of a town or city

**cor‑por‑eal** /kɔːˈpɔːriəl/ *NAmE* kɔːrˈp-/ *adj.* (*formal*) **1** that can be touched; physical rather than spiritual: *his corporeal presence* **2** of or for the body: *corporeal needs*

**corps** /kɔː(r)/ *noun* (*pl.* **corps** /kɔːz/ *NAmE* kɔːrz/) [C + sing. / pl. v.] **1** a large unit of an army, consisting of two or more DIVISIONS: *the commander of the third army corps* **2** one of the groups of an army with a special responsibility: *the Royal Army Medical Corps* **3** a group of people involved in a particular job or activity: *a corps of trained and experienced doctors* ⊃ see also DIPLOMATIC CORPS, PRESS CORPS

**corps de bal‑let** /ˌkɔː də ˈbæleɪ/ *NAmE* ˌkɔːr də bæˈleɪ/ *noun* [C + sing. / pl. v.] (from French) dancers in a BALLET company who dance together as a group

**corpse** /kɔːps/ *NAmE* kɔːrps/ *noun* a dead body, especially of a human

**cor‑pu‑lent** /ˈkɔːpjələnt/ *NAmE* ˈkɔːrp-/ *adj.* (*formal*) (of a person) fat. People say 'corpulent' to avoid saying 'fat'. ▶ **cor‑pu‑lence** /-ləns/ *noun* [U]

**cor‑pus** /ˈkɔːpəs/ *NAmE* ˈkɔːrp-/ *noun* (*pl.* **cor‑pora** /-pərə/ or **cor‑puses**) (*specialist*) a collection of written or spoken texts: *a corpus of 100 million words of spoken English* ◊ *the whole corpus of Renaissance poetry* ⊃ see also HABEAS CORPUS

**cor‑puscle** /ˈkɔːpʌsl/ *NAmE* ˈkɔːrp-/ *noun* (*anatomy*) any of the red or white cells found in blood: *red/white corpuscles*

**cor‑ral** /kəˈrɑːl/ *NAmE* -ˈræl/ *noun*, *verb*
■ *noun* (in North America) an area with a fence around it, for horses, cows, etc. on a farm or RANCH: *They drove the ponies into a corral.*
■ *verb* (-ll-, *US also* -l-) **1 ~ sth** to force horses or cows into a corral **2 ~ sb** to gather a group of people together and keep them in a particular place

**cor‑rect** ⓘ A1 Ⓦ /kəˈrekt/ *adj.*, *verb*
■ *adj.* **1** ⓘ A1 accurate or true, without any mistakes ⓢⓨⓝ **right**: *Do you have the correct time?* ◊ *the correct answer* ◊ *Please check that these details are correct.* ◊ *'Are you in charge here?' 'That's correct.'* ◊ *As always, your grandmother is absolutely correct.* ◊ *~ in (doing) sth Am I correct in saying that you know a lot about wine?* ⓞⓟⓟ **incorrect** ⊃ SYNONYMS at TRUE **2** ⓘ A1 right and suitable, so that sth is done as it should be done: *the correct procedure/approach* ◊ *Do you know the correct way to shut the machine down?* ◊ *I think you've made the correct decision.* ⊃ SYNONYMS at RIGHT **3** taking care to speak or behave in a way that follows the accepted standards or rules: *a correct young lady* ◊ *He is always very correct in his speech.* ⓞⓟⓟ **incorrect** ⊃ see also POLITICALLY CORRECT ▶ **cor‑rect‑ness** *noun* [U]: *The correctness of this decision may be doubted.* ⊃ see also POLITICAL CORRECTNESS ⓘⓓⓜ see PRESENT *adj.*
■ *verb* **1** ⓘ A1 to make sth right or accurate, for example by changing it or removing mistakes: **~ sth** *to correct an error* ◊ *Read through your work and correct any mistakes that you find.* ◊ *I thought we had corrected the problem.* ◊ *Their eyesight can be corrected in just a few minutes by the use of a laser.* ◊ *They issued a statement correcting the one they had made earlier.* ◊ **~ yourself** *He stopped and corrected*

# correction

▼ **EXPRESS YOURSELF**

### Correcting yourself
When you say something that was not quite what you intended, you can correct yourself in various ways:
- I'll be there at five fifteen, **I mean** five fifty—ten to six.
- It'll be Tuesday—sorry, **I meant to say** Thursday.
- **Sorry, what I mean is,** we need two handouts per person.
- We can meet in the conference centre—**or rather** in front of the centre.
- The painter—**or should I say,** the sculptor—was born in Padua.
- It's one t and double s—**no, sorry,** one s and double t.
- It's on the fifth floor—**no, actually,** it's the fourth.
- Can I get two lattes and an espresso—**no, scratch that**—three lattes? (NAmE, informal)
- There are three items on tonight's agenda. **Correction,** four items.

himself. 'I mean fifteen, not fifty.' **2** ~ **sth** (of a teacher) to mark the mistakes in a piece of work (and sometimes give a mark to the work): *I spent all evening correcting essays.* **3** to tell sb that they have made a mistake: ~ **sb** *Correct me if I'm wrong, but isn't this last year's brochure?* ◇ *Yes, you're right—I stand corrected* (= I accept that I made a mistake). ◇ ~ **sb + speech** *'It's Yates, not Wates,' she corrected him.*

**cor·rec·tion** /kəˈrekʃn/ *noun, exclamation*
- **noun 1** [C] ~ **(to sth)** a change that makes sth more accurate than it was before: *I've made a few small corrections to your report.* ◇ *The paper had to publish a correction to the story.* **2** [U] the act or process of correcting sth: *There are some programming errors that need correction.* **3** [U] (*old-fashioned*) punishment: *the correction of young offenders*
- **exclamation** (*informal*) used when you want to correct sth that you have just said: *I don't know. Correction—I do know, but I'm not going to tell you.*

**cor·rec·tion·al** /kəˈrekʃənl/ *adj.* [only before noun] (*especially NAmE*) connected with improving the behaviour of criminals, usually by punishing them: *a correctional center/institution/facility* (= a prison)

**cor'rection fluid** *noun* [U] a white liquid that you use to cover mistakes that you make when you are writing or typing, and that you can write on top of

**cor·rect·ive** /kəˈrektɪv/ *adj., noun*
- **adj.** (*formal*) designed to make sth right that was wrong before: *We need to take corrective action to halt this country's decline.* ◇ *corrective measures* ◇ *corrective surgery/glasses*
- **noun** ~ **(to sth)** (*formal*) something that helps to give a more accurate or fairer view of sb/sth: *I should like to add a corrective to what I have written previously.*

**cor·rect·ly** /kəˈrektli/ *adv.* **1** in a way that is accurate or true, without any mistakes: *Have you spelled it correctly?* ◇ *Students correctly identified 16 trees species found on their study sites.* ◇ *If I remember correctly, he was still the prime minister at that point.* ◇ *They reasoned, correctly, that she was away for the weekend.* **OPP incorrectly 2** in a way that is right and suitable, so that sth is done as it should be done: *When correctly applied, fake tan is difficult to tell from the real thing.* **OPP incorrectly 3** in a way that follows the accepted standards or rules: *He was looking correctly grave.*

**cor·rel·ate** /ˈkɒrəleɪt; NAmE ˈkɔːr-/ *verb* **1** [I] if two or more facts, figures, etc. **correlate** or if a fact, figure, etc. **correlates** with another, the facts are closely connected and affect or depend on each other: *The figures do not seem to correlate.* ◇ ~ **with sth** *A high-fat diet correlates with a greater risk of heart disease.* **2** [T] ~ **sth** to show that there is a close connection between two or more facts, figures, etc: *Researchers are trying to correlate the two sets of figures.* ▶ **cor·rel·ate** /-lət/ *noun*

**cor·rel·ation** /ˌkɒrəˈleɪʃn; NAmE ˌkɔːr-/ *noun* [C, U] a connection between two things in which one thing changes as the other does: ~ **between A and B** *There is a direct correlation between exposure to sun and skin cancer.* ◇ ~ **of A with B** *the correlation of social power with wealth* ⊃ see also RANK CORRELATION

**cor·rela·tive** /kəˈrelətɪv/ *noun* (*formal*) a fact or an idea that is closely related to or depends on another fact or idea ▶ **cor·rela·tive** *adj.*

**cor·re·spond** /ˌkɒrəˈspɒnd; NAmE ˌkɔːrəˈspɑːnd/ *verb* **1** [I] to be the same as or match sth **SYN agree, tally**: *Your account and hers do not correspond.* ◇ ~ **with sb** *Your account of events does not correspond with hers.* ◇ ~ **to sth** *The written record of the conversation doesn't correspond to* (= is different from) *what was actually said.* **2** [I] ~ **(to sth)** to be similar to or the same as sth else: *The British job of Lecturer corresponds roughly to the US Associate Professor.* **3** [I] ~ **(with sb)** (*formal*) to write letters or emails, etc. to sb and receive letters or emails, etc. from them

**cor·res·pond·ence** /ˌkɒrəˈspɒndəns; NAmE ˌkɔːrəˈspɑːn-/ *noun* (*formal*) **1** [U] the letters, emails, etc. a person sends and receives: *personal/private correspondence* ◇ *The editor welcomes correspondence from readers on any subject.* ◇ *the correspondence column/page* (= in a newspaper) ◇ *Jane Austen's correspondence with her sister* **2** [U, C] the activity of writing letters: ~ **(with sb)** *I refused to enter into any correspondence* (= to exchange letters) *with him about it.* ◇ **in ~** *We have been in correspondence for months.* ◇ *We kept up a correspondence for many years.* **3** [C, U] ~ **(between A and B)** a connection between two things; the fact of two things being similar: *There is a close correspondence between the two extracts.*

**corre'spondence course** *noun* a course of study that you do at home, communicating with your teacher by post or email and sometimes using materials on the internet

**cor·res·pond·ent** /ˌkɒrəˈspɒndənt; NAmE ˌkɔːrəˈspɑːn-/ *noun* **1** a person who reports news from a particular country or on a particular subject for a newspaper or a television or radio station: *the BBC's political correspondent* ◇ *a foreign/war/sports correspondent* ◇ *our Delhi correspondent* ⊃ WORDFINDER NOTE at JOURNALIST **2** (used with an adjective) a person who writes letters, emails, etc. to another person: *She's a poor correspondent* (= she does not write regularly).

**cor·res·pond·ing** /ˌkɒrəˈspɒndɪŋ; NAmE ˌkɔːrəˈspɑːn-/ *adj.* matching or connected with sth that you have just mentioned **SYN equivalent**: *A change in the money supply brings a corresponding change in expenditure.* ◇ *Profits have risen by 15 per cent compared with the corresponding period last year.* ◇ *The Redskins lost to the Cowboys in the corresponding game last year.* ◇ ~ **to sth** *Give each picture a number corresponding to its position on the page.* ▶ **cor·res·pond·ing·ly** *adv.*: *a period of high demand and correspondingly high prices*

**corresponding 'angles** *noun* [pl.] (*geometry*) equal angles formed on the same side of a line that crosses two PARALLEL lines ⊃ picture at ANGLE ⊃ compare ALTERNATE ANGLES

**cor·ri·dor** /ˈkɒrɪdɔː(r); NAmE ˈkɔːr-/ *noun* **1** (*NAmE also* **hall·way**) a long narrow passage in a building, with doors that open into rooms on either side: *His room is along the corridor.* **2** a long narrow piece of land belonging to one country that passes through the land of another country; a part of the sky over a country that planes, for example from another country, can fly through ⊃ see also AIR CORRIDOR **3** a long narrow piece of land that follows the course of an important road or river: *the electronics industry in the M4 corridor* **4** (*BrE*) a passage along the side of some railway trains, from which doors lead into separate COMPARTMENTS
**IDM the corridors of 'power** (*sometimes humorous*) the higher levels of government, where important decisions are made

**cor·rie** /ˈkɒri; NAmE ˈkɔːri/ *noun* (*geology*) a round hollow area in the side of a mountain, especially in Scotland

**cor·rob·or·ate** /kəˈrɒbəreɪt; NAmE -ˈrɑːb-/ verb [T, I, often passive] ~ (sth) (formal) to provide evidence or information that supports a statement, theory, etc. **SYN** **confirm**: *The evidence was corroborated by two independent witnesses.* ◊ *corroborating evidence* ▶ **cor·rob·or·ation** /kəˌrɒbəˈreɪʃn; NAmE -ˌrɑːb-/ noun [U]

**cor·rob·ora·tive** /kəˈrɒbərətɪv; NAmE -ˈrɑːbəreɪt-/ adj. (formal) [usually before noun] giving support to a statement or theory: *Is there any corroborative evidence for this theory?*

**cor·rode** /kəˈrəʊd/ verb **1** [T, I] ~ (sth) to slowly destroy or damage metal, stone or other materials by chemical action; to be destroyed in this way: *Acid corrodes metal.* ◊ *The copper pipework has corroded in places.* **2** [T] ~ sth to slowly destroy or make sth weaker: *Corruption corrodes public confidence in a political system.* ▶ **cor·ro·sion** /-ˈrəʊʒn/ noun [U]: *Look for signs of corrosion.* ◊ *Clean off any corrosion before applying the paint.*

**cor·ro·sive** /kəˈrəʊsɪv/ adj. **1** tending to destroy sth slowly by chemical action: *the corrosive effects of salt water* ◊ *corrosive acid* **2** (formal) tending to damage sth gradually: *Unemployment is having a corrosive effect on our economy.*

**cor·ru·gated** /ˈkɒrəgeɪtɪd; NAmE ˈkɔːr-/ adj. having the shape of a series of regular folds that look like waves: *a corrugated iron roof* ◊ *corrugated cardboard*

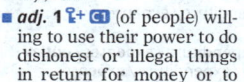
corrugated
corrugated iron

**cor·rupt** ͫ+ 🅲🅵 /kəˈrʌpt/ adj., verb

■ adj. **1** ͫ+ 🅲🅵 (of people) willing to use their power to do dishonest or illegal things in return for money or to get an advantage: *a corrupt regime* ◊ *corrupt officials accepting bribes* ͫ+ 🅲🅵 (of behaviour) not honest or moral: *corrupt practices* ◊ *The whole system is inefficient and corrupt.* **3** (computing) containing changes or faults, and no longer in the original state: *corrupt software* ◊ *The file on the disk seems to be corrupt.* ▶ **cor·rupt·ly** adv.

■ verb **1** [T, I] ~ (sb) to have a bad effect on sb and make them behave in a way that is not honest or moral: *He was corrupted by power and ambition.* ◊ *the corrupting effects of great wealth* **2** [T, often passive] ~ sth to change the original form of sth, so that it is damaged or made less good in some way: *a corrupted form of Buddhism* **3** [T, I] ~ (sth) (computing) to cause mistakes to appear in a computer file, etc. with the result that the information in it is no longer correct; (of a computer file, etc.) to start containing mistakes: *The program has somehow corrupted the system files.* ◊ *corrupted data* ◊ *The disk will corrupt if it is overloaded.*

**cor·rupt·ible** /kəˈrʌptəbl/ adj. that can be corrupted **OPP** **incorruptible**

**cor·rup·tion** ͫ+ 🅲🅵 /kəˈrʌpʃn/ noun **1** ͫ+ 🅲🅵 [U] dishonest or illegal behaviour, especially of people in authority: *allegations of bribery and corruption* ◊ *The new district attorney has promised to fight police corruption.* **2** ͫ+ 🅲🅵 [U] the act or effect of making sb change from moral to **IMMORAL** standards of behaviour: *He claimed that sex and violence on TV led to the corruption of young people.* **3** [C, usually sing., U] the form of a word or phrase that has become changed from its original form in some way; the process by which a word or phrase changes form in this way: *The word 'holiday' is a corruption of 'holy day'.* **4** [U] (computing) the effect when data is changed by accident in a computer system due to **HARDWARE** or software failure

**cor·sage** /kɔːˈsɑːʒ; NAmE kɔːr's-/ noun a small bunch of flowers that is worn on a woman's dress, for example at a wedding

**cor·set** /ˈkɔːsɪt; NAmE ˈkɔːrs-/ noun a piece of women's underwear, fitting the body tightly, worn especially in the past to make the middle part look smaller

**cor·tège** (also **cor·tege** especially in US) /kɔːˈteʒ, -ˈteɪʒ; NAmE kɔːrˈteʒ/ noun a line of cars or people moving along slowly at a **FUNERAL** (= ceremony for a dead person) **SYN** **funeral procession**

**cor·tex** /ˈkɔːteks; NAmE ˈkɔːrt-/ noun (pl. **cor·ti·ces** /-tɪsiːz/) (anatomy) the outer layer of an organ in the body, especially the brain: *the cerebral/renal cortex* (= around the brain/ **KIDNEY**) ▶ **cor·tic·al** /-tɪkl/ adj.

**cor·ti·sone** /ˈkɔːtɪzəʊn; NAmE ˈkɔːrt-/ noun [U] (medical) a **HORMONE** used in the treatment of diseases such as **ARTHRITIS**, to reduce **SWELLING** (= the condition of being larger than normal)

**cor·us·cate** /ˈkɒrəskeɪt; NAmE ˈkɔːr-/ verb (literary) **1** [I] (of light) to flash **2** [I] (of a person) to be full of life, enthusiasm or humour ▶ **cor·us·cat·ing** adj.: *coruscating wit* **cor·us·cat·ing·ly** adv.: *coruscatingly brilliant*

**cor·vette** /kɔːˈvet; NAmE kɔːrˈv-/ noun a small fast ship used in war to protect other ships from attack

**cos¹** (also **'cos**, **'cause**, **coz**) /kəz; BrE also kɒz/ conj. (BrE, informal) because: *I can't see her at all, cos it's too dark.*

**cos²** abbr. (in writing) **COSINE**

**COSATU** /kəʊˈsɑːtuː/ abbr. the Congress of South African Trade Unions (= a political organization in South Africa that represents many unions)

**cosh** /kɒʃ; NAmE kɑːʃ/ noun, verb

■ noun (BrE) a short thick heavy stick, for example a piece of metal or solid rubber, that is used as a weapon **IDM** **under the 'cosh** (BrE, informal) experiencing a lot of pressure: *Our side was under the cosh for most of the second half.*

■ verb ~ sb (BrE) to hit sb hard with a cosh or sth similar

**co-sign** /ˌkəʊ ˈsaɪn/ verb [I, T] (NAmE) ~ (sth) (for sb) to sign a legal document for sb else, in addition to their own **SIGNATURE**, in order to promise that an agreement will be kept: *Her dad co-signed the lease for her apartment.*

**co-ˈsignatory** noun (pl. **-ies**) one of two or more people who sign a formal document: *co-signatories of/to the treaty*

**co·sine** /ˈkəʊsaɪn/ noun (abbr. **cos**) (mathematics) the **RATIO** of the length of the side next to an **ACUTE ANGLE** in a **RIGHT-ANGLED TRIANGLE** to the length of the longest side (= the **HYPOTENUSE**) ⇒ compare **SINE**, **TANGENT**

**cos lettuce** /ˌkɒs ˈletɪs, ˌkɒz; NAmE ˌkɑːs/ (BrE) (NAmE **ro·maine**) noun [C, U] a type of **LETTUCE** with long, narrow leaves that form a tall **HEAD**

**cos·met·ic** /kɒzˈmetɪk; NAmE kɑːz-/ noun, adj.

■ noun [usually pl.] a substance that you put on your face or body to make it more attractive: *the cosmetics industry* ◊ *a cosmetic company* ◊ *cosmetic products*

■ adj. **1** improving only the outside appearance of sth and not its basic character: *These reforms are not merely cosmetic.* ◊ *She dismissed the plan as a cosmetic exercise to win votes.* **2** connected with medical treatment that is intended to improve a person's appearance: *cosmetic surgery* ◊ *cosmetic dental work* ▶ **cos·met·ic·al·ly** /-kli/ adv.

**cos·mic** /ˈkɒzmɪk; NAmE ˈkɑːz-/ adj. [usually before noun] **1** connected with the whole universe: *Do you believe in a cosmic plan?* ⇒ **WORDFINDER NOTE** at **UNIVERSE** **2** very great and important: *This was disaster on a cosmic scale.*

**cosmic ˈrays** noun [pl.] **RAYS** that reach the earth from outer space

**cos·mol·ogy** /kɒzˈmɒlədʒi; NAmE kɑːzˈmɑːl-/ noun [U] the scientific study of the universe and its origin and development ▶ **cosmo·logic·al** /ˌkɒzməˈlɒdʒɪkl; NAmE ˌkɑːzməˈlɑːdʒ-/ adj. **cos·molo·gist** /kɒzˈmɒlədʒɪst; NAmE kɑːzˈmɑːl-/ noun

**cosmo·naut** /ˈkɒzmənɔːt; NAmE ˈkɑːz-/ noun an **ASTRONAUT** from the former Soviet Union

**cosmo·pol·itan** /ˌkɒzməˈpɒlɪtən; NAmE ˌkɑːzməˈpɑːl-/ adj., noun

■ adj. (approving) **1** containing people of different types or from different countries, and influenced by their culture: *a cosmopolitan city/resort* ◊ *The club has a cosmopolitan atmosphere.* **2** having or showing a wide experience of people and things from many different countries: *people*

# cosmos 348

with a truly cosmopolitan outlook ◊ cosmopolitan young people
- **noun** a person who has a wide experience of people and things from many different countries: *She's a real cosmopolitan.*

**cos·mos** /ˈkɒzmɒs; NAmE ˈkɑːzməʊs, -məs/ **the cosmos** *noun* [sing.] the universe, especially when it is thought of as an ordered system: *the structure of the cosmos ◊ our place in the cosmos*

**cos·play** /ˈkɒspleɪ, ˈkɔzpleɪ; NAmE ˈkɑːspleɪ, ˈkɑːzpleɪ/ *noun, verb*
- **noun** [U] the activity of dressing up as a character from a film, book or video game
- **verb** [I, T] ~ (as) sb/sth to take part in cosplay (= dressing up as a character from a film, book or video game): *Two guys cosplayed as Chinese fantasy characters.* ▶ **cos·player** *noun*

**cos·set** /ˈkɒsɪt; NAmE ˈkɑːs-/ *verb* ~ **sb** (*often disapproving*) to treat sb with a lot of care and give them a lot of attention, sometimes too much ⓢⓨⓝ **pamper**

**cost** 🅐 🔠 /kɒst; NAmE kɔːst/ *noun, verb*
- **noun 1** 🔠 [C, U] the amount of money that you need in order to buy, make or do sth: **~ of sth** *the high/low cost of housing* ◊ **at a ~ of sth** *A new computer system has been installed at a cost of £80000.* ◊ *You could buy a used car at a* **fraction of the cost** *of a new one.* ◊ *We did not even make enough money to* **cover the cost** *of the food.* ◊ *Consumers will have to* **bear the full cost** *of these pay increases.* ◊ **~ to sb** *The* **total cost** *to you* (= the amount you have to pay) *is £3000.* ⊃ see also FIRST COST, LOW-COST, PRIME COST ⊃ SYNONYMS at PRICE **2** 🔠 **costs** [pl.] the total amount of money that needs to be spent by a business: *The use of cheap labour helped to keep costs down.* ◊ *to* **cut/reduce costs** ◊ *The company is focused on lowering its* **operating costs.** ◊ *We have had to raise our prices because of* **rising costs.** **3** 🔠 [U, sing.] the effort, loss or damage that is involved in order to do or achieve sth: **the ~ of sth** *the terrible cost of the war in death and suffering* ◊ **at the ~ of sth** *She saved him from the fire* **at the cost of her own life** (= she died). ◊ **at … ~ (in sth)** *Victory came at a high cost.* ◊ **at (a) ~ to sth** *He worked non-stop for three months, at considerable cost to his health.* ◊ **~ in sth** *I felt a need to please people, whatever the cost in time and energy.* **4 costs** (*also* **'court costs**) [pl.] the sum of money that sb is ordered to pay for lawyers, etc. in a legal case: *He was ordered to pay £2000 costs.*
- ⓘⓓⓜ **at ˌall cost/ˈcosts** whatever is needed to achieve sth: *You must stop the press from finding out at all costs.* **at ˌany ˈcost** under any circumstances: *He is determined to win at any cost.* **at ˈcost** for only the amount of money that is needed to make or get sth, without any profit being added on: *goods sold at cost* **know/learn/find sth to your ˈcost** to know sth because of sth unpleasant that has happened to you: *He's a ruthless businessman, as I know to my cost.* ⊃ more at COUNT v.
- **verb** (**cost, cost**) 🅗🅔🅛🅟 In sense 4 **costed** is used for the past tense and past participle. **1** 🔠 if sth **costs** a particular amount of money, you need to pay that amount in order to buy, make or do it: **~ sth** *How much did it cost? ◊ I didn't get it because it cost too much. ◊ Tickets cost ten dollars each. ◊ Calls to the helpline cost 45p per minute. ◊ Don't use too much of it—it* **cost a lot of money.** ◊ *All these reforms will* **cost money** (= be expensive). ◊ *Good food need not* **cost a fortune** (= cost a lot of money). ◊ **~ sb sth** *The meal cost us about £40.* ◊ *This is costing the taxpayer £10 billion a year.* ◊ **~ sth to do sth** *The hospital will cost an estimated £2 billion to build.* ◊ *It* **costs a fortune** *to fly first class.* **2** 🔠 to cause the loss of sth: **~ sb sth** *That one mistake almost* **cost him his life.** ◊ *A late penalty cost United the game* (= meant that they did not win the game). ◊ **~ sth** *The closure of the factory is likely to cost 1000 jobs.* **3 ~ sb sth** to involve you in making an effort or doing sth unpleasant: *The accident cost me a visit to the doctor.* ◊ *Financial worries cost her many sleepless nights.* **4** (**costed, costed**) to estimate how much money will be needed for sth or the price that

should be charged for sth: **~ sth** *The project needs to be costed in detail.* ◊ **~ sth at sth** *Their accountants have costed the project at $8.1 million.* ◊ **~ sth out** *Have you costed out these proposals yet?* ⊃ see also COSTING
- ⓘⓓⓜ **ˌcost sb ˈdear 1** to cost sb a lot of money: *The campaign for the presidency has cost him dear.* **2** to make sb suffer a lot: *That one mistake has cost him dear over the years.* **it will ˈcost you** (*informal*) used to say that sth will be expensive: *There is a deluxe model available, but it'll cost you.* ⊃ more at ARM *n*.

**ˈcost accounting** *noun* [U] (*business*) the process of recording and analysing the costs involved in running a business

**cos·tal** /ˈkɒstl; NAmE ˈkɑːs-/ *adj.* (*anatomy*) relating to the RIBS

**ˈco-star** *noun, verb*
- **noun** one of two or more famous actors who appear together in a film or play
- **verb** (**-rr-**) **1** [I] **~ (with sb)** to appear as one of the main actors with sb in a play or film: *a movie in which Jennifer Lawrence co-stars with Joel Edgerton* **2** [T] **~ sb** (of a film or play) to have two or more famous actors acting in it: *a movie co-starring Jennifer Lawrence and Joel Edgerton*

**ˈcost–benefit** *noun* [U] (*economics*) the relationship between the cost of doing sth and the value of the benefit that results from it: *cost–benefit analysis*

**ˈcost-cutting** *noun* [U] the reduction of the amount of money spent on sth, especially because of financial difficulty: *Deliveries of mail could be delayed because of cost-cutting.* ◊ *a cost-cutting exercise/measure/programme*

**ˌcost-ˈeffect·ive** (*also* **ˌcost-ˈefficient**) *adj.* giving the best possible profit or benefits in comparison with the money that is spent ▶ **ˌcost-ˈeffectively** (*also* **ˌcost-ˈefficiently**) *adv.* **ˌcost-ˈeffect·ive·ness** (*also* **ˌcost-ˈefficiency**) *noun* [U]

---

▼ SYNONYMS

### costs
spending • expenditure • expenses • overheads • outlay

These are all words for money spent by a government, an organization or a person.

**costs** the total amount of money that needs to be spent by a business: *labour/production costs ◊ rising costs*

**spending** the amount of money that is spent, especially by a government or an organization: *public spending ◊ More spending on health was promised.*

**expenditure** (*rather formal*) an amount of money spent by a government, an organization or a person: *expenditure on education*

**expenses** money that has to be spent by a person or an organization; money that you spend while you are working that your employer will pay back to you later: *legal expenses ◊ travel expenses*

**overhead(s)** the regular costs of running a business or an organization, such as rent, electricity and wages: *High overheads mean small profit margins.*

**outlay** the money that you have to spend in order to start a new business or project, or in order to save yourself money or time later: *The best equipment is costly but is well worth the outlay.*

PATTERNS
- spending/expenditure/outlay **on** sth
- **high/low** costs/spending/expenditure/expenses/overheads
- **total** costs/spending/expenditure/expenses/overheads/outlay
- **capital** costs/spending/expenditure/expenses/outlay
- **household** costs/spending/expenditure/expenses
- **government/public/education/health** costs/spending/expenditure
- to **increase/reduce** costs/spending/expenditure/expenses/overheads/the outlay

**cost·ing** /ˈkɒstɪŋ; NAmE ˈkɔːs-/ noun an estimate of how much money will be needed for sth: *Here is a detailed costing of our proposals.* ◇ *You'd better do some costings.*

**cost·ly** B1 /ˈkɒstli; NAmE ˈkɔːst-/ adj. (**cost·li·er**, **cost·li·est**) HELP It is also very common to use **more costly** and **most costly**. **1** costing a lot of money, especially more than you want to pay SYN **expensive**: *Buying new furniture may prove too costly.* ⇒ SYNONYMS at EXPENSIVE **2** causing problems or the loss of sth SYN **expensive**: *a costly mistake/failure* ◇ *Mining can be costly in terms of lives* (= too many people can die). ▸ **cost·li·ness** noun [U]

**the ˌcost of ˈliving** noun [sing.] the amount of money that people need to pay for food, clothing and somewhere to live: *a steady rise in the cost of living* ◇ *Despite the high cost of living, London is a great place to live.*

**ˌcost ˈprice** noun [U, C] the cost of producing sth or the price at which it is sold without profit: *Essential medicines must be available at cost price.* ⇒ compare ASKING PRICE, PURCHASE PRICE, SELLING PRICE

**cos·tume** B1 /ˈkɒstjuːm; NAmE ˈkɑːstuːm/ noun **1** [C, U] the clothes worn by people from a particular place or during a particular historical period: *She wore a traditional costume of bright pink silk.* ◇ *in... ~ a painting of an old woman in Welsh costume* ⇒ see also NATIONAL COSTUME **2** B1 [C, U] the clothes worn by actors in a play or film, or worn by sb to make them look like sb/sth else: **in a ~** *He went to the party in a giant chicken costume.* ◇ *in ~ The actors were still in costume and make-up.* ◇ *a costume designer* ⇒ WORDFINDER NOTE at STAGE **3** [C] (*BrE*) = SWIMMING COSTUME

**cos·tumed** /ˈkɒstjuːmd; NAmE ˈkɑːstuːmd/ adj. [usually before noun] wearing a costume

**ˈcostume drama** noun [C, U] a play or film set in the past, in which the actors wear clothes that are typical of the period

**ˈcostume jewellery** (*US* **ˈcostume jewelry**) noun [U] large heavy jewellery that can look expensive but is made with cheap materials

**ˈcostume party** noun (*especially NAmE*) a party where all the guests wear special clothes, in order to look like a different person, an animal, etc. ⇒ compare FANCY DRESS

**cos·tu·mier** /kɒsˈtjuːmiə(r); NAmE kɑːsˈtuːmiər/ (*NAmE* **cos·tu·mer**) noun a person or company that makes costumes or has costumes to hire, especially for the theatre: *a firm of theatrical costumiers*

**cosy** (*BrE*) (*NAmE* **cozy**) /ˈkəʊzi/ adj., verb
■ adj. (**cosi·er**, **cosi·est**) **1** warm, comfortable and safe, especially in a small space SYN **snug**: *a cosy little room* ◇ *a cosy feeling* ◇ *I felt warm and cosy sitting by the fire.* **2** friendly and private: *a cosy chat with a friend* **3** (*often disapproving*) easy and convenient, but not always honest or right: *The firm has a cosy relationship with the Ministry of Defence.* ◇ *The danger is that things get too cosy.* ▸ **cosi·ly** /-zɪli/ (*BrE*) (*NAmE* **cozi·ly**) *adv*.: *sitting cosily by the fire* **cosi·ness** (*BrE*) (*NAmE* **cozi·ness**) noun [U]: *the warmth and cosiness of the kitchen*
■ verb (**cosies**, **cosy·ing**, **cosied**, **cosied**)
PHRV **ˌcosy ˈup to sb** (*BrE*) (*NAmE* **ˌcozy ˈup to sb**) (*informal*) to act in a friendly way towards sb, especially sb who will be useful to you

**cot** /kɒt; NAmE kɑːt/ noun **1** (*BrE*) (*NAmE* **crib**) a small bed with high sides for a baby or young child: *a travel cot* (= one that can be moved around when travelling) ⇒ see also CARRYCOT **2** (*NAmE*) (*BrE* **ˈcamp bed**) a light narrow bed that you can fold up and carry easily

**ˈcot death** (*BrE*) (*NAmE* **ˈcrib death**) noun [U, C] the sudden death while sleeping of a baby that appears to be healthy (officially called 'sudden infant death syndrome') ⇒ see also SIDS

**co·terie** /ˈkəʊtəri/ noun [C + sing./pl. v.] (*formal, often disapproving*) a small group of people who have the same interests and do things together but do not like to include others

349

**co·ter·min·ous** /kəʊˈtɜːmɪnəs; NAmE -ˈtɜːrm-/ adj. [not usually before noun] (*formal*) **1** **~ (with sth)** (of countries or areas) sharing a border **2** **~ (with sth)** (of things or ideas) having so much in common that they are almost the same as each other

**cot·tage** B1 /ˈkɒtɪdʒ; NAmE ˈkɑːt-/ noun a small house, especially in the country: *a thatched cottage* ◇ (*BrE*) *a holiday cottage*

**ˌcottage ˈcheese** noun [U] soft white cheese with small thick pieces in it

**ˌcottage ˈhospital** noun (*BrE*, *becoming old-fashioned*) a small hospital in a country area

**ˌcottage ˈindustry** noun a small business in which the work is done by people in their homes: *Weaving and knitting are traditional cottage industries.*

**ˌcottage ˈpie** noun [C, U] a dish of beef cut into very small pieces and covered with a layer of MASHED potato ⇒ compare SHEPHERD'S PIE

**cot·tager** /ˈkɒtɪdʒə(r); NAmE ˈkɑːt-/ noun (*BrE*) (*especially in the past*) a person who lives in a small house or cottage in the country

**cot·ton** B1 /ˈkɒtn; NAmE ˈkɑːtn/ noun, verb
■ noun [U] **1** B1 a plant grown in warm countries for the soft white hairs around its seeds that are used to make cloth and THREAD: *bales of cotton* ◇ *cotton fields/plantations/plants* **2** B1 the cloth made from the cotton plant: *The sheets are 100 per cent pure cotton.* ◇ *a cotton shirt/skirt* ◇ *printed cotton cloth* ◇ *the cotton industry* ◇ *a cotton mill* **3** (*especially BrE*) THREAD that is used for SEWING: *sewing cotton* ◇ *a cotton reel* **4** (*NAmE*) (*BrE* **ˌcotton ˈwool**) a soft mass of white material that is used for cleaning the skin or a wound: *Use a cotton ball to apply the lotion.*
■ verb
PHRV **ˌcotton ˈon (to sth)** (*informal*) to begin to understand or realize sth without being told: *I suddenly cottoned on to what he was doing.* **ˈcotton (up) to sb/sth** (*NAmE*, *informal*) to make an attempt to be friendly to sb

**ˈcotton bud** (*BrE*) (*also* **ˈcotton swab** *NAmE*, **Q-tip**™ *NAmE*, *BrE*) noun a small stick with COTTON WOOL at each end, used for cleaning inside the ears, etc.

**ˌcotton ˈcandy** (*NAmE*) (*BrE* **candy-floss**) noun [U] a type of sweet in the form of a mass of sticky THREADS made from melted sugar and served on a stick, especially at FAIRGROUNDS

**ˈcotton gin** (*also* **gin**) noun a machine for separating the seeds of a cotton plant from the cotton

**ˈcotton-mouth** /ˈkɒtnmaʊθ; NAmE ˈkɑːt-/ (*also* **ˌcotton-mouth ˈmoccasin**, **ˈwater moccasin**) noun a poisonous snake that lives near water in the US

**ˈcot·ton·wood** /ˈkɒtnwʊd; NAmE ˈkɑːt-/ (*also* **ˈcottonwood tree**) noun a type of North American POPLAR tree, with seeds that are covered in hairs that look like white cotton

**ˌcotton ˈwool** (*BrE*) (*US* **(abˈsorbent) ˈcotton**) noun [U] a soft mass of white material that is used for cleaning the skin or a wound: *cotton wool balls*

**couch** /kaʊtʃ/ noun, verb
■ noun **1** a long comfortable seat for two or more people to sit on SYN **settee**, **sofa** **2** a long piece of furniture like a bed, especially in a doctor's office: *on the psychiatrist's couch*
■ verb [usually passive] (*formal*) to say or write words in a particular style or manner: **be couched (in sth)** *The letter was deliberately couched in very vague terms.*

**couch·ette** /kuːˈʃet/ noun a narrow bed on a train that folds down from the wall

**ˈcouch potato** noun (*informal, disapproving*) a person who spends a lot of time sitting and watching television

**cou·gar** /ˈkuːɡə(r)/ noun **1** (*especially NAmE*) = PUMA **2** (*informal*) an older woman who seeks a sexual relationship with a much younger man

# cough

**cough** /kɒf; NAmE kɔːf/ verb, noun
- **verb 1** [I] to force out air suddenly and noisily through your throat, for example when you have a cold: *I couldn't stop coughing.* ◇ *to cough nervously/politely/discreetly* **2** [T] ~ **sth (up)** to force sth out of your throat or lungs by coughing: *Sometimes she coughed (up) blood.* **3** [I] (of an engine) to make a sudden noise, especially as a sign that the engine is not working correctly
  **PHRV cough 'up | cough sth↔'up** (*informal*) to give sth, especially money, unwillingly: *Steve finally coughed up the money he owed us.*
- **noun 1** an act or a sound of coughing: *She gave a little cough to attract my attention.* **2** an illness or infection that makes you cough often: *to have a dry/persistent cough* ◇ *My cold's better, but I can't seem to shake off this cough.* ⊃ see also HACKING COUGH, WHOOPING COUGH

**cough·ing** /'kɒfɪŋ/ NAmE 'kɔːf-/ noun [U] the action or sound of coughing: *Another fit of coughing seized him.*

**'cough mixture** (*BrE*) (*also* **'cough syrup, 'cough medicine** *BrE*, *NAmE*) noun [U] liquid medicine that you take for a cough

**could** ⓘ A1 /kəd, strong form kʊd/ modal verb (negative **could not**, short form **couldn't** /'kʊdnt/) **1** ⓘ A1 used as the past tense of 'can': *She said that she couldn't come.* ◇ *I couldn't hear what they were saying.* ◇ *Sorry, I couldn't get any more.* ⊃ note at CAN¹ **2** ⓘ A1 used to ask if you can do sth: *Could I use your phone, please?* ◇ *Could we stop by next week?* **3** ⓘ A1 used to politely ask sb to do sth for you: *Could you babysit for us on Friday?* **4** ⓘ B1 used to show that sth is or might be possible: *I could do it now, if you like.* ◇ *Don't worry—they could have just forgotten to call.* ◇ *You couldn't have left it on the bus, could you?* ◇ *'Have some more cake.' 'Oh, I couldn't, thank you* (= I'm too full).' **5** ⓘ B1 used to suggest sth: *We could write a letter to the director.* ◇ *You could always try his home number.* **6** used to show that you are annoyed that sb did not do sth: *They could have let me know they were going to be late!* **7** (*informal*) used to emphasize how strongly you want to express your feelings: *I'm so fed up I could scream!* ⊃ note at MODAL
**IDM could do with sth** (*informal*) used to say that you need or would like to have sth: *I could do with a drink!* ◇ *Her hair could have done with a wash.*

**cou·lis** /'kuːli; NAmE kuː'liː/ noun (pl. **cou·lis**) (from French) a thin fruit sauce

**cou·lomb** /'kuːlɒm; NAmE -lɑːm, -loʊm/ noun (abbr. **C**) (*physics*) a unit for measuring electric charge

**coun·cil** ⓘ B2 /'kaʊnsl/ noun [C + sing./pl. v.] (*often* **the Council**) **1** ⓘ B2 a group of people who are elected to govern an area such as a city or county: *a city/town/district/borough council* ◇ *on the ~ She's on the local council.* ◇ *a council member/leader* ◇ *a council meeting/chamber* ⊃ see also BAND COUNCIL, COUNTY COUNCIL **2** ⓘ B2 (*BrE*) the organization that provides services in a city or county, for example education, houses, libraries, etc: *Residents have complained to the council about the noise.* ◇ *council workers/staff/officials/officers* ◇ *cuts to council services* **3** a group of people chosen to give advice, make rules, do research, provide money, etc: *the Medical Research Council* ◇ *In Britain, the Arts Council gives grants to theatres.* ⊃ see also SCHOOL COUNCIL, STUDENT COUNCIL, WORKS COUNCIL **4** (*formal*) (especially in the past) a formal meeting to discuss what action to take in a particular situation: *The king held a council at Nottingham from 14 to 19 October 1330.* ⊃ see also PRIVY COUNCIL

**'council chamber** noun (*BrE*) a large room in which a council meets

**'council estate** noun (*BrE*) a large group of houses built and rented out by a local council

**'council house, 'council flat** noun (*BrE*) a house or flat rented from the local council

**coun·cil·lor** ⓘ C1 (*NAmE also* **coun·cil·or**) /'kaʊnsələ(r)/ noun (*abbr.* **Cllr**) a member of a city or county council: *Councillor Ann Jones* ◇ *Talk to your local councillor about the problem.* ⊃ see also COUNCILMAN, COUNCILWOMAN

**coun·cil·man** /'kaʊnslmən/ noun (pl. **-men** /-mən/) (*US*) = COUNCILLOR

**council of 'war** noun (pl. **councils of war**) (*BrE*) a meeting to discuss how to deal with a difficult situation that requires immediate action

**'council tax** noun (*often* **the council tax**) [U, sing.] (in Britain) a tax charged by local councils to pay for local services, based on the value of a person's home

**coun·cil·woman** /'kaʊnslwʊmən/ noun (pl. **-women** /-wɪmɪn/) (*US*) = COUNCILLOR

**coun·sel** /'kaʊnsl/ noun, verb
- **noun 1** [U, C] (*formal*) advice, especially given by older people or experts; a piece of advice: *Listen to the counsel of your elders.* ◇ *In the end, wiser counsels prevailed.* **2** (*law*) a lawyer or group of lawyers representing sb in court: *to be represented by counsel* ◇ *the counsel for the defence/prosecution* ◇ *defence/prosecuting counsel* ◇ *The court then heard counsel for the dead woman's father.* ⊃ WORDFINDER NOTE at TRIAL ⊃ see also QUEEN'S COUNSEL ⊃ note at LAWYER
  **IDM a counsel of des'pair** (*formal*) advice not to try to do sth because it is too difficult **keep your own 'counsel** (*formal*) to keep your opinions, plans, etc. secret
- **verb** (**-ll-**, *US* **-l-**) **1** ~ **sb** to listen to and give support or professional advice to sb who needs help: *Therapists were brought in to counsel the bereaved.* **2** (*formal*) to advise sb to do sth: ~ **sth** *Most experts counsel caution in such cases.* ◇ ~ **sb to do sth** *He counselled them to give up the chase.*

**coun·sel·ling** ⓘ+ C1 (*US* **coun·sel·ing**) /'kaʊnsəlɪŋ/ noun [U] professional advice about a problem: *relationship/bereavement counselling* ◇ *a student counselling service*

**coun·sel·lor** ⓘ+ C1 (*US* **coun·sel·or**) /'kaʊnsələ(r)/ noun **1** ⓘ+ C1 a person who has been trained to advise people with problems, especially personal problems: *a debt counsellor* **2** (*NAmE, IrishE*) a lawyer **3** (*NAmE*) a person who is in charge of young people at a summer camp ⊃ see also GUIDANCE COUNSELOR

**count** ⓘ A2 /kaʊnt/ verb, noun
- **verb**
- • SAY NUMBERS **1** ⓘ A2 [I] to say numbers in the correct order: *Billy can't count yet.* ◇ ~ **(up) to sth** *She can count up to 10 in Italian.* ◇ ~ **from sth (to/up to sth)** *to count from 1 to 10*
- • FIND TOTAL **2** ⓘ A2 [T, I] to calculate the total number of people, things, etc. in a particular group: ~ **sth (up)** *They're still counting votes in Texas.* ◇ *I can't count the number of times I've eaten there* ◇ *I've eaten there very many times).* ◇ ~ **(up) how many…** *She began to count up how many guests they had to invite.* ◇ ~ **from…** *There are twelve weeks to go, counting from today.*
- • INCLUDE **3** ⓘ B1 [T] ~ **sb/sth** to include sb/sth when you calculate a total: *We have invited 50 people, not counting the children.*
- • MATTER **4** ⓘ B1 [I] (not used in the progressive tenses) to be important SYN matter: *It is going to be a close election, so every vote counts.* ◇ *It's the thought that counts* (= used about a small but kind action or gift). ◇ ~ **for sth** *The fact that she had apologized counted for nothing with him.*
- • ACCEPT OFFICIALLY **5** ⓘ B2 [I, T] to be officially accepted; to accept sth officially: *Don't go over that line or your throw won't count.* ◇ ~ **sth** *Applications received after 1 July will not be counted.*
- • CONSIDER **6** [T, I] to consider sb/sth in a particular way; to be considered in a particular way: ~ **(sb/sth) as sb/sth** *For tax purposes that money counts/is counted as income.* ◇ ~ **sb/sth/yourself among sb/sth** *I count him among my closest friends.* ◇ ~ **sb/sth/yourself + adj.** *I count myself lucky to have known him.* ◇ ~ **sb/sth/yourself + noun** *She counts herself one of the lucky ones.*
  **IDM …and 'counting** used to say that a total is continuing to increase: *The movie's ticket sales add up to $39 million, and counting.* **be able to count sb/sth on (the fingers of) one 'hand** used to say that the total number of sb/sth is very small **count your 'blessings** to be grateful for the good things in your life **count the cost (of sth)** to feel the bad effects of a mistake, an accident, etc: *The town is now counting the cost of its failure to provide adequate flood*

protection. **count ˈsheep** to imagine that sheep are jumping over a fence and to count them, as a way of getting to sleep **don't count your ˈchickens (before they are ˈhatched)** (*saying*) you should not be too confident that sth will be successful, because sth may still go wrong **stand up and be ˈcounted** to say publicly that you support sb or you agree with sth **who's ˈcounting?** (*informal*) used to say that you do not care how many times sth happens: *I've seen the film five times, but who's counting?*

**PHRV** ˌcount aˈgainst sb | ˌcount sth aˈgainst sb to be considered or to consider sth to be a disadvantage in sb: *For that job her lack of experience may count against her.* ˌcount ˈdown (to sth) to think about a future event with pleasure or excitement and count the minutes, days, etc. until it happens: *She's already counting down to the big day.* ⊃ related noun COUNTDOWN ˌcount sb ˈin to include sb in an activity: *I hear you're organizing a trip to the game next week? Count me in!* ˈcount on sb/sth to trust sb to do sth or to be sure that sth will happen **SYN** **bank on**: *'I'm sure he'll help.' 'Don't count on it.'* ◇ **count on sb/sth to do sth** *I'm counting on you to help me.* ◇ **count on doing sth** *Few people can count on having a job for life.* ◇ **count on sb/sth doing sth** *We can't count on this warm weather lasting.* ⊃ SYNONYMS at TRUST ˌcount sb/sth↔ˈout to count things one after the other as you put them somewhere: *She counted out $70 in $10 bills.* ˌcount sb ˈout to not include sb in an activity: *If you're going out tonight you'll have to count me out.* ˌcount toˈwards/toˈward sth to be included as part of sth that you hope to achieve in the future: *Students gain college credits which count towards their degree.*

■ *noun*
- TOTAL **1** ?+ **B1** [usually sing.] an act of counting to find the total number of sb/sth: *If the election result is close, there will be a second count.* ◇ *The bus driver did a quick count of the empty seats.* ◇ **by sb's ~** *By my count there are eight tracks here that aren't on the band's three albums.* ⊃ see also BODY COUNT, HEADCOUNT
- SAYING NUMBERS **2** ?+ **B1** [usually sing.] an act of saying numbers in order beginning with 1: **~ of...** *Raise your leg and hold for a count of ten.* ◇ *He was knocked to the ground and stayed down for a count of eight* (= in boxing). ◇ **on a/the ~ of...** *On the count of three, take one step forward.*
- MEASUREMENT **3** [usually sing.] (*specialist*) a measurement of the amount of sth contained in a particular substance or area: *a raised white blood cell count* ⊃ see also BLOOD COUNT, POLLEN COUNT
- CRIME **4** (*law*) a crime that sb is accused of committing: *They were found guilty on all counts.* ◇ *to be charged with two counts of murder*
- IN DISCUSSION/ARGUMENT **5** [usually pl.] a point made during a discussion or an argument: *I disagree with you on both counts.*
- RANK/TITLE **6** (in some European countries, but not the UK) a NOBLEMAN of high rank, similar to an EARL in the UK: *Count Tolstoy* ⊃ see also COUNTESS

**IDM** **at the last ˈcount** according to the latest information about the numbers of sth: *She'd applied for 30 jobs at the last count.* **keep (a) count (of sth)** to remember or keep a record of numbers or amounts of sth over a period of time: *Keep a count of your calorie intake for one week.* **lose count (of sth)** to forget the total of sth before you have finished counting it: *I lost count and had to start again.* ◇ *She had lost count of the number of times she'd told him to be careful* (= she could not remember because there were so many). **out for the ˈcount** (*BrE*) (*NAmE* ˌdown for the ˈcount) **1** (of a boxer) unable to get up again within ten seconds after being knocked down **2** in a deep sleep

**count·able** /ˈkaʊntəbl/ *adj.* (*grammar*) a noun that is **countable** can be used in the plural and with *a* or *an*, for example *table*, *cat* and *idea* **OPP** **uncountable**

**count·down** /ˈkaʊntdaʊn/ *noun* **1** [sing., U] **~ (to sth)** the action of counting numbers backwards to zero, for example before a SPACECRAFT is launched ⊃ WORDFINDER NOTE at SPACE **2** [sing.] **~ (to sth)** the period of time just before sth important happens: *the countdown to the wedding*

**coun·ten·ance** /ˈkaʊntənəns/ *noun*, *verb*
■ *noun* (*formal* or *literary*) a person's face or their expression

■ *verb* ~ **sth** | ~ **(sb) doing sth** (*formal*) to support sth or agree to sth happening **SYN** **consent to**: *The committee refused to countenance his proposals.*

**coun·ter** ?+ **B2** /ˈkaʊntə(r)/ *noun*, *verb*, *adv.*
■ *noun* **1** ?+ **B2** a long flat surface over which goods are sold or business is done in a shop, bank, etc: *behind the ~ I asked the woman behind the counter if they had any postcards.* ⊃ WORDFINDER NOTE at SHOP **2** ?+ **B2** (*also* **counter-top**) (*both NAmE*) (*BrE* ˈwork·top, ˈwork surface) a flat surface in a kitchen for preparing food on **3** a small disc used for playing or scoring in some board games ⊃ see also BARGAINING COUNTER at BARGAINING CHIP **4** (*especially in compounds*) an electronic device for counting sth: *The needle on the rev counter soared.* ⊃ see also GEIGER COUNTER **5** a person who counts sth, for example votes in an election ⊃ see also BEAN COUNTER **6** [usually sing.] **~ (to sb/sth)** (*formal*) a response to sb/sth that opposes their ideas, position, etc: *The employers' association was seen as a counter to union power.*

**IDM** **over the ˈcounter** goods, especially medicines, for sale **over the counter** can be bought without a PRESCRIPTION (= written permission from a doctor to buy a medicine) or special licence: *These tablets are available over the counter.* ⊃ see also OVER-THE-COUNTER **under the ˈcounter** goods that are bought or sold **under the counter** are sold secretly and sometimes illegally ⊃ see also UNDER-THE-COUNTER

■ *verb* **1** ?+ **C1** [T, I] to reply to sb by trying to prove that what they said is not true: **~ sb/sth** *Such arguments are not easily countered.* ◇ **~ that...** *I tried to argue but he countered that the plans were not yet finished.* ◇ **~ (sb) + speech** *'But I was standing right here!' he countered.* ◇ **~ (sb/sth) with sth** *Butler has countered with a lawsuit against the firm.* **2** ?+ **C1** [T] **~ sth** to do sth to reduce or prevent the bad effects of sth **SYN** **counteract**: *Businesses would like to see new laws to counter late payments of debts.*

■ *adv.* **~ to sth** in the opposite direction to sth; in opposition to sth: *The company's plans run counter to local development guidelines.*

**counter-** /ˈkaʊntə(r)/ *combining form* (in nouns, verbs, adjectives and adverbs) **1** against; opposite: *counterterrorism* ◇ *counter-accusations* **2** corresponding: *counterpart*

**coun·ter·act** /ˌkaʊntərˈækt/ *verb* **~ sth** to do sth to reduce or prevent the bad or harmful effects of sth **SYN** **counter**: *These exercises aim to counteract the effects of stress and tension.*

**coun·ter·argu·ment** /ˈkaʊntərəːɡjumənt; *NAmE* -ɑːrɡjuː-/ *noun* **~ (to sth)** an argument or set of reasons that you put forward to oppose an idea or theory: *Meyer offers a strong counterargument to these claims.*

**ˈcounter-attack** *noun*, *verb*
■ *noun* an attack made in response to the attack of an enemy or opponent in war, sport or an argument
■ *verb* [I, T] **~ (sb)** to make an attack in response to the attack of an enemy or opponent in war, sport or an argument **SYN** **retaliate**

**coun·ter·bal·ance** *verb*, *noun*
■ *verb* /ˌkaʊntəˈbæləns; *NAmE* -tərˈb-/ **~ sth** (*formal*) to have an equal but opposite effect to sth else **SYN** **offset**: *Parents' natural desire to protect their children should be counterbalanced by the child's need for independence.*
■ *noun* /ˈkaʊntəbæləns; *NAmE* -tərb-/ (*also* **ˌcounter·weight**) [usually sing.] **~ (to sth)** a thing that has an equal but opposite effect to sth else and can be used to limit the bad effects of sth: *The accused's right to silence was a vital counterbalance to the powers of the police.*

**coun·ter·claim** /ˈkaʊntəkleɪm; *NAmE* -tərk-/ *noun* a claim made in reply to another claim and different from it

**coun·ter·clock·wise** /ˌkaʊntəˈklɒkwaɪz; *NAmE* -tərˈklɑːk-/ (*NAmE*) (*BrE* ˌanti·clock·wise) *adv.*, *adj.* in the opposite direction to the movement of the hands of a clock **OPP** **clockwise**

**coun·ter·cul·ture** /ˈkaʊntəkʌltʃə(r); *NAmE* -tərk-/ *noun* [C, U] a way of life and set of ideas that are opposed to those accepted by most of society; a group of people who share such a way of life and set of ideas

**counter-'espion-age** noun [U] secret action taken by a country to prevent an enemy country from finding out its secrets

**coun·ter·fac·tual** /ˌkaʊntəˈfæktʃuəl; NAmE -tərˈf-/ adj. (formal) connected with what did not happen or what is not the case: *counterfactual questions such as 'What if the President had not been assassinated?'* ◇ *an interesting exercise in counterfactual history* ▸ **coun·ter·fac·tual** noun: *'What if' questions involving counterfactuals are familiar in historical speculations.*

**coun·ter·feit** /ˈkaʊntəfɪt; NAmE -tərf-/ adj., verb
■ adj. (formal) (of money and goods for sale) made to look exactly like sth in order to trick people into thinking that they are getting the real thing SYN **fake**: *counterfeit watches* ◇ *Are you aware these notes are counterfeit?* OPP **genuine** ▸ **coun·ter·feit** noun ⊃ compare FORGERY
■ verb ~ sth (formal) to make an exact copy of sth in order to trick people into thinking that it is the real thing ⊃ compare FORGE ▸ **coun·ter·feit·ing** noun [U]

**coun·ter·feit·er** /ˈkaʊntəfɪtə(r); NAmE -tərf-/ noun a person who COUNTERFEITS money or goods ⊃ compare FORGER

**counter-in'surgency** noun [U] action taken against a group of people who are trying to take control of a country by force

**counter-in'telli·gence** noun [U] secret action taken by a country to prevent an enemy country from finding out its secrets, for example by giving them false information; the department of a government, etc. that is responsible for this

**counter-in'tuitive** adj. the opposite of what you would expect or what seems to be obvious: *These results seem counter-intuitive.* ▸ **counter-in'tuitive·ly** adv.

**coun·ter·mand** /ˌkaʊntəˈmɑːnd; NAmE ˈkaʊntərmænd/ verb ~ sth (formal) to cancel an order that has been given, especially by giving a different order

**coun·ter·meas·ure** /ˈkaʊntəmeʒə(r); NAmE -tərm-/ noun a course of action taken to protect against sth that is considered bad or dangerous

**coun·ter·of·fen·sive** /ˈkaʊntərəfensɪv/ noun an attack made in order to defend against enemy attacks

**coun·ter·part** /ˈkaʊntəpɑːt; NAmE -tərpɑːrt/ noun a person or thing that has the same position or function as sb/sth else in a different place or situation: *The Foreign Minister held talks with his Chinese counterpart.* ◇ *The women's shoe, like its male counterpart, is specifically designed for the serious tennis player.* ⊃ compare YOUR OPPOSITE NUMBER

**coun·ter·point** /ˈkaʊntəpɔɪnt; NAmE -tərp-/ noun, verb
■ noun 1 [U] (*music*) the combination of two or more tunes played together to form a single piece of music SYN **polyphony**: *The two melodies are played in counterpoint.* ⊃ see also CONTRAPUNTAL 2 [C] ~ (to sth) (*music*) a tune played in combination with another one 3 [U, C] (*formal*) an effective or interesting contrast: *This work is in austere counterpoint to that of Gaudi.*
■ verb ~ sth (with/against sth) (*formal*) to contrast sth with sth else; to form a contrast with sth

**coun·ter·pro·duct·ive** /ˌkaʊntəprəˈdʌktɪv; NAmE -tərp-/ adj. having the opposite effect to the one that was intended: *counterproductive behaviour/policies/effects* ⊃ compare PRODUCTIVE

**counter-revo'lution** noun [C, U] opposition to or violent action against a government that came to power as a result of a revolution, in order to destroy and replace it

**counter-revo'lution·ary** noun a person involved in a counter-revolution ▸ **counter-revo'lution·ary** adj.

**coun·ter·sign** /ˈkaʊntəsaɪn; NAmE -tərs-/ verb ~ sth (specialist) to sign a document that has already been signed by another person, especially in order to show that it is legally or officially acceptable

**coun·ter·tenor** /ˈkaʊntətenə(r); NAmE -tərt-/ noun a man who is trained to sing with a very high voice; a male ALTO ⊃ compare ALTO

**counter·terror·ism** /ˌkaʊntəˈterərɪzəm; NAmE -tərˈt-/ noun [U] action taken to prevent the activities of political groups who use violence to try to achieve their aims ▸ **counter·terror·ist** /-ˈterərɪst/ adj.

**coun·ter·top** /ˈkaʊntətɒp; NAmE -tərtɑːp/ noun (NAmE) = COUNTER (2)

**coun·ter·vail·ing** /ˈkaʊntəveɪlɪŋ; NAmE -tərv-/ adj. [only before noun] (formal) having an equal but opposite effect

**coun·ter·weight** /ˈkaʊntəweɪt; NAmE -tərw-/ noun [usually sing.] = COUNTERBALANCE

**count·ess** /ˈkaʊntəs, -tes/ noun 1 a woman who has the rank of a COUNT or an EARL 2 the wife of a COUNT or an EARL: *the Earl and Countess of Rosebery*

**count·less** /ˈkaʊntləs/ adj. [usually before noun] very many; too many to be counted or mentioned: *I've warned her countless times.* ◇ *The new treatment could save Emma's life and the lives of countless others.* ⊃ compare UNCOUNTABLE

**'count noun** noun (*grammar*) a countable noun OPP **uncount noun**

**coun·tri·fied** /ˈkʌntrɪfaɪd/ adj. (often disapproving) like the countryside or the people who live there

**coun·try** /ˈkʌntri/ noun (pl. -ies) 1 [C] an area of land that has or used to have its own government and laws: *European countries* ◇ *developing countries* ◇ **in a ~** *She didn't know what life in a foreign country would be like.* ◇ **across the ~** *House prices are rising across the whole country.* ◇ **from a ~** *people from other countries* ⊃ see also MOTHER COUNTRY, NORTH-COUNTRY, OLD COUNTRY 2 **the country** [sing.] any area outside towns and cities, with fields, woods, farms, etc: **in the ~** *I live in the country.* ◇ *We spent a pleasant day in the country.* ◇ *country roads/lanes* ⊃ see also UP-COUNTRY 3 [U] (often following an adjective) an area of land, especially with particular physical features, suitable for a particular purpose or connected with a particular person or people: *open country* ◇ *superb walking country* ◇ *Explore Thomas Hardy country.* ⊃ see also BACKCOUNTRY 4 **the country** [sing.] the people of a country; the nation as a whole: *They have the support of most of the country.* ◇ *The rich benefited from the reforms, not the country as a whole.* 5 [U] = COUNTRY MUSIC: *pop, folk and country*
IDM **across 'country** directly across fields, etc.; not by a main road: *riding across country* ⊃ see also CROSS-COUNTRY adj. **go to the 'country** (BrE) (of a government) to hold an election to choose a new parliament ⊃ more at FREE adj.

> **WHICH WORD?**
>
> **country / state**
> • **Country** is the most usual, neutral word for a geographical area that has or used to have its own government.
> • **State** emphasizes the political organization of an area under an independent government. Especially in BrE, it can also mean the government: *the member states of the EU* ◇ *The state provides free education.* In NAmE **the state** usually refers to one of the 50 states of the US, not to the government of the country as a whole.

**country and 'western** (abbr. **C & W**) noun [U] = COUNTRY MUSIC: *a country and western singer*

**country 'bumpkin** (also **bump·kin**) noun (disapproving) a person from the countryside who seems stupid

**'country club** noun a club in the country, or on the edge of a town, where people can play sports and go to social events

**country 'dance** noun (BrE) a type of traditional dance, especially one in which couples dance in long lines or circles ▸ **country 'dancing** noun [U]

## ▼ SYNONYMS

**country**
landscape • countryside • terrain • land • scenery
These are all words for areas away from towns and cities, with fields, woods and farms.

**country** (often **the country**) an area that is away from towns and cities, especially one with particular natural features: *She lives in the country.* ◊ *an area of wooded country*

**landscape** everything that you can see when you look across a large area of land, especially in the country: *This pattern of woods and fields is typical of the English landscape.*

**countryside** land outside towns and cities, with fields, woods and farms. NOTE **Countryside** is usually used when you are talking about the beauty or peacefulness of a country area: *a little village in the French countryside.*

**terrain** (*formal*) land. NOTE **Terrain** is used when you are describing the natural features of an area, for example if it is rough, flat, etc: *The truck bumped its way over the rough terrain.*

**land** (usually **the land**) the countryside; the way people live in the country as opposed to in towns and cities: *Many younger people are leaving the land to find work in the cities.*

**scenery** the natural features of an area, such as mountains, valleys, rivers and forests, especially when these are attractive to look at: *We stopped on the mountain pass to admire the scenery.*

**PATTERNS**
- **mountainous / mountain / wild / rugged** country / landscape / countryside / terrain / scenery
- **beautiful / glorious / dramatic** country / landscape / countryside / scenery
- **open** country / landscape / countryside / terrain / land
- **rolling** country / landscape / countryside
- to **protect** the landscape / countryside / land

,country 'house *noun* (*BrE*) a large house in the country, especially one that belongs or used to belong to a rich important family

**coun·try·made** /'kʌntrimeɪd/ *adj.* (*IndE*) not made by a professional person: *a countrymade pistol*

**coun·try·man** /'kʌntrimən/ *noun* (*pl.* **-men** /-mən/) **1** a person born in or living in the same country as sb else SYN **compatriot**: *The champion looks set to play his fellow countryman in the final.* **2** a man living or born in the country, not in the town

,country 'mile *noun* [sing.] (*especially BrE*) a long distance: *He won the race by a country mile.*

'country ,music (*also* country, ,country and 'western) *noun* [U] a type of popular music in the style of the traditional music of the southern US, with singing and dance tunes played on VIOLIN, guitar and BANJO

,country 'seat (*also* seat) *noun* (*BrE*) a large house in the country that belongs to a member of the upper class

**coun·try·side** ⓞ B1 /'kʌntrisaɪd/ *noun* [U] land outside towns and cities, with fields, woods, etc: *The surrounding countryside is windswept and rocky.* ◊ *magnificent views over open countryside* ◊ **in the ~** *the quieter pace of life in the countryside* ⇒ SYNONYMS at COUNTRY

**coun·try·wide** /ˌkʌntri'waɪd/ *adj., adv.* over the whole of a country SYN **nationwide**: *a countrywide mail-order service*

**coun·try·woman** /'kʌntriwʊmən/ *noun* (*pl.* **-women** /-wɪmɪn/) **1** a woman living or born in the country, not the town **2** a woman born or living in the same country as sb else

**county** ⓞ B2 /'kaʊnti/ *noun, adj.*

■ *noun* ⓘ B2 (*pl.* **-ies**) (*abbr.* **Co.**) one of a number of areas that some countries are divided into, each with its own local government: *rural counties west of the Mississippi* ◊ *Oxfordshire and neighbouring counties* ◊ *Orange County* ◊ *county boundaries* ⇒ see also HOME COUNTIES

■ *adj.* (*BrE, usually disapproving*) typical of English upper-class people

,county 'clerk *noun* (in the US) an elected county official who is responsible for elections and who keeps records of who owns buildings in the county, etc.

,county 'council *noun* [C + sing. / pl. v.] **1** (in England and Wales) a group of people elected to the local government of a county: *a member of Lancashire County Council* **2** (in England and Wales) the organization that provides services in a county, for example education, housing, etc: *He works for the county council.* ▸ ,county 'councillor *noun*

,county 'court *noun* a local court. In the UK county courts only deal with private DISAGREEMENTS but in the US they also deal with criminal cases. ⇒ compare CROWN COURT

,county 'town (*BrE*) (*NAmE* ,county 'seat) *noun* the main town of a county, where its government is

**coun·ty·wide** /ˌkaʊnti'waɪd/ *adj.* over the whole of a county ▸ **coun·ty·wide** *adv.*

**coup** ⓘ+ C1 /kuː/ *noun* (*pl.* **coups** /kuːz/) **1** ⓘ+ C1 (*also* **coup d'état**) a sudden change of government that is illegal and often violent: *He seized power in a military coup in 2008.* ◊ *to stage/mount a coup* ◊ *an attempted coup* ◊ *a failed/an abortive coup* ◊ *She lost her position in a boardroom coup* (= a sudden change of power among senior managers in a company). ⇒ see also PALACE COUP **2** ⓘ+ C1 the fact of achieving sth that was difficult to do: *Getting this contract has been quite a coup for us.*

**coup de grâce** /ˌkuː də 'grɑːs/ *noun* [sing.] (*from French, formal*) **1** an action or event that finally ends sth that has been getting weaker or worse: *My disastrous exam results dealt the coup de grâce to my university career.* **2** a hit or shot that finally kills a person or an animal, especially to stop them from suffering SYN **death blow**

**coup d'état** /ˌkuː deɪ'tɑː/ *noun* (*pl.* **coups d'état** /ˌkuː deɪ'tɑː/) = COUP (1)

**coupé** /'kuːpeɪ; *NAmE* kuː'peɪ/ (*NAmE also* **coupe** /kuːp/) *noun* a car with two doors and usually a sloping back

**couple** ⓞ A2 /'kʌpl/ *noun, verb*

■ *noun* HELP In *BrE* a plural verb is usually used in all 3 senses. **1** ⓘ A2 [sing. + sing. / pl. v.] **~ (of sb / sth)** two people or things: *I saw a couple of men get out.* **2** ⓘ A2 [sing. + sing. / pl. v.] **~ (of sb / sth)** a small number of people or things: *We went there a couple of years ago.* ◊ *a couple of people / friends / guys* ◊ *I've seen her a couple of times before.* ◊ *I'll be with you in a minute. There are a couple of things I have to do first.* ◊ *We can do it in the next couple of weeks.* ◊ *There have been some new developments in the past couple of days.* ◊ *There are a couple more files to read first.* **3** ⓘ A2 [C + sing. / pl. v.] two people who are seen together, especially if they are married or in a romantic or sexual relationship: *married couples* ◊ *same-sex / gay / lesbian couples* ◊ *a young couple* ◊ *an elderly couple* ◊ *Several couples were on the dance floor.* ◊ *The couple was / were married in 2016.* ⇒ see also POWER COUPLE IDM see SHAKE *n.* ▸ **a couple** *pron.*: '*How many drinks have you had?' 'Only a couple.'* ◊ *Do you need any more glasses? I've got a couple I can lend you.* **a couple** *det.* (*NAmE, informal*): *It's only a couple blocks away.*

■ *verb* **1** [T, usually passive] to join together two parts of sth, for example two vehicles or pieces of equipment: **be coupled together** *The two railway trucks had been coupled together.* ◊ **be coupled to sth** *This energy is converted into electrical energy by the generator that is coupled to the turbine.* **2** [I] (*formal*) (of two people or animals) to have sex PHRV **couple 'up (with sb)** (of people) to join to form a pair, especially to have a romantic or sexual relationship **(be) coupled with sb / sth** (of one thing, situation, etc.) to be linked to another thing, situation, etc: *Overproduction, coupled with falling sales, has led to huge losses for the company.*

# couplet

**coup·let** /ˈkʌplət/ *noun* two lines of poetry of equal length one after the other: *a poem written in rhyming couplets* ⇒ WORDFINDER NOTE at POETRY

**coup·ling** /ˈkʌplɪŋ/ *noun* **1** [usually sing.] an action of joining or combining two things: *a coupling of Mozart's Prague Symphony and Schubert's Unfinished Symphony* (= for example, on the same CD) **2** (*formal*) an act of having sex: *illicit couplings* **3** (*specialist*) a thing that joins together two parts of sth, two vehicles or two pieces of equipment

**cou·pon** /ˈkuːpɒn; *NAmE* -pɑːn, ˈkjuː-/ *noun* **1** a small piece of printed paper that you can exchange for sth or that gives you the right to buy sth at a cheaper price than normal: *money-off coupons ◊ clothing coupons ◊ an international reply coupon* **2** a printed form, often cut out from a newspaper, that is used to enter a competition, order goods, etc: *Fill in and return the attached coupon.*

**cour·age** ❶ B2 /ˈkʌrɪdʒ; *NAmE* ˈkɜːr-/ *noun* [U] the ability to do sth dangerous, or to face pain or opposition, without showing fear SYN **bravery**: *He showed great courage and determination. ◊ moral/physical courage ◊* **~to do sth** *They had the courage to stand up and fight for what they believed in. ◊ I haven't yet* **plucked up the courage** *to ask her. ◊ It* **takes courage** *to sing in public. ◊ courage in the face of danger* ⇒ see also DUTCH COURAGE
IDM **have/lack the courage of your con'victions** to be/not be brave enough to do what you feel to be right **take courage (from sth)** to begin to feel happier and more confident because of sth **take your courage in both 'hands** to make yourself do sth that you are afraid of: *Taking her courage in both hands, she opened the door and walked in.* ⇒ more at SCREW *v.*

**cour·age·ous** /kəˈreɪdʒəs/ *adj.* showing courage SYN **brave**: *a very courageous decision ◊ I hope people will be courageous enough to speak out against this injustice.* OPP **cowardly** ▸ **cour·age·ous·ly** *adv.*

**cour·gette** /kʊəˈʒet, kɔː-; *NAmE* kʊrˈʒ-/ (*BrE*) (*NAmE* **zuc·chini**) *noun* a long vegetable with dark green skin that is white inside ⇒ VISUAL VOCAB page V5

**cour·ier** /ˈkʊriə(r)/ *noun* **1** a person or company whose job is to take packages or important papers somewhere: *We sent the documents by courier.* **2** (*BrE*) a person who is employed by a travel company to give advice and help to a group of tourists on holiday ▸ **cour·ier** *verb*: **~ sth** *Courier that letter—it needs to get there today* (= send it by courier).

**course** ❶ A1 S /kɔːs; *NAmE* kɔːrs/ *noun, verb*
■ *noun*
- EDUCATION **1** B2 [C] a series of lessons or lectures on a particular subject: *a French/chemistry course ◊* **~ in sth** *to take/do a course in art and design ◊ The department offers short courses in drama, fiction, and poetry. ◊* **on a ~** *to go on a management training course* ⇒ see also ACCESS COURSE, CORRESPONDENCE COURSE, CRASH *adj.*, FOUNDATION COURSE, INDUCTION COURSE, REFRESHER COURSE, SURVEY COURSE ⇒ HOMOPHONES at COARSE **2** A1 [C] (*especially BrE*) a period of study at a college or university that leads to an exam or a qualification: *a degree course ◊ a two-year postgraduate course leading to a master's degree* ⇒ compare PROGRAMME ⇒ WORDFINDER NOTE at STUDY
- FOR GOLF **3** B1 [C] = GOLF COURSE: *He set a new course record.*
- FOR RACES **4** B1 [C] an area of land or water where races are held: *She was overtaken on the last stretch of the course.* ⇒ see also ASSAULT COURSE, OBSTACLE COURSE, RACECOURSE
- PART OF MEAL **5** B1 [C] any of the separate parts of a meal: *a four-course dinner ◊ The* **main course** *was roast duck.* ⇒ WORDFINDER NOTE at RESTAURANT
- DIRECTION **6** B2 [U, C, usually sing.] a direction or route followed by a ship or an aircraft: *He radioed the pilot to* **change course.** *◊* **on/off~** *The plane was off course* (= not going in the right direction). *◊ We're on course for our destination.* **7** B2 [C, usually sing.] the general direction in which sb's ideas or actions are moving or in which things are developing: *to change/reverse course ◊ Her career followed a similar course to her sister's.*
- ACTION **8** B2 (*also* **course of 'action**) [C] a way of acting in or dealing with a particular situation: *There are various courses open to us. ◊ What course of action would you recommend? ◊ The wisest course would be to say nothing.*
- DEVELOPMENT **9** B2 [sing.] the way sth develops or should develop: **~ of sth** *an event that changed* **the course of history** *◊* **during the ~ of sth** *She repeatedly raised the issue during the course of the campaign.*
- OF RIVER **10** [C, usually sing.] the direction a river moves in: *The path follows the course of the river.* ⇒ WORDFINDER NOTE at RIVER
- MEDICAL TREATMENT **11** [C] **~ (of sth)** a series of medical treatments, tablets, etc: *to prescribe a course of antibiotics*
- IN WALL **12** [C] A continuous layer of BRICK, stone or other building material in a wall: *A new damp-proof course could cost £1000 or more.* ⇒ see also DAMP COURSE
IDM **in course of sth** (*formal*) going through a particular process: *The new textbook is in course of preparation.* **in/over the course of …** (used with expressions for periods of time) during: *He's seen many changes in the course of his long life. ◊ The company faces major challenges over the course of the next few years.* **in the course of 'time** when enough time has passed SYN **eventually**: *It is possible that in the course of time a cure for cancer will be found.* **in the ordinary, normal, etc. course of events, things, etc.** as things usually happen SYN **normally**: *In the normal course of things we would not treat her disappearance as suspicious.* **of course 1** A1 (*also informal* **course**) used to emphasize that what you are saying is true or correct: *'Don't you like my mother?' 'Of course I do!' ◊ 'Will you be there?' 'Course I will.'* **2** A1 (*also informal* **course**) used as a polite way of giving sb permission to do sth: *'Can I come, too?' 'Course you can.' ◊ 'Can I have one of those pens?' 'Of course—help yourself.'* **3** A2 used as a polite way of agreeing with what sb has just said: *'I did all I could to help.' 'Of course,' he murmured gently.*

▼ **BRITISH/AMERICAN**

### course / program
- In *BrE* **course** is used for a series of lessons or lectures on a particular subject: *a physics course ◊ a course of ten lectures.* In *NAmE* you would say: *a physics course/program ◊ a program of ten lectures.*
- In *NAmE* a **course** is usually an individual unit that forms part of a longer period of study: *I have to take a physics course/class.* This is called a **module** in Britain, especially in a college or university.
- In *BrE* **course** can also mean a period of study at a college or university: *a two-year college course.* In *NAmE* you would say: *a two-year college program.*

▼ **MORE ABOUT …**

### of course
- **Of course** is often used to show that what you are saying is not surprising or is generally known or accepted. For this reason, and because it can be difficult to get the right intonation, you may not sound polite if you use **of course** or **of course not** when you answer a request for information or permission. It can be safer to use a different word or phrase.
- *'Is this the right room for the English class?' 'Yes, it is.' ◊ 'Of course.' or 'Of course it is.'*
- *'Can I borrow your dictionary?' 'Certainly.' (formal) ◊ 'Sure.' (informal)*
- *'Do you mind if I borrow your dictionary?' 'Not at all.' ◊ 'Go ahead.' (informal).*
- If you say **of course/of course not** it may sound as though you think the answer to the question is obvious and that the person should not ask. In the same way, **of course** should not be used as a reply to a statement of fact or when someone expresses an opinion: *'It's a lovely day.' 'It certainly is.'/'Yes it is.' ◊ 'Of course it is.' ◊ 'I think you'll enjoy that play.' 'I'm sure I will.'/'Yes, it sounds really good.' ◊ 'Of course.'*

**4** [A2] used to show that what you are saying is not surprising or is generally known or accepted: *Ben, of course, was the last to arrive.* ◇ *Of course, there are other ways of doing this.* ⊃ LANGUAGE BANK at NEVERTHELESS **of ˈcourse ˈnot** (*also* **ˈcourse not**) used to emphasize the fact that you are saying 'no': *'Are you going?' 'Of course not.'* ◇ *'Do you mind?' 'No, of course not.'* **on ˈcourse for sth/to do sth** likely to achieve or do sth because you have already started to do it: *The American economy is on course for higher inflation than Britain by the end of the year.* **run/take its ˈcourse** to develop in the usual way and come to the usual end: *When her tears had run their course, she felt calmer and more in control.* ◇ *With minor ailments the best thing is often to let nature take its course.* ⊃ more at COLLISION, DUE *adj.*, HORSE *n.*, MATTER *n.*, MIDDLE *adj.*, NATURE, PAR, PERVERT *v.*, STAY *v.*
- *verb* [I] + *adv./prep.* (*literary*) (of liquid) to move or flow quickly

**course-book** /ˈkɔːsbʊk; *NAmE* ˈkɔːrs-/ *noun* (*BrE*) a book for studying from, used regularly on a particular course of study

**course of ˈaction** *noun* (*pl.* **courses of action**) = COURSE (8)

**course-ware** /ˈkɔːsweə(r); *NAmE* ˈkɔːrswer/ *noun* [U] (*computing*) computer programs that are designed to be used to teach a subject

**course-work** /ˈkɔːswɜːk; *NAmE* ˈkɔːrswɜːrk/ *noun* [U] work that students do during a course of study, not in exams, that is included in their final mark: *Coursework accounts for 40 per cent of the final marks.*

**cours·ing** /ˈkɔːsɪŋ; *NAmE* ˈkɔːrs-/ *noun* [U] the sport of hunting animals with dogs, using sight rather than smell: *hare coursing*

**court** ❶ [B1] /kɔːt; *NAmE* kɔːrt/ *noun, verb*
- *noun*
- LAW **1** [B1] [C, U] the place where legal trials take place and where crimes, etc. are judged: *the civil/criminal courts* ◇ *Her lawyer made a statement outside the court.* ◇ *in* ~ *She will appear in court tomorrow.* ◇ *to* ~ *They took their landlord to court for breaking the contract.* ◇ *The case took five years to come to court* (= to be heard by the court). ◇ *There wasn't enough evidence to bring the case to court* (= start a trial). ◇ *out of* ~ *The case was settled out of court* (= a decision was reached without a trial). ◇ *He won the court case and was awarded damages.* ◇ *She can't pay her tax and is facing court action.* ⊃ see also COURTHOUSE, COURTROOM, LAW COURT ⊃ WORDFINDER NOTE at LAW ⊃ note at SCHOOL **2** [B1] **the court** [usually sing.] the people in a court, especially those who make the decisions, such as the judge and JURY: *Please tell the court what happened.* ◇ *The court heard how the man collapsed after being stabbed.* ◇ *before the* ~ *This evidence was not put before the court.* ◇ *Airlines could face huge compensation bills following a court ruling on flight delays.* ⊃ see also APPEAL COURT, CONTEMPT OF COURT, COUNTY COURT, CROWN COURT, HIGH COURT, JUVENILE COURT, MOOT COURT, SUPREME COURT
- FOR SPORT **3** [B1] [C] a place where games such as tennis and basketball are played: *a tennis/squash/basketball court* ◇ *on/off* ~ *He won after only 52 minutes on court.* ⊃ see also CLAY COURT, GRASS COURT, HALF-COURT, HARD COURT
- KINGS/QUEENS **4** [C, U] the official place where kings and queens live: *the court of Queen Victoria* ◇ *at* ~ *He was presented to the queen at court.* **5 the court** [sing.] the king or queen, their family, and the people who work for them and/or give advice to them: *The painting shows the emperor with his court.*
- BUILDINGS **6** [C] = COURTYARD **7** (*abbr.* **Ct**) [C] used in the names of blocks of flats or apartment buildings, or of some short streets, (in the UK) used in the names of some large houses **8** [C] a large open section of a building, often with a glass roof: *the food court at the shopping mall*

IDM **hold ˈcourt (with sb)** to entertain people by telling them interesting or funny things **rule/throw sth out of ˈcourt** to say that sth is completely wrong or not worth considering, especially in a trial: *The charges were thrown out of court.* ◇ *Well that's my theory ruled out of court.* ⊃ more at BALL *n.*, LAUGH *v.*, PAY *v.*

- *verb*
- TRY TO PLEASE **1** [T] ~ **sb** to try to please sb in order to get sth you want, especially the support of a person, an organization, etc. SYN **cultivate**: *Both candidates have spent the last month courting the media.*
- TRY TO GET **2** [T] ~ **sth** (*formal*) to try to obtain sth: *He has never courted popularity.*
- INVITE STH BAD **3** [T] ~ **sth** (*formal*) to do sth that might result in sth unpleasant happening: *to court danger/death/disaster* ◇ *As a politician he has often courted controversy.*
- HAVE RELATIONSHIP **4** [T, I] ~ **(sb)** (*old-fashioned*) to have a romantic relationship with sb that you hope to marry: *At that time they had been courting for several years.* ⊃ see also COURTSHIP
- ANIMALS **5** ~ **sth** (of a male bird or other animal) to try to attract a female

▼ **WHICH WORD?**

**court / law court / court of law**
- All these words can be used to refer to a place where legal trials take place. **Court** and (*formal*) **court of law** usually refer to the actual room where cases are judged. **Courtroom** is also used for this. **Law court** (*BrE*) is more often used to refer to the building: *The prison is opposite the law court.* **Courthouse** is used for this in *NAmE*.

**ˈcourt card** (*BrE*) (*also* **ˈface card** *NAmE, BrE*) *noun* a PLAYING CARD with a picture of a king, queen or JACK on it

**ˈcourt costs** *noun* [pl.] = COSTS

**cour·te·ous** /ˈkɜːtiəs; *NAmE* ˈkɜːrt-/ *adj.* polite, especially in a way that shows respect: *a courteous young man* ◇ *The hotel staff are friendly and courteous.* OPP **discourteous**
▶ **cour·te·ous·ly** *adv.*

**cour·te·san** /ˌkɔːtɪˈzæn; *NAmE* ˈkɔːrtɪzn/ *noun* (in the past) a PROSTITUTE, especially one with rich customers

**cour·tesy** [C1] /ˈkɜːtəsi; *NAmE* ˈkɜːrt-/ *noun, adj.*
- *noun* (*pl.* **-ies**) **1** [C1] [U] polite behaviour that shows respect for other people SYN **politeness**: *I was treated with the utmost courtesy by the staff.* ◇ *It's only common courtesy to tell the neighbours that we'll be having a party* (= the sort of behaviour that people would expect). **2** [C, usually pl.] (*formal*) a polite thing that you say or do when you meet people in formal situations: *an exchange of courtesies before the meeting*
IDM **courtesy of sb/sth 1** (*also* **by courtesy of sb/sth**) with the official permission of sb/sth and as a favour: *The pictures have been reproduced by courtesy of the British Museum.* **2** given as a prize or provided free by a person or an organization: *Win a weekend in Rome, courtesy of Fiat.* **3** as the result of a particular thing or situation: *Viewers can see the stadium from the air, courtesy of a camera fastened to the plane.* **do sb the courtesy of doing sth** to be polite by doing the thing that is mentioned: *Please do me the courtesy of listening to what I'm saying.* **have the courtesy to do sth** to know when you should do sth in order to be polite: *You think he'd at least have the courtesy to call to say he'd be late.*
- *adj.* [only before noun] (of a bus, car, etc.) provided free, at no cost to the person using it: *A courtesy bus operates between the hotel and the beach.* ◇ *The dealer will provide you with a courtesy car while your vehicle is being repaired.*

**ˈcourtesy call** *noun* **1** (*also* **ˈcourtesy visit**) a formal or official visit, usually by one important person to another, just to be polite, not to discuss important business **2** a phone call from a company to one of its customers, for example to see if they are satisfied with the company's service

**court·house** /ˈkɔːthaʊs; *NAmE* ˈkɔːrt-/ *noun* **1** (*especially NAmE*) a building containing courts of law ⊃ note at COURT **2** (in the US) a building containing the offices of a county government

**court·ier** /ˈkɔːtiə(r); *NAmE* ˈkɔːrt-/ *noun* (especially in the past) a person who is part of the COURT of a king or queen

# courtly

**court·ly** /ˈkɔːtli; NAmE ˈkɔːrt-/ adj. (formal or literary) extremely polite and full of respect, especially in an old-fashioned way

**courtly ˈlove** noun [U] a tradition in literature, especially in Medieval times, involving the love of a KNIGHT for his married LADY, with whom he can never have a relationship

**court ˈmartial** noun [C, U] (pl. courts martial) a military court that deals with members of the armed forces who break military law; a trial at such a court: *He was convicted at a court martial.* ◊ *All the men now face court martial.*

**court-ˈmar·tial** verb [often passive] (-ll-, US -l-) to hold a trial of sb in a military court: **be court-martialled (for sth)** *He was court-martialled for desertion.*

**court of apˈpeal** noun **1** (also **appeal court**) (pl. **courts of appeal**) a court that people can go to in order to try and change decisions that have been made by a lower court ⊃ see also APPELLATE COURT **2 Court of Apˈpeal** (also **Appeal Court**) [sing.] the highest court in England and Wales (apart from the SUPREME COURT), which can change decisions made by a lower court **3 court of apˈpeals** (also **apˈpeals court**) [C] (US) one of the courts in the US that can change decisions made by a lower court

**court of ˈclaims** noun (pl. **courts of claims**) (US) a court in the US that hears claims made against the government

**court of inˈquiry** (also **court of enˈquiry**) noun (pl. **courts of inquiry / enquiry**) (BrE) a special official group of people that investigates a particular problem

**court of ˈlaw** noun (pl. **courts of law**) (formal) (also **law court**) a room or building where legal cases are judged ⊃ note at COURT

**Court of ˈSession** noun in Scotland, the highest court that deals with CIVIL cases (= not criminal cases)

**ˈcourt order** noun a decision that is made in court about what must happen in a particular situation

**ˈcourt reporter** noun **1** (NAmE) a person whose job is to create the official written record of what is said in court **2** a journalist who goes to court to report on what happens there

**court·room** /ˈkɔːtruːm, -rʊm; NAmE ˈkɔːrt-/ noun a room in which trials or other legal cases are held ⊃ note at COURT

**court·ship** /ˈkɔːtʃɪp; NAmE ˈkɔːrtʃ-/ noun **1** [C, U] (old-fashioned) the time when two people have a romantic relationship before they get married; the process of developing this relationship: *They married after a short courtship.* ◊ *Mr Elton's courtship of Harriet* **2** [U] the special way animals behave in order to attract a MATE (= sexual partner): *courtship displays* **3** [U] **~ (of sb/sth)** (formal) the process or act of attracting a business partner, etc: *the company's courtship by the government*

**ˈcourt shoe** (BrE) (NAmE **pump**) noun a woman's formal shoe that is plain and does not cover the top part of the foot

**court·yard** /ˈkɔːtjɑːd; NAmE ˈkɔːrtjɑːrd/ (also **court**) noun an open space that is partly or completely surrounded by buildings and is usually part of a castle, a large house, etc: *the central/inner courtyard*

**cous·cous** /ˈkʊskʊs, ˈkuːskuːs/ noun [U] a type of North African food made from WHEAT in very small round pieces; a dish of meat and/or vegetables with couscous

**cousin** ⓘ **A1** /ˈkʌzn/ noun **1 A1** (also **first ˈcousin**) a child of your aunt or uncle: *She's my cousin.* ◊ *We're cousins.* ◊ **~ to sb** *He claims to be a cousin to the Queen.* ⊃ see also SECOND COUSIN **2 B1** a person who is in your wider family but who is not closely related to you: *She's some sort of cousin, I think.* ◊ **~ of sb/sb's** *He's a distant cousin of mine.* **3** [usually pl.] a way of describing people from another country who are similar in some way to people in your own country: *our American cousins* **4** [usually pl.] a way of describing things that are similar or related in some way: *Asian elephants are smaller than their African cousins.*

356

**ˈcousin brother** noun (IndE, informal) a male cousin of your own generation

**ˈcousin sister** noun (IndE, informal) a female cousin of your own generation

**cou·ture** /kuˈtjʊə(r); NAmE -ˈtʊr/ noun [U] (from French) the design and production of expensive and fashionable clothes; these clothes: *a couture evening dress* ⊃ see also HAUTE COUTURE

**cou·tur·ier** /kuˈtjʊəriər; NAmE -ˈtʊr-/ noun (from French) a person who designs, makes and sells expensive, fashionable clothes, especially for women SYN **fashion designer**

**co·va·lent** /ˌkəʊˈveɪlənt; adj. (chemistry) (of a chemical BOND) sharing a pair of ELECTRONS ⊃ compare IONIC

**cove** /kəʊv/ noun **1** a small BAY (= an area of sea that is partly surrounded by land): *a secluded cove* **2** (BrE, old-fashioned, informal) a man

**coven** /ˈkʌvn/ noun a group or meeting of WITCHES

**cov·en·ant** /ˈkʌvənənt/ noun a promise to sb, or a legal agreement, especially one to pay a regular amount of money to sb/sth: *God's covenant with Abraham* ◊ *a covenant to a charity* ▸ **cov·en·ant** verb: **~ sth (to sb/sth)** *All profits are covenanted to medical charities.*

**Cov·en·try** /ˈkɒvəntri; NAmE ˈkʌv-, ˈkɑːv-/ noun IDM **send sb to ˈCoventry** (BrE) to refuse to speak to sb, as a way of punishing them for sth that they have done

## cover ⓘ A2 /ˈkʌvə(r)/ verb, noun

■ verb
- HIDE/PROTECT **1** A2 [T] to place sth over or in front of sth in order to hide, protect or decorate it: **~ sth with sth** *Cover the chicken loosely with foil.* ◊ *She covered her face with her hands.* ◊ **~ sth** *I covered my mouth to stifle a yawn.* ◊ (figurative) *He laughed to cover (= hide) his nervousness.* ⊃ SYNONYMS at HIDE
- SPREAD OVER SURFACE **2** A2 [T] to lie or spread over the surface of sth: **~ sth** *Snow covered the ground.* ◊ **be covered with/in sth** *Its head, body, and tail are completely covered with brown fur.* **3** A2 [T] to put or spread a layer of liquid, dust, etc. on sb/sth: **~ sb/sth with/in sth** *The wind blew in from the desert and covered everything with sand.* ◊ **be covered with/in sth** *The players were soon covered in mud.*
- INCLUDE **4** B1 [T] **~ sth** to include sth; to deal with sth: *The lectures covered a lot of ground* (= a lot of material, subjects, etc.). ◊ *the sales team covering the northern part of the country* (= selling to people in that area) ◊ *Do the rules cover* (= do they apply to) *a case like this?* ◊ *Don't worry. I've got it covered* (= I'm dealing with it).
- MONEY **5** B2 [T] **~ sth** to be or provide enough money for sth: *$100 should cover your expenses.* ◊ *The show barely covered its costs.* ◊ *Your parents will have to cover your tuition fees.*
- DISTANCE/AREA **6** [T] **~ sth** to travel the distance mentioned: *By sunset we had covered thirty miles.* ◊ *They walked for a long time and covered a good deal of ground.* **7** [T] **~ sth** to spread over the area mentioned: *The reserve covers an area of some 1140 square kilometres.*
- REPORT NEWS **8** [T] **~ sth** to report on an event for television, a newspaper, etc.; to show an event on television: *She's covering the party's annual conference.* ◊ *The BBC will cover all the major games of the tournament.*
- FOR SB **9** [I] **~ for sb** to do sb's work or duties while they are away: *I'm covering for Jane while she's on leave.* **10** [I] **~ for sb** to invent a lie or an excuse that will stop sb from getting into trouble: *I have to go out for a minute—will you cover for me if anyone asks where I am?*
- WITH INSURANCE **11** [T] to protect sb against loss, injury, etc. by insurance: **~ sb/sth (against/for sth)** *Are you fully covered for fire and theft?* ◊ **~ sb/sth to do sth** *Does this policy cover my husband to drive?*
- AGAINST BLAME **12** [T] **~ yourself (against sth)** to take action in order to protect yourself against being blamed for sth: *Many firms put money aside to cover themselves against possible legal claims.*
- WITH GUN **13** [T] **~ sb** to protect sb by threatening to shoot at anyone who tries to attack them: *Cover me while I move forward.* **14** [T] **~ sb/sth** to aim a gun at a place or person so that nobody can escape or shoot: *The police covered the exits to the building.* ◊ *Don't move—we've got you covered!*

- SONG **15** [T] ~ sth to record a new version of a song that was originally recorded by another band or singer: *They've covered an old Rolling Stones number.*

**IDM** ,cover all the 'bases to consider and deal with all the things that could happen or could be needed when you are arranging sth ,cover your 'back (*informal*) (*NAmE also* ,cover your 'ass *taboo, slang*) to realize that you may be blamed or criticized for sth later and take action to avoid this: *Get everything in writing in order to cover your back.* ,cover your 'tracks to try and hide what you have done, because you do not want other people to find out about it: *He had attempted to cover his tracks by making her death appear like suicide.* ⇒ more at MULTITUDE

**PHRV** ,cover sth↔ 'in to put a cover or roof over an open space ,cover sth↔ 'over to cover sth completely so that it cannot be seen **SYN** conceal: *The Roman remains are now covered over by office buildings.* ,cover 'up | ,cover yourself 'up to put on clothes or more clothes ,cover sth↔ 'up **1** to cover sth completely so that it cannot be seen: *He covered up the body with a sheet.* **2** (*disapproving*) to try to stop people from knowing the truth about a mistake, a crime, etc. ⇒ related noun COVER-UP

■ *noun*
- PROTECTION/SHELTER **1** [C] a thing that is put over or on another thing, usually to protect it or to decorate it: *a cushion cover* ◇ **~ for sth** *a plastic waterproof cover for the pushchair* ⇒ see also DUST COVER, LOOSE COVER **2** [U] **(for)** ~ shelter from bad weather or protection from an attack: *Everyone ran for cover when it started to rain.* ◇ *The climbers took cover from the storm in a cave.*
- OF BOOK **3** [C] the outside of a book or a magazine: *the front/back cover* ◇ *on the ~ Her face was on the cover* (= the front cover) *of every magazine.* ◇ *He always reads the paper from cover to cover* (= everything in it).
- INSURANCE **4** (*BrE*) (*NAmE* cov·er·age) [U] protection that an insurance company provides by promising to pay you money if a particular event happens: *accident cover* ◇ *~ against sth cover against accidental damage* ⇒ WORDFINDER NOTE at INSURANCE
- WITH WEAPONS **5** [U] support and protection that is provided when sb is attacking or in danger of being attacked: *The ships needed air cover* (= protection by military planes) *once they reached enemy waters.*
- TREES/PLANTS **6** [U] trees and plants that grow on an area of land: *The total forest cover of the earth is decreasing.* ⇒ see also GROUND COVER
- CLOUD/SNOW **7** [U] the fact of the sky being covered with cloud or the ground with snow: *Fog and low cloud cover are expected this afternoon.* ◇ *In this area there is snow cover for six months of the year.*
- ON BED **8** the covers [pl.] the sheets, BLANKETS, etc. on a bed: *She threw back the covers and leapt out of bed.*
- SONG **9** [C] (*also* cover version) a new recording of an old song by a different band or singer: *They started out singing covers of country songs.* ◇ *a Beatles cover band* (= a band that plays songs originally recorded by the Beatles).
- HIDING STH **10** [C, usually sing.] ~ **(for sth)** activities or behaviour that seem honest or true but that hide sb's real identity or feelings, or that hide sth illegal: *His work as a civil servant was a cover for his activities as a spy.* ◇ *Her over-confident attitude was a cover for her nervousness.* ◇ *It would only take one phone call to blow their cover* (= make known their true identities and what they were really doing).
- FOR SB'S WORK **11** [U] the fact of sb doing a job when the person who usually does it is away or when there are not enough staff: *It's the manager's job to organize cover for staff who are absent.* ◇ *Ambulance drivers provided only emergency cover during the dispute.*

**IDM** break 'cover to leave a place that you have been hiding in, usually at a high speed under 'cover **1** pretending to be sb else in order to do sth secretly: *a police officer working under cover* **2** under a structure that gives protection from the weather under (the) cover of sth hidden or protected by sth: *Later, under cover of darkness, they crept into the house.* under separate 'cover (*business*) in a separate ENVELOPE: *The information you requested is being forwarded to you under separate cover.* ⇒ more at JUDGE *v.*

**cov·er·age** /ˈkʌvərɪdʒ/ *noun* **1** [U] the reporting of news and sport in the media: *media/newspaper/press coverage* ◇ *tonight's live coverage of the hockey game* ⇒ WORDFINDER NOTE at JOURNALIST **2** [U] the range or quality of information that is included in a book or course of study, on television, etc: *magazines with extensive coverage of diet and health topics* ◇ *The volume offers incomplete coverage of the history of philosophy.* **3** [U, C, usually sing.] the amount of sth that sth provides; the extent to which sth covers an area or a group of people: *Immunization coverage against fatal diseases has increased to 99 per cent in some countries.* ◇ *The service has a coverage of 90 per cent of the UK population.* **4** (*NAmE*) (*BrE* cover) [U] protection that an insurance company provides by promising to pay you money if a particular event happens: *insurance coverage* ◇ *Medicaid health coverage for low-income families*

**cover·all** /ˈkʌvərɔːl/ *noun* [usually pl.] (*NAmE*) (*BrE* overalls [pl.]) a loose piece of clothing like a shirt and trousers in one piece, made of heavy cloth and usually worn over other clothing by workers doing dirty work ⇒ picture at OVERALL

'cover charge *noun* [usually sing.] an amount of money that you pay in some restaurants or clubs in addition to the cost of the food and drink

**covered** /ˈkʌvəd; *NAmE* -vərd/ *adj.* **1** [not before noun] ~ **in / with sth** having a layer or amount of sth on it: *His face was covered in blood.* ◇ *I was completely covered in mud.* ◇ *The walls were covered with pictures.* ⇒ see also SNOW-COVERED **2** having a roof over it: *a covered walkway/bridge* ◇ *a covered area of the stadium with seats* **3** -covered having a layer of the thing mentioned on or around sth: *chocolate-covered banana slices*

,covered 'wagon *noun* a large wooden vehicle pulled by horses, with a curved roof made of cloth, used especially in the past in North America by people travelling across the land to the west

'cover girl *noun* a young woman whose photograph is on the front of a magazine

**cov·er·ing** /ˈkʌvərɪŋ/ *noun* **1** a layer of sth that covers sth else: *a thick covering of snow on the ground* **2** a layer of material such as carpet or WALLPAPER, used to cover, decorate and protect floors, walls, etc: *floor/wall coverings* **3** a piece of material that covers sth: *He pulled the plastic covering off the dead body.*

'covering letter (*BrE*) (*NAmE* 'cover letter) *noun* a letter that you send with sth explaining the contents of the document, etc. that you are sending

'cover story *noun* **1** the main story in a magazine that goes with the picture shown on the front cover **2** a story that is invented in order to hide sth, especially a person's identity or their reasons for doing sth

**cov·ert** *adj., noun*
■ *adj.* /ˈkʌvət, ˈkəʊvɜːt; *NAmE* ˈkoʊvɜːrt/ (*formal*) secret or hidden, making it difficult to notice: *covert operations/surveillance* ◇ *He stole a covert glance at her across the table.* ⇒ compare OVERT ▶ cov·ert·ly *adv.*: *She watched him covertly in the mirror.*
■ *noun* /ˈkʌvət; *NAmE* ˈkʌvərt/ an area of thick low bushes and trees where animals can hide

'cover-up *noun* [usually sing.] action that is taken to hide a mistake or an illegal activity from the public: *Government sources denied there had been a deliberate cover-up.*

'cover version *noun* = COVER (9)

**covet** /ˈkʌvət/ *verb* ~ sth (*formal*) to want sth very much, especially sth that belongs to sb else: *He had long coveted the chance to work with a famous musician.* ◇ *They are this year's winners of the coveted trophy* (= that everyone would like to win).

**cov·et·ous** /ˈkʌvətəs/ *adj.* (*formal*) having a strong desire for the things that other people have ▶ cov·et·ous·ness *noun* [U]

# COW

**cow** /kaʊ/ noun, verb
- **noun 1** a large animal kept on farms to produce milk or beef: *to milk a cow* ◊ *cow's milk* ◊ *a herd of dairy cows* (= cows kept for their milk) ⇒ see also MAD COW DISEASE ⇒ compare BULL, CALF, HEIFER ⇒ see also CATTLE **2** the female of the elephant, WHALE and some other large animals ⇒ compare BULL **3** (*slang, disapproving*) an offensive word for a woman: *You stupid cow!* **4** (*AustralE, NZE*) an unpleasant person, thing or situation ⇒ see also CASH COW, SACRED COW
  **IDM** **have a 'cow** (*NAmE, informal*) to become very angry or anxious about sth: *Don't have a cow—it's no big deal.* **till the 'cows come home** (*informal*) for a very long time; forever
- **verb** [usually passive] to frighten sb in order to make them obey you **SYN** **intimidate**: **be cowed (by sb/sth)** *She was easily cowed by people in authority.*

**cow·ard** /ˈkaʊəd; *NAmE* -ərd/ *noun* (*disapproving*) a person who is not brave or who does not have the courage to do things that other people do not think are especially difficult: *You coward! What are you afraid of?* ◊ *I'm a real coward when it comes to going to the dentist.* ▸ **cow·ard·ly** *adj.*: *a cowardly attack on a defenceless man*

▾ **HOMOPHONES**

**coward • cowered** /ˈkaʊəd; *NAmE* -ərd/
- **coward** *noun*: *He was both a bully and a coward, as bullies often are.*
- **cowered** *verb* (*past tense, past participle* of **COWER**): *They boarded up the windows and cowered in the basement.*

**cow·ard·ice** /ˈkaʊədɪs; *NAmE* -ərd-/ *noun* [U] (*disapproving*) fear or lack of courage **OPP** **bravery, courage**

**cow·bell** /ˈkaʊbel/ *noun* a bell that is put around a cow's neck so that the cow can easily be found

**cow·boy** /ˈkaʊbɔɪ/ *noun* **1** a man who rides a horse and whose job is to take care of CATTLE in the western parts of the US **2** a man like this as a character in a film about the American West: *old Hollywood cowboy movies* **3** (*BrE, informal, disapproving*) a dishonest person in business, especially sb who produces work of bad quality or charges too high a price

**'cowboy boot** *noun* a type of leather boot with a high heel and a pointed toe, originally worn by cowboys

**'cowboy hat** *noun* a hat with a wide BRIM, worn by American cowboys

**cowed** /kaʊd/ *adj.* made to feel afraid and that you are not as good as sb else ⇒ see also COW *verb*

**cower** /ˈkaʊə(r)/ *verb* [I] to bend low and/or move backwards because you are frightened: *A gun went off and people cowered behind walls and under tables.* ⇒ HOMOPHONES at COWARD

**cow·girl** /ˈkaʊɡɜːl; *NAmE* -ɡɜːrl/ *noun* a female COWBOY in the American West

**cow·hide** /ˈkaʊhaɪd/ *noun* [U] strong leather made from the skin of a cow

**'co-wife** *noun* (in some cultures) a fellow wife of the same man

**cowl** /kaʊl/ *noun* **1** a large loose piece of cloth that covers the head, worn especially by MONKS **2** a cover for a CHIMNEY, etc., usually made of metal. Cowls often turn with the wind and are designed to improve the flow of air or smoke.

**cowl·ing** /ˈkaʊlɪŋ/ *noun* (*specialist*) a metal cover for an engine, especially on an aircraft

**'co-worker** *noun* a person that sb works with, doing the same kind of job **SYN** **colleague**

**cow·pea** /ˈkaʊpiː/ *noun* a type of bean that is white with a black spot and is grown for food: *Cowpeas are an important crop in many African countries.*

**cow·rie** /ˈkaʊri/ *noun* a small shiny shell that was used as money in the past in parts of Africa and Asia

**cow·shed** /ˈkaʊʃed/ *noun* a farm building in which cows are kept

**cow·slip** /ˈkaʊslɪp/ *noun* a small wild plant with yellow flowers with a sweet smell

**cox** /kɒks; *NAmE* kɑːks/ *noun, verb*
- **noun** (also **cox·swain**) the person who controls the direction of a ROWING BOAT while other people are ROWING
- **verb** [T, I] ~ **(sth)** to control the direction of a ROWING BOAT while other people are ROWING; to act as a cox

**cox·swain** /ˈkɒksn; *NAmE* ˈkɑːk-/ *noun* **1** the person who is in charge of a LIFEBOAT and who controls its direction **2** = COX

**coy** /kɔɪ/ *adj.* **1** shy or pretending to be shy and innocent, especially about love or sex, and sometimes in order to make people more interested in you: *She gave me a coy smile.* **2** ~ **(about sth)** not willing to give information about sth, or answer questions that tell people too much about you **SYN** **reticent**: *She was a little coy about how much her dress cost.* ▸ **coy·ly** *adv.* **coy·ness** *noun* [U]

**coy·ote** /ˈkaɪəʊti; *BrE also* kɔɪ-; *NAmE also* ˈkaɪoʊt/ (*also* **'prairie wolf**) *noun* a North American wild animal of the dog family

**coy·pu** /ˈkɔɪpuː/ *noun* (*pl.* **coy·pus, coy·pu**) a large South American animal, like a BEAVER, that lives near water

**coz** *conj.* = $\cos^1$

**cozy** (*NAmE*) (*BrE* **cosy**) /ˈkəʊzi/ *adj., verb*
- *adj.* (**cozi·er, cozi·est, cosi·er, cosi·est**) **1** warm, comfortable and safe, especially in a small space **SYN** **snug**: *a cozy little room* ◊ *a cozy feeling* ◊ *I felt warm and cozy sitting by the fire.* **2** friendly and private: *a cozy chat with a friend* **3** (*often disapproving*) easy and convenient, but not always honest or right: *The firm has a cozy relationship with the Department of Defense.* ◊ *The danger is that things get too cozy.* ▸ **cozi·ly** /-zɪli/ (*NAmE*) (*BrE* **cosi·ly**) *adv.*: *sitting cozily by the fire* **cozi·ness** (*NAmE*) (*BrE* **cosi·ness**) *noun* [U]: *the warmth and coziness of the kitchen*
- *verb* (**cozies, cozy·ing, cozied, cozied**)
  **PHRV** **'cozy up to sb** (*NAmE*) (*BrE* **'cosy 'up to sb**) (*informal*) to act in a friendly way towards sb, especially sb who will be useful to you: *He was accused of cozying up to the people in power.*

**cp.** *abbr.* (in writing) compare

**CPE** /ˌsiː piː ˈiː/ *noun* [U] a British test, now called 'C2 Proficiency', that measures a person's ability to speak and write English at a very advanced level (the abbreviation for 'Certificate of Proficiency in English')

**CPI** /ˌsiː piː ˈaɪ/ *abbr.* CONSUMER PRICE INDEX

**Cpl** (*BrE*) (*NAmE* **Cpl.**) *abbr.* (in writing) CORPORAL

**CPR** /ˌsiː piː ˈɑː(r)/ *noun* [U] breathing air into the mouth of an unconscious person and pressing on their chest to keep them alive by sending air around their body (the abbreviation for 'cardiopulmonary resuscitation')

**CPU** /ˌsiː piː ˈjuː/ *abbr.* (*computing*) central processing unit (the part of a computer that controls all the other parts of the system)

**CRA** /ˌsiː ɑːr ˈeɪ/ *abbr.* Canada Revenue Agency (the department of the Canadian government that deals with personal income tax)

**crab** /kræb/ *noun* **1** [C] a sea creature with a hard shell, eight legs and two PINCERS (= curved and pointed arms for catching and holding things). Crabs move SIDEWAYS (= towards the side) on land. ⇒ **VISUAL VOCAB** page V3 ⇒ see also HERMIT CRAB **2** [U] meat from a crab, used for food: *dressed crab* **3** **crabs** (*informal*) the condition caused by having LICE (called **'crab lice**) in the hair around the GENITALS

**'crab apple** *noun* a tree that produces fruit like small hard apples with a bitter sharp taste, also called crab apples

**crabbed** /ˈkræbɪd, kræbd/ *adj.* (*literary*) **1** (of sb's writing) small and difficult to read **2** = CRABBY

**crabby** /ˈkræbi/ adj. (informal) (of people) angry and unpleasant

**crab·grass** /ˈkræbgrɑːs; NAmE -græs/ noun [U] (especially NAmE) a type of grass that grows where it is not wanted, spreads quickly and is hard to get rid of

**crack** /kræk/ verb, noun, adj.
■ verb
- **BREAK** 1 [I, T] to break without dividing into separate parts; to break sth in this way: *The ice cracked as I stepped onto it.* ◇ ~ **sth** *He has cracked a bone in his arm.* 2 [I, T] to break open or into pieces; to break sth in this way: **+ adv./prep.** *A chunk of the cliff had cracked off in a storm.* ◇ (figurative) *His face cracked into a smile.* ◇ ~ **sth** *to crack a nut* ◇ ~ **sth + adv./prep.** *She cracked an egg into the pan.*
- **HIT** 3 [T] ~ **sth/sb (on/against sth)** to hit sth/sb in a short hard manner: *I cracked my head on the low ceiling.* ◇ *He cracked me on the head with a ruler.*
- **MAKE SOUND** 4 [I, T] to make a sharp sound; to make sth do this: *A shot cracked across the ridge.* ◇ [no passive] ~ **sth** *He cracked his whip and galloped away.*
- **OF VOICE** 5 [I] if your voice **cracks**, it changes in depth, volume, etc. suddenly and in a way that you cannot control: *In a voice cracking with emotion, he told us of his son's death.*
- **UNDER PRESSURE** 6 [I] to no longer be able to function normally because of pressure: *Things are terrible at work and people are cracking under the strain.* ◇ *They questioned him for days before he cracked.* ◇ *The old institutions are cracking.*
- **FIND SOLUTION** 7 [T] ~ **sth** to find the solution to a problem, etc; to find the way to do sth difficult: *to crack the enemy's code* ◇ (informal) *After a year in this job I think I've got it cracked!*
- **STOP SB/STH** 8 [T] ~ **sth** to find a way of stopping or defeating a criminal or an enemy: *Police have cracked a major drugs ring.*
- **OPEN BOTTLE** 9 [T] ~ **(open) a bottle** (informal) to open a bottle, especially of wine, and drink it
- **A JOKE** 10 [T] ~ **a joke** (informal) to tell a joke

**IDM** **crack the ˈwhip** to use your authority or power to make sb work very hard, usually by treating them in a strict way **get ˈcracking** (informal) to begin immediately and work quickly **SYN** **get going**: *There's a lot to be done, so let's get cracking.* **not all, everything, etc. sb's cracked ˈup to be** (informal) not as good as people say: *He's not nearly such a good writer as he's cracked up to be.* ⊃ more at **NUT** n., **SLEDGEHAMMER**

**PHRV** **crack ˈdown (on sb/sth)** to try harder to prevent an illegal activity and deal more severely with those who are caught doing it: *Police are cracking down on drug dealers.* ⊃ related noun **CRACKDOWN** **crack ˈon (with sth)** (BrE, informal) to work hard at sth so that you finish it quickly; to pass or continue quickly: *If we crack on with the painting we should finish it today.* ◇ *Time was cracking on and we were nowhere near finished.* **crack ˈup** (informal) 1 to become ill, either physically or mentally, because of pressure: *You'll crack up if you carry on working like this.* 2 to start laughing a lot: *He walked in and everyone just cracked up.* **crack sb ˈup** (informal) to make sb laugh a lot: *Gill's so funny—she just cracks me up.*

■ noun
- **BREAK** 1 [C] ~ **(in sth)** a line on the surface of sth where it has broken but not split into separate parts: *This cup has a crack in it.* ◇ *Cracks began to appear in the walls.* ◇ (figurative) *The cracks (= faults) in the government's economic policy are already beginning to show.* ⊃ picture at **BROKEN**
- **NARROW OPENING** 2 [C] a narrow space or opening: *She peeped through the crack in the curtains.* ◇ *The door opened a crack (= just a small amount).*
- **SOUND** 3 [C] a sudden loud noise: *a crack of thunder* ◇ *the sharp crack of a rifle shot*
- **HIT** 4 [C] ~ **(on sth)** a sharp, hard hit that can be heard: *She fell over and got a nasty crack on the head.*
- **ATTEMPT** 5 [C] ~ **(at sth)** | ~ **(at doing sth)** (informal) an occasion when you try to do sth **SYN** **attempt**: *She hopes to have another crack at the world record this year.*

359

# crackle

- **DRUG** 6 (also **ˌcrack coˈcaine**) [U] a powerful, illegal drug that is a form of **COCAINE**: *a crack addict*
- **JOKE** 7 [C] (informal) a joke, especially a critical one: *He made a very unfair crack about her looks.*
- **CONVERSATION** 8 (also **craic**) [U, sing.] (IrishE, informal) a good time; friendly, lively talk: *Where's the crack tonight?* ◇ *He's a person who enjoys a drink and a bit of crack.*

**IDM** **at the crack of ˈdawn** (informal) very early in the morning ⊃ more at **FAIR** adj., **SLIP** v

■ adj. [only before noun] expert and highly trained; excellent at sth: *crack troops* ◇ *He's a crack shot (= accurate and skilled at shooting).*

**crack·down** /ˈkrækdaʊn/ noun ~ **(on sb/sth)** severe action taken to limit the activities of criminals or of people opposed to the government or sb in authority: *a military crackdown on student protesters* ◇ *a crackdown on crime*

**cracked** /krækt/ adj. 1 damaged with lines in its surface but not completely broken: *a cracked mirror/mug* ◇ *He suffered cracked ribs and bruising.* ◇ *Her lips were dry and cracked.* ⊃ picture at **BROKEN** 2 (of sb's voice) sounding rough with sudden changes in how loud or high it is, because the person is upset: *'I'm just fine,' she said in a cracked voice.* 3 [not before noun] (informal) crazy: *I think he must be cracked, don't you?*

**crackers**

**crack·er** /ˈkrækə(r)/ noun 1 a thin dry biscuit that often tastes of salt and is usually eaten with cheese ⊃ see also **GRAHAM CRACKER** 2 (also **ˌChristmas ˈcracker**) a tube of coloured paper that makes a loud **EXPLOSIVE** sound when it is pulled open by two people. Crackers usually contain a paper hat, a small present and a joke, and are used in the UK at Christmas parties and meals: *Who wants to pull this cracker with me?* ⊃ see also **FIRECRACKER** 3 (BrE, informal) something that you think is very good, funny, etc: *It was a cracker of a goal.* ◇ *I've got a joke for you. It's a real cracker!* 4 (NAmE, slang) an offensive word for a poor white person with little education from the southern US 5 (informal) a person who illegally finds a way of looking at or stealing information on sb else's computer system 6 (BrE, old-fashioned, informal) an attractive woman

**crack·er·jack** /ˈkrækədʒæk; NAmE -kərdʒ-/ noun (NAmE, informal) an excellent person or thing ▶ **crack·er·jack** adj.

**crack·ers** /ˈkrækəz; NAmE -kərz/ adj. [not before noun] (BrE, old-fashioned, informal) crazy: *That noise is driving me crackers.*

**crack·head** /ˈkrækhed/ noun (slang) a person who uses the illegal drug **CRACK**

**ˈcrack house** noun a place where people sell **CRACK** (= a type of illegal drug)

**crack·ing** /ˈkrækɪŋ/ noun, adj.
■ noun [U] 1 lines on a surface where it is damaged or beginning to break: *All planes are being inspected for possible cracking and corrosion.* 2 the sound of sth cracking: *the cracking of thunder/twigs*
■ adj. [usually before noun] (BrE, informal) excellent: *That was a cracking goal.* ◇ *She's in cracking form at the moment.* ◇ *We set off at a cracking pace (= very quickly).*

**IDM** **ˈcracking good** (BrE, informal) extremely good: *a cracking good dinner*

**crackle** /ˈkrækl/ verb, noun
■ verb [I] to make short sharp sounds like sth that is burning in a fire: *A log fire crackled in the hearth.* ◇ *The radio crackled into life.* ◇ (figurative) *The atmosphere crackled with tension.*
■ noun [U, C] a series of short sharp sounds: *the distant crackle of machine-gun fire* ▶ **crack·ly** /-kli/ adj.: *She*

**O** Oxford Phrasal Academic Lexicon (OPAL) written and spoken word lists | **W** OPAL written word list | **S** OPAL spoken word list

picked up the phone and heard a crackly voice saying: 'Sue here.'

**crack·ling** /ˈkræklɪŋ/ noun **1** [U, sing.] a series of sharp sounds: *He could hear the crackling of burning trees.* **2** [U] (*BrE*) (*US* **crack·lings** [pl.]) the hard skin of PORK (= meat from a pig) that has been cooked in the oven

**crack·pot** /ˈkrækpɒt; *NAmE* -pɑːt/ noun (*informal*) a person with strange or crazy ideas ▶ **crack·pot** adj. [only before noun]: *crackpot ideas/theories*

**-cracy** /krəsi/ combining form (in nouns) the government or rule of: *democracy* ◇ *bureaucracy*

**cra·dle** /ˈkreɪdl/ noun, verb
■ noun **1** a small bed for a baby that can be pushed gently from side to side: *She rocked the baby to sleep in its cradle.* **2** [usually sing.] **~ of sth** the place where sth important began: *Greece, the cradle of Western civilization* **3** (*BrE*) a small platform that can be moved up and down the outside of a high building, used by people cleaning windows, etc. **4** the part of a phone on which the HANDSET rests
IDM **from the ˌcradle to the ˈgrave** a way of referring to the whole of a person's life, from birth until death ⇒ more at ROB
■ verb **~ sb/sth** to hold sb/sth gently in your arms or hands: *The old man cradled the tiny baby in his arms.*

**ˈcradle-snatcher** (*BrE*) (*NAmE* **ˈcradle-robber**) noun (*disapproving*) a person who has a sexual relationship with a much younger person ▶ **ˈcradle-snatching** (*BrE*) (*NAmE* **ˈcradle-robbing**) noun [U]

**craft** 🔊+ 🅱2 /krɑːft; *NAmE* kræft/ noun, verb
■ noun **1** 🔊+ 🅱2 [C, U] an activity involving a special skill at making things with your hands: *traditional crafts like basket-weaving* ◇ *a craft fair/workshop* ⇒ see also ARTS AND CRAFTS **2** 🔊+ 🅱2 [sing.] all the skills needed for a particular activity: *chefs who learned their craft in top hotels* ◇ *the writer's craft* **3** [U] (*formal, disapproving*) skill in making people believe what you want them to believe: *He knew how to win by craft and diplomacy what he could not gain by force.* **4** [C] (*pl.* **craft**) (*formal*) a boat or ship: *Hundreds of small craft bobbed around the liner as it steamed into the harbour.* ◇ *a landing/pleasure craft* ⇒ see also LANDING CRAFT **5** [C] (*pl.* **craft**) an aircraft or SPACECRAFT
■ verb 🔊+ 🅲1 [usually passive] to make sth using special skills, especially with your hands 🔁 **fashion**: **be crafted (from sth)** *All the furniture is crafted from natural materials.* ◇ *a carefully crafted speech* ⇒ see also HANDCRAFTED

**ˌcraft ˈbeer** noun a beer that is made in a traditional way by a small company

**crafts·man** /ˈkrɑːftsmən; *NAmE* ˈkræfts-/ (*also* **crafts·person**) noun (*pl.* **-men** /-mən/) a person with a special skill, especially one who makes beautiful things by hand: *rugs handmade by local craftsmen* ◇ *It is clearly the work of a master craftsman.* ⇒ see also CRAFTSWOMAN

**crafts·man·ship** /ˈkrɑːftsmənʃɪp; *NAmE* ˈkræfts-/ noun [U] **1** the level of skill shown by sb in making sth beautiful with their hands: *The whole house is a monument to her craftsmanship.* **2** the quality of design and work shown by sth that has been made by hand: *the superb craftsmanship of the carvings*

**crafts·person** /ˈkrɑːftspɜːsn; *NAmE* ˈkræftspɜːrsn/ noun (*pl.* **-people** /-piːpl/) = CRAFTSMAN

**crafts·woman** /ˈkrɑːftswʊmən; *NAmE* ˈkræfts-/ noun (*pl.* **-women** /-wɪmɪn/) a woman with a special skill, especially one who makes beautiful things by hand ▶ note at GENDER

**craft·work** /ˈkrɑːftwɜːk; *NAmE* ˈkræftwɜːrk/ noun [U] work done by a CRAFTSMAN

**crafty** /ˈkrɑːfti; *NAmE* ˈkræf-/ adj. (**craft·ier, crafti·est**) (*usually disapproving*) clever at getting what you want, especially by indirect or dishonest methods 🔁 **cunning, wily**: *He's a crafty old devil.* ◇ *one of the party's craftiest political strategists* ▶ **craft·ily** /-tɪli/ adv. **crafti·ness** noun [U]

**crag** /kræg/ noun a high, steep, rough mass of rock: *a castle set on a crag above the village*

**craggy** /ˈkrægi/ adj. **1** having many crags: *a craggy coastline* **2** (*usually approving*) (of a man's fa ⁀) having strong features and deep lines

**craic** noun [U, sing.] (*IrishE*) = CRACK (8)

**cram** /kræm/ verb (**-mm-**) **1** [T, I] to push or force sb/sth into a small space; to move into a small space with the result that it is full: **~sb/sth into/onto sth** *He crammed eight people into his car.* ◇ **~sth in** *I could never cram in all that she does in a day.* ◇ **~sth + adv./prep.** *I managed to cram down a few mouthfuls of food.* ◇ **~sth** *Supporters crammed the streets.* ◇ **~sth full** *I bought a large basket and crammed it full of presents.* ◇ **~into/onto sth** *We all managed to cram into his car.* **2** [I] **~(for sth)** (*NAmE, informal* or *BrE, old-fashioned*) to learn a lot of things in a short time, in preparation for an exam 🔁 **swot**: *He's been cramming for his exams all week.*

**crammed** /kræmd/ adj. **1 ~(with sb/sth)** full of things or people 🔁 **packed**: *All the shelves were crammed with books.* ◇ *The room was crammed full of people.* ◇ *The article was crammed full of ideas.* **2** [not before noun] if people are **crammed** into a place, there is not much room for them in it 🔁 **packed**: *We were crammed four to an office.*

**cramp** /kræmp/ noun, verb
■ noun **1** [U, C] a sudden pain that you get when the muscles in a particular part of your body contract, usually caused by cold or too much exercise: (*BrE*) **to get cramp in your leg** ◇ (*NAmE*) **to get a cramp in your leg** ⇒ see also WRITER'S CRAMP **2 cramps** [pl.] severe pain in the stomach
■ verb **~ sth** to prevent the development or progress of sb/sth 🔁 **restrict**: *Tighter trade restrictions might cramp economic growth.*
IDM **ˌcramp sb's ˈstyle** (*informal*) to stop sb from behaving in the way they want to

**cramped** /kræmpt/ adj. **1** a **cramped** room, etc. does not have enough space for the people in it: *working in cramped conditions* **2** (of people) not having room to move freely **3** (of sb's writing) with small letters close together and therefore difficult to read

**cram·pon** /ˈkræmpɒn; *NAmE* -pɑːn/ noun [usually pl.] a metal plate with pointed pieces of metal on the bottom, worn on sb's shoes when they are walking or climbing on ice and snow

**cran·berry** /ˈkrænbəri; *NAmE* -beri/ noun (*pl.* **-ies**) a small red BERRY with a bitter, sharp taste that grows on a small bush and is used in cooking: *cranberry sauce*

**crane** /kreɪn/ noun, verb
■ noun **1** a tall machine with a long arm, used to lift and move building materials and other heavy objects **2** a large bird with long legs and a long neck ⇒ see also BLUE CRANE
■ verb [I, T] to lean or stretch over sth in order to see sth better; to stretch your neck: **(+ adv./prep.)** *People were craning out of the windows and waving.* ◇ **~sth** *She craned her neck to get a better view of the stage.*

**ˈcrane fly** (*also informal* **ˌdaddy-ˈlong-legs**) noun a flying insect with very long legs

**cra·nium** /ˈkreɪniəm/ noun (*pl.* **cra·ni·ums** *or* **cra·nia** /-niə/) (*anatomy*) the bone structure that forms the head and surrounds and protects the brain 🔁 **skull** ⇒ VISUAL VOCAB page V1 ▶ **cra·nial** /-əl/ adj. [only before noun]: *cranial nerves/injuries*

**crank** /kræŋk/ noun, verb
■ noun **1** (*disapproving*) a person with ideas that other people find strange 🔁 **eccentric**: *Vegans are no longer dismissed as cranks.* **2** (*NAmE*) a person who easily gets angry or annoyed **3** a bar and handle in the shape of an L that you pull or turn to produce movement in a machine, etc.
■ verb **~ sth (up)** to make sth turn or move by using a crank: *to crank an engine* ◇ (*figurative*) *He has a limited time to crank the reforms into action.*
PHRV **ˌcrank sth ↔ ˈout** (*informal*) to produce a lot of sth quickly, especially things of low quality 🔁 **turn sb/sth out ˌcrank sth ↔ ˈup** (*informal*) **1** to make a machine, etc. work or work at a higher level **2** to make music, etc. louder 🔁 **turn sth up**: *Crank up the volume!*

**crank·shaft** /'kræŋkʃɑːft; NAmE -ʃæft/ noun (specialist) a long piece of metal in a vehicle that connects the engine to the wheels and helps turn the engine's power into movement

**cranky** /'kræŋki/ adj. (informal) **1** (BrE) strange SYN **eccentric**: *cranky ideas/schemes* **2** (especially NAmE) easily annoyed: *The kids were getting tired and a little cranky.*

**cranny** /'kræni/ noun (pl. **-ies**) a very small hole or opening, especially in a wall IDM see NOOK

**crap** /kræp/ noun, adj., verb
■ **noun** (taboo, slang) **1** [U] ideas, statements or beliefs that you think are silly or not true SYN **nonsense**: *He's so full of crap.* ◊ *Let's cut the crap and get down to business.* ◊ (BrE) *You're talking a load of crap!* **2** [U] something of bad quality: *This work is complete crap.* ◊ (BrE) *Her latest film is a load of crap.* ◊ (NAmE) *Her latest movie is a bunch of crap.* HELP More acceptable words are **rubbish**, **garbage**, **trash** or **junk**. **3** [U] criticism or unfair treatment: *I'm not going to take this crap any more.* **4** [U] solid waste matter from the BOWELS SYN **excrement 5** [sing.] an act of emptying solid waste matter from the BOWELS: *to have a crap* IDM see BUG v.
■ **adj.** (BrE, taboo, slang) bad; of very bad quality: *a crap band* ◊ *The concert was crap.* ▶ **crap** adv.: *The team played crap yesterday.*
■ **verb** [I] (**-pp-**) (taboo, slang) to empty solid waste from the BOWELS SYN **defecate** HELP A more polite way of expressing this is 'to go to the toilet/lavatory' (BrE), 'to go to the bathroom' (NAmE), or 'to go'. A more formal expression is 'to empty the bowels'.

**crappy** /'kræpi/ adj. (**crap·pier**, **crap·pi·est**) [usually before noun] (slang) of very bad quality: *a crappy novel*

**craps** /kræps/ noun [U] (NAmE) a GAMBLING game played with two DICE: *to shoot craps* (= play this game) ▶ **crap** adj. [only before noun]: *a crap game*

**crap·shoot** /'kræpʃuːt/ noun (NAmE) **1** a game of CRAPS **2** (informal) a situation whose success or result is based on luck rather than on effort or careful organization

**crash** ⓘ B2 /kræʃ/ noun, verb, adj.
■ **noun**
• VEHICLE ACCIDENT **1** ⓘ B2 (NAmE also **wreck**) an accident in which a vehicle hits sth, for example another vehicle, usually causing damage and often injuring or killing the passengers: *a car/plane crash* ◊ *a fatal crash on the motorway* ◊ *It is not clear what caused the crash.* ◊ *in a ~ A girl was killed yesterday in a crash involving a stolen car.* ◊ *There were no other vehicles involved in the crash.* ⟹ see also CAR CRASH
• LOUD NOISE **2** ⓘ B2 [usually sing.] a sudden loud noise made, for example, by sth falling or breaking: *The tree fell with a great crash.* ◊ *The first distant crash of thunder shook the air.* ◊ *She heard the crash of shattering glass as the vehicles collided.*
• IN FINANCE/BUSINESS **3** ⓘ B2 a sudden serious fall in the price or value of sth; the occasion when a business, etc. fails SYN **collapse**: *Some economists have been predicting another crash for years.* ◊ *the 2008 stock market crash* ◊ *~ of … the crash of 2008* ◊ *~ in sth a crash in share prices*
• COMPUTING **4** ⓘ B2 a sudden failure of a machine or system, especially of a computer or computer system: *Users won't lose important data if a hardware problem causes a crash.* ◊ *a computer crash*
■ **verb**
• OF VEHICLE **1** ⓘ B2 [I, T] if a vehicle **crashes** or the driver **crashes** it, it hits an object or another vehicle, causing damage: *I was terrified that the plane would crash.* ◊ *We're going to crash, aren't we?* ◊ *~ into sth A truck went out of control and crashed into the back of a bus.* ◊ *~ sth (into sth) He crashed his car into a wall.*
• HIT HARD/LOUD NOISE **2** ⓘ B2 [I, T] to hit sth hard while moving, causing noise and/or damage; to make sth hit sb/sth in this way: *~ + adv./prep. A brick crashed through the window.* ◊ *The huge tree came crashing down during the storm.* ◊ *~ + adj. The door crashed open.* ◊ *~ sth + adj. She stormed out of the room and crashed the door shut behind her.* **3** ⓘ B2 [I] to make a loud noise: *Thunder crashed overhead.*

361

• IN FINANCE/BUSINESS **4** ⓘ B2 [I] (of prices, a business, shares, etc.) to lose value or fail suddenly and quickly: *Share prices crashed to an all-time low yesterday.* ◊ *We were badly affected when the stock market crashed in 2008.*
• COMPUTING **5** ⓘ B2 [I, T] if a computer **crashes** or you **crash** a computer, it stops working suddenly: *Files can be lost if the system suddenly crashes.* ◊ *Their website crashed repeatedly on Tuesday.* ◊ *~ sth A surge of traffic crashed their servers.*
• PARTY **6** [T] *~ sth* (informal) = GATECRASH
• IN SPORT **7** [I] (+ adv./prep.) (especially BrE) to lose very badly in a sports game: *The team crashed to their worst defeat this season.*
• SLEEP **8** [I] *~ (out)* (informal) to go to sleep, especially suddenly or in a place where you do not usually sleep: *I was so tired I crashed out on the sofa.* ◊ *I've come to crash on your floor for a couple of nights.*
• MEDICAL **9** [I] if sb **crashes**, their heart stops beating
IDM **crash and 'burn** (informal) to go wrong or to fail badly and suddenly: *His career crashed and burned after he threatened a journalist.*
PHR V **crash 'out (of sth)** (BrE, sport) to lose a game with the result that you have to stop playing in a competition: *They crashed out of the World Cup after a 2–1 defeat to Brazil.*
■ **adj.** [only before noun] involving hard work or a lot of effort over a short period of time in order to achieve quick results: *a crash course in computer programming* ◊ *a crash diet*

▼ SYNONYMS
**crash**
slam • collide • smash • wreck
These are all words that can be used when sth, especially a vehicle, hits sth else very hard and is damaged or destroyed.
**crash** to hit an object or another vehicle, causing damage; to make a vehicle do this: *I was terrified that the plane would crash.*
**slam (sth) into/against sb/sth** to crash into sth with a lot of force; to make sth do this: *The car skidded and slammed into a tree.*
**collide** (rather formal) (of two vehicles or people) to crash into each other; (of a vehicle or person) to crash into sb/sth else: *The car and the van collided head-on in thick fog.*
**smash** (rather informal) to crash into sth with a lot of force; to make sth do this; to crash a car: *Ram-raiders smashed a stolen car through the shop window.*
CRASH, SLAM OR SMASH?
**Crash** is used especially to talk about vehicles and can be used without a preposition: *We're going to crash, aren't we?* In this meaning **slam** and **smash** always take a preposition: We're going to slam/smash, aren't we? They are used for a much wider range of things than just vehicles.
**wreck** to crash a vehicle and damage it so badly that it is not worth repairing
PATTERNS
• two vehicles crash/collide
• two vehicles crash/slam/smash **into each other**
• to crash/smash/wreck a **car**

**'crash barrier** (BrE) (NAmE **'guard rail**) noun a strong low fence or wall at the side of a road or between the two halves of a major road such as a MOTORWAY or INTERSTATE

**crash·er** /'kræʃə(r)/ noun (especially NAmE, informal) a GATECRASHER

**'crash helmet** noun a hat made of very strong material and worn to protect the head when riding a motorcycle or driving a racing car

**crash-land** verb [I, T] ~ (sth) if a plane **crash-lands** or a pilot **crash-lands** it, the pilot lands it roughly in an emergency, usually because it is damaged and cannot land normally ▸ **crash ˈlanding** noun: *to make a crash landing*

**ˈcrash team** noun (*BrE*) a team of people in a hospital who are ready to make patients start breathing or become conscious again after they have almost died

**ˈcrash-test** verb ~ sth to deliberately crash a new vehicle under carefully CONTROLLED conditions in order to test how it reacts or to improve its safety ▸ **ˈcrash test** noun

**crass** /kræs/ adj. very stupid and showing no sympathy or understanding SYN **insensitive**: *the crass questions all disabled people get asked* ◇ *an act of crass* (= great) *stupidity* ▸ **crass·ly** adv. **crass·ness** noun [U]

**-crat** /kræt/ combining form (in nouns) a member or supporter of a particular type of government or system: *democrat* ◇ *bureaucrat* ▸ **-cratic** /krætɪk/ (in adjectives): *aristocratic*

**crate** /kreɪt/ noun, verb
■ noun **1** a large wooden container for transporting goods: *a crate of bananas* **2** a container made of plastic or metal divided into small sections, for transporting or storing bottles: *a beer crate* **3** the amount of sth contained in a crate: *They drank two crates of beer.*
■ verb ~ (up) to pack sth in a crate

**crater** /ˈkreɪtə(r)/ noun **1** a large hole in the top of a VOLCANO ⊃ picture at VOLCANO **2** a large hole in the ground caused by the explosion of a bomb or by sth large hitting it: *a meteorite crater*

**cra·vat** /krəˈvæt/ (*NAmE also* **ascot**) noun a short wide piece of silk, etc. worn by men around the neck, folded inside the COLLAR of a shirt

**crave** /kreɪv/ verb **1** [T, I] ~ (for) sth to have a very strong desire for sth SYN **long for**: *She has always craved excitement.* **2** [T] ~ sth (*BrE, old use*) to ask for sth seriously: *I must crave your pardon.*

**cra·ven** /ˈkreɪvn/ adj. (*formal, disapproving*) not having or showing courage SYN **cowardly** OPP **brave** ▸ **craven·ly** adv.

**crav·ing** /ˈkreɪvɪŋ/ noun a strong desire for sth: ~ (for sth) *a craving for chocolate* ◇ ~ **to do sth** *a desperate craving to be loved*

**craw** /krɔː/ noun the part of a bird's throat where food is kept IDM see STICK v.

**craw·fish** /ˈkrɔːfɪʃ/ noun (*especially NAmE*) = CRAYFISH

**crawl** A2+ B1 /krɔːl/ verb, noun
■ verb **1** A2+ B1 [I] (+ adv./prep.) to move forward on your hands and knees or with your body close to the ground: *Our baby is just starting to crawl.* ◇ *A man was crawling away from the burning wreckage.* **2** B1 [I] (+ adv./prep.) when an insect, a spider, etc. **crawls**, it moves forward on its legs: *There's a spider crawling up your leg.* **3** [I] (+ adv./prep.) to move forward very slowly: *The traffic was crawling along.* ◇ *The weeks dragged by.* **4** [I] ~ **(to sb)** (*informal, disapproving*) to be too friendly or helpful to sb in authority, in a way that is not sincere, especially in order to get an advantage from them: *She's always crawling to the boss.* IDM see SKIN n., WOODWORK
PHRV ▸ **be ˈcrawling with sth** (*informal*) to be full of or completely covered with people, insects or animals, in a way that is unpleasant: *The place was crawling with journalists.* ◇ *Her hair was crawling with lice.*
■ noun **1** [sing.] a very slow speed: *The traffic slowed to a crawl.* ⊃ see also PUB CRAWL **2** (*often* **the crawl**) [sing., U] a fast swimming STROKE that you do lying on your front moving one arm over your head, and then the other, while kicking with your feet: *a swimmer doing the crawl*

**crawl·er** /ˈkrɔːlə(r)/ noun (*informal*) **1** (*BrE, disapproving*) a person who tries to get sb's favour by praising them, doing what will please them, etc. **2** a thing or person that crawls, such as a vehicle, an insect or a baby ⊃ see also KERB-CRAWLER

**cray·fish** /ˈkreɪfɪʃ/ (*especially BrE*) (*also* **craw·fish** *especially in NAmE*) noun [C, U] (*pl.* **cray·fish, craw·fish**) an animal like a small LOBSTER that lives in rivers and lakes and can be eaten, or one like a large lobster that lives in the sea and can be eaten

**crayon** /ˈkreɪən; *BrE also* ˈkreɪɒn; *NAmE also* ˈkreɪɑːn/ noun a coloured pencil or stick of soft coloured CHALK or WAX, used for drawing ▸ **crayon** verb [I, T] ~ **(sth)**

**craze** /kreɪz/ noun ~ **(for sth)** an enthusiastic interest in sth that is shared by many people but that usually does not last very long; a thing that people have a craze for SYN **fad**: *the latest fitness craze to sweep the country*

**crazed** /kreɪzd/ adj. ~ **(with sth)** (*formal*) full of strong feelings and out of control: *crazed with fear/grief/jealousy* ◇ *a crazed killer roaming the streets*

**crazy** 🔑 A2 /ˈkreɪzi/ adj., noun, adv.
■ adj. (**cra·zier, crazi·est**) (*informal*) **1** A2 not sensible; stupid: *Are you crazy? We could get killed doing that.* ◇ *I'd never do anything like that. That's just crazy.* ◇ *What a crazy idea!* ◇ **be ~ to do sth** *She must be crazy to lend him money.* ◇ **it is ~ to do sth** *It's crazy to think he'll ever change.* **2** A2 very angry: *That noise is driving me crazy.* ◇ *Marie says he went crazy, and smashed the room up.* **3** A2 (*often in compounds*) very enthusiastic or excited about sth: *The crowd went crazy when the band came on stage.* ◇ *You're so beautiful you're driving me crazy.* ◇ ~ **about sth** *Rick is crazy about football.* ◇ *He's football-crazy.* ◇ *I'm not crazy about Chinese food* (= I don't like it very much). **4** A2 ~ **about sb** liking sb very much; in love with sb: *I've been crazy about him since the first time I saw him.* **5** A2 mentally ill; INSANE: *I'd go crazy if I lived here.* ⊃ SYNONYMS at MAD ▸ **crazi·ly** /-zɪli/ adv. **cra·zi·ness** noun [U]
IDM **like ˈcrazy / ˈmad** (*informal*) very fast, hard, much, etc.: *We worked like crazy to get it done on time.*
■ noun (*pl.* **-ies**) (*especially NAmE, informal*) a crazy person
■ adv. (*NAmE, informal*) extremely: *My job continues to be crazy busy.*

**ˈcrazy golf** noun [U] (*BrE*) a type of golf in which people go around a small course hitting a ball through or over little tunnels, hills, bridges and other objects ⊃ compare MINIGOLF

**creak** /kriːk/ verb, noun
■ verb [I] to make the sound that a door sometimes makes when you open it or that a wooden floor sometimes makes when you step on it: *She heard a floorboard creak upstairs.* ◇ *a creaking bed/gate/stair* ◇ **The table creaked and groaned under the weight.** ◇ **+ adj.** *The door creaked open.*
IDM **ˌcreak under the ˈstrain** if a system or service **creaks under the strain**, it cannot deal effectively with all the things it is expected to do or provide
■ noun [C] (*also* **creak·ing** [U, C]) a sound, for example that sometimes made by a door when it opens or shuts, or by a wooden floor when you step on it: *the creak/creaking of the door* ◇ *Distant creaks and groans echoed eerily along the dark corridors.*

**creaky** /ˈkriːki/ adj. **1** making creaks: *a creaky old chair* **2** old and not in good condition: *the country's creaky legal machinery*

**cream** 🔑 A1 /kriːm/ noun, adj., verb
■ noun **1** A1 [U] the thick white or pale yellow FATTY liquid that rises to the top of milk, used in cooking or as a type of sauce to put on fruit, etc: *strawberries and cream* ◇ *whipped cream* ◇ (*BrE*) *cream cakes* (= containing cream) ⊃ see also CLOTTED CREAM, DOUBLE CREAM, FULL-CREAM, ICE CREAM, SINGLE CREAM, SOUR CREAM, WHIPPING CREAM **2** [C] (in compounds) a sweet that has a soft substance like cream inside: *a chocolate/peppermint cream* **3** B1 [U, C] a soft substance or thick liquid used on your skin to protect it or make it feel soft; a similar substance used for cleaning things: *moisturizing cream* ◇ *antiseptic cream* ◇ *a cream cleaner* ⊃ see also COLD CREAM, FACE CREAM, HAND CREAM, SHAVING CREAM, SUN CREAM **4** B1 [U] a pale colour between yellow and white: *Do you have this blouse in cream?* **5 the ~ of sth** the best people or things in a particular group: *the cream of New York society* ◇ *the cream of the crop of this season's movies* IDM see CAT

- **adj.** [B1] between yellow and white in colour: *a cream linen suit*
- **verb 1** ~ sth (together) to mix things together into a soft smooth mixture: *Cream the butter and sugar together.* **2** ~ sb (NAmE, *informal*) to completely defeat sb: *We got creamed in the first round.*
- **PHRV** **cream sb/sth↔off** to take sth away, usually the best people or things or an amount of money, in order to get an advantage for yourself: *The best students were creamed off by the grammar schools.*

**cream 'cheese** *noun* [U, C] soft white cheese containing a lot of cream

**cream·er** /ˈkriːmə(r)/ *noun* **1** [U] a liquid or powder that you can put in coffee, etc. instead of cream or milk: *non-dairy creamer* **2** [C] (NAmE) a small container for holding and pouring cream

**cream·ery** /ˈkriːməri/ *noun* (*pl.* **-ies**) a place where milk and cream are made into butter and cheese

**cream puff** *noun* (NAmE) **1** a cake made of light PASTRY filled with cream ⊃ compare ECLAIR, PROFITEROLE **2** (*slang, disapproving*) a person who is not strong or brave **SYN** wimp

**cream 'soda** *noun* [U, C] (*especially* NAmE) a FIZZY drink (= one with bubbles) that tastes of VANILLA

**cream 'tea** *noun* (BrE) a special meal eaten in the afternoon, consisting of tea with SCONES, jam and thick cream ⊃ compare HIGH TEA

**creamy** /ˈkriːmi/ *adj.* (**cream·ier**, **creami·est**) **1** thick and smooth like cream; containing a lot of cream: *a creamy sauce/soup* ⊃ WORDFINDER NOTE at CRISP **2** between yellow and white in colour: *creamy skin*

**crease** /kriːs/ *noun, verb*
- **noun 1** an untidy line that is made in cloth or paper when it is pressed or folded without care: *She smoothed the creases out of her skirt.* ◇ *a shirt made of crease-resistant material* **2** a neat line that you make in sth, for example when you fold paper or iron clothes: *trousers with a sharp crease in the legs* **3** a line in the skin, especially on the face: *creases around the eyes* **4** (in CRICKET) a white line on the ground near each WICKET that marks the position of the BOWLER and the BATSMAN: **at the ~** *He spent six hours at the crease* (= he was BATTING) *for six hours.*
- **verb 1** [T, I] ~(sth) to make lines on cloth or paper by folding or pressing it; to develop lines in this way: *Pack your suit carefully so that you don't crease it.* **2** [T, I] ~(sth) to make lines in the skin; to develop lines in the skin: *A frown creased her forehead.* ◇ *Her face creased into a smile.* ▶ **creased** *adj.*: *I can't wear this blouse. It's creased.*
- **PHRV** **crease 'up** | **crease sb 'up** (BrE, *informal*) to start laughing or make sb start laughing **SYN** crack up, crack sb up: *Ed creased up laughing.* ◇ *Her jokes really creased me up.*

**cre·ate** 🔊 [A1] 🔊 /kriˈeɪt/ *verb* **1** [A1] ~ sth to make sth happen or exist: *Scientists disagree about how the universe was created.* ◇ *The government plans to create more jobs for young people.* ◇ *Create a new directory and put all your files into it.* ◇ *Severe storms created some travel problems.* ◇ *the newly created position of executive editor* ⊃ SYNONYMS at MAKE **2** [B1] ~ sth to produce a particular feeling or impression: *He's eager to create a good impression at work.* ◇ *The announcement only succeeded in creating confusion.* ◇ *We work hard to create a pleasant environment for patients, visitors and staff.* **3** to give sb a particular rank or title: *~ sth The government has created eight new peers.* ◇ *~ sth + noun He was created a baronet in 1715.* **IDM** see RIPPLE *n.*

**cre·ation** 🔊 [B2] 🔊 /kriˈeɪʃn/ *noun* **1** [B2] [U] the act or process of making sth that is new, or of causing sth to exist that did not exist before: *job/wealth creation* ◇ *~ of sth the creation of an independent state* ◇ *He had been with the company since its creation in 1989.* ⊃ see also JOB CREATION **2** [C] (*often humorous*) a thing that sb has made, especially sth that shows ability or imagination: *a literary creation* ◇ *The cake was a delicious creation of sponge, cream and fruit.* **3** (*usually* **the Creation**) [sing.] the making

of the world, especially by God as described in the Bible **4** (*often* **Creation**) [U] the world and all the living things in it

**cre·ation·ism** /kriˈeɪʃənɪzəm/ *noun* [U] the belief that the universe was made by God exactly as described in the Bible ▶ **cre·ation·ist** /-ɪst/ *adj., noun*

**cre'ation science** *noun* [U] science that tries to find proof that God created the world

**cre·ative** 🔊 [A2] 🔊 /kriˈeɪtɪv/ *adj., noun*
- **adj. 1** [A2] [only before noun] involving the use of skill and the imagination to produce sth new or a work of art: *a course on creative writing* (= writing stories, plays and poems) ◇ *creative thinking* (= thinking about problems in a new way or thinking of new ideas) ◇ *the company's creative team/director* ◇ *the creative process* ◇ *~ with sth* (*informal*) *You can get creative with this recipe and add whatever fruit you like.* **2** [A2] having the skill and ability to produce sth new, especially a work of art; showing this ability: *She's very creative—she writes poetry and paints.* ◇ *a highly creative artist* ▶ **cre·ative·ly** *adv.*
- **noun** [C] a person whose job involves creative work: *The exhibition features the paintings of local creatives.* ◇ *the advertising agency creatives*

**cre,ative ac'counting** *noun* [U] (*disapproving*) a way of doing or presenting the accounts of a business that might not show what the true situation really is

**cre·ativ·ity** 🔊 [B2] 🔊 /ˌkriːeɪˈtɪvəti/ *noun* [U] the use of skill and imagination to produce sth new or to produce art: *Creativity and originality are more important than technical skill.*

**cre·ator** 🔊 [C1] 🔊 /kriˈeɪtə(r)/ *noun* **1** 🔊 [C1] [C] a person who has made or invented a particular thing: *Walt Disney, the creator of Mickey Mouse* **2 the Creator** [sing.] God

**crea·ture** 🔊 [B2] 🔊 /ˈkriːtʃə(r)/ *noun* **1** [B2] a living thing, real or imaginary, that can move around, such as an animal: *respect for all living creatures* ◇ *alien/strange/mythical creatures* ◇ *octopuses and other sea creatures* **2** (*especially following an adjective*) a person, considered in a particular way: *You pathetic creature!* ◇ *She was an exotic creature with long red hair and brilliant green eyes.* ◇ *He always goes to bed at ten—he's a creature of habit* (= he likes to do the same things at the same time every day). **IDM** **a/the creature of sb** | **sb's creature** (*formal, disapproving*) a person or thing that depends completely on sb else and is controlled by them

**creature 'comforts** *noun* [pl.] all the things that make life, or a particular place, comfortable, such as good food, comfortable furniture or modern equipment

**crèche** (*also* **creche**) /kreʃ/ *noun* **1** (BrE) a place where babies and young children are taken care of while their parents are working, studying, shopping, etc. ⊃ compare DAY NURSERY **2** (NAmE) (BrE **crib**) a model of the scene of Jesus Christ's birth, placed in churches and homes at Christmas

**cred** /kred/ *noun* [U] = STREET CRED

**cre·dence** /ˈkriːdns/ *noun* (*formal*) **1** a quality that an idea or a story has that makes you believe it is true: *Historical evidence lends credence to his theory.* **2** belief in sth as true: *They could give no credence to the findings of the survey.* ◇ *Alternative medicine has been gaining credence* (= becoming more widely accepted) *recently.*

**cre·den·tial** /krəˈdenʃl/ *verb* [usually passive] (NAmE) **be credentialed** to be provided with credentials: *Faculty members needed to be properly credentialed in their respective disciplines.*

**cre·den·tials** /krəˈdenʃlz/ *noun* [pl.] **1** ~ (as/for sth) the qualities, training or experience that make you suitable to do sth: *He has all the credentials for the job.* ◇ *She will first have to establish her leadership credentials.* **2** documents such as letters that prove that you are who you claim to be, and can therefore be trusted

**cred·ibil·ity** 🔊 [C1] 🔊 /ˌkredəˈbɪləti/ *noun* [U] the quality that sb/sth has that makes people believe or trust them: *to gain/lack/lose credibility* ◇ *The prosecution did its best*

# credible

to *undermine the credibility of the witness.* ◊ *Newspapers were talking of a credibility gap between what he said and what he did.* ➔ see also STREET CRED

**cred·i·ble** /ˈkredəbl/ *adj.* **1** that can be believed or trusted SYN **convincing**: *a credible explanation/witness* ◊ *It is just not credible that she would cheat.* **2** that can be accepted, because it seems possible that it could be successful SYN **viable**: *Community service is seen as the only credible alternative to imprisonment.* ▸ **cred·ibly** /-bli/ *adv.*: *The 1920s period is portrayed very credibly.*

**credit** /ˈkredɪt/ *noun, verb*

■ *noun*

- **BUY NOW—PAY LATER 1** [U] an arrangement that you make, with a shop for example, to pay later for sth you buy: *to get credit* ◊ *on~ We bought the dishwasher on credit.* ◊ *to offer interest-free credit* (= allow sb to pay later, without any extra charge) ◊ *Someone with a bad credit history is less likely to be lent money.* ◊ *a credit facility* ◊ *He's a bad credit risk* (= he is unlikely to pay the money later). ◊ *Your credit limit is now £2000.* ◊ *The credit crisis is far from over.* ➔ compare HIRE PURCHASE
- **MONEY BORROWED 2** [U, C] money that you borrow from a bank; a loan: *The bank refused further credit to the company.* ◊ *Local lenders are more likely to extend credit* (= lend money) *to smaller, more marginal borrowers.* ➔ see also CONSUMER CREDIT, LINE OF CREDIT, LETTER OF CREDIT ➔ WORDFINDER NOTE at BANK **3** [U] the status of being trusted to pay back money to sb who lends it to you: *Her credit isn't good anywhere now.*
- **MONEY IN BANK 4** [U] money that you have in your bank account; if you or your bank account are **in credit**, there is money in the account: *You have a credit balance of £250.* ◊ *My account is in credit.* **5** [C, U] a sum of money paid into a bank account; a record of the payment: *a credit of £50* ◊ *You'll be paid by direct credit into your bank account.* OPP **debit**
- **MONEY PAID IN ADVANCE 6** [U] the right to use a service up to a certain limit, paid for in advance: *My phone's run out of credit.*
- **MONEY BACK 7** [C, U] (*specialist*) a payment that sb has a right to for a particular reason ➔ see also TAX CREDIT, UNIVERSAL CREDIT
- **PRAISE 8** [U] praise or approval because you are responsible for sth good that has happened: *to get/deserve/receive/take/claim the credit* ◊ *We did all the work and she gets all the credit!* ◊ *~for (doing) sth I can't take all the credit for the show's success—it was a team effort.* ◊ *At least give him credit for trying* (= praise him because he tried, even if he did not succeed) ➔ compare BLAME, DISCREDIT **9** [*sing.*] *~to sb/sth* a person or thing whose qualities or achievements are praised and who therefore earns respect for sb/sth else: *She is a credit to the school.*
- **MOVIE/TV PROGRAMME 10** [C, usually pl.] the act of mentioning sb who worked on a project such as a film or a television programme: *She was given a programme credit for her work on the costumes for the play.* ◊ *The credits* (= the list of all the people involved) *seemed to last almost as long as the film!* **11** a film, play, television programme, etc. that sb has worked on: *His film credits included 'The Witches' and 'Halloween III'.*
- **UNIT OF STUDY 12** [C] a unit of study at a college or university (in the US, also at a school); the fact of having successfully completed a unit of study: *My math class is worth three credits.* ➔ see also CARBON CREDIT

IDM **do sb credit | do credit to sb/sth** if sth **does credit** to a person or an organization, they deserve to be praised for it: *Your honesty does you great credit.* **give credit where credit is ˈdue** to give sb the praise they deserve, even if you do not really want to **have sth to your credit** to have achieved sth: *He's only 30, and he already has four novels to his credit.* **on the ˈcredit side** used to introduce the good points about sb/sth, especially after the bad points have been mentioned **to sb's credit** making sb deserve praise or respect: *To his credit, Jack never told anyone exactly what had happened.*

■ *verb*

- **PUT MONEY IN BANK 1** to add an amount of money to sb's bank account: *~A (with B) Your account has been credited with $50000.* ◊ *~B (to A) $50000 has been credited to your account.* OPP **debit**
- **WITH ACHIEVEMENT 2** [usually passive] to believe or say that sb is responsible for doing sth, especially sth bad: **be credited (as sb/sth)** *She has been wrongly credited as the author.* ◊ **be credited with/for (doing) sth** *The group has been widely credited with creating the sound of heavy metal.* ◊ **be credited to sth** *The invention of the industrial robot is credited to the company.*
- **WITH QUALITY 3** *~A with B* to believe that sb/sth has a particular good quality or feature: *I credited you with a little more sense.* **4** [usually passive] to believe that sb/sth is of a particular type or quality: **be credited as sth** *The cheetah is generally credited as the world's fastest animal.*
- **BELIEVE 5** *~sth | ~what, how, etc ... | ~that ...* (*BrE*) (used mainly in questions and negative sentences) to believe sth, especially sth surprising or unexpected: *He's been promoted—would you credit it?*

**cred·it·able** /ˈkredɪtəbl/ *adj.* (*formal*) **1** of a quite good standard and deserving praise or approval SYN **praiseworthy**: *It was a very creditable result for the team.* **2** morally good SYN **admirable**: *There was nothing very creditable in what he did.* ▸ **cred·it·ably** /-bli/ *adv.*

ˈcredit account *noun* (*BrE*) = ACCOUNT (6)

ˈcredit agency *noun* (*BrE*) (*NAmE* ˈcredit bureau) *noun* a company that collects information about people's CREDIT RATINGS and makes it available to credit card companies, financial institutions, etc.

ˈcredit card *noun* a small plastic card that you can use to buy goods and services and pay for them later: *All major credit cards are accepted at our hotels.* ◊ *~by~ picture at* MONEY ➔ see also CHARGE CARD, DEBIT CARD, STORE CARD

ˈcredit crunch *noun* [usually *sing.*] (*economics*) an economic condition in which it suddenly becomes difficult and expensive to borrow money

ˈcredit line *noun* = LINE OF CREDIT

ˈcredit note *noun* (*BrE*) a letter that a shop gives you when you have returned sth and that allows you to have goods of the same value in exchange

**cred·it·or** /ˈkredɪtə(r)/ *noun* a person, company, etc. that sb owes money to ➔ compare DEBTOR

ˈcredit rating *noun* a judgement made by a bank, etc. about how likely sb is to pay back money that they borrow, and how safe it is to lend money to them

ˈcredit score *noun* (*especially NAmE*) a number given to sb to show how likely they are to pay back money that they borrow from a bank, a company, etc.

ˈcredit union *noun* an organization that lends money to its members at low rates of interest

**credit·worthy** /ˈkredɪtwɜːði; *NAmE* -wɜːrði/ *adj.* able to be trusted to pay back money that is owed; safe to lend money to ▸ **credit·worthi·ness** *noun* [U]

**credo** /ˈkriːdəʊ, ˈkreɪd-/ *noun* (*pl.* **-os**) (*formal*) a set of beliefs SYN **creed**

**cre·du·lity** /krɪˈdjuːləti; *NAmE* -ˈduː-/ *noun* [U] (*formal*) the ability or the wish to believe that sth is real or true: *The plot of the novel stretches credulity to the limit* (= it is almost impossible to believe).

**credu·lous** /ˈkredʒələs/ *adj.* (*formal*) too ready to believe things and therefore easy to trick SYN **gullible** ➔ compare INCREDULOUS

**Cree** /kriː/ *noun* (*pl.* **Cree** or **Crees**) a member of a Native American people, many of whom live in central Canada

**creed** /kriːd/ *noun* **1** [C] a set of principles or religious beliefs: *people of all races, colours and creeds* ◊ *discrimination on the basis of race, colour or creed* ◊ *What is his political creed?* **2 the Creed** [*sing.*] a statement of Christian belief that is spoken as part of some church services

**Creek** /kriːk/ *noun* (*pl.* **Creek** or **Creeks**) a member of a Native American people, many of whom now live in the US state of Oklahoma

**creek** /kriːk/ noun **1** (BrE) a narrow area of water where the sea flows into the land SYN **inlet 2** (NAmE, AustralE, NZE) a small river or stream
IDM **up the ˈcreek (without a ˈpaddle)** (informal) in a difficult or bad situation: *If they won't accept my credit card, I'll really be up the creek.*

**creep** ⓘ+ C1 /kriːp/ verb, noun
■ verb (**crept, crept** /krept/) HELP In the phrasal verb **creep sb out**, **creeped** is used for the past simple and past participle. **1** ⓘ+ C1 [I] (+ adv./prep.) (of people or animals) to move slowly, quietly and carefully, because you do not want to be seen or heard: *I crept up the stairs, trying not to wake my parents.* **2** [I] (+ adv./prep.) (NAmE) to move with your body close to the ground; to move slowly on your hands and knees SYN **crawl 3** [I] (+ adv./prep.) to move or develop very slowly: *Her arms crept around his neck.* ◊ *A slight feeling of suspicion crept over me.* **4** [I] (+ adv./prep.) (of plants) to grow along the ground or up walls using long STEMS or roots ⊃ see also CREEPER **5** [I] **~(to sb)** (BrE, informal, disapproving) to be too friendly or helpful to sb in authority in a way that is not sincere, especially in order to get an advantage from them IDM see FLESH *n*.
PHRV **ˌcreep ˈin/ˈinto sth** to begin to happen or affect sth: *As she became more tired, errors began to creep into her work.* **ˌcreep sb ˈout** (**creeped, creeped**) (informal) to give sb an unpleasant feeling of fear or worry: *He said the empty streets creeped him out.* **ˌcreep ˈup** to gradually increase in amount, price, etc: *House prices are creeping up again.* **ˌcreep ˈup on sb 1** to move slowly nearer to sb, usually from behind, without being seen or heard: *Don't creep up on me like that!* **2** to begin to affect sb, especially before they realize it: *Tiredness can easily creep up on you while you're driving.*
■ noun **1** [C] (informal) a person that you dislike very much and find very unpleasant: *He's a nasty little creep!* **2** [C] (BrE, informal) a person who is not sincere but tries to win your approval by being nice to you **3** [U] (often in compounds) (often disapproving) the development of a project beyond the goal that was originally agreed: *The World Bank has been accused of **mission creep** when seeking to address these concerns.* ◊ **~ of sth** *We need to prevent this slow creep of costs.*
IDM **give sb the ˈcreeps** (informal) to make sb feel nervous and slightly frightened, especially because sb/sth is unpleasant or strange

**creep·er** /ˈkriːpə(r)/ noun a plant that grows along the ground, up walls, etc., often winding itself around other plants

**creep·ing** /ˈkriːpɪŋ/ adj. [only before noun] (of sth bad) happening or moving gradually and not easily noticed: *creeping inflation*

**creepy** /ˈkriːpi/ adj. (**creep·ier, creepi·est**) (informal) **1** causing an unpleasant feeling of fear or slight horror SYN **scary**: *a creepy ghost story* ◊ *It's kind of creepy down in the cellar!* **2** strange in a way that makes you feel nervous SYN **spooky**: *What a creepy coincidence.*

**creepy-crawly** /ˌkriːpi ˈkrɔːli/ noun (pl. **-ies**) (informal) an insect, a WORM, etc. when you think of it as unpleasant

**cre·mate** /krəˈmeɪt; NAmE ˈkriːmeɪt/ verb [often passive] **~ sb/sth** to burn a dead body, especially as part of a FUNERAL ceremony

**cre·ma·tion** /krəˈmeɪʃn/ noun **1** [U] the act of cremating sb **2** [C] a FUNERAL at which the dead person is cremated
⊃ WORDFINDER NOTE at DIE

**cre·ma·tor·ium** /ˌkreməˈtɔːriəm; NAmE ˌkriːm-/ noun (pl. **crema·toria** /-riə/ or **cre·ma·tor·iums**) (NAmE also **crema·tory** /ˈkremətəri; NAmE ˈkriːmətɔːri/ pl. **-ies**) a building in which the bodies of dead people are burned

**crème brûlée** /ˌkrem bruːˈleɪ/ noun [C, U] (pl. **crèmes brûlées** /ˌkrem bruːˈleɪ/) (from French) a cold DESSERT (= a sweet dish) made from cream, with burnt sugar on top

**crème caramel** /ˌkrem ˈkærəmel/ noun [C, U] (pl. **crèmes caramel** /ˌkrem ˈkærəmel/ **crème caramels** /-ˈmelz/) (BrE, from French) (NAmE **flan**) a cold DESSERT (= a sweet dish) made from milk, eggs and sugar

**crème de la crème** /ˌkrem də lɑː ˈkrem/ noun [sing.] (from French, formal or humorous) the best people or things of their kind: *This school takes only the crème de la crème.*

**crème fraîche** /ˌkrem ˈfreʃ/ noun [U] (from French) thick cream with a slightly SOUR taste

**Cre·ole** /ˈkriːəʊl/ (also **creole**) noun **1** [C] a person of mixed European and African race, especially one who lives in the West Indies **2** [C] a person whose ANCESTORS were among the first Europeans who settled in the West Indies or South America, or one of the French or Spanish people who settled in the southern states of the US: *Creole cookery* **3** [U, C] a language formed when a mixture of a European language with a local language (especially an African language spoken by slaves in the West Indies) is spoken as a first language ⊃ compare PIDGIN

**creo·sote** /ˈkriːəsəʊt/ noun, verb
■ noun [U] a thick brown liquid that is made from COAL TAR, used to preserve wood
■ verb **~ sth** to paint or preserve sth with creosote

**crêpe** (also **crepe**) /kreɪp/ noun **1** [U] a type of light thin cloth, made especially from cotton or silk, with a surface that is covered in lines and folds: *a black crêpe dress* ◊ *a crêpe bandage* **2** [U] a type of strong rubber with a rough surface, used for making the SOLES of shoes: *crêpe-soled shoes* **3** /krep/ [C] a thin PANCAKE

**ˈcrêpe paper** (also **crepe paper**) noun [U] a type of thin brightly coloured paper that stretches and has a surface covered in lines and folds, used especially for making decorations

**crept** /krept/ past tense, past part. of CREEP

**cres·cendo** /krəˈʃendəʊ/ noun (pl. **-os**) [C, U] **1** (music, from Italian) a slow steady increase in how loudly a piece of music is played or sung **2** a slow steady increase in noise; the loudest point of a period of continuous noise SYN **swell**: *Voices rose in a crescendo and drowned him out.* ◊ (figurative) *The advertising campaign reached a crescendo just before Christmas.*

**cres·cent** /ˈkresnt; BrE also ˈkreznt/ noun **1** [C] a curved shape that is wide in the middle and pointed at each end: *a crescent moon* **2** [C] (often used in street names) a curved street with a row of houses on it: *I live at 7 Park Crescent.* **3 the Crescent** [sing.] the curved shape that is used as a symbol of Islam ⊃ see also RED CRESCENT

**cress** /kres/ noun [U] a small plant with thin STEMS and very small leaves, often eaten in salads and sandwiches ⊃ see also WATERCRESS

**crest** /krest/ noun, verb
■ noun **1** [usually sing.] **~ (of sth)** the top part of a hill or wave: *surfers riding the crest of the wave* **2** a design used as the symbol of a particular family, organization, etc., especially one that has a long history: *the university crest* **3** a group of feathers that stand up on top of a bird's head
⊃ VISUAL VOCAB page V2
IDM **the crest of a/the ˈwave** a situation in which sb is very successful, happy, etc. ⊃ more at RIDE *v*.
■ verb **1** [T] **~ sth** (formal) to reach the top of a hill, mountain or wave: *He slowed the pace as he crested the ridge.* **2** [I] (NAmE) (of a flood, wave, etc.) to reach its highest level before it falls again: (figurative) *The level of debt crested at a massive $290 billion in 2009.*

**crest·ed** /ˈkrestɪd/ adj. **1** marked with a crest: *crested notepaper* **2** used especially in names of birds or animals that have a crest: *crested newts*

**crest·fall·en** /ˈkrestfɔːlən/ adj. sad and disappointed because you have failed and you did not expect to

**Cret·aceous** /krɪˈteɪʃəs/ adj. (geology) belonging to the period between around 146 and 65 million years ago, when DINOSAURS lived (until they died out); relating to the rocks formed during this time ▸ **the Cret·aceous** noun [sing.]

**cre·tin** /ˈkretɪn; NAmE ˈkriːtn/ noun (informal, offensive) a very stupid person: *Why did you do that, you cretin?* ▸ **ˌcret·inˈous** /ˈkretɪnəs; NAmE ˈkriːtn-/ adj.

# Creutzfeldt-Jakob disease

**Creutzfeldt-Jakob disease** /ˌkrɔɪtsfelt ˈjækɒb dɪziːz/ NAmE -kɔːb-/ noun [U] (abbr. **CJD**) a brain disease that causes slow loss of control of the mind and body and, finally, death. It is believed to be caused by PRIONS and is linked to BSE in cows.

**cre·vasse** /krəˈvæs/ noun a deep opening, especially in ice, for example in a GLACIER

**crev·ice** /ˈkrevɪs/ noun a narrow opening in a rock or wall

**crew** 🔊 B2 /kruː/ noun, verb
■ noun
• ON SHIPS AND PLANES **1** 🔊 [C + sing./pl. v.] all the people working on a ship, plane, etc.: *crew members* ◇ *in a ~* ◇ *all the men and women in the crew* ⊃ see also AIRCREW, CABIN CREW, FLIGHT CREW **2** 🔊 [C + sing./pl. v.] all the people working on a ship, plane etc. except the officers who are in charge: *the officers and crew*
• SKILLED PEOPLE **3** 🔊 B2 [C + sing./pl. v.] a group of people with special skills working together: *a film/camera/TV crew* ◇ *a fire/an emergency/an ambulance crew* ⊃ see also GROUND CREW ⊃ HOMOPHONES at CRUISE
• GROUP **4** [sing.] (*usually disapproving*) a group of people: *The people she invited were a pretty motley crew* (= a strange mix of types of people).
• ROWING AND SAILING **5** [C + sing./pl. v.] a team of people who row boats in races: *a member of the Cambridge crew* **6** [U] (NAmE) the sport of ROWING with other people in a boat: *I'm thinking of going out for crew this semester* (= joining the ROWING team). **7** [C + sing./pl. v.] a person or team of people who sail boats in races or for pleasure (usually not including the captain)
■ verb [T, I] to be part of a crew, especially on a ship: *~ (sth) Normally the boat is crewed by five people.* ◇ *~ (for sb) I crewed for him on his yacht last summer.* ⊃ HOMOPHONES at CRUISE

**crew cut** noun a HAIRSTYLE for men in which the hair is cut very short ▶ **crew-cut** adj.: *crew-cut teenagers*

**crew·man** /ˈkruːmən/ noun (pl. -men /-mən/) a member of a crew, usually a man

**crew 'neck** noun a round neck on a sweater, etc.; a sweater with a round neck

**crib** /krɪb/ noun, verb
■ noun **1** (NAmE) (BrE **cot**) a small bed with high sides for a baby or young child **2** a long open box that horses and cows can eat from SYN **manger 3** (BrE) (NAmE **crèche**) a model of the scene of Jesus Christ's birth, placed in churches and homes at Christmas **4** (*informal*) = CRIB SHEET: *crib notes* **5** = CRIBBAGE **6** (NAmE, *informal*) the house, flat, etc. where sb lives
■ verb (-bb-) **1** [I, T] ~ **(sth) (from sb)** (*old-fashioned*) to dishonestly copy work from another student or from a book **2** [I] ~ **(about sth)** (BrE, *old-fashioned* or IndE) to complain about sb/sth in an angry way

**crib·bage** /ˈkrɪbɪdʒ/ (also **crib**) noun [U] a card game in which players score points by collecting different combinations of cards. The score is kept by putting small PEGS in holes in a board.

**'crib death** (NAmE) (BrE **'cot death**) noun [U, C] the sudden death while sleeping of a baby that appears to be healthy

**'crib sheet** (also **crib**) noun (*informal*) a set of notes to help you remember important information, especially one taken secretly into an exam room SYN **cheat sheet**: *She was caught using a crib sheet in the exam.*

**crick** /krɪk/ (NAmE also **kink**) noun [usually sing.] a sudden painful stiff feeling in the muscles of your neck or back ▶ **crick** verb: *~ sth I suffered a cricked neck during a game of tennis.*

**cricket** /ˈkrɪkɪt/ noun **1** [U] a game played on grass by two teams of 11 players. Players score points (called RUNS) by hitting the ball with a wooden BAT and running between two sets of VERTICAL wooden sticks, called STUMPS: *a cricket match/team/club/ball* **2** [C] a small brown jumping insect that makes a loud high sound by rubbing its wings together: *the chirping of crickets* IDM **not 'cricket** (*old-fashioned*, BrE, *informal*) unfair; not HONOURABLE

**crick·et·er** /ˈkrɪkɪtə(r)/ noun a cricket player

**cricket·ing** /ˈkrɪkɪtɪŋ/ adj. [only before noun] playing cricket; connected with cricket: *cricketing nations* ◇ *a cricketing jersey*

**cried** /kraɪd/ past tense, past part. of CRY

**crier** /ˈkraɪə(r)/ noun = TOWN CRIER

**cri·key** /ˈkraɪki/ *exclamation* (BrE, *old-fashioned*, *informal*) used to show that sb is surprised or annoyed: *Crikey, is that the time?*

**crime** 🔊 A2 /kraɪm/ noun **1** 🔊 A2 [U] activities that involve breaking the law: *an increase in violent crime* ◇ *the fight against crime* ◇ *Stores spend more and more on crime prevention every year.* ◇ *serious crime* ◇ *gun/knife crime* ◇ *a rise in street crime* ◇ *the connection between drugs and organized crime* ◇ *He turned to crime when he dropped out of school.* ◇ *The crime rate is rising.* ◇ *crime fiction/novels* (= stories about crime) ◇ *She's a crime writer* (= she writes stories about crime). ⊃ see also HATE CRIME, TRUE CRIME ▶ WORDFINDER NOTE at LAW **2** A2 [C] an illegal act or activity that can be punished by law: *to commit a crime* (= do sth illegal) ◇ *~ against sth/sb The massacre was a crime against humanity.* ⊃ see also HATE CRIME, SCENE-OF-CRIME, WAR CRIME **3 a crime** [sing.] (*informal*) an act that you think is morally wrong or is a big mistake: *It's a crime to waste so much money.*

**'crime lab** noun (NAmE) the place in a police department where the physical evidence of a crime is examined

**'crime wave** noun [sing.] a situation in which there is a sudden increase in the number of crimes that are committed

**crim·inal** 🔊 A2 /ˈkrɪmɪnl/ noun, adj.
■ noun 🔊 A2 a person who commits a crime: *a convicted criminal* ◇ *Police sometimes put themselves in danger when arresting violent criminals.* ⊃ see also WAR CRIMINAL
■ adj. **1** 🔊 B1 [*usually before noun*] (*rather formal* or *law*) connected with or involving crime: *criminal offences/activities* ◇ *criminal damage* (= the crime of damaging sb's property deliberately). ◇ *criminal negligence* (= the illegal act of sb failing to do sth that they should do, with the result that sb else is harmed) **2** B1 [only before noun] connected to the laws that deal with crime: *the criminal justice system* ◇ *to bring criminal charges against sb* ◇ *a criminal investigation* ◇ *a criminal case* ⊃ compare CIVIL **3** morally wrong: *This is a criminal waste of resources.*

**crim·in·al·ity** /ˌkrɪmɪˈnæləti/ noun [U] the fact of people being involved in crime; criminal acts

**crim·in·al·ize** (BrE also **-ise**) /ˈkrɪmɪnəlaɪz/ verb **1 ~ sth** to make sth illegal by passing a law: *The use of opium was not criminalized until fairly recently.* **2 ~ sb** to make sb a criminal by making their activities illegal: *The law criminalized parents who took their children out of school to go on holiday.* ▶ **crim·in·al·iza·tion**, **-isa·tion** /ˌkrɪmɪnəlaɪˈzeɪʃn; NAmE -ləˈz-/ noun [U]

**criminal 'law** noun [U] law that deals with the punishment of people who commit crimes ⊃ compare CIVIL LAW

**crim·in·al·ly** /ˈkrɪmɪnəli/ adv. according to the laws that deal with crime: *criminally insane*

**criminal 'record** noun = RECORD (5)

**crim·in·ology** /ˌkrɪmɪˈnɒlədʒi; NAmE -ˈnɑːl-/ noun [U] the scientific study of crime and criminals ▶ **crim·ino·logic·al** /ˌkrɪmɪnəˈlɒdʒɪkl; NAmE -ˈlɑːdʒ-/ adj. **crim·in·olo·gist** /ˌkrɪmɪˈnɒlədʒɪst; NAmE -ˈnɑːl-/ noun

**crimp** /krɪmp/ verb, noun
■ verb **1 ~ sth** to make CURLS in sb's hair by pressing it with a heated tool: *crimped blonde hair* **2 ~ sth** to press cloth, paper, etc. into small folds **3 ~ sth** (NAmE, *informal*) to limit the growth or development of sth

■ noun

IDM **put a ˈcrimp in/on sth** (*NAmE*, *informal*) to have a bad or negative effect on sth

**crim·son** /ˈkrɪmzn/ *adj.* dark red in colour: *She went crimson* (= her face became very red because she was embarrassed). ▶ **crim·son** *noun* [U]

**cringe** /krɪndʒ/ *verb* **1** [I] to move back and/or away from sb because you are afraid **SYN** **cower**: *a child cringing in terror* **2** [I] to feel very embarrassed and uncomfortable about sth: *I cringe when I think of the poems I wrote then.*

**cringe·worthy** /ˈkrɪndʒwɜːði; *NAmE* -wɜːrði/ (*also* **ˈcringe-making**) *adj.* (*both BrE*, *informal*) making you feel embarrassed or uncomfortable: *It was a cringeworthy performance from start to finish.*

**crin·kle** /ˈkrɪŋkl/ *verb*, *noun*
■ *verb* [I, T] to become covered with or to form a lot of thin folds or lines, especially in skin, cloth or paper: *Her face crinkled up in a smile.* ◇ *He smiled, his eyes crinkling* (= the skin around his eyes). ◇ **be crinkled** *The binding had faded and the pages were crinkled.*
■ *noun* a very thin fold or line made on paper, cloth or skin

**crin·kly** /ˈkrɪŋkli/ *adj.* **1** having a lot of thin folds or lines: *crinkly silver foil* **2** (of hair) having a lot of small CURLS or waves

**crin·ol·ine** /ˈkrɪnəlɪn/ *noun* a frame that was worn under a skirt by some women in the past in order to give the skirt a very round full shape

**cripes** /kraɪps/ *exclamation* (*informal*) used to show that sb is surprised or annoyed

**crip·ple** /ˈkrɪpl/ *verb*, *noun*
■ *verb* **1** [usually passive] to damage sb's body so that they are no longer able to walk or move normally **SYN** **disable**: **be crippled (by sth)** *He was crippled by polio as a child.* ◇ **be crippled with sth** *She's eighty and crippled with arthritis.* **2** [usually passive] to seriously damage or harm sb/sth: **be crippled (by sth)** *The industry has been financially crippled by these policies.* ◇ *The pilot tried to land his crippled plane.* ▶ **crip·pling** /-plɪŋ/ *adj.*: *a crippling disease* ◇ *crippling debts*
■ *noun* (*old-fashioned* or *offensive*) a person who is unable to walk or move normally because of a disease or injury; (*figurative*) *He's an emotional cripple* (= he cannot express his feelings). **HELP** People now use **disabled person** instead of 'cripple'.

**cri·sis** ⓘ **B2** /ˈkraɪsɪs/ *noun* [C, U] (*pl.* **cri·ses** /ˈkraɪsiːz/) **1** **B2** a time of great danger, difficulty or doubt when problems must be solved or important decisions must be made: *an economic/a financial/a debt crisis* ◇ *The government is facing a political crisis.* ◇ *to resolve/solve/address a crisis* ◇ **in ~** *The business is still in crisis but it has survived the worst of the recession.* ◇ *The Labour Party was facing an identity crisis.* ◇ *an expert in crisis management* ◇ *I know which friends I can turn to in times of crisis.* ◇ **~ of sth** *The party was suffering a crisis of confidence among its supporters* (= they did not trust it any longer). ⇨ see also MIDLIFE CRISIS **2** **B2** a time when a problem, a bad situation or an illness is at its worst point: *Their marriage has reached crisis point.* ◇ *The fever has passed its crisis.* ⇨ see also CRITICAL

**crisp** /krɪsp/ *adj.*, *noun*, *verb*
■ *adj.* (**crisp·er**, **crisp·est**) **1** (*approving*) (of food) (*also* **crispy**) pleasantly hard and dry: *Bake until the pastry is golden and crisp.*

**WORDFINDER** chewy, creamy, crunchy, greasy, juicy, mushy, rubbery, tender, tough

**2** (*also* **crispy**) (*approving*) (of fruit and vegetables) fairly hard and fresh: *a crisp apple/lettuce* **3** (*approving*) (of paper or cloth) fresh and clean; new and slightly stiff without any folds in it: *a crisp new $5 bill* ◇ *a crisp white shirt* **4** (*approving*) (of the air or the weather) pleasantly dry and cold: *a crisp winter morning* ◇ *The air was crisp and clear and the sky was blue.* **5** (*approving*) (of snow, leaves, etc.) hard or dry and making a pleasant noise under pressure: *deep, crisp snow* **6** (*approving*) (of sounds, images, etc.) pleasantly clear and sharp: *The*

367 **critically**

*recording sounds very crisp, considering its age.* **7** (*sometimes disapproving*) (of a person's way of speaking) quick and confident in a way that suggests that the person is busy or is not being friendly: *Her answer was crisp, and she gave no details.* ▶ **crisp·ly** *adv.*: *crisply fried potatoes* ◇ *'Take a seat,' she said crisply.* **crisp·ness** *noun* [U]: *The salad had lost its crispness.*
■ *noun* **1** (*also* **poˌtato ˈcrisp**) (*both BrE*) (*NAmE* **chip**, **poˌtato ˈchip**) [C] a thin round slice of potato that is fried until hard then dried and eaten cold. Crisps are sold in bags and are made to taste of many different foods. **2** (*NAmE*) (*BrE* **crum·ble**) [U, C] a DESSERT (= a sweet dish) made from fruit that is covered with a rough mixture of flour, butter and sugar, cooked in the oven and usually served hot: *apple crisp* IDM⇨ see BURN *v.*
■ *verb* [T, I] **~ (sth)** to give food a crisp surface by putting it in an oven or under a GRILL; to develop a crisp surface in this way

**crispy** /ˈkrɪspi/ *adj.* (*approving*) = CRISP: *crispy batter*

**criss-cross** /ˈkrɪs krɒs; *NAmE* krɔːs/ *adj.*, *verb*
■ *adj.* [usually before noun] with many straight lines that cross each other: *a criss-cross pattern* ▶ **criss-cross** *noun* [sing.]: *a criss-cross of streets*
■ *verb* [T, I] to make a pattern on sth with many straight lines that cross each other: *The smaller streets criss-cross in a grid pattern.* ◇ **be criss-crossed with sth** *The city is criss-crossed with canals.*

**cri·ter·ion** ⓘ **B2** **W** /kraɪˈtɪəriən; *NAmE* -ˈtɪr-/ *noun* (*pl.* **cri·teria** /-riə/) a standard or principle by which sth is judged, or with the help of which a decision is made: *The main criterion is value for money.* ◇ *She failed to meet the strict selection criteria.* ◇ **~ for sth** *the criteria for inclusion*

**crit·ic** ⓘ **B2** /ˈkrɪtɪk/ *noun* **1** **B2** a person who expresses opinions about the good and bad qualities of books, music, etc.: *a film/an art/a music critic* ◇ *Bradley Cooper's gripping performance has been praised by critics.* ⇨ WORDFINDER NOTE at WRITE **2** **B2** a person who expresses dislike of sb/sth and talks about their bad qualities, especially publicly: *She has become one of the ruling party's most outspoken critics.* ◇ **~ of sth/sb** *a critic of private healthcare*

**crit·ic·al** ⓘ **B2** ⓞ /ˈkrɪtɪkl/
• EXPRESSING DISAPPROVAL **1** **B2** saying what you think is bad about sb/sth: *You should just ignore any critical comments.* ◇ *The supervisor is always very critical.* ◇ **~ of sb/sth** *Some parents are highly critical of the school.* ⇨ see also SELF-CRITICAL
• IMPORTANT **2** **B2** extremely important because a future situation will be affected by it **SYN** **crucial**: *a critical issue/factor* ◇ *The kidneys play a critical role in overall health.* ◇ **~ to/for sth** *Your decision is critical to our future.* ⇨ see also MISSION-CRITICAL ⇨ SYNONYMS at ESSENTIAL
• SERIOUS/DANGEROUS **3** **B2** serious, uncertain and possibly dangerous: *One of the victims of the fire remains in a critical condition.* ◇ *a critical moment in our country's history* ◇ *He's at a critical point in his life.* ◇ *a critical step in the process* ⇨ see also CRISIS
• MAKING CAREFUL JUDGEMENTS **4** **B2** involving making fair, careful judgements about the good and bad qualities of sb/sth: *Students are encouraged to develop critical thinking instead of accepting opinions without questioning them.*
• OF ART/MUSIC/BOOKS, ETC. **5** [only before noun] according to the judgement of critics of art, music, literature, etc.: *the film director's greatest critical success* ◇ *In her day she never received the critical acclaim* (= praise from the critics) *she deserved.*

**ˌcritical ˈcare** *noun* [U] = INTENSIVE CARE

**crit·ic·al·ly** **B2** **W** /ˈkrɪtɪkli/ *adv.* **1** **B2** in a way that says what you think is bad about sb/sth: *She spoke critically of her father.* **2** **B2** in a way that is extremely important because a future situation will be affected by it: *a critically important decision* **3** **B2** in a way that is serious, uncertain and possibly dangerous: *He is critically ill in intensive care.* **4** **B2** in a way that involves making fair, careful judgements about the good and bad qualities of sb/sth: *I looked at myself critically in the mirror.* **5** ?+ C1 in a way that is connected with the judgement of critics of art, music, literature, etc: *a critically acclaimed artist*

,critical 'mass noun [U, sing.] **1** (*physics*) the smallest amount of a substance that is needed for a nuclear CHAIN REACTION to take place **2** the minimum amount of resources, number of customers, etc. needed to start or support a project or an activity, or the minimum size that a project or activity needs to be in order to be successful: *The company needs one million customers to reach critical mass and start making a profit.* ◊ *TV via internet could only be developed once a critical mass of households had broadband access.*

,critical 'path noun [sing.] (*specialist*) the order of work that should be followed to complete a project as fast and as cheaply as possible

,critical 'theory noun [U] (*specialist*) a way of thinking about and examining culture and literature by considering the social, historical and IDEOLOGICAL forces that affect it and make it the way it is

,critical 'thinking noun [U] the process of analysing information in order to make a logical decision about the extent to which you believe sth to be true or false: *Critical thinking skills enable students to evaluate information.*

**criti·cism** 🔊 B2 /ˈkrɪtɪsɪzəm/ *noun* **1** ?+ B2 [U, C] the act of expressing DISAPPROVAL of sb/sth and opinions about their faults or bad qualities; a statement showing this DISAPPROVAL: *to draw/face/attract/receive criticism* ◊ *Ben is very sensitive—he just can't take criticism.* ◊ *to offer sb constructive criticism* (= that is meant to be helpful) ◊ *harsh/sharp/heavy criticism* ◊ *I didn't mean it as a criticism.* ◊ *criticisms levelled at* (= aimed at) *journalists* ◊ **~ of sb/sth** *There is widespread criticism of the government's handling of the disaster.* ◊ **~ over/for/about sth** *The former minister is facing growing criticism over his remark.* ◊ **~ against sb/sth** *The past five years has seen growing criticism against the regime.* ⊃ see also SELF-CRITICISM **OPP** praise **2** ?+ B2 [U] the work or activity of making fair, careful judgements about the good and bad qualities of sb/sth, especially books, music, etc: *literary criticism*

**criti·cize** 🔊 B2 Ⓦ (*BrE also* **-ise**) /ˈkrɪtɪsaɪz/ *verb* **1** ?+ B2 [I, T] to say that you think sb/sth is bad; to say what you do not like or think is wrong about sb/sth: *All you ever do is criticize!* ◊ *a heavily criticized plan* ◊ **~ sb/sth (for/over sth)** *She has been sharply criticized for her comments.* ◊ **~ sb/sth as sth/as + adj.** *The law was widely criticized as racist.* **OPP** praise **2** ?+ B2 [T] **~ sth** to judge the good and bad qualities of sth: *We were taught how to criticize poems.*

**cri·tique** ?+ C1 /krɪˈtiːk/ *noun, verb*
- *noun* ?+ C1 a piece of written criticism of a set of ideas, a work of art, etc: *a feminist critique of Freud's theories*
- *verb* **~ sth** to write or give your opinion of, or reaction to, a set of ideas, a work of art, etc: *Her job involves critiquing designs by fashion students.*

**crit·ter** /ˈkrɪtə(r)/ *noun* (*NAmE, informal*) a living creature: *wild critters*

**croak** /krəʊk/ *verb, noun*
- *verb* **1** [I] to make a rough low sound, like the sound a frog makes **2** [I, T] to speak or say sth with a rough low voice: *I had a sore throat and could only croak.* ◊ **~ sth** *He managed to croak a greeting.* ◊ **+ speech** *'I'm fine,' she croaked.* **3** [I] (*slang*) to die
- *noun* a rough low sound made in the throat, like the sound made by a frog

**croaky** /ˈkrəʊki/ *adj.* (*informal*) (of sb's voice) deep and rough, especially because of a SORE throat (= one that is painful because of an infection)

**croc** /krɒk; *NAmE* kraːk/ *noun* (*informal*) = CROCODILE (1)

**cro·chet** /ˈkrəʊʃeɪ; *NAmE* krəʊˈʃeɪ/ *noun, verb*
- *noun* [U] a way of making clothes, etc. from wool or cotton using a special thick needle with a HOOK at the end to make a pattern of connected THREADS
- *verb* [T, I] (**cro·chet·ing**, **cro·cheted**) **~ (sth)** to make sth using crochet: *a crocheted shawl*

**crock** /krɒk; *NAmE* kraːk/ *noun* **1 crocks** [pl.] (*old-fashioned*) cups, plates, dishes, etc. **2** [C] a large pot made of baked CLAY **3** [C] (*BrE, informal*) an old person **4** [C] (*BrE, informal*) an old car in bad condition
**IDM** a ,crock of 'shit (*taboo, slang, especially NAmE*) something that is not true ⊃ more at GOLD *n*.

**crocked** /krɒkt; *NAmE* kraːkt/ *adj.* [not before noun] (*NAmE, slang*) drunk

**crock·ery** /ˈkrɒkəri; *NAmE* ˈkraːk-/ *noun* **1** (*especially BrE*) plates, cups, dishes, etc. **2** (*NAmE*) dishes, etc. that you use in the oven

**croco·dile** /ˈkrɒkədaɪl; *NAmE* ˈkraːk-/ *noun* **1** (*also informal* **croc**) [C] a large REPTILE with a long tail, hard skin and very big JAWS. Crocodiles live in rivers and lakes in hot countries. **2** [U] crocodile skin made into leather: *crocodile shoes* **3** [C] (*BrE*) a long line of people, especially children, walking in pairs
**IDM** ,crocodile 'tears if sb SHEDS (= cries) **crocodile tears**, they pretend to be sad about sth, but they are not really sad at all

'**crocodile clip** (*especially BrE*) (*also* '**alligator clip** *especially NAmE*) *noun* an object with sharp teeth that is used for holding things together. It is held closed by a spring and you press the ends of it together to open it: *Use the crocodile clips to attach the cables to the battery.*

**Crocs™** /krɒks; *NAmE* kraːks/ *noun* [pl.] shoes made from a soft comfortable material that fits the wearer's feet

**cro·cus** /ˈkrəʊkəs/ *noun* a small yellow, purple or white flower that appears in early spring

**croft** /krɒft; *NAmE* krɔːft/ *noun* (*BrE*) a small rented farm or the house on it, especially in Scotland

**croft·er** /ˈkrɒftə(r); *NAmE* ˈkrɔːf-/ *noun* (*BrE*) a person who rents or owns a small family farm, especially in Scotland

**Crohn's disease** /ˈkrəʊnz dɪziːz/ (*also* **Crohn's**) *noun* [U] a disease affecting the lower INTESTINES, in which they develop many painful areas. The disease lasts for many years and is difficult to cure.

**crois·sant** /ˈkwæsɒ̃; *NAmE* kwaːˈsɑːnt, krəˈs-/ *noun* (*from French*) a small sweet roll with a curved shape, eaten especially at breakfast

**crone** /krəʊn/ *noun* (*literary*) an ugly old woman

**crony** /ˈkrəʊni/ *noun* [usually pl.] (*pl.* **-ies**) (*informal, often disapproving*) a person that sb spends a lot of time with: *He was playing cards with his cronies.*

**cro·ny·ism** /ˈkrəʊniɪzəm/ *noun* [U] (*disapproving*) the situation in which people in power give jobs to their friends

**crook** /krʊk/ *noun, verb, adj.*
- *noun* **1** (*informal*) a dishonest person **SYN** criminal: *That salesman is a real crook.* **2 ~ of your arm/elbow** the place where your arm bends at the ELBOW **3** a long stick with a HOOK (= a curved part) at one end, used by SHEPHERDS for catching sheep **IDM** see HOOK *n*.
- *verb* **~ sth** to bend your finger or arm
- *adj.* [not usually before noun] (*AustralE, NZE, informal*) ill

**crooked** /ˈkrʊkɪd/ *adj.* **1** not in a straight line; bent or TWISTED: *a crooked nose/smile* ◊ *a village of crooked streets* ◊ *Your glasses are on crooked.* **OPP** straight **2** dishonest: *a crooked businessman/deal* **3 ~ (on sb)** (*AustralE, informal*) annoyed: *It's not you I'm crooked on, it's him.* ▶ **crook·ed·ly** *adv.*

**croon** /kruːn/ *verb* [T, I] **~ (sth)** to sing sth quietly and gently: *She gently crooned a lullaby.*

**croon·er** /ˈkruːnə(r)/ *noun* (*old-fashioned*) a male singer who sings slow romantic songs

**crop** /krɒp; NAmE krɑːp/ noun, verb

■ noun
- **PLANTS FOR FOOD 1** [C] a plant that is grown in large quantities, especially as food: *What are the benefits of growing GM crops?* ◊ *crop yield/production* ◊ *to grow/plant/harvest crops* ⊃ WORDFINDER NOTE at FARM ⊃ see also CASH CROP

**WORDFINDER** blight, cereal, genetically modified, grain, harvest, monoculture, organic, staple, yield

**2** [C] the amount of grain, fruit, etc. that is grown in one season **SYN** harvest: *a fall in this year's coffee crop* ◊ *We are looking forward to a bumper crop* (= a very large one).
- **GROUP OF PEOPLE 3** [sing.] **a ~ of sth** a group of people who do sth at the same time; a number of things that happen at the same time: *the current crop of trainees* ◊ *She is really the cream of the crop* (= the best in her group). ◊ *a crop of disasters/injuries*
- **WHIP 4** [C] a short WHIP used by horse riders: *a riding crop*
- **HAIR 5** [C] a very short HAIRSTYLE: *She has her hair cut in a short crop.* **6** [sing.] **a ~ of dark, fair, etc. hair/curls** hair that is short and thick: *He had a thick crop of black curly hair.*
- **OF BIRD 7** (*specialist*) a part of a bird's throat that has the shape of a bag where food is stored before it passes into the stomach

■ verb (-pp-)
- **HAIR 1** [T] **~ sth (+ adj.)** to cut sb's hair very short: *closely cropped hair*
- **IMAGE 2** [T] **~ sth** (*specialist*) to cut off part of a photograph, picture or image
- **OF ANIMALS 3** [T] **~ sth** to bite off and eat the tops of plants, especially grass
- **PLANTS 4** [I] (*of plants*) to produce a crop: *The potatoes cropped well this year.* **5** [T] **~ sth** to use land to grow crops: *The river valley is intensively cropped.*

**PHR V** ,**crop 'up** to appear or happen, especially when it is not expected **SYN** come up: *His name just cropped up in conversation.* ◊ *I'll be late—something's cropped up at home.*

**'crop circle** (*also* **'corn circle**) *noun* a round area in a field of crops that has suddenly become flat. Some people say that crop circles are made by creatures from outer space.

**'crop dusting** *noun* [U] the practice of SPRAYING crops with chemicals from a plane

**crop·per** /ˈkrɒpə(r); NAmE ˈkrɑːp-/ noun
**IDM** ,**come a 'cropper** (*BrE, informal*) **1** (of a person) to fall over **2** to have a failure or near disaster: *We nearly came a cropper in the second half of the game.*

**'crop top** *noun* a woman's informal piece of clothing for the upper body, cut short so that the stomach can be seen

**cro·quet** /ˈkrəʊkeɪ; NAmE kroʊˈkeɪ/ *noun* [U] a game played on grass in which players use MALLETS (= sticks with a block of wood at one end) to knock wooden balls through a series of HOOPS (= curved wires)

**cro·quette** /krɒˈket; NAmE kroʊˈk-/ *noun* a small amount of MASHED potato, fish, etc., shaped into a ball or tube, covered with BREADCRUMBS and fried

**crore** /krɔː(r)/ *number* (*plural verb*) (*pl.* **crore** or **crores**) (*IndE*) ten million; one hundred LAKH

**cros·ier** = CROZIER

**cross** /krɒs; NAmE krɔːs/ verb, noun, adj.

■ verb
- **GO/PUT ACROSS 1** [I, T] to go across; to pass or stretch from one side to the other: *As soon as traffic slowed down enough to safely cross, I started walking.* ◊ **~ over** *I waved and she crossed over* (= crossed the road towards me). ◊ **~ (over) from …** *He crossed over from the other side of the road.* ◊ **~ (over) from … to/into …** *We crossed from Dover to Calais.* ◊ **~ (over) to/into …** *She crossed to the other side of the room.* ◊ **~ sth** *to cross the road/street* ◊ *to cross the sea/mountains* ◊ *He was caught trying to cross the border illegally.* ◊ *A look of annoyance crossed her face.* ◊ **~ over sth** *He crossed over the road and joined me.* **2** [I, T] to pass across each other: *The roads cross just outside the town.* ◊ **~ over** *The straps cross over at the back and are tied at the waist.* **3** [T] **~ sth** to put or place sth across or over sth else: *to cross your arms/legs* (= place one arm or leg over the other) ◊ *She sat with her legs crossed.* ◊ *a flag with a design of two crossed keys*
- **OPPOSE 4** [T] **~ sb** to oppose sb or speak against them or their plans or wishes: *She's really nice until you cross her.* ◊ (*literary*) *He had been crossed in love* (= the person he loved was not faithful to him).
- **MIX ANIMALS/PLANTS 5** [T] **~ A with B | ~ A and B** to make two different types of animal BREED (= produce young) together; to mix two types of plant to form a new one: *A mule is the product of a horse crossed with a donkey.* ◊ (*figurative*) *He behaved like an army officer crossed with a professor.*
- **IN SPORT 6** [I, T] **~ (sth)** (in football (soccer) or hockey ) to kick or pass a ball to the side across the field
- **DRAW LINE 7** [T] **~ sth** to draw a line across sth: *to cross your t's* (= the letters in writing)
- **MAKE CHRISTIAN SYMBOL 8** [T] **~ yourself** to make the sign of the cross (= the Christian symbol) on your chest

**IDM** ,**cross your 'fingers** to hope that your plans will be successful (sometimes putting one finger across another as a sign of hoping for good luck): *I'm crossing my fingers that my proposal will be accepted.* ◊ *Keep your fingers crossed!* ,**cross my 'heart (and hope to 'die)** (*informal*) used to emphasize that you are telling the truth or will do what you promise: *I saw him do it—cross my heart.* ,**cross a/the 'line** to do sth that is not considered to be acceptable behaviour: *He crossed the line by making details of their very private conversation public.* ,**cross your 'mind** (of thoughts, etc.) to come into your mind **SYN** occur to sb: *It never crossed my mind that she might lose* (= I was sure that she would win). ,**cross sb's palm with 'silver** to give sb money so that they will do you a favour, especially tell your FORTUNE ,**cross sb's 'path | people's paths 'cross** if sb **crosses sb's path** or **their paths cross**, they meet by chance: *I hope I never cross her path again.* ◊ *Our paths were to cross again many years later.* ,**cross 'swords (with sb)** to fight or argue with sb ,**cross that 'bridge when you 'come to it** to worry about a problem when it actually happens and not before ⊃ more at DOT *v.*, WIRE *n.*

**PHR V** ,**cross sb/sth↔'off | ,cross sb/sth 'off sth** to draw a line through a person's name or an item on a list because they/it is no longer required or involved: *We can cross his name off; he's not coming.* ,**cross sth↔'out/'through** to draw a line through a word, usually because it is wrong ,**cross 'over (to/into sth)** to move or change from one type of culture, music, political party, etc. to another: *a cult movie that has crossed over to mass appeal* ⊃ related noun CROSSOVER

■ noun
- **MARK ON PAPER 1** [C] a mark or an object formed by two lines crossing each other (X or +); the mark (X) is often used on paper to show sth: *I've put a cross on the map to show where the hotel is.* ◊ *Put a tick if the answer is correct and a cross if it's wrong.* ◊ *Sign your name on the form where I've put a cross.* ◊ *Those who could not write signed with a cross.* ⊃ see also NOUGHTS AND CROSSES ⊃ compare TICK
- **FOR PUNISHMENT 2** [C] a long straight piece of wood with one end in the ground and a shorter piece joined across it from side to side near the top. In the past people were hung on crosses and left to die as a punishment.
- **CHRISTIAN SYMBOL 3 the Cross** [sing.] the cross that Jesus Christ died on, used as a symbol of Christianity **4** [C] an object, a design, a piece of jewellery, etc. in the shape of a cross, used as a symbol of Christianity: *She wore a small gold cross on a chain around her neck.*
- **MEDAL 5** (*usually* **Cross**) [C] a small decoration in the shape of a cross that is given to sb as an honour for doing sth very brave
- **MIXTURE 6** [C, usually sing.] **~ (between A and B)** a mixture of two different things, BREEDS (= types) of animal, etc: *The play was a cross between a farce and a tragedy.* ◊ *A*

ʊ actual | aɪ my | aʊ now | eɪ say | əʊ go | ɔɪ boy | ɪə near | eə hair | ʊə pure

mule is a cross between a horse and a donkey. ⇒ see also HYBRID
- **IN SPORT 7** [C] (in football (soccer) or hockey) a kick or hit of the ball across the field rather than up or down it ⇒ see also RED CROSS

**IDM** **have a (heavy) ˈcross to bear** to have a difficult problem that makes you worried or unhappy but that you have to deal with: *We all have our crosses to bear.*

- **adj.** (**cross·er, cross·est**) ~ **(with sb)** (especially *BrE*) annoyed or quite angry: *I was cross with him for being late.* ◇ *Please don't get cross. Let me explain.* **SYNONYMS** at ANGRY ▶ **ˈcross·ly** *adv.*: '*Well what did you expect?' she said crossly.*

**cross-** /krɒs; *NAmE* krɔːs/ *combining form* (in nouns, verbs, adjectives and adverbs) involving movement or action from one thing to another or between two things: *cross-Channel ferries* ◇ *cross-fertilize* ◇ *crossfire*

**ˈcross·bar** /ˈkrɒsbɑː(r); *NAmE* ˈkrɔːs-/ *noun* **1** the bar across the top that joins the two VERTICAL posts of a goal ⇒ picture at BAR **2** the bar between the seat and the HANDLEBARS of a man's bicycle

**ˈcross-bencher** *noun* (*BrE*) a member of the British House of Lords who does not belong to a particular political party ▶ **ˈcross benches** *noun* [pl.]: *members who sit on the cross benches*

**ˈcross·bones** /ˈkrɒsbəʊnz; *NAmE* ˈkrɔːs-/ *noun* [pl.] ⇒ SKULL AND CROSSBONES

**ˈcross-border** *adj.* [only before noun] involving activity across a border between two countries: *a cross-border raid by guerrillas* ⇒ **WORDFINDER NOTE** at ALLY

**ˈcross·bow** /ˈkrɒsbəʊ; *NAmE* ˈkrɔːs-/ *noun* a weapon which consists of a BOW that is fixed onto a larger piece of wood, and that shoots short heavy ARROWS (called BOLTS) ⇒ picture at BOLT

**ˈcross-breed** *verb, noun*
- *verb* [T, I] ~ **(sth)** to make an animal or a plant BREED (= produce young animals/new plants) with a different type; to BREED with an animal or a plant of a different type: *cross-bred sheep* ▶ **ˈcross-ˈbreeding** *noun* [U]
- *noun* an animal or a plant that is a result of cross-breeding ⇒ compare HYBRID

**ˈcross-ˈcheck** *verb* to make sure that information, figures, etc. are correct by using a different method or system to check them: ~ **sth** *Cross-check your answers with a calculator.* ◇ ~ **sth against sth** *Baggage should be cross-checked against the names of individual passengers.* ▶ **ˈcross-check** *noun*

**ˌcross-con·tamˈin·ation** *noun* [U] the process by which harmful bacteria spread from one substance to another

**ˌcross-ˈcountry** *adj., adv., noun*
- *adj.* [usually before noun], *adv.* **1** across fields or open country rather than on roads or a track: *cross-country running* ◇ *We rode cross-country.* **2** from one part of a country to the other, especially not using main roads or routes: *cross-country train journeys* **3** involving two or more countries: *The report contains the findings of a cross-country comparison of crime statistics.*
- *noun* **1 the cross-country** [sing.] a cross-country running or skiing race **2** [U] the sport of running or skiing across country ⇒ compare DOWNHILL

**ˌcross-country ˈskiing** *noun* [U] the sport of skiing across the countryside, rather than down mountains

**ˈcross-ˈcultural** *adj.* involving or containing ideas from two or more different countries or cultures

**ˈcross-current** *noun* **1** a current of water in a river or in the sea that flows across the main current **2** [usually pl.] (*formal*) a set of beliefs or ideas that are different from others, especially from those that most people hold

**ˌcross-curˈricu·lar** *adj.* (*BrE*) affecting or connected with different parts of the school CURRICULUM

**ˌcross-disciˈplinary** *adj.* involving different areas of knowledge or study **SYN** **interdisciplinary**: *a cross-disciplinary approach to research*

**ˈcross-ˈdressing** *noun* [U] the practice of wearing clothes usually worn by a person of the opposite sex **SYN** **transvestism** ▶ **ˈcross-ˈdresser** *noun*

**ˈcross-eˈxamine** *verb* ~ **sb** to question sb carefully and in a lot of detail about answers that they have already given, especially in court: *The witness was cross-examined for over two hours.* ▶ **ˈcross-ˌexamiˈnation** *noun* [U, C]: *He broke down under cross-examination* (= while he was being cross-examined) *and admitted his part in the assault.*

**ˈcross-ˈeyed** *adj.* having one or both eyes looking towards the nose

**ˈcross-ˈfertilize** (*BrE also -***ise**) *verb* **1** ~ **sth** (*biology*) to FERTILIZE a plant using POLLEN from a different plant of the same species **2** ~ **sth** to help sth develop in a useful or positive way by mixing ideas from a different area: *The study of psychology has recently been widely cross-fertilized by new discoveries in genetics.* ▶ **ˈcross-ˌfertiliˈzation, -iˈsation** *noun* [U, sing.]

**ˈcross·fire** /ˈkrɒsfaɪə(r); *NAmE* ˈkrɔːs-/ *noun* [U] the firing of guns from two or more directions at the same time, so that the bullets cross: *The doctor was killed in crossfire as he went to help the wounded.* ◇ (*figurative*) *When two industrial giants clash, small companies can get* **caught in the crossfire** (= become involved and suffer as a result).

**ˈcross hairs** (*BrE*) (*NAmE* **ˈcross-hairs**) *noun* [pl.] a pair of very thin wires in the shape of a cross that you see when you look through a GUNSIGHT, MICROSCOPE, etc.

**IDM** **(caught) in the ˈcross hairs** in a situation in which you are the target or victim of sb's anger, violence or blame: *In the fight over immigration, it's kids who are really getting caught in the cross hairs.*

**ˈcross-inˈfection** *noun* [U] (*medical*) an occasion an infection is passed to sb who has a different infection or to a different species of animal or plant

**ˈcross·ing** /ˈkrɒsɪŋ; *NAmE* ˈkrɔːs-/ *noun* **1** a place where you can safely cross a road, a river, etc., or from one country to another: *The child was killed when a car failed to stop at the crossing.* ◇ *The next crossing point is a long way downstream.* ◇ *He was arrested by guards at the border crossing.* ⇒ see also LEVEL CROSSING, PEDESTRIAN CROSSING, PELICAN CROSSING, RAILROAD CROSSING, ZEBRA CROSSING **2** a journey across a sea or a wide river: *a three-hour ferry crossing* ◇ *a rough crossing from Dover to Calais* ◇ *the first Atlantic crossing* **3** an act of going from one side to another: *attempted crossings of the border*

**ˈcross-ˈlegged** /ˌkrɒs ˈlegd, ˈlegɪd; *NAmE* ˌkrɔːs-/ *adv., adj.* sitting on the floor with your legs pulled up in front of you and with one leg or foot over the other: *the cross-legged figure of the Hindu god*

**ˈcross·over** /ˈkrɒsəʊvə(r); *NAmE* ˈkrɔːs-/ *noun* [C, U] the process or result of changing from one area of activity or style of doing sth to another: *The album was an exciting jazz-pop crossover.*

**ˈcross·piece** /ˈkrɒspiːs; *NAmE* ˈkrɔːs-/ *noun* (*specialist*) a piece of a structure or a tool that lies or is fixed across another piece

**ˈcross-ˈplatform** *adj.* (of a computer program or an electronic device) that can be used with different types of computers or programs

**ˈcross-ˈpollinˌate** *verb* ~ **sth** (*biology*) to move POLLEN from a flower or plant onto another flower or plant so that it produces seeds ▶ **ˈcross-ˌpolliˈnation** *noun* [U]

**ˈcross post** *noun* (*also* **cross-post**) a message, an image, an article, etc. that has been put at two or more online locations: *I ran a cross post from the site.* ◇ *One of your cross-posts sparked a debate.*

**ˈcross-ˈpost** *verb* [T, I] to put a message, an image, an article, etc. at two or more online locations: *You can cross-post items from/to your own blog.*

**ˈcross-proˈmotion** *noun* [C, U] (*business*) a set of advertisements or other activities that are designed to help a company sell two different products, or to help two companies sell their products or services together

**cross ˈpurposes** noun [pl.] if two people are **at cross purposes**, they do not understand each other because they are talking about or aiming at different things, without realizing it: *I think we're talking at cross purposes; that's not what I meant at all.*

**cross-ˈquestion** verb ~ sb to question sb carefully and in great detail and often in a way that seems aggressive

**cross-reˈfer** verb [T, I] (-rr-) ~ (sth) to sth to refer to another text or part of a text, especially to give more information about sth: *The entry for 'polygraph' is cross-referred to the entry for 'lie detector'.*

**cross ˈreference** noun ~ (to sth) a note that tells a reader to look in another part of a book or file for further information

**cross-ˈreference** verb ~ sth to give cross references to another text or part of a text: *The book is fully cross-referenced and has a useful thematic index.*

**cross·roads** /ˈkrɒsrəʊdz; NAmE also **cross-road**/ noun (pl. **cross·roads**) a place where two roads meet and cross each other: *At the next crossroads, turn right.* ◇ (figurative) *He has reached a career crossroads* (= he must decide which way to go next in his career). ⊃ see also INTERSECTION, JUNCTION
**IDM** **at a/the ˈcrossroads** at an important point in sb's life or development

**ˈcross section** noun 1 [C, U] what you see when you cut through the middle of sth so that you can see the different layers it is made of; a drawing of this view: *a diagram representing a cross section of the human eye* ◇ **in** ~ : *the human eye in cross section* 2 [C, usually sing.] a group of people or things that are typical of a larger group: *a representative cross section of society*

**cross-ˈselling** noun [U] (business) the activity of selling a different extra product to a customer who is already buying a product from a company

**ˈcross stitch** noun [C, U] a STITCH in EMBROIDERY formed by two STITCHES crossing each other; SEWING in which this stitch is used

**ˈcross street** noun (NAmE) a street that crosses another street

**ˈcross-talk** /ˈkrɒstɔːk; NAmE ˈkrɔːs-/ noun [U] (specialist) a situation in which a communications system is picking up the wrong signals

**cross·town** /ˌkrɒsˈtaʊn; NAmE ˌkrɔːs-/ adj. (NAmE) going from one side of a town or city to the other: *a crosstown bus*

**ˈcross-training** noun [U] the activity of training in sports other than your main sport in order to make yourself fitter and able to do your main sport better

**cross·walk** /ˈkrɒswɔːk; NAmE ˈkrɔːs-/ noun (NAmE) (BrE **peˌdestrian ˈcrossing**) noun a part of a road where vehicles must stop to allow people to cross ⊃ see also ZEBRA CROSSING

**cross·wind** /ˈkrɒswɪnd; NAmE ˈkrɔːs-/ noun a wind that is blowing across the direction that you are moving in

**cross·wise** /ˈkrɒswaɪz; NAmE ˈkrɔːs-/ adv. 1 across, especially from one corner to the opposite one: *Cut the fabric crosswise.* 2 in the form of a cross

**cross·word** /ˈkrɒswɜːd; NAmE ˈkrɔːswɜːrd/ (also **ˈcrossword puzzle**) noun a game in which you have to fit words across and downwards into spaces with numbers in a square diagram. You find the words by solving clues: *to do a/the crossword* ◇ *I've finished the crossword apart from 3 across and 10 down.*

**crotch** /krɒtʃ; NAmE krɑːtʃ/ (also **crutch**) noun 1 the part of the body where the legs join at the top, including the area around the GENITALS 2 the part of a pair of trousers, etc. that covers the crotch: *There's a hole in the crotch.*

**crot·chet** /ˈkrɒtʃɪt; NAmE ˈkrɑːtʃ-/ (BrE) (NAmE **ˈquarter note**) noun (music) a note that lasts half as long as a MINIM ⊃ picture at MUSIC

371

**crot·chety** /ˈkrɒtʃəti; NAmE ˈkrɑːtʃ-/ adj. (informal) easily upset; angry: *He was tired and crotchety.*

**crouch** /kraʊtʃ/ verb, noun
■ verb [I] (+ adv./prep.) to put your body close to the ground by bending your legs under you **SYN** squat: *He crouched down beside her.* ◇ *Doyle crouched behind a hedge.* ▸ **crouched** adj.: *She sat crouched in a corner.*
**PHRV** **ˈcrouch over sb/sth** to bend over sb/sth so that you are very close to them or it: *He crouched over the papers on his desk.*
■ noun [sing.] a crouching position: *She dropped to a crouch.*

**croup** /kruːp/ noun [U] a disease of children that makes them COUGH (= force air through the throat noisily) a lot and have difficulty breathing

**croup·ier** /ˈkruːpieɪ; NAmE also ˈkruːpiər/ noun a person whose job is to be in charge of a game in a CASINO and collect and pay out money, give out cards, etc. ⊃ WORDFINDER NOTE at GAMBLING

**crou·ton** /ˈkruːtɒn; NAmE -tɑːn/ noun a small piece of cold dry fried bread served in soup or as part of a salad

**Crow** /krəʊ/ noun (pl. **Crow** or **Crows**) a member of a Native American people, many of whom live in the US state of Montana

**crow** /krəʊ/ noun, verb
■ noun 1 a large bird, completely or mostly black, with a rough unpleasant call 2 a sound like that of a ROOSTER (= an adult male chicken) crowing: *She gave a little crow of triumph.*
**IDM** **as the ˈcrow flies** in a straight line: *The villages are no more than a mile apart as the crow flies.* ⊃ more at EAT
■ verb 1 [I] (of a ROOSTER) to make repeated loud high sounds, especially early in the morning 2 [I, T] (disapproving) to talk too proudly about sth you have achieved, especially when sb else has been unsuccessful **SYN** boast, gloat: ~ (about/over sth) *He won't stop crowing about his victory.* ◇ **+ speech** '*I've won, I've won!' she crowed.* ◇ ~ that … *He crowed that they had sold out in one day.*

**crow·bar** /ˈkrəʊbɑː(r)/ noun a straight iron bar, usually with a curved end, used for forcing open boxes and moving heavy objects

# crowd ⓘ A2 /kraʊd/ noun, verb
■ noun 1 A2 [C + sing./pl. v.] a large number of people gathered together in a public place, for example in the streets or at a sports game: *He pushed his way through the crowd.* ◇ *A small crowd had gathered outside the church.* ◇ ~ **of sb/sth** *Crowds of people poured into the street.* ◇ *Several speakers addressed the crowd at the rally.* ◇ *a large/huge crowd* ◇ *The match attracted a capacity crowd of 80000* (= the maximum number of people who could attend). ◇ **before a** ~ *The President spoke before a crowd of more than 50000 in the city's football stadium.* ◇ **among a** ~ *The mayor of Paris was among the crowd that had gathered for the street celebration.* ◇ **to attract/draw a crowd** ◇ **crowd control** *A whole crowd of us* (= a lot of us) *are going to the ball.* 2 [C + sing./pl. v.] (informal, often disapproving) a particular group of people: *Bob introduced her to some of the usual crowd* (= people who often meet each other). ◇ *the bright young theatrical crowd* ⊃ see also IN-CROWD 3 **the crowd** [sing.] (sometimes disapproving) ordinary people, not special or unusual in any way: *We all like to think we **stand out from the crowd*** (= are different from and better than other people). ◇ *He prefers to be **one of the crowd**.* ◇ *She's quite happy to **follow the crowd**.*
■ verb 1 ~ sth to fill a place so there is little room to move: *Thousands of people crowded the narrow streets.* 2 ~ sth to fill your mind so that you can think of nothing else: *Memories crowded his mind.* 3 ~ sb (informal) to stand very close to sb so that they feel uncomfortable or nervous
**PHRV** **ˌcrowd aˈround (sb/sth)** (also **ˌcrowd ˈround (sb/sth)** especially in BrE) to gather in large numbers around sb/sth: *We all crowded around the stove to keep warm.* ◇ *Photographers were crowding around outside.* **ˌcrowd ˈin (on sb)**, **ˌcrowd ˈinto sth** (of thoughts, questions, etc.) to fill your mind so that you can think of nothing else: *Too many uncomfortable thoughts were crowding in on her.* ◇

# crowded

Memories came crowding into her mind. **crowd 'into/ 'onto sth** | **crowd 'in** to move in large numbers into a small space: *We all crowded into her office to sing 'Happy Birthday'.* ▶ **crowd sb/sth 'into/'onto sth** | **crowd sb/ sth 'in** to put many people or things into a small space: *Guests were crowded into the few remaining rooms.* ▶ **crowd sb/sth 'out** to fill a place so that other people or things are kept out ▶ **crowd 'round (sb/sth)** (especially BrE) = CROWD AROUND (SB/STH)

**crowd·ed** ❶ **A2** /ˈkraʊdɪd/ *adj.* **1** **A2** having a lot of people or too many people: *crowded streets* ◊ *a crowded bar* ◊ *The main beach can get really crowded in summer.* ◊ *~ with sb In the spring the place is crowded with skiers.* ⟹ compare UNCROWDED **2** ~ (**with sth**) full of sth: *a room crowded with books* ◊ *We have a very crowded schedule.*

**crowd·fund·ing** /ˈkraʊdfʌndɪŋ/ *noun* [U] the practice of funding a project or an activity by raising many small amounts of money from a large number of people, usually using the internet: *They raised the money for the film through crowdfunding.* ▶ **crowd·fund** *verb:* ~ **sth** *She's planning to crowdfund her next research project.*

**ˈcrowd-pleaser** *noun* (*informal*) a person or performance that always pleases an audience

**ˈcrowd-puller** *noun* (*informal*) a person or thing that always attracts a large audience

**crowd·sour·cing** /ˈkraʊdsɔːsɪŋ; NAmE -sɔːrs-/ *noun* [U] the activity of getting information or help for a project or a task from a large number of people, typically using the internet: *The newspaper uses crowdsourcing to gather information for its website.* ▶ **crowd·source** *verb* ~ **sth**

**crown** ❶⁺ **C1** /kraʊn/ *noun, verb*
■ *noun*
- OF KING/QUEEN **1** ❶⁺ **C1** [C] an object in the shape of a circle, usually made of gold and precious stones, that a king or queen wears on his or her head on official occasions⟹ WORDFINDER NOTE at KING **2** ❶⁺ **C1** **the Crown** [*sing.*] the government of a country, thought of as being represented by a king or queen: *land owned by the Crown* ◊ *a Minister of the Crown* ◊ *Who's appearing for the Crown (= bringing a criminal charge against sb on behalf of the state) in this case?* **3** ❶⁺ **C1** **the crown** [*sing.*] the position or power of a king or queen: *She refused the crown (= refused to become queen).* ◊ *his claim to the French crown*
- OF FLOWERS/LEAVES **4** [C] a circle of flowers, leaves, etc. that is worn on sb's head, sometimes as a sign of victory
- IN SPORTS COMPETITION **5** [C, usually *sing.*] (*informal*) the position of winning a sports competition: *She is determined to retain her Wimbledon crown.*
- OF HEAD/HAT **6** (*usually* **the crown**) [*sing.*] the top part of the head or a hat
- HIGHEST PART **7** (*usually* **the crown**) [*sing.*] the highest part of sth: *the crown of a hill*
- OF A PLANT **8** [C] the part of a plant just above and below the ground **9** [C] the top of a tree or other plant
- ON TOOTH **10** [C] an artificial cover for a damaged tooth **SYN** cap⟹ WORDFINDER NOTE at DENTIST
- SHAPE **11** [C] anything in the shape of a crown, especially as a decoration or a BADGE
- MONEY **12** [C] a unit of money in several European countries: *Czech crowns* **13** [C] an old British coin worth five SHILLINGS (= now 25p) **IDM** see JEWEL
■ *verb*
- KING/QUEEN **1** [often passive] to put a crown on the head of a new king or queen as a sign of royal power in a ceremony at which they officially become king or queen: **be crowned** *Queen Elizabeth was crowned in 1953.* ◊ **be crowned + noun** *The prince was soon to be crowned King of England.*
- COVER TOP **2** [usually passive] to form or cover the top of sth: **be crowned with sth** *His head was crowned with a mop of brown curls.*
- MAKE COMPLETE **3** [often passive] to make sth complete or perfect, especially by adding an achievement, a success, etc: ~ **sth** *The award of the Nobel Prize has crowned a glorious career in physics.* ◊ **be crowned with sth** *Their efforts were finally crowned with success.*
- HIT ON HEAD **4** ~ **sb** (*old-fashioned, informal*) to hit sb on the head
- TOOTH **5** [often passive] to put an artificial cover on a tooth **SYN** cap: **have sth/be crowned** *I've had one of my teeth crowned.*
**IDM** **to crown it ˈall** (*BrE, informal*) used to say that sth is the final and worst event in a series of unpleasant or annoying events: *It was cold and raining, and, to crown it all, we had to walk home.*

**ˌCrown ˈColony** *noun* a COLONY ruled directly by the British government

**ˌCrown ˈCourt** *noun* (in England and Wales) a court that deals with serious criminal cases, with a judge and JURY, and with cases referred from a MAGISTRATES' COURT⟹ compare COUNTY COURT

**crown·ing** /ˈkraʊnɪŋ/ *adj.* [only before noun] making sth perfect or complete: *The cathedral is the crowning glory of the city.* ◊ *His 'Beethoven' sculpture is seen as the crowning achievement of his career.*

**ˌcrown ˈjewels** *noun* [*pl.*] **1** the CROWN and other objects worn or carried by a king or queen on formal occasions **2** things that are considered very valuable, especially in terms of their cultural value

**ˌcrown ˈprince** *noun* (in some countries) a prince who will become king when the present king or queen dies

**ˌcrown ˈprincess** *noun* **1** the wife of a crown prince **2** (in some countries) a princess who will become queen when the present king or queen dies

**ˌCrown ˈprosecutor** *noun* (in England and Wales) a lawyer who works for the state

**ˈcrow's feet** *noun* [*pl.*] lines in the skin around the outer corner of a person's eye

**ˈcrow's nest** *noun* a platform at the top of a ship's MAST (= the post that supports the sails) from which sb can see a long way and watch for land, danger, etc.

**croz·ier** (*also* **cro·sier**) /ˈkrəʊziə(r); NAmE ˈkroʊʒər/ *noun* a long stick, usually curved at one end, carried by a BISHOP (= a Christian priest of high rank) at religious ceremonies

**cru·cial** ❶ **B2** ❂ /ˈkruːʃl/ *adj.* extremely important, because it will affect other things **SYN** **critical, essential**: *Private security cameras can prove crucial in some investigations.* ◊ *Parents play a crucial role in preparing their child for school.* ◊ *This step is a crucial part of the process.* ◊ *a crucial moment/step/point* ◊ ~ **to/for sth** *Winning this contract is absolutely crucial to our long term success.* ◊ **it is ~ that …** *It is crucial that we get this right.* ◊ ~ **in doing sth** *The summit was crucial in shaping the reform process.* ⟹ SYNONYMS at ESSENTIAL ⟹ LANGUAGE BANK at EMPHASIS, VITAL▶ **cru·cial·ly** /-ʃəli/ *adv.: crucially important*

**cru·cible** /ˈkruːsɪbl/ *noun* **1** a pot in which substances are heated to high temperatures, metals are melted, etc. **2** (*formal or literary*) a place or situation in which people or ideas are tested severely, often creating sth new or exciting in the process

**cru·ci·fix** /ˈkruːsəfɪks/ *noun* a model of a cross with a figure of Jesus Christ on it, as a symbol of the Christian religion

**cru·ci·fix·ion** /ˌkruːsəˈfɪkʃn/ *noun* (*sometimes* **Crucifixion**) **1** [C, U] the act of killing sb by fastening them to a cross: *the Crucifixion (= of Jesus)* **2** [C] a painting or other work of art representing the crucifixion of Jesus Christ

**cru·ci·form** /ˈkruːsɪfɔːm; NAmE -fɔːrm/ *adj.* (*specialist*) (especially of buildings) in the shape of a cross

**cru·cify** /ˈkruːsɪfaɪ/ *verb* (**cru·ci·fies, cru·ci·fy·ing, cru·ci·fied, cru·ci·fied**) **1** ~ **sb** to kill sb as a punishment by fastening them to a wooden cross **2** ~ **sb** (*informal*) to criticize or punish sb very severely: *The prime minister was crucified in the press for his handling of the affair.*

**crud** /krʌd/ *noun* [U] (*informal*) any dirty or unpleasant substance

**cruddy** /ˈkrʌdi/ *adj.* (**crud·dier, crud·di·est**) (*informal*) bad, dirty or of low quality: *We got really cruddy service in that restaurant last time.*

**crude** /kruːd/ *adj., noun*
- *adj.* (**cruder, crudest**) **1** [usually before noun] (of oil and other natural substances) in its natural state, before it has been processed or REFINED: *crude oil/metal* **2** (*statistics*) (of figures) not changed or corrected **3** (of people or the way they behave) offensive or rude, especially about sex SYN **vulgar**: *crude jokes/language* **4** simple and not very accurate but giving a general idea of sth: *In crude terms, the causes of mental illness seem to be of three main kinds.* **5** (of objects or works of art) simply made, not showing much skill or attention to detail: *a crude drawing of a face* ▸ **crudely** *adv.*: *a crudely drawn ship* ◇ *To put it crudely, the poor are going without food so that the rich can drive cars.* **crudeness** *noun* [U]
- *noun* (also **crude 'oil**) [U] oil in its natural state, before it has been processed or REFINED: *50000 barrels of crude*

**crudity** /ˈkruːdəti/ *noun* [U, C] (*pl.* **-ies**) the fact of being CRUDE; an example of sth CRUDE: *Despite the crudity of their methods and equipment, the experiment was a considerable success.* ◇ *the novel's structural crudities* ◇ *The crudity of her language shocked him.*

**cruel** /ˈkruːəl/ *adj., verb*
- *adj.* (**crueller, cruellest**, *US* **crueler, cruelest**) **1** having a desire to cause physical or mental pain and make sb suffer: *a cruel dictator* ◇ *~ to sb/sth I can't stand people who are cruel to animals.* ◇ *Her eyes were cruel and hard.* ◇ *Sometimes you have to be cruel to be kind* (= make sb suffer because it will be good for them later). OPP **kind 2** causing physical or mental pain and making sb suffer: *a cruel joke/hoax* ◇ *It was a cruel irony that he, being gravely ill, would survive his family.* ▸ **cruelly** /-əli/ *adv.*: *The dog had been cruelly treated.* ◇ *I was cruelly deceived.*
- *verb* (**-ll-**) ~ **sth** (*AustralE, informal*) to negatively affect an opportunity or a chance of success: *He cruelled his interview by arriving late and being completely unprepared.*

**cruelty** /ˈkruːəlti/ *noun* (*pl.* **-ies**) **1** [U] ~ **(to sb/sth)** behaviour that causes physical or mental pain to others and makes them suffer, especially deliberately: *cruelty to animals* ◇ *The deliberate cruelty of his words cut her like a knife.* OPP **kindness 2** [C, usually pl.] a cruel action **3** [C, U] something that happens that seems unfair: *the cruelties of life*

**cruise** /kruːz/ *noun, verb*
- *noun* a journey by sea, visiting different places, especially as a holiday: *I'd love to go on a round-the-world cruise.* ◇ *a luxury cruise ship* ⇒ WORDFINDER NOTE at HOLIDAY
- *verb* **1** [I, T] to travel in a ship or boat visiting different places, especially as a holiday: **(+ *adv./prep.*)** *They cruised down the Nile.* ◇ *~ sth We spent two weeks cruising the Bahamas.* **2** [I] **(+ *adv./prep.*)** (of a car, plane, etc.) to travel at a steady speed: *a light aircraft cruising at 4000 feet* ◇ *a cruising speed of 50 miles an hour* **3** [I, T] (of a car, etc. or its driver) to drive along slowly, especially when you are looking at or for sth: **+ *adv./prep.*** *She cruised around the block looking for a parking space.* ◇ *~ sth Taxis cruised the streets, looking for fares.* **4** [I] **+ *adv./prep.*** to win or achieve sth easily: *The home team cruised to victory.* **5** [I, T] **~(sth)** (*slang*) to go around in public places looking for a sexual partner

▽ **HOMOPHONES**

**crews ♦ cruise** /kruːz/
- **crews** *noun* (*plural* of CREW): *Fire crews were called to the scene.*
- **crews** *verb* (*third person* of CREW): *He crews for a billionaire on his yacht.*
- **cruise** *noun*: *We're taking a cruise around the Mediterranean.*
- **cruise** *verb*: *I'd love to cruise down the Nile.*

**'cruise control** *noun* [U] a device in a vehicle that allows it to stay at the speed that the driver has chosen

**'cruise 'missile** *noun* a large weapon with a WARHEAD that flies close to the ground and is guided by its own computer to an exact place

373

# crunch

**cruiser** /ˈkruːzə(r)/ *noun* **1** a large fast ship used in war **2** (also **'cabin cruiser**) a boat with a motor and room for people to sleep, used for pleasure trips **3** (*NAmE*) a police car

**'cruiserweight** /ˈkruːzəweɪt; *NAmE* -zərw-/ *noun* [U, C] = LIGHT HEAVYWEIGHT

**crumb** /krʌm/ *noun* **1** a very small piece of food, especially of bread or cake, that has fallen off a larger piece: *She stood up and brushed the crumbs from her sweater.* **2** a small piece or amount: *a few crumbs of useful information* ◇ *The government's only crumb of comfort is that their opponents are as confused as they are.*

**crumble** /ˈkrʌmbl/ *verb, noun*
- *verb* **1** [I, T] to break or break sth into very small pieces: *Rice flour makes the cake less likely to crumble.* ◇ *~ sth Crumble the cheese over the salad.* **2** [I] if a building or piece of land **is crumbling**, parts of it are breaking off: *buildings crumbling into dust* ◇ *crumbling stonework* ◇ *The cliff is gradually crumbling away.* **3** [I] to begin to fail or get weaker or to come to an end: *a crumbling business/relationship* ◇ *~ away All his hopes began to crumble away.* ◇ *~ into/to sth The empire finally crumbled into dust.* IDM see WAY *n.*
- *noun* (*BrE*) (*NAmE* **crisp** /krɪsp/) [U, C] a DESSERT (= a sweet dish) made from fruit that is covered with a rough mixture of flour, butter and sugar, cooked in the oven and usually served hot: *apple crumble and custard*

**crumbly** /ˈkrʌmbli/ *adj.* that easily breaks into very small pieces: *crumbly soil/cheese*

**crumbs** /krʌmz/ *exclamation* (*BrE, old-fashioned, informal*) used to show that you are surprised: *Oh crumbs! Is that the time?*

**crummy** /ˈkrʌmi/ *adj.* (*informal*) of very bad quality: *Most of his songs are pretty crummy.*

**crumpet** /ˈkrʌmpɪt/ *noun* (*BrE*) **1** [C] a small flat round cake with small holes in the top, eaten hot with butter **2** [U] (*slang*) an offensive way of referring to people who are sexually attractive, usually women

**crumple** /ˈkrʌmpl/ *verb* **1** [T, I] ~ **(sth) (up) (into sth)** to press or CRUSH sth into folds; to become pressed, etc. into folds: *She crumpled the letter up into a ball and threw it on the fire.* ◇ *This material crumples very easily.* ⇒ picture at SQUEEZE **2** [I] ~ **(up)** if your face **crumples**, you look sad and disappointed, as if you might cry **3** [I] ~ **(up)** to suddenly fall down with no control of your body because you are injured, unconscious, drunk, etc. SYN **collapse**: *He crumpled up in agony.* ▸ **crumpled** /-pld/ *adj.*: *crumpled clothes/papers* ◇ *A crumpled figure lay motionless in the doorway.*

**crunch** /krʌntʃ/ *noun, verb, adj.*
- *noun* **1** [C, usually sing.] a noise like the sound of sth hard being pressed or CRUSHED: *the crunch of feet on snow* ◇ *The car drew up with a crunch of gravel.* **2 the crunch** [sing.] (*informal*) an important and often unpleasant situation or piece of information: *The crunch came when she returned from America.* ◇ *He always says he'll help but when it comes to the crunch* (= when it is time for action) *he does nothing.* ◇ *The crunch is that we can't afford to go abroad this year.* **3** [C, usually sing.] a situation in which there is suddenly not enough of sth, especially money: *the budget/energy/housing crunch* ⇒ see also CREDIT CRUNCH **4** [C] = SIT-UP
- *verb* **1** [T, I] ~ **(on) sth** to bite sth noisily between your teeth when you are eating: *She crunched her apple noisily.* **2** [I, T] ~ **(sth)** to make a noise like sth hard being pressed or CRUSHED; to cause sth to make a noise like this SYN **scrunch**: *The snow crunched under our feet.* **3** [I] **+ *adv./prep.*** to move over a surface, making a noise like the sound of sth hard being pressed or CRUSHED: *I crunched across the gravel to the front door.* **4** [T] ~ **sth** (*computing*) to deal with large amounts of data very quickly ⇒ see also NUMBER CRUNCHING

PHRV **crunch sth↔up** to press or CRUSH sth completely: *He crunched up the empty pack and threw it out of the window.*

# crunch time

- **adj.** [only before noun] (*informal*) a **crunch** meeting, sports game, etc. is very important and may be the last chance to succeed: *Sunday's crunch game with Leeds*

**ˈcrunch time** *noun* [U] (*informal*) an important moment or busy time when you must make a decision or take action: **it is ~ (for sb/sth)** *It's crunch time for students who want to graduate early.*

**crunchy** /ˈkrʌntʃi/ *adj.* (**crunch·ier**, **crunchi·est**) (*approving*) (especially of food) hard and making a sharp sound when you bite it: *a crunchy salad* ⇨ WORDFINDER NOTE at CRISP

**crunk** /krʌŋk/ *noun* [U] a type of music, similar to RAP or HIP-HOP, that contains phrases that are repeated many times and has a strong BASS beat

**cru·sade** /kruːˈseɪd/ *noun*, *verb*
- *noun* **1** ~ (for/against sth) | ~ (to do sth) a long and determined effort to achieve sth that you believe to be right or to stop sth that you believe to be wrong SYN **campaign**: *to lead a crusade against crime* ◊ *a moral crusade* **2** (*sometimes* **Crusade**) any of the wars fought in Palestine by European Christian countries against the Muslims in the Middle Ages
- *verb* [I] to make a long and determined effort to achieve sth that you believe to be right or to stop sth you believe to be wrong SYN **campaign**: *a crusading environmentalist*

**cru·sader** /kruːˈseɪdə(r)/ *noun* **1** a person who makes a long and determined effort to achieve sth that they believe to be right or to stop sth they believe to be wrong SYN **campaigner**: *moral crusaders* **2** *often* **Crusader** a fighter in the Crusades in the Middle Ages

**crush** 🔑+ C1 /krʌʃ/ *verb*, *noun*
- *verb* **1** 🔑+ C1 [T] ~ sb/sth to press sth so hard that it is damaged or injured, or loses its shape: *The car was completely crushed under the truck.* ◊ *Several people were crushed to death in the accident.* **2** 🔑+ C1 ~ sth to break sth into small pieces or into a powder by pressing hard: *Add two cloves of crushed garlic.* ◊ *They crush the olives with a heavy wooden press.* ⇨ picture at SQUEEZE **3** 🔑+ C1 [T] ~ sb/sth + adv./prep. to push or press sb/sth into a small space: *Over twenty prisoners were crushed into a small dark cell.* **4** [T, I] ~ (sth) to make sth full of folds or lines; to become full of folds or lines: *She crushed the scrap of paper in her hand.* **5** [T] ~ sb to use violent methods to defeat people who are opposing you SYN **put down**, **quash**: *The army was sent in to crush the rebellion.* **6** ~ sb to destroy sb's confidence or happiness: *She felt completely crushed by the teacher's criticism.* IDM **ˈcrush it** (*informal*) to do sth very well or be very successful SYN **smash it**: *She got up on stage and absolutely crushed it—the audience was going wild!*
- *noun* **1** [C, usually sing.] a crowd of people pressed close together in a small space: *a big crush in the theatre bar* ◊ *I couldn't find a way through the crush.* **2** [C] ~ (on sb) a strong feeling of love, that usually does not last very long, that a young person has for sb older: *a schoolgirl crush* ◊ *I had a huge crush on her.* **3** [U, C] a drink made from fruit juice

**crush·er** /ˈkrʌʃə(r)/ *noun* (often in compounds) a machine or tool for crushing sth: *a garlic crusher*

**crush·ing** /ˈkrʌʃɪŋ/ *adj.* [usually before noun] used to emphasize how bad or severe sth is: *a crushing defeat in the election* ◊ *The shipyard has been dealt another crushing blow with the failure to win this contract.* ▶ **crush·ing·ly** *adv.*

**crust** /krʌst/ *noun*
- *noun* [C, U] **1** the hard outer surface of bread: *sandwiches with the crusts cut off* **2** a layer of PASTRY, especially on top of a PIE: *Bake until the crust is golden.* **3** the outer layer of rock that forms the surface of the earth or another planet: *the earth's crust* **4** a hard layer or surface, especially above or around sth soft or liquid: *a thin crust of ice* ⇨ see also UPPER CRUST, UPPER-CRUST IDM see EARN
- *verb* [I, T] to form a hard layer; to cover sth with a hard layer: ~ (over) (with sth) *Water was beginning to crust over with ice as temperatures dropped.* ◊ *warm rolls crusted with poppy seeds* ◊ ~ sth *Dirt crusted her cheek.*

**crust·acean** /krʌˈsteɪʃn/ *noun* (*specialist*) any creature with a soft body that is divided into sections, and a hard outer shell. Most crustaceans live in water. CRABS, LOBSTERS and SHRIMPS are all crustaceans. ⇨ VISUAL VOCAB page V3 ⇨ compare SHELLFISH

**crusty** /ˈkrʌsti/ *adj.*, *noun*
- *adj.* (**crust·ier**, **crusti·est**) **1** (of food) having a hard outer layer: *fresh crusty bread* **2** (*informal*) (especially of older people) easily made angry: *a crusty old man*
- *noun* (*also* **crustie**) (*pl.* **-ies**) (*BrE*, *informal*) a person who usually has no permanent home, has a dirty or untidy appearance, and rejects the way that most people live in Western society

**crutch** /krʌtʃ/ *noun* **1** one of two long sticks that you put under your arms to help you walk after you have injured your leg or foot: *After the accident I spent six months on crutches.* **2** (*usually disapproving*) a person or thing that gives you help or support but often makes you depend on them too much **3** = CROTCH

**crux** /krʌks/ *noun* [sing.] **the ~ (of sth)** the most important or difficult part of a problem or an issue SYN **nub**: *Now we come to the crux of the matter.*

**cry** 🔑 A2 /kraɪ/ *verb*, *noun*
- *verb* (**cries**, **cry·ing**, **cried**, **cried**) **1** 🔑 A2 [I, T] to produce tears from your eyes because you are unhappy or hurt: *It's all right. Don't cry.* ◊ ~ **for sb/sth** *The baby was crying for* (= because it wanted) *its mother.* ◊ ~ **about/over sth** *There's nothing to cry about.* ◊ ~ **with sth** *He felt like crying with rage.* ◊ *She threw her arms around his neck crying tears of joy.* ◊ **+ speech** *'Waaa!' she cried.* ◊ (*informal*) *I found him crying his eyes out* (= crying very much). ◊ *That night she cried herself to sleep.* **2** 🔑 B1 [I, T] to shout loudly: ~ **for sth** *She ran to the window and cried for help.* ◊ **+ speech** *'You're safe!' Tom cried in delight.* ⇨ SYNONYMS at SHOUT **3** [I] (of a bird or an animal) to make a loud noise: *Seagulls followed the boat, crying loudly.* IDM **ˌcry ˈfoul** (*informal*) to complain that sb else has done sth wrong or unfair **ˌcry over spilt ˈmilk** (*BrE*) (*US* **ˌcry over spilled ˈmilk**) to waste time worrying about sth that has happened that you cannot do anything about: *As the saying goes—it's no use crying over spilt milk.* **ˌcry ˈwolf** to call for help when you do not need it, with the result that when you do need it people do not believe you **for ˌcrying out ˈloud** (*informal*) used to show you are angry or surprised: *For crying out loud! Why did you have to do that?* ⇨ more at LAUGH *v.*, SHOULDER *n.* PHRV **ˌcry ˈoff** (*BrE*, *informal*) to say that you cannot do sth that you promised to do: *She said she was coming to the party, but cried off at the last moment.* **ˌcry ˈout** to make a loud sound without words because you are hurt, afraid, surprised, etc: *She tried to stop herself from crying out.* ◊ *to cry out in fear/alarm/pain* **ˌcry ˈout/ˌcry ˈout sth** to shout sth loudly: *She cried out for help.* ◊ *She cried out his name.* ◊ **+ speech** *'Help!' he cried out.* ⇨ SYNONYMS at CALL **ˌcry ˈout for sth** (usually used in the progressive tenses) to

▼ **VOCABULARY BUILDING**

### Cry

To **cry** is the most general word for producing tears when you are unhappy or hurt, or when you are extremely happy.

- To **sob** means to cry noisily, taking sudden, sharp breaths.
- To **wail** means to cry in a loud high voice.
- To **whimper** means to cry making low, weak noises.
- To **weep** (*literary* or *formal*) means to cry quietly for a long time.

All these verbs can be used like 'say': *'I don't want you to go,' she cried/wailed/sobbed.*
- To **be in tears** means to be crying.
- To **burst into tears** means to suddenly begin to cry.
- To **cry your eyes out** means to cry a lot or for a long time, because you are very sad.

need sth very much: *The company is crying out for fresh new talent.*
- **noun** (*pl.* **cries**) **1** [C] ~ **(of sth)** a loud sound without words that expresses a strong feeling: *to give a cry of anguish/despair/pain/joy/alarm, etc.* ◇ *a baby's cries* **2** [C] a loud shout: *With a cry of 'Stop thief!' he ran after the boy.* ◇ *Her answer was greeted with cries of outrage.* **3** [C] the sound made by a bird or an animal: *the cry of gulls circling overhead* **4** [C] ~ **(for sth)** a demand or request for sth that is needed immediately: *Her suicide attempt was really a cry for help.* **5** [sing.] an action or a period of crying: *I felt a lot better after a good long cry.* **6** [C] (especially in compounds) a word or phrase that expresses a group's beliefs and calls people to action: *a battle cry* ⇨ see also WAR CRY
- **IDM** **in full 'cry** talking or shouting loudly and in an enthusiastic way: *The Leeds supporters were in full cry.* ⇨ more at FAR *adj.*, HUE

**cry·ba·by** /ˈkraɪbeɪbi/ *noun* (*pl.* **-ies**) (*informal, disapproving*) a person, especially a child, who cries too often or without good reason: *Don't be such a crybaby.*

**cry·ing** /ˈkraɪɪŋ/ *adj., noun*
- **adj.** [only before noun] (*informal*)
- **IDM** **be a crying 'shame** used to emphasize that you think sth is extremely bad or that it shocks you: *It's a crying shame to waste all that food.* **a crying 'need (for sth)** a great and desperate need for sth
- **noun** [U] the sound or act of crying: *the crying of terrified children*

**cryo·gen·ic** /ˌkraɪəˈdʒenɪk/ *adj.* (*physics*) involving the use of very low temperatures: *a cryogenic storage system*

**cryo·gen·ics** /ˌkraɪəˈdʒenɪks/ *noun* [U] (*physics*) the scientific study of the production and effects of very low temperatures ⇨ compare CRYONICS

**cry·on·ics** /kraɪˈɒnɪks; *NAmE* -ˈɑːn-/ *noun* [U] the process of freezing a body at the moment of its death with the hope that it will be brought back to life at some future time ⇨ compare CRYOGENICS

**crypt** /krɪpt/ *noun* a room under the floor of a church, used especially in the past as a place for burying people

**cryp·tic** /ˈkrɪptɪk/ *adj.* with a meaning that is hidden or not easily understood **SYN** **mysterious**: *a cryptic message/remark/smile* ◇ *a cryptic crossword clue* ▸ **cryp·tic·al·ly** /-kli/ *adv.*: *'Yes and no,' she replied cryptically.*

**crypto-** /ˈkrɪptəʊ, krɪptɒ; *BrE also* krɪptə; *NAmE also* krɪpˈtɑː/ *combining form* (in nouns) secret: *a crypto-communist*

**crypto·cur·rency** /ˈkrɪptəʊkʌrənsi; *NAmE* -kɜːr-/ *noun* [U, C] (*pl.* **-ies**) any system of electronic money, used for buying and selling online and without the need for a central bank

**crypt·og·raphy** /krɪpˈtɒɡrəfi; *NAmE* -ˈtɑːɡ-/ *noun* [U] the art of writing or solving codes

**crypto·spor·id·ium** /ˌkrɪptəʊspəˈrɪdiəm/ *noun* a PARASITE found in water that causes infections inside the body

**crys·tal** [B2] /ˈkrɪstl/ *noun* **1** [C] a small piece of a substance with many even sides, that is formed naturally when the substance becomes solid: *ice/salt crystals* **2** [U, C] a clear mineral, such as QUARTZ, used in making jewellery and attractive objects: *crystal earrings* **3** [U] glass of very high quality: *a crystal chandelier/vase* **4** [C] a small piece of a mineral that some people believe has the power to bring health or happiness **5** [C] a piece of glass or plastic that covers the face of a watch **6** = METH

**crystal 'ball** *noun* a clear glass ball used by people who claim they can predict what will happen in the future by looking into it: *Without a crystal ball, it's impossible to say where we'll be next year.*

**crystal 'clear** *adj.* **1** (of glass, water, etc.) completely clear and bright **2** very easy to understand; completely obvious: *I want to make my meaning crystal clear.*

**crys·tal·line** /ˈkrɪstəlaɪn/ *adj.* **1** (*specialist*) made of or similar to crystals: *crystalline structure/rocks* **2** (*formal*) very clear **SYN** **transparent**: *water of crystalline purity*

**crys·tal·lize** (*BrE also* **-ise**) /ˈkrɪstəlaɪz/ *verb* **1** [I, T] (of thoughts, plans, beliefs, etc.) to become clear and fixed; to make thoughts, beliefs, etc. clear and fixed: *Our ideas began to crystallize into a definite plan.* ◇ ~ **sth** *The final chapter crystallizes all the main issues.* **2** [I, T] ~ **(sth)** (*specialist*) to form or make sth form into CRYSTALS: *The salt crystallizes as the water evaporates.* ▸ **crys·tal·liza·tion, -isa·tion** /ˌkrɪstəlaɪˈzeɪʃn; *NAmE* -ləˈz-/ *noun* [U, sing.]

**crys·tal·lized** (*BrE also* **-ised**) /ˈkrɪstəlaɪzd/ *adj.* (especially of fruit) preserved in and covered with sugar

**crystal·log·raphy** /ˌkrɪstəˈlɒɡrəfi; *NAmE* -ˈlɑːɡ-/ *noun* [U] the branch of science that deals with CRYSTALS ▸ **crystal·log·raph·er** /ˌkrɪstəˈlɒɡrəfə(r); *NAmE* -ˈlɑːɡ-/ *noun*

**crystal 'meth** *noun* = METH

**C-section** *noun* (*especially NAmE*) = CAESAREAN SECTION

**CS gas** /ˌsiː es ˈɡæs/ *noun* [U] a gas that STINGS (= causes sharp pain) in the eyes, producing tears and making it difficult to breathe. CS gas is sometimes used to control crowds. ⇨ see also TEAR GAS

**CST** /ˌsiː es ˈtiː/ *abbr.* CENTRAL STANDARD TIME

**Ct** (*also* **Ct.** *especially in NAmE*) *abbr.* (used in written addresses) COURT: *30 Willow Ct*

**ct** (*also* **ct.** *especially in NAmE*) *abbr.* **1** (in writing) CARAT: *an 18ct gold ring* **2** (in writing) CENT(S): *50 cts*

**CTO** /ˌsiː tiː ˈəʊ/ *noun* (*pl.* **CTOs**) the person in a company who is responsible for managing the company's technology requirements (the abbreviation for 'chief technology officer')

**CT scan** /ˌsiː ˈtiː skæn/ *noun* = CAT SCAN

**cu.** *abbr.* (in writing) CUBIC: *a volume of 2 cu. m* (= 2 cubic metres)

**cub** /kʌb/ *noun* **1** [C] a young bear, lion, FOX, etc.: *a lioness guarding her cubs* **2** the **Cubs** (*US* the **'Cub Scouts**) [pl.] a branch of the SCOUT ASSOCIATION for boys and girls between the ages of 8 and 10 or 11: *to join the Cubs* **3** **Cub** (*also* **'Cub Scout**) [C] a member of the Cubs ⇨ compare BROWNIE

**cub·by·hole** /ˈkʌbihəʊl/ *noun* **1** a small room or a small space: *My office is a cubbyhole in the basement.* **2** (*SAfrE*) a small space or shelf facing the front seats of a car where you can keep papers, maps, etc. ⇨ compare GLOVE COMPARTMENT

**cube** /kjuːb/ *noun, verb*
- **noun 1** a solid or hollow figure with six equal square sides ⇨ see also RUBIK'S CUBE™ ⇨ picture at SOLID **2** a piece of sth, especially food, with six sides: *Cut the meat into cubes.* ⇨ see also ICE CUBE, SUGAR CUBE **3** (*mathematics*) the number that you get when you multiply a number by itself twice: *The cube of 5 (5³) is 125 (5×5×5).*
- **verb 1** [usually passive] (*mathematics*) to multiply a number by itself twice: **(be) cubed** *10 cubed is 1000.* **2** ~ **sth** to cut food into cubes **SYN** **dice**

**cube 'root** *noun* (*mathematics*) a number that, when multiplied by itself twice, produces a particular number: *The cube root of 64 (∛64) is 4.* ⇨ compare SQUARE ROOT

**cubic** /ˈkjuːbɪk/ *adj.* **1** (*abbr.* **cu.**) [only before noun] used to show that a measurement is the volume of sth, that is the height multiplied by the length and the WIDTH: *cubic centimetres/inches/metres* **2** measured or expressed in cubic units: *the cubic capacity of a car's engine* **3** having the shape of a cube: *a cubic figure*

**cu·bicle** /ˈkjuːbɪkl/ *noun* a small area of a room that is separated off by curtains or by thin or low walls: *a shower cubicle* ◇ (*BrE*) *a changing cubicle* (= for example at a public swimming pool) ◇ (*especially NAmE*) *an office cubicle*

**cu·bism** /ˈkjuːbɪzəm/ (*also* **Cubism**) *noun* [U] a style and movement in early 20th century art in which objects and people are represented as GEOMETRIC shapes, often shown from many different angles at the same time ▸ **cu·bist** (*also* **Cubist**) /-bɪst/ *adj.* [usually before noun]: *cubist paintings*

**cubit** /ˈkjuːbɪt/ noun an ancient measurement of length, about 45cm or the length from the ELBOW to the end of the fingers

**cu·boid** /ˈkjuːbɔɪd/ noun, adj.
- noun (geometry) a solid object that has six RECTANGULAR sides at RIGHT ANGLES to each other
- adj. having a shape that is approximately like a CUBE

**ˌcub reˈporter** noun a young newspaper reporter without much experience

**cuck·old** /ˈkʌkəʊld/ noun, verb
- noun (old use, disapproving) a man whose wife has sex with another man
- verb (old use) **1** ~ sb (of a man) to make another man a cuckold by having sex with his wife **2** ~ sb (of a woman) to make her husband a cuckold by having sex with another man

**cuckoo** /ˈkʊkuː/ noun (pl. -oos) a bird with a call that sounds like its name. Cuckoos leave their eggs in the NESTS of other birds. ⇒ see also CLOUD CUCKOO LAND

**ˈcuckoo clock** noun a clock that has a small toy bird inside that comes out every hour and marks the hours with a sound like that of a cuckoo

**cu·cum·ber** /ˈkjuːkʌmbə(r)/ noun [C, U] a long vegetable with dark green skin that is light green inside, usually eaten raw ⇒ VISUAL VOCAB page V5 ⇒ see also SEA CUCUMBER IDM see COOL adj.

**cud** /kʌd/ noun [U] the food that cows and similar animals bring back from the stomach into the mouth to chew again: *cows chewing the cud*

**cud·dle** /ˈkʌdl/ verb, noun
- verb [I, T] to hold sb/sth close in your arms to show love SYN hug: *A couple of teenagers were kissing and cuddling on the doorstep.* ◊ ~ sth (+ adj.) *The little boy cuddled the teddy bear close.*
- PHRV **cuddle ˈup (to/against sb/sth) | ˌcuddle ˈup (together)** to sit or lie very close to sb/sth: *She cuddled up against him.* ◊ *We cuddled up together under the blanket.*
- noun [usually sing.] the action of holding sb close in your arms to show love SYN hug: *to give sb a cuddle*

**cud·dly** /ˈkʌdli/ adj. (informal) (**cud·dli·er**, **cud·dli·est**) **1** (approving) if a person or an animal is **cuddly**, they make you want to cuddle them **2** [only before noun] (of a child's toy) soft and designed to be cuddled: *a cuddly rabbit*

**cud·gel** /ˈkʌdʒl/ noun, verb
- noun a short thick stick that is used as a weapon
- verb (BrE) (-ll-, US -l-) ~ sb to hit sb with a cudgel

**cue** /kjuː/ noun, verb
- noun **1** an action or event that is a signal for sb to do sth: ~ **(for sth)** *Jon's arrival was a cue for more champagne.* ◊ ~ **to do sth** *I think that's my cue to explain why I'm here.* **2** ~ **(to do sth)** a few words or an action in a play that is a signal for another actor to do sth: *She stood in the wings and waited for her cue to go on.* ⇒ WORDFINDER NOTE at PERFORMANCE **3** a long wooden stick with a leather tip, used for hitting the ball in the games of BILLIARDS, POOL and SNOOKER
- IDM **(right) on ˈcue** at exactly the moment you expect or that is appropriate: *'Where is that boy?' As if on cue, Simon appeared in the doorway.* **take your ˈcue from sb/sth** to copy what sb else does as an example of how to behave or what to do: *Investors are taking their cue from the big banks and selling dollars.*
- verb (**cue·ing**, **cued**, **cued**) ~ sb to give sb a signal so they know when to start doing sth: *Can you cue me when you want me to begin speaking?*

▼ HOMOPHONES
**cue ♦ queue** /kjuː/
- **cue** noun: *I took this as my cue to leave.*
- **queue** noun: *There was a long queue at the ticket office.*
- **queue** verb: *I had to queue for ages before it was my turn.*

**ˈcue ball** noun the ball that is hit with the cue in games such as BILLIARDS and SNOOKER

**ˈcue card** noun a large card held up behind a television camera so that it can be read by actors or television PRESENTERS but cannot be seen on television ⇒ compare AUTOCUE™

**cuff** /kʌf/ noun, verb
- noun **1** [C] the lower end of a coat or shirt SLEEVE at the WRIST: *a collar and cuffs of white lace* **2 cuffs** [pl.] (informal) = HANDCUFFS **3** (NAmE) (BrE **ˈturn-up**) [C] the bottom of the leg of a pair of trousers that has been folded over on the outside **4** [C] a light hit with an open hand: *to give sb a friendly cuff*
- IDM **off the ˈcuff** (of speaking, remarks, etc.) without previous thought or preparation: *I'm just speaking off the cuff here—I haven't seen the results yet.* ◊ *an off-the-cuff remark*
- verb **1** ~ sb to hit sb quickly and lightly with your hand, especially in a way that is not serious: *She cuffed him lightly around his head.* **2** ~ sb (informal) to put HANDCUFFS on sb

**ˈcuff link** /ˈkʌflɪŋk/ noun [usually pl.] one of a pair of small objects used for fastening shirt cuffs together: *a pair of gold cufflinks*

**cuis·ine** /kwɪˈziːn/ noun [U, C] (from French) **1** a style of cooking: *Italian cuisine* **2** the food served in a restaurant (usually an expensive one): *The hotel restaurant is noted for its excellent cuisine.* ⇒ see also HAUTE CUISINE, NOUVELLE CUISINE ⇒ WORDFINDER NOTE at RESTAURANT

**cul-de-sac** /ˈkʌl də sæk/ noun (pl. **culs-de-sac** /ˈkʌl də sæks/ or **culs-de-sac** /ˈkʌl də sæk/) (from French) a street that is closed at one end

**cu·lin·ary** /ˈkʌlɪnəri; NAmE -neri/ adj. [only before noun] (formal) connected with cooking or food: *culinary skills* ◊ *Savour the culinary delights of Mexico.*

**cull** /kʌl/ verb, noun
- verb ~ sth to kill a number of wild animals from a group, especially in order to stop the group from becoming too large
- PHRV **ˈcull sth from sth** to choose or collect sth from a source or several different sources: *an exhibition of paintings culled from regional art galleries*
- noun the act of killing some wild animals from a group, especially in order to prevent the group from getting too large: *the annual seal cull*

**cul·min·ate** /ˈkʌlmɪneɪt/ verb [I] ~ **(in/with sth)** (formal) to end with a particular result, or at a particular point: *a gun battle which culminated in the death of two police officers* ◊ *Months of hard work culminated in success.* ◊ *Their summer tour will culminate at a spectacular concert in London.*

**cul·min·ation** /ˌkʌlmɪˈneɪʃn/ noun [sing.] (formal) the highest point or end of sth, usually happening after a long time: *The reforms marked the successful culmination of a long campaign.*

**cu·lottes** /kjuːˈlɒts; NAmE kuːˈlɑːts/ noun [pl.] women's wide short trousers that are made to look like a skirt: *a pair of culottes*

**culp·able** /ˈkʌlpəbl/ adj. (formal) responsible and deserving blame for having done sth wrong ▶ **culp·abil·ity** /ˌkʌlpəˈbɪləti/ noun [U] **culp·ably** /ˈkʌlpəbli/ adv.

**ˌculpable ˈhomicide** noun [U] (law) in some countries, the crime of killing sb illegally but not deliberately ⇒ compare JUSTIFIABLE HOMICIDE

**cul·prit** /ˈkʌlprɪt/ noun **1** a person who has done sth wrong or against the law: *The police quickly identified the real culprits.* **2** a person or thing responsible for causing a problem: *The main culprit in the current crisis seems to be modern farming techniques.*

**cult** /kʌlt/ noun, adj.
- noun **1** [usually sing.] ~ **(of sth)** a way of life, an attitude, an idea, etc. that has become very popular: *the cult of physical fitness* ⇒ see also PERSONALITY CULT **2** a small group of people who have extreme religious beliefs and who are not part of any established religion: *Their son ran away from home and joined a cult.* **3** (formal) a system of religious beliefs and practices: *the Chinese cult of ancestor worship*

■ *adj.* [only before noun] very popular with a particular group of people: *a cult movie/book* ◊ *The singer has become a cult figure in America.* ◊ *The cartoon has achieved cult status.* ◊ *The TV series has a cult following among young people.*

**cul·tiv·able** /ˈkʌltɪvəbl/ *adj.* (of land) that can be used to grow crops

**cul·ti·var** /ˈkʌltɪvɑː(r)/ *noun* (*specialist*) a type of plant that has been deliberately developed to have particular features

**cul·ti·vate** /ˈkʌltɪveɪt/ *verb* 1 ~ sth to prepare and use land for growing plants or crops: *The land around here has never been cultivated.* ⇒ WORDFINDER NOTE at FARM 2 ~ sth to grow plants or crops SYN grow: *The people cultivate mainly rice and beans.* 3 ~ sb/sth (*sometimes disapproving*) to try to get sb's friendship or support: *He purposely tried to cultivate good relations with the press.* ◊ *It helps if you go out of your way to cultivate the local people.* 4 ~ sth to develop an attitude, a way of talking or behaving, etc: *She cultivated an air of sophistication.*

**cul·ti·vated** /ˈkʌltɪveɪtɪd/ *adj.* 1 (of people) having a high level of education and showing good manners SYN **cultured** 2 (of land) used to grow crops: *cultivated fields* 3 (of plants that are also wild) grown on a farm, etc. in order to be sold: *cultivated mushrooms* OPP **wild**

**cul·ti·va·tion** /ˌkʌltɪˈveɪʃn/ *noun* [U] 1 the preparation and use of land for growing plants or crops: *under ~ fertile land that is under cultivation* (= being CULTIVATED) ◊ *rice/wheat cultivation* 2 the deliberate development of a particular relationship, quality or skill: *the cultivation of a good relationship with local firms*

**cul·ti·va·tor** /ˈkʌltɪveɪtə(r)/ *noun* 1 a person who cultivates (= grows crops on) the land 2 a machine for breaking up soil and destroying WEEDS (= plants growing where they are not wanted)

**cult of perˈsonality** *noun* (*disapproving*) = PERSONALITY CULT

**cul·tural** /ˈkʌltʃərəl/ *adj.* [usually before noun] 1 connected with the culture of a particular society or group, its customs, beliefs, etc: *Teachers need to be aware of cultural differences.* ◊ *a cultural institution/centre* ⇒ see also CROSS-CULTURAL 2 connected with art, literature, music, etc: *a cultural event* ◊ *Europe's cultural heritage* ◊ *The orchestra is very important for the cultural life of the city.* ▶ **cul·tur·al·ly** /-rəli/ *adv.*

**culˌtural appropriˈation** *noun* [U] (*disapproving*) the act of copying or using the customs and traditions of a particular group or culture, by sb from a more DOMINANT (= powerful) group in society: *The novelist has been accused of cultural appropriation for basing the story on a Navajo legend.*

**cul·ture** /ˈkʌltʃə(r)/ *noun, verb*
■ *noun*
• WAY OF LIFE 1 [U] the customs and beliefs, art, way of life and social organization of a particular country or group: *African/American/European/Islamic culture* ◊ *working-class culture* 2 [C] a country, group, etc. with its own beliefs, etc: *The children are taught to respect different cultures.* ◊ *the effect of technology on traditional cultures* ⇒ WORDFINDER NOTE at SOCIETY
• ART/MUSIC/LITERATURE 3 [U] art, music, literature, etc., thought of as a group: *Venice is a beautiful city, full of culture and history.* ◊ *the Minister for Culture* ⇒ see also POP CULTURE
• BELIEFS/ATTITUDES 4 [C, U] the beliefs and attitudes about sth that people in a particular group or organization share: *We are living in a consumer culture.* ◊ *Corporate culture has become the dominant culture.* ◊ *You can't change the culture of an organization overnight.* ◊ ~ **of sth** *She believes the media have created a culture of fear.*
• GROWING/BREEDING 5 [U] (*specialist*) the growing of plants or producing of particular animals in order to get a particular substance or crop from them: *the culture of silkworms* (= for silk)
• CELLS/BACTERIA 6 [C] (*biology, medical*) a group of cells or bacteria, especially one taken from a person or an animal

# cunning

and grown for medical or scientific study, or to produce food; the process of obtaining and growing these cells: *a culture of cells from the tumour* ◊ *Yogurt is made from active cultures.* ◊ *to do/take a throat culture*
■ *verb* ~ sth (*biology, medical*) to grow a group of cells or bacteria for medical or scientific study

**cul·tured** /ˈkʌltʃəd; *NAmE* -tʃərd/ *adj.* 1 (of people) well educated and able to understand and enjoy art, literature, etc. SYN **cultivated** OPP **uncultured** 2 (of cells or bacteria) grown for medical or scientific study 3 (of PEARLS) grown artificially

**ˈculture shock** *noun* [C, U] a feeling of being confused and worried that sb may get when they visit another country or experience a different way of life or set of attitudes, because the experience is so different from what they are used to

**ˈculture vulture** *noun* (*humorous*) a person who is very interested in serious art, music, literature, etc.

**cul·vert** /ˈkʌlvət; *NAmE* -vərt/ *noun* a tunnel that carries a river or a pipe for water under a road

**cum** /kʌm/ *prep.* (used for linking two nouns) and; as well as: *a bedroom-cum-study*

**cum·ber·some** /ˈkʌmbəsəm; *NAmE* -bərs-/ *adj.* 1 large and heavy; difficult to carry SYN **bulky**: *cumbersome machinery* 2 slow and complicated: *cumbersome legal procedures* 3 (of words or phrases) long or complicated: *The organization changed its cumbersome title to something easier to remember.*

**cumin** /ˈkjuːmɪn; ˈkʌm-/ *noun* [U] the dried seeds of the cumin plant, used in cooking as a SPICE (= to give a strong taste and smell to the dish): *cumin seeds* ⇒ VISUAL VOCAB page V8

**cum laude** /ˌkʊm ˈlɔːdi, ˈlaʊdeɪ/ *adv., adj.* (from Latin) (in the US) at the third of the three highest levels of achievement that students can reach when they finish their studies at college: *He graduated cum laude.* ⇒ compare MAGNA CUM LAUDE, SUMMA CUM LAUDE

**cum·mer·bund** /ˈkʌməbʌnd; *NAmE* -mərb-/ *noun* a wide band of silk, etc. worn around the middle part of the body, especially under a DINNER JACKET

**cu·mu·la·tive** /ˈkjuːmjələtɪv; *NAmE* -leɪt-/ *adj.* 1 having a result that increases in strength or importance each time more of sth is added: *the cumulative effect of human activity on the world environment* 2 including all the amounts that have been added previously: *the monthly sales figures and the cumulative total for the past six months* ▶ **cu·mu·la·tive·ly** *adv.*

**cu·mu·lo·nim·bus** /ˌkjuːmjələʊˈnɪmbəs/ *noun* [U] (*specialist*) a high mass of thick cloud with a flat base, often seen during THUNDERSTORMS

**cu·mu·lus** /ˈkjuːmjələs/ *noun* [U] (*specialist*) a type of thick white cloud

**cu·nei·form** /ˈkjuːnɪfɔːm; *NAmE* -fɔːrm/ *noun* [U] an ancient system of writing used in Persia and Assyria

**cun·ni·lin·gus** /ˌkʌnɪˈlɪŋɡəs/ *noun* [U] the act of touching a woman's sex organs with the mouth and tongue in order to give sexual pleasure

**cun·ning** /ˈkʌnɪŋ/ *adj., noun*
■ *adj.* 1 (*disapproving*) able to get what you want in a clever way, especially by tricking or cheating sb SYN **crafty, wily**: *a cunning liar* ◊ *He was as cunning as a fox.* 2 clever and showing skill SYN **ingenious**: *It was a cunning piece of detective work.* ▶ **cun·ning·ly** *adv.*: *The microphone was cunningly concealed in the bookcase.*
■ *noun* [U] the ability to achieve sth by tricking or cheating other people in a clever way SYN **craftiness**: *It took energy and cunning just to survive.* ◊ *She used low cunning* (= dishonest behaviour) *to get what she wanted.*

**cunt** /kʌnt/ *noun* (*taboo, slang*) 1 a woman's VAGINA and outer sexual organs 2 a very offensive word used to show great anger or dislike: *You stupid cunt!*

Oxford Phrasal Academic Lexicon (OPAL) written and spoken word lists | OPAL written word list | OPAL spoken word list

# cup

**cup** 🔊 A1 /kʌp/ *noun, verb*

■ *noun* **1** 🔊 A1 [C] a small container that is like a bowl in shape, usually with a handle, used for drinking tea, coffee, etc: *He filled the cup with water.* ◊ *a coffee cup* ◊ *a cup and saucer* ◊ *a plastic/paper cup* ⊃ see also SIPPY CUP **2** 🔊 A1 [C] the contents of a cup: *She drank the whole cup.* ◊ **~of sth** *Would you like a cup of tea?* **3** 🔊 A2 [C] a gold or silver cup on a STEM, often with two handles, that is given as a prize in a competition: *She's won several cups for skating.* ◊ *He lifted the cup* (= won) *for the fifth time this year.* ⊃ picture at MEDAL **4** 🔊 [sing.] (*usually* **Cup**) a sports competition in which a cup is given as a prize: *the World Cup* **5** [C] a unit for measuring quantity used in cooking mainly in the US; a metal or plastic container used to measure this quantity: *two cups of flour and half a cup of butter* ⊃ see also MEASURING CUP **6** [C] a thing that has the shape of a cup: *an egg cup* **7** [C] one of the two parts of a BRA that cover the breasts: *a C cup* **8** [C, U] a drink made from wine mixed with, for example, fruit juice ⊃ see also FRUIT CUP **9** [C] (in *golf*) the hole on the green, or the metal container inside it, that you must get the ball into **10** [C] (*NAmE*) a piece of plastic that a man wears over his sex organs to protect them while he is playing a sport ⊃ compare BOX (10)
 ▫ **in your ˈcups** (*old-fashioned*) having drunk too much alcohol: *He gets very maudlin when he's in his cups.* **ˌnot sb's ˌcup of ˈtea** (*informal*) not what sb likes or is interested in: *An evening at the opera isn't everyone's cup of tea.* ◊ *He's nice enough but not really my cup of tea.* ⊃ more at SLIP *n.*

■ *verb* (-pp-) **1 ~ your hand(s) (around / over sth)** to make your hands into the shape of a bowl: *He held the bird gently in cupped hands.* **2 ~ sth (in your hands)** to hold sth, making your hands into a round shape: *He cupped her face in his hands and kissed her.*

**cup·board** 🔊 A2 /ˈkʌbəd; NAmE -bərd/ *noun* **1** 🔊 A2 a piece of furniture with doors and shelves used for storing dishes, food, clothes, etc: *kitchen cupboards* **2** 🔊 A2 (*BrE*) (*NAmE* **closet**) a space in a wall with a door that reaches the ground, used for storing things: *built-in cupboards* ⊃ see also AIRING CUPBOARD, BROOM CUPBOARD
 ▫ **the ˌcupboard is ˈbare** (*BrE*) used to say that there is no money for sth: *They are seeking more funds but the cupboard is bare.* ORIGIN This expression refers to a children's nursery rhyme about Old Mother Hubbard, who had nothing in her cupboard to feed her dog. **a ˌskeleton in the ˈcupboard** (*BrE*) (*also* **a ˌskeleton in the ˈcloset** *NAmE, BrE*) (*informal*) something SHOCKING, embarrassing, etc. that has happened to you or your family in the past that you want to keep secret ⊃ more at SKELETON

**cup·cake** *noun* /ˈkʌpkeɪk/ (*especially NAmE*) (*BrE also* **ˈfairy cake**) *noun* a small cake, baked in a paper container that is like a cup in shape and often with ICING on top

**ˈcup final** (*also* **Cup Final**) *noun* (*BrE*) (*especially in football (soccer)*) the last match in a series of matches in a competition that gives a cup as a prize to the winners: *cup final tickets* ◊ *the FA Cup Final*

**cup·ful** /ˈkʌpfʊl/ *noun* the amount that a cup will hold: *3 cupfuls of water* ⊃ see also CUP *noun*

**Cupid** /ˈkjuːpɪd/ *noun* **1** the Roman god of love who is shown as a beautiful baby boy with wings, carrying a BOW and ARROW **2 cupid** [C] a picture or statue of a baby boy who looks like Cupid
 ▫ **play ˈCupid** to try to start a romantic relationship between two people: *She played Cupid to her two best friends when she set them up on a date together.*

**cu·pola** /ˈkjuːpələ/ *noun* a round part on top of a building (like a small DOME)

**cuppa** /ˈkʌpə/ *noun* (*BrE, informal*) a cup of tea: *Do you fancy a cuppa?*

**cup·ping** /ˈkʌpɪŋ/ *noun* [U] a way of treating pain by putting special cups on the skin and heating them so that the flow of blood to the skin increases

**ˈcup tie** *noun* (*BrE*) (*especially in football (soccer)*) a match between two teams in a competition that gives a cup as a prize to the winner

**cur** /kɜː(r)/ *noun* (*old-fashioned, disapproving*) an aggressive dog, especially a MONGREL

**cur·able** /ˈkjʊərəbl; NAmE ˈkjʊr-/ *adj.* (of an illness) that can be cured: *Most skin cancers are curable if treated early.* OPP INCURABLE

**cur·acy** /ˈkjʊərəsi; NAmE ˈkjʊr-/ *noun* (*pl.* **-ies**) the position of a curate; the time that sb is a curate

**cur·ate**[1] /ˈkjʊərət; NAmE ˈkjʊr-/ *noun* (in the Anglican Church) an assistant to a priest, who is in charge of the church or churches in a particular area)
 ▫ **the/a ˌcurate's ˈegg** (*BrE*) something that has some good parts and some bad ones

**cur·ate**[2] /kjʊəˈreɪt; NAmE kjʊˈr-/ *verb* **1 ~ sth** to select, organize and look after the objects or works of art in a museum or an ART GALLERY, etc. **2 ~ sth** to collect, select and present information or items such as pictures, video, music, etc. for people to use or enjoy, using your professional or expert knowledge: *A UK rock band are curating the BBC's digital music station for a week.*

**cura·tive** /ˈkjʊərətɪv; NAmE ˈkjʊr-/ *adj.* (*formal*) able to cure illness SYN **healing**: *the curative properties of herbs* ⊃ compare PREVENTIVE

**cur·ator** /kjʊəˈreɪtə(r); NAmE ˈkjʊreɪtər/ *noun* **1** a person whose job is to be in charge of the objects or works of art in a museum or an ART GALLERY, etc. **2** a person who uses their knowledge to select and present information or items such as pictures, video, music, etc. for people to use and enjoy, especially on the internet

**curb** /kɜːb; NAmE kɜːrb/ *verb, noun*

■ *verb* **~ sth** to control or limit sth, especially sth bad SYN **check**: *He needs to learn to curb his temper.* ◊ *a new law designed to curb harmful emissions from factories*

■ *noun* **1 ~ (on sth)** something that controls and puts limits on sth: *curbs on government spending* **2** (*NAmE*) (*BrE* **kerb**) the edge of the raised path at the side of a road, usually made of long pieces of stone: *The bus mounted the curb* (= went onto the SIDEWALK) *and hit a tree.*

**curb·side** (*NAmE*) (*also* **kerb·side** *BrE*) /ˈkɜːbsaɪd; NAmE ˈkɜːrb-/ *noun* [U] the side of the street or path near the CURB

**curb·stone** (*NAmE*) (*also* **kerb·stone** *BrE*) /ˈkɜːbstəʊn; NAmE ˈkɜːrb-/ *noun* a block of stone or CONCRETE in a CURB

**curd** /kɜːd; NAmE kɜːrd/ *noun* [U] (*also* **curds** [pl.]) a thick soft substance that is formed when milk turns SOUR (= not fresh) ⊃ see also BEAN CURD, LEMON CURD

**cur·dle** /ˈkɜːdl; NAmE ˈkɜːrdl/ *verb* **1** [I, T] **~ (sth)** when a liquid, especially milk, **curdles** or sth **curdles** it, it separates into solid and liquid parts **2** [I, T] **~ (sth)** if sth **curdles** your blood or makes your blood **curdle**, it makes you extremely frightened or shocked ⊃ see also BLOOD-CURDLING

**cure** 🔊 B2 /kjʊə(r); NAmE kjʊr/ *verb, noun*

■ *verb* **1** 🔊 B2 to make a person or an animal healthy again after an illness: **~ sb** *Will you be able to cure him, Doctor?* ◊ **~ sb of sth** *The doctor managed to cure her of her illness.* ⊃ WORDFINDER NOTE at DOCTOR

> WORDFINDER chemotherapy, disease, drug, injection, medication, osteopathy, palliative, physiotherapy, radiotherapy

**2** 🔊 B2 **~ sth (with sth)** to make an illness go away: *It is better to prevent rather than cure diseases.* **3 ~ sth (with sth)** to deal with a problem successfully: *I finally managed to cure the rattling noise in my car.* **4 ~ sb of sth** to stop sb from behaving in a particular way, especially a way that is bad or annoying: *I thought I had finally cured him of this annoying habit.* **5 ~ sth** to treat food or TOBACCO with smoke, salt or heat, etc. in order to preserve it: *cured ham/bacon* ▫ see KILL *v.*

■ *noun* **1** 🔊 B2 **~ (for sth)** a medicine or medical treatment that cures an illness: *the search for a cure for cancer* ◊

Researchers are working to **find a cure** for the disease. ◊ There is no **miracle cure** for this condition. **2** the act of curing sb of an illness or the process of being cured: *Doctors cannot effect a cure if the disease has spread too far.* ◊ *The cure took six weeks.* **3** ~ **(for sth)** something that will solve a problem, improve a bad situation, etc: *a cure for poverty* **IDM** see PREVENTION

**ˈcure-all** *noun* something that people believe can cure any problem or any disease **SYN** panacea

**curˈfew** /ˈkɜːfjuː; *NAmE* ˈkɜːrfjuː/ *noun* [C, U] **1** a law that says that people must not go outside after a particular time at night until the morning; the time after which nobody must go outside: *The army imposed a dusk-to-dawn curfew.* ◊ *You must get home before curfew.* **2** *(especially NAmE)* a time when children must be home in the evening: *I have a 10 o'clock curfew.*

**curio** /ˈkjʊəriəʊ; *NAmE* ˈkjʊr-/ *noun* (*pl.* **-os**) a small object that is rare or unusual, often sth that people collect

**curiˈosity** 🔑+ **C1** /ˌkjʊəriˈɒsəti; *NAmE* ˌkjʊriˈɑːs-/ *noun* (*pl.* **-ies**) **1** 🔑+ **C1** [U, sing.] ~ **(about sth)** | ~ **(to do sth)** a strong desire to know about sth: *Children show curiosity about everything.* ◊ *a certain curiosity to see what would happen next* ◊ *The letter wasn't addressed to me but I opened it out of curiosity.* ◊ *His answer did not satisfy my curiosity at all.* ◊ *Sophie's curiosity was aroused by the mysterious phone call.* ◊ *intellectual curiosity* ◊ *'Why do you ask?' 'Oh, just idle curiosity'* (= no particular reason). **2** [C] an unusual and interesting thing: *The museum is full of historical curiosities.* **IDM** **curiosity killed the ˈcat** *(saying)* used to tell sb not to ask questions or try to find out about things that do not involve them

**curiˈous** 🔑+ **B2** /ˈkjʊəriəs; *NAmE* ˈkjʊr-/ *adj.* **1** 🔑+ **B2** having a strong desire to know about sth **SYN** inquisitive: *He is such a curious boy, always asking questions.* ◊ ~ **about sth** *They were very curious about the people who lived upstairs.* ◊ ~ **as to sth** *Everyone was curious as to why Mark was leaving.* ◊ ~ **to do sth** *I was curious to find out what she had said.* **2** 🔑+ **B2** strange and unusual: *There was a curious mixture of people in the audience.* ◊ *It was a curious feeling, as though we were floating on air.* ◊ **it is ~ that …** *It was curious that she didn't tell anyone.* ▶ **curiˈously** *adv.*: *'Are you really an artist?' Sara asked curiously.* ◊ *His clothes were curiously old-fashioned.* ◊ *Curiously enough, a year later exactly the same thing happened again.*

**curl** /kɜːl; *NAmE* kɜːrl/ *verb, noun*
- *verb* **1** [I, T] ~ **(sth)** to form or make sth form into a curl or curls: *His hair curls naturally.* **2** [I, T] to form or make sth form into a curved shape: (+ *adv./prep.*) *The cat curled into a ball and went to sleep.* ◊ ~ **sth** (+ *adv./prep.*) *She curled her legs up under her.* **3** [I, T] to move while forming into a TWISTED or curved shape; to make sth do this: (+ *adv./prep.*) *The smoke curled steadily upwards.* ◊ ~ **sth** (+ *adv./prep.*) *He turned and curled the ball around the goalkeeper.* **4** [T, I] ~ **(sth)** if you **curl** your lip or your lip **curls**, you move your lip upwards and to the side to show that you think sb/sth is stupid or that you are better than they are **IDM** see TOE *n.*
**PHRV** **curl ˈup** | **be ˌcurled ˈup** to lie or sit with your back curved and your arms and legs bent close to your body: *She curled up and closed her eyes.* | **curl ˈup** | **curl sb ˈup** (*BrE, informal*) to become or make sb become very embarrassed | **ˌcurl ˈup** | **curl sth↔ˈup** to form or make sth form into a curly shape: *The paper started to shrivel and curl up in the heat.*
- *noun* **1** [C] a small bunch of hair that forms a curved or round shape: *Her hair was a mass of curls.* ◊ *The baby had dark eyes and dark curls.* **2** [C, U] the way that sb's hair tends to form curved or round shapes: *His hair had a natural curl.* **3** [C] a thing that forms a curved or round shape: *a curl of smoke* ◊ *Decorate the cake with curls of chocolate.* ◊ *a contemptuous curl of the lip* (= an expression showing disapproval)

**ˈcurler** /ˈkɜːlə(r); *NAmE* ˈkɜːrl-/ *noun* [usually pl.] a small plastic or metal tube that you can wrap wet hair around in order to make it curly **SYN** roller

---

379

## curriculum vitae

**ˈcurlew** /ˈkɜːljuː; *NAmE* ˈkɜːrluː/ *noun* (*pl.* **ˈcurlew** or **ˈcurlews**) a bird with a long thin BEAK that curves downwards, that lives near water

**ˈcurliˌcue** /ˈkɜːlɪkjuː; *NAmE* ˈkɜːrl-/ *noun* (*specialist*) an attractive curve or TWIST in writing or in a design

**ˈcurling** /ˈkɜːlɪŋ; *NAmE* ˈkɜːrl-/ *noun* [U] a game played on ice, in which players slide heavy flat stones towards a mark

**ˈcurling tongs** *noun* (*also* **tongs**) [pl.] (*both BrE*) (*NAmE* **ˈcurling iron** [C]) a tool that is heated and used to curl hair

**curly** 🔑 **A2** /ˈkɜːli; *NAmE* ˈkɜːrli/ *adj.* (**curlier, curliest**) having a lot of curls or a curved shape: *long curly hair* ◊ *a curly-haired girl* ◊ *a dog with a curly tail* **OPP** straight

**curly ˈendive** *noun* [C, U] = CHICORY (2)

**ˈcurmudgeon** /kɜːˈmʌdʒən; *NAmE* kɜːrˈm-/ *noun* (*old-fashioned*) a person who gets annoyed easily, often an old person ▶ **curˈmudgeonly** *adj.*

**ˈcurrant** /ˈkʌrənt; *NAmE* ˈkɜːr-/ *noun* **1** a small dried GRAPE, used in cakes, etc: *a currant bun* **2** (usually in compounds) a small black, red or white BERRY that grows in bunches on bushes: *blackcurrants* ◊ *currant bushes*

**ˈcurrency** 🔑 **B1** /ˈkʌrənsi; *NAmE* ˈkɜːr-/ *noun* (*pl.* **-ies**) **1** 🔑 **B1** [C, U] the system of money that a country uses: *trading in foreign currencies* ◊ *the single European currency* ◊ *You'll need some cash in local currency but you can also use your credit card.* ⊃ see also HARD CURRENCY **2** [U] the fact that sth is used or accepted by a lot of people: *The term 'post-industrial' now has wide currency.* ◊ *The qualification has gained currency all over the world.*

**ˈcurrent** 🔑 **B1** 🅦 /ˈkʌrənt; *NAmE* ˈkɜːr-/ *adj., noun*
- *adj.* **1** 🔑 **B1** [only before noun] happening now; of the present time: *current prices* ◊ *the current situation* ◊ *the current year* ⊃ note at ACTUAL **2** 🔑 being used by or accepted by most people: *words that are no longer current*
- *noun* **1** 🔑 **B2** the movement of water in the sea or a river; the movement of air in a particular direction: **with the ~** *It's easier to go with the current.* ◊ **against the ~** *He swam to the shore against a strong current.* ◊ *ocean/air currents* ⊃ see also CROSS-CURRENT, RIP CURRENT ⊃ WORDFINDER NOTE at RIVER **2** 🔑 **B2** the flow of electricity through a wire, etc: *wires carrying electric currents* ⊃ see also AC, ALTERNATING CURRENT, DC, DIRECT CURRENT **3** the fact of particular ideas, opinions or feelings being present in a group of people: *Ministers are worried by this current of anti-government feeling.*

**ˈcurrent acˈcount** (*BrE*) (*US* **ˈchecking account**, *CanE* **ˈchequing account**) *noun* a type of bank account that you can take money out of at any time, and that provides you with a DEBIT CARD and (sometimes) a CHEQUEBOOK ⊃ compare DEPOSIT ACCOUNT

**ˌcurrent afˈfairs** (*especially BrE*) (*also* **ˌcurrent eˈvents** *especially in NAmE*) *noun* [pl.] events of political or social importance that are happening now

**ˈcurrently** 🔑 **B1** 🅦 /ˈkʌrəntli; *NAmE* ˈkɜːr-/ *adv.* at the present time: *The hourly charge is currently £35.* ◊ *Currently, over 500 students are enrolled on the course.* ◊ *All the options are currently available.* ◊ *She's currently working on a book about painters.*

**curˈricular** /kəˈrɪkjələ(r)/ *adj.* connected with the curriculum of a school, etc. ⊃ see also CROSS-CURRICULAR, EXTRACURRICULAR

**curˈriculum** 🔑+ **B2** /kəˈrɪkjələm/ *noun* (*pl.* **curˈricula** /-lə/ or **curˈriculums**) the subjects that are included in a course of study or taught in a school, college, etc: *the school curriculum* ◊ **on the ~** (*BrE*) *Spanish is on the curriculum.* ◊ **in the ~** (*NAmE*) *Spanish is in the curriculum.* ⊃ compare SYLLABUS

**curˌriculum ˈvitae** /kəˌrɪkjələm ˈviːtaɪ/ (*abbr.* **CV**) *noun* **1** (*BrE*) (*NAmE* **réˈsumé**) a written record of your education and the jobs you have done that you send when you are

**cur·ried** /ˈkʌrid/; NAmE ˈkɜːr-/ adj. [only before noun] cooked in a hot spicy sauce: *curried chicken/beef/eggs, etc.*

**curry** /ˈkʌri/; NAmE ˈkɜːri/ noun, verb
- noun [C, U] a South Asian dish of meat, vegetables, etc. cooked in a hot spicy sauce, often served with rice: *a chicken curry* ◊ *Would you like some more curry?*
- verb (**cur·ries, curry·ing, cur·ried, cur·ried**) ~ **sth** to make curry out of meat or vegetables
- IDM **curry ˈfavour (with sb)** (*disapproving*) to try to get sb to like or support you by praising or helping them a lot

**ˈcurry leaf** noun [C, U] a type of SHRUB (= a large plant) or small tree grown in India and Sri Lanka; the leaf of this tree, widely used as a SPICE in Indian cooking to give a strong taste and smell to the food

**ˈcurry powder** noun [U] a powder made from a mixture of SPICES, used to make food taste hot, especially curry

**curse** /kɜːs; NAmE kɜːrs/ noun, verb
- noun **1** [C] a rude or offensive word or phrase that some people use when they are very angry SYN **oath, swear word**: *He muttered a curse at the other driver.* **2** [C] a word or phrase that has a magic power to make sth bad happen: *The family thought that they were under a curse.* ⇒ compare HEX **3** [C] something that causes harm or evil: *the curse of drug addiction* ◊ *Noise is a curse of modern city life.* **4** **the curse** [sing.] (*old-fashioned, informal*) = MENSTRUATION
- verb **1** [I] to swear: *He hit his head as he stood up and cursed loudly.* **2** [T] to say rude things to sb or think rude things about sb/sth: ~ **sb/sth/yourself (that)** *She cursed her bad luck.* ◊ ~ **sb/sth/yourself for sth** *He cursed himself for his stupidity.* **3** [T] ~ **sb/sth** to use a magic word or phrase against sb in order to harm them: *Legend has it that the whole village had been cursed by a witch.* ⇒ compare HEX
- PHRV **be ˈcursed with sth** to continuously suffer from or be affected by sth bad: *She seems cursed with bad luck.*

**cursed** adj. **1** /kɜːst; NAmE kɜːrst/ having a curse on it; suffering from a curse: *The necklace was cursed.* ◊ *The whole family seemed cursed.* **2** /ˈkɜːsɪd; NAmE ˈkɜːrs-/ [only before noun] (*old-fashioned*) unpleasant; annoying

**cur·sive** /ˈkɜːsɪv; NAmE ˈkɜːrs-/ adj. (*specialist*) (of HANDWRITING) with the letters joined together

**cur·sor** /ˈkɜːsə(r); NAmE ˈkɜːrs-/ noun a small mark on a computer screen that can be moved and that shows the position on the screen where, for example, text will be added ⇒ WORDFINDER NOTE at KEYBOARD

**curs·ory** /ˈkɜːsəri; NAmE ˈkɜːrs-/ adj. (*often disapproving*) done quickly and without giving enough attention to details SYN **brief, perfunctory**: *a cursory glance/examination/inspection* ▶ **cur·sor·ily** /-rəli/ adv.

**curt** /kɜːt; NAmE kɜːrt/ adj. (of a person's manner or behaviour) appearing rude because very few words are used, or because sth is done in a very quick way SYN **abrupt, brusque**: *a curt reply* ◊ *a curt nod* ◊ *His tone was curt and unfriendly.* ▶ **curt·ly** adv. **curt·ness** noun [U]

**cur·tail** /kɜːˈteɪl; NAmE kɜːrˈt-/ verb (*formal*) to limit sth or make it last for a shorter time: *Spending on books has been severely curtailed.* ◊ *The lecture was curtailed by the fire alarm going off.* ▶ **cur·tail·ment** noun [U]: *the curtailment of civil liberties*

**cur·tain** /ˈkɜːtn; NAmE ˈkɜːrtn/ noun, verb
- noun **1** [C] a piece of cloth that is hung to cover a window: *to draw/pull/close the curtains* (= to pull them across the window so they cover it) ◊ *She opened her curtains and looked out.* ◊ *It was ten in the morning but the curtains were still drawn* (= closed). ◊ *a pair of curtains* ⇒ see also DRAPE noun **2** [C] (NAmE) (BrE **net ˈcurtain**) a very thin piece of cloth that you hang at a window and that allows light to enter but stops people outside from being able to see inside **3** [C] a piece of cloth that is hung up as a screen in a room or around a bed, for example: *a shower curtain* ⇒ see also IRON CURTAIN **4** [sing.] a piece of thick, heavy cloth that hangs in front of the stage in the theatre: *The audience was waiting for the curtain to rise* (= for the play to begin). ◊ *There was tremendous applause when the curtain came down* (= the play ended). ◊ *We left just before the final curtain* (= the end of a play). ◊ (*figurative*) *It's time to face the final curtain* (= the end; death). ◊ (*figurative*) *The curtain has fallen on her long and distinguished career* (= her career has ended). ⇒ WORDFINDER NOTE at STAGE **5** [C, usually sing.] a thing that covers, hides or protects sth: *a curtain of rain/smoke* ◊ *She pushed back the curtain of brown hair from her eyes.*
- IDM **be ˈcurtains (for sb)** (*informal*) to be a situation without hope or that you cannot escape from: *When I saw he had a gun, I thought it was curtains for me.* **bring down the ˈcurtain on sth | bring the ˈcurtain down on sth** to finish or mark the end of sth: *His sudden decision to retire brought down the curtain on a distinguished career.*
- verb ~ **sth** to provide curtains for a window or a room
- PHRV **ˌcurtain sth↔ˈoff** to separate an area of a room with a curtain or curtains

**ˈcurtain call** noun the time in the theatre when the actors come to the front of the stage at the end of a play to receive the APPLAUSE of the audience

**ˈcurtain-raiser** noun **1** ~ **(to sth)** a small event that prepares for a more important one **2** ~ **(to sth)** a short performance before the main performance in a theatre, etc.

**curtsy** (also **curt·sey**) /ˈkɜːtsi; NAmE ˈkɜːrt-/ noun (*pl.* **-ies** or **-eys**) a formal movement made by a woman in a dance or to say hello or goodbye to an important person, by bending her knees with one foot in front of the other ▶ **curtsy** verb (**curt·sies, curt·sy·ing, curt·sied, curt·sied**) (also **curt·sey**) [I]: ~ **(to sb)** *She curtsied to the Queen.*

**curv·aceous** /kɜːˈveɪʃəs; NAmE kɜːrˈv-/ adj. (*informal*) used in newspapers, etc. to describe a woman whose body has attractive curves

**curv·ature** /ˈkɜːvətʃə(r); NAmE ˈkɜːrv-/ noun [U, C] (*specialist*) the state of being curved; the amount by which sth is curved: *the curvature of the earth* ◊ *curvature of the spine*

**curve** /kɜːv; NAmE kɜːrv/ noun, verb
- noun **1** a line or surface that bends gradually; a smooth bend: ~ **of sth** *the delicate curve of her ear* ◊ *a pattern of straight lines and curves* ◊ ~ **in sth** (*especially NAmE*) *a curve in the road* ◊ **on a ~** (*especially NAmE*) *The driver lost control on a curve and the vehicle hit a tree.* ◊ *to plot a curve on a graph* ⇒ see also BELL CURVE, LEARNING CURVE **2** = CURVEBALL **3** **curves** [pl.] curving shapes that form part of a woman's body
- IDM **ahead of/behind the ˈcurve** (*especially NAmE, business*) in advance of or behind a particular trend: *Our expert advice will help you stay ahead of the curve.* ◊ *We've fallen behind the curve when it comes to developing new digital products.*
- verb **1** [I, T] to move or make sth move in the shape of a curve; to be in the shape of a curve: *a curving staircase* ◊ + **adv./prep.** *The road curved around the bay.* ◊ *The ball curved through the air.* ◊ ~ **sth** *A smile curved his lips.*

**curve·ball** /ˈkɜːvbɔːl; NAmE ˈkɜːrvbɔːl/ (also **curve**) noun **1** (in baseball) a ball that moves in a curve when it is thrown to the BATTER: *His curveball has lost its bite.* **2** (NAmE, *informal*) something that is unexpected and difficult to deal with: *One of the journalists threw the senator a curveball* (= surprised him/her by asking a difficult question).

**curved** /kɜːvd; NAmE kɜːrvd/ adj. having a round shape: *a curved edge/surface* ◊ *a gently curved bay* ◊ *The knife has a curved blade.* ⇒ picture at LINE

**curvi·lin·ear** /ˌkɜːvɪˈlɪniə(r); NAmE ˌkɜːrv-/ adj. (*formal*) consisting of a curved line or lines

**curvy** /ˈkɜːvi; NAmE ˈkɜːrvi/ adj. (*informal*) having curves: *a curvy body* ◊ *curvy lines*

**cush·ion** /ˈkʊʃn/ noun, verb
- **noun 1** (NAmE also **pil·low**) a cloth bag filled with soft material or feathers that is used, for example, to make a seat more comfortable: *matching curtains and cushions* ◊ *a floor cushion* (= a large cushion that you put on the floor to sit on) ◊ *(figurative) a cushion of moss on a rock* ⊃ see also SCATTER CUSHION **2** a layer of sth between two surfaces that keeps them apart: *A hovercraft rides on a cushion of air.* **3** [usually sing.] **~ (against sth)** something that protects you against sth unpleasant that might happen: *His savings were a comfortable cushion against financial problems.* ◊ *The team built up a safe cushion of two goals in the first half.* **4** (in the game of BILLIARDS, etc.) the soft inside edge along each side of the table that the balls BOUNCE off
- **verb** [I, T] **~ sth** to make the effect of a fall or hit less severe: *My fall was cushioned by the deep snow.* **2 ~ sb/sth (against/from sth)** to protect sb/sth from being hurt or damaged or from the unpleasant effects of sth: *The south of the country has been cushioned from the worst effects of the recession.* ◊ *He broke the news of my brother's death to me, making no effort to cushion the blow* (= make the news less shocking).

**cush·ioned** /ˈkʊʃnd/ adj. made soft with cushions: *a cushioned seat*

**cushy** /ˈkʊʃi/ adj. (**cush·ier**, **cushi·est**) (informal, often disapproving) very easy and pleasant; needing little or no effort: *a cushy job*
IDM **a cushy ˈnumber** (BrE) an easy job; a pleasant situation that other people would like

**cusp** /kʌsp/ noun [C] (specialist) a pointed end where two curves meet: *the cusp of a leaf* **2** [sing.] the time of change between two different states: **on the ~ of sth** *two girls on the cusp of adulthood* **3** [sing.] the time when one sign of the ZODIAC ends and the next begins: **on the ~ between A and B** *I was born on the cusp between Virgo and Libra.*

**cuss** /kʌs/ verb, noun
- **verb** [I, T] **~ (sb/sth)** (old-fashioned, informal) to swear at sb: *My dad used to come home drunk, shouting and cussing.*
- **noun** (old-fashioned, informal) **1** used with a negative adjective to describe a person: *He's an awkward cuss.* **2** = CURSE (1): *cuss words*

**cussed** /ˈkʌsɪd/ adj. (old-fashioned, informal) (of people) not willing to be helpful SYN **stubborn** ▸ **cuss·ed·ly** adv. **cuss·ed·ness** noun [U]

**cus·tard** /ˈkʌstəd/ NAmE -stərd/ noun **1** [U] (especially BrE) (NAmE usually **custard ˈsauce**) a sweet yellow sauce made from milk, sugar, eggs and flour, usually served hot with cooked fruit, PUDDINGS, etc: *apple pie and custard* **2** [C, U] a mixture of eggs, milk and sugar baked until it is thick and fairly solid: *a custard tart*

**ˈcustard apple** noun a large tropical fruit that is yellow-white inside

**ˈcustard ˈpie** noun a flat PIE filled with sth soft and wet that looks like custard, that performers throw at each other to make people laugh

**cus·to·dial** /kʌˈstəʊdiəl/ adj. [usually before noun] (law) **1** involving sending sb to prison: *The judge gave him a custodial sentence* (= sent him to prison). **2** connected with the right or duty of taking care of sb; having CUSTODY: *The mother is usually the custodial parent after a divorce.* OPP **non-custodial**

**cus·to·dian** /kʌˈstəʊdiən/ noun **1** a person who takes responsibility for taking care of or protecting sth: *the museum's custodians* ◊ *a self-appointed custodian of public morals* **2** (NAmE) (BrE **care·taker**) (also **jani·tor** NAmE, ScotE) a person whose job is to take care of a building such as a school or a block of flats or an apartment building

**cus·tody** /ˈkʌstədi/ noun [U] **1** the legal right or duty to take care of or keep sb/sth; the act of taking care of sth/sb: *Who will have custody of the children?* ◊ *The divorce court awarded custody to the child's mother.* ◊ *The parents were locked in a bitter battle for custody.* ◊ *The bank provides safe custody for valuables.* ◊ **in the ~ of sb/sth** *The castle is now in the custody of the state.* **2** the state of being in prison, especially while waiting for trial: *After the riot, 32 people were taken into police custody.* ◊ (BrE) *He was remanded in custody, charged with the murder of a policeman.* ⊃ see also PROTECTIVE CUSTODY, YOUTH CUSTODY

**cus·tom** /ˈkʌstəm/ noun, adj.
- **noun** ⊃ see also CUSTOMS **1** [C, U] an accepted way of behaving or of doing things in a society or a community: *It's a local custom.* ◊ *an ancient custom* **according to ~** *According to custom, one son inherited all the family property.* ◊ **of doing sth** *Widows observed the custom of wearing black* ⊃ WORDFINDER NOTE at SOCIETY [sing.] (formal or literary) the way a person always behaves SYN **habit, practice**: *It was her custom to rise early.* ◊ *As was his custom, he knocked three times.* **3** [U] (BrE, formal) (also **business** NAmE, BrE) the fact of a person or people buying goods or services at a shop or business: *Thank you for your custom. Please call again.* ◊ *We've lost a lot of custom since prices went up.*
- **adj.** [only before noun] (especially NAmE) = CUSTOM-BUILT, CUSTOM-MADE: *a custom motorcycle*

**cus·tom·ary** /ˈkʌstəməri; NAmE -meri/ adj. **1** if sth is **customary**, it is what people usually do in a particular place or situation SYN **usual**: *Is it customary to tip hairdressers in this country?* **2** typical of a particular person SYN **habitual**: *She arranged everything with her customary efficiency.* ▸ **cus·tom·ar·ily** /ˈkʌstəmərəli; NAmE ˌkʌstəˈmerəli/ adv.

**ˌcustom-ˈbuilt** (also **cus·tom** especially in NAmE) adj. designed and built for a particular person

**cus·tom·er** /ˈkʌstəmə(r)/ noun **1** a person or an organization that buys goods or services from a shop or business: *marketing strategies to target potential customers* ◊ *the customer service department* ◊ *Improving customer satisfaction is a core company strategy.* ◊ *How do you attract new online customers?* ⊃ WORDFINDER NOTE at COMPANY **2** (old-fashioned, informal) used after an adjective to describe a particular type of person: *an awkward customer*

**ˈcustomer base** noun [usually sing.] (business) all the people who buy or use a particular product or service: *We need to appeal to a wider customer base.*

**ˈcustomer-facing** adj. [only before noun] (business) dealing directly with customers or used by customers: *customer-facing operations such as call centres* ◊ *customer-facing software applications*

**ˌcus·tom·er ˈser·vice** noun [U] **1** the help and advice that a company gives people who buy or use its products or services: *Our main concern is to provide quality customer service.* **2** the department in a company that provides **customer service**: *to phone customer service* ◊ *the customer service department* **3** the activity of serving people in hotels, restaurants and shops: *Votes were based on quality of food, customer service and atmosphere.*

**cus·tom·iz·able** (BrE also **cus·tom·is·able**) /ˈkʌstəmaɪzəbl/ adj. able to be made or changed in ways that suit individual people or tasks: *The app is fully customizable and allows users to create their own word lists.*

**cus·tom·ize** (BrE also **-ise**) /ˈkʌstəmaɪz/ verb **~ sth** to make or change sth to suit the needs of the owner or user: *You can customize the software in several ways.* ▸ **cus·tom·ized, -ised** adj.: *a customized car*

**ˌcustom-ˈmade** (also **cus·tom** especially in NAmE) adj. designed and made for a particular person ⊃ see also BESPOKE

**cus·toms** /ˈkʌstəmz/ noun [pl.] **1** (usually **Customs**) (BrE also **Revenue and ˈCustoms**) the government department that collects taxes on goods bought and sold and on goods brought into the country, and that checks what is brought in: *French Customs have arrested two men.* ◊ *a customs officer* HELP NAmE uses a singular verb with **customs** in this meaning. **2** the place at a port or an airport where your bags are checked as you come into a country: *to go through customs and passport control* **3** the taxes that must be paid to the government when goods are brought in from other

# customs union

countries: *to pay customs on sth* ⋄ **customs duty/duties** ⋄ SYNONYMS at TAX ⋄ compare EXCISE¹

**'customs union** *noun* a group of states that agree to have the same taxes on imported goods and usually to allow FREE TRADE between themselves

**cut** ❶ A1 /kʌt/ *verb, noun*

■ *verb* (**cut·ting, cut, cut**)
- **WOUND/HOLE 1** A1 [T, I] to make an opening or a wound in sth, especially with a sharp tool such as a knife or SCISSORS: *~ sth She cut her finger on a piece of glass.* ⋄ *~ yourself He cut himself (= his face) shaving.* ⋄ *~ sth + adj. She had fallen and cut her head open.* ⋄ *~ into sth She picked up the knife and cut into the meat.* ⋄ *~ through sth You need a powerful saw to cut through metal.*
- **DIVIDE 2** A1 [T] to divide sth into two or more pieces with a knife, etc.: *~ sth Don't cut the string, untie the knots.* ⋄ *The bus was cut in two by the train.* ⋄ *Now cut the tomatoes in half.* ⋄ *~ sth into sth He cut the loaf into thick slices.* ⋄ see also PRE-CUT
- **HAIR/NAILS/GRASS, ETC. 3** A1 [T] to make sth shorter by cutting: *~ sth She cuts hair for a living.* ⋄ *to cut the grass/lawn/hedge* ⋄ *~ sth + adj. He's had his hair cut really short.*
- **REMOVE WITH KNIFE 4** A2 [T] to remove sth or a part of sth, using a knife, etc.: *~ sth (from sth) He cut four thick slices from the loaf.* ⋄ *a bunch of cut flowers* ⋄ *~ sb sth I cut them all a piece of birthday cake.* ⋄ *~ sth for sb I cut a piece of birthday cake for them all.* **5** A2 [T] to make or form sth by removing material with a knife, etc.: *~ sth (in sth) Workmen cut a hole in the pipe.* ⋄ *~ sth into sth homemade biscuits cut into heart shapes*
- **ABLE TO CUT/BE CUT 6** A2 [I] to be capable of cutting: *This knife won't cut.* **7** [I] to be capable of being cut: *Sandstone cuts easily.*
- **REDUCE 8** B1 [T] to reduce sth by removing a part of it: *~ sth to cut costs/prices/spending/taxes* ⋄ *a plan to drastically cut emissions* ⋄ *~ sth by … His salary has been cut by ten per cent.* ⋄ *~ sth (from …) to … The Bank of England has cut interest rates to 1.5 per cent.*
- **RELEASE 9** [T] to allow sb to escape from somewhere by cutting the rope, object, etc. that is holding them: *~ sb (from sth) The injured driver had to be cut from the wreckage.* ⋄ *~ sb + adj. Two survivors were cut free after being trapped for twenty minutes.*
- **CLOTHING 10** [T, usually passive] to design and make a piece of clothing in a particular way: *be cut + adj. The swimsuit was cut high in the leg.* ⋄ see also BIAS-CUT, LOW-CUT
- **REMOVE 11** [T] *~ sth (from sth)* to remove sth from sth: *This scene was cut from the final version of the movie.*
- **COMPUTING 12** [I, T] *~ (sth)* to DELETE (= remove) part of a text on a computer screen in order to place it somewhere else: *You can cut and paste between different programs.*
- **STOP 13** [T] *~ sth (informal)* used to tell sb to stop doing sth: *Cut the chatter and get on with your work!*
- **END 14** [T] *~ sth* to completely end a relationship or all communication with sb SYN **sever**: *She has cut all ties with her family.*
- **IN MOVIE/TV 15** [T] *~ sth* to prepare a film or tape by removing parts of it or putting them in a different order SYN **edit** ⋄ see also DIRECTOR'S CUT **16** [I] (usually used in orders) to stop filming or recording: *The director shouted 'Cut!'* **17** [I] *~ (from sth) to sth* (in films, radio or television) to move quickly from one scene to another: *The scene cuts from the bedroom to the street.*
- **MISS CLASS 18** [T] *~ sth (informal, especially NAmE)* to stay away from a class that you should go to: *He's always cutting class.*
- **UPSET 19** [T] *~ sb* to hurt sb emotionally: *His cruel remarks cut her deeply.*
- **IN CARD GAMES 20** [I, T] *~ (sth)* to divide a PACK of PLAYING CARDS by lifting a section from the top, in order to reveal a card to decide who is to play first, etc: *Let's cut for dealer.* ⋄ WORDFINDER NOTE at CARD
- **GEOMETRY 21** [T] *~ sth* (of a line) to cross another line: *The line cuts the circle at two points.*
- **A TOOTH 22** [T] *~ a tooth* to have a new tooth beginning to appear through the GUM: *When did she cut her first tooth?*
- **A DISC, ETC. 23** [T] *~ a disc, etc.* to make a sound recording on a record, CD, etc: *The Beatles cut their first disc in 1962.*
- **DRUG 24** [T] *~ sth (with sth)* to mix an illegal drug such as HEROIN with another substance

IDM HELP Most idioms containing **cut** are at the entries for the nouns and adjectives in the idioms, for example **cut your losses** is at **loss**. **,cut and 'run** (*informal*) to make a quick or sudden escape **(not) 'cut it** (*informal*) to (not) be as good as is expected or needed: *He won't cut it as a professional singer.*

PHRV **,cut a'cross sth 1** to affect or be true for different groups that usually remain separate: *Opinion on this issue cuts across traditional political boundaries.* **2** to go across sth in order to make your route shorter: *I usually cut across the park on my way home.*
**,cut sth↔a'way (from sth)** to remove sth from sth by cutting: *They cut away all the dead branches from the tree.*
**,cut sth↔'back 1** (*also* **,cut 'back (on sth)**) to reduce sth: *If we don't sell more we'll have to cut back production.* ⋄ *to cut back on spending* ⋄ related noun CUTBACK **2** to make a bush, etc. smaller by cutting branches off SYN **prune**: *to cut back a rose bush*
**,cut sb↔'down** (*formal*) to kill sb: *He was cut down by an assassin's bullet.* **,cut sth↔'down** to make sth fall down by cutting it at the base: *to cut down a tree* **,cut sth↔'down (to …)** | **,cut 'down (on sth)** to reduce the size, amount or number of sth: *We need to cut the article down to 1000 words.* ⋄ *The doctor told him to cut down on his drinking.* ⋄ *I won't have a coffee thanks—I'm trying to cut down* (= drink less coffee).
**,cut 'in 1** if a motor or an engine **cuts in**, it starts working: *Emergency generators cut in.* **2** (*especially NAmE*) (*BrE usually* **,push 'in**) to go in front of other people who are waiting in a way that is rude and unfair **,cut 'in (on sb/sth) 1** to interrupt sb when they are speaking SYN **butt in (on sb/sth)**: *She kept cutting in on our conversation.* ⋄ *+ speech 'Forget it!' she cut in.* **2** (of a vehicle or its driver) to move suddenly in front of another vehicle, leaving little space between the two vehicles **,cut sb 'in (on sth)** (*informal*) to give sb a share of the profit in a business or an activity
**,cut sb↔'off 1** [often passive] to interrupt sb who is speaking on the phone by breaking the connection: *We were cut off in the middle of our conversation.* **2** to refuse to let sb receive any of your property after you die SYN **disinherit**: *He cut his son off without a penny.* **,cut sb/sth↔'off 1** to interrupt sb and stop them from speaking: *My explanation was cut off by loud protests.* **2** [often passive] to stop the supply of sth to sb: *Our water supply has been cut off.* ⋄ *They were cut off for not paying their phone bill.* **,cut sth↔'off 1** (*also* **,cut sth 'off sth**) to remove sth from sth larger by cutting: *He had his finger cut off in an accident at work.* ⋄ (*figurative*) *The winner cut ten seconds off (= ran the distance ten seconds faster than) the world record.* ⋄ see also CUT-OFF *noun* **2** to block or get in the way of sth: *They cut off the enemy's retreat.* ⋄ *The new factory cuts off our view of the hills.* **,cut sb/sth 'off (from sb/sth)** [often passive] to prevent sb/sth from leaving or reaching a place or communicating with people outside a place: *The army was cut off from its base.* ⋄ *She feels very cut off living in the country.* ⋄ *He cut himself off from all human contact.*
**,cut 'out** if a motor or an engine **cuts out**, it suddenly stops working ⋄ related noun CUT-OUT **,cut sb↔'out (of sth)** to not allow sb to be involved in sth: *Don't cut your parents out of your lives.* ⋄ *Furious, his mother cut him out of her will* (= refused to let him receive any of her property after she died). **,cut sth↔'out 1** to make sth by cutting: *She cut the dress out of some old material.* **2** (*figurative*) *He's cut out a niche for himself* (= found a suitable job) *in journalism.* ⋄ related noun CUT-OUT **2** to leave sth out of a piece of writing, etc. SYN **omit**: *I would cut out the bit about working as a waitress.* **3** (*informal*) used to tell sb to stop doing or saying sth annoying: *I'm sick of you two arguing—just cut it out!* **4** to block sth, especially light: *Tall trees cut out the sunlight.* **,cut sth↔'out (of sth) 1** to remove sth from sth larger by cutting, usually with SCISSORS: *I cut this article out of the newspaper.* **2** to stop doing, using or eating sth: *I've been advised to cut sugar out of my*

diet. **be ˌcut ˈout for sth** | **be ˌcut ˈout to be sth** (*informal*) to have the qualities and abilities needed for sth: *He's not cut out for teaching.* ◊ *He's not cut out to be a teacher.* **ˌcut ˈthrough sth 1** to go through sth in order to make your route shorter: *I cut through the building site to the river.* **2** (*also* **ˌcut sth ˈthrough sth**) to make a path or passage through sth by cutting: *They used a machete to cut through the bush.* ◊ *The prisoners cut their way through the barbed wire.* **ˌcut ˈup** (*NAmE, informal*) to behave in a noisy and silly way **ˌcut sb↔ˈup** (*informal*) **1** to injure sb badly by cutting or hitting them: *He was very badly cut up in the fight.* **2** [usually passive] to upset sb emotionally: *She was pretty cut up about them leaving.* **ˌcut sb/sth↔ˈup** (*BrE*) to suddenly drive in front of another vehicle in a dangerous way **ˌcut sth↔ˈup** to divide sth into smaller pieces with a knife, etc: *He cut up the meat on his plate.*

■ *noun*
- **WOUND 1** 🔑 B1 a wound caused by sth sharp: *cuts and bruises on the face* ◊ *Blood poured from the **deep cut** on his arm.*
- **HOLE 2** 🔑 B1 a hole or an opening in sth, made with sth sharp: *Using sharp scissors, **make a small cut in** the material.*
- **REDUCTION 3** 🔑 B1 a reduction in amount, size, supply, etc: *tax/budget/price/funding cuts* ◊ *The company has made another round of job cuts this year.* ◊ *~ **in sth** They announced cuts in public spending.* ➪ see also POWER CUT, SHORTCUT
- **OF HAIR 4** 🔑 B1 [usually sing.] an act of cutting sb's hair; the style in which it is cut: *Your hair could do with a cut* (= it is too long). ◊ *a cut and blow-dry* ➪ see also BUZZ CUT
- **OF CLOTHING 5** [usually sing.] the shape and style that a piece of clothing has because of the way the cloth is cut: *the elegant cut of her dress* ➪ see also BIAS-CUT, LOW-CUT
- **SHARE OF MONEY 6** a share in sth, especially money: *They were rewarded with a cut of 5% from the profits.*
- **OF FILM/PLAY, ETC. 7** ~ **(in sth)** an act of removing part of a film, play, piece of writing, etc: *The director objected to the cuts ordered by the censor.* ◊ *She made some cuts before handing over the finished novel.*
- **MEAT 8** a piece of meat cut from an animal: *a lean cut of pork* ◊ *cheap cuts of stewing lamb* ➪ see also COLD CUTS

IDM **a ˌcut aˈbove sb/sth** better than sb/sth: *His latest novel is a cut above the rest.* **the ˌcut and ˈthrust (of sth)** (*BrE*) the lively or aggressive way that sth is done: *the cut and thrust of political debate* **make the ˈcut 1** to reach or maintain the required standard: *I had to explain to the applicants why they didn't make the cut.* **2** (in golf) to achieve a good enough score to be able to take part in the next stage of a competition: *Woods needed a 69 to make the cut.* **3** (of a film, play, piece of writing, etc.) to be included after parts have been removed: *When a book is made into a movie not every scene will make the cut.*

**ˌcut and ˈdried** *adj.* [not usually before noun] decided in a way that cannot be changed or argued about: *The inquiry is by no means cut and dried.*

**cu·ta·ne·ous** /kjuːˈteɪniəs/ *adj.* (*anatomy*) relating to the skin ➪ see also SUBCUTANEOUS

**cut·away** /ˈkʌtəweɪ/ *adj., noun*
■ *adj.* [only before noun] (of a model or diagram) with some outside parts left out, in order to show what the inside looks like: *a cutaway picture of the inside of a nuclear reactor*
■ *noun* **1** ~ **(to sb/sth)** (on television, in a film, etc.) a picture that shows sth different from the main thing that is being shown: *There was a cutaway to the guests in the royal box.* **2** a model or diagram with some outside parts left out, in order to show what the inside looks like **3** (*NAmE*) (*BrE* **ˈmorning coat**) a black or grey jacket for men, short at the front and very long at the back, worn as part of morning dress

**cut·back** /ˈkʌtbæk/ *noun* [usually pl.] ~ **(in sth)** a reduction in sth: *cutbacks in public spending* ◊ *staff cutbacks*

**ˌcut-ˈdown** *adj.* [only before noun] reduced in length, size or range: *a cut-down version of the program*

**cute** 🔑+ B2 /kjuːt/ *adj.* (**cuter**, **cutest**) **1** 🔑 B2 pretty and attractive: *a cute little baby* ◊ *She's so cute!* ◊ (*BrE*) *an unbearably cute picture of two kittens* (= it seems SENTIMENTAL) **2** (*especially NAmE, informal*) sexually attractive: *Check out those cute guys over there!* **3** (*especially NAmE, informal*) clever, sometimes in an annoying way because a person is trying to get an advantage for himself or herself: *She had a really cute idea.* ◊ *Don't get cute with me!*
▶ **cute·ly** *adv.*: *to smile cutely* **cute·ness** *noun* [U]

**cutesy** /ˈkjuːtsi/ *adj.* (*informal*) too pretty or attractive in a way that is annoying or not realistic

**ˌcut ˈglass** *noun* [U] glass with patterns cut in it: *a cut-glass vase*

**cut·icle** /ˈkjuːtɪkl/ *noun* an area of hard skin at the base of the nails on the fingers and toes

**cutie** /ˈkjuːti/ *noun* (*informal*) a person who is attractive or kind: *He's a real cutie.*

**cut·lass** /ˈkʌtləs/ *noun* a short SWORD with a curved metal cutting edge that was used as a weapon by sailors and PIRATES in the past

**cut·lery** /ˈkʌtləri/ *noun* [U] **1** (*especially BrE*) (*NAmE usually* **flat·ware**, **sil·ver·ware**) knives, forks and spoons, used for eating and serving food **2** (*NAmE*) knives, etc. that are sharp

**cut·let** /ˈkʌtlət/ *noun* **1** a thick slice of meat, especially LAMB or PORK (= meat from a pig), that is cooked and served with the bone still attached **2** (in compounds) pieces of meat, fish, vegetables, etc. that are cut up and pressed together into a flat piece, covered with BREADCRUMBS and cooked: *nut cutlets*

---

▼ **SYNONYMS**

**cut**
slash • cut sth back • scale sth back • rationalize • downsize

These words all mean to reduce the amount or size of sth, especially of an amount of money or a business.

**cut** to reduce sth, especially an amount of money that is demanded, spent, earned, etc. or the size of a business: *The President has promised to cut taxes significantly.* ◊ *Buyers will bargain hard to cut the cost of the house they want.* ◊ *His salary has been cut by ten per cent.* ◊ *Could you cut your essay from 5 000 to 3 000 words?*

**slash** [often passive] (*rather informal*) (often used in newspapers) to reduce sth by a large amount: *The workforce has been slashed by half.*

**cut sth back/cut back on sth** to reduce sth, especially an amount of money or business: *We had to cut back production.*

**scale sth back** (*especially NAmE or business*) to reduce sth, especially an amount of money or business: *The IMF has scaled back its growth forecasts for the next decade.*

**rationalize** (*BrE, business*) to make changes to a business or system, in order to make it more efficient, especially by spending less money.

**downsize** (*business*) to make a company or an organization smaller by reducing the number of jobs in it, in order to reduce costs. NOTE **Downsize** is often used by people who want to avoid saying more obvious words like 'dismiss' or 'make redundant' because they sound too negative.

**PATTERNS**
- to cut/slash/cut back on/scale back/rationalize **spending/production**
- to cut/slash/cut back on **jobs**
- to cut/slash/downsize **the workforce**
- to cut/slash/rationalize **the cost** of sth
- to cut/slash **prices/taxes/the budget**
- to cut sth/slash sth/cut sth back **drastically**

## cut-off

**'cut-off** noun, adj.
- noun 1 a point or limit when you stop sth: *Is there a cut-off point between childhood and adulthood?* 2 the act of stopping the supply of something: *The government announced a cut-off in overseas aid.* 3 **cut-offs** [pl.] trousers that have been made shorter by cutting off part of the legs: *wearing frayed cut-offs*
- adj. [only before noun] (of trousers) made shorter by cutting off part of the legs: *cut-off jeans*

**'cut-out** noun 1 a shape cut out of paper, wood, etc: *a cardboard cut-out* 2 a piece of safety equipment that stops an electric current from flowing through sth: *A cut-out stops the kettle boiling dry.*

**cut-'price** adj. [only before noun] (*especially BrE*) (*NAmE usually* **cut-'rate**) 1 sold at a reduced price: *cut-price goods/fares* 2 selling goods at a reduced price: *a cut-price store/supermarket*

**cut·scene** /ˈkʌtsiːn/ noun a short scene in a video game that the player cannot control, and that usually develops the story

**cut·ter** /ˈkʌtə(r)/ noun 1 (usually in compounds) a person or thing that cuts: *a pastry cutter* 2 **cutters** [pl.] (usually in compounds) a tool for cutting: *a pair of wire cutters* 3 a small fast ship 4 a ship's boat, used for travelling between the ship and land

**'cut-throat** adj. [usually before noun] (of an activity) in which people compete with each other in aggressive and unfair ways: *the cut-throat world of politics*

**cut·ting** ⚫ B1 /ˈkʌtɪŋ/ noun, adj.
- noun 1 ⚫ B1 (*also* **'press cutting**) (*both BrE*) (*also* **clipping**, **'press clipping** *NAmE, BrE*) an article or a story that you cut from a newspaper or magazine and keep: *newspaper/press cuttings* 2 a piece cut off a plant that will be used to grow a new plant 3 (*BrE*) a narrow open passage that is dug through high ground for a road, railway or CANAL ⊃ see also COST-CUTTING
- adj. [usually before noun] 1 unkind and likely to hurt sb's feelings SYN biting: *a cutting remark* 2 (of winds) cold in a sharp and unpleasant way SYN biting

**'cutting board** (*NAmE*) (*BrE* **'chopping board**) noun a board made of wood or plastic used for cutting meat or vegetables on

**'cutting 'edge** noun [sing.] 1 **the ~ (of sth)** the newest, most advanced stage in the development of sth: *working at the cutting edge of computer technology* ⊃ compare BLEEDING EDGE 2 an aspect of sth that gives it an advantage: *We're relying on him to give the team a cutting edge.* ▶ **'cutting-'edge** adj.: *cutting-edge technology/research/science/design*

**'cutting grass** noun = GRASSCUTTER

**'cutting room** noun a room in which the different parts of a film are cut and put into order: *The scene with the elephant ended up* **on the cutting room floor** (= was not included in the final version of the film).

**cuttle·fish** /ˈkʌtlfɪʃ/ noun (*pl.* **cuttle·fish**) a sea creature with eight arms, two TENTACLES (= long thin parts like arms) and a wide flat shell inside its body. It produces a black substance like INK when it is attacked.

**CV** /ˌsiː ˈviː/ noun 1 (*BrE*) (*NAmE* **résumé**) a written record of your education and the jobs you have done, that you send when you are applying for a job (the abbreviation for 'curriculum vitae'): *Send a full CV with your job application.* ⊃ WORDFINDER NOTE at APPLY 2 (*US*) a record of a college teacher's education, where they have worked, the books and articles they have published and the courses they have taught, used when they are applying for a job (the abbreviation for 'curriculum vitae')

**'C-word** noun [usually sing.] (*informal*) used to replace a word beginning with C that you do not want to say, for example the offensive swear word 'cunt', or 'cancer': *An employee who uses the C-word to a colleague will be suspended.* ⋄ *I hate it when people refer to cancer as the C-word.* ⊃ compare F-WORD

**cwt** abbr. (*pl.* **cwt**) (in writing) HUNDREDWEIGHT

**-cy** /si/, **-acy** /əsi/ suffix (in nouns) 1 the state or quality of: *infancy* ⋄ *accuracy* 2 the status or position of: *chaplaincy*

**cyan** /ˈsaɪæn, ˈsaɪən/ noun [U] (*specialist*) a blue-green colour, used in printing

**cy·an·ide** /ˈsaɪənaɪd/ noun [U] a highly poisonous chemical

**cyber-** /ˈsaɪbə(r)/ combining form (in nouns and adjectives) connected with electronic communication networks, especially the internet: *cybernetics* ⋄ *cybercafe*

**'cyber·attack** /ˈsaɪbərətæk/ noun the act of trying to damage or destroy a computer network, computer system or website by secretly changing information on it without permission: *Fourteen people were arrested for launching a cyberattack on the company's website.* ⊃ compare CYBERTHREAT

**'cyber·bully** /ˈsaɪbəbʊli; *NAmE* -bɜːrb-/ noun (*pl.* **-ies**) a person who uses messages on SOCIAL MEDIA, emails, text messages, etc. to frighten or upset sb

**'cyber·bully·ing** /ˈsaɪbəbʊliɪŋ; *NAmE* -bɜːrb-/ noun [U] the activity of using messages on SOCIAL MEDIA, emails, text messages, etc. to frighten or upset sb: *The school provides guidance for parents on how to deal with issues such as cyberbullying.*

**'cyber·cafe** /ˈsaɪbəkæfeɪ; *NAmE* -bɜːrk-/ noun a cafe with computers on which customers can use the internet, send emails, etc.

**'cyber·crime** /ˈsaɪbəkraɪm; *NAmE* -bɜːrk-/ noun [U, C] crime that is committed using the internet, for example by stealing sb's personal or bank details or by INFECTING their computer with a virus

**cy·ber·net·ics** /ˌsaɪbəˈnetɪks; *NAmE* -bɜːrˈn-/ noun [U] the scientific study of communication and control systems, which involves comparing human and animal brains with machines and electronic devices ▸ **cy·ber·net·ic** adj.

**'cyber·punk** /ˈsaɪbəpʌŋk; *NAmE* -bɜːrp-/ noun [U] stories set in an unpleasant imaginary future world controlled by technology and computers

**'cyber·sex** /ˈsaɪbəseks; *NAmE* -bɜːrs-/ noun [U] communication between people using the internet that makes them sexually excited

**'cyber·space** /ˈsaɪbəspeɪs; *NAmE* -bɜːrs-/ noun [U] the internet considered as an imaginary space without a physical location in which communication over computer networks takes place: *Many more business functions will move into cyberspace.*

**'cyber·squat·ting** /ˈsaɪbəskwɒtɪŋ; *NAmE* -bɜːrskwɑːt-/ noun [U] the illegal activity of buying and officially recording an address on the internet that is the name of an existing company or a well-known person, with the intention of selling it to the owner in order to make money ▸ **'cyber·squat·ter** noun

**'cyber·threat** /ˈsaɪbəθret; *NAmE* -bɜːrθ-/ noun the possibility that sb will try to damage or destroy a computer network, computer system or website by secretly changing information on it without permission: *The company isn't doing enough to secure its systems against cyberthreats.* ⊃ compare CYBERATTACK

**cy·borg** /ˈsaɪbɔːɡ; *NAmE* -bɔːrɡ/ noun (in SCIENCE FICTION stories) a creature that is part human, part machine

**cyc·la·men** /ˈsɪkləmən; *NAmE* ˈsaɪ-/ noun (*pl.* **cyc·la·men** or **cyc·la·mens**) a plant with pink, purple or white flowers that grow on long STEMS pointing downwards, often grown indoors

**cycle** ⚫ A2 ⚫ /ˈsaɪkl/ noun, verb
- noun 1 A2 a bicycle or motorcycle: *We went for a cycle ride on Sunday.* ⋄ **on a ~** *Lots of people arrived in cars or on cycles.* ⊃ see also BIKE noun 2 B1 **~ (of sth)** the fact of a series of events being repeated many times, always in the same order: *the cycle of the seasons* ⋄ *They could not break the cycle of harvest failure, food shortage, price increase and misery.* ⋄ *different phases of the cell cycle* ⊃ see also CARBON CYCLE, LIFE CYCLE, LUNAR CYCLE, WATER CYCLE 3 a complete set or series, for example of movements in a

machine: *eight cycles per second* ◊ *the rinse cycle* (= in a washing machine)
- **verb** [I] (*especially BrE*) (+ **adv./prep.**) to ride a bicycle; to travel by bicycle: *I usually cycle home through the park.* ⊃ compare BICYCLE, BIKE

'**cycle lane** (*BrE*) (*NAmE* '**bicycle lane**, *informal* '**bike lane**) *noun* a part of a road that only bicycles are allowed to use

'**cycle path** (*also* '**cycle track**, **cycle·way** /ˈsaɪklweɪ/) *noun* (*BrE*) a path or track that only people on bicycles are allowed to use

'**cycle rickshaw** (*also* **cycle-rickshaw**) *noun* a vehicle like a bicycle with three wheels, with a covered seat for passengers behind the driver, used especially in some Asian countries

**cyc·lic** /ˈsaɪklɪk, ˈsɪ-/ (*also* **cyc·lic·al** /ˈsaɪklɪkl, ˈsɪ-/) *adj.* [usually before noun] repeated many times and always happening in the same order: *the cyclic processes of nature* ◊ *Economic activity often follows a cyclical pattern.* ▶ **cyc·lic·al·ly** /ˈsaɪklɪkli, ˈsɪ-/ *adv.*: *events that occur cyclically*

**cyc·ling** /ˈsaɪklɪŋ/ *noun* [U] the sport or activity of riding a bicycle: *to go cycling* ◊ *Cycling is Europe's second most popular sport.* ◊ *cycling shorts*

**WORDFINDER** back-pedal, dismount, handlebar, pedal, ride, saddle, speed, tandem, velodrome

**cyc·list** /ˈsaɪklɪst/ *noun* a person who rides a bicycle ⊃ compare BICYCLIST

**cyclo-cross** /ˈsaɪkləʊ krɒs; *NAmE* krɔːs/ *noun* [U] the sport of racing bicycles over rough ground, which in places is too difficult to ride on so you have to carry your bicycle and run

**cyc·lone** /ˈsaɪkləʊn/ *noun* a violent tropical storm in which strong winds move in a circle ⊃ compare HURRICANE, TYPHOON ⊃ **WORDFINDER NOTE** at DISASTER ▶ **cyc·lon·ic** /saɪˈklɒnɪk; *NAmE* -ˈklɑːn-/ *adj.*

**Cy·clops** /ˈsaɪklɒps; *NAmE* -klɑːps/ *noun* (in ancient Greek stories) a giant with only one eye in the middle of his face

**cyclo·tron** /ˈsaɪklətrɒn; *NAmE* -trɑːn/ *noun* (*physics*) a machine that makes ATOMS or ELECTRONS move more quickly, using electrical and MAGNETIC FIELDS

**cyg·net** /ˈsɪɡnət/ *noun* a young SWAN (= a large white bird with a long neck that lives on or near water)

**cy·lin·der** /ˈsɪlɪndə(r)/ *noun* **1** a solid or hollow figure with round ends and long straight sides ⊃ picture at SOLID **2** an object like a cylinder in shape, especially one used as a container: *a gas/oxygen cylinder* **3** the hollow tube in an engine, like a cylinder in shape, inside which the PISTON moves: *a six-cylinder engine*
IDM **working/firing on all ˈcylinders** (*informal*) using all your energy to do sth; working as well as possible

**cy·lin·dric·al** /səˈlɪndrɪkl/ *adj.* having a shape like a cylinder: *huge cylindrical gas tanks*

**cym·bal** /ˈsɪmbl/ *noun* a musical instrument in the form of a round metal plate. It is hit with a stick, or two cymbals are hit against each other: *a clash/crash of cymbals*

**Cymru** /ˈkʌmri/ *noun* the name for 'Wales' in the Welsh language ⊃ see also PLAID CYMRU

▼ **HOMOPHONES**

**cymbal** ◆ **symbol** /ˈsɪmbl/
- **cymbal** *noun*: *The final cymbal rings out.*
- **symbol** *noun*: *The owl is a well-recognized symbol of wisdom.*

**cynic** /ˈsɪnɪk/ *noun* **1** a person who believes that people only do things to help themselves, rather than for good or sincere reasons **2** a person who does not believe that sth good will happen or that sth is important: *Cynics will say that there is not the slightest chance of success.* ▶ **cyni·cism** /-nɪsɪzəm/ *noun* [U]: *In a world full of cynicism she was the one person I felt I could trust.*

**cyn·ic·al** /ˈsɪnɪkl/ *adj.* **1** believing that people only do things to help themselves rather than for good or honest reasons: *a cynical view/smile* ◊ **~ about sth** *Do you have to be so cynical about everything?* **2** **~ (about sth)** not believing that sth good will happen or that sth is important: *I'm a bit cynical about the benefits of the plan.* **3** not caring that sth might hurt other people, if there is some advantage for you: *a cynical disregard for the safety of others* ◊ *a deliberate and cynical foul* ▶ **cyn·ic·al·ly** /-kli/ *adv.*

**cyn·o·sure** /ˈsaɪnəzjʊə(r); *NAmE* -nəʃʊr/ *noun* [sing.] (*formal*) a person or thing that is the centre of attention: *Ruth was the cynosure of all eyes.*

**cy·pher** /ˈsaɪfə(r)/ = CIPHER

**cy·press** /ˈsaɪprəs/ *noun* a tall straight EVERGREEN tree ⊃ see also LEYLAND CYPRESS

**Cy·ril·lic** /səˈrɪlɪk/ *adj.* the Cyrillic alphabet is used to write Russian, Bulgarian, Serbian, Ukrainian and some other Slavic languages ▶ **Cy·ril·lic** *noun* [U]

**cyst** /sɪst/ *noun* a GROWTH containing liquid that forms in or on a person's or an animal's body and may need to be removed

**cys·tic fi·bro·sis** /ˌsɪstɪk faɪˈbrəʊsɪs/ *noun* [U] a serious medical condition that some people are born with, in which GLANDS in the lungs and other organs do not work correctly, causing the production of extra thick MUCUS. It often leads to infections and can result in early death.

**cyst·itis** /sɪˈstaɪtɪs/ *noun* [U] an infection of the BLADDER, especially in women, that causes painful URINATION which happens often

**cy·tol·o·gy** /saɪˈtɒlədʒi; *NAmE* -ˈtɑːl-/ *noun* [U] the scientific study of the structure and function of cells from living things

**cyto·megalo·virus** /ˌsaɪtəʊˈmeɡələʊvaɪrəs/ *noun* (*medical*) a virus that usually causes mild infections, but that can be serious for people with AIDS or for new babies

**cy·to·plasm** /ˈsaɪtəʊplæzəm/ *noun* [U] (*biology*) all the living material in a cell, not including the NUCLEUS ▶ **cy·to·plas·mic** /ˌsaɪtəʊˈplæzmɪk/ *adj.* ⊃ compare PROTOPLASM

**czar, czar·ina, czar·ism, czar·ist** = TSAR, TSARINA, TSARISM, TSARIST

# Dd

**D** /diː/ noun, abbr., symbol
- noun (also **d**) [C, U] (pl. **Ds**, **D's**, **d's** /diːz/) **1** the fourth letter of the English alphabet: 'Dog' begins with (a) D/'D'. **2 D** (music) the second note in the SCALE of C MAJOR **3 D ~ (in/for sth)** a grade that a student can get for a piece of work or course of study, showing that it is not very good: He got (a) D in geography. ⇒ see also D-DAY
- abbr. (also **D.** especially in NAmE) (in politics in the US) DEMOCRAT; DEMOCRATIC
- symbol the number 500 in ROMAN NUMERALS

**d.** abbr. (in writing) **1** died: Emily Clifton, d. 1865 **2 d** (in the system of money used in the past in the UK) a PENNY

**-d** suffix ⇒ -ED

**DA** (BrE) (US **D.A.**) /ˌdiː ˈeɪ/ noun = DISTRICT ATTORNEY

**dab** /dæb/ verb, noun
- verb (**-bb-**) **1** to touch sth lightly, usually several times: **~ sth** She dabbed her eyes and blew her nose. ◇ **~ at sth** He dabbed at the cut with his handkerchief. **2 ~ sth + adv./prep.** to put sth on a surface with quick light movements: She dabbed a little perfume behind her ears.
- noun **1** a small amount of a liquid, cream or powder that is put on a surface in a quick gentle movement: She put a dab of perfume behind her ears. **2** an act of gently touching or pressing sth without rubbing: He gave the cut a quick dab with a towel. **3** a small flat fish

**dabba** /ˈdʌbə/ noun (IndE) a lunch box; a container with a meal or SNACK

**dab·ble** /ˈdæbl/ verb **1** [I] **~ (in/with sth)** to take part in a sport, an activity, etc. but not very seriously: He dabbles in local politics. **2** [T] **~ sth (in sth)** to move your hands, feet, etc. around in water: She dabbled her toes in the stream.

**ˌdab ˈhand** noun (BrE, informal) a person who is very good at doing sth or using sth: He's a dab hand at cooking spaghetti. ◇ She's a dab hand with a paintbrush.

**dacha** /ˈdætʃə/; NAmE /ˈdɑːtʃə/ noun a Russian country house

**dachs·hund** /ˈdæksnd/; NAmE /ˈdɑːkshʊnd/ (also BrE, informal **ˈsausage dog**) noun a small dog with a long body, long ears and very short legs

**da·coit** /dəˈkɔɪt/ noun (IndE) a member of a group of armed thieves

**dad** 🔊 **A1** /dæd/ noun (informal) (often used as a name) father: That's my dad over there. ◇ Do you live with your mum or your dad? ◇ Is it OK if I borrow the car, Dad?

**Dada** /ˈdɑːdɑː/ noun [U] an early 20th century movement in art, literature, music and film that made fun of social and artistic behaviour and traditions ▶ **Dada·ism** noun [U] **Dada·ist** noun

**dada** /ˈdɑːdɑː/ noun (IndE) **1** an older brother or male cousin **2** used after the first name of an older man as a polite way of addressing him **3** the father of your father **4** a leader of a gang

**daddy** /ˈdædi/ noun (pl. **-ies**) used especially by and to young children, and often as a name, to mean 'father': What does your daddy look like? ◇ Daddy, where are you? ◇ Come to Daddy. ⇒ see also SUGAR DADDY

**ˌdaddy-ˈlong-legs** noun (pl. **daddy-long-legs**) (informal) **1** = CRANE FLY **2** (NAmE) a small creature like a spider with very long legs

**dado** /ˈdeɪdəʊ/ noun (pl. **-os**, NAmE **-oes**) the lower part of the wall of a room when it is a different colour or material from the top part

**dae·mon** /ˈdiːmən/ noun a creature in stories from ancient Greece that is half man and half god

**daf·fo·dil** /ˈdæfədɪl/ noun a tall yellow spring flower that is like a TRUMPET in shape. It is a national symbol of Wales. ⇒ VISUAL VOCAB page V7

**daffy** /ˈdæfi/ adj. (**daf·fier**, **daf·fi·est**) (informal) silly

**daft** /dɑːft/; NAmE /dæft/ adj. (**daft·er**, **daft·est**) (informal) silly, often in a way that is funny: Don't be so daft! ◇ She's not as daft as she looks. ◇ What a daft thing to say! ▶ **daft·ness** noun [U]
**IDM** ˌdaft as a ˈbrush (BrE, informal) very silly

**dag** /dæg/ noun (informal) **1** (AustralE, NZE) a person who is strange or different in a way that is funny **2** (AustralE) a person who is not fashionable **3** (AustralE, NZE) a dirty piece of wool that hangs down from a sheep's bottom

**dagaa** /ˈdɑːɡɑː/ EAfrE /ˈdæɡɑː/ noun [C, U] (pl. **dagaa**) (EAfrE) small fish that are dried to preserve them, and often fried and then cooked with tomatoes and milk to make a STEW

**dagga** /ˈdæxə/ SAfrE /ˈdʌxə/ noun [U] (SAfrE) = MARIJUANA: She was arrested for smoking dagga.

**dag·ger** /ˈdæɡə(r)/ noun a short pointed knife that is used as a weapon ⇒ picture at SWORD ⇒ see also CLOAK-AND-DAGGER
**IDM** ˌat daggers ˈdrawn (BrE) if two people are **at daggers drawn**, they are very angry with each other **glare/look ˈdaggers at sb** to look at sb in a very angry way

**daggy** /ˈdæɡi/ adj. (AustralE, informal) **1** not fashionable: a daggy restaurant **2** untidy or dirty

**da·guerre·otype** /dəˈɡerətaɪp/ (also **da·guerro·type**) noun a photograph taken using an early process that used a silver plate and MERCURY gas

**dah·lia** /ˈdeɪliə, ˈdɑːl-/; NAmE also /ˈdæl-/ noun a large brightly coloured garden flower, often like a ball in shape

**dai·kon** /ˈdaɪkɒn/; NAmE /-kɑːn/ noun [U, C] = MOOLI

**the Dáil** /ðə ˈdɔɪl/ noun [sing. + sing./pl. v.] one of the parts of the parliament of the Republic of Ireland, whose members are elected by the people

**daily** 🔊 **A2** /ˈdeɪli/ adj., adv., noun
- adj. [only before noun] **1** 🔊 **A2** happening, done or produced every day: Many people still read a daily newspaper. ◇ events affecting the daily lives of millions of people ◇ your daily routine/activities ◇ Invoices are signed **on a daily basis**. **2** connected with one day's work: They charge a daily rate.
**IDM** your daily ˈbread the basic things that you need to live, especially food
- adv. 🔊 **B1** every day: The machines are inspected twice daily. ◇ News stories are updated daily.
- noun (pl. **-ies**) **1** a newspaper published every day except Sunday: The story was in all the dailies. **2** (also ˌdaily ˈhelp) (BrE, old-fashioned) a person employed to come to sb's house each day to clean it and do other jobs

**dainty** /ˈdeɪnti/ adj. (**dain·tier**, **dain·ti·est**) **1** (of people and things) small and pretty in a way that people find attractive **SYN** delicate: dainty feet ◇ a dainty porcelain cup **2** (of movements) careful, often in a way that suggests good manners **SYN** delicate: She took a dainty little bite of the apple. ▶ **dain·tily** /-tɪli/ adv.: She blew her nose as daintily as possible. **dain·ti·ness** noun [U]

**dai·quiri** /ˈdækɪri/; BrE also /ˈdaɪk-/ noun an alcoholic drink made from RUM mixed with fruit juice, sugar, etc.

**dairy** 🔊 **B2** /ˈdeəri/; NAmE /ˈderi/ noun, adj.
- noun (pl. **-ies**) **1** 🔊 **B2** [U] milk, cheese and other milk products: The doctor told me to eat less red meat and dairy. ⇒ see also NON-DAIRY **2** [C] a place on a farm where milk is kept and where butter and cheese are made ⇒ WORDFINDER NOTE at FARM **3** [C] a company that sells milk, cheese and other milk products **4** [C] (NZE) a small local shop: I went to buy a paper at the corner dairy.
- adj. [only before noun] **1** 🔊 **B2** made from milk: dairy products/produce **2** 🔊 **B2** connected with the production of milk rather than meat: the dairy industry ◇ dairy cattle/farmers ◇ a dairy cow/farm

**dairy·man** /ˈdeərimən/; NAmE /ˈder-/ noun (pl. **-men** /-mən/) **1** a man who works in a dairy **2** a man who owns or manages a dairy and sells the products

**dais** /ˈdeɪs/ noun a stage, especially at one end of a room, on which people stand to make speeches to an audience

**daisy** /ˈdeɪzi/ noun (pl. **-ies**) a small wild flower with white PETALS around a yellow centre; a taller plant with similar but larger flowers IDM see PUSH v. ⊃ VISUAL VOCAB page V7

**daisy chain** noun a string of daisies tied together to wear around the neck, etc.

**dal** (also **dhal**) /dɑːl/ noun [U] A South Asian dish made from LENTILS or other PULSES (= seeds from certain plants)

**dala-dala** /ˌdɑːləˈdɑːlə/ EAfrE [dalaˈdala] noun (EAfrE) (in Tanzania) a privately owned road vehicle with seats for about twelve people that carries passengers and has a driver that you pay to take you somewhere, usually along a fixed route with other stops for people to get on and off

**the Dalai Lama** /ðə ˌdælaɪ ˈlɑːmə; NAmE ˌdɑːli/ noun [sing.] the leader of Tibetan Buddhism and, in former times, the ruler of Tibet

**dale** /deɪl/ noun (literary or dialect) a valley, especially in northern England: *the Yorkshire Dales*

**Dalit** /ˈdʌlɪt/ noun (in the traditional Indian CASTE system) a member of the caste that is considered the lowest and that has the fewest advantages: *the Dalits' struggle for social and economic rights*

**dal·li·ance** /ˈdæliəns/ noun [U, C] (old-fashioned or humorous) **1** the behaviour of sb who is dallying with sb/sth: *It turned out to be his last dalliance with the education system.* **2** a sexual relationship that is not serious

**dally** /ˈdæli/ verb (**dal·lies, dally·ing, dal·lied, dal·lied**) [I] (old-fashioned) to do sth too slowly; to take too much time making a decision ⊃ see also DILLY-DALLY
PHRV **ˈdally with sb/sth** (old-fashioned) to treat sb/sth in a way that is not serious enough

**Dal·ma·tian** /dælˈmeɪʃn/ noun a large dog that has short white hair with black spots

**dam** /dæm/ noun, verb
▪ noun **1** a barrier that is built across a river in order to stop the water from flowing, used especially to make a RESERVOIR (= a lake for storing water) or to produce electricity ⊃ WORDFINDER NOTE at RIVER **2** (SAfrE) an artificial lake where rain or spring water is collected and stored: *The dam was full of water.* **3** (specialist) the mother of some animals, especially horses ⊃ compare SIRE
▪ verb (**-mm-**) ~ **sth (up)** to build a dam across a river, especially in order to make an artificial lake for use as a water supply, etc.

**dam·age** /ˈdæmɪdʒ/ noun, verb
▪ noun **1** [U] physical harm caused to sth which makes it less attractive, useful or valuable: *serious/severe/extensive damage ◊ permanent/irreparable/irreversible damage ◊ She suffered minor brain damage at birth. ◊ liver/nerve/kidney damage ◊ ~ to sth The earthquake caused damage to property estimated at $6 billion. ◊ The storm didn't do much damage. ◊ It could take years to repair the damage. ◊ Make sure you insure your camera against loss or damage.* **2** [U] harmful effects on sb/sth: *The children suffered psychological and emotional damage. ◊ irreparable/permanent/lasting damage ◊ ~ to sth This could cause serious damage to the country's economy. ◊ It will be hard to repair the damage to his reputation. ◊ Don't you think you've done enough damage already?* **3 damages** [pl.] an amount of money that a court decides should be paid to sb by the person, company, etc. that has caused them harm or injury: *He was ordered to pay damages totalling £30000. ◊ They intend to sue for damages. ◊ Ann was awarded £6000 (in) damages.*
IDM **what's the ˈdamage?** (informal) a way of asking how much sth costs
▪ verb ~ **sth/sb** to have a bad or harmful effect on sth/sb: *The church was badly damaged by the 1997 earthquake. ◊ Smoking seriously damages your health. ◊ to be severely/heavily damaged in the fire ◊ Our car was damaged beyond repair in the crash. ◊ She fears the allegations could permanently damage her reputation. ◊ She was psychologically damaged by her experiences.*

387

▼ **SYNONYMS**

**damage**
hurt • harm • impair
These words all mean to have a bad effect on sb/sth.
**damage** to cause physical harm to sth, making it less attractive, useful or valuable; to have a bad effect on sb/sth's life, health, happiness or chances of success: *The fire badly damaged the town hall. ◊ emotionally damaged children*
**hurt** (rather informal) to have a bad effect on sb/sth's life, health, happiness or chances of success: *Hard work never hurt anyone.*
**harm** to have a bad effect on sb/sth's life, health, happiness or chances of success: *Pollution can harm marine life.*
DAMAGE, HURT OR HARM?
**Hurt** is slightly less formal than **damage** or **harm**, especially when it is used in negative statements: *It won't hurt him to have to wait a bit. ◊ It won't damage/harm him to have to wait a bit.* **Harm** is also often used to talk about ways in which things in the natural world such as *wildlife* and the *environment* are affected by human activity.
**impair** (rather formal) to damage sb's health, abilities or chances: *Even one drink can impair driving performance.*
PATTERNS
• to damage/hurt/harm/impair sb's **chances**
• to damage/hurt/harm sb's **interests/reputation**
• to damage/harm/impair sb's **health**
• to **seriously/greatly** damage/hurt/harm/impair sb/sth
• to **badly/severely** damage/hurt/impair sb/sth

**damage limiˈtation** (also ˌdamage conˈtrol especially in NAmE) noun [U] the process of trying to limit the amount of damage that is caused by sth

**dam·aging** /ˈdæmɪdʒɪŋ/ adj. causing damage; having a bad effect on sb/sth: *damaging consequences/effects ◊ ~to sb/sth Lead is potentially damaging to children's health.*

**Da·mas·cus** /dəˈmæskəs/ noun
IDM **the road to Daˈmascus** an experience that results in a great change in a person's attitudes or beliefs: *Spending a night in jail was his road to Damascus.* ORIGIN From the story in the Bible in which St Paul hears the voice of God on the road to Damascus and becomes a Christian.

**dam·ask** /ˈdæməsk/ noun [U] a type of thick cloth, usually made from silk or LINEN, with a pattern that can be seen on both sides: *a damask tablecloth*

**dame** /deɪm/ noun **1 Dame** (in the UK) a title given to a woman as a special honour because of the work she has done: *Dame Maggie Smith* **2** (NAmE, old-fashioned, informal) a woman **3** (BrE) = PANTOMIME DAME

**damn** /dæm/ exclamation, adj., verb, adv., noun
▪ **exclamation** (also old-fashioned **damˈmit** /ˈdæmɪt/, ˈdamn it) (informal) a swear word that people use to show that they are annoyed, disappointed, etc: *Oh damn! I forgot he was coming.*
▪ **adj.** (also **damned**) [only before noun] (informal) **1** a swear word that people use to show that they are annoyed with sb/sth: *Where's that damn book! ◊ The damned thing won't start! ◊ It's none of your damn business! ◊ He's a damn nuisance!* **2** a swear word that people use to emphasize what they are saying: *What a damn shame!* IDM see THING
▪ **verb 1** ~ **sb/sth** (informal) used when swearing at sb/sth to show that you are angry: *Damn you! I'm not going to let you bully me. ◊ Damn this machine! Why won't it work?* **2** ~ **sb** (of God) to decide that sb must suffer in hell **3** ~ **sb/sth** to criticize sb/sth very strongly: *The film was damned by the critics for its mindless violence.*
IDM **damn the consequences, expense, etc.** (informal) used to say that you are going to do sth even though you know it may be expensive, have bad results, etc: *Let's celebrate and damn the expense!* **damn sb/sth with faint**

# damnable

**'praise** to praise sb/sth only a little, in order to show that you do not really like them/it **I'll be damned!** (*old-fashioned, informal*) used to show that you are very surprised about sth **I'm damned if …** (*informal*) used to show that you refuse to do sth or do not know sth: *I'm damned if I'll apologize!* ◊ *I'm damned if I know who he is.* ⊃ more at NEAR *adv.*
- **adv.** (*also* **damned**) (*informal*) **1** a swear word that people use to show that they are annoyed with sb/sth: *Don't be so damn silly!* ◊ *What a damn stupid question!* ◊ *You know damn well* (= you know very well) *what I mean!* ◊ *I'll damn well leave tonight* (= I am determined to). **2** a swear word that people use to emphasize what they are saying: *damn good* ◊ *We got out pretty damned fast!* ◊ *I'm damn sure she had no idea.*
  - IDM **damn 'all** (*BrE*) nothing: *I know damn all about computers.*
- **noun**
  - IDM **not care/give a 'damn (about sb/sth)** (*informal*) to not care at all about sb/sth

**dam·na·ble** /ˈdæmnəbl/ *adj.* (*old-fashioned*) bad or annoying ▸ **dam·nably** /-bli/ *adv.*

**dam·na·tion** /dæmˈneɪʃn/ *noun* [U] the state of being in hell; the act of sending sb to hell: *eternal damnation*

**damned** /dæmd/ *adj., adv., noun*
- **adj., adv.** = DAMN IDM see THING
- **noun the damned** [pl.] people who are forced to live in hell after they die

**damned·est** /ˈdæmdɪst/ *noun, adj.* (*informal*)
  - IDM **the damnedest …** (*especially NAmE, informal*) the most surprising …: *It's the damnedest thing I ever saw.* **do/try your 'damnedest (to do sth)** (*informal*) to try as hard as you can (to do sth): *She did her damnedest to get it done on time.*

**damn·ing** /ˈdæmɪŋ/ *adj.* critical of sb/sth; suggesting that sb is guilty: *damning criticism/evidence* ◊ *a damning conclusion/report* ◊ *Her report is expected to deliver a damning indictment of education standards.*

**Damo·cles** /ˈdæməkliːz/ *noun* IDM see SWORD

**damp** /dæmp/ *adj., noun, verb*
- **adj.** (**damp·er**, **damp·est**) slightly wet, often in a way that is unpleasant: *The cottage was cold and damp.* ◊ *It feels damp in here.* ◊ *damp clothes* ◊ *Wipe the surface with a damp cloth.* ⊃ SYNONYMS at WET ▸ **damp·ly** *adv.*: *The blouse clung damply to her skin.*
  - IDM **a damp 'squib** (*BrE, informal*) an event that is disappointing because it is not as exciting or impressive as expected
- **noun** [U] (*BrE*) the state of being slightly wet; areas on a wall, etc. that are slightly wet: *The old house smells of damp.* ◊ *Those marks above the window look like damp to me.*
- **verb** ~ **sth** = DAMPEN: *She damped a towel and wrapped it round his leg.*
  - PHRV **damp sth↔'down 1** to make a fire burn more slowly or stop burning **2** to make an emotion or a feeling less strong

**'damp course** (*also* **'damp-proof course**) *noun* (*BrE*) a layer of material near the bottom of a wall that is used to stop DAMP rising from the ground

**damp·en** /ˈdæmpən/ *verb* **1** (*also less frequent* **damp**) ~ **sth** to make sth slightly wet: *Perspiration dampened her face and neck.* ◊ *He dampened his hair to make it lie flat.* **2** ~ **sth** to make sth such as a feeling or a reaction less strong: *None of the setbacks could dampen his enthusiasm for the project.* ◊ *She wasn't going to let anything dampen her spirits today.*

**damp·er** /ˈdæmpə(r)/ *noun* **1** a piece of metal that can be moved to allow more or less air into a fire so that the fire burns more or less strongly **2** a device in a piano that is used to reduce the level of the sound produced **3** (*BrE also* **dampener**) ~ **(on sth)** (*informal*) a thing that makes sth less pleasant, successful, etc: *Lily isn't letting motherhood put a damper on her social life.*

**damp·ness** /ˈdæmpnəs/ *noun* [U] the fact or state of being slightly wet: *To avoid dampness, air the room regularly.*

**'damp-proof course** *noun* = DAMP COURSE

**dam·sel** /ˈdæmzl/ *noun* (*old use*) a young woman who is not married
  - IDM **a ˌdamsel in diˈstress** (*humorous*) a woman who needs help

**dam·sel·fly** /ˈdæmzlflaɪ/ *noun* (*pl.* **-ies**) an insect with a long thin body and two pairs of wings, similar to a DRAGONFLY but smaller

**dam·son** /ˈdæmzn/ *noun* a small purple fruit, like a PLUM: *a damson tree*

**dan** /dæn/ *noun* **1** one of the levels in KARATE or JUDO **2** a person who has reached a particular level in KARATE or JUDO

**dance** 🔊 A1 /dɑːns; *NAmE* dæns/ *noun, verb*
- **noun 1** 🔊 A1 [C] a series of movements and steps that are usually performed to music; a particular example of these movements and steps: *Do you know any other Latin American dances?* ◊ *The next dance will be a waltz.* ◊ *a dance class/routine* ◊ *Find a partner and practise these new dance steps.*

  > **WORDFINDER** ballet, ballroom, band, choreograph, floor, folk dance, music, partner, step

  **2** 🔊 A1 [U] the art of dancing, especially for entertainment: *an evening of drama, music and dance* ◊ *classical/contemporary/traditional dance* ◊ *a dance company/troupe* ⊃ see also MODERN DANCE **3** 🔊 A2 [C] an act of dancing: *Let's have a dance.* ◊ *He did a little dance of triumph.* **4** 🔊 [C] a social event at which people dance: *We hold a dance every year to raise money for charity.* ⊃ see also BARN DANCE, DINNER DANCE, TEA DANCE **5** 🔊 A2 [C] a piece of music for dancing to: *The band finished with a few slow dances.* IDM see LEAD¹ *v.*, SONG
- **verb 1** 🔊 A1 [I] to move your body to the sound and rhythm of music: *Do you want to dance?* ◊ *He asked me to dance.* ◊ *They stayed up all night singing and dancing.* ◊ **~ to sth** *They danced to the music of a string quartet.* ◊ **~ with sb** *Ruth danced all evening with Richard.* ◊ **~ together** *Ruth and Richard danced together all evening.* **2** 🔊 A2 [T] **~ sth** to do a particular type of dance: *to dance the tango* ◊ *to dance a waltz* **3** [I] to move in a lively way: *The children danced around her.* ◊ *The sun shone on the sea and the waves danced and sparkled.* ◊ *The words danced before her tired eyes.*
  - IDM ˌdance the 'night away to dance for the whole evening or night **dance to sb's 'tune** to do whatever sb tells you to

**'dance band** *noun* a group of musicians who play music at dances

**'dance floor** *noun* an area where people can dance in a hotel, club, etc.

**'dance hall** *noun* a large public room where people pay to go and dance (more common in the past than now) ⊃ compare BALLROOM

**dan·cer** 🔊 A1 /ˈdɑːnsə(r); *NAmE* ˈdæn-/ *noun* a person who dances or whose job is dancing: *She's a fantastic dancer.* ◊ *a ballet dancer* ◊ *He's a principal dancer with the Royal Ballet.* ⊃ see also BELLY DANCER, EXOTIC DANCER, ICE DANCER, MORRIS DANCER, POLE DANCER, TAP DANCER

**dan·cing** 🔊 A1 /ˈdɑːnsɪŋ; *NAmE* ˈdæn-/ *noun* [U] moving your body to music: *There was music and dancing till two in the morning.* ◊ *dancing classes* ⊃ see also BALLROOM DANCING, BELLY DANCING, COUNTRY DANCING, ICE DANCING, LAP DANCING, LINE DANCING, MORRIS DANCING, POLE DANCING, TAP-DANCING

**dan·de·lion** /ˈdændɪlaɪən/ *noun* a small wild plant with a bright yellow flower that becomes a soft white ball of seeds called a **ˈdandelion clock** ⊃ VISUAL VOCAB page V7

**dan·di·fied** /ˈdændɪfaɪd/ *adj.* (*old-fashioned, disapproving*) (of a man) caring a lot about his clothes and appearance

**dan·druff** /ˈdændrʌf; *NAmE* -drəf/ *noun* [U] very small pieces of dead skin, seen as a white dust in a person's hair

**dandy** /ˈdændi/ noun, adj.
- **noun** (pl. **-ies**) (old-fashioned) a man who cares a lot about his clothes and appearance
- **adj.** (especially NAmE, old-fashioned) very good

**dang** /dæŋ/ adj., adv., exclamation (NAmE, informal) a mild swear word, used instead of DAMN: *It's just dang stupid!*

**dan·ger** ❶ A2 /ˈdeɪndʒə(r)/ noun 1 ⓕ A2 [U] the possibility of sth happening that will injure, harm or kill sb, or damage or destroy sth: *Danger! Keep Out!* ◊ *Firefighters face danger every day.* ◊ **in** ~ *Children's lives are in danger every time they cross this road.* ◊ **in grave/mortal danger** ◊ **in ~ of** *sth species in imminent danger of extinction* ◊ **out of ~** *Doctors said she is now out of danger* (= not likely to die). 2 ⓕ A2 [C, U] the possibility of sth bad or unpleasant happening: **~ of sth** *There is no danger of a bush fire now.* ◊ **~ of doing sth** *They reminded residents of the potential dangers of living so near an active volcano.* ◊ **in ~ of doing sth** *The building is in danger of collapsing.* ◊ *How many people are in danger of losing their jobs?* ◊ **~ that** … *There is a danger that the political disorder of the past will return.* ◊ *Most people are aware of the **dangers posed by** online fraudsters.* 3 ⓕ A2 [C] a person or thing that may cause damage, or harm sb: *the hidden dangers in your home* ◊ **~ to sb/sth** *Smoking is a serious danger to health.* ◊ *Police said the man was a danger to the public.* ⊃ see also ENDANGER
- IDM **be on/off the ˈdanger list** (BrE) to be so ill that you may die; to no longer be very ill

**ˈdanger money** (BrE) (US **ˈhazard pay**, **ˈdanger pay**) noun [U] extra pay for doing work that is dangerous

**dan·ger·ous** ❶ A1 /ˈdeɪndʒərəs/ adj. 1 A1 likely to injure or harm sb, or to damage or destroy sth: *The situation is extremely dangerous.* ◊ *potentially dangerous levels of pesticides* ◊ *It's one of the most dangerous places in the world.* ◊ (BrE) *a conviction for **dangerous driving*** ◊ **~for sb** *Poor air quality is particularly dangerous for young children.* ◊ **~for sb to do sth** *It would be dangerous for you to stay here.* ◊ **~to sb/sth** *The evidence is clear that smoking is dangerous to health.* 2 likely to cause problems or have a bad result: *This ruling sets a dangerous precedent.* ◊ **~to do sth** *As always, it's dangerous to generalize.* ▸ **dan·ger·ous·ly** adv.: *She was standing dangerously close to the fire.* ◊ *His father is dangerously ill* (= so ill that he might die). ◊ *Mel enjoys **living dangerously*** (= doing things that involve risk or danger).
- IDM **a ˌdangerous ˈgame** a situation in which sb takes risks, usually hoping to gain an advantage: *Both gangs are playing a very dangerous game.* **ˌdangerous ˈground** a situation or subject that is likely to make sb angry, or that involves risk: *We'd be **on dangerous ground** if we asked about race or religion.*

**dan·gle** /ˈdæŋɡl/ verb 1 [I, T] to hang or move freely; to hold sth so that it hangs or moves freely: **+adv./prep.** *Gold charms dangled from her bracelet.* ◊ *A single light bulb dangled from the ceiling.* ◊ *He sat on the edge with his legs dangling over the side.* ◊ **~sth + adv./prep.** *She dangled her car keys nervously as she spoke.* 2 [T] **~sth (before/in front of sb)** to offer sb sth good in order to persuade them to do sth: *He had a company directorship dangled in front of him.* ▸ **dan·gly** /-ɡli/ adj.: *a pair of dangly earrings*
- IDM **keep/leave sb ˈdangling** (informal) to keep sb in an uncertain state by not telling them sth that they want to know: *She kept him dangling for a week before making her decision.*

**Dan·ish** /ˈdeɪnɪʃ/ adj., noun
- **adj.** from or connected with Denmark
- **noun 1** [U] the language of Denmark **2** [C] = DANISH PASTRY

**ˌDanish ˈpastry** (especially BrE) (also **ˈDan·ish** NAmE, BrE) noun a sweet cake made of light PASTRY, often containing apple, nuts, etc. and/or covered with ICING

**dank** /dæŋk/ adj. (especially of a place) slightly wet, cold and unpleasant: *a dark dank cave* ▸ **dank·ness** noun [U]

**dap·per** /ˈdæpə(r)/ adj. (of a man) small with a neat appearance and nice clothes

---

**dap·pled** /ˈdæpld/ adj. marked with spots of a different colour; with areas of light and shade: *the cool dappled light under the trees*

**dare** ⓕ+ B2 /deə(r); NAmE der/ verb, noun
- **verb 1** ⓕ+ B2 (not usually used in the progressive tenses) to be brave enough to do sth: *She said it as loudly as she dared.* ◊ **~(to) do sth** *He didn't dare (to) say what he thought.* ◊ *They daren't ask for any more money.* ◊ (literary) *She dared not breathe a word of it to anybody.* ◊ *There was something, **dare I say it**, a little unusual about him.* **2** ⓕ+ C1 [T] to persuade sb to do sth dangerous, difficult or embarrassing so that they can show that they are not afraid: **~sb** *Go on! Take it! I dare you.* ◊ **~sb to do sth** *Some of the older boys had dared him to do it.* ⊃ note at MODAL
- IDM **ˈdon't you ˈdare!** (informal) used to tell sb strongly not to do sth: *'I'll tell her about it.' 'Don't you dare!'* ◊ *Don't you dare say anything to anybody.* **how ˈdare you, etc.** used to show that you are angry about sth that sb has done: *How dare you talk to me like that?* ◊ *How dare she imply that I was lying?* **I ˈdare say** (also **I ˈdaresay** especially in BrE) used when you are saying that sth is likely: *I dare say you know about it already.*
- **noun** [usually sing.] something dangerous, difficult or embarrassing that you try to persuade sb to do, to see if they will do it: **for a ~** (BrE) *He climbed onto the roof for a dare.* ◊ **on a ~** (NAmE) *She learned to fly on a dare.*

▼ **GRAMMAR POINT**

**dare**
- **Dare** (sense 1) usually forms negatives and questions like an ordinary verb and is followed by an infinitive with *to*. It is most common in the negative: *I didn't dare to ask.* ◊ *He won't dare to break his promise.* ◊ *You told him? How did you dare?* ◊ *I hardly dared to hope she'd remember me.* In positive sentences a phrase like **not be afraid** is often used instead: *She wasn't afraid* (= she dared) *to tell him the truth.*
- It can also be used like a modal verb especially in present tense negative forms in BrE, and is followed by an infinitive without *to*: *I daren't tell her the truth.*
- In spoken English, the forms of the ordinary verb are often used with an infinitive without *to*: *Don't you dare tell her what I said!* ◊ *I didn't dare look at him.*

**dare·devil** /ˈdeədevl/ NAmE /ˈderd-/ noun a person who enjoys doing dangerous things, in a way that other people may think is stupid: *a reckless daredevil* ▸ **dare·devil** adj. [only before noun]: *Don't try any daredevil stunts.*

**dar·ing** /ˈdeərɪŋ/ NAmE /ˈder-/ adj., noun
- **adj.** brave; willing to do dangerous or unusual things; involving danger or taking risks: *a daring walk in space* ◊ *There are plenty of activities at the resort for the less daring.* ◊ *The gallery was known for putting on daring exhibitions.* ◊ *a daring strapless dress in black silk* ▸ **dar·ing·ly** adv.
- **noun** [U] courage and the quality of being willing to take risks if necessary: *the skill and daring of the mountain climbers*

**dark** ❶ A1 /dɑːk/ NAmE /dɑːrk/ adj., noun
- **adj.** (**dark·er**, **dark·est**)
- • **WITH LITTLE LIGHT 1** ⓕ A1 with no or very little light, especially because it is night: *a dark room/street/forest/night* ◊ *What time does it get dark in summer?* ◊ *It was dark outside and I couldn't see much.* OPP **light** ⊃ see also PITCH-DARK
- • **COLOURS 2** ⓕ A1 not light; closer in shade to black than to white: *dark blue/green/red/brown* ◊ *Darker colours are more practical and don't show stains.* OPP **light**, **pale 3** ⓕ A1 having a colour that is close to black: *a dark suit* ◊ *dark-coloured wood* ◊ *The dark clouds in the sky meant that a storm was coming.*
- • **HAIR/SKIN/EYES 4** ⓕ A1 brown or black in colour: *Sue has long dark hair.* ◊ *Even if you have dark skin, you still need protection from the sun.* **5** ⓕ A1 (of a person) having dark

# the dark ages

hair, eyes, etc: *a dark handsome stranger* **OPP** **fair** ⇒ **WORD-FINDER NOTE** at **BLONDE**
- **MYSTERIOUS** **6** mysterious; hidden and not known about: *There are no dark secrets in our family.*
- **EVIL** **7** evil or frightening: *There was a **darker side** to his nature.* ◊ *the dark forces of the imagination*
- **WITHOUT HOPE** **8** unpleasant and without any hope that sth good will happen: *the darkest days of Fascism* ◊ *The film is a dark vision of the future.*
- **PHONETICS** **9** (of a speech sound) produced with the back part of the tongue close to the back of the mouth. In many ACCENTS of (= ways of pronouncing) English, dark /l/ is used after a vowel, as in *ball*. **OPP** **clear**

**IDM** **a dark ˈhorse** **1** (*BrE*) a person who does not tell other people much about their life, and who surprises other people by having interesting qualities **2** a person taking part in a race, etc. who surprises everyone by winning **keep sth ˈdark** (*BrE*, *informal*) to keep sth secret and not tell people about it

■ **noun**
- **NO LIGHT** **1** 🔊 **A2** **the dark** [sing.] the lack of light in a place, especially because it is night: *Are the children afraid of the dark?* ◊ **in ~** *All the lights went out and we were left in the dark.* ◊ *animals that can see in the dark*
- **COLOUR** **2** 🔊 **A2** [U] an amount of sth that is dark in colour: *patterns of light and dark*

**IDM** **ˌafter/beˈfore dark** after/before the sun goes down and it is night: *Try to get home before dark.* ◊ *Don't go out alone after dark.* **in the ˈdark (about sth)** knowing nothing about sth: *Workers were kept in the dark about the plans to sell the company.* ◊ *She arrived at the meeting as much in the dark as everyone else.* **a ˌshot/stab in the ˈdark** a guess; sth you do without knowing what the result will be: *The figure he came up with was really just a shot in the dark.* ⇒ more at **LEAP** *n*.

**the ˌdark ˈages** *noun* [pl.] **1** **the Dark Ages** the period of European history between the end of the Roman Empire and the end of the 10th century AD **2** (*often humorous*) a period of history or a time when sth was not developed or modern: *Back in the dark ages of computing, in about 1980, they started a software company.*

**ˌdark ˈchocolate** (*BrE also* **ˌplain ˈchocolate**) *noun* [U] dark-brown chocolate with a slightly bitter taste, made without milk being added ⇒ compare **MILK CHOCOLATE**, **WHITE CHOCOLATE**

**darkˑen** /ˈdɑːkən; *NAmE* ˈdɑːrk-/ *verb* **1** [I, T, usually passive] to become dark; to make sth dark: *The sky began to darken as the storm approached.* ◊ **darkened ~ noun** *We walked quickly through the darkened streets.* ◊ *a darkened room* **2** [I, T] to become unhappy or angry; to make sb unhappy or angry: *Her mood darkened at the news.* ◊ *Luke's face darkened* (= he looked angry). ◊ **~ sth** *It was a tragedy that darkened his later life.*

**IDM** **never ˌdarken my ˈdoor again** (*old-fashioned*, *humorous*) used to tell sb never to come to your home again

**ˌdark ˈglasses** *noun* [pl.] glasses that have dark-coloured LENSES ⇒ see also **SUNGLASSES**

**darkˑly** /ˈdɑːkli; *NAmE* ˈdɑːrk-/ *adv.* **1** in a THREATENING or unpleasant way: *He hinted darkly that all was not well.* **2** showing a dark colour: *Her eyes burned darkly.*

**ˌdark ˈmatter** *noun* [U] (*astronomy*) according to some theories, material that exists in space but does not reflect any light

**ˌdark ˈmeat** *noun* [U] meat from the legs of a chicken or other bird that is dark when it has been cooked ⇒ compare **WHITE MEAT**

**darkˑness** 🔊+ **B2** /ˈdɑːknəs; *NAmE* ˈdɑːrk-/ *noun* [U] **1** 🔊+ **B2** the state of being dark, without any light: *After a few minutes our eyes got used to the darkness.* ◊ *The house was plunged into **total darkness** when the electricity was cut off.* ◊ *The sun went down and **darkness fell** (= it became night).* ◊ *There is an extra hour of darkness on winter mornings.* ◊ *Parking is not allowed during the **hours of darkness**.* ◊ *Her face was **in darkness**.* ◊ *They managed to escape **under cover of darkness**.* **2** 🔊+ **B2** the quality or state of

being dark in colour: *It depends on the darkness of your skin.* **3** (*literary*) evil: *the forces of darkness*

**darkˑroom** /ˈdɑːkruːm, -rʊm; *NAmE* ˈdɑːrk-/ *noun* a room that can be made completely dark, where you can take film out of a camera and develop photographs

**ˈdark star** *noun* (*astronomy*) an object in space similar to a star, that produces no light or very little light

**the ˌDark ˈWeb** /ðə ˌdɑːk ˈweb; *NAmE* ˌdɑːrk-/ *noun* [sing.] the part of the **WORLD WIDE WEB** that you can only get access to with special software, allowing users and website owners to remain secret, used especially for criminal activities: *Dealers are also selling drugs through the Dark Web.*

**darˑling** /ˈdɑːlɪŋ; *NAmE* ˈdɑːrl-/ *noun*, *adj.*
■ *noun* **1** (*informal*) a way of addressing sb that you love: *What's the matter, darling?* **2** a person who is very friendly and kind: *You are a darling, Hugo.* **3** **the ~ of sb/sth** a person who is especially liked and very popular: *She is the darling of the newspapers and can do no wrong.*
■ *adj.* [only before noun] (*informal*) much loved; very attractive, special, etc: *My darling daughter.* ◊ *'Darling Henry,' the letter began.*

**darn** /dɑːn; *NAmE* dɑːrn/ *verb*, *noun*, *adj.*, *adv.*
■ *verb* [T, I] **~ (sth)** to repair a hole in a piece of clothing by SEWING STITCHES across the hole: *to darn socks*

**IDM** **ˈdarn it!** (*informal*, *especially NAmE*) used as a mild swear word to show that you are angry or annoyed about sth, to avoid saying 'damn': *Darn it! I've lost my keys!* **I'll be ˈdarned!** (*informal*, *especially NAmE*) used to show that you are surprised about sth
■ *noun* a place on a piece of clothing that has been repaired by darning
■ *adj.* (*also* **darned**) (*informal*) used as a mild swear word, to emphasize sth: *Why don't you switch the darn thing off and listen to me!*
■ *adv.* (*also* **darned**) (*informal*) used as a mild swear word, instead of saying 'damn', to mean 'extremely' or 'very': *You had a darn good try.* ◊ *It's darn cold tonight.*

**darned** /dɑːnd; *NAmE* dɑːrnd/ *adj.*, *adv.* = DARN: *That's a darned good idea!* ▸ **ˌdarnedˈest** *adj.*, *noun*

**dart** /dɑːt; *NAmE* dɑːrt/ *noun*, *verb*
■ *noun* **1** [C] a small pointed object, sometimes with feathers to help it fly, that is shot as a weapon or thrown in the game of darts: *a poisoned dart* **2** **darts** [U] a game in which darts are thrown at a round board marked with numbers for scoring. Darts is often played in British pubs: *a darts match* **3** [sing.] a sudden quick movement **SYN** **dash**: *She made a dart for the door.* **4** [sing.] (*literary*) a sudden feeling of a strong emotion: *Nina felt a sudden dart of panic.* **5** [C] a pointed fold that is SEWN in a piece of clothing to make it fit better
■ *verb* **1** [I] + *adv./prep.* to move suddenly and quickly in a particular direction: *A dog darted across the road in front of me.* ◊ *Her eyes darted around the room, looking for Greg.* **2** [T] to look at sb suddenly and quickly: **~a glance/look (at sb)** *He darted an impatient look at Vicky.* ◊ **~ sb a glance/look** *He darted Vicky an impatient look.*

**dartˑboard** /ˈdɑːtbɔːd; *NAmE* ˈdɑːrtbɔːrd/ *noun* a round board used in the game of darts

**Darˑwinˑism** /ˈdɑːwɪnɪzəm; *NAmE* ˈdɑːrw-/ *noun* [U] (*biology*) the theory that living things EVOLVE by NATURAL SELECTION, developed by Charles Darwin in the 19th century ▸ **Darˑwinˑian** /dɑːˈwɪniən; *NAmE* dɑːrˈw-/ *adj.*: *Darwinian ideas*

**dash** /dæʃ/ *noun*, *verb*
■ *noun*
- **STH DONE QUICKLY** **1** [sing.] **a ~ (for sth)** an act of going somewhere suddenly and/or quickly: *When the doors opened, there was a **mad dash** for seats.* ◊ *a 60-mile dash to safety* ◊ *He jumped off the bus and **made a dash** for the nearest bar.* ◊ *We waited for the police to leave then **made a dash for it** (= left quickly in order to escape).* **2** [sing.] an act of doing sth quickly because you do not have enough time: *a last-minute dash to buy presents*
- **SMALL AMOUNT** **3** [C, usually sing.] **~ (of sth)** a small amount of sth that is added to sth else: *Add a dash of lemon juice.* ◊

*The rug adds a dash of colour to the room.* ➔ compare SPLASH
- **SYMBOL** 4 [C] the mark (—) used to separate parts of a sentence, often instead of a colon or in pairs instead of brackets ➔ compare HYPHEN
- **RACE** 5 [C, usually sing.] (*especially NAmE*) a race in which the people taking part run very fast over a short distance **SYN** sprint: *the 100-meter dash*
- **WAY OF BEHAVING** 6 [U] (*old-fashioned, approving*) a way of behaving that combines style, enthusiasm and confidence
- **PART OF CAR** 7 [C] (*especially NAmE, informal*) = DASHBOARD
**IDM** **cut a ˈdash** (*old-fashioned*) to look attractive in a particular set of clothes, especially in a way that makes other people notice you: *He cut quite a dash in his uniform.*
■ verb
- **GO QUICKLY** 1 [I] to go somewhere very quickly **SYN** rush: *I must dash* (= leave quickly), *I'm late.* ◇ + *adv./prep.* *She dashed off to keep an appointment.* ◇ *He dashed along the platform and jumped on the train.*
- **THROW / BEAT** 2 [T, I] to throw sth, push sb or make sth fall violently onto a hard surface; to beat against a surface: *sth/sb + adv./prep. The boat was dashed repeatedly against the rocks.* ◇ + *adv./prep. The waves were dashing against the harbour wall.*
**IDM** **dash (it)!** | **dash it all!** (*old-fashioned, BrE*) used to show that you are annoyed about sth **dash sb's ˈhopes** to destroy sb's hopes by making what they were hoping for impossible
**PHRV** **dash sth ↔ ˈoff** to write or draw sth very quickly: *I dashed off a note to my brother.*

**dash·board** /ˈdæʃbɔːd; NAmE -bɔːrd/ noun 1 (*also* fa·scia) (*also informal* dash *especially in NAmE*) the part of a car in front of the driver that has instruments and controls in it 2 a diagram that shows important information, typically one that gives an outline of a business: *an executive dashboard showing key performance indicators* 3 a page on a website where you can access information about its various functions

**dash·cam** /ˈdæʃkæm/ noun a camera that is fixed to a car's DASHBOARD (= the part in front of the driver, with the instruments and controls)

**dash·ed** /dæʃt/ adj. [only before noun] (*BrE, old-fashioned, informal*) 1 used as a mild swear word by some people to emphasize sth or to show they are annoyed 2 (of a line on paper or a screen) made of dashes with spaces in between ➔ compare DOTTED LINE

**dash·iki** /dæˈʃiːki/ noun a loose shirt or longer piece of clothing worn by men in West Africa, often made from cloth with brightly coloured patterns

**dash·ing** /ˈdæʃɪŋ/ adj. (*old-fashioned*) 1 (usually of a man) attractive and full of confidence: *a dashing young officer* ◇ *his dashing good looks* 2 (of a thing) attractive and fashionable: *his dashing red waistcoat*

**das·tard·ly** /ˈdæstədli; NAmE -stərd-/ adj. (*old-fashioned*) evil and cruel: *My first part was Captain O'Hagarty, a dastardly villain in a children's play.*

**data** ❶ **A2** ⊙ /ˈdeɪtə; BrE also ˈdɑːtə; NAmE also ˈdætə/ noun (used as a plural noun in technical English, when the singular is datum) 1 ? **A2** [U, pl.] facts or information, especially when examined and used to find out things or to make decisions: *We collected data over a 10-day period.* ◇ *to gather/obtain data* ◇ *~ on/for sth Researchers analysed the data on 2515 patient visits at the Children's Hospital.* ◇ *Our model is based on experimental data.* ◇ *published/unpublished data* ◇ *raw data* (= that has not been analysed) ◇ *Multiple data collection methods were used.* ◇ (*specialist*) *These data show that most cancers are detected as a result of clinical follow-up.* ➔ see also BIG DATA 2 ? **A2** [U] information that is stored by a computer: *All this data is stored on hundreds of servers in San Francisco.* ◇ *data storage/transfer* ➔ **WORDFINDER NOTE** at FILE **IDM** see MINE *n.*

**data·bank** /ˈdeɪtəbæŋk; BrE also ˈdɑːt-; NAmE also ˈdæt-/ noun a large amount of data on a particular subject that is stored in a computer

**data·base** ? + **B2** /ˈdeɪtəbeɪs; BrE also ˈdɑːt-; NAmE also ˈdæt-/ noun an organized set of data that is stored in a computer and can be looked at and used in various ways ➔ see also RELATIONAL DATABASE

ˌdatabase ˈmanagement system noun (*abbr.* DBMS) (*computing*) a system for organizing and managing a large amount of data

**dat·able** (*also* date·able) /ˈdeɪtəbl/ adj. 1 that can be dated to a particular time: *pottery that is datable to the second century* 2 (*informal*) (of a person) attractive in a romantic way; available for a date

ˈdata capture noun [U] the action or process of collecting data, especially using computers

ˈdata centre (*US* ˈdata center) (*also* ˈserver farm) noun a large network of computer SERVERS, typically used by organizations for storing, processing or sharing large amounts of data

ˈdata-driven adj. based on or decided by collecting and analysing data: *We use a data-driven approach.*

ˈdata mining noun [U] (*computing*) looking at large amounts of information that has been collected on a computer and using it to provide new information

ˌdata ˈprocessing noun [U] (*computing*) a series of actions that a computer performs on data to produce an OUTPUT (= results)

ˈdata projector (*also* projector) noun a piece of equipment that takes data and images from a computer and shows them on a wall or large screen ➔ compare OVERHEAD PROJECTOR, SLIDE PROJECTOR

ˌdata proˈtection noun [U] legal controls that keep information stored on computers private and that limit who can read it or use it: *data protection legislation*

ˈdata set noun (*computing*) a collection of data that is treated as a single unit by a computer

ˈdata warehouse noun a large amount of data that comes from different parts of a business and that is stored together ▸ ˌdata ˈwarehousing noun [U]

**date** ❶ **A1** /deɪt/ noun, verb
■ noun
- **PARTICULAR DAY/YEAR** 1 ? **A1** [C] a particular day of the month, sometimes in a particular year, given in numbers and words: *'What's the date today?' 'The 10th.'* ◇ *Write today's date at the top of the page.* ◇ *They haven't set a date for the wedding yet.* ◇ *We need to fix a date for the next meeting.* ◇ *I can't come on that date.* ◇ *Please give your name, address and date of birth.* ◇ (*especially NAmE*) *name, address and birth date* ◇ *There's no word yet on a UK release date for the film.* ➔ see also BEST-BEFORE DATE, CLOSING DATE, DUE DATE, EXPIRY DATE, EXPIRATION DATE, PULL DATE, RAIN DATE, SELL-BY DATE 2 ? **A1** a particular day or year when a particular event happened or will happen: *1066 is the most famous date in English history.* ◇ *the biggest date in the country music calendar*
- **PAST TIME / FUTURE** 3 ? **B1** [sing., U] a time in the past or future that is not a particular day: *The details can be added at a later date.* ◇ *The work will be carried out at a future date.* ◇ *This was an important trade route from an early date.*
- **ARRANGEMENT TO MEET** 4 ? **A2** [C] an arrangement to meet sb at a particular time: *Call me next week and we'll try and make a date.* ◇ *Next Friday? Fine—it's a date!* ➔ see also PLAY DATE
- **ROMANTIC MEETING** 5 ? **A2** [C] a meeting that you have arranged with a boyfriend or girlfriend or with sb who might become a boyfriend or girlfriend: *a ~ with sb I've got a date with Lucy tomorrow night* ◇ *on a ~ We agreed to go out on a date.* ◇ *Paul's not coming. He's got a hot date* (= an exciting one). ➔ see also BLIND DATE, DOUBLE DATE 6 [C] a boyfriend or girlfriend with whom you have arranged a date: *My date is meeting me at seven.* ➔ **WORDFINDER NOTE** at LOVE
- **FRUIT** 7 [C] a sweet sticky brown fruit that grows on a tree called a ˈdate palm, common in North Africa and West Asia ➔ **VISUAL VOCAB** page V4

# dateable

**IDM** **to ˈdate** until now: *To date, we have received over 200 replies.* ◊ *The exhibition contains some of his best work to date.* ⇨ see also OUT OF DATE, UP TO DATE
- verb
- **WRITE DATE 1** 🔑 **B2** [T, often passive] ~ sth to write or print the date on sth: *Thank you for your letter dated 24th March.* ⇨ see also POST-DATE
- **FIND AGE 2** 🔑 **B2** [T, often passive] to say when sth old existed or was made: *~ sth It has not yet been possible to date the paintings accurately.* ◊ *~ sth at/to sth The skeleton has been dated at about 2000 BC.* ⇨ see also POST-DATE, PREDATE
- **OF CLOTHES/WORDS 3** [I] to become old-fashioned: *She designs classic clothes that do not date.*
- **PERSON 4** [T] ~ sb if sth **dates** you, it shows that you are fairly old or older than the people you are with: *I was at the Woodstock festival—that dates me, doesn't it?*
- **HAVE RELATIONSHIP 5** [T, I] ~ **(sb)** to have a romantic relationship with sb: *She's been dating Ron for several months.* ⇨ see also DOUBLE-DATE

**PHRV** **ˌdate ˈback (to …)** | **ˈdate from …** | **ˈdate to …** to have existed since a particular time in the past or for the length of time mentioned: *The college dates back to medieval times.* ◊ *The custom dates back hundreds of years.* ◊ *a law dating from the 17th century*

**ˈdate·able** = DATABLE

**dated** /ˈdeɪtɪd/ *adj.* old-fashioned; belonging to a time in the past: *These ideas seem a bit dated now.* ⇨ compare UNDATED

**ˈDate Line** *noun* = INTERNATIONAL DATE LINE

**ˈdate rape** *noun* [U, C] the crime of RAPING sb, committed by a person he or she has gone out with on a DATE

**ˈdat·ing agency** (*also* **ˈdat·ing service**) *noun* a service that arranges meetings between single people who want to begin a romantic relationship: *The couple met through an online dating agency.*

**dat·ive** /ˈdeɪtɪv/ *noun* (*grammar*) (in some languages) the form of a noun, a pronoun or an adjective when it is the INDIRECT OBJECT of a verb or is connected with the INDIRECT OBJECT: *In the sentence, 'I sent her a postcard', the word 'her' is in the dative.* ⇨ compare ACCUSATIVE, GENITIVE, INSTRUMENTAL (2), LOCATIVE, NOMINATIVE, VOCATIVE
▸ **dat·ive** *adj.*: *the dative case*

**datum** /ˈdeɪtəm/ *noun* (*pl.* **data**) (*specialist*) a fact or piece of information ⇨ see also DATA

**daub** /dɔːb/ *verb, noun*
- verb to spread a substance such as paint, mud, etc. thickly and/or carelessly onto sth: *~ A with B The walls of the building were daubed with red paint.* ◊ *~ B on A They used spray paint to daub slogans on the walls.*
- noun **1** [U] a mixture of CLAY, etc. that was used in the past for making walls: *walls made of wattle and daub* **2** [C] a small amount of a substance such as paint that has been spread carelessly: *a daub of lipstick* **3** [C] a badly painted picture

**daugh·ter** 🔑 **A1** /ˈdɔːtə(r)/ *noun* **1** 🔑 **A1** a person's female child: *We have two sons and a daughter.* ◊ *a baby/teenage/grown-up daughter* ◊ *She's the eldest daughter of an Oxford professor.* ◊ *our younger/youngest daughter* ⇨ see also GOD-DAUGHTER, GRANDDAUGHTER, STEPDAUGHTER **2** (*literary*) a woman who belongs to a particular place or country, etc: *one of the town's most famous daughters*

**ˈdaughter-in-law** *noun* (*pl.* **daughters-in-law**) the wife of your son or daughter ⇨ compare SON-IN-LAW

**daunt** /dɔːnt/ *verb* ~ sb to make sb feel nervous and less confident about doing sth **SYN** intimidate: *She was a brave woman but she felt daunted by the task ahead.*
▸ **daunt·ing** *adj.* **SYN** intimidating: *She has the daunting task of cooking for 20 people every day.* ◊ *Starting a new job can be a daunting prospect.* **daunt·ing·ly** *adv.*

**daunt·less** /ˈdɔːntləs/ *adj.* (*literary*) not easily frightened or stopped from doing sth difficult **SYN** resolute

**dau·phin** /ˈdəʊfæ̃, ˈdəʊfæn/ *noun* (*old use*) the oldest son of the king of France

**David and Goliath** /ˌdeɪvɪd ən ɡəˈlaɪəθ/ *adj.* used to describe a situation in which a small or weak person or organization tries to defeat another much larger or stronger opponent: *The match looks like a David and Goliath contest.* **ORIGIN** From the Bible story in which Goliath, a giant, is killed by the boy David with a stone.

**daw·dle** /ˈdɔːdl/ *verb* [I] to take a long time to do sth or go somewhere: *Stop dawdling! We're going to be late!* ◊ *+ adv./prep. They dawdled along by the river, laughing and talking.*

**dawn** 🔑+ **C1** /dɔːn/ *noun, verb*
- noun **1** 🔑+ **C1** [U, sing.] the time of day when light first appears **SYN** daybreak: *at~ They start work at dawn.* ◊ *It's almost dawn.* ◊ *We arrived in Sydney as dawn broke* (= as the first light could be seen). ◊ *I woke up just before dawn.* ◊ *summer's early dawns* ◊ *He works from dawn till dusk* (= from morning till night). ⇨ compare DUSK, SUNRISE **2** 🔑+ **C1** [sing.] ~ **(of sth)** the beginning or first signs of sth: *the dawn of civilization/time/history* ◊ *Peace marked a new dawn in the country's history.* ⇨ see also FALSE DAWN **IDM** see BREAK *n.*, CRACK *n.*
- verb **1** [I] (of a day or a period of time) to begin: *The following morning dawned bright and warm.* ◊ *A new technological age had dawned.* **2** [I] to become obvious or easy to understand: *Slowly the awful truth dawned.* **IDM** see LIGHT *n.*

**PHRV** **ˈdawn on sb** [no passive] if sth **dawns on you**, you begin to realize it for the first time: *it dawns on sb that … Suddenly it dawned on me that they couldn't possibly have met before.*

**the ˌdawn ˈchorus** *noun* [sing.] the sound of birds singing very early in the morning

**day** 🔑 **A1** /deɪ/ *noun* **1** 🔑 **A1** [C] a period of 24 hours: *'What day is it today?' 'Monday.'* ◊ *I go to the gym every day.* ◊ *We spent five days in Paris.* ◊ *I saw Tom three days ago.* ◊ *We're going away in a few days.* ◊ *The situation has been deteriorating for the past few days.* ◊ *On that day Rosa Parks did something that changed history.* ◊ *I saw her again the next day.* ◊ *They left the day before yesterday* (= two days ago). ◊ *We're meeting the day after tomorrow* (= in two days). ◊ *New Year's Day* ◊ *a/per~ Take the medicine three times a day.* ◊ *The helpline is open 24 hours a day.* **2** 🔑 **A1** [C, U] the time between when it becomes light in the morning and when it becomes dark in the evening: *What a beautiful day!* ◊ *The sun was shining all day.* ◊ *I could sit and watch the river all day long.* ◊ *We spent the day gardening.* ◊ *during the~ He works at night and sleeps during the day.* ◊ *by~ Nocturnal animals sleep by day and hunt by night.* ◊ *on a …~ On a sunny day in June …* **3** 🔑 **A1** [C, usually sing.] the hours of the day when you are active, working, etc., not sleeping: *a seven-hour working day* ◊ (*especially NAmE*) *Have a nice day!* ◊ *Did you have a good day?* ◊ *Our waiter seemed to be having a bad day.* ◊ *It's been a long day* (= I've been very busy). ◊ *She didn't do a full day's work.* ◊ *I took a half day off yesterday.* ⇨ see also SCHOOL DAY (2), WORKDAY **4** 🔑 **B1** [C, usually pl.] a particular period of time or history: *in sb's~ in Queen Victoria's day* ◊ *in the days of sth in the days of the industrial revolution* ◊ *back in the early days of computers* ◊ *in those days He was the biggest star in Hollywood in those days.* ◊ (*informal*) *in the old days* (= in the past) ⇨ see also GLORY DAYS, HEYDAY, NOWADAYS, PRESENT DAY ⇨ **HOMOPHONES** at DAZE **HELP** There are many other compounds ending in **day**. You will find them at their place in the alphabet. **5** **days** [pl.] (usually in compounds) a particular period in sb's life or career: *I have many happy memories from my student days.* ◊ *She cared for him for the rest of his days* (= the rest of his life).

**IDM** **ˌall in a ˈday's ˈwork** part of your normal working life and not unusual **ˌany ˈday (ˈnow)** | **ˌany ˈtime ˈnow** (*informal*) very soon: *The letter should arrive any day now.* **ˌcarry/win the ˈday** (*formal*) to be successful against sb/sth: *Despite strong opposition, the ruling party carried the day.* **ˌday after ˈday** each day repeatedly (used especially when sth is boring or annoying): *She hates doing the same work day after day.* **ˌday by ˈday** all the time; a little at a time and gradually: *Day by day his condition improved.* **ˌday in, ˌday**

**'out** every day for a long period of time **a day of 'reckoning** the time when sb will have to deal with the result of sth that they have done wrong, or be punished for sth bad that they have done **sb's/sth's days are 'numbered** a person or thing will not continue to live, exist or be successful for much longer: *His days as leader of the party are numbered.* **from day 'one** (*informal*) from the beginning: *It's never worked from day one.* **from day to 'day 1** with no thoughts or plans for the future: *They live from day to day, looking after their sick daughter.* **2** if a situation changes **from day to day**, it changes often: *A baby's need for food can vary from day to day.* **from ,one day to the 'next** if a situation changes **from one day to the next**, it is uncertain and not likely to stay the same each day: *I never know what to expect from one day to the next.* **have had your 'day** to no longer be successful, powerful, etc: *She's had her day as a supermodel.* **have seen/known better 'days** (*humorous*) to be in poor condition: *Our car has seen better days!* **if he's, she's, etc. a 'day** (*informal*) (used when talking about sb's age) at least: *He must be 70 if he's a day!* **in sb's 'day 1** during the part of sb's life when they were most successful, famous, etc: *She was a great dancer in her day.* **2** when sb was young: *In my day, there were plenty of jobs when you left school.* **in 'this day and age** now, in the modern world **it's not sb's 'day** (*informal*) used when several bad or unpleasant things happen on the same day: *My car broke down and then I locked myself out — it's just not my day!* **make sb's 'day** to make sb feel very happy on a particular day: *The phone call from Mike really made my day.* **make a day/night of it** (*informal*) to make a particular activity that you enjoy last for a whole day/evening instead of only part of it **not have all 'day** to not have much time: *Come on! We don't have all day!* **of sb's 'day** during a particular period of time when sb lived: *the best player of his day ◊ Bessie Smith was the Madonna of her day.* **of the 'day 1** of the present time: *the political issues of the day* **2** that is served on a particular day in a restaurant: *soup of the day* **,one 'day** [A1] at some time in the future, or on a particular day in the past: *One day, I want to leave the city and move to the country. ◊ One day, he walked out of the house with a small bag and never came back.* **,one of these 'days** before a long time has passed: *One of these days you'll come back and ask me to forgive you.* **,one of those 'days** (*informal*) a day when there are a lot of mistakes and a lot of things go wrong: *It's been one of those days!* **'some day** at an unknown time in the future: *Some day I'll be famous.* **,take it/things one day at a 'time** (*informal*) to not think about what will happen in the future: *I don't know if he'll get better. We're just taking it one day at a time.* **'that'll be the day** (*informal, ironic*) used when you are saying that sth is very unlikely to happen: *Paul? Apologize? That'll be the day!* **'these days** [A2] (*informal*) used to talk about the present, especially when you are comparing it with the past: *These days kids grow up so quickly.* **'those were the days** (*informal*) used to suggest that a time in the past was happier or better than now **to the 'day** exactly: *It's been three years to the day since we met.* **to this 'day** even now, when a lot of time has passed: *To this day, I still don't understand why he did it.* ⊃ more at BACK *adv.*, BORN v., BREAK *n.*, CALL v., CLEAR *adj.*, COLD *adj.*, DEED, DOG *n.*, EARLY *adj.*, END *n.*, END v., EVIL *adj.*, FORTH, GIVE v., LATE *adv.*, LIVE¹, LIVELONG, NICE, NIGHT, NINE, OLD, OLDEN, ORDER *n.*, OTHER, PASS v., PLAIN *adj.*, RAINY, ROME, SALAD, SAVE v., TIME *n.*

**'day·break** /'deɪbreɪk/ *noun* [U] the time of day when light first appears ⓈⓎⓃ **dawn**: *We left before daybreak.*

**'day care** *noun* [U] care for young children, or for old or sick people, away from home, during the day: *Day care is provided by the company she works for.*

**'day care center** (*NAmE*) (*BrE* **'day nursery, nursery**) *noun* a place where young children are cared for while their parents are at work ⊃ compare NURSERY SCHOOL ⊃ compare DAY CENTRE

**'day centre** (*also* **'day care centre**) (*both BrE*) (*US* **'day center**) *noun* a place that provides care during the day for people who cannot be fully independent ⊃ compare DAY CARE CENTER

**'day·dream** /'deɪdriːm/ *noun* pleasant thoughts that make you forget about the present: *She stared out of the window, lost in a daydream.* ▶ **day·dream** *verb* [I]: **~(about sb/sth)** *I would spend hours daydreaming about a house of my own.*

**Day-Glo™** /'deɪ gləʊ/ *adj.* having a very bright orange, yellow, green or pink colour: *Day-Glo cycling shorts*

**'day job** *noun* [sing.] the paid work that sb normally does ⒾⒹⓂ **don't give up the 'day job** (*informal, humorous*) used to tell sb that they should continue doing what they are used to, rather than trying sth new that they are likely to fail at: *So you want to be a writer? Well my advice is, don't give up the day job.*

**'day·light** /'deɪlaɪt/ *noun* [U] the light that comes from the sun during the day: *They emerged from the church into the bright daylight. ◊ The street looks very different* **in daylight**. *◊ They left* **before daylight** (= before the sun had risen). ⊃ **WORDFINDER NOTE** at SUN
ⒾⒹⓂ **,daylight 'robbery** (*also* **,highway 'robbery** especially in *NAmE*) (*informal*) the fact of sb charging too much money for sth: *You wouldn't believe some of the prices they charge; it's daylight robbery.* ⊃ more at BROAD *adj.*

**'day·lights** /'deɪlaɪts/ *noun* [pl.]
ⒾⒹⓂ **beat/knock the (living) 'daylights out of sb** (*informal*) to hit sb very hard several times and hurt them very much **frighten/scare the (living) 'daylights out of sb** (*informal*) to frighten sb very much

**,daylight 'saving time** (*abbr.* DST) (*also* **'daylight time**) (*both NAmE*) (*BrE* **'summer time**) *noun* [U] the period during which in some countries the clocks are put forward one hour, so that it is light for an extra hour in the evening

**'day-long** *adj.* [only before noun] lasting for a whole day: *a day-long meeting*

**'day nursery** (*also* **nursery**) (*both BrE*) (*NAmE* **'day care center**) *noun* a place where young children are cared for while their parents are at work ⊃ compare CRÈCHE, NURSERY SCHOOL

**the Day of A'tonement** /ðə ,deɪ əv əˈtəʊnmənt/ *noun* [sing.] = YOM KIPPUR

**'day off** *noun* (*pl.* **days off**) a day on which you do not have to work: *Most weeks, Sunday is my only day off.*

**the ,Day of 'Judgement** (*also* **the Day of Judgment** especially in *NAmE*) *noun* [sing.] = JUDGEMENT DAY

**,day 'out** *noun* (*pl.* **days out**) a trip or visit somewhere for a day: *We had a day out in the country.* ⊃ **SYNONYMS** at TRIP

**,day re'lease** *noun* (*BrE*) [U] a system of allowing employees days off work for education: *time off for study on day release ◊ a day release course*

**,day re'turn** *noun* (*BrE*) a ticket at a reduced price for a journey to a place and back again on the same day

**'day room** *noun* a room in a hospital or other institution where people can sit, relax, watch television, etc. during the day

**'day school** *noun* **1** (*old-fashioned*) a private school with students who live at home and only go to school during the day ⊃ compare BOARDING SCHOOL **2** (*BrE*) a course of education lasting one day, at which a particular topic is discussed: *a day school at Leeds University on women in Victorian times*

**'day·time** /'deɪtaɪm/ *noun* [U] the period during the day between the time when it gets light and the time when it gets dark: **in (the)** ~ *You don't often see this bird in (the) daytime. ◊* **during (the)** ~ *The park is open during (the) daytime. ◊ Daytime temperatures never fell below 30°C. ◊ Please give your name and daytime phone number.*

**,day-to-'day** *adj.* [only before noun] **1** planning for only one day at a time: *I have organized the cleaning* **on a day-to-day basis**, *until our usual cleaner returns.* **2** involving the usual events or tasks of each day: *She has been looking after the* **day-to-day running** *of the school.*

**'day trading** *noun* [U] (*finance*) buying and selling shares very quickly on the same day using the internet in order to make a profit from small price changes ▶ **'day trader** *noun*

# day trip 394

**day trip** noun a trip or visit completed in one day: *a day trip to France* ▶ **ˈday tripper** noun (BrE)

**ˈday·wear** /ˈdeɪweə(r); NAmE -wer/ noun [U] clothes for wearing every day, for example for working or shopping, not for special occasions

**daze** /deɪz/ noun
IDM **in a daze** in a confused state: *I've been in a complete daze since hearing the news.*

▼ **HOMOPHONES**

**days • daze** /deɪz/
- **days** noun (plural of DAY): *His glory days in 1970s Hollywood felt long behind him.*
- **daze** noun: *The day had passed in a dreamy daze.*

**dazed** /deɪzd/ adj. unable to think clearly, especially because of a shock or because you have been hit on the head: *Survivors waited for the rescue boats, dazed and frightened.* ◇ *Jimmy was still dazed by the blow to his head.*

**daz·zle** /ˈdæzl/ verb, noun
■ verb [often passive] **1** [T, I] ~ (sb) if a strong light **dazzles** you, it is so bright that you cannot see for a short time SYN **blind**: *He was momentarily dazzled by the strong sunlight.* **2** [T] ~ **sb** to impress sb a lot with your beauty, skill, etc: *He was dazzled by the warmth of her smile.* ▶ **daz·zling** /ˈdæzlɪŋ/ adj. SYN **brilliant**: *a dazzling display of oriental dance* **daz·zlingly** adv.: *She was dazzlingly beautiful.*
■ noun [U, sing.] **1** the quality that bright light has that stops you from seeing clearly **2** a thing or quality that impresses you but may prevent you from understanding or thinking clearly

**d.b.a.** /ˌdiː biː ˈeɪ/ abbr. (US) doing business as: *Philip Smith, d.b.a. Phil's Signs*

**DBMS** /ˌdiː biː em ˈes/ abbr. DATABASE MANAGEMENT SYSTEM

**DBS** /ˌdiː biː ˈes/ abbr. (in the UK) Disclosure and Barring Service (called the Criminal Records Bureau in the past), a government body that checks to see whether people have committed crimes that make them unsuitable for certain jobs, e.g. working with children, or to adopt children: *a DBS check*

**DC** /ˌdiː ˈsiː/ abbr. **1** DIRECT CURRENT ⊃ compare ALTERNATING CURRENT **2** District of Columbia in the US: *Washington, DC*

**DD** /ˌdiː ˈdiː/ abbr. (informal) (especially in text messages, on SOCIAL MEDIA, etc.) darling daughter: *My DD is nearly a year old now.*

**ˈD-Day** noun [U] a date on which sth important is expected to happen ORIGIN From the name given to 6 June 1944, the day on which the British, US and other armies landed on the beaches of northern France in the Second World War.

**DDT** /ˌdiː diː ˈtiː/ noun [U] a chemical used, especially in the past, for killing insects that harm crops

**de-** /diː/ prefix (in verbs and related nouns, adjectives and adverbs) **1** the opposite of: *decentralization* **2** removing sth: *to defrost the refrigerator* (= remove layers of ice from it)

**dea·con** /ˈdiːkən/ noun **1** (in the Roman Catholic, Anglican and Orthodox Churches) a religious leader just below the rank of a priest **2** (in some Nonconformist Churches) a person who is not a member of the CLERGY, but who helps a minister with church business affairs

**dea·con·ess** /ˌdiːkəˈnes; NAmE ˈdiːkənəs/ noun (in some Christian Churches) a woman who has duties that are similar to those of a deacon

**de·act·iv·ate** /diːˈæktɪveɪt/ verb ~ **sth** to make sth such as a device or chemical process stop working: *Do you know how to deactivate the alarm?*

**dead** 🌐 A2 /ded/ adj., noun, adv.
■ adj.
• NOT ALIVE **1** 🅰 A2 no longer alive: *My mother's dead; she died in 2017.* ◇ *a dead person/animal* ◇ *dead leaves/wood/* skin ◇ *Catherine's **dead body** lay peacefully on the bed.* ◇ *He was **shot dead** by a gunman outside his home.* ◇ *A high school shooting has **left six students dead**.* ◇ *The poor child looks **more dead than alive**.* ◇ (informal) *He **dropped dead** (= died suddenly) last week.*
• MACHINE **2** 🅰 A2 (of machines or equipment) not working because of a lack of power: *a dead battery* ◇ *Suddenly the phone went dead.*
• IDEA/BELIEF/PLAN **3** [not before noun] no longer believed in or aimed for: *Many believe the peace plan is dead.* ◇ *Unfortunately racism is not yet dead.* ◇ *Though the idea may be dead, it is far from being buried* (= people still talk about it, even though there is nothing new to say). ⊃ see also STONE DEAD
• NOT USED **4** belonging to the past; no longer practised or fashionable: *Is the Western a dead art form?* ◇ *a dead language* (= one that is no longer spoken, for example Latin)
• FINISHED **5** (informal) finished; not able to be used any more: *dead matches* ◇ *There were two dead bottles of wine on the table.*
• PLACE **6** (informal, disapproving) very quiet, without activity or interest: *There were no theatres, no cinemas, no coffee bars. It was **dead as anything**.*
• BUSINESS **7** (informal, disapproving) without activity; with nobody buying or selling anything: *'The market is absolutely dead this morning,' said one foreign exchange trader.* ◇ *Winter is traditionally the dead season for the housing market.*
• TIRED **8** [not usually before noun] (informal) extremely tired; not well: *half dead with cold and hunger* ◇ *She felt dead on her feet and didn't have the energy to question them further.*
• WITHOUT FEELING **9** [not before noun] (of a part of the body) unable to feel because of cold, etc. SYN **numb**: *My left arm had gone dead.* **10** ~ **to sth** unable to feel or understand emotions SYN **insensitive**: *He was dead to all feelings of pity.* **11** (especially of sb's voice, eyes or face) showing no emotion SYN **expressionless**: *She said, 'I'm sorry, too,' in a quiet, dead voice.* ◇ *His usually dead grey eyes were sparkling.*
• COMPLETE/EXACT **12** [only before noun] complete or exact: *a dead silence/calm* ◇ *the dead centre of the target* ◇ *The car gave a sudden jerk and came to a dead stop.* ◇ (informal) *Her face was a dead giveaway* (= made it very obvious) *that something was going on.* ◇ (BrE) *This horse is a dead cert for* (= will certainly win) *the race tomorrow.*
• NEVER ALIVE **13** never having been alive: *dead matter* (= for example rock) ◇ *a dead planet* (= one with no life on it)
• IN SPORT **14** (of the ball) outside the playing area
IDM **be dead and ˈgone** (informal) to be dead: *You'll be sorry you said that when I'm dead and gone.* **be a dead ˈringer for sb** (informal) to look very like sb: *She's a dead ringer for a girl I used to know.* **(as) dead as a/the ˈdodo** (BrE, informal) completely dead; no longer interesting or relevant **a dead ˈduck** (informal) a plan, an event, etc. that has failed or is certain to fail and that is therefore not worth discussing **the dead hand of sth** an influence that controls or limits sth: *We need to free business from the dead hand of bureaucracy.* **dead in the ˈwater** a person or plan that is **dead in the water** has failed and has little hope of succeeding in the future: *His leadership campaign is dead in the water.* **dead ˈmeat** (informal) in serious trouble: *If anyone finds out, you're dead meat.* **dead on arˈrival** (abbr. **DOA**) **1** (of an accident victim or other patient) already dead when arriving at a hospital: *She was pronounced dead on arrival.* **2** (NAmE, informal) very unlikely to be successful; not working when it is delivered: *The bill was dead on arrival in the Senate.* ◇ *The software was DOA.* **dead to the ˈworld** in a deep sleep **flog a dead ˈhorse** (NAmE also **beat a dead ˈhorse**) (informal) to waste your effort by trying to do sth that is no longer possible **over ˌmy dead ˈbody** (informal) used to show you are strongly opposed to sth: *She moves into our home over my dead body.* **sb wouldn't be ˌseen/ˌcaught ˈdead ...** (informal) used to say that you would not like to wear particular clothes, or to be in a particular situation: *She wouldn't be seen dead in a hat.* ◇ *He wouldn't be caught dead going to a club with his mother.* ⊃ more at KNOCK v.
■ noun **the dead 1** [pl.] people who have died: *The dead and wounded in that one attack amounted to 6000.* ⊃ see also

**LIVING DEAD 2** [sing.] the state of being dead: *Christians believe that God raised Jesus from the dead.* ◊ *(figurative) In nine years he has brought his party back from the dead almost to the brink of power.*

**IDM** **in the ˌdead of ˈnight** (*BrE also* **at ˌdead of ˈnight**) in the quietest part of the night: *I crept out of bed in the dead of night and sneaked downstairs.* **in the ˌdead of ˈwinter** in the coldest part of winter

■ *adv.* (*informal*)
• **COMPLETELY 1** completely; exactly: *You're dead right!* ◊ (*BrE*) *a dead straight road* ◊ (*BrE*) *The train was dead on time.* ◊ *He's dead against the idea.* ◊ *The sight made him* **stop dead in his tracks** (= stop suddenly). ◊ *She's* **dead set on getting** (= determined to get) *this new job.*
• **VERY 2** (*BrE, informal*) very; extremely: *The instructions are dead easy to follow.* ◊ *You were dead lucky to get that job.* ◊ *I was dead scared.*

**IDM** **cut sb ˈdead** (*BrE*) to pretend not to have seen sb; to refuse to say hello to sb: *She saw me, recognized me and cut me dead.* ⊃ more at RIGHT *n*.

**ˌdead·ˈbeat** /ˈdedbiːt/ *noun* (*informal*) **1** (*especially NAmE*) a lazy person; a person with no job and no money, who is not part of normal society **2** (*NAmE*) a person or company that tries to avoid paying their debts **3** (*also* **ˌdeadbeat ˈdad**) (*NAmE*) a father who does not live with his children and does not pay their mother any money to take care of them

**ˌdead ˈbeat** (*also* **beat**) *adj.* [not before noun] (*informal*) very tired: *You look dead beat.*

**ˈdead·bolt** /ˈdedbəʊlt/ (*especially NAmE*) (*BrE usually* **ˌdead-ˈlock**) *noun* a type of lock on a door that needs a key to open or close it

**dead·en** /ˈdedn/ *verb* ~ **sth** to make sth such as a sound, a feeling, etc. less strong **SYN** **dull**: *He was given drugs to deaden the pain.* ▶ **ˈdead·en·ing** /ˈdednɪŋ/ *adj.* [only before noun]: *the deadening effect of alcohol on your reactions*

**ˌdead ˈend** *noun* **1** a road, passage, etc. that is closed at one end: *The first street we tried turned out to be a dead end.* **2** a point at which you can make no further progress in what you are doing: *We had come to a dead end in our research.* ◊ *He's in a* **dead-end job** *in the local factory* (= one with low wages and no hope of promotion). ◊ *These negotiations are a* **dead-end street** (= they have reached a point where no further progress is possible).

**ˌdead ˈheat** *noun* **1** (*especially BrE*) a result in a race when two of those taking part finish at exactly the same time **2** (*NAmE*) a situation during a race or competition, etc. when two or more people are at the same level: *The two candidates are* **in a dead heat** *in the polls.*

**ˌdead ˈletter** *noun* **1** [usually sing.] a law or an agreement that still exists but that is ignored **2** (*especially NAmE*) a letter that cannot be delivered to an address or to the person who sent it

**dead·line** /ˈdedlaɪn/ *noun* a point in time by which sth must be done: *I prefer to* **work to a deadline**. ◊ ~ **for sth** *The deadline for applications is 30 April.*

**dead·lock** /ˈdedlɒk/; *NAmE* -lɑːk/ *noun* **1** [sing., U] a complete failure to reach agreement or settle an argument **SYN** **stalemate**: *European agriculture ministers failed to* **break the deadlock** *over farm subsidies.* ◊ (*BrE*) *The strike appeared to have reached deadlock.* ◊ (*NAmE, BrE*) *The strike has reached a deadlock.* **2** (*BrE*) (*also* **ˌdead·ˈbolt** *NAmE, BrE*) [C] a type of lock on a door that needs a key to open or close it ▶ **dead·locked** *adj.* [not before noun]: *Despite months of discussion the negotiations remained deadlocked.*

**ˌdead ˈloss** *noun* [usually sing.] (*BrE, informal*) a person or thing that is not helpful or useful: *He may be a very talented designer, but as a manager he's a dead loss.*

**dead·ly** /ˈdedli/ *adj., adv.*
■ *adj.* (**dead·li·er, dead·li·est**) **HELP** More **deadly** and **deadliest** are the usual forms. You can also use **most deadly**. **1** causing or likely to cause death **SYN** **lethal**: *a deadly weapon/disease* ◊ *deadly poison* ◊ *The cobra is one of the world's deadliest snakes.* ◊ *The terrorists have chosen to play a deadly game with the civilian population.* **2** [only before noun] extreme; complete: *I'm* **in deadly earn-**

395

**est.** ◊ *We sat* **in deadly silence**. ◊ *They are deadly enemies* (= are full of hatred for each other). **3** extremely effective, so that no defence is possible: *His aim is deadly* (= so accurate that he can kill easily). ◊ *It was the deadly striker's 11th goal of the season.* **4** (*informal*) very boring: *The lecture was absolutely deadly.* **5** = DEATHLY
■ *adv.* **1** (*informal*) extremely: **deadly serious/dull 2** = DEATHLY: *deadly pale/cold*

**ˌdead·ly ˈnight·shade** /ˌdedli ˈnaɪtʃeɪd/ (*also* **bella·donna**) *noun* [U] a very poisonous plant with purple flowers and black berries

**ˌdeadly ˈsin** *noun* one of the seven actions for which you can go to hell, in Christian tradition: *Greed is one of the seven deadly sins.*

**dead·pan** /ˈdedpæn/ *adj.* without any expression or emotion; often pretending to be serious when you are joking: *deadpan humour*

**ˌdead ˈweight** *noun* [usually sing.] **1** a thing that is very heavy and difficult to lift or move **2** a person or thing that makes it difficult for sth to succeed or change

**ˌdead ˈwood** *noun* [U] people or things that are no longer useful or necessary in an organization

**ˈdead zone** *noun* **1** a place or a period of time in which nothing happens: *The town is a cultural dead zone.* **2** an area that separates two places, groups of people, etc: *The UN is trying to maintain a dead zone between the warring groups.* **3** a place where a mobile phone does not work because no signal can be received **4** (*biology*) an area of water in which animals cannot live because there is not enough OXYGEN

**deaf** /def/ *adj.* (**deaf·er, deaf·est**) **1** unable to hear anything or unable to hear very well: *to* **become/go deaf** ◊ *She was born deaf.* ⊃ see also TONE-DEAF **2** **the deaf** *noun* [pl.] people who cannot hear: *television subtitles for the deaf and hard of hearing* **3** [not before noun] ~ **to sth** not willing to listen or pay attention to sth: *He was deaf to my requests for help.* ▶ **deaf·ness** *noun* [U]

**IDM** (**as**) **ˌdeaf as a ˈpost** (*informal*) very deaf **fall on deaf ˈears** to be ignored or not noticed by other people: *Her advice fell on deaf ears.* **turn a ˌdeaf ˈear** (**to sb / sth**) to ignore or refuse to listen to sb/sth: *He turned a deaf ear to the rumours.*

**deaf·en** /ˈdefn/ *verb* ~ **sb** to make sb unable to hear, either permanently or for a short time: *The noise of the siren was deafening her.*

**deaf·en·ing** /ˈdefnɪŋ/ *adj.* very loud: *deafening applause* ◊ *The noise of the machine was deafening.* ◊ *The government's response to the report has been a* **deafening silence** (= it was very noticeable that nothing was said or done).
▶ **deaf·en·ing·ly** *adv.*

**ˌdeaf ˈmute** *noun* (*old-fashioned* or *offensive*) a person who is unable to hear or speak **HELP** In modern use the term **deaf mute** is considered offensive because it suggests, wrongly, that such people cannot communicate at all. Use a different term such as **profoundly deaf**.

**deal** ❶ **A2** /diːl/ *verb, noun*
■ *verb* (**dealt, dealt** /delt/)
• **CARDS 1** [I, T] to give cards to each player in a game of cards: *Whose turn is it to deal?* ◊ ~ **(sth) (out) (to sb)** *Start by dealing out ten cards to each player.* ◊ ~ **sb sth** *He dealt me two aces.* ⊃ WORDFINDER NOTE at CARD
• **DRUGS 2** [I, T] ~ **(sth)** to buy and sell illegal drugs: *You can often see people dealing openly on the streets.* ⊃ WORDFINDER NOTE at DRUG

**IDM** **ˌdeal sb / sth a ˈblow** | **ˌdeal a ˈblow to sb / sth** (*formal*) **1** to shock sb/sth very much; to be very harmful to sb/sth: *Her sudden death dealt a blow to the whole country.* **2** to hit sb/sth **ˌdeal ˈwith it** used to tell sb that they cannot change a situation so they must accept it: *That's the way it is, so deal with it!* ⊃ more at WHEEL *v.*

**PHRV** **ˈdeal in sth 1** to buy and sell a particular product: *The company deals in computer software.* **2** to accept sth as a basis for your decisions, attitudes or actions: *We don't deal in rumours or guesswork.* **ˌdeal sb ˈin** (*especially*

---

**O** Oxford Phrasal Academic Lexicon (OPAL) written and spoken word lists | **W** OPAL written word list | **S** OPAL spoken word list

## deal-breaker

NAmE, informal) to include sb in an activity: *That sounds great. Deal me in!* **deal sth↔out 1** to share sth out among a group of people SYN **distribute**: *The profits were dealt out among the investors.* **2** to say what punishment sb should have: *Many judges deal out harsher sentences to men than to women.* **deal with sb** A2 to take appropriate action in a particular situation or according to who you are talking to, managing, etc. SYN **handle**: *She is used to dealing with all kinds of people in her job.* **deal with sb/sth** B1 to do business with a person, a company or an organization **deal with sth** A2 to solve a problem, perform a task, etc: *to deal with enquiries/issues/complaints* ◊ *Have you dealt with these letters yet?* ◊ *He's good at dealing with pressure.* **2** B2 to be about sth: *Her poems often deal with the subject of death.* ⇨ LANGUAGE BANK at ABOUT

■ **noun**
• BUSINESS AGREEMENT **1** B1 [C] an agreement, especially in business, on particular conditions for buying or doing sth: *to sign/strike/finalize/close a deal* ◊ *to negotiate/broker/agree/reach a deal* ◊ *She is travelling to New York to seal the deal* (= conclude it). ◊ *a deal with sb We did a deal with the management on overtime.* ◊ *I'll make a deal with you—I'll work evenings if you'll work weekends.* ◊ (*informal*) *He is trying to cut a deal* (= make one) *with the rebels.* ◊ *The deal fell through* (= no agreement was reached). ◊ *I got a good deal on the car* (= bought it cheaply). ◊ *They were hoping for a better pay deal.* ◊ *Listen. This is the deal* (= this is what we have agreed and are going to do). ⇨ see also PACKAGE *noun*

WORDFINDER acquisition, bid, broker, contract, merger, negotiation, offer, proposal, takeover

• TREATMENT **2** B2 [C, usually sing.] the way that sb/sth is treated: *If elected, the party has promised a new deal* (= better and fairer treatment) *for teachers.* ◊ *They knew they'd been given a raw deal* (= been treated unfairly). ◊ *We tried to ensure that everyone got a fair deal.* ⇨ see also BIG DEAL
• IN CARD GAMES **3** [C, usually sing.] the action of giving out cards to the players: *It's your deal.*
• WOOD **4** [U] (*especially BrE*) the soft pale wood of FIR or PINE trees, especially when it is cut into boards for making things: *a deal table*
IDM **a good/great deal (of sth)** B1 much; a lot: *She's feeling a good deal better.* ◊ *We don't see them a great deal* (= often) *these days.* ◊ *They spent a great deal of money.* **it's a deal!** (*informal*) used to say that you agree to sb's terms **what's the 'deal?** (*informal*) what is happening in the present situation?: *What's the deal? Do you want to go out or not?* ⇨ more at BIG DEAL, DONE *adj.*, STRIKE *v.*

**'deal-breaker** *noun* something that causes sb to reject a deal in politics or business: *The candidate's support for the war is the deal-breaker* (= people will not vote for the candidate because of it).

**deal·er** /ˈdiːlə(r)/ *noun* **1** a person whose business is buying and selling a particular product: *an art/antique dealer* ◊ *~ in sth He's a dealer in second-hand cars.* ⇨ see also BROKER-DEALER, DOUBLE-DEALER, WHEELER-DEALER **2** a person who sells illegal drugs: *a crack dealer* ⇨ see also DRUG DEALER **3** the person who gives out the cards in a card game

**deal·er·ship** /ˈdiːləʃɪp/ *NAmE* -lərʃ-/ *noun* a business that buys and sells products, especially cars, for a particular company; the position of being a dealer who can buy and sell sth: *a Ford dealership*

**deal·ing** /ˈdiːlɪŋ/ *noun* **1 dealings** [pl.] business activities; the relations that you have with sb in business: *I knew nothing of his business dealings.* ◊ *~ with sb/sth Have you had any previous dealings with this company?* ◊ *She has always been very polite in her dealings with me.* **2** [U] a way of doing business with sb: *a reputation for fair/honest dealing* **3** [U, C] buying and selling: *drug dealing* ◊ *dealings in shares*

---

**dealt** /delt/ past tense, past part. of DEAL

**dean** /diːn/ *noun* **1** (in the Anglican Church) a priest of high rank who is in charge of the other priests in a CATHEDRAL **2** (*also* **rural 'dean**) (*BrE*) a priest who is in charge of the priests of several churches in an area **3** a person in a university who is in charge of a department of studies **4** (in a college or university, especially at Oxford or Cambridge) a person who is responsible for the discipline of students **5** (*NAmE*) = DOYEN

**dean·ery** /ˈdiːnəri/ *noun* (*pl.* **-ies**) **1** a group of PARISHES controlled by a dean **2** the office or house of a dean (1,2)

**dean's 'list** *noun* (in the US) a list that is published every year of the best students in a college or university

**dear** ① A1 /dɪə(r); *NAmE* dɪr/ *adj., exclamation, noun, adv.*
■ *adj.* (**dear·er, dear·est**) **1** A1 **Dear** used at the beginning of a letter before the name or title of the person that you are writing to: *Dear Sir or Madam* ◊ *Dear Mrs Jones* ◊ *Dear Beth/Dad/Aunt Susan* **2** B1 loved by or important to sb: *He's one of my dearest friends.* ◊ *~ to sb Her daughter is very dear to her.* ⇨ HOMOPHONES at DEER **3** [only before noun] (*old-fashioned*) used in speech or writing to address sb in a polite or friendly way: *Martin, my dear fellow …* **4** [not usually before noun] (*BrE*) expensive; costing a lot of money: *Everything's so dear now, isn't it?* OPP **cheap**
IDM **dear old/little …** used to describe sb in a way that shows love: *Dear old Sue! I knew she'd help.* ◊ *Their baby's a dear little thing.* **hold sb/sth 'dear** (*formal*) to care very much for sb/sth; to value sb/sth highly: *He had destroyed everything we held dear.* ⇨ more at HEART *n.*, LIFE, NEAR *adj.*
■ *exclamation* A2 used in expressions that show that you are surprised, upset, annoyed or worried: *Oh dear! I think I've lost my purse!* ◊ *Oh dear! What a shame.* ◊ *Dear me! What a mess!* ◊ *Dear oh dear! What are you going to do now?*
■ *noun* **1** (*informal*) a kind person: *Isn't he a dear?* ◊ *Be a dear and fetch me my coat.* ⇨ see also OLD DEAR **2** used when speaking to sb you love: *Would you like a drink, dear?* ◊ *Come here, my dear.* ⇨ HOMOPHONES at DEER **3** used when speaking to sb in a friendly way, for example by an older person to a young person or a child: *What's your name, dear?* ⇨ compare DUCK
■ *adv.* (*BrE*) at a high price: *to buy cheap and sell dear* IDM see COST *v.*

**dear·est** /ˈdɪərɪst/ *NAmE* ˈdɪr-/ *adj., noun*
■ *adj.* (*old-fashioned*) used when writing to sb you love: *'Dearest Nina', the letter began.* **2** [usually before noun] that you feel deeply: *It was her dearest wish to have a family.*
■ *noun* (*old-fashioned*) used when speaking to sb you love: *Come (my) dearest, let's go home.* IDM see NEAR *adj.*

**dearie** /ˈdɪəri/ *NAmE* ˈdɪri/ *noun* (*BrE, old-fashioned, informal*) used to address sb in a friendly way: *Sit down, dearie.*

**dear·ly** /ˈdɪəli/ *NAmE* ˈdɪrli/ *adv.* **1** very much: *She loves him dearly.* ◊ *I would dearly like/love to know what he was thinking.* ◊ *dearly beloved* (= used by a minister at a Christian church service to address people) **2** in a way that causes a lot of pain, difficulty or damage, or that costs a lot of money: *Success has cost him dearly.* ◊ *She paid dearly for her mistake.*

**dearth** /dɜːθ; *NAmE* dɜːrθ/ *noun* [sing.] **~ (of sth)** (*formal*) a lack of sth; the fact of there not being enough of sth SYN **scarcity**: *There was a dearth of reliable information on the subject.*

**death** ① A2 /deθ/ *noun* **1** A2 [C] the fact of sb dying or being killed: *his sudden/untimely/premature death* ◊ *the tragic death of a child* ◊ *The jury returned a verdict of accidental death.* ◊ *It is believed she died a violent death.* ◊ *~ from sth an increase in deaths from cancer* ⇨ see also BRAIN DEATH, COT DEATH, CRIB DEATH, SUDDEN DEATH **2** A2 [U] the end of life; the state of being dead: *Police are trying to establish the cause of death.* ◊ *The disease can cause death unless the patient is treated promptly.* ◊ *Do you believe in life after death?* ◊ *He was sentenced to death* (= to be EXECUTED). ◊ *to ~ Millions of people starved to death* (= were killed by lack of food). ⇨ see also LIVING DEATH **3** [U] the stopping of BIOCHEMICAL processes of life

in a cell or TISSUE, in a way that cannot be REVERSED: *cell death* ⇨ see also BRAIN DEATH **4** [U] **~ of sth** the permanent end or DESTRUCTION of sth: *the death of all my plans* ◊ *the death of fascism* **5** (*also* **Death**) [U] (*literary*) the power that destroys life, imagined as human in form: *Death is often shown in paintings as a human skeleton.* ⇨ see also SUDDEN DEATH
- **IDM** **at death's ˈdoor** (*often humorous*) so ill that you may die **be the ˈdeath of sb** (*informal*) to worry or upset sb very much: *Those kids will be the death of me.* **do sth to ˈdeath** to do or perform sth so often that people become tired of seeing or hearing it: *That joke's been done to death.* **frighten/scare sb to ˈdeath** (*informal*) to frighten sb very much **look/feel like death warmed ˈup** (*BrE*) (*NAmE* **like death warmed ˈover**) (*informal*) to look or feel very ill or tired **put sb to ˈdeath** to kill sb as a punishment **SYN** execute: *The prisoner will be put to death at dawn.* **to ˈdeath** extremely; very much: *to be bored to death* ◊ *I'm sick to death of your endless criticism.* **to the ˈdeath** until sb is dead: *a fight to the death* ⇨ more at CATCH *v.*, CHEAT *v.*, DICE *v.*, DIE *v.*, FATE, FIGHT *v.*, FLOG, GRIM, KISS *n.*, LIFE, MATTER *n.*

ˈ**death·bed** /ˈdeθbed/ *noun* [usually sing.] the bed in which sb is dying or dies: *a deathbed confession/conversion* ◊ *He told me the truth on his deathbed* (= as he lay dying). ◊ *She was on her deathbed* (= going to die very soon). ◊ (*humorous*) *You'd have to be practically on your deathbed before the doctor would come and see you!*

ˈ**death blow** *noun* an event that destroys or puts an end to sth: *They thought the arrival of television would deal a death blow to mass cinema audiences.*

ˈ**death certificate** *noun* an official document, signed by a doctor, that states the cause and time of sb's death

ˈ**death duty** *noun* [usually pl.] (*BrE, old-fashioned*) = INHERITANCE TAX

ˈ**death knell** (*also* **knell**) *noun* [sing.] an event that means that the end or DESTRUCTION of sth will come soon

**death·less** /ˈdeθləs/ *adj.* never dying or forgotten **SYN** immortal: (*ironic*) *written in his usual deathless prose* (= very bad)

**death·ly** /ˈdeθli/ (*also less frequent* **dead·ly**) *adv.* like a dead person; suggesting death: *Her face was deathly pale.* ◊ *The house was deathly still.* ▶ **death·ly** *adj.*: *A deathly hush fell over the room as he walked in.*

ˈ**death mask** *noun* a model of the face of a person who has just died, made by pressing a soft substance over their face and removing it when it becomes hard

**the ˈdeath penalty** *noun* [sing.] the punishment of being killed that is used in some countries for very serious crimes: *the abolition/return of the death penalty* ◊ *The two men are facing the death penalty.*

ˈ**death rate** *noun* **1** the number of deaths every year for every 1000 people in the population of a place: *a high/low death rate* **2** the number of deaths every year from a particular disease or in a particular group: *Death rates from heart disease have risen considerably in recent years.*

ˈ**death rattle** *noun* [sing.] a sound sometimes heard in the throat of a dying person

ˌ**death ˈrow** *noun* [U] the cells in a prison for prisoners who are waiting to be killed as punishment for a serious crime: *prisoners on death row* ⇨ WORDFINDER NOTE at PRISON

ˈ**death sentence** *noun* the legal punishment of being killed for a serious crime: *to be given/to receive the death sentence for murder*

ˈ**death's head** *noun* a human SKULL (= the bone structure of the head) used as a symbol of death

ˈ**death squad** *noun* a group of people who are ordered by a government, the police, etc. to kill other people, especially their political opponents

ˈ**death throes** *noun* [pl.] **1** the final stages of sth just before it comes to an end: *The regime is now in its death throes.* **2** violent pains and movements at the moment of death

ˈ**death toll** *noun* the number of people killed in an accident, a war, a disaster, etc.

ˈ**death trap** (*also* **death-trap**) *noun* (*informal*) a building, vehicle, etc. that is dangerous and could cause sb's death: *The cars blocking the exits could turn this place into a death trap.* ◊ *Oil slicks, overhead cables and pollution are all death traps for birds.*

ˈ**death warrant** *noun* an official document stating that sb should receive the punishment of being killed for a crime that they have committed: *The president signed the death warrant.* ◊ *If you pay the ransom, you may be signing your son's death warrant.* ◊ (*figurative*) *By withdrawing the funding, the government signed the project's death warrant.*

ˈ**death wish** *noun* [sing.] a desire to die, often that sb is not aware of

**deb** /deb/ *noun* (*informal*) = DEBUTANTE (1)

**de·ba·cle** /dɪˈbɑːkl; *BrE also* deɪ-/ *noun* an event or a situation that is a complete failure and causes people to feel ashamed or embarrassed

**debar** /dɪˈbɑː(r)/ *verb* [usually passive] (**-rr-**) (*formal*) to officially prevent sb from doing sth, joining sth, etc: **be debarred (from sth/from doing sth)** *He was debarred from holding public office.*

**de·base** /dɪˈbeɪs/ *verb* **~ sb/sth** to make sb/sth less valuable or respected **SYN** devalue: *Sport is being debased by commercial sponsorship.* ▶ **de·base·ment** *noun* [U, C]

**de·bat·able** /dɪˈbeɪtəbl/ *adj.* not certain because people can have different ideas and opinions about the thing being discussed **SYN** arguable, questionable: *a debatable point* ◊ **it is ~ whether…** *It is highly debatable whether conditions have improved for low-income families.*

**de·bate** 🔊 **B2** 🔊 /dɪˈbeɪt/ *noun, verb*
- *noun* [C, U] **1** 🔊 **B2** a formal discussion of an issue at a public meeting or in a parliament. In a debate two or more speakers express opposite views and then there is often a vote on the issue: *the first ever televised presidential debate* ◊ *The minister opened the debate* (= was the first to speak). ◊ *After a long debate, Congress approved the proposal.* ◊ **~ on sth** *a debate on transport policy* ◊ **under ~** *The motion under debate* (= being discussed) *was put to a vote.* ⇨ SYNONYMS at DISCUSSION

**WORDFINDER** argument, ayes, chair, the floor, motion, propose, second, speak, vote

**2** 🔊 **B2** an argument or a discussion expressing different opinions: *The issue has sparked debate across the industry.* ◊ *to provoke/stimulate debate* ◊ *a fierce/vigorous debate* ◊ *The theatre's future is a subject of lively public debate.* ◊ *Intense political debate focused on the merits of the two alternative schemes.* ◊ **~ about/on/over sth** *There has been heated debate about whether the film should be allowed.* ◊ *Whether he deserved what happened to him is open to debate* (= cannot be certain or decided yet). ◊ **under ~** *The issue is still under debate.*
- *verb* **1** 🔊 **B2** [T, I] to discuss sth, especially formally, before making a decision or finding a solution **SYN** discuss: **~(sth)** *Politicians will be debating the bill later this week.* ◊ *It is time to debate the issue of school funding.* ◊ *They debated endlessly, without ever reaching a decision.* ◊ *The question of the origin of the universe is still hotly debated* (= strongly argued about) *by scientists.* ◊ *to be openly/widely/publicly debated* ◊ **~ whether, what, etc…** *The committee will debate whether to lower the age of club membership to 16.* ⇨ SYNONYMS at TALK **2** [I, T] to think carefully about sth before making a decision: **~(with yourself)** *She debated with herself for a while, and then picked up the phone.* ◊ **~ whether, what, etc…** *We're debating whether or not to go skiing this winter.* ◊ **~ doing sth** *For a moment he debated going after her.* ▶ **de·bat·ing** *noun* [U]: *a debating society at a school*

**de·bater** /dɪˈbeɪtə(r)/ *noun* a person who is involved in a formal debate

# debauched

**de·bauched** /dɪˈbɔːtʃt/ *adj.* a **debauched** person is not moral in their sexual behaviour, drinks a lot of alcohol, takes drugs, etc. SYN **depraved, dissolute**

**de·bauch·ery** /dɪˈbɔːtʃəri/ *noun* [U] behaviour involving too much sex, alcohol or drugs

**de·ben·ture** /dɪˈbentʃə(r)/ *noun* (*finance*) **1** (*BrE*) an arrangement to invest money in a company in return for a fixed rate of interest. The money is secured against property owned by the company. **2** (*also* **debenture bond**) (*NAmE*) an UNSECURED loan to a company with a fixed rate of interest

**de·bili·tate** /dɪˈbɪlɪteɪt/ *verb* (*formal*) **1** ~ sb/sth to make sb's body or mind weaker **2** ~ sth to make a country, an organization, etc. weaker: *Prolonged strike action debilitated the industry.*

**de·bili·tat·ing** /dɪˈbɪlɪteɪtɪŋ/ *adj.* **1** making sb's body or mind weaker: *a debilitating disease* **2** making a country, an organization, etc. weaker: *a long and debilitating recession*

**de·bil·ity** /dɪˈbɪləti/ *noun* [U, C] (*pl.* **-ies**) (*formal*) physical weakness, especially as a result of illness

**debit** /ˈdebɪt/ *noun, verb*
- *noun* **1** a written note in a bank account or other financial record of a sum of money owed or spent: *on the debit side of an account* ◇ (*figurative*) *On the debit side* (= a negative result will be that) *the new shopping centre will increase traffic problems.* **2** a sum of money taken from a bank account OPP **credit** ⇒ see also DIRECT DEBIT ⇒ WORDFINDER NOTE at BANK
- *verb* when a bank **debits** an account or **debits** money from an account, it takes money from the account: **~ sth (from sth)** *The money will be debited from your account each month.* ◇ **~ sth (with sth)** *The bank will debit your account with any withdrawals made using your payment card.* OPP **credit**

**ˈdebit card** (*US also* **ˈcheck card**) *noun* a plastic card that can be used to take money directly from your bank account when you pay for sth ⇒ compare CREDIT CARD ⇒ picture at MONEY

**de·bon·air** /ˌdebəˈneə(r)/; *NAmE* -ˈner/ *adj.* (*old-fashioned*) (usually of men) fashionable and confident

**de·brief** /ˌdiːˈbriːf/ *verb* **~ sb (on sth)** to ask sb questions officially, in order to get information about the task that they have just completed: *He was taken to a US airbase to be debriefed on the mission.* ⇒ compare BRIEF ▸ **de·brief·ing** *noun* [U, C]: *a debriefing session*

**deb·ris** /ˈdebriː, ˈdeɪb-/; *NAmE* dəˈbriː/ *noun* [U] **1** pieces of wood, metal, building materials, etc. that are left after sth has been destroyed: *Emergency teams are still clearing the debris from the plane crash.* **2** (*formal*) rubbish or pieces of material that are left somewhere and are not wanted: *Clear away leaves and other garden debris from the pond.*

**debt** /det/ *noun* **1** [C] a sum of money that sb owes: *to pay/repay a debt* ◇ *I need to pay off all my debts.* ◇ *an outstanding debt of £300* ◇ *He had run up huge credit card debts.* ⇒ see also CARBON DEBT, NATIONAL DEBT ⇒ WORDFINDER NOTE at LOAN **2** [U] the situation of owing money, especially when you cannot pay: **in ~** *He died heavily in debt.* ◇ *The club is £4 million in debt.* ◇ *We were poor but we never got into debt.* ◇ **out of ~** *It's hard to stay out of debt when you are a student.* ◇ *The country's debt burden is increasing.* ⇒ see also BAD DEBT **3** [C, usually sing.] the fact that you should feel grateful to sb because they have helped you or been kind to you: *I owe them a debt of gratitude that I can never repay.* ◇ *I would like to acknowledge my debt to my teachers.* IDM **be in sb's ˈdebt** (*formal*) to feel grateful to sb for their help, kind behaviour, etc.

**ˈdebt ceiling** *noun* the upper limit on the amount of money that a government can borrow: *They will either have to make cuts somewhere or raise the debt ceiling.*

**debt·or** /ˈdetə(r)/ *noun* a person, a country or an organization that owes money OPP **creditor**

**ˈdebt relief** *noun* the act of cancelling all or part of the money that a person, organization or country owes: *The intention was to provide debt relief to poor countries that had suffered natural disasters.*

**debug** /ˌdiːˈbʌɡ/ *verb* (**-gg-**) **~ sth** (*computing*) to look for and remove the faults in a computer program ▸ **debug** /ˈdiːbʌɡ/ *noun* [U, C]: *The new website is in its final stages of debug and will launch next month.*

**de·bug·ger** /ˌdiːˈbʌɡə(r)/ *noun* a computer program that helps to find and correct mistakes in other programs

**de·bunk** /ˌdiːˈbʌŋk/ *verb* **~ sth** to show that an idea, a belief, etc. is false; to show that sth is not as good as people think it is: *His theories have been debunked by recent research.*

**debut** /ˈdeɪbjuː, ˈdeb-/; *NAmE* deɪˈbjuː/ *noun, verb*
- *noun* the first public appearance of a performer or sports player: *He will make his debut for the first team this week.* ◇ *the band's debut album*
- *verb* **1** [I] (of a performer or show) to make a first public appearance: *The ballet will debut next month in New York.* **2** [I, T] **~ sth** (*especially NAmE, business*) (of a product or advertising campaign) to be presented to the market for the first time; to present a new product or advertising campaign to the market: *The model is expected to debut at $19000.* ◇ *They will debut the products at the trade show.*

**debu·tant** /ˈdebjutɑːnt/ *noun* a person who is making their first public appearance, especially in sport or films

**debu·tante** /ˈdebjutɑːnt/ *noun* **1** (*also informal* **deb**) (especially in the past) a young, rich or UPPER-CLASS woman who is going to fashionable social events for the first time **2** a woman who is making her first public appearance, especially in sport or films; a female DEBUTANT

**deca-** /ˈdekə, dɪˈkæ/ *combining form* (in nouns) ten; having ten: *decathlon* ⇒ compare DECI-

**dec·ade** /ˈdekeɪd, dɪˈkeɪd/ *noun* a period of ten years, especially a continuous period, such as 1910–1919 or 2000–2009: *the early decades of the nineteenth century* ◇ *The nineties were a decade of rapid advances.* ◇ *a career spanning five decades* ◇ **over a ~** *He's changed a lot over the past decade.* ◇ **for decades** *The war may be short but the environmental impacts could last for decades.*

**deca·dence** /ˈdekədəns/ *noun* [U] (*disapproving*) behaviour, attitudes, etc. that show a fall in standards, especially moral ones, and an interest in pleasure and fun rather than more serious things: *the decadence of modern Western society*

**deca·dent** /ˈdekədənt/ *adj.* (*disapproving*) having or showing low standards, especially moral ones, and an interest only in pleasure and fun rather than serious things: *the decadent rich* ◇ *a decadent lifestyle/society*

**de·caf·fein·ated** /ˌdiːˈkæfɪneɪtɪd/ *adj.* (of coffee or tea) with most or all of the CAFFEINE removed ▸ **de·caf·fein·ated** *noun* [U, C]

**De·caf**™ (*also* **de·caff**) (*both BrE*) (*NAmE* **decaf**) /ˈdiːkæf/ *noun* [U, C] (*informal*) decaffeinated coffee: (*BrE*) *Regular coffee or Decaf?* ◇ *I'll have a decaff, please.*

**decal** /ˈdiːkæl/ *noun* (*NAmE*) (*BrE* **transfer**) a picture or design that can be removed from a piece of paper and stuck onto a surface, for example by being pressed or heated

**de·camp** /dɪˈkæmp/ *verb* [I] **~ (from ...) (to ...)** to leave a place suddenly, often secretly

**de·cant** /dɪˈkænt/ *verb* **~ sth (into sth)** to pour liquid, especially wine, from one container into another

**de·cant·er** /dɪˈkæntə(r)/ *noun* a special glass bottle with a STOPPER (= an object that fits into the top of the bottle to close it) that wine and other alcoholic drinks are poured into from an ordinary bottle before serving

**de·capi·tate** /dɪˈkæpɪteɪt/ *verb* **~ sb/sth** to cut off sb's head SYN **behead**: *His decapitated body was found floating in a canal.* ▸ **de·capi·ta·tion** /dɪˌkæpɪˈteɪʃn/ *noun* [U, C]

---

æ cat | ɑː father | e bed | ɜː fur | ə about | ɪ sit | iː see | i happy | ɒ got (*BrE*) | ɔː saw | ʌ cup | ʊ put | uː too

**de·car·bon·ize** (*BrE* also **-ise**) /ˌdiːˈkɑːbənaɪz; *NAmE* -ˈkɑːrb-/ *verb* ~ **sth** to replace FOSSIL FUELS with a fuel that is less harmful to the environment: *If we decarbonize electricity then through electric cars we can decarbonize transport.* ▶ **de·car·bon·iz·ation**, **-isa·tion** /ˌdiːˌkɑːbənaɪˈzeɪʃn; *NAmE* -ˌkɑːrbənəˈz-/ *noun* [U]

**dec·ath·lete** /dɪˈkæθliːt/ *noun* a person who competes in a decathlon

**dec·ath·lon** /dɪˈkæθlən/ *noun* a sporting event in which people compete in ten different sports ⊃ compare BIATHLON, HEPTATHLON, PENTATHLON, TRIATHLON

**decay** /dɪˈkeɪ/ *noun*, *verb*
■ *noun* [U] **1** the process or result of being destroyed by natural causes or by not being cared for (= of decaying): *tooth decay* ◊ *The landlord had let the building fall into decay.* ◊ *The smell of death and decay hung over the town.* **2** the process of a society, an institution, a system, etc. being gradually destroyed: *economic/moral/urban decay* ◊ *the decay of the old industries* **3** (*physics*) the process by which a RADIOACTIVE substance changes to a different form by sending out RADIATION ⊃ see also BETA DECAY
■ *verb* **1** [I, T] ~ **(sth)** to be destroyed gradually by natural processes; to destroy sth in this way SYN **rot**: *decaying leaves/teeth/food* **2** [I] if a building or an area **decays**, its condition slowly becomes worse: *decaying inner city areas* **3** [I] to become less powerful and lose influence over people, society, etc: *decaying standards of morality*

**de·cease** /dɪˈsiːs/ *noun* [U] (*law* or *formal*) the death of a person

**de·ceased** /dɪˈsiːst/ *adj.* (*law* or *formal*) **1** dead: *her deceased parents* **2 the deceased** *noun* (*pl.* **the deceased**) a person who has died, especially recently

**de·ceit** /dɪˈsiːt/ *noun* [U, C] dishonest behaviour that is intended to make sb believe sth that is not true; an example of this behaviour SYN **deception**: *He was accused of lies and deceit.* ◊ *Everyone was involved in this web of deceit.* ◊ *Their marriage was an illusion and a deceit.*

**de·ceit·ful** /dɪˈsiːtfl/ *adj.* (*formal*) behaving in a dishonest way by telling lies and making people believe things that are not true SYN **dishonest** ▶ **de·ceit·ful·ly** /-fəli/ *adv.* **de·ceit·ful·ness** *noun* [U]

**de·ceive** /dɪˈsiːv/ *verb* **1** [T] to make sb believe sth that is not true: ~ **sb** *Her husband had been deceiving her for years.* ◊ ~ **sb into doing sth** *She deceived him into handing over all his savings.* ⊃ SYNONYMS ⊃ CHEAT **2** [T] ~ **yourself (that …)** to refuse to admit to yourself that sth unpleasant is true: *You're deceiving yourself if you think he'll change his mind.* **3** [T, I] ~ **(sb)** to make sb have a wrong idea about sb/sth SYN **mislead**: *Unless my eyes deceive me, that's his wife.* ◊ see also DECEPTIVE ▶ **de·ceiver** *noun* IDM see FLATTER

WORD FAMILY
**deceive** verb
**deceit** noun
**deceitful** adj.
**deception** noun
**deceptive** adj.

**de·cel·er·ate** /ˌdiːˈseləreɪt/ *verb* (*formal*) **1** [I, T] ~ **(sth)** to reduce the speed at which a vehicle is travelling **2** [I, T] ~ **(sth)** to become or make sth become slower SYN **slow down**: *Economic growth decelerated sharply in June.* OPP **accelerate** ▶ **de·cel·er·ation** /ˌdiːseləˈreɪʃn/ *noun* [U, C]

**De·cem·ber** 🔊 **A1** /dɪˈsembə(r)/ *noun* [U, C] (*abbr.* **Dec.**) the 12th and last month of the year HELP To see how **December** is used, look at the examples at **April**.

**de·cency** /ˈdiːsnsi/ *noun* **1** [U] honest, polite behaviour that follows accepted moral standards and shows respect for others: *Her behaviour showed a total lack of common decency.* ◊ *Have you no sense of decency?* ◊ *He might have had the decency to apologize.* **2** **the decencies** [pl.] (*formal*) standards of behaviour in society that people think are acceptable: *the basic decencies of civilized society*

**de·cent** 🔊 **B2** /ˈdiːsnt/ *adj.* **1 B2** of a good enough standard or quality: *a decent meal/place to live* ◊ *Mark did a decent job as a replacement for Turner.* ◊ *a decent pension/wage/standard of living* ◊ (*informal*) *The acting in the film is actually pretty decent.* **2** 🔊 **B2** (of people or behaviour) honest and fair; treating people with respect: *ordinary, decent, hard-working people* ◊ *Everyone said he was a decent sort of guy.* **3** acceptable to people in a particular situation: *a decent burial* ◊ *That dress isn't decent.* ◊ *She ought to have waited for a decent interval before getting married again.* **4** (*informal*) wearing enough clothes to allow sb to see you: *I can't go to the door—I'm not decent.* ⊃ compare INDECENT ▶ **de·cent·ly** *adv.* IDM **to do the decent thing** to do what people or society expect, especially in a difficult situation: *He did the decent thing and resigned.*

**de·cen·tral·ize** (*BrE* also **-ise**) /ˌdiːˈsentrəlaɪz/ *verb* [T, I] ~ **(sth)** to give some of the power of a central government, organization, etc. to smaller parts or organizations around the country: *decentralized authority/administration* OPP **centralize** ▶ **de·cen·tral·iza·tion**, **-isa·tion** /ˌdiːˌsentrəlaɪˈzeɪʃn; *NAmE* -ləˈz-/ *noun* [U, sing.]

**de·cep·tion** /dɪˈsepʃn/ *noun* **1** [U] the act of deliberately making sb believe sth that is not true (= of DECEIVING them) SYN **deceit**: *a drama full of lies and deception* ◊ *He was accused of obtaining property by deception.* **2** [C] a trick intended to make sb believe sth that is not true SYN **deceit**: *The whole episode had been a cruel deception.*

**de·cep·tive** /dɪˈseptɪv/ *adj.* likely to make you believe sth that is not true SYN **misleading**: *a deceptive advertisement* ◊ *Appearances can often be deceptive* (= things are not always what they seem to be). ◊ *the deceptive simplicity of her writing style* (= it seems simple but is not really) ▶ **de·cep·tive·ly** *adv.*: *a deceptively simple idea*

**deci-** /ˈdesɪ/ *combining form* (in nouns, often used in units of measurement) one tenth: *decilitre* ⊃ compare DECA-

**deci·bel** /ˈdesɪbel/ *noun* a unit for measuring how loud a sound is

**de·cide** 🔊 ❶ **A1** /dɪˈsaɪd/ *verb* **1** 🔊 **A1** [I, T] to think carefully about the different possibilities that are available and choose one of them: *You will have to decide soon.* ◊ ~ **to do sth** *We've decided not to go away after all.* ◊ ~ **(that) …** *The government has already decided that the law needs to be changed.* ◊ ~ **what, whether, etc. …** *You have the right to decide what you want to do.* ◊ ~ **between A and B** *It was difficult to decide between the two candidates.* ◊ ~ **against sth/against doing sth** *She finally decided against a career in medicine.* ◊ ~ **sth** *Sales figures will ultimately decide the future of these types of games.* ◊ **it is decided (that) …** *It was decided that the school should purchase new software.* **2** [T, I] (*law*) to make an official or legal judgement: ~ **sth** *The case will be decided by a jury.* ◊ ~ **for/in favour of sb** | ~ **in sb's favour** *The Appeal Court decided in their favour.* ◊ ~ **against sb** *It is always possible that the judge may decide against you.* ◊ ~ **on sth** *He challenged her right as governor to decide on the matter.* **3** [T] to affect the result of sth: ~ **sth** *A mixture of skill and good luck decided the outcome of the game.* ◊ ~ **if, whether, etc. …** *A number of factors decide whether a movie will be successful or not.* **4** [T] to be the reason why sb does sth: *For most customers, price is the deciding factor.* ◊ ~ **sb (to do sth)** *They offered me free accommodation for a year, and that decided me.* ◊ ~ **sth (for sb)** *That decided it for me: I wasn't carrying my bike back up those stairs.*
PHRV **de'cide on/upon sth** 🔊 **B1** to choose sth from a number of possibilities: *We're still trying to decide on a venue.*

WORD FAMILY
**decide** verb
**decision** noun (≠ indecision)
**decisive** adj. (≠ indecisive)
**undecided** adj.

**de·cided** /dɪˈsaɪdɪd/ *adj.* **1** [only before noun] obvious and definite: *His height was a decided advantage in the job.* **2** (*especially BrE*) having very strong opinions: *She was a very decided young woman, eager to do some good in the world.* ◊ *The child is very decided about what she wants and doesn't want.* ⊃ compare UNDECIDED

**de·cid·ed·ly** /dɪˈsaɪdɪdli/ adv. **1** (used with an adjective or adverb) definitely and in an obvious way: *Amy was looking decidedly worried.* **2** in a way that shows that you are sure and determined about sth: *'I won't go,' she said decidedly.*

**de·cider** /dɪˈsaɪdə(r)/ noun [usually sing.] the game, race, etc. that will decide who the winner is in a competition

**de·cidu·ous** /dɪˈsɪdʒuəs/ adj. (of a tree, bush etc.) that loses its leaves every year ➲ compare EVERGREEN ➲ VISUAL VOCAB page V6

**decile** /ˈdesaɪl; NAmE also -sl/ noun (statistics) one of ten equal groups into which a collection of things or people can be divided according to the DISTRIBUTION of a particular VARIABLE: *families in the top decile of income* (= the 10 per cent of families with the highest income)

**deci·litre** (*US* **deci·liter**) /ˈdesɪliːtə(r)/ noun (abbr. **dl**) a unit for measuring liquids. There are 10 decilitres in a LITRE.

**deci·mal** /ˈdesɪml/ adj., noun
- **adj.** (*mathematics*) based on or counted in tens or tenths: *the decimal system* ➲ compare BINARY, HEXADECIMAL
- **noun** (*mathematics*) **1** (also ˌdecimal ˈfraction) [C] a FRACTION (= a number less than one) that is shown as a point followed by the number of tenths, HUNDREDTHS, etc: *The decimal 0.61 stands for 61 hundredths.* **2** [U] the system of numbers that counts in tens or tenths: *The computer converts the data from decimal to binary.* ➲ compare BINARY, HEXADECIMAL

**deci·mal·ize** (*BrE also* **-ise**) /ˈdesɪməlaɪz/ verb **1** ~ sth to change a system of coins or weights and measurements to a decimal system **2** ~ sth to express an amount using the decimal system instead of the system it is already expressed in: *The question asks you to decimalize the fraction ⅞.* ▶ **deci·mal·iza·tion**, **-isa·tion** /ˌdesɪməlaɪˈzeɪʃn; *NAmE* -ləˈz-/ noun [U]

ˌdecimal ˈplace noun the position of a number after a decimal point: *The figure is accurate to two decimal places.*

ˌdecimal ˈpoint noun a small round mark used to separate the whole number from the tenths, HUNDREDTHS, etc. of a decimal, for example in 0.61

**deci·mate** /ˈdesɪmeɪt/ verb **1** [usually passive] to kill large numbers of animals, plants or people in a particular area: *be decimated (by sth) The rabbit population was decimated by the disease.* **2** ~ sth (*informal*) to severely damage sth or make sth weaker: *Cheap imports decimated the British cycle industry.* ▶ **deci·ma·tion** /ˌdesɪˈmeɪʃn/ noun [U]

**de·cipher** /dɪˈsaɪfə(r)/ verb **1** ~ sth to convert sth written in code into normal language: *They were able to decipher the French military codes.* **2** ~ sth to succeed in finding the meaning of sth that is difficult to read or understand: *Can anyone decipher his handwriting?* ➲ see also INDECIPHERABLE

**de·ci·sion** 🔊 **A2** ⊙ /dɪˈsɪʒn/ noun **1** **A2** [C] a choice or judgement that you make after thinking and talking about what is the best thing to do: *I think I've made the right decision.* ◊ (*BrE*) *No decisions have yet been taken.* ◊ *to reach/come to a decision* ◊ *~ on sth We need a decision on this by next week.* ◊ *~ about sth I will consult colleagues before making a final decision about how to proceed.* ◊ *to do sth Who made the decision to go ahead with the project?* ◊ *a difficult/tough/hard decision* ◊ *It is almost impossible for the average person to make an informed decision* (= one based on evidence). ◊ *The government plans to appeal the decision in the High Court.* ◊ *to reverse/overturn a decision on appeal* **2** [U] the process of deciding sth: *The moment of decision had arrived.* **3** (also de·ci·sive·ness) [U] the ability to decide sth clearly and quickly: *This is not a job for someone who lacks decision.* **OPP** indecision **IDM** see RESERVE v.

de·ci·sion-mak·ing 🔊 **C1** noun [U] the process of deciding about sth important, especially in a group of people or in an organization ▶ de·ci·sion-mak·er noun: *Mary is the decision-maker in the house.*

**de·ci·sive** 🔊 **C1** /dɪˈsaɪsɪv/ adj. **1** 🔊 **C1** very important for the final result of a particular situation: *a decisive factor/victory/battle* ◊ *She has played a decisive role in the peace negotiations.* ◊ *a decisive step* (= an important action that will change a situation) *towards a cleaner environment* ➲ SYNONYMS at ESSENTIAL **2** 🔊 **C1** able to decide sth quickly and with confidence: *decisive management* ◊ *The government must take decisive action on gun control.* **OPP** indecisive ▶ **de·cisive·ly** adv.

**de·cisive·ness** /dɪˈsaɪsɪvnəs/ noun [U] = DECISION (3)

**deck** 🔊 **B2** /dek/ noun, verb
- **noun 1** 🔊 **B2** the top outside floor of a ship or boat: *on ~ I was the only person on deck at that time of night.* ◊ *below deck(s) As the storm began, everyone disappeared below deck(s).* **2** 🔊 **B2** one of the floors of a ship or a bus: *the upper/lower/main deck of a ship* ◊ *We sat on the top deck of the bus.* ◊ *My cabin is on deck C.* ➲ see also DOUBLE-DECKER, FLIGHT DECK, SINGLE-DECKER, SUN DECK, VOID DECK **3** a floor or platform similar to the deck of a ship: *There is an open-air observation deck on the building's top floor.* **4** 🔊 **C1** (also ˌdeck of ˈcards) (*both especially NAmE*) (*BrE usually* **pack**) a complete set of 52 PLAYING CARDS **5** 🔊 **C1** (*especially NAmE*) a wooden floor that is built outside the back of a house where you can sit and relax: *After dinner we sat out on the deck.* **6** a part of a SOUND SYSTEM that records and/or plays sounds on a disc or tape: *a cassette/tape deck* **7** a set of slides (= pages created on a computer that contain text and images) that are used to accompany a person's presentation **IDM** see CLEAR v., HAND n., HIT v.
- **verb 1** [often passive] to decorate sb/sth with sth: **be decked out in/with sth** *The room was decked out in flowers and balloons.* **2** ~ **sb** (*informal*) to hit sb very hard so that they fall to the ground

**deck·chair** /ˈdektʃeə(r); *NAmE* -tʃer/ noun a folding chair with a seat made from a long piece of material on a wooden or metal frame, used for example on a beach

**deck·hand** /ˈdekhænd/ noun a worker on a ship who does work that does not need special skills

**deck·ing** /ˈdekɪŋ/ noun [U] wood used to build a floor (called a DECK) in the garden next to or near a house

ˈdeck shoe noun a flat shoe made of strong cloth or soft leather, with a sole that does not slip

**de·claim** /dɪˈkleɪm/ verb [T, I] ~ (**against**) **sth** | ~ **that** … | + **speech** (*formal*) to say sth loudly; to speak loudly and with force about sth you feel strongly about, especially in public: *She declaimed the famous opening speech of the play.* ◊ *He declaimed against the evils of alcohol.*

**dec·lam·ation** /ˌdekləˈmeɪʃn/ noun (*formal*) **1** [U] the act of speaking or of expressing sth to an audience in a formal way **2** [C] a speech or piece of writing that strongly expresses feelings and opinions

**de·clama·tory** /dɪˈklæmətəri; *NAmE* -tɔːri/ adj. (*formal*) expressing feelings or opinions in a strong way in a speech or a piece of writing

**dec·lar·ation** 🔊 **C1** /ˌdekləˈreɪʃn/ noun **1** 🔊 **C1** [C, U] an official or formal statement, especially about the plans of a government or an organization; the act of making such a statement: *to issue/sign a declaration* ◊ *the declaration of war* ◊ *the Declaration of Independence* (= of the United States) **2** [C] a written or spoken statement, especially about what people feel or believe: *a declaration of love/faith/guilt* ➲ SYNONYMS at STATEMENT **3** [C] an official written statement giving information: *a declaration of income* ◊ *customs declarations* (= giving details of goods that have been brought into a country)

**de·clara·tive** /dɪˈklærətɪv/ adj. (*grammar*) (of a sentence) in the form of a simple statement

**de·clare** 🔊 **B2** /dɪˈkleə(r); *NAmE* -ˈkler/ verb **1** 🔊 **B2** [T] to say sth officially or publicly: ~ **sth** *The government has declared a state of emergency.* ◊ *Germany declared war on France on 1 August 1914.* ◊ *The government has declared war on* (= officially stated its intention to stop) *illiteracy.* ◊ ~ **that** … *The court declared that strike action was illegal.* ◊ ~ **sth/sb** + **noun** *In the end, they were both* *declared winners of the tournament.* ◊ ~ **sth to be sth** *The painting was declared to be a forgery.* ◊ ~ **sth as sth** *Excess weight has been declared as one of the top ten health risks in the world.* ◊ ~ **sth/sb + adj.** *I declare this bridge open.* ◊ *Kenya was officially declared independent on December 12, 1963.* **2** [T] to state sth clearly and definitely: + **speech** *'I'll do it!' Tom declared.* ◊ ~ **that** … *He declared that he was in love with her.* ◊ ~ **sth** *Few people dared to declare their opposition to the regime.* ◊ ~ **yourself + adj./noun** *She declared herself extremely hurt by his lack of support.* **3** [T] ~ **yourself (to sb)** to say clearly and openly who you are or what you intend to do: *Only two candidates have declared themselves so far.* **4** [T] ~ **sth** to tell the tax authorities how much money you have earned: *All income must be declared.* **5** [T] ~ **sth** to tell CUSTOMS officers (= at the border of a country) that you are carrying goods on which you should pay tax: *Do you have anything to declare?* **6** [I] (in CRICKET) to decide to end your INNINGS (= the period during which your team is BATTING) before all your players have BATTED: *England declared at 224 for 4* (= 4 BATSMEN had scored 224 RUNS).

**PHRV** de‚clare a'gainst sb/sth (*formal*) to say publicly that you do not support sb/sth  de'clare for sb/sth (*formal*) to say publicly that you support sb/sth

▼ SYNONYMS
**declare**
state • indicate • announce
These words all mean to say sth, usually clearly and definitely and often in public.
**declare** (*rather formal*) to say sth officially or publicly; to state sth clearly and definitely: *to declare war* ◊ *The painting was declared to be a forgery.*
**state** (*rather formal*) to formally write or say sth, especially in a careful and clear way: *He has already stated his intention to run for election.*
**indicate** (*rather formal*) to state sth, sometimes in a way that is slightly indirect: *During our meeting, he indicated his willingness to cooperate.*
**announce** to tell people officially about a decision or plans; to give information about sth in a public place, especially through a loudspeaker; to say sth in a loud and/or serious way: *They haven't formally announced their engagement yet.* ◊ *Has our flight been announced yet?*
DECLARE OR ANNOUNCE?
• **Declare** is used more often for giving judgements; **announce** is used more often for giving facts: *The painting was announced to be a forgery.* ◊ *They haven't formally declared their engagement yet.*
PATTERNS
• to declare/state/indicate/announce **that** …
• to declare/state sb/sth **to be** sth
• to declare/state/indicate/announce **your intention** to do sth
• to declare/state/announce sth **formally/publicly/officially**
• to declare/state/announce sth **firmly/confidently**

**de·clared** /dɪˈkleəd; *NAmE* -ˈklerd/ *adj.* [only before noun] stated in an open way so that people know about it **SYN** **professed**: *the government's declared intention to reduce crime*

**de·clas·sify** /ˌdiːˈklæsɪfaɪ/ *verb* (**de·clas·si·fies**, **de·clas·si·fy·ing**, **de·clas·si·fied**, **de·clas·si·fied**) ~ **sth** to state officially that secret government information is no longer secret: *declassified information/documents* **OPP** **classify** ► **de·clas·si·fi·ca·tion** /ˌdiːˌklæsɪfɪˈkeɪʃn/ *noun* [U]

**de·clen·sion** /dɪˈklenʃn/ *noun* (*grammar*) **1** [C] (in some languages) a set of nouns, adjectives or pronouns that change in the same way to show CASE, number and GENDER **2** [U] (in some languages) the way in which some sets of nouns, adjectives and pronouns change their form or endings to show CASE, number or GENDER

**de·cline** ⓘ B2 ⓞ /dɪˈklaɪn/ *verb*, *noun*
▪ *verb* **1** ⓘ B2 [I] (*rather formal*) to become smaller, fewer, weaker, etc: *Support for the party continues to decline.* ◊ ~ **by sth** *Sales of whole milk declined by 4 per cent.* ◊ ~ **in sth** *The city declined in importance in the nineteenth century.* ◊ *Jobs in manufacturing have steadily declined.* ◊ *to decline sharply/significantly/dramatically* ◊ *Her health began to decline.* **2** [I, T] (*formal*) to refuse politely to accept or to do sth **SYN** **refuse**[1]: *I offered to give them a lift but they declined.* ◊ ~ **sth** *to decline an offer/invitation* ◊ *We politely declined her invitation.* ◊ ~ **to do sth** *Their spokesman declined to comment on the allegations.* **3** [I, T] ~ **(sth)** (*grammar*) if a noun, an adjective or a pronoun **declines**, it has different forms according to whether it is the subject or the object of a verb, whether it is in the singular or plural, etc. When you **decline** a noun, etc., you list these forms. ⊃ compare **CONJUGATE**
▪ *noun* ⓘ B2 [C, usually sing., U] a continuous decrease in the number, value, quality, etc. of sth: ~ **in sth** *There has been a 5 per cent decline in student numbers.* ◊ ~ **of sth** *the decline of seabird populations* ◊ *a sharp/steep/rapid decline* ◊ *a steady/gradual decline* ◊ *They have experienced decades of economic decline.* ◊ **in** ~ *Industry in Britain has been in decline since the 1970s.* ⊃ **WORDFINDER NOTE** at **TREND**

**de·clin·ing** /dɪˈklaɪnɪŋ/ *adj.* becoming lower, smaller or weaker: *The declining birth rate is common to all developed countries.* ◊ *declining sales/revenues* ◊ *Declining health forced him to retire from business.*
**IDM** **sb's declining ˈyears** (*literary*) the last years of sb's life

**de·clut·ter** (*also* **de-clutter**) /ˌdiːˈklʌtə(r)/ *verb* [I, T] to remove things that you do not use so that you have more space and can easily find things when you need them: *Moving is a good opportunity to declutter.* ◊ ~ **sth** *a 7-step plan to help you declutter your home*

**de·code** /ˌdiːˈkəʊd/ *verb* **1** ~ **sth** to convert sth written in code into normal language **SYN** **decipher**: *I was involved in decoding enemy documents.* **2** ~ **sth** to find the meaning of sth that is difficult to understand **SYN** **decipher**: *I struggled to decode all the jargon he used.* **3** ~ **sth** to receive an electronic signal and change it into a different form, for example pictures that can be shown on a television screen: *decoding equipment* **4** ~ **sth** (*linguistics*) to understand the meaning of sth in a foreign language ⊃ compare **ENCODE**

**de·coder** /ˌdiːˈkəʊdə(r)/ *noun* a device that changes an electronic signal into a form that people can understand, such as sound and pictures: *a satellite/video decoder*

**dé·col·le·tage** /ˌdeɪkɒlˈtɑːʒ; *NAmE* -kɑːlˈt-/ (*also* **dé·col·leté** /ˈdeɪkɒlteɪ; *NAmE* ˌdeɪkɑːlˈteɪ/) *noun* (*from French*) the top edge of a woman's dress, etc. that is designed to be very low in order to show her shoulders and the top part of her breasts ► **dé·col·leté** *adj.*

**de·col·on·iza·tion** (*BrE also* **-isa·tion**) /ˌdiːˌkɒlənaɪˈzeɪʃn; *NAmE* -ˌkɑːlənəˈz-/ *noun* [U] the process of a COLONY or COLONIES becoming independent

**de·com·mis·sion** /ˌdiːkəˈmɪʃn/ *verb* **1** ~ **sth** to officially stop using weapons or military equipment **2** ~ **sth** to stop using a nuclear power station and take it apart safely

**de·com·pose** /ˌdiːkəmˈpəʊz/ *verb* **1** [I, T] to be destroyed gradually after death by natural processes **SYN** **decay**, **rot**: *a decomposing corpse* ◊ ~ **sth** *a decomposed body* **2** [I, T] ~ **(sth) (into sth)** (*chemistry*) (of a chemical compound) to break down sth into smaller and simpler parts; to break a substance down into smaller and simpler parts: *Water decomposes into oxygen and hydrogen.* ► **de·com·pos·ition** /ˌdiːˌkɒmpəˈzɪʃn; *NAmE* -ˌkɑːm-/ *noun* [U]: *the decomposition of organic waste*

**de·com·press** /ˌdiːkəmˈpres/ *verb* **1** [I, T] ~ **(sth)** to have the air pressure in sth reduced to a normal level or to reduce it to its normal level **2** [T] ~ **sth** (*computing*) to return files, etc. to their original size after they have been COMPRESSED **OPP** **compress** **3** [I] (*NAmE*, *informal*) to calm down and relax **SYN** **unwind**

**de·com·pres·sion** /ˌdiːkəmˈpreʃn/ *noun* [U] **1** a reduction in air pressure; the act of reducing the pressure of the air: *decompression of the aircraft cabin* **2** a reduction in air pressure on a person who has experienced high pressure

# decompression sickness

while DIVING deep UNDERWATER **3** (*computing*) the process of expanding computer data to its normal size so that it can be read by a computer

**de·com'pres·sion sickness** *noun* [U] severe pain and difficulty in breathing experienced by DIVERS who come back to the surface of deep water too quickly SYN **the bends**: *Symptoms of decompression sickness include visual disturbances and severe headaches.*

**de·con·gest·ant** /ˌdiːkənˈdʒestənt/ *noun* a medicine that helps sb with a cold to breathe more easily by UNBLOCKING their nose: *a nasal decongestant*

**de·con·struct** /ˌdiːkənˈstrʌkt/ *verb* **1** ~ sth (*specialist*) (in literature and philosophy) to analyse a text in order to show that there is no fixed meaning within the text but that the meaning is created each time in the act of reading **2** ~ sth (into sth) to separate sth into the parts from which it is made up and put them together again in a different way: *Picasso deconstructed his subjects into cubes and colours.*

**de·con·struc·tion** /ˌdiːkənˈstrʌkʃn/ *noun* [U] (*specialist*) (in literature and philosophy) a theory that states that it is impossible for a text to have one fixed meaning, and emphasizes the role of the reader in the production of meaning ⊃ compare STRUCTURALISM ▶ **de·con·struc·tion·ist** /-ʃənɪst/ *noun, adj.*: *a deconstructionist critic/approach*

**de·con·tam·in·ate** /ˌdiːkənˈtæmɪneɪt/ *verb* ~ sth to remove harmful substances from a place or thing: *the process of decontaminating areas exposed to radioactivity* ▶ **de·con·tam·in·ation** /ˌdiːkənˌtæmɪˈneɪʃn/ *noun* [U]

**decor** /ˈdeɪkɔː(r); *NAmE* deɪˈkɔːr/ *noun* [U, C, usually sing.] the style in which the inside of a building is decorated: *interior decor* ◊ *the restaurant's elegant new decor*

**dec·or·ate** 🔑 B1 /ˈdekəreɪt/ *verb* **1** 🔑 B1 [T] to make sth look more attractive by putting things on it: ~ sth with sth *They decorated the room with flowers and balloons.* ◊ ~ sth *The cake was decorated to look like a car.* **2** 🔑 B1 [I, T] (*especially BrE*) to put paint, WALLPAPER, etc. on the walls and ceilings of a room or house: *I hate decorating.* ◊ *He has his own painting and decorating business.* ◊ ~ sth *to decorate a room/a wall/a house/an apartment* ◊ ~ sth in sth *The room is decorated in pale blues and greens.* **3** [T] ~ sth to be placed on sth in order to make it look more attractive SYN **adorn**: *Photographs of actors decorated the walls of the restaurant.* **4** [T, usually passive] to give sb an award or MEDAL as a sign of respect for sth they have done: **be decorated (for sth)** *She was decorated for her efforts during the war.* ◊ *decorated war heroes/veterans*

**dec·or·ation** 🔑 B2 /ˌdekəˈreɪʃn/ *noun* **1** 🔑 B2 [C, usually pl.] a thing that makes sth look more attractive on special occasions: *Christmas/festive decorations* ◊ *cake/table decorations* **2** 🔑 B2 [U, C] a pattern, etc. that is added to sth and that stops it from being plain: *the elaborate decoration on the carved wooden door* ▶ **for** ~ *Rings are worn both for decoration and also as signs of status.* **3** 🔑 B2 [U] the style in which sth is decorated: *a Chinese theme in the* **interior decoration** ⊃ see also INTERIOR DECORATION **4** [U] (*BrE*) the act or process of decorating sth such as the inside of a house by painting it, etc. **5** [C] an award or MEDAL that is given to sb as an honour

**dec·ora·tive** /ˈdekərətɪv; *NAmE* -reɪt-/ *adj.* (of an object or a building) decorated in a way that makes it attractive; intended to look attractive or pretty: *The mirror is functional yet decorative.* ◊ *purely decorative arches* ▶ **dec·ora·tive·ly** *adv.*: *decoratively painted plates*

**decorative arts** *noun* [pl.] artistic activities that produce objects that are useful and beautiful at the same time

**dec·or·ator** /ˈdekəreɪtə(r)/ *noun* **1** (*especially BrE*) a person whose job is painting the inside walls of buildings and putting up WALLPAPER **2** (*especially NAmE*) a person whose job is designing the inside of houses by choosing colours, carpets, furniture, etc; an INTERIOR DECORATOR

**dec·or·ous** /ˈdekərəs/ *adj.* (*formal*) polite and appropriate in a particular social situation SYN **proper**: *a decorous kiss* ▶ **dec·or·ous·ly** *adv.*

**de·corum** /dɪˈkɔːrəm/ *noun* [U] (*formal*) polite behaviour that is appropriate in a social situation SYN **propriety**

**dé·coup·age** (*especially NAmE* **de·coup·age**) /ˌdeɪkuːˈpɑːʒ/ *noun* [U] (*art*) the art of decorating furniture or other objects by cutting out pictures or designs on paper and sticking them onto the surface

**de·couple** /ˌdiːˈkʌpl/ *verb* ~ sth (from sth) (*formal*) to end the connection or relationship between two things

**decoy** /ˈdiːkɔɪ/ *noun* [C] **1** an animal or a bird, or a model of one, that attracts other animals or birds, especially so that they can be shot by people who are hunting them **2** a thing or a person that is used to trick sb into doing what you want them to do, going where you want them to go, etc. ▶ **decoy** /dɪˈkɔɪ/ *verb* ~ sth

**de·crease** 🔑 B2 w *verb, noun*
- *verb* 🔑 B2 /dɪˈkriːs/ [I, T] (*rather formal*) to become smaller in size, number, etc.; to make sth smaller in size, number, etc. *Donations have decreased significantly over the past few years.* ◊ *a decreasing population* ◊ ~ (from sth) (to sth) *The number of new students decreased from 210 to 160 this year.* ◊ ~ by sth *The price of wheat has decreased by 5 per cent.* ◊ ~ in sth *This species of bird is decreasing in numbers every year.* ◊ ~ with sth *Fertility decreases with age.* ◊ ~ sth *The drug did not significantly decrease the risk of heart attack.* OPP **increase**
- *noun* 🔑 B2 /ˈdiːkriːs/ [C, U] the process of reducing sth; the amount that sth is reduced by SYN **reduction**: ~ in sth *There has been some decrease in military spending this year.* ◊ ~ of sth (in sth) *a decrease of nearly 6 per cent in the number of visitors to the museum* ◊ **on the** ~ *Marriage is still on the decrease* (= decreasing). OPP **increase**

**de·cree** /dɪˈkriː/ *noun, verb*
- *noun* **1** [C, U] an official order from a leader or a government that becomes the law: *to issue/sign a decree* ◊ *a leader who rules by decree* (= not in a DEMOCRATIC way) **2** [C] a decision that is made in court
- *verb* [T, I] (**de·cree·ing, de·creed, de·creed**) to decide, judge or order sth officially: ~ (sth) *The government decreed a state of emergency.* ◊ ~ what, how, etc… *We cannot decree what the committee should do.* ◊ **it is decreed that…** *It was decreed that the following day would be a holiday.*

**de·cree abˈsolute** *noun* [sing.] (*BrE, law*) an order from a court that finally ends a marriage, making the two people divorced: *The period between the decree nisi and the decree absolute was six weeks.*

**decree ˈnisi** /dɪˌkriː ˈnaɪsaɪ/ *noun* [sing.] (*BrE, law*) an order from a court that a marriage will end after a fixed amount of time unless there is a good reason why it should not

**de·crep·it** /dɪˈkrepɪt/ *adj.* (of a thing or person) very old and not in good condition or health

**de·crepi·tude** /dɪˈkrepɪtjuːd; *NAmE* -tuːd/ *noun* [U] (*formal*) the state of being old and in poor condition or health

**de·crim·in·al·ize** (*BrE also* **-ise**) /ˌdiːˈkrɪmɪnəlaɪz/ *verb* ~ sth to change the law so that sth is no longer illegal: *There are moves to decriminalize some soft drugs.* OPP **criminalize** ▶ **de·crim·in·al·iza·tion**, **-isa·tion** /ˌdiːˌkrɪmɪnəlaɪˈzeɪʃn; *NAmE* -lə'z-/ *noun* [U]

**decry** /dɪˈkraɪ/ *verb* (**de·cries, de·cry·ing, de·cried, de·cried**) ~ sth/sb (as sth) (*formal*) to strongly criticize sb/sth, especially publicly SYN **condemn**: *The measures were decried as useless.*

**de·crypt** /ˌdiːˈkrɪpt/ *verb* ~ sth to change information that is in code into ordinary language so that it can be understood by anyone OPP **encrypt** ▶ **de·cryp·tion** /-ˈkrɪpʃn/ *noun* [U] OPP **encryption**

**dedi·cate** /ˈdedɪkeɪt/ *verb* **1** to give a lot of your time and effort to a particular activity or purpose because you think it is important SYN **devote**: ~ yourself/sth to sth *She dedicates herself to her work.* ◊ ~ yourself/sth to doing sth *He dedicated his life to helping the poor.* **2** ~ sth to sb to say at the beginning of a book, a piece of music or a performance, or when receiving an award, that you are doing it for sb, as a way of thanking them or showing respect: *This book is dedicated to my parents.* **3** to hold an official ceremony to say that a building or an object has a special purpose or is special to the memory of a particular person: **~ sth** *The chapel was dedicated in 1880.* ◊ **~ sth to sb/sth** *A memorial stone was dedicated to those who were killed in the war.*

**ded·i·cated** /ˈdedɪkeɪtɪd/ *adj.* **1** working hard at sth because it is very important to you **SYN committed**: *a dedicated teacher* ◊ **~ to (doing) sth** *She is dedicated to her job.* **2** [only before noun] designed to do only one particular type of work; used for one particular purpose only: *Software is exported through a dedicated satellite link.*

**ded·i·ca·tion** /ˌdedɪˈkeɪʃn/ *noun* **1** [U] (approving) the hard work and effort that sb puts into an activity or a purpose because they think it is important **SYN commitment**: *hard work and dedication* ◊ **~ to sb/sth** *I really admire Gina for her dedication to her family.* **2** [C, U] a ceremony that is held to show that a building or an object has a special purpose or is special to the memory of a particular person **3** [C] the words that are used at the beginning of a book, piece of music, a performance, etc., or when receiving an award, to offer it to sb as a sign of thanks or respect

**de·duce** /dɪˈdjuːs; *NAmE* -ˈduːs/ *verb* (*formal*) to form an opinion about sth based on the information or evidence that is available **SYN infer**: **~ sth (from sth)** *We can deduce a lot from what people choose to buy.* ◊ **~ (from sth) that, what, how, etc** *Can we deduce from your silence that you do not approve?* ⇒ see also DEDUCTION ▶ **de·du·cible** /dɪˈdjuːsəbl; *NAmE* -ˈduː-/ *adj.*

**de·duct** /dɪˈdʌkt/ *verb* [often passive] to take away money, points, etc. from a total amount **SYN subtract**: **be deducted** *Ten points will be deducted for a wrong answer.* ◊ **be deducted from sth** *The cost of your uniform will be deducted from your wages.*

**de·duct·ible** /dɪˈdʌktəbl/ *adj., noun*
▪ *adj.* **~ (from sth)** that can be taken away from an amount of money you earn, from tax, etc: *These costs are deductible from profits.* ◊ *tax-deductible expenses (= that you do not have to pay tax on)*
▪ *noun* (*NAmE*) (*BrE* **ex·cess**) the part of an insurance claim that a person has to pay while the insurance company pays the rest: *a policy with a very high deductible*

**de·duc·tion** /dɪˈdʌkʃn/ *noun* **1** [U, C] the process of using information you have in order to understand a particular situation or to find the answer to a problem: *He arrived at the solution by a simple process of deduction.* ◊ *If my deductions are correct, I can tell you who the killer was.* ⇒ compare INDUCTION (3) ⇒ see also DEDUCE **2** [U, C] the process of taking an amount of sth, especially money, away from a total; the amount that is taken away: *The dividend will be paid without deduction of tax.* ◊ **~ from sth** *deductions from your pay for tax, etc.* ◊ *tax deductions* ⇒ **WORDFINDER NOTE** at PAY

**de·duct·ive** /dɪˈdʌktɪv/ *adj.* [usually before noun] using knowledge about things that are generally true in order to think about and understand particular situations or problems: *deductive logic/reasoning* ⇒ compare INDUCTIVE ▶ **de·duct·ive·ly** *adv.*

**deed** /diːd/ *noun* **1** (*formal, literary*) a thing that sb does that is usually very good or very bad **SYN act**: *a tale of heroic deeds* ◊ *She tried to do a good deed every day.* ◊ *They will be punished for their evil deeds.* **2** (often plural in BrE) a legal document that you sign, especially one that proves that you own a house or a building: *the deeds of the house* ⇒ **WORDFINDER NOTE** at DOCUMENT ⇒ see also TITLE DEED
**IDM** **your good deed for the day** a helpful, kind thing that you do

**deed poll** *noun* [U, sing.] (*BrE*) a legal document signed by only one person, especially in order to change their name: *Smith changed his name by deed poll to Jervis-Smith.*

**dee·jay** (*also* **DJ**) /ˈdiːdʒeɪ/ *noun, verb*
▪ *noun* (*informal*) = DISC JOCKEY
▪ *verb* [I] to perform as a DISC JOCKEY, especially in a club

---

403 **deep**

**deem** /diːm/ *verb* (not usually used in the progressive tenses) **~ sb/sth + noun/adj. | ~ sb/sth to be sth | ~ (that) …** (*formal*) to have a particular opinion about sb/sth **SYN consider**: *The evening was deemed a great success.* ◊ *She deemed it prudent not to say anything.* ◊ *They would take any action deemed necessary.*

**deemed uni'versity** *noun* (*IndE*) an institution of higher education that is officially ACCREDITED (= approved) as a university

**deep** /diːp/ *adj., adv., noun*
▪ *adj.* (**deep·er, deep·est**)
• TOP TO BOTTOM **1** having a large distance from the top or surface to the bottom: *a deep hole/well/river* ◊ *deep water/snow* ◊ *The water looks quite deep there.* **OPP shallow**

WORD FAMILY
deep *adj., adv.*
deeply *adv.*
deepen *verb*
depth *noun*

• FRONT TO BACK **2** having a large distance from the front edge to the furthest point inside: *a deep cut/wound* ◊ *deep space* **OPP shallow**
• MEASUREMENT **3** used to describe or ask about the depth of sth: *The water is only a few centimetres deep.* ◊ *How deep is the wound?*
• -DEEP **4** (in adjectives) as far up or down as the point mentioned: *The water was only waist-deep so I walked ashore.* **5** (in adjectives) in the number of rows mentioned, one behind the other: *They were standing three-deep at the bar.*
• BREATH/SIGH **6** [usually before noun] taking in or giving out a lot of air: *She took a deep breath.* ◊ *He gave a deep sigh.*
• SLEEP **7** a person in a deep sleep is difficult to wake: *She fell into a deep sleep.* **OPP light**
• COLOURS **8** strong and dark: *a rich deep red* **OPP pale**
• SOUNDS **9** low: *I heard his deep warm voice filling the room.* ◊ *a deep roar/groan*
• EMOTIONS **10** strongly felt **SYN sincere**: *deep respect/regret* ◊ *a deep sense of loss* ◊ *We extend our deepest sympathies to his family.*
• SERIOUS **11** extreme or serious: *He's in deep trouble.* ◊ *a deep economic recession* ◊ *The affair had exposed deep divisions within the party.*
• KNOWLEDGE **12** showing great knowledge or understanding: *She had reached a deep understanding of the local culture.*
• DIFFICULT TO UNDERSTAND **13** difficult to understand **SYN profound**: *This discussion's getting too deep for me.* ◊ *He always sought for a deeper meaning in everything.*
• INVOLVED **14 ~ in sth** fully involved in an activity or a state: *to be deep in thought/conversation* ◊ *He is often so deep in his books that he forgets to eat.* ◊ *The firm ended up deep in debt.*
• PERSON **15** if a person is **deep**, they hide their real feelings and opinions: *She's always been a deep one, trusting no one.*
• IN SPORT **16** to or from a position far down or across the field: *a deep ball from Brown* ⇒ see also DEPTH
**IDM** **in deep 'water(s)** (*informal*) in trouble or difficulty ⇒ more at DEVIL, SHIT *n.*

▪ *adv.* (**deep·er, deep·est**) a long way below the surface of sth or a long way inside or into sth: *Dig deeper!* ◊ **+ adv./prep.** *The miners were trapped deep underground.* ◊ *whales that feed deep beneath the waves* ◊ *deep in the forest* ◊ *He stood with his hands deep in his pockets.* ◊ *He gazed deep into her eyes.* ◊ *They sat and talked deep into the night (= until very late).*
**IDM** **deep 'down 1** if you know sth **deep down**, you know your true feelings about sth, although you may not admit them to yourself: *Deep down I still loved him.* **2** if sth is true **deep down**, it is really like that, although it may not be obvious to people: *He seems confident but deep down he's quite insecure.* **go/run 'deep** (of emotions, beliefs, etc.) to be felt in a strong way, especially for a long time: *Dignity and pride run deep in this community.* ⇒ more at DIG *v.*, STILL *adj.*

# Deepavali

**noun 1 the deep** [sing.] (*literary*) the sea **2 the deep** [sing.], **the deeps** [pl.] a deep part of sth; the deepest part of sth: *in the deep of night/winter* (= in the middle of the night/of winter) ◊ (*figurative*) *the deeps of sorrow* ◊ *the deeps of Loch Ness*

▼ **WHICH WORD?**

### deep / deeply

- The adverbs **deep** and **deeply** can both mean 'a long way down or into something'. **Deep** can only mean this and is more common than **deeply** in this sense. It is usually followed by a word like *into* or *below*: *We decided to go deeper into the jungle.*
- **Deeply** usually means 'very much': *deeply in love* ◊ *deeply shocked*. You can use **deep down** (but not **deeply**) to talk about a person's real nature: *She can seem stern, but deep down she's a very kind person.* ◊ *She can seem stern, but deeply she's a very kind person.*

**Dee·pa·vali** noun /ˌdiːpəˈvɑːli/ = DIWALI

**deep·en** /ˈdiːpən/ verb **1** [I, T] ~ (sth) (into sth) if an emotion or a feeling **deepens**, or if sth **deepens** it, it becomes stronger: *Their friendship soon deepened into love.* **2** [I, T] ~ (sth) to become worse; to make sth worse: *Warships were sent in as the crisis deepened.* ◊ *a deepening economic recession* **3** [I, T] to become deeper; to make sth deeper: *The water deepened gradually.* ◊ *His frown deepened.* ◊ ~ **sth** *There were plans to deepen a stretch of the river.* **4** [T] ~ **sth** to improve your knowledge or understanding of sth: *an opportunity for students to deepen their understanding of different cultures* **5** [I, T] ~ (sth) if colour or light **deepens** or if sth **deepens** it, it becomes darker: *deepening shadows* **6** [I, T] ~ (sth) (to sth) if a sound or voice **deepens** or if you **deepen** it, it becomes lower or you make it lower: *His voice deepened to a growl.* **7** [I] if your breathing **deepens**, you breathe more deeply than usual

**ˈdeep end** noun [sing.] the part of a swimming pool where the water is deepest
**IDM** **go off the ˈdeep end** (*informal*) to suddenly become very angry or emotional **jump/be thrown in at the ˈdeep end** (*informal*) to start or be made to start a new and difficult activity that you are not prepared for: *Junior hospital doctors are thrown in at the deep end in their first jobs.*

**ˌdeep ˈfreeze** /ˈdiːp ˈfriːz/ noun (*BrE*) (*US* **Deep-freeze**™, **ˌdeep ˈfreezer**) noun = FREEZER

**deep-ˈfrozen** adj. preserved at an extremely low temperature

**deep-ˈfry** verb [usually passive] ~ **sth** to cook food in oil that covers it completely: *deep-fried chicken pieces*

**deep·ly** ⓣ 🅱🅲 /ˈdiːpli/ adv. **1** 🅱🅲 very; very much: *She is deeply religious.* ◊ *His art was deeply personal.* ◊ *This is a deeply disturbing film.* ◊ *a deeply unpopular decision* ◊ *I deeply regret my error.* ◊ *Farmers care deeply for their land.* **2** 🅱🅲 used with some verbs to show that sth is done in a very complete way: *to breathe/inhale deeply* (= filling your lungs with air) ◊ *Leila sighed deeply and said, 'I know'.* ◊ *We need to think deeply about these questions.* **3** to a depth that is quite a long way from the surface of sth: *to drill deeply into the wood* ◊ note at DEEP

**ˌdeep-ˈrooted**, **ˌdeep-ˈseated** adj. [usually before noun] very fixed and strong; difficult to change or to destroy: *a deep-rooted desire* ◊ *The country's political divisions are deep-seated.*

**ˌdeep-ˈsea** (*also less frequent* **ˌdeep-ˈwater**) adj. [only before noun] of or in the deeper parts of the sea: *a deep-sea diver* ◊ *deep-sea fishing/diving*

**ˌdeep-ˈset** adj. (*formal*) eyes that are **deep-set** seem to be quite far back in a person's face

**the ˌDeep ˈSouth** noun [sing.] the southern states of the US, especially Georgia, Alabama, Mississippi, Louisiana and South Carolina

**ˌdeep ˈstructure** (*also* **ˈD-structure**) noun [U] (*grammar*) the basic relationships between the different parts of a sentence that show how we think when we are using language ◊ compare SURFACE STRUCTURE

**ˌdeep vein thromˈbosis** noun [U, C] (*abbr.* **DVT**) (*medical*) a serious condition caused by a blood CLOT (= a thick mass of blood) forming in a VEIN: *Passengers on long-haul flights are being warned about the risks of deep vein thrombosis.*

**ˈdeep-water** adj. = DEEP-SEA

**deer** /dɪə(r); *NAmE* dɪr/ noun (*pl.* **deer**) an animal with long legs that eats grass, leaves, etc. and can run fast. Most male deer have ANTLERS (= parts on their heads that are like branches in shape). There are many types of deer: *a herd of deer* ◊ *a deer park* ◊ see also DOE, FALLOW DEER, FAWN *noun*, RED DEER, REINDEER, ROE DEER, STAG

▼ **HOMOPHONES**

### dear • deer /dɪə(r); *NAmE* dɪr/

- **dear** *adj.*: *Kate is a very dear friend of mine.*
- **dear** *noun*: *Congratulations, my dear!*
- **deer** *noun*: *The team is responsible for conserving red deer in the forest.*

**deer·stalk·er** /ˈdɪəstɔːkə(r); *NAmE* ˈdɪrs-/ noun a cap with two PEAKS, one in front and one behind, and two pieces of cloth that are usually tied together on top but can be folded down to cover the ears

**def** /def/ noun, adv. (*informal*)
**noun** definition: *You can now view the trailer in high def online.* ◊ see also HD
**adv.** definitely: *This will def be a good movie.*

**de·face** /dɪˈfeɪs/ verb ~ **sth** to damage the appearance of sth especially by drawing or writing on it ► **deˈface·ment** noun [U]

**de facto** /ˌdeɪ ˈfæktəʊ/
**adj.** [usually before noun] ► **de facto** adv.: *He continued to rule the country de facto.* ◊ compare DE JURE **1** (*from Latin, formal*) existing as a fact although it may not be legally accepted as existing: *The general took de facto control of the country.* **2** (*AustralE, NZE*) (of a relationship) in which two people live together as if they were married, without actually being married: *John was in a de facto relationship with Dawn for 22 years.* **3** (*AustralE, NZE*) (of a person or couple) living in a de facto relationship: *her de facto husband*
**noun** (*pl.* **-os**) (*AustralE, NZE*) a person who lives with sb as their husband or wife, although they are not officially married

**defae·cate**, **defae·ca·tion** /ˈdefəkeɪt, ˌdefəˈkeɪʃn/ (*BrE*) = DEFECATE, DEFECATION

**def·am·ation** /ˌdefəˈmeɪʃn/ noun [U, C] (*formal*) the act of damaging sb's reputation by saying or writing bad or false things about them: *The company sued for defamation.*

**de·fama·tory** /dɪˈfæmətri; *NAmE* -tɔːri/ adj. (*formal*) (of speech or writing) intended to harm sb by saying or writing bad or false things about them

**de·fame** /dɪˈfeɪm/ verb ~ **sb/sth** (*formal*) to harm sb by saying or writing bad or false things about them

**de·fault** 🅸+ 🅲🅱 noun, verb
**noun** /dɪˈfɔːlt; ˈdiːfɔːlt/ **1** 🅸+ 🅲🅱 [U, C, usually sing.] what happens or appears if you do not make any other choice or decision, especially in a computer program: *The default option is to save your work every five minutes.* **2** 🅸+ 🅲🅱 [U, C] failure to do sth that must be done by law, especially paying a debt: *in ~* (*on sth*) *The company is in default on the loan.* ◊ *Mortgage defaults have risen in the last year.*
**IDM** **by deˈfault 1** a game or competition can be won **by default** if there are no other people, teams, etc. taking part **2** if sth happens **by default**, it happens because you have not made any other decision or choices that would make things happen in a different way **in deˈfault of sth** (*formal*) because of a lack of sth: *They accepted what he had said in default of any evidence to disprove it.*

---

æ cat | ɑː father | e bed | ɜː fur | ə about | ɪ sit | iː see | i happy | ɒ got (*BrE*) | ɔː saw | ʌ cup | ʊ put | uː too

**defensive**

■ **verb** /dɪˈfɔːlt/ **1** [I] ~ **(on sth)** to fail to do sth that you legally have to do, especially by not paying a debt: *to default on a loan/debt* ◇ *defaulting borrowers/tenants* **2** [I] ~ **(to sth)** to happen when you do not make any other choice or change ▶ **deˈfault·er** *noun*: *mortgage defaulters*

## de·feat ⓘ B2 /dɪˈfiːt/ *verb, noun*

■ **verb 1** ⓘ B2 to win against sb in a war, competition, sports game, etc. SYN **beat**: ~ **sb/sth** *He defeated the champion in three sets.* ◇ *The goal is to defeat the enemy by whatever means possible.* ◇ *a defeated army* ◇ ~ **sb by sth** *The government was defeated by 200 votes to 83.* ◇ ~ **sb in sth** *Our team was narrowly defeated in the final.* **2** ⓘ B2 to stop sth from being successful: ~ **sth** *They are united in their determination to defeat global terrorism.* ◇ **be defeated by sth** *The motion was defeated by 19 votes.* ◇ *Writing down your password so you remember it defeats the purpose of having a password.* **3** ~ **sb** (*formal*) if sth **defeats** you, you cannot understand it: *The instruction manual completely defeated me.*

■ **noun 1** ⓘ B2 [U, C] failure to win or to be successful: *The party faces defeat in the election.* ◇ *They suffered a narrow defeat in the final.* ◇ *a heavy/humiliating/crushing defeat* ◇ *They finally had to admit defeat* (= stop trying to be successful). ◇ ~ **by/against sb** *their defeat by the Brazilians* ◇ **in** ~ *He was gracious in defeat, acknowledging his opponent's greater skill.* **2** ⓘ B2 [C, usually sing.] the act of winning a victory over sb/sth: *The army inflicted a heavy defeat on rebel forces.* ◇ *the defeat of fascism* IDM see SNATCH *v.*

**de·feat·ist** /dɪˈfiːtɪst/ *adj.* (*disapproving*) expecting not to succeed, and showing it in a particular situation: *a defeatist attitude/view* ▶ **deˈfeat·ist** *noun*: *He is a pessimist and a defeatist.* **deˈfeat·ism** *noun* [U]

**defe·cate** (*BrE also* **defae·cate**) /ˈdefəkeɪt, ˈdiːf-/ *verb* [I] (*formal*) to get rid of solid waste from your body through your BOWELS ▶ **defe·caˈtion** (*BrE also* **defae·caˈtion**) /ˌdefəˈkeɪʃn, ˌdiːf-/ *noun* [U]

## de·fect ᴵ⁺ C1 *noun, verb*

■ **noun** ᴵ⁺ C1 /ˈdiːfekt/ a fault in sth or in the way it has been made that means that it is not perfect: *a speech defect* ◇ *a defect in the glass*

■ **verb** /dɪˈfekt/ [I] ~ **(from sth) (to sth)** to leave a political party, country, etc. to join another that is considered to be an enemy ▶ **deˈfec·tion** /-ˈfekʃn/ *noun* [U, C]: ~ **(from sth) (to sth)** *There have been several defections from the ruling party.* **deˈfect·or** *noun*

**de·fect·ive** /dɪˈfektɪv/ *adj.* having a fault or faults; not perfect or complete SYN **faulty**: *defective goods* ◇ *Her hearing was found to be slightly defective.* ▶ **deˈfect·ive·ly** *adv.* **deˈfect·ive·ness** *noun* [U]

## de·fence ⓘ B2 (*US* **de·fense**) /dɪˈfens/ *noun*

- **PROTECTION AGAINST ATTACK 1** ⓘ B2 [U] the act of protecting sb/sth from attack, criticism, etc: **in** ~ **of sb/sth** *soldiers who died in defence of their country* ◇ *What points can be raised in defence of this argument?* ◇ **in sb's** ~ *I have to say in her defence that she knew nothing about it beforehand.* ◇ *When her brother was criticized she leapt to his defence.* ↪ see also CIVIL DEFENCE, SELF-DEFENCE **2** ⓘ B2 [C, U] something that provides protection against attack from enemies, the weather, illness, etc: *They are responsible for maintaining coastal flood defences.* ◇ *At this point the country had no effective air defences.* ◇ ~ **against sth** *The town walls were built as a defence against enemy attacks.* ◇ *a new missile defence system* (= for defence against MISSILES) ◇ *The body has natural defence mechanisms to protect it from disease.* **3** ⓘ B2 [U] the organization of the people and systems that are used by a government to protect a country from attack: (*BrE*) *the Ministry of Defence* ◇ (*US*) *the Department of Defense* ◇ *Further cuts in defence spending are being considered.*
- **SUPPORT 4** [C] something that is said or written in order to support sth: *a defence of Marxism*
- **LAW 5** [C, usually sing.] what is said in court to prove that a person did not commit a crime; the act of presenting this argument in court: *Her defence was that she was somewhere completely different at the time of the crime.* ◇ *He wanted to conduct his own defence.* **6 the defence** [sing. + sing./pl. v.] the lawyer or lawyers whose job is to prove in court that a person did not commit a crime: *The defence requested more time to prepare their case.* ◇ *the defence lawyer/counsel* ◇ (*US also*) *the defense attorney* ◇ *a witness for the defence* ↪ compare PROSECUTION
- **IN SPORT 7** /ˈdiːfens; *NAmE* ˈdiːfens/ [sing., U] the players who must prevent the other team from scoring; the position of these players on the sports field: *Welford cut through the defence to score the winning goal.* ◇ **in** ~ (*BrE*) *She plays in defence.* ◇ **on** ~ (*NAmE*) *She plays on defense.* ↪ compare ATTACK, OFFENSE **8** [C] a contest, game, etc. in which the previous winner or winners compete in order to try to win again: *Barcelona's defence of the Champions League title*

**de·fence·less** (*US* **de·fense·less**) /dɪˈfensləs/ *adj.* weak; not able to protect yourself; having no protection: *defenceless children* ◇ *The village is defenceless against attack.* ▶ **deˈfence·less·ness** (*US* **deˈfense·less·ness**) *noun* [U]

## de·fend ⓘ B2 /dɪˈfend/ *verb*

- **PROTECT AGAINST ATTACK/LOSS 1** ⓘ B2 [T, I] to protect sb/sth from attack: ~ **sb/sth** *The role of the military is to defend the country.* ◇ ~ **sb/sth against sb/sth** *The male birds defend their territory against other males.* ◇ ~ **sb/sth from sb/sth** *The cannons once defended the city from attack by sea.* ◇ ~ **yourself (from/against sb/sth)** *All our officers are trained to defend themselves against knife attacks.* ◇ ~ **against sb/sth** *It is impossible to defend against an all-out attack.* ↪ WORDFINDER NOTE at ARMY **2** ⓘ B2 [T] ~ **sth** to protect sth that you value and prevent it from being taken away: *The organization works to defend human rights wherever they are threatened.* ◇ *Freedom must always be defended.* ◇ *The ruling class will always defend its own interests.*
- **SUPPORT 3** ⓘ B2 [T] to say or write sth in support of sb/sth that has been criticized: *They defended their decision to pull out of the event.* ◇ ~ **sb/sth against/from sb/sth** *The article seeks to defend him against charges of hypocrisy.* ◇ ~ **yourself (from/against sb/sth)** *Politicians are skilled at defending themselves against their critics.*
- **IN SPORT 4** [I, T] ~ **(sth)** (in sports) to protect your own goal to stop your opponents from scoring OPP **attack**
- **IN COMPETITIONS 5** [T] ~ **sth** to take part in a competition that you won the last time and try to win it again: *He is defending champion.* ◇ *She will be defending her title at next month's championships.* ◇ (*politics*) *He intends to defend his seat in the next election.*
- **LAW 6** [T, I] ~ **(sb/yourself)** to act as a lawyer for sb who has been charged with a crime: *He has employed one of the UK's top lawyers to defend him.* ↪ compare PROSECUTE

**de·fend·ant** /dɪˈfendənt/ *noun* the person in a trial who is accused of committing a crime, or who is being SUED by another person ↪ WORDFINDER NOTE at TRIAL ↪ compare ACCUSED, PLAINTIFF

**de·fend·er** ᴵ⁺ /dɪˈfendə(r)/ *noun* **1** ᴵ⁺ B2 a player who must stop the other team from scoring in games such as football (soccer), hockey, etc. **2** ᴵ⁺ B2 a person who defends and believes in protecting sth: *a passionate defender of human rights* ↪ see also PUBLIC DEFENDER

**de·fense, de·fense·less, de·fense·less·ness** (*US*) = DEFENCE, DEFENCELESS, DEFENCELESSNESS

**de·fens·ible** /dɪˈfensəbl/ *adj.* **1** able to be supported by reasons or arguments that show that it is right or should be allowed: *Is abortion morally defensible?* OPP **indefensible 2** (of a place) able to be defended from an attack

## de·fen·sive ᴵ⁺ C1 /dɪˈfensɪv/ *adj., noun*

■ *adj.* **1** ᴵ⁺ C1 protecting sb/sth against attack: *a defensive measure* ◇ *Troops took up a defensive position around the town.* ↪ compare OFFENSIVE **2** ᴵ⁺ C1 behaving in a way that shows that you feel that people are criticizing you: *Don't ask him about his plans—he just gets defensive.* **3** ᴵ⁺ C1 (*sport*) connected with trying to prevent the other team or player from scoring points or goals: *defensive play* ↪ compare OFFENSIVE ▶ **deˈfen·sive·ly** *adv.* **deˈfen·sive·ness** *noun* [U]

# defensive medicine

**noun**

**IDM** **on/onto the de'fensive** acting in a way that shows that you expect to be attacked or criticized; having to defend yourself: *Their questions about the money put her on the defensive.* ◊ *Warnings of an enemy attack forced the troops onto the defensive.*

**de‧fensive 'medicine** *noun* [U] (*especially NAmE*) medical treatment that may involve more tests, operations, etc. than a person really needs because a doctor is worried that a claim or complaint may be made against them in court if they make a mistake in the treatment they give

**defer** /dɪˈfɜː(r)/ *verb* (-rr-) ~ **(doing) sth** (*formal*) to delay sth until a later time **SYN** **put off**: *The department deferred the decision for six months.* ◊ *She had applied for deferred admission to college.* ▸ **de‧fer‧ment**, **de‧fer‧ral** /-ˈfɜːrəl/ *noun* [U, C]

**PHRV** **de'fer to sb/sth** (*formal*) to agree to accept what sb has decided or what they think about sb/sth because you respect him or her: *We will defer to whatever the committee decides.*

**def‧er‧ence** /ˈdefərəns/ *noun* [U] behaviour that shows that you respect sb/sth: **in ~ to sb/sth** *The women wore veils in deference to the customs of the country.* ◊ **out of ~ to sb/sth** *The flags were lowered out of deference to the bereaved family.* ▸ **def‧er‧en‧tial** /ˌdefəˈrenʃl/ *adj.* **def‧er‧en‧tial‧ly** /-ʃəli/ *adv.*

**de‧fi‧ance** /dɪˈfaɪəns/ *noun* [U] the act of openly refusing to obey sb/sth: *a look/an act/a gesture of defiance* ◊ **in ~ of sth** *Nuclear testing was resumed in defiance of an international ban.*

**de'fiance campaign** *noun* (in South Africa in the past, especially in the period after 1952) a series of activities in which black people refused to obey laws that were not fair

**de‧fi‧ant** /dɪˈfaɪənt/ *adj.* openly refusing to obey sb/sth, sometimes in an aggressive way: *a defiant teenager* ◊ *The terrorists sent a defiant message to the government.* ▸ **de‧fi‧ant‧ly** *adv.*

**de‧fib‧ril‧la‧tion** /ˌdiːfɪbrɪˈleɪʃn/ *noun* [U] (*medical*) the use of a CONTROLLED electric shock from a defibrillator to return the heart to its natural rhythm

**de‧fib‧ril‧la‧tor** /ˌdiːfɪbrɪleɪtə(r)/ *noun* (*medical*) a piece of equipment used to control the movements of the heart muscles by giving the heart an electric shock in a carefully managed way

**de‧fi‧ciency** /dɪˈfɪʃnsi/ *noun* (*pl.* **-ies**) **1** [U, C] the state of not having, or not having enough of, sth that is essential **SYN** **shortage**: ~ **(in sth)** *Vitamin deficiency in the diet can cause illness.* ◊ **~of sth** *a deficiency of Vitamin B* **2** [C] ~ **(in sth)** a fault or a weakness in sth/sb that makes it or them less successful: *deficiencies in the computer system*

**de‧fi‧cient** /dɪˈfɪʃnt/ *adj.* **1** ~ **(in sth)** not having enough of sth, especially sth that is essential: *a diet that is deficient in vitamin A* **2** not good enough: *Deaf people are sometimes treated as being mentally deficient.*

**def‧icit** /ˈdefɪsɪt/ *noun* **1** (*economics*) the amount by which money spent or owed is greater than money earned in a particular period of time: *a budget/trade deficit* ◊ **in~** *The trade balance has been in deficit for the past five years.* ⊃ see also TRADE DEFICIT ⊃ compare SURPLUS **2** (*formal*) the amount by which sth, especially an amount of money, is too small or smaller than sth else: *There's a deficit of $3 million in the total needed to complete the project.* ◊ *The team has to come back from a 2–0 deficit in the first half.*

**de‧fied** /dɪˈfaɪd/ *past tense, past part.* of DEFY

**de‧file**[1] /dɪˈfaɪl/ *verb* ~ **sth** (*formal or literary*) to make sth dirty or no longer pure, especially sth that people consider important or holy: *Many victims of burglary feel their homes have been defiled.* ◊ *The altar had been defiled by vandals.* ▸ **de‧file‧ment** *noun* [U, C]

**de‧file**[2] /ˈdiːfaɪl, dɪˈfaɪl/ *noun* (*formal*) a narrow way through mountains

**de‧fine** /dɪˈfaɪn/ *verb* **1** to say or explain what the meaning of a word or phrase is: ~ **sth** *The term 'mental illness' is difficult to define.* ◊ ~ **sth as sth** *Life imprisonment is defined as 60 years under state law.* **2** to describe or show the nature or range of sb/sth: ~ **sth** *The goals of the project are clearly defined.* ◊ *The difficulty of a problem was defined in terms of how long it took to complete.* ◊ ~ **what, how, etc…** *It is difficult to define what makes him so popular.* ◊ ~ **yourself (as sth)** *He defines himself as an independent.* **3** ~ **sb/sth/yourself** to make or establish the essential character of sb/sth: *For some, the football club defines their identity.* **4** ~ **sth** to show clearly a line, shape or edge: *The mountain was sharply defined against the sky.* ▸ **de‧fin‧able** *adj.*

▼ LANGUAGE BANK

### define

Defining terms

- It is important to **clarify** what is meant by climate change.
- Climate change **can/may be defined as** 'the long-term fluctuations in temperature, precipitation, wind and other aspects of the earth's climate'.
- A generally accepted **definition of** global warming **is** the gradual increase in the overall temperature of the earth's atmosphere due to the greenhouse effect.
- The greenhouse effect **is defined by** the author **as** the process by which heat from the sun is trapped in the earth's atmosphere, causing the temperature of the earth to rise.
- The author **uses the term** climate change **to refer to** any significant change in measures of climate lasting for an extended period.
- **The term** 'carbon footprint' **refers to** the amount of carbon dioxide released into the atmosphere as a result of the activities of an individual or organization.
- Scientists suggest that increased carbon dioxide in the atmosphere will result in an increase in global temperatures, and **the term** 'global warming' **is used** to describe this phenomenon.

⊃ LANGUAGE BANK at FIRST

**de‧fined 'benefit** *noun* a fixed amount of money that will be paid by a PENSION PLAN, especially when this amount is based on your salary at the end of your working life and the number of years you worked

**de‧fined contri'bution** *noun* fixed payments that are made to a PENSION PLAN, where the amount that will be paid out can change

**de‧fin‧ing** /dɪˈfaɪnɪŋ/ *adj.* **1** that describes or shows the essential meaning of sth: *The EU referendum was a defining moment for our nation.* ◊ *Front porches are a defining characteristic of Garfield's architecture.* **2** = RESTRICTIVE (2)

**de'fining vocabulary** *noun* a set of carefully chosen words used to write the explanations in some dictionaries

**def‧in‧ite** /ˈdefɪnət/ *adj., noun*

■ *adj.* **1** sure or certain; unlikely to change: *Can you give me a definite answer by tomorrow?* ◊ ~ **that…** *Is it definite that he's leaving?* ◊ *I've heard rumours, but nothing definite.* ◊ ~ **for~** *I'm not sure—I can find out for definite if you like.* ◊ *That's definite then, is it?* ⊃ SYNONYMS at CERTAIN **2** easily or clearly seen or understood; obvious **SYN** **clear**: *The look on her face was a definite sign that something was wrong.* ◊ *There was a definite feeling that things were getting worse.* **3** [not before noun] (of a person) sure that sth is true or that sth is going to happen and stating it to other people: ~ **about sth** *I'm definite about this.* ◊ ~ **that…** *She was definite that they weren't coming till next week.*

■ *noun* [sing.] (*informal*) sth that you are certain about or that you know will happen; sb who is sure to do sth: *'We're moving our office to Glasgow.' 'That's a definite, is it?'* ◊ *'Is Sarah coming to the party?' 'Yes, she's a definite.'*

**definite 'article** *noun* (*grammar*) the word *the* in English, or a similar word in another language ⊃ compare INDEFINITE ARTICLE

**def·in·ite·ly** /ˈdefɪnətli/ adv. **1** a way of emphasizing that sth is true and that there is no doubt about it: *I definitely remember sending the letter.* ◊ *'Was it what you expected?' 'Yes, definitely.'* ◊ *'Do you plan to have children?' 'Definitely not!'* ◊ *Some old people want help; others most definitely do not.* **2** in a way that is certain or that shows that you are certain: *The date of the move has not been definitely decided yet* (= it may change). ◊ *Please say definitely whether you will be coming or not.*

**def·in·ition** /ˌdefɪˈnɪʃn/ noun **1** [C, U] an explanation of the meaning of a word or phrase, especially in a dictionary: *clear simple definitions* ◊ *~ of sth the dictionary definition of this term* ◊ *a precise/strict definition of a word* ⊃ LANGUAGE BANK at DEFINE ⊃ WORDFINDER NOTE at DICTIONARY **2** [C] *~ of sth* what an idea means: *What's your definition of happiness?* ◊ *a broad/narrow definition of the concept* **3** [U] the act of saying what a word or an idea means: *The term 'partner' requires careful definition.* ◊ *by~ Neighbours by definition live close by* (= this is what being a neighbour means). **4** [U] the quality of being clear and easy to see; the ability of a device to give clear images: *The clarity and definition of the images are excellent.* ◊ *The definition of this TV is very good.* ⊃ see also HIGH-DEFINITION

**de·fini·tive** /dɪˈfɪnətɪv/ adj. **1** final; not able to be changed: *a definitive agreement/answer/statement* ◊ *The definitive version of the text is ready to be published.* **2** [usually before noun] considered to be the best of its kind and almost impossible to improve: *the definitive biography of Einstein* ▶ **de·fini·tive·ly** adv.

**de·flate** verb **1** /dɪˈfleɪt, ˌdiːˈfleɪt/ [T, I] *~ (sth)* to let air or gas out of a tyre, BALLOON, etc.; to become smaller because of air or gas coming out **2** /dɪˈfleɪt/ [T, often passive] to make sb feel less confident; to make sb/sth feel or seem less important: *be/feel deflated All the criticism had left her feeling totally deflated.* **3** /ˌdiːˈfleɪt/ [T] *~ sth* (*economics*) to reduce the amount of money being used in a country so that prices fall or stay steady ⊃ compare INFLATE, REFLATE

**de·fla·tion** /ˌdiːˈfleɪʃn/ noun [U] **1** (*economics*) a reduction in the amount of money in a country's economy so that prices fall or remain the same **2** the action of air being removed from sth **OPP** inflation ▶ **de·fla·tion·ary** /ˌdiːˈfleɪʃənri/; *NAmE* -ʃəneri/ adj.: *deflationary policies*

**de·flect** /dɪˈflekt/ verb **1** [I, T] to change direction or make sth change direction, especially after hitting sth: *The ball deflected off Reid's body into the goal.* ◊ *~ sth He raised his arm to try to deflect the blow.* **2** [T] *~ sth* to succeed in preventing sth from being directed towards you **SYN** divert: *All attempts to deflect attention from his private life have failed.* ◊ *She sought to deflect criticism by blaming her family.* **3** [T] *~ sb (from sth)* to prevent sb from doing sth that they are determined to do: *The government will not be deflected from its commitments.*

**de·flec·tion** /dɪˈflekʃn/ noun [U, C, usually sing.] a sudden change in the direction that sth is moving in, usually after it has hit sth; the act of causing sth to change direction: *the angle of deflection* ◊ *the deflection of the missile away from its target* ◊ *O'Leary's shot took a deflection off a defender and finished in the net.*

**de·flower** /ˌdiːˈflaʊə(r)/ verb *~ sb* (*old-fashioned, literary*) to have sex with a woman who has not had sex before

**de·foli·ant** /ˌdiːˈfəʊliənt/ noun [C, U] a chemical that removes the leaves from plants, sometimes used as a weapon in war

**de·foli·ate** /ˌdiːˈfəʊlieɪt/ verb *~ sth* (*specialist*) to destroy the leaves of trees or plants, especially with chemicals ▶ **de·foli·ation** /ˌdiːˌfəʊliˈeɪʃn/ noun [U]

**de·for·est** /ˌdiːˈfɒrɪst/ verb [usually passive] *~ sth* to cut down and destroy all the trees in a place: *be deforested Two thirds of the region has been deforested in the past decade.*

**de·for·est·ation** /ˌdiːˌfɒrɪˈsteɪʃn/; *NAmE* -fɔːr-/ noun [U] the act of cutting down or burning the trees in an area ⊃ compare AFFORESTATION, REFORESTATION

# defy

**de·form** /dɪˈfɔːm; *NAmE* -ˈfɔːrm/ verb [T, I] *~ (sth)* to change or damage the usual or natural shape of sth; to become changed in shape: *The disease had deformed his spine.*

**de·form·ation** /ˌdiːfɔːˈmeɪʃn; *NAmE* -fɔːr'm-/ noun **1** [U] the process or result of changing or damaging the normal shape of sth **2** [C] a change in the normal shape of sth as a result of injury or illness: *a deformation of the spine*

**de·formed** /dɪˈfɔːmd; *NAmE* -ˈfɔːrmd/ adj. (of a person or a part of the body) having a shape that is not normal because it has grown wrongly: *She was born with deformed hands.*

**de·form·ity** /dɪˈfɔːməti; *NAmE* -ˈfɔːrm-/ noun [C, U] (*pl.* -ies) a condition in which a part of the body is not the normal shape because of injury, illness or because it has grown wrongly **SYN** malformation: *Drugs taken during pregnancy may cause physical deformity in babies.*

**de·frag·ment** /ˌdiːfrægˈment; *NAmE* ˌdiːˈfrægmənt/ (also *informal* **de·frag** /ˌdiːˈfræɡ/) verb *~ sth* (*computing*) to organize where data is stored on a computer HARD DISK in the most efficient way, in order to reduce the time taken to access the data ▶ **de·frag·men·ta·tion** /ˌdiːˌfrægmənˈteɪʃn; *NAmE* -mən-/ noun [U]

**de·fraud** /dɪˈfrɔːd/ verb [I, T] to get money illegally from a person or an organization by tricking them: *All three men were charged with conspiracy to defraud.* ◊ *~ sb (of sth) They were accused of defrauding the company of $14000.*

**de·fray** /dɪˈfreɪ/ verb *~ costs / expenses* (*formal*) to give sb back the money that they have spent on sth

**de·friend** /ˌdiːˈfrend/ verb = UNFRIEND

**de·frock** /ˌdiːˈfrɒk; *NAmE* -ˈfrɑːk/ verb [usually passive] *~ sb* to officially remove a priest from his or her job, because he or she has done sth wrong: *a defrocked priest*

**de·frost** /ˌdiːˈfrɒst; *NAmE* -ˈfrɔːst/ verb **1** [I, T] (of food) to become warmer so that it is no longer frozen; to make food warmer so that it is no longer frozen: *It will take about four hours to defrost.* ◊ *~ sth Make sure you defrost the chicken completely before cooking.* ⊃ compare DE-ICE, MELT, THAW, UNFREEZE **2** [T, I] *~ (sth)* when you defrost a fridge or FREEZER, or when it defrosts, you remove the ice from it **3** [T] *~ sth* to remove ice from the surface of a car's windows **SYN** de-ice ▶ **de·frost·er** noun

**deft** /deft/ adj. **1** (of a person's movements) quick and showing skill: *deft hands/fingers/footwork* ◊ *He finished off the painting with a few deft strokes of the brush.* ◊ *In one deft movement, he had her hand locked behind her back.* **2** clever and showing skill: *her deft command of the language* ▶ **deft·ly** adv.: *I threw her a towel which she deftly caught.* ◊ *They deftly avoided answering my questions.* **deft·ness** noun [U]

> **WORD FAMILY**
> **defy** verb
> **defiance** noun
> **defiant** adj.

**de·funct** /dɪˈfʌŋkt/ adj. (*formal*) no longer existing, operating or being used

**de·fuse** /ˌdiːˈfjuːz/ verb **1** *~ sth* to stop a possibly dangerous or difficult situation from developing, especially by making people less angry or nervous: *Local police are trying to defuse racial tension in the community.* **2** *~ sth* to remove the FUSE from a bomb so that it cannot explode

**defy** /dɪˈfaɪ/ verb (**de·fies**, **defy·ing**, **de·fied**, **de·fied**) **1** *~ sb/sth* to refuse to obey or show respect for sb in authority, a law, a rule, etc.: *I wouldn't have dared to defy my teachers.* ◊ *Hundreds of people today defied the ban on political gatherings.* **2** *~ sth* **belief, explanation, description, etc.** to be impossible or almost impossible to believe, explain, describe, etc.: *a political move that defies explanation* ◊ *The beauty of the scene defies description.* **3** *~ sth* to successfully resist sth to a very unusual degree: *The baby boy defied all the odds and survived* (= stayed alive when it seemed certain that he would die). **IDM** **I defy you / anyone to do sth** used to say that sb should try to do sth, as a way of emphasizing that you

---

● Oxford Phrasal Academic Lexicon (OPAL) written and spoken word lists | Ⓦ OPAL written word list | Ⓢ OPAL spoken word list

**deg.**

think it is impossible to do it: *I defy anyone not to cry at the end of the film.*

**deg.** *abbr.* DEGREE(S): 26 deg. C

**de·gen·er·ate** *verb, adj., noun*
- *verb* /dɪˈdʒenəreɪt/ [I] to become worse, for example by becoming lower in quality or weaker SYN **deteriorate**: *Her health degenerated quickly.* ◊ *~ into sth The march degenerated into a riot.*
- *adj.* /dɪˈdʒenərət/ having moral standards that have fallen to a level that is very low and unacceptable to most people: *a degenerate popular culture* ▶ **de·gen·er·acy** /-rəsi/ *noun* [U]
- *noun* /dɪˈdʒenrərət/ a person whose behaviour shows moral standards that have fallen to a very low level

**de·gen·er·ation** /dɪˌdʒenəˈreɪʃn/ *noun* [U] the process of becoming worse or less acceptable in quality or condition: *social/moral degeneration* ◊ *Intensive farming in the area has caused severe degeneration of the land.*

**de·gen·era·tive** /dɪˈdʒenərətɪv/ *adj. (specialist)* (of an illness) getting or likely to get worse as time passes: *degenerative diseases such as arthritis*

**deg·rad·ation** /ˌdegrəˈdeɪʃn/ *noun* [U] **1** a situation in which sb has lost all SELF-RESPECT and the respect of other people: *the degradation of being sent to prison* **2** *(specialist)* the process of sth being damaged or made worse: *environmental degradation*

**de·grade** /dɪˈɡreɪd/ *verb* **1** [T] *~ sb* to show or treat sb in a way that makes them seem not worth any respect or not worth taking seriously: *This poster is offensive and degrades women.* **2** [T] *~ sth (specialist)* to make sth become worse, especially in quality **3** [I, T] *~ (into sth)* | *~ sth (specialist)* to change or make sth change to a simpler chemical form

**de·grad·ing** /dɪˈɡreɪdɪŋ/ *adj.* treating sb as if they have no value, so that they lose their SELF-RESPECT and the respect of other people: *the inhuman and degrading treatment of prisoners*

**de·gree** 🔊 A2 ⊙ /dɪˈɡriː/ *noun* **1** A2 [C] *(abbr.* **deg.***)* a unit for measuring temperature: *at … degrees Water freezes at 32 degrees Fahrenheit (32°F) or zero/nought degrees Celsius (0°C).* **2** B1 [C] a unit for measuring angles: *an angle of ninety degrees (90°)* **3** B2 [C, U] the amount or level of sth: *~ of sth Her job demands a high degree of skill.* ◊ *with a ~ of sth The story has been staged several times before, with varying degrees of success.* ◊ *to a ~ I agree with you to a certain degree.* ◊ *These criticisms are, to a degree (= to some extent), well founded.* **4** A2 [C] the qualification obtained by students who successfully complete a university or college course: *My brother has a master's degree from Harvard.* ◊ *in sth She's pursuing a degree in biochemistry.* ◊ *an undergraduate/graduate/doctoral degree⊃* see also ASSOCIATE'S DEGREE, FIRST DEGREE, JOINT DEGREE, HIGHER DEGREE, MASTER'S DEGREE⊃ WORD-FINDER NOTE at UNIVERSITY **5** [C] (*BrE*) a university or college course, normally lasting three years or more: *I'm hoping to do a chemistry degree.* **6** [C] a level in a scale of how serious sth is: *murder in the first degree (= of the most serious kind)* ◊ *first-degree murder* ◊ *third-degree (= very serious) burns⊃* see also SECOND-DEGREE, THIRD DEGREE
**IDM** **by de'grees** slowly and gradually: *By degrees their friendship grew into love.* ⊃ more at NTH

**de·hu·man·ize** (*BrE also* **-ise**) /ˌdiːˈhjuːmənaɪz/ *verb ~ sb* to make sb lose their human qualities such as KINDNESS, PITY, etc.; to make people seem like objects rather than human beings: *the dehumanizing effects of poverty and squalor* ▶ **de·hu·man·iza·tion**, **-isa·tion** /ˌdiːˌhjuːmənaɪˈzeɪʃn; *NAmE* -nəˈz-/ *noun* [U]

**de·hu·midi·fier** /ˌdiːhjuːˈmɪdɪfaɪə(r)/ *noun* an electrical machine for removing water from the air ⊃ see also HUMIDIFIER

**de·hy·drate** /ˌdiːhaɪˈdreɪt; *NAmE* diːˈhaɪdreɪt/ *verb* **1** [T, usually passive] *~ sth* to remove the water from sth, especially food, in order to preserve it **2** [I, T] to lose too much water from your body; to make a person's body lose too

much water: *Runners can dehydrate very quickly in this heat.* ◊ *the dehydrating effects of alcohol* ▶ **de·hy·dra·tion** /ˌdiːhaɪˈdreɪʃn/ *noun* [U]: *to suffer from dehydration* **de·hy·drated** /ˌdiːhaɪˈdreɪtɪd; *NAmE* diːˈhaɪdreɪtɪd/ *adj.*: *Drink lots of water to avoid becoming dehydrated.*

**de-ice** /ˌdiːˈaɪs/ *verb ~ sth* to remove the ice from sth ⊃ compare DEFROST, MELT, THAW, UNFREEZE

**de-icer** /ˌdiːˈaɪsə(r)/ *noun* [C, U] a substance that is put on a surface to remove ice or to stop it from forming

**deify** /ˈdeɪɪfaɪ, ˈdiːɪfaɪ/ *verb* (**dei·fies**, **dei·fy·ing**, **dei·fied**, **dei·fied**) *~ sb (formal)* to treat sb as a god ▶ **dei·fi·ca·tion** /ˌdeɪɪfɪˈkeɪʃn, ˌdiːɪf-/ *noun* [U]: *the deification of medieval kings*

**deign** /deɪn/ *verb ~ to do sth (disapproving)* to do sth in a way that shows you think you are too important to do it SYN **condescend**: *She just grunted, not deigning to look up from the page.*

**deism** /ˈdeɪɪzəm, ˈdiːɪzəm/ *noun* belief in God, especially a God that created the universe but does not take part in it ▶ **deist** /ˈdeɪɪst, ˈdiːɪst/ *noun* **de·is·tic** /deɪˈɪstɪk, diːˈɪ-/ *adj.*

**deity** /ˈdeɪəti, ˈdiːəti/ *noun (pl.* **-ies***)* **1** [C] a god or GODDESS: *Greek/Roman/Hindu deities* **2 the Deity** [sing.] *(formal)* God

**déjà vu** /ˌdeɪʒɑː ˈvuː/ *noun* [U] (*from French*) the feeling that you have previously experienced sth that is happening to you now: *I had a strong sense of déjà vu as I entered the room.*

**de·ject·ed** /dɪˈdʒektɪd/ *adj.* unhappy and disappointed SYN **despondent**: *She looked so dejected when she lost the game.* ▶ **de·ject·ed·ly** *adv.*

**de·jec·tion** /dɪˈdʒekʃn/ *noun* [U] a sad or depressed state

**de jure** /ˌdeɪ ˈdʒʊəri; *NAmE* ˈdʒʊri/ *adj., adv. (from Latin, law)* according to the law: *He held power de jure and de facto (= both according to the law and in reality).* ⊃ compare DE FACTO

**delay** 🔊 B2 /dɪˈleɪ/ *noun, verb*
- *noun* **1** 🔊 B2 [C, U] a period of time when sb/sth has to wait because of a problem that makes sth slow or late: *Commuters will face long delays on the roads today.* ◊ *a delay of two hours/a two-hour delay* ◊ *~ in (doing) sth We apologize for the delay in answering your letter.* ◊ *~ to sth These issues have caused serious delays to the project.* ◊ *Flights to New York may be subject to delay.* **2** 🔊 B2 [U] failure to do sth quickly or at the right time; the act of delaying: *There's no time for delay.* ◊ *without ~ Report it to the police without delay (= immediately).*
- *verb* **1** 🔊 B2 [T] *~ sb/sth* to make sb/sth late or force them to do sth more slowly: *My flight was delayed.* ◊ *Thousands of commuters were delayed for over an hour.* ◊ *The government is accused of using delaying tactics (= deliberately doing sth to delay a process, decision, etc.).* **2** 🔊 B2 [I, T] to not do sth until a later time or to make sth happen at a later time SYN **defer**: *Don't delay—call us today!* ◊ *~ sth Heavy hail showers delayed the start of the race.* ◊ *She's suffering a delayed reaction (= a reaction that did not happen immediately) to the shock.* ◊ *~ sth until … The judge will delay his verdict until he receives medical reports on the offender.* ◊ *~ doing sth He delayed telling her the news, waiting for the right moment.*

**de·lect·able** /dɪˈlektəbl/ *adj.* **1** (of food and drink) extremely pleasant to taste, smell or look at SYN **delicious**: *the delectable smell of freshly baked bread* **2** *(humorous)* (of a person) very attractive: *his delectable body* ▶ **de·lect·ably** /-bli/ *adv.*

**de·lect·ation** /ˌdiːlekˈteɪʃn/ *noun* [U] *(formal or humorous)* pleasure or entertainment SYN **delight**

**dele·gate** 🔊 C1 *noun, verb*
- *noun* /ˈdelɪɡət/ **1** 🔊 C1 a person who is chosen or elected to represent the views of a group of people and vote and make decisions for them: *Congress delegates rejected the proposals.* **2** 🔊 C1 a person who attends a conference: *The conference was attended by delegates from 56 countries.* ⊃ WORDFINDER NOTE at CONFERENCE
- *verb* /ˈdelɪɡeɪt/ **1** [I, T] to give part of your work, power or authority to sb in a lower position than you: *Some*

*managers find it difficult to delegate.* ◇ *~(sth) (to sb) The job had to be delegated to an assistant.* ◇ [T] (usually passive) to choose sb to do sth: **be delegated to do sth** *I've been delegated to organize the Christmas party.*

**del·e·ga·tion** /ˌdelɪˈɡeɪʃn/ *noun* **1** [C + sing. / pl. v.] a group of people who represent the views of an organization, a country, etc: *the Dutch delegation to the United Nations* ◇ *a delegation of teachers* **2** [U] the process of giving sb work or responsibilities that would usually be yours: *delegation of authority/decision-making*

**de·lete** /dɪˈliːt/ *verb, noun*
- *verb* **~ sth (from sth)** to remove sth that has been written or printed, or that has been stored on a computer: *Your name has been deleted from the list.* ◇ *This command deletes files from the directory.* ◇ (BrE) *Mr/Mrs/Ms* (**delete as appropriate**) ⇒ WORDFINDER NOTE at FILE ▶ **de·le·tion** /-ˈliːʃn/ *noun* [U, C]: *He made several deletions to the manuscript.*
- *noun* [U] a key or command on a computer, phone, etc. that removes text, records or images: *If the caller asks for financial details, just hang up and press delete.*

**dele·teri·ous** /ˌdeləˈtɪəriəs; NAmE -ˈtɪr-/ *adj.* (*formal*) harmful and damaging

**deli** /ˈdeli/ *noun* = DELICATESSEN

**de·lib·er·ate** *adj., verb*
- *adj.* /dɪˈlɪbərət/ **1** done on purpose rather than by accident SYN **intentional, planned**: *a deliberate act of vandalism* ◇ *The speech was a deliberate attempt to embarrass the government.* OPP **unintentional 2** (of a movement or an action) done slowly and carefully: *She spoke in a slow and deliberate way.*
- *verb* /dɪˈlɪbəreɪt/ [I, T] (*formal*) to consider sth very carefully, usually before making a decision: *The jury deliberated for five days before finding him guilty.* ◇ *~(on) whether, what, etc ... They deliberated (on) whether to continue with the talks.*

**de·lib·er·ate·ly** /dɪˈlɪbərətli/ *adv.* **1** done in a way that was planned, not by chance SYN **intentionally, on purpose**: *an ad campaign that deliberately targets children* ◇ *The fire had been started deliberately.* ◇ *Her tone was deliberately insulting.* **2** slowly and carefully: *He packed up his possessions slowly and deliberately.*

**de·lib·er·ation** /dɪˌlɪbəˈreɪʃn/ *noun* (*formal*) **1** [U, C, usually pl.] the process of carefully considering or discussing sth: *After ten hours of deliberation, the jury returned a verdict of 'not guilty'.* ◇ *The deliberations of the committee are completely confidential.* **2** [U] the quality of being slow and careful in what you say or do: *She signed her name with great deliberation.*

**de·lib·era·tive** /dɪˈlɪbərətɪv; NAmE -reɪt-/ *adj.* (*formal*) involving or showing careful consideration or discussion: *We are engaged in a deliberative process.*

**deli·cacy** /ˈdelɪkəsi/ *noun* (*pl.* **-ies**) **1** [U] the fact of being, or appearing to be, easy to damage or break: *the delicacy of the fabric* **2** [U] the quality of being done carefully and gently: *the delicacy of his touch* **3** [U] very careful behaviour in a difficult situation so that nobody is offended SYN **tact**: *She handled the situation with great sensitivity and delicacy.* **4** [U] the fact that a situation is difficult and sb may be easily offended: *I need to talk to you about a matter of some delicacy.* **5** [C] a type of food considered to be very special in a particular place SYN **speciality**: *local delicacies*

**deli·cate** /ˈdelɪkət/ *adj.* **1** easily damaged or broken SYN **fragile**: *delicate china teacups* ◇ *The eye is one of the most delicate organs of the body.* ◇ *the delicate ecological balance of the rainforest* ◇ *Babies have very delicate skin.* ◇ *a cool wash cycle for delicate fabrics* **2** (of a person) not strong and easily becoming ill: *a delicate child/constitution* **3** small and having a beautiful shape or appearance: *his delicate hands* **4** made or formed in a very careful and detailed way: *the delicate mechanisms of a clock* **5** showing or needing careful or sensitive treatment: *I admired your delicate handling of the situation.* ◇ *a delicate problem* ◇ *The delicate surgical operation took five hours.* **6** (of colours, flavours and

409 **deliver**

smells) light and pleasant; not strong SYN **subtle**: *a delicate fragrance/flavour* ◇ *a river scene painted in delicate watercolours* ▶ **deli·cate·ly** *adv.*: *He stepped delicately over the broken glass.* ◇ *delicately balanced flavours*

**deli·ca·tes·sen** /ˌdelɪkəˈtesn/ (*also* **deli**) *noun* a shop or part of one that sells cooked meats and cheeses, and special or unusual foods that come from other countries

**de·li·cious** /dɪˈlɪʃəs/ *adj.* **1** having a very pleasant taste or smell: *Who cooked this? It's absolutely delicious.* ◇ *to taste/smell/look delicious* ◇ *a delicious meal/recipe/treat* **2** (*literary*) extremely pleasant: *the delicious coolness of the breeze* ▶ **de·li·cious·ly** *adv.*: *deliciously creamy soup*

**de·light** /dɪˈlaɪt/ *noun, verb*
- *noun* **1** [U, sing.] a feeling of great pleasure SYN **joy**: *a feeling of sheer/pure delight* ◇ *with ~ The children squealed with delight when they saw the puppy.* ◇ *to the ~ of sb* | *to sb's ~ She won the game easily, to the delight of all her fans.* ◇ *~ in (doing) sth He takes (great) delight in* (= enjoys) *proving others wrong.* ◇ *~ at (doing) sth She couldn't hide her delight at the news.* ⇒ SYNONYMS at PLEASURE **2** [C] something that gives you great pleasure SYN **joy**: *This guitar is a delight to play.* ◇ *~ of doing sth the delights of living in the country* ⇒ see also TURKISH DELIGHT
- *verb* **~ sb** to give sb a lot of pleasure and joy: *This news will delight his fans all over the world.*
- PHR V **deˈlight in (doing) sth** [no passive] to enjoy doing sth very much, especially sth that makes other people feel embarrassed, uncomfortable, etc.

**de·light·ed** /dɪˈlaɪtɪd/ *adj.* very pleased: *a delighted smile* ◇ *~ to do sth I'd be absolutely delighted to come.* ◇ *~ that ... I was delighted that you could stay.* ◇ *~ by/at sth She was delighted by/at the news of the wedding.* ◇ *~ with sth I was delighted with my presents.* ⇒ SYNONYMS at GLAD ▶ **de·light·ed·ly** *adv.*

**de·light·ful** /dɪˈlaɪtfl/ *adj.* very pleasant SYN **charming**: *a delightful book/restaurant/town* ◇ *a delightful child* ⇒ SYNONYMS at WONDERFUL ▶ **de·light·ful·ly** /-fəli/ *adv.*

**de·limit** /diːˈlɪmɪt/ *verb* **~ sth** (*formal*) to decide what the limits of sth are ▶ **de·limit·ation** /diːˌlɪmɪˈteɪʃn/ *noun* [U, C]

**de·lin·eate** /dɪˈlɪniett/ *verb* **~ sth** (*formal*) to describe, draw or explain sth in detail: *Our objectives need to be precisely delineated.* ◇ *The ship's route is clearly delineated on the map.* ▶ **de·lin·ea·tion** /dɪˌlɪniˈeɪʃn/ *noun* [U, C]

**de·lin·quency** /dɪˈlɪŋkwənsi/ *noun* [U, C] (*pl.* **-ies**) bad or criminal behaviour, usually of young people: *an increase in juvenile delinquency* ⇒ see also JUVENILE DELINQUENCY

**de·lin·quent** /dɪˈlɪŋkwənt/ *adj.* **1** (especially of young people or their behaviour) tending to commit crimes: *delinquent teenagers* **2** (NAmE, *finance*) having failed to pay money that is owed: *a delinquent borrower* **3** (NAmE, *finance*) (of a sum of money) not having been paid in time: *a delinquent loan* ▶ **de·lin·quent** *noun* ⇒ see also JUVENILE DELINQUENT

**de·li·ri·ous** /dɪˈlɪriəs; BrE also -ˈlɪər-/ *adj.* **1** in an excited state and not able to think or speak clearly, usually because of a high temperature: *He became delirious and couldn't recognize people.* **2** **~(with sth)** extremely excited and happy: *The crowds were delirious with joy.* ▶ **de·li·ri·ous·ly** *adv.*

**de·lir·ium** /dɪˈlɪriəm; BrE also -ˈlɪər-/ *noun* [U] a mental state where sb becomes excited and not able to think or speak clearly, usually because of illness: *fits of delirium*

**de·lir·ium tre·mens** /dɪˌlɪriəm ˈtriːmenz; BrE also -ˌlɪər-/ *noun* [U] (*medical*) = DTs

**de·liver** /dɪˈlɪvə(r)/ *verb*
- **TAKE GOODS/LETTERS 1** [T, I] to take goods, letters, etc. to the person or people they have been sent to: *~ sth I get my food delivered from the supermarket to save time.* ◇ *~ sth to sb/sth Leaflets have been delivered to every household.* ◇ *~ (to sb/sth) We promise to deliver within 48 hours.*

# deliverable 410

- **GIVE/SEND INFORMATION** 2 [B1] [T] to give or send information or ideas to sb: *~ sth Let me deliver the good news first.* ◊ *The video delivers a clear message about road safety.* ◊ *~ sth to sb/sth Online training sessions are delivered directly to your desktop.* ◊ *~ sth via sth Our courses are delivered via the internet.*
- **GIVE SPEECH** 3 [B2] [T] *~ sth* to give a speech, talk, performance, etc. or to make an official statement: *She will deliver a major speech on foreign policy tomorrow.* ◊ *to deliver an address/a lecture/a sermon* ◊ *The cast delivered the performances of a lifetime.* ◊ *The jury finally delivered its verdict.*
- **KEEP PROMISE** 4 [B2] [I, T] to do what you promised to do or what you are expected to do; to produce or provide what people expect you to: *He has promised to finish the job by June and I am sure he will deliver.* ◊ *on sth She always delivers on her promises.* ◊ *~ sth If you can't deliver improved sales figures, you're fired.* ◊ *The team delivered a stunning victory last night.* ◊ *~ sth to sb There have been major breakdowns in delivering services to elderly residents.*
- **GIVE TO SB'S CARE OR CONTROL** 5 [T] to take sb somewhere; to give sb into sb else's care or control: *~ sb (to sb/sth) The taxi delivered us to our hotel.* ◊ *~ sb (up/over) (to sb/sth) They delivered their prisoner over to the invading army.*
- **BABY** 6 [T] *~ a baby* to help a woman to give birth to a baby: *The baby was delivered by Caesarean section.* 7 [T] to give birth to a baby: *~ sth The number of women delivering their babies in hospital increased.* ◊ *be delivered of sth (formal) She was delivered of a healthy boy.* ⊃ **WORDFINDER NOTE** at BIRTH
- **THROW** 8 [T] *~ sth* to throw or aim sth: *He delivered the blow (= hit sb hard) with all his force.*
- **RESCUE** 9 [T] *~ sb (from sth) (old use)* to rescue sb from sth bad [SYN] **save** [IDM] see GOODS, SIGN *v.*

**de·liver·able** /dɪˈlɪvərəbl/ *adj., noun*
- *adj.* that can be delivered: *deliverable objectives*
- *noun* [usually pl.] a product that a company promises to have ready for a customer: *computer software deliverables*

**de·liver·ance** /dɪˈlɪvərəns/ *noun* [U] *~ (from sth) (formal)* the state of being rescued from danger, evil or pain

**de·liv·ery** ⓘ [B2] /dɪˈlɪvəri/ *noun (pl. -ies)* 1 [B2] [U, C] the act of taking goods, letters, etc. to the people they have been sent to: *Allow 28 days for delivery.* ◊ *We offer free delivery on orders over $200.* ◊ *on ~ Please pay for goods on delivery (= when you receive them).* ◊ *a delivery van* ⊃ see also RECORDED DELIVERY, SPECIAL DELIVERY 2 [B2] [U] the act of making a service or information available to people: *the delivery of public services* ◊ *We have invested to improve service delivery.* ◊ *Digital content delivery, especially music and video, is big business.* 3 [C, U] the process of giving birth to a baby: *an easy/a difficult delivery* ◊ *a delivery room/ward* (= in a hospital, etc.) 4 [sing.] the way in which sb speaks, sings a song, etc. in public: *The beautiful poetry was ruined by her poor delivery.* 5 [C] a ball that is thrown, especially in CRICKET or baseball: *a fast delivery* [IDM] see CASH *n.*

**dell** /del/ *noun (literary)* a small valley with trees growing in or around it

**Del·phic** /ˈdelfɪk/ *adj.* 1 relating to the ancient Greek ORACLE at Delphi (= the place where people went to ask the gods for advice or information about the future) 2 *(often delphic) (formal)* with a meaning that is deliberately hidden or difficult to understand: *a delphic utterance*

**del·phin·ium** /delˈfɪniəm/ *noun* a tall garden plant with blue or white flowers growing up its STEM

**delta** /ˈdeltə/ *noun* 1 the fourth letter of the Greek alphabet (Δ, δ) 2 an area of land, like a TRIANGLE in shape, where a river has split into several smaller rivers before entering the sea: *the Nile Delta*

**del·toids** /ˈdeltɔɪdz/ *(also informal* **delts** /delts/) *noun* [pl.] *(anatomy)* the thick muscles that are TRIANGULAR in shape and cover the shoulder JOINTS

**de·lude** /dɪˈluːd/ *verb* to make sb believe sth that is not true [SYN] **deceive**: *~ sb You poor deluded creature.* ◊ *~ yourself He's deluding himself if he thinks it's going to be easy.* ◊ *~ sb/yourself into doing sth Don't be deluded into thinking that we are out of danger yet.* ◊ *~ yourself that … She had been deluding herself that he loved her.* ⊃ see also DELUSION

**del·uge** /ˈdeljuːdʒ/ *noun, verb*
- *noun* [usually sing.] 1 a severe flood; a sudden very heavy fall of rain [SYN] **flood** 2 a large number of things that happen or arrive at the same time: *a deluge of calls/complaints/letters*
- *verb* 1 [usually passive] to send or give sb/sth a large number of things at the same time [SYN] **flood, inundate**: *be deluged (with sth) We have been deluged with applications for the job.* 2 *(often passive) (formal)* to flood a place with water: *be deluged (by sth) The campsite was deluged by a flash flood.*

**de·lu·sion** /dɪˈluːʒn/ *noun* 1 [C] a false belief or opinion about yourself or your situation: *the delusions of the mentally ill* ◊ *Don't go getting delusions of grandeur* (= a belief that you are more important than you actually are). 2 [U] the act of believing or making yourself believe sth that is not true ⊃ see also DELUDE

**de·lu·sion·al** /dɪˈluːʒənl/ *adj.* having ideas or beliefs that are not based in reality: *If you think that plan will work, you're delusional.*

**de·lu·sive** /dɪˈluːsɪv/ *(also* **de·lu·sory** /dɪˈluːsəri, -ˈluːzə-/) *adj. (formal)* not real or true [SYN] **deceptive**

**de·luxe** /dɪˈlʌks, -ˈlʊks/ *adj.* [usually before noun] of a higher quality and more expensive than usual [SYN] **luxury**: *a deluxe hotel*

**delve** /delv/ *verb* [I] + *adv./prep.* to reach inside a bag, container, etc. to search for sth [SYN] **dig**: *She delved in her handbag for a pen.*
[PHR V] **delve ˈinto sth** to try hard to find out more information about sth: *She had started to delve into her father's distant past.*

**Dem.** *abbr.* (in politics in the US) DEMOCRAT; DEMOCRATIC

**dema·gogue** /ˈdeməɡɒɡ; NAmE -ɡɑːɡ/ *noun (disapproving)* a political leader who tries to win support by using arguments based on emotion rather than reason ▶ **dema·gog·ic** /ˌdeməˈɡɒɡɪk; NAmE -ˈɡɑːɡ-/ *adj.* **dema·gogy** /ˈdeməɡɒɡi; NAmE -ɡɑːɡi/ *noun* [U]

**de·mand** ⓘ [B2] ⊙ /dɪˈmɑːnd; NAmE -ˈmænd/ *noun, verb*
- *noun* 1 [B2] [C] a very strong request for sth; sth that sb needs: *~ for sth a demand for higher pay* ◊ *~ that … demands that the law on gun ownership should be changed* ◊ *A federal judge rejected their demands.* 2 [B2] **demands** [pl.] things that sb/sth makes you do, especially things that are difficult, make you tired, worried, etc.: *Juggling the demands of work and family is never easy.* ◊ *~ on sb As a director he makes huge demands on his actors.* 3 [U, sing.] the desire or need of customers for goods or services that they want to buy or use: *Demand is exceeding supply.* ◊ *It is becoming more difficult for us to meet demand.* ◊ *~ for sth/sb Consumer demand for organic foods continues to increase rapidly.* ◊ *We are seeing an increased demand for housing in the area.* ⊃ see also PRINT ON DEMAND, SUPPLY AND DEMAND
[IDM] **by popular deˈmand** because a lot of people have asked for sth: *By popular demand, the play will run for another week.* **in deˈmand** wanted by a lot of people: *Good secretaries are always in demand.* **on deˈmand** done or happening whenever sb asks: *Feed the baby on demand.* ◊ *The service allows you to watch video on demand.* ⊃ see also ON-DEMAND ⊃ see also SUPPLY AND DEMAND
- *verb* 1 [B2] to make a very strong request for sth: *~ sth They are demanding the release of all political prisoners.* ◊ *~ that … The UN has demanded that all troops be withdrawn.* ◊ *(BrE also) They are demanding that all troops should be withdrawn.* ◊ *~ to do sth I demand to see the manager.* ◊ *~ sth of/from sb We demand a lot of our teachers.* ⊃ SYNONYMS at ASK 2 [B2] + **speech** to ask a question in an angry or aggressive way: *'Who the hell are you?' he demanded angrily.* 3 *~ sth* (of customers) to want or

need goods or services: *Today's consumers are demanding a greater variety of produce.* 4 ⚡ B2 **~ sth** to need sth in order to be successful at sth: *This sport demands both speed and strength.*

▼ **SYNONYMS**
**demand**
require • expect • insist • ask
These words all mean to say that sb should do or have sth.

**demand** to make a very strong request for sth; to say very definitely that sb should have or do sth: *She demanded an immediate explanation.*

**require** [often passive] (*rather formal*) to make sb do or have sth, especially because it is necessary according to a law or set of rules or standards: *All candidates will be required to take a short test.*

**expect** to demand that sb should do, have or be sth, especially because it is their duty or responsibility: *I expect to be paid promptly for the work.*

**insist** to demand that sth happens or that sb agrees to do sth: *I didn't want to go but he insisted.* ◊ *We insist on the highest standards at all times.*

**ask** to expect or demand sth: *You're asking too much of him.*

DEMAND, EXPECT OR ASK?
• **Ask** is not as strong as **demand** or **expect**, both of which can be more like a command.

PATTERNS
• to demand / require / expect / ask **of / from** sb
• to demand / require / expect / insist / ask **that** …
• to require / expect / ask sb **to do** sth
• to demand / require / expect / ask **a lot / too much / a great deal**
• to **be too much** to expect / ask

**de·'mand draft** *noun* (*IndE*) a printed form on which your bank account details are written that you can order from a bank in order to pay for sth. The money is taken from your account when you order it and the person you want to pay must then take the draft to a bank to receive the money.

**de·mand·ing** /dɪˈmɑːndɪŋ; *NAmE* -ˈmæn-/ *adj.* **1** (of a piece of work) needing a lot of skill, effort, etc: *The work is physically demanding.* ⊃ SYNONYMS at DIFFICULT **2** (of a person) expecting a lot of work or attention from others; not easily satisfied: *a demanding boss / child* OPP **undemanding**

**de·mar·cate** /ˈdiːmɑːkeɪt; *NAmE* -mɑːrk-/ *verb* **~ sth** (*formal*) to mark or establish the limits of sth: *Plots of land have been demarcated by barbed wire.*

**de·mar·ca·tion** /ˌdiːmɑːˈkeɪʃn; *NAmE* -mɑːrˈk-/ *noun* [U, C] a line or limit that separates two things, such as types of work, groups of people or areas of land: *social demarcations* ◊ **~ between A and B** *It was hard to draw clear lines of demarcation between work and leisure.*

**de·mean** /dɪˈmiːn/ *verb* **1 ~ yourself** to do sth that makes people have less respect for you: *I wouldn't demean myself by asking for charity.* **2 ~ sb / sth** to make people have less respect for sb / sth SYN **degrade**: *Such images demean women.*

**de·mean·ing** /dɪˈmiːnɪŋ/ *adj.* putting sb in a position that does not give them the respect that they should have SYN **humiliating**: *He found it demeaning to work for his former employee.*

**de·mean·our** (*US* **de·mean·or**) /dɪˈmiːnə(r)/ *noun* [C, U] (*formal*) the way that sb looks or behaves: *He maintained a professional demeanour throughout.*

**de·ment·ed** /dɪˈmentɪd/ *adj.* **1** (*especially BrE*) behaving in a crazy way because you are extremely upset or worried: *I've been nearly demented with worry about you.* **2** (*old-fashioned* or *medical*) suffering from dementia ▶ **de·ment·ed·ly** *adv.*

**de·men·tia** /dɪˈmenʃə/ *noun* [U] (*medical*) a serious mental DISORDER caused by brain disease or injury, that affects the ability to think, remember and behave normally: *patients with dementia* ◊ *a dementia sufferer / patient* ◊

---

411 **democracy**

*She was diagnosed with dementia.* ⊃ compare ALZHEIMER'S ⊃ see also SENILE DEMENTIA ⊃ WORDFINDER NOTE at CONDITION

**de·merge** /ˌdiːˈmɜːdʒ; *NAmE* -ˈmɜːrdʒ/ *verb* [T, I] **~ (sth)** (*BrE, business*) to separate a company into smaller companies, usually into the companies that had previously been joined together; to be split in this way

**de·mer·ger** /ˌdiːˈmɜːdʒə(r); *NAmE* -ˈmɜːrdʒ-/ *noun* [C, U] (*BrE, business*) the act of separating a company from a larger company, especially when they had previously been joined together

**de·merit** /diːˈmerɪt/ *noun* (*formal*) **1** [usually pl.] a fault in sth or a disadvantage of sth: *the merits and demerits of the scheme* **2** (*NAmE*) a mark on sb's school record showing that they have done sth wrong: *You'll get three demerits if you're caught smoking on school grounds.*

**de·mesne** /dɪˈmeɪn/ *noun* **1** (in the past) land attached to a MANOR (= large house) that was kept by the owners for their own use **2** (*old use*) a region or large area of land

**demi-** /ˈdemi/ *prefix* (in nouns) half; partly: *demigod*

**demi·god** /ˈdemigɒd; *NAmE* -gɑːd/ *noun* **1** a minor god, or a being that is partly a god and partly human **2** a leader or other person who is treated like a god

**de·mili·tar·ize** (*BrE also* **-ise**) /ˌdiːˈmɪlɪtəraɪz/ *verb* [usually passive] **~ sth** to remove military forces from an area: *a demilitarized zone* OPP **militarize** ▶ **de·mili·tar·iza·tion**, **-isa·tion** /ˌdiːˌmɪlɪtəraɪˈzeɪʃn; *NAmE* -rəˈz-/ *noun* [U]

**de·mise** /dɪˈmaɪz/ *noun* [usually sing.] **1** the end or failure of an institution, an idea, a company, etc. **2** (*formal* or *humorous*) death: *his imminent / sudden / sad demise*

**demi·urge** /ˈdemiɜːdʒ; *NAmE* -ɜːrdʒ/ *noun* (*literary*) **1** a being that is responsible for creating the world **2** a being that controls the part of the world that is not spiritual

**demo** /ˈdeməʊ/ *noun, verb*
■ *noun* (*pl.* **-os**) (*informal*) **1** (*especially BrE*) = DEMONSTRATION (1): *They all went on the demo.* **2** = DEMONSTRATION (2): *I'll give you a demo.* ⊃ WORDFINDER NOTE at SOFTWARE **3** a version of an app or computer program that you can try out before you buy the full program: *The full version costs £22.99, but there is a demo to try before you buy.* **4** a recording of an example of sb's music: *The band have uploaded three demo tracks recorded last month.* **5** (*US*) = DEMOGRAPHIC (2): *They're trying to appeal to a younger demo.*
■ *verb* **~ sth** to use sth, especially a piece of software, to show sb or to see for yourself how it works: *He demoed the new program he had just created.* ◊ *Can I demo the software before I buy it?*

**demo-** /ˈdemə; *BrE also* dɪˈmɒ; *NAmE also* dɪˈmɑː/ *prefix* (in nouns, adjectives and adverbs) connected with people or population: *democracy* ◊ *democratic*

**demob** /ˌdiːˈmɒb; *NAmE* -ˈmɑːb/ *verb* [usually passive] **(-bb-)** (*BrE, informal*) = DEMOBILIZE: **be demobbed** *He was demobbed in 1946.* ▶ **demob** *noun* [U]

**de·mo·bil·ize** (*BrE also* **-ise**) /ˌdiːˈməʊbəlaɪz/ *verb* **1** (*also BrE, informal* **demob**) [T] **~ sb** to release sb from military service, especially at the end of a war ⊃ compare MOBILIZE **2** [I] (of a country or group of soldiers) to stop military activities ▶ **de·mo·bil·iza·tion**, **-isa·tion** /ˌdiːˌməʊbəlaɪˈzeɪʃn; *NAmE* -ləˈz-/ *noun* [U]

**dem·oc·racy** ⚡+ B2 /dɪˈmɒkrəsi; *NAmE* -ˈmɑːk-/ *noun* (*pl.* **-ies**) **1** ⚡ B2 [U] a system of government in which the people of a country can vote to elect their representatives: *parliamentary democracy* ◊ *the principles of democracy* ⊃ see also SOCIAL DEMOCRACY

WORDFINDER candidate, constituency, contest, election, majority, manifesto, poll, referendum, swing vote

**2** ⚡ B2 [C] a country that has this system of government: *Western democracies* ◊ *I thought we were supposed to be living in a democracy.* **3** ⚡ C1 [U] fair and equal treatment of everyone in an organization, etc., and their right to take part in making decisions: *the fight for justice and democracy* ⊃ WORDFINDER NOTE at CAPITALISM

# democrat

**dem·o·crat** /ˈdeməkræt/ noun **1** a person who believes in or supports democracy ⇨ see also SOCIAL DEMOCRAT **2 Democrat** (abbr. **D**, **Dem.**) a member or supporter of the Democratic Party of the US ⇨ compare REPUBLICAN ⇨ see also SOCIAL DEMOCRACY

**dem·o·crat·ic** /ˌdeməˈkrætɪk/ adj. **1** (of a country, state, system, etc.) controlled by representatives who are elected by the people of a country; connected with this system: *a democratic country* ◊ *a democratic system* ◊ *democratic government* **2** based on the principle that all members have an equal right to be involved in running an organization, etc: *democratic participation* ◊ *a democratic decision* **3** based on the principle that all members of society are equal rather than divided by money or social class: *a democratic society* ◊ *democratic reforms* **4 Democratic** (abbr. **Dem.**, **D**) connected with the Democratic Party in the US: *the Democratic senator from Oregon* ▸ **dem·o·crat·ic·al·ly** /-kli/ adv.: *a democratically elected government* ◊ *democratically controlled* ◊ *The decision was taken democratically.*

**the Demoˈcratic Party** noun [sing.] one of the two main political parties in the US, usually considered to be in favour of changing society in order to improve it ⇨ compare REPUBLICAN PARTY

**dem·oc·ra·tize** (BrE also **-ise**) /dɪˈmɒkrətaɪz; NAmE -ˈmɑːk-/ verb ~ sth (formal) to make a country or an institution more democratic ▸ **dem·oc·ra·tiza·tion, -isa·tion** /dɪˌmɒkrətaɪˈzeɪʃn; NAmE -ˌmɑːkrətəˈz-/ noun [U]

**demo·graph·ic** /ˌdeməˈɡræfɪk/ noun, adj.
■ noun **1 demographics** [pl.] (*statistics*) data relating to the population and different groups within it: *the demographics of radio listeners* **2** (US also, informal **demo**) [C] a section of the population who are of a similar age, the same sex, etc: *The products are designed to appeal to a young demographic.* ◊ *the 18–30 demographic*
■ adj. relating to the population and different groups within it: *demographic changes/trends/factors* ▸ **demo·graph·ic·al·ly** /-kli/ adv.

**dem·og·raphy** /dɪˈmɒɡrəfi/ NAmE -ˈmɑːɡ-/ noun [U] the changing number of births, deaths, diseases, etc. in a community over a period of time; the scientific study of these changes: *the social demography of Africa* ▸ **dem·og·raph·er** /dɪˈmɒɡrəfə(r); NAmE -ˈmɑːɡ-/ noun

**de·mol·ish** /dɪˈmɒlɪʃ; NAmE -ˈmɑːl-/ verb **1** ~ sth to pull or knock down a building; to destroy sth: *The factory is due to be demolished next year.* ◊ *The car had skidded across the road and demolished part of the wall.* **2** ~ sth to show that an idea or theory is completely wrong: *A recent book has demolished this theory.* **3** ~ sb/sth to defeat sb easily and completely: *They demolished New Zealand 44–6 in the final.* **4** ~ sth (BrE, informal) to eat sth very quickly: *The children demolished their burgers and chips.* ▸ **demo·li·tion** /ˌdeməˈlɪʃn/ noun [U, C]: *The whole row of houses is scheduled for demolition.* ◊ *His speech did a very effective demolition job on the government's proposals.*

**demoˈlition ˈderby** noun [C] (NAmE) (BrE **ˈstock-car racing** [U]) a type of race in which the competing cars are allowed to hit each other

**demon** /ˈdiːmən/ noun **1** an evil spirit: *The people believed the girl was possessed by demons.* **2** something that causes a person to worry and makes them unhappy: *the demons of jealousy* **3** (*informal*) a person who does sth very well or with a lot of energy: *He skis like a demon.*
IDM **the demon ˈdrink** (BrE, humorous) alcoholic drink

**de·mon·ic** /dɪˈmɒnɪk; NAmE -ˈmɑːn-/ adj. connected with, or like, a demon: *demonic forces* ◊ *a demonic appearance*

**de·mon·ize** (BrE also **-ise**) /ˈdiːmənaɪz/ verb ~ sb/sth to describe sb/sth in a way that is intended to make other people think of them or it as evil or dangerous: *He was demonized by the right-wing press.* ▸ **de·mon·iza·tion, -isa·tion** /ˌdiːmənaɪˈzeɪʃn; NAmE -nəˈz-/ noun [U]

**dem·on·strable** /dɪˈmɒnstrəbl; ˈdemənstrəbl; NAmE dɪˈmɑːnstrəbl/ adj. (formal) that can be shown or proved: *a demonstrable need* ▸ **dem·on·strably** /-bli/ adv.: *demonstrably unfair*

**dem·on·strate** /ˈdemənstreɪt/ verb **1** [T] to show sth clearly by giving proof or evidence: ~ that … *New research convincingly demonstrates that age-related memory loss is not inevitable.* ◊ ~ sth *These paintings demonstrate his extraordinary ability as a portrait painter.* ◊ ~ how, what, etc … *This study clearly demonstrates how fishing can affect an ecosystem.* ◊ ~ sth to sb *Let me demonstrate to you some of the difficulties we are facing.* ◊ ~ sb/sth to be sth *The theories were demonstrated to be false.* ◊ **it is demonstrated that …** *It has been demonstrated that this drug is effective.* ⇨ LANGUAGE BANK at EVIDENCE **2** [T] ~ sth to show by your actions that you have a particular quality, feeling or opinion protest: *The team demonstrated breathtaking skills.* ◊ *We want to demonstrate our commitment to human rights.* **3** [T] to show and explain how sth works or how to do sth: ~ sth (to sb) *Her job involves demonstrating new educational software.* ◊ ~ (to sb) how, what, etc … *Let me demonstrate to you how it works.* **4** [I] to take part in a public meeting or MARCH (= an organized walk by many people), usually as a protest or to show support for sth protest: ~ against sth *students demonstrating against the war* ◊ ~ for sth *Their objective was to demonstrate peacefully for civil rights.* ⇨ WORDFINDER NOTE at PROTEST

**dem·on·stra·tion** /ˌdemənˈstreɪʃn/ noun **1** (also informal **demo** especially in BrE) [C] ~ (against sb/sth) a public meeting or a MARCH (= an organized walk by many people) at which people show that they are protesting against or supporting sb/sth: *to take part in/go on a demonstration* ◊ *to hold/stage a demonstration* ◊ *mass demonstrations in support of the exiled leader* ◊ *anti-government demonstrations* ◊ *a peaceful/violent demonstration* ⇨ compare MARCH **2** (also informal **demo**) [C, U] an act of showing or explaining how sth works or is done: *We were given a brief demonstration of the computer's functions.* ◊ *a practical demonstration* ◊ *Sandra and Nigel provided a demonstration of salsa dance steps.* **3** [C, U] an act of giving proof or evidence for sth: *a demonstration of the connection between the two sets of figures* ◊ *a demonstration of how something that seems simple can turn out to be very complicated* **4** [C] an act of showing a feeling or an opinion: *a public demonstration of affection* ◊ *a demonstration of support for the reforms*

**de·mon·stra·tive** /dɪˈmɒnstrətɪv; NAmE -ˈmɑːn-/ adj., noun
■ adj. **1** showing feelings openly, especially feelings of love: *Some people are more demonstrative than others.* ◊ *a demonstrative greeting* **2** (*grammar*) used to identify the person or thing that is being referred to: *'This' and 'that' are demonstrative pronouns.* ▸ **de·mon·stra·tive·ly** adv.
■ noun (*grammar*) a demonstrative pronoun or determiner

**dem·on·stra·tor** /ˈdemənstreɪtə(r)/ noun **1** a person who takes part in a public meeting or MARCH (= an organized walk by many people) in order to protest against sb/sth or to show support for sb/sth **2** a person whose job is to show or explain how sth works or is done

**de·mor·al·ize** (BrE also **-ise**) /dɪˈmɒrəlaɪz; NAmE -ˈmɔːr-/ verb ~ sb to make sb lose confidence or hope dishearten: *Constant criticism is enough to demoralize anybody.* ▸ **de·mor·al·ized, -ised** adj.: *The workers here seem very demoralized.* **de·mor·al·iz·ing, -is·ing** adj.: *the demoralizing effects of unemployment* **de·mor·al·iza·tion, -isa·tion** /dɪˌmɒrəlaɪˈzeɪʃn; NAmE -ˌmɔːrələˈz-/ noun [U]

**de·mote** /ˌdiːˈməʊt/ verb [often passive] ~ sb/sth (from sth) (to sth) to move sb/sth to a lower position or rank, often as a punishment promote ▸ **de·mo·tion** /-ˈməʊʃn/ noun [C, U]

**dem·ot·ic** /dɪˈmɒtɪk; NAmE -ˈmɑːt-/ adj. (formal) used by or typical of ordinary people

**de·mo·ti·vate** /ˌdiːˈməʊtɪveɪt/ verb ~ sb to make sb less keen to work or study: *Failure can demotivate students.*

▶ **de·mo·tiv·at·ing** adj. **de·mo·tiv·ated** adj. **de·mo·tiv·ation** /ˌdiːməʊtɪˈveɪʃn/ noun [U]

**demur** /dɪˈmɜː(r)/ verb, noun
- verb [I] (-rr-) (+ speech) (formal) to say that you do not agree with sth or that you refuse to do sth: *At first she demurred, but then finally agreed.*
- noun
  - IDM **without deˈmur** (formal) without objecting or hesitating: *They accepted without demur.*

**de·mure** /dɪˈmjʊə(r); NAmE -ˈmjʊr/ adj. **1** (of a woman or a girl) behaving in a way that does not attract attention to herself or her body; quiet and serious SYN **modest**: *a demure young lady* **2** suggesting that a woman or girl is demure SYN **modest**: *a demure smile* ◇ *a demure navy blouse with a white collar* ▶ **de·mure·ly** adv.

**de·mys·tify** /ˌdiːˈmɪstɪfaɪ/ verb (**de·mys·ti·fies**, **de·mys·ti·fy·ing**, **de·mys·ti·fied**, **de·mys·ti·fied**) ~ sth to make sth easier to understand and less complicated by explaining it in a clear and simple way ▶ **de·mys·ti·fi·ca·tion** /ˌdiːˌmɪstɪfɪˈkeɪʃn/ noun [U]

**den** /den/ noun **1** the hidden home of some types of wild animal: *a bear's/lion's den* **2** (*disapproving*) a place where people meet in secret, especially for some illegal activity: *a den of thieves* ◇ *a drinking/gambling den* ◇ *He thought of New York as a den of iniquity.* **3** (*NAmE*) a room in a house where people go to relax, watch television, etc. **4** (*BrE*, *old-fashioned*, *informal*) a room in a house where a person can work or study without being interrupted: *He would often retire to his den.* **5** a secret place, often made roughly with walls and a roof, where children play: *They made themselves a den in the woods.* IDM see BEARD v., LION

**de·nation·al·ize** (*BrE* also **-ise**) /ˌdiːˈnæʃnəlaɪz/ verb ~ sth to sell a company or an industry so that it is no longer owned by the state but becomes a private business SYN **privatize** OPP **nationalize** ▶ **de·nation·al·iza·tion**, **-isa·tion** /ˌdiːˌnæʃnəlaɪˈzeɪʃn; NAmE -ləˈz-/ noun [U]

**den·drite** /ˈdendraɪt/ (also **den·dron** /ˈdendrɒn/; NAmE -drɑːn/) noun (*biology*) a short branch at the end of a nerve cell that receives signals from other cells ↔compare AXON ▶ **den·drit·ic** /denˈdrɪtɪk/ adj.: *dendritic cells*

**den·gue** /ˈdeŋɡi/ (also ˌden·gue ˈfever, ˌbreak·bone ˈfever) noun [U] a disease caused by a virus carried by MOSQUITOES that is found in tropical areas and causes a high temperature and severe pain in the JOINTS

**deni·able** /dɪˈnaɪəbl/ adj. that can be denied OPP undeniable

**de·nial** /dɪˈnaɪəl/ noun **1** [C] a statement that sth is not true or does not exist; the action of denying sth: *~ (of sth)* *the prisoner's repeated denials of the charges against him* ◇ *The terrorists issued a denial of responsibility for the attack.* ◇ *that ... an official denial that there would be an election before the end of the year* ◇ *in ~ She shook her head in denial.* **2** [C, U] **(a)** ~ **of sth** an act of refusing to allow sb to have sth they have a right to expect: *the denial of basic human rights* **3** [U] the act of refusing to accept that sth unpleasant or painful is true: *in ~ The patient is still in denial.*

**den·ier¹** /ˈdeniə(r)/ noun (*especially BrE*) a unit for measuring how fine THREADS of NYLON, silk, etc. are: *15 denier tights*

**den·ier²** /dɪˈnaɪə(r)/ noun a person who publicly refuses to accept sth that most people accept, such as a historical event or scientific fact: *climate change/Holocaust deniers* ◇ *a denier of evolution*

**deni·grate** /ˈdenɪɡreɪt/ verb ~ sb/sth (*formal*) to criticize sb/sth unfairly; to say sb/sth does not have any value or is not important SYN **belittle**: *I didn't intend to denigrate her achievements.* ▶ **deni·gra·tion** /ˌdenɪˈɡreɪʃn/ noun [U, C]

**denim** /ˈdenɪm/ noun **1** [U] a type of strong cotton cloth that is usually blue and is used for making clothes, especially jeans: *a denim jacket* ORIGIN From the French *serge de Nîmes*, meaning 'serge (= a type of cloth) from the town of Nîmes'. **2** **denims** [pl.] trousers or other clothes made of denim SYN **jeans**

**deni·zen** /ˈdenɪzn/ noun (*formal or humorous*) a person, an animal or a plant that lives, grows or is often found in a particular place SYN **inhabitant**: *polar bears, denizens of the frozen north* ◇ *the denizens of the local pub*

**de·nom·in·ate** /dɪˈnɒmɪneɪt; NAmE -ˈnɑːm-/ verb **1** ~ sth **(in sth)** to express an amount of money using a particular unit: *The loan was denominated in US dollars.* **2** ~ **sb (as) sth** (*formal*) to give sth a particular name or description: *These payments are denominated as 'fees' rather than 'salary'.*

**de·nom·in·ation** /dɪˌnɒmɪˈneɪʃn; NAmE -ˌnɑːm-/ noun (*formal*) **1** a branch of the Christian Church: *Christians of all denominations attended the conference.* **2** a unit of value, especially of money: *coins and banknotes of various denominations*

**de·nom·in·ation·al** /dɪˌnɒmɪˈneɪʃənl; NAmE -ˌnɑːm-/ adj. belonging to a particular branch of the Christian Church OPP **non-denominational**

**de·nom·in·ator** /dɪˈnɒmɪneɪtə(r); NAmE -ˈnɑːm-/ noun (*mathematics*) the number below the line in a FRACTION showing how many parts the whole is divided into, for example 4 in ¾ ↔see also LEAST COMMON DENOMINATOR, LOWEST COMMON DENOMINATOR ↔compare NUMERATOR, COMMON DENOMINATOR

**de·no·ta·tion** /ˌdiːnəʊˈteɪʃn/ noun (*specialist*) the act of naming sth with a word; the actual object or idea to which the word refers ↔compare CONNOTATION ▶ **de·no·ta·tion·al** /-ʃənl/ adj.

**de·note** W /dɪˈnəʊt/ verb (*formal*) **1** ~ **sth** | **~ that ...** to be a sign of sth SYN **indicate**: *A very high temperature often denotes a serious illness.* **2** ~ **sth** | **~ what, when, etc ...** to mean sth SYN **represent**: *In this example 'X' denotes the time taken and 'Y' denotes the distance covered.* ◇ *The red triangle denotes danger.* ◇ *Here 'family' denotes mother, father and children.* ↔compare CONNOTE

**de·noue·ment** (also **dé·noue·ment**) /deɪˈnuːmɒ̃; NAmE ˌdeɪnuːˈmɑ̃/ noun (*from French*) the end of a play, book, etc., in which everything is explained or settled; the end result of a situation ↔WORDFINDER NOTE AT DRAMA

**de·nounce** /dɪˈnaʊns/ verb **1** to strongly criticize sb/sth that you think is wrong, illegal, etc: *~ sb/sth She publicly denounced the government's handling of the crisis.* ◇ *~ sb/sth as sth The project was denounced as a scandalous waste of public money.* **2** to tell the police, the authorities, etc. about sb's illegal political activities: *~ sb as sth They were denounced as spies.* ◇ *~ sb (to sb) Many people denounced their neighbours to the secret police.* ↔see also DENUNCIATION

**dense** /dens/ adj. (**dens·er**, **dens·est**) **1** containing a lot of people, things, plants, etc. with little space between them: *a dense crowd/forest* ◇ *areas of dense population* **2** difficult to see through SYN **thick**: *dense fog/smoke/fumes* **3** (*informal*) stupid: *How can you be so dense?* **4** difficult to understand because it contains a lot of information: *a dense piece of writing* **5** (*specialist*) heavy in relation to its size: *Less dense substances move upwards to form a crust.* ▶ **dense·ly** adv.: *a densely populated area* ◇ *densely covered/packed*

**dens·ity** /ˈdensəti/ noun (pl. **-ies**) **1** [U] the quality of being dense; the degree to which sth is dense: *population density* ◇ *low density forest* **2** [C, U] (*physics*) how thick a solid, liquid or gas is, measured by its mass per unit of volume: *the density of a gas* ↔see also RELATIVE DENSITY **3** [U] (*computing*) the amount of space available on a disk for recording data

**dent** /dent/ verb, noun
- verb **1** ~ **sth** to make a hollow place in a hard surface, usually by hitting it: *The back of the car was badly dented in the collision.* **2** ~ **sth** to damage sb's confidence, reputation, etc: *It seemed that nothing could dent his confidence.*
- noun a hollow place in a hard surface, usually caused by sth hitting it: *a large dent in the car door*
  - IDM **make, etc. a ˈdent in sth** to reduce the amount of sth, especially money: *The lawyer's fees will make a dent in our finances.*

---
◉ Oxford Phrasal Academic Lexicon (OPAL) written and spoken word lists | Ⓦ OPAL written word list | Ⓢ OPAL spoken word list

# dental

**dent·al** /ˈdentl/ adj. [only before noun] **1** connected with teeth: *dental disease/care/treatment/health* ◊ *a dental appointment* ◊ *dental records* ◊ (*BrE*) *a dental surgery* (= where a dentist sees patients) **2** (*phonetics*) (of a consonant) produced with the tongue against the upper front teeth, for example /θ/ and /ð/ in *thin* and *this*

**dental floss** (*also* **floss**) *noun* [U] a type of very thin string that is used for cleaning between the teeth

**dental hygienist** *noun* = HYGIENIST

**dental surgeon** *noun* (*formal*) a dentist, especially one who performs surgery inside the mouth

**den·tine** /ˈdentiːn/ (*NAmE also* **den·tin** /ˈdentɪn/) *noun* [U] (*biology*) the hard substance that forms the main part of a tooth under the ENAMEL

**den·tist** /ˈdentɪst/ *noun* **1** (*also formal* **dental surgeon**) a person whose job is to take care of people's teeth: *to see/visit/consult your dentist* ◊ *the dentist's chair/drill*

WORDFINDER anaesthetic, cavity, check-up, crown, dentures, drill, extract, filling, hygienist

**2** *often* **dentist's** *pl.* **dentists** a place where a dentist sees patients: *I hate going to the dentist.* ◊ *an appointment at the dentist's*

**den·tis·try** /ˈdentɪstri/ *noun* [U] **1** the medical study of the teeth and mouth **2** the work of a dentist: *preventive dentistry*

**den·ti·tion** /denˈtɪʃn/ *noun* [U, C] (*specialist*) the arrangement or condition of a person's or an animal's teeth

**den·tures** /ˈdentʃəz/ *NAmE* -tʃərz/ *noun* [pl.] artificial teeth on a thin piece of plastic (= a PLATE), worn by sb who no longer has all their own teeth ⊃ WORDFINDER NOTE at DENTIST ▶ **den·ture** *adj.*: *denture adhesive* ⊃ compare FALSE TEETH, PLATE

**de·nude** /dɪˈnjuːd/; *NAmE* -ˈnuːd/ *verb* [usually passive] (*formal*) to remove a top layer, the features, etc. from sth, so that it is exposed: **(be) denuded (of sth)** *hillsides denuded of trees*

**de·nun·ci·ation** /dɪˌnʌnsiˈeɪʃn/ *noun* [C, U] **~ (of sb/sth)** (*formal*) an act of criticizing sb/sth strongly in public: *an angry denunciation of the government's policies* ◊ *All parties joined in bitter denunciation of the terrorists.* ⊃ see also DENOUNCE

**Den·ver boot** /ˈdenvə ˈbuːt/; *NAmE* -vər/ (*also* **boot**) (*both NAmE*) (*BrE* **clamp**, **wheel clamp**) *noun* a device that is attached to the wheel of a car that has been parked illegally, so that it cannot be driven away

**deny** /dɪˈnaɪ/ *verb* (**de·nies**, **deny·ing**, **de·nied**, **de·nied**) **1 ~ sth** to say that sth is not true: *~ sth to deny an allegation/a charge/an accusation* ◊ *He has denied any involvement in the incident.* ◊ *A spokesperson refused to confirm or deny the reports.* ◊ **~ (that) …** *She denied that there had been a cover-up.* ◊ *It can't be denied that we need to devote more resources to this problem.* ◊ *There's no denying the fact that quicker action could have saved them.* ◊ **~ doing sth** *He denies attempting to murder his wife.* **2** **~ sth** to refuse to admit or accept sth: *She denied all knowledge of the incident.* ◊ *The department denies responsibility for what occurred.* ◊ *an anti-environmentalist campaign group that denies climate change* **3** (*formal*) to refuse to allow sb to have sth that they want or ask for: **~ sb sth** *They were denied access to the information.* ◊ **~ sth to sb** *Access to the information was denied to them.* **4 ~ yourself (sth)** (*formal*) to refuse to let yourself have sth that you would like to have, especially for moral or religious reasons

WORD FAMILY
**deny** *verb*
**denial** *noun*
**undeniable** *adj.*
**undeniably** *adv.*

**de·odor·ant** /diˈəʊdərənt/ *noun* [C, U] a substance that people put on their bodies to prevent or hide unpleasant smells: *(a) roll-on deodorant* ⊃ see also ANTIPERSPIRANT

**de·oxy·ribo·nucle·ic acid** /diːˌɒksiˌraɪbəʊnjuːˈkleɪɪk ˈæsɪd/; *NAmE* -ˌɑːksiˌraɪbəʊnuː-/ *noun* [U] = DNA

**dep.** *abbr.* (in writing) DEPARTS; departure ⊃ compare ARR.

**de·part** /dɪˈpɑːt/; *NAmE* -ˈpɑːrt/ *verb* (*rather formal*) **1** [I, T] to leave a place, especially to start a trip: **~ (for …) (from …)** *Flights for Rome depart from Terminal 3.* ◊ *She waited until the last of the guests had departed.* ◊ **~ sth** (*NAmE*) *The train departed Amritsar at 6.15 p.m.* OPP **arrive 2** [I, T] (*NAmE*) to leave your job: *the departing president* ◊ **~ sth** *He departed his job December 16.* ⊃ see also DEPARTURE
IDM **depart this life** to die. People say 'depart this life' to avoid saying 'die'.
PHRV **de·part from sth** to behave in a way that is different from usual: *Departing from her usual routine, she took the bus to work.*

**de·part·ed** /dɪˈpɑːtɪd/; *NAmE* -ˈpɑːrt-/ *adj.* [only before noun] (*formal*) **1** dead. People say 'departed' to avoid saying 'dead': *your dear departed brother* **2 the departed** *noun* (*pl.* **the de·part·ed**) the person who has died

**de·part·ment** /dɪˈpɑːtmənt/; *NAmE* -ˈpɑːrt-/ *noun* (*abbr.* **Dept**) a section of a large organization such as a government, business, university, etc.: **~ of sth** *the Department of Health* ◊ *a government/university, etc. department* ◊ *the marketing/sales, etc. department* ◊ *the children's department* (= in a large store) ◊ *the English department* ◊ **in a ~** *She used to work in the IT department.* ⊃ see also POLICE DEPARTMENT, STATE DEPARTMENT
IDM **be sb's department** (*informal*) to be sth that sb is responsible for or knows a lot about: *Don't ask me about it—that's her department.*

**de·part·ment·al** /ˌdiːpɑːtˈmentl/; *NAmE* -pɑːrt-/ *adj.* [only before noun] connected with a department rather than with the whole organization: *a departmental manager*

**de·partment store** *noun* a large shop that is divided into several parts, each part selling a different type of goods

**de·part·ure** /dɪˈpɑːtʃə(r)/; *NAmE* -ˈpɑːrtʃ-/ *noun* **1** [C, U] an act of leaving a place: *His sudden departure threw the office into chaos.* ◊ **~ from …** *They had received no news of him since his departure from the island.* ◊ **~ for/to …** *The day of their departure for London was growing closer.* ◊ **before ~** *Flights should be confirmed 48 hours before departure.* OPP **arrival** ⊃ WORDFINDER NOTE at JOURNEY **2** [C] a plane, train, etc. leaving a place at a particular time: *arrivals and departures* ◊ *All departures are from Manchester.* ◊ *the departure lounge/time/gate* ◊ *the departures board* OPP **arrival 3** **~ departures** [U] the part of an airport where you go before catching a plane: *There were long delays and queues in departures.* ⊃ compare ARRIVALS **4** [C] an action that is different from what is usual or expected: *Their latest single represents a new departure for the band.* ◊ **~ from sth** *It was a radical departure from tradition.* IDM see POINT *n.*

**de·pend** /dɪˈpend/ *verb*
IDM **de·pend·ing on** according to: *Starting salary varies from £26000 to £30500, depending on experience.* ◊ *He either resigned or was sacked, depending on who you talk to.* **that de·pends** | **it (all) de·pends** used to say that you are not certain about sth because other things have to be considered: *'Is he coming?' 'That depends. He may not have the time.'* ◊ *'I don't know if we can help—it all depends.'* ◊ *I might not go. It depends how tired I am.* ◊ *'Your job sounds fun.' 'It depends what you mean by "fun".'* ◊ *I shouldn't be too late. But it depends if the traffic's bad.*
PHRV **de·pend on/upon sb/sth 1** to rely on sb/sth and be able to trust them: *He was the sort of person you could depend on.* ◊ **depend on/upon sb/sth to do sth** *He knew he could depend upon her to deal with the situation.* ⊃ SYNONYMS at TRUST **2** to be sure or expect that sth will happen. SYN **count on sb/sth**: *Depend upon it* (= you can be sure) *we won't give up.* ◊ **depend on/upon sb/sth doing sth** *Can we depend on you coming in on Sunday?* (*formal*)

You can depend on his coming in on Sunday. **depend on/ upon sb/sth to do sth**: (*ironic*) *You can depend on her to be* (= she always is) *late.* **de'pend on/upon sb/sth (for sth)** [A2] (not usually used in the progressive tenses) to need money, help, etc. from sb/sth else for a particular purpose: *The community depends on the shipping industry for its survival.* ◊ *I don't want to depend too much on my parents.* **de'pend on/upon sth** [A2] (not used in the progressive tenses) to be affected or decided by sth: *Does the quality of teaching depend on class size?* ◊ *It would depend on the circumstances.* ◊ **depend on/upon how, what, etc** ... *Whether we need more food depends on how many people turn up.*

▼ **GRAMMAR POINT**

**depend on**
- In informal English, it is quite common to say **depend** rather than **depend on** before words like *what*, *how* or *whether*: *It depends what you mean by 'hostile'.* In formal written English, **depend** should always be followed by *on* or *upon*: *It depends on how you define the term 'hostile'. Upon* is more formal and less frequent than *on*.

**de·pend·able** /dɪˈpendəbl/ *adj.* that can be relied on to do what you want or need SYN **reliable** ▶ **de·pend·abil·ity** /dɪˌpendəˈbɪləti/ *noun* [U]

**de·pend·ant** /dɪˈpendənt/ (*BrE*) (*also* **de·pend·ent** *NAmE, BrE*) *noun* a person, especially a child, who depends on another person for a home, food, money, etc: *Married women received only the basic pension as their husband's dependant.*

**de·pend·ence** [B2+] [C1] W /dɪˈpendəns/ *noun* [U] [B2+] the state of needing the help and support of sb/sth in order to survive or be successful: *Our relationship was based on mutual dependence.* ◊ *financial/economic dependence* ◊ *~on/upon sb/sth his dependence on his parents* ◊ *the dependence of Europe on imported foods* OPP **independence 2** (*also* **de·pend·ency**) the state of being ADDICTED to sth (= unable to stop taking or using it): *drug/alcohol dependence* ◊ WORDFINDER NOTE *at* DRUG **3** *~ of A and B* (*specialist*) the fact of one thing being affected by another: *the close dependence of soil and landforms*

**de·pend·ency** /dɪˈpendənsi/ *noun* (*pl.* **-ies**) **1** [U] *~(on/ upon sb/sth)* the state of relying on sb/sth for sth, especially when this is not normal or necessary: *financial dependency* ◊ *Their aim is to reduce people's dependency on the welfare state.* ◊ *the dependency culture* (= a way of life in which people depend too much on money from the government) ⊃ compare CODEPENDENCY **2** [C] a country, an area, etc. that is controlled by another country **3** = DEPENDENCE (2)

**de·pend·ent** [B2+] [B2] W /dɪˈpendənt/ *adj., noun*
■ *adj.* **1** [B2+] [B2] needing sb/sth in order to survive or be successful: *a woman with several dependent children* ◊ *~on/ upon sb/sth You can't be dependent on your parents all your life.* ◊ *~on/upon sb/sth for sth The festival is heavily dependent on sponsorship for its success.* **2** *~on/upon sth* ADDICTED to sth (= unable to stop taking or using it): *to be dependent on drugs* **3** *~on/upon sth* (*formal*) affected or decided by sth: *A child's development is dependent on many factors.* ◊ *The price is dependent on how many extras you choose.*
■ *noun* = DEPENDANT

**de₁pendent ˈclause** *noun* (*grammar*) = SUBORDINATE CLAUSE

**de₁pendent ˈvariable** *noun* (*mathematics*) a VARIABLE whose value depends on another variable

**de·per·son·al·ize** (*BrE also* **-ise**) /diːˈpɜːsənəlaɪz; *NAmE* -ˈpɜːrs-/ *verb* [often passive] *~sth* to make sth less personal so that it does not seem as if humans with feelings and personality are involved ▶ **de·per·son·al·iza·tion** (*BrE also* **-isa·tion**) /diːˌpɜːsənəlaɪˈzeɪʃn; *NAmE* -ˌpɜːrsənələˈz-/ *noun* [U]

**de·pict** [B2+] [C1] /dɪˈpɪkt/ *verb* (*rather formal*) **1** [B2+] [C1] to show an image of sb/sth in a picture: *~sb/sth (as sb/sth) a painting depicting the Virgin and Child* ◊ *~sb/sth doing sth The artist had depicted her lying on a bed.* **2** [B2+] [C1] to describe sth in words, or give an impression of sth in words or with a picture: *~sb/sth The novel depicts French society in the 1930s.* ◊ *~sb/sth as sb/sth The advertisements depicted smoking as glamorous and attractive.* ▶ **de·pic·tion** /-ˈpɪkʃn/ *noun* [U, C]: *They object to the movie's depiction of gay people.*

**de·pila·tory** /dɪˈpɪlətri; *NAmE* -tɔːri/ *noun* (*pl.* **-ies**) a substance used for removing body hair ▶ **de·pila·tory** *adj.* [only before noun]: *depilatory creams*

**de·plane** /ˌdiːˈpleɪn/ *verb* [I] (*NAmE*) to get off a plane SYN **disembark**

**de·plete** /dɪˈpliːt/ *verb* [T, *usually passive*, I] *~(sth)* (*formal*) to reduce sth by a large amount so that there is not enough left; to be reduced by a large amount: *Food supplies were severely depleted.* ▶ **de·ple·tion** /-ˈpliːʃn/ *noun* [U, C]: *ozone depletion* ◊ *the depletion of fish stocks*

**de·plor·able** /dɪˈplɔːrəbl/ *adj.* (*formal*) very bad and unacceptable, often in a way that shocks people SYN **appalling**: *a deplorable incident* ◊ *They were living in the most deplorable conditions.* ◊ *The acting was deplorable.* ▶ **de·plor·ably** /-bli/ *adv.*: *They behaved deplorably.* ◊ *deplorably high/low/bad*

**de·plore** /dɪˈplɔː(r)/ *verb* *~sth* (*formal*) to criticize sth, especially publicly, because you think it is very bad: *Like everyone else, I deplore and condemn this killing.*

**de·ploy** [B2+] [C1] /dɪˈplɔɪ/ *verb* **1** [B2+] [C1] *~sb/sth* to move soldiers or weapons into a position where they are ready for military action: *2000 troops were deployed in the area.* ◊ *At least 5000 missiles were deployed along the border.* **2** *~sth* (*formal*) to use sth effectively: *to deploy arguments/ resources*

**de·ploy·ment** [B2+] [C1] /dɪˈplɔɪmənt/ *noun* **1** [B2+] [C1] [U, C] the act of moving soldiers or weapons into a position where they are ready for military action **2** [U] (*formal*) the act of using sth effectively

**de·popu·late** /ˌdiːˈpɒpjuleɪt; *NAmE* -ˈpɑːp-/ *verb* [*usually passive*] to reduce the number of people living in a place: *be depopulated Whole stretches of land were laid waste and depopulated.* ▶ **de·popu·la·tion** /diːˌpɒpjuˈleɪʃn; *NAmE* -ˌpɑːp-/ *noun* [U]

**de·port** /dɪˈpɔːt; *NAmE* -ˈpɔːrt/ *verb* *~sb* to force sb to leave a country, usually because they have broken the law or because they have no legal right to be there ▶ **de·port·ation** /ˌdiːpɔːˈteɪʃn; *NAmE* -pɔːrˈt-/ *noun* [C, U]: *Several of the asylum seekers now face deportation.* ◊ *a deportation order*

**de·port·ee** /ˌdiːpɔːˈtiː; *NAmE* -pɔːrˈtiː/ *noun* a person who has been deported or is going to be deported

**de·port·ment** /dɪˈpɔːtmənt; *NAmE* -ˈpɔːrt-/ *noun* [U] (*formal*) (*BrE*) the way in which a person stands and moves: *lessons for young ladies in deportment and etiquette*

**de·pose** /dɪˈpəʊz/ *verb* *~sb* to remove sb, especially a political leader, from power: *The president was deposed in a military coup.*

**de·posit** [B2+] [B2] /dɪˈpɒzɪt; *NAmE* -ˈpɑːz-/ *noun, verb*
■ *noun*
- MONEY **1** [B2+] [B2] [usually sing.] a sum of money that is given as the first part of a larger payment SYN **down payment**: *They normally ask you to pay $100 (as a) deposit.* ◊ *~on sth* (*BrE*) *We've put down a 5% deposit on the house.* ⊃ SYNONYMS at PAYMENT ⊃ WORDFINDER NOTE at LOAN **2** [B2+] [B2] [usually sing.] a sum of money that is paid by sb when they rent sth and that is returned to them if they do not lose or damage the thing they are renting: *to pay a deposit* ◊ *The landlord requires a security deposit of one month's rent.* **3** [B2+] [C1] a sum of money that is paid into a bank account: *Deposits can be made at any branch.* ◊ see also DIRECT DEPOSIT OPP **withdrawal** ⊃ WORDFINDER NOTE at BANK **4** (in the British political system) the amount of money that a candidate in an election to Parliament has to pay, and that is returned if he/she gets enough votes: *All the other candidates lost their deposits.*

## deposit account

- **SUBSTANCE** **5** ₹+ C1 a layer of a substance that has formed naturally underground: *mineral/gold/coal deposits* **6** ₹+ C1 a layer of a substance that has been left somewhere, especially by a river, flood, etc., or is found at the bottom of a liquid: *The rain left a deposit of mud on the windows.* ◊ *fatty deposits in the arteries of the heart*

■ **verb**

- **MONEY** **1** ₹+ C1 ~ **sth** to put money into a bank account: *Millions were deposited in Swiss bank accounts.* **2** ~ **sth** to pay a sum of money as the first part of a larger payment; to pay a sum of money that you will get back if you return in good condition sth that you have rented
- **PUT DOWN** **3** ~ **sb/sth** + *adv./prep.* to put or lay sb/sth down in a particular place: *She deposited a pile of books on my desk.* ◊ *(informal) I was whisked off in a taxi and deposited outside the hotel.*
- **LEAVE SUBSTANCE** **4** ~ **sth** (especially of a river or a liquid) to leave a layer of sth on the surface of sth, especially gradually and over a period of time: *Sand was deposited which hardened into sandstone.*
- **PUT IN SAFE PLACE** **5** ~ **sth (in sth)** | ~ **sth (with sb/sth)** to put sth valuable or important in a place where it will be safe: *Guests may deposit their valuables in the hotel safe.*

**de·pos·it ac·count** *noun* (*BrE*) (*also* **savings account** *BrE, NAmE*) a type of bank account that pays interest on the money that is left in it, but from which you cannot take the money out without giving notice or losing interest ⊃ compare CURRENT ACCOUNT

**de·pos·ition** /ˌdepəˈzɪʃn/ *noun* **1** [U, C] (*specialist*) the natural process of leaving a layer of a substance on rocks or soil; a substance left in this way: *marine/river deposition* **2** [U, C] the act of removing sb, especially a leader, from power: *the deposition of the King* **3** [C] (*law*) a formal statement, taken from sb and used in court

**de·pos·it·or** /dɪˈpɒzɪtə(r)/; *NAmE* -ˈpɑːz-/ *noun* a person who puts money in a bank account

**de·pos·it·ory** /dɪˈpɒzɪtri/; *NAmE* -ˈpɑːzɪtɔːri/ *noun* (*pl.* **-ies**) a place where things can be stored

**depot** /ˈdepəʊ/; *NAmE* ˈdiːp-/ *noun* **1** a place where large amounts of food, goods or equipment are stored: *an arms depot* **2** (*BrE*) a place where buses or other vehicles are kept and repaired **3** (*NAmE*) a small station where trains or buses stop

**de·prave** /dɪˈpreɪv/ *verb* ~ **sb** (*formal*) to make sb morally bad SYN **corrupt**: *In my view this book would deprave young children.*

**de·praved** /dɪˈpreɪvd/ *adj.* (*formal*) morally bad SYN **wicked**, **evil**: *This is the work of a depraved mind.*

**de·prav·ity** /dɪˈprævəti/ *noun* [U, C] (*formal*) the state of being morally bad; morally bad acts SYN **wickedness**: *a life of depravity*

**dep·re·cate** /ˈdeprəkeɪt/ *verb* ~ **sth** (*formal*) to feel and express strong DISAPPROVAL of sth ▶ **dep·re·cat·ing** (*also less frequent* **dep·re·ca·tory** /ˌdeprəˈkeɪtəri/; *NAmE* ˈdeprɪkətɔːri/) *adj.*: *a deprecating comment* **dep·re·cat·ing·ly** *adv.*

**de·pre·ci·ate** /dɪˈpriːʃieɪt/ *verb* **1** [I] to become less valuable over a period of time: *New cars start to depreciate as soon as they are on the road.* ◊ *Shares continued to depreciate on the stock markets today.* OPP **appreciate 2** [T] ~ **sth** (*business*) to reduce the value, as stated in the company's accounts, of a particular ASSET over a particular period of time: *The bank depreciates laptops over a period of five years.* **3** [T] ~ **sth** (*formal*) to make sth seem unimportant or of no value: *I had no intention of depreciating your contribution.* ▶ **de·pre·ci·ation** /dɪˌpriːʃiˈeɪʃn/ *noun* [U, C]: *currency depreciations* ◊ *the depreciation of fixed assets*

**dep·re·da·tion** /ˌdeprəˈdeɪʃn/ *noun* (*usually pl.*) (*formal*) an act that causes damage to people's property, lives, etc.

**de·press** /dɪˈpres/ *verb* **1** to make sb sad and without enthusiasm or hope: ~ **sb** *Wet weather always depresses me.* ◊ **it depresses sb to do sth** *It depresses me to see so many young girls smoking.* **2** ~ **sth** to make trade, business, etc. less active: *The recession has depressed the housing market.* **3** ~ **sth** to make the value of prices or wages lower: *to depress wages/prices* **4** ~ **sth** (*formal*) to press or push sth down, especially part of a machine: *to depress the clutch pedal* (= when driving)

**de·pres·sant** /dɪˈpresnt/ *noun* (*medical*) a drug that slows the rate of the body's functions ⊃ see also ANTIDEPRESSANT

**de·pressed** ⓘ B2 /dɪˈprest/ *adj.* **1** ₹ B2 very sad and without hope: *You mustn't let yourself get depressed.* ◊ ~ **about/over/at sth** *She felt very depressed about the future.* **2** ₹ B2 suffering from the medical condition of DEPRESSION: *She became severely depressed.* **3** (of a place or an industry) without enough economic activity or jobs for people: *an attempt to bring jobs to economically depressed areas* **4** having a lower amount or level than usual: *depressed prices*

**de·press·ing** ⓘ B2 /dɪˈpresɪŋ/ *adj.* making you feel very sad and without enthusiasm: *a depressing sight/thought/experience* ◊ *Looking for a job these days can be very depressing.* ▶ **de·press·ing·ly** *adv.*: *a depressingly familiar experience*

**de·pres·sion** ₹+ B2 /dɪˈpreʃn/ *noun* **1** ₹+ B2 [U] a medical condition in which a person feels very sad and anxious and often has physical symptoms such as being unable to sleep, etc: *clinical depression* ◊ *She suffered from severe depression after losing her job.* ⊃ WORDFINDER NOTE at CONDITION ⊃ see also MANIC DEPRESSION, POSTNATAL DEPRESSION, POST-PARTUM DEPRESSION **2** ₹+ B2 [U, C] the state of feeling very sad and without hope: *There was a feeling of gloom and depression in the office when the news of the job cuts was announced.* **3** ₹+ B2 [C, U] a period when there is little economic activity and many people are poor or without jobs: *The country was in the grip of (an) economic depression.* **4** [C] (*formal*) a part of a surface that is lower than the parts around it SYN **hollow**: *Rainwater collects in shallow depressions on the ground.* **5** [C] (*specialist*) a weather condition in which the pressure of the air becomes lower, often causing rain ⊃ compare ANTICYCLONE

**de·pres·sive** /dɪˈpresɪv/ *adj., noun*
■ *adj.* connected with the medical condition of depression: *depressive illness*
■ *noun* a person who is suffering from the medical condition of depression ⊃ see also MANIC-DEPRESSIVE

**de·pres·sor** /dɪˈpresə(r)/ *noun* an instrument for pressing sth down ⊃ see also TONGUE DEPRESSOR

**de·priv·ation** /ˌdeprɪˈveɪʃn/ *noun* [U, C] the fact of not having sth that you need, like enough food, money or a home; the process that causes this: *neglected children suffering from social deprivation* ◊ *sleep deprivation* ◊ *the deprivation of war* (= the suffering caused by not having enough of some things)

**de·prive** ₹+ C1 /dɪˈpraɪv/ *verb*
PHRV **de·prive sb/sth of sth** ₹+ C1 to prevent sb from having or doing sth, especially sth important: *They were imprisoned and deprived of their basic rights.* ◊ *Why should you deprive yourself of such simple pleasures?*

**de·prived** /dɪˈpraɪvd/ *adj.* **1** without enough food, education, and all the things that are necessary for people to live a happy and comfortable life: *a deprived childhood/background/area* ◊ *economically/emotionally/socially deprived* ⊃ SYNONYMS at POOR **2** **-deprived** suffering from a lack of the thing mentioned: *The American adult population is chronically sleep-deprived.*

**Dept** (*also* **Dept.** *especially in NAmE*) *abbr.* (in writing) department

**depth** ⓘ B2 /depθ/ *noun*
- **MEASUREMENT** **1** ₹ B2 [C, U] the distance from the top or surface to the bottom of sth; a particular distance down from the surface of sth: ~ **of sth** *What's the depth of the water here?* ◊ *the depth of a cut/wound/crack* ◊ **at a ~ of sth** *Water was found at a depth of 30 metres.* ◊ **to a ~ of sth** *They dug down to a depth of two metres.* ◊ **in ~** *The oil well extended several hundreds of feet in depth.* ◊ **at ~** *The camera must be strong enough to resist the immense water pressure at depth.* **2** [C, U] the distance from the front to

the back of sth: *The depth of the shelves is 30 centimetres.* ⊃ picture at DIMENSION
- **OF FEELINGS 3** ?B2 [U] the strength and power of feelings: *the depth of her love* ◇ *music of great emotional depth*
- **OF CHARACTER/QUALITIES 4** ?B2 [U, C] (*approving*) qualities that give sb/sth extra character and make them/it interesting: *The separate storylines really* **add depth** *and personality to the characters.* ◇ *Her paintings reveal* **hidden depths** (= unknown and interesting things about her character).
- **OF KNOWLEDGE 5** ?B2 [U] (*approving*) the quality of knowing or understanding a lot of details about sth; the ability to provide and explain these details: *a writer of great wisdom and depth* ◇ *His ideas lack depth.* ◇ ~ **of sth** *a job that doesn't require any great depth of knowledge* ⊃ see also IN-DEPTH
- **DEEPEST PART 6** [C, usually pl.] the deepest, most extreme or serious part of sth: *the* **depths of the ocean** ◇ *to live* **in the depths of the country** (= a long way from a town) ◇ *in the* **depths of winter** (= when it is coldest) ◇ *She was* **in the depths of despair.**
- **OF COLOUR 7** [U] the strength of a colour: *Strong light will affect the depth of colour of your carpets and curtains.*
- **PICTURE/PHOTOGRAPH 8** [U] (*specialist*) the quality in a work of art or a photograph that makes it appear not to be flat ⊃ see also DEEP *noun*

IDM **be out of your ˈdepth 1** (*BrE*) to be in water that is too deep to stand in with your head above water **2** to be unable to understand sth because it is too difficult; to be in a situation that you cannot control: *He felt totally out of his depth in his new job.* **in ˈdepth** in a detailed, careful and complete way: *I haven't looked at the report in depth yet.* ◇ *an in-depth study* ⊃ more at PLUMB *v.*, STRENGTH

**ˈdepth charge** *noun* a bomb that is set to explode UNDERWATER, used to destroy SUBMARINES

**ˌdepth of ˈfield** (*also* **ˌdepth of ˈfocus**) *noun* (*specialist*) the distance between the nearest and the furthest objects that a camera can produce a clear image of at the same time

**depu·ta·tion** /ˌdepjuˈteɪʃn/ *noun* [C + sing./pl. v.] a small group of people who are asked or allowed to act or speak for others

**de·pute** /dɪˈpjuːt/ *verb* [often passive] (*formal*) to give sb else the authority to represent you or do sth for you SYN **delegate**: **be deputed to do sth** *He was deputed to put our views to the committee.*

**depu·tize** (*BrE also* **-ise**) /ˈdepjutaɪz/ *verb* [I] ~ **(for sb)** to act or speak for sb else on a temporary basis: *Ms Green has asked me to deputize for her at the meeting.*

**dep·uty** ?+ /ˈdepjuti/ *noun* (*pl.* **-ies**) **1** ?+ C1 a person who is the next most important person below a business manager, a head of a school, a political leader, etc. and who does the person's job when he or she is away: *I'm acting as deputy till the manager returns.* ◇ *the deputy head of a school* **2** the name for a member of parliament in some countries **3** (in the US) a police officer who helps the SHERIFF of an area

**de·rail** /ˌdiːˈreɪl/ *verb* **1** [I, T] ~ **(sth)** (of a train) to leave the track; to make a train do this: *The train derailed and plunged into the river.* **2** [T] ~ **sth** to stop a process from continuing in the way it was intended to: *This latest incident could derail the peace process.* ▶ **de·rail·ment** *noun* [C, U]

**de·rail·leur** /dɪˈreɪljə(r); *NAmE* -ˈreɪlər/ *noun* (*specialist*) a type of GEAR on a bicycle that works by lifting the chain from one GEARWHEEL to another larger or smaller one

**de·ranged** /dɪˈreɪndʒd/ *adj.* unable to behave and think normally, especially because of mental illness: *mentally deranged* ◇ *a deranged attacker* ▶ **de·range·ment** *noun* [U]: *He seemed to be on the verge of total derangement.*

**derby** /ˈdɑːbi; *NAmE* ˈdɜːrbi/ *noun* (*pl.* **-ies**) **1** (*NAmE*) (*BrE* **bowler**, **bowler ˈhat**) a hard black hat with a curved BRIM and round top, worn, for example, in the past by men in business in England **2** (*BrE*) a sports competition between teams from the same area or town: *a local derby between the two North London sides* ◇ *a derby match* **3** a race or sports competition: *a motorcycle derby* ⊃ see also DEMOLITION DERBY **4 Derby** used in the name of several horse races that happen every year: *the Epsom Derby* ◇ *the Kentucky Derby*

**de·regu·late** /ˌdiːˈregjuleɪt/ *verb* [often passive] ~ **sth** to free a trade, a business activity, etc. from rules and controls: *deregulated financial markets* ▶ **de·regu·la·tion** /ˌdiːˌregjuˈleɪʃn/ *noun* [U] **de·regu·la·tory** /ˌdiːˈregjulətəri; *NAmE* -tɔːri/ *adj.* [only before noun]: *deregulatory reforms*

**dere·lict** /ˈderəlɪkt/ *adj.*, *noun*
- *adj.* **1** (especially of land or buildings) not used or cared for and in bad condition: *derelict land/buildings/sites* **2** ~ **in (doing) sth** (*especially NAmE*) failing completely to do your duty or perform your obligations: *They have been grossly derelict in their duty.*
- *noun* (*formal*) a person without a home, a job or property SYN **vagrant**: *derelicts living on the streets*

**dere·lic·tion** /ˌderəˈlɪkʃn/ *noun* (*formal*) **1** [U] the state of land or buildings not being used or cared for and in bad condition: *industrial/urban dereliction* ◇ *a house in a state of dereliction* **2** [U, sing.] ~ **of duty** (*formal or law*) the fact of deliberately not doing what you ought to do, especially when it is part of your job: *The police officers were found guilty of serious dereliction of duty.*

**de·ride** /dɪˈraɪd/ *verb* [often passive] (*formal*) to treat sb/sth as silly and not worth considering seriously SYN **mock**: **be derided (as sth)** *His views were derided as old-fashioned.*

**de ri·gueur** /də rɪˈɡɜː(r)/ *adj.* [not before noun] (*from French*) considered necessary if you wish to be accepted socially: *Evening dress is de rigueur at the casino.*

**de·ri·sion** /dɪˈrɪʒn/ *noun* [U] a strong feeling that sb/sth is silly and not worth considering seriously, shown by laughing in an unkind way or by making unkind remarks SYN **scorn**: *Her speech was greeted with howls of derision.* ◇ *He became an object of universal derision.*

**de·ri·sive** /dɪˈraɪsɪv/ (*also less frequent* **de·ri·sory**) *adj.* unkind and showing that you think sb/sth is silly: *She gave a short, derisive laugh.* ▶ **de·ri·sive·ly** *adv.*

**de·ri·sory** /dɪˈraɪsəri/ *adj.* (*formal*) **1** too small or of too little value to be considered seriously SYN **laughable**: *They offered us a derisory £50 a week.* **2** = DERISIVE

**der·iv·ation** /ˌderɪˈveɪʃn/ *noun* **1** [U, C] the origin or development of sth, especially a word: *a word of Greek derivation* **2** [U] the action of obtaining sth from a source or origin: *the derivation of scientific laws from observation*

**de·riva·tive** /dɪˈrɪvətɪv/ *noun*, *adj.*
- *noun* a word or thing that has been developed or produced from another word or thing: *'Happiness' is a derivative of 'happy'.* ◇ *Crack is a highly potent and addictive derivative of cocaine.*
- *adj.* (*usually disapproving*) copied from sth else; not having new or original ideas: *a derivative design/style*

**de·rive** ?+ B2 O /dɪˈraɪv/ *verb*
PHRV **de·ˈrive from sth** | **be de·ˈrived from sth** ?B2 to come or develop from sth: *The word 'politics' is derived from a Greek word meaning 'city'.* **de·ˈrive sth from sth 1** (*formal*) to get sth from sth: *He derived great pleasure from painting.* **2** (*specialist*) to obtain a substance from sth: *The new drug is derived from fish oil.*

**derma·ti·tis** /ˌdɜːməˈtaɪtɪs; *NAmE* ˌdɜːrm-/ *noun* [U] (*medical*) a skin condition in which the skin becomes red, SWOLLEN (= larger or rounder than normal) and painful

**derma·tolo·gist** /ˌdɜːməˈtɒlədʒɪst; *NAmE* ˌdɜːrməˈtɑːl-/ *noun* a doctor who studies and treats skin diseases
⊃ WORDFINDER NOTE at SPECIALIST

**derma·tol·ogy** /ˌdɜːməˈtɒlədʒi; *NAmE* ˌdɜːrməˈtɑːl-/ *noun* [U] the scientific study of skin diseases ▶ **derma·to·logi·cal** /ˌdɜːmətəˈlɒdʒɪkl; *NAmE* ˌdɜːrmətəˈlɑːdʒ-/ *adj.*

**der·mis** /ˈdɜːmɪs; *NAmE* ˈdɜːrm-/ *noun* [U] (in non-technical use) the skin

**dero·gate** /ˈderəɡeɪt/ *verb* ~ **sth** (*formal*) to state that sth or sb is without worth
PHRV **ˈderogate from sth** to ignore a responsibility or duty

**dero·ga·tion** /ˌderəˈɡeɪʃn/ *noun* (*formal*) **1** [C] an occasion when a rule or law is allowed to be ignored **2** [U, C] words

# derogatory

or actions that show that sb or sth is considered to have no worth: *the derogation of women*

**de·rog·a·tory** /dɪˈrɒgətri; *NAmE* -ˈrɑːgətɔːri/ *adj.* (*formal*) showing a critical attitude and lack of respect for sb **SYN** **insulting**: *derogatory remarks/comments*

**der·rick** /ˈderɪk/ *noun* **1** a tall machine used for moving or lifting heavy weights, especially on a ship; a type of CRANE **2** a tall structure over an OIL WELL for holding the DRILL (= the machine that makes the hole in the ground for getting the oil out)

**derring-do** /ˌderɪŋ ˈduː/ *noun* [U] (*old-fashioned* or *humorous*) brave actions, like those in adventure stories

**der·vish** /ˈdɜːvɪʃ; *NAmE* ˈdɜːrv-/ *noun* a member of a Muslim religious group whose members make a promise to stay poor and live without comforts or pleasures. They perform a fast lively dance as part of their religious ceremonies: *He threw himself around the stage like a **whirling dervish**.*

**de·sal·in·ation** /ˌdiːˌsælɪˈneɪʃn/ *noun* [U] the process of removing salt from SEAWATER: *a desalination plant* ▶ **de·sal·in·ate** /ˌdiːˈsælɪneɪt/ *verb* **~ sth**

**de·scale** /ˌdiːˈskeɪl/ *verb* **~ sth** (*BrE*) to remove the SCALE (= the hard white material left on pipes, etc. by water when it is heated) from sth

**des·cend** /dɪˈsend/ *verb* **1** [I, T] (*formal*) to come or go down from a higher to a lower level: *The plane began to descend.* ◊ *The results, ranked in **descending order** (= from the highest to the lowest) are as follows …* ◊ **~ sth** *She descended the stairs slowly.* **OPP** **ascend 2** [I] (*formal*) (of a hill, etc.) to slope downwards: *At this point the path descends steeply.* **OPP** **ascend 3** [I] (*literary*) (of night, DARKNESS, a mood, etc.) to arrive and begin to affect sb/sth **SYN** **fall**: *Night descends quickly in the tropics.* ◊ **~ on/upon sb/sth** *Calm descended on the crowd.*
**PHRV** **be desˈcended from sb** to be related to sb who lived a long time ago: *He claims to be descended from a Spanish prince.* **desˈcend into sth** [no passive] (*formal*) to gradually get into a bad state: *The country was descending into chaos.* **desˈcend on/upon sb/sth** to visit sb/sth in large numbers, sometimes unexpectedly: *Hundreds of football fans descended on the city.* **desˈcend to sth** [no passive] to do sth that makes people stop respecting you: *They descended to the level of personal insults.*

**des·cend·ant** /dɪˈsendənt/ *noun* **1** a person's **descendants** are their children, their children's children, and all the people who live after them who are related to them: *He was an O'Conor and a **direct descendant** of the last High King of Ireland.* ◊ *Many of them are descendants of the original settlers.* **2** something that has developed from sth similar in the past

**des·cent** /dɪˈsent/ *noun* **1** [C, usually sing.] an action of coming or going down: *The plane began its descent to Heathrow.* ◊ (*figurative*) *the country's swift descent into anarchy* **OPP** **ascent 2** [C] a slope going downwards: *There is a gradual descent to the sea.* **OPP** **ascent 3** [U] a person's family origins **SYN** **ancestry**: *to be of Scottish descent* ◊ **~ from sb** *He traces his line of descent from the Stuart kings.* ⇒ WORDFINDER NOTE AT RELATION

**de·scribe** /dɪˈskraɪb/ *verb* **1** to say what sb/sth is like: **~ sb/sth** *The next section describes our findings in detail.* ◊ **~ sb/sth to/for sb** *Can you describe him to me?* ◊ **~ sb/sth as sth** *The man was described as tall and dark, and aged about 20.* ◊ **~ how, what, etc.…** *Describe how you did it.* ◊ **~ doing sth** *Witnesses described seeing strange lights in the sky.* **2 ~ sth** (*formal* or *specialist*) to make a movement that has a particular shape; to form a particular shape: *The shark described a circle around the shoal of fish.* ▶ **de·scrib·able** *adj.*

**de·scrip·tion** /dɪˈskrɪpʃn/ *noun* [C, U] **1** a piece of writing or speech that says what sb/sth is like; the act of writing or saying in words what sb/sth is like: *Follow the link below for a more **detailed description**.* ◊ **~ of sth** *a brief description of the software* ◊ *The name means 'no trees' and it is an **accurate description** of the*

## ▼ EXPRESS YOURSELF
### Describing a picture
In some exams, you have to describe what you see in a picture or photograph. Here are some useful phrases:
- **The picture shows** *a family gathered around a kitchen table.*
- **This is a picture/photo of** *a busy city street.*
- **In the foreground/background, we can see** *a group of protesters.*
- **In the bottom right-hand corner/top left-hand corner,** *there's a child sitting alone.*
- **On the left/On the right/In the middle,** *someone is standing with a bottle in his hand.*
- **In the cartoon, we can see** *two people looking at a newspaper headline.*
- **The cartoonist has drawn the man** *to represent a typical businessman.*

*island.* ◊ *This is a film that **defies description** (= is difficult or impossible to describe).* ◊ *the novelist's powers of description* ◊ **beyond ~** *a personal pain that goes beyond description (= is too great to express in words)* **2 of some, all, every, etc. ~** of some, etc. type: *boats of every description/all descriptions* ◊ *Their money came from trade of some description.* ◊ *medals, coins and things of that description*
**IDM** **answer/fit/match a description (of sb/sth)** to be like a particular person or thing: *A child answering the description of the missing boy was found safe and well in London yesterday.* ⇒ more at BEGGAR *v.*

**de·scrip·tive** /dɪˈskrɪptɪv/ *adj.* **1** saying what sb/sth is like; describing sth: *the descriptive passages in the novel* ◊ *The term I used was meant to be purely descriptive (= not judging).* **2** (*linguistics*) saying how language is actually used, without giving rules for how it should be used **OPP** **prescriptive**

**de·scrip·tor** /dɪˈskrɪptə(r)/ *noun* (*linguistics*) **1** a word or expression used to describe or identify sth **2** (*computing*) a piece of additional information that describes the purpose and FORMAT of other data

**dese·crate** /ˈdesɪkreɪt/ *verb* **~ sth** to damage a holy thing or place or treat it without respect: *desecrated graves* ▶ **dese·cra·tion** /ˌdesɪˈkreɪʃn/ *noun* [U]: *the desecration of a cemetery* ◊ (*figurative*) *the desecration of the countryside by new roads*

**de·seg·re·gate** /ˌdiːˈsegrɪgeɪt/ *verb* **~ sth** to end the policy of SEGREGATION in a place in which people of different races are kept separate in public places, etc. ▶ **de·seg·re·ga·tion** /ˌdiːˌsegrɪˈgeɪʃn/ *noun* [U]

**de·select** /ˌdiːsɪˈlekt/ *verb* **1 ~ sb** if the local branch of a political party in the UK **deselects** the existing Member of Parliament, it does not choose him or her as a candidate at the next election **2 ~ sth** (*computing*) to remove sth from the list of possible choices on a computer menu ▶ **de·selec·tion** /-ˈlekʃn/ *noun* [U, C]

**de·sen·si·tize** (*BrE also* **-ise**) /ˌdiːˈsensətaɪz/ *verb* **1** [usually passive] to make sb/sth less aware of sth as a problem by making them become used to it: **be/become desensitized (to sth)** *People are increasingly becoming desensitized to violence on television.* **2 ~ sth** (*specialist*) to treat sb/sth so that they will stop being sensitive to physical or chemical changes, or to a particular substance ▶ **de·sen·si·tiza·tion, -isa·tion** /ˌdiːˌsensətaɪˈzeɪʃn; *NAmE* -təˈz-/ *noun* [U]

**des·ert** *noun, verb*
- **noun** /ˈdezət; *NAmE* -zərt/ ⇒ see also DESERTS [C, U] a large area of land that has very little water and very few plants growing on it. Many deserts are covered by sand: *the Sahara Desert* ◊ *Somalia is mostly desert.* ◊ *burning desert sands* ◊ (*figurative*) *a cultural desert (= a place without any culture)*
- **verb** /dɪˈzɜːt; *NAmE* -ˈzɜːrt/ **1** **~ sb** [T] to leave sb without help or support **SYN** **abandon**: *She was deserted by her husband.* **2** **~ sth** [T, often passive] to go away from a place and leave it empty **SYN** **abandon**: *The villages had been deserted.* ◊ *The owl seems to have deserted its nest.* **3** [I, T] to leave the armed forces without permission:

*Large numbers of soldiers deserted as defeat became inevitable.* ◇ **~ sth** *The rebels had deserted the US army to fight for Mexico.* **4** [T] to leave an organization or stop doing an activity, especially in a way that is considered bad and DISLOYAL: **~ sth** *Millions of voters are deserting the party.* ◇ **~ sth for sth** *Why did you desert teaching for politics?* **5** [T] **~ sb** if a particular quality **deserts** you, it is not there when you need it: *Her courage seemed to desert her for a moment.* ▶ **de·ser·tion** /dɪˈzɜːʃn/ *NAmE* -ˈzɜːrʃn/ *noun* [U, C]: *She felt betrayed by her husband's desertion.* ◇ *The army was badly affected by desertions.* **IDM** see SINK *v.*

▼ **HOMOPHONES**

desert • dessert /dɪˈzɜːt; *NAmE* -ˈzɜːrt/

- **desert** *verb*: *His companions desert him as he dies.*
- **dessert** *noun*: *Summer pudding has long been a favourite English dessert.*

**des·ert·ed** /dɪˈzɜːtɪd; *NAmE* -ˈzɜːrt-/ *adj.* **1** (of a place) with no people in it: *deserted streets* **2** left by a person or people who do not intend to return **SYN** **abandoned**: *a deserted village* ◇ *deserted wives*

**de·sert·er** /dɪˈzɜːtə(r); *NAmE* -ˈzɜːrt-/ *noun* a person who leaves the army, NAVY, etc. without permission

**desert·ifi·ca·tion** /dɪˌzɜːtɪfɪˈkeɪʃn; *NAmE* -,zɜːrt-/ *noun* [U] (*specialist*) the process of becoming or making sth a desert

**desert 'island** *noun* a tropical island where no people live

**des·erts** /dɪˈzɜːts; *NAmE* -ˈzɜːrts/ *noun* [pl.]
**IDM** **sb's (just) deserts** what sb deserves, especially when it is sth bad: *The family of the victim said that the killer had got his just deserts when he was jailed for life.*

**de·serve** 🅞 **B2** /dɪˈzɜːv; *NAmE* -ˈzɜːrv/ *verb* (not used in the progressive tenses) to do sth or show qualities that mean a particular reaction, reward or punishment is appropriate: **~ sth** *You deserve a rest after all that hard work.* ◇ *This idea deserves more attention.* ◇ *One player in particular deserves a mention.* ◇ *to deserve praise/respect/credit* ◇ *What have I done to deserve this?* ◇ *This was a well-deserved victory.* ◇ **~ to do sth** *They didn't deserve to win.* ◇ **~ doing sth** *Several other points deserve mentioning.*
**IDM** **sb de'serves a 'medal** (*informal*) used to say that you admire sb because they have done sth difficult or unpleasant | **get what you de'serve | de,serve all / everything you 'get | de,serve what's 'coming (to you)** (*informal*) used to say that you think sb has earned the bad things that happen to them: *He did wrong, and he got what he deserved.* ⊃ more at TURN *n.*

**de·served·ly** /dɪˈzɜːvɪdli; *NAmE* -ˈzɜːrv-/ *adv.* in the way that is deserved; correctly: *The restaurant is deservedly popular.* ◇ *He has just been chosen for the top job, and deservedly so.* **OPP** **undeservedly**

**de·serv·ing** /dɪˈzɜːvɪŋ; *NAmE* -ˈzɜːrv-/ *adj.* **~ (of sth)** (*formal*) that deserves help, praise, a reward, etc: *to give money to a deserving cause* ◇ *This family is one of the most deserving cases.* ◇ *an issue deserving of attention* **OPP** **undeserving**

**desi** (*also* **deshi**) /ˈdeɪsi, ˈdesi/ *adj., noun*
- *adj.* **1** local or belonging to a particular place; Indian, Pakistani, Bangladeshi, or Sri Lankan: *Many people in the city prefer desi food to the type that is sold by foreign fast food chains.* ◇ *a desi film* ⊃ compare VIDESHI **2** not mixed with other substances: *desi ghee* **3** (*disapproving*) typical of the country or country people; simple and basic: *Modern consumers weren't attracted by the desi images of rural life shown in the adverts.*
- *noun* a person of Indian, Pakistani, Bangladeshi or Sri Lankan birth or origin who lives abroad

**des·ic·cated** /ˈdesɪkeɪtɪd/ *adj.* **1** (of food) dried in order to preserve it: *desiccated coconut* **2** (*specialist*) completely dry: *treeless and desiccated soil*

**des·ic·ca·tion** /ˌdesɪˈkeɪʃn/ *noun* [U] (*specialist*) the process of becoming completely dry

**de·sid·er·atum** /dɪˌzɪdəˈrɑːtəm, -ˈreɪt-/ *noun* (*pl.* **de·sid·er·ata** /-tə/) (*from Latin, formal*) a thing that is wanted or needed

**de·sign** 🅞 **A1** 🅞 /dɪˈzaɪn/ *noun, verb*
- *noun*
  - **ARRANGEMENT** **1** 🅐 **A1** [U, C] the general arrangement of the different parts of sth that is made, such as a building, book, machine, etc: *The basic design of the car is very similar to that of earlier models.* ◇ *special new design features* ◇ *The magazine will appear in a new design from next month.*
  - **DRAWING/PLAN/MODEL** **2** 🅐 **A1** [U] the art or process of deciding how sth will look, work, etc. by drawing plans, making computer models, etc: *the design and development of new products* ◇ *a course in art and design* ◇ *web/set/product design* ◇ *computer-aided design* ◇ *a design studio* ⊃ see also INTERIOR DESIGN **3** 🅐 **A1** [C] a drawing or plan from which sth may be made: *new and original designs* ◇ **~ for sth** *designs for aircraft*
  - **PATTERN** **4** 🅐 **B1** [C] an arrangement of lines and shapes as a decoration **SYN** **pattern**: *floral/abstract/geometric designs* ◇ *The tiles come in a huge range of colours and designs.*
  - **INTENTION** **5** [U, C] a plan or an intention: *It happened—whether by accident or design—that the two of them were left alone after all the others had gone.* ◇ *It is all part of his grand design.*
  **IDM** **have designs on sb** (*formal* or *humorous*) to want to start a sexual relationship with sb | **have designs on sth** (*formal*) to be planning to get sth for yourself, often in a way that other people do not approve of: *Rumours spread that the Duke had designs on the crown* (= wanted to make himself king).
- *verb*
  - **DRAW PLANS** **1** 🅐 **A1** to decide how sth will look, work, etc., by drawing plans, making computer models, etc: **~ sth** *He designed and built his own house.* ◇ *to design a building/product/website* ◇ *a well designed kitchen* ◇ **~ sth for sb/sth** *They asked me to design a poster for the campaign.* ◇ **~ sb** *Could you design us a poster?*
  - **PLAN STH FOR SPECIAL PURPOSE** **2** 🅐 **B1** [often passive] to think of and plan a system, a way of doing sth, etc., usually for a particular purpose or use: **~ sth** *We need to design a comprehensive professional development programme.* ◇ **be designed for sth** *The method is specifically designed for use in small groups.* ◇ **be designed as sth** *This course is primarily designed as an introduction to the subject.* ◇ **be designed to do sth** *The system is designed to alert drivers to traffic jams ahead.*

**des·ig·nate** 🅐+ **C1** *verb, adj.*
- *verb* /ˈdezɪɡneɪt/ (*formal*) **1** 🅐+ **C1** [often passive] to say officially that sb/sth has a particular character or name; to describe sb/sth in a particular way: **be designated (as) sth** *This area has been designated (as) a National Park.* ◇ *The school has been designated a specialist science academy.* ◇ **be designated (as being/having sth)** *Several pupils were designated as having moderate or severe learning difficulties.* ◇ *a designated nature reserve* ◇ *designated seats for the elderly* **2** 🅐+ **C1** to choose or name sb for a particular job or position: **~ sb/sth** *The director is allowed to designate his/her successor.* ◇ **~ sb (as) sth** *Who has she designated (as) her deputy?* ◇ **~ sb to do sth** *the man designated to succeed the president* **3** [often passive] to show sth using a particular mark or sign: **be designated (by sth)** *The different types of designs are designated by the letters A, B and C.*
- *adj.* /ˈdezɪɡnət, -neɪt/ [after noun] (*formal*) chosen to do a job but not yet having officially started it: *an interview with the director designate*

**designated 'driver** *noun* the person who agrees to drive and not drink alcohol when people go to a party, a bar, etc.

**designated 'hitter** *noun* (in baseball) a player who is named at the start of the game as the person who will hit the ball in place of the PITCHER

**des·ig·na·tion** /ˌdezɪɡˈneɪʃn/ *noun* (*formal*) **1** [U] **~ (as sth)** the action of choosing a person or thing for a particular purpose, or of giving them or it a particular status: *The district is under consideration for designation as a conservation area.* **2** [C] a name, title or description: *Her official designation is Financial Controller.*

---

🅞 Oxford Phrasal Academic Lexicon (OPAL) written and spoken word lists | 🅦 OPAL written word list | 🅢 OPAL spoken word list

## designer

**de·sign·er** ❶ **A2** /dɪˈzaɪnə(r)/ *noun, adj.*
- *noun* ❶ **A2** a person whose job is to decide how things such as clothes, furniture, tools, etc. will look or work by making drawings, plans or patterns: *one of the country's top fashion designers* ◊ *a graphic/web/game designer* ⇨ see also INTERIOR DESIGNER
- *adj.* [only before noun] made by a famous designer; expensive and having a famous brand name: *designer clothes* ◊ *designer jeans* ◊ *designer water* ◊ *He had a trendy haircut, an earring and designer stubble* (= a short beard, grown for two or three days and thought to look fashionable).

**deˌsigner ˈbaby** *noun* (used especially in newspapers) a baby that is born from an EMBRYO that was selected from a number of embryos produced using IVF, in order to ensure the baby has or does not have particular GENES that can treat or cause disease

**deˌsigner ˈdrug** *noun* a drug produced artificially that is designed to have similar effects to an illegal drug

**deˌsigner ˈlabel** (*also* **label**) *noun* the name or TRADEMARK of a fashion company: *He'll only wear clothes with a designer label.*

**de·sir·able** ❓+ **C1** 𝕎 /dɪˈzaɪərəbl/ *adj.* ❶ ❓+ (*formal*) that you would like to have or do; worth having or doing: *She chatted for a few minutes about the qualities she considered desirable in a secretary.* ◊ *Such measures are desirable, if not essential.* ◊ *The house has many desirable features.* ◊ *highly desirable* ◊ **It is ~ that …** (*BrE*) *It is desirable that interest rates should be reduced.* ◊ (*especially NAmE*) *It is desirable that interest rates be reduced.* ◊ **It is ~ (for sb) (to do sth)** *It is no longer desirable for such young children to take formal written tests.* **OPP** undesirable **2** (of a person) causing other people to feel sexual desire
▶ **de·sir·abil·ity** /dɪˌzaɪərəˈbɪləti/ *noun* [U] (*formal*) *No one questions the desirability of cheaper fares.*

**de·sire** ❶ **B2** 𝕎 /dɪˈzaɪə(r)/ *noun, verb*
- *noun* ❶ ❓+ **B2** [C] a strong wish to have or do sth: *enough money to satisfy all your desires* ◊ **~ for sth** *a strong desire for power/revenge* ◊ **~ to do sth** *She has a burning desire to be an artist.* ◊ (*formal*) *I have no desire* (= I do not want) *to discuss the matter further.* ◊ *He has expressed a desire to see you.* **2** [U, C] a strong wish to have sex with sb: *sexual desire* ◊ **~ for sb** *She felt a surge of love and desire for him.* **3** [C, usually sing.] a person or thing that is wished for: *When she agreed to marry him, he felt he had achieved his heart's desire.*
- *verb* (not used in the progressive tenses) **1** ❓+ **B2** (*formal*) to want sth; to wish for sth: **~sth** *We all desire health and happiness.* ◊ *The house had everything you could desire.* ◊ *The medicine did not achieve the desired effect.* ◊ **~(sb) to do sth** *Fewer people desire to live in the north of the country.* **2** **~ sb** to be sexually attracted to sb: *He still desired her.*
- **IDM** **leave a lot, much, something, etc. to be deˈsired** to be bad or unacceptable

**de·sir·ous** /dɪˈzaɪərəs/ *adj.* [not before noun] **~ (of sth/of doing sth) | ~ (to do sth)** (*formal*) having a wish for sth; wanting sth: *At that point Franco was desirous of prolonging the war.*

**de·sist** /dɪˈzɪst, -ˈsɪst/ *verb* [I] **~ (from sth/from doing sth)** (*formal*) to stop doing sth: *They agreed to desist from the bombing campaign.*

**desk** ❶ **A1** /desk/ *noun* **1** **A1** a piece of furniture like a table, often with DRAWERS (= parts like boxes in it with handles on the front for pulling them open), that you sit at to read, write, work, etc: **at/behind a ~** *I spend all day sitting at a desk.* ◊ *He abandoned a career at sea for a desk job.* ⇨ see also MIXING DESK **2** **A1** a place where you can get information or be served at an airport, a hotel, etc: *the reception desk* ◊ **at a ~** *There was a long queue at the check-in desk.* ⇨ see also CASH DESK, FRONT DESK, HELP DESK **3** an office at a newspaper, television company, etc. that deals with a particular subject: *the sports desk* ⇨ see also CITY DESK, NEWS DESK

**ˈdesk clerk** *noun* (*NAmE*) = CLERK (2)

**ˈdesk job** *noun* a job working in an office: *He used to be a pilot but now he has a desk job.*

**ˈdesk-mate** /ˈdeskmeɪt/ *noun* (*EAfrE*) a person who sits or sat next to you in class at school

**ˈdesk-top** ❓+ **C1** /ˈdesktɒp; *NAmE* -tɑːp/ *noun* **1** ❓+ **C1** a screen on a computer that shows the ICONS of programs and files that can be used: *desktop icons* ⇨ WORDFINDER NOTE at COMMAND **2** the top of a desk **3** = DESKTOP COMPUTER

**ˌdesktop comˈputer** (*also* **desk·top**) *noun* a computer with a keyboard, screen and main processing unit that fits on a desk ⇨ compare LAPTOP, NOTEBOOK

**ˌdesktop ˈpublishing** *noun* [U] (*abbr.* **DTP**) the use of a small computer and a printer to produce a small book, a magazine or other printed material

**deso·late** *adj., verb*
- *adj.* /ˈdesələt/ **1** (of a place) empty and without people, making you feel sad or frightened: *a bleak and desolate landscape* **2** very lonely and unhappy **SYN** forlorn
- *verb* /ˈdesəleɪt/ [usually passive] (*literary*) to make sb feel sad and without hope: **be desolated (by sth)** *She had been desolated by the death of her friend.*

**deso·la·tion** /ˌdesəˈleɪʃn/ *noun* [U] (*formal*) **1** the feeling of being very lonely and unhappy **2** the state of a place that is badly damaged or destroyed and offers no joy or hope to people: *a scene of utter desolation*

**des·pair** /dɪˈspeə(r); *NAmE* -ˈsper/ *noun, verb*
- *noun* [U] the feeling of having lost all hope: *She uttered a cry of despair.* ◊ *A deep sense of despair overwhelmed him.* ◊ **in ~** *He gave up the struggle in despair.* ◊ *One harsh word would send her into* **the depths of despair.** ◊ *Eventually,* **driven to despair,** *he threw himself under a train.* ⇨ see also DESPERATE
- **IDM** **be the despair of sb** to make sb worried or unhappy, because they cannot help: *My handwriting was the despair of my teachers.* ⇨ more at COUNSEL *n.*
- *verb* [I] to stop having any hope that a situation will change or improve: *Don't despair! We'll think of a way out of this.* ◊ **~ of sth/sb** *I despair of him; he can't keep a job for more than six months.* ◊ **~ of doing sth** *They'd almost despaired of ever having children.*

**des·pair·ing** /dɪˈspeərɪŋ; *NAmE* -ˈsper-/ *adj.* showing or feeling the loss of all hope: *a despairing cry/look/sigh* ◊ *With every day that passed he became ever more despairing.* ▶ **des·pair·ing·ly** *adv.*: *She looked despairingly at the mess.*

**des·patch** /dɪˈspætʃ/ (*BrE*) = DISPATCH

**deˈspatch box** = DISPATCH BOX

**des·per·ado** /ˌdespəˈrɑːdəʊ; *NAmE* noun (*pl.* **-oes** or **-os**) (*old-fashioned*) a man who does dangerous and criminal things without caring about himself or other people

**des·per·ate** ❶ **B2** /ˈdespərət/ *adj.* **1** **B2** feeling or showing that you have little hope and are ready to do anything without worrying about danger to yourself or others: *The prisoners grew increasingly desperate.* ◊ *Stores are getting desperate after two years of poor sales.* ◊ *I heard sounds of a desperate struggle in the room.* **2** ❓+ **B2** [usually before noun] (of an action) giving little hope of success; tried when everything else has failed: *a desperate bid for freedom* ◊ *She clung to the edge in* **a desperate attempt** *to save herself.* ◊ *His increasing financial difficulties forced him to take* **desperate measures.** **3** ❓+ **B2** [not usually before noun] needing or wanting sth very much: **~ for sth** *He was so desperate for a job he would have done anything.* ◊ (*informal*) *I'm desperate for a cigarette.* ◊ **~ to do sth** *I was absolutely desperate to see her.* **4** ❓+ **B2** (of a situation) extremely serious or dangerous: *The children are* **in desperate need** *of love and attention.* ◊ *They face a desperate shortage of clean water.*

**des·per·ate·ly** ❓+ **B2** /ˈdespərətli/ *adv.* **1** ❓+ **B2** in a way that shows you have little hope and are ready to do anything without worrying about danger to yourself or others: *She looked desperately around for a weapon.* **2** ❓+ **B2** extremely, especially when talking about bad situations: *desperately ill/unhappy/lonely* ◊ *He grew up*

**desperately** poor. **3** very much, especially when talking about difficult or bad situations: *They desperately wanted a child.* ◇ *He took a deep breath, desperately trying to keep calm.*

**des·per·ation** /ˌdespəˈreɪʃn/ *noun* [U] the state of being desperate: **in ~** *In desperation, she called Louise and asked for her help.* ◇ *There was a note of desperation in his voice.* ◇ *an act of sheer desperation*

**des·pic·able** /dɪˈspɪkəbl, ˈdespɪkəbl/ *adj.* (*formal*) very unpleasant or evil: *a despicable act/crime* ◇ *I hate you! You're despicable.* ▸ **des·pic·ably** /-bli/ *adv.*

**des·pise** /dɪˈspaɪz/ *verb* (not used in the progressive tenses) to dislike and have no respect for sb/sth: **~ sb/sth** *She despised gossip in any form.* ◇ **~ sb/yourself for (doing) sth** *He despised himself for being so cowardly.* ⟹ SYNONYMS at HATE

**des·pite** ❶ B1 /dɪˈspaɪt/ *prep.* **1** B1 used to show that sth happened or is true although sth else might have happened to prevent it SYN **in spite of**: *Her voice was shaking despite all her efforts to control it.* ◇ *Despite applying for hundreds of jobs, he is still out of work.* ◇ *She was good at physics despite the fact that she found it boring.* ⟹ LANGUAGE BANK at HOWEVER **2 despite yourself** used to show that sb did not intend to do the thing mentioned SYN **in spite of**: *He had to laugh despite himself.*

**de·spoil** /dɪˈspɔɪl/ *verb* **~ sth (of sth)** (*literary*) to steal sth valuable from a place; to make a place less attractive by damaging or destroying it SYN **plunder**

**des·pond·ent** /dɪˈspɒndənt/ *NAmE* -ˈspɑːn-/ *adj.* **~ (about/over sth)** sad, without much hope SYN **dejected**: *She was becoming increasingly despondent about the way things were going.* ▸ **des·pond·ency** /-dənsi/ *noun* [U]: *a mood of despondency* ◇ *Life's not all gloom and despondency.* **des·pond·ent·ly** *adv.*

**des·pot** /ˈdespɒt/ *NAmE* -spɑːt/ *noun* a leader with great power, especially one who uses it in a cruel way: *an enlightened despot* (= one who tries to use his/her power in a good way) ▸ **des·pot·ic** /dɪˈspɒtɪk/ *NAmE* -ˈspɑːt-/ *adj.*: *despotic power/rule*

**des·pot·ism** /ˈdespətɪzəm/ *noun* [U] the rule of a despot

**des·sert** /dɪˈzɜːt; *NAmE* -ˈzɜːrt/ *noun* [U, C] sweet food eaten at the end of a meal: *What's for dessert?* ◇ *a rich chocolate dessert* ◇ *a dessert wine* ◇ (*BrE*) *the dessert trolley* (= a table on wheels from which you choose your dessert in a restaurant). ⟹ HOMOPHONES at DESERT ⟹ compare AFTERS, PUDDING, SWEET

**des·sert·spoon** /dɪˈzɜːtspuːn; *NAmE* -ˈzɜːrt-/ *noun* **1** a spoon of medium size **2** (*also* **des·sert·spoon·ful** /dɪˈzɜːtspuːnfʊl; *NAmE* -ˈzɜːrt-/) the amount a dessertspoon can hold

**de·sta·bil·ize** (*BrE also* **-ise**) /ˌdiːˈsteɪbəlaɪz/ *verb* **~ sth** to make a system, country, government, etc. become less well established or successful: *Terrorist attacks were threatening to destabilize the government.* ◇ *The news had a destabilizing effect on the stock market.* ⟹ compare STABILIZE ▸ **de·sta·bil·iza·tion, -isa·tion** /ˌdiːˌsteɪbəlaɪˈzeɪʃn; *NAmE* -ləˈz-/ *noun* [U]

**des·tin·ation** ❶ B1 /ˌdestɪˈneɪʃn/ *noun, adj.*
■ *noun* B1 a place to which sb/sth is going or being sent: *popular tourist/holiday destinations like the Bahamas* ◇ *to arrive at/reach your destination* ◇ *Our luggage was checked all the way through to our final destination.* ⟹ WORDFINDER NOTE at JOURNEY
■ *adj.* **~ hotel/store/restaurant, etc.** a hotel, store, etc. that people will make a special trip to visit

**des·tined** /ˈdestɪnd/ *adj.* (*formal*) **1** having a future that has been decided or planned at an earlier time, especially by FATE: **~ for sth** *He was destined for a military career, like his father before him.* ◇ **~ to do sth** *We seem destined never to meet.* **2 ~ for ...** on the way to or intended for a place SYN **bound**: *goods destined for Poland*

**des·tiny** /ˈdestəni/ *noun* (*pl.* **-ies**) **1** [C] what happens to sb or what will happen to them in the future, especially things that they cannot change or avoid: *the destinies of nations* ◇ *He wants to be in control of his own destiny.* **2** [U]

---

421      **detached**

the power believed to control events SYN **fate**: *I believe there's some force guiding us—call it God, destiny or fate.* ⟹ SYNONYMS at LUCK

**des·ti·tute** /ˈdestɪtjuːt; *NAmE* -tuːt/ *adj.* **1** without money, food and the other things necessary for life: *When he died, his family was left completely destitute.* **2 the destitute** *noun* [pl.] people who are destitute **3 ~ of sth** (*formal*) not having sth: *They seem destitute of ordinary human feelings.* ▸ **des·ti·tu·tion** /ˌdestɪˈtjuːʃn; *NAmE* -ˈtuː-/ *noun* [U]: *homelessness and destitution*

**de·stock** /ˌdiːˈstɒk; *NAmE* -ˈstɑːk/ *verb* [I, T] **~ (sth)** (*BrE, business*) to reduce the amount of goods in a shop, the amount of materials kept available for making sth in a factory, etc.

**de·stress** /ˌdiː ˈstres/ *verb* [I, T] **~ (sb/yourself)** to relax after working hard or experiencing stress; to reduce the amount of stress that you experience: *De-stress yourself with a relaxing bath.*

**de·stroy** ❶ A2 ⓢ /dɪˈstrɔɪ/ *verb* **1** **~ sth** to damage sth so badly that it no longer exists, works, etc: *The building was completely destroyed by fire.* ◇ *The earthquake damaged or destroyed countless homes.* ◇ *They've destroyed all the evidence.* **2 ~ sb/sth** to take all the value and pleasure from sb's life; to RUIN (= completely damage) sb's life or reputation: *Failure was slowly destroying him.* ◇ *She threatened to destroy my reputation.* ◇ *He wanted revenge on the man who had destroyed his life.* **3 ~ sth** to kill an animal deliberately, usually because it is sick or not wanted: *The injured horse had to be destroyed.* ⟹ see also SOUL-DESTROYING

> **WORD FAMILY**
> **destroy** *verb*
> **destroyer** *noun*
> **destruction** *noun*
> **destructive** *adj.*
> **indestructible** *adj.*

**de·stroy·er** /dɪˈstrɔɪə(r)/ *noun* **1** a small fast ship used in war, for example to protect larger ships **2** a person or thing that destroys: *Sugar is the destroyer of healthy teeth.*

**de·struc·tion** B2 /dɪˈstrʌkʃn/ *noun* [U] the act of destroying sth; the process of being destroyed: *the destruction of the rainforests* ◇ *a tidal wave bringing* **death and destruction** *in its wake* ◇ *The central argument is that capitalism sows the seeds of its own destruction* (= creates the forces that destroy it). ⟹ see also SELF-DESTRUCTION, WEAPON OF MASS DESTRUCTION

**de·struc·tive** C1 /dɪˈstrʌktɪv/ *adj.* **1** C1 causing destruction or damage: *the destructive power of modern weapons* ◇ *the destructive effects of anxiety* ⟹ see also SELF-DESTRUCTIVE ⟹ compare CONSTRUCTIVE **2** C1 negative or not helpful: *destructive behaviour/impulses/tendencies* ▸ **de·struc·tive·ly** *adv.* **de·struc·tive·ness** *noun* [U]

**des·ul·tory** /ˈdesəltri; *NAmE* -tɔːri/ *adj.* (*formal*) going from one thing to another, without a definite plan and without enthusiasm: *I wandered about in a desultory fashion.* ◇ *a desultory conversation* ▸ **des·ul·tor·ily** /ˈdesəltrɪli; *NAmE* ˌdesəlˈtɔːrəli/ *adv.*

**Det** *abbr.* (*BrE*) (in writing) detective: *Det Insp* (= Inspector) *Cox*

**de·tach** /dɪˈtætʃ/ *verb* **1** [T, I] to remove sth from sth larger; to become separated from sth: **~ sth** *Detach the coupon and return it as soon as possible.* ◇ **~ sth from sth** *One of the panels had become detached from the main structure.* ◇ **~ (from sth)** *The skis should detach from the boot if you fall.* ⟹ compare ATTACH **2** [T] **~ yourself (from sb/sth)** (*formal*) to leave or separate yourself from sb/sth: *She detached herself from his embrace.* ◇ (*figurative*) *I tried to detach myself from the reality of these terrible events.* **3** [T] **~ sb/sth** (*specialist*) to send a group of soldiers, etc. away from the main group, especially to do special duties

**de·tach·able** /dɪˈtætʃəbl/ *adj.* that can be taken off SYN **removable**: *a coat with a detachable hood*

**de·tached** /dɪˈtætʃt/ *adj.* **1** (of a house) not joined to another house on either side ⟹ compare SEMI-DETACHED

# detachment

**2** showing a lack of feeling SYN **indifferent**: *She wanted him to stop being so cool, so detached, so cynical.* **3** *(approving)* not influenced by other people or by your own feelings SYN **impartial**: *a detached observer*

**de·tach·ment** /dɪˈtætʃmənt/ *noun* **1** [U] the state of not being involved in sth in an emotional or personal way: *He answered with an air of detachment.* ◊ *She felt a sense of detachment from what was going on.* OPP **involvement** **2** [U] *(approving)* the state of not being influenced by other people or by your own feelings: *In judging these issues a degree of critical detachment is required.* **3** [C] a group of soldiers, ships, etc. sent away from a larger group, especially to do special duties: *a detachment of artillery* **4** [U] the act of detaching sth; the process of being detached from sth: *to suffer detachment of the retina*

**de·tail** ❶ A1 ⓞ /ˈdiːteɪl; NAmE also dɪˈteɪl/ *noun, verb*
■ *noun*
- **FACTS/INFORMATION 1** B A1 [C] a small individual fact or item; a less important fact or item: *an expedition planned down to the last detail* ◊ *The Ministry refused to reveal any more details of the attack.* ◊ *Tell me the main points now; leave the details till later.* ◊ *The finer details of the plan have still to be worked out.* **2** B A1 [U] the small facts or features of sth, when you consider them all together: *in ~ This issue will be discussed in more detail in the next chapter.* ◊ *The research has been carried out with scrupulous attention to detail.* ◊ *He had an eye for detail* (= noticed and remembered small details). **3** B A1 **details** [pl.] information about sth: *Please provide the following details: name, age and sex.* ◊ *Can you send me your contact details?* ◊ *For further details visit our website.* ◊ *~ about sth They didn't give any details about the game.*
- **SMALL PARTS 4** [C, U] a small part of a picture or painting; the smaller or less important parts of a picture, pattern, etc. when you consider them all together: *This is a detail from the 1844 Turner painting.* ◊ *a huge picture with a lot of fine detail in it*
- **SOLDIERS 5** [C] a group of soldiers given special duties
IDM **go into ˈdetail(s)** to explain sth fully: *I can't go into details now; it would take too long.*
■ *verb*
- **GIVE FACTS/INFORMATION 1** B B2 *~ sth* to give a list of facts or all the available information about sth: *The brochure details all the hotels in the area and their facilities.*
- **ORDER SOLDIER 2** [often passive] to give an official order to sb, especially a soldier, to do a particular task: *be detailed (to do sth) Several of the men were detailed to form a search party.*
- **CLEAN CAR 3** *~ sth (NAmE)* to clean a car carefully and completely: *He got work for a while detailing cars.*

**de·tailed** ❶ B2 Ⓦ /ˈdiːteɪld; NAmE also dɪˈteɪld/ *adj.* giving many details and a lot of information; paying great attention to details: *a detailed description of the events* ◊ *For more detailed information visit our website.* ◊ *a detailed analysis/examination/study*

**de·tail·ing** /ˈdiːteɪlɪŋ; NAmE also dɪˈteɪlɪŋ/ *noun* [U] small details put on a building, piece of clothing, etc., especially for decoration

**de·tain** B+ C1 /dɪˈteɪn/ *verb* **1** B+ C1 *~ sb* to keep sb in an official place, such as a police station, a prison or a hospital, and prevent them from leaving: *One man has been detained for questioning.* ⊃ WORDFINDER NOTE at POLICE **2** B+ C1 *~ sb (formal)* to delay sb or prevent them from going somewhere: *I'm sorry—he'll be late; he's been detained at a meeting.* ⊃ see also DETENTION

**de·tain·ee** /ˌdiːteɪˈniː/ *noun* a person who is kept in prison, usually because of his or her political opinions

**de·tect** ❶ B2 /dɪˈtekt/ *verb ~ sth* to discover or notice sth, especially sth that is not easy to see, hear, etc: *The tests are designed to detect the disease early.* ◊ *to detect a difference/change* ◊ *Do I detect a note of criticism?* ⊃ SYNONYMS at NOTICE ▶ **de·tect·able** *adj.*: *The noise is barely detectable by the human ear.* OPP **undetectable**

**de·tec·tion** B+ C1 /dɪˈtekʃn/ *noun* [U] the process of discovering or noticing sth, especially sth that is not easy to see, hear, etc.; the fact of being discovered or noticed: *crime prevention and detection* ◊ *Last year the detection rate for car theft was just 13 per cent.* ◊ *Many problems, however, escape detection.* ◊ *Early detection of cancers is vitally important.*

**de·tect·ive** ❶ A2 /dɪˈtektɪv/ *noun (abbr. Det)* **1** B A2 a person, especially a police officer, whose job is to investigate crimes and catch criminals: *a police/homicide/undercover detective* ◊ *detectives from the anti-terrorist squad* ◊ *a detective story/novel* ◊ *Detective Inspector (Roger) Brown* ⊃ WORDFINDER NOTE at POLICE **2** a person employed by sb to find out information about sb/sth ⊃ see also PRIVATE DETECTIVE

**de'tective work** *noun* [U] the activity of trying to discover more information about sth: *He did some detective work and figured out what had happened to his bike.*

**de·tect·or** /dɪˈtektə(r)/ *noun* a piece of equipment for discovering the presence of sth, such as metal, smoke, EXPLOSIVES or changes in pressure or temperature: *a smoke detector* ⊃ see also LIE DETECTOR, METAL DETECTOR

**de·tente** (*also* **dé·tente**) /ˌdeɪˈtɑːnt/ *noun* [U] *(from French, formal)* an improvement in the relationship between two or more countries which have been unfriendly towards each other in the past

**de·ten·tion** B+ C1 /dɪˈtenʃn/ *noun* **1** B+ C1 [U] the state of being kept in a place, especially a prison, and prevented from leaving: *a sentence of 12 months' detention in a young offender institution* ◊ *police powers of arrest and detention* ◊ *allegations of torture and detention without trial* ◊ *a detention camp* **2** B+ C1 [U, C] the punishment of being kept at school for a time after other students have gone home: *They can't give me (a) detention for this.* ⊃ see also DETAIN

**de'tention centre** (*BrE*) (*US* **de'tention center**) *noun* **1** a place where people who have entered a country without the necessary documents can be kept in detention for a short period of time **2** a prison for people who have been accused of a crime and are waiting for their trial or (in the UK in the past) for young people who have been found guilty of a crime

**de·tenu** (*also* **de·tenue**) /ˈdeɪtənuː/ *noun* (*IndE*) a person who is held in prison, especially while waiting for trial

**deter** /dɪˈtɜː(r)/ *verb* [T, I] (**-rr-**) *~ (sb) (from sth/from doing sth)* to make sb decide not to do sth or continue doing sth, especially by making them understand the difficulties and unpleasant results of their actions: *I told him I wasn't interested, but he wasn't deterred.* ◊ *The high price of the service could deter people from seeking advice.* ⊃ see also DETERRENT

**de·ter·gent** /dɪˈtɜːdʒənt; NAmE -ˈtɜːrdʒ-/ *noun* [U, C] a liquid or powder that helps remove dirt, for example from clothes or dishes

**de·teri·or·ate** B+ C1 /dɪˈtɪəriəreɪt; NAmE -ˈtɪr-/ *verb* [I] to become worse: *Her health deteriorated rapidly, and she died shortly afterwards.* ◊ *deteriorating weather conditions* ◊ *~ into sth The discussion quickly deteriorated into an angry argument.* ▶ **de·teri·or·ation** /dɪˌtɪəriəˈreɪʃn; NAmE -ˌtɪr-/ *noun* [U, C]: *a serious deterioration in relations between the two countries*

**de·ter·min·able** /dɪˈtɜːmɪnəbl; NAmE -ˈtɜːrm-/ *adj. (formal)* that can be found out or calculated: *During the third month of pregnancy the sex of the child becomes determinable.*

**de·ter·min·ant** Ⓦ /dɪˈtɜːmɪnənt; NAmE -ˈtɜːrm-/ *noun (formal)* a factor that decides whether or how sth happens

**de·ter·min·ate** /dɪˈtɜːmɪnət; NAmE -ˈtɜːrm-/ *adj. (formal)* fixed and definite: *a sentence with a determinate meaning* OPP **indeterminate**

**de·ter·min·ation** B+ B2 Ⓦ /dɪˌtɜːmɪˈneɪʃn; NAmE -ˌtɜːrm-/ *noun* **1** B+ B2 [U] the quality that makes you continue trying to do sth even when this is difficult: *fierce/grim/dogged determination* ◊ *He fought the illness with courage and determination.* ◊ *They had survived by sheer determination.* ◊ *~ to do sth I admire her determination to* *get it right.* **2** [U] (*formal*) the process of deciding sth officially: *factors influencing the determination of future policy* ⊃ see also SELF-DETERMINATION **3** [U, C] (*specialist*) the act of finding out or calculating sth: *Both methods rely on the accurate determination of the pressure of the gas.*

**de·ter·mine** ⊕ B1 ⊘ /dɪˈtɜːmɪn; NAmE -ˈtɜːrm-/ *verb* (*formal*) **1** ~ [T] to discover the facts about sth; to calculate sth exactly SYN **establish**: ~ *sth An inquiry was set up to determine the cause of the accident.* ◇ ~ *what, whether, etc … We set out to determine exactly what happened that night.* ◇ *it is determined that … It was determined that she had died of natural causes.* **2** ~ B2 [T] to make sth happen in a particular way or be of a particular type: ~ *sth Rural voters in key states will determine the outcome of the election.* ◇ ~ *where, whether, etc … The physical capabilities of a plant determine where it can and cannot live.* **3** [T] to officially decide and/or arrange sth: ~ *sth A date for the meeting has yet to be determined.* ◇ ~ *(that) … The court determined (that) the defendant should pay the legal costs.* **4** [T, I] ~ **to do sth** | ~ **on sth** | ~ *(that) …* to decide definitely to do sth: *They determined to start early.*

**de·ter·mined** ⊕ B1 /dɪˈtɜːmɪnd; NAmE -ˈtɜːrm-/ *adj.* **1** ~ B1 [not before noun] having made a definite decision to do sth and not letting anyone prevent you: ~ **to do sth** *I'm determined to succeed.* ◇ ~ *that … They were quite determined that he wasn't going to do it.* **2** ~ B1 showing determination: *a determined effort to stop smoking* ◇ *The proposal had been dropped in the face of determined opposition.* IDM see BOUND *adj.* ▶ **de·ter·mined·ly** *adv.*

**de·ter·miner** /dɪˈtɜːmɪnə(r); NAmE -ˈtɜːrm-/ *noun* (*grammar*) (abbreviation det. in this dictionary) a word such as *the, some, my,* etc. that comes before a noun to show how the noun is being used

**de·ter·min·ism** /dɪˈtɜːmɪnɪzəm; NAmE -ˈtɜːrm-/ *noun* [U] (*philosophy*) the belief that people are not free to choose what they are like or how they behave, because these things are decided by their environment and other things over which they have no control ▶ **de·ter·min·is·tic** /dɪˌtɜːmɪˈnɪstɪk; NAmE -ˌtɜːrm-/ *adj.*

**de·ter·rent** /dɪˈterənt; NAmE -ˈtɜːr-/ *noun* something that makes sb less likely to do sth (= that DETERS them): ~ **to sb/sth** *Hopefully his punishment will act as a deterrent to others.* ◇ ~ **against sth** *a deterrent against cheating* ⊃ see also NUCLEAR DETERRENT ▶ **de·ter·rence** /-rəns/ *noun* [U] (*formal*) **de·ter·rent** *adj.*: *a deterrent effect*

**de·test** /dɪˈtest/ *verb* (not used in the progressive tenses) ~ **sb/sth** | ~ **doing sth** to hate sb/sth very much SYN **loathe**: *They detested each other on sight.* ⊃ SYNONYMS at HATE ▶ **de·test·ation** /ˌdiːteˈsteɪʃn/ *noun* [U]

**de·test·able** /dɪˈtestəbl/ *adj.* that deserves to be hated: *All terrorist crime is detestable, whoever the victims.*

**de·throne** /diːˈθrəʊn/ *verb* ~ **sb** to remove a king or queen from power; to remove sb from a position of authority or power

**det·on·ate** /ˈdetəneɪt/ *verb* [I, T] ~ **(sth)** to explode, or to make a bomb or other device explode: *Two other bombs failed to detonate.* ⊃ SYNONYMS at EXPLODE

**det·on·ation** /ˌdetəˈneɪʃn/ *noun* [C, U] an explosion; the action of making sth explode

**det·on·ator** /ˈdetəneɪtə(r)/ *noun* a device for making sth, especially a bomb, explode

**de·tour** /ˈdiːtʊə(r), -tɔː(r)/ *noun*, *verb*
■ *noun* **1** a longer route that you take in order to avoid a problem or to visit a place: *We had to make a detour around the flooded fields.* ◇ *It's well worth making a detour to see the village.* **2** (*NAmE*) (*BrE* **diversion**) a road or route that is used when the usual one is closed
■ *verb* [I, T] (especially *NAmE*) ~ **(sb/sth)** (+ *adv./prep.*) to take a longer route in order to avoid a problem or to visit a place; to make sb/sth take a longer route: *The President detoured to Chicago for a special meeting.*

**detox** /ˈdiːtɒks; NAmE -tɑːks/ *noun*, *verb*
■ *noun* [U, C] (*informal*) **1** the process of removing harmful substances from your body by only eating and drinking

# Devanagari

particular things: *a 28-day detox plan* **2** = DETOXIFICATION: *a detox clinic* ◇ *He's gone into detox.*
■ *verb* [I, T] (*informal*) **1** ~ **(sb)** to stop drinking alcohol or taking drugs; to make sb do this **2** ~ **(sth)** to attempt to remove harmful substances from your body by only eating and drinking certain things: *Fasting is a great way to detox your body.*

**de·toxi·fi·ca·tion** /ˌdiːˌtɒksɪfɪˈkeɪʃn; NAmE -ˌtɑːk-/ *noun* [U] **1** (also informal **detox**) treatment given to people to help them stop drinking alcohol or taking drugs: *a detoxification unit* ⊃ WORDFINDER NOTE at DRUG **2** the process of improving the reputation of sth that has been seen as morally bad **3** the process of removing harmful substances or poisons from sth: *the detoxification of formaldehyde*

**de·toxi·fy** /ˌdiːˈtɒksɪfaɪ; NAmE -ˈtɑːk-/ *verb* [T, I] (**de·toxi·fies, de·toxi·fy·ing, de·toxi·fied, de·toxi·fied**) **1** ~ **(sth)** to remove harmful substances or poisons from sth; to become free from harmful substances **2** ~ **(sb) (from sth)** to stop drinking too much alcohol or taking drugs; to treat sb in order to help them do this

**de·tract** /dɪˈtrækt/ *verb*
**PHRV** **deˈtract from sth** | **deˈtract sth from sth** (not used in the progressive tenses) to make sth seem less good or fun SYN **take away from**: *He was determined not to let anything detract from his enjoyment of the trip.*

**de·tract·or** /dɪˈtræktə(r)/ *noun* [usually pl.] (*especially formal*) a person who tries to make sb/sth seem less good or valuable by criticizing them/it

**de·train** /ˌdiːˈtreɪn/ *verb* [I, T] ~ **(sb)** (*formal*) to leave a train or make sb leave a train

**det·ri·ment** /ˈdetrɪmənt/ *noun* [U, C, usually sing.] (*formal*) the act of causing harm or damage; sth that causes harm or damage
IDM **to the detriment of sb/sth** | **to sb's/sth's detriment** resulting in harm or damage to sb/sth: *He was engrossed in his job to the detriment of his health.* **without detriment (to sb/sth)** not resulting in harm or damage to sb/sth

**det·ri·ment·al** /ˌdetrɪˈmentl/ *adj.* ~ **(to sb/sth)** (*formal*) harmful SYN **damaging**: *the sun's detrimental effect on skin* ◇ *The policy will be detrimental to the peace process.* ▶ **det·ri·men·tal·ly** /-təli/ *adv.*

**de·tritus** /dɪˈtraɪtəs/ *noun* [U] **1** (*specialist*) natural waste material that is left after sth has been used or broken up: *organic detritus from fish and plants* **2** (*formal*) any kind of rubbish that is left after an event or when sth has been used SYN **debris**: *the detritus of everyday life*

**deuce** /djuːs; NAmE duːs/ *noun* **1** [U, C] (in tennis) the situation when both players have 40 as a score, after which one player must win two points one after the other in order to win the game **2** [C] (*NAmE*) a PLAYING CARD with two PIPS on it: *the deuce of clubs* **3** **the deuce** [sing.] (*old-fashioned, informal*) used in questions to show that you are annoyed: *What the deuce is he doing?*

**deur·me·kaar** /ˌdɪəməˈkɑː(r); NAmE ˌdɪrm-/ *adj.* (*SAfrE, informal*) confused state

**deus ex mach·ina** /ˌdeɪʊs eks ˈmækɪnə/ *noun* [sing.] (*literary*) an unexpected power or event that saves a situation that seems without hope, especially in a play or novel

**deu·ter·ium** /djuːˈtɪəriəm; NAmE duːˈtɪr-/ *noun* [U] (*symb.* D) (*chemistry*) an ISOTOPE (= a different form) of HYDROGEN with twice the mass of the usual isotope

**de·value** /ˌdiːˈvæljuː/ *verb* **1** [I, T] ~ **(sth) (against sth)** (*finance*) (of money) to reduce in value when it is exchanged for the money of another country; to reduce the value of money in this way OPP **revalue 2** [T] ~ **sth** to give a lower value to sth, making it seem less important than it really is: *Work in the home is often ignored and devalued.* ▶ **de·valu·ation** /ˌdiːvæljuˈeɪʃn/ *noun* [C, U]: *There has been a further small devaluation against the dollar.*

**Deva·nag·ari** /ˌdeɪvəˈnɑːɡəri, dev-/ *noun* [U] the alphabet used to write Sanskrit, Hindi and some other Indian languages

# devastate

**dev·as·tate** /ˈdevəsteɪt/ verb **1** ~ sth to completely destroy a place or an area: *The bomb devastated much of the old part of the city.* **2** [often passive] ~ sb to make sb feel very shocked and sad

**dev·as·tated** /ˈdevəsteɪtɪd/ adj. extremely upset and shocked: *His family is absolutely devastated.*

**dev·as·tat·ing** /ˈdevəsteɪtɪŋ/ adj. **1** causing a lot of damage and destroying things SYN **disastrous**: *a devastating explosion/fire/cyclone* ◊ *Oil spills are having a devastating effect on coral reefs in the ocean.* ◊ *He received devastating injuries in the accident.* ◊ *It will be a devastating blow to the local community if the factory closes.* **2** that shocks or upsets you very much: *the devastating news that her father was dead* **3** impressive and powerful: *his devastating performance in the 100 metres* ◊ *Her smile was devastating.* ◊ *a devastating attack on the President's economic record* ▶ **dev·as·tat·ing·ly** adv.: *a devastatingly handsome man*

**dev·as·ta·tion** /ˌdevəˈsteɪʃn/ noun [U] great DESTRUCTION or damage, especially over a wide area: *The bomb caused widespread devastation.*

**de·velop** /dɪˈveləp/ verb
- **GROW/IMPROVE 1** [I, T] to gradually grow or become bigger, more advanced, stronger, etc.; to make sth do this: *The child is developing normally.* ◊ ~ (from sth) (into sth) *The place has rapidly developed from a small fishing community into a thriving tourist resort.* ◊ ~ sth *The aim is to develop your personal skills.* ◊ ~ sth (from sth) (into sth) *She developed the company from nothing.* **2** [T, I] ~ (sth) to start to have a skill, ability, quality, etc. that becomes better and stronger; to become better and stronger: *He's developed a real flair for management.* ◊ *Their relationship has developed over a number of years.*
- **NEW IDEA/PRODUCT 3** [T] ~ sth to think of or produce a new idea, product, etc. and make it successful: *The company develops and markets new software.* ◊ *It takes time to develop new technology.* ⟹ SYNONYMS at MAKE
- **DISEASE/PROBLEM 4** [T, I] ~ (sth) to begin to have sth such as a disease or a problem; to start to affect sb/sth: *She developed lung cancer at the age of sixty.* ◊ *The car developed engine trouble and we had to stop.* ◊ *If symptoms develop, seek help quickly.*
- **HAPPEN/CHANGE 5** [I] to start to happen or change, especially in a bad way: *A crisis was rapidly developing in the Gulf.* ◊ *We need more time to see how things develop before we take action.* ◊ ~ **into** sth *The conflict quickly developed into full-scale war.*
- **BUILD HOUSES 6** [T] ~ sth to build new houses, factories, etc. on an area of land, especially land that was not being used effectively before: *The site is being developed by a French company.*
- **CREATE/IMPROVE FACILITIES 7** [T] ~ sth to build or improve a building or other facilities: *The company is developing a chain of hotels.*
- **BECOME ECONOMICALLY ADVANCED 8** [I] (*economics*) (of a country) to become economically and socially more advanced: *China is developing at a pace that is remarkable to behold.* ⟹ see also DEVELOPED (1)
- **IDEA/STORY/MUSICAL THEME 9** [T] ~ sth to add further explanation or details to an idea, story or musical theme SYN **elaborate**: *She develops the theme more fully in her later books.* ◊ *He began to develop these ideas in a series of paintings.*
- **PHOTOGRAPHS 10** [T] ~ sth to treat film that has been used to take photographs with chemicals so that the pictures can be seen

**de·vel·oped** /dɪˈveləpt/ adj. **1** (of a country, society, etc.) having many industries and a complex economic system: *financial aid to less developed countries* ◊ *The average citizen in the developed world uses over 155 kg of paper per year.* ⟹ compare UNDERDEVELOPED **2** in an advanced state: *children with highly developed problem-solving skills* ⟹ see also WELL DEVELOPED

**de·vel·op·er** /dɪˈveləpə(r)/ noun **1** [C] a person or company that buys land or buildings in order to build new houses, shops, etc., or to improve the old ones, and makes a profit from doing this: *property developers* **2** [C] a person or a company that designs and creates new products: *a software developer* **3** [U] a chemical substance that is used for developing photographs from a film

**de·vel·op·ing** /dɪˈveləpɪŋ/ adj. [only before noun] (of a country, society, etc.) poor, and trying to make its industry and economic system more advanced: *developing countries/nations/economies* ⟹ compare UNDERDEVELOPED

**de·vel·op·ment** /dɪˈveləpmənt/ noun
- **GROWTH 1** [U] the steady growth of sth so that it becomes more advanced, stronger, etc: *a baby's development in the womb* ◊ *This is a perfectly normal stage of development.* ◊ *the development of basic skills such as literacy and numeracy* ◊ *career development* ⟹ see also SELF-DEVELOPMENT **2** (*economics*) the growth of the economy of a country or region through increased business activity: *Increased tourism will promote job creation and economic development.* ◊ *International policies should support, not inhibit, sustainable development.* ◊ *community development projects* ◊ *a development plan/programme*
- **NEW PRODUCT OR IDEA 3** [U, C] the process of producing or creating sth new or more advanced; a new or advanced product or idea: *the development of new technology* ◊ *Pete is head of product development.* ◊ **in**/**under** ~ *A new vaccine is under development.* ◊ *This drug is an exciting new development.* ◊ ~ **in** sth *developments in aviation technology* ⟹ see also RESEARCH AND DEVELOPMENT
- **NEW EVENT 4** [C, usually pl.] a new event or stage that is likely to affect what happens in a continuing situation: *Have there been any further developments?* ◊ ~ **in** sth *the latest developments in the war*
- **NEW BUILDINGS 5** [C] a piece of land with new buildings on it: *I live in a brand-new housing development.* **6** [U] the process of using an area of land, especially to make a profit by building on it, etc: *He bought the land for development.*

**de·vel·op·men·tal** /dɪˌveləpˈmentl/ adj. **1** in a state of developing or being developed: *The product is still at a developmental stage.* **2** connected with the development of sb/sth: *developmental psychology* ▶ **de·vel·op·men·tal·ly** /-təli/ adv.

**de'velopment area** noun (*BrE*) an area where new industries are encouraged in order to create jobs

**Devi** /ˈdeɪvi/ noun (*IndE*) **1** [C] a female god **2** used after the first name of a Hindu woman as a polite way of addressing her

**de·vi·ant** /ˈdiːviənt/ adj. different from what most people consider to be normal and acceptable: *deviant behaviour/sexuality* ▶ **de·vi·ant** noun: *sexual deviants* **de·vi·ance** /-əns/, **de·vi·ancy** /-ənsi/ noun [U]: *a study of social deviance and crime*

**de·vi·ate** /ˈdiːvieɪt/ verb [I] ~ (**from** sth) to be different from sth; to do sth in a different way from what is usual or expected: *The bus had to deviate from its usual route because of a road closure.* ◊ *He never deviated from his original plan.*

**de·vi·ation** /ˌdiːviˈeɪʃn/ noun **1** [U, C] ~ (**from** sth) the act of moving away from what is normal or acceptable; a difference from what is expected or acceptable: *deviation from the previously accepted norms* ◊ *sexual deviation* ◊ *a deviation from the plan* **2** [C] ~ (**from** sth) (*specialist*) the amount by which a single measurement is different from the average: *a compass deviation of 5°* (= from true north) ⟹ see also STANDARD DEVIATION

**de·vice** /dɪˈvaɪs/ noun **1** an object or a piece of equipment that has been designed to do a particular job: *a tracking/recording/listening device* ◊ *The new devices will be installed at US airports.* ◊ *electrical labour-saving devices around the home* ⟹ see also INTRAUTERINE DEVICE, POINTING DEVICE **2** a piece of computer equipment, especially a small one such as a smartphone: *You can store thousands of photos on your device.* ◊ *a hand-held/portable/wireless device* ⟹ see also MOBILE DEVICE **3** a bomb or weapon that will explode: *A powerful device exploded outside the station.* ◊ *Two* bombers *detonated their devices* in the busy shopping centre. ⊃ see also IED **4** a method of doing sth that produces a particular result or effect: *Targeted advertising on social media is very successful as a marketing device.* **5** a plan or trick that is used to get sth that sb wants: *The report was a device used to hide rather than reveal problems.*

**IDM** **leave sb to their own de'vices** to leave sb alone to do as they wish, and not tell them what to do

**devil** ?+ **C1** /ˈdevl/ *noun* **1** ?+ **C1** **the Devil** (in the Christian, Jewish and Muslim religions) the most powerful evil being **SYN Satan 2** ?+ **C1** an evil spirit: *They believed she was possessed by devils.* **3** (*informal*) a person who behaves badly, especially a child: *a naughty little devil* **4** (*old-fashioned, informal*) used to talk about sb and to emphasize an opinion that you have of them: *I miss the old devil, now that he's gone.* ◇ *She's off to Greece for a month—lucky devil!* ⊃ see also DUST DEVIL

**IDM** **be a 'devil** (*BrE*) people say **Be a devil!** to encourage sb to do sth that they are not sure about doing: *Go on, be a devil, buy both of them.* **better the devil you 'know (than the devil you 'don't)** (*saying*) used to say that it is easier and wiser to stay in a bad situation that you know and can deal with rather than change to a new situation that may be much worse **between the devil and the deep blue 'sea** in a difficult situation where there are two equally unpleasant or unacceptable choices **the 'devil** (*old-fashioned*) very difficult or unpleasant: *These berries are the devil to pick because they're so small.* **a 'devil of a job/time** (*old-fashioned*) a very difficult or unpleasant job or time: *I've had a devil of a job finding you.* **go to the 'devil!** (*old-fashioned, informal*) used, in an unfriendly way, to tell sb to go away **like the 'devil** (*old-fashioned, informal*) very hard, fast, etc: *We ran like the devil.* **speak/talk of the 'devil** (*informal*) people say **speak/talk of the devil** when sb they have been talking about appears unexpectedly: *Well, speak of the devil—here's Alice now!* **what, where, who, why, etc. the 'devil ...** (*old-fashioned*) used in questions to show that you are annoyed or surprised: *What the devil do you think you're doing?* ⊃ more at PAY *v.*, SELL *v.*

**devil·ish** /ˈdevəlɪʃ/ *adj.* **1** cruel or evil: *a devilish conspiracy* **2** morally bad, but in a way that people find attractive: *He was handsome, with a devilish charm.*

**devil·ish·ly** /ˈdevəlɪʃli/ *adv.* (*old-fashioned*) extremely; very: *a devilishly hot day*

**dev·illed** (*BrE*) (*US* **dev·iled**) /ˈdevld/ *adj.* cooked in a thick liquid containing hot SPICES

**ˌdevil-may-ˈcare** *adj.* [usually before noun] cheerful and not worried about the future

**ˌdevil's 'advocate** *noun* a person who expresses an opinion that they do not really hold in order to encourage a discussion about a subject: *Often the interviewer will need to play devil's advocate in order to get a discussion going.*

**de·vi·ous** /ˈdiːviəs/ *adj.* **1** behaving in a dishonest or indirect way, or tricking people, in order to get sth **SYN deceitful, underhand:** *a devious politician* ◇ *He got rich by devious means.* **2** ~ **route/path** a route or path that is not straight but has many changes in direction; not direct: *a devious route from the airport* ▶ **de·vi·ous·ly** *adv.* **de·vi·ous·ness** *noun* [U]

**de·vise** ?+ **C1** /dɪˈvaɪz/ *verb* ~ **sth** to invent sth new or a new way of doing sth **SYN think up:** *A new system has been devised to control traffic in the city.*

**de·void** /dɪˈvɔɪd/ *adj.* ~ **of sth** completely without sth: *The letter was devoid of warmth and feeling.*

**de·vo·lu·tion** /ˌdiːvəˈluːʃn; *NAmE* ˌdevə-/ *noun* [U] the act of giving power from a central authority or government to an authority or a government in a local region

**de·volve** /dɪˈvɒlv; *NAmE* -ˈvɑːlv/ *verb*
**PHRV** **deˈvolve on/upon sb/sth** (*formal*) **1** if property, money, etc. **devolves on/upon** you, you receive it after sb else dies **2** if a duty, responsibility, etc. **devolves on/upon** you, it is given to you by sb at a higher level of authority **deˈvolve sth to/on/upon sb** to give a duty, responsibility, power, etc. to sb who has less authority than you: *The central government devolved most tax-raising powers to the regional authorities.*

**de·volved** /dɪˈvɒlvd; *NAmE* -ˈvɑːlvd/ *adj.* if power or authority is **devolved**, it has been passed to sb who has less power: *devolved responsibility* ◇ *a system of devolved government*

**de·vote** ?+ **B2** /dɪˈvəʊt/ *verb*
**PHRV** **deˈvote yourself to sb/sth** ?+ **B2** to give most of your time, energy, attention, etc. to sb/sth: *She devoted herself to her career.* **deˈvote sth to sth** ?+ **B2** to give an amount of time, attention, etc. to sth: *I could only devote two hours a day to the work.* ◇ *The amount of time devoted to leisure is dropping.*

**de·voted** /dɪˈvəʊtɪd/ *adj.* having great love for sb/sth and supporting them in everything: *a devoted son/friend/fan* ◇ ~ **to sb/sth** *They are devoted to their children.* ⊃ SYNONYMS at LOVE ▶ **de·voted·ly** *adv.*

**de·votee** /ˌdevəˈtiː/ *noun* **1** ~ **(of sb/sth)** a person who admires and is very enthusiastic about sb/sth: *a devotee of science fiction* **2** ~ **(of sb/sth)** a very religious person who belongs to a particular group: *devotees of Krishna*

**de·vo·tion** /dɪˈvəʊʃn/ *noun* **1** [U, sing.] ~ **(to sb/sth)** great love, care and support for sb/sth: *His devotion to his wife and family is touching.* **2** [U, sing.] ~ **(to sb/sth)** the action of spending a lot of time or energy on sth **SYN dedication:** *her devotion to duty* ◇ *Her devotion to the job left her with very little free time.* **3** [U] religious WORSHIP: *The statue of the emperor became an object of devotion.* **4** **devotions** [pl.] prayers and other religious practices

**de·vo·tion·al** /dɪˈvəʊʃənl/ *adj.* (of music, etc.) connected with or used in religious services

**de·vour** /dɪˈvaʊə(r)/ *verb* **1** ~ **sth** to eat all of sth quickly, especially because you are very hungry **SYN gobble 2** to read or look at sth with great interest and enthusiasm: *She devoured everything she could lay her hands on: books, magazines and newspapers.* **3** ~ **sb/sth** (*formal*) to destroy sb/sth **SYN engulf:** *Flames devoured the house.*
**IDM** **be devoured by sth** to be filled with a strong emotion that seems to control you: *She was devoured by envy and hatred.*

**de·vout** /dɪˈvaʊt/ *adj.* (of a person) believing strongly in a particular religion and obeying its laws and practices: *a devout Christian/Muslim* ▶ **de·vout·ly** *adv.*: *a devoutly Catholic region* ◇ *She devoutly (= very strongly) hoped he was telling the truth.*

**dew** /djuː; *NAmE* duː/ *noun* [U, sing.] the very small drops of water that form on the ground, etc. during the night: *The grass was wet with early morning dew.*

▼ **HOMOPHONES**
**dew • due** /djuː; *NAmE* duː/
- **dew** *noun*: *The dew sparkled in the morning sunlight.*
- **due** *adj.*: *The fourth soloist was absent due to an illness.*
- **due** *noun*: *Despite his talent, radio and TV have never given him his due.*
- **due** *adv.*: *They sailed due north.*

**Dewey ˌdeci·mal clas·si·fi·ca·tion**™ /ˌdjuːi ˌdesɪml ˌklæsɪfɪˈkeɪʃn; *NAmE* ˌduː-/ (*also* **Dewey**™ **ˈdeci·mal sys·tem**) *noun* [sing.] an international system for arranging books in a library

**ˈdew point** *noun* [sing.] (*specialist*) the temperature at which air can hold no more water. Below this temperature the water comes out of the air in the form of drops.

**dewy** /ˈdjuːi; *NAmE* ˈduːi/ *adj.* wet with DEW

**ˌdewy-ˈeyed** *adj.* (*often disapproving*) showing emotion about sth, perhaps with a few tears in the eyes **SYN sentimental**

**dex·ter·ity** /dekˈsterəti/ *noun* [U] skill in using your hands or your mind: *You need good manual dexterity to be a dentist.* ◇ *mental/verbal dexterity*

**dex·ter·ous** (also **dex·trous**) /ˈdekstrəs/ adj. (formal) showing or having skill, especially with your hands ▶ **dex·ter·ous·ly** (also **dex·trous·ly**) adv.

**dex·trose** /ˈdekstrəʊz, -strəʊs/ noun [U] (chemistry) a form of GLUCOSE (= a type of natural sugar)

**dhaba** /ˈdɑːbə/ noun (IndE) a small cheap restaurant where Punjabi food is served, with basic furniture and facilities, and often with an open front and tables outside

**dhal** = DAL

**dhania** /ˈdɑːniə/ noun [U] (EAfrE, IndE, SAfrE) the leaves or seeds of the CORIANDER plant, used in cooking as a SPICE

**dhan·sak** /ˈdʌnsɑːk, ˈdænsæk/ noun an Indian meat or vegetable dish cooked with LENTILS and CORIANDER

**dharma** /ˈdɑːmə; NAmE ˈdɑːrmə/ noun [U] (IndE) truth or law that affects the whole universe

**dharna** /ˈdɜːnə, -nɑː; NAmE ˈdɜːrnə, -nɑː/ noun (IndE) **1** an act of lying flat with your face down on the floor of a TEMPLE as a way of showing respect for God **2** a form of protest in which a group of people refuse to leave a factory, public place, etc.

**dhoti** /ˈdəʊti/ noun a long piece of cloth worn by Hindu men at weddings and other traditional occasions. It is worn on the lower part of the body, tied around the middle, with the lower part passed between the legs.

**dhow** /daʊ/ noun an Arab ship with one large sail in the shape of a TRIANGLE

**dhur·rie** (also **dur·rie**) /ˈdʌri; NAmE ˈdɜːri/ noun a heavy cotton RUG (= small carpet) from South Asia

**DI** /ˌdiː ˈaɪ/ noun a British police officer of middle rank (the abbreviation for 'Detective Inspector'): *DI Ross*

**di-** /daɪ/ combining form **1** twice; two; double: *dicotyledon* **2** (chemistry) (in nouns that are names of chemical COMPOUNDS) containing two ATOMS or groups of the type mentioned: *carbon dioxide*

**dia·betes** /ˌdaɪəˈbiːtiːz/ noun [U] a medical condition in which the body cannot produce enough INSULIN to control the amount of sugar in the blood

**dia·bet·ic** /ˌdaɪəˈbetɪk/ adj., noun
■ adj. **1** having or connected with diabetes: *She's diabetic.* ◇ *a diabetic patient* ◇ *diabetic complications* **2** suitable for or used by sb who has diabetes: *a diabetic diet*
■ noun a person who suffers from DIABETES

**dia·bol·ical** /ˌdaɪəˈbɒlɪkl; NAmE -ˈbɑːl-/ adj. **1** (especially BrE, informal) extremely bad or annoying SYN terrible: *The traffic was diabolical.* **2** (also less frequent **dia·bol·ic** /ˌdaɪəˈbɒlɪk; NAmE -ˈbɑːl-/) morally bad and evil; like a DEVIL ▶ **dia·bol·ic·ally** /-kli/ adv.

**dia·crit·ic** /ˌdaɪəˈkrɪtɪk/ noun (linguistics) a mark such as an ACCENT, placed over, under or through a letter in some languages, to show that the letter should be pronounced in a different way from the same letter without a mark ▶ **dia·crit·ical** /-tɪkl/ adj.: *diacritical marks*

**dia·dem** /ˈdaɪədem/ noun a small CROWN (= an object in the shape of a circle that is worn on the head, usually made of gold and precious stones), worn especially as a sign of royal power

**diag·nose** /ˈdaɪəɡnəʊz, ˌdaɪəɡˈnəʊz; NAmE ˌdaɪəɡˈnəʊs/ verb to say exactly what an illness or the cause of a problem is: ~ **sth** *The test is used to diagnose a variety of diseases.* ◇ ~ **sth as sth** *The illness was diagnosed as cancer.* ◇ ~ **sb with sth** *He has recently been diagnosed with angina.* ◇ ~ **sb/sth (as) sth** *I quickly diagnosed the problem as a faulty battery.* ◇ ~ **sb + adj./noun** *He was diagnosed (a) diabetic.* ⇨ WORDFINDER NOTE at EXAMINE

**diag·no·sis** /ˌdaɪəɡˈnəʊsɪs/ noun [C, U] (pl. **diag·noses** /-ˈnəʊsiːz/) ~ **(of sth)** the act of discovering or identifying the exact cause of an illness or a problem: *a diagnosis of lung cancer* ◇ *They are waiting for the doctor's diagnosis.* ◇ *An accurate diagnosis was made after a series of tests.*

**diag·nos·tic** /ˌdaɪəɡˈnɒstɪk; NAmE -ˈnɑːs-/ adj., noun
■ adj. **1** [usually before noun] (specialist) connected with identifying an illness or other problem: *to carry out diagnostic assessments/tests* ◇ *Get a low-cost car diagnostic tool to identify the fault.* ◇ ~ **of sth** *specific conditions which are diagnostic of AIDS* **2** connected with identifying what a student needs to learn: *diagnostic grammar tests* ▶ **diag·nos·tic·ally** /-kli/ adv.
■ noun **1** (also ˌdiagˈnostic program) [C] (computing) a program used for identifying a computer fault **2** [C] (computing) a message on a computer screen giving information about a fault **3** **diagnostics** [U] the practice or methods of diagnosis

**di·ag·onal** /daɪˈæɡənl/ adj., noun
■ adj. (of a straight line) at an angle; joining two opposite sides of sth at an angle: *diagonal stripes* ⇨ picture at LINE ▶ **di·ag·onal·ly** /-nəli/ adv.: *Walk diagonally across the field to the far corner and then turn left.*
■ noun a straight line that joins two opposite sides of sth at an angle; a straight line that is at an angle

**dia·gram** /ˈdaɪəɡræm/ noun a simple drawing using lines to explain where sth is, how sth works, etc: *The results are shown in diagram 2.* ◇ ~ **of sth** *a diagram of the wiring system* ⇨ see also VENN DIAGRAM ▶ **dia·gram·mat·ic** /ˌdaɪəɡrəˈmætɪk/ adj. **dia·gram·mat·ic·ally** /-kli/ adv.

**dial** /ˈdaɪəl/ noun, verb
■ noun **1** the face of a clock or watch, or a similar control on a machine, piece of equipment or vehicle that shows a measurement of time, amount, speed, temperature, etc: *an alarm clock with a luminous dial* ◇ *Check the tyre pressure on the dial.* ⇨ see also SUNDIAL **2** the round control on a radio, cooker, etc. that you turn in order to change sth, for example to choose a particular station or to choose a particular temperature **3** the round part on some older phones, with holes for the fingers, that you move around to call a particular number ⇨ see also SPEED DIAL
■ verb [T, I] (-ll-, NAmE -l-) ~ **(sth)** to use a phone by pushing buttons or turning the dial to call a number: *He dialled the number and waited.* ◇ *Dial 0033 for France.* ⇨ WORDFINDER NOTE at CALL
PHRV ˌdial sth↔ˈdown **1** to reduce the noise, heat, etc. produced by a piece of equipment by moving its controls: *The event organizers took the hint and dialled down the background music.* **2** (informal) to reduce the amount, degree or power of a quality: *He called on both sides to dial down the anger and start talking to each other.* ˌdial ˈin | ˌdial ˈinto sth to connect to a service or computer system using a phone line: *Remote users dial in from various locations worldwide.* ˌdial sb↔ˈin | ˌdial sb ˈinto sth to connect sb to a CONFERENCE CALL (= a phone call in which three or more people take part) ˌdial ˈup | ˌdial sth↔ˈup to connect to a computer system using a phone line ⇨ see also DIAL-UP ˌdial sth↔ˈup **1** to order sth by phone, to be delivered immediately: *If I'm too tired to cook, I just dial up a pizza.* **2** to increase the noise, heat, etc. produced by a piece of equipment by moving its controls **3** (informal) to increase the amount, degree or power of a quality: *She gradually dialled up the pressure on the rest of the team.*

**dia·lect** /ˈdaɪəlekt/ noun [C, U] the form of a language that is spoken in one area with grammar, words and pronunciation that may be different from other forms of the same language: *the Yorkshire dialect* ⇨ compare ACCENT ⇨ WORDFINDER NOTE at LANGUAGE ▶ **dia·lect·al** /ˌdaɪəˈlektl/ adj.

**dia·lec·tic** /ˌdaɪəˈlektɪk/ noun [sing.] (also less frequent **dia·lect·ics** [U]) **1** (philosophy) a method of discovering the truth of ideas by discussion and logical argument and by considering ideas that are opposed to each other **2** (formal) the way in which two aspects of a situation affect each other ▶ **dia·lect·ic·al** /-tɪkl/ adj.

**dia·lectical ma·terialism** noun [U] (philosophy) the Marxist theory that all change results from different social forces which come into conflict because of material needs

**dial·ler** (BrE) (NAmE **dial·er**) /ˈdaɪələ(r)/ noun a piece of computer software or a device for calling phone numbers, without needing a person to do it

**'dial·ling code** (also **code**) noun (BrE) the numbers that are used for a particular town, area or country, in front of an individual phone number: *international dialling codes* ⊃ compare AREA CODE

**'dial·ling tone** (BrE) (NAmE **'dial tone**) noun the sound that you hear from a phone that means you can make a call

**'dialog box** (BrE also **'dialogue box**) noun a box that appears on a computer screen asking the user to give information or choose what they want to do next

**dia·logue** ❶ 🅐🅛 (US also **dia·log**) /ˈdaɪəlɒɡ; NAmE -lɔːɡ/ noun [C, U] **1** 🅐🅛 a conversation in a book, play or film or in language teaching materials: *Learners are asked to listen to three short dialogues.* ◇ *Practise the dialogue with a partner.* ◇ *The novel has long descriptions and not much dialogue.* ⊃ SYNONYMS at DISCUSSION ⊃ WORDFINDER NOTE at FILM **2** 🅑🅞 a formal discussion between two groups or countries, especially when they are trying to solve a problem, end a DISAGREEMENT, etc: *The president told waiting reporters there had been a constructive dialogue.* ◇ **~ with sb** *The government refused to engage in direct dialogue with the terrorists.* ◇ **~ between A and B** *There needs to be a closer dialogue between management and staff.* ◇ **~ about sth** *an honest and open dialogue about racial identity in the US* ◇ **on sth** *a meaningful dialogue on pay and working conditions* ⊃ compare MONOLOGUE

**'dial-up** adj. [only before noun] using a phone line and a MODEM to connect your computer to the internet

**dia·ly·sis** /daɪˈæləsɪs/ noun [U] (specialist) a process for separating substances from a liquid, especially for taking waste substances out of the blood of people with damaged KIDNEYS: *kidney/renal dialysis* ◇ *a dialysis machine*

**dia·manté** /ˌdiːəˈmɒnteɪ; NAmE diːəmɑːnˈteɪ/ adj. decorated with glass that is cut to look like diamonds: *diamanté earrings*

**diam·eter** /daɪˈæmɪtə(r)/ noun **1** a straight line going from one side of a circle or any other round object to the other side, passing through the centre: *the diameter of a tree trunk* ◇ **in ~** *The dome is 42.3 metres in diameter.* ⊃ picture at CIRCLE ⊃ compare RADIUS **2** (specialist) a measurement of the power of an instrument to MAGNIFY sth: *a lens magnifying 300 diameters* (= making sth look 300 times larger than it really is)

**dia·met·ric·al** /ˌdaɪəˈmetrɪkl/ adj. [usually before noun] **1** used to emphasize that people or things are completely different: *He's the diametrical opposite of his brother.* **2** relating to the DIAMETER of sth

**dia·met·ric·al·ly** /ˌdaɪəˈmetrɪkli/ adv. **~opposed, opposite, different,** etc. completely different: *We hold diametrically opposed views.*

**dia·mond** ❶ 🅑🅛 /ˈdaɪmənd/ noun **1** 🅑🅛 [U, C] a clear PRECIOUS STONE of pure CARBON, the hardest substance known. Diamonds are used in jewellery and also in industry, especially for cutting glass: *a diamond ring/necklace* ◇ *She was wearing her diamonds* (= jewellery with diamonds in it). ◇ *The lights shone like diamonds.* ⊃ see also BLACK DIAMOND, BLOOD DIAMOND, CONFLICT DIAMOND, ROUGH DIAMOND **2** 🅑 🅛 [C] a shape with four straight sides of equal length and with angles that are not RIGHT ANGLES: *a sweater with a diamond pattern* **3** **diamonds** [pl., U] one of the four SUITS (= PACK of cards. The cards are marked with red diamond shapes: *the ten of diamonds* **4** [C] one card from the SUIT called diamonds: *You must play a diamond if you have one.* **5** [C] (in baseball) the space inside the lines that connect the four BASES; also used to mean the whole baseball field

**diamond in the 'rough** (NAmE) (BrE **rough 'diamond**) noun a person who has many good qualities even though they do not seem to be very polite, educated, etc.

**diamond ju'bilee** noun [usually sing.] the 60th anniversary of an important event, especially of sb becoming king/queen; a celebration of this event ⊃ compare GOLDEN JUBILEE, SILVER JUBILEE

**diamond 'wedding** (BrE) (NAmE **diamond anni'versary**) (also **diamond 'wedding anniversary** NAmE, BrE) noun the 60th anniversary of a wedding ⊃ compare GOLDEN WEDDING, RUBY WEDDING, SILVER WEDDING

**dia·mor·phine** /ˌdaɪəˈmɔːfiːn; NAmE -ˈmɔːrf-/ noun [U] a powerful drug that is made from OPIUM and used to reduce pain

**di·aper** /ˈdaɪpə(r)/ (NAmE) (BrE **nappy**) noun a piece of soft cloth or other thick material that is folded around a baby's bottom and between its legs to take in and hold its body waste: *I'll change her diaper.*

**di·aph·an·ous** /daɪˈæfənəs/ adj. (formal) (of cloth) so light and fine that you can almost see through it

**dia·phragm** /ˈdaɪəfræm/ noun **1** (anatomy) the layer of muscle between the lungs and the stomach, used especially to control breathing **2** (BrE also **cap**) a rubber or plastic device that a woman places inside her VAGINA before having sex to prevent SPERM from entering the WOMB and making her pregnant **3** any thin piece of material used to separate the parts of a machine, etc. **4** (specialist) a thin disc used to turn electronic signals into sound and sound into electronic signals in phones, LOUDSPEAKERS, etc.

**diar·ist** /ˈdaɪərɪst/ noun a person who writes a diary, especially one that is later published: *Samuel Pepys, the famous seventeenth-century diarist*

**diar·rhoea** (BrE) (NAmE **diar·rhea**) /ˌdaɪəˈrɪə; NAmE -ˈriːə/ (also informal **the runs**) noun [U] an illness in which waste matter is emptied from the BOWELS much more frequently than normal, and in liquid form: *Symptoms include diarrhoea and vomiting.*

**diary** ❶ 🅐🅜 /ˈdaɪəri/ noun (pl. **-ies**) **1** 🅐🅜 a book in which you can write down the experiences you have each day, your private thoughts, etc: *Do you keep a diary* (= write one regularly)? ◇ *the diaries of Samuel Pepys* ◇ *The writer's letters and diaries are being published next year.* ◇ **in a ~** *'It's all over,' he wrote in his diary for April 21.* ◇ *her diary entry for 9 December 2017* ⊃ see also JOURNAL, VIDEO DIARY **2** 🅐🅜 (BrE) (NAmE **appointment book**) a book or an app with spaces for each day of the year in which you can record things you have to do in the future: *a desk diary* ◇ **in a ~** *I've made a note in my diary.*

**dias·pora** /daɪˈæspərə/ noun [sing.] (formal) **1** **the diaspora** the movement of the Jewish people away from their own country to live and work in other countries; Jewish people living and working in other countries **2** the movement of people from any nation or group away from their own country; people who have moved away from their own country: *The Russian diaspora in London.*

**dia·stole** /daɪˈæstəli/ noun [U, C] (medical) the stage of the heart's rhythm when its muscles relax and the heart fills with blood ⊃ compare SYSTOLE ▸ **dia·stol·ic** /ˌdaɪəˈstɒlɪk; NAmE -ˈstɑːl-/ adj.

**dia·ton·ic** /ˌdaɪəˈtɒnɪk; NAmE -ˈtɑːn-/ adj. (music) using only the notes of the appropriate MAJOR or MINOR SCALE ⊃ compare CHROMATIC

**dia·tribe** /ˈdaɪətraɪb/ noun **~(against sb/sth)** (formal) a long and angry speech or piece of writing attacking and criticizing sb/sth: *He launched a bitter diatribe against the younger generation.*

**di·aze·pam** /daɪˈæzɪpæm/ noun [U] (medical) a drug that is used to make people feel less anxious and more relaxed

**dibs** /dɪbz/ noun [pl.] (informal) the right to have or choose sth before other people: *Jamie had first dibs and chose the top bunk.* ◇ *Dibs on* (= I claim) *the chocolate cake!*

# dice

**dice** /daɪs/ noun, verb
- **noun** (pl. **dice**) **1** (also **die** especially in NAmE) [C] a small CUBE of wood, plastic, etc., with a different number of spots on each of its sides, used in games of chance: *a pair of dice* ◇ *to roll/throw/shake the dice* **2** [U] a game played with dice: *We played dice all night.*
- **IDM** **no ˈdice** (especially NAmE, informal) used to show that you refuse to do sth, or that sth cannot be done: *He wanted $400 for it, so no dice.* ⇒ more at LOAD v.
- **verb** ~ **sth** to cut meat, vegetables, etc. into small square pieces: *diced carrots*
- **IDM** **dice with death** (informal) to risk your life by doing sth that you know is dangerous

**dicey** /ˈdaɪsi/ adj. (informal) dangerous and uncertain **SYN** risky

**di·chot·omy** /daɪˈkɒtəmi; NAmE -ˈkɑːt-/ noun [usually sing.] (pl. -ies) ~ **(between A and B)** (formal) a division or contrast between two groups or things that are completely opposite to and different from each other

**dick** /dɪk/ noun (taboo, slang) **1** a man's PENIS **2** = DICKHEAD

**dick·ens** /ˈdɪkɪnz/ noun **the dickens** (old-fashioned, informal) **1** used in questions instead of 'devil' to show that you are annoyed or surprised: *Where the dickens did he go?* **2** (NAmE) used when you are saying how attractive, etc. sb is: *cute as the dickens*

**Dick·ens·ian** /dɪˈkenziən/ adj. connected with or typical of the novels of Charles Dickens, which often describe bad social conditions: *a Dickensian slum*

**dicker** /ˈdɪkə(r)/ verb [I] ~ **(with sb) (over sth)** (especially NAmE) to argue about or discuss sth with sb, especially in order to agree on a price **SYN** bargain

**dick·head** /ˈdɪkhed/ (also **dick**) noun (taboo, slang) a very rude way of referring to sb, especially a man, that you think is stupid **SYN** idiot

**dicky** /ˈdɪki/ adj., noun
- **adj.** (BrE, old-fashioned, informal) not healthy; not working correctly: *a dicky heart*
- **noun** (also **dickey**) (pl. **dickies** or **dickeys**) (IndE) the BOOT of a car

**ˈdicky bird** noun (BrE) (used by or when speaking to young children) a bird
- **IDM** **not say, hear, etc. a dicky bird** (BrE, informal) to say, hear, etc. nothing: *He won't say a dicky bird, but we think he knows who did it.* **ORIGIN** This idiom is from rhyming slang, in which 'dicky bird' stands for 'word'.

**Dicta·phone™** /ˈdɪktəfəʊn/ noun a small machine used to record people speaking, so that their words can be played back later and written down

**dic·tate** ?+ **C1** verb, noun
- **verb** /dɪkˈteɪt; NAmE ˈdɪkteɪt/ **1** ?+ **C1** [T] to tell sb what to do, especially in an annoying way: ~ **sth (to sb)** *They are in no position to dictate terms* (= tell other people what to do). ◇ ~ **how, what, etc…/that…** *What right do they have to dictate how we live our lives?* **2** ?+ **C1** [T, I] to control or influence how sth happens ~ **(sth)** *When we take our vacations is very much dictated by Greg's work schedule.* ◇ ~ **where, what, etc…** *It's generally your job that dictates where you live now.* ◇ ~ **that…** *The social conventions of the day dictated that she should remain at home with her parents.* **3** ?+ **C1** [T, I] ~ **(sth) (to sb)** to say words for sb else to write down or to be recorded: *She dictated the letter to her assistant.* ◇ *OK, you write, I'll dictate.*
- **PHRV** **ˈdictate to sb** [often passive] to give orders to sb, often in a rude or aggressive way: *She refused to be dictated to by anyone.*
- **noun** /ˈdɪkteɪt/ [usually pl.] (formal) an order or a rule that you must obey: *to follow the dictates of fashion*

**dic·ta·tion** /dɪkˈteɪʃn/ noun **1** [U] the act of speaking or reading sth so that sb can write down the words or they can be recorded **2** [C, U] a test in which students write down what is being read to them, especially in language lessons

**dic·ta·tor** ?+ **C1** /dɪkˈteɪtə(r); NAmE ˈdɪkteɪtər/ noun (disapproving) **1** ?+ **C1** a political leader who have complete power over a country, especially one who has gained it using military force **2** a person who behaves as if they have complete power over other people, and tells them what to do

**dic·ta·tor·ial** /ˌdɪktəˈtɔːriəl/ adj. (disapproving) **1** connected with or controlled by a dictator: *a dictatorial ruler* ◇ *a dictatorial regime* **2** using power in an unreasonable way by telling people what to do and not listening to their views or wishes: *dictatorial behaviour* ▶ **dic·ta·tor·i·al·ly** /-əli/ adv.

**dic·ta·tor·ship** /dɪkˈteɪtəʃɪp; NAmE -tərʃ-/ noun [C, U] **1** government by a dictator **2** [C] a country that is ruled by a dictator ⇒ WORDFINDER NOTE at CAPITALISM

**dic·tion** /ˈdɪkʃn/ noun [U] **1** the way that sb pronounces words: *clear diction* **2** (specialist) the choice and use of words in literature

**dic·tion·ary** ❶ **A1** /ˈdɪkʃənri; NAmE -ʃəneri/ noun (pl. -ies) **1 A1** a book or electronic resource that gives a list of the words of a language in alphabetical order and explains what they mean, or gives a word for them in a foreign language: *a Spanish-English dictionary* ◇ *in a ~ Look it up in a dictionary!*

**WORDFINDER** alphabetical, definition, entry, example, headword, meaning, part of speech, pronunciation, register

**2** a book that explains the words that are used in a particular subject: *a dictionary of mathematics* **3** a list of words in electronic form, for example stored in a computer's SPELLCHECKER ⇒ WORDFINDER NOTE at WORD

**dic·tum** /ˈdɪktəm/ noun (pl. **dicta** /-tə/ or **dic·tums**) (formal) a statement that expresses sth that people believe is always true or should be followed

**did** /dɪd/ ⇒ DO¹ verb

**di·dac·tic** /daɪˈdæktɪk/ adj. (formal) **1** designed to teach people sth, especially a moral lesson: *didactic art* **2** (usually disapproving) telling people things rather than letting them find out for themselves ▶ **di·dac·tic·al·ly** /-kli/ adv.

**did·dle** /ˈdɪdl/ verb (informal) **1** [T] ~ **sb (out of sth)** (BrE) to get money or some advantage from sb by cheating them **SYN** cheat **2** [I] ~ **(around)** (NAmE) to waste time without having a purpose: *Sometimes I just diddle around all day.* **3** [I] ~ **(with sth)** (NAmE) to play with sth carelessly or without thinking: *He diddled with the graphics on his computer.*

**did·dly** /ˈdɪdli/ (also **diddly-ˈsquat**) noun (used in negative sentences) (NAmE, informal) not anything; nothing: *She doesn't know diddly about it.*

**diddy** /ˈdɪdi/ adj. (BrE, informal) very small: *a diddy little camera*

**didg·eri·doo** /ˌdɪdʒəriˈduː/ noun (pl. **-oos**) an Australian musical instrument consisting of a long wooden tube which you blow through to produce a variety of deep sounds

**didi** /ˈdiːdiː/ noun (IndE) **1** an older sister: *Didi taught me how to read.* **2** used after the name of an older female cousin of the same generation **3** used when speaking to an older female who is not related to you, as a title showing respect: *Didi, could you help me with this bag?*

**didn't** /ˈdɪdnt/ short form did not

**die** ❶ **A1** /daɪ/ verb, noun
- **verb** (**dies**, **dying**, **died**, **died**) **1** ?+ **A1** [I, T] to stop living: *My father died suddenly at the age of 48.* ◇ *At least six people have died in the accident.* ◇ *That plant's going to die if you don't water it!* ◇ ~ **of/from sth** *to die of/from cancer* ◇ ~ **for sth** *He was ready to die for his cause.* ◇ *I'll never forget it to my dying day* (= until I die). ◇ (informal) *I nearly died when I saw him there* (= it was very embarrassing). ◇ ~ **a…death** *to die a natural/slow/horrible/violent death* ◇ ~ **+ adj.** *She died young.* ◇ ~ **+ noun** *He died a hero.*

**WORDFINDER** ashes, cemetery, coffin, cremation, funeral, grave, hearse, morgue, mourn

**2** ?+ **B2** [I] to stop existing; to disappear: *The old customs are dying.* ◇ *His secret died with him* (= he never told anyone). ◇ *The words died on my lips* (= I stopped speaking).

| æ cat | ɑː father | e bed | ɜː fur | ə about | ɪ sit | iː see | i happy | ɒ got (BrE) | ɔː saw | ʌ cup | ʊ put | uː too |

**3** [I] (of a machine) to stop working: *My phone died and I had no way to contact you.* ◇ *The engine spluttered and died.* ◇ *My car just died on me.*
**IDM** be ˈdying for sth/to do sth (*informal*) to want sth or want to do sth very much: *I'm dying for a glass of water.* ◇ *I'm dying to know what happened.* die a/the ˈdeath (*BrE, informal*) to fail completely: *The play got terrible reviews and quickly died a death.* die in your ˈbed to die because you are old or ill die ˈlaughing to find sth extremely funny: *I nearly died laughing when she said that.* ˌold ˈhabits, traˈditions, etc. die ˈhard used to say that things change very slowly to ˈdie for (*informal*) if you think sth is to die for, you really want it, and would do anything to get it: *She was wearing a dress to die for.* ⇒ more at CROSS *v.*, FLY *n.*, SAY *v.*
**PHRV** ˌdie aˈway to become gradually weaker and finally disappear: *The sound of their laughter died away.* ˌdie ˈback if a plant **dies back**, it loses its leaves but remains alive ˌdie ˈdown to become gradually less strong, loud, easy to notice, etc: *The flames finally died down.* ◇ *When the applause had died down, she began her speech.* ˌdie ˈoff to die one after the other until there are none left ˌdie ˈout to stop existing: *This species has nearly died out because its habitat is being destroyed.*
■ **noun 1** a block of metal with a special shape, or with a pattern cut into it, that is used for shaping other pieces of metal such as coins, or for making patterns on paper or leather **2** (*especially NAmE*) = DICE
**IDM** the die is ˈcast (*saying*) used to say that an event has happened or a decision has been made that cannot be changed

**ˈdie-cast** *adj.* (of a metal object) made by pouring liquid metal into a MOULD and allowing it to cool

**die·hard** /ˈdaɪhɑːd; *NAmE* -hɑːrd/ *adj.* [only before noun] strongly opposing change and new ideas: *diehard supporters of the exiled king* ▶ **ˈdie-hard** *noun*: *A few diehards are trying to stop the reforms.*

**die·sel** /ˈdiːzl/ *noun* **1** (*also* ˈdie·sel fuel, ˈdie·sel oil) [U] a type of heavy oil used as a fuel instead of petrol: *a diesel engine* (= one that burns diesel) ◇ *diesel cars/locomotives/trains* ⇒ compare PETROL **2** [C] a vehicle that uses diesel fuel: *Our new car is a diesel.*

**diet** 🔑 **A1** /ˈdaɪət/ *noun, verb*
■ **noun 1** 🔑 **A1** [C, U] the food and drink that you eat and drink regularly: *to eat a healthy, balanced diet* ◇ *the Japanese diet of rice, vegetables and fish* ◇ *to receive advice on diet* ⇒ see also STAPLE DIET (1) ▶ WORDFINDER NOTE at EAT **2** [C, U] a limited variety or amount of food that you eat for medical reasons or because you want to lose weight; a time when you only eat this limited variety or amount: *He followed a strict low-fat diet.* ◇ *on a ~ I need to go on a diet* (= to lose weight) *before my holiday.* ◇ *She is trying to lose weight through diet and exercise.* ◇ *diet drinks* (= with fewer CALORIES than normal) ⇒ WORDFINDER NOTE at FIT **3** [sing.] **a ~ of sth** (*disapproving*) a large amount of a limited range of activities: *Children today are brought up on a diet of video games and TV on demand.* ⇒ see also STAPLE DIET (2) ▶ **dietˑary** /ˈdaɪətəri; *NAmE* -teri/ *adj.* [usually before noun]: *dietary advice/changes/habits* ◇ *dietary fibre*
■ **verb** [I] to eat less food or only food of a particular type in order to lose weight **SYN** be on a diet: *She's always dieting but she never seems to lose any weight.*

**dietˑer** /ˈdaɪətə(r)/ *noun* a person who is trying to lose weight on a diet

**dietˑetˑics** /ˌdaɪəˈtetɪks/ *noun* [U] the scientific study of diet and healthy eating ▶ **dietˑetˑic** *adj.*: *dietetic advice*

**dietˑician** (*also* **dietˑitian**) /ˌdaɪəˈtɪʃn/ *noun* a person whose job is to advise people on what kind of food they should eat to keep healthy

**difˑfer** **B2** /ˈdɪfə(r)/ *verb* **1** [I] to be different from sb/sth: *They hold differing views.* ◇ *A ~s from B French differs from English in this respect.* ◇ *A and B ~(from each other) French and English differ in this respect.* ◇ *~ between A and B Ideas on childcare may differ considerably between the parents.* ⇒ LANGUAGE BANK at CONTRAST **2** [I] to disagree with sb: *~(with sb)* (about/on/over sth) *I have to differ with you on that.* ◇ *~(as to sth) Medical opinion differs as to how to treat the disease.* **IDM** see AGREE, BEG

**difˑferˑence** **A1** /ˈdɪfrəns/ *noun* **1** [C, U] the way in which two people or things are not like each other; the way in which sb/sth has changed: *~between A and B There are no significant differences between the education systems of the two countries.* ◇ *He was studying the similarities and differences between humans and animals.* ◇ *I can never tell the difference* (= distinguish) *between the twins.* ◇ *~ in sth There's no difference in the results.* ◇ *There is a fundamental difference in approach to conservation in Japan.* ◇ *What a difference! You look great with your hair like that.* **OPP** similarity ⇒ LANGUAGE BANK at CONTRAST **2** **B1** [sing., U] the amount that sth is greater or smaller than sth else: *~ in sth We measured the difference in temperature.* ◇ *~ between A and B The difference between the two numbers gives you the profit.* ◇ *There's an age difference of six years between the boys* (= one is six years older than the other). ◇ *I'll lend you £500 and you'll have to find the difference* (= the rest of the money that you need). ⇒ see also GOAL DIFFERENCE **3** [C] a DISAGREEMENT between people: *We have our differences, but she's still my sister.* ◇ *Why don't you settle your differences and be friends again?* ◇ *There was a difference of opinion over who had won.*
**IDM** make a, no, some, etc. ˈdifference (to sb/to sth/in sth) **B1** to have an effect/no effect on sb/sth: *The rain didn't make much difference to the game.* ◇ *Your age shouldn't make any difference to whether you get the job or not.* ◇ *Changing schools made a big difference to my life.* ◇ *What difference will it make if he knows or not?* ◇ *I don't think it makes a lot of difference what colour it is* (= it is not important). ◇ *'Shall we go on Friday or Saturday?' 'It makes no difference (to me).'* make all the ˈdifference (to sb/sth) to have an important effect on sb/sth; to make sb feel better: *A few kind words at the right time make all the difference.* same ˈdifference (*informal*) used to say that you think the differences between two things are not important: *'That's not a xylophone, it's a glockenspiel.' 'Same difference.'* with a ˈdifference (*informal*) (after nouns) used to show that sth is interesting or unusual: *The traditional backpack with a difference—it's waterproof.* ⇒ more at BURY, DISTINCTION, SINK *v.*, SPLIT *v.*, WORLD

**difˑferˑent** 🔑 **A1** /ˈdɪfrənt/ *adj.* **1** **A1** not the same as sb/sth; not like sth/sb else: *~ from sb/sth American English is significantly different from British English.* ◇ *~ to sb/sth* (*especially BrE*) *It's slightly different to what I'm used to.* ◇ *~ than sb/sth* (*especially NAmE*) *He's different than the rest.* ◇ *It's completely different now then it was a year ago.* ◇ *People often give very different accounts of the same event.* ◇ *My son's terribly untidy; my daughter's no different.* **OPP** similar **2** **A1** [only before noun] separate and individual: *Each chapter deals with a different type of business.* ◇ *She offered us five different kinds of cake.* ◇ *We're helping society in many different ways.* ◇ *I looked it up in three different dictionaries.* **3** [not usually before noun] (*informal*)

▼ BRITISH/AMERICAN

**different from / to / than**

- **Different from** is the most common structure in both *BrE* and *NAmE*. **Different to** is also used, especially in *BrE*: *Paul's very different from/to his brother.* ◇ *This visit is very different from/to last time.*
- Especially in *NAmE* people also say **different than**: *Your trains are different than ours.* ◇ *You look different than before.*
- Use of **different than** is now becoming more common in *BrE* as well, especially before a clause because you don't need to use *what* or *how* after *than*. Compare: *She looked different than I'd expected.* ◇ *She looked different from what I'd expected.*

# differential

unusual; not like other people or things: *'Did you enjoy the play?' 'Well, it was certainly different!'* **IDM** **a different kettle of fish** (*informal*) a completely different situation or person from the one previously mentioned ⇒ more at COMPLEXION, KNOW v., MARCH v., MATTER n., PULL v., SING, TELL

**dif·fer·en·tial** /ˌdɪfəˈrenʃl/ *noun, adj.*
- *noun* **1** ~ **(between A and B)** a difference in the amount, value or size of sth, especially the difference in rates of pay for people doing different work in the same industry or profession: *wage/pay/income differentials* **2** (*also* **differential ˈgear**) a GEAR that makes it possible for a vehicle's back wheels to turn at different speeds when going around corners
- *adj.* [only before noun] (*formal*) showing or depending on a difference; not equal: *the differential treatment of prisoners based on sex and social class* ◊ *differential rates of pay*

**ˌdifferential eˈquation** *noun* (*mathematics*) an EQUATION that involves FUNCTIONS (= quantities that can vary) and their rates of change

**dif·fer·en·ti·ate** ?+ C1 W /ˌdɪfəˈrenʃieɪt/ *verb* **1** ?+ C1 [I, T] to recognize or show that two things are not the same **SYN** **distinguish**: ~ **(between) A and B** *It's difficult to differentiate between the two varieties.* ◊ ~ **A (from B)** *I can't differentiate one variety from another.* **2** ?+ C1 [T] ~ **sth (from sth)** to be the particular thing that shows that things or people are not the same **SYN** **distinguish**: *The male's yellow beak differentiates it from the female.* **3** ?+ C1 [I] ~ **(between A and B)** to treat people or things in a different way, especially in an unfair way **SYN** **discriminate 4** [I, T] ~ **(sth) (into sth)** (*biology*) (of a cell or TISSUE) to become more SPECIALIZED during growth and development; to make a cell or TISSUE more SPECIALIZED during growth and development: *The fertilized egg differentiates into several different cell types.* ▶ **dif·fer·en·ti·ation** /ˌdɪfəˌrenʃiˈeɪʃn/ *noun* [U]

**dif·fer·ent·ly** ? A2 W /ˈdɪfrəntli/ *adv.* in a different way from sb/sth: *He didn't like being **treated differently**.* ◊ *What will you **do differently** next time?* ◊ *The male bird has a differently shaped head.* **OPP** **similarly**

**dif·fi·cult** ? A1 O /ˈdɪfɪkəlt/ *adj.* **1** A1 not easy; needing effort or skill to do or to understand: *a difficult task/decision/question* ◊ ~ **for sb** *Asking for help is extremely difficult for some people.* ◊ **it is~to do sth** *It's really difficult to read your writing.* ◊ **sth is~to do** *Your writing is really difficult to read.* ◊ *She finds **it** very difficult to get up early.* ◊ **it is~for sb to do sth** *It's difficult for them to get here much before seven.* **2** ? A1 full of problems; causing a lot of trouble: *I found myself in a **difficult situation**.* ◊ *difficult conditions/circumstances* ◊ *a difficult time/year/month* ◊ *My boss is **making life** very **difficult** for me.* **3** ? B1 (of people) not easy to please; not helpful **SYN** **awkward**: *a difficult child/customer/boss* ◊ *Don't pay any attention to her—she's just being difficult.* **IDM** see JOB

**dif·fi·culty** ? B1 W /ˈdɪfɪkəlti/ *noun* (*pl.* **-ies**) **1** ? B1 [C, usually pl., U] a problem; a thing or situation that causes problems: *the difficulties of English syntax* ◊ *a patient with breathing difficulties* ◊ *to **experience/encounter difficulties*** ◊ *I think we've managed to **overcome** most of the practical difficulties.* ◊ *I know the kinds of difficulties faced by parents and teachers.* ◊ **with sth** *We've **run into difficulties** with the new project.* ◊ *I'm having difficulty with the engine.* ◊ **in~ | in difficulties** *He was often in financial difficulties.* ⇒ see also LEARNING DIFFICULTIES **2** ? B1 [U] the state or quality of being hard to do or to understand; the effort that sth involves: ~ **(in) doing sth** *I had considerable difficulty (in) persuading her to leave.* ◊ *I had no difficulty (in) making myself understood.* ◊ **with~** *He spoke slowly and with great difficulty.* ◊ *The changes were made with surprisingly little difficulty.* ◊ **without~** *We found the house without difficulty.* ◊ ~ **of doing sth** *They discussed the difficulty of studying abroad.* **HELP** You cannot say 'have difficulty to do sth': *I had difficulty to persuade her to leave.*

## ▼ SYNONYMS

### difficult
**hard • challenging • demanding • taxing**

These words all describe sth that is not easy and requires a lot of effort or skill to do.

**difficult** not easy; needing effort or skill to do or to understand: *The exam questions were quite difficult.* ◊ *It is difficult for young people to find jobs around here.*

**hard** not easy; needing effort or skill to do or understand: *I always found languages quite hard at school.* ◊ *It was one of the hardest things I ever did.*

**DIFFICULT OR HARD?**
**Hard** is slightly less formal than **difficult**. It is used particularly in the structure *hard to believe/say/find/take*, etc., although **difficult** can also be used in any of these examples.

**challenging** (*approving*) difficult in an interesting way that tests your ability.

**demanding** difficult to do or deal with and needing a lot of effort, skill, etc: *It is a technically demanding piece of music to play.*

**taxing** (often used in negative statements) difficult to do and needing a lot of mental or physical effort: *This shouldn't be too taxing for you.*

**PATTERNS**
- difficult/hard/challenging/demanding/taxing for sb
- difficult/hard **to do sth**
- **physically** difficult/hard/challenging/demanding/taxing
- **technically** difficult/challenging/demanding
- **mentally/intellectually** challenging/demanding/taxing

**3** ? B1 [U] how hard sth is: *the **degree/level of difficulty*** ◊ *questions of increasing difficulty*

**dif·fi·dent** /ˈdɪfɪdənt/ *adj.* ~ **(about sth)** not having much confidence in yourself; not wanting to talk about yourself **SYN** **shy**: *a diffident manner/smile* ◊ *He was modest and diffident about his own success.* ▶ **dif·fi·dence** /-dəns/ *noun* [U]: *She overcame her natural diffidence and spoke with great frankness.* **dif·fi·dent·ly** *adv.*

**dif·fract** /dɪˈfrækt/ *verb* ~ **sth** (*physics*) to break up a stream of light into a series of dark and light bands or into the different colours of the SPECTRUM ▶ **dif·frac·tion** /-ˈfrækʃn/ *noun* [U]

**dif·fuse** *adj., verb*
- *adj.* /dɪˈfjuːs/ **1** spread over a wide area: *diffuse light* ◊ *a diffuse community* **2** not clear or easy to understand; using a lot of words: *a diffuse style of writing* ▶ **dif·fuse·ly** *adv.* **dif·fuse·ness** *noun* [U]
- *verb* /dɪˈfjuːz/ **1** [T, I] ~ **(sth)** (*formal*) to spread sth or become spread widely in all directions: *The problem is how to diffuse power without creating anarchy.* ◊ *Technologies diffuse rapidly.* **2** [I, T] ~ **(sth)** (*specialist*) if a gas or liquid **diffuses** or **is diffused** in a substance, it becomes slowly mixed with that substance **3** [T] ~ **sth** (*formal*) to make light shine less brightly by spreading it in many directions: *The moon was fuller than the night before, but the light was diffused by cloud.* ▶ **dif·fu·sion** /-ˈfjuːʒn/ *noun* [U]

**dif·fu·ser** /dɪˈfjuːzə(r)/ *noun* **1** a device used in photography to avoid dark shadows or areas that are too bright **2** a part that is attached to a piece of equipment (for example a HAIRDRYER) to make air flow more slowly and over a wider area

**dig** ? B2 /dɪɡ/ *verb, noun*
- *verb* (**dig·ging**, **dug**, **dug** /dʌɡ/) **1** ? B2 [I, T] to make a hole in the ground or to move soil from one place to another using your hands, a tool or a machine: *I think I'll **do some digging** in the garden.* ◊ ~ **+ adv./prep.** *They dug deeper and deeper but still found nothing.* ◊ **for sth** *to dig for gold/treasure* ◊ ~ **sth** *to dig a hole/trench/grave* ◊ ~ **sth + adv./prep.** *They had obviously dug special tunnels beneath the city.* **2** [T] ~ **sth** to remove sth from the ground with a tool: *I'll dig some potatoes for lunch.* **3** [I] **(+ adv./prep.)** to

search in sth in order to find an object in sth: *I dug around in my bag for a pen.* **4** [T] ~ **sth** (*old-fashioned, slang*) to approve of or like sth very much
**IDM** **dig ˈdeep (into sth)** **1** to search for information in a careful and detailed way: *You'll need to dig deep into the records to find the figures you want.* **2** to try hard to provide the money, equipment, etc. that is needed: *We're asking you to dig deep for the earthquake victims.* **dig your ˈheels / ˈtoes in** to refuse to do sth or to change your mind about sth: *They dug in their heels and would not lower the price.* **dig (deep) in / into your ˈpocket(s), ˈsavings, etc.** to spend a lot of your own money on sth **dig sb in the ˈribs** to push your finger or your ELBOW into sb's side, especially to attract their attention **dig your own ˈgrave | dig a ˈgrave for yourself** to do sth that will have very harmful results for you **dig yourself into a ˈhole** to get yourself into a bad situation that will be very difficult to get out of
**PHRV** **ˌdig ˈin** (*informal*) **1** used to tell sb to start to eat: *Help yourselves, everybody! Dig in!* **2** to deal with a difficult situation or wait patiently: *There is nothing we can do except dig in and wait.* **ˌdig sth↔ˈin** **1** to mix soil with another substance by digging the two substances together: *The manure should be well dug in.* **2** to push sth into sth else: *He dug his feet in to gain his balance.* **ˌdig yourself ˈin** (of soldiers) to protect yourself against an attack by making a safe place in the ground **ˌdig ˈinto sth** **1** (*informal*) to start to eat food with enthusiasm: *She dug into her bowl of pasta.* **2** to push or rub against your body in a painful or uncomfortable way: *His fingers dug painfully into my arm.* **3** to find out information by searching or asking questions: *Will you dig a little into his past and see what you find?* **ˌdig sth ˈinto sth** **1** to mix soil with another substance by digging the two substances together **2** to push or press sth into sth else: *She dug her hands deeper into her pockets.* **ˌdig sb / sth↔ˈout (of sth)** **1** to remove sb/sth from somewhere by digging the ground around them or it: *More than a dozen people were dug out of the avalanche alive.* **2** to find sth that has been hidden or forgotten for a long time: *I went to the attic and dug out Grandad's medals.* **ˌdig sth↔ˈover** to prepare ground by digging the soil to remove stones, etc. **ˌdig sth↔ˈup** **1** to break the ground into small pieces before planting seeds, building sth, etc: *They are digging up the football field to lay a new surface.* **2** to remove sth from the ground by digging: *An old Roman vase was dug up here last month.* **3** to discover information about sb/sth **SYN** **unearth**: *Tabloid newspapers love to dig up scandal.*
■ *noun* ⊃ see also DIGS **1** a small push with your finger or ELBOW: *She gave him* ***a dig in the ribs.*** **2** ~ **(at sb/sth)** a remark that is intended to annoy or upset sb: *He kept making sly little digs at me.* ◊ *to* ***have a dig at sb/sth*** **3** an occasion when an organized group of people dig in the ground to discover old buildings or objects, in order to find out more about their history **SYN** **excavation**: *to go on a dig* ◊ *an archaeological dig*

**diˈgest** *verb, noun*
■ *verb* /daɪˈdʒest, dɪ-/ **1** [T, I] ~ **(sth)** when you **digest** food, or it **digests**, it is changed into substances that your body can use: *Humans cannot digest plants such as grass.* ◊ *You should allow a little time after a meal for the food to digest.* ⊃ WORDFINDER NOTE at EAT **2** [T] ~ **sth** to think about sth so that you fully understand it: *He paused, waiting for her to digest the information.*
■ *noun* /ˈdaɪdʒest/ a short report containing the most important facts of a longer report or piece of writing; a collection of short reports: *a monthly news digest*

**diˈgest·ible** /daɪˈdʒestəbl, dɪ-/ *adj.* **1** (of food) easy to digest **OPP** **indigestible** **2** (of information) easy to understand **OPP** **indigestible**

**diˈges·tion** /daɪˈdʒestʃən, dɪ-/ *noun* **1** [U] the process of digesting food ⊃ compare INDIGESTION **2** [C, usually sing.] the ability to digest food: *to have a good/poor digestion*

**diˈgest·ive** /daɪˈdʒestɪv, dɪ-/ *adj.* [only before noun] connected with the digestion of food; helping the process of digestion: *the digestive tract* ◊ *digestive problems*

**diˌgestive ˈbiscuit** (also **digestive**) *noun* (*BrE*) a round sweet biscuit made from WHOLEMEAL flour, sometimes covered with chocolate: *a packet of chocolate digestives*

---

431 **dignify**

**diˈgestive system** *noun* the series of organs inside the body that digest food

**dig·ger** /ˈdɪɡə(r)/ *noun* **1** a large machine that is used for digging up the ground **2** a person or an animal that digs ⊃ see also GOLD-DIGGER **3** (*AustralE, NZE, old-fashioned, informal*) a man

**digit** /ˈdɪdʒɪt/ *noun* **1** any of the numbers from 0 to 9: *The number 57306 contains five digits.* ◊ *a four-digit number* ⊃ see also DOUBLE-DIGIT **2** (*anatomy*) a finger, THUMB or toe

**digit·al** ⓘ **A2** **W** /ˈdɪdʒɪtl/ *adj., noun*
■ *adj.* **1** **A2** using a system of receiving and sending information as a series of the numbers one and zero, showing that an electronic signal is there or is not there: *a digital camera* ◊ *digital media/content/platforms* ◊ *These figures include digital downloads in addition to retail sales.* ◊ *He quickly realized that all film and video production would go digital.* ⊃ compare ANALOGUE (1) **2** **A2** connected with the use of computer technology, especially the internet: *communication in* **the digital age** ◊ *Digital technology continues to evolve rapidly.* ◊ *Advertisers are putting more and more money into* ***digital marketing.*** **3** **A2** (of clocks, watches, etc.) showing information by using figures, rather than with HANDS that point to numbers: *a digital clock/watch* ⊃ compare ANALOGUE (2) ⊃ picture at CLOCK ▶ **digit·al·ly** /-təli/ *adv.*: *digitally remastered audio*
■ *noun* [U] (*rather informal*) digital technology: *The world of digital is forever changing.*

**ˌdigital diˈvide** *noun* [sing.] the very large difference in opportunity between people who can easily access computers and the internet and people who cannot

**ˌdigital ˈfootprint** *noun* the information about a particular person that exists on the internet as a result of their online activities: *Everything you do online leaves a digital footprint that will always be there.*

**digi·talis** /ˌdɪdʒɪˈteɪlɪs; *NAmE also* -ˈtæl-/ *noun* [U] (*medical*) a drug made from the FOXGLOVE plant, that helps the heart muscle to work

**digit·al·ize** (*BrE also* **-ise**) /ˈdɪdʒɪtəlaɪz/ *verb* = DIGITIZE
▶ **digit·al·iza·tion, -isa·tion** /ˌdɪdʒɪtəlaɪˈzeɪʃn; *NAmE* -ləˈz-/ *noun* [U] = DIGITIZATION

**ˌdigital ˈnative** *noun* a person who was born or has grown up since the use of digital technology became common and so is familiar and comfortable with computers and the internet

**ˌdigital ˈpublishing** (*also* **electronic publishing, e-publishing**) *noun* [U] the business of publishing materials in a form that can be read on a computer, either online or on an E-READER or other device: *Digital publishing challenges traditional concepts of books.*

**ˌdigital reˈcording** *noun* [C, U] a recording in which sounds or pictures are represented by a series of numbers showing that an electronic signal is there or is not there; the process of making a recording in this way

**ˌdigital ˈsignature** *noun* (*computing*) a process that guarantees that the contents of a message have not been altered in the process of sending and delivering the message ⊃ compare ELECTRONIC SIGNATURE

**ˌdigital ˈtelevision** *noun* **1** [U] the system of broadcasting television using digital signals **2** [C] a television set that can receive digital signals

**digit·ize** (*BrE also* **-ise**) /ˈdɪdʒɪtaɪz/ (*also* **digit·al·ize**) *verb* ~ **sth** to change data into a digital form that can be easily read and processed by a computer: *a digitized map* ▶ **digit·iza·tion** (*also* **-isa·tion**) /ˌdɪdʒɪtaɪˈzeɪʃn; *NAmE* -təˈz-/ (*also* **digit·al·iza·tion, -isa·tion**) *noun* [U]

**dig·ni·fied** /ˈdɪɡnɪfaɪd/ *adj.* calm and serious and deserving respect: *a dignified person/manner/voice* ◊ *Throughout his trial he maintained a dignified silence.* **OPP** **undignified**

**dig·nify** /ˈdɪɡnɪfaɪ/ *verb* (**dig·ni·fies, dig·ni·fy·ing, dig·ni·fied**) (*formal*) **1** ~ **sb / sth** to make sb/sth seem impressive: *The mayor was there to dignify the celebrations.* **2** ~ **sth** to make sth appear important when it is not really: *I'm not going to dignify his comments by reacting to them.*

# dignitary

**dig·ni·tary** /ˈdɪɡnɪtəri; NAmE -teri/ noun (pl. **-ies**) a person who has an important official position **SYN** VIP

**dig·ni·ty** /ˈdɪɡnəti/ noun **1** [U, sing.] a calm and serious manner that deserves respect: *She accepted the criticism with quiet dignity.* **2** [U] the fact of being given honour and respect by people: *the dignity of work ◊ The terminally ill should be allowed to die with dignity.* **3** [U] a sense of your own importance and value: *It's difficult to preserve your dignity when you have no job and no home.*
**IDM be·neath your 'dignity** below what you see as your own importance or worth **,stand on your 'dignity** (*formal*) to demand to be treated with the respect that you think that you deserve

**di·graph** /ˈdaɪɡrɑːf; NAmE -ɡræf/ noun (*linguistics*) a combination of two letters representing one sound, for example 'ph' and 'sh' in English

**di·gress** /daɪˈɡres/ verb [I] (*formal*) to start to talk about sth that is not connected with the main point of what you are saying ▶ **di·gres·sion** /-ˈɡreʃn/ noun [C, U]: *After several digressions, he finally got to the point.*

**digs** /dɪɡz/ noun [pl.] (*old-fashioned, informal*) a room or rooms that you rent to live in **SYN** lodgings

**dike** /daɪk/ noun = DYKE

**dik·tat** /ˈdɪktæt; NAmE dɪkˈtæt/ noun [C, U] (*disapproving*) an order given by a government, for example, that people must obey: *an EU diktat from Brussels ◊ government by diktat*

**di·lapi·dated** /dɪˈlæpɪdeɪtɪd/ adj. (of furniture and buildings) old and in very bad condition **SYN** ramshackle
▶ **di·lapi·da·tion** /dɪˌlæpɪˈdeɪʃn/ noun [U]: *in a state of dilapidation*

**dila·ta·tion** /ˌdaɪləˈteɪʃn, dɪl-/ noun [U] (*medical*) the process of becoming wider (= of becoming dilated), or the action of making sth become wider

**di·late** /daɪˈleɪt/ verb [I, T] (of a part of the body) to become larger, wider or more open; to make a part of the body larger, wide or more open: *Her eyes dilated with fear. ◊ dilated pupils/nostrils ◊ ~ sth Red wine can help to dilate blood vessels.* **OPP** contract ▶ **dila·tion** /-ˈleɪʃn/ noun [U, C]

**dilated** /daɪˈleɪtɪd/ adj. (of a part of the body) larger, wider or more open than usual: *dilated pupils/nostrils*

**dila·tory** /ˈdɪlətəri; NAmE -tɔːri/ adj. **~ (in doing sth)** (*formal*) not acting quickly enough; causing delay: *The government has been dilatory in dealing with the problem of unemployment.*

**dildo** /ˈdɪldəʊ/ noun (pl. **dildos** or **dildoes**) an object that is like a PENIS in shape and is used for sexual pleasure

**di·lemma** /dɪˈlemə, daɪ-/ noun a situation that makes problems, often one in which you have to make a very difficult choice between things of equal importance **SYN** predicament: *I could see no way of resolving this moral dilemma. ◊* **in a ~** *They were caught in a real dilemma. ◊* **about/over sth** *She faced a dilemma about whether to accept the offer or not. ◊* **between A and B** *the perennial dilemma between work and family commitments*
**IDM** see HORN *n.*

**dil·et·tante** /ˌdɪləˈtænti/ noun (pl. **dil·et·tanti** /-ti/ or **dil·et·tan·tes**) (*disapproving*) a person who does or studies sth but is not serious about it and does not have much knowledge
▶ **dil·et·tante** adj.: *a dilettante artist*

**dili·gence** /ˈdɪlɪdʒəns/ noun [U] (*formal*) careful work or great effort: *She shows great diligence in her schoolwork.*
⇒ see also DUE DILIGENCE

**dili·gent** /ˈdɪlɪdʒənt/ adj. (*formal*) showing care and effort in your work or duties: *a diligent student/worker* ▶ **dili·gent·ly** adv.

**dill** /dɪl/ noun [U] a plant with yellow flowers whose leaves and seeds have a strong taste and are used in cooking and medicines. Dill is often added to vegetables kept in VINEGAR: *dill pickles* ⇒ VISUAL VOCAB page V8

**dilly-dally** /ˈdɪli dæli/ verb (**dilly-dallies**, **dilly-dallying**, **dilly-dallied**, **dilly-dallied**) [I] (*old-fashioned, informal*) to take too long to do sth, go somewhere or make a decision **SYN** dawdle

**di·lute** /daɪˈluːt/ verb, adj.
▶ *verb* **1** **~ sth (in/with sth)** to make a liquid weaker by adding water or another liquid to it **SYN** water down: *The paint can be diluted with water to make a lighter shade.* ⇒ WORDFINDER NOTE at LIQUID **2** **~ sth** to make sth weaker or less effective **SYN** water down: *Large classes dilute the quality of education that children receive.*
▶ **di·lu·tion** /-ˈluːʃn/ noun [U, C]: *the dilution of sewage ◊ This is a serious dilution of their election promises.*
▶ *adj.* **1** (*also* **di·luted**) (of a liquid) made weaker by adding water or another substance **2** (*chemistry*) (of a SOLUTION) having only a small amount of a substance DISSOLVED in it: *a dilute solution of acetic acid*

**dim** /dɪm/ adj., verb
▶ *adj.* (**dim·mer**, **dim·mest**)
• LIGHT **1** not bright: *the dim glow of the fire in the grate ◊ This light is too dim to read by.*
• PLACE **2** where you cannot see well because there is not much light: *a dim room/street*
• SHAPE **3** that you cannot see well because there is not much light: *the dim outline of a house in the moonlight ◊ I could see a dim shape in the doorway.*
• EYES **4** not able to see well: *His eyesight is getting dim.*
• MEMORIES **5** that you cannot remember or imagine clearly **SYN** vague: *dim memories ◊ She had a dim recollection of the visit. ◊* (*humorous*) *in the dim and distant past*
• PERSON **6** (*informal, especially BrE*) not intelligent: *He's very dim.*
• SITUATION **7** not giving any reason to have hope; not good: *Her future career prospects look dim.* ▶ **dim·ness** noun [U]: *It took a while for his eyes to adjust to the dimness.* ⇒ see also DIMLY
**IDM** **take a dim view of sb/sth** to think sb/sth is bad; to not have a good opinion of sb/sth: *She took a dim view of my suggestion.*
▶ *verb* (**-mm-**)
• LIGHT **1** [I, T] **~(sth)** if a light **dims** or if you **dim** it, it becomes or you make it less bright: *The lights in the theatre dimmed as the curtain rose.*
• FEELING/QUALITY **2** [I, T] **~(sth)** if a feeling or quality **dims**, or if sth **dims** it, it becomes less strong: *Her passion for dancing never dimmed over the years.*

**dime** /daɪm/ noun a coin of the US and Canada worth ten cents ⇒ see also FIVE-AND-DIME
**IDM** **a dime a 'dozen** (NAmE) (BrE **two/ten a 'penny**) very common and therefore not valuable

## dimensions

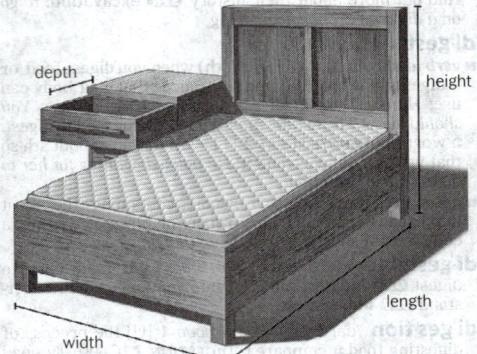

**di·men·sion** /daɪˈmenʃn, dɪ-/ noun **1** a measurement in space, for example how high, wide or long sth is: *We measured the dimensions of the kitchen. ◊ computer design tools that work in three dimensions* ⇒ see also FOURTH DIMENSION **2** [usually pl.] the size and extent of a situation: *a problem of considerable dimensions* **3** an aspect, or way of looking at or thinking about sth: *Her job added a new dimension to her life.* ◊ *the social dimension of unemployment*

**-dimensional** /daɪmenʃnəl, dɪmenʃnəl/ *combining form* (in adjectives) having the number of dimensions mentioned: *a multidimensional model* ⊃ see also FOUR-DIMENSIONAL, MULTIDIMENSIONAL, ONE-DIMENSIONAL, THREE-DIMENSIONAL, TWO-DIMENSIONAL

**'dime store** *noun* (*NAmE, old-fashioned*) = FIVE-AND-DIME

**di·min·ish** /dɪˈmɪnɪʃ/ *verb* **1** [I, T] to become smaller, weaker, etc.; to make sth become smaller, weaker, etc. **SYN** **decrease**: *The world's resources are rapidly diminishing.* ◊ *His influence has diminished with time.* ◊ *~ sth The new law is expected to diminish the government's chances.* **2** [T] *~ sb/sth* to make sb/sth seem less important than they really are: *I don't wish to diminish the importance of their contribution.*
**IDM** **(the law of) diminishing re'turns** used to refer to a point at which you start achieving less than the value of the time or money you put into sth: *Our efforts were producing diminishing returns.*

**di‚minished re'sponsi·bility** (*BrE*) (*NAmE* **di‚min·ished ca'pacity**) *noun* [U] (*law*) a state in which a person who is accused of a crime is not considered to be responsible for their actions, because they are mentally ill: *He was found not guilty of murder on the grounds of diminished responsibility.*

**dim·in·ution** /ˌdɪmɪˈnjuːʃn; *NAmE* -'nuː-/ *noun* **1** [U] *~ (of/in sth)* (*formal*) the act of reducing sth or of being reduced: *the diminution of political power* **2** [C, usually sing.] *~ (of/in sth)* (*formal*) a reduction; an amount reduced: *a diminution in population growth*

**di·minu·tive** /dɪˈmɪnjətɪv/ *adj., noun*
• *adj.* (*formal*) very small: *She was a diminutive figure beside her husband.*
• *noun* **1** a word or an ending of a word that shows that sb/sth is small, for example *piglet* (= a young pig), *kitchenette* (= a small kitchen) **2** a short informal form of a word, especially a name: *'Nick' is a common diminutive of 'Nicholas'.*

**dimly** /ˈdɪmli/ *adv.* not very brightly or clearly: *a dimly lit room* ◊ *I was dimly aware* (= only just aware) *of the sound of a car in the distance.* ◊ *I did remember, but only dimly.*

**'dim·mer switch** (also **'dim·mer**) *noun* **1** a switch that allows you to make an electric light brighter or less bright **2** (*NAmE*) (*BrE* **'dip switch**) a switch that allows you to make the front lights on a car point downwards

**dimple** /ˈdɪmpl/ *noun, verb*
• *noun* **1** a small hollow place in the skin, especially in the face: *He has a little round dimple in one cheek.* **2** any small hollow place in a surface: *a pane of glass with a dimple pattern* ▸ **dimpled** /-pld/ *adj.: a dimpled chin*
• *verb* [I] to make a hollow place appear on each side of your face, especially by smiling

**dim sum** /ˌdɪm ˈsʌm/ (*also* **dim sim** /ˌdɪm ˈsɪm/) *noun* [U] (*from Chinese*) a Chinese dish or meal consisting of small pieces of food wrapped in sheets of DOUGH

**dim-'witted** *adj.* (*informal*) stupid: *a dim-witted child* ▸ **'dim-wit** /ˈdɪmwɪt/ *noun*

**din** /dɪn/ *noun* [sing.] a loud, unpleasant noise that lasts for a long time **SYN** **racket**: *The children were making an awful din.*

**dinar** /ˈdiːnɑː(r)/ *noun* a unit of money in Serbia and various countries in the Middle East and North Africa

**dine** /daɪn/ *verb* [I] (*formal*) to eat dinner: *We dined with my parents at a restaurant in town.* **IDM** see WINE *v.*
**PHRV** **'dine on sth** (*formal*) to have a particular type of food for dinner  **‚dine 'out** (*formal*) to eat dinner in a restaurant or sb else's home  **‚dine 'out on sth** (*informal*) to tell other people about sth that has happened to you, in order to make them interested in you

**diner** /ˈdaɪnə(r)/ *noun* **1** a person eating a meal, especially in a restaurant: *a restaurant capable of seating 100 diners* **2** (in the US) a small, usually cheap, restaurant: *a roadside diner*

**din·ero** /dɪˈneərəʊ; *NAmE* -'ner-/ *noun* [U] (*especially NAmE, from Spanish, informal*) money

**din·ette** /daɪˈnet/ *noun* (*especially NAmE*) a small room or part of a room for eating meals

**ding** /dɪŋ/ *noun, verb*
• *noun* **1** (*especially NAmE*) a hit, especially one that causes slight damage to a car, etc.: *I got a ding in my rear fender.* **2** used to represent the sound made by a bell: *The lift came to a halt with a loud 'ding'.*
• *verb* **1** [I] to make a sound like a bell: *The computer just dings when I press a key.* **2** [T] *~ sth* (*NAmE*) to cause slight damage to a car, etc.: *I dinged my passenger door.* **3** [T] *~ sb* (*especially NAmE*) to hit sb: (*figurative*) *My department got dinged by the budget cuts.*

**ding·bat** /ˈdɪŋbæt/ *noun* (*NAmE, slang*) a stupid person

**ding-dong** /ˈdɪŋ dɒŋ; *NAmE* dɑːŋ/ *noun* **1** [U] used to represent the sound made by a bell: *I rang the doorbell. Ding-dong! No answer.* **2** [C] (*BrE, informal*) an argument or a fight: *They were having a real ding-dong on the doorstep.*

**dinghy** /ˈdɪŋi, ˈdɪŋɡi/ *noun* (*pl.* **-ies**) **1** a small open boat that you sail or ROW: *a sailing dinghy* ⊃ compare YACHT **2** a small open boat made of plastic or rubber that is filled with air ⊃ see also RUBBER DINGHY

**dingo** /ˈdɪŋɡəʊ/ *noun* (*pl.* **-oes**) a wild Australian dog

**dingy** /ˈdɪndʒi/ *adj.* (**din·gier, din·gi·est**) dark and dirty: *a dingy room/hotel* ◊ *dingy curtains/clothes* ▸ **din·gi·ness** *noun* [U]

**din·ing** /ˈdaɪnɪŋ/ *noun* [U] the activity of eating a meal: *The city has become a capital of fine dining* (= eating food of very high quality in a restaurant). ◊ *The dining area has an airy, open feel.*

**'dining car** (*BrE also* **'restaurant car**) *noun* a coach on a train in which meals are served

**'dining room** *noun* a room in a house or hotel that is used for eating meals in

**'dining table** *noun* a table for having meals on ⊃ compare DINNER TABLE

**dink** /dɪŋk/ *noun* (in sport) a soft hit that makes the ball land on the ground without BOUNCING much ▸ **dink** *verb* *~ sth*

**din·kum** /ˈdɪŋkəm/ *adj.* (*AustralE, NZE, informal*) (of an article or a person) real or saying only what is true: *If you're dinkum, I'll help you.* ⊃ see also FAIR DINKUM

**dinky** /ˈdɪŋki/ *adj.* (*informal*) **1** (*BrE, approving*) small and neat in an attractive way: *What a dinky little hat!* **2** (*NAmE, disapproving*) too small: *I grew up in a dinky little town that didn't even have a movie theater.*

**din·ner** /ˈdɪnə(r)/ *noun* **1** [U, C] the main meal of the day, eaten either in the middle of the day or in the evening: *It's time for dinner.* ◊ *When do you have dinner?* ◊ *for ~ What shall we have for dinner tonight?* ◊ *to ~ As I'm single, I tend to go out to dinner* (= eat in a restaurant) *a lot.* ◊ (*NAmE also*) *to go to dinner* ◊ *Let's invite them to dinner tomorrow.* ◊ *It's your turn to cook dinner.* ◊ *She didn't eat much dinner.* ◊ *Christmas/Thanksgiving dinner* ◊ *a three-course dinner* ◊ *a family sitting around the dinner table* ◊ (*BrE*) **school dinners** (= meals provided at school in the middle of the day) ⊃ see also TV DINNER ⊃ note at MEAL **2** [C] a large formal social gathering at which dinner is eaten: *The club's annual dinner will be held on 3 June.* ◊ *The winner will be announced at a gala dinner.* ⊃ see also DINNER PARTY
**IDM** **done like a 'dinner** (*AustralE, NZE, informal*) completely defeated ⊃ more at DOG *n.*

**'dinner dance** *noun* a social event in the evening that includes a formal meal and dancing

**'dinner jacket** (*also* **tux·edo** *especially in NAmE*) *noun* a black or white jacket worn with a BOW TIE at formal occasions in the evening ⊃ compare TAILCOAT

**'dinner lady** (*BrE*) (*US* **'lunch lady**) *noun* a woman whose job is to serve meals to children in schools

**dinner party** noun a social event at which a small group of people eat dinner at sb's house

**dinner service** noun a set of matching plates, dishes, etc. for serving a meal

**dinner suit** (BrE) (also **tux·edo** especially in NAmE) noun a DINNER JACKET and trousers, worn with a BOW TIE at formal occasions in the evening

**dinner table** noun (often **the dinner table**) [usually sing.] the table at which people are eating dinner; an occasion when people are eating together: *conversation at the dinner table* ⇒ compare DINING TABLE

**dinner theater** noun (NAmE) a theatre in which a meal is included in the price of a ticket

**dinner time** noun [U, C] the time at which dinner is normally eaten

**din·ner·ware** /ˈdɪnəweə(r); NAmE ˈdɪnərwer/ noun [U] (NAmE) plates, dishes, etc. used for serving a meal

**dino·saur** /ˈdaɪnəsɔː(r)/ noun 1 an animal that lived millions of years ago but is now EXTINCT (= it no longer exists). There were many types of dinosaur, some of which were very large. 2 (*disapproving*) a person or thing that is old-fashioned and cannot change in the changing conditions of modern life

**dint** /dɪnt/ noun
**IDM** **by dint of sth/of doing sth** (*formal*) by means of sth: *He succeeded by dint of hard work.*

**dio·cese** /ˈdaɪəsɪs/ noun (pl. **dio·ceses** /-əsiːz/) (in the Christian Church) a district for which a BISHOP is responsible ▸ **dio·cesan** /daɪˈɒsɪsn; NAmE -ˈɑːs-/ adj.

**diode** /ˈdaɪəʊd/ noun (*specialist*) an electronic device in which the electric current passes in one direction only, for example a SILICON CHIP

**di·op·trics** /daɪˈɒptrɪks; NAmE -ˈɑːp-/ noun [U] (*physics*) the scientific study of REFRACTION (= the way light changes direction when it goes through glass, etc.) ▸ **di·op·tric** adj.

**dio·rama** /ˌdaɪəˈrɑːmə; NAmE also -ˈræm-/ noun a model representing a scene with figures, especially in a museum

**di·ox·ide** /daɪˈɒksaɪd; NAmE -ˈɑːk-/ noun [U, C] (*chemistry*) a substance formed by combining two ATOMS of OXYGEN and one ATOM of another chemical element ⇒ see also CARBON DIOXIDE, NITROGEN DIOXIDE, SULPHUR DIOXIDE

**di·oxin** /daɪˈɒksɪn; NAmE -ˈɑːk-/ noun [C, U] a chemical (with a ring structure containing two OXYGEN ATOMS) that is formed as a result of some industrial processes. Dioxins are TOXIC (= poisonous) and cause harm to the environment.

**dip** /dɪp/ verb, noun
■ verb (-pp-) 1 [T] to put sth quickly into a liquid and take it out again: *~sth (into sth) He dipped the brush into the paint.* *~sth (in) Dip your hand in to see how hot the water is.* ◊ *The fruit had been dipped in chocolate.* 2 *~sth* [I, T] to go downwards or to a lower level; to make sth do this **SYN** **fall**: **(+ adv./prep.)** *The sun dipped below the horizon.* ◊ *Sales for this quarter have dipped from 38.7 million to 33 million.* ◊ *The road dipped suddenly as we approached the town.* ◊ *~sth (+ adv./prep.) The plane dipped its wings.* ⇒ WORDFINDER NOTE at TREND 3 [T] *~sth* (BrE) if you **dip** your HEADLIGHTS when driving a car at night, you make the light from them point down so that other drivers do not have the light in their eyes 4 [T] *~sth* when farmers **dip** animals, especially sheep, they put them in a bath of a liquid containing chemicals in order to kill insects, etc.
**IDM** **dip into your 'pocket** (*informal*) to spend some of your own money on sth **dip a 'toe in/into sth | dip a 'toe in/into the water** (*informal*) to start doing sth very carefully to see if it will be successful or not
**PHRV** **dip 'into sth** 1 to put your hand into a container to take sth out: *She dipped into her purse and took out some coins.* 2 to read or watch only parts of sth: *I have only had time to dip into the report.* 3 to take an amount from money that you have saved: *We took out a loan for the car because we didn't want to dip into our savings.*

■ noun 1 [C, usually sing.] (*informal*) a quick swim: *Let's go for a dip before breakfast.* 2 [C] a decrease in the amount or success of sth, usually for only a short period **SYN** **fall**: *Share prices have taken a slight dip.* ◊ *~in sth a sharp dip in profits* 3 [C] a place where a surface suddenly drops to a lower level and then rises again: *a dip in the road* ◊ *Puddles had formed in the dips.* 4 [C, U] a thick mixture into which pieces of food are dipped before being eaten 5 [U, C] a liquid containing a chemical into which sheep and other animals can be dipped in order to kill insects on them ⇒ see also SHEEP DIP 6 [sing.] *~into sth* a quick look at sth: *A brief dip into history serves to confirm this view.* 7 [C, usually sing.] a quick movement of sth down and up: *He gave a dip of his head.* ⇒ see also LUCKY DIP

**diph·theria** /dɪfˈθɪəriə, dɪpˈθ-; NAmE -ˈθɪr-/ noun [U] a serious disease of the throat that causes difficulty in breathing

**diph·thong** /ˈdɪfθɒŋ, ˈdɪpθ-; NAmE -θɔːŋ/ noun (*phonetics*) a combination of two vowel sounds or vowel letters, for example the sounds /aɪ/ in *pipe* /paɪp/ or the letters *ou* in *doubt* ⇒ WORDFINDER NOTE at PRONUNCIATION ▸ **diph·thong·al** /dɪfˈθɒŋgl, dɪpˈθ-; NAmE dɪfˈθɔːŋgl, dɪpˈθ-/ adj.

**dip·lod·ocus** /ˌdɪpləˈdəʊkəs; BrE also dɪˈplɒdəkəs; NAmE also -ˈplɑːd-/ noun a very large DINOSAUR with a long thin neck and tail

**dip·loid** /ˈdɪplɔɪd/ adj. (*biology*) (of a cell) containing two complete sets of CHROMOSOMES, one from each parent ⇒ compare HAPLOID

**dip·loma** /dɪˈpləʊmə/ noun 1 (BrE) a course of study at a college or university: *a two-year diploma course* ◊ *She is taking a diploma in management studies.* 2 a document showing that you have completed a course of study or part of your education: *a High School diploma*

**dip·lo·macy** /dɪˈpləʊməsi/ noun [U] 1 the activity of managing relations between different countries; the skill in doing this: *international diplomacy* ◊ *Diplomacy is better than war.* ⇒ see also SHUTTLE DIPLOMACY 2 skill in dealing with people in difficult situations without upsetting or offending them **SYN** **tact**

**dip·lo·mat** /ˈdɪpləmæt/ noun 1 a person whose job is to represent his or her country in a foreign country, for example, in an EMBASSY: *Washington's top diplomat in Havana* ⇒ WORDFINDER NOTE at ALLY 2 a person who shows skill at dealing with other people

**dip·lo·mat·ic** /ˌdɪpləˈmætɪk/ adj. 1 connected with managing relations between countries (= DIPLOMACY): *a diplomatic crisis* ◊ *Attempts are being made to settle the dispute by diplomatic means.* ◊ *to break off/establish/restore diplomatic relations with a country* 2 having or showing skill in dealing with people in difficult situations **SYN** **tactful**: *a diplomatic answer* ▸ **dip·lo·mat·ic·al·ly** /-kli/ adv.: *The country remained diplomatically isolated.* ◊ *'Why don't we take a break for coffee?' she suggested diplomatically.*

**diplo matic 'bag** (BrE) (US **diplo matic 'pouch**) noun a container that is used for sending official letters and documents between a government and its representatives in another country and that cannot be opened by CUSTOMS officers

**diplo matic 'corps** noun (usually **the diplomatic corps**) [C + sing./pl. v.] (*pl.* **diplomatic corps**) all the DIPLOMATS who work in a particular city or country

**diplo matic im'munity** noun [U] special rights given to DIPLOMATS working in a foreign country that mean they cannot be arrested, taxed, etc. in that country

**the Diplo matic 'Service** (*especially BrE*) (NAmE *usually* **the Foreign Service**) noun [sing.] the government department concerned with representing a country in foreign countries

**di·pole** /ˈdaɪpəʊl/ noun (*physics*) a pair of separated POLES, one positive and one negative

**dip·per** /ˈdɪpə(r)/ noun 1 a bird that lives near rivers ⇒ see also BIG DIPPER 2 [usually pl.] a piece of food intended for DIPPING into a sauce

**dippy** /ˈdɪpi/ adj. (informal) silly; strange but not dangerous: *dippy ideas*

**dipso·maniac** /ˌdɪpsəˈmeɪniæk/ noun a person who has a strong desire for alcoholic drink that they cannot control **SYN** alcoholic

**dip-stick** /ˈdɪpstɪk/ noun **1** a long straight piece of metal used for measuring the amount of liquid in a container, especially the amount of oil in an engine **2** (informal) a stupid person

**'dip switch** (BrE) (NAmE **'dim·mer switch**) noun a switch that allows you to make the front lights on a car point downwards

**dip·tych** /ˈdɪptɪk/ noun (specialist) a painting, especially a religious one, with two wooden panels that can be closed like a book

**dire** /ˈdaɪə(r)/ adj. (**direr**, **direst**) **1** [usually before noun] (formal) very serious: *living in dire poverty* ◇ **dire warnings/threats** ◇ *Such action may have dire consequences.* ◇ *We're in dire need of your help.* ◇ *The firm is in dire straits* (= in a very difficult situation) *and may go bankrupt*. **2** (BrE, informal) very bad: *The acting was dire*.

**dir·ect** ⓘ A2 ⓞ /dəˈrekt, daɪˈr-/ adj., verb, adv.

■ adj.
- **JOURNEY/ROUTE 1** ⓘ A2 going in the straightest line between two places without stopping or changing direction: *the most direct route* ◇ *This door allows **direct access** from the kitchen to the garage.* ◇ *a **direct flight*** (= a flight that does not stop) ◇ *There's a **direct train** to Leeds* (= it may stop at other stations but you do not have to change trains). ◇ *a **direct hit*** (= a hit that is accurate and does not touch sth else first) **OPP** indirect
- **NOBODY/NOTHING IN BETWEEN 2** ⓘ B1 [usually before noun] happening or done without involving other people, actions, etc. in between: *She has been in **direct contact** with the prime minister.* ◇ *a direct link/connection* ◇ *a direct result/effect/consequence* ◇ *Many farmers are developing direct access to consumers.* ◇ *He was cleared of any direct involvement in the case.* **OPP** indirect
- **HEAT/LIGHT 3** ⓘ B1 [only before noun] with nothing between sth and the source of the heat or light: *The plant should not be placed in **direct sunlight**.*
- **SAYING WHAT YOU MEAN 4** ⓘ B1 saying exactly what you mean in a way that nobody can pretend not to understand: *a direct answer/question* ◇ *Her response is refreshingly direct.* **OPP** indirect ➔ SYNONYMS at HONEST
- **EVIDENCE 5** [only before noun] (of evidence or proof) clearly showing sth: *There is no direct evidence for the beneficial effects of these herbs.* ◇ *This information **has a direct bearing on** (= is closely connected with) the case.* **OPP** indirect
- **EXACT 6** [only before noun] exact: *That's the **direct opposite** of what you told me yesterday.* ◇ *a **direct quote*** (= one using a person's exact words)
- **RELATIONSHIP 7** [only before noun] related through parents and children rather than brothers, sisters, aunts, etc.: *a direct descendant of the country's first president* **OPP** indirect

■ verb
- **CONTROL 1** ⓘ B1 [T] ~ sb/sth to control or be in charge of sb/sth: *He was asked to take command and **direct operations**.* ◇ *A police officer was directing traffic.* ◇ *How much should the teacher direct and the students?*
- **FILM/PLAY/MUSIC 2** ⓘ B1 [I, T] to be in charge of actors in a play or film, or musicians in a band, ORCHESTRA, etc.: *She prefers to act rather than direct.* ◇ ~ sb/sth *The film was written and directed by Sofia Coppola.* ◇ *She now directs a large choir.*
- **AIM 3** ⓘ B2 [T] to aim sth at a particular goal or person, or in a particular direction: ~ sth to sth/sb *He directed his attention to the next task.* ◇ ~ sth towards/toward sth/sb *All our efforts should be directed towards helping those who need it.* ◇ ~ sth at sth/sb *Her criticism was directed at her own superiors.* ◇ ~ sth against sth/sb *Most of his anger was directed against himself.* ◇ ~ sth + adv./prep. *He directed the light straight in her face.*
- **SHOW THE WAY 4** ⓘ B2 [T] to tell or show sb how to get to somewhere or where to go: ~ sb *It's not far—I'll direct you.* ◇ ~ sb to sth *Could you direct me to the station?* ➔ SYNONYMS at TAKE
- **GIVE ORDER 5** [T] (formal) to give an official order **SYN** order: ~ sb to do sth *The police officers had been directed to search the building.* ◇ ~ that … *The judge directed that the mother be given custody of the children.* ◇ (BrE also) *The judge directed that the mother should be given custody of the children.* ➔ SYNONYMS at ORDER
- **LETTER/COMMENT 6** [T] ~ sth to … (formal) to send a letter, etc. to a particular place or to a particular person: *Direct any complaints to the Customer Services department.*

■ adv.
- **JOURNEY/ROUTE 1** ⓘ B1 without stopping or changing direction or vehicle: ~ to sth *We flew direct to Hong Kong.* ◇ *The 10.40 goes direct to Leeds.*
- **NOBODY IN BETWEEN 2** ⓘ B2 without involving other people, or without anyone or anything in between: ~ to sb/sth *an online retailer selling direct to consumers* ◇ ~ from sb/sth *Customers can buy produce direct from the farmer.*

**di·rect 'access** noun [U] (computing) the ability to get data immediately from any part of a computer file

**di·rect 'action** noun [U, C] the use of strikes, protests, etc. instead of discussion in order to get what you want

**di·rect 'current** noun [C, U] (abbr. **DC**) an electric current that flows in one direction only ➔ compare ALTERNATING CURRENT

**di·rect 'debit** noun [U, C] (BrE) an instruction to your bank to allow sb else to take an amount of money from your account on a particular date, especially to pay bills: *We pay all our bills **by direct debit**.* ➔ compare STANDING ORDER

**di·rect de'posit** noun [U] (NAmE) the system of moving money electronically from one bank account to another

**dir·ec·tion** ⓘ A2 ⓞ /dəˈrekʃn, daɪˈr-/ noun
- **WHERE TO 1** ⓘ A2 [C, U] the general position a person or thing moves or points towards: *in the ~ of sth They headed in the direction of the village.* ◇ *in sb's ~ She pointed in my direction.* ◇ *in the/a … ~ They hit a truck coming in the opposite direction.* ◇ *in the right/wrong direction* ◇ *When the police arrived, the crowd scattered **in all directions**.* ◇ *Has the wind changed direction?* ◇ *I lost all **sense of direction*** (= I didn't know which way to go).
- **INSTRUCTIONS 2** ⓘ A2 [C, usually p.] instructions about how to do sth, where to go, etc: *Let's stop and ask for directions.* ◇ **directions to sth** *A farmer gave us directions to the town.* ◇ **directions for (doing) sth** *With all pesticides, follow the directions for use carefully.*
- **DEVELOPMENT 3** ⓘ B2 [C, U] the general way in which a person or thing develops: *The exhibition provides evidence of several new directions in her work.* ◇ *in a … ~ He wants to take the company in a different direction.* ◇ *It's only a small improvement, but at least it's **a step in the right direction**.*
- **WHERE FROM 4** [C] the general position a person or thing comes or develops from: *Support came from an unexpected direction.* ◇ *Let us approach the subject from a different direction.*
- **PURPOSE 5** [U] a purpose; an aim: *We are looking for somebody with a clear **sense of direction**.* ◇ *Once again her life felt lacking in direction.*
- **CONTROL 6** [U] the art of managing or guiding sb/sth: **under the ~ of sb** *All work was produced by the students under the direction of John Williams.*
- **FILM/MOVIE 7** [U] the instructions given by sb directing a film or play: *There is some clever direction and the film is very well shot.* ➔ see also STAGE DIRECTION **IDM** ➔ see PULL v.

**dir·ec·tion·al** /dəˈrekʃənl, daɪˈr-/ adj. (specialist) **1** producing or receiving signals, sound, etc. better in one particular direction: *a directional microphone/aerial* **2** connected with the direction in which sth is moving: *directional stability*

**dir·ec·tion·less** /dəˈrekʃnləs, daɪˈr-/ adj. (formal) without a direction or purpose

# directive

**di·rect·ive** /dəˈrektɪv, daɪˈr-/ *noun, adj.*
- *noun* an official instruction: *The EU has issued a new set of directives on pollution.*
- *adj.* (*formal*) giving instructions: *They are seeking a central, directive role in national energy policy.*

**di·rect·ly** 🔑 **B1** 🔊 /dəˈrektli, daɪˈr-/ *adv., conj.*
- *adv.* **1** 🔑 **B1** without stopping or changing direction: *The path leads directly to the river.* ◊ *He drove him directly to her hotel.* **2** 🔑 **B1** with nobody or nothing in between: *She speaks directly to camera.* ◊ *We have not been directly affected by the cuts.* ◊ *directly linked/connected/related* ◊ *The president was not directly involved.* ◊ *He was not directly responsible for the accident.* **OPP** **indirectly** **3** exactly in a particular position: *directly opposite/below/ahead* ◊ *They remain directly opposed to these new plans.* **4** immediately: *She left directly after the show.* **5** (*BrE, old-fashioned*) soon **SYN** **shortly**: *Tell them I'll be there directly.*
- *conj.* (*BrE*) as soon as: *I went home directly I had finished work.*

**diˌrect ˈmail** *noun* [U] advertisements that are sent to people through the post

**diˌrect ˈmarketing** *noun* [U] the business of selling products or services directly to customers who order by mail, phone or email, or over the internet, instead of going to a shop

**diˌrect ˈmessage** *noun* = DM

**di·rect·ness** /dəˈrektnəs, daɪˈr-/ *noun* [U] the quality of being simple and clear, so that it is impossible not to understand: *'What's that?' she asked with her usual directness.*

**diˌrect ˈobject** *noun* (*grammar*) a noun, noun phrase or pronoun that refers to a person or thing that is directly affected by the action of a verb: *In 'I met him in town', the word 'him' is the direct object.* ⊃ compare INDIRECT OBJECT

**dir·ect·or** 🔑 **A2** /dəˈrektə(r), daɪˈr-/ *noun* **1** 🔑 **A2** one of a group of senior managers who run a company: *a non-executive director* ◊ *He's on the board of directors.* ⊃ see also EXECUTIVE DIRECTOR, MANAGING DIRECTOR ⊃ WORDFINDER NOTE at COMPANY **2** 🔑 **A2** a person in charge of a film or play who tells the actors and staff what to do: *a famous film director* ⊃ compare PRODUCER ⊃ WORDFINDER NOTE at FILM **3** **A2** a person who is in charge of a particular activity or department in a company, a college, etc: *the artistic/musical director* ◊ *the deputy/assistant/associate director* ◊ *~ of sth the director of marketing/operations/communications* ◊ *a regional director*

**dir·ect·or·ate** /dəˈrektərət, daɪˈr-/ *noun* **1** a section of a government department in charge of one particular activity: *the environmental directorate* **2** the group of directors who run a company **SYN** **board**

**diˌrector ˈgeneral** *noun* (*especially BrE*) the head of a large organization, especially a public organization: *the director general of the BBC*

**dir·ect·or·ial** /ˌdaɪrekˈtɔːriəl/ *adj.* [only before noun] connected with the position or work of a director, especially of a director of films or plays: *The film marks her directorial debut.*

**Diˌrector of ˌPublic Proseˈcutions** *noun* (*abbr.* **DPP**) (in England and Wales) a public official whose job is to decide whether people who are suspected of a crime should be brought to trial

**diˈrector's chair** *noun* a folding wooden chair with crossed legs, a seat and back made of cloth, and sides on which you can rest your arms, typically used by film directors
**IDM** **in the director's chair** directing a film

**diˈrector's cut** *noun* a version of a film, usually released some time after the original is first shown, that is exactly how the director wanted it to be

**dir·ect·or·ship** /dəˈrektəʃɪp, daɪˈr-; *NAmE* -tərʃ-/ *noun* **1** the position of being in charge of an activity, department or organization: *His directorship has come under fierce attack.* **2** the position of a company director; the period during which this is held: *She has held a number of directorships.*

**di·rec·tory** 🔑 **C1** /dəˈrektəri, daɪˈr-/ *noun* (*pl.* **-ies**) **1** 🔑 **C1** a book or electronic resource containing lists of information, usually in alphabetical order, for example people's phone numbers or the names and addresses of businesses in a particular area: *a telephone/trade directory* ◊ *a directory of European Trade Associations* **2** a file containing a group of other files or programs in a computer ⊃ see also ROOT DIRECTORY **3** a board in an organization or large store listing the names of departments and where to find them

**diˌrectory enˈquiries** (*BrE*) (*NAmE* **diˌrectory asˈsistance**, or *informal* **inforˈmation**) *noun* [U + *sing./pl. v.*] a phone service that you can use to find out a person's phone number

**diˌrect ˈrule** *noun* [U] government of a region by a central government, when that region has had its own government in the past

**diˌrect ˈspeech** *noun* [U] (*grammar*) a speaker's actual words; the use of these in writing: *Only direct speech should go inside inverted commas.* ⊃ compare INDIRECT SPEECH, REPORTED SPEECH

**diˌrect ˈtax** *noun* (*specialist*) a tax that is collected directly from the person who pays it, for example income tax ⊃ compare INDIRECT TAX ▶ **diˌrect taxˈation** *noun* [U]

**dirge** /dɜːdʒ; *NAmE* dɜːrdʒ/ *noun* **1** a song sung in the past at a FUNERAL or for a dead person **2** (*informal, disapproving*) any song or piece of music that is too slow and sad

**diri·gible** /ˈdɪrɪdʒəbl/ *adj., noun*
- *adj.* (*formal*) able to be guided or moved in a particular direction: *a dirigible balloon*
- *noun* an AIRSHIP

**dirt** 🔑 **B1** /dɜːt; *NAmE* dɜːrt/ *noun* [U] **1** 🔑 **B1** any substance that makes sth dirty, for example dust, soil or mud: *His clothes were covered in dirt.* ◊ *First remove any grease or dirt from the surface.* **2** 🔑 **B1** (*especially NAmE*) loose earth or soil: *He picked up a handful of dirt and threw it at them.* ◊ *Pack the dirt firmly round the plants.* ◊ *They lived in a shack with a dirt floor.* ⊃ SYNONYMS at SOIL **3** (*informal*) unpleasant or harmful information about sb that could be used to damage their reputation, career, etc: *Do you have any dirt on the new guy?* **4** (*informal*) solid waste matter from the body **SYN** **excrement**: *dog dirt* **IDM** see DISH *v.*, DRAG *v.*, EAT, TREAT *v.*

**ˈdirt bike** *noun* a motorcycle designed for rough ground, especially for competitions

**dirt ˈcheap** *adj., adv.* (*informal*) very cheap: *It was dirt cheap.* ◊ *I got it dirt cheap.*

**dirt ˈpoor** *adj.* (*NAmE, informal*) extremely poor

**dirt ˈroad** (*also* **ˈdirt track**) *noun* a rough road in the country that is made from hard earth

**ˈdirt track** *noun* **1** = DIRT ROAD **2** a track made of CINDERS, soil, etc. used for motorcycle racing: *a dirt-track race*

**dirty** 🔑 **A1** /ˈdɜːti; *NAmE* ˈdɜːrti/ *adj., verb, adv.*
- *adj.* (**dirt·ier**, **dirti·est**)
- • NOT CLEAN **1** 🔑 **A1** not clean: *dirty hands/clothes/dishes* ◊ *a dirty mark* ◊ *Try not to get too dirty!* ◊ *I always get given the dirty jobs* (= jobs that make you become dirty).
- • OFFENSIVE **2** [usually before noun] connected with sex in an offensive way: *a dirty joke/book* ◊ *He's got a dirty mind* (= he often thinks about sex).
- • UNPLEASANT/DISHONEST **3** [usually before noun] (*informal*) unpleasant or dishonest: *a dirty lie* ◊ *They discovered her dirty little secret.* ◊ *He's a great man for doing the dirty jobs* (= jobs which are unpleasant because they involve being dishonest or mean to people).
- • COLOURS **4** [only before noun] not bright: *a dirty brown carpet*
- • DRUGS **5** (*NAmE, slang*) using illegal drugs
**IDM** **air/wash your dirty laundry/linen in ˈpublic** (*disapproving*) to discuss your personal affairs in public, especially sth embarrassing **(do sb's) ˈdirty work** (to do) the unpleasant or dishonest jobs that sb else does not want to do **do the ˈdirty on sb** (*BrE, informal*) to cheat sb who

trusts you; to treat sb badly or unfairly: *I'd never do the dirty on my friends.* **give/shoot sb a dirty ˈlook** (*informal*) to look at sb in a way that shows you are annoyed with them ⇨ more at DOWN *adv.*, HAND *n.*
- **verb** (dirt·ies, dirty·ing, dirt·ied, dirt·ied) ~ sth to make sth dirty
- **adv.**

**IDM** **dirty great/big** (*BrE*, *informal*) used to emphasize how large sth is: *When I turned round he was pointing a dirty great gun at me.* **play ˈdirty** (*informal*) to behave or play a game in an unfair way ⇨ more at TALK *v.*

▼ **SYNONYMS**

**dirty**
dusty • filthy • muddy • soiled • grubby • stained
These words all describe sb/sth that is not clean.
**dirty** not clean; covered with dust, soil, mud, oil, etc: *If your hands are dirty, go and wash them.*
**dusty** full of dust; covered with dust: *There were shelves full of dusty books.*
**filthy** very dirty and unpleasant: *It's absolutely filthy in here.*
**muddy** full of or covered in mud: *Don't you come in here with those muddy boots on!*
**soiled** (*rather formal*) dirty, especially with waste from the body: *soiled nappies/diapers*
**grubby** (*rather informal*) rather dirty, usually because it has not been washed: *He hoped she wouldn't notice his grubby shirt cuffs.*
**stained** (often in compounds) covered with stains; marked with a stain (= a dirty mark that is difficult to remove): *a pair of paint-stained jeans*

PATTERNS
- dirty/dusty/filthy/muddy/soiled/grubby/stained **clothes**
- dirty/dusty/filthy/grubby **hands**
- a dirty/dusty/filthy **room**
- to **get** dirty/dusty/filthy/muddy/stained

ˈdirty bomb *noun* a bomb that contains RADIOACTIVE material

ˌdirty old ˈman *noun* (*informal*) an older man whose interest in sex or in sexually attractive young people is considered to be offensive or not natural for sb of his age

ˌdirty ˈtrick *noun* **1** [usually pl.] dishonest, secret and often illegal activity by a political group or other organization that is intended to harm the reputation or success of an opponent: *a dirty tricks campaign* **2** an unpleasant and dishonest act: *What a dirty trick to play!*

ˌdirty weekˈend *noun* (*BrE*, *humorous*) a weekend spent away with a sexual partner, often in secret

ˌdirty ˈword *noun* a word connected with sex in an offensive way

**IDM** **be a dirty ˈword** to be a subject or an idea that people think is bad or morally wrong: *Profit is not a dirty word around here.*

**dis** (*also* **diss**) /dɪs/ *verb* (-ss-) ~ sb (*informal*) to show a lack of respect for sb, especially by saying offensive things to them

**dis-** /dɪs/ *prefix* (in adjectives, adverbs, nouns and verbs) not; the opposite of: *dishonest ◊ disagreeably ◊ disadvantage ◊ disappear*

**dis·abil·ity** ʕ+ B2 /ˌdɪsəˈbɪləti/ *noun* (*pl.* -ies) **1** ʕ+ B2 [C] a physical or mental condition that means you cannot use a part of your body completely or easily, or that you cannot learn easily: *a physical/mental disability ◊ with a ~ people with severe learning disabilities* **2** ʕ+ B2 [U] the state of not being able to use a part of your body completely or easily, or the state of not being able to learn easily: *learning to live with disability ◊ He qualifies for help on the grounds of disability.* ⇨ note at DISABLED

**dis·able** /dɪsˈeɪbl/ *verb* **1** ~ sb to injure or affect sb permanently so that, for example, they cannot walk or cannot use a part of their body: *He was disabled in a car accident. ◊ a disabling condition* **2** ~ sth to make sth unable to work

437

# disaffiliate

so that it cannot be used: *The burglars gained entry to the building after disabling the alarm.*

**dis·abled** ʕ+ B2 /dɪsˈeɪbld/ *adj.* **1** ʕ+ B2 unable to use a part of your body completely or easily because of a physical condition, an illness, an injury, etc.; unable to learn easily: *physically/mentally disabled ◊ severely disabled ◊ He was born disabled. ◊ facilities for disabled people* **2 the disabled** *noun* [pl.] people who are disabled: *caring for the sick, elderly and disabled*

▼ **WHICH WORD?**

**disabled / handicapped**
- **Disabled** is the most generally accepted term to refer to people with a permanent illness or injury that makes it difficult for them to use part of their body completely or easily. **Handicapped** is old-fashioned and many people now think it is offensive. The expressions **disabled people** or **people with disabilities** are preferred to **the disabled** because they sound more personal.
- **Disabled** and **disability** can be used with other words to talk about a mental condition: *mentally disabled ◊ learning disabilities*. In Britain the preferred term to use is **learning difficulties** because it emphasizes the difficulty experienced, rather than any lack of ability within the person. In North America the standard accepted term is **learning disability**.
- If somebody's ability to hear or see has been damaged but not destroyed completely, they have **hearing loss** or a **visual impairment**. They can be described as **hard of hearing, visually impaired** or **partially sighted**: *The museum has special facilities for blind and partially sighted visitors.*

**dis·able·ment** /dɪsˈeɪblmənt/ *noun* [U] (*formal*) the state of being DISABLED; the process of becoming DISABLED: *The insurance policy covers sudden death or disablement.*

**dis·abuse** /ˌdɪsəˈbjuːz/ *verb* ~ sb (of sth) (*formal*) to tell sb that what they think is true is, in fact, not true

**dis·ad·van·tage** ❶ B1 ⓦ /ˌdɪsədˈvɑːntɪdʒ; *NAmE* -ˈvæn-/ *noun* [C, U] something that causes problems and tends to stop sb/sth from succeeding or making progress: *a serious/severe/significant disadvantage ◊ One major disadvantage of the area is the lack of public transport. ◊ Each plan has its own* **advantages and disadvantages**. *◊ ~ to sth There are disadvantages to the plan. ◊* **at a ~** *The fact that he didn't speak a foreign language put him at a distinct disadvantage. ◊* **to sb's ~** | **to the ~ of sb** *I hope my lack of experience won't be to my disadvantage. ◊ The advantages of the scheme far outweighed the disadvantages. ◊ Many children in the class suffered severe social and economic disadvantage.* OPP advantage ▶ **dis·ad·van·tage** *verb*

**dis·ad·van·taged** /ˌdɪsədˈvɑːntɪdʒd; *NAmE* -ˈvæn-/ *adj.* **1** not having the things, such as education, or enough money, that people need in order to succeed in life SYN **deprived**: *disadvantaged groups/children ◊ a severely disadvantaged area* OPP **advantaged** ⇨ SYNONYMS at POOR **2 the disadvantaged** *noun* [pl.] people who are disadvantaged

**dis·ad·van·ta·geous** /ˌdɪsædvənˈteɪdʒəs/ *adj.* ~ (to/for sb) (*formal*) causing sb to be in a worse situation compared to other people: *The deal will not be disadvantageous to your company.* OPP **advantageous**

**dis·af·fect·ed** /ˌdɪsəˈfektɪd/ *adj.* no longer satisfied with your situation, organization, belief, etc. and therefore no longer supporting it: *Some disaffected members left to form a new party.* ▶ **dis·af·fec·tion** /-ˈfekʃn/ *noun* [U]: *There are signs of growing disaffection amongst voters.*

**dis·af·fili·ate** /ˌdɪsəˈfɪlieɪt/ *verb* [I, T] ~ (sth) (from sth) to end the link between a group, a company or an organization and a larger one: *The local club has disaffiliated from the National Athletic Association.* ▶ **dis·af·fili·ation** /ˌdɪsəfɪliˈeɪʃn/ *noun* [U]

Ⓞ Oxford Phrasal Academic Lexicon (OPAL) written and spoken word lists | Ⓦ OPAL written word list | Ⓢ OPAL spoken word list

# disaggregate

**dis·ag·gre·gate** /ˌdɪsˈæɡrəɡeɪt/ verb ~ sth to separate sth into the different parts that it is made up of: *One recommendation for future research is disaggregating the data according to age.*

**dis·agree** 🔊 **A2** /ˌdɪsəˈɡriː/ verb **1** **A2** [I] if two people **disagree** or one person **disagrees** with another about sth, they have a different opinion about it: *Even friends disagree sometimes.* ◊ *No, I disagree. I don't think it would be the right thing to do.* ◊ **~ with sb** *I must respectfully disagree with my colleague.* ◊ **~ with sb on/over/about sth** *He disagreed with his parents on most things.* ◊ **~ with sth** *I strongly disagree with this decision.* ◊ **~ that …** *Few would disagree that students learn best when they are interested in the topic.* **2** **B2** [I] if statements or reports **disagree**, they give different information **OPP** **agree** **IDM** see AGREE
**PHR V** **disaˈgree with sb** if sth, especially food, **disagrees** with you, it has a bad effect on you and makes you feel ill
**disaˈgree with (doing) sth** to believe that sth is bad or wrong; to DISAPPROVE of sth: *I disagree with violent protests.*

▼ **EXPRESS YOURSELF**

**Disagreeing**

In a discussion, you may think that what other people say is wrong, but there are polite ways to convey this. It is common to express support for something that the other person says before expressing disagreement.

- *I'm sorry, I don't agree / I have to disagree with you there.*
- *Well, actually, I'm not sure that that's true.*
- *I don't think that is exactly right.*
- *I wouldn't agree that that's the best solution.*
- *I have to say that I don't find that argument very convincing.*
- *I can't go along with that idea.*
- *I take / see your point, but I don't think it would work in practice.*
- *Actually, I think that would make the situation worse.*
- *Actually, I'm not sure that's the best plan.*
- *I understand where you're coming from, but I think we might want to take a different approach here.*
- *I can see why you might feel that way, but I think we need to handle this differently.*

**dis·agree·able** /ˌdɪsəˈɡriːəbl/ adj. (formal) **1** not nice or pleasant **SYN** **unpleasant**: *a disagreeable smell/experience/job* **2** (of a person) rude and unfriendly **SYN** **unpleasant**: *a disagreeable bad-tempered man* **OPP** **agreeable**
▶ **dis·agree·ably** /-bli/ adv.

**dis·agree·ment** 🔊 **B2** /ˌdɪsəˈɡriːmənt/ noun **1** **B2** [U, C] a situation where people have different opinions about sth and often argue: **~ (about/on/over/as to sth)** *Disagreement arose about exactly how to plan the show.* ◊ *disagreement on the method to be used* ◊ *There is considerable disagreement over the safety of the treatment.* ◊ **~ (between A and B)** *It was a source of disagreement between the two states.* ◊ **(among …)** *There is disagreement among archaeologists as to the age of the sculpture.* ◊ **~ (with sb)** *They have had several disagreements with their neighbours.* **OPP** **agreement** **2** **C1** [U, C] **~ between A and B** a difference between two things that should be the same: *The comparison shows considerable disagreement between theory and practice.*

**dis·allow** /ˌdɪsəˈlaʊ/ verb [often passive] **~ sth** to officially refuse to accept sth because it has not been done in the correct way: *to disallow a claim/an appeal* ◊ *The second goal was disallowed.* ⊃ compare ALLOW (6)

**dis·am·bigu·ate** /ˌdɪsæmˈbɪɡjueɪt/ verb **~ sth** (specialist) to show clearly the difference between two or more words, phrases, etc. which are similar in meaning

**dis·ap·pear** 🔊 **A2** /ˌdɪsəˈpɪə(r)/; NAmE -ˈpɪr/ verb **1** **A2** [I] to become impossible to see **SYN** **vanish**: *With that, Matt promptly disappeared.* ◊ **+ adv./prep.** *The plane disappeared behind a cloud.* ◊ *Lisa watched until the train disappeared from view.* **2** **A2** [I] to stop existing **SYN** **vanish**: *Her nervousness quickly disappeared once she was on stage.* ◊ *The problem won't just disappear.* ◊ **~ from sth** *Wildlife is fast disappearing from our countryside.* **3** **A2** [I] to be lost or impossible to find **SYN** **vanish**: *I can never find a pen in this house. They disappear as soon as I buy them.* ◊ **~ from sth** *The child disappeared from his home some time after four.* ▶ **dis·ap·pear·ance** /ˌdɪsəˈpɪərəns/; NAmE -ˈpɪr-/ noun [U, C]: *the disappearance of many species of plants and animals from our planet* ◊ *Police are investigating the disappearance of a young woman.* **IDM** see ACT *n.*, FACE *n.*, THIN *adj.*

**dis·ap·point** 🔊 **B2** /ˌdɪsəˈpɔɪnt/ verb **1** 🔊 **B2** [T, I] to make sb feel sad because sth that they hope for or expect to happen does not happen or is not as good as they hoped: **~ (sb)** *Her decision to cancel the concert is bound to disappoint her fans.* ◊ *I hate to disappoint you, but I'm just not interested.* ◊ *The movie had disappointed her* (= it wasn't as good as she had expected). ◊ *His latest novel does not disappoint.* ◊ **it disappoints sb that …** *It disappointed me that nobody bothered to say thank you.* **2** 🔊 **B2** [T] **~ sth** to prevent sth that sb hopes for from becoming a reality: *The new government had soon disappointed the hopes of many of its supporters.*

**dis·ap·point·ed** 🔊 **B1** /ˌdɪsəˈpɔɪntɪd/ adj. upset because sth you hoped for has not happened or been as good, successful, etc. as you expected: *The singer has promised to refund any disappointed fans.* ◊ **~ at/by/about sth** *They were bitterly disappointed at the result of the game.* ◊ **~ in/with sb/sth** *I'm disappointed in you—I really thought I could trust you!* ◊ **~ to see, hear, etc.** *He was disappointed to see she wasn't at the party.* ◊ **~ (that) …** *I'm disappointed (that) it was sold out.* ◊ **~ (not) to be …** *She was disappointed not to be chosen.* ▶ **dis·ap·point·edly** adv.: *'Is that it?' she asked disappointedly.*

**dis·ap·point·ing** 🔊 **B1** /ˌdɪsəˈpɔɪntɪŋ/ adj. not as good, successful, etc. as you had hoped; making you feel disappointed: *a disappointing result/performance/defeat* ◊ **~ for/to sb** *The outcome of the court case was disappointing for the family involved.* ◊ **~ to do sth** *We did a good job but it's still disappointing to only finish second.*
▶ **dis·ap·point·ing·ly** adv.: *The room was disappointingly small.*

**dis·ap·point·ment** 🔊 **B2** /ˌdɪsəˈpɔɪntmənt/ noun **1** 🔊 **B2** [U] the feeling of being sad because sth has not happened or been as good, successful, etc. as you expected or hoped: *Book early for the show to avoid disappointment.* ◊ *To our great disappointment, it rained every day of the trip.* ◊ *He found it difficult to hide his disappointment when she didn't arrive.* **2** 🔊 **B2** [C] a person or thing that is disappointing: *a bitter/major disappointment* ◊ *That new restaurant was a big disappointment.* ◊ **~ to sb** *I always felt I was a disappointment to my father.*

**dis·ap·pro·ba·tion** /ˌdɪsˌæprəˈbeɪʃn/ noun [U] (formal) DISAPPROVAL of sb/sth that you think is morally wrong

**dis·ap·proval** /ˌdɪsəˈpruːvl/ noun [U] a feeling that you do not like an idea, an action or sb's behaviour because you think it is bad, not suitable or going to have a bad effect on sb else: *to show/express disapproval* ◊ **~ of sb/sth** *disapproval of his methods* ◊ **in ~** *He shook his head in disapproval.* ◊ **with ~** *She looked at my clothes with disapproval.*
**OPP** **approval**

**dis·ap·prove** /ˌdɪsəˈpruːv/ verb [I, T] to think that sb/sth is not good or suitable; to not approve of sb/sth: *She wants to be an actress, but her parents disapprove.* ◊ **~ of sb/sth** *He strongly disapproved of the changes that had been made.* ◊ **~ sth** (NAmE) *A solid majority disapproves the way the president is handling the controversy.* **OPP** **approve**

**dis·ap·prov·ing** /ˌdɪsəˈpruːvɪŋ/ adj. showing that you do not approve of sb/sth: *a disapproving glance/tone/look* **OPP** **approving** ▶ **dis·ap·prov·ing·ly** adv.: *He looked disapprovingly at the row of empty wine bottles.*

**dis·arm** /dɪsˈɑːm/; NAmE -ˈɑːrm/ verb **1** [T] **~ sb** to take a weapon or weapons away from sb: *Most of the rebels were captured and disarmed.* **2** [I] (of a country or a group of people) to reduce the size of an army or to give up some or all weapons, especially nuclear weapons **3** [T] ~ **sb** to make sb feel less angry or critical: *He disarmed her immediately by apologizing profusely.* ⊃ compare ARM

**dis·arma·ment** /dɪsˈɑːməmənt; *NAmE* -ˈɑːrm-/ *noun* [U] the fact of a country reducing the size of its armed forces or the number of weapons, especially nuclear weapons, that it has: *nuclear disarmament* ◊ *disarmament talks* ⊃ compare ARMAMENT

**dis·arm·ing** /dɪsˈɑːmɪŋ; *NAmE* -ˈɑːrm-/ *adj.* making people feel less angry or likely to suspect sb than they were before: *a disarming smile* ▸ **dis·arm·ing·ly** *adv.*: *disarmingly frank*

**dis·array** /ˌdɪsəˈreɪ/ *noun* [U] a lack of order or organization in a situation or a place: **in/into** ~ *The peace talks broke up in disarray.* ◊ *Our plans were **thrown into disarray** by her arrival.*

**dis·as·sem·ble** /ˌdɪsəˈsembl/ *verb* **1** [T] ~ **sth** to take apart a machine or structure so that it is in separate pieces **SYN dismantle**: *We had to completely disassemble the engine to find the problem.* **OPP assemble 2** [T] ~ **sth** (*computing*) to translate sth from computer code into a language that can be read by humans **3** [I] (*formal*) (of a group of people) to move apart and go away in different directions: *The concert ended and the crowd disassembled.*

**dis·as·soci·ate** /ˌdɪsəˈsəʊsieɪt, -ˈsəʊʃi-/ *verb* = DISSOCIATE

**dis·as·ter** ⓘ **A2** /dɪˈzɑːstə(r); *NAmE* -ˈzæs-/ *noun* **1** **B2** [C] an unexpected event, such as a very bad accident, a flood or a fire, that kills a lot of people or causes a lot of damage **SYN catastrophe**: *the world's worst humanitarian disaster* ◊ *an environmental/ecological disaster* ◊ **in a ~** *Thousands died in the disaster.* ◊ *They provided more than $2.3 billion in **disaster relief**.* ⊃ see also NATURAL DISASTER

**WORDFINDER** avalanche, cyclone, earthquake, eruption, flood, hurricane, landslide, tornado, tsunami

**2** **A2** [C, U] a very bad situation that causes problems: *Losing your job doesn't have to be such a disaster.* ◊ *Disaster struck when the wheel came off.* ◊ *to avert/avoid disaster* ◊ **~ for sb** *The discovery of the disease among sheep spells financial disaster for farmers.* ◊ *Letting her organize the party is a **recipe for disaster** (= something that is likely to go badly wrong).* **3** **A2** [C] (*informal*) a complete failure: *As a teacher, he's a disaster.* ◊ *The play's first night was a total disaster.* **IDM** see WAIT *v.*

**diˈsaster area** *noun* **1** a place where a disaster has happened and that needs special help **2** (*informal*) a place or situation that has a lot of problems, is a failure, or is badly organized

**dis·as·trous** **B2+** **C1** /dɪˈzɑːstrəs; *NAmE* -ˈzæs-/ *adj.* very bad, harmful or unsuccessful **SYN catastrophic, devastating**: *a disastrous harvest/fire/result* ◊ *Lowering interest rates could have disastrous consequences for the economy.* ▸ **dis·as·trous·ly** *adv.*: *How could everything go so disastrously wrong?*

**dis·avow** /ˌdɪsəˈvaʊ/ *verb* ~ **sth** (*formal*) to state publicly that you have no knowledge of sth or that you are not responsible for sth/sb: *They disavowed claims of a split in the party.* ▸ **dis·avow·al** /-əl/ *noun* [C, U]

**dis·band** /dɪsˈbænd/ *verb* [T, I] ~ **(sb/sth)** to stop sb/sth from operating as a group; to separate or no longer operate as a group: *They set about disbanding the terrorist groups.* ◊ *The committee formally disbanded in August.* ▸ **dis·band·ment** *noun* [U]

**dis·bar** /dɪsˈbɑː(r)/ *verb* [usually passive] (**-rr-**) ~ **sb (from sth/from doing sth)** to stop a lawyer from working in the legal profession, especially because he or she has done sth illegal ▸ **dis·bar·ment** *noun* [U]

**dis·be·lief** /ˌdɪsbɪˈliːf/ *noun* [U] the feeling of not being able to believe sth: *He stared at me **in disbelief**.* ◊ *To enjoy the movie you have to **suspend your disbelief** (= pretend to believe sth, even if it seems very unlikely).* ⊃ compare BELIEF (3), UNBELIEF

**dis·be·lieve** /ˌdɪsbɪˈliːv/ *verb* (not used in the progressive tenses) ~ **sth** (*formal*) to not believe that sth is true or that sb is telling the truth: *Why should I disbelieve her story?* ▸ **dis·be·liev·ing** *adj.*: *a disbelieving look/smile/laugh* **dis·be·liev·ing·ly** *adv.*

**PHRV disbeˈlieve in sth** to not believe that sth exists

**dis·burse** /dɪsˈbɜːs; *NAmE* -ˈbɜːrs/ *verb* ~ **sth** (*formal*) to pay money to sb from a large amount that has been collected for a purpose ▸ **dis·burse·ment** *noun* [U, C]: *the disbursement of funds* ◊ *aid disbursements*

**disc** ⓘ **B2** (*also* **disk** *especially in NAmE*) /dɪsk/ **HELP** The usual spelling is **disc** in (*BrE*) and **disk** in (*NAmE*) but for senses connected with computers, the spelling is usually **disk**, even in (*BrE*). *noun* **1** **B2** a thin flat round object: *He wears an identity disc around his neck.* **2** a CD or DVD: **on ~** *This recording is available online or on disc.* ⊃ see also BLU-RAY DISC™ **3** (*BrE*) a disk for a computer **4** (*old-fashioned*) = RECORD (6) **5** a structure made of CARTILAGE between the bones of the back: *He's been off work with a **slipped disc** (= one that has moved from its correct position, causing pain).*

**dis·card** **B2+** **C1** *verb*, *noun*
■ *verb* /dɪˈskɑːd; *NAmE* -ˈskɑːrd/ **1** **B2+** **C1** [T] (*formal*) to get rid of sth that you no longer want or need: **~ sb/sth** *The room was littered with discarded newspapers.* ◊ *He had discarded his jacket because of the heat.* ◊ (*figurative*) *She could now discard all thought of promotion.* ◊ **~ sb/sth as sth** *10 per cent of the data was discarded as unreliable.* **2** [T, I] ~ **(sth)** (in card games) to get rid of a card that you do not want
■ *noun* /ˈdɪskɑːd; *NAmE* -skɑːrd/ a person or thing that is not wanted or that is thrown away, especially a card in a card game

**ˈdisc brake** *noun* [usually pl.] a BRAKE that works by two surfaces pressing onto a disc in the centre of a wheel

**dis·cern** /dɪˈsɜːn; *NAmE* -ˈsɜːrn/ *verb* (not used in the progressive tenses) (*formal*) **1** to know, recognize or understand sth, especially sth that is not obvious **SYN detect**: **~ sth** *It is possible to discern a number of different techniques in her work.* ◊ *He discerned a certain coldness in their welcome.* ◊ **~ how, whether, etc…** *It is often difficult to discern how widespread public support is.* ◊ **~ that…** *I quickly discerned that something was wrong.* **2** ~ **sth** to see or hear sth, usually with difficulty **SYN make out**: *We could just discern the house in the distance.* ▸ **dis·cern·ible** *adj.* (*formal*) **SYN perceptible**: *There is often no discernible difference between rival brands.* ◊ *His face was barely discernible in the gloom.*

**dis·cern·ing** /dɪˈsɜːnɪŋ; *NAmE* -ˈsɜːrn-/ *adj.* (*approving*) able to show good judgement about the quality of sb/sth: *The discerning customer will recognize this as a high-quality product.*

**dis·cern·ment** /dɪˈsɜːnmənt; *NAmE* -ˈsɜːrn-/ *noun* [U] (*formal*, *approving*) the ability to show good judgement about the quality of sb/sth **SYN discrimination**: *He shows great discernment in his choice of friends.*

**dis·charge** **B2+** **C1** *verb*, *noun*
■ *verb* /dɪsˈtʃɑːdʒ; *NAmE* -ˈtʃɑːrdʒ/ (*formal*)
• FROM THE POLICE/ARMY **1** **B2+** **C1** [T, usually passive] to give sb official permission to leave the police or the armed forces; to make sb leave the police or the armed forces: **be discharged from sth** *He was discharged from the army following his injury.* ◊ *She was discharged from the police force for bad conduct.*
• FROM HOSPITAL **2** **B2+** **C1** [T, often passive] to allow sb to leave hospital because they are well enough to leave: **be discharged (from sth)** *Patients were being discharged from the hospital too early.* ◊ **~ sb/yourself (from sth)** *She had discharged herself against medical advice.*
• FROM PRISON/COURT **3** [T, often passive] to allow sb to leave prison or court: **be discharged** *He was conditionally discharged after admitting the theft.* ⊃ WORDFINDER NOTE at PRISON **4** [T, often passive] ~ **sb/sth** to allow a member of a JURY to stop serving in a court case: *If the jury cannot agree, it should be discharged.*
• GAS/LIQUID **5** [I, T] when a gas or a liquid **discharges** or **is discharged**, or sb **discharges** it, it flows somewhere: **~ (into sth)** *The river is diverted through the power station before discharging into the sea.* ◊ **~ sth (from sth) (into sth)**

# disciple

*The factory was fined for discharging chemicals into the river.* **6** [T] ~ sth if part of the body **discharges** sth, a liquid such as PUS comes out of it
- **FORCE/POWER 7** [T, I] ~ (sth) (*specialist*) to release force or power: *Lightning is caused by clouds discharging electricity.*
- **DUTY 8** [T] ~ sth to do everything that is necessary to perform and complete a particular duty: *to discharge your duties/responsibilities/obligations* ◊ *to discharge a debt* (= to pay it)
- **GUN 9** [T, I] ~ (sth) to fire a gun, etc.; (of a gun, etc.) to be fired: *The police officer accidentally discharged a firearm while unloading it.*

■ **noun** /ˈdɪstʃɑːdʒ; NAmE -tʃɑːrdʒ/ (*formal*)
- **OF LIQUID/GAS 1** [U, C] the action of releasing a substance such as a liquid or gas; a substance that comes out from inside somewhere: *a ban on the discharge of toxic waste* ◊ *nasal/vaginal discharge* (= from the nose/VAGINA) ◊ ~ **from sth** *a thick discharge from the nose*
- **OF ELECTRICITY 2** [U, C] the release of electricity from a CHARGED object; a flow of electricity through air or other gas: *thunder and lightning caused by electrical discharges*
- **FROM THE POLICE/ARMY 3** [U, C] ~ **(from sth)** the act of officially allowing sb, or of telling sb, to leave the police or the army
- **FROM HOSPITAL 4** [U, C] ~ **from sth** the act of allowing sb to leave hospital because they are well enough to leave
- **FROM PRISON/COURT 5** [C] the act of allowing sb to leave prison or court: *The magistrate gave her a 12-month conditional discharge.*
- **OF DUTY 6** [U] the act of performing a task or a duty or of paying money that is owed: *the discharge of debts/obligations*
- **OF GUN 7** [C, U] ~ **(from sth)** the action of firing a gun, etc.

**dis·ciple** /dɪˈsaɪpl/ *noun* **1** a person who believes in and follows the teachings of a religious or political leader **SYN follower**: *a disciple of the economist John Maynard Keynes* **2** (*according to the Bible*) one of the people who followed Jesus Christ and his teachings when he was living on earth, especially one of the twelve APOSTLES

**dis·cip·lin·ar·ian** /ˌdɪsəplɪˈneəriən; NAmE -ˈner-/ *noun* a person who believes in using rules and punishments for controlling people: *She's a very strict disciplinarian.*

**dis·cip·lin·ary** /ˈdɪsəplɪnəri, ˈdɪsəplɪnəri; NAmE ˈdɪsəplɪneri/ *adj.* **1** connected with the punishment of people who break rules: *a disciplinary hearing* (= to decide if sb has done sth wrong) ◊ *The company will be taking disciplinary action against him.* **2** (*formal*) connected with an area of knowledge, especially a subject that people study in a university: *disciplinary knowledge* ⊃ see also CROSS-DISCIPLINARY, INTERDISCIPLINARY, MULTIDISCIPLINARY

**dis·cip·line** 0 B2 W /ˈdɪsəplɪn/ *noun, verb*
■ *noun* **1** B2 [U] the practice of training people to obey rules and orders and punishing them if they do not; the CONTROLLED behaviour or situation that is the result of this training: *The school has a reputation for high standards of discipline.* ◊ *Strict discipline is imposed on army recruits.* ◊ *She keeps good discipline in class.* **OPP indiscipline 2** [C] a method of training your mind or body or of controlling your behaviour; an area of activity where this is necessary: *Yoga is a good discipline for learning to relax.* **3** [U] the ability to control your behaviour or the way you live, work, etc: *He'll never get anywhere working for himself—he's got no discipline.* ⊃ see also SELF-DISCIPLINE **4** [C] (*formal*) an area of knowledge, a subject that people study or are taught, especially in a university: *The new recruits were drawn from a range of academic disciplines.*
■ *verb* **1** ~ **sb (for sth)** to punish sb for sth they have done: *The officers were disciplined for using racist language.* **2** ~ **sb** to train sb, especially a child, to obey particular rules and control the way they behave: *a guide to the best ways of disciplining your child* **3** to control the way you behave and make yourself do things that you believe you should do: ~ **yourself** *Dieting is a matter of disciplining yourself.* ◊ ~ **yourself to do sth** *He disciplined himself to*

*exercise at least three times a week.* ▶ **dis·cip·lined** *adj.: a disciplined army/team* ◊ *a disciplined approach to work*

**ˈdisc jockey** (*NAmE also* **disk jockey**) (*abbr.* **DJ**) (*also informal* **dee·jay**) *noun* a person whose job is to introduce and play recorded popular music, on radio or television or at a club, party, etc.

**dis·claim** /dɪsˈkleɪm/ *verb* (*formal*) **1** ~ **sth** to state publicly that you have no knowledge of sth, or that you are not responsible for sth **SYN deny**: *She disclaimed any knowledge of her husband's whereabouts.* ◊ *The rebels disclaimed all responsibility for the explosion.* **2** ~ **sth** to give up your right to sth, such as property or a title **SYN renounce**

**dis·claim·er** /dɪsˈkleɪmə(r)/ *noun* **1** (*formal*) a statement in which sb says that they are not connected with or responsible for sth, or that they do not have any knowledge of it **2** (*law*) a statement in which a person says officially that they do not claim the right to do sth

**dis·close** ⁺ C1 /dɪsˈkləʊz/ *verb* (*formal*) **1** ⁺ C1 to give sb information about sth, especially sth that was previously secret **SYN reveal**: ~ **sth (to sb)** *The spokesman refused to disclose details of the takeover to the press.* ◊ ~ **that…** *The report discloses that human error was to blame for the accident.* ◊ **it is disclosed that…** *It was disclosed that two women were being interviewed by the police.* ◊ ~ **what, whether, etc…** *I cannot disclose what we discussed.* **2** ~ **sth** to allow sth that was hidden to be seen **SYN reveal**: *The door swung open, disclosing a long dark passage.*

**dis·clo·sure** ⁺ C1 /dɪsˈkləʊʒə(r)/ *noun* (*formal*) **1** ⁺ C1 [U] the act of making sth known or public that was previously secret or private **SYN revelation**: *the newspaper's disclosure of defence secrets* **2** ⁺ C1 [C] information or a fact that is made known or public that was previously secret or private **SYN revelation**: *startling disclosures about his private life*

**disco** /ˈdɪskəʊ/ (*pl.* **-os**) *noun* **1** a club, party or event where people dance to recorded pop music: *disco dancing* ◊ *the youth club disco* **2** (*also* **ˈdisco music**) [U] a type of music intended for dancing at **discos**, that was especially popular in the 1970s. It is influenced by SOUL music but has electronic instruments and a strong regular beat. **3** the lights and sound equipment for a disco

**ˈdisco ball** *noun* a decoration for a party, NIGHTCLUB, etc. consisting of a hanging ball covered in small mirrors that shine in the lights

**dis·cog·raphy** /dɪˈskɒɡrəfi; NAmE -ˈskɑːɡ-/ *noun* (*pl.* **-ies**) **1** [C] all of the music that has been performed, written or collected by a particular person; a list of this music **2** [U] the study of musical recordings or collections

**dis·col·or·ation** (*BrE also* **dis·col·our·ation**) /dɪsˌkʌləˈreɪʃn/ *noun* **1** [U] the process of changing colour, or making sth change colour, in a way that makes it look less attractive: *discoloration caused by the sun* **2** [C] a place where sth has changed colour in a way that makes it look less attractive

**dis·col·our** (*US* **dis·color**) /dɪsˈkʌlə(r)/ *verb* [I, T] to change colour, or to make the colour of sth change, in a way that makes it look less attractive: *Plastic tends to discolour with age.* ◊ ~ **sth** *The pipes were beginning to rust, discolouring the water.*

**dis·com·fit** /dɪsˈkʌmfɪt/ *verb* [*often passive*] ~ **sb** (*literary*) to make sb feel confused or embarrassed ▶ **dis·com·fit·ure** /-fɪtʃə(r)/ *noun* [U]: *He was clearly taking delight in her discomfiture.*

**dis·com·fort** /dɪsˈkʌmfət; NAmE -fərt/ *noun, verb*
■ *noun* (*formal*) **1** [U] a feeling of slight pain or of being physically uncomfortable: *You will experience some minor discomfort during the treatment.* ◊ *abdominal discomfort* **2** [U] a feeling of worry or being embarrassed **SYN unease**: *John's presence caused her considerable discomfort.* **3** [C] something that makes you feel uncomfortable or causes you a slight feeling of pain
■ *verb* [*often passive*] ~ **sb** (*formal*) to make sb feel anxious or embarrassed

**ˈdisco music** = DISCO (2)

**dis·con·cert** /ˌdɪskənˈsɜːt; NAmE -ˈsɜːrt/ *verb* ~ **sb** to make sb feel anxious, confused or embarrassed **SYN disturb**:

His answer rather disconcerted her. ▸ **dis·con·cert·ed** adj.: I was disconcerted to find that everyone else already knew it. **dis·con·cert·ing** adj.: She had the disconcerting habit of saying exactly what she thought. **dis·con·cert·ing·ly** adv.

**dis·con·nect** verb, noun
- verb /ˌdɪskəˈnekt/ **1** [T] ~ **sth (from sth)** to remove a piece of equipment from a supply of gas, water or electricity: *First, disconnect the boiler from the water mains.* **2** [T] [usually passive] to officially stop the supply of phone lines, water, electricity or gas to a building: **be disconnected** *You may be disconnected if you do not pay the bill.* **3** [T, often passive] to separate sth from sth: **be/become disconnected (from sth)** *The ski had become disconnected from the boot.* **4** [T] [usually passive] to break the contact between two people who are talking on the phone: **be disconnected** *We were suddenly disconnected.* **5** [T, often passive, I] to end a connection to the internet: **be/get disconnected (from sth)** *I keep getting disconnected when I'm online.* ◇ ~ **(from sth)** *My computer crashes every time I disconnect from the internet.* **6** [T] ~ **sb (from sth)** to remove sb's connection to a piece of equipment, especially a life support machine: *It was the family's decision to disconnect her from the life support machine.* **OPP connect**
- noun (rather informal) /ˈdɪskənekt/ **1** ~ **(between A and B)** | ~ **(from/with sb/sth)** a difference or lack of connection: *There is a fundamental disconnect between union leaders and members.* **2** a lack of connection with a network, a supply of electricity, the internet, etc: *There might be a power failure or sudden network disconnect.*

**dis·con·nect·ed** /ˌdɪskəˈnektɪd/ adj. **1** not related to or connected with the things or people around: *disconnected images/thoughts/ideas* ◇ *I felt disconnected from the world around me.* **2** (of speech or writing) with the parts not connected in a logical order **SYN disjointed, incoherent**

**dis·con·nec·tion** /ˌdɪskəˈnekʃn/ noun **1** [U, C] the act of ending a connection, especially stopping the supply of phone lines, water, electricity or gas to a building: ~ **from sth** *Persistent copyright breaches would lead to disconnection from the internet.* **2** [C] a situation in which two things are not connected although they should be, and this causes problems: ~ **(between A and B)** *One problem is the disconnection between political leaders and ordinary people.* ◇ ~ **(from sth)** *our disconnection from nature*

**dis·con·so·late** /dɪsˈkɒnsələt/; NAmE -ˈkɑːn-/ adj. (formal) very unhappy and disappointed **SYN dejected** ▸ **dis·con·so·late·ly** adv.

**dis·con·tent** /ˌdɪskənˈtent/ (also **dis·con·tent·ment** /ˌdɪskənˈtentmənt/) noun [U, C] ~ **(at/over/with sth)** a feeling of being unhappy because you are not satisfied with a particular situation; sth that makes you have this feeling **SYN dissatisfaction**: *There is widespread discontent among the staff at the proposed changes to pay and conditions.* ⇒ compare CONTENTMENT

**dis·con·tent·ed** /ˌdɪskənˈtentɪd/ adj. ~ **(with sth)** unhappy because you are not satisfied with your situation **SYN dissatisfied OPP contented** ▸ **dis·con·tent·ed·ly** adv.

**dis·con·tinue** /ˌdɪskənˈtɪnjuː/ verb (formal) **1** ~ **(doing) sth** to stop doing, using or providing sth, especially sth that you have been doing, using or providing regularly: *It was decided to discontinue the treatment after three months.* **2** [usually passive] ~ **sth** to stop making a product: *a sale of discontinued china*

**dis·con·tinu·ity** /ˌdɪsˌkɒntɪˈnjuːəti/; NAmE -ˌkɑːntɪˈnuː-/ noun (pl. -**ies**) (formal) **1** [U] the state of not being continuous: *discontinuity in the children's education* **2** [C] a break or change in a continuous process: *Changes in government led to discontinuities in policy.* **OPP continuity**

**dis·con·tinu·ous** /ˌdɪskənˈtɪnjuəs/ adj. (formal) not continuous; stopping and starting again **SYN intermittent**

**dis·cord** /ˈdɪskɔːd/; NAmE -kɔːrd/ noun **1** [U] (formal) DISAGREEMENT, arguing: *marital/family discord* ◇ *A note of discord surfaced during the proceedings.* **OPP concord 2** [C, U] (music) a combination of musical notes that do not sound pleasant together ⇒ compare HARMONY

**dis·cord·ant** /dɪsˈkɔːdənt/; NAmE -ˈkɔːrd-/ adj. **1** (usually before noun) (formal) not in agreement; combining with other things in a way that is strange or unpleasant: *discordant views* **2** (of sounds) not sounding pleasant together **OPP harmonious**

**disco·theque** /ˈdɪskətek/ noun (old-fashioned) a club where people dance to recorded pop music **SYN disco**

**dis·count** 🔑 **B1** noun, verb
- noun ᛕ **B1** /ˈdɪskaʊnt/ [C, U] an amount of money that is taken off the usual cost of sth **SYN reduction**: *to get/offer a discount* ◇ *a 10, 20, 50, etc. per cent discount* ◇ ~ **for sb** *Do you give any discount for students?* ◇ ~ **on/off sth** *They're offering a 10% discount on all sofas this month.* ◇ **at a ~** *They were selling everything at a discount* (= at reduced prices). ◇ *We offer special discount rates for families.* ◇ *a discount store/retailer* (= one that regularly sells goods at reduced prices) ⇒ **WORDFINDER NOTE** at BUY
- verb **1** ᛕ **B2** /dɪsˈkaʊnt/ [usually passive] ~ **sth** to take an amount of money off the usual cost of sth; to sell sth at a discount **SYN reduce**: *Most of our stock has been discounted by up to 40 per cent.* ◇ *discounted rates/fares/tickets* ◇ *Aer Lingus is offering heavily discounted prices on flights to the US this month.* **2** /dɪsˈkaʊnt/ (formal) to think or say that sth is not important or not true **SYN dismiss**: ~ **sth** *We cannot discount the possibility of further strikes.* ◇ ~ **sth as sth** *The news reports were being discounted as propaganda.*

**dis·counter** /ˈdɪskaʊntə(r)/ (also **discount store**) noun a shop that sells things very cheaply, often in large quantities or from a limited range of goods

**discount rate** noun (finance) **1** the minimum rate of interest that banks in the US and some other countries must pay when they borrow money from other banks **2** the amount that the price of a BILL OF EXCHANGE is reduced by when it is bought before it reaches its full value

**dis·cour·age** ᛕ+ **B2** /dɪsˈkʌrɪdʒ/; NAmE -ˈkɜːr-/ verb **1** ᛕ+ **B2** to try to prevent sth or to prevent sb from doing sth, especially by making it difficult to do or by showing that you do not approve of it: ~ **(doing) sth** *a campaign to discourage smoking among teenagers* ◇ ~ **sb** *I leave a light on when I'm out to discourage burglars.* ◇ ~ **sb from doing sth** *His parents tried to discourage him from being an actor.* **2** ᛕ+ **B2** to make sb feel less confident or enthusiastic about doing sth **SYN dishearten**: ~ **sb/sth** *Don't be discouraged by the first failure—try again!* ◇ ~ **sb from doing sth** *The weather discouraged people from attending.* **OPP encourage** ▸ **dis·cour·aged** adj. [not usually before noun] **SYN disheartened**: *Learners can feel very discouraged if an exercise is too difficult.* **dis·cour·aging** adj.: *a discouraging experience/response/result* **dis·cour·aging·ly** adv.

**dis·cour·age·ment** /dɪsˈkʌrɪdʒmənt/; NAmE -ˈkɜːr-/ noun **1** [U] a feeling that you no longer have the confidence or enthusiasm to do sth: *an atmosphere of discouragement and despair* **2** [U] the action of trying to stop sth: *the government's discouragement of political protest* **3** [C] a thing that makes sb feel less confident or enthusiastic about doing sth: *Despite all these discouragements, she refused to give up.*

**dis·course** ᛕ+ **C1** noun, verb
- noun /ˈdɪskɔːs/; NAmE -kɔːrs/ **1** ᛕ+ **C1** [C, U] (formal) a long and serious treatment or discussion of a subject in speech or writing: ~ **on sth** *a discourse on issues of gender and sexuality* ◇ *He was hoping for some lively political discourse at the meeting.* **2** ᛕ+ **C1** [U] (linguistics) the use of language in speech and writing in order to produce meaning; language that is studied, usually in order to see how the different parts of a text are connected: *spoken/written discourse* ◇ *discourse analysis*
- verb /dɪsˈkɔːs/; NAmE -ˈkɔːrs/
  **PHRV dis'course on/upon sth** (formal) to talk or give a long speech about sth that you know a lot about

**dis·cour·teous** /dɪsˈkɜːtiəs/; NAmE -ˈkɜːrt-/ adj. (formal) having bad manners and not showing respect for other people **SYN impolite OPP courteous** ⇒ **SYNONYMS** at RUDE

**dis·cour·tesy** /dɪsˈkɜːtəsi/; NAmE -ˈkɜːrt-/ noun [U, C] (pl. -**ies**) (formal) behaviour or an action that is not polite

# discover

**dis·cover** /dɪˈskʌvə(r)/ verb 1 ~ sth to be the first person to become aware that a particular place or thing exists: *Cook is credited with discovering Hawaii.* ◊ *Scientists around the world are working to discover a cure for AIDS.* ◊ *a newly discovered snake species* ⊃ WORDFINDER NOTE AT EXPLORE 2 to find sb/sth that was hidden or that you did not expect to find: ~ sb/sth *Police discovered a large stash of drugs while searching the house.* ◊ *We discovered this beach while we were sailing around the island.* ◊ ~ sb/sth doing sth *He was discovered hiding in a shed.* ◊ ~ sb/sth + adj. *She was discovered dead at her home in Leeds.* 3 to find out about sth; to find some information about sth: ~ sth *She was determined to discover the truth about her neighbours.* ◊ *I've just discovered hang-gliding!* ◊ ~ (that) … *It was a shock to discover (that) he couldn't read.* ◊ ~ why, how, etc … *We never did discover why she gave up her job.* ◊ *it is discovered that … It was later discovered that the diaries were a fraud.* ◊ *sb/sth is discovered to be/have … He was later discovered to be seriously ill.* 4 [often passive] to be the first person to realize that sb is very good at singing, acting, etc. and help them to become successful and famous: **be discovered** *The singer was discovered while still at school.* ▶ **dis·cov·er·er** noun: *the discoverer of penicillin*

**dis·cov·er·able** /dɪˈskʌvərəbl/ adj. that you can find by searching or find easily ▶ **dis·cov·er·abil·ity** /dɪˌskʌvərəˈbɪləti/ noun [U]: *They are working to improve the discoverability of their e-books.*

**dis·cov·ery** /dɪˈskʌvəri/ noun (pl. -ies) 1 [C, U] an act of the process of finding sb/sth, or learning about sth that was not known about before: *Researchers in this field have made some important new discoveries.* ◊ *New scientific discoveries are being made all the time.* ◊ ~ of sth *the discovery of antibiotics in the twentieth century* ◊ *The discovery of a child's body in the river has shocked the community.* ◊ *He saw life as a voyage of discovery.* ◊ ~ that … *She was shocked by the discovery that he had been unfaithful.* ◊ *In 1974 Hawking made the discovery (= he discovered) that black holes give off radiation.* 2 [C] a thing, fact or person that is found or learned about for the first time: *The drug is not a new discovery—it's been known about for years.* ◊ ~ about sth *recent discoveries about sleep*

**dis·credit** /dɪsˈkredɪt/ verb, noun
■ verb 1 ~ sb/sth to make people stop respecting sb/sth: *The photos were deliberately taken to discredit the president.* ◊ *a discredited government/policy* 2 ~ sth to make people stop believing that sth is true; to make sth appear unlikely to be true: *These theories are now largely discredited among linguists.*
■ noun (formal) 1 [U] damage to sb's/sth's reputation; loss of respect: *Violent football fans bring discredit on the teams they support.* ◊ **to sb/sth's ~** *Britain, to its discredit, did not speak out against these atrocities.* ⊃ compare CREDIT 2 [C] ~ (**to sb/sth**) a person or thing that causes damage to sb's/sth's reputation or loss of respect: *They were a discredit to their country.*

**dis·cred·it·able** /dɪsˈkredɪtəbl/ adj. (formal) bad and unacceptable; causing people to lose respect

**dis·creet** /dɪˈskriːt/ adj. careful in what you say or do, in order to keep sth secret or to avoid causing difficulty for sb or making them feel embarrassed SYN **tactful**: *He was always very discreet about his love affairs.* ◊ *You ought to make a few discreet enquiries before you sign anything.* ▶ **dis·creet·ly** adv.: *She coughed discreetly to announce her presence.*

**WORD FAMILY**
discreet adj. (≠ indiscreet)
discretion noun (≠ indiscretion)

**dis·crep·ancy** /dɪsˈkrepənsi/ noun [C, U] (pl. -ies) a difference between two or more things that should be the same: ~ (**in sth**) *wide discrepancies in prices quoted for the work* ◊ ~ **between A and B** *What are the reasons for the discrepancy between girls' and boys' performance in school?*

**dis·crete** /dɪˈskriːt/ adj. (formal or specialist) independent of other things of the same type SYN **separate**: *The organisms can be divided into discrete categories.* ▶ **dis·crete·ly** adv. **dis·crete·ness** noun [U]

**dis·cre·tion** /dɪˈskreʃn/ noun [U] 1 the freedom or power to decide what should be done in a particular situation: *I'll leave it up to you to use your discretion.* ◊ *How much to tell terminally ill patients is left to the discretion of the doctor.* 2 care in what you say or do, in order to keep sth secret or to avoid causing difficulty for sb or making them feel embarrassed; the quality of being DISCREET: *This is confidential, but I know that I can rely on your discretion.* ⊃ compare INDISCRETION
IDM **at sb's di'scretion** according to what sb decides or wishes to do: *Bail is granted at the discretion of the court.* ◊ *There is no service charge and tipping is at your discretion.* **di'scretion is the ˌbetter part of ˈvalour** (saying) you should avoid danger and not take unnecessary risks

**dis·cre·tion·ary** /dɪˈskreʃənəri; NAmE -neri/ adj. [usually before noun] (formal) decided according to the judgement of a person in authority about what is necessary in each particular situation; not decided by rules: *You may be eligible for a discretionary grant for your university course.*

**dis·crim·in·ate** /dɪˈskrɪmɪneɪt/ verb 1 [I, T] to recognize that there is a difference between people or things; to show a difference between people or things SYN **differentiate, distinguish**: ~ (**between A and B**) *The computer program was unable to discriminate between letters and numbers.* ◊ ~ **sth** *When do babies learn to discriminate voices?* ◊ ~ **A from B** *A number of features discriminate this species from others.* 2 [I] to treat one person or group worse/better than another in an unfair way: ~ (**against sb**) | ~ (**in favour of sb**) *practices that discriminate against women and in favour of men* ◊ ~ **on the grounds of sth** *It is illegal to discriminate on the grounds of race, gender or religion.* ⊃ WORDFINDER NOTE AT EQUAL

**dis·crim·in·at·ing** /dɪˈskrɪmɪneɪtɪŋ/ adj. (approving) able to judge the quality of sth SYN **discerning**: *a discriminating audience/customer*

**dis·crim·in·ation** /dɪˌskrɪmɪˈneɪʃn/ noun 1 [U] the practice of treating sb or a particular group in society less fairly than others: *age/racial/gender/sex discrimination* (= because of sb's age, race or sex) ◊ ~ **against sb** *discrimination against the elderly* ◊ ~ **by sb** *They alleged discrimination by the authorities.* ◊ ~ **on the basis/grounds of sth** *to prohibit/outlaw/ban discrimination on the basis of race, gender or sexual orientation* ⊃ see also POSITIVE DISCRIMINATION, REVERSE DISCRIMINATION 2 [U] (approving) the ability to judge what is good, true, etc. SYN **discernment**: *He showed great discrimination in his choice of friends.* 3 (formal) [U, C] the ability to recognize a difference between one thing and another; a difference that is recognized: *to learn discrimination between right and wrong* ◊ *fine discriminations*

**dis·crim·in·atory** /dɪˈskrɪmɪnətəri; NAmE -tɔːri/ adj. unfair; treating sb or one group of people worse than others: *discriminatory practices/rules/measures* ◊ *sexually/racially discriminatory laws*

**dis·cur·sive** /dɪsˈkɜːsɪv; NAmE -ˈkɜːrs-/ adj. (formal) (of a style of writing or speaking) moving from one point to another without any strict structure: *the discursive style of the novel*

**dis·cus** /ˈdɪskəs/ noun 1 [C] a heavy flat round object thrown in a sporting event 2 often **the discus** [sing.] the event or sport of throwing a discus as far as possible

**dis·cuss** /dɪˈskʌs/ verb 1 to talk about sth with sb, especially in order to decide sth: ~ **sth with sb** *Have you discussed the problem with anyone?* ◊ ~ **sth** *I'm not prepared to discuss this on the phone.* ◊ *to discuss the issue/matter/topic* ◊ *to discuss a plan/proposal* ◊ ~ **when, what, etc** … *We need to discuss when we should go.* ◊ ~ **doing sth** *We briefly discussed buying a second car.* HELP People sometimes say '*discuss about sth*'. However, this is still considered incorrect by most people, teachers and in exams. Use **discuss** or **have a discussion about** instead: *I discussed my problem with my parents.* ◊ *I had* *a discussion about my problem with my parents.* ◇ *I discussed about my problem with my parents.* ⊃ SYNONYMS at TALK **2** 🄰🄰 to write or talk about sth in detail, showing the different ideas and opinions about it: *~ sth This topic will be discussed at greater length in the next chapter.* ◇ *~ what, how, etc... The article discusses how teachers can use technology in their classrooms.* ⊃ LANGUAGE BANK at ABOUT ⊃ SYNONYMS at EXAMINE

**dis·cus·sion** 🄾 🄰🄰 🄾 /dɪˈskʌʃn/ *noun* [C, U] **1** 🄰🄰 a conversation about sb/sth; the process of discussing sb/sth: *~ with sb (about sb/sth) We had a discussion with them about the differences between Britain and the US.* ◇ *~ about/on/around sb/sth A lively discussion followed about whether he should be allowed to join the club.* ◇ *~ of sth We want to encourage public discussion of mental health issues.* ◇ *~ among/between A and B (about sb/sth) There was some discussion among reviewers about this film.* ◇ *under ~ The plans have been under discussion (= being talked about) for a year now.* ◇ *for ~ a list of topics for discussion* **2** 🄰🄰 a speech or a piece of writing that discusses many different aspects of a subject: *I have chosen to focus my discussion on a single work.* ◇ *~ of sth Her article is a discussion of the methods used in research.*

▼ **SYNONYMS**
**discussion**
conversation • dialogue • talk • debate • consultation • chat • gossip

These are all words for an occasion when people talk about sth.

**discussion** a detailed conversation about sth that is considered to be important: *Discussions are still taking place between the two leaders.*

**conversation** a talk, usually a private or informal one, involving two people or a small group; the activity of talking in this way: *a telephone conversation*

**dialogue** conversations in a book, play or film: *The novel has long descriptions and not much dialogue.* A **dialogue** is also a formal discussion between two groups, especially when they are trying to solve a problem or end a dispute: *The President told waiting reporters there had been a constructive dialogue.*

**talk** a conversation or discussion, often one about a problem or sth important for the people involved: *I had a long talk with my boss about my career prospects.*

**debate** a formal discussion of an issue at a public meeting or in a parliament. In a debate two or more speakers express opposing views and then there is often a vote on the issue: *a debate on prison reform*

**consultation** a formal discussion between groups of people before a decision is made about sth: *There have been extensive consultations between the two countries.*

**chat** a friendly informal conversation; informal talking. NOTE The countable use of **chat** is especially British English: *I just called in for a chat about the kids.*

**gossip** a conversation about other people and their private lives: *We had a good gossip about the boss.*

PATTERNS
• a discussion/conversation/dialogue/talk/debate/consultation/chat/gossip **about** sth
• a discussion/conversation/dialogue/debate/consultation **on** sth
• **in (close)** discussion/conversation/dialogue/debate/consultation **with** sb
• to **have** a discussion/conversation/dialogue/talk/debate/consultation/chat/gossip **with** sb
• to **hold** a discussion/conversation/debate/consultation

**disˈcussion board** *noun* = MESSAGE BOARD

**dis·dain** /dɪsˈdeɪn/ *noun, verb*
▪ *noun* [U, sing.] the feeling that sb/sth is not good enough to deserve your respect or attention SYN **contempt: with ~** *She treated him with disdain.* ◇ **in ~** *He turned his head away in disdain.* ◇ **~ for sb/sth** *a disdain for the law*

443    **disembark**

▪ *verb* (*formal*) **1** *~ sb/sth* to think that sb/sth is not good enough to deserve your respect: *She disdained his offer of help.* **2** *~ to do sth* to refuse to do sth because you think that you are too important to do it: *He disdained to turn to his son for advice.*

**dis·dain·ful** /dɪsˈdeɪnfl/ *adj.* **~ (of sb/sth)** showing the feeling that sb/sth is not good enough to deserve your respect or attention SYN **contemptuous, dismissive**: *She's always been disdainful of people who haven't been to college.* ▶ **dis·dain·ful·ly** /-fəli/ *adv*

**dis·ease** 🄾 🄰🄰 /dɪˈziːz/ *noun* **1** 🄰🄰 [U, C] an illness affecting humans, animals or plants, often caused by infection: *heart/lung/liver disease* ◇ *an infectious disease* ◇ *health measures to prevent the spread of disease* ◇ *Smoking increases the risk of heart disease.* ◇ *It is not known what causes the disease.* ◇ *He suffers from a rare blood disease.* ◇ *Sailors who ate no fresh food contracted the disease.* ◇ *to treat/cure a disease* ◇ *to spread/transmit a disease* ⊃ WORDFINDER NOTE at CURE

WORDFINDER bacteria, epidemic, fever, illness, immunity, infection, spread, vaccinate, virus

**2** [C] (*formal*) something that is very wrong with people's attitudes, way of life or with society: *Greed is a disease of modern society.*

▼ **SYNONYMS**
**disease**
illness • disorder • infection • condition • ailment • bug

These are all words for a medical problem.

**disease** a medical problem affecting humans, animals or plants, often caused by infection: *He suffers from a rare blood disease.*

**illness** a medical problem, or a period of suffering from one: *She died after a long illness.*

DISEASE OR ILLNESS?
**Disease** is used to talk about more severe physical medical problems, especially those that affect the organs. **Illness** is used to talk about both more severe and more minor medical problems, and those that affect mental health: *heart/kidney/liver illness* ◇ *mental disease.* **Disease** is not used about a period of illness: *She died after a long disease.*

**disorder** (*rather formal*) an illness that causes a part of the body to stop functioning correctly: *a rare disorder of the liver.* NOTE A **disorder** is generally not infectious. **Disorder** is used most frequently with words relating to mental problems, for example *psychiatric personality, mental* and *eating*. When it is used to talk about physical problems, it is most often used with *blood, bowel* and *kidney*, and these are commonly *serious, severe* or *rare*.

**infection** an illness that is caused by bacteria or a virus and that affects one part of the body: *a throat infection*

**condition** a medical problem that you have for a long time because it is not possible to cure it: *a heart condition*

**ailment** (*rather formal*) an illness that is not very serious: *childhood ailments*

**bug** (*informal*) an infectious illness that is usually fairly mild: *a nasty flu bug*

PATTERNS
• to **have/suffer from** a(n) disease/illness/disorder/infection/condition/ailment/bug
• to **catch/contract/get/pick up** a(n) disease/illness/infection/bug

**dis·eased** /dɪˈziːzd/ *adj.* suffering from a disease: *diseased tissue* ◇ *the diseased social system*

**dis·em·bark** /ˌdɪsɪmˈbɑːk; *NAmE* -ˈbɑːrk/ *verb* [I, T] (*formal*) to leave a vehicle, especially a ship or an aircraft, at the end of a journey; to let or make people leave a vehicle: *We will be disembarking at midday.* ◇ *~ (from) sth They had just disembarked from their tour bus after a 12-hour*

# disembodied

*journey.* ◊ **~sb** *The passengers were disembarked safely.* **OPP** **embark** ▶ **dis·em·bark·ation** /ˌdɪsˌembɑːˈkeɪʃn; *NAmE* -bɑːrˈk-/ *noun* [U]

**dis·em·bod·ied** /ˌdɪsɪmˈbɒdid; *NAmE* -ˈbɑːd-/ *adj.* [usually before noun] **1** (of sounds) coming from a person or place that cannot be seen or identified: *a disembodied voice* **2** separated from the body: *disembodied spirits*

**dis·em·bowel** /ˌdɪsɪmˈbaʊəl/ *verb* (**-ll-**, *US* **-l-**) **~sb/sth** to take the stomach, BOWELS and other organs out of a person or animal ▶ **dis·em·bowel·ment** *noun* [U, C]

**dis·en·chant·ed** /ˌdɪsɪnˈtʃɑːntɪd; *NAmE* -ˈtʃæn-/ *adj.* **~(with sb/sth)** no longer feeling enthusiasm for sb/sth; not believing sth is good or worth doing **SYN** **disillusioned**: *He was becoming disenchanted with his job as a lawyer.* ▶ **dis·en·chant·ment** *noun* [U]: *a growing sense/feeling of disenchantment with his job*

**dis·en·fran·chise** /ˌdɪsɪnˈfræntʃaɪz/ *verb* [often passive] **~sb** (*formal*) to take away sb's rights, especially their right to vote **OPP** **enfranchise**

**dis·en·gage** /ˌdɪsɪnˈgeɪdʒ/ *verb* **1** [T, I] (*formal*) to free sb/sth from the person or thing that is holding them or it; to become free: **~yourself (from sb/sth)** *She gently disengaged herself from her sleeping son.* ◊ (*figurative*) *They wished to disengage themselves from these policies.* ◊ **~(sth/sb) (from sth/sb)** *to disengage the clutch* (= when driving a car) ◊ *We saw the booster rockets disengage and fall into the sea.* **2** [I, T] **~(sth)** (*specialist*) if an army **disengages** or sb **disengages** it, it stops fighting and moves away ⊃ compare ENGAGE ⊃ WORDFINDER NOTE at PEACE ▶ **dis·en·gage·ment** *noun* [U]

**dis·en·gaged** /ˌdɪsɪnˈgeɪdʒd/ *adj.* (*formal*) not involved with sb/sth or not interested in them/it: *Her father was emotionally disengaged.* ◊ **~from sb/sth** *The electorate is becoming increasingly disengaged from politics.*

**dis·en·tan·gle** /ˌdɪsɪnˈtæŋgl/ *verb* **1** **~sth (from sth)** to separate different arguments, ideas, etc. that have become confused: *It's not easy to disentangle the truth from the official statistics.* **2** **~sth/sb (from sth)** to free sb/sth from sth that has become wrapped or TWISTED around it or them: *He tried to disentangle his fingers from her hair.* ◊ (*figurative*) *She has just disentangled herself from a painful relationship.* **3** **~sth** to get rid of the TWISTS and KNOTS in sth: *He was sitting on the deck disentangling a coil of rope.* ⊃ compare ENTANGLE

**dis·equi·lib·rium** /ˌdɪsˌiːkwɪˈlɪbriəm, -ˌek-/ *noun* [U] (*formal* or *specialist*) a loss or lack of balance in a situation

**dis·es·tab·lish** /ˌdɪsɪˈstæblɪʃ/ *verb* **~sth** (*formal*) to end the official status of sth, especially a national Church: *a campaign to disestablish the Church of England* ▶ **dis·es·tab·lish·ment** *noun* [U]

**dis·favour** (*US* **dis·favor**) /dɪsˈfeɪvə(r)/ *noun* [U] (*formal*) the feeling that you do not like or approve of sb/sth: **with ~** *They looked upon the birth of a girl with disfavour.* ◊ **in/into ~(with sb)** *She seems to have fallen into disfavour with the director.*

**dis·fig·ure** /dɪsˈfɪgə(r); *NAmE* -ˈfɪgjər/ *verb* **~sb/sth** to damage the appearance of a person, thing or place: *Her face was disfigured by a long red scar.* ▶ **dis·fig·ure·ment** *noun* [U, C]: *He suffered permanent disfigurement in the fire.*

**dis·gorge** /dɪsˈgɔːdʒ; *NAmE* -ˈgɔːrdʒ/ *verb* (*formal*) **1** **~sth** to pour sth out in large quantities: *The pipe disgorges sewage into the sea.* **2** **~sb/sth** if a vehicle or building **disgorges** people, they come out of it in large numbers: *The bus disgorged a crowd of noisy children.*

**dis·grace** /dɪsˈgreɪs/ *noun, verb*
- *noun* **1** [U] the loss of other people's respect and approval because of the bad way sb has behaved **SYN** **shame**: *Her behaviour has brought disgrace on her family.* ◊ **in ~** *The swimmer was sent home from the Olympics in disgrace.* ◊ **in ~ with sb** *Sam was in disgrace with his parents.* ◊ **~in doing sth** *There is no disgrace in being poor.* **2** [sing.] a person or thing that is so bad that people connected with them or it feel or should feel ashamed: *Your homework is an absolute disgrace.* ◊ *The state of our roads is a national disgrace.* ◊ **a~to sb/sth** *That sort of behaviour is a disgrace to the legal profession.* ◊ *You are a disgrace to this school.* ◊ **it is a~that …** *It's a disgrace that* (= it is very wrong that) *they are paid so little.*
- *verb* **1** to behave badly in a way that makes you or other people feel ashamed: **~yourself** *I disgraced myself by drinking far too much.* ◊ **~sb/sth** *He had disgraced the family name.* **2** **be disgraced** to lose the respect of people, usually so that you lose a position of power: *He was publicly disgraced and sent into exile.*

**dis·graced** /dɪsˈgreɪst/ *adj.* having lost the respect of people, usually meaning you have also lost a position of power: *a disgraced politician/leader*

**dis·grace·ful** /dɪsˈgreɪsfl/ *adj.* very bad or unacceptable; that people should feel ashamed about: *His behaviour was absolutely disgraceful!* ◊ *It's disgraceful that none of the family tried to help her.* ◊ *a disgraceful waste of money* ▶ **dis·grace·ful·ly** /-fəli/ *adv.*

**dis·grun·tled** /dɪsˈgrʌntld/ *adj.* annoyed or disappointed because sth has happened to upset you: *disgruntled employees* ◊ **~at/with sb/sth** *I left feeling disgruntled at the way I'd been treated.*

**dis·guise** /dɪsˈgaɪz/ *verb, noun*
- *verb* **1** to change your appearance so that people cannot recognize you: **~sb** *The hijackers were heavily disguised.* ◊ **~sb as sb/sth** *They got in disguised as security guards.* ◊ **~yourself (as sb/sth)** *She disguised herself as a boy.* **2** **~sth** to hide sth or change it, so that it cannot be recognized **SYN** **conceal**: *She made no attempt to disguise her surprise.* ◊ *It was a thinly disguised attack on the president.* ◊ *She couldn't disguise the fact that she felt uncomfortable.* ⊃ SYNONYMS at HIDE
- *noun* **1** [C, U] something that you wear or use to change your appearance so that people do not recognize you: *She wore glasses and a wig as a disguise.* ◊ **in~** *The star travelled in disguise* (= wearing a disguise) **2** [U] the art of changing your appearance so that people do not recognize you: *He is a master of disguise.* **3** [C, U] a way of hiding the true nature of sth: *His angelic look is just a disguise.* ◊ **in~** *Her books can be history lessons in disguise.* **IDM** see BLESSING

**dis·gust** /dɪsˈɡʌst/ *noun, verb*
- *noun* [U] a strong feeling of dislike for sb/sth that you feel is unacceptable, or for sth that looks, smells, etc. unpleasant: *The film fills me with disgust.* ◊ *I can only feel disgust for these criminals.* ◊ **~at/with sth** *She expressed her disgust at the programme in a tweet.* ◊ **in~** *He walked away in disgust* ◊ *She wrinkled her nose in disgust at the smell.* ◊ **with~** *He regarded the cubes of fat with disgust.* ◊ **to sb's~** *Much to my disgust, they refused to help.*
- *verb* **~sb** if sth **disgusts** you, it makes you feel shocked and almost sick because it is so unpleasant: *The level of violence in the film really disgusted me.*

**dis·gust·ed** /dɪsˈɡʌstɪd/ *adj.* feeling or showing DISGUST: **~(at/by sb/sth)** *I was disgusted at/by the sight.* ◊ **~(with sb/sth/yourself)** *I was disgusted with myself for eating so much.* ◊ **~(to see, hear, etc…)** *He was disgusted to see such awful living conditions.* ▶ **dis·gust·ed·ly** *adv.*: *'This champagne is warm!', he said disgustedly.*

**dis·gust·ing** /dɪsˈɡʌstɪŋ/ *adj.* **1** extremely unpleasant **SYN** **revolting**: *The kitchen was in a disgusting state when she left.* ◊ *What a disgusting smell!* **2** making you feel shocked, upset or angry **SYN** **despicable, outrageous**: *I think it's disgusting that they're closing the local hospital.* ◊ *His language is disgusting* (= he uses a lot of offensive words).

**dis·gust·ing·ly** /dɪsˈɡʌstɪŋli/ *adv.* **1** (*sometimes humorous*) extremely (in a way that other people feel JEALOUS of): *He looked disgustingly healthy when he got back from the Bahamas.* **2** in a way that makes people feel shocked, upset or angry: *disgustingly dirty*

**dish** /dɪʃ/ *noun, verb*
- *noun* **1** [C] a flat shallow container for cooking food in or serving it from: *a baking/serving dish* ◊ **in a~** *Bake in a shallow dish for 45 mins.* ◊ **~of sth** *They helped themselves*

▼ **SYNONYMS**

### disgusting

foul • revolting • repulsive • offensive • gross

These words all describe sth, especially a smell, taste or habit, that is extremely unpleasant and often makes you feel slightly ill.

**disgusting** extremely unpleasant and making you feel slightly ill: *What a disgusting smell!*

**foul** dirty, and tasting or smelling bad: *She could smell his foul breath.*

**revolting** extremely unpleasant and making you feel slightly ill: *The stew looked revolting.*

DISGUSTING OR REVOLTING?

Both of these words are used to describe things that smell and taste unpleasant, unpleasant personal habits and people who have them. There is no real difference in meaning, but **disgusting** is more frequent, especially in spoken English.

**repulsive** (*rather formal*) extremely unpleasant in a way that offends you or makes you feel slightly ill. NOTE Repulsive usually describes people, their behaviour or habits, which you may find offensive for physical or moral reasons.

**offensive** (*formal*) (especially of smells) extremely unpleasant.

**gross** (*informal*) (of a smell, taste or personal habit) extremely unpleasant.

PATTERNS
- disgusting/repulsive/offensive **to** sb
- **to find** sb/sth disgusting/revolting/repulsive/offensive
- **to smell/taste** disgusting/foul/gross
- a(n) disgusting/foul/revolting/offensive/gross **smell**
- a disgusting/revolting/gross **habit**
- disgusting/offensive/gross **behaviour**
- a disgusting/revolting/repulsive **man/woman/person**

---

*from a large dish of pasta.* **2** ♀ A1 *often* **the dishes** [pl.] the plates, bowls, cups, etc. that have been used for a meal and need to be washed: *I'll do the dishes* (= wash them). ◇ *My first real job was washing dishes in a restaurant.* **3** ♀ A1 [C] food prepared in a particular way as part of a meal: *a vegetarian/fish/meat/pasta dish* ◇ *This makes an excellent hot main dish.* ◇ *to cook/prepare/serve a dish* ◇ **of sth** *a savoury dish of curried rice and lamb* ⊃ see also SIDE DISH **4** [C] any object that is like a dish or bowl in shape: *a soap dish* ⊃ see also EVAPORATING DISH, PETRI DISH, SATELLITE DISH **5** [C] (*old-fashioned, informal*) a sexually attractive person: *What a dish!*
■ *verb*
IDM **dish the 'dirt (on sb)** (*informal*) to tell people unkind or unpleasant things about sb, especially about their private life **dish it 'out** (*disapproving, informal*) to criticize other people: *He enjoys dishing it out, but he really can't take it* (= cannot accept criticism from other people).
PHRV **dish sth↔'out 1** (*informal*) to give sth, often to a lot of people or in large amounts: *Students dished out leaflets to passers-by.* ◇ *She's always dishing out advice, even when you don't want it.* **2** to serve food onto plates for a meal: *Can you dish out the potatoes, please?* | **dish 'up** | **dish sth↔'up** to serve food onto plates for a meal **dish sth↔'up** to offer sth to sb, especially sth that is not very good

**dis·har·mony** /dɪsˈhɑːməni; *NAmE* -ˈhɑːr-/ *noun* [U] (*formal*) a lack of agreement about important things, which causes bad feelings between groups of people: *marital/racial/social disharmony* OPP harmony

**dish·cloth** /ˈdɪʃklɒθ; *NAmE* -klɔːθ/ (*NAmE usually* **dish-rag**) *noun* a cloth for washing dishes

**dis·heart·en** /dɪsˈhɑːtn; *NAmE* -ˈhɑːrtn/ *verb* ~ **sb** to make sb lose hope or confidence SYN discourage: *Don't let this defeat dishearten you.* ▶ **dis·heart·ened** *adj.*: *a disheartened team* **dis·heart·en·ing** *adj.*: *a disheartening experience*

---

445

# disinformation

**dish·ev·elled** /dɪˈʃevld/ (*especially BrE*) (*NAmE usually* **dish·ev·eled**) *adj.* (of hair, clothes or sb's general appearance) very untidy SYN unkempt: *He looked tired and dishevelled.*

**dis·hon·est** ❶ B2 /dɪsˈɒnɪst; *NAmE* -ˈɑːn-/ *adj.* not honest; intending to trick people: *Beware of dishonest traders in the tourist areas.* ◇ **with sb** *She has been dishonest with voters.* ◇ **about sth** *He has been dishonest about his age and academic qualifications.* OPP honest ▶ **dis·hon·est·ly** *adv.* **dis·hon·esty** *noun* [U]

**dis·hon·our** (*US* **dis·honor**) /dɪsˈɒnə(r); *NAmE* -ˈɑːn-/ *noun, verb*
■ *noun* [U] (*formal*) a loss of honour or respect because you have done sth unacceptable or morally wrong
■ *verb* (*formal*) **1** ~ **sb/sth** to make sb/sth lose the respect of other people: *You have dishonoured the name of the school.* **2** ~ **sth** to refuse to keep an agreement or a promise: *He had dishonoured nearly all of his election pledges.* OPP honour

**dis·hon·our·able** (*US* **dis·hon·or·able**) /dɪsˈɒnərəbl; *NAmE* -ˈɑːn-/ *adj.* not deserving respect; unacceptable or morally wrong: *It would have been dishonourable of her not to keep her promise.* ◇ *He was given a* **dishonourable discharge** (= an order to leave the army for unacceptable behaviour). OPP honourable ▶ **dis·hon·our·ably** /-bli/ *adv.*

**dish·rag** /ˈdɪʃræɡ/ (*NAmE*) (*BrE* **dish·cloth**) *noun* a cloth for washing dishes

**dish·towel** /ˈdɪʃtaʊəl/ (*NAmE*) (*BrE* **ˈtea towel, ˈtea cloth**) *noun* a small towel used for drying cups, plates, knives, etc. after they have been washed

**dish·wash·er** /ˈdɪʃwɒʃə(r); *NAmE* -wɔːʃ-/ *noun* **1** a machine for washing plates, cups, etc: *to load/stack the dishwasher* **2** a person whose job is to wash plates, etc., for example in a restaurant

**ˈdishwashing liquid** (*NAmE*) (*BrE* **ˌwashing-ˈup liquid**) *noun* [U] liquid soap for washing dishes, pans, etc.

**dish·water** /ˈdɪʃwɔːtə(r)/ *noun* [U] water that sb has used to wash dirty plates, etc. IDM see DULL *adj.*

**dishy** /ˈdɪʃi/ *adj.* (**dish·ier, dishi·est**) (*especially BrE, old-fashioned, informal*) (of a person) physically attractive

**dis·il·lu·sion** /ˌdɪsɪˈluːʒn/ *verb* ~ **sb** to destroy sb's belief in or good opinion of sb/sth: *I hate to disillusion you, but not everyone is as honest as you.* ▶ **dis·il·lu·sion** *noun* [U] = DISILLUSIONMENT

**dis·il·lu·sioned** /ˌdɪsɪˈluːʒnd/ *adj.* ~ **(by/with sb/sth)** disappointed because the person you admired or the idea you believed to be good and true now seems without value SYN disenchanted: *I soon became disillusioned with the job.*

**dis·il·lu·sion·ment** /ˌdɪsɪˈluːʒnmənt/ (*also* **dis·il·lu·sion**) *noun* [U, sing.] ~ **(with sth)** the state of being disillusioned SYN disenchantment: *There is widespread disillusionment with the present government.*

**dis·in·cen·tive** /ˌdɪsɪnˈsentɪv/ *noun* [C] a thing that makes sb less willing to do sth OPP incentive

**dis·in·clin·ation** /ˌdɪsˌɪnklɪˈneɪʃn/ *noun* [sing., U] (*formal*) a lack of desire to do sth; a lack of enthusiasm for sth: *There was a general disinclination to return to the office after lunch.*

**dis·in·clined** /ˌdɪsɪnˈklaɪnd/ *adj.* [not before noun] ~ **(to do sth)** (*formal*) not willing SYN reluctant: *He was strongly disinclined to believe anything that she said.*

**dis·in·fect** /ˌdɪsɪnˈfekt/ *verb* **1** ~ **sth** to clean sth using a substance that kills bacteria: *to disinfect a surface/room/wound* **2** ~ **sth** to run a computer program to get rid of a computer virus ▶ **dis·in·fec·tion** /-ˈfekʃn/ *noun* [U]

**dis·in·fect·ant** /ˌdɪsɪnˈfektənt/ *noun* [U, C] a substance that kills bacteria, used for cleaning: *a strong smell of disinfectant*

**dis·in·for·ma·tion** /ˌdɪsˌɪnfəˈmeɪʃn; *NAmE* -fərˈm-/ *noun* [U] false information that is given deliberately: *The*

# disingenuous

*government launched a campaign of propaganda and disinformation.*

**dis·in·genu·ous** /ˌdɪsɪnˈdʒenjuəs/ *adj.* [not usually before noun] (*formal*) not sincere, especially when you pretend to know less about sth than you really do: *It would be disingenuous of me to claim I had never seen it.* ⊃ compare INGENUOUS ▶ **dis·in·genu·ous·ly** *adv.*

**dis·in·herit** /ˌdɪsɪnˈherɪt/ *verb* ~ **sb** to prevent sb, especially a member of your family, from receiving your money or property after your death ⊃ compare INHERIT (1)

**dis·in·hibit** /ˌdɪsɪnˈhɪbɪt/ *verb* ~ **sb** (*formal*) to help sb to stop feeling shy so that they can relax and show their feelings ▶ **dis·in·hib·ition** /ˌdɪsɪnhɪˈbɪʃn/ *noun* [U]

**dis·in·te·grate** /dɪsˈɪntɪɡreɪt/ *verb* **1** [I] to break into small parts or pieces and be destroyed: *The plane disintegrated as it fell into the sea.* **2** [I] to become much less strong or united and be gradually destroyed **SYN** **fall apart**: *The authority of the central government was rapidly disintegrating.* ▶ **dis·in·te·gra·tion** /dɪsˌɪntɪˈɡreɪʃn/ *noun* [U]: *the gradual disintegration of traditional values*

**dis·in·ter** /ˌdɪsɪnˈtɜː(r)/ *verb* (-rr-) (*formal*) **1** ~ **sth** to dig up sth, especially a dead body, from the ground **OPP** **inter** **2** ~ **sth (from sth)** to find sth that has been hidden or lost for a long time

**dis·in·ter·est** /dɪsˈɪntrəst, -trest/ *noun* [U] ~ **(in sth)** lack of interest: *His total disinterest in money puzzled his family.*

**dis·in·ter·est·ed** /dɪsˈɪntrəstɪd, -tres-/ *adj.* **1** not influenced by personal feelings, or by the chance of getting some advantage for yourself **SYN** **impartial, objective, unbiased**: *a disinterested onlooker/spectator* ◇ *Her advice appeared to be disinterested.* **2** (*informal*) not interested ⊃ note at INTERESTED ▶ **dis·in·ter·est·ed·ly** *adv.*

**dis·in·vest** /ˌdɪsɪnˈvest/ *verb* [I] ~ **(from sth)** (*business*) to stop investing money in a company, an industry or a country; to reduce the amount of money invested

**dis·in·vest·ment** /ˌdɪsɪnˈvestmənt/ *noun* [U] (*finance*) the process of reducing the amount of money that you have invested in a particular company, industry, etc.

**dis·joint·ed** /dɪsˈdʒɔɪntɪd/ *adj.* not communicated or described in a clear or logical way; not connected **SYN** **disconnected, incoherent**

**dis·junc·tion** /dɪsˈdʒʌŋkʃn/ (*also less frequent* **dis·junc·ture** /dɪsˈdʒʌŋktʃə(r)/) *noun* ~ **(between A and B)** (*formal*) a difference between two things that you would expect to be in agreement with each other

**disk** **①** **B2** /dɪsk/ *noun* **1** **B2** (*especially NAmE*) (*BrE usually* **disc**) a thin flat round object: *Red blood cells are roughly the shape of a disk.* **2** **B2** (*also* **magnetic 'disk**) (*computing*) a device for storing information on a computer, in the shape of a round flat plate that SPINS (= turns) to give access to all parts of its MAGNETIC surface, which records information received in electronic form ⊃ see also HARD DISK

**'disk drive** *noun* a device that passes data between a disk and the memory of a computer or from one disk or computer to another

**'disk jockey** (*NAmE*) = DISC JOCKEY

**dis·like** **①** **B1** /dɪsˈlaɪk/ *verb, noun*

- *verb* **B1** (*rather formal*) to not like sb/sth: ~ **sb/sth** *Why do you dislike him so much?* ◇ ~ **doing sth** *I dislike being away from my family.* ◇ **Much as she disliked** *going to funerals (= although she did not like it at all), she knew she had to be there.* ◇ ~ **sb/sth doing sth** *He disliked her staying away from home.* ◇ ~ **it when …** *He disliked it when she behaved badly in front of his mother.* ◇ ~ **sth about sb/sth** *What did you dislike about the movie?* ⊃ SYNONYMS at HATE **OPP** **like**
- *noun* **1** **B1** [U, sing.] a feeling of not liking sb/sth: ~ **of/for sb/sth** *He did not try to hide his dislike of his boss.* ◇ ~ **to sb/sth** *She took an instant dislike to the house and the neighbourhood.* **2** **B1** [C, usually pl.] a thing that you do not like: *I've told you all my likes and dislikes.*

**dis·lo·cate** /ˈdɪsləkeɪt; *NAmE* -loʊk-, dɪsˈloʊkeɪt/ *verb* **1** ~ **sth** to put a bone out of its normal position in a JOINT: *He dislocated his shoulder in the accident.* ◇ *a dislocated finger* **2** ~ **sth** to stop a system, plan etc. from working or continuing in the normal way **SYN** **disrupt** ▶ **dis·lo·ca·tion** /ˌdɪsləˈkeɪʃn; *NAmE* -loʊˈk-/ *noun* [C, U]: *a dislocation of the shoulder* ◇ *These policies could cause severe economic and social dislocation.*

**dis·lodge** /dɪsˈlɒdʒ; *NAmE* -ˈlɑːdʒ/ *verb* (*formal*) **1** ~ **sth (from sth)** to force or knock sth out of its position: *The wind dislodged one or two tiles from the roof.* **2** ~ **sb (from sth)** to force sb to leave a place, position or job: *The rebels have so far failed to dislodge the President.*

**dis·loyal** /dɪsˈlɔɪəl/ *adj.* ~ **(to sb/sth)** not LOYAL to (= not supporting) your friends, family, country, etc: *He was accused of being disloyal to the government.* ▶ **dis·loy·alty** /-ti/ *noun* [U]

**dis·mal** /ˈdɪzməl/ *adj.* **1** causing or showing the feeling of being sad **SYN** **gloomy, miserable**: *dismal conditions/surroundings/weather* **2** (*informal*) not successful; of very low quality: *The singer gave a dismal performance of some old songs.* ◇ *Their recent attempt to increase sales has been a dismal failure.* ▶ **dis·mal·ly** /-məli/ *adv.*: *I tried not to laugh but failed dismally (= was completely unsuccessful).*

**dis·man·tle** /dɪsˈmæntl/ *verb* **1** ~ **sth** to take apart a machine or structure so that it is in separate pieces: *I had to dismantle the engine in order to repair it.* ◇ *The steel mill was dismantled piece by piece.* **2** ~ **sth** to end an organization or a system gradually in an organized way: *The government was in the process of dismantling the state-owned industries.* ▶ **dis·mant·ling** *noun* [U] **dis·man·tle·ment** *noun* [U]

**dis·may** /dɪsˈmeɪ/ *noun, verb*

- *noun* [U] a worried, sad feeling after you have received an unpleasant surprise: ~ **at sth** *She could not hide her dismay at the result.* ◇ **in** ~ *He looked at her in dismay.* ◇ **with** ~ *I read of her resignation with some dismay.* ◇ **to sb's** ~ *To her dismay, her name was not on the list.*
- *verb* ~ **sb** to make sb feel shocked and disappointed: *Their reaction dismayed him.* ▶ **dis·mayed** *adj.*: ~ **(at/by sth)** *He was dismayed at the change in his old friend.* ◇ *The suggestion was greeted by a dismayed silence.* ◇ ~ **(to find, hear, see, etc …)** *They were dismayed to find that the ferry had already left.*

**dis·mem·ber** /dɪsˈmembə(r)/ *verb* **1** ~ **sth** to cut or tear the dead body of a person or an animal into pieces **2** ~ **sth** (*formal*) to divide a country, an organization, etc. into smaller parts ▶ **dis·mem·ber·ment** *noun* [U]

**dis·miss** **①** **B2** /dɪsˈmɪs/ *verb* **1** **B2** to decide that sb/sth is not important and not worth thinking or talking about **SYN** **wave sth↔aside/away**: ~ **sb/sth** *to dismiss a suggestion/a claim/an idea* ◇ *The criticisms were summarily dismissed by the government.* ◇ ~ **sb/sth as sth** *He dismissed the opinion polls as worthless.* ◇ *The suggestion should not be dismissed out of hand (= without thinking about it).* **2** **B2** to put thoughts or feelings out of your mind: ~ **sth** *Dismissing her fears, she climbed higher.* ◇ ~ **sb/sth from sth** *He dismissed her from his mind.* **3** **B2** ~ **sb (from sth)** to officially remove sb from their job **SYN** **fire, sack**: *She claims she was unfairly dismissed from her post.* ⊃ WORDFINDER NOTE at EMPLOY **4** ~ **sb** to send sb away or allow them to leave: *At 12 o'clock the class was dismissed.* **5** ~ **sth** (*law*) to say that a trial or legal case should not continue, usually because there is not enough evidence: *The judge dismissed the case for lack of evidence.* **6** ~ **sb** (in CRICKET) to end the INNINGS of a player or team

**dis·missal** **①** **C1** /dɪsˈmɪsl/ *noun* **1** **C1** [U, C] the act of dismissing sb from their job; an example of this: *He still hopes to win his claim against unfair dismissal.* ◇ *The dismissals followed the resignation of the chairman.* ⊃ see also CONSTRUCTIVE DISMISSAL **2** **C1** [U] the failure to consider sth as important: *Her casual dismissal of the threats seemed irresponsible.* **3** [U, C] (*law*) the act of not allowing a trial or legal case to continue, usually because there is not enough evidence: *the dismissal of the appeal* **4** [U, C] the act of sending sb away or allowing them to leave **5** [U, C] (in CRICKET) the end of the INNINGS of a player or team

**dis·mis·sive** /dɪsˈmɪsɪv/ *adj.* ~ **(of sb/sth)** showing that you do not believe a person or thing to be important or worth considering **SYN** **disdainful**: *a dismissive gesture/tone* ▶ **dis·mis·sive·ly** *adv.*: *to shrug/wave dismissively*

**dis·mount** *verb, noun*
- *verb* /dɪsˈmaʊnt/ [I] (*formal*) ~ **(from sth)** to get off a horse, bicycle or motorcycle **OPP** **mount** ⇒ **WORDFINDER NOTE** at CYCLING
- *noun* /ˈdɪsmaʊnt/ a move in which a GYMNAST jumps off a piece of equipment or finishes a set of exercises

**dis·obedi·ence** /ˌdɪsəˈbiːdiəns/ *noun* [U] the act of failing or refusing to obey: *an act of disobedience* ◊ ~ **to sb/sth** *their disobedience to the king* ⇒ see also CIVIL DISOBEDIENCE **OPP** **obedience**

**dis·obedi·ent** /ˌdɪsəˈbiːdiənt/ *adj.* failing or refusing to obey: *a disobedient child* ◊ ~ **to sb/sth** *I was very disobedient to my father.* **OPP** **obedient**

**dis·obey** /ˌdɪsəˈbeɪ/ *verb* [T, I] ~ **(sb/sth)** to refuse to do what a person, a law, an order, etc. tells you to do; to refuse to obey: *He was punished for disobeying orders.* **OPP** **obey**

**dis·obli·ging** /ˌdɪsəˈblaɪdʒɪŋ/ *adj.* (*formal*) deliberately not helpful: *a disobliging manner*

**dis·order** /dɪsˈɔːdə(r); NAmE -ˈɔːrd-/ *noun* 1 [C, U] (*medical*) an illness that causes a part of the body to stop functioning correctly: *a blood/bowel disorder* ◊ *eating disorders* ◊ *He was suffering from some form of psychiatric disorder.* ⇒ see also ATTENTION DEFICIT DISORDER, BIPOLAR DISORDER, PERSONALITY DISORDER, POST-TRAUMATIC STRESS DISORDER, SEASONAL AFFECTIVE DISORDER ⇒ SYNONYMS at DISEASE 2 [U] (*formal*) an untidy state; a lack of order or organization: *The room was in a state of disorder.* ◊ **in (…)** ~ *His financial affairs were in complete disorder.* **OPP** **order** 3 [U] (*formal*) violent behaviour of large groups of people: *an outbreak of rioting and* **public disorder** ⇒ compare ORDER

**dis·ordered** /dɪsˈɔːdəd; NAmE -ˈɔːrdərd/ *adj.* 1 showing a lack of order or control: *disordered hair* ◊ *a disordered state* **OPP** **ordered** 2 (*medical*) suffering from a mental or physical disorder: *emotionally disordered children*

**dis·order·ly** /dɪsˈɔːdəli; NAmE -ˈɔːrdərli/ *adj.* [usually before noun] (*formal*) 1 (of people or behaviour) showing lack of control; publicly noisy or violent 2 untidy: *newspapers in a disorderly pile by the door* **OPP** **orderly** **IDM** see DRUNK *adj.*

**dis·orderly ˈconduct** *noun* [U] (*law*) the crime of being noisy or violent in a public place

**dis·or·gan·ized** (*BrE also* **-ised**) /dɪsˈɔːɡənaɪzd; NAmE -ˈɔːrɡ-/ (*also less frequent* **un·or·gan·ized, -ised**) *adj.* badly planned; not able to plan or organize well: *It was a hectic disorganized weekend.* ◊ *She's so disorganized.* ⇒ compare ORGANIZED ▶ **dis·or·gan·iza·tion, -isa·tion** /dɪsˌɔːɡənaɪˈzeɪʃn; NAmE -ˌɔːrɡənəˈz-/ *noun* [U]

**dis·orien·tate** /dɪsˈɔːriənteɪt/ (*BrE*) (*also* **dis·orient** /dɪsˈɔːrient/; *NAmE, BrE*) *verb* 1 ~ **sb** to make sb unable to recognize where they are or where they should go: *The darkness had disorientated him.* 2 ~ **sb** to make sb feel confused: *Ex-soldiers can be disorientated by the transition to civilian life.* ⇒ compare ORIENT ▶ **dis·orien·tated** (*also* **dis·orient·ed** /-entɪd/) *adj.*: *She felt shocked and totally disorientated.* **dis·orien·ta·tion** /dɪsˌɔːriənˈteɪʃn/ *noun* [U]

**dis·own** /dɪsˈəʊn/ *verb* ~ **sb/sth** to decide that you no longer want to be connected with or responsible for sb/sth: *Her family disowned her for marrying a foreigner.*

**dis·par·age** /dɪˈspærɪdʒ/ *verb* ~ **sb/sth** (*formal*) to suggest that sb/sth is not important or valuable **SYN** **belittle**: *I don't mean to disparage your achievements.* ▶ **dis·par·age·ment** *noun* [U] **dis·para·ging** *adj.*: *disparaging remarks* **dis·para·ging·ly** *adv.*: *He spoke disparagingly of his colleagues.*

**dis·par·ate** /ˈdɪspərət/ *adj.* (*formal*) 1 made up of parts or people that are very different from each other: *a disparate group of individuals* 2 (of two or more things) so different from each other that they cannot be compared or cannot work together

447 **dispenser**

**dis·par·ity** /dɪˈspærəti/ *noun* [U, C] (*pl.* **-ies**) (*formal*) a difference, especially one connected with unfair treatment: ~ **between A and B** *the wide disparity between rich and poor* ◊ ~ **(in sth)**

**dis·pas·sion·ate** /dɪsˈpæʃənət/ *adj.* (*approving*) not influenced by emotion **SYN** **impartial**: *taking a calm, dispassionate view of the situation* ◊ *a dispassionate observer* ▶ **dis·pas·sion·ate·ly** *adv.*

**dis·patch** (*BrE also* **des·patch**) /dɪˈspætʃ/ *verb, noun*
- *verb* 1 ~ **sb/sth (to …)** (*formal*) to send sb/sth somewhere, especially for a special purpose: *Troops have been dispatched to the area.* ◊ *A courier was dispatched to collect the documents.* 2 ~ **sth (to sb/sth)** (*formal*) to send a letter, package or message somewhere: *Goods are dispatched within 24 hours of your order reaching us.* 3 ~ **sb/sth** (*formal*) to deal or finish with sb/sth quickly and completely: *He dispatched the younger player in straight sets.* 4 ~ **sb/sth** (*old-fashioned*) to kill a person or an animal
- *noun* 1 [U] (*formal*) the act of sending sb/sth somewhere: *More food supplies are ready for immediate dispatch.* 2 [C] a message or report sent quickly from one military officer to another or between government officials 3 [C] a report sent to a newspaper by a journalist who is working in a foreign country: *dispatches from the war zone* **IDM** **with diˈspatch** (*formal*) quickly and efficiently

**diˈspatch box** (*also* **deˈspatch box**) *noun* (*BrE*) 1 [C] a container for carrying official documents 2 **the Dispatch Box** [sing.] a box on a table in the centre of the House of Commons in the British parliament, which ministers stand next to when they speak

**dis·patch·er** /dɪˈspætʃə(r)/ *noun* a person whose job is to send vehicles to where they are needed

**diˈspatch rider** (*also* **deˈspatch rider**) *noun* (*both BrE*) a person whose job is to carry messages or packages by motorcycle

**dis·pel** /dɪˈspel/ *verb* (**-ll-**) ~ **sth** to make sth, especially a feeling or belief, go away or disappear: *His speech dispelled any fears about his health.*

**dis·pens·able** /dɪˈspensəbl/ *adj.* [not usually before noun] not necessary; that can be got rid of: *They looked on music and art lessons as dispensable.* **OPP** **essential, indispensable**

**dis·pens·ary** /dɪˈspensəri/ *noun* (*pl.* **-ies**) 1 a place in a hospital, shop, etc. where medicines are prepared for patients 2 (*old-fashioned*) a place where patients are treated, especially one run by a charity

**dis·pen·sa·tion** /ˌdɪspenˈseɪʃn/ *noun* 1 [C, U] special permission to do sth that is not usually allowed or legal: *She needed a special dispensation to remarry.* ◊ *The sport's ruling body gave him dispensation to compete in national competitions.* 2 [U] (*formal*) the act or process of providing sth, especially by sb in authority: *the dispensation of justice* 3 [C] (*specialist*) a political or religious system that operates in a country at a particular time

**dis·pense** /dɪˈspens/ *verb* 1 ~ **sth (to sb)** (*formal*) to give out sth to people: *The machine dispenses a range of drinks and snacks.* 2 ~ **sth (to sb)** (*formal*) to provide sth, especially a service, for people: *The organization dispenses free healthcare to the poor.* ◊ *to dispense justice/advice* 3 ~ **sth** to prepare medicine and give it to people, as a job: *to dispense a prescription* ◊ (*BrE*) *to dispense medicine* ◊ (*BrE*) *a dispensing chemist* ⇒ **WORDFINDER NOTE** at MEDICINE **PHRV** **diˈspense with sb/sth** to stop using sb/sth because you no longer need them or it **SYN** **do away with**: *Debit cards dispense with the need for cash altogether.* ◊ *I think we can dispense with the formalities* (= speak openly and naturally to each other).

**dis·pens·er** /dɪˈspensə(r)/ *noun* 1 a machine or container holding money, drinks, paper towels, etc. that you can obtain quickly, for example by pulling a handle or pressing buttons: *a soap dispenser* ⇒ see also CASH DISPENSER 2 (*formal*) a person who provides sth for people: *He saw himself as a dispenser of justice.* 3 a person who prepares medicines in a dispensary

## dispensing chemist 448

**dis·pensing chemist** noun (BrE) = CHEMIST (1)

**dis·pensing op·tician** noun (BrE) = OPTICIAN (2)

**dis·pers·al** /dɪˈspɜːsl; NAmE -ˈspɜːrsl/ noun [U, C] (formal) the process of sending sb/sth in different directions; the process of spreading sth over a wide area: *police trained in crowd dispersal* ◊ *the dispersal of seeds*

**dis·perse** /dɪˈspɜːs; NAmE -ˈspɜːrs/ verb **1** [I, T] to move apart and go away in different directions; to make sb/sth do this: *The fog began to disperse.* ◊ *The crowd dispersed quickly.* ◊ **~sb/sth** *Police dispersed the protesters with tear gas.* **2** [T, I] **~(sth)** to spread or to make sth spread over a wide area SYN **scatter**: *The seeds are dispersed by the wind.*

**dis·per·sion** /dɪˈspɜːʃn; NAmE -ˈspɜːrʒn/ noun [U] (specialist) the process by which people or things are spread over a wide area

**dis·pir·it·ed** /dɪˈspɪrɪtɪd/ adj. having no hope or enthusiasm: *She looked tired and dispirited.* ⇨ compare SPIRITED

**dis·pir·it·ing** /dɪˈspɪrɪtɪŋ/ adj. making sb lose their hope or enthusiasm: *a dispiriting experience/failure* ▸ **dis·pir·it·ing·ly** adv.

**dis·place** /dɪˈspleɪs/ verb [often passive] (formal) **1** **~sb/sth** to take the place of sb/sth SYN **replace**: *be displaced (by sb/sth) Gradually factory workers have been displaced by machines.* **2** **~sb/sth** to force people to move away from their home to another place: *be displaced (by sth) Around 10000 people have been displaced by the fighting.* **3** to move sth from its usual position: *be displaced (by sth) Check for roof tiles that have been displaced by the wind.* **4** **~sb** (especially NAmE) to remove sb from a job or position: *displaced workers* **5** **~sth** (physics) (especially of a ship) to take the place of an amount of liquid when put or floating in it, used as a way of measuring size: *The ship displaces 58 000 tonnes.*

**dis·placed ˈperson** noun (pl. **displaced persons**) (specialist) a person who has been forced to leave their country or home, because of war or cruel treatment SYN **refugee**

**dis·place·ment** /dɪsˈpleɪsmənt/ noun [U] **1** (formal) the act of forcing sb/sth away from their home or position: *the largest displacement of civilian population since World War Two* **2** [C] (physics) the amount of a liquid moved out of place by sth floating or put in it, especially a ship floating in water: *a ship with a displacement of 10 000 tonnes*

**dis·placement activity** noun [U, C] **1** things that you do in order to avoid doing what you are supposed to be doing **2** (biology, psychology) behaviour in animals or humans that does not seem to be useful in the situation in which it is performed, resulting from the presence of two opposing desires that cannot be resolved

**dis·play** /dɪˈspleɪ/ verb, noun
■ verb **1** [T] **~sth (to sb)** to put sth in a place where people can see it easily; to show sth to people SYN **exhibit**: *The exhibition gives local artists an opportunity to display their work.* ◊ *His football trophies were prominently displayed in the kitchen.* ⇨ see also PAY AND DISPLAY **2** [T] **~sth** to show a quality, feeling, skill or type of behaviour; to show signs of sth: *I have rarely seen her display any sign of emotion.* ◊ *to display your talent/skill* ◊ *These statistics display a definite trend.* **3** [T] **~sth** (of a computer, etc.) to show information: *Giant screens displayed images of cheering crowds.* ◊ *ways of displaying information on screen* **4** [I] (specialist) (of male birds and animals) to show a special pattern of behaviour that is intended to attract a female bird or animal
■ noun **1** [C] an arrangement of things in a public place to inform or entertain people or advertise sth for sale: *a beautiful floral display* ◊ *a window display* ◊ **~of sth** *a display of photographs* ◊ *a display cabinet* ⇨ WORDFINDER NOTE at SHOP **2** [C] an act of performing a skill or of showing sth happening, in order to entertain: *a spectacular firework display* ◊ **~of sth** *a stunning display of aerobatics* **3** [C] an occasion when you show a particular quality, feeling or ability by the way that you behave: *a display of affection/emotion/skill* **4** [C, U] the words, pictures, etc. shown on a computer screen; the process of showing words, pictures, etc. on a computer screen: *a high resolution colour display* ◊ *the processing and display of high volumes of information* ⇨ WORDFINDER NOTE at COMPUTER **5** [C] an electronic device for presenting words, pictures, etc: *The colour display now costs £400.* **6** [C] (specialist) a special pattern of behaviour by male birds and animals of some species that is intended to attract a female bird or animal: *Males perform courtship displays to attract mates.*
IDM **on diˈsplay** put in a place where people can look at it SYN **show**: *Designs for the new sports hall are on display in the library.* ◊ *to put sth on* **temporary/permanent display**

**dis·please** /dɪsˈpliːz/ verb **~sb** (formal) to make sb feel upset, annoyed or not satisfied OPP **please** ▸ **dis·pleased** adj.: **~(with sb/sth)** *Are you displeased with my work?* ◊ **~at sth** *She was not displeased at the effect she was having on the young man.* **dis·pleas·ing** adj.: **~(to sb/sth)** *His remarks were clearly not displeasing to her.*

**dis·pleas·ure** /dɪsˈpleʒə(r)/ noun [U] **~(at/with sb/sth)** (formal) the feeling of being upset and annoyed SYN **annoyance**: *She made no attempt to hide her displeasure at the prospect.* ⇨ compare PLEASURE

**dis·pos·able** /dɪˈspəʊzəbl/ adj. [usually before noun] **1** made to be thrown away after use: *disposable gloves/razors* ◊ (BrE) *disposable nappies* ◊ (NAmE) *disposable diapers* **2** (finance) available for use: *disposable assets/capital/resources* ◊ *a person's disposable income* (= money they are free to spend after paying taxes, etc.)

**dis·pos·ables** /dɪˈspəʊzəblz/ noun [pl.] items such as NAPPIES and CONTACT LENSES that are designed to be thrown away after use

**dis·pos·al** /dɪˈspəʊzl/ noun **1** [U] the act of getting rid of sth: *The council is responsible for* **waste disposal** *and street cleaning.* ◊ *sewage disposal systems* ◊ *the disposal of nuclear waste* ⇨ see also BOMB DISPOSAL **2** [C] (business) the sale of part of a business, property, etc. **3** [C] (NAmE) = WASTE DISPOSAL UNIT
IDM **at your/sb's diˈsposal** available for use as you prefer/sb prefers: *He will have a car at his disposal for the whole month.* ◊ *Well, I'm at your disposal* (= I am ready to help you in any way you can).

**dis·pose** /dɪˈspəʊz/ verb (formal) **1** **~sth/sb + adv./prep.** to arrange things or people in a particular way or position **2** **~sb to/toward(s) sth** | **~sb to do sth** to make sb want to behave in a particular way: *a drug that disposes the patient towards sleep*
PHRV **diˈspose of sb/sth** **1** to get rid of sb/sth that you do not want or cannot keep: *the difficulties of disposing of nuclear waste* ◊ *to dispose of stolen property* **2** to deal with a problem, question or threat successfully: *That seems to have disposed of most of their arguments.* **3** to defeat or kill sb: *It took her a mere 20 minutes to dispose of her opponent.*

**dis·posed** /dɪˈspəʊzd/ adj. [not before noun] (formal) **1** **~(to do sth)** willing or prepared to do sth: *I'm not disposed to argue.* ◊ *You're most welcome to join us if you feel so disposed.* ◊ *being naturally disposed towards speculation* **2** (following an adverb) **~to/towards sth/sb** having a good/bad opinion of a person or thing: *She seems favourably disposed to the move.* ⇨ see also ILL-DISPOSED, WELL DISPOSED

**dis·pos·ition** /ˌdɪspəˈzɪʃn/ noun **1** [C, usually sing.] (formal) the natural qualities of a person's character SYN **temperament**: *to have a cheerful disposition* ◊ *people of a nervous disposition* **2** [C, usually sing.] **~to/towards sth** | **~to do sth** (formal) a quality of tending to behave in a particular way: *to have/show a disposition towards violence* **3** [C, usually sing.] (formal) the way sth is placed or arranged SYN **arrangement** **4** [C, U] (law) a formal act of giving property or money to sb

**dis·pos·sess** /ˌdɪspəˈzes/ verb [usually passive] **~sb (of sth)** (formal) to take sb's property, land or house away from them ▸ **dis·pos·ses·sion** /-ˈzeʃn/ noun [U]

**the dis·pos·sessed** /ðə ˌdɪspəˈzest/ noun [pl.] people who have had property taken away from them

**dis·pro·por·tion** /ˌdɪsprəˈpɔːʃn; *NAmE* -ˈpɔːrʃn/ *noun* [U, C] (*formal*) the state of two things not being at an equally high or low level; an example of this: ~ **(between A and B)** *the disproportion between the extra responsibilities and the small salary increase* ◊ ~ **(of A to B)** *a profession with a high disproportion of male to female employees*

**dis·pro·por·tion·ate** /ˌdɪsprəˈpɔːʃənət; *NAmE* -ˈpɔːrʃ-/ *adj.* ~ **(to sth)** too large or too small when compared with sth else: *The area contains a disproportionate number of young middle-class families.* ⊃ compare PROPORTIONATE ▶ **dis·pro·por·tion·ate·ly** *adv.*: *The lower-paid spend a disproportionately large amount of their earnings on food.*

**dis·prove** /ˌdɪsˈpruːv/ *verb* ~ **sth** to show that sth is wrong or false: *The theory has now been disproved.* OPP **prove**

**dis·put·able** /dɪˈspjuːtəbl/ *adj.* (*formal*) that can or should be questioned or argued about ⊃ compare INDISPUTABLE

**dis·pu·ta·tion** /ˌdɪspjuˈteɪʃn/ *noun* [C, U] (*formal*) a discussion about sth that people cannot agree on

**dis·pute** 🔑+ 〇1 *noun, verb*
■ *noun* 🔑+ 〇1 /dɪˈspjuːt, ˈdɪspjuːt/ [C, U] an argument between two people, groups or countries; discussion about a subject on which people disagree: *industrial/pay disputes* ◊ ~ **between A and B** *a dispute between the two countries about the border* ◊ ~ **over/about sth** *the latest dispute over fishing rights* ◊ **in** ~ **with sb/sth** *The union is in dispute with management over working hours.* ◊ **in/under** ~ *The cause of the accident was still in dispute* (= being argued about). ◊ **beyond** ~ *The matter was settled beyond dispute by the court judgment* (= it could no longer be argued about). ◊ **open to** ~ *His theories are open to dispute* (= can be disagreed with).
■ *verb* /dɪˈspjuːt/ **1** 🔑+ 〇1 [T] to question whether sth is true or legally or officially acceptable: ~ **sth** *These figures have been disputed.* ◊ *to dispute a decision/claim* ◊ *The family wanted to dispute the will.* ◊ ~ **that** … *No one is disputing that there is a problem.* | **it is disputed whether, how, etc** … *It is disputed whether the law applies in this case.* **2** 🔑+ 〇1 [T, I] ~ **(sth)** to argue or disagree strongly with sb about sth, especially about who owns sth: *disputed territory* ◊ *The issue remains hotly disputed.* **3** [T] ~ **sth** to fight to get control of sth or to win sth: *On the last lap three runners were disputing the lead.*

**dis·qual·ify** /dɪsˈkwɒlɪfaɪ; *NAmE* -ˈkwɑːl-/ *verb* (**dis·qualifies, dis·quali·fy·ing, dis·quali·fied, dis·quali·fied**) **1** to stop sb from doing sth because they have broken a rule SYN **bar**: ~ **sb (from sth)** *He was disqualified from the competition for using drugs.* ◊ ~ **sb (from doing sth)** (*BrE*) *You could be disqualified from driving for up to three years.* ⊃ WORD-FINDER NOTE at COMPETITION **2** ~ **sb (for sth)** to make sb unsuitable for an activity or position: *A heart condition disqualified him from military service.* ▶ **dis·quali·fi·ca·tion** /dɪsˌkwɒlɪfɪˈkeɪʃn; *NAmE* -ˌkwɑːl-/ *noun* [C, U]: *Any form of cheating means automatic disqualification.*

**dis·quiet** /dɪsˈkwaɪət/ *noun* [U] ~ **(about/over sth)** (*formal*) feelings of worry and unhappiness about sth SYN **unease**: *There is considerable public disquiet about the safety of the new trains.*

**dis·quiet·ing** /dɪsˈkwaɪətɪŋ/ *adj.* (*formal*) causing worry and unhappiness

**dis·qui·si·tion** /ˌdɪskwɪˈzɪʃn/ *noun* (*formal*) a long complicated speech or written report on a particular subject

**dis·re·gard** /ˌdɪsrɪˈɡɑːd; *NAmE* -ˈɡɑːrd/ *verb, noun*
■ *verb* ~ **sth** (*formal*) to not consider sth; to treat sth as unimportant SYN **ignore**: *The board completely disregarded my recommendations.* ◊ *Safety rules were disregarded.*
■ *noun* [U, sing.] ~ **(for/of sb/sth)** (*formal*) the act of treating sb/sth as not important and not caring about them/it: *their reckless disregard for human life* ◊ *She shows a total disregard for other people's feelings.*

**dis·re·pair** /ˌdɪsrɪˈpeə(r); *NAmE* -ˈper/ *noun* [U] a building, road, etc. that is in a state of **disrepair** has not been taken care of and is broken or in bad condition: *The station quickly fell into disrepair after it was closed.*

**dis·rep·ut·able** /dɪsˈrepjətəbl/ *adj.* that people do not respect or trust; considered to be bad, dangerous or dishonest: *She spent the evening with her disreputable brother* *Stefan.* ◊ *a disreputable area of the city* OPP **respectable** ⊃ compare REPUTABLE

**dis·re·pute** /ˌdɪsrɪˈpjuːt/ *noun* [U] (*formal*) the fact that sb/sth loses the respect of other people: *The players' behaviour on the field is likely to bring the game into disrepute.*

**dis·re·spect** /ˌdɪsrɪˈspekt/ *noun, verb*
■ *noun* [U, C] ~ **(for/to sb/sth)** a lack of respect for sb/sth: *disrespect for the law/the dead* ◊ *No disrespect intended, sir. It was just a joke.* ▶ **dis·re·spect·ful** /-fl/ *adj.* ~ **(to sb/sth) dis·re·spect·ful·ly** /-fəli/ *adv.*
■ *verb* ~ **sb/sth** (*informal*) to speak about or treat sb/sth without respect: *They were accused of disrespecting the country's flag.* ⊃ compare DIS HELP Some people consider that it is not correct to use **disrespect** as a verb, and that you should use the noun instead, especially in formal and written English: *They were accused of treating the country's flag with disrespect.*

**dis·robe** /ˌdɪsˈrəʊb/ *verb* [I, T] ~ **(sb)** (*formal or humorous*) to take off your or sb else's clothes; to take off clothes worn for an official ceremony: *She went behind the screen to disrobe.*

**dis·rupt** 🔑+ 〇1 /dɪsˈrʌpt/ *verb* ~ **sth** to make it difficult for sth to continue in the normal way: *Demonstrators succeeded in disrupting the meeting.* ◊ *Bus services will be disrupted tomorrow because of the bridge closure.*

**dis·rup·tion** 🔑+ 〇1 /dɪsˈrʌpʃn/ *noun* [U, C] ~ **(to sb/sth)** a situation in which it is difficult for sth to continue in the normal way; the act of stopping sth from continuing in the normal way: *We aim to help you move house with minimum disruption to yourself.* ◊ *disruptions to rail services* ◊ *The strike caused serious disruptions.*

**dis·rup·tive** /dɪsˈrʌptɪv/ *adj.* **1** causing problems, noise, etc. so that sth cannot continue normally: *She had a disruptive influence on the rest of the class.* **2** new and original, in a way that causes major changes to how something is done: *disruptive companies/technologies*

**diss** = DIS

**dis·sat·is·fac·tion** /ˌdɪsˌsætɪsˈfækʃn/ *noun* **1** [U] ~ **(with/at sb/sth)** a feeling that you are not pleased or satisfied: *Many people have expressed their dissatisfaction with the arrangement.* OPP **satisfaction 2** [C, usually pl.] something that causes you to feel dissatisfied

**dis·sat·is·fied** /dɪsˈsætɪsfaɪd, dɪˈs-/ *adj.* not happy or satisfied with sb/sth: *dissatisfied customers* ◊ ~ **with sb/sth** *If you are dissatisfied with our service, please contact our customer service department.* OPP **satisfied** ⊃ compare UNSATISFIED

**dis·sect** /dɪˈsekt, daɪ-/ *verb* **1** ~ **sth** to cut up a dead person, animal or plant in order to study it **2** ~ **sth** to study sth closely and/or discuss it in great detail: *Her latest novel was dissected by the critics.* **3** ~ **sth** to divide sth into smaller pieces, areas, etc: *The city is dissected by a network of old canals.* ▶ **dis·sec·tion** /-ˈsekʃn/ *noun* [U, C]: *anatomical dissection* ◊ *Your enjoyment of a novel can suffer from too much analysis and dissection.*

**dis·sem·ble** /dɪˈsembl/ *verb* [I, T] ~ **(sth)** (*formal*) to hide your real feelings or intentions, often by pretending to have different ones: *She was a very honest person who was incapable of dissembling.* ▶ **dis·sem·bler** /-blə(r)/ *noun*

**dis·sem·in·ate** /dɪˈsemɪneɪt/ *verb* ~ **sth** (*formal*) to spread information, knowledge, etc. so that it reaches many people: *Their findings have been widely disseminated.* ▶ **dis·sem·in·ation** /dɪˌsemɪˈneɪʃn/ *noun* [U]

**dis·sen·sion** /dɪˈsenʃn/ *noun* [U, C] ~ **(between/among/within sb/sth)** (*formal*) DISAGREEMENT between people or within a group: *dissension within the government*

**dis·sent** /dɪˈsent/ *noun, verb*
■ *noun* (*formal*) **1** [U] the fact of having or expressing opinions that are different from those that are officially accepted: *political/religious dissent* **2** [U] (in sport) the offence of openly disagreeing with the REFEREE's decision: *He was sent off for dissent.* **3** [C] (*NAmE*) a judge's

# dissenter

statement giving reasons why he or she disagrees with a decision made by the other judges in a court case
- **verb** [I] ~ (from sth) (*formal*) to have or express opinions that are different from those that are officially or generally accepted: *Only two ministers dissented from the official view.* ▶ **dis·sent·ing** *adj.*: *dissenting groups/voices/views/opinion*

**dis·sent·er** /dɪˈsentə(r)/ *noun* a person who does not agree with opinions that are officially or generally accepted

**dis·ser·ta·tion** /ˌdɪsəˈteɪʃn; *NAmE* -sərˈt-/ *noun* ~ (on sth) a long piece of writing on a particular subject, especially one written for a university degree ⇒ **WORDFINDER NOTE** at UNIVERSITY

**dis·ser·vice** /dɪsˈsɜːvɪs, dɪˈs-; *NAmE* -ˈsɜːrv-/ *noun* [sing.]
**IDM** **do sb a dis'service** to do sth that harms sb and the opinion that other people have of them

**dis·si·dent** /ˈdɪsɪdənt/ *noun* a person who strongly disagrees with and criticizes their government, especially in a country where this kind of action is dangerous ▶ **dis·si·dence** /-dəns/ *noun* [U] **dis·si·dent** *adj.*

**dis·simi·lar** /dɪˈsɪmɪlə(r)/ *adj.* ~ (from/to sb/sth) (*formal*) not the same: *These wines are not dissimilar* (= are similar). **OPP** similar ▶ **dis·simi·lar·ity** /ˌdɪsɪmɪˈlærəti/ *noun* [C, U] (*pl.* -ies)

**dis·simu·late** /dɪˈsɪmjuleɪt/ *verb* [T, I] ~ (sth) (*formal*) to hide your real feelings or intentions, often by pretending to have different ones **SYN** dissemble ▶ **dis·simu·la·tion** /dɪˌsɪmjuˈleɪʃn/ *noun* [U]

**dis·si·pate** /ˈdɪsɪpeɪt/ *verb* **1** [I, T] to gradually become or make sth become weaker until it disappears: *Eventually, his anger dissipated.* ◊ *~sth Her laughter soon dissipated the tension in the air.* **2** [T] ~ sth to waste sth, such as time or money, especially by not planning the best way of using it **SYN** squander

**dis·si·pated** /ˈdɪsɪpeɪtɪd/ *adj.* (*disapproving*) enjoying activities that are harmful such as drinking too much alcohol

**dis·si·pa·tion** /ˌdɪsɪˈpeɪʃn/ *noun* [U] (*formal*) **1** the process of disappearing or of making sth disappear: *the dissipation of energy in the form of heat* **2** the act of wasting money or spending money until there is none left: *concerns about the dissipation of the country's wealth* **3** (*disapproving*) behaviour that is fun but has a harmful effect on you

**dis·so·ci·ate** /dɪˈsəʊsieɪt, -ˈsəʊʃi-/ *verb* **1** (*also* **dis·as·so·ci·ate**) ~ yourself/sb from sb/sth to say or do sth to show that you are not connected with or do not support sb/sth; to make it clear that sth is not connected with a particular plan, action, etc.: *He tried to dissociate himself from the party's more extreme views.* ◊ *They were determined to dissociate the UN from any agreement to impose sanctions.* **2** ~ sb/sth (from sth) (*formal*) to think of two people or things as separate and not connected with each other: *She tried to dissociate the two events in her mind.* **OPP** associate ▶ **dis·so·ci·ation** /dɪˌsəʊsiˈeɪʃn, -ˌsəʊʃi-/ *noun* [U]

**dis·sol·ute** /ˈdɪsəluːt/ *adj.* (*formal*, *disapproving*) enjoying IMMORAL activities and not caring about behaving in a morally acceptable way

**dis·sol·ution** /ˌdɪsəˈluːʃn/ *noun* [U] **1** ~ (of sth) (*formal*) the act of officially ending a marriage, a business agreement or a parliament; the act of breaking up an organization, etc. **2** ~ (of sth) the process in which sth gradually disappears: *the dissolution of barriers of class and race*

**dis·solve** /dɪˈzɒlv; *NAmE* -ˈzɑːlv/ *verb* **1** ~ (in sth) (of a solid) to mix with a liquid and become part of it: *Salt dissolves in water.* ◊ *Heat gently until the sugar dissolves.* ⇒ **WORDFINDER NOTE** AT LIQUID **2** [T] ~ sth (in sth) to make a solid become part of a liquid: *Dissolve the tablet in water.* **3** [T] ~ sth to officially end a marriage, business agreement or parliament: *Their marriage was dissolved in 1999.* ◊ *The election was announced and parliament was dissolved.* **4** [I, T] to disappear; to make sth disappear: *When the ambulance had gone, the crowd dissolved.* ◊ *~ sth His calm response dissolved her anger.* **5** [I] ~ into laughter, tears, etc. to suddenly start laughing, crying, etc.: *When the teacher looked up, the children dis-* solved into giggles. ◊ *Every time she heard his name, she dissolved into tears.* **6** [T, I] to remove or destroy sth, especially by a chemical process; to be destroyed in this way: *~ sth (away) a new detergent that dissolves stains* ◊ *~(away) All the original calcium had dissolved away.*

**dis·son·ance** /ˈdɪsənəns/ *noun* **1** [C, U] (*music*) a combination of musical notes that do not sound pleasant together **OPP** consonance **2** [U] (*formal*) lack of agreement ⇒ see also COGNITIVE DISSONANCE ▶ **dis·son·ant** /ˈdɪsənənt/ *adj.*: *dissonant voices/notes*

**dis·suade** /dɪˈsweɪd/ *verb* ~ sb (from sth/from doing sth) to persuade sb not to do sth: *I tried to dissuade him from giving up his job.* ◊ *They were going to set off in the fog, but were dissuaded.*

**dis·tal** /ˈdɪstl/ *adj.* (*anatomy*) located away from the centre of the body or at the far end of sth: *the distal end of the tibia*

**dis·tance** /ˈdɪstəns/ *noun*, *verb*
- **noun 1** [C, U] the amount of space between two places or things: *a short/long distance* ◊ *a ~ of sth to travel/cover a distance of 200 kilometres* ◊ *~ to sth She walked the short distance to her apartment.* ◊ *~ from sth Once she was a safe distance from the shop, Gina stopped.* ◊ *~ from A to B What's the distance from New York City to Boston?* ◊ *~ between A and B What's the distance between New York City and Boston?* ◊ *over a ~ (of sth) The wind carries pollen over considerable distances.* ◊ *within ... ~ (of sth) The beach is within walking distance of my house* (= you can walk there easily). ◊ *In the US, distance is measured in miles.* ◊ *~ away Our parents live some distance away* (= quite far away). ⇒ see also LONG-DISTANCE, MIDDLE DISTANCE, OUTDISTANCE **2** [U] being far away in space or in time: *Distance is no problem on the internet.* ◊ *problems of physical/geographical distance* **3** [sing.] a point that is a particular amount of space away from sth else: *from a ~ (of sth) You'll never get the ball in from that distance.* ◊ *at a ~ (of sth) A digital camera was positioned at a distance of 1.5 metres from the subject.* **4** [C, usually sing., U] a difference or lack of a connection between two things: *~ between A and B The distance between fashion and art remains as great as ever.* ◊ *~ from sth Sociologists must maintain critical distance from the ideas of society at any particular time.* ◊ (*BrE*) *Eddie is, by some distance* (= by a great amount), *the funniest character in the show.* **5** [U, C] a situation in which there is a lack of friendly feelings or of a close relationship between two people or groups of people: *The coldness and distance in her voice took me by surprise.*
**IDM** **at/from a 'distance** from a place or time that is not near; from far away: *She had loved him at a distance for years.* **go the (full) 'distance** to continue playing in a competition or sports contest until the end: *Nobody thought he would last 15 rounds, but he went the full distance.* **in/into the 'distance** far away but still able to be seen or heard: *We saw lights in the distance.* ◊ *Alice stood staring into the distance.* **keep sb at a 'distance** to refuse to be friendly with sb; to not let sb be friendly towards you **keep your 'distance (from sb/sth) 1** to make sure you are not too near sb/sth **2** to avoid getting too friendly or involved with a person, group, etc.: *She was warned to keep her distance from Charles if she didn't want to get hurt.* **within 'touching distance (of sth)** (*BrE also* **within 'spitting distance**) (*also* **within 'shouting distance** especially in *NAmE*) (*informal*) very close
- **verb 1** to become less involved or connected with sb/sth: *~ yourself from sb/sth When he retired, he tried to distance himself from politics.* ◊ *~ yourself It's not always easy for nurses to distance themselves emotionally.* **2** ~ sb/sth from sb/sth to make sb/sth less involved or connected with sb/sth: *Her mother wished to distance her from the rough village children.*

**distance 'learning** (*also* **distance edu'cation**) *noun* [U] a system of education in which people study at home with the help of special internet sites and send or email work to their teachers ⇒ **WORDFINDER NOTE** at STUDY

**dis·tant** /ˈdɪstənt/ *adj.* **1** far away in space or time: *the distant sound of music* ◊ *distant stars/planets*

The time we spent together is now a distant memory. ◊ (formal) The airport was about 20 kilometres distant. ◊ a star 30000 light years distant from the Earth ◊ (figurative) Peace was just a distant hope (= not very likely). **2 ~ (from sth)** not like sb else SYN **remote**: *Their life seemed utterly distant from his own.* **3** [only before noun] (of a person) related to you but not closely: *a distant cousin/aunt/relative* **4** not friendly; not wanting a close relationship with sb: *Pat sounded very cold and distant on the phone.* **5** not paying attention to sth but thinking about sth completely different: *There was a distant look in her eyes; her mind was obviously on something else.* ▶ **dis·tant·ly** *adv.*: *Somewhere, distantly, he could hear the sound of the sea.* ◊ *We're distantly related.* ◊ *Holly smiled distantly.*
IDM **the (ˌdim and) ˌdistant ˈpast** a long time ago: *stories from the distant past* **in the not too ˌdistant ˈfuture** not a long time in the future but fairly soon

**dis·taste** /dɪsˈteɪst/ *noun* [U, sing.] a feeling that sb/sth is unpleasant or offensive: **in/with ~** *He looked around the filthy room in distaste.* ◊ **~ (for sb/sth)** *a distaste for politics of any sort* ◊ **~ at (doing) sth** *He couldn't hide his distaste at having to sleep in such a filthy room.*

**dis·taste·ful** /dɪsˈteɪstfl/ *adj.* (*formal*) unpleasant or offensive

**dis·tem·per** /dɪsˈtempə(r)/ *noun* [U] **1** a disease of animals, especially dogs, that causes a high temperature and COUGHING (= forcing air through the throat suddenly and noisily) **2** (*BrE*) a type of paint that is mixed with GLUE (= a sticky substance) and used on walls

**dis·tend** /dɪˈstend/ *verb* [I, T] **~ (sth)** (*formal* or *medical*) to SWELL (= become larger and rounder than before) or make sth SWELL because of pressure from inside ▶ **dis·ten·sion** /-ˈstenʃn/ *noun* [U]: *distension of the stomach*

**dis·tend·ed** /dɪˈstendɪd/ *adj.* (*formal* or *medical*) (especially of part of the body) larger than normal due to pressure from inside: *starving children with huge distended bellies*

**dis·til** (*NAmE* **dis·till**) /dɪˈstɪl/ *verb* (**-ll-**) **1 ~ sth (from sth)** to make a liquid pure by heating it until it becomes a gas, then cooling it and collecting the drops of liquid that form: *to distil fresh water from seawater* ◊ *distilled water* **2 ~ sth** to make sth such as a strong alcoholic drink in this way: *The factory distils and bottles whisky.* **3 ~ sth (from/into sth)** (*formal*) to get the essential meaning or ideas from thoughts, information, experiences, etc: *The notes I made on my travels were distilled into a book.* ▶ **dis·til·la·tion** /ˌdɪstɪˈleɪʃn/ *noun* [C, U]: *the distillation process*

**dis·til·late** /ˈdɪstɪlət, -leɪt/ *noun* [U, C] (*specialist*) a substance that is formed by distilling a liquid

**dis·til·ler** /dɪˈstɪlə(r)/ *noun* a person or company that produces SPIRITS (= strong alcoholic drinks) such as WHISKY by distilling them

**dis·til·lery** /dɪˈstɪləri/ *noun* (*pl.* **-ies**) a factory where strong alcoholic drink is made by the process of distilling

**dis·tinct** /dɪˈstɪŋkt/ *adj.* **1** easily or clearly heard, seen, felt, etc: *There was a distinct smell of gas.* ◊ *His voice was quiet but every word was distinct.* **2** clearly different or of a different kind: *The results of the survey fell into two distinct groups.* ◊ **~from sth** *Jamaican reggae music is quite distinct from North American jazz or blues.* ◊ *rural areas, as distinct from major cities* **3** [only before noun] used to emphasize that you think an idea or situation definitely exists and is important SYN **definite**: *Being tall gave Tony a distinct advantage.* ◊ *I had the distinct impression I was being watched.* ◊ *A strike is now a distinct possibility.* ▶ **dis·tinct·ly** *adv.*: *I distinctly heard someone calling me.* ◊ *a distinctly Australian accent* ◊ *He could remember everything very distinctly.* **dis·tinct·ness** *noun* [U]

**dis·tinc·tion** /dɪˈstɪŋkʃn/ *noun* **1** [C] **~ (between A and B)** a clear difference or contrast especially between people or things that are similar or related: *distinctions between traditional and modern societies* ◊ *Philosophers did not use to make a distinction between arts and science.* ◊ *We need to draw a distinction between the two events.* **2** [U] the act of separating people or things into different groups: **~ (between A and B)** *The new law makes no distinction between adults and children* (= treats them equally). ◊ *without ~ All groups are entitled to this money without distinction.* **3** [sing.] the quality of being sth that is special: *She had the distinction of being the first woman to fly the Atlantic.* **4** [U] the quality of being excellent or important: *a writer of distinction* **5** [C, U] a special mark or award that is given to sb, especially a student, for excellent work: *Naomi got a distinction in maths.* ◊ **with ~** *He graduated with distinction.*

**dis·tinct·ive** /dɪˈstɪŋktɪv/ *adj.* having a quality or characteristic that makes sth different and easily noticed SYN **characteristic**: *clothes with a distinctive style* ◊ *The male bird has distinctive white markings on its head.* ▶ **dis·tinct·ive·ly** *adv.*: *a distinctively nutty flavour*

**dis·tin·guish** /dɪˈstɪŋɡwɪʃ/ *verb* **1** [I, T] to recognize the difference between two people or things SYN **differentiate**: **~ between A and B** *At what age are children able to distinguish between right and wrong?* ◊ **~ A from B** *It was hard to distinguish one twin from the other.* ◊ **~ A and B** *Sometimes reality and fantasy are hard to distinguish.* **2** [T] (not used in the progressive tenses) **~ A (from B)** to be a characteristic that makes two people, animals or things different: *What was it that distinguished her from her classmates?* ◊ *The male bird is distinguished from the female by its red beak.* ◊ *Does your cat have any distinguishing marks?* **3** [T] (not used in the progressive tenses) **~ sth** to be able to see or hear sth SYN **make out**: *I could not distinguish her words, but she sounded agitated.* **4** [T] **~ yourself (as sth)** to do sth so well that people notice and admire you: *She has already distinguished herself as an athlete.* ▶ **dis·tin·guish·able** /-ɡwɪʃəbl/ *adj.*: **~ (from sth)** *The male bird is easily distinguishable from the female.* ◊ *The coast was barely distinguishable in the mist.*

**dis·tin·guished** /dɪˈstɪŋɡwɪʃt/ *adj.* **1** very successful and admired by other people: *a distinguished career in medicine* **2** having an appearance that makes sb look important or that makes people admire or respect them: *I think grey hair makes you look very distinguished.*

**dis·tort** /dɪˈstɔːt; *NAmE* -ˈstɔːrt/ *verb* **1 ~ sth** to change the shape, appearance or sound of sth so that it is strange or not clear: *a fairground mirror that distorts your shape* ◊ *The loudspeaker seemed to distort his voice.* **2 ~ sth** to change facts, ideas, etc. so that they are no longer correct or true: *Newspapers are often guilty of distorting the truth.* ▶ **dis·tor·tion** /dɪˈstɔːʃn; *NAmE* -ˈstɔːrʃn/ *noun* [C, U]: *modern alloys that are resistant to wear and distortion* ◊ *a distortion of the facts*

**dis·tort·ed** /dɪˈstɔːtɪd; *NAmE* -ˈstɔːrt-/ *adj.* **1** pulled out of shape so that it looks strange; made to sound strange: *a distorted image* **2** (of facts or ideas) presented in a way that changes them so that they are no longer correct or true: *The article gave a distorted picture of his childhood.*

**dis·tract** /dɪˈstrækt/ *verb* **~ sb/sth (from sth)** to take sb's attention away from what they are trying to do SYN **divert**: *You're distracting me from my work.* ◊ *Don't talk to her—she's very easily distracted.* ◊ *It was another attempt to distract attention from the truth.* ▶ **dis·tract·ing** *adj.*: *distracting thoughts* ◊ *a distracting noise*

**dis·tract·ed** /dɪˈstræktɪd/ *adj.* **~ (by sb/sth)** unable to pay attention to sb/sth because you are worried or thinking about sth else ▶ **dis·tract·ed·ly** *adv.*

**dis·trac·tion** /dɪˈstrækʃn/ *noun* **1** [C, U] a thing that takes your attention away from what you are doing or thinking about: *I find it hard to work at home because there are too many distractions.* ◊ *cinema audiences looking for distraction* ◊ **~ from sth** *The TV provided a distraction from his work.* **2** [C] an activity that entertains you
IDM **to diˈstraction** so that you become upset, excited or angry, and not able to think clearly: *The children are driving me to distraction today.*

**dis·tract·or** /dɪˈstræktə(r)/ *noun* **1** a person or thing that takes your attention away from what you should be doing **2** one of the wrong answers in a MULTIPLE-CHOICE test

# distraught

**dis·traught** /dɪˈstrɔːt/ *adj.* extremely upset and anxious so that you cannot think clearly

**dis·tress** /dɪˈstres/ *noun, verb*
- *noun* [U] **1** a feeling of great worry or unhappiness; great mental pain: *The newspaper article caused the actor considerable distress.* ◊ *She sensed his deep emotional distress.* ◊ **in~** *She was obviously in distress after the attack.* **2** severe problems caused by not having enough money, food, etc. **SYN** hardship: *economic/financial distress* **3** a situation in which a ship, plane, etc. is in danger or difficulty and needs help: *a distress signal* (= a message asking for help) ◊ **in~** *It is a rule of the sea to help another boat in distress.* **4** (*medical*) a state of physical pain and effort, especially difficulty in breathing: **in~** *The baby was clearly in distress.* **IDM** see DAMSEL
- *verb* to make sb feel very worried or unhappy: **~sb** *It was clear that the letter had deeply distressed her.* ◊ **~yourself** *Don't distress yourself* (= don't worry).

**dis·tressed** /dɪˈstrest/ *adj.* **1** very upset and anxious: *He was too distressed and confused to answer their questions.* **2** suffering pain; in a poor physical condition: *When the baby was born, it was blue and distressed.* **3** (of a piece of clothing or furniture) made to look older and more worn than it really is: *a distressed leather jacket* **4** (*formal or business*) having problems caused by lack of money: *They buy up financially distressed companies.* ◊ *The charity helps kids in distressed situations.*

**dis·tress·ing** /dɪˈstresɪŋ/ *adj.* making you feel extremely upset, especially because sb is suffering ▶ **dis·tress·ing·ly** *adv.*

**dis·trib·ute** /dɪˈstrɪbjuːt; *BrE also* ˈdɪstrɪbjuːt/ *verb* **1** to give things to a large number of people; to share sth between a number of people: **~sth** *The leaflets have been widely distributed.* ◊ **~sth to sb/sth** *The organization distributed food to the earthquake victims.* ◊ **~sth among/between sb/sth** *The money was distributed among schools in the area.* **2** **~sth (+ adv./prep.)** to send goods to shops and businesses so that they can be sold: *Who distributes our products in the UK?* **3** [often passive] to spread sth, or different parts of sth, over an area: **be distributed + adv./prep.** *Make sure your weight is evenly distributed.* ◊ *Cases of the disease are widely distributed through Europe.*

**di·stributed ˈsystem** *noun* a number of individual computers that are linked to form a network

**dis·tri·bu·tion** /ˌdɪstrɪˈbjuːʃn/ *noun* **1** [U, C] the way that sth is spread or exists over a particular area or among a particular group of people: **~of sth** *They studied the geographical distribution of the disease.* ◊ *a more equitable distribution of wealth* ◊ **~(of sth) + adv./prep.** *The map shows the distribution of this species across the world.* ⊃ see also NORMAL DISTRIBUTION **2** [U, C] the act of giving or sharing sth out among a number of people: **~of sth** *the distribution of food and medicines* ◊ **~(of sth) to/among sb** *the distribution of profit among the partners* ◊ **for ~(to/among sb)** *The food was packed up for distribution to outlying communities.* **3** [U] (*business*) the system of transporting and delivering a product: *marketing, sales and distribution* ◊ *distribution channel/networks* ◊ *production and distribution systems* ▶ **dis·tri·bu·tion·al** /-ʃənl/ *adj.*

**distriˈbution board** *noun* (*BrE, physics*) a board that contains the connections for several electrical CIRCUITS

**dis·tribu·tive** /dɪˈstrɪbjətɪv/ *adj.* [usually before noun] (*business*) connected with distribution of goods

**dis·tribu·tor** /dɪˈstrɪbjətə(r)/ *noun* **1** a person or company that supplies goods to shops, etc.: *Japan's largest software distributor* **2** a device in an engine that sends electric current to the SPARK PLUGS

**dis·trict** /ˈdɪstrɪkt/ *noun* **1** an area of a country or town, especially one that has particular features: *the City of London's financial district* ◊ *Every city has its central business district.* ⊃ see also RED-LIGHT DIS-

TRICT **2** one of the areas that a country, town or state is divided into for purposes of organization, with official BOUNDARIES (= borders): *a tax/postal district* ◊ *a village in the Darjeeling district* ◊ *a district judge* ◊ *the district health authority* ⊃ see also CONGRESSIONAL DISTRICT, SCHOOL DISTRICT

**district atˈtorney** *noun* (*abbr.* **DA**) (in the US) a lawyer who is responsible for bringing criminal charges against sb in a particular area or state

**district ˈcourt** *noun* (in the US) a court that deals with cases in a particular area

**district ˈnurse** *noun* (in the UK) a nurse who visits patients in their homes

**dis·trust** /dɪsˈtrʌst/ *noun, verb*
- *noun* [U, sing.] a feeling of not being able to trust sb/sth: *They looked at each other with distrust.* ◊ **~of sb/sth** *He has a deep distrust of all modern technology.* ▶ **dis·trust·ful** /-fl/ *adj.*: *distrustful of authority*
- *verb* **~sb/sth** to feel that you cannot trust or believe sb/sth: *She distrusted his motives for wanting to see her again.* ⊃ compare MISTRUST

▼ **WHICH WORD?**

**distrust / mistrust**
- There is very little difference between these two words, but **distrust** is more common and perhaps slightly stronger. If you are sure that someone is acting dishonestly or cannot be relied on, you are more likely to say that you **distrust** them. If you are expressing doubts and suspicions, on the other hand, you would probably use **mistrust**.

**dis·turb** /dɪˈstɜːb; *NAmE* -ˈstɜːrb/ *verb* **1** **~sb/sth** to interrupt sb when they are trying to work, sleep, etc: *I'm sorry to disturb you, but can I talk to you for a moment?* ◊ *If you get up early, try not to disturb everyone else.* ◊ *Do not disturb* (= a sign placed on the outside of the door of a hotel room, office, etc.) ◊ *She awoke early after a disturbed night.* **2** to make sb worry: **~sb** *The letter shocked and disturbed me.* ◊ *it disturbs sb to do sth* *It disturbed her to realize that she was alone.* **3** **~sth** to move sth or change its position: *Don't disturb the papers on my desk.* **4** **~sth** to make sth function differently from normal: *During a magnetic storm, the earth's magnetic field is disturbed.*

**dis·turb·ance** /dɪˈstɜːbəns; *NAmE* -ˈstɜːrb-/ *noun* **1** [U, C, usually sing.] actions that make you stop what you are doing, or that upset the normal state that sth is in; the act of disturbing sb/sth or the fact of being disturbed: *The building work is creating constant noise, dust and disturbance.* ◊ *a disturbance in the usual pattern of events* ◊ *the disturbance of the local wildlife by tourists* **2** [C, U] a situation in which people behave violently in a public place: *serious disturbances in the streets* ◊ *He was charged with causing a disturbance after the game.* ◊ *The army is trained to deal with riots and civil disturbance.* **3** [U, C] a state in which sb's mind or a function of the body is upset and not working normally: *emotional disturbance*

**dis·turbed** /dɪˈstɜːbd; *NAmE* -ˈstɜːrbd/ *adj.* **1** mentally ill, especially because of very unhappy or unpleasant experiences: *a special school for emotionally disturbed children* ⊃ note at MENTAL HEALTH **2** unhappy and full of bad or horrible experiences: *The killer had a disturbed family background.* **3** very anxious and unhappy about sth: *I was severely disturbed and depressed by the news.* ⊃ compare UNDISTURBED

**dis·turb·ing** /dɪˈstɜːbɪŋ; *NAmE* -ˈstɜːrb-/ *adj.* making you feel anxious and upset or shocked: *a disturbing piece of news* ▶ **dis·turb·ing·ly** *adv.*

**dis·united** /ˌdɪsjuˈnaɪtɪd/ *adj.* (*formal*) (of a group of people) unable to agree with each other or work together: *a disunited political party*

**dis·unity** /dɪsˈjuːnəti/ *noun* [U] (*formal*) a lack of agreement between people: *disunity within the Conservative party* **OPP** unity

---

æ cat | ɑː father | e bed | ɜː fur | ə about | ɪ sit | iː see | i happy | ɒ got (*BrE*) | ɔː saw | ʌ cup | ʊ put | uː too

**dis·use** /dɪsˈjuːs/ noun [U] a situation in which sth is no longer being used: *The factory fell into disuse twenty years ago.*

**dis·used** /dɪsˈjuːzd/ adj. [usually before noun] no longer used: *a disused station* ⊃ compare UNUSED¹

**ditch** /dɪtʃ/ noun, verb
■ noun a long channel dug at the side of a field or road, to hold or take away water
■ verb 1 [T] ~ sth/sb (informal) to get rid of sth/sb because you no longer want or need it/them: *The new road building programme has been ditched.* ◊ *He ditched his girlfriend.* 2 [T, I] ~ (sth) if a pilot **ditches** an aircraft, or if it **ditches**, it lands in the sea in an emergency 3 [T] ~ **school** (NAmE, informal) to stay away from school without permission

**ditch·water** /ˈdɪtʃwɔːtə(r)/ noun [U] **IDM** see DULL adj.

**dither** /ˈdɪðə(r)/ verb, noun
■ verb [I] to hesitate about what to do because you are unable to decide: *Stop dithering and get on with it.* ◊ ~ **over sth** *She was dithering over what to wear.* ▶ **dither·er** noun
■ noun [sing.] (informal) 1 a state of not being able to decide what you should do: **in a ~ (about / over sth)** *I'm in a dither about who to invite.* 2 a state of excitement or worry: **in a ~ (about / over sth)** *Don't get yourself in a dither over everything.*

**ditsy** = DITZY

**ditto** /ˈdɪtəʊ/ noun, adv.
■ noun (abbr. **do.**) (symb. ″ ) used, especially in a list, below a particular word or phrase, to show that it is repeated and to avoid having to write it again
■ adv. (informal) used instead of a particular word or phrase, to avoid repeating it: *The waiters were rude and unhelpful, the manager ditto.*

**ditty** /ˈdɪti/ noun (pl. **-ies**) (often humorous) a short simple song

**ditzy** (also **ditsy**) /ˈdɪtsi/ adj. (especially NAmE, informal) (usually of a woman) silly; not able to be trusted to remember things or to think in an organized way

**di·ur·et·ic** /ˌdaɪjʊˈretɪk/ noun (medical) a substance that causes an increase in the flow of URINE ▶ **di·ur·et·ic** adj.: *diuretic drugs/effects*

**di·ur·nal** /daɪˈɜːnl; NAmE -ˈɜːrnl/ adj. 1 (biology) (of animals) active during the day **OPP** nocturnal 2 (astronomy) taking one day: *the diurnal rotation of the earth*

**Div.** abbr. (in writing) DIVISION: *League Div. 1* (= in football (soccer))

**diva** /ˈdiːvə/ noun 1 a famous woman singer, especially an OPERA singer ⊃ WORDFINDER NOTE at OPERA 2 a person who is difficult to please and demands a lot of attention

**Di·vali** = DIWALI

**divan** /dɪˈvæn/ noun 1 (also **di·van ˈbed**) (both BrE) a bed with a thick base and a MATTRESS 2 a long low soft seat without a back or arms

**dive** /daɪv/ verb, noun
■ verb (**dived**, **dived**, NAmE also **dove** /dəʊv/, **dived**)
• JUMP INTO WATER 1 [I] to jump into water with your head and arms going in first: ~ **(from / off sth) (into sth)** *We dived into the river to cool off.* ◊ ~ **in** *Sam walked to the deep end of the pool and dived in.* ⊃ WORDFINDER NOTE at SWIMMING
• UNDERWATER 2 (usually **go diving**) [I] to swim UNDERWATER wearing breathing equipment, collecting or looking at things: *to dive for pearls* ◊ *The main purpose of his holiday to Greece was to go diving.* ⊃ see also DIVING 3 [I] to go to a deeper level UNDERWATER: *The whale dived as the harpoon struck it.*
• OF BIRDS/AIRCRAFT 4 [I] to go steeply down through the air: *The seagulls soared then dived.* ⊃ see also NOSE-DIVE verb
• MOVE / JUMP / FALL 5 [I] (informal) to move or jump quickly in a particular direction, especially to avoid sth, to try to catch a ball, etc.: ~ **for sth** *We heard an explosion and dived for cover* (= got into a place where we would be protected). ◊ *The goalie dived for the ball, but missed it.* ◊ **+ adv. / prep.** *It started to rain so we dived into the nearest* 

453

**diversion**

*cafe.* 6 [I] (in football (soccer), hockey, etc.) to fall deliberately when sb TACKLES you
• OF PRICES 7 [I] to fall suddenly **SYN** plunge: *The share price dived from 75p to an all-time low of 50p.*
**PHR V** ˈdive in 1 (informal) to start eating with enthusiasm **SYN** dig in: *Dive in, everybody!* 2 (informal) to start doing sth without hesitating or with enthusiasm: *I didn't know what to expect at first but I just dived in.* ˈdive into sth 1 (informal) to put your hand quickly into sth such as a bag or pocket: *She dived into her bag and took out a couple of coins.* 2 (informal) to start or join in something without hesitating, or with enthusiasm: *Artists must be ready to dive into the unknown.*
■ noun
• JUMP INTO WATER 1 a jump into deep water with your head first and your arms in front of you: *a spectacular high dive* (= from high above the water)
• UNDERWATER 2 an act of going UNDERWATER and swimming there with special equipment: *a dive to a depth of 18 metres*
• OF BIRDS/AIRCRAFT 3 an act of suddenly flying downwards
• BAR / CLUB 4 (informal) a bar, music club, etc. that is cheap, and perhaps dark or dirty
• FALL 5 (in football (soccer), hockey, etc.) a deliberate fall that a player makes when sb TACKLES them: *Kane's dive won England a penalty.*
**IDM** (make) a ˈdive (for sth) to suddenly move or jump forward to do sth or reach sb/sth: *The goalkeeper made a dive for the ball.* take a ˈdive (informal) to suddenly get worse: *Profits really took a dive last year.*

**ˈdive-bomb** verb ~ **sb/sth** (of an aircraft, a bird, etc.) to dive steeply through the air and attack sb/sth

**diver** /ˈdaɪvə(r)/ noun 1 a person who swims UNDERWATER using special equipment, usually for their job: *a deep-sea diver* ⊃ compare FROGMAN 2 a person who jumps into the water with their head first and their arms in front of them, especially as a sport: *an Olympic diver*

**di·verge** /daɪˈvɜːdʒ; NAmE -ˈvɜːrdʒ/ verb (formal) 1 [I] to separate and go in different directions: *The parallel lines appear to diverge.* ◊ *We went through school and college together, but then our paths diverged.* ◊ ~ **from sth** *The coastal road diverges from the freeway just north of Santa Monica.* ◊ *Many species have diverged from a single ancestor.* 2 [I] ~ **(from sth)** (formal) (of opinions, views, etc.) to be different: *Opinions diverge greatly on this issue.* 3 [I] ~ **from sth** to be or become different from what is expected, planned, etc: *to diverge from the norm* ◊ *He diverged from established procedure.* **OPP** converge ▶ **di·ver·gence** /daɪˈvɜːdʒəns; NAmE -ˈvɜːrdʒ-/ noun [C, U]: *a wide divergence of opinion* **di·ver·gent** /-dʒənt/ adj.: *divergent paths/opinions*

**di·vers** /ˈdaɪvəz; NAmE -vərz/ adj. [only before noun] (old use) of many different kinds

**di·verse** /daɪˈvɜːs; NAmE -ˈvɜːrs/ adj. very different from each other and of various kinds: *people from diverse cultures* ◊ *My interests are very diverse.*
▶ **di·verse·ly** adv.: *a diversely talented group*

**di·ver·sify** /daɪˈvɜːsɪfaɪ; NAmE -ˈvɜːrs-/ verb (**di·ver·si·fies**, **di·ver·si·fy·ing**, **di·ver·si·fied**, **di·ver·si·fied**) 1 [I, T] ~ **(sth) (into sth)** (especially of a business or company) to develop a wider range of products, interests, skills, etc. in order to be more successful or reduce risk **SYN** branch out: *Farmers are being encouraged to diversify into new crops.* 2 [I, T] to change or to make sth change so that there is greater variety: *Opinions of family life are diversifying.* ◊ ~ **sth** *The culture has been diversified with the arrival of immigrants.*
▶ **di·ver·si·fi·ca·tion** /daɪˌvɜːsɪfɪˈkeɪʃn; NAmE -ˌvɜːrs-/ noun [U]

**di·ver·sion** /daɪˈvɜːʃn; NAmE -ˈvɜːrʒn/ noun 1 [C, U] the act of changing the direction that sb/sth is following, or what sth is used for: *a river diversion project* ◊ *We made a short diversion to go and look at the castle.* ◊ *the diversion of funds from the public to the private sector of industry* 2 [C] something that takes your attention away from sb/

# diversionary

sth while sth else is happening: *For the government, the war was a welcome diversion from the country's economic problems.* ◊ *A smoke bomb* **created a diversion** *while the robbery took place.* **3** [C] (*BrE*) (*NAmE* **de·tour**) a road or route that is used when the usual one is closed: *Diversions will be signposted.* ⇒ **WORDFINDER NOTE** at ROAD **4** [C] (*rather formal*) an activity that is done for pleasure, especially because it takes your attention away from sth else **SYN** **distraction**: *The party will make a pleasant diversion.* ◊ *~from sth TV provided a welcome diversion from our routine.*

**di·ver·sion·ary** /daɪˈvɜːʃənəri; *NAmE* -ˈvɜːrʒəneri/ *adj.* intended to take sb's attention away from sth

**di·ver·sity** /daɪˈvɜːsəti; *NAmE* -ˈvɜːrs-/ *noun* (*pl. -ies*) **1** [U, C, usually sing.] a range of many people or things that are very different from each other **SYN** **variety**: *the biological diversity of the rainforests* ◊ *a great/wide/rich diversity of opinion* **2** [U] the quality or fact of including a range of many people or things: *There is a need for greater diversity and choice in education.*

**di·vert** /daɪˈvɜːt; *NAmE* -ˈvɜːrt/ *verb* **1** [often passive] to make sb/sth change direction: **be diverted (from sth) (to/into/onto sth)** *Northbound traffic will have to be diverted onto minor roads.* **2** [often passive] to use money, materials, etc. for a different purpose from their original purpose: **be diverted (from sth) (to/into sth)** *More of the budget was diverted into promotions.* **3** *~sb/sth (from/away from sth) (to/onto sth)* to take sb's thoughts or attention away from sth **SYN** **distract**: *The war diverted people's attention away from the economic situation.* **4** [often passive] (*formal*) to entertain people: **be diverted** *Children are easily diverted.*

**di·vert·ing** /daɪˈvɜːtɪŋ; *NAmE* -ˈvɜːrt-/ *adj.* (*formal*) interesting and funny

**di·vest** /daɪˈvest/ *verb* (*formal*) **1** *~sb/yourself of sth* to remove clothes: *He divested himself of his jacket.* **2** *~yourself of sth* to get rid of sth: *The company is divesting itself of some of its assets.* **3** *~sb/sth of sth* to take sth away from sb/sth: *After her illness she was divested of much of her responsibility.*

**di·vest·ment** /daɪˈvestmənt/ *noun* (*also* **di·vesti·ture** /daɪˈvestɪtʃə(r)/) [U, C] (*finance*) the act of selling the shares you have bought in a company or of taking money away from where you have invested it

**div·ide**
/dɪˈvaɪd/ *verb, noun*

**WORD FAMILY**
divide *verb, noun*
division *noun*
divisive *adj.*

■ *verb*
• SEPARATE **1** [I, T] to separate into parts; to make sth separate into parts **SYN** **split up**: *The cells began to divide rapidly.* ◊ *~into sth The questions divide into two categories: easy and hard.* ◊ *~sth (into sth) I divided the class into four groups.* ◊ *~sth up (into sth) A sentence can be divided up into meaningful segments.* **2** [T] *~sth* to separate sth into parts and give a share to each of a number of different people, etc. **SYN** **share**: *~sth up Jack divided up the rest of the cash.* ◊ *~sth (up) between/among sb We divided the work between us.* **3** [T] *~sth (between A and B)* to use different parts of your time, energy, etc. for different activities, etc: *He divides his energies between politics and business.* **4** [I] (of a road or river) to separate into two or more parts that lead in different directions: *Where the path divides, keep right.* **5** [T] *~A from B* (*formal*) to separate two people or things: *Can it ever be right to divide a mother from her child?* **6** [T] *~sth (off)* | *~A from B* to be the real or imaginary line or barrier that separates two people or things **SYN** **separate**: *A fence divides off the western side of the grounds.*
• MATHEMATICS **7** [T, I] *~(sth) (by sth)* to find out how many times one number is contained in another: *~sth by sth 30 divided by 6 is 5 (=30÷6=5).* **8** [I, T] *~(sth) into sth* to be able to be multiplied to give another number: *5 divides into 30 6 times.*
• DISAGREEMENT **9** [T] to make people disagree **SYN** **split**: *~sb/sth to divide the nation/country* ◊ *The building divides opinion (=some people like it and some do not).* ◊ **be divided on/over sth** *The party is deeply divided on this question.* **10** [I] (*+ adv./prep.*) (of two or more people) to disagree: *Communities frequently divided along racial lines.*

**IDM** **di·vide and ˈrule** to keep control over people by making them disagree with and fight each other, therefore not giving them the chance to join together and oppose you: *a policy of divide and rule* ⇒ more at MIDDLE *n.*

■ *noun* [usually sing.]
• DIFFERENCE **1** a difference between two groups of people or two things that separates them from each other: *He offered advice on bridging cultural divides.* ◊ *~between A and B Will this deepen the divide between the country's rich and poor?* ⇒ see also DIGITAL DIVIDE, NORTH-SOUTH DIVIDE
• BETWEEN RIVERS **2** (especially *NAmE*) a line of high land that separates two systems of rivers **SYN** **watershed** **IDM** see BRIDGE *v.*

**div·ided** /dɪˈvaɪdɪd/ *adj.* (of a group or an organization) split by arguments or different opinions: *The government is divided on this issue.* ◊ *a deeply divided society* ◊ *The regime is profoundly divided against itself.*

**di·vided ˈhighway** (*NAmE*) (*BrE* **dual ˈcarriageway**) *noun* a road with a narrow piece of land in the middle that divides the lines of traffic moving in opposite directions

**divi·dend** /ˈdɪvɪdend/ *noun* **1** an amount of the profits that a company pays to people who own shares in the company: *dividend payments of 50 cents a share* ⇒ **WORDFINDER NOTE** at INVEST **2** great advantages or profits: *Exercising regularly will* **pay dividends** *in the end* ◊ *The company* **reaped rich dividends** *with its new strategy for packaging holidays.* ⇒ see also PEACE DIVIDEND **3** (*BrE*) a payment that is divided among a number of people, for example winners in the FOOTBALL POOLS or members of a COOPERATIVE **4** (*mathematics*) a number that is to be divided by another number ⇒ compare DIVISOR

**div·ider** /dɪˈvaɪdə(r)/ *noun* **1** [C] a thing that divides sth: *a room divider (=a screen or door that divides a room into two parts)* **2** **dividers** [pl.] an instrument made of two long thin metal parts joined together at the top, used for measuring lines and angles: *a pair of dividers* **3** an issue on which people disagree: *On the Labour side, the big divider was still nuclear weapons.*

**diˈviding line** *noun* [usually sing.] **1** something that marks the division or contrast between two things or ideas: *There is no clear dividing line between what is good and what is bad.* **2** a place that separates two areas: *The river was chosen as a dividing line between the two districts.*

**div·in·ation** /ˌdɪvɪˈneɪʃn/ *noun* [U] the act of finding out and saying what will happen in the future

**di·vine** /dɪˈvaɪn/ *adj., verb*

■ *adj.* **1** [usually before noun] coming from or connected with God or a god: *divine law/love/will* ◊ *divine intervention (=help from God to change a situation)* **2** (*old-fashioned*) wonderful; beautiful ▶ **di·vine·ly** *adv.*

■ *verb* **1** [T] *~what, whether, etc . . .* | *~sth* (*formal*) to find out sth by guessing: *She could divine what he was thinking just by looking at him.* **2** [T, I] *~(sth)* to search for underground water using a stick in the shape of a Y, called a **diˈvining rod**

**diˌvine ˈright** *noun* [U, sing.] **1** (in the past) the belief that the right of a king or queen to rule comes directly from God rather than from the agreement of the people **2** a right that sb thinks they have to do sth, without needing to ask anyone else: *No player has a divine right to be in this team.*

**div·ing** /ˈdaɪvɪŋ/ *noun* [U] **1** the sport or activity of diving into water with your head and arms first: *a diving competition* **2** the activity of swimming UNDERWATER using special breathing equipment: *I'd love to go diving in the Aegean.* ◊ *a diving suit* ⇒ see also SCUBA DIVING

**ˈdiving bell** *noun* a container that has a supply of air and that is open at the bottom, in which a person can be carried down to the deep ocean

**diving board** *noun* a board at the side of or above a swimming pool from which people can jump or DIVE into the water

**div·in·ity** /dɪˈvɪnəti/ *noun* (*pl.* **-ies**) **1** [U] the quality of being a god or like God or a god: *the divinity of Christ* **2** [C] a god or GODDESS: *Roman/Greek/Egyptian divinities* **3** [U] the study of the nature of God and religious belief ▶ **theology**: *a doctor of Divinity*

**div·is·ible** /dɪˈvɪzəbl/ *adj.* [not usually before noun] **1** ~ **(into sth)** that can be divided: *Plants are divisible into three main groups.* **2** ~ **(by sth)** (*mathematics*) that can be divided, usually with nothing left over: *8 is divisible by 2 and 4, but not by 3.* OPP **indivisible**

**div·ision** 🔊 B2 Ⓦ /dɪˈvɪʒn/ *noun*
- INTO SEPARATE PARTS **1** B2 [U, sing.] the process or result of dividing into separate parts; the process or result of dividing sth or sharing it out: *cell division* ◊ ~ **of sth** *a fair division of time and resources* ◊ ~ **(of sth) between A and B** *the division of labour between the sexes* ◊ ~ **(of sth) among sb** *His will detailed his assets and gave instructions for their division among his children.* ◊ ~ **(of sth) into sth** *the division of the population into age groups* ◊ *a distinction that cuts right across the familiar division into arts and sciences*
- MATHEMATICS **2** B2 [U] the process of dividing one number by another: *the division sign* (÷) ⮕ compare MULTIPLICATION ⮕ see also LONG DIVISION
- DISAGREEMENT/DIFFERENCE **3** B2 [C, U] a DISAGREEMENT or difference in opinion, way of life, etc., especially between members of a society or an organization: *class/racial/ethnic divisions* ◊ ~ **(in sth) (over sth)** *There are deep divisions in the party over the war.* ◊ ~ **within sth** *the work of healing the divisions within society* ◊ ~ **between A and B** *divisions between rich and poor* ◊ *The party was weakened by division between various factions.* ◊ ~ **among sb/sth** *He hopes to heal divisions among his people.*
- PART OF ORGANIZATION **4** B2 [C + sing./pl. v.] (*abbr.* **Div.**) a large and important unit or section of an organization: *the company's sales division* **5** [C] part of a city, county, or country that is regarded as a separate area for administration purposes: *Nagpur is the most eastern division in the state.*
- IN SPORT **6** [C + sing./pl. v.] (*abbr.* **Div.**) a group of teams or competitors in a sports competition who compete against each other. Divisions may be organized by ability, geography or weight, depending on the sport: *the premier division* ◊ *The club will finish second in Division One.* ◊ *a first-division team*
- PART OF ARMY **7** [C + sing./pl. v.] (*abbr.* **Div.**) a unit of an army, consisting of several BRIGADES or REGIMENTS: *the Guards Armoured Division*
- BORDER **8** [C] ~ **(between A and B)** a line that divides sth: *A hedge forms the division between their land and ours.* ◊ (*figurative*) *Sometimes there is no simple division between good and evil.*
- IN PARLIAMENT **9** [C] (*specialist*) the act of separating members of the British parliament into groups to vote for or against sth: *The Bill was read without a division.*

**div·ision·al** /dɪˈvɪʒənl/ *adj.* [only before noun] belonging to or connected with a DIVISION (= a section of the army or department of an organization): *the divisional commander/headquarters*

**div·isive** /dɪˈvaɪsɪv/ *adj.* (*disapproving*) causing people to be split into groups that disagree with or oppose each other: *He believes that unemployment is socially divisive.* ⮕ see also DIVIDE ▶ **div·isive·ly** *adv.* **div·isive·ness** *noun* [U]

**div·isor** /dɪˈvaɪzə(r)/ *noun* (*mathematics*) a number by which another number is divided ⮕ compare DIVIDEND (4)

**di·vorce** 🔊 B2 /dɪˈvɔːs; *NAmE* -ˈvɔːrs/ *noun, verb*
- *noun* **1** 🔊 B2 [U, C] the legal ending of a marriage: *The marriage ended in divorce in 1996.* ◊ *an increase in the divorce rate* (= the number of divorces in a year) ◊ *They have agreed to get a divorce.* ◊ *Divorce proceedings* (= the legal process of divorce) *started today.* ⮕ compare SEPARATION **2** [C, usually sing.] ~ **(between A and B)** (*formal*) an act of separating two things; the ending of a relationship between two things: *the divorce between religion and science*
- *verb* **1** 🔊 B2 [T, I] ~ **(sb)** to end your marriage to sb legally: *They're getting divorced.* ◊ *She's divorcing her husband.* ◊ *I'd heard they're divorcing.* **2** 🔊 C1 [T, often passive] ~ **sb/sth from sth** (*formal*) to separate a person, an idea, a subject, etc. from sth; to keep two things separate: *They believed that art should be divorced from politics.*

**di·vorcé** /dɪˌvɔːˈseɪ; *NAmE* -ˌvɔːrˈseɪ/ *noun* (*NAmE*) a man whose marriage has been legally ended

**di·vorced** 🔊 A2 /dɪˈvɔːst; *NAmE* -ˈvɔːrst/ *adj.* **1** 🔊 A2 no longer married because your marriage has been legally ended: *My parents are divorced.* ◊ *Many divorced men remarry and have second families.* **2** ~ **from sth** (*formal*) appearing not to be affected by sth; separate from sth: *He seems completely divorced from reality.*

**di·vor·cee** /dɪˌvɔːˈsiː; *NAmE* -ˌvɔːrˈseɪ/ *noun* (*BrE*) a person whose marriage has been legally ended, especially a woman

**di·vorcée** /dɪˌvɔːˈseɪ; *NAmE* -ˌvɔːrˈseɪ/ *noun* (*NAmE*) a woman whose marriage has been legally ended

**divot** /ˈdɪvət/ *noun* a piece of grass and earth that is dug out by accident, for example by a CLUB when sb is playing golf; the small hole in the earth that is made

**di·vulge** /daɪˈvʌldʒ/ *verb* ~ **sth (to sb)** | ~ **what, whether, etc. …** (*formal*) to give sb information that is supposed to be secret ▶ **reveal**: *Police refused to divulge the identity of the suspect.*

**divvy** /ˈdɪvi/ *verb* (**div·vies**, **divvy·ing**, **div·vied**, **div·vied**)
**PHRV divvy sth↔up** (*informal*) to divide sth, especially money into two or more parts

**Di·wali** /dɪˈwɑːli/ (*also* **Di·vali** /dɪˈvɑːli/) (*also* **Dee·pa·vali**) *noun* [U] a Hindu festival that is held in the autumn, celebrated by lighting CANDLES and CLAY lamps, and with FIREWORKS

**Dix·ie** /ˈdɪksi/ *noun* [U] an informal name for the southern states of the US that fought against the north in the American CIVIL WAR

**Dixie·land** /ˈdɪksilænd/ *noun* [U] a type of traditional jazz ⮕ see also TRAD

**DIY** /ˌdiː aɪ ˈwaɪ/ *noun* [U] the activity of making, repairing or decorating things in the home yourself, instead of paying sb to do it (the abbreviation for 'do-it-yourself'): *a DIY store*

**dizzy** /ˈdɪzi/ *adj.* (**diz·zier**, **diz·zi·est**) **1** feeling as if everything is turning around you and that you are not able to balance ▶ **giddy**: *Climbing so high made me feel dizzy.* ◊ *I suffer from dizzy spells* (= short periods when I am dizzy). **2** making you feel dizzy; making you feel that a situation is changing very fast ▶ **giddy**: *the dizzy descent from the summit* ◊ *the dizzy pace of life in Hong Kong* **3** (*especially NAmE, informal*) silly or stupid ▶ **giddy**: *a dizzy blonde* ▶ **diz·zily** /-zɪli/ *adv.* **diz·zi·ness** *noun* [U]
IDM **the dizzy ˈheights (of sth)** (*informal*) an important or impressive position: *She dreamed of reaching the dizzy heights of stardom.*

**dizzy·ing** /ˈdɪziɪŋ/ *adj.* making you feel dizzy: *The car drove past at a dizzying speed.*

**DJ** /ˈdiː dʒeɪ/ *noun, verb*
- *noun* **1** (*also* **deejay**) a person whose job is to introduce and play recorded popular music, on radio or television or at a club, party, etc. (the abbreviation for 'disc jockey') **2** (*BrE*) a black or white jacket worn with a BOW TIE at formal occasions in the evening (the abbreviation for 'dinner jacket')
- *verb* [I] (*also* **deejay**) (**DJ's, DJ'ing, DJ·d, DJ'd**) to perform as a DISC JOCKEY, especially in a club

**djinn** /dʒɪn/ *noun* (in Arabian stories) a spirit with magic powers ▶ **genie**

**DLC** /ˌdiː el ˈsiː/ *noun* [U, C] additional content for a computer game, which can be bought or obtained as a separate item (the abbreviation for 'downloadable content')

# DLitt

**DLitt** (*NAmE* **D.Litt**) /ˌdiː ˈlɪt/ *noun* a university degree at the highest level, awarded for a long record of academic research, or as an HONORARY degree to recognize sb's contribution to society (the abbreviation for 'Doctor of Letters')

**D-lock** *noun* a metal device for locking a bicycle or motorcycle that has the shape of a U with a bar across it

**DM** /ˌdiː ˈem/ *noun, verb*
- *noun* (*pl.* **DMs**) (*informal*) a private message that you send on TWITTER™ that will only be seen by the person that you send it to (the abbreviation for 'direct message')
- *verb* [T, I] (**DM's, DM'ing, DM'd**) (*informal*) to send sb a direct message (a private message that you send on TWITTER™ that will only be seen by the person you send it to): ~ **sb (sth)** *I DM'd him my email address.* ◇ ~ **(sth) (to sb)** *I'll DM the link to you.* ◇ ~ + **adv./prep.** *She DM'd back right away.*

**DNA** /ˌdiː en ˈeɪ/ *noun* [U] (*chemistry*) **1** the chemical in the cells of animals and plants that carries GENETIC information and is a type of NUCLEIC ACID (the abbreviation for 'deoxyribonucleic acid'): *A DNA test confirmed the suspect had been at the scene of the crime.* ⊃ WORDFINDER NOTE at BIOLOGY **2** the qualities and characteristics that are a fixed part of sb/sth: *The desire to win is part of his DNA.*

**DNA ˈfingerprinting** *noun* [U] = GENETIC FINGERPRINTING

**do¹** ⓘ A1 *verb, auxiliary verb, noun* ⊃ IRREGULAR VERBS ⊃ *see also* DO²
- *verb* /duː/
- ACTION **1** A1 [T] ~ **sth** used to refer to actions that you do not mention by name or do not know about: *What are you doing this evening?* ◇ *We will do what we can to help.* ◇ *Are you doing anything tomorrow evening?* ◇ *The company ought to do something about the poor service.* ◇ *What have you done to your hair?* ◇ *There's **nothing to do** (= no means of passing the time in an enjoyable way) in this place.* ◇ *There's **nothing we can do** about it (= we can't change the situation).* ◇ *What can I do for you (= how can I help)?*
- BEHAVE **2** A1 [I] to act or behave in the way mentioned: ~ **as** … *Do as you're told!* ◇ *They are free to do as they please.* ◇ + **adv./prep.** *You would do well to (= I advise you to) consider all the options before buying.*
- SUCCEED/PROGRESS **3** A1 [I] + **adv./prep.** used to ask or talk about the success or progress of sb/sth: *How is the business doing?* ◇ *She did well out of (= made a big profit from) the deal.* ◇ *He's doing very well at school (= his work is good).* ◇ *Both mother and baby are doing well (= after the birth of the baby).* ◇ (*informal*) *How are you doing (= how are you?)*
- TASK/ACTIVITY **4** A1 [T] ~ **sth** to work at or perform an activity or a task: *I'm doing some research on the subject.* ◇ *I have a number of things to do today.* ◇ *I do aerobics once a week.* ◇ *Let's do (= meet for) lunch.* ◇ (*informal*) *Sorry. I don't do funny (= I can't be funny).* **5** A1 [T] to perform the activity or task mentioned: ~ **the ironing, cooking, shopping, etc.** *I like listening to the radio when I'm doing the ironing.* ◇ ~ **some, a little, etc. acting, writing, etc.** *She did a lot of acting when she was at college.* **6** A2 [T] ~ **sth** used with nouns to talk about tasks such as cleaning, washing, arranging, etc: *to do (= wash) the dishes* ◇ *to do (= arrange) the flowers* ◇ *I like the way you've done your hair.*
- JOB **7** A1 [T] ~ **sth** (usually used in questions) to work at sth as a job: *What do you do (= what is your job)?* ◇ *What does she want to do when she leaves school?* ◇ *What did she do for a living?* ◇ *What's Tom doing these days?*
- STUDY **8** A1 [T] ~ **sth** to learn or study sth: *I'm doing physics, biology and chemistry.* ◇ *Have you done any (= studied anything by) Keats?*
- SOLVE **9** A2 [T] ~ **sth** to find the answer to sth; to solve sth: *I can't do this sum.* ◇ *Are you good at doing crosswords?*
- MAKE **10** A2 [T] ~ **sth** to produce, make or provide sth: ~ **sth** *to do a drawing/painting/sketch* ◇ *Does this pub do lunches?* ◇ *Who's doing the food for the wedding reception?* ◇ ~ **sth for sb** *I'll do a copy for you.* ◇ ~ **sb sth** *I'll do you a copy.* ⊃ SYNONYMS at MAKE
- BE SUITABLE/ENOUGH **11** B2 [I, T] to be suitable or be enough for sb/sth: *'Can you lend me some money?' 'Sure—will $20 do?'* ◇ ~ **for sb/sth** *These shoes won't do for the party.* ◇ ~ **as sth** *The box will do fine as a table.* ◇ ~ **sb (+ adv./prep.)** (*especially BrE*) *This room will do me nicely, thank you (= it has everything I need).*
- PERFORM **12** [T] ~ **sth** to perform or produce a play, an OPERA, etc: *The local dramatic society is doing 'Hamlet' next month.*
- COPY SB **13** [T] ~ **sb/sth** to copy sb's behaviour or the way sb speaks, sings, etc., especially in order to make people laugh: *He does a great Elvis Presley.* ◇ *Can you do a Welsh accent?*
- FINISH **14** **be/get sth done** [I, T] to finish sth: *Sit there and wait till I'm done.* ◇ **be done doing sth** *I've done talking—let's get started.* ◇ **get sth done** *Did you get your article done in time?*
- TRAVEL **15** [T] ~ **sth** to travel a particular distance: *How many miles did you do during your tour?* ◇ *My car does 40 miles to the gallon (= uses one GALLON of petrol to travel 40 miles).* **16** [T] ~ **sth** to complete a journey: *We did the round trip in two hours.*
- SPEED **17** [T] ~ **sth** to travel at or reach a particular speed: *The car was doing 90 miles an hour.*
- VISIT **18** [T] ~ **sth** (*informal*) to visit a place as a tourist: *We did Tokyo in three days.*
- SPEND TIME **19** [T] ~ **sth** to spend a period of time doing sth: *She did a year at college, but then dropped out.* ◇ *He did six years (= in prison) for armed robbery.*
- DEAL WITH **20** [T] ~ **sb/sth** to deal with or attend to sb/sth: *The hairdresser said she could do me (= cut my hair) at three.*
- COOK **21** [T] ~ **sth** to cook sth: *How would you like your steak done?*
- CHEAT **22** [T, usually passive] (*BrE, informal*) to cheat sb: **be done** *This isn't a genuine antique—you've been done.*
- PUNISH **23** [T] ~ **sb (for sth)** (*BrE, informal*) to punish sb: *They did him for tax evasion.* ◇ *She got done for speeding.*
- STEAL **24** [T] ~ **sth** (*informal*) to steal from a place: *The gang did a warehouse and a supermarket.*
- TAKE DRUGS **25** [T] ~ **sth** (*informal*) to take an illegal drug: *He doesn't smoke, drink or do drugs.*
- HAVE SEX **26** [T] ~ **sb/it** (*slang*) to have sex with sb

IDM HELP Most idioms containing **do** are at the entries for the nouns and adjectives in the idioms, for example **do a bunk** is at BUNK. **be/have (got) nothing/not much to do with sb/sth** to be sth that sb does not need to know about or should not get involved in: *It's my decision—it's nothing to do with you.* ◇ *'How much do you earn?' 'What's it got to do with you?'* ◇ *We don't have very much to do with our neighbours (= we do not speak to them very often).* ◇ *I'd have nothing to do with him, if I were you.* **be/have to do with sb/sth** B1 | **have (got) something, a lot, etc. to do with sb/sth** B1 to be about or connected with sb/sth: *'What do you want to see me about?' 'It's to do with that letter you sent me.'* ◇ *Her job has something to do with computers.* ◇ *Hard work has a lot to do with (= is an important reason for) her success.* **do right, well, etc. by sb** to treat sb in a way that is right, good, etc: *We need to do better by those suffering from mental illness.* **it won't 'do** (*especially BrE*) used to say that a situation is not acceptable and should be changed or improved: *This is the third time you've been late this week; it simply won't do.* **not 'do anything/a lot/much for sb** (*informal*) used to say that sth does not make sb look attractive: *That hairstyle doesn't do anything for her.* **nothing 'doing** (*informal*) used to refuse a request: *'Can you lend me ten dollars?' 'Nothing doing!'* **no you 'don't** (*informal*) used to show that you intend to stop sb from doing sth that they were going to do: *Sharon went to get into the taxi. 'Oh no you don't,' said Steve.* **that 'does it** (*informal*) used to show that you will not accept sth any longer: *That does it, I'm off. I'm not having you swear at me like that.* **that's 'done it** (*informal*) used to say that an accident, a mistake, etc. has had a very bad effect on sth: *That's done it. You've completely broken it this time.* **that will 'do** used to order sb to stop doing or saying sth: *That'll do, children—you're getting far too noisy.*

**what do you 'do for sth?** used to ask how sb manages to obtain the thing mentioned: *What do you do for entertainment out here?* **what is sb/sth 'doing …?** used to ask why sb/sth is in the place mentioned: *What are these shoes doing on my desk?*
**PHRV** **do a'way with sb/yourself** (*informal*) to kill sb/yourself **do a'way with sth** (*informal*) to stop doing or having sth; to make sth end **SYN** **abolish**: *He thinks it's time we did away with the monarchy.* **do sb/sth 'down** (*BrE, informal*) **1** to criticize sb/sth unfairly: *The media is always doing British industry down.* **2** to take an unfair advantage over sb **'do for sb/sth** [often passive] (*informal*) to destroy or kill sb/sth, or to have a very bad or harmful effect on them: *Without that contract, we're done for.* **do sb/yourself 'in** (*informal*) **1** to kill sb/yourself **2** [usually passive] to make sb very tired: *Come and sit down—you look done in.* **do sth↔'in** (*informal*) to injure a part of the body: *He did his back in lifting heavy furniture.* **do sb 'out of sth** (*informal*) to unfairly prevent sb from having what they ought to have: *She was done out of her promotion.* **do sth↔'out (in sth)** [usually passive] to decorate sth such as a room: *The rooms are done out in pale blue and white.* **do sb 'over** (*especially BrE, informal*) to attack and beat sb severely: *He was done over by a gang of thugs.* **do sth↔'over 1** to clean or decorate sth again: *The paintwork will need doing over soon.* **2** (*NAmE*) to do sth again: *She insisted that everything be done over.* **3** (*BrE, informal*) to enter a building by force and steal things: *He got home to find that his flat had been done over.* **do 'up** to be fastened: *The skirt does up at the back.* **do sth↔'up 1** to fasten a coat, skirt, etc.: *He never bothers to do his jacket up.* **OPP** **undo 2** to make sth into a package **SYN** **wrap**: *She was carrying a package done up in brown paper.* **3** to repair and decorate a house, etc.: *He makes money by buying old houses and doing them up.* **do yourself 'up** (*also* **get done 'up**) (*informal*) to make yourself more attractive by putting on MAKE-UP, attractive clothes, etc. **'do sth with sb/sth** (used in negative sentences and questions with *what*): *I don't know what to do with* (= how to use) *all the food that's left over.* ◊ *What have you done with* (= where have you put) *my umbrella?* ◊ *What have you been doing with yourselves* (= how have you been passing the time)? ⊃ see also **CAN'T BE DOING WITH** *at* **CAN**¹, **COULD DO WITH STH** *at* **COULD**. **do with'out (sb/sth)** to manage without sb/sth: *She can't do without a secretary.* ◊ *If they can't get it to us in time, we'll just have to do without.* ◊ **do without doing sth** (*ironic*) *I could have done without being* (= I wish I had not been) *woken up so early.*

■ **auxiliary verb** /də, du, *strong form* du:/ (**does** /dʌz/, **did** /dɪd/, **done** /dʌn/) **1** ⓘ used before a full verb to form negative sentences and questions: *I don't like fish.* ◊ *They didn't go to Paris.* ◊ *Don't forget to write.* ◊ *Does she speak French?* **2** ⓘ used to make QUESTION TAGS (= short questions at the end of statements): *You live in New York, don't you?* ◊ *She doesn't work here, does she?* **3** ⓘ used to avoid repeating a full verb: *He plays better than he did a year ago.* ◊ *She works harder than he does.* ◊ *'He put more feeling into the words than he had ever done before.'* ◊ *'Who won?' 'I did.'* ◊ *'I love peaches.' 'So do I.'* ◊ *'I don't want to go back.' 'Neither do I.'* **4** ⓘ used when no other auxiliary verb is present, to emphasize what you are saying: *He does look tired.* ◊ *She did at least write to say thank you.* ◊ (*BrE*) *Do shut up!* **5** used to change the order of the subject and verb when an adverb is moved to the front: *Not only does she speak Spanish, she's also good with computers.*

■ **noun** /du:/ (*pl.* **dos** *or* **do's** /du:z/) **1** (*BrE, informal*) a party; a social event: *Are you having a big do for your birthday?* **2** (*especially NAmE, informal*) the style in which a person's hair is arranged **SYN** **hairdo**
**IDM** **dos and don'ts** (*also* **do's and don'ts**) (*informal*) rules that you should follow: *Here are some dos and don'ts for exercise during pregnancy.* ⊃ more at **FAIR** *adj.*

**do²** = DOH ⊃ see also DO¹
**do.** *abbr.* DITTO
**DOA** /ˌdiː əʊ ˈeɪ/ *abbr.* = DEAD ON ARRIVAL
**do·able** /ˈduːəbl/ *adj.* (*informal*) **1** [not usually before noun] able to be done: *It's not doable by Friday.* ⊃ compare FEASIBLE **2** (*BrE*) sexually attractive

### 457

### docking station

▼ **VOCABULARY BUILDING**
**Household jobs: do or make?**
- To talk about jobs in the home you can use such phrases as **wash the dishes**, **clean the kitchen floor**, **set the table**, etc. In conversation the verb **do** is often used instead: *Let me do the dishes.* ◊ *Michael said he would do the kitchen floor.* ◊ *It's your turn to do the table.* **Do** is often used with nouns ending in *-ing*: *to do the shopping/cleaning/ironing/vacuuming.*
- The verb **make** is used especially in the phrase **make the beds** and when you are talking about preparing or cooking food: *He makes a great lasagne.* ◊ *I'll make breakfast while you're having a shower.* You can also say **get**, **get ready** and, especially in NAmE, **fix** for preparing meals: *Can you get dinner while I put the kids to bed?* ◊ *Sit down—I'll fix supper for you.*

**dob** /dɒb; *NAmE* dɑːb/ *verb* (**-bb-**) (*BrE, informal*)
**PHRV** **dob sb 'in (to sb) (for sth/for doing sth)** to tell sb about sth that another person has done wrong: *Sue dobbed me in to the teacher.*
**D.O.B.** *abbr.* date of birth
**Do·ber·mann** /ˈdəʊbəmən; *NAmE* -bərm-/ (*also* **Do·ber·mann pin·scher** /ˌdəʊbəmən ˈpɪnʃə(r); *NAmE* -bərm-/) (*both especially BrE*) (*NAmE usually* **Do·ber·man**, **Do·ber·man pin·scher**) *noun* a large dog with short dark hair, often used for guarding buildings
**doc** /dɒk; *NAmE* dɑːk/ *noun* (*informal*) **1** a way of addressing or talking about a doctor **2** a document
**do·cent** /ˈdəʊsnt/ *noun* (*NAmE*) a person whose job is to show tourists around a museum etc. and talk to them about it
**do·cile** /ˈdəʊsaɪl; *NAmE* ˈdɑːsl/ *adj.* quiet and easy to control: *a docile child/horse/temperament* ▶ **do·cile·ly** /ˈdəʊsaɪlli; *NAmE* ˈdɑːsəli/ *adv.* **do·cil·ity** /dəʊˈsɪləti/ *NAmE* dɑː-/ *noun* [U]

**dock** /dɒk; *NAmE* dɑːk/ *noun, verb*
■ *noun* **1** [C] a part of a port where ships are repaired, or where goods are put onto or taken off them: *dock workers* ◊ *in ~ The ship was in dock.* ⊃ see also DRY DOCK **2 docks** [pl.] a group of docks in a port and the buildings around them that are used for repairing ships, storing goods, etc. **3** [C] (*NAmE*) = JETTY **4** [C] a raised platform for loading vehicles or trains **5** [C] the part of a court where the person who has been accused of a crime stands or sits during a trial: **in the ~** *He's been in the dock* (= on trial for a crime) *several times already.* **6** [U] a wild plant of northern Europe with large thick leaves that can be rubbed on skin that has been STUNG by NETTLES to make it less painful: *dock leaves* **7** (*computing*) = DOCKING STATION
■ *verb* **1** [I, T] **~(sth)** if a ship **docks** or you **dock** a ship, it sails into a HARBOUR and stays there: *The ferry is expected to dock at 6.* **2** [I, T] **~(sth)** if two SPACECRAFT **dock**, or are **docked**, they are joined together in space: *Next year, a technology module will be docked on the space station.* ⊃ WORDFINDER NOTE *at* SPACE **3** [T] to take away part of sb's wages, etc.: **~ sth** *If you're late, your wages will be docked.* ◊ **~ sth from/off sth** *They've docked 15 per cent off my pay for this week.* **4** [T] **~ sth** (*computing*) to connect a computer to a DOCKING STATION: *I docked my laptop and started work.* **OPP** **undock 5** [T] **~ sth** to cut an animal's tail short
**dock·er** /ˈdɒkə(r); *NAmE* ˈdɑːk-/ (*especially BrE*) (*NAmE usually* **long·shore·man**) *noun* a person whose job is moving goods on and off ships ⊃ compare STEVEDORE
**docket** /ˈdɒkɪt; *NAmE* ˈdɑːk-/ *noun* **1** (*BrE, business*) a document or label that shows what is in a package, which goods have been delivered, which jobs have been done, etc. **2** (*NAmE*) (*also* **docket sheet**) a list of cases to be dealt with in a particular court **3** (*NAmE*) a list of items to be discussed at a meeting
**'docking station** (*also* **dock**) *noun* (*computing*) a piece of equipment to which a laptop, smartphone or other mobile

# dockland 458

device can be connected, to provide access to a power supply or so that it can be used with a printer, a keyboard, speakers, etc.

**dock·land** /ˈdɒklænd; NAmE ˈdɑːk-/ noun [U] (also **docklands** [pl.]) (BrE) the district near DOCKS (= the place where ships are loaded and unloaded in a port)

**dock·side** /ˈdɒksaɪd; NAmE ˈdɑːk-/ noun [sing.] the area around the DOCKS (= the place where ships are loaded and unloaded) in a port

**dock·yard** /ˈdɒkjɑːd; NAmE ˈdɑːkjɑːrd/ noun an area with DOCKS (= the place where ships are loaded and unloaded in a port) and equipment for building and repairing ships

**Doc ˈMartens**™ noun (informal) = DR MARTENS™

**doc·tor** 🔵 **A1** /ˈdɒktə(r); NAmE ˈdɑːk-/ noun, verb
- noun (abbr. **Dr**) **1** 🔵 **A1** a person who has been trained in medical science, whose job is to treat people who are ill or injured: *You'd better see a doctor about that cough.* ◊ *Dr Staples* (= as a title/form of address) ◊ *He's training to be a doctor.* ⊃ see also FAMILY DOCTOR, FLYING DOCTOR, JUNIOR DOCTOR, WITCH DOCTOR ⊃ **WORDFINDER NOTE** at HOSPITAL

> **WORDFINDER** cure, examine, medicine, patient, practice, prescribe, receptionist, specialist, surgeon

**2** 🔵 **A1** **doctor's** a place where a doctor sees patients: *an appointment at the doctor's* **3** a person who has received the highest university degree: *a Doctor of Philosophy/Law* ◊ *Dr Franks* (= as a title/form of address) **4** (especially NAmE) used as a title or form of address for a dentist or VET ⊃ see also SPIN DOCTOR
🔶 **just what the doctor ˈordered** (humorous) exactly what sb wants or needs
- verb **1** ~ **sth** to change sth in order to trick sb **SYN** falsify: *He was accused of doctoring the figures.* **2** ~ **sth** to add sth harmful to food or drink: *The wine had been doctored.* **3** ~ **sth** (informal) to remove part of the sex organs of an animal **SYN** neuter

**doc·tor·al** /ˈdɒktərəl; NAmE ˈdɑːk-/ adj. [only before noun] connected with a doctorate: (BrE) *a doctoral thesis* ◊ (NAmE) *a doctoral dissertation*

**doc·tor·ate** /ˈdɒktərət; NAmE ˈdɑːk-/ noun the highest university degree: *She's studying for her doctorate.*

**doc·trin·aire** /ˌdɒktrɪˈneə(r); NAmE ˌdɑːktrɪˈner/ adj. (disapproving) strictly following a theory in all circumstances, even if there are practical problems or people disagree: *a doctrinaire conservative* ◊ *doctrinaire attitudes/beliefs/policies*

**doc·trin·al** /dɒkˈtraɪnl; NAmE ˈdɑːktrənl/ adj. (formal) relating to a doctrine or doctrines: *the doctrinal position of the English church* ◊ (disapproving) *a rigidly doctrinal approach*
▶ **doc·trin·al·ly** /dɒkˈtraɪnəli/ NAmE ˈdɑːk-/ adv.

**doc·trine** 🔵+ **C1** /ˈdɒktrɪn; NAmE ˈdɑːk-/ noun **1** 🔵+ **C1** [C, U] a belief or set of beliefs held and taught by a Church, a political party, etc: *the doctrine of parliamentary sovereignty* ◊ *Christian doctrine* **2 Doctrine** [C] (US) a statement of government policy: *the Monroe Doctrine*

**docu·drama** /ˈdɒkjudrɑːmə; NAmE ˈdɑːk-/ noun a film, usually made for television, in which real events are shown in the form of a story

**docu·ment** 🔵 **A2** 🌐 noun, verb
- noun /ˈdɒkjumənt; NAmE ˈdɑːk-/ **1** 🔵 **A2** an official paper, book or electronic file that gives information about sth, or that can be used as evidence or proof of sth: *Please read and sign the attached document.* ◊ *This is an important legal document.* ◊ *court/travel documents* ◊ *According to documents released yesterday, he was paid over £1 million last year.* ◊ *Copies of the relevant documents must be filed at court.*

> **WORDFINDER** agreement, binding, certificate, clause, deed, draft, draw up, subsection, witness

**2** 🔵 **A2** a computer file that contains text that has a name that identifies it: *Save the document before closing.* ◊ *Click here to print your document.* ◊ *an XML/a PDF document*
- verb /ˈdɒkjument; NAmE ˈdɑːk-/ **1** 🔵+ **B2** ~ **sth** to record sth in the form of a written document, photograph, film, etc: *Urban life in the nineteenth century is well documented.* ◊ *The results are documented in Chapter 3.* **2** 🔵+ **B2** ~ **sth** to support or accompany sth with documents: *This is a meticulously documented biography.*

**docu·men·tary** 🔵 **B1** /ˌdɒkjuˈmentri; NAmE ˌdɑːk-/ noun, adj.
- noun 🔵 **B1** (pl. **-ies**) ~ **(about-/on sth)** a film or a radio or television programme giving facts about sth: *a television documentary about the future of nuclear power* ⊃ **WORDFINDER NOTE** at PROGRAMME
- adj. [only before noun] **1** consisting of documents: *documentary evidence/sources/material* **2** giving a record of or report on the facts about sth, especially by using pictures, recordings, etc. of people involved: *a documentary film about the war*

**docu·men·ta·tion** 🔵+ **C1** /ˌdɒkjumenˈteɪʃn; NAmE ˌdɑːk-/ noun [U] **1** 🔵+ **C1** the documents that are required for sth, or that give evidence or proof of sth: *I couldn't enter the country because I didn't have all the necessary documentation.* **2** 🔵+ **C1** written instructions for using a product, especially a computer program or equipment: *user documentation* **3** the act of recording sth in a document; the state of being recorded in a document: *the documentation of an agreement*

**dod·der·ing** /ˈdɒdərɪŋ; NAmE ˈdɑːd-/ (BrE also **dod·dery** /ˈdɒdəri; NAmE ˈdɑːd-/) adj. weak, slow and not able to walk in a steady way, especially because you are old

**dod·dle** /ˈdɒdl; NAmE ˈdɑːdl/ noun [sing.] (BrE, informal) a task or an activity that is very easy **SYN** cinch: *The first year of the course was an absolute doddle.* ◊ *The machine is a doddle to set up and use.*

**do·deca·he·dron** /ˌdəʊdekəˈhiːdrən/ noun (geometry) a solid shape with twelve flat sides

**dodge** /dɒdʒ; NAmE dɑːdʒ/ verb, noun
- verb **1** [T, I] to move quickly and suddenly to one side in order to avoid sb/sth: ~ **sth** *He ran across the road, dodging the traffic.* ◊ (+ adv./prep.) *The girl dodged behind a tree to hide from the other children.* **2** [T] (rather informal) to avoid doing sth, especially in a dishonest way: ~ **sth** *He dodged his military service.* ◊ ~ **doing sth** *She tried to dodge paying her taxes.*
🔶 **dodge a/the ˈbullet** | **dodge ˈbullets** (especially US, informal) to only just avoid getting hurt in a dangerous situation: *South Texas dodged a bullet with no direct hit from Hurricane Emily.*
- noun (informal) a clever and dishonest trick, played in order to avoid sth: *When it comes to getting off work, he knows all the dodges.* ⊃ see also TAX DODGE

**dodge·ball** /ˈdɒdʒbɔːl; NAmE ˈdɑːdʒ-/ noun [U] (NAmE) a game in which teams of players form circles and try to hit other teams with a large ball

**dodgem** /ˈdɒdʒəm; NAmE ˈdɑːdʒ-/ noun (BrE) **1 the dodgems** [pl.] a ride at a FUNFAIR in which people drive small electric cars around a track, trying to hit the other cars: *The kids wanted to go on the dodgems.* **2** (also **ˈdodgem car**) (also **bumper car** NAmE, BrE) one of the small electric cars that you drive in the dodgems

**dodgem / bumper car**

**dodger** /ˈdɒdʒə(r); NAmE ˈdɑːdʒ-/ noun (usually in compounds) (informal) a person who dishonestly avoids doing sth: *tax dodgers* ◊ *a crackdown on fare dodgers on trains* ⊃ see also DRAFT DODGER, TAX DODGER

**dodgy** /ˈdɒdʒi; NAmE ˈdɑːdʒi/ adj. (BrE, informal) (**dodgi·er**, **dodgi·est**) **1** seeming or likely to be dishonest **SYN** suspicious: *He made a lot of money, using some very dodgy methods.* ◊ *I don't want to get involved in anything dodgy.*

**2** not working well; not in good condition: *I can't play—I've got a dodgy knee.* ◊ *The marriage had been distinctly dodgy for a long time.* **3** involving risk, danger or difficulty: *If you get into any dodgy situations, call me.*

**dodo** /ˈdəʊdəʊ/ *noun* (*pl.* **-os**) **1** a large bird that could not fly and that is now EXTINCT (= no longer exists) **2** (*NAmE*) a stupid person IDM see DEAD *adj.*

**doe** /dəʊ/ *noun* a female DEER; a female of some other animals, including RABBITS and HARES ⇒ compare BUCK, HIND, STAG

**doek** /dʊk/ *noun* (*pl.* **doeks** or **doeke** /ˈdʊkə/) (*SAfrE*) a square piece of cloth tied around the head by women or girls

**doer** /ˈduːə(r)/ *noun* (*approving*) a person who does things rather than thinking or talking about them: *We need fewer organizers and more doers.* ⇒ see also EVIL-DOER

**does** /dʌz/ ⇒ DO¹ *verb*

**doesn't** /ˈdʌznt/ *short form* does not

**dof** /dɒf; *NAmE* dɑːf/ *SAfrE* [dɔf] *adj.* (**dofer, dofest**) (*SAfrE, informal*) stupid; not knowing very much: *Sometimes our guys appear a bit dof!*

**doff** /dɒf; *NAmE* dɔːf/ *verb* ~ **sth** to take off a piece of clothing; to take off your hat, especially to show respect for sb/sth

**dog** ⓘ A1 /dɒɡ; *NAmE* dɔːɡ/ *noun, verb*
■ *noun* **1** ⓘ A1 [C] an animal with four legs and a tail, often kept as a pet or trained for work, for example hunting or guarding buildings. There are many types of dog, some of which are wild: *I took the dog for a walk.* ◊ *I'm just going to walk the dog.* ◊ *I could hear a dog barking.* ◊ *dog walkers/owners* ◊ *dog food/biscuits* ⇒ see also BIRD DOG, GUARD DOG, GUIDE DOG, GUN DOG, HEARING DOG, LAPDOG, PRAIRIE DOG, SHEEPDOG, SNIFFER DOG **2** [C] a male dog, FOX, WOLF or OTTER ⇒ compare BITCH **3** **the dogs** [*pl.*] (*BrE, informal*) GREYHOUND racing **4** [C] (*especially NAmE, informal*) a thing of low quality; a failure: *Her last movie was an absolute dog.* **5** [C] (*informal*) an offensive way of describing a woman who is not considered attractive **6** [C] (*informal, disapproving*) used, especially after an adjective, to describe a man who has done sth bad: *You dirty dog!* ⇒ see also HOT DOG, TOP DOG, WATCHDOG
IDM **a ˌdog and ˈpony show** (*NAmE, informal, disapproving*) an event that is planned only in order to impress people so that they will support or buy sth (**a case of**) **ˌdog eat ˈdog** a situation in business, politics, etc. where there is a lot of competition and people are willing to harm each other in order to succeed: *I'm afraid in this line of work it's a case of dog eat dog.* ◊ *We're operating in a dog-eat-dog world.* **a ˌdog in the ˈmanger** (*NAmE*) a person who stops other people from enjoying what he or she cannot use or does not want **a ˌdog's ˈbreakfast/ˈdinner** (*BrE, informal*) a thing that has been done badly SYN mess: *He's made a real dog's breakfast of these accounts.* **a ˌdog's ˈlife** an unhappy life, full of problems or unfair treatment **ˌevery dog has his/its ˈday** (*saying*) everyone has good luck or success at some point in their life **ˌgive a dog a bad ˈname** (*saying*) when a person already has a bad reputation, it is difficult to change it because others will continue to blame or suspect him/her **go to the ˈdogs** (*NAmE also* **go to hell in a ˈhandbasket**) (*informal*) to get into a very bad state: *This firm's gone to the dogs since the new management took over.* **ˌlike a ˈdog** (*informal*) **1** extremely hard: *I've been working like a dog recently.* **2** in a very bad or cruel way: *They treated him like a dog.* **ˌlike a dog with a ˈbone** (*informal*) very determined and refusing to give up: *When she sensed a good story she was like a dog with a bone.* **ˌnot have a ˈdog's chance** to have no chance at all: *He hasn't a dog's chance of passing the exam.* **ˌthrow sb to the ˈdogs** to allow sb to suffer or be punished in an unfair way, as if they have no value **ˌwhy keep a ˌdog and bark yourˈself?** (*informal, saying*) if sb can do a task for you, there is no point in doing it yourself ⇒ more at HAIR, RAIN *v.*, SICK *adj.*, SLEEP *v.*, TAIL *n.*, TEACH
■ *verb* (**-gg-**) **1** [often passive] (of a problem or bad luck) to cause you trouble for a long time: **be dogged by sth** *He had been dogged by ill health all his life.* **2** ~ **sb/sth** to follow sb

closely: *She had the impression that someone was dogging her steps.*

**ˈdog biscuit** *noun* a small hard biscuit fed to dogs

**ˈdog-box** /ˈdɒɡbɒks; *NAmE* ˈdɔːɡbɑːks/ *noun*
IDM **be in the ˈdogbox** (*SAfrE, informal*) = BE IN THE DOGHOUSE at DOGHOUSE

**ˈdog-catcher** /ˈdɒɡkætʃə(r); *NAmE* ˈdɔːɡ-, -ketʃ-/ *noun* (*NAmE, becoming old-fashioned*) = DOG WARDEN

**ˈdog collar** *noun* **1** a COLLAR for a dog **2** (*informal*) a stiff white COLLAR fastened at the back and worn by some Christian priests

**ˈdog days** *noun* [*pl.*] the hottest period of the year

**ˈdog-eared** *adj.* (of a book) used so much that the corners of many of the pages are turned down

**ˈdog-end** *noun* (*BrE, informal*) the end of a cigarette that has been smoked

**ˈdog fight** /ˈdɒɡfaɪt; *NAmE* ˈdɔːɡ-/ *noun* **1** a fight between aircraft in which they fly around close to each other **2** a struggle between two people or groups in order to win sth **3** **dog fight** a fight between dogs, especially one that is arranged illegally, for entertainment ▶ **ˈdog fight·ing** *noun* [U]

**ˈdog·fish** /ˈdɒɡfɪʃ; *NAmE* ˈdɔːɡ-/ *noun* (*pl.* **dog·fish**) a small SHARK (= an aggressive sea fish with very sharp teeth)

**dog·ged** /ˈdɒɡɪd; *NAmE* ˈdɔːɡ-/ *adj.* [usually before noun] (*approving*) showing DETERMINATION; not giving up easily SYN **tenacious**: *dogged determination/persistence* ◊ *their dogged defence of the city* ▶ **ˈdog·ged·ly** *adv.* SYN **tenaciously** **ˈdog·ged·ness** *noun* [U] SYN **tenacity**

**dog·gerel** /ˈdɒɡərəl; *NAmE* ˈdɔːɡ-/ *noun* [U] poetry that is badly written or silly, sometimes because the writer has not intended it to be serious

**dog·gone** /ˈdɒɡɒn; *NAmE* ˈdɔːɡɔːn/ *adj.* [only before noun], *adv., exclamation* (*NAmE, informal*) used to show that you are annoyed or surprised: *Where's the doggone key?* ◊ *Don't drive so doggone fast.* ◊ *Well, doggone it!*

**doggy** /ˈdɒɡi; *NAmE* ˈdɔːɡi/ *noun, adj.*
■ *noun* (*also* **dog·gie**) (*pl.* **-ies**) (*informal*) a child's word for a dog
■ *adj.* [only before noun] of or like a dog: *a doggy smell*

**ˈdoggy bag** (*also* **ˈdoggie bag**) *noun* (*informal*) a bag for taking home any food that is left after a meal in a restaurant

**ˈdog handler** *noun* a person who works with trained dogs

**dog·house** /ˈdɒɡhaʊs; *NAmE* ˈdɔːɡ-/ (*NAmE*) (*BrE* **ken·nel**) *noun* a small shelter for a dog to sleep in
IDM **be in the ˈdoghouse** (*NAmE, BrE, informal*) if you are **in the doghouse**, sb is annoyed with you because of sth that you have done

**ˈdog-leg** (*especially BrE*) (*also* **ˈdogleg** *especially in NAmE*) *noun* a sharp bend, especially in a road or on a GOLF COURSE

**dogma** /ˈdɒɡmə; *NAmE* ˈdɔːɡ-/ *noun* [U, C] (*often disapproving*) a belief or set of beliefs held by a group or organization that others are expected to accept without argument: *political/religious/party dogma* ◊ *one of the central dogmas of the Church*

**dog·matic** /dɒɡˈmætɪk; *NAmE* dɔːɡ-/ *adj.* (*disapproving*) being certain that your beliefs are right and that others should accept them, without paying attention to evidence or other opinions: *a dogmatic approach* ◊ *There is a danger of becoming too dogmatic about teaching methods.* ▶ **dog·matic·al·ly** /-kli/ *adv.*

**dog·ma·tism** /ˈdɒɡmətɪzəm; *NAmE* ˈdɔːɡ-/ *noun* [U] (*disapproving*) behaviour and attitudes that are dogmatic

**ˈdo-gooder** *noun* (*informal, disapproving*) a person who tries to help other people but who does it in a way that is annoying

**dogs·body** /ˈdɒɡzbɒdi; *NAmE* ˈdɔːɡzbɑːdi/ *noun* (*pl.* **-ies**) (*BrE, informal*) a person who does all the boring jobs that nobody else wants to do, and who is treated as being less

# dogsled 460

important than other people: *I got myself a job as a general office dogsbody on a small magazine.*

**dog·sled** (*also* **dog sled**) /ˈdɒɡsled; NAmE ˈdɔːɡ-/ *noun* (NAmE) a SLEDGE (= a vehicle that slides over snow) pulled by dogs, used especially in Canada and Alaska

**ˈdog tag** *noun* **1** a small piece of metal attached to a dog's COLLAR, typically giving its name and the owner's address **2** (NAmE, *informal*) a small piece of metal that US soldiers wear round their necks with their name and number on it

**dog-ˈtired** *adj.* [not usually before noun] (*informal*) very tired SYN **exhausted**

**ˈdog warden** (NAmE *also*, *becoming old-fashioned* **dog-catch·er**, *formal* **animal control officer**) *noun* a person whose job is to catch dogs and cats that are walking freely in the streets and do not seem to have a home

**dog·wood** /ˈdɒɡwʊd; NAmE ˈdɔːɡ-/ *noun* [U, C] a bush or small tree with red or pink BERRIES and red STEMS, that grows in northern regions; the hard wood of this tree

**doh** /dəʊ/
- (*also* **do**) *noun* (*music*) the 1st and 8th note of a MAJOR SCALE
- *exclamation* (*also* **d'oh**) (*informal*) used when you have just said or done sth that you know is stupid: *Doh! That was the biggest mistake ever.* ORIGIN Used by Homer Simpson in *The Simpsons* television series.

**DOI** /ˌdiː əʊ ˈaɪ/ *abbr.* (*computing*) digital object identifier (a series of numbers and letters that identifies a particular text or document published in electronic form on the internet)

**doily** /ˈdɔɪli/ *noun* (*pl.* **-ies**) **1** a small circle of paper or cloth with a pattern of very small holes in it, that you put on a plate under a cake or sandwiches **2** (NAmE) a small attractive MAT that you put on top of a piece of furniture

**doing** /ˈduːɪŋ/ *noun* [C, usually pl., U] a thing done or caused by sb: *I've been hearing a lot about your doings recently.* ◇ *I promise you this was none of my doing* (= I didn't do it). IDM **take some ˈdoing** | **take a lot of ˈdoing** to be hard work; to be difficult: *Getting it finished by tomorrow will take some doing.*

**do-it-yourˈself** *noun* [U] (*especially BrE*) = DIY: *The materials you need are available from any good do-it-yourself store.*

**dojo** /ˈdəʊdʒəʊ/ *noun* (*pl.* **-os**) (*from Japanese*) a hall or school where JUDO or other similar MARTIAL ARTS (= fighting sports) are practised

**dol·drums** /ˈdɒldrəmz; NAmE ˈdəʊl-/ *noun* [pl.] (*usually* **the doldrums**) **1** the state of feeling sad or depressed: **in the ~** *He's been in the doldrums ever since she left him.* **2** a lack of activity or improvement: *The bond market normally revives after the summer doldrums.* ◇ **in the ~** *Despite these measures, the economy remains in the doldrums.* ORIGIN From the place in the ocean near the equator where there are sudden periods of calm. A sailing ship caught in this area can be stuck there because of a lack of wind.

**dole** /dəʊl/ *noun, verb*
- *noun* [sing.] (*usually* **the dole**) (*BrE*, *informal*) money paid by the state to unemployed people: **on the ~** *He's been on the dole* (= without a job) *for a year.* ◇ *The changes will affect about 80 per cent of those receiving the dole.* ◇ *We could all be in the dole queue on Monday* (= have lost our jobs). ⇒ compare BENEFIT (2)
- *verb* PHRV ˌdole sth↔ˈout (to sb) (*informal*) to give out an amount of food, money, etc. to a number of people in a group

**dole·ful** /ˈdəʊlfl/ *adj.* very sad SYN **mournful**: *a doleful expression/face/song* ◇ *a doleful looking man* ▶ **dole·ful·ly** /-fəli/ *adv.*

**doll** /dɒl; NAmE dɑːl/ *noun, verb*
- *noun* **1** a child's toy in the shape of a person, especially a baby or a child: *a rag doll* (= one made out of cloth) ⇒ see also BARBIE DOLL™, RUSSIAN DOLL **2** (NAmE, *informal*) a kind person: *Be a doll and help me out.*
- *verb* PHRV ˌdoll sb/yourˈself ˈup (*informal*) to make sb/yourself look attractive for a party, etc., with fashionable clothes: *Are you getting dolled up for the party?*

**dol·lar** /ˈdɒlə(r); NAmE ˈdɑːl-/ *noun* **1** [C] (*symb.* **$**) the unit of money in the US, Canada, Australia and several other countries: *You will be paid in American dollars.* ◇ *a dollar bill* ◇ *He sold the company in a multimillion-dollar deal.* ◇ **per ~** *The company generates an additional $4 in sales per dollar spent on ads.* ⇒ compare BUCK ⇒ see also SILVER DOLLAR, TOP DOLLAR **2 the dollar** [sing.] (*finance*) the value of the US dollar compared with the value of the money of other countries: *The dollar closed two cents down.* IDM see BET v., MILLION

**doll·house** /ˈdɒlhaʊs; NAmE ˈdɑːl-/ (NAmE) (BrE **ˈdoll's house**) *noun* a toy house with small furniture and sometimes DOLLS in it for children to play with

**dol·lop** /ˈdɒləp; NAmE ˈdɑːl-/ *noun* (*informal*) **1** a small amount of soft food, often dropped from a spoon: *a dollop of whipped cream* **2** an amount of sth: *A dollop of romance now and then is good for everybody.*

**ˈdoll's house** (BrE) (NAmE **doll·house**) *noun* a toy house with small furniture and sometimes DOLLS in it for children to play with

**dolly** /ˈdɒli; NAmE ˈdɑːli/ *noun* (*pl.* **-ies**) **1** a child's word for a DOLL **2** a low platform on wheels for moving heavy objects

**dol·men** /ˈdɒlmen; NAmE ˈdəʊl-/ *noun* a pair or group of standing stones, with a large flat stone lying across the top of them, built in ancient times to mark a place where sb was buried

**dol·phin** /ˈdɒlfɪn; NAmE ˈdɑːl-/ *noun* a sea animal (a MAMMAL) that looks like a large fish with a pointed mouth. Dolphins are very intelligent and often friendly towards humans. There are several types of dolphin: *a school of dolphins* ⇒ compare PORPOISE

**dolt** /dəʊlt/ *noun* (*disapproving*) a stupid person SYN **idiot** ▶ **dolt·ish** *adj.*

**-dom** /dəm/ *suffix* (in nouns) **1** the condition or state of: *freedom* ◇ *martyrdom* **2** the rank of; an area ruled by: *kingdom* **3** the group of: *officialdom*

**do·main** /dəˈmeɪn, dəʊ-; NAmE dəʊˈm-/ *noun* **1** an area of knowledge or activity; especially one that sb is responsible for: *Financial matters are her domain.* ◇ *Physics used to be very much a male domain.* ⇒ see also PUBLIC DOMAIN **2** (*computing*) a set of websites on the internet that end with the same group of letters, for example '.com', '.org': *top-level domains* ⇒ WORDFINDER NOTE at WEBSITE **3** lands owned or ruled by a particular person, government, etc., especially in the past: *The Spice Islands were within the Spanish domains.* ⇒ see also EMINENT DOMAIN **4** (*mathematics*) the range of possible values of a particular VARIABLE

**doˈmain name** *noun* (*computing*) a name that identifies a website or group of websites on the internet

**dome** /dəʊm/ *noun* **1** a round roof with a CIRCULAR base: *the dome of St Paul's Cathedral* ⇒ see also GEODESIC DOME **2** a thing or a building that is like a dome in shape: *his bald dome of a head* **3** (NAmE) (in names) a sports stadium whose roof is shaped like a dome: *the Houston Astrodome*

**domed** /dəʊmd/ *adj.* [usually before noun] having a dome, or like a dome in shape: *a domed forehead/ceiling*

**do·mes·tic** /dəˈmestɪk/ *adj., noun*
- *adj.* **1** [usually before noun] of or inside a particular country; not foreign or international: *domestic affairs/politics* ◇ *Output consists of both exports and sales on the domestic market.* ◇ *domestic flights* (= to and from places within a country) OPP **foreign 2** [only before noun] used in the home; connected with the home or family: *domestic appliances* ◇ *the growing problem of domestic violence* (= violence between members of the same family) ◇ *The vast majority of paid and unpaid domestic workers are women.* **3** (of animals) kept on farms or as

pets; not wild: *horses and other* **domestic** *animals* ◊ *Most domestic cats hate getting wet.* **4** liking home life; enjoying or good at cooking, cleaning the house, etc: *I'm not a very domestic sort of person.* ▸ **do·mes·tic·al·ly** /-kli/ *adv.*: *domestically produced goods*
■ *noun* **1** (*also* do̩mestic ˈhelp, do̩mestic ˈworker) a servant who works in sb's house, doing the cleaning and other jobs **2** (*BrE, informal*) a fight between two members of the same family: *The police were called to sort out a domestic.*

**do·mes·ti·cate** /dəˈmestɪkeɪt/ *verb* **1** [often passive] ~ *sth* to make a wild animal used to living with or working for humans **2** [often passive] ~ *sth* to grow plants or crops for human use, especially for the first time **3** ~ *sb* (*often humorous*) to make sb good at cooking, caring for a house, etc.; to make sb enjoy home life: *Some men are very hard to domesticate.* ▸ **do·mes·ti·cated** *adj.*: *domesticated animals* ◊ *They've become a lot more domesticated since they got married.* ▸ **do·mes·ti·ca·tion** /dəˌmestɪˈkeɪʃn/ *noun* [U]: *the domestication of cattle*

**do·mes·ti·city** /ˌdəʊmeˈstɪsəti; *BrE also* ˌdɒm-; *NAmE also* ˌdɑːm-/ *noun* [U] life at home with your family, taking care of the house, etc: *an atmosphere of happy domesticity*

do̩mestic ˈpartner *noun* (*NAmE*) the sexual partner that sb lives with, especially when they are not married

do̩mestic ˈscience *noun* (*BrE, old-fashioned*) = HOME ECONOMICS

**domi·cile** /ˈdɒmɪsaɪl; *NAmE* ˈdɑːm-, ˈdoʊm-/ *noun, verb*
■ *noun* **1** (*formal or law*) the country that a person treats as their permanent home, or lives in and has a strong connection with **2** (*especially NAmE, formal*) a person's home **3** (*formal or law*) the place where a company is registered for tax purposes
■ *verb* **be domiciled 1** (*formal or law*) to treat a particular country as your permanent home: *to be domiciled in the United Kingdom* **2** (*especially NAmE, formal*) to live or be based in a place

**domi·ciled** /ˈdɒmɪsaɪld; *NAmE* ˈdɑːm-, ˈdoʊm-/ *adj.* [not before noun] (*formal or law*) living in a particular place: *to be domiciled in the United Kingdom*

**domi·cil·iary** /ˌdɒmɪˈsɪliəri; *NAmE* ˌdɑːmɪˈsɪlieri, ˌdoʊm-/ *adj.* [only before noun] (*formal*) in sb's home: *a domiciliary visit* (= for example, by a doctor) ◊ *domiciliary care/services/treatment*

**dom·in·ance** 🎧 C1 Ⓦ /ˈdɒmɪnəns; *NAmE* ˈdɑːm-/ *noun* [U] **1** 🎧 C1 the fact of being more important, powerful or easy to notice than sb/sth else: *political/economic dominance* ◊ *America's rise to global dominance* ◊ ~ **over sb/sth** *to achieve/assert/establish dominance over sb* **2** ~ **(over sth)** (*biology*) the fact of being dominant: *In this situation one gene has dominance over the other gene.*

**dom·in·ant** 🎧 B2 Ⓦ /ˈdɒmɪnənt; *NAmE* ˈdɑːm-/ *adj.* **1** 🎧 B2 more important, powerful or easy to notice than other things: *The firm has achieved a dominant position in the world market.* ◊ *The dominant feature of the room was the large fireplace.* **2** (*biology*) a **dominant** GENE causes a person to have a particular physical characteristic, for example brown eyes, even if only one of their parents has passed on the GENE ⊃ compare RECESSIVE

**dom·in·ate** 🎧 B2 Ⓦ /ˈdɒmɪneɪt; *NAmE* ˈdɑːm-/ *verb* **1** 🎧 B2 [T, I] to control or have a lot of influence over sb/sth, especially in an unpleasant way: *She always says a lot in meetings, but she doesn't dominate.* ◊ ~ **sb/sth** *He tended to dominate the conversation.* ◊ *As a child he was dominated by his father.* ◊ *These two regions continue to dominate the market for orange juice.* **2** 🎧 [T] ~ **sth** to be the most important or NOTICEABLE feature of sth: *The train crash dominated the news.* ◊ *He dominates every scene he's in.* **3** [T] ~ **sth** to be the largest, highest or most obvious thing in a place: *The cathedral dominates the city.* **4** [T, I] ~ **(sth)** (*sport*) to play much better than your opponent in a game: *Arsenal dominated the first half of the match.*
▸ **dom·in·ation** /ˌdɒmɪˈneɪʃn; *NAmE* ˌdɑːm-/ *noun* [U]: *companies fighting for domination of the software market*

**dom·in·atrix** /ˌdɒmɪˈneɪtrɪks; *NAmE* ˌdɑːm-/ *noun* (*pl.* **dom·in·atri·ces** /-trɪsiːz/, **dom·in·atrixes**) a woman who controls a man during sex, often using violence to give sexual pleasure

**dom·in·eer·ing** /ˌdɒmɪˈnɪərɪŋ; *NAmE* ˌdɑːmɪˈnɪr-/ *adj.* (*disapproving*) trying to control other people without considering their opinions or feelings: *a cold and domineering father* ◊ *a domineering manner*

**Do·min·ic·an** /dəˈmɪnɪkən/ *noun* a member of a Christian group of FRIARS or NUNS following the rules of St Dominic
▸ **Do·min·ic·an** *adj.*

**do·min·ion** /dəˈmɪnjən/ *noun* **1** [U] ~ **(over sb/sth)** (*literary*) authority to rule; control: *Man has dominion over the natural world.* ◊ *Soon the whole country was under his sole dominion.* **2** [C] (*formal*) an area controlled by one political leader: *the vast dominions of the Roman Empire* **3** (*often* **Dominion**) [C] (in the past) any of the countries of the British Commonwealth that had their own government ⊃ compare COLONY, PROTECTORATE

**dom·ino** /ˈdɒmɪnəʊ; *NAmE* ˈdɑːm-/ *noun* (*pl.* **-oes**) **1** [C] a small flat block, often made of wood, with two groups of DOTS (= small round marks) representing numbers on one side, used for playing games **2 dominoes** [U] a game played with a set of dominoes, in which players take turns to put them onto a table

ˈdomino effect *noun* [usually sing.] a situation in which one event causes a series of similar events to happen one after the other ORIGIN From a comparison with the effect of standing a line of dominoes on end and then pushing one over, so that it falls and pushes the next one over, and so on, until all the dominoes fall in turn. ⊃ compare RIPPLE EFFECT

**dom·pas** /ˈdɒmpʌs; *NAmE* ˈdɑːmpæs/ *SAfrE* /ˈdɒmpəs/ *noun* (*SAfrE, informal, disapproving*) (in South Africa in the past) the official document that black people had to carry with them to prove their identity and where they could live or work

**don** /dɒn; *NAmE* dɑːn/ *noun, verb*
■ *noun* **1** (*BrE*) a teacher at a university, especially Oxford or Cambridge ⊃ see also DONNISH **2** (often used as a title) a Spanish gentleman **3** (*informal*) the leader of a group of criminals involved with the Mafia
■ *verb* (*formal*) (**-nn-**) ~ **sth** to put clothes, etc. on: *He donned his jacket and went out.*

**do·nate** 🎧 B1 /dəʊˈneɪt; *NAmE* ˈdoʊneɪt/ *verb* **1** 🎧 B1 [T, I] to give money, food, clothes, etc. to sb/sth, especially a charity: ~ **(sth) to sb/sth** *He donated thousands of pounds to charity.* ◊ ~ **sth** *The organization suggests ways to help besides donating money.* **2** 🎧 B1 to allow doctors to remove blood, a body organ, etc. in order to help sb who needs it: ~ **sth** *I've been donating blood regularly for a few years now.* ◊ **to donate organs/sperm/eggs** ◊ ~ **sth to sb** *He donated a kidney to his mother.*

**do·na·tion** 🎧 B2 /dəʊˈneɪʃn; *NAmE* doʊˈneɪʃn/ *noun* [C, U] **1** 🎧 B2 something that is given to a person or an organization such as a charity, in order to help them; the act of giving sth in this way: *a generous/large/small donation* ◊ ~ **to sb/sth** *to make a donation to charity* ◊ ~ **(of…)** *a donation of £200/a £200 donation* ◊ *The work of the charity is funded by voluntary donations.* ◊ *The campaign has raised £200000 through online donations.* ◊ *The project is funded by public donation.* ⊃ WORDFINDER NOTE at CHARITY **2** 🎧 C1 [U] the act of allowing doctors to remove blood or a body organ in order to help sb who needs it: *organ donation*

**don·cha** /ˈdəʊntʃə/ *short form* (*non-standard or humorous*) don't you: *The yearbook came out pretty good, doncha think?*

**done** /dʌn/ *adj., exclamation* ⊃ see also DO¹ *verb*
■ *adj.* [not before noun] **1** finished; completed: *When you're done, perhaps I can say something.* ◊ ~ **with** *I'll be glad when this job is over and done with.* **2** (of food) cooked enough: *The meat isn't quite done yet.* ⊃ see also WELL DONE **3** socially acceptable, especially among people who have a strict set of social rules: *At school, it simply wasn't done to show that you were upset.*
IDM **be ˈdone for** (*informal*) to be in a very bad situation; to be certain to fail: *Unless we start making some sales, we're*

**done for.** ◊ *When he pointed the gun at me, I thought I was done for* (= about to die). **be/get ˈdone for sth/for doing sth** (*BrE*, *informal*) to be caught and punished for doing sth illegal but not too serious: *I got done for speeding on my way back.* **be done ˈin** (*informal*) to be extremely tired **SYN exhausted** **be the ˌdone ˈthing** (*BrE*) to be socially acceptable behaviour **be/have ˈdone with sth** to have finished dealing with sb, or doing or using sth: *If you've done with that magazine, can I have a look at it?* **ˌdone and ˈdusted** (*BrE*, *informal*) completely finished: *That's my article for the magazine done and dusted.* **a ˌdone ˈdeal** an agreement or a plan that has been finally completed or agreed: *The merger is by no means a done deal yet.* **have ˈdone with it** (*BrE*) to do sth unpleasant as quickly as possible, so that it is finished: *Why not tell her you're quitting and have done with it?* ⇨ more at EASY *adv.*, HARD *adv.*, SOON

■ *exclamation* used to show that you accept an offer: *'I'll give you £800 for it.' 'Done!'*

**doner kebab** /ˌdɒnə kɪˈbæb; *NAmE* ˌdəʊnər kɪˈbɑːb/ *noun* (*BrE*) thin slices of cooked meat, usually served with PITTA bread ⇨ see also KEBAB

**donga** /ˈdɒŋɡə; *NAmE* ˈdɔːŋ-/ *SAfrE* [ˈdɒŋɡə] *noun* (*SAfrE*) a deep channel in the ground that is formed by the action of water: *The car slid into a donga at the side of the road.*

**donˑgle** /ˈdɒŋɡl; *NAmE* ˈdɑːŋ-/ *noun* (*computing*) a small device that is used with a computer, especially to access protected software or the internet

**Don Juan** /ˌdɒn ˈdʒuːən; *NAmE* ˌdɑːn ˈhwɑːn/ *noun* (*informal*) a man who has sex with a lot of women **ORIGIN** From the name of a character from Spanish legend who was skilled at persuading women to have sex with him.

**donˑkey** /ˈdɒŋki; *NAmE* ˈdɑːŋ-/ *noun* an animal of the horse family, with short legs and long ears. People ride donkeys or use them to carry heavy loads.
**IDM** **ˈdonkey's (years)** (*BrE*, *informal*) a very long time: *We've known each other for donkey's years.*

**ˈdonkey work** *noun* [U] (*informal*) the hard boring part of a job or task

**donˑnish** /ˈdɒnɪʃ; *NAmE* ˈdɑːn-/ *adj.* (*BrE*) (usually of a man) serious and interested in academic rather than practical matters: *He has a somewhat donnish air about him.*

**donor** /ˈdəʊnə(r); *NAmE* ˈdoʊ-/ *noun* **1** a person or an organization that makes a gift of money, clothes, food, etc. to a charity, etc: *international aid donors* (= countries that give money, etc. to help other countries) ◊ *She is one of the charity's main donors.* **2** a person who gives blood or a part of his or her body to be used by doctors in medical treatment: *a blood donor* ◊ *The heart transplant will take place as soon as a suitable donor can be found.* ◊ *donor organs* ◊ *a donor card* (= a card that you carry giving permission for doctors to use parts of your body after your death)

**don't** /dəʊnt/ *short form* do not

**don't-ˈknow** *noun* a person who does not have a strong opinion about a question that they are asked in an OPINION POLL: *A quarter of all the people surveyed were don't-knows.*

**donut** (*especially NAmE*) = DOUGHNUT

**doo-dah** /ˈduːdɑː/ (*BrE*) (*NAmE* **doo-dad** /ˈduːdæd/) *noun* (*informal*) a small object whose name you have forgotten or do not know

**dooˑdle** /ˈduːdl/ *verb* [I] to draw lines, shapes, etc., especially when you are bored or thinking about sth else: *I often doodle when I'm on the phone.* ▶ **dooˑdle** *noun*

**doo-fus** /ˈduːfəs/ *noun* (*NAmE*, *informal*) a stupid person

**doom** /duːm/ *noun*, *verb*
■ *noun* [U] death or DESTRUCTION; any terrible event that you cannot avoid: *to meet your doom* ◊ *She had a sense of impending doom* (= felt that sth very bad was going to happen).
**IDM** **ˌdoom and ˈgloom** | **ˌgloom and ˈdoom** a general feeling of having lost all hope, and of PESSIMISM (= expecting things to go badly): *Despite the obvious setbacks, it is not all doom and gloom for the England team.* **ˌprophet of ˈdoom** | **ˈdoom merchant** a person who predicts that things will go very badly: *The prophets of doom who said television would kill off the book were wrong.*
■ *verb* [usually passive] to make sb/sth certain to fail, suffer, die, etc: **be doomed to (do) sth** *The plan was doomed to failure.* ◊ **be doomed** *The marriage was doomed from the start.*

**doom-laden** *adj.* [usually before noun] predicting or leading to death, destruction or a bad situation: *doom-laden economic forecasts*

**doomˑsayer** /ˈduːmseɪə(r)/ (*especially NAmE*) (*BrE also* **doomˑster** /ˈduːmstə(r)/) *noun* a person who says that sth very bad is going to happen

**doomsˑday** /ˈduːmzdeɪ/ *noun* [sing.] the last day of the world when Christians believe that everyone will be judged by God
**IDM** **till ˈdoomsday** (*informal*) a very long time; forever: *This job's going to take me till doomsday.*

**doomy** /ˈduːmi/ *adj.* (**doomˑier**, **doomˑiest**) suggesting disaster and unhappiness: *doomy predictions* ◊ *Their new album is their doomiest.*

**Doona**™ /ˈduːnə/ *noun* (*AustralE*) a large cloth bag that is filled with feathers or other soft material and that you have on top of you in bed to keep yourself warm **SYN duvet**

**door** 🔊 **A1** /dɔː(r)/ *noun* **1** 🔊 **A1** [C] a piece of wood, glass, etc. that is opened and closed so that people can get in and out of a room, building, car, etc.; a similar thing in a cupboard: *Open the door!* ◊ *Close the door behind you, please.* ◊ *The door closed behind him.* ◊ *to shut/slam/lock/unlock the door* ◊ *a knock on/at the door* ◊ *to knock/bang on the door* ◊ *to answer the door* (= to go and open it because sb has knocked on it or rung the bell) ◊ *the front/back/side door* (= at the entrance at the front/back/side of a building) ◊ *the bedroom/kitchen/car/garage door* ◊ *~ to sth There are double doors to the rear garden.* ◊ *~ into/onto sth Each bedroom has one door onto the balcony.* ⇨ see also BACK-DOOR, CAT DOOR, DUTCH DOOR, FIRE DOOR, FRENCH DOOR, FRONT DOOR, OPEN DOOR, PATIO DOOR, REVOLVING DOOR, SLIDING DOOR, STAGE DOOR, SWING DOOR, TRAP-DOOR **2** 🔊 **A1** [C] the space when a door is open: *through a/the ~ Marc appeared through a door at the far end of the room.* ◊ *(informal)* **in the ~** *He's just arrived—she's just come in the door* ◊ *(informal)* **out the ~** *He walked out the door.* **3** 🔊 **A1** [C] the area close to the entrance of a building: *at the ~ There's somebody at the door* (= at the front door of a house). ◊ *'Can I help you?' asked the man at the door.* ⇨ see also DOORWAY **4** [C] a house, room, etc. that is a particular number of houses, rooms, etc. away from another: *the family that lives three doors up from us* ◊ *Our other branch is just a few doors down the road.* ⇨ see also NEXT DOOR *noun* **5** [U] (*BrE*) the amount of money made by selling tickets for an event **SYN gate**: *50% of the door will go to the Red Cross.*
**IDM** **be on/work the door** to work at the entrance to a theatre, club, etc., for example collecting tickets from people as they enter **ˌclose/shut the ˈdoor on sth** to make it unlikely that sth will happen: *She was careful not to close the door on the possibility of further talks.* **(from) ˌdoor to ˈdoor** from building to building: *The journey takes about an hour door to door.* ◊ *a door-to-door salesman* **(open) the ˈdoor to sth** (to provide) the means of getting or reaching sth; (to create) the opportunity for sth: *The agreement will open the door to increased international trade.* ◊ *Our courses are the door to success in English.* **ˌlay sth at sb's ˈdoor** (*formal*) to say that sb is responsible for sth that has gone wrong **ˌleave the door ˈopen (for sth)** to make sure that there is still the possibility of doing sth **ˌout of ˈdoors** not inside a building: *You should spend more time out of doors in the fresh air.* **ˌshut/ˌslam the door in sb's ˈface 1** to shut a door hard when sb is trying to come in **2** to refuse to meet or talk to sb, in a rude way **to sb's ˈdoor** directly to sb's house: *We promise to deliver to your door within 48 hours of you ordering.* ⇨ more at BACK DOOR,

BEAT v., CLOSE¹ v., CLOSED, DARKEN, DEATH, FOOT n., OPEN v., SHOW v., STABLE n., WOLF n.

**door·bell** /ˈdɔːbel; NAmE ˈdɔːrb-/ noun a bell with a button outside a house that you push to let the people inside know that you are there: *to ring the doorbell*

**do-or-ˈdie** adj. having or needing great DETERMINATION: *a do-or-die attitude*

**door·keep·er** /ˈdɔːkiːpə(r); NAmE ˈdɔːrk-/ noun a person who guards the entrance to a large building, especially to check on people going in

**door·knob** /ˈdɔːnɒb; NAmE ˈdɔːrnɑːb/ noun a type of round handle for a door that you turn in order to open the door ⊃ picture at KNOB

**ˈdoor knocker** noun = KNOCKER

**door·man** /ˈdɔːmən; NAmE ˈdɔːrm-/ noun (pl. -men /-mən/) a man, often in uniform, whose job is to stand at the entrance to a large building such as a hotel or a theatre, and open the door for visitors, find them taxis, etc. ⊃ compare PORTER (3)

**door·mat** /ˈdɔːmæt; NAmE ˈdɔːrm-/ noun 1 a small piece of strong material near a door that people can clean their shoes on 2 (*informal*) a person who allows other people to treat them badly but usually does not complain

**door·step** /ˈdɔːstep; NAmE ˈdɔːrs-/ noun, verb
■ noun 1 a step outside a door of a building, or the area that is very close to the door: *The police turned up on their doorstep at 3 o'clock this morning.* 2 (*BrE, informal*) a thick piece of bread, usually one that is made into a sandwich
IDM **on the/your ˈdoorstep** very close to where a person lives: *The nightlife is great with bars and clubs right on the doorstep.*
■ verb [T, I] (-pp-) ~ (sb) (*BrE*) when a journalist **doorsteps** sb, he or she goes to the person's house to try to speak to them, even if they do not want to say anything

**door·stop** /ˈdɔːstɒp; NAmE ˈdɔːrstɑːp/ noun a thing that is used to stop a door from closing or to prevent it from hitting and damaging a wall when it is opened

**door·way** /ˈdɔːweɪ; NAmE ˈdɔːrw-/ noun an opening into a building or a room, where the door is: *She stood in the doorway for a moment before going in.* ◇ *homeless people sleeping in shop doorways*

**doo·zy** (*also* **doo·zie**) /ˈduːzi/ noun (pl. -ies) (*NAmE, informal*) something that is very special or unusual

**dop** /dɒp; NAmE dɑːp/ *SAfrE* [dɔp] noun, verb (*SAfrE, informal*)
■ noun an alcoholic drink: *Let's have a dop.*
■ verb (-pp-) 1 [I, T] ~ (sth) to drink alcohol, especially in large amounts: *They lay around dopping all day.* 2 [T] ~ sth (*slang*) to not pass a test or an exam; to not be successful in completing a period of study at a school, university, etc: *I dopped my first year at varsity.*

**dopa·mine** /ˈdəʊpəmiːn/ noun [U] a chemical produced by nerve cells that has an effect on other cells

**dope** /dəʊp/ noun, verb
■ noun 1 [U] (*informal*) a drug that is used illegally for pleasure HELP In (*BrE*) **dope** usually means CANNABIS. In (*NAmE*) it can also refer to HEROIN. 2 [U] a drug that is taken by a person or given to an animal to affect their performance in a race or sport: *The athlete failed a dope test* (= a medical test showed that he had taken such drugs). 3 [C] (*informal*) a stupid person SYN idiot 4 [U] the ~ (on sb/sth) (*informal*) information on sb/sth, especially details that are not generally known: *Give me the dope on the new boss.*
■ verb 1 ~ sb/sth to give a drug to a person or an animal in order to affect their performance in a race or sport 2 ~ sb/sth to give sb a drug, often in their food or drink, in order to make them unconscious; to put a drug in food, etc: *Thieves doped a guard dog and stole $10000 worth of goods.* ◇ *The wine was doped.* 3 [usually passive] ~ sb (up) (*informal*) if sb is **doped** or **doped up**, they cannot think clearly or act normally because they are under the influence of drugs

**dopey** /ˈdəʊpi/ adj. (*informal*) (**dopi·er**, **dopi·est**) 1 rather stupid: *a dopey grin* 2 wanting to sleep or not thinking clearly, sometimes because you have taken a drug: *I felt dopey and drowsy after the operation.*

**dop·pel·gäng·er** /ˈdɒplgæŋə(r), -geŋ-; NAmE ˈdɑːp-/ noun (*from German*) a person's **doppelgänger** is another person who looks exactly like them

**the ˈDop·pler ef·fect** /ðə ˈdɒplər ɪfekt; NAmE ˈdɑːp-/ noun [sing.] (*physics*) the way that sound waves, light waves, etc. change in frequency depending on the direction that the source is moving in relative to the person who is observing

**ˈDop·pler shift** noun (*physics*) the change in PITCH (of sound), colour (of light), etc. caused by the Doppler effect

**Doric** /ˈdɒrɪk; NAmE ˈdɔːr-/ adj. [usually before noun] (*architecture*) used to describe the oldest style of architecture in ancient Greece that has thick plain columns and no decoration at the top: *a Doric column/temple*

**dork** /dɔːk; NAmE dɔːrk/ noun (*informal*) a stupid or boring person that other people laugh at ▸ **dorky** adj. (**dork·ier**, **dorki·est**)

**dorm** /dɔːm; NAmE dɔːrm/ noun 1 (*also* **dormitory**, ˈresidence hall) (*all NAmE*) (*BrE* ˈhall of ˈresidence, hall) a building for university or college students to live in: *There's not much space in my college dorm room.* 2 (*informal*) = DORMITORY (1)

**dor·mant** /ˈdɔːmənt; NAmE ˈdɔːrm-/ adj. not active or growing now but able to become active or to grow in the future SYN **inactive**: *a dormant volcano* ◇ *During the winter the seeds lie dormant in the soil.* OPP **active** ▸ **dor·mancy** /-mənsi/ noun [U]

**dormer ˈwindow** /ˈdɔːmə ˈwɪndəʊ; NAmE ˈdɔːrmər/ (*also* **dormer**) noun a VERTICAL window that sticks out of a room that is built into a sloping roof

**dor·mi·tory** /ˈdɔːmətri; NAmE ˈdɔːrmətɔːri/ noun (pl. -ies) 1 (*also informal* **dorm**) a room for several people to sleep in, especially in a school or other institution 2 (*NAmE*) = DORM (1)

**ˈdormitory town** (*BrE*) (*NAmE* ˈbedroom community, ˈbedroom suburb) noun a town that people live in and from where they travel to work in a bigger town or city

**dor·mouse** /ˈdɔːmaʊs; NAmE ˈdɔːrm-/ noun (pl. **dor·mice** /-maɪs/) a small animal like a mouse, with a tail covered in fur

**dorp** /dɔːp; NAmE dɔːrp/ *SAfrE* [dɔrp] noun (*SAfrE, informal*) a small town or village in the country

**dor·sal** /ˈdɔːsl; NAmE ˈdɔːrsl/ adj. [only before noun] (*specialist*) on or relating to the back of a fish or an animal: *a shark's dorsal fin* ⊃ compare VENTRAL ⊃ VISUAL VOCAB page V2 ▸ **dor·sally** /-səli/ adv.

**DOS** /dɒs; NAmE dɑːs/ abbr. (*computing*) disk operating system

**dosa** /ˈdəʊsə/ noun a southern Indian PANCAKE made with rice flour

**dos·age** /ˈdəʊsɪdʒ/ noun [C, U] [usually sing.] the amount of a medicine or drug that is taken regularly, and how often it is taken: *a high/low dosage* ◇ *to increase/reduce the dosage* ◇ *Do not exceed the recommended dosage.*

**dos and ˈdon'ts** ⊃ DOS AND DON'TS at DO¹ noun

**dose** /dəʊs/ noun, verb
■ noun 1 an amount of a medicine or a drug that is taken once, or regularly over a period of time: *a high/low/lethal dose* ◇ *Repeat the dose after 12 hours if necessary.* ⊃ WORDFINDER NOTE at MEDICINE 2 (*informal*) an amount of sth: *A dose of flu kept me off work.* ◇ *Workers at the nuclear plant were exposed to high doses of radiation.* ◇ *I can cope with her in small doses* (= for short amounts of time). IDM see MEDICINE
■ verb ~ sb/yourself (up) (with sth) to give sb/yourself a medicine or drug: *She dosed herself up with vitamin pills.* ◇ *He was heavily dosed with painkillers.*

**dosh** /dɒʃ; NAmE dɑːʃ/ noun [U] (*BrE, slang*) money

# doss

**doss** /dɒs; NAmE dɑːs/ *verb, noun*
■ *verb* (*BrE, informal*) **1** [I] ~ (**down**) to sleep somewhere, especially somewhere uncomfortable or without a real bed: *You can doss down on my floor.* **2** [I] ~ (**about/around**) to spend your time not doing very much: *We were just dossing about in lessons today.*
■ *noun* (*BrE, informal*) something that does not need much effort

**doss·er** /ˈdɒsə(r); NAmE ˈdɑːs-/ *noun* (*BrE, informal*) **1** a person who has no permanent home and who lives and sleeps on the streets or in cheap HOSTELS **2** (*disapproving*) a person who is very lazy

**doss-house** /ˈdɒshaʊs; NAmE ˈdɑːs-/ (*BrE*) (*NAmE* **flop-house**) *noun* (*informal*) a cheap place to stay for people who have no home

**dos·sier** /ˈdɒsieɪ; NAmE ˈdɔːs-/ *noun* (*formal*) a collection of documents that contain information about a person, an event or a subject SYN **file**: *to assemble/compile a dossier* ◇ ~ **on sb/sth** *We have a dossier on him.*

**dot** 🔊+ B2 /dɒt; NAmE dɑːt/ *noun, verb*
■ *noun* **1** 🔊+ B2 a small round mark, especially one that is printed: *There are dots above the letters i and j.* ◇ *Text and graphics are printed at 300 dots per inch.* ◇ *The helicopters appeared as two black dots on the horizon.* ⊃ see also POLKA DOT ⊃ SYNONYMS at PATCH ⊃ WORDFINDER NOTE at PATTERN **2** 🔊+ B2 (*computing*) a symbol like a full stop used to separate parts of a DOMAIN NAME, a URL or an email address **IDM** **on the ˈdot** (*informal*) exactly on time or at the exact time mentioned: *The taxi showed up on the dot.* ◇ *Breakfast is served at 8 on the dot.* ⊃ more at YEAR
■ *verb* (**-tt-**) **1** ~ **sth** to put a dot above or next to a letter or word: *Why do you never dot your i's?* **2** [usually passive] to spread things or people over an area; to be spread over an area: **be dotted with sth** *The countryside was dotted with small villages.* ◇ **be dotted around...** *There are lots of Italian restaurants dotted around London.* **3** to put very small amounts of sth in a number of places on a surface: ~ **A on/over B** *Dot the cream all over your face.* ◇ ~ **B with A** *Dot your face with the cream.*
**IDM** **dot your ˈi's and cross your ˈt's** to pay attention to the small details when you are finishing a task

**dot·age** /ˈdəʊtɪdʒ/ *noun* [sing.] the period of life when you are old and not always able to think clearly: **in sb's ~** *I need you to look after me in my dotage.*

**dot-com** (*also* **dot·com**) /ˌdɒt ˈkɒm; NAmE ˌdɑːt ˈkɑːm/ *noun* a company that sells goods and services on the internet, especially one whose address ends '.com': *The weaker dot-coms collapsed.* ◇ *a dot-com millionaire*

**dote** /dəʊt/ *verb*
**PHRV** **ˈdote on/upon sb** to feel and show great love for sb, ignoring their faults: *He dotes on his children.* ⊃ SYNONYMS at LOVE

**dot·ing** /ˈdəʊtɪŋ/ *adj.* [only before noun] showing a lot of love for sb, often ignoring their faults

**dot·ted** /ˈdɒtɪd; NAmE ˈdɑːt-/ *adj.* **1** covered in DOTS (= small round marks) ⊃ picture at LINE **2** [only before noun] (*music*) (of a musical note) followed by a DOT to show that it is one and a half times the length of the same note without the mark

**ˌdotted ˈline** *noun* a line made of DOTS (= small round marks): *Country boundaries are shown on this map as dotted lines.* ◇ *Fold along the dotted line.* ◇ *Write your name on the dotted line.* **IDM** see SIGN *v.*

**dotty** /ˈdɒti; NAmE ˈdɑːti/ *adj.* (**dot·tier, dot·ti·est**) (*BrE, old-fashioned, informal*) **1** slightly crazy or silly SYN **eccentric** **2** ~ **about sb/sth** having romantic feelings for sb; being enthusiastic about sth

**double** 🔊 A2 /ˈdʌbl/ *adj., det., pron., verb, adv., noun*
■ *adj.* [usually before noun]
• TWICE AS MUCH/MANY **1** 🔊 A2 twice as much or as many as usual: *a double helping* ◇ *two double whiskies*
• WITH TWO PARTS **2** 🔊 A2 having or made of two things or parts that are equal or similar: *double doors* ◇ *a double-*page *advertisement* ◇ *'Otter' is spelt with a double t.* ◇ *My extension is two four double 0 (2400).*
• FOR TWO PEOPLE **3** 🔊 A2 made for two people or things: *a double bed/room* ⊃ compare SINGLE
• COMBINING TWO THINGS **4** 🔊 A2 combining two things or qualities: *a double meaning/purpose/aim* ◇ *It has the double advantage of being both easy and cheap.*

▼ WHICH WORD?

**double / dual**

These adjectives are frequently used with the following nouns:

| double ~ | dual ~ |
|---|---|
| bed | purpose |
| doors | function |
| figures | role |
| standards | approach |
| thickness | citizenship |

• **Dual** describes something that has two parts, uses or aspects.
• **Double** can be used with a similar meaning, but when it is used to describe something that has two parts, the two parts are usually the same or very similar.
• **Double**, but not **dual**, can describe something that is made for two people or things, or is twice as big as usual.

■ *det.* 🔊 A2
• TWICE AS MUCH/MANY twice as much or as many as: *His income is double hers.* ◇ *He earns double what she does.* ◇ *We need double the amount we already have.*
■ *pron.* 🔊 A2
• TWICE AS MUCH/MANY a number or amount that is twice as much or as many as another number or amount: *He gets paid double for doing the same job I do.*
■ *verb*
• BECOME TWICE AS MUCH/MANY **1** 🔊 A2 [I, T] to become, or make sth become, twice as much or as many: *Membership almost doubled in two years.* ◇ ~ **in sth** *The town has approximately doubled in size since 1960.* ◇ ~ **sth** *The firm has promised to double the number of women promoted to partner by 2022.*
• FOLD **2** [T] ~ **sth (over)** to bend or fold sth so that there are two layers: *She doubled the blanket and put it under his head.*
• IN BASEBALL **3** [I] to hit the ball far enough for you to get to second BASE: *He doubled to left field.*
**PHRV** **ˈdouble as sth** | **ˌdouble ˈup as sth** to have another use or function as well as the main one: *The kitchen doubles as a dining room.* **ˌdouble ˈback** to turn back and go in the direction you have come from **ˌdouble ˈup (on sth/with sb)** (*informal*) to form a pair in order to do sth or to share sth: *We'll have to double up on books; there aren't enough to go around.* ◇ *They only have one room left: you'll have to double up with Peter.* **ˌdouble ˈup/ˈover** | **ˌdouble sb ˈup/ˈover** to bend or to make your body bend over quickly, for example because you are in pain: *Jo doubled up with laughter.* ◇ *I was doubled over with pain.*
■ *adv.*
• IN TWO PARTS **1** 🔊 B1 in twos or in two parts: *I thought I was seeing double* (= seeing two of sth). ◇ *Fold the blanket double.* ◇ *I had to bend double to get under the table.*
• TWICE AS MUCH **2** at twice the amount; to twice the extent: *You have to be careful, and this counts double for older people.*
■ *noun*
• ALCOHOLIC DRINK **1** [C] a glass of strong alcoholic drink containing twice the usual amount: *Two Scotches, please—and make those doubles, will you?*
• PERSON/THING **2** [C] a person or thing that looks exactly like another: *She's the double of her mother.* **3** [C] an actor who replaces another actor in a film to do dangerous or other special things ⊃ see also BODY DOUBLE
• BEDROOM **4** [C] = DOUBLE ROOM: *Is that a single or a double you want?* ⊃ compare SINGLE

---

| æ cat | ɑː father | e bed | ɜː fur | ə about | ɪ sit | iː see | i happy | ɒ got (*BrE*) | ɔː saw | ʌ cup | ʊ put | uː too |

• **IN SPORT 5** **doubles** [U + sing./pl. v.] a game, especially of tennis, in which one pair plays another: *mixed doubles* (= in which each pair consists of a man and a woman) ⊃ compare SINGLES **6 the double** [sing.] the fact of winning two important competitions or beating the same player or team twice, in the same season or year
**IDM** **at the 'double** (*BrE*) (*NAmE* **on the 'double**) (*informal*) quickly; hurrying **,double or 'quits** (*BrE*) (*NAmE* **,double or 'nothing**) (in gambling) a risk in which you could win twice the amount you pay, or you could lose all your money

**'double act** *noun* two people who work together, usually to entertain an audience

**,double-'action** *adj.* [usually before noun] **1** working in two ways: *double-action tablets* **2** (of a gun) needing two separate actions for preparing to fire and firing

**,double 'agent** *noun* a person who is a SPY for a particular country, and also for another country that is an enemy of the first one

**'double 'bar** *noun* (*music*) a pair of straight lines up and down at the end of a piece of music

**,double-'barrelled** (*US* **,double-'barreled**) *adj.* [usually before noun] **1** (of a gun) having two BARRELS (= places where the bullets come out) **2** (*BrE*) (of a family name) having two parts, sometimes joined by a hyphen, for example 'Day-Lewis' **3** (of a plan, etc.) having two parts, and therefore likely to be effective

**,double 'bass** (*also* **bass**) *noun* the largest musical instrument in the VIOLIN family, which plays very low notes

**,double 'bill** (*NAmE also* **,double 'feature**) *noun* two films, television programmes, etc. that are shown one after the other

**,double 'bind** *noun* [usually sing.] a situation in which it is difficult to choose what to do because whatever you choose will have negative results

**,double-'blind** *adj.* [only before noun] (of a test) conducted so that neither the organizer nor any other people involved know any information that might influence the results: *A randomized double-blind study was carried out to test the drug's effectiveness.*

**,double 'bluff** *noun* a way of trying to trick sb by telling them the truth while hoping that they think you are lying

**,double-'book** *verb* [often passive] **~sth** to promise the same room, seat, table, etc. to two different people at the same time ⊃ compare OVERBOOK ▸ **,double-'booking** *noun* [C, U]

**,double-'breasted** *adj.* a **double-breasted** jacket or coat has two front parts so that one part covers the other when the buttons are done up, and two rows of buttons can be seen ⊃ compare SINGLE-BREASTED

**,double-'check** *verb* [T, I] **~(sth)** | **~(that)...** to check sth for a second time or with great care: *I'll double-check the figures.* ▸ **,double-'check** *noun*

**,double 'chin** *noun* a fold of fat under a person's CHIN (= part of the face below the mouth), which looks like another CHIN

**,double-'click** *verb* [I, T] **~(on) sth** (*computing*) to choose a particular function or item on a computer screen, etc. by pressing one of the buttons on a mouse twice quickly: *To run an application, just double-click on the icon.*

**,double 'cream** (*BrE*) (*NAmE* **heavy cream**) *noun* [U] thick cream that contains a lot of fat and can be mixed so that it is no longer liquid ⊃ compare SINGLE CREAM

**,double-'cross** *verb* **~sb** to cheat or trick sb who trusts you (usually in connection with sth illegal or dishonest): *He double-crossed the rest of the gang and disappeared with all the money.* ▸ **,double-'cross** *noun* [usually sing.]

**,double 'date** *noun* an occasion when two couples go out together on a DATE ▸ **,double-'date** *verb* [I]

**,double-'dealer** *noun* (*informal*) a dishonest person who cheats other people ▸ **,double-'dealing** *noun* [U]

## double quick

**,double-'decker** *noun* **1** a bus with two floors, one on top of the other ⊃ compare SINGLE-DECKER **2** (*NAmE*) a sandwich made from three pieces of bread with two layers of food between them

**,double 'digits** *noun* [pl.] (especially *NAmE*) = DOUBLE FIGURES ▸ **,double-'digit** *adj.* [only before noun]: *a double-digit growth rate*

**,double 'Dutch** *noun* [U] (*BrE*, *informal*) speech or writing that is impossible to understand, and that seems to have no meaning or make no sense

**,double-'edged** (*also less frequent* **two-edged**) *adj.* **1** (of a knife, etc.) having two cutting edges **2** (of a remark) having two possible meanings **SYN** **ambiguous 3** having two different parts or uses, often parts that contrast with each other: *the double-edged quality of life in a small town—security and boredom*
**IDM** **be a double-edged/two-edged 'sword/'weapon** to be sth that has both advantages and disadvantages

**,double en·ten·dre** /ˌduːbl ɒ̃ˈtɒ̃drə; *NAmE* ɑːˈtɑːdrə/ *noun* (from French) a word or phrase that can be understood in two different ways, one of which usually refers to sex

**,double-entry 'bookkeeping** *noun* [U] (*business*) a system of keeping financial records in which each piece of business is recorded as a CREDIT in one account and a DEBIT in another

**,double 'fault** *noun* (in tennis) the loss of a point caused by a player making two bad SERVES, one after the other ▸ **,double-'fault** *verb* [I]

**,double 'feature** *noun* (*NAmE*) = DOUBLE BILL

**,double 'figures** (especially *BrE*) (*also* **,double 'digits** especially in *NAmE*) *noun* [pl.] used to describe a number that is not less than 10 and not more than 99: *in ~ Inflation is in double figures.* ▸ **,double-'figure** (especially *BrE*) (*also* **,double-'digit** *BrE*, *NAmE*) *adj.* [only before noun]: *a double-figure pay rise*

**,double 'glazing** *noun* [U] (especially *BrE*) windows that have two layers of glass with a space between them, designed to make the room warmer and to reduce noise ▸ **,double-'glaze** *verb* **~sth** **,double-'glazed** *adj.*: *double-glazed windows*

**,double-'header** *noun* (*NAmE*) a sports event in which two games are played on the same day, traditionally on a Sunday, and usually by the same two teams

**,double 'helix** *noun* (*biology*) the structure of DNA, consisting of two connected long thin pieces that form a SPIRAL shape

**,double 'jeopardy** *noun* [U] (in US law) the fact of taking sb to court twice for the same crime, or punishing sb twice for the same reason. This is not allowed under the Fifth AMENDMENT of the US Constitution.

**,double-'jointed** *adj.* having JOINTS in your fingers, arms, etc. that allow you to bend them both backwards and forwards

**,double 'life** *noun* a life of a person who leads two different lives that are kept separate from each other, usually because one of them involves secret, often illegal, activities: *to live/lead a double life*

**,double 'negative** *noun* (*grammar*) a negative statement containing two negative words. 'I didn't say nothing' is a double negative because it contains two negative words, 'didn't' and 'nothing'. This use is not considered correct in standard English.

**,double-'park** *verb* [T, usually passive, I] to park a car or other vehicle next to one that is already parked in a street: **be double-parked** *I'll have to rush—I'm double-parked.* ◊ *A car stood double-parked almost in the middle of the road.*

**,double 'play** *noun* (*NAmE*) (in baseball) a situation in which two players are put out (= made to finish their attempt at scoring a RUN)

**,double 'quick** *adv.* (*BrE*, *informal*) very quickly ▸ **,double-'quick** *adj.* [only before noun]: *The TV was repaired in double-quick time.*

**double room**

**double room** (also **double**) noun a bedroom for two people

**double·speak** /ˈdʌblspiːk/ (also **double-talk**) noun [U] language that is intended to make people believe sth that is not true, or that can be understood in two different ways

**double standard** noun a rule or moral principle that is unfair because it is used in one situation, but not in another, or because it treats one group of people in a way that is different from the treatment of another

**doub·let** /ˈdʌblət/ noun a short, tightly fitting jacket worn by men from the fourteenth to the seventeenth century: *dressed in doublet and hose*

**double take** noun if you **do a double take**, you wait for a moment before you react to sth that has happened, because it is very surprising

**double-talk** noun [U] = DOUBLESPEAK

**double·think** /ˈdʌblθɪŋk/ noun [U] the act of holding two opposite opinions or beliefs at the same time; the ability to do this

**double time** noun [U] twice sb's normal pay, that they earn for working at times that are not normal working hours

**double vision** noun [U] if you have **double vision**, you can see two things where there is actually only one

**doubly** /ˈdʌbli/ adv. (used before adjectives) **1** more than usual: *doubly difficult/hard/important* ◊ *I made doubly sure I locked all the doors when I went out.* **2** in two ways; for two reasons: *I was doubly attracted to the house—by its size and its location.*

**doubt** 🔑 **B1** /daʊt/ noun, verb

■ noun 🔑 **B1** [U, C] a feeling of being uncertain about sth or not believing sth: *a feeling of doubt and uncertainty* ◊ *New evidence has cast doubt on the guilt of the man jailed for the crime.* ◊ *He was starting to have some serious doubts.* ◊ *~ about sth The article raised doubts about how effective the new drug really was.* ◊ *~(that) ... There is no doubt at all that we did the right thing.* ◊ *~ as to sth She leaves no doubt as to her own view of Picasso's work.* ◊ *~ over sth Medical experts have expressed doubt over how the scientist died.* ◊ *She knew without a shadow of a doubt that he was lying to her.* ⊃ see also SELF-DOUBT ⊃ LANGUAGE BANK at IMPERSONAL
IDM **be in doubt** to be uncertain: *The success of the system is not in doubt.* **beyond (any) doubt** in a way that shows that sth is completely certain: *The research showed beyond doubt that smoking contributes to heart disease.* ◊ *(law) The prosecution was able to establish beyond reasonable doubt that the woman had been lying.* **have your doubts (about sth)** to have reasons why you are not certain about whether sth is good or whether sth good will happen: *I've had my doubts about his work since he joined the firm.* ◊ *It may be all right. Personally, I have my doubts.* **if in doubt** used to give advice to sb who cannot decide what to do: *If in doubt, wear black.* **no doubt 1 B2** used when you are saying that sth is likely: *No doubt she'll call us when she gets there.* **2 B2** used when you are saying that sth is certainly true: *He's made some great movies. There's no doubt about it.* **put/throw sth into doubt** to make sth uncertain: *The proposed development has been thrown into doubt by the decision.* **without/beyond (a) doubt** used when you are giving your opinion and emphasizing the point that you are making: *This meeting has been, without doubt, one of the most useful we have had so far.* ⊃ more at BENEFIT *n.*

■ verb **1** 🔑 **B1** to feel uncertain about sth; to feel that sth is not true, will probably not happen, etc: *~ sth There seems no reason to doubt her story.* ◊ *'Do you think England will win?'—'I doubt it.'* ◊ *~(that) ... I never doubted (that) she would come.* ◊ *She seriously doubted he would still be waiting for her.* ◊ *~ whether, if, etc ... I doubt whether the new one will be any better.* **2** *~ sb/sth* to not trust sb/sth; to not believe sb: *I had no reason to doubt him.* ▶ **doubt·er** noun

**doubt·ful** /ˈdaʊtfl/ adj. **1** (of a person) not sure; uncertain and feeling doubt SYN dubious: *~(about sth) Rose was doubtful about the whole idea.* ◊ *~(about doing sth) He was doubtful about accepting extra work.* **2** unlikely; not PROBABLE: *~(if ...) It's doubtful if this painting is a Picasso.* ◊ *~(that ...) With her injuries it's doubtful that she'll ever walk again.* ◊ *~(whether ...) It's doubtful whether the car will last another year.* ◊ *~(for sth) He is injured and is doubtful for the game tomorrow* (= unlikely to play). **3** [not usually before noun] (of a thing) uncertain and likely to get worse: *At the beginning of the war things were looking very doubtful.* **4** [only before noun] of low value; probably not what sb claims it is or of a quality that you can rely on SYN dubious: *This wine is of doubtful quality.* ▶ **doubt·ful·ly** /-fəli/ adv.

**doubt·ing Thomas** /ˌdaʊtɪŋ ˈtɒməs; NAmE ˈtɑːm-/ noun [usually sing.] a person who is unlikely to believe sth until they see proof of it ORIGIN From St Thomas in the Bible, who did not believe that Jesus Christ had risen from the dead until he saw and touched his wounds.

**doubt·less** /ˈdaʊtləs/ adv. (also less frequent **doubt·less·ly**) almost certainly SYN **without/beyond (a) doubt**: *He would doubtless disapprove of what Kelly was doing.*

**douche** /duːʃ/ noun a method of washing inside a woman's VAGINA using a stream of water ▶ **douche** verb [I, T] *~(sth)*

**dough** /dəʊ/ noun **1** [U, sing.] a mixture of flour, water, etc. that is made into bread and PASTRY: *Knead the dough on a floured surface.* **2** [U] (old-fashioned, slang) money

**dough·nut** (also **donut** especially in NAmE) /ˈdəʊnʌt/ noun a small cake made of fried dough, usually in the shape of a ring, or round and filled with JAM, fruit, cream, etc.

**doughty** /ˈdaʊti/ adj. (old-fashioned) brave and strong

**doula** /ˈduːlə/ noun a woman whose role is to give support, help and advice to a woman who is having a baby ⊃ compare MIDWIFE

**dour** /ˈdaʊə(r); BrE also dʊə(r); NAmE also dʊr/ adj. **1** (of a person) giving the impression of being unfriendly and severe **2** (of a thing, a place, or a situation) not pleasant; with no features that make it lively or interesting: *The city, drab and dour by day, is transformed at night.* ◊ *The game proved to be a dour struggle, with both men determined to win.* ▶ **dour·ly** adv.

**douse** /daʊs/ verb **1** *~ sth (with sth)* to stop a fire from burning by pouring water over it; to put out a light **2** *~ sb/ sth (in/with sth)* to pour a lot of liquid over sb/sth; to SOAK sb/sth in liquid: *The car was doused in petrol and set alight.*

**dove¹** /dʌv/ noun **1** a bird of the PIGEON family. The white dove is often used as a symbol of peace: *A dove cooed softly.* ◊ *He wore a dove-grey suit.* ⊃ see also TURTLE DOVE **2** a person, especially a politician, who prefers peace and discussion to war OPP hawk

**dove²** /dəʊv/ (NAmE) past tense of DIVE

**dove·cote** /ˈdʌvkəʊt; BrE also -kɒt; NAmE also -kɑːt/ (also **dove·cot** /ˈdʌvkɒt; NAmE -kɑːt/) noun a small building for doves or PIGEONS to live in

dovetail        mitre

**dove·tail** /ˈdʌvteɪl/ verb, noun

■ verb [I, T] (formal) *~(sth) (with/into sth)* if two things **dovetail** or if one thing **dovetails** with another, they fit together well: *My plans dovetailed nicely with hers.*

■ noun (also **dovetail joint**) a JOINT for fixing two pieces of wood together

**dov·ish** /ˈdʌvɪʃ/ adj. preferring to use peaceful discussion rather than military action in order to solve a political problem OPP hawkish

**dow·ager** /ˈdaʊədʒə(r)/ noun **1** a woman of high social rank who has a title from her dead husband: *the dowager Duchess of Norfolk* **2** (informal) an impressive, usually rich, old woman

**dowdy** /ˈdaʊdi/ adj. (**dow·dier**, **dow·di·est**) **1** (of a woman) not attractive or fashionable **2** (of a thing) boring and not attractive **SYN** **drab**: *a dowdy dress*

**dow·el** /ˈdaʊəl/ (*also* **dowel rod**) *noun* a small piece of wood, plastic, etc. in the shape of a CYLINDER, used to fix larger pieces of wood, plastic, etc. together

**the Dow Jones Index** /ðə ˌdaʊ dʒəʊnz ˈɪndeks/ (*also* ˌDow Jones ˈaverage, **the ˈDow**) *noun* [sing.] a list of the share prices of 30 US industrial companies that can be used to compare the prices to previous levels

**down** ❶ **A1** /daʊn/ *adv.*, *prep.*, *verb*, *adj.*, *noun*

■ *adv.* **HELP** For the special uses of **down** in phrasal verbs, look at the entries for the verbs. For example **climb down** is in the phrasal verb section at **climb**. **1** **A1** to or at a lower place or position: *She jumped down off the chair.* ◇ *He looked down at her.* ◇ *We watched as the sun went down.* ◇ *She bent down to pick up her glove.* ◇ *Mary's not down yet* (= she is still upstairs). ◇ *The baby can't keep any food down* (= in her body). **2** **A1** from a standing position to a sitting or lying position: *Please sit down.* ◇ *He had to go and lie down for a while.* **3** **A2** at a lower level or rate: *Prices have gone down recently.* ◇ *We're already two goals down* (= the other team has two goals more). ⇒ LANGUAGE BANK at FALL **4** **A2** used to show that the amount or strength of sth is lower, or that there is less activity: *Turn the music down!* ◇ *The class settled down and she began the lesson.* **5** **A2** on paper; on a list: *Did you get that down?* ◇ *I always write everything down.* ◇ *Have you got me down for the trip?* **6** (in a CROSSWORD) reading from top to bottom, not from side to side: *I can't do 3 down.* **7** to or in the south of a country: *They flew down to Texas.* ◇ *Houses are more expensive down south.* **8** used to show the limits in a range or an order: *Everyone will be there, from the Principal down.* **9** having lost the amount of money mentioned: *At the end of the day we were £20 down.* **10** if you pay an amount of money **down**, you pay that to start with, and the rest later **11** (*informal*) used to say how far you have got in a list of things you have to do: *Well, I've seen six apartments so far. That's six down and four to go!* **12** (*informal*) to or at a local place such as a shop, pub, etc: *I'm just going down to the post office.* ◇ *I saw him down at the shops.* **HELP** In informal British English, **to** and **at** are often left out after **down** in this sense: *He's gone down the shops.* **13** used to tell an animal or person to sit or lie: *'Down, boy!' she laughed as the dog jumped up to greet her.*

**IDM** **be down to sb** (*informal*) to be the responsibility of sb: *It's down to you to check the door.* **be down to sb/sth** to be caused by a particular person or thing: *She claimed her problems were down to the media.* **be down to sth** to have only a little money left: *I'm down to my last dollar.* **be/go down with sth** to have or catch an illness ˌdown and ˈdirty (*NAmE*, *informal*) **1** behaving in an unfair or aggressive way, especially because you want to win: *The candidate again got down and dirty with his rival.* **2** rude and making you feel shocked: *The singer got down and dirty at the club last night and made headlines again.* ˌdown through sth (*formal*) during a long period of time: *Down through the years this town has seen many changes.* ˌdown to the last, smallest, final, etc. sth including every small part or detail of sth: *She organized everything down to the last detail.* ˌdown ˈunder (*informal*) in or to Australia and/or New Zealand ˌdown with sb/sth used to say that you are opposed to sth, or to a person: *The crowds chanted 'Down with NATO!'* ˌhave/get sth ˈdown to be able to do sth easily or well: *She's young and she hasn't really got it down yet.* ⇒ more at MAN *n.*

■ *prep.* **1** **A1** from a high or higher point on sth to a lower one: *The stone rolled down the hill.* ◇ *Tears ran down her face.* ◇ *Her hair hung down her back to her waist.* **2** **A2** along; towards the direction in which you are facing: *He lives just down the street.* ◇ *Go down the road till you reach the traffic lights.* ◇ *There's a bridge a mile down the river from here.* **3** all through a period of time: *an exhibition of costumes down the ages* (= from all periods of history)

■ *verb* **1** ~ **sth** to finish a drink or eat sth quickly: *We downed our coffees and left.* **2** ~ **sb/sth** to force sb/sth down to the ground: *to down a plane*

467

**IDM** ˌdown ˈtools (*BrE*) (of workers) to stop work; to go on strike

■ *adj.* **1** [only before noun] moving or directed downwards or away from a place: *Click the down arrow.* **2** [not before noun] (*informal*) sad or depressed: *I feel a bit down today.* **3** [not before noun] (of a computer or computer system) not working: *The system was down all morning.* ⇒ see also DOWNTIME **IDM** see HIT *v.*, KICK *v.*, LUCK *n.*, MOUTH *n.*

■ *noun* ⇒ see also DOWNS **1** [U] the very fine soft feathers of a bird: *duck down* **2** [U] fine soft hair ⇒ see also DOWNY **3** [C, usually pl.] (*informal*) a period of feeling sad or depressed, or when things are not going well **4** [C] (in AMERICAN FOOTBALL) one of a series of four chances to carry the ball forward ten yards that a team is allowed. These series continue until the team loses the ball or fails to go forward ten yards in four downs.

**IDM** ˌhave a ˈdown on sb/sth (*BrE*, *informal*) to have a bad opinion of a person or thing ⇒ more at UP *n.*

ˌdown-and-ˈout *noun* a person without money, a home or a job, who lives on the streets

ˌdown and ˈout *adj.* (of a person) **1** without money, a home or a job, and living on the streets: *a novel about being down and out in London* **2** certain to be defeated

ˌdown at ˈheel *adj.* looking less attractive and fashionable than before, usually because of a lack of money: *The town has become very down at heel.* ◇ *a down-at-heel hotel*

**down·beat** /ˈdaʊnbiːt/ *adj.* **1** depressing; not having much hope for the future: *The overall mood of the meeting was downbeat.* **OPP** **upbeat** **2** not showing strong feelings or enthusiasm

**down·cast** /ˈdaʊnkɑːst; *NAmE* -kæst/ *adj.* **1** (of eyes) looking down: *Eyes downcast, she continued eating.* **2** (of a person or an expression) sad or depressed **SYN** **dejected**: *A group of downcast men stood waiting for food.*

**down·draught** (*BrE*) (*NAmE* **down·draft**) /ˈdaʊndrɑːft; *NAmE* -dræft/ *noun* a movement of air going downwards, for example down a CHIMNEY **OPP** **updraught**

**down·er** /ˈdaʊnə(r)/ *noun* (*informal*) **1** [usually pl.] a drug, especially a BARBITURATE, that relaxes you or makes you want to sleep ⇒ compare UPPER **2** an experience that makes you feel sad or depressed: *Not getting the promotion was a real downer.* ◇ **on a ~** *He's really on a downer* (= very depressed).

**down·fall** /ˈdaʊnfɔːl/ *noun* [sing.] the loss of a person's money, power, social position, etc.; the thing that causes this: *The sex scandal finally led to his downfall.* ◇ *Greed was her downfall.*

**down·grade** /ˌdaʊnˈɡreɪd/ *verb* **1** ~ **sb/sth (from sth) (to sth)** to move sb/sth down to a lower rank or level: *She's been downgraded from principal to vice-principal.* **2** ~ **sth/sb** to make sth/sb seem less important or valuable than it/they really are ⇒ compare UPGRADE ▸ **down·grad·ing** *noun* [U, C, usually sing.]: *a downgrading of diplomatic relations*

**down·heart·ed** /ˌdaʊnˈhɑːtɪd; *NAmE* -ˈhɑːrt-/ *adj.* [not usually before noun] feeling depressed or sad: *We're disappointed by these results but we're not downhearted.*

**down·hill** *adv.*, *adj.*, *noun*

■ *adv.* /ˌdaʊnˈhɪl/ towards the bottom of a hill; in a direction that goes down: *to run/walk/cycle downhill* **OPP** **uphill**

**IDM** ˌgo downˈhill to get worse in quality, health, etc. **SYN** **deteriorate**: *Their marriage went downhill after the first child was born.*

■ *adj.* /ˌdaʊnˈhɪl/ going or sloping towards the bottom of a hill: *a downhill path* **OPP** **uphill**

**IDM** ˌbe (all) ˈdownhill | ˌbe ˌdownhill all the ˈway (*informal*) **1** to be easy compared with what came before: *It's all downhill from here. We'll soon be finished.* **2** to become worse or less successful: *It's been all downhill for his career since then, with four defeats in five games.* ◇ *I started work as a journalist and it was downhill all the way for my health.*

**downhill**

**O** Oxford Phrasal Academic Lexicon (OPAL) written and spoken word lists | **W** OPAL written word list | **S** OPAL spoken word list

# down-home

**noun** /ˈdaʊnhɪl/ [U] the type of skiing in which you go directly down a mountain; a race in which people ski down a mountain ⊃ compare CROSS-COUNTRY

**ˌdown-ˈhome** *adj.* (NAmE) used to describe a person or thing that reminds you of a simple way of life, typical of the country, not the town

**ˈDowning Street** /ˈdaʊnɪŋ striːt/ *noun* [U] (not used with *the*) a way of referring to the British prime minister and government, taken from the name of the street where the prime minister lives: *Downing Street issued a statement late last night.*

**down·link** /ˈdaʊnlɪŋk/ *noun* a communications link by which information is received from space or from an aircraft ▶ **down·link** *verb*: ~ *sth Any organization can downlink the program without charge.*

**down·load** ⓘ A1 *verb, noun*
- **verb** A2 /ˌdaʊnˈləʊd/ to get data from another computer, usually using the internet: ~ *sth to download files/music/software* ◊ *You can download the app for free.* ◊ ~ *sth to/onto sth a small program you can download to your desktop* ◊ ~ *sth from sth If you download pictures from the internet, check the terms of use.* OPP **upload** ⊃ compare LOAD
- **noun** /ˈdaʊnləʊd/ **1** A2 [C] data that is downloaded from another computer system: *A staggering 99.9 % of digital music downloads are to mobile handsets.* ◊ *This book is available as a free download.* **2** A2 [C, U] the act or process of downloading data from another computer system: *app/file downloads* ◊ ~ *from sth More songs will soon be available for download from Xbox live.* ◊ *Faster download speeds make it easier for employees to work from remote locations.* ▶ **down·load·able** /ˌdaʊnˈləʊdəbl/ *adj.*

**down·mark·et** /ˌdaʊnˈmɑːkɪt; NAmE -ˈmɑːrk-/ (BrE) (NAmE **down·scale**) *adj.* (*disapproving*) cheap and of poor quality: *The company wants to break away from its downmarket image.* OPP **upmarket** ▶ **down·mark·et** *adv.*: *To get more viewers the TV station was forced to go downmarket.*

**ˌdown ˈpayment** *noun* a sum of money that is given as the first part of a larger payment: *We are saving for a down payment on a house.*

**down·pipe** /ˈdaʊnpaɪp/ *noun* (BrE) a pipe for carrying water from a roof down to the ground or to a DRAIN

**down·play** /ˌdaʊnˈpleɪ/ *verb* ~ *sth* to try to make sth seem less important than it really is SYN **play down**: *The coach is downplaying the team's poor performance.*

**down·pour** /ˈdaʊnpɔː(r)/ *noun* [usually sing.] a heavy fall of rain that often starts suddenly ⊃ WORDFINDER NOTE at RAIN

**down·right** /ˈdaʊnraɪt/ *adj.* [only before noun] used as a way of emphasizing sth negative or unpleasant: *There was suspicion and even downright hatred between them.* ▶ **down·right** *adv.*: *She couldn't think of anything to say that wasn't downright rude.* ◊ *It's not just stupid—it's downright dangerous.*

**down·river** /ˌdaʊnˈrɪvə(r)/ *adv.* = DOWNSTREAM

**downs** /daʊnz/ *noun* **the downs** [pl.] an area of open land with low hills, especially in southern England

**down·scale** /ˌdaʊnˈskeɪl/ (NAmE) (BrE **down·mark·et**) *adj.* (*disapproving*) cheap and of poor quality OPP **upscale** ▶ **down·scale** *adv.*

**down·shift** /ˈdaʊnʃɪft/ *verb* **1** [I] (NAmE) to change to a lower GEAR in a vehicle **2** [I] to change to a job or style of life where you may earn less but which puts less pressure on you and involves less stress ▶ **down·shift** *noun* [C, U]

**down·side** /ˈdaʊnsaɪd/ *noun* the disadvantages or less positive aspects of sth OPP **upside**

**down·size** /ˈdaʊnsaɪz/ *verb* **1** [I, T] ~ (sth) (*business*) to reduce the number of people who work in a company, business, etc. in order to reduce costs ⊃ SYNONYMS at CUT **2** [I] ~ (to sth) to move to a smaller home ▶ **down·siz·ing** *noun* [U]

**down·spout** /ˈdaʊnspaʊt/ *noun* (NAmE) = DRAINPIPE

**ˈDown's syndrome** (also **Down's**) (both especially BrE) (NAmE usually **ˈDown syndrome**) *noun* [U] a medical condition, caused by a fault with one CHROMOSOME, in which a person is born with particular physical characteristics and a mental ability that is below average

**down·stage** /ˌdaʊnˈsteɪdʒ/ *adv.* towards the front of the stage in a theatre ▶ **down·stage** *adj.* OPP **upstage**

**down·stairs** ⓘ A1 /ˌdaʊnˈsteəz; NAmE -ˈsterz/ *adv., noun*
- *adv.* A1 down the stairs; on or to a floor of a house or building lower than the one you are on, especially the one at ground level: *I couldn't sleep so I went downstairs and watched TV.* ◊ *Wait downstairs in the hall.* OPP **upstairs**
- *adj.* A2 [only before noun] on a floor of a house or building lower than the one you are on, especially the one at ground level: *a downstairs bathroom* OPP **upstairs**
- *noun* [sing.] the lower floor of a house or building, especially the one at ground level: *We're painting the downstairs.* OPP **upstairs**

**down·state** /ˌdaʊnˈsteɪt/ *adv.* (US) in or to a part of a state that is far from its main cities, especially a southern part: *They moved downstate from New York City.* OPP **upstate** ▶ **down·state** *adj.* [only before noun]: *downstate Illinois*

**down·stream** /ˌdaʊnˈstriːm/ *adv., adj.*
- *adv.* (also less frequent **down·river**) ~ (of/from sth) in the direction in which a river flows: *to drift/float downstream* ◊ *downstream of/from the bridge* OPP **upstream** ⊃ WORDFINDER NOTE at RIVER
- *adj.* **1** (also less frequent **down·river**) in a position along a river which is nearer the sea: *downstream areas* OPP **upstream 2** happening as a consequence of sth that has happened earlier: *downstream effects*

**down·swing** /ˈdaʊnswɪŋ/ *noun* [usually sing.] **1** ~ (in sth) a situation in which sth gets worse or decreases over a period of time: *the current downswing in the airline industry* ◊ *He is on a career downswing.* OPP **upswing 2** (in golf) the movement of a CLUB going downwards when a player is about to hit the ball

**ˈDown syndrome** *noun* [U] (NAmE) = DOWN'S SYNDROME

**down·tick** /ˈdaʊntɪk/ *noun* [C, usually sing.] (NAmE, *economics*) a small decrease in the level or value of sth, especially in the price of shares: *The shares were bought on a downtick.* OPP **uptick**

**down·time** /ˈdaʊntaɪm/ *noun* [U] **1** the time during which a machine, especially a computer, is not working ⊃ compare UPTIME **2** (*especially NAmE*) the time when sb stops working and is able to relax: *Everyone needs a little downtime.*

**ˌdown to ˈearth** *adj.* (*approving*) sensible and practical, in a way that is helpful and friendly

**down·town** ⓘ+ B2 /ˌdaʊnˈtaʊn/ *adv., adj., noun*
- *adv.* ⓘ+ B2 in or towards the centre of a city, especially its main business area: *to go/work downtown* ⊃ compare MIDTOWN, TOWN CENTRE, UPTOWN
- *adj.* ⓘ+ B2 [only before noun] (*especially NAmE*) in, towards or typical of the centre of a city, especially its main business area: *a downtown store* ⊃ compare UPTOWN
- *noun* ⓘ+ B2 [U] (*especially NAmE*) the centre of a city, especially its main business area: *a hotel in the heart of downtown*

**down·trend** /ˈdaʊntrend/ *noun* [usually sing.] a situation in which business activity or performance decreases or becomes worse over a period of time OPP **uptrend**

**down·trod·den** /ˈdaʊntrɒdn; NAmE -trɑːdn/ *adj.* **downtrodden** people are treated so badly by the people with authority and power that they no longer have the energy or ability to fight back

**down·turn** /ˈdaʊntɜːn; NAmE -tɜːrn/ *noun* [C, U] ~ (in sth) a fall in the amount of business that is done; a time when the economy becomes weaker: *the recent economic downturns* ◊ *a downturn in sales/trade/business* ◊ *the economic downturn of 2008/2009* OPP **upturn**

**down·vote** /ˈdaʊnvəʊt/ *verb, noun*
- *verb* [T, I] **~ (sth)** to show that you disagree with an online article or comment by using a particular ICON: *If five people downvote a post, it will disappear.* ◊ *Someone will probably disagree and downvote.* **OPP** upvote
- *noun* an act of showing that you disagree with an online article or comment by using a particular ICON: *I don't see why this comment should get a downvote.* **OPP** upvote

**down·ward** /ˈdaʊnwəd/; *NAmE* -wərd/ *adj.* [usually before noun] moving or pointing towards a lower level: *the downward slope of a hill* ◊ *the downward trend in inflation* ◊ *She was trapped in a downward spiral* (= continuous increase) *of personal unhappiness.* **OPP** upward ▶ **down·ward·ly** *adv.*

**down·wards** 🅒 **B2** /ˈdaʊnwədz/; *NAmE* -wərdz/ (*also* **down·ward** *especially in NAmE*) *adv.* **1** 🅑 **B2** towards the ground; towards a lower place or position: *She was lying face downwards on the grass.* ◊ *The garden sloped gently downwards to the river.* **OPP** upwards ⊃ LANGUAGE BANK at FALL **2** 🅙 **B2** towards a lower level, amount or price: *Nine per cent of commuters used public transport in 2018 and the trend is downwards.* ◊ *It was a policy welcomed by world leaders from the US president downwards.* **OPP** upwards

**down·wind** /ˌdaʊnˈwɪnd/ *adv., adj.* in the direction in which the wind is blowing: *sailing downwind* ◊ **~ of sth** *Warnings were issued to people living downwind of the fire to stay indoors.* **OPP** upwind

**downy** /ˈdaʊni/ *adj.* covered in sth very soft, especially hair or feathers ⊃ see also DOWN *noun*

**dowry** /ˈdaʊri/ *noun* (*pl.* **-ies**) **1** money and/or property that, in some societies, a wife or her family must pay to her husband when they get married **2** money and/or property that, in some societies, a husband must pay to his wife's family when they get married

**doyen** /ˈdɔɪən/ (*NAmE usually* **dean**) *noun* the most respected or most experienced member of a group or profession: *Richard Dawkins, the doyen of evolutionary biologists*

**doy·enne** /dɔɪˈen/ *noun* the most respected or most experienced woman member of a group or profession: *Martha Graham, the doyenne of American modern dance*

**doz.** *abbr.* (in writing) DOZEN: *2 doz. eggs*

**doze** /dəʊz/ *verb, noun*
- *verb* [I] to sleep lightly for a short time ⊃ SYNONYMS at SLEEP ⊃ WORDFINDER NOTE at SLEEP **PHRV** ▶ **doze 'off** to go to sleep, especially during the day: *She dozed off in front of the fire.*
- *noun* [sing.] a short period of sleep, usually during the day: *I had a doze on the train.*

**dozen** 🅒 **B2** /ˈdʌzn/ *noun, det.* (*pl.* **dozen**) **1** 🅑 **B2** [C] (*abbr.* **doz.**) a group of twelve of the same thing: *Give me a dozen, please.* ◊ *two dozen eggs* ◊ *half a dozen bottles of wine* ⊃ *a half-dozen bottles of wine* ⊃ see also BAKER'S DOZEN **2** 🅙 **B2** [C] a group of approximately twelve people or things: *several dozen/a few dozen people* ◊ *The company employs no more than a couple of dozen people.* ◊ *Only about half a dozen people turned up.* ◊ *There was only space for a half-dozen tables.* **3** 🅙 **B2** **dozens** [pl.] (*informal*) a lot of people or things: **~ of sth** *I've been there dozens of times.* ◊ **in dozens** *They arrived in dozens* (= in large numbers). **IDM** see NINETEEN, PENNY, SIX

**dozy** /ˈdəʊzi/ *adj.* (*informal*) **1** looking or feeling as if you are going to sleep **2** (*BrE*) stupid; not intelligent

**DPhil** /ˌdiː ˈfɪl/ *noun* (*BrE*) a university degree of a very high level that is given to sb who has done research in a particular subject (the abbreviation for 'Doctor of Philosophy'): *to be/have/do a DPhil* ◊ *James Mendelssohn DPhil*

**dpi** /ˌdiː piː ˈaɪ/ *abbr.* (*computing*) dots per inch (a measure of how clear the images produced by a printer, SCANNER, etc. are)

**DPP** /ˌdiː piː ˈpiː/ *abbr.* = DIRECTOR OF PUBLIC PROSECUTIONS

**Dr** (*BrE*) (*also* **Dr.** *NAmE, BrE*) *abbr.* **1** (in writing) Doctor: *Dr (Jane) Walker* **2** (in street names) DRIVE

**drab** /dræb/ *adj.* (**drab·ber, drab·best**) without interest or colour; boring: *a cold drab little office* ◊ *drab women, dressed in browns and greys* ▶ **drab·ness** *noun* [U]

**drabs** /dræbz/ *noun* **IDM** see DRIBS

**dra·co·nian** /drəˈkəʊniən/ *adj.* (*formal*) (of a law, punishment, etc.) extremely cruel and severe **ORIGIN** From *Draco*, a legislator in ancient Athens who gave severe punishments for crimes, especially the punishment of being killed.

**Drac·ula** /ˈdrækjələ/ *noun* a character in many horror films who is a VAMPIRE. Vampires appear at night and bite their victims and drink their blood. **ORIGIN** From the novel *Dracula* by Bram Stoker.

**draft** 🅒 **B2** /drɑːft; *NAmE* dræft/ *noun, verb, adj.*
- *noun* **1** 🅑 **B2** [C] a rough written version of sth that is not yet in its final form: *This is only the first draft of my speech.* ◊ *I've made a rough draft of the letter.* ◊ *the final draft* (= the final version) ◊ *a draft report/plan/bill/resolution* ⊃ WORDFINDER NOTE at MESSAGE **2** [C] (*finance*) a written order to a bank to pay money to sb: *Payment must be made by bank draft drawn on a UK bank.* **3** **the draft** [sing.] (*especially US*) (*BrE usually* **conscription**) the practice of ordering people by law to join the armed forces **4** [sing.] (*NAmE*) a system in which professional teams in some sports choose players each year from among college students: *He was the fourth player chosen in the 2017 draft, but the first of his class to reach the major leagues.* **5** (*NAmE*) [C] = DRAUGHT: *Can you shut the door? There's a draft in here.*
- *verb* (*also* **draught** *especially in BrE*) **1** 🅙 **B2** **~ sth** to write the first rough version of sth such as a letter, speech, book or law: *I'll draft a letter for you.* ◊ *The military began drafting a new constitution.* ⊃ WORDFINDER NOTE at DOCUMENT **2** **~ sb + adv./prep.** to choose people and send them somewhere for a special task: *Extra police are being drafted in to control the crowds.* **3** [usually passive] (*NAmE*) = CONSCRIPT: *be drafted (into sth) They were drafted into the army.*
- *adj.* (*especially NAmE*) = DRAUGHT

**'draft dodger** *noun* (*NAmE, disapproving*) a person who illegally tries to avoid doing military service ⊃ compare CONSCIENTIOUS OBJECTOR

**draft·ee** /ˌdrɑːfˈtiː; *NAmE* ˌdræf-/ (*US* **conscript**) *noun* a person who has been ordered by law to join the armed forces

**draft·er** /ˈdrɑːftə(r)/; *NAmE* ˈdræf-/ *noun* **1** a person who prepares a rough version of a plan, document, etc. **2** (*NAmE*) = DRAFTSMAN (2)

**drafts·man** /ˈdrɑːftsmən/; *NAmE* ˈdræfts-/, **drafts·woman** /ˈdrɑːftswʊmən/; *NAmE* ˈdræfts-/ *noun* (*pl.* **-men** /-mən/, **-women** /-wɪmɪn/) **1** (*NAmE*) = DRAUGHTSMAN, DRAUGHTSWOMAN **2** (*NAmE also* **drafter**) a person who writes official or legal documents: *the draftsmen of the constitution*

**drafts·man·ship** (*NAmE*) = DRAUGHTSMANSHIP

**drafts·per·son** (*NAmE*) = DRAUGHTSPERSON

**drafty** (*NAmE*) = DRAUGHTY

**drag** 🅒 **B2** /dræɡ/ *verb, noun*
- *verb* (**-gg-**)
- • PULL **1** 🅙 **B2** [T] to pull sb/sth along with effort and difficulty: **~ sb/sth** *The sack is too heavy to lift—you'll have to drag it.* ◊ **~ sb/sth + adv./prep.** *I dragged the chair over to the window.* ◊ **~ sb/sth + adj.** *She managed to drag him clear of the wreckage.* ⊃ SYNONYMS at PULL **2** [I] **~ adv./prep.** to take hold of sth and pull it: *Desperately, Jinny dragged at his arm.*
- • MOVE SLOWLY **3** [T, I] to move yourself slowly and with effort: **~ yourself + adv./prep.** *I managed to drag myself out of bed.* ◊ **~ + adv./prep.** *She always drags behind when we walk anywhere.*
- • PERSUADE SB TO GO **4** [T] **~ sb/yourself + adv./prep.** to persuade sb to come or go somewhere they do not really want to come or go to: *I'm sorry to drag you all this way in the heat.* ◊ *The party was so good I couldn't drag myself away.*

# drag-and-drop

- **OF TIME** 5 [I] (of time or an event) to pass very slowly: *Time dragged terribly.* ◇ *The meeting really dragged.* ⊃ see also DRAG ON
- **TOUCH GROUND** 6 [I, T] to move, or make sth move, partly touching the ground: *This dress is too long—it drags on the ground when I walk.* ◇ *~sth He was dragging his coat in the mud.*
- **SEARCH RIVER** 7 [T] ~sth (for sb/sth) to search the bottom of a river, lake, etc. with nets or HOOKS: *They dragged the canal for the murder weapon.*
- **COMPUTING** 8 [T] ~sth + adv./prep. to move some text, an ICON, etc. across the screen of a computer using the mouse ⊃ WORDFINDER NOTE at COMMAND

IDM **drag your 'feet/'heels** to be deliberately slow in doing sth or in making a decision **drag sb/sb's name through the 'mud/'dirt** (*informal*) to criticize or say bad things about sb in public, in a way that is unfair: *The paper has dragged his name through the mud.* ⊃ more at KICK v., BOOTSTRAP n.

PHRV **drag 'by** (of time) to pass very slowly: *The last few weeks of the summer really dragged by.* **drag sb↔'down** to make sb feel weak or unhappy **drag sb/sth↔'down (to sth)** to bring sb/sth to a lower social or economic level, a lower standard of behaviour, etc: *If he fails, he'll drag us all down with him.* **drag sth/sb 'into sth** | **drag sth/sb↔'in** 1 to start to talk about sth/sb that has nothing to do with what is being discussed: *Do you have to drag politics into everything?* 2 to try to get sb who is not connected with a situation involved in it: *Don't drag the children into our argument.* **drag 'on** (*disapproving*) to go on for too long: *The dispute has dragged on for months.* **drag sth↔'out** to make sth last longer than necessary SYN prolong: *Let's not drag out this discussion—we need to reach a decision.* **drag sth 'out of sb** to make sb say sth they do not want to say: *We dragged a confession out of him.* **drag sth↔'up** to mention an unpleasant story, fact, etc. that people do not want to remember or talk about: *Why do you have to keep dragging up my divorce?*

■ *noun*
- **BORING PERSON/THING** 1 [sing.] (*informal*) a boring person or thing; sth that is annoying: *He's such a drag.* ◇ *Walking's a drag—let's drive there.* ◇ *Having to work late every day is a drag.*
- **SB/STH STOPPING PROGRESS** 2 [sing.] **a ~ on sb/sth** (*informal*) a person or thing that makes progress difficult: *He came to be seen as a drag on his own party's prospects.*
- **ON CIGARETTE** 3 [C] (*informal*) an act of breathing in smoke from a cigarette, etc. SYN draw: *She took a long drag on her cigarette.*
- **WOMEN'S CLOTHES** 4 [U] (*informal*) clothes that are usually worn by the opposite sex (usually women's clothes worn by men): *in~ He performed in drag.* ◇ *a drag queen* (= a man who dresses in women's clothes, usually in order to entertain people)
- **PHYSICS** 5 [U] the force of the air that acts against the movement of an aircraft or other vehicle ⊃ compare LIFT ⊃ see also MAIN DRAG

**drag-and-'drop** *adj.* (*computing*) relating to the moving of ICONS, etc. on a screen using the mouse

**drag·net** /'drægnet/ *noun* 1 a net that is pulled through water to catch fish, or along the ground to catch animals ⊃ WORDFINDER NOTE at FISHING 2 a careful and complete search, especially for a criminal

**dragon** /'drægən/ *noun* 1 (in stories) a large aggressive animal with wings and a long tail, that can breathe out fire 2 (*disapproving, especially BrE*) a woman who behaves in an aggressive and frightening way

**'dragon boat** *noun* a long, narrow boat of traditional Chinese design that is used for racing and that is moved through the water by a lot of people using PADDLES. It is decorated to look like a dragon.

**dragon·fly** /'drægənflaɪ/ *noun* (*pl.* -ies) an insect with a long, thin body, often brightly coloured, and two pairs of large TRANSPARENT wings. Dragonflies are often seen over water. ⊃ VISUAL VOCAB page V3

**dra·goon** /drə'guːn/ *noun, verb*
■ *noun* a soldier in the past who rode a horse and carried a gun
■ *verb*
PHRV **dra'goon sb into sth/into doing sth** (*formal*) to force or persuade sb to do sth that they do not want to do SYN coerce

**'drag race** *noun* a race between powerful, specially adapted cars over a short distance ▸ **'drag racing** *noun* [U]

**drag·ster** /'drægstə(r)/ *noun* a car that is used in a drag race

**drain** /dreɪn/ *verb, noun*
■ *verb* 1 [T, I] ~(sth) to make sth empty or dry by removing the liquid from it; to become empty or dry in this way: *Drain and rinse the pasta.* ◇ *The marshes have been drained.* ◇ *You will need to drain the central heating system before you replace the radiator.* ◇ *The swimming pool drains very slowly.* ◇ *Leave the dishes to drain.* 2 [T, I] to make liquid flow away from sth; to flow away: *~sth (from/out of sth) We had to drain the oil out of the engine.* ◇ *~sth away/off Drain off the excess fat from the meat.* ◇ *~away/off She pulled out the plug and the water drained away.* ◇ (*figurative*) *My anger slowly drained away.* ◇ *~into sth The river drains into a lake.* ◇ *~from/out of sth All the colour drained from his face when I told him the news.* ◇ *~of sth His face drained of colour.* 3 [T] *~sth* to empty a cup or glass by drinking everything in it: *In one gulp, he drained the glass.* ◇ *She quickly drained the last of her drink.* 4 [T] to make sb/sth weaker, poorer, etc. by using up their/its strength, money, etc: *~sb/sth My mother's hospital expenses were slowly draining my income.* ◇ *an exhausting and draining experience* ◇ *~sb/sth of sth I felt drained of energy.*
■ *noun* 1 [C] a pipe that carries away dirty water or other liquid waste: *We had to call in a plumber to unblock the drain.* ◇ *The drains (= the system of pipes) date from the beginning of the century.* ⊃ WORDFINDER NOTE at WASTE 2 [C] (*BrE*) (*US* **grate, 'sewer grate**) a frame of metal bars over the opening to a drain in the ground 3 (*US*) (*BrE* **plug-hole**) [C] a hole in a bath, SINK, etc. where the water flows away and into which a PLUG fits 4 [sing.] **a ~ on sb/sth** a thing that uses a lot of the time, money, etc. that could be used for sth else: *Military spending is a huge drain on the country's resources.* 5 [U] **the ~ of sb/sth** the fact of resources, people, etc. being lost or wasted: *the drain of talented staff to the United States* ⊃ see also BRAIN DRAIN

IDM **(go) down the 'drain** (*BrE also* **(go) down the 'plug-hole**) (*informal*) (to be) wasted; (to get) very much worse: *It's just money down the drain, you know.* ◇ *Safety standards have gone down the drain.* ⊃ more at LAUGH v.

**drain·age** /'dreɪnɪdʒ/ *noun* [U] 1 the process by which water or liquid waste is drained from an area: *a drainage system/channel/ditch* ◇ *The area has good natural drainage.* 2 a system of drains

**drained** /dreɪnd/ *adj.* [not usually before noun] very tired and without energy: *She suddenly felt totally drained.* ◇ *The experience left her emotionally drained.*

**'draining board** (*BrE*) (*NAmE* **drain·board** /'dreɪnbɔːd; *NAmE* -bɔːrd/) *noun* the area next to a kitchen SINK where cups, plates, etc. are put for the water to run off, after they have been washed

**drain·pipe** /'dreɪnpaɪp/ *noun* 1 (*NAmE also* **down·spout**) a pipe that carries RAINWATER from the roof of a building to a DRAIN ⊃ picture at PIPE 2 a pipe that carries dirty water or other liquid waste away from a building

**drake** /dreɪk/ *noun* a male DUCK

**dram** /dræm/ *noun* (*especially ScotE*) a small amount of alcoholic drink, especially WHISKY

**drama** /'drɑːmə/ *noun* 1 [C] a play for the theatre, television or radio: *a costume/period/courtroom/crime drama* ◇ *a powerful television drama about city life* ◇ *a drama series set in an American dance academy* ⊃ WORDFINDER NOTE at PLAY

**WORDFINDER** comedy, denouement, dialogue, dramatic irony, play, scene, set, soliloquy, speech

**2** [U] plays considered as a form of literature: *classical/modern drama* ◇ *a drama critic* ◇ *a drama school/group* ◇ *I studied English and Drama at college.* ⊃ **WORDFINDER NOTE** at **WRITE** **3** [C] an exciting event: *A powerful human drama was unfolding before our eyes.* **4** [U] the fact of being exciting: *You couldn't help being thrilled by the drama of the situation.*
**IDM** **make a drama out of sth** to make a small problem or event seem more important or serious than it really is

**'drama queen** *noun* (*informal, disapproving*) a person who behaves as if a small problem or event is more important or serious than it really is

**dra·mat·ic** /drəˈmætɪk/ *adj.* **1** (of a change, an event, etc.) sudden, very great and often surprising: *a dramatic increase/change/improvement/shift* ◇ *There has been a dramatic rise in reported crime.* ◇ *The announcement had a dramatic effect on house prices.* **2** exciting and impressive: *a dramatic victory* ◇ *They watched dramatic pictures of the police raid on TV.* ◇ *This scene lacked the dramatic impact that it should have had.* ⊃ **SYNONYMS** at **EXCITING** **3** [usually before noun] connected with the theatre or plays: *a local dramatic society* **4** EXAGGERATED in order to create a special effect and attract people's attention: *He flung out his arms in a dramatic gesture.* ◇ *Don't be so dramatic!*

**dra·mat·ic·al·ly** /drəˈmætɪkli/ *adv.* **1** very suddenly and to a very great and often surprising degree: *Prices have fallen dramatically.* ◇ *Events could have developed in a dramatically different way.* **2** in a way that is exciting and impressive **3** in a way that is connected with the theatre or plays: *The opera does not compare musically or dramatically with the composer's best work.* **4** in a way that is EXAGGERATED in order to create a special effect and attract people's attention: *'At last!' she cried dramatically.*

**dra,matic 'irony** *noun* [U] (*specialist*) a situation in a play when a character's words carry an extra meaning to the audience because they know more than the character, especially about what is going to happen ⊃ **WORDFINDER NOTE** at **DRAMA**

**dra·mat·ics** /drəˈmætɪks/ *noun* [pl.] **1** [sing. or pl. v.] the study or practice of acting in plays or putting on plays: *Her love for dramatics began when she started appearing in plays at the age of 13.* ⊃ see also **AMATEUR DRAMATICS** **2** behaviour that does not seem sincere because it is EXAGGERATED or too emotional

**dra·ma·tis per·son·ae** /ˌdræmətɪs pəˈsəʊnaɪ; NAmE pərˈsoʊni/ *noun* [pl.] (*from Latin, specialist*) all the characters in a play in the theatre

**dra·ma·tist** /ˈdræmətɪst/ *noun* a person who writes plays for the theatre, television or radio **SYN** *playwright*: *a TV dramatist*

**dra·ma·tize** (*BrE also* **-ise**) /ˈdræmətaɪz/ *verb* **1** [T] ~ sth to present a book, an event, etc. as a play or a film **2** [T, I] ~ (sth) to make sth seem more exciting or important than it really is: *Don't worry too much about what she said—she tends to dramatize things.* ▸ **dra·ma·tiza·tion, -isa·tion** /ˌdræmətaɪˈzeɪʃn; NAmE -təˈz-/ *noun* [U, C]: *a television dramatization of the trial*

**dra·ma·turgy** /ˈdræmətɜːdʒi; NAmE -tɜːrdʒi/ *noun* [U] (*specialist*) the study or activity of writing dramatic texts

**dram·edy** /ˈdrɑːmədi/ *noun* (*pl.* **-ies**) (*NAmE*) a television programme that is intended to be both humorous and serious

**drank** /dræŋk/ *past tense of* **DRINK**

**drape** /dreɪp/ *verb, noun*
- *verb* **1** [T] ~ sth around/over/across, etc. sth to hang clothes, materials, etc. loosely on sb/sth: *She had a shawl draped around her shoulders.* ◇ *He draped his coat over the back of the chair.* ◇ *She draped a cover over the old sofa.* **2** [I] (of clothes or materials) to hang loosely: *Some silk fabrics will drape beautifully.* **3** [T] ~ sb/sth in/with sth to cover or decorate sth with material: *walls draped in ivy* **4** [T] ~ sth around/round/over, etc. sth to allow part of your body to rest on sth in a relaxed way: *His arm was draped casually around her shoulders.*
- *noun* (*especially NAmE*) (*NAmE also* **dra·pery**) [usually pl.] a long thick curtain: *blue velvet drapes*

**draper** /ˈdreɪpə(r)/ *noun* (*BrE, old-fashioned*) **1** a person who owns or manages a shop that sells cloth, curtains, etc. **2** **draper's** (*pl.* **drapers**) a shop that sells cloth, curtains, etc.

**dra·pery** /ˈdreɪpəri/ *noun* (*pl.* **-ies**) **1** [U] (*also* **dra·per·ies** [pl.]) cloth or clothing hanging in loose folds: *a cradle swathed in draperies and blue ribbon* **2** [C, usually pl.] (*NAmE*) = **DRAPE** **3** [U] (*old-fashioned*) cloth and materials for sewing sold by a draper ⊃ compare **DRY GOODS**

**dras·tic** /ˈdræstɪk/ *adj.* extreme in a way that has a sudden, serious or violent effect on sth: *drastic measures/changes* ◇ *The government is threatening to take drastic action.* ◇ *a drastic shortage of food* ◇ *Talk to me before you do anything drastic.* ▸ **dras·tic·al·ly** /-kli/ *adv.*: *Output has been drastically reduced.* ◇ *Things have started to go drastically wrong.*

**drat** /dræt/ *exclamation* (*old-fashioned, informal*) used to show that you are annoyed: *Drat! I forgot my key.* ▸ **drat·ted** /ˈdrætɪd/ *adj.* [only before noun] (*BrE, old-fashioned, informal*): *This dratted pen won't work.*

**draught** /drɑːft; NAmE dræft/ *noun, adj., verb*
- *noun* (*BrE*) (*NAmE* **draft**) **1** [C] a flow of cool air in a room or other small space: *There's a draught in here.* ◇ *A cold draught of air blew in from the open window.* ◇ **in a ~** *I was sitting in a draught.* **2** [C] (*formal*) one continuous action of SWALLOWING liquid (= making it go down your throat); the amount SWALLOWED: *He took a deep draught of his beer.* **3** [C] (*old use or literary*) medicine in a liquid form: *a sleeping draught* (= one that makes you sleep) **4** **draughts** (*BrE*) (*NAmE* **check·ers**) [U] a game for two players using 24 round pieces on a board marked with black and white squares **5** [C] (*BrE*) (*NAmE* **check·er**) one of the round pieces used in a game of draughts
**IDM** **on 'draught** (*BrE*) (of beer) taken from a large container (= a BARREL): *This beer is not available on draught* (= it is available only in bottles or cans).
- *adj.* (*BrE*) (*also* **draft** *especially in NAmE*) **1** [usually before noun] served from a large container (= a BARREL) rather than in a bottle: *draught beer* **2** [only before noun] used for pulling heavy loads: *a draught horse*
- *verb* (*especially BrE*) = **DRAFT**

**draught·board** /ˈdrɑːftbɔːd; NAmE ˈdræftbɔːrd/ (*BrE*) (*NAmE* **'check·er·board**) *noun* a board with black and white squares, used for playing DRAUGHTS

**draughts·man** (*BrE*) (*NAmE* **drafts·man**) /ˈdrɑːftsmən; NAmE ˈdræfts-/ *noun* (*pl.* **-men** /-mən/) **1** a person whose job is to draw detailed plans of machines, buildings, etc. **2** a person who draws: *He's a poor draughtsman.* ⊃ see also **DRAUGHTSWOMAN, DRAUGHTSPERSON**

**draughts·man·ship** (*BrE*) (*NAmE* **drafts·man·ship**) /ˈdrɑːftsmənʃɪp; NAmE ˈdræfts-/ *noun* [U] the ability to draw well: *You have to admire her superb draughtsmanship.*

**draughts·person** (*BrE*) (*NAmE* **drafts·person**) /ˈdrɑːftspɜːsn; NAmE ˈdræftspɜːrsn/ *noun* a draughtsman or draughtswoman

**draughts·woman** (*BrE*) (*NAmE* **drafts·woman**) /ˈdrɑːftswʊmən; NAmE ˈdræfts-/ *noun* (*pl.* **-women** /-wɪmɪn/) **1** a woman whose job is to draw detailed plans of machines, buildings, etc. ⊃ note at **GENDER** **2** a woman who draws ⊃ see also **DRAUGHTSMAN**

**draughty** /ˈdrɑːfti; NAmE ˈdræf-/ (*BrE*) (*NAmE* **drafty**) *adj.* (**draught·ier, draughti·est**) (of a room, etc.) uncomfortable because cold air is blowing through: *a draughty room/corridor*

**Dra·vid·ian** /drəˈvɪdiən/ *adj.* connected with a group of languages spoken in southern India and in Sri Lanka, or with the people who speak these languages

# draw

**draw** ❶ **A1** **S** /drɔː/ *verb, noun*

■ **verb** (**drew** /druː/, **drawn** /drɔːn/)

- **MAKE PICTURES 1** **A1** [I, T] to make pictures, or a picture of sth, with a pencil, pen or CHALK (but not paint): *You draw beautifully.* ◇ *~sth to draw a picture/map/diagram* ◇ *She drew a house.* ◇ *~sth with sth He drew a circle in the sand with a stick.*
- **DESCRIBE IN WORDS 2** **B1** [T] *~sth* to describe sth in words in a way that produces an image in sb's mind: *The report drew a grim picture of inefficiency and corruption.* ◇ *She writes lively stories with sharply drawn characters.*
- **CONCLUSION 3** **B2** [T] *~sth (from sth)* to have a particular idea after you have studied sth or thought about it: *What conclusions did you draw from the report?* ◇ *We can draw some lessons for the future from this accident.*
- **COMPARISON/LIMITS 4** **B2** [T] *~sth* to express a comparison or a contrast; to define the limits of sth: *to draw a comparison/a parallel/an analogy/a distinction between two events* ◇ *He attempted to draw a contrast between himself and the prime minister.* ◇ *The site's boundaries were tightly drawn by the Department of the Environment.*
- **GET REACTION 5** **B2** [T] to produce a reaction or response: *~sth The plan has drawn a lot of criticism.* ◇ *~sth from sb The announcement drew loud applause from the audience.* **6** **B2** [T] to direct or attract sb's attention to sth: *Our aim is to draw attention to the plight of these children.* ◇ *My eyes were drawn to the man in the corner.*
- **ATTRACT 7** [T] to attract or interest sb: *~sth The movie is drawing large audiences.* ◇ *The events continue to draw huge crowds.* ◇ *~sb to sth Her screams drew passers-by to the scene.*
- **MOVE 8** [I] + *adv./prep.* to move in the direction mentioned: *The train drew into the station.* ◇ *The train drew in.* ◇ *The figures in the distance seemed to be drawing closer.* ◇ *Their car drew alongside ours.* ◇ *(figurative) Her retirement is drawing near.* ◇ *(figurative) The meeting was drawing to a close.*
- **PULL 9** [T] *~sth/sb + adv./prep.* to move sth/sb by pulling it or them gently: *He drew the cork out of the bottle.* ◇ *I drew my chair up closer to the fire.* ◇ *She drew me onto the balcony.* ◇ *I tried to draw him aside* (= for example where I could talk to him privately). ⇒ **SYNONYMS** at **PULL** **10** [T, often passive] (of horses, etc.) to pull a vehicle such as a CARRIAGE: *be drawn by sth The Queen's coach was drawn by six horses.* ◇ *a horse-drawn carriage*
- **CURTAINS 11** [T] *~sth* to open or close curtains, etc: *The blinds were drawn.* ◇ *It was getting dark so I switched on the light and drew the curtains.* ◇ *She drew back the curtains and let the sunlight in.*
- **WEAPON 12** [T, I] *~(sth) (on sb)* to take out a weapon, such as a gun or a SWORD, in order to attack sb: *She drew a revolver on me.* ◇ *He came towards them with his sword drawn.*
- **MAKE SB TALK 13** [T] [often passive] to make sb say more about sth: *be drawn (about/on sth) Spielberg refused to be drawn on his next movie.*
- **CHOOSE 14** [I, T] to decide sth by picking cards, tickets or numbers by chance: *~for sth We drew for partners.* ◇ *~sth He drew the winning ticket.* ◇ *~sth (from sth) Names were drawn from a hat for the last few places.* ◇ *be drawn against sb/sth Italy has been drawn against Spain in the first round.* ◇ *~sb/sth to do sth Italy has been drawn to play Spain.* ⇒ see also DRAW/CAST LOTS (FOR STH/TO DO STH) at LOT *noun*
- **GAME 15** [I, T] to finish a game without either team winning: *England and France drew.* ◇ *England and France drew 3–3.* ◇ *~with/against sb England drew with/against France.* ◇ *~sth England drew their game against France.*
- **MONEY 16** [T] to take money or payments from a bank account or post office **SYN** **withdraw**: *~sth out (of sth) I drew out £200.* ◇ *Can I draw $80 out of my account?* ◇ *~sth (from sth) She went to the post office to draw her pension.* ◇ *~sth on sth The cheque was drawn on his personal account.*
- **LIQUID/GAS 17** [T] *~sth (+adv./prep.)* to take or pull liquid or gas from somewhere: *to draw water from a well* ◇ *The device draws gas along the pipe.*
- **SMOKE/AIR 18** [I, T] to breathe in smoke or air: *~at/on sth He drew thoughtfully on his pipe.* ◇ *~sth in Sh_ breathed deeply, drawing in the fresh mountain air.*

**IDM** **draw a ˈblank** to get no response or result: *So far, the police investigation has drawn a blank.* **ˌdraw ˈblood** to make sb BLEED **draw ˈbreath** (*BrE*) (*US* **draw a ˈbreath**) **1** to stop doing sth and rest: *She talks all the time and hardly stops to draw breath.* **2** (*literary*) to live; to be alive: *He was as kind a man as ever drew breath.* **draw sb's ˈfire** to make sb direct their anger, criticism, etc. at you, so that others do not have to face it **draw a ˈline under sth** (*BrE*) to say that sth is finished and not worth discussing any more **draw the ˈline (at sth/at doing sth)** to refuse to do sth; to set a limit: *I don't mind helping, but I draw the line at doing everything myself.* ◇ *We would have liked to invite all our relatives, but you have to draw the line somewhere.* **draw the ˈline (between sth and sth)** to make a difference between two closely related ideas: *Where do you draw the line between genius and madness?* **draw the short ˈstraw** (*BrE*) (*NAmE* **get the ˌshort end of the ˈstick**) to be the person in a group who is chosen or forced to perform an unpleasant duty or task: *I drew the short straw and had to clean the toilets.* **draw ˈstraws (for sth)** to use a method of choosing sb to do or have sth in which each person takes a piece of paper, etc. from a container and the one whose paper has a special mark is chosen: *We drew straws for who went first.* ⇒ more at BATTLE *n.*, BEAD, DAGGER, HEIGHT, HORN *n.*, LOT *n.*, SIDE *n.*

**PHRV** **ˌdraw ˈback** to move away from sb/sth: *He came close but she drew back.* **ˌdraw ˈback (from sth/from doing sth)** to choose not to take action, especially because you feel nervous: *We drew back from taking our neighbours to court.* **ˌdraw sth↔ˈdown** | **ˌdraw ˈdown** (*especially NAmE*) to reduce a supply of sth that has been created over a period of time; to be reduced: *There are many life events that can unexpectedly draw down savings.* ◇ *If we don't cut costs our reserves will draw down.* ⇒ related noun DRAWDOWN **ˌdraw sth↔ˈdown (from sth)** | **ˌdraw ˈdown on sth** (*especially NAmE*) (*finance*) to take money from a fund that a bank, etc. has made available: *The company has already drawn down €600 million of its €725 million credit line.* ◇ *They can draw down on the loan at any time.* ⇒ related noun DRAWDOWN **ˌdraw sth from sb/sth** to take or obtain sth from a particular source: *to draw support/comfort/strength from your family* ◇ *She drew her inspiration from her childhood experiences.* **ˌdraw ˈin** to become dark earlier in the evening as winter gets nearer: *The nights/days are drawing in.* **ˌdraw sb ˈinto (doing) sth** | **ˌdraw sb↔ˈin** to involve sb or make sb take part in sth, although they may not want to take part at first: *youngsters drawn into a life of crime* ◇ *The book starts slowly, but it gradually draws you in.* **ˌdraw sth↔ˈoff** to remove some liquid from a container or the body: *The doctor drew off some fluid to relieve the pressure.* **ˌdraw ˈon** if a time or a season **draws on**, it passes: *Night was drawing on.* **ˌdraw ˈon/upon sth** to use a supply of sth that is available to you: *I'll have to draw on my savings.* ◇ *The novelist draws heavily on her personal experiences.* **ˌdraw ˈout** to become lighter in the evening as summer gets nearer: *The days/evenings are drawing out.* **ˌdraw sb↔ˈout** to encourage sb to talk or express themselves freely **ˌdraw sth↔ˈout** to make sth last longer than usual or necessary: *She drew the interview out to over an hour.* ⇒ see also LONG-DRAWN-OUT **ˌdraw ˈup** if a vehicle **draws up**, it arrives and stops: *The cab drew up outside the house.* ◇ *She waved to me as I drew up.* **ˌdraw sth↔ˈup** to make or write sth that needs careful thought or planning: *to draw up a contract/list* ⇒ WORDFINDER NOTE at DOCUMENT

■ **noun**

- **CHOOSING 1** (*US also* **draw·ing**) [usually sing.] *~(for sth)* the act of choosing sth, for example the winner of a prize or the teams who play each other in a competition, usually by taking pieces of paper, etc. out of a container without being able to see what is written on them: *the draw for the second round of the Champions League* ◇ *The draw for the raffle takes place on Saturday.* **2** (*NAmE usually* **draw·ing**) a competition in which the winners are chosen in a draw: *a prize draw* ⇒ compare LOTTERY

- **SPORTS/GAMES 3** (*especially BrE*) a game in which both teams or players finish with the same number of points: *The match ended in a two-all draw.* ◊ *He managed to hold Smith to a draw* (= to stop him from winning when he seemed likely to do so). ⊃ compare TIE **4** (*BrE*) a sports match for which the teams or players are chosen in a draw: *Liverpool have an away draw against Manchester United.* **5** [usually sing.] a set of matches for which the teams or players are chosen in a draw: *There are only two seeded players left in the top half of the draw.*
- **ATTRACTION 6** a person, a thing or an event that attracts a lot of people SYN **attraction**: *She is currently one of the biggest draws on the Irish music scene.*
- **SMOKE 7** an act of breathing in the smoke from a cigarette SYN **drag**

IDM **be quick/fast on the ˈdraw 1** (*informal*) to be quick to understand or react in a new situation: *You can't fool him —he's always quick on the draw.* **2** to be quick at pulling out a gun in order to shoot it ⊃ more at LUCK *n.*

**draw·back** /ˈdrɔːbæk/ *noun* ~ (of/to sth) | ~ (of/to doing sth) a disadvantage or problem that makes sth a less attractive idea SYN **disadvantage, snag**: *The main drawback to it is the cost.* ◊ *This is the one major drawback of the new system.*

**draw·bridge** /ˈdrɔːbrɪdʒ/ *noun* a bridge that can be pulled up, for example to stop people from entering a castle or to allow ships to pass under it

**draw·down** /ˈdrɔːdaʊn/ *noun* [C, U] **1** ~ (on sth) the act of reducing a supply of sth that has been created over a period of time; the amount used: *The cold winter has led to a larger-than-expected drawdown on oil stocks.* **2** ~ (on sth) (*finance*) the act of using money that is available to you; the amount used: *a drawdown of cash from the company's reserves*

**drawer** *noun* /drɔː(r)/ a part of a piece of furniture such as a desk, used for keeping things in. It is like a box in shape and has a handle on the front for pulling it out: *in the top/middle/bottom drawer of the desk* ⊃ see also APP DRAWER, CHEST OF DRAWERS, TOP DRAWER

**drawers** /drɔːz; *NAmE* drɔːrz/ *noun* [pl.] (*old-fashioned*) KNICKERS *or* UNDERPANTS, especially ones that cover the upper parts of the legs

**draw·ing** 🔊 A2 /ˈdrɔːɪŋ/ *noun* **1** 🔊 A2 [C] a picture made using a pencil or pen rather than paint: *a pencil/pen-and-ink/charcoal drawing* ◊ *He did a drawing of the old farmhouse.* ◊ *The children were asked to make a drawing of a dinosaur.* ◊ ~ by sb *a drawing by Paul Klee* ⊃ SYNONYMS at PICTURE ⊃ see also LIFE DRAWING (2), LINE DRAWING **2** 🔊 A2 [U] the art or skill of making pictures, plans, etc. using a pen or pencil: *I'm not very good at drawing.* ◊ *technical drawing* ⊃ see also LIFE DRAWING (1) **3** [usually sing.] (*NAmE*) = DRAW (1) **4** (*NAmE*) = DRAW (2)

**ˈdrawing board** *noun* a large flat board used for holding a piece of paper while a drawing or plan is being made IDM **(go) back to the ˈdrawing board** to start thinking about a new way of doing sth after a previous plan or idea has failed **on the ˈdrawing board** being prepared or considered: *It's just one of several projects on the drawing board.*

**ˈdrawing pin** (*BrE*) (*NAmE* **thumb·tack, tack**) *noun* a short pin with a large round, flat head, used especially for fastening paper to a board or wall

**ˈdrawing power** (*NAmE*) (*BrE* **ˈpulling power**) *noun* [U] the ability of sb/sth to attract people

**ˈdrawing room** *noun* (*formal or old-fashioned*) a room in a large house in which people relax and guests are entertained ⊃ compare LIVING ROOM

**drawl** /drɔːl/ *verb* [T, I] + *speech* | ~ (sth) to speak or say sth slowly with vowel sounds that are longer than usual: *'Hi there!' she drawled lazily.* ◊ *He had a smooth drawling voice.* ▶ **drawl** *noun* [sing.]: *She spoke in a slow southern drawl.*

**drawn** /drɔːn/ *adj., verb*
- *adj.* (of a person or their face) looking pale and thin because the person is ill, tired or worried
- *verb past part.* of DRAW

**drawn-ˈout** (*also* **ˈlong-drawn, ˌlong-drawn-ˈout**) *adj.* lasting a very long time, often too long SYN **protracted**: *They had all the stress of a drawn-out legal process.*

**draw·string** /ˈdrɔːstrɪŋ/ *noun* a piece of string SEWN inside the material at the top of a bag, pair of trousers, etc. that can be pulled tighter in order to make the opening smaller: *They fasten with a drawstring.*

**dread** /dred/ *verb, noun, adj.*
- *verb* to be very afraid of sth; to fear that sth bad is going to happen: ~ sth *This was the moment he had been dreading.* ◊ ~ doing sth *I dread being sick.* ◊ ~ sb doing sth *She dreads her husband finding out.* ◊ ~ to do sth *I dread to think what would happen if there really was a fire here.* ◊ ~ that … *I both hoped and dreaded that he would come.*
- *noun* **1** [U, C, usually sing.] a feeling of great fear about sth that might or will happen in the future; a thing that causes this feeling: *The prospect of growing old fills me with dread.* ◊ *She has an irrational dread of hospitals.* ◊ *The committee members live in dread of* (= are always worried about) *anything that may cause a scandal.* ◊ *My greatest dread is that my parents will find out.* **2 dreads** [pl.] (*informal*) = DREADLOCKS
- *adj.* (*formal*) = DREADED

**dread·ed** /ˈdredɪd/ (*also formal* **dread**) *adj.* [only before noun] causing fear: *The dreaded moment had finally arrived.* ◊ (*humorous*) *Did I hear the dreaded word 'homework'?*

**dread·ful** /ˈdredfl/ *adj.* (*especially BrE*) **1** very bad or unpleasant: *What dreadful weather!* ◊ *What a dreadful thing to say!* ◊ *It's dreadful the way they treat their staff.* ◊ *How dreadful!* ◊ *Jane looked dreadful* (= looked ill or tired). ⊃ SYNONYMS at TERRIBLE **2** [only before noun] used to emphasize how bad sth is SYN **terrible**: *She's making a dreadful mess of things.* ◊ *I'm afraid there's been a dreadful mistake.* **3** [usually before noun] causing fear, pain or difficulty SYN **terrible**: *a dreadful accident* ◊ *They suffered dreadful injuries.*

**dread·ful·ly** /ˈdredfəli/ *adv.* (*especially BrE*) **1** extremely; very much: *I'm dreadfully sorry.* ◊ *I miss you dreadfully.* **2** very badly: *They suffered dreadfully during the war.*

**dread·locks** /ˈdredlɒks; *NAmE* -lɑːks/ (*also informal* **dreads** /dredz/) *noun* [pl.] hair that is TWISTED into long thick pieces that hang down from the head, worn especially by RASTAFARIANS

**dread·nought** /ˈdrednɔːt/ *noun* a type of ship used in war in the early 20th century

**dream** 🔊 A2 /driːm/ *noun, verb*
- *noun* **1** 🔊 A2 [C] a series of images, events and feelings that happen in your mind while you are asleep: *I had a really weird dream last night.* ◊ *'Goodnight. Sweet dreams.'* ◊ *Don't think about it. You'll only give yourself bad dreams.* ◊ ~ about sb/sth/about doing sth *a vivid dream about my old school.* ◊ *in a/sb's ~ His dead mother appeared to him in a dream.* ⊃ compare NIGHTMARE ⊃ see also WET DREAM ⊃ WORDFINDER NOTE at SLEEP **2** 🔊 A2 [C] a wish to have or be sth, especially one that seems difficult to achieve: *Her lifelong dream was to be a famous writer.* ◊ *He wanted to be rich but it was an impossible dream.* ◊ *a chance to fulfil a childhood dream* ◊ *to realize/achieve a dream* ◊ *If I win, it will be a dream come true.* ◊ *It was the end of all my hopes and dreams.* ◊ ~ of (doing) sth *He left his job to pursue his dream of opening a restaurant.* ◊ *of sb's dreams I've finally found the man of my dreams.* ◊ *Being a TV presenter would be my dream job.* ⊃ see also PIPE DREAM **3** 🔊 A2 [sing.] a state of mind or a situation in which things do not seem real or part of normal life: *in a ~ She walked around in a dream all day.* ⊃ see also DAYDREAM **4** [sing.] (*informal*) a beautiful or wonderful person or thing: *That meal was an absolute dream.*

# dreamboat

**IDM** **go/work like a ˈdream** **1** to work very well: *My new car goes like a dream.* **2** to happen without problems, in the way that you had planned **in your ˈdreams** (*informal*) used to tell sb that sth they are hoping for is not likely to happen: *'I'll be a manager before I'm 30.' 'In your dreams.'* **like a bad ˈdream** (of a situation) so unpleasant that you cannot believe it is true: *In broad daylight the events of the night before seemed like a bad dream.* ⊃ more at LIVE[1], WILD *adj.*

■ *verb* (**dreamed, dreamed** or **dreamt, dreamt** /dremt/) **1** [AZ] [I, T] to experience a series of images, events and feelings in your mind while you are asleep: *Did I talk in my sleep? I must have been dreaming.* ◊ *~ of/about sb/sth I dreamed about you last night.* ◊ *~ sth Did it really happen or did I just dream it?* ◊ *~ (that)... I dreamt (that) I got the job.* **2** [AZ] [I, T] to imagine and think about sth that you would like to happen: *It might never happen, but I can dream can't I?* ◊ *~ of/about sth It was the kind of trip most of us only dream about.* ◊ *~ of/about doing sth She dreams of running her own business.* ◊ *I wouldn't dream of going without you* (= I would never go without you). ◊ *~ (that)... I never dreamt (that) I'd actually get the job.*

**PHR V** **ˌdream sth aˈway** to waste time just thinking about things you would like to do without actually doing anything **ˌdream ˈon** (*informal*) you say **dream on** to tell sb that an idea is not practical or likely to happen **ˌdream sth↔ˈup** (*informal*) to have an idea, especially a very unusual or silly one **SYN** **think up**: *Trust you to dream up a crazy idea like this!*

**ˈdream·boat** /ˈdriːmbəʊt/ *noun* (*old-fashioned, informal*) a person who is very attractive, especially a man

**ˈdream·catch·er** /ˈdriːmkætʃə(r); *NAmE also* -ketʃ-/ *noun* a ring containing a decorated net, originally made by Native Americans, and thought to give its owner good dreams

**dreamcatcher**

**dream·er** /ˈdriːmə(r)/ *noun* **1** (*sometimes disapproving*) a person who has ideas or plans that are not practical or realistic **2** (*usually disapproving*) a person who does not pay attention to what is happening around them, but thinks about other things instead **3** a person who dreams: *Dreamers do not always remember their dreams.*

**dream·land** /ˈdriːmlænd/ *noun* [U] (*especially BrE, disapproving*) a pleasant but not very realistic situation that only exists in your mind: *You must be living in dreamland if you think he'll change his mind.*

**dream·less** /ˈdriːmləs/ *adj.* (of sleep) without dreams; deep and peaceful

**dream·like** /ˈdriːmlaɪk/ *adj.* as if existing or happening in a dream

**ˈdream team** *noun* [usually sing.] the best possible combination of people for a particular competition or activity

**ˈdream ticket** *noun* [sing.] (used especially in newspapers about candidates for an election) a combination of people who, together, are considered to be the best

**Dream·time** /ˈdriːmtaɪm/ *noun* [U] = ALCHERINGA

**dream·world** /ˈdriːmwɜːld; *NAmE* -wɜːrld/ *noun* a world that is not like the real world; a person's idea of reality that is not realistic: *If he thinks it's easy to get a job, he's living in a dreamworld.*

**dreamy** /ˈdriːmi/ *adj.* (**dream·ier, dreami·est**) **1** looking as though you are thinking about other things and not paying attention to what is happening around you: *She had a dreamy look in her eyes.* **2** (of a person or an idea) having a lot of imagination, but not very realistic: *Paul was dreamy and not very practical.* **3** as if you are asleep or in a dream: *He moved in the dreamy way of a man in a state of shock.* **4** (*informal*) pleasant and gentle; that makes you feel relaxed: *a slow, dreamy melody* **5** (*informal*) beautiful; wonderful: *What's he like? I bet he's really dreamy.* ▶ **dream·ily** /-mɪli/ *adv.* **dreami·ness** *noun* [U]

**dreary** /ˈdrɪəri; *NAmE* ˈdrɪri/ *adj.* (**drear·ier, dreari·est**) that makes you feel sad; not bright or interesting **SYN** **dull**: *a dreary winter's day* ◊ *a dreary film* ◊ *a long and dreary journey on the train* ▶ **drear·ily** /ˈdrɪərəli; *NAmE* ˈdrɪr-/ *adv.* **dreari·ness** /ˈdrɪərinəs; *NAmE* ˈdrɪr-/ *noun* [U]

**dreck** /drek/ *noun* [U] (*slang, especially NAmE*) something that you think is of very bad quality: *The movie is utter dreck.*

**dredge** /dredʒ/ *verb* **1** [T, I] to remove mud, stones, etc. from the bottom of a river, CANAL, etc. using a boat or special machine, to make it deeper or to search for sth: *~ (sth) They're dredging the harbour so that larger ships can use it.* ◊ *~ (sth) for sth They dredge the bay for gravel.* **2** [T] *~ sth (up) (from sth)* to bring sth up from the bottom of a river, etc. using a boat or special machine: *waste dredged (up) from the seabed* **3** [T] *~ sth in/with sth* to cover food lightly with sugar, flour, etc: *Dredge the top of the cake with icing sugar.*

**PHR V** **ˌdredge sth↔ˈup** **1** (*usually disapproving*) to mention sth that has been forgotten, especially sth unpleasant or embarrassing: *The papers keep trying to dredge up details of his past love life.* **2** to manage to remember sth, especially sth that happened a long time ago: *Now she was dredging up memories from the depths of her mind.*

**dredg·er** /ˈdredʒə(r)/ *noun* a boat or machine that is used to clear mud, etc. from the bottom of a river, or to make the river wider

**dregs** /dregz/ *noun* [pl.] **1** the last drops of a liquid, mixed with little pieces of solid material that are left in the bottom of a container: *coffee dregs* **2** the worst parts of sth that have no use or value: *the dregs of society* **3** (*literary*) the last parts of sth: *the last dregs of daylight*

**drench** /drentʃ/ *verb* [often passive] to make sb/sth completely wet **SYN** **soak**: *be/get drenched We were caught in the storm and got drenched to the skin.* ◊ *be drenched in/with sth His face was drenched with sweat.* ◊ *drench sb/sth/yourself in/with sth* (*figurative*) *She drenched herself in perfume.* ⊃ SYNONYMS at WET

**dress** ❶ [A1] /dres/ *noun, verb*

■ *noun*
- **CLOTHES** **1** [A1] [C] a piece of women's clothing that is made in one piece and covers the body down to the legs, sometimes reaching to below the knees, or to the ankles: *a long white dress* ◊ *to wear/put on/take off a dress* ◊ *a ~ a young woman in a pink silk dress* ⊃ see also COCKTAIL DRESS, EVENING DRESS, SUNDRESS, WEDDING DRESS **2** [B2] [U] clothes for either men or women: *formal/casual/formal dress* ◊ *in ...~ men and women in traditional Tibetan dress* ◊ *He has no dress sense* (= no idea of how to dress well). ⊃ SYNONYMS at CLOTHES ⊃ see also EVENING DRESS, FANCY DRESS, HEADDRESS, MORNING DRESS

■ *verb*
- **CLOTHES** **1** [A1] [I, T] to put clothes on yourself/sb: *I dressed quickly.* ◊ *Get up and get dressed!* ◊ *~ in sth He had dressed in a black T-shirt and jeans.* ◊ *~ sb/yourself (in sth) She dressed the children in their best clothes.* **OPP** **undress** **2** [B1] [I] to wear a particular type or style of clothes: *to dress smartly/casually* ◊ *~ for sth You should dress for cold weather today.* ◊ *~ in sth She always dressed entirely in black.* **3** [T] to put on formal clothes: *Do they expect us to dress for dinner?* **4** [T] *~ sb* to provide clothes for sb famous: *He dresses many of Hollywood's most famous young stars.*
- **WOUND** **5** [T] *~ sth* to clean, treat and cover a wound: *The nurse will dress that cut for you.*
- **FOOD** **6** [T] *~ sth* to prepare food for cooking or eating: *to dress a salad* (= put oil or VINEGAR, etc. on it) ◊ *to dress a chicken* (= take out the parts you cannot eat)
- **DECORATE/ARRANGE** **7** [T] *~ sth* (*formal*) to decorate or arrange sth: *to dress a shop window* (= arrange a display of clothes or goods in it)
- **STONE/WOOD/LEATHER** **8** [T] *~ sth* to prepare a material such as stone, wood, leather, etc. for use **IDM** SEE MUTTON, PART *n.*

**PHR V** **dress 'down** to wear clothes that are more informal than those you usually wear, for example in an office **dress sb 'down** to criticize or be angry with sb because they have done sth wrong ⊃ related noun DRESSING-DOWN **dress sb 'up** to wear clothes that are more formal than those you usually wear **dress 'up (as sb/sth) | be dressed 'up (as sb/sth)** to put on special clothes, especially to pretend to be sb/sth different: *Kids love dressing up.* ◇ *The boys were all dressed up as pirates.* ◇ (BrE) *dressing-up clothes* ◇ (NAmE) *dress-up clothes* **dress sth 'up** to present sth in a way that makes it seem better or different: *However much you try to dress it up, office work is not glamorous.*

**dress·age** /'dresɑːʒ/ *noun* [U] a set of movements which a rider trains a horse to perform with care and control; a competition in which these movements are performed

**'dress circle** (*especially BrE*) (*NAmE usually* **first 'balcony**) *noun* the first level of seats above the ground floor in a theatre

**'dress code** *noun* rules about what clothes people should wear at work, at school, in a restaurant or club, etc: *The company has a strict dress code—all male employees are expected to wear suits.*

**dressed** ⓘ B1 /drest/ *adj.* [not before noun] **1** ⓘ B1 wearing clothes and not NAKED or wearing clothes for sleeping: *Hurry up and get dressed.* ◇ *I can't go to the door—I'm not dressed yet.* **2** ⓘ wearing clothes of a particular type: *She is always so smartly dressed.* ◇ **~ in sth** *The bride was dressed in white.* ◇ *He was casually dressed in jeans and a T-shirt.* ◇ **~ for sth** *She was dressed for a business meeting.* ◇ **as sth** *He was dressed as a woman* (= he was wearing women's clothes). ◇ **~ like sth** *You can't go out dressed like that* (= wearing those clothes)! **3** cleaned and prepared for cooking or eating: *dressed crab* **IDM** **dressed to 'kill** (*informal*) wearing the kind of clothes that will make people notice and admire you **dressed (up) to the 'nines** (*informal*) wearing very attractive or formal clothes ⊃ more at MUTTON

**dress·er** /'dresə(r)/ *noun* **1** (*also* **Welsh 'dresser**) (*BrE*) a large piece of wooden furniture with shelves in the top part and cupboards below, used for displaying and storing cups, plates, etc. **2** (*NAmE*) = CHEST OF DRAWERS **3** (used with an adjective) a person who dresses in the way mentioned: *a snappy dresser* ⊃ see also CROSS-DRESSER **4** (in a theatre) a person whose job is to take care of an actor's clothes for a play and help him/her to get dressed ⊃ WORD-FINDER NOTE at PERFORMANCE

**dress·ing** /'dresɪŋ/ *noun* **1** (*also* **'salad dressing**) [C, U] a thin sauce added to salads, usually made from oil, VINEGAR, salt, pepper, etc. ⊃ see also FRENCH DRESSING **2** [U] (*NAmE*) = STUFFING (1) **3** [C] a piece of soft material placed over a wound in order to protect it **4** [U] the act of putting on clothes: *Many of our patients need help with dressing.* ⊃ see also CROSS-DRESSING, POWER DRESSING, WINDOW DRESSING

**dressing-'down** *noun* [sing.] (*old-fashioned, informal*) an occasion when sb speaks angrily to a person because they have done sth wrong

**'dressing gown** (*BrE*) (*NAmE* **bath·robe**, **robe**) *noun* a long loose piece of clothing, usually with a belt, worn indoors over night clothes, for example when you first get out of bed ⊃ picture at GOWN

**'dressing room** *noun* **1** a room for changing your clothes in, especially for actors or, in British English, for sports players **2** a small room next to a bedroom in some large houses, in which clothes are kept and people get dressed **3** (*NAmE*) = FITTING ROOM

**'dressing table** (*also* **'vanity table**, *NAmE also* **van·ity**) *noun* a piece of bedroom furniture like a table with DRAWERS (= parts like boxes in it with handles on the front for pulling them open) and a mirror on top

**dress·maker** /'dresmeɪkə(r)/ *noun* a person who makes women's clothes, especially as a job ▶ **dress·mak·ing** *noun* [U]

---

475 **drift**

**dress re'hearsal** *noun* the final practice of a play in the theatre, using the clothes and lights that will be used for the real performance: (*figurative*) *The earlier protests had just been dress rehearsals for full-scale revolution.*

**'dress shirt** *noun* **1** a white shirt worn on formal occasions with a BOW TIE and suit **2** (*NAmE*) a smart shirt with long SLEEVES that can be worn with a tie

**'dress uniform** *noun* [U, C] a uniform that army, NAVY, etc. officers wear for formal occasions and ceremonies

**dressy** /'dresi/ *adj.* (**dress·ier**, **dressi·est**) **1** (of clothes) attractive and formal **2** (of people) liking to wear attractive or fashionable clothes

**drew** /druː/ *past tense of* DRAW

**drib·ble** /'drɪbl/ *verb, noun*
▪ *verb* **1** [I, T] **~ (sth)** to let SALIVA or another liquid come out of your mouth and run down your CHIN **SYN** drool **2** [I] **+ adv./prep.** to fall in small drops or in a thin stream: *Melted wax dribbled down the side of the candle.* **3** [T] **~ sth (into/over/onto sth)** to pour sth slowly, in drops or a thin stream **SYN** drizzle, trickle: *Dribble a little olive oil over the salad.* **4** [T, I] **~ (sth) (+ adv./prep.)** (in football (soccer) and some other sports) to move the ball along with several short kicks, hits or BOUNCES: *She dribbled the ball the length of the field.* ◇ *He dribbled past two defenders and scored a magnificent goal.*
▪ *noun* **1** [C] a very small amount of liquid, in a thin stream: *a dribble of blood* ◇ *Add just a dribble of oil.* **2** [U] (*especially BrE*) SALIVA (= liquid) from a person's mouth: *There was dribble all down the baby's front.* **3** [C] the act of dribbling the ball in a sport

**dribs** /drɪbz/ *noun* [pl.]
**IDM** **in ,dribs and 'drabs** (*informal*) in small amounts or numbers over a period of time: *She paid me in dribs and drabs, not all at once.*

**dried** /draɪd/ *adj., verb*
▪ *adj.* with all the liquid removed in order to preserve sth: *dried flowers/apricots*
▪ *verb past tense, past part.* of DRY

**dried 'fruit** *noun* [U, C] fruit (for example, CURRANTS or RAISINS) that has been dried to be used in cooking or eaten on its own

**drier** = DRYER ⊃ see also DRY

**dri·est** /'draɪɪst/ ⊃ DRY *adj.*

**drift** ⓘ+ C1 /drɪft/ *verb, noun*
▪ *verb*
• MOVE SLOWLY **1** ⓘ+ C1 [I] **(+ adv./prep.)** to move along smoothly and slowly in water or air: *Clouds drifted across the sky.* ◇ *The empty boat drifted out to sea.* **2** ⓘ+ C1 [I] **+ adv./prep.** to move or go somewhere slowly: *The crowd drifted away from the scene of the accident.* ◇ *Her gaze drifted around the room.*
• WITHOUT PURPOSE **3** [I] **(+ adv./prep.)** to do sth, happen or change without a particular plan or purpose: *I didn't intend to be a teacher—I just drifted into it.* ◇ *He hasn't decided what to do yet—he's just drifting.* ◇ *The conversation drifted onto politics.*
• INTO STATE/SITUATION **4** [I] **~ in/into sth** to go from one situation or state to another without realizing it: *Finally she drifted into sleep.* ◇ *The injured man tried to speak but soon drifted into unconsciousness.*
• OF SNOW/SAND **5** [I] to be blown into large piles by the wind: *drifting sand* ◇ *Some roads are closed because of drifting.*
• FLOAT **6** [T] **+ adv./prep.** to make sth float somewhere: *The logs are drifted downstream to the mill.*
**PHR V** **drift a'part** to become less friendly or close to sb: *As children we were very close, but as we grew up we just drifted apart.* **,drift 'off (to sleep)** to fall asleep: *I didn't hear the storm. I must have drifted off by then.*
▪ *noun*
• SLOW MOVEMENT **1** [sing., U] a slow steady movement from one place to another; a slow change or development from one situation to another, especially to sth bad: *a population*

# drifter

*drift away from rural areas* ◇ *attempts to halt the drift towards war* • **OF SHIP 2** [U] the movement of a ship or plane away from its direction because of currents or wind • **OF SEA/AIR 3** [U, C] the movement of the sea or air SYN **current**: *the general direction of drift on the east coast* ◇ *He knew the hidden drifts in that part of the river.* • **OF SNOW 4** [C] a large pile of sth, especially snow, made by the wind: *The road was blocked by deep drifts of snow.* ⊃ see also SNOWDRIFT⊃ WORDFINDER NOTE at SNOW • **OF FLOWERS 5** [C] a large mass of sth, especially flowers: *Plant daffodils in informal drifts.* • **MEANING 6** [sing.] the general meaning of what sb says or writes SYN **gist**: *Do you catch my drift?* ◇ *My German isn't very good, but I got the drift of what she said.* ⊃ see also CONTINENTAL DRIFT

**drift·er** /ˈdrɪftə(r)/ *noun* (*disapproving*) a person who moves from one job or place to another with no real purpose

**drift net** *noun* a very large net used by fishing boats. The net has weights at the bottom and FLOATS at the top and is allowed to hang in the sea.

**drift·wood** /ˈdrɪftwʊd/ *noun* [U] wood that the sea carries up onto land, or that floats on the water

**drill** /drɪl/ *noun, verb*
■ *noun* **1** [C] a tool or machine with a pointed end for making holes: *an electric drill* ◇ *a hand drill* ◇ *a dentist's drill* ◇ *a drill bit* (= the pointed part at the end of the drill) ⊃ picture at PLANE⊃ see also PNEUMATIC DRILL⊃ WORDFINDER NOTE at DENTIST **2** [C, U] a way of learning sth by means of repeated exercises **3** [C, U] a practice of what to do in an emergency, for example if there is a fire: *a fire drill* **4** [U] military training in MARCHING, the use of weapons, etc: *rifle drill* **5 the drill** [sing.] (*old-fashioned*) the correct or usual way to do sth SYN **procedure**: *What's the drill for claiming expenses?* **6** [U] a type of strong cotton cloth **7** [C] a machine for planting seeds in rows: *a seed drill*
■ *verb* **1** [T, I] to make a hole in sth, using a drill: ~ **sth** *Drill a series of holes in the frame.* ◇ *The dentist started drilling my tooth.* ◇ **~(through sth)** *He drilled through the wall by mistake.* **2** [I] **~(for sth)** to try to get oil or water by drilling in the ground or sea bed: *They're drilling for oil off the Irish coast.* **3** [T] to teach sb to do sth by making them repeat it a lot of times: **~ sb to do sth** *The children were drilled to leave the classroom quickly when the fire bell rang.* ◇ **~ sb** *a well-drilled team* ◇ **~ sb in sth** *Recruits are drilled in basic techniques over the five-day course.* **4** [T] **~ sb** to train soldiers to perform military actions **5** [T] **~ sth + adv./prep.** to hit or kick a ball hard and in a straight line: *She drilled the ball into the back of the net.*
PHR V **,drill ˈdown** (*computing or business*) to go to deeper levels of an organized set of data in order to find more detail, especially on a computer or a website: *Navigation is good and there's a display to show how far you've drilled down.* **ˈdrill sth into sb** to make sb remember or learn sth by repeating it often: *It was drilled into us at an early age never to drop litter.*

**drily** (*especially BrE*) (*also* **dryly** *NAmE, BrE*) /ˈdraɪli/ *adv.* ⊃ see also DRY *adj.* **1** if sb speaks **drily**, they are being humorous, but not in an obvious way: '*That's a lovely purple suit you're wearing,' she said drily.* **2** in a way that shows no emotion: *He smiled drily and leaned back in his chair.* **3** in a way that shows that there is no liquid present: *She coughed drily.* ◇ *He swallowed drily and nodded.*

**drink** 🔑 A1 /drɪŋk/ *noun, verb*
■ *noun* **1** 🔑 A1 [C, U] a liquid for drinking; an amount of a liquid that you drink: *Can I have a drink?* ◇ *a hot/cold drink* ◇ *Passengers were left without food and drink for hours.* ◇ **~of sth** *a drink of water* ◇ **~from sth** *She took a drink from the glass and then put it down.* ⊃ see also ENERGY DRINK, SOFT DRINK, SPORTS DRINK **2** 🔑 A2 [C, U] alcohol or an alcoholic drink; sth that you drink on a social occasion: **for a~** *They went for a drink together.* ◇ *The drinks are on me* (= I'll pay for them)*.* ◇ *her battle with drink and drugs* ◇ (*BrE*) *He's got a drink problem.* ◇ (*NAmE*) *He has a drinking problem.* ◇ (*humorous*) *The children are enough to drive me to drink.* ◇ (*BrE*) *They came home the worse for drink* (= drunk)*.* ◇ *She took to drink* (= often drank too much alcohol) *after her marriage broke up.* ⊃ see also LONG DRINK **3 drinks** [pl.] a social occasion where you have alcoholic drinks: *Would you like to come for drinks on Sunday?* ◇ *a drinks party*
IDM see DEMON
■ *verb* (**drank** /dræŋk/, **drunk** /drʌŋk/) **1** 🔑 A1 [T, I] to take liquid into your mouth and then down your throat into your stomach: **~ sth** *I don't drink coffee.* ◇ *What would you like to drink?* ◇ **~ (from sth)** *She drank from a tall glass.* ◇ *She opened the can and drank thirstily.* **2** 🔑 A2 [I, T] to drink alcohol, especially when it is done regularly: *He doesn't drink.* ◇ *to drink heavily* ◇ *Don't drink and drive* (= drive a car after drinking alcohol)*.* ◇ **~ sth** *I drank far too much last night.* ◇ **~yourself + adj.** *He had drunk himself unconscious on vodka.* ◇ **~yourself to sth** *His father drank himself to death*⊃ see also DRUNK
IDM **,drink sb's ˈhealth** (*BrE*) to wish sb good health as you lift your glass, and then drink from it **drink like a ˈfish** (*informal*) to drink a lot of alcohol regularly **drink a ˈtoast to sb** to wish sb good luck, health or success as you lift your glass and then drink from it **,drink sb under the ˈtable** (*informal*) to drink more alcohol than sb else without becoming as drunk as they are **I'll, we'll, etc. ˌdrink to ˈthat** (*informal*) used to say that you like or agree with an idea, or would like it to happen: '*I hope you have a peaceful New Year.' 'I'll drink to that!'* ⊃ more at EAT, HORSE *n.*
PHR V **ˈdrink sth↔ˈin** to look at or listen to sth with great interest and pleasure: *We just stood there drinking in the scenery.* **ˈdrink to sb/sth** to wish sb good luck, health or success as you lift your glass and then drink from it SYN **toast**: *All raise your glasses and drink to Katie and Tom!* **,drink ˈup** | **,drink (sth)↔ˈup** to drink all of sth: *Drink up and let's go.* ◇ *Come on, drink up your juice.*

**drink·able** /ˈdrɪŋkəbl/ *adj.* **1** clean and safe to drink **2** pleasant to drink: *a very drinkable wine*

**drink-ˈdriver** (*BrE*) (*also* **drunk ˈdriver** *NAmE, BrE*) *noun* a person who drives a vehicle after drinking too much alcohol

**drink-ˈdriving** (*BrE*) (*also* **drunk ˈdriving**, **drunken ˈdriving** (*especially in NAmE*)) *noun* [U] driving a vehicle after drinking too much alcohol

**drink·er** /ˈdrɪŋkə(r)/ *noun* **1** a person who drinks alcohol regularly, especially sb who drinks too much: *a heavy/moderate drinker* **2** (after a noun) a person who regularly drinks the particular drink mentioned: *a coffee drinker*

**drink·ing** /ˈdrɪŋkɪŋ/ *noun* [U] the act of drinking alcohol: *Drinking is not advised during pregnancy.* ◇ *There are tough penalties for drinking and driving.*

**ˈdrinking box** *noun* (*CanE*) a small box of juice, etc. made of stiff card that has a drinking straw with it that can be pushed through a small hole in the top

**ˈdrinking chocolate** *noun* [U, C] (*BrE*) a sweet chocolate powder; a hot drink made from this powder mixed with hot milk and/or water⊃ compare COCOA

**ˈdrinking fountain** (*especially BrE*) (*NAmE usually* **ˈwater fountain**) *noun* a device that supplies water for drinking in public places

**ˈdrinking straw** *noun* = STRAW (3)

**ˈdrinking water** *noun* [U] water that is safe for drinking

**drip** /drɪp/ *verb, noun*
■ *verb* (**-pp-**) **1** [I] **(+ adv./prep.)** (of liquid) to fall in small drops: *She was hot and sweat dripped into her eyes.* ◇ *Water was dripping down the walls.* **2** [I, T] to produce or let fall drops of liquid: *The tap was dripping.* ◇ **+ adv./prep.** *Her hair dripped down her back.* ◇ **~with sth** *Her hands were dripping with blood.* ◇ **~sth (+adv./prep.)** *Be careful, you're dripping paint everywhere!* **3** [I, T] to contain or hold a lot of sth: **~with sth** *The trees were dripping with fruit.* ◇ **~sth** *His voice dripped sarcasm.*
■ *noun* **1** [sing.] the sound or action of small drops of liquid falling continuously: *The silence was broken only by the steady drip, drip of water from the roof.* **2** [C] a small drop of liquid that falls from sth: *Put a bucket under the hole in the roof to catch the drips.* **3** (*also* **IV** *especially in NAmE*) [C] (*medical*) a piece of equipment that passes liquid food,

medicine or blood very slowly through a tube into a patient's VEIN: *on a* ~ *She's been put on a drip.* **4** [C] (*old-fashioned*, *informal*) a boring or stupid person with a weak personality SYN **wimp**: *Don't be such a drip—come and join in the fun!*

**drip-dry** *adj.* made of a type of cloth that will dry quickly without CREASES when you hang it up wet

**drip-feed** *verb* (**drip-fed, drip-fed**) ~ **sb/sth** to give sb sth in separate small amounts ▶ **'drip feed** *noun* [U, C]: *the steady drip feed of leaked documents in the papers*

**drip·ping** /ˈdrɪpɪŋ/ *adj., noun*
- *adj.* ~ **(with sth)** very wet: *Her face was dripping with sweat.* ◊ *His clothes were still dripping wet.* ◊ (*figurative*) *His wife came in, dripping with diamonds.*
- *noun* [U] (*BrE*) (*NAmE* **drip·pings** [pl.]) fat that comes out of meat when it is cooked, often kept for frying other food in

**drip·py** /ˈdrɪpi/ *adj.* (**drip·pier, drip·pi·est**) (*informal*) **1** boring, stupid and weak or SENTIMENTAL: *her drippy boyfriend* **2** in a liquid state, and likely to fall in drops: *drippy paint* ◊ *a drippy nose* (= with drops of liquid falling from it)

## drive ⓘ A1 /draɪv/ *verb, noun*
- *verb* (**drove** /drəʊv/, **driven** /ˈdrɪvn/)
  - • VEHICLE **1** A1 [I, T] to operate a vehicle so that it goes in a particular direction: *Can you drive?* ◊ *Don't drive so fast!* ◊ *I drove to work this morning.* ◊ *Shall we drive* (= go there by car) *or go by train?* ◊ ~ **sth** *He drives a taxi* (= that is his job). ⇒ see also FLY-DRIVE **2** A2 [T] ~ **sb (+adv./prep.)** to take sb somewhere in a car, taxi, etc: *Could you drive me home?* ⇒ SYNONYMS at TAKE **3** A2 [I] + **adv./prep.** (of a vehicle) to travel under the control of a driver: *A stream of black cars drove by.* **4** A2 [T] ~ **sth** to own or use a particular type of vehicle: *What car do you drive?*
  - • MAKE SB DO STH **5** B1 [T] to make sb very angry, crazy, etc. or to make them do sth extreme: ~ **sb + adj.** *to drive sb crazy/mad/nuts/insane* ◊ ~ **sb to sth** *Hunger drove her to steal.* ◊ ~ **sb to sth** *Those kids are driving me to despair.* ◊ (*humorous*) *It's enough to drive you to drink* (= to make you start drinking too much alcohol). **6** [T] ~ **sb/yourself (+ adv./prep.)** to force sb to act in a particular way: *The urge to survive drove them on.* ◊ *You're driving yourself too hard.*
  - • MACHINE **7** [T] ~ **sth** to provide the power that makes a machine work; to operate a device: *a steam-driven locomotive* ◊ *The interface can be used to drive a printer.*
  - • MAKE SB/STH MOVE **8** [T] ~ **sb/sth + adv./prep.** to force sb/sth to move in a particular direction: *to drive sheep into a field* ◊ *The enemy was driven back.*
  - • CAUSE STH TO MAKE PROGRESS **9** [T] ~ **sth** to influence sth or cause it to make progress: *This is the main factor driving investment in the area.*
  - • HIT/PUSH **10** [T] ~ **sth + adv./prep.** to force sth to go in a particular direction or into a particular position by pushing it, hitting it, etc: *to drive a nail into a piece of wood*
  - • MAKE A HOLE **11** [T] ~ **sth + adv./prep.** to make an opening in or through sth by using force: *They drove a tunnel through the solid rock.*
  - • IN SPORT **12** [T, I] ~ **(sth) (+ adv./prep.)** to hit a ball with force, sending it forward: *to drive the ball into the rough* (= in golf)
  - • WIND/WATER **13** [T] ~ **sth (+ adv./prep.)** to carry sth along: *Huge waves drove the yacht onto the rocks.* **14** [I] **(+ adv./prep.)** to fall or move rapidly and with great force: *The waves drove against the shore.*
  - IDM **drive a coach and horses through sth** to cause sth to fail, for example a plan **drive sth 'home (to sb)** to make sb understand or accept sth by saying it often, loudly, angrily, etc: *You will really need to drive your point home.* **drive a 'wedge between A and B** to make two people start disliking each other: *I don't want to drive a wedge between the two of you.* **what sb is 'driving at** (*informal*) the thing sb is trying to say: *I wish I knew what they were driving at.* ⇒ more at GROUND *n.*, HARD *adj.*, SNOW *n.*
  - PHRV **drive a'way** | **drive sb/sth a'way** to leave in a vehicle; to take sb away in a vehicle: *We heard him drive away.* ◊ *Someone drove the car away in the night.* **drive sb a'way** to make sb not want to stay or not want to go somewhere: *Her constant nagging drove him away.* ◊ *Terrorist threats are driving away tourists.* **drive sth↔'down** to

make sth such as prices fall quickly **drive 'off 1** (of a driver, car, etc.) to leave: *The robbers drove off in a stolen vehicle.* **2** (in golf) to hit the ball to begin a game **drive sb/sth↔'off** to force sb/sth to go back or away: *The defenders drove off each attack.* **drive 'on** to continue driving: *Don't stop—drive on!* **drive sb/sth↔'out (of sth)** to make sb/sth disappear or stop doing sth: *New fashions drive out old ones.* **drive sth↔'up** to make sth such as prices rise quickly

- *noun*
  - • IN/OF VEHICLE **1** A2 [C] a journey in a car or other vehicle: *Let's go for a drive.* ◊ *It's a three-hour drive to London.* **2** [C, U] the equipment in a vehicle that takes power from the engine to the wheels: *the drive shaft* ◊ *a car with four-wheel drive* ◊ *a left-/right-hand drive car* (= a car where the driver and the controls are on the left/right)
  - • OUTSIDE HOUSE **3** (also **drive·way**) [C] a wide hard path or a private road that leads from the street to a house: *in/on the* ~ *There were two cars parked in the drive.*
  - • EFFORT **4** [C] an organized effort by a group of people to achieve sth: *The company is launching a big recruitment drive.* ◊ ~ **for sth** *a drive for greater efficiency* ◊ ~ **to do sth** *the government's drive to reduce energy consumption* ⇒ see also BLOOD DRIVE ⇒ SYNONYMS at CAMPAIGN
  - • DESIRE/ENERGY **5** [C, U] a strong desire or need in people: *a strong sex drive* **6** [U] (*approving*) a strong desire to do things and achieve sth; great energy: *He'll do very well—he has tremendous drive.*
  - • IN SPORT **7** [C] a long hard hit or kick: *She has a strong forehand drive* (= in tennis). ◊ *He scored with a brilliant 25-yard drive.*
  - • COMPUTING **8** [C] a type of computer STORAGE that stores large amounts of data on a SPINNING (= turning) disk: *a CD drive* ⇒ WORDFINDER NOTE at COMPUTER ⇒ see also DISK DRIVE, HARD DRIVE, PEN DRIVE, USB DRIVE
  - • GAMES **9** [C] (*BrE*) a social occasion when a lot of people compete in a game such as WHIST or BINGO
  - • ANIMALS/ENEMY **10** [C] an act of going after animals or the enemy and making them go into a smaller area, especially in order to kill or capture them
  - • ROAD **11** Drive (*abbr.* **Dr**) used in the names of roads: *21 Island Heights Drive*

**'drive bay** *noun* (*computing*) a space inside a computer for a DISK DRIVE

**'drive-by** *adj.* [only before noun] a **drive-by** shooting, etc. is done from a moving car: *a drive-by killing* ▶ **'drive-by** *noun* (*pl.* **drive-bys**)

**'drive-in** *noun* a place where you can watch films, eat, etc. without leaving your car: *We stopped at a drive-in for a hamburger.* ▶ **'drive-in** *adj.*: *drive-in movies*

**driv·el** /ˈdrɪvl/ *noun* [U] (*informal, disapproving*) ideas, statements or beliefs that you think are silly or not true SYN **nonsense**: *How can you watch that drivel on TV?*

**driv·en** /ˈdrɪvn/ *adj., verb*
- *adj.* **1** (of a person) determined to succeed, and working very hard to do so **2** -**driven** (in compounds) influenced or caused by a particular thing: *a market-driven economy* ◊ *a character-driven movie* ⇒ see also DATA-DRIVEN IDM see SNOW *n.*
- *verb* past part. of DRIVE

## driver ⓘ A1 /ˈdraɪvə(r)/ *noun* **1** A1 a person who drives a vehicle: *a bus/train/taxi driver* ◊ *a good/careful driver* ◊ *She climbed into the driver's seat.* ◊ (*BrE*) *a learner driver* (= one who has not yet passed a driving test) ◊ (*NAmE*) *a student driver* ◊ (*BrE*) *a lorry driver* ◊ (*especially NAmE*) *a truck driver* ⇒ see also CO-DRIVER, DESIGNATED DRIVER, DRINK-DRIVER, DRUNK DRIVER, ENGINE DRIVER **2** (in golf) a CLUB with a large head, used for hitting the ball long distances from the TEE **3** (*computing*) software that controls the sending of data between a computer and a piece of equipment that is attached to it, such as a printer **4** one of the main things that influence sth or cause it to make progress: *Housing is a key driver of the economy.* ⇒ see also SLAVE-DRIVER IDM see SEAT *n.*

# driverless

**'driver·less** /'draɪvələs; *NAmE* -vərl-/ *adj.* = SELF-DRIVING

**'driver's license** (*NAmE*) (*BrE* **'driving licence**) *noun* an official document that shows that you are qualified to drive

**'drive·shaft** /'draɪvʃɑːft; *NAmE* -ʃæft/ *noun* a long thin part of a machine that turns round and round and sends power from the engine to another part of the machine

**'drive-through** (*also* **'drive-thru**) *noun* (*NAmE*) a restaurant, bank, etc. where you can be served without having to get out of your car

**'drive time** *noun* [U] a time during the day when many people are driving their cars, for example to or from work ▶ **'drive-time** *adj.* [only before noun]: *a drive-time radio show*

**'drive·way** /'draɪvweɪ/ *noun* = DRIVE: *in/on the ~ There was a car parked in/on the driveway.*

**driv·ing** 🔑 **A2** /'draɪvɪŋ/ *noun, adj.*

■ *noun* 🔑 **A2** [U] the way that sb drives a vehicle; the act of driving: *dangerous/careless/reckless driving* ◊ *a driving lesson/instructor* ⊃ see also DRINK-DRIVING, DRUNK DRIVING, DRUNKEN DRIVING **IDM** see SEAT *n.* ⊃ **WORDFINDER NOTE** at CAR

■ *adj.* [only before noun] **1** 🔑 **C1** strong and powerful; having a strong influence in making sth happen: *Who was the driving force* (= the person with the strongest influence) *in the band?* **2** (of rain, snow, etc.) falling very fast and at an angle

**'driving licence** (*BrE*) (*NAmE* **'driver's license**) *noun* an official document that shows that you are qualified to drive

**'driving range** *noun* a place where people can practise hitting golf balls

**'driving school** *noun* a business that gives people lessons in how to drive a car, etc.

**'driving test** (*NAmE also* **'road test**) *noun* a test that must be passed before you are qualified to drive a car, etc.

**driving under the 'influence** *noun* [U] (*abbr.* **DUI**) (*US*) (in some states in the US) the crime of driving a vehicle after drinking too much alcohol or taking drugs that affect your ability to drive. It is a less serious crime than 'driving while intoxicated'.

**driving while in'toxicated** *noun* [U] (*abbr.* **DWI**) (*US*) the crime of driving a vehicle after drinking too much alcohol or taking drugs that affect your ability to drive

**driz·zle** /'drɪzl/ *verb, noun*

■ *verb* **1** [I] when **it is drizzling**, it is raining lightly **2** [T] *~ sth* **(over sth)** to pour a small amount of liquid over the surface of sth **SYN** dribble

■ *noun* [U, sing.] light fine rain ▶ **driz·zly** /'drɪzli/ *adj.*: *a dull, drizzly morning*

**DRM** /ˌdiː ɑːr 'em/ *abbr.* (*computing*) digital rights management (actions and devices that are used by the owners of software or information to prevent people from accessing or copying it from the internet without permission)

**Dr Mar·tens**™ /ˌdɒktə 'mɑːtənz; *NAmE* ˌdɑːktər 'mɑːrtnz/ (*also informal* **Doc Martens**™) *noun* [pl.] a type of comfortable heavy boot or shoe with LACES

**droid** /drɔɪd/ *noun* (in science fiction) a robot ⊃ compare ANDROID

**droll** /drəʊl/ *adj.* (*old-fashioned or ironic*) funny, but not in a way that you expect ▶ **drolly** /'drəʊlli/ *adv.*

**drom·ed·ary** /'drɒmədəri; *NAmE* 'drɑːməderi/ *noun* (*pl.* **-ies**) an animal of the CAMEL family, with only one HUMP, that lives in desert countries

**drone** /drəʊn/ *noun, verb*

■ *noun* **1** [usually sing.] a continuous low noise: *the distant drone of traffic* **2** [usually sing.] a continuous low sound made by some musical instruments, for example the BAGPIPES, over which other notes are played or sung; the part of the instrument that makes this noise **3** an aircraft without a pilot, controlled from the ground, used for taking photographs, dropping bombs, delivering goods, etc: *aerial/surveillance drones* ◊ *unmanned drones* ◊ *drone strikes/attacks* ◊ *Drone strikes killed 20 people in rebel-held areas.* ⊃ **WORDFINDER NOTE** at AIRCRAFT **4** a male bee that does not work ⊃ compare QUEEN BEE, WORKER **5** a person who is lazy and gives nothing to society while others work

■ *verb* [I] to make a continuous low noise: *A plane was droning in the distance.* ◊ *a droning voice*

**PHRV** **drone 'on (about sth)** to talk for a long time in a boring way

**drongo** /'drɒŋɡəʊ; *NAmE* 'drɑːŋ-/ *noun* (*pl.* **-os** *or* **-oes**) **1** a shiny black bird with a long tail **2** (*AustralE, NZE, slang*) a stupid person

**drool** /druːl/ *verb* **1** [I] to let SALIVA (= liquid) come out of your mouth **SYN** dribble: *The dog was drooling at the mouth.* **2** [I] *~ (over sb/sth)* (*disapproving*) to show in a silly or EXAGGERATED way that you want or admire sb/sth very much: *teenagers drooling over photos of movie stars*

**droop** /druːp/ *verb* **1** [I] to bend, hang or move downwards, especially because of being weak or tired: *She was so tired, her eyelids were beginning to droop.* **2** [I] to become sad or depressed: *Our spirits drooped when we heard the news.* ▶ **droop** *noun* [sing.]: *the slight droop of her mouth* **droopy** /'druːpi/ *adj.*: *a droopy moustache*

**drop** 🔑 **A2** /drɒp; *NAmE* drɑːp/ *verb, noun*

■ *verb* (-pp-)

• **FALL 1** 🔑 **A2** [T, I] to allow sth to fall by accident; to fall by accident: *~ sth Be careful not to drop that plate.* ◊ *to sth The climber slipped and dropped to his death.* **2** 🔑 **B1** [T, I] to make sth fall deliberately; to let yourself fall: *~ sth You can never be sure whether the planes will be dropping bombs or food parcels.* ◊ *~ sth + adv./prep. Medical supplies are being dropped into the stricken area.* ◊ (*BrE*) *He dropped his trousers* (= undid them and let them fall). ◊ (*NAmE*) *He dropped his pants.* ◊ *~ (+ adv./prep.) Catch me when I drop.* **3** [I] (*informal*) to fall down or be no longer able to stand because you are extremely tired: *I feel ready to drop.* ◊ *~ + adv./prep. He staggered in and dropped into a chair.*

• **BECOME WEAKER/LESS 4** 🔑 **B1** [I, T] to become or make sth weaker, lower or less **SYN** fall: *The temperature has dropped considerably.* ◊ *At last the wind dropped.* ◊ *~ to sth His voice dropped to a whisper.* ◊ *~ by sth The price of shares dropped by 14p.* ◊ *~ in sth* (*sb/sth*) *Shares dropped in price by 14p.* ◊ *~ against sth The dollar dropped sharply against the euro.* ◊ *~ sth You must drop your speed in built-up areas.* ⊃ **LANGUAGE BANK** at FALL

• **IN SPORT 5** [T] *~ sth* to fail to win sth: *They didn't drop any points until halfway through the season.*

• **EYES 6** [I, T] *your eyes/gaze ~ | ~ your eyes/gaze* (*formal*) to look down: *Her eyes dropped to her lap.*

• **SLOPE DOWNWARDS 7** [I] *~ (away) (from sth)* to slope steeply downwards: *In front of them the valley dropped sharply away from the road.*

• **DELIVER/SEND 8** [T] to stop so that sb can get out of a car, etc.; to deliver or leave sth in a particular place, especially on the way to somewhere else: *~ sb/sth Can you drop me near the bank?* ◊ *~ sb/sth off You left your jacket, but I can drop it off on my way to work tomorrow.* ◊ *~ sth + adv./prep. Just drop it in the mail when you have time.* ⊃ related noun DROP-OFF (2) **9** [T] *~ sb a line/a note/an email* to send a short letter or email to sb: *Drop me a line when you get there.*

• **ON A COMPUTER SCREEN 10** [T] *~ sth (+ adv./prep.)* to put some text, an ICON, etc. into a file, FOLDER or place on a computer screen, using the mouse: *You can easily drag and drop files onto your memory stick.*

• **LEAVE OUT 11** [T] to leave sb/sth out by accident or deliberately: *~ sb/sth from sth She's been dropped from the team because of injury.* ◊ *~ sb/sth He spoke with a cockney accent and dropped his aitches* (= did not pronounce the letter 'h' at the start of words).

• **FRIENDS 12** [T] *~ sb* to stop seeing sb socially: *She's dropped most of her old friends.*

- **STOP 13** [T] ~ sth to stop doing or discussing sth; to not continue with sth: *I dropped German* (= stopped studying it) *when I was 14.* ◊ *Drop everything and come at once!* ◊ *Look, can we just drop it* (= stop talking about it)? ◊ *I think we'd better drop the subject.* ◊ *The police decided to drop the charges against her.*
- **HINT 14** [T] ~ a hint to say or do sth in order to show sb, in an indirect way, what you are thinking ⊃ see also NAME-DROP
- **IN KNITTING 15** [T] ~ a stitch to let a STITCH go off the needle

**IDM** **drop the ˈball** (*NAmE*, *informal*) to make a mistake and cause sth that you are responsible for to fail **drop a ˈbrick/ˈclanger** (*BrE*, *informal*) to say sth that offends or embarrasses sb, although you did not intend to **drop your ˈbundle** (*AustralE*, *NZE*, *informal*) to suddenly not be able to think clearly; to act in a stupid way because you have lost control over yourself **drop ˈdead 1** (*informal*) to die suddenly and unexpectedly **2** (*informal*) used to tell sb, rudely, to stop annoying you, INTERFERING, etc. ⊃ see also DROP-DEAD **drop your ˈguard** to stop being careful and preparing yourself for possible danger or difficulty: *You can never drop your guard with a two-year-old.* **drop sb ˈin it** (*BrE*, *informal*) to put sb in an embarrassing situation, especially by telling a secret that you should not have told **drop ˈnames** to mention famous people you know or have met in order to impress others ⊃ related noun NAME-DROPPING **let sb/sth ˈdrop 1** to do or say nothing more about sb/sth: *I suggest we let the matter drop.* **2** to mention sb/sth in a conversation, by accident or as if by accident: *He let it drop that the prime minister was a close friend of his.* ⊃ more at BOTTOM *n.*, FLY *n.*, HEAR, JAW *n.*, LAP *n.*, PENNY

**PHRV** **drop aˈway** to become weaker or less: *She could feel the tension drop away.* **drop ˈback/beˈhind | drop beˈhind sb** to move or fall into position behind sb else: *We cannot afford to drop behind our competitors.* **drop ˈby/ˈin | drop ˈin on sb | drop ˈinto sth** (*BrE also* **drop ˈround**) to pay an informal visit to a person or a place: *Drop by sometime.* ◊ *I thought I'd drop in on you while I was passing.* ◊ *Sorry we're late—we dropped into the pub on the way.* **drop ˈoff** (*informal*) **1** to fall into a light sleep: *I dropped off and missed the end of the film.* **2** to become fewer or less: *Traffic in the town has dropped off since the bypass opened.* **drop ˈout (of sth) 1** to no longer take part in or be part of sth: *He has dropped out of active politics.* ◊ *a word that has dropped out of the language* **2** to leave school, college, etc. without finishing your studies: *to drop out of school/college* ◊ *She started a degree but dropped out after only a year.* ⊃ related noun DROPOUT (1) **3** to reject the ideas and ways of behaving that are accepted by the rest of society ⊃ related noun DROPOUT (2) **drop ˈround** (*BrE*) = DROP BY/IN

■ *noun*
- **OF LIQUID 1** [C] ~ (of sth) a very small amount of liquid that forms a round shape: *The first drops of rain fell.* ◊ *a drop of blood* ⊃ see also RAINDROP, TEARDROP **2** [C, usually *sing.*] a small quantity of a liquid: *Could I have a drop more milk in my coffee, please?* ◊ ~ of sth *Would you like a drop of brandy?*
- **FALL 3** [C, usually *sing.*] a fall or reduction in the amount, level or number of sth: ~ in sth *a sharp/steep drop in profits* ◊ *We've seen a 15 per cent drop in price since May.* ◊ ~ against sth *The pound has suffered a big drop against the euro.* ⊃ LANGUAGE BANK at FALL
- **DISTANCE DOWN 4** [C, usually *sing.*] a distance straight down from a high point to a lower point: *There was a sheer drop of fifty metres to the rocks below.* ◊ *a twenty-foot drop*
- **MEDICINE 5 drops** [pl.] a liquid medicine that you put one drop at a time into your eyes, ears or nose: *eye drops*
- **DELIVERING 6** [C] the act of delivering sb/sth in a vehicle or by plane; the act of dropping sth: *Aid agencies were organizing food drops to civilians in the war zone.* ◊ *a parachute drop* ⊃ see also MAIL DROP, MIC DROP
- **SWEET/CANDY 7** [C] a small round sweet of the type mentioned: *fruit drops* ◊ *cough drops* (= sweets to help a cough)

**IDM** **at the drop of a ˈhat** immediately; without hesitating: *The company can't expect me to move my home and family at the drop of a hat.* **a ˌdrop in the ˈocean** (*BrE*) (*NAmE* **a ˌdrop in the ˈbucket**) an amount of sth that is too small or unimportant to make any real difference to a situation

**ˈdrop cloth** (*NAmE*) (*BrE* **ˈdust sheet**) *noun* a large sheet that is used to protect floors, furniture, etc. from dust or paint

**ˌdrop-ˈdead** *adv.* (*informal*) used before an adjective to emphasize that sb/sth is attractive in a way that is very easy to notice: *a drop-dead gorgeous Hollywood star*

**ˌdrop-down ˈmenu** (*also* **ˈdrop-down**, **ˈdrop-down ˈlist**) *noun* (*computing*) a menu that appears on a computer screen when you choose it, and that stays there until you choose one of the functions on it

**ˈdrop goal** *noun* (in rugby) a goal scored by dropping the ball onto the ground and kicking it over the CROSSBAR as it BOUNCES

**ˌdrop ˈhandlebars** *noun* [pl.] low curved handles on a bicycle

**ˈdrop-in** *adj.* [only before noun] able to be visited without arranging a fixed time first: *a drop-in clinic*

**ˈdrop kick** *noun* (especially in rugby) a kick made by dropping the ball onto the ground and kicking it as it BOUNCES ▶ **ˈdrop-kick** *verb* ~ sth

**ˈdrop·let** /ˈdrɒplət; *NAmE* ˈdrɑːp-/ *noun* a small drop of a liquid

**ˈdrop-off** *noun* **1** a reduction or fall: *Sales suffered a 53 per cent drop-off.* ◊ ~ in sth *What has caused the drop-off in performance?* **2** the action of stopping your car so that sb can get out; the action of delivering sb/sth to a place: *The area outside the airport terminal is for pickups and drop-offs only.* **3** (*NAmE*) a very steep slope downwards: *a path with sheer drop-offs to either side*

**ˈdrop-out** /ˈdrɒpaʊt; *NAmE* ˈdrɑːp-/ *noun* **1** a person who leaves school or college before they have finished their studies: *college dropouts* ◊ *a university with a high dropout rate* **2** a person who rejects the ideas and ways of behaving that are accepted by the rest of society

**ˈdrop·per** /ˈdrɒpə(r); *NAmE* ˈdrɑːp-/ *noun* a short glass tube with a hollow rubber end used for measuring medicine or other liquids in drops

**drop·pings** /ˈdrɒpɪŋz; *NAmE* ˈdrɑːp-/ *noun* [pl.] the solid waste matter of birds and animals (usually small animals)

**ˈdrop shot** *noun* (in tennis) a soft hit that makes the ball land on the ground without BOUNCING much **SYN** dink

**ˈdrop zone** *noun* the area in which sb/sth should land after being dropped from an aircraft

**dros·oph·ila** /drəˈsɒfɪlə; *NAmE* -ˈsɑːf-/ (*pl.* **dros·oph·ila**) *noun* a small fly that feeds on fruit and is often used in scientific research

**dross** /drɒs; *NAmE* drɑːs/ *noun* [U] **1** (*especially BrE*) something of very low quality; the least valuable part of sth: *mass-produced dross* ◊ *The well-written dialogue separates this film from the usual teenage dross.* **2** (*specialist*) a waste substance, especially that separated from a metal when it is melted

**drought** /draʊt/ *noun* [U, C] **1** a long period of time when there is little or no rain: *two years of severe drought* ◊ *one of the worst droughts on record* ⊃ WORDFINDER NOTE at RAIN **2** a long period of time when there is a lack of sth that is needed or wanted

**drove** /drəʊv/ *noun*, *verb* [usually pl.]
■ *noun* a large number of people or animals, often moving or doing sth as a group: *droves of tourists* ◊ *People were leaving the countryside in droves to look for work in the cities.*
■ *verb* past tense of DRIVE

**drov·er** /ˈdrəʊvə(r)/ *noun* (in the past) a person who moved groups of cows or sheep from one place to another, especially to market, travelling on foot or on HORSEBACK

**drown** /draʊn/ *verb* **1** [I, T] to die because you have been UNDERWATER too long and you cannot breathe; to kill sb by holding them underwater: *Two children drowned after falling into the river.* ◊ *He had attempted to rescue the*

# drowse

drowning man. ◊ ~ **sb/sth/yourself** *She tried to drown herself.* ◊ *They had drowned the unwanted kittens.* ◊ **be drowned** *He was drowned at sea.* **2** [T] ~ **sth (in sth)** to make sth very wet; to completely cover sth in water or another liquid **SYN** **drench**: *The fruit was drowned in cream.* **3** [T] ~ **sb/sth (out)** (of a sound) to be louder than other sounds so that you cannot hear them: *She turned up the radio to drown out the noise from next door.* ▸ **drowning** *noun* [U, C]: *death by drowning* ◊ *Alcohol plays a part in an estimated 30% of drownings.*
**IDM** **drown your ˈfears/ˈloneliness/ˈsorrows, etc.** (especially humorous) to get drunk in order to forget your problems

**drowse** /draʊz/ *verb* [I] to be in a light sleep or almost asleep

**drow·sy** /ˈdraʊzi/ *adj.* (**drows·ier**, **drowsi·est**) **1** tired and wanting to sleep **SYN** **sleepy**: *The tablets may make you feel drowsy.* ⇨ WORDFINDER NOTE at SLEEP **2** making you feel relaxed and tired: *a drowsy afternoon in the sunshine* ▸ **drows·ily** /-zɪli/ *adv.* **drow·si·ness** *noun* [U]: *The drugs tend to cause drowsiness.*

**drub·bing** /ˈdrʌbɪŋ/ *noun* (*informal*) (in a sport) a situation where one team easily beats another: *We gave them a drubbing in the match on Saturday.*

**drudge** /drʌdʒ/ *noun* a person who has to do long hard boring jobs

**drudg·ery** /ˈdrʌdʒəri/ *noun* [U] hard boring work

**drug** ⓘ A2 /drʌɡ/ *noun*, *verb*
■ *noun* **1** A2 an illegal substance that some people smoke, INJECT, etc. for the physical and mental effects it has: *He does not smoke or take drugs.* ◊ *to use/abuse drugs* ◊ (*informal*) *I don't do drugs* (= use them). ◊ *to smuggle/supply/sell drugs* ◊ *He was charged with possessing drugs.* ◊ *illegal/illicit drugs* ◊ *a drug dealer/trafficker/smuggler* ◊ *drug use/abuse* ◊ *She was a drug addict.* ◊ *The actor struggled with drug addiction.* ⇨ see also CLASS A DRUG, RECREATIONAL DRUG

**WORDFINDER** abuse, addict, deal, dependence, detoxification, hallucinate, overdose, rehab, withdrawal

**2** A2 a substance used as a medicine or used in a medicine: *to prescribe/administer a drug* ◊ *a prescription drug* (= one that must be PRESCRIBED by a doctor) ◊ *a new cancer drug* ◊ *a major drug company* ◊ *He's taking drugs for depression.* ⇨ WORDFINDER NOTE at CURE ⇨ see also DESIGNER DRUG
■ *verb* (**-gg-**) **1** ~ **sb/sth** to give a person or an animal a drug, especially to make them unconscious, or to affect their performance in a race or competition: *He was drugged and bundled into the back of the car.* ◊ *It's illegal to drug horses before a race.* **2** ~ **sth** to add a drug to sb's food or drink to make them unconscious or SLEEPY: *Her drink must have been drugged.*
**IDM** **be drugged up to the ˈeyeballs** (*informal*) to have taken or been given a lot of drugs

**ˈdrug dealer** *noun* a person who sells illegal drugs

**drug·gie** (*BrE also* **drug·gy**) /ˈdrʌɡi/ *noun* (*pl.* **-ies**) (*informal*) a person who takes illegal drugs regularly

**drug·ging** /ˈdrʌɡɪŋ/ *noun* [U] the act of taking a drug, especially an illegal one: *They were feeling the effects of drinking and drugging all night.*

**drug·gist** /ˈdrʌɡɪst/ *noun* (*NAmE, old-fashioned*) = PHARMACIST (1)

**drug·gy** /ˈdrʌɡi/ *adj.*, *noun*
■ *adj.* (**drug·gier**, **drug·gi·est**) (*informal*) using or involving illegal drugs
■ *noun* (*informal*) (*BrE*) = DRUGGIE

**drug·store** /ˈdrʌɡstɔː(r)/ *noun* (*NAmE*) a shop that sells medicines and also other types of goods, for example COSMETICS ⇨ compare PHARMACY ⇨ see also CHEMIST'S

**Druid** /ˈdruːɪd/ *noun* a priest of an ancient Celtic religion

**drum** ⓘ B1 /drʌm/ *noun*, *verb*
■ *noun* **1** ⓘ B1 a musical instrument made of a hollow round frame with plastic or skin stretched tightly across one or both ends. You play it by hitting it with sticks or with your hands: *to play the drum* ◊ *I used to play drums in a band.* ◊ **on drums** *Tony Cox on drums* ◊ *a slow drum beat* ⇨ see also BASS DRUM, KICK DRUM, SNARE DRUM, STEEL DRUM **2** a large container for oil or chemicals that is like a CYLINDER in shape: *a 50 gallon drum* ◊ *an oil drum* **3** a thing that is like a drum in shape, especially part of a machine: *The mixture flows to a revolving drum where the water is filtered out.*
**IDM** **beat/bang the ˈdrum (for sb/sth)** (*especially BrE*) to speak with enthusiasm in support of sb/sth ⇨ more at MARCH *v.*
■ *verb* (**-mm-**) **1** [I] to play a drum: *Then they started chanting and drumming and stamping their feet.* **2** [T, I] ~ **(sth) on sth** to make a sound by hitting a surface again and again: *Impatiently, he drummed his fingers on the table.*
**IDM** **ˈdrum sth into sb's head** = DRUM STH INTO SB
**PHRV** **ˈdrum sth into sb** to make sb remember sth by repeating it a lot of times: *We had it drummed into us that we should never talk to strangers.* **ˌdrum sb ˈout (of sth)** [usually passive] to force sb to leave an organization as a punishment for doing sth wrong **ˌdrum sth↔ˈup** to try hard to get support or business: *He had flown to the north of the country to drum up support for the campaign.*

**ˌdrum and ˈbass** (*also* **drum ˈn' bass**) *noun* [U] a type of electronic dance music developed in the UK in the early 1990s, which has a fast drumbeat and a strong slower BASS beat

**drum·beat** /ˈdrʌmbiːt/ *noun* the sound that a beat on a drum makes: *a regular drumbeat*

**ˈdrum kit** *noun* a set of drums

**ˈdrum machine** *noun* an electronic musical instrument that produces the sound of drums

**ˈdrum major** *noun* the leader of a MARCHING BAND of musicians, especially in the army

**ˌdrum majorˈette** (*especially BrE*) (*NAmE usually* **maj·or·ette**) *noun* a girl in special brightly coloured clothes who walks in front of a MARCHING BAND, turning, throwing and catching a long stick (called a BATON)

**drum·mer** /ˈdrʌmə(r)/ *noun* a person who plays a drum or drums **IDM** see MARCH *v.*

**drum·ming** /ˈdrʌmɪŋ/ *noun* [U, sing.] **1** the act of playing a drum; the sound of a drum being played **2** a continuous sound or feeling like the BEATS (= hits) of a drum: *the steady drumming of the rain on the tin roof*

**drum ˈn' ˈbass** = DRUM AND BASS

**drum·stick** /ˈdrʌmstɪk/ *noun* **1** a stick used for playing a drum **2** the lower part of the leg of a chicken or other bird that is cooked and eaten as food: *a chicken/turkey drumstick*

**drunk** ⓘ B1 /drʌŋk/ *adj.*, *noun*, *verb*
■ *adj.* **1** ⓘ B1 [not usually before noun] having drunk so much alcohol that it is impossible to think or speak clearly: *She was too drunk to remember anything about the party.* ◊ *His only way of dealing with his problems was to go out and get drunk.* ◊ ~ **on sth** *They got drunk on vodka.* **OPP** **sober** **2** ~ **with sth** (*formal*) very excited, tired, etc. because of a particular emotion or situation: *drunk with success* ⇨ see also PUNCH-DRUNK
**IDM** **ˌdrunk and disˈorderly** (*law*) behaving in a noisy or violent way in a public place because you are drunk **(as) drunk as a ˈlord** (*old-fashioned, BrE*) (*NAmE* **(as) drunk as a ˈskunk**) (*informal*) very drunk ⇨ more at BLIND *adv.*, ROARING
■ *noun* a person who is drunk or who often gets drunk
■ *verb past part.* of DRINK

**drunk·ard** /ˈdrʌŋkəd/ *NAmE* -kərd/ *noun* (*old-fashioned*) a person who gets drunk very often **SYN** **alcoholic**

**drunk ˈdriver** (*especially NAmE*) (*BrE usually* **drink-ˈdriver**) *noun* a person who drives a vehicle after drinking too much alcohol

**drunk 'driving** (also **drunken 'driving**) (both especially NAmE) (BrE usually **drink-'driving**) noun [U] driving a vehicle after drinking too much alcohol

**drunk·en** /ˈdrʌŋkən/ adj. [only before noun] **1** drunk or often getting drunk: *a drunken driver* ◇ *She was often beaten by her drunken husband.* **2** showing the effects of too much alcohol; involving people who are drunk: *He came home to find her in a drunken stupor.* ◇ *a drunken brawl* ▸ **drunk·en·ly** adv.: *He staggered drunkenly to his feet.* **drunk·en·ness** /-kənnəs/ noun [U]

**drunken 'driving** noun [U] (especially NAmE) = DRINK-DRIVING

**drunk tank** noun (especially NAmE, informal, humorous) a place where people are put by the police because they are drunk: *He spent the night in the drunk tank.*

**dry** 🔊 **A2** /draɪ/ adj., verb
■ adj. (**dri·er**, **dri·est**)
- NOT WET **1** 🔊 **A2** not wet or sticky; without water or MOISTURE: *Is my shirt dry yet?* ◇ *Store onions in a cool dry place.* ◇ *I'm afraid this cake has turned out very dry.* ◇ *When the paint is completely dry, apply another coat.* ◇ *It was high summer and the rivers were dry* (= had no water in them). ⊃ see also BONE DRY **OPP** wet
- LITTLE RAIN **2** 🔊 **A2** with very little rain: *weeks of hot, dry weather* ◇ *the dry season* ◇ *I hope it stays dry for our picnic.* ◇ *Rattlesnakes occur in the warmer, drier parts of North America.* **OPP** wet
- SKIN/HAIR **3** without the natural oils that makes it soft and healthy: *a shampoo for dry hair*
- COUGH **4** that does not produce any PHLEGM (= the thick liquid that forms in the nose and throat): *a dry hacking cough*
- BREAD **5** eaten on its own without any butter, jam, etc.: *Breakfast consisted of dry bread and a cup of tea.*
- WINE **6** not sweet: *a crisp dry white wine* ◇ *a dry sherry* **OPP** sweet
- HUMOUR **7** (approving) very clever and expressed in a quiet way that is not obvious; often using IRONY: *He was a man of few words with a delightful dry sense of humour.*
- WITHOUT EMOTION **8** not showing emotion: *a dry voice*
- BORING **9** not interesting: *Government reports tend to make dry reading.*
- WITHOUT ALCOHOL **10** without alcohol; where it is illegal to buy, sell or drink alcohol: *We had a dry wedding* (= no alcoholic drinks were served). ◇ *a dry county/state*
- THIRSTY **11** (informal, especially BrE) thirsty; that makes you thirsty: *I'm a bit dry.* ◇ *This is dry work.* ▸ **dryly** adv. = DRILY **dry·ness** noun [U]
**IDM** **milk/suck sb/sth 'dry** to get from sb/sth all the money, help, information, etc. they have, usually giving nothing in return **not a dry eye in the 'house** (humorous) used to say that everyone was very emotional about sth: *There wasn't a dry eye in the house when they announced their engagement.* **run 'dry** to stop supplying water; to be all used so that none is left: *The wells in most villages in the region have run dry.* ◇ *Vaccine supplies started to run dry as the flu outbreak reached epidemic proportions.* ⊃ more at BLEED, HIGH adj., HOME adv., POWDER n., SQUEEZE v.
■ verb 🔊 **A2** (**dries**, **dry·ing**, **dried**, **dried**) [I, T] to become dry; to make sth dry: *Be careful. The paint hasn't dried yet.* ◇ *You wash the dishes and I'll dry.* ◇ *~sth Use this towel to dry your hands.* ◇ *to dry your hair* ◇ *First, wash and dry the vegetables.* ◇ *to dry your eyes/tears* (= stop crying) ⊃ see also BLOW-DRY, DRIP-DRY
**PHRV** **dry 'off** | **dry sb/sth↔'off** to become dry or make sth dry: *We went swimming and then lay in the sun to dry off.* ◇ *We dried our boots off by the fire.* **dry 'out** | **dry sb↔'out** (informal) to stop drinking alcohol after you have continuously been drinking too much; to cure sb of drinking too much alcohol: *He went to an expensive clinic to dry out.* **dry 'out** | **dry sth↔'out** to become or to allow sth to become dry, often in a way that is not wanted: *Water the plant regularly, never letting the soil dry out.* ◇ *Hot sun and cold winds can soon dry out your skin.* **dry 'up 1** (of rivers, lakes, etc.) to become completely dry: *During the drought the river dried up.* **2** if a supply of sth **dries up**, there is gradually less of it until there is none left: *As she got older, offers of modelling work began to dry*

481

up. **dry 'up** | **dry sth↔'up** (BrE) to dry dishes with a towel after you have washed them: *I'll wash and you can dry up.*

**dry·ad** /ˈdraɪæd/ noun (in stories) a female spirit who lives in a tree

**dry-'clean** (also **clean**) verb ~sth to clean clothes using chemicals instead of water: *This garment must be dry-cleaned only.* ⊃ SYNONYMS at CLEAN ▸ **dry-'cleaning** noun [U]

**dry-'cleaner's** noun = CLEANER'S

**dry 'dock** noun [C, U] an area in a port from which the water can be removed, used for building or repairing ships

**dryer** (also **drier**) /ˈdraɪə(r)/ noun (especially in compounds) a machine for drying sth: *a hairdryer* ⊃ see also TUMBLE DRYER, WASHER-DRYER

**dry-'eyed** adj. [not before noun] not crying: *She remained dry-eyed throughout the trial.*

**dry goods** noun [pl.] **1** (BrE) types of food that are solid and dry, such as tea, coffee and flour **2** (NAmE, old-fashioned) cloth and things that are made out of cloth, such as clothes and sheets: *a dry goods store* ⊃ compare DRAPERY

**dry 'ice** noun [U] solid CARBON DIOXIDE used for keeping food, etc. cold or for producing special effects in the theatre

**dry 'land** noun [U] land, rather than sea **SYN** terra firma: *It was a great relief to be back on dry land after such a rough crossing.*

**dry·ly** = DRILY

**dry 'milk** (US) (BrE **'milk powder**, **powdered 'milk**) noun [U] dried milk in the form of a powder

**dry-'roasted** adj. cooked in an oven without adding oil or fat: *dry-roasted peanuts*

**dry 'rot** noun [U] **1** wood that has DECAYED (= been destroyed by natural causes) and turned to powder **2** any FUNGUS that causes this DECAY

**dry 'run** noun [usually sing.] a complete practice of a performance or way of doing sth, before the real one **SYN** dummy run

**dry 'slope** (also **dry 'ski slope**) noun a steep slope with an artificial surface for practising skiing

**dry·stone wall** /ˌdraɪstəʊn ˈwɔːl/ noun (BrE) a stone wall built without MORTAR (= a substance used to hold building materials together) between the stones

**dry·suit** /ˈdraɪsuːt/ noun a piece of clothing that fits the whole body and keeps water out, worn by people swimming UNDERWATER or sailing ⊃ compare WETSUIT

**dry·wall** /ˈdraɪwɔːl/ noun [U] (NAmE) = PLASTERBOARD

**DSL** /ˌdiː es ˈel/ abbr. (computing) digital subscriber line (= a way of sending electronic data at high speed along ordinary phone lines, used for supplying the internet to homes, businesses, etc.)

**DST** /ˌdiː es ˈtiː/ abbr. DAYLIGHT SAVING TIME

**DT** /ˌdiː ˈtiː/ noun [U] (BrE) a school subject in which students learn about the role of technology in modern life and also design and make things for themselves (the abbreviation for 'design and technology')

**DTP** /ˌdiː tiː ˈpiː/ abbr. DESKTOP PUBLISHING

**DTs** (BrE) (US **D.T.'s**) /ˌdiː ˈtiːz/ noun [pl.] a physical condition that affects people who regularly drink too much alcohol when they stop drinking alcohol for a while; they feel their body shaking and imagine that they are seeing things that are not really there (the abbreviation for 'delirium tremens')

**dual** 🔊+ **C1** /ˈdjuːəl; NAmE ˈduː-/ adj. [only before noun] having two parts or aspects: *his dual role as composer and conductor* ◇ *She has dual nationality* (= is a citizen of two different countries). ◇ *The piece of furniture serves a dual purpose as a cupboard and as a table.* ⊃ note at DOUBLE ⊃ see also DUAL-PURPOSE

**dual**

**dual carriageway** (*BrE*) (*NAmE* **divided highway**) *noun* a road with a narrow piece of land in the middle that divides the lines of traffic moving in opposite directions

**dual con‌trols** *noun* [pl.] two sets of instruments for controlling a vehicle or aircraft, so that a teacher, for example, can take control from the driver ▶ **dual con‌trol** *adj.*: *a dual-control vehicle*

**dual‧ism** /ˈdjuːəlɪzəm; *NAmE* ˈduː-/ *noun* [U] **1** (*philosophy*) the theory that there are two opposite principles in everything, for example good and evil **2** (*formal*) the state of having two parts ▶ **dual‧ist, dual‧ist‧ic** /djuːəˈlɪstɪk; *NAmE* ˌduː-/ *adj.* **dual‧ist** *noun*

**dual‧ity** /djuˈæləti; *NAmE* duː-/ *noun* [U, C] (*pl.* **-ies**) (*formal*) the state of having two parts or aspects

**dual-ˈpurpose** *adj.* that can be used for two different purposes: *a dual-purpose vehicle* (= for carrying passengers or goods)

**dub** ᴮ¹+ 🄲 /dʌb/ *verb*, *noun*
- *verb* (**-bb-**) **1** ᴮ¹+ 🄲 **~ sb + noun** to give sb/sth a particular name, often in a humorous or critical way: *The media dubbed anorexia 'the slimming disease'.* **2** ᴮ¹+ 🄲 **~ sth (into sth)** to replace the original speech in a film or television programme with words in another language: *an American movie dubbed into Italian* ⇒ compare SUBTITLE ⇒ WORDFINDER NOTE at FILM **3** **~ sth** (*especially BrE*) to make a piece of music by mixing sounds from different recordings
- *noun* [U] a type of West Indian music or poetry with a strong beat

**du‧bi‧ous** /ˈdjuːbiəs; *NAmE* ˈduː-/ *adj.* **1** [not usually before noun] **~ (about sth) / (about doing sth)** (of a person) not certain about sth and suspecting that sth may be wrong; not knowing whether sth is good or bad ⓢʏɴ **doubtful**: *I was rather dubious about the whole idea.* **2** (*disapproving*) probably not honest ⓢʏɴ **suspicious**: *They indulged in some highly dubious business practices to obtain their current position in the market.* **3** that you cannot be sure about; that is probably not good: *They consider the plan to be of dubious benefit to most families.* ◊ (*ironic*) *She had the dubious honour of being the last woman to be hanged in England* (= it was not an honour at all). ▶ **du‧bi‧ous‧ly** *adv.*

**dub‧step** /ˈdʌbstep/ *noun* [U] a type of electronic dance music, developed in England in the late 1990s, that has a strong BASS beat and drum patterns that are repeated many times, and that sometimes contains singing

**ducal** /ˈdjuːkl; *NAmE* ˈduː-/ *adj.* [only before noun] of or belonging to a DUKE

**ducat** /ˈdʌkət/ *noun* (in the past) a gold coin used in many European countries

**duch‧ess** /ˈdʌtʃəs/ *noun* **1** the wife of a DUKE: *the Duchess of York* **2** a woman who has the rank of a DUKE

**duchy** /ˈdʌtʃi/ *noun* (*pl.* **-ies**) (*also* **duke‧dom**) an area of land that is owned and controlled by a DUKE or DUCHESS

**duck** /dʌk/ *noun*, *verb*
- *noun* **1** (*pl.* **ducks** or **duck**) [C] a common bird that lives on or near water and has short legs, WEBBED feet (= feet with thin pieces of skin between the toes) and a wide BEAK. There are many types of duck, some of which are kept for their meat or eggs: *wild ducks* ◊ *duck eggs* ⇒ see also RUBBER DUCK ⇒ VISUAL VOCAB page V2 **2** [C] a female duck ⇒ compare DRAKE **3** [U] meat from a duck: *roast duck with orange sauce* **4** (*also* **duckie, ducks**) [C, usually sing.] (*BrE, informal*) a friendly way of speaking to sb: *Anything else, duck?* ⇒ compare DEAR, LOVE **5** a duck [sing.] (in CRICKET) a BATSMAN's score of zero: *He was out for a duck.* ⇒ see also LAME DUCK, SITTING DUCK
ɪᴅᴍ **get / have (all) your ˈducks in a ˈrow** (*especially NAmE*) to have made all the preparations needed to do sth; to be well organized **(take to sth) like a ˌduck to ˈwater** (to become used to sth) very easily, without any problems or fears: *She has taken to teaching like a duck to water.* ⇒ more at DEAD *adj.*, WATER *n.*
- *verb* **1** [I, T] to move your head or body downwards to avoid being hit or seen: *He had to duck as he came through the door.* ◊ **~ (down) (behind / under sth)** *We ducked down behind the wall so they wouldn't see us.* ◊ *He just managed to duck out of sight.* ◊ **~ sth** *She ducked her head and got into the car.* **2** [T] **~ sth** to avoid sth by moving your head or body out of the way ⓢʏɴ **dodge**: *He ducked the first few blows then started to fight back.* **3** [I] + **adv. / prep.** to move somewhere quickly, especially in order to avoid being seen: *She ducked into the adjoining room as we came in.* **4** [I, T] (*rather informal*) to avoid a difficult or unpleasant duty or responsibility: **~ out of sth** *It's his turn to cook dinner, but I bet he'll try to duck out of it.* ◊ **~ sth** *The government is ducking the issue.* **5** (*especially NAmE* **dunk**) [T] **~ sb** to push sb UNDERWATER and hold them there for a short time: *The kids were ducking each other in the pool.*

**duck-billed ˈplatypus** *noun* = PLATYPUS

**duck‧ling** /ˈdʌklɪŋ/ *noun* [C, U] a young duck; the meat of a young duck ⇒ see also UGLY DUCKLING

**duct** /dʌkt/ *noun* **1** a pipe or tube carrying liquid, gas, electric or phone wires, etc.: *a heating/ventilation duct* **2** a tube in the body or in plants through which liquid passes ⇒ see also BILE DUCT, TEAR DUCT

**duc‧tile** /ˈdʌktaɪl/ *adj.* (*specialist*) (of a metal) that can be made into a thin wire

**duct‧ing** /ˈdʌktɪŋ/ *noun* [U] **1** a system of ducts **2** material in the form of a duct or ducts: *a short piece of ducting*

**ˈduct tape** *noun* [U] very strong cloth tape that is WATERPROOF and sticky on one side, often used for repairing things or covering holes in pipes

**dud** /dʌd/ *noun*, *adj.*
- *noun* **1** [C] (*informal*) a thing that has no use, especially because it does not work correctly: *Two of the fireworks in the box were duds.* **2** **duds** [pl.] (*slang*) clothes
- *adj.* [only before noun] that has no use; that does not work correctly: *a dud battery*

**dude** /duːd/ *noun* (*especially NAmE, informal*) a man: *He's a real cool dude.* ◊ *Hey, dude, what's up?*

**ˈdude ranch** *noun* an American RANCH (= a large farm) where people can go on holiday and do the sort of activities that COWBOYS do ᴏʀɪɢɪɴ From an old meaning of the word *dude*, a man from the city who wears fashionable clothes.

**dudgeon** /ˈdʌdʒən/ *noun* ɪᴅᴍ see HIGH *adj.*

**due** 🄰 🄱¹ 🅆 /djuː; *NAmE* duː/ *adj., noun, adv.*
- *adj.*
- • CAUSED BY **1** ᴮ¹ [not before noun] **~ to sb / sth** caused by sb/sth; because of sb/sth: *The team's success was largely due to her efforts.* ◊ *The delay to the flight was due to the fact that there was ice on the runway.* ◊ *Due to staff shortages, we are unable to offer a full buffet service on this train.* ⇒ HOMOPHONES at DEW ⇒ LANGUAGE BANK at BECAUSE OF
- • EXPECTED **2** ᴮ² [not before noun] arranged or expected: *When's the baby due?* ◊ *The next train is due in five minutes.* ◊ *My essay's due next Friday* (= it has to be given to the teacher by then). ◊ **~ to do sth** *Rose is due to start school in January.* ◊ **for sth** *The band's first album is due for release later this month.*
- • OWED **3** ᴮ² [not usually before noun] when a sum of money is **due**, it must be paid immediately: *Payment is due on 1 October.* **4** [not before noun] **~ (to sb)** owed to sb as a debt, because it is their right or because they have done sth to deserve it: *Have they been paid the money that is due to them?* ◊ *Our thanks are due to the whole team.* **5** [not before noun] owed sth; deserving sth: **~ sth** *I'm still due 15 days' leave.* ◊ **~ for sth** *She's due for promotion soon.*
- • SUITABLE / RIGHT **6** [only before noun] (*formal*) that is suitable or right in the circumstances: *After due consideration, we have decided to appoint Mr Davis to the job.* ◊ *to make due allowance for sth* ◊ (*BrE*) *He was charged with driving without due care and attention.* ⇒ compare UNDUE
ɪᴅᴍ **in due ˈcourse** at the right time and not before: *Your request will be dealt with in due course.* ⇒ more at CREDIT *n.*, RESPECT *n.*
- *noun* **1 your / sb's ~** [U] a thing that should be given to sb by right: *He received a large reward, which was no more than his due* (= than what he deserved). ◊ *She's a slow worker, but to give her her due* (= to be fair to her), *she does*

try very hard. ⇨ HOMOPHONES at DEW **2 dues** [pl.] charges, for example to be a member of a club: *to pay your dues* **IDM** see PAY v.
■ *adv.* ~ **north / south / east / west** exactly; in a straight line: *to sail due east* ◇ *The village lies five miles due north of York.* ⇨ HOMOPHONES at DEW

**'due date** *noun* [usually sing.] the date by or on which sth is expected, especially the payment of a bill or the birth of a baby

**due 'diligence** *noun* [U] **1** (*law*) reasonable steps taken by a person or an organization to avoid committing a TORT or an offence **2** (*business*) a careful investigation of the state of a business by a person or organization that is thinking of buying it or investing in it

**duel** /ˈdjuːəl; *NAmE* ˈduː-/ *noun* **1** (in the past) a formal fight with weapons between two people who disagreed, especially over a matter of honour: *to fight/win a duel* ◇ *to challenge sb to a duel* **2** a competition or struggle between two people or groups: *a verbal duel* ▶ **duel** *verb* (**-ll-**, *US* **-l-**) [I]: *The two men duelled to the death.*

**du·el·ling** (*US* **du·el·ing**) /ˈdjuːəlɪŋ; *NAmE* ˈduː-/ *noun* [U] the practice of fighting duels

**due 'process of 'law** (*also* **due 'process**) *noun* [U] (*law*) (in the US) the right of a citizen to be treated fairly, especially the right to a fair trial

**duet** /djuˈet; *NAmE* duː-/ (*also less frequent* **duo**) *noun* a performance by two musicians or singers; a piece of music for two players or singers: *a piano duet* ⇨ compare SOLO, TRIO

**duff** /dʌf/ *adj.*, *noun*, *verb*
■ *adj.* (*BrE*, *informal*) that does not work as it should; false or INCORRECT: *He sold me a duff radio.* ◇ *She played some duff notes.*
■ *noun* (*NAmE*, *informal*) a person's bottom
**IDM** **up the 'duff** (*BrE*, *slang*) pregnant
■ *verb*
**PHRV** **duff sb↔'up** (*BrE*, *informal*) to hit or kick sb severely **SYN** beat up

**duf·fel bag** (*also* **duf·fle bag**) /ˈdʌfl bæɡ/ *noun* **1** a bag made out of cloth that is like a tube in shape and is closed by a string around the top. It is usually carried over the shoulder. **2** (*NAmE*) (*BrE* **hold-all**) a large bag made of strong cloth or soft leather, used when you are travelling for carrying clothes, etc.

**duf·fel coat** (*also* **duf·fle coat**) /ˈdʌfl kəʊt/ *noun* a heavy coat made of wool, usually with a HOOD and fastened with TOGGLES

**duf·fer** /ˈdʌfə(r)/ *noun* (*BrE*, *informal*) a person who is stupid or unable to do anything well

**dug** /dʌɡ/ past tense, past part. of DIG

**du·gong** /ˈduːɡɒŋ; *NAmE* -ɡɑːŋ/ *noun* a large sea animal with thick grey skin that lives mainly in the Indian Ocean and eats plants

**dug·out** /ˈdʌɡaʊt/ *noun* **1** a rough shelter made by digging a hole in the ground and covering it, used by soldiers **2** a shelter by the side of a football (soccer) or baseball field where a team's manager, etc. can sit and watch the game **3** (*also* **dugout ca'noe**) a CANOE (= type of light narrow boat) made by cutting out the inside of a tree TRUNK

**duh** /dʌ; *BrE also* dɜː/ *exclamation* (*informal*) used to comment on a statement you think is stupid or obvious: '*You should always lock up your bike.*' '*Well, duh!*'

**DUI** /ˌdiː juː ˈaɪ/ *abbr.* (*NAmE*) DRIVING UNDER THE INFLUENCE

**du jour** /duː ˈʒʊə(r); *NAmE* ˈʒʊr/ *adj.* [after noun] (*informal*, *humorous*) very popular or important now: ◇ *What are the hot social media platforms du jour?* **ORIGIN** From French, meaning 'of the day'.

**duke** /djuːk; *NAmE* duːk/ *noun*, *verb*
■ *noun* **1** a NOBLEMAN of the highest rank: *the Duke of Edinburgh* **2** (in some parts of Europe, especially in the past) a male ruler of a small independent state ⇨ see also ARCHDUKE, DUCHESS, DUCHY, GRAND DUKE
■ *verb*
**IDM** **duke it 'out** (*NAmE*, *informal*) to fight or argue until an argument has been settled

---

483    **dumb animal**

**duke·dom** /ˈdjuːkdəm; *NAmE* ˈduːk-/ *noun* **1** the rank or position of a duke **2** = DUCHY

**dul·cet** /ˈdʌlsɪt/ *adj.* [only before noun] (*humorous or ironic*) sounding sweet and pleasant: *I thought I recognized your* **dulcet tones** (= the sound of your voice).

**dul·ci·mer** /ˈdʌlsɪmə(r)/ *noun* **1** a musical instrument that you play by hitting the metal strings with two HAMMERS **2** a musical instrument with strings, popular in American traditional music, that you lay on your knee and play with your fingers

**dull** /dʌl/ *adj.*, *verb*
■ *adj.* (**dull·er**, **dull·est**)
• BORING **1** not interesting or exciting **SYN** dreary: *Life in a small town could be deadly dull.* ◇ *The countryside was flat, dull and uninteresting.* ◇ *The first half of the game was pretty dull.* ◇ *There's **never a dull moment** when John's around.* ⇨ SYNONYMS at BORING
• LIGHT/COLOURS **2** not bright or shiny: *a dull grey colour* ◇ *dull, lifeless hair* ◇ *Her eyes were dull.* ◇ *The fire died down to a dull glow.*
• WEATHER **3** not bright, with a lot of clouds **SYN** overcast: *It was a dull, grey day.*
• SOUNDS **4** not clear or loud: *The gates shut behind him with a dull thud.*
• PAIN **5** not very severe, but continuous: *a dull ache/pain*
• PERSON **6** slow in understanding **SYN** stupid: *a dull pupil*
• TRADE **7** (*especially NAmE*) not busy; slow: *Don't sell into a dull market.* ▶ **dull·ness** *noun* [U] **dully** /ˈdʌli/ *adv.*: '*I suppose so,*' *she said dully.* ◇ *His leg ached dully.*
**IDM** **(as) dull as 'ditchwater** (*BrE*) (*US* **(as) dull as 'dishwater**) (*informal*) extremely boring ⇨ more at WORK *n.*
■ *verb*
• PAIN **1** [T, I] ~**(sth)** to make a pain or an emotion weaker or less severe; to become weaker or less severe: *The tablets they gave him dulled the pain for a while.* ◇ *The pain of loss never dulls.*
• PERSON **2** [T] ~**sb** to make a person slower or less lively: *He felt dulled and stupid with sleep.*
• COLOURS/SOUNDS **3** [I, T] to become less bright, clean or sharp; to make sth less bright, clean or sharp: *His eyes dulled and he slumped to the ground.* ◇ *~sth The endless rain seemed to dull all sound.*

**dull·ard** /ˈdʌlɑːd; *NAmE* -lɑːrd/ *noun* (*old-fashioned*) a stupid person with no imagination

**duly** /ˈdjuːli; *NAmE* ˈduː-/ *adv.* **1** (*formal*) in the correct or expected manner: *The document was duly signed by the inspector.* **2** at the expected and correct time: *They duly arrived at 9.30 in spite of torrential rain.* ⇨ compare UNDULY

**dumb** /dʌm/ *adj.*, *verb*
■ *adj.* (**dumb·er**, **dumb·est**) **1** (*especially NAmE*, *informal*) stupid: *That was a pretty dumb thing to do.* ◇ *If the police question you,* **act dumb** (= pretend you do not know anything). ◇ *In her early movies she played a dumb blonde.* **2** (*old-fashioned*, *sometimes offensive*) unable to speak: *She was born deaf and dumb.* **HELP** **Dumb** used in this meaning is old-fashioned and can be offensive. It is better to use **speech-impaired** instead. **3** temporarily not speaking or refusing to speak: *We were all **struck dumb** with amazement.* ◇ *We sat there in dumb silence.* ▶ **dumb·ly** *adv.*: '*Are you all right?*' *Laura nodded dumbly.* **dumb·ness** *noun* [U]
■ *verb*
**PHRV** **dumb 'down | dumb sth↔'down** (*disapproving*) to make sth less accurate or educational, and of worse quality, by trying to make it easier for people to understand ▶ **dumbing 'down** *noun* [U]

**dumb 'animal** *noun* [usually pl.] (*BrE*) an animal, especially when seen as deserving sympathy or help

**'dumb-ass** *adj.* [only before noun] (*NAmE*, *taboo*, *slang*) stupid

---

u **actual** | aɪ **my** | aʊ **now** | eɪ **say** | əʊ **go** | ɔɪ **boy** | ɪə **near** | eə **hair** | ʊə **pure**

# dumb-bell

**'dumb-bell** noun **1** a short bar with a weight at each end, used for making the arm and shoulder muscles stronger ⊃ picture at EXERCISE BIKE **2** (NAmE, informal) a stupid person

**dumb·found** /dʌmˈfaʊnd/ verb ~ sb to surprise or shock sb so much that they are unable to speak: *His reply dumbfounded me.*

**dumb·found·ed** /dʌmˈfaʊndɪd/ (also less frequent **dumb-struck** /ˈdʌmstrʌk/) adj. unable to speak because of surprise: *The news left her dumbfounded.*

**dumbo** /ˈdʌmbəʊ/ noun (pl. **-oes**) (informal) a stupid person

**dummy** /ˈdʌmi/ noun, adj., verb
- noun (pl. **-ies**) **1** [C] a model of a person, used especially when making clothes or for showing them in a shop window: *a tailor's dummy* ⊃ see also MANNEQUIN **2** [C] a thing that seems to be real but is only a copy of the real thing **3** [C] (NAmE, informal) a stupid person: *Don't just stand there, you dummy.* **4** [C] (in some sports) an occasion when you pretend to make a particular move and then do not do so **5** [C] (BrE) (NAmE **paci·fier**) a rubber or plastic object with a special shape that a baby SUCKS on with its lips and tongue ⊃ WORDFINDER NOTE at BABY **6** [U] (in card games, especially BRIDGE) the cards that are placed facing upwards on the table and which can be seen by all the players
- *adj.* [only before noun] made to look real, although it is actually a copy that does not work SYN **replica**: *a dummy bomb*
- *verb* [T, I] (especially in football (soccer) and rugby) to pretend to make a particular move in order to confuse your opponent: ~ sth *She dummied a shot that brought the goalie to her knees.* ◊ + adv./prep. *He dummied past five defenders, then shot at the near post.*

**dummy 'run** noun (BrE) a practice attack, performance, etc. before the real one SYN **dry run**

**dump** ⚡+ B2 /dʌmp/ verb, noun
- *verb*
  - GET RID OF **1** ⚡+ B2 ~ sth to get rid of sth you do not want, especially in a place that is not suitable: *Too much toxic waste is being dumped at sea.* ◊ *The dead body was just dumped by the roadside.* ⊃ WORDFINDER NOTE at WASTE **2** ~ sb/sth (on sb) (informal) to get rid of sb/sth or leave them for sb else to deal with: *He's got no right to keep dumping his problems on me.* **3** ~ sth (business) to get rid of goods by selling them at a very low price, often in another country
  - PUT DOWN **4** ⚡+ C1 ~ sth/sb (informal) to put sth/sb down in a careless or untidy way: *Just dump your stuff over there— we'll sort it out later.*
  - END RELATIONSHIP **5** ⚡+ C1 ~ sb (informal) to end a romantic relationship with sb: *Did you hear he's dumped his girlfriend?*
  - COMPUTING **6** ~ sth to copy information and move it somewhere to store it IDM ▶ see LAP n.
- PHRV **'dump on sb** (especially NAmE, informal) to criticize sb severely or treat them badly
- *noun* ⊃ see also DUMPS
  - FOR WASTE **1** a place where waste or rubbish is taken and left: (BrE) *a rubbish dump* ◊ (NAmE) *a garbage dump* ◊ *the municipal dump* ◊ *a toxic/nuclear waste dump* **2** (also **'mine dump**) (SAfrE) a hill that is formed when waste sand from the mining of gold is piled in one place over a period of time
  - DIRTY PLACE **3** (informal, disapproving) a dirty or unpleasant place: *How can you live in this dump?*
  - FOR WEAPONS **4** a temporary store for military supplies: *an ammunition dump*
  - COMPUTING **5** an act of copying data stored in a computer; a copy or list of the contents of this data
  - WASTE FROM BODY **6** [C] (slang) an act of passing waste matter from the body through the BOWELS: *to have a dump*

**dump·er** /ˈdʌmpə(r)/ noun (especially NAmE) a person who throws away dangerous or harmful things, especially in the wrong place

**'dumper truck** (BrE) (NAmE **'dump truck**) noun a vehicle for carrying earth, stones, etc. in a container that can be lifted up for the load to fall out

**dump·ing** /ˈdʌmpɪŋ/ noun [U] the act or practice of dumping sth , especially dangerous substances: *a ban on the dumping of radioactive waste at sea*

**'dumping ground** noun [usually sing.] a place where sth that is not wanted is dumped

**dump·ling** /ˈdʌmplɪŋ/ noun **1** a small ball of DOUGH (= a mixture of flour, fat and water) that is cooked and served with meat dishes or in soup: *chicken with herb dumplings* **2** a small ball of PASTRY, often with fruit in it, eaten as a DESSERT: *apple dumplings*

**dumps** /dʌmps/ noun [pl.]
IDM **down in the 'dumps** (informal) feeling unhappy SYN **depressed**

**Dump·ster**™ /ˈdʌmpstə(r)/ (NAmE) (BrE **skip**) noun a large open container for putting old bricks, rubbish, etc. in. The Dumpster is then loaded on a lorry and taken away.

**'dump truck** (NAmE) (BrE **'dumper truck**) noun a vehicle for carrying earth, stones, etc. in a container that can be lifted up for the load to fall out

**dumpy** /ˈdʌmpi/ adj. (especially of a person) short and fat

**dun** /dʌn/ adj. grey-brown in colour ▶ **dun** noun [U]

**dunce** /dʌns/ noun (old-fashioned) a person, especially a child at school, who is stupid or slow to learn

**'dunce's cap** (NAmE also **'dunce cap**) noun a pointed hat that was sometimes given in the past to a child in a class at school who was slow to learn

**dune** /djuːn; NAmE duːn/ (also **'sand dune**) noun a small hill of sand formed by the wind, near the sea or in a desert ⊃ WORDFINDER NOTE at COAST

**'dune buggy** noun = BEACH BUGGY

**dung** /dʌŋ/ noun [U] solid waste from animals, especially from large ones SYN **manure**: *cow dung*

**dun·ga·rees** /ˌdʌŋgəˈriːz/ noun [pl.] **1** (BrE) (NAmE **overalls**, **'bib overalls**) a piece of clothing that consists of trousers with an extra piece of cloth covering the chest, held up by long narrow pieces of cloth over the shoulders: *a pair of dungarees* ◊ *His dungarees were covered in grease.* ⊃ picture at OVERALL **2** (NAmE) heavy cotton trousers for working in

**dun·geon** /ˈdʌndʒən/ noun a dark underground room used as a prison, especially in a castle

**'dung·heap** /ˈdʌŋhiːp/ (also **dung·hill** /ˈdʌŋhɪl/) noun a large pile of dung, especially on a farm

**dunk** /dʌŋk/ verb **1** [T] ~ sth (in/into sth) to put food quickly into liquid before eating it: *She sat reading a magazine, dunking cookies in her coffee.* **2** [T] ~ sb/sth (especially NAmE) to push sb UNDERWATER for a short time, as a joke; to put sth into water: *The camera survived being dunked in the river.* **3** [I, T] ~ (sth) (in basketball) to jump very high and put the ball through the BASKET with great force from above ⊃ see also SLAM-DUNK

**dunno** /dəˈnəʊ/ (non-standard) a way of writing the informal spoken form of 'I don't know'

**dunny** /ˈdʌni/ noun (pl. **-ies**) (AustralE, NZE, informal) a toilet

**duo** ⚡+ C1 /ˈdjuːəʊ; NAmE ˈduː-/ noun (pl. **-os**) **1** ⚡+ C1 two people who perform together or are often seen or thought of together: *the comedy duo Laurel and Hardy* ⊃ compare TRIO **2** = DUET

**duo·de·num** /ˌdjuːəˈdiːnəm; NAmE ˌduː-/ noun (pl. **duo·de·nums** or **duo·dena** /-nə/) (anatomy) the first part of the small INTESTINE, next to the stomach ⊃ VISUAL VOCAB page V1 ⊃ compare ILEUM, JEJUNUM ▶ **duo·denal** /-nl/ adj.: *a duodenal ulcer*

**du·op·oly** /djuˈɒpəli; NAmE duˈɑːp-/ noun (pl. **-ies**) (business) a situation in which only two companies or organizations do all the trade in a particular product or service ⊃ compare MONOPOLY, OLIGOPOLY

**the DUP** /ðə ˌdiː juː ˈpiː/ abbr. the Democratic Unionist Party (a political party in Northern Ireland that wants it to remain a part of the United Kingdom)

**du·patta** /dʊˈpʌtə/ *noun* a long piece of material worn around the head and neck by women in South Asia, usually with a SALWAR or GHAGRA

**dupe** /djuːp; *NAmE* duːp/ *verb, noun*
▪ *verb* to trick or cheat sb: **~ sb** *They soon realized they had been duped.* ◇ **~ sb into doing sth** *He was duped into giving them his credit card.*
▪ *noun* (*formal*) a person who is tricked or cheated

**du·plex** /ˈdjuːpleks; *NAmE* ˈduː-/ *noun* **1** (*NAmE*) a building divided into two homes or apartments with separate entrances **2** (*BrE*) a flat with rooms on two floors **3** (*AustralE, NAmE*) a house that is joined to another house by a wall on one side that is shared; a SEMI-DETACHED house

**du·pli·cate** *verb, adj., noun*
▪ *verb* /ˈdjuːplɪkeɪt; *NAmE* ˈduː-/ **1** [often passive] **~ sth** to make an exact copy of sth: *a duplicated form* **2 ~ sth** to do sth again, especially when it is unnecessary: *There's no point in duplicating work already done.* ▶ **du·pli·ca·tion** /ˌdjuːplɪˈkeɪʃn; *NAmE* ˌduː-/ *noun* [U, C]
▪ *adj.* /ˈdjuːplɪkət; *NAmE* ˈduː-/ [only before noun] exactly like sth else; made as a copy of sth else: *a duplicate invoice*
▪ *noun* /ˈdjuːplɪkət; *NAmE* ˈduː-/ one of two or more things that are the same in every detail; a copy of an original **SYN** **copy**: *Books may be disposed of if they are duplicates.* ◇ *Is this a duplicate or the original?*
**IDM** **in duplicate** (of documents, etc.) as two copies that are exactly the same in every detail: *to prepare a contract in duplicate* ⊃ compare TRIPLICATE

**du·pli·city** /djuːˈplɪsəti; *NAmE* duː-/ *noun* [U, C] (*pl.* **-ies**) (*formal*) dishonest behaviour that is intended to make sb believe sth that is not true **SYN** **deceit** ▶ **du·pli·ci·tous** /-sɪtəs/ *adj.*

**dur·able** /ˈdjʊərəbl; *NAmE* ˈdʊr-/ *adj.* likely to last for a long time without breaking or getting weaker: *durable plastics* ◇ *negotiations for a durable peace* ▶ **dur·abil·ity** /ˌdjʊərəˈbɪləti; *NAmE* ˌdʊr-/ *noun* [U]: *the durability of gold* ⊃ see also CONSUMER DURABLES

**ˌdurable ˈgoods** (*NAmE*) (*BrE* conˌsumer ˈdurables, ˌdurables) *noun* [pl.] (*business*) goods that are expected to last for a long time after they have been bought, such as cars, televisions, etc.

**dur·ables** /ˈdjʊərəblz; *NAmE* ˈdʊr-/ *noun* [pl.] (*NAmE*) = CONSUMER DURABLES

**dur·ation** /djuˈreɪʃn; *NAmE* duˈ-/ *noun* [U] (*formal*) the length of time that sth lasts or continues: *The school was used as a hospital for the duration of the war.* ◇ *a contract of three years' duration*
**IDM** **for the duration** (*informal*) until the end of a particular situation, especially a war

**dur·ess** /djuˈres; *NAmE* duˈ-/ *noun* [U] (*formal*) threats or force that are used to make sb do sth: *He signed the confession under duress.*

**Durex™** /ˈdjʊəreks; *NAmE* ˈdʊr-/ *noun* (*pl.* **Durex**) (*BrE*) a CONDOM

**dur·ian** /ˈdʊəriən; *NAmE* ˈdʊr-/ *noun* a large tropical fruit with a strong unpleasant smell but a sweet taste ⊃ VISUAL VOCAB page V4

**dur·ing** /ˈdjʊərɪŋ; *NAmE* ˈdʊr-/ *prep.* **1** all through a period of time: *during the 1990s* ◇ *There are extra flights to Colorado during the winter.* ◇ *Please remain seated during the performance.* **2** at some point in a period of time: *He was taken to the hospital during the night.* ◇ *I only saw her once during my stay in Rome.* **HELP** *During* is used to say when something happens; *for* answers the question 'how long?': *I stayed in London for a week.* ◇ *I stayed in London during a week.*

**durrie** = DHURRIE

**durum** /ˈdjʊərəm; *NAmE* ˈdʊr-/ *noun* (*also* ˌdurum ˈwheat) *noun* [U] a type of hard WHEAT, used to make PASTA

**dusk** /dʌsk/ *noun* [U] the time of day when the light has almost gone, but it is not yet dark: **at ~** *The street lights go on at dusk.* ⊃ compare DAWN, TWILIGHT

**dusky** /ˈdʌski/ *adj.* (*literary*) not very bright; dark or soft in colour: *the dusky light inside the cave* ◇ *dusky pink*

485 **Dutch auction**

**dust** /dʌst/ *noun, verb*
▪ *noun* **1** [U] a fine powder that consists of very small pieces of sand, earth, etc: *A cloud of dust rose as the truck drove off.* ◇ *The workers wear masks to avoid inhaling the dust.* ⊃ SYNONYMS at SOIL **2** the fine powder of dirt that forms in buildings, on furniture, floors, etc: *The books were all covered with dust.* ◇ *There wasn't a speck of dust anywhere in the room.* ◇ *That guitar's been sitting gathering dust* (= not being used) *for years now.* ⊃ see also DUSTY **3** a fine powder that consists of very small pieces of a particular substance: *coal dust* ⊃ see also GOLD DUST
**IDM** **collect/gather ˈdust** to not be used for a long time | **leave sb in the ˈdust** (*NAmE*) to leave sb far behind | **let the dust settle** | **wait for the dust to settle** to wait for a situation to become clear or certain ⊃ more at BITE *v.*
▪ *verb* **1** [I, T] to clean furniture, a room, etc. by removing dust from surfaces with a cloth: *I broke the vase while I was dusting.* ◇ **~ sth** *Could you dust the sitting room?* **2** [T] **~ sth (+ adv./prep.)** to remove dirt from sb/sth/yourself with your hands or a brush: *She dusted some ash from her sleeve.* **3** [T] **~ sth (with sth)** to cover sth with fine powder: *Dust the cake with sugar.* **IDM** see DONE *adj.*
**PHRV** **ˌdust sb/sthˈdown** (especially *BrE*) to remove dust, dirt, etc. from sb/sth: *Mel stood up and dusted herself down.* **ˌdust sb/sthˈoff 1** to remove dust, dirt, etc. from sb/sth **2** to use sth again after a long period of not using it: *For the concert, he dusted off some of his old hits.*

**dust·bin** /ˈdʌstbɪn/ (*BrE*) (*NAmE* ˈgarbage can, ˈtrash can) *noun* a large container with a LID (= cover), used for putting rubbish in, usually kept outside the house ⊃ note at RUBBISH

**ˈdust bowl** *noun* an area of land that has been turned into desert by lack of rain or too much farming

**ˈdust bunny** *noun* (*NAmE*, *informal*) a mass of dust and small pieces of wool, cotton, hair, etc.

**dust·cart** /ˈdʌstkɑːt; *NAmE* -kɑːrt/ *noun* (*BrE*, *old-fashioned*) = BIN LORRY

**ˈdust cover** *noun* **1** = DUST JACKET **2** a hard or soft plastic cover on a piece of equipment, etc. that protects it when it is not being used **3** (*BrE*) = DUST SHEET

**ˈdust devil** *noun* a small column of dust over land, caused by the wind

**dust·er** /ˈdʌstə(r)/ *noun* **1** a cloth for removing dust from furniture ⊃ picture at BROOM ⊃ see also FEATHER DUSTER **2** (*also* ˈduster coat) (*NAmE*) a long, light coat

**ˈdust jacket** (*also* ˈdust cover) *noun* a paper cover on a book that protects it but that can be removed

**dust·man** /ˈdʌstmən/ *noun* (*pl.* **-men** /-mən/) (*also informal* ˈbin·man, *formal* ˈrefuse colˌlector) (*all BrE*) (*NAmE* ˈgarbage man) a person whose job is to remove waste from outside houses, etc. ⊃ note at RUBBISH

**ˈdust mite** (*also* ˈhouse dust mite) *noun* a very small creature that lives in houses and can cause ALLERGIES

**dust·pan** /ˈdʌstpæn/ *noun* a small flat container with a handle into which dust is brushed from the floor ⊃ picture at BROOM

**ˈdust sheet** (*also* **dust cover**) (*both BrE*) (*NAmE* ˈdrop cloth) *noun* a large sheet that is used to protect floors, furniture, etc. from dust or paint

**ˈdust storm** *noun* a storm that carries clouds of dust in the wind over a wide area

**ˈdust-up** *noun* (*BrE*, *informal*) an argument or a fight

**dusty** /ˈdʌsti/ *adj.* (**dust·ier**, **dusti·est**) **1** full of dust; covered with dust: *a dusty road* ◇ *piles of dusty books* ⊃ SYNONYMS at DIRTY **2** (of a colour) not bright or shiny: *dusty pink*

**Dutch** /dʌtʃ/ *adj.* of or connected with the Netherlands, its people or its language ⊃ see also DOUBLE DUTCH
**IDM** **go Dutch (with sb)** to share the cost of sth with sb

**Dutch ˈauction** *noun* a sale in which the price of an item is reduced until sb offers to buy it

**Dutch courage**

**Dutch 'courage** noun [U] (BrE, informal) the false courage or confidence that a person gets from drinking alcohol

**Dutch 'door** (NAmE) (BrE ˌstable 'door) noun a door that is divided into two parts so that the top part can be left open while the bottom part is kept shut

**duti·ful** /ˈdjuːtɪfl; NAmE ˈduː-/ adj. doing everything that you are expected to do; willing to obey and to show respect SYN **obedient**: *a dutiful daughter/son/wife* ▸ **duti·ful·ly** /-fəli/ adv.

**duty** ❶ B1 S /ˈdjuːti; NAmE ˈduː-/ noun (pl. **-ies**) **1** ❓ B1 [C, U] something that you feel you have to do because it is your moral or legal responsibility: *~ to do sth It is my duty to report it to the police.* ◇ *Local councillors have a duty to serve the community.* ◇ *to do your duty for your country* ◇ *~ to sb/sth He has failed in his duty to his client.* ◇ *as sb your duties as a parent* ◇ *~ of (doing) sth The company owes a duty of care to its employees.* ◇ *I don't want you to visit me simply out of a sense of duty.* **2** ❓ B2 [U] the work that is your job: *Report for duty at 8 a.m.* ◇ *He was the duty manager that day.* ⊃ see also JURY DUTY, NIGHT DUTY, TOUR OF DUTY **3** ❓ B2 **duties** [pl.] tasks that are part of your job: *The princess has taken on her mother's official duties.* ◇ *to perform/fulfil/discharge your duties* ◇ *Your duties will include greeting visitors and answering the phone.* ⊃ see also HEAVY-DUTY **4** [C, U] a tax that you pay on things that you buy, especially those that you bring into a country: *customs/excise/import duties* ◇ *~ on sth duty on wine and beer* ⊃ SYNONYMS at TAX ⊃ see also DEATH DUTY, STAMP DUTY
IDM **on/off duty** (of nurses, police officers, etc.) working/not working at a particular time: *Who's on duty today?* ◇ *What time do you go off duty?* ⊃ see also OFF-DUTY ⊃ more at BOUNDEN, CALL *v.*, LINE *n.*

**duty-'bound** adj. [not before noun] (formal) having to do sth because it is your duty: *I felt duty-bound to help her.*

**duty-'free** adj. (of goods) that you can bring into a country without paying tax on them: *duty-free cigarettes* ▸ **duty-'free** adv. **duty-'free** noun (BrE, informal): *We bought a load of duty-frees* (= duty-free goods) *at the airport.*

**duty-'free shop** (BrE) (NAmE **duty-'free store**) (also **duty-'free** BrE and NAmE) noun a shop in an airport or on a ship, etc. that sells goods such as cigarettes, alcohol, PERFUME, etc. without tax on them

**duty of 'care** noun [sing.] **~ (to sb)** (especially BrE) a moral or legal obligation to ensure that other people are safe from physical or mental harm: *Employers have a duty of care to their employees.*

**'duty officer** noun the officer, for example in the police, army, etc., who is on duty at a particular time in a particular place

**duvet** /ˈduːveɪ; NAmE also duːˈveɪ/ (NAmE also **comforter**) noun a large cloth bag that is filled with feathers or other soft material and that you have on top of you in bed to keep yourself warm: *a duvet cover* (= a cover that you can wash, that you put over a duvet)

**dux** /dʌks/ noun (ScotE, AustralE) the top student in a school or class

**DVD** ❶ A1 /ˌdiː viː ˈdiː/ noun a disk on which large amounts of information, especially films, photographs and video, can be stored, for use on a **DVD player** or computer (the abbreviation for 'digital versatile disc' or 'digital videodisc'): *Let's just stay in and watch a DVD.* ◇ *on ~ Is it available on DVD yet?*

**DVR** /ˌdiː viː ˈɑː(r)/ noun [C, U] a device or system for storing video data (the abbreviation for 'digital video recorder' or 'digital video recording') SYN **PVR**

**DVT** /ˌdiː viː ˈtiː/ abbr. DEEP VEIN THROMBOSIS

**DW** abbr. (informal) **1** /ˌdiː ˈdʌbljuː/ (especially in text messages, on SOCIAL MEDIA, etc.) darling wife or dear wife **2** (especially in text messages, on SOCIAL MEDIA, etc.) don't worry

**dwaal** /dwɑːl/ noun (SAfrE) a confused or very relaxed state of mind: *I was in a complete dwaal.*

**dwarf** /dwɔːf; NAmE dwɔːrf/ noun, adj., verb
▪ noun (pl. **dwarfs** or **dwarves** /dwɔːvz; NAmE dwɔːrvz/) **1** (in stories) a creature like a small man, who has magic powers and who is usually described as living and working under the ground, especially working with metal **2** (offensive) a person who is very short because of the medical condition DWARFISM HELP People who have this condition usually prefer the terms **little person** or **person of short stature**. ⊃ see also BROWN DWARF, RED DWARF, WHITE DWARF
▪ adj. [only before noun] (of a plant or an animal) much smaller than the normal size: *dwarf conifers*
▪ verb **~ sth** to make sth seem small or unimportant compared with sth else: *The old houses were dwarfed by the huge new tower blocks.*

**dwarf·ism** /ˈdwɔːfɪzəm; NAmE ˈdwɔːrf-/ noun a medical condition that causes sb to have an unusually small adult height.

**dwarf 'planet** noun a round object in space that goes around the sun but is not as large as a planet: *the dwarf planets Pluto, Ceres, Eris, Makemake and Haumea*

**dweeb** /dwiːb/ noun (especially NAmE, slang) a person, especially a boy or a man, who does not have good social skills and is not fashionable

**dwell** /dwel/ verb [I] (**dwelt, dwelt** or **dwelled, dwelled**) + adv./prep. (formal or literary) to live somewhere: *For ten years she dwelled among the nomads of North America.*
PHRV **dwell 'on/upon sth 1** to think or talk a lot about sth, especially sth it would be better to forget: *So you made a mistake, but there's no need to dwell on it.* **2** to look at sth for a long time

**dwell·er** /ˈdwelə(r)/ noun (especially in compounds) a person or an animal that lives in the particular place that is mentioned: *apartment dwellers*

**dwell·ing** /ˈdwelɪŋ/ noun (formal) a house, flat, etc. where a person lives: *The development will consist of 66 dwellings and a number of offices.*

**'dwelling house** noun (BrE, law) a house that people live in, not one that is used as an office, etc.

**'dwelling place** noun (old-fashioned) the place where sb lives

**DWI** /ˌdiː dʌbljuː ˈaɪ/ abbr. (US) DRIVING WHILE INTOXICATED

**dwin·dle** /ˈdwɪndl/ verb [I] to become gradually less or smaller: *dwindling audiences* ◇ *~ (away) (to sth) Support for the party has dwindled away to nothing.* ◇ *~ (from sth) (to sth) Membership of the club has dwindled from 70 to 20.*

**dyad** /ˈdaɪæd/ noun **1** (specialist) something that consists of two parts: *the mother-child dyad* **2** (mathematics) an OPERATOR that is the combination of two VECTORS ▸ **dyad·ic** /daɪˈædɪk/ adj.

**dye** /daɪ/ verb, noun
▪ verb (**dyes, dye·ing, dyed, dyed**) to change the colour of sth, especially by using a special liquid or substance: *~ sth to dye fabric* ◇ *~ sth + adj. She dyed her hair blonde.* ⊃ see also TIE-DYE
▪ noun [C, U] a substance that is used to change the colour of things such as cloth or hair: *black dye* ◇ *hair dye* ◇ *natural/chemical/vegetable dyes*

**ˌdyed in the 'wool** adj. [usually before noun] (usually disapproving) having strong beliefs or opinions that are never going to change: *dyed-in-the-wool traditionalists* ORIGIN From the idea that wool which was dyed in its raw state gave a more even and lasting colour.

**dying** /ˈdaɪɪŋ/ adj. **1** [only before noun] connected with or happening at the time of sb's death: *I will remember it to my dying day.* ◇ *her dying wishes/words* **2** **the dying** noun [pl.] people who are dying: *doctors who care for the dying* ⊃ see also ASSISTED DYING **3** gradually disappearing; that will soon no longer exist: *Letter-writing is a dying art.* **4** [only before noun] coming at the end of a period of time or an activity SYN **closing**: *the dying moments of the match* ⇒ see also DIE IDM see BREATH

**dyke** (*also* **dike**) HELP The spelling **dike** is preferred in (*NAmE*) in senses 1 and 2. /daɪk/ *noun* **1** a long thick wall that is built to stop water flooding onto a low area of land, especially from the sea **2** (*especially BrE*) a channel that carries water away from the land SYN **ditch 3** (*taboo*, *slang*) a word for a LESBIAN that is usually offensive

**dy·nam·ic** /daɪˈnæmɪk/ *adj., noun*
- *adj.* **1** (*approving*) (of a person) having a lot of energy and a strong personality: *a dynamic leader* **2** (of a process, relationship or system) always changing and making progress: *The business has managed to change and remain dynamic.* OPP **static 3** (*physics*) (of a force or power) producing movement OPP **static 4** (*linguistics*) (of verbs) describing an action rather than a state. **Dynamic** verbs (for example *eat, grow, knock, die*) can be used in the progressive tenses. ⇒ compare STATIVE ▸ **dy·nam·ic·al·ly** /-kli/ *adv.*
- *noun* **1** **dynamics** [pl.] the way in which people or things behave and react to each other in a particular situation: *the dynamics of political change* ◊ *group dynamics* (= the way in which members of a group react to each other) **2 dynamics** [U] the science of the forces involved in movement: *fluid dynamics* ⇒ compare STATIC **3** [sing.] (*formal*) a force that produces change, action or effects **4 dynamics** [pl.] (*music*) changes in volume in music

**dyna·mism** /ˈdaɪnəmɪzəm/ *noun* (*approving*) energy and enthusiasm to make new things happen or to make things succeed

**dyna·mite** /ˈdaɪnəmaɪt/ *noun, verb*
- *noun* [U] **1** a powerful EXPLOSIVE: *a stick of dynamite* **2** a thing that is likely to cause a violent reaction or a lot of trouble: *The abortion issue is political dynamite.* **3** (*informal, approving*) an extremely impressive or exciting person or thing: *Their new album is dynamite.*
- *verb* ~ sth to destroy or damage sth using dynamite

**dy·namo** /ˈdaɪnəməʊ/ *noun* (*pl.* **-os**) **1** a device for turning MECHANICAL energy (= energy from movement) into electricity; a GENERATOR **2** (*informal*) a person with a lot of energy: *the team's midfield dynamo* ◊ *She's a human dynamo.*

**dyn·asty** /ˈdɪnəsti/; *NAmE* /ˈdaɪ-/ *noun* (*pl.* **-ies**) **1** a series of leaders of a country who all belong to the same family: *the Nehru-Gandhi dynasty* ⇒ WORDFINDER NOTE at RELATION **2** a period of years during which members of a particular family rule a country ▸ **dyn·as·tic** /dɪˈnæstɪk/; *NAmE* /daɪ-/ *adj.* [usually before noun]: *dynastic history*

**dys·en·tery** /ˈdɪsəntri/; *NAmE* -teri/ *noun* [U] an infection of the BOWELS that causes severe DIARRHOEA with loss of blood

**dys·func·tion** /dɪsˈfʌŋkʃn/ *noun* [U, C] **1** (*medical*) the fact of a part of the body not working normally: *He's suffering from sexual dysfunction caused by depression.* **2** the situation when the relationships within a society, family, etc. are not working normally: *a tale of loneliness and family dysfunction*

**dys·func·tion·al** /dɪsˈfʌŋkʃənl/ *adj* (*specialist*) not working normally or properly: *children from dysfunctional families*

**dys·lexia** /dɪsˈleksiə/ *noun* [U] a slight DISORDER of the brain that causes difficulty in reading and spelling, for example, but does not affect intelligence ▸ **dys·lex·ic** /-sɪk/ *adj.*: *He's dyslexic.* **dys·lex·ic** *noun*: *writing courses for dyslexics*

**dys·mor·phia** /dɪsˈmɔːfiə/; *NAmE* -ˈmɔːrf-/ *noun* [U] (*medical*) a condition in which a part of the body grows larger than and a different shape from normal ▸ **dys·morph·ic** /-fɪk/ *adj.*

**dys·pep·sia** /dɪsˈpepsiə/; *NAmE* -ˈpepʃə/ *noun* [U] (*medical*) pain caused by difficulty in DIGESTING food SYN **indigestion**

**dys·pep·tic** /dɪsˈpeptɪk/ *adj.* **1** (*medical*) connected with or suffering from dyspepsia **2** (*formal*) easily annoyed

**dys·phoria** /dɪsˈfɔːriə/ *noun* [U] (*medical*) a state of worry or general unhappiness ⇒ compare EUPHORIA ▸ **dys·phor·ic** /dɪsˈfɒrɪk/; *NAmE* -ˈfɔːr-/ *adj.*

**dys·praxia** /dɪsˈpræksiə/ *noun* [U] (*medical*) a condition of the brain that develops in childhood causing difficulties with physical movement and writing neatly, for example

**dys·to·pia** /dɪsˈtəʊpiə/ *noun* an imaginary place or state in which everything is extremely bad or unpleasant ⇒ compare UTOPIA ▸ **dys·to·pian** /-piən/ (*also* **dys·top·ic** /dɪsˈtɒpɪk/; *NAmE* -ˈtɑːp-/) *adj.*

**dys·trophy** /ˈdɪstrəfi/ *noun* [U] (*medical*) a medical condition in which an organ or body tissue gradually becomes weaker ⇒ see also MUSCULAR DYSTROPHY

# E e

**E** /iː/ noun, abbr.
- noun (also **e**) [C, U] (pl. **Es**, **E's**, **e's** /iːz/) **1** the fifth letter in the English alphabet: *'Egg' begins with (an) E/'E'.* **2 E** (music) the third note in the SCALE of C MAJOR **3 E ~ (in / for sth)** a grade that a student can get for a piece of work or course of study, showing that it is very bad: *He got (an) E in French.* ⊃ see also E-NUMBER
- abbr. **1** (in writing) East; Eastern: *E Asia* **2** (slang) the drug ECSTASY: *She had taken an E.*

**e-** /iː/ combining form (in nouns and verbs) connected with the use of electronic communication, especially the internet, for sending information, doing business, etc: *e-commerce* ◊ *e-business* ⊃ see also EMAIL

**each** 🔑 **A1** /iːtʃ/ det., pron., adv. used to refer to every one of two or more people or things, when you are thinking about them separately: *Each answer is worth 20 points.* ◊ *Each of the answers is worth 20 points.* ◊ *The answers are worth 20 points each.* ◊ *'Red or blue?' 'I'll take one of each, please.'* ◊ *Look at the pictures and answer the questions about each one.* ◊ *We each have our own car.* ◊ *There aren't enough books for everyone to have one each.* ◊ *They lost $40 each.* ◊ *Each day that passed he grew more and more desperate.*
**IDM** **each and every** (used for emphasis) every single one: *I look forward to seeing each and every one of you as we celebrate our 50th year.*

▼ **GRAMMAR POINT**

**each / every**
- **Each** is used in front of a singular noun and is followed by a singular verb: *Each student has been given his or her own email address.* The use of *his* or *her* sometimes sounds slightly formal and it is more common to use the plural pronoun *their*: *Each student has been given their own email address.*
- When **each** is used after a plural subject, it has a plural verb: *They each have their own email address.*
- **Every** is always followed by a singular verb: *Every student in the class is capable of passing the exam.*
- **Each of, each one of** and **every one of** are followed by a plural noun or pronoun, but the verb is usually singular: *Each (one) of the houses was slightly different.* ◊ *I bought a dozen eggs and every one of them was bad.*

**each 'other** pron. used as the object of a verb or preposition to show that each member of a group does sth to or for the other members **SYN** **one another**: *Don and Susie really loved each other* (= he loved her and she loved him). ◊ *They looked at each other and laughed.* ◊ *We can wear each other's clothes.*

**each 'way** adv., adj. (BrE) if you bet money **each way** on a race, you win if your horse, etc. comes first, second or third in the race: *She put £5 each way on the favourite.* ◊ *an each-way bet*

**eager** 🔑+ **C1** /ˈiːɡə(r)/ adj. very interested and excited by sth that is going to happen or about sth that you want to do; showing this **SYN** **keen**: *eager crowds outside the stadium* ◊ *Small eager faces looked up and listened.* ◊ **~ for sth** *She is eager for* (= wants very much to get) *her parents' approval.* ◊ **~ to do sth** *Everyone in the class seemed eager to learn.* ◊ *They're eager to please* (= wanting to be helpful).
▶ **eager·ly** adv.: *the band's eagerly awaited new album* **eager·ness** noun [U, sing.]: *I couldn't hide my eagerness to get back home.*

**eagle** /ˈiːɡl/ noun **1** a large BIRD OF PREY (= a bird that kills other creatures for food) with a sharp curved BEAK and very good sight: *eagles soaring overhead* ⊃ see also BALD EAGLE, GOLDEN EAGLE **2** (in golf) a score of two STROKES (= hits of the ball) less than the standard score for a hole (= two under PAR) ⊃ compare BIRDIE, BOGEY ⊃ see also LEGAL EAGLE

**ˌeagle 'eye** noun [usually sing.] if sb has an **eagle eye**, they watch things carefully and are good at noticing things: *Nothing escaped our teacher's eagle eye.* ▶ **ˌeagle-'eyed** adj. **SYN** **hawk-eyed**: *An eagle-eyed tourist found the suspicious package.*

**eag·let** /ˈiːɡlət/ noun a young eagle

**EAL** /ˌiː eɪ ˈel/ abbr. (in the UK and Ireland) English as an additional language (refers to the teaching of English in schools to children whose first language is not English) ⊃ compare EFL, ESL, ESOL

**EAP** /ˌiː eɪ ˈpiː/ abbr. ENGLISH FOR ACADEMIC PURPOSES

**ear** 🔑 **A1** /ɪə(r); NAmE ɪr/ noun **1** 🔑 **A1** [C] either of the organs on the sides of the head that you hear with: *the left / right ear* ◊ *He put his hands over his ears.* ◊ *She's had her ears pierced.* ◊ **in sb's ~** *She whispered something in his ear.* ◊ *He was always there with a sympathetic ear* (= was always willing to listen to people). ◊ *an ear infection* ⊃ VISUAL VOCAB page V1 ⊃ see also EXTERNAL EAR, INNER EAR, MIDDLE EAR **2** **-eared** (in adjectives) having the type of ears mentioned: *a long-eared owl* **3** [sing.] an ability to recognize and copy sounds well: *You need a good ear to master the piano.* **4** [C] the top part of a grain plant, such as WHEAT, that contains the seeds: *ears of corn* ⊃ VISUAL VOCAB page V8
**IDM** **be all 'ears** (informal) to be waiting with interest to hear what sb has to say: *'Do you know what he said?' 'Go on —I'm all ears.'* **be out on your 'ear** (informal) to be forced to leave (a job, etc.) **be up to your ears in sth** (informal) to have a lot of sth to deal with: *We're up to our ears in work.* **sth comes to / reaches sb's 'ears** somebody hears about sth, especially when other people already know about it: *News of his affair eventually reached her ears.* **sb's 'ears are burning** a person thinks that other people are talking about them, especially in an unkind way: *'I bumped into your ex-wife last night.' 'I thought I could feel my ears burning!'* **sb's 'ears are flapping** (BrE, informal) a person is trying to listen to sb else's conversation **go in ˌone ear and out the 'other** (informal) (of information, etc.) to be forgotten quickly: *Everything I tell them just goes in one ear and out the other.* **have sth coming out of your 'ears** (informal) to have a lot of sth, especially more than you need **have sb's ear** | **have the ear of sb** to be able to give sb advice, influence them, etc. because they trust you: *He had the ear of the monarch.* **keep / have your ear to the 'ground** to make sure that you always find out about the most recent developments in a particular situation **play (sth) by 'ear** to play music by remembering how it sounds rather than by reading it **play it by 'ear** (informal) to decide how to deal with a situation as it develops rather than by having a plan to follow: *I'm not sure how many people are expected—we'll just have to play it by ear.* **shut / close your 'ears to sth** to refuse to listen to sth: *She decided to shut her ears to all the rumours.* **smile / grin / beam from ear to 'ear** to be smiling, etc. a lot because you are very pleased about sth **with half an 'ear** without giving your full attention to what is being said, etc. ⊃ more at BELIEVE, BEND v., BOX n., BOX v., COCK v., DEAF, EASY adj., FLEA, LEND, MUSIC, OPEN adj., PIG n., PRICK v., RING² v., SILK, THICK adj., WALL n., WET adj., WORD n.

**ear·ache** /ˈɪəreɪk; NAmE ˈɪr-/ noun [U, C] pain inside the ear: *have (an) earache*

**ear·bud** /ˈɪəbʌd; NAmE ˈɪrb-/ noun [usually pl.] a very small HEADPHONE that is worn inside the ear

**'ear drops** noun [pl.] liquid medicine that can be put into the ears

**ear·drum** /ˈɪədrʌm; NAmE ˈɪrd-/ noun the piece of thin tightly stretched skin inside the ear that is moved by sound waves, making you able to hear: *a perforated eardrum*

**ear·ful** /ˈɪəfʊl; NAmE ˈɪrf-/ noun [sing.] (informal) if sb gives you an **earful**, they tell you for a long time how angry they are about sth

**ear·hole** /ˈɪəhəʊl; NAmE ˈɪrh-/ noun (informal) the outer opening of the ear

**earl** /ɜːl; NAmE ɜːrl/ noun a British NOBLEMAN of high rank: *the Earl of Essex* ⊃ see also COUNTESS

**ˌEarl 'Grey** noun [U] a type of tea with BERGAMOT added

---

æ cat | ɑː father | e bed | ɜː fur | ə about | ɪ sit | iː see | i happy | ɒ got (BrE) | ɔː saw | ʌ cup | ʊ put | uː too

**earli·est** /'ɜːliɪst; NAmE 'ɜːrl-/ noun [sing.] **the earliest** the time before which sth cannot happen: *The earliest we can finish is next Friday.* ◊ *We can't finish before next Friday at the earliest.*

**ear·lobe** /'ɪələʊb; NAmE 'ɪrl-/ (also **lobe**) noun the soft part at the bottom of the ear

**early** ⓘ A1 ⓞ /'ɜːli; NAmE 'ɜːrli/ adj., adv.
■ **adj.** (**earl·ier**, **earli·est**) **1** A1 near the beginning of a period of time, an event etc: *the early morning* ◊ *my earliest memories* ◊ *The project is still in the early stages.* ◊ *the early 1990s* ◊ *in the early days of space exploration* (= when it was just beginning) ◊ *it is too ~ to do sth It is too early to tell how badly the economy will be affected.* ◊ *He's in his early twenties.* ◊ *Mozart's early works* (= those written at the beginning of his career) ◊ *Early booking is essential, as space is limited.* ◊ *The earliest possible date I can make it is the third.* **2** A1 arriving, or done before the usual, expected or planned time: *You're early! I wasn't expecting you till seven.* ◊ *The bus was ten minutes early.* ◊ *an early breakfast* ◊ *He learnt to play the piano at an early age.* ◊ *Let's make an early start tomorrow.* **3** A1 belonging to the beginning of a period of history or a cultural movement: *The gallery has an unrivalled collection of early twentieth-century art.* ◊ *the early modern period from the fifteenth to the eighteenth century* OPP **late** ▸ **earli·ness** noun [U]
IDM **an ˈearly bird** (*humorous*) a person who gets up, arrives, etc. very early **at your earliest conˈvenience** (*business*) as soon as possible: *Please contact us at your earliest convenience.* **the ˌearly bird catches the ˈworm** (*saying*) the person who takes the opportunity to do sth before other people will have an advantage over them **it's early ˈdays (yet)** | **it's still early ˈdays** (*BrE*) used to say that it is too soon to be sure how a situation will develop ⊃ more at BRIGHT *adj.*, HOUR, NIGHT
■ **adv.** (**earl·ier**, **earli·est**) **1** A1 near the beginning of a period of time, an event, a piece of work, etc: *We arrived early the next day.* ◊ *in sth early in the week/year/season/morning* ◊ *as ~ as sth He started writing music as early as 1989.* ◊ *The best rooms go to those who book earliest.* OPP **late 2** A1 before the usual, expected or planned time: *Why don't you go home early if you're not feeling well?* ◊ *The bus came five minutes early.* ◊ *I woke up early this morning.* ◊ *The baby arrived earlier than expected.* OPP **late 3** A2 **earlier** before the present time or the time mentioned: *As I said earlier…* ◊ *As mentioned/noted/described earlier…* ◊ *a week earlier* ◊ *She had seen him earlier in the day.* OPP **later**
IDM **early ˈon** at an early stage of a situation, relationship, period of time, etc: *I knew quite early on that I wanted to marry her.*

**ˌearly ˈclosing** noun [U] (*BrE*) the practice of closing shops on a particular afternoon every week (now no longer very common)

**ˌearly ˈwarning** noun [U, sing.] a thing that tells you in advance that sth serious or dangerous is going to happen: *an early warning of heart disease* ◊ *an early warning system* (= of enemy attack)

**ear·mark** /'ɪəmɑːk; NAmE 'ɪrmɑːrk/ verb, noun
■ **verb** [usually passive] to decide that sth will be used for a particular purpose, or to state that sth will happen to sb/sth in the future: **be earmarked (for sb/sth)** *The money had been earmarked for spending on new school buildings.* ◊ **be earmarked as sb/sth** *She was earmarked early as a possible champion.*
■ **noun** [usually pl.] (*especially NAmE*) a feature or quality that is typical of sth/sb: *The incident has all the earmarks of a terrorist attack.*

**ear·muffs** /'ɪəmʌfs; NAmE 'ɪrm-/ noun [pl.] a pair of soft thick covers for the ears connected by a band across the top of the head, and worn to protect the ears, especially from cold: *a pair of earmuffs*

**earn** ⓘ A2 /ɜːn; NAmE ɜːrn/ verb **1** ~ (**sth**) [T, I] to get money for work that you do: ~ (**sth**) *He earns about $40000 a year.* ◊ *to earn an income/a wage/a salary* ◊ *She earned a living as a part-time secretary.* ◊ *She must earn a fortune* (= earn a lot of money). ◊ *All the children are earning now.* ◊ **~sb sth** *His victory in the tournament earned him $50000.* ⊃ WORDFINDER NOTE at PAY ⊃ see also HARD-EARNED **2** [T] to get money as profit or interest on money you lend, have in a bank, etc: ~**sth** *Your money would earn more in a*

489

*high-interest account.* ◊ **~ sth from sth** *interest earned from investments* **3** B2 [T] to get sth that you deserve, usually because of sth good you have done or because of the good qualities you have: ~**sth** *He earned a reputation as an expert on tax law.* ◊ *As a teacher, she had earned the respect of her students.* ◊ *Their supporters have certainly earned the right to celebrate.* ◊ *I need a rest. I think I've earned it, don't you?* ◊ (*especially NAmE*) *She earned a degree in music.* ◊ **~ sb sth** *His outstanding ability earned him a place on the team.* ⊃ see also HARD-EARNED, WELL EARNED
IDM **earn a/your ˈcrust** (*BrE, informal*) to earn enough money to live on **earn your ˈkeep 1** to do useful or helpful things in return for being allowed to live or stay somewhere **2** to be worth the amount of time or money that is being spent: *He felt he no longer deserved such a high salary. He just wasn't earning his keep.* **earn your ˈstripes** (*informal*) to get a position or reputation you deserve through work or achievements ⊃ more at SPUR *n.*

**ˌearned ˈrun** noun (in baseball) a RUN scored without the help of errors by the other team

**earn·er** /'ɜːnə(r); NAmE 'ɜːrn-/ noun **1** a person who earns money for a job that they do: *high/low earners* ⊃ see also WAGE EARNER **2** an activity or a business that makes a profit: *Tourism is the country's biggest foreign currency earner.* ◊ (*BrE, informal*) *Her new business has turned out to be a nice little earner.*

**earn·est** /'ɜːnɪst; NAmE 'ɜːrn-/ *adj.* very serious and sincere: *an earnest young man* ▸ **earn·est·ly** *adv.* **earn·est·ness** noun [U]
IDM **in ˈearnest 1** more seriously and with more force or effort than before: *The work on the house will begin in earnest on Monday.* **2** very serious and sincere about what you are saying and about your intentions; in a way that shows that you are serious: *You may laugh but I'm in deadly earnest.* ◊ *I could tell she spoke in earnest.*

**earn·ings** ⓘ+ C1 /'ɜːnɪŋz; NAmE 'ɜːrn-/ noun [pl.] **1** ⓘ+ C1 the money that you earn for the work that you do: *a rise in average earnings* ◊ *compensation for loss of earnings caused by the accident* ⊃ SYNONYMS at INCOME **2** ⓘ+ C1 the profit that a company makes: *export earnings*

**earnings-reˈlated** *adj.* (*BrE*) (of payments, etc.) connected to and changing according to the amount of money that you earn: *an earnings-related pension scheme*

**ear·phones** /'ɪəfəʊnz; NAmE 'ɪrf-/ noun [pl.] a piece of equipment worn in or over the ears that makes it possible to listen to music, the radio, etc. without other people hearing it ⊃ compare HEADPHONES

**ear·piece** /'ɪəpiːs; NAmE 'ɪrp-/ noun the part of a phone or piece of electrical equipment that you hold next to or put into your ear so that you can listen

**ˈear-piercing** *adj., noun*
■ *adj.* [only before noun] (of a sound) very high, loud and unpleasant: *an ear-piercing scream*
■ *noun* [U] the practice of making small holes in sb's ears so jewellery can be put in them

**ear·plug** /'ɪəplʌg; NAmE 'ɪrp-/ noun [usually pl.] a piece of soft material that you put into your ear to keep out noise or water

**ear·ring** /'ɪərɪŋ; NAmE 'ɪr-/ noun a piece of jewellery that you fasten in or on your ear: *a pair of earrings*

**ear·shot** /'ɪəʃɒt; NAmE 'ɪrʃɑːt/ noun
IDM **out of ˈearshot (of sb/sth)** too far away to hear sb/sth or to be heard: *We waited until Ted was safely out of earshot before discussing it.* **within ˈearshot (of sb/sth)** near enough to hear sb/sth or to be heard

**ˈear-splitting** *adj.* (of a sound) extremely loud

**earth** ⓘ A2 /ɜːθ; NAmE ɜːrθ/ noun, verb
■ *noun* **1** ⓘ A2 (also **Earth**, **the Earth**) [U, sing.] the world; the planet that we live on: *the planet Earth* ◊ *The earth revolves around the sun.* ◊ *a satellite orbiting the earth* ◊ *the earth's surface/crust* ◊ **on ~** *the history of life on earth* ◊ *I must be the happiest person on earth!*
WORDFINDER climate, equator, equinox, hemisphere, International Date Line, latitude, map, planet, tropic

# earthbound

**2** [U, sing.] land; the hard surface of the world that is not the sea or the sky; the ground: *After a week at sea, it was good to feel the earth beneath our feet again.* ◊ **above the ~** *fifty feet above the earth* ◊ **under/below/beneath the ~** *in mines deep under the earth* ⇨ see also SCORCHED EARTH POLICY ⇨ SYNONYMS at FLOOR **3** [U] the substance that plants grow in: *a clod/mound of earth* ◊ *I cleaned off the earth clinging to my boots.* ⇨ SYNONYMS at SOIL **4** [C] the hole under the ground where an animal, especially a FOX, lives **5** (*BrE*) (*NAmE* **ground**) [C, usually sing.] a wire that connects an electric CIRCUIT with the ground and makes it safe ⇨ see also RARE EARTH

**IDM** **be, feel, look, taste, etc. like nothing on 'earth** (*informal*) to be, feel, look, taste, etc. very bad **charge, cost, pay, etc. the 'earth** (*BrE*, *informal*) to charge, etc. a lot of money: *I'd love that dress but it costs the earth.* **come back/down to 'earth (with a 'bang/'bump) | bring sb (back) down to 'earth (with a 'bang/'bump)** (*informal*) to return, or to make sb return, to a normal way of thinking or behaving after a time when you/they have been very excited, not very practical, etc. ⇨ see also DOWN TO EARTH **go to 'earth/'ground** (*BrE*) to hide, especially to escape from sb **how, why, where, who, etc. on 'earth** (*informal*) used to emphasize the question you are asking when you are surprised or angry or cannot think of an obvious answer: *What on earth are you doing?* ◊ *How on earth can she afford that?* **on 'earth** used after negative nouns or pronouns to emphasize what you are saying: *Nothing on earth would persuade me to go with him.* **run sb/sth to 'earth/'ground** (*BrE*) to find sb/sth after looking hard for a long time ⇨ more at END *n.*, FACE *n.*, MOVE *v.*, PROMISE *v.*, SALT *n.*, WIPE *v.*

▪ *verb* (*BrE*) (*NAmE* **ground**) [usually passive] **~ sth** to make electrical equipment safe by connecting it to the ground with a wire

**earth·bound** /ˈɜːθbaʊnd; *NAmE* ˈɜːrθ-/ *adj.* **1** unable to leave the surface of the earth: *birds and their earthbound predators* **2** (*literary*) not spiritual or having much imagination

**earth·en** /ˈɜːθn; *NAmE* ˈɜːrθn/ *adj.* [only before noun] **1** (of floors or walls) made of earth **2** (of objects) made of baked CLAY: *earthen pots*

**earth·en·ware** /ˈɜːθnweə(r); *NAmE* ˈɜːrθnwer/ *noun* [U] an object or objects made of very hard baked CLAY: *an earthenware bowl*

**earth·ling** /ˈɜːθlɪŋ; *NAmE* ˈɜːrθ-/ *noun* (in SCIENCE FICTION stories) a word used by creatures from other planets to refer to a person living on the earth

**earth·ly** /ˈɜːθli; *NAmE* ˈɜːrθ-/ *adj.* [usually before noun] **1** (*literary*) connected with life on earth and not with any spiritual life: *the sorrows of this earthly life* **2** (often used in questions and negatives for emphasis) possible: *There's no earthly reason why you shouldn't go.* ◊ *What earthly difference is my opinion going to make?* ◊ *He didn't have an earthly chance of getting the job.*

**ˈearth mother** *noun* **1** (*also* **Earth Mother**) a GODDESS who represents the earth as the source of life; a GODDESS of FERTILITY **2** (*informal*) a woman who seems to have all the qualities needed to be a good mother

**ˈearth mover** *noun* a vehicle or machine that digs up large quantities of soil

**earth·quake** 🔑 B1 /ˈɜːθkweɪk; *NAmE* ˈɜːrθ-/ (*also informal* **quake**) *noun* a sudden, violent shaking of the earth's surface: *a devastating/massive/powerful earthquake* ◊ *I was asleep when the earthquake struck.* ◊ *in a/the ~* *Much of the town was destroyed in the earthquake.* ◊ *earthquake victims/survivors* ⇨ WORDFINDER NOTE at DISASTER

**ˈearth science** *noun* [C, U] a science that involves studying the earth or part of it. Geography and GEOLOGY are both earth sciences. ⇨ compare LIFE SCIENCE, NATURAL SCIENCE

**ˈearth-shatter·ing** *adj.* having a very great effect on or of great importance: *an earth-shattering discovery*

**earth·work** /ˈɜːθwɜːk; *NAmE* ˈɜːrθwɜːrk/ *noun* [usually pl.] a large bank of earth that was built long ago in the past and used as a defence

**earth·worm** /ˈɜːθwɜːm; *NAmE* ˈɜːrθwɜːrm/ *noun* a common long thin WORM that lives in soil

**earthy** /ˈɜːθi; *NAmE* ˈɜːrθi/ *adj.* (**earth·ier**, **earthi·est**) **1** connected with the body, sex , etc. in an open and direct way that some people find rude or embarrassing: *an earthy sense of humour* **2** of or like earth or soil: *earthy colours* ▸ **earthi·ness** *noun* [U]

**ear·wax** /ˈɪəwæks; *NAmE* ˈɪrw-/ *noun* [U] the yellow substance produced inside the ear to protect it

**ear·wig** /ˈɪəwɪɡ; *NAmE* ˈɪrwɪɡ/ *noun* a small brown insect with a long body and two curved pointed parts called PINCERS that stick out at the back end of its body

**ear·worm** /ˈɪəwɜːm; *NAmE* ˈɪrwɜːrm/ *noun* a song or tune that stays in your head for a long time after you have heard it

**ease** 🔑+ C1 /iːz/ *noun*, *verb*

▪ *noun* [U] **1** 🔑+ C1 lack of difficulty: **with ~** *He passed the exam with ease.* ◊ *The ease with which he learns languages is astonishing.* ◊ **for ~ of sth** *All important points are numbered for ease of reference* (= so that you can find them easily). ◊ *This computer is popular for its good design and ease of use.* **2** the state of feeling relaxed or comfortable without worries, problems or pain: *In his retirement, he lived a life of ease.*

**IDM** **(stand) at 'ease** used as a command to soldiers to tell them to stand with their feet apart and their hands behind their backs ⇨ compare ATTENTION **at (your) 'ease** relaxed and confident and not nervous or embarrassed: *I never feel completely at ease with him.* **put sb at (their) 'ease** to make sb feel relaxed and confident, not nervous or embarrassed ⇨ more at ILL *adj.*, MIND *n.*

▪ *verb* **1** 🔑+ C1 [I, T] to become less unpleasant, painful or severe; to make sth less unpleasant, etc. SYN **alleviate**: *The pain immediately eased.* ◊ **~ sth** *This should help ease the pain.* ◊ *The plan should ease traffic congestion in the town.* ◊ *It would ease my mind* (= make me less worried) *to know that she was settled.* **2** 🔑+ C1 [T] **~ sth** to make sth easier: *Ramps have been built to ease access for the disabled.* **3** [I, T] to move slowly and carefully; to move sb/sth slowly and carefully: **+ adv./prep.** *He eased slowly forwards.* ◊ **~ sb/sth + adv./prep.** *She eased herself into a chair.* ◊ *He eased off* (= took off) *his shoes.* **4** [T, I] **~(sth)** to make sth less tight and more relaxed; to become less tight and more relaxed SYN **relax**: *Ease your grip on the wheel a little.* **5** [I, T] **~(sth)** to become or make sth lower in price or value SYN **reduce**: *Share prices eased back from yesterday's levels.*

**PHRV** **ˈease into sth | ˈease yourself/sb into sth** to become or help sb to become familiar with sth new, especially a new job **ˌease ˈoff** to become less strong, unpleasant, etc.; to: *We waited until the traffic had eased off.* **ˌease ˈoff (on) sth** to do, eat, drink, etc. less of sth SYN **ease ˈup on**: *Ease off the training a few days before the race.* **ˌease sb↔ˈout (of sth)** to force sb to leave a job or position of authority, especially by making it difficult or unpleasant for them over a period of time **ˌease ˈup** **1** to reduce the speed at which you are travelling **2** to become less strong, unpleasant, etc. **ˌease ˈup on sth** to do, eat, drink, etc. less of sth SYN **ease off**: *You need to ease up on all this travelling.*

**easel** /ˈiːzl/ *noun* a wooden frame to hold a picture while it is being painted

**ease·ment** /ˈiːzmənt/ *noun* [U] **1** (*law*) the right to cross or use sb's land for a particular purpose **2** (*literary*) a state or feeling of peace or happiness

**eas·ily** 🔑 A2 S /ˈiːzəli/ *adv.* **1** 🔑 A2 without problems or difficulty: *The museum is easily accessible by car.* ◊ *I can easily finish it tonight.* ◊ *Learning languages doesn't come easily to him.* **2** very probably; very likely: *Are you sure you locked the gate? You could easily have forgotten.* ◊ *The situation might all too easily have become a disaster.* **3 ~ the best, nicest, etc.** without doubt; definitely: *It's easily the best play I've seen this year.* **4** quickly; more quickly than is usual: *I get bored easily.* ◊ *He's easily distracted.*

**east** 🔑 A1 /iːst/ *noun*, *adj.*, *adv.*

▪ *noun* [U, sing.] (*abbr.* **E**) **1** 🔑 A1 *usually* **the east** the direction that you look towards to see the sun rise; one of the four

main points of the COMPASS: *Which way is east?* ◊ *A gale was blowing from the east.* ◊ **to the ~ (of …)** *a town to the east of* (= further east than) *Chicago* ⊃ picture at COMPASS ⊃ compare NORTH, SOUTH, WEST **2** 🔑 **A1 the east, the East** the eastern part of a country, region or city: *The east of the country is especially popular with tourists.* ◊ **in the ~** *I was born in the East, but now live in San Francisco.* **3** 🔑 **A1 the East** the countries of Asia, especially China, Japan and India **4 the East** (in the past) the Communist countries of Central and Eastern Europe: *East–West relations*
- *adj.* [only before noun] **1** 🔑 **A1** (also **East**) (*abbr.* **E**) in or towards the east: *East Africa* ◊ *They live on the east coast.* **2 an east wind** blows from the east ⊃ compare EASTERLY
- *adv.* **1** 🔑 **A1** towards the east: *The house faces east.* **2** 🔑 **A1** **~ of sth** nearer to the east than sth: *They live five miles east of Oxford.*

**east·bound** /ˈiːstbaʊnd/ *adj.* travelling or leading towards the east: *eastbound traffic* ◊ *the eastbound carriageway of the motorway*

**East Coast ˈFever** *noun* [U] a disease that cows in Africa can get by being bitten by a TICK (= a small insect) and that can kill them

**the ˌEast ˈEnd** *noun* an area of East London traditionally connected with working people ▶ **East ˈEnder** *noun*: *He's a real East Ender.*

**Easter** /ˈiːstə(r)/ *noun* **1** [U, C] (also **Easter Day**, **Easter ˈSunday**) (in the Christian religion) a Sunday in March or April when Christians remember the death of Christ and his return to life **2** (also **Easter·time**) the period that includes Easter Day and the days close to it: *the Easter holidays/vacation*

**Easter egg** *noun* **1** chocolate in the shape of an egg that is given as a present and eaten at Easter **2** an egg with a shell that is painted and decorated at Easter

**east·er·ly** /ˈiːstəli; *NAmE* -stərli/ *adj., noun*
- *adj.* **1** [only before noun] in or towards the east: *travelling in an easterly direction* **2** [usually before noun] (of winds) blowing from the east: *a cold easterly wind* ⊃ compare EAST
- *noun* (*pl.* -ies) a wind that blows from the east

**east·ern** 🕛 **B1** /ˈiːstən; *NAmE* -stərn/ *adj.* **1** 🔑 **B1 Eastern** (*abbr.* **E**) [only before noun] located in the east or facing east: *eastern Spain* ◊ *Eastern Europe* ◊ *the eastern slopes of the mountain* **2** 🔑 **B1** usually **Eastern** connected with the part of the world that is to the east of Europe: *Eastern culture/cookery*

**ˌEastern ˈDaylight ˌTime** *noun* [U] (*abbr.* **EDT**) the time used in the summer in the eastern US and Canada, which is four hours earlier than UTC

**east·ern·er** /ˈiːstənə(r); *NAmE* -stərn-/ *noun* a person who comes from or lives in the eastern part of a country, especially the US

**east·ern·most** /ˈiːstənməʊst; *NAmE* -stərn-/ *adj.* furthest east: *the easternmost city in Europe*

**the ˌEastern ˈOrthodox ˈChurch** *noun* = ORTHODOX CHURCH

**ˌEastern ˈStandard ˌTime** *noun* [U] (*abbr.* **EST**) (also **Eastern time**) the time used in the winter in the eastern US and Canada, which is five hours earlier than UTC

**ˈEastern time** *noun* [U] the standard time in the eastern US and parts of Canada

**East·er·time** /ˈiːstətaɪm; *NAmE* -stərt-/ *noun* [U, C] = EASTER (2)

**east-north-ˈeast** *noun* [sing.] (*abbr.* **ENE**) the direction at an equal distance between east and north-east ▶ **east-north-ˈeast** *adv.*

**east-south-ˈeast** *noun* [sing.] (*abbr.* **ESE**) the direction at an equal distance between east and south-east ▶ **east-south-ˈeast** *adv.*

**east·wards** /ˈiːstwədz; *NAmE* -wərdz/ (*especially BrE*) (also **east·ward** *especially in NAmE*) *adv.* towards the east: *to go/look/turn eastwards* ▶ **east·ward** *adj.*: *in an eastward direction*

**easy** 🕛 **A1** /ˈiːzi/ *adj., adv.*
- *adj.* (**eas·ier**, **easi·est**) **1** 🔑 **A1** not difficult; done or obtained without a lot of effort or problems: *an easy way to make 

---

491 **eat**

bread* ◊ *an easy win/victory* ◊ *It's much easier if you speak the language.* ◊ **~ to do sth** *It's easy to forget how we lived before the internet.* ◊ *The tool is quick and easy to use.* ◊ *Several schools are within easy reach* (= not far away). ◊ **~ for sb (to do sth)** *It's easy for you to criticize.* ◊ *He didn't make it easy for me to leave.* **OPP hard 2** 🔑 **A2** comfortable, relaxed and not worried: *He has not had an easy life.* ◊ *I don't feel easy about letting the kids go out alone.* **OPP uneasy 3** [only before noun] open to attack; not able to defend yourself: *She's an easy target for their criticisms.* ◊ *The baby fish are easy prey for birds.* **4** [only before noun] pleasant and friendly **SYN easy-going**: *He had an easy manner.* **OPP awkward 5** [not usually before noun] (*informal, disapproving*) (of women) willing to have sex with many different people ⊃ see also EASILY ▶ **easi·ness** *noun* [U]

**IDM** **as ˌeasy as ˈanything/as ˈpie/as ABˈC/as ˌfalling off a ˈlog** (*informal*) very easy or very easily **ˌeasy ˈmeat** a person who seems easy to defeat or cheat: *Rogue traders saw elderly people as easy meat for overcharging.* **ˌeasy ˈmoney** (*informal*) money that you get without having to work very hard for it **ˌeasy on the ˈear/ˈeye** (*informal*) pleasant to listen to or look at **have an ˌeasy ˈtime (of it)** to have no difficulties or problems **I'm ˈeasy** (*informal*) used to say that you do not have a strong opinion when sb has offered you a choice: *'Do you want to watch this or the news?' 'Oh, I'm easy. It's up to you.'* **on ˈeasy street** (*old-fashioned, informal*) enjoying a comfortable way of life with plenty of money **take the ˌeasy way ˈout** to end a difficult situation by choosing the simplest solution even if it is not the best one ⊃ more at FREE *adj.*, OPTION *n.*, REACH *n.*, RIDE *n.*, TOUCH *n.*
- *adv.* (**eas·ier**, **easi·est**) used to tell sb to be careful when doing sth: *Easy with that chair—one of its legs is loose.*

**IDM** **be ˌeasier ˌsaid than ˈdone** (*saying*) to be much more difficult to do than to talk about: *'Why don't you get yourself a job?' 'That's easier said than done.'* **ˌbreathe/ˌrest/ˌsleep ˈeasy** to relax and stop worrying: *You can rest easy—I'm not going to tell anyone.* **ˌeasy ˌcome, ˌeasy ˈgo** (*saying*) used to mean that sb does not care very much about money or possessions especially if they spend it or lose sth **ˌeasy ˈdoes it** (*informal*) used to tell sb to do sth, or move sth, slowly and carefully **go ˌeasy on sb** (*informal*) used to tell sb to treat a person in a gentle way and not to be too angry or severe: *Go easy on her—she's having a really hard time at the moment.* **go ˌeasy on/with sth** (*informal*) used to tell sb not to use too much of sth: *Go easy on the sugar.* **not come ˈeasy (to sb)** to be difficult for sb to do: *Talking about my problems doesn't come easy to me.* **ˌstand ˈeasy** used as a command to soldiers who are already STANDING AT EASE to tell them that they can stand in an even more relaxed way **take it ˈeasy** (*informal*) used to tell sb not to be worried or angry: *Take it easy! Don't panic.* **take it/things ˈeasy** to relax and avoid working too hard or doing too much: *The doctor told me to take it easy for a few weeks.*

**ˈeasy chair** *noun* a large comfortable chair, usually an ARMCHAIR: *to sit in an easy chair*

**ˌeasy-ˈgoing** *adj.* relaxed and happy to accept things without worrying or getting angry

**ˌeasy ˈlistening** *noun* [U] music that is pleasant and relaxing but that some people think is not very interesting

**easy-peasy** /ˌiːzi ˈpiːzi/ *adj.* (*BrE, informal*) (used especially by children) very easy

**eat** 🕛 **A1** /iːt/ *verb* (**ate** /et, eɪt; *NAmE* eɪt/, **eaten** /ˈiːtn/) **1** 🔑 **A1** [I, T] to put food in your mouth, bite it and SWALLOW it: *I was too nervous to eat.* ◊ *to eat well/healthily* ◊ *She doesn't eat properly* (= doesn't eat food that is good for her). ◊ **~ sth** *I don't eat meat.* ◊ *to eat breakfast/lunch/dinner* ◊ *Would you like something to eat?* ◊ *I couldn't eat another thing* (= I have had enough food). **2** 🔑 **A1** [I] to have a meal: *Where shall we eat tonight?* ◊ *We ate at a pizzeria.*

**WORDFINDER** binge, calorie, diet, digest, fattening, food, meal, restaurant, taste

---

🅞 Oxford Phrasal Academic Lexicon (OPAL) written and spoken word lists | 🅦 OPAL written word list | 🅢 OPAL spoken word list

# eatable

**IDM** **eat sb aˈlive** (*informal*) **1** to criticize or punish sb severely because you are extremely angry with them: *He'll eat you alive if he ever finds out.* **2** to defeat sb completely in an argument, a competition, etc: *The defence lawyers are going to eat you alive tomorrow.* **3** [usually passive] (of insects, etc.) to bite sb many times: *I was being eaten alive by mosquitoes.* **eat dirt** (*NAmE*) to accept bad treatment and being made to feel small or stupid: *Her mother ate dirt in poorly-paid jobs just so the family could stay in the country.* **eat, drink and be ˈmerry** (*saying*) said to encourage sb to enjoy life now, while they can, and not to think of the future **eat your ˈheart out!** (*informal*) used to compare two things and say that one of them is better: *Look at him dance! Eat your heart out, Fred Astaire* (= he dances even better than Fred Astaire). **eat your ˈheart out (for sb/sth)** to feel very unhappy, especially because you want sb/sth you cannot have **eat humble ˈpie** (*NAmE also* **eat ˈcrow**) to say and show that you are sorry for a mistake that you made **ORIGIN** From a pun on the old word **umbles**, meaning 'offal', which was considered to be food for poor people. **eat like a ˈhorse** (*informal*) to eat a lot: *She may be thin, but she eats like a horse.* **eat out of your/sb's ˈhand** to trust sb and be willing to do what they say: *She'll have them eating out of her hand in no time.* **eat sb out of house and ˈhome** (*informal, often humorous*) to eat a lot of sb else's food **eat your ˈwords** to admit that what you said was wrong: *When he told her she would fail, she swore she would make him eat his words.* **I could eat a ˈhorse** (*informal*) used to say that you are very hungry **I'll eat my ˈhat** (*informal*) used to say that you think sth is very unlikely to happen: *If she's here on time, I'll eat my hat!* **what's ˈeating him, etc?** (*informal*) used to ask what sb is annoyed or worried about ⊃ more at CAKE *n.*, DOG *n.*

**PHRV** **ˌeat sth ↔ aˈway** to reduce or destroy sth gradually **SYN** erode: *The coastline is being eaten away year by year.* **ˌeat aˈway at sb** to worry sb over a period of time: *The thought of her child left helpless and alone ate away at her.* **ˌeat aˈway at sth** to reduce or destroy sth gradually: *Woodworm had eaten away at the door frame.* ◊ *His constant criticism ate away at her self-confidence.* **ˌeat ˈin** to eat food in a restaurant rather than buying it to take away **ˈeat into sth** **1** to use up a part of sth, especially sb's money or time: *Those repair bills have really eaten into my savings.* **2** to destroy or damage the surface of sth: *Rust had eaten into the metal.* **ˌeat ˈout** to have a meal in a restaurant, etc. rather than at home: *Do you feel like eating out tonight?* **ˌeat ˈup** | **ˌeat sth ↔ ˈup** to eat all of sth: *Eat up! We've got to go out soon.* ◊ *Come on. Eat up your potatoes.* **ˌeat sb ˈup** [usually passive] to fill sb with a particular emotion so that they cannot think of anything else: *She was eaten up by regrets.* **ˌeat sth ↔ ˈup** to use sth in large quantities: *Legal costs had eaten up all the savings she had.*

**eatˈable** /ˈiːtəbl/ *adj.* good enough to be eaten ⊃ see also EDIBLE

**eater** /ˈiːtə(r)/ *noun* (usually after an adjective or a noun) a person or an animal that eats a particular thing or in a particular way: *We're not great meat eaters.* ◊ *He's a big eater* (= he eats a lot).

**eatery** /ˈiːtəri/ (*pl.* **-ies**) *noun* (*informal*) a restaurant or other place that serves food

**ˈeat-in** *adj.* [only before noun] (of a kitchen) big enough for eating in as well as cooking in

**eating** /ˈiːtɪŋ/ *noun* [U] the act of eating sth: *healthy eating* ⊃ see also MAN-EATING **IDM** SEE PROOF *n.*

**ˈeating disorder** *noun* an emotional DISORDER that causes eating habits that are not normal, for example ANOREXIA

**eats** /iːts/ *noun* [pl.] (*informal*) food, especially at a party or social event

**eau de cologne** /ˌəʊ də kəˈləʊn/ *noun* [U] = COLOGNE

**eau de toilette** /ˌəʊ də twɑːˈlet/ *noun* [U] a kind of PERFUME (= a pleasant-smelling liquid for the skin) that contains a lot of water and does not smell very strong **SYN** toilet water

---

**eaves** /iːvz/ *noun* [pl.] the lower edges of a roof that stick out over the walls: *birds nesting under the eaves*

**eavesˈdrop** /ˈiːvzdrɒp/; *NAmE* -drɑːp/ *verb* [I] (-pp-) ~ **(on sb/sth)** to listen secretly to what other people are saying: *We caught him eavesdropping outside the window.* ▶ **eavesˈdropper** *noun*

**eavesˈtrough** /ˈiːvztrɒf/; *NAmE* -trɔːf/ *noun* (*CanE*) = GUTTER (1)

**eBay™** /ˈiːbeɪ/ *noun* [U] a website on the internet where people can sell goods to other users of the website, usually to the one who offers the most money: *He buys rare baseball cards on eBay.* ▶ **eBay** *verb* **~ sth**

**ebb** /eb/ *noun, verb*
■ *noun* **the ebb** [usually sing.] the period of time when the sea flows away from the land: *the ebb tide*
**IDM** **the ˌebb and ˈflow (of sth/sb)** the repeated, often regular, movement from one state to another; the repeated change in level, numbers or amount: *the ebb and flow of the seasons* ◊ *She sat in silence enjoying the ebb and flow of conversation.* ⊃ more at LOW *adj.*
■ *verb* **1** [I] (*formal*) (of the TIDE in the sea) to move away from the land **SYN** go out **OPP** flow **2** [I] **~ (away)** to become gradually weaker or less **SYN** decrease: *The pain was ebbing.* ◊ *As night fell, our enthusiasm began to ebb away.*

**ˈe-bike** (*also* **eˌlectric ˈbike**) *noun* a type of bicycle that you can ride by pushing the PEDALS with your feet or by using a small electric motor

**Ebola** /iˈbəʊlə/ (*also* **Eˌbola ˈfever**) *noun* a very serious disease, caused by a virus, that causes internal parts of the body to lose blood and usually ends in death

**ebony** /ˈebəni/ *noun, adj.*
■ *noun* [U] the hard black wood of various tropical trees: *an ebony carving*
■ *adj.* black in colour: *ebony skin*

**ˈe-book** *noun* a book that is displayed on a computer screen or on an electronic device that is held in the hand, instead of being printed on paper

**ebulˈlient** /ɪˈbʌliənt, ɪˈbʊl-/ *adj.* (*formal*) full of confidence, energy and good humour: *The Prime Minister was in ebullient mood.* ▶ **ebulˈlience** /-əns/ *noun* [U] **ebulˈliently** *adv.*

**ˈe-business** *noun* [U] = E-COMMERCE

**ˈe-card** *noun* a message that is like a card that you send to sb on their birthday, etc., but that is displayed on a screen instead of being printed on paper and usually opened through a HYPERLINK in an email

**ecˈcentric** /ɪkˈsentrɪk/ *adj.* considered by other people to be strange or unusual: *eccentric behaviour/clothes* ◊ *an eccentric aunt* ⊃ WORDFINDER NOTE at BEHAVIOUR ▶ **ecˈcentric** *noun*: *Most people considered him a harmless eccentric.* **ecˈcentrically** /-kli/ *adv.*

**eccentricity** /ˌeksenˈtrɪsəti/ (*pl.* **-ies**) *noun* **1** [U] behaviour that people think is strange or unusual; the quality of being unusual and different from other people: *As a teacher, she had a reputation for eccentricity.* ◊ *Arthur was noted for the eccentricity of his clothes.* **2** [C, usually pl.] an unusual act or habit: *We all have our little eccentricities.*

**eccleˈsiastic** /ɪˌkliːziˈæstɪk/ *noun* (*formal*) a priest or minister in the Christian Church

**eccleˈsiastical** /ɪˌkliːziˈæstɪkl/ *adj.* [usually before noun] connected with the Christian Church

**ECG** /ˌiː siː ˈdʒiː/ (*NAmE also* **EKG**) *noun* a medical test that measures and records electrical activity of the heart (the abbreviation for 'electrocardiogram')

**echelon** /ˈeʃəlɒn/; *NAmE* -lɑːn/ *noun* **1** [usually pl.] a rank or position of authority in an organization or a society: *the lower/upper/top/higher echelons of the Civil Service* **2** an arrangement of soldiers, planes, etc. in which each one is behind and to the side of the one in front

**echidna** /ɪˈkɪdnə/ (*also* **ˌspiny ˈanteater**) *noun* an Australasian insect-eating animal that has a long nose, sharp CLAWS on its feet, and sharp SPINES on its body

**echinacea** /ˌekɪˈneɪʃə/; *BrE also* -ˈneɪsiə/ *noun* [U, C] a plant similar to a DAISY that is thought to help the body recover if sb is ill and to fight infection

**echo** /ˈekəʊ/ verb, noun
■ **verb** (**echoes**, **echo·ing**, **echoed**, **echoed**) **1** [I] if a sound **echoes**, it is reflected off a wall, the side of a mountain, etc. so that you can hear it again SYN **reverberate**: *Her footsteps echoed in the empty room.* ◊ *The gunshot echoed through the forest.* **2** [I, T] to send back and repeat a sound; to be full of a sound SYN **reverberate**: *The whole house echoed.* ◊ *~ to / with sth The street echoed with the cries of children.* ◊ *~ sth (back) The valley echoed back his voice.* **3** [T] *~ sth* to repeat an idea or opinion because you agree with it: *This is a view echoed by many on the right of the party.* **4** [T] *+ speech* | *~ sth* to repeat what sb else has just said, especially because you find it surprising: *'He's gone!' Viv echoed.*
■ **noun** (*pl.* **-oes**) **1** [C] the reflecting of sound off a wall or inside a particular space so that a noise appears to be repeated; a sound that is reflected back in this way: *There was an echo on the phone and I couldn't hear clearly.* ◊ *The hills sent back a faint echo.* ◊ *the echo of footsteps running down the corridor* **2** the fact of an idea, event, etc. being like another and reminding you of it; sth that reminds you of sth else: *Yesterday's crash has grim echoes of previous disasters.* **3** an opinion or attitude that agrees with or repeats one already expressed or thought: *His words were an echo of what she had heard many times before.* ◊ *The speech found an echo in the hearts of many of the audience* (= they agreed with it).

ˈ**echo chamber** *noun* an environment in which sb encounters only opinions and beliefs similar to their own, and does not have to consider alternatives

**echo·lo·ca·tion** /ˌekəʊləʊˈkeɪʃn/ *noun* [U] the use of reflected sound waves for finding things, especially by creatures such as DOLPHINS and BATS

ˈ**e-cigarette** (*also* **electronic cigarette**) *noun* an electronic device, like a cigarette in shape, that contains NICOTINE that you can take into your lungs through your mouth, and that produces VAPOUR that looks like cigarette smoke

**eclair** /ɪˈkleə(r)/; *NAmE* ɪˈkler/ *noun* a long thin cake for one person, made of light PASTRY, filled with cream and usually with chocolate on top ⊃ compare CREAM PUFF (1), PROFITEROLE

**eclamp·sia** /ɪˈklæmpsɪə/ *noun* [U] (*medical*) a condition in which a pregnant woman has high blood pressure and CONVULSIONS, which can be dangerous to the woman and the baby ⊃ compare PRE-ECLAMPSIA

**eclec·tic** /ɪˈklektɪk/ *adj.* (*formal*) not following one style or set of ideas but choosing from or using a wide variety: *She has very eclectic tastes in literature.* ▶ **eclec·tic·al·ly** /-kli/ *adv.* **eclec·ti·cism** /-tɪsɪzəm/ *noun* [U]

**eclipse** /ɪˈklɪps/ *noun*, *verb*
■ **noun 1** [C] an occasion when the moon passes between the earth and the sun so that you cannot see all or part of the sun for a time; an occasion when the earth passes between the moon and the sun so that you cannot see all or part of the moon for a time: *an eclipse of the sun/moon* ◊ *a total/partial eclipse* ⊃ WORDFINDER NOTE at SUN **2** [sing., U] a loss of importance, power, etc. especially because sb/sth else has become more important, powerful, etc: *The election result marked the eclipse of the right wing.* ◊ *in ~ Her work was in eclipse for most of the 20th century.*
■ **verb 1** [often passive] *~ sth* (of the moon or the earth) to cause an eclipse of the sun or the moon **2** *~ sb/sth* to make sb/sth seem neither exciting nor important by comparison SYN **outshine**, **overshadow**: *Though a talented player, he was completely eclipsed by his brother.*

**eco-** /iːkəʊ, iːkə; *BrE also* iːˈkɒ; *NAmE also* iːˈkɑː/ combining form (in nouns, adjectives and adverbs) connected with the environment: *eco-friendly* ◊ *eco-clothing* (= clothes made from environmentally friendly materials) ⊃ see also ECOTERRORISM

ˌ**eco-ˈfriend·ly** *adj.* not harmful to the environment: *eco-friendly products*

**E. coli** /ˌiː ˈkəʊlaɪ/ *noun* [U] a type of bacteria that lives inside humans and some animals, some forms of which can cause FOOD POISONING

**eco·logic·al** /ˌiːkəˈlɒdʒɪkl/; *NAmE* -ˈlɑːdʒ-/ *adj.* **1** connected with the relation of plants and living creatures to each other and to their environment: *We risk upsetting the ecological balance of the area.* ◊ *an ecological disaster* (= one that alters the whole balance of ecology in an area) **2** interested in and concerned about the ecology of a place: *the ecological movement* ▶ **eco·logic·al·ly** /-kli/ *adv.*: *The system is both practical and ecologically sound.*

ˌ**eco·logical ˈfootprint** (*also* **footprint**) *noun* a measure of the amount of the earth's resources used by a person or a population that lives in a particular way: *the ecological footprint of the average Canadian*

**ecol·o·gist** /iˈkɒlədʒɪst; *NAmE* iˈkɑːl-/ *noun* **1** a scientist who studies ecology **2** a person who is interested in ecology and believes the environment should be protected

**ecol·ogy** /iˈkɒlədʒi; *NAmE* iˈkɑːl-/ *noun* [U, C] (*pl.* **-ies**) the relation of plants and living creatures to each other and to their environment; the study of this: *plant/animal/human ecology* ◊ *the ecology movement* ◊ *Oil pollution could damage the fragile ecology of the coral reefs.*

ˌ**e-ˈcommerce** (*also* **e-business**) *noun* [U] business that is conducted on the internet: *Travel companies have moved from the traditional bricks and mortar environment to e-commerce.*

**eco·nom·ic** /ˌiːkəˈnɒmɪk, ˌek-; *NAmE* -ˈnɑːm-/ *adj.* **1** [only before noun] connected with the trade, industry and development of wealth of a country, an area or a society: *They discussed social, economic and political issues.* ◊ *economic growth/development* ◊ *the worst economic crisis since the war* ◊ *There will be no quick economic recovery.* ◊ *the government's economic policy* ◊ *the current economic climate* ⊃ see also SOCIO-ECONOMIC **2** (especially in negative sentences) (of a process, a business or an activity) producing enough profit to continue SYN **profitable**: *The college was not achieving the numbers of students needed to make it economic.* ◊ *it is ~ (for sb/sth) to do sth They found it was not economic to sell their milk to the supermarkets.* OPP **uneconomic**
⊃ SYNONYMS at SUCCESSFUL

▼ SYNONYMS

**economic**
financial • commercial • monetary • budgetary
These words all describe activities or situations that are connected with the use of money, especially by a business or country.

**economic** connected with the trade, industry and development of wealth of a country, an area or a society: *This book deals with the social, economic and political issues of the period.*

**financial** connected with money and finance: *She had got into financial difficulties.* ◊ *Tokyo is a major financial centre.*

**commercial** connected with the buying and selling of goods and services.

**monetary** (*formal or finance*) connected with money, especially all the money in a country: *closer European monetary union*

**budgetary** (*finance*) connected with a budget (= the money available or a plan of how it will be spent).

PATTERNS
- economic / financial / commercial / monetary / budgetary affairs / decisions
- the economic / financial / commercial / budgetary climate
- the economic / financial / commercial side of sth
- a(n) economic / financial / commercial centre

**eco·nom·ic·al** /ˌiːkəˈnɒmɪkl, ˌek-; *NAmE* -ˈnɑːm-/ *adj.* **1** providing good service or value in relation to the amount of time or money spent: *an economical car to run* (= one that does not use too much petrol) ◊ *It would be more economical to buy the bigger size.* OPP **uneconomical 2** using no more of sth than is necessary: *an economical use of space* ◊ *an economical prose style* (= one that uses no unnecessary words) OPP **uneconomical 3** not spending more money than necessary SYN **frugal**: *He was economical in all areas of his life.*
IDM **be economical with the ˈtruth** if you say that sb has been economical with the truth, you mean that they left

# economically

▼ **WHICH WORD?**

**economic / economical**
- **Economic** means 'connected with the economy of a country or an area, or with the money that a society or an individual has': *the government's economic policy* ◇ *the economic aspects of having children.*
  - ⇨ see also ECONOMY (1)
- **Economical** means 'spending money or using something in a careful way that avoids waste': *It is usually economical to buy washing powder in large quantities.*
  - ⇨ see also ECONOMY (3)

out some important facts, but you do not want to say that they were lying

**eco·nom·ic·al·ly** W /ˌiːkəˈnɒmɪkli, ˌek-; NAmE -ˈnɑːm-/ *adv.* **1** in a way connected with the trade, industry and development of wealth of a country, an area or a society: *The factory is no longer economically viable.* ◇ *Economically, the centre of Spain has lost its dominant role.* ◇ *the economically active/inactive population* (= those who are employed or available for work/those who are not) **2** in a way that provides good service or value in relation to the amount of time or money spent: *I'll do the job as economically as possible.* **3** in a way that uses no more of sth than is necessary: *The design is intended to use space as economically as possible.* ◇ *She writes elegantly and economically.*

**eˌconomic ˈmigrant** *noun* a person who moves from one country or area to another in order to improve their standard of living: *They claimed they were political refugees and not economic migrants.*

**eco·nom·ics** B2 /ˌiːkəˈnɒmɪks, ˌek-; NAmE -ˈnɑːm-/ *noun* **1** [U] the study of how a society organizes its money, trade and industry: *He studied politics and economics at Yale.* ◇ *Keynesian/Marxist economics* ⇨ see also HOME ECONOMICS **2** C1 [pl., U] the way in which money influences, or is organized within, an area of business or society: *The economics of the project are very encouraging.*

**econ·o·mist** B2 /ɪˈkɒnəmɪst; NAmE ɪˈkɑːn-/ *noun* a person who studies or writes about economics: *the World Bank's* **chief economist**

**econ·o·mize** (*BrE also* **-ise**) /ɪˈkɒnəmaɪz; NAmE ɪˈkɑːn-/ *verb* [I] ~ (**on sth**) to use less money, time, etc. than you normally use: *Old people often try to economize on heating, thus endangering their health.* ⇨ SYNONYMS at SAVE

**econ·omy** B1 /ɪˈkɒnəmi; NAmE ɪˈkɑːn-/ *noun* (*pl.* **-ies**) **1** B1 (*often* **the economy**) [C] the relationship between production, trade and the supply of money in a particular country or region: *the world/global economy* ◇ *He favours tax cuts to* **stimulate the economy**. ◇ *to boost/revive/grow the economy* ◇ *Over the past few years, the country's economy has grown at a record pace.* ⇨ see also BLACK ECONOMY, CONTROLLED ECONOMY, GIG ECONOMY, MARKET ECONOMY, MIXED ECONOMY, PLANNED ECONOMY, POLITICAL ECONOMY, SHARING ECONOMY, UNDERGROUND ECONOMY ⇨ WORDFINDER NOTE at MONEY **2** B2 [C] a country, when you are thinking about its economic system: *Ireland was one of the fastest-growing economies in Western Europe in the 1990s.* **3** B2 [C, U] the use of resources in a way that avoids waste: *The company has improved the* **fuel economy** *of all its vehicles.* ◇ *It's a* **false economy** *to buy cheap clothes* (= it seems cheaper but it is not really since they do not last very long). **4** [U] (in compound nouns) offering good value for money: *Buy the large* **economy pack**. **5 economies** [pl.] ways of saving money: *We need to* **make substantial economies**. **6** ~ **of sth** [U, sing.] a way of using as little of sth as possible: *a technique based on* **economy of effort** ◇ *She writes with a great* **economy of words** (= using only the necessary words). **7** (*also* **economy class**) [U] the cheapest class of air travel: *We flew economy.* ◇ *an economy fare/ticket/seat/passenger*

**eco·sys·tem** /ˈiːkəʊsɪstəm/ *noun* all the plants and living creatures in a particular area considered in relation to their physical environment

**eco·ter·ror·ism** /ˈiːkəʊterərɪzəm/ *noun* [U] **1** violent activities that are carried out in order to draw attention to issues relating to the environment **2** deliberate damage to the environment, done in order to draw attention to a political issue ▶ **eco·ter·ror·ist** /-terərɪst/ *noun*

**eco·tour·ism** /ˈiːkəʊtʊərɪzəm, -tɔːr-; NAmE -tʊr-/ *noun* [U] organized holidays that are designed so that the tourists damage the environment as little as possible, especially when some of the money they pay is used to protect the local environment and animals ▶ **eco·tour·ist** /-rɪst/ *noun*

**eco·type** /ˈiːkəʊtaɪp/ *noun* (*biology*) the type or race of a plant or animal that has adapted to live in particular local conditions

**ec·stasy** /ˈekstəsi/ *noun* (*pl.* **-ies**) **1** [U, C] a feeling or state of very great happiness SYN **bliss 2** (*also* **Ecstasy**) [U] (*abbr.* **E**) an illegal drug, taken especially by young people at parties, clubs, etc.

**ec·stat·ic** /ɪkˈstætɪk/ *adj.* very happy, excited and enthusiastic; feeling or showing great enthusiasm SYN **delighted**: *Sally was ecstatic about her new job.* ◇ *ecstatic applause/praise/reviews* ⇨ SYNONYMS at EXCITED ▶ **ec·stat·ic·al·ly** /-kli/ *adv.*

**ECT** /ˌiː siː ˈtiː/ *abbr.* ELECTROCONVULSIVE THERAPY

**-ec·tomy** /ektəmi/ *combining form* (in nouns) a medical operation in which part of the body is removed: *appendectomy* (= removal of the APPENDIX)

**ec·top·ic ˈpregnancy** /ekˌtɒpɪk ˈpreɡnənsi; NAmE -ˌtɑːp-/ *noun* (*medical*) a PREGNANCY in which the baby starts to develop outside the mother's WOMB

**ecto·plasm** /ˈektəʊplæzəm/ *noun* [U] **1** (*old-fashioned, biology*) the outer layer of the JELLY-like substance inside cells **2** a substance that is said to come from the body of sb who is communicating with the spirit of a dead person, allowing the spirit to have a form

**ecu·men·ic·al** /ˌekjuːˈmenɪkl; BrE also ˌiːk-/ *adj.* involving or joining together members of different branches of the Christian Church ▶ **ecu·men·ic·ally** /-kli/ *adv.*

**ecu·men·ism** /ɪˈkjuːmənɪzəm/ *noun* [U] the principle or aim of joining different branches of the Christian Church together

**ec·zema** /ˈeksmə; NAmE ɪɡˈziːmə, ˈeksɪmə/ *noun* [U] a skin condition in which areas of skin become red, rough and ITCHY

**ed.** (*also* **Ed.**) *abbr.* (in writing) EDITED (BY), EDITION, EDITOR: *'Eighteenth Century Women Poets', Ed. Lonsdale* ◇ *7th ed.*

**-ed, -d** HELP The pronunciation is formed by adding /d/ after vowels and voiced consonants, /t/ after voiceless consonants, and /ɪd/ after /t/ or /d/. *suffix* **1** (in adjectives) having; having the characteristics of: *talented* ◇ *bearded* ◇ *diseased* **2** (makes the past tense and past participle of regular verbs): *hated* ◇ *walked* ◇ *loved*

**Edam** /ˈiːdæm/ *noun* [U, C] a type of round yellow Dutch cheese that is covered with red WAX

**eda·mame** /ˌedəˈmɑːmeɪ, -mi/ *noun* [pl.] fresh green SOYA BEANS

**eddy** /ˈedi/ *noun, verb*
- *noun* (*pl.* **-ies**) a movement of air, dust or water in a circle
- *verb* [I] (**ed·dies, eddy·ing, ed·died, ed·died**) (of air, dust, water, etc.) to move around in a circle SYN **swirl**: *The waves swirled and eddied around the rocks.*

**edema** /ɪˈdiːmə/ (*NAmE*) (*BrE* **oe·dema**) *noun* [U] (*medical*) a condition in which liquid collects in the spaces inside the body and makes it SWELL (= become larger or rounder than normal)

**Eden** /ˈiːdn/ (*also* **the ˌGarden of ˈEden**) *noun* [sing.] (in the Bible) the beautiful garden where Adam and Eve, the first humans, lived before they did sth God had told them not to and were sent away, often seen as a place of happiness and INNOCENCE

---

æ cat | ɑː father | e bed | ɜː fur | ə about | ɪ sit | iː see | i happy | ɒ got (*BrE*) | ɔː saw | ʌ cup | ʊ put | uː too

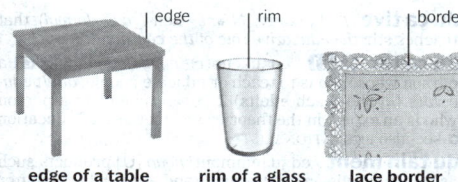

edge of a table   rim of a glass   lace border

## edge ⓘ B1 /edʒ/ noun, verb

■ **noun 1** B1 [C] the outside limit of an object, a surface or an area; the part furthest from the centre: *I gripped the edge of my desk to steady myself.* ◊ **on the ~ of sth** *He stood on the edge of the cliff.* ◊ **Stand the coin on its edge.** ◊ **at the ~ of sth** *a big house on/at the edge of town* ◊ *I sat down at the water's edge.* ➪ see also BLEEDING EDGE, CUTTING EDGE, LEADING EDGE, STRAIGHT EDGE, TRAILING EDGE **2** [C] the sharp part of a knife, BLADE or SWORD that is used for cutting: *Be careful—it has a **sharp edge.*** ➪ see also KNIFE-EDGE **3** (*usually* **the edge**) [sing.] the point at which sth, especially sth bad, may begin to happen SYN **brink**, **verge**: *They had brought the country to the edge of disaster.* **4** [sing.] a slight advantage over sb/sth: *The company needs to improve its **competitive edge**.* ◊ **~ on/over sb/sth** *They have the edge on us.* **5** [sing.] a strong, often exciting, quality: *Her show now has a hard political edge to it.* **6** [sing.] a sharp tone of voice, often showing anger: *He did his best to remain calm, but there was a distinct edge to his voice.* **7 -edged** (in adjectives) having the type of edge or edges mentioned: *a lace-edged handkerchief* ➪ see also GILT-EDGED
IDM **be on ˈedge** to be nervous, excited or easily made angry ➪ SYNONYMS at NERVOUS **on the edge of your ˈseat** very excited and giving your full attention to sth: *The game had the crowd on the edge of their seats.* **take the ˈedge off (sth)** to make sth less strong, less bad, etc: *The sandwich took the edge off my appetite.* ➪ more at FRAY v., PUSH v., RAZOR, ROUGH adj., TEETER, TOOTH
■ **verb 1** [I, T] to move or to move sth slowly and carefully in a particular direction: **+ adv./prep.** *She edged a little closer to me.* ◊ *I edged nervously past the dog.* ◊ **~sth + adv./prep.** *Emily edged her chair forward.* **2** [T, usually passive] to put sth around the edge of sth: **be edged (with/ in sth)** *The handkerchief is edged with lace.* **3** [I] **+ adv./ prep.** to increase or decrease slightly: *Prices edged up 2 per cent in the year to December.*
PHRV ˌedge sb/sth↔ˈout (of sth) to move sb from their position or job gradually, especially when they are not fully aware of what is happening: *She was edged out of the company by the new director.*

**ˈedge ˌcity** *noun* (*NAmE*) a large area of buildings on the edge of a city, usually near a main road

**edgeˌways** /ˈedʒweɪz/ (*BrE*) (*NAmE* **edgeˌwise** /ˈedʒwaɪz/) *adv.* with the edge upwards or forwards; on one side: *You'll only get the desk through the door if you turn it edgeways.*
IDM see WORD n.

**edging** /ˈedʒɪŋ/ *noun* [U, C] something that forms the border or edge of sth, added to make it more attractive, etc.

**edgy** /ˈedʒi/ *adj.* (**edgiˈer**, **edgiˈest**) (*informal*) **1** nervous, especially about what might happen: *She's been very edgy lately.* ◊ *After the recent unrest there is an edgy calm in the capital.* **2** (of a film, book, piece of music, etc.) having a sharp exciting quality: *a clever, edgy film* ▶ **edgiˈly** /-dʒɪli/ *adv.*: *'I'm not sure I can make it tomorrow,' he said edgily.* **ˈedgiˌness** *noun* [U, sing.]

**EDI** /ˌiː diː ˈaɪ/ *noun* [U] (*computing*) a system that is used in business for sending information between different companies' computer systems (the abbreviation for 'electronic data interchange')

**ˈedible** /ˈedəbl/ *adj.* fit or suitable to be eaten; not poisonous: *The food at the hotel was barely edible.* ◊ *edible fungi/ snails/flowers*

**edict** /ˈiːdɪkt/ *noun* [C, U] (*formal*) an official order or statement given by sb in authority SYN **decree**

**edifiˈcation** /ˌedɪfɪˈkeɪʃn/ *noun* [U] (*formal* or *humorous*) the improvement of sb's mind or character: **for the ~ of sb | for sb's ~** *The books were intended for the edification of the masses.*

**edifice** /ˈedɪfɪs/ *noun* (*formal*) a large impressive building: *an imposing edifice* ◊ (*figurative*) *The **whole edifice** of our civilization is built on hard work, trust and decency.* ◊ (*figurative*) *an edifice of lies*

**edify** /ˈedɪfaɪ/ *verb* [I, T] (**ediˈfies**, **edifyˈing**, **ediˈfied**, **ediˈfied**) **~ sb** (*formal*) to improve people's minds or characters by teaching them about sth

**edifying** /ˈedɪfaɪɪŋ/ *adj.* (*formal* or *humorous*) likely to improve your mind or your character

## edit ⓘ B2 /ˈedɪt/ verb 1 B2 [T, I] ~(sth) to prepare a
piece of writing, a book, etc. to be published by correcting the mistakes, making improvements to it, etc: *This draft text will need to be edited.* ◊ *This is the edited version of my speech* (= some parts have been taken out). ◊ *Students will be taught how to edit and proofread.* ➪ see also COPY-EDIT **2** B2 [I, T] (*computing*) to make changes to text or data on screen: *Press F2 to edit directly in the cell.* ◊ **~sth** *You can download the file and edit it on your computer.* **3** [T] **~sth** when sb **edits** a film, television programme, etc. they take what has been filmed or recorded and decide which parts to include and in which order: *They're showing the **edited highlights** of last month's game.* **4** [T] **~sth** to prepare a book to be published by collecting together and arranging pieces of writing by one or more authors: *He's editing a book of essays by Isaiah Berlin.* **5** [T] **~sth** to be responsible for planning and publishing a newspaper, magazine, etc. (= to be the EDITOR): *She used to edit a women's magazine.* ▶ **edit** *noun*: *I had time to do a quick edit of my essay before handing it in.*
PHRV ˌedit sth↔ˈout (of sth) to remove words, phrases or scenes from a book, programme, etc. before it is published or shown: *They edited out references to her father in the interview.*

**editable** /ˈedɪtəbl/ *adj.* (*computing*) (of text or software) that can be edited by the user: *an editable document*

**edition** ⓘ B2 /ɪˈdɪʃn/ *noun* 1 B2 the form in which a book, newspaper, etc. is published: *a paperback/hardback edition* ◊ *the print/online edition* 2 B2 a version of a book or other text that is regularly revised: *A second edition appeared in 1824.* ◊ *The dictionary is now **in its tenth edition**.* ◊ *a revised/an updated/an expanded edition* ➪ see also FIRST EDITION, SPECIAL EDITION **3** B2 a particular newspaper or magazine, or radio or television programme, especially one in a regular series: *Tonight's edition of 'Panorama' looks at unemployment.* ◊ **in an~ of sth** *The article appeared in the evening edition of 'The Mercury'.* **4** (*abbr.* **ed.**) the total number of copies of a book, newspaper or magazine, etc. published at one time ➪ see also LIMITED EDITION ➪ compare IMPRESSION (7)

**editor** ⓘ B1 /ˈedɪtə(r)/ *noun* 1 B1 a person who is in charge of a newspaper, magazine, etc., or part of one, and who decides what should be included: *the editor of the Washington Post* ◊ *a newspaper/magazine editor* ◊ *the sports/financial/fashion editor* ➪ see also CITY EDITOR ➪ WORDFINDER NOTE at JOURNALIST **2** B1 a person who prepares a book or other written material to be published, for example by checking and correcting the text, making improvements, etc: *Jenny Cook is a freelance writer and editor based in New York.* ➪ see also COPY EDITOR, SUBEDITOR ➪ WORDFINDER NOTE at BOOK **3** a person who prepares a film, radio or television programme for being shown or broadcast by deciding what to include, and what order it should be in **4** a person who works as a journalist for radio or television reporting on a particular area of news: *our economics editor* **5** a person who chooses texts written by one or by several writers and prepares them to be published in a book: *She's the editor of a new collection of ghost stories.* **6** (*computing*) a program that allows you to change stored text or data: *There are hundreds of different web editors on the market.* ➪ see also TEXT EDITOR ▶ **ˈeditorˌship** *noun* [U, C]: *the editorship of 'The Times'*

**editorial** B2+ B2 /ˌedɪˈtɔːriəl/ *adj., noun*
■ *adj.* B2+ B2 [usually before noun] connected with the task of preparing sth such as a newspaper, a book or a television or radio programme, to be published or broadcast: *the magazine's **editorial staff*** ◊ *an editorial decision*

**editorialize**

■ *noun* (*BrE also* **lead·er**, **leading 'article**) an important article in a newspaper that expresses the editor's opinion about an item of news or an issue; in the US also a comment on radio or television that expresses the opinion of the STATION or network ⊃ WORDFINDER NOTE at NEWSPAPER

**edi·tor·ial·ize** (*BrE also* **-ise**) /ˌedɪˈtɔːriəlaɪz/ *verb* **1** [I] to express your opinions rather than just reporting the news or giving the facts: *He accused the BBC of editorializing in its handling of the story.* **2** [I] (*NAmE*) to express an opinion in an editorial: *Yesterday the Washington Post editorialized on this subject.*

**EDM** /ˌiː diː ˈem/ *noun* [U] a type of popular music with a strong beat that people dance to in clubs (the abbreviation for 'electronic dance music')

**EDT** /ˌiː diː ˈtiː/ *abbr.* EASTERN DAYLIGHT TIME

**Ed·Tech** /ˈedtek/ *noun* [U] educational technology (creating and using technology for education and study)

**edu·cate** /ˈedʒukeɪt/ *verb* **1** [T, often passive] to teach sb over a period of time at a school, university, etc: *She was educated in the US.* ◊ *He was educated at his local comprehensive school and then at Oxford.* **2** [T, I] to teach sb about sth or how to do sth: *He believed the BBC's purpose was 'to inform, educate and entertain'.* ◊ *~ sb* *The industry wants to* **educate the public**, *but not cause undue concern.* ◊ *~ sb on/about sth* *Children need to be educated on the dangers of drug-taking.* ⊃ see also RE-EDUCATE

**edu·cated** /ˈedʒukeɪtɪd/ *adj.* **1** (*also* **-educated**) (in compounds) having had the kind of education mentioned; having been to the school, college or university mentioned: *privately educated children* ◊ *a British-educated lawyer* ◊ *He's a Princeton-educated Texan.* ⊃ see also SELF-EDUCATED **2** having had a high standard of education; showing a high standard of education: *He seemed intelligent and* **well educated**. ◊ *a highly educated workforce* ◊ *the educated elite* ◊ *He spoke in an educated voice.*
**IDM** **an educated 'guess** a guess that is based on some degree of knowledge, and is therefore likely to be correct

**edu·ca·tion** /ˌedʒuˈkeɪʃn/ *noun* **1** [U, C] a process of teaching, training and learning, especially in schools, colleges or universities, to improve knowledge and develop skills: *primary/elementary education* ◊ *post-secondary education* ◊ *a college/university education* ◊ *She completed her* **formal education** *in 2019.* ◊ *to continue/further/pursue your education* ◊ *to get/receive an education* ◊ *in ~* *students in full-time education* ◊ *a man of little education* ◊ *the British* **education system** ◊ *a bilingual* **education program** **HELP** There are many compounds ending in **education**. You will find them at their place in the alphabet. ⊃ WORDFINDER NOTE at STUDY **2** [U, sing.] a particular kind of teaching or training: *sex education in schools* ◊ *health education* ◊ *~ about sth* *education about danger on the roads* ⊃ see also PUBLIC EDUCATION (2) **3** (*also* **Education**) [U] the institutions or people involved in teaching and training: *the Education Department* ◊ *the Department of Education* ◊ *There should be closer links between education and industry.* **4** (*usually* **Education**) [U] the subject of study that deals with how to teach: *a College of Education* ◊ *a Bachelor of Education degree* ◊ *She's an education major.* **5** [sing.] (*often humorous*) an interesting experience that teaches you sth: *The rock concert was quite an education for my parents!*

**edu·ca·tion·al** /ˌedʒuˈkeɪʃənl/ *adj.* **1** connected with education: *children with special educational needs* ◊ *educational attainment/achievement* ◊ *an educational psychologist* ⊃ see also CO-EDUCATIONAL **2** providing education: *educational institutions* ◊ *an educational visit* ◊ *educational games/toys* (= that teach you sth as well as amusing you) ◊ *Watching television can be very educational.* ▸ **edu·ca·tion·al·ly** /-nəli/ *adv.*: *Children living in inner-city areas may be educationally disadvantaged.*

**edu·ca·tion·al·ist** /ˌedʒuˈkeɪʃənəlɪst/ (*also* **edu·ca·tion·ist** /ˌedʒuˈkeɪʃnɪst/) *noun* a specialist in theories and methods of teaching

**edu·ca·tive** /ˈedʒukətɪv; *NAmE* -keɪt-/ *adj.* (*formal*) that teaches sb: *the educative role of the community*

**edu·ca·tor** /ˈedʒukeɪtə(r)/ *noun* (*formal*) **1** a person whose job is to teach or educate people: *adult educators* (= who teach adults) **2** (*especially NAmE*) a person who is an expert in the theories and methods of education ⊃ see also EDUCATIONALIST

**edu·tain·ment** /ˌedʒuˈteɪnmənt/ *noun* [U] products such as books, television programmes and especially computer software that both educate and entertain

**Ed·ward·ian** /edˈwɔːdiən; *NAmE* -ˈwɔːrd-/ *adj.* from the time of the British king Edward VII (1901–1910): *an Edwardian terraced house* ▸ **Ed·ward·ian** *noun*

**-ee** /iː/ *suffix* (in nouns) **1** a person affected by an action: *employee* ⊃ compare -ER, -OR **2** a person described as sth or doing an action: *absentee* ◊ *refugee*

**EEG** /ˌiː iː ˈdʒiː/ *noun* a medical test that measures and records electrical activity in the brain (the abbreviation for 'electroencephalogram')

**eejit** /ˈiːdʒɪt/ *noun* (*IrishE, ScotE, informal, disapproving*) a way of saying IDIOT that represents the way it is pronounced by some people

**eek** /iːk/ *exclamation* used to express fear or surprise: *Eek! It moved.*

**eel** /iːl/ *noun* [C, U] a long thin sea or FRESHWATER fish that looks like a snake. There are several types of eel, some of which are used for food: *jellied eels*

**e'en** /iːn/ *adv.* (*literary*) even

**e'er** /eə(r); *NAmE* er/ *adv.* (*literary*) ever

**-eer** /ɪə(r); *NAmE* ɪr/ *suffix* **1** (in nouns) a person connected with sth or doing an activity: *auctioneer* ◊ *mountaineer* **2** (in verbs) (*often disapproving*) to be connected with sth or doing an activity: *profiteer* ◊ *commandeer*

**eerie** /ˈɪəri; *NAmE* ˈɪri/ *adj.* strange, mysterious and frightening **SYN** **uncanny**: *an eerie yellow light* ◊ *I found the silence underwater really eerie.* ▸ **eer·ily** /-rəli/ *adv.* **eeri·ness** *noun* [U]

**eff** /ef/ *verb*
**IDM** **eff and 'blind** (*BrE, informal*) to use swear words: *There was a lot of effing and blinding going on.*
**PHRV** **eff 'off** (*BrE, taboo*) a rude way of telling sb to go away, used instead of 'fuck off' ⊃ see also EFFING

**ef·face** /ɪˈfeɪs/ *verb* (*formal*) **1** *~ sth* to make sth disappear; to remove sth **2** *~ yourself* to not attract attention to yourself; to make yourself seem unimportant ⊃ see also SELF-EFFACING

**ef·fect** /ɪˈfekt/ *noun*, *verb*

■ *noun* **1** [C, U] a change that sb/sth causes in sb/sth else; a result: *the beneficial effects of exercise* ◊ *The results show a statistically significant effect.* ◊ *~ on sb/sth* *Her tears had no effect on him.* ◊ *the effect of heat on metal* ◊ *Modern farming methods can have an adverse effect on the environment.* ◊ *Despite her ordeal, she seems to have suffered no ill effects.* ◊ *to examine/study/investigate the effect of sth* ◊ *I can certainly feel the effects of too many late nights.* ◊ *~ of doing sth* *Her criticisms had the effect of discouraging him completely.* ◊ *to learn to distinguish between cause and effect* ⊃ LANGUAGE BANK at CONSEQUENTLY ⊃ note at EFFECT ⊃ see also AFTER-EFFECT, DOMINO EFFECT, DOPPLER EFFECT, GREENHOUSE EFFECT, KNOCK-ON, NETWORK EFFECT, RIPPLE EFFECT, SIDE EFFECT **2** [C, U] a particular look, sound or impression that sb, such as an artist or a writer, wants to create: *The overall effect of the painting is overwhelming.* ◊ *The stage lighting gives the effect of a moonlit scene.* ◊ *She uses glass to achieve a variety of visual effects.* ◊ *to produce/create an effect* ◊ *for ~* *He only behaves like that for effect* (= in order to impress people). **3** effects [pl.] lights, sounds, special SCENERY, computer images, etc. used in a play or film, especially in order to show things that do not normally exist or happen: *The production relied too much on spectacular effects.* ⊃ compare SOUND EFFECT, SPECIAL EFFECTS **4** effects [pl.] (*formal*) your personal possessions **SYN** **belongings**: *The insurance policy covers all baggage and personal effects.*
**IDM** **bring/put sth into effect** to cause sth to come into use: *The recommendations will soon be put into effect.* **come into effect** to come into use; to begin to apply: *New controls come into effect next month.* **in effect**

**1** used when you are stating what the facts of a situation are: *In effect, the two systems are identical.* ◇ *His wife had, in effect, run the government for the past six months.* **2** (of a law or rule) in use: *These laws are in effect in twenty states.* **take effect 1** to start to produce the results that are intended: *The aspirins soon take effect.* **2** to come into use; to begin to apply: *The new law takes effect from tomorrow.* **to the effect that … | to this/that ef·fect** used to show that you are giving the general meaning of what sb has said or written rather than the exact words: *He left a note to the effect that he would not be coming back.* ◇ *She told me to get out—or* **words to that effect.** **to good, great, dramatic, etc. ef·fect** producing a good, successful, dramatic, etc. result or impression **to no ef·fect** not producing the result you intend or hope for: *We warned them, but to no effect.* **with effect from …** (*formal*) starting from …: *The government has cut interest rates with effect from the beginning of next month.* ⇒ more at IMMEDIATE
■ *verb* ~ **sth** (*formal*) to make sth happen: *to effect a cure/change/recovery* ⇒ note at AFFECT

**ef·fect·ive** ⓘ B1 ○ /ɪˈfektɪv/ *adj.* **1** B1 producing the result that is wanted or intended; producing a successful result: *Aspirin is a simple but* **highly effective** *treatment.* ◇ *an effective way/means/strategy/tool/method* ◇ *I admire the effective use of colour in her paintings.* ◇ *The system has* **proved less effective** *than hoped.* ◇ **~ against sth** *drugs that are effective against cancer* OPP **ineffective** ⇒ see also COST-EFFECTIVE **2** [only before noun] in reality, although not officially intended: *the effective, if not the actual, leader of the party* ◇ *He has now taken effective control of the country.* **3** (*formal*) (of laws and rules) coming into use: *The new speed limit on this road becomes effective from 1 June.*

**ef·fect·ive·ly** ⓘ B1 ○ /ɪˈfektɪvli/ *adv.* **1** B1 in a way that produces the intended result or a successful result: *The company must reduce costs to compete effectively.* ◇ *You dealt with the situation very effectively.* OPP **ineffectively** ⇒ see also COST-EFFECTIVE **2** used when you are saying what the facts of a situation are: *The government has now effectively ruled out tax cuts.*

**ef·fect·ive·ness** B1+ C1 Ⓦ /ɪˈfektɪvnəs/ (*also less frequent* **ef·fect·iv·ity** /ɪˌfekˈtɪvəti/) *noun* [U] the fact of producing the result that is wanted or intended; the fact of producing a successful result: *to check the effectiveness of the security system* ⇒ see also COST-EFFECTIVENESS OPP **ineffectiveness**

**ef·fect·or** /ɪˈfektə(r)/ *noun* (*biology*) an organ or a cell in the body that is made to react by sth outside the body

**ef·fec·tual** /ɪˈfektʃuəl/ *adj.* (*formal*) (of things, not people) producing the result that was intended SYN **effective**: *an effectual remedy* ⇒ compare INEFFECTUAL ▶ **ef·fec·tual·ly** /-əli/ *adv.*

**ef·fec·tu·ate** /ɪˈfektʃueɪt/ *verb* ~ **sth** (*formal*) to make sth happen SYN **cause**

**ef·fem·in·ate** /ɪˈfemɪnət/ *adj.* (*disapproving*) (of a man or a boy) looking, behaving or sounding like a woman or a girl ▶ **ef·fem·in·acy** /-nəsi/ *noun* [U]

**ef·fer·ves·cent** /ˌefəˈvesnt/ ; *NAmE* ˌefərˈv-/ *adj.* **1** (*approving*) (of people and their behaviour) excited, enthusiastic and full of energy **bubbly 2** (of a liquid) having or producing small bubbles of gas SYN **fizzy** ▶ **ef·fer·ves·cence** /-sns/ *noun* [U]

**ef·fete** /ɪˈfiːt/ *adj.* (*disapproving*) **1** (of a person) with manners and interests that other people consider silly, unimportant and not sincere: *They despised us as effete art students.* **2** weak; without the power that it once had **3** (*sometimes offensive*) (of a man) behaving in a way that is regarded as weak or typical of a woman

**ef·fi·ca·cious** /ˌefɪˈkeɪʃəs/ *adj.* (*formal*) (of things, not of people) producing the result that was wanted or intended SYN **effective**: *They hope the new drug will prove especially efficacious in the relief of pain.*

**ef·fi·cacy** Ⓦ /ˈefɪkəsi/ *noun* [U] (*formal*) the ability of sth to produce the results that are wanted SYN **effectiveness**

**ef·fi·ciency** B1+ C1 Ⓦ /ɪˈfɪʃnsi/ *noun* **1** B1+ C1 [U] the quality of doing sth well with no waste of time or money: *improvements in efficiency at the factory* ◇ *I was impressed by the efficiency with which she handled the crisis.* **2** B1+ C1 **efficiencies** [pl.] ways of wasting less time

and money or of saving time or money: *We are looking at our business to see where savings and efficiencies can be made.* **3** [U] the relationship between the amount of energy that goes into a machine or an engine, and the amount that it produces: *energy/fuel efficiency* ◇ *What is the efficiency percentage of solar panels?* **4** [C] = EFFICIENCY APARTMENT

**ef·ficiency apartment** (*also* **ef·fi·ciency unit**, **ef·fi·ciency**) *noun* (*NAmE*) a small apartment with one main room for living, cooking and sleeping in and a separate bathroom

**ef·fi·cient** ⓘ B2 Ⓦ /ɪˈfɪʃnt/ *adj.* doing sth in a good, careful and complete way with no waste of time, money or energy: *a highly efficient worker* ◇ *efficient heating equipment* ◇ *more* **efficient use** *of energy* ◇ **fuel-efficient cars** (= that do not use much fuel) ◇ *This is simply the most efficient way to do it.* ◇ **~ at (doing) sth** *As we get older, our bodies become less efficient at burning up calories.* OPP **inefficient**

**ef·fi·cient·ly** B1+ B2 Ⓦ /ɪˈfɪʃntli/ *adv.* in a good and careful way, with no waste of time, money or energy: *a very efficiently organized event* ◇ *Resources must be used efficiently to avoid waste.* ◇ *If markets fail or do not work efficiently, government has a role to play.*

**ef·figy** /ˈefɪdʒi/ *noun* (*pl.* **-ies**) **1** a statue of a famous person, a SAINT or a god: *stone effigies in the church* **2** a model of a person that makes them look ugly: *The demonstrators burned a crude effigy of the president.* ◇ **in ~** *The president was burnt in effigy.*

**eff·ing** (*also* **f-ing**) /ˈefɪŋ/ *adj.* [only before noun], *adv.* (*taboo, slang*) a swear word that many people find offensive that is used to emphasize a comment or an angry statement; used instead of saying 'fucking'

**ef·flor·es·cence** /ˌefləˈresns/ *noun* [U, C] **1** (*formal*) the most developed stage of sth **2** (*chemistry*) the powder that appears on the surface of BRICKS, rocks, etc. when water EVAPORATES

**ef·flu·ent** /ˈefluənt/ *noun* [U, C] (*formal*) liquid waste, especially chemicals produced by factories, or SEWAGE ⇒ WORDFINDER NOTE at WASTE

**ef·fort** ⓘ B1 Ⓦ /ˈefət/; *NAmE* ˈefərt/ *noun* **1** B1 [C] an attempt to do sth especially when it is difficult to do: *The project was a* **team effort.** ◇ **~ to do sth** *Please make an effort to be on time.* ◇ *The local clubs are* **making every effort** *to interest more young people.* ◇ *We need to make a* **concerted effort** *to finish on time.* ◇ *You need to* **focus your efforts** *on critical areas first.* ◇ *to* **coordinate/redouble your efforts** ◇ *I'm glad to hear that many of you* **support our efforts.** ◇ **in an ~ to do sth** *The company has laid off 150 workers in an effort to save money.* ◇ **despite sb's efforts** *Despite our best efforts, we didn't manage to win the game.* **2** B1 [U, C] the physical or mental energy that you need to do sth; sth that takes a lot of energy: *You should* **put more effort into** *your work.* ◇ *A great deal of* **time and effort** *has gone into making this event a success.* ◇ *It's a long climb to the top, but* **well worth the effort.** ◇ *Getting up this morning was quite an effort* (= it was difficult). ◇ *The task* **required almost no effort.** ◇ **with (an)~** (*BrE*) *With an effort* (= with difficulty) *she managed to stop herself laughing.* **3** [C] (usually after a noun) a particular activity that a group of people organize in order to achieve sth: *the Russian space effort* ◇ *the United Nations' peacekeeping effort* **4** [C] the result of an attempt to do sth: *I'm afraid this essay is a poor effort.* IDM see BEND *v.*

**ef·fort·less** /ˈefətləs/; *NAmE* ˈefərt-/ *adj.* needing little or no effort, so that it seems easy: *She dances with effortless grace.* ◇ *He made playing the guitar look effortless.* ▶ **ef·fort·less·ly** *adv.* **ef·fort·less·ness** *noun* [U]

**ef·front·ery** /ɪˈfrʌntəri/ *noun* [U] (*formal*) behaviour that is confident and very rude, without any feeling of shame SYN **nerve**

**ef·fu·sion** /ɪˈfjuːʒn/ *noun* [C, U] **1** (*specialist*) something, especially a liquid or gas, that flows out of sb/sth; the act of flowing out **2** (*formal*) the expression of feelings in an EXAGGERATED way; feelings that are expressed in this way

---

Ⓞ Oxford Phrasal Academic Lexicon (OPAL) written and spoken word lists | Ⓦ OPAL written word list | Ⓢ OPAL spoken word list

**ef·fu·sive** /ɪˈfjuːsɪv/ adj. showing much or too much emotion: *an effusive welcome* ◊ *He was effusive in his praise.* ▶ **ef·fu·sive·ly** adv.

**EFL** /ˌiː ef ˈel/ abbr. (BrE) English as a foreign language (refers to the teaching of English to people for whom it is not the first language) ⊃ compare EAL, EAP, ESL, ESOL

**e-float** noun [U] (in Kenya) money that exists in an account that you can access to make payments, transfer money, etc. on your mobile phone, and that you can add to or exchange for cash by visiting an agent

**EFTA** /ˈeftə/ abbr. European Free Trade Association (an economic association of some European countries)

**e.g.** /ˌiː ˈdʒiː/ abbr. for example (from Latin 'exempli gratia'): *popular pets, e.g. cats and dogs*

▼ LANGUAGE BANK

**e.g.**
Giving examples

- The website has a variety of interactive exercises (**e.g.** *matching games, crosswords and quizzes*).
- The website has a variety of interactive exercises, **including** *matching games, crosswords and quizzes.*
- Internet technologies, **such as** *wikis, blogs and social networking sites*, have changed the way that people find information and interact with it.
- Many websites allow users to contribute information. **A good example of this is** *the 'wiki', a type of website that anyone can edit.*
- Wikis vary in how open they are. **For example**, *some wikis allow anybody to edit content, while others only allow registered users to do this.*
- Wikis vary in how open they are. Some wikis, **for example/for instance**, *allow anybody to edit content, while others only allow registered users to do this.*
- More and more people read their news on the internet. **To take one example**, *over 14 million people now read the online version of 'The Oxford Herald'.*
- Online newspapers are now more popular than paper ones. *'The Oxford Herald'* **is a case in point**. *Its print circulation has fallen in recent years, while its website attracts millions of users every month.*

⊃ note at EXAMPLE
⊃ LANGUAGE BANK at ADDITION, ARGUE, EVIDENCE, ILLUSTRATE

**egal·i·tar·ian** /ɪˌɡælɪˈteəriən/ NAmE -ˈter-/ adj. based on, or holding, the belief that everyone is equal and should have the same rights and opportunities: *an egalitarian society* ◊ *a highly egalitarian system of taxation* ▶ **egal·i·tar·ian** noun: *He described himself as 'an egalitarian'.* **egal·i·tar·ian·ism** noun [U].

**egg** /eɡ/ noun, verb
■ noun **1** [C] a small OVAL object with a thin hard shell produced by a female bird and containing a young bird; a similar object (without a hard shell) produced by a female fish, insect, etc: *The female sits on the eggs until they hatch.* ◊ *The fish lay thousands of eggs at one time.* ◊ *crocodile eggs* ⊃ VISUAL VOCAB pages V2, V3 **2** [C, U] a bird's egg, especially one from a chicken, that is eaten as food: *a boiled egg* ◊ *bacon and eggs* ◊ *fried/poached/scrambled eggs* ◊ *You've got some egg on your shirt.* ◊ *egg yolks/whites* ◊ *hen's/duck/quail eggs* ◊ *a chocolate egg* (= made from chocolate in the shape of an egg) ⊃ see also EASTER EGG, SCOTCH EGG **3** [C] (in women and female animals) a cell that combines with a SPERM to create a baby or young animal SYN **ovum**: *The male sperm fertilizes the female egg.* ◊ *an egg donor* ⊃ see also GARDEN EGG, GOOSE EGG, NEST EGG
IDM a ˌgood/ˌbad ˈegg (old-fashioned, informal) a person who you know will behave well/badly ˌhave/be left with ˈegg on/all over your face (informal) to be made to look stupid: *They were left with egg on their faces when only ten people showed up.* put all your ˈeggs in one ˈbasket to rely on one particular course of action for success rather than giving yourself several different possibilities ⊃more at CHICKEN n., CURATE¹, KILL v., OMELETTE, SURE adv., TEACH

■ verb
PHRV ˌegg sb↔ˈon (informal) to encourage sb to do sth, especially sth that they should not do: *He hit the other boy again and again as his friends egged him on.*

**ˌegg-and-ˈspoon race** noun (BrE) a race, usually run by children, in which those taking part have to hold an egg balanced in a spoon

**ˈegg cup** noun a small cup for holding a boiled egg

**ˈegg·head** /ˈeɡhed/ noun (informal, disapproving or humorous) a person who is very intelligent and is only interested in studying

**ˈegg·nog** /ˈeɡnɒɡ; NAmE -nɑːɡ/ (BrE also **ˈegg flip**) noun [U, C] an alcoholic drink made by mixing eggs, milk and sugar with alcohol such as RUM or BRANDY

**ˈegg plant** /ˈeɡplɑːnt; NAmE -plænt/ (NAmE) (BrE **auˈber·gine**) noun [C, U] a vegetable with shiny dark purple skin that is soft and white inside ⊃ VISUAL VOCAB page V5

**ˈegg ˌroll** noun (NAmE) a type of SPRING ROLL in which the PASTRY is made with eggs

**ˈegg·shell** /ˈeɡʃel/ noun [C, U] the hard thin outside of an egg

**ego** /ˈiːɡəʊ; BrE also ˈeɡ-/ noun (pl. -os) **1** your sense of your own value and importance: *He has the biggest ego of anyone I've ever met.* ◊ *Winning the prize really boosted her ego.* **2** (psychology) the part of the mind that is responsible for your sense of who you are (= your identity) ⊃ compare ID, SUPEREGO ⊃ see also ALTER EGO
IDM see MASSAGE v.

**ego·cen·tric** /ˌiːɡəʊˈsentrɪk; BrE also ˌeɡ-/ adj. thinking only about yourself and not about what other people need or want SYN **selfish**

**ego·ism** /ˈiːɡəʊɪzəm; BrE also ˈeɡ-/ (also **ego·tism** /ˈiːɡətɪzəm; BrE also ˈeɡ-/) noun [U] (disapproving) the fact of thinking that you are better or more important than anyone else ▶ **ego·is·tic** /ˌiːɡəʊˈɪstɪk; BrE also ˌeɡ-/ (also **ego·tis·tic·al** /ɪˈɡətɪstɪkl; BrE also ˌeɡ-/, **ego·tis·tic** /-stɪk/) adj. **ego·tis·tic·al·ly** /-kli/ adv.

**ego·ist** /ˈiːɡəʊɪst; BrE also ˈeɡ-/ (also **egot·ist** /ˈiːɡətɪst; BrE also ˈeɡ-/) noun (disapproving) a person who thinks that he or she is better than other people and who thinks and talks too much about himself or herself

**ego·mania** /ˌiːɡəʊˈmeɪniə; BrE also ˌeɡ-/ noun [U] a mental condition in which sb is interested in themselves or concerned about themselves in a way that is not normal ▶ **ego·maniac** /-niæk/ noun **ego·ma·ni·acal** /ˌiːɡəʊməˈnaɪəkl; BrE also ˌeɡ-/ adj.

**ˈego trip** noun (usually disapproving) an activity that sb does because it makes them feel good and important

**egre·gious** /ɪˈɡriːdʒəs/ adj. (formal) extremely bad

**e·gress** /ˈiːɡres/ noun [U] (formal) the act of leaving a place ⊃ compare ACCESS, INGRESS

**egret** /ˈiːɡrət/ noun a bird of the HERON family, with long legs and long white tail feathers

**Egypt·ology** /ˌiːdʒɪpˈtɒlədʒi; NAmE -ˈtɑːl-/ noun [U] the study of the language, history and culture of ancient Egypt ▶ **Egypt·olo·gist** noun

**eh** /eɪ/ exclamation (especially BrE) (NAmE usually **huh**) **1** the sound that people make when they want sb to repeat sth: *'I'm not hungry.' 'Eh?' 'I said I'm not hungry.'* **2** the sound that people make when they want sb to agree or reply: *So what do you think, eh?* **3** the sound people make when they are surprised: *Another new dress, eh!*

**Eid** (also **Id**) /iːd/ noun one of the two main Muslim festivals, either **Eid ul-Fitr** /ˌiːd ʌl ˈfɪtə(r)/ at the end of Ramadan, or **Eid ul-Adha** /ˌiːd ʌl ˈʌdə/, which celebrates the end of the PILGRIMAGE to Mecca and Abraham's SACRIFICE of a sheep

**eight** /eɪt/ **1** number 8 HELP There are examples of how to use numbers at the entry for **five**. **2** noun a team of eight people who ROW a long narrow boat in races; the boat they row ⊃ see also FIGURE OF EIGHT

**eight·een** /ˌeɪˈtiːn/ number 18 ▶ **eight·eenth** /-ˈtiːnθ/ ordinal number, noun

**eighth** /eɪtθ/ ordinal number, noun
■ ordinal number 8th HELP There are examples of how to use ordinal numbers at the entry for **fifth**.
■ noun each of eight equal parts of sth

**eighth note** (*NAmE*) (*BrE* **qua·ver**) *noun* (*music*) a note that lasts half as long as a CROTCHET/QUARTER NOTE ⊃ picture at MUSIC

**eighty** ⓘ A1 /ˈeɪti/ 1 A1 *number* 80 2 *noun* **the eight·ies** [pl.] numbers, years or temperatures from 80 to 89 ▶ **eight·ieth** /-əθ/ *ordinal number, noun* HELP There are examples of how to use ordinal numbers at the entry for **fifth**.
IDM **in your eighties** between the ages of 80 and 89

**eina** /ˈeɪnɑː/ *SAfrE* [ˈeɪnə] *exclamation* (*SAfrE*) used to express sudden pain: *Eina! That was sore!*

**eish** /eɪʃ/ *exclamation* (*SAfrE, informal*) used to express surprise, pain, being annoyed, etc: *Eish man, love at first sight!*

**ei·stedd·fod** /aɪˈsteðvɒd; *NAmE* -vɑːd/ *noun* (*from Welsh*) a type of festival, held in Wales, in which there are singing, music and poetry competitions

**ei·ther** ⓘ A2 /ˈaɪðə(r), ˈiːð-; *NAmE* ˈiːð-, ˈaɪð-/ *det., pron., adv.*
▪ *det., pron.* 1 A2 one or the other of two; it does not matter which: *You can park on either side of the street.* ◇ *You can keep one of the photos. Either of them—whichever you like.* ◇ *There are two types of qualification—either is acceptable.* ⊃ note at NEITHER 2 B2 each of two: *The offices on either side were empty.* ◇ *There's a door at either end of the corridor.*
▪ *adv.* 1 A2 used after negative phrases to state that a feeling or situation is similar to one already mentioned: *Pete can't go and I can't either.* ◇ (*especially NAmE, informal*) '*I don't like it.' 'Me either.'* (= Neither do I). 2 A2 **either … or …** used to show a choice of two things: *Well, I think she's either Czech or Slovak.* ◇ *I'm going to buy either the blue one or the red one—I can't decide.* ◇ *Either he could not come or he did not want to.* 3 B1 used to add extra information to a statement: *I know a good Italian restaurant. It's not far from here, either.* ⊃ note at NEITHER ⊃ compare OR

**ejacu·late** /iˈdʒækjuleɪt/ *verb* 1 [I, T] **~ (sth)** when a man or a male animal **ejaculates**, SEMEN comes out through the PENIS 2 [T] **+ speech** (*old-fashioned*) to say or shout sth suddenly SYN **exclaim**

**ejacu·la·tion** /iˌdʒækjuˈleɪʃn/ *noun* 1 [C, U] the act of ejaculating; the moment when SPERM comes out of a man's PENIS: *premature ejaculation* 2 [C] (*formal*) a sudden shout or sound that you make when you are angry or surprised SYN **exclamation**

**eject** /iˈdʒekt/ *verb* 1 [T] **~ sb (from sth)** (*formal*) to force sb to leave a place or position SYN **throw sb out (of …)**: *Police ejected a number of violent protesters from the hall.* 2 [T] **~ sth (from sth)** to push sth out suddenly and with a lot of force: *Used cartridges are ejected from the gun after firing.* 3 [I] (of a pilot) to escape from an aircraft that is going to crash, sometimes using an EJECTOR SEAT 4 [T, I] **~ (sth)** when you **eject** a disk, tape, etc., or when it **ejects**, it comes out of the machine after you have pressed a button ▶ **ejec·tion** /iˈdʒekʃn/ *noun* [U, C]

**eject·or seat** /iˈdʒektə siːt; *NAmE* -tər/ (*especially BrE*) (*also* **ejec·tion seat** *especially in NAmE*) *noun* a seat that allows a pilot to be thrown out of an aircraft in an emergency

**eke** /iːk/ *verb*
PHRV **eke sth↔out** 1 to make a small supply of sth such as food or money last longer by using only small amounts of it: *She managed to eke out her student loan till the end of the year.* 2 **eke out a living, etc.** to manage to live with very little money

**EKG** /ˌiː keɪ ˈdʒiː/ *noun* (*NAmE*) = ECG

**elab·or·ate** ⓘ+ B2 *adj., verb*
▪ *adj.* ⓘ+ C1 /iˈlæbərət/ [*usually before noun*] very complicated and detailed; carefully prepared and organized: *elaborate designs* ◇ *She had prepared a very elaborate meal.* ◇ *an elaborate computer system* ▶ **elab·or·ate·ly** *adv.*: *an elaborately decorated room* **elab·or·ate·ness** *noun* [U]
▪ *verb* /iˈlæbəreɪt/ 1 [I, T] to explain or describe sth in a more detailed way: **~ (on/upon sth)** *He said he was resigning but did not elaborate on his reasons.* ◇ **~ sth** *She went on to elaborate her argument.* 2 [T] **~ sth** to develop a plan, an idea, etc. and make it complicated or detailed: *In his plays* he takes simple traditional tales and elaborates them. ▶ **elab·or·ation** /iˌlæbəˈreɪʃn/ *noun* [U, C]: *The importance of the plan needs no further elaboration.*

**elan** /eɪˈlɒ̃, eɪˈlæn; *NAmE* -ˈlɑːn/ *noun* [U] (*from French, literary*) great enthusiasm and energy, style and confidence

**elapse** /iˈlæps/ *verb* [I] (not usually used in the progressive tenses) (*formal*) if a period of time **elapses**, it passes SYN **go by**: *Many years elapsed before they met again.*

**e·lapsed ˈtime** *noun* [U] (*specialist*) used to describe the time that passes between the start and end of a project or a computer operation, in contrast to the actual time needed to do a particular task that is part of the project

**elas·tic** /iˈlæstɪk/ *noun, adj.*
▪ *noun* [U] material made with rubber, that can stretch and then return to its original size: *This skirt needs some new elastic in the waist.*
▪ *adj.* 1 made with elastic: *an elastic headband* 2 able to stretch and return to its original size and shape: *elastic materials* 3 that can change or be changed: *Our plans are fairly elastic.*

**elas·ti·cated** /iˈlæstɪkeɪtɪd/ (*BrE*) (*NAmE* **elas·ti·cized** /iˈlæstɪsaɪzd/) *adj.* (of clothing, or part of a piece of clothing) made using elastic material that can stretch: *a skirt with an elasticated waist*

**eˌlastic ˈband** *noun* (*BrE*) = RUBBER BAND

**elas·ti·city** /ˌiːlæˈstɪsəti, ˌɪlæ-/ *noun* [U] the quality that sth has of being able to stretch and return to its original size and shape (= of being elastic)

**elas·tin** /iˈlæstɪn/ *noun* [U] (*biology*) a natural substance that stretches easily, found in the skin, the heart and other body TISSUES

**elasto·mer** /iˈlæstəmə(r)/ *noun* (*chemistry*) a natural or artificial chemical that behaves like rubber

**elated** /iˈleɪtɪd/ *adj.* **~ (at/by sth)** very happy and excited because of sth good that has happened, or will happen: *They were elated at the result.* ◇ *I was elated by the prospect of the new job ahead.* ⊃ SYNONYMS at EXCITED

**ela·tion** /iˈleɪʃn/ *noun* [U] a feeling of great happiness and excitement

**elbow** ⓘ+ B2 /ˈelbəʊ/ *noun, verb*
▪ *noun* 1 ⓘ+ B2 the JOINT between the upper and lower parts of the arm where it bends in the middle: *She jabbed him with her elbow.* ◇ *He's fractured his elbow.* ⊃ VISUAL VOCAB page V1 2 ⓘ+ B2 the part of a piece of clothing that covers the elbow: *The jacket was worn at the elbows.* 3 a part of a pipe, CHIMNEY, etc. where it bends at a sharp angle
IDM **get the ˈelbow** (*BrE, informal*) to be told by sb that they no longer want to have a relationship with you; to be told to go away **give sb the ˈelbow** (*BrE, informal*) to tell sb that you no longer want to have a relationship with them; to tell sb to go away ⊃ more at KNOW *v.*, POWER *n.*, RUB *v.*
▪ *verb* **~ sb/sth (+adv./prep.)** to push sb with your elbow, usually in order to get past them: *She elbowed me out of the way to get to the front of the line.* ◇ *He elbowed his way through the crowd.*

**ˈelbow grease** *noun* [U] (*informal*) the effort used in physical work, especially in cleaning or POLISHING sth (= rubbing it until it is smooth and shiny)

**ˈelbow room** *noun* [U] (*informal*) enough space to move or walk in

**elder** /ˈeldə(r)/ *adj., noun*
▪ *adj.* 1 [*only before noun*] (of people, especially two members of the same family) older: *my elder brother* ◇ *his elder sister* 2 **the elder** used without a noun immediately after it to show who is the older of two people: *the elder of their two sons* 3 **the elder** (*formal*) used before or after sb's name to show that they are the older of two people who have the same name: *the elder Pitt* ◇ *Pitt the elder* ⊃ note at OLD ⊃ compare THE YOUNGER
▪ *noun* 1 **elders** [pl.] people of greater age, experience and authority: *Children have no respect for their elders nowadays.* ◇ *the village elders* (= the old and respected people of the village) 2 **my, etc. elder** [sing.] (*formal*) a person older than me, etc: *He is her elder by several years.* 3 [C] an official in some Christian churches 4 [C] a small tree

# elder abuse

with white flowers with a sweet smell (**elderflowers**) and bunches of small black BERRIES (**elderberries**)
**IDM** **your elders and betters** people who are older and wiser than you and whom you should respect

**'elder abuse** *noun* [U] the crime of harming or stealing from an old person, committed by sb who is trusted to care for or help them

**elder·ber·ry** /'eldəberi; *NAmE* -derb-/ *noun* (*pl.* **-ies**) a small black BERRY that grows in bunches on an elder tree

**elder·care** /'eldəkeə(r); *NAmE* -derker/ *noun* [U] (*especially NAmE*) help for old people, especially services such as special homes and medical care: *nursing homes and other eldercare facilities*

**elder·flower** /'eldəflaʊə(r); *NAmE* -derf-/ *noun* the flower of the elder tree, used to make wines and other drinks

**eld·er·ly** 🔑 **B2** /'eldəli; *NAmE* -dərli/ *adj.* **1** 🔑 **B2** (of people) used as a polite word for 'old': *an elderly man/woman/lady* ◇ *an elderly couple* ◇ *elderly relatives* ◇ *elderly patients/residents* ⮕ SYNONYMS at OLD **2 the elderly** *noun* [pl.] people who are old ⮕ WORDFINDER NOTE at AGE

**elder 'statesman** (*also* **elder 'stateswoman**) *noun* **1** an old and respected politician or former politician whose advice is still valued because of his or her long experience **2** any experienced and respected person whose advice or work is valued: *an elder statesman of golf*

**eld·est** /'eldɪst/ *adj.* **1** (of people, especially of three or more members of the same family) oldest: *Tom is my eldest son.* **2 the eldest** used without a noun immediately after it to show who is the oldest of three or more people: *the eldest of their three children* ⮕ note at OLD

**'e-learning** *noun* [U] a system of learning that uses electronic media, typically over the internet: *We use e-learning to deliver online training to our employees.* ◇ *an e-learning course/module/platform* ⮕ compare DISTANCE LEARNING

**elect** 🔑 **B2** /ɪ'lekt/ *verb, adj.*
■ *verb* **1** 🔑 **B2** to choose sb to do a particular job by voting for them: *~sb/sth Voters will elect a new president on 30 March next year.* ◇ *the newly/democratically elected government* ◇ *an elected representative/official/assembly* ◇ *What changes will he make if he gets elected?* ◇ *~sb to sth She became the first black woman to be elected to the Senate.* ◇ *~sb (as) sth He was elected (as) MP for Oxford East.* **2 ~to do sth** (*formal*) to choose to do sth: *Increasing numbers of people elect to work from home nowadays.*
■ *adj.* **1 -elect** used after nouns to show that sb has been chosen for a job, but is not yet doing that job: *the president-elect* ⮕ see also PRESIDENT-ELECT **2 the elect** *noun* [pl.] (*religion*) people who have been chosen to be saved from punishment after death

**elect·able** /ɪ'lektəbl/ *adj.* (of a politician or political party) having the qualities that make it likely or possible that they will win in an election ▶ **elect·abil·ity** /ɪ,lektə'bɪləti/ *noun* [U]

**elec·tion** 🔑 **B1** /ɪ'lekʃn/ *noun* **1** 🔑 **B1** [C, U] the process of choosing a person or a group of people for a position, especially a political position, by voting: *presidential/parliamentary/local elections* ◇ *The prime minister is about to call* (= announce) *an election.* ◇ *Elections will be held later this year.* ◇ *to vote in an election* (*especially BrE*) *How many candidates are standing for election?* ◇ (*especially NAmE*) *to run for election* ◇ *to win/lose an election* ◇ *the 2020 US election campaign* ◇ *an election result/victory* ⮕ see also BY-ELECTION, GENERAL ELECTION, RE-ELECTION **2** 🔑 **B2** [U] the fact of having been chosen by election: *~(as sth) We welcome his election as president.* ◇ *~to sth a year after her election to the committee* ⮕ see also BY-ELECTION, GENERAL ELECTION ⮕ WORDFINDER NOTE at DEMOCRACY

**elec·tion·eer·ing** /ɪ,lekʃə'nɪərɪŋ; *NAmE* -'nɪr-/ *noun* [U] the activity of making speeches and visiting people to try to persuade them to vote for a particular politician or political party in an election

▼ SYNONYMS

### election
vote • poll • referendum • ballot

These are all words for an event in which people choose a representative or decide sth by voting.

**election** an occasion on which people officially choose a political representative or government by voting: *Who did you vote for in the last election?*

**vote** an occasion on which a group of people vote for sb/sth: *They took a vote on who should go first.*

**poll** (*journalism*) the process of voting in an election: *They suffered a defeat at the polls.*

**referendum** an occasion on which all the adults in a country can vote on a particular issue

**ballot** the system of voting by marking an election paper, especially in secret; an occasion on which a vote is held: *The leader will be chosen by secret ballot.* NOTE **Ballot** is usually used about a vote within an organization rather than an occasion on which the public vote.

PATTERNS
- a **national/local** election/vote/poll/referendum/ballot
- to **have/hold/conduct** a(n) election/vote/poll/referendum/ballot

**elect·ive** /ɪ'lektɪv/ *adj., noun*
■ *adj.* [usually before noun] (*formal*) **1** using or chosen by election: *an elective democracy* ◇ *an elective assembly* ◇ *an elective member* ◇ *He had never held elective office* (= a position that is filled by election). **2** having the power to elect: *an elective body* **3** (of medical treatment) that you choose to have; that does not require immediate attention SYN **optional**: *elective surgery* **4** (of a course or subject) that a student can choose SYN **optional**
■ *noun* (*especially NAmE*) a course or subject at a college or school that a student can choose to do

**elect·or** /ɪ'lektə(r)/ *noun* **1** a person who has the right to vote in an election **2** (in the US) a member of the Electoral College

**elect·or·al** 🔑 **C1** /ɪ'lektərəl/ *adj.* [only before noun] connected with elections: *electoral systems/reforms* ▶ **elect·or·al·ly** /-rəli/ *adv.*: *an electorally effective campaign*

**e,lectoral 'college** *noun* **1 the Electoral College** (in the US) a group of people who come together to elect the President and Vice-President, based on the votes of people in each state ⮕ WORDFINDER NOTE at CONGRESS **2** (*BrE*) a group of people who are chosen to represent the members of a political party, etc. in the election of a leader

**e,lectoral 'register** (*also* **e,lectoral 'roll**) *noun* (in the UK) the official list of people who have the right to vote in a particular area

**e,lectoral 'vote** *noun* **1** [C] (in the US) a vote cast by a member of the ELECTORAL COLLEGE: *Arizona's 11 electoral votes were won by Trump.* **2** [sing.] (in the US) the choice made by all the members of the ELECTORAL COLLEGE, which determines the winner in the election of the president and vice-president: *He became president by winning the electoral vote 304 to 227.* ⮕ compare THE POPULAR VOTE

**elect·or·ate** /ɪ'lektərət/ *noun* **1** [C + sing./pl. v.] the people in a country or an area who have the right to vote, thought of as a group: *Only 60 per cent of the electorate voted in the last election.* **2** [C] (*AustralE, NZE*) = CONSTITUENCY (1)

**elec·tric** 🔑 **A2** /ɪ'lektrɪk/ *adj., noun*
■ *adj.* **1** 🔑 **A2** [usually before noun] connected with electricity; using, produced by or producing electricity: *an electric car/vehicle* ◇ *an electric guitar* ◇ *an electric light/motor* ◇ *an electric current/charge* ⮕ see also ELECTRIC SHOCK, ELECTRICAL STORM **2** full of excitement; making people excited SYN **electrifying**: *The atmosphere was electric.*
■ *noun* **1 electrics** [pl.] (*BrE, informal*) the system of electrical wires in a house, car or machine: *There's a problem with the electrics.* **2** [U] (*informal*) used to refer to the supply of electricity to a building: *The electric will be off tomorrow.*

---

æ cat | ɑː father | e bed | ɜː fur | ə about | ɪ sit | iː see | i happy | ɒ got (*BrE*) | ɔː saw | ʌ cup | ʊ put | uː too

# electronics

> **▼ WHICH WORD?**
>
> **electric / electrical**
> These adjectives are frequently used with the following nouns:
>
> | electric ~ | electrical ~ |
> |---|---|
> | light | equipment |
> | guitar | wiring |
> | drill | signal |
> | chair | engineer |
> | shock | shock |
>
> - **Electric** is usually used to describe something that uses or produces electricity. You use **electrical** with more general nouns such as *equipment* and *wiring* and things that are concerned with electricity: *an electrical fault.* However, the difference is not always so clear now: *an electric/electrical company ◊ an electric/electrical current ◊ an electric/electrical shock.*

**elec·tric·al** ❶ A2 /ɪˈlektrɪkl/ *adj.* connected with electricity; using or producing electricity: *an electrical fault in the engine ◊ electrical equipment/appliances ◊ electrical power/energy* ▸ **elec·tric·al·ly** /-kli/ *adv.*: *a car with electrically operated windows ◊ electrically charged particles*

**e‚lectrical engiˈneering** *noun* [U] the design and building of machines and systems that use or produce electricity; the study of this subject ▸ **e‚lectrical engiˈneer** *noun*

**e‚lectrical ˈstorm** (*BrE also* **e‚lectric ˈstorm**) *noun* a violent storm in which electricity is produced in the atmosphere

**e‚lectric ˈbike** *noun* = E-BIKE

**e‚lectric ˈblanket** *noun* a BLANKET for a bed that is heated by electricity passing through the wires inside it (usually used under the bottom sheet of the bed)

**e‚lectric ˈblue** *noun* [U] a bright or METALLIC blue colour

**e‚lectric ˈchair** (*usually* **the electric chair**) (*also informal* **the chair**) *noun* [sing.] (especially in the US) a chair in which criminals are killed by having a powerful electric current passed through their bodies; the method of EXECUTION that uses this chair: *He was sent to the electric chair. ◊ They face death by the electric chair.*

**e‚lectric ˈfence** *noun* a wire fence through which an electric current can be passed, giving an electric shock to any person or animal touching it

**elec·tri·cian** /ɪˌlekˈtrɪʃn/ *noun* a person whose job is to connect, repair, etc. electrical equipment

**elec·tri·city** ❶ A2 /ɪˌlekˈtrɪsəti/ *noun* 1 ⚡ A2 [U] a form of energy from charged ELEMENTARY PARTICLES, usually supplied as electric current through cables, wires, etc. for lighting, heating, driving machines, etc: *materials that conduct electricity ◊ to produce/supply electricity ◊ The wind farm will generate enough electricity for some 30 000 homes. ◊ electricity supply/generation ◊ The electricity is off* (= there is no electric power supply). ⊃ *see also* STATIC ELECTRICITY

> **WORDFINDER** battery, charge, conduct, connect, generate, insulate, power, switch, wire

2 [U, *sing.*] a feeling of great emotion, excitement, etc.

**e‚lectric ˈrazor, e‚lectric ˈshaver** *noun* = SHAVER

**elec·trics** /ɪˈlektrɪks/ *noun* [pl.] (*BrE, informal*) the system of electrical wires in a house, car or machine: *There's a problem with the electrics.*

**e‚lectric ˈshock** (*also* **shock**) *noun* a sudden flow of electricity through a part of the body, causing pain and sometimes death

**elec·tri·fi·ca·tion** /ɪˌlektrɪfɪˈkeɪʃn/ *noun* [U] the process of changing sth so that it works by electricity

**elec·trify** /ɪˈlektrɪfaɪ/ *verb* (**elec·tri·fies**, **elec·tri·fy·ing**, **elec·tri·fied**, **elec·tri·fied**) **1** [usually passive] to make sth work by using electricity; to pass an electrical current through sth: **be electrified** *The railway line was electrified in the 1950s. ◊ He had all the fences around his home electrified.*

**2 ~ sb** to make sb feel very excited and enthusiastic about sth: *Her performance electrified the audience.*

**elec·tri·fy·ing** /ɪˈlektrɪfaɪɪŋ/ *adj.* very exciting: *The dancers gave an electrifying performance.*

**elec·tro-** /ɪˈlektrəʊ, ɪˌlektrə; *BrE also* ɪlekˈtrɒ; *NAmE also* ɪlekˈtrɑː/ *combining form* (in nouns, adjectives, verbs and adverbs) connected with electricity: *electromagnetism*

**elec·tro·car·dio·gram** /ɪˌlektrəʊˈkɑːdiəʊɡræm; *NAmE* -ˈkɑːrd-/ *noun* = ECG

**elec·tro·con·vul·sive ther·apy** /ɪˌlektrəʊkənˌvʌlsɪv ˈθerəpi/ *noun* (*abbr.* **ECT**) [U] a medical treatment of mental illness in which electricity is passed through the patient's brain

**elec·tro·cute** /ɪˈlektrəkjuːt/ *verb* [usually passive] to injure or kill sb by passing electricity through their body: **be electrocuted** *The boy was electrocuted when he wandered onto a railway track. ◊ He was electrocuted in Virginia in 2006* (= punished by being killed in the electric chair). ▸ **elec·tro·cu·tion** /ɪˌlektrəˈkjuːʃn/ *noun* [U, C]: *Six people were drowned; five died from electrocution. ◊ He was sentenced to death by electrocution.*

**elec·trode** /ɪˈlektrəʊd/ *noun* either of two points (or TERMINALS) by which an electric current enters or leaves a battery or other electrical device ⊃ *see also* ANODE, CATHODE

**elec·tro·dy·nam·ics** /ɪˌlektrəʊdaɪˈnæmɪks/ *noun* [U] (*physics*) the study of the way that electric currents and MAGNETIC FIELDS affect each other

**elec·tro·enceph·alo·gram** /ɪˌlektrəʊɪnˈsefələɡræm; *BrE also* -ˈke-/ *noun* = EEG

**elec·troly·sis** /ɪˌlekˈtrɒləsɪs; *NAmE* -ˈtrɑːl-/ *noun* **1** the DESTRUCTION of the roots of hairs by means of an electric current, as a beauty treatment **2** (*chemistry*) the process of separating a liquid (or electrolyte) into its chemical parts by passing an electric current through it

**elec·tro·lyte** /ɪˈlektrəlaɪt/ *noun* (*chemistry*) a liquid that an electric current can pass through, especially in an electric cell or battery ▸ **elec·tro·ly·tic** /ɪˌlektrəˈlɪtɪk/ *adj.*

**elec·tro·mag·net** /ɪˈlektrəʊmæɡnət/ *noun* (*physics*) a piece of metal that becomes MAGNETIC when electricity is passed through it

**elec·tro·mag·net·ic** /ɪˌlektrəʊmæɡˈnetɪk/ *adj.* (*physics*) having both electrical and MAGNETIC characteristics (or PROPERTIES): *an electromagnetic wave/field*

**elec·tro·mag·net·ism** /ɪˌlektrəʊˈmæɡnətɪzəm/ *noun* [U] (*physics*) the production of a MAGNETIC FIELD by means of an electric current, or of an electric current by means of a MAGNETIC FIELD

**elec·tron** /ɪˈlektrɒn; *NAmE* -trɑːn/ *noun* (*physics*) a very small piece of matter (= a substance) with a negative electric charge, found in all ATOMS ⊃ *see also* NEUTRON, PROTON ⊃ **WORDFINDER NOTE** at ATOM

**elec·tron·ic** ❶ A2 /ɪˌlekˈtrɒnɪk; *NAmE* -ˈtrɑːn-/ *adj.* [usually before noun] **1** ⚡ A2 (of a device) having or using many small parts, such as MICROCHIPS, that control and direct a small electric current: *an electronic device/gadget ◊ electronic voting machines* **2** ⚡ A2 done or produced by means of a computer or other electronic device: *electronic dance music ◊ electronic medical records ◊ electronic communication/banking/payments* ⊃ *see also* E- **3** A2 involving or connected with electronic equipment: *an electronic engineer*

**elec·tron·ic·ally** /ɪˌlekˈtrɒnɪkli; *NAmE* -ˈtrɑːn-/ *adv.* in an electronic way, or using a device that works in an electronic way: *to process data electronically* (= using a computer)

**e‚lectronic ciˈgarette** *noun* = E-CIGARETTE

**e‚lectronic ˈmail** *noun* [U] (*formal*) email

**e‚lectronic ˈpublishing** (*also* **e-publishing**) *noun* [U] = DIGITAL PUBLISHING

**elec·tron·ics** ⚡+ B2 /ɪˌlekˈtrɒnɪks; *NAmE* -ˈtrɑːn-/ *noun* **1** ⚡+ B2 [U] the branch of science and technology that studies electric currents in electronic equipment **2** ⚡+ B2 [U] the use of electronic technology, especially in

# electronic signature

developing new equipment: *the electronics industry* ⇒ see also CONSUMER ELECTRONICS **3** [pl.] the electronic CIRCUITS and components (= parts) used in electronic equipment: *a fault in the electronics*

**e,lectronic 'signature** *noun* (*also* **e-signature**) a piece of digital data attached to a document sent electronically that is used to confirm the identity of the sender ⇒ compare DIGITAL SIGNATURE

**e,lectronic 'tagging** *noun* [U] the system of attaching an electronic device to a person, animal or object so that the police, etc. know where the person, animal or object is

**e,lectron 'microscope** *noun* a very powerful MICROSCOPE that uses ELECTRONS instead of light

**elec·tro·stat·ic** /ɪˌlektrəʊˈstætɪk/ *adj.* (*physics*) used to talk about electric charges that are not moving, rather than electric currents

**ele·gant** /ˈelɪɡənt/ *adj.* **1** (of people or their behaviour) attractive and showing a good sense of style **SYN** stylish: *She was tall and elegant.* **2** (of clothes, places and things) attractive and designed well **SYN** stylish: *an elegant dress ◇ an elegant room/restaurant* **3** (of a plan or an idea) clever but simple: *an elegant solution to the problem* ▶ **ele·gance** /-ɡəns/ *noun* [U, sing.]: *She dresses with casual elegance. ◇ His writing combines elegance and wit.* **ele·gant·ly** *adv.*: *elegantly dressed ◇ elegantly furnished*

**ele·giac** /ˌelɪˈdʒaɪək/ *adj.* (*formal or literary*) expressing sad feelings, especially about the past or people who have died

**elegy** /ˈelədʒi/ *noun* (*pl.* **-ies**) a poem or song that expresses sad feelings, especially for sb who has died

## elem·ent /ˈelɪmənt/ *noun*

- PART/AMOUNT **1** [C] a necessary or typical part of sth; one of several parts that sth contains: *There are three important elements to consider. ◇ ~ in sth Cost was a key element in our decision. ◇ ~ of sth The story has all the elements of a soap opera. ◇ ~ to sth Police say there may have been a racial element to the attacks.* **2** [C, usually sing.] **~ of surprise, truth, risk, etc.** a small amount of a quality or feeling: *We need to preserve the element of surprise. ◇ These rumours do contain an element of truth.*
- CHEMISTRY **3** (*also* **chemical element**) [C] a simple chemical substance that consists of ATOMS of only one type and cannot be split by chemical means into a simpler substance. Gold, OXYGEN and CARBON are all elements: *All chemical substances, whether elements, compounds or mixtures, are made up of three types of particles.* ⇒ compare COMPOUND
- EARTH/AIR/FIRE/WATER **4** [C] one of the four substances: earth, air, fire and water, which people used to believe everything else was made of
- WEATHER **5 the elements** [pl.] the weather, especially bad weather: *Are we going to brave the elements and go for a walk? ◇ to be exposed to the elements*
- BASIC PRINCIPLES **6 elements** [pl.] the basic principles of a subject that you have to learn first **SYN** basics: *He taught me the elements of map-reading.*
- GROUP OF PEOPLE **7** [C, usually pl.] a group of people who form a part of a larger group or society: *moderate/radical elements within the party ◇ unruly elements in the school*
- ENVIRONMENT **8** [C, usually sing.] a natural or suitable environment, especially for an animal: *Water is a fish's natural element.*
- ELECTRICAL PART **9** [C] the part of a piece of electrical equipment that gives out heat

**IDM** **in your 'element** doing what you are good at and enjoy: *She's really in her element at parties.* **out of your 'element** in a situation that you are not used to and that makes you feel uncomfortable

**elem·en·tal** /ˌelɪˈmentl/ *adj.* [usually before noun] (*formal*) **1** wild and powerful; like the forces of nature: *the elemental fury of the storm* **2** basic and important: *an elemental truth*

**elem·en·tary** /ˌelɪˈmentri/ *adj.* **1** in or connected with the first stages of a course of study: *an elementary English course ◇ a book for elementary students ◇ at an elementary level* ⇒ compare PRIMARY, SECONDARY **2** of the most basic kind: *the elementary laws of economics ◇ an elementary mistake* **3** very simple and easy: *elementary questions*

**ele,mentary 'particle** (*also* **fundamental particle**) *noun* (*physics*) a very small piece of MATTER (= a substance), such as a QUARK, that does not contain within it any even smaller pieces of matter ⇒ compare SUBATOMIC PARTICLE

**ele'mentary school** (*also informal* **'grade school**) *noun* (in the US) a school for children between the ages of about 6 and 12

**ele·phant** /ˈelɪfənt/ *noun* a very large animal with thick grey skin, large ears, two curved outer teeth called TUSKS and a long nose called a TRUNK. There are two types of elephant, the African and the Asian: *herds of elephants ◇ a bull elephant ◇ a baby elephant* ⇒ see also WHITE ELEPHANT

**IDM** **the ,elephant in the 'room** a problem or question that everyone knows about but does not mention because it is easier not to discuss it: *The elephant in the room was the money that had to be paid in bribes.*

**ele·phan·tine** /ˌelɪˈfæntaɪn; NAmE -tiːn/ *adj.* (*formal or humorous*) very large and CLUMSY; like an elephant

**ele·vate** /ˈelɪveɪt/ *verb* **1** (*formal*) to give sb/sth a higher position or rank, often more important than they deserve **SYN** raise, promote: *~ sb/ sth (to sth) He elevated many of his friends to powerful positions within the government. ◇ ~sth (into/to sth) It was an attempt to elevate football to a subject worthy of serious study.* **2** **~sth** (*specialist or formal*) to lift sth up or put sth in a higher position: *It is important that the injured leg should be elevated.* **3 ~sth** (*specialist*) to make the level of sth increase: *Smoking often elevates blood pressure.* **4 ~sth** (*formal*) to improve a person's mood, so that they feel happy: *The song never failed to elevate his spirits.*

**ele·vated** /ˈelɪveɪtɪd/ *adj.* [usually before noun] **1** high in rank: *an elevated status* **2** (*formal*) having a high moral or INTELLECTUAL level: *elevated language/sentiments/thoughts* **3** higher than the area around; above the level of the ground: *The house is in an elevated position, overlooking the town. ◇ an elevated highway/railway/road* (= one that runs on a bridge above the ground or street) **4** (*specialist*) higher than normal: *elevated blood pressure*

**ele·vat·ing** /ˈelɪveɪtɪŋ/ *adj.* making people think about serious and interesting subjects: *Reading this essay was an elevating experience.*

**ele·va·tion** /ˌelɪˈveɪʃn/ *noun* **1** [U] (*formal*) the process of sb getting a higher or more important rank: *his elevation to the presidency* **2** [C, usually sing.] (*specialist*) the height of a place, especially its height above sea level: *The city is at an elevation of 2 000 metres.* **3** [C] (*formal*) a piece of ground that is higher than the area around **4** [C] (*architecture*) one side of a building, or a drawing of this by an architect: *the front/rear/side elevation of a house* ⇒ compare PLAN **5** [U, sing.] (*specialist*) an increase in the level or amount of sth: *elevation of blood sugar levels*

**ele·va·tor** /ˈelɪveɪtə(r)/ *noun* **1** (*NAmE*) (*BrE* **lift**) a machine that carries people or goods up and down to different levels in a building or a mine: *It's on the fifth floor, so we'd better take the elevator.* **2** (*NAmE*) = GRAIN ELEVATOR **3** a part in the tail of an aircraft that is moved to make it go up and down

**eleven** /ɪˈlevn/ **1** *number* 11 **HELP** There are examples of how to use numbers at the entry for **five**. **2** *noun* a team of eleven players for football (soccer), CRICKET or hockey: *She was chosen for the first eleven.* ▶ **elev·enth** /-vnθ/ *ordinal number*, *noun* **HELP** There are examples of how to use ordinal numbers at the entry for **fifth**.

**IDM** **at the e,leventh 'hour** at the last possible moment; just in time

**e,leven-'plus** *noun* (*usually* **the eleven-plus**) [sing.] an exam that all children used to take in the UK at the age of eleven to decide which type of SECONDARY SCHOOL they should go to. It is still taken in a few areas.

**ELF** /elf/ *abbr.* (*linguistics*) English as a lingua franca (English used as a shared language of communication between people whose main languages are different)

**elf** /elf/ *noun* (*pl.* **elves** /elvz/) (in stories) a creature like a small person with pointed ears, who has magic powers

**elfin** /ˈelfɪn/ adj. (of a person or their features) small and attractive: *an elfin face*

**elicit** /ɪˈlɪsɪt/ verb ~ **sth (from sb)** (formal) to get information or a reaction from sb, often with difficulty: *I could elicit no response from him.* ◊ *Her tears elicited great sympathy from her audience.* ▶ **elic·it·a·tion** /ɪˌlɪsɪˈteɪʃn/ noun [U]

**elide** /ɪˈlaɪd/ verb ~ **sth** (phonetics) to leave out the sound of part of a word when you are pronouncing it: *The 't' in 'often' may be elided.* ⇨ see also ELISION ⇨ WORDFINDER NOTE at PRONUNCIATION

**eli·gible** ⓘ+ C1 /ˈelɪdʒəbl/ adj. 1 ⓘ+ C1 a person who is eligible for sth or to do sth, is able to have or do it because they have the right qualifications, are the right age, etc: ~ **(for sth)** *Only those over 70 are eligible for the special payment.* ◊ ~ **(to do sth)** *When are you eligible to vote in your country?* OPP **ineligible** 2 an eligible young man or woman is thought to be a good choice as a husband/wife, usually because they are rich or attractive ▶ **eli·gi·bil·ity** /ˌelɪdʒəˈbɪləti/ noun [U]

**elim·in·ate** ⓘ+ B2 Ⓦ /ɪˈlɪmɪneɪt/ verb 1 ⓘ+ B2 to remove or get rid of sth: ~ **sth** *Credit cards eliminate the need to carry a lot of cash.* ◊ ~ **sth from sth** *This diet claims to eliminate toxins from the body.* 2 ⓘ+ C1 to stop considering that sb/sth might be responsible for sth or chosen for sth: ~ **sb/sth from sth** *The police have eliminated two suspects from their investigation.* ◊ ~ **sb/sth (as sth)** *Malaria was eliminated as a cause of death.* 3 ⓘ+ C1 [usually passive] to defeat a person or a team so that they no longer take part in a competition, etc. SYN **knock out: be eliminated (from sth)** *All the English teams were eliminated in the early stages of the competition.* 4 ~ **sb** (formal) to kill sb, especially an enemy or opponent: *Most of the regime's left-wing opponents were eliminated.* ▶ **elim·in·ation** /ɪˌlɪmɪˈneɪʃn/ noun [U, C]: *the elimination of disease/poverty/crime* ◊ *There were three eliminations in the first round of the competition.* ◊ *the elimination of toxins from the body*

**eli·sion** /ɪˈlɪʒn/ noun [U, C] (phonetics) the act of leaving out the sound of part of a word when it is spoken, for example the pronunciation of *sixth* as /sɪks/ ⇨ see also ELIDE

**elite** ⓘ+ C1 /eɪˈliːt, ɪ-/ noun [C + sing./pl. v.] 1 ⓘ+ C1 a small group of people in a society, etc. who are powerful and have a lot of influence, because they are rich, intelligent, etc: *a member of the ruling/intellectual elite* ◊ *Public opinion is influenced by the small elite who control the media.* ◊ *In these countries, only the elite can afford an education for their children.* 2 ⓘ+ C1 a group of people with the greatest ability at the highest level of competition, especially in sport: *The club has returned to the elite of European football.* ⇨ WORDFINDER NOTE at SOCIETY ▶ **elite** adj. [only before noun]: *an elite group of senior officials* ◊ *an elite military academy* ◊ *an elite athlete/swimmer/runner*

**elit·ism** /eɪˈliːtɪzəm, ɪ-/ noun [U] (often disapproving) 1 a way of organizing a system, society, etc. so that only a few people (= an elite) have power or influence: *Many people believe that private education encourages elitism.* 2 the feeling of being better than other people that being part of an elite encourages ▶ **elit·ist** adj.: *an elitist model of society* ◊ *She accused him of being elitist.* **elit·ist** noun

**elixir** /ɪˈlɪksə(r); BrE also -sɪə(r)/ noun (literary) a magic liquid that is believed to cure illnesses or to make people live forever: *the elixir of life/youth*

**Eliza·bethan** /ɪˌlɪzəˈbiːθn/ adj. connected with the time when Queen Elizabeth I was queen of England (1558–1603) ▶ **Eliza·bethan** noun: *Shakespeare was an Elizabethan.*

**elk** /elk/ noun (pl. **elk** or **elks**) 1 (BrE) a large DEER that lives in the north of Europe, Asia and North America. In North America it is called a MOOSE. 2 (NAmE) = WAPITI 3 **Elk** a member of the Benevolent and Protective Order of Elks, a US social organization that gives money to charity

**ELL** /ˌiː el ˈel/ noun (US) English language learner (a student who is learning English as a second or foreign language)

**el·lipse** /ɪˈlɪps/ noun (specialist) a regular OVAL shape, like a circle that has been pressed on two sides ⇨ picture at CONIC SECTION

**el·lip·sis** /ɪˈlɪpsɪs/ noun (pl. **el·lip·ses** /ɪˈlɪpsiːz/) [C, U] 1 (grammar) the act of leaving out a word or words from a sentence deliberately, when the meaning can be under-

elk/moose

wapiti

stood without them 2 three small marks (…) used to show that a word or words have been left out

**el·lip·tic·al** /ɪˈlɪptɪkl/ adj. 1 (grammar) with a word or words left out of a sentence deliberately: *an elliptical remark* (= one that suggests more than is actually said) 2 (also less frequent **el·lip·tic** /ɪˈlɪptɪk/) (geometry) connected with or in the form of an ELLIPSE ▶ **el·lip·tic·al·ly** /-kli/ adv.: *to speak/write elliptically*

**elm** /elm/ noun 1 [C, U] (also **elm tree**) a tall tree with broad leaves: *a line of stately elms* ◊ *The avenue was planted with elm.* 2 [U] the hard wood of the elm tree

**El Niño** /ˌel ˈniːnjəʊ/ noun [U] a set of changes in the weather system near the coast of northern Peru and Ecuador that happens every few years, causing the surface of the Pacific Ocean there to become warmer and having severe effects on the weather in many parts of the world ⇨ compare LA NIÑA (1)

**elo·cu·tion** /ˌeləˈkjuːʃn/ noun [U] the ability to speak clearly and correctly, especially in public and pronouncing the words in a way that is considered to be socially acceptable

**elong·ate** /ˈiːlɒŋɡeɪt; NAmE ɪˈlɔːŋɡeɪt/ verb [I, T] ~ **(sth)** to become longer; to make sth longer SYN **lengthen** ▶ **elonga·tion** /ˌiːlɒŋˈɡeɪʃn; NAmE -lɔːŋ-/ noun [U]: *the elongation of vowel sounds*

**elong·ated** /ˈiːlɒŋɡeɪtɪd; NAmE ɪˈlɔːŋɡeɪtɪd/ adj. long and thin, often in a way that is not normal: *Modigliani's women have strangely elongated faces.*

**elope** /ɪˈləʊp/ verb [I] ~ **(with sb)** to run away with sb in order to marry them secretly ▶ **elope·ment** noun [C, U]

**elo·quent** /ˈeləkwənt/ adj. 1 able to use language and express your opinions well, especially when you are speaking in public: *an eloquent speech/speaker* 2 (of a look or movement) able to express a feeling: *His eyes were eloquent.* ▶ **elo·quence** /-kwəns/ noun [U]: *a speech of passionate eloquence* ◊ *the eloquence of his smile* **elo·quent·ly** adv.: *She spoke eloquently on the subject.* ◊ *His face expressed his grief more eloquently than any words.*

**else** ⓘ A1 /els/ adv. (used in questions or after *nothing, nobody, something, anything,* etc.) 1 ⓘ A1 in addition to sth already mentioned: *What else did he say?* ◊ *I don't want anything else, thanks.* ◊ *I'm taking a few clothes and some books, not much else.* 2 ⓘ A1 different: *Ask somebody else to help her.* ◊ *Haven't you got anything else to wear?* ◊ *Why didn't you come? Everybody else was there.* ◊ *Yes I did give it to her. What else could I do?* 3 (informal) if not SYN **or else**: *Keep your mouth shut, else we'll be in trouble.*

IDM **or else 1** if not SYN **otherwise**: *Hurry up or else you'll be late.* ◊ *They can't be coming or else they'd have called.* **2** used to introduce the second of two possibilities: *He either forgot or else decided not to come.* **3** (informal) used to threaten or warn sb: *Just shut up, or else!*

**else·where** ⓘ B2 Ⓦ /ˌelsˈweə(r); NAmE -ˈwer/ adv. in, at or to another place or other places: *Dissatisfied*

Ⓘ Oxford Phrasal Academic Lexicon (OPAL) written and spoken word lists  |  Ⓦ OPAL written word list  |  Ⓢ OPAL spoken word list

# ELT

customers will **look elsewhere**. ◊ *The site contains information not found elsewhere*. ◊ *Our favourite restaurant was closed, so we had to go elsewhere*. ◊ *Prices are higher here than elsewhere*.

**ELT** /ˌiː el ˈtiː/ *abbr.* (*BrE*) English Language Teaching (the teaching of English to people for whom it is not the first language)

**elu·ci·date** /ɪˈluːsɪdeɪt/ *verb* [T, I] (*formal*) to make sth clearer by explaining it more fully SYN **explain**: ~(**sth**) *He elucidated a point of grammar.* ◊ *Let me elucidate.* ◊ *~ what, how, etc* ... *I will try to elucidate what I think the problems are.* ▶ **elu·ci·da·tion** /ɪˌluːsɪˈdeɪʃn/ *noun* [U, C]: *Their objectives and methods require further elucidation.*

**elude** /ɪˈluːd/ *verb* **1** ~ **sb/sth** to manage to avoid or escape from sb/sth, especially in a clever way: *The two men managed to elude the police for six weeks.* **2** ~ **sb** if sth **eludes you**, you are not able to achieve it, or not able to remember or understand it: *He was extremely tired but sleep eluded him.* ◊ *They're a popular band but chart success has eluded them so far.* ◊ *Finally he remembered the tiny detail that had eluded him the night before.*

**elu·sive** /ɪˈluːsɪv/ *adj.* difficult to find, define or achieve: *Eric, as elusive as ever, was nowhere to be found.* ◊ *the elusive concept of 'literature'* ◊ *A solution to the problem of toxic waste is proving elusive.* ▶ **elu·sive·ly** *adv.* **elu·sive·ness** *noun* [U]

**elver** /ˈelvə(r)/ *noun* a young EEL

**elves** /elvz/ *pl.* of ELF

**Ely·sian** /ɪˈlɪziən/ *NAmE* ɪˈlɪːʒən/ *adj.* (*literary*) relating to heaven or to a place of perfect happiness
IDM **the Elysian Fields** (in ancient Greek stories) a wonderful place where some people were taken by the gods after death

**em-** /ɪm/ ⇒ EN-

**'em** /əm/ *pron.* (*informal*) a way of saying 'them' in informal speech: *Don't let 'em get away.* HELP You should not write this form unless you are copying sb's speech.

**ema·ci·ated** /ɪˈmeɪsieɪtɪd, ɪˈmeɪʃi-/ *adj.* thin and weak, usually because of illness or lack of food ▶ **ema·ci·ation** /ɪˌmeɪsiˈeɪʃn/ *noun* [U]: *She was very thin, almost to the point of emaciation.*

**email** (also **e-mail**) /ˈiːmeɪl/ *noun, verb*
■ *noun* **1** [U] a way of sending messages and data to other people by means of computers connected together in a network: *They use email, conference calls and chat rooms to discuss business.* ◊ *by ~ to send a message by email* ◊ *via ~ Automated notifications will be sent via email or text message.* ◊ *What's your email address?* **2** (also **mail**) [C, U] a message sent by email: *to send/receive/read an email* ◊ *I have to check my email.* ◊ *unsolicited/spam/junk email* ⇒ WORDFINDER NOTE at MESSAGE
■ *verb* (also **mail**) [T, I] to send a message to sb by email: *~ sb Patrick emailed me yesterday.* ◊ *~ sth (to sb) I'll email the documents to her.* ◊ *~ sb sth I'll email her the documents.* ◊ *~ for sth Call or email for a free information pack.*

**em·an·ate** /ˈeməneɪt/ *verb* ~**sth** (*formal*) to produce or show sth: *He emanates power and confidence.* ▶ **em·an·ation** /ˌeməˈneɪʃn/ *noun* [C, U]
PHRV **emanate from sth** (*formal*) to come from sth or somewhere SYN **issue from**: *The sound of loud music emanated from the building.* ◊ *The proposal originally emanated from the UN.*

**eman·ci·pate** /ɪˈmænsɪpeɪt/ *verb* [often passive] (*formal*) to free sb, especially from legal, political or social controls that limit what they can do SYN **free**: **be emancipated (from sth)** *Slaves were not emancipated until 1863 in the United States.* ▶ **eman·ci·pated** *adj.*: *Are women now fully emancipated* (= with the same rights and opportunities as men)? ◊ *an emancipated young woman* (= one with modern ideas about women's place in society) **eman·ci·pa·tion** /ɪˌmænsɪˈpeɪʃn/ *noun* [U]: *the emancipation of slaves*

**emas·cu·late** /ɪˈmæskjuleɪt/ *verb* [often passive] (*formal*)
**1** ~ **sb/sth** to make sb/sth less powerful or less effective
**2** ~ **sb** to make a man feel that he has lost his male role or qualities ▶ **emas·cu·la·tion** /ɪˌmæskjuˈleɪʃn/ *noun* [U]

**em·balm** /ɪmˈbɑːm/ *verb* ~ **sb/sth** to prevent a dead body from DECAYING (= being destroyed by natural processes) by treating it with special substances to preserve it ▶ **em·balm·er** *noun*

**em·bank·ment** /ɪmˈbæŋkmənt/ *noun* a wall or bank of stone or earth made to keep water back or to carry a road or railway over low ground

**em·bargo** /ɪmˈbɑːɡəʊ; *NAmE* -ˈbɑːrɡ-/ *noun, verb*
■ *noun* (*pl.* **-oes**) **1** an official order that bans trade with another country SYN **boycott**: *an arms embargo* ◊ *to impose/enforce/lift an embargo* ◊ *~ on sth an embargo on arms sales to certain countries* ◊ *~ against sth a trade embargo against certain countries* ⇒ WORDFINDER NOTE at TRADE **2** an official ban on any activity: *~ on (doing) sth There is a complete embargo on taking photographs in court.*
■ *verb* (**em·bar·goes, em·bar·go·ing, em·bar·goed, em·bar·goed**) **1** ~ **sth** to officially ban trade with another country SYN **boycott**: *There have been calls to embargo all arms shipments to the region.* **2** [usually passive] to officially ban publication of sth: **be embargoed (for sth)** *The report is strictly embargoed for publication until Friday.*

**em·bark** /ɪmˈbɑːk; *NAmE* -ˈbɑːrk/ *verb* [I, T] (*formal*) to get onto a ship or plane; to put sb/sth onto a ship or plane: *We stood on the pier and watched as they embarked.* ◊ *~ sb They embarked the troops by night.* OPP **disembark** ▶ **em·bark·ation** /ˌembɑːˈkeɪʃn; *NAmE* -bɑːrˈk-/ *noun* [U, C]: *Embarkation will be at 14:20 hours.*
PHRV **em·bark on/upon sth** (*formal*) to start to do sth new or difficult: *She is about to embark on a diplomatic career.*

**em·bar·rass** /ɪmˈbærəs/ *verb* **1** to make sb feel shy, uncomfortable or ashamed, especially in a social situation: *~ sb Her questions about my private life embarrassed me.* ◊ *I didn't want to embarrass him by kissing her in front of his friends.* ◊ **it embarrasses sb to do sth** *It embarrasses her to meet strange men in the corridor at night.* **2** ~ **sb** to cause problems or difficulties for sb: *The speech was deliberately designed to embarrass the prime minister.*

**em·bar·rassed** /ɪmˈbærəst/ *adj.* **1** (of a person or their behaviour) shy, uncomfortable or ashamed, especially in a social situation: *I've never felt so embarrassed in my life!* ◊ *Her remark was followed by an embarrassed silence.* ◊ *~ about (doing) sth She's embarrassed about her weight.* ◊ *~ at (doing) sth He felt embarrassed at being the centre of attention.* ◊ *~ to do sth I'm embarrassed to admit it, but I laughed.* ⇒ note at ASHAMED ⇒ WORDFINDER NOTE at SORRY **2** **financially ~** (*informal*) not having any money; in a difficult financial situation

**em·bar·rass·ing** /ɪmˈbærəsɪŋ/ *adj.* **1** making you feel shy, uncomfortable or ashamed: *an embarrassing moment/situation* ◊ *~ (for sb) (to do sth) It can be embarrassing for children to tell complete strangers about such incidents.* ◊ *~ doing sth It was so embarrassing having to sing in public.* **2** *~ (to/for sb)* causing sb to look stupid, dishonest, etc: *The report is likely to prove highly embarrassing to the government.* ▶ **em·bar·rass·ing·ly** *adv.*: *The play was embarrassingly bad.*

**em·bar·rass·ment** /ɪmˈbærəsmənt/ *noun* **1** [U] shy, uncomfortable or guilty feelings; a feeling of being embarrassed: *I nearly died of embarrassment when he said that.* ◊ *~ of (doing) sth I'm glad you offered—it saved me the embarrassment of having to ask.* ◊ **to sb's ~** *Much to her embarrassment, she realized that everybody had been listening to her singing.* **2** [C] *~ (to/for sb)* a situation that causes problems for sb: *Her resignation will be a severe embarrassment to the party.* **3** [C] *~ (to sb)* a person who causes problems for another person or other people and makes them feel embarrassed
IDM **an embarrassment of 'riches** so many good things that it is difficult to choose just one

**em·bassy** /ˈembəsi/ *noun* (*pl.* **-ies**) **1** a group of officials led by an AMBASSADOR who represent their government in a foreign country; **embassy officials** ◊ *to inform the embassy of the situation* **2** the building in which an embassy works: *a demonstration outside the Russian Embassy* ⇒ compare CONSULATE, HIGH COMMISSION ⇒ WORDFINDER NOTE at ALLY

**em·bat·tled** /ɪmˈbætld/ *adj.* **1** surrounded by problems and difficulties: *the embattled party leader* **2** (of an army, a city, etc.) involved in war; surrounded by the enemy

**embed** /ɪmˈbed/ (*also* **imbed**) *verb* (**-dd-**) [usually passive] **1** to fix sth in a substance or solid object: **be embedded in sth** *an operation to remove glass that was embedded in his leg* ◊ (*figurative*) *These attitudes are deeply embedded in our society* (= felt very strongly and difficult to change). ◊ **~ sth/itself (in sth)** *The bullet embedded itself in the wall.* **2 ~ sb** to send a journalist, photographer, etc. to an area where there is fighting, so that he or she can travel with the army and report what is happening: *embedded reporters in the war zone* **3 ~ sth** (*linguistics*) to place a sentence inside another sentence. In the sentence 'I'm aware that she knows', *she knows* is an embedded sentence.

**em·bel·lish** /ɪmˈbelɪʃ/ *verb* (*formal*) **1 ~ sth** to make sth more beautiful by adding decoration to it SYN **decorate** **2 ~ sth** to make a story more interesting by adding details that are not always true SYN **embroider** ▸ **em·bel·lish·ment** *noun* [U, C]: *Good fresh food needs very little embellishment.* ◊ *a sixteenth-century church with eighteenth-century embellishments*

**ember** /ˈembə(r)/ *noun* [usually pl.] a piece of wood or coal that is not burning but is still red and hot after a fire has died

**em·bez·zle** /ɪmˈbezl/ *verb* [T, I] **~ (sth)** to steal money that you are responsible for or that belongs to your employer: *He was found guilty of embezzling $150 000 of public funds.* ▸ **em·bezzle·ment** *noun* [U]: *She was found guilty of embezzlement.* **em·bez·zler** /-ˈbezlə(r)/ *noun*

**em·bit·ter** /ɪmˈbɪtə(r)/ *verb* **~ sb** to make sb feel angry or disappointed about sth over a long period of time ▸ **em·bit·tered** *adj.*: *a sick and embittered old man* ◊ *an embittered laugh*

**em·bla·zon** /ɪmˈbleɪzn/ *verb* (*also* **bla·zon**) *verb* [usually passive] to decorate sth with a design, a symbol or words so that people will notice it easily: **~ A with B** *baseball caps emblazoned with the team's logo* ◊ **~ B on, across,** etc. **A** *The team's logo was emblazoned on the baseball caps.*

**em·blem** /ˈembləm/ *noun* **1 ~ (of sth)** a design or picture that represents a country or an organization: *America's national emblem, the bald eagle* ◊ *the club emblem* **2 ~ (of sth)** something that represents a perfect example or a principle: *The dove is an emblem of peace.*

**em·blem·at·ic** /ˌembləˈmætɪk/ *adj.* **1 ~ (of sth)** (*formal*) that represents or is a symbol of sth SYN **representative** **2 ~ (of sth)** (*formal*) that is considered typical of a situation, an area of work, etc. SYN **typical**: *The violence is emblematic of what is happening in our inner cities.*

**em·bodi·ment** /ɪmˈbɒdimənt; NAmE -ˈbɑː-/ *noun* [usually sing.] **~ of sth** (*formal*) a person or thing that represents or is a typical example of an idea or a quality SYN **epitome**: *He is the embodiment of the young successful businessman.*

**em·body** /ɪmˈbɒdi; NAmE -ˈbɑː-/ *verb* (**em·bod·ies, em·body·ing, em·bod·ied, em·bod·ied**) **1** to express or represent an idea or a quality SYN **represent**: **~ sth** *a politician who embodied the hopes of black youth* ◊ **be embodied in sth** *the principles embodied in the Declaration of Human Rights* **2 ~ sth** (*formal*) to include or contain sth: *This model embodies many new features.*

**em·bold·en** /ɪmˈbəʊldən/ *verb* **1** [usually passive] (*formal*) to make sb feel braver or more confident: **(be) emboldened by sth** *Emboldened by the wine, he went over to introduce himself to her.* ◊ **be emboldened to do sth** *With such a majority, the administration was emboldened to introduce radical new policies.* **2 ~ sth** (*specialist*) to make a piece of text appear in BOLD print

**em·bol·ism** /ˈembəlɪzəm/ *noun* [C, U] (*medical*) a condition in which a BLOOD CLOT or air bubble blocks an ARTERY in the body

**em·bolus** /ˈembələs/ *noun* (*pl.* **em·boli** /ˈembəlaɪ, -liː/) (*medical*) a BLOOD CLOT, air bubble, or small object that causes an embolism

**em·boss** /ɪmˈbɒs; NAmE -ˈbɔːs/ *verb* [usually passive] to put a raised design or piece of writing on paper, leather, etc.: **A (is) embossed with B** *stationery embossed with the hotel's name* ◊ **B (is) embossed on A** *The hotel's name was embossed on the stationery.* ▸ **em·bossed** *adj.*: *embossed stationery*

**em·brace** /ɪmˈbreɪs/ *verb* (*formal*) **1** [I, T] to put your arms around sb as a sign of love or friendship SYN **hug**: *They embraced and promised to keep in touch.* ◊ **~ sb** *She embraced her son warmly.* **2** [T] **~ sth** to accept an idea, a proposal, a set of beliefs, etc., especially when it is done with enthusiasm: *to embrace democracy/feminism/Islam* **3** [T] **~ sth** to include sth: *The talks embraced a wide range of issues.* ▸ **em·brace** *noun* [C, U]: *He held her in a warm embrace.* ◊ *There were tears and embraces as they said goodbye.* ◊ *the country's eager embrace of modern technology*

**em·broi·der** /ɪmˈbrɔɪdə(r)/ *verb* **1** [T, I] to decorate cloth with a pattern of STITCHES usually using coloured THREAD: **~ A on B** *She embroidered flowers on the cushion covers.* ◊ **~ B with A** *She embroidered the cushion cover with flowers.* ◊ **~ (sth)** *an embroidered blouse* ◊ *She sat in the window, embroidering.* **2** [T] **~ sth** to make a story more interesting by adding details that are not always true SYN **embellish**

**em·broi·dery** /ɪmˈbrɔɪdəri/ *noun* **1** [U, C] patterns that are SEWN onto cloth using THREADS of various colours; cloth that is decorated in this way: *a beautiful piece of embroidery* ◊ *Indian embroideries* **2** [U] the skill or activity of decorating cloth in this way ⊃ WORDFINDER NOTE at SEW

**em·broil** /ɪmˈbrɔɪl/ *verb* [often passive] (*formal*) to involve sb/yourself in an argument or a difficult situation: **be/become embroiled (in sth)** *He became embroiled in a dispute with his neighbours.* ◊ **~ sb/yourself (in sth)** *I was reluctant to embroil myself in his problems.*

**em·bryo** /ˈembriəʊ/ *noun* (*pl.* **-os**) **1** a young animal or plant in the very early stages of development before birth, or before coming out of its egg or seed, especially a human egg in the first eight weeks after FERTILIZATION: *human embryos* ⊃ compare FETUS **2** a thing at a very early stage of development: *the embryo of an idea* ◊ *an embryo central bank*
**IDM** ▸ **in embryo** existing but not yet fully developed: *The idea already existed in embryo in his earlier novels.*

**em·bry·ology** /ˌembriˈɒlədʒi; NAmE -ˈɑːl-/ *noun* [U] the scientific study of the development of embryos ▸ **em·bryo·logic·al** /ˌembriəˈlɒdʒɪkl; NAmE -ˈlɑːdʒ-/ *adj.* **em·bry·olo·gist** /ˌembriˈɒlədʒɪst; NAmE -ˈɑːl-/ *noun*

**em·bry·on·ic** /ˌembriˈɒnɪk; NAmE -ˈɑːn-/ *adj.* [usually before noun] **1** (*formal*) in an early stage of development: *The plan, as yet, only exists in embryonic form.* **2** (*specialist*) of an embryo: *embryonic cells*

**emcee** /ˌemˈsiː/ *noun* (*especially NAmE, informal*) **1** a person who introduces guests or people who provide entertainment at a formal occasion SYN **compère, master of ceremonies** **2** an MC at a club or party ▸ **emcee** *verb* [I, T] **~ (sth)**

**emend** /iˈmend/ *verb* **~ sth** (*formal*) to remove the mistakes in a piece of writing, especially before it is printed SYN **correct**

**emend·ation** /ˌiːmenˈdeɪʃn/ *noun* [C, U] (*formal*) a letter or word that has been changed or corrected in a text; the act of making changes to a text

**em·er·ald** /ˈemərəld/ *noun* **1** [C, U] a bright green PRECIOUS STONE: *an emerald ring* **2** (*also* **emerald 'green**) [U] a bright green colour ▸ **em·er·ald** (*also* **emerald 'green**) *adj.*

**the Emerald 'Isle** *noun* [sing.] (*literary*) a name for Ireland

**emerg** /ɪˈmɜːdʒ; NAmE ɪˈmɜːrdʒ/ *noun* [U] (*CanE, informal*) = EMERGENCY ROOM

**emerge** /ɪˈmɜːdʒ; NAmE ɪˈmɜːrdʒ/ *verb* **1** [I] to move out of or away from sth and become possible to see: *The crabs emerge at low tide to look for food.* ◊ **~ from sth** *She finally emerged from her room at noon.* ◊ **~ into sth** *We emerged into bright sunlight.* **2** [I, T] (of facts, ideas, etc.) to become known SYN **transpire**: *No new evidence emerged during the investigation.* ◊ **~ from sth** *A clear picture emerges from this complex set of data.* ◊ **it emerges that…** *It emerged that the company*

# emergence

was going to be sold. **3** [B2] [I] to start to exist; to appear or become known: *After the elections opposition groups began to emerge.* ◊ *~ as sth He emerged as a key figure in the campaign* ⊃ see also RE-EMERGE **4** [I] *~* **(from sth)** to survive a difficult situation or experience: *She emerged from the scandal with her reputation intact.*

**emer·gence** [+] [C1] [W] /ɪˈmɜːdʒəns; NAmE ɪˈmɜːrdʒ-/ noun [U] **1** [+] [C1] *~* **(of sb/sth) (from sth)** the fact of sb/sth moving out of or away from sth and becoming possible to see: *the island's emergence from the sea 3000 years ago* ◊ *Albania's emergence from its long period of isolation* **2** [+] [C1] the fact of starting to exist or becoming known for the first time: *the emergence of new technologies*

**emer·gency** [🔊] [B1] /ɪˈmɜːdʒənsi; NAmE ɪˈmɜːrdʒ-/ noun (pl. **-ies**) [C, U] a sudden serious and dangerous event or situation that needs immediate action to deal with it: *This is a medical emergency needing urgent treatment with antibiotics.* ◊ *The government has declared a state of emergency following the earthquake.* ◊ **in an** *~ This door should only be used in an emergency.* ◊ **for emergencies** *I always have some extra cash with me for emergencies.* ◊ *the emergency exit* (= to be used in an emergency) ◊ *The pilot made an emergency landing in a field.* ◊ *The emergency response team was on the scene within eight minutes.* ⊃ see also ACCIDENT AND EMERGENCY

**eˈmergency brake** *noun* **1** (*NAmE*) = HANDBRAKE **2** a BRAKE on a train that can be pulled in an emergency

**eˈmergency room** *noun* (*abbr.* **ER**) (*NAmE*) [C] **accident and eˈmergency**, *CanE*, *informal* **emerg** [U] the part of a hospital where people who need immediate treatment are taken

**eˈmergency services** *noun* [pl.] (*BrE*) the public organizations that deal with emergencies: *the police, fire,* AMBULANCE and COASTGUARD *services* ⊃ compare FIRST RESPONDER

**emer·gent** /ɪˈmɜːdʒənt; NAmE ɪˈmɜːrdʒ-/ adj. [usually before noun] new and still developing: *emergent nations/ states*

**emerging** /ɪˈmɜːdʒɪŋ; NAmE ɪˈmɜːrdʒ-/ adj. [only before noun] starting to exist, grow or become known: *the emerging markets of South Asia* ◊ *an emerging artist/talent* ◊ *newly emerging areas of science*

**emeri·tus** /ɪˈmerɪtəs/ adj. (often **Emeritus**) used before or after a title to show that a person, usually a university teacher, keeps the title as an honour, although he or she has stopped working: *the Emeritus Professor of Biology* [HELP] In *NAmE* the form **Emerita** /ɪˈmerɪtə/ is used for women: *Professor Emerita Mary Judd*

**emery** /ˈeməri/ noun [U] a hard mineral used especially in powder form for POLISHING things and making them smooth

**emet·ic** /ɪˈmetɪk/ noun (*medical*) a substance that makes you VOMIT (= bring up food from the stomach) ▶ **emet·ic** *adj.*

**emi·grant** /ˈemɪɡrənt/ noun a person who leaves their country to live permanently in another: *emigrant workers* ◊ *emigrants to Canada* ⊃ compare IMMIGRANT

**emi·grate** /ˈemɪɡreɪt/ verb [I] *~* **(from …) (to …)** to leave your own country to go and live permanently in another country ⊃ compare IMMIGRATE ▶ **emi·gra·tion** /ˌemɪˈɡreɪʃn/ noun [U, C]: *the mass emigration of Jews from Eastern Europe* ⊃ compare IMMIGRATION

**émi·gré** /ˈemɪɡreɪ/ noun (*from French*) a person who has left their own country, usually for political reasons [SYN] **exile**

**emi·nence** /ˈemɪnəns/ noun **1** [U] (*formal*) the quality of being famous and respected, especially in a profession: *a man of political eminence* **2** [C] **His/Your Eminence** a title used in speaking to or about a CARDINAL (= a priest of the highest rank in the Roman Catholic Church): *Their Eminences will see you now.* **3** [C] (*old-fashioned* or *formal*) an area of high ground

**emi·nent** /ˈemɪnənt/ adj. [usually before noun] **1** (of people) famous and respected, especially in a particular profession: *an eminent architect* **2** (of good qualities) unusual; excellent: *a man of eminent good sense*

**ˈeminent doˌmain** *noun* [U] (*especially NAmE, law*) the right to force sb to sell land or a building if it is needed by the government

**emi·nent·ly** /ˈemɪnəntli/ adv. (*formal*) (used to emphasize a positive quality) very; extremely: *She seems eminently suitable for the job.*

**emir** (*also* **amir**) /eˈmɪə(r), ˈeɪmɪə(r); NAmE eˈmɪr, eɪˈm-/ noun the title given to some Muslim rulers: *the Emir of Kuwait*

**emir·ate** /ˈemɪrət, ˈemɪr-; NAmE ˈemər-/ noun **1** the position of an emir **2** an area of land that is ruled over by an emir: *the United Arab Emirates* **3** the period of time that an emir rules

**emis·sary** /ˈemɪsəri; NAmE -seri/ noun (pl. **-ies**) (*formal*) a person who is sent to deliver an official message, especially from one country to another, or to perform a special task [SYN] **envoy**

**emis·sion** [+] [B2] /iˈmɪʃn; NAmE ɪˈmɪʃn/ noun **1** [+] [B2] the production or sending out of light, heat, gas, etc: *the emission of carbon dioxide into the atmosphere* ◊ *emission controls* **2** [+] [B2] [C] gas, etc. that is sent out into the air: *The government has pledged to clean up industrial emissions.*

**eˈmissions ˌtrading** *noun* = CARBON TRADING

**emit** /iˈmɪt/ verb **(-tt-)** *~* **sth** (*formal*) to send out sth such as light, heat, sound, gas, etc: *The metal container began to emit a clicking sound.* ◊ *Sulphur gases were emitted by the volcano.*

**Emmy** /ˈemi/ noun (pl. **-ys**) one of the awards given every year in the US for achievement in the making of television programmes

**emo** /ˈiːməʊ/ noun (pl. **emos**) **1** [U] a style of rock music that developed from PUNK, but has more complicated musical arrangements and deals with more emotional subjects: *an emo band* **2** [C] a person who likes emo music and often follows emo fashion, wearing tight jeans and having long black hair. Emos are typically supposed to be emotional and sensitive.

**emoji** /ɪˈməʊdʒi/ noun (pl. **emoji** or **emojis**) (*from Japanese*) a small digital image used to express an idea or emotion in emails, on the internet, on social media, etc: *He responded with a red heart emoji.*

**emol·li·ent** /ɪˈmɒliənt; NAmE ɪˈmɑːl-/ adj., noun
■ *adj.* (*formal*) **1** making a person or situation calmer in the hope of keeping relations peaceful [SYN] **soothing**: *an emollient reply* **2** (*specialist*) used for making your skin soft or less painful [SYN] **soothing**: *an emollient cream*
■ *noun* [C, U] (*specialist*) a liquid or cream that is used to make the skin soft

**emolu·ment** /ɪˈmɒljumənt; NAmE ɪˈmɑːl-/ noun [usually pl.] (*formal*) money paid to sb for work they have done, especially to sb who earns a lot of money

**emote** /iˈməʊt/ verb [I] to show emotion in a very obvious way

**emoti·con** /ɪˈməʊtɪkɒn; NAmE -kɑːn/ noun a short set of keyboard symbols that represents the expression on sb's face, used in email, etc. to show the feelings of the person sending the message. For example :-) represents a smiling face (when you look at it with your head on one side).
⊃ WORDFINDER NOTE at MESSAGE

**emo·tion** [🔊] [B1] /iˈməʊʃn/ noun [C, U] a strong feeling such as love, fear or anger; the part of a person's character that consists of feelings: **to show/express your emotions** ◊ *They expressed mixed emotions at the news.* ◊ *Fear is a normal human emotion.* ◊ *Emotions are running high* (= people are feeling very excited, angry, etc.). ◊ *She showed no emotion at the verdict.* ◊ *Mary was overcome with emotion.*

**emo·tion·al** [🔊] [B2] [W] /iˈməʊʃənl/ adj. **1** [B2] [usually before noun] connected with people's feelings (= with the emotions): *emotional problems/stress* ◊ *an emotional impact/connection* ◊ *a child's emotional and intellectual development* ◊ *Mothers are often the ones who provide emotional support for the family.* **2** [B2] causing people to feel strong emotions [SYN] **emotive**: *emotional language* ◊ *~ for sb The anniversary of the accident was very emotional* for him. ◇ It was obviously an emotional moment for everyone involved. **3** ? B2 (*sometimes disapproving*) showing strong emotions, sometimes in a way that other people think is unnecessary: *an emotional response/reaction* ◇ *She was* **in a very emotional state**. ◇ *He tends to* **get emotional** *on these occasions*.

**e‧motional in'telligence** *noun* [U] the ability to understand your emotions and those of other people and to behave appropriately in different situations

**emo‧tion‧al‧ly** ?+ B2 /ɪˈməʊʃənəli/ *adv.* **1** ?+ B2 in a way that is connected with people's feelings (= with the emotions): *emotionally disturbed children* ◇ *I try not to become emotionally involved.* ◇ *They have suffered physically and emotionally.* **2** ?+ B2 in a way that causes people to feel strong emotions: *an emotionally charged atmosphere*

**emo‧tion‧less** /ɪˈməʊʃənləs/ *adj.* not showing any emotion: *an emotionless voice*

**emo‧tive** /ɪˈməʊtɪv/ *adj.* causing people to feel strong emotions SYN **emotional**: *emotive language/words* ◇ *Capital punishment is a highly emotive issue.*

**em‧pa‧nada** /ˌempəˈnɑːdə/ *noun* a Spanish or Latin American PASTRY filled with meat, vegetables, etc. and baked or fried

**em‧panel** (*also* **im‧panel**) /ɪmˈpænl/ *verb* (**-ll-**, *US* **-l-**) **~ sb/sth** to choose the members of a JURY in a court case; to choose sb as a member of a JURY

**em‧path‧et‧ic** /ˌempəˈθetɪk/ (*also* **em‧path‧ic** /emˈpæθɪk/) *adj.* able to understand how sb else feels because you can imagine what it is like to be that person: *an empathetic listener* ◇ **~ to/towards sb/sth** *His personal history makes him especially empathetic to workers' need for a fair wage.*
▶ **em‧path‧et‧ic‧al‧ly** /ˌempəˈθetɪkli/ (*also* **em‧path‧ic‧al‧ly** /emˈpæθɪkli/) *adv.*: *to listen empathetically*

**em‧pa‧thize** (*BrE also* **-ise**) /ˈempəθaɪz/ *verb* [I] **~ (with sb/sth)** to understand another person's feelings and experiences, especially because you have been in a similar situation

**em‧pathy** /ˈempəθi/ *noun* [U] the ability to understand another person's feelings, experience, etc.: **~ (with sb/sth)** *the writer's imaginative empathy with his subject* ◇ **~ (for sb/sth)** *empathy for other people's situations* ◇ **~ (between A and B)** *The empathy between the two women was obvious.*

**em‧peror** /ˈempərə(r)/ *noun* the ruler of an EMPIRE: *the Roman emperors* ◇ *the Emperor Napoleon* ⊃ *see also* EMPRESS
IDM **the ˌemperor's new ˈclothes** (*also* **the ˌemperor has no ˈclothes**) used to describe a situation in which everybody suddenly realizes that they were wrong to believe that sb/sth was very good, important, etc.: *Soon investors will realize that the emperor has no clothes and there will be a big sell-off in stocks.* ORIGIN From the story of *The Emperor's New Clothes* by Hans Christian Andersen, in which the emperor is tricked into thinking he is wearing beautiful new clothes and everyone pretends to admire them, until a little boy points out that he is naked.

**em‧phasis** ? B2 ○ /ˈemfəsɪs/ *noun* (*pl.* **em‧phases** /-fəsiːz/) [U, C] **1** ? B2 special importance that is given to sth SYN **stress**: **~ on/upon sth** *to put/lay/place emphasis on sth* ◇ *to put particular/special/strong emphasis on sth* ◇ *Increased emphasis is now being placed on corporate image.* ◇ **~ on/upon doing sth** *The emphasis is very much on learning the spoken language.* ◇ **with an ~ on sth** *We provide all types of information, with an emphasis on legal advice.* ◇ *There has been a shift of emphasis from manufacturing to service industries.* ◇ *The course has a vocational emphasis.* **2** ? B2 the extra force given to a word or phrase when spoken, especially in order to show that it is important; a way of writing a word (for example drawing a line below it) to show that it is important SYN **stress**: **~on sth** *You're placing the emphasis on the wrong syllable.* ◇ **with ~** *'I can assure you,' she added with emphasis, 'the figures are correct.'*

**em‧pha‧size** ? B2 ○ (*BrE also* **-ise**) /ˈemfəsaɪz/ *verb* **1** ? B2 to give special importance to sth SYN **stress**: **~ sth** *His speech emphasized the importance of attracting industry to the town.* ◇ **that …** *She emphasized that their plan would mean sacrifices and hard work.* ◇ **~ how, what,**

507

# employ

▼ LANGUAGE BANK

### emphasis

Highlighting an important point

- This case **emphasizes/highlights** the importance of honest communication between managers and employees.
- Effective communication skills are **essential/crucial/vital**.
- **It should be noted that** this study considers only verbal communication. Non-verbal communication is not dealt with here.
- **It is important to remember that/An important point to remember is that** non-verbal communication plays a key role in getting your message across.
- Communication is not only about the words you use but also your body language and, **especially/above all**, the effectiveness with which you listen.
- I would like to **draw attention to** the role of listening in effective communication.
- Choose your words carefully: **in particular**, avoid confusing and ambiguous language.
- Finally, and perhaps **most importantly**, you must learn to listen as well as to speak.

⊃ note at ESSENTIAL
⊃ LANGUAGE BANK at VITAL

**etc …** *He emphasized how little was known about the disease.* ◇ **it must/should be emphasized that …** *It should be emphasized that this is only one possible explanation.* ◇ **+ speech** *'This must be our top priority,' he emphasized.* ⊃ LANGUAGE BANK at EMPHASIS **2** ? B2 **~ sth** to make sth easier to notice: *She swept her hair back from her face to emphasize her high cheekbones.* **3** ? B2 **~ sth** to give extra force to a word or phrase when you are speaking, especially to show that it is important: *'Let nothing … nothing,' he emphasized the word, 'tempt you.'* ⊃ SYNONYMS at STRESS

**em‧phat‧ic** /ɪmˈfætɪk/ *adj.* **1** an **emphatic** statement, answer, etc. is given with force to show that it is important: *an **emphatic** denial/rejection* **2** (of a person) making it very clear what you mean by speaking with force: *He was emphatic that he could not work with her.* **3** an **emphatic** victory, win, or defeat is one in which one team or player wins by a large amount ▶ **em‧phat‧ic‧al‧ly** /-kli/ *adv.*: *'Certainly not,' he replied emphatically.* ◇ *She is emphatically opposed to the proposals.* ◇ *He has always emphatically denied the allegations.* ◇ *The proposal was emphatically defeated.*

**em‧phy‧se‧ma** /ˌemfɪˈsiːmə/ *noun* [U] (*medical*) a condition that affects the lungs, making it difficult to breathe

**em‧pire** ?+ /ˈempaɪə(r)/ *noun* **1** ?+ B2 a group of countries or states that are controlled by one leader or government: *the Roman Empire* **2** ?+ C1 a group of commercial organizations controlled by one person or company: *a business empire* **3** an area of activity controlled by one person or group: *All the bureaucrats jealously guarded their own little empires.*

**ˈempire-building** *noun* [U] (*usually disapproving*) the process of obtaining extra land, authority, etc. in order to increase your own power or position

**em‧pir‧ic‧al** ?+ C1 W /ɪmˈpɪrɪkl/ *adj.* [usually before noun] (*formal*) based on experiments or experience rather than ideas or theories: *empirical evidence/knowledge/research* ◇ *an empirical study* OPP **theoretical** ▶ **em‧pir‧ic‧al‧ly** /-kli/ *adv.*: *Such claims need to be tested empirically.*

**em‧pir‧icism** /ɪmˈpɪrɪsɪzəm/ *noun* [U] (*philosophy*) the use of experiments or experience as the basis for your ideas; the belief in these methods ▶ **em‧pir‧icist** /-sɪst/ *adj.*: *an empiricist theory* **em‧pir‧icist** *noun*: *the English empiricist, John Locke*

**em‧place‧ment** /ɪmˈpleɪsmənt/ *noun* (*specialist*) a position that has been specially prepared so that a large gun can be fired from it

**em‧ploy** ? A2 W /ɪmˈplɔɪ/ *verb, noun*
■ *verb* **1** ? A2 to give sb a job to do for payment: **~ sb** *How many people does the company employ?* ◇ *to employ workers/staff* ◇ **~ sb as sth** *For the past three years he has been*

# employable

employed as a firefighter. ◊ **~ sb to do sth** A number of people have been employed to deal with the backlog of work. ⊃ **WORDFINDER NOTE** at **COMPANY** ⊃ see also **SELF-EMPLOYED, UNEMPLOYED**

> **WORDFINDER** apply, appoint, contract, dismiss, job, pay, retire, work, workforce

**2** [B2] (*formal*) to use sth such as a skill, method, etc. for a particular purpose: **~ sth** *to employ a technique/strategy/tactic* ◊ *He criticized the repressive* **methods employed** *by the country's government.* ◊ *The police had to employ force to enter the building.*

**IDM** **be employed (in) doing sth** if a person or their time is **employed in doing sth**, the person spends time doing that thing: *She was employed in making a list of all the jobs to be done.*
■ *noun* [U]
**IDM** **in sb's em'ploy** | **in the em'ploy of sb** (*formal*) working for sb; employed by sb

**em·ploy·able** /ɪmˈplɔɪəbl/ *adj.* having the skills and qualifications that will make sb want to employ you ▸ **em·ploy·abil·ity** /ɪmˌplɔɪəˈbɪləti/ *noun* [U]

**em·ploy·ee** ❶ [A2] /ɪmˈplɔɪiː/ *noun* a person who is paid to work for sb: *The firm has over 500 employees.* ◊ *They have eight* **full-time** *and two* **part-time employees.** ◊ *government/state/federal employees* ◊ *employee benefits/morale*

**em·ploy·er** ❶ [A2] /ɪmˈplɔɪə(r)/ *noun* a person or company that pays people to work for them: *They're very* **good employers** *(= they treat the people that work for them well).* ◊ *one of the largest employers in the area* ◊ *a potential/prospective employer*

**em·ploy·ment** ❶ [B1] /ɪmˈplɔɪmənt/ *noun* **1** [B1] [U, C] work, especially when it is done to earn money; the state of being employed: *full-time/part-time employment* ◊ *people* **seeking employment** ◊ *They are finding it more and more difficult to* **find employment.** ◊ **in** ~ *Most of last year's graduates are now in* **paid employment.** ◊ *There are limited* **employment opportunities** *here.* ◊ **conditions/terms of employment** ◊ (*formal*) *pensions from previous employments* ⊃ **SYNONYMS** at **WORK** **2** [B1] [U] the situation in which people have work: *The government is aiming at* **full employment.** ◊ *Changes in farming methods have badly affected employment in the area.* **OPP** **unemployment** **3** [U] the act of employing sb: *The law prevented the employment of children under ten in the cotton mills.* **4** [U] (*formal*) the use of sth: *the employment of artillery in the capture of the town*

**em'ployment agency** *noun* a business that helps people to find work and employers to find workers

**em·ploy·ment equity** /ɪmˌplɔɪmənt ˈekwəti/ *noun* [U] (*CanE, SAfrE*) the use of employment practices that encourage fair treatment of employees from all groups in society

**em'ployment tribunal** (*also* **in,dustrial tri'bunal**) *noun* (*BrE*) a type of court that can decide on **DISAGREEMENTS** between employees and employers: *She took her case to an employment tribunal.*

**em·por·ium** /emˈpɔːriəm/ *noun* (*pl.* **em·por·iums** *or* **em·poria** /-riə/) **1** (*old-fashioned*) a large shop **2** a shop that sells a particular type of goods: *an arts and crafts emporium*

**em·power** ❓+ [C1] Ⓦ /ɪmˈpaʊə(r)/ *verb* **1** ❓+ [C1] [often passive] (*formal*) to give sb the power or authority to do sth **SYN** **authorize**: **be empowered (to do sth)** *The courts were empowered to impose the death sentence for certain crimes.* **2** ❓+ [C1] ~ **sb (to do sth)** to give sb more control over their own life or the situation they are in: *The movement actively empowered women and gave them confidence in themselves.* ▸ **em·power·ment** *noun* [U]: *the empowerment of the individual*

**em·press** /ˈemprəs/ *noun* **1** a woman who is the ruler of an **EMPIRE**: *the Empress of Egypt* **2** the wife of an **EMPEROR**

**emp·ties** /ˈemptiz/ *noun* [pl.] empty bottles or glasses

**emp·ti·ness** /ˈemptinəs/ *noun* [U, sing.] **1** a feeling of being sad because nothing seems to have any value: *There was an aching emptiness in her heart.* **2** the fact that there

is nothing or nobody in a place: *The silence and emptiness of the house did not scare her.* **3** (*formal*) a place that is empty: *He stared out at the vast emptiness of the sea.*

**empty** ❶ [A2] /ˈempti/ *adj., verb*
■ *adj.* (**emp·tier**, **emp·ti·est**) **1** ❓ [A2] with no people or things inside: *an empty box/glass/bottle* ◊ *an empty plate (= with no food on it)* ◊ *I noticed an* **empty space** *on the bookshelf.* ◊ *I couldn't see any* **empty seats** *(= with nobody sitting in them).* ◊ *The theatre was* **half empty.** ◊ *an empty house/room/bus* ◊ *The house had been* **standing empty** *(= without people living in it) for some time.* ◊ *It's not good to drink alcohol on an* **empty stomach** *(= without having eaten something).* ◊ **~ of sth** (*formal*) *The room was empty of furniture.* **2** ❓ [B2] [usually before noun] (of sth that sb says or does) with no meaning; not meaning what is said **SYN** **hollow**: *empty words* ◊ *an empty promise* ◊ *an empty gesture aimed at pleasing the crowds* **3** (of a person, or a person's life) unhappy because life does not seem to have a purpose, usually after sth sad has happened: *Three months after his death, she still felt empty.* ◊ *My life seems empty without you.* **4** ~ **of sth** without a quality that you would expect to be there: *words that were empty of meaning* ▸ **emp·ti·ly** /-tɪli/ *adv.*: *She stood staring emptily into space.*
■ *verb* (**emp·ties**, **empty·ing**, **emp·tied**, **emp·tied**) **1** ❓ [B1] [T] to remove everything that is in a container, etc.: **~ sth** *She emptied the bins, washed the glasses and went to bed.* ◊ *He emptied his glass and asked for a refill.* ◊ ~ **sth out** *I emptied out my pockets but could not find my keys.* ◊ **~ sth of sth** *The room had been emptied of all furniture.* ◊ (*figurative*) *She emptied her mind of all thoughts of home.* **2** ❓ [B1] [I] to become empty: *The streets soon emptied when the rain started.* ◊ **~ of sb/sth** *The beach gradually emptied of people.* ◊ **~ out** *The tank empties out in five minutes.* **3** ❓ [B1] [T] to take out the contents of sth and put them somewhere else: **~ sth** *He stepped outside to empty the trash.* ◊ **~ sth + adv./prep.** *She emptied the contents of her bag onto the table.* **4** [T] **~ sth** to make sure that everyone leaves a room, building, etc. **SYN** **evacuate**: *Police had instructions to empty the building because of a bomb threat.* **5** [I] to flow or move out from one place to another: **~ into/onto sth** *The Rhine empties into the North Sea.* ◊ **~ out into/onto sth** *Fans emptied out onto the streets after the concert.*

**empty-'handed** *adj.* [not usually before noun] without getting what you wanted; without taking sth to sb: *The robbers fled empty-handed.* ◊ *She visited every Sunday and never arrived empty-handed.*

**empty-'headed** *adj.* (*disapproving*) unable to think or behave in an intelligent way

**empty 'nest** *noun* the situation or the home of parents whose children have grown up and left

**empty 'nester** *noun* [usually pl.] a parent whose children have grown up and left home

**EMT** /ˌiː em ˈtiː/ *noun* (*NAmE*) a person who is trained to provide emergency medical treatment to people who are not in a hospital (the abbreviation for 'emergency medical technician') ⊃ compare **PARAMEDIC**

**EMU** /ˌiː em ˈjuː/ *abbr.* Economic and Monetary Union (of the European Union)

**emu** /ˈiːmjuː/ *noun* a large Australian bird that can run fast but cannot fly

**emu·late** /ˈemjuleɪt/ *verb* **1** ~ **sb/sth** (*formal*) to try to do sth as well as sb else because you admire them: *She hopes to emulate her sister's sporting achievements.* **2** ~ **sth** (*computing*) (of a computer program, etc.) to work in the same way as another computer, etc. and perform the same tasks ▸ **emu·la·tion** /ˌemjuˈleɪʃn/ *noun* [U, C]

**emu·la·tor** /ˈemjuleɪtə(r)/ *noun* **1** (*formal*) a person who tries to do sth as well as sb else that they admire **2** (*computing*) a device or piece of software that makes it possible to use programs, etc. on one type of computer even though they have been designed for a different type

**emul·si·fier** /ɪˈmʌlsɪfaɪə(r)/ *noun* (*chemistry*) a substance that is added to sth, especially food, to make the different substances in it combine to form a smooth mixture

**emul·sify** /ɪˈmʌlsɪfaɪ/ *verb* [I, T] (**emul·si·fies**, **emul·si·fy·ing**, **emul·si·fied**, **emul·si·fied**) **~ (sth)** (*specialist*) if two liquids, one of which is thicker than the other, **emulsify** or **are emulsified**, they combine to form a smooth mixture

**emul·sion** /ɪˈmʌlʃn/ noun [C, U] **1** any mixture of liquids that do not normally mix together, such as oil and water **2** (also **eˈmulsion paint**) (BrE) a type of paint used on walls and ceilings that dries without leaving a shiny surface **3** (specialist) a substance on the surface of PHOTOGRAPHIC film that makes it sensitive to light

**en-** /ɪn/ HELP Before 'b', 'm', or 'p', the form is **em-** /ɪm/. prefix (in verbs) **1** to put into the thing or condition mentioned: *encase* ◊ *endanger* ◊ *empower* **2** to cause to be: *enlarge* ◊ *embolden*

**-en** /ən, n/ suffix **1** (in verbs) to make or become: *blacken* ◊ *sadden* **2** (in adjectives) made of; looking like: *wooden* ◊ *golden*

**en·able** 🅞 B2 🅦 /ɪˈneɪbl/ verb **1** 🅣 B2 **~ sb/sth to do sth** to make it possible for sb/sth to do sth **SYN** allow: *a new programme to enable older people to study at college* ◊ *This approach enables the company to focus on its core business.* ◊ *Insulin enables the body to use and store sugar.* **2** 🅣 B2 **~ sth** to make it possible for sth to happen or exist by creating the necessary conditions **SYN** allow: *a new train line to enable easier access to the stadium* ⊃ LANGUAGE BANK at PROCESS¹ **3 ~ sth** (computing) to make a system, device or feature ready to use **4 -enabled** (in compound adjectives) (computing) that can be used with a particular system or technology: *Bluetooth-enabled devices* ⊃ see also WEB-ENABLED

**-enabled** /ɪneɪbld/ adj. (computing) (in compound adjectives) that can be used with a particular system or technology, especially the internet: *internet-enabled devices* ⊃ see also WEB-ENABLED

**en·able·ment** /ɪˈneɪblmənt/ noun [U] **1** the act of making it possible for sth to happen or for sb to do sth: *The surprising benefit of the changes has been the enablement of innovation.* **2** (computing) the act of making a system, device or feature ready to use: *Most of the hardware enablement is now complete.*

**en·abler** /ɪˈneɪblə(r)/ noun **1** a person or thing that makes sth possible: *Air transport is a key enabler of world trade.* **2** a person or thing that encourages or makes it possible for sb to engage in behaviour that is negative or that does them harm: *If you buy drugs for a friend, you are an enabler.*

**enact** 🅣+ C1 /ɪˈnækt/ verb **1** 🅣+ C1 [often passive] (law) to pass a law: **(be) enacted (by sb/sth)** *legislation enacted by parliament* **2** [often passive] (formal) to perform a play or act a part in a play: **(be) enacted (by sb)** *scenes from history enacted by local residents* **3 be enacted** (formal) to take place ⊃ see also RE-ENACT **SYN** play out: *They seemed unaware of the drama being enacted a few feet away from them.* **4 ~ sth** (formal) to put sth into practice: *This involves identifying problems and enacting solutions.*

**en·act·ment** /ɪˈnæktmənt/ noun [U, C] (law) the process of a law becoming official; a law which has been made official ⊃ see also RE-ENACTMENT

**en·amel** /ɪˈnæml/ noun **1** [U, C] a substance made from glass powder that is melted onto metal, pots, etc. and forms a hard shiny surface to protect or decorate them; an object made from enamel: *a chipped enamel bowl* ◊ *a handle inlaid with enamel* ◊ *an exhibition of enamels and jewellery* **2** [U] the hard white outer layer of a tooth **3** (also **eˈnamel ˈpaint**) [U, C] a type of paint that dries to leave a hard shiny surface

**en·am·elled** (US **en·am·eled**) /ɪˈnæmld/ adj. [usually before noun] covered or decorated with enamel

**en·am·oured** (US **en·amored**) /ɪˈnæməd; NAmE -mərd/ adj. **1** (formal) (often in negative sentences) liking sth a lot: **~ of sth** *He was less than enamoured of the music.* ◊ **~ with sth** *I'm not exactly enamoured with the idea of spending a whole day with them.* **2 ~ of/with sb** (literary) in love with sb

**en bloc** /ˌɒn ˈblɒk; NAmE ˌɑː ˈblɑːk/ adv. (from French) as a group rather than separately: *There are reports of teachers resigning en bloc.*

**enc.** = ENCL.

**en·camp** /ɪnˈkæmp/ verb [I, T] (formal) if a group of people **encamp** or **are encamped** somewhere, they set up a camp or have set up a camp there

**en·camp·ment** /ɪnˈkæmpmənt/ noun a group of tents, HUTS, etc. where people live together, usually for only a short period of time: *a military encampment*

**en·cap·su·late** /ɪnˈkæpsjuleɪt/ verb **~ sth (in sth)** (formal) to express the most important parts of sth in a few words, a small space or a single object **SYN** sum up: *The poem encapsulates many of the central themes of her writing.* ▶ **en·cap·su·la·tion** /ɪnˌkæpsjuˈleɪʃn/ noun [U, C]

**en·case** /ɪnˈkeɪs/ verb [often passive] (formal) to surround or cover sth completely, especially to protect it: **be encased (in sth)** *The reactor is encased in concrete and steel.*

**-ence** ⊃ -ANCE

**en·ceph·al·itis** /ˌensefəˈlaɪtɪs; BrE also -keˈ-/ noun [U] (medical) a condition in which the brain becomes SWOLLEN (= larger than normal), caused by an infection or ALLERGIC reaction

**en·ceph·al·op·athy** /enˌsefəˈlɒpəθi, -keˈ-; NAmE -ˌsefəˈlɑːp-/ noun [U] (medical) a disease in which the functioning of the brain is affected by infection, BLOOD POISONING, etc. ⊃ see also BSE

**en·chant** /ɪnˈtʃɑːnt; NAmE -ˈtʃænt/ verb **1 ~ sb** (formal) to attract sb strongly and make them feel very interested, excited, etc. **SYN** delight **2 ~ sb/sth** to place sb/sth under a magic SPELL (= magic words that have special powers) **SYN** bewitch

**en·chant·ed** /ɪnˈtʃɑːntɪd; NAmE -ˈtʃæn-/ adj. **1** placed under a SPELL (= magic words that have special powers): *an enchanted forest/kingdom* **2** (formal) filled with great pleasure **SYN** delighted: **~ (to do sth)** *He was enchanted to see her again after so long.*

**en·chant·er** /ɪnˈtʃɑːntə(r); NAmE -ˈtʃæn-/ noun (in stories) a man who has magic powers that he uses to control people

**en·chant·ing** /ɪnˈtʃɑːntɪŋ; NAmE -ˈtʃæn-/ adj. attractive and pleasant **SYN** delightful: *an enchanting view* ▶ **en·chant·ing·ly** adv.

**en·chant·ment** /ɪnˈtʃɑːntmənt; NAmE -ˈtʃænt-/ noun **1** [U] (formal) a feeling of great pleasure **2** [U] the state of being under a magic SPELL: *It was a place of deep mystery and enchantment.* **3** [C] (literary) a magic SPELL: *They had been turned to stone by an enchantment.*

**en·chant·ress** /ɪnˈtʃɑːntrəs; NAmE -ˈtʃæn-/ noun **1** (in stories) a woman who has magic powers that she uses to control people **2** (literary) a woman that men find very attractive and interesting

**en·chil·ada** /ˌentʃɪˈlɑːdə/ noun (from Spanish) a Mexican dish consisting of a TORTILLA filled with meat and covered with a spicy sauce

**IDM** **the whole enchiˈlada** (informal) the whole thing; everything ⊃ more at BIG adj.

**en·cir·cle** /ɪnˈsɜːkl; NAmE -ˈsɜːrkl/ verb **~ sb/sth** (formal) to surround sb/sth completely in a circle: *Jack's arms encircled her waist.* ◊ *The island is encircled by a coral reef.* ▶ **en·circle·ment** noun [U]

**encl.** (also **enc.**) abbr. (business) enclosed (used on business letters to show that another document is being sent in the same ENVELOPE)

**en·clave** /ˈenkleɪv/ noun an area of a country or city where the people have a different religion, culture or NATIONALITY from those who live in the country or city that surrounds it

**en·close** /ɪnˈkləʊz/ verb **1** [usually passive] to build a wall, fence, etc. around sth: **be enclosed (with sth)** *The yard had been enclosed with iron railings.* ◊ **be enclosed in sth** (figurative) *All translated words should be enclosed in brackets.* **2 ~ sth** (especially of a wall, fence, etc.) to surround sth: *Low hedges enclosed the flower beds.* ◊ (figurative) *She felt his arms enclose her.* **3** [usually passive] (in England in the past) to build a wall or fence around COMMON (= public) land and make it private property: **be enclosed** *The land was enclosed in the seventeenth century.* **4 ~ sth (with sth)** to put sth in the same ENVELOPE, package, etc. as sth else: *Please return the completed form, enclosing a recent photograph.*

🅞 Oxford Phrasal Academic Lexicon (OPAL) written and spoken word lists | 🅦 OPAL written word list | 🅢 OPAL spoken word list

# enclosed 510

**en·closed** /ɪnˈkləʊzd/ *adj.* **1** with walls, etc. all around: *Do not use this substance in an enclosed space.* **2** (*abbr.* **encl.**) sent with a letter, etc: *Please complete the enclosed application form.* ◊ *Please find enclosed a cheque for £100.* **3** (of religious communities) having little contact with the outside world

**en·clos·ure** /ɪnˈkləʊʒə(r)/ *noun* **1** [C] a piece of land that is surrounded by a fence or wall and is used for a particular purpose: *a wildlife enclosure* **2** [U, C] the act of placing a fence or wall around a piece of land: *the enclosure of common land in the seventeenth century* HELP In this meaning, **enclosure** refers especially to the enclosure of COMMON (= public) land in England in the past, turning it into private property. **3** [C] something that is placed in an ENVELOPE with a letter

**en·code** W /ɪnˈkəʊd/ *verb* **1** ~ sth to change ordinary language into letters, symbols, etc. in order to send secret messages **2** ~ sth (*computing*) to change information into a form that can be processed by a computer **3** ~ sth (*linguistics*) to express the meaning of sth in a foreign language ⊃ compare DECODE

**en·co·mium** /enˈkəʊmiəm/ *noun* (*pl.* **en·co·miums** or **en·co·mia** /-ˈkəʊmiə/) (*formal*) a speech or piece of writing that praises sb or sth highly

**en·com·pass** ?+ C1 /ɪnˈkʌmpəs/ *verb* (*formal*) **1** ?+ C1 ~ sth to include a large number or range of things: *The job encompasses a wide range of responsibilities.* ◊ *The group encompasses all ages.* **2** ~ sth to surround or cover sth completely: *The fog soon encompassed the whole valley.*

**en·core** /ˈɒŋkɔː(r)/, *NAmE* /ˈɑːŋk-/ *noun, exclamation*
■ *noun* an extra short performance given at the end of a concert or other performance; a request for this made by an audience calling out: *She played a Chopin waltz as an encore.* ◊ *The group got three encores.*
■ *exclamation* an audience calls out **encore!** at the end of a concert to ask the performer to play or sing another piece of music

**en·coun·ter** ❶ B2 W /ɪnˈkaʊntə(r)/ *verb, noun*
■ *verb* **1** ?+ B2 ~ sth to experience sth, especially sth unpleasant or difficult, while you are trying to do sth else SYN **meet**, **run into**: *We encountered a number of difficulties in the first week.* ◊ *to encounter problems* ◊ *I had never encountered such resistance before.* **2** ?+ B2 ~ sb/sth (*formal*) to meet sb, or discover or experience sth, especially sb/sth new, unusual or unexpected SYN **come across**: *She was the most remarkable woman he had ever encountered.*
■ *noun* **1** ?+ B2 a meeting, especially one that is sudden, unexpected or violent: *a chance encounter* ◊ *~ with sb/sth Three of them were killed in the subsequent encounter with the police.* ◊ *~ between A and B The story describes the extraordinary encounter between a man and a dolphin.* ◊ *I've had a number of close encounters (= situations that could have been dangerous) with bad drivers.* ◊ *It was his first sexual encounter (= first experience of sex).* **2** a sports match against a particular player or team: *She has beaten her opponent in all of their previous encounters.* **3** (*IndE*) an incident in which police shoot dead a suspected criminal

**en·cour·age** ❶ B1 W /ɪnˈkʌrɪdʒ/; *NAmE* /-ˈkɜːr-/ *verb* **1** ?+ B1 to give sb support, courage or hope: *~ sb We were greatly encouraged by the positive response of the public.* ◊ *~ sb in sth My parents have always encouraged me in my choice of career.* ◊ *+ speech 'You're doing fine,' he encouraged her.* **2** ?+ B1 to persuade sb to do sth by making it easier for them and making them believe it is a good thing to do: *~ sb to do sth Banks actively encouraged people to borrow money.* ◊ *I strongly encourage everyone to go and see this important film.* ◊ *~ (doing) sth Speaking your mind is highly encouraged at these sessions.* **3** ?+ B1 to make sth more likely to happen or develop: *~ sth There is a clear case for spending public money on encouraging participation in sport.* ◊ *to encourage development/investment/growth* ◊ *~ sth in sb/sth They claim that some computer games encourage violent behaviour in young children.* ◊ *~ sb to do sth Music and lighting are used to encourage shoppers to buy more.* OPP **discourage**

**en·cour·age·ment** ?+ C1 /ɪnˈkʌrɪdʒmənt; *NAmE* -ˈkɜːr-/ *noun* [U, C, usually sing.] the act of encouraging sb to do sth; something that encourages sb: *a few words of encouragement* ◊ *He needs all the support and encouragement he can get.* ◊ *With a little encouragement from his parents he should do well.* ◊ *~ (to sb) (to do sth) She was given every encouragement to try something new.* ◊ *Her words were a great encouragement to them.* OPP **discouragement**

**en·cour·ag·ing** ?+ C1 /ɪnˈkʌrɪdʒɪŋ/; *NAmE* -ˈkɜːr-/ *adj.* that gives sb support, courage or hope: *This month's unemployment figures are not very encouraging.* ◊ *You could try being a little more encouraging.* ◊ *Despite the encouraging findings, we remain cautious.* OPP **discouraging** ▶ **en·cour·ag·ing·ly** *adv.*: *to smile encouragingly* ◊ *The attendance was encouragingly high.*

**en·croach** /ɪnˈkrəʊtʃ/ *verb* (*formal*) **1** [I] ~ (on/upon sth) (*disapproving*) to begin to affect or use up too much of sb's time, rights, personal life, etc: *I won't encroach on your time any longer.* ◊ *He never allows work to encroach upon his family life.* **2** [I] ~ (on/upon sth) to slowly begin to cover more and more of an area: *The growing town soon encroached on the surrounding countryside.* ◊ *the encroaching tide (= that is coming in)* ▶ **en·croach·ment** *noun* [U, C]: *~ (on/upon sth) the regime's many encroachments on human rights*

**en·crust·ation** (*also* **in·crust·ation**) /ˌɪnkrʌˈsteɪʃn/ *noun* [U, C] the process of forming a hard outer layer over sth; the layer that is formed

**en·crust·ed** /ɪnˈkrʌstɪd/ *adj.* ~ (with/in sth) covered with a thin hard layer of sth; forming a thin hard layer on sth: *a crown encrusted with diamonds* ◊ *encrusted blood*

**en·crypt** /ɪnˈkrɪpt/ *verb* ~ sth to put information into a special code, especially in order to prevent people from looking at it without authority: *All data is encrypted before it is sent.* OPP **decrypt** ▶ **en·cryp·tion** /-ˈkrɪpʃn/ *noun* [U] OPP **decryption**

**en·cum·ber** /ɪnˈkʌmbə(r)/ *verb* [*usually passive*] (*formal*) **1** to make it difficult for sb to do sth or for sth to happen: *be encumbered by sb/sth The police operation was encumbered by crowds of reporters.* ◊ *be encumbered with sth The business is encumbered with debt.* **2** to be large and/or heavy and make it difficult for sb to move: *be encumbered by sth The frogmen were encumbered by their diving equipment.*

**en·cum·brance** /ɪnˈkʌmbrəns/ *noun* (*formal*) a person or thing that prevents sb from moving easily or from doing what they want SYN **burden**: *I felt I was being an encumbrance to them.*

**-ency** ⊃ -ANCY

**en·cyc·lic·al** /ɪnˈsɪklɪkl/ *noun* an official letter written by the Pope and sent to all Roman Catholic BISHOPS

**en·cyc·lo·pe·dia** (*BrE also* **-pae·dia**) /ɪnˌsaɪkləˈpiːdiə/ *noun* a book or set of books giving information about all areas of knowledge or about different areas of one particular subject, usually arranged in alphabetical order; a similar collection of information in digital form: *an online encyclopedia*

**en·cyclo·pe·dic** (*BrE also* **-pae·dic**) /ɪnˌsaɪkləˈpiːdɪk/ *adj.* **1** connected with encyclopedias or the type of information found in them: *encyclopedic information* ◊ *an encyclopedic dictionary* **2** having a lot of information about a wide variety of subjects; containing complete information about a particular subject: *She has an encyclopedic knowledge of natural history.*

**end** ❶ A1 S /end/ *noun, verb*
■ *noun*
• **FINAL PART 1** ?+ A1 the final part of a period of time, an event, an activity or a story: *It's the end of an era.* ◊ *the end of the book* ◊ *at the ~ of sth at the end of the week* ◊ *at the ~ There'll be a chance to ask questions at the end.* ◊ *by the ~ of sth He wants the reports by the end of the month.* ◊ *to the ~ of sth She remained active as an artist to the end of her life.* ◊ *until the ~ (of sth) We didn't leave until the very end.* ◊ *We had to hear about the whole journey from beginning to end.* ⊃ see also BACK END (1), FRONT END (3)
• **FINISH 2** ?+ A1 a situation in which sth does not exist any more: *the end of all his dreams* ◊ *at an ~ The war was finally at an end.* ◊ *The meeting came to an end (= finished).* ◊ *The coup brought his corrupt regime to an end.* ◊ *an ~ to sth They have called for an end to violence.* ◊ *an end to the*

b **b**ad | d **d**id | f **f**all | g **g**et | h **h**at | j **y**es | k **c**at | l **l**eg | m **m**an | n **n**ow | p **p**en | r **r**ed

*conflict/war* ◊ *There's no **end in sight** to the present crisis.* ◊ *to **mark/signal the end of** sth*
- **FURTHEST PART 3** the part of an object or a place that is the furthest away from its centre: *I joined the end of the queue.* ◊ *Go to the end of the line!* ◊ **at the ~ of sth** *Turn right at the end of the road.* ◊ *That's his wife sitting at **the far end of** the table.* ◊ **on the ~ of sth** *You've got something on the end of your nose.* ◊ *Tie the ends of the string together.* ◊ *These two products are from **opposite ends** of the price range.* ◊ *We've travelled from one end of Mexico to the other.* ◊ *They live in the end house.* ⊃ see also BUSINESS END (1), DEAD END, EAST END, FRONT END (1), REAR END, SPLIT END, TAIL END
- **AIM 4** an aim or a purpose: *They are prepared to use violence in pursuit of their ends.* ◊ *She is exploiting the current situation for her own ends.* ◊ **With this end in view** (= in order to achieve this) *they employed 50 new staff.* ◊ *We are willing to make any concessions necessary **to this end** (= in order to achieve this).* ⊃ SYNONYMS at TARGET
- **PART OF ACTIVITY 5** [usually sing.] a part of an activity with which sb is involved, especially in business: *We need somebody to handle the marketing end of the business.* ◊ *Are there any problems at your end?* ◊ *I have kept my end of the bargain.* ⊃ see also BUSINESS END (2), FRONT END (2)
- **OF PHONE LINE/JOURNEY 6** [usually sing.] either of two places connected by a phone call, journey, etc: *I answered the phone but there was no one **at the other end**.* ◊ *Jean is going to meet me **at the other end**.*
- **OF SPORTS FIELD 7** one of the two halves of a sports field: *The teams changed ends at half-time.*
- **PIECE LEFT 8** (*BrE*) a small piece that is left after sth has been used: *a cigarette end* ⊃ see also DOG-END, FAG END, LOOSE END, ODDS AND ENDS
- **DEATH 9** [usually sing.] a person's death. People say 'end' to avoid saying 'death': *She came to **an untimely end** (= died young).* ◊ *I was with him at the end (= when he died).* ◊ *(literary) He **met his end** (= died) at the Battle of Waterloo.*
**10** (in AMERICAN FOOTBALL) a LINEMAN who is nearest to the side of the field: *a defensive end* ⊃ see also TIGHT END ⊃ see also FRONT-END, HIGH-END, LOW-END, REAR-END, TOP-END

**IDM** **at the ˌend of the ˈday** (*informal*) used to introduce the most important fact after everything has been considered: *At the end of the day, he'll still have to make his own decision.* **a ˌbad/ˈsticky ˌend** (*BrE, informal*) something unpleasant that happens to sb, for example punishment or a violent death, usually because of their own actions: *He'll **come to a sticky end** one of these days if he carries on like that.* **be at the ˌend of sth** to have almost nothing left of sth: *I'm at the end of my patience.* ◊ *They are at the end of their food supply.* **be at the ˌend of your ˈtether** (*BrE*) (*NAmE* **be at the end of your ˈrope**) (*informal*) to feel that you cannot deal with a difficult situation any more because you are too tired, worried, etc. **be the ˈend** (*BrE, informal*) when you say that people or situations are **the end**, you mean that you are annoyed with them **an ˌend in itˈself** a thing that is itself important and not just a part of sth more important **the ˌend justifies the ˈmeans** (*saying*) bad or unfair methods of doing sth are acceptable if the result of that action is good or positive **(reach) the end of the ˈline/ˈroad** (to reach) the point at which sth can no longer continue in the same way: *A defeat in the second round marked the end of the line for last year's champion.* **end of ˈstory** (*informal*) (*BrE also* **end ˈof**) used when you are stating that there is nothing more that can be said or done about sth ˌend to ˈend in a line, with the ends touching: *They arranged the tables end to end.* **ˌget/ˌhave your ˈend away** (*BrE, slang*) to have sex **ˌgo to the ˌends of the ˈearth** to do everything possible, even if it is difficult, in order to get or achieve sth: *I'd go to the ends of the earth to see her again.* **ˌin the ˈend 1** after a long period of time or series of events: *He tried various jobs and in the end became an accountant.* **2** after everything has been considered: *You can try your best to impress the interviewers but in the end it's often just a question of luck.* **ˌkeep your ˈend up** (*BrE, informal*) to continue to be cheerful in a difficult situation **ˌmake (both) ends ˈmeet** to earn just enough money to be able to buy the things you need: *Many families struggle to make ends meet.* **no ˈend** (*informal*) very much: *It upset me no end to hear they'd split up.* **no ˈend of sth** (*informal*) a lot of sth: *We had no end of trouble getting them to agree.* **not the end of the ˈworld** (*informal*) not the worst thing that could

---

511    **endeavour**

happen to sb: *Failing one exam is not the end of the world.* **ˌon ˈend 1** in a position standing UPRIGHT rather than lying flat: *It'll fit if you stand it on end.* **2** for the stated length of time, without stopping: *He would disappear for weeks on end.* **ˌput an ˈend to yourself** | **ˌput an ˈend to it all** to kill yourself ⊃ more at BEGINNING, BITTER *adj.*, BURN *v.*, DEEP END, HAIR, HEAR, LIGHT *n.*, LOOSE END, MEANS, RECEIVE, ROUGH *adj.*, SHARP *adj.*, SHORT *adj.*, THIN *adj.*, WIT, WRONG *adj.*

■ *verb* [I, T] to finish; to reach a point and go no further; to make sth finish: *At last the war ended.* ◊ *The road ends here.* ◊ *How does the story end?* ◊ **~ with sth** *Her note ended with the words: 'See you soon.'* ◊ **~ by doing sth** *The speaker ended by suggesting some topics for discussion.* ◊ **~ sth** *They decided to end their relationship.* ◊ **~ sth with sth** *The team ended the season with a 4–0 win.* ◊ **+ speech** *'And that was that,' she ended.* ⊃ EXPRESS YOURSELF at FINISH **IDM ˌa/the sth to ˌend all ˈsths** used to emphasize how large, important, exciting, etc. you think sth is: *The movie has a car chase to end all car chases.* **ˌend your ˈdays/ˈlife (in sth)** to spend the last part of your life in a particular state or place: *He ended his days in poverty.* **ˌend in ˈtears** (*BrE, informal*) if you say that sth will **end in tears**, you are warning sb that what they are doing will have an unhappy or unpleasant result **ˌend it ˈall** | **ˌend your ˈlife** to kill yourself **PHRV ˌend in ˈsth** [no passive] **1** to have sth as an ending: *The word I'm thinking of ends in '-ous'.* **2** to have sth as a result: *The game ended in a draw.* ◊ *Their long struggle ended in failure.* ◊ *The debate ended in uproar.* **ˌend ˈup** to find yourself in a place or situation at the end of a process or period of time: **end up doing sth** *I ended up doing all the work myself.* ◊ **+ adv./prep.** *If you go on like this you'll end up in prison.* ◊ **+ adj.** *If he carries on driving like that, he'll end up dead.*

▼ EXPRESS YOURSELF

**Ending a conversation**

When you stop talking to someone, there are polite ways to end a conversation:
- It's been lovely/so nice/good talking to you.
- I'm so glad we got to talk.
- I'm sorry, I have to rush off.
- It was nice to meet you. I'm sorry I have to go now.
- Will you excuse me? There's someone I've got to speak to.

**en·dan·ger** /ɪnˈdeɪndʒə(r)/ *verb* **~ sb/sth** to put sb/sth in a situation in which they could be harmed or damaged: *The health of our children is being endangered by exhaust fumes.* ◊ *That one mistake seriously endangered the future of the company.* ⊃ WORDFINDER NOTE at GREEN ▶ **en·dan·ger·ment** /ɪnˈdeɪndʒəmənt/ *NAmE* -dʒɚrn-/ *noun* [U]

**en·dan·gered** /ɪnˈdeɪndʒəd; *NAmE* -dʒɚd/ *adj.* (used especially about groups of animals, plants, etc.) at risk of no longer existing: *The sea turtle is an endangered species.* ◊ *These orang-utans are critically endangered due to habitat loss.*

**en·dear** /ɪnˈdɪə(r)/; *NAmE* -ˈdɪr/ *verb* **PHRV en·dear sb/yourself to sb** to make sb/yourself popular: *Their policies on taxation didn't endear them to voters.* ◊ *She was a talented teacher who endeared herself to all who worked with her.*

**en·dear·ing** /ɪnˈdɪərɪŋ/; *NAmE* -ˈdɪr-/ *adj.* causing people to feel love **SYN** **lovable**: *an endearing habit* ▶ **en·dear·ing·ly** *adv.*

**en·dear·ment** /ɪnˈdɪəmənt/; *NAmE* -ˈdɪrm-/ *noun* [C, U] a word or an expression that is used to show love: *They were whispering endearments to each other.* ◊ *'Darling' is a term of endearment.*

**en·deav·our** (*US* **en·deav·or**) /ɪnˈdevə(r)/ *noun, verb*
■ *noun* [U, C] (*formal*) an attempt to do sth, especially sth new or difficult: *advances in the field of scientific endeavour* ◊ **~ to do sth** *Please make every endeavour to arrive on time.* ◊ **in an ~ to do sth** *The public bombarded the company with complaints in an endeavour to have the price increases revoked.*

# endemic

■ *verb* ~ **to do sth** (*formal*) to try very hard to do sth **SYN** **strive**: *I will endeavour to do my best for my country.*

**en·dem·ic** /enˈdemɪk/ *adj.* regularly found in a particular place or among a particular group of people and difficult to get rid of: ~ **(in ...)** *Malaria is endemic in many hot countries.* ◊ *Corruption is endemic in the system.* ◊ **(among ...)** *an attitude endemic among senior members of the profession* ◊ ~ **(to ...)** *species endemic to* (= only found in) *Madagascar* ◊ *the endemic problem of racism* ➔ compare PANDEMIC

**end·game** /ˈendɡeɪm/ *noun* **1** the final stage of a game of CHESS **2** the final stage of a political process or contest between people

**end·ing** ❶ **A2** /ˈendɪŋ/ *noun* **1** ⚡ **A2** the last part of a story, film, etc: *His stories usually have a happy ending.* ◊ ~ **to sth** *It's a beautiful ending to the scene.* **OPP** **opening** ➔ see also HOLLYWOOD ENDING ➔ WORDFINDER NOTE at PLOT **2** ⚡ **A2** the act of finishing sth; the last part of sth: *the anniversary of the ending of the Pacific War* ◊ ~ **to sth** *It was the perfect ending to the perfect day.* **3** ⚡ **A2** the last part of a word, that is added to a main part: *verb endings* ◊ *a masculine/feminine ending*

**en·dive** /ˈendaɪv, -dɪv/ *noun* [C, U] **1** (*BrE*) (*NAmE* **chic·ory**, **curly ˈendive**, **fri·sée** [U]) a plant with green curly leaves that are eaten raw as a vegetable **2** (*also* **Belgian endive**) (*both NAmE*) (*BrE* **chic·ory**) a small pale green plant with bitter leaves that are eaten raw or cooked as a vegetable. The root can be dried and used with or instead of coffee.

**end·less** ⚡+ **C1** /ˈendləs/ *adj.* **1** ⚡+ **C1** very large in size or amount and seeming to have no end **SYN** **limitless**: *endless patience* ◊ *endless opportunities for making money* ◊ *The possibilities are endless.* ◊ *an endless list of things to do* ◊ *We don't have an endless supply of money, you know.* ◊ *I've had enough of their endless arguing.* **2** ⚡+ **C1** continuing for a long time and seeming to have no end: *an endless round of parties and visits* ◊ *The journey seemed endless.* **3** (*specialist*) (of a LOOP, etc.) having the ends joined together so it forms one piece: *an endless loop of tape* ▶ **end·less·ly** *adv.*: *She talks endlessly about her problems.* ◊ *an endlessly repeated pattern*

**end·note** /ˈendnəʊt/ *noun* a note printed at the end of a book or section of a book

**endo·crine** /ˈendəʊkrɪn, -kraɪn; *NAmE* -dəkrɪn/ *adj.* (*biology*) relating to GLANDS that put HORMONES and other products directly into the blood: *the endocrine system* ➔ compare EXOCRINE

**endo·crin·ology** /ˌendəʊkrɪˈnɒlədʒi; *NAmE* -ˈnɑːl-/ *noun* [U] (*medical*) the branch of medicine that is the study of the endocrine system and HORMONES ▶ **endo·crin·olo·gist** *noun*

**en·dog·en·ous** /enˈdɒdʒənəs; *NAmE* -ˈdɑːdʒ-/ *adj.* **1** ~ **(to sth)** (*formal*) having a cause that is inside itself ➔ compare EXOGENOUS (1) **2** (*medical*) (of a disease or symptom) having a cause that is inside the body ➔ compare EXOGENOUS

**en·dor·phin** /enˈdɔːfɪn; *NAmE* -ˈdɔːrf-/ *noun* (*biology*) a HORMONE produced in the brain that reduces the feeling of pain

**en·dorse** ⚡+ **C1** /ɪnˈdɔːs; *NAmE* -ˈdɔːrs/ *verb* **1** ⚡+ **C1** ~ **sth** to say publicly that you support a person, statement or course of action: *I wholeheartedly endorse his remarks.* ◊ *Members of all parties endorsed a ban on land mines.* **2** ~ **sth** to say in an advertisement that you use and like a particular product so that other people will want to buy it **3** [usually passive] (*BrE*) to put details of a driving offence on sb's driving record: **have sth/be endorsed** *You risk having your licence endorsed.*

**en·dorse·ment** ⚡+ **C1** /ɪnˈdɔːsmənt; *NAmE* -ˈdɔːrs-/ *noun* [C, U] **1** ⚡+ **C1** a public statement or action showing that you support sb/sth: *The election victory is a clear endorsement of their policies.* ◊ *a letter of endorsement* **2** a statement made in an advertisement, usually by sb famous or important, saying that they use and like a particular product **3** (*BrE*) details of a driving offence recorded on sb's DRIVING LICENCE

**en·do·scope** /ˈendəskəʊp/ *noun* an instrument used in medical operations that consists of a very small camera on a long thin tube that can be put into a person's body so that the parts inside can be seen

**en·dos·copy** /enˈdɒskəpi; *NAmE* -ˈdɑːs-/ *noun* [C, U] (*pl.* **-ies**) (*medical*) a medical operation in which an endoscope is put into a person's body so that the parts inside can be seen

**endo·sperm** /ˈendəʊspɜːm; *NAmE* -spɜːrm/ *noun* [U] (*biology*) the part of the plant seed that provides food for the EMBRYO

**endo·ther·mic** /ˌendəʊˈθɜːmɪk; *NAmE* -ˈθɜːrm-/ *adj.* (*chemistry*) (of a chemical reaction) needing heat in order to take place ➔ compare EXOTHERMIC

**en·dow** /ɪnˈdaʊ/ *verb* ~ **sth** to give a large sum of money to a school, a college or another institution to provide it with an income

**PHRV** **be enˈdowed with sth** (*formal*) to naturally have a particular feature, quality, etc: *She was endowed with intelligence and wit.* ➔ see also WELL ENDOWED **enˈdow sb/sth with sth** (*formal*) **1** to believe or imagine that sb/sth has a particular quality: *She had endowed Marcus with the qualities she wanted him to possess.* **2** to give sth to sb/sth: *to endow sb with a responsibility*

**en·dow·ment** /ɪnˈdaʊmənt/ *noun* (*formal*) **1** [C, U] money that is given to a school, a college or another institution to provide it with an income; the act of giving this money **2** [C, usually pl.] a quality or an ability that you are born with

**enˈdowment mortgage** *noun* (*BrE*) a type of MORTGAGE (= money borrowed to buy property) in which money is regularly paid into an endowment policy. At the end of a particular period of time this money is then used to pay back the money that was borrowed. ➔ compare REPAYMENT MORTGAGE

**enˈdowment policy** *noun* (*BrE*) a type of life insurance in which a person regularly pays money to an insurance company, and receives a sum of money from them at the end of a particular period of time

**ˈend product** *noun* something that is produced by a particular activity or process

**ˌend reˈsult** *noun* [usually sing.] the final result of a particular activity or process

**ˌend ˈrun** *noun* (in AMERICAN FOOTBALL) an attempt by the person carrying the ball to run around the end of the line of defending players

**en·dur·ance** /ɪnˈdjʊərəns; *NAmE* -ˈdʊr-/ *noun* [U] the ability to continue doing sth painful or difficult for a long period of time without giving up: *He showed remarkable endurance throughout his illness.* ◊ *This event tests both physical and mental endurance.* ◊ *powers of endurance* ◊ **beyond** ~ *They were humiliated beyond endurance.* ◊ *The party turned out to be more of an endurance test than a pleasure.*

**en·dure** ⚡+ **C1** /ɪnˈdjʊə(r); *NAmE* -ˈdʊr/ *verb* (*formal*) **1** ⚡+ **C1** [T] to experience and deal with sth that is painful or unpleasant without giving up **SYN** **bear**: ~ **sth** *They had to endure a long wait before the case came to trial.* ◊ *She could not endure the thought of parting.* ◊ *The pain was almost too great to endure.* ◊ (*formal*) *a love that endures all things and never fails* ◊ ~ **doing sth** *He can't endure being defeated.* ◊ ~ **to do sth** *He can't be endured.* **2** [I] to continue to exist for a long time **SYN** **last**¹: *a success that will endure* ▶ **en·dur·able** /ɪnˈdjʊərəbl; *NAmE* -ˈdʊr-/ *adj.*: *I felt that life was no longer endurable.* **OPP** **unendurable**

**en·dur·ing** /ɪnˈdjʊərɪŋ; *NAmE* -ˈdʊr-/ *adj.* lasting for a long time: *enduring memories* ◊ *What is the reason for the game's enduring appeal?* ▶ **en·dur·ing·ly** *adv.*: *an enduringly popular style*

**ˌend ˈuser** *noun* a person who actually uses a product rather than one who makes or sells it, especially a person who uses a product connected with computers

**end·ways** /ˈendweɪz/ (*also* **end·wise** /ˈendwaɪz/) *adv.* **1** (*also* **ˌendways/ˌendwise ˈon**) (of an object) with one end facing up, forwards, or towards the person who is looking at it: *We turned the table endways to get it through the doors.* ◊ *The first picture was taken from the side of the building,* and the second one endways on. **2** with the end of one thing touching the end of another: *The stones are laid down endways to make a path.*

**ˈend zone** *noun* the area at the end of an AMERICAN FOOTBALL field into which the ball must be carried or passed in order to score points

**enema** /ˈenəmə/ *noun* a liquid that is put into a person's RECTUM (= the opening through which solid waste leaves the body) in order to clean out the BOWELS, especially before a medical operation; the act of cleaning out the BOWELS in this way

**enemy** 🔊 **B1** /ˈenəmi/ *noun* (*pl.* **-ies**) **1** 🔊 **B1** [C] a person who hates sb or who acts or speaks against sb/sth: *She didn't have an enemy in the world.* ◇ *After just one day, she had already made an enemy of her manager.* ◇ *They united in the face of a common enemy.* ◇ *They used to be friends but they are now sworn enemies* (= are determined not to become friends again). ◇ *Birds are the natural enemies of many insect pests* (= they kill them). ⊃ see also ENMITY **2** 🔊 **B1** **the enemy** [sing. + sing. / pl. v.] a country or group that you are fighting a war against; the soldiers, etc. of this country or group: *The enemy was/were forced to retreat.* ◇ *to fight/defeat the enemy* ◇ *enemy forces/combatants* ◇ *The men came under enemy fire.* ◇ *They were dropped by parachute behind enemy lines* (= in the area controlled by the enemy) **3** [C] (*formal*) anything that harms sb or prevents it from being successful: *Poverty and ignorance are the enemies of progress.* **IDM** see WORST *adj.*

**en·er·get·ic** /ˌenəˈdʒetɪk/; *NAmE* ˌenərˈdʒ-/ *adj.* having or needing a lot of energy and enthusiasm: *He knew I was energetic and dynamic and would get things done.* ◇ *an energetic supporter* ◇ *The heart responds well to energetic exercise.* ◇ *For the more energetic* (= people who prefer physical activities), *we offer windsurfing and diving.* ▶ **en·er·get·ic·al·ly** /-kli/ *adv.*

**en·er·gize** (*BrE also* **-ise**) /ˈenədʒaɪz/; *NAmE* ˈenərdʒ-/ *verb* **1** ~ **sb** to make sb enthusiastic about sth **2** ~ **sb** to give sb more energy, strength, etc: *a refreshing and energizing fruit drink* **3** ~ **sth** (*specialist*) to supply power or energy to a machine, an ATOM, etc.

**en·ergy** 🔊 **A2** 🅦 /ˈenədʒi; *NAmE* ˈenərdʒi/ *noun* **1** 🔊 **A2** [U] the strength, effort and enthusiasm required for physical or mental activity, work, etc: *It's a waste of time and energy.* ◇ *She's always full of energy.* ◇ *I don't seem to have any energy these days.* **2 energies** [pl.] the physical and mental effort that you use to do sth: *She put all her energies into her work.* ◇ *He focused his energies on preparing the lectures.* **3** 🔊 **A2** [U] a source of power, such as fuel, used for driving machines, providing heat, etc: *solar/wind/renewable energy* ◇ *to save/conserve energy* ◇ *to generate/produce energy* ◇ *The £500 million programme is centred around energy efficiency and renewable power sources.* ◇ *an energy crisis* (= for example when fuel is not freely available). ⊃ see also ALTERNATIVE ENERGY, NUCLEAR ENERGY

**WORDFINDER** fossil fuel, fracking, fuel, hydroelectric, nuclear, oil, power station, solar, wind farm

**4** [U] (*physics*) the ability of matter or RADIATION to work because of its MASS, movement, electric charge, etc: *potential/kinetic/electrical energy* ⊃ see also POTENTIAL ENERGY ⊃ WORDFINDER NOTE at PHYSICS **IDM** see BALL *n.*

**ˈenergy drink** *noun* a drink that contains a lot of sugar, CAFFEINE or other substance that makes you feel more active

**ener·vate** /ˈenəveɪt/; *NAmE* ˈenərv-/ *verb* ~ **sb** (*formal*) to make sb feel weak and tired: *an enervating disease/climate* ▶ **en·er·va·tion** /ˌenəˈveɪʃn/; *NAmE* ˌenərˈv-/ *noun* [U]

**en·fee·ble** /ɪnˈfiːbl/ *verb* ~ **sb/sth** (*formal*) to make sb/sth weak ▶ **en·fee·bled** *adj.*

**en·fold** /ɪnˈfəʊld/ *verb* (*literary*) **1** ~ **sb/sth (in sth)** to hold sb in your arms in a way that shows love **SYN** embrace: *She lay quietly, enfolded in his arms.* **2** ~ **sb/sth (in sth)** to surround or cover sb/sth completely: *Darkness spread and enfolded him.*

**en·force** 🔊+ **C1** /ɪnˈfɔːs/; *NAmE* -ˈfɔːrs/ *verb* **1** 🔊+ **C1** to make sure that people obey a particular law or rule: ~ **sth** *It's the job of the police to enforce the law.* ◇ *The legislation will be difficult to enforce.* ◇ *United Nations troops enforced a ceasefire in the area.* **2** ~ **sth (on sb)** to make sth happen or force sb to do sth: *You can't enforce cooperation between the players.* ▶ **en·force·able** *adj.*: *A gambling debt is not legally enforceable.*

**en·forced** /ɪnˈfɔːst/; *NAmE* -ˈfɔːrst/ *adj.* that sb is forced to do or experience without being able to control it: *a period of enforced absence*

**en·force·ment** 🔊+ **C1** /ɪnˈfɔːsmənt/; *NAmE* -ˈfɔːrs-/ *noun* [U] the act of making people obey a particular law or rule: *strict enforcement of regulations* ◇ *law enforcement officers*

**en·for·cer** /ɪnˈfɔːsə(r)/; *NAmE* -ˈfɔːrs-/ *noun* a person whose responsibility is to make sure that other people perform the actions they are supposed to, especially in a government

**en·fran·chise** /ɪnˈfræntʃaɪz/ *verb* [*usually passive*] ~ **sb** (*formal*) to give sb the right to vote in an election **OPP** disenfranchise ▶ **en·fran·chise·ment** /ɪnˈfræntʃɪzmənt/; *NAmE* -tʃaɪz-/ *noun* [U]

**eng.** *abbr.* (*BrE*) (in writing) engineer; engineering

**en·gage** 🔊 **B2** 🅦 /ɪnˈɡeɪdʒ/ *verb* **1** 🔊 **B2** [T] ~ **sth/sb** (*formal*) to succeed in attracting and keeping sb's attention and interest: *It is a movie that engages both the mind and the eye.* ◇ *It was difficult to engage the students at first.* **2** 🔊 **B2** [T] (*formal*) to employ a person, company, etc. to do a particular job: ~ **sb/sth (as sth)** *He was immediately engaged as a consultant.* ◇ ~ **sb/sth to do sth** *Karl Böhm engaged her to sing in Vienna.* **3** [I] ~ **(with sth/sb)** to become involved with and try to understand sth/sb: *She has the ability to engage with young minds.* **4** [T, I] ~ **(with) sb** (*formal*) to begin fighting with sb: *to engage (with) the enemy* **5** [I, T] when a part of a machine **engages**, or when you **engage** it, it fits together with another part of the machine and the machine begins to work: *The cogwheels are not engaging.* ◇ ~ **with sth** *One cogwheel engages with the next.* ◇ ~ **sth** *Engage the clutch before selecting a gear.* **OPP** disengage

**PHRV** **enˈgage in sth** 🔊 **B2** | **enˈgage sb in sth** (*formal*) to take part in sth; to make sb take part in sth: *Even in prison, he continued to engage in criminal activities.* ◇ *She tried desperately to engage him in conversation.*

**en·gaged** 🔊 **B1** /ɪnˈɡeɪdʒd/ *adj.* **1** 🔊 **B1** having agreed to marry sb: *When did you get engaged?* ◇ *an engaged couple* ◇ ~ **to sb** *She's engaged to Peter.* ◇ *They are engaged to be married* (= to each other). ◇ WORDFINDER NOTE at WEDDING **2** 🔊 **B2** (*formal*) busy doing sth; involved with sb/sth in an active and interested way: *I can't come to dinner on Tuesday—I'm otherwise engaged* (= I have already arranged to do something else). ◇ ~ **in sth** *They were engaged in conversation.* ◇ ~ **on sth** *She is actively engaged on several projects.* ◇ ~ **with sth** *We need to become more engaged with our history as a nation.* ⊃ compare DISENGAGED **3** (*BrE*) (*also* **busy** *especially in NAmE*) (of a phone line) being used: *I couldn't get through—the line's engaged.* ◇ *I phoned earlier but you were engaged* (= using your phone). ◇ *the engaged tone/signal* ⊃ WORDFINDER NOTE at CALL **4** (*BrE*) (of a public toilet/bathroom) being used **OPP** vacant

**en·gage·ment** 🔊+ **C1** /ɪnˈɡeɪdʒmənt/ *noun*
- BEFORE MARRIAGE **1** 🔊+ **C1** [C] an agreement to marry sb; the period during which two people are engaged: *Their engagement was announced in the local paper.* ◇ ~ **(to sb)** *She has broken off her engagement to Charles.* ◇ *an engagement party* ◇ *a long/short engagement*
- ARRANGEMENT TO DO STH **2** 🔊+ **C1** [C] an arrangement to do sth at a particular time, especially sth official or sth connected with your job: *an engagement book/diary* ◇ *He has a number of social engagements next week.* ◇ *It was her first official engagement.* ◇ *I had to refuse because of a prior engagement.*
- BEING INVOLVED **3** 🔊+ **C1** [U] (*formal*) being involved with sb/sth in an attempt to understand them/it: ~ **(with sb/sth)** *Her views are based on years of engagement with the problems of the inner city.*

# engagement ring 514

- **FIGHTING** 4 [C, U] (*specialist*) fighting between two armies, etc: *The general tried to avoid an engagement with the enemy.*
- **EMPLOYMENT** 5 [U, C] (*BrE*) an arrangement to employ sb; the process of employing sb: *The terms of engagement are to be agreed in writing.*

**en'gagement ring** *noun* a ring that a man traditionally gives to a woman when they agree to get married

**en·gag·ing** 🔑+ B1 /ɪnˈɡeɪdʒɪŋ/ *adj.* interesting or pleasant in a way that attracts your attention: *an engaging smile* ▶ **en·ga·ging·ly** *adv.*

**en·gen·der** /ɪnˈdʒendə(r)/ *verb* ~ sth (*formal*) to make a feeling or situation exist: *The issue engendered controversy.*

**en·gine** 🔑 A2 /ˈendʒɪn/ *noun* **1** 🔑 A2 the part of a vehicle that produces power to make the vehicle move: *a diesel/petrol engine* ◊ *I got in the car and started the engine.* ◊ *engine trouble/failure* ⇒ see also INTERNAL-COMBUSTION ENGINE, JET ENGINE, TRACTION ENGINE **2** a thing that has an important role in making a particular process happen: **~ of sth** *Agriculture is a key engine of growth in most developing countries.* ◊ **~ for (doing) sth** *Great newspapers serve as an engine for positive change.* **3** (*also* **loco·mo·tive**) a vehicle that pulls a train ⇒ see also TANK ENGINE, TRACTION ENGINE **4 -engined** (in adjectives) having the type or number of engines mentioned: *a twin-engined speedboat* ⇒ see also FIRE ENGINE, SEARCH ENGINE

**'engine driver** (*BrE, becoming old-fashioned*) (*NAmE* **en·gin·eer**) *noun* a person whose job is driving a railway engine

**en·gin·eer** 🔑 A2 /ˌendʒɪˈnɪə(r)/ *NAmE* -ˈnɪr/ *noun, verb*
- *noun* **1** 🔑 B1 a person whose job involves designing and building engines, machines, roads, bridges, etc: *a team of scientists and engineers* ⇒ see also CHEMICAL ENGINEER, CIVIL ENGINEER, ELECTRICAL ENGINEER, LIGHTING ENGINEER, MECHANICAL ENGINEER, SOFTWARE ENGINEER, SOUND ENGINEER, STRUCTURAL ENGINEER **2** A2 a person who is trained to repair machines and electrical equipment: *They're sending an engineer to fix the problem with the heating.* **3** a person whose job is to control and repair engines, especially on a ship or an aircraft: *a flight engineer* ◊ *the chief engineer on a cruise liner* **4** (*NAmE*) (*BrE* **'engine driver**) a person whose job is driving a railway engine **5** a soldier trained to design and build military structures
- *verb* **1** ~ sth (*often disapproving*) to arrange for sth to happen or take place, especially when this is done secretly in order to give yourself an advantage SYN **contrive**: *She engineered a further meeting with him.* **2** (*usually passive*) to design and build sth: **be ... engineered** *The car is beautifully engineered and a pleasure to drive.* **3** ~ sth to change the GENETIC structure of sth: *genetically engineered crops*

**en·gin·eer·ing** 🔑 B1 /ˌendʒɪˈnɪərɪŋ/ *NAmE* -ˈnɪr-/ *noun* [U] **1** 🔑 B1 the activity of applying scientific knowledge to the design, building and control of machines, roads, bridges, electrical equipment, etc: *The bridge is a triumph of modern engineering.* ◊ *an engineering firm/company* ⇒ see also REVERSE ENGINEERING **2** B1 (*also* **engin·eer·ing 'science**) the study of engineering as a subject: *a degree in engineering* ◊ *an engineering student* ⇒ see also CHEMICAL ENGINEERING, CIVIL ENGINEERING, ELECTRICAL ENGINEERING, GENETIC ENGINEERING, MECHANICAL ENGINEERING, SOCIAL ENGINEERING

**'engine room** *noun* **1** the part of a ship where the engines are **2** the part of an organization where most of the important activity takes place or important decisions are made

**Eng·lish** /ˈɪŋɡlɪʃ/ *noun, adj.*
- *noun* **1** [U, C] the language, originally of England, now spoken in many other countries and used as a language of international communication throughout the world: *She speaks good English.* ◊ *I need to improve my English.* ◊ *world Englishes* ⇒ see also BASIC ENGLISH, BRITISH ENGLISH, KING'S ENGLISH, MIDDLE ENGLISH, MODERN ENGLISH, OLD ENGLISH, QUEEN'S ENGLISH, WORLD ENGLISH **2** [U] English language or literature as a subject of study: *a degree in English* ◊ *English is my best subject.* **3** **the English** [pl.] the people of England (sometimes wrongly used to mean the British, including the Scots, the Welsh and the Northern Irish) IDM see PLAIN *adj.*
- *adj.* connected with England, its people or its language: *the English countryside* ◊ *an English man/woman* ◊ *typically English attitudes* ◊ *an English dictionary* ⇒ note at BRITISH

**English 'breakfast** *noun* [C, U] a large breakfast of hot cooked food including BACON and eggs ⇒ compare CONTINENTAL BREAKFAST

**English for Academic 'Purposes** (*abbr.* **EAP**) *noun* [U] the teaching of English for people who are using English for study, but whose first language is not English

**English 'horn** *noun* (*especially NAmE*) = COR ANGLAIS

**Eng·lish·man** /ˈɪŋɡlɪʃmən/ *noun* (*pl.* **-men** /-mən/) a man from England
IDM **an Englishman's home is his 'castle** (*BrE*) (*US* **a man's home is his 'castle**) (*saying*) a person's home is a place where they can be private and safe and do as they like

**English 'muffin** (*NAmE*) (*BrE* **muf·fin**) *noun* a type of round flat bread roll, usually TOASTED and eaten hot with butter

**English 'rose** *noun* an attractive girl with fair skin and an appearance that is thought to be typical of English people

**Eng·lish·woman** /ˈɪŋɡlɪʃwʊmən/ *noun* (*pl.* **-women** /-wɪmɪn/) a woman from England

**en·gorge** /ɪnˈɡɔːdʒ; *NAmE* -ˈɡɔːrdʒ/ *verb* [usually passive] ~ sth (with sth) (*specialist*) to cause sth to become filled with blood or another liquid and to SWELL (= become larger or rounder than normal)

**en·grained** /ɪnˈɡreɪnd/ *adj.* = INGRAINED

**en·grave** /ɪnˈɡreɪv/ *verb* [often passive] to cut words or designs on wood, stone, metal, etc: **A is engraved (with B)** *The silver cup was engraved with his name.* ◊ **B is engraved on A** *His name was engraved on the silver cup.*
IDM **be engraved on/in your 'heart, 'memory, 'mind, etc.** to be sth that you will never forget because it affected you so strongly

**en·graver** /ɪnˈɡreɪvə(r)/ *noun* a person whose job is to cut words or designs on wood, stone, metal, etc.

**en·grav·ing** /ɪnˈɡreɪvɪŋ/ *noun* **1** [C] a picture made by cutting a design on a piece of metal and then printing the design on paper **2** [U] the art or process of cutting designs on wood, stone, metal, etc.

**en·gross** /ɪnˈɡrəʊs/ *verb* ~ sb if sth **engrosses** you, it is so interesting that you give it all your attention and time ▶ **en·gross·ing** *adj.*: *an engrossing problem*

**en·grossed** /ɪnˈɡrəʊst/ *adj.* **~ (in/with sth)** so interested or involved in sth that you give it all your attention: *She was engrossed in conversation.*

**en·gulf** /ɪnˈɡʌlf/ *verb* (*formal*) **1** ~ sb/sth to surround or to cover sb/sth completely: *He was engulfed by a crowd of reporters.* ◊ *The vehicle was engulfed in flames.* **2** ~ sb/sth to affect sb/sth very strongly: *Fear engulfed her.*

**en·hance** 🔑 B2 W /ɪnˈhɑːns; *NAmE* -ˈhæns/ *verb* ~ sth to increase or further improve the good quality, value or status of sb/sth: *This is an opportunity to enhance the reputation of the company.* ◊ *the skilled use of make-up to enhance your best features* ◊ *The techniques should greatly enhance the prospects for children with learning difficulties.* ▶ **en·hanced** *adj.*: *enhanced efficiency* **en·hance·ment** *noun* [U, C]: *equipment for the enhancement of sound quality* ◊ *software enhancements*

**en·hancer** /ɪnˈhɑːnsə(r); *NAmE* -ˈhæn-/ *noun* (*specialist*) a substance or device that is designed to improve sth: *flavour enhancers*

**en·igma** /ɪˈnɪɡmə/ *noun* a person, thing or situation that is mysterious and difficult to understand SYN **mystery**, **puzzle**

**en·ig·mat·ic** /ˌenɪɡˈmætɪk/ *adj.* mysterious and difficult to understand: *an enigmatic smile* ▶ **en·ig·mat·ic·al·ly** /-kli/ *adv.*: *'I might,' he said enigmatically.*

**en·join** /ɪnˈdʒɔɪn/ verb 1 ~ sb to do sth | ~ sth (on sb) (formal) to order or strongly advise sb to do sth; to say that a particular action or quality is necessary 2 ~ sb from doing sth (law) to legally prevent sb from doing sth, for example with an INJUNCTION

**enjoy** 🔑 A1 /ɪnˈdʒɔɪ/ verb 1 A1 [T] to get pleasure from sth: ~ sth *We thoroughly enjoyed our time in New York.* ◊ *Thanks for a great evening. I really enjoyed it.* ◊ ~ doing sth *I enjoy playing tennis and squash.* 2 A2 [T] ~ yourself to be happy and get pleasure from what you are doing: *They all enjoyed themselves at the party.* 3 [T] ~ sth (formal) to have sth good that is an advantage to you: *People in this country enjoy a high standard of living.* ◊ *He's always enjoyed good health.* 4 [I] enjoy! (informal) used to say that you hope sb gets pleasure from sth that you are giving them or recommending to them: *Here's that book I promised you. Enjoy!*

▼ GRAMMAR POINT

**enjoy**

Note the following patterns:
- *I enjoyed myself at the party.* ◊ ~~*I enjoyed at the party.*~~
- *Thanks. I really enjoyed it.* ◊ ~~*Thanks. I really enjoyed.*~~
- *I enjoy playing basketball.* ◊ ~~*I enjoy to play basketball.*~~
- *I enjoy reading very much.* ◊ ~~*I enjoy very much reading.*~~
- *I hope you enjoy your trip.* ◊ ~~*I hope you enjoy with your trip.*~~

**en·joy·able** 🔑+ B2 /ɪnˈdʒɔɪəbl/ adj. giving pleasure: *an enjoyable weekend/experience* ◊ *highly/really/thoroughly/very enjoyable* ▶ **en·joy·ably** /-bli/ adv.: *The evening passed enjoyably.*

**en·joy·ment** /ɪnˈdʒɔɪmənt/ noun 1 [U] the pleasure that you get from sth: *He spoiled my enjoyment of the game by talking all through it.* ◊ *The rules are there to ensure everyone's safety and enjoyment.* ◊ *I get a lot of enjoyment from my grandchildren.* ◊ ~ in (doing) sth *Children seem to have lost their enjoyment in reading.* ⇒ SYNONYMS at FUN 2 [C] something that gives you pleasure: *Children like to share interests and enjoyments with their parents.* 3 [U] ~ of sth (formal) the fact of having and using sth: *the enjoyment of equal rights*

**en·large** /ɪnˈlɑːdʒ; NAmE -ˈlɑːrdʒ/ verb 1 [T, I] ~ (sth) to make sth bigger; to become bigger: *There are plans to enlarge the recreation area.* ◊ *Reading will enlarge your vocabulary.* 2 [T, usually passive] to make a bigger copy of a photograph or document: have sth/be enlarged *We're going to have this picture enlarged.* ▶ **en·larged** adj.: *an enlarged heart*
PHRV **en·large on/upon sth** (formal) to say or write more about sth that has been mentioned SYN elaborate

**en·large·ment** /ɪnˈlɑːdʒmənt; NAmE -ˈlɑːrdʒ-/ noun 1 [U, sing.] ~ (of sth) the process or result of sth becoming or being made larger: *the enlargement of the company's overseas business activities* ◊ *There was widespread support for EU enlargement* (= the fact of more countries joining). 2 [C] something that has been made larger, especially a photograph: *If you like the picture I can send you an enlargement of it.* OPP reduction

**en·larg·er** /ɪnˈlɑːdʒə(r); NAmE -ˈlɑːrdʒ-/ noun a piece of equipment for making photographs larger or smaller

**en·light·en** /ɪnˈlaɪtn/ verb ~ sb (formal) to give sb information so that they understand sth better: *She didn't enlighten him about her background.* ▶ **en·light·en·ing** adj.: *It was a very enlightening interview.*

**en·light·ened** /ɪnˈlaɪtnd/ adj. [usually before noun] (approving) having or showing an understanding of people's needs, a situation, etc. that is not based on old-fashioned attitudes and PREJUDICE: *enlightened opinions/attitudes/ideas*

**en·light·en·ment** /ɪnˈlaɪtnmənt/ noun 1 [U] knowledge about and understanding of sth; the process of understanding sth or making sb understand it: *The newspapers provided little enlightenment about the cause of the accident.* ◊ *spiritual enlightenment* 2 **the Enlightenment** [sing.] the period in the 18th century in Europe when many writers and scientists began to argue that science and reason were more important than religion and tradition

**en·list** /ɪnˈlɪst/ verb 1 [T] to persuade sb to help you or to join you in doing sth: ~ sth/sb (in sth) *They hoped to enlist the help of the public in solving the crime.* ◊ ~ sb (as sth) *We* were enlisted as helpers. ◊ ~ sb to do sth *We were enlisted to help.* 2 [I, T] to join the armed forces; to make sb join the armed forces: *They both enlisted in 1915.* ◊ ~ as sth to enlist as a soldier ◊ ~ sb (in/into/for/as sth) *He was enlisted into the US Navy.* ⇒ compare CALL UP, CONSCRIPT, DRAFT
▶ **en·list·ment** noun [U, C]: *the enlistment of expert help* ◊ *his enlistment in the Royal Air Force*

**en·list·ed** /ɪnˈlɪstɪd/ adj. (especially US) (of a member of the army, etc.) having a rank that is below that of an officer: *enlisted men and women* ◊ *enlisted personnel*

**en·liven** /ɪnˈlaɪvn/ verb ~ sth (formal) to make sth more interesting or more fun

**en masse** /ˌɒ̃ ˈmæs; NAmE ɑː-/ adv. (from French) all together, and usually in large numbers

**en·mesh** /ɪnˈmeʃ/ verb [usually passive] ~ sb/sth (in sth) (formal) to involve sb/sth in a bad situation that it is not easy to escape from

**en·mity** /ˈenməti/ noun [U, C] (pl. -ies) feelings of hate towards sb: *personal enmities and political conflicts* ◊ *Her action earned her the enmity of two or three colleagues.* ◊ ~ between A and B *the traditional problem of the enmity between Protestants and Catholics* ⇒ see also ENEMY

**en·noble** /ɪˈnəʊbl/ verb (formal) 1 [usually passive] ~ sb to make sb a member of the NOBILITY 2 ~ sb/sth to give sb/sth a better moral character: *In a strange way she seemed ennobled by her grief.* ▶ **en·noble·ment** noun [U]

**ennui** /ɒnˈwiː; NAmE ɑːn-/ noun [U] (from French, literary) feelings of being bored and not satisfied because nothing interesting is happening

**en·or·mity** /ɪˈnɔːməti; NAmE ɪˈnɔːrm-/ noun (pl. -ies) 1 [U] the ~ of sth (of a problem, etc.) the very great size, effect, etc. of sth; the fact of sth being very serious: *the enormity of the task* ◊ *People are still coming to terms with the enormity of the disaster.* ◊ *The full enormity of the crime has not yet been revealed.* 2 [C, usually pl.] (formal) a very serious crime: *the enormities of the Hitler regime*

**enor·mous** 🔑 A2 /ɪˈnɔːməs; NAmE ɪˈnɔːrm-/ adj. extremely large SYN huge, immense: *an enormous house/dog* ◊ *an enormous amount of time* ◊ *Universities are under enormous pressure financially.* ◊ *Their house is absolutely enormous!*

**enor·mous·ly** /ɪˈnɔːməsli; NAmE ɪˈnɔːrm-/ adv. very; very much: *enormously rich/powerful/grateful* ◊ *The price of wine varies enormously depending on where it comes from.* ◊ *She was looking forward to the meeting enormously.*

**enough** 🔑 A1 /ɪˈnʌf/ det., pron., adv.

■ **det.** 🔑 A1 used before plural or uncountable nouns to mean 'as many or as much as sb needs or wants' SYN sufficient: *Have you made enough copies?* ◊ *Is there enough room for me?* ◊ *I didn't have enough clothes to last a week.* ◊ *Don't ask me to do it. I've got enough problems as it is.* ◊ (old-fashioned) *There was food enough for all.* HELP Although enough after a noun now sounds old-fashioned, time enough is still fairly common: *There'll be time enough to relax when you've finished your work.*

■ **pron.** 🔑 A1 as many or as much as sb needs or wants: *Six bottles should be enough.* ◊ *Have you had enough* (= to eat)? ◊ *If enough of you are interested, we'll organize a trip to the theatre.* ◊ *There was nowhere near enough for everybody.* ◊ *We've nearly run out of paper. Do you think there's enough for today?*
IDM **e'nough already** (especially NAmE, informal) used to say that sth is annoying or boring and that you want it to stop **e·nough is e·nough** (saying) used when you think that sth should not continue any longer **e·nough 'said** used to say that you understand a situation and there is no need to say any more: *'He's a politician, remember.' 'Enough said.'* **have had e'nough (of sth/sb)** used when sth/sb is annoying you and you no longer want to do, have or see it or them: *I've had enough of driving the kids around.*

■ **adv.** (used after verbs, adjectives and adverbs) 1 🔑 A1 to the necessary degree: *I hadn't trained enough for the game.* ◊ *This house isn't big enough for us.* ◊ *She's old enough to decide for herself.* ◊ *They've been in this business*

# enquire

long enough to know what they're doing. ◊ *Tell them it's just not good enough.* **2** to an acceptable degree, but not to a very great degree: *He seemed pleasant enough to me.* **3** to a degree that you do not wish to get any greater: *I hope my job's safe. Life is hard enough as it is.* **IDM** **curiously, funnily, oddly, strangely, etc. e'nough** used to show that sth is surprising: *Funnily enough, I said the same thing myself only yesterday.* ⟹ more at **FAIR** *adj.*, **FAR** *adv.*, **LIKE** *adv.*, **MAN** *n.*, **NEAR** *adv.*, **RIGHT** *adj.*, **SURE** *adv.*

**en·quire** (especially *BrE*) (also **in·quire** *NAmE*, *BrE*) /ɪnˈkwaɪə(r)/ *verb* [I, T] (*rather formal*) to ask sb for some information: ~ *about sb/sth I called the station to enquire about train times.* ◊ ~ *why, where, etc… Might I enquire why you have not mentioned this until now?* ◊ ~ *sth He enquired her name.* ◊ + **speech** '*What is your name?*' *he enquired.* ⟹ SYNONYMS at **ASK** **HELP** In British English people sometimes distinguish between **enquire** and **inquire**, using **enquire** for the general meaning of 'ask for information' and **inquire** for the more particular meaning of 'officially investigate': *I called to enquire about train times.* ◊ *A committee will inquire into the allegations.* However, you can use either spelling in either meaning. In American English **inquire** is usually used in both meanings.
**PHRV** **en'quire after sb** (*formal*) to ask for information about sb, especially about their health or about what they are doing **en'quire into sth** to find out more information about sth **SYN** **investigate**: *A committee was appointed to enquire into the allegations.* **en'quire sth of sb** (*formal*) to ask sb sth: + **speech** '*Will you be staying for lunch?*' *she enquired of Charles.*

**en·quir·er** (especially *BrE*) (also **in·quirer** *NAmE*, *BrE*) /ɪnˈkwaɪərə(r)/ *noun* (*formal*) a person who asks for information

**en·quir·ing** (especially *BrE*) (also **in·quir·ing** *NAmE*, *BrE*) /ɪnˈkwaɪərɪŋ/ *adj.* [usually before noun] **1** showing an interest in learning new things: *a child with an enquiring mind* **2** asking for information: *an enquiring look* ▶ **en·quir·ing·ly** (especially *BrE*) (also **in·quir·ing·ly** *NAmE*, *BrE*) *adv.*

**en·quiry** (especially *BrE*) (also **in·quiry** *NAmE*, *BrE*) /ɪnˈkwaɪəri; *NAmE* ˈɪŋkwəri, ɪnˈkwaɪəri/ *noun* (*pl.* **-ies**) **1** [C] an official process to find out the cause of sth or to find out information about sth: *a murder enquiry* ◊ ~ *into sth a public enquiry into the environmental effects of the proposed new road* ◊ *to hold/conduct/launch an enquiry into the affair* **2** [C] a request for information about sb/sth; a question about sb/sth: ~ (*from sb*) (*about sth*) *enquiries from prospective students about courses* ◊ *I'll have to make a few enquiries* (= try to find out about it) *and get back to you.* ◊ *For further enquiries, please call…* ◊ (*BrE*) *Two men have been helping police with their enquiries* (= are being questioned about a crime, but have not been charged with it). **3** [U] the act of asking questions or collecting information about sth: *scientific enquiry* ◊ *The police are following several lines of enquiry.* ◊ *a commission/committee of enquiry* **4 enquiries** [pl.] (*BrE*) a place where you can get information: *Ask at enquiries to see if your bag has been handed in.* ⟹ see also **DIRECTORY ENQUIRIES** **HELP** In British English people sometimes distinguish between **enquiry** and **inquiry**, using **enquiry** for the general meaning of 'a request for information' and **inquiry** for the more particular meaning of 'official investigation': *enquiries from prospective students* ◊ *a murder inquiry*. However, you can use either spelling in either meaning. In American English **inquiry** is usually used in both meanings.

**en·rage** /ɪnˈreɪdʒ/ *verb* [often passive] ~ *sb* to make sb very angry **SYN** **infuriate**

**en·rap·ture** /ɪnˈræptʃə(r)/ *verb* [usually passive] ~ *sb* (*formal*) to give sb great pleasure or joy **SYN** **enchant**

**en·rap·tured** /ɪnˈræptʃəd; *NAmE* -tʃərd/ *adj.* (*formal*) filled with great pleasure or joy **SYN** **enchanted**

**en·rich** /ɪnˈrɪtʃ/ *verb* **1** ~ *sth* to improve the quality of sth, often by adding sth to it: *The study of science has enriched all our lives.* **2** ~ *sth* (*with sth*) to improve the quality of food by adding vitamins or NUTRIENTS: *Most breakfast cereals are enriched with vitamins.* **3** ~ *sb/sth* to make sb/sth rich or richer: *a nation enriched*

516

*by oil revenues* ◊ *He used his position to enrich himself.* ▶ **en·rich·ment** *noun* [U]

**enrol** (*US* **en·roll**) /ɪnˈrəʊl/ *verb* (**-ll-**) [I, T] to arrange for yourself or for sb else to officially join a course, school, etc: *You need to enrol before the end of August.* ◊ (*BrE*) *to enrol on a course* ◊ (*NAmE*) *to enroll in a course* ◊ ~ *sb The centre will soon be ready to enrol candidates for the new programme.*

**en·rol·lee** /ɪnrəʊˈliː/ *noun* (*NAmE*) a person who has officially joined a course, an organization, etc.

**en·rol·ment** (*US* **en·roll·ment**) /ɪnˈrəʊlmənt/ *noun* [U, C] the act of officially joining a course, school, etc.; the number of people who do this: *Enrolment is the first week of September.* ◊ *School enrolments are currently falling.*

**en route** /ˌɒn ˈruːt; *NAmE* ˌɑːn ˈruːt/ *adv.* (from French) on the way; while travelling from/to a particular place: *We stopped for a picnic en route.* ◊ ~ (*from*…) (*to*…) *The bus broke down en route from Boston to New York.* ◊ (*BrE*) ~ (*for*…) *a plane en route for Heathrow*

**en·sconce** /ɪnˈskɒns; *NAmE* -ˈskɑːns/ *verb* **be ensconced** (+ *adv./prep.*) | ~ *yourself* (+ *adv./prep.*) (*formal*) if you are ensconced or ensconce yourself somewhere, you are made or make yourself comfortable and safe in that place or position

**en·sem·ble** /ɒnˈsɒmbl; *NAmE* ɑːnˈsɑːm-/ *noun* **1** [C + sing./pl. v.] a small group of musicians, dancers or actors who perform together: *a brass/wind/string, etc. ensemble* ◊ *The ensemble is/are based in Lyons.* **2** [C, usually sing.] (*formal*) a number of things considered as a group **3** [C, usually sing.] a set of clothes that are worn together

**en·shrine** /ɪnˈʃraɪn/ *verb* [usually passive] (*formal*) to make a law, right, etc. respected or official, especially by stating it in an important written document: **be enshrined (in sth)** *These rights are enshrined in the country's constitution.*

**en·shroud** /ɪnˈʃraʊd/ *verb* ~ *sth* (*literary*) to cover or surround sth completely so that it cannot be seen or understood

**en·sign** /ˈensən/ *noun* **1** a flag flown on a ship to show which country it belongs to: *the White Ensign* (= the flag of the British NAVY) **2** an officer of low rank in the US NAVY: *Ensign Marshall*

**en·slave** /ɪnˈsleɪv/ *verb* [usually passive] **1** ~ *sb* to make sb a slave **2** ~ *sb/sth* (*to sth*) (*formal*) to make sb/sth completely depend on sth so that they cannot manage without it ▶ **en·slave·ment** *noun* [U]

**en·snare** /ɪnˈsneə(r); *NAmE* -ˈsner/ *verb* ~ *sb/sth* (*formal*) to make sb/sth unable to escape from a difficult situation or from a person who wants to control them **SYN** **trap**: *young homeless people who become ensnared in a life of crime*

**ensue** /ɪnˈsjuː; *NAmE* -ˈsuː/ *verb* [I] (*formal*) to happen after or as a result of another event **SYN** **follow**: *An argument ensued.* ▶ **en·su·ing** *adj.*: *He had become separated from his parents in the ensuing panic.*

**en suite** /ˌɒn ˈswiːt; *NAmE* ˌɑː/ *adj., adv.* (*BrE*, from French) (of a bathroom) joined onto a bedroom and for use only by people in that bedroom: *Each bedroom in the hotel has a bathroom en suite/an en-suite bathroom.* ◊ *an en-suite bedroom* (= a bedroom with a bathroom en suite) ◊ *en-suite facilities* ▶ **en·suite** *noun*: *The en-suite has a power shower.* ◊ *Both bedrooms have tiled en-suites.*

**en·sure** (also **in·sure** especially in *NAmE*) /ɪnˈʃʊə(r); -ˈʃɔː(r); *NAmE* -ˈʃʊr/ *verb* to make sure that sth happens or is definite: ~ *sth We are working to ensure the safety of people in the city.* ◊ ~ *sb Victory ensured them a place in the final.* ◊ ~ *sth for sb The system ensures equal access to education for all children.* ◊ ~ (*that*)… *The government needs to ensure (that) workers' rights are respected.*

**ENT** /ˌiː en ˈtiː/ *abbr.* ear, nose and throat (as a department in a hospital or a branch of medicine): *the ENT department* ◊ *an ENT surgeon/specialist*

**-ent** ⟹ -ANT

**en·tail** /ɪnˈteɪl/ *verb* to involve sth that cannot be avoided **SYN** **involve**: ~ *sth The job entails a lot of hard work.* ◊ **be entailed in sth** *The girls learn exactly what is entailed in*

---

b **b**ad | d **d**id | f **f**all | g **g**et | h **h**at | j **y**es | k **c**at | l **l**eg | m **m**an | n **n**ow | p **p**en | r **r**ed

caring for a newborn baby. ◇ ~ **(sb) doing sth** It will entail driving a long distance every day.

**en·tan·gle** /ɪnˈtæŋgl/ verb [usually passive] **1** to make sb/sth become caught or TWISTED in sth: **be/become entangled (in/with sth)** The bird had become entangled in the wire netting. **2** to involve sb in a difficult or complicated situation: **be/become entangled in sth** He became entangled in a series of conflicts with the management. ◇ **be/get entangled with sb** She didn't want to get entangled (= emotionally involved) with him.

**en·tangle·ment** /ɪnˈtæŋglmənt/ noun **1** [C] a difficult or complicated relationship with another person or country **2** [U] the act of becoming caught or TWISTED in sth; the state of being caught or TWISTED in sth: Many dolphins die each year from entanglement in fishing nets. **3 entanglements** [pl.] (specialist) barriers made of BARBED WIRE, used to stop an enemy from getting close

**en·tente** /ɒnˈtɒnt; NAmE ɑːnˈtɑːnt/ noun [U, sing.] (from French) a friendly relationship between two countries: the Franco-Russian entente

**enter** ⓘ **A2** ⓢ /ˈentə(r)/ verb
- COME/GO IN **1** ⓘ **A2** [I, T] (not usually used in the passive) (formal) to come or go into sth: Knock before you enter. ◇ ~ **sth** Someone entered the room behind me. ◇ people who **enter the country** illegally ◇ Where did the bullet enter the body? ◇ (figurative) A note of defiance entered her voice. ◇ (figurative) It never entered my head (= I never thought) that she would tell him about me.
- EXAM/COMPETITION **2** ⓘ **B1** [T, I] to put your name on the list for an exam, a race, a competition, etc.; to do this for sb: ~ **sth** Over a thousand children **entered the competition**. ◇ ~ **sb/sth in sth** Irish trainers have entered several horses in the race. ◇ ~ **sb/sth for sth** How many students have been entered for the exam? ◇ ~ **(for sth)** Only four British players have entered for the championship.
- BEGIN ACTIVITY **3** ⓘ **B1** [T] ~ **sth** to begin or become involved in an activity, a situation, etc: Several new firms have now entered the market. ◇ The US entered the war in 1917. ◇ The investigation has entered a new phase. ◇ The strike is entering its fourth week.
- JOIN INSTITUTION/START WORK **4** ⓘ **B1** [T, no passive] ~ **sth** (formal) to become a member of an institution; to start working in an organization or a profession: to enter a school/college/university ◇ to enter politics ◇ to enter Parliament (= become an MP) ◇ to enter the Church (= become a priest) ◇ to enter the legal/medical profession
- WRITE INFORMATION **5** [T] to put names, numbers, details, etc. in a list, book or computer: ~ **sth (in sth)** Enter your name and occupation in the boxes (= on a form). ◇ ~ **sth into sth** to enter data into a computer ◇ ~ **sth on sth** to enter figures on a spreadsheet ⊃ WORDFINDER NOTE at COMMAND
- SAY OFFICIALLY **6** [T] ~ **sth** (formal) to say sth officially so that it can be recorded: to enter a plea of not guilty (= at the beginning of a court case) ◇ to enter an offer ⊃ see also ENTRANCE¹, ENTRY ⓘⓓⓜ see FORCE n., NAME n.
**PHR V** ˈenter into sth (formal) **1** to begin to discuss or deal with sth: Let's not enter into details at this stage. **2** to take an active part in sth: They entered into the spirit of the occasion (= began to enjoy and feel part of it). **3** [no passive] to form part of sth or have an influence on sth: This possibility never entered into our calculations. ◇ Your personal feelings shouldn't enter into this at all. ˈenter into sth (with sb) to begin sth or become involved in sth: to enter into an agreement ◇ to enter into negotiations ˈenter on/upon sth (formal) to start to do sth or become involved in it: to enter on a new career

**en·ter·ic** /enˈterɪk/ adj. (medical) connected with the INTESTINES

**en·ter·itis** /ˌentəˈraɪtɪs/ noun [U] (medical) a painful infection in the INTESTINES that usually causes DIARRHOEA ⊃ see also GASTROENTERITIS

**en·ter·prise** ⓘ+ **C1** /ˈentəpraɪz; NAmE -tərp-/ noun **1** ⓘ+ **C1** [C] a company or business: an enterprise with a turnover of $26 billion ◇ state-owned/public enterprises ◇ small and medium-sized enterprises **2** ⓘ+ **C1** [C] a large project, especially one that is difficult ⓢⓨⓝ **venture**: his latest business enterprise ◇ a joint enterprise **3** ⓘ+ **C1** [U] the development of businesses by the people of a country rather than by the government: grants to encourage enterprise in the region ◇ an enterprise culture (= in which people are encouraged to develop small businesses) ⊃ see also FREE ENTERPRISE, PRIVATE ENTERPRISE **4** ⓘ+ **C1** [U] (approving) the ability to think of new projects and make them successful ⓢⓨⓝ **initiative**: a job in which enterprise is rewarded

**enterprise ˈbargaining** noun [U] (AustralE) discussions between employers and employees about pay and working conditions

**en·ter·pris·ing** /ˈentəpraɪzɪŋ; NAmE -tərp-/ adj. (approving) having or showing the ability to think of new projects or new ways of doing things and make them successful

**en·ter·tain** ⓘ **B1** /ˌentəˈteɪn; NAmE -tərˈt-/ verb **1** ⓘ **B1** [T, I] to interest sb or make sb laugh in order to please them: The aim of the series is both to entertain and inform. ◇ ~ **sb/yourself (with sth)** He entertained us for hours with his stories and jokes. **2** ⓘ **B2** [I, T] to invite people to eat or drink with you as your guests, especially in your home: Do you entertain a lot? ◇ ~ **sb** Barbecues are a favourite way of entertaining friends. ◇ ~ **sb to sth** They entertained us to lunch in their new house. **3** [T] (not used in the progressive tenses) ~ **sth** (formal) to consider or allow yourself to think about an idea, a hope, a feeling, etc: He had entertained hopes of a reconciliation. ◇ to entertain a doubt/suspicion

**en·ter·tain·er** /ˌentəˈteɪnə(r); NAmE -tərˈt-/ noun a person whose job is to sing, dance or perform for people so that they enjoy themselves

**en·ter·tain·ing** ⓘ+ **B2** /ˌentəˈteɪnɪŋ; NAmE -tərˈt-/ adj. that you enjoy watching, listening to, doing or experiencing: an entertaining speech/evening ◇ I found the talk both informative and entertaining. ◇ She was always so funny and entertaining. ⊃ SYNONYMS at FUNNY ▶ **en·ter·tain·ing·ly** adv.

**en·ter·tain·ment** ⓘ **B1** /ˌentəˈteɪnmənt; NAmE -tərˈt-/ noun **1** ⓘ **B1** [U, C] films, music, etc. used to entertain people; an example of this: radio, television and other forms of entertainment ◇ There will be live entertainment at the party. ◇ It was typical family entertainment. ◇ A folk band provided the entertainment. ◇ Local entertainments are listed in the newspaper. ◇ the entertainment industry/business ◇ The show was good entertainment value. ⊃ SYNONYMS on page 518 **2** [U] the act of providing people with sth to interest them or make them laugh: Ladies and gentlemen, for your entertainment, we present Magic Man. **3** [U] the act of inviting people to eat or drink with you as your guests: a budget for the entertainment of clients

**en·thral** (BrE) (NAmE **en·thrall**) /ɪnˈθrɔːl/ verb (-ll-) [T, often passive, I] if sth **enthrals** you, it is so interesting, beautiful, etc. that you give it all your attention ⓢⓨⓝ **entrance**²: **(be) enthralled (by sth)** The child watched, enthralled by the bright moving images. ◇ ~ **(sb)** The story never fails to enthral. ▶ **en·thral·ling** adj.: an enthralling performance

**en·throne** /ɪnˈθrəʊn/ verb [usually passive] ~ **sb** when a king, queen or important member of a Church is enthroned, they sit on a THRONE (= a special chair) in a ceremony to mark the beginning of their rule ▶ **en·throne·ment** noun [U, C]

**en·thuse** /ɪnˈθjuːz; NAmE -ˈθuːz/ verb **1** [I, T] to talk in an enthusiastic and excited way about sth: ~ **(about/over sth/sb)** The article enthused about the benefits that the new system would bring. ◇ + **speech** 'It's a wonderful idea', he enthused. ◇ ~ **that…** The organizers enthused that it was their most successful event yet. **2** [usually passive] to make sb feel very interested and excited: **be enthused (by/with sth)** Everyone present was enthused by the idea.

**en·thu·si·asm** ⓘ **B2** /ɪnˈθjuːziæzəm; NAmE -ˈθuː-/ noun **1** ⓘ **B2** [U, sing.] a strong feeling of excitement and interest in sth and a desire to become involved in it: full of enthusiasm ◇ The news was greeted with a lack of enthusiasm by those at the meeting. ◇ Bella responded with great enthusiasm. ◇ ~ **for (doing) sth** I can't say I share your enthusiasm for the idea. ◇ He had a real enthusiasm for the work. **2** [C] (formal) something that you are very interested in and spend a lot of time doing ⊃ WORDFINDER NOTE at ADVENTURE

**en·thu·si·ast** ⓘ+ **C1** /ɪnˈθjuːziæst; NAmE -ˈθuː-/ noun **1** ⓘ+ **C1** ~ **(for/of sth)** a person who is very interested in

# enthusiastic

## SYNONYMS

### entertainment
fun • recreation • relaxation • play • pleasure • amusement

These are all words for things or activities used to entertain people when they are not working.

**entertainment** films, television, music, etc. used to entertain people: *There are three bars, with live entertainment seven nights a week.*

**fun** (*rather informal*) behaviour or activities that are not serious but are meant to be enjoyed: *It wasn't serious—it was all done in fun.* ◊ *We didn't mean to hurt him. We were just* **a bit of fun**. ◊ *The lottery provides* **harmless fun** *for millions.*

**recreation** (*rather formal*) things people do for pleasure when they are not working: *His only form of recreation is playing football.*

**relaxation** (*rather formal*) things people do to rest and enjoy themselves when they are not working; the ability to relax: *I go hill-walking for relaxation.*

**RECREATION OR RELAXATION?**
Both these words can be used for a wide range of activities, physical and mental, but **relaxation** is sometimes used for gentler activities than **recreation**: *I play the flute in a wind band for recreation.* ◊ *I listen to music for relaxation.*

**play** things that people, especially children, do for pleasure rather than as work: *the happy sounds of children at play*

**pleasure** the activity of enjoying yourself, especially in contrast to working: *Are you in Paris* **for business or pleasure***?*

**amusement** the fact of being entertained by sth: *What do you do for amusement round here?*

**PATTERNS**
- to do sth **for** entertainment/fun/recreation/relaxation/pleasure/amusement
- to **provide** entertainment/fun/recreation/relaxation/amusement

sth and spends a lot of time doing it: *a football enthusiast* ◊ *an enthusiast of jazz* **2** ⓘ⁺ ◘ ~ **(for/of sth)** a person who approves of sth and shows enthusiasm for it: *enthusiasts for a united Europe*

**en·thu·si·as·tic** ⓘ B2 /ɪnˌθjuːziˈæstɪk; NAmE -ˌθuː-/ adj. feeling or showing a lot of excitement and interest about sb/sth: *an enthusiastic supporter* ◊ *an enthusiastic reception/welcome* ◊ ~ **about sb/sth** *You don't sound very enthusiastic about the idea.* ◊ ~ **about doing sth** *She was still really enthusiastic about going to Spain.* ▶ **en·thu·si·as·tic·al·ly** /-kli/ adv.

**en·tice** /ɪnˈtaɪs/ verb to persuade sb/sth to go somewhere or to do sth, usually by offering them sth **SYN** **persuade**: ~ **sb/sth (+ adv./prep.)** *The bargain prices are expected to entice customers away from other stores.* ◊ *The animal refused to be enticed from its hole.* ◊ ~ **sb into doing sth** *He was not enticed into parting with his cash.* ◊ ~ **sb to do sth** *Try and entice the child to eat by offering small portions of their favourite food.* ▶ **en·tice·ment** *noun* [C, U]: *The party is offering low taxation as its main enticement.*

**en·ti·cing** /ɪnˈtaɪsɪŋ/ adj. something that is **enticing** is so attractive and interesting that you want to have it or know more about it: *The offer was too enticing to refuse.* ▶ **en·ti·cing·ly** adv.

**en·tire** ⓘ B2 /ɪnˈtaɪə(r)/ adj. [only before noun] (used when you are emphasizing that the whole of sth is involved) including everything, everyone or every part **SYN** **whole**: *You two are her favourite people in the entire world.* ◊ *The film is perfect for the entire family.* ◊ *I have never in my entire life heard such nonsense!* ◊ *The disease threatens to wipe out the entire population.*

**en·tire·ly** ⓘ B2 ⓢ /ɪnˈtaɪəli; NAmE -ərli/ adv. in every way possible; completely: *The experience was entirely new to me.* ◊ *That's an entirely different matter.* ◊ *The approach taken will depend entirely on the individual.* ◊ *The audience consisted almost entirely of children.* ◊ *I entirely agree with you.*

**en·tir·ety** /ɪnˈtaɪərəti/ noun [sing.] **the ~ of sth** (*formal*) the whole of sth
**IDM** **in its/their en'tirety** as a whole, rather than in parts: *The poem is too long to quote in its entirety.*

**en·title** ⓘ⁺ C1 /ɪnˈtaɪtl/ verb **1** ⓘ⁺ C1 [often passive] to give sb the right to have or to do sth: **be entitled to sth** *You will be entitled to your pension when you reach 65.* ◊ *Everyone's entitled to their own opinion.* ◊ ~ **sb to do sth** *This ticket does not entitle you to travel first class.* **2** ⓘ⁺ C1 [usually passive] to give a title to a book, play, etc: **be entitled +  noun** *He read a poem entitled 'Salt'.*

**en·titled** /ɪnˈtaɪtld/ adj. (usually disapproving) feeling that you have a right to the good things in life without necessarily having to work for them: *He's so entitled!* ◊ *the entitled children of wealthy parents*

**en·title·ment** /ɪnˈtaɪtlmənt/ noun (*formal*) **1** [U] ~ **(to sth)** the official right to have or do sth: *This may affect your entitlement to compensation.* **2** [C] something that you have an official right to; the amount that you have the right to receive: *Your contributions will affect your pension entitlements.* **3** [C] (*NAmE*) a government system that provides financial support to a particular group of people: *a reform of entitlements* ◊ *Medicaid, Medicare and other entitlement programs* **4** [U] (*usually disapproving*) the feeling of having a right to the good things in life without necessarily having to work for them: *I can't stand the sense of entitlement among these kids.*

**en·tity** ⓘ⁺ C1 ⓦ /ˈentəti/ noun (pl. -ies) (*formal*) something that exists separately from other things and has its own identity: *The unit has become part of a larger department and no longer exists as a* **separate entity**. ◊ *These countries can no longer be viewed as a* **single entity**.

**en·tomb** /ɪnˈtuːm/ verb [usually passive] (*formal*) **1** ~ **sb/sth (in sth)** to bury or completely cover sb/sth so that they cannot get out, be seen, etc. **2** ~ **sb/sth (in sth)** to put a dead body in a TOMB

**en·to·mol·ogy** /ˌentəˈmɒlədʒi; NAmE -ˈmɑːl-/ noun [U] the scientific study of insects ▶ **en·to·mo·logic·al** /ˌentəməˈlɒdʒɪkl; NAmE -ˈlɑːdʒ-/ adj. **en·to·mo·lo·gist** /ˌentəˈmɒlədʒɪst; NAmE -ˈmɑːl-/ noun

**en·tour·age** /ˈɒntʊrɑːʒ; NAmE ˌɑːntʊˈrɑːʒ/ noun [C + sing./pl. v.] a group of people who travel with an important person

**en·trails** /ˈentreɪlz/ noun [pl.] the organs inside the body of a person or an animal, especially their INTESTINES **SYN** **innards**, **inside**

**en·trance¹** ⓘ B1 /ˈentrəns/ noun ◊ see also ENTRANCE²
- **DOOR/GATE 1** ⓘ B1 [C] a door, gate, passage, etc. used for entering a room, building or place: *the front/back/side entrance of the house* ◊ ~ **to sth** *Protesters blocked the entrance to the building.* ◊ *A lighthouse marks the entrance to the harbour.* ◊ **at the~** *I'll meet you at the main entrance.* ◊ *an entrance hall* ◊ compare EXIT
- **GOING IN 2** [C, usually sing.] the act of entering a room, building or place, especially in a way that attracts the attention of other people: *His sudden entrance took everyone by surprise.* ◊ *A fanfare signalled the entrance of the king.* ◊ *She* **made her entrance** *after all the other guests had arrived.* ◊ *The hero* **makes his entrance** (= walks onto the stage) *in Scene 2.* ◊ WORDFINDER NOTE at PLAY **3** [U] ~ **(to sth)** the right or opportunity to enter a building or place: *They were refused entrance to the exhibition.* ◊ *The police were unable to* **gain entrance** *to the house.* ◊ *an* **entrance fee** (= money paid to go into a museum, etc.)
- **BECOMING INVOLVED 4** [C] ~ **(into sth)** the act of becoming involved in sth: *The company made a dramatic entrance into the export market.*
- **TO CLUB/INSTITUTION 5** [U] permission to become a member of a club, society, university, etc: *a university entrance exam* ◊ *entrance requirements* ◊ ~ **(to sth)** *Entrance to the golf club is by sponsorship only.* ◊ compare ENTRY

**en·trance²** /ɪnˈtrɑːns; NAmE -ˈtræns/ verb [usually passive] ~ sb (formal) to make sb admire and like sb/sth very much, so they give them/it all their attention SYN **enthral**: *He listened to her, entranced.* ⊃ see also ENTRANCE¹ ▶ **en·tran·cing** adj.: *entrancing music*

**ˈentrance hall** noun a large room inside the entrance of a large or public building

**en·trant** /ˈentrənt/ noun **1** ~ (to sth) a person or group that has recently joined a profession, university, business, etc: *new women entrants to the police force* ◇ *university entrants* **2** ~ (to sth) a person or an animal that enters a race or a competition; a person that enters an exam **3** ~ (in/into/to sth) a company that starts operating in an area of business where other companies already operate: *The company is a new entrant into the multimedia market.*

**en·trap** /ɪnˈtræp/ verb [often passive] (-pp-) **1** ~ sb/sth (formal) to put or catch sb/sth in a place or situation from which they cannot escape SYN **trap 2** ~ sb (into doing sth) (law) to trick sb, and encourage them to do sth, especially to commit a crime, so that they can be arrested for it

**en·trap·ment** /ɪnˈtræpmənt/ noun [U] (law) the illegal act of tricking sb into committing a crime so that they can be arrested for it

**en·treat** /ɪnˈtriːt/ verb (formal) to ask sb to do sth in a serious and often emotional way SYN **beg, implore**: ~ sb *Please help me, I entreat you.* ◇ ~ sb to do sth *She entreated him not to go.* ◇ ~ (sb) + speech '*Please don't go,'* she entreated (him).

**en·treaty** /ɪnˈtriːti/ noun [C, U] (pl. -ies) (formal) a serious and often emotional request

**en·trée** /ˈɒntreɪ; NAmE ˈɑːn-/ noun (from French) **1** [C] (NAmE) (in a restaurant) the main dish of a meal **2** [U, C] ~ (into/to sth) (formal) the right or ability to enter a social group or institution

**en·trench** /ɪnˈtrentʃ/ verb [usually passive] (sometimes disapproving) to establish sth very strongly so that it is very difficult to change: **be entrenched (in sth)** *Sexism is deeply entrenched in our society.* ◇ *entrenched attitudes/interests/opposition*

**en·trench·ment** /ɪnˈtrentʃmənt/ noun **1** [U] the fact of sth being strongly established **2** [C, usually pl.] a system of TRENCHES (= long narrow holes dug in the ground by soldiers to provide defence)

**entre·pre·neur** /ˌɒntrəprəˈnɜː(r); NAmE ˌɑːn-/ noun a person who makes money by starting or running businesses, especially when this involves taking financial risks ⊃ WORDFINDER NOTE at BUSINESSMAN ▶ **en·tre·pre·neur·ial** /-ˈnɜːriəl/ adj.: *entrepreneurial skills* **entre·pre·neur·ship** noun [U]

**en·tropy** /ˈentrəpi/ noun [U] **1** (specialist) a way of measuring the lack of order that exists in a system **2** (physics) (symb. S) a measurement of the energy that is present in a system or process but is not available to do work **3** a complete lack of order: *In the business world, entropy rules.* ▶ **en·trop·ic** /enˈtrɒpɪk, -ˈtrəʊp-; NAmE -ˈtrɑːp-/ adj. **en·trop·ical·ly** /-kli/ adv.

**en·trust** /ɪnˈtrʌst/ verb (formal) to make sb responsible for doing sth or taking care of sb: ~ **A (to B)** *He entrusted the task to his nephew.* ◇ ~ **B with A** *He entrusted his nephew with the task.*

**entry** ⓪ B1 ⓔ /ˈentri/ noun (pl. -ies)
• GOING IN **1** ⓘ B1 [C, U] an act of going into or getting into a place: *She made her entry to the sound of thunderous applause.* ◇ *The children were surprised by the sudden entry of their teacher.* ◇ ~ **into sth** *How did the thieves gain entry into the building?* ◇ *Drugs come into the country through five main entry points.* ⊃ see also FORCED ENTRY, RE-ENTRY **2** ⓘ B1 [U] the right or opportunity to enter a place: *No Entry* (= for example, on a sign) ◇ ~ **to sth** *Entry to the museum is free.* ◇ ~ **into sth** *to be granted/refused entry into the country*
• IN COMPETITION **3** ⓘ B1 [C] something that you do, write or make to take part in a competition, for example answering a set of questions: *There have been some impressive entries in the wildlife photography section* (= impressive photographs). ◇ *The closing date for entries is 31 March.* ◇ *The winning entry will be published in next month's issue.*

**4** [U] the act of taking part in a competition, race, etc: *Entry is open to anyone over the age of 18.* ◇ **an entry form/fee 5** [sing.] the total number of people who are taking part in a competition, race, etc: *There's a record entry for this year's marathon.*
• WRITTEN INFORMATION **6** ⓘ B1 [C] an item, for example a piece of information, that is written or printed in a dictionary, an account book, a diary, etc: *an encyclopedia entry* ◇ *a blog/diary/journal entry* ◇ ~ **in sth** *There is no entry in his diary for that day.* ⊃ WORDFINDER NOTE at DICTIONARY **7** [U] the act of recording information in a computer, book, etc: *The job involves filing and data entry.*
• JOINING GROUP/ACTIVITY **8** ⓘ B2 [U] the right or opportunity to take part in sth or become a member of a group: ~ **into sth** *countries seeking entry into the European Union* ◇ *It is extremely difficult for new companies to gain entry into the market.* ◇ ~ **to sth** *She applied for entry to Nottingham University.* **9** [U] the act of taking part in an activity or becoming a member of a group: ~ **into sth** *the entry of women into the workforce* ◇ *American entry into the war*
• DOOR/GATE **10** (also **entry·way** /ˈentriweɪ/) (both especially NAmE) [C] a door, gate or passage where you enter a building; an entrance hall: *You can leave your umbrella in the entry.*

**ˈentry-level** adj. [usually before noun] **1** (of a product) basic and suitable for new users who may later move on to a more advanced product: *an entry-level computer* **2** (of a job) at the lowest level in a company

**ˈentry point** noun **1** a particular place where a person or thing can enter sth or somewhere: ~ **to sth** *The emergency services closed all entry points to the square.* ◇ ~ **for sb/sth** *An open wound is an easy entry point for germs.* **2** ~ **(to/into sth)** something that helps you start an activity: *Dance education may be an entry point to other kinds of learning.*

**en·twine** /ɪnˈtwaɪn/ verb [usually passive] **1** to TWIST or wind sth around sth else: **be entwined (with sth)** *The balcony was entwined with roses.* ◇ *They strolled through the park, with arms entwined.* **2 be entwined (with sth)** to be very closely involved or connected with sth: *Her destiny was entwined with his.*

**ˈE-number** noun (BrE) a number with the letter E in front of it that is printed on packs and containers to show what artificial tastes and colours have been added to food and drink; an artificial taste, colour, etc. added to food and drink: *This sauce is full of E-numbers.*

**enu·mer·ate** /ɪˈnjuːməreɪt; NAmE ˈnuː-/ verb ~ **sth** (formal) to name things on a list one by one ▶ **enu·mer·ation** /ɪˌnjuːməˈreɪʃn; NAmE ɪˌnuː-/ noun [U, C]

**enun·ci·ate** /ɪˈnʌnsieɪt/ verb **1** [T, I] ~ **(sth)** | + speech to say or pronounce words clearly: *She enunciated each word slowly and carefully.* **2** [T] ~ **sth** (formal) to express an idea clearly and exactly: *He enunciated his vision of the future.* ▶ **enun·ci·ation** /ɪˌnʌnsiˈeɪʃn/ noun [U, C]

**en·velop** /ɪnˈveləp/ verb ~ **sb/sth (in sth)** (formal) to wrap sb/sth up or cover them or it completely: *She was enveloped in a huge white towel.* ◇ *Clouds enveloped the mountain tops.* ▶ **en·velop·ment** noun [U]

**en·ve·lope** ⓘ B2 /ˈenvələʊp; BrE also ˈɒn-; NAmE also ˈɑːn-/ noun **1** ⓘ B2 a flat paper container used for sending letters in, with a part that you stick down to close it: *writing paper and envelopes* ◇ *a padded/prepaid envelope* ⊃ see also PAY ENVELOPE, SAE, SASE **2** ⓘ C1 a flat container made of plastic for keeping papers in IDM see BACK n., PUSH v.

**en·vi·able** /ˈenviəbl/ adj. something that is **enviable** is the sort of thing that is good and that other people want to have too: *He is in the enviable position of having two job offers to choose from.* OPP **unenviable** ⊃ related noun ENVY ▶ **en·vi·ably** /-bli/ adv.: *an enviably mild climate*

**en·vi·ous** /ˈenviəs/ adj. ~ **(of sb/sth)** wanting to be in the same situation as sb else; wanting sth that sb else has: *Everyone is so envious of her.* ◇ *They were envious of his success.* ◇ *He saw the envious look in the other boy's eyes.* ⊃ related noun ENVY ▶ **en·vi·ous·ly** adv.: *They look enviously at the success of their European counterparts.*

**en·vir·on·ment** ⓪ A2 ⓔ /ɪnˈvaɪrənmənt/ noun
**1** ⓘ A2 **the environment** [sing.] the natural world in which

# environmental

people, animals and plants live: *to protect/preserve/pollute/harm the environment* ◊ *damage to the* **natural environment** ◊ *protection/destruction of the marine environment* ◊ *The environment minister expressed concern over pollution levels.* ⇒ **WORDFINDER NOTE** at GREEN 2 [C, U] the conditions in which a person, animal or plant lives or operates or in which an activity takes place: *a pleasant work/learning environment* ◊ *Hospitals have a duty to provide a safe working environment for all staff.* ◊ *They have* **created an environment** *in which productivity should flourish.* ◊ *Polar bears are totally adapted to their hostile environment.* ◊ *We operate in a highly competitive business environment.* **3** [C] (*computing*) the complete structure (including HARDWARE and software) within which a user, computer or program operates: *a desktop development environment*

▼ SYNONYMS

**environment**
setting • surroundings • background

These are all words for the type of place in which sb/sth exists or is located.

**environment** the conditions in a place that affect the behaviour and development of sb/sth: *An unhappy home environment can affect children's behaviour.* ◊ *a pleasant working environment*

**setting** a place or situation of a particular type, in which sth happens or exists: *The island provided an idyllic setting for the concert.*

**surroundings** everything that is around or near sb/sth: *The huts blend in perfectly with their surroundings.*

**background** the things or area behind or around the main objects or people that are in a place or picture: *The mountains in the background were capped with snow.*

PATTERNS
- in (a/an) environment/setting/surroundings
- (a/an) new/unfamiliar environment/setting/surroundings
- sb/sth's immediate environment/surroundings
- (a) dramatic setting/background

**en·vir·on·men·tal** /ɪnˌvaɪrənˈmentl/ *adj.* [usually before noun] **1** connected with the natural conditions in which people, animals and plants live; connected with the environment: *the environmental impact of pollution* ◊ *Their main objective is to promote environmental protection.* ◊ *environmental issues/problems/concerns* ◊ *an environmental group/movement* (= that aims to improve or protect the natural environment) **2** connected with the conditions that affect the behaviour and development of sb/sth: *the environmental factors that affect insect development* ◊ *She is the director of environmental health at the council.* ▶ **en·vir·on·men·tal·ly** /-təli/ *adv.*: *an environmentally sensitive area* (= one that is easily damaged or that contains rare animals, plants, etc.) ◊ *environmentally damaging*

**en·vir·on·men·tal·ist** /ɪnˌvaɪrənˈmentəlɪst/ *noun* a person who is interested in the natural environment and wants to improve and protect it ▶ **en·vir·on·men·tal·ism** /-lɪzəm/ *noun* [U]

**en·vir·on·men·tal·ly ˈfriendly** (*also* **en·vir·on·ment-ˈfriendly**) *adj.* (of products) not harming the environment: *environmentally friendly packaging*

**en·vir·ons** /ɪnˈvaɪrənz/ *noun* [pl.] (*formal*) the area surrounding a place: *Berlin and its environs* ◊ *people living in the immediate environs of a nuclear plant*

**en·vis·age** /ɪnˈvɪzɪdʒ/ (*especially BrE*) (*NAmE usually* **en·vi-sion**) *verb* to imagine what will happen in the future: ~ **sth** *What level of profit do you envisage?* ◊ ~ **(sb) doing sth** *I can't envisage her coping with this job.* ◊ **it is envisaged that …** *It is envisaged that the talks will take place in the spring.* ◊ ~ **that …** *I envisage that the work will be completed next year.* ◊ ~ **how, where, etc …** *It is difficult to envisage how people will react.* ⇒ SYNONYMS at IMAGINE

**en·vi·sion** /ɪnˈvɪʒn/ *verb* **1** ~ **sth** (*formal*) to imagine what a situation will be like in the future, especially a situation you intend to work towards: *They envision an equal society, free of poverty and disease.* ⇒ SYNONYMS at IMAGINE **2** (*especially NAmE*) = ENVISAGE: *They didn't envision any problems with the new building.*

**envoy** /ˈenvɔɪ/ *noun* a person who represents a government or an organization and is sent as a representative to talk to other governments and organizations SYN **emissary**

**envy** /ˈenvi/ *noun, verb*
■ *noun* [U] the feeling of wanting to be in the same situation as sb else; the feeling of wanting sth that sb else has SYN **jealousy**: ~ **(of sb)** *He couldn't conceal his envy of me.* ◊ ~ **(at/of sth)** *She felt a pang of envy at the thought of his success.* ◊ *They looked* **with envy** *at her latest purchase.* ◊ *Her colleagues were* **green with envy** (= they had very strong feelings of envy).
IDM **be the envy of sb/sth** to be a person or thing that other people admire and that causes feelings of envy: *British television is the envy of the world.* ⇒ see also ENVIABLE, ENVIOUS
■ *verb* (**en·vies**, **envy·ing**, **en·vied**, **en·vied**) **1** to wish you had the same qualities, possessions, opportunities, etc. as sb else: ~ **sb** *He envied her—she seemed to have everything she could possibly want.* ◊ ~ **sth** *She has always envied my success.* ◊ ~ **sb (for) sth** *I envied him his good looks.* ◊ ~ **sb doing sth** *I envy you having such a close family.* **2** to be glad that you do not have to do what sb else has to do: **not** ~ **sb** *It's a difficult situation you're in. I don't envy you.* ◊ **not** ~ **sb sth** *I don't envy her that job.*

**en·zyme** /ˈenzaɪm/ *noun* (*biology*) a substance that is produced by all living things and that helps a chemical change happen or happen more quickly, without being changed itself ⇒ see also PROTEIN

**eo·lian** (*US*) = AEOLIAN

**eon** (*NAmE or specialist*) (*BrE usually* **aeon**) /ˈiːən; *BrE also* ˈiːɒn; *NAmE also* ˈiːɑːn/ *noun* **1** (*formal*) an extremely long period of time; thousands of years **2** (*geology*) a major division of time, divided into ERAS: *eons of geological history*

**ep·aul·ette** (*especially BrE*) (*NAmE usually* **ep·aulet**) /ˈepəlet/ *noun* a decoration on the shoulder of a coat, jacket, etc., especially when part of a military uniform

**épée** /ˈeɪpeɪ, ˈepeɪ/ *noun* **1** [C] a SWORD used in the sport of FENCING **2** [U] (*NAmE*) the sport of FENCING with an épée

epaulette

**ephem·era** /ɪˈfemərə/ *noun* [pl.] things that are important or used for only a short period of time: *a collection of postcards, tickets and other ephemera*

**ephem·eral** /ɪˈfemərəl/ *adj.* (*formal*) lasting or used for only a short period of time SYN **short-lived**

**epic** /ˈepɪk/ *noun, adj.*
■ *noun* **1** [C, U] a long poem about the actions of great men and women or about a nation's history; this style of poetry: *one of the great Hindu epics* ◊ *the creative genius of Greek epic* ⇒ compare LYRIC **2** [C] a long film or book that contains a lot of action, usually about a historical subject **3** [C] (*sometimes humorous*) a long and difficult job or activity that you think people should admire: *Their four-hour match on Centre Court was an epic.*
■ *adj.* [usually before noun] **1** having the features of an epic: *an epic poem* ⇒ compare LYRIC **2** taking place over a long period of time and involving a lot of difficulties: *an epic journey/struggle* **3** very great and impressive: *a tragedy of epic proportions* **4** (*informal*) very good, impressive or great fun: *The party was epic!* ◊ *I went to an epic festival last summer.*

**epi·centre** (*US* **epi·cen·ter**) /ˈepɪsentə(r)/ *noun* **1** the point on the earth's surface where the effects of an earthquake are felt most strongly **2** (*formal*) the central point of sth

**epi·cur·ean** /ˌepɪkjʊəˈriːən; *NAmE* -kjʊˈr-/ *adj.* (*formal*) taking great pleasure in things, especially food and drink, and enjoying yourself

**ep·i·dem·ic** /ˌepɪˈdemɪk/ noun **1** a large number of cases of a particular disease or medical condition happening at the same time in a particular community: *the outbreak of a flu epidemic* ◊ *an epidemic of measles* ⊃ WORDFINDER NOTE at DISEASE **2** a sudden rapid increase in how often sth bad happens: *an epidemic of crime in the inner cities* ▶ **ep·i·dem·ic** *adj.*: *Car theft is now reaching epidemic proportions.* ⊃ compare PANDEMIC

**ep·i·demi·ology** /ˌepɪˌdiːmiˈɒlədʒi/ NAmE -ˈɑːl- noun [U] the scientific study of the spread and control of diseases ▶ **ep·i·demi·olog·ic·al** /ˌepɪˌdiːmiəˈlɒdʒɪkl/ NAmE -ˈlɑːdʒ- adj. **ep·i·demi·olo·gist** /ˌepɪˌdiːmiˈɒlədʒɪst/ NAmE -ˈɑːl- noun

**ep·i·der·mis** /ˌepɪˈdɜːmɪs/ NAmE -ˈdɜːrm- noun [sing., U] (anatomy) the outer layer of the skin

**ep·i·dural** /ˌepɪˈdjʊərəl/ NAmE -ˈdʊr- noun (medical) an ANAESTHETIC that is put into the lower part of the back so that no pain is felt below the middle part of the body: *Some mothers choose to have an epidural when giving birth.*

**epi·glot·tis** /ˌepɪˈɡlɒtɪs/ NAmE -ˈɡlɑːt- noun (anatomy) a thin piece of TISSUE behind the tongue that prevents food or drink from entering the lungs

**epi·gram** /ˈepɪɡræm/ noun a short poem or phrase that expresses an idea in a clever or humorous way ▶ **epi·gram·mat·ic** /ˌepɪɡrəˈmætɪk/ adj.

**epi·graph** /ˈepɪɡrɑːf/ NAmE -ɡræf/ noun a line of writing, short phrase, etc. on a building or statue, or as an introduction to part of a book

**epi·lepsy** /ˈepɪlepsi/ noun [U] a DISORDER of the nervous system that causes a person to become unconscious suddenly, often with violent movements of the body ▶ **epi·lep·tic** /ˌepɪˈleptɪk/ adj.: *an epileptic fit* **epi·lep·tic** noun: *Is she an epileptic?*

**epi·logue** (US also **epi·log**) /ˈepɪlɒɡ/ NAmE -lɔːɡ/ noun a speech, etc. at the end of a play, book, or film that comments on or acts as a conclusion to what has happened ⊃ compare PROLOGUE

**epiph·any** /ɪˈpɪfəni/ noun **1** (also **Epiphany**) [U] a Christian festival, held on the 6 January, in memory of the time when the MAGI came to see the baby Jesus at Bethlehem **2 epiphany** [C] a sudden and surprising moment of understanding: *She had an epiphany and realized it was time to leave her job and become a full-time artist.*

**epis·cop·acy** /ɪˈpɪskəpəsi/ noun [U] government of a church by BISHOPS

**epis·cop·al** /ɪˈpɪskəpl/ adj. **1** connected with a BISHOP or BISHOPS: *episcopal power* **2** (usually **Episcopal**) (also **Epis·co·pa·lian**) (of a Christian Church) that is governed by BISHOPS: *the Episcopal Church* (= the Anglican Church in Scotland and the US)

**Epis·co·pa·lian** /ɪˌpɪskəˈpeɪliən/ noun a member of the Episcopal Church

**epis·co·pate** /ɪˈpɪskəpət/ noun [usually sing.] (religion) **1** the **episcopate** the BISHOPS of a particular church or area **2** the job of BISHOP or the period of time during which sb is bishop

**epi·si·ot·omy** /ɪˌpiːsiˈɒtəmi/ NAmE -ˈɑːt- noun (pl. **-ies**) (medical) a cut that is sometimes made at the opening of a woman's VAGINA to make the birth of a baby easier or safer

**epi·sode** /ˈepɪsəʊd/ noun **1** one part of a story that is broadcast on television or radio in several parts: *I watched a few episodes of seasons one and two.* **in an~** *It happened in the final episode of 'Star Trek'.* **2** an event, a situation, or a period of time in sb's life, a novel, etc. that is important or interesting in some way SYN **incident**: *I'd like to try and forget the whole episode.* ◊ *One of the funniest episodes in the book occurs in Chapter 6.*

**epi·sod·ic** /ˌepɪˈsɒdɪk/ NAmE -ˈsɑːd- adj. (formal) **1** happening occasionally and not at regular INTERVALS **2** (of a story, etc.) containing or consisting of many separate and different events: *My memories of childhood are hazy and episodic.*

**epi·stem·ic** /ˌepɪˈstiːmɪk, -ˈstem-/ adj. (formal) relating to knowledge

**epis·te·mol·ogy** /ɪˌpɪstəˈmɒlədʒi/ NAmE -ˈmɑːl- noun [U] the part of philosophy that deals with knowledge ▶ **epis·temo·logic·al** /ɪˌpɪstəməˈlɒdʒɪkl/ NAmE -ˈlɑːdʒ- adj. [usually before noun] **epis·temo·logic·al·ly** /-kli/ adv.

**epis·tle** /ɪˈpɪsl/ noun **1 Epistle** any of the letters in the New Testament of the Bible, written by the first people who followed Christ: *the Epistles of St Paul* **2** (formal or humorous) a long, serious letter on an important subject

**epis·tol·ary** /ɪˈpɪstələri/ NAmE -leri/ adj. (formal) written or expressed in the form of letters: *an epistolary novel*

**epi·taph** /ˈepɪtɑːf/ NAmE -tæf/ noun **1** words that are written or said about a dead person, especially words on a GRAVESTONE **2 ~ (to sb/sth)** something that is left to remind people of a particular person, a period of time or an event: *These slums are an epitaph to the housing policy of the 1960s.*

**epi·thet** /ˈepɪθet/ noun **1** an adjective or phrase that is used to describe sb/sth's character or most important quality, especially in order to give praise or criticism: *The film is long and dramatic but does not quite earn the epithet 'epic'.* **2** (especially NAmE) an offensive word or phrase that is used about a person or group of people: *Racial epithets were scrawled on the walls.*

**epit·ome** /ɪˈpɪtəmi/ noun [sing.] **the ~ of sth** (formal) a perfect example of sth SYN **embodiment**: *He is the epitome of a modern young man.* ◊ *clothes that are the epitome of good taste*

**epit·om·ize** (BrE also **-ise**) /ɪˈpɪtəmaɪz/ verb **~ sth** to be a perfect example of sth: *The fighting qualities of the team are epitomized by the captain.* ◊ *These movies seem to epitomize the 1950s.*

**epoch** /ˈiːpɒk; NAmE ˈepək/ noun **1** (formal or literary) a period of time in history, especially one during which important events or changes happen SYN **era**: *The death of the emperor marked the end of an epoch in the country's history.* **2** (geology) a length of time that is a division of a period: *geological epochs*

**epoch-making** adj. (formal) having a very important effect on people's lives and on history

**epony·mous** /ɪˈpɒnɪməs/ NAmE ɪˈpɑːn- adj. [only before noun] the **eponymous** character of a book, play, film, etc. is the one mentioned in the title SYN **titular**: *Don Quixote, eponymous hero of the great novel by Cervantes*

**epoxy** /ɪˈpɒksi/ NAmE ɪˈpɑːk- noun [U, C] (pl. **-ies**) (also **eˌpoxy ˈresin**) a type of strong GLUE (= a sticky substance used for joining things together)

**ep·si·lon** /ˈepsɪlɒn, epˈsaɪlən/ NAmE ˈepsɪlɑːn/ noun the fifth letter of the Greek alphabet (E, ε)

**Epsom salts** /ˈepsəm sɔːlts/ noun [pl.] a white powder that can be mixed with water and used as a medicine or LAXATIVE

**e-publishing** noun [U] = DIGITAL PUBLISHING

**equ·able** /ˈekwəbl/ adj. (formal) **1** calm and not easily upset or annoyed: *an equable temperament* **2** (of weather) keeping a steady temperature with no sudden changes ▶ **equ·ably** /-bli/ adv.

## equal

**equal** /ˈiːkwəl/ adj., verb, noun

■ *adj.* **1** the same in size, quantity, value, etc. as sth else: *There is an equal number of boys and girls in the class.* ◊ *Cut it into four equal parts.* ◊ *~ in sth The two countries are roughly equal in size.* ◊ *~ to sb/sth One unit of alcohol is equal to half a pint of beer.* HELP *You can use exactly, precisely, approximately,* etc. with **equal** in this meaning. **2** having the same rights or being treated the same as other people, without differences such as race, religion or sex being considered: *I believe everyone is born equal.* ◊ *a society where women and men are equal partners* HELP *You can use more with equal in this meaning.*

WORDFINDER bias, discriminate, feminism, homophobia, human right, marginalize, persecute, race, society

**3** [usually before noun] giving people the same rights and opportunities, without differences such as race, religion or sex being considered: *equal rights/pay* ◊ *The company has an equal opportunities policy* (= gives the same chances of employment to everyone). ◊ *the desire for a more equal society* (= in which everyone has the same

# equality

rights and chances) **4** ~ **to sth** (*formal*) having the necessary strength, courage and ability to deal with sth successfully: *I hope that he proves equal to the challenge.* ⇒ see also EQUALLY

**IDM** **on equal 'terms (with sb)** having the same advantages and disadvantages as sb else: *Can our industry compete on equal terms with its overseas rivals?* **some (people, members, etc.) are more equal than 'others** (*saying*) although the members of a society, group, etc. appear to be equal, some, in fact, get better treatment than others **ORIGIN** This phrase is used by one of the pigs in the book 'Animal Farm' by George Orwell: 'All animals are equal but some animals are more equal than others.' ⇒ more at THING

■ *verb* (**-ll-**, *US* **-l-**) **1** B1 *linking verb* + **noun** to be the same in size, quantity, value, etc. as sth else: *2x plus y equals 7 (= 2x+y=7)* ◊ *A metre equals 39.38 inches.* **2** B2 ~ **sth** to be as good as sth else or do sth to the same standard as sb else: *This achievement is unlikely ever to be equalled.* ◊ *Her hatred of religion is equalled only by her loathing for politicians.* ◊ *With his last jump he equalled the world record.* **3** ~**sth** to lead to or result in sth: *Cooperation equals success.*

■ *noun* B2 a person or thing of the same quality or with the same status, rights, etc. as another: *She treats the people who work for her as her equals.* ◊ **be the** ~**of sb/sth** *Our cars are the equal of those produced anywhere in the world.*

**IDM** **be without 'equal | have no 'equal | have no/few 'equals** (*formal*) to be better than anything else or anyone else of the same type: *He is a player without equal.* ⇒ more at FIRST *n.*

**equal·ity** B1+ C1 /i'kwɒləti; *NAmE* i'kwɑː-/ *noun* [U] the fact of being equal in rights, status, advantages, etc: *racial/social/gender equality* ◊ *equality of opportunity* ◊ *the principle of equality before the law* (= the law treats everyone the same) ◊ *Don't you believe in equality between men and women?* **OPP** **inequality** ⇒ see also MARRIAGE EQUALITY ⇒ WORDFINDER NOTE at SOCIETY

**equal·ize** (*BrE also* **-ise**) /'iːkwəlaɪz/ *verb* **1** [T] ~**sth** to make things equal in size, quantity, value, etc. in the whole of a place or group: *a policy to equalize the distribution of resources throughout the country* **2** [I] (*BrE*) (especially in football (soccer)) to score a goal that makes the score of both teams equal: *Kane equalized early in the second half.*
▶ **equal·iza·tion, -isa·tion** /ˌiːkwəlaɪˈzeɪʃn; *NAmE* -ləˈz-/ *noun* [U]

**equal·izer** (*BrE also* **-iser**) /'iːkwəlaɪzə(r)/ *noun* [usually sing.] (*BrE*) (especially in football (soccer)) a goal that makes the score of both teams equal: *Kane scored the equalizer.* ⇒ see also GRAPHIC EQUALIZER

**equal·ly** ❶ B1 Ⓦ /'iːkwəli/ *adv.* **1** B1 to the same degree, in the same or in a similar way: *Diet and exercise are equally important.* ◊ *This job could be done equally well by a computer.* ◊ *Everyone should be treated equally.* ◊ *The findings of the survey apply equally to adults and children.* **2** B1 in equal parts, amounts, etc: *The money was divided equally among her four children.* ◊ *They share the housework equally.* **3** used to introduce another phrase or idea that adds to and is as important as what you have just said: *I'm trying to do what is best, but equally I've got to consider the cost.*

**equal 'marriage** (*also* **marriage e'quality**) *noun* [U] the situation in which same-sex couples have the same legal right to marry as opposite-sex couples

**equal oppor'tunities** *noun* [pl.] (*also* **equal opportunity** [U]) the right to be treated equally, whatever your sex, race, age, etc: *Segregation laws denied equal opportunities to black people.* ◊ *We are an equal opportunities employer.*

**'equals sign** (*also* **'equal sign**) *noun* the symbol (=), used in mathematics

**equa·nim·ity** /ˌekwəˈnɪməti/ *noun* [U] (*formal*) a calm state of mind that means that you do not become angry or upset, especially in difficult situations: *She accepted the prospect of her operation with equanimity.*

**equate** /ɪˈkweɪt/ *verb* ~**sth (with sth)** to think that sth is the same as sth else or is as important: *Some parents equate education with exam success.* ◊ *I don't see how you can equate the two things.*
**PHRV** **e'quate to sth** to be equal to sth else: *A £5000 rise equates to 25 per cent.*

**equa·tion** B1+ C1 /ɪˈkweɪʒn/ *noun* **1** B1+ C1 [C] (*mathematics*) a statement showing that two amounts or values are equal, for example 2x+y = 54 ⇒ see also DIFFERENTIAL EQUATION ⇒ WORDFINDER NOTE at MATHS **2** B1+ C1 [U, sing.] the act of making sth equal or considering sth as equal (= of equating them): *The equation of wealth with happiness can be dangerous.* **3** B1+ C1 [C, usually sing.] a problem or situation in which several things must be considered and dealt with: *When children enter the equation, further tensions may arise within a marriage.*

**equa·tor** /ɪˈkweɪtə(r)/ (*usually* **the equator**) *noun* [sing.] an imaginary line around the earth at an equal distance from the North and South Poles ⇒ WORDFINDER NOTE at EARTH

**equa·tor·ial** /ˌekwəˈtɔːriəl; *NAmE also* ˌiːk-/ *adj.* near the equator or typical of a country that is near the equator: *equatorial rainforests* ◊ *an equatorial climate* ⇒ WORDFINDER NOTE at CLIMATE

**equer·ry** /ɪˈkweri, ˈekwəri/ *noun* (*pl.* **-ies**) a male officer who acts as an assistant to a member of a royal family

**eques·trian** /ɪˈkwestriən/ *adj.* [usually before noun] connected with riding horses, especially as a sport: *equestrian events at the Olympic Games*

**eques·tri·an·ism** /ɪˈkwestriənɪzəm/ *noun* [U] the skill or sport of riding horses. As an Olympic sport it consists of three events: SHOWJUMPING, DRESSAGE and THREE-DAY EVENTING.

**equi-** /ˈiːkwɪ, ˈekwɪ/ *combining form* (in nouns, adjectives and adverbs) equal; equally: *equidistant* ◊ *equilibrium*

**equi·dis·tant** /ˌiːkwɪˈdɪstənt, ˌek-/ *adj.* [not before noun] ~**(from sth)** (*formal*) equally far from two or more places: *All points on a circle are equidistant from the centre.*

**equi·lat·eral 'tri·angle** /ˌiːkwɪˌlætərəl ˈtraɪæŋgl/ *noun* (*geometry*) a flat shape with three straight sides that are all the same length ⇒ picture at TRIANGLE

**equi·lib·rium** /ˌiːkwɪˈlɪbriəm, ˌek-/ *noun* [U, sing.] **1** a state of balance, especially between different forces or influences: *Any disturbance to the body's state of equilibrium can produce stress.* ◊ **in** ~ *The point at which the solid and the liquid are in equilibrium is called the freezing point.* ◊ *We have achieved an equilibrium in the economy.* **2** a calm state of mind and a balance of emotions: *He sat down to try and recover his equilibrium.*

**equine** /ˈekwaɪn, ˈiːk-; *NAmE* ˈiːk-/ *adj.* (*formal*) connected with horses; like a horse

**equi·noc·tial** /ˌiːkwɪˈnɒkʃl, ˌek-; *NAmE* -ˈnɑːk-/ *adj.* connected with an equinox

**equi·nox** /ˈiːkwɪnɒks, ˈek-; *NAmE* -nɑːks/ *noun* one of the two times in the year (around 20 March and 22 September) when the sun is above the EQUATOR and day and night are of equal length: *the spring/autumn equinox* ⇒ WORDFINDER NOTE at EARTH

**equip** B1+ B2 /ɪˈkwɪp/ *verb* (**-pp-**) **1** B1+ B2 to provide yourself/sb/sth with the things that are needed for a particular purpose or activity **SYN** **kit out/up**: ~**sth** *to be fully/poorly equipped* ◊ *She got a bank loan to rent and equip a small workshop.* ◊ ~**yourself/sb/sth (with sth) (for sth)** *He equipped himself with a street plan.* ◊ **be equipped for/with sth** *The centre is well equipped for canoeing and mountaineering.* **2** B1+ B2 ~**sb (for sth) | ~sb (to do sth)** to prepare sb for an activity or task, especially by teaching them what they need to know: *The course is designed to equip students for a career in nursing.*

**equip·ment** ❶ A2 /ɪˈkwɪpmənt/ *noun* [U] **1** A2 the things that are needed for a particular purpose or activity: *a useful piece of equipment for the kitchen* ◊ *electrical/electronic/communications/computer equipment* ◊ *military equipment and supplies* ◊ *office equipment* ◊ *They have installed state-of-the-art medical equipment to help improve early diagnosis of the condition.* **2** the process of providing a place or person with necessary things: *The equipment of the photographic studio was expensive.*

> **SYNONYMS**
>
> **equipment**
> material • gear • kit • apparatus
>
> These are all words for the things that you need for a particular purpose or activity.
>
> **equipment** the things that are needed for a particular purpose or activity: *camping equipment ◊ a piece of equipment*
>
> **material** things that are needed for a particular activity: *household cleaning materials ◊ teaching material*
>
> EQUIPMENT OR MATERIAL?
> **Equipment** is usually solid things, especially large ones. **Materials** may be liquids, powders or books, software, etc. containing information, as well as small solid items.
>
> **gear** the equipment or clothes needed for a particular activity: *Skiing gear can be expensive.*
>
> **kit** a set of tools or equipment that you use for a particular purpose: *a first-aid kit ◊ a tool kit*
>
> **apparatus** the tools or other pieces of equipment that are needed for a particular activity or task: *breathing apparatus for firefighters ◊ laboratory apparatus* NOTE **Apparatus** is used especially for scientific, medical or technical purposes.
>
> PATTERNS
> - electrical / electronic equipment / gear / apparatus
> - sports equipment / gear / kit
> - camping equipment / gear
> - a piece of equipment / apparatus

**equi·poise** /ˈekwɪpɔɪz, ˈiːk-/ *noun* [U] (*formal*) a state of balance

**equit·able** /ˈekwɪtəbl/ *adj.* (*formal*) fair and reasonable; treating everyone in an equal way SYN **fair** OPP **inequitable** ▶ **equit·ably** /-bli/ *adv.*

**equity** /ˈekwəti/ *noun* 1 [U] (*finance*) the value of a company's shares ⊃ see also PRIVATE EQUITY ⊃ WORDFINDER NOTE at INVEST 2 [U] the value of a property after all charges and debts have been paid ⊃ see also NEGATIVE EQUITY 3 **equities** [pl.] (*finance*) shares in a company that do not pay a fixed amount of interest 4 [U] (*formal*) a situation in which everyone is treated equally SYN **fairness** OPP **inequity** ⊃ see also EMPLOYMENT EQUITY 5 [U] (*law, especially BrE*) a system of natural justice allowing a fair judgement in a situation which is not covered by the existing laws

**equiva·lency** /ɪˈkwɪvələnsi/ *noun* (*pl.* **-ies**) 1 [C, U] ~ (between A and B) EQUIVALENCE (= the fact or state of being equal in value, amount, meaning, importance, etc.): *You are creating a false equivalency between the two parties.* 2 (in the US and Canada) short for 'General Equivalency Diploma' ⊃ see also GED

**equiva·lent** B2 ⊙ /ɪˈkwɪvələnt/ *noun, adj.*
■ *noun* B2 a thing, amount, word, etc. that is equal in value, meaning or purpose to sth else: *Send €20 or the equivalent in your own currency.* ◊ **~ of (doing) sth** *the modern equivalent of the Roman baths* ◊ **~ to sth** *The German 'Gymnasium' is the closest equivalent to the grammar school in England.*
■ *adj.* B2 equal in value, amount, meaning, importance, etc: *250 grams or an equivalent amount in ounces* ◊ **~ to sth** *Eight kilometres is roughly equivalent to five miles.* ▶ **equiva·lence** /-ləns/ *noun* [U] (*formal*): *There is no straightforward equivalence between economic progress and social well-being.*

**equivo·cal** /ɪˈkwɪvəkl/ *adj.* (*formal*) 1 (of words or statements) not having one clear or definite meaning or intention; able to be understood in more than one way SYN **ambiguous**: *She gave an equivocal answer, typical of a politician.* 2 (of actions or behaviour) difficult to understand or explain clearly or easily: *The experiments produced equivocal results.* ⊃ see also UNEQUIVOCAL

**equivo·cate** /ɪˈkwɪvəkeɪt/ *verb* [I, T] (+ *speech*) (*formal*) to talk about sth in a way that is deliberately not clear in order to avoid or hide the truth

**equivo·ca·tion** /ɪˌkwɪvəˈkeɪʃn/ *noun* [C, U] (*formal*) a way of behaving or speaking that is not clear or definite and is intended to avoid or hide the truth

**-er** /ə(r)/ *suffix* 1 (in nouns) a person or thing that performs the action: *lover ◊ computer* ⊃ compare -EE, -OR 2 (in nouns) a person or thing that has the thing or quality mentioned: *three-wheeler ◊ foreigner* 3 (in nouns) a person studying or expert in: *astronomer ◊ philosopher* 4 (in nouns) a person belonging to: *New Yorker* 5 (makes comparative adjectives and adverbs): *wider ◊ bigger ◊ happier ◊ sooner* ⊃ compare -EST

**ER** /ˌiː ˈɑː(r)/ *abbr.* (*NAmE*) EMERGENCY ROOM (= the part of a hospital where people who need immediate treatment are taken)

**er** /ɜː(r)/ (*also* **erm**) *exclamation* (*BrE*) the sound that people make when they are deciding what to say next: '*Will you do it?*' '*Er, yes, I suppose so.*'

**era** B2 /ˈɪərə; *NAmE* ˈɪrə, ˈerə/ *noun* 1 B2 a period of time, usually in history, that is different from other periods because of particular characteristics or events: *the Victorian / modern / post-war era* ◊ *When she left the firm, it was the end of an era* (= things were different after that). ⊃ see also CHRISTIAN ERA, COMMON ERA 2 (*geology*) a length of time that is a division of an AEON

**eradi·cate** /ɪˈrædɪkeɪt/ *verb* to destroy or get rid of sth completely, especially sth bad SYN **wipe out**: **~ sth** *Diphtheria has been virtually eradicated in the United States.* ◊ **~ sth from sth** *We are determined to eradicate racism from our sport.* ▶ **eradi·ca·tion** /ɪˌrædɪˈkeɪʃn/ *noun* [U]

**erase** /ɪˈreɪz; *NAmE* ɪˈreɪs/ *verb* 1 to remove sth completely: **~ sth** *She tried to erase the memory of that evening.* ◊ **~ sth from sth** *All doubts were suddenly erased from his mind.* ◊ *You cannot erase injustice from the world.* 2 **~ sth** to make a mark or sth you have written disappear, for example by rubbing it, especially in order to correct it: *He had erased the wrong word.* ◊ *All the phone numbers had been erased.* 3 **~ sth** to remove a recording from a tape or information from a computer's memory: *Parts of the recording have been erased.*

**eraser** /ɪˈreɪzə(r); *NAmE* ɪˈreɪsər/ (*NAmE or formal*) (*BrE also* **rubber**) *noun* a small piece of rubber or a similar substance, used for removing pencil marks from paper; a piece of soft material used for removing CHALK marks from a BLACKBOARD

**eras·ure** /ɪˈreɪʒə(r)/ *noun* [U, C] (*formal*) 1 the act of removing writing, drawing, recorded material or data: *the accidental erasure of important computer files* 2 the act of removing or destroying all signs of sth: *the erasure of the past*

**ere** /eə(r); *NAmE* er/ *conj., prep.* (*old use or literary*) before: *Ere long* (= soon) *they returned.*

**e-reader** *noun* a small device on which you can store and read texts taken from the internet; an APPLICATION on a device that enables you to do this

**erect** B2 C1 /ɪˈrekt/ *verb, adj.*
■ *verb* (*formal*) 1 B2 C1 **~ sth** to build sth: *The church was erected in 1582.* ⊃ SYNONYMS at BUILD 2 B2 C1 **~ sth** to put sth in position so that it stands upright SYN **put up**: *Police had to erect barriers to keep crowds back.* ◊ *to erect a tent* ⊃ SYNONYMS at BUILD 3 **~ sth** to create or establish sth: *to erect trade barriers*
■ *adj.* 1 (*formal*) in a straight position pointing upwards SYN **straight**: *Stand with your arms by your side and your head erect.* 2 (of the PENIS or NIPPLES) larger than usual, stiff and standing up because of sexual excitement

**erect·ile** /ɪˈrektaɪl; *NAmE also* -tl/ *adj.* (*biology*) (of a part of the body) able to become stiff and stand up: *erectile tissue*

**erec·tion** /ɪˈrekʃn/ *noun* 1 [C] if a man has an **erection**, his PENIS is hard and stands up because he is sexually excited: *to get / have an erection* 2 [U] (*formal*) the act of building sth or putting it in a standing or UPRIGHT position: *the erection of scaffolding around the building* 3 [C] (*formal*) a structure or building, especially a large one

**erf** /ɜːf; *NAmE* ɜːrf/ *noun* (*pl.* **erfs** *or* **erven** /ˈɜːvn; *NAmE* ˈɜːrvn/) (*SAfrE*) a plot of land

**erg** /ɜːg; *NAmE* ɜːrg/ *noun* (*physics*) a unit of work or energy

**ergo** /ˈɜːɡəʊ; *NAmE* ˈerɡ-/ *adv.* (from Latin, *formal or humorous*) therefore

# ergonomic 524

**er·go·nom·ic** /ˌɜːɡəˈnɒmɪk; NAmE ˌɜːrɡəˈnɑːm-/ adj. designed to make people's working environment more comfortable and to help them work more efficiently: *ergonomic design* ◇ *an ergonomic keyboard/chair* ▶ **er·go·nom·ic·al·ly** /-kli/ adv.: *The layout is hard to fault ergonomically.*

**er·go·nom·ics** /ˌɜːɡəˈnɒmɪks; NAmE ˌɜːrɡəˈnɑːm-/ noun [U] the study of working conditions, especially the design of equipment and furniture, in order to help people work more efficiently

**erm** /ɜːm; NAmE ɜːrm/ exclamation (BrE) = ER: '*Shall we go?*' '*Erm, yes, let's.*'

**er·mine** /ˈɜːmɪn; NAmE ˈɜːrm-/ noun **1** [U] the white winter fur of the STOAT, used especially to decorate the formal clothes of judges, kings, etc. **2** [C] a STOAT, especially when in its white winter coat

**erode** /ɪˈrəʊd/ verb [often passive] **1** [T, I] to gradually destroy the surface of sth through the action of wind, rain, etc.; to be gradually destroyed in this way SYN **wear away**: *be eroded (away)* *The cliff face has been steadily eroded by the sea.* ◇ *~(away)* *The rocks have eroded away over time.* **2** [T, I] to gradually destroy sth or make it weaker over a period of time; to be destroyed or made weaker in this way: *be eroded (by sth)* *Her confidence has been slowly eroded by repeated failures.* ◇ *Mortgage payments have been eroded (= decreased in value) by inflation.* ◇ *~(away)* *All my security has slowly eroded away.*

**er·ogen·ous zone** /ɪˈrɒdʒənəs zəʊn; NAmE ɪˈrɑːdʒ-/ noun an area of the body that gives sexual pleasure when it is touched

**Eros** /ˈɪərɒs; NAmE ˈɪrɑːs, ˈer-/ noun [U] (formal) sexual love or desire ORIGIN *Eros was the ancient Greek god of love.*

**erot·ic** /ɪˈrɒtɪk; NAmE ɪˈrɑːt-/ adj. showing or involving sexual desire and pleasure; intended to make sb feel sexual desire: *erotic art* ◇ *an erotic fantasy* ▶ **erot·ic·al·ly** /-kli/ adv.

**erot·ica** /ɪˈrɒtɪkə; NAmE ɪˈrɑːt-/ noun [U] books, pictures, etc. that are intended to make sb feel sexual desire

**eroti·cism** /ɪˈrɒtɪsɪzəm; NAmE ɪˈrɑːt-/ noun [U] the fact of expressing or describing sexual feelings and desire, especially in art, literature, etc.

**err** /ɜː(r); NAmE er/ verb [I] (old-fashioned, formal) to make a mistake: *To err is human…*
IDM **err on the side of sth** to show too much of a good quality in order to avoid showing too little: *I thought it was better to err on the side of caution (= to be too careful rather than take a risk).*

**er·rand** /ˈerənd/ noun a job that you do for sb that involves going somewhere to take a message, to buy sth, deliver goods, etc: *He often runs errands for his grandmother.* ◇ *Her boss sent her on an errand into town.* ⇒ see also FOOL'S ERRAND

**er·rant** /ˈerənt/ adj. [only before noun] (formal or humorous) **1** doing sth that is wrong; not behaving in an acceptable way **2** (of a husband or wife) not sexually FAITHFUL

**er·rat·ic** /ɪˈrætɪk/ adj., noun
■ *adj.* (often disapproving) not happening at regular times; not following any plan or regular pattern; that you cannot rely on SYN **unpredictable**: *The electricity supply here is quite erratic.* ◇ *She had learnt to live with his sudden changes of mood and erratic behaviour.* ◇ *Mary is a gifted but erratic player (= she does not always play well).* ▶ **er·rat·ic·al·ly** /-kli/ adv.: *He was obviously upset and was driving erratically.*
■ *noun* (also **er·ratic ˈblock, er·ratic ˈboulder**) (geology) a large rock that is different from the rock around it and was left behind when a large mass of ice melted

**er·ratum** /eˈrɑːtəm/ noun [usually pl.] (pl. **er·rata** /-tə/) (specialist) a mistake in printing or writing (printed in a list or posted in a list on a website)

**er·ro·ne·ous** /ɪˈrəʊniəs/ adj. (formal) not correct; based on wrong information: *erroneous conclusions/assumptions* ▶ **er·ro·ne·ous·ly** adv.

**error** ⓘ A2 ⓞ /ˈerə(r)/ noun [C, U] a mistake, especially one that causes problems or affects the result of sth: *spelling/typographical/grammatical errors* ◇ *The report contains some factual errors that must be corrected.* ◇ *~in sth* *There are too many errors in your work.* ◇ *~in doing sth* *I think you have made an error in calculating the total.* ◇ *~of sth* *A simple error of judgement meant that there was not enough food to go around.* ◇ *a serious/grave error* ◇ *in ~* *The computer system was switched off in error (= by mistake.)* ◇ *I get an error message whenever I try to log on.* ⇒ SYNONYMS at MISTAKE ⇒ see also HUMAN ERROR, MARGIN OF ERROR, SAMPLING ERROR, STANDARD ERROR
IDM **see, realize, etc. the ˈerror of your ˈways** (formal or humorous) to realize or admit that you have done sth wrong and decide to change your behaviour ⇒ more at TRIAL n.

**ˈerror message** noun (computing) a message that appears on a computer screen that tells you that you have done sth wrong or that the program cannot do what you want it to do

**er·satz** /ˈeəzæts; NAmE ˈersɑːts/ adj. artificial and not as good as the real thing or product: *ersatz coffee*

**Erse** /ɜːs; NAmE ɜːrs/ noun [U] (old-fashioned) the Scottish or Irish Gaelic language ⇒ compare GAELIC, IRISH

**erst·while** /ˈɜːstwaɪl; NAmE ˈɜːrst-/ adj. [only before noun] (formal) former; that until recently was the type of person or thing described but is not any more: *an erstwhile opponent* ◇ *His erstwhile friends turned against him.*

**eru·dite** /ˈeruːdaɪt; NAmE ˈerjəd-/ adj. (formal, approving) having or showing great knowledge that is gained from academic study SYN **learned**

**eru·di·tion** /ˌeruːˈdɪʃn; NAmE ˌerjəˈd-/ noun [U] (formal, approving) great academic knowledge

**erupt** ⓘ B2 /ɪˈrʌpt/ verb **1** ⓘ B2 [I, T] when a VOLCANO **erupts** or burning rocks, smoke, etc. **erupt** or **are erupted**, the burning rocks, etc. are thrown out from the volcano: *The volcano could erupt at any time.* ◇ *~from sth* *Ash began to erupt from the crater.* ◇ *~sth* *An immense volume of rocks and molten lava was erupted.* ⇒ SYNONYMS at EXPLODE **2** ⓘ C1 [I] to start happening, suddenly and violently SYN **break out**: *Violence erupted outside the embassy gates.* ◇ *~into sth* *The unrest erupted into revolution.* **3** [I, T] to suddenly express your feelings very strongly, especially by shouting loudly: *When Davis scored for the third time the crowd erupted.* ◇ *~in/into sth* *My father just erupted into fury.* ◇ *~with sth* *The room erupted with laughter.* ◇ *+ speech* *'How dare you!' she erupted.* **4** [I] (of spots, etc.) to suddenly appear on your skin: *A rash had erupted all over his chest.* ▶ **erup·tion** /ɪˈrʌpʃn/ noun [C, U]: *a major volcanic eruption* ◇ *an eruption of violent protest* ◇ *skin rashes and eruptions* ⇒ WORDFINDER NOTE at DISASTER

**erup·tive** /ɪˈrʌptɪv/ adj. (specialist) relating to or produced by the eruption of a VOLCANO

**erven** /ˈɜːvn; NAmE ˈɜːrvn/ pl. of ERF

**-ery** /əri/, **-ry** /ri/ suffix (in nouns) **1** the group or class of: *greenery* ◇ *gadgetry* **2** the state or character of: *bravery* ◇ *rivalry* **3** the art or practice of: *cookery* ◇ *archery* **4** a place where sth is made, grows, lives, etc: *bakery* ◇ *orangery*

**eryth·ro·cyte** /ɪˈrɪθrəsaɪt/ noun (biology) = RED BLOOD CELL

**-es** suffix ⇒ -S

**es·cal·ate** ⓘ C1 /ˈeskəleɪt/ verb [I, T] to become greater, worse, more serious, etc.; to make sth greater, worse, more serious, etc: *the escalating costs of healthcare* ◇ *~into sth* *The fighting escalated into a full-scale war.* ◇ *~sth (into sth)* *We do not want to escalate the war.* ▶ **es·cal·ation** /ˌeskəˈleɪʃn/ noun [C, U]: *an escalation in food prices* ◇ *further escalation of the conflict*

**es·cal·ator** /ˈeskəleɪtə(r)/ noun moving stairs that carry people between different floors of a large building: *to take/ride the escalator* ◇ *an up/a down escalator*

**es·cap·ade** /ˈeskəpeɪd/ noun an exciting adventure (often one that people think is dangerous or stupid): *Isabel's latest romantic escapade* ⇒ WORDFINDER NOTE at ADVENTURE

**es·cape** ⓘ B1 /ɪˈskeɪp/ verb, noun
■ *verb* **1** ⓘ B1 [I] to get away from a place where you have been kept as a prisoner or not allowed to leave: *Two prisoners have escaped.* ◇ *They were caught trying to escape.* ◇ *~from sb/sth* *He escaped from prison this morning.* ◇ *~sb/sth* *She managed to escape her captors.* **2** ⓘ B1 [I, T] to get away from or avoid sth unpleasant or

dangerous: ~ **(from sth)** *She managed to escape from the burning car.* ◊ ~ **into/to sth** *(figurative) As a child he would often escape into a dream world of his own.* ◊ ~ **with sth** *I escaped with only minor injuries.* ◊ + *adj. Both drivers escaped unhurt.* ◊ ~ **sth** *She was lucky to escape punishment.* ◊ *They were glad to have escaped the clutches of winter for another year.* ◊ *The pilot escaped death by seconds.* ◊ *There was no escaping the fact that he was overweight.* ◊ ~ **doing sth** *He narrowly escaped being killed.*
**3** [T, no passive] ~ **sb/sth** to be forgotten or not noticed: *Her name escapes me* (= I can't remember it). ◊ *It might have escaped your notice, but I'm very busy at the moment.*
**4** [I] (of gases, liquids, etc.) to get out of a container, especially through a hole: *Put a lid on to prevent heat escaping.* ◊ ~ **into sth** *toxic waste escaping into the sea* **5** [T, I] ~ **(sth)** (of a sound) to come out from your mouth without you intending it to: *A groan escaped her lips.* IDM - see STABLE *n.*
■ *noun* **1** [C, U] the act or a method of escaping from a place or an unpleasant or dangerous situation: *I had a narrow escape* (= I was lucky to have escaped). ◊ *He had a lucky escape when his car skidded out of control.* ◊ *As soon as he turned his back, she would make her escape.* ◊ ~ **from sth** *an escape from a prisoner of war camp* ◊ *There was no hope of escape from her disastrous marriage.* ◊ *He took an elaborate escape route from South Africa to Britain.* ⊃ see also FIRE ESCAPE **2** [sing., U] a way of forgetting sth unpleasant or difficult for a short time: *Craig finds escape in dreams.* ◊ ~ **from sth** *For her, travel was an escape from the boredom of her everyday life.* **3** [C] the fact of a liquid, gas, etc. coming out of a pipe or container by accident; the amount that comes out: *an escape of gas* **4** [U] (*also* **e'scape key** [C]) (*computing*) a button on a computer keyboard that you press to stop a particular operation or leave a program: *Press escape to get back to the menu.* ⊃ WORDFINDER NOTE at KEYBOARD
IDM **make good your e'scape** (*formal*) to manage to escape completely

**es·cape clause** *noun* a part of a contract that states the conditions under which the contract may be broken

**es·caped** /ɪˈskeɪpt/ *adj.* [only before noun] having escaped from a place: *an escaped prisoner/lion*

**es·capee** /ɪˌskeɪˈpiː/ *noun* (*formal*) a person or an animal that has escaped from somewhere, especially sb who has escaped from prison

**es·cap·ism** /ɪˈskeɪpɪzəm/ *noun* [U] an activity, a form of entertainment, etc. that helps you avoid or forget unpleasant or boring things: *the pure escapism of adventure movies* ◊ *For John, books are a form of escapism.* ▶ **es·cap·ist** /-pɪst/ *adj.*

**es·carp·ment** /ɪˈskɑːpmənt; *NAmE* ɪˈskɑːrp-/ *noun* a steep slope that separates an area of high ground from an area of lower ground

**ES cell** /ˌiː es ˈsel/ *noun* (*biology*) a STEM CELL taken from an EMBRYO soon after it is formed (the abbreviation for 'embryonic stem cell')

**eschat·ology** /ˌeskəˈtɒlədʒi/ *NAmE* -ˈtɑːl-/ *noun* [U] (*religion*) the branch of THEOLOGY that is about death and judgement ▶ **eschat·ological** /ˌeskətəˈlɒdʒɪkl/ *NAmE* -ˈlɑːdʒ-/ *adj.*

**es·chew** /ɪsˈtʃuː/ *verb* ~ **sth** (*formal*) to deliberately avoid or keep away from sth

**es·cort** *noun, verb*
■ *noun* /ˈeskɔːt; *NAmE* ˈeskɔːrt/ **1** [C, U] a person or group of people or vehicles that travels with sb/sth in order to protect or guard them: *Armed escorts are provided for visiting heads of state.* ◊ *Prisoners are taken to court under police escort.* **2** [C] (*formal or old-fashioned*) a person, especially a man, who takes sb to a particular social event **3** [C] a person, especially a woman, who is paid to go out socially with sb HELP **Escort** is sometimes used as a polite word for a PROSTITUTE. ⊃ *an escort service/agency*
■ *verb* /ɪˈskɔːt; *NAmE* ɪˈskɔːrt/ ~ **sb** (+ *adv./prep.*) to go with sb to protect or guard them or to show them the way: *The president arrived, escorted by twelve soldiers.* ⊃ SYNONYMS at TAKE

**-ese** /iːz/ *suffix* **1** (in adjectives and nouns) of a country or city; a person who lives in a country or city; the language spoken there: *Chinese* ◊ *Viennese* **2** (in nouns) (*often disapproving*) the style or language of: *journalese* ◊ *officialese*

**e-signature** *noun* = ELECTRONIC SIGNATURE

**esikuti** /ˌesiˈkuːti/ *EAfrE* [esiˈkuti] (*also* **isikuti**) *noun* [U] (*EAfrE*) a quick dance with a lot of movement, accompanied by singing and the sound of drums

**Es·kimo** /ˈeskɪməʊ/ *noun* (*pl.* **Es·kimo** *or* **Es·kimos**) (*sometimes offensive*) a member of a race of people from northern Canada, and parts of Alaska, Greenland and Siberia. Some of these people prefer to use the name Inuit. ⊃ compare INUIT

**Esky**™ /ˈeski/ *noun* (*pl.* **-ies**) (*AustralE*) a bag or box that keeps food or drinks cold and that can be used for a PICNIC

**ESL** /ˌiː es ˈel/ *abbr.* English as a second language (refers to the teaching of English as a foreign language to people who are living in a country in which English is either the first or second language) ⊃ compare EAL, EFL, ESOL

**ESOL** /ˈiːsɒl; *NAmE* -sɑːl/ *abbr.* English for speakers of other languages (used especially in the UK and Ireland to refer to the teaching of English as a foreign language to people who are living in a country in which English is either the first or second language) HELP The term **ESOL** may be preferred to **ESL** (English as a second language) because many people learn English as a third or even fourth language. ⊃ compare EAL, EFL, ESL

**esopha·gus** (*NAmE*) (*BrE* **oe·sopha·gus**) /iˈsɒfəgəs; *NAmE* iˈsɑːf-/ *noun* (*anatomy*) (*pl.* **-pha·guses** *or* **-ph·agi** /-gaɪ/) the tube through which food passes from the mouth to the stomach SYN **gullet**

**eso·ter·ic** /ˌiːsəˈterɪk, ˌes-; *NAmE* ˌes-/ *adj.* (*formal*) likely to be understood or enjoyed by only a few people with a special knowledge or interest

**ESP** /ˌiː es ˈpiː/ *abbr.* **1** English for specific/special purposes (the teaching of English for scientific, technical, etc. purposes to people whose first language is not English) **2** extrasensory perception (the ability to know things without using the senses of sight, hearing, etc., for example to know what people are thinking or what will happen in the future)

**esp.** *abbr.* (in writing) especially

**espa·drille** /ˈespədrɪl/ *noun* a light shoe made of strong cloth with a SOLE made of rope

**es·pe·cial** /ɪˈspeʃl/ *adj.* [only before noun] (*formal*) greater or better than usual; special in some way or for a particular group: *a matter of especial importance* ◊ *The lecture will be of especial interest to history students.* ⊃ compare SPECIAL

**es·pe·cial·ly** /ɪˈspeʃəli/ *adv.* (*abbr.* **esp.**)
**1** more with one person, thing, etc. than with others, or more in particular circumstances than in others SYN **particularly**: *Teenagers are very fashion conscious, especially girls.* ◊ ~ + *adv./prep. I love Rome, especially in the spring.* ◊ ~ *if ... The car is quite small, especially if you have children.* ⊃ LANGUAGE BANK at EMPHASIS **2** for a particular purpose, person, etc: *I got up early especially.* ◊ ~ **for sb/sth** *I made it especially for you.* **3** very much; to a particular degree: *A plentiful supply of water is especially important in summer.* ◊ *especially useful/interesting* ◊ *'Do you like his novels?' 'Not especially.'*

▼ **WHICH WORD?**

**especially / specially**

- **Especially** usually means 'particularly': *She loves all sports, especially swimming.* It is not placed first in a sentence: *I especially like sweet things.* ◊ ~~*Especially I like sweet things.*~~
- **Specially** usually means 'for a particular purpose' and is often followed by a past participle, such as *designed, developed* or *made*: *a course specially designed to meet your needs* ◊ *She has her clothes specially made in Paris.*
- In *BrE*, **especially** and **specially** are often used in the same way and it can be hard to hear the difference when people speak. **Specially** is less formal: *I bought this especially/specially for you.* ◊ *It is especially/specially important to remember this.*
- The adjective for both **especially** and **specially** is usually **special**.

# Esperanto

**Es·per·an·to** /ˌespəˈræntəʊ/ noun [U] an artificial language invented in 1887 as a means of international communication, based on the main European languages but with easy grammar and pronunciation

**es·pi·on·age** /ˈespiənɑːʒ/ noun [U] the activity of secretly getting important political or military information about another country or of finding out another company's secrets by using SPIES [SYN] **spying**: *Some of the commercial activities were a cover for espionage.* ◊ *She may call it research; I call it industrial espionage.* ⊃ see also COUNTER-ESPIONAGE

**es·plan·ade** /ˌespləˈneɪd; NAmE ˈesplənɑːd, -neɪd/ noun a level area of open ground in a town for people to walk along, often by the sea or a river

**es·pouse** /ɪˈspaʊz/ verb ~ **sth** (*formal*) to give your support to a belief, policy, etc: *They espoused the notion of equal opportunity for all in education.* ▶ **es·pous·al** /ɪˈspaʊzl/ noun [U, sing.]: ~ **of sth** *his recent espousal of populism*

**es·pres·so** /eˈspresəʊ/ noun (*pl.* -os) **1** [U] strong black coffee made by forcing STEAM or boiling water through GROUND coffee: *an espresso machine* **2** [C] a cup of espresso

**espy** /ɪˈspaɪ/ verb (espies, espy·ing, espied, espied) ~ **sb/sth** (*literary*) to see sb/sth suddenly [SYN] **sight, spy**

**Esq.** abbr. **1** (*old-fashioned, especially BrE*) Esquire (a polite title written after a man's name, especially on an official letter addressed to him. If Esq. is used, Mr. is not then used): *Edward Smith, Esq.* **2** (*NAmE*) used as a title after the name of a female or male lawyer

**-esque** /esk/ *suffix* (in adjectives) in the style of: *statuesque* ◊ *Kafkaesque*

**-ess** /es, əs/ *suffix* (in nouns) female: *lioness* ◊ *actress* ⊃ note at GENDER

**essay** ❶ **A2** noun, verb
■ *noun* /ˈeseɪ/ **1** **A2** a short piece of writing by a student as part of a course of study: *I have to write an essay this weekend.* ◊ ~ **on/about sb/sth** *an essay on the causes of the First World War* ◊ **in an** ~ *He made some very good points in his essay.* **2** **A2** a short piece of writing on a particular subject, written in order to be published: ~ **(by sb)** *a collection of essays by prominent African American writers* ◊ ~ **on/about sb/sth** *The book contains a number of interesting essays on women in politics.* ◊ **in an** ~ *I discuss this in a forthcoming essay.* **3 (in sth)** (*formal*) an attempt to do sth: *His first essay in politics was a complete disaster.*
■ *verb* /eˈseɪ/ ~ **sth** (*literary*) to try to do sth

**es·say·ist** /ˈeseɪɪst/ noun a person who writes essays to be published

**es·sence** ❷+ **C1** **W** /ˈesns/ noun **1** ❷+ **C1** [U] the most important quality or feature of sth, that makes it what it is: *His paintings capture the essence of France.* ◊ **in~** *In essence* (= when you consider the most important points), *your situation isn't so different from mine.* **2** ❷+ **C1** [U, C] a liquid taken from a plant, etc. that contains its smell and taste in a very strong form: *essence of rose* ◊ (*BrE*) *coffee/vanilla/almond essence* ⊃ see also EXTRACT noun
**IDM** **of the 'essence** necessary and very important: *In this situation time is of the essence* (= we must do things as quickly as possible).

**es·sen·tial** ❶ **B1** ⦿ /ɪˈsenʃl/ *adj., noun*
■ *adj.* **1** ⦿ **B1** completely necessary; extremely important in a particular situation or for a particular activity [SYN] **vital**: *an essential part/feature of sth* ◊ *an essential element/ingredient/component of sth* ◊ *essential services such as gas, water and electricity* ◊ *Vitamins play an essential role in many body processes.* ◊ *All events are free, but booking is essential.* ◊ ~ **to sth** *Money is not essential to happiness.* ◊ ~ **for sth** *Experience is essential for this job.* ◊ **it is essential (for sb/sth) to do sth** *It is essential to keep the two groups separate.* ◊ **it is essential that …** *It is essential that you have some experience.* ⊃ compare INESSENTIAL, NON-ESSENTIAL [OPP] **dispensable** ⊃ LANGUAGE BANK at EMPHASIS, VITAL **2** ⦿ **B2** [only before noun] connected with the most important aspect or basic nature of sb/sth [SYN] **fundamental**: *The essential difference between Sara and me is in our attitude to money.* ◊ *He describes what he thinks is the essential nature of America.* ◊ *The essential character of the town has been destroyed by the new road.*
■ *noun* [usually pl.] **1** something that is needed in a particular situation or in order to do a particular thing: *I only had time to pack the bare essentials* (= the most necessary things). ◊ *The studio had all the essentials like heating and running water.* ◊ *The relief agencies are trying to provide food and other basic essentials.* **2** an important basic fact or piece of knowledge about a subject: *the essentials of English grammar*

**es·sen·tial·ly** ❷+ **B2** ⦿ /ɪˈsenʃəli/ *adv.* when you think about the true, important or basic nature of sb/sth [SYN] **basically, fundamentally**: *There are three essentially different ways of tackling the problem.* ◊ *The pattern is essentially the same in all cases.* ◊ *Essentially, what we are suggesting is that the firm needs to change.* ◊ *He was, essentially, a teacher, not a manager.* ◊ *The article was essentially concerned with her relationship with her parents* (= it dealt with other things, but this was the most important).

**es·sential 'oil** *noun* an oil taken from a plant, used because of its strong smell for making PERFUME and in AROMATHERAPY

**EST** /ˌiː es ˈtiː/ *abbr.* EASTERN STANDARD TIME

---

## SYNONYMS

### essential
**vital • crucial • critical • decisive • indispensable**

These words all describe sb/sth that is extremely important and completely necessary because a particular situation or activity depends on them.

**essential** extremely important and completely necessary, because without it sth cannot exist, be made or be successful: *Experience is essential for this job.*

**vital** essential: *The police play a vital role in our society.*

**ESSENTIAL OR VITAL?**
These words have the same meaning but there can be a slight difference in tone. **Essential** is used to state a fact or opinion with authority. **Vital** is often used when there is some worry felt about sth, or a need to persuade sb that a fact or opinion is true, right or important. **Vital** is less often used in negative statements: *It was vital to show that he was not afraid.* ◊ *Money is not vital to happiness.*

**crucial** extremely important because a particular situation or activity depends on it: *It is crucial that we get this right.*

**critical** extremely important because a particular situation or activity depends on it: *Your decision is critical to our future.*

**CRUCIAL OR CRITICAL?**
These words have the same meaning but there can be a slight difference in context. **Critical** is often used in technical matters of business or science; **crucial** is often used to talk about matters that may cause worry or other emotions.

**decisive** of the greatest importance in affecting the final result of a particular situation: *She has played a decisive role in the peace negotiations.*

**indispensable** essential; too important to be without: *Cars have become an indispensable part of our lives.*

**PATTERNS**
- essential / vital / crucial / critical / decisive / indispensable **for** sth
- essential / vital / crucial / critical / indispensable **to** sth
- essential / vital / crucial / critical **that …**
- essential / vital / crucial / critical **to do** sth
- a(n) essential / vital / crucial / critical / decisive / indispensable **part / factor**
- **of** vital / crucial / critical / decisive **importance**
- **absolutely** essential / vital / crucial / critical / decisive / indispensable

**-est** /ɪst/ suffix (makes superlative adjectives and adverbs): widest ◊ biggest ◊ happiest ◊ soonest ⊃ compare -ER

**es·tab·lish** /ɪˈstæblɪʃ/ verb 1 ~ sth to start or create an organization, a system, etc. that is meant to last for a long time SYN set up: *The committee was established in 1912.* ◊ *They now hope to establish a centre in Cuba.* ◊ *to establish standards/rules/principles* ◊ *The proposal would establish a system of inspections of prisons worldwide.* 2 ~ sth to start having a relationship, especially a formal one, with another person, group or country: *to establish relations/links/contacts/connections* ◊ *The school is trying to establish a relationship with the local community.* 3 to hold a position for long enough or succeed in sth well enough to make people accept and respect you: ~ sb/sth/yourself *He has just set up his own business but it will take him a while to get established.* ◊ ~ sb/sth/yourself (in sth) (as sth) *The exhibition helped to establish her as an artist.* 4 ~ sth to make people accept a belief, claim, custom etc: *This success helped to establish the practice of vaccination.* ◊ *Traditions get established over time.* 5 to discover or prove the facts of a situation SYN ascertain: ~ sth *Police are still trying to establish the cause of the accident.* ◊ *There will be an investigation to establish the facts.* ◊ ~ that… *They have established that his injuries were caused by a fall.* ◊ ~ where, what, etc… *We need to establish where she was at the time of the shooting.* ◊ **it is established that…** *It has since been established that the horse was drugged.*

**es·tab·lished** /ɪˈstæblɪʃt/ adj. [only before noun] 1 respected or given official status because it has existed or been used for a long time: *They are an established company with a good reputation.* ◊ *This unit is now an established part of the course.* ⊃ see also WELL ESTABLISHED 2 (of a person) well known and respected in a job, etc. that they have been doing for a long time: *an established actor* 3 (of a Church or a religion) made official for a country

**es·tab·lish·ment** /ɪˈstæblɪʃmənt/ noun 1 [C] (formal) an organization, a large institution or a hotel: *an educational establishment* ◊ *a research establishment* ◊ *The hotel is a comfortable and well-run establishment.* 2 (usually **the Establishment**) [sing. + sing./pl. v.] (often disapproving) the people in a society or a profession who have influence and power and who usually do not support change: *the medical/military/political, etc. establishment* ◊ *young people rebelling against the Establishment* 3 [U] the act of starting or creating sth that is meant to last for a long time: *The speaker announced the establishment of a new college.* ◊ *the establishment of diplomatic relations between the countries*

**es·tate** /ɪˈsteɪt/ noun 1 [C] (BrE) an area of land with a lot of houses or factories of the same type on it: **on an~** *She lives in a tower block on an estate in London.* ⊃ see also COUNCIL ESTATE, HOUSING ESTATE, INDUSTRIAL ESTATE, TRADING ESTATE 2 [C] a large area of land, usually in the country, that is owned by one person or family: **on an~** *The poet's childhood was spent on a country estate.* 3 (law) [C, U] all the money and property that a person owns, especially everything that is left when they die: *Her estate was left to her daughter.* 4 [C] (BrE) = ESTATE CAR ⊃ see also FOURTH ESTATE, REAL ESTATE

**eˈstate agent** (BrE) (NAmE **Realtor**™, ˈreal estate agent) noun a person whose job is to sell houses and land for people

**eˈstate car** (also **estate**) (both BrE) (NAmE ˈstation wagon) noun a car with a lot of space behind the back seats and a door at the back for loading large items

**eˈstate sale** noun (NAmE) a sale of the possessions of a person who has died or is moving to another house

**eˈstate tax** noun [U] (especially in the US) tax that must be paid on the money or property of sb who dies ⊃ compare INHERITANCE TAX

**es·teem** /ɪˈstiːm/ noun, verb
- noun [U] (formal) great respect and approval; a good opinion of sb: *She is held in high esteem by her colleagues.* ◊ *Please accept this small gift as a token of our esteem.* ⊃ see also SELF-ESTEEM
- verb (formal) (not used in the progressive tenses) 1 [usually passive] to respect and admire sb/sth very much: **be esteemed (by sb)** *Many of these qualities are esteemed by managers.* ◊ *a highly esteemed scientist* 2 ~ sb/sth + noun (old-fashioned, formal) to think of sb/sth in a particular way: *We esteem it a privilege to have you with us.*

**ester** /ˈestə(r)/ noun (chemistry) a chemical that is formed by the reaction between an ACID and an alcohol. Esters made from acids that contain CARBON are generally sweet-smelling.

**es·thete, es·thet·ic** (NAmE) = AESTHETE, AESTHETIC

**es·tim·able** /ˈestɪməbl/ adj. (old-fashioned or formal) deserving respect and approval

**es·ti·mate** verb, noun
- verb /ˈestɪmeɪt/ [often passive] to form an idea of the cost, size, value etc. of sth, but without calculating it exactly: *to estimate the cost/value/number of sth* ◊ *The satellite will cost an estimated £400 million.* ◊ ~ sth at sth *Police estimate the crowd at 30000.* ◊ ~ sth to do sth *The deal is estimated to be worth around $1.5 million.* ◊ ~ (that)… *We estimated (that) it would cost about €5000.* ◊ **it is estimated (that)…** *It is estimated (that) the project will last four years.* ◊ ~ how, large, etc… *It is hard to estimate how many children suffer from dyslexia.*
- noun /ˈestɪmət/ 1 a judgement that you make without having the exact details or figures about the size, amount, cost, etc. of sth: *to provide/obtain an estimate* ◊ ~ of sth *I can give you a rough estimate of the amount of wood you will need.* ◊ *a ballpark estimate* (= an approximate estimate) ◊ *At least 5000 people were killed, and that's a conservative estimate* (= the real figure will be higher). ◊ **according to an~** *Losses totalled $1.87 billion last year, according to estimates.* 2 a statement of how much a piece of work will probably cost: *We got estimates from three firms and accepted the lowest.* ◊ ~ of sth *an estimate of £300*

**es·ti·ma·tion** /ˌestɪˈmeɪʃn/ noun (formal) 1 [sing.] a judgement or opinion about the value or quality of sb/sth: *Who is the best candidate in your estimation?* ◊ *Since he left his wife he's certainly gone down in my estimation* (= I have less respect for him). ◊ *She went up in my estimation* (= I have more respect for her) *when I discovered how much charity work she does.* 2 [C] A judgement about the levels or quantity of sth: *Estimations of our total world sales are around 50 million.*

**es·tranged** /ɪˈstreɪndʒd/ adj. (formal) 1 [usually before noun] no longer living with your husband, wife or partner: *his estranged wife Emma* 2 ~ (from sb) no longer friendly or in contact with sb: *He became estranged from his family after the argument.* 3 ~ (from sth) no longer involved in or connected with sth, especially sth that used to be important to you: *She felt estranged from her former existence.*

**es·trange·ment** /ɪˈstreɪndʒmənt/ noun [U, C] (formal) 1 the fact of no longer living with your husband, wife or partner: ~ from sb/sth *a period of estrangement from his wife* ◊ **between A and B** *the bitter estrangement between husband and wife* 2 the fact of no longer being friendly or in contact with sb: ~ from sb/sth *her estrangement from her family* ◊ **between A and B** *The misunderstanding had caused a seven-year estrangement between them.*

**es·tro·gen** (NAmE) (BrE **oes·tro·gen**) /ˈiːstrədʒən; NAmE ˈes-/ noun [U] a HORMONE produced in women's OVARIES that causes them to develop the physical and sexual features that are characteristic of females and that causes them to prepare their body to have babies ⊃ compare PROGESTERONE, TESTOSTERONE

**es·trus** (NAmE) (BrE **oes·trus**) /ˈiːstrəs; NAmE ˈes-/ noun [U] (specialist) a period of time in which a female animal is FERTILE and ready to have sex ⊃ compare BE ON HEAT

**es·tu·ary** /ˈestʃuəri; NAmE -tʃueri -ies/ noun the wide part of a river where it flows into the sea: *the Thames estuary* ⊃ WORDFINDER NOTE at RIVER

# ETA

**ETA** /ˌiː tiː ˈeɪ/ abbr. estimated time of arrival (the time at which an aircraft, a ship, etc. is expected to arrive) ⇨ compare ETD

**eta** /ˈiːtə/ noun the 7th letter of the Greek alphabet (Η, η)

**ˈe-tailing** noun [U] the business of selling goods to the public over the internet: *E-tailing in the US broke all records last year.* ▶ **ˈe-tailer** noun: *America's leading e-tailers*

**et al.** /ˌet ˈæl; NAmE ˈɑːl/ abbr. (used especially after names) and other people or things (from Latin 'et alii/alia'): *research by West et al., 2012*

**etc.** /ˌet ˈsetərə, ˌɪt/ abbr. used after a list to show that there are other things that you could have mentioned (the abbreviation for 'et cetera'): *Remember to take some paper, a pen, etc.* ⋄ *We talked about the contract, pay, etc.*

**et cetˈera** /ˌet ˈsetərə, ˌɪt/ adv. = ETC.

**etch** /etʃ/ verb [usually passive] **1** to cut lines into a piece of glass, metal, etc. in order to make words or a picture: **A (is) etched in/into/on B** *a glass tankard with his initials etched on it* ⋄ **B (is) etched with A** *a glass tankard etched with his initials* **2** (*literary*) if a feeling is **etched** on sb's face, or sb's face is **etched** with a feeling, that feeling can be seen very clearly: **A is etched in/into/on B** *Tiredness was etched on his face.* ⋄ **B is etched with A** *His face was etched with tiredness.* **3** to make a strong clear mark or pattern on sth: **(be) etched + adv./prep.** *a mountain etched (= having a clear outline) against the sky*
**IDM** **be etched on your ˈheart/ˈmemory/ˈmind** if sth is etched on your heart, memory, etc. you remember it because it has made a strong impression on you

**etchˈing** /ˈetʃɪŋ/ noun [C, U] a picture that is printed from an etched piece of metal; the art of making these pictures

**ETD** /ˌiː tiː ˈdiː/ abbr. estimated time of departure (the time at which an aircraft, ship, etc. is expected to leave) ⇨ compare ETA

**eterˈnal** ?+ C1 /ɪˈtɜːnl; NAmE ɪˈtɜːrnl/ adj. **1** ?+ C1 without an end; existing or continuing forever: *the promise of eternal life in heaven* ⋄ *She's an eternal optimist (= she always expects that the best will happen).* ⋄ *eternal truths (= ideas that are always true and never change)* ⋄ *You have my eternal gratitude (= very great GRATITUDE).* **2** ?+ C1 [only before noun] (*disapproving*) happening often and seeming never to stop **SYN** **constant**: *I'm tired of your eternal arguments.* ▶ **eterˈnalˈly** /-nəli/ adv.: *I'll be eternally grateful to you for this.* ⋄ *women trying to look eternally young*
**IDM** see HOPE n.

**eterˈnity** /ɪˈtɜːnəti; NAmE ɪˈtɜːrn-/ noun **1** [U] time without end, especially life continuing without end after death: *There will be rich and poor for all eternity.* ⋄ *They believed that their souls would be condemned to burn in hell for eternity.* **2** **an eternity** [sing.] (*informal*) a period of time that seems to be very long or to never end: *After what seemed like an eternity the nurse returned with the results of the test.*

**ethˈane** /ˈiːθeɪn/ noun [U] (*symb.* C₂H₆) (*chemistry*) a gas that has no colour or smell and that can burn. Ethane is found in natural gas and mineral oil.

**ethaˈnol** /ˈeθənɒl; NAmE -nɔːl, -nəʊl/ (*also* ˌethyl ˈalcohol) noun [U] (*chemistry*) the type of alcohol in alcoholic drinks, also used as a fuel or SOLVENT

**ethˈene** /ˈeθiːn/ noun [U] = ETHYLENE

**ether** /ˈiːθə(r)/ noun **1** a clear liquid made from alcohol, used in industry as a SOLVENT and, in the past, in medicine to make people unconscious before an operation **2** **the ether** (*old use* or *literary*) the upper part of the sky: *Her words disappeared into the ether.* **3** **the ether** the air, when it is thought of as the place in which radio or electronic communication takes place: *The messages simply vanish into the ether after 24 hours.*

**etherˈeal** /ɪˈθɪəriəl; NAmE ɪˈθɪr-/ adj. (*formal*) extremely light and beautiful; seeming to belong to another, more spiritual, world: *ethereal music* ⋄ *her ethereal beauty*

**Etherˈnet** /ˈiːθənet; NAmE -θərn-/ noun [sing.] (*computing*) a system for connecting a number of computer systems to form a network

**ethic** ?+ B2 W /ˈeθɪk/ noun **1** ?+ B2 **ethics** [pl.] moral principles that control or influence a person's behaviour: *professional/business/medical ethics* ⋄ *to draw up a code of ethics* ⋄ *He began to question the ethics of his position.* **2** ?+ B2 [sing.] a system of moral principles or rules of behaviour ⇨ see also WORK ETHIC **3** **ethics** [U] the branch of philosophy that deals with moral principles

**ethˈical** ❶ B2 W /ˈeθɪkl/ adj. **1** ?+ B2 connected with beliefs and principles about what is right and wrong: *ethical issues/standards/questions/dilemmas* ⋄ *the ethical problems of human embryo research* **2** ?+ B2 morally correct or acceptable: *it is ~(for sb) to do sth Is it ethical to keep animals in zoos?* ⋄ *ethical investment (= investing money in businesses that are considered morally acceptable)* ▶ **ethˈicalˈly** /-kli/ adv.: *The committee judged that he had not behaved ethically.*

**ethˈnic** ?+ B2 /ˈeθnɪk/ adj., noun
■ **adj.** **1** ?+ B2 connected with or belonging to a nation or people that shares a cultural tradition: *ethnic groups/communities* ⋄ *ethnic strife/tensions/violence (= between people from different races or peoples)* ⋄ *ethnic Albanians living in Germany* ⇨ see also MULTI-ETHNIC **2** ?+ B2 typical of a country or culture that is very different from modern Western culture and therefore interesting for people in Western countries: *ethnic clothes/jewellery/cooking* ▶ **ethˈnicˈally** /-kli/ adv.: *an ethnically divided region*
■ **noun** (*especially NAmE, old-fashioned, often offensive*) a person from an ETHNIC MINORITY

**ˌethnic ˈcleansing** noun [U] (used especially in news reports) the policy of forcing the people of a particular race or religion to leave an area or a country

**ethˈnicity** W /eθˈnɪsəti/ noun [U, C] (*pl.* **-ies**) (*specialist*) the fact of belonging to a particular nation or people that shares a cultural tradition: *Many factors are important, for example class, gender, age and ethnicity.* ⋄ *the diverse experience of women of different ethnicities*

**ˌethnic miˈnority** noun a group of people from a particular culture or of a particular race living in a country where the main group is of a different culture or race

**ethnoˈcentric** /ˌeθnəʊˈsentrɪk/ adj. based on the ideas and beliefs of one particular culture and using these to judge other cultures: *a white, ethnocentric school curriculum* ▶ **ethnoˈcentrism** /-trɪzəm/ noun [U]

**ethˈnographer** /eθˈnɒɡrəfə(r); NAmE -ˈnɑːɡ-/ noun a person who studies different peoples and cultures, with their customs, habits and differences

**ethˈnography** /eθˈnɒɡrəfi; NAmE -ˈnɑːɡ-/ noun [U] the scientific description of different peoples and cultures, with their customs, habits and differences ▶ **ethnoˈgraphic** /ˌeθnəˈɡræfɪk/ adj.: *ethnographic research*

**ethˈnology** /eθˈnɒlədʒi; NAmE -ˈnɑːl-/ noun [U] the study of the characteristics of different peoples and the differences and relationships between them ▶ **ethnoˈlogical** /ˌeθnəˈlɒdʒɪkl; NAmE -ˈlɑːdʒ-/ adj. **ethˈnologist** /eθˈnɒlədʒɪst; NAmE -ˈnɑːl-/ noun

**ethos** /ˈiːθɒs; NAmE -θɑːs/ noun [sing.] (*formal*) the moral ideas and attitudes that belong to a particular group, society or person: *an ethos of public service* ⋄ *Teaching was central to his ethos.*

**ethyl** /ˈeθɪl, ˈiːθaɪl/ adj. [only before noun] (*chemistry*) containing the group of ATOMS C₂H₅, formed from ETHANE: *ethyl acetate*

**ˌethyl ˈalcohol** noun [U] (*chemistry*) = ETHANOL

**ˈethylˈene** /ˈeθɪliːn/ (*also* **ethˈene**) noun [U] (*symb.* C₂H₄) (*chemistry*) a gas that is present in coal, CRUDE OIL and NATURAL GAS

**ˈe-ticket** (*US* **ˈE-ticket**™) noun a ticket, for example a plane ticket, that you buy over the internet and receive on your computer or phone. Your purchase details are stored on computer so you do not need a paper ticket.

**etiˈology** (NAmE) (BrE **aetiˈology**) /ˌiːtiˈɒlədʒi; NAmE -ˈɑːl-/ noun (*pl.* **-ies**) (*medical*) **1** [C, U] the cause of a disease or medical condition **2** [U] the scientific study of the causes of disease

**etiˈquette** /ˈetɪkət, -ket/ noun [U] the formal rules of correct or polite behaviour in society, among members of a particular profession or in a particular area of activity: *advice on etiquette* ⋄ *medical/legal/professional etiquette*

◇ Students need to be aware of cell phone etiquette. ▶ **WORDFINDER NOTE** at BEHAVIOUR

**e-toll** noun (SAfrE) **1** [U] (also **e-tolls** [pl.]) the system of collecting TOLLS (= money that you pay to use a particular road) using equipment that recognizes vehicles through electronic TAGS **2** [C] the charge for using this system: *Motorists are fined if they fail to pay their e-tolls within a week.* ▶ **e-tolling** noun [U]: *the e-tolling system*

**Eton·ian** /iˈtəʊniən/ noun a person who is or was a student at the English private school Eton College

**-ette** /et/ suffix (in nouns) **1** small: *kitchenette* **2** female: *usherette*

**étude** /ˈeɪtjuːd; NAmE also -tuːd/ (especially NAmE) (BrE also **study**) noun (music, from French) a piece of music designed to give a player practice in technical skills

**ety·mol·ogy** /ˌetɪˈmɒlədʒi; NAmE -ˈmɑːl-/ noun (pl. **-ies**) **1** [U] the study of the origin and history of words and their meanings **2** [C] the origin and history of a particular word ⊃ see also FOLK ETYMOLOGY, POPULAR ETYMOLOGY ▶ **etymo·logic·al** /ˌetɪməˈlɒdʒɪkl; NAmE -ˈlɑːdʒ-/ adj.: *an etymological dictionary*

**EU** /ˌiː ˈjuː/ abbr. EUROPEAN UNION: *the member states of the EU* ◇ *The EU is under pressure from the US to lift the ban.* ◇ *EU laws/regulations*

**eu·ca·lyp·tus** /ˌjuːkəˈlɪptəs/ noun [C, U] (pl. **eu·ca·lyp·tuses** or **eu·ca·lyp·ti** /-taɪ/) (also **euca'lyptus tree**, **'gum tree**) a tall straight tree with leaves that produce an oil with a strong smell, that is used in medicine. There are several types of eucalyptus and they grow especially in Australasia.

**Eu·char·ist** /ˈjuːkərɪst/ noun [sing.] a ceremony in the Christian Church during which people eat bread and drink wine in memory of the last meal that Christ had with his DISCIPLES; the bread and wine taken at this ceremony ⊃ see also COMMUNION, MASS

**Eu·clid·ean geom·etry** /juːˌklɪdiən dʒiˈɒmətri; NAmE -ˈɑːm-/ noun [U] the system of GEOMETRY based on the work of Euclid

**eu·gen·ics** /juːˈdʒenɪks/ noun [U] the study of methods to improve the mental and physical characteristics of the human race by choosing who may become parents ▶ **eu·gen·ic** adj. **eu·geni·cist** /-nɪsɪst/ (also **eu·gen·ist** /-ˈdʒiːnɪst/) noun, adj.

**eu·lo·gize** (BrE also **-ise**) /ˈjuːlədʒaɪz/ verb ~ **sb/sth (as sth)** (formal) to praise sb/sth very highly: *He was eulogized as a hero.* ▶ **eu·lo·gis·tic** /ˌjuːləˈdʒɪstɪk/ adj.

**eu·logy** /ˈjuːlədʒi/ noun [C, U] (pl. **-ies**) **1** ~ **(of/to sb/sth)** a speech or piece of writing praising sb/sth very much: *a eulogy to marriage* **2** ~ **(for/to sb)** a speech given at a FUNERAL praising the person who has died

**eu·nuch** /ˈjuːnək/ noun **1** a man whose TESTICLES have been removed, especially one who guarded women in some Asian countries in the past **2** (formal) a person without power or influence: *a political eunuch*

**eu·phem·ism** /ˈjuːfəmɪzəm/ noun ~ **(for sth)** an indirect word or phrase that people often use to refer to sth embarrassing or unpleasant, sometimes to make it seem more acceptable than it really is: *'Pass away' is a euphemism for 'die'.* ◇ *'User fees' is just a politician's euphemism for taxes.* ⊃ **WORDFINDER NOTE** at IMAGE ▶ **eu·phem·is·tic** /ˌjuːfəˈmɪstɪk/ adj.: *euphemistic language* **eu·phem·is·tic·al·ly** /-kli/ adv.: *The prison camps were euphemistically called 'retraining centres'.*

**eu·pho·nium** /juːˈfəʊniəm/ noun a large BRASS musical instrument like a TUBA

**eu·phoria** /juːˈfɔːriə/ noun [U] an extremely strong feeling of happiness and excitement that usually lasts only a short time ▶ **eu·phor·ic** /juːˈfɒrɪk; NAmE -ˈfɔːr-/ adj.: *My euphoric mood could not last.* ⊃ SYNONYMS at EXCITED

**Eur·asian** /jʊˈreɪʒn; BrE also -ˈreɪʃn/ adj., noun
■ **adj. 1** of or connected with both Europe and Asia: *the Centre for Russian and Eurasian Studies* **2** having one Asian parent and one parent who is white or from Europe
■ **noun** a person with one Asian parent and one parent who is white or from Europe: *Singapore Eurasians*

**eur·eka** /jʊˈriːkə/ exclamation used to show pleasure at having found sth, especially the answer to a problem

eu'reka moment noun the moment when you suddenly understand sth important, have a great idea, or find the answer to a problem

**Euro** /ˈjʊərəʊ; NAmE ˈjʊr-/ adj. (informal) (used especially in newspapers) connected with Europe, especially the European Union: *Euro rules*

**euro** 🔑 A1 /ˈjʊərəʊ; NAmE ˈjʊr-/ noun (symb. €) (pl. **euros** or **euro**) **1** A1 [C] the unit of money of some countries of the European Union: *I paid five euros for it.* ◇ *10 million euro* ◇ **in euros** *The price is given in euros.* ◇ *a 30-million-euro deal* **2** **the euro** or **the Euro** [sing.] (finance) euros as a system of money; the value of the euro compared with the value of the money of other countries: *What if the UK had joined the Euro in 1999?* ◇ *the value of the euro against the dollar*

**Euro-** /ˈjʊərəʊ; NAmE jʊrəʊ/ combining form (in nouns and adjectives) connected with Europe or the European Union: *a Euro-MP* ◇ *Euro-elections*

**euro·land** /ˈjʊərəʊlænd; NAmE ˈjʊr-/ noun [U] (informal) = EUROZONE

**Eur·ope** /ˈjʊərəp; NAmE ˈjʊr-/ noun [U] **1** the continent next to Asia in the east, the Atlantic Ocean in the west, and the Mediterranean Sea in the south: *western/eastern/central Europe* **2** the European Union: *countries wanting to join Europe* ◇ *He's very pro-Europe.* **3** (BrE) all of Europe except for the UK: *British holidaymakers in Europe*

**Euro·pean** /ˌjʊərəˈpiːən; NAmE ˌjʊr-/ adj., noun
■ **adj. 1** of or connected with Europe: *European languages* ⊃ see also INDO-EUROPEAN, MIDDLE-EUROPEAN **2** of or connected with the European Union: *European law*
■ **noun 1** a person from Europe, or whose ANCESTORS came from Europe **2** (BrE) a person who supports the principles and aims of the European Union: *a good European*

**the European Com'mission** noun [sing.] the group of people who are responsible for the work of the European Union and for suggesting new laws

**the European 'Parliament** noun [sing.] the group of people who are elected in the countries of the European Union to make and change its laws

**the European 'Union** noun [sing.] (abbr. EU) an economic and political organization, based in Brussels, that many European countries belong to

**Euro·scep·tic** /ˌjʊərəʊˈskeptɪk; ˌjʊərəʊskeptɪk; NAmE ˌjʊrəʊˈskeptɪk; ˌjʊərəʊskeptɪk/ noun a person who is opposed to closer links with the European Union **HELP** Since the UK voted to leave the EU in 2016, British Eurosceptics are more often referred to as BREXITEERS (= people who support the departure of the UK from the EU). ▶ **Euro·scep·tic** adj.

**the euro·zone** /ðə ˈjʊərəʊzəʊn; NAmE ˈjʊr-/ noun [sing.] (also informal **euro·land**) the countries in the European Union that use the euro as a unit of money

**Eus·ta·chian tube** /juːˈsteɪʃn tjuːb; NAmE tuːb/ noun (anatomy) a narrow tube that joins the throat to the middle ear

**eu·tha·nasia** /ˌjuːθəˈneɪziə; NAmE -ˈneɪʒə/ noun [U] the practice of killing without pain a person or animal who is suffering from a disease that cannot be cured. Euthanasia of people is illegal in most countries. **SYN** **mercy killing**: *They argued in favour of legalizing voluntary euthanasia (= people being able to ask for euthanasia themselves).*

**eu·than·ize** (BrE also **-ise**) /ˈjuːθənaɪz/ verb ~ **sb/sth** (especially NAmE) to kill a sick or injured animal or person by giving them drugs so that they die without pain **SYN** **put down**, **put to sleep**

**EV** /ˌiː ˈviː/ noun (especially NAmE) a vehicle that uses one or more electric motors (the abbreviation for 'electric vehicle')

**evacu·ate** 🔑+ C1 /ɪˈvækjueɪt/ verb **1** 🔑+ C1 [T] to move people from a place of danger to a safer place: ~ **sth** *Police evacuated nearby buildings.* ◇ ~ **sb (from …) (to …)** *Children were evacuated from London to escape the bombing.* **2** 🔑+ C1 [T, I] ~ **(sth)** to move out of a place because of danger, and leave the place empty: *Employees were urged to evacuate their offices immediately.* ◇ *Locals were told to evacuate.* **3** [T] ~ **sth** (formal) to empty your BOWELS

# evacuee

▶ **evac·u·ation** /ɪˌvækjuˈeɪʃn/ *noun* [U, C]: *the emergency evacuation of thousands of people after the earthquake*

**evac·uee** /ɪˌvækjuˈiː/ *noun* a person who is sent away from a place because it is dangerous, especially during a war

**evade** /ɪˈveɪd/ *verb* **1** ~ **(doing) sth** to escape from sb/sth or avoid meeting sb: *For two weeks they evaded the press.* ◇ *He managed to evade capture.* **2** ~ **(doing) sth** to find a way of not doing sth, especially sth that legally or morally you should do: *to evade payment of taxes* ◇ *She is trying to evade all responsibility for her behaviour.* **3** to avoid dealing with or talking about sth: ~**sth** *Come on, don't you think you're evading the issue?* ◇ ~**doing sth** *to evade answering a question* **4** ~ **sb** (*formal*) to not come or happen to sb SYN **elude**: *The answer evaded him* (= he could not think of it).
⊃ see also EVASION, EVASIVE

**evalu·ate** ⓘ B2 W /ɪˈvæljueɪt/ *verb* to form an opinion of the amount, value or quality of sth after thinking about it carefully SYN **assess**: ~**sth** *The trial will evaluate the effectiveness of the different drugs.* ◇ ~**how, whether, etc ...** *The study will critically evaluate whether this technology is useful.* ⊃ WORDFINDER NOTE at SCIENCE
⊃ see also RE-EVALUATE ▶ **evalu·ative** /-jʊətɪv/ *adj.*: *We need to make some evaluative judgements of this relationship.*

**evalu·ation** ⓘ+ B2 W /ɪˌvæljuˈeɪʃn/ *noun* [C, U] the act of forming an opinion of the amount, value or quality of sth after thinking about it carefully: *an evaluation of the healthcare system* ◇ *The technique is not widely practised and requires further evaluation.* ◇ *The discussion includes a critical evaluation of the documentary sources.* ⊃ see also RE-EVALUATION

**evan·es·cent** /ˌevəˈnesnt, ˌiːv-/ *adj.* (*literary*) disappearing quickly from sight or memory ▶ **evan·es·cence** /-sns/ *noun* [U]

**evan·gel·ic·al** /ˌiːvænˈdʒelɪkl/ *adj., noun*
■ *adj.* **1** of or belonging to a Christian group that emphasizes the authority of the Bible and the importance of people being saved through faith: *They're evangelical Christians.* **2** wanting very much to persuade people to accept your views and opinions: *He delivered his speech with evangelical fervour.* ▶ **evan·gel·ic·al·ism** /-kəlɪzəm/ *noun* [U]
■ *noun* a member of the evangelical branch of the Christian Church

**evan·gel·ist** /ɪˈvændʒəlɪst/ *noun* **1** a person who tries to persuade people to become Christians, especially by travelling around the country holding religious meetings or speaking on radio or television ⊃ see also TELEVANGELIST **2 Evangelist** one of the four writers (Matthew, Mark, Luke, John) of the books called the GOSPELS in the Bible
▶ **evan·gel·ism** /-lɪzəm/ *noun* [U] **evan·gel·ist·ic** /ɪˌvændʒəˈlɪstɪk/ *adj.*: *an evangelistic meeting*

**evan·gel·ize** (*BrE also* **-ise**) /ɪˈvændʒəlaɪz/ *verb* [T, I] ~ **(sb/ sth)** to try to persuade people to become Christians

**evap·or·ate** /ɪˈvæpəreɪt/ *verb* **1** [I, T] if a liquid **evaporates** or if sth **evaporates** it, it changes into a gas, especially STEAM: *Heat until all the water has evaporated.* ◇ ~**sth** *The sun is constantly evaporating the earth's moisture.*
⊃ WORDFINDER NOTE at LIQUID **2** [I] to disappear, especially by gradually becoming less and less: *Her confidence had now completely evaporated.* ▶ **evap·or·ation** /ɪˌvæpəˈreɪʃn/ *noun* [U]

**eˌvaporated ˈmilk** *noun* [U] thick milk sold in cans that has had some of its water content removed

**eˈvaporating dish** *noun* (*specialist*) a dish in which scientists heat a liquid, so that it leaves a solid when it has disappeared

**eva·sion** /ɪˈveɪʒn/ *noun* [C, U] **1** the act of avoiding sb or of avoiding sth that you are supposed to do: *His behaviour was an evasion of his responsibilities as a father.* ◇ *She's been charged with tax evasion.* ⊃ see also TAX EVASION **2** a statement that sb makes that avoids dealing with sth or talking about sth honestly and directly: *His speech was full of evasions and half-truths.* ⊃ see also EVADE

**eva·sive** /ɪˈveɪsɪv/ *adj.* not willing to give clear answers to a question SYN **cagey**: *evasive answers/comments/replies* ◇ *Tessa was evasive about why she had not been at home that night.* ▶ **eva·sive·ly** *adv.*: *'I'm not sure,' she replied evasively.* **eva·sive·ness** *noun* [U]
IDM **take evasive action** to act in order to avoid danger or an unpleasant situation

**eve** /iːv/ *noun* **1** the day or evening before an event, especially a religious festival or holiday: *Christmas Eve* (= 24 December) ◇ *a New Year's Eve party* (= on 31 December) ◇ *on the eve of the election* **2** (*old use or literary*) evening

**even** ⓘ A1 /ˈiːvn/ *adv., adj., verb*
■ *adv.* **1** ⓘ A1 used to emphasize sth unexpected or surprising: *She didn't even call to say she wasn't coming.* ◇ *He never even opened the letter* (= so he certainly didn't read it). ◇ *It was cold there even in summer* (= so it must have been very cold in winter). ◇ *Even a child can understand it* (= so adults certainly can). **2** ⓘ A2 used when you are comparing things, to make the comparison stronger: *You know even less about it than I do.* ◇ *She's even more intelligent than her sister.* **3** used to introduce a more exact description of sb/sth: *It's an unattractive building, ugly even.*
⊃ note at ALTHOUGH
IDM **even as** (*formal*) just at the same time as sb does sth or as sth else happens: *Even as he shouted the warning the car skidded.* **even if 1** B1 despite the possibility that; no matter whether: *I'll get there, even if I have to walk.* **2** B1 despite the fact that; even though: *He is a great leader, even if he has many enemies.* **even ˈnow/ˈthen 1** despite what has/had happened: *I've shown him the photographs but even now he won't believe me.* ◇ *Even then she would not admit her mistake.* **2** (*formal*) at this or that exact moment: *The troops are even now preparing to march into the city.* **even ˈso** despite that: *There are a lot of spelling mistakes; even so, it's quite a good essay.* **even ˈthough/if**
⓵ B1 despite the fact that: *I like her, even though she can be annoying at times.* ⊃ note at ALTHOUGH
■ *adj.*
• NUMBERS **1** ⓘ B2 that can be divided exactly by two: *4, 6, 8 and 10 are all even numbers.* OPP **odd**
• EQUAL **2** ⓘ B2 (of an amount of sth) equal or the same for each person, team, place, etc: *Our scores are now even.* ◇ *the even distribution of food* OPP **uneven 3** ⓘ B2 (of two people or teams) equally balanced or of an equal standard: *an even contest* ◇ *The two players were pretty even.* OPP **uneven**
• NOT CHANGING **4** ⓘ B2 not changing very much in amount, speed, etc: *Children do not learn at an even pace.* ◇ *Try to keep your baby's room at an even temperature.* OPP **uneven**
• SMOOTH/LEVEL **5** smooth, level and flat: *You need an even surface to work on.* OPP **uneven**
• SAME SIZE **6** equally spaced and the same size: *even features/teeth* OPP **uneven**
• CALM **7** calm; not changing or becoming upset: *She has a very even temperament.* ◇ *He spoke in a steady, even voice.*
• **even·ness** /-vənnəs/ *noun* [U]
IDM **be ˈeven** (*informal*) to no longer owe sb money or a favour **be/get ˈeven (with sb)** (*informal*) to cause sb the same amount of trouble or harm as they have caused you: *I'll get even with you for this, just you wait.* **break ˈeven** to complete a piece of business, etc. without either losing money or making a profit: *The company just about broke even last year.* **have an even ˈchance (of doing sth)** to be equally likely to do or not do sth: *She has more than an even chance of winning tomorrow.* **on an even ˈkeel** living, working or happening in a calm way, with no sudden changes, especially after a difficult time ⊃ more at HONOUR *n.*
■ *verb*
IDM **even the ˈscore** to harm or punish sb who has harmed or cheated you in the past
PHRV **even ˈout** to become level or steady, usually after varying a lot: *House prices keep rising and falling but they should eventually even out.* **ˌeven sth↔ˈout** to spread things equally over a period of time or among a number of people: *He tried to even out the distribution of work among his employees.* **ˌeven sth↔ˈup** to make a situation or a competition more equal

**ˌeven-ˈhanded** *adj.* completely fair, especially when dealing with different groups of people

**even·ing** ⓘ A1 /ˈiːvnɪŋ/ *noun* **1** ⓘ A1 [C, U] the part of the day between the afternoon and the time you go to bed: *this/yesterday/tomorrow evening* ◇ *Come over on*

Thursday evening. ◊ **in the ~** What do you usually do in the evening? ◊ **for the ~** She's going to her sister's for the evening. ◊ **on the ~ of** on the evening of May 15 ◊ We spent many enjoyable summer evenings together. ◊ The **evening meal** is served at 7 p.m. ⇨ see also GOOD EVENING **2** [C] an event of a particular type happening in the evening: *a musical evening at school* (= when music is performed) ◊ *the school parents' evening* (= when parents are invited to talk to teachers about their children's progress) ▶ **even·ings** *adv.*: *He works evenings.* **IDM** see OTHER

**'evening class** *noun* a course of study for adults in the evening: *an evening class in car maintenance* ◊ *to go to/attend evening classes*

**'evening dress** *noun* **1** [U] smart clothes worn for formal occasions in the evening: *Everyone was in evening dress.* **2** (*also* **'evening gown**) [C] a woman's long formal dress ⇨ picture at GOWN

**'evening 'primrose** *noun* [C, U] a plant with yellow flowers that open in the evening, sometimes used as a medicine

**the 'evening 'star** *noun* [sing.] the planet Venus, when it is seen in the western sky after the sun has set

**even·ly** /'iːvnli/ *adv.* **1** in a smooth, regular or equal way: *Make sure the paint covers the surface evenly.* ◊ *She was fast asleep, breathing evenly.* ◊ *evenly spaced at four cm apart* **2** with equal amounts for each person or in each place: *evenly distributed/divided* ◊ *Incidence of the disease is fairly evenly spread across Europe.* ◊ *The two teams are very evenly matched* (= are equally likely to win). **3** calmly; without showing any emotion: *'I warned you not to phone me,' he said evenly.*

**even 'money** *noun* [U] (*BrE also* **evens** [pl.]) (in betting) ODDS that give an equal chance of winning or losing and that mean a person has the chance of winning the same amount of money that he or she has bet

**even·song** /'iːvnsɒŋ; *NAmE* -sɔːŋ/ *noun* [U] the service of evening prayer in the Anglican Church ⇨ compare MATINS, VESPERS

**event** ❶ 🅰🅱 ⊙ /ɪ'vent/ *noun* **1** 🅰🅱 a thing that happens, especially sth important: *recent/current/world events* ◊ *The tragic events of last Monday occurred only 200 metres from the shore.* ◊ *a dramatic turn of events* (= change in what is happening) ◊ *a sequence/chain/series of events* ◊ *Why should we believe his version of events* (= description of what happened from his point of view)? ◊ *The decisions we take now may influence the course of events* (= the way things happen) *in the future.* ◊ *In the normal course of events* (= if things had happened as expected) *she would have gone with him.* **2** 🅰🅱 a planned public or social occasion: *Is the city ready to host such a major sporting event?* ◊ *The hospital is organizing a special fundraising event.* ⇨ see also NON-EVENT **3** one of the races or competitions in a sports programme: *The 800 metres is the fourth event of the afternoon.* ⇨ see also FIELD EVENT, TRACK EVENT

**IDM** **after the e'vent** (*BrE*) after sth has happened: *I knew nothing about it until after the event.* **in 'any event | at 'all events** used to emphasize or show that sth is true or will happen despite other circumstances **SYN** **in any case**: *I think she'll agree to do it but in any event, all she can say is 'no'.* **in the e'vent** when the situation actually happened: *I got very nervous about the exam, but in the event, I needn't have worried; it was really easy.* **in the event of sth** | **in the event that sth happens** if sth happens: *In the event of an accident, call this number.* ◊ *Sheila will inherit everything in the event of his death.* **in 'that event** if that happens: *In that event, we will have to reconsider our offer.* ⇨ more at HAPPY, WISE *adj.*

**even-'tempered** *adj.* not easily made angry or upset

**event·ful** /ɪ'ventfl/ *adj.* full of things that happen, especially exciting, important or dangerous things: *an eventful day/life/journey*

**event·ing** /ɪ'ventɪŋ/ *noun* (*also* **three-day e'venting**) *noun* [U] the sport of taking part in competitions riding horses. These are often held over three days and include riding across country, jumping and DRESSAGE.

**even·tual** /ɪ'ventʃuəl/ *adj.* [only before noun] happening at the end of a period of time or of a process: *the eventual winner of the tournament* ◊ *It is impossible to predict what the eventual outcome will be.* ◊ *The village school may face eventual closure.*

**even·tu·al·ity** /ɪˌventʃu'æləti/ *noun* (*pl.* **-ies**) (*formal*) something that may possibly happen, especially sth unpleasant: *We were prepared for every eventuality.* ◊ *The money had been saved for just such an eventuality.*

**even·tu·al·ly** ❶ 🅱🅸 /ɪ'ventʃuəli/ *adv.* at the end of a period of time or a series of events: *Our flight eventually left five hours late.* ◊ *I'll get round to mending it eventually.* ◊ *She hopes eventually to attend medical school and become a doctor.* **HELP** Use **finally** for the last in a list of things: *Finally, I'd like to thank my parents …* ◊ ⊘*Eventually, I'd like to thank my parents …*

**even·tu·ate** /ɪ'ventʃueɪt/ *verb* [I] (*formal*) to happen as a result of sth

**ever** ❶ 🅰🅱 /'evə(r)/ *adv.* **1** 🅰🅱 used in negative sentences and questions, or sentences with *if* to mean 'at any time': *Nothing ever happens here.* ◊ *Don't you ever get tired?* ◊ *If you're ever in Miami, come and see us.* ◊ '*Have you ever been to Rome?' 'Yes, I have, actually. Not long ago.'* ◊ *'Have you ever thought of changing your job?' 'No, never/No I haven't.'* ◊ *She hardly ever* (= almost never) *goes out.* ◊ *We see them very seldom, if ever.* ◊ (*informal*) *I'll never ever do that again!* ◊ *I'm never speaking to you ever again!* **2** 🅱🅸 used for emphasis when you are comparing things: *It was raining harder than ever.* ◊ *Consumers today have more choices than ever before.* ◊ *It's my best-ever score.* ◊ *It's the worst film I've ever seen.* ⇨ see also FIRST-EVER **3** (*rather formal*) all the time or every time; always: *Paul, ever the optimist, agreed to try again.* ◊ *She married the prince and they lived happily ever after.* ◊ *He said he would love her for ever (and ever).* ◊ *Their debts grew ever larger* (= kept increasing). ◊ *the ever-growing problem* ◊ *an ever-present danger* ⇨ see also FOREVER **4** used after *when, why,* etc. to show that you are surprised or shocked: *Why ever did you agree?*

**IDM** **all sb ever does is …** used to emphasize that sb does the same thing very often, usually in an annoying way: *All he ever does is grumble about things.* **did you 'ever ( …)!** (*old-fashioned, informal*) used to show that you are surprised or shocked: *Did you ever hear anything like it?* **ever since ( …)** 🅱🅸 continuously since the time mentioned: *He's had a car ever since he was 18.* ◊ *I was bitten by a dog once and I've been afraid of them ever since.* **'ever so | 'ever such a** (*informal, especially BrE*) very; really: *He looks ever so smart.* ◊ *She's ever such a nice woman.* ◊ *It's ever so easy.* **if ever there 'was (one)** (*informal*) used to emphasize that sth is certainly true: *That was a disaster if ever there was one!* **was/is/does, etc. sb 'ever!** (*informal, especially NAmE*) used to emphasize sth you are talking about: *'You must have been upset by that.' 'Was I ever!'* **yours 'ever/ever 'yours** sometimes used at the end of an informal letter, before you write your name

**ever·green** /'evəɡriːn; *NAmE* 'evərɡ-/ *noun* a tree or bush that has green leaves all through the year ⇨ compare CONIFER, DECIDUOUS ⇨ VISUAL VOCAB page V6 ▶ **ever·green** *adj.* [usually before noun]: *evergreen shrubs* ◊ (*figurative*) *a new production of Rossini's evergreen* (= always popular) *opera*

**ever·last·ing** /ˌevə'lɑːstɪŋ; *NAmE* ˌevər'læs-/ *adj.* **1** continuing forever; never changing **SYN** **eternal**: *everlasting life/love* ◊ *an everlasting memory of her smile* ◊ *To his everlasting credit, he never told anyone what I'd done.* **2** (*disapproving*) continuing too long; repeated too often **SYN** **constant, interminable, never-ending**: *I'm tired of your everlasting complaints.* ▶ **ever·last·ing·ly** *adv.*

**ever·more** /ˌevə'mɔː(r); *NAmE* ˌevər'm-/ (*also* **for ever 'more**) *adv.* (*literary*) always

**every** ❶ 🅰🅱 /'evri/ *det.* **1** 🅰🅱 used with singular nouns to refer to all the members of a group of things or people: *She knows every student in the school.* ◊ *I could hear every word they said.* ◊ *We enjoyed every minute of our stay.* ◊ *I go to the gym every day.* ◊ *I get that wrong every single time.* ◊ *I read every last article in the newspaper* (= all of them). ◊ *They were watching her every movement.* ◊ *Every one of their songs has been a hit.* ⇨ note at EACH **2** 🅱🅸 used to say how often sth happens or is done: *The buses go every 10 minutes.* ◊ *We had to stop*

# everybody

*every few miles.* ◊ *One in every three marriages ends in divorce.* ◊ *He has every third day off* (= he works for two days, then has one day off, then works for two days and so on). ◊ *We see each other every now and again.* ◊ *Every now and then he regretted his decision.* **3** all possible: *We wish you every success.* ◊ *He had every reason to be angry.*
**IDM** **every other** each ALTERNATE one (= the first, third, fifth, etc. one, but not the second, fourth, sixth, etc.): *They visit us every other week.* ⊃ more at EACH

**eve·ry·body** ⓘ **A1** /ˈevribɒdi; NAmE -baːdi, -bʌdi/ *pron.* = EVERYONE: *Everybody knows Tom.* ◊ *Have you asked everybody?* ◊ *Didn't you like it? Everybody else did.* ⊃ compare ANYBODY, NOBODY, SOMEBODY

**eve·ry·day** ⓘ **A2** /ˈevrideɪ/ *adj.* [only before noun] used or happening every day or regularly; ordinary: *everyday objects* ◊ *Change is a part of everyday life in business.*

**Every·man** (also **everyman**) /ˈevrimæn/ *noun* [sing.] an ordinary or typical person: *a story of Everyman*

**eve·ry·one** ⓘ **A1** /ˈevriwʌn/ (also **every·body**) *pron.* every person; all people: *Everyone cheered and clapped.* ◊ *Everyone has a chance to win.* ◊ *Everyone brought their partner to the party.* ◊ (*formal*) *Everyone brought his or her partner to the party.* ◊ *The police questioned everyone in the room.* ◊ *The teacher commented on everyone's work.* ◊ *Everyone else was there.*

**eve·ry·place** /ˈevripleɪs/ *adv.* (*NAmE*) = EVERYWHERE

**eve·ry·thing** ⓘ **A1** /ˈevriθɪŋ/ *pron.* (with a singular verb) **1** ⓘ **A1** all things: *Everything had gone.* ◊ *When we confronted him, he denied everything.* ◊ *Take this bag, and leave everything else to me.* ◊ *She seemed to have everything—looks, money, intelligence.* **2** ⓘ **A2** the situation now; life generally: *Everything in the capital is now quiet.* ◊ *'How's everything with you?' 'Fine, thanks.'* **3** ⓘ **B1** the most important thing: *Money isn't everything.* ◊ *My family means everything to me.*
**IDM** **and everything** (*informal*) and so on; and other similar things: *Have you got his name and address and everything?* ◊ *She told me about the baby and everything.*

**eve·ry·where** ⓘ **A2** /ˈevriweə(r); NAmE -wer/ (*NAmE also* **every·place**) *adv., pron., conj.* in, to or at every place; all places: *I've looked everywhere.* ◊ *He follows me everywhere.* ◊ *We'll have to eat here—everywhere else is full.* ◊ *Everywhere we went was full of tourists.*

**'eve-teasing** *noun* (*IndE*) physical contact, comments about sex, etc. by a man to a woman in a public place, that the woman finds annoying and offensive ⊃ compare SEXUAL HARASSMENT ▶ **'eve-teaser** *noun*

**evict** /ɪˈvɪkt/ *verb* ~ **sb** (**from sth**) to force sb to leave a house or land, especially when you have the legal right to do so: *A number of tenants have been evicted for not paying the rent.* ▶ **evic·tion** /ɪˈvɪkʃn/ *noun* [U, C]: *to face eviction from your home*

**evi·dence** ⓘ **A2** ⓞ /ˈevɪdəns/ *noun, verb*
■ *noun* **1** ⓘ **A2** [U] the facts, signs or objects that make you believe that sth is true: **~ (of sth)** *Researchers have found clear scientific evidence of a link between exposure to sun and skin cancer.* ◊ **~ for sth** *There is a growing body of evidence for the existence of black holes that are ten times as massive as the Sun.* ◊ **~ that ...** *There is not a shred of evidence that the meeting actually took place.* ◊ **~ to suggest, support, show, etc.** *Have you any evidence to support this allegation?* ◊ *The study provides empirical evidence* (= based on experiments or experience) *to prove that the drug has no long-term side effects.* ◊ *Anecdotal evidence* (= based on personal accounts) *suggests that drivers over the age of 70 find it difficult to get insurance.* ◊ **on the ~ of sth** *On the evidence of their recent matches, it is unlikely the Spanish team will win.* **HELP** *In general English,* **evidence** *is always uncountable. However, in academic English the plural* **evidences** *is sometimes used:* (*specialist*) *The cave contained evidences of prehistoric settlement.* ⊃ WORDFINDER NOTE at SCIENCE **2** ⓘ **B2** [U] the information that is used in court to try to prove sth: *I was asked to give evidence* (= to say what I knew, describe what I had seen, etc.) *at the trial.* ◊ *The defence accused the prosecution of withholding several key pieces of evidence.* ◊ **circumstantial/forensic evidence** ◊ **~ against sb** *Despite a lack of evidence against him, Burton will appear in court next week.* ◊ **as ~ of sth** *The emails were presented as evidence of his involvement in the fraud.* ⊃ WORDFINDER NOTE at TRIAL ⊃ see also CIRCUMSTANTIAL, KING'S EVIDENCE, QUEEN'S EVIDENCE, STATE'S EVIDENCE
**IDM** **(be) in 'evidence** (to be) present and clearly seen: *The police were much in evidence at today's demonstration.* ⊃ more at BALANCE *n.*
■ *verb* [usually passive] (*formal*) to prove or show sth; to be evidence of sth: **as evidenced by sth** *The legal profession is still a largely male world, as evidenced by the small number of women judges.* ◊ **be evidenced in sth** *The scale of the problem is not evidenced in police statistics.*

> ▼ **LANGUAGE BANK**
>
> **evidence**
> Giving proof
>
> - There is clear **evidence that** TV advertising influences what children buy.
> - **It is clear** from numerous studies **that** TV advertising influences what children buy.
> - Recent research **demonstrates** that TV advertising influences children's spending habits.
> - Many parents think that TV advertising influences their children. This view **is supported by** the findings of a recent study, which **show** a clear link between television advertisements and children's spending habits.
> - The findings also **reveal** that most children are unaware of the persuasive purpose of advertising.
> - There is little **evidence that** children understand the persuasive intent of advertising.
> - The results **contradict** claims that advertising is unrelated to children's spending habits.
> - Manufacturers argue that it is difficult to **prove** that advertising alone influences what children buy.
>
> ⊃ LANGUAGE BANK at ARGUE, E.G., ILLUSTRATE

**evi·dent** ⓡ **B2 W** /ˈevɪdənt/ *adj.* clear; easily seen **SYN** **obvious**: *The orchestra played with evident enjoyment.* ◊ **~ (to sb) (that ...)** *It has now become evident to us that a mistake has been made.* ◊ **~ in/from sth** *The growing interest in history is clearly evident in the number of people visiting museums and country houses.* ⊃ SYNONYMS at CLEAR ⊃ see also SELF-EVIDENT

**evi·den·tial** /ˌevɪˈdenʃl/ *adj.* [usually before noun] (*formal*) providing or connected with evidence: *The necessary evidential basis for her claim is lacking.*

**evi·dent·ly** /ˈevɪdəntli/ *adv.* **1** clearly; that can be seen or understood easily **SYN** **obviously**: *She walked slowly down the road, evidently in pain.* ◊ *'I'm afraid I couldn't finish the work last night.' 'Evidently not.'* ⊃ see also SELF-EVIDENTLY **2** according to what people say **SYN** **apparently**: *Evidently, she had nothing to do with the whole affair.*

**evil** ⓘ **B2** /ˈiːvl; BrE also -vɪl/ *adj., noun*
■ *adj.* **1** ⓘ **B2** (of people) enjoying harming others; morally bad and cruel: *an evil man* ◊ *an evil grin* **2** ⓘ **B2** having a harmful effect on people; morally bad: *evil deeds* ◊ *the evil effects of racism* **3** ⓘ **B2** connected with the DEVIL and with what is bad in the world: *evil spirits* **4** extremely unpleasant: *an evil smell*
**IDM** **the evil 'hour/'day** (*often humorous*) the time when you have to do sth difficult or unpleasant ⊃ more at BREW *n.*, GENIUS
■ *noun* (*formal*) **1** ⓘ **B2** [U] a force that causes bad things to happen; morally bad behaviour: *the eternal struggle between good and evil* ◊ *the forces of evil* ◊ *He was a good man who was forced to do evil.* **OPP** **good 2** [C, usually pl.] a bad or harmful thing; the bad effect of sth: *the evils of drugs/alcohol* ◊ *social evils* **IDM** see LESSER, NECESSARY

**'evil-doer** *noun* (*formal*) a person who does very bad things

**the ˌevil 'eye** *noun* [sing.] the magic power to harm sb by looking at them

**evil·ly** /ˈiːvəli/ *adv.* in a morally bad or very unpleasant way: *to grin evilly* ◊ *to look evilly at sb*

**evince** /ɪˈvɪns/ verb ~ sth (formal) to show clearly that you have a feeling or quality: *He evinced a strong desire to be reconciled with his family.*

**evis·cer·ate** /ɪˈvɪsəreɪt/ verb ~ sth (formal) to remove the inner organs of a body SYN **disembowel**

**evoca·tive** /ɪˈvɒkətɪv; NAmE ɪˈvɑːk-/ adj. (approving) making you think of or remember a strong image or feeling, in a pleasant way: *evocative smells/sounds/music* ◇ ~ **of sth** *Her new book is wonderfully evocative of village life.* ▶ **evoca·tive·ly** adv.

**evoke** ?+ C1 /ɪˈvəʊk/ verb ~ sth (formal) to bring a feeling, a memory or an image into your mind: *The music evoked memories of her youth.* ◇ *His case is unlikely to evoke public sympathy.* ▶ **evo·ca·tion** /ˌiːvəʊˈkeɪʃn/ noun [C, U]: *a brilliant evocation of childhood in the 1940s*

**evo·lu·tion** ?+ B2 W /ˌiːvəˈluːʃn, ˌev-; NAmE ˌev-/ noun **1** ?+ B2 [U] (biology) the slow steady development of plants, animals, etc. during the history of the earth, as they adapt to changes in their environment: *the evolution of the human species* ◇ *Darwin's theory of evolution* **2** ?+ B2 [U, C] the slow steady development of sth: *In politics Britain has preferred evolution to revolution* (= slow steady development to sudden violent change) ◇ *cultural trends and evolutions*

**evo·lu·tion·ary** ?+ C1 W /ˌiːvəˈluːʃənri, ˌev-; NAmE ˌevəˈluːʃəneri/ adj. connected with evolution; connected with slow steady development and change: *evolutionary theory* ◇ *evolutionary change* ▶ **evo·lu·tion·ar·ily** /ˌiːvəˈluːʃənərəli, ˌev-; NAmE ˌevəˌluːʃəˈnerɪli/ adv.

**evo·lu·tion·ist** /ˌiːvəˈluːʃənɪst, ˌev-; NAmE ˌev-/ noun, adj.
■ noun a person who believes in the theories of EVOLUTION and NATURAL SELECTION
■ adj. relating to the theories of EVOLUTION and NATURAL SELECTION ▶ **evo·lu·tion·ism** noun [U]

**evolve** ?+ B2 W /ɪˈvɒlv; NAmE ɪˈvɑːlv/ verb **1** ?+ B2 [I, T] to develop gradually, especially from a simple to a more complicated form; to develop sth in this way: ~ **(from sth) (into sth)** *The idea evolved from a drawing I discovered in the attic.* ◇ *The company has evolved into a major chemical manufacturer.* ◇ ~ **sth (from sth)** *Each school must evolve its own way of working.* **2** ?+ B2 [I, T] (biology) (of plants, animals, etc.) to develop over time, often many generations, into forms that are better adapted to survive changes in their environment: ~ **(from sth)** *The three species evolved from a single ancestor.* ◇ ~ **sth** *The dolphin has evolved a highly developed jaw.*

**ewe** /juː/ noun a female sheep ⊃ compare RAM

**eww** (also **ew**) /ˈiːuː/ exclamation the way of writing the sound that people make when they think that sth is horrible or unpleasant: *Eww! There's a fly in my lemonade!*

**ex** /eks/ noun, prep.
■ noun (pl. **exes**) (informal) a person's former wife, husband or partner: *The children are spending the weekend with my ex and his new wife.*
■ prep. (BrE) not including sth: *The price is £1500 ex VAT.*

**ex-** /eks/ prefix **1** (in nouns) former: *ex-wife* ◇ *ex-president* **2** out: *exodus* ◇ *export*

**ex·acer·bate** /ɪɡˈzæsəbeɪt; NAmE -sərb-/ verb ~ **sth** (formal) to make sth worse, especially a disease or problem SYN **aggravate**: *The symptoms may be exacerbated by certain drugs.* ▶ **ex·acer·ba·tion** /ɪɡˌzæsəˈbeɪʃn; NAmE -sər-/ noun [U, C]

**exact** ⓞ A2 /ɪɡˈzækt/ adj., verb
■ adj. **1** ?+ A2 correct in every detail SYN **precise**: *The new palace is an exact replica of the original building.* ◇ *The model is exact in every detail.* ◇ *For now they are keeping the exact date and location of the wedding a secret.* ◇ *The exact nature of her illness* (= precisely what her illness is) *has not been made public.* ◇ *Her second husband was the exact opposite of her first* (= completely different). ◇ *The colours were an almost exact match.* ◇ *She's in her mid-thirties—thirty-six to be exact.* ◇ (informal) *I had the exact same problem as you when I first started.* **2** (of people) very accurate and careful about details SYN **meticulous**, **precise 3** (of a science) using accurate measurements and following set rules SYN **precise**: *Assessing insurance risk can never be an exact science.* ▶ **exact·ness** noun [U]

■ verb (formal) **1** ~ **sth (from sb)** to demand and get sth from sb: *She was determined to exact a promise from him.* **2** to make sth bad happen to sb: ~ **sth** *He exacted* (= took) *a terrible revenge for their treatment of him.* ◇ ~ **sth from sb** *Stress can exact a high price from workers* (= can affect them badly). ▶ **exac·tion** /-ˈzækʃn/ noun [C, U] (formal)

**exact·ing** /ɪɡˈzæktɪŋ/ adj. needing or demanding a lot of effort and care about details SYN **demanding**: *exacting work* ◇ *products designed to meet the exacting standards of today's marketplace* ◇ *He was an exacting man to work for.*

**exac·ti·tude** /ɪɡˈzæktɪtjuːd; NAmE -tuːd/ noun [U] (formal) the quality of being very accurate and exact

**exact·ly** ⓞ A2 ⓢ /ɪɡˈzæktli/ adv. **1** ?+ A2 used to emphasize that sth is correct in every way or in every detail SYN **precisely**: *It's exactly nine o'clock.* ◇ *It happened almost exactly a year ago.* ◇ *Your answer is exactly right.* ◇ *It was a warm day, if not exactly hot.* ◇ ~ **how, what, why, etc …** *I know exactly how she felt.* ◇ ~ **as …** *Do exactly as I tell you.* ◇ *You haven't changed at all—you still look exactly the same.* ◇ *His words had exactly the opposite effect.* **2** ?+ A2 (informal) used to ask for more information about sth: *Where exactly did you stay in France?* ◇ (disapproving) *Exactly what are you trying to tell me?* **3** ?+ B1 used as a reply, agreeing with what sb has just said, or emphasizing that it is correct: *'You mean somebody in this room must be the murderer!' 'Exactly.'*
IDM **not exactly** (informal) **1** used when you are saying the opposite of what you really mean: *He wasn't exactly pleased to see us—in fact he refused to open the door.* ◇ *It's not exactly beautiful, is it?* (= it's ugly) **2** used when you are correcting sth that sb has said: *'So he told you you'd got the job?' 'Not exactly, but he said they were impressed with me.'*

**ex·ag·ger·ate** ?+ C1 /ɪɡˈzædʒəreɪt/ verb [I, T] to make sth seem larger, better, worse or more important than it really is: *The hotel was really filthy and I'm not exaggerating.* ◇ ~ **sth** *He tends to exaggerate the difficulties.* ◇ *I'm sure he exaggerates his Irish accent* (= tries to sound more Irish than he really is). ◇ *Demand for the product has been greatly exaggerated.*

**ex·ag·ger·ated** /ɪɡˈzædʒəreɪtɪd/ adj. **1** made to seem larger, better, worse or more important than it really is or needs to be: *to make greatly/grossly/wildly exaggerated claims* ◇ *She has an exaggerated sense of her own importance.* **2** (of an action) done in a way that makes people notice it: *He looked at me with exaggerated surprise.* ▶ **ex·ag·ger·ated·ly** adv.

**ex·ag·ger·ation** /ɪɡˌzædʒəˈreɪʃn/ noun [C, usually sing., U] a statement or description that makes sth seem larger, better, worse or more important than it really is; the act of making a statement like this: *a slight/gross/wild exaggeration* ◇ *It would be an exaggeration to say I knew her well—I only met her twice.* ◇ *It's no exaggeration to say that most students have never read a complete Shakespeare play.* ◇ *He told his story simply and without exaggeration.*

**exalt** /ɪɡˈzɔːlt/ verb (formal) **1** ~ **sb (to sth)** to make sb rise to a higher rank or position, sometimes to one that they do not deserve **2** ~ **sb/sth** to praise sb/sth very much

**exalt·ation** /ˌeɡzɔːlˈteɪʃn/ noun [U] (formal) **1** a feeling of very great joy or happiness **2** an act of raising sth/sb to a high position or rank: *the exaltation of emotion above logical reasoning*

**exalt·ed** /ɪɡˈzɔːltɪd/ adj. **1** (formal or humorous) of high rank, position or great importance: *She was the only woman to rise to such an exalted position.* ◇ *You're moving in very exalted circles!* **2** (formal) full of great joy and happiness: *I felt exalted and newly alive.*

**exam** ⓞ A1 ⓢ /ɪɡˈzæm/ (also formal **exam·in·ation**) noun **1** ?+ A1 a formal written, spoken or practical test, especially at school or college, to see how much you know about a subject, or what you can do: *to take an exam* ◇ *to pass/fail an exam* ◇ (BrE) *I hate doing exams.* ◇ (BrE, formal) *to sit an exam* ◇ (BrE) *to mark an exam* ◇ (NAmE) *to grade an exam* ◇ ~ **in sth** *Every term we would have exams in maths,*

# examination

*English, French, etc.* ◊ **in an ~** (*BrE*) *She did well in her exams.* ◊ **on an ~** (*NAmE*) *She did well on her exams.* ◊ *an exam paper* ◊ *I got my exam results today.* **HELP** Use: *take/do/sit an exam* not: *write an exam*. ⊃ see also EXIT EXAM
⊃ WORDFINDER NOTE at STUDY

**WORDFINDER** candidate, grade, invigilate, mark, oral, paper, practical, resit, revise

**2** (*NAmE*) a medical test of a particular part of the body: *an eye exam*

▼ **MORE ABOUT ...**

**exams**
- **Exam** is the usual word for a written, spoken or practical test at school or college, especially an important one that you need to do in order to get a qualification. **Examination** is a very formal word. A **test** is something that students might be given in addition to, or sometimes instead of, regular exams, to see how much they have learned. A very short informal test is called a **quiz** in *NAmE*. **Quiz** in both *NAmE* and *BrE* also means a contest in which people try to answer questions: *a trivia quiz* ◊ *a quiz show*.

**ex·am·in·a·tion** 🔊 B2 W /ɪɡˌzæmɪˈneɪʃn/ *noun*
**1** B2 [C] (*formal*) = EXAM: *successful candidates in GCSE examinations* ◊ **~ in sth** *to sit an examination in mathematics* ◊ **~ for sth** *In 1864 he passed the examination for the Indian Civil Service.* **HELP** Use: *take/do/sit an examination* not: *write an examination*. **2** B2 [U, C] the act of looking at or considering sth very carefully: *Careful examination of the ruins revealed an even earlier temple.* ◊ *The issue needs further examination.* ◊ **after (an) ~** *After a thorough examination, they announced that the suspicious device was harmless.* ◊ **on ~** *On closer examination it was found that the signature was not genuine.* ◊ **under ~** *Your proposals are still under examination.* **3** B2 [C, U] a close look at sth/sb, especially to see if there is anything wrong or to find the cause of a problem: *a medical/physical examination* ◊ *Regular breast examination is advised.* ◊ *A specialist should carry out an examination of the patient.*
⊃ see also CROSS-EXAMINATION, RE-EXAMINATION, SELF-EXAMINATION

**ex·am·ine** 🔊 B1 W /ɪɡˈzæmɪn/ *verb* **1** B1 to consider or study an idea, a subject, etc. very carefully: **~ sth** *This study sets out to examine in detail the possible effects of climate change.* ◊ *Her new show critically examines the relationship between the arts and popular culture.* ◊ *This important issue must be carefully examined.* ◊ **~ how, what, etc ...** *It is necessary to examine how the proposals can be carried out.* ⊃ see also RE-EXAMINE ⊃ LANGUAGE BANK at ABOUT **2** B1 to look at sb/sth closely, to see if there is anything wrong or to find the cause of a problem: **~ sb/sth** *The doctor examined her carefully but could find nothing wrong.* ◊ **~ yourself** *She examined herself closely in the mirror.* ◊ **~ sth/sb for sth** *The samples were examined under the microscope for the presence of damaged cells.* ⊃ WORDFINDER NOTE at DOCTOR ⊃ SYNONYMS at CHECK

**WORDFINDER** biopsy, diagnose, sample, scan, swab, symptom, test, ultrasound, X-ray

**3** [usually passive] (*formal*) to give sb a test to see how much they know about a subject or what they can do: **be examined (in sth)** *The students will be examined in all subjects at the end of term.* ◊ **be examined on sth** *You are only being examined on this semester's work.* **4 ~ sb** (*law*) to ask sb questions formally, especially in court ⊃ see also CROSS-EXAMINE **IDM** see NEED *v.*

**ex·am·in·ee** /ɪɡˌzæmɪˈniː/ *noun* a person who is being tested to see how much they know about a subject or what they can do; a person who is taking an exam

**ex·am·in·er** /ɪɡˈzæmɪnə(r)/ *noun* **1** a person who writes the questions for, or marks, a test of knowledge or ability: *The papers are sent to external examiners* (= ones not connected with the students' school or college). **2** (*especially NAmE*) a person who has the official duty to check that things are being done correctly and according to the rules of an organization; a person who officially examines sth ⊃ see also MEDICAL EXAMINER

▼ **SYNONYMS**

**examine**
analyse • review • study • discuss

These words all mean to think about, study or describe sb/sth carefully, especially in order to understand them, form an opinion of them or make a decision about them.

**examine** to think about, study or describe an idea, subject or piece of work very carefully: *These ideas will be examined in more detail in Chapter 10.*

**analyse/analyze** to examine the nature or structure of sth, especially by separating it into its parts, in order to understand or explain it: *The job involves gathering and analysing data.* ◊ *He tried to analyse his feelings.*

**review** to examine sth again, especially so that you can decide if it is necessary to make changes: *The government will review the situation later in the year.*

**study** to examine sb/sth in order to understand them or it: *We will study the report carefully before making a decision.*

**EXAMINE OR STUDY?**
You **examine** sth in order to understand it or to help other people understand it, for example by describing it in a book; you **study** sth in order to understand it yourself.

**discuss** to write or talk about sth in detail, showing the different ideas and opinions about it: *This topic will be discussed at greater length in the next chapter.*

**PATTERNS**
- to examine/analyse/review/study/discuss **what/how/whether ...**
- to examine/analyse/review/study/discuss the **situation/evidence**
- to examine/analyse/review/study/discuss sth **carefully/critically/systematically/briefly**

**ex·am·ple** 🔊 A1 🔊 /ɪɡˈzɑːmpl; *NAmE* -ˈzæm-/ *noun*
**1** A1 something such as an object, a fact or a situation that shows, explains or supports what you say: *Let me give you an example.* ◊ *It is important to cite examples to support your argument.* ◊ *to provide/offer an example* ◊ **~ of sth** *Can you show me an example of what you mean?* ◊ *The progress the students have made serves as an example of the benefit of small class sizes.* ◊ *By way of example, we'll look at our most recent advertising campaign.* ⊃ LANGUAGE BANK at E.G. ⊃ WORDFINDER NOTE at DICTIONARY **2** A1 **~ (of sth)** a thing that is typical of or represents a particular group or set: *This is a good example of the artist's early work.* ◊ *It is a perfect example of this type of architecture.* ◊ *Japan is often quoted as the prime example of a modern industrial nation.* ◊ *It is a classic example of how not to design a new city centre.* **3** B1 a person or their behaviour that is thought to be a good model for others to copy: **~ to sb** *Her courage is an example to us all.* ◊ **~ for sb** *He sets an example for the other students.* ◊ **~ of sth** *She is a shining example of what people with disabilities can achieve.* ◊ **by ~** *He is a captain who leads by example.* **4** a person's behaviour, either good or bad, that other people copy: *It would be a mistake to follow his example.*
**IDM** **for example** A1 (*abbr.* **e.g.**) used to emphasize sth that explains or supports what you are saying; used to give an example of what you are saying: *There is a similar word in many languages, for example in French and Italian.* ◊ *The report is incomplete; it does not include sales in France, for example.* ◊ *It is possible to combine computer science with other subjects, for example physics.* ⊃ LANGUAGE BANK at E.G. **make an example of sb** to punish sb as a warning to others not to do the same thing

**ex·as·per·ate** /ɪɡˈzæspəreɪt; *BrE also* -ˈzɑːs-/ *verb* **~ sb** to annoy sb very much **SYN** **infuriate** ▶ **ex·as·per·ation** /ɪɡˌzæspəˈreɪʃn; *BrE also* -ˌzɑːs-/ *noun* [U]: *a groan/look/sigh of exasperation* ◊ **in ~** *He shook his head in exasperation.*

**ex·as·per·ated** /ɪɡˈzæspəreɪtɪd; *BrE also* -ˈzɑːs-/ *adj.* extremely annoyed, especially if you cannot do anything

▼ SYNONYMS

## example
case • instance • specimen • illustration

These are all words for a thing or situation that is typical of a particular group or set, and is sometimes used to support an argument.

**example** something such as an object, a fact or a situation that shows, explains or supports what you say; a thing that is typical of or represents a particular group or set: *Can you give me an example of what you mean?*

**case** a particular situation or a situation of a particular type; a situation that relates to a particular person or thing: *In some cases people have had to wait several weeks for an appointment.*

**instance** (*rather formal*) a particular situation or a situation of a particular type: *The report highlights a number of instances of injustice.*

**specimen** an example of sth, especially an animal or plant: *The aquarium has some interesting specimens of unusual tropical fish.*

**illustration** (*rather formal*) a story, an event or an example that clearly shows the truth about sth: *The statistics are a clear illustration of the point I am trying to make.*

### EXAMPLE OR ILLUSTRATION?
- An **illustration** is often used to show that sth is true. An **example** is used to help to explain sth.

### PATTERNS
- a(n) example/case/instance/specimen/illustration **of** sth
- **in** a particular case/instance
- **for** example/instance

---

to improve the situation ⓢⓨⓝ **infuriate**: *'Why won't you answer me?' he asked in an exasperated voice.* ◇ *She was becoming exasperated with all the questions they were asking.* ▶ **ex·as·per·at·ed·ly** *adv.*

**ex·as·per·at·ing** /ɪɡˈzæspəreɪtɪŋ; *BrE also* -ˈzɑːs-/ *adj.* extremely annoying ⓢⓨⓝ **infuriating**

**ex·cav·ate** /ˈekskəveɪt/ *verb* **1** to dig in the ground to look for old buildings or objects that have been buried for a long time; to find sth by digging in this way: *~ sth The site has been excavated by archaeologists.* ◇ *~ sth from sth pottery and weapons excavated from the burial site* **2** *~ sth* (*formal*) to make a hole, etc. in the ground by digging: *The body was discovered when builders excavated the area.*

**ex·cav·ation** /ˌekskəˈveɪʃn/ *noun* **1** [C, U] the activity of digging in the ground to look for old buildings or objects that have been buried for a long time **2** [C, usually pl.] a place where people are digging to look for old buildings or objects: *The excavations are open to the public.* **3** [U] the act of digging, especially with a machine

**ex·cav·ator** /ˈekskəveɪtə(r)/ *noun* **1** a large machine that is used for digging and moving earth **2** a person who digs in the ground to look for old buildings and objects

**ex·ceed** 🅱️2 🆆 /ɪkˈsiːd/ *verb* (*formal*) **1** 🅱️2 *~ sth* to be greater than a particular number or amount: *The price will not exceed £100.* **2** *~ sth* to do more than the law or an order, etc. allows you to do: *She was exceeding the speed limit (= driving faster than is allowed).* ◇ *The officers had exceeded their authority.* ➔ see also **EXCESS** **3** 🅲1 *~ expectations* to be better than expected ⓢⓨⓝ **surpass**: *His achievements have exceeded expectations.*

**ex·ceed·ing·ly** /ɪkˈsiːdɪŋli/ *adv.* (*formal, becoming old-fashioned*) extremely; very; very much ⓢⓨⓝ **exceptionally**

**excel** /ɪkˈsel/ *verb* (**-ll-**) **1** [I] to be very good at doing sth: *~ (in/at sth) She has always excelled in foreign languages.* ◇ *As a child he excelled at music and art.* ◇ *~ (at doing sth) The team excels at turning defence into attack.* **2** [T] *~ yourself* (*BrE*) to do extremely well and even better than you usually do: *Rick's cooking was always good, but this time he really excelled himself.*

---

535

# exception

**ex·cel·lence** 🅲1 /ˈeksələns/ *noun* [U] the quality of being extremely good: *a reputation for academic excellence* ◇ *~ in sth The hospital is recognized as a centre of excellence in research and teaching.* ➔ see also **PAR EXCELLENCE**

**Ex·cel·lency** /ˈeksələnsi/ *noun* **His/Her/Your Excellency** (*pl.* **-ies**) a title used when talking to or about sb who has a very important official position, especially an AMBASSADOR: *Good evening, your Excellency.* ◇ *their Excellencies the French and Spanish Ambassadors*

**ex·cel·lent** 🅰️2 /ˈeksələnt/ *adj.* **1** 🅰️2 extremely good: *an excellent book/article* ◇ *excellent results/work* ◇ *Both the food and the service were truly excellent.* ◇ *She has done an excellent job of adapting the novel for the screen.* ◇ *The apartment is in excellent condition and is ready to move into.* ◇ *~ at (doing) sth Our staff are excellent at advising small businesses.* ◇ *~ for (doing) sth The experience was excellent for students' self-confidence.* **2** 🅰️2 used to show that you are very pleased about sth or that you approve of sth: *You can all come? Excellent!* ▶ **ex·cel·lent·ly** *adv.*

▼ SYNONYMS

## excellent
outstanding • perfect • superb

These words all describe sth that is extremely good.

**excellent** extremely good. 🅽🅾🆃🅴 **Excellent** is used especially about standards of service or of sth that sb has worked to produce: *The rooms are excellent value at $20 a night.* ◇ *He speaks excellent English.* 🅽🅾🆃🅴 **Excellent** is also used to show that you are very pleased about sth or that you approve of sth: *You can all come? Excellent!*

**outstanding** extremely good. 🅽🅾🆃🅴 **Outstanding** is used especially about how well sb does sth or how good sb is at sth: *an outstanding achievement*

**perfect** so good that it could not be better. 🅽🅾🆃🅴 **Perfect** is used especially about conditions or how suitable sth is for a purpose: *Conditions were perfect for walking.* ◇ *She came up with the perfect excuse.*

**superb** (*informal*) extremely good or impressive: *The facilities at the hotel are superb.*

### PATTERNS
- a(n) excellent/outstanding/perfect/superb **job/performance**
- a(n) excellent/outstanding/superb **achievement**
- **really/absolutely/quite** excellent/outstanding/perfect/superb

---

**ex·cept** 🅰️2 /ɪkˈsept/ *prep., conj., verb*

■ *prep.* 🅰️2 (*also* **ex'cept for**) used before you mention the only thing or person about which a statement is not true ⓢⓨⓝ **apart from**: *We work every day except Sunday.* ◇ *They all came except Matt.* ◇ *I had nothing on except for my socks.* ➔ **LANGUAGE BANK** on page 536 ➔ note at **BESIDES**

■ *conj.* 🅱️1 *~ (that)...* used before you mention sth that makes a statement not completely true: *I didn't tell him anything except that I needed the money.* ◇ *Our dresses were the same except mine was red.*

■ *verb* [often passive] (*formal*) to not include sb/sth: **be excepted (from sth)** *Children under five are excepted from the survey.* ◇ *Tours are arranged all year round (January excepted).* 🅸🅳🅼 see **PRESENT** *adj.*

**ex·cept·ing** /ɪkˈseptɪŋ/ *prep.* (*formal*) except for; apart from: *The sanctions ban the sale of any products excepting medical supplies and food.*

**ex·cep·tion** 🅱️2 🆆 /ɪkˈsepʃn/ *noun* **1** 🅱️2 a person or thing that is not included in a general statement: *Most of the buildings in the town are modern, but the church is an exception.* ◇ *With very few exceptions, private schools get the best exam results.* ◇ *Nobody had much money at the time and I was no exception.* ➔ **LANGUAGE BANK** at **EXCEPT** **2** 🅱️2 a thing that does not follow a rule: *Good writing is unfortunately the exception rather than the rule (= it is unusual).* ◇ *There are always a lot of exceptions to grammar rules.*

---

s **see** | t **tea** | v **van** | w **wet** | z **zoo** | ʃ **shoe** | ʒ **vision** | tʃ **chain** | dʒ **jam** | θ **thin** | ð **this** | ŋ **sing**

# exceptional

### ▼ LANGUAGE BANK

**except**

Making an exception

- She wrote all of the songs on the album **except for** the final track.
- **Apart from / aside from** the final track, all of the songs on the album were written by her.
- The songwriting—**with a few minor exceptions**—is of a very high quality.
- With only **one or two exceptions**, the songwriting is of a very high quality.
- The majority of the compositions are less than three minutes long, **with the notable exception of** the title track.
- **With the exception of** the title track, this album is a huge disappointment.
- Here is a list of all the band's CDs, **excluding** unofficial 'bootleg' recordings.

**IDM** **the exception that proves the ˈrule** (saying) people say that sth is **the exception that proves the rule** when they are stating sth that seems to be different from the normal situation, but they mean that the normal situation remains true in general: *Most electronics companies have not done well this year, but ours is the exception that proves the rule.* **make an exˈception** to allow sb not to follow the usual rule on one occasion or for one particular reason: *Children are not usually allowed in, but I'm prepared to make an exception in this case.* **take exˈception to sth** to object strongly to sth; to be angry about sth: *I take great exception to the fact that you told my wife before you told me.* ◇ *No one could possibly take exception to his comments.* **with the exˈception of sb/sth** except; not including: *All his novels are set in Italy with the exception of his last.* ⇨ LANGUAGE BANK at EXCEPT **without exˈception** used to emphasize that the statement you are making is always true and everyone or everything is included: *All students without exception must take the English examination.*

**ex·cep·tion·al** ?+ **C1** /ɪkˈsepʃənl/ *adj.* **1** ?+ **C1** unusually good **SYN** **outstanding**: *At the age of five he showed exceptional talent as a musician.* ◇ *The quality of the recording is quite exceptional.* **2** ?+ **C1** very unusual: *This deadline will be extended only in exceptional circumstances.* **OPP** **unexceptional**

**ex·cep·tion·al·ly** /ɪkˈsepʃənəli/ *adv.* **1** used before an adjective or adverb to emphasize how strong or unusual the quality is: *The weather, even for January, was exceptionally cold.* ◇ *I thought Bill played exceptionally well.* **2** only in unusual circumstances: *Exceptionally, students may be accepted without formal qualifications.*

**ex·cerpt** /ˈeksɜːpt; NAmE -sɜːrpt/ *noun* ~ **(from sth)** a short piece of writing, music, film, etc. taken from a longer whole▸ **ex·cerpt** /ekˈsɜːpt; NAmE -ˈsɜːrpt/ *verb*: ~ **sth (from sth)** *The document was excerpted from an unidentified FBI file.*

**ex·cess** ?+ **C1** **W** *noun, adj.*

- *noun* /ɪkˈses/ ?+ **C1** [sing., U] more than is necessary, reasonable or acceptable: *You can throw away any excess.* ◇ ~ **of sth** *Are you suffering from an excess of stress in your life?* ◇ *In an excess of enthusiasm I agreed to work late.* ◇ **to** ~ *He started drinking to excess after losing his job.* ◇ **in** ~ **of sth** *The increase will not be in excess of (= more than) two per cent.* **2** ?+ **C1** [C, usually sing., U] an amount by which sth is larger than sth else: *We cover costs up to £600 and then you pay the excess.* **3** [C, usually sing.] *(BrE)* (*NAmE* **de·duct·ible**) the part of an insurance claim that a person has to pay while the insurance company pays the rest: *There is an excess of £100 on each claim under this policy.* ⇨ WORD-FINDER NOTE at INSURANCE **4** [U] *(disapproving)* the fact of doing too much of sth, especially eating or drinking: *He gave in to bouts of alcoholic excess.* **5** **excesses** [pl.] *(disapproving)* extreme behaviour that is unacceptable, illegal or morally wrong: *We need a free press to curb government excesses.*
- *adj.* /ˈekses/ [only before noun] ?+ **C1** in addition to an amount that is necessary, usual or legal: *Excess food is stored as fat.* ◇ *Driving with excess alcohol in the blood is*

*a serious offence.* **2** *(BrE)* required as extra payment: *The full excess fare had to be paid.*

**excess ˈbaggage** *noun* [U] bags, cases, etc. taken on to a plane that weigh more than the amount each passenger is allowed to carry without paying extra

**ex·ces·sive** ?+ **B2** **W** /ɪkˈsesɪv/ *adj.* greater than what seems reasonable or appropriate: *They complained about the excessive noise coming from the upstairs flat.* ◇ *The amounts she borrowed were not excessive.* ◇ *Excessive drinking can lead to stomach disorders.* ▸ **ex·ces·sive·ly** *adv.*: *excessively high prices*

**ex·change** ⓘ **B1** ⓞ /ɪksˈtʃeɪndʒ/ *noun, verb*

- *noun*
- **GIVING AND RECEIVING 1** ?+ **B1** [C, U] an act of giving sth to sb or doing sth for sb and receiving sth in return: *The exchange of prisoners took place this morning.* ◇ *We need to promote an open exchange of ideas and information.* ◇ *an exchange of fire* (= between enemy soldiers) ◇ *I buy you lunch and you fix my computer. Is that a fair exchange?* ◇ **in** ~ **for sth** *Wool and timber were sent to Egypt in exchange for linen or papyrus.* ◇ **in** ~ *I'll type your report if you'll baby-sit in exchange.* ⇨ see also BILL OF EXCHANGE, PART EXCHANGE
- **OF MONEY 2** ?+ **B1** [U] the process of changing an amount of one currency for an equal value of another: *currency exchange facilities* ◇ *Where can I find the best exchange rate/rate of exchange?* ⇨ see also FOREIGN EXCHANGE
- **BETWEEN TWO COUNTRIES 3** ?+ **B1** [C] an arrangement when two people or groups from different countries visit each other's homes or do each other's jobs for a short time: ~ **(with sb/sth)** *Our school does an exchange with a school in France.* ◇ *trade and cultural exchanges with China* ◇ **on an** ~ *Nick went on the French exchange.*
- **CONVERSATION/ARGUMENT 4** [C] a conversation or an argument: *There was only time for a brief exchange.* ◇ ~ **with sb** *The prime minister was involved in a heated exchange with Opposition MPs.* ◇ ~ **between A and B** *There was an angry exchange between the two players.*
- **BUILDING 5** *(often* **Exchange***)* [C] (in compounds) a building where business people met in the past to buy and sell a particular type of goods: *the old Corn Exchange* ⇨ see also CORN EXCHANGE, STOCK EXCHANGE
- **TELEPHONE 6** [C] = TELEPHONE EXCHANGE
- *verb*
- **GIVE AND RECEIVE 1** ?+ **B1** [T] to give sth to sb and at the same time receive the same type of thing from them: ~ **sth** *to exchange ideas/news/information* ◇ *Juliet and David exchanged glances* (= they looked at each other). ◇ *Everyone in the group exchanged email addresses.* ◇ ~ **sth with sb** *I shook hands and exchanged a few words with the manager.* ◇ **(be) exchanged between A and B** *He read the letters exchanged between Anna and her friend.*
- **MONEY 2** ?+ **B1** [T] to change an amount of one currency for an equal value of another **SYN** **change**: ~ **sth** *Where can I exchange my money?* ◇ ~ **A for B** *You can exchange your currency for dollars in the hotel.*
- **GOODS 3** [T] to give or return sth that you have and get sth different or better instead: ~ **sth** *If it doesn't fit, take it back and the store will exchange it.* ◇ ~ **A for B** *I need to exchange this for a larger size.* ⇨ see also PART-EXCHANGE
- **CONTRACTS 4** [T, I] ~ **(contracts) (on sth)** *(especially BrE)* when a buyer and seller **exchange contracts**, especially on the sale of a house or land, they each sign a copy of the contract and give it to the other person **IDM**▸ see WORD n.

**ex·change·able** /ɪksˈtʃeɪndʒəbl/ *adj.* ~ **(for sth)** that can be exchanged: *The vouchers are exchangeable for goods at selected stores.*

**ex·chequer** /ɪksˈtʃekə(r)/ *noun* [sing.] **1** *(often* **the Exchequer***)* (in the UK in the past) the government department that controlled public money. This department is now called THE TREASURY. ⇨ see also CHANCELLOR OF THE EXCHEQUER **2** the public or national supply of money: *This resulted in a considerable loss to the exchequer.*

**ex·cise**[1] /ˈeksaɪz/ *noun* [U] a government tax on some goods made, sold or used within a country: *new excise duties on low-alcohol drinks* ◇ *a sharp increase in vehicle excise* ◇ *an excise officer* (= an official whose job is to collect excise) ⇨ compare CUSTOMS

**ex·cise²** /ɪkˈsaɪz/ verb ~ **sth (from sth)** (formal) to remove sth completely: *Certain passages were excised from the book.* ◊ *The sensor improves the precision with which surgeons can excise brain tumours.*

**ex·ci·sion** /ɪkˈsɪʒn/ noun [U, C] (formal or specialist) the act of removing sth completely from sth; the thing removed

**ex·cit·able** /ɪkˈsaɪtəbl/ adj. (of people or animals) likely to become easily excited: *a class of excitable ten-year-olds* ▶ **ex·cit·abil·ity** /ɪkˌsaɪtəˈbɪləti/ noun [U]

**ex·cite** /ɪkˈsaɪt/ verb **1** ~ **sb** to make sb feel very pleased, interested or enthusiastic, especially about sth that is going to happen: *The prospect of a year in India greatly excited her.* **2** to make sb nervous or upset and unable to relax: *~ sb Try not to excite your baby too much before bedtime.* ◊ *~ yourself Don't excite yourself* (= keep calm). **3** to make sb feel a particular emotion or react in a particular way SYN **arouse**: *~ sth to excite attention/curiosity/admiration* ◊ *The news has certainly excited comment* (= made people talk about it). ◊ *~ sth in sb The advertising campaign failed to excite much interest in consumers.* **4** ~ **sb** to make sb feel sexual desire SYN **arouse 5** ~ **sth** (specialist) to make a part of the body or part of a physical system more active

**ex·cit·ed** ❶ A1 /ɪkˈsaɪtɪd/ adj. **1** A1 feeling or showing happiness and enthusiasm: *Staff got excited when they heard they were getting a bonus.* ◊ *~ about sth/about doing sth I am really excited about the opportunity to work with her.* ◊ *~ at sth/at doing sth I'm really excited at the prospect of working abroad.* ◊ *~ by sth Don't get too excited by the sight of your name in print.* ◊ *~ for sb I'm so excited for you!* ◊ *~ to do sth He was very excited to be asked to play for Wales.* ◊ *~ (that) ... He is very excited that he will get to meet his idol.* ◊ *The new restaurant is nothing to get excited about* (= not particularly good). ◊ *An excited crowd of people gathered around her.* **2** nervous or upset and unable to relax: *Some horses become excited when they're in traffic.* **3** feeling sexual desire SYN **aroused** ▶ **ex·cit·ed·ly** adv.: *She waved excitedly as the car approached.*

▼ SYNONYMS

**excited**
ecstatic • elated • euphoric • rapturous • exhilarated
These words all describe feeling or showing happiness and enthusiasm.

**excited** feeling or showing happiness and enthusiasm: *The kids were excited about the holiday.*
**ecstatic** very happy, excited and enthusiastic; showing this enthusiasm: *Sally was ecstatic about her new job.*
**elated** happy and excited because of sth good that has happened or will happen: *I was elated with the thrill of success.*
**euphoric** very happy and excited, but usually only for a short time: *My euphoric mood could not last.*
**rapturous** expressing extreme pleasure or enthusiasm: *He was greeted with rapturous applause.*
**exhilarated** happy and excited, especially after physical activity: *She felt exhilarated with the speed.*

PATTERNS
- to feel excited/elated/euphoric/exhilarated
- to be excited/ecstatic/elated/euphoric **at** sth
- to be excited/ecstatic/elated **about** sth
- to be excited/elated/exhilarated **by** sth
- to be ecstatic/elated/exhilarated **with** sth

**ex·cite·ment** ❶ B1 /ɪkˈsaɪtmənt/ noun **1** B1 [U] the state of feeling or showing happiness and enthusiasm: *The news caused great excitement among her friends.* ◊ *~ about (doing) sth He did not share their excitement about the project.* ◊ *~ at (doing) sth She told of her excitement at the prospect of a new career as a pilot.* ◊ *~ of (doing) sth I can remember the excitement of winning that game.* ◊ *with ~ You'll jump up from your seat with excitement.* ◊ *in ~ The dog leapt and wagged its tail in excitement.* ◊ *in sb's ~ In her excitement she dropped her glass.* ⊃ WORDFINDER NOTE at ADVENTURE **2** [C] (formal) something that you find exciting: *The new job was not without its excitements.* **3** [U] The state of feeling sexual desire SYN **arousal**

**ex·cit·ing** ❶ A1 /ɪkˈsaɪtɪŋ/ adj. causing great interest or excitement: *This is an exciting opportunity for me.* ◊ *It's an exciting time for the entire industry.* ◊ *They waited and waited for something exciting to happen.* ◊ *~ for sb That's what makes the game so exciting for the fans.* ◊ *it is ~ (for sb) to do sth It was really exciting for them to see him in person.* ▶ **ex·cit·ing·ly** adv.

▼ SYNONYMS

**exciting**
dramatic • heady • thrilling • exhilarating
These words all describe an event, experience or feeling that causes excitement.

**exciting** causing great interest or excitement: *This is one of the most exciting developments in biology in recent years.*
**dramatic** (of events or scenes) exciting and impressive: *They watched dramatic pictures of the police raid on TV.*
**heady** having a strong effect on your senses; making you feel excited and full of hope: *the heady days of youth*
**thrilling** exciting and a lot of fun: *Don't miss next week's thrilling episode!*
**exhilarating** very exciting and great fun: *My first parachute jump was an exhilarating experience.*

EXCITING, THRILLING OR EXHILARATING?
**Exhilarating** is the strongest of these words and **exciting** the least strong. **Exciting** is the most general and can be used to talk about any activity, experience, feeling or event that excites you. **Thrilling** is used especially for contests and stories where the ending is uncertain. **Exhilarating** is used especially for physical activities that involve speed and/or danger.

PATTERNS
- a(n) exciting/dramatic/heady/thrilling/exhilarating **experience/moment**
- a(n) exciting/dramatic/heady **atmosphere**
- a(n) exciting/dramatic/thrilling **finish/finale/victory/win**

**ex·claim** /ɪkˈskleɪm/ verb [I, T] to say sth suddenly and loudly, especially because of strong emotion or pain: *She opened her eyes and exclaimed in delight at the scene.* ◊ *+ speech 'It isn't fair!', he exclaimed angrily.* ◊ *~ that ... She exclaimed that it was useless.* ⊃ SYNONYMS at CALL

**ex·clam·ation** /ˌekskləˈmeɪʃn/ noun a short sound, word or phrase spoken suddenly to express an emotion. *Oh!*, *Look out!* and *Ow!* are exclamations: *He gave an exclamation of surprise.*

**excla'mation mark** (especially BrE) (NAmE usually **excla'mation point**) noun the mark (!) that is written after an exclamation

**ex·clama·tory** /ɪkˈsklæmətri/ NAmE -tɔːri/ adj. (formal) (of language) expressing surprise or strong feelings

**ex·clude** B2 W /ɪkˈskluːd/ verb **1** B2 ~ **sth (from sth)** to deliberately not include sth in what you are doing or considering: *The cost of borrowing has been excluded from the inflation figures.* ◊ *Try excluding fat from your diet.* ◊ *Buses run every hour, Sundays excluded.* OPP **include 2** B2 ~ **sb/sth (from sth)** to prevent sb/sth from entering a place or taking part in sth: *Women are still excluded from some London clubs.* ◊ *(BrE) Concern is growing over the number of children excluded from school* (= not allowed to attend because of bad behaviour). ◊ *She felt excluded by the other girls* (= they did not let her join in what they were doing). **3** B2 ~ **sth** to decide that sth is not possible: *We should not exclude the possibility of negotiation.* ◊ *The police have excluded theft as a motive for the murder.* OPP **include**

**ex·clud·ing** /ɪkˈskluːdɪŋ/ prep. not including: *Lunch costs £20 per person, excluding drinks.* ⊃ LANGUAGE BANK at EXCEPT

**ex·clu·sion** C1 W /ɪkˈskluːʒn/ noun **1** C1 [U] the act of preventing sb/sth from entering a place or taking part in sth: *~ (of sb/sth) (from sth) He was disappointed with his exclusion from the England squad.* ◊ *Exclusion of air creates a vacuum in the bottle.* ◊ *to the ~ of sth Memories*

# exclusionary

*of the past filled her mind to the exclusion of all else.* **OPP inclusion 2** [C] a person or thing that is not included in sth: *Check the list of exclusions in the insurance policy.* **3** [U] **~ (of sth)** the act of deciding that sth is not possible: *the exclusion of robbery as a motive* **4** [U, C] (*BrE*) a situation in which a child is banned from attending school because of bad behaviour: *the exclusion of disruptive students from school* ◇ *Two exclusions from one school in the same week is unusual.*

**ex·clu·sion·ary** /ɪkˈskluːʒənri; *NAmE* -ʒəneri/ *adj.* (*formal*) designed to prevent a particular person or group of people from taking part in sth or doing sth

**ex'clusion order** *noun* (*BrE*) an official order not to go to a particular place: *The judge placed an exclusion order on him, banning him from city centre shops.*

**ex'clusion zone** *noun* an area where people are not allowed to enter because it is dangerous or is used for secret activities

**ex·clu·sive** /ɪkˈskluːsɪv/ *adj., noun*
- *adj.* **1** only to be used by one particular person or group; only given to one particular person or group: *The hotel has exclusive access to the beach.* ◇ *exclusive rights to televise the World Cup* ◇ *His mother has told 'The Times' about his death in an exclusive interview* (= not given to any other newspaper). **WORDFINDER NOTE** at JOURNALIST **2** (of a group, society, etc.) not very willing to allow new people to become members, especially if they are from a lower social class: *He belongs to an exclusive club.* **3** of a high quality and expensive and therefore not often bought or used by most people: *an exclusive hotel* ◇ *exclusive designer clothes* **4** not including anything else: *He had an exclusive focus on success and making money.* ◇ *This list is not exclusive.* **5** **~ of sb/sth** not including sb/sth: *The price is for accommodation only, exclusive of meals.* **OPP inclusive** **6** not able to exist or be a true statement at the same time as sth else: *The two options are not mutually exclusive* (= you can have them both). ▶ **ex·clu·sive·ness** (*also* **exclusivity**) *noun* [U]
- *noun* an item of news or a story about famous people that is published in only one newspaper or magazine or broadcast on only one TV or radio station

**ex·clu·sive·ly** /ɪkˈskluːsɪvli/ *adv.* **1** for only one particular person, group or use: *The resort caters almost exclusively for a high-society public.* ◇ *Some products are labelled exclusively for indoor or outdoor use.* **2** completely; without including anybody or anything else: *a charity that relies almost exclusively on voluntary contributions*

**ex·clu·siv·ity** /ˌeksklu:ˈsɪvəti/ (*also* **ex·clu·sive·ness** /ɪkˈskluːsɪvnəs/) *noun* [U] **1** the fact of being of a high quality and expensive and therefore not often bought or used by most people: *The resort still preserves a feeling of exclusivity.* ◇ *a designer whose clothes have not lost their exclusiveness* **2** the practice in a group or society of not allowing other people from different groups to become members or be included: *The club has been criticized for its exclusivity and elitism.*

**ex·com·mu·ni·cate** /ˌekskəˈmjuːnɪkeɪt/ *verb* **~ sb (for sth)** to punish sb by officially stating that they can no longer be a member of a Christian Church, especially the Roman Catholic Church ▶ **ex·com·mu·ni·ca·tion** /ˌekskəˌmjuːnɪˈkeɪʃn/ *noun* [U, C]

**ex·cori·ate** /ɪkˈskɔːrieɪt/ *verb* **1 ~ sth** (*medical*) to make a person's skin painful, and often red, so that it starts to come off **2 ~ sb/sth** (*formal*) to criticize sb/sth severely ▶ **ex·cori·ation** /ɪkˌskɔːriˈeɪʃn/ *noun* [U, C]

**ex·cre·ment** /ˈekskrɪmənt/ *noun* [U] (*formal*) solid waste matter that is passed from the body through the BOWELS **SYN faeces**: *the pollution of drinking water by untreated human excrement* ▶ **ex·cre·men·tal** /ˌekskrɪˈmentl/ *adj.*

**ex·creta** /ɪkˈskriːtə/ *noun* [U, pl.] (*specialist*) solid and liquid waste matter passed from the body: *human excreta*

**ex·crete** /ɪkˈskriːt/ *verb* [I] (*specialist*) to pass solid or liquid waste matter from the body ▶ **ex·cre·tion** /-ˈskriːʃn/ *noun* [U, C]

**ex·cre·tory** /ɪksˈkriːtəri; *NAmE* ˈekskrətɔːri/ *adj.* (*specialist*) connected with getting rid of waste matter from the body: *the excretory organs*

**ex·cru·ci·at·ing** /ɪkˈskruːʃieɪtɪŋ/ *adj.* extremely painful or bad: *The pain in my back was excruciating.* ◇ *She groaned at the memory, suffering all over again the excruciating embarrassment of those moments.* **SYNONYMS** at **PAINFUL** ▶ **ex·cru·ci·at·ing·ly** *adv.*: *excruciatingly uncomfortable* ◇ *excruciatingly painful/boring/embarrassing*

**ex·cul·pate** /ˈekskʌlpeɪt/ *verb* **~ sb** (*formal*) to prove or state officially that sb is not guilty of sth ▶ **ex·cul·pa·tion** /ˌekskʌlˈpeɪʃn/ *noun* [U]

**ex·cur·sion** /ɪkˈskɜːʃn; *NAmE* -ˈskɜːrʒn/ *noun* **1** a short journey made for pleasure, especially one that has been organized for a group of people: **on an~** *They've gone on an excursion to York.* **SYNONYMS** at **TRIP** **WORDFINDER NOTE** at **JOURNEY** **2 ~ into sth** (*formal*) a short period of trying a new or different activity: *After a brief excursion into drama, he concentrated on his main interest, which was poetry.*

**ex·cus·able** /ɪkˈskjuːzəbl/ *adj.* [not usually before noun] that can be excused **SYN forgivable**: *Doing it once was just about excusable—doing it twice was certainly not.* **OPP inexcusable**

**ex·cuse** *noun, verb*
- *noun* /ɪkˈskjuːs/ **1** a reason, either true or invented, that you give to explain or defend your behaviour: *Late again! What's your excuse this time?* ◇ *I tried desperately to think of a good excuse.* ◇ *I know I missed the deadline, but I have an excuse.* ◇ **~ for (doing) sth** *There's no excuse for such behaviour.* ◇ *You don't have to make excuses for her* (= try to think of reasons for her behaviour). ◇ *It's late. I'm afraid I'll have to make my excuses* (= say I'm sorry, give my reasons and leave). **SYNONYMS** at **REASON** **2** a good reason that you give for doing sth that you want to do for other reasons: **~ for (doing) sth** *It's just an excuse for a party.* ◇ **~ to do sth** *It gave me an excuse to take the car.* **3** a very bad example of sth: *Why get involved with that pathetic excuse for a human being?* **4** (*NAmE*) a note written by a parent or doctor to explain why a student cannot go to school or sb cannot go to work
- *verb* /ɪkˈskjuːz/ **1** to forgive sb for sth that they have done, for example not being polite or making a small mistake: **~ sth** *Please excuse the mess.* ◇ **~ sb** *You must excuse my father—he's not always that rude.* ◇ **~ sb for (doing) sth** *I hope you'll excuse me for being so late.* ◇ (*BrE*) *You might be excused for thinking that Ben is in charge* (= he is not, but it is an easy mistake to make). ◇ **~ sb doing sth** *Excuse me interrupting you.* **2** to make your or sb else's behaviour seem less offensive by finding reasons for it **SYN justify**: **~ sth** *Nothing can excuse such rudeness.* ◇ **~ sth as sth** *He tried to excuse his behaviour as 'a bit of harmless fun'.* ◇ **~ sb/yourself (for sth/for doing sth)** *I could try to excuse myself, but why bother?* **3 ~ sb/yourself (from sth)** to allow sb to leave; to say in a polite way that you are leaving: *Now if you'll excuse me, I'm a very busy man.* ◇ *She excused herself and left the meeting early.* **4** [usually passive] to allow sb to not do sth that they should normally do: **be excused (from sth/from doing sth)** *She was excused from giving evidence because of her age.* ◇ **be excused sth** *He was excused military service because of poor health.*
- **IDM** **ex'cuse me 1** used to politely get sb's attention, especially sb you do not know: *Excuse me, is this the way to the station?* **2** used to politely ask sb to move so that you can get past them: *Excuse me, could you let me through?* **3** used to say that you are sorry for interrupting sb or behaving in a slightly rude way: *Guy sneezed loudly. 'Excuse me,' he said.* **4** used to disagree politely with sb: *Excuse me, but I don't think that's true.* **5** used to politely tell sb that you are going to leave or talk to sb else: *'Excuse me for a moment,' she said and left the room.* **6** (*especially NAmE*) used to say sorry for pushing sb or doing sth wrong: *Oh, excuse me. I didn't see you there.* **7 excuse me?** (*NAmE*) used when you did not hear what sb said and you want them to repeat it **⊃** more at **FRENCH** *n.*

**exec** /ɪɡˈzek/ *noun* (*informal*) an executive in a business

**exe·crable** /ˈeksɪkrəbl/ *adj.* (*formal*) very bad **SYN terrible**

**exe·cut·able** /ˌeksɪˈkjuːtəbl/ *adj.* (*computing*) (of a file or program) that can be run by a computer

**ex·e·cute** /ˈeksɪkjuːt/ verb **1** [usually passive] to kill sb, especially as a legal punishment: **be executed (for sth)** *He was executed for treason.* ◊ **be executed by sth** *The prisoners were executed by firing squad.* ⊃ WORDFINDER NOTE at ATTACK **2** ~ sth (*formal*) to do a piece of work, perform a duty, put a plan into action, etc: *They drew up and executed a plan to reduce fuel consumption.* ◊ *The crime was very cleverly executed.* ◊ *Check that the computer has executed your commands.* **3** ~ sth (*formal*) to successfully perform an action or movement that requires skill: *The pilot executed a perfect landing.* **4** ~ sth (*formal*) to make or produce a work of art: *Picasso also executed several landscapes at Horta de San Juan.* **5** ~ sth (*law*) to follow the instructions in a legal document; to make a document legally acceptable

**ex·e·cu·tion** /ˌeksɪˈkjuːʃn/ noun **1** [U, C] the act of killing sb, especially as a legal punishment: *He faced execution by hanging for murder.* ◊ *Over 200 executions were carried out last year.* **2** [U] (*formal*) the act of doing a piece of work, performing a duty, or putting a plan into action: *He had failed in the execution of his duty.* ◊ *The idea was good, but the execution was poor.* **3** [U] (*formal*) skill in performing or making sth, such as a piece of music or work of art: *Her execution of the piano piece was perfect.* **4** [U] (*law*) the act of following the instructions in a legal document, especially those in sb's WILL IDM see STAY n.

**ex·e·cu·tion·er** /ˌeksɪˈkjuːʃənə(r)/ noun a person whose job or role is to kill people as a punishment, especially a public official who executes criminals

**ex·ecu·tive** /ɪɡˈzekjətɪv/ noun, adj.
■ noun **1** [C] a person who has an important job as a manager of a company or an organization: *company/corporate/business/industry executives* ◊ *marketing/advertising executives* ◊ *a senior/top executive in a computer firm* ⊃ see also ACCOUNT EXECUTIVE, CHIEF EXECUTIVE ⊃ WORDFINDER NOTE at BUSINESSMAN **2** [C + sing./pl. v.] a group of people who run a company or an organization: *The union's executive has/have yet to reach a decision.* **3 the executive** [sing. + sing./pl. v.] the part of a government responsible for putting laws into effect ⊃ compare JUDICIARY, LEGISLATURE
■ adj. [only before noun] **1** connected with managing a business or an organization, and with making plans and decisions: *She has an executive position in a finance company.* ◊ *executive decisions/duties/jobs* ◊ *the executive dining room* **2** having or using the power to put important laws and decisions into effect: *an executive vice-president/chairman/officer* ◊ *an executive producer/editor* ◊ *an executive committee/board/member* ◊ *The boss took an executive decision* (= used his/her power to decide) *to cancel the project.* ◊ *Executive power is held by the president.* ⊃ see also NON-EXECUTIVE **3** expensive; for the use of sb who is considered important: *an executive car/home* ◊ *an executive suite* (= in a hotel) ◊ *an executive lounge* (= at an airport)

**the eˈxecutive branch** noun [sing.] (in the US) the part of the government that is controlled by the president

**eˌxecutive diˈrector** noun the most senior person in an organization or department with responsibility for making daily business decisions (often used to refer to sb who has these responsibilities in a NON-PROFIT organization) ⊃ compare CHIEF EXECUTIVE (1)

**eˌxecutive ˈorder** noun (*law*) (in the US) an official order from the president that becomes the law

**eˌxecutive ˈprivilege** noun [U] (in the US) the right of the president and the executive part of the government to keep official documents secret

**eˌxecutive ˈsecretary** noun (*NAmE*) a secretary who manages the business activities of an executive or an organization

**eˌxecutive ˈsummary** (also ˈmanagement summary) noun a short statement that gives the important facts, conclusions and suggestions of a report, usually printed at the beginning of a report

**ex·ecu·tor** /ɪɡˈzekjətə(r)/ noun (*law*) a person, bank, etc. that is chosen by sb who is making their WILL to follow the instructions in it

---

**exercise**

**exe·gesis** /ˌeksɪˈdʒiːsɪs/ noun [U, C] (*pl.* **exe·geses** /-ˈdʒiːsiːz/) (*formal*) the detailed explanation of a piece of writing, especially religious writing

**ex·em·plar** /ɪɡˈzemplɑː(r)/ noun (*formal*) a person or thing that is a good or typical example of sth **SYN** model

**ex·em·plary** /ɪɡˈzempləri/ adj. **1** providing a good example for people to copy: *Her behaviour was exemplary.* ◊ *a man of exemplary character* **2** [usually before noun] (*law or formal*) (of punishment) severe; used especially as a warning to others

**ex·em·plify** /ɪɡˈzemplɪfaɪ/ verb (ex·em·pli·fies, ex·em·pli·fy·ing, ex·em·pli·fied, ex·em·pli·fied) (*formal*) **1** ~ sth to be a typical example of sth: *Her early work is exemplified in her book, 'A Study of Children's Minds'.* ◊ *His food exemplifies Italian cooking at its best.* **2** ~ sth to give an example in order to make sth clearer **SYN** illustrate: *She exemplified each of the points she was making with an amusing anecdote.* ▸ **ex·em·pli·fi·ca·tion** /ɪɡˌzemplɪfɪˈkeɪʃn/ noun [U, C]

**ex·empt** /ɪɡˈzempt/ adj., verb
■ adj. [not before noun] ~ **(from sth)** if sb/sth is **exempt** from sth, they are not affected by it, do not have to do it, pay it, etc: *The interest on the money is exempt from tax.* ◊ *Some students are exempt from certain exams.* ▸ **-exempt** (in compounds, forming adjectives): *tax-exempt donations to charity*
■ verb (*formal*) to give sb official permission not to do sth or not to pay sth they would normally have to do or pay; to cause sb to get this official permission: **~sb/sth (from doing sth)** *Charities were exempted from paying the tax.* ◊ **~sb/sth from sth** *His bad eyesight exempted him from military service.*

**ex·emp·tion** /ɪɡˈzempʃn/ noun **1** [U, C] ~ **(from sth)** official permission not to do sth or pay sth that you would normally have to do or pay: *She was given exemption from the final examination.* **2** [C] a part of your income that you do not have to pay tax on: *a tax exemption on money donated to charity* ⊃ see also MATRIC EXEMPTION, PERSONAL EXEMPTION

**ex·er·cise** /ˈeksəsaɪz; *NAmE* -sərs-/ noun, verb
■ noun
• ACTIVITY/MOVEMENTS **1** [U] physical or mental activity that you do to stay healthy or become stronger: *Swimming is good exercise.* ◊ *the importance of regular exercise* ◊ *health problems resulting from a lack of physical exercise* ◊ *I don't get much exercise sitting in the office all day.* ◊ *John never does any exercise.* ◊ (*BrE*) *to take exercise* ⊃ WORDFINDER NOTE at FIT **2** [C] a set of movements or activities that you do to stay healthy or develop a skill: *breathing/relaxation/stretching exercises* ◊ *to do/perform an exercise* ◊ **an~for sth** *exercises for the piano*
• QUESTIONS **3** [C] a set of questions in a book that tests your knowledge or practises a skill: *grammar exercises* ◊ *Do exercise one for homework.*
• USE OF POWER/RIGHT/QUALITY **4** [U] ~ **of sth** the use of power, a skill, a quality or a right to make sth happen: *the exercise of power by the government* ◊ *the exercise of discretion*
• FOR PARTICULAR RESULT **5** [C] an activity that is designed to achieve a particular result: *a public consultation exercise* ◊ *In the end it proved a pointless exercise.* ◊ **~in sth** *an exercise in public relations* ◊ *Staying calm was an exercise in self-control.*
• FOR SOLDIERS **6** [C, usually pl.] a set of activities for training soldiers: *military exercises* ◊ *He was injured in a training exercise.*
• CEREMONIES **7** **exercises** [pl.] (*NAmE*) ceremonies: *college graduation exercises*
■ verb
• DO PHYSICAL ACTIVITY **1** [I, T] to do sports or other physical activities in order to stay healthy or become stronger; to make an animal do this: *How often do you exercise?* ◊ **~sth** *Horses need to be exercised regularly.* **2** [T] ~ sth to give a part of the body the movement and activity it needs to keep strong and healthy: *These movements will exercise your arms and shoulders.*

# exercise ball

- USE POWER/RIGHT/QUALITY **3** [T] ~ sth (formal) to use your power, rights or personal qualities in order to achieve sth: *to exercise power/authority/control* ◇ *When she appeared in court she exercised the right to remain silent.* ◇ *The roads are very slippery, so drivers should exercise caution.*
- BE ANXIOUS **4** [usually passive] (formal) if sb is **exercised about sth**, they are very anxious about it

**'exercise ball** *noun* a large ball that you can sit on when doing exercises to make your muscles work in a different way

exercise bike    barbell    dumb-bell

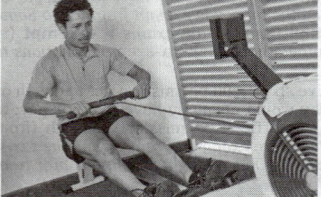  

rowing machine    treadmill

**'exercise bike** *noun* a bicycle that does not move forward but is used for getting exercise indoors

**'exercise book** *noun* **1** (*BrE*) (*NAmE* **note-book**) a small book for students to write their work in **2** = WORKBOOK

**exert** /ɪgˈzɜːt; *NAmE* -ˈzɜːrt/ *verb* **1** ~ sth to use power or influence to affect sb/sth: *He exerted all his authority to make them accept the plan.* ◇ *The moon exerts a force on the earth that causes the tides.* **2** ~ **yourself** to make a big physical or mental effort: *In order to be successful he would have to exert himself.*

**ex-er-tion** /ɪgˈzɜːʃn; *NAmE* -ˈzɜːrʃn/ *noun* **1** [U] (also **exer-tions** [pl.]) physical or mental effort; the act of making an effort: *She was hot and breathless from the exertion of cycling uphill.* ◇ *He needed to relax after the exertions of a busy day at work.* **2** [sing.] the use of power to make sth happen: *the exertion of force/strength/authority*

**ex-foli-ate** /eksˈfəʊlieɪt/ *verb* [I, T] ~ (**sth**) to remove dead cells from the surface of skin in order to make it smoother ▸ **ex-foli-ation** /eksˌfəʊliˈeɪʃn/ *noun* [U]

**ex gra·tia** /ˌeks ˈɡreɪʃə/ *adj.* (*from Latin*) given or done as a gift or favour, not because there is a legal duty to do it: *ex gratia payments* ▸ **ex gra·tia** *adv.*: *The sum was paid ex gratia.*

**ex-hale** /eksˈheɪl/ *verb* [I, T] (*formal*) to breathe out the air or smoke, etc. in your lungs: *He sat back and exhaled deeply.* ◇ ~ **sth** *She exhaled the smoke through her nose.* **OPP** inhale ▸ **ex-hal-ation** /ˌekshəˈleɪʃn/ *noun* [U, C]

**ex-haust** /ɪgˈzɔːst/ *noun, verb*
- *noun* **1** [U] waste gases that come out of a vehicle, an engine or a machine: *car exhaust fumes/emissions* ⇨ WORD-FINDER NOTE at WASTE **2** [C] the system in a vehicle through which exhaust gases come out: *My car needs a new exhaust.*
- *verb* **1** to make sb feel very tired **SYN** **wear out**: ~ **sb** *Even a short walk exhausted her.* ◇ ~ **yourself** *There's no need to exhaust yourself clearing up—we'll do it.* **2** ~ **sth** to use all of sth so that there is none left: *Within three days they had exhausted their supply of food.* ◇ *Don't give up until you have exhausted all the possibilities.* **3** ~ **sth** to talk about or study a subject until there is nothing else to say about it: *I think we've exhausted that particular topic.*

**ex·haust·ed** /ɪgˈzɔːstɪd/ *adj.* **1** very tired: *I'm exhausted!* ◇ *to feel completely/utterly exhausted* ◇ *The exhausted climbers were rescued by helicopter.* **2** completely used or finished: *You cannot grow crops on exhausted land.*

**ex·haust·ing** /ɪgˈzɔːstɪŋ/ *adj.* making you feel very tired: *an exhausting day at work* ◇ *I find her exhausting—she never stops talking.*

**ex·haus·tion** /ɪgˈzɔːstʃən/ *noun* [U] **1** the state of being very tired: *suffering from physical/mental/nervous exhaustion* ◇ *Her face was grey with exhaustion.* **2** (*formal*) the act of using sth until it is completely finished: *the exhaustion of natural resources*

**ex·haust·ive** /ɪgˈzɔːstɪv/ *adj.* including everything possible; very careful or complete: *exhaustive research/tests* ◇ *This list is not intended to be exhaustive.* ▸ **ex·haust·ive-ly** *adv.*: *Every product is exhaustively tested before being sold.*

**exˈhaust pipe** (also **tailpipe** *especially in NAmE*) *noun* a pipe through which waste gases come out of a vehicle

**ex·hibit** /ɪɡˈzɪbɪt/ *verb, noun*
- *verb* **1** [T, I] to show sth in a public place for people to enjoy or to give them information: ~ **sth** (**at/in** …) *They will be exhibiting their new designs at the trade fairs.* ◇ ~ (**at/in** …) *He exhibits regularly in local art galleries.* **2** [T] ~ **sth** (*formal*) to show clearly that you have or feel a particular quality, ability, feeling or symptom **SYN** **display**: *The patient exhibited signs of fatigue and memory loss.*
- *noun* **1** an object or a collection of objects put in a public place, for example a museum, so that people can see it **2** (*NAmE*) = EXHIBITION (1): *The new exhibit will tour a dozen US cities next year.* **3** a thing that is used in court to prove that sb is guilty or not guilty: *The first exhibit was a knife which the prosecution claimed was the murder weapon.*

**ex·hib·ition** /ˌeksɪˈbɪʃn/ *noun* **1** (*especially BrE*) (*NAmE usually* **ex·hibit**) [C] a collection of things, for example works of art, that are shown to the public: *Have you seen the Picasso exhibition?* ◇ *to hold/organize an exhibition* ◇ *an art exhibition* ◇ ~ **of sth** *an exhibition of paintings/photographs* ◇ ~ **on sb/sth** *She is currently preparing an exhibition on Van Gogh and Expressionism.* ⇨ WORDFINDER NOTE at CONFERENCE ⇨ WORDFINDER NOTE at PAINTING **2** [U] ~ **of sth** the act of showing sth, for example works of art, to the public: *She refused to allow the exhibition of her husband's work.* **3** [sing.] **an ~ of sth** (*formal*) the act of showing a skill, a feeling, or a kind of behaviour: *We were treated to an exhibition of the footballer's speed and skill.* ◇ *an appalling exhibition of bad manners* **4** [C] (*BrE*) an amount of money that is given as a prize to a student
- **IDM** **make an exhiˈbition of yourself** (*disapproving*) to behave in a bad or stupid way in public

**ex·hib·ition·ism** /ˌeksɪˈbɪʃənɪzəm/ *noun* [U] **1** (*disapproving*) behaviour that is intended to make people notice or admire you **2** (*psychology*) the mental condition that makes sb want to show their sexual organs in public

**ex·hib·ition·ist** /ˌeksɪˈbɪʃənɪst/ *noun, adj.*
- *noun* **1** (*usually disapproving*) a person who likes to make other people notice him or her: *Children are natural exhibitionists.* **2** (*psychology*) a person suffering from a mental condition that makes them want to show their sexual organs in public
- *adj.* **1** (*usually disapproving*) deliberately behaving in a way that will make other people notice you: *He was a confident child with an exhibitionist streak, always showing off.* **2** (*psychology*) suffering from a mental condition that makes sb want to show their sexual organs in public: *exhibitionist tendencies* ◇ *an exhibitionist streak*

**ex·hib·it·or** /ɪɡˈzɪbɪtə(r)/ *noun* a person or a company that shows their work or products to the public

**ex·hil·ar·ate** /ɪɡˈzɪləreɪt/ *verb* ~ **sb** to make sb feel very happy and excited: *Speed had always exhilarated him.* ▸ **ex·hil·ar·ated** *adj.*: *I felt exhilarated after a morning of skiing.* ⇨ SYNONYMS at EXCITED **ex·hil·ar·ation** /ɪɡˌzɪləˈreɪʃn/ *noun* [U]: *the exhilaration of performing on stage*

**ex·hil·ar·at·ing** /ɪɡˈzɪləreɪtɪŋ/ *adj.* very exciting and great fun: *My first parachute jump was an exhilarating experience.* ⇨ SYNONYMS at EXCITING

**ex·hort** /ɪɡˈzɔːt; NAmE -ˈzɔːrt/ verb (formal) to try hard to persuade sb to do sth **SYN** urge: ~ **sb to do sth** *The party leader exhorted his members to start preparing for government.* ◊ ~ **sb to sth** *They had been exhorted to action.* ◊ ~**(sb) + speech** *'Come on!' he exhorted (them).* ▶ **ex·hort·ation** /ˌeɡzɔːˈteɪʃn; NAmE -zɔːrˈt-/ noun [C, U]

**ex·hume** /eksˈhjuːm, ɪɡˈzjuːm; NAmE ɪɡˈzuːm/ verb [usually passive] ~ **sth** (formal) to remove a dead body from the ground especially in order to examine how the person died **SYN** dig up ▶ **ex·hum·ation** /ˌekshjuːˈmeɪʃn/ noun [U]

**exi·gency** /ˈeksɪdʒənsi, ɪɡˈzɪdʒənsi/ noun [C, usually pl., U] (pl. **-ies**) (formal) a need or demand that you must deal with immediately **SYN** demand

**exile** ⚡+ **C1** /ˈeksaɪl, ˈeɡzaɪl/ noun, verb
■ noun **1** ⚡+ **C1** [U, sing.] the state of being sent to live in another country that is not your own, especially for political reasons or as a punishment: *a place of exile* ◊ *He returned after 40 years of exile.* ◊ **in ~** *He has lived in exile since 1989.* ◊ **into ~** *The whole family went into exile.* ◊ *to be forced/sent into exile* **2** [C] a person who chooses, or is forced, to live away from his or her own country: *political exiles* ⇒ see also TAX EXILE
■ verb [usually passive] to force sb to leave their country, especially for political reasons or as a punishment; to send sb into exile: **be exiled (from …) (to …)** *He was exiled to Siberia.* ◊ *the party's exiled leaders*

**exist** ❶ **A2** ◯ /ɪɡˈzɪst/ verb **1** **A2** [I] (not used in the progressive tenses) to be real; to be present in a place or situation: *Few of these monkeys still exist in the wild.* ◊ *Major differences continue to exist between the two countries.* ◊ *A solution has been found and the problem no longer exists.* ◊ *On his retirement the post will cease to exist.* ◊ ~ **to do sth** *The charity exists to support victims of crime.* ⇒ see also PRE-EXIST **2** [I] ~ **(on sth)** to live, especially in a difficult situation or with very little money: *We existed on a diet of rice.* ◊ *They can't exist on the money he's earning.*

**ex·ist·ence** ❶ **B2** ◯ /ɪɡˈzɪstəns/ noun **1** ⚡+ **B2** [U] the state or fact of being real or living or of being present: *The continued existence of the industry depends on the investment of public money.* ◊ *The peasants depend on a good harvest for their very existence* (= in order to continue to live). ◊ *Some groups in the industry seek to **deny the existence** of a global warming problem.* ◊ **in ~** *The company has been in existence since 1924.* ◊ **as sth** *Pakistan came into existence as an independent country in 1947.* ◊ *Several species are in danger of being hunted out of existence.* **OPP** non-existence **2** ⚡ **B2** [C] a way of living, especially when this is difficult or boring: *The family endured a miserable existence in a cramped apartment.* ◊ *They eke out a precarious existence* (= they have hardly enough money to live on).

**ex·ist·ent** /ɪɡˈzɪstənt/ adj., noun
■ **adj.** (formal) existing; real: *creatures existent in nature* **OPP** non-existent ⇒ see also PRE-EXISTENT
■ **noun** (philosophy) a thing that is real and exists: *The self is the only knowable existent.*

**ex·ist·en·tial** /ˌeɡzɪˈstenʃl/ adj. [only before noun] **1** (formal) connected with human existence **2** (philosophy) connected with the theory of existentialism

**ex·ist·en·tial·ism** /ˌeɡzɪˈstenʃəlɪzəm/ noun [U] (philosophy) the theory that humans are free and responsible for their own actions in a world without meaning ▶ **ex·ist·en·tial·ist** /-lɪst/ noun: *Sartre was an existentialist.* **ex·ist·en·tial·ist** adj.: *existentialist theory*

**ex·ist·ing** /ɪɡˈzɪstɪŋ/ adj. [only before noun] found or used now: *New laws will soon replace existing legislation.*

**exit** ⚡+ **B2** /ˈeksɪt, ˈeɡzɪt/ noun, verb
■ noun **1** ⚡+ **B2** [C] a door or way out of a public building or vehicle: *Where's the exit?* ◊ *There is a fire exit on each floor of the building.* ◊ *The emergency exit is at the back of the bus.* ⇒ compare ENTRANCE¹ **2** ⚡+ **B2** a place where vehicles can leave a road to join another road: *Leave the roundabout at the second exit.* ◊ *Take the exit for Brno.* **3** ⚡+ **C1** an act of leaving, especially of an actor from the stage: *The heroine made her exit to great applause.* ◊ *He made a quick exit to avoid meeting her.* ◊ *an exit visa* (= a stamp in a passport giving sb permission to leave a particular country) ⇒ WORDFINDER NOTE at PLAY **4** ⚡+ **C1** the fact of leaving a

particular situation or activity: ~ **from sth** *They were disappointed by the team's early exit from the World Cup.*
■ verb **1** ⚡+ **C1** [I, T] (formal) to go out; to leave a building, stage, vehicle, etc.: **(+ adv./prep.)** *The bullet entered her back and exited through her chest.* ◊ *We exited via a fire door.* ◊ ~ **sth** *As the actors exited the stage the lights went on.* **2** [I, T] to finish using a computer program: ~ **(from sth)** *To exit from this page, press the return key.* ◊ ~ **sth** *I exited the database and switched off the computer.* **3** [I] **exit** … used in the instructions printed in a play to say that an actor must leave the stage

**ˈexit exam** (also formal **ˈexit exam·in·ation**) noun (especially NAmE) an exam that you take at the end of the last year in school or at the end of a period of training: *a high school exit exam*

**ˈexit interview** noun an interview with an employee leaving their job, a student finishing a study programme, etc. in order to find out why they are leaving or what their experience was like

**ˈexit poll** noun in an **exit poll** immediately after an election, people are asked how they voted, in order to predict the result of the election

**ˈexit strategy** noun a plan for getting safely out of a situation that may become difficult or unpleasant: *Part of starting a business is to have an exit strategy.*

**exo·crine** /ˈeksəʊkraɪn, -krɪn; NAmE -səkrɪn/ adj. (biology) connected with GLANDS that do not put substances directly into the blood but export their product through tubes for use outside the body: *exocrine glands* ⇒ compare ENDOCRINE

**exo·dus** /ˈeksədəs/ noun [sing.] ~ **(from …) (to …)** (formal or humorous) a situation in which many people leave a place at the same time: *the mass exodus from Paris to the country in the summer*

**ex of·fi·cio** /ˌeks əˈfɪʃiəʊ/ adj. (from Latin, formal) included or allowed because of your job, position or rank: *an ex officio member of the committee* ▶ **ex of·fi·cio** adv.

**ex·ogen·ous** /ekˈsɒdʒənəs; NAmE -ˈsɑːdʒ-/ adj. **1** ~ **(to sth)** having a cause that is outside itself ⇒ compare ENDOGENOUS **(1) 2** (medical) (of a disease or symptom) having a cause that is outside the body ⇒ compare ENDOGENOUS

**ex·on·er·ate** /ɪɡˈzɒnəreɪt; NAmE -ˈzɑːn-/ verb ~ **sb (from/of sth)** (formal) to officially state that sb is not responsible for sth that they have been blamed for: *The police report exonerated Lewis from all charges of corruption.* ▶ **ex·on·er·ation** /ɪɡˌzɒnəˈreɪʃn; NAmE -ˌzɑːn-/ noun [U]

**ex·or·bi·tant** /ɪɡˈzɔːbɪtənt; NAmE -ˈzɔːrb-/ adj. (formal) (of a price) much too high: *exorbitant costs/fares/fees/prices/rents* ▶ **ex·or·bi·tant·ly** adv.: *Prices are exorbitantly high in this shop.*

**ex·or·cise** (also **-ize**) /ˈeksɔːsaɪz; NAmE -sɔːrs-/ verb **1** ~ **sth (from sb/sth)** | ~ **sb/sth (of sth)** to make an evil spirit leave a place or sb's body by special prayers or magic **2** ~ **sth (from sth)** (formal) to remove sth that is bad or painful from your mind: *She had managed to exorcise these unhappy memories from her mind.*

**ex·or·cism** /ˈeksɔːsɪzəm; NAmE -sɔːrs-/ noun [U, C] **1** the act of getting rid of an evil spirit from a place or a person's body by prayers or magic; a ceremony where this is done **2** (formal) the act of making yourself forget a bad experience or memory

**ex·or·cist** /ˈeksɔːsɪst; NAmE -sɔːrs-/ noun a person who makes evil spirits leave a place or a person's body by prayers or magic

**exo·skel·eton** /ˈeksəʊskelɪtn/ noun (biology) a hard outer layer that protects the bodies of certain animals, such as insects

**exo·ther·mic** /ˌeksəʊˈθɜːmɪk; NAmE -ˈθɜːrm-/ adj. (chemistry) (of a chemical reaction) producing heat ⇒ compare ENDOTHERMIC

**ex·ot·ic** ⚡+ **B2** /ɪɡˈzɒtɪk; NAmE -ˈzɑːt-/ adj. from or in another country, especially a tropical one; seeming exciting and unusual because it seems to be connected with foreign countries: *brightly-coloured exotic flowers/plants/birds* ◊ *She travels to all kinds of exotic locations all over*

# exotica

the world. ▶ **exot·ic·al·ly** /-kli/ *adv.*: *rainbows of exotically coloured blooms*

**exot·ica** /ɪgˈzɒtɪkə; *NAmE* -ˈzɑːt-/ *noun* [U] unusual and exciting things, especially from other countries

**eˌxotic ˈdancer** *noun* a person who dances with very few clothes on, or who removes clothes while dancing

**exoti·cism** /ɪgˈzɒtɪsɪzəm; *NAmE* -ˈzɑːt-/ *noun* [U] (*formal*) the quality of being exciting and unusual that sth has because it seems to be connected with foreign countries

**EXP** (*also* **Exp**) = XP

**ex·pand** ⓘ B1 Ⓦ /ɪkˈspænd/ *verb* **1** Ⓑ1 [I, T] to become greater in size, number or importance; to make sth greater in size, number or importance: *Metals expand when they are heated.* ◊ *Student numbers are expanding rapidly.* ◊ *a greatly expanded version of his earlier book* ◊ **~ to do sth** *The waist expands to fit all sizes.* ◊ **~ (from sth) to sth** *By 1999, the event had expanded from two to three days.* ◊ **~ sth** *They are continuing to expand the range of goods and services they offer.* ◊ *to expand a programme/service* OPP **contract 2** Ⓑ1 [I, T] if a business **expands** or **is expanded**, new branches are opened, it makes more money, etc: *an expanding economy* (= with more businesses starting and growing) ◊ *The organic market is rapidly expanding among middle-class shoppers.* ◊ **~ into sth** *They have recently expanded into the Middle East.* ◊ **~ sth** *We've expanded the business by opening two more stores.* ◊ *The company is planning to expand its American operations.* **3** [I] to talk more; to add details to what you are saying: *I repeated the question and waited for her to expand.*
PHRV **exˈpand on/upon sth** to say more about sth and add some details: *Could you expand on that point, please?*

**ex·pand·able** /ɪkˈspændəbl/ *adj.* (*specialist*) that can be expanded: *an expandable briefcase* ◊ **~ to sth** *The system has 4GB RAM, expandable to 32GB.*

**ex·panse** /ɪkˈspæns/ *noun* **~ (of sth)** a wide and open area of sth, especially land or water: *a wide/vast expanse of blue sky* ◊ *flat expanses of open farmland*

**ex·pan·sion** B2+ Ⓦ /ɪkˈspænʃn/ *noun* [U, C] an act of increasing or making sth increase in size, amount or importance: *a period of rapid economic expansion* ◊ *Despite the recession the company is confident of further expansion.* ◊ *The book is an expansion of a series of lectures given last year.*

**ex·pan·sion·ary** /ɪkˈspænʃənri; *NAmE* -ʃəneri/ *adj.* (*formal*) encouraging economic or political expansion: *This budget will have a net expansionary effect on the economy.*

**ex·pan·sion·ism** /ɪkˈspænʃənɪzəm/ *noun* [U] (*sometimes disapproving*) the belief in and process of increasing the size and importance of sth, especially in a country or a business: *the economic expansionism of America* ◊ *military/territorial expansionism* ▶ **ex·pan·sion·ist** /-ʃənɪst/ *adj.*: *expansionist policies*

**ex·pan·sive** /ɪkˈspænsɪv/ *adj.* **1** covering a large amount of space: *She opened her arms wide in an expansive gesture of welcome.* ◊ *landscape with expansive skies* **2** covering a large subject area, rather than trying to be exact and use few words: *We need to look at a more expansive definition of the term.* ◊ *The piece is written in his usual expansive style.* **3** friendly and willing to talk a lot: *She was clearly relaxed and in an expansive mood.* **4** (*especially of a period of time*) encouraging economic EXPANSION: *In the expansive 1990s bright graduates could advance rapidly.* ▶ **ex·pan·sive·ly** *adv.*: *He waved his arms expansively.* **ex·pan·sive·ness** *noun* [U]

**ex·patri·ate** /ˌeksˈpætriət; *NAmE* -ˈpeɪt-/ (*also informal* **expat** /ˈekspæt/) *noun* a person living in a country that is not their own: *American expatriates in Paris* ⇨ SYNONYMS at IMMIGRANT ▶ **ex·patri·ate** *adj.* [only before noun]: *expatriate Britons in Spain* ◊ *expatriate workers* ⇨ SYNONYMS at IMMIGRANT

**ex·pect** ⓘ A2 Ⓦ /ɪkˈspekt/ *verb* **1** A2 [T] to think or believe that sth will happen or that sb will do sth: **~ sth** *The company is expecting record sales this year.* ◊ *Change often happens when you least expect it.* ◊ **~ sth from sb/sth** *Don't expect sympathy from me!* ◊ **~ sth of sb/sth** *That's not the sort of behaviour I expect of you!* ◊ **~ to do sth** *They never expected to find their dream home.* ◊ *I looked back, half expecting to see someone following me.* ◊ **~ sb/sth to do sth** *Analysts expect the company to announce growth of at least 5 per cent.* ◊ *I fully expected her to refuse my offer.* ◊ **~ (that)…** *House prices are expected to rise sharply.* ◊ **~ (that)…** *Many people were expecting (that) the peace talks would break down.* ◊ *it is expected that…* *It is widely expected that interest rates will rise.* **2** A2 [T] (often used in the progressive tenses) to be waiting for sb/sth to arrive, as this has been arranged: **~ sb/sth** *to expect a visit/call/letter from sb* ◊ *We were expecting him yesterday.* ◊ *They are not expected until tomorrow.* ◊ **~ sb to do sth** *We were expecting him to arrive yesterday.* **3** Ⓑ1 [T] to demand that sb will do sth because it is their duty or responsibility: **~ sth** *It is reasonable to expect changes in the way we work.* ◊ *These are the high standards that hotel guests have come to expect.* ◊ **~ sth from sb** *He's still getting over his illness, so it's unrealistic to expect too much from him.* ◊ **~ sth of sb** *Are you clear what is expected of you?* ◊ **~ sb to do sth** *You can't reasonably expect people to pay such high taxes.* ◊ **~ to do sth** *I expect to be paid promptly for the work.* ⇨ SYNONYMS at DEMAND **4** B2 [I] **expect** [I, T] (*especially BrE, informal*) (not used in the progressive tenses) used when you think sth is probably true: *'Will you be late?' 'I expect so.'* ◊ *'Are you going out tonight?' 'I don't expect so.'* ◊ **~ (that…)** *'Who's eaten all the cake?' 'Tom, I expect/I expect it was Tom.'* HELP *'That' is nearly always left out.* ⇨ *compare* UNEXPECTED
IDM **be exˈpecting (a baby/child)** (*informal*) to be pregnant: *Ann's expecting a baby in June.* **be (only) to be exˈpected** to be likely to happen; to be quite normal: *A little tiredness after taking these drugs is to be expected.* **what (else) do you exˈpect?** (*informal*) used to tell sb not to be surprised by sth: *She swore at you? What do you expect when you treat her like that?*

---

▼ **LANGUAGE BANK**

**expect**
Discussing predictions

- By 2050, one in six people on the planet **will be aged** 65 or over.
- The number of people globally aged 65 and over is **expected/likely** to more than double by 2050.
- Experts have **predicted/forecast** that the over-65s will make up 17 per cent of the global population by 2050.
- World population **is set to** reach 9.8 billion by 2050.
- Net migration into Britain over the last decade was higher **than expected**.
- Overall population growth in Britain has been **in line with predictions**.

⇨ LANGUAGE BANK *at* FALL, ILLUSTRATE, INCREASE, PROPORTION

---

**ex·pect·ancy** /ɪkˈspektənsi/ *noun* [U] the state of expecting or hoping that sth, especially sth good or exciting, will happen: *There was an air of expectancy among the waiting crowd.* ⇨ *see also* LIFE EXPECTANCY

**ex·pect·ant** /ɪkˈspektənt/ *adj.* **1** hoping for sth, especially sth good and exciting: *children with expectant faces waiting for the fireworks to begin* ◊ *A sudden roar came from the expectant crowd.* **2** **~ mother/father/parent** used to describe sb who is going to have a baby soon or become a father ▶ **ex·pect·ant·ly** *adv.*: *She looked at him expectantly.* ◊ *waiting expectantly*

**ex·pect·ation** ⓘ B2 Ⓦ /ˌekspekˈteɪʃn/ *noun* **1** B2 [U, C] a belief that sth will happen because it is likely: **~ of sth** *We are confident in our expectation of a full recovery.* ◊ **~ that…** *There was a general expectation that he would win.* ◊ *The expectation is that property prices will rise.* ◊ **in ~ (of sth)** *Buyers are holding back in expectation of further price cuts.* ◊ *Contrary to expectations, interest rates did not rise.* ◊ *Against all expectations, she was enjoying herself.* **2** B2 [C, usually pl., U] a hope that sth good will happen: *She went to college with great expectations.* ◊ *to have high/low expectations* ◊ *I don't want to raise your expectations too much.* ◊ *The results exceeded our expectations.* ◊ *The event did not live up to expectations.* ◊ *There was an air of expectation and great curiosity.* ◊ **expectations for sb/sth** *He has high expectations for the team.*

**3** [C, usually pl.] a strong belief about the way sth should happen or how sb should behave: *Unfortunately the new software has failed to meet expectations.* ◇ **expectations of sb** *Some parents have unrealistic expectations of their children.*

**ex·pec·ta·tion of ˈlife** *noun* [U] = LIFE EXPECTANCY

**ex·pect·ed** ❶ **B1** /ɪkˈspektɪd/ *adj.* that you think will happen: *Double the expected number of people came to the meeting.* ◇ *this year's expected earnings* ⇒ compare UNEXPECTED

**ex·pe·di·ent** /ɪkˈspiːdiənt/ *noun, adj.*
■ *noun* an action that is useful or necessary for a particular purpose, but not always fair or right: *The disease was controlled by the simple expedient of not allowing anyone to leave the city.*
■ *adj.* [not usually before noun] (of an action) useful or necessary for a particular purpose, but not always fair or right: *The government has clearly decided that a cut in interest rates would be politically expedient.* **OPP** inexpedient
▶ **ex·pe·di·ency** /-ənsi/ *noun* [U]: *He acted out of expediency, not principle.* **ex·pe·di·ent·ly** *adv.*

**ex·pe·dite** /ˈekspədaɪt/ *verb* ~ **sth** (*formal*) to make a process happen more quickly **SYN** **speed up**: *We have developed rapid order processing to expedite deliveries to customers.*

**ex·pe·di·tion** ❶ **B1** /ˌekspəˈdɪʃn/ *noun* **1** **B1** an organized journey with a particular purpose, especially to find out about a place that is not well known: *to plan/lead/go on an expedition* ◇ ~ **to sth** *Captain Scott's expedition to the South Pole* ◇ **on an~** *Hawkins had died on the same expedition a few weeks earlier.* ⇒ WORDFINDER NOTE at JOURNEY **2** the people who go on an expedition: *Three members of the Everest expedition were killed.* **3** (*sometimes humorous*) a short trip that you make when you want or need sth: *a shopping expedition* ⇒ SYNONYMS at TRIP ⇒ see also FISHING EXPEDITION

**ex·pe·di·tion·ary force** /ˌekspəˈdɪʃənri fɔːs; *NAmE* -ʃəneri fɔːrs/ *noun* [C + sing./pl. v.] a group of soldiers who are sent to another country to fight in a war

**ex·pe·di·tious** /ˌekspəˈdɪʃəs/ *adj.* (*formal*) that works well without wasting time, money, etc. **SYN** **efficient** ▶ **ex·pe·di·tious·ly** *adv.*

**expel** /ɪkˈspel/ *verb* (-ll-) **1** ~ **sb** (**from sth**) to officially make sb leave a school or an organization: *She was expelled from school at 15.* ◇ *Olympic athletes expelled for drug-taking* **2** ~ **sb** (**from sth**) to force sb to leave a country: *Foreign journalists are being expelled.* **3** ~ **sth** (**from sth**) (*specialist*) to force air or water out of a part of the body or from a container: *to expel air from the lungs* ⇒ see also EXPULSION

**ex·pend** /ɪkˈspend/ *verb* ~ **sth** (**in/on sth**) | ~ **sth** (**in/on**) **doing sth** (*formal*) to use or spend a lot of time, money, energy, etc.: *She expended all her efforts on the care of home and children.*

**ex·pend·able** /ɪkˈspendəbl/ *adj.* (*formal*) if you consider people or things to be **expendable**, you think that you can get rid of them when they are no longer needed, or think it is acceptable if they are killed or destroyed **SYN** **dispensable**

**ex·pend·iture** ❶ **C1** /ɪkˈspendɪtʃə(r)/ *noun* [U, C] **1** the act of spending or using money; an amount of money spent: *a reduction in public/government/military expenditure* ◇ *plans to increase expenditure on health* ◇ *The budget provided for a total expenditure of £27 billion.* ⇒ SYNONYMS at COST **2** the use of energy, time, materials, etc: *the expenditure of emotion* ◇ *This study represents a major expenditure of time and effort.* ⇒ compare INCOME

**ex·pense** ❶ **B2** /ɪkˈspens/ *noun* **1** **B2** [U] the money that you spend on sth: *The garden was transformed at great expense.* ◇ *No expense was spared* (= they spent as much money as was needed) *to make the party a success.* ◇ *She always travels first-class regardless of expense.* ◇ *The results are well worth the expense.* ⇒ WORDFINDER NOTE at MONEY ⇒ SYNONYMS at PRICE **2** **B2** [C, usually sing.] something that makes you spend money: *Running a car is a big expense.* **3** **B2** **expenses** [pl.] money spent in doing a particular job, or for a particular purpose: *living/medical/travel expenses* ◇ *The company has cut operating expenses*

---

543    **experience**

*to their lowest levels in three years* ◇ *Can I give you something towards expenses?* ◇ *The payments he gets barely cover his expenses.* ⇒ SYNONYMS at COST **4** **B2** **expenses** [pl.] money that you spend while you are working and that your employer will pay back to you later: *You can claim back your travelling/travel expenses.* ◇ *We paid their expenses, but nothing more.* ◇ *an all-expenses-paid trip* ◇ **on expenses** (*BrE*) *to take a client out for a meal on expenses* ⇒ SYNONYMS at COST

**IDM** **at sb's expense 1** paid for by sb: *We were taken out for a meal at the company's expense.* **2** if you make a joke **at sb's expense**, you laugh at them and make them feel silly **at the expense of sb/sth** with loss or damage to sb/sth: *He built up the business at the expense of his health.* **go to the expense of sth/of doing sth** | **go to a lot of, etc. expense** to spend money on sth: *They went to all the expense of redecorating the house and then they moved.* **put sb to the expense of sth/of doing sth** | **put sb to a lot of, etc. expense** to make sb spend money on sth: *Their visit put us to a lot of expense.*

**exˈpense account** *noun* an arrangement by which money spent by sb while they are at work is later paid back to them by their employer; a record of money spent in this way

**ex·pen·sive** ❶ **A1** /ɪkˈspensɪv/ *adj.* costing a lot of money: *an expensive car/restaurant/holiday* ◇ *I can't afford it—it's too expensive.* ◇ *Making the wrong decision could prove expensive.* ◇ *That dress was an expensive mistake.* ◇ ~ **to do** *Art books are expensive to produce.* ◇ ~ **for sb** *The new regulations are likely to be very expensive for employers.* ◇ **it is ~ (for sb) to do sth** *It's expensive to live in London.* **OPP** **cheap, inexpensive** ▶ **ex·pen·sive·ly** *adv.*: *expensively dressed/furnished* ◇ *There are other restaurants where you can eat less expensively.*

▼ SYNONYMS
**expensive**
costly • overpriced • pricey • dear
These words all describe sth that costs a lot of money.
**expensive** costing a lot of money; charging high prices: *I can't afford it—it's just too expensive for me.* ◇ *an expensive restaurant*
**costly** (*rather formal*) costing a lot of money, especially more than you want to pay: *You want to avoid costly legal proceedings if you can.*
**overpriced** too expensive; costing more than it is worth: *ridiculously overpriced designer clothes*
**pricey** (*informal*) expensive: *Houses in the village are now too pricey for local people to afford.*
**dear** [not usually before noun] (*BrE*) expensive: *Everything's so dear now, isn't it?* **NOTE** This word is starting to become rather old-fashioned.
PATTERNS
• expensive/costly/overpriced/pricey for sb/sth
• expensive/costly to do sth
• very/too/fairly/quite/pretty expensive/costly/pricey

**ex·peri·ence** ❶ **A2** ❶ /ɪkˈspɪəriəns; *NAmE* -ˈspɪr-/ *noun, verb*
■ *noun* **1** **A2** [U] the knowledge and skill that you have gained through doing sth for a period of time; the process of gaining this: *My lack of practical experience was a disadvantage.* ◇ ~ **of sth** *Do you have any previous experience of this type of work?* ◇ ~ **in doing sth** *a doctor with experience in dealing with patients suffering from stress* ◇ ~ **in sth** *He gained extensive experience in the field of artificial intelligence whilst working on the project.* ◇ **as sth** *I have over ten years' experience as a teacher.* ◇ ~ **with sth** *The course provides hands-on experience with various systems.* ◇ *We all learn by experience.* ⇒ see also WORK EXPERIENCE ⇒ WORDFINDER NOTE at APPLY **2** **A2** [U] the things that have happened to you that influence the way you think and behave: *Experience has taught me that life can be very unfair.* ◇ *The book is based on personal experience.* ◇ **from ~** *It is important to try and learn from experience.* ◇ *She knew from past experience that Ann would not give up*

# experienced

easily. ◊ in sb's ~ *In my experience, very few people really understand the problem.* ◊ **~ of sth** *He had first-hand experience of poverty.* **3** [C] *an event or activity that affects you in some way:* *a unique/positive/wonderful experience* ◊ **~ of sth** *Share your experiences of parenthood by emailing the address below.* ◊ **~ of doing sth** *It was her first experience of living alone.* ◊ *The play is based loosely on his own life experiences.* ◊ *Losing four matches in a row proved a valuable **learning experience** (= it showed the players what they need to improve).* ⇒ see also NEAR-DEATH EXPERIENCE, OUT-OF-BODY EXPERIENCE **4** [sing.] *(often in compounds)* what it is like for sb to use a service, do an activity, attend an event, etc: *We are continually looking for ways to improve the **customer experience**.* ◊ *Enjoy a fine dining experience with quality service.* ⇒ see also USER EXPERIENCE **5** **the … experience** [sing.] *events or knowledge shared by all the members of a particular group in society, that influences the way they think and behave: musical forms like jazz that emerged out of the Black American experience*

**IDM** **put sth down to ex'perience** *(also* **chalk sth up to ex'perience)** *used to say that sb should think of a failure as being sth that they can learn from: We lost a lot of money, but we just put it down to experience.*

- verb **1** ~ **sth** *to have a particular situation affect you or happen to you: Many people have never experienced these difficulties first-hand.* ◊ *We are currently experiencing problems with our IT systems.* ◊ *They had the opportunity to experience life at sea.* **2** ~ **sth** *to have and be aware of a particular emotion or physical feeling: I have never experienced such pain before.* ◊ *I experienced a moment of panic as I boarded the plane.*

**ex·peri·enced** /ɪkˈspɪəriənst/; *NAmE* -ˈspɪr-/ *adj.* **1** having knowledge or skill in a particular job or activity: *an experienced player/teacher* ◊ **~ in (doing) sth** *He's very experienced in looking after animals.* **2** having knowledge as a result of doing sth for a long time, or having had a lot of different experiences: *She's very young and not very experienced.* ◊ *an experienced traveller (= sb who has travelled a lot)* **OPP** inexperienced

**ex'perience points** *noun* [pl.] *(abbr.* **XP, XPs, EXP, Exp, EXPs, Exps)** *points that you earn in a computer game for completing tasks, collecting items, etc: You get experience points for each enemy you defeat.*

**ex·peri·en·tial** /ɪkˌspɪəriˈenʃl/; *NAmE* -ˌspɪr-/ *adj. (formal or specialist)* based on or involving experience: *experiential knowledge* ◊ *experiential learning methods*

**ex·peri·ment** *noun, verb*

- *noun* /ɪkˈsperɪmənt/ [C, U] **1** *a scientific test that is done in order to study what happens and to gain new knowledge: to do/perform/conduct an experiment* ◊ *laboratory experiments* ◊ **in an ~** *The 30 subjects in each experiment were divided into two groups.* ◊ **on sb/sth** *Many people do not like the idea of experiments on animals.* ◊ **~ with sb/sth** *The experiment with cells from other species was unsuccessful.* ◊ **by …** *Facts can be established by observation and experiment.* ⇒ WORDFINDER NOTE at SCIENCE **2** *a new activity, idea or method that you try out to see what happens or what effect it has: I've never cooked this before so it's an experiment.* ◊ **in sth** *the country's brief experiment in democracy* ◊ **~ with sth** *His experiments with narrative form were very influential.*

- *verb* /ɪkˈsperɪment/ **1** [I] *to do a scientific experiment or experiments:* **~ on sb/sth** *Some people feel that experimenting on animals is wrong.* ◊ **~ with sth** *The country had secretly experimented with biological weapons for years.* **2** [I] *to try or test new ideas, methods, etc. to find out what effect they have: I experimented until I got the recipe just right.* ◊ **~ with sth** *She had experimented with drugs when she was at college.* ▸ **ex·peri·ment·er** *noun*

**ex·peri·men·tal** /ɪkˌsperɪˈmentl/ *adj.* **1** *based on new ideas, forms or methods that are used to find out what effect they have: experimental teaching methods* ◊ *experimental theatre/art/music* ◊ *The equipment is still at the experimental stage.* **2** *connected with scientific experiments: experimental conditions/data/evidence* ▸ **ex·peri·men·tal·ly** /-təli/ *adv.: This theory can be confirmed experimentally.* ◊ *The new drug is being used experimentally on some patients.* ◊ *He moved his shoulder experimentally to see if it still hurt.*

**ex·peri·men·ta·tion** /ɪkˌsperɪmenˈteɪʃn/ *noun* [U] *(formal)* **1** **~ (on sth)** *the activity or process of doing scientific experiments: Many people object to experimentation on embryos.* **2** **~ (with sth)** *the activity or process of trying or testing new ideas, methods, etc. to find out what effect they have:* **~ with sth** *experimentation with new teaching methods*

**ex·pert** /ˈekspɜːt/; *NAmE* -pɜːrt/ *noun, adj.*

- *noun* *a person with special knowledge, skill or training in sth: a legal/security/medical/computer expert* ◊ **according to an ~** *According to our panel of leading industry experts, a downturn is inevitable.* ◊ **~ at/in/on sth** *Experts in the field of child psychology warn of the dangers of social media.* ◊ *I don't pretend to be an **expert on the subject** .* ◊ **~ at/in/on doing sth** *You will need to **become an expert** in analysing data.*

- *adj.* *done with, having or involving great knowledge or skill:* **to seek expert advice** ◊ *Only a fully qualified doctor can give an **expert opinion**.* ◊ *an **expert witness*** ◊ **~ at/in/on sth** *They are expert in these matters.* ◊ **~ at/in/on doing sth** *She's expert at making cheap but stylish clothes.* ⇒ compare INEXPERT ▸ **ex·pert·ly** *adv.: The roads were icy but she stopped the car expertly.* ◊ *The music was expertly performed.*

**ex·pert·ise** /ˌekspɜːˈtiːz/; *NAmE* -pɜːrt-/ *noun* [U] *expert knowledge or skill in a particular subject, activity or job: professional/scientific/technical, etc. expertise* ◊ *We have the expertise to help you run your business.* ◊ **~ in sth/in doing sth** *They have considerable expertise in dealing with oil spills.*

**expert 'system** *noun (computing)* *a computer system that can provide information and expert advice on a particular subject. The program asks users a series of questions about their problem and gives them advice based on its store of knowledge.*

**ex·pir·ation** /ˌekspəˈreɪʃn/ *noun* [U] *(NAmE)* = EXPIRY

**expi'ration date** *(NAmE)* *(BrE* **ex'piry date)** *noun the date after which an official document, agreement, etc. is no longer legally acceptable, or after which sth should not be used or eaten: Check the expiration date on your passport.* ◊ *The expiration date on this yogurt was November 20.*

**ex·pire** /ɪkˈspaɪə(r)/ *verb* **1** [I] *(of a document, an agreement, etc.) to be no longer legally acceptable because the period of time for which it could be used has ended* **SYN** **run out:** *When does your driving licence expire?* **2** [I] *(of a period of time, especially one during which sb holds a position of authority) to end: His term of office expires at the end of June.* **3** [I] *(literary) to die* ▸ **ex·pired** *adj.: an expired passport* ⇒ see also UNEXPIRED

**ex·piry** /ɪkˈspaɪəri/ *(especially BrE) (NAmE usually* **ex·pir·ation)** *noun* [U] *an ending of the period of time when an official document can be used, or when an agreement is legally acceptable: the expiry of a fixed-term contract* ◊ **on ~** *The licence can be renewed on expiry.*

**ex'piry date** *(BrE)* *(NAmE* **expi'ration date)** *noun the date after which an official document, agreement, etc. is no longer legally acceptable, or after which sth should not be used or eaten: Check the expiry date of your credit cards.*

**ex·plain** /ɪkˈspleɪn/ *verb* **1** [T, I] *to tell sb about sth in a way that makes it easy to understand:* **~ (sth)** *He was trying to explain the difference between hip hop and rap.* ◊ *'Let me explain!' he added helpfully.* ◊ **~ (sth) to sb** *It was difficult to explain the concept to beginners.* ◊ **~ that …** *I explained that an ambulance would be coming soon.* ◊ **~ who, how, etc …** *He explained who each person in the photo was.* ◊ **~ to sb who, how, etc …** *She explained to the children exactly what to do in an emergency.* ◊ **+ speech** *'It works like this,' she explained.* ◊ **it is explained that …** *It was explained that attendance was compulsory.* **2** [I, T] *to give a reason, or be a reason, for sth: She tried to explain but he wouldn't listen.* ◊ **~ that …** *Alex explained that his car had broken*

**WORD FAMILY**
explain *verb*
explanation *noun*
explanatory *adj.*
explicable *adj.*
(≠ inexplicable)

down. ◊ **~why, how, etc…** *Well, that doesn't explain why you didn't phone.* ◊ **~sth** *Please* **explain** *your reasons.* ◊ (*informal*) *Oh well then, that* **explains** *it* (= I understand now why sth happened). ◊ **~sth to sb** *The government now has to explain its decision to the public.* ◊ **+ speech** *'It was like this,' she explained.* HELP You cannot say 'explain me, him, her, etc.': *Can you explain the situation to me?* ◊ ~~Can you explain me the situation?~~ ◊ *I'll explain to you why I like it.* ◊ ~~I'll explain you why I like it.~~
IDM ex'plain yourself **1** to give sb reasons for your behaviour, especially when they are angry or upset because of it: *I really don't see why I should have to explain myself to you.* **2** to say what you mean in a clear way: *Could you explain yourself a little more—I didn't understand.*
PHR V ex,plain sth↔a'way to give reasons why sth is not your fault or why sth is not important

▼ EXPRESS YOURSELF
**Asking for clarification**
When you are given some information or asked to do something, you may need to check that you have understood correctly. Here are some ways of asking people to clarify what they said:
• *I'm sorry, I didn't quite understand.*
• *Would you mind explaining that again? I'm not sure that I've understood correctly.*
• *Sorry, I don't quite follow (you).*
• *Can I just check that I've got this right?*
• *I'm not quite/exactly clear about/really sure what I'm supposed to do.*
• *Sorry, could you repeat that? I didn't hear what you said.*
• *Sorry, would you mind repeating what you just said?*
• *If I understand you correctly, you want me to phone the customer and apologise?*
• *Do you mean (to say) that the deal's off?*
• *What exactly are you saying?*
• *So you're saying that the meeting's cancelled?*
• *Sorry, did you mean that I should wait here or come back later?*
• *Can you just confirm your date of birth for me, please?*

**ex·plain·er** /ɪkˈspleɪnə(r)/ *noun* **1** a person who explains a concept, topic, situation, etc: *to be a good explainer* **2** a video or a piece of text that explains a concept, topic, situation, etc: *Here's a video explainer on how the nervous system works.*

**ex·plan·ation** ⓘ A2 ⓞ /ˌekspləˈneɪʃn/ *noun*
**1** A2 [C, U] a statement, fact, or situation that tells you why sth happened; a reason given for sth: *The most likely explanation is that his plane was delayed.* ◊ *to offer/provide an explanation* ◊ *I can't think of any possible explanation for his absence.* ◊ *I'm sure there's a perfectly simple explanation for this.* ◊ **~for doing sth** *She didn't give an adequate explanation for being late.* ◊ **~of sth** *The book opens with an explanation of why some drugs are banned.* ◊ **~as to why…** *an explanation as to why he had left early* ◊ **without~** *She left the room abruptly without explanation.* ⮕ SYNONYMS at REASON **2** A2 [C] **~(of how, what, etc ….)** a statement or piece of writing that tells you how sth works or makes sth easier to understand: *For a full explanation of how the machine works, turn to page 5.*

**ex·plana·tory** Ⓦ /ɪkˈsplænətri; *NAmE* -tɔːri/ *adj.* [usually before noun] giving the reasons for sth; intended to describe how sth works or to make sth easier to understand: *There are explanatory notes at the back of the book.*
⮕ see also SELF-EXPLANATORY

**ex·ple·tive** /ɪkˈspliːtɪv; *NAmE* ˈeksplətɪv/ *noun* (*formal*) a word, especially a rude word, that you use when you are angry, or in pain SYN **swear word**

**ex·plic·able** /ɪkˈsplɪkəbl, ˈeksplɪkəbl/ *adj.* [not usually before noun] (*formal*) that can be explained or understood: *His behaviour is only explicable in terms of (= because of) his recent illness.* OPP **inexplicable**

**ex·pli·cate** /ˈeksplɪkeɪt/ *verb* **~sth** (*formal*) to explain an idea or a work of literature in a lot of detail ▸ **ex·pli·ca·tion** /ˌeksplɪˈkeɪʃn/ *noun* [C, U]

**ex·pli·cit** Ⓣ C1 Ⓦ /ɪkˈsplɪsɪt/ *adj.* **1** Ⓣ C1 (of a statement or piece of writing) clear and easy to understand, so that

545 **explode**

you have no doubt what is meant: *He gave me very explicit directions on how to get there.* ◊ *The reasons for the decision should be made explicit.* ◊ *She made some very explicit references to my personal life.* ⮕ compare IMPLICIT (1) **2** Ⓣ C1 (of a person) saying sth clearly, exactly and openly SYN **frank**: *She was quite explicit about why she had left.* **3** (*usually disapproving*) describing or showing sth, especially sexual activity, with a lot of detail: *a sexually explicit film* ▸ **ex·pli·cit·ness** *noun* [U]

**ex·pli·cit·ly** Ⓣ C1 Ⓦ /ɪkˈsplɪsɪtli/ *adv.* **1** Ⓣ C1 clearly or directly, so that the meaning is easy to understand: *The report states explicitly that the system was to blame.* ◊ *The text does not explicitly mention him by name.* ⮕ compare IMPLICITLY **2** (*usually disapproving*) with a lot of detail, especially in describing or showing sexual activity: *the explicitly sexual content of the image*

▼ SYNONYMS
**explode**
blow up • go off • burst • erupt • detonate
These are all words that can be used when sth breaks apart violently, causing damage or injury.
**explode** to BURST (= to break open or apart) loudly and violently, causing damage; to make sth BURST in this way: *The jet smashed into a hillside and exploded.* ◊ *The bomb was exploded under controlled conditions.*
**blow (sth) up** to be destroyed by an explosion; to destroy sth by an explosion: *A police officer was killed when his car blew up.*
**go off** (of a bomb) to explode; (of a gun) to be fired: *The bomb went off in a crowded street.* NOTE When used about guns, the choice of **go off** (instead of 'be fired') can suggest that the gun was fired by accident.
**burst** to break open or apart, especially because of pressure from inside; to make sth break in this way: *That balloon's going to burst.*
**erupt** (of a volcano) to throw out burning rocks and smoke; (of burning rocks and smoke) to be thrown out of a volcano.
**detonate** (*rather formal*) (of a bomb) to explode; to make a bomb explode: *Two other bombs failed to detonate.*
PATTERNS
• a **bomb** explodes/blows up/goes off/bursts/detonates
• a **car/plane/vehicle** explodes/blows up
• a **firework/rocket** explodes/goes off
• a **gun** goes off

**ex·plode** ⓘ B1
/ɪkˈspləʊd/ *verb*
• BREAK APART VIOLENTLY
**1** Ⓣ B1 [I, T] to BURST (= break apart) or make sth BURST loudly and violently, causing damage SYN **blow up**: *A second bomb exploded in a crowded market.* ◊ **~sth** *Bomb disposal experts exploded the device under controlled conditions.* ⮕ compare IMPLODE
• GET ANGRY/DANGEROUS **2** [I, T] (of a person or situation) to suddenly become very angry or dangerous: **~with sth** *Suddenly Charles exploded with rage.* ◊ **~into sth** *The protest exploded into a riot.* ◊ **+ speech** *'Of course there's something wrong!' Jem exploded.*
• EXPRESS EMOTION **3** [I] **~(into/with sth)** to suddenly express an emotion: *We all exploded into wild laughter.*
• MOVE SUDDENLY **4** [I] **~(into/to sth)** to suddenly and quickly do sth; to move suddenly with a lot of force: *After ten minutes the game exploded into life.*
• MAKE LOUD NOISE **5** [I] to make a sudden very loud noise: *Thunder exploded overhead.*
• INCREASE QUICKLY **6** [I] to increase suddenly and very quickly in number: *the exploding world population*
• SHOW STH IS NOT TRUE **7** [T] **~sth** to show that sth is not true, especially sth that people believe: *At last, a women's magazine to explode the myth that thin equals beautiful.*

WORD FAMILY
**explode** *verb*
**explosion** *noun*
**explosive** *adj., noun*
**unexploded** *adj.*

Ⓞ Oxford Phrasal Academic Lexicon (OPAL) written and spoken word lists | Ⓦ OPAL written word list | Ⓢ OPAL spoken word list

**ex·plod·ed** /ɪkˈspləʊdɪd/ *adj.* (*specialist*) (of a drawing or diagram) showing the parts of sth separately but also showing how they are connected to each other ⇨ compare UNEXPLODED

exploded diagram

**ex·ploit** ⓘ B2 Ⓦ *verb, noun*
▪ *verb* /ɪkˈsplɔɪt/ **1** ⓘ B2 ~ **sth** (*disapproving*) to treat a person or situation as an opportunity to gain an advantage for yourself: *He exploited his father's name to get himself a job.* ◇ *She realized that her youth and inexperience were being exploited.* **2** ⓘ B2 ~ **sb** (*disapproving*) to treat sb unfairly by making them work and not giving them much in return: *What is being done to stop employers from exploiting young people?* **3** ⓘ C1 ~ **sth** to use sth well in order to gain as much from it as possible: *She fully exploits the humour of her role in the play.* **4** ⓘ C1 to develop or use sth for business or industry: ~ **sth** *No minerals have yet been exploited in Antarctica.* ◇ ~ **sth for sth** *countries exploiting the rainforests for hardwood* ▶ **ex·ploit·er** *noun*
▪ *noun* /ˈeksplɔɪt/ [usually pl.] a brave, exciting or interesting act: *the daring exploits of Roman heroes*

**ex·ploit·ation** ⓘ+ C1 Ⓦ /ˌeksplɔɪˈteɪʃn/ *noun* [U, C] **1** ⓘ+ C1 (*disapproving*) a situation in which sb treats sb else in an unfair way, especially in order to make money from their work: *the exploitation of children* **2** ⓘ+ C1 the use of land, oil, minerals, etc: *commercial exploitation of the mineral resources in Antarctica* **3** ⓘ+ C1 (*disapproving*) the fact of using a situation in order to get an advantage for yourself: *exploitation of the situation for his own purposes*

**ex·ploit·ative** /ɪkˈsplɔɪtətɪv/ (*NAmE also* **ex·ploit·ive** /ɪkˈsplɔɪtɪv/) *adj.* (*disapproving*) treating sb unfairly in order to gain an advantage or to make money

**ex·plor·ation** ⓘ B2 Ⓦ /ˌekspləˈreɪʃn/ *noun* [C, U] **1** ⓘ B2 the act of travelling through a place in order to find out about it or look for sth in it: *Budgets for space exploration have been cut back.* ◇ *oil exploration* (= searching for oil in the ground) **2** ⓘ B2 an examination of sth in order to find out about it: *These findings merit further exploration.* ◇ *the book's explorations of the human mind*

**ex·plora·tory** /ɪkˈsplɒrətri; NAmE -ˈsplɔːrətɔːri/ *adj.* done with the intention of examining sth in order to find out more about it: *exploratory surgery* ◇ *exploratory drilling for oil*

**ex·plore** ⓘ B1 Ⓞ /ɪkˈsplɔː(r)/ *verb* **1** ⓘ B1 [I, T] to travel to or around an area or a country in order to learn about it: *As soon as we arrived on the island we were eager to explore.* ◇ ~ **sth (for sth)** *They explored the land to the south of the Murray River.* ◇ *The city is best explored on foot.* ◇ ~ **for sth** *companies exploring for* (= searching for) *oil* ⇨ WORDFINDER NOTE at ADVENTURE

| WORDFINDER colonize, discover, pioneer, reconnaissance, scout, settle, terrain, territory, voyage |
|---|

**2** ⓘ B2 [T] ~ **sth** to examine a subject or a possibility completely or carefully in order to find out more about it ⓢⓨⓝ **analyse**: *to explore a theme/an issue* ◇ *We will explore these ideas in more detail in chapter 7.* ◇ *to explore the possibilities/options* ◇ *The firm will explore possible joint development projects.* ⇨ LANGUAGE BANK at ABOUT **3** [T] ~ **sth (with sth)** to feel sth with your hands or another part of the body: *She explored the sand with her toes.* ⇨ see also UNEXPLORED

**ex·plor·er** /ɪkˈsplɔːrə(r)/ *noun* a person who travels to unknown places in order to find out more about them

**Ex'plorer Scout** (*also* **Explorer**) *noun* (in the UK) a member of the senior branch of the SCOUT ASSOCIATION for young people between the ages of 14 and 18

**ex·plo·sion** ⓘ B1 /ɪkˈspləʊʒn/ *noun* **1** ⓘ B1 [C, U] the sudden violent BURSTING and loud noise of sth such as a bomb exploding; the act of deliberately causing sth to explode: *a bomb/nuclear/gas explosion* ◇ *There were two loud explosions and then the building burst into flames.* ◇ *a huge/massive explosion* ◇ *Bomb Squad officers carried out a controlled explosion of the device.* ◇ *in an ~ 300 people were injured in the explosion.* **2** ⓘ B2 [C] a large, sudden or rapid increase in the amount or number of sth: *a population explosion* ◇ ~ **of sth** *an explosion of interest in learning Japanese* ◇ ~ **in sth** *an explosion in oil prices* **3** [C] (*formal*) a sudden, violent expression of emotion, especially anger ⓢⓨⓝ **outburst**

**ex·plo·sive** ⓘ+ C1 /ɪkˈspləʊsɪv, -ˈspləʊzɪv/ *adj., noun*
▪ *adj.* **1** ⓘ+ C1 easily able or likely to explode: *an explosive device* (= a bomb) ◇ *an explosive mixture of chemicals* **2** ⓘ+ C1 likely to cause violence or strong feelings of anger or hate: *a potentially explosive situation* **3** often having sudden violent or angry feelings: *an explosive temper* **4** increasing suddenly and rapidly: *the explosive growth of the export market* **5** (of a sound) sudden and loud ▶ **ex·plo·sive·ly** *adv.*
▪ *noun* ⓘ+ C1 a substance that is able or likely to cause an explosion [C, U]: *plastic explosives* ◇ *The bomb was packed with several pounds of high explosive.* ⇨ see also HIGH EXPLOSIVE, PLASTIC EXPLOSIVE

**expo** /ˈekspəʊ/ *noun* (*pl.* **expos**) a large exhibition: *The expo will bring together more than 900 exhibitors from the food industry.*

**ex·po·nent** /ɪkˈspəʊnənt/ *noun* **1** a person who supports an idea, theory, etc. and persuades others that it is good ⓢⓨⓝ **proponent**: *She was a leading exponent of free trade during her political career* **2** a person who is able to perform a particular activity with skill: *the most famous exponent of the art of mime* **3** (*mathematics*) a raised figure or symbol that shows how many times a quantity must be multiplied by itself, for example the figure 4 in $a^4$

**ex·po·nen·tial** /ˌekspəˈnenʃl/ *adj.* **1** (*mathematics*) of or shown by an exponent: $2^4$ *is an exponential expression.* ◇ *an exponential curve/function* **2** (*formal*) (of a rate of increase) becoming faster and faster: *exponential growth/increase* ▶ **ex·po·nen·ti·al·ly** /-ʃəli/ *adv.*: *to increase exponentially*

**ex·port** ⓘ B1 *noun, verb*
▪ *noun* /ˈekspɔːt; NAmE -pɔːrt/ **1** ⓘ B1 [U] the selling and transporting of goods to another country: *a ban on the export of live cattle* ◇ **for** ~ *Then the fruit is packaged for export.* ◇ *an export licence* ◇ *Their main export market is the United States.* **2** ⓘ B1 [C, usually pl.] a product that is sold to another country: *the country's major exports* ◇ *a fall in the value of exports* ◇ *Oil exports have risen steadily.* ◇ **exports (from sth) (to sth)** *exports from the United States to the European Union* ⓞⓟⓟ **import**
▪ *verb* /ɪkˈspɔːt; NAmE -ˈspɔːrt/ **1** ⓘ B1 [T, I] to sell and send goods to another country: ~ **(sth)** *The islands export sugar and fruit.* ◇ *Most US manufacturers both import and export.* ◇ ~ **sth (from sth) (to sth)** *90 per cent of the engines are exported to Europe.* **2** [T] ~ **sth (+ adv./prep.)** to introduce an idea or activity to another country or area: *American pop music has been exported around the world.* **3** [T] ~ **sth** (*computing*) to send data to another program, changing its form so that the other program can read it ⓞⓟⓟ **import**

**ex·port·ation** /ˌekspɔːˈteɪʃn; NAmE -pɔːrˈt-/ *noun* [U] the process of sending goods to another country for sale ⓞⓟⓟ **importation**

**ex·port·er** /ekˈspɔːtə(r); NAmE -ˈspɔːrt-/ *noun* a person, company or country that sells goods to another country: *the world's largest/major/leading exporter of cars* ◇ *The country is now a net exporter of fuel* (= it exports more than it imports). ⓞⓟⓟ **importer**

**ex·pose** ⓘ B2 Ⓦ /ɪkˈspəʊz/ *verb*
• **SHOW STH HIDDEN 1** ⓘ B2 to show sth that is usually hidden ⓢⓨⓝ **reveal**: ~ **sth** *He smiled suddenly, exposing a set of amazingly white teeth.* ◇ *Miles of sand are exposed at low tide.* ◇ *My job as a journalist is to expose the truth.* ◇ ~ **sth to sb** *He did not want to expose his fears and insecurity to anyone.*
• **SHOW TRUTH 2** ⓘ B2 to tell the true facts about a person or a situation, and show them/it to be dishonest, illegal, etc: ~ **sb/sth** *He threatened to expose the racism that existed*

within the police force. ◊ ~sb/sth as sth She was exposed as a liar and a fraud.
- **TO STH HARMFUL 3** [B2] to put sb/sth in a place or situation where they are not protected from sth harmful or unpleasant: ~sb/sth/yourself This tactic allowed the rebels to attack without the risk of exposing themselves. ◊ ~sb/sth/yourself to sth Children are being exposed to new dangers on the internet. ◊ Do not expose babies to strong sunlight.
- **GIVE EXPERIENCE 4** ~ sb to sth to let sb find out about sth by giving them experience of it or showing them what it is like: We want to expose the kids to as much art and culture as possible.
- **PHOTOGRAPH 5** ~sth to allow light into a camera when taking a photograph
- **YOURSELF 6** ~yourself a person who **exposes** himself or herself, shows their sexual organs in public in a way that is offensive to other people ⊃ see also EXPOSURE

**ex·po·sé** /ek'spəʊzeɪ; NAmE ˌekspoʊ'zeɪ/ noun an account of the facts of a situation, especially when these shock people or have deliberately been kept secret

**ex·posed** /ɪk'spəʊzd/ adj. **1** (of a place) not protected from the weather by trees, buildings or high ground **2** (of a person) not protected from attack or criticism: She was left feeling exposed and vulnerable. **3** (finance) likely to experience financial losses

**ex·pos·ition** /ˌekspə'zɪʃn/ noun (formal) **1** [C, U] a full explanation of a theory, plan, etc: a clear and detailed exposition of their legal position **2** [C] an event at which people, businesses, etc. show and sell their goods; a TRADE FAIR

**ex·posi·tory** /ɪk'spɒzətri; NAmE -'spɑːzətɔːri/ adj. (formal) intended to explain or describe sth: The film suffers from too much expository dialogue.

**ex·pos·tu·late** /ɪk'spɒstʃəleɪt; NAmE -'spɑːs-/ verb [I, T] (+ speech) (formal) to argue, disagree or protest about sth ▸ **ex·pos·tu·la·tion** /ɪkˌspɒstʃə'leɪʃn; NAmE -ˌspɑːs-/ noun [U, C]

**ex·pos·ure** [B2] /ɪk'spəʊʒə(r)/ noun
- **TO STH HARMFUL 1** [+ B2] [U, C] ~ (to sth) the state of being in a place or situation where there is no protection from sth harmful or unpleasant: prolonged exposure to harmful radiation ◊ (finance) the company's exposure on the foreign exchange markets (= to the risk of making financial losses)
- **SHOWING TRUTH 2** [+ C1] [U, C] the fact of having the true facts about sb/sth told after they have been hidden because they are bad, dishonest or illegal: his exposure as a liar and a fraud ◊ the exposure of illegal currency deals
- **ON TV/IN NEWSPAPERS, ETC. 3** [U] the fact of being discussed or mentioned on television, in newspapers, etc. SYN **publicity**: Her new movie has had a lot of exposure in the media.
- **TO STH NEW 4** [U] ~ **to sth** the fact of experiencing sth new or different: We try to give our children exposure to other cultures.
- **MEDICAL CONDITION 5** [U] a medical condition caused by being out in very cold weather for too long without protection: Two climbers were brought in suffering from exposure.
- **PHOTOGRAPHS 6** [C] the length of time for which light is allowed into the camera when taking a photograph: I used a long exposure for this one. **7** [C] a length of film in a camera that is used to take a photograph: There were three exposures left on the roll of film.
- **SHOWING STH HIDDEN 8** [U] the act of showing sth that is usually hidden ⊃ see also INDECENT EXPOSURE

**ex·pound** /ɪk'spaʊnd/ verb [T, I] (formal) to explain sth by talking about it in detail: ~sth (to sb) He expounded his views on the subject to me at great length. ◊ ~on sth We listened as she expounded on the government's new policies.

**ex·press** [B2] /ɪk'spres/ verb, adj., adv., noun
- **verb 1** [A2] to show or make known a feeling, an opinion, etc. by words, looks or actions: ~sth Teachers have expressed concern about the changes. ◊ to express a view/an opinion ◊ to express a hope/desire ◊ to express fears/doubts ◊ ~sth to sb I'd like to express my gratitude to everyone who helped us. ◊ ~how, what, etc... Words cannot express how pleased I am. ⊃ see also UNEXPRESSED **2** [B1]

~**yourself** to speak, write or communicate in some other way what you think or feel: Teenagers often have difficulty expressing themselves. ◊ ~**yourself + adv./ prep.** Perhaps I have not expressed myself very well. ◊ She expresses herself most fully in her paintings. ◊ (formal) ~**yourself + adj.** They expressed themselves delighted. **3** ~**itself (+ adv./ prep.)** (formal) (of a feeling) to become obvious in a particular way: Their pleasure expressed itself in a burst of applause. **4** (mathematics) to represent sth in a particular way, for example by symbols: ~**sth as sth** The figures are expressed as percentages. ◊ ~**sth in sth** Educational expenditure is often expressed in terms of the amount spent per student. **5** ~**sth (from sth)** to remove air or liquid from sth by pressing: Coconut milk is expressed from grated coconuts. **6** ~**sth (to sb/sth)** (NAmE) to send sth by express post: As soon as I receive payment I will express the book to you.
- **adj.** [only before noun] **1** travelling very fast; operating very quickly: an express bus/coach/train ◊ express delivery services **2** (of a letter, package, etc.) sent by express service: express mail **3** (NAmE) (of a company that delivers packages) providing an express service: an air express company **4** (formal) (of a wish or an aim) clearly and openly stated SYN **definite**: It was his express wish that you should have his gold watch after he died. ◊ I came here with the express purpose of speaking with the manager.
- **adv.** using a special fast service: I'd like to send this express, please.
- **noun 1** (also ex'press train) [C] a fast train that does not stop at many places: the 8.27 express to Edinburgh ◊ the Trans-Siberian Express (BrE also special de'livery) [U] a service for sending or transporting things quickly

**ex·pres·sion** [A2] /ɪk'spreʃn/ noun
- **WORDS 1** [A2] [C] a word or phrase: What's the meaning of the expression 'on cloud nine'? ◊ Keep a list of useful **words and expressions**. ◊ (informal) He's a pain in the butt, **if you'll pardon the expression**. ⊃ SYNONYMS at WORD
- **SHOWING FEELINGS/IDEAS 2** [B1] [U, C] things that people say, write or do in order to show their feelings, opinions and ideas: **Freedom of expression** (= freedom to say what you think) is a basic human right. ◊ (formal) The poet's anger finds expression in (= is shown in) the last verse of the poem. ◊ He describes drawing as a very personal form of artistic expression. ◊ ~**of sth** the expression of emotion/feelings ◊ expressions of concern/sympathy/support ◊ We are calling for expressions of interest from people wanting to take part in the project. ⊃ see also SELF-EXPRESSION
- **ON FACE 3** [+ B1] [C] a look on a person's face that shows their thoughts or feelings SYN **look**: facial expressions ◊ He had a pained expression on his face. ◊ The blank expression in her eyes showed that she hadn't understood. ◊ ~**of sth** She wore an expression of anger.

**WORDFINDER** beam, frown, grimace, grin, leer, scowl, smirk, sneer, wince

- **IN MUSIC/ACTING 4** [U] a strong show of feeling when you are playing music, speaking, acting, etc: Try to put a little more expression into it!
- **MATHEMATICS 5** [C] a group of signs that represent an idea or a quantity

**ex·pres·sion·ism** (also **Expressionism**) /ɪk'spreʃənɪzəm/ noun [U] a style and movement in early 20th century art, theatre, cinema and music that tries to express people's feelings and emotions rather than showing events or objects in a realistic way ⊃ see also ABSTRACT EXPRESSIONISM ▸ **ex·pres·sion·ist** /-nɪst/ (also **Expressionist**) noun, adj.

**ex·pres·sion·less** /ɪk'spreʃənləs/ adj. not showing feelings, thoughts, etc: an expressionless face/tone/voice ⊃ compare EXPRESSIVE

**ex·pres·sive** /ɪk'spresɪv/ adj. **1** showing or able to show your thoughts and feelings: She has wonderfully expressive eyes. ◊ the expressive power of his music ⊃ compare EXPRESSIONLESS **2** [not before noun] ~**of sth** (formal) showing sth; existing as an expression of sth: Every word and gesture is expressive of the artist's sincerity. ▸ **ex·pres·sive·ly** adv. **ex·pres·sive·ness** noun [U]

**ex·press lane** *noun* (*especially NAmE*) **1** part of a road on which certain vehicles can travel faster because there is less traffic **2** a place in a shop where customers can pay without having to wait for a long time: *Customers with ten items or less can use the express lane.* ⇨ compare CHECK-OUT (1), TILL (2)

**ex·press·ly** /ɪkˈspresli/ *adv.* (*formal*) **1** clearly; definitely: *She was expressly forbidden to touch my papers.* **2** for a special and deliberate purpose SYN **especially**: *The rule was introduced expressly for this purpose.*

**ex·press·way** /ɪkˈspreswei/ *noun* a wide road that allows traffic to travel fast through a city or other area where many people live

**ex·pro·pri·ate** /ˌeksˈprəʊprieɪt/ *verb* **1** ~ **sth** (*formal or law*) (of a government or an authority) to officially take away private property from its owner for public use **2** ~ **sth** (*formal*) to take sb's property and use it without permission ► **ex·pro·pri·ation** /ˌeksˌprəʊpriˈeɪʃn/ *noun* [U]

**ex·pul·sion** /ɪkˈspʌlʃn/ *noun* **1** [U, C] ~ (**from** …) the act of forcing sb to leave a place; the act of EXPELLING sb: *These events led to the expulsion of senior diplomats from the country.* **2** [U, C] ~ (**from** …) the act of sending sb away from a school or an organization, so that they can no longer belong to it; the act of EXPELLING sb: *The headteacher threatened the three girls with expulsion.* ◇ *The club faces expulsion from the football league.* **3** [U] ~ (**from** …) (*formal*) the act of sending or driving a substance out of your body or a container

**ex·punge** /ɪkˈspʌndʒ/ *verb* ~ **sth** (**from sth**) (*formal*) to remove or get rid of sth, such as a name, piece of information, or a memory, from a book or list, or from your mind SYN **erase**: *Details of his criminal activities were expunged from the file.* ◇ *What happened just before the accident was expunged from his memory.*

**ex·quis·ite** /ɪkˈskwɪzɪt, ˈekskwɪzɪt/ *adj.* **1** extremely beautiful or carefully made: *exquisite craftsmanship* **2** (*formal*) (of a feeling) strongly felt SYN **acute**: *exquisite pain/pleasure* **3** (*formal*) very sensitive: *The room was decorated in exquisite taste.* ◇ *an exquisite sense of timing* ► **ex·quis·ite·ly** *adv.*

**ex-ˈservice** *adj.* (*BrE*) having previously been a member of the army, NAVY, etc: *ex-service personnel*

**ex-service·man** /ˌeks ˈsɜːvɪsmən; *NAmE* ˈsɜːrv-/, **ex-service·woman** /ˌeks ˈsɜːvɪswʊmən; *NAmE* ˈsɜːrv-/ *noun* (*pl.* -men /-mən/, -women /-wɪmɪn/) (*BrE*) a person who used to be in the army, NAVY, etc.

**ext.** *abbr.* (used as part of a phone number) EXTENSION: *Ext. 4299*

**ex·tant** /ekˈstænt, ˈekstənt/ *adj.* (*formal*) (of sth very old) still in existence: *extant remains of the ancient wall*

**ex·tem·pore** /ɪkˈstempəri/ *adj.* spoken or done without any previous thought or preparation SYN **impromptu** ► **ex·tem·pore** *adv.*

## ex·tend 🔵 B2 Ⓦ /ɪkˈstend/ *verb*

- **MAKE LONGER/LARGER/WIDER 1** 🔵 B2 [T] ~ **sth** to make sth longer or larger: *to extend a fence/road/house* ◇ *There are plans to extend the children's play area.* ◇ *The Democratic candidate extended her early lead in the polls.* **2** 🔵 B2 [T] to make sth last longer: ~ **sth** *to extend a deadline/visa* ◇ *Careful maintenance can extend the life of your car.* ◇ ~ **sth for sth** *The show has been extended for another six weeks.* ◇ ~ **sth** (**from sth**) (**to sth**) *The repayment period will be extended from 20 years to 25 years.* **3** 🔵 B2 [T] to make a business, an idea, an influence, etc. cover more areas or operate in more places: ~ **sth** *The school is extending the range of subjects taught.* ◇ ~ **sth to/into sth** *The company plans to extend its operations into Europe.*
- **INCLUDE 4** [I] + *adv./prep.* to relate to or include sb/sth: *The offer does not extend to employees' partners.* ◇ *His willingness to help did not extend beyond making a few phone calls.*
- **COVER AREA/TIME/DISTANCE 5** [I] + *adv./prep.* to cover a particular area, distance or length of time: *Our land extends as far as the river.* ◇ *His writing career extended over a period of 40 years.* **6** [T] ~ **sth** + *adv./prep.* to make sth reach sth or stretc: *to extend a rope between two posts*
- **PART OF BODY 7** [T] ~ **sth** to stretch part of your body, especially an arm or a leg, away from yourself: *He extended his hand to* (= offered to shake hands with) *the new employee.* ◇ (*figurative*) *to* **extend the hand of friendship** *to* (= try to have good relations with) *another country*
- **OFFER/GIVE 8** [T] (*formal*) to offer or give sth to sb: ~ **sth to sb** *I'm sure you will join me in extending a very warm welcome to our visitors.* ◇ *to* **extend your sympathy/congratulations/thanks** *to sb* ◇ *The bank refused to extend credit to them* (= to lend them money). ◇ ~ **sb sth** *to extend sb an invitation*
- **USE EFFORT/ABILITY 9** [T] ~ **sb/sth/yourself** to make sb/sth use all their effort, abilities, supplies, etc: *Jim didn't really have to extend himself in the exam.* ◇ *Hospitals were already fully extended because of the epidemic.* ⇨ see also EXTENSION, EXTENSIVE

**ex·tend·able** (*also* **ex·tend·ible**) /ɪkˈstendəbl/ *adj.* that can be made longer, or made legally acceptable for a longer time: *an extendable ladder* ◇ *The visa is for 14 days, extendable to one month.*

**ex·tend·ed** /ɪkˈstendɪd/ *adj.* [only before noun] long or longer than usual or expected: *an extended lunch hour*

**ex·tended ˈfamily** *noun* [C + sing./pl. v.] a family group with a close relationship among the members that includes not only parents and children but also uncles, aunts, grandparents, etc. ⇨ compare NUCLEAR FAMILY

**ex·ten·sion** 🔵+ B2 Ⓦ /ɪkˈstenʃn/ *noun*
- **INCREASING INFLUENCE 1** 🔵+ B2 [U, C] ~ (**of sth**) the act of increasing the area of activity, group of people, etc. that is affected by sth: *the extension of new technology into developing countries* ◇ *a gradual extension of the powers of central government* ◇ *The bank plans various extensions to its credit facilities.*
- **OF BUILDING 2** 🔵+ C1 [C] ~ (**to sth**) (*NAmE also* **ad·di·tion**) a new room or rooms that are added to a house **3** 🔵+ C1 [C] a new part that is added to a building: *a planned two-storey extension to the hospital*
- **EXTRA TIME 4** [C] ~ (**of sth**) an extra period of time allowed for sth: *He's been granted an extension of the contract for another year.* ◇ *a visa extension* ◇ *She was given an extension to finish writing her thesis.*
- **PHONE 5** [C] (*abbr.* **ext.**) an extra phone line connected to a central phone in a house or to a SWITCHBOARD in a large building. In a large building, each extension usually has its own number: *We have an extension in the bedroom.* ◇ *What's your extension number?* ◇ *Can I have extension 4332 please?*
- **MAKING STH LONGER/LARGER 6** [U, C] the act of making sth longer or larger; the thing that is made longer and larger: *The extension of the subway will take several months.* ◇ *extensions to the original railway track*
- **HAIR 7** [C, usually pl.] = HAIR EXTENSION
- **COLLEGE/UNIVERSITY 8** [C] (used before another noun) a part of a college or university that offers courses to students who are not studying FULL-TIME; a programme of study for these students: *La Salle Extension University* ◇ *extension courses*
- **COMPUTING 9** [C] the set of three letters that are placed after the DOT (= small round mark) at the end of the name of a file and that show what type of file it is
- **ELECTRICAL 10** [C] (*BrE*) = EXTENSION LEAD

IDM **by exˈtension** (*formal*) taking the argument or situation one stage further: *The blame lies with the teachers and, by extension, with the Education Service.*

**exˈtension agent** *noun* (in the US) a person who works for a state university in a country area, and whose job is to give advice to farmers, do research into farming, etc.

**exˈtension lead** /ɪkˈstenʃn liːd/ (*also* **extension**) (*both BrE*) (*NAmE* **exˈtension cord**) *noun* an extra length of electric wire, used when the wire on an electrical device is not long enough

**ex·ten·sive** 🔵+ B2 Ⓦ /ɪkˈstensɪv/ *adj.* **1** 🔵+ B2 covering a large area; great in amount: *The house has extensive grounds.* ◇ *The fire caused extensive damage.* ◇ *She suffered extensive injuries in the accident.* ◇ *Extensive repair work is being carried out.* ◇ *an extensive range of wines* **2** 🔵+ B2 including or dealing with a wide range of information SYN **far-reaching**: *Extensive research has been done into this disease.* ◇ *His knowledge of music is extensive.*

**ex·ten·sive·ly** /ɪkˈstensɪvli/ adv. **1** in a way that covers a large area: *She has travelled extensively.* **2** in a way that includes or deals with a wide range of information: *He has written extensively on contemporary art.* **3** to a large degree; a great amount: *a spice used extensively in Eastern cooking*

**ex·ten·sor** /ɪkˈstensə(r)/ (also **ex·ten·sor muscle**) noun (anatomy) a muscle that allows you to make part of your body straight or stretched out ⊃ compare FLEXOR

**ex·tent** /ɪkˈstent/ noun [C, usually sing., U] **1** how large, important, serious, etc. sth is: *It is difficult to assess the **full extent** of the damage.* ◊ *She was exaggerating the true extent of the problem.* ◊ *We don't know the extent of his injuries at this point.* **2** the physical size of an area: *You can't see the **full extent** of the beach from here.* ◊ **in ~** *The island is 300 square kilometres in extent.*
IDM **to ... extent** used to show how far sth is true or how great an effect it has: *To a **certain extent**, we are all responsible for this tragic situation.* ◊ *He had changed to **such an extent** (= so much) that I no longer recognized him.* ◊ *To **some extent** what she argues is true.* ◊ *The pollution of the forest has seriously affected plant life and, **to a lesser extent**, wildlife.* ◊ *To what extent is this true of all schools?* ◊ *The book discusses **the extent to which** (= how much) family life has changed over the past 50 years.* ⊃LANGUAGE BANK at GENERALLY

**ex·tenu·at·ing** /ɪkˈstenjueɪtɪŋ/ adj. [only before noun] (formal) showing reasons why a wrong or illegal act, or a bad situation, should be judged less seriously or excused: *There were **extenuating circumstances** and the defendant did not receive a prison sentence.*

**ex·ter·ior** /ɪkˈstɪəriə(r)/ NAmE -ˈstɪr-/ noun, adj.
▪ noun **1** [C] the outside of sth, especially a building: *The exterior of the house needs painting.* OPP **interior 2** [sing.] the way that sb appears or behaves, especially when this is very different from their real feelings or character: *Beneath his confident exterior, he was desperately nervous.*
▪ adj. [usually before noun] on the outside of sth; done or happening outdoors: *exterior walls/surfaces* ◊ *The filming of the exterior scenes was done on the moors.* OPP **interior**

**ex͵terior ˈangle** noun (geometry) an angle formed between the side of a shape and the side next to it, when this side is made longer ⊃ picture at ANGLE

**ex·ter·min·ate** /ɪkˈstɜːmɪneɪt; NAmE -ˈstɜːrm-/ verb **~ sb/sth** to kill all the members of a group of people or animals SYN **wipe out** ▸ **ex·ter·min·ation** /ɪkˌstɜːmɪˈneɪʃn; NAmE -ˌstɜːrm-/ noun [U, C]

**ex·ter·min·ator** /ɪkˈstɜːmɪneɪtə(r); NAmE -ˈstɜːrm-/ noun a person whose job is to kill particular types of insects and small animals that are not wanted in a building

**ex·tern**
▪ noun /ˈekstɜːn; NAmE -stɜːrn/ (NAmE) a person who works in an institution but does not live there, especially a doctor or other worker in a hospital
▪ verb /ekˈstɜːn; NAmE -ˈstɜːrn/ **~ sb (from sth)** (IndE) to order sb to leave a region or district as a punishment ⊃compare INTERN

**ex·ter·nal** /ɪkˈstɜːnl; NAmE -ˈstɜːrnl/ adj.
**1** connected with or located on the outside of sth/sb: *the external walls of the building* ◊ *The lotion is **for external use** only (= only for the skin and must not be eaten).* **2** happening or coming from outside a place, an organization, your particular situation, etc.: *A combination of internal and external factors caused the company to close down.* ◊ *our perception of the external world* ◊ *Many external influences can affect your state of mind.* ◊ **~ to sb/sth** *The information has come from reliable sources external to the government.* **3** coming from or arranged by sb from outside a school, a university or an organization: (BrE) *external examiners/assessors* ◊ *An external auditor will verify the accounts.* **4** connected with foreign countries: *The government is committed to reducing the country's external debt.* ◊ *the Minister of State for External Affairs* OPP **internal** ▸ **ex·ter·nal·ly** /-nəli/ adv.: *The building has been restored externally and internally.* ◊ *The university has many externally funded research projects.*

**ex͵ternal ˈear** noun (anatomy) the parts of the ear outside the EARDRUM

**ex·ter·nal·ity** /ˌekstɜːˈnæləti; NAmE -stɜːrˈn-/ noun **1** [C] (economics) a consequence of an industrial or commercial activity that affects other people or things without this being reflected in market prices: *Pollution is a negative externality that imposes a cost—reduced happiness—on the victims.* **2** [U] (philosophy) the fact of existing outside the person or thing that is aware of it: *man's externality to an indifferent natural world*

**ex·ter·nal·ize** (BrE also **-ise**) /ɪkˈstɜːnəlaɪz; NAmE -ˈstɜːrn-/ verb **~ sth** (formal) to show what you are thinking and feeling by what you say or do ⊃ compare INTERNALIZE ▸ **ex·ter·nal·iza·tion, -isa·tion** /ɪkˌstɜːnəlaɪˈzeɪʃn; NAmE -ˌstɜːrnələˈz-/ noun [U]

**ex·ter·nals** /ɪkˈstɜːnlz; NAmE -ˈstɜːrn-/ noun [pl.] (formal) the outer appearance of sth

**ex·tinct** /ɪkˈstɪŋkt/ adj. **1** (of a type of plant, animal, etc.) no longer in existence: *an **extinct species*** ◊ *to become extinct* ⊃ WORDFINDER NOTE at GREEN **2** (of a type of person, job or way of life) no longer in existence in society: *Servants are now almost extinct in modern society.* **3** (of a VOLCANO) no longer active OPP **active**

**ex·tinc·tion** /ɪkˈstɪŋkʃn/ noun [U, C] a situation in which a plant, an animal, a way of life, etc. stops existing: *a tribe threatened with extinction/in danger of extinction* ◊ *The mountain gorilla is **on the verge of extinction**.* ◊ *We know of several mass extinctions in the earth's history.*

**ex·tin·guish** /ɪkˈstɪŋɡwɪʃ/ verb (formal) **1 ~ sth** to make a fire stop burning or a light stop shining SYN **put out**: *Firefighters tried to extinguish the flames.* ◊ *All lights had been extinguished.* **2 ~ sth** to destroy sth: *News of the bombing extinguished all hope of peace.*

**ex·tin·guish·er** /ɪkˈstɪŋɡwɪʃə(r)/ noun = FIRE EXTINGUISHER

**ex·tir·pate** /ˈekstəpeɪt; NAmE -stɜːrp-/ verb **~ sth** (formal) to destroy or get rid of sth that is bad or not wanted ▸ **ex·tir·pa·tion** /ˌekstəˈpeɪʃn; NAmE -stɜːrˈp-/ noun [U, C]

**extol** /ɪkˈstəʊl/ verb (-ll-) (formal) to praise sb/sth very much: **~ sb/sth** *Doctors often **extol the virtues** of eating less fat.* ◊ **~ sb/sth as sth** *She was extolled as a genius.*

**ex·tort** /ɪkˈstɔːt; NAmE -ˈstɔːrt/ verb **~ sth (from sb)** to make sb give you sth by threatening them: *The gang extorted money from over 30 local businesses.* ▸ **ex·tor·tion** /ɪkˈstɔːʃn; NAmE -ˈstɔːrʃn/ noun [U, C]: *He was arrested and charged with extortion.*

**ex·tor·tion·ate** /ɪkˈstɔːʃənət; NAmE -ˈstɔːrʃ-/ adj. (rather informal, disapproving) (of prices, etc.) much too high SYN **excessive, outrageous**: *They are offering loans at extortionate rates of interest.* ▸ **ex·tor·tion·ate·ly** adv.: *extortionately priced*

**extra** /ˈekstrə/ adj., noun, adv.
▪ adj. more than is usual, expected, or than exists already SYN **additional**: *extra money/cash/funding* ◊ *Breakfast is provided at **no extra charge**.* ◊ *The rate for a room is £60, but breakfast is extra.* ◊ *Employees are expected to put in **extra hours** without pay.* ◊ *The DVD comes with lots of **extra features**.* ◊ *extra help for single parents* ◊ *The government has promised an extra £1 billion for healthcare.* ⊃ see also EXTRA TIME
▪ noun **1** a thing that is added to sth that is not usual, standard or necessary and that costs more: *The monthly fee is fixed and there are no hidden extras (= unexpected costs).* ◊ *While I was saving I had no money for little extras or luxuries.* ◊ (BrE) *Metallic paint is an **optional extra** (= a thing you can choose to have or not, but must pay more for if you have it).* **2** a person who is employed to play a very small part in a film, usually as a member of a crowd
▪ adv. **1** in addition; more than is usual, expected or exists already: *to pay/cost extra* ◊ *We don't charge extra for the activities—everything is included in the admission fee.* **2** (with an adjective or adverb) more than usually: *You need to be **extra careful** not to make any mistakes.* ◊ *an extra large T-shirt* ◊ *She tried extra hard.* ◊ *He wanted to cook something extra special for dinner that night.*

**extra-** /ˈekstrə; ˌekstrə/ prefix (in adjectives) **1** outside; beyond: *extramarital sex* ◊ *extraterrestrial beings* **2** (informal) very; more than usual: *extra-thin* ◊ *extra-special*

# extract

**ex·tract** /ɪkˈstrækt/ *noun, verb*
- *noun* /ˈekstrækt/ **1** [C] ~ (from sth) a short passage from a book, piece of music, etc. that gives you an idea of what the whole thing is like: *The following extract is taken from her new novel.* **2** [U, C] a substance that has been obtained from sth else using a particular process: *yeast extract* ◊ *face cream containing natural plant extracts* ◊ *(NAmE) vanilla extract* ⇒ see also ESSENCE, YEAST EXTRACT
- *verb* /ɪkˈstrækt/ **1** ~ sth (from sth) to remove or obtain a substance from sth, for example by using an industrial or a chemical process: *a machine that extracts excess moisture from the air* ◊ *to extract essential oils from plants* **2** ~ sth (from sb/sth) to obtain information, money, etc., often by taking it from sb who is unwilling to give it: *Journalists managed to extract all kinds of information about her private life.* **3** ~ sth (from sth) to choose information, etc. from a book, a computer, etc. to be used for a particular purpose: *This article is extracted from his new book.* **4** ~ sth (from sb/sth) (*formal* or *specialist*) to take or pull sth out, especially when this needs force or effort: *The dentist may decide that the wisdom teeth need to be extracted.* ◊ *He rifled through his briefcase and extracted a file.* ⇒ WORDFINDER NOTE at DENTIST **5** ~ sth (from sth) (*formal*) to get a particular feeling or quality from a situation **SYN derive**: *They are unlikely to extract much benefit from the trip.*

**ex·trac·tion** /ɪkˈstrækʃn/ *noun* **1** [U, C] the act or process of removing or obtaining sth from sth else: *oil/mineral/coal, etc. extraction* ◊ *the extraction of salt from the sea* **2** [U] of ... extraction (*formal*) having a particular family origin: *an American of Hungarian extraction* **3** [C] (*specialist*) the process of removing a tooth

**ex·tract·ive** /ɪkˈstræktɪv/ *adj.* (*specialist*) relating to the process of removing or obtaining sth, especially minerals: *extractive industries*

**ex·tract·or** /ɪkˈstræktə(r)/ *noun* **1** (*also* ex'tractor fan) a device that removes hot air, unpleasant smells, etc. from a room **2** a device or machine that removes sth from sth else: *a juice extractor*

**extra-cur·ricu·lar** /ˌekstrəkəˈrɪkjələ(r)/ *adj.* [usually before noun] not part of the usual course of work or studies at a school or college: *She's involved in many extracurricular activities.*

**ex·tra·dite** /ˈekstrədaɪt/ *verb* ~ sb (to ...) (from ...) to officially send back sb who has been accused or found guilty of a crime to the country where the crime was committed: *The British government attempted to extradite the suspects from Belgium.* ▶ **extra·di·tion** /ˌekstrəˈdɪʃn/ *noun* [U, C]: *the extradition of terrorist suspects* ◊ *an extradition treaty* ◊ *to start extradition proceedings*

**extra·judi·cial** /ˌekstrədʒuˈdɪʃl/ *adj.* happening outside the normal power of the law

**extra·mar·it·al** /ˌekstrəˈmærɪtl/ *adj.* happening outside marriage: *an extramarital affair*

**extra·mural** /ˌekstrəˈmjʊərəl/; *NAmE* -ˈmjʊr-/ *adj.* [usually before noun] **1** (*BrE*) arranged by a university, college, etc. for people who only study PART-TIME: *extramural education/studies/departments* ⇒ see also EXTENSION (8) **2** (*formal*) happening or existing outside or separate from a place, an organization, etc: *The hospital provides extramural care to patients who do not need to be admitted.*

**ex·tra·ne·ous** /ɪkˈstreɪniəs/ *adj.* (*formal*) not directly connected with the particular situation you are in or the subject you are dealing with **SYN irrelevant**: *We do not want any extraneous information on the page.* ◊ ~ to sth *We shall ignore factors extraneous to the problem.*

**extra·or·din·aire** /ɪkˌstrɔːdɪˈneə(r)/; *NAmE* -ˌstrɔːrdɪˈner/ *adj.* (from French, approving, often humorous) used after nouns to say that sb is a good example of a particular kind of person: *Houdini, escape artist extraordinaire*

**extra·or·din·ary** /ɪkˈstrɔːdnri/; *NAmE* -ˈstrɔːrdəneri/ *adj.* **1** unexpected, surprising or strange **SYN incredible**: *What an extraordinary thing to say!* ◊ *We are a normal family dealing with extraordinary circumstances.* ◊ it is ~ that ... *It's extraordinary that he managed to sleep through the party.* **2** not normal or ordinary; greater or better than usual: *an extraordinary achievement* ◊ *She was a truly extraordinary woman.* ◊ *The response from the public has been quite extraordinary.* ⇒ compare ORDINARY **3** [only before noun] (*formal*) (of a meeting, etc.) arranged for a special purpose and happening in addition to what normally or regularly happens: *An extraordinary meeting was held to discuss the problem.* **4** (following nouns) (*specialist*) (of an official) employed for a special purpose in addition to the usual staff: *an envoy extraordinary* ▶ **extra·or·din·ar·ily** /ɪkˈstrɔːdnrəli/; *NAmE* ɪkˌstrɔːrdəˈnerəli/ *adv.*: *He behaves extraordinarily for someone in his position.* ◊ *extraordinarily difficult* ◊ *She did extraordinarily well.*

**ex·traordinary ren'dition** *noun* = RENDITION (2)

**ex·trapo·late** /ɪkˈstræpəleɪt/ *verb* [I, T] (*formal*) to estimate sth or form an opinion about sth, using the facts that you have now and that are relevant to one situation and supposing that they will be relevant to the new one: ~ (from/to sth) *The figures were obtained by extrapolating from past trends.* ◊ ~ sth (from/to sth) *We have extrapolated these results from research done in other countries.* ▶ **ex·trapo·la·tion** /ɪkˌstræpəˈleɪʃn/ *noun* [U, C]: *Their age can be determined by extrapolation from their growth rate.*

**extra-sens·ory per·cep·tion** /ˌekstrəˌsensəri pəˈsepʃn; *NAmE* pərˈs-/ *noun* [U] = ESP (2)

**extra-solar** /ˌekstrəˈsəʊlə(r)/ *adj.* [usually before noun] (*specialist*) (of a planet, etc.) located outside our SOLAR SYSTEM

**extra-ter·res·trial** /ˌekstrətəˈrestriəl/ *noun, adj.*
- *noun* (in stories) a creature that comes from another planet; a creature that may exist on another planet
- *adj.* connected with life existing outside the planet Earth: *extraterrestrial beings/life*

**extra-ter·ri·tor·ial** /ˌekstrəterəˈtɔːriəl/ *adj.* (of a law) that also applies outside the country where the law was made

**extra 'time** (*BrE*) (*NAmE* over·time) *noun* [U] (*sport*) a set period of time that is added to the end of a sports game, etc., if there is no winner at the end of the normal period: *They won by a single goal after extra time.*

**ex·trava·gance** /ɪkˈstrævəɡəns/ *noun* **1** [U] the act or habit of spending more money than you can afford or than is necessary **2** [C] something that you buy although it costs a lot of money, perhaps more than you can afford or than is necessary: *Going to the theatre is our only extravagance.* **3** [C, U] something that is impressive or likely to attract attention because it is unusual or extreme: *the extravagance of Strauss's music*

**ex·trava·gant** /ɪkˈstrævəɡənt/ *adj.* **1** spending a lot more money or using a lot more of sth than you can afford or than is necessary: *I felt very extravagant spending £200 on a dress.* ◊ *She's got very extravagant tastes.* ◊ ~ with sth *Residents were warned not to be extravagant with water, in view of the low rainfall this year.* **2** costing a lot more money than you can afford or is necessary: *an extravagant present* **3** (of ideas, speech or behaviour) very extreme or impressive but not reasonable or practical **SYN exaggerated**: *the extravagant claims/promises of politicians* ▶ **ex·trava·gant·ly** *adv.*: *extravagantly expensive* ◊ *extravagantly high hopes*

**ex·trava·ganza** /ɪkˌstrævəˈɡænzə/ *noun* a large, expensive and impressive entertainment

**ex·tra·vert** *noun* = EXTROVERT

**extra 'virgin** *adj.* used to describe good quality oil obtained the first time that OLIVES are pressed: *extra virgin olive oil*

# ex·treme /ɪkˈstriːm/ *adj., noun*
- *adj.* **1** [usually before noun] very great in degree: *We are working under extreme pressure at the moment.* ◊ *people living in extreme poverty* ◊ *The heat in the desert was extreme.* **2** not ordinary or usual; serious or severe: *extreme weather events such as floods and heatwaves* ◊ *Children will be removed from their parents only in extreme circumstances.* ◊ *It can cause nausea and, in extreme cases, death.* ◊ *Don't go doing anything extreme like leaving the country.* **3** (of people, political organizations, opinions, etc.) far from what most people consider to be normal, reasonable or acceptable: *extreme left-wing/right-wing views* ◊ *Their ideas are too extreme for*

me. **OPP** **moderate 4** [only before noun] as far as possible from the centre, the beginning or in the direction mentioned: *Kerry is in the extreme west of Ireland.* ◊ *She sat on the extreme edge of her seat.*
- **noun 1** [C] **B2** a feeling, situation, way of behaving, etc. that is as different as possible from another or is opposite to it: *extremes of love and hate* ◊ *He used to be very shy, but now he's gone to the opposite extreme* (= changed from one extreme kind of behaviour to another). ◊ *At the other extreme, the top 10 per cent receives 30 per cent of the nation's income.* **2** [U] **B2** the greatest or highest degree of sth: *The climate is mild with no extremes of temperature.* ◊ *Many of these plants won't tolerate temperature extremes.*
**IDM** ▶ **go, etc. to ex'tremes / an ex'treme** | **take sth to ex'tremes / an ex'treme** to act or be forced to act in a way that is far from normal or reasonable: *It's embarrassing the extremes he'll go to in order to impress his boss.* ◊ *Taken to extremes, this kind of behaviour can be dangerous.* **in the ex'treme** (*formal*) to a great degree: *The journey would be dangerous in the extreme.*

**ex·treme 'fighting** noun [U] = ULTIMATE FIGHTING™

**ex·treme·ly** ⓘ **A2** ⓢ /ɪkˈstriːmli/ adv. (with adjectives and adverbs) to a very high degree: *She found it extremely difficult to get a job.* ◊ *It's still an extremely rare occurrence.* ◊ *Their new tablet is selling extremely well.*

**ex·treme 'sport** noun [C, U] a sport that is extremely exciting to do and often dangerous, for example SKYDIVING and BUNGEE JUMPING

**ex·tre·mis** ⊃ IN EXTREMIS

**ex·trem·ism** /ɪkˈstriːmɪzəm/ noun [U] (*disapproving*) political, religious, etc. ideas or actions that are extreme and not normal, reasonable or acceptable to most people: *political/religious extremism* ◊ *New global threats include international terrorism and violent extremism.*

**ex·trem·ist** [C+] **C1** /ɪkˈstriːmɪst/ noun (*disapproving*) a person whose opinions, especially about religion or politics, are extreme, and who may do things that are violent or illegal for what they believe: *left-wing/right-wing/political/religious extremists* ▶ WORDFINDER NOTE at ATTACK ▶ **ex'trem·ist** adj. [usually before noun] (*disapproving*): *extremist groups* ◊ *violent extremist ideology*

**ex·trem·ity** /ɪkˈstreməti/ noun (pl. **-ies**) **1** [C] the furthest point, end or limit of sth: *The lake is situated at the eastern extremity of the mountain range.* **2** [C, U] the degree to which a situation, a feeling, an action, etc. is extreme, difficult or unusual: *the extremities/extremity of pain* **3 extremities** [pl.] (*formal*) the parts of your body that are furthest from the centre, especially your hands and feet

**ex·tri·cate** /ˈekstrɪkeɪt/ verb (*formal*) **1** ~ **sb / sth / yourself (from sth)** to escape or enable sb to escape from a difficult situation: *He had managed to extricate himself from most of his official duties.* **2** ~ **sb / sth / yourself (from sth)** to free sb/sth or yourself from a place where they/it or you have been stuck and unable to move: *They managed to extricate the pilot from the tangled control panel.*

**ex·trin·sic** /eksˈtrɪnzɪk/ adj. (*formal*) not belonging naturally to sb/sth; coming from or existing outside sb/sth rather than within them: *extrinsic factors* ⊃ compare INTRINSIC

**ex·tro·vert** (also less frequent **ex·tra·vert**) /ˈekstrəvɜːt; NAmE -vɜːrt/ noun a lively and confident person who enjoys being with other people **OPP** introvert ▶ **ex·tro·ver·sion** (also **ex·tra·ver·sion**) /ˌekstrəˈvɜːʃn; NAmE -ˈvɜːrʒn/ noun [U] **ex·tro·vert·ed** /ˈekstrəvɜːtɪd; NAmE -vɜːrt-/ (also **ex·tro·vert**) adj.

**ex·trude** /ɪkˈstruːd/ verb **1** [T, I] ~ **(sth) (from sth)** (*formal*) to force or push sth out of sth; to be forced or pushed in this way: *Lava is extruded from the volcano.* **2** [T] ~ **sth** (*specialist*) to shape metal or plastic by forcing it through a hole ▶ **ex·tru·sion** /-ˈstruːʒn/ noun [U, C]

**ex·tru·sive** /ɪkˈstruːsɪv/ adj. (*geology*) (of rock) that has been pushed out of the earth by a VOLCANO

**ex·uber·ant** /ɪɡˈzjuːbərənt; NAmE -ˈzuː-/ adj. **1** full of energy, excitement and happiness: *She gave an exuberant performance.* ◊ *an exuberant personality/imagination* ◊ *a picture painted in exuberant reds and yellows* **2** (of plants, etc.) strong and healthy; growing quickly and well

# eye

▶ **ex·uber·ance** /-rəns/ noun [U]: *We can excuse his behaviour as youthful exuberance.* **ex·uber·ant·ly** adv.

**exude** /ɪɡˈzjuːd; NAmE -ˈzuːd/ verb **1** [T, I] ~ **(sth)** | ~ **(from sb)** if you **exude** a particular feeling or quality, or it **exudes** from you, people can easily see that you have it: *She exuded confidence.* **2** [T, I] if sth **exudes** a liquid or smell, or a liquid or smell **exudes** from somewhere, the liquid, etc. comes out slowly: ~ **sth** *The plant exudes a sticky fluid.* ◊ ~ **(from sth)** *An awful smell exuded from the creature's body.*

**exult** /ɪɡˈzʌlt/ verb [I, T] (*formal*) to feel and show that you are very excited and happy because of sth that has happened: ~ **(at / in sth)** *He leaned back, exulting at the success of his plan.* ◊ + **speech** '*We won!*' *she exulted.*

**ex·ult·ant** /ɪɡˈzʌltənt/ adj. ~ **(at sth)** (*formal*) feeling or showing that you are very proud or happy, especially because of sth exciting that has happened **SYN** triumphant ▶ **ex·ult·ant·ly** adv.

**ex·ult·ation** /ˌeɡzʌlˈteɪʃn/ noun [U] (*formal*) a feeling of being very proud or happy, especially because of sth exciting that has happened

**-ey** ⊃ -Y

**eye** ⓘ **A1** /aɪ/ noun, verb
- noun
- **PART OF BODY 1** [C] **A1** either of the two organs on the face that you see with: *The suspect has dark hair and green eyes.* ◊ *to close/open your eyes* ◊ *She rolled her eyes in disgust.* ◊ *Keep your eyes shut!* ◊ *in sb's eyes / eye There were tears in his eyes.* ◊ *I could see a pair of blue eyes peering out at me.* ◊ *Her eyes widened in disbelief.* ◊ *to make / avoid eye contact with sb* (= to look/avoid looking at them at the same time as they look at you) **HELP** The organ of vision in many insects and other INVERTEBRATES is also called an **eye**: *insect compound eyes* ⊃ VISUAL VOCAB page V1 ⊃ see also BLACK EYE, COMPOUND EYE, LAZY EYE, SHUT-EYE **2 -eyed** (in adjectives) having the type or number of eyes mentioned: *a blue-eyed blonde* ◊ *a one-eyed monster*
- **ABILITY TO SEE 3** [sing.] the ability to see: *A surgeon needs a good eye and a steady hand.* ⊃ see also EAGLE EYE
- **WAY OF SEEING 4** [C, usually sing.] a particular way of seeing sth: *with the ~ of sb He looked at the design with the eye of an engineer.* ◊ *with a …~ She viewed the findings with a critical eye.* ◊ *to sb's~ To my eye, the windows seem out of proportion.*
- **OF NEEDLE 5** [C] the hole in the end of a needle that you put the THREAD through
- **ON CLOTHES 6** [C] a small thin piece of metal curved round, that a small HOOK fits into, used for fastening clothes: *It fastens with a hook and eye.*
- **OF STORM 7** [sing.] **the ~ of a / the storm, tornado, hurricane, etc.** a calm area at the centre of a storm, etc.
- **ON POTATO 8** [C] a dark mark on a potato from which another plant will grow ⊃ see also BULLSEYE, CATSEYE™, EVIL EYE, FISHEYE, RED-EYE, RIB-EYE

**IDM** **be all 'eyes** to be watching sb/sth carefully and with a lot of interest **before / in front of sb's (very) eyes** in sb's presence; in front of sb: *He had seen his life's work destroyed before his very eyes.* **be up to your eyes in sth** (*informal*) to have a lot of sth to deal with: *We're up to our eyes in work.* **cast / run an eye / your eyes over sth** to look at or examine sth quickly: *Could you just run your eyes over this report?* **clap / lay / set eyes on sb / sth** (*informal*) (usually used in negative sentences) to see sb/sth: *I haven't clapped eyes on them for weeks.* ◊ *I hope I never set eyes on this place again!* **an 'eye for an 'eye (and a 'tooth for a 'tooth)** (*saying*) used to say that you should punish sb by doing to them what they have done to you or to sb else **sb's eyes are bigger than their 'stomach** used to say that sb has been GREEDY by taking more food than they can eat **for sb's eyes 'only** to be seen only by a particular person: *I'll lend you the letters but they're for your eyes only.* **get your 'eye in** (*BrE*) to practise so that you are able to make good judgements about a task or activity that you are doing **have an eye for sth** to be able to judge if things look attractive, valuable, etc.: *I've never had much of an eye for fashion.* ◊ *She has an eye for a bargain.* **have your 'eye on sb 1** to be watching sb carefully, especially to check

---

ⓞ Oxford Phrasal Academic Lexicon (OPAL) written and spoken word lists | ⓦ OPAL written word list | ⓢ OPAL spoken word list

# eyeball

that they do not do anything wrong **2** to be thinking about asking sb out, offering sb a job, etc. because you think they are attractive, good at their job, etc: *He's got his eye on the new girl in your class.* **have your 'eye on sth** to be thinking about buying sth **have eyes in the back of your 'head** to be aware of everything that is happening around you, even things that seem difficult or impossible to see **have (got) eyes like a 'hawk** to be able to notice or see everything: *She's bound to notice that chipped glass. The woman has eyes like a hawk!* **have your eye/half an eye on sth** to look at or watch sth while doing sth else, especially in a secret way so that other people do not notice: *During his talk, most of the delegates had one eye on the clock.* **in 'sb's eyes** (*BrE also* **to 'sb's eyes**) in sb's opinion or according to the way that they see the situation: *She can do no wrong in her father's eyes.* **in the eyes of the 'law, 'world, etc.** according to the law, most people in the world, etc.: *In the eyes of the law she is guilty, though few ordinary people would think so.* **keep an eye on sb/sth** to take care of sb/sth and make sure that they are not harmed, damaged, etc: *We've asked the neighbours to keep an eye on the house for us while we are away.* **keep your eye on the 'ball** to continue to give your attention to what is most important **keep an eye open/out (for sb/sth)** to look for sb/sth while you are doing other things: *Police have asked residents to keep an eye out for anything suspicious.* **keep your 'eyes peeled/skinned (for sb/sth)** (*informal*) to look out for sb/sth that you might see: *We kept our eyes peeled for any signs of life.* **look sb in the 'eye(s)/'face** (usually used in negative sentences and questions) to look straight at sb without feeling embarrassed or ashamed: *Can you look me in the eye and tell me you're not lying?* ◊ *I'll never be able to look her in the face again!* **make 'eyes at sb** | **give sb the 'eye** (*informal*) to look at sb in a way that shows that you find them sexually attractive: *He's definitely giving you the eye!* **my 'eye!** (*old-fashioned, informal*) used to show that you do not believe sb/sth: *'It's an antique.' 'An antique, my eye!'* **not see eye to 'eye with sb (on sth)** to not share the same views as sb about sth **not (be able to) take your 'eyes off sb/sth** to find sb/sth so interesting, attractive, etc. that you watch them all the time **one in the eye (for sb/sth)** (*informal*) a result, action, etc. that is disappointing or a defeat for sb/sth: *The appointment of a woman was one in the eye for male domination.* **only have eyes for/have eyes only for sb** to be in love with only one particular person: *He's only ever had eyes for his wife.* **see, look at, etc. sth through sb's eyes** to think about or see sth the way that another person sees it: *Try looking at it through her eyes for a change.* **shut/close your eyes to sth** to pretend that you have not noticed sth so that you do not have to deal with it **take your eye off the 'ball** to stop giving your attention to what is most important **under the (watchful) eye of sb** being watched carefully by sb: *The children played under the watchful eye of their father.* **what the eye doesn't 'see (the heart doesn't 'grieve over)** (saying) if a person does not know about sth that they would normally think was bad, then it cannot hurt them: *What does it matter if I use his flat while he's away? What the eye doesn't see …!* **with an eye for/on/to the main chance** (*BrE, usually disapproving*) with the hope of using a particular situation in order to gain some advantage for yourself **with your eyes 'open** fully aware of the possible problems or results of a particular course of action: *I went into this with my eyes open so I guess I only have myself to blame.* **with your eyes 'shut/'closed** very easily, without thinking about it: *I've made this trip so often, I could do it with my eyes shut.* **with an eye to sth/to doing sth** with the intention of doing sth: *He bought the warehouse with an eye to converting it into a hotel.* ⊃ more at APPLE, BAT v., BEAUTY, BELIEVE, BIRD n., BLIND adj., BLINK n., CATCH v., CLOSE² adj., COCK v., CORNER n., DRY adj., EASY adj., FAR adv., FEAST v., HIT v., MEET v., MIND n., NAKED, OPEN adj., PLEASE v., PUBLIC adj., PULL v., ROVING, SIGHT n., TWINKLING, WEATHER n.

■ **verb** (**eye·ing**, **eying**, **eyed**, **eyed**) ~ **sb/sth** (+ *adv./prep.*) to look at sb/sth carefully, especially because you want sth or you suspect that sth is wrong: *to eye sb suspiciously* ◊ *He couldn't help eyeing the cakes hungrily.* ◊ *They eyed us with alarm.*

**PHRV** **eye sb ↔ 'up** (*informal*) to look at sb in a way that shows you have a special interest in them, especially a sexual interest

**'eye-ball** /ˈaɪbɔːl/ *noun, verb*
■ **noun 1** [C] the whole of the eye, including the round part inside the head that cannot be seen **2 eyeballs** [pl.] (*informal*) used to refer to the number of people who visit a website, watch a television programme, read a magazine, etc., especially when considering how much money they may bring in: *It's a sad fact that bad news grabs more eyeballs than good news.*
IDM **be up to your eyeballs in sth** (*informal*) to have a lot of sth to deal with: *They're up to their eyeballs in work.* **eyeball to 'eyeball (with sb)** (*informal*) very close to sb and looking at them, especially during an angry conversation, meeting, etc: *The protesters and police stood eyeball to eyeball.* ◊ *an eyeball-to-eyeball confrontation* ⊃ more at DRUG v.
■ **verb** ~ **sb/sth** (*informal*) to look at sb/sth in a way that is very direct and not always polite or friendly

**'eye-brow** /ˈaɪbraʊ/ (*also* **brow**) *noun* [usually pl.] the line of hair above the eye
IDM **be up to your eyebrows in sth** (*informal*) to have a lot of sth to deal with: *He's in it (= trouble) up to his eyebrows.* ⊃ more at RAISE v.

**'eyebrow pencil** *noun* a type of MAKE-UP in the form of a pencil, used for emphasizing or improving the shape of the eyebrows

**'eye candy** *noun* [U] (*informal*) a person or thing that is attractive but not intelligent or useful

**'eye-catching** *adj.* (of a thing) immediately likely to attract attention because it is particularly interesting, bright or attractive: *an eye-catching advertisement*

**'eye·ful** /ˈaɪfʊl/ *noun* **1** an amount of sth such as liquid or dust that has been thrown, or blown into your eye **2** (*informal*) a person or thing that is beautiful or interesting to look at
IDM **have/get an eyeful (of sth)** (*BrE, informal*) to look carefully at sth that is interesting or unusual

**'eye·glass** /ˈaɪɡlɑːs; *NAmE* -ɡlæs/ *noun* **1** a LENS for one eye used to help you see more clearly with that eye **2 eyeglasses** [pl.] (*NAmE*) = GLASSES

**'eye·lash** /ˈaɪlæʃ/ (*also* **lash**) *noun* [usually pl.] one of the hairs growing on the edge of the eyelids: *false eyelashes* ◊ *She just flutters her eyelashes and the men come running!*
IDM **bat** v.

**'eye·let** /ˈaɪlət/ *noun* a hole with a metal ring around it in a piece of cloth or leather, normally used for passing a rope or string through

**'eye level** *noun* [U] the height of a person's eyes: *Computer screens should be at eye level.* ◊ *an eye-level grill*

**'eye·lid** /ˈaɪlɪd/ (*also* **lid**) *noun* either of the pieces of skin above and below the eye that cover it when you BLINK or close the eye IDM see BAT v.

**'eye·line** /ˈaɪlaɪn/ *noun* the direction that sb is looking in

**'eye·liner** /ˈaɪlaɪnə(r)/ *noun* [U, C] a type of MAKE-UP, usually black, that is put around the edge of the eyes to make them more attractive and likely to attract attention ⊃ WORDFINDER NOTE at MAKE-UP

**'eye-opener** *noun* [usually sing.] an event, experience, etc. that is surprising and shows you sth that you did not already know: *Travelling around India was a real eye-opener for me.* ▸ **'eye-opening** *adj.*

**'eye-patch** /ˈaɪpætʃ/ *noun* a piece of material worn over one eye, usually because the eye is damaged

**'eye-piece** /ˈaɪpiːs/ *noun* the piece of glass (= a LENS) at the end of a TELESCOPE or MICROSCOPE that you look through ⊃ picture at BINOCULARS

**'eye-popping** *adj.* so exciting, large or impressive that it is very surprising or difficult to believe; amazing: *The special effects in the film were truly eye-popping.*

**'eye-rolling** *noun, adj.*
■ **noun** [U] the action of rolling your eyes, usually because you are annoyed or you do not believe or approve of sth: *There's been a lot of eye-rolling in the office about the latest announcements.*

■ *adj.* causing sb to roll their eyes, usually because they are annoyed or because they do not believe or approve of sth: *There were a few eye-rolling moments during the presentation.* ▶ **eye-rollingly** *adv.*

**eye·shadow** /ˈaɪʃædəʊ/ *noun* [C, U] a type of coloured MAKE-UP that is put on the EYELIDS (= the skin above the eyes) to make them look more attractive ⇒ WORDFINDER NOTE at MAKE-UP

**eye·sight** /ˈaɪsaɪt/ *noun* [U] the ability to see: *to have good/bad/poor eyesight* ◇ *an eyesight test*

**eye·sore** /ˈaɪsɔː(r)/ *noun* a building, an object, etc. that is unpleasant to look at: *That old factory is a real eyesore!*

**ˈeye strain** *noun* [U] a condition of the eyes caused, for example, by a long period of reading or looking at a computer screen

**ˈeye teeth** *noun* [pl.]
IDM **give your eye teeth for sth / to do sth** (*BrE, informal*) used when you are saying that you want sth very much: *I'd give my eye teeth to own a car like that.*

**eye·wash** /ˈaɪwɒʃ; *NAmE* -wɑːʃ/ *noun* [U] (*old-fashioned, informal*) words, promises, etc. that are not true or sincere

**ˈeye-watering** *adj.* (*informal, especially BrE*) so high or extreme that it is difficult or painful to think about it: *eye-watering fare increases* ▶ **ˈeye-wateringly** *adv.*: *eye-wateringly high interest rates*

**eye·wear** /ˈaɪweə(r); *NAmE* -wer/ *noun* [U] (*formal*) things worn on the eyes such as glasses or CONTACT LENSES

**eye·wit·ness** /ˈaɪwɪtnəs/ *noun* a person who has seen a crime, accident, etc. and can describe it afterwards: *an eyewitness account of the suffering of the refugees* ⇒ SYNONYMS at WITNESS ⇒ see also WITNESS *noun*

**eyrie** (*especially BrE*) (*NAmE usually* **aerie**) /ˈɪəri, -ˈeə-, -ˈaɪə-; *NAmE* ˈɪri, ˈeri/ *noun* **1** a NEST that is built high up among rocks by a BIRD OF PREY (= a bird that kills other creatures for food) such as an EAGLE **2** a room or building in a high place, especially one that is difficult to reach and from which sb can see what is happening below

**ˈe-zine** (*also* **ezine**) *noun* a magazine published in electronic form on the internet

# Ff

**F** /ef/ noun, abbr.
- **noun** (also **f**) [C, U] (pl. **Fs**, **F's**, **f's**/efs/) **1** the 6th letter of the English alphabet: *'Fox' begins with (an) F/'F'.* **2 F** (*music*) the fourth note in the SCALE of C MAJOR **3** ~ **(in/for sth)** a grade that a student can get for a piece of work or course of study, showing that it is very bad and the student has failed: *He got an F in chemistry.* ⊃ see also F-WORD
- **abbr. 1** FAHRENHEIT: *Water freezes at 32°F.* **2** (*BrE*) (in academic titles) FELLOW of: *FRCM* (= Fellow of the Royal College of Music)

**f** (also **f.**) abbr. **1** female **2** (*grammar*) feminine **3** (*music*) loudly (from Italian *'forte'*)

**F-1 visa** /,ef wʌn 'viːzə/ noun a document that allows sb from another country to enter the US as a student

**FA** /,ef 'eɪ/ abbr. [sing.] **the FA** Football Association (the organization that controls the sport of football (soccer) in England and Wales)

**fa** = FAH

**fab** /fæb/ adj. (*BrE, informal*) extremely good

**fable** /'feɪbl/ noun **1** [C, U] a traditional short story that teaches a moral lesson, especially one with animals as characters; these stories considered as a group: *Aesop's Fables* ◇ *a land rich in fable* **2** [U, C] a statement, or an account of sth, that is not true

**fabled** /'feɪbld/ adj. (*literary or humorous*) famous and often talked about, but rarely seen **SYN** legendary: *a fabled monster* ◇ *For the first week he never actually saw the fabled Jack.*

**fab·ric** /'fæbrɪk/ noun **1** [U, C] material made by WEAVING wool, cotton, silk, etc., used for making clothes, curtains, etc. and for covering furniture: *cotton fabric* ◇ *furnishing fabrics* **2** [sing.] **the ~ (of sth)** (*formal*) the basic structure of a society, an organization, etc. that enables it to function successfully: *a trend which threatens the very fabric of society* ⊃ SYNONYMS at STRUCTURE **3** [sing.] **the ~ (of sth)** the basic structure of a building, such as the walls, floor and roof

**fab·ri·cate** /'fæbrɪkeɪt/ verb [often passive] **1** ~ **sth** to invent false information in order to trick people **SYN** make up: *The evidence was totally fabricated.* **2** ~ **sth** (*specialist*) to make or produce goods, equipment, etc. from various different materials **SYN** manufacture ▶ **fab·ri·ca·tion** /ˌfæbrɪ'keɪʃn/ noun [C, U] (*formal*): *Her story was a complete fabrication from start to finish.*

**fabu·list** /'fæbjəlɪst/ noun (*formal*) **1** a person who invents or tells FABLES (= traditional moral stories) **2** a person who tells lies, especially in the form of long and unlikely stories

**fabu·lous** /'fæbjələs/ adj. **1** (*informal*) extremely good: *a fabulous performance* ◇ *Jana is a fabulous cook.* ⊃ SYNONYMS at GREAT **2** (*formal*) very great: *fabulous wealth/riches/beauty* **3** [only before noun] (*literary*) appearing in FABLES: *fabulous beasts*

**fabu·lous·ly** /'fæbjələsli/ adv. **1** (*informal*) extremely well: *We got on fabulously.* **2** (*formal*) extremely: *fabulously wealthy/rich*

**fa·cade** (also **fa·çade**) /fə'sɑːd/ noun **1** the front of a building **2** [usually sing.] the way that sb/sth appears to be, which is different from the way sb/sth really is: *She managed to maintain a facade of indifference.* ◇ *Squalor and poverty lay behind the city's glittering facade.*

**face** /feɪs/ noun, verb
- **noun**
- **FRONT OF HEAD 1** the front part of the head, where the eyes, nose and mouth are: *a pretty/pale/round face* ◇ *He buried his face in his hands.* ◇ **on sb's ~** *You should have seen the look on her face when I told her!* ◇ **in the ~** *She was red in the face with embarrassment.* ⊃ VISUAL VOCAB page V1 ⊃ see also FULL FACE
- **EXPRESSION 2** an expression that is shown on sb's face: *a smiling/happy/sad face* ◇ *Her face lit up* (= showed happiness) *when she spoke of the past.* ◇ *His face fell* (= showed disappointment, sadness, etc.) *when he read the headlines.* ◇ *I could tell by his face it hadn't gone well.* ⊃ see also GAME FACE, POKER FACE
- **PERSON 3** (in compounds) used to refer to a person of the type mentioned: *She looked around for a familiar face.* ◇ *He's a fresh face* (= somebody new) *at the company.* ◇ *It's nice to see some new faces here this evening.* ◇ *The movie is full of famous faces.*
- **-FACED 4** (in adjectives) having the type of face or expression mentioned: *pale-faced* ◇ *grim-faced* ⊃ see also BABY-FACED, FRESH-FACED, HARD-FACED, RED-FACED, SHAMEFACED, STONY-FACED, STRAIGHT-FACED
- **SIDE/SURFACE 5** a side or surface of sth: *the north face of the mountain* ◇ *A steep path zigzags down the cliff face.* ◇ *We could see tiny figures climbing the rock face.* ◇ *How many faces does a cube have?* ⊃ picture at SOLID ⊃ see also COALFACE, ROCK FACE
- **FRONT OF CLOCK 6** the front part of a clock or watch ⊃ picture at CLOCK
- **CHARACTER/ASPECT 7** the particular character of sth: **~ of sth** *the changing face of Britain* ◇ *This discovery changed the whole face of science.* ◇ *with a … ~ bureaucracy with a human face* **8 ~ of sth** a particular aspect of sth: *the unacceptable face of capitalism* ⊃ see also IN-YOUR-FACE, TYPEFACE, VOLTE-FACE

**IDM** **disappear/vanish off the face of the 'earth** to disappear completely: *Keep looking—they can't just have vanished off the face of the earth.* **sb's face fits/doesn't fit** (*BrE*) used to say that sb will/will not get a particular job or position because they have/do not have the appearance, personality, etc. that the employer wants, even when this should not be important: *It doesn't matter how well qualified you are; if your face doesn't fit, you don't stand a chance.* **sb's face is like 'thunder** | **sb has a face like 'thunder** somebody looks very angry **face to 'face (with sb)** close to and looking at sb: *The two have never met face*

---

æ cat | ɑː father | e bed | ɜː fur | ə about | ɪ sit | iː see | i happy | ɒ got (*BrE*) | ɔː saw | ʌ cup | ʊ put | uː too

to face before. **face to ˈface with sth** in a situation where you have to accept that sth is true and deal with it: *She was at an early age brought face to face with the horrors of war.* **ˌface ˈup/ˈdown 1** (of a person) with your face and stomach facing upwards/downwards: *She lay face down on the bed.* **2** with the front part or surface facing upwards/downwards: *Place the card face up on the pile.* **have the ˈface to do sth** (*BrE, informal*) to do sth that other people think is rude or shows a lack of respect, without feeling embarrassed or ashamed **in sb's ˈface** (*informal*) annoying sb by criticizing them or telling them what to do all the time **in the face of ˈsth 1** despite problems, difficulties, etc: *She showed great courage in the face of danger.* **2** as a result of sth: *He was unable to deny the charges in the face of new evidence.* **lose ˈface** to be less respected or look stupid because of sth you have done: *Many leaders don't want to lose face by admitting failures.* **on the ˈface of it** used to say that sth seems to be good, true, etc. but that this opinion may need to be changed when you know more about it: *On the face of it, it seems like a great deal.* **pull/make ˈfaces/a ˈface (at sb)** to produce an expression on your face to show that you do not like sb/sth or in order to make sb laugh: *What are you pulling a face at now?* **put your ˈface on** (*informal*) to put on MAKE-UP **set your face against sth/sth** (*especially BrE*) to be determined to oppose sb/sth: *Her father had set his face against the marriage.* **to sb's ˈface** if you say sth **to sb's face**, you say it to them directly rather than to other people ⇒ compare BEHIND SB'S BACK **what's his/her face** (*informal*) used to refer to a person whose name you cannot remember: *Are you still working for what's her face?* ⇒ more at BLOW v., BLUE adj., BRAVE adj., DOOR, EGG n., EYE n., FEED v., FLAT adv., FLY v., LAUGH v., LONG adj., LOSS, NOSE n., PLAIN adj., PRETTY adj., SAVE v., SHOW v., SHUT v., SLAP n., STARE v., STRAIGHT adj., WIPE v., WRITE

▪ **verb**

• BE OPPOSITE **1** B1 [T, I] to be opposite sb/sth; to have your face or front pointing towards sb/sth or in a particular direction: **~ sb/sth** *She turned and faced him.* ◇ *Most of the rooms face the sea.* ◇ **+ adv./prep.** *The terrace faces south.* ◇ *a north-facing wall* ◇ *Lie with your palms facing upwards.* ◇ *Which direction are you facing?*

• SB/STH DIFFICULT **2** B1 [T] if you **face** a particular situation, or it **faces** you, you have to deal with it: **~ sth** *Farmers face serious challenges in these conditions.* ◇ *to face charges/trial* ◇ *the problems faced by homeless people* ◇ *We look at the issues facing schools today.* ◇ **be faced with sth** *We are faced with the prospect of defeat.* **3** B1 [T] **~ sth** to accept that a difficult situation exists, although you would prefer not to: *It's time to face reality—we failed.* ◇ *She had to face the fact that her life had changed forever.* ◇ *Face facts—she isn't coming back.* ◇ *Let's face it, we're not going to win.* **4** B1 [T] if you **can't face** sth unpleasant, you feel unable or unwilling to deal with it: **~ sth** *I just can't face work today.* ◇ **~ doing sth** *I can't face seeing them.* **5** [T] **~ sb** to talk to or deal with sb, even though this is difficult or unpleasant: *How can I face Tom? He'll be so disappointed.*

• COVER SURFACE **6** [T, usually passive] to cover a surface with another material: **(be) faced with sth** *a brick building faced with stone*

IDM **face the ˈmusic** (*informal*) to accept and deal with criticism or punishment for sth you have done: *The others all ran off, leaving me to face the music.*

PHRV **face sb⇿ˈdown** to oppose or beat sb by dealing with them directly and confidently **face ˈoff 1** to start a game such as ICE HOCKEY: *Both teams are ready to face off.* **2** to argue, fight or compete with sb, or to get ready to do this: *The candidates are preparing to face off on TV tonight.* ⇒ related noun FACE-OFF **face ˈup to sth** to accept and deal with sth that is difficult or unpleasant: *She had to face up to the fact that she would never walk again.*

**Face·book**™ /ˈfeɪsbʊk/ *noun* a very popular SOCIAL MEDIA website: **on~** *Are you on Facebook?* ◇ *They posted the picture on the team's Facebook page.*

**ˈface card** (*especially NAmE*) (*BrE usually* **ˈcourt card**) *noun* a PLAYING CARD with a picture of a king, queen or JACK on it

**face·cloth** /ˈfeɪsklɒθ; *NAmE* -klɔːθ/ *noun* (*BrE*) = FLANNEL

---

555

# face-to-face

▼ **VOCABULARY BUILDING**

**Expressions on your face**

- To **beam** is to have a big happy smile on your face.
- To **frown** is to make a serious, angry or worried expression by bringing your eyebrows closer together so that lines appear on your forehead
- To **glare** or **glower** is to look in an angry, aggressive way.
- To **grimace** is to make an ugly expression with your face to show pain, disgust, etc.
- To **scowl** is to look at someone in an angry or annoyed way.
- To **smirk** is to smile in a silly or unpleasant way that shows that you are pleased with yourself, know something that other people do not know, etc.
- To **sneer** is to show that you have no respect for someone by turning your upper lip upwards.

These words can also be used as nouns: *She looked up with a puzzled frown.* ◇ *He gave me an icy glare.* ◇ *a grimace of pain*

**ˈface cream** *noun* [U, C] a thick cream that you put on your face to clean the skin or keep it soft

**face·less** /ˈfeɪsləs/ *adj.* [usually before noun] (*disapproving*) having no characteristics or identity that are easy to notice: *faceless bureaucrats* ◇ *faceless high-rise apartment blocks*

**face·lift** /ˈfeɪslɪft/ *noun* [usually sing.] **1** a medical operation in which the skin on a person's face is made tighter in order to make them look younger: *to have a facelift* **2** changes made to a building or place to make it look more attractive: *The town has recently been given a facelift.*

**ˈface-off** *noun* **1** (*informal*) an argument or a fight: *a face-off between the presidential candidates* **2** the way of starting play in a game of ICE HOCKEY

**ˈface pack** *noun* (*BrE*) a substance that you put on your face and take off after a short period of time, used to clean your skin

**face·palm** /ˈfeɪspɑːm/ *noun* (*informal*) the action of covering your face with your hand, usually because you are shocked, embarrassed, annoyed, etc. ▶ **facepalm** *exclamation* (in emails, comments on SOCIAL MEDIA, etc.): *I fell over right outside the restaurant—facepalm!* **facepalm** *verb* [I]: *I just facepalmed when he arrived wearing that ridiculous suit.*

**ˈface plant** (*also* **ˈface-plant**) *noun* (*informal*) a fall that leaves you lying on your front with your face on the ground: *She tripped on the step and did a face plant.*

**ˈface-plant** (*also* **face·plant**) *verb* [I] (*informal*) to fall so that you are lying on your front with your face on the ground: *Then Tom lost control and face-planted in the dirt.*

**ˈface powder** *noun* powder that you put on your face to make it look less shiny

**ˈface-saving** *adj.* [only before noun] intended to protect sb's reputation and to avoid making them feel embarrassed: *a face-saving compromise*

**facet** /ˈfæsɪt/ *noun* **1** ~ (**of sth**) a particular part or aspect of sth: *Now let's look at another facet of the problem.* **2** one of the flat sides of a JEWEL

**ˈface time** *noun* [U] (*especially NAmE, informal*) time that you spend talking face-to-face (= in person) to people you work with, rather than speaking on the phone or sending emails

**fa·cetious** /fəˈsiːʃəs/ *adj.* (*disapproving*) trying to appear funny and clever at a time when other people do not think it is appropriate, and when it would be better to be serious SYN **flippant**: *a facetious comment/remark* ◇ *Stop being facetious; this is serious.* ▶ **fa·cetious·ly** *adv.* **fa·cetious·ness** *noun* [U]

**face-to-ˈface** *adj.* involving people who are close together and looking at each other: *a face-to-face conversation* ▶ **face to face** *adv.*: *He opened the door and came*

# face value

*face to face with a burglar.* ◊ *I deal with customers on the phone and rarely meet them face to face.* ◊ (*figurative*) *She was brought face to face with the horrors of war.*

**face ˈvalue** *noun* [U, sing.] the value of a stamp, coin, ticket, etc. that is shown on the front of it
**IDM** **take sth at face ˈvalue** to believe that sth is what it appears to be, without questioning it: *Taken at face value, the figures look very encouraging.* ◊ *You shouldn't take anything she says at face value.*

**fa·cia** = FASCIA

**fa·cial** /ˈfeɪʃl/ *adj., noun*
- *adj.* [usually before noun] connected with a person's face; on a person's face: *a facial expression* ▸ *facial hair* ▸ **fa·cial·ly** /-ʃəli/ *adv.*: *Facially the two men were very different.*
- *noun* a beauty treatment in which a person's face is cleaned using creams, STEAM (= gas produced when water boils), etc. in order to improve the quality of the skin

**fa·cile** /ˈfæsaɪl; *NAmE* -sl/ *adj.* (*disapproving*) **1** produced without effort or careful thought **SYN** **glib**: *a facile remark/generalization* **2** [only before noun] (*formal*) obtained too easily and having little value: *a facile victory*

**fa·cili·tate** ▸+ **C1** **W** /fəˈsɪlɪteɪt/ *verb* ~ **sth** (*formal*) to make an action or a process possible or easier: *The new trade agreement should facilitate more rapid economic growth.* ◊ *Structured teaching facilitates learning.* ▸ **fa·cili·ta·tion** /fəˌsɪlɪˈteɪʃn/ *noun* [U, sing.]

**fa·cili·ta·tor** /fəˈsɪlɪteɪtə(r)/ *noun* **1** a person who helps sb do sth more easily by discussing problems, giving advice, etc. rather than telling them what to do: *The teacher acts as a facilitator of learning.* **2** (*formal*) a thing that helps a process take place

**fa·cil·ity** ❶ **B2** **W** /fəˈsɪləti/ *noun* **1** ▸ **B2** **facilities** [pl.] buildings, services, equipment, etc. that are provided for a particular purpose: *leisure/sports facilities* ◊ *medical/recreational/educational facilities* ◊ *Recycling facilities are provided.* ◊ *They provide facilities management services to corporations, hospitals and universities.* ◊ *~ for sb/sth There are not enough facilities for families with young children.* ◊ *All rooms have private facilities* (= a private bathroom). **2** [C] a place, usually including buildings, used for a particular purpose or activity: *the world's largest nuclear waste facility* ◊ *a new healthcare facility* **3** [C] a special feature of a machine, service, etc. that makes it possible to do sth extra: *a bank account with an overdraft facility* ◊ *~ for doing sth a facility for checking spelling* **4** [sing., U] *~ (for sth)* a natural ability to learn or do sth easily: *She has a facility for languages.*

**fa·cing** /ˈfeɪsɪŋ/ *noun* **1** [C, U] an outer layer that covers the surface of a wall to make it look more attractive **2** [C, U] a layer of stiff material SEWN around the inside of the neck, ARMHOLES, etc. of a piece of clothing to make them stronger **3** **facings** [pl.] the COLLAR, CUFFS, etc. of a piece of clothing that are made in a different colour or material

**fac·sim·ile** /fækˈsɪməli/ *noun* an exact copy of sth: *a facsimile edition* ◊ *in ~ a manuscript reproduced in facsimile*

**fact** ❶ **A1** ❷ /fækt/ *noun* **1** ▸ **A1** [C] a thing that is known to be true, especially when it can be proved: *~ about sth First, some basic facts about healthy eating.* ◊ *~ (that)... Isn't it a fact that the firm is losing money?* ◊ *It's a well-known fact that dogs have an acute sense of smell.* ◊ *I know for a fact* (= I am certain) *that she's involved in something illegal.* ◊ *The report is based on hard facts* (= information that can be proved to be true). ◊ *Get your facts right* (= make sure your information is correct) *before you start making accusations.* ◊ *It's about time you learnt to face (the) facts* (= accept the truth about the situation). ◊ *(informal) We didn't get on well, and that's a fact.* **2** ▸ **A2** [U] things that are true rather than things that have been invented: *The story is based on fact.* ◊ *Is the account fact or fiction?* **3** ▸ **B1** [sing.] used to refer to a particular situation that exists: *the ~ that ... I could no longer ignore the fact that he was unhappy.* ◊ *I did everything I could, and she acknowledged the fact.* ◊ **despite the ~ that ...** *Despite the fact that she was wearing a seat belt, she was thrown sharply forward.* ◊ **due to the ~ that ...** *Due to the fact that they did not read English, the prisoners were unaware of what they were signing.* ◊ **apart from the ~ that ...** *She was happy apart from the fact that she could not return home.* ◊ **the ~ of sth** *We want to celebrate the simple fact of their being here.* ◊ *The mere fact of being poor makes such children criminals in the eyes of the police.* ◊ *The fact remains that we are still two teachers short.* ⇒ LANGUAGE BANK at HOWEVER

**IDM** **after the ˈfact** after sth has happened or been done, when it is too late to prevent it or change it: *On some vital decisions employees were only informed after the fact.* **the fact (of the matter) is (that) ...** used to emphasize a statement, especially one that is the opposite of what has just been mentioned: *A new car would be wonderful but the fact of the matter is that we can't afford one.* **a ˌfact of ˈlife** a situation that cannot be changed, especially one that is unpleasant: *Illness is just a fact of life.* **ˌfacts and ˈfigures** accurate and detailed information: *I've asked to see all the facts and figures before I make a decision.* **the ˌfacts of ˈlife** the details about sex and about how babies are born, especially as told to children **the ˌfacts speak for themˈselves** it is not necessary to give any further explanation about sth because the information that is available already proves that it is true **in (actual) fact 1** ▸ **A1** used to give extra details about sth that has just been mentioned: *I used to live in France; in fact, not far from where you're going.* **2** ▸ **A1** used to emphasize a statement, especially one that is the opposite of what has just been mentioned: *I thought the work would be difficult. In actual fact, it's very easy.* ⇒ LANGUAGE BANK at HOWEVER **Is that a ˈfact?** (*informal*) used to reply to a statement that you find interesting or surprising, or that you do not believe: *'She says I'm one of the best students she's ever taught.' 'Is that a fact?'* ⇒ more at MATTER *n.*, POINT *n.*

**ˈfact-finding** *adj.* [only before noun] done in order to find out information about a country, an organization, a situation, etc.: *a fact-finding mission/visit*

**fac·tion** ▸+ **C1** /ˈfækʃn/ *noun* **1** ▸+ **C1** [C] a small group of people within a larger one, whose members have some different aims and beliefs to those of the larger group: *rival factions within the administration* **2** [U] (*formal*) opposition, DISAGREEMENT, etc. that exists between small groups of people within an organization or political party: *a party divided by faction and intrigue* **3** [U] films, books, etc. that combine fact with fiction (= imaginary events)

**fac·tion·al** /ˈfækʃənl/ *adj.* [only before noun] connected with the factions of an organization or political party: *factional conflict* ▸ **fac·tion·al·ism** /-nəlɪzəm/ *noun* [U]

**fac·ti·tious** /fækˈtɪʃəs/ *adj.* (*formal*) not real but created deliberately and made to appear to be true

**fac·toid** /ˈfæktɔɪd/ *noun* (*often disapproving*) **1** something that is widely accepted as a fact, although it is probably not true **2** a small piece of interesting information, especially about sth that is not very important: *Here's a pop factoid for you.*

**fac·tor** ❶ **A2** ❷ /ˈfæktə(r)/ *noun, verb*
- *noun* **1** ▸ **A2** [C] one of several things that cause or influence sth: *Obesity is a major risk factor for heart disease.* ◊ *the key/crucial/deciding factor* ◊ *The result will depend on a number of different factors.* ◊ *~ in sth The closure of the mine was the single most important factor in the town's decline.* ⇒ see also WOW FACTOR, X FACTOR ⇒ LANGUAGE BANK at CAUSE **2** [C] (*mathematics*) a number that divides into another number exactly: *1, 2, 3, 4, 6 and 12 are the factors of 12.* ⇒ see also HIGHEST COMMON FACTOR **3** [C] the amount by which sth increases or decreases: *The real wage of the average worker has increased by a factor of over ten in the last 70 years.* **4** [C] a particular level on a scale of measurement: *a suntan lotion with a protection factor of 10* ◊ *The wind-chill factor will make it seem colder.* ⇒ see also CHILL FACTOR, SPF **5** [U] (*medical*) a substance in the blood that helps the CLOTTING process. There are several types of this substance: *Haemophiliacs have no factor 8 in their blood.* ⇒ see also CLOTTING FACTOR **IDM** see FEEL-GOOD

■ verb

**PHRV** **factor sth ↔ 'in** | **factor sth 'into sth** to include a particular fact or situation when you are thinking about or planning sth: *Remember to factor in staffing costs when you are planning the project.*

**fac·tor VIII** (*also* **factor 8, factor eight**) /ˌfæktər ˈeɪt/ *noun* [U] (*biology*) a substance in the blood that helps it to CLOT (= become thick)

**fac·tor·ial** /fækˈtɔːriəl/ *noun* (*mathematics*) the result when you multiply a whole number by all the numbers below it: *5! (= factorial 5) is 120 (=5×4×3×2×1).*

**fac·tor·ize** (*BrE also* **-ise**) /ˈfæktəraɪz/ *verb* ~ **sth** (*mathematics*) to express a number in terms of its FACTORS

**fac·tory** ❶ ■ **A2** /ˈfæktri, -təri/ *noun* (*pl.* **-ies**) ■ **A2** a building or group of buildings where goods are made, mainly by machine: *a car factory ◇ in/at a ~ She works in the local textile factory.* ◇ *factory workers*

> **WORDFINDER** assembly line, capacity, foreman, plant, process, production, shift, shop floor, workforce

▼ **SYNONYMS**

**factory**
plant • mill • works • yard • workshop • foundry

These are all words for buildings or places where things are made or where industrial processes take place.

**factory** a building or group of buildings where goods are made, mainly by machine: *a chocolate/cigarette/clothing factory*

**plant** a factory or place where power is produced or an industrial process takes place: *a nuclear power plant ◇ a manufacturing plant*

**mill** a factory that produces a particular type of material: *a cotton/paper/textile/woollen mill*

**works** (often in compounds) a place where things are made or an industrial process takes place: *a brickworks ◇ a steelworks ◇ Raw materials were carried to the works by barge.*

**yard** (usually in compounds) an area of land used for building sth: *a shipyard*

**workshop** a room or building in which things are made or repaired using hand tools or machinery (usually individual items or small numbers of items): *a car repair workshop*

**foundry** a factory where metal or glass is melted and made into different shapes or objects: *an iron foundry*

PATTERNS
- a **car**/**chemical**/**munitions** factory/plant
- an **engineering** plant/works
- to **manage**/**run** a factory/plant/mill/works/yard/workshop/foundry
- to **work in**/**at** a factory/plant/mill/yard/workshop/foundry
- factory/mill/foundry **owners**/**managers**/**workers**

ˈfactory farm *noun* a type of farm in which animals are kept inside in small spaces and are fed special food so that a large amount of meat, milk, etc. is produced as quickly and cheaply as possible ⊃ *compare* BATTERY FARM ▶ ˈ**factory farming** *noun* [U]

ˈfactory ˈfloor *noun* (*often* **the factory floor**) [sing.] the part of a factory where the goods are actually produced: *Jobs are at risk, not just on the factory floor (= among the workers, rather than the managers) but throughout the business.*

ˈfactory ship *noun* a large ship with equipment on board for cleaning and freezing fish that have just been caught

ˈfactory shop (*BrE*) (*also* ˈ**factory store**, ˈ**factory outlet** *NAmE, BrE*) *noun* a shop in which goods are sold directly by the company that produces them at a cheaper price than normal

**fac·to·tum** /fækˈtəʊtəm/ *noun* (*formal or humorous*) a person employed to do a wide variety of jobs for sb

557

**fag**

ˈfact sheet *noun* a piece of paper or an electronic document giving information about a subject, especially (in the UK) one discussed on a radio or television programme

**fac·tual** /ˈfæktʃuəl/ *adj.* based on or containing facts: *a factual account of events ◇ factual information ◇ The essay contains a number of factual errors.* ▶ **fact·ual·ly** /-əli/ *adv.*: *factually correct*

**fac·ulty** ⓘ ■ **C1** /ˈfækəlti/ *noun* (*pl.* **-ies**) **1** ⓘ ■ **C1** [C] a department or group of related departments in a college or university: *the Faculty of Law ◇ the Arts Faculty* **2** ⓘ ■ **C1** [C + sing./pl. v.] all the teachers in a faculty of a college or university: *the Law School faculty ◇ a faculty meeting ◇ faculty members* **3** [C, U] (*often* **the faculty**) (*NAmE*) all the teachers of a particular university or college: *faculty members ◇ She joined the faculty of the University of Maryland.* **4** [C, usually pl.] any of the physical or mental abilities that a person is born with: *the faculty of sight ◇ She retained her mental faculties (= the ability to think and understand) until the day she died. ◇ to be in full possession of your faculties (= be able to speak, hear, see, understand, etc.)* **5** [sing.] **~ of/for (doing) sth** (*formal*) a particular ability for doing sth: *the faculty of understanding complex issues ◇ He had a faculty for seeing his own mistakes.*

**fad** /fæd/ *noun* something that people are interested in for only a short period of time **SYN** **craze**: *the latest/current fad ◇ a fad for physical fitness ◇ Rap music proved to be more than just a passing fad.*

**faddy** /ˈfædi/ *adj.* (*BrE, informal, disapproving*) liking some things and not others, especially food, in a way that other people think is unreasonable: *a faddy eater* ▶ **fad·di·ness** *noun* [U]

**fade** ⓘ ■ **C1** /feɪd/ *verb* **1** ⓘ ■ **C1** [I, T] to become or to make sth become paler or less bright: *The curtains had faded in the sun.* ◇ ~ **from sth** *All colour had faded from the sky.* ◇ ~ **sth** *The sun had faded the curtains.* ◇ *He was wearing faded blue jeans.* **2** ⓘ ■ **C1** [I] to disappear gradually: *Her smile faded.* ◇ ~ **away** *Hopes of reaching an agreement seem to be fading away. ◇ The laughter faded away. ◇* ~ **to/into sth** *His voice faded to a whisper (= gradually became quieter). ◇ All other issues fade into insignificance compared with the struggle for survival.* **3** [I] if a sports player, team, actor, etc. **fades**, they stop playing or performing as well as they did before: *Black faded on the final bend.*
**IDM** be ˌfading ˈfast to be disappearing quickly: *Hopes of a peace settlement were fading fast.* ⊃ *more at* WOODWORK
**PHRV** ˌfade aˈway (of a person) to become very weak or ill and die: *In the last weeks of her life she simply faded away.*
ˌfade ˈin/ˈout to become clearer or louder/less clear or quieter: *George saw the monitor black out and then a few words faded in.* ˌfade sth ˈin/ˈout to make a picture or a sound clearer or louder/less clear or quieter: *Fade out the music at the end of the scene.*

ˈfade-out *noun* [U, C] (in cinema, broadcasting, etc.) the process of making a sound or an image gradually disappear; an occasion when this happens

**fader** /ˈfeɪdə(r)/ *noun* (*specialist*) a piece of equipment used to make sounds or images gradually appear or disappear

**fae·ces** (*BrE*) (*NAmE* **feces**) /ˈfiːsiːz/ *noun* [pl.] (*formal*) solid waste material that leaves the body through the ANUS **SYN** **excrement** ▶ **fae·cal** (*BrE*) (*NAmE* **fecal**) /ˈfiːkl/ *adj.* [only before noun]

**faff** /fæf/ *verb, noun*
■ *verb*
**PHRV** ˌfaff aˈbout/aˈround (*BrE, informal*) to spend time doing things in a way that is not well organized and that does not achieve much: *Stop faffing about and get on with it!*
■ *noun* [U, sing.] (*BrE, informal*) a lot of activity that is not well organized and that may cause problems or be annoying: *There was the usual faff of finding somewhere to park the car.*

**fag** /fæɡ/ *noun* **1** [C] (*BrE, informal*) a cigarette **2** (*also* **fag-got**) [C] (*NAmE, taboo, slang*) an offensive word for a GAY man **3** [sing.] (*BrE, informal*) something that is boring to do and

# fag end

makes you tired: *It's too much of a fag to go out.* **4** [C] (*BrE*) (especially in the past) a boy at a PUBLIC SCHOOL who has to do jobs for an older boy

**fag end** *noun* (*BrE, informal*) **1** [C] /ˈfæɡ end/ the last part of a cigarette that is left after it has been smoked **2** [sing.] /ˈfæɡ ˈend/ **the ~ of sth** the last part of sth, especially when it is less important or interesting: *I only caught the fag end of their conversation.*

**fagged** /fæɡd/ (*also* **fagged ˈout**) *adj.* [not before noun] (*BrE, informal*) very tired SYN **exhausted**
IDM **I ˈcan't be ˈfagged (to do sth)** used to say that you are too tired or bored to do sth

**fag·got** /ˈfæɡət/ *noun* **1** (*BrE*) meat cut into small pieces and mixed with bread to form a ball, then baked or fried and eaten hot **2** (*NAmE, taboo, slang*) = FAG (2) **3** a bunch of sticks tied together, used for burning on a fire

**fah** (*also* **fa**) /fɑː/ *noun* (*music*) the fourth note of a MAJOR SCALE

**ˈfah-fee** *noun* [U] (*SAfrE*) an illegal game in which you risk money on a particular number being chosen

**Fahr·en·heit** /ˈfærənhaɪt/ *adj.* (*abbr.* **F**) of or using a scale of temperature in which water freezes at 32° and boils at 212°: *fifty degrees Fahrenheit* ▸ **Fahr·en·heit** *noun* [U]: *to give the temperature in Fahrenheit*

**fail** ⓘ A2 ⓞ /feɪl/ *verb, noun*
■ *verb*
- NOT SUCCEED **1** A2 [I, T] to not be successful in achieving sth: *Many diets fail because they are boring.* ◇ *Ultimately all their efforts failed.* ◇ **~ in sth** *I failed in my attempt to persuade her.* ◇ **to do sth** *The department failed to meet its sales targets.* ◇ *The song can't fail to be a hit* (= definitely will be a hit). OPP **succeed**
- TEST/EXAM **2** A2 [T, I] to not pass a test or an exam; to decide that sb/sth has not passed a test or an exam: *What will you do if you fail?* ◇ **~ sth** *He failed his driving test.* ◇ *Students who fail the exam can retake it.* ◇ **~ sb** *The examiners failed over half the candidates.* OPP **pass**
- NOT DO STH **3** B1 [I] to not do sth: **~ to do sth** *People failed to recognize her talent.* ◇ *Such comments never failed to annoy him.* ◇ *I fail to see* (= I don't understand) *why you won't even give it a try.* ◇ *She cannot fail to* (= must) *be aware of the situation.* ◇ **~ in sth** *They failed in their duty to protect the public.*
- OF MACHINES/PARTS OF BODY **4** B2 [I] to stop working: *The brakes on my bike failed half way down the hill.*
- OF HEALTH/SIGHT/LIGHT **5** [I] (especially in the progressive tenses) to become weak: *Her eyesight is failing.*
- DISAPPOINT SB **6** [T] **~ sb** to DISAPPOINT sb; to be unable to help when needed: *When he lost his job, he felt he had failed his family.* ◇ *She tried to be brave, but her courage failed her.* ◇ (*figurative*) *Words fail me* (= I cannot express how I feel).
- NOT BE ENOUGH **7** [I] to not be enough when needed or expected: *The crops failed again last summer.* ◇ *The rains had failed and the rivers were dry.*
- OF COMPANY/BUSINESS **8** [I] to be unable to continue: *Several banks failed during the recession.*
IDM **if all else ˈfails** used to suggest sth that sb can do if nothing else they have tried is successful: *If all else fails, you can always sell your motorbike.*
■ *noun* **1** [C] the result of an exam in which a person is not successful: *I got three passes and one fail.* OPP **pass 2** [C, U] (*informal*) a mistake or lack of success in doing sth: *The show was an epic fail.*
IDM **without ˈfail 1** when you tell sb to do sth **without fail**, you are telling them that they must do it: *I want you here by two o'clock without fail.* **2** always: *He hands in his assignment every week without fail.*

**failed** B1+ B2 /feɪld/ *adj.* [only before noun] not successful: *a failed writer* ◇ *a failed coup*

**failed ˈstate** *noun* a country in which the government is so weak that it has lost control of the structures of the state

▼ GRAMMAR POINT
**fail / failure**
This use of **fail** as a noun instead of **failure** in a sense that does not just apply to exams has become more common in informal language in the 21st century. A similar case is **reveal**: *We have to wait for the final chapter for the big reveal.*

**fail·ing** /ˈfeɪlɪŋ/ *noun, adj., prep.*
■ *noun* [usually pl.] a weakness or fault in sb/sth: *She is aware of her own failings.* ◇ *The inquiry acknowledges failings in the judicial system.*
■ *adj.* **1** not achieving sth; unsuccessful: *More support is needed to improve failing schools.* **2** becoming weak: *His last months in office were marred by failing health.*
■ *prep.* used to introduce a suggestion that could be considered if the one just mentioned is not possible: *Ask a friend to recommend a doctor or, failing that, ask for a list in your local library.*

**ˈfail-safe** *adj.* [usually before noun] (of machinery or equipment) designed to stop working if anything goes wrong: *a fail-safe device/mechanism/system*

**fail·ure** ⓘ B2 ⓞ /ˈfeɪljə(r)/ *noun*
- NOT SUCCESSFUL **1** B2 [U, C] lack of success in doing or achieving sth: *The success or failure of the plan depends on you.* ◇ *She is still coming to terms with the failure of her marriage.* ◇ *The attempt was doomed to failure.* ◇ *All my efforts ended in failure.* ◇ *The decision to withdraw funding represents a failure of imagination.* OPP **success 2** B2 [C] a person or thing that is not successful: *The whole thing was a complete failure.* ◇ **~ as sth** *He was a failure as a teacher.* OPP **success**
- NOT DOING STH **3** B2 [U, C] **~ to do sth** an act of not doing sth, especially sth that you are expected to do: *Failure to comply with the regulations will result in prosecution.* ◇ *the city's failure to provide an efficient public transport system*
- OF MACHINE/PART OF BODY **4** B2 [U, C] the state of not working correctly or as expected; an occasion when this happens: *patients suffering from heart/kidney/liver failure* ◇ *A power failure plunged everything into darkness.* ◇ *The cause of the crash was given as engine failure.*
- OF BUSINESS **5** [C, U] a situation in which a business has to close because it is not successful: *an alarming increase in business failures*
- OF CROP/HARVEST **6** [U, C] **crop/harvest ~** a situation in which crops do not grow correctly and do not produce food

**fain** /feɪn/ *adv.* (*old use*) willingly or with pleasure: *I would fain do as you ask.*

**faint** /feɪnt/ *adj., verb, noun*
■ *adj.* (**faint·er, faint·est**) **1** that cannot be clearly seen, heard or smelt: *a faint glow/glimmer/light* ◇ *a faint smell of perfume* ◇ *We could hear their voices growing fainter as they walked down the road.* ◇ *His breathing became faint.* **2** very small; possible but unlikely SYN **slight**: *There is still a faint hope that she may be cured.* ◇ *They don't have the faintest chance of winning.* **3** not enthusiastic: *a faint show of resistance* ◇ *a faint smile* **4** [not before noun] feeling weak and tired and likely to become unconscious: *She suddenly felt faint.* ◇ *The walkers were faint from hunger.*
▶ **faint·ly** *adv.*: *She smiled faintly.* ◇ *He looked faintly embarrassed.*
IDM **not have the ˈfaintest (idea)** (*informal*) to not know anything at all about sth: *I didn't have the faintest idea what you meant.* ⊃ more at DAMN *v.*
■ *verb* [I] to become unconscious when not enough blood is going to your brain, usually because of the heat, a shock, etc. SYN **pass out**: *to faint from hunger* ◇ *Suddenly the woman in front of me fainted.* ◇ (*informal*) *I almost fainted* (= I was very surprised) *when she told me.*
■ *noun* [sing.] the state of becoming unconscious: *He fell to the ground in a dead faint.*

**the ˌfaint-ˈhearted** *noun*
IDM **ˌnot for the ˌfaint-ˈhearted** not suitable for people who lack confidence or who get frightened easily: *The climb is not for the faint-hearted* (= is only for people who are brave).

**faint-hearted** *adj.* not being confident or brave enough; afraid of failing SYN **cowardly**

**faint·ness** /ˈfeɪntnəs/ *noun* [U] the state of feeling weak and tired and likely to become unconscious

**fair** ❶ A2 /feə(r); NAmE fer/ *adj., adv., noun*
■ *adj.* (**fair·er, fair·est**)
- **ACCEPTABLE/APPROPRIATE 1** ⓘ A2 acceptable and appropriate in a particular situation: *a fair deal/wage/price* ◇ *The punishment was very fair.* ◇ *~ to sb (to do sth) Was it really fair to him to ask him to do all the work?* ◇ *~ on sb (to do sth) It's not fair on the students to keep changing the timetable.* ◇ *it is ~ to do sth It's only fair to add that they were not told about the problem until the last minute.* ◇ *I think it is fair to say that they are pleased with this latest offer.* ◇ *it is ~ that … It's fair that they should give us something in return.* ◇ *To be fair, she behaved better than we expected.* ◇ (*especially BrE*) *'You should really have asked me first.' 'Right, okay, fair comment.'* OPP **unfair**
- **TREATING PEOPLE EQUALLY 2** ⓘ A2 treating everyone equally and according to the rules or law: *She has always been scrupulously fair.* ◇ *demands for a fairer distribution of wealth* ◇ *The new tax is fairer than the old system.* ◇ *~ to sb We have to be fair to both players.* ◇ *to receive a fair trial* ◇ *free and fair elections* ◇ *It's not fair! He always gets more than me.* OPP **unfair**
- **HAIR/SKIN 3** ⓘ B1 pale in colour: *a fair complexion* ◇ *She has long fair hair.* ◇ *All her children are fair* (= they all have fair hair). OPP **dark** ⊃ WORDFINDER NOTE at **BLONDE**
- **QUITE LARGE 4** [only before noun] quite large in number, size or amount: *There's been a fair amount of research on this topic.* ◇ *a fair-sized town* ◇ *We've still got a fair bit* (= quite a lot) *to do.*
- **QUITE GOOD 5** (*especially BrE*) quite good: *There's a fair chance that we might win this time.* ◇ *It's a fair bet that they won't turn up.* ◇ *I have a fair idea of what happened.* ◇ *His knowledge of French is only fair.*
- **WEATHER 6** bright and not raining SYN **fine**: *a fair and breezy day* **7** (*literary*) (of winds) not too strong and blowing in the right direction: *They set sail with the first fair wind.*
- **BEAUTIFUL 8** (*literary or old use*) beautiful: *a fair maiden*

IDM **all's fair in love and war** (*saying*) in some situations any type of behaviour is acceptable to get what you want **be ˈfair!** (*informal*) used to tell sb to be reasonable in their judgement of sb/sth: *Be fair! She didn't know you were coming.* **by fair means or ˈfoul** using dishonest methods if honest ones do not work **a fair crack of the ˈwhip** (*BrE, informal*) a reasonable opportunity to show that you can do sth: *I felt we weren't given a fair crack of the whip.* **fair eˈnough** (*informal, especially BrE*) used to say that an idea or suggestion seems reasonable: *'We'll meet at 8.' 'Fair enough.'* ◇ *If you don't want to come, fair enough, but let Bill know.* **(give sb) a fair ˈhearing** (to allow sb) the opportunity to give their opinion of sth before deciding if they have done sth wrong, often in court: *I'll see that you get a fair hearing.* **fair's ˈfair** (*BrE also* **fair ˈdos / ˈdo's**) (*informal*) used to ask for fair treatment or to claim that a situation is fair: *Fair's fair—we were here first.* **Come on, fair's fair—you've had your chance, now let me try.** **(give sb/get) a fair ˈshake** (*NAmE*) (*informal*) (to give sb/get) fair treatment that gives you the same chance as sb else **(more than) your fair share of sth** (more than) an amount of sth that is considered to be reasonable or acceptable: *He has more than his fair share of problems.* ◇ *I've had my fair share of success in the past.* **fair to ˈmiddling** not particularly good or bad **it's a fair ˈcop** (*BrE, informal, humorous*) used by sb who is caught doing sth wrong, to say that they admit that they are wrong ⊃ more at **FEW** *pron.*

■ *adv.* according to the rules; in a way that is considered to be acceptable and appropriate: *Come on, you two, fight fair!* ◇ *They'll respect you as long as you play fair* (= behave honestly).

IDM **fair and ˈsquare | fairly and ˈsquarely 1** honestly and according to the rules: *We won the election fair and square.* **2** (*BrE*) in a direct way that is easy to understand: *I told him fair and square to pack his bags.* **3** (*BrE*) exactly in the place you were aiming for: *I hit the target fair and square.* **set fair (to do sth / for sth)** (*BrE*) having the necessary qualities or conditions to succeed: *She seems set fair to win the championship.* ◇ *Conditions were set fair for stable economic development.* ⊃ more at **SAY** *v.*

■ *noun*
- **ENTERTAINMENT 1** (*BrE also* **fun·fair**) (*NAmE also* **car·ni·val**) a type of entertainment in a field or park at which people can ride on large machines and play games to win prizes: *Let's take the kids to the fair.* ◇ *all the fun of the fair* **2** (*NAmE*) a type of entertainment in a field or park at which farm animals and products are shown and take part in competitions: *the county/state fair* **3** (*BrE*) = **FETE** (1)
- **BUSINESS 4** an event at which people, businesses, etc. show and sell their goods: *a world trade fair* ◇ *a craft/a book/an antique fair* ⊃ see also **TRADE FAIR**
- **ANIMAL MARKET 5** (*BrE*) (in the past) a market at which animals were sold: *a horse fair*
- **JOBS 6 job/careers ~** an event at which people who are looking for jobs can get information about companies who might employ them ⊃ see also **SCIENCE FAIR**

**ˌfair ˈcopy** *noun* (*BrE*) a piece of writing that has been printed or written out neatly after all final changes have been made

**ˌfair ˈdinkum** *adj., adv.* (*AustralE, NZE, informal*) **1** used to emphasize that sth is real or true, or to ask whether it is: *It's a fair dinkum Aussie wedding.* ◇ *'Burt's just told me he's packing up in a month.' 'Fair dinkum?'* **2** used to emphasize that behaviour is acceptable: *They were asking a lot for the car, but fair dinkum considering how new it is.*

**the ˌfairer ˈsex** *noun* = **FAIR SEX**

**ˌfair ˈgame** *noun* [U] if a person or thing is said to be **fair game**, it is considered acceptable to play jokes on them, criticize them, etc.: *The younger teachers were considered fair game by most of the kids.*

**fair·ground** /ˈfeəɡraʊnd; NAmE ˈferɡ-/ *noun* **1** an outdoor area where a FAIR with entertainments is held **2** [usually pl.] (*NAmE*) a place where a FAIR showing farm animals, farm products, etc. is held: *the Ohio State Fairgrounds* **3** [usually pl.] (*NAmE*) a place where companies and businesses hold a FAIR to show their products: *the Milan trade fairgrounds*

**ˌfair-ˈhaired** *adj.* with light or blonde hair

**fair·ly** ❶ B1 ⓢ /ˈfeəli; NAmE ˈferli/ *adv.* **1** ⓘ B1 (before adjectives and adverbs) to some extent but not very: *fairly simple/easy/straightforward* ◇ *This is a fairly common problem.* ◇ *It's fairly obvious what's going on here.* ◇ *a fairly typical reaction* ◇ *I know him fairly well, but I wouldn't say we were really close friends.* ◇ *We'll have to leave fairly soon* (= before very long). ◇ *I'm fairly certain I can do the job.* ◇ *I think you'll find it fairly difficult* (= you do not want to say that it is very difficult). ⊃ note at **QUITE 2** ⓘ B1 in a fair and reasonable way; honestly: *He has always treated me very fairly.* ◇ *Her attitude could fairly be described as hostile.* **3** (*old-fashioned*) used to emphasize sth that you are saying: *The time fairly raced by.*

IDM **fairly and squarely** = **FAIR AND SQUARE** at **FAIR** *adv.*

**fair-ˈminded** *adj.* (of people) looking at and judging things in a fair and open way

**fair·ness** ⓘ+ C1 /ˈfeənəs; NAmE ˈfern-/ *noun* [U] **1** ⓘ+ C1 the quality of treating people equally or in a way that is reasonable: *the fairness of the judicial system* **2** a pale colour of skin or hair: *A tan emphasized the fairness of her hair.*

IDM **in (all) fairness (to sb)** used to introduce a statement that defends sb who has just been criticized, or that explains another statement that may seem unreasonable: *In all fairness to him, he did try to stop her leaving.*

**ˌfair ˈplay** *noun* [U] the fact of playing a game or acting honestly, fairly and according to the rules: *a player admired for his sense of fair play* ◇ *The task of the organization is to ensure fair play when food is distributed to the refugees.*

IDM **ˌfair ˈplay to sb** (*BrE, informal*) used to express approval when sb has done sth that you think is right or reasonable

**the ˌfair ˈsex** (also **the ˌfairer ˈsex**) noun [sing. + sing./pl. v.] (old-fashioned or humorous) a way of referring to women as a group

**ˌfair ˈtrade** noun [U] the set of business practices that support producers in developing countries by doing things like paying fair prices and making sure that workers have good working conditions and fair pay ▶ **ˌfair-ˈtrade** adj.: a range of fair-trade foods

**fair·way** /ˈfeəweɪ; NAmE ˈferw-/ noun [C, U] (in golf) the long area of short grass that you must hit the ball along before you get to the GREEN and the hole ⊃ compare ROUGH

**ˈfair-weather** adj. [only before noun] (disapproving) (of people) behaving in a particular way or doing a particular activity only when it is pleasant for them: a fair-weather friend (= sb who stops being a friend when you are in trouble)

**fairy** /ˈfeəri; NAmE ˈferi/ noun (pl. -ies) **1** (in stories) a creature like a small person, who has magic powers: a good/wicked fairy ⊃ see also TOOTH FAIRY **2** (slang, disapproving) an offensive word for a GAY man

**ˈfairy cake** (BrE) (also **ˈcup-cake** NAmE, BrE) noun a small cake, baked in a paper container that is like a cup in shape and often with ICING on top

**ˌfairy ˈgodmother** noun (also **ˌgood ˈfairy**) **1** (in stories) a female character who has magic powers and brings good luck to the main character **2** a person who rescues you when you most need help

**fairy·land** /ˈfeərilænd; NAmE ˈfer-/ noun **1** [U] (in stories) the home of FAIRIES **2** [sing.] a beautiful, special or unusual place: The toyshop is a fairyland for young children.

**ˈfairy lights** noun [pl.] (BrE) small white or coloured electric lights used for decoration, especially on a tree at Christmas

**ˈfairy tale** (also **ˈfairy story**) noun **1** a story about magic or FAIRIES, usually for children **2** a story that sb tells that is not true; a lie: Now tell me the truth: I don't want any more of your fairy stories.

**ˈfairy-tale** adj. typical of sth in a story about magic for children: a fairy-tale castle on an island ◊ a fairy-tale wedding in the cathedral ◊ Life doesn't always have a fairy-tale ending.

**fait ac·com·pli** /ˌfeɪt əˈkɒmpliː; NAmE -ˈkɑːm-/ noun [usually sing.] (pl. **faits ac·com·plis** /ˌfeɪz əˈkɒmpliː; NAmE -ˈkɑːm-/) (from French) something that has already happened or been done and that you cannot change

**faith** /feɪθ/ noun **1** [U] ~ (in sb/sth) trust in sb's ability or knowledge; trust that sb/sth will do what has been promised: I have faith in you—I know you'll do well. ◊ We've lost faith in the government's promises. ◊ Her friend's kindness has restored her faith in human nature. ◊ He has blind faith (= unreasonable trust) in doctors' ability to find a cure. **2** [U, sing.] strong religious belief: to have faith ◊ to lose your faith ◊ a woman of strong religious faith ◊ ~ in sb/sth He started questioning his faith in God. **3** [C] a particular religion: the Christian/Catholic/Islamic/Muslim/Jewish faith ◊ The children are learning to understand people of different faiths. **4** [U] **good/bad ~** the intention to do sth right/wrong: They handed over the weapons as a gesture of good faith. IDM **break/keep faith with sb** to break/keep a promise that you have made to sb; to stop/continue supporting sb **in bad faith** knowing that what you are doing is wrong **in good faith** believing that what you are doing is right; believing that sth is correct: We printed the report in good faith but have now learnt that it was incorrect. ⊃ more at LEAP n., PIN n.

**faith·ful** /ˈfeɪθfl/ adj. **1** staying with or supporting a particular person, organization or belief SYN **loyal**: a faithful servant/friend/dog ◊ She was rewarded for her 40 years' faithful service with the company. ◊ I have been a faithful reader of your newspaper for many years. ◊ ~ **to sb/sth** He remained faithful to the ideals of the party. **2 the faithful** noun [pl.] people who believe in a religion; strong supporters of a political party who will not change their views: The president will keep the support of the party faithful. **3** (of a wife, husband or partner) ~ (**to sb**) not having a sexual relationship with anyone else OPP **unfaithful 4** true and accurate; not changing anything: a faithful copy/account/description ◊ ~ **to sth** His translation manages to be faithful to the spirit of the original. **5** [only before noun] able to be trusted; that you can rely on: my faithful old car ▶ **faith·ful·ness** noun [U]: faithfulness to tradition ◊ She had doubts about his faithfulness.

**faith·ful·ly** /ˈfeɪθfəli/ adv. **1** accurately; carefully: to follow instructions faithfully ◊ The events were faithfully recorded in her diary. **2** in a way that shows true commitment; in a way that you can rely on: He had supported the local team faithfully for 30 years. ◊ She promised faithfully not to tell anyone my secret. IDM **Yours faithfully** (BrE) used at the end of a formal letter before you sign your name, when you have addressed sb as 'Dear Sir/Dear Madam, etc.' and not by their name

**ˈfaith healing** noun [U] a method of treating a sick person through the power of belief and prayer ▶ **ˈfaith healer** noun

**faith·less** /ˈfeɪθləs/ adj. (formal) that you cannot rely on or trust: a faithless friend

**ˈfaith school** noun (BrE) a school especially for children of a particular religion: He called for new faith schools to be created. ⊃ compare PAROCHIAL SCHOOL

**fa·jitas** /fəˈhiːtəz/ noun [pl.] (from Spanish) a Mexican dish of long thin pieces of meat and/or vegetables wrapped in a soft TORTILLA and often served with SOUR CREAM

**fake** /feɪk/ adj., noun, verb
- adj. **1** (disapproving) not what sb claims it is; appearing to be sth it is not SYN **counterfeit**: fake designer clothing ◊ a fake American accent **2** made to look like sth else SYN **imitation**: a fake fur jacket ◊ Don't go out in the sun—get a fake tan from a bottle. ⊃ SYNONYMS at ARTIFICIAL
- noun **1** an object such as a work of art, a coin or a piece of jewellery that is not what sb claims it is but has been made to look as if it is: All the paintings proved to be fakes. **2** a person who pretends to be what they are not in order to cheat people
- verb **1** [T] ~ **sth** to make sth false appear to be real, especially in order to cheat sb: She faked her mother's signature on the document. ◊ He arranged the accident in order to fake his own death. **2** [T, I] ~ (**sth**) to pretend to have a particular feeling, illness, etc: She's not really sick—she's just faking it. ◊ He faked a yawn. ▶ **faker** noun

**ˌfake ˈnews** noun [U] false reports of events, written and read on websites ⊃ compare POST-TRUTH

**fakir** (also **faquir**) /ˈfeɪkɪə(r); NAmE fəˈkɪr/ noun a Muslim (or sometimes a Hindu) holy man who lives without possessions and survives by receiving food and money from other people

**fala·fel** (also **fela·fel**) /fəˈlæfl; NAmE -ˈlɑːfl/ noun [U, C] (pl. **fala·fel** or **fala·fels**) a Middle Eastern dish consisting of small balls formed from CHICKPEAS, usually eaten with flat bread; one of these balls

**fal·con** /ˈfɔːlkən; NAmE ˈfæl-/ noun a BIRD OF PREY (= a bird that kills other creatures for food) with long pointed wings

**fal·con·er** /ˈfɔːlkənə(r); NAmE ˈfæl-/ noun a person who keeps and trains falcons, often for hunting

**fal·con·ry** /ˈfɔːlkənri; NAmE ˈfæl-/ noun [U] the art or sport of keeping falcons and training them to hunt other birds or animals ⊃ WORDFINDER NOTE at HUNT

**fall** /fɔːl/ verb, noun
- verb (**fell** /fel/, **fall·en** /ˈfɔːlən/)
• **DROP DOWN 1** [I] to drop down from a higher level to a lower level: The rain was falling steadily. ◊ They were injured by falling rocks. ◊ + **adv./prep**. Several of the books had fallen onto the floor. ◊ The label must have **fallen off**. ◊ One of the kids fell into the river. ◊ + **noun** He fell 20 metres onto the rocks below.

- **STOP STANDING** 2 [A1] [I] to suddenly stop standing: *She slipped on the ice and fell.* ◊ *~ + adv./prep. I fell over and cut my knee.* ◊ *The house looked as if it was about to fall down.* ⇒ see also FALLEN
- **DECREASE** 3 [A2] [I] to decrease in amount, number or strength: *Prices continued to fall on the stock market today.* ◊ *The temperature fell sharply in the night.* ◊ *falling birth rates* ◊ ~ **by sth** *Their profits have fallen by 30 per cent.* ◊ ~ **+ noun** *Share prices fell 30p.* ◊ ~ **to sth** *Her voice fell to a whisper.* **OPP** rise
- **BECOME** 4 [B1] [I] to pass into a particular state; to begin to be sth: ~ **+ adj.** *He had fallen asleep on the sofa.* ◊ *She fell ill soon after and did not recover.* ◊ *The room had fallen silent.* ◊ *When the rent fell due, she couldn't pay.* ◊ ~ **into sth** *I had fallen into conversation with a man on the train.* ◊ *The house had fallen into disrepair.*
- **OF HAIR/MATERIAL** 5 [I] + **adv./prep.** to hang down: *Her hair fell over her shoulders in a mass of curls.*
- **SLOPE DOWNWARDS** 6 [I] ~ **(away/off)** to slope downwards: *The land falls away sharply towards the river.*
- **BE DEFEATED** 7 [I] to be defeated or captured: *The coup failed but the government fell shortly afterwards.* ◊ ~ **to sb** *Troy finally fell to the Greeks.*
- **DIE IN BATTLE** 8 [I] (*literary*) to die in battle; to be shot: *a memorial to those who fell in the two world wars*
- **HAPPEN/OCCUR** 9 [I] (*literary*) to come quickly and suddenly **SYN** descend: *A sudden silence fell.* ◊ *Darkness falls quickly in the tropics.* ◊ ~ **on sb/sth** *An expectant hush fell on the guests.* 10 [I] + **adv./prep.** to happen or take place: *My birthday falls on a Monday this year.* 11 [I] + **adv./prep.** to move in a particular direction or come in a particular position: *My eye fell on* (= I suddenly saw) *a curious object.* ◊ *Which syllable does the stress fall on?* ◊ *A shadow fell across her face.*
- **BELONG TO GROUP** 12 [I] + **adv./prep.** to belong to a particular class, group or area of responsibility: *Out of over 400 staff there are just seven that fall into this category.* ◊ *This case falls outside my jurisdiction.* ◊ *This falls under the heading of scientific research.* **HELP** Idioms containing **fall** are at the entries for the nouns and adjectives in the idioms, for example **fall by the wayside** is at **wayside**.

**PHRV** ˌfall aˈbout (*BrE*, *informal*) to laugh a lot: **fall about doing sth** *We all fell about laughing.*
ˌfall aˈpart 1 to be in very bad condition so that parts are breaking off: *My car is falling apart.* 2 to have so many problems that it is no longer possible to exist or function: *Their marriage finally fell apart.* ◊ *The deal fell apart when we failed to agree on a price.*
ˌfall aˈway to become gradually fewer or smaller; to disappear: *His supporters fell away as his popularity declined.* ◊ *The market for their products fell away to almost nothing.* ◊ *All our doubts fell away.* ◊ *The houses fell away as we left the city.*
ˌfall ˈback 1 to move or turn back **SYN** retreat: *The enemy fell back as our troops advanced.* 2 to decrease in value or amount ˌfall ˈback on sb/sth [no passive] to go to sb for support; to have sth to use when you are in difficulty: *I have a little money in the bank to fall back on.* ◊ *She fell back on her usual excuse of having no time.* ⇒ related noun FALLBACK
ˌfall beˈhind (sb/sth) to fail to keep level with sb/sth: *She soon fell behind the leaders.* ˌfall beˈhind with sth (*also* ˌfall beˈhind on sth *especially in NAmE*) to not pay or do sth at the right time: *They had fallen behind on their mortgage repayments.* ◊ *He's fallen behind with his school work again.*
ˌfall ˈdown to be shown to be not true or not good enough: *And that's where the theory falls down.* ⇒ see also FALL *verb*
ˈfall for sb [no passive] (*informal*) to be strongly attracted to sb; to fall in love with sb: *They fell for each other instantly.* ˈfall for sth [no passive] (*informal*) to be tricked into believing sth that is not true: *I'm surprised you fell for that trick.*
ˌfall ˈin if soldiers **fall in**, they form lines: *The sergeant ordered his men to fall in.* ˌfall ˈin with sb/sth 1 [no passive] (*BrE*) to agree to sth: *She fell in with my idea at once.* 2 to meet a person or group by chance and then become involved with them: *He ended up falling in with a crowd of musicians and actors.*

▼ **LANGUAGE BANK**

**fall**
Describing a decrease
- *Car crime in Oxford **fell significantly** last year.*
- *Car crime **fell** by about a quarter over a 12-month period.*
- *The number of stolen vehicles **dropped** from 1013 to 780, **a fall of** 26 per cent.*
- *According to this data, 780 vehicles were stolen, 26 per cent **down** on the previous year.*
- *There was an 11 per cent **drop** in reported thefts from motor vehicles, from 1971 to 1737.*
- *These figures show that, as far as car crime is concerned, **the main trend is downwards**.*

⇒ LANGUAGE BANK at EXPECT, ILLUSTRATE, INCREASE, PROPORTION

ˌfall ˈinto sth 1 to be able to be divided into sth: *My talk falls naturally into three parts.* 2 to start doing sth that you had not planned to do: *He says that he fell into politics by chance.*
ˌfall ˈoff to decrease in quantity or quality: *Attendance at my lectures has fallen off considerably.* **OPP** rise
ˌfall ˈon/uˈpon sb/sth [no passive] (*especially BrE*) 1 to attack or take hold of sb/sth with a lot of energy and enthusiasm: *They fell on him with sticks.* ◊ *The children fell on the food and ate it greedily.* 2 to be the responsibility of sb: *The full cost of the wedding fell on us.*
ˌfall ˈout 1 to become loose and drop: *His hair is falling out.* 2 if soldiers **fall out**, they leave their lines and move away ˌfall ˈout (with sb) to have an argument with sb so that you are no longer friendly with them
ˌfall ˈover (*informal*) (of a computer or program) to stop working suddenly: *My spreadsheet keeps falling over.* ˌfall ˈover sth/sb [no passive] to hit your foot against sth/sb when you are walking and fall, or almost fall **SYN** trip: *I rushed for the door and fell over the cat in the hallway.* ⇒ see also FALL *verb* ˌfall ˈover yourself to do sth (*informal*) to try very hard or want very much to do sth: *He was falling over himself to be nice to me.*
ˌfall ˈthrough to not be completed, or not happen: *Our plans fell through because of lack of money.*
ˈfall to sb to become the duty or responsibility of sb: *With his partner away, all the work now fell to him.* ◊ **it falls to sb to do sth** *It fell to me to inform her of her son's death.* ˈfall to sth (*literary*) to begin to do sth **fall to doing sth** *She fell to brooding about what had happened to her.*

■ *noun*
- **ACT OF FALLING** 1 [A2] [C] an act of falling: *I had a bad fall and broke my arm.* ◊ ~ **from sth** *She was killed in a fall from a horse.*
- **OF SNOW/RAIN/ROCKS** 2 [A2] [C] ~ **(of sth)** an amount of snow, rain, rocks, etc. that falls or has fallen: *a heavy fall of snow* ◊ *a rock fall*
- **AUTUMN** 3 [A2] [C, U] (*NAmE*) (*also especially BrE* **autumn**) the season of the year between summer and winter, when leaves change colour and the weather becomes colder: *in the fall of 2019* ◊ *last fall* ◊ *fall weather*
- **DECREASE** 4 [A2] [C] ~ **(in sth)** a decrease in size, number, rate or level: *a sharp fall in prices* ◊ *a steep/dramatic fall in profits* ◊ *a 3 per cent fall in unemployment* **OPP** rise
- **DEFEAT** 5 [sing.] ~ **(of sth)** a loss of political, economic, etc. power or success; the loss or defeat of a city, country, etc. in war: *the fall of the Roman Empire* ◊ *the rise and fall of British industry* ◊ *the fall of Berlin*
- **LOSS OF RESPECT** 6 [sing.] a situation in which a person, an organization, etc. loses the respect of other people because they have done sth wrong: *the TV preacher's spectacular fall from grace*
- **OF WATER** 7 **falls** [pl.] (*especially in names*) a large amount of water falling down from a height **SYN** waterfall: *The falls upstream are full of salmon.* ◊ *Niagara Falls*
- **WAY STH FALLS/HAPPENS** 8 [sing.] ~ **of sth** the way in which sth falls or happens: *the fall of the dice* ◊ *the dark fall of her hair* (= the way her hair hangs down)

# fallacious

- **IN BIBLE** **9** **the Fall** [sing.] the occasion when Adam and Eve did not obey God and had to leave the Garden of Eden

**IDM** **break sb's 'fall** to stop sb from falling onto sth hard: *Luckily, a bush broke his fall.* **take the 'fall (for sb/sth)** (*informal, especially NAmE*) to accept responsibility or punishment for sth that you did not do, or did not do alone: *He took the fall for his boss and resigned.* ⊃ more at PRIDE *n.*, RIDE *v.*

**fal·la·cious** /fəˈleɪʃəs/ *adj.* (*formal*) wrong; based on a false idea: *a fallacious argument*

**fal·lacy** /ˈfæləsi/ *noun* (*pl.* **-ies**) **1** [C] a false idea that many people believe is true: *It is a fallacy to say that the camera never lies.* **2** [U, C] a false way of thinking about sth: *He detected the fallacy of her argument.* ⊃ see also PATHETIC FALLACY

**fall·back** /ˈfɔːlbæk/ *noun* a plan or course of action that is ready to be used in an emergency if other things fail: *What's our fallback if they don't come up with the money?* ◊ *We need a fallback position if they won't do the job.*

**fall·en** /ˈfɔːlən/ *adj.*, *verb*
- *adj.* [only before noun] **1** lying on the ground, after falling: *a fallen tree* **2** (*formal*) (of a soldier) killed in a war
- *verb* past part. of FALL

**fallen 'woman** *noun* (*old-fashioned*) a way of describing a woman in the past who had a sexual relationship with sb who was not her husband

**'fall guy** *noun* (*especially NAmE*) a person who is blamed or punished for sth wrong that another person has done **SYN** scapegoat

**fall·ible** /ˈfæləbl/ *adj.* able to make mistakes or be wrong: *Memory is selective and fallible.* ◊ *All human beings are fallible.* **OPP** infallible ▸ **fal·li·bil·ity** /ˌfæləˈbɪləti/ *noun* [U]: *human fallibility*

**falling-'off** *noun* [sing.] (*BrE*) = FALL-OFF

**falling-'out** *noun* (*informal*) [sing.] a situation where people are no longer friends, because they disagree or have had an argument: *Dave and I had a falling-out.*

**falling 'star** *noun* = SHOOTING STAR

**'fall-off** (*BrE also, less frequent* **falling-'off**) *noun* [sing.] **~ (in sth)** a reduction in the number, amount or quality of sth: *a recent fall-off in sales*

**fal·lo·pian tube** /fəˈləʊpiən tjuːb; *NAmE* tuːb/ *noun* (*anatomy*) one of the two tubes in the body of a woman or female animal along which eggs pass from the OVARIES to the UTERUS

**fall·out** /ˈfɔːlaʊt/ *noun* [U] **1** dangerous RADIOACTIVE dust that is in the air after a nuclear explosion **2** the bad results of a situation or an action

**fal·low** /ˈfæləʊ/ *adj.* **1** (of farm land) not used for growing crops, especially so that the quality of the land will improve: *Farmers are now paid to let their land lie fallow.* ⊃ WORDFINDER NOTE at FARM **2** (of a period of time) when nothing is created or produced; not successful: *Contemporary dance is coming onto the arts scene again after a long fallow period.*

**'fallow deer** *noun* a small European DEER with white spots on its back

**false** /fɔːls/ *adj.*
- **NOT TRUE** **1** wrong; not correct or true: *A whale is a fish. True or false?* ◊ *He used a false name to get the job.* ◊ *a false accusation/allegation/claim/statement*
- **NOT NATURAL** **2** not natural **SYN** artificial: *false teeth/eyelashes* ◊ *a false beard* ⊃ SYNONYMS at ARTIFICIAL
- **NOT REAL** **3** [U] not real or what sb claims it is, but made to look real to cheat people: *a false passport*
- **WRONG/NOT ACCURATE** **4** [usually before noun] wrong or not accurate, because it is based on sth that is not true or correct: *a false argument/assumption/belief* ◊ *to give a false impression of wealth* ◊ *to lull sb into a false sense of security* (= make sb feel safe when they are really in danger) ◊ *They didn't want to raise any false hopes, but they believed her husband had escaped capture.* ◊ *Buying a cheap computer is a false economy* (= will not actually save you money).
- **NOT SINCERE** **5** (of people's behaviour) not real or sincere: *false modesty* ◊ *She flashed him a false smile of congratulation.*
- **NOT FAITHFUL** **6** (*literary*) (of people) not FAITHFUL: *a false lover* ▸ **false·ly** *adv.*: *to be falsely accused of sth* ◊ *She smiled falsely at his joke.*

**IDM** **by/under/on false pre'tences** by pretending to be sth that you are not, in order to gain some advantage for yourself: *She was accused of obtaining money under false pretences.* ⊃ more at RING² *v.*

**false a'larm** *noun* a warning about a danger that does not happen; a belief that sth bad is going to happen, when it is not: *The fire service was called out but it was a false alarm.*

**false be'ginner** *noun* a person who has a basic knowledge of a language, but has started to study it again from the beginning

**false 'dawn** *noun* [usually sing.] (*formal*) a situation in which you think that sth good is going to happen but it does not: *a false dawn for the economy*

**false 'friend** *noun* **1** a person who seems to be your friend, but who in fact cannot be trusted **2** a word in a foreign language that looks similar to a word in your own language, but has a different meaning: *The English word 'sensible' and the French word 'sensible' are false friends.*

**false·hood** /ˈfɔːlshʊd/ *noun* (*formal*) **1** [U] the state of not being true; the act of telling a lie: *to test the truth or falsehood of her claims* **2** [C] a statement that is not true **SYN** lie²

**false im'prisonment** *noun* [U] (*law*) the crime of illegally keeping sb as a prisoner somewhere

**false 'memory** *noun* (*psychology*) a memory of sth that did not actually happen

**false 'move** *noun* [usually sing.] an action that is not allowed or not recommended and that may cause a bad result: *One false move and the bomb might blow up.*

**false 'rib** *noun* = FLOATING RIB

**false 'start** *noun* **1** an unsuccessful attempt to begin sth: *After a number of false starts, she finally found a job she liked.* **2** (*sport*) a situation when sb taking part in a race starts before the official signal has been given

**false 'teeth** *noun* [pl.] a set of artificial teeth used by sb who has lost their natural teeth ⊃ compare DENTURES

**fal·setto** /fɔːlˈsetəʊ/ *noun* (*pl.* **-os**) an unusually high voice, especially the voice that men use to sing very high notes

**fals·ify** /ˈfɔːlsɪfaɪ/ *verb* (**fal·si·fies**, **fal·si·fy·ing**, **fal·si·fied**, **fal·si·fied**) **~ sth** (*formal*) to change a written record or information so that it is no longer true ▸ **fal·si·fi·ca·tion** /ˌfɔːlsɪfɪˈkeɪʃn/ *noun* [U, C]: *the deliberate falsification of the company's records*

**fal·sity** /ˈfɔːlsəti/ *noun* [U, C] (*pl.* **-ties**) the state of not being true or real; sth that is not true or real **OPP** truth

**fal·ter** /ˈfɔːltə(r)/ *verb* **1** [I] to become weaker or less effective **SYN** waver: *The economy shows no signs of faltering.* ◊ *Her courage never faltered.* **2** [I, T] (**+ speech**) to speak in a way that shows that you are not confident: *His voice faltered as he began his speech.* **3** [I] to walk or behave in a way that shows that you are not confident: *She walked up to the platform without faltering.* ◊ *He never faltered in his commitment to the party.* ▸ **fal·ter·ing** *adj.*: *the faltering peace talks* ◊ *the baby's first faltering steps*

**fam** /fæm/ *noun* (*informal*) a person's family: *Had a great time relaxing with friends and fam!*

**fame** /feɪm/ *noun* [U] the state of being known and talked about by many people: *to achieve/win instant fame* ◊ *Daisy Ridley of 'Star Wars' fame* (= famous for 'Star Wars') ◊ *The town's only claim to fame is that there was once a riot there.* ◊ *She went to Hollywood in search of fame and fortune.* ⊃ see also FAMOUS **IDM** see MINUTE¹ *n.*, SHOOT *v.*

**famed** /feɪmd/ *adj.* **~ (for sth)** very well known **SYN** renowned: *Las Vegas, famed for its casinos* ◊ *a famed poet and musician* ⊃ see also FAMOUS

**fa·mil·ial** /fəˈmɪliəl/ adj. [only before noun] **1** (formal) related to or typical of a family **2** (medical) (of diseases, conditions, etc.) affecting several members of a family: *familial left-handedness.*

**fa·mil·iar** 🅞 🅱🅱 🅢 /fəˈmɪliə(r)/ adj. **1** 🅱🅱 well known to you; often seen or heard and therefore easy to recognize: *to look/sound/seem familiar* ◊ *I couldn't see any familiar faces in the room.* ◊ *The song was vaguely familiar.* ◊ *~ to sb The smell is very familiar to everyone who lives near a bakery.* ◊ *Violent attacks are becoming all too familiar* (= sadly familiar). **OPP** **unfamiliar** **2** 🅱🅱 *~ with sth* knowing sth very well: *an area with which I had been familiar since childhood* ◊ *You will soon become familiar with the different activities.* **OPP** **unfamiliar** **3** *~ (with sb)* (of a person's behaviour) very informal, sometimes in a way that is unpleasant: *You seem to be on very familiar terms with your tutor.* ◊ *After a few drinks her boss started getting too familiar for her liking.*

**fa·mil·iar·ity** /fəˌmɪliˈærəti/ noun [U, sing.] **1** *~ (with sth)* | *~ (to sb)* the state of knowing sb/sth well; the state of recognizing sb/sth: *His familiarity with the language helped him enjoy his stay.* ◊ *When she saw the house, she had a feeling of familiarity.* **2** a friendly informal manner: *She addressed me with an easy familiarity that made me feel at home.*
**IDM** **familiarity breeds conˈtempt** (saying) knowing sb/sth very well may cause you to lose respect for them/it

**fa·mil·iar·ize** (BrE also **-ise**) /fəˈmɪliəraɪz/ verb *~ yourself / sb (with sth)* to learn about sth or teach sb about sth, so that you/they start to understand it **SYN** **acquaint**: *You'll need time to familiarize yourself with our procedures.* ▶ **fa·mil·iar·iza·tion, -isa·tion** /fəˌmɪliərəˈzeɪʃn; NAmE -rəˈz-/ noun [U]

**fa·mil·iar·ly** /fəˈmɪliəli; NAmE -ərli/ adv. **1** in a friendly and informal manner, sometimes in a way that is too informal to be pleasant: *John Hunt, familiarly known to his friends as Jack* ◊ *He touched her cheek familiarly.* **2** in the way that is well known to people: *The elephant's nose or, more familiarly, trunk, is the most versatile organ in the animal kingdom.*

**fam·ily** 🅞 🅐🅐 /ˈfæməli/ noun, adj.
■ noun (pl. **-ies**) **1** 🅐🅐 [C + sing./pl. v.] a group consisting of one or two parents and their children: *the other members of my family* ◊ *the entire/whole family* ◊ *one-parent/single-parent families* ◊ *a ~ of four/five*, etc *Taking a family of four to the cinema is expensive.* ◊ *families with young children* ◊ *He's a friend of the family* (= he is known and liked by the parents and the children). ⊃ see also BLENDED FAMILY, NUCLEAR FAMILY

> **WORDFINDER** adopt, child, generation, heir, in-laws, parent, relation, stepfamily, surrogate mother

**2** 🅐🅐 [C + sing./pl. v., U] a group consisting of one or two parents, their children and close relations: *The support of family and friends is vital.* ◊ *We've only told the immediate family* (= the closest relations). ◊ *the royal family* (= the children and close relations of the king or queen) ◊ *I always think of you as one of the family.* ◊ *in a ~ There are a lot of girls in our family.* ◊ *We all knew her so well that we felt she was almost part of the family.* ⊃ see also EXTENDED FAMILY, FIRST FAMILY, JOINT FAMILY **3** 🅐🅐 [C + sing./pl. v.] all the people who are related to each other, including those who are now dead: *Some families have farmed in this area for hundreds of years.* ◊ *This painting has been in our family for generations.* **4** 🅐🅐 [C + sing./pl. v., U] a couple's or a person's children, especially young children: *They have a large family.* ◊ *Do they plan to start a family* (= have children)? ◊ *to raise a family* **5** 🅐🅐 [C] a group into which animals, plants, etc. that have similar characteristics are divided, smaller than an ORDER and larger than a GENUS: *Lions belong to the cat family.* ◊ *This bird is a member of the crow family.* ⊃ **VISUAL VOCAB** page V3 **6** a group of related languages: *the Germanic family of languages*
**IDM** **(be/get) in the ˈfamily way** (old-fashioned, informal) (to be/become) pregnant **run in the ˈfamily** to be a common feature in a particular family: *Heart disease runs in the family.*
■ adj. [only before noun] **1** 🅐🅐 connected with the family or a particular family: *family life* ◊ *Only close family members called her 'Sally'.* **2** 🅐🅐 owned by a family: *the family home* **3** 🅐🅐 suitable for all members of a family, both adults and children: *a family show*

**family ˈdoctor** noun = GENERAL PRACTITIONER

**family ˈleave** noun [U] (NAmE) time when you are allowed to be away from work to deal with family matters, especially the birth of a child or to care for a relative: *Last year she took paid family leave to look after her sick mother.* ⊃ compare MATERNITY LEAVE, PARENTAL LEAVE, PATERNITY LEAVE

**ˈfamily man** noun a man who has a wife or partner and children; a man who enjoys being at home with his wife or partner and children: *I see he's become a family man.* ◊ *a devoted family man*

**family ˈmedicine** noun [U] (NAmE) the branch of medicine that is designed to provide general HEALTHCARE to families and people of all ages

**ˈfamily name** noun the part of your name that shows which family you belong to ⊃ compare SURNAME

**family ˈplanning** noun [U] the process of controlling the number of children you have by using CONTRACEPTION

**family ˈpractice** (NAmE) (also **general practice** especially in BrE) noun the work of a doctor who treats people in the community rather than at a hospital and who is not a specialist in one particular area of medicine; a place where a doctor like this works: *Dr. Simon is part of a family practice in our neighborhood.*

**family pracˈtitioner** noun = GENERAL PRACTITIONER

**ˈfamily room** noun **1** (especially NAmE) a room in a house where the family can relax, watch television, etc. **2** a room in a hotel for three or four people to sleep in, especially parents and children

**family ˈtree** noun a diagram that shows the relationship between members of a family over a long period of time: *How far back can you trace your family tree?* ⊃ **WORDFINDER NOTE** at RELATION

**family ˈvalues** noun [pl.] beliefs about what is right, wrong or important in life that people often learn from their families, typically the importance of high moral standards and the traditional family unit of mother, father and children. In the US, family values are strongly associated with conservative Christian values.

**fam·ine** /ˈfæmɪn/ noun [C, U] a lack of food during a long period of time in a region: *a severe famine* ◊ *disasters such as floods and famine* ◊ *the threat of widespread famine in the area* ◊ *to raise money for famine relief*

**fam·ished** /ˈfæmɪʃt/ adj. [not usually before noun] (informal, becoming old-fashioned) very hungry **SYN** **starve**: *When's lunch? I'm famished!*

**fam·ous** 🅞 🅐🅐 🅢 /ˈfeɪməs/ adj. **1** 🅐🅐 known about by many people: *a famous artist/actor* ◊ *The actor was one of many famous faces at the party.* ◊ *Many rich and famous people have stayed at the hotel.* ◊ *The song was made famous by Frank Sinatra.* ◊ *~ for sth He became internationally famous for his novels.* ◊ *~ as sth She was more famous as a writer than as a singer.* ⊃ see also FAME, INFAMOUS, NOTORIOUS, WORLD-FAMOUS **2 the famous** noun [pl.] people who are known about by many people: *the lifestyles of the rich and famous*
**IDM** **ˌfamous last ˈwords** (saying) people sometimes say **Famous last words!** when they think sb is being too confident about sth that is going to happen: *'Everything's under control.' 'Famous last words!'* **ORIGIN** This phrase refers to a collection of quotations of the dying words of famous people.

**fam·ous·ly** /ˈfeɪməsli/ adv. in a way that is famous: *Some newspapers, most famously the New York Times, refused to print the word Ms.*

# fan

**IDM** **get on/along ˈfamously** (*old-fashioned*, *informal*) to have a very good relationship

**fan** ❶ **A2** /fæn/ *noun*, **fans** *verb*

■ *noun* **1** **A2** a person who admires sb/sth or enjoys watching or listening to sb/sth very much: *sports/music fans* ◇ *crowds of football fans* ◇ *~ of sb/sth I'm a big fan of her books.* ◇ *I'm not a great fan of bushy beards* (= I don't like them). ◇ *fan mail* (= letters from fans to the person they admire) **2** a machine that creates a current of air: *to switch on the electric fan* ◇ *a fan heater* ⊃ see also EXTRACTOR **3** a thing that you hold in your hand and wave to create a current of cool air **IDM** see SHIT *n.*

■ *verb* (**-nn-**) **1** ~ **sb/sth/yourself** to make air blow onto sb/sth by waving a fan, your hand, etc: *He fanned himself with a newspaper to cool down.* **2** ~ **sth** to make a fire burn more strongly by blowing on it: *Fanned by a westerly wind, the fire spread rapidly through the city.* **3** ~ **sth** (*literary*) to make a feeling, an attitude, etc. stronger **SYN** **fuel**: *His reluctance to answer her questions simply fanned her curiosity.*

**IDM** **fan the ˈflames (of sth)** to make a feeling such as anger, hate, etc. worse: *His writings fanned the flames of racism.*

**PHRV** **ˌfan ˈout | ˌfan sth↔ˈout** to spread out or spread sth out over an area: *The police fanned out to surround the house.* ◇ *The bird fanned out its tail feathers.*

**fan·at·ic** /fəˈnætɪk/ *noun* **1** (*disapproving*) a person who holds extreme or dangerous opinions **SYN** **extremist**: *religious fanatics* **2** (*informal*) a person who is extremely enthusiastic about sth **SYN** **enthusiast**: *a fitness/crossword fanatic* ▶ **fan·at·ic·al** /-tɪkl/ *adj*.: *fanatical anti-royalists* ◇ *a fanatical supporter* ◇ *a fanatical interest in football* ◇ *She's fanatical about healthy eating.* **fan·at·ic·al·ly** /-kli/ *adv.*: *fanatically devoted to exercise*

**fan·ati·cism** /fəˈnætɪsɪzəm/ *noun* [U] (*disapproving*) extreme beliefs or behaviour, especially in connection with religion or politics **SYN** **extremism**

**ˈfan belt** *noun* a belt that operates the machines that cool a car engine

**fan·boy** /ˈfænbɔɪ/ *noun* (*informal*) a person, especially a boy or young man, who is extremely interested in sth such as a particular type of music or software: *a Nintendo fanboy* ◇ *Linux fanboys*

**fan·cier** /ˈfænsiə(r)/ *noun* (usually in compounds) a person who has a special interest in sth, especially sb who keeps a particular type of bird or animal: *a pigeon fancier*

**fan·ci·ful** /ˈfænsɪfl/ *adj*. **1** (*often disapproving*) based on imagination and not facts or reason **2** (of things) decorated in an unusual style that shows imagination: *a fanciful gold border* ▶ **fan·ci·ful·ly** /-fəli/ *adv.*

**ˈfan club** *noun* an organization that a person's fans belong to and that sends them information, etc. about that person ⊃ compare FAN SITE

**fancy** ❶ **B1** /ˈfænsi/ *verb*, *adj*., *noun*

■ *verb* (**fan·cies**, **fancy·ing**, **fan·cied**, **fan·cied**) **1** ❶ **B1** [T] (*BrE*, *informal*) to want sth or want to do sth **SYN** **feel like**: ~ **sth** *Fancy a drink?* ◇ *She didn't fancy* (= did not like) *the idea of going home in the dark.* ◇ ~ **doing sth** *Do you fancy going out this evening?* **2** ❷ **B1** [T] ~ **sb** (*BrE*, *informal*) to be sexually attracted to sb: *I think she fancies me.* **3** [T] ~ **yourself** (*BrE*, *informal*, *disapproving*) to think that you are very popular, attractive or intelligent: *He started to chat to me and I could tell that he really fancied himself.* **4** [T] ~ **yourself** 

**(as) sth | ~ yourself + adv./prep.** (*BrE*) to like the idea of being sth or to believe, often wrongly, that you are sth: *She fancies herself as a serious actress.* **5** [I, T] **Fancy!** (*informal*, *becoming old-fashioned*) used to show that you are surprised or shocked by sth: *Fancy! She's never been in a plane before.* ◇ **~ doing sth** *Fancy meeting you here!* ◇ **~ sth** *'She remembered my name after all those years.' 'Fancy that!'* **6** [T] (*BrE*) ~ **sb/sth** to think that sb/sth will win or be successful at sth, especially in a race: *Which horse do you fancy in the next race?* ◇ *He's hoping to get the job but I don't fancy his chances.* **7** [T] ~ **(that) ...** (*literary*) to believe or imagine sth: *She fancied (that) she could hear footsteps.*

■ *adj*. (**fan·cier**, **fan·ci·est**) **1** ❶ **B1** unusually complicated, often in an unnecessary way; intended to impress other people: *a kitchen full of fancy gadgets* ◇ *They added a lot of fancy footwork to the dance.* **OPP** **simple** **2** [only before noun] (especially of small things) with a lot of decorations or bright colours: *fancy goods* (= things sold as gifts or for decoration) ⊃ compare PLAIN **3** (*sometimes disapproving*) expensive or connected with an expensive way of life: *fancy restaurants with fancy prices* ◇ *Don't come back with any fancy ideas.* **4** (*NAmE*) (of food) of high quality

■ *noun* (*pl.* **-ies**) **1** [C, U] something that you imagine; your imagination **SYN** **fantasy**: *night-time fancies that disappear in the morning* ◇ *a child's wild flights of fancy* **2** [sing.] a feeling that you would like to have or to do sth **SYN** **whim**: *She said she wanted a dog but it was only a passing fancy.* **3** [C, usually *pl.*] (*BrE*) a small decorated cake

**IDM** **as/whenever, etc. the fancy ˈtakes you** as/whenever, etc. you feel like doing sth: *We bought a camper van so we could go away whenever the fancy took us.* **catch/take sb's ˈfancy** to attract or please sb: *She looked through the hotel advertisements until one of them caught her fancy.* **take a ˈfancy to sb/sth** (*especially BrE*) to start liking sb/sth, often without an obvious reason ⊃ more at TICKLE *v.*

**ˌfancy ˈdress** *noun* [U] (*BrE*) clothes that you wear, especially at parties, to make you appear to be a different character: *guests in fancy dress* ◇ *a fancy-dress party* ⊃ see also COSTUME, MASQUERADE *noun*

**ˌfancy-ˈfree** *adj*. free to do what you like because you are not emotionally involved with anyone: *I was still footloose and fancy-free* (= free to enjoy myself) *in those days.*

**ˌfancy ˈman, ˌfancy ˈwoman** *noun* (*old-fashioned*, *informal*, *disapproving*) the man/woman with whom a person is having a romantic relationship, especially when one or both of them is married to sb else

**fan·dango** /fænˈdæŋɡəʊ/ *noun* (*pl.* **fan·dan·goes** or **fan·dangos**) [C] a lively Spanish dance; a piece of music for this dance

**fan·dom** /ˈfændəm/ *noun* **1** [U] the state of being a fan of sb/sth: *my 17 years of football fandom* **2** [C] the fans of a particular person, team, TV show, etc. considered together as a community: *This US comedy show has a really strong fandom.*

**fan·fare** /ˈfænfeə(r); NAmE -fer/ *noun* **1** [C] a short loud piece of music that is played to celebrate sb/sth important arriving **2** [U, C] a large amount of activity and discussion in the media to celebrate sb/sth: *The product was launched amid much fanfare worldwide.*

**ˈfan fiction** (*also informal* **fan·fic**) /ˈfænfɪk/ *noun* [U] a type of literature, usually written on the internet, by people who admire a particular novel, film, etc., with characters taken from these stories

**fang** /fæŋ/ *noun* [usually *pl.*] either of two long sharp teeth at the front of the mouths of some animals, such as a snake or dog ⊃ VISUAL VOCAB page V3

**fan·girl** /ˈfæŋɡɜːl; NAmE -ɡɜːrl/ *noun* (*informal*) a girl or young woman who is extremely enthusiastic about sth such as a particular singer, type of music, game, product, etc: *The singer was mobbed by crazed fangirls.*

**fan·light** /ˈfænlaɪt/ (*NAmE also* **tran·som**) *noun* a small window above a door or another window

**fanny** /ˈfæni/ *noun* (*pl.* **-ies**) **1** (*BrE*, *taboo*, *slang*) the female sex organs **2** (*informal*, *especially NAmE*) a person's bottom

**fanny pack** (*NAmE*) (*BrE* **bum-bag**) *noun* (*informal*) a small bag attached to a belt and worn around the middle part of the body, to keep money, etc. in

**fan site** *noun* a place on the internet where fans can find and share information about sb/sth

**fan·ta·sia** /fænˈteɪziə; *NAmE* -ˈteɪʒə/ *noun* a piece of music in a free form, often based on well-known tunes

**fan·ta·size** (*BrE also* **-ise**) /ˈfæntəsaɪz/ *verb* [I, T] ~ **(about sth)** | ~ **(that …)** | ~ **sth** to imagine that you are doing sth that you would like to do, or that sth that you would like to happen is happening, even though this is very unlikely: *He sometimes fantasized about winning the gold medal.* ▸ **fan·ta·sist** /-sɪst/ *noun*

**fan·tas·tic** ⓘ **A1** /fænˈtæstɪk/ *adj.* **1** **A1** (*informal*) extremely good; excellent **SYN** **great**, **brilliant**: *He's done a fantastic job.* ◇ *This was a fantastic opportunity for students.* ◇ *You look fantastic!* ◇ *a fantastic achievement* ◇ *The weather was absolutely fantastic.* ◇ *You've got the job. Fantastic!* ◇ **it is ~ to do sth** *It was fantastic to see so many families enjoying themselves.* ⇒ SYNONYMS at GREAT **2** (*informal*) very large; larger than you expected **SYN** **enormous**, **amazing**: *The response to our appeal was fantastic.* ◇ *The car costs a fantastic amount of money.* **3** (*also less frequent* **fan·tas·tic·al**) [usually before noun] strange and showing a lot of imagination **SYN** **weird**: *fantastic dreams of forests and jungles* **4** impossible to put into practice; impossible to believe: *a fantastic scheme/project* ▸ **fan·tas·tic·al·ly** /-kli/ *adv.*: *fantastically successful* ◇ *a fantastically shaped piece of stone*

**fan·tasy** **B2+** /ˈfæntəsi/ *noun* (*pl.* **-ies**) **1** **B2+** [C] a pleasant situation that you imagine but that is unlikely to happen: *his childhood fantasies about becoming a famous football player* **2** **B2+** [C] a product of your imagination: *Her books are usually escapist fantasies.* **3** **B2+** [U] the act of imagining things; a person's imagination: *a work of fantasy* ◇ *Stop living in a fantasy world.* **4** [U] a type of story that is set in a world, or a version of our world, that does not really exist and involves magic, MONSTERS, etc: *She wrote a series of fantasy novels filled with wizards, witches and dragons.*

**fantasy ˈfootball** *noun* [U] a competition in which you choose players to make your own imaginary team, and score points according to the performance of the real players

**fan·zine** /ˈfænziːn/ *noun* a magazine that is written and read by fans of a musician, sports team, etc.

**FAO** /ˌef eɪ ˈəʊ/ *abbr.* (*BrE*) used in writing to mean 'for the attention of' (written on a document or letter to say who should deal with it) ⇒ *see also* ATTN

**FAQ** /ˌef eɪ ˈkjuː; fæk/ *abbr.* used in writing to mean 'frequently asked questions' (a list of questions and answers about a particular subject, especially one giving basic information for users of a website)

**fa·quir** = FAKIR

**far** ⓘ **A1** /fɑː(r)/ *adv., adj.*

■ *adv.* (**far·ther**, **far·thest** *or* **fur·ther**, **fur·thest**)
- DISTANCE **1** **A1** a long distance away: *We didn't go far.* ◇ *Have you come far?* ◇ *It's not far to the beach.* ◇ *There's not far to go now.* ◇ *It's too far to walk.* ◇ **+ adv./prep.** *The restaurant is not far from here.* ◇ *countries as far apart as Japan and Brazil* ◇ *He looked down at the traffic far below.* ◇ *Far away in the distance, a train whistled.* ◇ *The farther north they went, the colder it became.* ◇ *a concert of music from near and far* **HELP** In positive sentences it is more usual to use **a long way**: *We went a long way.* ◇ *We went far.* *The restaurant is a long way from here.* **2** **A1** used when you are asking or talking about the distance between two places or the distance that has been travelled or is to be travelled: *How far is it to your house from here?* ◇ *How much further is it?* ◇ *I'm not sure I can walk so far.* ◇ **as ~ as sb/sth** *We'll go by train as far as London, and then take a bus.* ◇ *We didn't go as far as the others.*
- TIME **3** **B1** a long time from the present; for a large part of a particular period of time: *~ back The band had their first hit as far back as 2012.* ◇ *~ ahead Let's try to plan further ahead.* ◇ *~ into sth We worked far into the night.*

- DEGREE **4** **B1** very much; to a great degree: *That's a far better idea.* ◇ *There are far more opportunities for young people than there used to be.* ◇ *She always gives us far too much homework.* ◇ *The results far exceeded my expectations.* ◇ **~beyond (sth)** *It had been a success far beyond their expectations.* ◇ **~behind (sth)** *He's fallen far behind in his work.* **5** **B2** used when you are asking or talking about the degree to which sth is true or possible: *How far can we trust him?* ◇ **as ~ as …** *His parents supported him as far as they could.* ◇ *Plan your route in advance, using main roads as far as possible.*
- PROGRESS **6** **B2** used to talk about how much progress has been made in doing or achieving sth: *How far have you got with that report?* ◇ **as/so ~ as (doing) sth** *I read as far as the third chapter.* ⇒ *note at* FARTHER

**IDM** **as far as the eye can/could ˈsee** to the HORIZON (= where the sky meets the land or sea): *The bleak moorland stretched on all sides as far as the eye could see.* **as/so far as ˈI am concerned** **B2** used to give your personal opinion on sth: *As far as I am concerned, you can do what you like.* **as far as I ˈknow** | **as far as I can reˈmember**, **ˈsee**, **ˈtell, etc.** used to say that you think you know, remember, understand, etc. sth but you cannot be completely sure, especially because you do not know all the facts: *As far as we knew, there was no cause for concern.* ◇ *As far as I can see, you've done nothing wrong.* ◇ *She lived in Chicago, as far as I can remember.* ⇒ *see also* AFAIK **as/so far as sb/sth is concerned** (*also* **as/so far as sb/sth goes**) used to give facts or an opinion about a particular aspect of sth **as/so far as it ˈgoes** to a limited degree, usually less than is enough: *It's a good plan as far as it goes, but there are a lot of things they haven't thought of.* **by ˈfar** (used with comparative or superlative adjectives or adverbs) by a great amount: *The last of these reasons is by far the most important.* ◇ *Amy is the smartest by far.* **carry/take sth too ˈfar** to continue doing sth beyond reasonable limits **far and aˈway** (followed by comparative or superlative adjectives) by a very great amount: *She's far and away the best player.* **far and ˈwide** over a large area: *They searched far and wide for the missing child.* **far be it from me to do sth (but …)** (*informal*) used when you are just about to disagree with sb or to criticize them and you would like them to think that you do not really want to do this: *Far be it from me to interfere in your affairs but I would like to give you just one piece of advice.* **far from sth/from doing sth** **B2** almost the opposite of sth or of what is expected: *It is far from clear* (= it is not clear) *what he intends to do.* ◇ *Computers, far from destroying jobs, can create employment.* **far ˈfrom it** (*informal*) used to say that the opposite of what sb says is true: *'You're not angry then?' 'Far from it. I've never laughed so much in my life.'* **go ˈfar** (of people) to be very successful in the future: *She is very talented and should go far.* **go far eˈnough** (used in questions and negative sentences) to achieve all that is wanted: *The new legislation is welcome but does not go far enough.* ◇ *Do these measures go far enough?* ◇ (*disapproving*) *Stop it now. The joke has gone far enough* (= it has continued too long). **go so/as far as to …** to be willing to go to extreme or surprising limits in dealing with sth: *I wouldn't go as far as to say that he's a liar* (= but I think he may be slightly dishonest). **go too ˈfar** | **go ˈthis/ˈthat far** to behave in an extreme way that is not acceptable: *He's always been quite crude, but this time he's gone too far.* ◇ *I never thought she'd go this far.* **in so/as ˈfar as** to the degree that: *That's the truth, in so far as I know it.* **not far ˈoff/ˈout/ˈwrong** (*informal*) almost correct: *Your guess wasn't far out at all.* **not go far** **1** (of money) to not be enough to buy a lot of things: *Five pounds doesn't go very far these days.* **2** (of a supply of sth) to not be enough for what is needed: *Four bottles of wine won't go far among twenty people.* **ˈso far** **B1** (*also formal* **ˈthus far**) until now; up to this point: *What do you think of the show so far?* ◇ *Detectives are so far at a loss to explain the reason for his death.* **ˈso far** (*informal*) only to a limited degree: *I trust him only so far.* **ˈso far, so ˈgood** (*saying*) used to say that things have been successful until now and you hope that they will continue to be successful, but you know that the

# faraway

task, etc. is not finished yet ⊃ more at AFIELD, FEW det., NEAR adv.
- **adj.** (**far·ther**, **far·thest** or **fur·ther**, **fur·thest**) [only before noun] **1** B1 at a greater distance away from you: *I saw her on the far side of the road.* ◊ *at the far end of the room* ◊ *They made for an empty table in the far corner.* **2** B1 at the furthest point in a particular direction: *the far north of Scotland* ◊ *Who is that on the far left of the photograph?* ◊ *She is on the far right of the party* (= holds extreme RIGHT-WING political views). **3** (*old-fashioned* or *literary*) a long distance away: *a far country*
- IDM **a far cry from sth** a very different experience from sth SYN **remote**

**far·away** /ˈfɑːrəweɪ/ *adj.* [only before noun] **1** a long distance away SYN **distant**: *a war in a faraway country* **2** *a ~look/expression* an expression on your face that shows that your thoughts are far away from your present situation SYN **distant**

**farce** /fɑːs; *NAmE* fɑːrs/ *noun* [C, U] **1** a funny play for the theatre based on silly and unlikely situations and events; this type of writing or performance: *a bedroom farce* (= a funny play about sex) **2** a situation or an event that is so unfair or badly organized that it becomes silly: *The trial was a complete farce.*

**far·ci·cal** /ˈfɑːsɪkl; *NAmE* ˈfɑːrs-/ *adj.* silly and not worth taking seriously: *It was a farcical trial.* ◊ *a situation verging on the farcical*

**fare** ⓘ B2 /feə(r); *NAmE* fer/ *noun, verb*
- **noun 1** ⓘ B2 [C, U] the money that you pay to travel by bus, plane, taxi, etc: *bus/taxi fares* ◊ *train/rail fares* ◊ *Children travel (at) half fare.* ◊ *When do they start paying full fare?* ⊃ see also AIRFARE ⊃ SYNONYMS at RATE **2** [C] a passenger in a taxi: *The taxi driver picked up a fare at the station.* **3** (*also* **fayre**) [U] a range of food of a particular type: *The restaurant provides good traditional fare.* ⊃ see also BILL OF FARE **4** [U] something that is offered to the public, especially as a form of entertainment: *This movie is perfect family fare.*
- **verb** [I] *~ well, badly, better, etc.* to be successful/unsuccessful in a particular situation SYN **get on**: *The party fared very badly in the last election.*

**the ˌFar ˈEast** *noun* China, Japan and other countries of East and south-east Asia ⊃ compare MIDDLE EAST ▶ **ˌFar ˈEastern** *adj.*

**fare·well** /ˌfeəˈwel; *NAmE* ˌferˈw-/ *noun, exclamation, verb*
- **noun** [C, U] the act of saying goodbye to sb: *She said her farewells and left.* ◊ *a farewell party/drink, etc.*
- **exclamation** (*old use* or *formal*) goodbye
- **verb** *~ sb* (*AustralE*) to arrange a ceremony or party for sb because they are leaving: *The troops were farewelled at a ceremony in Darwin.*

**ˌfar-ˈfetched** *adj.* very difficult to believe: *The whole story sounds very far-fetched.* ⊃ WORDFINDER NOTE at STORY

**ˌfar-ˈflung** *adj.* [usually before noun] (*literary*) **1** a long distance away: *expeditions to the far-flung corners of the world* **2** spread over a wide area: *a newsletter that helps to keep all our far-flung graduates in touch*

**ˌfar ˈgone** *adj.* [not before noun] (*informal*) very ill, crazy or drunk: *She was too far gone to understand anything we said to her.*

**farm** ⓘ A1 /fɑːm; *NAmE* fɑːrm/ *noun, verb*
- **noun 1** ⓘ A1 an area of land, and the buildings on it, used for growing crops and/or keeping animals: *a dairy farm* ◊ *an organic farm* ◊ *a pig/sheep/poultry farm* ◊ *on a ~ to live on a farm* ◊ *She works on the family farm.* ◊ *a farm worker/labourer* ◊ *farm animals*
  - WORDFINDER arable, barn, crop, cultivate, dairy, fallow, graze, livestock, tractor
  **2** (*also* **ˈfarm-house**) the main house on a farm, where the farmer lives **3** (*especially in compounds*) a place where particular fish or animals are kept in order to produce young: *a trout/mink farm* ⊃ see also BATTERY FARM, COL-LECTIVE FARM, DAIRY *noun*, FACTORY FARM, FISH FARM, SERVER FARM, SEWAGE FARM, SOLAR FARM, TRUCK FARM, WIND FARM, WINE FARM IDM see BET *v.*, BUY *v.*
- **verb 1** ⓘ [I, T] to use land for growing crops and/or keeping animals: *The family has farmed in Kent for over two hundred years.* ◊ *~ sth They farm dairy cattle.* ◊ *He farmed 200 acres of prime arable land.* ◊ *organically farmed produce* **2** [T] *~ sth* to keep fish or birds in order to produce young and sell them for food: *Salmon are farmed in net pens near coasts.* ◊ *farmed salmon/trout*
- PHRV **ˌfarm sb↔ˈout (to sb)** (*disapproving*) to arrange for sb to be cared for by other people | **ˌfarm sth↔ˈout to sb** to send out work for other people to do: *The company farms out a lot of work to freelancers.*

**farm·er** ⓘ A1 /ˈfɑːmə(r); *NAmE* ˈfɑːrm-/ *noun* a person who owns or manages a farm: *My parents are dairy farmers.* ◊ *The land is owned by a local farmer.* ⊃ see also TRUCK FARMER

**ˈfarmers' market** *noun* a place where farmers and growers sell food directly to the public

**farm·hand** /ˈfɑːmhænd; *NAmE* ˈfɑːrm-/ (*NAmE also* **ˈfield hand**) *noun* a person who works for a farmer

**farm·house** /ˈfɑːmhaʊs; *NAmE* ˈfɑːrm-/ *noun* the main house on a farm, usually where the farmer lives

**farm·ing** ⓘ A2 /ˈfɑːmɪŋ; *NAmE* ˈfɑːrm-/ *noun* [U] the business of managing or working on a farm: *to take up farming* ◊ *organic farming* ◊ *sheep/fish/salmon farming* ◊ *a farming community* ◊ *the British farming industry* ⊃ see also BATTERY FARMING, FACTORY FARMING, MIXED FARMING, TRUCK FARMING

**farm·land** /ˈfɑːmlænd; *NAmE* ˈfɑːrm-/ *noun* [U, pl.] land that is used for farming: *250 acres of farmland* ◊ *the prosperous farmlands of Picardy*

**farm·stead** /ˈfɑːmsted; *NAmE* ˈfɑːrm-/ *noun* (*NAmE* or *formal*) a FARMHOUSE and the buildings near it

**farm·yard** /ˈfɑːmjɑːd; *NAmE* ˈfɑːrmjɑːrd/ *noun* an area that is surrounded by farm buildings

**ˈfar-off** *adj.* [only before noun] **1** a long distance away SYN **distant**, **faraway**, **remote**: *a far-off land* **2** a long time ago SYN **distant**: *memories of those far-off days*

**far·rago** /fəˈrɑːɡəʊ/ *noun* [usually sing.] (*pl.* **-oes** or **-os**) (*formal, disapproving*) a confused mixture of different things SYN **hotchpotch**

**ˌfar-ˈreaching** *adj.* likely to have a lot of influence or many effects: *far-reaching consequences/implications* ◊ *far-reaching changes/reforms*

**far·rier** /ˈfæriə(r)/ *noun* a person whose job is making and fitting HORSESHOES for horses' feet

**far·row** /ˈfærəʊ/ *noun, verb*
- **noun 1** a group of baby pigs that are born together to the same mother SYN **litter 2** an act of giving birth to pigs
- **verb** [I] (of a female pig) to give birth

**Farsi** /ˈfɑːsiː; *NAmE* ˈfɑːrsiː/ *noun* [U] the modern Persian language, the official language of Iran

**ˌfar-ˈsighted** (*US* **ˈfar·sighted**) *adj.* **1** having or showing an understanding of the effects in the future of actions that you take now, and being able to plan for them: *the most far-sighted of politicians* ◊ *a far-sighted decision* **2** [not usually before noun] (*NAmE*) = LONG-SIGHTED ▶ **ˌfar-ˈsighted·ness** *noun* [U]

**fart** /fɑːt; *NAmE* fɑːrt/ *verb, noun*
- **verb** [I] (*taboo, slang*) to let air from the BOWELS come out through the ANUS, especially when it happens loudly HELP A more polite way of expressing this is 'to break wind'.
- PHRV **ˌfart aˈround** (*BrE also* **ˌfart aˈbout**) (*taboo, slang*) to waste time by behaving in a silly way
- **noun** (*taboo, slang*) **1** an act of letting air from the BOWELS come out through the ANUS, especially when it happens loudly **2** an unpleasant, boring or stupid person

**far·ther** /ˈfɑːðə(r); *NAmE* ˈfɑːrð-/ (*also* **further**) *adv., adj.*
- **adv.** (comparative of *far*) at or to a greater distance in space or time: *farther north/south* ◊ *farther along the road* ◊ *I can't*

go *any* farther. ◊ As a family we grew **farther and farther** apart. ◊ We watched their ship moving gradually **farther away**. ◊ How much farther is it? ◊ They hadn't got *any* farther with the work (= they had made no progress). **IDM** see AFIELD

■ *adj.* (comparative of *far*) at a greater distance in space, direction or time: *the farther shore of the lake*

▼ **WHICH WORD?**

**farther / further / farthest / furthest**

- These are the comparative and superlative forms of **far**.
- To talk about distance, use either **farther**, **farthest** or **further**, **furthest**. In *BrE*, **further**, **furthest** are the more common forms and in *NAmE*, **farther** and **farthest**: *I have to travel further/farther to work now.*
- To talk about the degree or extent of something, **further/furthest** are usually preferred: *Let's consider this point further.*
- **Further**, but not **farther**, can also mean 'more' or 'additional': *Are there any further questions?* This sounds very formal in *NAmE*.

**far·thest** /ˈfɑːðɪst; *NAmE* ˈfɑːrð-/ (*also* **fur·thest**) *adv., adj.*

■ *adv.* (superlative of *far*) at or to the greatest distance in space or time: *a competition to see who could throw (the) farthest* ◊ **~ (away) (from sth)** *the house farthest away from the road*

■ *adj.* (superlative of *far*) at the greatest distance in space or time: *the farthest point of the journey* ◊ **~ from sth** *the part of the garden farthest from the house*

**far·thing** /ˈfɑːðɪŋ; *NAmE* ˈfɑːrð-/ *noun* in the past, a British coin worth one quarter of an old penny

**fa·scia** (*BrE also* **facia**) /ˈfeɪʃə/ *noun* **1** (*BrE*) = DASHBOARD **2** (*also* **fascia board**) a board on the roof of a house, at the end of the RAFTERS **3** (*BrE*) a board above the entrance of a shop, with the name of the shop on it **4** the hard cover on a mobile phone

**fas·cin·ate** /ˈfæsɪneɪt/ *verb* [T, I] **~ (sb)** to attract or interest sb very much: *China has always fascinated me.* ◊ *It was a question that had fascinated him since he was a boy.* ◊ *The private lives of movie stars never fail to fascinate.*

**fas·cin·ated** /ˈfæsɪneɪtɪd/ *adj.* very interested: *The children watched, fascinated, as the picture began to appear.* ◊ **~ by sth** *I've always been fascinated by his ideas.* ◊ **~ to see, learn, etc.** *They were fascinated to see that it was similar to one they had at home.*

**fas·cin·at·ing** ⓘ B1 /ˈfæsɪneɪtɪŋ/ *adj.* extremely interesting and attractive: *a fascinating story* ◊ *Her letters offer a fascinating insight into early Victorian family life.* ◊ **~ to do** *I fail to see what women find so fascinating about him.* ◊ **~ to do** *His performance is fascinating to watch.* ◊ **it is~to do sth** *It's fascinating to see how different people approach the problem.* ⇒ SYNONYMS *at* INTERESTING ▶ **fas·cin·at·ing·ly** *adv.*

**fas·cin·ation** /ˌfæsɪˈneɪʃn/ *noun* **1** [C, usually sing.] a very strong attraction, that makes sth very interesting: *London has a fascination all of its own.* ◊ **~ for sb** *Water holds a fascination for most children.* **2** [U, sing.] the state of being very attracted to and interested in sb/sth: **in ~** *The girls listened in fascination as the story unfolded.* ◊ **~ with sb/sth** *the public's enduring fascination with the Royal Family* **HELP** You usually have a **fascination with** sth you are very interested in; something interesting holds a **fascination for** you. In informal language, the preposition **for** is sometimes used in both meanings, but it is better to keep the difference between them in careful writing.

**fas·cin·ator** /ˈfæsɪneɪtə(r)/ *noun* a decoration for the head, like a very small hat, worn by women on special occasions and made from feathers, artificial flowers, etc.

**fas·cism** /ˈfæʃɪzəm/ *noun* [U] **1** (*also* **Fas·cism**) an extreme RIGHT-WING political system or attitude that is in favour of strong central government, aggressively promoting your own country or race above others, and that does not allow any opposition ⇒ WORDFINDER NOTE *at* CAPITALISM **2** (*in compounds*) (*disapproving*) extreme views or practices that try to make other people think and behave in the same way: *They claimed the smoking ban amounted to health fascism.*

**fas·cist** (*also* **Fas·cist**) /ˈfæʃɪst/ *noun* **1** a person who supports fascism **2** (*disapproving, offensive*) a way of referring to sb that you think is bad because they have RIGHT-WING attitudes ▶ **fas·cist** *adj.*: *a fascist state* ◊ *fascist sympathies*

**fash·ion** ⓘ A2 /ˈfæʃn/ *noun, verb*

■ *noun* **1** ⓘ A2 [U, C] a popular style of clothes, hair, etc. at a particular time or place; the state of being popular: *the latest fashion trends* ◊ *the new season's fashions* ◊ **in ~** *Jeans are always in fashion.* ◊ *Long skirts have* **come into fashion** *again.* ◊ *Some styles never* **go out of fashion.** **2** ⓘ A2 [U] the business of making or selling clothes in new and different styles: *They all want to work in fashion.* ◊ *the world of fashion* ◊ *a fashion magazine* ◊ *the fashion industry* ⇒ WORDFINDER NOTE *at* STORE **3** ⓘ B1 [C] a popular way of behaving, doing an activity, etc.: **~ (in sth)** *Fashions in art and literature come and go.* ◊ **~ for (doing) sth** *The fashion at the time was for teaching mainly the written language.*

**IDM** **after a ˈfashion** to some extent, but not very well: *I can play the piano, after a fashion.* **after the fashion of sb/sth** (*formal*) in the style of sb/sth: *The new library is very much after the fashion of Nash.* **in (a) … ˈfashion** (*formal*) in a particular way: *How could they behave in such a fashion?* ◊ *She was proved right, in dramatic fashion, when the whole department resigned.* **like it's going out of ˈfashion** (*informal*) used to emphasize that sb is doing sth or using sth a lot: *She's been spending money like it's going out of fashion.*

■ *verb* to make or shape sth, especially with your hands: **~ A (from/out of B)** *She fashioned a pot from the clay.* ◊ **~ B (into A)** *She fashioned the clay into a pot.*

**fash·ion·able** ⓘ B1 /ˈfæʃnəbl/ *adj.* **1** ⓘ B1 following a style that is popular at a particular time: *fashionable clothes/ideas/styles* ◊ *He was laughed at by his more fashionable friends.* ◊ **it is~to do sth** *It's becoming fashionable to have long hair again.* ◊ **~ among sb** *Such thinking is currently fashionable among right-wing politicians.* **2** ⓘ B1 used or visited by people following a current fashion, especially by rich people: *a fashionable address/resort/restaurant* ◊ *She lives in a very fashionable part of London.* **OPP** unfashionable ⇒ compare OLD-FASHIONED ▶ **fash·ion·ably** /-bli/ *adv.*: *fashionably dressed* ◊ *His wife was blonde and fashionably thin.*

ˈ**fashion-conscious** *adj.* aware of the latest fashions and wanting to follow them: *fashion-conscious teenagers*

ˈ**fashion designer** *noun* a person who designs fashionable clothes

ˈ**fashion-ˈforward** *adj.* more modern than the current fashion: *We tend to be traditional rather than fashion-forward in our designs.*

**fash·ion·ista** /ˌfæʃnˈiːstə/ *noun* (used especially in the media) a fashion designer, or a person who is always dressed in a fashionable way

ˈ**fashion show** *noun* an occasion where people can see new designs of clothes being worn by fashion models

ˈ**fashion statement** *noun* something that you wear or own that is new or unusual and is meant to draw attention to you: *This shirt is great for anyone who wants to* **make a fashion statement.**

ˈ**fashion victim** *noun* (*informal, disapproving*) a person who always wears the newest fashions even if they do not suit him or her

**fast** ⓘ A1 /fɑːst; *NAmE* fæst/ *adj., adv., verb, noun*

■ *adj.* (**fast·er, fast·est**)

• QUICK **1** ⓘ A1 moving or able to move quickly: *a fast car/horse* ◊ *the world's fastest runner* **2** ⓘ A1 happening in a short time or without delay: *the fastest rate of increase for years* ◊ *a fast response time* ◊ *Technology was expanding at a fast pace.* **3** ⓘ A1 able to do sth quickly: *a fast learner* ◊ *a fast internet connection*

• SURFACE **4** producing or allowing quick movement: *a fast road* ⇒ see also FAST LANE

# fastball 568

- **WATCH/CLOCK 5** [not before noun] showing a time later than the true time: *I'm early—my watch must be fast.* ◊ *That clock's ten minutes fast.*
- **PHOTOGRAPHIC FILM 6** (*specialist*) very sensitive to light, and therefore useful when taking photographs in poor light or of sth that is moving very quickly
- **FIXED 7** (of a boat, etc.) safely fixed in position: *He made the boat fast.*
- **COLOURS IN CLOTHES 8** not likely to change or to come out when washed ⊃ see also COLOUR FAST **HELP** There is no noun related to **fast**. Use **speed** in connection with vehicles, actions, etc.; **quickness** is used about thinking.

**IDM** **ˌfast and ˈfurious** (of films/movies, shows, etc.) full of rapid action and sudden changes: *In his latest movie, the action is fast and furious.* **a fast ˈtalker** a person who can talk very quickly and easily, but who cannot always be trusted **a fast ˈworker** (*informal*) a person who knows how to get what they want quickly, especially when beginning a sexual relationship with sb ⊃ more at BUCK *n.*, DRAW *n.*, HARD *adj.*, PULL *v.*

■ *adv.* (**ˈfast·er**, **ˈfast·est**)
- **QUICKLY 1** quickly: *Don't drive so fast!* ◊ *How fast were you going?* ◊ *I can't go any faster.* ◊ *The water was rising fast.* ◊ *Her heart beat faster.* ◊ (*formal*) *Night was fast approaching.* ⊃ note at QUICK **2** in a short time; without delay: *Children grow up so fast these days.* ◊ *Britain is fast becoming a nation of fatties.* ◊ *Ben knew he had to move fast.*
- **FAST- 3** (in compound adjectives) doing the thing mentioned quickly: *a fast-flowing stream* ◊ *fast-growing crops*
- **COMPLETELY 4** completely: *Within a few minutes she was fast asleep* = sleeping deeply). ◊ *The boat was stuck fast* (= unable to move) *in the mud.* **HELP** There is no noun related to **fast**. Use **speed** in connection with vehicles, actions, etc.; **quickness** is used about thinking.

**IDM** **as fast as your ˈlegs can ˈcarry you** as quickly as you can **hold ˈfast to sth** (*formal*) to continue to believe in an idea, etc. despite difficulties **play fast and ˈloose (with sb/sth)** (*old-fashioned*) to treat sb/sth in a way that shows that you feel no responsibility or respect for them **stand ˈfast/ˈfirm** to refuse to move back; to refuse to change your opinions ⊃ more at FADE, THICK *adv.*

■ *verb* [I] to eat little or no food for a period of time, especially for religious or medical reasons: *Muslims fast during Ramadan.*

■ *noun* a period during which you do not eat food, especially for religious or health reasons: *to go on a fast* ◊ *to break* (= end) *your fast*

**fast·ball** /ˈfɑːstbɔːl; NAmE ˈfæst-/ *noun* (in baseball) a ball that is thrown at the PITCHER's fastest speed

**ˌfast ˈbowler** (*also* ˈpace bowler, ˈpace·man) *noun* (in CRICKET) a person who BOWLS very fast

**ˌfast ˈbreeder** (*also* ˌfast ˌbreeder reˈactor) *noun* a REACTOR in a nuclear power station in which the reaction that produces energy is not made slower

**fas·ten** /ˈfɑːsn; NAmE ˈfæsn/ *verb* **1** [T, I] to close or join together the two parts of sth; to become closed or joined together **SYN** do up: *~ sth Fasten your seat belts, please.* ◊ *~ sth up He fastened up his coat and hurried out.* ◊ *~ sth with sth The garment is fastened with a sash.* ◊ *~ + adv./prep. The dress fastens at the back.* **OPP** unfasten **2** [T, I] *~ (sth)* to close sth so that it will not open; to be closed in this way: *Fasten the gates securely so that they do not blow open.* ◊ *The window wouldn't fasten.* **OPP** unfasten **3** [T] *~ sth + adv./prep.* to fix sth in a particular position: *He fastened back the shutters.* **4** [T] to attach or tie one thing to another thing: *~ A and B together He fastened the papers together with a paper clip.* ◊ *~ A to B She fastened the rope to a tree.* **5** [T, I] if you fasten your arms around sb, your teeth into sth, etc., or if your arms, teeth, etc. **fasten** around, into, etc. sb/sth, you hold the person/thing strongly with your arms, etc: *~ sth + adv./prep. The dog fastened its teeth in his leg.* ◊ *+ adv./prep. His hand fastened on her arm.* **6** [T, I] *~ (sth) (on sb/sth)* if you **fasten** your eyes on sb/

sth or your eyes **fasten** on sb/sth, you look at them for a long time: *He fastened his gaze on her face.*
**PHRV** **ˈfasten on(to) sb/sth** to choose or follow sb/sth in a determined way **SYN** latch on(to)

**fas·ten·er** /ˈfɑːsnə(r); NAmE ˈfæs-/ (*also* **fas·ten·ing**) *noun* a device, such as a button or a ZIP, used to close a piece of clothing; a device used to close a window, bag, etc. tightly

**fas·ten·ing** /ˈfɑːsnɪŋ; NAmE ˈfæs-/ *noun* **1** = FASTENER **2** the place where sth, especially a piece of clothing, fastens; the way sth fastens: *The trousers have a fly fastening.*

**ˌfast ˈfood** *noun* [U] hot food, such as HAMBURGERS and chips, that is served very quickly and can be taken away to be eaten in the street: *fast-food restaurants* ⊃ compare SLOW FOOD

**fast-ˈforward** *verb* **1** [T, I] *~ (sth)* to move a recording forwards to a later point without playing it **2** [I] *~ to sth + adv./prep.* to move quickly forwards in time, especially to a later point in a story: *The action then fast-forwards to Ettore as a young man.* ▶ **fast ˈforward** *noun* [U]: *I pressed fast forward when the ads came on.* ◊ *the fast-forward button*

**fas·tidi·ous** /fæˈstɪdiəs/ *adj.* **1** being careful that every detail of sth is correct **SYN** meticulous: *Everything was planned in fastidious detail.* ◊ *He was fastidious in his preparation for the big day.* **2** (*sometimes disapproving*) not liking things to be dirty or untidy: *The child seemed fastidious about getting her fingers dirty.* ▶ **fas·tidi·ous·ly** *adv.* **fas·tidi·ous·ness** *noun* [U]

**ˈfast lane** *noun* [sing.] the part of a major road such as a MOTORWAY or INTERSTATE where vehicles drive fastest **IDM** **in the ˈfast lane** where things are most exciting and where a lot is happening: *He had a good job, plenty of money and he was enjoying life in the fast lane.*

**fast·ness** /ˈfɑːstnəs; NAmE ˈfæst-/ *noun* (*literary*) a place that is thought to be safe because it is difficult to get to or easy to defend **SYN** stronghold

**fast-ˈpaced** *adj.* moving, changing or happening very quickly: *a fast-paced thriller* ◊ *She enjoys working in a fast-paced environment.*

**ˈfast track** *noun* [sing.] a quick way to achieve sth, for example a high position in a job: *the ~ (to sth) She is on the fast track to promotion.* ▶ **ˈfast-track** *adj.*: *the fast-track route to promotion* ◊ *fast-track graduates*

---

**▼ WHICH WORD?**

**fast / quick / rapid**
These adjectives are frequently used with the following nouns:

| fast ~ | quick ~ | rapid ~ |
|---|---|---|
| car | glance | change |
| train | look | growth |
| bowler | reply | increase |
| pace | decision | decline |
| lane | way | progress |

- **Fast** is used especially to describe a person or thing that moves or is able to move at great speed.
- **Quick** is more often used to describe something that is done in a short time or without delay.
- **Rapid**, **swift** and **speedy** are more formal words.
- **Rapid** is most commonly used to describe the speed at which something changes. It is not used to describe the speed at which something moves or is done: *a rapid train* ◊ *We had a rapid coffee.*
- **Swift** usually describes something that happens or is done quickly and immediately: *a swift decision* ◊ *The government took swift action.*
- **Speedy** has a similar meaning: *a speedy recovery.* It is used less often to talk about the speed at which something moves: *a speedy car.*
- For the use of **fast** and **quick** as adverbs, ⊃ note at QUICK.

**fast-track** verb ~ sb/sth to make sb's progress in achieving sth, for example a high position in a job, quicker than usual

**fat** ❶ A1 /fæt/ adj., noun

WORD FAMILY
fat adj.
fatty adj.
fatten verb
fattening adj.

■ adj. (fat·ter, fat·test) **1** A1 (of a person's or an animal's body) having too much FLESH on it and weighing too much: *a big fat man/woman* ◇ *You'll get fat if you eat so much chocolate.* ◇ *He grew fatter and fatter.* ◇ *fat flabby legs* OPP **thin 2** (of meat) containing a lot of fat: *fat bacon/sausages* **3** thick or wide: *a fat volume on American history* **4** [only before noun] (informal) large in quantity; worth a lot of money: *a fat sum/profit* ◇ *He gave me a nice fat cheque.* ▸ **fat·ness** noun [U]: *Fatness tends to run in families.* IDM **(a) fat ˈchance (of sth/doing sth)** (informal) used for saying that you do not believe sth is likely to happen: *'They might let us in without tickets.' 'Fat chance of that!'* **a fat lot of good, use, etc.** (informal) not at all good or useful: *Paul can't drive so he was a fat lot of use when I broke my arm.* **it's not ˌover until the fat ˌlady ˈsings** (saying) used for saying that a situation may still change, for example that a contest, election, etc. is not finished yet, and sb still has a chance to win it

■ noun **1** A2 [U] a white or yellow substance in the bodies of animals and humans, stored under the skin: *excess body fat* ◇ *This ham has too much fat on it.* **2** A2 [C, U] a solid or liquid substance from animals or plants, treated so that it becomes pure for use in cooking: *Cook the meat in shallow fat.* **3** A2 [C, U] animal and vegetable fats, when you are thinking of them as part of what a person eats: *You should cut down on fats and carbohydrates.* ◇ *foods that are low in fat* ◇ *Is your diet high in fat?* ⊃ see also FULL-FAT, LOW-FAT, MONOUNSATURATED FAT, POLYUNSATURATED FAT, SATURATED FAT, UNSATURATED FAT IDM see CHEW v., LIVE[1]

▼ **VOCABULARY BUILDING**
**Saying that somebody is fat**
• **Fat** is the most common and direct word, but it is not polite to say to someone that they are fat: *Does this dress make me look fat?* ◇ ~~You're looking fat now.~~
• **Overweight** is a more neutral word: *I'm a bit overweight.* It can also mean too fat, especially so that you are not fit.
• **Large** or **heavy** is less offensive than **fat**: *She's a rather large woman.* **Big** describes someone who is tall as well as fat: *Her sister is a big girl, isn't she?*
• **Plump** means slightly fat in an attractive way, often used to describe women.
• **Chubby** is used mainly to describe babies and children who are fat in a pleasant, healthy-looking way: *the baby's chubby cheeks*
• **Tubby** (informal) is used in a friendly way to describe people who are short and round, especially around the stomach.
• **Stocky** is a neutral word and means fairly short, broad and strong.
• **Stout** is often used to describe older people who have a round and heavy appearance: *a short stout man with a bald head*
• **Flabby** describes body parts that are fat and loose: *exercises to firm up flabby thighs*
• **Obese** is used by doctors to describe people who are so fat that they are unhealthy. It is also used in a general way to mean 'really fat'.
Note that although people talk a lot about their own size or weight, it is generally not considered polite to refer to a person's large size or their weight when you talk to them.
⊃ note at THIN

**fatal** B2 C1 /ˈfeɪtl/ adj. **1** B2 C1 causing or ending in death: *a fatal accident/blow/illness* ◇ *a potentially fatal form of cancer* ◇ *If she gets ill again it could prove fatal.* ⊃ compare MORTAL **2** B2 C1 causing disaster or failure: *a fatal error/mistake* ◇ *Any delay would be fatal.* ◇ *There was a fatal flaw in the plan.* ◇ *It'd be fatal to try and stop them now.*

▸ **fa·tal·ly** /-təli/ adv.: *fatally injured/wounded* ◇ *The plan was fatally flawed from the start.*

**fa·tal·ism** /ˈfeɪtəlɪzəm/ noun [U] the belief that events are decided by FATE and that you cannot control them; the fact of accepting that you cannot prevent sth from happening ▸ **fa·tal·ist** /-lɪst/ noun: *I'm a fatalist.*

**fa·tal·is·tic** /ˌfeɪtəˈlɪstɪk/ adj. showing a belief in FATE and feeling that you cannot control events or stop them from happening ▸ **fa·tal·is·tic·al·ly** /-kli/ adv.

**fa·tal·ity** /fəˈtæləti; NAmE feɪˈt-/ noun (pl. **-ies**) **1** [C] a death that is caused in an accident or a war, or by violence or disease: *Several people were injured, but there were no fatalities.* **2** [U] the fact that a particular disease will result in death: *to reduce the fatality of certain types of cancer* ◇ *Different forms of cancer have different fatality rates.* **3** [U] the belief or feeling that we have no control over what happens to us: *A sense of fatality gripped her.*

**ˈfat camp** noun [U, C] an organized holiday for fat children during which they are helped to lose weight

**ˈfat cat** noun (informal, disapproving) a person who earns, or who has, a lot of money (especially when compared to people who do not earn so much)

**fate** B2 C1 /feɪt/ noun **1** B2 C1 [C] the things, especially bad things, that will happen or have happened to sb/sth: *The fate of the three men is unknown.* ◇ *She sat outside, waiting to find out her fate.* ◇ *The court will decide our fate/fates.* ◇ *Each of the managers suffered the same fate.* ◇ *The government had abandoned the refugees to their fate.* ◇ *From that moment our fate was sealed* (= our future was decided). **2** B2 C1 [U] the power that is believed to control everything that happens and that cannot be stopped or changed: *Fate was kind to me that day.* ◇ *By a strange twist of fate, Andy and I were on the same plane.* ⊃ SYNONYMS at LUCK ⊃ WORDFINDER NOTE at LUCK IDM **a fate worse than ˈdeath** (often humorous) a terrible thing that could happen ⊃ more at TEMPT

**fated** /ˈfeɪtɪd/ adj. **1** ~ (to do sth) unable to escape a particular fate; certain to happen because everything is controlled by fate SYN **destined**: *We were fated never to meet again.* ◇ *He believes that everything in life is fated.* **2** (formal) = ILL-FATED

**fate·ful** /ˈfeɪtfl/ adj. [usually before noun] having an important, often very bad, effect on future events: *She looked back now to that fateful day in December.*

**fat-ˈfree** adj. not containing any fat SYN **nonfat**: *fat-free yogurt*

**father** ❶ A1 /ˈfɑːðə(r)/ noun, verb

■ noun **1** A1 a male parent of a child or an animal; a person who is acting as the father to a child: *My father died in 2017.* ◇ *Ben's a wonderful father.* ◇ *Our new boss is a father of three* (= he has three children). ◇ **~to sb** *You've been like a father to me.* ◇ (old-fashioned) *Father, I cannot lie to you.* ⊃ see also GODFATHER, GRANDFATHER, STEPFATHER **2 fathers** [pl.] (literary) a person's ANCESTORS (= people who are related to you who lived in the past): *the land of our fathers* ⊃ see also FOREFATHER **3 ~ (of sth)** the first man to introduce a new way of thinking about sth or of doing sth: *Henry Moore is considered to be the father of modern British sculpture.* ⊃ see also FOUNDING FATHER, CITY FATHER **4 Father** used by Christians to refer to God: *Father, forgive us.* ◇ *God the Father* **5 Father** (abbr. **Fr**) the title of a priest, especially in the Roman Catholic Church and the Orthodox Church: *Father Dominic* ⊃ see also HOLY FATHER IDM **from ˌfather to ˈson** from one generation of a family to the next **like ˌfather, like ˈson** (saying) used to say that a son's character or behaviour is similar to that of his father ⊃ more at OLD, WISH n.

■ verb **1** ~ **sb** to become the father of a child by making a woman pregnant: *He claims to have fathered over 20 children.* **2** ~ **sth** to create new ideas or a new way of doing sth

**Father ˈChristmas** noun (BrE) = SANTA CLAUS

**ˈfather figure** noun an older man that sb respects because he will advise and help them like a father

# fatherhood

**father·hood** /ˈfɑːðəhʊd; NAmE -ðərh-/ noun [U] the state of being a father

**ˈfather-in-law** noun (pl. **fathers-in-law**) the father of your husband or wife ⊃ compare MOTHER-IN-LAW

**father·land** /ˈfɑːðəlænd; NAmE -ðərl-/ noun [usually sing.] (old-fashioned) (used especially about Germany) the country where a person, or their family, was born, especially when they feel very proud of it

**father·less** /ˈfɑːðələs; NAmE -ðərl-/ adj. [usually before noun] without a father, either because he has died or because he does not live with his children: *fatherless children/families*

**father·ly** /ˈfɑːðəli; NAmE -ðərli/ adj. typical of a good father: *fatherly advice* ◊ *He keeps a fatherly eye on his players.*

**ˈFather's Day** noun (in some countries) a day when fathers receive cards and gifts from their children, usually the third Sunday in June

**Father ˈTime** noun an imaginary figure who represents time and looks like an old man carrying a SCYTHE and an HOURGLASS

**fathom** /ˈfæðəm/ verb, noun
- verb (usually in negative sentences) to understand or find an explanation for sth: ~ **sb/sth (out)** *She knew he was angry with her, for some reason she couldn't fathom.* ◊ ~ **(out) what, where, etc.** ... *He couldn't fathom out what the man could possibly mean.*
- noun a unit for measuring the depth of water, equal to 6 feet or 1.8 metres: *The ship sank in 20 fathoms.* ◊ *(figurative) She kept her feelings hidden fathoms deep.*

**fa·tigue** /fəˈtiːg/ noun 1 [U] a feeling of being extremely tired, usually because of hard work or exercise **SYN** exhaustion, tiredness: *physical and mental fatigue* ◊ *Driver fatigue was to blame for the accident.* ◊ *I was dropping with fatigue and could not keep my eyes open.* 2 [U] (usually after another noun) a feeling of not wanting to do a particular activity any longer because you have done too much of it: *battle fatigue* 3 [U] weakness in metal or wood caused by repeated bending or stretching: *The wing of the plane showed signs of metal fatigue.* 4 **fatigues** [pl.] loose clothes worn by soldiers 5 **fatigues** [pl.] (especially NAmE) duties, such as cleaning and cooking, that soldiers have to do, especially as a punishment

**fa·tigued** /fəˈtiːgd/ adj. [not usually before noun] (formal) very tired, both physically and mentally **SYN** exhausted

**fa·tigu·ing** /fəˈtiːgɪŋ/ adj. (formal) making you very tired, both physically and mentally **SYN** exhausting

**fatso** /ˈfætsəʊ/ noun (pl. **-oes**) = FATTY

**fat·ten** /ˈfætn/ verb [T, I] ~ **(sb/sth) (up)** to make sb/sth fatter, especially an animal before killing it for food; to become fatter: *The piglets are taken from the sow to be fattened for market.* ◊ *She's very thin after her illness—but we'll soon fatten her up.*

**fat·ten·ing** /ˈfætnɪŋ/ adj. (of food) likely to make you fat: *fattening cakes* ⊃ **WORDFINDER NOTE** at EAT

**fatty** /ˈfæti/ adj., noun
- adj. (**fat·tier, fat·ti·est**) containing a lot of fat; consisting of fat: *fatty foods* ◊ *fatty tissue*
- noun (pl. **-ies**) (also **fatso**) (informal, offensive) a fat person: *Britain is fast becoming a nation of fatties.*

**ˌfatty ˈacid** noun (chemistry) an ACID that is found in fats and oils

**fatu·ous** /ˈfætʃuəs/ adj. (formal) stupid: *a fatuous comment/grin* ▶ **fatu·ous·ly** adv.

**fatwa** /ˈfætwɑː/ noun a decision or order made under Islamic law

**fau·cet** /ˈfɔːsɪt/ (NAmE) (also **tap** especially in BrE) noun a device that controls the flow of water from a pipe: *the hot/cold faucet* ◊ *to turn a faucet on/off* ⊃ picture at PLUG

**fault** ❶ B2 /fɔːlt/ noun, verb
- noun
  - RESPONSIBILITY 1 B2 [U] the responsibility for sth wrong that has happened or been done: *Why should I say sorry when it's not my fault?* ◊ *It's nobody's fault.* ◊ ~ **(that)** ... *It was his fault that we were late.* ◊ ~ **for doing sth** *It's your own fault for being careless.* ◊ **at** ~ *I think the owners are at fault (= responsible) for not warning us.* ◊ *Many people live in poverty through no fault of their own.* ⊃ see also NO-FAULT
  - IN SB'S CHARACTER 2 B2 [C] a bad or weak aspect of sb's character **SYN** shortcoming: *He's proud of his children and blind to their faults.* ◊ *I love her for all her faults (= in spite of them).*
  - STH WRONG 3 B2 [C] something that is wrong or not perfect; something that is wrong with a machine or system that stops it from working correctly **SYN** defect: *The book's virtues far outweigh its faults.* ◊ *an electrical/a mechanical/a technical fault* ◊ *The system, for all its faults, is the best available at the moment.* ◊ ~ **in/with sth** *a major fault in the design* ◊ **without** ~ *The film is not without fault.*
  - IN TENNIS 4 [C] a mistake made when SERVING: *He has served a number of double faults in this set.* ⊃ see also DOUBLE FAULT, DOUBLE-FAULT
  - GEOLOGY 5 [C] a place where there is a break that is longer than usual in the layers of rock in the earth's CRUST: *the San Andreas fault* ◊ *a fault line*
  - **IDM** **to a ˈfault** used to say that sb has a lot, or even too much, of a particular good quality: *She is generous to a fault.* ⊃ more at FIND v.
- verb (usually used in negative sentences with *can* and *could*) ~ **sb/sth** to find a mistake or a weakness in sb/sth **SYN** criticize: *Her colleagues could not fault her dedication to the job.* ◊ *He had always been polite—she couldn't fault him on that.*

**ˈfault-finding** noun [U] constant criticism, especially about things that are not important

**fault·less** /ˈfɔːltləs/ adj. having no mistakes **SYN** perfect: *faultless English* ▶ **fault·less·ly** adv.

**ˈfault line** noun 1 (geology) a place where there is a long break in the rock that forms the surface of the earth and where earthquakes are more likely to happen 2 an issue that people disagree about and may, as a result, lead to conflict: *The two men are from opposite sides of the nation's political fault line.*

**faulty** /ˈfɔːlti/ adj. 1 not perfect; not working or made correctly **SYN** defective: *Ask for a refund if the goods are faulty.* ◊ *faulty workmanship* ◊ *an accident caused by a faulty signal* 2 (of a way of thinking) wrong or containing mistakes, often resulting in bad decisions: *faulty reasoning*

**faun** /fɔːn/ noun (in ancient Roman stories) a god of the woods, with a man's face and body and a GOAT's legs and HORNS

**fauna** /ˈfɔːnə/ noun [U, C] all the animals living in an area or in a particular period of history: *the local flora and fauna (= plants and animals)* ◊ *(specialist) land and marine faunas*

**Faust·ian** /ˈfaʊstiən/ adj. ~ **bargain/pact/agreement** (formal) an agreement in which sb agrees to do sth bad or dishonest, in return for money, success or power **ORIGIN** From **Faust**, who, according to the German legend, sold his soul to the Devil in return for many years of power and pleasure.

**faux** /fəʊ/ adj. (from French) artificial, but intended to look or seem real: *The chairs were covered in faux animal skin.* ◊ *His accent was so faux.*

**ˌfaux ˈpas** /ˌfəʊ ˈpɑː/ noun (pl. **faux pas** /-ˈpɑːz/) (from French) an action or a remark that causes sb to feel embarrassed because it is not socially correct

**ˈfava bean** /ˈfɑːvə biːn/ (NAmE) (also ˌbroad ˈbean especially in BrE) noun a type of round, pale green bean. Several fava beans grow together inside a fat POD.

**fave** /feɪv/ noun (informal) a favourite person or thing: *That song is one of my faves.* ▶ **fave** adj. [only before noun]: *her fave TV show*

**fa·vela** /fəˈvelə/ noun (from Portuguese) a poor area in or near a Brazilian city, with many small houses that are close together and in bad condition ⊃ compare SHANTY TOWN

## fa·vour (US favor) /ˈfeɪvə(r)/ noun, verb

■ **noun**
- **HELP 1** [C] a thing that you do to help sb: *Could you do me a favour* and pick up Sam from school today? ◊ *I'll ask Steve to take it. He owes me a favour.* ◊ *Thanks for helping me out. I'll return the favour* (= help you because you have helped me) *some time.* ◊ *as a ~ (to sb) I'm going as a favour to Ann, not because I want to.* ◊ *Do yourself a favour* (= help yourself) *and wear a helmet on the bike.* ⊃ EXPRESS YOURSELF at PERMISSION
- **APPROVAL 2** [U] approval or support for sb/sth: *~ with sb The suggestion to close the road has found favour with* (= been supported by) *local people.* ◊ *to gain/win/lose favour with sb* ◊ *in~ (with sb) She's not in favour with* (= supported or liked by) *the media just now.* ◊ *out of ~ (with sb) Reality TV has begun to fall out of favour with viewers.* ◊ *an athlete who fell from favour after a drugs scandal* ◊ *(formal) The government looks with favour upon* (= approves of) *the report's recommendations.*
- **BETTER TREATMENT 3** [U] treatment that is generous to one person or group in a way that seems unfair to others **SYN** bias: *As an examiner, she showed no favour to any candidate.* ⊃ see also GRACE AND FAVOUR
- **PARTY GIFT 4** [C, usually pl.] (NAmE) = PARTY FAVOR
- **SEX 5 favours** [pl.] (old-fashioned) agreement to have sex with sb: *demands for sexual favours*

**IDM** **do me a 'favour!** (*informal*) used in reply to a question that you think is silly: *'Do you think they'll win?' 'Do me a favour! They haven't got a single decent player.'* **do sb no 'favours** to do sth that is not helpful to sb or that gives a bad impression of them: *You're not doing yourself any favours, working for nothing.* ◊ *The orchestra did Beethoven no favours.* **in favour (of sb/sth) 1** if you are in favour of sb/sth, you support and agree with them/it: *He argued in favour of a strike.* ◊ *There were 247 votes in favour (of the motion) and 152 against.* ◊ *I'm all in favour of* (= completely support) *equal pay for equal work.* ◊ *Most of the 'don't knows' in the opinion polls came down in favour of* (= eventually chose to support) *the Democrats.* **2** in exchange for another thing (because the other thing is better or you want it more): *He abandoned teaching in favour of a career as a musician.* **in sb's favour 1** if sth is **in sb's favour**, it gives them an advantage or helps them: *The exchange rate is in our favour at the moment.* ◊ *She was willing to bend the rules in Mary's favour.* **2** a decision or judgement that is **in sb's favour** benefits that person or says that they were right ⊃ more at CURRY v., FEAR n., STACKED

■ **verb**
- **PREFER 1** to prefer one system, plan, way of doing sth, etc. to another: *~ sth Many countries favour a presidential system of government.* ◊ *~ sth over sth She favours hugs over handshakes.* ◊ *~ doing sth Most patients favour seeing the same GP for all their health needs.*
- **TREAT BETTER 2** to treat one person, group or organization better than you treat others, especially in an unfair way: *~ sb/sth The treaty seems to favour the US.* ◊ *~ sth over sb/sth News coverage should not favour one party over another.*
- **HELP 3** *~ sth* to provide suitable conditions for a particular person, group, etc: *The warm climate favours many types of tropical plants.*
- **LOOK LIKE PARENT 4** *~ sb* (*old-fashioned* or *NAmE, informal*) to look like one of your parents or older relations: *She definitely favours her father.*

## fa·vour·able (US fa·vor·able) /ˈfeɪvərəbl/ adj.

**1** making people have a good opinion of sb/sth: *She made a favourable impression on his parents.* ◊ *The biography shows him in a favourable light.* **2** positive and showing your good opinion of sb/sth: *favourable comments* **3** expressing your agreement; giving permission: *Their demands received a favourable response.* **4** good for sth and making it likely to be successful or have an advantage **SYN** advantageous: *favourable economic conditions* ◊ *~ to/for sb/sth The terms of the agreement are favourable to both sides.* **5** fairly good and not too expensive: *They offered me a loan on very favourable terms.* **6** (of a wind) blowing in the direction of travel **OPP** unfavourable ▶ **fa·vour·abil·ity** (*US* **fa·vor·abil·ity**)

/ˌfeɪvərəˈbɪləti/ noun [U] **fa·vour·ably** (*US* **fa·vor·ably**) /ˈfeɪvərəbli/ adv.: *He speaks very favourably of your work.* ◊ *I was very favourably impressed with her work.* ◊ *These figures compare favourably with last year's.*

## fa·voured (US favored) /ˈfeɪvəd; NAmE -vərd/ adj.

**1** treated in a special way or receiving special help or advantages in a way that may seem unfair: *a member of the President's favoured circle of advisers* **2** preferred by most people: *the favoured candidate* **3** (*formal*) particularly pleasant and worth having: *Their house is in a very favoured position near the park.*

## fa·vour·ite (US fa·vor·ite) /ˈfeɪvərɪt/ adj., noun

■ **adj.** liked more than others of the same kind: *It's one of my favourite movies.* ◊ *What is your all-time favourite song?* ◊ *January is my least favourite month.* ⊃ SYNONYMS at CHOICE

**IDM** **sb's favourite 'son 1** a performer, politician, sports player, etc., who is popular where they were born **2** (in the US) a candidate for president who is supported by his or her own state in the first part of a campaign

■ **noun 1** a person or thing that you like more than the others of the same type: *Which one's your favourite?* ◊ *The band played all my old favourites.* ◊ *~ of sb's This song is a particular favourite of mine.* ◊ *~ with sb The programme has become a firm favourite with young people.* **2** a person who is liked better by sb and receives better treatment than others: *She loved all her grandchildren but Ann was her favourite.* ◊ *~ with sb She was an extremely good student and a great favourite with the nuns.* **3** a record of a section of an app or the address of a website that enables you to find it quickly: *Add the website as a favourite.* ⊃ compare BOOKMARK (2) **4** the horse, runner, team, etc. that is expected to win: *The favourite came third.* ◊ *~ for sth Her horse is the hot favourite for the race.* ◊ *~ to do sth The Brazilians still look firm favourites to take the title.* **5** the person who is expected by most people to get a particular job or position: *~ for sth She's the favourite for the job.* ◊ *~ to do sth She's the favourite to succeed him as leader.*

## fa·vour·it·ism (US fa·vor·it·ism) /ˈfeɪvərɪtɪzəm/ noun [U]

(*disapproving*) the act of unfairly treating one person better than others because you like them better: *The students accused the teacher of favouritism.*

## fawn /fɔːn/ adj., noun, verb

■ **adj.** light yellow-brown in colour: *a fawn coat*
■ **noun 1** [C] a DEER less than one year old **2** [U] a light yellow-brown colour
■ **verb** [I] *~ (on/over sb)* (*disapproving*) to try to please sb by praising them or paying them too much attention

## fax /fæks/ noun, verb

■ **noun 1** (*also* **'fax machine**) [C] a machine that sends and receives documents in an electronic form along phone wires and then prints them **2** [U] a system for sending documents using scanned images over a phone line or the internet: **by** ~ *In those days we often sent documents by fax.* **3** [C] a letter or message sent by fax: *You can still send faxes via email.*
■ **verb** to send sb a document, message, etc. by fax: *~ sb Could you fax me the latest version?* ◊ *~ sth to sb Could you fax it to me?* ◊ *~ sth I faxed the list of hotels through to them.*

## fayre /feə(r); NAmE fer/ noun (BrE) **HELP** Fayre is an old spelling of either **fair** or **fare** that is sometimes used in (BrE) to suggest sth that is simple and traditional. **1** [C] = FETE (1): *Every year the school holds a summer fayre.* **2** [U] = FARE (3): *Visitors to the farmers' market can sample fresh local fayre.*

## faze /feɪz/ verb *~ sb* (*informal*) to make you feel confused or shocked, so that you do not know what to do **SYN** disconcert: *She wasn't fazed by his comments.* ◊ *He looked as if nothing could faze him.*

## FBI /ˌef biː ˈaɪ/ abbr. Federal Bureau of Investigation (the police department in the US that is controlled by the national government and that is responsible for dealing with crimes that affect more than one state)

**FC** /ˌef ˈsiː/ abbr. (BrE) football club: *Liverpool FC*

**FCE** /ˌef si: ˈiː/ noun [U] a British test, now called 'B2 First', that measures a person's ability to speak and write English as a foreign language at an upper-INTERMEDIATE level (the abbreviation for 'First Certificate in English')

**FCO** /ˌef si: ˈəʊ/ abbr. FOREIGN AND COMMONWEALTH OFFICE

**FDA** /ˌef di: ˈeɪ/ abbr. Food and Drug Administration (the US government department that is responsible for making sure that food and drugs are safe to be sold)

**FE** /ˌef ˈiː/ abbr. (in the UK) FURTHER EDUCATION

**fealty** /ˈfiːəlti/ noun [U] (old use) a promise to be LOYAL to sb and show them your support, especially a king or queen

**fear** 🔑 A2 /fɪə(r); NAmE fɪr/ noun, verb
■ noun 1 🔑 B1 [U, C] the bad feeling that you have when you are in danger or when a particular thing frightens you: *Her eyes showed no fear.* ◇ *The child was shaking with fear.* ◇ *He managed to overcome his fears.* ◇ **~ of sb/sth** *Fear of crime can affect people's lives.* ◇ **in ~ of sb/sth** *We lived in constant fear of losing our jobs.* 2 🔑 A2 [C] a feeling of concern about sb's safety or about sth bad that might happen: *The doctor's report confirmed our worst fears.* ◇ **for sb/sth** *her fears for her son's safety* ◇ *Alan spoke of his fears for the future.* ◇ **~ that …** *the fear that he had cancer*
IDM **for fear of sth/of doing sth | for fear (that) …** to avoid the danger of sth happening: *We spoke quietly for fear of waking the guards.* ◇ *I had to run away for fear (that) he might one day kill me.* **in fear of your ˈlife** feeling frightened that you might be killed **no ˈfear** (BrE, informal) used to say that you definitely do not want to do sth: *'Are you coming climbing?' 'No fear!'* **put the fear of ˈGod into sb** to make sb very frightened, especially in order to make them do sth **without fear or ˈfavour** (formal) in a fair way ⊃ more at STRIKE v.
■ verb 1 🔑 B1 [T] to be frightened of sb/sth or frightened of doing sth: **~ sb/sth** *All his employees fear him.* ◇ *to fear death/persecution/the unknown* ◇ *Don't worry, you have nothing to fear from us.* ◇ **~ to do sth** (formal) *She feared to tell him the truth.* ◇ **~ doing sth** (formal) *She feared going out at night.* 2 🔑 B1 [T, I] to feel that sth bad might have happened or might happen in the future: **~ sth** *She has been missing for five days now and police are beginning to fear the worst* (= think that she is dead). ◇ **~ (that) …** *Experts fear that terrorists could use the internet to launch attacks.* ◇ **~ doing sth** *The company feared losing its tax breaks.* ◇ **be feared to be/have sth** *Women and children are feared to be among the victims.* ◇ **it is feared (that) …** *It is feared (that) he may have been kidnapped.* ◇ **~ sb/sth + adj.** *Hundreds of people are feared dead.* 3 **I fear** [I] (formal) used to tell sb that you think that sth bad has happened or is true: *They are unlikely to get here on time, I fear.* ◇ *'He must be dead then?' 'I fear so.'* ◇ *'She's not coming back?' 'I fear not.'*
IDM see FOOL n.
PHRV ˈfear for sb/sth to be worried about sb/sth: *We fear for his safety.* ◇ *They feared for their lives.*

**fear·ful** /ˈfɪəfl; NAmE ˈfɪrfl/ adj. 1 (formal) nervous and afraid: **~ (for sb)** *Parents are ever fearful for their children.* ◇ **~ (of sth/of doing sth)** *fearful of an attack* ◇ **~ (about sth)** *They were understandably fearful about the future.* ◇ **~ (that …)** *She was fearful that she would fail.* 2 [only before noun] (formal) terrible and frightening 3 (old-fashioned, informal) extremely bad: *We made a fearful mess of the room.* ▸ **fear·ful·ly** /-fəli/ adv.: *We watched fearfully.* ◇ *fearfully* (= extremely) *expensive* **fear·ful·ness** noun [U]

**fear·less** /ˈfɪələs; NAmE ˈfɪrl-/ adj. (approving) not afraid, in a way that people admire: *a fearless mountaineer* ▸ **fear·less·ly** adv. **fear·less·ness** noun [U]

**fear·some** /ˈfɪəsəm; NAmE ˈfɪrs-/ adj. (formal) making people feel very frightened

**feas·ible** /ˈfiːzəbl/ adj. that is possible and likely to be achieved SYN practicable: *a feasible plan/suggestion/idea* ◇ *It's just not feasible to manage the business on a part-time basis.* OPP unfeasible ▸ **feasi·bil·ity** /ˌfiːzəˈbɪləti/ noun [U]: *a feasibility study on the proposed new airport* ◇ *I doubt the feasibility of the plan.*

---

▼ SYNONYMS
**fear**
terror • panic • alarm • fright
These are all words for the bad feeling you have when you are afraid.
**fear** the bad feeling that you have when you are in danger or when a particular thing frightens you: *(a) fear of flying* ◇ *She showed no fear.*
**terror** a feeling of extreme fear: *Her eyes were wild with terror.*
**panic** a sudden feeling of great fear that cannot be controlled and prevents you from thinking clearly: *I had a sudden moment of panic.*
**alarm** fear or worry that sb feels when sth dangerous or unpleasant might happen: *The doctor said there was **no cause for alarm**.*
**fright** a feeling of fear, usually sudden: *She cried out in fright.*
FEAR OR FRIGHT?
• **Fright** is a reaction to sth that has just happened or is happening now. Use **fear**, but not **fright**, to talk about things that always frighten you and things that may happen in the future: *I have a fright of spiders.* ◇ *his fright of what might happen*
PATTERNS
• a fear/terror **of** sth
• **in** fear/terror/panic/alarm/fright
• fear/terror/panic/alarm **that** …
• to be **filled with** fear/terror/panic/alarm
• a **feeling of** fear/terror/panic/alarm

**feast** /fiːst/ noun, verb
■ noun 1 a large or special meal, especially for a lot of people and to celebrate sth: *a wedding feast* 2 a day or period of time when there is a religious festival: *the feast of Christmas* ◇ *a feast day* 3 [usually sing.] a thing or an event that brings great pleasure: *a feast of colours* ◇ *The evening was a real feast for music lovers.*
■ verb [I] **~ (on sth)** to eat a large amount of food with great pleasure
IDM **feast your ˈeyes (on sb/sth)** to look at sb/sth and get great pleasure

**feat** 🔑 C1 /fiːt/ noun (approving) an action or a piece of work that needs skill, strength or courage: *The tunnel is a remarkable feat of engineering.* ◇ *to accomplish/achieve/perform astonishing feats* ◇ *That was **no mean feat*** (= it was difficult to do).

▼ HOMOPHONES
**feat • feet** /fiːt/
• **feat** noun: *The birds' flight south is an amazing feat of endurance.*
• **feet** noun (plural of FOOT): *The audience rose to their feet in appreciation.*

**fea·ther** 🔑 B2 /ˈfeðə(r)/ noun, verb
■ noun 🔑 B2 one of the many soft light parts covering a bird's body: *a peacock feather* ◇ *a feather pillow* (= one containing feathers) ⊃ VISUAL VOCAB page V2
IDM **a ˈfeather in your cap** an action that you can be proud of ORIGIN This idiom comes from the Native American custom of giving a feather to sb who had been very brave in battle. ⊃ more at BIRD n., KNOCK v., RUFFLE v., SMOOTH v.
■ verb
IDM **feather your (own) ˈnest** to make yourself richer, especially at sb else's expense, by spending money on yourself that should be spent on sb/sth else ⊃ more at TAR v.

**feather-ˈbed** verb (-dd-) **~ sb/sth** (BrE) to make things easy for sb, especially by giving them money or good conditions of work

**feather 'boa** (also **boa**) noun a long thin piece of clothing like a SCARF, made of feathers and worn over the shoulders by women, especially in the past

**feather 'duster** noun a stick with feathers on the end of it that is used for cleaning ⊃ picture at BROOM

**fea·thered** /ˈfeðəd; NAmE -ðərd/ adj. covered with feathers or having feathers

**fea·ther·weight** /ˈfeðəweɪt; NAmE -ðərw-/ noun [U, C] a weight in BOXING and other sports, between BANTAMWEIGHT and LIGHTWEIGHT, in BOXING usually between 54 and 57 KILOGRAMS; a BOXER or other competitor in this class

**fea·thery** /ˈfeðəri/ adj. light and soft; like feathers

**fea·ture** 🛈 A2 ⊙ /ˈfiːtʃə(r)/ noun, verb
■ noun [C] **1** A2 something important, interesting or typical of a place or thing: *An interesting feature of the city is the old market.* ◊ *Teamwork is a key feature of the training programme.* ◊ *I've added some new features to my website.* ◊ *new safety/security features* ◊ *There are a number of special features included on the disc.* ⊃ see also WATER FEATURE **2** B1 [usually pl.] a part of sb's face such as their nose, mouth and eyes: *facial features* ◊ *Her eyes are her most striking feature.* **3** ~ **(on sb/sth)** (in the media) a special article or programme about sb/sth: *a special feature on education* ◊ *There are in-depth feature articles in every issue.* ◊ *She is a feature writer for the 'Evening Standard'.* ⊃ see also DOUBLE FEATURE ⊃ WORDFINDER NOTE at NEWSPAPER **4** (old-fashioned) the main film in a cinema programme
■ verb **1** B1 [T] to include a particular person or thing as a special feature: *~ sb/sth as sb/sth The film features Cary Grant as a professor.* ◊ *~ sb/sth The latest model features alloy wheels and an electronic alarm.* ◊ **be featured in/on sth** *The actress was featured on the cover of Time magazine last month.* **2** B1 [I] *~ (in/on sth)* to have an important part in sth: *Olive oil and garlic feature prominently in his recipes.*

**'feature film** noun a main film with a story, rather than a DOCUMENTARY, etc.

**'feature-length** adj. [usually before noun] of the same length as a typical film

**fea·ture·less** /ˈfiːtʃələs; NAmE -tʃərl-/ adj. without any qualities or characteristics that are easy to notice: *The countryside is flat and featureless.*

**'feature phone** noun a mobile phone that can do some important things such as connect to the internet, play and store music, etc. but does not have all the functions of a smartphone

**fe·brile** /ˈfiːbraɪl, ˈfeb-/ adj. **1** (formal) nervous, excited and very active: *a product of her febrile imagination* **2** (medical) (of an illness) caused by FEVER (= a high temperature)

**Feb·ru·ary** 🛈 A1 /ˈfebruəri; NAmE -brueri/ noun [U, C] (abbr. **Feb.**) the 2nd month of the year, between January and March HELP To see how **February** is used, look at the examples at **April**.

**feces** (NAmE) (BrE **fae·ces**) /ˈfiːsiːz/ noun [pl.] (formal) solid waste material that leaves the body through the ANUS SYN **excrement** ▶ **fecal** (NAmE) (BrE **fae·cal**) /ˈfiːkl/ adj. [only before noun]

**feck·less** /ˈfekləs/ adj. (disapproving) having a weak character; not behaving in a responsible way: *Her husband was a charming, but lazy and feckless man.* ▶ **feck·less·ness** noun [U]

**fec·und** /ˈfiːkənd, ˈfek-/ adj. (formal) **1** able to produce a lot of children, crops, etc. SYN **fertile** **2** producing new and useful things, especially ideas ▶ **fe·cund·ity** /fɪˈkʌndəti/ noun [U]

**Fed** /fed/ noun (US, informal) **1** [C] an officer of the FBI or another FEDERAL organization: *The Feds raided his home and found a gun.* **2** **the Fed** [sing.] = FEDERAL RESERVE SYSTEM

**fed** /fed/ past tense, past part. of FEED ⊃ see also WELL FED

**fed·eral** 🛈+ B2 ⊙ /ˈfedərəl/ adj. **1**+ B2 having a system of government in which the individual states of a country

---

have control over their own affairs, but are controlled by a central government for national decisions, etc: *a federal republic* **2** 🛈+ B2 (within a federal system, for example the US and Canada) connected with national government rather than the local government of an individual state: *a federal law* ◊ *state and federal income taxes* ⊃ WORDFINDER NOTE at GOVERNMENT ▶ **fed·er·al·ly** /-rəli/ adv.: *federally funded healthcare*

**the Federal Bureau of Investiˈgation** noun [sing.] = FBI

**fed·er·al·ist** /ˈfedərəlɪst/ noun a supporter of a FEDERAL system of government ▶ **fed·er·al·ism** noun [U]: *European federalism* **fed·er·al·ist** adj.: *a federalist future in Europe*

**the Federal Reˈserve System** (also **the Federal Reˈserve**) noun (abbr. **the FRS**) (also informal **the Fed**) [sing.] the organization that controls the supply of money in the US

**fed·er·ate** /ˈfedəreɪt/ verb [I] (specialist) (of states, organizations, etc.) to join together under a central government or organization while keeping some local control

**fed·er·ation** /ˌfedəˈreɪʃn/ noun **1** [C] a country consisting of a group of individual states that have control over their own affairs but are controlled by a central government for national decisions, etc: *the Russian Federation* **2** [C] a group of clubs, trade unions, etc. that have joined together to form an organization: *the International Tennis Federation* **3** [U] the act of forming a federation: *Australia's centenary of federation in 2001*

**fe·dora** /fɪˈdɔːrə/ noun a low soft hat with a wide BRIM

fedora

**fed ˈup** adj. [not before noun] (informal) bored or unhappy, especially with a situation that has continued for too long: *You look fed up. What's the matter?* ◊ *~ with sb/sth People are fed up with all these traffic jams.* ◊ *In the end, I just got fed up with his constant complaining.* ◊ *I wish he'd get a job. I'm fed up with it* (= with the situation). ◊ *~ with doing sth I'm fed up with waiting for her.* HELP Some people say 'fed up of sth' in informal British English, but this is not considered correct in standard English.

**fee** 🛈 B2 /fiː/ noun **1** 🛈 B2 an amount of money that you pay for professional advice or services: *legal fees* ◊ *school/tuition fees* ◊ *~ for (doing) sth Does the bank charge a fee for setting up the account?* ◊ *for a ~ Users can block ads for a small monthly fee.* ⊃ see also CONTINGENCY FEE, USER FEE ⊃ SYNONYMS at RATE **2** 🛈 B2 an amount of money that you pay to join an organization, or to do sth: *a membership/subscription fee* ◊ *You have to pay a fee to enter the race.* ◊ *~ for sth The registration fee for the event is £35.*

**fee·ble** /ˈfiːbl/ adj. (**fee·bler** /-blə(r)/, **feeb·lest** /-blɪst/) **1** very weak: *a feeble old man* ◊ *The heartbeat was feeble and irregular.* **2** not effective; not showing energy or effort: *a feeble argument/excuse/joke* ◊ *a feeble attempt to explain* ◊ *Don't be so feeble! Tell her you don't want to go.* ▶ **feeble·ness** noun **feebly** /-bli/ adv.

**feeble-ˈminded** adj. **1** (old use, offensive) having less than usual intelligence **2** weak and unable to make decisions

**feed** 🛈 A2 /fiːd/ verb, noun
■ verb (**fed**, **fed** /fed/)
• GIVE/EAT FOOD **1** 🛈 A2 [T] to give food to a person or an animal: *~ sb/sth/yourself Have you fed the cat yet?* ◊ *The baby can't feed itself yet* (= can't put food into its own mouth). ◊ *~ sb/sth (on) sth The cattle are fed (on) barley.* ◊ *~ sth to sb/sth The barley is fed to the cattle.* ⊃ see also BOTTLE-FEED, FORCE-FEED ⊃ WORDFINDER NOTE at BABY **2** 🛈 B1 [I] (of a baby or an animal) to eat food: *Slugs and snails feed at night.* ⊃ see also FEED ON/OFF STH **3** 🛈 B1 [T] *~ sb* to provide food for a person or group of people: *They have a large family to feed.* ◊ *Have they been feeding you well?*
• PLANT **4** [T] *~ sth* to give a plant a special substance to make it grow: *Feed the plants once a week.*

# feedback

- **GIVE ADVICE/INFORMATION** 5 [T, often passive] to give advice, information, etc. to sb/sth: **be fed (with) sth** *We are constantly fed gossip and speculation by the media.* ◇ **be fed to sb** *Gossip and speculation are constantly fed to us by the media.* ⊃ see also DRIP-FEED, SPOON-FEED
- **SUPPLY** 6 [T, usually passive] to supply sth to sb/sth: **A is fed (with) B** *The electricity line is fed with power through an underground cable.* ◇ **B is fed into A** *Power is fed into the electricity line through an underground cable.*
- **PUT INTO MACHINE** 7 [T] to put or push sth into or through a machine: ~**A (with B)** *He fed the meter with coins.* ◇ ~**B into A** *He fed coins into the meter.* ◇ ~**sth into/through sth** *The fabric is fed through the machine.*
- **SATISFY NEED** 8 [T] ~**sth** to satisfy a need, desire, etc. and keep it strong: *For drug addicts, the need to feed the addiction takes priority over everything else.*

**IDM** **feed your 'face** (*informal, usually disapproving*) to eat a lot of food or too much food ⊃ more at BITE *v*.

**PHRV** **feed 'back (into/to sth)** to have an influence on the development of sth by reacting to it in some way: *What the audience tells me feeds back into my work.* **feed (sth)↔'back (to sb)** to give information or opinions about sth, especially so that it can be improved: *Test results will be fed back to the schools.* ⊃ related noun FEEDBACK (1) **'feed into sth** to have an influence on the development of sth: *The report's findings will feed into company policy.* **'feed on/off sth** 1 (of an animal) to eat sth: *Butterflies feed on the flowers of garden plants.* 2 (*often disapproving*) to become stronger because of sth else: *Racism feeds on fear.* **feed 'through (to sb/sth)** to reach sb/sth after going through a process or system: *It will take time for the higher rates to feed through to investors.* **feed sb/sth↔'up** (*BrE*) to give a lot of food to a person or an animal to make them fatter or stronger

■ **noun**
- **MEAL FOR BABY/ANIMAL** 1 [C] a meal of milk for a young baby; a meal for an animal: *her morning feed*
- **FOR ANIMALS/PLANTS** 2 [U] food for animals or plants: *a sack of animal feed*
- **FOR MACHINE** 3 [U] material supplied to a machine 4 [C] a pipe, device, etc. that supplies a machine with sth: *The printer has an automatic paper feed.* ◇ **to sth** *the cold feed to the water cylinder*
- **LARGE MEAL** 5 [C, usually sing.] (*informal*) a large meal: *They needed a bath and a good feed.*
- **TELEVISION PROGRAMMES** 6 [U] television programmes that are sent from a central station to other stations in a network; the system of sending out these programmes: *network feed* ⊃ see also LIVE FEED
- **WEBSITE** 7 a special feature on a blog, news website, SOCIAL MEDIA site, etc. that allows you to see new information that has been added without having to visit the website, usually using a FEED READER (= a piece of software that displays this information): *an RSS feed* ◇ *the film's official Twitter feed* ⊃ see also NEWSFEED ⊃ see also CHICKEN FEED, DRIP FEED

**feed·back** /ˈfiːdbæk/ *noun* [U] 1 advice, criticism or information about how good or useful sth or sb's work is: *customer/user feedback* ◇ *to provide/give feedback* ◇ *to receive/get feedback* ◇ ~**on sth** *I'd appreciate some feedback on my work.* ◇ **from sb** *We need both positive and negative feedback from our customers.* 2 the unpleasant noise produced by electrical equipment such as an AMPLIFIER when some of the power returns to the system

**feed·er** /ˈfiːdə(r)/ *noun, adj.*

■ **noun** 1 (used with an adjective or a noun) an animal or plant that eats a particular thing or eats in a particular way: *plankton feeders* 2 a part of a machine that supplies sth to another part of the machine 3 a container filled with food for birds or animals ⊃ see also BIRD FEEDER, BOTTOM FEEDER

■ **adj.** [only before noun] 1 (of roads, rivers, etc.) leading to a bigger road, etc: *a feeder road to the motorway/freeway* 2 supplying goods, services, etc. to a large organization

3 (*NAmE*) (of animals on a farm) kept to be killed and used for meat

**feed·ing** /ˈfiːdɪŋ/ *noun* [U] the act of giving food to a person, an animal or a plant: *breast/bottle feeding* ◇ *The cubs' feeding time at the zoo is 2 p.m.*

**'feeding bottle** *noun* (*BrE*) a plastic bottle with a rubber top that a baby or young animal can drink milk through

**'feeding frenzy** *noun* [usually sing.] 1 an occasion when a group of SHARKS or other fish attack sth 2 a situation in which a lot of people compete with each other in an excited way because they want to get sth

**'feed reader** *noun* a piece of software that you use to see new information that has been added on a blog, news website, SOCIAL MEDIA site, etc. without having to visit the website

**feed·stuff** /ˈfiːdstʌf/ *noun* [usually pl.] food for farm animals, especially food that has been processed **SYN** feed: *animal feedstuffs* ⊃ compare FOODSTUFF

**feel** /fiːl/ *verb, noun*

■ **verb** (**felt, felt** /felt/)
- **WELL/SICK/HAPPY/SAD, ETC.** 1 *linking verb* to experience a particular feeling or emotion: + **adj.** *The bus ride made me feel sick.* ◇ *Are you feeling comfortable?* ◇ *I was feeling guilty.* ◇ *You'll feel better after a good night's sleep.* ◇ *I feel sorry for him.* ◇ + **adv./prep.** *How are you feeling today?* ◇ *I know exactly how you feel* (= I feel sympathy for you). ◇ *Luckily I was feeling in a good mood.* ◇ ~**sth** *I felt the need to explain.* ◇ *I felt a sense of relief.* ◇ ~**like sth** *I felt like a complete idiot.* ◇ **as if/though…** *I feel as if nobody cares.* ◇ + **noun** *I felt like an idiot/a fool*
- **BE/BECOME AWARE** 2 [T] (not usually used in the progressive tenses) to notice or be aware of sth because it is touching you or having a physical effect on you **SYN** sense: ~**sth** *I could feel the warm sun on my back.* ◇ *She felt a sharp pain in her hand.* ◇ *She could not feel her legs.* ◇ ~**sb/sth/yourself doing sth** *He felt a hand touching his shoulder.* ◇ *She could feel herself blushing.* ◇ ~**sb/sth/yourself do sth** *I felt something crawl up my arm.* ◇ *We felt the ground give way under our feet.* 3 [T] (not usually used in the progressive tenses) ~**sth** to become aware of sth even though you cannot see it, hear it, etc. **SYN** sense: *Can you feel the tension in this room?*
- **GIVE IMPRESSION** 4 *linking verb* (not used in the progressive tenses) to give you a particular feeling or impression: + **adj.** *This situation doesn't feel right.* ◇ *You need to go somewhere that feels safe.* ◇ **it feels + adj. to do sth** *It felt strange to be back in my old school.* ◇ ~**like sth** *The place still feels like a small fishing village.* ◇ **it feels like sth** *The interview only took ten minutes, but it felt like hours.* ◇ ~**as if/though…** *Her head felt as if it would burst.* ◇ **it feels as if/though…** *It felt as though he had run a marathon.* **HELP** In spoken English people often use **like** instead of **as if** or **as though** in this meaning, especially in *NAmE*: *He felt like he'd run a marathon.* This is not considered correct in written *BrE*.
- **TOUCH** 5 *linking verb* (not used in the progressive tenses) to have a particular physical quality that you become aware of by touching: + **adj.** *The water feels warm.* ◇ *Its skin feels really smooth.* ◇ ~**like sth** *This wallet feels like leather.* 6 [T] to deliberately move your fingers over sth in order to find out what it is like: ~**sth** *Can you feel the bump on my head?* ◇ *Try to tell what this is just by feeling it.* ◇ ~**how, what, etc…** *Feel how rough this is.*
- **THINK/BELIEVE** 7 [T, I] (not usually used in the progressive tenses) to think or believe that sth is the case; to have a particular opinion or attitude: ~**(that)…** *We all felt (that) we were unlucky to lose.* ◇ *We've always felt this was our home.* ◇ + **adv./prep.** *This is something I feel strongly about.* ◇ *How do you feel about inviting the children too?* ◇ ~**it (to be) + noun** *She felt it her duty to tell the police.* ◇ ~**it + (to be) adj.** *Why did you feel it necessary to do that?* ◇ *This decision is, I feel, a huge mistake.* ⊃ SYNONYMS at THINK
- **BE STRONGLY AFFECTED** 8 [T] ~**sth** to experience the effects or results of sth, often strongly: *He feels the cold a lot.* ◇ *We're all starting to feel the pressure at work.* ◇ *I was OK after my run, but I'll feel it tomorrow.* ◇ *She felt her*

mother's death very deeply. ◊ The effects of the recession are being felt everywhere.
- **SEARCH WITH HANDS 9** [I] ~ (+ adv./prep.) (for sth) to search for sth with your hands, feet, etc: *She felt in her bag and pulled out a pen.* ◊ *I had to feel about in the dark for the light switch.*

**IDM** ,feel your 'age to realize that you are getting old, especially compared with people you are with who are younger than you **feel 'free (to do sth)** (*informal*) used to tell sb that they are allowed to do sth: *Feel free to ask questions if you don't understand.* ◊ *'Can I use your phone?' 'Feel free.'* **feel 'good** to feel happy, confident, etc: *It makes me feel good to know my work is appreciated.* **feel (it) in your 'bones (that …)** (*informal*) to be certain about sth even though you do not have any direct proof and cannot explain why you are certain: *I know I'm going to fail this exam—I can feel it in my bones.* **feel like sth / like doing sth** (*informal*) to want to have or do sth: *I feel like a drink.* ◊ *We all felt like celebrating.* ◊ *We'll go for a walk if you feel like it.* **feel the 'pinch** (*informal*) to not have enough money: *Lots of people who have lost their jobs are starting to feel the pinch.* **feel your 'way 1** to move along carefully, for example when it is dark, by touching walls, objects, etc. **2** to be careful about how you do things, usually because you are in a situation that you are not familiar with: *She was new in the job, still feeling her way.* **not feel your'self** to not feel healthy and well ⊃ more at DEATH, FLATTER, HARD *adv.*, HONOUR *n.*, HONOUR *v.*, JELLY, MARK *n.*, MILLION, PRESENCE, SMALL *adj.*

**PHRV** 'feel for sb to have sympathy for sb: *I really felt for her when her husband died.* ◊ *I do feel for you, honestly.* ,feel sb↔'up (*informal*) to touch sb sexually, especially when they do not want you to **SYN** grope ,feel 'up to sth to have the strength and energy to do or deal with sth: *Do we have to go to the party? I really don't feel up to it.* ◊ **feel up to doing sth** *After the accident she didn't feel up to driving.*

■ **noun** [sing.]
- **TOUCH 1** **B2** the feel the feeling you get when you touch sth or are touched: *You can tell it's silk by the feel.* ◊ *The model has the look and feel of wood.* **2** an act of feeling or touching: *I had a feel of the material.*
- **IMPRESSION 3** **B2** the impression that is created by a place, situation, etc.; atmosphere: *It's a big city but it has the feel of a small town.* ◊ *~* **to sth** *The film has a documentary feel to it.*

**IDM** **get the feel of (doing) sth** to become familiar with sth or with doing sth: *I haven't got the feel of the brakes in this car yet.* **get/have a feel for sth** to get/have an understanding of sth or be naturally good at doing it: *She has a real feel for languages.*

**feel·er** /ˈfiːlə(r)/ *noun* [usually pl.] either of the two long thin parts on the heads of some insects and of some animals that live in shells that they use to feel and touch things with **SYN** antenna
**IDM** **put out 'feelers** (*informal*) to try to find out what people think about a particular course of action before you do it

'feel-good *adj.* making you feel happy and pleased about life: *a feel-good movie*
**IDM** **the ,feel-good 'factor** (*BrE*) (used especially in the media) the feeling of confidence in the future that is shared by many people

**feel·ing** ⓞ **A1** /ˈfiːlɪŋ/ *noun*
- **STH THAT YOU FEEL 1** **A1** [C] something that you feel through the mind or through the senses: **a ~ of sth** *a feeling of guilt/helplessness/anger/sadness* ◊ *a strange/horrible feeling* ◊ *I've got a tight feeling in my stomach.* ◊ (*informal*) *'I really resent the way he treated me.' 'I know the feeling (= I know how you feel).'* ◊ *'I'm going to miss you.' 'The feeling's mutual (= I feel exactly the same).'*
- **EMOTIONS 2** **A1** feelings [pl.] a person's emotions rather than their thoughts or ideas: *He hates talking about his feelings.* ◊ **to express/share your feelings** ◊ *I didn't mean to hurt your feelings (= offend you).* **3** **A2** [U, C] strong emotion: *Feeling runs deep (= people feel strongly) on this issue.* ◊ **~ about sth** *the depth/strength of feeling about an issue* ◊ **with ~** *She spoke with feeling about the plight of the*

575

# fell

*homeless.* ◊ *The debate aroused* **strong feelings** *on both sides.* ◊ **Feelings are running high** (= people are very angry or excited).
- **ATTITUDE/OPINION 4** **A2** [U, C] an attitude or opinion about sth: *The general feeling was against the decision.* ◊ *My own feeling is that we should buy the cheaper one.* ◊ **~ about/on sth** *I don't have any* **strong feelings** *about it one way or the other.* ◊ *She had* **mixed feelings** *about giving up her job.* ◊ **~ towards/toward sb/sth** *his complicated feelings towards his classmates*
- **IDEA/BELIEF 5** **B1** [sing.] the idea or belief that a particular thing is true or a particular situation is likely to happen **SYN** impression: *Our gut feeling tells us that this will work.* ◊ **~ (that) …** *I got the feeling he didn't like me much.* ◊ **~ of (doing) sth** *He suddenly had the feeling of being followed.* ◊ **~ about sth** *I have a* **bad feeling** *about this* (= I have the impression it is not going to go well).
- **SYMPATHY/LOVE 6** **B1** [pl., U] sympathy or love for sb/sth: *He never told her his feelings.* ◊ **~ for sb/sth** *You have no feeling for the sufferings of others.* ◊ *I still* **have feelings** *for her* (= feel attracted to her in a romantic way). ⊃ see also FELLOW FEELING
- **PHYSICAL 7** **B1** [U] the ability to feel physically: *I've lost all feeling in my legs.*
- **UNDERSTANDING 8** **B2** [U, sing.] the ability to understand sb/sth or to do sth in a sensitive way: *He played the piano with great feeling.* ◊ **~ for sb/sth** *She has a wonderful feeling for colour.*
- **ATMOSPHERE 9** [sing.] the atmosphere of a place, situation, etc: *They have managed to recreate the feeling of the original theatre.*

**IDM** **bad/ill 'feeling** (*also* **bad/ill 'feelings** *especially in NAmE*) anger between people, especially after an argument: *There was a lot of bad feeling between the two groups of students.* ⊃ more at HARD *adj.*, SINK *v.*, SPARE *v.*

**feel·ing·ly** /ˈfiːlɪŋli/ *adv.* with strong emotion **SYN** emotionally: *He spoke feelingly about his dead father.*

**feet** /fiːt/ *pl.* of FOOT ⊃ **HOMOPHONES** AT **FEAT**

**feign** /feɪn/ *verb* **~ sth | ~ to do sth** (*formal*) to pretend that you have a particular feeling or that you are ill, tired, etc: *He survived the massacre by feigning death.* ◊ *'Who cares?' said Alex, feigning indifference.*

**feint** /feɪnt/ *noun, verb*
■ **noun** (especially in sport) a movement that is intended to make your opponent think you are going to do one thing when you are really going to do sth else
■ **verb** [I] (especially in sport) to confuse your opponent by making them think you are going to do one thing when you are really going to do sth else

**feisty** /ˈfaɪsti/ *adj.* (**feisti·er**, **feisti·est**) (*informal*, *approving*) (of people) strong, determined and not afraid of arguing with people

**fela·fel** = FALAFEL

**feld·spar** /ˈfeldspɑː(r)/ *noun* [U, C] a type of white or red rock

**fe·li·ci·tous** /fəˈlɪsɪtəs/ *adj.* (*formal or literary*) chosen well; very suitable; giving a good result **SYN** apt, happy: *a felicitous turn of phrase* ▸ **fe·li·ci·tous·ly** *adv.*

**fe·li·city** /fəˈlɪsəti/ *noun* (*pl.* **-ies**) (*formal or literary*) **1** [U] great happiness **2** [U] the quality of being well chosen or suitable **3 felicities** [pl.] well-chosen or successful features, especially in a speech or piece of writing

**fe·line** /ˈfiːlaɪn/ *adj., noun*
■ *adj.* like a cat; connected with an animal of the cat family: *She walks with feline grace.*
■ *noun* (*formal*) a cat; an animal of the cat family

**fell** /fel/ *noun, verb, adj.*
■ *noun* a hill or an area of hills in northern England
■ *verb* **1** *past tense of* FALL **2 ~ sth** to cut down a tree **3 ~ sb** (*literary*) to make sb fall to the ground: *He felled his opponent with a single blow.*
■ *adj.* (*literary*) very evil or violent
**IDM** **at/in one fell 'swoop** all at the same time; in a single action, especially a sudden or violent one

# fella

**fella** (also **fell·er**) /ˈfelə(r)/ noun (informal) **1** an informal way of referring to a man **2** an informal way of referring to sb's boyfriend: *Have you met her new fella?*

**fel·late** /fəˈleɪt; NAmE also ˈfeleɪt/ verb ~ **sb** (formal) to perform FELLATIO on a man

**fel·la·tio** /fəˈleɪʃiəʊ/ noun [U] (formal) the practice of touching a man's PENIS with the tongue and lips to give sexual pleasure

**fel·low** ⓘ B2 /ˈfeləʊ/ adj., noun

■ adj. ⓘ B2 [only before noun] used to describe sb who is the same as you in some way, or in the same situation: *fellow citizens/students* ◇ *my fellow passengers on the train* ◇ *From the outset of his illness, he has been driven to help fellow sufferers.*

■ noun **1** (informal, becoming old-fashioned) a way of referring to a man or boy: *He's a nice old fellow.* ⮕ see also FELLA **2** [usually pl.] a person that you work with or that is like you; a thing that is similar to the one mentioned: *She has a very good reputation among her fellows.* ◇ *Many caged birds live longer than their fellows in the wild.* **3** (BrE) a senior member of some colleges or universities: *a fellow of New College, Oxford* **4** a member of an academic or professional organization: *a fellow of the Royal College of Surgeons* **5** a graduate student who holds a FELLOWSHIP: *a graduate fellow* ◇ *a research/teaching fellow*

**ˌfellow ˈfeeling** noun [U, C] a feeling of sympathy for sb because you have shared similar experiences

**fel·low·ship** /ˈfeləʊʃɪp/ noun **1** [U] (formal) a feeling of friendship between people who do things together or share an interest **2** [C] an organized group of people who share an interest, aim or belief **3** [C] (especially BrE) the position of being a senior member of a college or university **4** [C] an award of money to a graduate student to allow them to continue their studies or to do research **5** [C, U] the state of being a member of an academic or professional organization: *to be elected to fellowship of the British Academy*

**ˌfellow ˈtravel·ler** (US **ˌfellow ˈtraveler**) noun **1** a person who is travelling to the same place as another person **2** a person who agrees with the aims of a political party, especially the Communist party, but is not a member of it

**felon** /ˈfelən/ noun (especially NAmE, law) a person who has committed a serious crime such as murder or RAPE

**fe·loni·ous** /fəˈləʊniəs/ adj. (formal) relating to or involved in crime

**fel·ony** /ˈfeləni/ noun [C, U] (pl. **-ies**) (US or old-fashioned, law) the act of committing a serious crime such as murder or RAPE; a crime of this type: *a charge of felony* ⮕ compare MISDEMEANOUR

**felt** /felt/ noun, verb

■ noun [U] a type of soft thick cloth made from wool or hair that has been pressed tightly together: *a felt hat*

■ verb past tense, past part. of FEEL

**ˌfelt-tip ˈpen** (also ˌfelt ˈtip, ˌfelt-tipped ˈpen) noun a pen that has a point made of felt

**fem** = FEMME

**fe·male** ⓘ A2 ⓞ /ˈfiːmeɪl/ adj., noun

■ adj. **1** ⓘ A2 being a woman or a girl: *a female student/employee/artist/athlete* ◇ *He has excelled in building films around strong female characters.* **2** ⓘ A2 belonging to the sex that can lay eggs or give birth to babies: *a female cat* **3** ⓘ A2 of women; typical of women; affecting women: *female characteristics* ◇ *the female role* ⮕ compare FEMININE **4** (biology) (of plants and flowers) that can produce fruit **5** (specialist) (of electrical equipment) having a hole that another part fits into: *a female plug* OPP **male**

■ noun **1** ⓘ A2 an animal that can lay eggs or give birth to babies; a plant that can produce fruit: *One adult female can lay 400 to 500 eggs.* **2** ⓘ A2 (formal) a woman or a girl: *The body is that of a white female aged about 30.* OPP **male**

**femi·nine** /ˈfemənɪn/ adj., noun

■ adj. **1** having the qualities or appearance considered to be typical of women; connected with women: *That dress makes you look very feminine.* ◇ *He had delicate, almost feminine, features.* ◇ *the traditional feminine role* ⮕ compare FEMALE, MASCULINE **2** (grammar) belonging to a class of words that refer to female people or animals and often have a special form: *Some people prefer not to use the feminine form 'actress' and use the word 'actor' for both sexes.* **3** (grammar) (in some languages) belonging to a class of nouns, pronouns or adjectives that have feminine GENDER, not MASCULINE or NEUTER: *The French word for 'table' is feminine.*

■ noun (grammar) **1** **the feminine** [sing.] the feminine GENDER (= form of nouns, adjectives and pronouns) **2** [C] a feminine word or word form ⮕ compare MASCULINE, NEUTER

**femi·nin·ity** /ˌfeməˈnɪnəti/ noun [U] the fact of being a woman; the qualities that are considered to be typical of women

**femi·nism** /ˈfemənɪzəm/ noun [U] the belief and aim that women should have the same rights and opportunities as men; the struggle to achieve this aim ⮕ WORDFINDER NOTE at EQUAL

**femi·nist** ⓘ+ C1 /ˈfemənɪst/ adj., noun

■ adj. **1** [usually before noun] having or based on the belief that women should have the same rights and opportunities as men: *feminist demands/ideas/theories* ◇ *the feminist movement*

■ noun ⓘ+ C1 a person who supports the belief that women should have the same rights and opportunities as men

**femi·nize** (BrE also **-ise**) /ˈfemənaɪz/ verb **1** ~ **sb** to make sb more like a woman **2** ~ **sth** to make sth involve more women: *Offices became increasingly feminized during the 1960s.*

**femme** (also **fem**) /fem/ adj., noun

■ adj. (sometimes offensive) (of a LESBIAN) having qualities typical of a woman ⮕ compare BUTCH

■ noun (sometimes offensive) a LESBIAN who has qualities that are typical of a woman

**ˌfemme faˈtale** /ˌfæm fəˈtɑːl; NAmE ˌfem fəˈtæl/ noun (pl. **ˌfemmes faˈtales** /ˌfæm fəˈtɑːl; NAmE ˌfem fəˈtæl/) (from French) a very beautiful woman that men find sexually attractive but who brings them trouble or unhappiness

**femto-** /ˈfemtəʊ/ combining form (specialist) (in units of measurement) $10^{-15}$: *a femtosecond*

**femur** /ˈfiːmə(r)/ noun (pl. **fe·murs** or **fem·ora** /ˈfemərə/) (anatomy) the THIGH BONE ⮕ VISUAL VOCAB page V1 ▸ **fem·oral** /ˈfemərəl/ adj. [only before noun]

**fen** /fen/ noun [C, U] an area of low, flat, wet land, especially in the east of England

**fence** ⓘ B1 /fens/ noun, verb

■ noun **1** ⓘ B1 a structure made of wood or wire supported with posts that is put between two areas of land as a BOUNDARY, or around a garden, field, etc. to keep animals in, or to keep people and animals out: *The two women chatted over the garden fence.* ◇ *The footpath was blocked by a barbed wire fence.* ⮕ see also CHAIN-LINK FENCE, ELECTRIC FENCE **2** a structure that horses must jump over in a race or a competition **3** (informal) a criminal who buys and sells stolen goods ⮕ see also RING FENCE IDM see GRASS n., MEND v., SIDE n., SIT

■ verb **1** ~ **sth** to surround or divide an area with a fence: *His property is fenced with barbed wire.* ⮕ see also UNFENCED **2** [I] to take part in the sport of FENCING **3** [I] ~ **(with sb)** to speak to sb in a clever way in order to gain an advantage in the conversation

PHR V **fence sb/sth↔ˈin** [often passive] **1** to surround sb/sth with a fence **2** to limit sb's freedom SYN **hem in**: *She felt fenced in by domestic routine.* ⮕ see also RING-FENCE **fence sth↔ˈoff** [often passive] to divide one area from another with a fence

**ˈfence-mending** noun [U] an attempt to improve relations between two people or groups and to try to find a solution when they disagree

**fen·cer** /ˈfensə(r)/ noun a person who takes part in the sport of FENCING

**fen·cing** /ˈfensɪŋ/ noun [U] **1** the sport of fighting with long thin SWORDS **2** fences; wood, wire, or other material used for making fences: *The factory is surrounded by electric fencing.*

**fend** /fend/ verb
**PHRV** **fend for yourˈself** to take care of yourself without help from anyone else: *His parents agreed to pay the rent for his apartment but otherwise left him to fend for himself.* ˌfend sth/sb↔ˈoff **1** to defend or protect yourself from sth/sb that is attacking you **SYN** **fight off, ward off**: *The police officer fended off the blows with his riot shield.* **2** to protect yourself from difficult questions, criticisms, etc., especially by avoiding them **SYN** **ward off**: *She managed to fend off questions about new tax increases.*

**fend·er** /ˈfendə(r)/ noun **1** (*NAmE*) (*BrE* **wing**) a part of a car that is above a wheel **2** (*NAmE*) (*BrE* **mud-guard**) a curved cover over a wheel of a bicycle or motorcycle **3** a frame around a FIREPLACE to prevent burning coal or wood from falling out **4** a soft solid object such as an old tyre or a piece of rope that is hung over the side of a boat so the boat is not damaged if it touches another boat, a wall, etc.

**ˈfender bender** noun (*NAmE, informal*) a car accident in which there is not a lot of damage

**feng shui** /ˌfeŋ ˈʃuːi, ˌfʌŋ ˈʃweɪ/ noun [U] (*from Chinese*) a Chinese system for deciding the right position for a building and for placing objects inside a building in order to make people feel comfortable and happy

**Fen·ian** /ˈfiːniən/ noun **1** a member of an organization formed in the 1850s in the US and Ireland in order to end British rule in Ireland **2** (*informal, taboo*) (especially in Northern Ireland) an offensive word for a Catholic

**fen·land** /ˈfenlənd/ noun [U, C] an area of low, flat, wet land in the east of England

**fen·nel** /ˈfenl/ noun [U] a vegetable that has a thick round STEM with a strong taste. The seeds and leaves are also used in cooking. ⊃ VISUAL VOCAB page V5

**fenu·greek** /ˈfenjʊɡriːk/ noun [U] a plant with hard yellow-brown seeds that are used in South Asian cooking as a SPICE

**feral** /ˈferəl/ adj., noun
■ *adj.* (of animals) living wild, especially after escaping from life as a pet or on a farm: *feral cats*
■ *noun* (*AustralE, offensive*) a person with a lifestyle that society considers unusual or unacceptable

**fer·mata** /fɜːˈmɑːtə; *NAmE* fɜːrˈm-/ noun (especially *NAmE, music*) = PAUSE

**fer·ment** verb, noun
■ *verb* /fəˈment; *NAmE* fərˈm-/ [I, T] to experience a chemical change because of the action of YEAST or bacteria, often changing sugar to alcohol; to make sth change in this way: *Fruit juices ferment if they are kept for too long.* ◊ (*figurative*) *A blend of emotions fermented inside her.* ~ *sth Red wine is fermented at a higher temperature than white.* ▶ **fer·men·ta·tion** /ˌfɜːmenˈteɪʃn; *NAmE* ˌfɜːrm-/ noun [U]
■ *noun* /ˈfɜːment; *NAmE* ˈfɜːrm-/ [U, sing.] (*formal*) a state of political or social excitement and activity, often with a lack of order: *The country is in ferment.*

**fern** /fɜːn; *NAmE* fɜːrn/ noun [C, U] a plant with large attractive leaves and no flowers that grows in wet areas or is grown in a pot. There are many types of fern. ⊃ VISUAL VOCAB page V7 ▶ **ferny** adj.

**fer·ocious** /fəˈrəʊʃəs/ adj. very aggressive or violent; very strong **SYN** **savage**: *a ferocious beast/attack/storm* ◊ *a man driven by ferocious determination* ◊ *ferocious opposition to the plan* ▶ **fer·ocious·ly** adv.

**fer·ocity** /fəˈrɒsəti; *NAmE* -ˈrɑːs-/ noun [U, sing.] violence; aggressive behaviour: *The police were shocked by the ferocity of the attack.*

**fer·ret** /ˈferɪt/ noun, verb
■ *noun* a small aggressive animal with a long thin body, kept for catching RABBITS, killing RATS, etc.
■ *verb* **1** [I] ~ **(about/around) (for sth)** (*informal*) to search for sth that is lost or hidden among a lot of things: *She opened the drawer and ferreted around for her keys.* **2** [I] to hunt RABBITS, RATS, etc. using FERRETS
**PHRV** ˌferret sb/sth↔ˈout (*informal*) to discover information or to find sb/sth by searching carefully and completely, asking a lot of questions, etc.

**ˈFerris wheel** /ˈferɪs wiːl/ (especially *NAmE* usually ˈbig ˈwheel) noun a large VERTICAL wheel pointing into the sky at an AMUSEMENT PARK that turns round and round, with seats hanging at its edge for people to ride in

**fer·rite** /ˈferaɪt/ noun **1** [U, C] a chemical containing iron, used in electrical devices such as AERIALS **2** [U] a form of pure iron that is found in steel that contains low amounts of CARBON

**ferro·mag·net·ic** /ˌferəʊmæɡˈnetɪk/ adj. (*physics*) having the kind of MAGNETISM that iron has

**fer·rous** /ˈferəs/ adj. [only before noun] (*specialist*) containing iron; connected with iron

**fer·rule** /ˈferuːl; *NAmE* -rəl/ noun a piece of metal or rubber that covers the end of an umbrella or a stick to protect it

**ferry** /ˈferi/ noun, verb
■ *noun* (*pl.* **-ies**) a boat or ship that carries people, vehicles and goods across a river or across a narrow part of the sea: *a passenger/car ferry* ◊ *the Staten Island ferry* ◊ *the ferry terminal at Calais* ◊ *the Dover-Calais ferry crossing* ◊ *We boarded the ferry at Ostend.*
■ *verb* (**fer·ries, ferry·ing, fer·ried, fer·ried**) **1** ~ **sb/sth (+ adv./prep.)** to carry people or goods in a boat or ship, especially across a small area of water: *He offered to ferry us across the river in his boat.* **2** ~ **sb/sth + adv./prep.** to carry people or goods in a vehicle from one place to another on short or regular trips: *The children need to be ferried to and from school.*

**ˈferry boat** noun a boat that is used as a ferry

**ferry·man** /ˈferimən/ noun (*pl.* **-men** /-mən/) (especially in the past) a person in charge of a small ferry across a river

**fer·tile** /ˈfɜːtaɪl; *NAmE* ˈfɜːrtl/ adj. **1** (of land or soil) that plants grow well in: *a fertile region* **OPP** **infertile** ⊃ WORDFINDER NOTE at LANDSCAPE **2** (of people, animals or plants) that can produce babies, young animals, fruit or new plants: *The treatment has been tested on healthy fertile women under the age of 35.* **OPP** **infertile 3** [usually before noun] that produces good results; that encourages activity: *a fertile partnership* ◊ *The region at the time was fertile ground for revolutionary movements* (= there were the necessary conditions for them to develop easily). **4** [usually before noun] (of a person's mind or imagination) that produces a lot of new ideas: *the product of a fertile imagination* ⊃ compare STERILE

**fer·til·ity** /fəˈtɪləti; *NAmE* fərˈt-/ noun [U] **1** the quality in land or soil of making plants grow well: *the fertility of the soil/land* **OPP** **infertility 2** the ability to produce babies, young animals, fruit or new plants: *fertility treatment/drugs* (= given to a person to help them have a baby)

**fer·til·ize** (*BrE also* **-ise**) /ˈfɜːtəlaɪz; *NAmE* ˈfɜːrt-/ verb **1** ~ **sth** to put POLLEN into a plant so that a seed develops; to join SPERM with an egg so that a baby or young animal develops: *Flowers are often fertilized by bees as they gather nectar.* ◊ *a fertilized egg* ⊃ see also CROSS-FERTILIZE **2** ~ **sth** to add a substance to soil to make plants grow more successfully ▶ **fer·til·iza·tion, -isa·tion** /ˌfɜːtəlaɪˈzeɪʃn; *NAmE* ˌfɜːrtələˈz-/ noun [U]: *Immediately after fertilization, the cells of the egg divide.* ◊ *the fertilization of soil with artificial chemicals*

**fer·til·izer** (*BrE also* **-iser**) /ˈfɜːtəlaɪzə(r); *NAmE* ˈfɜːrt-/ noun [C, U] a substance added to soil to make plants grow more successfully: *artificial/chemical fertilizers*

**fer·vent** /ˈfɜːvənt; *NAmE* ˈfɜːrv-/ adj. [usually before noun] having or showing very strong and sincere feelings about sth **SYN** **ardent**: *a fervent admirer/believer/supporter* ◊ *a fervent belief/hope/desire* ▶ **fer·vent·ly** adv.

# fervid

**fer·vid** /ˈfɜːvɪd; NAmE ˈfɜːrv-/ adj. (formal, often disapproving) feeling sth too strongly; showing feelings that are too strong ▶ **fer·vid·ly** adv.

**fer·vour** (US **fer·vor**) /ˈfɜːvə(r); NAmE ˈfɜːrv-/ noun [U] very strong feelings about sth **SYN** enthusiasm: *She kissed him with unusual fervour.* ◇ *religious/patriotic fervour*

**fess** /fes/ verb
**PHRV** **fess 'up (to sth)** (informal) to admit that you have done sth wrong **SYN** own up

**fest** /fest/ noun (informal) **1** a festival or large meeting concerned with a particular activity or interest: *an annual food and wine fest* **2** **-fest** combining form (in nouns) an event involving a particular activity or with a particular atmosphere: *a jazzfest* ◇ *a talkfest* (= a session involving long discussions)

**fes·ter** /ˈfestə(r)/ verb **1** [I] (of a wound or cut) to become painful and INFECTED (= full of bacteria): *festering sores/wounds* **2** [I] (of bad feelings or thoughts) to become much worse because you do not deal with them successfully

**fes·ti·val** ❶ **A1** /ˈfestɪvl/ noun **1** ❓ **A1** a series of performances of music, plays, films, etc., usually organized in the same place once a year; a series of public events connected with a particular activity or idea: *a film/music festival* ◇ *the Edinburgh Festival* ◇ *The pub is holding its annual beer festival later this week.* ◇ *a rock festival* (= where bands perform, often outdoors and over a period of several days) **2** ❓ **A2** a day or period of the year when people stop working to celebrate a special event, often a religious one: *The family always celebrates the Jewish festivals.* ◇ *Holi, the Hindu festival to welcome spring* ⊃ see also HARVEST FESTIVAL

**fes·tive** /ˈfestɪv/ adj. **1** typical of a special event or celebration: *a festive occasion* ◇ *The whole town is in festive mood.* **2** (BrE) connected with the period when people celebrate Christmas: *the festive season/period* ◇ *festive decorations*

**fes·tiv·ity** /feˈstɪvəti/ noun **1** festivities [pl.] the activities that are organized to celebrate a special event **2** [U] the happiness and joy that exist when people celebrate sth: *The wedding was an occasion of great festivity.* ◇ *an air of festivity* ⊃ WORDFINDER NOTE at CELEBRATE

**fes·toon** /feˈstuːn/ verb, noun
■ verb [usually passive] ~ sb/sth (with sth) to decorate sb/sth with flowers, coloured paper, etc., often as part of a celebration
■ noun a chain of lights, coloured paper, flowers, etc., used to decorate sth

**feta cheese** /ˌfetə ˈtʃiːz/ (also **feta**) noun [U] a type of Greek cheese made from sheep's milk, or from a mixture of sheep's and GOAT's milk

**fetal** (BrE also **foe·tal**) /ˈfiːtl/ adj. [only before noun] connected with a fetus; typical of a fetus: *fetal abnormalities* ◇ *She lay curled up in a fetal position* (= like the position of a baby inside its mother before it is born).

**fetal 'alcohol syndrome** noun [U] (medical) a condition in which a child's mental and physical development is damaged because the mother drank too much alcohol while she was pregnant

**fetch** /fetʃ/ verb **1** (especially BrE) to go to where sb/sth is and bring them/it back: ~ sb/sth *to fetch help/a doctor* ◇ *The inhabitants have to walk a mile to fetch water.* ◇ *She's gone to fetch the kids from school.* ◇ ~ sb sth *Could you fetch me my bag?* **2** ~ sth to be sold for a particular price **SYN** sell for: *The painting is expected to fetch $10000 at auction.*
**IDM** **fetch and 'carry (for sb)** to do a lot of little jobs for sb as if you were their servant
**PHRV** **fetch 'up** (especially BrE, informal) to arrive somewhere without planning to: *And then, a few years later, he somehow fetched up in Rome.*

**fetch·ing** /ˈfetʃɪŋ/ adj. (informal) (especially of a person or their clothes) attractive ▶ **fetch·ing·ly** adv.

**fete** (also **fête**) /feɪt/ noun, verb
■ noun **1** (also **fair**) (both BrE) an outdoor entertainment at which people can play games to win prizes, buy food and drink, etc., usually arranged to make money for a special purpose: *the school/village/church fete* ⊃ compare CARNIVAL (3), FAYRE (1) **2** (NAmE) a special occasion held to celebrate sth: *a charity fete*
■ verb [usually passive] ~ sb (formal) to welcome, praise or entertain sb publicly

**fetid** (BrE also, less frequent **foe·tid**) /ˈfetɪd; BrE also ˈfiːt-/ adj. [usually before noun] (formal) smelling very unpleasant **SYN** stinking

**fet·ish** /ˈfetɪʃ/ noun **1** (usually disapproving) the fact that a person spends too much time doing or thinking about a particular thing or thinks that it is more important than it really is: *She has a fetish about cleanliness.* ◇ *He makes a fetish of his work.* **2** the fact of getting sexual pleasure from a particular object: *to have a leather fetish* **3** an object that some people WORSHIP because they believe that it has magic powers ▶ **fet·ish·ism** noun [U]: *a magazine specializing in rubber fetishism* ◇ *the importance of animal fetishism in the history of Egypt* **fet·ish·ist** noun: *a leather fetishist* **fet·ish·is·tic** /ˌfetɪˈʃɪstɪk/ adj.

**fet·ish·ize** (BrE also **-ise**) /ˈfetɪʃaɪz/ verb **1** ~ sth to spend too much time thinking about or doing sth **2** ~ sth to get sexual pleasure from thinking about or looking at a particular thing

**fet·lock** /ˈfetlɒk; NAmE -lɑːk/ noun the part at the back of a horse's leg, just above its HOOF, where long hair grows

**fet·ter** /ˈfetə(r)/ verb, noun
■ verb [usually passive] **1** ~ sb (literary) to limit sb's freedom to do what they want **2** ~ sb to put chains around a prisoner's feet **SYN** shackle
■ noun **1** [usually pl.] (literary) something that stops sb from doing what they want: *They were at last freed from the fetters of ignorance.* **2** fetters [pl.] chains that are put around a prisoner's feet **SYN** chain

**fet·tle** /ˈfetl/ noun
**IDM** **in fine/good 'fettle** (old-fashioned, informal) healthy; in good condition

**fetus** (BrE also **foe·tus**) /ˈfiːtəs/ noun a young human or animal before it is born, especially a human more than eight weeks after FERTILIZATION ⊃ compare EMBRYO (1) ⊃ WORDFINDER NOTE at PREGNANT

**feud** /fjuːd/ noun, verb
■ noun an angry and bitter argument between two people or groups of people that continues over a long period of time: ~ between A and B *a long-running feud between the two artists* ◇ ~ with sb *a feud with the neighbours* ◇ *a family feud* (= within a family or between two families) ◇ ~ over sb/sth *a feud over money*
■ verb [I] ~ (with sb) to have an angry and bitter argument with sb over a long period of time ▶ **feud·ing** noun [U]: *stories of bitter feuding between rival drug dealers*

**feu·dal** /ˈfjuːdl/ adj. [usually before noun] connected with or similar to feudalism: *the feudal system*

**feu·dal·ism** /ˈfjuːdəlɪzəm/ noun [U] the social system that existed during the Middle Ages in Europe in which people were given land and protection by a NOBLEMAN, and had to work and fight for him in return ▶ **feu·dal·is·tic** /ˌfjuːdəˈlɪstɪk/ adj.

**fever** ❓+ **B2** /ˈfiːvə(r)/ noun **1** ❓ **B2** [C, U] a medical condition in which a person has a temperature that is higher than normal: *He has a high fever.* ◇ *Aspirin should help reduce the fever.* ⊃ WORDFINDER NOTE at DISEASE ⊃ compare TEMPERATURE **2** [C, U] (old-fashioned) a type of disease in which sb has a high temperature: *She caught a fever on her travels in Africa, and died.* **HELP** This meaning of **fever** is old-fashioned when used on its own, but not when used as part of the name of particular disease such as GLANDULAR FEVER or YELLOW FEVER. ⊃ see also EAST COAST FEVER, EBOLA, GLANDULAR FEVER, HAY FEVER, LASSA FEVER, RHEUMATIC FEVER, SCARLET FEVER, YELLOW FEVER **3** [sing.] ~ (of sth) a state of nervous excitement: *He waited for her arrival in a fever of impatience.* **4** [U] (especially in compounds) great interest or excitement about sth: *election fever*

**ˈfever blister** *noun* (*NAmE*) = COLD SORE

**fe·vered** /ˈfiːvəd; *NAmE* -vərd/ *adj.* [only before noun] **1** showing great excitement or worry: *fevered excitement/speculation* ◊ *a fevered imagination/mind* (= that imagines strange things) **2** suffering from a FEVER (= a high temperature): *She mopped his fevered brow.*

**ˈfever·few** /ˈfiːvəfjuː; *NAmE* -vərf-/ *noun* [U] a plant of the DAISY family, sometimes used as a medicine

**fe·ver·ish** /ˈfiːvərɪʃ/ *adj.* **1** [usually before noun] showing strong feelings of excitement or worry, often with a lot of activity or quick movements: *The whole place was a scene of feverish activity.* ◊ *a state of feverish excitement* ◊ *feverish with longing* **2** suffering from a FEVER (= a high temperature); caused by a FEVER: *She was aching and feverish.* ◊ *a feverish cold/dream* ▶ **fe·ver·ish·ly** *adv.*: *The team worked feverishly to the November deadline.* ◊ *Her mind raced feverishly.*

**ˈfever pitch** *noun* [U, sing.] a very high level of excitement or activity: *Speculation about his future had reached fever pitch.* ◊ **at ~** *Excitement has been at fever pitch for days*

**few** 🔑 **A1** /fjuː/ *det., adj., pron.*
■ *det., adj.* (**fewer, few·est**) **1** 🔑 **A1** (usually **a few**) used with plural nouns and a plural verb to mean 'a small number', 'some': *We've had a few replies.* ◊ *I need a few things from the store.* ◊ *Quite a few people are going to arrive early.* ◊ *I try to visit my parents every few weeks.* **2** 🔑 **A2** used with plural nouns and a plural verb to mean 'not many': *Few people understand the difference.* ◊ *There seem to be fewer tourists around this year.* ◊ *Very few students learn Latin now.*
**IDM** **few and ˈfar beˈtween** not happening often
■ *pron.* **1** 🔑 **a few** a small number of people, things or places; some: *I recognized a few of the other people.* ◊ *I've seen most of his movies. Only a few are as good as his first one.* ◊ *Could you give me a few more details?* **2** 🔑 **A2** not many people, things or places: *Very few of his books are worth reading.* ◊ *You can pass with as few as 25 points.* ◊ (*formal*) *Few will argue with this conclusion.* **3** 🔑 **A2** **fewer** not as many as: *Fewer than 20 students passed all the exams.* ◊ *There are **no fewer than** 100 different species in the area.* **HELP** Look at the note at **less**. **4 the few** used with a plural verb to mean 'a small group of people': *Real power belongs to the few.* ◊ *She was one of **the chosen few** (= the small group with special rights).*
**IDM** **have ˈhad a few** (*informal*) to have had enough alcohol to make you drunk **quite a ˈfew** (*BrE also* **a good ˈfew, a fair ˈfew**) a fairly large number: *I've been there quite a few times.*

**fey** /feɪ/ *adj.* (*literary, sometimes disapproving*) (usually of a person) sensitive and rather mysterious or strange; not acting in a very practical way

**fez** /fez/ *noun* (*pl.* **fezzes**) a round red hat with a flat top and a TASSEL but no BRIM, worn by men in some Muslim countries

**ff** *abbr.* (*music*) very loudly (from Italian 'fortissimo')

**ff.** *abbr.* written after the number of a page or line to mean 'and the following pages or lines': *See pp. 96 ff.*

**FGM** /ˌef dʒiː ˈem/ *abbr.* female genital mutilation (the practice of cutting off part of the sex organs of a girl or woman for non-medical reasons, which is traditional in some cultures but illegal in most countries) ⇒ compare CIRCUMCISE (2)

**fi·ancé** /fiˈɒnseɪ; *NAmE* ˌfiːɑːnˈseɪ/ *noun* the man that sb is engaged to: *Linda and her fiancé were there.*

**fi·an·cée** /fiˈɒnseɪ; *NAmE* ˌfiːɑːnˈseɪ/ *noun* the woman that sb is engaged to: *Paul and his fiancée were there.*

**fi·asco** /fiˈæskəʊ/ *noun* (*pl.* **-os**, *NAmE also* **-oes**) (*informal*) something that does not succeed, often in a way that makes people feel embarrassed **SYN** **disaster**: *What a fiasco!*

**fiat** /ˈfiːæt, ˈfiːət; *NAmE* ˈfiːɑːt/ *noun* [C, U] (*formal*) an official order given by sb in authority **SYN** **decree**

**fib** /fɪb/ *noun, verb*
■ *noun* (*informal*) a lie, usually one that is not important: *Stop telling fibs.*

579 **fictionalize**

■ *verb* [I] (*informal*) (**-bb-**) to tell a lie, usually about sth that is not important: *Come on, don't fib! Where were you really last night?* ▶ **ˈfib·ber** *noun*: *You fibber!*

**Fiˈbo·nacci ser·ies** /ˌfiːbəˈnɑːtʃi ˌsɪəriːz; *NAmE* ˌsɪr-/ (*also* **Fiˈbonacci sequence**) *noun* (*mathematics*) a series of numbers in which each number is equal to the two numbers before it added together. Starting from 1, the series is 1,1,2,3,5,8,13, etc.

**fibre** 🔑+ **C1** (*US* **fiber**) /ˈfaɪbə(r)/ *noun* **1** 🔑+ **C1** [U] the part of food that helps to keep a person healthy by keeping the BOWELS working and moving other food quickly through the body **SYN** **roughage**: *dietary fibre* ◊ *Dried fruits are especially high in fibre.* ◊ *a high-/low-fibre diet* **2** 🔑+ **C1** [C, U] a material such as cloth or rope that is made from a mass of natural or artificial THREADS: *nylon and other man-made fibres* ⇒ see also GLASS FIBRE **3** 🔑+ **C1** [C] one of the many thin THREADS that form body TISSUE, such as muscle, and natural materials, such as wood and cotton: *cotton/wood/nerve/muscle fibres* ◊ (*literary*) *She loved him with every fibre of her being.* ⇒ see also MORAL FIBRE, OPTICAL FIBRE

**ˈfibre·board** (*US* **ˈfiber·board**) /ˈfaɪbəbɔːd; *NAmE* -bərbɔːrd/ *noun* [U] a building material made of wood or other plant fibres pressed together to form boards ⇒ see also MDF

**ˈfibre·glass** (*US* **ˈfiber·glass**) /ˈfaɪbəɡlɑːs; *NAmE* -bərɡlæs/ (*BrE also* ˌglass ˈfibre) *noun* [U] a strong light material made from glass fibres and plastic, used for making boats, etc.

**ˈfibre ˈoptics** (*US* **ˈfiber ˈoptics**) *noun* [U] the use of thin fibres of glass, etc. for sending information in the form of light signals ▶ **ˌfibre-ˈoptic** (*US* **ˌfiber-ˈoptic**) *adj.* [usually before noun]: *fibre-optic cables*

**fi·brin** /ˈfaɪbrɪn/ *noun* [U] (*biology*) a PROTEIN involved in the CLOTTING of blood, which forms a network that helps reduce the flow of blood from a wound

**fi·brino·gen** /faɪˈbrɪnədʒən/ *noun* [U] (*biology*) a PROTEIN in the blood from which fibrin is produced

**fibro** /ˈfaɪbrəʊ/ *noun* (*pl.* **-os**) (*AustralE*) **1** [U] a mixture of sand, CEMENT, and plant FIBRES, used as a building material **2** [C] a house that is built mainly of such material

**fi·broid** /ˈfaɪbrɔɪd/ *noun* (*medical*) a mass of cells that form a round shape, usually found in the wall of a woman's UTERUS

**fi·brous** /ˈfaɪbrəs/ *adj.* [usually before noun] (*specialist*) made of many FIBRES; looking like FIBRES: *fibrous tissue*

**fib·ula** /ˈfɪbjələ/ *noun* (*pl.* **fibu·lae** /-liː/ *or* **fibu·las**) (*anatomy*) the outer bone of the two bones in the lower part of the leg between the knee and the ankle ⇒ VISUAL VOCAB page V1 ⇒ see also TIBIA

**fickle** /ˈfɪkl/ *adj.* (*disapproving*) **1** changing often and suddenly: *The weather here is notoriously fickle.* ◊ *the fickle world of fashion* **2** (of a person) often changing their mind in an unreasonable way so that you cannot rely on them: *a fickle friend* ▶ **ˈfickle·ness** *noun* [U]: *the fickleness of the English climate*

**fic·tion** 🔑 **A2** /ˈfɪkʃn/ *noun* **1** 🔑 **A2** [U] a type of literature that describes imaginary people and events, not real ones: *a work of popular fiction* ◊ *historical/romantic/crime fiction* ◊ *to write/read fiction* **OPP** **non-fiction** ⇒ see also FAN FICTION, PULP FICTION, SCIENCE FICTION ⇒ WORDFINDER NOTE at WRITE **2** [U, C] **~ (that …)** a thing that is invented or imagined and is not true: *~ that … For years he managed to keep up the fiction that he was not married.* **IDM** see TRUTH

**fic·tion·al** /ˈfɪkʃənl/ *adj.* not real or true; existing only in stories; connected with fiction: *fictional characters* ◊ *a fictional account of life on a desert island* ◊ *fictional techniques* **OPP** **real-life**

**fic·tion·al·ize** (*BrE also* **-ise**) /ˈfɪkʃənəlaɪz/ *verb* [usually passive] **~ sth** to write a book or make a film about a true story, but changing some of the details, characters, etc: *a fictionalized account of his childhood*

# fictitious 580

**fic·ti·tious** /fɪkˈtɪʃəs/ *adj.* invented by sb rather than true: *All the places and characters in my novel are fictitious* (= they do not exist in real life).

**fid·dle** /ˈfɪdl/ *verb, noun*
- *verb* **1** [I] ~ **(with sth)** to keep touching or moving sth with your hands, especially because you are bored or nervous: *He was fiddling with his keys while he talked to me.* **2** [T] ~ **sth** (*informal*) to change the details or figures of sth in order to try to get money dishonestly or gain an advantage: *to fiddle the accounts* ◊ *She fiddled the books* (= changed a company's financial records) *while working as an accountant.* **3** [I] (*informal*) to play music on the VIOLIN
**PHRV fiddle aˈround** (*also* **fiddle aˈbout** *especially in BrE*) to spend your time doing things that are not important **fiddle aˈround with sth** | **ˈfiddle with sth** (*also* **fiddle aˈbout with sth** *especially in BrE*) **1** to keep touching sth or making small changes to sth because you are not satisfied with it: *I've been fiddling around with this design for ages.* **2** to touch or move the parts of sth in order to try to change it or repair it: *Who's been fiddling with the TV again?*
- *noun* (*informal*) **1** [C] = VIOLIN **2** [C] (*BrE*) something that is done dishonestly to get money **SYN** *fraud: an insurance/tax, etc. fiddle* **3** [sing.] (*BrE*) something that is difficult to do
**IDM be on the ˈfiddle** (*BrE*) to be doing sth dishonest to get money **play second ˈfiddle (to sb/sth)** to be treated as less important than sb/sth; to have a less important position than sb/sth else ⇒ *more at* FIT *adj.*

**fid·dler** /ˈfɪdlə(r)/ *noun* a person who plays the VIOLIN, especially to play FOLK MUSIC

**fid·dling** /ˈfɪdlɪŋ/ *adj.* [usually before noun] (*informal*) small, unimportant and often annoying

**fid·dly** /ˈfɪdli/ *adj.* (**fid·dli·er, fid·dli·est**) (*BrE, informal*) difficult to do or use because small objects are involved: *Changing a fuse is one of those fiddly jobs I hate.*

**fi·del·ity** /fɪˈdeləti/ *noun* [U] **1** ~ **(to sth)** (*formal*) the quality of being LOYAL to sb/sth: *fidelity to your principles* **2** ~ **(to sb)** the quality of being FAITHFUL to your husband, wife or partner by not having a sexual relationship with anyone else: *marital/sexual fidelity* **OPP infidelity 3** ~ **(of sth) (to sth)** (*formal*) the quality of being accurate: *the fidelity of the translation to the original text* ⇒ *see also* HIGH FIDELITY

**fidget** /ˈfɪdʒɪt/ *verb, noun*
- *verb* [I] ~ **(with sth)** to keep moving your body, your hands or your feet because you are nervous, bored, excited, etc: *Sit still and stop fidgeting!*
- *noun* a person who is always fidgeting

**fidgety** /ˈfɪdʒɪti/ *adj.* (*informal*) (of a person) unable to remain still or quiet, usually because of being bored or nervous **SYN restless**

**fidu·ciary** /fɪˈdjuːʃəri; *NAmE* -ˈduːʃieri/ *adj., noun* (*law*)
- *adj.* involving trust, especially in a situation where a person or company controls money or property belonging to others: *the company's fiduciary duty to its shareholders*
- *noun* (*pl.* **-ies**) a person or company that is in a position of trust, especially when it involves controlling money or property belonging to others

**fief** /fiːf/ (*also* **fief·dom** /ˈfiːfdəm/) *noun* **1** (*law, old use*) an area of land, especially a rented area for which the payment is work, not money **2** an area or a situation in which sb has control or influence: *She considers the office as her own private fiefdom.*

**field** /fiːld/ *noun, verb*
- *noun*
  - **AREA OF LAND 1** [C] an area of land in the country used for growing crops or keeping animals in, usually surrounded by a fence, etc: *a ploughed field* ◊ *in a~ We camped in a field near the village.* ◊ *People were working in the fields.* ◊ **~ of sth** *We saw golden fields of wheat.* ◊ *a rice/wheat field* ⇒ *see also* CORNFIELD **2** [C] (usually in compounds) an area of land used for the purpose mentioned: *a landing field* ⇒ *see also* AIRFIELD, MINEFIELD **3** [C] (usually in compounds) a large area of land covered with the thing mentioned; an area from which the thing mentioned is obtained: *ice fields* ◊ *gas fields* ⇒ *see also* COALFIELD, GOLDFIELD, ICE FIELD, OILFIELD, SNOWFIELD
  - **IN SPORT 4** (*BrE also* **pitch**) [C] an area of land used for playing a sport on: *a football/soccer/sports field* ◊ *on/off the~ Every player on the field did their best today.* ◊ *There was huge excitement as the teams came onto the field.* ⇒ *see also* CENTRE FIELD, LEFT FIELD, ON-FIELD, PLAYING FIELD, TRACK AND FIELD **5** [sing. + sing./pl. v.] (in CRICKET and baseball) the team that is trying to catch the ball rather than hit it **6** [sing. + sing./pl. v.] all the people or animals competing in a particular sports event
  - **IN WAR 7** *usually* **the field** [C, usually sing.] an area of land where a battle is fought: **in the~** *a medal for bravery in the field* ◊ **on the~** *to die on the field of battle* ◊ *a field ambulance/kitchen* ⇒ *see also* BATTLEFIELD
  - **SUBJECT/ACTIVITY 8** [C] a particular subject or activity that sb works in or is interested in **SYN area: in a~** *All of them are experts in their chosen field.* ◊ **in the~ of sth** *She works in the field of adult education.* ◊ **~ of sth** *This discovery has opened up a whole new field of study.*
  - **PRACTICAL WORK 9** [C] (especially in compounds) the fact of people doing practical work or study, rather than working in a library or laboratory: *a field study/experiment/trial* ◊ *field recordings/observations* ◊ **in the~** *tests carried out in the field* ⇒ *see also* FIELD TRIP, FIELDWORK
  - **IN BUSINESS 10** [sing. + sing./pl. v.] all the people or products competing in a particular area of business: *They lead the field in home entertainment systems.*
  - **PHYSICS 11** [C] (usually in compounds) an area within which the force mentioned has an effect: *the earth's gravitational field* ◊ *an electromagnetic field* ⇒ *see also* FORCE FIELD, MAGNETIC FIELD
  - **COMPUTING 12** [C] part of a record that is a separate item of data: *You will need to create separate fields for first name, surname and address.*
  **IDM play the ˈfield** (*informal*) to have sexual relationships with a lot of different people ⇒ *more at* LEVEL *v.*
- *verb*
  - **CANDIDATE/TEAM 1** [T] ~ **sb/sth** to provide a candidate, speaker, team, etc. to represent you in an election, a competition, etc: *Each of the main parties fielded more than 300 candidates.* ◊ *England fielded a young side in the World Cup.*
  - **IN CRICKET/BASEBALL 2** [I] to be the person or the team that catches the ball and throws it back after sb has hit it: *He won the toss and chose to field first.* **3** [T] ~ **sth** to catch the ball and throw it back: *He fielded the ball expertly.*
  - **QUESTIONS 4** [T] ~ **sth** to receive and deal with questions or comments: *The BBC had to field more than 300 phone calls after last night's programme.*

**ˈfield day** (*NAmE*) (*BrE* **ˈsports day**) *noun* a special day at school when there are no classes and children compete in sports events
**IDM have a ˈfield day** (*NAmE, BrE*) to be given the opportunity to do sth that you enjoy, especially sth that other people do not approve of: *The tabloid press had a field day with the latest government scandal.*

**field·er** /ˈfiːldə(r)/ *noun* (in CRICKET and baseball) a member of the team that is trying to catch the ball rather than hit it

**ˈfield event** *noun* [usually pl.] a sport done by athletes that is not a race, for example jumping or throwing the JAVELIN ⇒ *compare* TRACK EVENT

**ˈfield glasses** *noun* [pl.] (*specialist*) = BINOCULARS

**ˈfield goal** *noun* **1** (in AMERICAN FOOTBALL or rugby) a goal scored by kicking the ball over the bar of the goal **2** (in basketball) a goal scored by throwing the ball through the net during normal play

**ˈfield hand** *noun* (*NAmE*) = FARMHAND

**ˈfield hockey** *noun* (*NAmE*) (*BrE* **hockey**) *noun* [U] a game played on a field by two teams of 11 players, with curved sticks and a small hard ball. Teams try to hit the ball into the other team's goal.

**ˈfield hospital** *noun* a temporary hospital near a BATTLEFIELD

**field house** noun (NAmE) **1** a building at a sports field where people can change their clothes, have a shower, etc. **2** a building where sports events are held, with seats for people to watch

**field·ing** /ˈfiːldɪŋ/ noun [U] (in CRICKET and baseball) the activity of catching and returning the ball

**field marshal** noun (abbr. FM) an officer of the highest rank in the British army: *Field Marshal Montgomery*

**field officer** noun **1** a person in a company or other organization whose job involves practical work in a particular area or region **2** an officer of high rank in the army (= a MAJOR, LIEUTENANT COLONEL or COLONEL)

**field of ˈvision** (also **field of ˈview**, or specialist **visual ˈfield**) noun (pl. **fields of vision/view**, **visual fields**) the total amount of space that you can see from a particular point without moving your head

**field sports** noun [pl.] (BrE) outdoor sports such as hunting, fishing and shooting

**field-test** verb ~ sth to test sth, such as a piece of equipment, in the place where it will be used ▶ **ˈfield test** noun: *Laboratory and field tests have been conducted.*

**field trip** noun a journey made by a group of people, often students, to study sth in its natural environment: *We went on a geology field trip.*

**field·work** /ˈfiːldwɜːk/ NAmE -wɜːrk/ noun [U] research or study that is done in the real world rather than in a library or laboratory ▶ **ˈfield-worker** noun

**fiend** /fiːnd/ noun **1** a very cruel or unpleasant person **2** (informal) (used after another noun) a person who is very interested in the thing mentioned SYN **fanatic**: *a crossword fiend* **3** an evil spirit

**fiend·ish** /ˈfiːndɪʃ/ adj. [usually before noun] **1** cruel and unpleasant: *a fiendish act ◇ shrieks of fiendish laughter* **2** (informal) extremely clever and complicated, often in an unpleasant way: *a puzzle of fiendish complexity ◇ a fiendish plan* **3** (informal) extremely difficult: *a fiendish problem*

**fiend·ish·ly** /ˈfiːndɪʃli/ adv. (informal) very; extremely: *fiendishly clever/complicated*

**fierce** ▮+ C1 /fɪəs; NAmE fɪrs/ adj. (**fier·cer**, **fier·cest**) **1** ▮+ C1 (especially of people or animals) angry and aggressive in a way that is frightening: *a fierce dog ◇ Two fierce eyes glared at them. ◇ He suddenly looked fierce. ◇ She spoke in a fierce whisper.* **2** ▮+ C1 (especially of actions or emotions) showing strong feelings or a lot of activity, often in a way that is violent: *fierce loyalty ◇ the scene of fierce fighting ◇ He launched a fierce attack on the Democrats. ◇ Competition from abroad became fiercer in the 1990s.* **3** ▮+ C1 (of weather conditions or temperatures) very strong in a way that could cause damage: *fierce wind ◇ the fierce heat of the flames* ▶ **fierce·ly** adv.: *'Let go of me,' she said fiercely. ◇ fiercely competitive ◇ The aircraft was burning fiercely.* **fierce·ness** noun [U]
IDM **something ˈfierce** (NAmE, informal) very much; more than usual: *I sure do miss you something fierce!*

**fiery** /ˈfaɪəri/ adj. [usually before noun] (**fier·ier**, **fieri·est**) **1** looking like fire; consisting of fire: *fiery red hair ◇ The sun was now sinking, a fiery ball of light in the west.* **2** quickly or easily becoming angry: *She has a fiery temper. ◇ a fiery young man* **3** showing strong emotions, especially anger SYN **passionate**: *a fiery look* **4** (of food or drink) causing a part of your body to feel as if it is burning: *a fiery Mexican dish*

**fi·esta** /fiˈestə/ noun (from Spanish) a public event when people celebrate and are entertained with music and dancing, usually connected with a religious festival in countries where the people speak Spanish

**FIFA** /ˈfiːfə/ abbr. (from French) Fédération Internationale de Football Association (the international organization that controls the sport of football (soccer))

**fife** /faɪf/ noun a musical instrument like a small FLUTE that plays high notes and is used with drums in military music

**fif·teen** ❶ A1 /ˌfɪfˈtiːn/ ▮ A1 number 15 **2** noun a team of RUGBY UNION players: *He's in the first fifteen.* ▶ **fif-**

---

581    **fight**

**teenth** /-ˈtiːnθ/ ordinal number, noun HELP There are examples of how to use ordinal numbers at the entry for **fifth**.

**fifth** ❶ A1 /fɪfθ/ ordinal number, noun
■ ordinal number ▮ A1 5th: *Today is the fifth (of May). ◇ the fifth century BC ◇ It's her fifth birthday. ◇ My office is on the fifth floor. ◇ It's the fifth time that I've been to America. ◇ Her mother had just given birth to another child, her fifth. ◇ the world's fifth-largest oil exporter ◇ He finished fifth in the race. ◇ Edward V (= Edward the Fifth)*
■ noun each of five equal parts of sth: *She cut the cake into fifths. ◇ He gave her a fifth of the total amount.*
IDM **take/plead the ˈfifth** (US) to make use of the right to refuse to answer questions in court about a crime, because you may give information which will make it seem that you are guilty ORIGIN From the **Fifth Amendment** of the US Constitution, which guarantees this right.

**fifth ˈcolumn** noun a group of people working secretly to help the enemy of the country or organization they are in ▶ **fifth ˈcolumnist** noun

**fifth·ly** /ˈfɪfθli/ adv. used to introduce the fifth of a list of points you want to make in a speech or piece of writing: *Fifthly, we need to consider the effect on the local population.*

**fifty** ❶ A1 /ˈfɪfti/ **1** ▮ A1 number 50 **2** noun **the fifties** [pl.] numbers, years or temperatures from 50 to 59: *She was born in the fifties.* ▶ **fif·ti·eth** /-əθ/ ordinal number, noun HELP There are examples of how to use ordinal numbers at the entry for **fifth**.
IDM **in your ˈfifties** between the ages of 50 and 59: *He retired in his fifties.*

**fifty-ˈfifty** adj., adv. (informal) divided equally between two people, groups or possibilities: *Costs are to be shared on a fifty-fifty basis between the government and local businesses. ◇ She has a fifty-fifty chance of winning (= an equal chance of winning or losing). ◇ Let's split this fifty-fifty.*

**fifty pence ˈpiece** (also **fifty ˈpence**, **50p** /ˌfɪfti ˈpiː/) noun a British coin worth 50 pence: *Put a fifty pence piece in the machine. ◇ Have you got a 50p?*

**fig** /fɪɡ/ noun a soft sweet fruit that is full of small seeds and often eaten dried: *a fig tree* ➤ VISUAL VOCAB page V4
IDM **not care/give a ˈfig (for sb/sth)** (old-fashioned, BrE, informal) not to care at all about sth; to think that sth is not important

**fig.** abbr. **1** (in writing) FIGURE: *See fig. 3.* **2** (in writing) FIGURATIVE

**fight** ❶ A2 /faɪt/ verb, noun
■ verb (**fought**, **fought** /fɔːt/)
• IN WAR/BATTLE **1** ▮ A2 [I, T] to take part in a war or battle against an enemy: *soldiers trained to fight ◇ He fought in Vietnam. ◇ ~ against sb My grandfather fought against the Fascists in Spain. ◇ ~ sb/sth to fight a war/battle ◇ They gathered soldiers to fight the invading army. ◇ ~ (sb/sth) for sth They fought for control of the island. ◇ ~ (sb/sth) over sth They were fighting over disputed land.*
• STRUGGLE/HIT **2** ▮ A2 [I, T] to struggle physically with sb: *My little brothers are always fighting. ◇ ~ with sb Riot police fought with demonstrators. ◇ ~ sb She fought her attacker, eventually forcing him to flee. ◇ ~ (sb) over sth Children will fight even over small things. ◇ ~ against sb/sth She fought hard against his strong grip.*
• ARGUE **3** ▮ B1 [I] to have an argument with sb about sth: *~ about/over sth It's a trivial matter and not worth fighting about.*
• OPPOSE **4** ▮ B1 [T, I] to try hard to stop, deal with or oppose sth bad or sth that you disagree with: *We will continue to fight for as long as it takes. ◇ ~ sth to fight terrorism/crime/corruption/poverty ◇ Vitamin C helps your body to fight disease. ◇ She fought a long battle against cancer. ◇ ~ against sth They are committed to fighting against racism. ◇ ~ sth with sth We must fight hatred with love.*
• TRY TO GET/DO STH **5** ▮ B1 [I, T] to try very hard to get sth or to achieve sth: *~ for sth Women fought for the right to vote. ◇*

---

❶ Oxford Phrasal Academic Lexicon (OPAL) written and spoken word lists | Ⓦ OPAL written word list | Ⓢ OPAL spoken word list

# fightback

~ **to do sth** *Doctors fought for more than six hours to save his life.* ◊ *She fought hard to get this film made.* ◊ **~ your way …** *She gradually fought her way to the top of the company.* ⊃ SYNONYMS at CAMPAIGN
- **IN CONTEST** **6** [T, I] to take part in a contest against sb: *~ sb/sth (for sth)* *to fight an election/a campaign* ◊ *~ for sth She's fighting for a place in the national team.*
- **IN BOXING** **7** [I, T] **~(sb/sth)** to take part in a BOXING match: *Doctors fear he may never fight again.*
- **LAW** **8** [T, I] to try to get what you want in court: *~ (sb) for sth He fought his wife for custody of the children.* ◊ *~ sth I'm determined to fight the case.*

**IDM** **fight your/sb's 'corner** *(BrE)* to defend your/sb's position against other people **fight fire with 'fire** to use similar methods in a fight or an argument to those your opponent is using **fight for (your) 'life** to make a great effort to stay alive, especially when you are badly injured or seriously ill **fight your own battles** to be able to win an argument or get what you want without anyone's help: *I wouldn't get involved—he's old enough to fight his own battles.* **fight 'shy of sth/of doing sth** to be unwilling to accept sth or do sth, and to try to avoid it: *Successive governments have fought shy of such measures.* **fight to the 'death/'finish** to fight until one of the two people or groups is dead, or until one person or group defeats the other **fight tooth and 'nail** to fight in a very determined way for what you want: *The residents are fighting tooth and nail to stop the new development.* ⊃ more at BATTLE *n.*, LIVE¹

**PHR V** **fight 'back (against sb/sth)** to resist strongly or attack sb who has attacked you: *Don't let them bully you. Fight back!* ◊ *It is time to fight back against street crime.* **fight sth↔'back/'down** to try hard not to do or show sth, especially not to show your feelings: *I was fighting back the tears.* ◊ *He fought down his disgust.* **fight sb/sth↔'off** to resist sb/sth by fighting against them/it: *The jeweller was stabbed as he tried to fight the robbers off.* ◊ *(figurative) Vitamin A helps your body fight off infection.* **fight 'out sth | fight it 'out** to fight, argue or compete until an argument or competition has been settled: *The conflict is still being fought out.* ◊ *They hadn't reached any agreement so we left them to fight it out.*

■ noun
- **STRUGGLE** **1** B1 [C] a struggle against sb/sth using physical force: *a street/gang fight* ◊ **~ with sb/sth** *He got into a fight with a man in the bar.* ◊ **~ between A and B** *A fight broke out between rival groups of fans.*
- **SPORT** **2** an occasion when people fight as a sport, especially in BOXING: *a world title fight*
- **ARGUMENT** **3** B1 [C] **~ (with sb) (over/about sth)** *(especially NAmE)* an argument about sth: *Did you have a fight with him?* ◊ *We had a fight over money.*
- **TRYING TO GET/DO STH** **4** B1 [sing.] the work of trying to destroy, prevent or achieve sth: *~ against sth the fight against crime/terrorism* ◊ *~ for sth a fight for justice/survival* ◊ *~ to do sth Workers won their fight to stop compulsory redundancies.*
- **COMPETITION** **5** [sing.] a competition or an act of competing, especially in a sport: *The team put up a good fight (= they played well) but were finally beaten.* ◊ *~ between A and B This will be a straight fight between the two parties.* ⊃ SYNONYMS at CAMPAIGN
- **BATTLE/WAR** **6** [C] **~ (for sth)** a battle, especially for a particular place or position: *In the fight for Lemburg, the Austrians were defeated.*
- **DESIRE TO FIGHT** **7** [U] the desire or ability to keep fighting for sth: *In spite of many defeats, they still had plenty of fight left in them.*

**IDM** **a fight to the 'finish** a sports competition, election, etc. between sides that are so equal in ability that they continue fighting very hard until the end ⊃ more at PICK *v.*, SPOIL *v.*

**fight·back** /ˈfaɪtbæk/ *noun* [usually sing.] *(BrE)* an effort by a person, group or team to get back to a strong position that they have lost

**fight·er** /ˈfaɪtə(r)/ *noun* **1** *(also* **'fighter plane***)* a fast military plane designed to attack other aircraft: *a jet fighter/*

**fighter jet** ◊ *a fighter pilot* ◊ *fighter bases* ⊃ WORDFINDER NOTE at AIRCRAFT **2** a person who fights ⊃ see also FIRE-FIGHTER, FREEDOM FIGHTER, PRIZEFIGHTER **3** *(approving)* a person who does not give up hope or admit that they are defeated

**fighter-bomber** *noun* a military plane that can fight other planes in the air and also drop bombs

# fight·ing ❶ B1 /ˈfaɪtɪŋ/ *noun* [U] **1** B1 the activity of being involved in a battle against an enemy: *Fighting broke out in three districts of the city last night.* ◊ *The island was the scene of heavy fighting during World War II.* **~ with sb/sth** *At least 50 were killed in fierce fighting with local militia.* ◊ **~ between A and B** *The fighting between the rebels and our troops continues.* **2** B1 a physical struggle with sb: *outbreaks of street fighting* **3** B1 an argument or arguments with sb about sth: *He hated all the fighting at home.* **4** B1 **~ (for/against sth)** the activity of trying very hard to get sth or achieve sth: *years of fighting against the policy* **5** the activity of taking part in a BOXING match: *prize fighting (= matches for money)* ⊃ see also EXTREME FIGHTING, ULTIMATE FIGHTING™

**IDM** **a fighting 'chance** a small chance of being successful if a great effort is made **fighting 'fit** extremely fit or healthy **fighting 'spirit** a feeling that you are ready to fight very hard for sth or to try sth difficult **fighting 'talk** comments or remarks that show that you are ready to fight very hard for sth: *What we want from the management is fighting talk.*

**'fig leaf** *noun* **1** a leaf of a FIG tree, traditionally used for covering the sex organs of NAKED bodies in paintings and on statues **2** a thing that is used to hide an embarrassing fact or situation

**fig·ment** /ˈfɪɡmənt/ *noun* something that sb has imagined and that does not really exist: *Are you telling me that these symptoms are just a figment of my imagination?*

**fig·ura·tive** /ˈfɪɡərətɪv; *NAmE* ˈfɪɡjə-/ *adj.* [usually before noun] **1** (of language, words, phrases, etc.) used in a way that is different from the usual meaning, in order to create a particular mental picture. For example, 'He exploded with rage' shows a figurative use of the verb 'explode'. ⊃ compare LITERAL, METAPHORICAL **2** (of paintings, art, etc.) showing people, animals and objects as they really look: *a figurative artist* ⊃ compare ABSTRACT
▸ **fig·ura·tive·ly** *adv.*: *She is, figuratively speaking, holding a gun to his head.*

**fig·ure** ⓘ A2 /ˈfɪɡə(r)/; *NAmE* /ˈfɪɡjər/ *noun, verb*

■ *noun*
- **NUMBERS** **1** A2 [C, usually pl.] a number representing a particular amount, especially one given in official information: *the latest sales/crime/unemployment figures* ◊ *Figures for April show a slight improvement on previous months.* ◊ *Figures released by the hospital reveal a rise in the number of admissions.* ◊ *Experts put the real figure at closer to 75 per cent.* ◊ **according to ... figures** *According to government figures, 3.6 million children are living in poverty.* **2** A2 [C] a symbol rather than a word representing one of the numbers between 0 and 9: *Write the figure '7' on the board.* ◊ *a six-figure salary* (= over 100000 pounds or dollars) ◊ **in ... figures** *Her salary is now in six figures.* ⊃ see also DOUBLE-FIGURE, DOUBLE FIGURES, SINGLE FIGURES, SIX-FIGURE **3 figures** [pl.] (*informal*) the area of mathematics that deals with adding, multiplying, etc. numbers SYN **arithmetic**: *Are you any good at figures?* ◊ *I'm afraid I don't have a head for figures* (= I am not good at adding, etc.).
- **PERSON** **4** B2 [C] a person of the type mentioned: *a leading figure in the music industry* ◊ *a senior figure in the organization* ◊ *a public figure* ◊ *teachers and other authority figures* ⊃ see also FATHER FIGURE, MOTHER FIGURE **5** B2 [C] the shape of a person seen from a distance or not clearly: *a tall figure in black*
- **SHAPE OF BODY** **6** [C] the shape of the human body, especially a woman's body that is attractive: *She's always had a good figure.* ◊ *I'm watching my figure* (= trying not to get fat).
- **IN PAINTING/STORY** **7** [C] a person or an animal in a drawing, painting, etc., or in a story: *The central figure in the painting is the artist's daughter.* ⊃ see also STICK FIGURE
- **STATUE** **8** [C] a statue of a person or an animal: *a bronze figure of a horse* ⊃ see also ACTION FIGURE
- **PICTURE/DIAGRAM** **9** [C] (*abbr.* **fig.**) a picture, diagram, etc. in a book, that is referred to by a number or letter: *The results are illustrated in figure 3 opposite.*
- **GEOMETRY** **10** [C] a particular shape formed by lines or surfaces: *a five-sided figure* ◊ *a solid figure*
- **MOVEMENT ON ICE** **11** [C] a pattern or series of movements performed on ice

IDM **be/become a figure of ˈfun** to be/become sb that other people laugh at **cut a ... figure** (of a person) to have a particular appearance: *He cut a striking figure in his white dinner jacket.* **put a figure on sth** to say the exact price or number of sth ⊃ more at FACT

■ *verb*
- **BE IMPORTANT** **1** B2 [I] to be part of a process, situation, etc. especially an important part SYN **feature**: *My feelings about the matter didn't seem to figure at all.* ◊ **~in/on/among sth** *The question of the peace settlement is likely to figure prominently in the talks.* ◊ *It did not figure high on her list of priorities.*
- **THINK/DECIDE** **2** [T] (*informal*) to think or decide that sth will happen or is true: **~(that) ...** *I figured (that) if I took the night train, I could be in Scotland by morning.* ◊ *We figured the sensible thing to do was to wait.* ◊ **~sth** *That's what I figured.* ◊ **~why, whether, etc ...** *He tried to figure why she had come.*
- **CALCULATE** **3** [T] **~sth (at sth)** (*NAmE*) to calculate an amount or the cost of sth: *We figured the attendance at 150000.*

IDM **go ˈfigure** (*NAmE, informal*) used to say that you do not understand the reason for sth, or that you do not want to give an explanation for sth because you think it is obvious: *In Cambridge, 'May Balls' are always held in June. Go figure.* **it/that figures** used to say that sth was expected or seems logical: *'John called in sick.' 'That figures, he wasn't feeling well yesterday.'* ◊ (*disapproving*) *'She was late again.' 'Yes, that figures.'*

PHRV **ˈfigure on sth** | **ˈfigure on (sb/sth) doing sth** to plan sth or to do sth; to expect sth (to happen) SYN **plan**: *I hadn't figured on getting home so late.* **figure sb/sth↔ˈout 1** B2 to think about sb/sth until you understand them/it: *We couldn't figure her out.* ◊ *I'm trying to figure out a way to make this work.* **figure out how, what, etc ...** *I can't figure out how to do this.* **2** B2 to calculate an amount or the cost of sth: **figure out how, what, etc ...** *Have you figured out how much the trip will cost?*

**fig·ured** /ˈfɪɡəd; *NAmE* /ˈfɪɡjərd/ *adj.* [only before noun] (*specialist*) decorated with a small pattern: *figured pottery*

**fig·ure·head** /ˈfɪɡəhed; *NAmE* /ˈfɪɡjər-/ *noun* **1** a person who is in a high position in a country or an organization but who has no real power or authority **2** a large wooden statue, usually representing a woman, that used to be fixed to the front end of a ship

**ˈfigure-hugging** *adj.* [usually before noun] (of a piece of clothing) tight in an attractive way that shows the shape of sb's body, especially a woman's SYN **form-fitting**

**ˌfigure of ˈeight** (*BrE*) (*NAmE* ˌfigure ˈeight) *noun* (*pl.* figures of eight, figure eights) a pattern or movement that looks like the shape of the number 8

**ˌfigure of ˈspeech** *noun* (*pl.* figures of speech) a word or phrase used in a different way from its usual meaning in order to create a particular mental picture or effect ⊃ WORDFINDER NOTE at IMAGE

**ˈfigure skating** *noun* [U] a type of ICE SKATING in which you cut patterns in the ice and do jumps and turns ⊃ compare SPEED SKATING

**fig·ur·ine** /ˌfɪɡəˈriːn; *NAmE* ˌfɪɡjə-/ *noun* a small statue of a person or an animal

**fila·ment** /ˈfɪləmənt/ *noun* **1** a thin wire in a LIGHT BULB that produces light when electricity is passed through it **2** (*specialist*) a long thin piece of sth that looks like a THREAD: *glass/metal filaments*

**fil·bert** /ˈfɪlbət; *NAmE* -bərt/ *noun* (*especially NAmE*) a type of HAZEL tree that produces OVAL nuts, also called **filberts**

**filch** /fɪltʃ/ *verb* **~sth** (*informal*) to steal sth, especially sth small or not very valuable SYN **pinch**

**file** ⓘ B1 /faɪl/ *noun, verb*

■ *noun* **1** B1 a box or folded piece of card for keeping loose papers together and in order: *a box file* ◊ *A stack of files awaited me on my desk.* **2** B1 a collection of information stored together in a computer, under a particular name: *to create/delete/download/upload a file* ◊ *to open/access/copy/save a file* ◊ *The service converts **video files** from one format to another.* ◊ *You can transfer and edit files on your smartphone.* ⊃ see also PDF, ZIP FILE

WORDFINDER copy, data, delete, folder, icon, menu, open, password, print

**3** B1 a file and the information it contains, for example about a particular person or subject: *The film is based on real FBI case files.* ◊ **on ~** *Your application will be kept on file* (= in a file, to be used later). ◊ **on sb** to have/open/keep a confidential file on sb ◊ *Police have reopened the file* (= have started collecting information again) *on the missing girl.* **4** (*CanE*) a number of issues and responsibilities connected with a particular government policy area **5** a metal tool with a rough surface for cutting or shaping hard substances or for making them smooth ⊃ picture at SCREWDRIVER ⊃ see also NAIL FILE **6** a line of people or things, one behind the other: **in ~** *They set off in file behind the teacher.* ⊃ see also RANK AND FILE

IDM **(in) single ˈfile** (*also old-fashioned* **(in) Indian file**) (in) one line, one behind the other: *They made their way in single file along the cliff path.*

■ *verb* **1** B1 [T] to put and keep paper documents in a particular place and in a particular order so that you can find them easily; to put a paper document in a box, file, etc: **~sth (+ adv./prep.)** *The forms should be filed alphabetically.* ◊ *Please file it in my 'Research' file.* ◊ **~sth away** *I filed the letters away in a drawer.* **2** B1 [I, T] (*law*) to present sth so that it can be officially recorded and dealt with: **~for sth** *to file for divorce/bankruptcy* ◊ **~sth** *to file a lawsuit/complaint/petition* ◊ **~sth against sb/sth** *No criminal charges were filed against him.* **3** [T] **~sth** (of a journalist) to send a report or a story to your employer **4** [I] **+ adv./prep.** to walk in a line of people, one after the other, in a

# file cabinet

particular direction: *The doors of the museum opened and the visitors began to file in.* **5** [T] *~ sth (away/down, etc.)* to cut or shape sth or make sth smooth using a file: *to file your nails*

**'file cabinet** *(NAmE) (also* **'filing cabinet** *especially in BrE) noun* a large piece of office furniture that is used for storing files

**'file name** /'faɪlneɪm/ *noun (computing)* a name given to a computer file in order to identify it

**'file sharing** *noun* [U] the practice of sharing computer files with other people over the internet or another computer network: *Illegal music file-sharing sites have spread through the Net.*

**filet** *(especially NAmE)* = FILLET

**fil·ial** /'fɪliəl/ *adj.* [usually before noun] *(formal)* connected with the way children behave towards their parents: *filial affection/duty*

**fili·bus·ter** /'fɪlɪbʌstə(r)/ *noun (especially NAmE)* a long speech made in a parliament in order to delay or prevent a vote ▶ **fili·bus·ter** *verb* [I]

**fili·gree** /'fɪlɪgriː/ *noun* [U] beautiful decoration made from thin gold or silver wire

**fil·ing** /'faɪlɪŋ/ *noun* **1** [U] the act of putting documents, letters, etc. into a file **2** [C] *(especially NAmE)* something that is placed in an official record: *a bankruptcy filing* **3** filings [pl.] very small pieces of metal, made when a larger piece of metal is filed: *iron filings*

**'filing cabinet** *(NAmE usually* **'file cabinet***) noun* a large piece of office furniture that is used for storing files

**Filipina** /ˌfɪlɪˈpiːnə/ *noun* a woman from the Philippines

**Fi·li·pino** /ˌfɪlɪˈpiːnəʊ/ *noun, adj.*

■ *noun (pl.* **-os)** **1** [C] a person from the Philippines **2** [U] the language of the Philippines

■ *adj.* connected with the Philippines, its people or easy language

## fill 🔊 A1 /fɪl/ *verb, noun*

■ *verb*

- MAKE FULL **1** 🔊 A1 [T, I] to make sth full of sth; to become full of sth: *~ sth Please fill this glass for me.* ◊ *to fill a space/vacuum/void* ◊ *Smoke filled the room.* ◊ *Her image filled the screen.* ◊ *The wind filled the sails.* ◊ *A Disney film can always fill cinemas* (= attract a lot of people to see it). ◊ *The school is filled to capacity.* ◊ *~ sth with sth She filled the page with writing.* ◊ *~ sth + adj. Fill a pan half full of water.* ◊ *The room was filling quickly.* ◊ *~ with sth Her eyes suddenly filled with tears.* ◊ *The sails filled with wind.*
- BLOCK HOLE **2** 🔊 A1 [T] to block a hole with a substance: *~ sth They used putty to fill the holes.* ◊ *~ sth with sth The crack in the wall had been filled with plaster.*
- TOOTH **3** [T] *~ sth* to put a FILLING (= a small amount of special material) in a hole in a tooth
- WITH FEELING **4** 🔊 B1 [T, I] *~ (sb) (with sth)* to make sb have a strong feeling; to become full of a strong feeling: *We were all filled with admiration for his achievements.*
- WITH SMELL/SOUND/LIGHT **5** 🔊 B1 [T] if a smell, sound or light fills a place, it is very strong, loud or bright and easy to notice: *~ sth The sound of bells ringing filled the air.* ◊ *~ sth with sth Large windows fill the room with light.*
- -FILLED **6** (in adjectives) full of the thing mentioned: *a smoke-filled room* ◊ *a fun-filled day*
- A NEED/GAP **7** [T] *~ sth* to supply sth that is missing: *More nurseries will be built to fill the need for high-quality childcare.* ◊ *Choose the best word to fill the gap in each sentence.* ◊ *The product has filled a gap in the market.*
- JOB **8** [T] *~ sth* to do a job, have a role or position, etc: *The team needs someone to fill the role of manager.* ◊ *to fill a post/position* **9** [T] *~ sth* to choose sb for a job: *The vacancy has already been filled.*
- TIME **10** [T] *~ sth (up)* to use up a particular period of time doing sth: *How do you fill your day now that you've retired?*

- WITH FOOD **11** [T] *~ sb/yourself (up) (with sth) (informal)* to make sb/yourself feel unable to eat any more: *The kids filled themselves with snacks.*
- AN ORDER **12** [T] *~ sth* if sb fills an order or a PRESCRIPTION, they give the customer what they have asked for ⊃ see also UNFILLED

**IDM** **fill your boots** *(informal)* used to invite sb to take as much as they like of sth such as food, drink, etc; help yourself **fill sb's shoes/boots** to do sb's job in an acceptable way when they are not there ⊃ more at BILL *n.*

**PHR V** **fill 'in (for sb)** to do sb's job for a short time while they are not there ˌfill 'in ⇔ 1 🔊 A2 *(BrE) (also* ˌfill 'out *especially in NAmE)* to complete a form, etc. by writing information on it: *to fill in an application form* ◊ *To order, fill in the coupon on p54.* **2** 🔊 A2 to fill sth completely: *The hole has been filled in.* **3** to spend time doing sth while waiting for sth more important: *He filled in the rest of the day watching television.* **4** to complete a drawing, etc. by covering the space inside the outline with colour ˌfill sb 'in (on sth) to tell sb about sth that has happened ˌfill 'out to become larger, rounder or fatter ˌfill sth⇔'out *(especially NAmE) (BrE usually* ˌfill sth 'in) to complete a form, etc. by writing information on it ˌfill 'up (with sth) | ˌfill sth⇔'up (with sth) **1** to become completely full; to make sth completely full: *The ditches had filled up with mud.* **2** to fill the fuel tank of a car: *We need to fill up.* ◊ *to fill up the tank with oil* ˌfill 'up on sth to eat sth until you are full: *He filled up on potato, more bread and dessert.*

■ *noun* [sing.] **1** your *~ (of sth/sb)* as much of sth/sb as you are willing to accept: *I've had my fill of entertaining for one week.* **2** your *~ (of food/drink)* as much as you can eat/drink

**fill·er** /'fɪlə(r)/ *noun* **1** [U, C] a substance used to fill holes, especially in walls before painting them **2** [C] *(informal)* something that is not important but is used to complete sth else because nothing better is available: *The song was originally a filler on their first album.* ⊃ see also STOCKING FILLER

**fil·let** /'fɪlɪt; *NAmE* fɪˈleɪ/ *noun, verb*

■ *noun (also* **filet** *especially in NAmE)* [C, U] a piece of meat or fish that has no bones in it: *plaice fillets* ◊ *a fillet of cod* ◊ *fillet steak*

■ *verb ~ sth* to remove the bones from a piece of fish or meat; to cut fish or meat into fillets

**fill·ing** /'fɪlɪŋ/ *noun, adj.*

■ *noun* **1** [C] a small amount of metal or other material used to fill a hole in a tooth: *I had to have two fillings at the dentist's today.* ⊃ WORDFINDER NOTE at DENTIST **2** [C, U] food put inside a sandwich, cake, PIE, etc: *a sponge cake with cream and jam filling* ◊ *a wide range of sandwich fillings* **3** [C, U] soft material used to fill CUSHIONS, PILLOWS, etc.

■ *adj.* (of food) making your stomach feel full: *This cake is very filling.*

**'filling station** *noun* = PETROL STATION

**fil·lip** /'fɪlɪp/ *noun* [sing.] *a ~ (to/for sth) (formal)* a thing or person that causes sth to improve suddenly **SYN** boost: *A drop in interest rates gave a welcome fillip to the housing market.*

**'fill-up** *noun* an occasion when a car is completely filled up with petrol

**filly** /'fɪli/ *noun (pl.* **-ies)** a young female horse, especially one that is less than 4 years old ⊃ compare COLT, MARE

## film 🔊 A1 /fɪlm/ *noun, verb*

■ *noun*

- MOVING PICTURES **1** 🔊 A1 [C] *(especially BrE) (NAmE usually* **movie**) a series of moving pictures recorded with sound that tells a story, watched at a cinema or on a television or other device: *Let's stay in and watch a film.* ◊ *We're going out to see a film.* ◊ *There's a good film on tonight* (= showing at the cinema or on TV). ◊ *a horror/documentary/feature film* ◊ *a ~ about sth As a student he made a short film about his home town.* ◊ *to shoot/direct/produce a film* ◊ *a film crew/critic/director/producer* ◊ *an international film festival* ⊃ see also ACTION FILM, FEATURE FILM

**WORDFINDER** actor, cameraman, dialogue, director, dub, location, scenario, sound effect

**2** [A2] [U] (*especially BrE*) (*NAmE usually* **the movies** [pl.]) (*BrE also* **the cin·ema**) the art or business of making films: *jobs in film and television* ◊ *the film industry* ⊃ compare CINEMA **3** [B1] [U] moving pictures of real events, shown for example on television: *television news film of the riots* ◊ **on**~ *The accident was caught on film.* ◊ *a film clip* ⊃ compare FOOTAGE
• IN CAMERAS **4** [B1] [U, C] thin plastic that is sensitive to light, used especially in the past for taking photographs and making films; a roll of this plastic, used in cameras: *a roll of film* ◊ *a 35mm film* ◊ *There was no film in the camera.*
• THIN LAYER **5** [C, *usually sing.*] ~ **(of sth)** a thin layer of sth, usually on the surface of sth else SYN **coat, coating, layer**: *Everything was covered in a film of dust.* ⊃ see also CLING FILM

■ **verb** [A2] [I, T] to make a film of a story or a real event; to record sb/sth on film: *They are filming in Moscow right now.* ◊ ~ **sth/sb** *The show was filmed on location in New York.* ◊ ~ **sb/sth doing sth** *A young boy was filmed by the security camera stealing a pair of jeans.* ▶ **film·ing** *noun* [U]: *Filming was delayed because of bad weather.*

**film·goer** /ˈfɪlmɡəʊə(r)/ (*especially BrE*) (*NAmE usually* **movie·goer**) (*BrE also* **cin·ema·goer**) *noun* a person who goes to the cinema, especially when they do it regularly

**film·ic** /ˈfɪlmɪk/ *adj.* [only before noun] (*formal*) connected with films

**'film-maker** [C1] *noun* a person who directs or produces films ▶ **'film-making** *noun* [U]

**film noir** /ˌfɪlm ˈnwɑː(r)/ *noun* (*pl.* **films noirs** /ˌfɪlm ˈnwɑː(r)/) (*from French*) [U] a style of making films in which there are strong feelings of fear or evil; a film made in this style ⊃ compare NOIR

**film·og·raphy** /fɪlˈmɒɡrəfi; *NAmE* -ˈmɑːɡ-/ *noun* (*pl.* **-ies**) a list of films made by a particular actor or director, or a list of films that deal with a particular subject

**'film star** (*especially BrE*) (*NAmE usually* **'movie star**) *noun* a male or female actor who is famous for being in films

**film·strip** /ˈfɪlmstrɪp/ *noun* a series of images on a film, through which light is shone to show them on a screen

**filmy** /ˈfɪlmi/ *adj.* [usually before noun] thin and almost TRANSPARENT SYN **sheer**: *a filmy cotton blouse*

**filo pastry** (*BrE*) (*NAmE* **phyllo pastry**) /ˌfiːləʊ ˈpeɪstri/ (*BrE also* **filo**, *NAmE also* **phyllo**) *noun* a type of thin PASTRY, used in layers

**filters**

filter paper in a coffee pot | cigarette filter | filter on a set of traffic lights
red light, filter paper, filter, filter

**fil·ter** [C1] /ˈfɪltə(r)/ *noun, verb*

■ *noun* **1** [C1] a device containing paper, sand, chemicals, etc. that a liquid or gas is passed through in order to remove any materials that are not wanted: *an air/oil filter* ◊ *a coffee/water filter* ◊ *filter paper for the coffee machine* ◊ *He smokes cigarettes without filters.* **2** a device that allows only particular types of light or sound to pass through it **3** (*computing*) a program that processes information to leave out the types that are not wanted, or that stops particular types of electronic information, email, etc. from being sent to a computer: *Spam filters block out almost all threats.* **4** (*BrE*) a light on a set of TRAFFIC LIGHTS showing that traffic can turn left (or right) while traffic that wants to go straight ahead or turn right (or left) must wait

585

■ *verb* **1** [+] [C1] [T] ~ **sth** to pass liquid, light, etc. through a special device, especially to remove sth that is not wanted: *All drinking water must be filtered.* ◊ *Use a sun block that filters UVA effectively.* ◊ (*figurative*) *My secretary is very good at filtering my calls* (= making sure that calls that I do not want do not get through). ⊃ see also FILTRATION ⊃ **WORDFINDER NOTE** at LIQUID **2** [T] ~ **sth** to use a special program to check the content of emails or websites before they are sent to your computer **3** [I] + **adv./prep.** (of people) to move slowly in a particular direction: *The doors opened and people started filtering through.* **4** [I] + **adv./prep.** (of information, news, etc.) to slowly become known: *More details about the crash are filtering through.* **5** [I] + **adv./prep.** (of light or sound) to come into a place slowly or in small amounts: *Sunlight filtered in through the curtains.* **6** [I] (*BrE*) (of traffic at traffic lights) to turn left (or right) at traffic lights while other vehicles wanting to go straight ahead or turn right (or left) must wait

**PHRV** **filter sth**↔**out 1** to remove sth that you do not want from a liquid, light, etc. by using a special device or substance: *to filter out dust particles/light/impurities* **2** to remove sb/sth that you do not want from a large number of people or things using a special system, device, etc.: *The test is used to filter out candidates who may be unsuitable.* ◊ *The software filters out internet sites whose content is not suitable for children.*

**filth** /fɪlθ/ *noun* **1** [U] any very dirty and unpleasant substance: *The floor was covered in grease and filth.* **2** [U] videos, magazines, websites, etc. that are connected with sex and that are considered very rude and offensive: *How can you read such filth?* **3 the filth** [pl.] (*BrE, slang*) an offensive word for the police

**filthy** /ˈfɪlθi/ *adj., adv.*
■ *adj.* (**filth·ier, filthi·est**) **1** very dirty and unpleasant: *filthy rags/streets* ◊ *It's filthy in here!* ⊃ SYNONYMS at DIRTY **2** very rude and offensive and usually connected with sex: *filthy language/words* ◊ *He's got a filthy mind* (= is always thinking about sex). **3** (*informal*) showing anger: *He was in a filthy mood.* ◊ *She has a filthy temper.* ◊ *Ann gave him a filthy look.* **4** (*BrE, informal*) (of the weather) cold and wet: *Isn't it a filthy day?* ▶ **filth·ily** /-θɪli/ *adv.* **filthi·ness** *noun* [U]
■ *adv.* (*informal*) **1** ~ **dirty** extremely dirty **2** ~ **rich** so rich that you think the person is too rich and you find it offensive

**fil·trate** /ˈfɪltreɪt/ *noun* (*chemistry*) a liquid that has passed through a FILTER

**fil·tra·tion** /fɪlˈtreɪʃn/ *noun* [U] (*chemistry*) the process of FILTERING a liquid or gas

**fin** /fɪn/ *noun* **1** a thin flat part that sticks out from the body of a fish, used for swimming and keeping balance ⊃ VISUAL VOCAB page V2 **2** a thin flat part that sticks out from the body of a vehicle, an aircraft, etc., used for improving its balance and movement: *tail fins*

**fin·agle** /fɪˈneɪɡl/ *verb* [T, I] ~ **(sth)** (*informal*, *especially NAmE*) to behave dishonestly or to obtain sth dishonestly: *He finagled some tickets for tonight's big game.*

**final** [A1] S /ˈfaɪnl/ *adj., noun*
■ *adj.* **1** [A1] [only before noun] being or happening at the end of a series of events, actions, statements, etc: *his final act as party leader* ◊ *Jamie is in his final year at Stirling University.* ◊ *the final week/day/minutes of sth* ◊ *The referee blew the final whistle.* ◊ *The project is in its final stages.* ⊃ LANGUAGE BANK at PROCESS¹ **2** [A1] [only before noun] being the result of a particular process: *the final product/result* ◊ *No one could have predicted the final outcome.* **3** [A1] that cannot be argued with or changed: *The judge's decision is final.* ◊ *Who has the final say around here?* ◊ *I'm not coming, and that's final!* (= I will not change my mind) IDM see ANALYSIS, STRAW, WORD n.
■ *noun* **1** [A2] [C] the last of a series of games or competitions, in which the winner is decided: *She reached the final of the 100m hurdles.* ◊ *The winner of each contest goes through to the grand final.* ◊ ~ **against sb** *a nail-biting final against last year's victor* ⊃ see also CUP FINAL,

QUARTER-FINAL, SEMI-FINAL **2** [pl.] **finals** a series of games or performances that make up the last stage of a competition: *the 2022 World Cup Finals* ◇ *the regional/national finals* ◇ *They got into the finals of a singing competition.* **3 finals** [pl.] (*BrE*) the last exams taken by university students at the end of their final year: *to sit/take your finals* **4** [C] (*NAmE*) an exam taken by school, university or college students at the end of a SEMESTER or QUARTER, usually in a topic that they will not study again

**final 'clause** *noun* (*grammar*) a clause that expresses purpose or intention, for example one that follows 'in order that' or 'so that'

**fi·nale** /fɪˈnɑːli; *NAmE* -ˈnæli/ *noun* **1** the last part of a show or a piece of music: *the rousing finale of Beethoven's Ninth Symphony* ◇ *The festival ended with a grand finale in Hyde Park.* ⊃ see also SEASON FINALE **2** ~ **(to sth)** (after an adjective) an ending to sth of the type mentioned: *a fitting finale to the day's events*

**fi·nal·ist** /ˈfaɪnəlɪst/ *noun* a person who takes part in the final of a game or competition, either on their own or as a member of a team: *an Olympic finalist*

**fi·nal·ity** /faɪˈnæləti/ *noun* [U, sing.] the fact of being final and impossible to change; sth that is final and impossible to change: *the finality of death* ◇ *There was a note of finality in his voice.*

**fi·nal·ize** (*BrE also* **-ise**) /ˈfaɪnəlaɪz/ *verb* ~ **sth** to complete the last part of a plan, trip, project, etc: *to finalize your plans/arrangements* ◇ *They met to finalize the terms of the treaty.* ▶ **fi·nal·iza·tion, -isa·tion** /ˌfaɪnəlaɪˈzeɪʃn; *NAmE* -ləˈz-/ *noun* [U]

**fi·nal·ly** ❶ **A2** ⓢ /ˈfaɪnəli/ *adv.* **1** **A2** after a long time, especially when there has been some difficulty or delay SYN **eventually**: *The performance finally started half an hour late.* ◇ *The law was finally passed in May 2019.* ◇ *Two years of hard work and waiting were finally over.* ◇ *Here, finally, we come to the heart of the problem.* ◇ *Finally ready, they all set off.* **2 A2** used to introduce the last in a list of things SYN **lastly**: *And finally, I would like to thank you all for coming here today.* ⊃ LANGUAGE BANK at FIRST, PROCESS¹ **3 A2** in a way that ends all discussion about sth: *The matter was not finally settled until later.*

**fi·nance** ❶ **B2** /ˈfaɪnæns, faɪˈnæns, fəˈn-/ *noun, verb*
■ *noun* **1** **B2** (*especially BrE*) (*NAmE usually* **fi·nan·cing**) [U] money used to run a business, an activity or a project: *The project will only go ahead if they can raise the necessary finance.* ◇ ~ **for sth** *Finance for education comes from tax-payers.* **2 B2** [U] the activity of managing money, especially by a government or commercial organization: *the Minister of Finance* ◇ *the finance director/department/committee* ◇ *a diploma in banking and finance* ◇ *an expert in public/personal/corporate finance* **3** **B2 finances** [pl.] the money available to a person, an organization or a country; the way this money is managed: *government/public/personal finances* ◇ *They were unable to manage their finances.* ◇ *Moving house put a severe strain on our finances.* ⊃ WORDFINDER NOTE at MONEY
■ *verb* **B2** ~ **sth** to provide money for a project SYN **fund**: *He took a job to finance his stay in Germany.* ◇ *The building project will be financed by the government.*

**'finance company** (*BrE also* **'finance house**) *noun* a company that lends money to people or businesses

**fi·nan·cial** ❶ **B1** Ⓦ /faɪˈnænʃl, fəˈn-/ *adj.* [usually before noun] **1** **B1** connected with money and finance: *the world's major financial markets/institutions* ◇ *financial services* ◇ *financial support/aid/assistance* ◇ *an independent financial adviser* ◇ *The current financial crisis is global.* ⊃ SYNONYMS at ECONOMIC **2** (*AustralE, NZE, informal*) having money ▶ **fi·nan·cial·ly** /-ʃəli/ *adv.*: *She is still financially dependent on her parents.* ◇ *Financially, I'm much better off than before.* ◇ *Such projects are not financially viable without government funding.*

**fi,nancial 'aid** *noun* [U] (*NAmE*) money that is given or lent to students at a university or college who cannot pay the full cost of their education: *to apply for financial aid*

**fi·nan·cials** /faɪˈnænʃlz, fəˈn-/ *noun* [pl.] **1** the money situation of an organization or individual: *Reviewing the financials of a company will provide performance evaluations.* **2** shares in companies that deal in money: *The fund is invested in energy companies, financials and consumer stocks.*

**the Fi,nancial 'Times ˌindex** *noun* = FTSE INDEX™

**fi,nancial 'year** (*BrE*) (*BrE also* **ˈtax year**) (*NAmE* **ˈfiscal year**) *noun* [usually sing.] a period of twelve months over which the accounts and taxes of a company or a person are calculated. The British financial year begins on 6 April: *the current financial year*

**fi·nan·cier** /faɪˈnænsɪə(r), fəˈn-; *NAmE* ˌfɪnənˈsɪr/ *noun* a person who manages or lends large amounts of money for or to businesses or governments

**fi·nan·cing** /ˈfaɪnænsɪŋ, faɪˈnænsɪŋ, fəˈn-/ *noun* [U] (*NAmE*) = FINANCE: *The project will only go ahead if they can raise the necessary financing.*

**finch** /fɪntʃ/ *noun* (often in compounds) a small bird with a short BEAK. There are several types of finch. ⊃ see also CHAFFINCH, GOLDFINCH ⊃ VISUAL VOCAB page V2

**find** ❶ **A1** ⓢ /faɪnd/ *verb, noun*
■ *verb* (**found**, **found** /faʊnd/)
• BY CHANCE **1** **A1** [T] to discover sb/sth unexpectedly or by chance: ~ **sb/sth** *Look what I've found!* ◇ *We've found a great new restaurant near the office.* ◇ ~ **sb/sth + adj.** *A whale was found washed up on the shore.*
• BY SEARCHING **2** **A1** [T] to get back sth/sb that was lost after searching for it/them: ~ **sb/sth** *I can't find my keys.* ◇ ~ **sth for sb** *Can you find my bag for me?* ◇ ~ **sb sth** *Can you find me my bag?* ◇ ~ **sb/sth + adj.** *The child was eventually found safe and well.*
• BY STUDYING/THINKING **3** **A1** [T] to discover sth/sb by searching, studying or thinking carefully: ~ **sth/sb** *They found no evidence to support this claim.* ◇ *We found a way out.* ◇ *to find a solution/an answer* ◇ *to find work/a job* ◇ *Have they found anyone to replace her yet?* ◇ ~ **sth for sb** *I'll find that information for you.* ◇ ~ **sb sth** *I'll find you that information.*
• BY EXPERIENCE/TESTING **4** **A2** [T] to discover that sth is true after you have tried it, tested it or experienced it: ~ **(that)** … *I find (that) it pays to be honest.* ◇ *A study found that green tea could be beneficial.* ◇ ~ **sb/sth + adj./noun** *We found the beds very comfortable.* ◇ ~ **sb/sth to be/do sth** *They found him to be charming.* ◇ *Her blood was found to contain poison.* ◇ **it is found that** … *It was found that her blood contained poison.*
• HAVE OPINION/FEELING **5** **A2** [T] to have a particular feeling or opinion about sth: ~ **sth + adj.** *You may find it hard to accept your illness.* ◇ *You may find your illness hard to accept.* ◇ *I found the book very interesting.* ◇ ~ **sth + noun** *She finds it a strain to meet new people.* ⊃ SYNONYMS at REGARD
• EXIST/GROW **6** **B1** [T, often passive] used to say that sth exists, grows, etc. somewhere: **be found + adv./prep.** *These flowers are found only in Africa.* ◇ ~ **sth/sb + adv./prep.** *You find this style of architecture all over the town.*
• IN UNEXPECTED SITUATIONS **7** **B1** [T] to discover sb/sth/yourself doing sth or in a particular situation, especially when this is unexpected: ~ **sb/sth/yourself + adv./prep.** *She woke up and found herself in a hospital bed.* ◇ ~ **sb/sth/yourself + adj.** *We came home and found him asleep on the sofa.* ◇ ~ **sb/sth/yourself doing sth** *He looked up to find her watching him.* ◇ ~ **(that)** … *She was surprised to find that everyone had left.*
• HAVE/MAKE AVAILABLE **8** [T] ~ **sth** to have sth available so that you can use it: *I keep meaning to write, but never seem to find (the) time.* ◇ *How are we going to find £10 000 for a car?* **9** [T] ~ **sth** to show a quality in yourself, usually with an effort: *I found the courage to speak.*
• REACH **10** [T] ~ **sth/sb** (of things) to arrive at sth naturally; to reach sth/sb: *Water will always find its own level.* ◇ *Most of the money finds its way to the people who need it.* ◇ *The criticism found its mark* (= had the effect intended).

- **IN COURT 11** [T, I] (*formal*) to make a particular decision in a court case: *~ sb + adj. The jury found him guilty.* ◊ *How do you find the accused?* ◊ *~ in sb's favour The court found in her favour.*

**IDM** **all ˈfound** (*old-fashioned*, *BrE*) with free food and accommodation in addition to your wages **find fault (with sb/sth)** to look for and discover mistakes in sb/sth; to complain about sb/sth **find your ˈfeet** to become able to act independently and with confidence: *I only recently joined the firm so I'm still finding my feet.* **find it in your heart/yourself to do sth** (*literary*) to be able or willing to do sth: *Can you find it in your heart to forgive her?* ◊ *He couldn't find it in himself to trust anyone again.* **find your ˈvoice/ˈtongue** to be able to speak or express your opinion **find your way (to …)** to discover the right route (to a place): *I hope you can find your way home.* **find your/its ˈway (to/into …)** to come to a place or a situation by chance or without intending to: *He eventually found his way into acting.* **take sb as you ˈfind them** to accept sb as they are without expecting them to behave in a special way or have special qualities ⊃ more at MATCH *n*., NOWHERE

**PHR V** **ˈfind for/against sb** [no passive] (*law*) to make a decision in favour of/against sb in a court case: *The jury found for the defendant.* **find ˈout (about sth/sb) | ˌfind ˈout sth (about sth/sb)** 🔊 **A1** to get some information about sth/sb by asking, reading, etc: *She'd been seeing the boy for a while, but didn't want her parents to find out.* ◊ *I haven't found anything out about him yet.* ◊ *Visit our website to find out more.* ◊ **find out what, when, etc …** *Can you find out what time the meeting starts?* ◊ **find out that …** *We found out later that we had been at the same school.* **ˌfind sb ˈout** to discover that sb has done sth wrong: *He had been cheating the taxman but it was years before he was found out.*

- *noun* a thing or person that has been found, especially one that is interesting, valuable or useful; the act of finding a thing or person like this: *an important archaeological find* ◊ *Our new babysitter is a real find.* ◊ *He made his most spectacular finds in the Valley of the Kings.*

**find·er** /ˈfaɪndə(r)/ *noun* a person who finds sth ⊃ see also VIEWFINDER

**IDM** **ˌfinders ˈkeepers** (*saying*) (often used by children) anyone who finds sth has a right to keep it

**fin de siècle** /ˌfæ̃ də ˈsjeklə/ *adj.* (*from French*) typical of the end of the 19th century, especially of its art, literature and attitudes

**find·ing** 🅞 **B2** 🔊 /ˈfaɪndɪŋ/ *noun* **1** 🔊 **B2** [usually pl.] information that is discovered as the result of research into sth: *Our research findings indicate that pregnant women benefit from this treatment.* ◊ *This result confirms the findings of many previous studies.* ◊ *to report/present/publish your findings* **2** (*law*) a decision made by the judge or jury in a court case ⊃ see also FACT-FINDING, FAULT-FINDING

**fine** 🅞 **A1** /faɪn/ *adj., adv., noun, verb*

- *adj.* (**fin·er**, **fin·est**)
- **VERY WELL 1** 🔊 **A1** (of a person) in good health: *'How are you?' 'Fine, thanks.'* ◊ *I was feeling fine when I got up this morning.* ⊃ SYNONYMS at WELL
- **VERY GOOD 2** 🔊 **A2** [usually before noun] of high quality; good: *a very fine performance* ◊ *fine clothes/wines/workmanship* ◊ *a particularly fine example of Saxon architecture* ◊ *Jim has made a fine job of the garden.* ◊ *people who enjoy the finer things in life* (= for example art, good food, etc.) ◊ *It was his finest hour* (= most successful period) *as manager of the England team.* ◊ *This movie features some of her finest work.*
- **ACCEPTABLE/GOOD ENOUGH 3** 🔊 **A2** (also used as an exclamation) used to tell sb that an action, a suggestion or a decision is acceptable: *'I'll leave this here, OK?' 'Fine.'* ◊ **~ by/with sb** *Bob wants to know if he can come too.' 'That's fine by me.'* ◊ **~ with sth** *She has been virtually ignoring me but I'm fine with that.* **4** 🔊 **A2** used to say you are satisfied with sth: *Don't worry. Your speech was fine.* ◊ *You go on without me. I'll be fine.* ◊ *'Can I get you another drink?' 'No, thanks. I'm fine.'* ◊ *Never mind, Jake. Everything will be just fine.*

587

- **WEATHER 5** 🔊 **B1** (especially *BrE*) bright and not raining: *a fine day/evening* ◊ *I hope it stays fine for the picnic.*
- **ATTRACTIVE 6** 🔊 **B1** [usually before noun] pleasant to look at: *a fine view* ◊ *a fine-looking woman* ◊ *a fine figure of a man*
- **WITH SMALL GRAINS 7** 🔊 **B2** made of very small grains: *fine sand* ◊ *Use a finer piece of sandpaper to finish.* **OPP** coarse
- **ATTRACTIVE 8** [usually before noun] attractive and small or thin: *fine bone china* ◊ *She has inherited her mother's fine features* (= a small nose, mouth, etc.). **SYN** delicate
- **VERY THIN 9** very thin or narrow; made of very thin or narrow wires or THREADS: *fine blond hair* ◊ *a fine thread* ◊ *a brush with a fine tip* ◊ *a fine sieve/mesh*
- **DETAIL/DISTINCTIONS 10** [usually before noun] difficult to see or describe **SYN** subtle: *You really need a magnifying glass to appreciate all the fine detail.* ◊ *There's no need to make such fine distinctions.* ◊ *There's a fine line between love and hate* (= it is easy for one to become the other). ◊ *The finer points of the plot are pretty subtle.*
- **PERSON 11** [only before noun] that you have a lot of respect for: *He was a fine man.*
- **WORDS/SPEECHES 12** sounding important and impressive but unlikely to have any effect: *His speech was full of fine words which meant nothing.*
- **METALS 13** (*specialist*) containing only a particular metal and no other substances that reduce the quality: *fine gold*

**IDM** **not to put too fine a ˈpoint on it** used to emphasize sth that is expressed clearly and directly, especially a criticism: *Not to put too fine a point on it, I think you are lying.* ⊃ more at CHANCE *n.*, FETTLE, LINE *n.*

- *adv.* (*informal*) in a way that is acceptable or good enough: *Keep going like that—you're doing fine.* ◊ *Things were going fine until you showed up.* ◊ *That arrangement suits me fine.* ◊ (*BrE*) *An omelette will do me fine* (= will be enough for me).

**IDM** **cut it/things ˈfine** (*informal*) to leave yourself just enough time to do sth: *If we don't leave till after lunch we'll be cutting it very fine.*

- *noun* 🔊 + 🔊 **C1** a sum of money that must be paid as punishment for breaking a law or rule: *a parking fine* ◊ *Offenders will be liable to a heavy fine* (= one that costs a lot of money). ◊ *She has already paid over $2000 in fines.* ⊃ SYNONYMS at RATE
- *verb* 🔊 + 🔊 **C1** [often passive] to make sb pay money as an official punishment: **be fined (for sth/for doing sth) | be fined for (doing) sth** *She was fined for speeding.* ◊ **be fined sth (for sth/for doing sth)** *The company was fined £20000 for breaching safety regulations.*

**ˌfine ˈart** *noun* [U] (also **ˌfine ˈarts** [pl.]) forms of art, especially painting, drawing and sculpture, that are created to be beautiful rather than useful

**IDM** **get sth down to a ˌfine ˈart** (*informal*) to learn to do sth well and efficiently: *I spend so much time travelling that I've got packing down to a fine art.*

**fine·ly** /ˈfaɪnli/ *adv.* **1** into very small grains or pieces: *finely chopped herbs* **2** in a beautiful or impressive way: *a finely furnished room* **3** in a very careful or exact way: *a finely tuned engine* ◊ *The match was finely balanced throughout.*

**fine·ness** /ˈfaɪnnəs/ *noun* [U] **1** the quality of being made of thin THREADS or lines very close together: *fineness of detail* **2** (*specialist*) the quality of sth: *the fineness of the gold*

**the ˌfine ˈprint** (*NAmE*) (especially *BrE* **the ˈsmall print**) *noun* [U] the important details of an agreement or a legal document that are usually printed in small type and are therefore easy to miss

**fin·ery** /ˈfaɪnəri/ *noun* [U] (*formal*) brightly coloured and beautiful clothes and jewellery, especially those that are worn for a special occasion

**fi·nesse** /fɪˈnes/ *noun, verb*

- *noun* [U] **1** great skill in dealing with people or situations, especially in a light and careful way **2** great skill and style in doing sth
- *verb* **1 ~ sth** (especially *NAmE*) to deal with sth in a way that is clever but slightly dishonest: *to finesse a deal* **2 ~ sth** to do sth with a lot of skill or style

# finesse

# fine-tooth comb

**fine-tooth 'comb** (*also* **fine-toothed 'comb**) *noun* a COMB in which the pointed parts are thin and very close together

**IDM** **go over/through sth with a fine-tooth/fine-toothed comb** to examine or search sth very carefully

**fine-'tune** *verb* ~ **sth** to make very small changes to sth so that it is as good as it can possibly be ▶ **fine-'tuning** *noun* [U]: *The system is set up but it needs some fine-tuning.*

**f-ing** /'efɪŋ/ *adj.* [only before noun] (*taboo, slang*) = EFFING

**fin·ger** /'fɪŋgə(r)/ *noun, verb*
■ *noun* **1** one of the four long thin parts that stick out from the hand (or five, if the THUMB is included): *She ran her fingers through her hair.* ◇ *Hold the material between finger and thumb.* ◇ *He was about to speak but she raised a finger to her lips.* ⊃ see also BUTTERFINGERS, FIRST FINGER, FOREFINGER, GREEN FINGERS, INDEX FINGER, LITTLE FINGER, MIDDLE FINGER, RING FINGER **2** **-fingered** (in adjectives) having the type of fingers mentioned; having or using the number of fingers mentioned: *long-fingered* ◇ *nimble-fingered* ◇ *a four-fingered chord* ⊃ see also LIGHT-FINGERED **3** the part of a glove that covers the finger **4** a long narrow piece of bread, cake, land, etc: *chocolate fingers* ◇ **-of sth** *a finger of toast* ⊃ see also FISH FINGER
**IDM** **the ,finger of 'blame/sus'picion** if **the finger of blame/suspicion** points or is pointed at sb, they are suspected of having committed a crime, being responsible for sth, etc. **get, pull, etc. your 'finger out** (*BrE, informal*) used to tell sb to start doing some work or making an effort: *You're going to have to pull your finger out if you want to pass this exam.* **give sb the 'finger** (*especially NAmE, informal*) to raise your middle finger in the air with the back part of your hand facing sb, done to be rude to sb or to show them that you are angry **have a finger in every 'pie** (*informal*) to be involved in a lot of different activities and have influence over them, especially when other people think that this is annoying **have, etc. your 'fingers in the till** (*BrE, informal*) to be stealing money from the place where you work **have/keep your finger on the 'pulse (of sth)** to always be aware of the most recent developments in a particular situation **lay a 'finger on sb** (usually used in negative sentences) to touch sb with the intention of hurting them physically: *I never laid a finger on her.* **(not) put your finger on sth** to (not) be able to identify what is wrong or different about a particular situation: *There was something odd about him but I couldn't put my finger on it.* **put/stick two 'fingers up at sb** (*BrE, informal*) to form the shape of a V with the two fingers nearest your THUMB and raise your hand in the air with the back part of it facing sb, done to be rude to them or to show them that you are angry ⊃ see also V-SIGN **work your fingers to the 'bone** to work very hard ⊃ more at BURN *v.*, COUNT *v.*, CROSS *v.*, LIFT *v.*, POINT *v.*, SLIP *v.*, SNAP *v.*, STICKY *adj.*, THUMB *n.*
■ *verb* **1** ~ **sth** to touch or feel sth with your fingers: *Gary sat fingering his beard, saying nothing.* **2** ~ **sb (for sth)** | ~ **sb (as sth)** (*informal, especially NAmE*) to accuse sb of doing sth illegal and tell the police about it: *Who fingered him for the burglaries?*

**fin·ger·board** /'fɪŋgəbɔːd; *NAmE* -gərbɔːrd/ *noun* a flat area on the neck of a musical instrument such as a guitar or VIOLIN, against which the strings are pressed to play different notes

**'finger bowl** *noun* a small bowl of water for washing your fingers during a meal

**'finger food** *noun* [U, C] pieces of food that you can easily eat with your fingers

**fin·ger·ing** /'fɪŋgərɪŋ/ *noun* [U, C] the positions in which you put your fingers when playing a musical instrument

**fin·ger·less** /'fɪŋgələs; *NAmE* -gərl-/ *adj.* [usually before noun] (especially of gloves) without fingers

**fin·ger·mark** /'fɪŋgəmɑːk; *NAmE* -gərmɑːrk/ *noun* [usually pl.] (*especially BrE*) a mark made by a finger, for example on a clean surface

**fin·ger·nail** /'fɪŋgəneɪl; *NAmE* -gərn-/ *noun* the thin hard layer that covers the outer tip of each finger

**'finger-pointing** *noun* [U] the act of accusing sb of doing sth: *There was a lot of finger-pointing over who was to blame for the mistake.* ⊃ see also POINT A/THE FINGER (AT SB) at POINT *verb*

**fin·ger·print** /'fɪŋgəprɪnt; *NAmE* -gərp-/ *noun* a mark made by the pattern of lines on the tip of a person's finger, often used by the police to identify criminals ⊃ SYNONYMS at MARK ⊃ see also GENETIC FINGERPRINT ▶ **fin·ger·print** *verb*

**fin·ger·print·ing** /'fɪŋgəprɪntɪŋ; *NAmE* -gərp-/ *noun* [U] the practice of recording sb's fingerprints, often used by the police to identify criminals ⊃ see also DNA FINGERPRINTING, GENETIC FINGERPRINTING

**fin·ger·tip** /'fɪŋgətɪp; *NAmE* -gərt-/ *noun* (usually *pl.*) the end of the finger that is furthest from the hand
**IDM** **have sth at your 'fingertips** to have the information, knowledge, etc. that is needed in a particular situation and be able to find it easily and use it quickly **to your 'fingertips** (*BrE*) in every way: *She's a perfectionist to her fingertips.*

**fin·ial** /'fɪniəl/ *noun* **1** (*architecture*) a part that decorates the top of a roof, wall, etc. **2** a part that fits on the end of a curtain POLE and decorates it

**fin·icky** /'fɪnɪki/ *adj.* **1** (*disapproving*) too worried about what you eat, wear, etc.; disliking many things **SYN** **fussy**: *a finicky eater* **2** needing great care and attention to detail **SYN** **fiddly**: *It's a very finicky job.*

**fin·ish** /'fɪnɪʃ/ *verb, noun*
■ *verb* **1** [T, I] to stop doing sth or making sth because it is complete: ~ **(sth)** *Haven't you finished your homework yet?* ◇ *She finished law school last year.* ◇ *I thought you'd never finish!* ◇ ~ **what ...** *Let me just finish what I'm doing.* ◇ ~ **doing sth** *Be quiet! He hasn't finished speaking.* ◇ ~ **by doing sth** *He finished by telling us about his trip to Spain.* ◇ **+ speech** *'And that was all,' she finished.* **2** [I, T] to come to an end; to bring sth to an end: *The play finished at 10.30.* ◇ ~ **with sth** *The symphony finishes with a flourish.* ◇ ~ **sth** *A cup of coffee finished the meal perfectly.* **3** [T] to eat, drink or use what remains of sth: ~ **sth (off)** *He finished off his drink with one large gulp.* ◇ ~ **sth up** *We might as well finish up the cake.* **4** [I, T] to be in a particular state or position at the end of a race or a competition: **+ adj.** *She was delighted to finish second.* ◇ **+ adv./prep.** *He finished 12 seconds outside the world record.* ◇ ~ **sth + adv./prep.** *The team finished the season in ninth position.* ◇ ~ **sth + adj.** *The dollar finished the day slightly down.* **5** [T] ~ **sb (off)** (*informal*) to make sb so tired or impatient that they cannot do any more: ~ **sb off** *Climbing that hill really finished me off.*
**PHRV** **finish sb/sth↔'off** (*informal*) to destroy sb/sth, especially sb/sth that is badly injured or damaged: *The hunter moved in to finish the animal off.* **finish sth↔'off | finish 'off** to do the last part of sth; to make sth end by doing one last thing: *I need about an hour to finish off this report.* ◇ *He finished off by welcoming new arrivals to the school.* **finish 'up ...** (*BrE*) to be in a particular state or at a particular place after a series of events: **+ adj.** *If you're not careful, you could finish up seriously ill.* **'finish with sb 1** (*BrE*) to end a relationship with sb: *She finished with her boyfriend last week.* **2** to stop dealing with a person: *He'll regret he ever said it once I've finished with him.* **'finish with sth 1** to no longer need to use sth: *When you've finished with the book, can I see it?* **2** (*BrE, informal*) to stop doing sth: *I've finished with gambling.* **finish (up) with sth** to have sth at the end: *We had a five-course lunch and finished up with coffee and mints.* ◇ *To finish with, we'll listen to a few songs.*
■ *noun* **1** [C, usually sing.] the last part or the end of sth: *It was a close finish as they had predicted.* ◇ ~ **to sth** *a dramatic finish to the race* ◇ *The story was a lie from start to finish.* ◇ **to the~** *I want to see the job through to the finish.* ◇ **at the~** *Several runners needed medical attention at the finish.* ⊃ see also GRANDSTAND FINISH, PHOTO FINISH **2** [C, usually sing.] (usually in compounds) the position in

which a person or team finishes a competition: *a second-/third-/fourth-place finish* **3** [C, U] the last layer of paint, POLISH, etc. that is put onto the surface of sth; the condition of the surface: *a gloss/matt finish* **4** [C, U] the final details that are added to sth to make it complete: *The bows will give a feminine finish to the curtains.* IDM see FIGHT *n.*

▼ **EXPRESS YOURSELF**
**Wrapping up a discussion**
In a formal meeting or conference, you may have to bring the session to a close. Here are some ways to get people to stop speaking:
- *I'm afraid time is running out/we're running out of time,* so we'll have to make this the final question.
- *We've only got a couple of minutes left,* so can we summarize what we've agreed?
- *I'd like to close the session with a few final remarks …*
- *We'll have to leave it there,* but thank you all very much for your input.
- *Well, that's all we have time for today,* but we'll meet again on Tuesday.
- *I'd like to thank you all for coming* and for a very productive meeting.

**fin·ished** /ˈfɪnɪʃt/ *adj.* **1** [not before noun] no longer doing sth or dealing with sb/sth: *I won't be finished for another hour.* ◊ ~ **with sb/sth** *I'm not finished with you yet.* **2** [not before noun] no longer powerful, effective or able to continue: *If the newspapers find out, he's finished in politics.* ◊ *Their marriage was finished.* **3** [usually before noun] fully completed, especially in a particular way: *a beautifully finished suit* ◊ *the finished product/article*

**fin·ish·er** /ˈfɪnɪʃə(r)/ *noun* a person or an animal that finishes a race, etc.

**ˈfin·ish·ing line** (*BrE*) (*NAmE* **ˈfinish line**) *noun* the line across a sports track, etc. that marks the end of a race: *The two horses crossed the finishing line together.*

**ˈfin·ish·ing school** *noun* a private school where young women from rich families are taught how to behave in fashionable society

**ˈfinishing ˈtouch** *noun* [usually pl.] a final detail or action that completes a piece of work and makes it even better: *He put the finishing touches to his painting.*

**fi·nite** /ˈfaɪnaɪt/ *adj.* **1** having a definite limit or fixed size: *a finite number of possibilities* ◊ *The world's resources are finite.* OPP **infinite 2** (*grammar*) a **finite** verb form or clause shows a particular tense, PERSON and NUMBER: '*Am*', '*is*', '*are*', '*was*' and '*were*' are the finite forms of '*be*'; '*being*' and '*been*' are the non-finite forms. OPP **non-finite**

**fink** /fɪŋk/ *noun* (*especially NAmE, informal*) an unpleasant person

**fin·tech** /ˈfɪntek/ *noun* [U] computer programs and other technology used to provide BANKING and financial services: *fintech startups/entrepreneurs*

**fiord** = FJORD

**FIR** /ˌef aɪ ˈɑː(r)/ *noun* (*IndE*) a document prepared by the police on first receiving information about a crime (the abbreviation for 'first information report')

**fir** /fɜː(r)/ (*also* **ˈfir tree**) *noun* an EVERGREEN forest tree with leaves like needles ⊃ VISUAL VOCAB page V6

**ˈfir cone** (*BrE*) (*also* **cone** *NAmE, BrE*) *noun* the hard fruit of the fir tree ⊃ VISUAL VOCAB page V6

**fire** ⓪ A1 /ˈfaɪə(r)/ *noun, verb*
■ *noun*
- STH BURNING **1** A1 [U] the flames, light and heat, and often smoke, that are produced when sth burns: *Most animals are afraid of fire.* **2** A1 [U, C] flames that are out of control and destroy buildings, trees, etc: *Several youths had set fire to the police car* (= had made it start burning). ◊ **on ~** *The car was on fire.* ◊ *A candle had set the curtains on fire.* ◊ *These thatched roofs frequently catch fire* (= start to burn). ◊ *forest fires* ◊ *Five people died in a house fire.* ◊ *Fires were breaking out everywhere.* ◊ *The warehouse was destroyed by fire.* ◊ *It took two hours to put out the fire*

589 **fire alarm**

(= stop it burning). ◊ *Fire crews arrived and began to fight the flames.* ⊃ see also BUSH FIRE
- FOR HEATING/COOKING **3** A1 [C] a pile of burning fuel, such as wood or coal, used for cooking food or heating a room: *They cook on an open fire.* ◊ *a log/coal/wood fire* ◊ *Sam had lit a fire to welcome us home.* ◊ *to make/build a fire* ◊ *Come and get warm by the fire.* ⊃ see also BONFIRE, CAMPFIRE **4** B1 [C] (*especially BrE*) a piece of equipment for heating a room: *a gas/an electric fire* ◊ *Shall I put the fire on?* ⊃ see also HEATER
- FROM GUNS **5** B2 [U] shots from guns: *The gunmen opened fire on* (= started shooting at) *the police.* ◊ **under~** *Their vehicle came under fire* (= was being shot at). ◊ *He was hit by enemy fire.* ◊ *a burst of machine-gun fire* ◊ *to return fire* (= to fire back at sb who is shooting at you) ◊ *Protesters exchanged fire with the guards* (= they shot at each other). ◊ *A young girl was in the line of fire* (= between the person shooting and what he/she was shooting at). ⊃ see also FRIENDLY FIRE
- CRITICISM **6** [U] strong criticism: *She directed her fire against the new education policy.* ◊ **under~** *The health minister has come under fire from all sides.*
- ANGER/ENTHUSIASM **7** [U] very strong emotion, especially anger or enthusiasm: *Her eyes were full of fire.* ◊ *He returned with a new kind of fire in his belly,* determined to win.
IDM **hang/hold ˈfire** to delay or be delayed in taking action: *The project had hung fire for several years for lack of funds.* **on ˈfire** giving you a painful burning feeling: *He couldn't breathe. His chest was on fire.* **play with ˈfire** to act in a way that is not sensible and take dangerous risks ⊃ more at BALL *n.*, BAPTISM, DRAW *v.*, FIGHT *v.*, FRYING PAN, HOUSE *n.*, IRON *n.*, SMOKE *n.*, WORLD
■ *verb*
- SHOOT **1** B1 [I, T] to shoot bullets, etc. from a gun or other weapon: *The officer ordered his men to fire.* ◊ **~on sb/sth** *Soldiers fired on the crowd.* ◊ **~sth** *to fire missiles/rockets/bullets* ◊ *They ran away as soon as the first shot was fired.* ◊ **~(sth) into sth** *He fired the gun into the air.* ◊ **~(sth) at sb/sth** *She fired an arrow at the target.* ◊ *Missiles were fired at the enemy.* **2** B1 [I, T] (of a gun) to shoot bullets out: *We heard the sound of guns firing.* ◊ **~sth** *A starter's pistol fires only blanks.*
- FROM JOB **3** B1 [T] to force sb to leave their job SYN **sack**: **~sb** *We had to fire him for dishonesty.* ◊ *He was responsible for hiring and firing staff.* ◊ **~sb from sth** *She got fired from her first job.*
- MAKE SB ENTHUSIASTIC **4** [T] to make sb feel very excited about sth or interested in sth: **~sb with sth** *The talk had fired her with enthusiasm for the project.* ◊ **~sth** *The stories fired his imagination.*
- OF ENGINE **5** [I] when an engine **fires**, an electrical SPARK is produced that makes the fuel burn and the engine start to work
- -FIRED **6** (in adjectives) using the fuel mentioned in order to operate: *gas-fired central heating*
- CLAY OBJECTS **7** [T] **~sth** to heat a CLAY object to make it hard and strong: *to fire pottery* ◊ *to fire bricks in a kiln*
IDM **fire ˈquestions, ˈinsults, etc. at sb** to ask sb a lot of questions one after another or make a lot of comments very quickly: *The room was full of journalists, all firing questions at them.* ⊃ more at CYLINDER
PHR V **fire aˈway** (*informal*) used to tell sb to begin to speak or ask a question: '*I've got a few questions.*' '*OK then, fire away.*' **fire sth↔ˈoff 1** to shoot a bullet from a gun: *They fired off a volley of shots.* **2** to write or say sth to sb very quickly, often when you are angry: *He fired off a letter of complaint.* ◊ *She spent an hour firing off emails to all concerned.* **fire sb↔ˈup** to make sb excited or interested in sth: *She's all fired up about her new job.* **fire sth↔ˈup** (*informal*) to start a machine, piece of equipment, computer program, etc: *We need to fire up one of the generators.* ◊ *Let me fire up another window* (= on the computer screen).

**ˈfire alarm** *noun* **1** a bell or other device that gives people warning of a fire in a building: *Who set off the fire alarm?*

# firearm

**2** an occasion when a fire alarm goes off: *We had a fire alarm at work this morning.*

**fire·arm** ⚑+ C1 /ˈfaɪərɑːm; NAmE -ɑːrm/ noun (*formal*) a gun that can be carried: *The police were issued with firearms.*

**fire·ball** /ˈfaɪəbɔːl; NAmE -ərb-/ noun a bright ball of fire, especially one at the centre of an explosion

**fire·bomb** /ˈfaɪəbɒm; NAmE -ərbɑːm/ noun a bomb that makes a fire start burning after it explodes ▶ **fire·bomb** *verb* ~ *sth*

**fire·brand** /ˈfaɪəbrænd; NAmE -ərb-/ noun a person who is always encouraging other people to take strong political action, often causing trouble

**fire·break** /ˈfaɪəbreɪk; NAmE -ərb-/ noun a thing that stops a fire from spreading, for example a special door or a piece of land in a forest that has been cleared of trees ⊃ see also FIRE LINE

**fire brigade** (*also* ˈfire service) (*both BrE*) (*NAmE* ˈfire department, ˈfire company) noun [C + sing. / pl. v.] an organization of people who are trained and employed to put out fires and to rescue people from fires; the people who belong to this organization: *to call out the fire brigade* ◊ *The fire brigade were there in minutes.*

**fire·bug** /ˈfaɪəbʌɡ; NAmE -ərb-/ noun (*informal*) a person who deliberately starts fires SYN arsonist

**ˈfire chief** noun **1** a person who is in charge of a group of FIREFIGHTERS (= people whose job is to put out fires) **2** (*NAmE*) a person who is in charge of a FIRE DEPARTMENT (= the organization of people whose job is to put out fires)

**fire·crack·er** /ˈfaɪəkrækə(r); NAmE -ərk-/ noun a small FIREWORK that explodes with a loud noise

**ˈfire de·part·ment** (*also* ˈfire company) (*both NAmE*) (*BrE* ˈfire brigade, ˈfire service) noun an organization of people who are trained and employed to put out fires and to rescue people from fires; the people who belong to this organization

**ˈfire door** noun a heavy door that is used to prevent a fire from spreading in a building

**ˈfire drill** (*BrE also* ˈfire practice) noun [C, U] a practice of what people must do in order to escape safely from a fire in a building

**ˈfire-eater** noun a person who pretends to eat fire, especially to entertain people

**ˈfire engine** (*NAmE also* ˈfire truck) noun a special vehicle that carries equipment for fighting large fires

**ˈfire escape** noun metal stairs or a LADDER on the outside of a building that people can use to escape from a fire

**ˈfire extinguisher** (*also* ex·tin·guish·er) noun a metal container with water or chemicals inside for putting out small fires

**fire·fight** /ˈfaɪəfaɪt; NAmE -ərf-/ noun (*specialist*) a battle where guns are used, involving soldiers or the police

**fire·fight·er** ⚑+ B2 /ˈfaɪəfaɪtə(r); NAmE -ərf-/ noun a person whose job is to put out fires: *Firefighters were called to a house in Summertown.* ⊃ see also FIREMAN

**fire·fight·ing** /ˈfaɪəfaɪtɪŋ; NAmE -ərf-/ noun [U] **1** the job or activity of putting out fires: *firefighting equipment/ vehicles* **2** (*in business*) the practice of dealing with problems as they occur rather than planning carefully to avoid them

**fire·fly** /ˈfaɪəflaɪ; NAmE -ərf-/ noun (*pl.* -**ies**) (*NAmE also* ˈlightning bug) a flying insect with a tail that shines in the dark

**fire·guard** /ˈfaɪəɡɑːd; NAmE -ərɡɑːrd/ (*NAmE usually* ˈfire screen) noun a metal frame that is put in front of a fire in a room to prevent people from burning themselves

**ˈfire hose** noun a long tube that is used for directing water onto fires

**fire·house** /ˈfaɪəhaʊs; NAmE -ərh-/ noun (*US*) a FIRE STATION in a small town

**ˈfire hydrant** (*also* hy·drant) noun a pipe in the street through which water can be sent using a PUMP in order to put out fires or to clean the streets

**ˈfire-light** /ˈfaɪəlaɪt; NAmE -ərl-/ noun [U] the light that comes from a fire in a room

**ˈfire-light·er** /ˈfaɪəlaɪtə(r); NAmE -ərl-/ (*BrE*) (*NAmE* ˈfire start·er) noun [C, U] a block of material that burns easily and is used to help start a coal or wood fire

**ˈfire line** noun (*NAmE*) a piece of land that has been cleared in order to stop a fire from spreading ⊃ see also FIREBREAK

**fire·man** /ˈfaɪəmən; NAmE -ərm-/ noun (*pl.* -**men** /-mən/) a person, usually a man, whose job is to put out fires ⊃ see also FIREFIGHTER ⊃ note at GENDER

**fire·place** /ˈfaɪəpleɪs; NAmE -ərp-/ noun an open space for a fire in the wall of a room

**fire·power** /ˈfaɪəpaʊə(r); NAmE -ərp-/ noun [U] the number and size of guns that an army, a ship, etc. has available: (*figurative*) *The company has enormous financial firepower.*

**ˈfire practice** noun [C, U] (*BrE*) = FIRE DRILL

**fire·proof** /ˈfaɪəpruːf; NAmE -ərp-/ adj. able to resist great heat without burning or being badly damaged: *a fireproof door* ◊ *a fireproof dish* (= that can be heated in an oven)

**ˈfire-raiser** noun (*BrE*) a person who starts a fire deliberately SYN arsonist ▶ **ˈfire-raising** noun [U]

**fire-retard·ant** /ˈfaɪə rɪtɑːdənt; NAmE -ər rɪtɑːrd-/ (*also* ˈflame-retardant) adj. [usually before noun] that makes a fire burn more slowly

**ˈfire sale** noun **1** a sale at low prices of things that a company or person owns, usually in order to pay debts: *The company was forced to have a fire sale of its assets.* **2** a sale of goods at low prices because they have been damaged by a fire or because they cannot be stored after a fire

**ˈfire screen** noun **1** (*NAmE*) = FIREGUARD **2** a screen, often decorated, that is put in front of an open fire in a room to protect people from the heat or from SPARKS, or to hide it when it is not lit

**ˈfire service** noun [C + sing. / pl. v.] (*BrE*) = FIRE BRIGADE

**fire·side** /ˈfaɪəsaɪd; NAmE -ərs-/ noun [usually sing.] the part of a room next to the fire: **by the** ~ *sitting by the fireside*

**ˈfire start·er** noun **1** a device that allows you to start a fire, usually by hitting a piece of FLINT (= a hard grey stone) against a piece of steel **2** (*NAmE*) (*BrE* ˈfire-light·er) a block of material that burns easily and is used to help start a coal or wood fire **3** a person who commits the crime of deliberately setting fire to sth SYN arsonist

**ˈfire station** noun a building for a FIRE BRIGADE or FIRE DEPARTMENT and its equipment

**fire·storm** /ˈfaɪəstɔːm; NAmE -ərstɔːrm/ noun a very large fire, usually started by bombs, that is not under control and is made worse by the winds that it causes

**ˈfire trap** noun a building that would be very dangerous if a fire started there, especially because it would be difficult for people to escape

**ˈfire truck** noun (*NAmE*) = FIRE ENGINE

**fire·wall** /ˈfaɪəwɔːl; NAmE -ərw-/ noun (*computing*) a part of a computer system that prevents people from reaching information without permission, but still allows them to receive information that is sent to them

**fire·wood** /ˈfaɪəwʊd; NAmE -ərw-/ noun [U] wood that has been cut into pieces to be used for burning in fires

**fire·work** ⚑+ B2 /ˈfaɪəwɜːk; NAmE -ərwɜːrk/ noun **1** ⚑+ B2 [C] a small device containing powder that burns or explodes and produces bright coloured lights and loud noises, used especially at celebrations: (*BrE*) *to let off a few fireworks* ◊ (*NAmE*) *to set off a few fireworks* ◊ *a firework(s) display* **2** ⚑+ B2 **fireworks** [pl.] a display of fireworks: *When do the fireworks start?* **3 fireworks** [pl.] (*informal*) strong or angry words; exciting actions: *There'll be fireworks when he finds out!*

**fir·ing** /ˈfaɪərɪŋ/ noun **1** [U] the action of firing guns: *There was continuous firing throughout the night.* **2** [U, C] the action of forcing sb to leave their job: *teachers protesting* against the firing of a colleague ⋄ She's responsible for the hirings and firings.

**'firing line** noun
**IDM** **be in the 'firing line** (NAmE also **be on the 'firing line**) **1** to be in a position where you can be shot at **2** to be in a position where people can criticize or blame you: *The employment secretary found himself in the firing line over recent job cuts.*

**'firing squad** noun [C + sing. / pl. v., U] a group of soldiers who are ordered to shoot and kill sb who is found guilty of a crime: *He was executed by (a) firing squad.*

**firm** 🔊 **B2** /fɜːm; NAmE fɜːrm/ *noun, adj., adv., verb*
▪ *noun* **🔊 B2** a business or company: *a law/consulting/research firm* ⋄ **a ~ of sth** *a firm of solicitors/accountants/architects*
▪ *adj.* (**firm·er**, **firm·est**) **1** 🔊+ **B2** fairly hard; not easy to press into a different shape: *a firm bed/mattress* ⋄ *These peaches are still firm.* ⋄ *Bake the cakes until they are firm to the touch.* **2** 🔊+ **B2** not likely to change: *a firm believer in socialism* ⋄ *a firm agreement/date/decision/offer/promise* ⋄ *firm beliefs/conclusions/convictions/principles* ⋄ *She is a firm favourite with the children.* ⋄ *We have no firm evidence to support the case.* ⋄ *They remained firm friends.* **3** 🔊+ **B2** strongly fixed in place **SYN** **secure**: *Stand the fish tank on a firm base.* ⋄ *No building can stand without firm foundations, and neither can a marriage.* **4** 🔊+ **B2** (of sb's voice or hand movements) strong and steady: *'No,' she repeated, her voice firmer this time.* ⋄ *With a firm grip on my hand, he pulled me away.* ⋄ *Her handshake was cool and firm.* **5** 🔊+ **B2** (of sb's behaviour, position or understanding of sth) strong and in control: *to exercise firm control/discipline/leadership* ⋄ *Parents must be firm with their children.* ⋄ *The company now has a firm footing in the marketplace.* ⋄ *This book will give your students a firm grasp of English grammar.* ⋄ *We need to keep a firm grip on the situation.* **6** [usually before noun] **~ (against sth)** (of a country's money, etc.) not lower than another: *The euro remained firm against the dollar, but fell against the yen.* ⊃ see also FIRMLY ▶ **firm·ness** *noun* [U]
**IDM** **a firm 'hand** strong control or discipline: *Those children need a firm hand to make them behave.* **take a firm 'line / 'stand (on/against sth)** to make your beliefs known and to try to make others follow them: *We need to take a firm line on data privacy.* ⋄ *They took a firm stand against drugs in the school.* ⊃ more at GROUND *n.*
▪ *adv.*
**IDM** **hold 'firm (to sth)** (*formal*) to believe sth strongly and not change your mind: *She held firm to her principles.* **stand 'fast / 'firm** to refuse to move back; to refuse to change your opinions
▪ *verb* **1** [T] **~ sth** to make sth become stronger or harder: *Firm the soil around the plant.* ⋄ *This product claims to firm your body in six weeks.* **2** [I] **~ (to / at …)** (*finance*) (of shares, prices, etc.) to become steady or rise steadily: *The company's shares firmed 3p to 696p.*
**PHR V** **firm 'up** to become harder or more solid: *Put the mixture somewhere cool to firm up.* **firm sth↔'up 1** to make arrangements more final and fixed: *The company has not yet firmed up its plans for expansion.* ⋄ *The precise details still have to be firmed up.* **2** to make sth harder or more solid: *A few weeks of aerobics will firm up that flabby stomach.*

**firma·ment** /'fɜːməmənt; NAmE 'fɜːrm-/ *noun* **the firmament** [sing.] (*old use* or *literary*) the sky: (*figurative*) *a rising star in the literary firmament*

**firm·ly** 🔊+ **B2** /'fɜːmli; NAmE 'fɜːrm-/ *adv.* in a strong or definite way: *'I can manage,' she said firmly.* ⋄ *It is now firmly established as one of the leading brands in the country.* ⋄ *Keep your eyes firmly fixed on the road ahead.*

**firm·ware** /'fɜːmweə(r); NAmE 'fɜːrmwer/ *noun* [U] (*computing*) a type of computer software that is stored in such a way that it cannot be changed or lost

**first** 🔊 **A1** /fɜːst; NAmE fɜːrst/ *det., ordinal number, adv., noun*
▪ *det., ordinal number* **1** 🔊 **A1** happening or coming before all other similar things or people; 1st: *his first wife* ⋄ *the first turning on the right* ⋄ *I didn't take the first bus.* ⋄ *It was the first time they had ever met.* ⋄ *students in their first year at college* ⋄ *your first impressions* ⋄ *She resolved to do it at the first* (= earliest) *opportunity.* ⋄ *King Edward I* (= pronounced 'King Edward the First') ⋄ *the first of May/May 1st* ⋄ *His second book is better than his first.* **2** 🔊+ **A1** the most important or best: *Your first duty is to your family.* ⋄ *She won first prize in the competition.* ⋄ *an issue of the first importance* **HELP** Idioms containing **first** *det.* are at the entries for the nouns and adjectives in the idioms, for example **on first acquaintance** is at **acquaintance**.
▪ *adv.* **1** 🔊 **A1** before anyone or anything else; at the beginning: *'Do you want a drink?' 'I'll finish my work first.'* ⋄ *First I had to decide what to wear.* ⋄ *Who came first in the race* (= who won)*?* ⋄ *It plunged nose first into the river.* **2** 🔊+ **A1** for the first time: *When did you first meet him?* ⋄ *The book was first published in 1971.* **3** 🔊+ **A1** used to introduce the first of a list of points you want to make in a speech or piece of writing **SYN** **firstly**: *This method has two advantages: first it is cheaper and second it is quicker.* ⊃ LANGUAGE BANK at PROCESS[1] **4** used to emphasize that you are determined not to do sth: *She swore that she wouldn't apologize—she'd die first!*
**IDM** **at 'first** 🔊 **A2** at or in the beginning: *I didn't like the job much at first.* ⋄ *At first I thought he was shy, but then I discovered he was just not interested in other people.* ⋄ (*saying*) *If at first you don't succeed, try, try again.* ⊃ note at FIRSTLY **come 'first** to be considered more important than anything else: *In any decision she makes, her family always comes first.* **first and 'foremost** more than anything else: *He does a little teaching, but first and foremost he's a writer.* **first and 'last** in every way that is important; completely: *She regarded herself, first and last, as a musician.* **first ˌcome, first 'served** (*saying*) people will be dealt with, seen, etc. strictly in the order in which they arrive: *Tickets are available on a first come, first served basis.* **first of 'all 1** 🔊 **A2** before doing anything else; at the beginning: *First of all, let me ask you something.* ⊃ LANGUAGE BANK at PROCESS[1] **2** 🔊 **A2** as the most important thing: *The content of any article needs, first of all, to be relevant to the reader.* ⊃ note at FIRSTLY **First 'off** (*informal, especially BrE*) before anything else: *First off, let's see how much it'll cost.* **first 'up** (*BrE, informal*) to start with; before anything else: *First up is a report on the situation in Australia.* **put sb/sth 'first** to consider sb/sth to be more important than anyone/anything else: *She always puts her children first.* ⊃ more at FOOT *n.*, HEAD *n.*, SAFETY
▪ *noun* **1** 🔊 **A2** **the first** (*pl.* **the first**) **the ~ (to do sth)** the person or thing that comes or happens before all other similar people or things: *I was the first in my family to go to college.* ⋄ *Sheila and Jim were the first to arrive.* **2 the first** [sing.] the earliest: *The first I heard about the wedding* (= the first time I became aware of it) *was when I saw it in the local paper.* ⋄ *The first I knew of a problem was around 9.30 a.m. last Monday.* **3 the first** (*pl.* **the first**) **the ~ to do sth** the most likely: *I'd be the first to admit* (= I will most willingly admit) *I might be wrong.* ⋄ *The poorest will be the first to suffer.* **4** [C, usually sing.] **~ (for sb)** an important achievement, event, etc., never done or experienced

▼ **LANGUAGE BANK**
**first**
Ordering your points
• This study has **the following** aims: **first**, to investigate how international students in the UK use humour; **second**, to examine how jokes can help to establish social relationships; **and third**, to explore the role that humour plays in helping overseas students adjust to life in the UK.
• **Let us begin by** identifying some of the popular joke genres in the UK.
• **Next, let us turn to / Next, let us consider** the question of gender differences in the use of humour.
• **Finally / Lastly**, let us briefly examine the role of humour in defining a nation's culture.
⊃ note at FIRSTLY, LASTLY
⊃ LANGUAGE BANK at CONCLUSION, PROCESS[1]

# first aid

before: *We went on a cruise, a first for both of us.* **5** (*also* **first 'gear**) [U] the lowest GEAR on a car, bicycle, etc. that you use when you are moving slowly: **in ~** *He stuck the car in first and revved.* **6** [C] **~ (in sth)** the highest level of university degree at British universities: *She got a first in maths at Exeter.* ⊃ compare SECOND¹, THIRD
**IDM** **first among 'equals** the person or thing with the highest status in a group **from the (very) 'first** from the beginning: *They were attracted to each other from the first.* **from first to 'last** from beginning to end; during the whole time: *It's a fine performance that commands attention from first to last.*

**first 'aid** *noun* [U] simple medical treatment that is given to sb before a doctor comes or before the person can be taken to a hospital: *to give first aid* ◊ *a first-aid course*
⊃ WORDFINDER NOTE at ACCIDENT

**first-'aider** *noun* (*BrE*) a person who is trained to give first aid

**the First A'mendment** *noun* [sing.] the statement in the US Constitution that protects freedom of speech and religion and the right to meet in peaceful groups

**first 'balcony** (*NAmE*) (*also* **dress circle** *especially in BrE*) *noun* the first level of seats above the ground floor in a theatre

**first 'base** *noun* **1** (in baseball) the first of the four positions that players must reach in order to score points; the position of the player on the defending team near first base: *He didn't make it past first base.* ◊ *He hasn't* **played first base** *yet this season.* **2** (*informal, especially NAmE*) the first stage of sexual contact, usually referring to kissing: *He had never even* **got to first base** *with a girl.*
**IDM** **not get to first 'base (with sth/sb)** (*informal, especially NAmE*) to fail to make a successful start in a project, relationship, etc.; to fail to get through the first stage

**first-born** /ˈfɜːstbɔːn; *NAmE* ˈfɜːrstbɔːrn/ *noun* (*old-fashioned*) a person's first child ▶ **first-born** *adj.* [only before noun]: *their firstborn son*

**first 'class** *noun, adv.*
■ *noun* [U] **1** the best and most expensive seats or accommodation on a train, plane or ship: *There is more room in first class.* **2** (in the UK) the class of mail that is delivered most quickly: *First class costs more.* **3** (in the US) the class of mail that is used for letters **4** the highest standard of degree by a British university
■ *adv.* **1** using the best and most expensive seats or accommodation in a train, plane or ship: *to travel first class* **2** (in the UK) by the quickest form of mail: *I sent the package first class on Monday.* **3** (in the US) by the class of mail that is used for letters

**first-'class** *adj.* **1** [usually before noun] in the best group; of the highest standard **SYN** **excellent**: *a first-class novel* ◊ *a first-class writer* ◊ *The car was in first-class condition.* ◊ *I know a place where the food is first-class.* **2** [only before noun] connected with the best and most expensive way of travelling on a train, plane or ship: *first-class rail travel* ◊ *a first-class cabin/seat/ticket* **3** [only before noun] (in the UK) connected with letters, packages, etc. that are delivered most quickly, or that cost more to send: *first-class mail/post/postage/stamps* **4** [only before noun] used to describe a university degree of the highest class from a British university: *She was awarded a first-class degree in English.*

**first 'cost** *noun* [C, U] (*business*) = PRIME COST

**first 'cousin** *noun* = COUSIN (1)

**first de'gree** *noun* (*especially BrE*) an academic qualification given by a university or college, for example a BA or BSc, that is given to sb who does not already have a degree in that subject: *What was your first degree in?* ◊ *to study geography at first-degree level*

**first-de'gree** *adj.* [only before noun] **1** (*especially NAmE*) **~ murder, assault, robbery**, etc. murder, etc. of the most serious kind **2** **~ burns** burns of the least serious of three kinds, affecting only the surface of the skin ⊃ compare SECOND-DEGREE, THIRD-DEGREE

**first 'down** *noun* (in AMERICAN FOOTBALL) **1** the first of a series of four DOWNS (= chances to move the ball forward ten yards) **2** the chance to start a new series of four DOWNS because your team has succeeded in going forward ten yards

**first e'dition** *noun* one of the copies of a book that was produced the first time the book was printed

**first-'ever** *adj.* [only before noun] never having happened or been experienced before: *his first-ever visit to London* ◊ *the first-ever woman vice-president*

**the first 'family** *noun* [sing.] the family of the President of the United States

**first 'finger** *noun* = INDEX FINGER

**first 'floor** (*usually* **the first floor**) *noun* [sing.] **1** (*BrE*) the level of a building above the ground level: *Menswear is on the first floor.* **2** (*NAmE*) (*BrE* **ground floor**) the floor of a building that is at the same level as the ground outside ▶ **first-'floor** *adj.* [only before noun]: *a first-floor flat/apartment* ⊃ note at FLOOR

**first fruit** *noun* [usually pl.] the first result of sb's work or effort

**first gene'ration** *noun* [sing.] **1** people who have left their country to go and live in a new country; the children of these people **2** the first type of a machine or piece of software to be developed: *the first generation of personal computers* ▶ **first-gene'ration** *adj.* [usually before noun]: *first-generation Caribbeans in the UK*

**first-'hand** *adj.* [only before noun] obtained or experienced yourself: *to have first-hand experience of poverty* ⊃ compare SECOND-HAND ▶ **first-'hand** *adv.*: *to experience poverty first-hand*

**First 'Lady** *noun* [usually sing.] **1 the First Lady** (in the US) the wife of the President ⊃ see also FLOTUS **2** (*NAmE*) the wife of the leader of a state **3** (*usually* **first lady**) the woman who is thought to be the best in a particular profession, sport, etc: *the first lady of country music*

**first 'language** *noun* the language that you learn to speak first as a child; the language that you speak best: *His first language is Welsh.* ⊃ compare SECOND LANGUAGE

**first lieu'tenant** *noun* **1** an officer in the NAVY with responsibility for managing a ship, etc. under the GUIDANCE of the captain **2** an officer in the US army and AIR FORCE just below the rank of a captain **3** (*informal*) a person who is the next most important to sb

**first 'light** *noun* [U] the time when light first appears in the morning **SYN** **dawn**, **daybreak**: *We left at first light.*

**first-'line** *adj.* [only before noun] the first choice, especially when talking about choosing a treatment for an illness: *first-line drugs for treating malaria*

**first·ly** ❶ **A2** /ˈfɜːstli; *NAmE* ˈfɜːrst-/ *adv.* used to introduce the first of a list of points you want to make in a speech or piece of writing: *There are two reasons for this decision: firstly …* ⊃ LANGUAGE BANK at FIRST

▼ WHICH WORD?
**firstly / first of all / at first**
- **Firstly** and **first (of all)** are used to introduce a series of facts, reasons, opinions, etc: *The brochure is divided into two sections, dealing firstly with basic courses and secondly with advanced ones.* **Firstly** is more common in *BrE* than in *NAmE*.
- **At first** is used to talk about the situation at the beginning of a period of time, especially when you are comparing it with a different situation at a later period: *Maggie had seen him nearly every day at first. Now she saw him much less.*

**first 'mate** (*also* **first 'officer**) *noun* the officer on a commercial ship just below the rank of captain or MASTER

**first 'minister** (*also* **First Minister**) *noun* the leader of the ruling political party in some regions or countries, for example in Scotland

**first name** (also **given name**) noun a name that was given to you when you were born, that comes before your family name: *His first name is Tom and his surname is Green.* ◊ *Please give all your first names.* ◊ (*BrE*) *to be* **on first-name terms** *with sb* (= to call them by their first name as a sign of a friendly informal relationship) ◊ (*NAmE*) *to be on a first-name basis*

**First 'Nations** noun [pl.] (*CanE*) the races of people who were the original people living in what is now Canada, not including the Inuit or Metis ⇒ compare NATIVE CANADIAN

**first 'night** noun **1** the first public performance of a play, film, etc. **2** (*NAmE*) a public celebration of NEW YEAR'S EVE

**first of'fender** noun a person who has been found guilty of a crime for the first time

**first 'officer** noun **1** = FIRST MATE **2** the second in command to the captain on an aircraft

**first-past-the-'post** adj. [only before noun] (of a system of elections) in which only the person who gets the most votes is elected ⇒ compare PROPORTIONAL REPRESENTATION

**the first 'person** noun [sing.] **1** (*grammar*) a set of pronouns and verb forms used by a speaker to refer to himself or herself, or to a group including himself or herself: '*I am*' *is the first person singular of the present tense of the verb 'to be'.* ◊ '*I*', '*me*', '*we*' *and* '*us*' *are first-person pronouns.* **2** a way of writing a novel, etc. as if one of the characters is telling the story using the word *I*: **in~** *The novel is written in the first person.* ⇒ compare SECOND PERSON, THIRD PERSON

**first-person 'shooter** (also **first-person 'shooter game**) noun (abbr. **FPS**) a type of video game in which the player views the action through the eyes of a character and has to attack enemies

**first 'principles** noun [pl.] the basic ideas on which a theory, system or method is based: *I think we should go back to first principles.*

**first-'rate** adj. of the highest quality SYN **excellent**: *a first-rate swimmer* ◊ *The food here is absolutely first-rate.*

**first re'fusal** noun [U] the right to decide whether to accept or refuse sth before it is offered to others: *Will you give me first refusal on the car, if you decide to sell it?*

**first re'sponder** noun (especially *NAmE*) a person such as a member of the police or fire department in a position to arrive first at an emergency, who has been trained to give basic medical treatment ⇒ compare EMERGENCY SERVICES

**'first school** noun (in the UK) a school for children between the ages of 5 and 8 or 9

**first 'strike** noun an attack on an enemy made before they attack you

**'first-time** adj. [only before noun] doing or experiencing sth for the first time: *houses for first-time buyers* ◊ *a computer program designed for first-time users*

**first-'timer** noun a person who does sth for the first time: *conference first-timers*

**First 'World** noun [sing.] the rich industrial countries of the world ⇒ compare THIRD WORLD

**the First World 'War** (also **World War 'I**) noun [sing.] the war that was fought mainly in Europe between 1914 and 1918

**firth** /fɜːθ; *NAmE* fɜːrθ/ noun (especially in Scottish place names) a narrow area of the sea that runs a long way into the land, or a part of a river where it flows into the sea: *the Moray Firth* ◊ *the Firth of Clyde*

**fis·cal** /ˈfɪskl/ adj. connected with government or public money, especially taxes: *fiscal policies/reforms* ⇒ see also PROCURATOR FISCAL ▸ **fis·cal·ly** /ˈfɪskəli/ adv.

**fiscal 'year** (*NAmE*) (*BrE* **fi,nancial 'year**, **'tax year**) noun [usually sing.] a period of twelve months over which the accounts and taxes of a company or a person are calculated

593

**fishing**

**fish ⓘ A1** /fɪʃ/ noun, verb
▪ noun (pl. **fish** or **fishes**) HELP **Fish** is the usual plural form. The older form, **fishes**, can be used to refer to different kinds of fish. **1** ⓘ A1 [C] a creature that lives in water, breathes through GILLS, and uses FINS and a tail for swimming: *They caught several fish.* ◊ *tropical/marine/freshwater fish* ◊ *shoals* (= groups) *of fish* ◊ *There are about 30000 species of fish in the world.* ◊ *a fish tank/pond* ◊ *Fish stocks in the Baltic are in decline.* ⇒ VISUAL VOCAB page V2 ⇒ see also COARSE FISH, FLATFISH, FLYING FISH, SEA FISH, SHELLFISH **2** ⓘ [U] the soft part of fish that is eaten as food: *a regular diet of fresh fish* ◊ *fried/grilled/smoked/dried fish* ◊ *fish pie/soup* ⇒ see also WHITE FISH IDM **a ,fish out of 'water** a person who feels uncomfortable because he or she is in an environment that is not familiar **have bigger/other fish to 'fry** to have more important or more interesting things to do **neither fish nor 'fowl** neither one thing nor another **an odd/a queer 'fish** (old-fashioned, *BrE*) a person who is slightly strange or crazy **there are plenty more fish in the 'sea** used to comfort sb whose romantic relationship has ended by saying that there are many other people with whom they may have a successful relationship in the future ⇒ more at BIG adj., COLD adj., DIFFERENT, DRINK v., SHOOT v.
▪ verb **1** ⓘ A2 [I] to try to catch fish with nets, a fishing line, etc: *The trawler was fishing off the coast of Iceland.* ◊ **~for sth** *You can fish for trout in this stream.* **2** ⓘ A2 [I] **go fishing** to spend time fishing for pleasure: *Let's go fishing this weekend.* **3** [T] **~sth (for sth)** to try to catch fish in the area of water mentioned: *They fished the loch for salmon.* **4** [I] **+ adv./prep.** to search for sth, using your hands: *She fished around in her bag for her keys.* PHRV **'fish for sth** to try to get sth, or to find out sth, although you are pretending not to: *to fish for compliments/information* **,fish sth/sb↔'out** | **,fish sth/sb 'out of sth** to take or pull sth/sb out of a place: *She fished a piece of paper out of the pile on her desk.* ◊ *They fished a dead body out of the river.*

**fish and 'chips** noun [U] a dish of fish that has been fried in BATTER served with CHIPS, and usually bought in the place where it has been cooked and eaten at home, etc., especially in the UK: *Three portions of fish and chips, please.* ◊ *a fish and chip shop*

**'fish·bowl** /ˈfɪʃbəʊl/ noun = GOLDFISH BOWL

**'fish·cake** /ˈfɪʃkeɪk/ noun (especially *BrE*) pieces of fish mixed with MASHED POTATO made into a flat round shape, covered with BREADCRUMBS and fried

**fish·er** /ˈfɪʃə(r)/ noun (especially *NAmE*) = FISHERMAN

**'fish·er·man** /ˈfɪʃəmən; *NAmE* -ʃərm-/ noun (pl. **-men** /-mən/) a person who catches fish, either as a job or as a sport ⇒ compare ANGLER

**'fisher·woman** /ˈfɪʃəwʊmən; *NAmE* -ʃərw-/ noun (pl. **-women** /-wɪmɪn/) a woman who catches fish, either as a job or as a sport ⇒ compare ANGLER ⇒ note at GENDER

**fish·ery** /ˈfɪʃəri/ noun (pl. **-ies**) **1** a part of the sea or a river where fish are caught in large quantities: *a herring fishery* ◊ *coastal/freshwater fisheries* **2** = FISH FARM: *a trout fishery*

**'fish·eye** /ˈfɪʃaɪ/ (also **'fisheye ,lens**) noun a camera LENS with a wide angle that gives the view a curved shape

**'fish farm** (also **fish·ery**) noun a place where fish are BRED (= kept in order to produce young) as a business

**'fish ,finger** (*BrE*) (*NAmE* **'fish stick**) noun a long narrow piece of fish covered with BREADCRUMBS or BATTER, usually frozen and sold in packs

**'fish hook** noun a sharp metal HOOK for catching fish that has a point that curves backwards to make it difficult to pull out ⇒ picture at HOOK

**fish·ing ⓘ A2** /ˈfɪʃɪŋ/ noun [U] the sport or business of catching fish: *They often go fishing.* ◊ *deep-sea fishing* ◊ *a fishing boat/vessel* ◊ *the fishing industry* ⇒ see also COARSE FISHING, FLY FISHING

**WORDFINDER** bait, bite, dragnet, fly, hook, line, net, rod, trawl

Ⓞ Oxford Phrasal Academic Lexicon (OPAL) written and spoken word lists | Ⓦ OPAL written word list | Ⓢ OPAL spoken word list

# fishing expedition

**fishing expedition** *noun* a search or investigation carried out in order to discover any information about a person, organization, etc. that might be used to harm them:: *There's a danger that the system could be used to conduct fishing expeditions rather than targeted surveillance.*

**fishing line** *noun* [C, U] a long string with a sharp HOOK attached, used for catching fish

**fishing rod** (*also* **rod**) (*NAmE also* **fishing pole**) *noun* a long wooden or plastic stick with a FISHING LINE and HOOK attached, used for catching fish

**fishing tackle** *noun* [U] equipment used for catching fish

**fish·mon·ger** /ˈfɪʃmʌŋɡə(r); *NAmE* -mɑːŋ-/ *noun* (*especially BrE*) a person whose job is to sell fish in a shop **2 fish·mon·ger's** (*pl.* **fish·mon·gers**) a shop that sells fish

**fish·net** /ˈfɪʃnet/ *noun* **1** [U] a type of cloth made of THREADS that produce a pattern of small holes like a net: *fishnet stockings* **2 fishnets** [pl.] TIGHTS or STOCKINGS made of fishnet

**fish slice** (*BrE*) (*NAmE* **spat·ula**) *noun* a kitchen UTENSIL that has a broad flat part with narrow holes in it, attached to a long handle, used for turning and lifting food when cooking

**fish stick** (*NAmE*) (*BrE* **fish finger**) *noun* a long narrow piece of fish covered with BREADCRUMBS or BATTER, usually frozen and sold in packs

**fish·tail** /ˈfɪʃteɪl/ *verb* [I] if a vehicle **fishtails**, the back end slides from side to side

**fish·wife** /ˈfɪʃwaɪf/ *noun* (*pl.* **-wives** /-waɪvz/) (*disapproving*) a woman with a loud voice and bad manners

**fishy** /ˈfɪʃi/ *adj.* (**fish·ier**, **fishi·est**) **1** (*informal*) seeming or likely to be wrong, illegal or dishonest **SYN** **suspicious**: *There's something fishy going on here.* **2** smelling or tasting like a fish: *What's that fishy smell?*

**fis·sile** /ˈfɪsaɪl; *NAmE* -sl/ *adj.* (*physics*) capable of nuclear FISSION: *fissile material*

**fis·sion** /ˈfɪʃn/ *noun* [U] **1** (*also* **nuclear 'fission**) (*physics*) the act or process of splitting the NUCLEUS (= central part) of an ATOM, when a large amount of energy is released ⇒ compare FUSION ⇒ WORDFINDER NOTE at PHYSICS **2** (*biology*) the division of cells as a method of producing new cells

**fis·sure** /ˈfɪʃə(r)/ *noun* (*specialist*) a long deep opening in sth, especially in rock or in the earth ▶ **fis·sured** *adj.*

**fist** /fɪst/ *noun* a hand when it is tightly closed with the fingers bent into the PALM: *He punched me with his fist.* ◊ *She clenched her fists to stop herself trembling.* ◊ *He got into a fist fight in the bar.* ⇒ see also HAM-FISTED, TIGHT-FISTED
**IDM** **make a better, good, poor, etc. fist of sth** (*BrE*, old-fashioned, informal) to make a good, bad, etc. attempt to do sth ⇒ more at IRON *adj.*, MONEY

**fist bump** *noun* (*informal*) a way of saying 'hello' or of showing support or agreement, in which two people raise one FIST (= a hand when it is tightly closed) each and lightly hit them together: *do/give a fist bump* ▶ **'fist-bump** *verb* [T, I] *~(sb)*: *Several of the politician's supporters fist-bumped him as he left the stage.*

**fist·ful** /ˈfɪstfʊl/ *noun* a number or an amount of sth that can be held in a fist: *a fistful of coins*

**fisti·cuffs** /ˈfɪstɪkʌfs/ *noun* [pl.] (*old-fashioned* or *humorous*) a fight in which people hit each other with their fists

**'fist pump** *noun* (*informal*) an action to celebrate success or victory, or to show support, in which you raise your bent arm with your hand tightly closed and then move it quickly and strongly down towards your body: *When I saw the final score, I gave a fist pump and shouted out 'YES!'* ▶ **'fist-pump** *verb* [I]: *They sang, they fist-pumped and they cheered the speakers.* **'fist-pumping** *noun* [U]

**fis·tula** /ˈfɪstjʊlə/ *noun* (*medical*) an opening between two organs of the body, or between an organ and the skin, that would not normally exist, caused by injury, disease, etc.

---

**fit** **A2** /fɪt/ *verb*, *adj.*, *noun*

■ *verb* (**fit·ting**, **fit·ted**, **fit·ted**) (*NAmE usually* **fit·ting**, **fit**, **fit**)
**HELP** Fit is not used in *NAmE* as the past participle in the passive.

• RIGHT SIZE/TYPE **1** **B2** [I, T] (not used in the progressive tenses) to be the right shape and size for sb/sth: *I tried the dress on but it didn't fit.* ◊ *That jacket fits well.* ◊ *a close-fitting dress* ◊ *~sb/sth I can't find clothes to fit me.* ◊ *The key doesn't fit the lock.* **2** **A2** [I, T] to be of the right size, type or number to go somewhere: *I'd like to have a desk in the room but it won't fit.* ◊ *+ adv./prep. All the kids will fit in the back of the car.* **3** [T, often passive] to put clothes on sb and make them the right size and shape: **be fitted for sth** *I'm going to be fitted for my wedding dress today.*

• PUT STH SOMEWHERE **4** **B2** [T] to put or fix sth somewhere: *~sth + adv./prep. They fitted a smoke alarm to the ceiling.* ◊ *~sth with sth The rooms were all fitted with smoke alarms.* **5** **B2** [I, T] to put or join sth in the right place: *~ + adv./prep. The glass fits on top of the jug to form a lid.* ◊ *How do these two parts fit together?* ◊ *~sth + adv./prep. We fitted together the pieces of the puzzle.*

• AGREE/MATCH **6** **B2** [I, T] (not used in the progressive tenses) to agree with, match or be suitable for sth; to make sth do this: *Something doesn't quite fit here.* ◊ *~into sth His pictures don't fit into any category.* ◊ *~sth The facts certainly fit your theory.* ◊ *The punishment ought to fit the crime.* ◊ *~sth to sth We should fit the punishment to the crime.*

• MAKE SUITABLE **7** [T] (*especially BrE*) to make sb/sth suitable for a particular job or situation: *~sb/sth for/to sth His experience fitted him perfectly for the job.* ◊ *~sb/sth to do sth His experience fitted him to do the job.* ⇒ see also FITTED

**IDM** **fit (sb) like a 'glove** to be the perfect size or shape for sb ⇒ more at BILL *n.*, SHOE *n.*, DESCRIPTION, FACE *n.*
**PHRV** **fit sb/sth↔'in** | **fit sb/sth 'in/'into sth 1** to find time to see sb or to do sth: *I'll try and fit you in after lunch.* ◊ *I had to fit ten appointments into one morning.* **2** to find or have enough space for sb/sth in a place: *We can't fit in any more chairs.* **fit 'in (with sb/sth)** to live, work, etc. in an easy and natural way with sb/sth: *He's never done this type of work before; I'm not sure how he'll fit in with the other people.* ◊ *Where do I fit in?* ◊ *Do these plans fit in with your arrangements?* **fit sb/sth↔'out/'up (with sth)** to supply sb/sth with all the equipment, clothes, food, etc. they need **SYN** **equip**: *to fit out a ship before a long voyage* ◊ *The room has been fitted out with a stove and a sink.* (*figurative*) **fit sb↔'up (for sth)** (*BrE*, *informal*) to make it look as if sb is guilty of a crime they have not committed **SYN** **frame**: *I didn't do it—I've been fitted up!*

■ *adj.* (**fit·ter**, **fit·test**)
• HEALTHY **1** **A2** healthy and strong, especially because you do regular physical exercise: *Top athletes have to be very fit.* ◊ *She tries to keep fit by jogging every day.* ◊ *Hiking helps keep him physically fit.* : *~to do sth He won't be fit to play in the match on Saturday.* ◊ *~for sth (BrE) He's had a bad cold and isn't fit enough for work yet.* ◊ (*figurative*) *The government aims to make British industry leaner and fitter* (= employing fewer people and with lower costs).
**OPP** **unfit** ⇒ SYNONYMS at WELL ⇒ see also KEEP-FIT

> **WORDFINDER** diet, exercise, gym, health spa, nutrition, personal trainer, sport, stamina, workout

• SUITABLE **2** **B2** suitable; of the right quality; with the right qualities or skills: *~sb/sth The food was not fit for human consumption.* ◊ *It was a meal fit for a king* (= of very good quality). ◊ *~for doing sth The children seem to think I'm only fit for cooking and washing!* ◊ *~to do sth Your car isn't fit to be on the road!* ◊ *He's so angry he's in no fit state to see anyone.* ◊ (*formal*) *This is not a fit place for you to live.* **OPP** **unfit**

• READY **3** *~to do sth* (*BrE*, *informal*) ready or likely to do sth extreme: *They worked until they were fit to drop* (= so tired that they were likely to fall down). ◊ *I've eaten so much I'm fit to burst.* ◊ *She was laughing fit to burst* (= very much).

• ATTRACTIVE **4** (*BrE*, *informal*) sexually attractive
**IDM** **(as) fit as a 'fiddle** (*informal*) in very good physical condition **fit for purpose** (of an institution, a system, a

thing, etc.) suitable for the function or purpose that it was designed for see/think 'fit (to do sth) (*formal*) to consider it right or acceptable to do sth; to decide or choose to do sth: *You must do as you think fit* (= but I don't agree with your decision). ◇ *The newspaper did not see fit to publish my letter* (= and I criticize it for that). ⊃ more at FIGHTING, SURVIVAL

■ noun

- ILLNESS **1** ?+ C1 [C] a sudden attack of an illness, such as EPILEPSY, in which sb becomes unconscious and their body may make violent movements SYN **convulsion**: *to have an epileptic fit* ◇ *Her fits are now controlled by drugs.*
- OF COUGHING/LAUGHTER **2** ?+ C1 [C] a sudden short period of COUGHING (= forcing air through the throat noisily) or of laughing, that you cannot control SYN **bout**: *a fit of coughing* ◇ *He had us all in fits* (*of laughter*) *with his jokes.*
- OF STRONG FEELING **3** ?+ C1 [C] a short period of very strong feeling: *to act in a fit of anger/rage/temper/pique* ⊃ see also HISSY FIT
- HOW STH FITS **4** [C, U] (often with an adjective) the way that sth, especially a piece of clothing, fits; the way that sb/sth fits into sth: *The shoe has a special strap to ensure a good fit.* ◇ *It was a tight fit with six of us in the boat.*
- MATCH **5** [C] ~ (**between A and B**) the way that two things match each other or are suitable for each other: *a perfect fit between the recruit and the job*

IDM have/throw a 'fit (*informal*) to be very shocked, upset or angry: *Your mother would have a fit if she knew you'd been drinking!* ⊃ more at START *n.*

**fit·ful** /ˈfɪtfl/ *adj.* happening only for short periods; not continuous or regular: *a fitful night's sleep* ▶ **fit·ful·ly** /-fəli/ *adv.*: *to sleep fitfully*

**fit·ment** /ˈfɪtmənt/ *noun* [usually pl.] (*BrE, specialist*) a piece of furniture or equipment, especially one that is made for and fixed in a particular place

**fit·ness** ❶ B1 /ˈfɪtnəs/ *noun* [U] **1** B1 the state of being physically healthy and strong: *a magazine on health and fitness* ◇ *a fitness instructor/test/class* ◇ *a high level of physical fitness* **2** the state of being suitable or good enough for sth: ~ **for sth** *He convinced us of his fitness for the task.* ◇ ~ **to do sth** *There were doubts about her fitness to hold office.*

'fitness centre (*BrE*) (*NAmE* 'fitness center) *noun* a place where people go to do physical exercise in order to stay or become healthy and fit

'fitness tracker (*also* ac'tivity tracker) *noun* a device that you can wear that records your daily physical activity, as well as other information about your health, such as your heart rate

**fit·ted** /ˈfɪtɪd/ *adj.* **1** [only before noun] (*especially BrE*) (of furniture) built to be fixed into a particular space SYN **built-in**: *fitted wardrobes/cupboards* **2** [only before noun] (*especially BrE*) (of a room) with matching cupboards and other furniture built for the space and fixed in place: *a fitted kitchen/bedroom* **3** [only before noun] (of clothes) made to follow the shape of the body: *a fitted jacket* OPP **loose 4** ~ **for/to sth | ~ to do sth** (*especially BrE*) suitable; with the right qualities and skills: *She was well fitted to the role of tragic heroine.* **5** ~ **with sth** having sth as equipment: *Insurance costs will be reduced for houses fitted with window locks.*

,fitted 'carpet *noun* (*BrE*) a carpet that is cut and fixed to cover the floor of a room completely ⊃ see also WALL-TO-WALL (1)

**fit·ter** /ˈfɪtə(r)/ *noun* **1** a person whose job is to put together or repair equipment: *a gas fitter* **2** a person whose job is to cut and fit clothes or carpets, etc.

**fit·ting** /ˈfɪtɪŋ/ *adj., noun*

■ *adj.* **1** (*formal*) suitable or right for the occasion SYN **appropriate**: *The award was a fitting tribute to her years of devoted work.* ◇ *A fitting end to the meal would be a glass of port.* ◇ *It is fitting that the new centre for European studies should be in a university that teaches every European language.* **2** **-fitting** (in adjectives) having a particular FIT: *a tight-fitting dress* ⊃ see also CLOSE-FITTING, FORM-FITTING, ILL-FITTING, TIGHT-FITTING

595

fix

■ *noun* **1** [usually pl.] a small part on a piece of equipment or furniture: *light fittings* ◇ *a pine cupboard with brass fittings* **2** [usually pl.] (*BrE*) items in a house such as a cooker, lights or shelves that are usually fixed but that you can take with you when you move to a new house ⊃ compare FIXTURE **3** an occasion when you try on a piece of clothing that is being made for you to see if it fits

'fitting room (*NAmE also* 'dressing room) *noun* a room or CUBICLE in a shop where you can put on clothes to see how they look ⊃ WORDFINDER NOTE at SHOP

**five** ❶ A1 /faɪv/ *number* 5: *There are only five cookies left.* ◇ *five of Sweden's top financial experts* ◇ *Ten people were invited but only five turned up.* ◇ *Do you have change for five dollars?* ◇ *a five-month contract* ◇ *Look at page five.* ◇ *Five and four is nine.* ◇ *Three fives are fifteen.* ◇ *I can't read your writing—is this meant to be a five?* ◇ *The bulbs are planted in threes or fives* (= groups of three or five). ◇ *We moved to America when I was five* (= five years old). ◇ *Shall we meet at five* (= at five o'clock), *then?* ⊃ see also HIGH FIVE

IDM give sb 'five (*informal*) to hit the inside of sb's hand with your hand as a way of saying hello or to celebrate a victory: *Give me five!* ⊃ more at NINE

,five-and-'dime (*also* ,five-and-'ten, 'dime store) *noun* (in the US in the past) a type of store that sold a range of cheap goods

,five-a-'side *noun* [U] (*BrE*) a game of football (soccer) played indoors with five players on each team

**five·fold** /ˈfaɪvfəʊld/ *adj., adv.* ⊃ -FOLD

,five o'clock 'shadow *noun* [sing.] the dark colour that appears on the CHIN and sides of a man's face when the hair has grown a little during the day since he SHAVED in the morning

,five 'pence (*also* ,five pence 'piece, 5p /ˌfaɪv ˈpiː/) *noun* a British coin worth five pence: *Have you got a five pence?*

**fiv·er** /ˈfaɪvə(r)/ *noun* (*informal*) **1** (*BrE*) £5 or a five-pound note: *Can you lend me a fiver?* **2** (*NAmE, old-fashioned*) $5 or a five-dollar bill

'five-star *adj.* [usually before noun] **1** having five stars in a system that measures quality. Five stars usually represents the highest quality: *a five-star hotel* **2** (in the US) having the highest military rank, and wearing a uniform that has five stars on it: *a five-star general*

**fix** ❶ A2 /fɪks/ *verb, noun*

■ verb
- REPAIR **1** ?+ A2 ~ **sth** to repair or correct sth: *The car won't start—can you fix it?* ◇ *I've fixed the problem.* ◇ *to have/get your computer fixed*
- ARRANGE **2** ?+ B1 to decide on a date, a time, an amount, etc. for sth SYN **set**: ~ **sth** *Has the date of the next meeting been fixed?* ◇ *Their prices are fixed until the end of the year* (= will not change before then). ◇ ~ **sth at sth** *They fixed the rent at £200 a week.* **3** ?+ B2 to arrange or organize sth: ~ **sth** *I'll fix a meeting.* ◇ ~ **sth up (for sb)** *You have to fix visits up in advance with the museum.* ◇ ~ **sth with sb** (*informal*) *Don't worry, I'll fix it with Sarah.*
- ATTACH **4** ?+ B2 ~ **sth + adv./prep.** (*especially BrE*) to put sth in a place so that it will not move: *to fix a shelf to the wall* ◇ *to fix a post in the ground* ◇ (*figurative*) *He noted every detail so as to fix the scene in his mind.*
- POSITION/TIME **5** ~ **sth** to discover or say the exact position, time, etc. of sth: *We can fix the ship's exact position at the time the fire broke out.*
- FOOD/DRINK **6** (*especially NAmE*) to provide or prepare sth, especially food: ~ **sb/yourself sth** *Can I fix you a drink?* ◇ ~ **sth for sb/yourself** *Can I fix a drink for you?* ◇ ~ **sth** *I'll fix supper.*
- HAIR/FACE **7** ~ **sth** (*especially NAmE*) to make sth such as your hair or face neat and attractive: *I'll fix my hair and then I'll be ready.*
- RESULT **8** [often passive] ~ **sth** (*informal*) to arrange the result of sth in a way that is not honest or fair: *I'm sure the race was fixed.*

# fixable

- **PUNISH** 9 ~ sb (*informal*) to punish sb who has harmed you and stop them doing you any more harm: *Don't worry—I'll fix him.*
- **IN PHOTOGRAPHY** 10 ~ sth (*specialist*) to treat film for cameras, etc. with a chemical so that the colours do not change or become less bright
- **ANIMAL** 11 ~ sth (*NAmE, informal*) to make an animal unable to have young by means of an operation ⇒ see also NEUTER *verb*

**IDM** **fix sb with a 'look, 'stare, 'gaze, etc.** to look directly at sb for a long time: *He fixed her with an angry stare.* ⇒ more at AIN'T
**PHR V** **'fix on sb/sth** to choose sb/sth: *They've fixed on Paris for their honeymoon.* **'fix (sth) on sb/sth** to look at or think about sb/sth with great attention: *Her gaze fixed on Jess.* **fix sth↔'up** to repair, decorate or make sth ready: *They fixed up the house before they moved in.* **fix sb 'up (with sb)** (*informal*) to arrange for sb to have a meeting with sb who might become a boyfriend or girlfriend **fix sb 'up (with sth)** (*informal*) to arrange for sb to have sth; to provide sb with sth: *I'll fix you up with a place to stay.*

■ *noun*
- **SOLUTION** 1 🔊 B2 [C] ~ (for sth) (*informal*) a solution to a problem, especially an easy or temporary one: *There is no quick fix for the steel industry.*
- **DRUG** 2 [sing.] (*informal*) an amount of sth that you need and want frequently, especially an illegal drug such as HEROIN: *to get yourself a fix* ◊ *I need a fix of coffee before I can face the day.*
- **DIFFICULT SITUATION** 3 [sing.] a difficult situation **SYN** mess: *in a ~* We've got ourselves in a fix about this.
- **ON POSITION** 4 [sing.] ~ on sth the act of finding the position of a ship or an aircraft: *They managed to get a fix on the yacht's position.*
- **UNDERSTANDING** 5 [sing.] ~ on sth (*informal*) an act of understanding sth: *He tried to get a fix on the young man's motives, but he just couldn't understand him.*
- **DISHONEST RESULT** 6 [sing.] (*informal*) a thing that is dishonestly arranged; a trick: *Her promotion was a fix, I'm sure!*

**fix·able** /ˈfɪksəbl/ *adj.* possible to repair or resolve: *Computers are often surprisingly fixable.* ◊ *He said the problems were minor and readily fixable.*

**fix·ated** /fɪkˈseɪtɪd/ *adj.* [not before noun] ~ (on sb/sth) always thinking and talking about sb/sth in a way that is not normal

**fix·ation** /fɪkˈseɪʃn/ *noun* 1 [C] a very strong interest in sb/sth, that is not normal or natural: *a mother fixation* ◊ ~ with/on sb/sth *He's got this fixation with cleanliness.* 2 [U] (*specialist*) the process of a gas becoming solid: *nitrogen fixation*

**fixa·tive** /ˈfɪksətɪv/ *noun* [C, U] 1 a substance that is used to prevent colours or smells from changing or becoming weaker, for example in photography, art or the making of PERFUME 2 a substance used to preserve BIOLOGICAL material, for example before examining it under a MICROSCOPE 3 a substance that is used to stick things together or keep things in position

**fixed** 🔊 B1 /fɪkst/ *adj.* 1 🔊 B1 staying the same; not changing or able to be changed: *fixed prices* ◊ *a fixed rate of interest* ◊ *people living on fixed incomes* ◊ *Speeders risk a fixed penalty of £60.* ⇒ see also ABODE 2 🔊 B1 (*often disapproving*) (of ideas and wishes) held very strongly; not easily changed: *My parents had fixed ideas about what I should become.* 3 [only before noun] (of expressions on sb's face) not changing and not sincere: *He greeted all his guests with a fixed smile on his face.*
**IDM** **how are you, etc. 'fixed (for sth)?** (*informal*) used to ask how much of sth a person has, or to ask about arrangements: *How are you fixed for cash?* ◊ *How are we fixed for Saturday* (= have we arranged to do anything)?

**fixed 'assets** *noun* [pl.] (*business*) land, buildings and equipment that are owned and used by a company

**fixed 'costs** *noun* [pl.] (*business*) the costs that a business must pay that do not change even if the amount of work produced changes

**fixed-'line** *adj.* relating to phone or internet connections that use wires carried on POLES or under the ground, in contrast to WIRELESS connections: *fixed-line broadband*

**fix·ed·ly** /ˈfɪksɪdli/ *adv.* continuously, without looking away, but often with no real interest: *to stare/gaze fixedly at sb/sth*

**fixed-'term** *adj.* [only before noun] a **fixed-term** contract, etc. is one that only lasts for the agreed period of time

**fixed-'wing** *adj.* [only before noun] used to describe aircraft with wings that remain in the same position, rather than helicopters, etc.

**fixer** /ˈfɪksə(r)/ *noun* 1 (*informal*) a person who arranges things for other people, sometimes dishonestly: *a great political fixer* 2 a chemical substance used in photography to prevent a photograph from changing and becoming too dark

**fixer-'upper** *noun* (*especially NAmE, informal*) a house or flat that is cheap because it needs a lot of repair work when you buy it

**fix·ings** /ˈfɪksɪŋz/ *noun* [pl.] (*NAmE*) 1 [pl.] = TRIMMINGS: *a hamburger with all the fixings* 2 the ingredients necessary to make a dish or meal: *picnic fixings*

**fix·ity** /ˈfɪksəti/ *noun* [U] (*formal*) the quality of being permanent and not changing

**fix·ture** 🔊 C1 /ˈfɪkstʃə(r)/ *noun* 1 🔊 C1 (*BrE*) a sports event that has been arranged to take place on a particular date and at a particular place: *an annual fixture* ◊ *Saturday's fixture against Liverpool* ◊ *the season's fixture list* ⇒ WORDFINDER NOTE at SPORT 🔊 C1 2 a thing such as a bath or toilet that is fixed in a house and that you do not take with you when you move house: (*BrE*) *The price of the house includes fixtures and fittings.* ◊ (*figurative*) *He has stayed with us so long he seems to have become a permanent fixture.* ⇒ compare FITTING

**fizz** /fɪz/ *verb, noun*
■ *verb* 1 [I] when a liquid **fizzes**, it produces a lot of bubbles and makes a long sound like an 's': *Champagne was fizzing in the glass.* 2 [I] to move a lot in a way that is exciting; to show that you are excited: *Share prices are fizzing.* ◊ ~ with sth *He started to fizz with enthusiasm.*
■ *noun* 1 [U, sing.] the small bubbles of gas in a liquid 2 [U, sing.] the sound that is made by bubbles of gas in a liquid, or a sound similar to this: *the fizz of a firework* 3 [U] (*BrE, informal*) a drink that has a lot of bubbles of gas, especially CHAMPAGNE ⇒ see also BUCK'S FIZZ 4 [U] lively and exciting movement or activity: *There is plenty of fizz and sparkle in the show.* ◊ *The fizz has gone out of the market.*

**fizz·er** /ˈfɪzə(r)/ *noun* (*AustralE, NZE, informal*) a failure: *The party was a fizzer.*

**fiz·zle** /ˈfɪzl/ *verb* [I] when sth, especially sth that is burning, **fizzles**, it makes a weak sound like a long 's' **SYN** hiss
**PHR V** **fizzle 'out** (*informal*) to gradually become less successful and end in a disappointing way

**fizzy** /ˈfɪzi/ *adj.* (*BrE*) (**fizz·ier**, **fizzi·est**) (of a drink) having bubbles of gas in it **SYN** sparkling: *fizzy drinks* **OPP** still

**fjord** (*also* **fiord**) /fjɔːd; *NAmE* fjɔːrd/ *noun* a long narrow area of sea between high CLIFFS, especially in Norway

**flab** /flæb/ *noun* [U] (*informal, disapproving*) soft, loose fat covering a person's body

**flab·ber·gast·ed** /ˈflæbəɡɑːstɪd; *NAmE* -bərɡæs-/ *adj.* [not usually before noun] (*informal*) extremely surprised and/or shocked **SYN** astonished

**flabby** /ˈflæbi/ *adj.* (*informal, disapproving*) (**flab·bier**, **flab·bi·est**) 1 covered with soft, loose fat; fat: *flabby thighs* 2 weak; with no strength or force: *a flabby grip* ◊ *a flabby argument*

**flac·cid** /ˈflæsɪd/ *adj.* (*formal*) soft and weak; not hard: *flaccid breasts*

**flack** /flæk/ *noun* 1 [U] = FLAK 2 [C] (*NAmE, informal*) = PRESS AGENT

**flag** /flæg/ noun, verb

■ **noun 1** a piece of cloth with a special coloured design on it that may be the symbol of a particular country or organization, may be used to give a signal or may have a particular meaning. A flag can be attached to a POLE (= a long thin straight piece of wood or metal) or held in the hand: *the Italian flag* ◇ *the flag of Italy* ◇ *The hotel flies the European Union flag.* ◇ *The American flag was flying.* ◇ *Hundreds of people cheered and waved flags.* ◇ *The assistant referee had raised his flag for offside.* ⇒ see also BLACK FLAG, BLUE FLAG, CHEQUERED FLAG, RED FLAG, WHITE FLAG **2** used to refer to a particular country or organization and its beliefs and values: *to swear allegiance to the flag* ◇ *under a~ The team competed under the Olympic flag.* **3** a flower that is grown in a garden and that grows near water: *yellow flags* ⇒ see also YELLOW FLAG **4** = FLAGSTONE
**IDM** **fly/show/wave the ˈflag** to show your support for your country, an organization or an idea to encourage or persuade others to do the same **keep the ˈflag flying** to represent your country or organization: *Our exporters keep the flag flying at international trade exhibitions.* ⇒ more at WAVE *v.*

■ **verb** (**-gg-**) **1** [T] ~ **sth** to draw attention to information that you think is important, especially by putting a special mark next to it: *I've flagged the paragraphs that we need to look at in more detail.* **2** [I] to become tired, weaker or less enthusiastic: *It had been a long day and the children were beginning to flag.* ◇ *Her confidence had never flagged.* ◇ *flagging support/enthusiasm*
**PHRV** **ˌflag sb/sthˈdown** to signal to the driver of a vehicle to stop by waving at them **ˌflag sthˈoff** (*IndE, WAfrE*) to officially start an event ⇒ related noun FLAG-OFF **ˌflag sthˈup** (*BrE*) to draw attention to sth: *The report flagged up the dangers of under-age drinking.*

**ˈflag day** noun **1** (*BrE*) a day when money is collected in public places for a charity, and people who give money receive a small paper STICKER **2 Flag Day** 14 June, the anniversary of the day in 1777 when the **Stars and Stripes** became the national flag of the United States

**flaˈgelˈlate** /ˈflædʒəleɪt/ verb ~ **sb/yourself** (*formal*) to WHIP yourself or sb else, especially as a religious punishment or as a way of experiencing sexual pleasure ▶ **flaˌgelˈlation** /ˌflædʒəˈleɪʃn/ noun [U]

**ˈflag ˈfootball** noun [U] (*NAmE*) a type of AMERICAN FOOTBALL played without the usual form of TACKLING. A TACKLE is made instead by pulling a piece of cloth from an opponent's WAISTBAND. ⇒ compare TOUCH FOOTBALL

**flagged** /flægd/ adj. covered with large flat stones (called FLAGSTONES): *a flagged floor*

**ˌflag of conˈvenience** noun a flag of a foreign country that is used by a ship from another country for legal or financial reasons

**ˈflag-off** noun (*IndE, WAfrE*) the official start of an event

**ˈflag-pole** /ˈflægpəʊl/ (*also* **ˈflag-staff**) noun a tall thin straight piece of wood or metal on which a flag is hung

**flaˈgrant** /ˈfleɪɡrənt/ adj. (*disapproving*) (of an action) that shocks you because it is done in a very obvious way and shows no respect for people, laws, etc. **SYN** blatant: *a flagrant abuse of human rights* ◇ *He showed a flagrant disregard for anyone else's feelings.* ▶ **flaˈgrantˈly** adv.

**ˈflag-ship** /ˈflæɡʃɪp/ noun **1** the main ship in a FLEET of ships in the NAVY **2** [usually sing.] the most important product, service, building, etc. that an organization owns or produces: *The company is opening a new flagship store in London.*

**ˈflag-staff** /ˈflæɡstɑːf/ NAmE -stæf/ noun = FLAGPOLE

**ˈflag-stone** /ˈflæɡstəʊn/ (*also* **flag**) noun a large flat square piece of stone that is used for floors, paths, etc.

**ˈflag-waving** noun [U] (*disapproving*) the expression of strong national feelings, especially in a way that people think is bad

**flail** /fleɪl/ verb, noun

■ **verb 1** [I, T] ~ (**sth**) (**about/around**) to move violently without control; to move your arms and legs around without control: *The boys flailed around on the floor.* ◇ *He was running along, his arms flailing wildly.* **2** [T] ~ **sb/sth** to hit sb/sth very hard, especially with a stick

■ **noun** a tool that has a long handle with a short stick hanging from it, used especially in the past to separate grains of WHEAT from their dry outer layer, by beating the WHEAT

**flair** /fleə(r); NAmE fler/ noun **1** [sir g., U] ~ **for sth** a natural ability to do sth well **SYN** talent: *He has a flair for languages.* **2** [U] a quality showing the ability to do things in an interesting way that shows imagination: *artistic flair* ◇ *She dresses with real flair.*

**flak** (*also* **flack**) /flæk/ noun [U] **1** guns on the ground that are shooting at enemy aircraft; bullets from these guns **2** (*informal*) severe criticism: *He's taken a lot of flak for his left-wing views.* ◇ *She came in for a lot of flak from the press.*

**flake** /fleɪk/ noun, verb

■ **noun 1** a small, very thin layer or piece of sth, especially one that has broken off from sth larger: *flakes of snow/paint* ◇ *dried onion flakes* ⇒ see also CORNFLAKES, SNOWFLAKE **2** (*NAmE, informal*) a person who is strange or unusual or who forgets things easily

■ **verb 1** [I] ~ (**off**) to fall off in small thin pieces: *You could see bare wood where the paint had flaked off.* ◇ *His skin was dry and flaking.* **2** [T, I] ~ (**sth**) to break sth, especially fish or other food into small thin pieces; to fall into small thin pieces: *Flake the tuna and add to the sauce.* ◇ *flaked almonds*
**PHRV** **ˌflakeˈout 1** (*informal*) to lie down or go to sleep because you are extremely tired: *When I got home he'd already flaked out on the bed.* **2** (*NAmE, informal*) to begin to behave in a strange way

**ˈflak jacket** noun a heavy jacket without arms that has metal or other special material inside it to make it stronger, and is worn for example by soldiers and police officers to protect them from bullets, SHELLS, etc.

**flaky** (*also* **flakey**) /ˈfleɪki/ adj. (**flakˈier**, **flakiˈest**) **1** tending to break into small, thin pieces: *flaky pastry* ◇ *dry flaky skin* **2** (*informal*) (of a person) behaving in a strange or unusual way; tending to forget things **3** (*BrE, informal*) that does not work well or often stops working: *I found the software a bit flaky.* ◇ *I had problems with a flaky internet connection.* ▶ **flakiˈness** noun [U]

**flambé** /ˈflɒmbeɪ; NAmE flɑːmˈbeɪ/ adj. [after noun] (from French) (of food) covered with alcohol, especially BRANDY and allowed to burn for a short time ▶ **flambé** verb ~ **sth**

**flamˈboyant** /flæmˈbɔɪənt/ adj. **1** (of people or their behaviour) different, confident and exciting in a way that attracts attention: *a flamboyant gesture/style/personality* **2** brightly coloured and likely to attract attention: *flamboyant clothes/designs* ▶ **flamˈboyˈance** /-əns/ noun [U] **flamˈboyˈantˈly** adv.

**flame** /fleɪm/ noun, verb

■ **noun 1** [C, U] a hot bright stream of burning gas that comes from sth that is on fire: *the tiny yellow flame of a match* ◇ *The room was filled with smoke and flames.* ◇ **in flames** *The building was in flames* (= was burning). ◇ *The plane burst into flame(s)* (= suddenly began burning strongly). ◇ *Everything went up in flames* (= was destroyed by fire). ◇ (*NAmE*) *an open flame* **2** [U] a bright red or orange colour: *a flame-red car* **3** [C] (*literary*) a very strong feeling: *a flame of passion* ⇒ see also OLD FLAME **4** [C] (*informal*) an angry or offensive message sent to sb by email or on the internet, typically in quick response to another message **IDM** see FAN *v.*

■ **verb 1** [I] (+ **adj.**) (*literary*) to burn with a bright flame: *The logs flamed on the hearth.* ◇ (*figurative*) *Hope flamed in her.* **2** [I, T] (+ **adj.**) | ~ (**sth**) (*literary*) (of a person's face) to become red as a result of a strong emotion; to make sth become red: *Her cheeks flamed with rage.* **3** [T] ~ **sb** (*informal*) to send sb an angry or offensive message by email or on the internet

**flaˈmenco** /fləˈmeŋkəʊ/ noun (pl. **-os**) **1** [U, C] a fast exciting Spanish dance that is usually danced to music played

# flameproof

on a guitar: *flamenco dancing* ◊ *to dance flamenco* **2** [U] the guitar music that is played for this dance

**flame-proof** /ˈfleɪmpruːf/ *adj.* made of or covered with a special material that will not burn easily

**flame-retard-ant** /ˈfleɪm rɪtɑːdənt; *NAmE* -tɑːrd-/ *adj.* = FIRE-RETARDANT

**flame-throw-er** /ˈfleɪmθrəʊə(r)/ *noun* a weapon like a gun that shoots out burning liquid or flames and is often used for clearing plants from land

**flam-ing** /ˈfleɪmɪŋ/ *adj.* [only before noun] **1** full of anger: *a flaming argument/temper* **2** burning and covered in flames: *Flaming fragments were still falling from the sky.* **3** (*BrE, informal*) used to emphasize that you are annoyed: *You flaming idiot!* **4** bright red or orange in colour: *flaming (red) hair* ◊ *a flaming sunset*

**fla-mingo** /fləˈmɪŋɡəʊ/ *noun* (*pl.* **-oes** *or* **-os**) a large pink bird with long thin legs and a long neck, that lives near water in warm countries

**flam-mable** /ˈflæməbl/ (*also* **in-flam-mable** *especially in BrE*) *adj.* that can burn easily: *highly flammable liquids*

**flan** /flæn; *NAmE also* flɑːn/ *noun* [C, U] **1** (*especially BrE*) an open PIE or cake filled with eggs and cheese, fruit, etc.: *a mushroom/strawberry flan* ◊ *Have some more flan.* ⇒ compare QUICHE, TART **2** (*NAmE*) (*BrE* **crème caramel**) a cold DESSERT (= a sweet dish) made from milk, eggs and sugar

**flange** /flændʒ/ *noun* an edge that sticks out from an object and makes it stronger or (as in a wheel of a train) keeps it in the correct position

**flank** /flæŋk/ *noun, verb*
■ *noun* **1** the side of sth such as a building or mountain **2** the left or right side of an army during a battle, or a sports team during a game **3** the side of an animal between the RIBS and the HIP
■ *verb* **1 be flanked by sb/sth** to have sb/sth on one or both sides: *She left the courtroom flanked by armed guards.* **2 ~ sth** to be placed on one or both sides of sth: *They drove through the cotton fields that flanked Highway 17.*

**flank-er** /ˈflæŋkə(r)/ *noun* an attacking player in rugby or AMERICAN FOOTBALL

**flan-nel** /ˈflænl/ *noun* **1** [U] a type of soft light cloth, containing cotton or wool, used for making clothes: *a flannel shirt* ◊ *a grey flannel suit* **2** (*also* **face-cloth**) (*both BrE*) (*NAmE* **wash-cloth**) [C] a small piece of cloth used for washing yourself: *a face flannel* **3 flannels** [pl.] trousers made of flannel **4** [U] (*BrE, informal*) words that do not have much meaning and that avoid telling sb what they want to know

**flap** /flæp/ *noun, verb*
■ *noun*
• FLAT PIECE OF PAPER, ETC. **1** [C] a flat piece of paper, cloth, metal, etc. that is attached to sth along one side and that hangs down or covers an opening: *the flap of an envelope* ◊ *I zipped the tent flaps shut.* ⇒ see also CAT FLAP
• MOVEMENT **2** [C, usually sing.] a quick often noisy movement of sth up and down or from side to side: *With a flap of its wings, the bird was gone.* ◊ *the flap of the sails*
• WORRY/EXCITEMENT **3** [sing.] (*informal, especially BrE*) a state of worry and excitement: *She gets in a flap over the slightest thing.*
• PUBLIC ANGER/CRITICISM **4** [sing.] (*NAmE*) public anger or criticism caused by sth a public figure has said or done: *the flap around the President's business affairs*
• PART OF AIRCRAFT **5** [C] (*specialist*) a part of the wing of an aircraft, at the back of the wing, that can be moved up or down to control movement in either direction ⇒ compare SLAT (2)
• PHONETICS **6** [C] (*phonetics*) = TAP
■ *verb* (**-pp-**)
• MOVE QUICKLY **1** [T, I] **~ (sth)** if a bird **flaps** its wings, or if its wings **flap**, they move quickly up and down SYN **beat**: *The bird flapped its wings and flew away.* ◊ *The gulls flew off, wings flapping.* **2** [I, T] to move or to make sth move up and down or from side to side, often making a noise:

(+ *adv./prep.*) *The sails flapped in the breeze.* ◊ *Two large birds flapped (= flew) slowly across the water.* ◊ **~ sth** *She walked up and down, flapping her arms to keep warm.* ◊ *A gust of wind flapped the tents.*
• BE WORRIED/EXCITED **3** [I] (*BrE, informal*) to behave in an anxious or excited way: *There's no need to flap—I've got everything under control.*
• PHONETICS **4** [T] (*phonetics*) **~ sth** = TAP IDM see EAR

**flap-jack** /ˈflæpdʒæk/ *noun* **1** [U, C] (*BrE*) a thick soft biscuit made from OATS, butter, sugar and SYRUP **2** [C] (*NAmE*) a thick PANCAKE

**flap-per** /ˈflæpə(r)/ *noun* a fashionable young woman in the 1920s who was interested in modern ideas and was determined to enjoy herself

**flare** /fleə(r); *NAmE* fler/ *verb, noun*
■ *verb* **1** [I] to burn brightly, but usually for only a short time or not steadily: *The match flared and went out.* ◊ *The fire flared into life.* ◊ (*figurative*) *Colour flared in her cheeks.* **2** [I] **~ (up)** (especially of anger and violence) to suddenly start or become much stronger SYN **erupt**: *Violence flared when the police moved in.* ◊ *Tempers flared towards the end of the meeting.* ⇒ related noun FLARE-UP (1) **3** [T, I] (+ *speech*) to say sth in an angry and aggressive way: *'You should have told me!' she flared at him.* **4** [I] (of clothes) to become wider towards the bottom: *The sleeves are tight to the elbow, then flare out.* **5** [T, I] **~ (sth)** if a person or an animal **flares** their NOSTRILS (= the openings at the end of the nose), or if their NOSTRILS **flare**, they become wider, especially as a sign of anger: *The horse backed away, its nostrils flaring with fear.*
PHRV **flare 'up 1** (of flames, a fire, etc.) to suddenly start burning more brightly ⇒ related noun FLARE-UP (3) **2** (of a person) to suddenly become angry ⇒ related noun FLARE-UP (1) **3** (of an illness, injury, etc.) to suddenly start again or become worse ⇒ related noun FLARE-UP (2)
■ *noun* **1** [C, usually sing.] a bright but unsteady light or flame that does not last long: *The flare of the match lit up his face.* **2** [C] a device that produces a bright flame, used especially as a signal; a flame produced in this way: *The ship sent up distress flares to attract the attention of the coastguard.* **3** [C] a shape that becomes gradually wider: *a skirt with a slight flare* **4 flares** (*BrE also* **flared 'trousers**) [pl.] (*informal*) trousers that become very wide at the bottom of the legs: *a pair of flares*

**flared** /fleəd; *NAmE* flerd/ *adj.* (of clothes) wider at the bottom edge than at the top

**flare-up** *noun* [usually sing.] **1** a sudden expression of angry or violent feeling SYN **outburst**: *a flare-up of tension between the two sides* **2** (of an illness) a sudden painful attack, especially after a period without any problems or pain **3** the fact of a fire suddenly starting to burn again more strongly than before: *a flare-up of the bushfires*

**flash** /flæʃ/ *noun, verb, adj.*
■ *noun*
• LIGHT **1** [C] a sudden bright light that shines for a moment and then disappears: *a flash of lightning* ◊ *Flashes of light were followed by an explosion.* ◊ *There was a blinding flash and the whole building shuddered.*
• SIGNAL **2** [C] the act of shining a light on sth, especially as a signal: *The lighthouse gives out four flashes every 15 seconds.*
• IN PHOTOGRAPHY **3** [C, U] a piece of equipment that produces a bright light for a very short time, used for taking photographs indoors, when it is dark, etc.; the use of this when taking a photograph: *a camera with a built-in flash* ◊ *I'll need flash for this shot.* ◊ *flash photography*
• OF BRIGHT COLOUR **4** [C] **~ of sth** the sudden appearance for a short time of sth bright: *a flash of white teeth* ◊ *On the horizon, she saw a flash of silver—the sea!*
• SUDDEN IDEA/EMOTION **5** [C] **~ of sth** a particular idea or feeling that suddenly comes into your mind or shows in your face: *a flash of brilliance/anger*
• NEWS **6** [C] (*especially BrE*) = NEWSFLASH
• ON UNIFORM **7** [C] (*BrE*) a band or small piece of cloth worn on a military uniform to show a person's rank

- **ON BOOK/PACK** 8 [C] a band of colour or writing across a book, pack, etc.
- IDM **a flash in the ˈpan** a sudden success that lasts only a short time and is not likely to be repeated **in/like a ˈflash** very quickly and suddenly ⊃ more at QUICK *adv.*

■ *verb*

- **SHINE BRIGHTLY** 1 ? B2 [I, T] to shine very brightly for a short time; to make sth shine in this way: *Lightning flashed in the distance.* ◊ *the flashing blue lights of a police car* ◊ + *adv./prep. A neon sign flashed on and off above the door.* ◊ ~ *sth The guide flashed a light into the cave.*
- **GIVE SIGNAL** 2 ? B2 [T, I] to use a light to give sb a signal: ~ *sth (at sb) Red lights flashed a warning at them.* ◊ ~**sb (sth)** *Red lights flashed them a warning.* ◊ ~ **at sb** *Why is that driver flashing at us?*
- **SHOW QUICKLY** 3 [T] ~ *sth at sb* to show sth to sb quickly: *He flashed his pass at the security officer.*
- **MOVE QUICKLY** 4 [I] + *adv./prep.* to move or pass very quickly: *The countryside flashed past the train windows.* ◊ *A look of terror flashed across his face.*
- **OF THOUGHTS/MEMORIES** 5 [I] + *adv./prep.* to come into your mind suddenly: *A terrible thought flashed through my mind.*
- **ON SCREEN** 6 [I, T] to appear on a television screen, computer screen, etc. for a short time; to make sth do this: *A message was flashing on the screen.* ◊ ~**(sth) (up)** *His name was flashed up on the screen.*
- **SEND NEWS** 7 [T] ~ *sth* + *adv./prep.* to send information quickly by radio, computer, etc: *News of their triumph was flashed around the world.*
- **SHOW EMOTION** 8 [I] (+ *adv./prep.*) (*literary*) to show a strong emotion suddenly and quickly: *Her eyes flashed with anger.*
- **OF A MAN** 9 [I] (*informal*) if a man **flashes**, he shows his sexual organs in public

IDM **flash sb a ˈsmile, ˈlook, etc.** to smile, look, etc. at sb suddenly and quickly
PHR V **ˌflash sth aˈround** (*disapproving*) to show sth to other people in order to impress them: *He's always flashing his money around.* **ˌflash ˈback (to sth)** 1 if your mind **flashes back** to sth, you remember sth that happened in the past: *Her thoughts flashed back to their wedding day.* ⊃ related noun FLASHBACK (2) 2 if a film **flashes back** to sth, it shows things that happened at an earlier time, for example at an earlier part of sb's life ⊃ related noun FLASHBACK (1) 3 to reply very quickly and/or angrily **ˌflash ˈby/ˈpast** (of time) to go very quickly: *The morning has just flashed by.* **ˌflash on sb** (*US, informal*) [no passive] if sth **flashes on you**, you suddenly realize it: *It flashes on sb that … It flashed on me that he was the man I'd seen in the hotel.* **ˈflash on sth** (*US, informal*) to suddenly remember or think of sth: *I flashed on an argument I had with my sister when we were kids.*

■ *adj.* (BrE, *informal, disapproving*) attracting attention by being large or expensive, or by having expensive clothes, etc: *a flash car* ◊ *He's very flash, isn't he?*

**flash·back** /ˈflæʃbæk/ *noun* 1 [C, U] a part of a film, play, etc. that shows a scene that happened earlier in the main story: *The events that led up to the murder were shown in a series of flashbacks.* ◊ *The reader is told the story in flashback.* ⊃ WORDFINDER NOTE at PLOT 2 [C] a sudden, very clear, strong memory of sth that happened in the past that is so real you feel that you are living through the experience again

**flash·bulb** /ˈflæʃbʌlb/ *noun* a small electric BULB that can be attached to a camera to take photographs indoors or when it is dark

**ˈflash card** *noun* 1 a card with a word or picture on it, used by teachers during lessons 2 a feature in an app or online game that flashes up a word or picture, used as a teaching or learning aid

**ˈflash drive** (*also* ˌUSˈB drive, ˈpen drive) (NAmE *also* ˈthumb drive) *noun* (*computing*) a small memory device that can be used to store data from a computer or digital camera and to move it from one device to another SYN Memory Stick™

**flash·er** /ˈflæʃə(r)/ *noun* 1 (*informal*) a man who shows his sexual organs in public, especially in order to shock or frighten women 2 a device that turns a light on and off quickly 3 (NAmE) a light on a vehicle that you can turn on and off quickly as a signal: *four-way flashers* (= four lights that flash together to warn other drivers of possible danger)

**ˈflash flood** *noun* a sudden flood of water caused by heavy rain ⊃ WORDFINDER NOTE at RAIN

**flash·gun** /ˈflæʃɡʌn/ *noun* a piece of equipment that holds and operates a bright light that is used to take photographs indoors or when it is dark

**flash·ing** /ˈflæʃɪŋ/ *noun* [U] (*also* **flashings** [pl.]) a narrow piece of metal put on a roof where it joins a wall to prevent water getting through

**flash·light** /ˈflæʃlaɪt/ (*especially* NAmE) (BrE *usually* **torch**) *noun* a small electric lamp that you can hold in your hand and carry with you

**ˈflash memory** *noun* [U] (*computing*) computer memory that does not lose data when the power supply is lost

**ˈflash mob** *noun* a large group of people who arrange (by mobile phone or email) to gather together in a public place at exactly the same time, spend a short time doing sth there and then quickly all leave at the same time ▶ **ˈflash mob·ber** *noun* **ˈflash mob·bing** *noun* [U]

**flash·point** /ˈflæʃpɔɪnt/ *noun* [C, U] a situation or place in which violence or anger starts and cannot be controlled: *Tension in the city is rapidly reaching flashpoint.* ◊ *potential flashpoints in the south of the country*

**flashy** /ˈflæʃi/ *adj.* (**flash·ier**, **flashi·est**) (*informal, usually disapproving*) 1 (of things) attracting attention by being bright, expensive, large, etc: *a flashy hotel* ◊ *I just want a good reliable car, nothing flashy.* 2 (of people) attracting attention by wearing expensive clothes, etc. 3 intended to impress by appearing to show a lot of skill: *He specializes in flashy technique, without much depth.* ▶ **flash·ily** /-ʃɪli/ *adv.*: *flashily dressed*

**flask** /flɑːsk; NAmE flæsk/ *noun* 1 a bottle with a narrow top, used in scientific work for mixing or storing chemicals 2 (BrE) = VACUUM FLASK: *a flask of tea/coffee* ⊃ compare THERMOS™ 3 (*especially* NAmE) (*also* **hip flask** NAmE, BrE) a small flat bottle made of metal or glass and often covered with leather, used for carrying alcohol with you

**flat** ? A1 /flæt/ *noun, adj., adv., verb*

■ *noun*

- **ROOMS** 1 ? A1 [C] (BrE) (*also* **apartment** *especially in* NAmE) a set of rooms for living in, usually on one floor of a building: *They're renting a furnished flat on the third floor.* ◊ *to buy/sell a flat* ◊ **in a ~** *Do you live in a flat or a house?* ◊ *a basement/ground-floor/top-floor flat* ◊ *a two-bedroom flat* ◊ *a new block of flats* ◊ *Many large old houses have been converted into flats.* ⊃ see also GRANNY FLAT
- **LEVEL PART** 2 [sing.] **the ~ of sth** the flat level part of sth: *He beat on the door with the flat of his hand.* ◊ *the flat of a sword*
- **LAND** 3 [C, usually pl.] an area of low flat land, especially near water: *salt flats* ⊃ see also MUDFLAT
- **HORSE RACING** 4 **the flat, the Flat** [sing.] (BrE) the season for racing horses on flat ground with no jumps
- **IN MUSIC** 5 [C] a note played a SEMITONE lower than the note that is named. The written symbol is (♭): *There are no sharps or flats in the key of C major.* OPP **sharp** ⊃ compare NATURAL
- **TYRE** 6 [C] (*especially* NAmE) a tyre that has lost air, usually because of a hole: *We got a flat on the way home.* ◊ *We had to stop to fix a flat.*
- **IN THEATRE** 7 [C] (*specialist*) a VERTICAL section of SCENERY used on a theatre stage
- **SHOES** 8 **flats** (*also* **flat-ties**) [pl.] (*informal*) shoes with a very low heel: *a pair of flats*

IDM **on the ˈflat** (BrE) on level ground, without hills or jumps (= for example in horse racing)

# flatbed

■ **adj.** (**flat·ter**, **flat·test**)
- **LEVEL** **1** 🔑 A2 having a level surface, not curved or sloping, and without holes or any bits sticking out: *low buildings with flat roofs* ◊ *I need a **flat surface** to write on.* ◊ *A large flat screen was mounted on the wall.* ◊ *People used to think the earth was flat.* **2** 🔑 A2 (of land) without any slopes or hills: *The road stretched ahead across the flat landscape.* **3** 🔑 A2 (of an area of water) calm and without waves: *The sails hung limply in the flat calm (= conditions at sea when there is no wind and the water is completely level).*
- **NOT HIGH** **4** 🔑 A2 broad but not very high: *Chapattis are a kind of flat Indian bread.* ◊ *flat shoes (= with no heels or very low ones)*
- **NOT EXCITING** **5** not exciting; not feeling or showing interest or enthusiasm: *He felt very flat after his friends had gone home.*
- **VOICE** **6** not showing much emotion; not changing much in tone: *Her voice was flat and expressionless.*
- **COLOURS/PICTURES** **7** very smooth, with no contrast between light and dark, and giving no impression of depth: *Acrylic paints can be used to create large, flat blocks of colour.*
- **BUSINESS** **8** not very successful because very little is being sold; not changing or increasing: *The housing market has been flat for months.*
- **REFUSAL/DENIAL** **9** [only before noun] not allowing discussion or argument; definite: *Her request was met with a flat refusal.* ◊ *He gave a flat 'No!' to one reporter's question.*
- **IN MUSIC** **10** used after the name of a note to mean a note a SEMITONE lower: *That note should be B flat, not B.* ◊ picture at MUSIC **OPP sharp** ◊ compare NATURAL **11** below the correct PITCH (= how high or low a note sounds): *The high notes were slightly flat.* **OPP sharp**
- **DRINK** **12** no longer having bubbles in it; not fresh: *The soda was warm and had gone flat.*
- **BATTERY** **13** (BrE) unable to supply any more electricity
- **TYRE** **14** not containing enough air, usually because of a hole
- **FEET** **15** with no natural raised curves under the feet ◊ see also FLAT-FOOTED ▶ **flat·ness** *noun* [U]
- **IDM** **and that's 'flat!** (BrE, informal) that is my final decision and I will not change my mind: *You can't go and that's flat!* **as flat as a 'pancake** (informal) completely flat ◊ more at BACK *n.*, SPIN *n.*

■ **adv.** (*comparative* **flat·ter**, no *superlative*)
- **LEVEL** **1** spread out in a level, straight position, especially against another surface: *Lie flat and breathe deeply.* ◊ *They pressed themselves flat against the tunnel wall as the train approached.*
- **REFUSING/DENYING** **2** (NAmE, *flat* **out**) (informal) in a definite and direct way: *She told me flat she would not speak to me again.* ◊ *I made them a reasonable offer but they turned it down flat.*
- **IN MUSIC** **3** lower than the correct PITCH (= how high or low a note sounds): *He sings flat all the time.* **OPP sharp**
- **IDM** **fall 'flat** if a joke, a story, or an event **falls flat**, it completely fails to make people laugh or to have the effect that was intended **fall flat on your 'face** **1** to fall so that you are lying on your front **2** to fail completely, usually in an embarrassing way: *His next television venture fell flat on its face.* **flat 'broke** (BrE also **stony 'broke**) (informal) completely BROKE (= without money) **flat 'out** (informal) **1** as fast or as hard as possible: *Workers are working flat out to meet the rise in demand for new cars.* **2** (especially NAmE) in a definite and direct way; completely: *I told him flat out 'No'.* ◊ *It's a 30-year mortgage we just flat out can't handle.* ◊ see also FLAT-OUT **in … 'flat** (informal) used with an expression of time to say that sth happened or was done very quickly, in no more time than the time stated: *They changed the wheel in three minutes flat (= in only three minutes).*

■ *verb* [I] (AustralE, NZE) (**-tt-**) to live in or share a flat: *My sister Zoe flats in Auckland.*

**flat·bed** /ˈflætbed/ *noun* **1** (computing) = FLATBED SCANNER **2** (also **flatbed 'truck**, **flatbed 'trailer**) (especially NAmE) an open truck or TRAILER without high sides, used for carrying large objects

**flatbed 'scanner** (also **flatbed**) *noun* (computing) a SCANNER (= device for copying pictures and documents so that they can be stored on a computer) on which the picture or document can be laid flat for copying

**flat·bread** /ˈflætbred/ *noun* [U, C] a type of flat, thin bread made without any YEAST

**flat 'cap** *noun* (BrE) = CLOTH CAP

**flat·car** /ˈflætkɑː(r)/ *noun* (NAmE) a WAGON on a train without a roof or sides, used for carrying goods

**flat-'chested** *adj.* (of a woman) having small breasts

**flat·fish** /ˈflætfɪʃ/ *noun* (*pl.* **flat·fish**) any sea fish with a flat body, for example a PLAICE

**flat-'footed** *adj.* **1** without naturally raised curves (= ARCHES) under the feet **2** (especially NAmE) not prepared for what is going to happen: *They were caught flat-footed by the attack.*

**flat·head** /ˈflæthed/ *adj.* (of a SCREWDRIVER) with an end that is straight and not like a cross in shape ◊ compare PHILLIPS

**flat·line** /ˈflætlaɪn/ *verb* (*informal*) **1** [I] to be at a low level and fail to improve or increase **2** [I] to die; to become CLINICALLY dead even if you later recover

**flat·ly** /ˈflætli/ *adv.* **1** in a way that is very definite and will not be changed **SYN** **absolutely**: *to flatly deny/reject/oppose sth* ◊ *I flatly refused to spend any more time helping him.* **2** in a way that shows very little interest or emotion: *'Oh, it's you,' she said flatly.*

**flat·mate** /ˈflætmeɪt/ (BrE) (NAmE **room·mate**) *noun* a person who shares a flat with one or more others

**flat-'out** *adj.* [only before noun] (*especially NAmE*) definite and direct; complete: *His story was full of contradictions and flat-out lies.* ▶ **flat-'out** *adv.*: *She just flat-out hated me.* ◊ see also FLAT *adj.*

**flat-pack** *noun* (BrE) a piece of furniture that is sold in pieces in a flat box and that you have to build yourself

**flat-panel** *adj.* = FLAT-SCREEN

**flat 'racing** *noun* [U] the sport of horse racing over flat ground with no jumps ◊ compare STEEPLECHASE

**flat 'rate** *noun* a price that is the same for everyone and in all situations: *Interest is charged at a flat rate of 11 per cent.* ◊ *flat-rate charges/tariffs*

**flat-screen** (also **flat-panel**) *adj.* [only before noun] **~ television/TV/computer/monitor**, etc. a type of television or computer monitor that is very thin when compared with the original type

**flat 'spin** *noun* (*specialist*) a movement of an aircraft in which it goes gradually downwards while flying around in almost HORIZONTAL circles
**IDM** **in a flat 'spin** very confused, worried or excited

**flat·ten** /ˈflætn/ *verb* **1** [I, T] to become flat or flatter; to make sth flat or flatter: *The cookies will flatten slightly while cooking.* ◊ *~ sth These exercises will help to flatten your stomach.* ◊ *He flattened his hair down with gel.* **2** [T] **~ sth** to destroy or knock down a building, tree, etc: *Most of the factory was flattened by the explosion.* **3** [T] to press sth/your body against sb/sth: *~ sth against sb/sth She flattened her nose against the window and looked in.* ◊ *~ yourself against sb/sth Greg flattened himself against the wall to let me pass.* **4** [T] **~ sb** (*informal*) to defeat sb easily in a competition, an argument, etc. **SYN** **smash**, **thrash**: *Our team was flattened this evening!* **5** [T] **~ sb** (*informal*) to hit sb very hard so that they fall down: *He flattened the intruder with a single punch.* ◊ *I'll flatten you if you do that again!*
**PHR V** **flatten 'out** **1** to gradually become completely flat: *The hills first rose steeply then flattened out towards the sea.* **2** to stop growing or going up: *Export growth has started to flatten out.* **flatten sth ⇌ out** to make sth completely flat

**flat·ter** /ˈflætə(r)/ *verb* **1** [T] **~ sb** to say nice things about sb, often in a way that is not sincere, because you want them to do sth for you or you want to please them: *Are you trying to flatter me?* **2** [T] **~ yourself (that …)** to choose to believe sth good about yourself and your abilities, especially when other people do not share this opinion: *'How will you manage without me?' 'Don't flatter yourself.'* **3** [T] **~ sb/sth** to make sb look attractive; to make sb seem more attractive or better than they really are: *That colour doesn't flatter many people.* ◊ *The scoreline flattered England* (= they did not deserve to get such a high score). ▶ **flat·ter·er** *noun*

**IDM** **be/feel ˈflattered** to be pleased because sb has made you feel important or special: *He was flattered by her attention.* ◊ *I felt flattered at being asked to give a lecture.* **ˌflatter to deˈceive** (*BrE*) if sth **flatters to deceive**, it appears to be better, more successful, etc. than it really is

**flat·ter·ing** /ˈflætərɪŋ/ *adj.* **1** making sb look more attractive: *a flattering dress* **2** saying nice things about sb/sth: *flattering remarks* **3** making sb feel pleased and special: *I found it flattering that he still recognized me after all these years.*

**flat·tery** /ˈflætəri/ *noun* [U] praise that is not sincere, especially in order to obtain sth from sb: *You're too intelligent to fall for his flattery.*

**IDM** **ˌflattery will get you ˈeverywhere/ˈnowhere** (*informal, humorous*) praise that is not sincere will/will not get you what you want

**flat·ties** /ˈflætiz/ *noun* [pl.] (*informal*) = FLATS

**flatu·lence** /ˈflætʃələns/ *noun* [U] an uncomfortable feeling caused by having too much gas in the stomach

**flatu·lent** /ˈflætʃələnt/ *adj.* **1** (*disapproving*) sounding important and impressive in a way that EXAGGERATES the truth or facts **2** suffering from too much gas in the stomach

**flat·ware** /ˈflætweə(r); *NAmE* -wer/ *noun* [U] (*NAmE*) **1** = SILVERWARE **2** flat dishes such as plates and SAUCERS

**ˌflat ˈwhite** *noun* a cup of coffee made with hot milk, but without the FROTH of a CAPPUCCINO

**flat·worm** /ˈflætwɜːm; *NAmE* -wɜːrm/ *noun* a very simple WORM with a flat body

**flaunt** /flɔːnt/ *verb* (*disapproving*) **1 ~ sth** to show sth you are proud of to other people, in order to impress them: *He did not believe in flaunting his wealth.* ◊ *She openly flaunted her affair with the senator.* **2 ~ yourself** to behave in a confident and sexual way to attract attention

**IDM** **if you've got it, ˈflaunt it** (*humorous, saying*) used to tell sb that they should not be afraid of allowing other people to see their qualities and abilities

**flaut·ist** /ˈflɔːtɪst; *NAmE also* ˈflaʊt-/ (*BrE*) (*NAmE* **flut·ist**) *noun* a person who plays the FLUTE

**fla·von·oid** /ˈfleɪvənɔɪd/ *noun* (*chemistry*) a type of substance found in some plants such as tomatoes that is thought to protect against some types of cancer and heart disease

**fla·vour** ?+ B2 (*US* **fla·vor**) /ˈfleɪvə(r)/ *noun, verb*
■ *noun* **1** ?+ B2 [U] how food or drink tastes SYN taste: *The tomatoes give extra flavour to the sauce.* ◊ *in ~ It is stronger in flavour than other Dutch cheeses.* **2** ?+ B2 [C] a particular type of taste: *This yogurt comes in ten different flavours.* ◊ *a wine with a delicate fruit flavour* **3** [U, C] (*NAmE*) = FLAVOURING **4** ?+ C1 [sing.] a particular quality or atmosphere SYN **ambience**: *the distinctive flavour of South Florida* ◊ *Foreign visitors help to give a truly international flavour to the occasion.* **5** [sing.] **a/the ~ of sth** an idea of what sth is like: *I have tried to convey something of the flavour of the argument.* **6** (*computing*) a particular type of sth, especially computer software

**IDM** **ˌflavour of the ˈmonth** a person or thing that is very popular at a particular time
■ *verb* **~ sth (with sth)** to add sth to food or drink to give it more taste or a particular taste

**fla·voured** (*US* **fla·vored**) /ˈfleɪvəd; *NAmE* -vərd/ *adj.* **1 -flavoured** having the type of flavour mentioned: *lemon-flavoured sweets/candy* **2** having had flavour added to it: *flavoured yogurt*

**fla·vour·ing** (*US* **fla·vor·ing**) /ˈfleɪvərɪŋ/ (*NAmE also* **fla·vor**) *noun* [U, C] a substance added to food or drink to give it a particular taste: *orange/vanilla flavouring* ◊ *This food contains no artificial flavourings.*

**fla·vour·less** (*US* **fla·vor·less**) /ˈfleɪvələs; *NAmE* -vərl-/ *adj.* having no flavour: *The meat was tough and flavourless.*

**fla·vour·some** /ˈfleɪvəsəm; *NAmE* -vərs-/ (*BrE*) **fla·vour·ful**, *US* **fla·vor·ful** /ˈfleɪvəfʊl; *NAmE* -vərf-/) *adj.* having a lot of flavour

**flaw** ?+ C1 /flɔː/ *noun* **1** ?+ C1 a mistake in sth that means that it is not correct or does not work correctly SYN **defect**, **fault**: *The argument is full of fundamental flaws.* ◊ **in ~** *The report reveals fatal flaws in security at the airport.* **2** ?+ C1 **~ (in sb/sth)** a weakness in sb's character: *There is always a flaw in the character of a tragic hero.* **3 ~ (in sth)** a fault or small break in sth that makes it less attractive or valuable

**flawed** ?+ C1 /flɔːd/ *adj.* having a flaw; not perfect or correct: *seriously/fundamentally/fatally flawed* ◊ *a flawed argument* ◊ *the book's flawed heroine*

**flaw·less** /ˈflɔːləs/ *adj.* without flaws and therefore perfect SYN **perfect**: *a flawless complexion/performance* ◊ *Her English is almost flawless.* ▶ **flaw·less·ly** *adv.*

**flax** /flæks/ *noun* [U] **1** a plant with blue flowers, grown for its STEM that is used to make THREAD and its seeds that are used to make LINSEED OIL **2** THREADS from the STEM of the flax plant, used to make LINEN

**flax·en** /ˈflæksn/ *adj.* (*literary*) (of hair) pale yellow SYN **blonde**

**flax·seed** /ˈflæksiːd/ (*also* **linseed**) *noun* [U, C] the seeds of the flax plant, eaten as a health food or used to make LINSEED OIL

**ˈflaxseed oil** *noun* [U] = LINSEED OIL

**flay** /fleɪ/ *verb* **1 ~ sth/sb** to remove the skin from an animal or person, usually when they are dead **2 ~ sb** to hit or WHIP sb very hard so that some of their skin comes off **3 ~ sb/yourself** (*formal*) to criticize sb/yourself severely

**flea** /fliː/ *noun* a very small jumping insect without wings, that bites animals and humans and drinks their blood: *The dog has fleas.* ⊃ VISUAL VOCAB page V3

**IDM** **with a ˈflea in your ear** if sb sends a person away **with a flea in their ear**, they tell them angrily to go away

**flea·bag** /ˈfliːbæg/ *noun* (*informal*) **1** a person who looks poor and does not take care of their appearance **2** an animal that is in poor condition **3** (*especially NAmE*) a hotel that is cheap and dirty

**ˈflea-bitten** *adj.* (*informal*) in poor condition and with an unpleasant appearance

**ˈflea market** *noun* an outdoor market that sells SECOND-HAND (= old or used) goods at low prices

**fleck** /flek/ *noun, verb*
■ *noun* [usually pl.] **1 ~ (of sth)** a very small area of a particular colour: *His hair was dark, with flecks of grey.* ⊃ WORDFINDER NOTE at PATTERN **2 ~ (of sth)** a very small piece of sth: *flecks of dust/foam/dandruff*
■ *verb* [often passive] **~ sth (with sth)** to cover or mark sth with small areas of a particular colour or with small pieces of sth: *The fabric was red, flecked with gold.* ◊ *His hair was flecked with paint.*

**fled** /fled/ *past tense, past part.* OF FLEE

**fledged** /fledʒd/ *adj.* (of birds) able to fly ⊃ see also FULLY FLEDGED

**fledg·ling** (*BrE also* **fledge·ling**) /ˈfledʒlɪŋ/ *noun* **1** a young bird that has just learnt to fly **2** (usually before another noun) a person, an organization or a system that is new and without experience: *fledgling democracies*

**flee** ?+ C1 /fliː/ *verb* (**fled**, **fled** /fled/) [I, T, no passive] to leave a person or place very quickly, especially because you are afraid of possible danger: *She burst into tears and fled.* ◊ **~ from sb/sth** *a camp for refugees fleeing from the war* ◊ **~ to…/into…** *He fled to London after an argument with his family.* ◊ **~ sth** *He was caught trying to flee the country.* ⊃ compare FLY (13)

**fleece** /fliːs/ *noun, verb*
■ *noun* **1** [C] the wool coat of a sheep; this coat when it has been removed from a sheep (by SHEARING) **2** [U, C] a type

# fleecy

of soft warm cloth that feels like sheep's wool; a jacket or SWEATSHIRT that is made from this cloth: *a fleece lining* ◊ *a bright red fleece*
- **verb** ~ **sb** (*informal*) to take a lot of money from sb by charging them too much: *Some local shops have been fleecing tourists.*

**fleecy** /ˈfliːsi/ *adj.* [usually before noun] made of soft material, like the wool coat of a sheep; looking like this: *a fleecy sweatshirt* ◊ *a blue sky with fleecy clouds*

**fleet** /fliːt/ *noun, adj.*
- **noun** **1** [C] a group of military ships commanded by the same person: *a fleet of destroyers* ⇒ WORDFINDER NOTE at NAVY **2** [C] a group of ships fishing together: *a fishing/whaling fleet* **3 the fleet** [sing.] all the military ships of a particular country: *a reduction in the size of the British fleet* **4** [C] ~ **(of sth)** a group of planes, buses, taxis, etc. travelling together or owned by the same organization: *the company's new fleet of vans* ◊ *a fleet car/vehicle*
- **adj.** (*literary*) able to run fast: *fleet of foot* ◊ *fleet-footed*

**Fleet ˈAdmiral** (*US*) (*BrE* **Admiral of the ˈFleet**) *noun* an admiral of the highest rank in the navy: *Fleet Admiral William Hunter*

**fleet·ing** /ˈfliːtɪŋ/ *adj.* [usually before noun] lasting only a short time SYN **brief**: *a fleeting glimpse/smile* ◊ *a fleeting moment of happiness* ◊ *We paid a fleeting visit to Paris.*
▶ **fleet·ing·ly** *adv.*

**ˈFleet Street** *noun* [U] a street in central London where many national newspapers used to have their offices (now used to mean British newspapers and journalists in general)

**Flem·ish** /ˈflemɪʃ/ *noun, adj.*
- **noun 1** [U] the Dutch language as spoken in northern Belgium **2 the Flemish** [pl.] the people of Flanders in northern Belgium
- **adj.** of or connected with Flanders in northern Belgium, its people or its language

**flesh** /fleʃ/ *noun, verb*
- **noun 1** [U] the soft substance between the skin and bones of animal or human bodies: *The trap had cut deeply into the rabbit's flesh.* ◊ *Tigers are flesh-eating animals.* ◊ *the smell of rotting flesh* **2** [U] the skin of the human body: *His fingers closed around the soft flesh of her arm.* ◊ *flesh-coloured* (= a light brownish pink colour) **3** [U] the soft part of fruit and vegetables, especially when it is eaten ⇒ VISUAL VOCAB page V4 **4 the flesh** [sing.] (*literary*) the human body when considering its physical and sexual needs, rather than the mind or soul: *the pleasures/sins of the flesh*
IDM **flesh and ˈblood** when you say that sb is **flesh and blood**, you mean that they are a normal human with needs, emotions and weaknesses: *Listening to the cries was more than flesh and blood could stand.* **your ˌ(own) flesh and ˈblood** a person that you are related to **in the ˈflesh** if you see sb **in the flesh**, you are in the same place as them and actually see them rather than just seeing a picture of them **make your ˈflesh creep** to make you feel afraid or full of horror **put flesh on (the bones of) sth** to develop a basic idea, etc. by giving more details to make it more complete: *The strength of the book is that it puts flesh on the bare bones of this argument.* ⇒ more at POUND *n.*, PRESS *v.*, SPIRIT *n.*, THORN, WAY *n.*
- **verb**
PHRV **flesh sth↔ˈout** [often passive] to add more information or details to a plan, an argument, etc: *These points were fleshed out in the later parts of the speech.*

**flesh·ly** /ˈfleʃli/ *adj.* [only before noun] (*literary*) connected with physical and sexual desires: *fleshly temptations/pleasures*

**ˈflesh wound** *noun* an injury in which the skin is cut but the bones and organs inside the body are not damaged

**fleshy** /ˈfleʃi/ *adj.* **1** (of parts of the body or people) having a lot of flesh: *fleshy arms/lips* ◊ *a large fleshy man* **2** (of plants or fruit) thick and soft: *fleshy fruit/leaves*

**fleur-de-lis** (*also* **fleur-de-lys**) /ˌflɜː də ˈliːs, ˈliːz; *NAmE* ˌflɜːr/ *noun* (*pl.* **fleurs-de-lis** *or* **fleurs-de-lys** /ˌflɜː də ˈliːs, ˈliːz; *NAmE* ˌflɜːr/) (from French) a design representing a flower with three PETALS joined together at the bottom, often used in COATS OF ARMS

**flew** /fluː/ *past tense of* FLY ⇒ HOMOPHONES at FLU

**flex** /fleks/ *verb, noun*
- **verb** [T, I] ~ **(sth)** to bend, move or stretch an arm or a leg, or pull a muscle tight, especially in order to prepare for a physical activity: *to flex your fingers/feet/legs* ◊ *He stood on the side of the pool flexing his muscles.*
IDM **flex your ˈmuscles** to show sb how powerful you are, especially as a warning or threat
- **noun** (*BrE*) (*also* **cord** *NAmE*, *BrE*) [C, U] a piece of wire that is covered with plastic, used for carrying electricity to a piece of equipment: *an electric flex* ◊ *a length of flex* ⇒ picture at CORD

**flexi·bil·ity** /ˌfleksəˈbɪləti/ *noun* [U] **1** (*approving*) the ability to change to suit new conditions or situations: *The new system offers a much greater degree of flexibility in the way work is organized.* **2** the ability to bend easily without breaking: *exercises to develop the flexibility of dancers' bodies* OPP **inflexibility**

**flex·ible** /ˈfleksəbl/ *adj.* **1** (*approving*) able to change to suit new conditions or situations: *a more flexible approach* ◊ *flexible working hours/practices* ◊ *Our plans need to be flexible enough to cater for the needs of everyone.* ◊ *You need to be more flexible and imaginative in your approach.* **2** able to bend easily without breaking: *flexible plastic tubing* OPP **inflexible** ▶ **flex·ibly** /-bli/ *adv.*: *Managers must respond flexibly to new developments in business practice.*

**flex·ion** /ˈflekʃn/ *noun* [U] (*specialist*) the action of bending sth, especially an arm, a leg, etc.

**flexi·time** /ˈfleksitaɪm/ (*especially BrE*) (*NAmE usually* **flex-time** /ˈflekstaɪm/) *noun* [U] a system in which employees work a particular number of hours each week or month but can choose when they start and finish work each day: *She works flexitime.*

**flex·or** /ˈfleksə(r); *NAmE also* -sɔːr/ (*also* **ˈflexor muscle**) *noun* (*anatomy*) a muscle that allows you to bend part of your body ⇒ compare EXTENSOR

**flick** /flɪk/ *verb, noun*
- **verb 1** [T] ~ **sth** + **adv./prep.** to hit sth lightly with a sudden quick movement, especially using your finger and THUMB together, or your hand: *She flicked the dust off her collar.* ◊ *The horse was flicking flies away with its tail.* ◊ *James flicked a peanut at her.* ◊ *Please don't flick ash on the carpet!* **2** [I, T] to move or make sth move with sudden quick movements: + **adv./prep.** *The snake's tongue flicked out.* ◊ *Her eyes flicked from face to face.* ◊ ~ **sth** (+ **adv./prep.**) *He lifted his head, flicking his hair off his face.* ◊ *The horse moved off, flicking its tail.* **3** [T] to smile or look at sb suddenly and quickly: ~ **a smile/look, etc. at sb** *She flicked a nervous glance at him.* ◊ ~ **sb a smile/look, etc.** *She flicked him a nervous glance.* **4** [T] to press a button or switch quickly in order to turn a machine, etc. on or off SYN **flip**: ~ **sth** *He flicked a switch and all the lights went out.* ◊ ~ **sth on/off** *She flicked the TV on.* **5** [T] to move sth up and down with a sudden movement so that the end of it hits sb/sth: ~ **A (with B)** *He flicked me with a wet towel.* ◊ ~ **B (at A)** *He flicked a wet towel at me.* ◊ *to flick a whip* **6** [I, T] ~ **(sth)** to move your finger quickly across the screen of an electronic device such as a mobile phone or small computer in order to move text, pictures, etc: *Flick to the next photo and pinch to zoom in or out.* ◊ *She flicked the screen and searched through her emails.* ⇒ compare PINCH (3), SWIPE (4), TAP (7)
PHRV **flick ˈthrough sth** (*especially BrE*) **1** to look quickly through a book, magazine, website, etc. without reading everything SYN **flip through**: *I've only had time to flick through your report but it seems to be fine.* **2** to keep changing television channels quickly to see what programmes are on SYN **flip through**: *Flicking through the channels, I came across an old war movie.*
- **noun 1** [C, usually sing.] a small sudden, quick movement or hit, for example with a WHIP or part of the body: *Bell's*

*flick into the penalty area helped to create the goal.* ◊ *All this information is available* **at the flick of a switch** (= by simply turning on a machine). ◊ *He threw the ball back with a quick* **flick of the wrist.** **2** [sing.] **a ~ through sth** (*especially BrE*) a quick look through a book, magazine, website, etc. **SYN** **flip:** *I had a flick through the catalogue while I was waiting.* **3** [C] (*old-fashioned, informal*) a film ⊃ see also CHICK FLICK **4** **the flicks** [pl.] (*old-fashioned, BrE, informal*) the cinema

**flicker** /ˈflɪkə(r)/ *verb, noun*
■ *verb* **1** [I] (of a light or a flame) to keep going on and off as it shines or burns: *The lights flickered and went out.* ◊ *the flickering screen of the television* **2** [I] **+ adv./prep.** (of an emotion, a thought, etc.) to be expressed or appear somewhere for a short time: *Anger flickered in his eyes.* **3** [I] to move with small quick movements: *Her eyelids flickered as she slept.*
■ *noun* [usually sing.] **1** **~ (of sth)** a light that shines in an unsteady way: *the flicker of a television/candle* **2** **~ (of sth)** a small, sudden movement with part of the body: *the flicker of an eyelid* **3** **~ (of sth)** a feeling or an emotion that lasts for only a very short time: *a flicker of hope/doubt/interest* ◊ *A flicker of a smile crossed her face.*

**ˈflick knife** (*BrE*) (*also* **switch-blade** *NAmE, BrE*) *noun* a knife with a BLADE inside the handle that jumps out quickly when a button is pressed

**flier** = FLYER

**flies** /flaɪz/ *noun* [pl.] **1** *pl.* of FLY **2** (*BrE*) = FLY *noun* (3) **3 the flies** the space above the stage in a theatre, used for lights and for storing SCENERY

**flight** ⓞ **A1** /flaɪt/ *noun, verb*
■ *noun*
• JOURNEY BY AIR **1** ⓞ **A1** [C] a journey made by air, especially in a plane: *a smooth/comfortable/bumpy flight* ◊ *a domestic/an international flight* ◊ *The first prize is a* **return flight** *to Delhi.* ◊ *~ (from A) (to B) We met on a flight from London to Paris.* ⊃ see also IN-FLIGHT, TEST FLIGHT
• PLANE **2** ⓞ **A1** [C] a plane making a particular journey: *We're booked on the same flight.* ◊ *If we leave now, we can catch the earlier flight.* ◊ *After a few phone calls he* **boarded a flight** *to Bangkok.* ◊ *Flight BA 4793 is now* **boarding** *at Gate 17.* ◊ *~ (to A) (from B) At present there is no* **direct flight** *to Egypt from Namibia.* ⊃ see also CHARTER FLIGHT, SCHEDULED FLIGHT
• FLYING **3** ⓞ **A1** [U] the act of flying: *the age of supersonic flight* ◊ **in ~** *The bird is easily recognized in flight* (= when it is flying) *by the black band at the end of its tail.* ◊ *the stresses the body endures in space flight* ◊ *flight safety*
• MOVEMENT OF OBJECT **4** [U] the movement or direction of an object as it travels through the air: *the flight of a ball*
• OF STEPS **5** [C] a series of steps between two floors or levels: *She fell down a* **flight of stairs/steps** *and hurt her back.*
• RUNNING AWAY **6** [U, sing.] the act of running away from a dangerous or difficult situation: **~ (of sb) (from sb/sth)** *the flight of refugees from the advancing forces* ◊ **in ~ from sth** *The main character is a journalist in flight from a failed marriage.* ⊃ see also WHITE FLIGHT
• OF FANCY/IMAGINATION **7** [C] **~ of fancy/imagination** an idea or a statement that shows a lot of imagination but is not practical or sensible
• GROUP OF BIRDS/AIRCRAFT **8** [C] a group of birds or aircraft flying together: *a flight of geese* ◊ *an aircraft of the Queen's flight*
**IDM** **in the first/top ˈflight** among the best of a particular group ⊃ see also TOP-FLIGHT **put sb to ˈflight** (*old-fashioned*) to force sb to run away **take ˈflight** to run away: *The gang took flight when they heard the police car.*
■ *verb* [usually passive] **~ sth** (*BrE, sport*) to kick, hit or throw a ball through the air with skill: *He equalized with a beautifully flighted shot.*

**ˈflight attendant** *noun* a person whose job is to serve and take care of passengers on an aircraft

**ˈflight crew** *noun* [C + sing./pl. v.] the people who work on a plane during a flight

**ˈflight deck** *noun* **1** an area at the front of a large plane where the pilot sits to use the controls and fly the plane **2** a long flat surface on top of a ship that carries aircraft (= an AIRCRAFT CARRIER) where they take off and land

**ˈflight jacket** (*US*) (*BrE* **ˈflying jacket**) *noun* a short leather jacket with a warm LINING and COLLAR, originally worn by pilots

**ˈflight·less** /ˈflaɪtləs/ *adj.* [usually before noun] (of birds or insects) unable to fly

**ˈflight lieuˈtenant** *noun* (*abbr.* **Flt. Lt.**) an officer of fairly high rank in the British AIR FORCE: *Flight Lieutenant Richard Clarkson*

**ˈflight path** *noun* the route taken by an aircraft through the air ⊃ WORDFINDER NOTE at PLANE

**ˈflight recorder** *noun* = BLACK BOX

**ˈflight sergeant** *noun* a member of the British AIR FORCE, just below the rank of an officer: *Flight Sergeant Bob Andrews*

**ˈflight simulator** *noun* a device that creates the same conditions as those that exist when flying an aircraft, used for training pilots

**flighty** /ˈflaɪti/ *adj.* (*old-fashioned, informal*) a **flighty** woman is one who cannot be relied on because she is always changing activities, ideas and partners without treating them seriously

**flimsy** /ˈflɪmzi/ *adj.* (**flim·sier**, **flim·si·est**) **1** badly made and not strong enough for the purpose for which it is used **SYN** **rickety:** *a flimsy table* **2** (of material) thin and easily torn: *a flimsy piece of paper/fabric/plastic* **3** difficult to believe **SYN** **feeble:** *a flimsy excuse/explanation* ◊ *The evidence against him is pretty flimsy.* ▶ **flim·sily** /-zɪli/ *adv.* **flim·si·ness** *noun* [U]

**flinch** /flɪntʃ/ *verb* [I] **1** to make a sudden movement with your face or body as a result of pain, fear, surprise, etc: *He met my gaze without flinching.* ◊ **~ at sth** *He flinched at the sight of the blood.* ◊ **~ away** *She flinched away from the dog.* ⊃ see also UNFLINCHING
**PHRV** **ˈflinch from sth** | **ˈflinch from doing sth** (often used in negative sentences) to avoid thinking about or doing sth unpleasant: *He never flinched from facing up to trouble.*

**fling** /flɪŋ/ *verb, noun*
■ *verb* (**flung**, **flung** /flʌŋ/) **1** to throw or push sb/sth with force, especially because you are angry, or in a careless way **SYN** **hurl:** **~ sb/sth + adv./prep.** *Someone had flung a brick through the window.* ◊ *He flung her to the ground.* ◊ *I flung a few clothes into a bag.* ◊ *He had his enemies flung into prison.* ◊ **~ sth + adj.** *The door was suddenly flung open.* ⊃ SYNONYMS at THROW **2** **~ yourself/sth + adv./prep.** to move yourself or part of your body suddenly and with a lot of force: *She flung herself onto the bed.* ◊ *He flung out an arm to stop her from falling.* **3** **~ sth (at sb)** **+ speech** to say sth to sb in an aggressive way **SYN** **hurl:** *They were flinging insults at each other.* ⊃ see also FAR-FLUNG
**PHRV** **ˈfling yourself at sb** (*informal, disapproving*) to make it too obvious to sb that you want to have a sexual relationship with them **ˈfling yourself into sth** to start to do sth with a lot of energy and enthusiasm: *They flung themselves into the preparations for the party.* **ˌfling sth↔ˈoff/ˈon** (*informal*) to take off or put on clothing in a quick and careless way: *He flung off his coat and collapsed on the sofa.* **ˌfling sb↔ˈout** (*BrE, informal*) to make sb leave a place suddenly **SYN** **throw sb out** **ˌfling sth↔ˈout** (*BrE, informal*) to get rid of sth that you do not want any longer **SYN** **throw sth out**
■ *noun* [usually sing.] (*informal*) **1** a short period of fun when you do not allow yourself to worry or think seriously about anything: *He was determined to have one last fling before retiring.* **2** **~ (with sb)** a short sexual relationship with sb

**flint** /flɪnt/ *noun* **1** [U, C] a type of very hard grey stone that can produce a SPARK when it is hit against steel; a piece of this stone: *prehistoric flint implements* ◊ *His eyes were as hard as flint.* **2** [C] a piece of flint or hard metal that is used to produce a SPARK

# flintlock

**flint·lock** /ˈflɪntlɒk; NAmE -lɑːk/ noun a gun used in the past that produced a SPARK from a flint when the TRIGGER was pressed

**flinty** /ˈflɪnti/ adj. **1** showing no emotion: *a flinty look/gaze/stare* **2** containing flint: *flinty pebbles/soils*

**flip** /flɪp/ verb, noun, adj.
- verb (**-pp-**) **1** [I, T] to turn over into a different position with a sudden quick movement; to make sth do this: *The plane flipped and crashed.* ◊ (*figurative*) *She felt her heart flip* (= with excitement, etc.). ◊ *~ sth (+ adj.) He flipped the lid open and looked inside the case.* ⇒ see also FLIP OVER **2** [T] to press a button or switch in order to turn a machine, etc. on or off SYN flick: *~ sth to flip a switch* ◊ *~ sth on/off She reached over and flipped off the light.* **3** [T] to throw sth somewhere with a sudden quick movement, especially using your THUMB and/or fingers SYN toss: *~ a coin They flipped a coin to decide who would get the ticket.* ◊ *~ sth + prep. He flipped the keys onto the desk.* **4** [I] *~ (out)* (*informal*) to become very angry, excited or unable to think clearly: *She finally flipped under the pressure.*
- IDM **flip your ˈlid** (*informal*) to become very angry and lose control of what you are saying or doing
- PHRV **ˌflip ˈover** to turn onto the other side or into a position in which the top is where the bottom normally is: *The car hit a tree and flipped over.* ◊ *He flipped over and sat up.* **ˌflip sth↔ˈover** to turn sth onto the other side or into a position in which the top of it is where the bottom of it normally is: *The wind flipped over several cars.* **ˈflip through sth 1** to look quickly through a book, magazine, website, etc. without reading everything SYN flick through: *She flipped through the magazine looking for the letters page.* **2** (*especially NAmE*) to keep changing television channels quickly to see what shows are on SYN flick through: *Flipping through the channels, I came across an old war movie.*
- noun **1** [C] a small quick hit with a part of the body that causes sth to turn over: *The whole thing was decided on the flip of a coin.* **2** [C] a movement in which the body turns over in the air SYN somersault: *The handstand was followed by a back flip.* ◊ (*figurative*) *Her heart did a flip.* **3** [*sing.*] *~ through sth* a quick look through a book, magazine, website, etc. SYN flick: *I had a quick flip through the report while I was waiting.*
- adj. (*informal, disapproving*) = FLIPPANT: *a flip answer/comment* ◊ *Don't be flip with me.*

**ˈflip chart** noun large sheets of paper fixed at the top to a stand so that they can be turned over, used for presenting information at a talk or meeting

**ˈflip-flop** noun, verb
- noun (*BrE and NAmE*) (*NAmE also, AustralE, NZE* **thong**) a type of SANDAL (= open shoe), typically made of plastic or rubber, that has a piece that goes between the big toe and the toe next to it: *a pair of flip-flops*
- verb [I] (**-pp-**) *~ (on sth)* (*especially NAmE, informal*) to change your opinion about sth, especially when you then hold the opposite opinion: *The vice-president was accused of flip-flopping on several major issues.*

**ˈflip-flopper** noun (*informal, especially NAmE*) a person, especially a politician, who suddenly changes his or her opinion or policy ⇒ see also U-TURN

**flip·pant** /ˈflɪpənt/ (*also informal* **flip**) adj. (*disapproving*) showing that you do not take sth as seriously as other people think you should: *a flippant answer/attitude* ◊ *Sorry, I didn't mean to sound flippant.* ▶ **flip·pancy** /-pənsi/ noun [U] **flip·pant·ly** adv.

**ˌflipped ˈclassroom** noun [C, usually sing.] a method of teaching in which students study new material at home, for example with videos over the internet, and then discuss and practise it with teachers in class, instead of the usual method where teachers present new material in school and students practise at home ⇒ see also BLENDED LEARNING

**flip·per** /ˈflɪpə(r)/ noun [usually pl.] **1** a flat body part like an arm without fingers that some sea animals such as SEALS and TURTLES use for swimming ⇒ VISUAL VOCAB page V3 **2** a long flat piece of rubber or plastic that you wear on your foot to help you swim more quickly, especially below the surface of the water: *a pair of flippers* ⇒ WORDFINDER NOTE at SWIMMING

**ˈflip phone** noun a small mobile phone with a cover that opens upwards

**flip·ping** /ˈflɪpɪŋ/ adj., adv. (*BrE, informal*) used as a mild swear word by some people to emphasize sth or to show that they are annoyed: *I hate this flipping hotel!* ◊ *Flipping kids!* ◊ *It's flipping cold today!*

**ˈflip side** noun [usually sing.] **1** *~ (of/to sth)* different and less welcome aspects of an idea, argument or action **2** (*old-fashioned*) the side of a record that does not have the main song or piece of music on it

**flirt** /flɜːt; NAmE flɜːrt/ verb, noun
- verb [I] *~ (with sb)* to behave towards sb as if you find them sexually attractive, without seriously wanting to have a relationship with them
- PHRV **ˈflirt with sth 1** to think about or be interested in sth for a short time but not very seriously: *She flirted with the idea of becoming an actress when she was younger.* **2** to take risks or not worry about a dangerous situation that may happen: *to flirt with danger/death/disaster*
- noun [usually sing.] a person who flirts with a lot of people: *She's a real flirt.*

**flir·ta·tion** /flɜːˈteɪʃn; NAmE flɜːrˈt-/ noun **1** [C, U] *~ with sth* a short period of time during which sb is involved or interested in sth, often not seriously: *a brief and unsuccessful flirtation with the property market* **2** [U] behaviour that shows you find sb sexually attractive but are not serious about them: *Frank's efforts at flirtation had become tiresome to her.* **3** [C] *~ (with sb)* a short sexual relationship with sb that is not taken seriously

**flir·ta·tious** /flɜːˈteɪʃəs; NAmE flɜːrˈt-/ (*also informal* **flirty**) adj. behaving in a way that shows a sexual attraction to sb that is not serious: *a flirtatious young woman* ◊ *a flirtatious smile* ▶ **flir·ta·tious·ly** adv. **flir·ta·tious·ness** noun [U]

**flit** /flɪt/ verb, noun
- verb (**-tt-**) **1** [I] to move lightly and quickly from one place or thing to another: *~ from A to B Butterflies flitted from flower to flower.* ◊ *He flits from one job to another.* ◊ *~ + adv./prep. A smile flitted across his face.* ◊ *A thought flitted through my mind.* **2** [I] (*ScotE, NEngE*) to change the place where you live, especially secretly in order to avoid paying money that you owe to sb: *I had to change schools every time my parents flitted.*
- noun
- IDM **do a (moonlight/midnight) ˈflit** (*BrE, informal*) to leave a place suddenly and secretly, especially at night, usually in order to avoid paying money that you owe to sb

**float** /fləʊt/ verb, noun
- verb
- • ON WATER/IN AIR **1** [I] *+ adv./prep.* to move slowly on water or in the air SYN drift: *A group of swans floated by.* ◊ *The smell of new bread floated up from the kitchen.* ◊ *Beautiful music came floating out of the window.* ◊ (*figurative*) *People seem to float in and out of my life.* **2** [I] to stay on or near the surface of a liquid and not sink: *Wood floats.* ◊ *~ in/on sth She relaxed, floating gently in the water.* ◊ *A plastic bag was floating on the water.* **3** [T] to make sth move on or near the surface of a liquid: *~ sth There wasn't enough water to float the ship.* ◊ *~ sth + adv./prep. They float the logs down the river to the towns.*
- • WALK LIGHTLY **4** [I] *+ adv./prep.* (*literary*) to walk or move in a smooth and easy way SYN glide: *She floated down the steps to greet us.*
- • SUGGEST IDEA **5** [T] *~ sth* to suggest an idea or a plan for other people to consider: *They floated the idea of increased taxes on alcohol.*
- • BUSINESS/ECONOMICS **6** [T] *~ sth (business)* to sell shares in a company or business to the public for the first time: *The company was floated on the stock market in 2014.* ◊ *Shares were floated at 585p.* **7** [T, I] *~ (sth) (economics)* if a government **floats** its country's money or allows it to **float**, it allows its value to change freely according to the value of the money of other countries

**IDM** **float sb's 'boat** (informal) to be what sb likes: *You can listen to whatever kind of music floats your boat.* ➔ more at AIR n.
**PHR V** **float a'bout/a'round** (usually used in the progressive tenses) if an idea, etc. is **floating around**, it is talked about by a number of people or passed from one person to another
■ noun
• VEHICLE **1** a large vehicle on which people dressed in special costumes are carried in a festival: *a carnival float*
• IN FISHING **2** a small light object attached to a FISHING LINE that stays on the surface of the water and moves when a fish has been caught
• FOR SWIMMING **3** a light object that floats in the water and is held by a person who is learning to swim ➔ WORDFINDER NOTE at SWIMMING
• DRINK **4** (NAmE) a drink with ice cream floating in it: *a Coke float*
• MONEY **5** (especially BrE) a sum of money consisting of coins and notes of low value that is given to sb before they start selling things so that they can give customers change
• BUSINESS **6** [C, U] = FLOTATION

**float·er** /ˈfləʊtə(r)/ noun (medical) a very small object inside a person's eye that they see moving up and down

**float·ing** /ˈfləʊtɪŋ/ adj. [usually before noun] not fixed permanently in one particular position or place: *floating exchange rates* ◊ *a floating population* (= one in which people frequently move from one place to another) ◊ (medical) *a floating kidney*

**floating 'rib** (also **false 'rib**) noun (anatomy) any of the lower RIBS that are not attached to the BREASTBONE

**floating 'voter** (BrE) (NAmE ˌswing 'voter) noun a person who does not always vote for the same political party or who has not decided which party to vote for in an election

**floaty** /ˈfləʊti/ adj. (of cloth or clothing) very light and thin

**flock** /flɒk; NAmE flɑːk/ noun, verb
■ noun **1** [C + sing./pl. v.] ~ (of sth) a group of sheep, GOATS or birds of the same type ➔ compare HERD **2** [C + sing./pl. v.] a large group of people, especially of the same type: ~ (of sb) *a flock of children/reporters* ◊ *in flocks They came in flocks to see the procession.* **3** [C + sing./pl. v.] (literary) the group of people who regularly attend the church of a particular priest, etc. **4** [U] small pieces of soft material used for filling CUSHIONS, chairs, etc. **5** [U] small pieces of soft material on the surface of paper or cloth that produce a raised pattern: *flock wallpaper*
■ verb [I] to go or gather together somewhere in large numbers: + **adv./prep.** *Thousands of people flocked to the beach this weekend.* ◊ *Huge numbers of birds had flocked together by the lake.* ◊ ~ **to do sth** *People flocked to hear him speak.* **IDM** see BIRD n.

**floe** /fləʊ/ noun = ICE FLOE

**flog** /flɒg; NAmE flɑːg/ verb (-gg-) **1** [often passive] ~ sb to punish sb by hitting them many times with a WHIP or stick: *He was publicly flogged for breaking the country's alcohol laws.* **2** (BrE, informal) to sell sth to sb: ~ **sth (to sb)** *She flogged her guitar to another student.* ◊ ~ **sth (off)** *We buy them cheaply and then flog them off at a profit.* ◊ ~ **sb sth** *I had a letter from a company trying to flog me insurance.*
**IDM** **flog sth to 'death** (BrE, informal) to use an idea, a story, etc. so often that it is no longer interesting ➔ more at DEAD adj.

**flog·ging** /ˈflɒgɪŋ/ NAmE ˈflɑːg-/ noun [C, U] a punishment in which sb is hit many times with a WHIP or stick: *a public flogging*

## flood ❶ **B1** /flʌd/ noun, verb
■ noun
• WATER **1** **B1** [C, U] a large amount of water covering an area that is usually dry: *The heavy rain has caused floods in many parts of the country.* ◊ *Police have issued flood warnings for Nevada.* ◊ *Much had been done in recent years to improve flood defences.* ◊ **in ~** *The river is in flood* (= has more water in it than normal and has caused a flood).
➔ see also FLASH FLOOD ➔ WORDFINDER NOTE at DISASTER
• LARGE NUMBER **2** **B2** [C] ~ (of sth) a very large number of things or people that appear at the same time: *a flood of*

605 **floor**

*complaints* ◊ *a flood of refugees* ◊ *The child was in floods of tears* (= crying a lot).
■ verb
• FILL WITH WATER **1** **B1** [I, T] if a place **floods** or sth **floods** it, it becomes filled or covered with water: *The cellar floods whenever it rains heavily.* ◊ ~ **sth** *If the pipe bursts it could flood the whole house.*
• OF RIVER **2** **B2** [I, T] to become so full that it spreads out onto the land around it: *When the Ganges floods, it causes considerable damage.* ◊ ~ **sth** *The river flooded the valley.*
• LARGE NUMBERS **3** **B2** [I] ~ + **adv./prep.** to arrive or go somewhere in large numbers **SYN** **pour**: *Refugees continue to flood into neighbouring countries.* ◊ *Texts and tweets came flooding in from all over the country.* **4** [T, usually passive] to send sth somewhere in large numbers: **be flooded with sth** *The office was flooded with applications for the job.* **5** [T] to become or make sth become available in a place in large numbers: ~ **sth** *Cheap imported goods are flooding the market.* ◊ ~ **sth with sth** *A man who planned to flood Britain with cocaine was jailed for 15 years.*
• OF FEELING/THOUGHT **6** [I, T] to affect sb suddenly and strongly: + **adv./prep.** *A great sense of relief flooded over him.* ◊ *Memories of her childhood came flooding back.* ◊ ~ **sb with sth** *The words flooded him with self-pity.*
• OF LIGHT/COLOUR **7** [I, T] to spread suddenly into sth; to cover sth: + **adv./prep.** *She drew the curtains and the sunlight flooded in.* ◊ ~ **sth** *She looked away as the colour flooded her cheeks.* ◊ **be flooded with sth** *The room was flooded with evening light.*
• ENGINE **8** [I, T] ~ **(sth)** if an engine **floods** or if you **flood** it, it becomes so full of petrol that it will not start ▶ **flood·ed** adj.: *flooded fields* **flood·ing** noun [U]: *There will be heavy rain with flooding in some areas.*
**PHR V** **flood sb↔'out** [usually passive] to force sb to leave their home because of a flood

**flood·gate** /ˈflʌdgeɪt/ noun [usually pl.] a gate that can be opened or closed to control the flow of water on a river: (figurative) *If the case is successful, it may open the floodgates to more damages claims against the industry* (= start sth that will be difficult to stop).

**flood·light** /ˈflʌdlaɪt/ noun, verb
■ noun [C, usually pl., U] a large powerful lamp, used for lighting sports grounds, theatre stages and the outside of buildings; the light provided by floodlights: **under floodlights** *a match played under floodlights* ◊ **by ~** *a match played by floodlight* ▶ **flood·light·ing** noun [U]: *The floodlighting had been turned off.*
■ verb [usually passive] (**flood·lit**, **flood·lit** /ˈflʌdlɪt/) to light a place or a building using floodlights: **be floodlit** *The swimming pool is floodlit in the evenings.* ◊ *floodlit tennis courts*

**flood·plain** /ˈflʌdpleɪn/ noun an area of flat land next to a river that regularly floods when there is too much water in the river

**'flood tide** noun a very high rise in the level of the sea as it moves in towards the coast ➔ compare HIGH TIDE

**flood·water** /ˈflʌdwɔːtə(r)/ noun [U] (also **floodwaters** [pl.]) water that covers land after there has been a flood: *The floodwaters have now receded.*

## floor ❶ **A1** /flɔː(r)/ noun, verb
■ noun
• OF ROOM **1** **A1** [C, usually sing.] the surface of a room that you walk on: *a wooden/concrete/tiled floor* ◊ *His glass fell to the floor and broke.* ◊ **on the ~** *The body was lying on the kitchen floor.* ◊ *ceramic floor tiles* ◊ *The alterations should give us extra floor space.* ➔ WORDFINDER NOTE at DANCE
• OF VEHICLE **2** (NAmE also **floor·board**) [C, usually sing.] the bottom surface of a vehicle: *The floor of the car was covered in cigarette ends.*
• LEVEL OF BUILDING **3** **A2** [C] all the rooms that are on the same level of a building: *Their apartment occupies the top floor of the building.* ◊ **on the … ~** *Her office is on the second floor.* ◊ *the Irish guy who lives two floors above* ◊ *There is a lift to all floors.* ➔ note at STOREY ➔ see also FIRST FLOOR, GROUND FLOOR

❶ Oxford Phrasal Academic Lexicon (OPAL) written and spoken word lists | W OPAL written word list | S OPAL spoken word list

# floorboard

- **OF THE SEA/FORESTS 4** ⚓ B1 [C, usually sing.] the ground at the bottom of the sea, a forest, etc: *the ocean/sea/forest floor*
- **IN PARLIAMENT, ETC. 5 the floor** [sing.] the part of a building where discussions or debates are held, especially in a parliament; the people who attend a discussion or debate: *Opposition politicians registered their protest on the floor of the House.* ◇ *We will now take any questions from the floor.* ⇒ **WORDFINDER NOTE** at **DEBATE**
- **AREA FOR WORK 6** [C, usually sing.] an area in a building that is used for a particular activity: *on the floor of the Stock Exchange* (= where trading takes place) ⇒ see also **DANCE FLOOR, FACTORY FLOOR, SHOP FLOOR, TRADING FLOOR**
- **FOR WAGES/PRICES 7** [C, usually sing.] the lowest level allowed for wages or prices: *Prices have gone through the floor* (= fallen to a very low level). ⇒ compare **CEILING** (2) ⇒ see also **PELVIC FLOOR**

IDM ˌget/be ˌgiven/have the ˈfloor to get/be given/have the right to speak during a discussion or debate ˌhold the ˈfloor to speak during a discussion or debate, especially for a long time so that nobody else is able to say anything ˌtake (to) the ˈfloor to start dancing on a DANCE FLOOR: *Couples took the floor for the last dance of the evening.* ˌwipe/ˌmop the ˈfloor with sb (*informal*) to defeat sb completely in an argument or a competition ⇒ more at **GROUND FLOOR**

■ *verb*
- **SURPRISE/CONFUSE 1** ~ **sb** to surprise or confuse sb so that they are not sure what to say or do
- **HIT 2** [usually passive] to make sb fall down by hitting them, especially in a sport: **be floored by sb/sth** *He was floored by the first punch.*
- **BUILDING/ROOM 3** [usually passive] to provide a building or room with a floor: **be floored in/with sth** *All of the rooms are floored in solid pine.*
- **DRIVING 4** ~ **the accelerator** to press the ACCELERATOR pedal of a car hard

**floor·board** /ˈflɔːbɔːd; NAmE ˈflɔːrbɔːrd/ noun **1** a long flat piece of wood in a wooden floor: *bare/polished floorboards* **2** [usually sing.] (*NAmE*) = **FLOOR** (2): *a car floorboard* ◇ *He had his foot to the floorboard* (= was going very fast).

**floor·cloth** /ˈflɔːklɒθ; NAmE ˈflɔːrklɔːθ/ noun (*BrE*) a cloth for cleaning floors

**floor·ing** /ˈflɔːrɪŋ/ noun [U] material used to make the floor of a room: *vinyl/wooden flooring* ◇ *kitchen/bathroom flooring*

ˈfloor lamp (*BrE also* ˈstandard lamp) noun a tall lamp that stands on the floor

ˈfloor manager noun the person responsible for the lighting and other technical arrangements for a television production

ˈfloor plan noun a diagram of the shape of a room or building, as seen from above, showing the position of rooms or furniture

ˈfloor show noun a series of performances by singers, dancers, etc. at a restaurant or club, on the floor, not on a stage

**floozy** (*also* **floozie**) /ˈfluːzi/ noun (*pl.* **-ies**) (*old-fashioned, informal, disapproving*) a woman who has sexual relationships with many different men

**flop** /flɒp; NAmE flɑːp/ verb, noun
■ *verb* (**-pp-**) **1** [I] to sit or lie down in a heavy and sudden way because you are very tired: ~ (**down/back**) **into/on sth** *Exhausted, he flopped down into a chair.* ◇ ~ **down/back** *The young man flopped back, unconscious.* **2** [I] + **adv./prep.** to fall, move or hang in a heavy way, without control: *Her hair flopped over her eyes.* ◇ *The fish were flopping around in the bottom of the boat.* **3** [I] (*informal*) to be a complete failure: *The play flopped on Broadway.* ⇒ see also **FLIP-FLOP** *verb*
■ *noun* (*informal*) a thing or person that is not successful, especially a film, show or party **OPP** hit ⇒ see also **BELLY-FLOP, FLIP-FLOP** *noun*

---

▼ **SYNONYMS**

### floor
**ground · land · earth**

These are all words for the surface that you walk on.

**floor** the surface of a room that you walk on: *She was sitting on the floor watching TV.*

**ground** (*often* **the ground**) the solid surface of the earth that you walk on: *I found her lying on the ground.* ◇ *The rocket crashed a few seconds after it left the ground.*

**land** the surface of the earth that is not sea: *It was good to be back on* **dry land** *again.* ◇ *They fought both at sea and* **on land**.

**earth** (*often* **the earth**) the solid surface of the world that is made of rock, soil, sand, etc: *You could feel the earth shake as the truck came closer.*

**GROUND, LAND OR EARTH?**

- **Ground** is the normal word for the solid surface that you walk on when you are not in a building or vehicle. You can use **earth** if you want to draw attention to the rock, soil etc. that the ground is made of. **Land** is only used when you want to contrast it with the sea: *the land beneath our feet* ◇ *feel the land shake* ◇ *sight ground/earth* ◇ *travel by ground/earth*

**PATTERNS**
- **on/under** the floor/ground/earth
- **bare** floor/ground/earth
- to **drop/fall to** the floor/the ground/(the) earth
- to **reach** the floor/the ground/land

---

▼ **BRITISH/AMERICAN**

### floor

- In *BrE* the floor of a building at street level is the **ground floor**, the one above it is the **first floor** and the one below it is the **basement**, or **lower ground floor** in a public building.
- In *NAmE* the floor at street level is usually called the **first floor**, the one above it is the **second floor** and the one below it is the **basement**. In public buildings the floor at street level can also be called the **ground floor**.
⇒ note at **STOREY**

---

**flop·house** /ˈflɒphaʊs; NAmE ˈflɑːp-/ (*NAmE*) (*BrE* **doss-house**) noun (*informal*) a cheap place to stay for people who have no home

**floppy** /ˈflɒpi; NAmE ˈflɑːpi/ adj. (**flop·pier, flop·piest**) hanging or falling loosely; not hard and stiff: *a floppy hat*

**flora** /ˈflɔːrə/ noun [U] (*specialist*) the plants of a particular area, type of environment or period of time: *alpine flora* ◇ *rare species of flora and fauna* (= plants and animals)

**floral** /ˈflɔːrəl/ adj. [usually before noun] **1** consisting of pictures of flowers; decorated with pictures of flowers: *wallpaper with a floral design/pattern* ◇ *a floral dress* **2** made of flowers: *a floral arrangement/display* ◇ *Floral tributes were sent to the church.*

**floret** /ˈflɒrət; NAmE ˈflɔːr-/ noun a flower part of some vegetables, for example BROCCOLI and CAULIFLOWER. Each vegetable has several florets coming from one main STEM. ⇒ **VISUAL VOCAB** page V5

**florid** /ˈflɒrɪd; NAmE ˈflɔːr-/ adj. **1** (of a person's face) naturally fairly red in colour (not just because the person is hot, angry, etc.): *a florid complexion* **2** (*usually disapproving*) having too much decoration or detail: *florid language* ▶ **florid·ly** *adv.*

**florist** /ˈflɒrɪst; NAmE ˈflɔːr-/ noun **1** a person who owns or works in a shop that sells flowers and plants **2 florist's** (*pl.* **florists**) a shop that sells flowers and plants: *I've ordered some flowers from the florist's.*

**floss** /flɒs; NAmE flɑːs/ noun, verb
■ *noun* [U] **1** = **DENTAL FLOSS 2** thin silk THREAD ⇒ see also **CANDYFLOSS**

■ *verb* [I, T] ~ **(sth)** to clean between your teeth with DENTAL FLOSS

**flo·ta·tion** /fləʊˈteɪʃn/ *noun* **1** (*also* **float**) [C, U] (*business*) the process of selling shares in a company to the public for the first time in order to raise money: *plans for (a) flotation on the stock exchange* ◊ *a stock-market flotation* **2** [U] (*formal*) the act of floating on or in water: *All who remain missing are believed to be wearing flotation devices.*

**floˈtation tank** *noun* a container filled with salt water in which people float in the dark as a way of relaxing

**flo·til·la** /fləˈtɪlə; *NAmE* fləʊˈt-/ *noun* a group of boats or small ships sailing together

**flot·sam** /ˈflɒtsəm; *NAmE* ˈflɑːt-/ *noun* [U] **1** parts of boats, pieces of wood or rubbish, etc. that are found on land near the sea or floating on the sea; any kind of rubbish: *The beaches are wide and filled with interesting flotsam and jetsam.* ⊃ compare JETSAM **2** people who have no home or job and who move from place to place, often rejected by society: *the human flotsam of inner cities*

**FLOTUS** /ˈfləʊtəs/ *abbr.* (*especially US, informal*) First Lady of the United States (the wife of the President of the US) ⊃ see also POTUS, SCOTUS

**flounce** /flaʊns/ *verb, noun*
■ *verb* [I] + *adv./prep.* (*disapproving*) to move somewhere in a way that draws attention to yourself, for example because you are angry or upset: *She flounced out of the room.*
■ *noun* **1** a piece of cloth that is SEWN around the edge of a skirt, dress, curtain, etc. **2** [usually sing.] (*disapproving*) a quick and EXAGGERATED movement that you make when you are angry or want people to notice you: *She left the room with a flounce.* ▶ **flounced** *adj.: a flounced skirt*

**floun·der** /ˈflaʊndə(r)/ *verb, noun*
■ *verb* **1** [I, T] to struggle to know what to say or do or how to continue with sth: *His abrupt change of subject left her floundering helplessly.* ◊ + **speech** '*Well, I, er ...*' *he floundered.* **2** [I] to have a lot of problems and to be in danger of failing completely: *At that time the industry was floundering.* **3** [I] + *adv./prep.* to struggle to move or get somewhere in water, mud, etc.: *She was floundering around in the deep end of the swimming pool.*
■ *noun* (*pl.* **floun·der** *or* **floun·ders**) a small flat sea fish that is used for food

**flour** 🔊 **B1** /ˈflaʊə(r)/ *noun, verb*
■ *noun* [U] **1** 🔊 **B1** a fine white or brown powder made from grain, especially WHEAT, and used in cooking for making bread, cakes, etc: *Sift the flour and salt into a bowl.* ◊ *wheat/rice flour* ⊃ see also ALL-PURPOSE FLOUR, BAKING FLOUR, PLAIN FLOUR, SELF-RAISING FLOUR, SELF-RISING FLOUR, WHITE FLOUR **2** (especially in compounds) fine soft powder made from the seeds or roots of vegetables: *manioc flour* ⊃ see also CHICKPEA FLOUR, GRAM FLOUR
■ *verb* [usually passive] ~ **sth** to cover sth with a layer of flour: *Roll the dough on a lightly floured surface.*

▼ **HOMOPHONES**

**flour • flower** /ˈflaʊə(r)/
• **flour** *noun*: *The cake is made with equal parts of flour and sugar.*
• **flower** *noun*: *The butterflies flit from flower to flower.*
• **flower** *verb*: *Daffodils flower in early spring.*

**flour·ish** 🔊+ **C1** /ˈflʌrɪʃ; *NAmE* ˈflɜːr-/ *verb, noun*
■ *verb* **1** 🔊+ **C1** [I] to develop quickly and become successful or common **SYN** **thrive**: *Few businesses are flourishing in the present economic climate.* **2** 🔊+ **C1** [I] to grow well; to be healthy and happy **SYN** **thrive**: *These plants flourish in a damp climate.* ◊ (*especially BrE*) *I'm glad to hear you're all flourishing.* **3** [T] ~ **sth** to wave sth around in a way that makes people look at it
■ *noun* **1** [usually sing.] an EXAGGERATED movement that you make when you want sb to notice you: *He opened the door for her with a flourish.* ◊ *With a final flourish she laid down her pen.* **2** [usually sing.] an impressive act or way of doing sth: *The season ended with a flourish for Kane, when he scored in the final minute of the match.* **3** a detail or decoration that is used in speech or writing: *a speech full of rhetorical flourishes* **4** a curved line that is used as decoration, especially in writing **5** [usually sing.] a loud short piece of music that is usually played to announce an important person or event: *a flourish of trumpets*

**floury** /ˈflaʊəri/ *adj.* **1** covered with flour: *floury hands* **2** like flour; tasting of flour: *a floury texture* **3** (of potatoes) soft and light when they are cooked

**flout** /flaʊt/ *verb* ~ **sth** to show that you have no respect for a law, etc. by openly not obeying it **SYN** **defy**: *Motorists regularly flout the law.* ◊ *to flout authority/convention*

**flow** 🔊 **B1** 🔊 /fləʊ/ *noun, verb*
■ *noun* [C, usually sing., U]
• CONTINUOUS MOVEMENT **1** 🔊 **B1** the steady and continuous movement of sth/sb in one direction: ~ **(of sth) (from sth)** *She tried to stop the flow of blood from the wound.* ◊ ~ **(of sth) to sth** *Exercise increases blood flow to the brain.* ◊ ~ **(of sth) into sth** *an endless flow of refugees into the country* ◊ ~ **(of sth) through sth** *a steady flow of traffic through the city* ◊ *to improve traffic flow* (= make it move faster)
• PRODUCTION/SUPPLY **2** 🔊 **B1** the continuous production or supply of sth: *to encourage the free flow of information* ◊ *efforts to stem the flow of illegal drugs* ◊ ~ **of sth** *the flow of goods and services to remote areas* ⊃ see also CASH FLOW
• OF SPEECH/WRITING **3** continuous talk by sb: *You've interrupted my flow—I can't remember what I was saying.* ◊ *As usual, Tom was in full flow* (= talking confidently in a way that is hard to interrupt). **4** the way that words, ideas or themes are linked together in speech, writing or music: *Too many examples can interrupt the smooth flow of the text.*
• OF THE SEA **5** the movement of the sea towards the land: *the ebb and flow of the tide*
**IDM** **go with the ˈflow** (*informal*) to be relaxed and not worry about what you should do ⊃ more at EBB *n.*
■ *verb*
• MOVE CONTINUOUSLY **1** 🔊 **B1** [I] (of liquid, gas or electricity) to move steadily and continuously in one direction: *She lost control and the tears began to flow.* ◊ + *adv./prep.* *It's here that the river flows down into the ocean.* ◊ *Blood flowed from a cut on her head.* ◊ *This can prevent air from flowing freely to the lungs.* **2** 🔊 **B1** [I] (of people or things) to move or pass continuously from one place or person to another, especially in large numbers or amounts: *New orders are finally starting to flow.* ◊ + *adv./prep.* *Constant streams of traffic flowed past.* ◊ *Election results flowed in throughout the night.*
• OF IDEAS/CONVERSATION **3** [I] to develop or be produced in an easy and natural way: *Conversation flowed freely throughout the meal.*
• BE AVAILABLE EASILY **4** [I] to be available easily and in large amounts: *It was obvious that money flowed freely in their family.* ◊ *The party got livelier as the drink began to flow.*
• OF FEELING **5** [I] + *adv./prep.* to be felt strongly by sb: *Fear and excitement suddenly flowed over me.*
• OF CLOTHES/HAIR **6** [I] ~ **(down/over sth)** to hang loosely and freely: *Her hair flowed down over her shoulders.* ◊ *long flowing skirts*
• OF THE SEA **7** [I] (of the TIDE in the sea/ocean) to come in towards the land **OPP** **ebb**
**PHR V** **ˈflow from sth** (*formal*) to come or result from sth

**ˈflow chart** (*also* **ˈflow diagram**) *noun* a diagram that shows the connections between the different stages of a process or parts of a system ⊃ picture at CHART

**flower** 🔊 **A1** /ˈflaʊə(r)/ *noun, verb*
■ *noun* **1** 🔊 **A1** the coloured part of a plant from which the seed or fruit develops. Flowers usually grow at the end of a STEM and last only a short time: *The plant has a beautiful bright red flower.* ◊ **in ~** *The roses are in flower early this year.* ◊ *The crocuses are late coming into flower.* ⊃ HOMOPHONES at FLOUR ⊃ VISUAL VOCAB page V7 **2** 🔊 **A1** a plant grown or valued for the beauty of its flowers: *a garden full of flowers* ◊ *The forest floor was a carpet of wild flowers.*

**flower arranging** 608

◇ *a flower garden/show* **3** 🔑 **A1** a flower with its STEM that has been picked as a decoration: *I picked some flowers.* ◇ *a bouquet/bunch of flowers* ◇ *a flower arrangement* ⊃ see also BOUQUET
**IDM** **the flower of sth** *(literary)* the finest or best part of sth
■ *verb* **1** [I] (of a plant or tree) to produce flowers **SYN** bloom: *This particular variety flowers in July.* ◇ *early-flowering spring bulbs* ⊃ HOMOPHONES at FLOUR **2** [I] *(literary)* to develop and become successful **SYN** blossom

**ˈflower arranging** *noun* [U] the art of arranging cut flowers in an attractive way ▶ **ˈflower arranger** *noun*

**ˈflower bed** *noun* a piece of ground in a garden or park where flowers are grown

**flowered** /ˈflaʊəd; NAmE -ərd/ *adj.* [usually before noun] decorated with patterns of flowers

**flower·ing** /ˈflaʊərɪŋ/ *noun* **1** [U] the time when a plant has flowers **2** [C, *usually sing.*] **~ of sth** the time when sth, especially a period of new ideas in art, music, science, etc., reaches its most complete and successful stage of development

**ˈflower·pot** /ˈflaʊəpɒt; NAmE -ərpɑːt/ *noun* a small container made of plastic or CLAY for growing plants in ⊃ compare CONTAINER (3)

**ˈflower power** *noun* [U] the culture connected with young people of the 1960s and early 1970s who believed in love and peace and were against war

**flow·ery** /ˈflaʊəri/ *adj.* [usually before noun] **1** covered with flowers or decorated with pictures of flowers **2** smelling or tasting of flowers **3** (*usually disapproving*) (of speech or writing) too complicated; not expressed in a clear and simple way

**flown** /fləʊn/ *past part.* of FLY ⊃ see also HIGH-FLOWN

**ˈflow-on** *noun, adj.* (*AustralE, NZE*)
■ *noun* an increase in pay or an improvement in working conditions that is made because one has already been given in a similar job
■ *adj.* flow-on effects, etc. are ones that happen as a result of sth else

**fl oz** *abbr.* (*pl.* **fl oz**) (in writing) FLUID OUNCE: *Add 8 fl oz water.*

**Flt Lt** *abbr.* (in writing) FLIGHT LIEUTENANT (= an officer of fairly high rank in the British AIR FORCE): *Flt Lt Richard Clarkson*

**flu** 🔑 **A2** /fluː/ (*often* **the flu**) (*also formal* **in·flu·enza**) *noun* [U] a serious disease caused by a virus, that causes a high temperature, severe pains and weakness: *The whole family has the flu.* ◇ (*BrE*) *She's got flu.* ◇ *a flu outbreak/epidemic/pandemic* ◇ *a flu vaccine/vaccination* ◇ (*BrE, informal*) *a flu jab* ◇ (*especially NAmE, informal*) *a flu shot* ◇ *He is suffering from flu-like symptoms.* ⊃ see also AVIAN FLU, BIRD FLU, GASTRIC FLU, SWINE FLU

▼ **HOMOPHONES**

**flew** • **flu** /fluː/
• **flew** *verb* (*past tense of* FLY): *The project team flew to Denver to meet the company's board.*
• **flu** *noun*: *She's had a nasty dose of flu.*

**flub** /flʌb/ *verb* [T, I] (**-bb-**) **~ (sth)** (*NAmE, informal*) to do sth badly or make a mistake **SYN** fluff, bungle: *She flubbed the first line of the song.* ▶ **flub** *noun*

**fluc·tu·ate** /ˈflʌktʃueɪt/ *verb* [I] to change frequently in size, amount, quality, etc., especially from one extreme to another **SYN** vary: *fluctuating prices* ◇ **~ between A and B** *During the crisis, oil prices fluctuated between $20 and $40 a barrel.* ◇ **+ adv./prep.** *Temperatures can fluctuate as much as 10 degrees.* ◇ *My mood seems to fluctuate from day to day.* ⊃ WORDFINDER NOTE at TREND ▶ **fluc·tu·ation** /ˌflʌktʃuˈeɪʃn/ *noun* [C, U]: **~ (in/of sth)** *wild fluctuations in interest rates*

**flue** /fluː/ *noun* a pipe or tube that takes smoke, gas or hot air away from a fire, a HEATER or an oven

**flu·ency** /ˈfluːənsi/ *noun* [U, *sing.*] **1** the quality of being able to speak or write a language, especially a foreign language, easily and well: *Fluency in French is required for this job.* **2** the quality of doing sth in a way that is smooth and shows skill: *The team lacked fluency during the first half.*

**flu·ent** /ˈfluːənt/ *adj.* **1** **~ (in sth)** able to speak, read or write a language, especially a foreign language, easily and well: *She's fluent in Polish.* ◇ *a fluent speaker/reader* **2** (of a language, especially a foreign language) expressed easily and well: *He speaks fluent Italian.* **3** (of an action) done in a way that is smooth and shows skill: *fluent handwriting* ◇ *fluent movements* ▶ **flu·ent·ly** *adv.*

**fluff** /flʌf/ *noun, verb*
■ *noun* [U] **1** (*also* **lint**) small pieces of wool, cotton, etc. that gather on clothes and other surfaces **2** soft animal fur or bird feathers, found especially on young animals or birds **3** (*informal, especially NAmE*) entertainment that is not serious and is not considered to have great value
■ *verb* **~ sth** (*informal*) to do sth badly or to fail at sth **SYN** bungle: *He completely fluffed an easy shot* (= in sport). ◇ *Most actors fluff their lines occasionally.* **2** **~ sth (out/up)** to shake or brush sth so that it looks larger and/or softer: *The female sat on the eggs, fluffing out her feathers.* ◇ *Let me fluff up your pillows for you.*

**fluffy** /ˈflʌfi/ *adj.* (**fluf·fier**, **fluf·fiest**) **1** covered in very soft fur or feathers: *a little fluffy kitten* **2** (of food) soft, light and containing air: *Beat the butter and sugar until soft and fluffy.* **3** looking as if it is soft and light: *fluffy white clouds* **4** (*informal, disapproving*) light and not serious; having no substance, depth or power: *a fluffy film/movie* ◇ *a fluffy argument*

**flu·gel·horn** /ˈfluːɡlhɔːn; NAmE -hɔːrn/ *noun* a BRASS musical instrument like a small TRUMPET

**fluid** 🔑 **C1** /ˈfluːɪd/ *noun, adj.*
■ *noun* 🔑 **C1** [C, U] (*formal or specialist*) a liquid; a substance that can flow: *body fluids* (= for example, blood) ◇ *The doctor told him to drink plenty of fluids.* ◇ *cleaning fluid* ⊃ see also AMNIOTIC FLUID, BRAKE FLUID, CORRECTION FLUID
■ *adj.* **1** (*formal*) (of movements, designs, music, etc.) smooth and beautiful **SYN** flowing: *a loose, fluid style of dancing* ◇ *fluid guitar playing* ◇ *the fluid lines of the drawing* **2** (*formal*) (of a situation) likely to change; not fixed: *a fluid political situation* **3** (*specialist*) that can flow freely, as gases and liquids do: *a fluid consistency*

**flu·id·ity** /fluˈɪdəti/ *noun* [U] **1** (*formal*) the quality of being smooth and beautiful: *She danced with great fluidity of movement.* **2** (*formal*) the quality of being likely to change: *the fluidity of human behaviour* ◇ *social fluidity* **3** (*specialist*) the quality of being able to flow freely, as gases and liquids do

**ˌfluid ˈounce** *noun* (*abbr.* **fl oz**) a unit for measuring liquids, equal to 0.028 of a LITRE in the UK and some other countries, and 0.03 of a LITRE in the US. There are 20 fluid ounces in a British PINT and 16 in an American PINT.

**fluke** /fluːk/ *noun* [usually *sing.*] (*informal*) a lucky or unusual thing that happens by accident, not because of planning or skill: *They are determined to show that their last win was no fluke.* ◇ *a fluke goal* ▶ **fluky** (*also* **flukey**) *adj.*

**flume** /fluːm/ *noun* **1** a narrow channel made to carry water for use in industry **2** a water CHUTE (= a tube for sliding down) at an AMUSEMENT PARK or a swimming pool

**flum·mery** /ˈflʌməri/ *noun* [U] ideas, statements or procedures that you think are silly or have no real meaning, especially praise that is silly or not sincere **SYN** nonsense: *She hated the flummery of public relations.*

**flum·mox** /ˈflʌməks/ *verb* [usually passive] (not used in the progressive tenses) (*informal*) to confuse sb so that they do not know what to say or do: **be flummoxed (by sth)** *I was flummoxed by her question.* ▶ **flum·moxed** *adj.*

**flung** /flʌŋ/ *past tense, past part.* of FLING ⊃ see also FAR-FLUNG

**flunk** /flʌŋk/ *verb* (*informal, especially NAmE*) **1** [T, I] **~ (sth)** to fail an exam, a test or a course: *I flunked math in second grade.* **2** [T] **~ sb** to make sb fail an exam, a test, or a course by giving them a low mark: *She's flunked 13 of the 18 students.*

**PHRV** **flunk ˈout (of sth)** (*NAmE, informal*) to have to leave a school or college because your grades are not good enough

**flun·key** (*also* **flunky**) /ˈflʌŋki/ *noun* (*pl.* **-eys** *or* **-ies**) **1** (*disapproving*) a person who tries to please sb who is important and powerful by doing small jobs for them **2** (*old-fashioned*) a servant in uniform

**fluor·es·cent** /flə'resnt/ *adj.* **1** (of substances) producing bright light by using some forms of RADIATION: *a fluorescent lamp* (= one that uses such a substance) ◊ *fluorescent lighting* **2** (of a colour, material, etc.) appearing very bright when light shines on it; that can be seen in the dark: *cyclists wearing fluorescent orange and yellow armbands* ⊃ compare PHOSPHORESCENT ▶ **fluor·es·cence** /-sns/ *noun* [U]

**fluorid·ation** /ˌflɔːrɪˈdeɪʃn; *BrE also* ˌflʊər-; *NAmE also* ˌflʊr-/ *noun* [U] the practice of adding fluoride to drinking water to prevent tooth DECAY (= damage from natural causes or lack of care)

**fluor·ide** /ˈflɔːraɪd; *BrE also* ˈflʊər-; *NAmE also* ˈflʊr-/ *noun* a chemical containing fluorine that protects teeth from DECAY (= damage from natural causes or lack of care) and is often added to TOOTHPASTE and sometimes to drinking water

**fluor·ine** /ˈflɔːriːn; *BrE also* ˈflʊər-; *NAmE also* ˈflʊr-/ *noun* [U] (*symb.* **F**) a chemical element. Fluorine is a poisonous pale yellow gas and is very REACTIVE.

**flur·ried** /ˈflʌrid; *NAmE* ˈflɜːr-/ *adj.* nervous and confused, especially because there is too much to do **SYN** **flustered**

**flurry** /ˈflʌri; *NAmE* ˈflɜːri/ *noun* (*pl.* **-ies**) **1** [usually sing.] an occasion when there is a lot of activity, interest, excitement, etc. within a short period of time: *a sudden flurry of activity* ◊ *in a ~ (of sth) They arrived in a flurry of excitement.* ◊ *A flurry of shots rang out in the darkness.* **2** a small amount of snow, rain, etc. that falls for a short time and then stops: *snow flurries* ◊ *flurries of snow* ⊃ WORDFINDER NOTE at SNOW **3** a sudden short movement of paper or cloth, especially clothes: **in a ~ (of sth)** *The ladies departed in a flurry of silks and satins.*

**flush** /flʌʃ/ *verb, noun, adj.*

■ *verb* **1** [I, T] (of a person or their face) to become red, especially because you are embarrassed, angry or hot; to make sb's face become red: *She flushed with anger.* ◊ *+ adj. Sam felt her cheeks flush red.* ◊ *~sth A rosy blush flushed her cheeks.* **2** [I, T] **~(sth)** when a toilet **flushes** or you **flush** it, water passes through it to clean it, after a handle, etc. has been pressed **3** [T] to clean sth by causing water to pass through it: *~sth out (with sth) Flush the pipe out with clean water.* ◊ *~sth through sth Flush clean water through the pipe.* **4** [T] *~sth + adv./prep.* to get rid of sth with a sudden flow of water or other liquid: *They flushed the drugs down the toilet.* ◊ *Drinking lots of water will help to flush toxins out of the body.* **5** [T] *~sb/sth + adv./prep.* to force a person or an animal to leave the place where they are hiding: *They're trying to flush him out of hiding.*

■ *noun* **1** [C, usually sing.] a red colour that appears on your face or body because you are embarrassed, excited or hot: *A pink flush spread over his cheeks.* ⊃ see also HOT FLUSH **2** [C, usually sing.] a sudden strong feeling; the hot feeling on your face or body caused by this: *a flush of anger/embarrassment/enthusiasm/guilt* **3** [sing.] the act of cleaning a toilet with a sudden flow of water: *Give the toilet a flush.* **4** [C] (in card games) a set of cards that a player has that are all of the same SUIT: *a royal flush* (= the five highest cards of a SUIT)

**IDM** **(in) the first flush of sth** (*formal*) (at) a time when sth is new, exciting and strong: *in the first flush of youth/enthusiasm/romance*

■ *adj.* [not before noun] **1** (*informal*) having a lot of money, usually for a short time **2** *~with sth* (of two surfaces) completely level with each other: *Make sure the paving stones are flush with the lawn.*

**flushed** /flʌʃt/ *adj.* (of a person) red; with a red face: *flushed cheeks* ◊ *Her face was flushed with anger.* ◊

609

(*figurative*) *He was flushed with success* (= very excited and pleased) *after his first novel was published.*

**flus·ter** /ˈflʌstə(r)/ *verb, noun*

■ *verb* [often passive] *~sb* to make sb nervous and/or confused, especially by giving them a lot to do or by making them hurry ▶ **flus·tered** *adj.* **SYN** **flurried**: *She arrived late, looking hot and flustered.*

■ *noun* [sing.] (*BrE*) a state of being nervous and confused

**flute** /fluːt/ *noun* **1** a musical instrument of the WOODWIND group, like a thin pipe in shape. The player holds it to the side of his or her face and blows across a hole at one end. **2** **champagne ~** a tall narrow glass used for drinking CHAMPAGNE

**fluted** /ˈfluːtɪd/ *adj.* (especially of a round object) with a pattern of curves cut around the outside: *fluted columns* ▶ **flut·ing** *noun* [U]

**flut·ist** /ˈfluːtɪst/ (*NAmE*) (*BrE* **flaut·ist**) *noun* a person who plays the FLUTE

**flut·ter** /ˈflʌtə(r)/ *verb, noun*

■ *verb* **1** [I, T] to move lightly and quickly; to make sth move in this way: *Flags fluttered in the breeze.* ◊ *Her eyelids fluttered but did not open.* ◊ *~sth He fluttered his hands around wildly.* ◊ *She fluttered her eyelashes at him* (= tried to attract him in order to persuade him to do sth). **2** [I, T] **~(sth)** when a bird or an insect **flutters** its wings, or its wings **flutter**, the wings move lightly and quickly up and down **3** [I] *+ adv./prep.* (of a bird or an insect) to fly somewhere moving the wings quickly and lightly: *The butterfly fluttered from flower to flower.* **4** [I] (of your heart, etc.) to beat very quickly and not regularly: *I could feel a fluttering pulse.* ◊ (*figurative*) *The sound of his voice in the hall made her heart flutter.*

■ *noun* **1** [C, usually sing.] a quick, light movement: *the flutter of wings* ◊ *a flutter of her long, dark eyelashes* ◊ (*figurative*) *to feel a flutter of panic in your stomach* **2** [C, usually sing.] *~(on sth)* (*BrE, informal*) a small bet: *to have a flutter on the horses* **3** [sing.] a state of nervous or confused excitement: *Her sudden arrival caused quite a flutter.* **4** [C] a very fast HEARTBEAT, caused when sb is nervous or excited: *Her heart gave a flutter when she saw him.* **5** [U, C] (*medical*) a medical condition in which you have an unsteady HEARTBEAT **6** [U] (*specialist*) rapid changes in the PITCH or volume of recorded sound ⊃ compare WOW

**flu·vial** /ˈfluːviəl/ *adj.* (*specialist*) relating to rivers

**flux** /flʌks/ *noun* **1** [U] continuous movement and change: *Our society is in a state of flux.* **2** [C, usually sing., U] (*specialist*) a flow; an act of flowing: *a flux of neutrons*

# fly

/flaɪ/ *verb, noun, adj.*

■ *verb* (**flies, fly·ing, flew** /fluː/, **flown** /fləʊn/) **HELP** In sense 15 **flied** is used for the past tense and past participle.

• **OF BIRD/INSECT** **1** [I] to move through the air, using wings: *Penguins can't fly.* ◊ *+ adv./prep. A stork flew slowly past.* ◊ *A wasp had flown in through the window.*

• **AIRCRAFT/SPACECRAFT** **2** [I] (of an aircraft or a SPACECRAFT) to move through air or space: *~(from A) (to B) They were on a plane flying from London to New York.* ◊ *+ adv./prep. Enemy planes fly overhead.* **3** [I] to travel in an aircraft or a SPACECRAFT: *Is this the first time that you've flown?* ◊ *~(from A) (to B) I'm flying to Hong Kong tomorrow.* ◊ *+ noun I always fly business class.* ◊ *We're flying KLM.* **4** [T, I] to control an aircraft, etc. in the air: *He's learning to fly.* ◊ *~sth a pilot trained to fly large passenger planes* ◊ *children flying kites* **5** [T] *+ adv./prep.* to transport goods or passengers in a plane: *The stranded tourists were finally flown home.* ◊ *He had flowers specially flown in for the ceremony.* **6** [T] *~sth* to move through the air for a particular distance; to travel over an ocean or area of land in an aircraft: *Some birds fly huge distances when they migrate.* ◊ *to fly the Atlantic*

• **MOVE QUICKLY/SUDDENLY** **7** [I] *(+ adv./prep.)* to go or move quickly: *The train was flying along.* ◊ *She gasped and her hand flew to her mouth.* ◊ *It's late—I must fly.* **8** [I] to move suddenly and with force: *(+ adv./prep.) A large stone came flying in through the window.* ◊ *Several*

# flyaway

people were hit by flying glass. ◊ + adj. David gave the door a kick and it flew open.
- OF TIME **9** [I] to seem to pass very quickly: *Doesn't time fly?* ◊ *~by/past Summer has just flown by.*
- FLAG **10** [I, T] if a flag **flies**, or if you **fly** it, it is displayed, for example on a POLE (= a long piece of wood or metal): *Flags were flying at half mast on all public buildings.* ◊ *~ sth to fly the Stars and Stripes*
- MOVE FREELY **11** [I] to move around freely: *hair flying in the wind*
- OF STORIES/RUMOURS **12** [I] to be talked about by many people
- ESCAPE **13** [T, I] *~ (sth)* (*formal*) to escape from sb/sth: *Both suspects have flown the country.* ⊃ compare FLEE
- OF PLAN **14** [I] (*especially NAmE*) to be successful: *It remains to be seen whether his project will fly.*
- IN BASEBALL **15** (**flies, flying, flied, flied**) [I, T] *~ (sth)* to hit a ball high into the air

**IDM** **fly the ˈcoop** (*informal, especially NAmE*) to escape from a place **fly ˈhigh** to be successful **fly in the face of ˈsth** to oppose or be the opposite of sth that is usual or expected: *Such a proposal is flying in the face of common sense.* **fly into a ˈrage, ˈtemper, etc.** to become suddenly very angry **fly a ˈkite** (*informal*) to test out public opinion on a subject **fly the ˈnest 1** (of a young bird) to become able to fly and leave its NEST **2** (*informal*) (of sb's child) to leave home and live somewhere else **fly off the ˈhandle** (*informal*) to suddenly become very angry **go fly a/your ˈkite** (*NAmE, informal*) used to tell sb to go away and stop annoying you or INTERFERING **go ˈflying** (*informal*) to fall, especially as a result of not seeing sth under your feet: *Someone's going to go flying if you don't pick up these toys.* **let ˈfly (at sb/sth) (with sth)** to attack sb by hitting them or speaking angrily to them: *He let fly at me with his fist.* ◊ *She let fly with a stream of abuse.* ⊃ more at BIRD *n.*, CROW *n.*, FLAG *n.*, PIG *n.*, SEAT *n.*, TANGENT, TIME *n.*, WINDOW

**PHRV** **ˈfly at sb** (of a person or an animal) to attack sb suddenly

■ *noun* (*pl.* **flies**)
- INSECT **1** [C] a small flying insect with two wings. There are many different types of fly and many of them spread disease: *A fly was buzzing against the window.* ◊ *Flies rose in thick black swarms.* ⊃ see also CRANE FLY, FRUIT FLY, TSETSE FLY
- IN FISHING **2** [C] a fly or sth made to look like a fly, that is put on the end of a fishing line and used as BAIT to catch fish: *fly fishing* ⊃ WORDFINDER NOTE AT FISHING
- ON TROUSERS/PANTS **3** [*sing.*] (*BrE also* **flies**) an opening down the front of a pair of trousers that fastens with a ZIP or buttons and is usually covered over by a narrow piece of material: *Your fly is undone!* ◊ *Your flies are undone!*
- ON TENT **4** [C] a piece of material that covers the entrance to a tent ⊃ see also FLIES
- IN BASEBALL **5** = FLY BALL

**IDM** **die/fall/drop like ˈflies** (*informal*) to die or become ill and fall down in very large numbers: *People were dropping like flies in the intense heat.* **a/the fly in the ˈointment** a person or thing that makes a situation or an occasion less pleasant, successful, etc. **a fly on the ˈwall** a person who watches others without being noticed: *I'd love to be a fly on the wall when he tells her the news.* ◊ *fly-on-the-wall documentaries* (= in which people are filmed going about their normal lives as if the camera were not there) **(there are) no flies on ˈsb** (*informal*) the person mentioned is clever and not easily tricked **not harm/hurt a ˈfly** to be kind and gentle and unwilling to cause unhappiness **on the ˈfly 1** (*informal*) if you do sth **on the fly**, you do it quickly while sth else is happening, and without thinking about it very much **2** (*computing*) while a computer program or application is operating, without completely RESTARTING it

■ *adj.* (*informal*) **1** (*BrE*) clever and showing good judgement about people, especially so that you can get an advantage for yourself **2** (*NAmE, informal*) fashionable and attractive

**ˈfly·away** /ˈflaɪəweɪ/ *adj.* (especially of hair) soft and fine; difficult to keep tidy

**ˈfly ball** (*also* **fly**) *noun* (in baseball) a ball that is hit high into the air

**ˈfly-by** *noun* (*pl.* **fly-bys**) **1** the flight of a SPACECRAFT near a planet to record data **2** (*also* **ˈfly-over**) (*both NAmE*) (*BrE* **ˈfly-past**) a special flight by a group of aircraft, for people to watch at an important ceremony

**ˈfly-by-night** *adj.* [only before noun] (of a person or business) dishonest and only interested in making money quickly ▶ **ˈfly-by-night** *noun*

**ˈfly·catch·er** /ˈflaɪkætʃə(r); *NAmE also* -ketʃ-/ *noun* a small bird that catches insects while it is flying

**ˈfly-drive** *adj.*, *noun* (*BrE*)
■ *adj.* [only before noun] (of a holiday/vacation) organized by a travel company at a fixed price that includes your flight to a place, a car to drive while you are there and somewhere to stay: *a fly-drive break*
■ *noun* a fly-drive holiday

**flyer** (*also* **flier**) /ˈflaɪə(r)/ *noun* **1** [C] (*informal*) a person who flies an aircraft (usually a small one, not a passenger plane) **2** [C] a person who travels in a plane as a passenger: *frequent flyers* **3** [C] a person who operates sth such as a model aircraft or a KITE from the ground **4** [C] a thing, especially a bird or an insect, that flies in a particular way: *Butterflies can be strong flyers.* **5** [C] a small sheet of paper that advertises a product or an event and is given to a large number of people **6** [C] (*informal*) a person, an animal or a vehicle that moves very quickly: *Ford's flashy new flyer* **7** [*sing.*] = FLYING START ⊃ see also HIGH-FLYER

**ˈfly fishing** *noun* [U] the sport of fishing in a river or lake using an artificial fly at the end of the line to attract and catch the fish

**ˌfly ˈhalf** *noun* = STAND-OFF HALF

**fly·ing** /ˈflaɪɪŋ/ *adj.*, *noun*
■ *adj.* [only before noun] **1** able to fly: *flying insects* **2** moving rapidly through the air: *flying glass/debris*
**IDM** **with flying ˈcolours** very well; with a very high mark: *She passed the exam with flying colours.* **ORIGIN** In the past, a ship returned to port after a victory in battle decorated with flags (= colours).
■ *noun* [U] **1** travelling in an aircraft: *I'm terrified of flying.* **2** operating the controls of an aircraft: *flying lessons*

**ˈflying boat** *noun* a large plane that can take off from and land on water

**ˌflying ˈbuttress** *noun* (*architecture*) a half ARCH of stone that supports the outside wall of a large building such as a church

**ˌflying ˈdoctor** *noun* (especially in Australia) a doctor who travels in an aircraft to visit patients who live far from a town: *A flying doctor service operates in remote regions.*

**ˌflying ˈfish** *noun* (*pl.* **flying fish**) a tropical sea fish that can rise and move forwards above the surface of the water, using its FINS (= flat parts that stick out from its body) as wings

**ˌflying ˈfox** *noun* a large BAT (= an animal like a mouse with wings) that lives in hot countries and eats fruit

**ˈflying jacket** (*BrE*) (*US* **ˈflight jacket**) *noun* a short leather jacket with a warm LINING and COLLAR, originally worn by pilots

**ˌflying ˈleap** *noun* a long high jump made while you are running quickly: *to take a flying leap into the air*

**ˈflying machine** *noun* an aircraft, especially one that is unusual or was built a long time ago

**ˌflying ˈofficer** *noun* an officer of fairly low rank in the British AIR FORCE: *Flying Officer Ian Wall*

**ˌflying ˈsaucer** *noun* a round SPACECRAFT that some people claim to have seen and that some people believe comes from another planet ⊃ compare UFO

**ˈflying squad** *noun* (*usually* **the Flying Squad**) [C + *sing./pl. v.*] a group of police officers in the UK who are ready to travel very quickly to the scene of a serious crime

**flying 'squirrel** noun a small animal like a SQUIRREL that travels through the air between trees, spreading out the skin between its front and back legs to stop itself from falling too quickly

**flying 'start** (also less frequent **flyer**) noun [sing.] a very fast start to a race, competition, etc.
**IDM** **get off to a ˌflying 'start** | **get off to a 'flyer** to make a very good start; to begin sth well

**flying 'visit** noun (BrE) a very short visit

**fly·over** /ˈflaɪəʊvə(r)/ noun **1** (BrE) (NAmE **over·pass**) a bridge that carries one road over another one **2** (NAmE) = FLY-BY (2)

**'flyover country** noun [U] (also the ˌflyover 'states [pl.]) (informal, disapproving) (in the US) the area in the middle of the country between the states on the coasts: *It's an area most New Yorkers know as flyover country.*

**fly·paper** /ˈflaɪpeɪpə(r)/ noun [C, U] a long narrow piece of sticky paper that you hang in a room to catch flies

**'fly-past** (BrE) (NAmE **fly-by**, **'fly-over**) noun a special flight by a group of aircraft, for people to watch at an important ceremony

**fly·sheet** /ˈflaɪʃiːt/ noun (BrE) an extra sheet of material on the outside of a tent that keeps the rain out ⊃ picture at TENT

**'fly-tip** verb (**-pp-**) [I] (BrE) to leave waste somewhere illegally ⊃ WORDFINDER NOTE at WASTE ▶ **'fly-tipping** noun [U] **'fly-tipper** noun

**fly·weight** /ˈflaɪweɪt/ noun [U, C] a weight in BOXING and other sports, lighter than BANTAMWEIGHT, usually between 48 and 51 KILOGRAMS; a BOXER or other competitor in this class

**fly·wheel** /ˈflaɪwiːl/ noun a heavy wheel in a machine or an engine that helps to keep it working smoothly and at a steady speed

**FM** abbr. **1** /ˌef 'em/ frequency modulation (a method of broadcasting high-quality sound by radio): *Radio 1 FM* **2** (in writing) FIELD MARSHAL

**foal** /fəʊl/ noun, verb
- noun a very young horse or DONKEY
- **IDM** **in 'foal** (of a female horse) pregnant
- verb [I] to give birth to a foal

**foam** /fəʊm/ noun, verb
- noun **1** (also ˌfoam 'rubber) [U] a soft light rubber material, full of small holes, that is used for seats, MATTRESSES, etc.: *a foam mattress* ⬦ *foam packaging* **2** [U] a mass of very small air bubbles on the surface of a liquid **SYN** **froth**: *a glass of beer with a good head of foam* ⬦ *The breaking waves left the beach covered with foam.* **3** [U, C] a chemical substance that forms or produces a soft mass of very small bubbles, used for washing, SHAVING (= cutting hair from the skin), or putting out fires, for example: *shaving foam* ⊃ picture at FROTH
- verb [I] (of a liquid) to have or produce a mass of small bubbles **SYN** **froth**
- **IDM** **foam at the 'mouth 1** (especially of an animal) to have a mass of small bubbles in and around its mouth, especially because it is sick or angry **2** (informal) (of a person) to be very angry

**foamy** /ˈfəʊmi/ adj. consisting of or producing a mass of small bubbles; like foam

**fob** /fɒb; NAmE fɑːb/ verb, noun
- verb (**-bb-**)
- **PHRV** **ˌfob sb ↔ 'off (with sth) 1** to try to stop sb asking questions or complaining by telling them sth that is not true: *Don't let him fob you off with any more excuses.* ⬦ *She wouldn't be fobbed off this time.* **2** to give sb sth that is not what they want or is of worse quality than they want: *He was unaware that he was being fobbed off with out-of-date stock.*
- noun a small object that is attached to a KEY RING, etc. for decoration: *a key fob*

**focal** /ˈfəʊkl/ adj. [only before noun] central; very important; connected with or providing a focus

**'focal length** noun (physics) the distance between the centre of a mirror or a LENS and its FOCUS

**'focal point** noun **1** a thing or person that is the centre of interest or activity: *In rural areas, the school is often the focal point for the local community.* ⬦ *He quickly became the focal point for those who disagreed with government policy.* **2** (physics) = FOCUS (3)

**fo'c's'le** /ˈfəʊksl/ = FORECASTLE

**focus** 🅞 A2 🅞 /ˈfəʊkəs/ verb, noun
- verb (**-s-** or **-ss-**) **1** 🅑 A2 [I, T] to give attention, effort, etc. to one particular subject, situation or person rather than another: *~ on/upon sb/sth The discussion focused on three main issues.* ⬦ *Each exercise focuses on a different grammar point.* ⬦ *~ sth on/upon sb/sth The visit helped to focus world attention on the plight of the refugees.* ⬦ (figurative) *All eyes are focused on the presidential elections at the moment.* **2** 🅑 B2 [I, T] (of your eyes, a camera, etc.) to adapt or be changed so that things can be seen clearly; to change sth so that you can see things clearly: *It took a few moments for her eyes to focus in the dark.* ⬦ *~ on sb/sth Let your eyes focus on objects that are further away from you.* ⬦ *In this scene, the camera focuses on the actor's face.* ⬦ *~ sth (on sb/sth) He focused his blue eyes on her.* **3** [T] *~ sth (on sth)* to aim light onto a particular point using a LENS **4** [I] *~ on sb/sth* (of a light) to shine on sth
- noun (pl. **fo·cuses** or **foci** /ˈfəʊsaɪ, ˈfəʊkaɪ/) **1** 🅑 A2 [U, C, usually sing.] the thing or person that people are most interested in; the act of paying special attention to sth and making people interested in it: *~ of sth It was the main focus of attention at the meeting.* ⬦ *for sth His comments provided a focus for debate.* ⬦ *~ on sth We shall maintain our focus on the needs of the customer.* ⬦ *In today's lecture the focus will be on tax structures within the European Union.* ⬦ *The incident brought the problem of violence in schools into sharp focus.* ⬦ *What we need now is a change of focus* (= to look at things in a different way). **2** 🅑 B2 [U] a point or distance at which the outline of an object is clearly seen by the eye or through a LENS: **out of** *~ Some parts of the photograph are out of focus* (= blurred rather than clearly seen). ⬦ **into** *~ When I got glasses, suddenly the whole world came into focus.* ⊃ see also SOFT FOCUS **3** (also **'focal point**) [C] (physics) a point at which waves of light, sound, etc. meet after REFLECTION or REFRACTION; the point from which waves of light, sound, etc. seem to come **4** [C] (geology) the point at which an earthquake starts to happen

**fo·cused** (also **fo·cussed**) /ˈfəʊkəst/ adj. with your attention directed to what you want to do; with very clear aims: *She should do well in her studies this year—she's very focused.*

**'focus group** noun [C + sing./pl. v.] a small group of people, specially chosen to represent different social classes, etc., who are asked to discuss and give their opinions about a particular subject. The information obtained is used by people doing MARKET RESEARCH, for example about new products or for a political party.

**fod·der** /ˈfɒdə(r); NAmE ˈfɑːd-/ noun [U] **1** food for horses and farm animals **2** (disapproving) (often after a noun) people or things that are considered to have only one use: *Without education, these children will end up as factory fodder* (= only able to work in a factory). ⬦ *This story will be more fodder for the gossip columnists.* ⊃ see also CANNON FODDER

**foe** /fəʊ/ noun (old-fashioned or formal) an enemy: *She was unsure as yet whether he was friend or foe.*

**foe·tal** (BrE) = FETAL

**foe·tid** (BrE) = FETID

**foe·tus** (BrE) = FETUS

**fog** /fɒg; NAmE fɑːg/ noun, verb
- noun [U, C] **1** a thick cloud of very small drops of water in the air close to the land or sea that is very difficult to see through: *Dense/thick fog is affecting roads in the north and visibility is poor.* ⬦ *freezing fog* ⬦ *Patches of fog will clear by mid-morning.* ⬦ *We get heavy fogs on this coast in winter.* ⬦ *The town was covered in a thick blanket of fog.* ⬦ *The fog finally lifted* (= disappeared). ⊃ compare MIST **2** a state in which things are not clear and seem difficult to

---
🅞 Oxford Phrasal Academic Lexicon (OPAL) written and spoken word lists | 🅦 OPAL written word list | 🅢 OPAL spoken word list

# fogbound

understand: **in a ~** *He went through the day with his mind in a fog.*
- **verb** (-gg-) **1** [I, T] **~ (sth) (up)** if a glass surface **fogs** or is **fogged** up, it becomes covered in STEAM or small drops of water so that you cannot see through it **2** [T] **~ sth** to make sb/sth confused or less clear: *I tried to clear the confusion that was fogging my brain.* ◊ *The government was trying to fog the real issues before the election.*

**fog·bound** /ˈfɒɡbaʊnd; *NAmE* ˈfɑːɡ-/ *adj.* unable to operate because of fog; unable to travel or to leave a place because of fog: *a fogbound airport* ◊ *fogbound passengers* ◊ *She spent hours fogbound in Brussels.*

**fogey** (also **fogy**) /ˈfəʊɡi/ *noun* (*pl.* **fogeys**, **fo·gies**) (*informal*) a person with old-fashioned ideas that he or she is unwilling to change: *He sounds like such an old fogey!*

**foggy** /ˈfɒɡi; *NAmE* ˈfɑːɡi/ *adj.* (**fog·gier**, **fog·gi·est**) not clear because of FOG: *foggy conditions* ◊ *a foggy road*
- IDM **not have the ˈfoggiest (idea)** (*informal*) to not know anything at all about sth: '*Do you know where she is?*' '*Sorry, I haven't the foggiest.*'

**fog·horn** /ˈfɒɡhɔːn; *NAmE* ˈfɑːɡhɔːrn/ *noun* a device that makes a loud noise to warn ships of danger in FOG: *He's got a voice like a foghorn* (= a loud unpleasant voice).

**ˈfog lamp** (*BrE*) (also **ˈfog light** *NAmE, BrE*) *noun* a very bright light on the front or back of a car to help the driver to see or be seen in FOG

**fogy** = FOGEY

**foi·ble** /ˈfɔɪbl/ *noun* a silly habit or a strange or weak aspect of a person's character that is not considered serious by other people SYN **idiosyncrasy**: *We have to tolerate each other's little foibles.*

**foie gras** /ˌfwɑː ˈɡrɑː/ *noun* [U] (*from French*) **1** the LIVER of a GOOSE or DUCK that has been specially fed so that it becomes very fat, prepared as food **2** ⇨ PÂTÉ DE FOIE GRAS

**foil** /fɔɪl/ *noun, verb*
- **noun 1** (*also* **tinfoil**) [U] metal made into very thin sheets that is used for covering or wrapping things, especially food: (*BrE*) **aluminium foil** ◊ (*NAmE*) **aluminum foil 2** [U] paper that is covered in very thin sheets of metal: *The chocolates are individually wrapped in gold foil.* **3** [C] **~ (for sb/sth)** a person or thing that contrasts with, and therefore emphasizes, the qualities of another person or thing: *The pale walls provide a perfect foil for the furniture.* **4** [C] a long thin light SWORD used in the sport of FENCING
- **verb** [often passive] to stop sth from happening, especially sth illegal; to prevent sb from doing sth SYN **thwart**: **~ sth** *to foil a plan/crime/plot* ◊ *Customs officials foiled an attempt to smuggle the paintings out of the country.* ◊ **~ sb (in sth)** *They were foiled in their attempt to smuggle the paintings.*

**foist** /fɔɪst/ *verb*
- PHRV **ˈfoist sb/sth on/upon sb** to force sb to accept sb/sth that they do not want: *The title for her novel was foisted on her by the publishers.*

**fold** 🔊 B1 /fəʊld/ *verb, noun*
- **verb 1** 🔊 B1 [T] to bend sth, especially paper or cloth, so that one part lies on top of another part: **~ sth** *First, fold the paper in half/in two.* ◊ *The bird folded its wings.* ◊ *a pile of neatly folded clothes* ◊ **~ sth up** *He folded the map up and put it in his pocket.* ◊ **~ sth back, down, over, etc.** *The blankets had been folded down.* OPP **unfold** ⇨ see also FOLD-UP **2** 🔊 B1 [T, I] to bend sth so that it becomes smaller or flatter and can be stored or carried more easily; to bend or be able to bend in this way: **~ sth away, down, up, etc.** *The bed can be folded away during the day.* ◊ **~ away/up** *The table folds up when not in use.* ◊ **+ adj.** *The ironing board folds flat for easy storage.* ◊ (*figurative*) *When she heard the news, her legs just folded under her* (= she fell). **3** [T] to wrap sth around sb/sth: **~ A in B** *She gently folded the baby in a blanket.* ◊ **~ B around/round/over A** *She folded a blanket around the baby.* **4** [I] (of a company, a play, etc.) to close because it is not successful
- IDM **fold your ˈarms** to put one of your arms over the other one and hold them against your body **fold your ˈhands** to bring or hold your hands together: *She kept her hands folded in her lap.* **fold sb in your ˈarms** (*literary*) to put your arms around sb and hold them against your body
- PHRV **fold sth ↔ ˈin** | **fold sth ˈinto sth** (in cooking) to add one substance to another and gently mix them together: *Fold in the beaten egg whites.*
- **noun 1** 🔊 B2 [C, usually pl.] a part of sth, especially cloth, that is folded or hangs as if it had been folded: *the folds of her dress* ◊ *loose folds of skin* **2** [C] a mark or line made by folding sth, or showing where sth should be folded **3** [C] an area in a field surrounded by a fence or wall where animals, especially sheep, are kept for safety **4 the fold** [sing.] a group of people who share the same ideas or beliefs: *He called on former Republican voters to return to the fold.* **5** [C] (*geology*) a curve or bend in the line of the layers of rock in the earth's CRUST **6** [C] (*BrE*) a hollow place among hills or mountains
- IDM **aˌbove/beˌlow the ˈfold** in/not in a position where you see it first, for example in the top/bottom part of a newspaper page or web page: *Your ad will be placed above the fold for prominent exposure.*

**-fold** /fəʊld/ *suffix* (in adjectives and adverbs) multiplied by; having the number of parts mentioned: *to increase tenfold*

**fold·away** /ˈfəʊldəweɪ/ *adj.* (of a piece of furniture or equipment) that can be folded, especially so that it can be stored in a small space: *a foldaway bed*

**fold·er** /ˈfəʊldə(r)/ *noun* **1** a cover made of stiff card or plastic for holding loose papers, etc. **2** (in some computer systems) a way of organizing and storing computer files ⇨ WORDFINDER NOTE at FILE

**fold·ing** 🔊 B2 /ˈfəʊldɪŋ/ *adj.* [only before noun] (of a piece of furniture, a bicycle, etc.) that can be folded, so that it can be carried or stored in a small space: *a folding chair/bike/knife*

**ˈfold-out** *adj.* [only before noun] (of a piece of furniture or a page in a book or magazine) designed to be opened out for use and then folded away again so it can be stored easily: *a fold-out bed/map*

**ˈfold-up** *adj.* [only before noun] (of an object) that can be made smaller by closing or folding so that it takes up less space

**fo·li·age** /ˈfəʊliɪdʒ/ *noun* [U] the leaves of a tree or plant; leaves and branches together: *dense green foliage* ⇨ VISUAL VOCAB page V6

**fo·liar** /ˈfəʊliə(r)/ *adj.* (*specialist*) relating to leaves: *foliar colour*

**folic acid** /ˌfɒlɪk ˈæsɪd, ˌfəʊl-; *NAmE* ˌfəʊl-/ *noun* [U] a vitamin found in green vegetables, LIVER and KIDNEY, needed by the body for the production of red blood cells

**folio** /ˈfəʊliəʊ/ *noun* (*pl.* **-os**) **1** a book made with large sheets of paper, especially as used in early printing **2** (*specialist*) a single sheet of paper from a book

**folk** 🔊 B1 /fəʊk/ *noun, adj.*
- **noun 1** 🔊 (*also* **folks** especially in *NAmE*) [pl.] (*informal*) people in general: *ordinary working-class folk* ◊ *I'd like a job working with old folk or kids.* ◊ *the folks back home* (= from the place where you come from) **2 folks** [pl.] (*informal*) a friendly way of addressing more than one person: *Well, folks, what are we going to do today?* **3 folks** [pl.] (*informal, especially NAmE*) the members of your family, especially your parents: *How are your folks?* **4** [pl.] people from a particular country or region, or who have a particular way of life: *country folk* ◊ *townsfolk* ◊ *farming folk* **5** (*also* **ˈfolk music**) [U] music in the traditional style of a country or community: *a folk festival/concert*
- **adj.** [only before noun] **1** 🔊 B1 (of art, culture, etc.) traditional and typical of the ordinary people of a country or community: *folk art* ◊ *a folk museum* **2** 🔊 B1 based on the beliefs of ordinary people: *folk wisdom* ◊ *Garlic is widely used in Chinese folk medicine.*

**folk dance** noun [C, U] a traditional dance of a particular area or country; a piece of music for such a dance ⊃ WORD-FINDER NOTE at DANCE

**folk etymology** (also **popular ety'mology**) noun [U, C] **1** a popular but wrong belief about the origin of a word or phrase **2** a process by which a word is changed, for example because people believe that it is related to another word, even though it is not, or to make a foreign word sound more familiar: *Folk etymology has created the cheeseburger and the beanburger, but the first hamburgers were in fact named after the city of Hamburg.*

**folk hero** noun a person that the ordinary people of a country or region admire because of sth special he or she has done

**folk·lore** /ˈfəʊklɔː(r)/ noun [U] the traditions and stories of a country or community: *Irish/Indian folklore* ◊ *The story rapidly became part of family folklore.*

**folk·lor·ist** /ˈfəʊklɔːrɪst/ noun a person who studies folk-lore, especially as an academic subject

**folk memory** noun [C, U] a memory or collection of memories of sth in the past that the people of a country or community never forget

**folk music** noun [U] the traditional music of a country or community: *He drew his inspiration from traditional Hungarian folk music.*

**folk rock** noun [U] a style of music that combines elements of folk music and rock

**folk singer** noun a person who sings folk songs

**folk song** noun **1** [C, U] a song in the traditional style of a country or community; songs of this type **2** [C] a type of song that became popular in the US in the 1960s, played on a guitar and often about political topics

**folksy** /ˈfəʊksi/ (also **folky**) adj. **1** (especially NAmE) simple, friendly and informal: *They wanted the store to have a folksy small-town image.* **2** (sometimes disapproving) done or made in a traditional style that is supposed to be typical of simple customs in the past, but sometimes in a false or artificial way: *a folksy ballad*

**folk tale** noun a very old traditional story from a particular place that was originally passed on to people in a spoken form

**folky** /ˈfəʊki/ adj. = FOLKSY

**fol·licle** /ˈfɒlɪkl/ NAmE /ˈfɑːl-/ noun one of the very small holes in the skin that hair grows from

**fol·low** ❶ **A1** /ˈfɒləʊ/; NAmE /ˈfɑːl-/ verb
- GO AFTER **1** **A1** [T, I] to come or go after or behind sb/sth: *~sb/sth Follow me please.* ◊ *~sb + adv./prep. He followed her into the house.* ◊ *Wherever she led, they followed.* ◊ *Sam walked in, with the rest of the boys following closely behind.* **2** **A1** [T] ~sb/sth to come or go after or behind sb in order to watch where they go and what they do: *I think we're being followed.*
- HAPPEN/DO AFTER **3** **A2** [T, I] to come after sth/sb else in time or order; to happen as a result of sth else: ~(sth/sb) *I remember little of the days that followed the accident.* ◊ *The first two classes are followed by a break of ten minutes.* ◊ *to~ I'll have soup and fish to follow.* ◊ *A detailed news report will follow shortly.* ◊ *There follows … There followed a short silence.* ◊ *as follows … The opening hours are as follows …* ◊ *~on from sth A new proposal followed on from the discussions.* **4** **A2** [T] to do sth after sth else: ~**sth with sth** *Give your contact details and follow this with a brief profile of yourself.* ◊ *~sth up with sth They follow up their March show with four UK dates next month.*
- ADVICE/INSTRUCTIONS **5** **A2** [T] ~sth to accept advice, instructions, etc. and do what you have been told or shown to do: *to follow rules/procedures/guidelines* ◊ *They said they were just following orders.* ◊ *He has trouble following simple instructions.* ◊ *Why didn't you follow my advice?* ◊ *to follow a diet/recipe*
- ACCEPT/COPY **6** **A2** [T, I] to accept sb/sth as a guide, a leader or an example; to copy sb/sth: ~(**sb/sth**) *I encourage others to follow our example.* ◊ *The movie follows the book faithfully.* ◊ *They followed the teachings of Buddha.* ◊ *Where one airline leads, others follow.* ◊ *~sb into sth Laura followed her mother into the medical profession (= became a doctor like her mother).*
- WEBSITE **7 B1 A2** ~**sth** to click on a link in a website: *Follow the links to sign up for the webinar.*
- ROAD/PATH **8 B1** [T] ~**sth** to go along a road, path, etc: *Follow this road until you get to the school, then turn left.* **9 B1** [T] ~**sth** (of a road, path, etc.) to go in the same direction as sth or PARALLEL to sth: *The lane follows the edge of a wood for about a mile.*
- BE RESULT **10 B2** [I, T] (not usually used in the progressive tenses) to be the logical result of sth: ~(**on**) **from sth** *I don't see how that follows from what you've just said.* ◊ *it follows that … If a=b and b=c it follows that a=c.*
- UNDERSTAND **11 B2** [I, T] to understand an explanation or the meaning of sth: *Sorry, I don't follow.* ◊ *~sth Do you follow me?* ◊ *~sth The plot is almost impossible to follow.* ⊃ SYNONYMS at UNDERSTAND
- WATCH/LISTEN **12 B2** [T] ~**sb/sth** to watch or listen to sb/sth very carefully: *The children were following every word of the story intently.* ◊ *Her eyes followed him everywhere (= she was looking at him all the time).*
- BE INTERESTED IN **13 B2** [T] ~**sth** to take an active interest in sth and be aware of what is happening; to support a sports team: *We've been following this story for months.* ◊ *Millions of people followed the trial on TV.* ◊ *In his leisure time he follows West Ham United.* **14** [T] ~**sb** to choose to regularly receive messages from a person, company, etc. using a SOCIAL MEDIA service: *I don't follow many celebrities on Twitter any more.*
- OF BOOK/MOVIE **15** [T] ~**sth** to be about the life or development of sb/sth: *The novel follows the fortunes of a village community in Scotland.*
- PATTERN/COURSE **16** [T] ~**sth** to develop or happen in a particular way: *The day followed the usual pattern.*

**IDM** **follow in sb's ˈfootsteps** to do the same job, have the same style of life, etc. as sb else, especially sb in your family: *She works in television, following in her father's footsteps.* **follow your ˈnose 1** to be guided by your sense of smell **2** to go straight forward: *The garage is a mile ahead up the hill—just follow your nose.* **3** to act according to what seems right or reasonable, rather than following any particular rules **follow ˈsuit 1** (in card games) to play a card of the same SUIT that has just been played **2** to act or behave in the way that sb else has just done ⊃ more at ACT n.

**PHRV** **follow sb aˈround/aˈbout** to keep going with sb wherever they go: *Will you stop following me around!* **follow ˈon 1** to go somewhere after sb else has gone there: *You go to the beach with the kids and I'll follow on when I've finished work.* **2** (of a CRICKET team) to play a second INNINGS (= a period during which a team is BATTING) immediately after its first, because it has failed to reach a particular score **follow ˈon from sth** to come or happen after sth and as a result of it: *My second point follows on from this.* **follow ˈthrough** (in tennis, golf, etc.) to complete a single movement of the arm when hitting the ball by continuing to move the club, RACKET, etc. after hitting it ⊃ related noun FOLLOW-THROUGH (1) **follow ˈthrough (with sth)** | **follow sth↔ˈthrough** to finish sth that you have started ⊃ related noun FOLLOW-THROUGH (2) **follow sth↔ˈup 1** to add to sth that you have just done by doing sth else: *You should follow up your phone call with an email or a letter.* **2** to find out more about sth that sb has told you or suggested to you **SYN** investigate: *The police are following up several leads after their TV appeal for information.* ⊃ related noun FOLLOW-UP

**fol·low·er** /ˈfɒləʊə(r)/; NAmE /ˈfɑːl-/ noun **1** a person who supports and admires a particular person or set of ideas: *the followers of Mahatma Gandhi* ⊃ see also CAMP FOLLOWER **2** a person who is very interested in a particular activity and follows all the recent news about it: *keen followers of football* ◊ *a follower of fashion* **3** a person who does things after sb else has done them first: *She is a leader, not a follower.* **4** a person who chooses to regularly receive sb's messages using a SOCIAL MEDIA service: *a celebrity with thousands of followers on Twitter*

# following

**fol·low·ing** ⓘ **A2** Ⓢ /ˈfɒləʊɪŋ; NAmE ˈfɑːl-/ adj., noun, prep.
■ adj. **the following ... 1** ⚡ **A2** that is/are going to be mentioned next: *Answer the following questions.* ⇒ LANGUAGE BANK at FIRST **2** ⚡ **A2** next in time: *the following afternoon/month/year/week* ◇ *They arrived on Monday evening and we got there the following day.*
IDM **a ˈfollowing ˈwind** a wind blowing in the same direction as a ship or other vehicle that helps it move faster
■ noun **1** ⚡ **B1** **the following** (used with either a singular or a plural verb, depending on whether you are talking about one thing or person or several things or people) the thing or things that you will mention next; the person or people that you will mention next: *The following is a summary of events.* ◇ *The following have been chosen to take part: Watts, Hodges and Lennox.* **2** [usually sing.] a group of supporters: *The band has a huge following in Italy.*
■ prep. ⚡ **B2** after or as a result of a particular event: *He took charge of the family business following his father's death.*

**follow-ˈon** noun [sing.] (in CRICKET) a second INNINGS (= a period during which a team is BATTING) that a team is made to play immediately after its first, if it fails to reach a particular score

**ˈfollow-through** noun **1** [U, sing.] (in tennis, golf, etc.) the final part of the movement of the arm when hitting the ball after the ball has been hit **2** [U] the actions that sb takes in order to complete a plan: *The project could fail if there is inadequate follow-through.*

**ˈfollow-up** noun [C, U] an action or a thing that continues sth that has already started or comes after sth similar that was done earlier: *The book is a follow-up to her excellent television series.* ▶ **ˈfollow-up** adj. [only before noun]: *a follow-up study*

**folly** /ˈfɒli; NAmE ˈfɑːli/ noun (pl. **-ies**) **1** [U, C] a lack of good judgement; the fact of doing sth stupid; an activity or idea that shows a lack of judgement SYN **stupidity**: *an act of sheer folly* ◇ *Giving up a secure job seems to be the height of folly.* ◇ **(to do sth)** *It would be folly to turn the offer down.* ◇ *the follies of youth* **2** [C] a building that has no practical purpose but was built in the past for decoration, often in the garden of a large country house

**fo·ment** /fəˈment; NAmE foʊˈm-/ verb **~ sth** (formal) to create trouble or violence or make it worse SYN **incite**: *They accused him of fomenting political unrest.*

**FOMO** /ˈfəʊməʊ/ abbr. (informal) fear of missing out (a feeling of worry that an interesting or exciting event is happening somewhere else)

**fond** ⚡+ **B2** /fɒnd; NAmE fɑːnd/ adj. (**fond·er**, **fond·est**)
**1** ⚡+ **B2** **~ of sb** having warm or loving feelings for sb, especially sb you have known for a long time: *Over the years, I have grown quite fond of her.* ⇒ SYNONYMS at LOVE **2** ⚡+ **B2** **~ of (doing) sth** finding sth pleasant, especially sth you have liked or enjoyed for a long time: *fond of music/cooking* ◇ *We had grown fond of the house and didn't want to leave.* ⇒ SYNONYMS at LIKE **3** ⚡+ **C1** **~ of (doing) sth** liking to do sth that other people find annoying or unpleasant, and doing it often: *Sheila's very fond of telling other people what to do.* ◇ *He's rather too fond of the sound of his own voice* (= he talks too much). **4** ⚡+ **C1** [only before noun] kind and loving SYN **affectionate**: *a fond look/embrace/farewell* ◇ *I have very fond memories of my time in Spain* (= I remember it with affection and pleasure). **5** [only before noun] **~ hope** a hope about sth that is not likely to happen: *I waited all day in the fond hope that she would change her mind.* ▶ **fond·ness** noun [U, sing.]: *He will be remembered by the staff with great fondness.* ◇ ~ **for sb/sth**: *a fondness for animals* IDM see ABSENCE

**fon·dant** /ˈfɒndənt; NAmE ˈfɑːn-/ noun **1** [U] a thick sweet soft mixture made from sugar and water, used especially to cover cakes: *fondant icing* **2** [C] a soft sweet that melts in the mouth, made of fondant

**fon·dle** /ˈfɒndl; NAmE ˈfɑːn-/ verb **~ sb/sth** to touch and move your hand gently over sb/sth, especially in a sexual way, or in order to show love SYN **caress**

**fond·ly** /ˈfɒndli; NAmE ˈfɑːnd-/ adv. **1** in a way that shows love SYN **affectionately**: *He looked at her fondly.* ◇ *I fondly remember my first job as a reporter.* **2** in a way that shows hope that is not reasonable or realistic: *I fondly imagined that you cared for me.*

**fon·due** /ˈfɒnduː; NAmE fɑːnˈduː/ noun [C, U] **1** a Swiss dish of melted cheese and wine into which pieces of bread are DIPPED **2** a dish of hot oil into which small pieces of meat, vegetables, etc. are DIPPED

**font** /fɒnt; NAmE fɑːnt/ noun **1** a large stone bowl in a church that holds water for the ceremony of BAPTISM **2** (specialist) the particular size and style of a set of letters that are used in printing, etc.

**food** ⓘ **A1** /fuːd/ noun [U, C] things that people or animals eat: *food and drink* ◇ *Do you like Italian food?* ◇ *the food industry* ◇ *People worry about food safety* (= if food is safe to eat). ◇ *baby food* (= prepared especially for babies) ◇ *cat/dog/pet food* (= for a cat/dog/pet to eat) ◇ *fresh/frozen foods* ⇒ see also COMFORT FOOD, CONVENIENCE FOOD, FAST FOOD, FINGER FOOD, FUNCTIONAL FOOD, HEALTH FOOD, JUNK FOOD, SEAFOOD, SOUL FOOD, SLOW FOOD, WHOLEFOOD ⇒ WORDFINDER NOTE at EAT
IDM **food for ˈthought** an idea that makes you think seriously and carefully **off your ˈfood** not wanting to eat anything: *He's been off his food all week.*

**ˈfood bank** noun **1** (in the UK) a place where people in need can go to get free food **2** (in the US) an organization that stores basic food supplies for distribution to people in need. The food is often passed on to local FOOD PANTRIES, which give it to the people who need it.

**ˈfood chain** noun (usually **the food chain**) **1** a series of living creatures in which each type of creature feeds on the one below it in the series: *Insects are fairly low down (on) the food chain.* **2** the series of stages that food passes along as it goes from being grown or produced to being sold and then eaten

**ˈfood group** noun any one of the categories of foods that share similar characteristics in terms of how they affect the health of the human body: *The five basic food groups are meat, milk, fruit, vegetables and carbohydrates.*

**foodie** (also **foody**) /ˈfuːdi/ noun, adj.
■ noun (pl. **-ies**) (informal) a person who is very interested in cooking and eating different kinds of food
■ adj. having or showing great interest in cooking and eating different kinds of food: *a foodie blog*

**ˈfood inseˈcurity** noun [U] the state of not having reliable access to enough healthy food that you can afford OPP **food security**

**ˈfood mile** noun a measurement of the distance food has to be transported from the producer to the consumer and the fuel that this uses: *We keep food miles to a minimum by sourcing products locally.*

**ˈfood pantry** noun (NAmE) an organization that gives food to poor people who live in a particular area. Food pantries often distribute food that they receive from a FOOD BANK.

**ˈfood poisoning** noun [U] an illness of the stomach caused by eating food that contains harmful bacteria

**ˈfood processor** noun a piece of equipment that is used to mix or cut up food

**ˈfood science** noun [U] the scientific study of food, for example what it is made of, the effects it has on our body, and how to prepare it and store it safely

**ˈfood seˈcurity** noun [U] the state of having reliable access to enough healthy food that you can afford OPP **food insecurity**

**ˈfood stamp** noun (in the US) a piece of paper that is given by the government to people on low income, which they can exchange for food

**food·stuff** /ˈfuːdstʌf/ noun [usually pl.] (specialist) any substance that is used as food: *basic foodstuffs*

**ˈfood web** noun (specialist) a system of FOOD CHAINS that are related to and depend on each other

**foody** = FOODIE

**foo-foo** = FUFU

**fool** /fuːl/ noun, verb, adj.

■ **noun** 1 [C] a person who you think behaves or speaks in a way that lacks intelligence or good judgement **SYN idiot**: *Don't be such a fool!* ◇ *I felt a fool when I realized my mistake.* ◇ *He told me he was an actor and I was fool enough to believe him.* 2 [C] (in the past) a man employed by a king or queen to entertain people by telling jokes, singing songs, etc. **SYN jester** 3 [U, C] (*BrE*) (usually in compounds) a cold light DESSERT (= a sweet dish) made from fruit that is cooked to make it soft and mixed with cream or CUSTARD: *rhubarb fool* ⊃ see also APRIL FOOL

**IDM** **act/play the 'fool** to behave in a stupid way in order to make people laugh, especially in a way that may also annoy them: *Quit playing the fool and get some work done!* **any fool can/could …** (*informal*) used to say that sth is very easy to do: *Any fool could tell she was lying.* **be ˌno/ˈnobody's 'fool** to be too intelligent or know too much about sth to be tricked by other people: *She's nobody's fool when it comes to dealing with difficult patients.* **ˌfools rush ˈin (where angels fear to ˈtread)** (*saying*) people with little experience try to do the difficult or dangerous things that more experienced people would not consider doing **ˌmake a 'fool of sb** to say or do sth deliberately so that people will think that sb is stupid: *Can't you see she's making a fool of you?* ⊃ SYNONYMS at CHEAT **ˌmake a 'fool of yourself** to do sth stupid that makes other people think that you are a fool: *I made a complete fool of myself in front of everyone!* **ˌmore fool 'sb (for doing sth)** (*informal*) used to say that you think that sb was stupid to do sth, especially when it causes them problems: *'He's not an easy person to live with.' 'More fool her for marrying him!'* **(there's) ˌno fool like an 'old fool** (*saying*) an older person who behaves in a stupid way is worse than a younger person who does the same thing, because experience should have taught him or her not to do it ⊃ more at SUFFER

■ **verb** 1 [T] to trick sb into believing sth that is not true: *~ sb You don't fool me!* ◇ *She certainly had me fooled—I really believed her!* ◇ *~ yourself You're fooling yourself if you think none of this will affect you.* ◇ *~ sb into doing sth Don't be fooled into thinking they're going to change anything.* 2 [I] to say or do stupid or silly things, often in order to make people laugh: *~ (about/around) Stop fooling around and sit down!* ◇ *~ about/around with sth If you fool about with matches, you'll end up getting burned.*

**IDM** **you could have fooled 'me** (*informal*) used to say that you do not believe sth that sb has just told you: *'I'm trying as hard as I can!' 'You could have fooled me!'*

**PHRV** **ˌfool aˈround** 1 (*BrE also* **ˌfool aˈbout**) to waste time instead of doing sth that you should be doing **SYN mess around** 2 **fool around (with sb)** to have a sexual relationship with another person's partner; to have a sexual relationship with sb who is not your partner **SYN mess around**: *She's been fooling around with a married man.*

■ **adj.** [only before noun] (*informal*) showing a lack of intelligence or good judgement **SYN silly, stupid, foolish**: *That was a damn fool thing to do!*

**fool·hardy** /ˈfuːlhɑːdi; *NAmE* -hɑːrdi/ *adj.* (*disapproving*) taking unnecessary risks **SYN reckless**: *It would be foolhardy to sail in weather like this.* ▸ **ˌfool·hardi·ness** *noun* [U]

**fool·ish** /ˈfuːlɪʃ/ *adj.* 1 (of actions or behaviour) not showing good sense or judgement **SYN silly, stupid**: *She's just a vain, foolish woman.* ◇ *I was foolish enough to believe what Jeff told me.* ◇ *The accident was my fault—it would be foolish to pretend otherwise.* ◇ *How could she have been so foolish as to fall in love with him?* ◇ *a foolish idea/dream/mistake* ◇ *It was a very foolish thing to do.* 2 [not usually before noun] made to feel or look silly and embarrassed **SYN silly, stupid**: *I felt foolish and a failure.* ◇ *He's afraid of looking foolish in front of his friends.* ▸ **ˌfool·ish·ly** *adv.*: *We foolishly thought that everyone would speak English.* ◇ *Foolishly, I allowed myself to be persuaded to enter the contest.* **ˌfool·ish·ness** *noun* [U]: *Jenny had to laugh at her own foolishness.*

**fool·proof** /ˈfuːlpruːf/ *adj.* (of a plan, machine, method, etc.) very well designed and easy to use so that it cannot fail and you cannot use it wrongly **SYN infallible**: *This recipe is foolproof—it works every time.*

**ˌfool's 'errand** *noun* [sing.] a task that has no hope of being done successfully: *He sent me on a fool's errand.*

**ˌfool's 'gold** *noun* [U] 1 a yellow mineral found in rock, which looks like gold but is not valuable, also called **iron pyˈrites** ⊃ see also PYRITES 2 something that you think is valuable or will earn you a lot of money, but which has no chance of succeeding

**ˌfool's 'paradise** *noun* [usually sing.] a state of happiness that is based on sth that is false or cannot last although the happy person does not realize it

**foos·ball** /ˈfuːzbɔːl; *BrE also* ˈfuːsb-/ (*NAmE*) (*BrE* **ˈtable football**) *noun* [U] an indoor game for two people or teams, played by moving rows of small models of football (soccer) players in order to move a ball on a board that has marks like a football (soccer) field

**foot** /fʊt/ *noun, verb*

■ **noun** (*pl.* **feet** /fiːt/)

• **PART OF BODY** 1 [C] the lowest part of the leg, below the ankle, on which a person or an animal stands: *My feet are aching.* ◇ *your right/left foot* ◇ *The whole audience rose to its feet* (= stood up) *and cheered.* ◇ *to leap/jump/spring to your feet* (= to stand up quickly and easily) ◇ **on ~** *We came on foot* (= we walked). ◇ **on your feet** *I've been on my feet* (= standing or walking around) *all day.* ◇ *We were stamping our feet* (= hitting them on the ground) *to keep warm.* ◇ *He is currently resting a foot injury.* ◇ *a foot passenger* (= one who travels on a FERRY without a car) ⊃ HOMOPHONES at FEAT ⊃ SYNONYMS at STAND ⊃ VISUAL VOCAB page V1 ⊃ see also ATHLETE'S FOOT, BAREFOOT, CLUB FOOT, UNDERFOOT

• **-FOOTED** 2 (in adjectives and adverbs) having or using the type or number of foot/feet mentioned: *bare-footed* ◇ *four-footed* ◇ *a left-footed shot into the corner* ⊃ see also FLAT-FOOTED, SURE-FOOTED

• **PART OF SOCK** 3 [C, usually sing.] the part of a sock, STOCKING, etc. that covers the foot

• **MEASUREMENT** 4 (*pl.* **feet** *or* **foot**) (*abbr.* **ft**) (in Britain and North America) a unit for measuring length equal to 12 inches or 30.48 CENTIMETRES: *a six-foot high wall* ◇ *We're flying at 35 000 feet.* ◇ *'How tall are you?' 'Five foot nine'* (= five feet and nine inches). ◇ *~ of sth The town was under several feet of water* (= the water was several feet deep). ◇ *The store has 600 square feet of retail space.*

• **BASE/BOTTOM/END** 5 [sing.] **the ~ of sth** the lowest part of sth; the base or bottom of sth: *The city now reaches to the foot of the surrounding mountains.* ◇ (*BrE*) *The team remains stuck at the foot of the table* (= with fewer points than all the other teams). ⊃ SYNONYMS at BOTTOM 6 the further or lower end of sth: *The nurse hung a chart at the foot of the bed* (= the part of the bed where your feet normally are when you are lying in it). ◇ *He sat at the foot of the table.*

**IDM** **be rushed/run off your 'feet** to be extremely busy; to have too many things to do **fall/land on your 'feet** to be lucky in finding yourself in a good situation, or in getting out of a difficult situation **feet 'first** 1 with your feet touching the ground before any other part of your body: *He landed feet first.* 2 (*humorous*) if you leave a place **feet first**, you are carried out after you are dead: *You'll have to carry me out feet first!* **get your 'feet wet** (*especially NAmE, informal*) to start doing sth that is new for you: *At that time he was a young actor, just getting his feet wet.* **get/have a/your 'foot in the 'door** to manage to enter an organization, a field of business, etc. that could bring you success: *I always wanted to work in TV but it took me two years to get a foot in the door.* **get/start off on the right/wrong 'foot (with sb)** (*informal*) to start a relationship well/badly: *I seem to have got off on the wrong foot with the new boss.* **have feet of 'clay** to have a fault or weakness in your character **have/keep your 'feet on the ground** to have a sensible and realistic attitude to life **have/keep a foot in both 'camps** to be involved in or connected with two different groups, especially ones that oppose each other **have ˌone foot in the 'grave** (*informal*) to be so old or ill that you are not likely to live much longer **…my 'foot!** (*old-fashioned, informal, humorous*) a strong way of saying that you disagree completely with what has

# footage

just been said: 'Ian can't come because he's tired.' 'Tired my foot! Lazy more like!' **on your 'feet** completely well or in a normal state again after an illness or a time of trouble: *Sue's back on her feet again after her operation.* ◊ *The new chairman hopes to get the company back on its feet within six months.* ⊃ SYNONYMS at STAND **put your best foot 'forward** to make a great effort to do sth, especially if it is difficult or you are feeling tired **put your 'feet up** to sit down and relax, especially with your feet raised and supported: *After a hard day's work, it's nice to get home and put your feet up.* **put your 'foot down 1** to be very strict in opposing what sb wishes to do: *You've got to put your foot down and make him stop seeing her.* **2** (*BrE*) to drive faster: *She put her foot down and roared past them.* **put your 'foot in it** (*BrE*) (*also* **put your foot in your 'mouth** *NAmE, BrE*) to say or do sth that upsets, offends or EMBARRASSES sb: *I really put my foot in it with Ella—I didn't know she'd split up with Tom.* **put a foot 'wrong** (usually used in negative sentences) to make a mistake: *In the last two games he has hardly put a foot wrong.* **set 'foot in/on sth** to enter or visit a place: *the first man to set foot on the moon* ◊ *I vowed never to set foot in the place again.* **set sb/sth on their/its 'feet** to make sb/sth independent or successful: *His business sense helped set the club on its feet again.* **stand on your own (two) 'feet** to be independent and able to take care of yourself: *When his parents died he had to learn to stand on his own two feet.* **under your 'feet** in the way; stopping you from working, etc: *I don't want you kids under my feet while I'm cooking.* ⊃ more at BACK *adj.*, BOOT *n.*, COLD *adj.*, DRAG *v.*, FIND *v.*, GRASS *n.*, GROUND *n.*, HAND *n.*, HEAD *n.*, ITCHY, LEFT *adj.*, PATTER *n.*, PULL *v.*, SHOE *n.*, SHOOT *v.*, SIT, STOCKING, SWEEP *v.*, THINK *v.*, VOTE *v.*, WAIT *v.*, WALK *v.*, WEIGHT *n.*, WORLD
- *verb* ⊃ see also SIDE-FOOT, WRONG-FOOT
- IDM **foot the 'bill** (*informal*) to be responsible for paying the cost of sth: *Once again it will be the taxpayer who has to foot the bill.*

**foot·age** /ˈfʊtɪdʒ/ *noun* [U] **1** part of a film showing a particular event: *old film footage of the moon landing* **2** size or length measured in feet: *I moved from an apartment into a house with three times the* **square footage**.

**foot-and-'mouth disease** (*also* **foot-and-'mouth**) (*NAmE also* **hoof-and-'mouth disease**) *noun* [U] a disease of cows, sheep, etc., that causes painful places on the mouth and feet

**foot·ball** /ˈfʊtbɔːl/ *noun* **1** [U] (*also formal* **As·so·ci·ation 'football**) (*both BrE*) (*also* **soc·cer** *NAmE, BrE*) (*also BrE, informal* **footy, footie**) a game played by two teams of 11 players, using a round ball that players kick up and down the playing field. Teams try to kick the ball into the other team's goal: *to* **play football** ◊ *a football match* ◊ *a Premier League football team* ◊ *a football player* ⊃ see also FANTASY FOOTBALL, GAELIC FOOTBALL, TABLE FOOTBALL **2** [U] (*NAmE*) = AMERICAN FOOTBALL: *He played football for Iowa State University.* ◊ *a football game* ⊃ see also FLAG FOOTBALL, TOUCH FOOTBALL **3** [C] a large round ball made of leather or plastic and filled with air: *As a child he was always kicking a football.* **4** [C] (always used with an adjective) an issue or a problem that frequently causes people to disagree or argue: *Healthcare should not become a political football.*

**'football boot** *noun* (*BrE*) a leather shoe with STUDS (= pieces of plastic or metal) on the bottom to stop it from slipping, worn for playing football (soccer) ⊃ compare CLEAT

**foot·baller** /ˈfʊtbɔːlə(r)/ *noun* (*BrE*) a person who plays football, especially as a profession

**foot·ball·ing** /ˈfʊtbɔːlɪŋ/ *adj.* [only before noun] (*BrE*) connected with the game of football (soccer): *footballing skills*

**foot·brake** /ˈfʊtbreɪk/ *noun* a BRAKE in a vehicle that is operated using your foot

**foot·bridge** /ˈfʊtbrɪdʒ/ *noun* a narrow bridge used only by people who are walking

**foot·er** /ˈfʊtə(r)/ *noun* **1** a line or block of text that appears at the bottom of every page that is printed from a computer ⊃ compare HEADER **2** a line at the bottom of a page on the internet: *a website footer* **3 -footer** (in compound nouns) a person or thing that is a particular number of feet tall or long: *His boat is an eighteen-footer.*

**foot·fall** /ˈfʊtfɔːl/ *noun* **1** [C] (*literary*) the sound of the steps made by sb walking **2** [U] (*BrE, business*) the number of people that visit a particular shop, shopping centre, etc. over a period of time: *a campaign to increase footfall*

**foot·hill** /ˈfʊthɪl/ *noun* [usually pl.] a hill or low mountain at the base of a higher mountain or range of mountains: *the foothills of the Himalayas* ⊃ WORDFINDER NOTE at MOUNTAIN

**foot·hold** /ˈfʊthəʊld/ *noun* **1** a place where your foot can be safely supported when climbing **2** [usually sing.] a strong position in a business, profession, etc. from which sb can make progress and achieve success: *The company is eager to* **gain a foothold** *in Europe.*

**footie** /ˈfʊti/ *noun* [U] (*BrE, informal*) = FOOTBALL (1)

**foot·ing** /ˈfʊtɪŋ/ *noun* [sing.] **1** the position of your feet when they are safely on the ground or some other surface: *She* **lost her footing** *(= she slipped or lost her balance) and fell backwards into the water.* ◊ *I slipped and struggled to* **regain my footing**. **2** the basis on which sth is established or organized: *The company is now* **on a sound financial footing**. ◊ *The country has been* **on a war footing** *(= prepared for war) since March.* **3** the position or status of sb/sth in relation to others; the relationship between two or more people or groups: *The two groups must meet* **on an equal footing**. ◊ *They were demanding to be treated* **on the same footing** *as the rest of the teachers.*

**foot·lights** /ˈfʊtlaɪts/ *noun* [pl.] a row of lights along the front of the stage in a theatre ⊃ WORDFINDER NOTE at STAGE

**foot·loose** /ˈfʊtluːs/ *adj.* free to go where you like or do what you want because you have no responsibilities: *Bert was a footloose, unemployed actor.* ◊ *Ah, I was still* **footloose and fancy-free** *(= free to enjoy myself) in those days.*

**foot·man** /ˈfʊtmən/ *noun* (*pl.* **-men** /-mən/) a male servant in a house in the past, who opened the door to visitors, served food at table, etc.

**foot·note** /ˈfʊtnəʊt/ *noun* **1** an extra piece of information that is given at the bottom of a page, below the main text **2** an event or person that may be remembered but only as sth/sb that is not important

**foot·path** /ˈfʊtpɑːθ; *NAmE* -pæθ/ *noun* **1** (*especially BrE*) a path that is made for people to walk along, especially in the country: *a public footpath* **2** (*AustralE, NZE, BrE*) a flat part at the side of a road for people to walk on; a PAVEMENT

**foot·print** /ˈfʊtprɪnt/ *noun* **1** [usually pl.] a mark left on a surface by a person's foot or shoe or by an animal's foot: *footprints in the sand* ◊ *muddy footprints on the kitchen floor* ⊃ see also CARBON FOOTPRINT, DIGITAL FOOTPRINT **2** = ECOLOGICAL FOOTPRINT **3** the amount of space that sth fills **4** the area on the earth in which a signal from a communications satellite can be received

**foot·rest** /ˈfʊtrest/ *noun* a support for your foot or feet, for example on a motorcycle or when you are sitting down

**the Foot·sie**™ /ðə ˈfʊtsi/ *noun* = FTSE INDEX™

**foot·sie** /ˈfʊtsi/ *noun* (*informal*) IDM **play 'footsie with sb** to touch sb's feet lightly with your own feet, especially under a table, as an expression of romantic interest

**'foot soldier** *noun* **1** a soldier who fights on foot, not on a horse or in a vehicle **2** a person in an organization who does work that is important but boring, and who has no power or responsibility

**foot·step** /ˈfʊtstep/ *noun* [usually pl.] the sound or mark made each time your foot touches the ground when you are walking or running: *the sound of footsteps on the stairs* ◊ *footsteps in the snow* IDM see FOLLOW

**foot·stool** /'fʊtstuːl/ noun a low piece of furniture used for resting your feet on when you are sitting

**foot·way** /'fʊtweɪ/ noun (BrE, formal) a flat part at the side of a road for people to walk on SYN **pavement, sidewalk**

**foot·wear** /'fʊtweə(r); NAmE -wer/ noun [U] things that people wear on their feet, for example shoes and boots: *Be sure to wear the correct footwear to prevent injuries to your feet.*

**foot·work** /'fʊtwɜːk; NAmE -wɜːrk/ noun [U] **1** the way in which a person moves their feet when playing a sport or dancing: *Both dancers displayed some fancy footwork.* **2** the ability to react quickly and with skill to a difficult situation: *It was going to take some deft political footwork to save the situation.*

**footy** /'fʊti/ noun [U] (BrE, informal) = FOOTBALL (1)

**fop** /fɒp; NAmE fɑːp/ noun (old-fashioned) a man who is too interested in his clothes and the way he looks ▶ **fop·pish** /'fɒpɪʃ; NAmE 'fɑːp-/ adj.

**for** ❶ A1 /fə(r), strong form fɔː(r)/ prep., conj.

■ prep. HELP For the special uses of **for** in phrasal verbs, look at the entries for the verbs. For example **fall for sb** is in the phrasal verb section at **fall**. **1** A1 used to show who is intended to have or use sth or where sth is intended to be put: *There's a letter for you.* ◇ *It's a book for children.* ◇ *We got a new table for the dining room.* ◇ *This is the place for me* (= I like it very much). **2** A1 in order to help sb/sth: *What can I do for you* (= how can I help you)? ◇ *Can you translate this letter for me?* ◇ *I took her classes for her while she was sick.* ◇ *soldiers fighting for their country* **3** A1 used to show purpose or function: *a machine for slicing bread* ◇ *Let's go for a walk.* ◇ *Are you learning English for pleasure or for your work?* ◇ *What did you do that for* (= Why did you do that)? **4** A1 used to show a reason or cause: *The town is famous for its cathedral.* ◇ *She gave me a watch for my birthday.* ◇ *He got an award for bravery.* ◇ *I couldn't speak for laughing.* **5** A1 in order to obtain sth: *He came to me for advice.* ◇ *For more information, call this number.* ◇ *There were over fifty applicants for the job.* **6** A1 used to show a length of time: *I'm going away for a few days.* ◇ *That's all the news there is for now.* **7** A1 used to show a distance: *The road went on for miles and miles.* **8** A1 used to show where sb/sth is going: *Is this the bus for Chicago?* ◇ *She knew she was destined for a great future.* **9** A1 used to show that sth is arranged or intended to happen at a particular time: *an appointment for May 12* ◇ *We're invited for 7.30.* **10** A1 used to show the occasion when sth happens: *I'm warning you for the last time—stop talking!* **11** A1 in exchange for sth: *Copies are available for two dollars each.* ◇ *I'll swap these two bottles for that one.* **12** A1 employed by: *She's working for an insurance company.* **13** B1 about; in connection with sb/sth: *They are anxious for her safety.* ◇ *Fortunately for us, the weather changed.* **14** B1 as a representative of: *I am speaking for everyone in this department.* **15** B1 meaning: *Shaking your head for 'No' is not universal.* **16** B1 in support of sb/sth: *Are you for or against the proposal?* ◇ *They voted for independence in a referendum.* ◇ *There's a strong case for postponing the exam.* ◇ *I'm all for* (= strongly support) *people having fun.* ⊃ compare AGAINST (2) **17** B1 considering what can be expected from sb/sth: *The weather was warm for the time of year.* ◇ *She's tall for her age.* ◇ *That's too much responsibility for a child.* **18** B1 used to say how difficult, necessary, pleasant, etc. sth is that sb might do or has done: *It's useless for us to continue.* ◇ *There's no need for you to go.* ◇ *For her to have survived such an ordeal was remarkable.* ◇ *The box is too heavy for me to lift.* ◇ *Is it clear enough for you to read?* **19** used to show who can or should do sth: *It's not for me to say why he left.* ◇ *How to spend the money is for you to decide.* **20 better, happier, etc. ~ sth** better, happier, etc. following sth: *You'll feel better for a good night's sleep.* ◇ *This room would look more cheerful for a spot of paint.*

IDM **be 'in for it** (BrE also **be 'for it**) (informal) to be going to get into trouble or be punished: *We'd better hurry or we'll be in for it.* **for 'all 1** despite: *For all its clarity of style, the book is not easy reading.* **2** used to say that sth is not important or of no interest or value to you/sb: *For all I know she's still living in Boston.* ◇ *You can do what you like, for all I care.* ◇ *For all the good it's done we might as well not have bothered.* **there's / that's ... for you** (often ironic) used to say that sth is a typical example of its kind: *She might at least have called to explain. There's gratitude for you.*

■ conj. (old-fashioned or literary) used to introduce the reason for sth mentioned in the previous statement: *We listened eagerly, for he brought news of our families.* ◇ *I believed her —for surely she would not lie to me.*

**for·age** /'fɒrɪdʒ; NAmE 'fɔːr-/ verb, noun

■ verb **1** [I] **~ (for sth)** (of a person or an animal) to search widely for food **2** [I] **~ (for sth)** (of a person) to search for sth, especially using the hands SYN **rummage**

■ noun [U] food for horses and cows: *forage crops/grass*

**foray** /'fɒreɪ; NAmE 'fɔːr-/ noun **1 ~ (into sth)** an attempt to become involved in a different activity or profession: *the company's first foray into the computer market* **2 ~ (into sth)** a short sudden attack made by a group of soldiers **3 ~ (to/into ...)** a short journey to find a particular thing or to visit a new place SYN **expedition**: *weekend shopping forays to France*

**for·bade** /fə'bæd, -'beɪd/; NAmE fər'b-/ past tense of FORBID

**for·bear** verb, noun

■ verb /fɔː'beə(r); NAmE fɔːr'ber/ [I, T] (formal) (**for·bore** /fɔː'bɔː(r); NAmE fɔːr'b-/, **for·borne** /fɔː'bɔːn; NAmE fɔːr'bɔːrn/) to stop yourself from saying or doing sth that you could or would like to say or do: **~ (from sth / from doing sth)** *He wanted to answer back, but he forbore from doing so.* ◇ **~ to do sth** *She forbore to ask any further questions.*

■ noun [usually pl.] (formal or literary) = FOREBEAR

**for·bear·ance** /fɔː'beərəns; NAmE fɔːr'ber-/ noun [U] (formal) the quality of being patient and kind towards other people, especially when they have done sth wrong

**for·bear·ing** /fɔː'beərɪŋ; NAmE fɔːr'ber-/ adj. (formal) being patient and showing sympathy towards other people, especially when they have done sth wrong SYN **patient**: *Thank you for being so forbearing.*

**for·bid** ❶+ B2 /fə'bɪd; NAmE fər'b-/ verb (**for·bade** /-'bæd, -'beɪd/, **for·bid·den** /fə'bɪdn; NAmE fər'b-/) **1** ❶+ B2 to order sb not to do sth; to order that sth must not be done: **~ sb (from doing sth)** *He forbade them from mentioning the subject again.* ◇ **~ sth** *Her father forbade the marriage.* ◇ **~ sb to do sth** *You are all forbidden to leave.* ◇ **~ sb sth** *My doctor has forbidden me sugar.* ◇ **~ (sb) doing sth** *She knew her mother would forbid her going.* OPP **allow, permit 2 ~ sth | ~ sb to do sth** (formal) to make it difficult or impossible to do sth SYN **prohibit**: *Lack of space forbids further treatment of the topic here.*

IDM **God / Heaven for'bid (that ...)** (informal) used to say that you hope that sth will not happen: *'Maybe you'll end up as a lawyer, like me.' 'God forbid!'* HELP Some people find this use of **God** offensive.

▼ EXPRESS YOURSELF

**Forbidding somebody to do something**

When speaking to somebody, we usually use indirect language to ask them not to do something:
• **I'm sorry**, *smoking isn't allowed.* / **You're not allowed to** *smoke here.*
• **Would you mind not** *talking during the music?*
• **Could I ask you not to** *use your phone here, please?*
• **I'm afraid I have to ask you not to** *take pictures here.*

**for·bid·den** /fə'bɪdn; NAmE fər'b-/ adj. not allowed: *Photography is strictly forbidden in the museum.* ◇ *The conversation was in danger of wandering into forbidden territory* (= topics that they were not allowed to talk about).

IDM **for,bidden 'fruit** a thing that is not allowed and that therefore seems very attractive

**for·bid·ding** /fə'bɪdɪŋ; NAmE fər'b-/ adj. seeming unfriendly and frightening: *a forbidding appearance/look/*

# forbore

manner ◊ *The house looked dark and forbidding.* ▶ **for·bid·ding·ly** *adv.*

**for·bore** /fɔːˈbɔː(r); *NAmE* fɔːrˈb-/ *past tense* of FORBEAR

**for·borne** /fɔːˈbɔːn; *NAmE* fɔːrˈbɔːrn/ *past part.* of FORBEAR

**force** ❶ B1 ○ /fɔːs; *NAmE* fɔːrs/ *noun, verb*

**WORD FAMILY**
force *noun, verb*
forceful *adj.*
forcefully *adv.*
forced *adj.* (≠ unforced)
forcible *adj.*
forcibly *adv.*
enforce *verb*

■ **noun**
- **VIOLENT ACTION** **1** B1 [U] violent physical action used to obtain or achieve sth: *The release of the hostages could not be achieved without the use of force.* ◊ *If persuasion doesn't work, they use force.* ◊ **by~** *The rioters were taken away by force.* ◊ *The empire was held together by military force.*
- **PHYSICAL STRENGTH** **2** B1 [U] physical strength, especially as shown when sth hits sth else: *the force of the explosion/impact* ◊ *The shopping centre took the full force of the blast.* ◊ *You have to apply some force to move the lever.* ◊ **with~** *She hits the ball with amazing force for someone so small.*
- **STRONG EFFECT** **3** B2 [U] the strong effect or influence of sth: *They realized the force of her argument.* ◊ **by~ of sth** *He controlled himself by sheer force of will.* ◊ **with~** *Grant drove the point home with considerable force.*
- **SB/STH WITH POWER** **4** B2 [C] a person or thing that has a lot of power or influence: *the forces of good/evil* ◊ *They believe that market forces should determine prices.* ◊ *Ron is the driving force* (= the person who has the most influence) *behind the project.* ◊ *She's a force to be reckoned with* (= a person who has a lot of power and influence and should therefore be treated seriously). ◊ **a ~ for sth** *a force for good/evil* ◊ *The expansion of higher education should be a powerful force for change.*
- **AUTHORITY** **5** [U] the authority of sth: *The court ruled that these standards have force in English law.* ◊ **the ~ of sth** *These guidelines do not have the force of law.*
- **GROUP OF PEOPLE** **6** B1 [C + sing./pl. v.] a group of people who have been organized for a particular purpose: *a member of the sales force* ⊃ see also LABOUR FORCE, TASK FORCE (2), WORKFORCE
- **MILITARY** **7** B1 [C + sing./pl. v.] a trained and organized group of police, soldiers or other military PERSONNEL: *government/rebel forces* ◊ *a peacekeeping force* ◊ *The government deployed military forces to attack terrorist strongholds.* ⊃ see also AIR FORCE, POLICE FORCE, SECURITY FORCES, STRIKE FORCE, TASK FORCE (1) **8 the forces** [pl.] (*BrE*) the army, navy and AIR FORCE: *life in the forces* ⊃ see also ARMED FORCES **9 forces** [pl.] the weapons and soldiers that an army, etc. has, considered as things that may be used: *strategic nuclear forces.*
- **POLICE 10 the force** [sing.] the police force: *He joined the force twenty years ago.*
- **PHYSICS 11** B2 [C, U] an effect that causes things to move in a particular way: *The moon exerts a force on the earth.* ◊ *the force of gravity* ◊ *the sun's magnetic force* ⊃ see also CENTRIFUGAL FORCE, STRONG FORCE, WEAK FORCE ⊃ WORDFINDER NOTE at PHYSICS
- **OF WIND 12** [C, usually sing.] a unit for measuring the strength of the wind on the BEAUFORT SCALE: *a force 9 gale* ◊ *a gale force wind* ⊃ WORDFINDER NOTE at WIND¹ ⊃ see also TOUR DE FORCE ⊃ see also LIFE FORCE

**IDM** **bring sth into ˈforce** to cause a law, rule, etc. to start being used: *They are hoping to bring the new legislation into force before the end of the year.* **come / enter into ˈforce** (of a law, rule, etc.) to start being used: *When do the new regulations come into force?* **force of ˈhabit** if you do sth from or out of **force of habit**, you do it without thinking about it and in a particular way because you have always done it that way in the past **a force of ˈnature** a person with a very strong personality who is full of energy, very determined and difficult for others to resist **the forces of ˈnature** the power of the wind, rain, etc., especially when it causes damage or harm **in ˈforce 1** (of people) in large numbers: *Protesters turned out in force.* **2** (of a law, rule, etc.) being used: *The new regulations are now in force.* **join / combine ˈforces (with sb)** to work together in order to achieve a shared aim: *The two firms joined forces to win the contract.* ⊃ more at SPENT *adj.*

■ **verb**
- **MAKE SB DO STH 1** B1 [often passive] to make sb do sth that they do not want to do **SYN** compel: **be forced into doing sth** *The President was forced into resigning.* ◊ **be forced to do sth** *The President was forced to resign.* ◊ *I was forced to take a taxi because the last bus had left.* ◊ **~ sb / yourself to do sth** *She forced herself to be polite to them.* ◊ **be forced into sth** *He was forced into exile with his family.* ◊ **be forced out of sth** *Residents were forced out of their homes.* ◊ **~ sb** *He didn't force me—I wanted to go.* ◊ **~ yourself** (*informal, humorous*) *'I shouldn't really have any more.' 'Go on—force yourself!'* ◊ **~ sth** *Public pressure eventually forced a change in the government's position.*
- **USE PHYSICAL STRENGTH 2** B2 to use physical strength to move sb/sth into a particular position: **~ sth** *to force a lock/window/door* (= to break it open using force) ◊ *to force (an) entry* (= to enter a building using force) ◊ **~ sth + adv./prep.** *She forced her way through the crowd of reporters.* ◊ **~ sth + adj.** *The door had been forced open.*
- **MAKE STH HAPPEN 3** to make sth happen, especially before other people are ready: **~ sth** *He was in a position where he had to force a decision.* ◊ **~ sth + adv./prep.** *Building a new road here will force house prices down.*
- **A SMILE / LAUGH 4 ~ sth** to make yourself smile, laugh, etc. rather than doing it naturally: *She managed to force a smile.*
- **FRUIT / PLANTS 5 ~ sth** to make fruit, plants, etc. grow or develop faster than normal by keeping them in special conditions: *forced rhubarb* ◊ (*figurative*) *It is unwise to force a child's talent.*

**IDM** **force sb's ˈhand** to make sb do sth that they do not want to do or make them do it sooner than they had intended **ˈforce the issue** to do sth to make people take a decision quickly **force the ˈpace** (*especially BrE*) **1** to run very fast in a race in order to make the other people taking part run faster **2** to make sb do sth faster than they want to: *The demonstrations have succeeded in forcing the pace of change.* ⊃ more at THROAT

**PHRV** **ˌforce sth↔ˈback** to make yourself hide an emotion: *She swallowed hard and forced back her tears.* **ˌforce sth↔ˈdown 1** to make yourself eat or drink sth that you do not really want **2** to make a plane, etc. land, especially by threatening to attack it **ˌforce sb / sth ˈon / upon sb** to make sb accept sth that they do not want: *to force your attentions/opinions/company on sb* **ˌforce sth ˈout of sb** to make sb tell you sth, especially by threatening them: *I managed to force the truth out of him.*

**forced** /fɔːst; *NAmE* fɔːrst/ *adj.* **1** happening or done against sb's will: *victims of forced marriage* ◊ *forced relocation to a job in another city* ◊ *a forced sale of his property* **2** not sincere; not the result of real emotions: *She said she was enjoying herself but her smile was forced.* ⊃ see also UNFORCED

**ˌforced ˈentry** *noun* [U, C] an occasion when sb enters a building illegally, using force

**ˌforced ˈlabour** (*US* **ˌforced ˈlabor**) *noun* [U] **1** hard physical work that sb, often a prisoner or slave, is forced to do **2** prisoners or slaves who are forced to work: *The mines were manned by forced labour from conquered countries.*

**ˌforced ˈlanding** *noun* an act of having to land an aircraft unexpectedly in order to avoid a crash: *to make a forced landing*

**ˌforced ˈmarch** *noun* a long MARCH (= walk), usually made by soldiers in difficult conditions

**ˈforce-feed** *verb* (**force-fed, force-fed**) **~ sb / sth (sth)** to use force to make a person or an animal eat or drink by putting food or drink down their throat

**ˈforce field** *noun* (often used in stories about space travel) a barrier that you cannot see

**ˈforce·ful** /ˈfɔːsfl; *NAmE* ˈfɔːrs-/ *adj.* **1** (of people) expressing opinions strongly and clearly in a way that persuades other people to believe them **SYN** assertive: *a forceful*

**foreign**

*woman/speaker* ◊ *a forceful personality* **2** (of opinions, etc.) expressed strongly and clearly so that other people believe them: *a forceful argument/speech* **3** using force: *the forceful suppression of minorities* ▶ **force·ful·ly** /-fəli/ *adv.*: *He argued his case forcefully.* **force·ful·ness** *noun* [U]

**for·ceps** /ˈfɔːseps; *NAmE* ˈfɔːrs-/ *noun* [pl.] an instrument used by doctors or scientists, with two long thin parts for picking up and holding things: *a pair of forceps* ◊ *a forceps delivery* (= a birth in which the baby is delivered with the help of forceps)

**for·cible** /ˈfɔːsəbl; *NAmE* ˈfɔːrs-/ *adj.* [only before noun] involving the use of physical force: *forcible repatriation* ◊ *The police checked all windows and doors for signs of forcible entry.*

**for·cibly** /ˈfɔːsəbli; *NAmE* ˈfɔːrs-/ *adv.* **1** in a way that involves the use of physical force: *Supporters were forcibly removed from the court.* **2** in a way that makes sth very clear: *It struck me forcibly how honest he'd been.*

**ford** /fɔːd; *NAmE* fɔːrd/ *noun, verb*
■ *noun* a shallow place in a river where it is possible to drive or walk across
■ *verb* ~ sth to walk or drive across a river or stream

**fore** /fɔː(r)/ *noun, adj., adv.*
■ *noun*
**IDM** **bring sth to the ˈfore** to make sth become noticed by people **come to the ˈfore** (*BrE also* **be to the ˈfore**, *NAmE also* **be at the ˈfore**) to be/become important and noticed by people; to play an important part: *The problem has come to the fore again in recent months.* ◊ *She has always been to the fore at moments of crisis.*
■ *adj.* [only before noun] (*specialist*) located at the front of a ship, an aircraft or an animal ⊃ compare AFT, HIND
■ *adv.* **1** (*specialist*) at or towards the front of a ship or an aircraft ⊃ compare AFT **2 Fore!** used in the game of golf to warn people that they are in the path of a ball that you are hitting

**fore-** /fɔː(r)/ *combining form* (in nouns and verbs) **1** before; in advance: *foreword* ◊ *foretell* **2** in the front of: *the foreground of the picture*

**fore·arm¹** /ˈfɔːrɑːm; *NAmE* -ɑːrm/ *noun* the lower part of the arm between the ELBOW and the WRIST ⊃ **VISUAL VOCAB** page V1

**fore·arm²** /ˌfɔːrˈɑːm; *NAmE* -ˈɑːrm/ *verb* **IDM** see FOREWARN

**fore·bear** (*also* **for·bear**) /ˈfɔːbeə(r); *NAmE* ˈfɔːrber/ *noun* [usually pl.] (*formal or literary*) a person in your family who lived a long time ago **SYN** ancestor

**fore·bod·ing** /fɔːˈbəʊdɪŋ; *NAmE* fɔːrˈb-/ *noun* [U, C] a strong feeling that sth unpleasant or dangerous is going to happen: *She had a sense of foreboding that the news would be bad.* ◊ *He knew from her face that his forebodings had been justified.* ▶ **fore·bod·ing** *adj.* [only before noun]: *a foreboding feeling that something was wrong*

**fore·brain** /ˈfɔːbreɪn; *NAmE* ˈfɔːrb-/ *noun* (*anatomy*) the front part of the brain

**fore·cast** 🔑 B2 /ˈfɔːkɑːst; *NAmE* ˈfɔːrkæst/ *noun, verb*
■ *noun* 🔑+ B2 a statement about what will happen in the future, based on information that is available now: *sales forecasts* ◊ *The forecast said there would be sunny intervals and showers.* ⊃ see also WEATHER FORECAST
■ *verb* 🔑+ B2 (**fore·cast**, **fore·cast** or **fore·cast·ed**, **fore·cast·ed**) to say what you think will happen in the future based on information that you have now **SYN** **predict**: ~ sth *Experts are forecasting a recovery in the economy.* ◊ *Snow is forecast for tomorrow.* ◊ ~ sth to do sth *Temperatures were forecast to reach 40°C.* ◊ ~ that... *The report forecasts that prices will rise by 3 per cent next month.* ◊ **how, what, etc...** *It is difficult to forecast how the markets will react.* ⊃ LANGUAGE BANK at EXPECT

**fore·cast·er** /ˈfɔːkɑːstə(r); *NAmE* ˈfɔːrkæs-/ *noun* a person who says what is expected to happen, especially sb whose job is to predict the weather: *a weather forecaster* ◊ *an economic forecaster*

**fore·castle** (*also* **fo'c'sle**) /ˈfəʊksl/ *noun* the front part of a ship below the DECK, where the sailors live

**fore·close** /fɔːˈkləʊz; *NAmE* fɔːrˈk-/ *verb* **1** [I, T] ~ (on sb/sth) | ~ sth (*finance*) (especially of a bank) to take control of sb's property because they have not paid back money that they borrowed to buy it **2** [T] ~ sth (*formal*) to reject sth as a possibility **SYN** exclude

**fore·clos·ure** /fɔːˈkləʊʒə(r); *NAmE* fɔːrˈk-/ *noun* [U, C] (*finance*) the act of taking control of sb's property because they have not paid back money that they borrowed to buy it; an example of this

**fore·court** /ˈfɔːkɔːt; *NAmE* ˈfɔːrkɔːrt/ *noun* (*BrE*) a large open space in front of a building, for example a PETROL STATION or hotel, often used for parking cars on

**fore·father** /ˈfɔːfɑːðə(r); *NAmE* ˈfɔːrf-/ *noun* [usually pl.] (*formal or literary*) a person (especially a man) in your family who lived a long time ago **SYN** ancestor

**fore·fin·ger** /ˈfɔːfɪŋɡə(r); *NAmE* ˈfɔːrf-/ *noun* = INDEX FINGER

**fore·foot** /ˈfɔːfʊt; *NAmE* ˈfɔːrf-/ *noun* (*pl.* **fore·feet** /-fiːt/) either of the two front feet of an animal that has four feet

**fore·front** /ˈfɔːfrʌnt; *NAmE* ˈfɔːrf-/ *noun* [sing.]
**IDM** **at/in/to the ˈforefront (of sth)** in or into an important or leading position in a particular group or activity: *Women have always been at the forefront of the Green movement.* ◊ *The new product took the company to the forefront of the computer software field.* ◊ *The court case was constantly in the forefront of my mind* (= I thought about it all the time).

**fore·go** = FORGO

**fore·go·ing** /ˈfɔːɡəʊɪŋ; *NAmE* ˈfɔːrɡ-/ *adj.* [only before noun] (*formal*) **1** used to refer to sth that has just been mentioned: *the foregoing discussion* **2 the foregoing** *noun* [sing. + sing./pl. v.] what has just been mentioned **OPP** following

**fore·gone** /ˈfɔːɡɒn; *NAmE* ˈfɔːrɡɔːn/ *adj.*
**IDM** **a foregone conˈclusion** if you say that sth is a foregone conclusion, you mean that it is a result that is certain to happen

**fore·ground** /ˈfɔːɡraʊnd; *NAmE* ˈfɔːrɡ-/ *noun, verb*
■ *noun* **the foreground 1** [C, usually sing.] the part of a view, picture, etc. that is nearest to you when you look at it: *The figure in the foreground is the artist's mother.* ⊃ WORDFINDER NOTE at PAINTING ⊃ EXPRESS YOURSELF at DESCRIBE **2** [sing.] an important position that is noticed by people: *Inflation and interest rates will be very much in the foreground of their election campaign.* **3** [sing.] (*computing*) used to refer to tasks or processes that the user is actively working on at the present time: *Normally, the user runs the program in the foreground.* ⊃ compare BACKGROUND
■ *verb* ~ sth to give particular importance to sth: *The play foregrounds the relationship between father and daughter.*

**fore·hand** /ˈfɔːhænd; *NAmE* ˈfɔːrh-/ *noun* [usually sing.] (in tennis, etc.) a way of hitting a ball in which the inner part of the hand (= the PALM) faces the ball as it is hit: *She has a strong forehand.* ◊ *a forehand volley* ◊ *He served to his opponent's forehand.* ⊃ compare BACKHAND

**fore·head** /ˈfɔːhed; ˈfɒrɪd; *NAmE* ˈfɔːrhed; ˈfɔːrəd/ *noun* the part of the face above the eyes and below the hair **SYN** brow

**for·eign** 🔑 A2 🅢 /ˈfɒrən; *NAmE* ˈfɔːr-/ *adj.* **1** 🔑 A2 in or from a country that is not your own: *a foreign language/country/currency* ◊ *foreign holidays* ◊ *He spoke with a foreign accent.* ◊ *You could tell she was foreign by the way she dressed.* **2** 🔑 A2 [only before noun] dealing with or involving other countries: *foreign policy* ◊ *the Japanese foreign minister* ◊ *a foreign correspondent* (= one who reports on foreign countries in newspapers or on television) **OPP** domestic, home **3** ~ to sb/sth (*formal*) not typical of sb/sth; not known to sb/sth and therefore seeming strange: *Dishonesty is foreign to his nature.* **4** ~ object/body (*formal*) an object that has entered sth by accident and should not be there: *Tears help to protect the eye from potentially harmful foreign bodies.* ▶ **for·eign·ness** *noun* [U]

**the ˌForeign and ˈCommonwealth Office** *noun* [sing. + sing./pl. v.] (*abbr.* **FCO**) the British government

# foreigner

department that deals with relations with other countries. It used to be called **the Foreign Office** and it is still often referred to as this.

**for·eign·er** /ˈfɒrənə(r)/; *NAmE* ˈfɔːr-/ *noun* (*sometimes offensive*) **1** a person who comes from a different country: *The fact that I was a foreigner was a big disadvantage.* **2** a person who does not belong in a particular place: *I have always been regarded as a foreigner by the local folk.*

**foreign exˈchange** *noun* **1** [U, C] the system of exchanging the money of one country for that of another country; the place where money is exchanged: *The euro fell on the foreign exchanges yesterday.* **2** [U] money that is obtained using this system: *our largest source of foreign exchange*

**the ˈForeign Office** *noun* [sing. + sing. / pl. v.] = FOREIGN AND COMMONWEALTH OFFICE

**foreign-reˈturned** *adj.* (*IndE, informal*) (of a person) educated or trained in a foreign country, and having returned to India

**the Foreign ˈSecretary** *noun* the British government minister in charge of the department that deals with relations with other countries

**ˈForeign Service** *noun* (*NAmE*) = DIPLOMATIC SERVICE

**fore·ˈknow·ledge** /ˌfɔːˈnɒlɪdʒ; *NAmE* fɔːrˈnɑːl-/ *noun* [U] (*formal*) knowledge of sth before it happens

**fore·land** /ˈfɔːlənd; *NAmE* ˈfɔːrl-/ *noun* [sing., U] **1** an area of land that lies in front of sth **2** an area of land that sticks out into the sea

**fore·leg** /ˈfɔːleɡ; *NAmE* ˈfɔːrl-/ (*also* **fore·limb** /ˈfɔːlɪm; *NAmE* ˈfɔːrl-/) *noun* either of the two front legs of an animal that has four legs

**fore·lock** /ˈfɔːlɒk; *NAmE* ˈfɔːrlɑːk/ *noun* **1** a piece of hair that grows at the front of the head and hangs down over the FOREHEAD **2** a part of a horse's MANE that grows forwards between its ears
IDM **touch/tug your ˈforelock (to sb)** (*BrE, disapproving*) to show too much respect for sb of a higher class, especially because you are anxious about what they think of you ORIGIN In the past people of the lower classes either took off their hats or pulled on their forelocks to show respect.

**fore·man** /ˈfɔːmən; *NAmE* ˈfɔːrm-/, **fore·woman** /ˈfɔːwʊmən; *NAmE* ˈfɔːrw-/ (*pl.* **-men** /-mən/, **-women** /-wɪmɪn/) **1** a worker who is in charge of a group of other factory or building workers ⇨ WORDFINDER NOTE at FACTORY **2** a person who acts as the leader of a JURY in court ⇨ note at GENDER

**fore·most** /ˈfɔːməʊst; *NAmE* ˈfɔːrm-/ *adj., adv.*
■ *adj.* the most important or famous; in a position at the front: *the world's foremost authority on the subject* ◊ *The Prime Minister was foremost among those who condemned the violence.* ◊ *This question has been foremost in our minds recently.*
■ *adv.* more than anything else: *He does a little teaching, but first and foremost he's a writer.*

**fore·name** /ˈfɔːneɪm; *NAmE* ˈfɔːrn-/ *noun* (*formal*) a person's first name rather than the name that they share with the other members of their family (= their SURNAME): *Please check that your surname and forenames have been correctly entered.*

**fore·noon** /ˈfɔːnuːn; *NAmE* ˈfɔːrn-/ *noun* (*NAmE, ScotE*) the morning

**fo·ren·sic** /fəˈrenzɪk/ *adj.* [only before noun] connected with the scientific tests used by the police when trying to solve a crime: *forensic evidence/medicine/science/tests* ◊ *the forensic laboratory* ◊ *a forensic pathologist* ▶ **fo·ren·sic·al·ly** /-kli/ *adv.*

**fo·ren·sics** /fəˈrenzɪks/ *noun* **1** [U] the branch of science that uses scientific methods to help the police to solve crimes **2** [pl.] scientific tests that are used to help the police solve crimes; the results of those tests: *Forensics revealed that he had been murdered.* **3** [U + sing./pl. v.] (*informal*) the department that uses scientific tests to help

the police to solve crimes: *Forensics is/are examining the scene of a gangland shooting.*

**fore·play** /ˈfɔːpleɪ; *NAmE* ˈfɔːrp-/ *noun* [U] sexual activity, such as touching the sexual organs and kissing, that takes place before people have sex

**fore·run·ner** /ˈfɔːrʌnə(r)/ *noun* **~ (of sb/sth)** a person or thing that came before and influenced sb/sth else that is similar; a sign of what is going to happen: *Country music was undoubtedly one of the forerunners of rock and roll.*

**fore·sail** /ˈfɔːseɪl, -sl; *NAmE* ˈfɔːrs-/ *noun* [usually sing.] the main sail on the MAST of a ship that is nearest the front (called the **foremast** /ˈfɔːmɑːst; *NAmE* ˈfɔːrmæst/)

**fore·see** /fɔːˈsiː; *NAmE* fɔːrˈsiː/ *verb* (**fore·saw** /-ˈsɔː/, **fore·seen** /-ˈsiːn/) to think sth is going to happen in the future; to know about sth before it happens SYN **predict**: *~ sth We do not foresee any problems.* ◊ *The extent of the damage could not have been foreseen.* ◊ *~ (that)… No one could have foreseen (that) things would turn out this way.* ◊ *~ how, what, etc…* *It is impossible to foresee how life will work out.* ◊ *~ sb/sth doing sth I just didn't foresee that happening.* ⇨ compare UNFORESEEN

**fore·see·able** /fɔːˈsiːəbl; *NAmE* fɔːrˈs-/ *adj.* that you can predict will happen; that can be FORESEEN: *foreseeable risks/consequences* OPP **unforeseeable**
IDM **for/in the foreseeable ˈfuture** for/in the period of time when you can predict what is going to happen, based on the present circumstances: *The statue will remain in the museum for the foreseeable future.* ◊ *It's unlikely that the hospital will be closed in the foreseeable future* (= soon).

**fore·shadow** /fɔːˈʃædəʊ; *NAmE* fɔːrˈʃ-/ *verb* **~ sth** (*formal*) to be a sign of sth that will happen in the future

**fore·shore** /ˈfɔːʃɔː(r); *NAmE* ˈfɔːrʃ-/ *noun* [C, usually sing., U] **1** (on a beach or by a river) the part of the SHORE between the highest and lowest levels reached by the water **2** the part by the SHORE between the highest level reached by the water and the area of land that has buildings, plants, etc. on it

**fore·short·en** /fɔːˈʃɔːtn; *NAmE* fɔːrˈʃɔːrtn/ *verb* **1** **~ sth/sb** (*specialist*) to draw, photograph, etc. objects or people so that they look smaller or closer together than they really are **2** **~ sth** (*formal*) to end sth before it would normally finish SYN **curtail**: *a foreshortened education*

**fore·sight** /ˈfɔːsaɪt; *NAmE* ˈfɔːrs-/ *noun* [U] (*approving*) the ability to predict what is likely to happen and to use this to prepare for the future: *She had had the foresight to prepare herself financially in case of an accident.* ⇨ compare HINDSIGHT

**fore·skin** /ˈfɔːskɪn; *NAmE* ˈfɔːrs-/ *noun* the loose piece of skin that covers the end of a man's PENIS

**for·est** ⓘ A2 /ˈfɒrɪst; *NAmE* ˈfɔːr-/ *noun* **1** A2 [C, U] a large area of land that is thickly covered with trees: *a tropical/pine forest* ◊ *a forest fire* ◊ *Thousands of hectares of forest are destroyed each year.* ⇨ see also CLOUD FOREST, RAINFOREST **2** [C] **~ (of sth)** a mass of tall narrow objects that are close together: *a forest of cranes on the skyline*
IDM **not see the ˈforest for the ˈtrees** (*NAmE*) (*BrE* **not see the ˈwood for the ˈtrees**) to not see or understand the main point about sth, because you are paying too much attention to small details

**fore·stall** /fɔːˈstɔːl; *NAmE* fɔːrˈs-/ *verb* **~ sth/sb** (*formal*) to prevent sth from happening or sb from doing sth by doing sth first: *Try to anticipate what your child will do and forestall problems.*

**for·ested** /ˈfɒrɪstɪd; *NAmE* ˈfɔːr-/ *adj.* covered in forest: *thickly forested hills* ◊ *The province is heavily forested and sparsely populated.*

**for·est·er** /ˈfɒrɪstə(r); *NAmE* ˈfɔːr-/ *noun* a person who works in a forest, taking care of the trees, planting new ones, etc.

**for·est·ry** /ˈfɒrɪstri; *NAmE* ˈfɔːr-/ *noun* [U] the science or practice of planting and taking care of trees and forests

**fore·taste** /ˈfɔːteɪst; *NAmE* ˈfɔːrt-/ *noun* [sing.] **a ~ (of sth)** a small amount of a particular experience or situation that shows you what it will be like when the same thing

---

| æ cat | ɑː father | e bed | ɜː fur | ə about | ɪ sit | iː see | i happy | ɒ got (*BrE*) | ɔː saw | ʌ cup | ʊ put | uː too |

happens on a larger scale in the future: *They were unaware that the street violence was just a foretaste of what was to come.*

**fore·tell** /fɔːˈtel; NAmE fɔːrˈt-/ *verb* (**fore·told**, **fore·told** /-ˈtəʊld/) (*literary*) to know or say what will happen in the future, especially by using magic powers: ~ *sth to foretell the future* ◇ ~ **that** ... *The witch foretold that she would marry a prince.* ◇ ~ **what, when, etc** ... *None of us can foretell what lies ahead.*

**fore·thought** /ˈfɔːθɔːt; NAmE ˈfɔːrθ-/ *noun* [U] careful thought to make sure that things are successful in the future: *Some forethought and preparation are necessary before you embark on the project.* **IDM** see MALICE

**fore·told** /fɔːˈtəʊld; NAmE fɔːrˈt-/ *past tense*, *past part*. of FORETELL

**for·ever** 🅱 **B1** /fərˈevə(r)/ *adv.* **1** 🅱 **B1** (BrE also **for ever**) used to say that a particular situation or state will always exist: *I'll love you forever!* ◇ *After her death, their lives changed forever.* ◇ *Just keep telling yourself that it won't last forever.* **2** 🅱 **B2** (BrE also **for ever**) (*informal*) a very long time: *It takes her forever to get dressed.* **3** (*informal*) used with verbs in the progressive tenses to say that sb does sth very often and in a way that is annoying to other people: *She's forever going on about how poor they are.*

**fore·warn** /fɔːˈwɔːn; NAmE fɔːrˈwɔːrn/ *verb* [usually passive] (*formal*) to warn sb about sth bad or unpleasant before it happens: **be forewarned of sth** *The commander had been forewarned of the attack.* ◇ **be forewarned that** ... *They were forewarned that a storm was approaching.* ▸ **fore·warn·ing** *noun* [U, C]
**IDM** ▸ **fore,warned is fore'armed** (*saying*) if you know about problems, dangers, etc. before they happen, you can be better prepared for them

**fore·woman** /ˈfɔːwʊmən; NAmE ˈfɔːrw-/ *noun* ⊃ FOREMAN

**fore·word** /ˈfɔːwɜːd; NAmE ˈfɔːrwɜːrd/ *noun* a short introduction at the beginning of a book, usually by a person other than the author ⊃ compare PREFACE

**for·feit** /ˈfɔːfɪt; NAmE ˈfɔːrf-/ *verb*, *noun*, *adj*.
■ *verb* **1** ~ **sth** to lose sth or have sth taken away from you because you have done sth wrong: *He has forfeited his right to be taken seriously.* **2** ~ **sth** to lose or give sth up as a necessary consequence of sth that you have done: *If you cancel your flight, you will forfeit your deposit.*
■ *noun* something that a person has to pay, or sth that is taken from them, because they have done sth wrong, or as a necessary consequence of sth they have done
■ *adj.* [not before noun] (*formal*) taken away from sb as a consequence of sth that they have done

**for·feit·ure** /ˈfɔːfɪtʃə(r); NAmE ˈfɔːrf-/ *noun* [U, C] (*law*) the act of giving sth up as a consequence of sth that you have done: *the forfeiture of property*

**for·gave** /fəˈɡeɪv; NAmE fərˈɡ-/ *past tense* of FORGIVE

**forge** 🅱 **C1** /fɔːdʒ; NAmE fɔːrdʒ/ *verb*, *noun*
■ *verb* **1** 🅱 **C1** [T] ~ **sth** to put a lot of effort into making sth successful or strong so that it will last: *a move to forge new links between management and workers* ◇ *Strategic alliances are being forged with major European companies.* ◇ *She forged a new career in the music business.* **2** 🅱 **C1** [T] ~ **sth** to make an illegal copy of sth in order to cheat people: *to forge a passport/banknote/document* ◇ *He's getting good at forging his mother's signature.* ⊃ compare COUNTERFEIT **3** [T] ~ **sth (from sth)** to shape metal by heating it in a fire and hitting it with a HAMMER; to make an object in this way: *swords forged from steel* **4** [I] + **adv./prep.** (*formal*) to move forward in a steady but powerful way: *He forged through the crowds to the front of the stage.* ◇ *She forged into the lead* (= in a competition, race, etc.).
**PHRV** ▸ **forge a'head (with sth)** to move forward quickly; to make a lot of progress quickly: *The company is forging ahead with its plans for expansion.*
■ *noun* **1** a place where objects are made by heating and shaping pieces of metal, especially one where a BLACKSMITH works **2** a large piece of equipment used for heating metals in; a building or part of a factory where this is found

**for·ger** /ˈfɔːdʒə(r); NAmE ˈfɔːrdʒ-/ *noun* a person who makes illegal copies of money, documents, etc. in order to cheat people ⊃ compare COUNTERFEITER

**for·gery** /ˈfɔːdʒəri; NAmE ˈfɔːrdʒ-/ *noun* (*pl.* **-ies**) **1** [U] the crime of copying money, documents, etc. in order to cheat people **2** [C] something, for example a document, piece of paper money, etc., that has been copied in order to cheat people **SYN** **fake**: *Experts are dismissing claims that the painting is a forgery.* ⊃ compare COUNTERFEIT

**for·get** 🅱 **A1** /fəˈɡet; NAmE fərˈɡ-/ *verb* (**for·got** /fəˈɡɒt; NAmE fərˈɡɑːt/, **for·got·ten** /fəˈɡɒtn; NAmE fərˈɡɑːtn/) (US also **for·got**, **for·got**)
• **TO DO STH** **1** 🅱 **A1** [I, T] to not remember to do sth that you ought to do, or to bring or buy sth that you ought to bring or buy: *'Why weren't you at the meeting?' 'Sorry—I forgot.'* ◇ ~ **about sth** *In the excitement I forgot all about my little brother.* ◇ ~ **to do sth** *Take care, and don't forget to write.* ◇ ~ **sth/sb** *I forgot my purse* (= I did not remember to bring it). ◇ *'Hey, don't forget me!'* (= don't leave without me) ◇ *Aren't you forgetting something?* (= I think you have forgotten to do sth) **HELP** You cannot use **forget** if you want to mention the place where you have left something: *I've left my book at home.* ◇ *I've forgotten my book at home.*
• **EVENTS/FACTS** **2** 🅱 **A2** [I, T] (not usually used in the progressive tenses) to be unable to remember sth that has happened in the past or information that you knew in the past: *Oh, I almost forgot—there was a call for you.* ◇ ~ **about sth** *I'd completely forgotten about the money he owed me.* ◇ ~ **sth** *I never forget a face.* ◇ **(that)** ... *She keeps forgetting (that) I'm not a child any more.* ◇ *I was forgetting* (= I had forgotten) *(that) you've been here before.* ◇ ~ **where, how, etc** ... *I've forgotten where they live exactly.* ◇ *I forget how much they paid for it.* ◇ ~ **(sb) doing sth** *I'll never forget hearing this piece of music for the first time.* ◇ **it is forgotten that** ... *It should not be forgotten that people used to get much more exercise.*
• **STOP THINKING ABOUT STH** **3** 🅱 **A2** [I, T] to deliberately stop thinking about sb/sth: ~ **about sb/sth** *Try to forget about what happened.* ◇ *Could you possibly forget about work for five minutes?* ◇ ~ **sb/sth** *Forget him!* ◇ *Let's forget our differences and be friends.* ◇ ~ **(that)** ... *I said anything!* **4** [I, T] to stop thinking that sth is a possibility: ~ **about sth** *If I lose this job, we can forget about buying a new car.* ◇ ~ **sth** *'I was hoping you might be able to lend me the money.' 'You can forget that!'*
• **YOURSELF** **5** [T] ~ **yourself** to behave in a way that is not socially acceptable: *I'm forgetting myself. I haven't offered you a drink yet!*
**IDM** ▸ **and don't (you) for'get it** (*informal*) used to tell sb how they should behave, especially when they have been behaving in a way you do not like: *You're a suspect, not a detective, and don't you forget it.* ▸ **for'get it** (*informal*) **1** used to tell sb that sth is not important and that they should not worry about it: *'I still owe you for lunch yesterday.' 'Forget it.'* **2** used to tell sb that you are not going to repeat what you said: *'Now, what were you saying about John?' 'Forget it, it doesn't matter.'* **3** used to emphasize that you are saying 'no' to sth: *'Any chance of you helping out here?' 'Forget it, I've got too much to do.'* **4** used to tell sb to stop talking about sth because they are annoying you: *Just forget it, will you!* ▸ **not forgetting** ... (*BrE*) used to include sth in the list of things that you have just mentioned: *I share the house with Jim, Ian and Sam, not forgetting Spike, the dog.* ⊃ more at FORGIVE

**for·get·ful** /fəˈɡetfl; NAmE fərˈɡ-/ *adj.* **1** often forgetting things **SYN** **absent-minded**: *She has become very forgetful in recent years.* **2** ~ **of sb/sth** (*formal*) not thinking about sb/sth that you should be thinking about ▸ **for·get·ful·ly** /-fəli/ *adv.* **for·get·ful·ness** *noun* [U]

**for'get-me-not** *noun* a low-growing plant with small, light-blue flowers

# forgettable

**for·get·table** /fəˈgetəbl; NAmE fərˈg-/ adj. not interesting or special and therefore easily forgotten: *an instantly forgettable tune* OPP **unforgettable**

**for·giv·able** /fəˈgɪvəbl; NAmE fərˈg-/ adj. that you can understand and forgive SYN **excusable**: *His rudeness was forgivable in the circumstances.* OPP **unforgivable**

**for·give** ⓘ B2 /fəˈgɪv; NAmE fərˈg-/ verb (**for·gave** /-ˈgeɪv/, **for·given** /-ˈgɪvn/) **1** B2 [T, I] to stop feeling angry with sb who has done sth to harm, annoy or upset you; to stop feeling angry with yourself: **~ sb** *Can you ever forgive me?* ◊ **~ yourself** *I'd never forgive myself if she heard the truth from someone else.* ◊ **~ sb/yourself for sth/for doing sth** *I'll never forgive her for what she did.* ◊ **~ (sth)** *I can't forgive that type of behaviour.* ◊ *We all have to learn to forgive.* ◊ **~ sb sth** *She'd forgive him anything.* ⊃ WORDFINDER NOTE at SORRY **2** B2 [T] used to say in a polite way that you are sorry if what you are doing or saying seems rude or silly: **~ me** *Forgive me, but I don't see that any of this concerns me.* ◊ **~ me for doing sth** *Forgive me for interrupting, but I really don't agree with that.* ◊ **~ my ... ~** *Forgive my ignorance, but what exactly does the company do?* **3** [T] **~ (sb) sth** (*formal*) (of a bank, country, etc.) to say that sb does not need to pay back money that they have borrowed: *The government has agreed to forgive a large part of the debt.* IDM **sb could/might be forgiven for doing sth** used to say that it is easy to understand why sb does or thinks sth, although they are wrong: *Looking at the crowds out shopping, you could be forgiven for thinking that everyone has plenty of money.* **for give and for'get** to stop feeling angry with sb for sth they have done to you and to behave as if it had not happened

**for·give·ness** /fəˈgɪvnəs; NAmE fərˈg-/ noun [U] the act of forgiving sb; the quality of being willing to forgive sb: *to pray for God's forgiveness* ◊ *the forgiveness of sins* ◊ *He begged forgiveness for what he had done.*

**for·giv·ing** /fəˈgɪvɪŋ; NAmE fərˈg-/ adj. **1** willing to forgive: *She had not inherited her mother's forgiving nature.* ◊ **~ of sth** *The public was more forgiving of the president's difficulties than the press and fellow politicians.* **2** (of a thing) easy or safe to deal with: *Snow is a forgiving surface on which to fall.*

**forgo** (*also* **fore·go**) /fɔːˈgəʊ; NAmE fɔːrˈg-/ verb (**for·goes** /-ˈgəʊz/, **for·went** /-ˈwent/, **for·gone** /-ˈgɒn; NAmE fɔːrˈgɔːn/) **~ sth** (*formal*) to decide not to have or do sth that you would like to have or do: *No one was prepared to forgo their lunch hour to attend the meeting.* ⊃ see also A FOREGONE CONCLUSION at FOREGONE

**for·got** /fəˈgɒt; NAmE fərˈgɑːt/ past tense of FORGET

**for·got·ten** /fəˈgɒtn; NAmE fərˈgɑːtn/ past part. of FORGET

**fork** ⓘ A2 /fɔːk; NAmE fɔːrk/ noun, verb
■ noun **1** A2 a tool with a handle and three or four sharp points (called PRONGS), used for picking up and eating food: *to eat with a knife and fork* **2** a garden tool with a long or short handle and three or four sharp metal points, used for digging ⊃ see also PITCHFORK **3** a place where a road, river, etc. divides into two; either of these two parts: *Take the right fork.* ◊ **~ in sth** *Bear left at the fork in the road.* **4 ~ (of sth)** a thing that is like a fork in shape, with two or more long parts: *a jagged fork of lightning* ⊃ see also TUNING FORK **5** either of two metal supporting pieces into which a wheel on a bicycle or motorcycle is fitted
■ verb **1** [I] (not used in the progressive tenses) (**+ adv./prep.**) (of a road, river, etc.) to divide into two parts that lead in different directions: *The path forks at the bottom of the hill.* ◊ *The road forks right after the bridge.* **2** [I] **+ adv./prep.** (not used in the progressive tenses) (of a person) to turn left or right where a road, etc. divides into two: *Fork right after the bridge.* **3** [T] (**+ adv./prep.**) to move, carry or dig sth using a fork: *Clear the soil of weeds and fork in plenty of compost.* PHRV **fork ˈout (for sth)** | **fork ˈout sth (for/on sth)** (*informal*) to spend a lot of money on sth, especially unwillingly: *Why fork out for a taxi when there's a perfectly good bus service?* ◊ *We've forked out a small fortune on their education.*

**forked** /fɔːkt; NAmE fɔːrkt/ adj. with one end divided into two parts, like the shape of the letter 'Y': *a bird with a forked tail* ◊ *the forked tongue of a snake* ⊃ VISUAL VOCAB page V3

**ˌforked ˈlightning** noun [U] the type of LIGHTNING that is like a line that divides into smaller lines near the ground ⊃ compare SHEET LIGHTNING

**fork·ful** /ˈfɔːkfʊl; NAmE ˈfɔːrk-/ noun the amount that a fork holds

**ˈfork-lift truck** /ˌfɔːklɪft ˈtrʌk; NAmE ˌfɔːrk-/ (*also* **ˈfork-lift**) noun a vehicle with special equipment on the front for moving and lifting heavy objects

**for·lorn** /fəˈlɔːn; NAmE fərˈlɔːrn/ adj. **1** (of a person) appearing lonely and unhappy: *She looked so forlorn, standing there in the rain.* **2** (of a place) not cared for and with no people in it: *Empty houses quickly take on a forlorn look.* **3** unlikely to succeed, come true, etc: *She waited in the forlorn hope that he would one day come back to her.* ◊ *His father smiled weakly in a forlorn attempt to reassure him that everything was all right.* ▶ **for·lorn·ly** adv.

**form** ⓘ A1 ⓞ /fɔːm; NAmE fɔːrm/ noun, verb
■ noun
- TYPE **1** A1 [C] a type or variety of sth: *all the millions of different life forms on the planet today* ◊ **~ of sth** *forms of transport/government/entertainment* ◊ *one of the most common forms of cancer* ⊃ see also ART FORM
- OF WORD **2** A1 [C] a way of writing or saying a word that shows, for example, if it is plural or in a particular tense: *the infinitive form of the verb* ⊃ see also BASE FORM, COMBINING FORM, PRO-FORM
- WAY STH IS/LOOKS **3** B1 [C, U] the particular way sth is, seems, looks or is presented: *The disease can take several different forms.* ◊ *The training programme* **takes the form of** *a series of workshops.* ◊ *We need to come to* **some form of** *agreement.* ◊ **in the ~ of sth/sth** *Help* **in the form of** *money will be very welcome.* ◊ **in ... ~** *Most political questions involve morality* **in some form or other.** ◊ *We prefer applications* **in electronic form.** ◊ *I'm opposed to censorship* **in any shape or form.**
- DOCUMENT **4** A2 [C] an official document containing questions and spaces for answers: *an application/entry/order form* ◊ (*especially BrE*) **to fill in a form** ◊ (*especially NAmE*) **to fill out a form** ◊ **to complete a form** ◊ *We asked them to read and sign consent forms.* ◊ (*BrE*) *a booking form* ◊ (*NAmE*) *a reservation form* ⊃ see also ORDER FORM
- SHAPE **5** [C] the shape of sb/sth; a person or thing of which only the shape can be seen: *The human form has changed little over the last 30000 years.* ◊ *They made out a shadowy form in front of them.*
- ARRANGEMENT OF PARTS **6** [U] the arrangement of parts in a whole, especially in a work of art or piece of writing: *In a novel, form and content are equally important.* ⊃ SYNONYMS at STRUCTURE
- BEING FIT/HEALTHY **7** [U] (*BrE*) how fit and healthy sb is; the state of being fit and healthy: **in ... ~** *After six months' training the whole team is in superb form.* ◊ **in ~** *I really need to get back in form.* ◊ **out of ~** *The horse was clearly out of form.*
- PERFORMANCE **8** [U] how well sb/sth is performing; the fact that sb/sth is performing well: *Midfielder Elliott has shown disappointing form recently.* ◊ *She signalled her return to form with a convincing victory.* ◊ **on ~** (*BrE*) *He's right on form* (= performing well) *as a crazy science teacher in his latest movie.* ◊ **on ... ~** *The whole team was on good form and deserved the win.* ◊ **On current/present form** *the party is heading for another election victory.* ◊ **in ... ~** *She was* **in great form** (= happy and cheerful and full of energy) *at the wedding party.*
- WAY OF DOING THINGS **9** [U, C] (*especially BrE*) the usual way of doing sth: *What's the form when you apply for a research grant?* ◊ *conventional social forms* ◊ **True to form** (= as he usually does) *he arrived an hour late.* ◊ *Partners of employees are invited* **as a matter of form** (= because that is the usual way things are done). **10** [U] **good/bad ~** (*old-*

*fashioned*, *BrE*) the way of doing things that is socially acceptable/not socially acceptable
- **IN SCHOOL** **11** (*BrE*, *old-fashioned*) a class in a school: *Who's your form teacher?* ⊃ see also SIXTH FORM ⊃ compare YEAR (5) **12** **-former** (in compounds) (*BrE*, *old-fashioned*) a student in the form mentioned at school: *a third-former* ⊃ see also SIXTH-FORMER
- **IDM** take 'form (*formal*) to gradually form into a particular shape; to gradually develop: *In her body a new life was taking form.* ⊃ more at SHAPE *n*.

■ **verb**
- **MAKE SHAPE/FORM** **1** [T] to produce sth in a particular way or make it have a particular shape: *~sth Bend the wire so that it forms a 'V'.* ◊ *Rearrange the letters to form a new word.* ◊ *Do you know how to form the past tense?* ◊ *~sth into sth Form the dough into balls with your hands.* ◊ *be formed from/of sth The chain is formed from 136 links.* **2** [T, I] to move or arrange objects or people so that they are in a group with a particular shape; to become arranged in a group like this: *~(sb/sth) First get students to form groups of four.* ◊ *to form a line/queue/circle* ◊ *Queues were already forming outside the theatre.* ◊ *~(up) into sth The teams formed up into lines.*
- **START TO EXIST** **3** [I, T] (especially of natural things) to begin to exist and gradually develop into a particular shape; to make sth begin to exist in a particular shape: *Flowers appeared, but fruits failed to form.* ◊ *Storm clouds are forming on the horizon.* ◊ **be formed (by sth)** *These hills were formed by glaciation.* **4** [I, T] to start to exist and develop; to make sth start to exist and develop: *A plan formed in my head.* ◊ *~sth to form a relationship/bond/partnership with sb/sth* ◊ *I formed many close friendships at college.* ◊ *I didn't see enough of the play to form an opinion about it.* ◊ *The plan came in a flash of inspiration, fully formed.* ⊃ SYNONYMS at MAKE
- **ORGANIZATION** **5** [T, I] to start a group of people, such as an organization, a committee, etc.; to come together in a group of this kind: *~sth They hope to form the new government.* ◊ *He formed a band with some friends from school.* ◊ *a newly formed political party* ◊ *The band formed in 2017.*
- **HAVE FUNCTION/ROLE** **6** *linking verb* **+ noun** to be sth; to have a particular function or pattern: *The castle forms the focal point of the city.* ◊ *The survey formed part of a larger programme of research.* ◊ *These drawings will form the basis of the exhibition.* ◊ *The trees form a natural protection from the sun's rays.*
- **HAVE INFLUENCE ON** **7** [T] *~sth* to have an influence on the way that sth develops **SYN** mould: *Positive and negative experiences form a child's character.*

## for·mal
/'fɔːml/; *NAmE* 'fɔːrml/ *adj.* **1** (of a style of dress, speech, writing, behaviour, etc.) very correct and suitable for official or important occasions: *ladies in formal evening wear* ◊ *The dinner was a formal affair.* ◊ *He kept the tone of the letter formal and business-like.* **OPP** informal **2** official; following an agreed or official way of doing things: *formal legal processes* ◊ *to make a formal complaint* ◊ *There has been no formal announcement of her resignation yet.* ◊ *It is time to put these arrangements on a slightly more formal basis.* **3** (of education or training) received in a school, college or university, with lessons, exams, etc., rather than gained just through practical experience: *He has no formal teaching qualifications.* ◊ *Young children are beginning their formal education as early as four years old.* **4** connected with the way sth is done rather than what is done: *Getting approval for the plan is a purely formal matter; nobody will seriously oppose it.* ◊ *The monarch retains largely formal duties.* **5** (of a garden, room or building) arranged in a regular manner, according to a clear, exact plan: *delightful formal gardens, with terraced lawns and an avenue of trees* **OPP** informal ▶ **for·mal·ly** /-məli/ *adv.*: *'How do you do?' she said formally.* ◊ *The accounts were formally approved by the board.* ◊ *Although not formally trained as an art historian, he is widely respected for his knowledge of the period.*

## for·mal·de·hyde
/fɔː'mældɪhaɪd/; *NAmE* fɔːr'm-/ *noun* [U] **1** (*symb.* **CH₂O**) a gas with a strong smell **2** (*also specialist* **for·mal·in** /'fɔːməlɪn/; *NAmE* 'fɔːrm-/) a liquid made by mixing formaldehyde and water, used for preserving BIOLOGICAL SPECIMENS, making plastics and as a DISINFECTANT

## for·mal·ism
/'fɔːməlɪzəm/; *NAmE* 'fɔːrm-/ *noun* [U] a style or method in art, music, literature, etc. that pays more attention to the rules and the correct arrangement and appearance of things than to inner meaning and feelings ▶ **for·mal·ist** /-lɪst/ *noun*

## for·mal·ity
/fɔː'mæləti/; *NAmE* fɔːr'm-/ *noun* (*pl.* **-ies**) **1** [C, usually pl.] a thing that you must do as a formal or official part of a legal process, a social situation, etc: *to go through all the formalities necessary in order to get a gun licence* ◊ *Let's skip the formalities and get down to business.* **2** [C, usually sing.] a thing that you must do as part of an official process, but that has little meaning and will not affect what happens: *He already knows he has the job so the interview is a mere formality.* **3** [U] correct and formal behaviour: *Different levels of formality are appropriate in different situations.* ◊ *She greeted him with stiff formality.*

## for·mal·ize
(*BrE also* **-ise**) /'fɔːməlaɪz/; *NAmE* 'fɔːrm-/ *verb* **1** *~sth* to make an arrangement, a plan or a relationship official: *They decided to formalize their relationship by getting married.* **2** *~sth* to give sth a fixed structure or form by introducing rules: *The college has a highly formalized system of assessment.* ▶ **for·mal·iza·tion**, **-isa·tion** /ˌfɔːməlaɪ'zeɪʃn/; *NAmE* ˌfɔːrmələ'z-/ *noun* [U, sing.]

## for·mat
/'fɔːmæt/; *NAmE* 'fɔːrm-/ *noun, verb*
■ *noun* **1** the general arrangement, plan, design, etc. of sth: *The format of the new quiz show has proved popular.* **2** the shape and size of a book, magazine, etc: *They've brought out the magazine in a new format.* **3** (*computing*) the way in which data is stored or held to be worked on by a computer
■ *verb* (**-tt-**) **1** *~sth* (*specialist*) to arrange text in a particular way on a page or a screen **2** *~sth* (*computing*) to prepare a computer disk for storing digital information

## for·ma·tion
/fɔː'meɪʃn/; *NAmE* fɔːr'm-/ *noun* **1** [U] the action of forming sth; the process of being formed: *the formation of a new government* ◊ *evidence of recent star formation in the galaxy* **2** [C] a thing that has been formed, especially in a particular place or in a particular way: *rock formations* **3** [U, C] a particular arrangement or pattern: *formation flying* ◊ *in ~ aircraft flying in formation* ◊ *The team usually plays in a 4-4-2 formation.*

## for·ma·tive
/'fɔːmətɪv/; *NAmE* 'fɔːrm-/ *adj.* [only before noun] having an important and lasting influence on the development of sth or of sb's character: *the formative years of childhood*

## for·mer
/'fɔːmə(r)/; *NAmE* 'fɔːrm-/ *adj.*, *noun*
■ *adj.* [only before noun] **1** that existed in earlier times **SYN** past: *in former times* ◊ *This beautiful old building has been restored to its former glory.* **2** that used to have a particular position or status in the past **SYN** previous, one-time: *the former president/prime minister* ◊ *my former boss/colleague/wife* ◊ *the countries of the former Soviet Union* **3** the former … used to refer to the first of two things or people mentioned: *The former option would be much more sensible.* ⊃ compare LATTER ⊃ see also SIXTH-FORMER
- **IDM** be a shadow/ghost of your former 'self to not have the strength, influence, etc. that you used to have
■ *noun* **1 the former** (*pl.* **the former**) the first of two things or people mentioned: *He had to choose between giving up his job and giving up his principles. He chose the former.* ◊ *However, the former are excluded.* ⊃ compare LATTER **2** a person or thing that forms sth: *opinion formers and policy makers*

## for·mer·ly
/'fɔːməli/; *NAmE* 'fɔːrmərli/ *adv.* in the past: *Namibia, formerly known as South West Africa* ◊ *I learnt that the house had formerly been an inn.* ◊ *John Marsh, formerly of London Road, Leicester, now living in France*

## 'form-fitting
*adj.* (of clothing) fitting your body closely, so that the shape of your body can be clearly seen **SYN** figure-hugging

# formic acid 624

**for·mic acid** /ˌfɔːmɪk ˈæsɪd; *NAmE* ˌfɔːrm-/ *noun* [U] (*chemistry*) an ACID made from CARBON MONOXIDE and STEAM (= gas produced when water boils). It is also present in a liquid produced by some ANTS.

**For·mica™** /fəˈmaɪkə; *NAmE* fɔːrˈm-/ *noun* [U] a hard plastic that can resist heat, used for covering work surfaces, etc.

**for·mid·able** /fəˈmɪdəbl, ˈfɔːmɪdəbl; *NAmE* ˈfɔːrmɪdəbl, fərˈmɪdəbl/ *adj.* if people, things or situations are **formidable**, you feel fear and/or respect for them, because they are impressive or powerful, or because they seem very difficult: *In debate he was a formidable opponent.* ◊ *She has a formidable list of qualifications.* ◊ *The two players together make a formidable combination.* ◊ *The task was a formidable one.* ◊ *They had to overcome formidable obstacles.* ▸ **for·mid·ably** /-bli/ *adv.*: *He now has the chance to prove himself in a formidably difficult role.* ◊ *She's formidably intelligent.*

**form·less** /ˈfɔːmləs; *NAmE* ˈfɔːrm-/ *adj.* without a clear or definite shape or structure: *formless dreams* ▸ **form·less·ness** *noun* [U]

**for·mula** ℞+ **C1 W** /ˈfɔːmjələ; *NAmE* ˈfɔːrm-/ *noun* (*pl.* **for·mu·las** or **formulae** /-liː/) **HELP** Formulae is used especially in scientific language. **1** ℞+ **C1** [C] (*mathematics*) a series of letters, numbers or symbols that represent a rule or law: *This formula is used to calculate the area of a circle.* **2** ℞+ **C1** [C] (*chemistry*) letters and symbols that show the parts of a chemical COMPOUND, etc: *CO is the formula for carbon monoxide.* ⊃ WORDFINDER NOTE at CHEMISTRY **3** ℞+ **C1** [C] a particular method of doing or achieving sth: *They're trying to work out a **peace formula** acceptable to both sides in the dispute.* ◊ *~ **for sth/for doing sth** There's no **magic formula** for a perfect marriage.* **4** [C] a list of the things that sth is made from, giving the amount of each substance to use: *the secret formula for the blending of the whisky* **5** (*also* **formula milk**) [U, C] a type of liquid food for babies, given instead of breast milk **6** [C] a class of racing car, based on engine size, etc: *Formula One™ racing* **7** [C] a fixed form of words used in a particular situation: *legal formulae* ◊ *The minister keeps coming out with the same tired formulas.*

**for·mu·la·ic** /ˌfɔːmjuˈleɪɪk; *NAmE* ˌfɔːrm-/ *adj.* (*formal*) made up of fixed patterns of words or ideas: *Traditional stories make use of formulaic expressions like 'Once upon a time ...'.*

**for·mu·late** ℞+ **C1 W** /ˈfɔːmjuleɪt; *NAmE* ˈfɔːrm-/ *verb* **1** ℞+ **C1** to create or prepare sth carefully, giving particular attention to the details: *~ sth to formulate a policy/theory/plan/proposal* ◊ *The compost is specially formulated for pot plants.* ◊ *~ sth to do sth This new kitchen cleaner is formulated to cut through grease and dirt.* **2** ℞+ **C1** *~ sth* to express your ideas in carefully chosen words: *She has lots of good ideas, but she has difficulty formulating them.* ▸ **for·mu·la·tion** /ˌfɔːmjuˈleɪʃn; *NAmE* ˌfɔːrm-/ *noun* [U, C]: *the formulation of new policies*

**for·ni·cate** /ˈfɔːnɪkeɪt; *NAmE* ˈfɔːrn-/ *verb* [I] (*formal, disapproving*) to have sex with sb that you are not married to ▸ **for·ni·ca·tion** /ˌfɔːnɪˈkeɪʃn; *NAmE* ˌfɔːrn-/ *noun* [U] **for·ni·ca·tor** /ˈfɔːnɪkeɪtə(r); *NAmE* ˈfɔːrn-/ *noun*

**for·sake** /fəˈseɪk; *NAmE* fərˈs-/ *verb* (**for·sook** /-ˈsʊk/, **for·saken** /-ˈseɪkən/) (*literary*) **1** *~ sb/sth (for sb/sth)* to leave sb/sth, especially when you have a responsibility to stay with sb/sth **SYN** abandon: *He had made it clear to his wife that he would never forsake her.* **2** *~ sth (for sb/sth)* to stop doing sth, or leave sth, especially sth that you enjoy **SYN** renounce: *She forsook the glamour of the city and went to live in the wilds of Scotland.* ⊃ see also GODFORSAKEN

**for·swear** /fɔːˈsweə(r); *NAmE* fɔːrˈswer/ *verb* (**for·swore** /fɔːˈswɔː(r); *NAmE* fɔːrˈs-/, **for·sworn** /fɔːˈswɔːn; *NAmE* fɔːrˈswɔːrn/) *~ sth* (*formal or literary*) to stop doing or using sth; to make a promise that you will stop doing or using sth **SYN** renounce: *The group forswears all worldly possessions.* ◊ *The country has not forsworn the use of chemical weapons.*

**for·sythia** /fɔːˈsaɪθiə; *NAmE* fərˈsɪ-/ *noun* [U, C] a bush that has small bright yellow flowers in the early spring

**fort** /fɔːt; *NAmE* fɔːrt/ *noun* **1** a building or buildings built in order to defend an area against attack **2** (*NAmE*) a place where soldiers live and have their training: *Fort Drum* **IDM** **hold the ˈfort** (*BrE*) (*NAmE* **hold down the ˈfort**) (*informal*) to have the responsibility for sth or care of sb while other people are away or out: *Why not have a day off? I'll hold the fort for you.*

**forte** *noun, adv.*
■ *noun* /ˈfɔːteɪ; *NAmE* fɔːrt/ [sing.] a thing that sb does particularly well: *Languages were never my forte.*
■ *adv.* /ˈfɔːteɪ; *NAmE* ˈfɔːrteɪ/ (*music, from Italian*) played or sung loudly **OPP** piano ▸ **forte** *adj.*

**For·tean** /ˈfɔːtiən; *NAmE* ˈfɔːrt-/ *adj.* involving or relating to things that cannot be explained by science **SYN** paranormal

**forth** ℞+ **C1** /fɔːθ; *NAmE* fɔːrθ/ *adv.* (*literary except in particular idioms and phrasal verbs*) **HELP** For the special uses of **forth** in phrasal verbs, look at the entries for the verbs. For example **bring sb/sth forth** is in the phrasal verb section at **bring**. **1** ℞+ **C1** away from a place; out: *They set forth at dawn.* ◊ *Huge chimneys belched forth smoke and grime.* **2** towards a place; forwards: *Water gushed forth from a hole in the rock.*
**IDM** **from that ˈday/ˈtime forth** (*literary*) beginning on that day; from that time ⊃ more at BACK *adv.*, SO *adv.*

> **HOMOPHONES**
>
> **forth • fourth** /fɔːθ; *NAmE* fɔːrθ/
>
> - **forth** *adv.*: *The film cuts back and forth between the two stories.*
> - **fourth** *ordinal number*: *The fourth of July is Independence Day in the US.*
> - **fourth** *noun* (*especially NAmE*): *A fourth of the ski resorts in the Alps may not have enough snow this year.*

**the Forth ˈBridge** *noun*
**IDM** **like painting the Forth ˈBridge** (*BrE*) used to describe a job that never seems to end because by the time you get to the end you have to start at the beginning again **ORIGIN** From the name of a very large bridge over the River Forth in Scotland.

**forth·com·ing** ℞+ **C1** /ˌfɔːθˈkʌmɪŋ; *NAmE* ˌfɔːrθ-/ *adj.* **1** ℞+ **C1** [only before noun] going to happen, be published, etc. very soon: *the forthcoming elections* ◊ *a list of forthcoming books* ◊ *the band's forthcoming UK tour* **2** [not before noun] ready or made available when needed: *Financial support was not forthcoming.* **3** [not before noun] willing to give information about sth: *She's never very forthcoming about her plans.* **OPP** unforthcoming

**forth·right** /ˈfɔːθraɪt; *NAmE* ˈfɔːrθ-/ *adj.* direct and honest in manner and speech **SYN** frank: *a woman of forthright views* ▸ **forth·right·ly** *adv.* **forth·right·ness** *noun* [U]

**forth·with** /ˌfɔːθˈwɪθ, -ˈwɪð; *NAmE* ˌfɔːrθ-/ *adv.* (*formal*) immediately; at once: *The agreement between us is terminated forthwith.*

**for·ti·eth** ⊃ FORTY

**for·ti·fi·ca·tion** /ˌfɔːtɪfɪˈkeɪʃn; *NAmE* ˌfɔːrt-/ *noun* **1** [C, usually pl.] a tower, wall, gun position, etc. built to defend a place against attack: *the ramparts and fortifications of the Old Town* **2** [U] the act of fortifying or making sth stronger: *plans for the fortification of the city*

**for·tify** /ˈfɔːtɪfaɪ; *NAmE* ˈfɔːrt-/ *verb* (**for·ti·fies**, **for·ti·fy·ing**, **for·ti·fied**, **for·ti·fied**) **1** *~ sth (against sb/sth)* to make a place more able to resist attack, especially by building high walls: *a fortified town* **2** *~ sb/yourself (against sb/sth)* to make sb/yourself feel stronger, braver, etc: *He fortified himself against the cold with a hot drink.* **3** to make a feeling or an attitude stronger: *The news merely fortified their determination.* **4** [usually passive] to increase the strength or quality of food or drink by adding sth to it: **(be) fortified** *Sherry is fortified wine* (= wine with extra alcohol added). ◊ **(be) fortified with sth** *cereal fortified with extra vitamins*

**for·ti·ori** ⊃ A FORTIORI

**for·tis·si·mo** /fɔːˈtɪsɪməʊ; NAmE fɔːrˈt-/ adv. (abbr. **ff**) (music, from Italian) very loudly **OPP** pianissimo ▶ **for·tis·si·mo** adj.

**for·ti·tude** /ˈfɔːtɪtjuːd; NAmE ˈfɔːrtɪtuːd/ noun [U] (formal) courage shown by sb who is suffering great pain or facing great difficulties **SYN** **bravery, courage** ⇨ see also INTESTINAL FORTITUDE

**Fort Knox** /ˌfɔːt ˈnɒks; NAmE ˌfɔːrt ˈnɑːks/ noun **IDM** **be like/as safe as Fort ˈKnox** (of a building) to be strongly built, often with many locks, strong doors, guards, etc., so that it is difficult for people to enter and the things kept there are safe: *This home of yours is like Fort Knox.* **ORIGIN** From the name of the military base in Kentucky where most of the US's store of gold is kept.

**fort·night** /ˈfɔːtnaɪt; NAmE ˈfɔːrt-/ noun [usually sing.] (*BrE*) two weeks: *a fortnight's holiday* ◇ *a fortnight ago* ◇ *in a fortnight's time* ◇ *He's had three accidents in the past fortnight.*

**fort·night·ly** /ˈfɔːtnaɪtli; NAmE ˈfɔːrt-/ adj. (*BrE*) happening once a fortnight: *Meetings take place at fortnightly intervals.* ▶ **fort·night·ly** adv.: *The committee meets fortnightly.*

**fort·ress** /ˈfɔːtrəs; NAmE ˈfɔːrt-/ noun a building or place that has been made stronger and protected against attack: *a fortress town enclosed by four miles of ramparts* ◇ *Fear of terrorist attack has turned the conference centre into a fortress.*

**for·tu·it·ous** /fɔːˈtjuːɪtəs; NAmE fɔːrˈtuː-/ adj. (formal) happening by chance, especially a lucky chance that brings a good result ▶ **for·tu·it·ous·ly** adv.

**for·tu·nate** /ˈfɔːtʃənət; NAmE ˈfɔːrtʃ-/ adj. having or bringing an advantage, an opportunity, a piece of good luck, etc. **SYN** **lucky**: *Remember those less fortunate than yourselves.* ◇ *~ to do sth I have been fortunate enough to visit many parts of the world as a lecturer.* ◇ *~ in having … I was fortunate in having a good teacher.* ◇ *it is ~ (for sb) (that …) It was very fortunate for him that I arrived on time.* **OPP** **unfortunate**

**for·tu·nate·ly** /ˈfɔːtʃənətli; NAmE ˈfɔːrtʃ-/ adv. by good luck **SYN** **luckily**: *I was late, but fortunately the meeting hadn't started.* ◇ *~ for sb Fortunately for him, he was very soon offered another job.* **OPP** **unfortunately**

**for·tune** /ˈfɔːtʃuːn; NAmE ˈfɔːrtʃən/ noun **1** [C] a large amount of money: *He made a fortune in real estate.* ◇ *Her father made his fortune selling electronics.* ◇ *She inherited a share of the family fortune.* ◇ *A car like that costs a small fortune* (= a lot of money). ◇ *You don't have to spend a fortune to give your family tasty, healthy meals.* ◇ *She is hoping her US debut will be the first step on the road to fame and fortune.* **2** [U] chance or luck, especially in the way it affects people's lives: *I have had the good fortune to work with some brilliant directors.* ◇ *By a stroke of fortune he found work almost immediately.* ⇨ WORDFINDER NOTE at LUCK **3** [C, usually pl., U] the good and bad things that happen to a person, family, country, etc: *the changing fortunes of the film industry* ◇ *the fortunes of war* ◇ *a reversal of fortune* **4** [C] a person's FATE or future: *She can tell your fortune by looking at the lines on your hand.* **IDM** see HOSTAGE, SEEK ⇨ see also SOLDIER OF FORTUNE

**ˈfortune cookie** noun a thin hollow biscuit, served in Chinese restaurants, containing a short message that predicts what will happen to you in the future

**ˈfortune hunter** noun a person who tries to become rich by marrying sb with a lot of money **SYN** **gold-digger**

**ˈfortune teller** noun a person who claims to have magic powers and who tells people what will happen to them in the future

**forty** /ˈfɔːti; NAmE ˈfɔːrti/ **1** number 40 **2** noun **the forties** [pl.] numbers, years or temperatures from 40 to 49 ▶ **fortieth** /-əθ/ ordinal number, noun **HELP** There are examples of how to use ordinal numbers at the entry for FIFTH. **IDM** **in your forties** between the ages of 40 and 49

**forum** /ˈfɔːrəm/ noun **1** an event or medium where people can exchange opinions on a particular issue; a meeting organized for this purpose: *~(on sth)* to hold an international forum on drug abuse ◇ *~ for sth Television is now an important forum for political debate.* **2** a website or web page where users can put comments about a particular issue or topic and reply to other users' comments: *an internet forum* ◇ *Check out our online discussion forum.* **3** (in ancient Rome) a public place where meetings were held

**for·ward** /ˈfɔːwəd; NAmE ˈfɔːrwərd/ adv., adj., verb, noun

■ adv. **HELP** For the special uses of **forward** in phrasal verbs, look at the entries for the verbs. For example **look forward to sth** is in the phrasal verb section at **look**. **1** (also **forwards** especially in *BrE*) towards a place or position that is in front: *She leaned forward and kissed him on the cheek.* ◇ *He took two steps forwards.* ◇ *They ran forward to welcome her.* **OPP** **back, backwards 2** (also **forwards** especially in *BrE*) towards the future; ahead in time: *Looking forward, we hope to expand our operations in several of our overseas branches.* ◇ *The next scene takes the story forwards five years.* ◇ (old use) *from this day forward* **3** towards a good result: *We consider this agreement to be an important step forward.* ◇ *Cutting our costs is the only way forward.* ◇ *We are not getting any further forward with the discussion.* ◇ *The project will go forward* (= continue) *as planned.* **OPP** **backwards 4** earlier; sooner: *It was decided to bring the meeting forward two weeks.* **5** (specialist) in or towards the front part of a ship or plane: *~ of sth The main cabin is situated forward of* (= in front of) *the mast.* **IDM** **going/ˈmoving ˈforward** (formal or business) in the future, starting from now: *We have a very solid financial position going forward.* ⇨ more at BACKWARDS, CLOCK n., FOOT n.

■ adj. **1** [only before noun] directed or moving towards the front: *The door opened, blocking his forward movement.* ◇ *a forward pass* (= in a sports game) **2** [only before noun] (specialist) located in front, especially on a ship, plane or other vehicle: *the forward cabins* ◇ *A bolt may have fallen off the plane's forward door.* **3** relating to the future: *the forward movement of history* ◇ *A little forward planning at the outset can save you a lot of expense.* ◇ *The plans are still no further forward than they were last month.* ⇨ see also FASHION-FORWARD **4** behaving towards sb in a manner that is too confident or too informal: *I hope you don't think I'm being too forward.* ⇨ compare BACKWARD

■ verb **1** (formal) to send or pass goods or information to sb: *~ sth to sb We will be forwarding our new catalogue to you next week.* ◇ *~ sb sth We will be forwarding you our new catalogue next week.* ◇ *~ sth to forward a request/complaint/proposal* ⇨ WORDFINDER NOTE at MESSAGE **2** to send a letter, etc. received at the address a person used to live at to their new address **SYN** **send on**: *~ sth (to sb) Could you forward any mail to us in New York?* ◇ *~(sth) I put 'please forward' on the envelope.* **3** *~ sth* (formal) to help to improve or develop sth **SYN** **further**: *He saw the assignment as a way to forward his career.* ⇨ see also FAST-FORWARD

■ noun an attacking player whose position is near the front of a team in some sports ⇨ compare BACK ⇨ see also CENTRE FORWARD, FULL FORWARD

**ˈforwarding address** noun a new address to which letters should be sent on from an old address that sb has moved away from

**ˈforward-looking** (also ˌforward-ˈthinking) adj. (approving) planning for the future; willing to consider modern ideas and methods

**for·ward·ness** /ˈfɔːwədnəs; NAmE ˈfɔːrwərd-/ noun [U] behaviour that is too confident or too informal

**ˈforward slash** noun the symbol (/) used in computer commands and in internet addresses to separate the different parts ⇨ compare BACKSLASH

**for·went** /fɔːˈwent; NAmE fɔːrˈw-/ past tense of FORGO

**fos·sick** /ˈfɒsɪk; NAmE ˈfɑːs-/ verb (AustralE, NZE, informal) **1** [I] *~(through sth)* to search through sth: *He spent ages*

# fossil 626

*fossicking through the documents.* **2** [I] to search for gold in mines that are no longer used

**fos·sil** ◆ B2 /ˈfɒsl; NAmE ˈfɑːsl/ *noun* **1** ◆ B2 the parts of a dead animal or a plant that have become hard and turned into rock: *fossils over two million years old* **2** (*informal*, *disapproving*) an old person, especially one who is unable to accept new ideas or adapt to changes

**ˈfossil fuel** *noun* [C, U] fuel such as coal or oil that was formed over millions of years from parts of dead animals or plants ⇨ compare BIOMASS ⇨ **WORDFINDER NOTE** at ENERGY

**fos·sil·ize** (*BrE also* **-ise**) /ˈfɒsəlaɪz; NAmE ˈfɑːs-/ *verb* **1** [T, usually passive, I] ~ (sth) to make an animal or a plant become a fossil; to become a fossil **2** [I, T] ~ (sb/sth) (*disapproving*) to become, or make sb/sth become, fixed and unable to change or develop ▸ **fos·sil·iza·tion**, **-isa·tion** /ˌfɒsəlaɪˈzeɪʃn; NAmE ˌfɑːsələˈz-/ *noun* [U]

**fos·sil·ized** (*BrE also* **fos·sil·ised**) /ˈfɒsəlaɪzd; NAmE ˈfɑːs-/ *adj.* **1** preserved as a fossil: *fossilized bones* **2** (*disapproving*) old-fashioned, fixed and unable to change or develop: *a fossilized political system*

**fos·ter** ◆ C1 /ˈfɒstə(r); NAmE ˈfɑːs-/ *verb, adj.*
■ *verb* **1** ◆ C1 [T] ~ sth to encourage sth to develop SYN encourage, promote: *The club's aim is to foster better relations within the community.* **2** ◆ C1 [T, I] ~ (sb) (*especially BrE*) to take another person's child into your home for a period of time, without becoming his or her legal parents: *They have fostered over 60 children during the past ten years.* ◇ *We couldn't adopt a child, so we decided to foster.* ⇨ compare ADOPT
■ *adj.* [only before noun] used with some nouns in connection with the fostering of a child: *a foster mother/father/family* ◇ *foster parents* ◇ *a foster child* ◇ *a foster home* ◇ *The children were placed in foster care.*

**fought** /fɔːt/ *past tense, past part.* of FIGHT ⇨ see also HARD-FOUGHT

**foul** /faʊl/ *adj., verb, noun*
■ *adj.* (**fouler, foulest**) **1** dirty and smelling bad: *foul air/breath* ◇ *a foul-smelling prison* ▸ SYNONYMS at DISGUSTING **2** (*especially BrE*) very unpleasant; very bad: *She's in a foul mood.* ◇ *His boss has a foul temper.* ◇ *This tastes foul.* **3** (of language) including rude words and swearing SYN offensive: *foul language* ◇ *I'm sick of her foul mouth* (= habit of swearing). ◇ *He called her the foulest names imaginable.* **4** (of weather) very bad, with strong winds and rain: *a foul night* **5** (*literary*) very evil or cruel SYN **abominable**: *a foul crime/murder* ▸ **ˈfoul·ly** /ˈfaʊlli/ *adv.*: *He swore foully.* ◇ *She had been foully murdered during the night.* **ˈfoul·ness** *noun* [U]: *The air was heavy with the stink of damp and foulness.*
IDM **fall ˈfoul of sb/sth** to get into trouble with a person or an organization because of doing sth wrong or illegal: *to fall foul of the law* ▸ more at CRY v., FAIR *adj.*
■ *verb* **1** [T] ~ sb (in sport) to do sth to another player that is against the rules of the game: *He was fouled inside the penalty area.* **2** [I, T] ~ (sth) (in baseball) to hit the ball outside the playing area **3** [T] ~ sth to make sth dirty, especially with waste matter from the body: *Do not permit your dog to foul the grass.* **4** [T, I] to become caught or TWISTED in sth and stop it working or moving: ~ sth (up) *The rope fouled the propeller.* ◇ *The line became fouled in* (= became TWISTED in) *the propeller.* ◇ ~ (up) *A rope fouled up* (= became TWISTED) *as we pulled the sail down.*
PHRV **foul ˈup** (*informal*) to make a lot of mistakes; to do sth badly: *I've fouled up badly again, haven't I?* ⇨ related *noun* FOUL-UP **foul sth↔ˈup** (*informal*) to cause sth to fail, especially by doing sth wrong ⇨ related *noun* FOUL-UP
■ *noun* (in sport) an action that is against the rules of the game: *It was a clear foul by Ford on the goalkeeper.* ◇ (*NAmE*) *to hit a foul* (= in baseball, a ball that is too far left or right, outside the lines that mark the side of the field) ⇨ see also PROFESSIONAL FOUL, TECHNICAL FOUL

**ˈfoul ball** *noun* (in baseball) a hit that goes outside the allowed area

**ˈfoul line** *noun* **1** (in baseball) either of two lines that show the area inside which the ball must be hit **2** (in basketball) a line from which a player is allowed to try to throw the ball into the BASKET after a foul

**ˌfoul-ˈmouthed** *adj.* using rude, offensive language: *a foul-mouthed racist*

**ˌfoul ˈplay** *noun* [U] **1** criminal or violent activity that causes sb's death: *Police immediately began an investigation, but did not suspect foul play* (= did not suspect that the person had been murdered). **2** (*BrE*) dishonest or unfair behaviour, especially during a sports game

**ˈfoul-up** *noun* (*informal*) a problem caused by bad organization or a stupid mistake

**found** ⓘ B2 /faʊnd/ *verb* **1** B2 ~ sth to start sth, such as an organization or an institution, especially by providing money SYN **establish**: *to found a club/company/school* ◇ *Her family founded the college in 1895.* ◇ *the founding members of the European Union* **2** ~ sth to be the first to start building and living in a town or country: *The town was founded by English settlers in 1790.* **3** [usually passive] to base sth on sth: **be founded on sth** *Their marriage was founded on love and mutual respect.* ⇨ see also ILL-FOUNDED, UNFOUNDED, WELL FOUNDED **4** ~ sth (*specialist*) to melt metal and pour it into a MOULD; to make objects using this process **5** *past tense, past part.* of FIND

**foun·da·tion** ◆ B2 /faʊnˈdeɪʃn/ *noun* **1** ◆ B2 [C, U] a principle, an idea or a fact that sth is based on and that it grows from: *Respect and friendship provide a solid foundation for marriage.* ◇ *He laid the foundation of Japan's modern economy.* ◇ *These stories have no foundation* (= are not based on any facts). ◇ *without~ The rumour is totally without foundation* (= is not based on any facts). ⇨ SYNONYMS at BASIS **2** ◆ [C] an organization that is established to provide money for a particular purpose, for example for scientific research or charity: *The money will go to the San Francisco AIDS Foundation.* **3** ◆ [U] the act of starting a new institution or organization SYN **establishment**: *The organization has grown enormously since its foundation in 1955.* **4** ◆ C1 [C, usually pl.] a layer of stone, CONCRETE, etc. that forms the solid underground base of a building: *The builders are now beginning to lay the foundations of the new school.* ◇ *The explosion shook the foundations of the houses nearby.* ⇨ SYNONYMS at BOTTOM ⇨ **WORDFINDER NOTE** at CONSTRUCTION **5** [U] a skin-coloured cream that is put on the face under other MAKE-UP ⇨ **WORDFINDER NOTE** at MAKE-UP
IDM **shake/rock the ˈfoundations of sth** | **shake/rock sth to its ˈfoundations** to cause people to question their basic beliefs about sth: *This issue has shaken the foundations of French politics.*

**founˈdation course** *noun* (*BrE*) a general course at a college that prepares students for longer or more difficult courses

**founˈdation stone** *noun* **1** a large block of stone that is put at the base of an important new public building in a special ceremony: *to lay the foundation stone of the new museum* **2** a basic or essential element of sth: *Family life is one of the foundation stones of society.*

**foun·der** ◆ B2 /ˈfaʊndə(r)/ *noun, verb*
■ *noun* ◆ B2 a person who starts an organization, institution, etc. or causes sth to be built: *the founder and president of the company*
■ *verb* (*formal*) **1** [I] ~ (on sth) (of a plan, attempt, etc.) to fail, especially because of a particular problem or difficulty: ~ on sth *The peace talks foundered on a basic lack of trust.* **2** [I] ~ (on sth) (of a ship) to fill with water and sink: *Our boat foundered on a reef.*

**ˈfounder ˈmember** (*BrE*) (*NAmE* **charter ˈmember**, **ˈfounding ˈmember**) *noun* one of the first members of a society, an organization, etc., especially one who helped start it

**ˈfounding ˈfather** *noun* **1** (*formal*) a person who starts or develops a new movement, institution or idea **2** **Founding Father** a member of the group of people who wrote the Constitution of the US in 1787

**found·ling** /ˈfaʊndlɪŋ/ noun (old-fashioned) a baby who has been left by its parents and who is found and taken care of by sb else

**foun·dry** /ˈfaʊndri/ noun (pl. -ies) a factory where metal or glass is melted and made into different shapes or objects: *an iron foundry* ◊ *foundry workers* **SYNONYMS** at FACTORY

**fount** /faʊnt/ noun ~ **(of sth)** (literary or humorous) the place where sth important comes from **SYN** source: *She treats him as if he were the fount of all knowledge.*

**foun·tain** /ˈfaʊntən/ NAmE -tn/ noun **1** a structure from which water is sent up into the air: A PUMP, used to decorate parks and gardens **2** a strong flow of liquid or of another substance that is forced into the air: *The amplifier exploded in a fountain of sparks.* **3** a rich source or supply of sth: *Tourism is a fountain of wealth for the city.* ⊃ see also DRINKING FOUNTAIN, SODA FOUNTAIN, WATER FOUNTAIN

**foun·tain·head** /ˈfaʊntənhed; NAmE -tn-/ noun (literary) a source or origin

**fountain pen** noun a pen with a container that you fill with INK (= coloured liquid for writing) that flows to a NIB

**four** ❶ **A1** /fɔː(r)/ **1** ? **A1** *number* **4** **HELP** There are examples of how to use numbers at the entry for **five**. **2** *noun* a group of four people or things: *to make up a four at tennis* ◊ *a coach and four* (= four horses) **3** *noun* (in CRICKET) a hit that scores four RUNS (= points) **4** *noun* a team of four people who ROW a long narrow boat in races; the boat that they row **IDM** **on all fours** (of a person) bent over with hands and knees on the ground: *We were crawling around on all fours.* **these four walls** used when you are talking about keeping sth secret: *Don't let this go further than these four walls* (= Don't tell anyone else who is not in the room now).

**four-by-four** (also **4x4**) noun a vehicle with FOUR-WHEEL DRIVE (= a system in which power is given to all four wheels)

**four-colour 'process** (*US* **four-color process**) noun (*specialist*) a way of producing colours that look natural in photographs and printing using COLOUR SEPARATION

**four-di'mensional** adj. having four DIMENSIONS, usually length, WIDTH, depth, and time

**four·fold** /ˈfɔːfəʊld; NAmE ˈfɔːrf-/ adj., adv. ⊃ -FOLD

**four-letter 'word** noun a short word that is considered rude or offensive, especially because it refers to sex or other functions of the body **SYN** swear word

**four-poster 'bed** (also **four-'poster**) noun a large bed with a tall post at each of the four corners, a cover over the top and curtains around the sides

**four·some** /ˈfɔːsəm; NAmE ˈfɔːrs-/ noun [C + sing./pl. v.] a group of four people taking part in a social activity or sport together: *Can you make up a foursome for tennis tomorrow?*

**four-'square** adj. **1** (of a building) square in shape, solid and strong **2** (of a person) steady, determined and not likely to change ▶ **four-'square** adv.: *I stand four-square with the President on this issue.*

**four-star** adj. [usually before noun] **1** having four stars in a system that measures quality. The highest quality is shown by either four or five stars: *a four-star hotel* **2** (in the US) having the second-highest military rank, and wearing a uniform that has four stars on it: *a four-star general*

**four-stroke** adj. (specialist) (of an engine or vehicle) with a PISTON that makes four up and down movements in each power CYCLE ⊃ compare TWO-STROKE

**four·teen** ❶ **A1** /ˌfɔːˈtiːn; NAmE ˌfɔːrt-/ number **14**
▶ **four·teenth** /-ˈtiːnθ/ ordinal number, noun

**the Fourteenth A'mendment** noun [sing.] a change made to the US Constitution in 1866 that gave all Americans equal rights and allowed former slaves to become citizens

---

627

**fourth** ❶ **A1** /fɔːθ; NAmE fɔːrθ/ ordinal number, noun
■ *ordinal number* ? **A1** 4th **HELP** There are examples of how to use ordinal numbers at the entry for FIFTH. ⊃ HOMOPHONES at FORTH
■ *noun* (especially NAmE) = QUARTER ⊃ HOMOPHONES at FORTH

**the fourth di'mension** noun [sing.] (used by scientists and writers of SCIENCE FICTION) time

**the fourth e'state** noun [sing.] newspapers and journalists in general and the political influence that they have **SYN** press

**fourth·ly** /ˈfɔːθli; NAmE ˈfɔːrθ-/ adv. used to introduce the fourth of a list of points you want to make in a speech or piece of writing

**fourth of'ficial** noun (in football (soccer)) an official who helps the REFEREE before, during and after a match

**the Fourth of Ju'ly** noun [sing.] a national holiday in the US when people celebrate the anniversary of the Declaration of Independence (= the day in 1776 when Americans declared themselves independent of Britain) ⊃ see also INDEPENDENCE DAY

**fourth 'wall** noun [sing.] the imaginary barrier that separates the characters in a work of fiction from the people who are watching or reading the story they are in: *The actors break the fourth wall and talk directly to the audience.*

**four-way 'stop** (NAmE, SAfrE) (also **four-way 'intersection**) noun a place where two roads cross each other, at which there are signs indicating that all vehicles must stop before continuing

**four-wheel 'drive** (especially NAmE **all-wheel 'drive**) noun [U, C] a system in which power is applied to all four wheels of a vehicle, making it easier to control; a vehicle with this system: *a car with four-wheel drive* ◊ *We rented a four-wheel drive to get around the island.* ⊃ see also FOUR-BY-FOUR

**four-'wheeler** (NAmE) (BrE **quad bike**) noun a motorcycle with four large wheels, used for riding over rough ground, often for fun ⊃ see also ATV

**fowl** /faʊl/ noun **1** [C, U] (pl. **fowl** or **fowls**) a bird that is kept for its meat and eggs, for example a chicken: *fowl such as turkeys and ducks* **2** [C] (old use) see also GUINEA FOWL, WATERFOWL, WILDFOWL **IDM** ⊃ see FISH *n*.

**fox** /fɒks; NAmE fɑːks/ noun, verb
■ *noun* **1** [C] a wild animal of the dog family, with red-brown fur, a pointed face and a thick heavy tail ⊃ see also FLYING FOX, VIXEN **2** [U] the skin and fur of the fox, used to make coats, etc. **3** [C] (often disapproving) a person who is clever and able to get what they want by influencing or tricking other people: *He's a wily old fox.* **4** [C] (NAmE, informal) an attractive young woman
■ *verb* ~ **sb** (especially BrE, informal) to be too difficult for sb to understand or solve; to trick or confuse sb: *The last question foxed even our panel of experts.*

**foxed** /fɒkst; NAmE fɑːkst/ adj. **1** unable to understand or solve sth: *I must admit I'm completely foxed.* **2** (of the paper of old books or prints) covered with brown spots

**fox·glove** /ˈfɒksɡlʌv; NAmE ˈfɑːks-/ noun [C, U] a tall plant with purple or white flowers that are like bells in shape growing up its STEM

**fox·hole** /ˈfɒkshəʊl; NAmE ˈfɑːks-/ noun a hole in the ground that soldiers use as a shelter against the enemy or as a place to fire back from ⊃ compare HOLE

**fox·hound** /ˈfɒkshaʊnd; NAmE ˈfɑːks-/ noun a dog with a very good sense of smell, that is trained to hunt FOXES

**'fox hunting** (BrE also **hunt·ing**) noun [U] a sport in which FOXES are hunted by specially trained dogs and by people on horses. Fox hunting with dogs is now illegal in the UK: *to go fox hunting* ▶ **fox hunt** noun: *a ban on fox hunts*

**fox·trot** /ˈfɒkstrɒt; NAmE ˈfɑːkstrɑːt/ noun a formal dance for two people together, with both small fast steps and longer slow ones; a piece of music for this dance

# foxy

**foxy** /ˈfɒksi; *NAmE* ˈfɑːk-/ *adj.* **1** like a FOX in appearance **2** (*informal*) (of a woman) sexually attractive SYN **sexy** **3** clever at tricking others SYN **cunning**

**foyer** /ˈfɔɪeɪ; *NAmE* ˈfɔɪər/ *noun* **1** a large open space inside the entrance of a theatre or hotel where people can meet or wait SYN **lobby** ⇒ WORDFINDER NOTE at THEATRE **2** (*NAmE*) an entrance hall in a private house or flat

**FPS** /ˌef piː ˈes/ *abbr.* = FIRST-PERSON SHOOTER

**Fr** (*also* **Fr.** *especially in NAmE*) *abbr.* Father (used in front of the name of some Christian priests): *Fr (Paul) O'Connor*

**fra·cas** /ˈfrækɑː; *NAmE* ˈfreɪkəs/ *noun* (*pl.* **fra·cas** /ˈfrækɑːz; *NAmE* ˈfreɪkəs/, *NAmE* **fra·cases** /ˈfrækəzɪz; *NAmE* ˈfreɪkəsɪz/) [*usually sing.*] a noisy argument or fight, usually involving several people

**frack** /fræk/ *verb* [I, T] **~(sth) (for sth)** to force liquid at high pressure into rocks, deep holes in the ground, etc. in order to force open existing CRACKS (= narrow openings) and take out oil or gas: *They have been fracking for oil in South Dakota since the fifties.*

**frack·ing** /ˈfrækɪŋ/ (*also formal or specialist* **hy·draulic ˈfrac·turing**) *noun* [U] the process of forcing liquid at high pressure into rocks, deep holes in the ground, etc. in order to force open existing CRACKS (= narrow openings) and take out oil or gas ⇒ WORDFINDER NOTE at ENERGY

**frac·tal** /ˈfræktl/ *noun* (*mathematics*, *physics*) a curve or pattern that includes a smaller curve or pattern that has exactly the same shape

**frac·tion** /ˈfrækʃn/ *noun* **1** a small part or amount of sth: *Only a small fraction of a bank's total deposits will be withdrawn at any one time.* ◇ *She hesitated for the merest fraction of a second.* HELP If **fraction** is used with a plural noun, the verb is usually plural: : *Only a fraction of cars in the UK use leaded petrol.* If it is used with a singular noun that represents a group of people, the verb can be singular or plural in *BrE*, but is usually singular in *NAmE*: *A tiny fraction of the population never vote/votes.* **2** a division of a number, for example ⅝ ⇒ LANGUAGE BANK at PROPORTION ⇒ *compare* INTEGER

**frac·tion·al** /ˈfrækʃənl/ *adj.* **1** (*formal*) very small; not important SYN **minimal**: *a fractional decline in earnings* **2** (*mathematics*) of or in fractions: *a fractional equation*

**frac·tion·al·ly** /ˈfrækʃənəli/ *adv.* to a very small degree: *He was just fractionally ahead at the finishing line.*

**frac·tious** /ˈfrækʃəs/ *adj.* (*especially BrE*) **1** easily upset, especially by small things SYN **irritable**: *Children often get fractious and tearful when tired.* **2** (*formal*) making trouble and complaining: *The six fractious republics are demanding autonomy.*

**frac·ture** /ˈfræktʃə(r)/ *noun*, *verb*
- *noun* **1** [C] a break in a bone or other hard material: *a fracture of the leg/skull* ◇ *a **compound/simple** fracture* (= one in which the broken bone comes/does not come through the skin) ⇒ *see also* COMPOUND FRACTURE, SIMPLE FRACTURE ⇒ WORDFINDER NOTE at HURT **2** [U] the fact of sth breaking, especially a bone: *Old people's bones are more prone to fracture.*
- *verb* **1** [I, T] to break or CRACK; to make sth break or CRACK: *His leg fractured in two places.* ◇ *~sth She fell and fractured her skull.* **2** [I, T] (*formal*) (of a society, an organization, etc.) to split into several parts so that it no longer functions or exists; to split a society or an organization, etc. in this way: *Many people predicted that the party would fracture and split.* ◇ *~sth (into sth) The company was fractured into several smaller groups.* ▶ **frac·tured** *adj.* [*usually before noun*]: *He suffered a badly fractured arm.* ◇ *a fractured pipeline* ◇ (*figurative*) *They spoke a sort of fractured German.*

**fra·gile** /ˈfrædʒaɪl; *NAmE* -dʒl/ *adj.* **1** easily broken or damaged: *fragile china/glass/bones* **2** weak and uncertain; easy to destroy or harm: *a fragile alliance/ceasefire/relationship* ◇ *The economy remains extremely fragile.* **3** thin or light and often beautiful: *fragile beauty* ◇ *The woman's fragile face broke into a smile.* **4** not strong and likely to become ill: *Her father is now 86 and in fragile health.* ◇ (*BrE, informal*) *I'm feeling a bit fragile after last night* (= not well, perhaps because of drinking too much alcohol). ▶ **fra·gil·ity** /frəˈdʒɪləti/ *noun* [U]: *the fragility of the human body*

**frag·ment** *noun*, *verb*
- *noun* /ˈfrægmənt/ **1** a small part of sth that has broken off or comes from sth larger: *~(of sth) Police found fragments of glass near the scene.* ◇ **in fragments** *The shattered vase lay in fragments on the floor.* **2** *~(of sth)* a single part of sth; a part that is not complete: *I overheard a fragment of their conversation.*
- *verb* /frægˈment; *NAmE* ˈfrægment/ [I, T] *~(sth)* to break or make sth break into small pieces or parts ▶ **frag·men·ta·tion** /ˌfrægmenˈteɪʃn/ *noun* [U]: *the fragmentation of the country into small independent states* **frag·ment·ed** /frægˈmentɪd; *NAmE* ˈfrægmentɪd/ *adj.*: *a fragmented society*

**frag·men·tary** /ˈfrægməntri; *NAmE* -teri/ *adj.* (*formal*) made of small parts that are not connected or complete: *There is only fragmentary evidence to support this theory.*

**fra·grance** /ˈfreɪɡrəns/ *noun* **1** [C, U] a pleasant smell: *The bath oil comes in various fragrances.* **2** [C] a liquid that you put on your skin in order to make yourself smell nice SYN **perfume**, **scent**: *an exciting new fragrance from Dior*

**fra·grant** /ˈfreɪɡrənt/ *adj.* having a pleasant smell: *fragrant herbs/flowers/oils* ◇ *The air was fragrant with scents from the sea and the hills.* ▶ **fra·grant·ly** *adv.*

**fraidy cat** /ˈfreɪdi kæt/ *noun* (*NAmE, informal, disapproving*) = SCAREDY-CAT

**frail** /freɪl/ *adj.* (**frail·er**, **frail·est**) **1** (especially of an old person) physically weak and thin: *Mother was becoming too frail to live alone.* ⇒ WORDFINDER NOTE at OLD **2** weak; easily damaged or broken: *the frail stems of the flowers* ◇ *Human nature is frail.*

**frailty** /ˈfreɪlti/ *noun* (*pl.* **-ies**) **1** [U] weakness and poor health: *Increasing frailty meant that she was more and more confined to bed.* **2** [U, C] (*formal*) weakness in a person's character or moral standards: *human frailty* ◇ *the frailties of human nature*

## frames

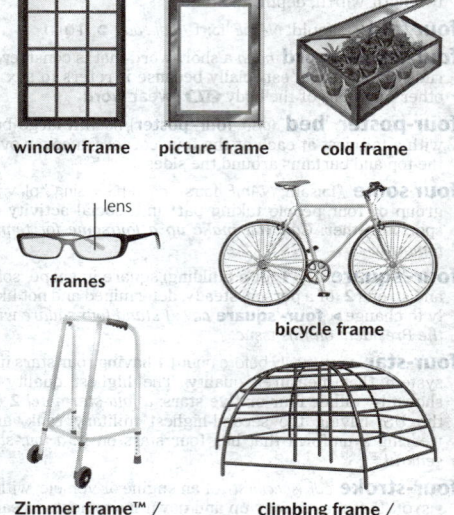

window frame    picture frame    cold frame

frames    bicycle frame

Zimmer frame™ / walker    climbing frame / jungle gym

**frame** /freɪm/ *noun*, *verb*
- *noun*
- BORDER **1** [C] a strong border or structure of wood, metal, etc. that holds a picture, door, piece of glass, etc. in position: *a picture/photo frame* ◇ *aluminium window frames* ◇ **in a ~** *pictures in gold frames*

- **STRUCTURE 2** [B1] [C] the supporting structure of a piece of furniture, a building, a vehicle, etc. that gives it its shape: *a bicycle frame* ◊ *The bed frame is made of pine.* ⊃ see also A-FRAME, CLIMBING FRAME ⊃ WORDFINDER NOTE at PAINTING
- **OF GLASSES 3** [C, usually pl.] a structure of plastic or metal that holds the LENSES in a pair of glasses: *gold-rimmed frames*
- **PERSON/ANIMAL'S BODY 4** [C, usually sing.] the form or structure of a person or animal's body: *to have a small/slender/large frame*
- **GENERAL IDEAS 5** [sing.] the general ideas or structure that form the background to sth: **in/within the ~ of sth** *In this course we hope to look at literature in the frame of its social and historical context.* ⊃ see also TIME FRAME
- **OF FILM 6** [C] one of the single photographs that a film or video is made of ⊃ see also FREEZE-FRAME
- **OF PICTURE STORY 7** [C] a single picture in a COMIC STRIP
- **COMPUTING 8** [C] one of the separate areas on an internet page that you can SCROLL through (= read by moving the text up or down)
- **IN GARDEN 9** [C] = COLD FRAME
- **IN SNOOKER/BOWLING 10** [C] a single section of play in the game of SNOOKER, etc., or in BOWLING ⊃ see also ZIMMER FRAME™

**IDM** **be in/out of the ˈframe (for sth)** (*BrE*) **1** be taking part/not taking part in sth: *We won our match, so we're still in the frame for the championship.* **2** be wanted/not wanted by the police because you are/are not suspected of having committed a crime: *He was always in the frame for the killing.*

■ *verb*
- **MAKE BORDER 1** [B1] [usually passive] to put or make a frame or border around sth: **be framed** *The photograph had been framed.* **2 ~ sth/sb** to surround sth/sb in a way that makes an attractive image: *Her blonde hair framed her face.*
- **PRODUCE FALSE EVIDENCE 3** [usually passive] to produce false evidence against an innocent person so that people think he or she is guilty **SYN** **fit up**: **be framed (for sth)** | **be framed** *He says he was framed.*
- **DEVELOP PLAN/SYSTEM 4 ~ sth** (*formal*) to create and develop sth such as a plan, a system or a set of rules
- **EXPRESS STH 5 ~ sth** to express sth in a particular way: *You'll have to be careful how you frame the question.*
▶ **framed** *adj.* (often in compounds): *a framed photograph* ◊ *a timber-framed house* (= with a supporting structure of wood)

**frame of ˈmind** *noun* [usually sing.] (*pl.* **frames of mind**) the way you feel or think about sth at a particular time: *We'll discuss this when you're in a better frame of mind.*

**frame of ˈreference** *noun* (*pl.* **frames of reference**) a particular set of beliefs, ideas or experiences in relation to which sth is measured or judged

**ˈframe-up** *noun* (*informal*) a situation in which false evidence is produced in order to make people think that an innocent person is guilty of a crime

**frame·work** [B2] 🔵 /ˈfreɪmwɜːk; *NAmE* -wɜːrk/ *noun* **1** [B2] the parts of a building or an object that support its weight and give it shape ⊃ SYNONYMS at STRUCTURE **2** [B2] a set of beliefs, ideas or rules that is used as the basis for making judgements, decisions, etc: *a theoretical/conceptual framework* ◊ **~ of/for sth** *The report provides a framework for further research.* **3** [B2] the structure of a particular system: *the basic framework of society* ◊ **~ for sth** *We need to establish a legal framework for the protection of the environment.*

**franc** /fræŋk/ *noun* the unit of money in Switzerland and several other countries (replaced in 2002 in France, Belgium and Luxembourg by the euro)

**fran·chise** [+] [C1] /ˈfræntʃaɪz/ *noun, verb*
■ *noun* **1** [+] [C1] [C, U] formal permission given by a company to sb who wants to sell its goods or services in a particular area; formal permission given by a government to sb who wants to operate a public service as a business: *a franchise agreement/company* ◊ *a catering/rail franchise* ◊ *In the reorganization, Southern Television lost their franchise.* ◊ *to operate a business* **under franchise 2** [+] [C1] [C] a

business or service run under franchise: *They operate franchises in London and Paris.* ◊ *a burger franchise* ⊃ WORDFINDER NOTE at COMPANY **3** [U] (*formal*) the right to vote in a country's elections: *universal adult franchise* **4** [C] a set of films in which the same characters appear in related stories ⊃ see also ENFRANCHISE
■ *verb* [usually passive] to give or sell a franchise to sb: **be franchised (out) (to sb/sth)** *Catering has been franchised (out) to a private company.* ◊ *franchised restaurants* ▶ **fran·chis·ing** *noun* [U]

**fran·chisee** /ˌfræntʃaɪˈziː/ *noun* a person or company that has been given a franchise

**ˈfranchise player** *noun* (*NAmE*) the best or most valuable player on a professional sports team

**fran·chiser** (*also* **fran·chisor**) /ˈfræntʃaɪzə(r)/ *noun* a company or an organization that gives sb a franchise

**Fran·cis·can** /frænˈsɪskən/ *noun, adj.*
■ *noun* a member of a religious organization started in 1209 by St Francis of Assisi in Italy
■ *adj.* relating to St Francis or to this organization: *a Franciscan monk*

**Franco-** /ˈfræŋkəʊ/ *combining form* (in nouns and adjectives) French; France: *the Franco-Prussian War* ◊ *Francophile*

**franco·phone** /ˈfræŋkəfəʊn/ *adj.* [only before noun] speaking French as the main language ▶ **franco·phone** *noun*: *Canadian francophones*

**fran·gi·pani** /ˌfrændʒɪˈpæni, -ˈpɑːni/ *noun* **1** [U, C] a tropical American tree or bush with groups of white, pink, or yellow flowers **2** [U] a PERFUME that is made from the frangipani plant

**frank** /fræŋk/ *adj., verb*
■ *adj.* (**frank·er**, **frank·est**) **HELP** **more frank** is also common. honest and direct in what you say, sometimes in a way that other people might not like: *a full and frank discussion* ◊ *a frank admission of guilt* ◊ *He was very frank about his relationship with the actress.* ◊ *To be frank with you, I think your son has little chance of passing the exam.* ⊃ SYNONYMS at HONEST ▶ **frank·ness** *noun* [U]: *They outlined their aims with disarming frankness.*
■ *verb* [often passive] **~ sth** to stamp a mark on an ENVELOPE, etc. to show that the cost of posting it has been paid or does not need to be paid

**Fran·ken·stein** /ˈfræŋkənstaɪn/ *noun* (*also* **Frankenstein's ˈmonster**, **Frankenstein ˈmonster**) used to talk about sth that sb creates or invents that goes out of control and becomes dangerous, often destroying the person who created it **ORIGIN** From the novel *Frankenstein* by Mary Shelley in which a scientist called Frankenstein makes a creature from pieces of dead bodies and brings it to life.

**frank·furt·er** /ˈfræŋkfɜːtə(r); *NAmE* -fɜːrt-/ (*NAmE also* **wie·ner**, *informal* **wee·nie**) *noun* a long thin smoked SAUSAGE with a red-brown skin, often eaten in a long bread roll as a HOT DOG

**frank·in·cense** /ˈfræŋkɪnsens/ *noun* [U] a substance that is burnt to give a pleasant smell, especially during religious ceremonies

**frank·ly** [+] [C1] /ˈfræŋkli/ *adv.* **1** [+] [C1] in an honest and direct way that people might not like: *He spoke frankly about the ordeal.* ◊ *They frankly admitted their responsibility.* **2** [+] [C1] used to show that you are being honest about sth, even though people might not like what you are saying: *Frankly, I couldn't care less what happens to him.* ◊ *Quite frankly, I'm not surprised you failed.*

**fran·tic** /ˈfræntɪk/ *adj.* **1** done quickly and with a lot of activity, but in a way that is not very well organized **SYN** **hectic**: *a frantic dash/search/struggle* ◊ *They made frantic attempts to revive him.* ◊ *Things are frantic in the office right now.* **2** unable to control your emotions because you are extremely frightened or worried about sth **SYN** **beside yourself**: *frantic with worry* ◊ *Let's go back. Your parents must be getting frantic by now.* ◊ *The children are driving me frantic* (= making me very annoyed). ▶ **fran·tic·al·ly** /-kli/ *adv.*: *They worked frantically to finish on time.*

# frappé

**frappé** /ˈfræpeɪ; NAmE fræˈpeɪ/ adj., noun (from French)
- adj. [after noun] (of drinks) served cold with a lot of ice: *coffee frappé*
- noun a drink or sweet food served cold with very small pieces of ice

**frat** /fræt/ noun (NAmE, informal) = FRATERNITY (2)

**ˈfrat boy** noun (NAmE, informal) a young man who behaves in a loud or stupid way, considered typical of members of some college FRATERNITIES (= clubs for male college students in the US): *frat-boy humour*

**fra·ter·nal** /frəˈtɜːnl; NAmE -ˈtɜːrnl/ adj. [usually before noun] **1** connected with the relationship that exists between people or groups that share the same ideas or interests: *a fraternal organization/society* **2** connected with the relationship that exists between brothers: *fraternal rivalry* ▸ **fra·ter·nal·ly** /-nəli/ adv.

**fra·ternal ˈtwin** noun either of two children or animals born from the same mother at the same time but not from the same egg ⇨ compare IDENTICAL TWIN

**fra·ter·nity** /frəˈtɜːnəti; NAmE -ˈtɜːrn-/ noun (pl. **-ies**) **1** [C + sing./pl. v.] a group of people sharing the same profession, interests or beliefs: *members of the medical/banking/racing, etc. fraternity* **2** (also NAmE, informal **frat**) [C] a club for a group of male students at an American college or university ⇨ compare SORORITY **3** [U] (formal) a feeling of friendship and support that exists between the members of a group: *the ideals of liberty, equality and fraternity*

**frat·er·nize** (BrE also **-ise**) /ˈfrætənaɪz; NAmE -tərn-/ verb [I] ~ (with sb) (often disapproving) to behave in a friendly manner, especially towards sb that you are not supposed to be friendly with: *She was accused of fraternizing with the enemy.* ▸ **frat·er·niza·tion, -isa·tion** /ˌfrætənaɪˈzeɪʃn; NAmE -tərnəˈz-/ noun [U]

**frat·ri·cide** /ˈfrætrɪsaɪd/ noun (formal) **1** [U, C] the crime of killing your brother or sister; a person who is guilty of this crime ⇨ compare MATRICIDE, PARRICIDE, PATRICIDE **2** [U, C] the crime of killing people of your own country or group; a person who is guilty of this crime **3** [U] (especially NAmE) the act of killing by accident your own forces in war SYN **friendly fire** ▸ **frat·ri·cid·al** /ˌfrætrɪˈsaɪdl/ adj.: *to be engaged in a fratricidal struggle*

**fraud** 0̶ B2 /frɔːd/ noun 1̶ B2 **1** [U, C] the crime of cheating sb in order to get money or goods illegally: *She was charged with credit card fraud.* ◇ *property that has been obtained by fraud* ◇ *a $100 million fraud* ⇨ see also WIRE FRAUD **2** 1̶ B2 [C] a person who pretends to have qualities, abilities, etc. that they do not really have in order to cheat other people: *He's nothing but a liar and a fraud.* ◇ *She felt a fraud accepting their sympathy* (= because she was not really sad). **3** [C] something that is not as good, useful, etc. as people claim it is

**ˈfraud squad** noun [sing. + sing./pl. v.] (BrE) part of a police force that investigates fraud

**fraud·ster** /ˈfrɔːdstə(r)/ noun (BrE) a person who commits fraud

**fraudu·lent** /ˈfrɔːdjələnt/ adj. (formal) intended to cheat sb, usually in order to make money illegally: *fraudulent advertising* ◇ *fraudulent insurance claims* ▸ **fraudu·lence** /-ləns/ noun [U] **fraudu·lent·ly** /-ləntli/ adv.

**fraught** /frɔːt/ adj. **1** ~ **with sth** filled with sth unpleasant: *a situation fraught with danger/difficulty/problems* **2** (especially BrE) causing or feeling worry and stress SYN **tense**: *She looked/sounded fraught.* ◇ *There was a fraught silence.* ◇ *Things are as fraught as ever in the office.*

**fray** /freɪ/ verb, noun
- verb **1** [I, T] if cloth **frays** or sth **frays** it, the THREADS in it start to come apart: *The cuffs of his shirt were fraying.* ◇ *This material frays easily.* ◇ *~ sth It was fashionable to fray the bottoms of your jeans.* **2** [I, T] ~ **(sth)** if sb's nerves or TEMPER **frays** or sth **frays** them, the person starts to get annoyed: *As the debate went on, tempers began to fray.* ▸ **frayed** adj.: *frayed denim shorts* ◇ *Tempers were getting very frayed.*

IDM **fray at/around the ˈedges/ˈseams** to start to come apart or to fail: *Support for the leader was fraying at the edges.*
- noun **the fray** [sing.] a fight, a competition or an argument, especially one that is exciting or seen as a test of your ability: *They were ready for the fray.* ◇ *to enter/join the fray* ◇ *At 71, he has now retired from the political fray.*

**fraz·zle** /ˈfræzl/ noun
IDM **be burnt, worn, etc. to a ˈfrazzle** (informal) to be completely burnt/extremely tired

**fraz·zled** /ˈfræzld/ adj. (informal) tired and easily annoyed: *They finally arrived home, hot and frazzled.*

**freak** /friːk/ noun, adj., verb
- noun **1** (informal) a person with a very strong interest in a particular subject: *a health/fitness/jazz, etc. freak* ⇨ see also CONTROL FREAK **2** (disapproving) a person who is considered to be unusual because of the way they behave, look or think: *She was treated like a freak because she didn't want children.* ◇ *He's going out with a real freak.* **3** (also **freak of ˈnature**) (sometimes offensive) a person, an animal, a plant or a thing that is not physically normal **4** a very unusual and unexpected event: *By some freak of fate they all escaped without injury.*
- adj. [only before noun] (of an event or the weather) very unusual and unexpected: *a freak accident/storm/occurrence* ◇ *freak weather conditions*
- verb [I, T] (informal) if sb **freaks** or if sth **freaks** them, they react very strongly to sth that makes them suddenly feel shocked, surprised, frightened, etc.: *~ (out) My parents really freaked when they saw my hair.* ◇ *~ sb (out) Snakes really freak me out.*

**freak·ing** /ˈfriːkɪŋ/ adv., adj. [only before noun] (NAmE, taboo, slang) a swear word that many people find offensive, used to emphasize a comment or an angry statement to avoid saying 'fucking'

**freak·ish** /ˈfriːkɪʃ/ adj. very strange, unusual or unexpected: *freakish weather/behaviour* ▸ **freak·ish·ly** adv.

**ˈfreak show** noun **1** a small show at a FAIR, where people pay to see people or animals with strange physical characteristics **2** (disapproving) an event that people watch because it is very strange

**freaky** /ˈfriːki/ adj. (informal) very strange or unusual

**freckle** /ˈfrekl/ noun [usually pl.] a small, pale brown spot on a person's skin, especially on their face, that often becomes darker after time spent in the sun ⇨ compare MOLE ▸ **freckled** adj.: *a freckled face/schoolgirl*

**free** 0̶ A1 S /friː/ adj., adv., verb
- adj. (**freer** /ˈfriːə(r)/, **freest** /ˈfriːɪst/)
- NOT BUSY **1** 1̶ A1 (of a person or time) without particular plans or arrangements; not busy: *Are you free on Saturday? We're having a barbecue.* ◇ *We try to keep Sundays free.* ◇ *~ for sth If Sarah is free for lunch I'll take her out.* ◇ *What do you like to do in your free time* (= when you are not working)?
- NOT BEING USED **2** 1̶ A2 not being used: *He held out his free hand and I took it.* ◇ *Is this seat free?*
- NO PAYMENT **3** 1̶ A2 costing nothing: *Admission is free.* ◇ *free software/tickets* ◇ *We even offer a free web design service.* ◇ *for ~ You can't expect people to work for free* (= without payment).
- NOT CONTROLLED **4** 1̶ B1 not under the control or in the power of sb else; able to do what you want: *I have no ambitions other than to have a happy life and be free.* ◇ *Students have a free choice of modules in their final year.* ◇ *~ to do sth You are free to leave at any time.* ◇ *~ from/of sth The organization wants to remain free from government control.* ◇ '*Can I sit here?*' '*Please, feel free* (= of course you can).' **5** 1̶ B1 not limited or controlled by anyone else: *A true democracy needs free speech and a free press.* ◇ *He called for free and fair elections.* ◇ *They gave me free access to all the files.*
- NOT PRISONER **6** 1̶ B1 (of a person) not a prisoner or slave: *He walked out of jail a free man.* ◇ *The hostages were all set free.*
- ANIMAL/BIRD **7** 1̶ B1 not tied up or in a CAGE: *The researchers set the birds free.*

- **NOT BLOCKED 8** clear; not blocked: *Ensure there is a free flow of air around the machine.*
- **WITHOUT STH 9** ~ **from/of sth** not containing or affected by sth harmful or unpleasant: *free from artificial colours and flavourings* ◊ *Beef producers want their herds free of disease.* ◊ *It was several weeks before he was completely free of pain.* **10** -**free** (in adjectives) without the thing mentioned: *pure, additive-free ingredients* ◊ *a trouble-free life* ◊ *After six months of treatment he is cancer-free.* ⊃ see also DUTY-FREE, FAT-FREE, INTEREST-FREE, LEAD-FREE, NUCLEAR-FREE, RENT-FREE, SMOKE-FREE, SUGAR-FREE, TAX-FREE
- **NOT ATTACHED/ABLE TO MOVE 11** not attached to sth; not stuck somewhere and unable to move: *Pull gently on the free end of the rope.* ◊ *She finally managed to* **pull** *herself free.* ◊ ~ **from sth** *They had to be* **cut** *free from their car after the accident.* ◊ ~ **of sth** *The boat had* **broken** *free of its moorings.*
- **READY TO GIVE 12** ~ **with sth** (*often disapproving*) ready to give sth, especially when it is not wanted: *He's too free with his opinions.*
- **TRANSLATION 13** a free translation is not exact but gives the general meaning ⊃ compare LITERAL

**IDM** **free and 'easy** *informal*; relaxed: *Life was never going to be so free and easy again.* **get, have, etc. a free 'hand** to get, have, etc. the opportunity to do what you want to do and to make your own decisions: *I was given a free hand in designing the syllabus.* **get, take, etc. a free 'ride** to get or take sth without paying because sb else is paying for it **it's a free 'country** (*informal*) used as a reply when sb suggests that you should not do sth, or when sb has asked permission or said they are going to do sth: *It's a free country; I'll say what I like!* **there's no such thing as a free 'lunch** (*informal*) used to say that it is not possible to get sth for nothing ⊃ more at HOME *adv.*, REIN *n.*, WALK *v.*

■ *adv.*
- **WITHOUT PAYMENT 1** (*also* **free of 'charge**) without payment: *Children under five travel free.*
- **NOT TIED 2** in a way that is not tied but is able to move about: *Attach the top and let the ends hang free.* ⊃ see also SCOT-FREE

**IDM** **make free with 'sth** (*disapproving*) to use sth a lot, even though it does not belong to you **run 'free** (of an animal) to be allowed to go where it likes; not tied to anything or kept in a CAGE

■ *verb*
- **PRISONER 1** to allow sb to leave prison or somewhere they have been kept against their will **SYN** **release**: ~ **sb** *The hijackers agreed to free a further ten hostages.* ◊ *By the end of May nearly 100 of an estimated 2000 political prisoners had been freed.* ◊ ~ **sb from sth** *They succeeded in freeing their friends from prison.*
- **SB/STH TRAPPED 2** to move sb/sth that is caught or fixed on sth **SYN** **release**: ~ **sb/sth/yourself** *She struggled to free herself.* ◊ ~ **sb/sth/yourself from sth** *Three people were freed from the wreckage.*
- **REMOVE STH 3** to remove sth that is unpleasant or not wanted from sb/sth **SYN** **rid**: ~ **sb/sth of sth/sth** *These exercises help free the body of tension.* ◊ *The police are determined to free the town of violent crime.* ◊ ~ **sb/sth from sth** *The centre aims to free young people from dependency on drugs.*
- **MAKE AVAILABLE 4** to make sb/sth available for a particular purpose: ~ **sb/sth (for sth)** *We freed time each week for a project meeting.* ◊ ~ **sb/sth up (for sth)** *The government has promised to free up more resources for education.* **5** to give sb the extra time to do sth that they want to do: ~ **sb to do sth** *Winning the prize freed him to paint full-time.* ◊ ~ **sb up (to do sth)** *Using the content management software frees up staff.*

**free 'agent** *noun* a person who can do whatever they want because they are not responsible to or for anyone else

**free·bie** /ˈfriːbi/ *noun* (*informal*) something that is given to sb without payment, usually by a company: *He took all the freebies that were on offer.* ◊ *a freebie holiday*

**free·born** /ˌfriːˈbɔːn; NAmE -ˈbɔːrn/ *adj.* [only before noun] (*formal*) not born as a slave

**Free 'Church** *noun* a Christian Church that does not belong to the ESTABLISHED (= official) Church in a particular country

**free·dom** /ˈfriːdəm/ *noun* **1** [U, C] the power or right to do or say what you want without anyone stopping you: *to defend/protect* **academic** *freedom* ◊ *Press freedom is under attack.* ◊ ~ **of sth** *We just want freedom of choice.* ◊ *Everyone has the right to freedom of expression.* ◊ *The government continues to restrict freedom of movement.* ◊ *rights and freedoms guaranteed by the constitution* ◊ ~ **to do sth** *complete freedom to do as you wish* ◊ ~ **in doing sth** *These proposals would give health authorities greater freedom in deciding how to spend their money.* **2** [U] the state of not being a prisoner or slave: *He finally won his freedom after twenty years in jail.*

> **WORDFINDER** allow, emancipation, imprisonment, independence, liberty, oppress, restriction, rule, slave

**3** [U] the state of not being ruled by a foreign or cruel government: *We believe in freedom and democracy.* **4** [U] the state of being able to move easily: *The skirt has a side split for* **freedom of movement**. ◊ ~ **to do sth** *Free-range hens have greater freedom to move about.* **5** [U] ~ **from sth** the state of not being affected by the thing mentioned: *All people should be guaranteed freedom from fear.* **6** [sing.] the ~ **of sth** permission to use sth without limits: *I was given the freedom of the whole house.*

**IDM** **the freedom of the 'city** (in the UK) an honour that is given to sb by a city as a reward for work they have done ⊃ see also FREEMAN ⊃ more at MANOEUVRE *n.*

**'freedom fighter** *noun* a person who takes part in a campaign to achieve greater political freedom **HELP** The term **freedom fighter** is used especially about sb who uses violence to try to remove a government from power, by people who support this. ⊃ compare GUERRILLA

**freedom of as'sembly** *noun* [U] the right to have public meetings which is guaranteed by law in the US

**freedom of as·soci'ation** *noun* [U] the right to meet people and to form organizations without needing permission from the government

**freedom of infor'mation** *noun* [U] the right to see any information that a government has about people and organizations

**free 'enterprise** *noun* [U] an economic system in which private businesses compete with each other without much government control ⊃ compare PRIVATE ENTERPRISE

**'free fall** *noun* [U] **1** the movement of an object or a person falling through the air without engine power or a PARACHUTE: *a free fall display* **2** a sudden drop in the value of sth that cannot be stopped: *Share prices have gone into free fall.*

**free-'floating** *adj.* not attached to or controlled by anything: *a free-floating exchange rate*

**Free·fone**™ /ˈfriːfəʊn/ *noun* [U] = FREEPHONE

**'free-for-all** *noun* [sing.] **1** a situation in which there are no rules or controls and everyone acts for their own advantage: *The lowering of trade barriers has led to a free-for-all among exporters.* **2** a noisy fight or argument in which a lot of people take part

**'free-form** *adj.* [only before noun] (of art or music) not created according to standard forms or structures: *a free-form jazz improvisation*

**'free·hand** /ˈfriːhænd/ *adj.* [only before noun] drawn without using a RULER (= a long straight piece of wood, plastic or metal) or other instruments: *a freehand drawing* ▸ **'free·hand** *adv.*: *to draw freehand*

**free·hold** /ˈfriːhəʊld/ *noun* [C, U] (*law, especially BrE*) the fact of owning a building or piece of land for a period of time that is not limited ▸ **'free·hold** *adj.*: *a freehold property* ▸ **'free·hold** *adv.*: *to buy a house freehold* ⊃ compare LEASEHOLD

# freeholder

**free·hold·er** /ˈfriːhəʊldə(r)/ *noun* (*law*, *especially BrE*) a person who owns the freehold of a building or piece of land ⇨ compare LEASEHOLDER

**free ˈhouse** *noun* (in the UK) a pub that can sell different types of beer because it is not owned and controlled by one particular BREWERY (= a company producing beer)

**free ˈkick** *noun* (in football (soccer) and rugby) an opportunity to kick the ball without any opposition, that is given to one team when the other team does sth wrong: *to take a free kick*

**free·lance** /ˈfriːlɑːns; *NAmE* -læns/ *adj.*, *verb*
- *adj.* earning money by selling your work or services to several different organizations rather than being employed by one particular organization: *a freelance journalist* ◊ *freelance work* ⇨ **WORDFINDER NOTE** at WORK ▶ **free·lance** *adv.* (*especially BrE*): *I work freelance from home.*
- *verb* [I] to earn money by selling your work to several different organizations

**free·lanc·er** /ˈfriːlɑːnsə(r)/; *NAmE* -læn-/ (*also* **free·lance**) *noun* a freelance worker

**free·load·er** /ˈfriːləʊdə(r)/ *noun* (*informal*, *disapproving*) a person who often accepts free food and accommodation from other people without giving them anything in exchange ▶ **free·load** *verb* [I] **free·load·ing** *adj.*, *noun* [U]

**free ˈlove** *noun* [U] (*old-fashioned*) the practice of having sex without being married or having several sexual relationships at the same time

**free·ly** ⁓+ 🄱🄲 /ˈfriːli/ *adv.* **1** ⁓+ 🄲 without anyone trying to prevent or control sth: *the country's first freely elected president* ◊ *EU citizens can travel freely between member states.* **2** ⁓+ 🄱🄲 without anything stopping the movement or flow of sth: *When the gate is raised, the water can flow freely.* ◊ *Traffic is now moving more freely following an earlier accident.* ◊ *The book is now freely available in the shops* (= it is not difficult to get a copy). ◊ (*figurative*) *The wine flowed freely* (= there was a lot of it to drink). **3** ⁓+ 🄱🄲 in an honest way without worrying about what people will say or do: *For the first time he was able to speak freely without the fear of reprisals against his family.* **4** ⁓+ 🄲 without trying to avoid the truth even though it might be unpleasant or embarrassing: *I freely admit that I made a mistake.* **5** in a willing and generous way: *Millions of people gave freely in response to the appeal for the victims of the earthquake.* **6** a piece of writing that is translated freely is not translated exactly but the general meaning is given

**free·man** /ˈfriːmən/ *noun* (*pl.* **-men** /-mən/) **1** (*BrE*) a person who has been given the FREEDOM of a particular city as a reward for the work that they have done **2** a person who is not a slave

**free ˈmarket** *noun* an economic system in which the price of goods and services is affected by supply and demand rather than controlled by a government: *She was a supporter of the free market economy.*

**free marke'teer** *noun* a person who believes that prices should be allowed to rise and fall according to supply and demand and not be controlled by a government

**Free·ma·son** /ˈfriːmeɪsn/ (*also* **Mason**) *noun* a man belonging to a secret society whose members help each other and communicate using secret signs

**Free·ma·son·ry** /ˈfriːmeɪsnri/ *noun* [U] **1** the system and practices of Freemasons **2 freemasonry** the friendship that exists between people who have the same profession or interests: *the freemasonry of actors*

**free ˈpardon** *noun* (*BrE*, *law*) = PARDON

**free ˈperiod** *noun* a period of time in a school day when a student or teacher does not have a class

**Free·phone** (*also* **Free·fone**™) /ˈfriːfəʊn/ *noun* [U] (in the UK) a system in which the cost of a phone call is paid for by the organization being called, rather than by the person making the call ⇨ compare TOLL-FREE

**free ˈport** *noun* a port at which tax is not paid on goods that have been brought there temporarily before being sent to a different country

**Free·post** /ˈfriːpəʊst/ *noun* [U] (in the UK) a system in which the cost of sending a letter is paid for by the organization receiving it, rather than by the person sending it

**free ˈradical** *noun* (*chemistry*) an ATOM or group of ATOMS that has an ELECTRON that is not part of a pair, causing it to take part easily in chemical reactions. Free radicals in the body are thought to be one of the causes of diseases such as cancer. ⇨ see also ANTIOXIDANT (1)

**free-range** *adj.* [usually before noun] connected with a system of farming in which animals are kept in natural conditions and can move around freely: *free-range chickens* ◊ *free-range eggs* ⇨ compare BATTERY (5), BATTERY FARM

**free ˈrunning** *noun* [U] the activity or art of moving through a city by running, jumping and climbing under, around and through things in a way that shows expression and style ⇨ compare PARKOUR

**free ˈsafety** *noun* (in AMERICAN FOOTBALL) a defending player who can try to stop any attacking player rather than one particular attacking player

**free ˈschool** *noun* a school in England that receives money from the government, but is organized and controlled independently ⇨ compare PRIVATE SCHOOL, STATE SCHOOL

**free·sia** /ˈfriːʒə; *BrE also* ˈfriːziə/ *noun* a plant with yellow, pink, white or purple flowers with a sweet smell, which are also called freesias

**free ˈspirit** *noun* a person who is independent and does what they want instead of doing what other people do

**free-ˈspirited** *adj.* independent and not wanting to do sth in the usual way

**free-ˈstanding** *adj.* **1** not supported by or attached to anything: *a free-standing sculpture* **2** not a part of sth else: *a free-standing adult education service*

**free·style** /ˈfriːstaɪl/ *noun*, *verb*
- *noun* [U] **1** a swimming race in which people taking part can use any STROKE (= swimming style) they want (usually the CRAWL): *the men's 400m freestyle* **2** (often used as an adjective) a sports competition in which people taking part can use any style that they want: *freestyle skiing*
- *verb* [I] to RAP, play music, dance, etc. by inventing it as you do it, rather than by planning it in advance or following fixed patterns **SYN** improvise

**free·think·er** /ˌfriːˈθɪŋkə(r)/ *noun* a person who forms their own ideas and opinions rather than accepting those of other people, especially in religious teaching ▶ **free·think·ing** *adj.* [only before noun]

**free ˈthrow** *noun* (in basketball) an attempt to throw a ball into the BASKET without any player trying to stop you, that you are allowed after a FOUL

**free-to-ˈair** *adj.* [usually before noun] (*BrE*) (of television programmes) that you do not have to pay to watch: *The company provides more than 20 free-to-air channels.*

**free ˈtrade** *noun* [U] a system of international trade in which there are no limits or taxes on imports and exports

**free ˈverse** *noun* [U] (*specialist*) poetry without a regular rhythm or RHYME ⇨ compare BLANK VERSE

**free ˈvote** *noun* (in the UK) a vote by members of parliament in which they can vote according to their own beliefs rather than following the policy of their political party

**free·ware** /ˈfriːweə(r); *NAmE* -wer/ *noun* [U] (*computing*) computer software that is offered free for anyone to use ⇨ compare SHAREWARE

**free·way** /ˈfriːweɪ/ (*also* **ex·press·way**) *noun* (in the US) a wide road where traffic can travel fast for long distances. You can only enter and leave freeways at special RAMPS: *a freeway exit* ◊ *an accident on the freeway*

**free·wheel** /ˌfriːˈwiːl/ *verb* [I] (+ **adv./prep.**) to ride a bicycle without using the PEDALS: *I freewheeled down the hill to the village.*

**free·wheel·ing** /ˌfriːˈwiːlɪŋ/ *adj.* [only before noun] (*informal*) not concerned about rules or the possible results of what you do: *a freewheeling lifestyle*

**free 'will** noun [U] the power to make your own decisions about what to do, without being controlled by God, FATE or circumstances
- **IDM of your own free 'will** because you want to do sth rather than because sb has told or forced you to do it: *She left of her own free will.*

## freeze ⓘ B1 /friːz/ verb, noun

■ **verb** (**froze** /frəʊz/, **fro·zen** /ˈfrəʊzn/)
- **BECOME ICE 1** B1 [I, T] to become hard, and often turn to ice, as a result of extreme cold; to make sth do this: *Water freezes at 0°C.* ◊ *It's so cold that even the river has frozen.* ◊ **~sth** *The cold weather had frozen the ground.* ◊ **~(sth) +adj.** *The clothes froze solid on the washing line.* **OPP** thaw
- **OF PIPE/LOCK/MACHINE 2** B1 [I, T] if a pipe, lock or machine **freezes**, or sth **freezes** it, it becomes blocked with frozen liquid and therefore cannot be used: **~(up)** *I kept the car running to stop the engine freezing up.* ◊ **~sth** *Ten degrees of frost had frozen the lock on the car.*
- **OF WEATHER 3** B1 [I] when **it freezes**, the weather is at or below 0° Celsius: *It may freeze tonight, so bring those plants inside.*
- **BE VERY COLD 4** B1 [I, T] to be very cold; to be so cold that you die: *Every time she opens the window we all freeze.* ◊ *Two men froze to death on the mountain.* ◊ **~sb** *Two men were frozen to death on the mountain.*
- **FOOD 5** B1 [T] **~sth** to keep something, especially food, at a very low temperature in order to preserve it: *Can you freeze this cake?* **6** [I] to be able to be kept at a very low temperature: *Some fruits freeze better than others.*
- **STOP MOVING 7** [I] to stop moving suddenly because of fear, etc: *I froze with terror as the door slowly opened.* ◊ *(figurative) The smile froze on her lips.* ◊ *The police officer shouted 'Freeze!' and the man dropped the gun.*
- **COMPUTER 8** [I] when a computer screen **freezes**, you cannot move any of the images, etc. on it, because there is a problem with the system
- **FILM/MOVIE 9** [T] **~sth** to stop a film or video in order to look at a particular picture: *Freeze the action there!* ⊃ see also FREEZE-FRAME
- **WAGES/PRICES 10** [T] **~sth** to hold wages, prices, etc. at a fixed level for a period of time **SYN** peg: *Salaries have been frozen for the current year.*
- **MONEY/BANK ACCOUNT 11** [T] **~sth** to prevent money, a bank account, etc. from being used by getting a court order which bans it: *The company's assets have been frozen.*
- **IDM freeze your 'blood | make your 'blood freeze** to make you extremely frightened or shocked ⊃ more at TRACK *n.*
- **PHRV freeze sb↔'out (of sth)** (*informal*) to be deliberately unfriendly to sb, creating difficulties, etc. in order to stop or DISCOURAGE them from doing sth or taking part in sth **freeze 'over** to become completely covered by ice: *The lake freezes over in winter.*

■ **noun**
- **OF WAGES/PRICES 1** the act of keeping wages, prices, etc. at a particular level for a period of time: *a wage/price freeze* ◊ **~on sth** *a freeze on bus fares*
- **STOPPING STH 2** [usually sing.] **~(on sth)** the act of stopping sth: *a freeze on imports*
- **COLD WEATHER 3** [usually sing.] (*BrE*) an unusually cold period of weather during which temperatures stay below 0° Celsius: *Farmers still talk about the big freeze of '99.* **4** (*NAmE*) a short period of time, usually at night, when the temperature is below 0° Celsius: *A freeze warning was posted for Thursday night.* ⊃ see also DEEP FREEZE

**'freeze-dry** verb [usually passive] **~sth** to preserve food or drink by freezing and drying it very quickly

**'freeze-frame** noun [U, C] the act of stopping a moving film at one particular FRAME (= picture)

**freez·er** /ˈfriːzə(r)/ (*BrE also* **deep 'freeze**) (*US also* **deep 'freezer**) noun a large piece of electrical equipment in which you can store food for a long time at a low temperature so that it stays frozen ⊃ see also FRIDGE-FREEZER

**freez·ing** /ˈfriːzɪŋ/ adj., noun
■ **adj. 1** (*also* **freezing cold**) extremely cold: *It's freezing in here!* ◊ *I'm freezing!* ◊ *It's freezing cold outside.* ⊃ SYNONYMS at COLD **2** [only before noun] having temperatures that are below 0° Celsius: *freezing fog* ◊ *freezing temperatures* ⊃ SYNONYMS at COLD
■ **noun** [U] = FREEZING POINT (1)

**'freezing point** noun **1** (*also* **freez·ing**) [U] 0° Celsius, the temperature at which water freezes: *Tonight temperatures will fall well below freezing (point).* **2** [C, usually sing.] the temperature at which a particular liquid freezes: *the freezing point of polar seawater*

**freight** /freɪt/ noun, verb
■ **noun** [U] goods that are transported by ships, planes, trains or lorries; the system of transporting goods in this way: *to send goods by air freight* ◊ *a freight business* ◊ *passenger and freight transportation services*
■ **verb 1 ~sth** to send or carry goods by air, sea or train **2** [usually passive] (*literary*) to fill sth with a particular mood or tone: **be freighted with sth** *Each word was freighted with anger.*

**'freight car** (*NAmE*) (*BrE* **wagon**) noun a railway truck for carrying goods ⊃ picture at WAGON

**freight·er** /ˈfreɪtə(r)/ noun a large ship or plane that carries goods

**'freight train** (*BrE also* **'goods train**) noun a train that carries only goods

**French** /frentʃ/ adj., noun
■ **adj.** of or connected with France, its people or its language
■ **noun 1** [U] the language of France and some other countries **2 the French** [pl.] the people of France
- **IDM excuse/pardon my 'French** (*informal*) used to say that you are sorry for swearing

**French 'bean** noun (*BrE*) = GREEN BEAN

**French 'bread** noun [U] white bread in the shape of a long thick stick

**French 'Canada** noun [U] the part of Canada where most French-speaking Canadians live, especially Quebec

**French Ca'nadian** noun a Canadian whose first language is French ▶ **French Ca'nadian** adj.

**French 'door** (*especially NAmE*) (*BrE also* **French window**) noun [usually pl.] a glass door, usually one of a pair that leads to a garden or BALCONY

**French 'dressing** noun [U, C] a mixture of oil, VINEGAR, etc. added to a salad **SYN** vinaigrette

**French 'fry** (*also* **fry**) (*both especially NAmE*) (*BrE usually* **chip**) noun [usually pl.] a long thin piece of potato fried in oil or fat

**French 'horn** (*also* **horn** *especially in BrE*) noun a BRASS musical instrument that consists of a long tube CURLED around in a circle with a wide opening at the end

**French 'kiss** noun a kiss during which people's mouths are open and their tongues touch

**French 'loaf** noun = BAGUETTE

**French 'press**™ (*NAmE*) (*BrE* **cafe·tière**) noun a special glass container for making coffee with a metal FILTER that you push down

**French 'stick** noun = BAGUETTE ⊃ picture at STICK

**French 'toast** noun [U] slices of bread that have been covered with a mixture of egg and milk and then fried

**French 'window** (*especially BrE*) (*NAmE usually* **French door**) noun [usually pl.] a glass door, usually one of a pair that leads to a garden or BALCONY

**fren·emy** /ˈfrenəmi/ noun (*pl.* **-ies**) a person or organization that you are friends with because it is useful or necessary to be their friend, even though you really dislike or disagree with them

**fre·net·ic** /frəˈnetɪk/ adj. involving a lot of energy and activity in a way that is not organized: *a scene of frenetic activity* ▶ **fre·net·ic·al·ly** /-kli/ adv.

**fren·zied** /ˈfrenzid/ adj. [usually before noun] involving a lot of activity and strong emotions in a way that is often violent or frightening and not under control: *a frenzied attack* ◊ *frenzied activity* ▶ **fren·zied·ly** /-zɪdli/ adv.

# frenzy

**fren·zy** /ˈfrenzi/ noun [C, usually sing., U] (pl. -ies) ~ (of sth) a state of great activity and strong emotion that is often violent or frightening and not under control: *in a frenzy of activity/excitement/violence* ◊ *The speaker worked the crowd up into a frenzy.* ◊ *an outbreak of patriotic frenzy* ◊ *a killing frenzy* ⊃ see also FEEDING FRENZY

**fre·quency** ❶ B2 /ˈfriːkwənsi/ noun (pl. -ies)
**1** B2 [U, C] the rate at which sth happens or is repeated: *Fatal road accidents have decreased in frequency over recent years.* ◊ *Dawn was then visiting New York with increasing frequency.* ◊ *a society with a high/low frequency* (= happening often/not very often) *of stable marriages* **2** B2 [U] the fact of sth happening often: *the alarming frequency of computer errors* ◊ *with … ~ Objects like this turn up at sales with surprising frequency.* **3** [C, U] (specialist) the rate at which a sound or ELECTROMAGNETIC wave VIBRATES (= moves up and down): *a high/low frequency* ⊃ WORDFINDER NOTE at PHYSICS **4** [C, U] (specialist) the number of radio waves for every second of a radio signal: *a frequency band* ◊ *an FM radio frequency* ⊃ see also ULTRA-HIGH FREQUENCY, VERY HIGH FREQUENCY

**fre·quent** ❶+ B2 W adj., verb
■ adj. ❶+ B2 /ˈfriːkwənt/ happening or doing sth often: *He is a frequent visitor to this country.* ◊ *Her calls became less frequent.* ◊ *There is a frequent bus service into the centre of town.* ◊ *How frequent is this word* (= how often does it occur in the language)? OPP infrequent
■ verb /friˈkwent/ ~ sth (formal) to visit a particular place often: *We met in a local bar much frequented by students.*

**fre·quent·ly** ❶ B1 W /ˈfriːkwəntli/ adv. often: *Buses run frequently between the city and the airport.* ◊ *some of the most frequently asked questions about the internet* OPP infrequently ⊃ see also FAQ

**fresco** /ˈfreskəʊ/ noun (pl. -oes or -os) [C, U] a picture that is painted on a wall while the PLASTER is still wet; the method of painting in this way ▶ WORDFINDER NOTE at PAINTING ⊃ see also AL FRESCO

**fresh** ❶ A2 /freʃ/ adj., adv.
■ adj. (fresh·er, fresh·est)
• FOOD **1** A2 (usually of food) recently produced or picked and not frozen, dried or preserved in tins or cans: *Is this milk fresh?* ◊ *fresh bread/flowers/fish* ◊ *Eat plenty of fresh fruit and vegetables.* ◊ *Our chefs use only the freshest produce available.* ◊ *~from/off sth vegetables fresh from the garden*
• CLEAN/COOL **2** B1 [usually before noun] pleasantly clean, pure or cool: *a toothpaste that leaves a nice fresh taste in your mouth* ◊ *Let's go and get some fresh air* (= go outside where the air is cooler).
• NEW **3** B2 made or experienced recently: *fresh tracks in the snow* ◊ *Let me write it down while it's still fresh in my mind.* **4** B2 [usually before noun] new or different in a way that adds to or replaces sth: *a fresh coat of paint* ◊ *fresh evidence* ◊ *This is the opportunity he needs to make a fresh start* (= to try sth new after not being successful at sth else). ◊ *The government is said to be taking a fresh look at the matter.*
• WATER **5** B2 [usually before noun] containing no salt: *There is a shortage of fresh water on the island.* ⊃ see also FRESHWATER
• WEATHER **6** (of the wind) quite strong and cold SYN brisk: *a fresh breeze* **7** (BrE) (of the weather) quite cold with some wind: *It's fresh this morning, isn't it?*
• CLEAR/BRIGHT **8** looking clear, bright and attractive: *He looked fresh and neat in a clean white shirt.* ◊ *a collection of summer dresses in fresh colours* ◊ *a fresh complexion*
• FULL OF ENERGY **9** [not usually before noun] full of energy: *Regular exercise will help you feel fresher and fitter.* ◊ *I managed to sleep on the plane and arrived feeling as fresh as a daisy.*
• JUST FINISHED **10** having just come from a particular place; having just had a particular experience: *~out of sth students fresh out of college* ◊ *~from/off sth fresh from her success at the Olympic Games*

• RUDE/CONFIDENT **11** [not before noun] ~ (with sb) (informal) rude and too confident in a way that shows a lack of respect for sb or a sexual interest in sb: *Don't get fresh with me!* ▶ **fresh·ness** noun [U, sing.]: *We guarantee the freshness of all our produce.* ◊ *the cool freshness of the water* ◊ *I like the freshness of his approach to the problem.*
IDM see BLOOD n., BREATH, HEART n.
■ adv. **fresh-** (in adjective compounds) freshly: *fresh-baked bread*
IDM **fresh out of sth** (especially NAmE, informal) having recently finished a supply of sth: *Sorry, we're fresh out of milk.*

**fresh·en** /ˈfreʃn/ verb **1** [T] ~ sth (up) to make sth cleaner, cooler, newer or more pleasant: *The walls need freshening up with white paint.* ◊ *The rain had freshened the air.* ◊ *Using a mouthwash freshens the breath.* **2** [T] ~ sth (up) (especially NAmE) to add more liquid to a drink, especially an alcoholic one ⊃ see also TOP STH UP **3** [I] (of the wind) to become stronger and colder: *The wind will freshen tonight.*
PHRV **freshen up | freshen yourself up** to wash and make yourself look clean and tidy: *I'll just go and freshen up before supper.*

**fresh·ener** /ˈfreʃnə(r)/ noun [U, C] (usually in compounds) a thing that makes sth cleaner, purer or more pleasant: *a breath freshener* ⊃ see also AIR FRESHENER

**fresh·er** /ˈfreʃə(r)/ noun (BrE, informal) a student who has just started his or her first term at a university ⊃ compare FRESHMAN (1)

**fresh-faced** adj. (approving) having a young, healthy-looking face: *fresh-faced kids*

**fresh·ly** /ˈfreʃli/ adv. usually followed by a past participle showing that sth has been made, prepared, etc. recently: *freshly brewed coffee*

**fresh·man** /ˈfreʃmən/ noun (pl. -men /-mən/) (NAmE) **1** a first-year student at a university or college: *college freshmen* ◊ *during my freshman year* ⊃ compare FRESHER **2** a first-year student at HIGH SCHOOL or JUNIOR HIGH SCHOOL: *high school freshmen* ⊃ compare SOPHOMORE

**fresh·water** /ˈfreʃwɔːtə(r)/ adj. [only before noun] **1** living in water that is not the sea and does not contain salt: *freshwater fish* **2** having water that does not contain salt: *freshwater lakes* ⊃ compare SALT WATER

**fret** /fret/ verb, noun
■ verb (-tt-) [I, T] ~ (about/over sth) | ~ (that …) to be worried or unhappy and not able to relax: *Her baby starts to fret as soon as she goes out of the room.* ◊ *Fretting about it won't help.*
■ noun **1** one of the bars on the long thin part of a guitar, etc. Frets show you where to press the strings with your fingers to produce particular sounds. **2** (also **sea fret**) (NEngE) MIST or FOG that comes in from the sea

**fret·ful** /ˈfretfl/ adj. behaving in a way that shows you are unhappy or uncomfortable SYN restless ▶ **fret·ful·ly** adv.

**fret·ted** /ˈfretɪd/ adj. (specialist) (especially of wood or stone) decorated with patterns

**fret·work** /ˈfretwɜːk; NAmE -wɜːrk/ noun [U] patterns cut into wood, metal, etc. to decorate it; the process of making these patterns

**Freud·ian** /ˈfrɔɪdiən/ adj. **1** connected with the ideas of Sigmund Freud about the way the human mind works, especially his theories of unconscious sexual feelings **2** (of sb's speech or behaviour) showing your secret thoughts or feelings, especially those connected with sex

**Freudian slip** noun something you say by mistake but that is believed to show your true thoughts ORIGIN This expression is named after Sigmund Freud and his theories of unconscious thought.

**Fri.** abbr. (in writing) Friday

**fri·able** /ˈfraɪəbl/ adj. (specialist) easily broken up into small pieces: *friable soil*

**friar** /ˈfraɪə(r)/ noun a member of one of several Roman Catholic religious communities of men who in the past travelled around teaching people about Christianity and lived by asking other people for food (= by begging) ⊃ compare MONK

**fri·ary** /ˈfraɪəri/ noun (pl. **-ies**) a building in which friars live

**fric·tion** /ˈfrɪkʃn/ noun **1** [U] the action of one object or surface moving against another: *Friction between moving parts had caused the engine to overheat.* **2** [U] (physics) the RESISTANCE (= the force that stops sth moving) of one surface to another surface or substance moving over or through it: *The force of friction slows the spacecraft down as it re-enters the earth's atmosphere.* **3** [U, C] a lack of friendship or agreement among people who have different opinions about sth **SYN tension**: *conflicts and frictions that have still to be resolved* ◇ *~ between A and B friction between neighbours*

**fric·tion·less** /ˈfrɪkʃnləs/ adj. **1** with no RESISTANCE between a surface or substance and sth that is moving along or through it: *The block moves on a frictionless surface.* **2** achieved with or involving little difficulty or effort: *You want the buying experience to be as frictionless as possible.*

**Fri·day** ⓞ A1 /ˈfraɪdeɪ, -di/ noun [C, U] (abbr. **Fri.**) the day of the week after Thursday and before Saturday HELP To see how **Friday** is used, look at the examples at **Monday**. ⊃ see also BLACK FRIDAY, GOOD FRIDAY ORIGIN Originally translated from the Latin for 'day of the planet Venus' *Veneris dies* and named after the Germanic goddess Frigga.

**fridge** ⓞ A2 /frɪdʒ/ (especially BrE) (NAmE or formal **re·frig·er·ator**) (US also, old-fashioned **ice-box**) noun a piece of electrical equipment in which food is kept cold so that it stays fresh: **in the ~** *There's no food in the fridge!*

**fridge-ˈfreezer** noun (BrE) a piece of kitchen equipment that consists of a fridge and a FREEZER together

**fried** /fraɪd/ past tense, past part. of FRY

**friend** ⓞ A1 /frend/ noun, verb
■ noun
• PERSON YOU LIKE **1** A1 a person you know well and like, and who is not usually a member of your family: *This is my friend Tom.* ◇ *Is he a friend of yours?* ◇ *She's an old friend* (= I have known her a long time). ◇ *He's one of my best friends.* ◇ *a close/good/dear friend* ◇ *a childhood/family/longtime friend* ◇ *We've been friends for years.* ◇ *to become/remain friends* ◇ *She has a wide circle of friends.* ⊃ see also BEFRIEND, BOSOM FRIEND, BOYFRIEND, FAIR-WEATHER, FALSE FRIEND, GIRLFRIEND, PENFRIEND, SCHOOL FRIEND

WORDFINDER acquaintance, bond, buddy, companion, comrade, mate, neighbour, platonic, playmate

• ON THE INTERNET **2** a person who is on your contacts list on a SOCIAL MEDIA website: *How many friends have you got on Facebook?* ◇ *Facebook friends*
• SUPPORTER **3** also **Friend** a person who supports an organization, a charity, etc., especially by giving or raising money; a person who supports a particular idea, etc: *the Friends of St Martin's Hospital* ◇ *a friend of democracy*
• NOT ENEMY **4** a person who has the same interests and opinions as yourself, and who will help and support you: *His eyes were moving from face to face: friend or foe?* ◇ **among friends** *You're among friends here—you can speak freely.*
• PERSON THAT YOU MEET/SPEAK TO **5** (often ironic) used to talk about or to sb that you meet who is not actually a friend: *I wish our friend at the next table would shut up.*
• IN PARLIAMENT/COURT **6** (in the UK) used by a member of parliament to refer to another member of parliament or by a lawyer to refer to another lawyer in a court of law: *my honourable friend, the member for Henley* (= in the House of Commons) ◇ *my noble friend* (= in the House of Lords) ◇ *my learned friend* (= in a court of law)
• IN RELIGION **7 Friend** a member of the Society of Friends SYN Quaker
IDM **be (just) good ˈfriends** used to say that two friends are not having a romantic relationship with each other **a ˌfriend in ˈneed (is a ˌfriend in ˈdeed)** (saying) a friend who gives you help when you need it (is a true friend) **have**

ˌfriends in high ˈplaces to know important people who can help you **make ˈfriends (with sb)** to become a friend of sb: *Simon finds it hard to make friends with other children.* ⊃ more at MAN n.
■ verb ~ **sb** to add sb to your list of contacts on a SOCIAL MEDIA website: *The chat system only allows you to communicate with those you have friended on the site.*

**friend·less** /ˈfrendləs/ adj. without any friends

**friend·ly** ⓞ A1 /ˈfrendli/ adj., noun
■ adj. (**friend·lier**, **friend·li·est**) **1** A1 behaving in a kind and pleasant way because you like sb or want to help them: *a warm and friendly person* ◇ *~ to/toward(s) sb Everyone was very friendly towards me.* OPP **unfriendly 2** A2 showing that sb is kind; making you feel relaxed and as though you are among friends: *a friendly smile/welcome* ◇ *a small hotel with a friendly atmosphere* OPP **unfriendly 3** B1 treating sb as a friend: *~ with sb We soon became friendly with the couple next door.* ◇ *She was on friendly terms with most of the hospital staff.* **4** A2 (especially of the relationship between countries) not treating sb/sth as an enemy: *to maintain friendly relations with all countries* OPP **hostile 5** B1 (often in compound adjectives) that is helpful and easy to use; that helps sb/sth or does not harm it: *This software is much friendlier than the previous version.* ◇ *child-friendly policies* ⊃ see also ECO-FRIENDLY, ENVIRONMENTALLY FRIENDLY, OZONE-FRIENDLY, USER-FRIENDLY **6** B1 [usually before noun] in which people are not arguing or competing in a serious or unpleasant way: *a friendly argument* ◇ *friendly rivalry* **7** [only before noun] (BrE) (of a game or match) not part of an important competition ▶ **friend·li·ness** noun [U]
■ noun (also **ˈfriendly match**) (both BrE) (pl. **-ies**) a game of football (soccer), rugby, etc. that is not part of an important competition

ˌfriendly ˈfire noun [U] in a war, if people are killed or injured by **friendly fire**, they are hit by a bomb or weapon that is fired by their own side SYN **fratricide**

ˈfriendly society noun (in the UK) an organization that people pay regular amounts of money to and that gives them money when they are ill or old

**friend·ship** ⓞ B1 /ˈfrendʃɪp/ noun **1** B1 [C] a relationship between friends: *They formed a close friendship at college.* ◇ *a lasting/lifelong friendship* ◇ *~ with sb He seemed to have already struck up* (= begun) *a friendship with Jo.* ◇ *~ between A and B It's the story of an extraordinary friendship between a boy and a seal.* **2** B1 [U] the feeling or relationship that friends have; the state of being friends: *Your friendship is very important to me.* ◇ *a conference to promote international friendship*

**frier** = FRYER

**Frie·sian** /ˈfriːʒn/ (BrE) noun a type of black and white cow that produces a lot of milk

**frieze** /friːz/ noun **1** a border that goes around the top of a room or building with pictures or CARVINGS on it **2** a long narrow picture, usually put up in a school, that children have made or that teaches them sth

**frig·ate** /ˈfrɪɡət/ noun a small fast ship in the NAVY that travels with other ships in order to protect them

**frig·ging** /ˈfrɪɡɪŋ/ adv., adj. [only before noun] (taboo, slang) a swear word that many people find offensive, used to emphasize a comment or an angry statement to avoid saying 'fucking': *It's frigging cold outside.* ◇ *Mind your own frigging business!*

**fright** /fraɪt/ noun **1** [U] a feeling of fear: *to cry out in fright* ◇ *He was shaking with fright.* ⊃ SYNONYMS at FEAR ⊃ see also STAGE FRIGHT **2** [C] an experience that makes you feel fear: *You gave me a fright jumping out at me like that.* ◇ *I got the fright of my life.*
IDM **look a ˈfright** (old-fashioned, BrE) to look ugly or silly **take ˈfright (at sth)** (formal) to be frightened by sth: *The birds took fright and flew off.*

# frighten 636

**fright·en** ❶ **B1** /ˈfraɪtn/ *verb* [T, I] to make sb suddenly feel afraid: **~ (sb)** *Sorry, I didn't mean to frighten you.* ◇ *She's not easily frightened.* ◇ *She doesn't frighten easily* (= it is not easy to make her afraid). ◇ **it frightens sb to think, see, hear, etc ...** *It really frightens me to think how this might have ended.* ◇ **it frightens sb that ...** *It frightened him that she could see so easily into his private thoughts.* **IDM** see DAYLIGHTS, DEATH, LIFE
**PHRV** **frighten sb/sth↔ˈaway/ˈoff** | **frighten sb/sth a ˈway from sth 1** to make a person or an animal go away by making them feel afraid: *He threatened the intruders with a gun and frightened them off.* **2** to make sb afraid or nervous so that they no longer want to do sth: *The high prices have frightened off many customers.* **ˈfrighten sb into sth/into doing sth** to make sb do sth by making them afraid

> ▼ SYNONYMS
>
> **frighten**
> scare • alarm • terrify
> These words all mean to make sb afraid.
> **frighten** to make sb feel afraid, often suddenly: *He brought out a gun and frightened them off.*
> **scare** to make sb feel afraid: *They managed to scare the bears away.*
> **alarm** to make sb anxious or afraid: *It alarms me that nobody takes this problem seriously.* **NOTE** Alarm is used when sb has a feeling that sth unpleasant or dangerous might happen in the future; the feeling is often more one of worry than actual fear.
> **terrify** to make sb feel extremely afraid: *Flying terrified her.*
> **FRIGHTEN OR SCARE?**
> **Scare** is slightly more informal than **frighten**.
> **PATTERNS**
> • to frighten / scare sb / sth **away / off**
> • to frighten / scare / terrify sb **into** doing sth
> • It frightens / scares / alarms / terrifies me **that** ...
> • It frightens / scares / alarms / terrifies me **to think, see,** etc.

**fright·ened** ❶ **B1** /ˈfraɪtnd/ *adj.* afraid; feeling fear: *a frightened child* ◇ *Don't be frightened.* ◇ **~ of sth** *What are you frightened of?* ◇ **~ of doing sth** *I'm frightened of walking home alone in the dark.* ◇ **~ to do sth** *I'm too frightened to ask him now.* ◇ **~ that ...** *She was frightened that the plane would crash.* ◇ **~ for sb** *I'm frightened for him* (= that he will be hurt, etc.). ◇ (*informal*) *I'd never do that. I'd be* **frightened to death**. ⇒ SYNONYMS at AFRAID **IDM** see SHADOW *n.*, WIT

**fright·en·ing** ❶ **B1** /ˈfraɪtnɪŋ/ *adj.* making you feel afraid: *a frightening experience/prospect/thought* ◇ **it is ~ to think, see, hear, etc ...** *It's frightening to think it could happen again.* ▶ **fright·en·ing·ly** *adv.*

**fright·ful** /ˈfraɪtfl/ *adj.* (*old-fashioned, especially BrE*) **1** (*informal*) used to emphasize how bad sth is **SYN** awful, terrible: *It was absolutely frightful!* ◇ *This room's in a frightful mess.* **2** very serious or unpleasant **SYN** awful, terrible: *a frightful accident*

**fright·ful·ly** /ˈfraɪtfəli/ *adv.* (*old-fashioned, especially BrE*) very; extremely **SYN** awfully, frightfully: *I'm frightfully sorry.*

**fri·gid** /ˈfrɪdʒɪd/ *adj.* **1** (of a woman) not able to enjoy sex **2** very cold: *frigid air* ⇒ WORDFINDER NOTE at CLIMATE **3** not showing any friendly or kind feelings **SYN** frosty: *a frigid voice* ◇ *There was a frigid atmosphere in the room.* ▶ **fri·gid·ly** *adv.*

**fri·gid·ity** /frɪˈdʒɪdəti/ *noun* [U] **1** (in a woman) the lack of the ability to enjoy sex **2** the lack of any friendly or kind feelings: *the film's emotional frigidity*

**frill** /frɪl/ *noun* **1** a narrow piece of cloth with a lot of folds that is attached to the edge of a dress, curtain, etc. to

decorate it: *a white blouse with frills at the cuffs* **SYN** ruffle **2** [*usually pl.*] things that are not necessary but are added to make sth more attractive or interesting: *a simple meal with no frills* ⇒ see also NO-FRILLS

**frilled** /frɪld/ *adj.* (*BrE*) decorated with frills **SYN** ruffled
**frilly** /ˈfrɪli/ *adj.* having a lot of frills: *a frilly blouse*
**fringe** /frɪndʒ/ *noun, verb*
■ *noun* **1** [C, *usually sing.*] (*BrE*) *NAmE* **bangs** [*pl.*]) the front part of sb's hair that is cut so that it hangs over their FOREHEAD **2** [C] a narrow border of hanging THREADS attached to the edge of sth to decorate it **3** [C] a narrow area of trees, buildings, etc. along the edge of sth: *a fringe of woodland* ◇ *Along the coast, an industrial fringe had already developed.* **4** [C] the outer edge of an area or a group: *on the northern fringe of the city* ◇ *the urban/rural fringe* ◇ *the fringes of society* ◇ *Nina remained on the fringe of the crowd.* **5** [*sing.*] (*usually* **the fringe**) groups of people, events and activities that are not part of the main group or activity: *Street musicians have been gathering as part of the festival fringe.* ◇ *fringe meetings at the party conference* **IDM** see LUNATIC *adj.*
■ *verb* [*usually passive*] to form a border around sth: **be fringed by sth** *The beach was fringed by coconut palms.* ▶ **fringed** *adj.*: *a carpet with a fringed edge*

**ˈfringe benefit** *noun* [*usually pl.*] something that an employer gives you as well as your wages: *The fringe benefits include free health insurance.*

**ˈfringe ˈtheatre** *noun* [U, C] (*BrE*) plays, often by new writers, that are unusual and question the way people think; a theatre where such plays are performed ⇒ compare OFF-BROADWAY

**frip·pery** /ˈfrɪpəri/ *noun* [C, *usually pl.*, U] (*pl.* **-ies**) (*especially BrE, disapproving*) objects, decorations and other items that are considered unnecessary and expensive

**Fris·bee**™ /ˈfrɪzbi/ *noun* a light plastic object, like a plate in shape, that is thrown from one player to another in a game

**fri·sée** /ˈfriːzeɪ; *NAmE* friːˈzeɪ/ *noun* (*NAmE*) = CHICORY (2)
**frisk** /frɪsk/ *verb* **1** [T] **~ sb** to pass your hands over sb's body to search them for hidden weapons, drugs, etc. **2** [I] **~ (around)** (of animals) to run and jump in a lively and happy way **SYN** gambol, skip: *Lambs frisked in the fields.*

**frisky** /ˈfrɪski/ *adj.* (**frisk·ier**, **friski·est**) **1** (of people or animals) full of energy; wanting to play: *a frisky puppy* **2** (*informal*) wanting to enjoy yourself in a sexual way

**fris·son** /ˈfriːsɒ̃; *NAmE* friːˈsɔːn/ *noun* [*usually sing.*] (*from French*) a sudden strong feeling, especially of excitement or fear

**fri·til·lary** /frɪˈtɪləri; *NAmE* ˈfrɪtəleri/ *noun* (*pl.* **-ies**) **1** a plant with flowers that have the shape of bells **2** a BUTTERFLY with orange-brown and black wings

**frit·ter** /ˈfrɪtə(r)/ *verb, noun*
■ *verb*
**PHRV** **fritter sth↔aˈway (on sth)** to waste time or money on things that are not important: *He frittered away the millions his father had left him.*
■ *noun* (*usually in compounds*) a piece of fruit, meat or vegetable that is covered with BATTER and fried

**fritz** /frɪts/ *noun*
**IDM** **on the ˈfritz** (*NAmE, informal*) not working: *The TV is on the fritz again.*

**fri·vol·ity** /frɪˈvɒləti; *NAmE* -ˈvɑː-/ *noun* (*pl.* **-ies**) (*often disapproving*) [U, C] behaviour that is silly or funny, especially when this is not suitable: *It was just a piece of harmless frivolity.* ◇ *I can't waste time on such frivolities.*

**frivo·lous** /ˈfrɪvələs/ *adj.* (*disapproving*) **1** (of people or their behaviour) silly or funny, especially when such behaviour is not suitable: *frivolous comments/suggestions* ◇ *Sorry, I was being frivolous.* **2** having no useful or serious purpose: *frivolous pastimes/pleasures* ▶ **frivo·lous·ly** *adv.*

**frizz** /frɪz/ *verb, noun*
■ *verb* [I, T] **~ (sth)** (*informal*) (of hair) to become very curly with lots of small tight CURLS; to make hair become like this ▶ **frizzy** *adj.* (**friz·zi·er**, **friz·zi·est**): *frizzy hair*

---

b **b**ad | d **d**id | f **f**all | g **g**et | h **h**at | j **y**es | k **c**at | l **l**eg | m **m**an | n **n**ow | p **p**en | r **r**ed

■ **noun** [U] (*disapproving*) hair that is very curly with lots of small tight CURLS

**friz·zled** /ˈfrɪzld/ *adj.* **1** (of food) fried until it CURLS at the edges or burns: *frizzled bacon* **2** (of hair) formed into tight CURLS

**fro** /frəʊ/ *adv.* IDM▶ see TO *adv.*

**frock** /frɒk; *NAmE* frɑːk/ *noun* (*old-fashioned, especially BrE*) a dress: *a party frock*

**ˈfrock coat** *noun* a long coat worn in the past by men, now worn only for special ceremonies

**frog** 🌐 A2 /frɒg; *NAmE* frɑːg/ *noun* **1** 🌐 A2 a small animal with smooth skin, that lives both on land and in water (= is an AMPHIBIAN). Frogs have very long back legs for jumping, and no tail: *the croaking of frogs* ⇒ see also TADPOLE ⇒ VISUAL VOCAB page V3 **2** **Frog** (*taboo, slang*) an offensive word for a French person
IDM▶ **have, etc. a ˈfrog in your throat** to lose your voice or be unable to speak clearly for a short time

**frog·man** /ˈfrɒgmən; *NAmE* ˈfrɑːg-/ *noun* (*pl.* **-men** /-mən/) a person who works UNDERWATER, wearing a rubber suit, FLIPPERS, and special equipment to help them breathe: *Police frogmen searched the lake for the murder weapon.* ⇒ compare DIVER

**frog·march** /ˈfrɒgmɑːtʃ; *NAmE* ˈfrɑːgmɑːrtʃ/ *verb* ~ **sb + adv./prep.** (*BrE*) to force sb to walk forward by holding their arms tightly from behind so they have to walk along with you: *He was grabbed by two men and frogmarched out of the hall.*

**frog·spawn** /ˈfrɒgspɔːn; *NAmE* ˈfrɑːg-/ *noun* [U] an almost clear substance that looks like JELLY and contains the eggs of a frog ⇒ VISUAL VOCAB page V3

**fro·ing** /ˈfrəʊɪŋ/ *noun* IDM▶ see TOING

**frolic** /ˈfrɒlɪk; *NAmE* ˈfrɑːl-/ *verb, noun*
■ *verb* [I] (**-ck-**) to play and move around in a lively, happy way: *children frolicking on the beach*
■ *noun* [C, U] (*old-fashioned*) a lively and fun activity during which people forget their problems and responsibilities: *It was just a harmless frolic.*

**from** 🌐 A1 /frəm; *BrE strong form* frɒm; *NAmE strong form* frɑːm/ *prep.* HELP▶ For the special uses of **from** in phrasal verbs, look at the entries for the verbs. For example **keep sth from sb** is in the phrasal verb section at **keep**. **1** 🌐 A1 used to show where sb/sth starts: *She began to walk away from him.* ◊ *Has the train from Bristol arrived?* **2** 🌐 A1 used to show what the origin of sb/sth is: *I'm from Italy.* ◊ *documents from the sixteenth century* ◊ *quotations from Shakespeare* ◊ *heat from the sun* **3** 🌐 A1 used to show who sent or gave sth/sb: *a letter from my brother* ◊ *information from witnesses* ◊ *the man from* (= representing) *the insurance company* **4** 🌐 A1 used to show when sth starts: *We're open from 8 a.m. to 7 p.m. every day.* ◊ *He was blind from birth.* **5** 🌐 A1 used to show how far apart two places are: *100 metres from the scene of the accident* **6** 🌐 A1 used to show sb's position or point of view: *You can see the island from here.* ◊ *From a financial point of view the project was a disaster.* **7** 🌐 A1 **~ sth (to sth)** used to show the range of sth: *The temperature varies from 30 degrees to minus 20.* ◊ *The store sells everything from shoelaces to computers.* ◊ *Conditions vary from school to school.* **8** 🌐 A1 **~ sth (to sth)** used to show the state or form of sth/sb before a change: *Things have gone from bad to worse.* ◊ *translating from English to Spanish* ◊ *You need a break from routine.* **9** 🌐 A1 used when making or recognizing a difference between two people or things: *Is Portuguese very different from Spanish?* ◊ *I can't tell one twin from the other.* **10** 🌐 A2 used to show the material that sth is made of: *Steel is made from iron.* **11** 🌐 A2 used to show that sb/sth is separated or removed: *The party was ousted from power after eighteen years.* **12** 🌐 A2 used to show that sth is prevented: *She saved him from drowning.* **13** 🌐 A2 used to show the reason for sth: *She felt sick from tiredness.* **14** 🌐 A2 used to show the reason for making a judgement: *You can tell a lot about a person from their handwriting.* ◊ *From what I heard the company's in deep trouble.*

637

IDM▶ **from ... ˈon** starting at the time mentioned and continuously after that: *From now on you can work on your own.* ◊ *She never spoke to him again from that day on.*

**frond** /frɒnd; *NAmE* frɑːnd/ *noun* **1** a long leaf of some plants or trees, especially PALMS or FERNS. Fronds are often divided into parts along the edge. **2** a long piece of SEAWEED that looks like one of these leaves

# front

**front** 🌐 A1 /frʌnt/ *noun, adj., verb*
■ **noun**
• FORWARD PART/POSITION **1** 🌐 A1 [C, usually sing.] (*usually* **the front**) the part or side of sth that faces forward; the side of sth that you look at first: *The front of the building was covered with ivy.* ◊ **on the ~** *The book has a picture of Rome on the front.* ◊ **up/down the ~** *The jacket zips up the front.* ⇒ see also SHOPFRONT, Y-FRONTS™ **2** 🌐 A1 **the front** [sing.] the position that is directly ahead of sb/sth: *I turned round to face the front.* ◊ **at the ~ of sth** *There's a garden at the front of the house.* **3** 🌐 A1 **the front** [sing.] the part of sth that is furthest forward: *The singer came to the front of the stage.* ◊ **at the ~ (of sth)** *She always sits at the front.* ◊ **in the ~** *I prefer to travel in the front* (= next to the driver in a car). ◊ **in the ~ of sth** *Write your name in the front of the book* (= the first few pages).
• CHEST **4** 🌐 B1 **sb's front** [sing.] the part of sb's body that faces forwards: **on your ~** *She was lying on her front.* ◊ **down your ~** *I spilled coffee down my front.*
• SIDE OF BUILDING **5** [C] **the west, north, south, east, etc. ~** the side of a large building, especially a church, that faces west, north, etc.: *the west front of the cathedral*
• EDGE OF SEA/LAKE **6** **the front** [sing.] (*BrE*) the road or area of land along the edge of the sea, a lake or a river: *Couples walked hand in hand along the front.* ⇒ see also SEAFRONT
• IN WAR **7** [C, usually sing.] an area where fighting takes place during a war: *More British troops have been sent to the front.* ◊ *to serve at the front* ◊ *fighting a war on two fronts* ⇒ see also FRONT LINE, HOME FRONT
• AREA OF ACTIVITY **8** [C] a particular area of activity: **on the ... ~** *Things are looking unsettled on the economic front.* ◊ *Progress has been made on all fronts.*
• HIDING TRUE FEELINGS **9** [sing.] behaviour that is not what it appears to be, done in order to hide sb's true feelings or opinions: *It's not always easy to put on a brave front for the family.* ◊ **~ for sth** *Rudeness is just a front for her shyness.*
• HIDING STH ILLEGAL **10** [C, usually sing.] **~ (for sth)** a person or an organization that is used to hide an illegal or secret activity: *The travel company is just a front for drug trafficking.*
• POLITICAL ORGANIZATION **11 Front** [sing.] used in the names of some political organizations: *the Animal Liberation Front* ⇒ see also POPULAR FRONT
• WEATHER **12** [C] the line where a mass of cold air meets a mass of warm air: *a cold/warm front*
IDM▶ **ˌfront and ˈcentre** (*US* **ˌfront and ˈcenter**) in or into the most important position **in ˈfront** *adv.* **1** in a position that is further forward than sb/sth but not very far away: *Their house is the one with the big garden in front.* **2** in first place in a race or competition: *The blue team is currently in front with a lead of six points.* **in ˈfront of** *prep.* **1** 🌐 A1 in a position that is further forward than sb/sth but not very far away: *The car in front of me stopped suddenly and I had to brake.* ◊ *The bus stops right in front of our house.* ◊ *He was standing in front of me in the line.* **2** 🌐 A1 in a position facing sb/sth: *to perform in front of a big crowd/audience* ◊ *She spends all day sitting in front of* (= working at) *her computer.* ◊ *She's a natural in front of the camera* (= being filmed/photographed). **3** if you do sth **in front of sb**, you do it when they are there: *Please don't talk about it in front of the children.* **4 in front of sb** (of time) still to come; not yet passed: *Don't give up. You still have your whole life in front of you.* **out ˈfront 1** in the part of a theatre, restaurant, etc. where the public sits: *There's only a small audience out front tonight.* **2** (*also BrE, informal* **out the ˈfront**) in the area near to the entrance to a building: *I'll wait for you out (the) front.* **ˌup ˈfront** (*informal*) **1** as payment in advance: *We'll pay you half up front and the other half when you've finished the job.* **2** (in sports) in a

# frontage

forward position: *to play up* **front** ◊ see also UPFRONT ◊ more at BACK *n.*, CASH *n.*, EYE *n.*, LEAD¹ *v.*, UNITED
- **adj.** [only before noun] **1** on or at the front of sth: (*BrE*) *the front garden* ◊ (*NAmE*) *the front yard* ◊ *the front wheels of the car* ◊ *the front cover of the book* ◊ *We had seats in the front row.* ◊ *an animal's front legs* ◊ *front teeth* ◊ *a front-seat passenger* ◊ compare BACK, HIND **2** (*phonetics*) (of a vowel) produced with the front of the tongue in a higher position than the back, for example /iː/ in English ◊ compare BACK, CENTRAL
- **IDM** on the 'front burner (*informal, especially NAmE*) (of an issue, a plan, etc.) being given a lot of attention because it is considered important: *Anything that keeps education on the front burner is good.* ◊ compare ON THE BACK BURNER
- **verb**
  - FACE STH **1** [T, I] to face sth or be in front of sth; to have the front pointing towards sth: *~ sth The cathedral fronts the city's main square.* ◊ *~ onto sth The line of houses fronted straight onto the road.*
  - -FRONTED **2** -fronted having the front made of or covered with sth: *a glass-fronted bookcase*
  - LEAD GROUP **3** [T] *~ sth* to lead or represent an organization, a group, etc: *He fronts a multinational company.* ◊ *A former art student fronted the band* (= was the main singer).
  - PRESENT TV PROGRAMME **4** [T] *~ sth* (*especially BrE*) to present a television programme, a show, etc.
  - GRAMMAR **5** [T] *~ sth* (*linguistics*) to give more importance to a part of a sentence by placing it at or near the beginning of the sentence, as in 'That I would like to see.'
- **PHRV** 'front for sb/sth to represent a group or an organization and try to hide its secret or illegal activities: *He fronted for them in several illegal property deals.* ,front 'up (*AustralE, NZE*) (of a person) to arrive or appear in a place SYN turn up

▼ **WHICH WORD?**

**in front of / in the front of**
- **In front of** can mean the same as **outside**, but not **opposite**: *I'll meet you in front of/outside your hotel.* ◊ *There's a bus stop in front of the house* (= on the same side of the road). ◊ *There's a bus stop opposite the house* (= on the other side of the road).
- **In/at the front (of sth)** means 'in the most forward part of something': *The driver sits at the front of the bus.* ◊ *Put the shortest flowers in the front (of the bunch).*

**front·age** /ˈfrʌntɪdʒ/ *noun* **1** [C, U] the front of a building, especially when this faces a road or river: *the baroque frontage of Milan Cathedral* **2** [U] land that is next to a building, a street or an area of water: *They bought two miles of river frontage along the Colorado.*

**frontage road** *noun* (*NAmE*) = SERVICE ROAD

**front·al** /ˈfrʌntl/ *adj.* [only before noun] **1** connected with the front of sth: *Airbags protect the driver in the event of a severe frontal impact.* **2** (*also* full-'frontal) a **frontal** attack is very strong and direct: *They launched a frontal attack on company directors.* **3** connected with a weather FRONT: *a cold frontal system* **4** (*medical*) connected with the front part of the head: *the frontal lobes of the brain* ▶ **front·al·ly** /-təli/ *adv.*

**frontal 'lobe** *noun* (*anatomy*) either of the two parts at the front of the brain that are connected with behaviour, learning and personality

**the ,front 'bench** *noun* [C + sing./pl. v.] the most important members of the government and the opposition in the British parliament, who sit in the front rows of seats: *an Opposition front-bench spokesman on defence* ◊ compare BACK BENCH

**front·bench·er** /ˌfrʌntˈbentʃə(r)/ *noun* an important member of the government or the opposition in the British parliament, who sits in the front rows of seats ◊ compare BACKBENCHER

**'front desk** *noun usually* **the front desk** the desk inside the entrance of a hotel, an office building, etc. where guests or visitors go when they first arrive ◊ compare RECEPTION

**,front 'door** *noun* the main entrance to a house, usually at the front: *There's someone at the front door.* ◊ picture at POSTBOX

**,front 'end** *noun* **1** the part of a car or other vehicle that faces forward: *I could hear a crunching noise coming from the front end of the car.* **OPP** rear end **2** (*computing*) the part of a computer system that the user sees and uses directly: *One of our designers created the graphics for the front end of the website.* ◊ compare BACK END (3) **3** the first part of a process, period of time, etc: *We need to focus on the front end of the process.* ◊ *I'm spending two nights in Kyoto at the front end of the trip.* **OPP** back end

**'front-end** *adj.* [only before noun] **1** (*computing*) (of a device or program) directly used by a user, and allowing the user to use other devices or programs ◊ compare BACK-END (2) **2** relating to the part of a vehicle that faces forward: *The vehicle sustained significant front-end damage.*

**,front-,end 'loader** *noun* (*especially NAmE*) a large vehicle with equipment for digging at the front, worked by a system of HYDRAULICS

**fron·tier** /ˈfrʌntɪə(r); *NAmE* frʌnˈtɪr/ *noun* **1** [C] a line that separates two countries, etc.; the land near this line: *~ (between A and B) the frontier between the land of the Saxons and that of the Danes* ◊ *~ (with sth) a customs post on the frontier with Italy* ◊ *a frontier town/zone/post* ◊ SYNONYMS at BORDER **2** the frontier [sing.] the edge of land where people have settled and built towns, beyond which the country is wild and unknown, especially in the western US in the 19th century: *a remote frontier settlement* **3** [C, usually pl.] *~ (of sth)* the limit of sth, especially the limit of what is known about a particular subject or activity: *to push back the frontiers of science* (= to increase knowledge of science) ◊ *to roll back the frontiers of government* (= to limit the powers of the government)

**fron·tiers·man** /ˈfrʌntɪəzmən; *NAmE* frʌnˈtɪrzmən/ *noun* (*pl.* -men /-mən/) a man living on the frontier especially one who lived in the western US during the 19th century

**fron·tis·piece** /ˈfrʌntɪspiːs/ *noun* [usually sing.] a picture at the beginning of a book, on the page opposite the page with the title on it

**the ,front 'line** *noun* [sing.] **1** an area where the enemies are facing each other during a war and where fighting takes place: *in/on ~ The regiment was sent to fight in the front line.* ◊ *front-line troops* **2** the most important position in a debate or an area of work: *in/on ~ (of sth) a life spent in the front line of research*

**front-'load** *verb* **1** *~ sth* (*business*) to spread the costs of a project so that more of the money is spent in the earlier stages: *a need to front-load budget spending* ◊ *the positive effects of front-loading funds* **2** *~ sth* to organize work on a project or information in a document so that the more important work or information is done or placed first: *Teach your students to front-load their research.*

**front·man** /ˈfrʌntmæn/ *noun* (*pl.* -men /-men/) **1** a person who represents an organization and tries to make its activities seem acceptable to the public, although in fact they may be illegal or dishonest: *He acted as a frontman for a drugs cartel.* **2** a man who is the main singer in a pop or rock band **3** (*BrE*) a person who presents a television programme

**,front 'office** *noun* [sing.] (*especially NAmE*) the people in a business who deal with the public

**,front of 'house** *noun, adv.*
- **noun** [U] (*BrE*) **1** the parts of a theatre that are used by the audience **2** (often used as an adjective) the business of dealing with an audience at a theatre, for example selling tickets and programmes
- **adv.** (*BrE*) in the parts of a theatre that are used by the audience: *There was an expectant atmosphere front of house.*

**,front 'page** *noun* the first page of a newspaper, where the most important news is printed: *The story was on the front pages of all the tabloids.* ▶ **front-page** *adj.* [only before noun]: *The divorce made front-page news.*

**front runner** *noun* a person, an animal or an organization that seems most likely to win a race or competition

**front-running** *adj.* [only before noun] (of a person, an animal or an organization) that seems most likely to win a race or competition: *Wilson was the front-running candidate in the run-up to the elections.*

**front-wheel drive** *noun* [U] a system in which power from the engine is sent to the front wheels of a vehicle ⊃ compare REAR-WHEEL DRIVE

**front·woman** /ˈfrʌntwʊmən/ *noun* (*pl.* **-women** /-wɪmɪn/) a woman who is the main singer in a pop or rock band

**frost** /frɒst; NAmE frɔːst/ *noun, verb*
- *noun* **1** [U, C] a weather condition in which the temperature drops below 0° Celsius (= FREEZING POINT) so that a thin white layer of ice forms on the ground and other surfaces, especially at night: *It will be a clear night with some ground frost.* ◊ *a sharp/hard/severe frost* ◊ *There were ten degrees of frost* (= the temperature dropped to -10° Celsius) *last night.* ◊ *frost damage* **2** [U] the thin white layer of ice that forms when the temperature drops below 0° Celsius: *The car windows were covered with frost.* ⊃ see also HOAR FROST
- *verb* **1** [T, I] to cover sth or to become covered with a thin white layer of ice: ~ *sth* (**over/up**) *The mirror was frosted up.* ◊ ~ (**over/up**) *The windows had frosted over.* **2** [T] ~ *sth* (*especially NAmE*) to cover a cake with FROSTING

**frost·bite** /ˈfrɒstbaɪt; NAmE ˈfrɔːst-/ *noun* [U] a medical condition in which parts of the body, especially the fingers and toes, become damaged as a result of extremely cold temperatures ▸ **frost·bit·ten** /-bɪtn/ *adj.*

**frost·ed** /ˈfrɒstɪd; NAmE ˈfrɔːs-/ *adj.* **1** [only before noun] (of glass) that has been given a rough surface, so that it is difficult to see through **2** (*especially NAmE*) (of cakes, etc.) covered with FROSTING **3** covered with FROST: *the frosted garden* **4** containing very small shiny pieces: *frosted eyeshadow*

**frost·ing** /ˈfrɒstɪŋ; NAmE ˈfrɔːs-/ *noun* [U] **1** (*NAmE*) = ICING **2** (*BrE*) the crime of stealing a vehicle that has been left with the engine running in cold weather so that the engine warms up **IDM** see ICING

**frosty** /ˈfrɒsti; NAmE ˈfrɔːs-/ *adj.* (**frost·ier, frosti·est**) **1** (of the weather) extremely cold; cold with FROST: *a frosty morning* ◊ *He breathed in the frosty air.* **2** covered with FROST: *frosty fields* **3** unfriendly, in a way that suggests that sb does not approve of sth: *a frosty look/reply* ◊ *The latest proposals were given a frosty reception.* ▸ **frost·ily** /-stɪli/ *adv.*: *'No, thank you,' she said frostily.*

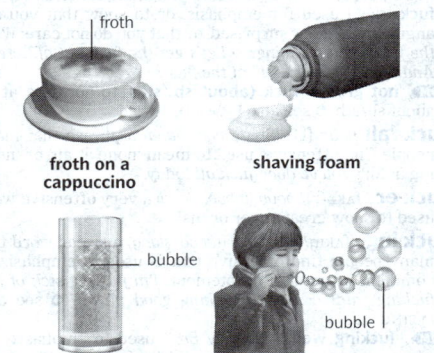

froth on a cappuccino
shaving foam
bubble
bubble
bubbles in a drink
blowing bubbles

**froth** /frɒθ; NAmE frɔːθ/ *noun, verb*
- *noun* **1** [U] a mass of small bubbles, especially on the surface of a liquid **SYN** foam: *a glass of beer with thick froth on top* **2** [U] ideas, activities, etc. that seem attractive and fun but have no real value **3** [sing.] ~ **of sth** something that looks like a mass of small bubbles on liquid: *a froth of black lace*
- *verb* **1** [I, T] ~ (**sth**) if a liquid froths, or if sb/sth froths it, a mass of small bubbles appears on the surface: *a cup of frothing coffee* **2** [I] to produce a lot of SALIVA (= liquid in your mouth): *The dog was frothing at the mouth.* ◊ (*figurative*) *He frothed at the mouth* (= was very angry) *when I asked for more money.*

**frothy** /ˈfrɒθi; NAmE ˈfrɔːθi/ *adj.* (**froth·ier, frothi·est**) **1** (of liquids) having a mass of small bubbles on the surface: *frothy coffee* **2** seeming attractive and fun but having no real value: *frothy romantic novels* **3** (of clothes or cloth) light and attractive

**frown** /fraʊn/ *verb, noun*
- *verb* [I, T] to make a serious, angry or worried expression by bringing your EYEBROWS closer together so that lines appear on your FOREHEAD: ~ (**at sb/sth**) *What are you frowning at me for?* ◊ + *speech* '*I don't understand*,' *she frowned.* ⊃ WORDFINDER NOTE at EXPRESSION
**PHRV** ˈ**frown on/upon sb/sth** to think sb/sth is bad: *In her family, any expression of feeling was frowned upon.*
- *noun* [usually sing.] a serious, angry or worried expression on a person's face that causes lines on their FOREHEAD: *She looked up with a puzzled frown on her face.* ◊ *a slight frown of disapproval/concentration, etc.*

**froze** /frəʊz/ *past tense* of FREEZE

**fro·zen** ❶ **B1** /ˈfrəʊzn/ *adj., verb*
- *adj.* **1** **B1** [usually before noun] (of food) kept at a very low temperature in order to preserve it: *frozen peas/fish/pizza* **2** **B1** [not usually before noun] (of people or parts of the body) extremely cold: *I'm absolutely frozen!* ◊ *My hands are frozen.* **3** **B1** (of rivers, lakes, etc.) with a layer of ice on the surface **4** **B1** (especially of ground) covered with ice; so cold that it has become very hard: *The ground was frozen solid.* **5** ~ **with/in sth** unable to move because of a strong emotion such as fear or horror: *She stared at him, frozen with shock.*
- *verb past part.* of FREEZE

**FRS** /ˌef ɑː ˈes/ *abbr.* **1** (*NAmE*) FEDERAL RESERVE SYSTEM **2** (*BrE*) Fellow of the Royal Society (a title given to important British scientists)

**fruc·tose** /ˈfrʌktəʊs, -təʊz/ *noun* [U] (*chemistry*) a type of sugar found in fruit juice and HONEY

**fru·gal** /ˈfruːɡl/ *adj.* **1** using only as much money or food as is necessary: *a frugal existence/life* **OPP** extravagant **2** (of meals) small, plain and not costing very much **SYN** meagre: *a frugal lunch of bread and cheese* ▸ **fru·gal·ity** /fruːˈɡæləti/ *noun* [U] **fru·gal·ly** /ˈfruːɡəli/ *adv.*: *to live/eat frugally*

**fruit** ❶ **A1** /fruːt/ *noun, verb*
- *noun* **1** **A1** [C, U] the part of a plant that consists of one or more seeds and a soft inner part, can be eaten as food and usually tastes sweet: *tropical fruits, such as bananas and pineapples* ◊ *Eat plenty of fresh fruit and vegetables.* ◊ *a piece of fruit* (= an apple, an orange, etc.) ◊ *fruit juice* ◊ *fruit trees* ⊃ compare VEGETABLE ⊃ see also DRIED FRUIT, FIRST FRUIT, KIWI FRUIT, LOW-HANGING FRUIT, PASSION FRUIT, SOFT FRUIT ⊃ VISUAL VOCAB page V4 **2** [C] (*specialist*) a part of a plant or tree that is formed after the flowers have died and in which seeds develop **3** [C, usually pl.] (*literary*) all the natural things that the earth produces
**IDM** **the fruit/fruits of sth** the good results of an activity or a situation: *to enjoy the fruits of your labours* (= the rewards for your hard work) ◊ *The book is the fruit of years of research.* ⊃ more at BEAR *v.*, FORBIDDEN
- *verb* [I] (*specialist*) (of a tree or plant) to produce fruit

ˈ**fruit bat** *noun* a BAT (= an animal like a mouse with wings) that lives in hot countries and eats fruit

ˈ**fruit cake** *noun* **1** [C, U] a cake containing dried fruit **2 fruitcake** [C] (*informal*) a person who behaves in a strange or crazy way: *She's nutty as a fruitcake.*

ˈ**fruit ˈcocktail** *noun* [U] a mixture of pieces of fruit in liquid, sold in tins

ˈ**fruit cup** *noun* [U, C] **1** (*BrE*) a drink consisting of fruit juices and pieces of fruit **2** (*NAmE*) = FRUIT SALAD

ˈ**fruit fly** *noun* a small fly that eats plants that are DECAYING, especially fruit

# fruitful

**fruit·ful** /ˈfruːtfl/ adj. **1** producing many useful results SYN **productive**: *a fruitful collaboration/discussion* OPP **fruitless 2** (*literary*) (of land or trees) producing a lot of crops ▶ **fruit·ful·ly** /-fəli/ adv. **fruit·ful·ness** noun [U]

**fruiti·ness** /ˈfruːtinəs/ noun [U] (*especially of wine*) the quality of tasting or smelling strongly of fruit

**fru·ition** /fruˈɪʃn/ noun [U] (*formal*) the successful result of a plan, a process or an activity: *After months of hard work, our plans finally came to fruition.* ◊ *His extravagant ideas were never brought to fruition.*

**fruit·less** /ˈfruːtləs/ adj. producing no useful results SYN **unproductive**: *a fruitless attempt/search* ◊ *Our efforts to persuade her proved fruitless.* OPP **fruitful** ▶ **fruit·less·ly** adv.

ˈ**fruit machine** (*BrE*) (*also* ˌone-armed ˈbandit, ˈslot machine *NAmE, BrE*) noun a GAMBLING machine that you put coins into and that gives money back if particular pictures appear together on the screen; a similar game, played online

ˌfruit ˈsalad (*NAmE also* ˈfruit cup) noun [U, C] a cold DESSERT (= a sweet dish) consisting of small pieces of different types of fruit

**fruity** /ˈfruːti/ adj. (**fruit·ier**, **fruiti·est**) **1** smelling or tasting strongly of fruit: *The wine from this region is rich and fruity.* **2** (of a voice or laugh) deep and pleasant in quality **3** (*NAmE, informal*) (of people) slightly crazy

**frump** /frʌmp/ noun (*disapproving*) a woman who wears clothes that are not fashionable ▶ **frumpy** (*also less frequent* **frump·ish**) adj.: *frumpy clothes* ◊ *a frumpy housewife*

**frus·trate** /frʌˈstreɪt; *NAmE* ˈfrʌstreɪt/ verb **1** ~ **sb** to make sb feel annoyed or impatient because they cannot do or achieve what they want: *What frustrates him is that there's too little money to spend on the project.* **2** ~ **sb/sth** to prevent sb from doing sth; to prevent sth from happening or succeeding SYN **thwart**: *The rescue attempt was frustrated by bad weather.*

**frus·trated** /-/ /frʌˈstreɪtɪd/ adj. **1** feeling annoyed and impatient because you cannot do or achieve what you want: *It's very easy to get frustrated in this job.* ◊ ~ **at/with sth** *They felt frustrated at the lack of progress.* **2** (of an emotion) having no effect; not being satisfied: *He stamped his foot in frustrated rage.* ◊ *frustrated desires* **3** [only before noun] unable to be successful in a particular career: *a frustrated artist* **4** not satisfied sexually

**frus·trat·ing** /-/ /frʌˈstreɪtɪŋ; *NAmE* ˈfrʌstreɪtɪŋ/ adj. causing you to feel annoyed and impatient because you cannot do or achieve what you want: *It's frustrating to have to wait so long.* ▶ **frus·trat·ing·ly** adv.: *Progress was frustratingly slow.*

**frus·tra·tion** /-/ /frʌˈstreɪʃn/ noun **1** /-/ [U] the feeling of being frustrated: **in** ~ *Dave thumped the table in frustration.* ◊ ~ **of (doing) sth** *She couldn't stand the frustration of not being able to help.* ◊ *sexual frustration* **2** /-/ [C, usually pl.] something that causes you to feel frustrated: *Every job has its difficulties and frustrations.* ◊ *She took out her frustrations on the children.* **3** ~ **of sth** (*formal*) the fact that sth is preventing sth/sb from succeeding: *the frustration of all his ambitions*

**fry** /fraɪ/ verb, noun
■ verb (**fries**, **fry·ing**, **fried**, **fried**) **1** [T, I] to cook sth in hot fat or oil; to be cooked in hot fat or oil: ~ (**sth**) *fried fish* ◊ *the smell of bacon frying* ◊ ~ **sth in sth** *Fry the onions gently in oil.* ⇨ related noun FRY-UP ⇨ see also DEEP-FRY, PAN-FRY, STIR-FRY verb **2** [I] (*informal*) to be burnt by the sun: *You'll fry on the beach if you're not careful.* IDM see FISH n.
■ noun **1** [pl.] very small young fish ⇨ see also SMALL FRY **2** [C] (*usually* **fries** [pl.]) (*especially NAmE*) = FRENCH FRY: *Would you like ketchup with your fries?*

**fryer** (*also* **frier**) /ˈfraɪə(r)/ noun **1** a large deep pan used for frying food in: *a deep-fat fryer* **2** (*NAmE*) a young chicken that is suitable for frying

ˈ**frying pan** (*NAmE also* ˈ**fry-pan** /ˈfraɪpæn/, **skil·let**) noun a large shallow pan with a long handle, used for frying food in
IDM **out of the** ˈ**frying pan into the** ˈ**fire** (*saying*) from a bad situation to one that is worse

**fry-up** noun (*BrE, informal*) a meal of fried food, such as BACON and eggs

**FT** (*also* **F/T**) abbr. (in writing) FULL-TIME: *The course is 1 year FT, 2 years PT.* ⇨ compare PT

**Ft** (*also* **Ft.** *especially in NAmE*) abbr. FORT: *Ft William*

**ft** (*also* **ft.** *NAmE, BrE*) abbr. (in writing measurements) feet; foot: *The room is 12ft × 9ft.*

**FTP** /ˌef tiː ˈpiː/ abbr. file transfer protocol (a set of rules for sending files from one computer to another on the internet) ⇨ see also ANONYMOUS FTP

**the FTSE index™** /ðə ˈfʊtsi ɪndeks/ (*also* **the FT index** /ðiː ˌef tiː ˈɪndeks/, **the Fiˌnancial Times ˈindex**, **the Foot·sie™**) noun [sing.] a figure that shows the relative prices of shares on the London Stock Exchange

**fuch·sia** /ˈfjuːʃə/ noun [C, U] a small bush with flowers in two colours of red, purple or white, that hang down

**fuck** /fʌk/ verb, noun
■ verb (*taboo, slang*) **1** [I, T] ~ (**sb**) to have sex with sb **2** [I, T] a swear word that many people find offensive that is used to express anger, horror or surprise: *Oh, fuck! I've lost my keys.* ◊ ~ **sb/sth** *Fuck you—I'm leaving.* ◊ *Fuck it! We've missed the train.*
IDM **fuck ˈme** used to express surprise
PHRV **fuck aˈround** (*BrE also* **fuck aˈbout**) to waste time by behaving in a silly way HELP A more polite, informal way of saying this is **mess about** (*BrE*) or **mess around** (*NAmE*, *BrE*). **fuck sb aˈround** (*BrE also* **fuck sb aˈbout**) to treat sb in a way that is deliberately not helpful to them or wastes their time HELP A more polite, informal way of saying this is **mess sb about/around** (*BrE*). **fuck ˈoff** (usually used in orders) to go away: *Why don't you just fuck off?* **fuck ˈup** to do sth badly or make a bad mistake: *You've really fucked up this time!* HELP A more polite way to express this is **mess up**. **fuck sb↔ˈup** to upset or confuse sb so much that they are not able to deal with problems in their life: *My parents' divorce really fucked me up.* HELP A more polite way to express this is **mess sb up**. **fuck sth↔ˈup** to do sth badly or cause sth to fail: *I completely fucked up my exams.* HELP A more polite, informal way of saying this is **mess sth up**. **ˈfuck with sb** to treat sb badly in a way that makes them annoyed: *Don't fuck with him.* HELP A more polite way to express this is **mess with sb**.
■ noun (*taboo, slang*) **1** [C, usually sing.] an act of sex **2** **the fuck** [sing.] used for emphasis, or to show that you are angry, annoyed or surprised, or that you do not care: *What the fuck are you doing?* ◊ *Let's get the fuck out of here!* ◊ *And then I thought—what the fuck?*
IDM **not give a ˈfuck (about sb/sth)** to not care at all about sb/sth ⇨ see also F-WORD

**fuck ˈall** noun [U] (*BrE, taboo, slang*) a phrase that many people find offensive, used to mean 'none at all' or 'nothing at all': *You've done fuck all today.*

**fuck·er** /ˈfʌkə(r)/ noun (*taboo, slang*) a very offensive word used to show great anger or dislike

**fuck·ing** /ˈfʌkɪŋ/ adj., adv. (*taboo, slang*) a swear word that many people find offensive that is used to emphasize a comment or an angry statement: *I'm fucking sick of this fucking rain!* ◊ *He's a fucking good player.* ⇨ see also EFFING

IDM ˈ**fucking well** (*especially BrE*) used to emphasize an angry statement or an order: *You're fucking well coming whether you want to or not.*

**fud·dled** /ˈfʌdld/ adj. unable to think clearly, usually as a result of being old or drinking alcohol

**fuddy-duddy** /ˈfʌdi dʌdi/ noun (pl. **fuddy-duddies**) (*old-fashioned, informal*) a person who has old-fashioned ideas or habits ▶ **fuddy-duddy** adj.

**fudge** /fʌdʒ/ noun, verb
■ noun **1** [U] a type of soft brown sweet made from sugar, butter and milk **2** [C, usually sing.] (*especially BrE, rather informal*) a way of dealing with a situation that does not

really solve the problems but is intended to appear to do so: *This solution is a fudge rushed in to win cheers at the party conference.*
- **verb** [T, I] (*rather informal*) to present or deal with sth in a way that avoids giving clear and accurate information: *~ sth Politicians are often very clever at fudging the issue.* ◊ *~ on sth They simply fudged on the details.*

**fuel** 🔑 **B1** /ˈfjuːəl/ *noun, verb*
- **noun 1** 🔑 **B1** [U, C] any material that produces heat or power, usually when it is burnt: *diesel/jet/rocket fuel* ◊ *solid fuel* (= wood, coal, etc.) ◊ *The car has a 65-litre fuel tank.* ◊ *a car with high fuel consumption* ◊ *steadily rising fuel prices* ⇒ see also ALTERNATIVE FUEL, FOSSIL FUEL, NUCLEAR FUEL ⇒ **WORDFINDER NOTE** at ENERGY **2** [U] a thing that is said or done that makes sth, especially an argument, continue or get worse: *The new information adds fuel to the debate over safety procedures.* ◊ *His remarks simply added fuel to the fire/flames of her rage.*
- **verb** (-ll-, *US* -l-) **1** 🔑 **B2** [T] ~ sth to supply sth with material that can be burnt to produce heat or power: *Uranium is used to fuel nuclear plants.* ◊ *oil-fuelled power stations* **2** [T, I] ~ **(sth) (up)** to put petrol into a vehicle: *The helicopter was already fuelled (up) and ready to go.* **3** 🔑 **B2** [T] ~ sth to increase sth; to make sth stronger **SYN** *stoke*: *Yesterday's meeting is likely to fuel further speculation about a takeover.* ◊ *Higher salaries helped to fuel inflation.*

ˈ**fuel cell** *noun* a device that produces electricity directly from a fuel, such as HYDROGEN, by its reaction with another chemical, such as OXYGEN, without any burning, in order to supply power to a vehicle or machine

ˈ**fuel injection** *noun* [U] a system of putting fuel into the engine of a car under pressure as a way of improving its performance

ˈ**fuel poverty** *noun* [U] (*especially BrE*) the state of not being able to afford to heat your home

ˈ**fuel rod** *noun* (*specialist*) a long thin part containing fuel used in a nuclear power station

**fufu** (*also* **foo-foo**) /ˈfuːfuː/ *WAfrE* [fùfú] *noun* (*WAfrE*) a smooth white food often eaten with soups or STEWS and made by boiling and pressing together the roots of plants such as COCOYAMS and CASSAVA

**fug** /fʌɡ/ *noun* [sing.] (*BrE, informal*) air in a room that is hot and smells unpleasant because there are too many people in the room or because people are smoking

**fugal** /ˈfjuːɡl/ *adj.* (*music*) similar to or related to a FUGUE

**fu·gi·tive** /ˈfjuːdʒətɪv/ *noun, adj.*
- **noun** ~ **(from sb/sth)** a person who has escaped or is running away from somewhere and is trying to avoid being caught: *a fugitive from justice*
- **adj.** [only before noun] **1** trying to avoid being caught: *a fugitive criminal* **2** (*literary*) lasting only for a very short time **SYN** *fleeting*: *a fugitive idea/thought*

**fugue** /fjuːɡ/ *noun* (*music*) a piece of music in which one or more tunes are introduced and then repeated in a complicated pattern

**-ful** *suffix* **1** /fl/ (in adjectives) full of; having the qualities of; tending to: *sorrowful* ◊ *masterful* ◊ *forgetful* **2** /fʊl/ (in nouns) an amount that fills sth: *handful* ◊ *spoonful*

**ful·crum** /ˈfʊlkrəm, ˈfʌl-/ *noun* (*pl.* **ful·crums** *or* **ful·cra** /-krə/) **1** (*physics*) the point on which a LEVER turns or is supported **2** [usually sing.] the most important part of an activity or a situation

**ful·fil** 🔑 **B2** (*BrE*) (*NAmE* **ful·fill**) /fʊlˈfɪl/ *verb* (**ful·fill·ing, ful·filled, ful·filled**) **1** 🔑 **B2** ~ sth to do or achieve what was hoped for or expected: *to fulfil your dream/ambition/potential* **2** 🔑 **B2** ~ sth (*formal*) to do or have what is required or necessary: *to fulfil a duty/an obligation/a promise* ◊ *to fulfil the terms/conditions of an agreement* ◊ *No candidate fulfils all the criteria for this position.* **3** 🔑 **B2** ~ sth to have a particular role or purpose: *Nursery schools should fulfil the function of preparing children for school.* **4** 🔑 **B2** ~ sb/yourself to make sb feel happy and satisfied with what they are doing or have done: *I need a job that really fulfils me.* ◊ *He was able to fulfil himself through his painting.* **5** ~ sth to pack and send sth that a customer has ordered:

We aim to fulfil all orders within seven days. ▶ **ful·fil·ment** (*BrE*) (*NAmE* **ful·fill·ment**) *noun* [U]: *the fulfilment of a dream* ◊ *to find personal fulfilment* ⇒ SYNONYMS at SATISFACTION

**ful·filled** /fʊlˈfɪld/ *adj.* feeling happy and satisfied that you are doing sth useful with your life: *He doesn't feel fulfilled in his present job.* **OPP** *unfulfilled*

**ful·fil·ling** /fʊlˈfɪlɪŋ/ *adj.* causing sb to feel satisfied and useful: *a fulfilling experience* **OPP** *unfulfilling* ⇒ see also SELF-FULFILLING ⇒ SYNONYMS at SATISFYING

**ful'filment centre** (*US* **fulˈfillment center**) *noun* (*especially NAmE*) a place where items are packed and then sent to the customers who ordered them

**full** 🔑 **A1** /fʊl/ *adj., adv.*
- **adj.** (**full·er, full·est**)
- WITH NO EMPTY SPACE **1** 🔑 **A1** containing or holding as much or as many as possible; having no empty space: *a full bottle of wine* ◊ *She could only nod, because her mouth was full.* ◊ *The theatre was less than half full.* ◊ *~ of sth My suitcase was full of books.* ◊ *There were cardboard boxes stuffed full of clothes.*
- HAVING A LOT **2** 🔑 **A2** ~ **of sth/sb** having or containing a large number or amount of sth/sb: *The sky was full of brightly coloured fireworks.* ◊ *The gallery was full of people.* ◊ *He's always full of energy.* ◊ *She was so bubbly and full of life.* ◊ *She was full of admiration for the care she had received.*
- WITH FOOD **3** 🔑 **B1** (*BrE also* **full up**) having had enough to eat: *No more for me, thanks—I'm full up.* ◊ *The kids still weren't full, so I gave them an ice cream each.* ◊ *You can't run on a full stomach.*
- COMPLETE **4** 🔑 **A2** [usually before noun] complete; with nothing missing: *Full details are available on request.* ◊ *They sell a full range of hair and beauty products.* ◊ *I still don't think we've heard the full story.* ◊ *a full English breakfast* ◊ *Fill in your full name and address.*
- AS MUCH AS POSSIBLE **5** 🔑 **B1** [usually before noun] to the highest level or greatest amount possible **SYN** *maximum*: *Many people don't use their computers to their full potential.* ◊ *measures to achieve full employment* ◊ *Students should take full advantage of the university's facilities.* ◊ *She came round the corner at full speed.*
- BUSY **6** 🔑 **B1** busy; involving a lot of activities: *He'd had a very full life.* ◊ *Her life was too full to find time for hobbies.*
- TALKING A LOT **7** ~ **of sth** (of a person) thinking or talking a lot about a particular thing: *He was full of his new job and everything he'd been doing.*
- FOR EMPHASIS **8** [only before noun] used to emphasize an amount or a quantity: *She is a full four inches shorter than her sister.*
- MOON **9** appearing as a complete circle: *The moon was full, the sky clear.* ⇒ see also FULL MOON
- FAT **10** (of a person or part of the body) large and round. 'Full' is sometimes used to avoid saying 'fat': *He kissed her full sensual lips.* ◊ *They specialize in clothes for women with a fuller figure.*
- CLOTHES **11** made with plenty of cloth; fitting loosely: *a full skirt*
- TONE/VOICE/FLAVOUR **12** deep, strong and rich: *He draws a unique full sound from the instrument.* ◊ *the full fruity flavour of the wine*
**IDM** **HELP** Most idioms containing **full** are at the entries for the nouns and verbs in the idioms, for example **full of the joys of spring** is at joy. ˈ**full of it** (*informal, disapproving*) (of a person) not telling the truth; tending to make things seem better, worse or more important than they actually are: *'You are so full of it!' she retorted furiously.* ˈ**full of yourself** (*disapproving*) very proud; thinking only of yourself **in full** including the whole of sth: *The address must be printed in full.* **to the full** (*NAmE usually* **to the fullest**) to the greatest possible degree: *I've always believed in living life to the full.*
- **adv.** ~ **in/on sth** directly: *She looked him full in the face.*

**full back** (*NAmE* **full·back**) *noun* **1** [C] one of the defending players in football (soccer), hockey or rugby whose position is near the goal they are defending. In soccer, they play on the left and right sides of the field. **2** [C] the attacking player in AMERICAN FOOTBALL whose position is behind the QUARTERBACK and next to the HALF BACKS **3** [U] the position a full back plays at: *Hunter is at full back.*

**full ˈbeam** *noun* [U] (*BrE*) the brightest light that a vehicle's HEADLIGHTS can give, usually used when there are no street lights and no other traffic: **on~** *Even with the lights on full beam I couldn't see very far.*

**full-ˈblooded** *adj.* [only before noun] **1** involving very strong feelings or actions; done in an enthusiastic way: *a full-blooded attack* **2** having parents, grandparents, etc. from only one race or country: *a full-blooded Scotsman*

**full-ˈblown** *adj.* [only before noun] having all the characteristics of sb/sth; fully developed: *full-blown AIDS ◊ The border dispute turned into a full-blown crisis.*

**full ˈboard** (*BrE*) (*NAmE* **Aˌmerican ˈplan**) *noun* [U] a type of accommodation in a hotel, etc. that includes all meals: *Do you require full or half board?* ➔ WORDFINDER NOTE at HOTEL ➔ compare BED AND BREAKFAST, HALF BOARD

**full-ˈbodied** *adj.* having a pleasantly strong taste or sound: *a full-bodied red wine ◊ a full-bodied string section*

**full-ˈcolour** (*US* **full-ˈcolor**) *adj.* [only before noun] using colours rather than just black and white

**full-court ˈpress** *noun* [sing.] (*NAmE*) **1** (in basketball) a way of attacking in which the members of a team stay close to their opponents over the whole area of play **2** (*informal*) a strong effort to influence sb or a group of people by putting pressure on them

**full-ˈcream** *adj.* (*BrE*) (of milk) with none of the fat taken away

**full ˈface** *adj., adv.* showing the whole of sb's face; not in PROFILE: *a full-face view/portrait*

**full-ˈfat** *adj.* [usually before noun] (*especially BrE*) (of milk, cheese, etc.) without any of the fat removed

**full-ˈfledged** (*especially NAmE*) (*BrE usually* **fully ˈfledged**) *adj.* completely developed; with all the qualifications necessary for sth

**full ˈforward** *noun* (in AUSTRALIAN RULES football) an attacking player who plays near the other team's goal

**full-ˈfrontal** *adj., noun*
■ *adj.* [only before noun] **1** showing the whole of the front of a person's body: *full-frontal nudity* **2** = FRONTAL (2)
■ *noun* a picture or a scene in a film that shows the NAKED body of a person from the front

**full-ˈgrown** *adj.* (of people, animals or plants) having reached the greatest size to which they can grow and stopped growing

**full ˈhouse** *noun* **1** an occasion in a theatre, cinema, etc. when there are no empty seats: *They played to a full house.* **2** (in the card game of POKER) three cards of one kind and two of another kind

**full ˈlength** *adv.* a person who is lying **full length** is lying flat with their legs straight: *He was sprawled full-length across the bed.*

**full-ˈlength** *adj.* [only before noun] **1** (of a mirror or picture) showing the whole of a person's body: *a full-length portrait* **2** (of a book, play, etc.) not made shorter; of the usual length: *a full-length novel* **3** (of curtains or a window) reaching the ground **4** (of clothing) reaching a person's ankles: *a full-length skirt*

**full ˈmarks** *noun* [pl.] (*BrE*) the highest mark in a test, etc. (when you get nothing wrong): *She got full marks in the exam. ◊* (*figurative*) *Full marks to Bill for an excellent idea!* (= he deserves praise)

**full ˈmoon** *noun* [C, usually sing., U] the moon when it appears as a full circle; a time when this happens ➔ compare HALF-MOON, HARVEST MOON, NEW MOON

**fullˈness** /ˈfʊlnəs/ *noun* [U, sing.] **1** (of the body or part of the body) the quality of being large and round: *the fullness of her lips* **2** (of colours, sounds and flavours) the quality of being deep and rich **3** the quality of being complete and giving pleasure: *the fullness of life*

**IDM** **in the ˌfullness of ˈtime** when the time is appropriate, usually after a long period

**full-ˈon** *adj.* (*informal*) used to say that sth is done to the greatest possible degree: *It was a full-on night out with the boys.*

**full-ˈpage** *adj.* [only before noun] filling a complete page of a newspaper or magazine: *a full-page ad*

**full ˈpoint** *noun* = FULL STOP

**full proˈfessor** *noun* (*NAmE*) = PROFESSOR (1)

**full-ˈscale** *adj.* [only before noun] **1** that is as complete and careful as possible: *a full-scale attack* **2** that is the same size as sth that is being copied: *a full-scale model*

**full-ˈsize** (*also* **full-ˈsized**) *adj.* [usually before noun] not made smaller; of the usual size: *a full-size model ◊ a full-size snooker table*

**full ˈstop** *noun, adv.*
■ *noun* (*also less frequent* **stop**) (*also* **full ˈpoint**) (*all BrE*) (*NAmE* **period**) the mark (.) used at the end of a sentence and in some abbreviations, for example *e.g.*
**IDM** **come to a full ˈstop** to stop completely
■ *adv.* (*BrE*) (*also* **period** *NAmE, BrE*) (*informal*) used at the end of a sentence to emphasize that there is nothing more to say about a subject: *I've already told you—we can't afford it, full stop!*

**full-ˈterm** *adj.* (*specialist*) **1** (of a PREGNANCY) lasting the normal length of time **2** (of a baby) born after a PREGNANCY lasting the normal length of time

**full ˈtime** *noun* [U] (*BrE*) the end of a sports game: *The referee blew his whistle for full time. ◊ The full-time score was 1–1.* ➔ compare HALF-TIME

**full-ˈtime** ⚡+ **B2** *adj., adv.* (*abbr.* **FT**) for all the hours of a week during which people normally work or study, rather than just for a part of it: *students in full-time education ◊ a full-time employee ◊ a full-time job ◊ Looking after a child is a full-time job* (= hard work that takes a lot of time). *◊ She works full-time and still manages to run a home.* ➔ compare PART-TIME

**full-ˈtimer** *noun* a person who works full-time

**fully** 🅘 **B2** 🅦 /ˈfʊli/ *adv.* **1** ⚡ completely: *I fully understand your motives. ◊ She never fully recovered from the accident. ◊ We are fully aware of the dangers. ◊ Everyone cooperated fully with the investigation.* **2** (*formal*) used to emphasize an amount; the whole of; as much as: *The disease affects fully 30 per cent of the population.*

**fully ˈfledged** (*BrE*) (*also* **full-ˈfledged** *NAmE, BrE*) *adj.* [usually before noun] completely developed; with all the qualifications necessary for sth: *the emergence of a fully fledged market economy ◊ She was now a fully fledged member of the teaching profession.*

**ful·min·ate** /ˈfʊlmɪneɪt, ˈfʌl-/ *verb* [I] **~ against (sb/sth)** (*formal*) to criticize sb/sth angrily ▶ **ful·min·ation** /ˌfʊlmɪˈneɪʃn, ˌfʌl-/ *noun* [C, U]

**ful·some** /ˈfʊlsəm/ *adj.* (*disapproving*) too generous in praising or thanking sb, or in saying sorry, so that you do not sound sincere: *a fulsome apology ◊ He was fulsome in his praise of the Prime Minister.* ▶ **ful·some·ly** *adv.*

**fum·ble** /ˈfʌmbl/ *verb, noun*
■ *verb* **1** [I, T] to use your hands in a way that is not smooth or steady or careful when you are doing sth or looking for sth: **~ (at/with/in sth) (for sth)** *She fumbled in her pocket for a handkerchief. ◊ He fumbled with the buttons on his shirt. ◊ ~ around She was fumbling around in the dark looking for the light switch. ◊ ~ sth + adv./prep. He fumbled the key into the ignition. ◊ ~ to do sth I fumbled to zip up my jacket.* **2** [I, T] to have difficulty speaking clearly or finding the right words to say: **~ (for sth)** *During the interview, she fumbled helplessly for words. ◊ ~ sth to fumble an announcement* **3** [T] **~ sth** (especially in sport) to drop a ball or to fail to stop or kick it
■ *noun* **1** [sing.] (*also* **fum·bling** [C, usually pl.]) an action using the hands that is not smooth or steady or careful **2** [C] (*NAmE*) the action of dropping the ball while it is in play in

American football **3** [C] (*NAmE*) the action of failing to pick up a ball that is rolling on the ground in baseball

**fum·bling** /ˈfʌmblɪŋ/ *adj.* hesitating or uncertain: *a fumbling schoolboy*

**fume** /fjuːm/ *verb* **1** [I, T] to be very angry about sth: **~ (at/over/about sb/sth)** *She sat in the car, silently fuming at the traffic jam.* ◊ **~ (with sth)** *He was fuming with indignation.* ◊ **+ speech** *'This is intolerable!' she fumed.* **2** [I] to produce smoke or fumes

**fumes** /fjuːmz/ *noun* [pl.] (*also less frequent* **fume** [U]) smoke, gas, or sth similar that smells strongly or is dangerous to breathe in: *diesel/petrol/exhaust fumes*: *to be overcome by smoke and fumes* ◊ *Clouds of toxic fumes escaped in a huge chemical factory blaze.* ◊ *The body of a man was found in a fume-filled car yesterday.*

**fu·mi·gate** /ˈfjuːmɪɡeɪt/ *verb* **~ sth** to use special chemicals, smoke or gas to destroy the harmful insects or bacteria in a place: *to fumigate a room* ▶ **fu·mi·ga·tion** /ˌfjuːmɪˈɡeɪʃn/ *noun* [U, C]

**fun** ❶ 🅰🄸 /fʌn/ *noun, adj.*
■ *noun* [U] **1** 🅰🄸 the feeling of enjoying yourself; activities that you enjoy: *We had a lot of fun at Sarah's party.* ◊ *Sailing is good fun.* ◊ *It was great fun! You should have come too.* ◊ *Have fun!* (= Enjoy yourself) ◊ **for ~** *I decided to learn Spanish, just for fun.* ◊ *I didn't do all that work just for the fun of it.* ◊ **it is ~ doing sth** *It's not much fun going to a party on your own.* ◊ *Walking three miles in the pouring rain is not my idea of fun.* **2** behaviour or activities that are not serious but are meant to be enjoyed: *She's very lively and full of fun.* ◊ *We didn't mean to hurt him. It was just a bit of fun.* ◊ **in ~** *It wasn't serious—it was all done in fun.* ⇒ SYNONYMS at ENTERTAINMENT
ⒾⒹⓂ **fun and ˈgames** (*informal*) activities that are not serious and that other people may think are bad **make ˈfun of sb/sth** to laugh at sb/sth or make other people laugh at them, usually in an unkind way: *It's cruel to make fun of people who stammer.* ⇒ more at FIGURE *n.*, POKE *v.*
■ *adj.* **?** that you enjoy: *She's really fun to be with.* ◊ *a film that's great fun to watch* ◊ *This game looks fun!* ◊ *There are lots of fun things for young people to do here.*

▼ SYNONYMS

**fun**

pleasure • (a) good time • enjoyment • (a) great time

These are all words for the feeling of enjoying yourself, or activities or time that you enjoy.

**fun** (*rather informal*) the feeling of enjoying yourself; activities that you enjoy: *We had a lot of fun at Sarah's party.* ◊ *Sailing is good/great fun.*

**pleasure** (*rather formal*) the feeling of enjoying yourself or being satisfied: *Reading for pleasure and reading for study are not the same.*

**(a) good time** (*rather informal*) a time that you spend enjoying yourself: *We had a good time in Spain.*

**enjoyment** (*rather formal*) the feeling of enjoying yourself: *I get a lot of enjoyment from music.*

PLEASURE OR ENJOYMENT?

**Enjoyment** usually comes from an activity that you do; **pleasure** can come from sth that you do or sth that happens: *He beamed with pleasure at seeing her.* ◊ *He beamed with enjoyment at seeing her.*

**(a) great time** (*rather informal*) a time that you spend enjoying yourself very much: *We had a really great time together.*

PATTERNS
- to do sth **for** fun/pleasure/enjoyment
- **great** fun/pleasure/enjoyment
- to **have** fun/a good time/a great time
- to **get** pleasure/enjoyment **from** sth
- to **spoil** the fun/sb's pleasure/sb's enjoyment

**func·tion** ❶ 🅱🄱 ◎ /ˈfʌŋkʃn/ *noun, verb*
■ *noun* **1** 🅱🄱 [C, U] a special activity or purpose of a person or thing: *The club serves a useful function as a meeting place.* ◊ *to fulfil/perform a function* ◊ *What is your function in the department?* ◊ *bodily functions* (= for example eating, sex, using the toilet) ◊ *This design aims for harmony of form and function.* **2** [C] a social event or official ceremony: *The hall provided a venue for weddings and other functions.* **3** [C] **~ (of sth)** (*mathematics*) a quantity whose value depends on the varying values of others. In the statement 2x=y, y is a function of x: (*figurative*) *Salary is a function of age and experience.* **4** [C] (*computing*) a part of a program, etc. that performs a basic operation
■ *verb* **?** 🄱🄱 [I] (*rather formal*) to work in the correct way 🅂🅈🄽 **operate**: *We now have a functioning shower.* ◊ **+ adv./prep.** *Despite the power cuts, the hospital continued to function normally.* ◊ *Many children can't function effectively in large classes.*
ⓅⒽⓇⓋ ▶ **ˈfunction as sb/sth** to perform the action or the job of the thing or person mentioned: *The sofa also functions as a bed.*

**func·tion·al** ❷ 🄲🄸 🆆 /ˈfʌŋkʃənl/ *adj.* **1** ❷ 🄲🄸 practical and useful; with little or no decoration 🅂🅈🄽 **utilitarian**: *Bathrooms don't have to be purely functional.* ◊ *The office was large and functional rather than welcoming.* **2** ❷ 🄲🄸 having a special purpose; making it possible for sb to do sth or for sth to happen: *a functional disorder* (= an illness caused when an organ of the body fails to perform its function) ◊ *a functional approach to language learning* ◊ *These units played a key functional role in the military operation.* **3** ❷ 🄲🄸 (especially of a machine, an organization or a system) working; able to work: *The hospital will soon be fully functional.* ▶ **func·tion·al·ly** /-nəli/ *adv.*

**ˈfunctional food** *noun* [C, U] (*also* **nutra·ceut·ical** [C]) food that has had substances that are good for your health specially added to it

**func·tion·al·ism** /ˈfʌŋkʃənəlɪzəm/ *noun* [U] (*specialist*) the idea or belief that the most important thing about the style or design of a building or object is how it is going to be used, not how it will look ▶ **func·tion·al·ist** /-lɪst/ *noun* **func·tion·al·ist** *adj.* [usually before noun]

**func·tion·al·ity** /ˌfʌŋkʃəˈnæləti/ *noun* (*pl.* **-ies**) **1** [U] the quality in sth of being very suitable for the purpose it was designed for 🅂🅈🄽 **practicality 2** [U] the purpose that sth is designed for or expected to perform: *Manufacturing processes may be affected by the functionality of the product.* **3** [U, C] (*computing*) the range of functions that a computer or other electronic system can perform: *new software with additional functionality* ⇒ WORDFINDER NOTE at PROGRAM

**func·tion·ary** /ˈfʌŋkʃənəri/ *NAmE* -neri/ *noun* (*pl.* **-ies**) (*often disapproving*) a person with official duties 🅂🅈🄽 **official**: *party/state/government functionaries*

**ˈfunction key** *noun* (*computing*) one of several keys on a computer keyboard, each marked with 'F' and a number, that can be used to do sth, such as save a file or get to the 'help' function in a program

**func·tor** /ˈfʌŋktə(r)/ *noun* (*mathematics*) a FUNCTION or a symbol such as + or ×

**fund** ❶ 🄱🄲 🆆 /fʌnd/ *noun, verb*
■ *noun* **1** ❷ 🄱🄲 [C] an amount of money that has been saved or has been made available for a particular purpose: *a disaster relief fund* ◊ *the company's pension fund* ◊ *the International Monetary Fund* ⇒ see also SLUSH FUND, SOCIAL FUND, TRUST FUND ⇒ WORDFINDER NOTE at INVEST **2** ❷ 🄱🄲 [pl.] money that is available to be spent: *government/federal funds* ◊ *The hospital is trying to raise funds for a new kidney machine.* ◊ *to provide/use funds for sth* ◊ *More funds should be allocated to housing.* ◊ *The project has been cancelled because of lack of funds.* **3** [C] (*finance*) a company that manages money for people by investing it; the money managed by such a company: *She is a fund manager for an Asian bank.* ⇒ see also HEDGE FUND, MUTUAL FUND **4** [sing.] **~ of sth** an amount or a supply of sth: *a fund of knowledge*
■ *verb* **?** 🄱🄲 **~ sth** to provide money for sth, usually sth official: *Who is funding this research?* ◊ *to fund a project/study/*

# funda

*scheme* ◇ *a government-funded programme* ◇ **publicly funded** *healthcare* ◇ *The museum is privately funded.*

**fun·da** /ˈfʌndə/ *noun* (*IndE*) a fundamental principle that is the basis of sth but that is not always easily noticed: *The artist explained the funda behind her exhibits.*

**fun·da·men·tal** 🔑 **B2** 🅞 /ˌfʌndəˈmentl/ *adj.*, *noun*
■ *adj.* **1** 🔑 **B2** serious and very important; affecting the most central and important parts of sth **SYN** basic: *the fundamental principles of scientific method* ◇ *You have a fundamental right to privacy.* ◇ *a fundamental question/problem/issue* ◇ *This principle is absolutely fundamental.* **2** ~ (to sth) central; forming the necessary basis of sth **SYN** essential: *Hard work is fundamental to success.* **3** [only before noun] (*physics*) forming the source or base from which everything else is made; not able to be divided any further: *a fundamental particle*
■ *noun* [usually pl.] a basic rule or principle; an essential part: *the fundamentals of modern physics* ◇ *He taught me the fundamentals of the job.*

**fundamental ˈforce** *noun* (*specialist*) a force that is a property (= characteristic) of everything in the universe. There are four fundamental forces including GRAVITY and ELECTROMAGNETISM.

**fun·da·men·tal·ism** /ˌfʌndəˈmentəlɪzəm/ *noun* [U] **1** a form of a religion, especially Islam or Protestant Christianity, based on the belief that everything that is written in the SCRIPTURES (= holy books) is completely true **2** the practice of following very strictly the basic principles of any subject or IDEOLOGY: *free-market fundamentalism* ▶ **fun·da·men·tal·ist** /-lɪst/ *noun* **fun·da·men·tal·ist** *adj.*

**fun·da·men·tal·ly** 🔑+ **B2** 🅦 /ˌfʌndəˈmentəli/ *adv.* **1** 🔑 **B2** in every way that is important; completely: *The two approaches are fundamentally different.* ◇ *By the 1960s the situation had changed fundamentally.* ◇ *They remained fundamentally opposed to the plan.* **2** 🔑+ **B2** used when you are introducing a topic and stating sth important about it **SYN** basically: *Fundamentally, there are two different approaches to the problem.* **3** 🔑+ **B2** used when you are saying what is the most important thing about sb/sth **SYN** basically: *She is fundamentally a nice person, but she finds it difficult to communicate.*

**fundamental ˈparticle** *noun* = ELEMENTARY PARTICLE

**fun·der** /ˈfʌndə(r)/ *noun* a person or an organization that provides money for a particular purpose

**fundi** /ˈfʊndi/ *noun* (*SAfrE*) a person who shows a lot of skill at sth or who has gained a lot of knowledge about a particular subject: *a computer fundi* ◇ *He's become quite a fundi on wine.*

**fund·ing** 🔑 **B2** 🅦 /ˈfʌndɪŋ/ *noun* [U] money for a particular purpose; the act of providing money for such a purpose: *federal/state funding* ◇ ~ **for sth** *There have been large cuts in government funding for scientific research.* ◇ *Alex originally struggled to secure funding for the project.* ◇ *to provide/allocate funding for sth*

**fund-raiser** /ˈfʌndreɪzə(r)/ *noun* **1** a person who collects money for a charity or an organization **2** a social event or an entertainment held in order to collect money for a charity or an organization ⸺ WORDFINDER NOTE at CHARITY

**fund-raising** 🔑+ **C1** /ˈfʌndreɪzɪŋ/ *noun* [U] the activity of collecting money for a charity or organization, often by organizing social events or entertainments: *a fundraising event* ▶ **fund-raise** *verb* [I]: ~ **(for sth)** *We're looking at new ways to fundraise for the charity.*

**fu·neral** 🔑+ **C1** /ˈfjuːnərəl/ *noun* a ceremony, often a religious one, for burying or CREMATING (= burning) a dead person: *Hundreds of people attended the funeral.* ◇ *a funeral procession* ◇ *a funeral march* (= a sad piece of music suitable for funerals) ⸺ WORDFINDER NOTE at DIE
**IDM** **it's ˈyour funeral** (*informal*) used to tell sb that they, and nobody else, will have to deal with the unpleasant results of their own actions

**ˈfuneral director** *noun* (*formal*) = UNDERTAKER

**ˈfuneral parlour** (*US* **ˈfuneral parlor**) (*also* **ˈfuneral home** *NAmE*, *BrE*) (*NAmE also* **ˈmor·tu·ary**) *noun* a place where dead people are prepared for being buried or CREMATED (= burned) and where visitors can see the body

**fu·ner·ary** /ˈfjuːnərəri; *NAmE* -reri/ *adj.* [only before noun] (*formal*) connected with a funeral (= ceremony for a dead person) or remembering the dead: *funerary rites/monuments*

**fu·ner·eal** /fjuːˈnɪəriəl; *NAmE* -ˈnɪr-/ *adj.* (*formal*) suitable for a FUNERAL (= ceremony for a dead person); sad: *a funereal atmosphere*

**fun·fair** /ˈfʌnfeə(r); *NAmE* -fer/ *noun* (*BrE*) = FAIR

**fun·gal** /ˈfʌŋgl/ *adj.* of or caused by FUNGUS: *a fungal infection*

**fun·gi·cide** /ˈfʌŋgɪsaɪd, ˈfʌndʒɪ-/ *noun* [C, U] a substance that kills fungus

**fun·gus** /ˈfʌŋgəs/ *noun* (*pl.* **fungi** /ˈfʌŋgiː, -gaɪ, ˈfʌndʒaɪ/) **1** [C] an ORGANISM (= a living thing) that is similar to a plant without leaves, flowers or green colouring, and that usually grows on plants or on DECAYING matter. MUSHROOMS and MILDEW are both fungi. **2** [U, C] a layer of MOULD or a similar fungus, for example on a plant or wall; an infection caused by a fungus: *fungus infections*

**fun·house** /ˈfʌnhaʊs/ *noun* (*especially NAmE*) a building at an AMUSEMENT PARK containing mirrors that produce strange images, moving floors, and other devices that frighten people and make them laugh

**fu·nicu·lar** /fjuːˈnɪkjələ(r)/ (*also* **fuˌnicular ˈrailway**) *noun* a railway on a steep slope, used to transport passengers up and down in special cars by means of a moving cable

**funk** /fʌŋk/ *noun* [U] [U] a type of dance music with a strong rhythm, developed by African American musicians in the 1960s

**funky** /ˈfʌŋki/ *adj.* (**funk·ier**, **funki·est**) (*informal*) **1** (of pop music) with a strong rhythm that is easy to dance to: *a funky disco beat* **2** (*approving*) fashionable and unusual: *She wears really funky clothes.* **3** (*NAmE*) having a strong unpleasant smell

**ˈfun-loving** *adj.* (of people) liking to enjoy themselves

**fun·nel** /ˈfʌnl/ *noun*, *verb*
■ *noun* **1** a device that is wide at the top and narrow at the bottom, used for pouring liquids or powders into a small opening **2** (*also* **smoke·stack**) a metal CHIMNEY, for example on a ship or an engine, through which smoke comes out
■ *verb* [I, T] (**-ll-**, *US* **-l-**) to move or make sth move through a narrow space, or as if through a funnel: **(+ adv./prep.)** *Wind was funnelling through the gorge.* ◇ ~ **sth (+ adv./prep.)** *Huge pipes funnel the water down the mountainside.* ◇ *Barricades funnelled the crowds towards the square.* ◇ (*figurative*) *Some $10 million in aid was funnelled into the country through government agencies.*

**fun·nily** /ˈfʌnəli/ *adv.* in a strange way
**IDM** **funnily eˈnough** used to show that you expect people to find a particular fact surprising: *Funnily enough, I met her only yesterday.*

**funny** 🔑 **A1** /ˈfʌni/ *adj.* (**fun·nier**, **fun·ni·est**)
• AMUSING **1** 🔑 **A1** making you laugh: *a funny story/joke* ◇ *That's the funniest thing I've ever heard.* ◇ *It's not funny! Someone could have been hurt.* ◇ *I was really embarrassed, but then I saw the funny side of it.* ◇ (*ironic*) *Oh very funny! You expect me to believe that?* ◇ *'What's so funny?' she demanded.* ⸺ WORDFINDER NOTE at COMEDY **HELP** Note that **funny** does not mean 'enjoyable': *The party was great fun.* ◇ *The party was very funny.*
• STRANGE **2** 🔑 **B1** difficult to explain or understand; strange and not as you expect **SYN** strange, peculiar: *A funny thing happened to me today.* ◇ *It's funny how things never happen the way you expect them to.* ◇ *That's funny*—he was here a moment ago and now he's gone. ◇ *The funny thing is it never happened again after that.* ◇ *I'm pleased I didn't get that job, in a funny sort of way.* ◇ *This wine tastes funny.*
• WRONG/ILLEGAL **3** (*informal*) seeming or likely to be wrong, illegal or dishonest: *I suspect there may be something*

*funny going on.* ◊ *If there has been any **funny business**, we'll soon find out.*
- **WITHOUT RESPECT 4** (*BrE*) humorous in a way that shows a lack of respect for sb **SYN** **cheeky**: *Don't you get funny with me!*
- **ILL/SICK 5** (*informal*) slightly ill: *I feel a bit funny today—I don't think I'll go to work.*
- **CRAZY 6** (*BrE, informal*) slightly crazy; not like other people **SYN** **strange**, **peculiar**: *That Dave's a funny chap, isn't he?* ◊ *She went a bit funny after her husband died.*
- **MACHINE 7** (*informal*) not working as it should: *My computer keeps going funny.*

**IDM** ˌfunny haˈha (*informal*) used to show that 'funny' is being used with the meaning of 'making you laugh' ˌfunny peˈculiar (*BrE*) (*US* ˌfunny ˈweird/ˈstrange) (*informal*) used to show that 'funny' is being used with the meaning of 'strange'

▼ **SYNONYMS**

**funny**

amusing • entertaining • witty • humorous • comic • hilarious

These words all describe sb/sth that makes you laugh or smile.

**funny** that makes you laugh: *a funny story* ◊ *He was a very funny guy.*

**amusing** funny and giving pleasure: *It's a very amusing game to play.*

**entertaining** that you enjoy watching, listening to, doing or experiencing: *It was a very entertaining evening.*

**witty** clever and amusing; able to say or write clever and amusing things: *a witty remark* ◊ *a witty public speaker*

**humorous** funny and entertaining; showing a sense of humour: *a humorous look at the world of fashion*

**comic** that makes you laugh: *Many of the scenes in the book are richly comic.*

**hilarious** extremely funny

FUNNY, AMUSING, HUMOROUS OR COMIC?

- **Amusing** is the most general of these words because it includes the idea of being fun as well as making people laugh and can be used to describe events, activities and occasions: *an amusing party/game/evening* ◊ *a funny/humorous/comic party/game/evening*. **Humorous** is more about showing that you see the humour in a situation, than actually making people laugh out loud. **Comic** is used especially to talk about writing and drama or things that are funny in a deliberate and theatrical way. It is not used to describe people (except for *comic writers/actors*). **Funny** can describe people, jokes and stories, things that happen, or anything that makes people laugh.

PATTERNS
- a(n) funny/amusing/entertaining/witty/humorous/comic **story**
- a(n) funny/amusing/entertaining/witty/humorous **speech**
- a(n) funny/entertaining/witty/humorous/comic **writer**
- a(n) funny/amusing/hilarious **joke**
- to **find** sth funny/amusing/entertaining/witty/humorous/hilarious

ˈfunny bone *noun* [usually sing.] (*informal*) the part of the ELBOW (= place where the arm bends) containing a very sensitive nerve that is painful if you hit it against sth

ˌfunny ˈmoney *noun* [U] (*informal, disapproving*) **1** a currency (= the money used in one country) that is not worth much and whose value can change quickly **2** money that has been illegally printed, stolen or has come from illegal activities; money that is not real because it has been created for a game

ˈfun run *noun* (*especially BrE*) an event in which people run a long distance, for fun, and to collect money for charity

**fur** 🔊 **B1** /fɜː(r)/ *noun* **1** 🔊 **B1** [U] the soft thick mass of hair that grows on the body of some animals: *The cat carefully licked its fur.* **2** 🔊 **B1** [U] the skin of an animal with the fur still on it, used especially for making clothes: *a fur coat* ◊ *the fur trade* ◊ *a fur farm* (= where animals are bred and killed for their fur) ◊ *The animal is hunted for its fur.* **3** [U] an artificial material that looks and feels like fur **4** [C] a piece of clothing, especially a coat or jacket, made of real or artificial fur: *elegant ladies in furs* **5** [U] (*BrE*) = SCALE (9) **6** [U] a grey-white layer that forms on a person's tongue, especially when they are ill ⊃ see also FURRED

**furious** 🔊+ **B2** /ˈfjʊəriəs; *NAmE* ˈfjʊr-/ *adj.* **1** 🔊+ **B2** very angry: *~(at sth/sb) She was absolutely furious at having been deceived.* ◊ *~with sb/yourself He was furious with himself for letting things get so out of control.* ◊ *~that… I'm furious that I wasn't told about it.* **2** 🔊+ **C1** with great energy, speed or anger: *a furious debate* ◊ *She drove off at a furious pace.* ⊃ see also FURY ▶ **furiously** *adv.*: *furiously angry* ◊ *'Damn!' he said furiously.* ◊ *They worked furiously all weekend, trying to get it finished on time.* **IDM** see FAST *adj.*

**furl** /fɜːl; *NAmE* fɜːrl/ *verb* ~ **sth** to roll and fasten sth such as a sail, a flag or an umbrella **OPP** **unfurl**

**furlong** /ˈfɜːlɒŋ; *NAmE* ˈfɜːrlɔːŋ/ *noun* (especially in horse racing) a unit for measuring distance, equal to 220 yards or 201 metres; one eighth of a mile

**furlough** /ˈfɜːləʊ; *NAmE* ˈfɜːrl-/ *noun.* [U, C] **1** permission to leave your duties for a period of time, especially for soldiers working in a foreign country **2** (*NAmE*) permission for a prisoner to leave prison for a period of time **3** (*NAmE*) a period of time during which workers are told not to come to work, usually because there is not enough money to pay them ▶ **furlough** *verb*: *~ sb*

**furnace** /ˈfɜːnɪs; *NAmE* ˈfɜːrn-/ *noun* **1** a space surrounded on all sides by walls and a roof for heating metal or glass to very high temperatures: *It's like a furnace* (= very hot) *in here!* ⊃ see also BLAST FURNACE **2** (*especially NAmE*) = BOILER

**furnish** /ˈfɜːnɪʃ; *NAmE* ˈfɜːrn-/ *verb* **1** ~ **sth** to put furniture in a house, room, etc: *The room was furnished with antiques.* **2** ~ **sb/sth with sth** | ~ **sth** (*formal*) to supply or provide sb/sth with sth; to supply sth to sb: *She furnished him with the facts surrounding the case.*

**furnished** /ˈfɜːnɪʃt; *NAmE* ˈfɜːrn-/ *adj.* (of a house, room, etc.) containing furniture: *furnished accommodation* (= to rent complete with furniture) ◊ *The house was simply furnished.*

**furnishings** /ˈfɜːnɪʃɪŋz; *NAmE* ˈfɜːrn-/ *noun* [pl.] the furniture, carpets, curtains, etc. in a room or house: *soft furnishings* ◊ *The wallpaper should match the furnishings.* ⊃ see also SOFT FURNISHINGS ⊃ WORDFINDER NOTE at STORE

**furniture** 🔊 **A2** /ˈfɜːnɪtʃə(r); *NAmE* ˈfɜːrn-/ *noun* [U] objects that can be moved, such as tables, chairs and beds, that are put into a house or an office to make it suitable for living or working in: *garden/office furniture* ◊ *a piece of furniture* ◊ *We need to buy some new furniture.* ⊃ see also STREET FURNITURE **IDM** see PART *n.*

ˈfurniture van *noun* (*BrE*) = REMOVAL VAN

**furore** /fjʊˈrɔːri; ˈfjʊərɔː(r); *NAmE* ˈfjʊrɔːr/ (*BrE*) (*NAmE* **furor** /ˈfjʊərɔː(r); *NAmE* ˈfjʊr-/) *noun* [sing.] great anger or excitement shown by a number of people, usually caused by a public event **SYN** **uproar**: *~(among sb) His novel about Jesus caused a furore among Christians.* ◊ *~about/over sth the recent furore over the tax increases*

**furphy** /ˈfɜːfi; *NAmE* ˈfɜːrfi/ *noun* (*pl.* **-ies**) (*AustralE*) a piece of information or a story that people talk about but that may not be true **SYN** **rumour**

**furred** /fɜːd; *NAmE* fɜːrd/ *adj.* covered with fur or with sth that looks like fur: *a furred tongue*

**furrier** /ˈfʌriə(r); *NAmE* ˈfɜːriər/ *noun* a person who prepares or sells clothes made from fur

**furrow** /ˈfʌrəʊ; *NAmE* ˈfɜːr-/ *noun, verb.*
■ *noun* **1** a long narrow cut in the ground, especially one made by a PLOUGH for planting seeds in **2** a deep line in the skin of the face **IDM** see PLOUGH *v.*

# furry

- **verb** [I, T] ~ (sth) (formal) if your BROWS or EYEBROWS **furrow** or **are furrowed**, you pull them together, usually because you are worried, and so produce lines on your face

**furry** /ˈfɜːri/ adj. (**fur·ri·er** /ˈfɜːriə(r)/, **fur·ri·est**) **1** covered with fur: *small furry animals* **2** like fur: *The moss was soft and furry to the touch.*

**fur·ther** ❶ A2 W /ˈfɜːðə(r)/; NAmE ˈfɜːrð-/ adj., adv., verb

- **adj.** ❷ A2 more; additional: *Cook for a further 2 minutes.* ◊ *For further details call this number.* ◊ *Can you give me any further information?* ◊ *further investigation/research/study/analysis* ◊ *We have decided to take no further action.* ◊ *The museum is closed until further notice* (= until we say that it is open again). ⊃ LANGUAGE BANK at ADDITION
- **adv. 1** ❷ B1 (comparative of *far*) **SYN farther**: *We had walked a bit further than I had realized.* ◊ *I'm too tired to go any further.* ◊ *further north/south/east/west* ◊ *Two miles further on we came to a small town.* ◊ *The hospital is further down the road.* ◊ *Can you stand a bit further away?* **2** ❷ B2 a longer way in the past or the future: *Think further back into your childhood.* ◊ *How will the company be doing ten years further on?* **3** ❷ B2 to a greater degree or extent: *to develop/increase/enhance/improve sth further* ◊ *Costs must be further reduced.* ◊ *The police decided to investigate further.* ◊ *She was getting further and further into debt.* ◊ *Nothing could be further from the truth.* **4** (formal) in addition to what has just been said **SYN furthermore**: *Further, it is important to consider the cost of repairs.* ⊃ note at FARTHER
- IDM **go ˈfurther 1** to say more about sth, or make a more extreme point about it: *I would go even further and suggest that the entire government is corrupt.* **2** to last longer; to serve more people: *They watered down the soup to make it go further.* **go no ˈfurther | not go any ˈfurther** if you tell sb that a secret will **go no further**, you promise not to tell it to anyone else **take sth ˈfurther** to take more serious action about sth or speak to sb at a higher level about it: *I am not satisfied with your explanation and intend to take the matter further.* ⊃ more at AFIELD, LOOK v.
- **verb** ~ **sth** to help sth to develop or be successful: *They hoped the new venture would further the cause of cultural cooperation in Europe.* ◊ *She took the new job to further her career.*

**fur·ther·ance** /ˈfɜːðərəns/; NAmE ˈfɜːrð-/ noun [U] (formal) the process of helping sth to develop or to be successful **SYN advancement**: *He took these actions purely in (the) furtherance of his own career.*

**further eduˈcation** noun [U] (abbr. **FE**) (BrE) education that is provided for people after leaving school, but not at a university ⊃ compare HIGHER EDUCATION, TERTIARY EDUCATION ⊃ WORDFINDER NOTE at STUDY

**fur·ther·more** ❶ B2 W /ˌfɜːðəˈmɔː(r)/; NAmE ˌfɜːrðərˈm-/ adv. (formal) in addition to what has just been stated. **Furthermore** is used especially to add a point to an argument. **SYN moreover**: *He said he had not discussed the matter with her. Furthermore, he had not even contacted her.* ⊃ LANGUAGE BANK at ADDITION

**fur·ther·most** /ˈfɜːðəməʊst/; NAmE ˈfɜːrðərm-/ adj. (formal) located at the greatest distance from sth: *at the furthermost end of the street*

**ˈfurther to** prep. (formal) used in letters, emails, etc. to refer to a previous letter, email, conversation, etc: *Further to our conversation of last Friday, I would like to book the conference centre for 26 June.*

**fur·thest** /ˈfɜːðɪst/; NAmE ˈfɜːrð-/ adj. = FARTHEST

**fur·tive** /ˈfɜːtɪv/; NAmE ˈfɜːrt-/ adj. (*disapproving*) behaving in a way that shows that you want to keep sth secret and do not want to be noticed **SYN stealthy**: *She cast a furtive glance over her shoulder.* ◊ *He looked sly and furtive.* ▶ **fur·tive·ly** adv. **fur·tive·ness** noun [U]

**fury** /ˈfjʊəri/; NAmE ˈfjʊri/ noun **1** [U] extreme anger that often includes violent behaviour **SYN rage**: *Her eyes blazed with fury.* ◊ *Fury over tax increases* (= as a newspaper headline) ◊ (*figurative*) *There was no shelter from the fury of the storm.* **2** [sing.] a state of being extremely angry about sth **SYN rage**: *He flew into a fury when I refused.* **3 the Furies** [pl.] (in ancient Greek stories) three GODDESSES who punish people for their crimes ⊃ see also FURIOUS

IDM **like ˈfury** (*informal*) with great effort, power, speed, etc. ⊃ more at HELL

**furze** /fɜːz/; NAmE fɜːrz/ noun [U] (BrE) = GORSE

**fuse** /fjuːz/ noun, verb

- **noun 1** a small wire or device inside a piece of electrical equipment that breaks and stops the current if the flow of electricity is too strong: *to change a fuse* ◊ *Check whether a fuse has blown.* **2** (NAmE also **fuze**) a long piece of string or paper that is lit to make a bomb or a FIREWORK explode **3** (NAmE also **fuze**) a device that makes a bomb explode when it hits sth or at a particular time: *He set the fuse to three minutes.* ◊ *The bombs inside were on a one-hour fuse.*
  IDM see BLOW v., SHORT adj.
- **verb 1** [I, T] (formal or specialist) when one thing **fuses** with another, or two things **fuse** or **are fused**, they are joined together to form a single thing: ~ **(together)** *As they heal, the bones will fuse together.* ◊ ~ **(into sth)** *Our different ideas fused into a plan.* ◊ ~ **with sth** *The sperm fuses with the egg to begin the process of fertilization.* ◊ ~ **sth (into sth)** *The two companies have been fused into a single organization.* ◊ *Atoms of hydrogen are fused to make helium.* **2** [I, T] ~ **(sth) (to sth)** (*specialist*) when a substance, especially metal, **fuses**, or you **fuse** it, it is heated until it melts and joins with sth else **3** [I, T] ~ **(sth)** (BrE) to stop working or to make sth stop working because a fuse melts: *The lights have fused.* ◊ *I've fused the lights.* **4** [T, usually passive] to put a fuse in a CIRCUIT or in a piece of equipment: *be fused Is this plug fused?*

**ˈfuse box** noun a small box or cupboard that contains the fuses of the electrical system of a building

**fu·sel·age** /ˈfjuːzəlɑːʒ/; NAmE ˈfjuːsə-/ noun the main part of an aircraft in which passengers and goods are carried

**fu·si·lier** /ˌfjuːzəˈlɪə(r)/; NAmE -ˈlɪr/ noun (in the past) a soldier who carried a light gun

**fu·sil·lade** /ˌfjuːzəˈleɪd/; NAmE ˈfjuːsəlɑːd, -leɪd/ noun a rapid series of shots fired from one or more guns; a rapid series of objects that are thrown **SYN barrage**: *a fusillade of bullets/stones* ◊ (*figurative*) *He faced a fusillade of questions from the waiting journalists.*

**fu·sion** /ˈfjuːʒn/ noun **1** [U, sing.] ~ **(of A and B)** the process or result of joining two or more things together to form one: *the fusion of copper and zinc to produce brass* ◊ *The movie displayed a perfect fusion of image and sound.* **2** (also ˌnuclear ˈfusion) [U] (*physics*) the act or process of combining the NUCLEI (= central parts) of ATOMS to form a heavier NUCLEUS, with energy being released ⊃ compare FISSION ⊃ see also COLD FUSION **3** [U] music that is a mixture of different styles, especially jazz and rock **4** [U] cooking that is a mixture of different styles: *French–Thai fusion*

**fuss** /fʌs/ noun, verb

- **noun 1** [U, sing.] unnecessary excitement, worry or activity: *I heard all that fuss and bother.* ◊ *He does what he's told without any fuss.* ◊ ~ **over sth** *All that fuss over a few pounds!* ◊ ~ **about sth** *It was all a fuss about nothing.* ◊ *It's a very ordinary movie—I don't know what all the fuss is about* (= why other people think it is so good). **2** [sing.] anger or complaints about sth, especially sth that is not important: *Steve kicks up a fuss every time I even suggest seeing you.* ◊ ~ **about sth** *I'm sorry for making such a fuss about the noise.*
  IDM **make a fuss of sb** (BrE) (also **make a fuss over sb** *especially in NAmE*) to pay a lot of attention to sb, usually to show how much you like them: *They made a great fuss of the baby.* ◊ *The dog loves being made a fuss of.*
- **verb 1** [I] to do things, or pay too much attention to things, that are not important or necessary: ~ **(around)** *Stop fussing around and find something useful to do!* ◊ ~ **(with/over sth)** *Don't fuss with your hair!* **2** [I] ~ **(about sth)** to worry about things that are not very important: *Don't fuss, Mum, everything is all right.*

**IDM** **not be fussed (about sth)** (*BrE, informal*) to not mind about sth; to not have feelings about sth **SYN** **not be bothered**: *It'd be good to be there, but I'm not that fussed.*
**PHRV** **ˈfuss over sb** to pay a lot of attention to sb

**fuss·pot** /ˈfʌspɒt; *NAmE* -pɑːt/ (*BrE*) (*NAmE* **fuss-budget** /ˈfʌsbʌdʒɪt/) *noun* (*informal*) a person who is often worried about unimportant things and is difficult to please

**fussy** /ˈfʌsi/ *adj.* (**fuss·ier, fussi·est**) (*disapproving*) **1** too concerned about having things exactly as you want them; hard to please: *fussy parents* ◊ *She's such a fussy eater.* ◊ *'Where do you want to go for lunch?' 'I'm not fussy (= I don't mind).'* ◊ **~ about sth** *Our teacher is very fussy about punctuation.* **2** doing sth with small, quick, nervous movements: *a fussy manner* **3** having too much detail or decoration: *The costume designs are too fussy.* ▶ **fuss·ily** /-səli/ *adv.* **fussi·ness** *noun* [U]

**fusty** /ˈfʌsti/ *adj.* (*disapproving*) **1** smelling old, slightly wet or not fresh **SYN** **musty**: *a dark fusty room* **2** old-fashioned: *fusty ideas* ◊ *a fusty old professor*

**fu·tile** /ˈfjuːtaɪl; *NAmE* -tl/ *adj.* having no purpose because there is no chance of success **SYN** **pointless**: *a futile attempt/exercise/gesture* ◊ *Their efforts to revive him were futile.* ◊ *It would be futile to protest.* ◊ *My appeal proved futile.* ▶ **fu·tile·ly** /ˈfjuːtaɪli; *NAmE* -təli/ *adv.* **fu·til·ity** /fjuːˈtɪləti/ *noun* [U]: *a sense of futility* ◊ *the futility of war*

**fu·ton** /ˈfuːtɒn; *NAmE* -tɑːn/ *noun* a Japanese MATTRESS, often on a wooden frame, that can be used for sitting on or rolled out to make a bed

**fut·sal** /ˈfʊtsɔːl, ˈfʌt-/ *noun* [U] a version of football (soccer) that is usually played indoors on a smaller pitch with five players on each team

**fu·ture** **①** **A1** **W** /ˈfjuːtʃə(r)/ *noun, adj.*
■ *noun* **1** **A1** **the future** [sing.] the time that will come after the present or the events that will happen then: *We need to plan for the future.* ◊ **in the ~** *The movie is set in the future.* ◊ *I don't expect any of these things to happen* **in the near future** *(= soon).* ◊ *Nobody can predict the future.* ◊ **of the ~** *What will the cities of the future look like?* **2** **A2** [C] what will happen to sb/sth at a later time: *The company faces a very uncertain future.* ◊ *We must seize the opportunity to shape our future.* ◊ *This deal could secure the futures of 2 000 employees.* **3** **B1** [sing., U] the possibility of being successful or surviving at a later time: *They have* **a bright future** *ahead of them.* ◊ *I can't see any future in this relationship.* ◊ *Children are the future of this country (= the country's future depends on children).* **4 futures** [pl.] (*finance*) goods or shares that are bought at agreed prices but will be delivered and paid for at a later time: *oil futures* ◊ *the futures market* **5** **the future** [sing.] (*grammar*) (*also* **the ˌfuture ˈtense**) the form of a verb that expresses what will happen after the present
**IDM** **in future** (*BrE*) (*NAmE* **in the future**) from now on: *Please be more careful in future.* ◊ *In future, make sure the door is never left unlocked.* ⊃ more at DISTANT, FORESEEABLE
■ *adj.* **A2** [only before noun] taking place or existing at a time after the present: *future generations* ◊ *at a future date* ◊ *future developments in artificial intelligence* ◊ *He met his future wife at law school.* ◊ *I wrote down the name of the hotel for future reference (= because it might be useful in the future).*

**the ˌfuture ˈperfect** (*also* **the ˌfuture perfect ˈtense**) *noun* [sing.] (*grammar*) the form of a verb that expresses an action completed before a particular point in the future, formed in English with *will have* or *shall have* and the past participle

**ˈfuture-proof** *adj., verb*
■ *adj.* (*business* or *specialist*) designed to continue working or to be effective after changes that may happen in the future: *future-proof website design*
■ *verb* **~ sth** to make sth future-proof: *The firm claims that it future-proofs its software.*

**Fu·tur·ism** /ˈfjuːtʃərɪzəm/ *noun* [U] a movement in art and literature in the 1920s and 30s that did not try to show realistic figures and scenes but aimed to express confidence in the modern world, particularly in modern machines ▶ **Fu·tur·ist** /-rɪst/ *noun* **Fu·tur·ist** *adj.*: *Futurist sculpture/paintings* ◊ *Futurist poets*

**fu·tur·is·tic** /ˌfjuːtʃəˈrɪstɪk/ *adj.* **1** extremely modern and unusual in appearance, as if belonging to a future time: *futuristic design* **2** imagining what the future will be like: *a futuristic novel*

**fu·tur·ity** /fjuːˈtjʊərəti; *NAmE* -ˈtʊr-/ *noun* [U] (*formal*) the time that will come after the present and what will happen then: *a vision of futurity*

**fu·tur·olo·gist** /ˌfjuːtʃəˈrɒlədʒɪst; *NAmE* -ˈrɑːl-/ *noun* a person who is an expert in futurology

**fu·tur·ology** /ˌfjuːtʃəˈrɒlədʒi; *NAmE* -ˈrɑːl-/ *noun* the study of how people will live in the future

**fuze** (*NAmE*) = FUSE (2), FUSE (3)

**fuzz** /fʌz/ *noun* **1** [U] short soft fine hair or fur that covers sth, especially a person's face or arms **SYN** **down** **2** [sing.] a mass of curly hair: *a fuzz of blonde hair* **3** **the fuzz** [sing. + sing./pl. v.] (*old-fashioned, slang*) the police **4** something that you cannot see clearly **SYN** **blur**: *I saw it as a dim fuzz through the binoculars.*

**fuzzy** /ˈfʌzi/ *adj.* (**fuzz·ier, fuzzi·est**) **1** covered with short soft fine hair or fur **SYN** **downy** **2** (of hair) in a mass of tight CURLS **3** not clear in shape or sound **SYN** **blurred**: *a fuzzy image* ◊ *The soundtrack is fuzzy in places.* **4** confused and not expressed clearly: *fuzzy ideas/thinking* ▶ **fuzz·ily** /-zəli/ *adv.* **fuzzi·ness** *noun* [U]

**ˌfuzzy ˈlogic** *noun* [U] (*computing*) a type of LOGIC with values other than 0 and 1 (for example, cold, warm and hot) so that computers and machines can more easily handle real-world applications

**FWIW** *abbr.* (*informal*) used in writing to mean 'for what it's worth'

**ˈF-word** *noun* [usually sing.] (*informal*) used instead of the offensive swear word 'fuck' because you do not want to say it: *He was shocked at how often she used the F-word.* ⊃ compare C-WORD

**FX** *abbr.* **1** /ˌef ˈeks/ a short way of writing SPECIAL EFFECTS **2** a short way of writing FOREIGN EXCHANGE

**-fy** ⊃ -IFY

**FYI** *abbr.* used mainly in writing to mean 'for your information'

# Gg

**G** /dʒiː/ noun, abbr.
- **noun** (also **g**) [C, U] (pl. **Gs**, **G's**, **g's** /dʒiːz/) **1** the 7th letter of the English alphabet: *'Gold' begins with (a) G/'G'.* **2 G** (*music*) the fifth note in the SCALE of C MAJOR ⇒ see also G AND T, G-STRING
- **abbr. 1** (in the US) general audiences (a label for a movie that is suitable for anyone, including children) ⇒ compare NC-17, PG-13, R (5) **2** (in units of measurement) giga-: *a download bandwidth of 1.5 Gbits per second* **3** (*NAmE, informal*) $1000

**g** abbr., symbol
- **abbr.** GRAM(S): *400g flour*
- **symbol** /dʒiː/ (*specialist*) GRAVITY or a measurement of the force with which sth moves faster through space because of GRAVITY: *Spacecraft which are re-entering the earth's atmosphere are affected by g forces.*

**gab** /gæb/ verb, noun
- **verb** [I] (*informal*) (**-bb-**) to talk for a long time about things that are not important
- **noun** IDM see GIFT *n*.

**gab·ble** /ˈgæbl/ verb, noun
- **verb** [I, T] (*informal*) to talk quickly so that people cannot hear you clearly or understand you: *She was nervous and started to gabble.* ◊ *~on/away They were gabbling on about the past.* ◊ *~sth He was gabbling nonsense.* ◊ *+ speech 'No, no, not all,' she gabbled.*
- **noun** [sing.] fast speech that is difficult to understand, especially when a lot of people are talking at the same time

**gabby** /ˈgæbi/ *adj.* (*informal, disapproving*) talking a lot, especially about things that are not important

**gab·fest** /ˈgæbfest/ *noun* (*NAmE, informal*) an informal meeting to talk and exchange news; a long conversation

**ga·bion** /ˈgeɪbiən/ *noun* a large square container made of wire in which rocks are packed. Gabions are used for building structures outdoors, for example to support pieces of ground or control a flow of water.

**gable** /ˈgeɪbl/ *noun* the upper part of the end wall of a building, between the two sloping sides of the roof, that is like a TRIANGLE in shape

**gabled** /ˈgeɪbld/ *adj.* having one or more GABLES: *a gabled house/roof*

**gad** /gæd/ *verb* (**-dd-**)
- PHRV **gad aˈbout/aˈround** (*especially BrE, informal*) to visit different places and have fun, especially when you should be doing sth else

**gad·fly** /ˈgædflaɪ/ *noun* (pl. **-ies**) (*usually disapproving*) a person who annoys or criticizes other people in order to make them do sth

**gadget** /ˈgædʒɪt/ *noun* a small tool or device that does sth useful

**gadget·ry** /ˈgædʒɪtri/ *noun* [U] (*sometimes disapproving*) a collection of modern tools and devices: *His desk is covered with electronic gadgetry.*

**gado·lin·ium** /ˌgædəˈlɪniəm/ *noun* [U] (*symb.* **Gd**) a chemical element. Gadolinium is a soft silver-white metal.

**Gael·ic** *noun* [U] **1** /ˈgælɪk, ˈgeɪl-/ the Celtic language of Scotland ⇒ compare SCOTS **2** /ˈgeɪlɪk/ (also **Irish ˈGaelic**) the Celtic language of Ireland ⇒ compare IRISH, ERSE ▶ **Gael·ic** *adj.*

**Gaelic football** /ˌgeɪlɪk ˈfʊtbɔːl/ *noun* [U] a game played mainly in Ireland between two teams of 15 players. The players of one team try to kick or hit a round ball into or over the other team's goal.

**the Gael·tacht** /ðə ˈgeɪltæxt/ *noun* the region of Ireland where Gaelic is spoken by a large part of the population

**gaff** /gæf/ *noun* **1** a stick with a HOOK (= a curved piece of metal) on the end used to pull large fish out of the water **2** (*BrE, slang*) the house, flat, etc. where sb lives IDM see BLOW *v*.

**gaffe** /gæf/ *noun* a mistake that a person makes in public or in a social situation, especially sth embarrassing SYN faux pas

**gaf·fer** /ˈgæfə(r)/ *noun* **1** (*BrE, informal*) a person who is in charge of a group of people, for example, workers in a factory, a sports team, etc. SYN boss **2** the person who is in charge of the electrical work and the lights when a film or television programme is being made

**gag** /gæg/ *noun*, *verb*
- **noun 1** a piece of cloth that is put over or in sb's mouth to stop them speaking **2** an order that prevents sth from being publicly reported or discussed: *a press gag* ◊ *a gag rule/order* (= one given by a court of law) **3** (*informal*) a joke or a funny story, especially one told by a professional COMEDIAN SYN joke: *to tell/crack a gag* ◊ *a running gag* (= one that is regularly repeated during a performance) **4** (*especially NAmE*) a trick you play on sb: *It was just a gag—we didn't mean to upset anyone.*
- **verb** (**-gg-**) **1** [T] **~sb** to put a piece of cloth in or over sb's mouth to prevent them from speaking or shouting: *The hostages were bound and gagged.* **2** [T] **~sb/sth** to prevent sb from speaking freely or expressing their opinion: *The new laws are seen as an attempt to gag the press.* ⇒ see also GAGGING ORDER **3** [I] **~(on sth)** to have the unpleasant feeling in your mouth and stomach as if you are going to VOMIT SYN retch: *She gagged on the blood that filled her mouth.*
- IDM **be gagging for sth/to do sth** (*BrE, slang*) to want sth or want to do sth very much **be ˈgagging for it** (*BrE, slang*) to want very much to have sex

**gaga** /ˈgɑːgɑː/ *adj.* [not usually before noun] (*informal*) **1** (*offensive*) confused and not able to think clearly, especially because you are old: *He has gone completely gaga.* **2** slightly crazy because you are very excited about sb/sth, or very much in love: *The fans went totally gaga over the band.*

**gage** (*US*) = GAUGE

**ˈgagging order** (*BrE*) (*NAmE* **ˈgag order**) *noun* an order by a court that prevents people from talking or writing about a particular matter, especially about what is happening in a court case: *to impose/issue/lift/obtain a gagging order* ⇒ see also GAG *verb* (2)

**gag·gle** /ˈgægl/ *noun* **1** a group of noisy people: *a gaggle of tourists/schoolchildren* **2** a group of GEESE

**ˈgag order** (*NAmE*) = GAGGING ORDER

**Gaia** /ˈgaɪə/ *noun* [sing.] the Earth, considered as a single natural system that organizes and controls itself

**gai·ety** /ˈgeɪəti/ *noun* [U] (*old-fashioned*) the state of being cheerful and full of fun: *The colourful flags added to the gaiety of the occasion.* ⇒ compare GAYNESS ⇒ see also GAILY, GAY *noun*

**gaily** /ˈgeɪli/ *adv.* **1** in a bright and attractive way: *a gaily decorated room* **2** in a cheerful way: *gaily laughing children* ◊ *She waved gaily to the little crowd.* **3** without thinking or caring about the effect of your actions on other people: *She gaily announced that she was leaving the next day.* ⇒ see also GAIETY, GAY

**gain** ❶ B2 ❷ /geɪn/ *verb*, *noun*
- **verb**
- • OBTAIN/WIN **1** ❷ B2 [T] to obtain or win sth, especially sth that you need or want: *~sth to gain access/entry to sth* ◊ *The country gained its independence ten years ago.* ◊ *The party gained over 50 per cent of the vote.* ◊ *Police officers quickly gained control of the situation.* ◊ *I gained an insight into the work of a journalist.* ◊ *~sb sth Her unusual talent gained her worldwide recognition.* **2** ❷ B2 [T, I] to obtain an advantage or benefit from sth or from doing sth: *~sth (by/from sth) The firm is hoping to gain an advantage over its competitors.* ◊ *~sth by/from (doing) sth There is nothing to be gained from delaying the decision.* ◊ *~(by/from sth) Consumers have gained from the increased competition.* ◊ *If the proposal goes ahead, we all stand to gain.*
- • GET MORE **3** ❷ B2 [T] **~sth** to gradually get more of sth: *As you gain experience, you will grow in confidence.* ◊ *I've*

gained weight recently. ◇ The campaign continues to gain momentum. **OPP** lose
- OF WATCH/CLOCK **4** [T, I] ~(sth) to go too fast (by a particular amount of time): My watch gains two minutes every 24 hours. **OPP** lose
- OF CURRENCIES/SHARES **5** [T, I] to increase in value: ~ sth The shares gained 14p to 262p. ◇ ~ against sth The euro gained against the dollar again today.
- REACH PLACE **6** [T] ~ sth (formal) to reach a place, usually after a lot of effort: At last she gained the shelter of the forest.
**IDM** gain ˈground to become more powerful or successful: Sterling continues to gain ground against the dollar. gain ˈtime to delay sth so that you can have more time to make a decision, deal with a problem, etc. ⊃ more at VENTURE v.
**PHR V** ˈgain in sth to get more of a particular quality: to gain in confidence ◇ His books have gained in popularity in recent years. ˈgain on sb/sth to get closer to sb/sth that you are going after or following
- noun
- INCREASE **1** [C, U] an increase in the amount of sth, especially in wealth or weight: The opposition made unexpected gains in the last election. ◇ efficiency gains ◇ Regular exercise helps prevent weight gain. ◇ ~ from sth a £3000 gain from our investment ◇ ~ of sth The party had a net gain of nine seats on the local council. ◇ ~ in sth significant gains in crop yield
- ADVANTAGE **2** [C] an advantage or improvement: Our loss is their gain. ◇ ~ in sth These policies have resulted in great gains in public health. **OPP** loss
- PROFIT **3** [U] (often disapproving) financial profit: He only seems to be interested in personal gain. ◇ for ~ It's amazing what some people will do for gain. ⊃ see also CAPITAL GAIN
**IDM** see PAIN n.

**gain·er** /ˈgeɪnə(r)/ noun a person or organization that benefits or improves as a result of a situation or process: Software developers were among the biggest gainers after the government said it would support emerging industries.

**gain·ful** /ˈgeɪnfl/ adj. (formal) used to describe useful work that you are paid for: gainful employment ▸ **gain·ful·ly** /-fəli/ adv.: gainfully employed

**gain·say** /ˌgeɪnˈseɪ/ verb (often used in negative sentences) (gain·says /-ˈsez/, gain·said, gain·said /-ˈsed/) ~ sth (formal) to say that sth is not true; to disagree with or deny sth **SYN** deny: Nobody can gainsay his claims.

**gait** /geɪt/ noun [usually sing.] a way of walking or running: He walked with a rolling gait.

**gai·ter** /ˈgeɪtə(r)/ noun [usually pl.] a piece of clothing made from cloth or leather that covers the leg between the knee and the ankle. Gaiters were worn by men in the past and are now mainly worn by people who go walking or climbing: a pair of gaiters

**gal** /gæl/ noun (especially NAmE, old-fashioned, informal) a girl or woman

**gal.** abbr. (in writing) GALLON/GALLONS

**gala** /ˈgɑːlə; NAmE ˈgeɪlə/ noun **1** a special public celebration or entertainment: a charity gala ◇ a gala dinner/night **2** (BrE) a sports competition, especially in swimming: a swimming gala

**ga·lac·tic** /gəˈlæktɪk/ adj. relating to a galaxy

**galah** /gəˈlɑː/ noun (AustralE, informal) a stupid person

**galamsey** /ˌgæləmˈseɪ/ WAfrE [galamse] noun (WAfrE) **1** [U] (in Ghana) illegal gold MINING **2** [C] (in Ghana) an illegal gold MINER

**gal·axy** /ˈgæləksi/ noun (pl. -ies) **1** [C] any of the large systems of stars, etc. in outer space ⊃ WORDFINDER NOTE at UNIVERSE **2** the Galaxy [sing.] the system of stars that contains our sun and its planets, seen as a band of light in the night sky ⊃ compare MILKY WAY, THE MILKY WAY **3** [C] (informal) a group of famous people, or people with a particular skill: a galaxy of Hollywood stars

**gale** /geɪl/ noun an extremely strong wind: The gale blew down hundreds of trees. ◇ gale-force winds ◇ (BrE) It's blowing a gale outside (= there's a strong wind is blowing). ⊃ WORDFINDER NOTE at WIND¹

# gallon

**IDM** ˌgale(s) of ˈlaughter the sound of people laughing very loudly: His speech was greeted with gales of laughter.

**gall** /gɔːl/ noun, verb
- noun **1** [U] rude behaviour showing a lack of respect that is surprising because the person behaving badly is not embarrassed **SYN** impudence: Then they had the gall to complain! **2** [U] (formal) a bitter feeling full of hate **SYN** resentment **3** [C] a SWELLING (= an area that is larger and rounder than normal) on plants, trees and the skin of animals, caused by insects, disease, etc. **4** [U] (old-fashioned) = BILE
- verb ~ sb | it galls sb to do sth | it galls sb that … to make sb feel upset and angry, especially because sth is unfair: It galls me to have to apologize to her. ⊃ see also GALLING

**gal·lant** adj., noun
- adj. /ˈgælənt/ **1** (old-fashioned or literary) brave, especially in a very difficult situation **SYN** heroic: gallant soldiers ◇ She made a gallant attempt to hide her tears. **2** (of a man) giving polite attention to women ▸ **gal·lant·ly** adv.: She gallantly battled on alone. ◇ He bowed and gallantly kissed my hand.
- noun /gəˈlænt, ˈgælənt/ (old-fashioned) a fashionable young man, especially one who gives polite attention to women

**gal·lant·ry** /ˈgæləntri/ noun [U] (formal) **1** courage, especially in a battle: a medal for gallantry **2** polite attention given by men to women

**ˈgall bladder** noun an organ attached to the LIVER in which BILE is stored ⊃ VISUAL VOCAB page V1

**gal·leon** /ˈgæliən/ noun a large sailing ship, used between the 15th and the 18th centuries, especially by Spain

**gal·ler·ied** /ˈgælərid/ adj. (of a building or room) having a gallery (4); in the form of a gallery: a galleried hall/landing

**gal·lery** /ˈgæləri/ noun (pl. -ies) **1** a room or building for showing works of art, especially to the public: a picture gallery ◇ at a ~ The painting is now on display at the National Gallery in London. ⊃ see also ART GALLERY **2** a collection of pictures: Visit the photo gallery on our website to see pictures from the event. **3** a small private shop where you can see and buy works of art **4** an upstairs area at the back or sides of a large hall where people can sit: Relatives of the victim watched from the public gallery as the murder charge was read out in court. ⊃ see also PRESS GALLERY **5** the highest level in a theatre where the cheapest seats are **6** a long narrow room, especially one used for a particular purpose ⊃ see also SHOOTING GALLERY **7** a level passage under the ground in a mine or CAVE
**IDM** ˌplay to the ˈgallery to behave in an EXAGGERATED way to attract people's attention

**gal·ley** /ˈgæli/ noun **1** a long flat ship with sails, usually ROWED by slaves or criminals, especially one used by the ancient Greeks or Romans in war **2** the kitchen on a ship or plane

**Gal·lic** /ˈgælɪk/ adj. connected with or considered typical of France or its people: Gallic charm

**gall·ing** /ˈgɔːlɪŋ/ adj. [not usually before noun] (of a situation or fact) making you angry because it is unfair: It was galling to have to apologize to a man she hated.

**gal·lium** /ˈgæliəm/ noun [U] (symb. Ga) a chemical element. Gallium is a soft silver-white metal.

**gal·li·vant** /ˈgælɪvænt/ verb [I] (usually used in the progressive tenses) (informal, old-fashioned or humorous) ~ (about/around) to go from place to place enjoying yourself **SYN** gad: You're too old to go gallivanting around Europe.

**gal·lon** /ˈgælən/ noun (abbr. gal.) (in Britain and North America) a unit for measuring liquid. In the UK, Canada and other countries it is equal to about 4.5 LITRES; in the US it is equal to about 3.8 LITRES. There are four QUARTS in a gallon: The tankers carried 130000 gallons of fuel.

# gallop 650

**gal·lop** /ˈɡæləp/ *verb, noun*

■ *verb* **1** [I] (+ *adv./prep.*) when a horse or similar animal **gallops**, it moves very fast and each STRIDE includes a stage when all four feet are off the ground together ⇒ compare CANTER ⇒ WORDFINDER NOTE at HORSE **2** [I, T] to ride a horse very fast, usually at a gallop: (+ *adv./prep.*) *Jo galloped across the field towards him.* ◇ ~ *sth* (+ *adv./prep.*) *He galloped his horse home.* ⇒ compare CANTER **3** [I] (+ *adv./prep.*) (*informal*) (of a person) to run very quickly SYN **charge**: *She came galloping down the street.*

■ *noun* **1** [sing.] the fastest speed at which a horse can run, with a stage in which all four feet are off the ground together: **at a ~** *He rode off at a gallop.* ◇ *My horse suddenly broke into a gallop.* **2** [C] a ride on a horse at its fastest speed: *to go for a gallop* **3** [sing.] an unusually fast speed; the act of doing sth at an unusually fast speed: **at a ~** *She always lives life at a gallop.*

**gal·lop·ing** /ˈɡæləpɪŋ/ *adj.* [only before noun] increasing or spreading rapidly: *galloping inflation*

**gal·lows** /ˈɡæləʊz/ *noun* (*pl.* **gal·lows**) a structure on which people, for example criminals, are killed by hanging: *to send a man to the gallows* (= to send him to his death by hanging)

**ˈgallows humour** (*US* **ˈgallows humor**) *noun* [U] jokes about unpleasant things like death

**gall·stone** /ˈɡɔːlstəʊn/ *noun* a hard mass that can form in the GALL BLADDER and cause severe pain

**gal·ore** /ɡəˈlɔː(r)/ *adj.* [after noun] (*informal*) in large quantities: *There will be games and prizes galore.*

**gal·oshes** /ɡəˈlɒʃɪz; *NAmE* -ˈlɑːʃ-/ *noun* [pl.] rubber shoes (no longer very common) that are worn over normal shoes in wet weather: *a pair of galoshes*

**gal·umph** /ɡəˈlʌmf/ *verb* [I] + *adv./prep.* (*informal*) to move in a heavy, careless or noisy way

**gal·van·ic** /ɡælˈvænɪk/ *adj.* **1** (*specialist*) producing an electric current by the action of a chemical on metal **2** (*formal*) making people react in a sudden and dramatic way

**gal·van·ize** (*BrE also* **-ise**) /ˈɡælvənaɪz/ *verb* **1** to make sb take action by shocking them or by making them excited: *The win galvanized the whole team.* ◇ **~ sb into (doing) sth** *The urgency of his voice galvanized them into action.* **2** ~ *sth* (*specialist*) to cover metal with ZINC in order to protect it from RUST: *a galvanized bucket* ◇ *galvanized steel*

**gam·bit** /ˈɡæmbɪt/ *noun* **1** a thing that sb does, or sth that sb says at the beginning of a situation or conversation, that is intended to give them some advantage: *an opening gambit* (= the first thing you say) **2** a move or moves made at the beginning of a game of CHESS in order to gain an advantage later

**gam·ble** /ˈɡæmbl/ *verb, noun*

■ *verb* **1** [I, T] to risk money on a card game, horse race, etc: **~ (at/on sth)** *to gamble at cards* ◇ *to gamble on the horses* ◇ **~ sth (at/on sth)** *I gambled all my winnings on the last race.* **2** [T, I] to risk losing sth in the hope of being successful: **~ sth (on sth)** *He's gambling his reputation on this deal.* ◇ **~ with sth** *It was wrong to gamble with our children's future.* ▶ **gam·bler** /-blə(r)/ *noun*: *He was a compulsive gambler* (= found it difficult to stop).
PHRV **gamble sth↔aˈway** to lose sth such as money, possessions, etc. by gambling **ˈgamble on sth/on doing sth** to take a risk with sth, hoping that you will be successful: *He gambled on being able to buy a ticket at the last minute.*

■ *noun* [sing.] an action that you take when you know there is a risk but when you hope that the result will be a success: *She knew she was taking a gamble but decided it was worth it.* ◇ *They invested money in the company right at the start and the gamble paid off* (= brought them success).

**gam·bling** ⓘ+ ⒸⒷ /ˈɡæmblɪŋ/ *noun* [U] the activity of playing games of chance for money and of BETTING on horses, etc: *online/internet gambling* ◇ *heavy gambling debts* ⇒ WORDFINDER NOTE at CARD

**WORDFINDER** bet, casino, chip, croupier, lottery, odds, roulette, stake, streak

**gam·bol** /ˈɡæmbl/ *verb* [I] (**-ll-**, *US also* **-l-**) (+ *adv./prep.*) to jump or run about in a lively way: *lambs gambolling in the meadow*

**game** ⓘ ⒶⒹ /ɡeɪm/ *noun, verb, adj.*

■ *noun*
- FUN **1** ⓘ ⒶⒹ [C] an activity that you do to have fun, often one that has rules and that you can win or lose; the equipment used for a game: *The kids were playing a game with their balloons.* ◇ *a video/computer game* ◇ *I play online games with my friends.* ◇ *a game of chance/skill* ◇ *Buy your games and software from us.* ⇒ see also BOARD GAME, CARD GAME, COMPUTER GAME, PARLOUR GAME, SHELL GAME, VIDEO GAME, WAR GAME ⇒ SYNONYMS at INTEREST
- SPORT **2** ⓘ ⒶⒹ [C] a sport with rules in which people or teams compete against each other: *ball games, such as football or tennis* ◇ *How I hated team games at school!* ◇ **the ~ of sth** *the game of football/golf/cricket/basketball* **3** ⓘ ⒶⒹ [C] an occasion of playing a game: *to win/lose a game* ◇ *a baseball/basketball game* (*especially NAmE*) *a football game* HELP In *BrE* it is more usual to say *a football match*, unless you are talking about American football.: *Are you coming to watch the game?* ◇ **a ~ of sth** *to play a game of chess* ◇ **~ against/with sb** *Saturday's League game against Swansea* ◇ *They're in training for the big game.* ⇒ see also BALL GAME **4** [sing.] *sb's* **~** the way in which sb plays a game: *Maguire raised his game to collect the £40000 first prize.* ◇ *Stretching exercises can help you avoid injury and improve your game.*
**5** ⓘ **Games** [pl.] a large organized sports event: *the Olympic Games* **6 games** [pl.] (*old-fashioned, BrE*) sport as a lesson or an activity at school: *I always hated games at school.* **7** ⓘ ⒶⒹ [C] a section of some games, such as tennis, which forms a unit in scoring: *two games all* (= both players have won two games)
- ACTIVITY/BUSINESS **8** [C] a type of activity or business: *How long have you been in this game?* ◇ *the game of politics* ◇ *I'm new to this game myself.* ◇ *Getting dirty was all part of the game to the kids.* ⇒ see also WAITING GAME
- SECRET PLAN **9** [sing.] (*informal*) a secret and clever plan; a trick: *So that's his game* (= now I know what he has been planning). ⇒ see also MIND GAME
- WILD ANIMALS/BIRDS **10** [U] wild animals or birds that people hunt for sport or food ⇒ VISUAL VOCAB page V2 ⇒ WORDFINDER NOTE at HUNT ⇒ see also BIG GAME, FAIR GAME

IDM **be a ˈgame** to not be considered to be serious: *For her the whole project was just a game.* **be on the ˈgame** (*BrE, slang*) to be a PROSTITUTE **be out of the ˈgame** to no longer have a chance of winning a game or succeeding in an activity that you are taking part in **be still/back in the ˈgame** to still/once again have a good chance of winning a game or succeeding in an activity that you are taking part in: *The team was still in the game, just one goal down.* **the game is ˈup** (*informal*) said to sb who has done sth wrong, when they are caught and the crime or trick has been discovered **game ˈon** (*informal*) used after sth has happened that makes it clear that a contest is not yet decided and anyone could still win: *We were losing 2–0 with ten minutes to go, and then we scored. It was game on!* **game ˈover** (*informal*) used to say that it is no longer possible for sb/sth to succeed, survive or continue: *The slightest mistake and it's game over for him.* **give the ˈgame away** to tell a secret, especially by accident; to show sth that should be kept hidden **off/on your ˈgame** performing badly/well, especially when compared with how well you usually perform **the only game in ˈtown** (*informal*) the most important thing of a particular type, or the only thing that is available **play sb's ˈgame** to do sth that helps sb else's plans, especially by accident, when you did not intend to help them **play the ˈgame** to behave in a fair and honest way **play (silly) games (with sb)** not to treat a situation seriously, especially in order to cheat sb: *Don't play silly games with me; I know you did it.* **two can play at ˈthat game** (*saying*) used to tell sb who has played a trick on you that you can do the same thing to them

---
æ cat | ɑː father | e bed | ɜː fur | ə about | ɪ sit | iː see | i happy | ɒ got (*BrE*) | ɔː saw | ʌ cup | ʊ put | uː too

**what's sb's / your ˈgame?** (*informal*) used to ask why sb is behaving as they are ⇒ more at BEAT *v.*, CAT, *n.*, MUG *n.*, NAME *n.*, NUMBER *n.*, RULE *n.*, TALK *v.*, WORTH *adj.*
- **verb 1** [I] to risk money playing a game of chance **2** [I] to play video games **3** [T] **~ sth** to use sth in a way that is unfair but legal, in order to get what you want: *Some companies only received a government grant because they gamed the system.* ◊ *The government finance programme is being gamed by some high-profile banks.* **4** [T] **~ sb** to treat sb who trusts you in an unfair way in order to get what you want: *He gamed his publishers, his family and his friends in order to make a success of his autobiography.*
- *adj.* **~ (for sth / to do sth)** ready and willing to do sth new, difficult or dangerous: *She's game for anything.* ◊ *We need a volunteer for this exercise. Who's game to try?*

ˈ**game bird** *noun* a bird that people hunt for sport or food

ˈ**game changer** *noun* a person, an idea or an event that completely changes the way a situation develops ▶ ˈ**game-changing** *adj.*: *a game-changing technology*

ˈ**game face** *noun* (*especially NAmE*) a serious expression on sb's face, typical of sb trying to win in a sport or game: *I put my game face on and didn't let them see I was injured.*

ˈ**game·keep·er** /ˈɡeɪmkiːpə(r)/ *noun* a person whose job is to take care of wild animals and birds that are kept on private land in order to be hunted **IDM** see POACHER

ˈ**game·lan** /ˈɡæməlæn/ *noun* a traditional group of Indonesian musicians, playing instruments such as XYLOPHONES and GONGS

ˈ**game·ly** /ˈɡeɪmli/ *adv.* in a way that is brave, usually when a lot of effort is involved: *She tried gamely to finish the race.*

ˈ**game·pad** /ˈɡeɪmpæd/ *noun* an electronic device, usually held with two hands, that is used to control video games via a computer or similar device

ˈ**game plan** *noun* a plan for success in the future, especially in sport, politics or business

ˈ**game·play** /ˈɡeɪmpleɪ/ *noun* [U] the features of a computer game, such as its story or the way it is played, rather than the images or sounds it uses

ˈ**game ˈpoint** *noun* (especially in tennis) a point that, if won by a player, will win them the game

ˈ**gamer** /ˈɡeɪmə(r)/ *noun* (*informal*) **1** a person who likes playing computer games **2** (*NAmE*) (in sports) a player who is enthusiastic and works hard

ˈ**game reserve** (*also* ˈ**game park**) (*both BrE*) (*NAmE* ˈ**game preserve**) *noun* a large area of land where wild animals can live in safety

ˈ**games console** *noun* = CONSOLE² (2)

ˈ**game show** *noun* a television programme in which people play games or answer questions to win prizes ⇒ WORDFINDER NOTE at PROGRAMME

ˈ**games·man·ship** /ˈɡeɪmzmənʃɪp/ *noun* [U] (*usually disapproving*) the ability to win games by making your opponent less confident and using rules to your advantage ⇒ compare SPORTSMANSHIP

ˈ**gam·ete** /ˈɡæmiːt/ *noun* (*biology*) a male or female cell that joins with a cell of the opposite sex to form a ZYGOTE (= a single cell that develops into a person, animal or plant)

ˈ**game theory** *noun* [U] the part of mathematics that deals with situations in which people compete with each other, for example war or business

ˈ**game-time** *noun* (*NAmE*) the time when a sports game starts: *Game-time is at 4 p.m.* ◊ *a game-time decision* (= a decision made at the start of a game, usually about whether a particular player will play)

ˈ**game warden** *noun* a person whose job is to manage and take care of the wild animals in a GAME RESERVE

ˈ**gamey** (*also* **gamy**) /ˈɡeɪmi/ *adj.* (of meat that has been hunted) having a strong taste or smell as a result of being kept for some time before cooking

ˈ**gami·fi·ca·tion** /ˌɡeɪmɪfɪˈkeɪʃn/ *noun* [U] the use of elements of game-playing in another activity, usually in order to make that activity more interesting: *The supermarket chain has started using gamification to make food shopping*

# gangmaster

*online fun.* ▶ **gam·ify** /ˈɡeɪmɪfaɪ/ *verb*: **~ sth** *We gamified the online survey by awarding virtual rewards at the end of each section.*

**gam·ine** /ˈɡæmiːn/ *adj.* (*formal*) (of a young woman) thin and attractive; looking like a boy ▶ **gam·ine** *noun*

**gam·ing** /ˈɡeɪmɪŋ/ *noun* [U] **1** playing computer games: *online/mobile/console gaming* ⇒ see also SOCIAL GAMING **2** (*old-fashioned* or *law*) = GAMBLING: *He spent all night at the gaming tables*

**gamma** /ˈɡæmə/ *noun* the third letter of the Greek alphabet (Γ, γ)

**gamma ˈglobulin** /ˌɡæmə ˈɡlɒbjulɪn; *NAmE* ˈɡlɑːb-/ *noun* (*biology*) [U] a type of PROTEIN in the blood that gives protection against some types of diseases

**gamma radiˈation** *noun* [U] (*also* ˈ**gamma rays** [pl.]) (*physics*) high-energy RAYS of very short WAVELENGTH sent out by some RADIOACTIVE substances

**gam·mon** /ˈɡæmən/ *noun* [U] (*BrE*) meat from the back leg or side of a pig that has been CURED (= preserved using salt or smoke), usually served in thick slices ⇒ compare BACON, HAM, PORK

**the ˈgamut** /ðə ˈɡæmət/ *noun* [sing.] the complete range of a particular kind of thing: *The network will provide the gamut of computer services to your home.* ◊ *She felt she had run the (whole) gamut of human emotions from joy to despair.*

**gamy** = GAMEY

**Gan** /ɡæn/ *noun* [U] a form of Chinese, spoken mainly in Jiangxi

**gan·der** /ˈɡændə(r)/ *noun* a male GOOSE (= a bird like a large DUCK)
**IDM** ˈ**have / take a ˈgander (at sth)** (*informal*) to look at sth ⇒ more at SAUCE

**G and ˈT** /ˌdʒiː ən ˈtiː/ *noun* gin and tonic (= a drink consisting of GIN mixed with TONIC)

**gang** /ɡæŋ/ *noun*, *verb*
- *noun* [C + sing. / pl. v.] **1** an organized group of criminals: *criminal gangs* ◊ **~ of sb** *a gang of thieves* ◊ *Several gang members have been arrested.* **2** a group of young people who spend a lot of time together and often cause trouble or fight against other groups: *to join a gang* ◊ *a street gang* ◊ **~ of sb** *a gang of youths* ◊ **in a ~** *We were all in the same gang.* ◊ *Many gang members are just children.* ◊ *gang warfare* **3** (*informal*) a group of friends who meet regularly: *The whole gang will be there.* **4** an organized group of workers or prisoners doing work together ⇒ see also CHAIN GANG, PRESS GANG
- *verb*
**PHRV** ˌ**gang toˈgether** (*informal*) to join together in a group in order to have more power or strength ˌ**gang ˈup (on / against sb)** (*informal*) to join together in a group to hurt, frighten or oppose sb: *At school the older boys ganged up on him and called him names.*

ˈ**gang bang** *noun* (*slang*) **1** an occasion when a number of people have sex with each other in a group **2** RAPE of a person by a number of people one after the other ▶ ˈ**gang-bang** *verb*: **~ sb**

**gang·bust·ers** /ˈɡæŋbʌstəz; *NAmE* -stərz/ *noun*
**IDM** ˈ**go (like) ˈgangbusters** (*NAmE, informal*) with a lot of energy and enthusiasm

**gang·land** /ˈɡæŋlænd/ *noun* [sing.] the world of organized and violent crime: *gangland killings*

**gan·gling** /ˈɡæŋɡlɪŋ/ (*also* **gan·gly** /ˈɡæŋɡli/) *adj.* (of a person) tall, thin and not moving in an easy way **SYN** lanky: *a gangling youth/adolescent*

**gan·glion** /ˈɡæŋɡliən/ *noun* (*pl.* **gan·glia** /-liə/) (*medical*) **1** a mass of nerve cells **2** a SWELLING (= an area that is larger and rounder than normal) in a TENDON, often at the back of the hand

**gang·mas·ter** /ˈɡæŋmɑːstə(r); *NAmE* -mæs-/ *noun* (*BrE*) a person or company that organizes groups of workers on a

# gangplank

temporary basis to do MANUAL work (= physical work using their hands), especially work on farms

**gang·plank** /ˈɡæŋplæŋk/ noun a board placed between the side of a boat and land so people can get on and off

**ˈgang rape** noun [U, C] the RAPE of a person by a number of people one after the other ▶ **ˈgang-rape** verb ~ sb

**gan·grene** /ˈɡæŋɡriːn/ noun [U] the DECAY (= a process of being destroyed) that takes place in a part of the body when the blood supply to it has been stopped because of an illness or injury: *Gangrene set in and he had to have his leg amputated.* ▶ **gan·gren·ous** /-ɡrɪnəs/ adj.

**gang·sta** /ˈɡæŋstə/ noun 1 [C] (*especially NAmE, slang*) a member of a street gang 2 (*also* **gangsta ˈrap**, **ˈgangster rap**) [U] a type of RAP music, typically with words about violence, guns, drugs and sex

**gang·ster** /ˈɡæŋstə(r)/ noun a member of a group of violent criminals: *Chicago gangsters*

**gang·way** /ˈɡæŋweɪ/ noun 1 (*BrE*) a passage between rows of seats in a theatre, an aircraft, etc. ⊃ compare AISLE 2 a bridge placed between the side of a ship and land so people can get on and off

**ganja** /ˈɡændʒə/, ˈɡɑːn-/ noun [U] (*slang*) = CANNABIS

**gan·net** /ˈɡænɪt/ noun a large bird that lives near the sea and that catches fish by DIVING

**gan·try** /ˈɡæntri/ noun (*pl.* **-ies**) a tall metal frame that is used to support a CRANE, road signs, a SPACECRAFT while it is still on the ground, etc.

**gaol** /dʒeɪl/, **gaoler** /ˈdʒeɪlə(r)/ noun (*BrE, old-fashioned*) = JAIL, JAILER

**gap** ❶ **A2** **w** /ɡæp/ noun 1 **A2** a space where sth is missing: *~ in sth Fill the gaps in these sentences.* ◇ *There are huge gaps in their knowledge.* ◇ *His death left an enormous gap in my life.* ◇ *We think we've identified a gap in the market* (= a business opportunity to make or sell sth that is not yet available). 2 **B1** a space between two things or in the middle of sth, especially because there is a part missing: *~ in sth a gap in a hedge* ◇ *~ between A and B Leave a gap between your car and the next.* ◇ **through a~** *I managed to squeeze through the gap.* 3 **B1** a period of time when sth stops, or between two events: *~ in sth a gap in the conversation* ◇ *~ between A and B He wrote his first novel in the gap between school and university.* ◇ *~ of sth They met again after a gap of twenty years.* ◇ *There's a big age gap between them* (= a big difference in their ages). 4 **B1** *~* **(between A and B)** a difference that separates people, or their opinions, situation, etc: *the gap between rich and poor* ◇ *the gap between theory and practice* ◇ *to bridge the gap between urban and rural communities* ⊃ see also CREDIBILITY, GENDER GAP, GENERATION GAP, PAY GAP, WAGE GAP

**gape** /ɡeɪp/ verb 1 [I] *~* **(at sb/sth)** to stare at sb/sth with your mouth open because you are shocked or surprised 2 [I] to be or become wide open: *a gaping hole/mouth/wound* ◇ *~* **open** *He stood yawning, his pyjama jacket gaping open.* ▶ **gape** noun

**gap-toothed** adj. (*usually before noun*) having a wide space between two of your teeth

**ˈgap year** noun (*BrE*) a year that a young person spends working and/or travelling, often between leaving school and starting university: *I'm planning to take a gap year and go backpacking in India.*

**gar·age** ❶ **B1** /ˈɡærɑːʒ, -rɑːdʒ, -rɪdʒ; *NAmE* ɡəˈrɑːʒ, -ˈrɑːdʒ/ *noun, verb*
■ *noun* 1 **B1** [C] a building for keeping one or more cars or other vehicles in: *a double garage* (= one for two cars) ◇ *a bus garage* ◇ *an underground garage* (= for example under an office building) ◇ *in a~ Don't forget to put the car in the garage.* ⊃ see also PARKING GARAGE 2 **B1** [C] a place where vehicles are repaired and/or where you can buy a car or buy petrol and oil: *I had to take the car to the garage.* ◇ **at a~** *The car's still at the garage.* ⊃ compare PETROL STATION 3 (*also* **garage rock**) [U] a style of rock music played with great energy but not necessarily great technique, popular in the 1960s 4 (*also* **UK garage**) [U] a type of electronic dance music with elements of DRUM AND BASS, HOUSE MUSIC and SOUL
■ *verb* ~ sth to put or keep a vehicle in a garage

**ˈgarage rock** noun [U] a type of rock music played with a lot of energy, often by musicians who are not professionals

**ˈgarage sale** noun a sale of used clothes, furniture, etc., held in the garage of sb's house ⊃ compare RUMMAGE SALE, YARD SALE

**garam masala** /ˌɡʌrəm məˈsɑːlə; *NAmE* məˈsɑːlɑː/ noun [U] a mixture of SPICES with a strong taste, used in South Asian cooking

**garb** /ɡɑːb; *NAmE* ɡɑːrb/ noun [U] (*formal or humorous*) clothes, especially unusual clothes or those worn by a particular type of person: *prison garb*

**gar·bage** /ˈɡɑːbɪdʒ; *NAmE* ˈɡɑːrb-/ noun [U] 1 (*especially NAmE*) waste food, paper, etc. that you throw away: *garbage collection* ◇ *Don't forget to take out the garbage.* 2 (*especially NAmE*) a place or container where waste food, paper, etc. can be placed: *Throw it in the garbage.* 3 (*informal*) something stupid or not true **SYN** **rubbish** ⊃ note at RUBBISH

**ˈgarbage can** (*also* **ˈtrash can**, **ˈgarbage bin**) (*all NAmE*) (*BrE* **ˈdust·bin**) noun a large container with a LID (= cover), used for putting rubbish in, usually kept outside the house ⊃ note at RUBBISH

**ˈgarbage disposal** noun (*NAmE*) = WASTE DISPOSAL UNIT

**ˈgarbage man** (*also formal* **ˈgarbage collector**) (*both NAmE*) (*BrE* **ˈdust·man**, *informal* **ˈbin·man**, *formal* **ˈrefuse collector**) noun a person whose job is to remove waste from outside houses, etc. ⊃ note at RUBBISH

**ˈgarbage truck** (*NAmE*) (*BrE* **ˈbin lorry**, **ˈrubbish truck**, *old-fashioned*, *BrE* **ˈdust-cart**) noun a vehicle for collecting rubbish from outside houses, etc.

**gar·banzo** /ɡɑːˈbænzəʊ; *NAmE* ɡɑːrˈbɑːn-, -ˈbæn-/ (*also* **garˈbanzo bean**) (*both NAmE*) noun (*pl.* **-os**) = CHICKPEA ⊃ VISUAL VOCAB page V5

**garbed** /ɡɑːbd; *NAmE* ɡɑːrbd/ adj. [not before noun] (*formal*) *~* **(in sth)** dressed in a particular way: *brightly garbed*

**gar·bled** /ˈɡɑːbld; *NAmE* ˈɡɑːrb-/ adj. (of a message or story) told in a way that confuses the person listening, usually by sb who is shocked or in a hurry **SYN** **confused**: *He gave a garbled account of what had happened.* ◇ *There was a garbled message from her on my voicemail.*

**garbo** /ˈɡɑːbəʊ; *NAmE* ˈɡɑːrb-/ noun (*pl.* **-os**) (*AustralE, informal*) a person whose job is to remove waste from outside houses, etc. **SYN** **dustman**, **garbage collector**

**Garda** /ˈɡɑːdə; *NAmE* ˈɡɑːrdə/ noun 1 **the Garda** [U] the police force of the Republic of Ireland 2 [C] (*also* **garda**) (*pl.* **gardai** /-diː/) a police officer of the Republic of Ireland

**gar·den** ❶ **A1** /ˈɡɑːdn; *NAmE* ˈɡɑːrdn/ *noun, verb*
■ *noun* 1 **A1** [C] (*BrE*) (*NAmE* **yard**) a piece of land next to or around your house where you can grow flowers, fruit, vegetables, etc., usually with a LAWN (= an area of grass): *a front/back/rear garden* ◇ *a vegetable garden* ◇ *a rose garden* (= where only ROSES are grown) ◇ *The main bedroom overlooks the garden.* ◇ **in the~** *children playing in the garden* ◇ *a garden shed* ◇ *garden flowers/plants* ⊃ see also COMMUNITY GARDEN, KITCHEN GARDEN, MARKET GARDEN, ROCK GARDEN, ROOF GARDEN 2 **A2** [C] (*NAmE*) an area in a yard where you grow flowers or plants: *These flowers brighten up backyard gardens all over the country.* ⊃ see also BEER GARDEN 3 **A2** [C] (*usually* **gardens**) a public park: *Thousands of people now visit the gardens every year.* ◇ **in the gardens** *The concert will take place in the gardens.* ⊃ see also BOTANICAL GARDEN, ZOOLOGICAL GARDEN 4 **gardens** [sing.] (*abbr.* **Gdns**) (*BrE*) used in the name of streets: *39 Belvoir Gardens*
**IDM** **everything in the garden is ˈrosy** (*BrE, saying*) everything is fine ⊃ more at COMMON adj., LEAD v.
■ *verb* [I] to work in a garden ▶ **gar·den·er** /ˈɡɑːdnə(r); *NAmE* ˈɡɑːrd-/ noun: *My wife's a keen gardener.* ◇ *We employ a gardener two days a week.* **gar·den·ing** /-nɪŋ/

noun [U]: *organic gardening* ◊ *gardening gloves* ◊ *a gardening programme on TV*

**'garden centre** (*BrE*) (*US* **'garden center**) *noun* a place that sells plants, seeds, garden equipment, etc.

**garden 'city, garden 'suburb** *noun* (*BrE*) a city or part of a city that has been specially designed to have a lot of open spaces, parks and trees

**'garden egg** *noun* [C, U] (*WAfrE*) a type of AUBERGINE with purple, white or yellow-green skin

**gar·denia** /gɑːˈdiːniə/ *NAmE* gɑːrˈd-/ *noun* a bush with shiny leaves and large white or yellow flowers with a sweet smell, also called gardenias

**'gardening leave** *noun* [U] (*BrE*) a period during which sb who has given notice that they want to leave their job does not work but remains employed by the company in order to prevent them from accessing CONFIDENTIAL (= secret) information: *She handed in her resignation and was put on three months' gardening leave.*

**the ,Garden of 'Eden** *noun* [sing.] = EDEN

**'garden party** *noun* a formal social event that takes place in the afternoon in a large garden

**,garden 'salad** *noun* [U, C] (*NAmE*) a salad containing a variety of raw vegetables, especially LETTUCE

**'garden-variety** (*NAmE*) (*BrE* **,common or 'garden**) *adj.* [only before noun] ordinary; with no special features: *He is not one of your garden-variety criminals.*

**gar·gan·tuan** /gɑːˈɡæntʃuən/ *NAmE* gɑːrˈɡ-/ *adj.* [usually before noun] extremely large **SYN** **enormous**: *a gargantuan appetite/meal*

**gar·gle** /ˈɡɑːɡl/ *NAmE* ˈɡɑːrɡl/ *verb, noun*
- *verb* [I] ~ (with sth) to wash inside your mouth and throat by moving a liquid around at the back of your throat and then SPITTING it out
- *noun* **1** [C, U] a liquid used for gargling: *an antiseptic gargle* **2** [sing.] an act of gargling or a sound like that made when gargling: *to have a gargle with salt water*

**gar·goyle** /ˈɡɑːɡɔɪl/ *NAmE* ˈɡɑːrɡ-/ *noun* an ugly figure of a person or an animal that is made of stone and through which water is carried away from the roof of a building, especially a church

**gar·ish** /ˈɡeərɪʃ/ *NAmE* ˈɡer-/ *adj.* (*disapproving*) very brightly coloured in an unpleasant way **SYN** **gaudy**: *garish clothes/colours* ▸ **gar·ish·ly** *adv.*: *garishly decorated/lit/painted*

**gar·land** /ˈɡɑːlənd/ *NAmE* ˈɡɑːrl-/ *noun, verb*
- *noun* a circle of flowers and leaves that is worn on the head or around the neck or is hung in a room as decoration
- *verb* [usually passive] ~ sb/sth (with sth) (*literary*) to decorate sb/sth with a garland or garlands

**gar·lic** /ˈɡɑːlɪk/ *NAmE* ˈɡɑːrl-/ *noun* [U] a vegetable of the onion family with a very strong taste and smell, used in cooking to add taste to food: *a clove of garlic* (= one section of it) ⊃ VISUAL VOCAB page V5 ▸ **gar·licky** /-lɪki/ *adj.*: *garlicky breath/food*

**,garlic 'bread** *noun* [U] bread, usually in the shape of a stick, containing or spread with butter and garlic and heated in an oven

**'garlic press** (*BrE also* **'garlic crusher**) *noun* a small kitchen tool used to CRUSH garlic

**gar·ment** /ˈɡɑːmənt/ *NAmE* ˈɡɑːrm-/ *noun* (*formal*) a piece of clothing: *a strange shapeless garment that had once been a jacket* ◊ *woollen/winter/outer garments* ⊃ SYNONYMS at CLOTHES ⊃ see also UNDERGARMENT

**gar·ner** /ˈɡɑːnə(r)/ *NAmE* ˈɡɑːrn-/ *verb* ~ sth (*formal*) to obtain or collect sth such as information, support, etc. **SYN** **gather, acquire**

**gar·net** /ˈɡɑːnɪt/ *NAmE* ˈɡɑːrn-/ *noun* a clear dark red SEMI-PRECIOUS stone that is fairly valuable

**gar·nish** /ˈɡɑːnɪʃ/ *NAmE* ˈɡɑːrn-/ *verb, noun*
- *verb* ~ sth (with sth) to decorate a dish of food with a small amount of another food
- *noun* [C, U] a small amount of food that is used to decorate a larger dish of food

**gar·otte** = GARROTTE

**gar·ret** /ˈɡærət/ *noun* a room, often a small dark unpleasant one, at the top of a house, especially in the roof ⊃ compare ATTIC ⊃ see also LOFT *noun*

**garri** /ˈɡæri/ *WAfrE* [gàrí] *noun* [U] (*WAfrE*) a type of flour made from the roots of the CASSAVA plant

**gar·rison** /ˈɡærɪsn/ *noun, verb*
- *noun* [C + sing. / pl. v.] a group of soldiers living in a town or FORT to defend it; the buildings these soldiers live in: *a garrison of 5000 troops* ◊ *a garrison town* ◊ *Half the garrison is/are on duty.*
- *verb* to put soldiers in a place in order to defend it from attack: ~ sth *Two regiments were sent to garrison the town.* ◊ ~ sb + adv./prep. *100 soldiers were garrisoned in the town.*

**gar·rotte** (*also* **gar·otte**) (*US also* **gar·rote**) /ɡəˈrɒt/ *NAmE* -ˈrɑːt/ *verb, noun*
- *verb* ~ sb to kill sb by putting a piece of wire, etc. around their neck and pulling it tight
- *noun* a piece of wire, etc. used for garrotting sb

**gar·rul·ous** /ˈɡærələs/ *adj.* talking a lot, especially about unimportant things **SYN** **talkative** ▸ **gar·rul·ous·ly** *adv.*

**gar·ter** /ˈɡɑːtə(r)/ *NAmE* ˈɡɑːrt-/ *noun* **1** a band, usually made of ELASTIC, that is worn around the leg to keep up a sock or STOCKING **2** (*NAmE*) (*BrE* **sus·pend·er**) a piece of ELASTIC attached to a belt and fastened to the top of a STOCKING to hold it up **IDM** see GUT *n.*

**'garter belt** (*NAmE*) (*BrE* **su'spender belt**) *noun* a piece of women's underwear like a belt, worn around the middle part of the body, used for holding STOCKINGS up

**'garter snake** *noun* an American snake that is not dangerous, with coloured lines along its back

**gas** /ɡæs/ *noun, verb*
- *noun* (*pl.* **gases** *or less frequent* **gas·ses**)
- • NOT SOLID/LIQUID **1** [C, U] any substance like air that is neither a solid nor a liquid, for example HYDROGEN or OXYGEN: *Air is a mixture of gases.* ◊ *Carbon monoxide is a poisonous gas.* ⊃ see also GREENHOUSE GAS, INERT GAS, NOBLE GAS, RARE GAS **2** [U] a particular type of gas or mixture of gases used as fuel for heating and cooking: *Can you smell gas?* ◊ *a gas cooker/stove/fire* ◊ *gas central heating* ◊ *a gas leak/explosion* ◊ *plans to build a new gas pipeline* ◊ *Gas prices have risen sharply.* ⊃ see also CALOR GAS™, COAL GAS, NATURAL GAS, SHALE GAS **3** [U] a particular type of gas used during a medical operation, to make the patient unconscious or to make the pain less: *an anaesthetic gas* ◊ *During the birth she was given gas and air.* ⊃ see also LAUGHING GAS **4** [U] a particular type of gas used in war to kill or injure people, or used by the police to control people: *a gas attack* ⊃ see also CS GAS, MUSTARD GAS, NERVE GAS, TEAR GAS
- • IN VEHICLE **5** (*also* **gas·oline**) (*both NAmE*) (*BrE* **pet·rol**) [U] a liquid obtained from PETROLEUM, used as fuel in car engines, etc: *to run out of gas* ◊ *a gas pump* ◊ *to fill up the gas tank* ⊃ see also GAS STATION (1) **6 the gas** [sing.] (*especially NAmE*) = GAS PEDAL: *Step on the gas, we're late.*
- • FUN **7** [sing.] (*especially NAmE*) a person or an event that is fun: *The party was a real gas.*
- • IN STOMACH **8** (*NAmE*) (*BrE* **wind**) [U] air that you SWALLOW with food or drink; gas that is produced in your stomach or INTESTINES that makes you feel uncomfortable **IDM** see COOK *v.*
- *verb* (-ss-)
- • KILL/HARM WITH GAS **1** [T] ~ sb/yourself to kill or harm sb by making them breathe poisonous gas
- • TALK **2** [I] (usually used in the progressive tenses) (*old-fashioned, informal*) to talk for a long time about things that are not important **SYN** **chat**

**'gas·bag** /ˈɡæsbæɡ/ *noun* (*informal, humorous*) a person who talks a lot

**'gas chamber** *noun* a room that can be filled with poisonous gas for killing animals or people

**gas-cooled** adj. [only before noun] using gas to keep the temperature cool: *gas-cooled nuclear reactors*

**gas·eous** /ˈgæsiəs; *BrE also* ˈgeɪs-; *NAmE also* ˈgæʃəs/ adj. [usually before noun] like or containing gas: *a gaseous mixture* ◊ *in gaseous form*

**gas-fired** adj. [usually before noun] (*BrE*) using gas as a fuel: *gas-fired central heating*

**gas giant** noun (*astronomy*) a large planet made mostly of the gases HYDROGEN and HELIUM, for example Jupiter or Saturn

**gas guzzler** noun (*informal, especially NAmE*) a car or other vehicle that needs a lot of petrol ▶ **gas-guzzling** adj. [only before noun]

**gash** /gæʃ/ noun, verb
■ noun ~ (in/on sth) a long deep cut in the surface of sth, especially a person's skin
■ verb ~ sth/sb to make a long deep cut in sth, especially a person's skin: *He gashed his hand on a sharp piece of rock.*

**gas·ket** /ˈgæskɪt/ noun a flat piece of rubber, etc. placed between two metal surfaces in a pipe or an engine to prevent STEAM, gas or oil from escaping: *The engine had blown a gasket* (= had allowed STEAM, etc. to escape) ◊ (*figurative, informal*) *He blew a gasket at the news* (= became very angry).

**gas lamp** (*also* **gas light**) noun a lamp in the street or in a house, that produces light from burning gas

**gas·light** /ˈgæslaɪt/ noun **1** [U] light produced from burning gas: *In the gaslight she looked paler than ever.* **2** [C] = GAS LAMP

**gas mask** noun a piece of equipment worn over the face as protection against poisonous gas

**gas oil** noun [U] a type of oil obtained from PETROLEUM that is used as a fuel

**gas·oline** (*also* **gas·olene**) /ˈgæsəliːn, ˌgæsəˈliːn/ noun (*NAmE*) = GAS (5): *I fill up the tank with gasoline about once a week.* ◊ *leaded/unleaded gasoline*

**gasp** /gɑːsp; *NAmE* gæsp/ verb, noun
■ verb **1** [I, T] to take a quick deep breath with your mouth open, especially because you are surprised or in pain: ~ (at sth) *She gasped at the wonderful view.* ◊ *They gasped in astonishment at the news.* ◊ + speech '*What was that noise?*' *he gasped.* **2** [I, T] to have difficulty breathing or speaking: ~ (for sth) *He came to the surface of the water gasping for air.* ◊ ~ (sth) (out) *She managed to gasp out her name.* ◊ + speech '*Can't breathe,*' *he gasped.* **3 be gasping (for sth)** [I] (*BrE, informal*) to want or need sth very badly, especially a drink or a cigarette
■ noun a quick deep breath, usually caused by a strong emotion: *to give a gasp of horror/surprise/relief* ◊ *His breath came in short gasps.* **IDM** see LAST¹ *det.*

**gas pedal** (*especially NAmE*) (*also* **ac·cel·er·ator** *BrE and NAmE*) noun the PEDAL in a car or other vehicle that you press with your foot to control the speed of the engine

**gas ring** noun (*BrE*) a round piece of metal with holes in it on the top of a gas cooker, where the gas is lit to produce the flame for cooking ⊃ picture at RING¹

**gas station** (*NAmE*) (*BrE* **petrol station**) (*also* **filling station**, **service station** *NAmE, BrE*) noun a place at the side of a road where you can stop to buy petrol, oil, etc.

**gassy** /ˈgæsi/ adj. **1** (*BrE, disapproving*) (of drinks) containing too much gas in the form of bubbles **2** (*NAmE*) (of people) having a lot of gas in your stomach, etc.

**gas·tric** /ˈgæstrɪk/ adj. [only before noun] (*medical*) connected with the stomach: *a gastric ulcer* ◊ *gastric juices* (= the acids in your stomach that help you to DIGEST food)

**gastric band** noun a device made of SILICONE that is put around the upper section of a person's stomach to help them lose weight by reducing the amount of food that they are able to eat

**gastric bypass** noun [usually sing.] surgery that reduces the size of sb's stomach so that they will eat less food: *gastric bypass surgery*

**gastric flu** noun [U] an illness affecting the stomach, which does not last long and is thought to be caused by a virus

**gas·tri·tis** /gæˈstraɪtɪs/ noun [U] (*medical*) an illness in which the inside of the stomach becomes SWOLLEN (= larger or rounder than normal) and painful

**gastro-enter·itis** /ˌgæstrəʊˌentəˈraɪtɪs/ noun [U] (*medical*) an illness of the stomach and other food passages that causes DIARRHOEA and VOMITING

**gas·tro·intest·inal** /ˌgæstrəʊɪnˈtestɪnl; *BrE also* -ˌinteˈstaɪ-/ adj. (*medical*) of or related to the stomach and INTESTINES

**gas·tro·nom·ic** /ˌgæstrəˈnɒmɪk; *NAmE* -ˈnɑːm-/ adj. [only before noun] connected with cooking and eating good food ▶ **gas·tro·nom·ic·al·ly** /-kli/ adv.

**gas·tron·omy** /gæˈstrɒnəmi; *NAmE* -ˈstrɑːn-/ noun [U] (*formal*) the art and practice of cooking and eating good food

**gas·tro·pod** /ˈgæstrəpɒd; *NAmE* -pɑːd/ noun (*biology*) a MOLLUSC such as a SNAIL or SLUG, that moves on one large foot ⊃ VISUAL VOCAB page V3

**gas·tro·pub** /ˈgæstrəʊpʌb/ noun (*BrE*) a pub that is well known for serving good food

**gas·works** /ˈgæswɜːks; *NAmE* -wɜːrks/ noun (*pl.* **gas·works**) [C + sing./pl. v.] a factory where gas for lighting and heating is made from coal

**gate** 🅘 **A2** /geɪt/ noun **1** 🔑 **A2** [C] a barrier like a door that is used to close an opening in a fence or a wall outside a building: *the front/main gate* ◊ *He pushed open the garden gate.* ◊ **outside a ~** *Students were still standing outside the school gates.* ◊ **at a ~** *A crowd gathered at the factory gates.* ◊ **~ to sth** *Someone was waiting by the gate to his house.* ⊃ see also STARTING GATE, TOLL GATE **2** 🔑 **A2** [C] an opening that can be closed by a gate or gates: **through a ~** *We drove through the palace gates.* **3** 🔑 **A2** [C] a way out of an airport through which passengers go to get on their plane: **at a ~** *BA flight 726 to Paris is now boarding at gate 16.* ⊃ WORDFINDER NOTE at AIRPORT **4** [C] a barrier that is used to control the flow of water on a river or CANAL: *a lock/sluice gate* **5** [C] the number of people who attend a sports event: *Tonight's game has attracted the largest gate of the season.* **6** (*also* **gate money**) [U] the amount of money made by selling tickets for a sports event: *Today's gate will be given to charity.* **7 -gate** (forming nouns from the names of people or places; used especially in newspapers) a political SCANDAL connected with the person or place mentioned **ORIGIN** From **Watergate**, the scandal in the United States that brought about the resignation of President Nixon in 1974. **8** (*computing*) = LOGIC GATE

**gat·eau** /ˈgætəʊ; *NAmE* gæˈtoʊ/ noun [C, U] (*pl.* **gat·eaux** /ˈgætəʊ; *NAmE* gæˈtoʊ/) (*especially BrE*) a large cake filled with cream and usually decorated with fruit, nuts, etc: *a strawberry gateau* ◊ *Is there any gateau left?*

**gate·crash** /ˈgeɪtkræʃ/ (*also informal* **crash**) verb [T, I] ~ (sth) to go to a party or social event without being invited ▶ **gate·crash·er** (*especially NAmE, informal* **crash·er**) noun

**gated** /ˈgeɪtɪd/ adj. [usually before noun] having gates to control the movement of traffic, people or animals: *a gated road*

**gated com·mun·ity** noun a group of houses surrounded by a wall or fence, with gates at the entrance to control the movement of traffic and people into and out of the area

**gate·fold** /ˈgeɪtfəʊld/ noun a large page folded to fit a book or magazine that can be opened out for reading

**gate·house** /ˈgeɪthaʊs/ noun a house built at or over a gate, for example at the entrance to a park or castle

**gate·keep·er** /ˈgeɪtkiːpə(r)/ noun **1** a person whose job is to check and control who is allowed to go through a gate **2** a person, system, etc. that decides whether sb/sth will be allowed, or allowed to reach a particular place or person: *His secretary acts as a gatekeeper, reading all mail before it reaches her boss.*

**gate money** *noun* [U] = GATE (6)

**gate-post** /ˈɡeɪtpəʊst/ *noun* a post to which a gate is attached or against which it is closed
**IDM** **between you, me and the ˈgatepost** (*BrE, informal*) used to show that what you are going to say next is a secret

**gate-way** /ˈɡeɪtweɪ/ *noun* **1** an opening in a wall or fence that can be closed by a gate: *They turned through the gateway on the left.* **2** [usually sing.] **~ to/into ...** a place through which you can go to reach another larger place: *Perth, the gateway to Western Australia* **3** [usually sing.] **~ to sth** a means of getting or achieving sth: *A good education is the gateway to success.* **4** (*computing*) an INTERMEDIATE link in the connection between two computers or networks that can provide facilities such as additional security

**gather** 🔊 **B1** /ˈɡæðə(r)/ *verb*
- **COME/BRING TOGETHER 1** 🔊 **B1** [I, T] to come together, or bring people together, in one place to form a group: *A crowd soon gathered.* ◊ **+ adv./prep.** *His supporters gathered in the main square.* ◊ *Can you all gather round? I've got something to tell you.* ◊ *The whole family gathered together at Ray's home.* ◊ **be gathered + adv./prep.** *They were all gathered round the TV.* ◊ *A large crowd was gathered outside the studio.* **2** 🔊 **B1** [T] to bring things together that have been spread around: **~ sth** *People slowly gathered their belongings and left the hall.* ◊ **~ sth together / up | ~ sth up** *I waited while he gathered up his papers.* ⊃ SYNONYMS at COLLECT
- **COLLECT 3** 🔊 **B1** [T] **~ sth** to collect information from different sources: *to gather information/data/intelligence* ◊ *Detectives have spent months gathering evidence.* ⊃ SYNONYMS at COLLECT **4** 🔊 **B1** [T] **~ sth** to collect plants, fruit, etc. from a wide area: *to gather wild flowers*
- **CROPS/HARVEST 5** [T] **~ sth (in)** (*formal* or *literary*) to pick or cut and collect crops to be stored: *It was late August and the harvest had been safely gathered in.*
- **BELIEVE/UNDERSTAND 6** [T] (not used in the progressive tenses) to believe or understand that sth is true because of information or evidence you have: **~(that)** *... I gather (that) you wanted to see me.* ◊ *I gather from your letter that you're not enjoying your job.* ◊ **~(sth)** *'There's been a delay.' 'I gathered that.'* ◊ *'She won't be coming.' 'So I gather.'* ◊ *You're self-employed, I gather.* ◊ *As far as I can gather, he got involved in a fight.* ◊ *From what I can gather, there's been some kind of problem.*
- **INCREASE 7** [T] **~ sth** to increase in speed, force, etc: *The truck gathered speed.* ◊ *During the 1980s the green movement gathered momentum.* ◊ *Thousands of these machines are gathering dust* (= not being used) *in stockrooms.*
- **OF CLOUDS / DARKNESS 8** [I] to gradually increase in number or amount: *The storm clouds were gathering.* ◊ *the gathering gloom of a winter's afternoon*
- **CLOTHING 9** [T] to pull a piece of clothing tighter to your body: **~ sth around you / sth** *He gathered his cloak around him.* ◊ **~ sth up** *She gathered up her skirts and ran.* **10** [T] **~ sth (in)** to pull parts of a piece of clothing together in folds and SEW them in place: *She wore a skirt gathered (in) at the waist.*
- **HOLD SB 11** [T] **~ sb + adv./prep.** to pull sb towards you and put your arms around them: *She gathered the child in her arms and held him close.* ◊ *He gathered her to him.*
- **PREPARE YOURSELF 12** [T] **~ sth / yourself** to prepare yourself to do sth that requires effort: *I sat down for a moment to gather my strength.* ◊ *She was still trying to gather her thoughts together when the door opened.* ◊ *Fortunately the short delay gave him time to gather himself.* **IDM** see DUST *n.*, ROLL *v.*

**gath-er-er** /ˈɡæðərə(r)/ *noun* a person who collects sth
⊃ see also HUNTER-GATHERER

**gath-er-ing** 🔊+ **C1** /ˈɡæðərɪŋ/ *noun* **1** 🔊+ **C1** [C] a meeting of people for a particular purpose: *a social/family gathering* ◊ *a gathering of religious leaders* **2** 🔊+ **C1** [U] the process of collecting sth: *methods of information gathering*

---

655

# gavial

**gathers** /ˈɡæðəz; *NAmE* -ðərz/ *noun* [pl.] small folds that are SEWN into a piece of clothing

**ga·tor** /ˈɡeɪtə(r)/ *noun* (*NAmE, informal*) = ALLIGATOR

**gat·vol** /ˈxætfɒl; *NAmE* ˈxɑːtfɔːl; *SAfrE* [ˈxætfəl] *adj.* [not usually before noun] (*SAfrE*) (*informal*) very upset or extremely unhappy or bored with a situation: **~ (of sb / sth)** *I am gatvol of travelling on a jarring road, picking up punctures.* ◊ **~ (with sb / sth)** *I'm gatvol with this traffic.*

**gauche** /ɡəʊʃ/ *adj.* shy or uncomfortable when dealing with people and often saying or doing the wrong thing: *a gauche schoolgirl / manner* ▸ **gauche·ness** (also **gauch·erie** /ˈɡəʊʃəri; *NAmE* ˌɡəʊʃəˈriː/) *noun* [U]: *the gaucheness of youth*

**gau·cho** /ˈɡaʊtʃəʊ/ *noun* (*pl.* **-os**) a South American COWBOY

**gaudy** /ˈɡɔːdi/ *adj.* (**gaud·ier**, **gaudi·est**) (*disapproving*) too brightly coloured in a way that lacks taste **SYN** **garish**: *gaudy clothes / colours* ▸ **gaud·ily** /-dɪli/ *adv.*: *gaudily dressed / painted* **gaudi·ness** *noun* [U]

**gauge** (*US also* **gage**) /ɡeɪdʒ/ *noun, verb*
▪ *noun* **1** (often in compounds) an instrument for measuring the amount or level of sth: *a fuel / pressure / temperature gauge* **2** a measurement of how wide or thick sth is: *What gauge of wire do we need?* **3** (*also* **bore** especially in *BrE*) a measurement of how wide the BARREL of a gun is: *a 12-gauge shotgun* **4** the distance between the RAILS of a railway track or the wheels of a train: *standard gauge* (= 56½ inches in Britain) ◊ *a narrow gauge* (= narrower than standard) *railway* ⊃ see also NARROW GAUGE **5** [usually sing.] **~ (of sth)** a fact or an event that can be used to estimate or judge sth: *Tomorrow's game against Arsenal will be a good gauge of their promotion chances.*
▪ *verb* **1** to make a judgement about sth, especially people's feelings or attitudes: **~ sth** *They interviewed employees to gauge their reaction to the changes.* ◊ *He tried to gauge her mood.* ◊ **~ whether, how, etc...** *It was difficult to gauge whether she was angry or not.* **2** **~ sth** to measure sth accurately using a special instrument: *precision instruments that can gauge the diameter to a fraction of a millimetre* **3** **~ sth | ~ how, what, etc...** to calculate sth approximately: *We were able to gauge the strength of the wind from the movement of the trees.*

**gaunt** /ɡɔːnt/ *adj.* **1** (of a person) very thin, usually because of illness, not having enough food, or worry: *a gaunt face* **2** (of a building) not attractive and without any decoration
▸ **gaunt·ness** *noun* [U]

**gaunt·let** /ˈɡɔːntlət/ *noun* **1** a metal glove worn as part of a suit of ARMOUR by soldiers in the Middle Ages **2** a strong glove that covers and protects the hand and WRIST, used for example when driving: *motorcyclists with leather gauntlets*
**IDM** **run the ˈgauntlet** to be criticized or attacked by a lot of people, especially a group of people that you have to walk through: *Some of the witnesses had to run the gauntlet of television cameras and reporters.* **ORIGIN** This phrase refers to an old army punishment where a man was forced to run between two lines of soldiers hitting him. **take up the ˈgauntlet** to accept sb's invitation to fight or compete **ORIGIN** In the Middle Ages a knight threw his gauntlet at the feet of another knight as a challenge to fight. If he accepted the challenge, the other knight would pick up the glove. **throw down the ˈgauntlet** to invite sb to fight or compete with you

**gauze** /ɡɔːz/ *noun* **1** [U] a type of light cloth that you can see through, usually made of cotton or silk **2** [U] a type of thin cotton cloth used for covering and protecting wounds: *a gauze dressing* **3** [U, C] material made of a network of wire; a piece of this: *wire gauze* ▸ **gauzy** *adj.* [usually before noun]: *a gauzy material*

**gave** /ɡeɪv/ *past tense of* GIVE

**gavel** /ˈɡævl/ *noun* a small HAMMER used by a person in charge of a meeting or an AUCTION or by a judge in court, in order to get people's attention

**ga·vial** /ˈɡeɪviəl/ *noun* = GHARIAL

---

s see | t tea | v van | w wet | z zoo | ʃ shoe | ʒ vision | tʃ chain | dʒ jam | θ thin | ð this | ŋ sing

# gawk

**Gawd** /gɔːd/ noun, exclamation (informal) used in written English to show that the word 'God' is being pronounced in a particular way to express surprise, anger or fear: *For Gawd's sake hurry up!* HELP Some people find this use of 'God' offensive.

**gawk** /gɔːk/ verb [I] ~ **(at sb/sth)** (informal) to stare at sb/sth in a rude or stupid way SYN **gape**

**gawky** /ˈgɔːki/ adj. (especially of a tall young person) not easy or comfortable in the way they move or behave SYN **awkward** ▸ **gawki·ness** noun [U]

**gawp** /gɔːp/ verb [I] ~ **(at sb/sth)** (BrE, informal) to stare at sb/sth in a rude or stupid way SYN **gape**

**gay** 🔑+ B2 /geɪ/ adj., noun
■ adj. **1** 🔑+ B2 (of people, especially men) sexually attracted to people of the same sex SYN **homosexual**: *gay men ◇ I didn't know he was gay. ◇ Is she gay?* OPP **straight 2** 🔑+ B2 [only before noun] connected with people who are gay: *a gay club/bar ◇ the lesbian and gay community* **3** [not before noun] (*slang, disapproving, offensive*) (used especially by young people) boring and not fashionable or attractive: *She didn't like the ringtone—said it was gay. ◇ That is so gay!* **4** (**gayer, gayest**) (*old-fashioned*) happy and full of fun: *gay laughter* **5** (*old-fashioned*) brightly coloured: *The garden was gay with red geraniums.* ⊃ see also GAIETY, GAILY
IDM **with ˌgay abˈandon** without thinking about the results or effects of a particular action
■ noun a person who is gay, especially a man

**gay·dar** /ˈgeɪdɑː(r)/ noun [U] (informal) the ability that a gay person is supposed to have to recognize other people who are gay

**gay·ness** /ˈgeɪnəs/ noun [U] the state of being HOMOSEXUAL ⊃ compare GAIETY

**ˌgay ˈpride** noun [U] the feeling that GAY people should not be ashamed of telling people that they are gay and should feel proud of themselves

**gaze** 🔑+ C1 /geɪz/ verb, noun
■ verb 🔑+ C1 [I] + adv./prep. to look steadily at sb/sth for a long time, either because you are very interested or surprised, or because you are thinking of sth else SYN **stare**: *She gazed at him in amazement. ◇ He sat for hours just gazing into space.* ⊃ SYNONYMS at STARE
■ noun 🔑+ C1 [usually sing.] a long, steady look at sb/sth: *He met her gaze (= looked at her while she looked at him). ◇ She dropped her gaze (= stopped looking).* ⊃ SYNONYMS at LOOK

## gazebos

**gaz·ebo** /gəˈziːbəʊ/ noun (pl. **-os**) **1** a small building with open sides in a garden, especially one with a view **2** a temporary structure like a large tent with open sides that is used to provide shelter at an outdoor event

**gaz·elle** /gəˈzel/ noun (pl. **gaz·elle** or **gaz·elles**) a small ANTELOPE

**gaz·ette** /gəˈzet/ noun **1** an official newspaper published by a particular organization containing important information about decisions that have been made and people who have been employed **2 Gazette** used in the titles of some newspapers: *the Evening Gazette*

**gaz·et·teer** /ˌgæzəˈtɪə(r)/; NAmE -ˈtɪr/ noun a list of place names published as a book, at the end of a book or as an online resource

**ga·zil·lion** /gəˈzɪljən/ noun (informal) a very large number: *gazillion-dollar houses ◇ gazillions of copies*

**gaz·pa·cho** /gəˈspætʃəʊ; NAmE -ˈspɑːtʃ-/ noun [U] a cold Spanish soup made with tomatoes, peppers, CUCUMBERS, etc.

**gaz·ump** /gəˈzʌmp/ verb [usually passive] ~ **sb** (BrE) when sb who has made an offer to pay a particular price for a house and who has had this offer accepted is **gazumped**, their offer is no longer accepted by the person selling the house, because sb else has made a higher offer ▸ **gaz·ump·ing** noun [U]

**GB** abbr. **1** /ˌdʒiː ˈbiː/ Great Britain **2** (in writing) GIGABYTE: *a 750GB hard drive*

**Gb** abbr. (in writing) GIGABIT

**GBH** /ˌdʒiː biː ˈeɪtʃ/ abbr. (BrE, law) GRIEVOUS BODILY HARM

**GCE** /ˌdʒiː siː ˈiː/ noun [C, U] a British exam taken by students in England and Wales and some other countries in any of a range of subjects. GCE O levels were replaced in 1988 by GCSE exams. GCE A levels are still the main exams taken in England and Wales at age 18. (the abbreviation for 'General Certificate of Education') ⊃ compare O LEVEL, A LEVEL

**GCSE** /ˌdʒiː siː es ˈiː/ noun [C, U] a British exam taken by students in England and Wales and some other countries, usually around the age of 16. GCSEs can be taken in a range of subjects. (GCSE is the abbreviation for 'General Certificate of Secondary Education'.): *She's got 10 GCSEs. ◇ He's doing German at GCSE.* ⊃ compare A LEVEL

**gˈday** /gəˈdeɪ/ exclamation (AustralE, NZE) hello

**Gdns** abbr. (BrE) (used in written addresses) Gardens: *7 Windsor Gdns*

**GDP** /ˌdʒiː diː ˈpiː/ noun [U, C] the total value of all the goods and services produced by a country in one year (the abbreviation for 'gross domestic product') ⊃ compare GNP

**GDR** /ˌdʒiː diː ˈɑː(r)/ abbr. German Democratic Republic

**gear** 🔑+ C1 /gɪə(r); NAmE gɪr/ noun, verb
■ noun
• IN VEHICLE **1** 🔑+ C1 [C, usually pl.] equipment in a vehicle that changes the relation between engine speed (or PEDAL speed on a bicycle) and the speed of the wheels moving forwards or backwards: *Careless use of the clutch may damage the gears.* **2** 🔑+ C1 [U, C] a particular position of the gears in a vehicle that gives a particular range of speed and power: *first/second, etc. gear ◇ reverse gear ◇ low/high gear ◇* (BrE) *bottom/top gear ◇* (BrE) *to change gear ◇* (NAmE) *to shift gear ◇ in~ When parking on a hill, leave the car in gear. ◇ What gear are you in?* ⊃ see also HIGH GEAR, TOP GEAR
• EQUIPMENT/CLOTHES **3** 🔑+ C1 [U] the equipment or clothing needed for a particular activity: *climbing/fishing/sports gear* ⊃ see also HEADGEAR, RIOT GEAR ⊃ SYNONYMS at EQUIPMENT **4** 🔑+ C1 [U] (informal) clothes: *wearing the latest gear* ⊃ SYNONYMS at CLOTHES
• POSSESSIONS **5** [U] (informal) the things that a person owns: *I've left all my gear at Dave's house.*
• MACHINERY **6** [U] (often in compounds) a machine used for a particular purpose: *lifting/towing/winding gear* ⊃ see also LANDING GEAR
• SPEED/EFFORT **7** [U, C] used to talk about the speed or effort involved in doing sth: (BrE) *The party organization is moving into top gear as the election approaches.* ◇ (NAmE) *to move into high gear ◇ Coming out of the final bend, the runner stepped up a gear to overtake the rest of the pack. ◇ He found it hard to switch gears when he retired.*
• DRUGS **8** [U] (slang) illegal drugs
IDM **get into ˈgear | get sth into ˈgear** to start working, or to start sth working, in an efficient way **(slip/be thrown) out of ˈgear** (of emotions or situations) (to become) out of control: *She said nothing in case her temper slipped out of gear.* ⊃ more at ASS
■ verb
PHRV **ˈgear sth to/towards sth** [usually passive] to make, change or prepare sth so that it is suitable for a particular purpose: *The course had been geared towards the specific needs of its members.* **ˌgear ˈup (for/to sth) | ˌgear sb/**

| æ cat | ɑː father | e bed | ɜː fur | ə about | ɪ sit | iː see | i happy | ɒ got (BrE) | ɔː saw | ʌ cup | ʊ put | uː too |

**sth⇌ˈup (for/to sth)** to prepare yourself/sb/sth to do sth: *Cycle organizations are gearing up for National Bike Week.* ⇒ see also GEARED

**gear·box** /ˈgɪəbɒks; *NAmE* ˈgɪrbɑːks/ *noun* the part containing the gears of a vehicle

**geared** /gɪəd; *NAmE* gɪrd/ *adj.* [not before noun] **1 ~to/towards sth** | **~to do/doing sth** designed or organized to achieve a particular purpose, or to be suitable for a particular group of people: *The programme is geared to preparing students for the world of work.* ◊ *The resort is geared towards children.* **2 ~ up (for sth)** | **~ up (to do sth)** prepared and ready for sth: *We have people on board geared up to help with any problems.*

**gear·head** /ˈgɪəhed; *NAmE* ˈgɪrh-/ *noun* (*informal*) a person who is very enthusiastic about cars or new technical devices and equipment: *He's a total gearhead—can't keep away from the race track.*

**gear·ing** /ˈgɪərɪŋ; *NAmE* ˈgɪr-/ *noun* [U] **1** (*BrE*) (also **lever·age** *BrE and NAmE*) (*finance*) the relationship between the amount of money that a company owes and the value of its shares **2** a particular set or arrangement of GEARS in a machine or vehicle

**ˈgear lever** (also **gear·stick** /ˈgɪəstɪk; *NAmE* ˈgɪrs-/) (both *BrE*) (*NAmE* **gearshift**, **ˈstick shift**) *noun* a handle used to change the GEARS of a vehicle

**gearshift** /ˈgɪəʃɪft; *NAmE* ˈgɪrʃ-/ *noun* = STICK SHIFT

**gecko** /ˈgekəʊ/ *noun* (*pl.* **-os** or **-oes**) a small LIZARD (= a type of REPTILE) that lives in warm countries

**GED** /ˌdʒiː iː ˈdiː/ *noun* **1** (in the US and Canada) an official CERTIFICATE that people who did not finish high school can get, after taking classes and passing a test (the abbreviation for 'General Equivalency Diploma') **2** (in the US and Canada) the test that people take in order to get the GED certificate (the abbreviation for 'General Educational Development')

**gedˈdit?** /ˈgedɪt/ *abbr.* (*informal*) Do you get it? (= Do you understand the joke?)

**gee** /dʒiː/ *exclamation, verb*
■ *exclamation* (especially *NAmE*) (also old-fashioned **gee whiz**) a word that some people use to show that they are surprised, impressed or annoyed: *Gee, what a great idea!*
■ *verb* (*BrE*)
PHRV **gee sb⇌ˈup** | **gee sb⇌ˈon** to encourage sb to work harder, perform better, etc. **gee sth⇌ˈup** to tell a horse to start moving or to go faster **gee ˈup** *exclamation* used to tell a horse to start moving or to go faster

**ˈgee-gee** *noun* (*BrE, informal*) (used especially by and to young children) a horse

**geek** /giːk/ *noun, verb* (*informal*)
■ *noun* **1** a person who is boring, wears clothes that are not fashionable, does not know how to behave in social situations, etc. SYN nerd **2** a person who is very interested in and who knows a lot about a particular subject SYN nerd: *a computer geek* ▸ **geeky** *adj.*
■ *verb* **1** [I] **~(out) (over sth)** to do or discuss computer tasks with great enthusiasm and attention to technical detail: *We geeked out for 50 minutes looking at code.* **2** [I, T] to be or become extremely excited about sth, especially sth that only a few people are interested in: **~(out) (about/over sth)** *We chatted and geeked about pop culture we both like.* ◊ **be geeked (out/up) (about/over sth)** *So we're all totally geeked up about the second half of the college football season.*

**geese** /giːs/ *pl.* of GOOSE

**gee whiz** /ˌdʒiː ˈwɪz/ *exclamation* (especially *NAmE*, old-fashioned) = GEE

**gee·zer** /ˈgiːzə(r)/ *noun* (*informal*) **1** (*BrE*) a man: *Some geezer called Danny did it.* **2** (*NAmE, disapproving*) an old man, especially one who is rather strange

**Geiˈger count·er** /ˈgaɪgə kaʊntə(r); *NAmE* -gər-/ *noun* a device used for finding and measuring RADIOACTIVITY

**gei·sha** /ˈgeɪʃə/ (also **ˈgeisha girl**) *noun* a Japanese woman who is trained to entertain men with conversation, dancing and singing

**gel** /dʒel/ *noun, verb*
■ *noun* [U, C] a thick, clear, slightly sticky substance, especially one used in products for the hair or skin: *hair/shower gel* ◊ *shaving gel* ⇒ see also SILICA GEL
■ *verb* (**-ll-**) **1** [I] (*BrE*) (also **jell** *NAmE*) (of two or more people) to work well together; to form a successful group: *We just didn't gel as a group.* **2** [I] (*ErE*) (also **jell** *NAmE, BrE*) (of an idea, a thought, a plan, etc.) to become clearer and more definite; to work well: *Ideas were beginning to gel in my mind.* ◊ *That day, everything gelled.* **3** [I] (also **jell** especially in *NAmE*) (*specialist*) (of a liquid) to become thicker and more solid; to form a gel **4** [T, usually passive] **~sth** to put gel on your hair

**gel·atin** /ˈdʒelətɪn/ (also **gel·atine** /ˈdʒelətiːn/) *noun* [U] a clear substance without any taste that is made from boiling animal bones and is used to make JELLY, film for cameras, etc.

**gel·at·in·ous** /dʒəˈlætɪnəs/ *adj.* thick and sticky, like JELLY: *a gelatinous substance*

**geld** /geld/ *verb* [usually passive] **~sth** (*specialist*) to remove the TESTICLES of a male animal, especially a horse SYN **castrate**

**geld·ing** /ˈgeldɪŋ/ *noun* a horse that has been CASTRATED ⇒ compare STALLION

**gel·ig·nite** /ˈdʒelɪgnaɪt/ *noun* [U] a powerful EXPLOSIVE

**gem** /dʒem/ *noun* **1** (also less frequent **gem·stone** /ˈdʒemstəʊn/) a PRECIOUS STONE that has been cut and POLISHED and is used in jewellery SYN **jewel, precious stone**: *a crown studded with gems* **2** a person, place or thing that is especially good: *This picture is the gem (= the best) of the collection.* ◊ *a gem of a place* ◊ *She's a real gem!* ⇒ compare JEWEL

**Gem·ini** /ˈdʒemɪnaɪ, -niː/ *noun* **1** [U] the third sign of the ZODIAC, the Twins **2** [C] a person born when the sun is in this sign, that is between 22 May and 21 June

**Gen.** *abbr.* (in writing) GENERAL: *Gen. (Stanley) Armstrong*

**gen** /dʒen/ *noun, verb*
■ *noun* (*informal*) [U] **~(on sth)** (*BrE, old-fashioned*) information
■ *verb* (**-nn-**)
PHRV **ˌgen ˈup (on sth)** | **ˌgen sb/ yourself ˈup (on sth)** (*BrE, old-fashioned, informal*) to find out or give sb information about sth

**gen·darme** /ˈʒɒndɑːm; *NAmE* ˈʒɑːndɑːrm/ *noun* (from French) a member of the French police force

**gen·der** /ˈdʒendə(r)/ *noun* **1** [U, C] the fact of being male or female, especially when considered with reference to social and cultural differences, rather than differences in biology; members of a particular gender as a group: *issues of class, race and gender* ◊ *traditional concepts of gender* ◊ *Levels of physical activity did not differ between genders.* ◊ **gender differences/relations/roles/equality** ⇒ compare SEX ⇒ see note on page 658 HELP The term **gender** is also used more broadly to mean a range of identities that do not necessarily fit in with the usual division between male and female. ⇒ see also INTERSEX, TRANSGENDER, TRANSSEXUAL **2** [C, U] (*grammar*) (in some languages) each of the classes (MASCULINE, FEMININE and sometimes NEUTER) into which nouns, pronouns and adjectives are divided; the division of nouns, pronouns and adjectives into these different genders. Different genders may have different endings, etc: *In French the adjective must agree with the noun in number and gender.* ⇒ WORD-FINDER NOTE at GRAMMAR

**gen·dered** /ˈdʒendəd; *NAmE* -dərd/ *adj.* specific to people of one particular gender: *All these toy colour schemes remain gendered: pink for girls, blue for boys.*

**ˈgender gap** *noun* the difference that separates men and women, in terms of attitudes, opportunities and status: *Women have closed the gender gap in education in recent years.*

**ˈgender identity** *noun* [C, U] the way sb considers their own gender (= whether they are male or female), which

# gender-neutral

### ▼ MORE ABOUT...

**gender**

Ways of talking about men and women

- When you are writing or speaking English it is important to use language that includes both men and women equally. Some people may be very offended if you do not.

The human race

- **Man** and **mankind** have traditionally been used to mean 'all men and women'. Many people now prefer to use **humanity**, **the human race**, **human beings** or **people**.

Jobs

- The suffix **-ess** in names of occupations such as **actress**, **hostess** and **waitress** shows that the person doing the job is a woman. Many people now avoid these. Instead you can use **actor** or **host** (although **actress** and **hostess** are still very common), or a neutral word, such as **server** for **waiter** and **waitress**.
- Neutral words like **assistant**, **worker**, **person** or **officer** are now often used instead of *-man* or *-woman* in the names of jobs. For example, you can use **police officer** instead of *policeman* or *policewoman*, and **spokesperson** instead of *spokesman* or *spokeswoman*. Neutral words are very common in newspapers, on television and radio and in official writing, in both *BrE* and *NAmE*.
- When talking about jobs that are traditionally done by the other sex, some people say: **a male secretary / nurse / model** (NOT *man*) or **a woman / female doctor / barrister / driver**. However this is now not usually used unless you need to emphasize which sex the person is, or it is still unusual for the job to be done by a man/woman: *My daughter prefers to see a woman doctor.* ◊ *They have a male nanny for their kids.* ◊ *a female racing driver*

Pronouns

- **He** used to be considered to cover both men and women: *Everyone needs to feel he is loved.* This is not now acceptable. Instead, after **everybody**, **everyone**, **anybody**, **anyone**, **somebody**, **someone**, etc. one of the plural pronouns **they**, **them**, and **their** is often used: *Does everybody know what they want?* ◊ *Somebody's left their coat here.* ◊ *I hope nobody's forgotten to bring their passport with them.*
- Some people prefer to use **he or she**, **his or her**, or **him or her** in speech and writing: *Everyone knows what's best for him- or herself.* **He / she** or **(s)he** can also be used in writing: *If in doubt, ask your doctor. He/she can give you more information.* (You may find that some writers just use 'she'.) These uses can seem awkward when they are used a lot. It is better to try to change the sentence, using a plural noun. Instead of saying: *A baby cries when he or she is tired* you can say: *Babies cry when they are tired.*

may be different from their BIOLOGICAL sex: *Different influences may help shape a child's gender identity.*

**gender-'neutral** *adj.* **1** suitable for or shared by people of both sexes; not making a difference between men and women: *gender-neutral toys/washrooms* ◊ *She argued that the law should always be gender-neutral.* **2** (of language) that does not refer specifically to men or women, and so can be understood to include both sexes: *'They' may be used as a gender-neutral pronoun instead of 'he' or 'she'.*

**gender reas'signment** *noun* [U] the act of changing a person's sex by a medical operation in which parts of their body are changed so that they become like a person of the opposite sex

**gender-spe'cific** *adj.* connected with women only or with men only: *The report was redrafted to remove gender-specific language.*

**gene** /dʒiːn/ *noun* (*biology*) a unit inside a cell that controls a particular quality in a living thing that has been passed on from its parents: *a dominant/recessive gene* ◊ *genes that code for the colour of the eyes* ⇒ see also GENETIC ⊃ **WORDFINDER NOTE** at BIOLOGY

**IDM** **be in the 'genes** to be a quality that your parents have passed on to you: *I've always enjoyed music—it's in the genes.*

**ge·neal·o·gist** /ˌdʒiːniˈælədʒɪst/ *noun* a person who studies family history

**ge·neal·o·gy** /ˌdʒiːniˈælədʒi/ *noun* (*pl.* **-ies**) **1** [U] the study of family history, including the study of who the ANCESTORS of a particular person were **2** [C] a particular person's line of ANCESTORS; a diagram that shows this ⊃ **WORDFINDER NOTE** at RELATION ▶ **ge·nea·logic·al** /ˌdʒiːniəˈlɒdʒɪkl/; *NAmE* -ˈlɑːdʒ-/ *adj.* [only before noun]: *a genealogical chart/table/tree* (= a chart with branches that shows a person's ANCESTORS)

**'gene pool** *noun* (*biology*) all of the genes that are available within BREEDING populations of a particular species of animal or plant

**gen·era** /ˈdʒenərə/ *pl.* of GENUS

**gen·eral** ⬥ A2 ⬥ /ˈdʒenrəl/ *adj.*, *noun*

■ *adj.*

- **AFFECTING ALL 1** A2 affecting all or most people, places or things: *books of general interest* (= of interest to most people) ◊ *The general feeling was one of relief.* ◊ *There is general agreement on that point.* ◊ *The general trend has been a slow decline in output.* ◊ *The bad weather has been fairly general* (= has affected most areas).
- **USUAL 2** A2 [usually before noun] normal; usual: *There is one exception to this general principle.* ◊ *As a general rule* (= usually) *he did what he could to be helpful.* ◊ *This opinion is common among the general population* (= ordinary people).
- **NOT EXACT 3** A2 including the most important aspects of sth; not exact or detailed **SYN** overall: *I check the bookings to get a general idea of what activities to plan.* ◊ *I know how it works in general terms.* **4** the ~ direction / area approximately, but not exactly, the direction/area mentioned: *They fired in the general direction of the enemy.*
- **NOT LIMITED 5** B1 not limited to a particular subject, use or activity: *a general hospital* ◊ *general education* ◊ *We shall keep the discussion fairly general.* **6** not limited to one part or aspect of a person or thing: *a general anaesthetic* ◊ *The building was in a general state of disrepair.*
- **HIGHEST IN RANK 7** [only before noun] (*also* **General** [after noun]) highest in rank; chief: *the general manager* ◊ *the Inspector General of Police* ⇒ see also ADJUTANT GENERAL, ATTORNEY GENERAL, DIRECTOR GENERAL, GOVERNOR GENERAL, SECRETARY GENERAL, SOLICITOR GENERAL, SURGEON GENERAL

**IDM** **in 'general 1** B1 usually; mainly: *In general, Japanese cars are very reliable and breakdowns are rare.* ⊃ **LANGUAGE BANK** at CONCLUSION, GENERALLY **2** B1 as a whole: *This is a crucial year for your relationships in general and your love life in particular.*

■ *noun* (*abbr.* **Gen.**) an officer of very high rank in the army or (in the US) the AIR FORCE; the officer with the highest rank in the MARINES: *a four-star general* ◊ *General Tom Parker* ⊃ see also BRIGADIER GENERAL, MAJOR GENERAL

**General A'merican** *noun* [U] the way people speak English in most parts of the US, without the regional characteristics often found in New England, New York and the South

**General Cer'tificate of Edu'cation** *noun* = GCE

**General Cer'tificate of Secondary Edu'cation** *noun* = GCSE

**general 'counsel** *noun* (in the US) the main lawyer who gives legal advice to a company

**general e'lection** *noun* an election in which all the adults of a country can vote to choose people to represent them in parliament ⊃ compare BY-ELECTION

**general head'quarters** *noun* [U + sing. / pl. v.] = GHQ

**gen·er·al·ist** /ˈdʒenrəlɪst/ *noun* a person who has knowledge of several different subjects or activities **OPP** specialist

**gen·er·al·i·ty** /ˌdʒenəˈræləti/ noun (pl. **-ies**) **1** [C, usually pl.] a statement that discusses general principles or issues rather than details or particular examples: *to speak in broad generalities* ◊ *As usual, he confined his comments to generalities.* **2 the generality** [sing. + sing./pl. v.] (*formal*) most of a group of people or things: *This view is held by the generality of leading scholars.* **3** [U] (*formal*) the fact of being general rather than detailed or exact: *An account of such generality is of little value.*

**gen·er·al·i·za·tion** Ⓦ (*BrE also* **-isa·tion**) /ˌdʒenrəlaɪˈzeɪʃn; NAmE -lə-z-/ noun [C, U] a general statement that is based on only a few facts or examples; the act of making such statements: *a speech full of broad/sweeping generalizations* ◊ *to make generalizations about sth* ◊ *Try to avoid generalization.*

**gen·er·al·ize** Ⓦ (*BrE also* **-ise**) /ˈdʒenrəlaɪz/ verb **1** [I] ~ **(from sth)** to use a particular set of facts or ideas in order to form an opinion that is considered relevant to a different situation: *It would be foolish to generalize from a single example.* **2** [I] ~ **(about sth)** to make a general statement about sth and not look at the details: *It is dangerous to generalize about the poor.* **3** [T, often passive] ~ **sth (to sth)** (*formal*) to apply a theory, idea, etc. to a wider group or situation than the original one: *These conclusions cannot be generalized to the whole country.*

**gen·er·al·ized** (*BrE also* **-ised**) /ˈdʒenrəlaɪzd/ adj. [usually before noun] not detailed; not limited to one particular area: *a generalized discussion* ◊ *a generalized disease/rash* (= affecting the whole body)

**general ˈknowledge** noun [U] knowledge of facts about a lot of different subjects: *a general knowledge quiz*

**gen·er·al·ly** 🅣 🅱🅱 🔵 /ˈdʒenrəli/ adv. **1** 🅱🅱 by or to most people: *The initiative was generally considered a success.* ◊ *It is generally accepted/agreed/believed that…* ◊ *The new drug will be generally available from January.* **2** ⓘ 🅱🅱 in most cases 🆂🆈🅽 **as a rule**: *These systems generally use solar power.* ◊ *The male is generally larger with a shorter beak.* **3** ⓘ 🅱🅱 without discussing the details of sth: *Let's talk just about investment generally.*

▼ **LANGUAGE BANK**

**generally**
Ways of saying 'in general'

- Women **generally** earn less than men.
- **Generally speaking**, jobs traditionally done by women are paid at a lower rate than those traditionally done by men.
- **In general/By and large**, women do not earn as much as men.
- Certain jobs, like nursing and cleaning, are still **mainly** carried out by women.
- Senior management posts are **predominantly** held by men.
- Most senior management posts **tend to** be held by men.
- Women are, **for the most part**, still paid less than men.
- Economic and social factors are, **to a large extent**, responsible for women being concentrated in low-paid jobs.

➲ LANGUAGE BANK at CONCLUSION, EXCEPT, SIMILARLY

**general ˈpractice** noun [U, C] **1** (*especially BrE*) (*NAmE usually* **family practice**) the work of a doctor who treats people in the community rather than at a hospital and who is not a specialist in one particular area of medicine; a place where a doctor like this works: *to be in general practice* ◊ *She runs a general practice in Hull.* **2** (*especially NAmE*) the work of a lawyer who deals with all kinds of legal cases and who is not a specialist in one particular area of law; the place where a lawyer like this works

**general pracˈtitioner** (*abbr.* **GP**) (*also* **family ˈdoctor**, **family pracˈtitioner**) (*all especially BrE*) (*NAmE usually* **primary ˈcare physician**, **PCP**) noun a doctor who is trained in general medicine and who treats patients in a local community rather than at a hospital

**the general ˈpublic** noun [sing. + sing./pl. v.] ordinary people who are not members of a particular group or organization: *At that time, the general public was/were not aware of the health risks.* ◊ *The exhibition is not open to the general public.*

---

659

---

**general-ˈpurpose** adj. [only before noun] having a wide range of different uses: *a general-purpose farm vehicle*

**general ˈsecretary** noun (in some organizations) a title that is given to the person who is in charge of administration: *He is general secretary of the teachers' union.*

**gen·er·al·ship** /ˈdʒenrəlʃɪp/ noun [U] the skill or practice of leading an army during a battle

**general ˈstaff** (*often* **the general staff**) noun [sing. + sing./pl. v.] officers who advise a military leader and help to plan a military operation

**general ˈstore** noun (*BrE also* **general ˈstores**) a shop that sells a wide variety of goods, especially one in a small town or village

**general ˈstrike** noun a period of time when most or all of the workers in a country go on strike

**gen·er·ate** 🅣 🅱🄷 🔵 /ˈdʒenəreɪt/ verb **1** 🅱🄷 ~ **sth** to produce energy, especially electricity: *The wind turbines are used to generate electricity.* ◊ *to generate heat/power/energy* ➲ WORDFINDER NOTE at ELECTRICITY **2** ⓘ 🅱🄷 ~ **sth** to produce or create sth: *to generate revenue/income/profit* ◊ *We need someone to generate new ideas.* ◊ *The proposal has generated a lot of interest.* ➲ SYNONYMS at MAKE

**gen·er·a·tion** 🅣 🅱🄷 🔵 /ˌdʒenəˈreɪʃn/ noun **1** ⓘ 🅱🄷 [C + sing./pl. v.] all the people who were born at about the same time: *the younger/older generation* ◊ *My generation have grown up with the internet.* ◊ *I often wonder what future generations will make of our efforts.* ◊ ~ **of sb** *Her books have delighted generations of children.* ➲ WORDFINDER NOTE at AGE **2** ⓘ 🅱🄷 [C] the average time in which children grow up, become adults and have children of their own, (usually considered to be about 30 years): *a generation ago* ◊ ~ **for a** *My family have lived in this house for generations* **3** ⓘ 🅱🄷 [C, U] a single stage in the history of a family: *stories passed down from generation to generation* ◊ *Five generations of his family had been farmers.* ➲ see also FIRST GENERATION, FIRST-GENERATION, SECOND-GENERATION ➲ WORDFINDER NOTE at FAMILY, RELATION **4** ⓘ 🅱🄷 [C, usually sing.] a group of people of similar age involved in a particular activity: *He influenced my generation more than any other actor.* ◊ ~ **of sb** *the current generation of writers* ◊ *She has inspired a whole generation of fashion school graduates.* ➲ see also BEAT GENERATION **5** [C, usually sing.] a stage in the development of a product, usually a technical one: *fifth-generation computing* ◊ *a new generation of vehicle* ➲ see also THIRD-GENERATION **6** [U] the production of sth, especially electricity, heat, etc: *the generation of electricity* ◊ *methods of income generation*

**gen·er·a·tion·al** /ˌdʒenəˈreɪʃənl/ adj. [usually before noun] connected with a particular generation or with the relationship between different generations: *generational conflict*

**the geneˈration gap** noun [sing.] the difference in attitude or behaviour between young and older people that causes a lack of understanding: *a movie that is sure to bridge the generation gap*

**Generation ˈX** (*also informal* **Gen X**) noun [U + sing./pl. v.] the group of people who were born between the middle of the 1960s and the late 1970s, who seem to lack a sense of direction in life and to feel that they have no part to play in society

**Generation ˈY** (*also informal* **Gen Y**) noun [U + sing./pl. v.] the group of people who were born between the early 1980s and the late 1990s, who are mainly the children of the BABY BOOMERS and who are regarded as being very familiar with computers and electronic technology

**gen·era·tive** /ˈdʒenərətɪv/ adj. (*formal*) that can produce sth: *generative processes*

**gen·er·ator** /ˈdʒenəreɪtə(r)/ noun **1** a machine for producing electricity: *The factory's emergency generators were used during the power cut.* ◊ *a wind generator* (= a machine that uses the power of the wind to produce electricity) **2** a machine for producing a particular substance: *The museum uses smells and smoke generators to create*

---

Ⓞ Oxford Phrasal Academic Lexicon (OPAL) written and spoken word lists | Ⓦ OPAL written word list | Ⓢ OPAL spoken word list

# generic

*atmosphere.* **3** a person or thing that creates sth: *The company is a major generator of jobs.* **4** (*BrE*) a company that produces electricity to sell to the public: *the UK's major electricity generator*

**gen·er·ic** /dʒəˈnerɪk/ *adj., noun*
- *adj.* **1** shared by, including or typical of a whole group of things; not specific: *'Vine fruit' is the generic term for currants and raisins.* **2** (of a product, especially a drug) not using the name of the company that made it: *The doctor offered me a choice of a branded or a generic drug.* **3** (*disapproving*) (of a film, song, story, etc.) lacking imagination and so not original: *The movie was pretty boring, with a generic storyline and emotionless characters.* ▶ **gen·er·ic·al·ly** /-kli/ *adv.*
- *noun* a version of an existing product that is not made by a well-known company: *Generics are copycat versions of brand-name prescription drugs.*

**gen·er·os·ity** /ˌdʒenəˈrɒsəti; *NAmE* -ˈrɑːs-/ *noun* [U, sing.] ~ (to/towards sb) the fact of being generous (= willing to do kind things or give sb money, gifts or time freely): *He treated them with generosity and thoughtfulness.*

**gen·er·ous** /ˈdʒenərəs/ *adj.* (*approving*) **1** giving or willing to give freely; given freely: *a generous benefactor* ◇ *a generous donation/gift/offer* ◇ ~ **with sth** *You've been incredibly generous with your time.* ◇ ~ **to sb** *He was generous to his friends and family.* ◇ ~ **in (doing) sth** *They were very generous in giving help* ◇ **it is ~ of sb (to do sth)** *It was extremely generous of him to offer to pay for us both.* **OPP** mean **2** more than is necessary; large **SYN** lavish: *a generous helping of meat* ◇ *The car has a generous amount of space.* **3** kind in the way you treat people; willing to see what is good about sb/sth: *a generous mind* ◇ *He wrote a very generous assessment of my work.* ▶ **gen·er·ous·ly** *adv.*: *Please give generously.* ◇ *a dress that is generously cut* (= uses plenty of material)

**gen·esis** /ˈdʒenəsɪs/ *noun* [sing.] (*formal*) the beginning or origin of sth

**'gene therapy** *noun* [U] (*medical*) a treatment in which normal GENES are put into cells to replace ones that are missing or not normal

**gen·et·ic** /dʒəˈnetɪk/ *adj.* connected with GENES (= the units in the cells of a living thing that control its physical characteristics) or GENETICS (= the study of GENES): *genetic and environmental factors* ◇ *genetic abnormalities* ◇ *genetic research/techniques* ▶ **gen·et·ic·al·ly** /-kli/ *adv.*: *genetically engineered/determined/transmitted*

**ge,netically 'modified** *adj.* (*abbr.* **GM**) (of a plant, etc.) having had its genetic structure changed artificially, so that it will, for example, produce more fruit or not be affected by disease: *genetically modified foods* (= made from plants that have been changed in this way) ⊃ WORDFINDER NOTE at CROP

**ge,netic 'code** *noun* the arrangement of GENES that controls how each living thing will develop

**ge,netic engi'neering** *noun* [U] the science of changing how a living creature or plant develops by changing the information in its GENES

**ge,netic 'fingerprinting** (*also* **DNA 'fingerprinting**) *noun* [U] the method of finding the particular pattern of GENES in an individual person, particularly to identify sb or find out if sb has committed a crime ▶ **ge,netic 'fingerprint** *noun*

**gen·eti·cist** /dʒəˈnetɪsɪst/ *noun* a scientist who studies genetics

**gen·et·ics** /dʒəˈnetɪks/ *noun* [U] the scientific study of the ways in which different characteristics are passed from each generation of living things to the next

**Geneva Convention** /dʒəˌniːvə kənˈvenʃn/ *noun* [sing.] an international agreement that states how PRISONERS OF WAR, sick and wounded soldiers, and CIVILIANS should be treated in WARTIME

**gen·ial** /ˈdʒiːniəl/ *adj.* friendly and cheerful **SYN** affable: *a genial person* ◇ *a genial smile* ▶ **geni·al·ity** /ˌdʒiːniˈæləti/

*noun* [U]: *an atmosphere of warmth and geniality* **geni·al·ly** /ˈdʒiːniəli/ *adv.*: *to smile genially*

**genie** /ˈdʒiːni/ *noun* (*pl.* **gen·ies** or **genii** /-aɪ/) (in Arabian stories) a spirit with magic powers, especially one that lives in a bottle or a lamp **SYN** djinn
- **IDM** **let the 'genie out of the bottle** to do sth that has a big effect and after which it is very difficult or impossible to go back to how things were before: *When guns were invented, the genie was let out of the bottle.* **HELP** This idiom can be expressed in various different ways. Other versions include **the genie is out of the bottle** and opposite form **put the genie back in the bottle**.

**geni·tal** /ˈdʒenɪtl/ *adj.* [only before noun] connected with the outer sexual organs of a person or an animal: *the genital area* ◇ *genital infections*

**geni·tals** /ˈdʒenɪtlz/ (*also* **geni·talia** /ˌdʒenɪˈteɪliə/) *noun* [pl.] a person's sex organs that are outside their body

**geni·tive** /ˈdʒenətɪv/ *noun* (*grammar*) (in some languages) the special form of a noun, a pronoun or an adjective that is used to show possession or close connection between two things ⊃ compare ACCUSATIVE, DATIVE, INSTRUMENTAL (2), LOCATIVE, NOMINATIVE, POSSESSIVE, VOCATIVE ▶ **geni·tive** *adj.*

**ge·nius** /ˈdʒiːniəs/ *noun* (*pl.* **gen·iuses**) **1** [U] unusually great intelligence, skill or artistic ability: *the genius of Shakespeare* ◇ *a statesman of genius* ◇ *Her idea was a stroke of genius.* **2** [C] a person who is unusually intelligent or artistic, or who has a very high level of skill, especially in one area: *a mathematical/comic, etc. genius* ◇ *He's a genius at organizing people.* ◇ *You don't have to be a genius to see that they are in love!* **3** [sing.] ~ **for sth/for doing sth** a special skill or ability: *He had a genius for making people feel at home.* ▶ **ge·nius** *adj.* (*informal*): *a genius idea*
- **IDM** **sb's good/evil 'genius** (especially *BrE*) a person or spirit who is thought to have a good/bad influence over you

**geno·cide** /ˈdʒenəsaɪd/ *noun* [U, C] the murder of a large number of people from a particular nation or ETHNIC group, with the aim of destroying that nation or group ▶ **geno·cidal** /ˌdʒenəˈsaɪdl/ *adj.*

**gen·ome** /ˈdʒiːnəʊm/ *noun* (*biology*) the complete set of GENES in a cell or living thing: *the human genome*

**ge·nom·ics** /dʒiːˈnɒmɪks; *NAmE* -ˈnɑːm-/ *noun* [U] (*biology*) the study of the structure, function and development of GENOMES and how they are arranged and organized

**geno·type** /ˈdʒenətaɪp, ˈdʒiːn-/ *noun* (*biology*) the combination of GENES that a particular living thing carries, some of which may not be noticed from its appearance ⊃ compare PHENOTYPE

**genre** /ˈʒɒ̃rə, ˈʒɒnrə; *NAmE* ˈʒɑːn-/ *noun* (*formal*) a particular type or style of literature, art, film or music that you can recognize because of its special features: *literary/musical genres* ◇ *the horror/action/fantasy genre* ◇ *genre fiction* ⊃ WORDFINDER NOTE at WRITE

**'genre painting** *noun* [U, C] (*art*) a style of painting showing scenes from ordinary life, especially associated with 17th century Dutch and Flemish artists; a painting done in this style

**gent** /dʒent/ *noun* **1** (*old-fashioned or humorous*) a man; a gentleman: *a gent's hairdresser* ◇ *This way please, ladies and gents!* **2** **a/the gents, a/the Gents** [sing.] (*BrE, informal*) a public toilet for men: *Is there a gents near here?* ◇ *Where's the gents?*

**gen·teel** /dʒenˈtiːl/ *adj.* (*sometimes disapproving*) **1** (of people and their way of life) quiet and polite, often in an EXAGGERATED way; from, or pretending to be from, a high social class: *a genteel manner* ◇ *Her genteel accent irritated me.* ◇ *He lived in genteel poverty* (= trying to keep the style of a high social class, but with little money). **2** (of places) quiet and old-fashioned and perhaps slightly boring ▶ **gen·teel·ly** /-ˈtiːlli/ *adv.*

**gen·tian** /ˈdʒenʃn/ *noun* [C, U] a small plant with bright blue flowers that grows in mountain areas

**gen·tile** /ˈdʒentaɪl/ (*also* **Gentile**) *noun* a person who is not Jewish ▶ **gen·tile** (*also* **Gentile**) *adj.* [only before noun]

**gen·til·i·ty** /dʒenˈtɪləti/ noun [U] (formal) **1** very good manners and behaviour; the fact of belonging to a high social class: *He took her hand with discreet gentility.* ◇ *She thinks expensive clothes are a mark of gentility.* **2** the fact of being quiet and old-fashioned: *the faded gentility of the town*

**gen·tle** 🔑 B1 /ˈdʒentl/ adj. (**gen·tler** /ˈdʒentlə(r)/, **gen·tlest** /-lɪst/) **1** 🔑 B1 calm and kind; doing things in a quiet and careful way: *a kind and gentle man* ◇ *Terry was a gentle soul.* ◇ *He looks scary but he's really a gentle giant.* ◇ *She was the gentlest of nurses.* ◇ *a gentle voice/laugh/touch* ◇ ~ **with sb/sth** *Be gentle with her!* **2** 🔑 B1 (of weather, temperature, etc.) not strong or extreme: *a gentle breeze* ◇ *the gentle swell of the sea* ◇ *Cook over a gentle heat.* **3** 🔑 B1 having only a small effect; not strong or violent: *The doctor recommended a little gentle exercise.* ◇ **~ on sth** *This soap is very gentle on the hands.* **4** 🔑 B2 not steep or sharp: *a gentle slope/curve* ⇨ see also GENTLY ▸ **gentle·ness** /ˈdʒentlnəs/ noun [U]

**gentle·folk** /ˈdʒentlfəʊk/ noun [pl.] (*old-fashioned*) (in the past) people belonging to respected families of the higher social classes

**gentle·man** 🔑 B1 /ˈdʒentlmən/ noun (pl. **-men** /-mən/) **1** 🔑 B1 [C] a man who is polite and well educated, who has excellent manners and always behaves well: *You acted like a true gentleman.* ◇ *He was always the perfect gentleman.* ⇨ compare LADY **2** 🔑 B1 [C, usually pl.] (*formal*) used to address or refer to a man, especially sb you do not know: *Ladies and gentlemen! Can I have your attention, please?* ◇ *She was talking to an elderly gentleman.* ◇ *Can I help you, gentlemen?* ◇ *There's a gentleman to see you.* **HELP** In more informal speech, you could say: *Can I help you?* ◇ *There's someone to see you.* **3** (*NAmE*) used to address or refer to a male member of a LEGISLATURE, for example the House of Representatives **4** (*old-fashioned*) a man from a high social class, especially one who does not need to work: *a country gentleman* ◇ *a gentleman farmer* (= one who owns a farm for pleasure, not as his main job) **IDM** see LEISURE

**gentle·man·ly** /ˈdʒentlmənli/ adj. (*approving*) behaving very well and showing very good manners; like a gentleman: *gentlemanly behaviour* ◇ *So far, the election campaign has been a very gentlemanly affair.*

**gentleman's aˈgreement** (*also* **gentlemen's aˈgreement**) noun an agreement made between people who trust each other, which is not written down and which has no legal force

**gentle·woman** /ˈdʒentlwʊmən/ noun (pl. **-women** /-wɪmɪn/) **1** (*old use*) a woman who belongs to a high social class; a woman who is well educated and has excellent manners **2** (*NAmE*) used to address or refer to a female member of a LEGISLATURE, for example the House of Representatives

**gen·tly** /ˈdʒentli/ adv. **1** in a way that is soft and light, not strong, extreme or violent: *She held the baby gently.* ◇ *Massage the area gently but firmly.* ◇ *Simmer the soup gently for 30 minutes.* ◇ *leaves moving gently in the breeze* **2** in a calm and quiet way: *'You miss them, don't you?' he asked gently.* **3** in a way that slopes very gradually: *The path ran gently down to the sea.* **4** **Gently!** (*BrE, informal*) used to tell sb to be careful: *Gently! You'll hurt the poor thing!* ◇ *Don't go too fast—gently does it!*

**gen·tri·fy** /ˈdʒentrɪfaɪ/ verb [usually passive] (**gen·tri·fies**, **gen·tri·fy·ing**, **gen·tri·fied**, **gen·tri·fied**) to improve an area of a town or city so that it attracts people of a higher social class than before: *be gentrified* *Old working-class areas of the city are being gentrified.* ▸ **gen·tri·fi·ca·tion** /ˌdʒentrɪfɪˈkeɪʃn/ noun [U]

**gen·try** /ˈdʒentri/ noun [pl.] (*usually* **the gentry**) (*old-fashioned*) people belonging to a high social class: *the local gentry* ◇ *the landed gentry* (= those who own a lot of land)

**genu·flect** /ˈdʒenjuflekt/ verb (*formal*) **1** [I] to move your body into a lower position by bending one or both knees, as a sign of respect in a church **2** [I] **~ (to sb/sth)** (*disapproving*) to show too much respect to sb/sth ▸ **genu·flec·tion** (*BrE also* **genu·flex·ion**) /ˌdʒenjuˈflekʃn/ noun [C, U]

# geology

**genu·ine** 🔑 B2 /ˈdʒenjuɪn/ adj. **1** 🔑 B2 real; exactly what it appears to be; not artificial **SYN** **authentic**: *Is the painting a genuine Picasso?* ◇ *Fake designer watches are sold at a fraction of the price of the genuine article.* ◇ *Only genuine refugees will be granted asylum.* **2** 🔑 B2 sincere and honest; that can be trusted: *He made a genuine attempt to improve conditions.* ◇ *genuine concern for others* ◇ *a very genuine person* ▸ **genu·ine·ness** /-ɪnnəs/ noun [U]

**genu·ine·ly** 🔑 B2 /ˈdʒenjuɪnli/ adv. **1** 🔑 B2 truly; in a way that is exactly what it appears to be and is not artificial: *There are some genuinely funny moments in the film.* ◇ *The election result was genuinely democratic.* ◇ *a genuinely new kind of politician* **2** 🔑 B2 in a sincere and honest way that can be trusted: *She was genuinely sorry.*

**genus** /ˈdʒiːnəs/ noun (pl. **gen·era** /ˈdʒenərə/) (*biology*) a group into which animals, plants, etc. that have similar characteristics are divided, smaller than a FAMILY and larger than a species ⇨ compare CLASS, KINGDOM, ORDER, PHYLUM ⇨ **WORDFINDER NOTE** at BREED ⇨ **VISUAL VOCAB** page V3 ⇨ see also GENERIC

**Gen X** /ˌdʒen ˈeks/ noun [U + sing./pl. v.] (*informal*) = GENERATION X

**Gen Y** /ˌdʒen ˈwaɪ/ noun [U + sing./pl. v.] (*informal*) = GENERATION Y

**geo-** /ˈdʒiːəʊ, dʒiːə; *BrE also* dʒiːˈɒ; *NAmE also* dʒiːˈɑː/ *combining form* (in nouns, adjectives and adverbs) of the earth: *geochemical* ◇ *geoscience*

**geo·caching** /ˈdʒiːəʊkæʃɪŋ/ noun [U] an activity in which people go out to look for a hidden object (usually a box containing a small item and a record of who has found it) using GPS (= a system that uses signals from satellites to show sb/sth's position on earth)

**geo·cen·tric** /ˌdʒiːəʊˈsentrɪk/ adj. (*specialist*) with the earth as the centre

**geo·chem·is·try** /ˌdʒiːəʊˈkemɪstri/ noun [U] the study of the different chemical substances that combine to form the earth and its rocks and minerals: *soil geochemistry* ▸ **geo·chem·ical** /-mɪkl/ adj.: *geochemical sampling/analysis*

**geo·des·ic** /ˌdʒiːəʊˈdesɪk, -ˈdiːs-/ adj. (*specialist*) relating to the shortest possible line between two points on a curved surface

**geoˌdesic ˈdome** noun (*architecture*) a DOME that is built from panels whose edges form geodesic lines

**geog·raph·er** /dʒiˈɒɡrəfə(r); *NAmE* -ˈɑːɡ-/ noun a person who studies geography; an expert in geography

**geog·raphy** 🔑 A1 /dʒiˈɒɡrəfi; *NAmE* -ˈɑːɡ-/ noun (pl. **-ies**) **1** 🔑 A1 [U] the scientific study of the earth's surface, physical features, divisions, products, population, etc: *recent work in economic geography* ◇ *a geography lesson/class/teacher* ◇ *a degree in geography* ⇨ see also HUMAN GEOGRAPHY, PHYSICAL GEOGRAPHY **(1) 2** 🔑 A2 [sing.] the way in which the physical features of a place are arranged: *the geography of New York City* ◇ *Kim knew the geography of the building and strode along the corridor.* **3** [sing.] the way in which a particular aspect of life or society is influenced by geography or varies according to geography: *The geography of poverty and the geography of voting are connected.* **4** [C] (*business*) a country, area or region: *We are now operational across multiple geographies.* ▸ **geo·graph·ical** /ˌdʒiːəˈɡræfɪkl/ (*also* **geo·graph·ic** /-fɪk/) adj.: *The survey covers a wide geographical area.* ◇ *The importance of the town is due to its geographical location.* **geo·graph·ic·al·ly** /-kli/ adv.: *geographically remote areas*

**geo·lo·ca·tion** /ˌdʒiːəʊləʊˈkeɪʃn/ noun [U] the process or technique of finding the exact location of a person or device using the internet

**geolo·gist** /dʒiˈɒlədʒɪst; *NAmE* -ˈɑːl-/ noun a scientist who studies geology

**geol·ogy** /dʒiˈɒlədʒi; *NAmE* -ˈɑːl-/ noun **1** [U] the scientific study of the physical structure of the earth, including the origin and history of the rocks and soil of which the earth is made **2** [sing.] the origin and history of the rocks and soil

# geometric

of a particular area: *the geology of the British Isles* ▶ **geo·log·ic·al** /ˌdʒiːəˈlɒdʒɪkl/; *NAmE* -ˈlɑːdʒ-/ (*also* **geo·logic** /-dʒɪk/) *adj.*: *a geological survey* **geo·log·ic·al·ly** /-kli/ *adv.*

**geo·met·ric** /ˌdʒiːəˈmetrɪk/ (*also less frequent* **geo·met·ric·al** /ˌdʒiːəˈmetrɪkl/) *adj.* **1** connected with geometry: *geometric methods* **2** of or like the lines, shapes, etc. used in GEOMETRY, especially because of having regular shapes or lines: *a geometric design* ▶ **geo·met·ric·al·ly** /-kli/ *adv.*

**geoˌmetric ˈmean** *noun* (*mathematics*) the central number in a geometric progression

**geoˌmetric proˈgression** (*also* **geoˌmetric ˈseries**) *noun* (*mathematics*) a series of numbers in which each is multiplied or divided by a fixed number to produce the next, for example 1, 3, 9, 27, 81 ⊃ compare ARITHMETIC PROGRESSION

**geom·etry** /dʒiˈɒmətri; *NAmE* -ˈɑːm-/ *noun* **1** [U] the branch of mathematics that deals with the measurements and relationships of lines, angles, surfaces and solids **2** [sing.] the measurements and relationships of lines, angles, etc. in a particular object or shape: *the geometry of a spider's web* ⊃ WORDFINDER NOTE at MATHS

**geo·phys·ics** /ˌdʒiːəʊˈfɪzɪks/ *noun* [U] the scientific study of the physics of the earth, including its atmosphere, climate ▶ **geo·phys·ic·al** /-zɪkl/ *adj.*: *geophysical data* **geo·physi·cist** /-zɪsɪst/ *noun*

**geo·pol·it·ics** /ˌdʒiːəʊˈpɒlətɪks; *NAmE* -ˈpɑːl-/ *noun* [U + sing./pl. v.] the political relations between countries and groups of countries in the world, as influenced by their geography; the study of these relations ▶ **geo·pol·it·ical** /ˌdʒiːəʊpəˈlɪtɪkl/ *adj.*

**Geor·die** /ˈdʒɔːdi; *NAmE* ˈdʒɔːrdi/ *noun* (*BrE*, *informal*) **1** [C] a person from Tyneside in north-east England **2** [U] a way of speaking typical of people from Tyneside in north-east England ▶ **Geor·die** *adj.*: *a Geordie accent*

**Geor·gian** /ˈdʒɔːdʒən; *NAmE* ˈdʒɔːrdʒ-/ *adj.* (especially of architecture and furniture) from the time of the British kings George I–IV (1714–1830): *a fine Georgian house*

**geo·sci·ence** /ˌdʒiːəʊˈsaɪəns/ *noun* [U] (*also* **geo·sci·ences** [pl.]) the sciences concerned with studying the earth or part of it, especially GEOLOGY

**geo·spa·tial** /ˌdʒiːəʊˈspeɪʃl/ *adj.* [only before noun] relating to information that is associated with a particular location: *geospatial data/information*

**geo·ther·mal** /ˌdʒiːəʊˈθɜːml; *NAmE* -ˈθɜːrml/ *adj.* (*geology*) connected with the natural heat of rock deep in the ground: *geothermal energy*

**ge·ra·nium** /dʒəˈreɪniəm/ *noun* a garden plant with a mass of red, pink or white flowers on the end of each STEM

**ger·bil** /ˈdʒɜːbɪl; *NAmE* ˈdʒɜːrb-/ *noun* a small desert animal like a mouse, one type of which is often kept as a pet

**geri·at·ric** /ˌdʒeriˈætrɪk/ *noun* **1** geriatrics [U] the branch of medicine that deals with the diseases and care of old people **2** [C] (*informal, offensive*) an old person, especially one with poor physical or mental health: *I'm not a geriatric yet, you know!* ▶ WORDFINDER NOTE at OLD ▶ **geri·at·ric** *adj.*: *the geriatric ward* (= in a hospital) ◊ *a geriatric vehicle* (= old and in bad condition)

**geria·tri·cian** /ˌdʒeriəˈtrɪʃn/ *noun* a doctor who studies and treats the diseases of old people

**germ** /dʒɜːm; *NAmE* dʒɜːrm/ *noun* **1** [C, usually pl.] a very small living thing that can cause infection and disease: *Disinfectant kills germs.* ◊ *Dirty hands can be a breeding ground for germs.* **2** [sing.] ~ **of sth** an early stage of the development of sth: *Here was the germ of a brilliant idea.* **3** [C] (*biology*) the part of a plant or an animal that can develop into a new one

**Ger·man** /ˈdʒɜːmən; *NAmE* ˈdʒɜːrm-/ *adj., noun*
■ *adj.* from or connected with Germany
■ *noun* **1** [C] a person from Germany **2** [U] the language of Germany, Austria and parts of Switzerland

**ger·mane** /dʒɜːˈmeɪn; *NAmE* dʒɜːrˈm-/ *adj.* [not usually before noun] **~ (to sth)** (*formal*) (of ideas, remarks, etc.) connected with sth in an important or appropriate way SYN **relevant**: *remarks that are germane to the discussion*

**Ger·man·ic** /dʒɜːˈmænɪk; *NAmE* dʒɜːrˈm-/ *adj.* **1** connected with or considered typical of Germany or its people: *She had an almost Germanic regard for order.* **2** connected with the language family that includes German, English, Dutch and Swedish among others

**ger·ma·nium** /dʒɜːˈmeɪniəm; *NAmE* dʒɜːrˈm-/ *noun* [U] (*symb.* **Ge**) a chemical element. Germanium is a shiny grey element that is similar to a metal (= is a METALLOID).

**ˌGerman ˈmeasles** (*also* **ru·bella**) *noun* [U] a mild disease that causes a SORE throat (= a painful throat because of an infection) and red spots all over the body. It can seriously affect babies born to women who catch it soon after they become pregnant.

**ˌGerman ˈshepherd** (*BrE also* **Al·sa·tian**) *noun* a large dog, often trained to help the police, to guard buildings or (especially in the US) to help blind people find their way

**ger·mi·cide** /ˈdʒɜːmɪsaɪd; *NAmE* ˈdʒɜːrm-/ *noun* [C, U] a substance that destroys bacteria, etc. ▶ **ger·mi·cidal** /ˌdʒɜːmɪˈsaɪdl; *NAmE* ˌdʒɜːrm-/ *adj.*

**ger·min·ate** /ˈdʒɜːmɪneɪt; *NAmE* ˈdʒɜːrm-/ *verb* [I, T] **~ (sth)** when the seed of a plant **germinates** or **is germinated**, it starts to grow: (*figurative*) *An idea for a novel began to germinate in her mind.* ▶ **ger·min·ation** /ˌdʒɜːmɪˈneɪʃn; *NAmE* ˌdʒɜːrm-/ *noun* [U]

**ˌgerm ˈwarfare** *noun* [U] the use of weapons of war that spread disease SYN **biological warfare**

**ger·ont·olo·gist** /ˌdʒerɒnˈtɒlədʒɪst; *NAmE* -rənˈtɑːl-/ *noun* (especially *NAmE*) a person who studies the process of people growing old

**ger·on·tol·ogy** /ˌdʒerɒnˈtɒlədʒi; *NAmE* -rənˈtɑːl-/ *noun* [U] the scientific study of OLD AGE and the process of growing old

**ger·ry·man·der** /ˈdʒerimændə(r)/ *verb* **~ sth** (*disapproving*) to change the size and borders of an area for voting in order to give an unfair advantage to one party in an election ▶ **ger·ry·man·der·ing** *noun* [U]

**ger·und** /ˈdʒerənd/ *noun* (*grammar*) a noun in the form of the present participle of a verb (that is, ending in *-ing*) for example *travelling* in the sentence *I preferred travelling alone.*

**ge·stalt** /ɡəˈʃtælt; *NAmE also* -ˈʃtɑːlt/ *noun* (*psychology, from German*) a set of things, such as a person's thoughts or experiences, that is considered as a single system that is different from the individual thoughts, experiences, etc. within it

**ges·tate** /dʒeˈsteɪt; *NAmE* ˈdʒesteɪt/ *verb* **~ sth** (*biology or medical*) to carry a young human or animal inside the WOMB until it is born

**ges·ta·tion** /dʒeˈsteɪʃn/ *noun* **1** [U, C] the time that the young of a person or an animal develops inside its mother's body until it is born; the process of developing inside the mother's body: *a baby born at 38 weeks' gestation* ◊ *The gestation period of a horse is about eleven months.* **2** [U] (*formal*) the process by which an idea or a plan develops SYN **development**

**ges·ticu·late** /dʒeˈstɪkjuleɪt/ *verb* [I] to move your hands and arms about in order to attract attention or make sb understand what you are saying: *He gesticulated wildly at the clock.* ▶ **ges·ticu·la·tion** /dʒeˌstɪkjuˈleɪʃn/ *noun* [C, U]: *wild/frantic gesticulations*

**ges·ture** /ˈdʒestʃə(r)/ *noun, verb*
■ *noun* **1** [C, U] a movement that you make with your hands, your head or your face to show a particular meaning: *He made a rude gesture at the driver of the other car.* ◊ *She finished what she had to say with a gesture of despair.* ◊ *They communicated entirely by gesture.* **2** [C] something that you do or say to show a particular feeling or intention: *They sent some flowers as a gesture of sympathy to the parents of the child.* ◊ *It was a nice gesture* (= it was kind) *to invite his wife too.* ◊ *We do not accept responsibility but we will refund the money as a gesture of goodwill.* ◊ *The*

---

æ cat | ɑː father | e bed | ɜː fur | ə about | ɪ sit | iː see | i happy | ɒ got (*BrE*) | ɔː saw | ʌ cup | ʊ put | uː too

government has made a gesture towards public opinion (= has tried to do sth that the public will like).

■ *verb* [I, T] to move your hands, head, face, etc. as a way of expressing what you mean or want: **+ adv./prep.** '*I see you read a lot,*' *he said, gesturing at the wall of books.* ◇ **~ to sb (to do sth)** *He gestured to the guards and they withdrew.* ◇ **for sb to do sth** *She gestured for them to come in.* ◇ **~ (to sb) (that)** *... He gestured (to me) that it was time to go.* ◇ *They gestured that I should follow.*

**ge·sund·heit** /gəˈzʊndhaɪt/ *exclamation* (*NAmE*, *from German*) used when sb has SNEEZED to wish them good health

**get** 🔊 **A1** /get/ *verb* (**getting**, **got**, **got** /gɒt/; *NAmE* gɑːt/) **HELP** In spoken *NAmE* the past participle **gotten** /ˈgɒtn; *NAmE* ˈgɑːtn/ is almost always used.

- **RECEIVE/OBTAIN 1** 🔊 **A1** [T, no passive] **~ sth** to receive sth: *I got a call from Dave this morning.* ◇ *What* (= What presents) *did you get for your birthday?* ◇ *He gets* (= earns) *about $40 000 a year.* ◇ *This room gets very little sunshine.* ◇ *I got a shock when I saw the bill.* ◇ *I will report back when I get a chance.* ◇ *I get the impression that he is bored with his job.* ◇ *Where did you get the idea from?* **2** 🔊 **A1** [T, no passive] to obtain sth: *He has just got a new job.* ◇ *I'll get the money somehow.* ◇ *She opened the door wider to get a better look.* ◇ *Try to get some sleep.* **3** 🔊 **A1** [T] to buy sth: **~ sth** *Where did you get that skirt?* ◇ (*NAmE*) *Can I get a Coke?* **HELP** For example, when ordering in a cafe or restaurant. In (*BrE*), we are more likely to say: *Can I have a Coke?*: **~ sth for sb** *Did you get a present for your mother?* ◇ **~ sb/yourself sth** *Did you get your mother a present?* ◇ *Why don't you get yourself a car?* **4** 🔊 **A1** [T, no passive] **~ sth (for sth)** to obtain or receive an amount of money by selling sth: *How much did you get for your car?*
- **BRING 5** 🔊 **A1** [T] to go to a place and bring sb/sth back **SYN** fetch: **~ sb/sth** *Quick—go and get a cloth!* ◇ *Somebody get a doctor!* ◇ *She went to get help.* ◇ *I have to go and get my mother from the airport* (= collect her). ◇ **~ sth for sb** *Get a drink for John.* ◇ **~ sb/yourself sth** *Get John a drink.*
- **MARK/GRADE 6** 🔊 **A1** [T, no passive] **~ sth** to achieve or be given a particular mark or grade in an exam: *He got a 'C' in Chemistry and a 'B' in English.*
- **ILLNESS 7** 🔊 **A1** [T, no passive] **~ sth** to start to develop an illness; to suffer from a pain, etc: *I got this cold off* (= from) *you!* ◇ *She gets* (= often suffers from) *really bad headaches.*
- **PUNISHMENT 8** [T, no passive] **~ sth** to receive sth as a punishment: *He got ten years* (= was sent to prison for ten years) *for armed robbery.*
- **INTERNET/PHONE/BROADCASTS 9** [T, no passive] **~ sth** to connect to the internet or a phone network; to receive broadcasts from a particular television or radio station: *95 per cent of the UK can now get superfast broadband.* ◇ *I couldn't get any mobile phone reception.*
- **CONTACT 10** [T, no passive] **~ sb** to be connected with sb by phone: *I wanted to speak to the manager but I got his secretary instead.*
- **ARRIVE 11** 🔊 **A1** [I] **+ adv./prep.** to arrive at or reach a place or point: *We got to San Diego at 7 o'clock.* ◇ *You got in very late last night.* ◇ *Let me know when you get there.* ◇ *I haven't got very far with the book I'm reading.*
- **MOVE/TRAVEL 12** 🔊 **A1** [I, T] to move to or from a particular place or in a particular direction, sometimes with difficulty; to make sb/sth do this: **+ adv./prep.** *The bridge was destroyed so we couldn't get across the river.* ◇ *She got into bed.* ◇ *He got down from the ladder.* ◇ *We didn't get* (= go) *to bed until 3 a.m.* ◇ *Where do we get on the bus?* ◇ *I'm getting off* (= leaving the train) *at the next station.* ◇ *Where have they got to* (= where are they)? ◇ *We must be getting home; it's past midnight.* ◇ **~ sb/sth + adv./prep.** *We couldn't get the piano through the door.* ◇ *We'd better call a taxi and get you home.* ◇ *I can't get the lid off.* **13** 🔊 **A1** [T, no passive] **~ sth** to use a bus, taxi, plane, etc: *We're going to be late—let's get a taxi.* ◇ *I usually get the bus to work.*
- **STATE/CONDITION 14** 🔊 **A2** *linking verb* to reach a particular state or condition; to make sb/sth/yourself reach a particular state or condition: **+ adj.** *to get angry/bored/hungry/fat* ◇ *to get better/worse* ◇ *You'll soon get used to the climate here.* ◇ *We ought to go; it's getting late.* ◇ *They plan to get married in the summer.* ◇ *She's upstairs getting ready.* ◇ *As he's got older his tastes have changed.* ◇ *I wouldn't go there alone; you might get* (= be) *mugged.* ◇ **~ sb/sth + adj.** *Don't get your dress dirty!* ◇ *He got his fingers caught in the door.* ◇ *She soon got the children ready for school.* **15** 🔊 **B1** [I] **~ to do sth** to reach the point at which you feel, know, are, etc. sth: *After a time you get to realize that these things don't matter.* ◇ *You'll like her once you get to know her.* ◇ *His drinking is getting to be a problem.* ◇ *She's getting to be an old lady now.*
- **GET STH DONE 16** 🔊 **B1** [T] **~ sth done** to cause sth to happen or be done: *I must get my hair cut.* ◇ *I'll never get all this work finished.* ◇ *She has a reputation for getting things done.*
- **MAKE/PERSUADE 17** 🔊 **B2** [T] to make, persuade, etc. sb/sth to do sth: **~ sb/sth to do sth** *I couldn't get the car to start this morning.* ◇ *He got his sister to help him with his homework.* ◇ *You'll never get him to understand.* ◇ **~ sb/sth doing sth** *It's not hard to get him talking—the problem is stopping him!*
- **START 18** [T] **~ doing sth** to start doing sth: *I got talking to her.* ◇ *We need to get going soon.*
- **OPPORTUNITY 19** [I] **~ to do sth** (*informal*) to have the opportunity to do sth: *He got to try out all the new software.* ◇ *It's not fair—I never get to go first.*
- **MEAL 20** [T] (*especially BrE*) to prepare a meal: **~ sth** *Who's getting the lunch?* ◇ **~ sth for sb/yourself** *I must go home and get tea for the kids.* ◇ **~ sb/yourself sth** *I must go home and get the kids their tea.*
- **TELEPHONE/DOOR 21** [T, no passive] **~ sth** (*informal*) to answer the phone or a door when sb calls, knocks, etc: *Will you get the phone?*
- **CATCH/HIT 22** [T] **~ sb** to catch or take hold of sb, especially in order to harm or punish them: *He was on the run for a week before the police got him.* ◇ *to get sb by the arm/wrist/throat* ◇ *She fell overboard and the sharks got her.* ◇ *He thinks everybody is out to get him* (= trying to harm him). ◇ (*informal*) *I'll get you for that!* **23** [T] **~ sb + adv./prep.** to hit or wound sb: *The bullet got him in the neck.*
- **UNDERSTAND 24** [T, no passive] **~ sb/sth** (*informal*) to understand sb/sth: *I don't get you.* ◇ *She didn't get the joke.* ◇ *I don't get it—why would she do a thing like that?* ◇ *I get the message—you don't want me to come.* ⊃ SYNONYMS at UNDERSTAND
- **HAPPEN/EXIST 25** [T, no passive] **~ sth** (*informal*) used to say that sth happens or exists: *You get* (= There are) *all these kids hanging around in the street.* ◇ *They still get cases of typhoid there.*
- **CONFUSE/ANNOY 26** [T, no passive] **~ sb** (*informal*) to make sb feel confused because they do not understand sth **SYN** puzzle: *'What's the capital of Bhutan?' 'You've got me there!'* (= *I don't know*) **27** [T, no passive] **~ sb** (*informal*) to annoy sb: *What gets me is having to do the same thing all day long.* **HELP** Get is one of the most common words in English, but some people try to avoid it in formal writing.

**IDM** **HELP** Most idioms containing **get** are at the entries for the nouns and adjectives in the idioms, for example **get sb's goat** is at **goat**. **be getting ˈon** (*informal*) **1** (of a person) to be becoming old **2** (of time) to be becoming late: *The time's getting on—we ought to be going.* **be getting ˈon for ...** (*especially BrE*) to be nearly a particular time, age or number: *It must be getting on for midnight.* ◇ *He's getting on for eighty.* **ˌcan't get ˈover sth** (*informal*) used to say that you are shocked, surprised, etc. by sth: *I can't get over how rude she was.* **get a ˈway from it ˈall** (*informal*) to have a short holiday in a place where you can relax **get ˈgoing** (*informal*) **1** to leave a place in order to go somewhere else: *It's been lovely to see you, but it's probably time we got going.* **2** to start happening or being done: *The project hasn't really got going yet.* **get sb ˈgoing** (*informal*) to make sb angry, worried or excited **get sth ˈgoing** to succeed in starting a machine, vehicle, process, etc: *We finally managed to get the car going.* **ˈget it** (*NAmE also* **catch ˈhell**) (*BrE also* **catch ˈit**) (*informal*) to be punished or spoken to angrily about sth: *If your dad finds out you'll really get it!* **ˌget it ˈon (with sb)** (*especially NAmE, slang*) to have sex

# get

with sb **get it 'up** (*slang*) (of a man) to have an ERECTION **get nowhere/not get sb anywhere** to not help sb make progress or succeed: *This line of investigation is getting us nowhere.* ◇ *Being rude to me won't get you anywhere.* **get somewhere/anywhere/nowhere** to make some progress/no progress: *After six months' work on the project, at last I feel I'm getting somewhere.* ◇ *I don't seem to be getting anywhere with this letter.* **get 'there** to achieve your aim or complete a task: *I'm sure you'll get there in the end.* ◇ *It's not perfect but we're getting there* (= making progress). **get 'this!** (*informal, especially NAmE*) used to say that you are going to tell sb sth that they will find surprising or interesting: *OK, get this guys—there are only two left!* **how selfish, stupid, ungrateful, etc. can you 'get?** (*informal*) used to express surprise or DISAPPROVAL that sb has been so SELFISH, stupid, etc. **there's no getting a'way from sth** | **you can't get a'way from sth** you have to admit that sth unpleasant is true **what are you, was he, etc. 'getting at?** (*informal*) used to ask, especially in an angry way, what sb is/was suggesting: *I'm partly to blame? What exactly are you getting at?* **what has got into sb?** (*informal*) used to say that sb has suddenly started to behave in a strange or different way: *What's got into Alex? He never used to worry like that.*

**PHR V** **get a'bout** = GET AROUND
**get a'bove yourself** (*especially BrE*) to have too high an opinion of yourself
**get a'cross (to sb)** | **get sth ↔ a'cross (to sb)** to be communicated or understood; to succeed in communicating sth: *Your meaning didn't really get across.* ◇ *He's not very good at getting his ideas across.*
**get a'head (of sb)** to make progress (further than others have done): *She wants to get ahead in her career.* ◇ *He soon got ahead of the others in his class.*
**get a'long** 1 (usually used in the progressive tenses) to leave a place: *It's time we were getting along.* 2 = GET ON
**get a'round** (*BrE also* **get a'bout**) 1 to move from place to place or from person to person: *She gets around with the help of a stick.* ◇ *News soon got around that he had resigned.* 2 (*informal*) to go to a lot of different places: *Stuart really gets around—last week he was in Dubai and this week he's in Paris.* **get a'round sb** (*especially NAmE*) = GET ROUND SB **get a'round sth** (*especially NAmE*) = GET ROUND STH **get a'round to sth** (*especially NAmE*) = GET ROUND TO STH
**get at sb** (usually used in the progressive tenses) to keep criticizing sb: *He's always getting at me.* ◇ *She feels she's being got at.* **get at sb/sth** to reach sb/sth; to gain access to sb/sth: *The files are locked up and I can't get at them.* **get at sth** to learn or find out sth: *The truth is sometimes difficult to get at.*
**get a'way** 1 to have a holiday: *We're hoping to get away for a few days at Easter.* ⊃ related noun GETAWAY 2 (*BrE, informal*) used to show that you do not believe or are surprised by what sb has said: *'These tickets didn't cost me a thing.' 'Get away!'* **get a'way (from ...)** to succeed in leaving a place: *I won't be able to get away from the office before 7.* **get a'way (from sb/ ...)** to escape from sb or a place **get a'way with sth** 1 to steal sth and escape with it: *Thieves got away with computer equipment worth $30000.* ⊃ related noun GETAWAY 2 to receive a relatively light punishment: *He was lucky to get away with only a fine.* 3 to do sth wrong and not be punished for it: *Don't be tempted to cheat—you'll never get away with it.* ◇ **get away with doing sth** *Nobody gets away with insulting me like that.* 4 to manage with less of sth than you might expect to need: *After the first month, you should be able to get away with one lesson a week.*
**get 'back** ⁊ **A2** to return, especially to your home: *What time did you get back last night?* ⊃ SYNONYMS at RETURN **get sth ↔ back** to obtain sth again after having lost it: *She's got her old job back.* ◇ *I never lend books—you never get them back.* **get 'back (in)** (of a political party) to win an election after having lost the previous one **get 'back at sb** (*informal*) to do sth bad to sb who has done sth bad to you; to get REVENGE on sb: *I'll find a way of getting back at him!* **get 'back to sb** (*informal*) to speak or write to sb

again later, especially in order to give a reply: *I'll find out and get back to you.* **get 'back to sth** to ret n to sth: *Could we get back to the question of funding?* **get back to'gether (with sb)** to start a relationship with sb again, especially a romantic relationship, after having finished a previous relationship with the same person: *I just got back together with my ex-girlfriend.*
**get be'hind (with sth)** to fail to make enough progress or to produce sth at the right time: *I'm getting behind with my work.* ◇ *He got behind with the payments for his car.* **get be'hind sb/sth** (*informal*) to help or support sb/sth: *Prince Harry has appealed to the public to get behind the project.*
**get 'by (on/in/with sth)** to manage to live or do a particular thing using the money, knowledge, equipment, etc. that you have: *How does she get by on such a small salary?* ◇ *I can just about get by in German* (= I can speak basic German).
**get 'down** (of children) (*BrE*) to leave the table after a meal **get sb 'down** (*informal*) to make sb feel sad or depressed **get sth ↔ down** 1 to SWALLOW sth, usually with difficulty 2 to make a note of sth **SYN** **write down**: *Did you get his number down?* **get 'down to sth** to begin to do sth; to give serious attention to sth: *Let's get down to business.* ◇ *I like to get down to work by 9.* ◇ **get down to (doing) sth** *It's time I got down to thinking about that essay.*
**get 'in** | **get 'into sth** 1 ⁊ **B2** to arrive at a place: *The train got in late.* ◇ *What time do you get into Heathrow?* 2 to win an election: *The Republican candidate stands a good chance of getting in.* ◇ *She first got into Parliament* (= became an MP) *in 2005.* 3 to be admitted to a school, university, etc.: *She's got into Durham to study law.* **get sb ↔ 'in** to call sb to your house to do a job **get sth ↔ 'in** 1 to collect or gather sth: *to get the crops/harvest in* 2 to buy a supply of sth: *Remember to get in some beers for this evening.* 3 to manage to do or say sth: *I got in an hour's work while the baby was asleep.* ◇ *She talks so much it's impossible to get a word in.* **get 'in on sth** to take part in an activity: *He's hoping to get in on any discussions about the new project.* **get 'in with sb** (*informal*) to become friendly with sb, especially in order to gain an advantage
**get 'into sth** 1 to put on a piece of clothing, especially with difficulty: *I can't get into these shoes—they're too small.* 2 to start a career in a particular profession: *What's the best way to get into journalism?* 3 to become involved in sth; to start sth: *I got into conversation with an Italian student.* ◇ *to get into a fight* 4 to develop a particular habit: *Don't let yourself get into bad habits.* ◇ *You should get into the routine of saving the document you are working on every ten minutes.* ◇ *How did she get into* (= start taking) *drugs?* 5 (*informal*) to become interested in sth: *I'm really getting into jazz these days.* 6 to become familiar with sth; to learn sth: *I haven't really got into my new job yet.* **get 'into sth** | **get yourself/sb 'into sth** to reach a particular state or condition; to make sb reach a particular state or condition: *He got into trouble with the police while he was still at school.* ◇ *Three people were rescued from a yacht which got into difficulties.* ◇ *She got herself into a real state* (= became very anxious) *before the interview.*
**get 'off** | **get 'off sb** used especially to tell sb to stop touching you or another person: *Get off me, that hurts!* **get 'off** | **get 'off sb** 1 to leave a place or start a journey; to help sb do this: *We got off straight after breakfast.* ◇ *He got the children off to school.* 2 (*BrE*) to go to sleep; to make sb do this: *I had great difficulty getting off to sleep.* ◇ *They couldn't get the baby off till midnight.* **get 'off** | **get 'off sth** to leave work with permission: *Could you get off (work) early tomorrow?* **get 'off sth** | **get sb 'off sth** to stop discussing a particular subject; to make sb do this: *Please can we get off the subject of dieting?* ◇ *I couldn't get him off politics once he had started.* **get sth 'off** to send sth by post or email: *I must get that email off.* **get 'off on sth** (*informal*) to be excited by sth, especially in a sexual way **get 'off (with sth)** to have no or almost no injuries in an accident: *She was lucky to get off with just a few bruises.* **get 'off (with sth)** | **get sb 'off (with sth)** to receive no or almost no punishment; to help sb do this: *He was lucky to get off with a small fine.* ◇ *A good lawyer might be able to get you off.* **get 'off with sb** (*informal, especially*

*BrE*) to have a sexual or romantic experience with sb; to start a sexual relationship with sb: *Steve got off with Tracey at the party.*

**get ˈon** **1** (*also* **get aˈlong**) used to talk or ask about how well sb is doing in a particular situation: *He's getting on very well at school.* ◊ **How did you get on** *at the interview?* **2** to be successful in your career, etc: *Parents are always anxious for their children to get on.* ◊ *I don't know how he's going to* **get on in life**. **3** (*also* **get aˈlong**) to manage or survive: *We can get on perfectly well without her.* ◊ *I just can't get along without a secretary.* **get ˈon to sb** **1** to contact sb by phone, letter or email: *The heating isn't working; I'll get on to the landlord about it.* **2** to become aware of sb's activities, especially when they have been doing sth bad or illegal: *He had been stealing money from the company for years before they got on to him.* **get ˈon to sth** to begin to talk about a new subject: *It's time we got on to the question of costs.* **get ˈon with sb** ?**B1** | **get ˈon (together)** (*both BrE*) (*also* **get aˈlong with sb**, **get aˈlong (together)** *NAmE, BrE*) to have a friendly relationship with sb: *She's never really got on with her sister.* ◊ *She and her sister have never really got on.* ◊ *We get along just fine together.* **get ˈon with sth** **1** (*also* **get aˈlong with sth**) used to talk or ask about how well sb is doing a task: *I'm not getting on very fast with this job.* **2** to continue doing sth, especially after you have been interrupted: *Be quiet and get on with your work.* ◊ (*informal*) *Get on with it! We haven't got all day.*

**get ˈout** to become known: *If this gets out there'll be trouble.* **get sth↔ˈout** **1** to produce or publish sth: *Will we get the book out by the end of the year?* **2** to say sth with difficulty: *She managed to get out a few words of thanks.* **get ˈout (of sth)** ?**A2** to leave or go out of a place: *You ought to get out of the house more.* ◊ *She screamed at me to get out.* **get ˈout of sth** **1** to avoid a responsibility or duty: *We promised we'd go—we can't get out of it now.* ◊ **get out of doing sth** *I wish I could get out of going to that meeting.* **2** to stop having a particular habit: *I can't get out of the habit of waking at six in the morning.* **get sth ˈout of sb** to persuade sb to tell or give you sth, especially by force: *The police finally got a confession out of her.* **get sth ˈout of sb/sth** to gain or obtain sth good from sb/sth: *She seems to get a lot out of life.* ◊ *He always gets the best out of people.*

**get ˈover sth** to deal with or gain control of sth SYN **overcome**: *She can't get over her shyness.* ◊ *I think the problem can be got over without too much difficulty.* **get ˈover sth/sb** ?**B2** to return to your usual state of health, happiness, etc. after an illness, a shock, the end of a relationship, etc: *He was disappointed at not getting the job, but he'll get over it.* **get ˈover yourself** (*informal*) to stop thinking that you are so important; to stop being so serious: *Just get over yourself and stop moaning!* ◊ *He needs to grow up a bit and get over himself.* **get sth↔ˈover to sb** to make sth clear to sb: *He didn't really get his meaning over to the audience.* **get sth ˈover (with)** (*informal*) to complete sth unpleasant but necessary: *I'll be glad to get the exam over and done with.*

**get ˈround sb** (*BrE*) (*also* **get aˈround sb** *especially in NAmE*) to persuade sb to agree to or to do what you want, usually by doing nice things for them: *She knows how to get round her dad.* **get ˈround sth** (*BrE*) (*also* **get aˈround sth** *especially in NAmE*) to deal with a problem successfully SYN **overcome**: *A clever lawyer might find a way of getting round that clause.* **get ˈround to sth** (*BrE*) (*also* **get aˈround to sth** *especially in NAmE*) to find the time to do sth: *I meant to do the ironing but I didn't get round to it.* ◊ **get round to doing sth** *I hope to get round to answering your letter next week.*

**get ˈthrough sth** **1** to use up a large amount of sth: *We got through a fortune while we were in New York!* **2** to manage to do or complete sth: *Let's start—there's a lot to get through.* **get ˈthrough (sth)** (*BrE*) to be successful in an exam, etc. **get sb ˈthrough sth** to help sb to be successful in an exam: *She got all her students through the exam.* **get ˈthrough (sth)** | **get sth ˈthrough (sth)** to be officially accepted; to make sth be officially accepted: *They got the bill through Congress.* **get ˈthrough (to sb)** **1** to make contact with sb by phone: *I tried calling you several times but I couldn't get through.* **2** to reach sb: *Thousands of refugees will die if these supplies don't get through to them.* **get ˈthrough (to sth)** (of a player or team) to reach the next stage of a competition: *Gulbis has got through to the final.* **get ˈthrough to sb** to make sb understand or accept what you say, especially when you are trying to help them: *I find it impossible to get through to her.* **get ˈthrough with sth** to finish or complete a task

**get to sb** (*informal*) to annoy or affect sb: *The pressure of work is beginning to get to him.*

**get sb/sth toˈgether** to collect people or things in one place: *I'm trying to get a team together for Saturday.* **get toˈgether (with sb)** (*informal*) to meet with sb socially or in order to discuss sth: *We must get together for a drink sometime.* ◊ *Management should get together with the union.* ⊃ related noun GET-TOGETHER

**get ˈup** **1** ?**A1** to stand up after sitting, lying, etc. SYN **rise**: *The class got up when the teacher came in.* ⊃ SYNONYMS at STAND **2** if the sea or wind **gets up**, it increases in strength and becomes violent **get ˈup** ?**B1** **get sb ˈup** to get out of bed; to make sb get out of bed: *He always gets up early.* ◊ *Could you get me up at 6.30 tomorrow?* **get yourˈself/sb ˈup as sth** [*often passive*] (*BrE*) to dress yourself/sb as sb/sth else: *She was got up as an Indian princess.* ⊃ related noun GET-UP **get sth↔ˈup** to arrange or organize sth: *We're getting up a party for her birthday.* **get ˈup to sth** **1** to reach a particular point: *We got up to page 72 last lesson.* **2** to be busy with sth, especially sth surprising or unpleasant: *What on earth will he get up to next?* ◊ *She's been getting up to her old tricks again!*

**getˈaway** /ˈɡetəweɪ/ *noun* [*usually sing.*] **1** an escape from a difficult situation, especially after committing a crime: *to* **make a** *quick* **getaway** ◊ *a* **getaway** *car* **2** (*informal*) a short holiday; a place that is suitable for a holiday: *a romantic weekend getaway in New York* ◊ *the popular island getaway of Penang*

**ˈget-go** *noun* (*informal*) the beginning: **from the~** *He's covered this case from the get-go.*

**ˈget-out** *noun* [*usually sing.*] (*BrE*) a way of avoiding sth, especially a responsibility or duty: *He said he'd come but he's looking for a get-out.* ◊ *a* **get-out** *clause in the contract*

**getˈting** /ˈɡetɪŋ/ *noun* [*sing.*]
IDM **while the ˈgetting is ˈgood** (*NAmE*) (*also* **while the ˈgoing is ˈgood** *especially in BrE*) before a situation changes and it is no longer possible to do sth

**ˈget-together** *noun* (*informal*) an informal meeting; a party

**ˈget-up** *noun* (*old-fashioned, informal*) a set of clothes, especially strange or unusual ones

**ˈget-up-and-ˈgo** *noun* [U] (*informal*) energy and a strong wish to get things done

**geyˈser** /ˈɡiːzə(r)/ *NAmE* ˈɡaɪz-/ *noun* **1** a natural SPRING that sometimes sends hot water or STEAM up into the air ⊃ picture at VOLCANO **2** (*BrE*) a piece of equipment in a kitchen or bathroom that heats water, usually by gas **3** (*SAfrE*) a large container in which water is stored and heated, usually by electricity, in order to provide hot water in a building

**GF** (*also* **gf**) /ˌdʒiː ˈef/ *abbr.* (*especially in text messages, on* SOCIAL MEDIA, *etc.*) girlfriend

**ghagra** (*also* **ghaghra**) /ˈɡʌɡrɑː/ *NAmE* ˈɡɑːɡ-/ *noun* a long skirt, worn by women in South Asia

**ghaˈrara** /ɡəˈrɑːrə/ *noun* loose wide trousers, worn with a KAMEEZ and DUPATTA by women in South Asia

**gharˈial** /ˈɡæriɑːl, ˌɡʌriˈɑːl/ *NAmE* ˈɡeriəl/ (*also* **gaˈvial**) *noun* a South Asian CROCODILE

# ghastly

**ghastly** /ˈɡɑːstli/ *NAmE* ˈɡæst-/ *adj.* (**ghastˈlier**, **ghastˈliest**) **1** (of an event) very frightening and unpleasant, because it involves pain, death, etc. SYN **horrible**: *a ghastly crime/ murder* **2** (*informal*) (of an experience or a situation) very bad; unpleasant SYN **terrible**: *The weather was ghastly.* ◊ *It's all been a ghastly mistake.* **3** (*informal*) (of a person or*

---

Oxford Phrasal Academic Lexicon (OPAL) written and spoken word lists | **W** OPAL written word list | **S** OPAL spoken word list

thing) that you find unpleasant and dislike very much **SYN horrible**: *her ghastly husband* ◊ *This lipstick is a ghastly colour.* **4** [not usually before noun] ill or upset **SYN terrible**: *I felt ghastly the next day.* **5** (*literary*) very pale in appearance, like a dead person: *His face was ghastly white.*

**ghat** /gɑːt/ *noun* (*IndE*) **1** [C] steps leading down to a river or lake **2** [C] a road or way over or through mountains **3 Ghats** [pl.] the mountains near the eastern and western coasts of India

**gha·zal** /ˈɡʌzʌl; *NAmE* ˈɡæzəl/ *noun* (*IndE*) a type of poem, typically on the theme of love, and normally set to music

**ghee** /ɡiː/ *noun* [U] a type of butter used in South Asian cooking

**ghe·rao** /ɡeˈraʊ/ *noun* (*pl.* **ghe·raos**) (*IndE*) a protest in which workers prevent employers from leaving a place of work until they are given what they want ▶ **ghe·rao** *verb* (**ghe·raoes** or **ghe·raos**, **ghe·raoing**, **ghe·raoed**, **ghe·raoed**): *~ sb The protesters are threatening to gherao the vice chancellor.*

**gher·kin** /ˈɡɜːkɪn; *NAmE* ˈɡɜːrkɪn/ *noun* **1** (*BrE*) (*NAmE* **pickle**) a small CUCUMBER that has been preserved in VINEGAR before being eaten **2** (*NAmE*) a small CUCUMBER

**ghetto** /ˈɡetəʊ/ *noun* (*pl.* **-os** or **-oes**) **1** an area of a city where many people of the same race or background live, separately from the rest of the population. Ghettos are often crowded, with bad living conditions: *a poor kid growing up in the ghetto* ◊ *The south coast of Spain has become something of a tourist ghetto.* ⊃ **WORDFINDER NOTE** at CITY **2** the area of a town where Jews were forced to live in the past: *the Warsaw ghetto*

**ghil·lie** = GILLIE

**ghost** ❶ **B1** /ɡəʊst/ *noun, verb*
■ *noun* **1** ❷ **B1** [C] the spirit of a dead person that a living person believes they can see or hear: *Do you believe in ghosts* (= believe that they exist)*?* ◊ *~ of sb The ghost of her father had come back to haunt her.* ◊ *He looked as if he had seen a ghost* (= looked very frightened) **2** [C] the memory of sth, especially sth bad: *The ghost of anti-Semitism still haunts Europe.* **3** [sing.] *~ of sth* a very slight amount of sth that is left behind or that you are not sure really exists: *There was a ghost of a smile on his face.* ◊ *You don't have a ghost of a chance* (= you have no chance). **4** [sing.] a second image on a television screen that is not as clear as the first, caused by a fault
**IDM** **give up the ˈghost 1** to die **2** (*humorous*) (of a machine) to stop working: *My car finally gave up the ghost.* ⊃ more at FORMER *adj.*
■ *verb* **1** [T, usually passive, I] = GHOSTWRITE **2** [I] **+ adv./prep.** (*literary*) to move without making a sound: *They ghosted up the smooth waters of the river.* **3** [T] *~ sb* to suddenly stop all communication with sb, usually online, in order to end a relationship

**ghost·ing** /ˈɡəʊstɪŋ/ *noun* [U] the appearance of a pale second image next to an image on a television screen, computer screen, etc.

**ghost·ly** /ˈɡəʊstli/ *adj.* (**ghost·lier**, **ghost·li·est**) looking or sounding like a ghost; full of ghosts: *a ghostly figure* ◊ *ghostly footsteps* ◊ *the ghostly churchyard*

**ˈghost story** *noun* a story about ghosts that is intended to frighten you

**ˈghost town** *noun* a town that used to be busy and have a lot of people living in it, but is now empty

**ˈghost train** *noun* (*BrE*) a small train at a FUNFAIR that goes through a dark tunnel full of frightening things

**ghost·write** /ˈɡəʊstraɪt/ *verb* (**ghost·wrote** /-rəʊt/, **ghost·written** /-rɪtn/) (*also* **ghost**) [T, often passive, I] to write a book, an article, etc. for another person who publishes it as their own work: **be ghostwritten** *Her memoirs were ghostwritten.*

**ghost·writer** /ˈɡəʊstraɪtə(r)/ *noun* a person who writes a book, etc. for another person, under whose name it is then published

**ghoul** /ɡuːl/ *noun* **1** (in stories) an evil spirit that opens GRAVES and eats the dead bodies in them **2** (*disapproving*) a person who is too interested in unpleasant things such as death and disaster ▶ **ghoul·ish** *adj.*: *ghoulish laughter*

**GHQ** /ˌdʒiː eɪtʃ ˈkjuː/ *abbr.* general headquarters (the main centre of a military organization): *He was posted to GHQ Cairo.*

**GHz** *abbr.* (in writing) GIGAHERTZ

**GI** /ˌdʒiː ˈaɪ/ *noun, abbr.*
■ *noun* (*pl.* **GIs**) a soldier in the US armed forces
■ *abbr.* GLYCAEMIC INDEX (= a system for measuring the effect of foods containing CARBOHYDRATES on the level of sugar in the blood): *The diet is based mainly on low GI foods.*

**giant** ❶ **B1** /ˈdʒaɪənt/ *adj., noun*
■ *adj.* ❷ **B1** [only before noun] very large; much larger or more important than similar things usually are: *The match was shown on a giant screen outside the town hall.* ◊ *a giant step towards achieving independence* ◊ *a giant squid*
■ *noun* **1** ❷ **B1** (in stories) a very large strong person who is often cruel and stupid: *tales of giants and ogres* ⊃ see also GIANTESS **2** ❷ **B1** a person or thing that is unusually large: *He's a giant of a man.* ◊ *He is described as a gentle giant.* **3** ❷ **B2** a very large and powerful organization: *These are boom times for the software giant.* **4** a person who is very good at sth: *literary giants* ⊃ see also GAS GIANT, RED GIANT

**giant·ess** /ˌdʒaɪənˈtes; *NAmE* ˈdʒaɪəntəs/ *noun* (in stories) a female giant

**giant·ism** /ˈdʒaɪəntɪzəm/ *noun* [U] = GIGANTISM

**ˈgiant-killer** *noun* (*BrE*) (especially in sports) a person or team that defeats another much stronger opponent

**ˌgiant ˈpanda** *noun* = PANDA (1)

**ˌgiant ˈslalom** *noun* a SLALOM skiing competition over a long distance, with wide fast turns

**GiB** *abbr.* (in writing) GIBIBYTE

**Gib** *abbr.* (in writing) GIBIBIT

**gib·ber** /ˈdʒɪbə(r)/ *verb* [I, T] **(+ speech)** to speak quickly in a way that is difficult to understand, often because of fear: *He cowered in the corner, gibbering with terror.* ◊ *By this time I was a gibbering wreck.*

**gib·ber·ish** /ˈdʒɪbərɪʃ/ *noun* [U, sing.] (*informal*) words that have no meaning or are impossible to understand **SYN nonsense**: *You were talking gibberish in your sleep.*

**gib·bet** /ˈdʒɪbɪt/ *noun* (in the past) a wooden structure on which criminals were hanged **SYN gallows**

**gib·bon** /ˈɡɪbən/ *noun* a small APE — an animal like a large monkey without a tail with long arms that lives in south-east Asia

**gibe** = JIBE

**gibi·bit** /ˈɡɪbɪbɪt/ *noun* (*abbr.* **Gib**) (*computing*) = GIGABIT (2)

**gibi·byte** /ˈɡɪbɪbaɪt/ *noun* (*abbr.* **GiB**) (*computing*) = GIGABYTE (2)

**gib·lets** /ˈdʒɪbləts/ *noun* [pl.] the inside parts of a chicken or other bird, including the heart and LIVER, that are usually removed before it is cooked

**giddy** /ˈɡɪdi/ *adj.* (**gid·dier**, **gid·di·est**) **1** [not usually before noun] feeling that everything is moving and that you are going to fall **SYN dizzy**: *When I looked down from the top floor, I felt giddy.* **2** [not usually before noun] *~ (with sth)* so happy and excited that you cannot behave normally: *She was giddy with happiness.* **3** [usually before noun] making you feel as if you are about to fall: *The kids were pushing the roundabout at a giddy speed.* ◊ (*figurative*) *the giddy heights of success* **4** (*old-fashioned*) (of people) not serious **SYN silly**: *Isabel's giddy young sister* ▶ **gid·dily** /-dɪli/ *adv.*: *She swayed giddily across the dance floor.* **gid·di·ness** *noun* [U]: *Symptoms include nausea and giddiness.*

**GIF** /ɡɪf, dʒɪf/ *noun* (*computing*) a type of computer file that contains images and is used especially to make them appear to move (the abbreviation for 'Graphic Interchange Format'): *Send it as a GIF.*

**gift** /gɪft/ noun, verb
- **noun 1** a thing that you give to sb, especially on a special occasion or to say thank you *present*: *to give/receive a gift* ◊ *a Christmas/birthday/wedding gift* ◊ *~ from sb The watch was a gift from my mother.* ◊ *for sb a free gift for every reader* ◊ *to sb The golf clubs were her gift to her husband.* ◊ *of sth (figurative) the gift of life* ◊ *(formal) The family made a gift of his paintings to the gallery.* ◊ *as a ~ She gave me the book as a gift.* **2** a natural ability *talent*: *He knew from an early age he had a special gift.* ◊ *for sth She showed a natural gift for comedy.* ◊ *for doing sth He has a gift for making friends easily.* **3** [usually sing.] (*informal*) a thing that is very easy to do or cheap to buy: *Their second goal was an absolute gift.* ◊ *At £500 it's a gift.*
- IDM **be in the gift of sb | be in sb's gift** (*especially BrE*) if sth such as an important job or a special right or advantage is **in sb's gift**, that person can decide who to give it to: *All such posts are in the gift of the managing director* (= only given by the managing director). *the gift of the 'gab* (*BrE*) (*US* **a gift for/of 'gab**) (*informal, sometimes disapproving*) the ability to speak easily and to persuade other people with your words **look a gift horse in the 'mouth** (usually with negatives) (*informal*) to refuse or criticize sth that is given to you for nothing → more at GOD
- **verb** (*BrE*) (used especially in JOURNALISM) to give sth to sb without their having to make any effort to get it: *~ sb sth They gifted their opponents a goal.* ◊ *~ sth to sb They gifted a goal to their opponents.*

**'gift card** noun a card that is worth a particular amount of money that can be exchanged for goods or services → compare GIFT VOUCHER

**'gift certificate** (*especially NAmE*) (*BrE usually* **'gift voucher, 'gift token**) noun a piece of paper that is worth a particular amount of money and that can be exchanged for goods in a store → compare GIFT CARD

**gift·ed** /ˈɡɪftɪd/ adj. **1** having a lot of natural ability or intelligence: *a gifted musician/player, etc.* ◊ *gifted children* **2 ~ with sth** having sth pleasant: *He was gifted with a charming smile.*

**'gift shop** noun a shop that sells SOUVENIRS and small items that are suitable for giving as presents

**'gift voucher** (*also* **'gift token**) (*both BrE*) (*also* **'gift certificate** *especially in NAmE*) noun a piece of paper that is worth a particular amount of money and that can be exchanged for goods in a shop

**'gift wrap** noun [U] attractive coloured or patterned paper used for wrapping presents in *wrapping paper*

**'gift-wrap** verb [often passive] (-pp-) **~ sth** to wrap sth as a present for sb, especially in a shop: *Would you like the chocolates gift-wrapped?* ◊ *The store offers a gift-wrapping service.*

**gig** /ɡɪɡ/ noun, verb
- **noun 1** a performance by musicians playing popular music or jazz in front of an audience; a similar performance by a COMEDIAN: *to do a gig* ◊ *an Arctic Monkeys gig* **2 ~ (as sth)** (*especially NAmE, informal*) a job, especially a temporary one: *a gig as a basketball coach* **3** (*informal*) (*abbr.* **GB**) (*computing*) = GIGABYTE **4** a small light CARRIAGE with two wheels, pulled by one horse
- **verb** [I] (-gg-) to give musical performances in front of audiences, especially of modern music like rock, pop or jazz: *We were gigging two or three nights a week.*

**giga-** /ˈɡɪɡə/ *combining form* (in nouns; used in units of measurement) **1** $10^9$, or 1000000000: *gigahertz* **2** $2^{30}$, or 1073741824

**giga·bit** /ˈɡɪɡəbɪt/ noun (*abbr.* **Gb**) (*computing*) **1** a unit of computer memory or data, equal to $10^9$, or $1000^3$, (= 1000000000) BITS **2** (*also* **gibi·bit**) a unit of computer memory or data, equal to $2^{30}$, or $1024^3$, (= 1073741824) BITS

**giga·byte** /ˈɡɪɡəbaɪt/ (*also informal* **gig**) noun (*abbr.* **GB**) (*computing*) **1** a unit of computer memory or data, equal to $10^9$, or $1000^3$, (= 1000000000) BYTES **2** (*also* **gibi·byte**) a unit of computer memory or data, equal to $2^{30}$, or $1024^3$, (= 1073741824) BYTES

**giga·hertz** /ˈɡɪɡəhɜːts; *NAmE* -hɜːrts/ noun (*pl.* **giga·hertz**) (*abbr.* **GHz**) (*computing, physics*) a unit for measuring radio waves and the speed at which a computer operates; 1000000000 HERTZ

**gi·gan·tic** /dʒaɪˈɡæntɪk/ adj. extremely large *enormous, huge*

**gi·gant·ism** /dʒaɪˈɡæntɪzəm, ˈdʒaɪɡæntɪzəm/ (*also* **giant·ism**) noun [U] (*medical*) a condition in which sb grows to an unusually large size

**'gig economy** noun [usually sing.] an economic system in which many short periods of work are available rather than permanent jobs

**gig·gle** /ˈɡɪɡl/ verb, noun
- **verb** [I, T] **~ (at/about sb/sth) | (+ speech)** to laugh in a silly way because you are embarrassed or nervous or you think that sth is funny: *The girls giggled at the joke.* ◊ *They giggled nervously as they waited for their turn.*
- **noun 1** [C] a slight, silly, repeated laugh: *She gave a nervous giggle.* ◊ *Matt collapsed into giggles and hung up the phone.* **2** [sing.] (*BrE, informal*) a thing that you think is funny: *We only did it for a giggle.* **3 the giggles** [pl.] (*informal*) continuous giggling that you cannot control or stop: *I get the giggles when I'm nervous.* ◊ *She had a fit of the giggles and had to leave the room.*

**gig·gly** /ˈɡɪɡli/ adj. laughing a lot in a silly, nervous way

**gig·olo** /ˈdʒɪɡələʊ, ˈʒɪ-/ noun (*pl.* **-os**) a man who is paid to be the sexual partner of an older woman, usually one who is rich

**gild** /ɡɪld/ verb **1 ~ sth** (*literary*) to make sth look bright, as if covered with gold: *The golden light gilded the sea.* **2 ~ sth** to cover sth with a thin layer of gold or gold paint
- IDM **gild the 'lily** to cause sth to be less good or beautiful than it already is by trying to improve it

**gild·ed** /ˈɡɪldɪd/ adj. [only before noun] **1** covered with a thin layer of gold or gold paint **2** (*literary*) rich and belonging to the upper classes: *the gilded youth* (= rich, upper-class young people) *of the Edwardian era*

**gild·ing** /ˈɡɪldɪŋ/ noun [U] a layer of gold or gold paint; the surface that this makes

**gilet** /ˈʒiːleɪ; *NAmE* ʒəˈleɪ/ noun a light thick jacket without arms

**gill**[1] /ɡɪl/ noun [usually pl.] one of the openings on the side of a fish's head that it breathes through → VISUAL VOCAB page V2
- IDM **to the 'gills** (*informal*) until completely full: *I was stuffed to the gills with chocolate cake.*

**gill**[2] /dʒɪl/ noun a unit for measuring liquids, equal to 0.142 of a LITRE in the UK and some other countries, and 0.118 of a LITRE in the US. There are four gills in a PINT.

**gil·lie** (*also* **ghil·lie**) /ˈɡɪli/ noun (*ScotE*) a man or boy who helps sb who is shooting or fishing for sport in Scotland

**gilt** /ɡɪlt/ noun **1** [U] a thin layer of gold, or sth like gold that is used on a surface for decoration: *gilt lettering* **2 gilts** [pl.] (*BrE, finance*) documents offering a fixed rate of interest on money lent to the UK government; gilt-edged investments

**gilt-'edged** adj. (*finance*) very safe: **gilt-edged securities/shares/stocks** (= investments that are considered safe because they have been sold by the government)

**gim·let** /ˈɡɪmlət/ noun a small tool for making holes in wood to put SCREWS into: *(figurative) eyes like gimlets* (= looking very hard at things and noticing every detail)

**gimme** /ˈɡɪmi/ *short form, noun (informal)*
- **short form** a way of writing the way that the words 'give me' are sometimes spoken: *Gimme back my bike!*
- **noun** [usually sing.] something that is very easy to do or achieve

**gim·mick** /ˈɡɪmɪk/ noun (*often disapproving*) an unusual trick or unnecessary device that is intended to attract attention or to persuade people to buy sth: *a promotional/publicity/sales gimmick* ▸ **gim·micky** *adj.*: *a gimmicky idea*

**gim·mick·ry** /ˈɡɪmɪkri/ noun [U] (*disapproving*) the use of gimmicks in selling, etc.

**gin** /dʒɪn/ noun **1** [U, C] an alcoholic drink made from grain and with JUNIPER BERRIES added. Gin is usually drunk mixed with TONIC or fruit juice. ⊃ see also PINK GIN **2** [C] a glass of gin: *I'll have a gin and tonic, please.* **3** = COTTON GIN

**gin·ger** /ˈdʒɪndʒə(r)/ noun, adj., verb
- noun [U] **1** the root of the ginger plant used in cooking as a SPICE: *a teaspoon of ground ginger* ◊ (*BrE*) *ginger biscuits* ⊃ VISUAL VOCAB page V8 **2** a light orange-brown colour
- adj. (*BrE*) light orange-brown in colour: *ginger hair* ◊ *a ginger cat* ⊃ WORDFINDER NOTE at BLONDE
- verb

PHRV **ginger sth/sb⇌up** (*BrE*) to make sth/sb more active or exciting SYN **liven up**

**ˌginger ˈale** noun **1** [U, C] a clear FIZZY drink (= with bubbles) that does not contain alcohol, tastes of ginger and is often mixed with alcoholic drinks **2** [C] a bottle or glass of ginger ale

**ˌginger ˈbeer** noun **1** [U, C] a FIZZY drink (= with bubbles) that tastes of GINGER. Some types of ginger beer contain a small amount of alcohol. **2** [C] a bottle or glass of ginger beer

**gin·ger·bread** /ˈdʒɪndʒəbred; *NAmE* -dʒərb-/ noun [U] a sweet cake or soft biscuit that is made with GINGER: *a gingerbread man* (= a gingerbread biscuit in the shape of a person)

**gin·ger·ly** /ˈdʒɪndʒəli; *NAmE* -dʒərli/ adv. in a careful way, because you are afraid of being hurt, of making a noise, etc: *He opened the box gingerly and looked inside.*

**ging·ham** /ˈɡɪŋəm/ noun [U] a type of cotton cloth with a pattern of white and coloured squares: *a blue and white gingham dress*

**gin·gi·vitis** /ˌdʒɪndʒɪˈvaɪtɪs/ noun [U] (*medical*) a condition in which the GUMS around the teeth become painful, red and SWOLLEN (= larger or rounder than normal)

**gink·go** (*also* **gingko**) /ˈɡɪŋkəʊ; *NAmE* -koʊ/ noun (*pl.* -**os** *or* -**oes**) a Chinese tree with yellow flowers

**gi·nor·mous** /dʒaɪˈnɔːməs; *NAmE* -ˈnɔːrm-/ adj. (*BrE*, *informal*) extremely large

**gin·seng** /ˈdʒɪnseŋ/ noun [U] a medicine obtained from a plant root that some people believe helps you stay young and healthy

**Gipsy** = GYPSY

**gir·affe** /dʒəˈrɑːf; *NAmE* -ˈræf/ noun a tall African animal with a very long neck, long legs, and dark marks on its coat

**gird** /ɡɜːd; *NAmE* ɡɜːrd/ verb (*literary*) ~ **sb/sth (with sth)** to surround sth with sth; to fasten sth around sb/sth
IDM **gird (up) your ˈloins** (*literary or humorous*) to get ready to do sth difficult: *The company is girding its loins for a plunge into the overseas market.*
PHRV **gird (yourself/sb/sth) (up) for sth** (*literary*) to prepare for sth difficult, especially a fight, contest, etc.

**gird·er** /ˈɡɜːdə(r); *NAmE* ˈɡɜːrd-/ noun a long strong iron or steel bar used for building bridges and the FRAMEWORK of large buildings ⊃ WORDFINDER NOTE at CONSTRUCTION

**gir·dle** /ˈɡɜːdl; *NAmE* ˈɡɜːrdl/ noun, verb
- noun **1** a piece of women's underwear that fits closely around the lower part of the body down to the top of the legs, designed to make a woman look thinner ⊃ see also PANTIE GIRDLE, PANTY GIRDLE **2** (*literary*) a thing that surrounds sth else: *carefully tended lawns set in a girdle of trees* **3** (*old-fashioned*) a belt or thick string fastened around the middle part of the body to keep clothes in position
- verb ~ **sth** (*literary*) to surround sth: *A chain of volcanoes girdles the Pacific.*

**girl** ❶ A1 /ɡɜːl; *NAmE* ɡɜːrl/ noun **1** A1 [C] a female child: *a little girl of six* ◊ *a baby/young/teenage girl* ◊ *The poor girl was scared out of her wits.* ◊ *Hello, girls and boys!* ⊃ see also HEAD GIRL, POSTER CHILD **2** A1 [C] a daughter: *They have two girls and a boy.* **3** A1 [C] (*sometimes offensive*) a young woman: *He married the girl next door.* ◊ *It's a* great way to meet girls. ⊃ see also VALLEY GIRL **4** [C] (*usually in compounds*) (*old-fashioned*, *offensive*) a female worker: *an office girl* ⊃ see also CALL GIRL, CHORUS GIRL, COVER GIRL, WORKING GIRL **5** [C] (*old-fashioned*) a girlfriend **6** **girls** [*pl.*] (used especially as a form of address by women) the women in a group: *I'm having a night out with the girls.* ◊ *Good morning, girls!* **7** [*sing.*] **old ~** (*often offensive*) an old woman, especially sb's wife or mother: *How is the old girl these days?* ⊃ see also OLD GIRL IDM see BIG adj.

**ˈgirl band** (*also* **ˈgirl group**) noun a group of young women who sing pop music and dance, whose music and image are designed to appeal to a young teenage audience

**girl·friend** ❶ A1 /ˈɡɜːlfrend; *NAmE* ˈɡɜːrl-/ noun **1** A1 a girl or a woman that sb is having a romantic relationship with: *He's got a new girlfriend.* **2** A2 a woman's female friend: *I had lunch with a girlfriend.*

**ˈGirl Guide** noun (*BrE*, *old-fashioned*) = GUIDE

**girl·hood** /ˈɡɜːlhʊd; *NAmE* ˈɡɜːrl-/ noun [U] (*old-fashioned*) the time when sb is a girl; the fact of being a girl

**girl·ish** /ˈɡɜːlɪʃ; *NAmE* ˈɡɜːrl-/ adj. like a girl; of a girl: *a girlish giggle* ◊ *a girlish figure*

**ˈgirl power** noun [U] the idea that women should take control of their careers and lives and be independent and confident

**ˌGirl ˈScout** (*US*) (*BrE* **Guide**, *old-fashioned* **ˌGirl ˈGuide**) noun a member of an organization (called **the Girl Scouts** or **the Guides**) that is similar to THE SCOUTS and that trains girls in practical skills and does a lot of activities with them, for example camping

**girly** (*also* **girlie**) /ˈɡɜːli; *NAmE* ˈɡɜːrli/ adj., noun (*informal*)
- adj. [only before noun] **1** (*usually disapproving*) suitable for or like girls, not boys: *girly games* **2** *usually* **girlie** containing photographs of women wearing few or no clothes, that are intended to make men sexually excited: *girlie magazines*
- noun a way of referring to a girl or young woman, that many women find offensive

**girn** = GURN

**giro** /ˈdʒaɪrəʊ; *NAmE* -roʊ/ noun (*pl.* -**os**) [U] (*finance*) a system in which money can be moved from one bank or post office account to another electronically: *to pay by giro* ◊ *a giro credit/payment/transfer*

**girth** /ɡɜːθ; *NAmE* ɡɜːrθ/ noun **1** [U, C] the measurement around sth, especially the middle part of a person's body: *a man of enormous girth* ◊ *a tree one metre in girth/with a girth of one metre* **2** [C] a narrow piece of leather or cloth that is fastened around the middle of a horse to keep the seat (called a SADDLE) or a load in place

**gismo** = GIZMO

**gist** /dʒɪst/ noun (*usually* **the gist** [*sing.*]) **~ (of sth)** the main or general meaning of a piece of writing, a speech or a conversation: *to get* (= understand) *the gist of an argument* ◊ *I missed the beginning of the lecture—can you give me the gist of what he said?* ◊ *I'm afraid I don't quite follow your gist* (= what you really mean).

**git** /ɡɪt/ noun (*BrE*, *slang*) a stupid or unpleasant man

**githeri** /ɡɪˈðeəri; *NAmE* -ˈðeri/ *EAfrE* /ɡiˈðeri/ noun [U] (*EAfrE*) an East African dish of MAIZE and KIDNEY BEANS cooked slowly in liquid and served hot, usually eaten as a main meal

**give** ❶ A1 /ɡɪv/ verb, noun
- verb (**gave** /ɡeɪv/, **given** /ˈɡɪvn/)
- HAND/PROVIDE **1** A1 [T] to hand sth to sb so that they can look at it, use it or keep it for a time: **~ sth to sb** *Give the letter to your mother when you've read it.* ◊ *She gave her ticket to the woman at the check-in desk.* ◊ **~ sb sth** *Give your mother the letter.* ◊ *They were all given a box to carry.* **2** A1 [T, I] to hand sth to sb as a present; to allow sb to have sth as a present: **~ sth to sb** *What are you giving your father for his birthday?* ◊ *Did you give the waiter a tip?* ◊ **~ sth to sb** *She gave a couple of pounds to the beggar.* ◊ **~ (sth)** *We all agreed not to give presents this year.* ◊ *They say it's better to give than to receive.* **3** A1 [T] to provide

sb with sth: **~sb sth** *They were all thirsty so I gave them a drink.* ◇ *Give me your name and address.* ◇ *We've been given a 2 per cent pay increase.* ◇ *I was hoping you would give me a job.* ◇ *He was given a new heart in a five-hour operation.* ◇ **Give me** some time to decide. ◇ *We should at least **give him the opportunity** to explain why he did this.* ◇ *She wants a job that **gives** her more **responsibility**.* ◇ *Can I give you a ride to the station?* ◇ *I'll give you (= allow you to have) ten minutes to prepare your answer.* ◇ **~sth to sb** *He gives Italian lessons to his colleagues.* ◇ **~sth** *She gave some helpful **advice**.* ◇ *She gives the **impression** of being very busy.*
- **MONEY 4** [I, T] to pay money to a charity, etc., to help people: *We need your help—please give generously.* ◇ **~to sb** *They both gave regularly to charity.* ◇ **~sth (to sb)** *I gave a small donation.* **5** [T] to pay in order to have or do sth: **~sb sth (for sth)** *I'll give you £100 and not a penny more!* ◇ *How much will you give me for the car?* ◇ **~sth** *I'd give anything to see him again.* ◇ **~sth for sth** *I gave £50 for the lot.*
- **DO/PRODUCE STH 6** [T] used with a noun to describe a particular action, giving the same meaning as the related verb: **~sth** *She gave a **shrug** of her shoulders* (= SHRUGGED). ◇ *He turned to us and gave a big **smile*** (= smiled broadly). ◇ *Her work has given **pleasure** to* (= pleased) *millions of readers.* ◇ **~sb sth** *He gave her a **kiss*** (= kissed her). ◇ *He gave me a suspicious **look*** (= looked at me suspiciously). **HELP** For other similar expressions, look up the nouns in each. For example, you will find **give your approval** at **approval**. **7** [T] **~sb sth** to produce a particular feeling in sb: *All that driving has given me a **headache**.* ◇ *Go for a walk. It'll give you an **appetite**.*
- **TELEPHONE CALL 8** [T] **~sb sth** to make a phone call to sb: *Give me a call tomorrow.*
- **MARK/GRADE 9** [T] to judge sb/sth to be of a particular standard: **~sb/sth sth** *She had given the assignment an A.* ◇ *I give it ten out of ten for originality.* ◇ **~sth (to sb/sth)** | **~sth** *He virtually never gives a grade of less than C.*
- **ILLNESS 10** [T] to pass an illness onto sb and make them ill: **~sb sth** *You've given me your cold.* ◇ **~sth to sb** *She'd given the bug to all her colleagues.*
- **PUNISHMENT 11** [T] to make sb suffer a particular punishment: **~sb sth** *The judge gave him a nine-month suspended sentence.* ◇ **~sth to sb** *We discussed what punishment should be given to the boys.*
- **PARTY/EVENT 12** [T] **~sth** if you **give** a party, you organize it and invite people: *We're giving a party to celebrate our silver wedding.* **13** [T] to perform sth in public: **~sth** *He gave a rousing **performance** of the Bob Marley song.* ◇ **~sth to sb** *She gave a fine **speech** to the waiting crowd.*
- **TREAT AS IMPORTANT 14** [T] to use time, energy, etc. for sb/sth: **~sb/sth sth** *I gave the matter a lot of thought.* ◇ **~sth to sb/sth** *I gave a lot of thought to the matter.* ◇ *The government has given top priority to reforming the tax system.*
- **PREDICT HOW LONG 15** [T] **~sb/sth sth** to predict that sth will last a particular length of time: *That marriage won't last. I'll give them two years at the outside.*
- **IN SPORT 16** [T] **~sb/sth sth (+ adj.)** to say that a player or the ball is in a particular position or that a goal has been scored: *The umpire gave the ball out.*
- **BEND 17** [I] to bend or stretch under pressure: *The branch began to give under his weight.* ◇ (*figurative*) *We can't go on like this—something's got to give.* **18** [I] to agree to change your mind or give up some of your demands: *You're going to have to give a little.*

**IDM** **HELP** Most idioms containing **give** are at the entries for the nouns and adjectives in the idioms, for example, **give rise to sth** is at **rise** *n.* **don't give me 'that** (*informal*) used to tell sb that you do not accept what they say: '*I didn't have time to do it.' 'Oh, don't give me that!'* **give and 'take** to be willing, in a relationship, to accept what sb else wants and to give up some of what you want: *You're going to have to learn to give and take.* **give as good as you 'get** to react with equal force when sb attacks or criticizes you: *She can give as good as she gets.* **give it 'up (for sb)** (*informal*) to show your approval of sb by CLAPPING your hands: *Give it up for Ed Sheeran!* **give me sth/sb (any day/time)**

(*informal*) used to say that you prefer a particular thing or person to the one that has just been mentioned: *We don't go out much. Give me a quiet night in front of the TV any day!* **give or 'take (sth)** if sth is correct **give or take** a particular amount, it is approximately correct: *It'll take about three weeks, give or take a day or so.* **give sb to believe/understand (that) …** [often passive] (*formal*) to make sb believe/understand sth: *I was given to understand that she had resigned.* **I give you …** used to ask people to drink a TOAST to sb: *Ladies and gentlemen, I give you Geoff Ogilby!* **I/'ll give you 'that** (*informal*) used when you are admitting that sth is true **what 'gives?** (*informal*) what is happening?; what is the news?

**PHRV** **give sb↔ a'way** (in a marriage ceremony) to lead the bride to the BRIDEGROOM and formally allow her to marry him: *The bride was given away by her father.* **give sth↔ a'way 1** to give sth as a gift: *He gave away most of his money to charity.* ◇ (*informal*) *Check out the prices of our pizzas—we're virtually giving them away!* ⊃ related noun GIVEAWAY **2** to present sth: *The mayor gave away the prizes at the school sports day.* **3** to carelessly allow sb to have an advantage: *They've given away two goals already.* **give sth/sb↔ a'way** to make known sth that sb wants to keep secret **SYN** **betray**: *She gave away state secrets to the enemy.* ◇ *It was supposed to be a surprise but the children gave the game away.* ◇ *His voice gave him away* (= showed who he really was). ⊃ related noun GIVEAWAY **give sb sth↔ 'back** | **give sth↔ 'back (to sb) 1** to return sth to its owner: *Could you give me back my pen?* ◇ *Could you give me my pen back?* ◇ *I picked it up and gave it back to him.* ◇ (*informal*) *Give it me back!* **2** to allow sb to have sth again: *The operation gave him back the use of his legs.*
**give 'in (to sb/sth) 1** to admit that you have been defeated by sb/sth: *The rebels were forced to give in.* **2** to agree to do sth that you do not want to do: *The authorities have shown no signs of giving in to the kidnappers' demands.* **give sth 'in (to sb)** (*BrE*) (*also* **hand sth↔ 'in (to sb)** *BrE, NAmE*) to hand over sth to sb in authority: *Please give your work in before Monday.*
**give 'off sth** to produce sth such as a smell, heat, light, etc: *The flowers gave off a fragrant perfume.*
**give on to/onto sth** [no passive] (*BrE*) to have a view of sth; to lead directly to sth: *The bedroom windows give on to the street.* ◇ *This door gives onto the hall.*
**give 'out 1** to come to an end; to be completely used up: *After a month their food supplies gave out.* ◇ *Her patience finally gave out.* **2** to stop working: *One of the plane's engines gave out in mid-air.* ◇ *Her legs gave out and she collapsed.* **give sth↔ 'out** to give sth to a lot of people: *The teacher gave out the exam papers.* **give 'out sth 1** to produce sth such as heat, light, etc: *The radiator gives out a lot of heat.* **2** [often passive] (*especially BrE*) to tell people about sth or broadcast sth
**give 'over** (*BrE, informal*) used to tell sb to stop doing sth: *Give over, Chris! You're hurting me.* ◇ **give over doing sth** *Give over complaining!* **give yourself 'over/'up to sth** to spend all your time doing sth or thinking about sth; to allow sth to completely control your life **give sth↔ 'over to sth** [usually passive] to use sth for one particular purpose: *The gallery is given over to British art.*
**give 'up** [T] to stop trying to do sth: *They gave up without a fight.* ◇ *She doesn't give up easily.* ◇ *I give up—tell me the answer.* **give sb↔ 'up 1** (*also* **give 'up on sb**) to believe that sb is never going to arrive, get better, be found, etc: *There you are at last! We'd given you up.* ◇ *We hadn't heard from him for so long, we'd **given him up for dead**.* **2** to stop having a relationship with sb: *Why don't you give him up?* **give sth↔ 'up 1** [no passive] to stop doing or having sth: *She didn't give up work when she had the baby.* ◇ *We'd **given up hope** of ever having children.* ◇ **give up doing sth** *You ought to give up smoking.* **2** to spend time on a task that you would normally spend on sth else: *I gave up my weekend to help him paint his apartment.* **give sth↔ 'up (to sb)** to hand sth over to sb else: *We had to give our passports up to the authorities.* ◇ *He gave up his seat to a pregnant woman* (= stood up to allow her to sit down).

# giveaway

**give yourself / sb 'up (to sb)** to offer yourself/sb to be captured by sb in authority: *After a week on the run he gave himself up to the police.* **give yourself 'up to sth** = GIVE YOURSELF OVER / UP TO STH **give 'up on sb 1** to stop hoping or believing that sb will change, get better, etc: *His teachers seem to have given up on him.* **2** = GIVE SB UP

- **noun** [U] the ability of sth to bend or stretch under pressure: *The shoes may seem tight at first, but the leather has plenty of give in it.*

**IDM** **give and 'take 1** the quality of being willing to accept what sb else wants and give up some of what you want **2** an exchange of words or ideas: *to encourage a lively give and take*

**give·a·way** /ˈɡɪvəweɪ/ *noun, adj.*
- **noun** (*informal*) **1** something that a company gives free, usually with sth else that is for sale **2** something that makes you guess the real truth about sth/sb: *She pretended she wasn't excited but the expression on her face was a **dead** (= obvious) giveaway.*
- **adj.** [only before noun] (*informal*) (of prices) very low

**give·back** /ˈɡɪvbæk/ *noun* (*NAmE*) a situation in which workers agree to accept lower wages or fewer benefits at a particular time, in return for more money or benefits later

**given** 🌕 /ˈɡɪvn/ *adj., prep., noun*
- **adj.** [usually before noun] **1** already arranged: *They were to meet at a given time and place.* **2** that you have stated and are discussing; particular: *We can find out how much money is spent on food in any given period.* ⊃ see also GOD-GIVEN

**IDM** **be given to sth / to doing sth** (*formal*) to do sth often or regularly: *He's given to going for long walks on his own.*
- **prep.** when you consider sth: *Given his age* (= considering how old he is), *he's remarkably active.* ◇ *Given her interest in children, teaching seems the right job for her.* ▸ **given that** *conj.*: *It was surprising the government was re-elected, given that they had raised taxes so much.*
- **noun** something that is accepted as true, for example when you are discussing sth, or planning sth

**given name** *noun* = FIRST NAME

**giver** /ˈɡɪvə(r)/ *noun* (often in compounds) a person or an organization that gives: *gift-givers* ◇ *~ to sb/sth They are very generous givers to charity.*

**gizmo** (*also* **gismo**) /ˈɡɪzməʊ/ *noun* (*pl. -os*) (*informal*) a general word for a small piece of equipment, often one that does sth in a new and clever way

**giz·zard** /ˈɡɪzəd; NAmE -zərd/ *noun* the part of a bird's stomach in which food is broken up into smaller pieces before being DIGESTED

**glacé** /ˈɡlæseɪ; NAmE ɡlæˈseɪ/ *adj.* [only before noun] (of fruit) preserved in sugar: *glacé fruits* ◇ *glacé cherries*

**gla·cial** /ˈɡleɪʃl; BrE also ˈɡleɪsiəl/ *adj.* **1** [usually before noun] (*geology*) connected with the Ice Age: *the glacial period* (= the time when much of the northern half of the world was covered by ice) **2** (*specialist*) caused or made by glaciers; connected with glaciers: *a glacial landscape* ◇ *glacial deposits / erosion* **3** (*formal*) very cold; like ice **SYN** ICY: *glacial winds / temperatures* **4** (*formal*) (of people) cold and unfriendly; not showing feelings **SYN** ICY: *Her expression was glacial.* ◇ *Relations between the two countries had always been glacial.*

**gla·ci·ation** /ˌɡleɪsiˈeɪʃn; NAmE ˌɡleɪʃi-/ *noun* [U] (*geology*) the process or result of land being covered by glaciers

**gla·cier** /ˈɡlæsiə(r); NAmE ˈɡleɪʃər/ *noun* a slow-moving mass or river of ice, formed from snow on mountains or near the North Pole or South Pole

**glad** 🌕 **B1** /ɡlæd/ *adj.* **1** **B1** [not before noun] pleased; happy: *'I passed the test!' 'I'm so glad.'* ◇ *She was glad when the meeting was over.* ◇ *~ about sth 'He doesn't need the pills any more.' 'I'm glad about that.'* ◇ *~ to know, hear, see … I'm glad to hear you're feeling better.* ◇ *~ (that) … I'm glad (that) you're feeling better.* ◇ *He was glad he'd come.* ◇ *I'm just glad you're safe!* ◇ *~ to do sth I've never been so glad to see anyone in my life!* ◇ *I'm glad to meet you. I've heard a lot about you.* ◇ *~ for sb I'm so glad for him because he's such a nice lad.* **2** grateful for sth: *~ of sth She was very glad of her warm coat in the biting wind.* ◇ *I'd be glad of your help.* ◇ *~ if … I'd be glad if you could help me.* **3** *~ to do sth* very willing to do sth: *I'd be glad to lend you the money.* ◇ *If you'd like me to help you, I'd **be only too glad to.*** **4** [only before noun] (*old-fashioned*) bringing joy; full of joy: *glad tidings*

**IDM** **I'm glad to say (that …)** (*informal*) used when you are commenting on a situation and saying that you are happy about it: *Most teachers, I'm glad to say, take their jobs very seriously.*

▼ SYNONYMS

**glad**
happy • pleased • delighted • proud • relieved • thrilled

These words all describe people feeling happy about sth that has happened or is going to happen.

**glad** [not usually before noun] happy about sth or grateful for it: *He was glad he'd come.* ◇ *She was glad when the meeting was over.*

**happy** pleased about sth nice that you have to do or sth that has happened to sb: *We are happy to announce the engagement of our daughter.*

**pleased** [not before noun] happy about sth that has happened or sth that you have to do: *She was very pleased with her exam results.* ◇ *You're coming? I'm so pleased.*

**GLAD, HAPPY OR PLEASED?**
Feeling **pleased** can suggest that you have judged sb/sth and approve of them. Feeling **glad** can be more about feeling grateful for sth. You cannot be 'glad with sb': *The boss should be glad with you.* **Happy** can mean glad, pleased or satisfied.

**delighted** very pleased about sth; very happy to do sth; showing your delight: *I'm delighted at your news.* **NOTE** Delighted is often used to accept an invitation: *'Can you stay for dinner?' 'I'd be delighted (to).'*

**proud** pleased and satisfied about sth that you own or have done, or are connected with: *proud parents* ◇ *He was proud of himself for not giving up.*

**relieved** feeling happy because sth unpleasant has stopped or has not happened; showing this: *You'll be relieved to know your jobs are safe.*

**thrilled** [not before noun] (*rather informal*) extremely pleased and excited about sth: *I was thrilled to be invited.*

**DELIGHTED OR THRILLED?**
- **Thrilled** may express a stronger feeling than **delighted**, but **delighted** can be made stronger with *absolutely*, *more than* or *only too*. **Thrilled** can be made negative and ironic with *not exactly* or *less than*: *She was not exactly thrilled at the prospect of looking after her niece.*

**PATTERNS**
- glad / happy / pleased / delighted / relieved / thrilled **about** sth
- pleased / delighted / relieved / thrilled **at** sth
- glad / happy / pleased / delighted / thrilled **for** sb
- glad / happy / pleased / delighted / proud / relieved / thrilled **that … / to see / hear / find / know …**
- **very** glad / happy / pleased / proud / relieved
- **absolutely** delighted / thrilled

**glad·den** /ˈɡlædn/ *verb* (*literary*) to make sb feel pleased or happy: *~ sth The sight of the flowers gladdened her heart.* ◇ *it gladdens sb to do sth It gladdened him to see them all enjoying themselves.*

**glade** /ɡleɪd/ *noun* (*literary*) a small open area of grass in a wood or a forest

**gladi·ator** /ˈɡlædieɪtə(r)/ *noun* (in ancient Rome) a man trained to fight other men or animals in order to entertain the public ▸ **gladi·ator·ial** /ˌɡlædiəˈtɔːriəl/ *adj.*: *gladiatorial combat*

**gladi·olus** /ˌglædiˈəʊləs/ noun (pl. **gladi·oli** /-laɪ/) a tall garden plant with long thin leaves and brightly coloured flowers growing up the STEM

**glad·ly** /ˈglædli/ adv. **1** willingly: *I would gladly pay extra for a good seat.* **2** happily; with thanks: *When I offered her my seat, she accepted it gladly.* IDM see SUFFER

**glad·ness** /ˈglædnəs/ noun [U] (*literary*) joy; happiness

**glam·or·ize** (*BrE also* **-ise**) /ˈglæməraɪz/ verb ~ **sb/sth** (*usually disapproving*) to make sb/sth appear attractive or exciting, especially sth that is actually bad: *Television tends to glamorize violence.*

**glam·or·ous** /ˈglæmərəs/ (*also informal* **glam**) *adj.* especially attractive and exciting, and different from ordinary things or people: *glamorous movie stars* ◊ *a glamorous job* OPP **unglamorous** ▶ **glam·or·ous·ly** *adv.*: *glamorously dressed*

**glam·our** (*NAmE also* **glamor**) /ˈglæmə(r)/ noun [U, sing.] **1** the attractive and exciting quality that makes a person, a job or a place seem special, often because of wealth or status: *hopeful young actors dazzled by the glamour of Hollywood* ◊ *Now that she's a flight attendant, foreign travel has lost its glamour for her.* **2** physical beauty that also suggests wealth or success: *Her long dark hair lent her a certain glamour.*

**ˈglamour model** noun (*especially BrE*) a person, especially a woman, who is photographed wearing very few or no clothes in order to make the person looking at the photographs sexually excited

**glamp·ing** /ˈglæmpɪŋ/ noun [U] a type of camping, using tents and other kinds of accommodation, facilities, etc. that are more comfortable and expensive than those usually used for camping ORIGIN From **glamour** and **camping**.

**glam rock** /ˌglæm ˈrɒk; *NAmE* ˈrɑːk/ noun [U] a style of music popular in the 1970s, in which male singers wore unusual clothes and MAKE-UP

**glance** /glɑːns; *NAmE* glæns/ verb, noun
■ verb **1** [I] + adv./prep. to look quickly at sth/sb: *She glanced at her watch.* ◊ *He glanced around the room.* ◊ *I glanced up quickly to see who had come in.* **2** [I] ~ **at/down/over/through sth** to read sth quickly and not carefully or completely SYN **scan**: *I only had time to glance at my emails.* ◊ *He glanced briefly down the list of names.* ◊ *She glanced through the report.*
PHRV **ˌglance ˈon/ˈoff sth** (of light) to flash on a surface or be reflected off sth **ˌglance ˈoff (sth)** to hit sth at an angle and move off it in a different direction: *The ball glanced off the post into the net.*
■ noun ~ (**at sb/sth**) a quick look: *to take/have a glance at the newspaper headlines* ◊ *a cursory/brief/casual/furtive glance* ◊ *The sisters exchanged glances* (= looked at each other). ◊ *She shot him a sideways glance.* ◊ *He walked away without a backward glance.* ◊ *She stole a glance* (= looked secretly) *at her watch.* ➲ SYNONYMS at LOOK
IDM **at a (single) ˈglance** immediately; with only a quick look: *He could tell at a glance what was wrong.* **at ˈfirst ˈglance** when you first look at or think about sth, often rather quickly: *At first glance the problem seemed easy.*

**glan·cing** /ˈglɑːnsɪŋ; *NAmE* ˈglæn-/ *adj.* [only before noun] hitting sth/sb at an angle, not with full force: *to strike somebody a glancing blow*

**gland** /glænd/ noun an organ in a person's or an animal's body that produces a substance for the body to use; part of the body that is similar to this, especially a LYMPH NODE: *a snake's poison glands* ◊ *Her glands are swollen.* ➲ see also ADRENAL GLAND, PINEAL, PITUITARY, PROSTATE, THYMUS, THYROID ▶ **glan·du·lar** /ˈglændʒələ(r)/ *adj.* [usually before noun]: *glandular tissue*

**ˌglandular ˈfever** (*BrE*) (*NAmE* **mononucleosis**, *informal* **mono**) noun [U] a disease that causes the LYMPH GLANDS to SWELL (= become large, round and painful) and makes the person feel very weak for a long time

**glans** /glænz/ noun (pl. **glan·des** /ˈglændiːz/) (*anatomy*) the round part at the end of a man's PENIS or a woman's CLITORIS

**glare** /gleə(r); *NAmE* gler/ verb, noun
■ verb **1** [I] ~ (**at sb/sth**) to look at sb/sth in an angry way SYN **glower**: *He didn't shout, he just glared at me silently.* **2** [I] to shine with a very bright, unpleasant light IDM see DAGGER
■ noun **1** [U, sing.] a very bright, unpleasant light: *the glare of the sun* ◊ *The rabbit was caught in the glare of the car's headlights.* ◊ *These sunglasses are designed to reduce glare.* ◊ (*figurative*) *The divorce was conducted in the full glare of publicity* (= with continuous attention from newspapers and television). **2** [C] a long, angry look: *to give sb a hostile glare* ➲ SYNONYMS at LOOK, STARE

**glar·ing** /ˈgleərɪŋ; *NAmE* ˈgler-/ *adj.* **1** [usually before noun] (of sth bad) very easily seen SYN **blatant**: *a glaring error/omission/inconsistency* ◊ *the most glaring example of this problem* **2** (of a light) very bright and unpleasant **3** angry; aggressive: *glaring eyes* ▶ **glar·ing·ly** *adv.*: *glaringly obvious*

**glass** ⓘ A1 /glɑːs; *NAmE* glæs/ noun, verb
■ noun
• CLEAR SUBSTANCE **1** A1 [U] a hard, usually clear, substance used, for example, for making windows and bottles: *a sheet/pane of glass* ◊ *I cut myself on a piece of broken glass.* ◊ *a glass bottle/jar* ◊ *sliding glass doors* ◊ *under ~* *The vegetables are grown under glass* (= in a GREENHOUSE). ➲ see also CUT GLASS, PLATE GLASS, SAFETY GLASS, STAINED GLASS, GLAZIER
• FOR DRINKING **2** A1 [C] (often in compounds) a container made of glass, used for drinking out of: *He poured orange juice into a glass.* ◊ *a champagne/beer glass* ◊ *a shot glass* ◊ *a pint glass* ➲ see also WINE GLASS **3** A1 [C] the contents of a glass: *He drank three whole glasses.* ◊ *~ of sth a glass of wine/water*
• FOR EYES **4** A1 **glasses** (*NAmE also* **eye·glasses**) (*also oldfashioned or formal* **spec·tacles**, *informal* **specs** *especially in BrE*) [pl.] two LENSES in a frame that rests on the nose and ears. People wear glasses in order to be able to see better or to protect their eyes from bright light: *a pair of glasses* ◊ *reading glasses* ◊ *I wear glasses for driving.* ➲ see also DARK GLASSES, FIELD GLASSES, MAGNIFYING GLASS, SUNGLASSES
• GLASS OBJECTS **5** [U] objects made of glass: *We keep all our glass and china in this cupboard.* **6** [sing.] a protecting cover made of glass on a watch, picture or photograph frame, FIRE ALARM, etc: *In case of emergency, break the glass and press the button.*
• MIRROR **7** [C, usually sing.] (*old-fashioned*) a mirror ➲ see also LOOKING GLASS
• BAROMETER **8** **the glass** [sing.] a BAROMETER IDM see PEOPLE *n.*, RAISE *v.*
■ verb ~ **sb** (*BrE*, *informal*) to hit sb in the face with a glass
PHRV **ˌglass sth ˈin/ˈover** [usually passive] to cover sth with a roof or wall made of glass: *a glassed-in pool* ➲ compare GLAZE

**ˈglass-blowing** noun [U] the art or activity of blowing hot glass into shapes using a special tube ▶ **ˈglass-blower** noun

**ˈglass ˈceiling** noun [usually sing.] the way in which unfair attitudes can stop women, or other groups, from getting the best jobs in a company, etc. although there are no official rules to prevent them from getting these jobs: *to hit/break the glass ceiling*

**ˈglass ˈfibre** (*US* **glass fiber**) noun **1** [C] a very thin THREAD of glass **2** [U] (*BrE*) = FIBREGLASS

**glass·ful** /ˈglɑːsfʊl; *NAmE* ˈglæs-/ noun the amount that a drinking glass will hold

**glass·house** /ˈglɑːshaʊs; *NAmE* ˈglæs-/ noun (*BrE*) **1** a building with glass sides and a glass roof, for growing plants in; a type of large GREENHOUSE **2** (*slang*) a military prison

**glass·ware** /ˈglɑːsweə(r); *NAmE* ˈglæswer/ noun [U] objects made of glass

**glassy** /ˈglɑːsi; *NAmE* ˈglæsi/ *adj.* (**glass·ier**, **glassi·est**) **1** like glass; smooth and shiny: *a glassy lake* ◊ *a glassy material*

# Glaswegian

**2** showing no feeling or emotion: *glassy eyes* ◇ *a glassy look/stare* ◇ *He looked flushed and glassy-eyed.*

**Glas·we·gian** /glæzˈwiːdʒən/ *noun* a person from Glasgow in Scotland ▶ **Glas·we·gian** *adj.*

**glau·coma** /glaʊˈkəʊmə, glɔːˈk-/ *noun* [U] an eye disease involving increased pressure in the eye that makes you gradually lose your sight

**glaze** /gleɪz/ *verb, noun*
- *verb* **1** [I] ~ **(over)** if a person's eyes **glaze** or **glaze over**, the person begins to look bored or tired: *A lot of people's eyes glaze over if you say you are a feminist.* ◇ *'I'm feeling rather tired,' he said, his eyes glazing.* **2** [T] ~ *sth* to fit sheets of glass into sth: *to glaze a window/house* ⊃ compare GLASS ⊃ see also DOUBLE GLAZING, DOUBLE-GLAZE **3** [T] ~ *sth* **(with sth)** to cover sth with a glaze to give it a shiny surface: *Glaze the pie with beaten egg.*
- *noun* [C, U] **1** a thin clear liquid put on CLAY objects such as cups and plates before they are finished, to give them a hard shiny surface **2** a thin liquid, made of egg, milk or sugar, for example, that is put on cake, bread, etc. to make it look shiny

**glazed** /gleɪzd/ *adj.* **1** fitted with sheets of glass: *a glazed door* **2** covered with glaze to give a shiny surface: *glazed tiles/pottery* ◇ *(NAmE) a glazed doughnut* **3** (especially of the eyes) showing no feeling or emotion; not bright: *She had a glazed look in her eyes.*

**glaz·ier** /ˈgleɪziə(r); NAmE ˈgleɪzər/ *noun* a person whose job is to fit glass into the frames of windows, etc.

**gleam** /gliːm/ *verb, noun*
- *verb* **1** [I] to shine with a pale clear light: *The moonlight gleamed on the water.* ◇ *Her eyes gleamed in the dark.* ⊃ SYNONYMS at SHINE **2** [I] to look very clean or bright: ~ **(with sth)** *The house was gleaming with fresh white paint.* ◇ + *adj. Her teeth gleamed white against the tanned skin of her face.* **3** [I] if a person's eyes **gleam** with a particular emotion, or an emotion **gleams** in a person's eyes, the person shows that emotion: ~ **(with sth)** *His eyes gleamed with amusement.* ◇ ~ **(in sth)** *Amusement gleamed in his eyes.*
- *noun* [usually sing.] **1** a pale clear light, often reflected from sth: *the gleam of moonlight on the water* ◇ *A few gleams of sunshine lit up the gloomy afternoon.* ◇ *I saw the gleam of the knife as it flashed through the air.* **2** a small amount of sth: *a faint gleam of hope* ◇ *a serious book with an occasional gleam of humour* **3** an expression of a particular feeling or emotion that shows in sb's eyes SYN **glint**: *a gleam of triumph in her eyes* ◇ *a mischievous gleam in his eye* ◇ *The gleam in his eye made her uncomfortable* (= as if he was planning sth secret or unpleasant).

**gleam·ing** /ˈgliːmɪŋ/ *adj.* shining brightly because of being very clean: *gleaming white teeth*

**glean** /gliːn/ *verb* ~ *sth* **(from sb/sth)** to obtain information, knowledge, etc., sometimes with difficulty and often from various different places: *These figures have been gleaned from a number of studies.*

**glean·ings** /ˈgliːnɪŋz/ *noun* [pl.] information, knowledge, etc., that you obtain from various different places, often with difficulty

**glee** /gliː/ *noun* [U] a feeling of happiness, usually because sth good has happened to you, or sth bad has happened to sb else SYN **delight**: *He rubbed his hands in glee as he thought of all the money he would make.* ◇ ~ **at sth** *She couldn't disguise her glee at their embarrassment.*

**ˈglee club** *noun* (*NAmE*) a group of people who meet regularly to sing and perform short songs together

**glee·ful** /ˈgliːfl/ *adj.* happy because of sth good you have done or sth bad that has happened to sb else: *a gleeful laugh* ▶ **glee·ful·ly** /-fəli/ *adv.*

**glen** /glen/ *noun* a deep narrow valley, especially in Scotland or Ireland

**glib** /glɪb/ *adj.* (*disapproving*) (of speakers and speech) using words that are clever, but are not sincere, and do not show much thought: *a glib salesman* ◇ *glib answers* ▶ **glib·ly** *adv.*

**glide** /glaɪd/ *verb, noun*
- *verb* **1** [I] (+ **adv./prep.**) to move smoothly and quietly, especially as though it takes no effort: *Swans went gliding past.* ◇ *The skaters were gliding over the ice.* **2** [I] (+ **adv./prep.**) (of birds or aircraft) to fly using air currents, without the birds moving their wings or the aircraft using the engine: *An eagle was gliding high overhead.* ◇ *The plane managed to glide down to the runway.*
- *noun* **1** [sing.] a continuous smooth movement: *the graceful glide of a skater* **2** [C] (*phonetics*) a speech sound made while moving the tongue from one position to another ⊃ compare DIPHTHONG

**glider** /ˈglaɪdə(r)/ *noun* a light aircraft that flies without an engine ⊃ see also HANG-GLIDER

**glid·ing** /ˈglaɪdɪŋ/ *noun* [U] the sport of flying in a glider ⊃ see also HANG-GLIDING

**glim·mer** /ˈglɪmə(r)/ *noun, verb*
- *noun* **1** a small unsteady light: *We could see a glimmer of light on the far shore.* **2** (*also* **glim·mer·ing**) a small sign of sth: *a glimmer of hope* ◇ *I caught the glimmer of a smile in his eyes.* ◇ *the glimmering of an idea*
- *verb* [I] to shine with a small unsteady light: *The candles glimmered in the corner.* ◇ (*figurative*) *Amusement glimmered in his eyes.*

**glimpse** /glɪmps/ *noun, verb*
- *noun* [usually sing.] **1** a sight of sb/sth for a very short time, when you do not see the person or thing completely: ~ **(of sb/sth)** *He caught a glimpse of her in the crowd.* ◇ *I came up on deck to get my first glimpse of the island.* ◇ ~ **at sb/sth** *I just got a glimpse at the baby, but she was very cute.* ⊃ SYNONYMS at LOOK, SEE **2** a short experience of sth that helps you to understand it: ~ **(of sth)** *The programme gives us a rare glimpse of a great artist at work.* ◇ ~ **into sth** *Take a glimpse into the future of rail travel.* ◇ ~ **at sth** *The exhibition offers a fascinating glimpse at life beneath the waves.*
- *verb* **1** ~ *sb/sth* to see sb/sth for a moment, but not very clearly SYN **catch**, **spot**: *He'd glimpsed her through the window as he passed.* **2** ~ *sth* to start to understand sth: *Suddenly she glimpsed the truth about her sister.*

**glint** /glɪnt/ *verb, noun*
- *verb* **1** [I] (+ **adv./prep.**) to produce small bright flashes of light: *The sea glinted in the moonlight.* ◇ *The sun glinted on the windows.* ⊃ SYNONYMS at SHINE **2** [I] + **adv./prep.** if a person's eyes **glint** with a particular emotion, or an emotion **glints** in a person's eyes, the person shows that emotion, which is usually a strong one: *Her eyes glinted angrily.* ◇ *Hostility glinted in his eyes.*
- *noun* **1** a sudden flash of light or colour shining from a bright surface: *the glint of the sun on the water* ◇ *golden glints in her red hair* ◇ *She saw a glint of silver in the grass.* **2** an expression in sb's eyes showing a particular emotion, often a negative one: *He had a wicked glint in his eye.*

**glis·sando** /glɪˈsændəʊ/ *noun* (*pl.* **glis·san·dos** *or* **glis·sandi** /-diː/) (*from Italian, music*) a way of playing a series of notes so that each one slides into the next, making a smooth continuous sound

**glis·ten** /ˈglɪsn/ *verb* [I] (of sth wet) to shine: *Her eyes were glistening with tears.* ◇ *Sweat glistened on his forehead.* ◇ + *adj. The road glistened wet after the rain.* ⊃ SYNONYMS at SHINE IDM see GOLD *n.*

**glis·ter** /ˈglɪstə(r)/ *verb* [I] (*literary*) to shine brightly with little flashes of light, like a diamond SYN **glitter** IDM see GOLD *n.*

**glitch** /glɪtʃ/ *noun, verb* (*informal*)
- *noun* a small problem or fault that stops sth working successfully
- *verb* [I] (of a machine or system) to suffer a sudden fault and fail to work correctly

**glitchy** /ˈglɪtʃi/ *adj.* (**glitch·ier**, **glitchi·est**) (*informal*) (of a machine or system) tending to GLITCH (= suffer a sudden fault and fail to work correctly): *The game is so buggy and glitchy it is barely playable.*

**glit·ter** /ˈglɪtə(r)/ *verb, noun*
- *verb* **1** [I] to shine brightly with little flashes of light, like a diamond SYN **sparkle**: *The ceiling of the cathedral*

glittered with gold. ◊ *The water glittered in the sunlight.* ⊃ SYNONYMS at SHINE **2** [I] ~ **(with sth)** (of the eyes) to shine brightly with a particular emotion, usually a strong one: *His eyes glittered with greed.* IDM see GOLD *n.*
■ *noun* **1** [U] bright light consisting of many little flashes: *the glitter of diamonds* **2** [sing.] a bright expression in sb's eyes showing a particular emotion SYN **glint**: *There was a triumphant glitter in his eyes.* **3** [U] the attractive, exciting qualities that sb/sth, especially a rich and famous person or place, seems to have SYN **glamour**: *the superficial glitter of show business* **4** [U] very small shiny pieces of thin metal or paper that are stuck to things as a decoration: *gold/silver glitter*

**glit·ter·ati** /ˌɡlɪtəˈrɑːti/ *noun* [pl.] (used in newspapers) fashionable, rich and famous people

**glit·ter·ing** /ˈɡlɪtərɪŋ/ *adj.* [usually before noun] **1** very impressive and successful: *He has a glittering career ahead of him.* **2** very impressive and involving rich and successful people: *a glittering occasion/ceremony* ◊ *a glittering array of stars* **3** shining brightly with many small flashes of light SYN **sparkling**: *glittering jewels*

**glit·tery** /ˈɡlɪtəri/ *adj.* shining brightly with many little flashes of light: *a glittery suit*

**glitz** /ɡlɪts/ *noun* [U] (*sometimes disapproving*) the fact of appearing very attractive, exciting and impressive, in a way that is not always real: *the glitz and glamour of the music scene* ▶ **glitzy** *adj.*: *a glitzy, Hollywood-style occasion*

**the gloam·ing** /ðə ˈɡləʊmɪŋ/ *noun* [sing.] (*ScotE or literary*) the light that remains after the sun sets SYN **twilight, dusk**

**gloat** /ɡləʊt/ *verb* [I] ~ **(about/at/over sth)** to show that you are happy about your own success or sb else's failure, in an unpleasant way SYN **crow**: *She was still gloating over her rival's disappointment.* ▶ **gloat·ing** *adj.*: *a gloating look*

**glob** /ɡlɒb; *NAmE* ɡlɑːb/ *noun* (*informal*) a small amount of a liquid or substance in a round shape: *thick globs of paint on the floor*

**global** ⓘ B1 ◉ /ˈɡləʊbl/ *adj.* [usually before noun] **1** B1 covering or affecting the whole world: *This year the global economy will grow by about 4 per cent.* ◊ *a global financial/economic crisis* ◊ *the struggle to stay competitive in global markets* ◊ *the country's ability to compete on a global scale* **2** considering or including all parts of sth: *They sent a global email to all staff.* **3** (*computing*) operating or applying through the whole of a file, program, etc: *global searches on the database* ▶ **glob·al·ly** /-bəli/ *adv.*: *We need to start thinking globally.*

**glob·al·iza·tion** ⓘ B2 (*BrE also* **-isa·tion**) /ˌɡləʊbəlaɪˈzeɪʃn; *NAmE* -ləˈz-/ *noun* [U] the fact that different cultures and economic systems around the world are becoming connected and similar to each other because of the influence of large MULTINATIONAL companies and of improved communication

**glob·al·ize** (*BrE also* **-ise**) /ˈɡləʊbəlaɪz/ *verb* [I, T] ~ **(sth)** (*economics*) if sth, for example a business company, **globalizes** or **is globalized**, it operates all around the world

**the ˌGlobal ˈSouth** *noun* [sing.] = THE SOUTH

**global ˈvillage** *noun* [sing.] the whole world, looked at as a single community that is connected by electronic communication systems

**global ˈwarming** *noun* [U] the increase in temperature of the earth's atmosphere that is caused by the increase of particular gases, especially CARBON DIOXIDE ⊃ compare CLIMATE CHANGE ⊃ see also GREENHOUSE EFFECT

**globe** ⓘ B2 /ɡləʊb/ *noun* **1** ⓘ B2 **the globe** [sing.] the world (used especially to emphasize its size): *tourists from every corner of the globe* **2** [C] an object like a ball in shape with a map of the world on its surface, usually on a stand so that it can be turned ⊃ WORDFINDER NOTE at MAP **3** [C] a thing that is like a ball in shape

**ˌglobe ˈartichoke** *noun* = ARTICHOKE (1)

**globe·trot·ting** /ˈɡləʊbtrɒtɪŋ; *NAmE* -trɑːt-/ *adj.* (*informal*) travelling in many countries all over the world: *a globe-trotting journalist* ▶ **globe·trot·ter** *noun* **globe·trot·ting** *noun* [U]

**globu·lar** /ˈɡlɒbjələ(r); *NAmE* ˈɡlɑːb-/ *adj.* having the shape of a ball, GLOBE or globule; consisting of globules

**glob·ule** /ˈɡlɒbjuːl; *NAmE* ˈɡlɑːb-/ *noun* a very small drop or ball of a liquid or of a solid that has been melted: *a globule of fat*

**glock·en·spiel** /ˈɡlɒkənʃpiːl; *NAmE* ˈɡlɑːk-/ *noun* a musical instrument made of a row of metal bars of different lengths, that you hit with two small HAMMERS ⊃ compare XYLOPHONE

**glom** /ɡlɒm; *NAmE* ɡlɑːm/ *verb* (**-mm-**) ~ **sth** (*NAmE, informal*) to steal
PHRV **ˌglom ˈonto sth 1** to develop a strong interest in sth: *Kids soon glom onto the latest trend.* **2** to become attached or stuck to sth

**gloom** /ɡluːm/ *noun* **1** [U, sing.] a feeling of being sad and without hope SYN **depression**: *The gloom deepened as the election results came in.* **2** [U] (*literary*) almost total DARKNESS: *We watched the boats come back in the gathering gloom.* IDM see DOOM *n.*, PILE *v.*

**gloomy** /ˈɡluːmi/ *adj.* (**gloom·ier, gloomi·est**) **1** nearly dark, or badly lit in a way that makes you feel sad SYN **depressing**: *a gloomy room/atmosphere* ◊ *It was a wet and gloomy day.* **2** sad and without hope SYN **glum**: *a gloomy expression* ◊ *We sat in gloomy silence.* **3** without much hope of success or happiness in the future SYN **depressing**: *a gloomy picture of the country's economic future* ◊ *Suddenly, the future didn't look so gloomy after all.* ▶ **gloom·ily** /-mɪli/ *adv.*: *He stared gloomily at the phone.* **gloomi·ness** *noun* [U]

**gloop** /ɡluːp/ (*BrE*) (*NAmE* **glop** /ɡlɒp; *NAmE* ɡlɑːp/) *noun* [U] (*informal*) a thick wet substance that looks, tastes or feels unpleasant ▶ **gloopy** (*BrE*) (*NAmE* **gloppy**) *adj.*

**glori·fied** /ˈɡlɔːrɪfaɪd/ *adj.* [only before noun] making sb/sth seem more important or better than they are: *The restaurant was no more than a glorified fast-food cafe.*

**glor·ify** /ˈɡlɔːrɪfaɪ/ *verb* (**glori·fies, glori·fy·ing, glori·fied, glori·fied**) **1** ~ **sth** (*often disapproving*) to make sth seem better or more important than it really is: *He denies that the movie glorifies violence.* **2** ~ **sb** (*formal*) to praise and WORSHIP God ▶ **glori·fi·ca·tion** /ˌɡlɔːrɪfɪˈkeɪʃn/ *noun* [U]: *the glorification of war*

**glori·ous** ⓘ C1 /ˈɡlɔːriəs/ *adj.* **1** ⓘ C1 (*formal*) deserving or bringing great success and making sb/sth famous: *a glorious victory* ◊ *a glorious chapter in our country's history* ⊃ compare INGLORIOUS **2** ⓘ C1 very beautiful and impressive SYN **splendid**: *a glorious sunset* **3** ⓘ C1 (of weather) hot, with the sun shining: *They had three weeks of glorious sunshine.* **4** extremely pleasant SYN **wonderful**: *a glorious trip to Rome* ▶ **glori·ous·ly** *adv.*

**glory** ⓘ C1 /ˈɡlɔːri/ *noun, verb*
■ *noun* **1** ⓘ C1 [U] great success that brings sb praise and honour and makes them famous: *Olympic glory in the 100 metres* ◊ *I do all the work and he gets all the glory.* ◊ *She wanted to enjoy her moment of glory.* ◊ *He came home a rich man, covered in glory.* **2** ⓘ C1 [U] praise and WORSHIP of God: *'Glory to God in the highest'* **3** ⓘ C1 [U] great beauty: *The city was spread out beneath us in all its glory.* ◊ *The house has now been restored to its former glory.* **4** [C] something that is beautiful, impressive, or deserves praise: *The temple is one of the glories of ancient Greece.* ◊ *Her long black hair is her crowning glory* (= most impressive feature). ⊃ see also REFLECTED GLORY
■ *verb* (**glor·ies, glory·ing, glor·ied, glor·ied**)
PHRV **ˈglory in sth** to get great pleasure from sth SYN **revel**: *She gloried in her new-found independence.*

**ˈglory days** *noun* [pl.] a time in the past which people look back on as being better than the present

**gloss** /ɡlɒs; *NAmE* ɡlɑːs/ *noun, verb*
■ *noun* **1** [U, sing.] a shine on a smooth surface: *paper with a high gloss on one side* ◊ *The gel gives your hair a gloss.* ◊ *You can have the photos with either a gloss or a matt finish.* **2** [U] (often in compounds) a substance designed to make

# glossary

sth shiny: *lip gloss* **3** (*also* **gloss 'paint**) [U] paint which, when dry, has a hard shiny surface: *two coats of gloss* **4** [U, sing.] an attractive appearance that is only on the surface and hides what is not so attractive: *Beneath the gloss of success was a tragic private life.* ◊ *This scandal has taken the gloss off the occasion.* **5** [C] ~ **(on sth)** a way of explaining sth to make it seem more attractive or acceptable: *The director puts a Hollywood gloss on the civil war.* **6** [C] ~ **(on sth)** a note or comment added to a piece of writing to explain a difficult word or phrase
- *verb* ~ **sth (as sth)** to add a note or comment to a piece of writing to explain a difficult word or idea

**PHRV** **gloss 'over sth** to avoid talking about sth unpleasant or embarrassing by not dealing with it in detail: *to gloss over a problem* ◊ *He glossed over any splits in the party.*

**gloss·ary** /ˈglɒsəri; NAmE ˈglɑːs-/ *noun* (*pl.* **-ies**) a list of technical or special words, especially those in a particular text, explaining their meanings

**glossy** /ˈglɒsi; NAmE ˈglɑːsi/ *adj., noun*
- *adj.* (**gloss·ier**, **glossi·est**) **1** smooth and shiny: *glossy hair* ◊ *a glossy brochure/magazine* (= printed on shiny paper) **2** giving an appearance of being important and expensive: *the glossy world of fashion*
- *noun* (*pl.* **-ies**) (*informal*) an expensive magazine printed on glossy paper, with a lot of colour photographs, etc.

**glot·tal** /ˈglɒtl; NAmE ˈglɑːtl/ *noun* (*phonetics*) a speech sound produced by the glottis ▸ **glot·tal** *adj.*

**glottal 'stop** *noun* (*phonetics*) a speech sound made by closing and opening the glottis, which in English is sometimes used for /t/, for example in *atlas*

**glot·tis** /ˈglɒtɪs; NAmE ˈglɑːt-/ *noun* (*anatomy*) the part of the throat that contains the VOCAL CORDS and the narrow space between them

**glove** ⓘ B1 /glʌv/ *noun* a piece of clothing for the hand, made of wool, leather, etc. with separate parts for each finger and the THUMB: *a pair of gloves* ◊ *rubber/latex gloves* ◊ *gardening/boxing gloves* ⊃ compare MITTEN ⊃ see also BOXING, OVEN GLOVE

**IDM** **the gloves are off** used to say that sb is ready for a fight or an argument ⊃ more at FIT *v.*, HAND *n.*, IRON *adj.*, KID *n.*

**glove com'partment** (*also* **glove-box** /ˈglʌvbɒks; NAmE -bɑːks/) *noun* a small space or shelf facing the front seats of a car, used for keeping small things in

**gloved** /glʌvd/ *adj.* [usually before noun] wearing a glove or gloves

**glove puppet** (*BrE*) (*also* **hand puppet** *especially in NAmE*) *noun* a type of PUPPET that you put over your hand and move using your fingers

**glow** /ɡləʊ/ *verb, noun*
- *verb* **1** [I] (especially of sth hot or warm) to produce a steady light that is not very bright: *The embers still glowed in the hearth.* ◊ *The strap has a fluorescent coating that glows in the dark.* ◊ + *adj.* *A cigarette end glowed red in the darkness.* ⊃ SYNONYMS at SHINE **2** [I] (of a person's body or face) to look or feel warm or pink, especially after exercise or because you are excited, embarrassed, etc: *Her cheeks were glowing.* ◊ ~ **with sth** *His face glowed with embarrassment.* **3** [I] ~ **(with sth)** to look very pleased or satisfied: *She was positively glowing with pride.* ◊ *He gave her a warm glowing smile.* **4** [I] to appear a strong, warm colour: ~ **(with sth)** *The countryside glowed with autumn colours.* ◊ + *adj.* *The brick walls glowed red in the late afternoon sun.*
- *noun* [sing.] **1** a steady light that is not too bright, like the light from a fire that has stopped producing flames: *The city was just a red glow on the horizon.* ◊ *There was no light except for the occasional glow of a cigarette.* **2** the pink colour in your face when you have been doing exercise or feel happy and excited: *The fresh air had brought a healthy glow to her cheeks.* **3** a gold or red colour: *the glow of autumn leaves* **4** a feeling of pleasure: *When she looked at her children, she felt a glow of pride.*

**glow·er** /ˈɡlaʊə(r)/ *verb* [I] ~ **(at sb/sth)** to look in an angry, aggressive way **SYN** glare ▸ **glow·er** *noun*

**glow·ing** /ˈɡləʊɪŋ/ *adj.* giving enthusiastic praise: *a glowing account/report/review* ◊ *He spoke of her performance in the film in glowing terms* (= praising her highly). ▸ **glow·ing·ly** *adv.*

**'glow stick** (*also* **'light stick**) *noun* a plastic tube filled with chemicals that shines like a lamp when you bend it

**glow-worm** *noun* a type of insect. The female has no wings and produces a green light at the end of the tail.

**glu·cose** /ˈɡluːkəʊs, -kəʊz/ *noun* [U] a simple type of sugar that is an important energy source in living things and that is a part of many CARBOHYDRATES

**glue** /ɡluː/ *noun, verb*
- *noun* [U, C] a sticky substance that is used for joining things together: *a tube of glue* ◊ *He sticks to her like glue* (= never leaves her). ◊ (*figurative*) *These sports were the glue that held the community together.*
- *verb* (**glues**, **glu·ing** *or* **glue·ing**, **glued**, **glued**) to join two things together using glue **SYN** stick: ~ **A (to/onto B)** *She glued the label onto the box.* ◊ ~ **A and B (together)** *Glue the two pieces of cardboard together.* ◊ *Make sure the edges are glued down.*

**IDM** **be 'glued to sth** (*informal*) to give all your attention to sth; to stay very close to sth: *He spent the whole trip glued to his phone.* ◊ *Her eyes were glued to the screen* (= she did not stop watching it). ⊃ more at SPOT *n.*

**'glue-sniffing** *noun* [U] the habit of breathing in the gases from some kinds of GLUE (= a sticky substance used for joining things together) in order to produce a state of excitement

**gluey** /ˈɡluːi/ *adj.* sticky like GLUE (= a substance used for joining things together); covered with GLUE

**glug** /ɡlʌɡ/ *verb, noun* (*informal*)
- *verb* (**-gg-**) **1** [I] + *adv./prep.* (of liquid) to pour out quickly and noisily, especially from a bottle **2** [T] ~ **sth (down)** to drink sth quickly: *She glugged down a glass of water.*
- *noun* a small amount of a drink or liquid poured out quickly and noisily; the sound it makes

**glum** /ɡlʌm/ *adj.* sad, quiet and unhappy **SYN** gloomy: *The players sat there with glum looks on their faces.* ▸ **glum·ly** *adv.*: *The three of us sat glumly looking out to sea.*

**glut** /ɡlʌt/ *noun, verb*
- *noun* [usually sing.] ~ **(of sth)** a situation in which there is more of sth than is needed or can be used **SYN** surfeit: *a glut of cheap imported goods on the market* **OPP** shortage
- *verb* (**-tt-**) [usually passive] to supply or provide sth with too much of sth: **be glutted (with sth)** *The market has been glutted with foreign cars.*

**glu·ten** /ˈɡluːtn/ *noun* [U] a sticky substance that is a mixture of two PROTEINS and is left when starch is removed from flour, especially WHEAT flour: *We sell a range of gluten-free products* (= not containing gluten).

**glutes** /ɡluːts/ *noun* [pl.] (*informal*) the muscles in the BUTTOCKS that move the top of the leg; the gluteus muscles

**glu·teus** /ˈɡluːtiəs/ (*also* **'gluteus muscle**) *noun* (*anatomy*) any of the three muscles in each BUTTOCK

**glu·tin·ous** /ˈɡluːtənəs/ *adj.* sticky: *glutinous rice*

**glut·ton** /ˈɡlʌtn/ *noun* **1** (*disapproving*) a person who eats too much **2** ~ **for punishment/work** a person who enjoys doing difficult or unpleasant tasks ▸ **glut·ton·ous** /-tənəs/ *adj.* **SYN** greedy

**glut·tony** /ˈɡlʌtəni/ *noun* [U] (*disapproving*) the habit of eating and drinking too much **SYN** greed

**gly·caem·ic index** (*BrE*) (*NAmE* **gly·cem·ic index**) /ɡlaɪˌsiːmɪk ˈɪndeks/ *noun* = GI

**gly·cer·ine** /ˈɡlɪsərɪn; *BrE also* -riːn/ (*especially BrE*) (*US usually* **gly·cerin** /ˈɡlɪsərɪn/) *noun* [U] an alternative name for GLYCEROL, frequently used in labels showing ingredients

**gly·cerol** /ˈɡlɪsərɒl; NAmE -rɔːl, -roʊl/ *noun* [U] a thick sweet COLOURLESS liquid made from fats and oils and used in medicines and EXPLOSIVES ⊃ compare GLYCERINE

---

æ cat | ɑː father | e bed | ɜː fur | ə about | ɪ sit | iː see | i happy | ɒ got (*BrE*) | ɔː saw | ʌ cup | ʊ put | uː too

**glyph** /glɪf/ noun **1** a symbol or picture that represents a word, especially one from an ancient writing system **2** (computing) a small symbol

**GM** /ˌdʒiː ˈem/ abbr. (BrE) GENETICALLY MODIFIED: *GM foods or 'Frankenstein foods' as they are popularly called*

**gm** (also **gm.**) abbr. (in writing) (pl. **gm** or **gms**) GRAM(S)

**GMAT** /ˈdʒiːmæt/ abbr. Graduate Management Admissions Test (a test taken by graduate students in the US who want to study for a degree in Business)

**GMO** /ˌdʒiː em ˈəʊ/ noun (pl. **GMOs**) a plant, etc. that has had its genetic structure changed artificially, so that, for example, it will produce more fruit or not be affected by disease (the abbreviation for 'genetically modified organism')

**GMT** /ˌdʒiː em ˈtiː/ abbr. [U] Greenwich Mean Time (the time at Greenwich in England on the line of 0° LONGITUDE, used in the past for calculating time everywhere in the world) ⊃ compare UTC

**gnarled** /nɑːld/; *NAmE* nɑːrld/ (also **gnarly** *NAmE*) adj. **1** (of a tree) TWISTED and rough; with hard parts growing all over it: *a gnarled oak/branch/trunk* **2** (of a person or part of the body) bent or TWISTED because of age or illness: *gnarled hands*

**gnarly** /ˈnɑːli; *NAmE* ˈnɑːrli/ adj. (*NAmE*) **1** = GNARLED **2** (*slang*) difficult or dangerous **3** (*slang*) very good; excellent: *Wow, man! That's totally gnarly!*

**gnash** /næʃ/ verb
**IDM** **gnash your ˈteeth** to press or hit your teeth together because you feel angry; to feel very angry and upset about sth, especially because you cannot get what you want: *He'll be gnashing his teeth when he hears that we lost the contract.*

**gnat** /næt/ noun a very small fly with two wings that bites and often flies in large groups

**gnaw** /nɔː/ verb [T, I] to keep biting sth: ~ **sth** *The dog was gnawing a bone.* ◇ ~ **through sth** *Rats had gnawed through the cable.* ◇ ~ **at/on sth** *She gnawed at her fingernails.* ◇ ~ **away at/on sth** (*figurative*) *Self-doubt began to gnaw away at her confidence.*
**PHRV** **ˈgnaw at sb** to make sb feel anxious, frightened or uncomfortable over a long period of time: *The problem had been gnawing at him for months.*

**gnaw·ing** /ˈnɔːɪŋ/ adj. [only before noun] making you feel worried over a period of time: *gnawing doubts*

**gneiss** /naɪs/ noun [U] (*geology*) a type of METAMORPHIC rock formed at high pressure and temperature deep in the ground

**gnoc·chi** /ˈnjɒki; *NAmE* ˈnjɑːki/ noun [pl.] an Italian dish consisting of small balls of potato mixed with flour and boiled, usually eaten with a sauce

**gnome** /nəʊm/ noun **1** (in stories) a creature like a small man with a pointed hat, who lives under the ground and guards gold and TREASURE **2** a plastic or stone figure of a gnome, used to decorate a garden

**gno·mic** /ˈnəʊmɪk/ adj. (*formal*) (of a person or a remark) clever and wise but sometimes difficult to understand

**GNP** /ˌdʒiː en ˈpiː/ noun [U, C] the total value of all the goods and services produced by a country in one year, including the total income from foreign countries (the abbreviation for 'gross national product') ⊃ compare GDP

**gnu** /nuː, njuː/ noun (pl. **gnu** or **gnus**) = WILDEBEEST

**go** /gəʊ/ verb, noun
■ verb (**goes** /gəʊz/, **went** /went/, **gone** /ɡɒn; *NAmE* ɡɔːn/)
**HELP** **Been** is used as the past participle of **go** when sb has gone somewhere and come back.
• MOVE/TRAVEL **1** [I] to move or travel from one place to another: + adv./prep. *She went into her room and shut the door behind her.* ◇ *I have to go to Rome on business.* ◇ *She has gone to China* (= is now in China or is on her way there). ◇ *She has been to China* (= she went to China and has now returned). ◇ *Are you going home for Christmas?* ◇ ~ **to do sth** *She has gone to see her sister this weekend.*
**HELP** In spoken English **go** can be used with **and** plus another verb to show purpose or to tell sb what to do: *I'll go and answer the door.* ◇ *Go and get me a drink!* The **and** is sometimes left out, especially in *NAmE*: *Go ask your mom!* **2** [I] to move or travel, especially with sb else, to a particular place or in order to be present at an event: ~ (**to sth**) *Are you going to Dave's party?* ◇ *Who else is going?* ◇ ~ **with sb** *His dog goes everywhere with him.* **3** [I] to move or travel in a particular way or over a particular distance: + adv./prep. *He's going too fast.* ◇ + noun *We had gone about fifty miles when the car broke down.* **4** [I] ~ **flying, skidding, etc. (+ adv./prep.)** to move in a particular way or while doing sth else: *She crashed into a waiter and his tray of drinks went flying.* ◇ *The car went skidding off the road into a ditch.* ◇ *She went sobbing up the stairs.*
• LEAVE **5** [I] to leave one place in order to reach another **SYN** **depart**: *I must be going now.* ◇ *They came at six and went at nine.* ◇ *Has she gone yet?* ◇ *He's been gone an hour* (= he left an hour ago). ◇ *When does the train go?* **6** [I] ~ **on sth** to leave a place and do sth different: *to go on a journey/tour/trip/cruise* ◇ *Richard has gone on leave for two weeks.* ◇ (*BrE*) *to go on holiday* ◇ (*NAmE*) *to go on vacation*
• VISIT/ATTEND **7** [I] ~ **to sth** to visit or attend a place for a particular purpose: *to go to school/college/university* ◇ (*BrE*) *I have to go to hospital for an operation.* ◇ (*NAmE*) *I have to go to the hospital.* ◇ (*BrE*) *to go to the cinema* ◇ (*NAmE*) *to go to the movies* ◇ *to go to prison/jail* (= to be sent there as punishment for a crime) ◇ *Do you go to church* (= regularly attend church services)? **8** [I] ~ **on sth** to look at a particular page or website: ~ **on sth** *She went on Facebook and changed her relationship status.* ◇ ~ **to sth** *To find out what the terms mean, go to the glossary.*
• SWIMMING/FISHING/JOGGING, ETC. **9** [I] to leave a place or travel to a place in order to take part in an activity or a sport: ~ **for sth** *to go for a walk* ◇ *to go for a ride/drive/run/swim* ◇ *Shall we go for a drink* (= at a pub or bar) *after work?* ◇ ~ **doing** *to go swimming/fishing/jogging* ◇ *I have to go shopping this afternoon.*
• BE SENT **10** [I] + adv./prep. to be sent or passed somewhere: *I want this memo to go to all managers.*
• TIME **11** [I] + adv./prep. used to talk about how quickly or slowly time seems to pass: *Hasn't the time gone quickly?* ◇ *Half an hour went past while we were sitting there.*
• DISAPPEAR **12** [I] to stop existing; to be lost or stolen **SYN** **disappear**: *Has your headache gone yet?* ◇ *I left my bike outside the library and when I came out again it had gone.*
• LEAD **13** [I] to lead or extend in a particular direction: + adv./prep. *Where does this road go?* ◇ ~ **from sth to sth** *I want a rope that will go from the top window to the ground.*
• PLACE/SPACE **14** [I] + adv./prep. to have as a usual or correct position; to be placed: *This dictionary goes on the top shelf.* ◇ *Where do you want the piano to go* (= be put)? **15** [I] **will/would not** ~ (**in/into sth**) used to say that sth did/does not fit into a particular place or space: *My clothes won't all go in that one suitcase.* ◇ *He tried to push his hand through the gap but it wouldn't go.*
• PROGRESS **16** [I] + adv./prep. used to talk about how well or badly sth makes progress or succeeds: *'How did the interview go?' 'It went well, thank you.'* ◇ *Did everything go smoothly?* ◇ *How's it going* (= is your life enjoyable, successful, etc. at the moment)? ◇ *The way things are going, the company will be bankrupt by the end of the year.*
• STATE/CONDITION **17** [I] used in many expressions to show that sb/sth has reached a particular state/is no longer in a particular state: ~ **to sth** *She went to sleep.* ◇ *The US and Mexico went to war in 1846.* ◇ ~ **on sth** *Shares went on sale this morning.* ◇ *They're threatening to go on strike again.* ◇ ~ **out of sth** *That colour has gone out of fashion.* **18** [I] linking verb + adj. to become different in a particular way, especially a bad way: *to go crazy/mad/nuts/insane* ◇ *The company went bankrupt last year.* ◇ *Her hair is going grey.* ◇ *The children went wild with excitement.* ⊃ note at BECOME **19** [I] + adj. to live or move around in a particular state: *to go naked/barefoot* ◇ *She cannot bear the thought of children going hungry.* **20** [I] to spend a period of time in a particular way: *They went for two*

# go

weeks without receiving any news. **21** [I] ~ **unnoticed, unreported, etc.** to not be noticed, reported, etc: *In these traditional stories, no crime goes unpunished.* ◊ *Customer service calls went unanswered.*

- **SOUND/MOVEMENT 22** [B1] [I] to make a particular sound or movement: **+ noun** *The gun went 'bang'.* ◊ **+ adv./prep.** *She went like this with her hand.* **23** [I] to be sounded as a signal or warning: *The whistle went for the end of the game.*
- **NUMBERS 24** [I] if a number will **go into** another number, it is contained in that number an exact number of times: **(+ adj.)** *3 into 12 goes 4 times.* ◊ *7 into 15 won't go.* ◊ *(NAmE) 7 into 15 doesn't go.* ◊ **~ into sth** *7 won't go into 15.*
- **COMBINE WELL 25** to combine well with sth [SYN] **match**: *~ with sth Does this jacket go with this skirt?* ◊ *~ (together) Those colours don't really go (together).*
- **SONG/STORY 26** [I, T] used to talk about what tune or words a song or poem has or what happens in a story: **+ adv./prep.** *How does that song go?* ◊ *I forget how the next line goes.* ◊ *~ that ... The story goes that she's been married five times.*
- **SAY 27** [T] **+ speech** (*informal*) (used when telling a story) to say: *I asked 'How much?' and he goes, 'Fifty' and I go, 'Fifty? You must be joking!'*
- **START 28** [I] (often used as an order) to start an activity: *I'll say 'One, two, three, go!' as a signal for you to start.* ◊ *As soon as he gets here we're ready to go.*
- **MACHINE 29** [I] if a machine **goes**, it works: *This clock doesn't go.*
- **BE THROWN OUT 30** [I] **sb/sth must/has to/can ~** used to talk about wanting to get rid of sb/sth: *The old sofa will have to go.* ◊ *He's useless—he'll have to go.*
- **NOT WORK 31** [I] to get worse; to become damaged or stop working correctly: *Her sight is beginning to go.* ◊ *His mind is going (= he is losing his mental powers).* ◊ *I was driving home when my brakes went.*
- **DIE 32** [I] to die. People say 'go' to avoid saying 'die': *You can't take your money with you when you go.*
- **MONEY 33** [I] when money **goes**, it is spent or used for sth: *I don't know where the money goes!* ◊ **~ on sth** *Most of my salary goes on the rent.* ◊ **~ to do sth** *The money will go to finance a new community centre.* **34** [I] **~ (to sb) (for sth)** to be sold: *We won't let the house go for less than $200000.* ◊ *There was usually some bread going cheap (= being sold cheaply) at the end of the day.* **35** [I] **+ adv./prep.** to be willing to pay a particular amount of money for sth: *He's offered £3000 for the car and I don't think he'll go any higher.* ◊ *I'll go to $1000 but that's my limit.*
- **HELP 36** [I] **~ to do sth** to help; to play a part in doing sth: *This all goes to prove my theory.* ◊ *It (= what has just happened) just goes to show you can't always tell how people are going to react.*
- **BE AVAILABLE 37 be going** [I] (*informal*) to be available: *There just aren't any jobs going in this area.*
- **USE TOILET 38** [I] (*informal*) to use a toilet: *Do you need to go, Billy?*

[IDM] [HELP] Most idioms containing **go** are at the entries for the nouns and adjectives in the idioms, for example **go it alone** is at **alone**. **anything goes** (*informal*) anything that sb says or does is accepted or allowed, even if it shocks or surprises people: *Almost anything goes these days.* **as people, things, etc. go** in comparison with the average person, thing, etc: *As teachers go, he's not bad.* **be going on (for) sth** (*BrE*) to be nearly a particular age, time or number: *It was going on (for) midnight.* **be going to do sth 1** [A1] used to show what sb intends to do in the future: *We're going to buy a house when we've saved enough money.* **2** [A1] used to show that sth is likely to happen very soon or in the future: *I think I'm going to faint.* ◊ *If the drought continues there's going to be a famine.* **don't go doing sth** (*informal*) used to tell or warn sb not to do sth: *Don't go getting yourself into trouble.* **enough/something to be going 'on with** (*BrE*) something that is enough for a short time: *£50 should be enough to be going on with.* **go all 'out for sth**|**go all out to 'do sth** to make a very great effort to get sth or do sth **go and do sth** used to show that you are angry or annoyed that sb has done sth stupid:

*Trust him to go and mess things up!* ◊ *Why did you have to go and upset your mother like that?* ◊ **You've really gone and done it (= done sth very stupid) now! go 'off on one** (*BrE, informal*) to suddenly become very angry **go 'on (with you)** (*old-fashioned*) used to express the fact that you do not believe sth, or that you think sth is bad **(have) a lot, nothing, etc. 'going for you** (to have) many/not many advantages: *You're young, intelligent, attractive—you have a lot going for you!* **no 'go** (*informal*) not possible or allowed: *If the bank won't lend us the money it's no go, I'm afraid.* ⊃ see also NO-GO AREA **not (even) 'go there** (*informal*) used to say that you do not want to talk about sth in any more detail because you do not even want to think about it: *Don't ask me to choose. I don't want to go there.* ◊ *'There was a problem with his parents, wasn't there?' 'Don't even go there!'* **to 'go 1** that remains; still left: *I only have one exam to go.* **2** (*NAmE, informal*) if you buy cooked food **to go** in a restaurant or shop, you buy it to take away and eat somewhere else: *Two pizzas to go, please.* **what goes around 'comes around** (*saying*) **1** the way sb behaves towards other people will affect the way those people behave towards them in the future **2** something that is not fashionable now will become fashionable again in the future **where does sb ˌgo from 'here?** used to ask what action sb should take, especially in order to improve the difficult situation that they are in **who goes 'there?** used by a soldier who is guarding a place to order sb to say who they are: *Halt, who goes there?*

[PHRV] **ˌgo a'bout** (*BrE*) = GO AROUND (3) **ˌgo about sth** to continue to do sth; to keep busy with sth: *Despite the threat of war, people went about their business as usual.* **ˌgo a'bout sth** to start working on sth [SYN] **tackle**: *You're not going about the job in the right way.* ◊ **go about doing sth** *How should I go about finding a job?*

**ˌgo 'after sb** to run after or follow sb: *He went after the burglars.* ◊ *She left the room in tears so I went after her.* **ˌgo 'after sb/sth** to try to get sb/sth: *We're both going after the same job.*

**ˌgo a'gainst sb** to not be in sb's favour or not to their advantage: *The jury's verdict went against him.* **ˌgo a'gainst sb/sth** to resist or oppose sb/sth: *He would not go against his parents' wishes.* **ˌgo a'gainst sth** to be opposed to sth; to not fit or agree with sth: *Paying for hospital treatment goes against her principles.* ◊ *His thinking goes against all logic.*

**ˌgo a'head 1** [B1] to travel in front of other people in your group and arrive before them: *I'll go ahead and tell them you're on the way.* **2** [B1] to happen; to be done [SYN] **proceed**: *The building of the new bridge will go ahead as planned.* ⊃ related noun GO-AHEAD **ˌgo a'head (with sth)** [B1] to begin to do sth, especially when sb has given permission or has expressed doubts or opposition: *'May I start now?' 'Yes, go ahead.'* ◊ *The government intends to go ahead with its tax cutting plans*

**ˌgo a'long 1** to continue with an activity: *He made up the story as he went along.* **2** to make progress; to develop: *Things are going along nicely.* **ˌgo a'long with sb/sth** to agree with sb/sth: *I don't go along with her views on private medicine.* ⊃ SYNONYMS at AGREE

**ˌgo a'round** (*also* **ˌgo 'round** *especially in BrE*) **1** to turn round in a circle: *to go around in a circle* **2** to be enough for everyone to have one or some: *There aren't enough chairs to go around.* **3** (*BrE also* **ˌgo a'bout**) to often be in a particular state or behave in a particular way: *She often goes around barefoot.* ◊ **go around doing sth** *It's unprofessional to go around criticizing your colleagues.* **4** (*also* **ˌgo a'bout**) to spread from person to person: *There's a rumour going around that they're having an affair.* **ˌgo a'round (to ...)** (*also* **ˌgo 'round (to ...)** *especially in BrE*) to visit sb or a place that is near: *I went around to the post office.* ◊ *I'm going around to my sister's (= her house) later.* **ˌgo a'round with sb** (*also* **ˌgo 'round with sb** *especially in BrE*) to spend time with sb, especially in different places: *He goes around with some of the local lads.*

**ˌgo at sb** to attack sb: *They went at each other furiously.* **ˌgo at sth** to make great efforts to do sth; to work hard at sth: *They went at the job as if their lives depended on it.*

**ˌgo a'way 1** [A2] to leave a person or place: *Just go away!* ◊ *Go away and think about it, then let me know.*

**2** to leave home for a period of time, especially for a holiday: *They've gone away for a few days.* ◇ *I'm going away on business.* **3** to disappear: *The smell still hasn't gone away.*

**go ˈback 1** if two people **go back** a period of time (usually a long time), they have known each other for that time: *Dave and I go back twenty years.* **2** when the clocks **go back** at the end of SUMMER TIME, the time on them is changed so that it is one hour earlier: *Don't forget—the clocks go back tonight.* **OPP** go forward ˌgo ˈback (to …) to return to a place: *She doesn't want to go back to her husband* (= to live with him again). ◇ *This toaster will have to go back* (= be taken or sent back to the shop it was bought from)—*it's faulty.* ◇ *Of course we want to go back some day—it's our country, our real home.* ⟹ SYNONYMS at RETURN ˌgo ˈback (to sth) **1** to consider sth that happened or was said at an earlier time: *Can I go back to what you said at the beginning of the meeting?* ◇ *Once you have made this decision, there will be no going back* (= you will not be able to change your mind). **2** to have existed since a particular time or for a particular period: *Their family goes back to the time of the Pilgrim Fathers.* ˌgo ˈback on sth to fail to keep a promise; to change your mind about sth: *He never goes back on his word* (= never fails to do what he has said he will do). ˌgo ˈback to sth to start doing sth again that you had stopped doing: *The kids go back to school next week.* ◇ **go back to doing sth** *She's decided to go back to teaching.*

ˌgo beˈfore to exist or happen in an earlier time: *The present crisis is worse than any that have gone before.* ˌgo beˈfore sb/sth to be presented to sb/sth for discussion, decision or judgement: *My application goes before the planning committee next week.*

ˌgo beˈyond sth to be more than sth **SYN** exceed: *This year's sales figures go beyond all our expectations* (= are much better than we thought they would be).

ˌgo ˈby (of time) to pass: *Things will get easier as time goes by.* ◇ *The weeks went slowly by.* ˌgo ˈby sth **1** to be guided by sth; to form an opinion from sth: *That's a good rule to go by.* ◇ *If past experience is anything to go by, they'll be late.* **2** (*also* ˌgo ˈunder sth) to be known or called by a particular name: *He goes by the name of King Creole.*

ˌgo ˈdown **1** if the price of sth, the temperature, etc. **goes down**, it becomes lower **SYN** fall: *The price of oil is going down.* ◇ *Oil is going down in price.* **OPP** go up **2** to fall to the ground: *She tripped and went down with a bump.* **3** if a ship, etc. **goes down**, it disappears below the water **SYN** sink **4** when the sun or moon **goes down**, it disappears below the HORIZON **SYN** set **5** if food or drink will/will not **go down**, it is easy/difficult to SWALLOW: *A glass of wine would go down very nicely* (= I would very much like one). **6** (*informal*) to get worse in quality: *The neighbourhood has gone down a lot recently.* **7** (*computing*) to stop working temporarily: *The system is going down in ten minutes.* **8** (*NAmE, informal*) to happen: *You really don't know what's going down?* **9** (*BrE, informal*) to be sent to prison: *She went down for ten years.* ˌgo ˈdown (from …) (*BrE, formal*) to leave a university, especially Oxford or Cambridge, at the end of a term or after finishing your studies: *She went down (from Cambridge) in 2018.* **OPP** go up (to …) ˌgo ˈdown (in sth) to be written in sth; to be recorded or remembered in sth: *It all goes down* (= she writes it all) *in her notebook.* ◇ *He will go down in history as a great statesman.* ˌgo ˈdown (on sb) (*slang*) to perform ORAL sex on sb (= to use the mouth to give sb sexual pleasure) ˌgo ˈdown (to sb) to be defeated by sb, especially in a game or competition: *Italy went down to Brazil by three goals to one.* ˌgo ˈdown (to …) (from …) to go from one place to another, especially further south or from a city or large town to a smaller place: *They've gone down to Brighton for a couple of days.* **OPP** go up (to …) (from …) ˌgo ˈdown (with sth) (*also* ˌgo ˈover (with sb)) *especially in NAmE*) to be received in a particular way by sb: *The suggestion didn't go down very well with her boss.* ˌgo ˈdown with sth (*especially BrE*) to become ill with sth **SYN** catch: *Our youngest boy has gone down with chickenpox.*

ˌgo ˈfor sb to attack sb: *She went for him with a knife.* ˌgo ˈfor sb/sth **1** to apply to sb/sth: *What I said about Peter goes for you, too.* ◇ *They have a high level of unemployment* —*but the same goes for many other countries.* **2** to go to a place and bring sb/sth back: *She's gone for some milk.* **3** (*informal*) to be attracted by sb/sth; to like or prefer sb/sth: *She goes for tall slim men.* ◇ *I don't really go for modern art.* ˌgo ˈfor sth **1** to choose sth: *I think I'll go for the fruit salad.* ⟹ SYNONYMS at CHOOSE **2** to apply for a job: *I'm going for a job in sales.* **3** to put a lot of effort into sth, so that you get or achieve sth: *Go for it, John! You know you can beat him.* ◇ *It sounds a great idea. Go for it!*

ˌgo ˈforward when the clocks **go forward** at the beginning of SUMMER TIME, the time on them is changed so that it is one hour later: *Remember, the clocks go forward tonight.* **OPP** go back

ˌgo ˈin **1** to enter a room, house, etc: *Let's go in, it's getting cold.* **2** if the sun or moon **goes in**, it disappears behind a cloud ˌgo ˈin for sth (*BrE*) to take an exam or enter a competition: *She's going in for the Cambridge B2 First exam.* **2** to have sth as an interest or a hobby: *She doesn't go in for team sports.* ˌgo ˈin with sb to join sb in starting a business: *My brothers are opening a garage and they want me to go in with them.*

ˌgo ˈinto sth **1** (of a vehicle) to hit sth violently: *The car skidded and went into a tree.* **2** (of a vehicle or driver) to start moving in a particular way: *The plane went into a nosedive.* **3** to join an organization, especially in order to have a career in it: *to go into the Army/the Church/Parliament* ◇ *to go into teaching* **4** to begin to do sth or behave in a particular way: *He went into a long explanation of the affair.* **5** to examine sth carefully: *We need to go into the question of costs.* **6** (of money, time, effort, etc.) to be spent on sth or used to do sth: *More government money needs to go into the project.* ◇ **go into sth doing sth** *Years of work went into researching the book.*

ˌgo ˈoff **1** to leave a place, especially in order to do sth: *She went off to get a drink.* **2** to be fired; to explode: *The gun went off by accident.* ◇ *The bomb went off in a crowded street.* ⟹ SYNONYMS at EXPLODE **3** if an alarm, etc. **goes off**, it makes a sudden loud noise **4** if a light, the electricity, etc. **goes off**, it stops working: *Suddenly the lights went off.* ◇ *The heating goes off at night.* **OPP** go on **5** (*BrE, informal*) to go to sleep: *Hasn't the baby gone off yet?* **6** (*BrE*) if food or drink **goes off**, it becomes bad and not fit to eat or drink **7** (*BrE*) to get worse in quality: *Her books have gone off in recent years.* **8** to happen in a particular way: *The meeting went off well.* ˌgo ˈoff (on sb) (*NAmE, informal*) to suddenly become angry with sb ˌgo ˈoff sb/sth (*BrE, informal*) to stop liking sb/sth or lose interest in sth/him: *Jane seems to be going off Paul.* ◇ *I've gone off beer.* ˌgo ˈoff with sb to leave your husband, wife, partner, etc. in order to have a relationship with sb else: *He went off with his best friend's wife.* ˌgo ˈoff with sth to take away from a place sth that does not belong to you: *He went off with $10000 of the company's money.*

ˌgo ˈon **1** when a performer **goes on**, they begin their performance: *She doesn't go on until Act 2.* **2** (in sport) to join a team as a SUBSTITUTE during a game: *Maguire went on in place of Cahill just before half-time.* **3** when a light, the electricity, etc. **goes on**, it starts to work: *Suddenly all the lights went on.* **OPP** go off **4** (of time) to pass: *She became more and more talkative as the evening went on.* **5** *usually* **be going on** to happen: *What's going on here?* **6** if a situation **goes on**, it continues without changing: *This cannot be allowed to go on.* ◇ *How much longer will this hot weather go on for?* ◇ *We can't go on like this—we seem to be always arguing.* **7** to continue speaking, often after stopping for a short time: *She hesitated for a moment and then went on.* ◇ **+ speech** *'You know,' he went on, 'I think my brother could help you.'* **8** used to encourage sb to do sth: *Go on! Have another drink!* ◇ *Go on—jump!* ˌgo ˈon (ahead) to travel in front of sb else: *You go on ahead—I'll catch you up in a few minutes.* ˌgo ˈon sth (used in negative sentences and questions) to base an opinion or a judgement on sth: *The police don't have much to go on.* ˌgo ˈon (about sb/sth) (*informal*) to talk about sb/sth for a long time, especially in a boring or complaining way: *He went on and on about how poor he was.* ◇ *She does go on sometimes!* ˌgo ˈon (at sb) (*especially BrE,*

**goad**

*informal*) to complain to sb about their behaviour, work, etc. **SYN** criticize: *She goes on at him continually.* **go 'on (with sth)** to continue an activity, especially after a break: *That's enough for now—let's go on with it tomorrow.* **go 'on doing sth** to continue an activity without stopping: *He said nothing but just went on working.* **go 'on to sth** to pass from one item to the next: *Let's go on to the next item on the agenda.* **go 'on to do sth** **B2** to do sth after completing sth else: *The book goes on to describe his experiences in the army.* **go 'out 1** **A1** to leave your house to go to a social event: *She goes out a lot.* ◊ **go out doing sth** *He goes out drinking most evenings.* ◊ when the TIDE **goes out**, it moves away from the land **SYN** ebb **OPP** come in **3** to be sent: *Have the invitations gone out yet?* **4** (*BrE*) when a radio or television programme **goes out**, it is broadcast **5** when news or information **goes out**, it is announced or published: *~ that… Word went out that the director had resigned.* **6** if a fire or light **goes out**, it stops burning or shining **go 'out (of sth) 1** to fail to reach the next stage of a competition, etc: *She went out of the tournament in the first round.* **2** to be no longer fashionable or generally used: *Those skirts went out years ago.* **go 'out of sb/sth** (of a quality or a feeling) to be no longer present in sb/sth; to disappear from sb/sth: *All the fight seemed to go out of him.* **go 'out to sb** if your thoughts, etc. **go out to sb**, you think about them in a kind way and hope that the difficult situation that they are in will get better **go 'out with sb** | **go 'out (together)** (especially of young people) to spend time with sb and have a romantic or sexual relationship with them: *Tom has been going out with Lucy for six weeks.* ◊ *How long have Tom and Lucy been going out together?* ⇒ WORDFINDER NOTE at LOVE
**go 'over sth 1** to examine or check sth carefully: *Go over your work before you hand it in.* ⇒ SYNONYMS at CHECK **2** to study sth carefully, especially by repeating it: *He went over the events of the day in his mind (= thought about them carefully).* **go 'over (to …)** to move from one place to another, especially when this means crossing sth such as a room, town or city: *He went over and shook hands with his guests.* ◊ *Many Irish people went over to America during the famine.* **go 'over to sb/sth** (in broadcasting) to change to a different person or place for the next part of a broadcast: *We are now going over to the news desk for an important announcement.* **go 'over to sth** to change from one side, opinion, habit, etc. to another: *Two Conservative MPs have gone over to the Liberal Democrats.* **go 'over (with sb)** (especially NAmE) = GO DOWN (WITH SB)
**go 'round** = GO AROUND **go 'round (to …)** = GO AROUND (TO …) **go 'round with sb** = GO AROUND WITH SB
**go 'through** if a law, contract, etc. **goes through**, it is officially accepted or completed: *The deal did not go through.* **go through sth 1** **B2** to look at or examine sth carefully, especially in order to find sth: *She went through the company's accounts, looking for evidence of fraud.* **2** **B2** to study or consider sth in detail, especially by repeating it: *Let's go through the arguments again.* ◊ *Could we go through (= practise) Act 2 once more?* **3** **B2** to perform a series of actions; to follow a method or procedure: *Certain formalities have to be gone through before you can emigrate.* **4** **B2** to experience or suffer sth: *She's been going through a bad patch recently.* ◊ *He's amazingly cheerful considering all he's had to go through.* **5** to use up or finish sth completely: *The boys went through two whole loaves of bread.* **go 'through with sth** to do what is necessary to complete a course of action, especially one that is difficult or unpleasant: *She decided not to go through with (= not to have) the operation.*
**go to sb/sth** to be given to sb/sth: *Proceeds from the concert will go to charity.* ◊ *All her property went to her eldest son (= when she died).*
**go to'gether** = GO WITH STH (3)
**go 'towards sth** to be used as part of the payment for sth: *The money will go towards a new car.* ◊ **go towards doing sth** *Part of my pay goes towards paying off my student loans.*
**go 'under 1** (of sth that floats) to sink below the surface **2** (*informal*) to become BANKRUPT (= be unable to pay what you owe): *The firm will go under unless business improves.*
**go under sth** = GO BY STH (2)
**go 'up 1** **A2** if the price of sth, the temperature, etc. **goes up**, it becomes higher **SYN** rise: *The price of cigarettes is going up.* ◊ *Cigarettes are going up in price.* **OPP** go down **2** to be built: *New office buildings are going up everywhere.* **3** when the curtain across the stage in a theatre **goes up**, it is raised or opened **4** to be destroyed by fire or an explosion: *The whole building went up in flames.* **go 'up (to …)** (*BrE*, *formal*) to arrive at a university, especially Oxford or Cambridge, at the beginning of a term or in order to begin your studies **OPP** go down (from …) **go 'up (to …) (from …)** to go from one place to another, especially further north or to a city or large town from a smaller place: *When are you next going up to Scotland?* ◊ *We went up to London last weekend.* **OPP** go down (to …) (from …)
**go 'with sb 1** (*old-fashioned, informal*) to have a sexual or romantic relationship with sb **2** (*informal*) to have sex with sb **go 'with sth 1** to be included with or as part of sth: *A car goes with the job.* **2** to agree to accept sth, for example a plan or an offer: *You're offering £500? I think we can go with that.* **3** (*also* **go to'gether**) to exist at the same time or in the same place as sth; to be found together: *Disease often goes with poverty.* ◊ *Disease and poverty often go together.*
**go wi'thout (sth)** to manage without sth that you usually have or need: *There wasn't time for breakfast, so I had to go without.* ◊ *How long can a human being go (= survive) without sleep?* ◊ **go without doing sth** *She went without eating for three days.*

▪ *noun* (*pl.* **goes** /gəʊz/) **1** **B1** [C] (*BrE*) (*also* turn *NAmE*, *BrE*) a person's turn to move or play in a game or an activity: *Whose go is it?* ◊ *It's your go.* ◊ *How much is it to play?* 'It's 50p a go.' ◊ **~ on sth** *Can I have a go on your new bike?* **2** **B2** [C] (*also* try) an attempt at doing sth: *It took three goes to get it right.* ◊ *I doubt if he'll listen to advice from me, but I'll give it a go (= I'll try but I don't think I will succeed).* **3** [U] (*BrE*) energy and enthusiasm: *Mary's always got plenty of go.* ⇒ see also GET-UP-AND-GO
**IDM** **at a/one 'go** | **at/in a single 'go** (*BrE*) in one single attempt or try: *She blew out the candles at one go.* **be a 'go** (*NAmE*, *informal*) to be planned and possible or allowed: *I'm not sure if Friday's trip is a go.* **be all 'go** (*BrE*, *informal*) to be very busy or full of activity: *It was all go in the office today.* **be on the 'go** (*also* **be on the 'move**) (*informal*) to be very active and busy: *I've been on the go all day.* ◊ *Having four children keeps her on the go.* **first, second, etc. 'go** (*BrE*) at the first, second, etc. attempt: *I passed my driving test first go.* **have a 'go** (*informal*, *especially BrE*) to attack sb physically: *There were about seven of them standing round him, all waiting to have a go.* **have a 'go (at sth/at doing sth)** to make an attempt to do sth: '*I can't start the engine.' 'Let me have a go.'* ◊ *I'll have a go at fixing it tonight.* **have a 'go at sb** (*informal*, *BrE*) to criticize sb or complain about sb: *The boss had a go at me for being late for work.* **have sth on the 'go** (*BrE*, *informal*) to be in the middle of an activity or a project: *The award-winning novelist often has three or four books on the go at once.* **in one 'go** (*informal*) all together on one occasion: *I'd rather do the journey in one go, and not stop on the way.* ◊ *They ate the packet of biscuits all in one go.* **make a 'go of sth** (*informal*) to be successful in sth: *We've had a few problems in our marriage, but we're both determined to make a go of it.* ⇒ more at FAIR *adj.*, LEAVE *v.*, LET *v.*

**goad** /ɡəʊd/ *verb, noun*

▪ *verb* to keep annoying sb/sth until they react: **~ sb/sth** *Goaded beyond endurance, she turned on him and hit out.* ◊ **~ sb/sth into (doing) sth** *He finally goaded her into answering his question.* ◊ **~ sb/sth to do sth** *She felt a needle of annoyance goading her to hit back.*
**PHRV** **goad sb** ↔ **'on** to drive or encourage sb to do sth: *The boxers were goaded on by the shrieking crowd.*

- **noun 1** a pointed stick used for making cows, etc. move forwards **2** something that makes sb do sth, usually by annoying them

**'go-ahead** noun, adj.
- **noun the go-ahead** [sing.] (*informal*) permission for sb to start doing sth: **the ~ to do sth** *The council has given the go-ahead to start building.* ◇ **the ~ for sth** *Union leaders have now got the go-ahead for new talks with management.*
- **adj.** [usually before noun] willing to try new ideas, methods, etc. and therefore likely to succeed: *a go-ahead company*

**goal** ❶ **A2 W** /ɡəʊl/ noun **1** **A2** (in sports) a frame with a net into which players must kick or hit the ball in order to score a point: *He headed the ball into an open goal* (= one that had nobody defending it). ◇ **in ~** *Nicky Roberts was outstanding in goal* (= as GOALKEEPER). **2** **A2** the act of kicking or hitting the ball into the goal; a point that is scored for this: *She scored twenty goals in her first season.* ◇ *Liverpool won by three goals to one.* ◇ *The winning goal came in the 71st minute.* ⊃ see also DROP GOAL, FIELD GOAL, GOLDEN GOAL, OWN GOAL **3** **A2** something that you hope to achieve **SYN** **aim**: *to achieve/accomplish/reach a goal* ◇ *My job is to help businesses meet their goals.* ◇ *You need to set yourself some long-term goals.* ◇ *Our ultimate goal must be the preservation of the environment.* ◇ **toward/towards a ~** *We are all working towards a common goal.* ⊃ SYNONYMS at TARGET

**'goal difference** noun [U] (in football (soccer), hockey, etc.) the difference between the number of goals that a team has scored and the number of goals that have been scored against them over a series of games, sometimes used to decide the team's position in the league table

**'goal·keep·er** /'ɡəʊlkiːpə(r)/ (*also informal* **goalie** /'ɡəʊli/, *informal* **keeper**, *NAmE also* **goal·tend·er**) noun (in football (soccer), hockey, etc.) a player whose job is to stop the ball from going into his or her own team's goal ▶ **'goal·keep·ing** noun [U]: *goalkeeping techniques*

**'goal kick** noun **1** (in football (soccer)) a kick taken by one team after the ball has been kicked over their GOAL LINE by the other team without a goal being scored **2** (in rugby) an attempt to kick a goal

**'goal·less** /'ɡəʊləs/ adj. [usually before noun] without either team scoring a goal: *The match ended in a goalless draw.*

**'goal line** noun (in football (soccer), hockey, etc.) the line at either end of a sports field on which the goal stands or which the ball must cross to score a goal or TOUCHDOWN

**'goal·mouth** /'ɡəʊlmaʊθ/ noun the area directly in front of a goal

**'goal poacher** noun = POACHER (3)

**'goal·post** /'ɡəʊlpəʊst/ (*also* **post**) noun one of the two posts that form part of a goal ⊃ picture at BAR
**IDM** **move, etc. the 'goalposts** (*informal, disapproving*) to change the rules for sth, or conditions under which it is done, so that the situation becomes more difficult for sb

**'goal·scorer** /'ɡəʊlskɔːrə(r)/ noun a player in a sports game who scores a goal

**'goal·tend·er** /'ɡəʊltendə(r)/ noun (*NAmE*) = GOALKEEPER

**'go-around** (*also* **'go-round**) noun **1** (*specialist*) a path taken by a plane after an unsuccessful attempt at landing, in order to get into a suitable position to try to land again **2** (*NAmE, informal*) an argument

**goat** /ɡəʊt/ noun **1** an animal with HORNS and a coat of hair, that lives wild in mountain areas or is kept on farms for its milk or meat: *a mountain goat* ◇ *goat's milk* ⊃ see also BILLY GOAT, KID noun, NANNY GOAT **2 old ~** (*informal*) an unpleasant old man who is annoying in a sexual way
**IDM** **get sb's 'goat** (*informal*) to annoy sb very much ⊃ more at SHEEP

**'goat cheese** (*NAmE*) (*BrE* **goat's cheese**) noun cheese made from the milk of a goat

**goatee** /ɡəʊ'tiː/ noun a small pointed BEARD (= hair growing on a man's face) that is grown only on the CHIN

**goat·herd** /'ɡəʊthɜːd; *NAmE* -hɜːrd/ noun a person whose job is to take care of a group of GOATS

**goat·skin** /'ɡəʊtskɪn/ noun [U] leather made from the skin of a goat

**gob** /ɡɒb; *NAmE* ɡɑːb/ noun, verb
- **noun** (*slang*) **1** (*BrE*) a rude way of referring to a person's mouth: *Shut your gob!* (= a rude way of telling sb to be quiet) **2** a small amount of a thick wet substance: *Gobs of spittle ran down his chin.* **3** [usually pl.] (*NAmE*) a large amount of sth: *great gobs of cash*
- **verb** [I] (*BrE, slang*) (-**bb**-) to blow SALIVA out of your mouth **SYN** **spit**

**gob·ble** /'ɡɒbl; *NAmE* 'ɡɑːbl/ verb **1** [T, I] to eat sth very fast, in a way that people consider rude or GREEDY **SYN** **wolf**: **~ (sth)** *Don't gobble your food like that!* ◇ **~ sth up/down** *They gobbled down all the sandwiches.* **2** [I] when a TURKEY **gobbles**, it makes a noise in its throat
**PHRV** **gobble sth ↔ up** (*informal*) **1** to use sth very quickly: *Hotel costs gobbled up most of their holiday budget.* **2** if a business company, etc. **gobbles up** a smaller one, it takes control of it

**gobble·de·gook** (*also* **gobble·dy·gook**) /'ɡɒbldiɡuːk; *NAmE* 'ɡɑːb-/ noun (*informal*) complicated language that is difficult to understand, especially when used in official documents: *It's all gobbledegook to me.*

**'go-between** noun [C, U] a person who takes messages between one person or group and another: *to act as (a) go-between*

**gob·let** /'ɡɒblət; *NAmE* 'ɡɑːb-/ noun a cup for wine, usually made of glass or metal, with a STEM and base but no handle

**gob·lin** /'ɡɒblɪn; *NAmE* 'ɡɑːb-/ noun (in stories) a small ugly creature that likes to trick people or cause trouble

**gob·smacked** /'ɡɒbsmækt; *NAmE* 'ɡɑːbs-/ adj. (*BrE, informal*) so surprised that you do not know what to say

**goby** /'ɡəʊbi/ noun (*pl.* **goby** *or* **gob·ies**) a small sea fish with a SUCKER on the UNDERSIDE of its body

**'go-cart** = GO-KART

**god** ❶ **A2** /ɡɒd; *NAmE* ɡɑːd/ noun **1** **A2 God** [sing.] (not used with *the*) (in Christianity, Islam and Judaism) the being or spirit that is WORSHIPPED and is believed to have created the universe: *Do you believe in God?* ◇ *Good luck and God bless you.* **2** **A2** [C] (in some religions) a being or spirit who is believed to have power over a particular part of nature or who is believed to represent a particular quality: *Greek gods* ◇ *the sun/rain god* ◇ **~ of sth** *Mars was the Roman god of war.* ⊃ see also GODDESS **3** [C] a person who is loved or admired very much by other people: *To her fans she's a god.* ⊃ see also GODDESS **4** [C] something to which too much importance or attention is given: *Money is his god.* **5 the gods** [pl.] (*BrE, informal*) the seats that are high up at the back of a theatre
**IDM** **by 'God!** (*old-fashioned, informal*) used to emphasize a feeling of surprise or that you are determined to do sth **HELP** Some people find this use of **God** offensive. **God | God al'mighty | God in 'heaven | good 'God | my 'God | oh (dear) 'God** (*informal*) used to emphasize what you are saying when you are surprised, shocked or annoyed: *God, what a stupid thing to do!* **HELP** Some people find this use of **God** offensive. **God 'bless** used when you are leaving sb, to say that you hope they will be safe, etc: *Goodnight, God bless.* **God ,rest his/her 'soul | God ,rest him/her** (*old-fashioned, informal*) used to show respect when you are talking about sb who is dead **God's gift (to sb/sth)** (*ironic*) a person who thinks that they are particularly good at sth or who thinks that sb will find them particularly attractive: *He seems to think he's God's gift to women.* **God 'willing** (*informal*) used to say that you hope that things will happen as you have planned and that there will be no problems: *I'll be back next week, God willing.* **play 'God** to behave as if you control events or other people's lives: *It is unfair to ask doctors to play God and end someone's life.* **to 'God/'goodness/'Heaven** used after a verb to emphasize a particular hope, wish, etc: *I wish to God you'd learn to pay attention!* **HELP** Some people find this

# godchild

use of **God** offensive. **ye ˈgods!** (*old-fashioned*, *informal*) used to show surprise, lack of belief, etc. ⇨ more at ACT *n.*, FEAR *n.*, FORBID, GRACE *n.*, HELP *v.*, HONEST, KNOW *v.*, LAP *n.*, LOVE *n.*, MAN *n.*, NAME *n.*, PLEASE *v.*, THANK

**ˈgod-awful** (*also* **god-awful**) /ˈɡɒdɔːfl; NAmE ˈɡɑːd-/ *adj.* [usually before noun] (*informal*) extremely bad: *He made a godawful mess of it.* **HELP** Some people find this use offensive.

**ˈgod-child** /ˈɡɒdtʃaɪld; NAmE ˈɡɑːd-/ *noun* (*pl.* **ˈgod-chil-dren** /-tʃɪldrən/) a child that a GODPARENT at a Christian BAPTISM ceremony promises to be responsible for and to teach about the Christian religion

**ˈgod-dam** (*also* **god-damn**) /ˈɡɒddæm; NAmE ˈɡɑːd-/ (*also* **god-damned** /ˈɡɒddæmd; NAmE ˈɡɑːd-/) *adj.*, *adv.* (*taboo*, *slang*) a swear word that many people find offensive, used to show that you are angry or annoyed: *There's no need to be so goddam rude!* ◊ *Where's that goddamned pen?*

**ˈgod-daughter** *noun* a female GODCHILD

**ˈgod-dess** /ˈɡɒdes, -dəs; NAmE ˈɡɑːdəs/ *noun* **1** a female god: *Diana, the goddess of hunting* **2** a woman who is loved or admired very much by other people: *a screen goddess* (= a female film star)

**ˈgod-father** /ˈɡɒdfɑːðə(r); NAmE ˈɡɑːd-/ *noun* **1** a male GODPARENT **2** (*often* **Godfather**) a very powerful man in a criminal organization, especially the Mafia **3** ~ **of sth** a person who began or developed sth: *He's the godfather of punk.*

**ˈGod-fearing** *adj.* [usually before noun] (*old-fashioned*) living a moral life based on religious principles

**god-for-saken** /ˈɡɒdfəseɪkən; NAmE ˈɡɑːdfərs-/ *adj.* [only before noun] (*of places*) boring, depressing and ugly: *I can't stand living in this godforsaken hole.*

**ˈGod-given** *adj.* [usually before noun] given or created by God: *a God-given talent* ◊ *What gives you a God-given right to know all my business?*

**god-head** /ˈɡɒdhed; NAmE ˈɡɑːd-/ *noun* **the Godhead** [sing.] (*formal*) used in the Christian religion to mean God, including the Father, Son and HOLY SPIRIT

**god-less** /ˈɡɒdləs; NAmE ˈɡɑːd-/ *adj.* [usually before noun] (*often disapproving*) not believing in or respecting God: *a godless generation/world* ▸ **god-less-ness** *noun* [U]

**god-like** /ˈɡɒdlaɪk; NAmE ˈɡɑːd-/ *adj.* like God or a god in some quality: *his godlike beauty*

**godly** /ˈɡɒdli; NAmE ˈɡɑːd-/ *adj.* [usually before noun] (*old-fashioned*) living a moral life based on religious principles: *a godly man* ▸ **god-li-ness** *noun* [U]

**ˈgod-man** *noun* (*pl.* **god-men**) (*IndE, often disapproving*) a holy man; a religious teacher or leader: *The god-men in the village claim to have special powers.*

**god-mother** /ˈɡɒdmʌðə(r); NAmE ˈɡɑːd-/ *noun* a female GODPARENT ⇨ see also FAIRY GODMOTHER

**go-down** /ˈɡəʊdaʊn/ *noun* (*IndE*) a WAREHOUSE (= building where goods are stored)

**god-par-ent** /ˈɡɒdpeərənt; NAmE ˈɡɑːdper-/ *noun* a person who promises at a Christian BAPTISM ceremony to be responsible for a child (= his or her GODCHILD) and to teach them about the Christian religion

**ˈGod Save the ˈKing/ˈQueen** *noun* [U] the British national ANTHEM (= song)

**ˈGod's country** (*also* **ˈGod's own country**) *noun* a beautiful and peaceful area that people love. Americans often use the expression to mean the US, especially the western states.

**god-send** /ˈɡɒdsend; NAmE ˈɡɑːd-/ *noun* [sing.] ~ **(for/to sb/sth)** something good that happens unexpectedly and helps sb/sth when they need help: *This new benefit has come as a godsend for low-income families.*

**god-son** /ˈɡɒdsʌn; NAmE ˈɡɑːd-/ *noun* a male GODCHILD

**goer** /ˈɡəʊə(r)/ *noun* **1** -**goer** (in compounds) a person who regularly goes to the place or event mentioned: *a cinema-goer* ◊ *a moviegoer* ⇨ see also CINEMAGOER, FILMGOER, PARTY-GOER **2** (*BrE, informal*) a woman who enjoys having sex frequently, especially with different men

**gofer** (*also* **go-pher**) /ˈɡəʊfə(r)/ *noun* (*informal*) a person whose job is to do small boring tasks for other people, especially in an office or on a film SET **SYN** dogsbody: *They call me the gofer—go for this, go for that…*

**ˈgo-getter** *noun* (*informal*) a person who is determined to succeed, especially in business

**gogga** /ˈxɔxa; NAmE ˈxɑːxə/ SAfrE [ˈxɔxa] *noun* (*SAfrE, informal*) an insect

**gog-gle** /ˈɡɒɡl; NAmE ˈɡɑːɡl/ *verb* [I] ~ **(at sb/sth)** (*informal*) to look at sb/sth with your eyes wide open, especially because you are surprised or shocked

**ˈgoggle-eyed** *adj.* with your eyes wide open, staring at sth, especially because you are surprised

**gog-gles** /ˈɡɒɡlz; NAmE ˈɡɑːɡ-/ *noun* [pl.] a pair of glasses that fit closely to the face to protect the eyes from wind, dust, water, etc. or give extra visual powers: *a pair of swimming/ski/safety goggles* ◊ *night-vision goggles* ⇨ see also BEER GOGGLES ▸ WORDFINDER NOTE at SWIMMING

**gogo** /ˈɡəʊɡəʊ/ SAfrE *noun* (*SAfrE*) **1** a grandmother **2** the title for an older woman that is polite and shows respect

**ˈgo-go** *adj.* **1** connected with a style of dancing to pop music in which the dancers wear very few clothes: *a go-go dancer* **2** (*NAmE, informal*) of a period of time when businesses are growing and people are making money fast: *the go-go years of the 1990s*

**going** /ˈɡəʊɪŋ/ *noun*, *adj.*

■ *noun* **1** [sing.] (*formal*) an act of leaving a place **SYN** departure: *We were all sad at her going.* **2** [U] (used with an adjective) the speed with which sb does sth; how difficult it is to do sth: *Walking four miles in an hour is pretty good going for me.* ◊ *She had her own company by 25—not bad going!* ◊ *It was hard going getting up at five every morning.* **3** [U] the condition of the ground, especially in horse racing: *The going is good to firm.* ⇨ see also OUTGOINGS

**IDM when the ˈgoing gets ˈtough (the ˌtough get ˈgoing)** (*saying*) when conditions or progress become difficult (strong and determined people work even harder to succeed) **while the ˌgoing is ˈgood** (*BrE*) (*NAmE usually* **while the ˌgetting is ˈgood**) before a situation changes and it is no longer possible to do sth: *Don't you think we should quit while the going is good?* ⇨ more at COMING *n.*, HEAVY *adj.*

■ *adj.* **-going** (in compounds) going regularly to the place or event mentioned: *the theatre-going public* ⇨ see also EASY-GOING, OCEAN-GOING, ONGOING, OUTGOING

**IDM a ˌgoing conˈcern** a business or an activity that is making a profit and is expected to continue to do well: *He sold the cafe as a going concern.* **the ˌgoing ˈrate (for sth)** the usual amount of money paid for goods or services at a particular time: *They pay slightly more than the going rate.*

**ˌgoing-ˈover** *noun* [sing.] (*informal*) **1** a complete examination or cleaning of sb/sth: *The garage gave the car a thorough going-over.* **2** a serious physical attack on sb: *The gang gave him a real going-over.*

**goings-ˈon** *noun* [pl.] (*informal*) activities or events that are strange, surprising or dishonest: *There were some strange goings-on next door last night.*

**goitre** (*US* **goi-ter**) /ˈɡɔɪtə(r)/ *noun* [U, C] a SWELLING of the throat caused by a disease of the THYROID

**go-kart** (*also* **go-cart**) /ˈɡəʊ kɑːt; NAmE kɑːrt/ *noun* a vehicle like a small low car with no roof or doors, used for racing

**gold** /ɡəʊld/ *noun*, *adj.*

■ *noun* **1** [U] (*symb.* **Au**) a chemical element. Gold is a yellow PRECIOUS METAL used for making coins, jewellery, beautiful objects, etc: *gold coins/jewellery* ◊ *a gold ring/watch/necklace/bracelet* ◊ *18-carat gold* ◊ *made of solid/pure gold* ⇨ see also FOOL'S GOLD **2** [U] money, jewellery, etc. that is made of gold: *His wife was dripping with* (= wearing a lot of) *gold.* ◊ *the country's gold reserves* **3** [U, C] = GOLD MEDAL: *The team look set to win Olympic*

**gold.** ◇ *He won three golds and a bronze.* **4** [U, C] the colour of gold: *I love the reds and golds of autumn.*
**IDM** **all that glitters/ glistens/ glisters is not 'gold** (*saying*) not everything that seems good, attractive, etc. is actually good, etc. **a crock/pot of 'gold** a large prize or reward that sb hopes for but is unlikely to get **(as) good as 'gold** (*informal*) behaving in a way that other people approve of: *The kids have been as good as gold all day.* ◇ more at HEART *n.*, STREET *n.*, STRIKE *v.*, WORTH *adj.*
■ **adj.** [only before noun] bright yellow in colour, like gold: *The company name was spelled out in gold letters.*

**'Gold Card™** *noun* a type of credit card that offers more benefits and enables a person to buy more goods and services than a normal card does

**'gold-digger** *noun* (*informal, disapproving*) a person who uses the fact that he or she is attractive to get money from a relationship with sb

**'gold dust** *noun* [U] gold in the form of powder
**IDM** **like 'gold dust** (*BrE*) difficult to find or obtain: *Tickets for the final are like gold dust.*

**gold·en** /ˈɡəʊldən/ *adj.* **1** (*especially literary*) made of gold: *a golden crown* **2** bright yellow in colour like gold: *golden hair* ◇ *miles of golden beaches* **3** special; wonderful: *golden memories* ◇ *Businesses have a golden opportunity to expand into new markets.* ◇ *Hollywood's golden boy*
**IDM** **be 'golden** (*NAmE, informal*) to be in a situation where you are successful or do not have any problems: *He thinks once he gets the money he'll be golden.* ◇ more at KILL *v.*, MEAN *n.*, SILENCE *n.*

**'golden age** *noun* [usually sing.] ~ **(of sth)** a period during which sth is very successful, especially in the past: *the golden age of cinema*

**golden anni'versary** *noun* (*US*) **1** (*BrE* **golden jubilee**) the 50th anniversary of an important event **2** (*BrE* **golden wedding**) (*also* **golden wedding anniversary** *NAmE, BrE*) the 50th anniversary of a wedding

**golden 'eagle** *noun* a large BIRD OF PREY (= a bird that kills other creatures for food) of the EAGLE family, with brown feathers, that lives in northern parts of the world ◇ VISUAL VOCAB page V2

**golden 'goal** *noun* (in some football (soccer) competitions) the first goal scored during EXTRA TIME, which ends the game and gives victory to the team that scores the goal

**golden 'goose** *noun* something that provides sb with a lot of money, that they must be very careful with in order not to lose it: *An increase in crime could kill the golden goose of tourism.*

**golden 'handshake** *noun* (*informal*) a large sum of money that is given to sb when they leave their job, or to persuade them to leave their job

**golden ju'bilee** (*BrE*) (*US* **golden anni'versary**) *noun* the 50th anniversary of an important event: *Queen Victoria's Golden Jubilee celebrations* ◇ *a party to mark the company's golden jubilee* ◇ compare DIAMOND JUBILEE, SILVER JUBILEE

**golden 'oldie** *noun* (*informal*) **1** a thing that is quite old but still well known and popular, especially a song or film **2** a person who is no longer young but still successful in their particular career, sport, etc.

**golden 'parachute** *noun* (*informal*) part of a work contract in which a business person is promised a large amount of money if they have to leave their job

**golden 'raisin** (*NAmE*) (*BrE* **sul·tana**) *noun* a small dried GRAPE without seeds, used in cakes, etc.

**golden re'triever** *noun* a large dog with thick yellow hair, of a type used in hunting to bring back birds that have been shot

**golden 'rule** *noun* [usually sing.] an important principle that should be followed when doing sth in order to be successful: *The golden rule in tennis is to keep your eye on the ball.*

**golden 'section** *noun* (*specialist*) the PROPORTION (= relationship in size between two parts) that is considered to be the most attractive to look at when a line is divided into two

**golden 'syrup** (*also* **trea·cle**) (*both BrE*) *noun* [U] a very sweet thick yellow liquid made from sugar

**golden 'wedding** (*US* **golden anni'versary**) (*also* **golden 'wedding anniversary** *NAmE, BrE*) *noun* the 50th anniversary of a wedding: *The couple celebrated their golden wedding in January.* ◇ compare DIAMOND WEDDING, RUBY WEDDING, SILVER WEDDING

**'gold·field** /ˈɡəʊldfiːld/ *noun* an area where gold is found in the ground

**'gold·finch** /ˈɡəʊldfɪntʃ/ *noun* a small brightly coloured European bird of the FINCH family, with yellow feathers on its wings

**'gold·fish** /ˈɡəʊldfɪʃ/ *noun* (*pl.* **gold·fish** or **gold·fishes**) a small orange or red fish. Goldfish are kept as pets in bowls or PONDS.

**'goldfish bowl** *noun* **1** (*also* **fish-bowl**) a glass bowl for keeping fish in as pets **2** a situation in which people can see everything that happens and nothing is private: *Living in this goldfish bowl of publicity would crack the strongest marriage.*

**Goldi·locks** /ˈɡəʊldɪlɒks; *NAmE* -lɑːks/ *adj.* without extremes; just right: *The planet is in what astronomers call the Goldilocks zone: neither too hot, nor too cold.* **ORIGIN** From the story *Goldilocks and the Three Bears* where a girl finds a house and tries things out until she finds the one that is just right: the chair that is neither too big nor too small, the porridge that is not too hot and not too cold, and the bed that is neither too hard nor too soft.

**gold 'leaf** (*also* **gold 'foil**) *noun* [U] gold that has been made into a very thin sheet and is used for decoration

**gold 'medal** *noun* [C] (*also* **gold** [U, C]) a MEDAL made of or coloured gold that is given to the winner of a race or competition: *an Olympic gold medal winner* ◇ compare BRONZE MEDAL, SILVER MEDAL ▶ **gold 'medallist** (*BrE*) (*NAmE* **gold 'medalist**) *noun*: *an Olympic gold medallist*

**'gold mine** *noun* **1** a place where gold is dug out of the ground **2** a business or an activity that makes a large profit: *This restaurant is a potential gold mine.*

**gold 'plate** *noun* [U] **1** dishes, etc. made of gold **2** a thin layer of gold used to cover another metal; objects made in this way

**gold-'plated** *adj.* covered with a thin layer of gold: *gold-plated earrings*

**'gold reserve** *noun* [usually pl.] an amount of gold kept by a country's bank in order to support the supply of money

**'gold rush** *noun* a situation in which a lot of people suddenly go to a place where gold has recently been discovered

**'gold·smith** /ˈɡəʊldsmɪθ/ *noun* a person who makes or repairs things made of gold

**'gold standard** *noun* **1** (*usually* **the gold standard**) [sing.] an economic system in which the value of money is based on the value of gold **2** [usually sing.] a high level of quality that others try to copy: *Articles like his are the gold standard of news reporting.*

**golem** /ˈɡəʊləm; *BrE also* ˈɡɔɪl-/ *noun* **1** (in Jewish stories) a figure made of CLAY that comes to life **2** a machine that behaves like a human

**golf** /ɡɒlf; *NAmE* ɡɑːlf/ *noun* [U] a game played over a large area of ground using sticks with a special shape to hit a small hard ball (a **'golf ball**) into a series of 9 or 18 holes, using as few shots as possible: *I play golf every weekend.* ◇ *He enjoyed a round of golf on a Sunday morning.* ◇ see also CRAZY GOLF, MINIGOLF

**'golf cart** (*BrE also* **'golf buggy**) *noun* a small vehicle, often without a roof or doors, used especially to carry players and equipment around a golf course

**golf club** noun **1** (also **club**) a long metal stick with a piece of metal or wood at one end, used for hitting the ball in golf: *a set of golf clubs* **2** an organization whose members play golf; the place where these people meet and play golf: *Pine Ridge Golf Club* ◊ *We're going for lunch at the golf club.*

**golf course** (also **course**) noun a large area of land that is designed for playing golf on

**golf·er** /ˈɡɒlfə(r)/ NAmE /ˈɡɑːl-/ noun a person who plays golf

**golf·ing** /ˈɡɒlfɪŋ/ NAmE /ˈɡɑːl-/ adj. [only before noun] playing golf; connected with golf: *a golfing holiday* ▶ **golf·ing** noun [U]: *a week's golfing with friends*

**golf links** (also **links**) noun (pl. **golf links**) a golf course, especially one by the sea

**golf shirt** noun (NAmE) = POLO SHIRT

**Gol·iath** /ɡəˈlaɪəθ/ noun a person or thing that is very large or powerful: *a Goliath of a man* ◊ *a Goliath of the computer industry* ORIGIN From **Goliath**, a giant in the Bible who is killed by the boy David with a stone. ⊃ see also DAVID AND GOLIATH

**gol·li·wog** /ˈɡɒliwɒɡ/ NAmE /ˈɡɑːliwɑːɡ/ (also informal **golly** /ˈɡɒli/ NAmE /ˈɡɑːli/ pl. **-ies**) noun a DOLL (= a model of a person for a child to play with) made of cloth with a black face and short black hair, now often considered offensive to black people

**golly** /ˈɡɒli/ NAmE /ˈɡɑːli/ exclamation (old-fashioned, informal) used to express surprise: *Golly, you're early!*

**gonad** /ˈɡəʊnæd/ noun (anatomy) a male sex organ that produces SPERM; a female sex organ that produces eggs

**gon·dola** /ˈɡɒndələ/ NAmE /ˈɡɑːn-, ɡɑːnˈdəʊlə/ noun **1** a long boat with a flat bottom and high parts at each end, used on CANALS in Venice **2** the part on a CABLE CAR or SKI LIFT where the passengers sit **3** (especially NAmE) the part of a hot air BALLOON or AIRSHIP where the passengers sit

**gon·do·lier** /ˌɡɒndəˈlɪə(r)/ NAmE /ˌɡɑːndəˈlɪr/ noun a person whose job is to move and control the direction of a gondola in Venice

**Gon·dwana** /ɡɒnˈdwɑːnə/ NAmE /ɡɑːn-/ (also **Gon·dwana·land** /ɡɒnˈdwɑːnəlænd/ NAmE /ɡɑːn-/) noun [sing.] (geology) a very large area of land that existed in the southern HEMISPHERE millions of years ago. It was made up of the present Arabia, Africa, South America, Antarctica, Australia and India.

**gone** /ɡɒn/ NAmE /ɡɔːn/ adj., prep., verb
■ adj. [not before noun] **1** (of a thing) used up: *'Where's the coffee?' 'It's all gone.'* **2** (of a person) having left a place; away from a place: *'Is Tom here?' 'No, he was gone before I arrived.'* **3** (formal) used to say that a particular situation no longer exists: *The days are gone when you could leave your door unlocked at night.* **4** (BrE, informal) having been pregnant for the length of time mentioned: *She's seven months gone.* ◊ *How far gone are you?*
IDM **going, going, gone** (also **going 'once, going 'twice, 'sold**) said by an AUCTIONEER to show that an item has been sold ⊃ more at DEAD adj.
■ prep. (BrE, informal) later than the time mentioned SYN past: *It's gone six already.*
■ verb past part. of GO

**goner** /ˈɡɒnə(r)/ NAmE /ˈɡɔːn-/ noun (informal) a person or animal who is going to die soon; sb/sth that cannot be saved from a dangerous situation: *We were frantic. We thought you were a goner.*

**gong** /ɡɒŋ/ NAmE /ɡɔːŋ/ noun **1** a round piece of metal that hangs in a frame and makes a loud deep sound when it is hit with a stick. Gongs are used as musical instruments or to give signals, for example that a meal is ready. **2** (BrE, informal) an award or MEDAL given to sb for the work they have done

**gonna** /ˈɡənə/ (informal, non-standard) a way of saying or writing 'going to' in informal speech, when it refers to the future: *What's she gonna do now?* HELP You should not write this form unless you are copying somebody's speech.

**go·nor·rhoea** (BrE) (NAmE **go·nor·rhea**) /ˌɡɒnəˈriːə/ NAmE /ˌɡɑːnəˈriːə/ noun [U] a disease of the sexual organs, caught by having sex with a person who already has the disease ⊃ see also VENEREAL DISEASE

**goo** /ɡuː/ noun [U] (informal) any unpleasant sticky wet substance ⊃ see also GOOEY

**good** 🔊 A1 /ɡʊd/ adj., noun, adv.
■ adj. (**bet·ter** /ˈbetə(r)/, **best** /best/)
• HIGH QUALITY **1** 🔊 A1 of high quality or an acceptable standard: *a good book* ◊ *good food* ◊ *The piano was in really good condition.* ◊ *Your work is just not good enough.* ◊ *The results were pretty good.* ◊ *Sorry, my English is not very good.* ◊ *They've done a reasonably good job.* ◊ *It's a good way to make friends.* ◊ *Things are looking good at the moment.* ⊃ see also NO-GOOD
• PLEASANT **2** 🔊 A1 pleasant; that you enjoy or want: *Did you have a good time in London?* ◊ *This is very good news.* ◊ *Let's hope we have good weather tomorrow.* ◊ *it is~to do sth It's good to see you again.* ◊ *It's a good thing* (= it's lucky) *you came early.* ◊ *There are loads of good things about working here.* ◊ *We are still friends, though, which is good.* ⊃ see also FEEL-GOOD
• SENSIBLE/STRONG **3** 🔊 A1 sensible, logical or strongly supporting what is being discussed: *Thank you, good question.* ◊ *Yes, that's a good point.* ◊ *I have good reason to be suspicious.* ◊ *What a good idea!* ◊ *This is a good example of what I mean.*
• FAVOURABLE **4** 🔊 A1 showing or getting approval or respect: *The play had good reviews.* ◊ *The hotel has a good reputation.* ◊ *He comes from a good family.*
• SKILFUL **5** 🔊 A1 able to do sth well: *a good player* ◊ *a good actor/cook* ◊ *~ at sth to be good at languages/your job* ◊ *~ at doing sth Nick has always been good at finding cheap flights.* **6** 🔊 A1 *~ with sth/sb* able to use sth or deal with people well: *She's good with her hands* (= able to make things, etc.). ◊ *He's very good with children.*
• MORALLY RIGHT **7** 🔊 A1 morally right; behaving in a way that is morally right: *She has tried to lead a good life.* ◊ *a good deed* ◊ *Giving her that money was a good thing to do.*
• FOLLOWING RULES **8** 🔊 A1 following strictly a set of rules or principles: *It is good practice to supply a written report to the buyer.* ◊ *She was a good Catholic girl.*
• KIND **9** 🔊 A1 willing to help; kind to other people: *You've always been such a good friend.* ◊ *~ to sb He was very good to me when I was ill.* ◊ *~ of sb (to do sth) It was very good of you to come.* ◊ *~ about sth I had to take a week off work but my colleagues were very good about it.*
• CHILD/ANIMAL **10** 🔊 A1 behaving well or politely: *You can stay up late if you're good.* ◊ *Get dressed now, there's a good girl.*
• HEALTHY **11** 🔊 A1 healthy or strong: *Can you speak into my good ear?* ◊ *I don't feel too good today.* ◊ *'How are you?' 'I'm good.'* (= used as a general reply to a greeting)
• USEFUL/HELPFUL **12** 🔊 A1 having a useful or helpful effect on sb/sth: *~ for sb/sth Too much sun isn't good for you.* ◊ *policies that are good for business* ◊ *it is~for sb to do sth It's probably good for you to get some criticism now and then.*
• SUITABLE **13** 🔊 A1 suitable or appropriate: *Now is a good time to buy a house.* ◊ *Do you really think this is a good use of your time?* ◊ *for sth/to do sth She would be good for the job.* ◊ *~ for sb Can we change our meeting? Monday isn't good* (= convenient) *for me.* ◊ *This is as good a place as any to spend the night.*
• SHOWING APPROVAL **14** 🔊 A1 used in speaking to show that you approve of or are pleased about sth that has been said or done, or to show that you want to move on to a new topic of conversation: *'Dinner's ready.' 'Good—I'm starving.'* ◊ *'I got the job.' 'Oh, good.'* ◊ *Good, I think we've come to a decision.* **15** 🔊 A1 [only before noun] (informal) used as a form of praise: *Good old Jack!* ◊ *I've ordered some drinks.' 'Good man!'*
• IN EXCLAMATIONS **16** (informal) used in exclamations: *Good heavens!* ◊ *Good God!*
• LARGE **17** [only before noun] great in number, amount or degree: *a good number of people* ◊ *The kitchen is a good*

size. ◊ *We spent a good while* (= quite a long time) *looking for the house.* ◊ *There's* **a good chance** (= it is likely) *that I won't be here next year.*
- **AT LEAST 18** not less than; rather more than: *We waited for a good hour.* ◊ *It's a good three miles to the station.*
- **COMPLETE 19** [only before noun] done to a high level or a great degree; complete: *We had a good laugh about it afterwards.* ◊ *You'll feel better after a good sleep.*
- **AMUSING 20** [usually before noun] funny or clever: *a good story/joke* ◊ (*informal*) *That's a good one!*
- **FOR PARTICULAR TIME/DISTANCE 21** ~ **for sth** having enough energy, health, strength, etc. to last for a particular length of time or distance: *You're good for* (= you will live) *a few years yet.* **22** ~ **for sth** acceptable for sth: *The ticket is good for three months.*
- **LIKELY TO PROVIDE 23** ~ **for sth** likely to provide sth: *He's always good for a laugh.* ◊ *Bobby should be good for a few drinks.*

**IDM** **HELP** Most idioms containing **good** are at the entries for the nouns and verbs in the idioms, for example **(as) good as gold** is at **gold**. **as ˈgood as** very nearly: *The matter is as good as settled.* ◊ *He as good as called me a coward* (= suggested that I was a coward without actually using the word 'coward'). **as ˌgood as it ˈgets** used when you are saying that a situation is not going to get any better **be ˌgood to ˈgo** (of a thing) to be prepared and ready for use; (of a person) to be prepared and ready to do something: *By tomorrow afternoon the document will be good to go.* ◊ *I've spent several months training for this race so now I'm good to go.* **good and…** (*informal*) *completely: I won't go until I'm good and ready.* **a ˌgood ˈfew** (*also* **quite a ˈfew**) several: *There are still a good few empty seats.* **a ˌgood ˈmany** a lot of sb/sth: *There were a good many people there.* **ˌgood for ˈyou, ˈsb, ˈthem, etc.** (*especially AustralE* **good ˈon you, etc.**) (*informal*) used to praise sb for doing sth well: *'I passed first time.' 'Good for you!'*

■ *noun* ⊃ see also **GOODS**
- **MORALLY RIGHT 1 ⦁ A2** [U] behaviour that is morally right or acceptable: *the difference between good and evil* ◊ *Is religion always a force for good?* **2** **the good** [pl.] people who live a moral life; people who are admired for the work they do to help other people: *a gathering of the great and the good*
- **STH HELPFUL 3 ⦁ B1** [U] something that helps sb/sth: **for the ~ of sb/sth** *Cuts have been made for the good of the company.* ◊ *I'm only telling you this for your own good.* ◊ *The results of the research should be used for the common good* (= the advantage of everyone). ◊ *What's the good of* (= how does it help you) *earning all that money if you don't have time to enjoy it?* ◊ *What good is it redecorating if you're thinking of moving?* ⊃ see also **DO-GOODER**

**IDM** **all to the ˈgood** used to say that if sth happens, it will be good, even if it is not exactly what you were expecting: *If these measures also reduce unemployment, that is all to the good.* **be no ˈgood (doing sth/to sb)** | **not be any/much ˈgood 1** to not be useful; to have no useful effect: *This gadget isn't much good.* ◊ *It's no good complaining—they never listen.* ◊ *This book is no good to me: I need the new edition.* ◊ *Was his advice ever any good?* **2** to not be interesting or fun: *His latest film isn't much good.* **do ˈgood 1** to do things that are morally good, especially by helping others: *It's nice to get recognition for doing good in the community.* **2** (*also* **do sb good**) to have a useful effect; to help sb: *Do you think these latest changes will do any good?* ◊ *It will do you good to get out of the house more often.* **for ˈgood** (*BrE also* **for ˌgood and ˈall**) permanently: *This time she's leaving for good* (= she will never return). **to the ˈgood** used to say that sb now has a particular amount of money that they did not have before: *We are £500 to the good.* **up to no ˈgood** (*informal*) doing sth wrong or dishonest: *Those kids are always up to no good.* ⊃ more at **ILL** *adj.*, **POWER** *n.*, **WORLD**

■ *adv.* (*especially NAmE, informal*) well: *'How's it going?' 'Pretty good.'* ◊ *Now, you listen to me good!*

**good afterˈnoon** *exclamation* used to say hello politely when people first see each other in the afternoon (in informal use people often just say *Afternoon* in this case); sometimes also used formally when people leave each other in the afternoon

---

683 **good morning**

▼ **VOCABULARY BUILDING**

**Good and very good**

Instead of saying that something is **good** or **very good**, try to use more precise and interesting adjectives to describe things:
- **delicious/tasty** food
- an **exciting/entertaining/absorbing** movie
- an **absorbing/a fascinating/an informative** book
- a **pleasant/an enjoyable** trip
- a **skilful/talented/fine** player
- **impressive/high-quality** acting
- **useful/helpful** advice

In conversation you can use words like **great**, **super**, **wonderful**, **lovely** and **excellent**. ⊃ note at **NICE**

▼ **WHICH WORD?**

**good / goodness**
- The noun **good** means actions and behaviour that are morally right. You can talk about a person doing **good**: *The charity does a lot of good.* ◊ *the difference between good and evil.*
- **Goodness** is the quality of being good. You can talk about a person's **goodness**: *Her goodness shone through.*

**good·bye 🕪 A1** /ˌɡʊdˈbaɪ/ *exclamation, noun* used when you are leaving sb or when sb else is leaving: *Goodbye! It was great to meet you.* ◊ *She didn't even say goodbye to her mother.* ◊ *We waved them goodbye.* ◊ *We've already said our goodbyes.* ◊ *Kiss me goodbye!* ◊ (*figurative*) *Take out our service contract and say goodbye to costly repair bills.* ⊃ compare **BYE** **IDM** see **KISS** *v.*

**good ˈday** *exclamation* (*old-fashioned*) used to say hello or goodbye politely when people first see each other or leave each other during the day: *Good day to you.* ⊃ compare **G'DAY**

**good ˈevening** *exclamation* used to say hello politely when people first see each other in the evening (in informal use people often just say *Evening* in this case); sometimes also used formally when people leave each other in the evening

**good ˈfairy** *noun* = **FAIRY GODMOTHER**

**good ˈfaith** *noun* [U] the intention to be honest and helpful: *a gesture of good faith* ◊ *He acted in good faith.*

**good-for-ˈnothing** *noun* (*informal*) a person who is lazy and has no skills: *an idle good-for-nothing* ▶ **ˈgood-for-nothing** *adj.* [usually before noun]: *Where's that good-for-nothing son of yours?*

**Good ˈFriday** *noun* [U, C] the Friday before Easter, the day when Christians remember the Crucifixion of Christ (= when Jesus Christ was killed by being fastened to a cross)

**good-ˈhearted** *adj.* kind; willing to help other people

**good ˈhumour** (*US* **good ˈhumor**) *noun* [U, sing.] a cheerful mood: *Everyone admired her patience and unfailing good humour.* **OPP** **ill humour** ▶ **good-ˈhumoured** (*US* **good-ˈhumored**) *adj.*: *a good-humoured atmosphere* **good-ˈhumoured·ly** (*US* **good-ˈhumored·ly**) *adv.*

**goodie** = **GOODY**

**good-ˈlooking** *adj.* (especially of people) physically attractive **OPP** **ugly**: *a good-looking man/couple* ◊ *She's strikingly good-looking.* ⊃ **SYNONYMS** at **BEAUTIFUL**

**good ˈlooks** *noun* [pl.] the physical beauty of a person: *an actor famous for his rugged good looks*

**good·ly** /ˈɡʊdli/ *adj.* [only before noun] **1** (*old-fashioned, formal*) quite large in size or amount: *a goodly number* **2** (*old use*) physically attractive; of good quality

**good ˈmorning** (*also informal* **morning**) *exclamation* used to say hello politely when people first see each other in the morning; sometimes also used formally when people leave each other in the morning

---

◉ Oxford Phrasal Academic Lexicon (OPAL) written and spoken word lists | Ⓦ OPAL written word list | Ⓢ OPAL spoken word list

# good name

**ˌgood ˈname** noun [usually sing.] the good opinion that people have of sb/sth **SYN** reputation: *He told the police he didn't know her, to protect her good name.* ◊ *My election chances are not as important as the good name of the party.*

**ˌgood ˈnature** noun [U] the quality of being kind, friendly and patient when dealing with people

**ˌgood-ˈnatured** adj. kind, friendly and patient when dealing with people: *a good-natured person/discussion* ▶ **ˌgood-ˈnaturedly** adv.: *to smile good-naturedly*

**goodˈness** ?+ B2 /ˈɡʊdnəs/ noun 1 ?+ B2 the quality of being good: *the essential goodness of human nature* ◊ *evidence of God's goodness* ◊ (formal) *At least have the goodness* (= good manners) *to look at me when I'm talking to you.* ⊃ see also HONEST-TO-GOODNESS ⊃ note at GOOD 2 ?+ C1 the part of sth that has a useful effect on sb/sth, especially sb's health: *These vegetables have had all the goodness boiled out of them.* **IDM** ˈGoodness! | ˈGoodness ˈme! | ˌMy ˈgoodness! | ˌGoodness ˈgracious! (informal) used to express surprise: *Goodness, what a big balloon!* ◊ *My goodness, you have been busy!* ◊ *Goodness me, no!* **out of the goodness of your ˈheart** because of kind feelings, without thinking about what advantage there will be for you: *You're not telling me he offered to lend you the money out of the goodness of his heart?* ⊃ more at GOD, HONEST, KNOW v., THANK

**ˈgood-night** (also **good night**) /ˌɡʊdˈnaɪt/ exclamation used when you are saying goodbye to sb late in the evening, or when they or you are going to bed; in informal use people often just say *Night*

**goodo** /ˈɡʊdəʊ/ adj. (AustralE, NZE, informal) good

**ˌgood old ˈboy** noun (NAmE, informal) a man who is considered typical of white men in the southern states of the US

**goods** ? B1 /ɡʊdz/ noun [pl.] 1 ?+ B1 things that are produced to be sold: *to produce/buy/sell goods* ◊ *manufactured/imported goods* ◊ *luxury goods* ◊ *electrical/sporting goods* ◊ *tax on goods and services* ⊃ see also BAKED GOODS, CAPITAL GOODS, CONSUMER GOODS, DRY GOODS, DURABLE GOODS, WHITE GOODS ⊃ SYNONYMS at PRODUCT 2 ?+ B1 possessions that can be moved: *stolen goods* ◊ *household goods* ◊ *The plastic bag contained all his worldly goods* (= everything he owned). ⊃ SYNONYMS at THING 3 (BrE) things (not people) that are transported by railway or road: *a goods train* ◊ *a heavy goods vehicle* ⊃ compare FREIGHT **IDM** be the ˈgoods (BrE, informal) to be very good or impressive deˌliver the ˈgoods | ˌcome up with the ˈgoods (informal) to do what you have promised to do or what people expect or want you to do: *We expected great things of the England team, but on the day they simply failed to deliver the goods.*

**ˌgood ˈsense** noun [U] ~ **(to do sth)** the ability to make the right decision about sth; good judgement: *a man of honour and good sense* ◊ *Keeping to a low-fat diet makes very good sense* (= is a sensible thing to do).

**ˈgoods train** noun (BrE) = FREIGHT TRAIN

**ˌgood-ˈtempered** adj. cheerful and not easily made angry

**ˈgood-time** adj. [only before noun] only interested in pleasure, and not in anything serious or important: *I was too much of a good-time girl to do any serious studying.*

**ˈgood-will** /ˌɡʊdˈwɪl/ noun [U] 1 friendly or helpful feelings towards other people or countries: *a spirit of goodwill in international relations* ◊ *a goodwill gesture/a gesture of goodwill* 2 the good relationship between a business and its customers that is calculated as part of its value when it is sold

**ˌgoodwill amˈbassador** noun a famous person who represents an organization by educating the public or promoting a good relationship with the public: *The singer is a goodwill ambassador for the American Heart Association.*

**goody** /ˈɡʊdi/ noun, exclamation
- noun (also **goodie**) [usually pl.] (*-ies*) (informal) 1 a thing that is very nice to eat: *a basket of goodies for the children* 2 anything that is attractive and that people want to have: *We're giving away lots of free goodies—T-shirts, hats and posters!* 3 a good person, especially in a book or film: *It's sometimes difficult to tell who are the goodies and who are the baddies.* **OPP** baddy ⊃ WORDFINDER NOTE at CHARACTER
- exclamation (old-fashioned) a word children use when they are excited or pleased about sth

**ˈgoody bag** (also **ˈgoodie bag**) noun 1 a bag containing sweets and small presents, given to children to take home at the end of a party 2 a bag containing examples of a company's products, given away in order to advertise them

**ˌgoody-ˈgoody** noun (pl. **goody-goodies**) (informal, disapproving) (used especially by and about children) a person who behaves very well to please people in authority such as parents or teachers

**gooey** /ˈɡuːi/ adj. (informal) soft and sticky: *a gooey mess* ◊ *gooey cakes*

**goof** /ɡuːf/ verb, noun
- verb [I] (especially NAmE, informal) to make a stupid mistake: *Sorry, guys. I goofed.* **PHR V** ˌgoof aˈround (especially NAmE, informal) to spend your time doing silly or stupid things **SYN** mess around ˌgoof ˈoff (NAmE, informal) to spend your time doing nothing, especially when you should be working
- noun (especially NAmE, informal) 1 a stupid mistake 2 a silly or stupid person

**ˈgoof-ball** /ˈɡuːfbɔːl/ noun (NAmE, informal) a stupid person ▶ **ˈgoof-ball** adj. [only before noun]: *This is just another of his goofball ideas.*

**goofy** /ˈɡuːfi/ adj. (informal) silly; stupid: *a goofy grin*

**Google™** /ˈɡuːɡl/ a very popular internet SEARCH ENGINE (= a website that helps you to search for information on the internet)

**google** /ˈɡuːɡl/ verb [T, I] ~ **(sb/sth)** to type words into the SEARCH ENGINE Google™ in order to find information about sb/sth: *I just googled her and found her blog.* ◊ *I tried googling but couldn't find anything relevant.* ⊃ WORDFINDER NOTE at WEB

**googly** /ˈɡuːɡli/ noun (pl. *-ies*) (in CRICKET) a ball that is BOWLED so that it looks as if it will turn in one direction, but that actually turns the opposite way: (figurative) *He bowled the prime minister a googly* (= asked him a difficult question).

**gook** /ɡuːk/ noun 1 [U] (informal) any unpleasant sticky wet substance 2 [C] (NAmE, taboo, slang) an offensive word for a person from south-east Asia

**goon** /ɡuːn/ noun 1 (especially NAmE) a criminal who is paid to frighten or injure people 2 (especially BrE, old-fashioned) a stupid or silly person

**goonda** /ˈɡuːndə/ noun (IndE) a person who is paid to frighten or hurt sb: *The politician hired a group of goondas to intimidate rival candidates.*

**goop** /ɡuːp/ noun (especially NAmE, informal) a thick soft sticky substance that looks, tastes or feels unpleasant: *Everything was covered in sticky brown goop.*

**goose** /ɡuːs/ noun, verb
- noun (pl. **geese** /ɡiːs/) 1 [C] a bird like a large DUCK with a long neck. Geese either live wild or are kept on farms. ⊃ see also CANADA GOOSE 2 [U] meat from a goose: *roast goose* 3 [C] a female goose ⊃ compare GANDER 4 [C] (old-fashioned, informal) a silly person ⊃ see also GOLDEN GOOSE, WILD GOOSE CHASE **IDM** see COOK v., KILL v., SAUCE, SAY v.
- verb (informal) 1 ~ **sb** to touch or press sb's bottom quickly 2 ~ **sth (along/up)** (NAmE) to make sth move or work faster

**goose-berry** /ˈɡʊzbəri; NAmE ˈɡuːsberi/ noun (pl. *-ies*) a small green fruit that grows on a bush with THORNS. Gooseberries have a bitter sharp taste and are usually cooked to make jam, PIES, etc. Children are sometimes told that babies come from 'under the gooseberry bush': *a gooseberry bush* ⊃ VISUAL VOCAB page V4

**ˈgoose-bumps** /ˈɡuːsbʌmps/ noun (also **ˈgoose pimples** especially in BrE**) [pl.] a condition in which there are raised spots on your skin because you feel cold, frightened or excited: *It gave me goosebumps just to think about it.*

**ˈgoose egg** noun (NAmE, informal) a score of zero in a game

**ˈgoose pimples** noun [pl.] (especially BrE) = GOOSEBUMPS

**goose-step** noun [sing.] (often disapproving) a way of MARCHING (= walking), used by soldiers in some countries, in which the legs are raised high and straight ▶ **goose-step** verb (-pp-) [I]

**GOP** /ˌdʒiː əʊ ˈpiː/ abbr. Grand Old Party (the Republican political party in the US)

**go·pher** /ˈɡəʊfə(r)/ noun **1** a North American animal like a RAT, that lives in holes in the ground **2** (NAmE) = GROUND SQUIRREL **3** (informal) = GOFER

**gora** /ˈɡɔːrə/ noun (pl. **goras** or **goray** /-reɪ/) a word used by people from South Asia for a white person

**Gor·dian knot** /ˌɡɔːdiən ˈnɒt; NAmE ˌɡɔːrdiən ˈnɑːt/ noun a very difficult or impossible task or problem: *to cut/untie the Gordian knot* (= to solve a problem by taking action) ORIGIN From the legend in which King Gordius tied a very complicated knot and said that whoever undid it would become the ruler of Asia. Alexander the Great cut through the knot with his sword.

**gore** /ɡɔː(r)/ verb, noun
■ verb ~ sb/sth (of an animal) to wound a person or another animal with a HORN or TUSK: *He was gored by a bull.*
■ noun [U] thick blood that has flowed from a wound, especially in a violent situation: *The movie is not just blood and gore* (= scenes of violence); *it has a thrilling story.* ⊃ see also GORY

**gorge** /ɡɔːdʒ; NAmE ɡɔːrdʒ/ noun, verb
■ noun a deep narrow valley with steep sides SYN canyon: *the Rhine Gorge*
■ verb [T, I] ~ (yourself) (on sth) (sometimes disapproving) to eat a lot of sth, until you are too full to eat any more SYN stuff

**gor·geous** 🔊 B2 /ˈɡɔːdʒəs; NAmE ˈɡɔːrdʒ-/ adj. **1** 🔊 B2 (informal) very beautiful and attractive; giving great pleasure SYN lovely: *a gorgeous girl/man ◊ a gorgeous view ◊ gorgeous weather* (= warm and with a lot of sun) *◊ You look gorgeous! ◊ It was absolutely gorgeous.* ⊃ SYNONYMS at BEAUTIFUL **2** [usually before noun] (of colours, clothes, etc.) with very deep colours; impressive: *exotic birds with feathers of gorgeous colours* ▶ **gor·geous·ly** adv.

**gor·gon** /ˈɡɔːɡən; NAmE ˈɡɔːrɡ-/ noun **1** (in ancient Greek stories) one of three sisters with snakes on their heads instead of hair, who can change anyone that looks at them into stone **2** an ugly woman who behaves in an aggressive and frightening way

**gor·illa** /ɡəˈrɪlə/ noun **1** a very large powerful African APE (= an animal like a large monkey without a tail) covered with black or brown hair **2** (informal) a large aggressive man

**gorm·less** /ˈɡɔːmləs; NAmE ˈɡɔːrm-/ adj. (BrE, informal) stupid: *a gormless boy ◊ Don't just stand there looking gormless—do something!*

**go-round** noun = GO-AROUND

**gorse** /ɡɔːs; NAmE ɡɔːrs/ (BrE also **furze**) noun [U] a bush with thin leaves with sharp points and small yellow flowers. Gorse often grows on land that is not used or cared for.

**gory** /ˈɡɔːri/ adj. (**gor·ier**, **gori·est**) **1** (informal) involving a lot of blood or violence; showing or describing blood and violence: *a gory accident ◊ the gory task of the pathologist ◊ a gory movie ◊* (humorous) *He insisted on telling us all the gory details about their divorce* (= the unpleasant facts). **2** (literary) covered with blood SYN **bloodstained**: *a gory figure*

**gosh** /ɡɒʃ; NAmE ɡɑːʃ/ exclamation (old-fashioned, informal) people say '**Gosh!**' when they are surprised or shocked: *Gosh, is that the time?*

**gos·hawk** /ˈɡɒshɔːk; NAmE ˈɡɑːs-/ noun a large HAWK with short wings

**gos·ling** /ˈɡɒzlɪŋ; NAmE ˈɡɑːz-/ noun a young GOOSE (= a bird like a large DUCK)

**go-slow** (BrE) (NAmE **slow-down**) noun a protest that workers make by doing their work more slowly than usual ⊃ compare WORK-TO-RULE

**gos·pel** /ˈɡɒspl; NAmE ˈɡɑːs-/ noun **1** [C] (also **Gospel**) one of the four books in the Bible about the life and teaching of Jesus: *the Gospel according to St John ◊ St Mark's Gospel* **2** [sing.] (also **the Gospel**) the life and teaching of Jesus as explained in the Bible: *preaching/spreading the gospel* **3** [C, usually sing.] a set of ideas that sb believes in and tries to persuade others to accept: *He preached a gospel of military strength.* **4** (also **gospel truth**) [U] (informal) the complete truth: *Is that gospel? ◊ Don't take his word as gospel.* **5** (also **gospel music**) [U] a style of religious singing developed by African Americans: *a gospel choir*

**gos·samer** /ˈɡɒsəmə(r); NAmE ˈɡɑːs-/ noun [U] **1** the very fine THREAD made by spiders **2** (literary) any very light fine material: *a gown of gossamer silk ◊ the gossamer wings of a dragonfly*

**gos·sip** /ˈɡɒsɪp; NAmE ˈɡɑːs-/ noun, verb
■ noun **1** [U] (disapproving) informal talk or stories about other people's private lives, which may be unkind or not true: *Don't believe all the gossip you hear. ◊ Tell me all the latest gossip! ◊ The gossip was that he had lost a fortune on the stock exchange. ◊ He knows all the juicy gossip. ◊ It was common gossip* (= everyone said so) *that they were having an affair. ◊ She's a great one for idle gossip* (= she enjoys spreading stories about other people that are probably not true). **2** [C, usually sing.] a conversation about other people and their private lives: *I love a good gossip.* ⊃ SYNONYMS at DISCUSSION **3** [C] (disapproving) a person who enjoys talking about other people's private lives ⊃ SYNONYMS at SPEAKER ▶ **gos·sipy** adj.: *a gossipy letter/neighbour*
■ verb [I] to talk about other people's private lives, often in an unkind way: *I can't stand here gossiping all day. ◊ ~ about sb/sth She's been gossiping about you.*

**gossip column** noun a piece of writing in a newspaper about social events and the private and personal lives of famous people ▶ **gossip columnist** noun

**got** /ɡɒt; NAmE ɡɑːt/ past tense, past part. of GET

**gotcha** /ˈɡɒtʃə; NAmE ˈɡɑːtʃə/ exclamation (non-standard) the written form of the way some people pronounce 'I've got you', which is not considered to be correct: '*Gotcha!' I yelled as I grabbed him by the arm* (= used when you have caught sb, or have beaten them at sth). *◊ 'Don't let go.' 'Yeah, gotcha.'* (= Yes, I understand.) HELP You should not write this form unless you are copying sb's speech.

**goth** /ɡɒθ; NAmE ɡɑːθ/ noun **1** [U] a style of rock music, popular in the 1980s, that developed from PUNK music. The words often expressed ideas about the end of the world, death or the DEVIL. **2** [C] a member of a group of people who listen to goth music and wear black clothes and black and white MAKE-UP **3** **Goth** [C] a member of a Germanic people who fought against the Roman Empire ▶ **goth** (also **goth·ic**) adj.

**Gotham** /ˈɡɒθəm; NAmE ˈɡɑːθ-/ (also **Gotham City**) noun (informal) a way of referring to New York City

**Goth·ic** /ˈɡɒθɪk; NAmE ˈɡɑːθ-/ adj., noun
■ adj. **1** connected with the Goths (= a Germanic people who fought against the Roman Empire) **2** (architecture) built in the style that was popular in western Europe from the 12th to the 16th centuries, and which has pointed ARCHES and windows and tall thin PILLARS: *a Gothic church* **3** (of a novel, etc.) written in the style popular in the 18th and 19th centuries, which described romantic adventures in mysterious or frightening places or situations **4** (of type and printing) having pointed letters with thick lines and sharp angles. German books used to be printed in this style. **5** **gothic** connected with goths
■ noun [U] **1** the Gothic style of architecture **2** Gothic printing type or printed letters

**go-to** adj. [only before noun] used to refer to the person or place that sb goes to for help, advice or information: *He's the president's go-to guy on Asian politics.*

**gotta** /ˈɡɒtə; NAmE ˈɡɑːtə/ (informal, non-standard) the written form of the word some people use to mean '(have) got to' or '(have) got a', which is not considered to be correct: *He's gotta go. ◊ Gotta cigarette?* HELP You should not write this form unless you are copying somebody's speech.

**got·ten** /ˈɡɒtn; NAmE ˈɡɑːtn/ (NAmE) past part. of GET ⊃ see also ILL-GOTTEN

**gou·ache** /guˈɑːʃ, gwɑːʃ/ noun **1** [U] a method of painting using colours that are mixed with water and made thick with white paint or other substances; the paints used in this method **2** [C] a picture painted using this method

**gouge** /ɡaʊdʒ/ verb, noun
- verb **1** ~ sth (in sth) to make a hole or cut in sth with a sharp object in a rough or violent way: *The lion's claws had gouged a wound in the horse's side.* ◇ *He had gouged her cheek with a screwdriver.* **2** ~ sb / sth (NAmE) to force sb to pay an unfairly high price for sth; to raise prices unfairly: *Price gouging is widespread.*
- PHRV **gouge sth↔out (of sth)** to remove or form sth by digging into a surface: *The man's eyes had been gouged out.* ◇ *Glaciers gouged out valleys from the hills.*
- noun **1** a sharp tool for making hollow areas in wood **2** a deep, narrow hole or cut in a surface

**gou·jons** /ˈɡuːʒɒnz, ˈɡuːʒənz/ noun [pl.] (BrE from French) small pieces of fish or chicken fried in oil

**gou·lash** /ˈɡuːlæʃ; NAmE -lɑːʃ/ noun [C, U] a hot spicy Hungarian dish of meat that is cooked slowly in liquid with PAPRIKA

**gourd** /ɡʊəd, ɡɔːd; NAmE ɡʊrd, ɡɔːrd/ noun a type of large fruit with hard skin and a soft inner part. Gourds are often dried and used as containers. ⊃ see also CALABASH

**gour·mand** /ˈɡʊəmənd; NAmE ˈɡʊrmɑːnd/ noun (often disapproving) a person who enjoys eating and eats large amounts of food

**gour·met** /ˈɡʊəmeɪ; NAmE ˈɡʊrm-/ noun a person who knows a lot about good food and wines and is careful in choosing, eating and drinking them ▶ **gour·met** adj. [only before noun]: *gourmet food* (= of high quality and often expensive)

**gout** /ɡaʊt/ noun [U] a disease that causes painful SWELLING (= the condition of being larger or rounder than normal) in the JOINTS, especially of the toes, knees and fingers

**gov·ern** /ˈɡʌvn; NAmE -vərn/ verb **1** [T, I] ~ (sth) to legally control a country or its people and be responsible for introducing new laws, organizing public services, etc: *The country is governed by elected representatives of the people.* ◇ *He accused the opposition party of being unfit to govern.* **2** [T, often passive] ~ sth to control or influence sb/sth or how sth happens, functions, etc: *We need changes in the law governing school attendance.* ◇ *Prices are governed by market demand.* ◇ *All his decisions have been entirely governed by self-interest.* **3** [T] ~ sth (grammar) if a word **governs** another word or phrase, it affects how that word or phrase is formed or used

**gov·ern·ance** /ˈɡʌvənəns; NAmE -vərn-/ noun [U] (formal) the activity of governing a country or controlling a company or an organization; the way in which a country is governed or a company or institution is controlled: *He emphasized the company's commitment to high standards of corporate governance.*

**gov·ern·ess** /ˈɡʌvənəs; NAmE -vərn-/ noun (especially in the past) a woman employed to teach the children of a rich family in their home and to live with them ⊃ compare TUTOR

**gov·ern·ing** /ˈɡʌvənɪŋ; NAmE -vərn-/ adj. [only before noun] having the right and the authority to control sth such as a country or an institution: *The Conservatives were then the governing party.* ◇ *The school's governing body* (= the group of people who control the organization of the school) *took responsibility for the decision.* ⊃ see also SELF-GOVERNING

**gov·ern·ment** /ˈɡʌvnmənt; NAmE -vərn-/ noun **1** [C + sing./pl. v.] (often **the Government**) (abbr. **govt**) the group of people who are responsible for controlling a country or a state: *to lead/form a government* ◇ *She has resigned from the Government.* ◇ *The Government have/have been considering income tax cuts.* ◇ *the last Conservative government* ◇ *EU national governments* ◇ *the Nebraska state government* ◇ *The country still has an interim government.* ◇ *the government of the day* ◇ *government officials/ministers/employees* ◇ *a government department/agency* ⊃ WORDFINDER NOTE at KING **2** [U] a particular system or method of controlling a country: *Democratic government has now replaced military rule.* ◇ *communist/totalitarian government* ◇ *a federal system of government* ⊃ see also CENTRAL GOVERNMENT, LOCAL GOVERNMENT, MINORITY GOVERNMENT, SELF-GOVERNMENT, STUDENT GOVERNMENT **3** [U] the activity or the manner of controlling a country: *strong government* ◇ *The army retained a strong role in the government of the country.* ◇ **in ~** *At that time the Democrats were in government.* ⊃ see also BIG GOVERNMENT

WORDFINDER cabinet, checks and balances, constitution, federal, minister, the Opposition, parliament, politics, system

**gov·ern·men·tal** /ˌɡʌvnˈmentl; NAmE ˌɡʌvərn-/ adj. connected with government; of a government: *governmental agencies* ◇ *governmental actions* ⊃ compare NON-GOVERNMENTAL

**government ˈhealth warning** noun **1** (in the UK) a notice that must by law appear on a product, especially a pack of cigarettes, that warns people that it is dangerous to their health **2** (also **ˈhealth warning**) (BrE) a warning that sth should be treated carefully because it may cause problems: *These figures should come with a government health warning.*

**gov·ern·or** /ˈɡʌvənə(r); NAmE -vərn-/ noun **1** (also **Governor**) a person who is the official head of a country or region that is governed by another country: *the former governor of the colony* ◇ *a provincial governor* **2** (also **Governor**) a person who is chosen to be in charge of the government of a state in the US: *the governor of Arizona* ◇ *the Arizona governor* ◇ *Governor Bev Perdue* **3** (especially BrE) a member of a group of people who are responsible for controlling an institution such as a school, a college or a hospital: *a school governor* ◇ *the board of governors of the college* **4** (BrE) a person who is in charge of an institution: *a prison governor* ◇ *the governor of the Bank of England* ◇ (informal) *I can't decide. I'll have to ask the governor* (= the man in charge, who employs sb). ⊃ see also GUV'NOR

**governor ˈgeneral** noun (pl. **governors general** or **governor generals**) the official representative in a country of the country that has or had political control over it, especially the representative of the British King or Queen in a Commonwealth country

**govt** (also **govt.** especially in NAmE) abbr. (in writing) government

**go ˈwell** exclamation (SAfrE) used to say goodbye to sb: *I hope you enjoy your holiday. Go well!*

**gown** /ɡaʊn/ noun **1** a woman's dress, especially a long one for special occasions: *an evening/a wedding gown* **2** a long loose piece of clothing that is worn over other clothes by judges and (in the UK) by other lawyers, and by members of universities (at special ceremonies): *a graduation gown* ⊃ see also TOWN AND GOWN **3** a piece of clothing worn in a hospital, either by medical staff during surgery or by a patient, especially as protection against infection: *a surgeon's gown* ⊃ see also DRESSING GOWN

**gowned** /ɡaʊnd/ adj. wearing a gown

**gowns**

surgical gown

academic gown

evening gown

dressing gown / bathrobe

**goy** /gɔɪ/ noun (pl. **goy·im** /ˈgɔɪɪm/ or **goys**) (informal, often offensive) a word used by Jewish people for a person who is not Jewish

**GP** /ˌdʒiː ˈpiː/ noun (especially BrE) a doctor who is trained in general medicine and who works in the local community, not in a hospital (the abbreviation for 'general practitioner'): *Go and see your GP as soon as possible.* ◊ *There are four GPs in our local practice.*

**GPA** /ˌdʒiː piː ˈeɪ/ abbr. (NAmE) GRADE POINT AVERAGE: *He graduated with a GPA of 3.8.*

**Gp Capt** abbr. GROUP CAPTAIN

**GPRS** /ˌdʒiː piː ɑːr ˈes/ abbr. general packet radio services (a way of sending electronic data as radio signals, used especially between mobile phones and the internet)

**GPS** /ˌdʒiː piː ˈes/ noun a system by which signals are sent from satellites to a special device, used to show the position of a person or thing on the surface of the earth very accurately (the abbreviation for 'global positioning system'): *The drivers all have GPS in the van.* ⇨ compare SAT-NAV ⇨ WORDFINDER NOTE at MAP

**grab** 🔑 B2 /græb/ verb, noun
■ verb (-bb-) **1** 🔑 B2 [T, I] to take or hold sb/sth with your hand suddenly or roughly SYN seize: ~ sb/sth *She grabbed his arm as he got up to leave.* ◊ *He grabbed hold of me and wouldn't let go.* ◊ ~ sb/sth by sth *He grabbed Tom by the collar and dragged him outside.* ◊ ~ sth from sb/sth *Jim grabbed a cake from the plate.* ◊ *Don't grab—there's plenty for everyone.* **2** [I] to try to take hold of sth: ~ at sth *She grabbed at the branch, missed and fell.* ◊ ~ for sth *Kate grabbed for the robber's gun.* **3** [T, I] to take advantage of an opportunity to do or have sth SYN seize: ~ sth *This was my big chance and I grabbed it with both hands.* ◊ ~ at sth *He'll grab at any excuse to avoid doing the dishes.* **4** [T] ~ sth to have or take sth quickly, especially because you are in a hurry: *Let's grab a sandwich before we go.* ◊ *I managed to grab a couple of hours' sleep on the plane.* ◊ *Grab a seat, I won't keep you a moment.* **5** [T] ~ sth to take sth for yourself, especially in a SELFISH or GREEDY way: *By the time we arrived, someone had grabbed all the good seats.* **6** [T] ~ sb/sth to get sb's attention: *I'll see if I can grab the waitress and get the bill.* ◊ *Glasgow's drugs problem has grabbed the headlines tonight* (= been published as an important story in the newspapers).
IDM **how does ... grab you?** (informal) used to ask sb whether they are interested in sth or in doing sth: *How does the idea of a trip to Rome grab you?*
■ noun **1** [usually sing.] ~ (at/for sb/sth) a sudden attempt to take or hold sb/sth: *He made a grab for her bag.* ⇨ see also LAND GRAB, POWER GRAB, SMASH-AND-GRAB **2** (computing) a picture taken from a television or video film, or from a computer screen, stored as an image on a computer: *a frame grab from CCTV* ◊ *I posted the screen grab on Twitter.* **3** a piece of equipment that lifts and holds goods, for example the equipment that hangs from a CRANE
IDM **up for ˈgrabs** (informal) available for anyone who is interested: *There are £25 000 worth of prizes up for grabs in our competition!*

**ˈgrab bag** noun (NAmE) **1** (BrE **lucky ˈdip**) a game in which people choose a present from a container of presents without being able to see what it is going to be **2** (informal) a mixed collection of things: *He offered a grab bag of reasons for his decision.*

**grabber** /ˈgræbə(r)/ noun (especially in compounds) a person or thing that demands money, attention, etc: *The World Cup is always a big headline grabber.* ⇨ see also LAND GRABBER

**grace** 🔑+ C1 /greɪs/ noun, verb
■ noun
• OF MOVEMENT **1** 🔑+ C1 [U] an attractive quality of movement that is smooth and done with control; a simple and beautiful quality: *She moves with the natural grace of a ballerina.*
• BEHAVIOUR **2** 🔑+ C1 [U] a quality of behaviour that is polite and pleasant and deserves respect: *He conducted himself with grace and dignity throughout the trial.* ⇨ see also SAVING GRACE **3 graces** [pl.] (especially BrE) ways of behaving that people think are polite and acceptable: *He was not particularly well versed in the social graces.*
• EXTRA TIME **4** [U] extra time that is given to sb to enable them to pay a bill, finish a piece of work, etc: *They've given me a month's grace to get the money.*
• OF GOD **5** [U] the love that God shows towards the human race: *It was only by the grace of God that they survived.*
• PRAYER **6** [U, C] a short prayer that is usually said before a meal to thank God for the food: *Let's say grace.*
• TITLE **7 His/Her/Your Grace** [C] used as a title of respect when talking to or about an ARCHBISHOP, a DUKE or a DUCHESS: *Good Morning, Your Grace.* ◊ *Their Graces the Duke and Duchess of Kent.* ⇨ see also COUP DE GRÂCE, SAVING GRACE
IDM **be in sb's good ˈgraces** (formal) to have sb's approval and be liked by them **fall from ˈgrace** to lose the trust or respect that people have for you, especially by doing sth bad or morally wrong **sb's ˌfall from ˈgrace** a situation in which sb loses the trust or respect that people have for them, especially because they have done sth that is bad or morally wrong **have the (good) grace to do sth** to be polite enough to do sth, especially when you have done sth wrong: *He didn't even have the grace to look embarrassed.* **there but for the grace of ˈGod (go I)** (saying) used to say that you could easily have been in the same difficult or unpleasant situation that sb else is in **with (a) bad ˈgrace** in an unwilling and/or rude way: *He handed over the money with typical bad grace.* **with (a) good ˈgrace** in a willing and pleasant way: *You must learn to accept defeat with good grace.* ⇨ more at AIR *n.*, STATE *n.*, YEAR
■ verb (formal) **1** ~ sth to make sth more attractive; to decorate sth: *The table had once graced a duke's drawing room.* **2** to bring honour to sb/sth; to be kind enough to attend or take part in sth: ~ sb/sth *She is one of the finest players ever to have graced the game.* ◊ ~ sb/sth with sth (ironic) *Will you be gracing us with your presence tonight?*

**ˌgrace and ˈfavour** adj. [only before noun] (BrE) used to describe a house or flat that a king, queen or government has allowed sb to use

**grace·ful** /ˈgreɪsfl/ adj. **1** moving in an attractive way that shows control; having a smooth, attractive form: *The dancers were all tall and graceful.* ◊ *He gave a graceful bow to the audience.* ◊ *the graceful curves of the hills* **2** polite and kind in your behaviour, especially in a difficult situation: *His father had always taught him to be graceful in defeat.*
▶ **grace·ful·ly** /-fəli/ adv.: *The cathedral's white towers climb gracefully into the sky.* ◊ *I think we should just give in gracefully.* **grace·ful·ness** noun [U]

**grace·less** /ˈgreɪsləs/ adj. **1** not knowing how to be polite and pleasant to other people: *a graceless, angry young man* **2** not pleasant or attractive to look at: *the graceless architecture of the 1960s* **3** moving in a way that is not smooth, attractive or easy: *She swam with a graceless stroke.* OPP graceful ▶ **grace·less·ly** adv.

**ˈgrace note** noun (music) an extra note that is not a necessary part of a tune but that is played before one of the notes of the tune as decoration

**gra·cious** /ˈgreɪʃəs/ adj. **1** (of people or behaviour) kind, polite and generous, especially to sb of a lower social position: *a gracious smile* ◊ *He has not yet learned how to be gracious in defeat.* **2** [usually before noun] showing the comfort and easy way of life that wealth can bring: *gracious living* **3** [only before noun] (BrE, formal) used as a very polite word for royal people or their actions: *her gracious Majesty the Queen* **4** ~ (to sb) (of God) being kind and showing MERCY: *a gracious act of God* **5** (becoming old-fashioned) used for expressing surprise: *Goodness gracious!* ◊ *'I hope you didn't mind my phoning you.' 'Good gracious, no, of course not.'* ▶ **gra·cious·ly** adv.: *She graciously accepted our invitation.* **gra·cious·ness** noun [U]

**grad** /græd/ noun (informal, especially NAmE) = GRADUATE: *I'm 22 and a recent college grad.* ◊ *an ambitious grad student from Harvard*

**grad·ation** /grəˈdeɪʃn/ noun **1** [C, U] (formal) any of the small changes or levels that sth is divided into; the

# grade

process or result of sth changing gradually: *gradations of colour* ◇ *gradation in size* **2** (*also* **gradu‧ation**) [C] a mark showing a division on a scale: *the gradations on a thermometer*

**grade** 🔑 **B1** /greɪd/ *noun, verb*
- *noun* **1** 🔑 **B1** a mark given in an exam or for a piece of school work: (*BrE*) *She got good grades in her exams.* ◇ (*NAmE*) *She got good grades on her exams.* ◇ *70 per cent of students achieved Grade C or above.* ⇨ WORDFINDER NOTE at EXAM **2** (in the US school system) one of the levels in a school with children of similar age: *Sam is in (the) second grade.* ⇨ see also STANDARD GRADE **3** the quality of a particular product or material: *All the materials used were of the highest grade.* ⇨ see also HIGH-GRADE, LOW-GRADE **4** a level of ability or rank that sb has in an organization: *salary/pay grades* (= levels of pay) ◇ *She's still only on a secretarial grade.* **5** (*specialist*) how serious an illness is: *low/high grade fever* **6** (*especially NAmE*) = GRADIENT (1) **7** (*BrE*) a level of exam in musical skill
  - **IDM** **make the ˈgrade** (*informal*) to reach the necessary standard; to succeed: *About 10 per cent of trainees fail to make the grade.*
- *verb* **1** 🔑 **B2** (*especially NAmE*) to give a grade to a student or to a piece of their written work: ~ *sb/sth* *I spent all weekend grading papers.* ◇ ~ *sb/sth* + *noun* *The best students are graded A.* ⇨ compare MARK **2** [usually passive] to arrange people or things in groups according to their ability, quality, size, etc.: **be graded (by/according to sth)** *The containers are graded according to size.* ◇ **be graded from … to …** *Eggs are graded from small to extra large.* ◇ *Responses were graded from 1 (very satisfied) to 5 (not at all satisfied).* ◇ **be graded (as) sth** *Ten beaches were graded as acceptable.*

ˈ**grade crossing** *noun* (*NAmE*) = RAILROAD CROSSING

**graded** /ˈɡreɪdɪd/ *adj.* arranged in order or in groups according to difficulty, size, etc: *graded tests for language students* ◇ *graded doses of a drug*

ˈ**grade point average** *noun* [usually sing.] (*abbr.* **GPA**) the average of a student's grades over a period of time in the US education system

**grader** /ˈɡreɪdə(r)/ *noun* (*NAmE*) **1** **first, second,** etc. ~ a student who is in the grade mentioned: *The play is open to all seventh and eighth graders.* **2** (*BrE* **mark‧er**) a person who marks students' work or exam papers

ˈ**grade school** *noun* (*informal*) = ELEMENTARY SCHOOL

**gra‧di‧ent** /ˈɡreɪdiənt/ *noun* **1** (*also* **grade** *especially in NAmE*) a slope on a road or railway; the degree to which the ground slopes: *a steep gradient* ◇ *a hill with a gradient of 1 in 4 (or 25 per cent)* **2** (*specialist*) the rate at which temperature, pressure, etc. changes, or increases and decreases, between one region and another

ˈ**grad‧ing** /ˈɡreɪdɪŋ/ *noun* [U] (*NAmE*) = MARKING (3)

ˈ**grad school** *noun* (*NAmE, informal*) = GRADUATE SCHOOL

**grad‧ual** /ˈɡrædʒuəl/ *adj.* **1** happening slowly over a long period; not sudden: *a gradual change in the climate* ◇ *Recovery from the disease is very gradual.* **OPP** **sudden** **2** (of a slope) not steep

**grad‧ual‧ism** /ˈɡrædʒuəlɪzəm/ *noun* [U] a policy of slow steady change in society rather than sudden change or revolution ▶ **grad‧ual‧ist** *adj., noun*

**grad‧ual‧ly** 🔑 **B1** /ˈɡrædʒuəli/ *adv.* slowly, over a long period of time: *to gradually increase/decrease* ◇ *The weather gradually improved.* ◇ *Gradually, the children began to understand.*

**gradu‧ate** 🔑 **B1** /ˈɡrædʒuət/ *noun, verb*
- *noun* /ˈɡrædʒuət/ (*also informal* **grad** *especially in NAmE*) **1** 🔑 **B1** a person who has a university degree: *job prospects for graduates* ◇ *a university/college graduate* ◇ *an Oxford/a Yale graduate* ◇ ~ *of sth* *a graduate of Oxford/Yale* ◇ *engineering/science graduates* ◇ **in sth** *a graduate in history* ◇ *a graduate student* ◇ (*NAmE*) *graduate programs/degrees/studies* **HELP** In *BrE* **postgraduate** is usually used in these phrases: *postgraduate courses/degrees/studies* **2** 🔑 **B1** (*NAmE*) a person who has completed their school studies: *a high school graduate* ⇨ note at STUDENT
- *verb* /ˈɡrædʒueɪt/ **1** 🔑 **B1** [I, T] to get a degree, especially your first degree, from a university or college: *She taught in France after she graduated.* ◇ ~ **in sth** *Only three students graduated in Czech studies last year.* ◇ ~ **from sth** *She graduated from Harvard this year.* ◇ ~ **with sth** *He graduated with a BA in English in 2018.* ◇ (*NAmE*) *She graduated college last year.* ⇨ WORDFINDER NOTE at UNIVERSITY ⇨ WORDFINDER NOTE at STUDY **2** 🔑 **B1** [I, T] (*NAmE*) to complete a course in education, especially at HIGH SCHOOL: *He flunked math and never graduated.* ◇ ~ **from sth** *Martha graduated from high school two years ago.* ◇ ~ **sth** *Martha graduated high school two years ago.* **3** [T] (*NAmE*) to give a degree, DIPLOMA, etc. to sb: *The college graduated 50 students last year.* **4** [I] ~ **(from sth) to sth** to start doing sth more difficult or important than what you were doing before: *She recently graduated from being a dancer to having a small role in a movie.*

ˈ**graduate asˈsistant** *noun* (*especially NAmE*) a graduate student at a university who is paid to help with teaching or research

**gradu‧ated** /ˈɡrædʒueɪtɪd/ *adj.* **1** divided into groups or levels on a scale: *graduated lessons/tests* **2** (of a container or measure) marked with lines to show measurements **SYN** **calibrate**: *a graduated jar*

**ˈGraduate Manageˈment Adˈmissions Test** ⇨ GMAT

ˈ**graduate school** (*also informal* ˈ**grad school**) (*both NAmE*) *noun* a part of a college or university where you can study for a second or further degree

**gradu‧ation** /ˌɡrædʒuˈeɪʃn/ *noun* **1** [U] the act of successfully completing a university degree, or studies at an American HIGH SCHOOL: *It was my first job after graduation.* **2** [U, C] (*also* **graduˈation ceremony** [C]) a ceremony at which degrees, etc. are officially given out: *graduation day* ◇ *My whole family came to my graduation.* **3** [C] = GRADATION (2): *The graduations are marked on the side of the flask.*

**Graeco-** (*BrE*) (*also* **Greco-** *BrE and NAmE*) /ˈɡriːkəʊ; *NAmE* ˈɡrekoʊ/ *combining form* (in adjectives) Greek

**graf‧fiti** /ɡrəˈfiːti/ *noun* [U, pl.] drawings or writing on a wall, etc. in a public place: *The subway was covered in graffiti.* ◇ *a fashionable graffiti artist*

**graft** /ɡrɑːft; *NAmE* ɡræft/ *noun, verb*
- *noun* **1** [C] a piece cut from a living plant and fixed in a cut made in another plant, so that it grows there; the process or result of doing this **2** [C] a piece of skin, bone, etc. removed from a living body and placed in another part of the body that has been damaged; the process or result of doing this: *a skin graft* ⇨ WORDFINDER NOTE at OPERATION **3** [U] (*BrE, informal*) hard work: *Their success was the result of years of hard graft.* **4** [U] (*especially NAmE*) the use of illegal or unfair methods, especially BRIBERY, to gain advantage in business, politics, etc.; money obtained in this way
- *verb* **1** [T] ~ **sth (onto/to/into sth)** | ~ **sth (on) (from sth)** to take a piece of skin, bone, etc. from a living body and attach it to a damaged part: *newly grafted tissue* ◇ *New skin had to be grafted on from his back.* **2** [T] ~ **sth (onto sth)** to cut a piece from a living plant and attach it to another plant **3** [T] ~ **sth (onto sth)** to make one idea, system, etc. become part of another one: *Old values are being grafted onto a new social class.* **4** [I] (*BrE, informal*) to work hard

ˈ**graham cracker** /ˈɡreɪəm krækə(r); *NAmE also* ˈɡræm/ *noun* (*NAmE*) a slightly sweet RECTANGULAR biscuit made with WHOLEMEAL flour

**grail** /ɡreɪl/ (*also* **the ˌHoly ˈGrail**) *noun* **1** [sing.] the cup or bowl believed to have been used by Jesus Christ before he died, that became a holy thing that people wanted to find **2** [C, usually sing.] a thing that you try very hard to find or achieve, but never will

**grain** 🔑 **B1** /ɡreɪn/ *noun* **1** 🔑 **B1** [U, C] the small hard seeds of food plants such as WHEAT, rice, etc.; a single seed of such a plant: *Russia sold 12 million tons of grain abroad last year.* ◊ *America's grain exports* ◊ *~ of sth a few grains of rice* ⊃ **WORDFINDER NOTE** at CROP ⊃ see also WHOLEGRAIN ⊃ **VISUAL VOCAB** page V8 **2** B2 [C] *~ (of sth)* a small hard piece of particular substances: *a grain of salt/sand/sugar* **3** [C] (used especially in negative sentences) a very small amount SYN **iota**: *There isn't **a grain of truth** in those rumours.* **4** [C] a small unit of weight, equal to 0.00143 of a pound or 0.0648 of a GRAM, used for example for weighing medicines **5** [U, sing.] the natural direction of lines in wood, cloth, etc. or of layers of rock; the pattern of lines that you can see: **along/across the** *~ to cut a piece of wood along/across the grain* ◊ *This wood has a beautiful natural grain.* **6** [U, C] how rough or smooth a surface feels: *wood of coarse/fine grain*

IDM **be/go against the 'grain** to be or do sth different from what is normal or natural: *It really goes against the grain to have to work on a Sunday.* ⊃ more at SALT *n.*

**grained** /greɪnd/ *adj.* (of wood, stone, etc.) **1** having a clear and definite pattern or lines on the surface **2 -grained** having a TEXTURE of the type mentioned: *fine-grained stone*

**'grain elevator** (*also* **elevator**) *noun* (*NAmE*) a tall building used to store grain and that contains equipment to move it

**grainy** /ˈgreɪni/ *adj.* (**grain·i·er, grain·i·est**) **1** (especially of photographs) not having completely clear images because they look as if they are made of a lot of small marks: *The film is shot in grainy black and white.* **2** having a rough surface or containing small bits, seeds, etc: *grainy texture*

**gram** /græm/ *noun* **1** (*BrE also, less frequent* **gramme**) (*abbr.* **g, gm**) a unit for measuring weight. There are 1000 grams in one KILOGRAM. **2 -gram** a thing that is written or drawn: *telegram* ◊ *hologram*

**'gram flour** (*also* **besan** /ˈbeɪsʌn/, **'chickpea flour**) *noun* [U] flour made from CHICKPEAS

**'gram·mar** /ˈgræmə(r)/ *noun* **1** [U] the rules in a language for changing the form of words and joining them into sentences: *the basic rules of grammar* ◊ *English grammar* ⊃ **WORDFINDER NOTE** at LANGUAGE

**WORDFINDER** case, conjugate, gender, inflect, noun, part of speech, singular, subject, tense

**2** [U] a person's knowledge and use of a language: *His grammar is appalling.* ◊ *bad grammar* **3** [C] a book containing a description of the rules of a language: *a French grammar*

**gram·mar·ian** /grəˈmeəriən; *NAmE* -ˈmer-/ *noun* a person who is an expert in the study of grammar

**'grammar school** *noun* **1** (in England, Wales and Northern Ireland, especially in the past) a school for young people between the ages of 11 and 18 who are good at academic subjects **2** (*old-fashioned*) = ELEMENTARY SCHOOL

**gram·mat·ical** /grəˈmætɪkl/ *adj.* **1** connected with the rules of grammar: *a grammatical error* **2** correctly following the rules of grammar: *That sentence is not grammatical.* ▶ **gram·mat·ical·ly** /-kli/ *adv.*: *a grammatically correct sentence*

**gramme** (*BrE*) = GRAM

**Grammy** /ˈɡræmi/ *noun* (*pl.* **Gram·mies** *or* **Grammys**) one of the awards for achievement in the music industry given every year by the US National Academy of Recording Arts and Sciences

**gramo·phone** /ˈɡræməfəʊn/ *noun* (*old-fashioned*) = RECORD PLAYER

**gramps** /græmps/ (*also* **gramp** /græmp/, **grampy** /ˈɡræmpi/) *noun* [sing.] (*NAmE, informal*) grandfather

**gran** /ɡræn/ *noun* (*BrE, informal*) grandmother: *Do you want to go to your gran's?* ◊ *Gran, can I have some more?*

**Gran·ary**™ /ˈɡrænəri/ *adj.* [only before noun] (*BrE*) (of bread) containing whole grains of WHEAT

**gran·ary** /ˈɡrænəri; *NAmE* ˈɡreɪn-, ˈɡræn-/ *noun* (*pl.* **-ies**) a building where grain is stored

689

# grandiose

**grand** ⊕ B2 /grænd/ *adj., noun*

■ *adj.* (**grand·er, grand·est**) **1** B2 impressive and large or important: *It's not a very grand house.* ◊ *The wedding was a very grand occasion.* **2 Grand** [only before noun] used in the names of impressive or very large buildings, etc: *the Grand Canyon* ◊ *We stayed at the Grand Hotel.* **3** B2 needing a lot of effort, money or time to succeed but intended to achieve impressive results: *a **grand plan/strategy/scheme*** ◊ *The gallery had its **grand opening** on 18 January.* ◊ *New Yorkers built their city **on a grand scale**.* **4** used to describe the largest or most important item of its kind: *The film won the **grand prize** at the Berlin Film Festival.* ◊ *Tomorrow is the **grand final** with just 12 contestants left from the hundreds who entered.* **5** (of people) behaving in a proud way because they are rich or from a high social class **6** (*dialect or informal*) very good or great fun; excellent: *I had a grand day out at the seaside.* ◊ *Thanks. That'll be grand!* ◊ *Fred did a grand job of painting the house.* **7 Grand** used in the titles of people of very high social rank: *the Grand Duchess Elena* ⊃ see also GRANDEUR ▶ **grand·ly** *adv.*: *He described himself grandly as a 'landscape architect'.* **'grand·ness** *noun* [U]

IDM **a/the 'grand old 'age (of …)** a great age: *She finally learned to drive at the grand old age of 70.* **a/the 'grand old 'man (of sth)** a man who is respected in a particular profession that he has been involved in for a long time: *James Lovelock, the grand old man of environmental science*

■ *noun* **1** (*pl.* **grand**) (*informal*) $1000; £1000: *It'll cost you five grand!* **2** = GRAND PIANO ⊃ see also BABY GRAND, CONCERT GRAND

**gran·dad** (*also* **grand·dad** *especially in NAmE*) /ˈɡrændæd/ *noun* (*informal*) grandfather

**gran·daddy** (*also* **grand·daddy**) /ˈɡrændædi/ *noun* (*pl.* **-ies**) (*NAmE, informal*) **1** = GRANDFATHER **2 the grandaddy** the first or greatest example of sth

**grand·child** /ˈɡræntʃaɪld/ *noun* (*pl.* **grand·chil·dren**) a child of your son or daughter

**grand·daugh·ter** /ˈɡrændɔːtə(r)/ *noun* a daughter of your son or daughter ⊃ compare GRANDSON

**grand 'duchess** *noun* **1** the wife of a grand duke **2** (in some parts of Europe, especially in the past) a female leader of a small independent state **3** (in Russia in the past) a daughter of the TSAR

**grand 'duke** *noun* **1** (in some parts of Europe, especially in the past) a male leader of a small independent state: *The Grand Duke of Tuscany* **2** (in Russia in the past) a son of the TSAR ⊃ compare ARCHDUKE

**gran·dee** /ɡrænˈdiː/ *noun* **1** (in the past) a Spanish or Portuguese NOBLEMAN of high rank **2** a person of high social rank and importance

**grand·eur** /ˈɡrændʒə(r), -djə(r)/ *noun* [U] **1** the quality of being great and impressive in appearance SYN **splendour**: *the grandeur and simplicity of Roman architecture* ◊ *The hotel had an air of faded grandeur.* **2** the importance or social status that people think they have: *He has a sense of grandeur about him.* ◊ *She is clearly suffering from **delusions of grandeur** (= thinks she is more important than she really is).* ⊃ see also GRAND *adj.*

**grand·father** ⊕ A1 /ˈɡrænfɑːðə(r)/ *noun* the father of your father or mother: *The firm had been founded by his grandfather.* ⊃ see also GRANDAD, GRANDADDY, GRANDPA ⊃ compare GRANDMOTHER

**'grandfather 'clock** *noun* an old-fashioned type of clock in a tall wooden case that stands on the floor ⊃ picture at CLOCK

**grand·ilo·quent** /ɡrænˈdɪləkwənt/ *adj.* (*formal, disapproving*) using long or complicated words in order to impress people SYN **pompous** ▶ **grand·ilo·quence** /-kwəns/ *noun* [U]

**gran·di·ose** /ˈɡrændiəʊs/ *adj.* (*disapproving*) seeming very impressive but too large, complicated, expensive, etc. to be practical or possible: *The grandiose scheme for a*

# grand jury

*journey across the desert came to nothing.* ◊ *a grandiose opera house*

**grand ˈjury** *noun* (*law*) (in the US) a JURY that has to decide whether there is enough evidence against an accused person for a trial in court

**grand·kid** /ˈɡrænkɪd/ *noun* (*NAmE, informal*) a GRANDCHILD: *I have 10 kids and 34 grandkids.*

**grand·ma** /ˈɡrænmɑː/ *noun* (*informal*) grandmother

**grand·mas·ter** /ˌɡrændˈmɑːstə(r)/; *NAmE* -ˈmæs-/ *noun* a CHESS player of the highest standard

**grand·mother** 🔊 **A1** /ˈɡrænmʌðə(r)/ *noun* the mother of your father or mother: *I always loved going to visit my grandmother.* ⇨ see also GRAN, GRANDMA, GRANNY ⇨ compare GRANDFATHER **IDM** see TEACH

**grand ˈopera** *noun* [U, C] OPERA in which everything is sung and there are no spoken parts

**grand·pa** /ˈɡrænpɑː/ *noun* (*informal*) grandfather ⇨ see also GRANDAD

**grand·par·ent** 🔊 **A1** /ˈɡrænpeərənt; *NAmE* -per-/ *noun* [usually pl.] the father or mother of your father or mother: *The children are staying with their grandparents.*

**grand piˈano** (*also* **grand**) *noun* a large piano in which the strings are HORIZONTAL ⇨ compare UPRIGHT PIANO

**Grand Prix** /ˌɡrɒ̃ ˈpriː/; *NAmE* ˌɡrɑː/ *noun* (*pl.* **Grands Prix** /ˌɡrɒ̃ ˈpriː/; *NAmE* ˌɡrɑː/) one of a series of important international races for racing cars or motorcycles

**grand ˈslam** *noun* **1 Grand Slam** a set of very important competitions in a particular sport in the same year in tennis, golf or rugby; one of the individual competitions that make up a Grand Slam: *a Grand Slam tournament/cup/title* **2** the winning of every part of a sports contest or all the main contests in a year for a particular sport: *Will France win the grand slam this year* (= in rugby)? **3** (*also* ˌgrand slam ˈhome ˈrun) (in baseball) a HOME RUN that is worth four points **4** (in card games, especially BRIDGE) the winning of all the TRICKS in a single game

**grand·son** /ˈɡrænsʌn/ *noun* a son of your son or daughter ⇨ compare GRANDDAUGHTER

**grand·stand** /ˈɡrænstænd/ *noun* the main STAND (= a large covered structure with rows of seats) at a sports event with the best view: *The game was played to a packed grandstand.* ◊ *From her house, we had a grandstand view* (= very good view) *of the celebrations.*

**grandstand ˈfinish** *noun* (*BrE*) (in sport) a close or exciting finish to a race or competition

**grand·stand·ing** /ˈɡrænstændɪŋ/ *noun* [U] (especially in business, politics, etc.) the fact of behaving or speaking in a way that is intended to make people impressed in order to gain some advantage for yourself

**grand ˈtheft** *noun* [U] (*law*) the crime of stealing a lot of money or sth very valuable ⇨ compare PETTY (1)

**grand ˈtotal** *noun* the final total when a number of other totals have been added together

**grand ˈtour** *noun* **1** (*often humorous*) a visit around a building or house in order to show it to sb: *Steve took us on a grand tour of the house and garden.* **2** (*also* **Grand Tour**) a visit to the main cities of Europe made by rich young British or American people as part of their education in the past

**grand ˌunified ˈtheory** *noun* (*physics*) a single theory that tries to explain all the behaviour of SUBATOMIC PARTICLES

**grange** /ɡreɪndʒ/ *noun* (often as part of a name) a country house with farm buildings: *Thrushcross Grange*

**gran·ita** /ɡrəˈniːtə/ *noun* [U, C] (*from Italian*) a drink or sweet dish made with CRUSHED ice (= that has been broken into very small pieces)

**gran·ite** /ˈɡrænɪt/ *noun* [U] a type of hard grey stone, often used in building

**granny** (*also less frequent* **gran·nie**) /ˈɡræni/ *noun* (*pl.* **-ies**) (*informal*) grandmother ⇨ see also GRANDMA ▶ **granny** (*also less frequent* **gran·nie**) *adj.*: *a pair of granny glasses*

**ˈgranny flat** *noun* (*BrE*) (*informal*) a set of rooms for an old person, especially in a relative's house

**gran·ola** /ɡrəˈnəʊlə/ *noun, adj.*
■ *noun* [U] (*especially NAmE*) a type of breakfast CEREAL made of grains, nuts, etc. that have been TOASTED
■ *adj.* [only before noun] (*NAmE, informal, usually disapproving*) (of a person) eating healthy food, supporting the protection of the environment and having LIBERAL views

**grant** 🔊 **B2** /ɡrɑːnt; *NAmE* ɡrænt/ *verb, noun*
■ *verb* **1** 🔊 **B2** [often passive] to agree to give sb what they ask for, especially formal or legal permission to do sth: **~ sth** *My request was granted.* ◊ **~ sb sth** *I was granted permission to visit the palace.* ◊ *She was granted a divorce.* ◊ *The court granted him leave to appeal.* ◊ **~ sth to sb/sth** *These lands had been granted to the family in perpetuity.* **2** to admit to sb that sth is true, although you may not like or agree with it: **~ sb** *She's a smart woman, I grant you, but she's no genius.* ◊ **~ (sb) (that) …** *I grant you (that) it looks good, but it's not exactly practical.*
**IDM** ˌtake it for ˈgranted (that …) to believe sth is true without first making sure that it is: *I just took it for granted that he'd always be around.* ˌtake sb/sth for ˈgranted to be so used to sb/sth that you do not recognize their true value any more and do not show that you are grateful: *Her husband was always there and she just took him for granted.* ◊ *We take having an endless supply of clean water for granted.*
■ *noun* 🔊 **B2** a sum of money that is given by the government or by another organization to be used for a particular purpose: *government/federal grants* ◊ *There is a lot of competition for research grants.* ◊ *to apply for a grant* ◊ *a grant application* ◊ **~ to sb/sth** *The money is used for small grants to deserving organizations.* ◊ **~ from sb/sth** *The study was supported by a grant from the National Science Foundation.* ◊ **~ to do sth** *The school has received a large grant to improve its buildings.*

**ˈgrant aid** *noun* [U] (*BrE*) money given by the government to organizations or local areas ▶ **ˌgrant-ˈaided** *adj.*: *a grant-aided school*

**grant·ed** /ˈɡrɑːntɪd; *NAmE* ˈɡræn-/ *adv., conj.*
■ *adv.* used to show that you accept that sth is true, often before you make another statement about it: 'You could have done more to help.' 'Granted.' ◊ *Granted, it's not the most pleasant of jobs but it has to be done.*
■ *conj.* **~ (that …)** because of the fact that: *Granted that it is a simple test to perform, it should be easy to get results quickly.*

**ˌgrant-in-ˈaid** *noun* [C, U] (*pl.* **grants-in-aid**) a sum of money given to a local government or an institution, or to a particular person to allow them to study sth

**granu·lar** /ˈɡrænjələ(r)/ *adj.* consisting of small granules; looking or feeling like a collection of granules

**ˌgranulated ˈsugar** /ˌɡrænjuleɪtɪd ˈʃʊɡə(r)/ *noun* [U] white sugar in the form of small grains ⇨ compare CASTER SUGAR

**gran·ule** /ˈɡrænjuːl/ *noun* [usually pl.] a small, hard piece of sth; a small grain: *instant coffee granules*

**grape** /ɡreɪp/ *noun* a small green or purple fruit that grows in bunches on a climbing plant (called a VINE). Wine is made from grapes: *a bunch of grapes* ◊ *black/white grapes* (= grapes that are actually purple/green in colour) ⇨ VISUAL VOCAB page V4 **IDM** see SOUR *adj.*

**grape·fruit** /ˈɡreɪpfruːt/ *noun* (*pl.* **grape·fruit** *or* **grape·fruits**) [C, U] a large round yellow CITRUS fruit with juice that has a slightly sharp bitter taste ⇨ VISUAL VOCAB page V4

**ˈgrape·shot** /ˈɡreɪpʃɒt/; *NAmE* -ʃɑːt/ *noun* [U] a number of small iron balls that are fired together from a CANNON

**grape·vine** /ˈɡreɪpvaɪn/ *noun* a climbing plant that produces grapes

**IDM** **on/through the 'grapevine** by talking in an informal way to other people: *I heard on the grapevine that you're leaving.*

**graph** /grɑːf; NAmE græf/ *noun* a diagram consisting of a line or lines, showing how two or more sets of numbers are related to each other: *Plot a graph of height against age.* ◊ *The graph shows how house prices have risen since the 1980s.* ⊃ see also LINE GRAPH ⊃ LANGUAGE BANK at ILLUSTRATE

**graph·eme** /'græfiːm/ *noun* (*linguistics*) any one of the set of smallest units in a writing system that represents a speech sound and can make the difference between one word and another. In English, the 's' in *sip* and the 'sh' in *ship* represent two different graphemes. ⊃ compare PHONEME

**graph·ene** /'græfiːn/ *noun* [U] a very strong, light form of CARBON

**graph·ic** ?+ B2 /'græfɪk/ *adj., noun*
■ *adj.* 1 ?+ B2 [only before noun] connected with drawings and design, especially in the production of books, magazines, websites, etc: *graphic design* ◊ *a graphic designer* 2 ?+ C1 (of descriptions, etc.) very clear and full of details, especially about sth unpleasant **SYN** **vivid**: *a graphic account/description* of a battle ◊ *He kept telling us about his operation, in the most graphic detail.*
■ *noun* a diagram or picture, especially one that appears on a computer screen or in a newspaper or book ⊃ compare GRAPHICS

**graph·ic·al** /'græfɪkl/ *adj.* 1 [only before noun] connected with art or computer graphics: *The system uses an impressive graphical interface.* 2 in the form of a diagram or graph: *a graphical presentation of results*

**graph·ic·al·ly** /'græfɪkli/ *adv.* 1 in the form of drawings or diagrams: *This data is shown graphically on the opposite page.* 2 very clearly and in great detail **SYN** **vividly**: *The murders are graphically described in the article.*

**graphic 'arts** *noun* [U] art based on the use of lines and SHADING, rather than THREE-DIMENSIONAL work or the use of colour ▶ **graphic 'artist** *noun*

**graphic e'qualizer** *noun* (*specialist*) an electronic device or computer program that allows you to control the strength and quality of particular sound frequencies separately

**graphic 'novel** *noun* a novel in the form of a COMIC STRIP

**graph·ics** ?+ B2 /'græfɪks/ *noun* 1 ?+ B2 [pl.] designs, drawings or pictures that are used especially in the production of books, magazines, websites, etc: *Text and graphics are prepared separately and then combined.* 2 ?+ B2 [U] the activity of making these designs, drawings or pictures or the use of these images: *expertise in computer graphics*

**'graphics card** *noun* (*computing*) a CIRCUIT BOARD that allows a computer to show images on its screen

**graph·ite** /'græfaɪt/ *noun* [U] a soft black mineral that is a form of CARBON. Graphite is used to make pencils, to LUBRICATE machines and in nuclear REACTORS.

**'graph paper** *noun* [U] paper with small squares of equal size printed on it, used for drawing GRAPHS and other diagrams

**-graphy** /ɡrəfi/ *combining form* (in nouns) 1 a type of art or science: *choreography* ◊ *geography* 2 a method of producing images: *radiography* 3 a form of writing or drawing: *calligraphy* ◊ *biography*

**grappa** /'græpə; NAmE 'grɑːpə/ *noun* [U, C] a strong alcoholic drink from Italy, made from GRAPES

**grap·ple** /'græpl/ *verb* 1 [I, T] to take a strong hold of sb/sth and struggle with them: *~(with sb/sth) Passers-by grappled with the man after the attack.* ◊ *~sb/sth (+ adv./prep.) They managed to grapple him to the ground.* 2 [I] to try hard to find a solution to a problem: *~with sth The new government has yet to grapple with the problem of air pollution.* ◊ *~ to do sth I was grappling to find an answer to his question.*

# grass snake

**'grappling iron** (*also* **'grappling hook**) *noun* a tool with several HOOKS attached to a long rope, used for dragging sth along or holding a boat still

**grasp** ?+ C1 /ɡrɑːsp; NAmE ɡræsp/ *verb, noun*
■ *verb* 1 ?+ C1 *~sb/sth* to take a strong hold of sb/sth **SYN** **grip**: *He grasped my hand and shook it warmly.* ◊ *Kay grasped him by the wrist.* ⊃ SYNONYMS at HOLD 2 ?+ C1 to understand sth completely: *~sth They failed to grasp the importance of his words.* ◊ *~ how, why, etc... She was unable to grasp how to do it.* ◊ *~ that... It took him some time to grasp that he was now a public figure.* ⊃ SYNONYMS at UNDERSTAND *~ a chance/an opportunity* to take an opportunity without hesitating and use it: *I grasped the opportunity to work abroad.*
**IDM** **grasp the 'nettle** (*BrE*) to deal with a difficult situation without hesitating ⊃ more at STRAW
**PHRV** **'grasp at sth** 1 to try to take hold of sth in your hands: *She grasped at his coat as he rushed past her.* 2 to try to take an opportunity
■ *noun* [usually sing.] 1 ?+ C1 a strong hold of sb/sth or control over sb/sth **SYN** **grip**: *I grabbed him, but he slipped from my grasp.* ◊ *She felt a firm grasp on her arm.* ◊ *Don't let the situation escape from your grasp.* 2 ?+ C1 a person's understanding of a subject or of difficult facts: *He has a good grasp of German grammar.* ◊ *beyond sb's ~ These complex formulae are beyond the grasp of the average pupil.* 3 *within sb's ~* the ability to get or achieve sth: *Success was within her grasp.*

**grasp·ing** /'ɡrɑːspɪŋ; NAmE 'ɡræs-/ *adj.* (*disapproving*) always trying to get money, possessions, power, etc. for yourself **SYN** **greedy**: *a grasping landlord*

**grass** ⓘ A2 /ɡrɑːs; NAmE ɡræs/ *noun, verb*
■ *noun* 1 ?+ A2 [U] a common wild plant with narrow green leaves and STEMS that are eaten by cows, horses, sheep, etc: *a blade of grass* ◊ *The dry grass caught fire.* 2 [C] any type of grass: *ornamental grasses* ⊃ see also LEMONGRASS 3 ?+ A2 [sing., U] (*usually* **the grass**) an area of ground covered with grass: *to cut/mow the grass* ◊ *on the ~ Don't walk on the grass.* ◊ *Keep off the grass.* (= on a sign) ◊ *on ~ He plays better on grass* (= on a grass court, when playing tennis). 4 [U] (*informal*) MARIJUANA 5 [C] (*BrE, informal, usually disapproving*) a person, usually a criminal, who tells the police about sb's criminal activities and plans ⊃ compare SUPERGRASS ⊃ see also CUTTING GRASS
**IDM** **the grass is (always) greener on the other side (of the fence)** (*saying*) said about people who never seem happy with what they have and always think they could be happier in a different place or situation **not let the grass grow under your feet** to not delay in getting things done **put sb out to 'grass** (*informal*) to force sb to stop doing their job, especially because they are old ⊃ more at KICK *v.*, SNAKE *n.*
■ *verb* [I] *~(on sb)* (*also* **grass sb ↔ up**) (*both BrE, informal*) to tell the police about sb's criminal activities
**PHRV** **grass sth ↔ over** to cover an area with grass

**grass 'court** *noun* a tennis COURT with a grass surface

**'grass-cutter** /'ɡrɑːskʌtə(r); NAmE 'ɡræs-/ (*also* **cutting grass**) *noun* (*WAfrE*) a CANE RAT (= type of large RODENT) that is used for food

**grassed** /ɡrɑːst; NAmE ɡræst/ *adj.* covered with grass

**'grass·hop·per** /'ɡrɑːshɒpə(r); NAmE 'ɡræshɑːp-/ *noun* an insect with long back legs, that can jump very high and that makes a sound with its legs ⊃ VISUAL VOCAB page V3
**IDM** see KNEE-HIGH

**'grass·land** /'ɡrɑːslænd; NAmE 'ɡræs-/ *noun* [U] (*also* **grasslands** [pl.]) a large area of open land covered with wild grass

**'grass·roots** /'ɡrɑːsruːts; NAmE 'ɡræs-/ *noun* [pl.] ordinary people in society or in an organization, rather than the leaders or people who make decisions: *the grassroots of the party* ◊ *We need support at grassroots level.*

**'grass skirt** *noun* a skirt made of long grass, worn by dancers in the Pacific islands

**'grass snake** *noun* a small snake that is not dangerous

# grass widow

**grass ˈwidow** *noun* a woman whose husband is away from home for long periods of time

**grassy** /ˈgrɑːsi; *NAmE* ˈgræsi/ *adj.* (**grass·i·er**, **grass·i·est**) covered with grass

**grate** /greɪt/ *noun*, *verb*
- *noun* **1** a metal frame for holding the wood or coal in a FIREPLACE **2** (also **sewer grate**) (*both US*) (*BrE* **drain**) a frame of metal bars over the opening to a DRAIN in the ground ⊃ see also GRATING *noun*
- *verb* **1** [T] ~ **sth** to rub food against a GRATER in order to cut it into small pieces: *grated apple/carrot/cheese, etc.* **2** [I] to annoy sb: ~ **(on sb)** *Her voice really grates on me.* ◊ ~ **(with sb)** *It grated with him when people implied he wasn't really British.* **3** [I, T] when two hard surfaces **grate** as they rub together, they make a sharp unpleasant sound; sb can also make one thing **grate** against another: *The rusty hinges grated as the gate swung back.* ◊ ~ **sth (+ adv./prep.)** *He grated his knife across the plate.*

▼ HOMOPHONES

**grate** • **great** /greɪt/
- **grate** *verb*: *Grate the apples and carrots and add to the mixture.*
- **grate** *noun*: *A small fire was burning in the grate.*
- **great** *adj.*: *She is a young player with great potential.*

**grate·ful** 🔊 B1
/ˈgreɪtfl/ *adj.* **1** B1 feeling or showing thanks because sb has done sth kind for you or has done as you asked: ~ **(to sb) (for sth)** *I am extremely grateful to all the teachers for their help.* ◊ ~ **to do sth** *She seems to think I should be grateful to have a job at all.* ◊ ~ **(that …)** *He was grateful that she didn't tell his parents about the incident.* ◊ *Grateful thanks are due to the following people for their help …* ◊ *Kate gave him a grateful smile.* ▶ EXPRESS YOURSELF at THANK **2** 🔊 B1 used to make a request, especially in a letter or in a formal situation: *I would be grateful if you could send the completed form back as soon as possible.* ◊ ~ **for sth** *We would be grateful for any information you can give us.* ▶ **grate·ful·ly** /-fəli/ *adv.*: *He nodded gratefully.* ◊ *All donations will be gratefully received.* IDM see SMALL *adj.*

WORD FAMILY
**grateful** *adj.*
(≠ ungrateful)
**gratefully** *adv.*
**gratitude** *noun*
(≠ ingratitude)

**grater** /ˈgreɪtə(r)/ *noun* a kitchen UTENSIL (= a tool) with a rough surface, used for GRATING food into very small pieces: *a cheese/nutmeg grater*

**grat·ifi·ca·tion** /ˌgrætɪfɪˈkeɪʃn/ *noun* [U, C] (*formal*) the state of feeling pleasure when sth goes well for you or when your desires are satisfied; sth that gives you pleasure SYN **satisfaction**: *sexual gratification* ◊ *A feed will usually provide instant gratification to a crying baby.*

**grat·ify** /ˈgrætɪfaɪ/ *verb* (**grati·fies**, **grati·fy·ing**, **grati·fied**, **grati·fied**) **1** (*formal*) to please or satisfy sb: *it gratifies sb to do sth It gratified him to think that it was all his work.* ◊ ~ **sth** *I was gratified by their invitation.* **2** (*formal*) to satisfy a wish, need, etc: *He only gave his consent in order to gratify her wishes.* ▶ **grati·fied** *adj.* [not usually before noun]: ~ **(at sth)** | ~ **(to find, hear, see, etc.)** *She was gratified to find that they had followed her advice.*

**grati·fy·ing** /ˈgrætɪfaɪɪŋ/ *adj.* (*formal*) giving pleasure and making you feel satisfied: *It is gratifying to see such good results.* ⊃ SYNONYMS at SATISFYING ▶ **grati·fy·ing·ly** *adv.*

**gra·tin** /ˈgrætæn; *NAmE* -tn/ *noun* (*from French*) a cooked dish that is covered with a layer of cheese or BREADCRUMBS

**grat·ing** /ˈgreɪtɪŋ/ *noun*, *adj.*
- *noun* a flat frame with metal bars across it, used to cover a window, a hole in the ground, etc. ⊃ see also GRATE *noun*
- *adj.* (of a sound or sb talking) unpleasant or annoying to listen to

**gra·tis** /ˈgrætɪs; *BrE also* ˈgrɑːt-/ *adv.* done or given without having to be paid for SYN **free**: *I knew his help wouldn't be given gratis.* ▶ **gra·tis** *adj.*: *a gratis copy of a book*

**grati·tude** /ˈgrætɪtjuːd; *NAmE* -tuːd/ *noun* [U] the feeling of being grateful and wanting to express your thanks: *a deep sense of gratitude* ◊ ~ **with** ~ *He smiled at them with gratitude.* ◊ ~ **(to sb) (for sth)** *I would like to express my gratitude to everyone for their hard work.* ◊ ~ **in ~ for sth** *She was presented with the gift in gratitude for her long service.* ◊ *I owe you a great debt of gratitude* (= feel extremely grateful). OPP **ingratitude**

**gra·tuit·ous** /grəˈtjuːɪtəs; *NAmE* -ˈtuː-/ *adj.* (*disapproving*) done without any good reason or purpose and often having harmful effects SYN **unnecessary**: *gratuitous violence on television* ▶ **gra·tuit·ous·ly** *adv.*

**gra·tu·ity** /grəˈtjuːəti; *NAmE* -ˈtuː-/ *noun* (*pl.* -**ies**) **1** (*formal*) money that you give to sb who has provided a service for you SYN **tip 2** (*BrE*) money that is given to employees when they leave their job

**grave**[1] 🔊+ C1 /greɪv/ *noun*, *adj.* ⊃ see also GRAVE[2]
- *noun* **1** 🔊+ C1 a place in the ground where a dead person is buried: *We visited Grandma's grave.* ◊ **in a ~** *The plague victims were buried in a mass grave.* **2** 🔊+ C1 [sing.] (*often* **the grave**) (*usually literary*) a way of referring to death or a person's death: *Is there life beyond the grave* (= life after death)*?* ◊ *He followed her to the grave* (= died soon after her)*.* ◊ *She smoked herself into an early grave* (= died young as a result of smoking)*.* ⊃ WORDFINDER NOTE at DIE IDM **turn in his / her ˈgrave** (*BrE*) (*NAmE also* **roll (over) in his / her ˈgrave**) (of a person who is dead) likely to be very shocked or angry: *My father would turn in his grave if he knew.* ⊃ more at CRADLE *n.*, DIG *v.*, FOOT *n.*
- *adj.* (**graver**, **grav·est**) (*formal*) **1** 🔊+ C1 (of situations, feelings, etc.) very serious and important; giving you a reason to feel worried: *The police have expressed grave concern about the missing child's safety.* ◊ *The consequences will be very grave if nothing is done.* ◊ *We were in grave danger.* **2** (of people) serious in manner, as if sth sad or important has just happened: *He looked very grave as he entered the room.* ⊃ see also GRAVITY ⊃ SYNONYMS at SERIOUS ▶ **grave·ly** *adv.*: *She is gravely ill.* ◊ *Local people are gravely concerned.* ◊ *He nodded gravely as I poured out my troubles.*

**grave**[2] /grɑːv/ (*also* ˌgrave ˈaccent) *noun* a mark placed over a vowel in some languages to show how it should be pronounced, as over the *e* in the French word *père* ⊃ compare ACUTE ACCENT, CIRCUMFLEX, TILDE, UMLAUT ⊃ see also GRAVE[1]

**grave·dig·ger** /ˈgreɪvdɪgə(r)/ *noun* a person whose job is to dig graves

**gravel** /ˈgrævl/ *noun* [U] small stones, often used to make the surface of paths and roads: *a gravel path* ◊ *a gravel pit* (= a place where gravel is taken from the ground)

**grav·elled** (*US* **grav·eled**) /ˈgrævld/ *adj.* (of a road, etc.) covered with gravel

**grav·el·ly** /ˈgrævəli/ *adj.* **1** full of or containing many small stones: *a dry gravelly soil* **2** (of a voice) deep and with a rough sound

**gra·ven image** /ˌgreɪvn ˈɪmɪdʒ/ *noun* (*disapproving*) a statue or image that people WORSHIP as a god or as if it were a god

**grave·side** /ˈgreɪvsaɪd/ *noun* the area around the edge of a GRAVE: *a graveside service*

**grave·stone** /ˈgreɪvstəʊn/ *noun* a stone that is put on a GRAVE, showing the name, etc. of the person buried there SYN **headstone** ⊃ compare TOMBSTONE

**grave·yard** /ˈgreɪvjɑːd; *NAmE* -jɑːrd/ *noun* **1** an area of land, often near a church, where people are buried ⊃ compare CEMETERY, CHURCHYARD **2** a place where things or people that are not wanted are sent or left

**ˈgraveyard shift** *noun* a period of time working at night or in the very early morning

**gravid** /ˈgrævɪd/ *adj.* (*specialist*) pregnant

**grav·itas** /ˈɡrævɪtɑːs, -tæs/ noun [U] (formal) the quality of being serious SYN **seriousness**: *a book of extraordinary gravitas*

**gravi·tate** /ˈɡrævɪteɪt/ verb (formal)
PHRV **ˈgravitate to/toward(s) sb/sth** to move towards sb/sth that you are attracted to: *Many young people gravitate to the cities in search of work.*

**gravi·ta·tion** /ˌɡrævɪˈteɪʃn/ noun [U] (physics) a force of attraction that causes objects to move towards each other

**gravi·ta·tion·al** /ˌɡrævɪˈteɪʃənl/ adj. connected with or caused by the force of gravity: *a gravitational field* ◊ *the gravitational pull of the moon*

**grav·ity** ⓘ+ 🅒🅘 /ˈɡrævəti/ noun [U] **1** ⓘ+ 🅒🅘 (abbr. **g**) the force that attracts objects in space towards each other, and that on the earth pulls them towards the centre of the planet, so that things fall to the ground when they are dropped: *Newton's law of gravity* ⓓ see also CENTRE OF GRAVITY, SPECIFIC GRAVITY, ZERO GRAVITY ⓦ WORDFINDER NOTE at PHYSICS **2** ⓘ+ 🅒🅘 (formal) extreme importance and a cause for worry SYN **seriousness**: *I don't think you realise the gravity of the situation.* ◊ *Punishment varies according to the gravity of the offence.* **3** (formal) serious behaviour, speech or appearance: *They were asked to behave with the gravity that was appropriate in a court of law.* ⓓ see also GRAVE¹ adj.

**gravy** /ˈɡreɪvi/ noun (pl. **-ies**) **1** [U, C] a brown sauce made by adding flour to the juices that come out of meat while it is cooking **2** [U] (NAmE, informal) something, especially money, that is obtained when you do not expect it

**ˈgravy train** noun (informal) a situation where people seem to be making a lot of money without much effort

**gray** (US) = GREY
**ˈgray·beard** (US) = GREYBEARD
**gray·ish** (US) = GREYISH
**ˈgray·scale** (US) = GREYSCALE

**graze** /ɡreɪz/ verb, noun
■ verb **1** [I, T] (of cows, sheep, etc.) to eat grass that is growing in a field: *There were cows grazing beside the river.* ◊ *~ on sth The horses were grazing on the lush grass.* ◊ *~ sth The field had been grazed by sheep.* ⓦ WORDFINDER NOTE at FARM **2** [T] *~ sth* to put cows, sheep, etc. in a field so that they can eat the grass there: *The land is used by local people to graze their animals.* **3** [I] *~ (on sth)* (informal) to eat small amounts of food many times during the day, often while doing other things, instead of eating three meals: *I have this really bad habit of grazing on junk food.* **4** [T] *~ sth (on sth)* to break the surface of your skin by rubbing it against sth rough: *I fell and grazed my knee.* **5** [T] *~ sth* to touch sth lightly while passing it: *The bullet grazed his cheek.*
■ noun a small injury where the surface of the skin has been slightly broken by rubbing against sth: *Adam walked away from the crash with just cuts and grazes.*

**gra·zier** /ˈɡreɪziə(r); NAmE ˈɡreɪʒər/ noun a farmer who keeps animals that eat grass

**graz·ing** /ˈɡreɪzɪŋ/ noun [U] land with grass that cows, sheep, etc. can eat

**GRE**™ /ˌdʒiː ɑːr ˈiː/ abbr. Graduate Record Examination (an examination taken by students who want to study for a further degree in the US)

**grease** /ɡriːs/ noun, verb
■ noun [U] **1** any thick OILY substance, especially one that is used to make machines run smoothly: *Grease marks can be removed with liquid detergent.* ◊ *Her hands were covered with oil and grease.* ◊ *the grease in his hair* ⓓ see also ELBOW GREASE **2** animal fat that has been made softer by cooking or heating: *plates covered with grease*
■ verb *~ sth* to rub grease or fat on sth: *to grease a cake tin/pan*
IDM **grease sb's ˈpalm** (old-fashioned, informal) to give sb money in order to persuade them to do sth dishonest SYN **bribe** **grease the ˈwheels** (NAmE) (BrE **oil the ˈwheels**) to help sth to happen easily and without problems, especially in business or politics

**ˈgrease·paint** /ˈɡriːspeɪnt/ noun [U] a thick substance used by actors as MAKE-UP

**ˌgrease·proof ˈpaper** /ˌɡriːspruːf ˈpeɪpə(r)/ (BrE) noun [U] paper that does not let GREASE, oil, etc. pass through it, used in cooking and for wrapping food in ⓓ compare WAXED PAPER

**greasy** /ˈɡriːsi, ˈɡriːzi/ adj. (**greas·ier**, **greasi·est**) **1** covered in a lot of GREASE or oil: *greasy fingers/marks/overalls* **2** (disapproving) (of food) cooked with too much oil or fat: *greasy chips* ⓓ WORDFINDER NOTE at CRISP **3** (disapproving) (of hair or skin) producing too much natural oil: *long greasy hair* **4** (informal, disapproving) (of people or their behaviour) friendly in a way that does not seem sincere SYN **smarmy**
IDM **the greasy ˈpole** (informal) used to refer to the difficult way to the top of a profession

**ˌgreasy ˈspoon** noun (informal, often disapproving) a small cheap cafe or restaurant that serves greasy fried food

**great** ⓘ 🅐🅘 /ɡreɪt/ adj., noun, adv.
■ adj. (**great·er**, **great·est**)
• GOOD **1** ⓘ 🅐🅘 (informal) very good or pleasant: *He's a great bloke.* ◊ *What a great goal!* ◊ *We had a great time in Madrid.* ◊ *You should have come along. It was great fun.* ◊ *You've done a great job.* ◊ *I think that's a great idea.* ◊ *it is~to do sth It's great to see you again.* ◊ *~ with sb/sth He's great with the kids.* ◊ *'I'll pick you up at seven.' 'That'll be great, thanks.'* ◊ (ironic) *Oh great, they left without us.*
• LARGE **2** ⓘ 🅐🅘 much more than average in degree or quantity: *a matter of great importance* ◊ *The concert had been a great success.* ◊ *Her death was a great shock to us all.* ◊ *Take great care of it.* ◊ *You've been a great help.* ◊ (ironic) *You've been a great help, I must say* (= no help at all). ◊ *We are all to a great extent the products of our culture.* ⓓ HOMOPHONES at GRATE **3** ⓘ 🅐🅘 [usually before noun] very large; much bigger than average in size or quantity: *A great crowd had gathered.* ◊ *People were arriving in great numbers.* ◊ *He must have fallen from a great height.* ◊ *She lived to a great age.* **4** ⓘ 🅐🅘 [only before noun] (informal) used to emphasize an adjective of size or quality: *There was a great big pile of books on the table.* ⓓ note at BIG
• ADMIRED **5** ⓘ 🅐🅘 extremely good in ability or quality and therefore admired by many people: *the greatest chess player of all time* ◊ *Sherlock Holmes, the great detective* ◊ *Great art has the power to change lives.* ◊ *This represents a great achievement.*
• IMPORTANT/IMPRESSIVE **6** ⓘ 🅐🅘 [only before noun] important and impressive: *The wedding was a great occasion.* ◊ *This is a great day for the city of Chicago.* ◊ *The great thing is to get it done quickly.* ◊ *One great advantage of this metal is that it doesn't rust.*
• WITH INFLUENCE **7** ⓘ 🅐🅘 having high status or a lot of influence: *the great powers* (= important and powerful countries) ◊ *We can make this country great again.* ◊ *Alexander the Great*
• IN GOOD HEALTH **8** ⓘ 🅐🅘 in a very good state of physical or mental health: *She seemed in great spirits* (= very cheerful). ◊ *I feel great today.* ◊ *Everyone's in great form.*
• SKILLED **9** [not usually before noun] *~at (doing) sth* (informal) able to do sth well: *She's great at chess.*
• USEFUL **10** *~for (doing) sth* (informal) very suitable or useful for sth: *This gadget's great for opening jars.*
• FOR EMPHASIS **11** [only before noun] used when you are emphasizing a particular description of sb/sth: *We are great friends.* ◊ *I've never been a great reader* (= I do not read much).
• FAMILY **12 great-** added to words for family members to show a further stage in relationship: *my great-aunt* (= my father's or mother's aunt) ◊ *her great-grandson* (= the grandson of her son or daughter) ◊ *my great-great-grandfather* (= the grandfather of my grandfather)
• LARGER ANIMALS/PLANTS **13** [only before noun] used in the names of animals or plants that are larger than similar kinds: *the great tit*
• CITY NAME **14 Greater** used with the name of a city to describe an area that includes the centre of the city and

# great ape

a large area all round it: *Greater London* ▶ **great·ness** *noun* [U]

**IDM** ▶ **be going great 'guns** (*informal*) to be doing sth quickly and successfully: *Work is going great guns now.* **be a 'great one for (doing) sth** to do sth a lot; to enjoy sth: *He's never been a great one for keeping in touch.* ◇ *You're a great one for quizzes, aren't you?* **be no great 'shakes** (*informal*) to be not very good, efficient, suitable, etc. **great and 'small** of all sizes or types: *all creatures great and small* **the great … in the 'sky** (*humorous*) used to refer to where a particular person is imagined to go when they die or a thing when it is no longer working, similar to the place they were connected with on earth: *Their pet rabbit had gone to the great rabbit hutch in the sky.* **great 'minds think a'like** (*informal, humorous*) used to say that you and another person must both be very clever because you have had the same idea or agree about sth ⊃ more at DEAL *n.*, OAK, PAINS, SUM *n.*

- *noun* [usually pl.] (*informal*) a very well-known and successful person: *He was one of boxing's all-time greats.*
- *adv.* (*informal, non-standard*) very well: *Well done. You did great.*

▼ **SYNONYMS**

**great**
cool • fantastic • fabulous • terrific • brilliant • awesome • epic

These are all informal words that describe sb/sth that is very good, impressive, great fun, etc.

**great** (*informal*) very good; giving a lot of pleasure: *We had a great time in Madrid.*

**cool** (*informal*) used to show that you admire or approve of sth, often because it is fashionable, attractive or different: *I think their new song's really cool.*

**fantastic** (*informal*) extremely good; giving a lot of pleasure: *'How was your holiday?' 'Fantastic!'*

**fabulous** (*informal*) extremely good: *Jane's a fabulous cook.* (**Fabulous** is slightly more old-fashioned than the other words in this set.)

**terrific** (*informal*) extremely good; wonderful: *She's doing a terrific job.*

**brilliant** (*BrE, informal*) extremely good; wonderful: *'How was the show?' 'Brilliant!'*

**awesome** (*informal, especially NAmE*) very good, impressive or great fun: *The show was just awesome.*

**epic** (*informal*) very good, impressive or great fun: *The adventure and action are truly epic in scope.*

PATTERNS
- to have a(n) great/cool/fantastic/fabulous/terrific/brilliant/awesome **time**
- to **look/sound** great/cool/fantastic/fabulous/terrific/brilliant/awesome
- **really** great/cool/fantastic/fabulous/terrific/brilliant/awesome
- **absolutely** great/fantastic/fabulous/terrific/brilliant/awesome/epic

**great 'ape** *noun* [usually pl.] one of the large animals that are most similar to humans (including CHIMPANZEES, GORILLAS and ORANGUTANS)

**Great 'Britain** *noun* [U] England, Scotland and Wales, when considered as a unit **HELP** Sometimes 'Great Britain' (or 'Britain') is wrongly used to refer to the political state, officially called the 'United Kingdom of Great Britain and Northern Ireland' or the 'UK'.

**great·coat** /ˈgreɪtkəʊt/ *noun* a long heavy coat, especially one worn by soldiers

**Great Dane** /ˌgreɪt ˈdeɪn/ *noun* a type of very large dog with short hair

**great·ly** ⚡+ **B2** /ˈgreɪtli/ *adv.* (*formal*) (usually before a verb or participle) very much: *People's reaction to the film* has varied greatly. ◇ *a greatly increased risk* ◇ *Your help would be greatly appreciated.*

**the Great 'War** *noun* [sing.] (*old-fashioned*) = FIRST WORLD WAR

**great white 'shark** *noun* a large aggressive SHARK with a brown or grey back, found in warm seas

**the Great White 'Way** *noun* (*informal*) a name for Broadway in New York City that refers to the many bright lights of its theatres

**grebe** /ɡriːb/ *noun* a bird like a DUCK, that can also swim UNDERWATER: *a great crested grebe*

**Gre·cian** /ˈɡriːʃn/ *adj.* from ancient Greece or like the styles of ancient Greece: *Grecian architecture*

**Greco-** = GRAECO-

**greed** /ɡriːd/ *noun* [U] (*disapproving*) **1** a strong desire for more wealth, possessions, power, etc. than a person needs: *His actions were motivated by greed.* ◇ **~ for sth** *Nothing would satisfy her greed for power.* **2** a strong desire for more food or drink when you are no longer hungry or thirsty: *I had another helping of ice cream out of pure greed.*

**greedy** /ˈɡriːdi/ *adj.* (**greed·ier**, **greedi·est**) (*disapproving*) wanting more money, power, food, etc. than you really need: *You greedy pig! You've already had two helpings!* ◇ *He stared at the diamonds with greedy eyes.* ◇ **~ for sth** *The shareholders are greedy for profit.* ▶ **greed·ily** /-dɪli/ *adv.*: *She ate noisily and greedily.*

**IDM** ▶ **greedy 'guts** (*BrE, informal*) used to refer to sb who eats too much

**Greek** /ɡriːk/ *noun, adj.*
- *noun* **1** [C] a person from modern or ancient Greece **2** [U] the language of modern or ancient Greece **3** [C] (*NAmE*) a member of a FRATERNITY or a SORORITY at a college or university

**IDM** ▶ **it's all 'Greek to me** (*informal, saying*) I cannot understand it: *She tried to explain how the system works, but it's all Greek to me.*

- *adj.* of or connected with Greece, its people or their language

**Greek 'salad** *noun* [C, U] a salad that is made with tomatoes, OLIVES and FETA CHEESE

**green** ⓘ **A1** /ɡriːn/ *adj., noun, verb*
- *adj.* (**green·er**, **green·est**)
- COLOUR **1** **A1** having the colour of grass or the leaves of most plants and trees: *green grass/leaves/vegetables* ◇ *his piercing green eyes* ◇ *Wait for the light to turn green* (= on traffic lights). ⊃ see also BOTTLE-GREEN, LIME-GREEN, PEA-GREEN, SEA-GREEN
- COVERED WITH GRASS **2** **A1** covered with grass or other plants: *green fields/pastures/hills* ◇ *It's just two minutes' walk to the nearest public green space.*
- FRUIT **3** **A1** not yet ready to eat: *green tomatoes*
- POLITICS **4** **B1** connected with the protection of the environment; supporting the protection of the environment as a political principle: *green energy* ◇ *green politics* ◇ *Try to adopt a greener lifestyle.* ◇ *the Green Party*

**WORDFINDER** biodiversity, conservation, endanger, the environment, extinct, managed, species, sustainable, toxic

- PERSON **5** (*informal*) (of a person) young and without experience: *The new trainees are still very green.* **6** (of a person or their skin) being a pale colour, as if the person is going to VOMIT: *It was a rough crossing and most of the passengers looked distinctly green.* ▶ **green·ness** /ˈɡriːnnəs/ *noun* [U]: *the greenness of the countryside* ◇ *Supermarkets have started proclaiming the greenness of their products.*

**IDM** ▶ **green with 'envy** very JEALOUS (= angry or unhappy because you wish you had sth that sb else has) ⊃ more at GRASS *n.*

- *noun*
- COLOUR **1** **A1** [U, C] the colour of grass and the leaves of most plants and trees: *dark/light/pale/bright/emerald green* ◇ *the green of the countryside in spring* ◇ *She was dressed all in green.* ◇ *The room was decorated in a*

*combination of greens and blues.* ⊃ see also BOTTLE GREEN, LIME GREEN, PEA GREEN, SEA GREEN
- **VEGETABLES 2 greens** [pl.] vegetables with dark green leaves, for example CABBAGE or SPINACH: *Eat up your greens.*
- **AREA OF GRASS 3** [C] (*BrE*) an area of grass, especially in the middle of a town or village: *Children were playing on the village green.* **4** [C] (in golf) an area of grass cut short around a hole on a GOLF COURSE: *the 18th green* ◊ *Did the ball land on the green?* ⊃ see also BOWLING GREEN, PUTTING GREEN
- **POLITICS 5 the Greens** [pl.] the Green Party (= the party whose main aim is the protection of the environment)

■ *verb*
- **CREATE PARKS 1 ~ sth** to create parks and other areas with trees and plants in a city: *projects for greening the cities*
- **POLITICS 2 ~ sb/sth** to make sb more aware of issues connected with the environment; to make sth appear friendly towards the environment: *an attempt to green industry bosses* ▶ **green·ing** *noun* [U]: *the greening of British politics*

**green·back** /ˈɡriːnbæk/ *noun* (*NAmE*, *informal*) an American dollar note

**green ˈbean** (*BrE also* **French ˈbean**) (*NAmE also* **string ˈbean**) *noun* a type of bean that is a long thin green POD, cooked and eaten whole as a vegetable ⊃ VISUAL VOCAB page V5

**ˈgreen belt** *noun* [U, C, usually sing.] (*especially BrE*) an area of open land around a city where there are strict controls about building: *New roads are cutting into the green belt.*

**Green Beˈret** *noun* a member of the US army Special Forces

**ˈgreen card** *noun* **1** a document that legally allows sb from another country to live and work in the US **2** (*BrE*) an insurance document that you need when you drive your car in another country

**green·ery** /ˈɡriːnəri/ *noun* [U] attractive green leaves and plants: *The room was decorated with flowers and greenery.*

**the ˌgreen-eyed ˈmonster** *noun* (*informal*) used as a way of talking about being JEALOUS (= angry or unhappy because sb has sth you wish you had or because sb you love shows interest in sb else)

**green·field** /ˈɡriːnfiːld/ *adj.* [only before noun] used to describe an area of land that has not yet had buildings on it, but for which building development may be planned: *a greenfield site* ⊃ compare BROWNFIELD

**green ˈfingers** *noun* [pl.] (*BrE*) (*NAmE* **ˌgreen ˈthumb**) if you are said to have **green fingers**, you are good at making plants grow ▶ **ˌgreen-ˈfingered** *adj.* (*BrE*)

**green·fly** /ˈɡriːnflaɪ/ *noun* [C, U] (*pl.* **green·flies** *or* **green·fly**) a small flying insect that is harmful to plants: *The roses have got greenfly.*

**green·gro·cer** /ˈɡriːnɡrəʊsə(r)/ *noun* (*especially BrE*) **1** a person who owns, manages or works in a shop selling fruit and vegetables **2 green·gro·cer's** (*pl.* **green·gro·cers**) a shop that sells fruit and vegetables

**green·horn** /ˈɡriːnhɔːn; *NAmE* -hɔːrn/ *noun* (*informal*, *especially NAmE*) a person who has little experience and can be easily tricked **SYN** **tenderfoot**

**green·house** ?+ B2 /ˈɡriːnhaʊs/ *noun* a building with glass sides and a glass roof for growing plants in

**the ˈgreenhouse effect** *noun* [sing.] the problem of the slow steady rise in temperature of the earth's atmosphere, caused by an increase of gases around the earth, which TRAP the heat of the sun ⊃ see also GLOBAL WARMING

**ˌgreenhouse ˈgas** *noun* any of the gases that are thought to cause the greenhouse effect, especially CARBON DIOXIDE: *a government commitment to reduce greenhouse gas emissions*

**green·ing** /ˈɡriːnɪŋ/ *noun* [U] ⊃ GREEN *noun*

**green·ish** /ˈɡriːnɪʃ/ *adj.* fairly green in colour

695

**green·keep·er** /ˈɡriːnkiːpə(r)/ (*NAmE also* **greens·keep·er**) *noun* a person whose job is to take care of a GOLF COURSE

**green ˈlight** *noun* [sing.] permission for a project, etc. to start or continue **SYN** **go-ahead**: *The government has decided to give the green light to the plan.*

**green-ˈlight** *verb* (**green-lighted**, **green-lighted** *or* **green-lit**, **green-lit**) ~ **sth** to give permission for a project, etc. to start or continue: *A sixth season of the show has been green-lit.*

**green maˈnure** *noun* [U, C] plants that are dug into the soil in order to improve its quality

**green ˈonion** (*also* **scalˈlion**) (*both NAmE*) (*BrE* **spring ˈonion**) *noun* a type of small onion with a long green STEM and leaves. Green onions are often eaten raw in salads. ⊃ VISUAL VOCAB page V5

**Green ˈPaper** *noun* (in the UK) a document containing government proposals on a particular subject, intended for general discussion ⊃ compare WHITE PAPER

**green ˈpepper** *noun* a hollow green fruit that is eaten, raw or cooked, as a vegetable ⊃ compare SWEET PEPPER

**green ˈroof** (*also* **living ˈroof**) *noun* a type of roof that has plants growing on it that help to keep the building cool in summer and warm in winter

**ˈgreen room** *noun* a room in a theatre, television studio, etc. where the performers can relax when they are not performing

**green ˈsalad** *noun* [C, U] a salad that is made with raw green vegetables, especially LETTUCE: *Serve with a green salad.*

**greens·keep·er** /ˈɡriːnzkiːpə(r)/ *noun* (*NAmE*) = GREENKEEPER

**green ˈtea** *noun* [U] a pale tea made from leaves that have been dried but not FERMENTED

**green ˈthumb** (*NAmE*) (*BrE* **green ˈfingers**) *noun* [sing.] if you are said to have a **green thumb**, you are good at making plants grow

**green ˈvegetable** *noun* [C, usually pl.] (*BrE also* **greens** [pl.]) a vegetable with dark green leaves, for example CABBAGE or SPINACH

**ˈgreen wall** *noun* a structure covered in plants that can be attached to the wall of a building

**green·wash** /ˈɡriːnwɒʃ; *NAmE* -wɔːʃ/ (*also* **green·wash·ing**) *noun* [U] (*disapproving*) activities by a company or an organization that are intended to make people think that it is concerned about the environment, even if its real business actually harms the environment

**Greenwich Mean Time** /ˌɡrenɪtʃ ˈmiːn taɪm, -nɪdʒ/ ⊃ GMT

**greet** ① A2 /ɡriːt/ *verb* **1** ? A2 to say hello to sb or to welcome them: ~**sb** *He greeted all the guests warmly as they arrived.* ◊ ~**sb with sth** *She greeted us with a smile.* ⊃ see also MEET-AND-GREET, MEET AND GREET **2** [often passive] to react to sb/sth in a particular way: ~**sb/sth** *Loud cheers greeted the news.* ◊ **be greeted with sth** *The changes were greeted with suspicion.* ◊ **be greeted as sth** *The team's win was greeted as a major triumph.* **3** [usually passive] (of sights, sounds or smells) to be the first thing that you see, hear or smell at a particular time: **be greeted by sth** *When she opened the door she was greeted by a scene of utter confusion.*

**greet·er** /ˈɡriːtə(r)/ *noun* (*especially in the US*) a person whose job is to meet and welcome people in a public place such as a restaurant or shop

**greet·ing** /ˈɡriːtɪŋ/ *noun* **1** [C, U] something that you say or do to greet sb: *She waved a friendly greeting.* ◊ *They exchanged greetings and sat down to lunch.* ◊ *He raised his hand in greeting.* **2 greetings** [pl.] a message of good wishes for sb's health, happiness, etc: *Christmas/birthday, etc. greetings* ◊ *My mother sends her greetings to you all.* **IDM** see SEASON *n.*

**greetings card** (*BrE*) (*NAmE* **greeting card**) *noun* a card with a picture on the front and a message inside that you send to sb on a particular occasion such as their birthday

**gre·gar·i·ous** /grɪˈɡeəriəs; *NAmE* -ˈɡer-/ *adj.* **1** liking to be with other people SYN **sociable 2** (*biology*) (of animals or birds) living in groups ▸ **gre·gar·i·ous·ly** *adv.* **gre·gar·i·ous·ness** *noun* [U]

**Gre·gor·ian cal·en·dar** /ɡrɪˌɡɔːriən ˈkælɪndə(r)/ *noun* [sing.] the system used since 1582 in Western countries of arranging the months in the year and the days in the months and of counting the years from the birth of Christ ⇒ compare JULIAN CALENDAR

**Gre·gor·ian chant** *noun* [U, C] a type of church music for voices alone, used since the Middle Ages

**grem·lin** /ˈɡremlɪn/ *noun* an imaginary creature that people blame when a machine suddenly stops working

**gren·ade** /ɡrəˈneɪd/ *noun* a small bomb that can be thrown by hand or fired from a gun ⇒ see also HAND GRENADE, STUN GRENADE

**grena·dier** /ˌɡrenəˈdɪə(r); *NAmE* -ˈdɪr/ *noun* a soldier in the part of the British army known as the **Grenadiers** or **Grenadier Guards**

**grena·dine** /ˈɡrenədiːn/ *noun* [U] a sweet red liquid that is made from POMEGRANATES (= a fruit with many seeds). It is drunk mixed with water or alcoholic drinks.

**grew** /ɡruː/ *past tense* of GROW

**grey** ❶ A1 (*US usually* **gray**) /ɡreɪ/ *adj., noun, verb*
■ *adj.* **1** A1 having the colour of smoke or ASHES: *grey eyes/hair* ◇ *Her hair was turning grey.* ◇ *wisps of grey smoke* ◇ *a grey suit* **2** A2 (of the sky or weather) not bright; full of clouds: *grey skies* ◇ *I hate these grey days.* **3** [not usually before noun] having grey hair: *He's gone very grey.* ⇒ WORDFINDER NOTE at BLONDE **4** (of a person's skin colour) pale, because they are ill, tired or sad **5** without interest or variety; making you feel sad: *Life seems grey and pointless without him.* **6** (*disapproving*) not interesting or attractive: *The company was full of faceless grey men who all looked the same.* **7** [only before noun] connected with old people: *the grey vote* ◇ *grey power* ▸ **grey·ness** (*US usually* **gray·ness**) *noun* [U, sing.]
■ *noun* **1** A1 [U, C] the colour of smoke or ASHES: *the dull grey of the sky* ◇ *dressed in grey* ◇ *light/pale grey* ◇ *His eyes are a dark grey.* **2** [C] a grey or white horse: *She's riding the grey.*
■ *verb* [I] (of hair) to become grey: *His hair was greying at the sides.* ◇ *a tall woman with greying hair*

**grey area** (*US usually* **gray area**) *noun* an area of a subject or situation that is not clear or does not fit into a particular group and is therefore difficult to define or deal with: *Exactly what can be called an offensive weapon is still a grey area.*

**grey·beard** (*US usually* **gray·beard**) /ˈɡreɪbɪəd; *NAmE* -bɪrd/ *noun* (*informal*) an old man: *the greybeards of the art world*

**grey-'haired** (*US usually* **gray-'haired**) *adj.* with grey hair

**grey·hound** /ˈɡreɪhaʊnd/ *noun* a large thin dog with smooth hair and long thin legs, that can run very fast and is used in the sport of **greyhound racing**

**grey·ish** (*US usually* **gray·ish**) /ˈɡreɪɪʃ/ *adj.* fairly grey in colour: *greyish hair*

**grey 'market** (*US usually* **gray 'market**) *noun* [usually sing.] **1** a system in which products are imported into a country and sold without the permission of the company that produced them **2** (*BrE*) old people, when they are thought of as customers for goods

**grey matter** (*US usually* **gray matter**) *noun* [U] (*informal*) a person's intelligence

**grey·scale** (*US usually* **gray·scale**) /ˈɡreɪskeɪl/ *noun* (*specialist*) a range of shades of grey, not colour: **in** ~ *I've printed out the pictures in greyscale.* ◇ *a greyscale scanner*

**grid** ❷ C1 /ɡrɪd/ *noun* **1** ❷ C1 a pattern of straight lines, usually crossing each other to form squares: *New York's grid of streets* **2** a frame of metal or wooden bars that are PARALLEL or cross each other ⇒ see also CATTLE GRID **3** ❷ C1 a pattern of squares on a map that are marked with letters or numbers to help you find the exact position of a place: *The grid reference is C8.* ⇒ WORDFINDER NOTE at MAP **4** ❷ C1 (*especially BrE*) a system of electric wires or pipes carrying gas, for sending power over a large area: *the national grid* (= the electricity supply in a country) ⇒ see also NATIONAL GRID **5** (*also* **starting grid**) (in motor racing) a pattern of lines marking the starting positions for the racing cars **6** (*often* **the Grid**) [sing.] (*computing*) a number of computers that are linked together using the internet so that they can share power, data, etc. in order to work on difficult problems
IDM **off the 'grid** (*especially NAmE*) not using the public supplies of electricity, water, gas, etc.: *The mountain cabin is entirely off the grid.* ⇒ see also OFF-THE-GRID

**grid·dle** /ˈɡrɪdl/ *noun* a flat iron plate that is heated and used for cooking food ▸ **griddle** *verb* ~ **sth**

**grid·iron** /ˈɡrɪdaɪən; *NAmE* -ərn/ *noun* **1** a frame made of metal bars that is used for cooking meat or fish on, over an open fire **2** (*NAmE*) a field used for AMERICAN FOOTBALL marked with a pattern of straight lines

**grid·lock** /ˈɡrɪdlɒk; *NAmE* -lɑːk/ *noun* [U, C] **1** a situation in which there are so many cars in the streets of a town that the traffic cannot move at all **2** (usually in politics) a situation in which people with different opinions are not able to agree with each other and so no action can be taken: *Congress is in gridlock.* ▸ **grid·locked** *adj.*

**grief** ❷ C1 /ɡriːf/ *noun* **1** ❷ C1 [U, C] ~ (**for sb/sth**) | ~ (**over/at sth**) a very sad feeling, especially when sb dies: *She was overcome with grief when her husband died.* ◇ *They were able to share their common joys and griefs.* **2** [C, usually sing.] something that makes you feel very sad: *It was a grief to them that they had no children.* **3** [U] (*informal*) problems and worry: *He caused his parents a lot of grief.*
IDM **come to 'grief** (*informal*) **1** to end in total failure **2** to be harmed in an accident: *Several pedestrians came to grief on the icy pavement.* **give sb 'grief (about/over sth)** (*informal*) to be annoyed with sb and criticize their behaviour **good 'grief!** (*informal*) used to express surprise or shock: *Good grief! What a mess!*

**'grief-stricken** *adj.* feeling extremely sad because of sth that has happened, especially the death of sb

**griev·ance** /ˈɡriːvəns/ *noun* something that you think is unfair and that you complain or protest about; a feeling that you have been badly treated: *Parents were invited to air their grievances* (= express them) *at the meeting.* ◇ ~ **against sb** *He had been nursing a grievance against his boss for months.* ◇ *Does the company have a formal **grievance procedure*** (= a way of dealing with your complaints at work)?

**grieve** /ɡriːv/ *verb* **1** [I, T] to feel very sad, especially because sb has died: ~ (**for/over sb/sth**) *They are still grieving for their dead child.* ◇ *grieving relatives* ◇ ~ **sb/sth** *She grieved the death of her husband.* **2** [T] (*formal*) to make you feel very sad SYN **pain**: *it grieves sb that … It grieved him that he could do nothing to help her.* ◇ ~ **sb** *Their lack of interest grieved her.* ◇ **it grieves sb to do sth** *It grieved her to leave.* IDM see EYE *n.*

**griev·ous** /ˈɡriːvəs/ *adj.* (*formal*) very serious and often causing great pain or difficulty: *He had been the victim of a grievous injustice.* ▸ **griev·ous·ly** *adv.*: *grievously hurt/wounded*

**grievous bodily 'harm** *noun* [U] (*abbr.* **GBH**) (*BrE, law*) the crime of causing sb serious physical injury ⇒ compare ACTUAL BODILY HARM

**grif·fin** /ˈɡrɪfɪn/ (*also* **grif·fon, gry·phon** /ˈɡrɪfən/) *noun* (in stories) a creature with a lion's body and an EAGLE's wings and head, and with eagle's legs for the front legs

**grift·er** /ˈɡrɪftə(r)/ *noun* (*especially US*) a person who tricks people into giving them money, etc.

**grill** /grɪl/ noun, verb
- **noun 1** (BrE) the part of a cooker that directs heat downwards to cook food that is placed under it ⇨ compare BROILER **2** a flat metal frame that you put food on to cook over a fire ⇨ see also BARBECUE noun **3** a dish of grilled food, especially meat ⇨ see also MIXED GRILL **4** (especially in names) a restaurant serving grilled food: *Harry's Bar and Grill* **5** = GRILLE
- **verb 1** ~ sth (BrE) to cook food under a very strong heat: *Grill the sausages for ten minutes.* ◊ *grilled bacon* ⇨ compare BROIL **2** ~ sth to cook food over a fire, especially outdoors: *grilled meat and shrimp* ◊ ~ sb (about sth) to ask sb a lot of questions about their ideas, actions, etc., often in an unpleasant way: *They grilled her about where she had been all night.* ⇨ see also GRILLING

**grille** (also **grill**) /grɪl/ noun a screen made of metal bars or wire that is placed in front of a window, door or machine in order to protect it: *a radiator grille* (= at the front of a car) ◊ *a security grille*

**grill·ing** /ˈgrɪlɪŋ/ noun [C, usually sing., U] a period of being questioned closely about your ideas, actions, etc: *The minister faced a tough grilling at today's press conference.*

**grim** /grɪm/ adj. (**grim·mer, grim·mest**) **1** looking or sounding very serious: *a grim face/look/smile* ◊ *She looked grim.* ◊ *with a look of grim determination on his face* ◊ *grim-faced policemen* **2** unpleasant and depressing: *grim news* ◊ *We face the grim prospect of still higher unemployment.* ◊ *The outlook is pretty grim.* ◊ *Things are looking grim for workers in the building industry.* **3** (of a place or building) not attractive; depressing: *The house looked grim and dreary in the rain.* ◊ *the grim walls of the prison* **4** [not before noun] (BrE, informal) ill: *I feel grim this morning.* **5** [not usually before noun] (BrE, informal) of very low quality: *Their performance was fairly grim, I'm afraid!* ▶ **grim·ly** adv.: *'It won't be easy,' he said grimly.* ◊ *grimly determined* **grim·ness** noun [U]
IDM **hang/hold on for/like grim ˈdeath** (BrE) (also **hang/hold on for dear ˈlife** NAmE, BrE) (informal) to hold sb/sth very tightly or keep sth in a very determined way because you are afraid

**grim·ace** /ˈgrɪməs, grɪˈmeɪs/ verb, noun
- **verb** [I] ~ (at sb/sth) to make an ugly expression with your face to show pain, dislike, etc: *He grimaced at the bitter taste.* ◊ *She grimaced as the needle went in.* ⇨ WORDFINDER NOTE at EXPRESSION
- **noun** an ugly expression made by TWISTING your face, used to show pain, dislike, etc. or to make sb laugh: *to make/give a grimace of pain* ◊ *'What's that?' she asked with a grimace.*

**grime** /graɪm/ noun [U] **1** dirt that forms a layer on the surface of sth SYN dirt: *a face covered with grime and sweat* **2** a type of electronic dance music that developed from DRUM AND BASS, UK GARAGE and other styles

**the ˌGrim ˈReaper** noun an imaginary figure who represents death. It looks like a SKELETON, wears a long CLOAK and carries a SCYTHE.

**grimy** /ˈgraɪmi/ adj. (**grimi·er, grimi·est**) covered with dirt SYN **dirty**: *grimy hands/windows*

**grin** /grɪn/ verb, noun
- **verb** [I, T] (-nn-) to smile widely: *They grinned with delight when they heard our news.* ◊ ~ at sb *She grinned amiably at us.* ◊ ~ sth *He grinned a wide grin.* ⇨ WORDFINDER NOTE at EXPRESSION
IDM **grin and ˈbear it** (only used as an infinitive and in orders) to accept pain or bad luck without complaining: *There's nothing we can do about it. We'll just have to grin and bear it.* ⇨ see also EAR
- **noun** a wide smile: *She gave a broad grin.* ◊ *a wry/sheepish grin* ◊ *with a ~ 'No,' she said with a grin.* IDM see WIPE v.

**grind** /graɪnd/ verb, noun
- **verb** (**ground, ground** /graʊnd/)
- FOOD/FLOUR/COFFEE **1** [T] ~ sth (down/up) | ~ sth (to/into sth) to break or press sth into very small pieces between two hard surfaces or using a special machine: *to grind coffee/corn* ⇨ see also GROUND adj. **2** [T] ~ sth to produce sth such as flour by grinding: *The flour is ground using traditional methods.* **3** [T] ~ sth (NAmE) = MINCE
- MAKE SHARP/SMOOTH **4** [T] ~ sth to make sth sharp or smooth by rubbing it against a hard surface: *a special stone for grinding knives*
- PRESS INTO SURFACE **5** [T] to press or rub sth into a surface: ~ sth into sth *He ground his cigarette into the ashtray.* ◊ ~ sth in *The dirt on her hands was ground in.*
- RUB TOGETHER **6** [I, T] to rub together, or to make hard objects rub together, often producing an unpleasant noise: ~ (together) *Parts of the machine were grinding together noisily.* ◊ ~ sth (together) *She grinds her teeth when she is asleep.* ◊ *He ground the gears on the car.*
- MACHINE **7** [T] ~ sth to turn the handle of a machine that grinds sth: *to grind a pepper mill*
IDM **bring sth to a ˈgrinding ˈhalt** to make sth gradually go slower until it stops completely | **grind to a ˈhalt** | **come to a grinding ˈhalt** to go slower gradually and then stop completely: *Production ground to a halt during the strike.* ⇨ more at AXE n.
PHRV **grind sb↔ˈdown** to treat sb in a cruel unpleasant way over a long period of time, so that they become very unhappy: *Don't let them grind you down.* ◊ *Years of oppression had ground the people down.* **ˌgrind ˈon** to continue for a long time, when this is unpleasant: *The argument ground on for almost two years.* **grind sth↔ˈout** to produce sth in large quantities, often sth that is not good or interesting SYN **churn sth ~ out**: *She grinds out romantic novels at the rate of five a year.*
- **noun**
- BORING ACTIVITY **1** [sing.] (informal) an activity that is boring or makes you tired and takes a lot of time: *the daily grind of family life* ◊ *It's a long grind to the top of that particular profession.*
- OF MACHINES **2** [sing.] the unpleasant noise made by machines
- SWOT **3** (US) (BrE **swot**) [C] (informal, disapproving) a person who spends too much time studying

**grind·er** /ˈgraɪndə(r)/ noun **1** a machine or tool for grinding a solid substance into a powder: *a coffee grinder* ⇨ see also MEAT GRINDER **2** a person whose job is to make knives sharper; a machine which does this ⇨ see also ORGAN GRINDER

**grind·ing** /ˈgraɪndɪŋ/ adj. [only before noun] **1** (of a difficult situation) that never ends or improves: *grinding poverty* **2** (of a sound) rough and unpleasant to listen to: *a loud grinding noise*

**grind·stone** /ˈgraɪndstəʊn/ noun a round stone that is turned like a wheel and is used to make knives and other tools sharp IDM see NOSE n.

**gringo** /ˈgrɪŋgəʊ/ noun (pl. **-os**) (informal, disapproving) used in Latin American countries and communities to refer to a person, especially an American, who is not of Latin American origin

**griot** /ˈgriːəʊ/ noun (in West Africa, especially in the past) a person who sings or tells stories about the history and traditions of their people and community

**grip** /grɪp/ noun, verb
- **noun**
- HOLDING TIGHTLY **1** [C, usually sing.] ~ (on sb/sth) an act of holding sb/sth tightly; a particular way of doing this SYN **grasp**: *Keep a tight grip on the rope.* ◊ *to loosen/release/relax your grip* ◊ *She tried to get a grip on the icy rock.* ◊ *The climber slipped and lost her grip.* ◊ *She struggled from his grip.* ◊ *Try adjusting your grip on the racket.*
- CONTROL/POWER **2** [sing.] ~ (on sb/sth) control or power over sb/sth: *The home team took a firm grip on the game.* ◊ *We need to tighten the grip we have on the market.*
- UNDERSTANDING **3** [sing.] ~ (on sth) an understanding of sth SYN **grasp**: *I couldn't get a grip on what was going on.* ◊ *You need to keep a good grip on reality in this job.*
- MOVING WITHOUT SLIPPING **4** [U, sing.] the ability of sth to move over a surface without slipping: *These tyres give the bus better grip in slippery conditions.*

# gripe

- **PART OF OBJECT 5** [C] a part of sth that has a special surface so that it can be held without the hands slipping: *the grip on a golf club*
- **FOR HAIR 6** [C] (*BrE*) = HAIRGRIP
- **JOB IN THE MOVIES 7** [C] a person who prepares and moves the cameras, and sometimes the lighting equipment, when a film is being made
- **BAG 8** [C] (*old-fashioned*) a large soft bag, used when travelling

IDM **come / get to ˈgrips with sth** to begin to understand and deal with sth difficult: *I'm slowly getting to grips with the language.* **get / take a ˈgrip (on yourself)** to improve your behaviour or control your emotions after being afraid, upset or angry: *I have to take a grip on myself, he told himself firmly.* ◊ (*informal*) *Get a grip!* (= make an effort to control your emotions) **in the ˈgrip of sth** experiencing sth unpleasant that cannot be stopped: *a country in the grip of recession* **lose your ˈgrip (on sth)** to become unable to understand or control a situation: *Sometimes I feel I'm losing my grip.*

- **verb (-pp-)**
- **HOLD TIGHTLY 1** [T, I] to hold sth tightly SYN grasp: *~ sth 'Please don't go,' he said, gripping her arm.* ◊ *~ on to sth She gripped on to the railing with both hands.* ⇒ SYNONYMS at HOLD
- **INTEREST / EXCITE 2** [T] to interest or have a strong effect on sb; to hold sb's attention: *The book grips you from start to finish.* ◊ *I was totally gripped by the story.* ◊ *The campaign gripped people's imagination.* ⇒ see also GRIPPING
- **HAVE POWERFUL EFFECT 3** [T] *~ sb/sth* (of an emotion or a situation) to have a powerful effect on sb/sth: *I was gripped by a feeling of panic.* ◊ *Terrorism has gripped the country for the past two years.*
- **MOVE / HOLD WITHOUT SLIPPING 4** [T, I] *~ (sth)* to hold onto or to move over a surface without slipping: *tyres that grip the road*

**gripe** /graɪp/ *noun, verb*
- **noun** (*informal*) a complaint about sth: *My only gripe about the hotel was the food.*
- **verb** [I] *~ (about sb/sth)* (*informal*) to complain about sb/sth in an annoying way: *He's always griping about the people at work.*

**grip·ing** /ˈgraɪpɪŋ/ *adj.* [only before noun] a griping pain is a sudden strong pain in your stomach

**grip·ping** /ˈgrɪpɪŋ/ *adj.* exciting or interesting in a way that keeps your attention ⇒ SYNONYMS at INTERESTING ⇒ WORDFINDER NOTE at STORY

**grisly** /ˈgrɪzli/ *adj.* [usually before noun] (**gris·lier, gris·li·est**) extremely unpleasant and frightening and usually connected with death and violence: *a grisly crime*

**grist** /grɪst/ *noun* [U] *~ (for sb/sth)* useful ideas or material: *Pearl Harbor has provided the grist for more than 100 books and at least seven movies.*
IDM **(all) grist to the / sb's ˈmill** (*BrE*) (*NAmE*) **(all) grist for the / sb's ˈmill** something that is useful to sb for a particular purpose: *Political sex scandals are all grist to the mill of the tabloid newspapers.*

**gris·tle** /ˈgrɪsl/ *noun* [U] a hard substance in meat that is unpleasant to eat: *a lump of gristle*

**grit** /grɪt/ *noun, verb*
- **noun** [U] **1** very small pieces of stone or sand: *I had a piece of grit in my eye.* ◊ *They were spreading grit and salt on the icy roads.* **2** the courage and strength of mind that makes it possible for sb to continue doing sth difficult or unpleasant
- **verb (-tt-)** *~ sth* to spread grit, salt or sand on a road that is covered with ice
IDM **grit your ˈteeth 1** to bite your teeth tightly together: *She gritted her teeth against the pain.* ◊ *'Stop it!' he said through gritted teeth.* **2** to be determined to continue to do sth in a difficult or unpleasant situation: *It started to rain harder, but we gritted our teeth and carried on.*

**grits** /grɪts/ *noun* [pl.] CORN (MAIZE) that is pressed into small pieces before cooking, often eaten for breakfast or as part of a meal in the southern US

**grit·ter** /ˈgrɪtə(r)/ (*BrE*) (*US* **salt truck**) *noun* a large vehicle used for putting salt, sand or GRIT on the roads in winter when there is ice on them

**gritty** /ˈgrɪti/ *adj.* (**grit·ti·er, grit·ti·est**) **1** containing or like GRIT: *a layer of gritty dust* **2** showing the courage and strength of mind to continue doing sth difficult or unpleasant: *gritty determination* ◊ *a gritty performance from the British player* **3** showing sth unpleasant as it really is; having a lot of unpleasant features: *a gritty description of urban violence* ◊ *gritty realism* ◊ (*especially NAmE*) *a gritty neighborhood of flophouses and bars* ⇒ see also NITTY-GRITTY ▶ **grit·tily** /-tɪli/ *adv.* **grit·ti·ness** *noun* [U]

**griz·zle** /ˈgrɪzl/ *verb* [I] (*BrE, informal*) (especially of a baby or child) to cry or complain continuously in a way that is annoying

**griz·zled** /ˈgrɪzld/ *adj.* (*literary*) having hair that is grey or partly grey

**griz·zly bear** /ˌgrɪzli ˈbeə(r); *NAmE* ˈber/ (*also* **ˈgriz·zly** *pl.* **-ies**) *noun* a large brown bear that lives in North America and parts of Russia

**groan** /ɡrəʊn/ *verb, noun*
- **verb 1** [I, T] to make a long deep sound because you are annoyed, upset or in pain, or with pleasure SYN **moan**: *He lay on the floor groaning.* ◊ *~ with sth to groan with pain/pleasure* ◊ *~ at sth We all groaned at his terrible jokes.* ◊ *+ speech 'It's a complete mess!' she groaned.* **2** [I, T] to complain about sth, especially in an annoying way SYN **grumble**: *~ about sth They were all moaning and groaning about the amount of work they had.* ◊ *+ speech 'It's not fair!' she groaned.* **3** [I] to make a sound like a person groaning SYN **moan**: *The trees creaked and groaned in the wind.*
IDM **groan under the weight of sth** (*formal*) used to say that there is too much of sth
PHRV **ˈgroan with sth** (*formal*) to be full of sth: *tables groaning with food*
- **noun 1** a long deep sound made when sb/sth groans SYN **moan**: *She let out a groan of dismay.* ◊ *He fell to the floor with a groan.* ◊ *The house was filled with the cello's dismal squeaks and groans.* **2** a complaint: *I don't have time to listen to your moans and groans.*

▼ HOMOPHONES

**groan · grown** /ɡrəʊn/

- **groan** *verb*: *The awful jokes made us all groan.*
- **groan** *noun*: *He let out a groan of pain.*
- **grown** (*past participle* of GROW): *The business has grown hugely in the last ten years.*
- **grown** *adj.*: *Although he's a grown man, he'll always be our little boy.*

**groat** /ɡrəʊt/ *noun* a silver coin used in Europe in the past

**gro·cer** /ˈɡrəʊsə(r)/ *noun* **1** a person who owns, manages or works in a shop selling food and other things used in the home **2** **ˈgro·cer's** (*pl.* **gro·cers**) a shop that sells these things

**gro·cery** /ˈɡrəʊsəri/ *noun* (*pl.* **-ies**) **1** (*especially BrE*) (*NAmE usually* **ˈgrocery store**) [C] a shop that sells food and other things used in the home. In American English 'grocery store' is often used to mean 'supermarket'. **2** **groceries** [pl.] food and other goods sold by a grocer or at a supermarket ▶ **gro·cery** *adj.* [only before noun]: *the grocery bill*

**grog** /ɡrɒɡ; *NAmE* ɡrɑːɡ/ *noun* [U] **1** a strong alcoholic drink, originally RUM, mixed with water **2** (*AustralE, NZE, informal*) any alcoholic drink, especially beer

**groggy** /ˈɡrɒɡi; *NAmE* ˈɡrɑːɡi/ *adj.* [not usually before noun] (**grog·gier, grog·gi·est**) (*informal*) weak and unable to think or move well because you are ill or very tired

**groin** /ɡrɔɪn/ *noun* the part of the body where the legs join the main part of the body, including the area around the GENITALS (= sex organs): *She kicked her attacker in the groin.* ◊ *He's been off all season with a groin injury.* ⇒ VISUAL VOCAB page V1

---

æ cat | ɑː father | e bed | ɜː fur | ə about | ɪ sit | iː see | i happy | ɒ got (*BrE*) | ɔː saw | ʌ cup | ʊ put | uː too

**grok** /grɒk; NAmE grɑːk/ verb (-kk-) ~ sth (US, informal) to understand sth completely using your feelings rather than considering the facts: *Kids grok this show immediately but their parents take longer to get it.*

**grom·met** /ˈɡrɒmɪt; NAmE ˈɡrɑːm-/ noun **1** a small metal or rubber ring placed around a hole for a rope or wire to pass through, in order to make the hole stronger **2** (*BrE*) (*NAmE* **tube**) a small tube placed in a child's ear in order to DRAIN liquid from it when there is an infection

**groom** /ɡruːm/ verb, noun
■ *verb* **1** ~ sth to clean or brush an animal: *to groom a horse/dog/cat* ◇ *The horses are all well fed and groomed.* **2** ~ sth (of an animal) to clean the fur or skin of another animal or itself: *a female ape grooming her mate* **3** to prepare or train sb for an important job or position: ~ sb (for/as sth) *Our junior employees are being groomed for more senior roles.* ◇ ~ sb to do sth *The eldest son is being groomed to take over when his father dies.* **4** ~ sb (of a person who is sexually attracted to children) to prepare a child for a meeting, especially using SOCIAL MEDIA, with the intention of performing an illegal sexual act
■ *noun* **1** a person whose job is to feed and take care of horses, especially by brushing and cleaning them **2** = BRIDEGROOM

**groomed** /ɡruːmd/ adj. (usually following an adverb) used to describe the way in which a person cares for their clothes and hair: *She is always perfectly groomed.* ⊃ see also WELL GROOMED

**groom·ing** /ˈɡruːmɪŋ/ noun [U] **1** the things that you do to keep your clothes and hair clean and neat, or to keep an animal's fur or hair clean: *You should always pay attention to personal grooming.* **2** the process in which an adult develops a friendship with a child, particularly through the internet, with the intention of having an illegal sexual relationship

**grooms·man** /ˈɡruːmzmən/ noun (pl. **-men** /-mən/) (*especially NAmE*) one of the male friends of the BRIDEGROOM at a wedding who have special duties ⊃ compare BEST MAN, USHER (3)

**groove** /ɡruːv/ noun **1** a long narrow cut in the surface of sth hard **2** (*informal*) a particular type of musical rhythm: *a jazz groove*
**IDM** ▶ **be (stuck) in a ˈgroove** (*BrE*) to be unable to change sth that you have been doing the same way for a long time and that has become boring

**grooved** /ɡruːvd/ adj. having a groove or grooves

**groovy** /ˈɡruːvi/ adj. (*informal, old-fashioned or humorous*) fashionable, attractive and interesting

**grope** /ɡrəʊp/ verb, noun
■ *verb* **1** [I] ~ (around) (for sth) to try and find sth that you cannot see, by feeling with your hands: *He groped around in the dark for his other sock.* ◇ (*figurative*) *'It's so ..., so ...' I was groping for the right word to describe it.* **2** [T, I] to try and reach a place by feeling with your hands because you cannot see clearly: ~ your way + adv./prep. *He groped his way up the staircase in the dark.* ◇ + adv./prep. *She groped through the darkness towards the doors.* **3** [T] ~ sb (*informal*) to touch sb sexually, especially when they do not want you to
■ *noun* (*informal*) an act of groping sb (= touching them sexually)

**gross** /ɡrəʊs/ adj., adv., verb, noun
■ *adj.* (**gross·er, gross·est**) **1** [only before noun] being the total amount of sth before anything is taken away: *gross weight* (= including the container or wrapping) ◇ *gross income/wage* (= before taxes, etc. are taken away) ◇ *Investments showed a gross profit of 26 per cent.* ⊃ compare NET **2** [only before noun] (*formal or law*) (of a crime, etc.) very obvious and unacceptable: *gross negligence/misconduct* ◇ *a gross violation of human rights* **3** (*informal*) very unpleasant **SYN** disgusting: *'He ate it with mustard.' 'Oh, gross!'* ⊃ SYNONYMS at DISGUSTING **4** very rude **SYN** crude: *gross behaviour* **5** very fat and ugly: *She's not just fat, she's positively gross!* ▶ **gross·ness** noun [U]
■ *adv.* in total, before anything is taken away: *She earns £25000 a year gross.* ⊃ compare NET

---

699

■ *verb* ~ sth to earn a particular amount of money before tax has been taken off it: *It is one of the biggest grossing movies of all time.*
**PHR V** ˌgross sb ˈout (*informal*) to be very unpleasant and make sb feel strong dislike **SYN** disgust: *His bad breath really grossed me out.*
■ *noun* **1** (*pl.* **gross**) a group of 144 things: *two gross of apples* ◇ *to sell sth by the gross* **2** (*pl.* **grosses**) (*especially US*) a total amount of money earned by sth, especially a film, before any costs are taken away

**gross doˈmestic ˈproduct** noun [U, C] = GDP

**gross·ly** /ˈɡrəʊsli/ adv. (*disapproving*) (used to describe unpleasant qualities) extremely: *grossly overweight/unfair/inadequate* ◇ *Press reports have been grossly exaggerated.*

**gross ˈnational ˈproduct** noun [U, C] = GNP

**ˈgross-out** noun (*especially NAmE, informal*) something horrible: *They eat flies? What a gross-out!* ▶ **ˈgross-out** adj. [only before noun]: *gross-out movie scenes*

**gro·tesque** /ɡrəʊˈtesk/ adj., noun
■ *adj.* **1** strange in a way that is unpleasant or offensive: *a grotesque distortion of the truth* ◇ *It's grotesque to expect a person of her experience to work for so little money.* **2** extremely ugly in a strange way that is often frightening or funny: *a grotesque figure* ◇ *tribal dancers wearing grotesque masks* ▶ **gro·tesque·ly** adv.
■ *noun* **1** [C] a person who is extremely ugly in a strange way, especially in a book or painting **2** **the grotesque** [sing.] a style of art or sculpture using grotesque figures and designs

**grotto** /ˈɡrɒtəʊ; NAmE ˈɡrɑːt-/ noun (*pl.* **-oes** or **-os**) a small CAVE, especially one that has been made artificially, for example in a garden

**grotty** /ˈɡrɒti; NAmE ˈɡrɑːti/ adj. (*BrE, informal*) (**grot·tier, grot·ti·est**) unpleasant or of poor quality: *a grotty little hotel* ◇ *I'm feeling pretty grotty* (= ill).

**grouch** /ɡraʊtʃ/ noun (*informal*) **1** a person who complains a lot **2** a complaint about sth unimportant ▶ **grouch** verb [I]

**grouchy** /ˈɡraʊtʃi/ adj. (*informal*) easily annoyed and often complaining

**ground** /ɡraʊnd/ noun, verb, adj.
■ *noun*
• **SURFACE OF EARTH 1** (*often* **the ground**) [U] the solid surface of the earth: **on the ~** *I found her lying on the ground.* ◇ **to the ~** *He fell to the ground, crying out in pain.* ◇ **above/below (the) ~** *The adult insects live above ground.* ◇ *Most of the monkey's food is found at ground level.* ⊃ SYNONYMS at FLOOR **2** [U] (especially in noun compounds) used to describe activities that take place on the ground, not in the air or at sea: *ground forces/troops* ◇ *a ground and air attack*
• **AREA OF LAND 3** [U] an area of open land: *The kids were playing on waste ground behind the school.* **4** [C] (often in compounds) an area of land that is used for a particular purpose, activity or sport: *a football/cricket ground* ◇ *The atmosphere inside the ground was electric.*
⊃ SYNONYMS at LAND ⊃ see also BREEDING GROUND, BURIAL GROUND, DUMPING GROUND, HOME GROUND, HUNTING GROUND, PARADE GROUND, RECREATION GROUND, STAMPING GROUND, TESTING GROUND, TRAINING GROUND **5 grounds** [pl.] a large area of land or sea that is used for a particular purpose: *fishing grounds* ◇ *feeding grounds for birds*
• **SOIL 6** [U] soil on the surface of the earth: *fertile ground for planting crops* ◇ **in/into the ~** *You can sow the seeds directly into the ground.* ⊃ SYNONYMS at SOIL
• **GARDENS 7 grounds** [pl.] the land or gardens around a large building: *the hospital grounds*
• **AREA OF KNOWLEDGE/IDEAS 8** [U] an area of interest, knowledge or ideas: *He managed to cover a lot of ground in a short talk.* ◇ *We had to go over the same ground* (= talk about the same things again) *in class the next day.* ◇ **on ... ~** *I thought I was on safe ground* (= not likely to offend or upset sb) *talking about music.* ◇ *Legal scholars say the president is on shaky ground.* ◇ **~ for sth** *Paris in the 1920s*

# ground ball

was *fertile ground for artistic experimentation.* ⊃ see also COMMON GROUND, HIGH GROUND, MIDDLE GROUND
- **GOOD REASON 9** [C, usually pl.] a good or true reason for saying, doing or believing sth: **~(s) for sth** *You have no grounds for complaint.* ◊ **~(s) for doing sth** *What were his grounds for wanting a divorce?* ◊ **~(s) to do sth** *There are reasonable grounds to believe that a crime has been committed.* ◊ **on the ~(s) that ...** *The case was dismissed on the ground that there was insufficient evidence.* ◊ **on~s of sth** *Employers cannot discriminate on grounds of age.* ◊ **on ...~s** *He retired early on health grounds.* ⊃ SYNONYMS at REASON
- **IN LIQUID 10 grounds** [pl.] the small pieces of solid matter in a liquid that have fallen to the bottom: *coffee grounds*
- **ELECTRICAL WIRE 11** (*NAmE*) (*BrE* **earth**) [C, usually sing.] a wire that connects an electric CIRCUIT with the ground and makes it safe: *Don't forget to connect the ground wire.*
- **BACKGROUND 12** [C] a background that a design is painted or printed on: *pink roses on a white ground*

**IDM** **be on firm/solid 'ground** to be in a strong position in an argument, etc. because you know the facts: *Everyone agreed with me, so I knew I was on firm ground.* **cut the ground from under sb's 'feet** to suddenly cause sb's idea or plan to fail by doing sth to stop them from continuing with it **from the ground 'up** (*informal*) completely, or including everything, starting with the most basic things: *We need to rebuild the system from the ground up.* **gain/make up 'ground (on sb/sth)** to gradually get closer to sb/sth that is moving or making progress in an activity: *The police car was gaining ground on the suspects.* ◊ *They needed to make up ground on their competitors.* **get (sth) off the 'ground** to start happening successfully; to make sth start happening successfully: *Without more money, the movie is unlikely to get off the ground.* ◊ *to get a new company off the ground* **give/lose 'ground (to sb/sth)** to allow sb/sth to have an advantage; to lose an advantage for yourself: *They are not prepared to give ground on tax cuts.* ◊ *The Conservatives lost a lot of ground to the Liberal Democrats at the election.* **go to 'ground** (*BrE*) to hide, especially to escape from sb **hold/stand your 'ground 1** to continue with your opinions or intentions when sb is opposing you and wants you to change: *Don't let him persuade you—stand your ground.* **2** to face a situation and refuse to run away: *It is not easy to hold your ground in front of someone with a gun.* **on sb's own ground** in an area where sb has a lot of power, knowledge or experience: *They are fighting the Conservatives on their own ground.* **on the 'ground** in the place where sth is happening and among the people who are in the situation, especially a war: *On the ground, there are hopes that the fighting will soon stop.* ◊ *There's a lot of support for the policy on the ground.* **run/drive/work yourself into the 'ground** to work so hard that you become extremely tired **run sb/sth into the 'ground** to make sb work so hard that they are no longer able to work; to use sth so much that it is broken **thick/thin on the 'ground** (*BrE*) if people or things are **thick/thin on the ground**, there are a lot/not many of them in a place: *Customers are thin on the ground at this time of year.* **to the 'ground** completely, so that there is nothing left: *The hotel burned to the ground.* ◊ *The city was razed to the ground* (= completely destroyed). ⊃ more at EAR, FOOT *n.*, GAIN *v.*, HIT *v.*, MORAL *adj.*, NEUTRAL *adj.*, NEW, PREPARE, SHIFT *v.*, STONY, SUIT *v.*

■ *verb*
- **BOAT 1** [T, I] **~ (sth)** when a boat **grounds** or sth **grounds** it, it touches the ground in shallow water and is unable to move: *The fishing boat had been grounded on rocks off the coast of Cornwall.*
- **AIRCRAFT 2** [T, often passive] to prevent an aircraft from taking off: **be grounded (by sth)** *The balloon was grounded by strong winds.* ◊ *All planes out of Heathrow have been grounded by the strikes.*
- **CHILD 3** [T, usually passive] to punish a child or young person by not allowing them to go out with their friends for a period of time: **be grounded** *You're grounded for a week!*
- **ELECTRICITY 4** (*NAmE*) (*BrE* **earth**) [T, usually passive] **~ sth** to make electrical equipment safe by connecting it to the ground with a wire **5** *past tense, past part.* of GRIND ⊃ see also GROUNDED, GROUNDING

■ *adj.* [only before noun] (of food) cut or CRUSHED into very small pieces or powder: *ground coffee* ◊ (*US*) *ground pork* ⊃ see also HAMBURGER (2)

**'ground ball** *noun* = GROUNDER

**'ground 'beef** *noun* [U] (*NAmE*) = HAMBURGER (2)

**'ground·break·ing** /'graʊndbreɪkɪŋ/ *adj.* [only before noun] making new discoveries; using new methods: *a groundbreaking piece of research*

**'ground cloth** (*US*) (*BrE* **'ground·sheet**) *noun* a large piece of material that does not let water through that is placed on the ground inside a tent ⊃ picture at TENT

**'ground control** *noun* [U + sing./pl. v.] the people and equipment on the ground that make sure that planes or SPACECRAFT take off and land safely and monitor flights while they are in progress

**'ground cover** *noun* [U, C] low-growing plants that cover the soil and help to stop WEEDS (= wild plants growing where they are not wanted)

**'ground crew** (*also* **'ground staff**) *noun* [C + sing./pl. v.] the people at an airport whose job is to take care of aircraft while they are on the ground

**'ground·ed** /'graʊndɪd/ *adj.* having a sensible and realistic attitude to life: *Away from Hollywood, he relies on his family and friends to keep him grounded.* ⊃ see also WELL GROUNDED

**IDM** **(be) 'grounded in/on sth** (to be) based on sth: *His views are grounded on the assumption that all people are equal.*

**'ground·er** /'graʊndə(r)/ (*also* **'ground ball**) *noun* (in baseball) a ball that runs along the ground after it has been hit

**'ground 'floor** (*BrE*) (*NAmE* **first 'floor**) *noun* the floor of a building that is at the same level as the ground outside: *a ground-floor window* ◊ *I live on the ground floor.*

**IDM** **be/get in on the ground 'floor** to become involved in a plan, project, etc. at the beginning

**'ground·hog** /'graʊndhɒɡ; *NAmE* -hɑːɡ/ *noun* = WOODCHUCK

**'Groundhog Day** *noun* **1** (in North America) February 2, when it is said that the GROUNDHOG comes out of its hole at the end of winter. If the sun shines and the groundhog sees its shadow, it is said that there will be another six weeks of winter. **2** an event that is repeated without changing: *The Government lost the vote then and it can expect a Groundhog Day next time.* **ORIGIN** From the film *Groundhog Day* about a man who lives the same day many times.

**'ground·ing** /'graʊndɪŋ/ *noun* **1** [sing.] **~ (in sth)** the teaching of the basic parts of a subject: *a good grounding in grammar* **2** [U, C] the act of keeping a plane on the ground or a ship in a port, especially because it is not in a good enough condition to travel

**'ground·less** /'graʊndləs/ *adj.* not based on reason or evidence **SYN** **unfounded**: *groundless allegations* ◊ *Our fears proved groundless.* ▸ **'ground·less·ly** *adv.*

**'ground·nut** /'graʊndnʌt/ *noun* (*BrE*) = PEANUT

**'ground·out** /'graʊndaʊt/ *noun* (in baseball) a situation in which a player hits the ball along the ground but a FIELDER touches first BASE with it before the player reaches the base

**'ground plan** *noun* **1** a plan of the ground floor of a building ⊃ compare PLAN **2** a plan for future action

**'ground rent** *noun* [U, C] (in the UK) rent paid by the owner of a building to the owner of the land on which it is built

**'ground rule** *noun* **1 ground rules** [pl.] the basic rules on which sth is based: *The new code of conduct lays down the ground rules for management-union relations.* **2** [C] (*NAmE*, *sport*) a rule for the playing of a game on a particular field, etc.

**'ground·sheet** /'graʊndʃiːt/ (*BrE*) (*US* **'ground cloth**) *noun* a large piece of material that does not let water through that is placed on the ground inside a tent ⊃ picture at TENT

**grounds·man** /ˈgraʊndzmən/ noun (pl. **-men** /-mən/) (especially BrE) (NAmE usually **grounds·keeper** /ˈgraʊndzkiːpə(r)/) a person whose job is to take care of a sports ground or large garden

**ˈground speed** noun the speed of an aircraft relative to the ground ⊃ compare AIRSPEED

**ˈground squirrel** (NAmE also **gopher**) noun a type of SQUIRREL that lives in holes in the ground

**ˈground staff** noun [C + sing./pl. v.] **1** (BrE) the people at a sports ground whose job it is to take care of the grass, equipment, etc. **2** = GROUND CREW

**ˈground·stroke** /ˈgraʊndstrəʊk/ noun (in tennis) a hit that is made after the ball has BOUNCED ⊃ compare VOLLEY (1)

**ˈground·swell** /ˈgraʊndswel/ noun [sing.] **~ (of sth)** (formal) the sudden increase of a particular feeling among a group of people: *a groundswell of support* ◊ *There was a groundswell of opinion that he should resign.*

**ˈground·water** /ˈgraʊndwɔːtə(r)/ noun [U] water that is found under the ground in soil, rocks, etc.

**ˈground·work** /ˈgraʊndwɜːk; NAmE -wɜːrk/ noun [U] **~ (for sth)** work that is done as preparation for other work that will be done later: *Officials are laying the groundwork for a summit conference of world leaders.*

**ˌground ˈzero** noun **1** [U, C] the point on the earth's surface where a nuclear bomb explodes **2 Ground Zero** [U] the site of the Twin Towers in New York, destroyed on 11 September 2001 **3** [U] the beginning; a starting point for an activity

**group** 🄾 **A1** 🄾 /gruːp/ noun, verb

■ *noun* [C + sing./pl. v.] **1** **A1** a number of people or things that are together in the same place or that are connected in some way: **~ of sb/sth** *a group of people/students/friends* ◊ *A group of us are going to the theatre this evening.* ◊ *English is a member of the Germanic group of languages.* ◊ **in groups** *People were standing around in small groups.* ◊ *different ethnic groups* ◊ *a minority group* ⊃ see also AGE GROUP, BLOOD GROUP, FOOD GROUP, PEER GROUP, SUB-GROUP **HELP** There are many other compounds ending in **group**. You will find them at their place in the alphabet. **2** **A1** a number of people who work or do sth together or share particular beliefs: *The residents formed a community action group.* ◊ *I've joined a writing group.* ◊ **of sb** *She leads a group of scientists at the Medical Research Centre.* ◊ **in a ~** *There are fifteen of us in the group.* ◊ **into groups** *The students were divided into groups of four.* ◊ *Classes will involve both individual and group activities.* **3** (*business*) a number of companies that are owned by the same person or organization: *a newspaper group* ◊ *the Burton group* ◊ *the group sales director* **4** (*rather old-fashioned*) a number of musicians who perform together, especially to play pop music: *She sings in a rock group.*

■ *verb* **1** [T, I] to gather into a group; to make sb/sth form a group: **~ sb/sth/yourself (round/around sb/sth)** *The children grouped themselves around their teacher.* ◊ **~ round/around sb/sth** *We all grouped around the tree for a photograph.* ◊ **(sb/sth) together** *The colleges grouped together to offer a wider range of courses.* **2** [T] to divide people or things into groups of people or things that are similar in some way: **~ sb/sth (together) (by sth)** *The books are grouped together by subject.* ◊ **~ sb/sth + adv./prep.** *Contestants were grouped according to age and ability.*

**ˌgroup ˈcaptain** noun (abbr. **Gp Capt**) an officer of high rank in the British AIR FORCE: *Group Captain (Jonathan) Sutton*

**groupie** /ˈgruːpi/ noun a person, especially a young woman, who follows pop or rock musicians or other famous people around and tries to meet them

**group·ing** /ˈgruːpɪŋ/ noun **1** [C] a number of people or organizations that have the same interests, aims or characteristics and are often part of a larger group: *These small nations constitute an important grouping within the EU.* **2** [U] the act of forming sth into a group

# grow

**ˌgroup ˈpractice** noun a group of several doctors or other medical workers who work together in the community and use the same building to see patients

**ˌgroup ˈtherapy** noun [U] a type of PSYCHIATRIC treatment in which people with similar personal problems meet together to discuss them

**group·think** /ˈgruːpθɪŋk/ noun [U] (*disapproving*) the practice of thinking or making decisions as a group, especially when this results in bad decisions being made

**group·ware** /ˈgruːpweə(r); NAmE -wer/ noun [U] (*computing*) software that is designed to help a group of people on different computers to work together

**ˈgroup work** noun [U] work done by a group of people working together, for example students in a classroom

**grouse** /graʊs/ noun, verb
■ *noun* **1** [C, U] (*pl.* **grouse**) a bird with a fat body and feathers on its legs, which people shoot for sport and food; the meat of this bird: *grouse shooting* ◊ *grouse moors* ◊ *roast grouse* **2** [C] (*informal*) a complaint
■ *verb* [I, T] **~ (about sb/sth) | (+ speech)** (*informal*) to complain about sb/sth in a way that other people find annoying **SYN** grumble

**grout** /graʊt/ (also **grout·ing**) noun [U] a substance that is used between the TILES on the walls and floors of kitchens, bathrooms, etc. ▸ **grout** verb **~ sth**

**grove** /grəʊv/ noun **1** (*literary*) a small group of trees: *a grove of birch trees* **2** a small area of land with fruit trees of particular types on it: *an olive grove* **3** used in the names of streets: *Elm Grove*

**grovel** /ˈɡrɒvl; NAmE ˈɡrʌvl/ verb (-ll-, US -l-) **1** [I] **~ (to sb) (for sth)** (*disapproving*) to show too much respect to sb who is more important than you or who can give you sth you want **SYN** crawl **2** [I] **~ + adv./prep.** to move along the ground on your hands and knees, especially because you are looking for sth ▸ **grov·el·ling** (US **grov·el·ing**) adj. [only before noun]: *a grovelling letter of apology*

**grow** 🄾 **A1** 🅢 /grəʊ/ verb (**grew** /gruː/, **grown** /grəʊn/)

• INCREASE **1** **A1** [I] to increase in size, number, strength or quality: *Opposition to the latest proposals is growing steadily.* ◊ *The market is growing rapidly.* ◊ **~ by sth** *The economy is growing by roughly 2 per cent a year.* ◊ **~ in sth** *The family has grown in size recently.* ◊ *She is growing in confidence all the time.* ◊ **~ (from sth) (to sth)** *The city's population has grown from about 50000 to over a million in 20 years.* ◊ **+ adj.** *to grow larger/stronger* ⊃ HOMOPHONES at GROAN

• OF PERSON/ANIMAL **2** **A1** [I] to become bigger or taller and develop into an adult: *You've grown since the last time I saw you!* ◊ **+ noun** *Nick's grown almost an inch in the last month.* ◊ **+ adj.** *to grow bigger/taller/older*

• OF PLANT **3** **A1** [I, T] to exist and develop in a particular place; to make plants grow: *The region is too dry for plants to grow.* ◊ *Tomatoes grow best in direct sunlight.* ◊ **~ sth** *The land is used to grow crops.* ◊ *We need to grow our food more efficiently.* ⊃ see also HOME-GROWN

• OF HAIR/NAILS **4** **A1** [I, T] to become longer; to allow sth to become longer by not cutting it: *I've decided to let my hair grow.* ◊ **~ sth** *I've decided to grow my hair.* ◊ *I didn't recognize him—he's grown a beard.*

• BECOME/BEGIN **5** **A2** linking verb **+ adj.** to begin to have a particular quality or feeling over a period of time: *He had grown old and fat.* ◊ *They were growing tired of her unreasonable behaviour.* ◊ *As time went on he grew more and more impatient.* ◊ *The skies grew dark and it began to rain.* **6** [I] **~ to do sth** to gradually begin to do sth: *I'm sure you'll grow to love him in time.*

• DEVELOP SKILLS **7** [I] **~ (as sth)** (of a person) to develop and improve particular qualities or skills: *She continues to grow as an artist.*

• BUSINESS **8** [T] **~ sth** to increase the size, quality or number of sth: *We are trying to grow the business.*

**IDM** **it/money doesn't grow on ˈtrees** (*saying*) used to tell sb not to use sth or spend money carelessly because you do not have a lot of it ⊃ more at ABSENCE, GRASS n., OAK

# grower

**PHR V** **grow a'part (from sb)** to stop having a close relationship with sb over a period of time **grow a'way from sb** [no passive] to become less close to sb; to depend on sb or care for sb less: *When she left school she grew away from her mother.* **grow back** to begin growing again after being cut off or damaged **grow 'into sth** [no passive] **1** to gradually develop into a particular type of person or thing over a period of time: *The town grew into a city.* **2** (of a child) to grow big enough to fit into a piece of clothing that used to be too big: *The dress is too long for her now but she'll grow into it.* **3** to become more confident in a new job, etc. and learn to do it better: *She's still growing into her new role as a mother.* **grow on sb** [no passive] if sb/sth **grows on** you, you start to like them or it more and more **grow 'out** (of a HAIRSTYLE, etc.) to disappear as your hair grows: *I had a perm a year ago and it still hasn't grown out.* **grow sth↔'out** to allow your hair to grow in order to change the style: *I've decided to grow my layers out.* **grow 'out of sth** [no passive] **1** (of a child) to become too big to fit into a piece of clothing **SYN** **outgrow**: *He's already grown out of his school uniform.* **2** to stop doing sth as you become older **SYN** **outgrow**: *Most children suck their thumbs but they grow out of it.* **3** to develop from sth: *The idea for the book grew out of a visit to India.* **grow 'up** **1** **A1** (of a person) to develop into an adult: *She grew up in Boston* (= lived there as a child). ◊ *Their children have all grown up and left home now.* ◊ **grow up to do sth** *He grew up to become a famous pianist.* ⊃ related noun GROWN-UP[2] **2** used to tell sb to stop behaving in a silly way: *Why don't you grow up?* ◊ *It's time you grew up.* **3** to develop gradually: *A closeness grew up between the two girls.*

**grow·er** /'grəʊə(r)/ *noun* **1** a person or company that grows plants, fruit or vegetables to sell: *a tobacco grower* ◊ *All our vegetables are supplied by local growers.* **2** a plant that grows in the way mentioned: *a fast/slow grower*

**grow·ing** /'grəʊɪŋ/ *adj.* [only before noun] **1** increasing in size, amount or degree: *A growing number of people are returning to full-time education.* ◊ *one of the country's fastest growing industries* ◊ *There is growing concern over the safety of the missing teenager.* **2** becoming bigger and taller and developing into an adult: *A growing child needs plenty of sleep.*

**'growing pains** *noun* [pl.] **1** pains that some children feel in their arms and legs when they are growing **2** emotional worries felt by young people as they grow up **3** problems that are experienced by a company, organization, etc. when it begins operating but that are not likely to last

**'growing season** *noun* [usually sing.] the period of the year during which the weather conditions are right for plants to grow

**growl** /graʊl/ *verb, noun*
- *verb* **1** [I] ~ (at sb/sth) (of animals, especially dogs) to make a low sound in the throat, usually as a sign of anger **2** [T] to say sth in a low angry voice: **+ speech** (at sb) '*Who are you?*' *he growled at the stranger.* ◊ ~ **sth** (at sb) *She growled a sarcastic reply.*
- *noun* a deep angry sound made when sb/sth GROWLS

**grown** /grəʊn/ *adj.* [only before noun] (of a person) mentally and physically an adult: *It's pathetic that grown men have to resort to violence like this.* ⊃ see also FULL-GROWN, GROW, HOME-GROWN ⊃ HOMOPHONES at GROAN

**grown-up**[1] *adj.* **1** (of a person) mentally and physically an adult: *What do you want to be when you're grown-up?* ◊ *She has a grown-up son.* **2** suitable for or typical of an adult: *The child was clearly puzzled at being addressed in such a grown-up way.*

**'grown-up**[2] *noun* (used especially by and to children) an adult person **SYN** **adult**: *If you're good you can eat with the grown-ups.*

**growth** **⊕** **B1** **⊙** /grəʊθ/ *noun* **1** **A1** [U] the process in people, animals or plants of growing physically, mentally or emotionally: *Lack of water will stunt the plant's growth.* ◊ *Remove dead leaves to encourage new growth.* ◊ *a concern with personal* (= mental and emotional) *growth* ◊ *growth hormones* (= that make sb/sth grow faster) **2** **B1** [U] an increase in the size, amount or degree of sth: *population growth* ◊ *revenue/earnings/sales/productivity growth* ◊ ~ **in sth** *the rapid growth in violent crime* **3** **B1** [U] an increase in economic activity: *policies aimed at sustaining economic growth* ◊ *a period of slow growth* ◊ *to stimulate/promote/drive growth* ◊ *an annual growth rate of 10 per cent* **4** [C] a mass of cells caused by a disease that forms on or inside a person, an animal or a plant: *a malignant/cancerous growth* **5** [U, C] something that has grown: *The forest's dense growth provides nesting places for a wide variety of birds.* ◊ *several days' growth of beard*

**'growth ring** *noun* a layer of wood, shell or bone developed in one year, or in another regular period of growth, that an expert can look at to find out how old sth is

**grub** /grʌb/ *noun, verb*
- *noun* **1** [C] the young form of an insect, that looks like a small fat WORM **2** [U] (*informal*) food: *Grub's up!* (= the meal is ready) ◊ *They serve good pub grub* (= food in a pub) *there.*
- *verb* [I] (**-bb-**) ~ (**around/about**) (**for sth**) to look for sth, especially by digging or by looking through or under other things: *birds grubbing for worms*
**PHR V** **grub sth↔'up/'out** to dig sth out of the ground

**grub·ber** /'grʌbə(r)/ *noun* **1** (in CRICKET) a ball that is BOWLED along the ground **2** (*also* **'grubber kick**) (in rugby) a forward kick of the ball along the ground ⊃ see also MONEY-GRUBBER

**grubby** /'grʌbi/ *adj.* (**grub·bier**, **grub·bi·est**) **1** rather dirty, usually because it has not been washed or cleaned: *grubby hands/clothes* ⊃ SYNONYMS at DIRTY **2** unpleasant because it involves activities that are not honest or moral **SYN** **sordid**: *a grubby scandal* ▸ **grub·bi·ness** *noun* [U]

**'Grub Street** *noun* used to refer as a group to writers and journalists who do not earn much, or to the life they live **ORIGIN** From the name of a street in London where many poor writers lived in the 17th century.

**grudge** /grʌdʒ/ *noun, verb*
- *noun* ~ (**against sb**) a feeling of anger or dislike towards sb because of sth bad they have done to you in the past: *I bear him no grudge.* ◊ *He has a grudge against the world.* ◊ *I don't hold any grudges now.* ◊ *He's a man with a grudge.* ◊ *England beat New Zealand in a grudge match* (= a match where there is strong dislike between the teams).
- *verb* **1** to do or give sth unwillingly **SYN** **begrudge**: ~ **doing sth** *I grudge having to pay so much tax.* ◊ *I grudge the time he spends travelling to work.* **2** ~ **sb sth** to think that sb does not deserve to have sth **SYN** **begrudge**: *You surely don't grudge her her success?*

**grudg·ing** /'grʌdʒɪŋ/ *adj.* (usually before noun) given or done unwillingly **SYN** **reluctant**: *He could not help feeling a grudging admiration for the old lady.* ▸ **grudg·ing·ly** (*also less frequent* **be·grudg·ing·ly**) *adv.*: *She grudgingly admitted that I was right.*

**gruel** /'gru:əl/ *noun* [U] a simple dish made by boiling OATS in milk or water, eaten especially in the past by poor people

**gruel·ling** (*especially* BrE) (NAmE *usually* **gruel·ing**) /'gru:əlɪŋ/ *adj.* very difficult and making you very tired, needing great effort for a long time **SYN** **punishing**: *a gruelling journey/schedule* ◊ *I've had a gruelling day.*

**grue·some** /'gru:səm/ *adj.* very unpleasant and filling you with horror, usually because it is connected with death or injury: *a gruesome murder* ◊ *gruesome pictures of dead bodies* ◊ (*humorous*) *We spent a week in a gruesome apartment in Miami.* ▸ **grue·some·ly** *adv.*

**gruff** /grʌf/ *adj.* **1** (of a voice) deep and rough, and often sounding unfriendly **2** (of a person's behaviour) impatient and unfriendly: *Beneath his gruff exterior, he's really very kind-hearted.* ▸ **gruff·ly** *adv.*

**grum·ble** /'grʌmbl/ *verb, noun*
- *verb* **1** [I, T] to complain about sb/sth, especially sth that is not really very serious: ~ (**at/to sb**) (**about/at sth**) *She's always grumbling to me about how badly she's*

treated at work. ◇ **+ speech** 'I'll just have to do it myself,' he grumbled. ◇ **~ that …** They kept grumbling that they were cold. ⊃ SYNONYMS at COMPLAIN **2** [I] to make a deep continuous sound SYN **rumble**: *Thunder grumbled in the distance.* ▶ **grum·bler** /-blə(r)/ *noun*
■ *noun* **1** ~ (**about sth**) | ~ (**that …**) something that you complain about because you are not satisfied: *My main grumble is about the lack of privacy.* **2** a long low sound SYN **rumble**: *a distant grumble of thunder*

**grum·bling** /'grʌmblɪŋ/ *noun* **1** [U] the act of complaining about sth: *We didn't hear any grumbling about the food.* **2 grumblings** [pl.] protests about sth that come from a number of people but that are not expressed very clearly

**grump** /grʌmp/ *noun* (*informal*) an angry person

**grumpy** /'grʌmpi/ *adj.* (**grump·ier**, **grumpi·est**) (*informal*) easily annoyed; in a bad mood ▶ **grump·ily** /-pɪli/ *adv.*

**grunge** /grʌndʒ/ *noun* [U] **1** (*informal*) dirt of any kind SYN **grime 2** (*also* **'grunge music**) a type of loud rock music, which was popular in the early 1990s **3** a style of fashion worn by people who like grunge music, usually involving clothes that look untidy

**grungy** /'grʌndʒi/ *adj.* (**grungier**, **grungiest**) (*informal*) dirty in an unpleasant way

**grunt** /grʌnt/ *verb*, *noun*
■ *verb* **1** [I] (of animals, especially pigs) to make a short, low sound in the throat **2** [I, T] (of people) to make a short, low sound in your throat, especially to show that you are in pain, annoyed or not interested; to say sth using this sound: *He pulled harder on the rope, grunting with the effort.* ◇ *When I told her what had happened she just grunted and turned back to her book.* ◇ **~ sth** *He grunted something about being late and rushed out.* ◇ **+ speech** 'Thanks,' he grunted.
■ *noun* **1** a short, low sound made by a person or an animal (especially a pig): *to give a* **grunt** *of effort/pain* **2** (*NAmE*, *informal*) a worker who does boring tasks for low pay **3** (*NAmE*, *informal*) a soldier of low rank

**'grunt work** *noun* [U] (*informal*) hard boring work: *She has assistants to do the grunt work like research and proofreading.*

**gryphon** = GRIFFIN

**GSM** /ˌdʒiː es 'em/ *noun* an international system for digital communication by mobile phone (the abbreviation for 'Global System/Standard for Mobile Communication(s)')

**GSOH** /ˌdʒiː es əʊ 'eɪtʃ/ *abbr.* good sense of humour (used in personal advertisements)

**GST** /ˌdʒiː es 'tiː/ *noun* [U] (*CanE*) goods and services tax (a tax that is added to the price of goods and services)

**'G-string** *noun* a narrow piece of cloth that covers the sexual organs and is held up by a string around the middle part of the body

**Gt** (*also* **Gt.** *especially in NAmE*) *abbr.* (in names of places) Great: *Gt Britain* ◇ *Gt Yarmouth*

**gua·ca·mole** /ˌɡwækə'məʊleɪ, -li/ *noun* [U] (*from Spanish*) a Mexican dish made from AVOCADO mixed with onion, tomatoes, CHILLIES, etc.

**guano** /'ɡwɑːnəʊ/ *noun* [U] the waste substance passed from the bodies of birds that live near the sea, used to make plants and crops grow well

**guanxi** /ɡwæn'ʃiː; *SEAsianE* [kwænçi/ *noun* [U] (*SEAsianE*) (in China) the system of social networks and the relationships between people that are helpful and useful in business: *The main reason for his company's success is that he has good guanxi with the authorities.* ▶ **guanxi** *adj.* [only before noun]

**guar·an·tee** ⓞ B2 /ˌɡærən'tiː/ *verb*, *noun*
■ *verb* **1** B2 to promise to do sth; to promise sth will happen: ~ **sth** *Basic human rights, including freedom of speech, are now guaranteed.* ◇ ~ (**that**) … *We cannot guarantee (that) our flights will never be delayed.* ◇ ~ **sb sth** *The ticket will guarantee you free entry.* ◇ **to do sth** *We guarantee to deliver your goods within a week.* **2** B2 ~ **sth** (**against sth**) to give a written promise to replace or repair a product free if it goes wrong: *This iron is guaranteed for a year against faulty workmanship.* **3** B2 to make sth certain to happen: ~ **sth** *Tonight's victory guarantees the team's place*

703 **guard**

*in the final.* ◇ ~ **sb sth** *These days getting a degree doesn't guarantee you a job.* **4** ~ (**that**) … to be certain that sth will happen: *You can guarantee (that) the children will start being naughty as soon as they have to go to bed.* **5** to agree to be legally responsible for sth or for doing sth, especially for paying back money that sb else owes if they cannot pay it back themselves: ~ **sth** *to guarantee a bank loan* ◇ ~ **to do sth** *to guarantee to pay sb's debts* ◇ ~ **that** … *I guarantee that he will appear in court.*
IDM **be guaran'teed to do sth** to be certain to have a particular result: *If we try to keep it a secret, she's guaranteed to find out.* ◇ *That kind of behaviour is guaranteed to make him angry.* ⊃ SYNONYMS at CERTAIN
■ *noun* **1** B2 a formal promise that you will do sth or that sth will happen SYN **assurance**: *They are demanding certain guarantees before they sign the treaty.* ◇ ~ **of sth** *to give a guarantee of good behaviour* ◇ ~ (**that** …) *He gave me a guarantee that it would never happen again.* **2** B2 a written promise given by a company that sth you buy will be replaced or repaired without payment if it goes wrong within a particular period SYN **warranty**: *The television comes with a year's guarantee.* ◇ ~ **against sth** *We provide a 5-year guarantee against rust.* ◇ **under** ~ *The watch is still under guarantee.* ⊃ see also MONEY-BACK GUARANTEE **3** B2 (used especially in negative sentences) something that makes sth else certain to happen: ~ **of** (**doing**) **sth** *Career success is no guarantee of happiness.* ◇ ~ (**that** …) *There's no guarantee that she'll come* (= she may not come). **4** money or sth valuable that you give or promise to a bank, for example, to make sure that you will do what you have promised: *We had to offer our house as a guarantee when getting the loan.* **5** a written promise to pay back money that sb else owes, or do sth that sb else promised to do, if they cannot do it themselves: *A close relative, usually a parent, can provide a guarantee for the loan.*

**guar·an·tor** /ˌɡærən'tɔː(r)/ *noun* (*formal or law*) a person who agrees to be responsible for sb or for making sure that sth happens or is done: *The United Nations will act as guarantor of the peace settlement.*

**guard** ⓞ B1 /ɡɑːd; *NAmE* ɡɑːrd/ *noun*, *verb*
■ *noun*
• PEOPLE WHO PROTECT **1** B1 [C] a person, such as a soldier, a police officer or a prison officer, who protects a place or people, or prevents prisoners from escaping: *prison/border guards* ◇ *armed guards* ◇ *The prisoner slipped past the guards on the gate and escaped.* ⊃ compare WARDER ⊃ see also BODYGUARD, COASTGUARD, LAND GUARD, LIFEGUARD, SECURITY GUARD **2** B2 [U] the act or duty of protecting property, places or people from attack or danger; the act or duty of preventing prisoners from escaping: **on** ~ *a sentry on guard* (= at his or her post, on duty) ◇ *to be* **on guard duty** ◇ **under** ~ *The escaped prisoner was brought back under armed guard.* **3** [C + sing. / pl. v.] a group of people, such as soldiers or police officers, who protect sb/sth: *the captain of the guard* ◇ *the changing of the guard* (= when one group replaces another) ◇ *Fellow airmen provided a* **guard of honour** *at his wedding.* ◇ *The president always travels with an* **armed guard**. ⊃ see also ADVANCE GUARD, NATIONAL GUARD, OLD GUARD, REARGUARD **4 the Guards** [pl.] (in the UK and some other countries) special REGIMENTS of soldiers whose original duty was to protect the king or queen
• AGAINST INJURY **5** [C] (often in compounds) something that covers a part of a person's body or a dangerous part of a machine to prevent injury: *All players wear helmets and face guards.* ◇ *Ensure the guard is in place before operating the machine.* ⊃ see also FIREGUARD, MUDGUARD, SAFEGUARD, SHIN GUARD
• ON TRAIN **6** [C] (*BrE*, *becoming old-fashioned*) = CONDUCTOR (2)
• IN BOXING / FENCING **7** [U] a position you take to defend yourself, especially in a sport such as BOXING or FENCING: *to drop/keep up your guard* ◇ (*figurative*) *In spite of the awkward questions the minister never let his guard fall for a moment.*

# guard dog

- **IN BASKETBALL 8** [C] one of the two players on a basketball team who are mainly responsible for staying close to players of the other team to stop them from scoring ⇒ see also POINT GUARD, SHOOTING GUARD
- **IN AMERICAN FOOTBALL 9** [C] one of the two players on an AMERICAN FOOTBALL team who play either side of the CENTRE FORWARD

**IDM** **be on your ˈguard** to be very careful and prepared for sth difficult or dangerous **mount/stand/keep ˈguard (over sb/sth)** to watch or protect sb/sth: *Four soldiers stood guard over the coffin.* **off (your) ˈguard** not careful or prepared for sth difficult or dangerous: *The lawyer's apparently innocent question was designed to* **catch** *the witness* **off (his) guard.** ⇒ more at DROP v.

- **verb 1** ~ **sb/sth** to protect property, places or people from attack or danger: *Armed officers guarded the entrance.* ◊ *political leaders guarded by the police* ◊ *You can't get in; the whole place is guarded.* ◊ *(figurative) a closely guarded secret* **2** ~ **sb** to prevent prisoners from escaping: *The prisoners were guarded by soldiers.*

**PHRV** **ˈguard against sth** to take care to prevent sth or to protect yourself from sth: *to guard against accidents/disease*

**ˈguard dog** *noun* a dog that is kept to guard a building

**guard·ed** /ˈɡɑːdɪd; NAmE ˈɡɑːrd-/ *adj.* (of a person or a remark they make) careful; not showing feelings or giving much information **SYN** **cautious**: *a guarded reply* ◊ *You should be more guarded in what you say to reporters.* ◊ *They gave the news a guarded welcome* (= did not show great enthusiasm about it). **OPP** **unguarded** ▸ **ˈguard·ed·ly** *adv.*

**ˈguard·house** /ˈɡɑːdhaʊs; NAmE ˈɡɑːrd-/ *noun* a building for soldiers who are guarding the entrance to a military camp or for keeping military prisoners in

**guard·ian** /ˈɡɑːdiən; NAmE ˈɡɑːrd-/ *noun* **1** a person who protects sth **SYN** **custodian**: *Farmers should be guardians of the countryside.* ◊ *The police are guardians of law and order.* **2** a person who is legally responsible for the care of another person, especially a child whose parents have died

**guardian ˈangel** *noun* a spirit that some people believe protects and guides them, especially when they are in danger: *(figurative) A delightful guide was my guardian angel for the first week of the tour.*

**guard·ian·ship** /ˈɡɑːdiənʃɪp; NAmE ˈɡɑːrd-/ *noun* [U] (formal or law) the state or position of being responsible for sb/sth

**ˈguard rail** *noun* **1** a bar placed on the edge of a path, a boat, etc. to protect people and prevent them falling over the edge **2** (*NAmE*) (*BrE* **ˈcrash barrier**) a strong low fence or wall at the side of a road or between the two halves of a major road such as a MOTORWAY or INTERSTATE

**guards·man** /ˈɡɑːdzmən; NAmE ˈɡɑːrdz-/ *noun* (*pl.* **-men** /-mən/) a soldier in the Guards or in the National Guard in the US

**guava** /ˈɡwɑːvə/ *noun* the fruit of a tropical American tree that has yellow skin and is pink or yellow inside

**gub·bins** /ˈɡʌbɪnz/ *noun* [U] (*BrE, informal*) various things that are not important: *All the gubbins that came with the computer is still in the box.*

**gu·ber·na·tor·ial** /ˌɡuːbənəˈtɔːriəl; NAmE -bərn-/ *adj.* (*formal*) connected with the job of state GOVERNOR in the US: *a gubernatorial candidate* ◊ *gubernatorial duties*

**Guern·sey** /ˈɡɜːnzi; NAmE ˈɡɜːrn-/ *noun* **1** a type of cow kept for its rich milk **2** **ˈguernsey** a thick sweater made with dark blue wool that has been specially treated so that it does not let water through, worn originally by FISHERMEN **3** **guernsey** (*AustralE*) a football sweater, especially one of the type without arms worn by Australian Rules players

**IDM** **get a ˈguernsey** (*AustralE, informal*) to be recognized as being good (originally meaning to be chosen for a football team)

**guer·rilla** (also **guer·illa**) /ɡəˈrɪlə/ *noun, adj.*
- *noun* a member of a small group of soldiers who are not part of an official army and who fight against official soldiers, usually to try to change the government: *urban guerrillas* (= those who fight in towns) ◊ *guerrilla war/warfare* (= fought by guerrillas on one or both sides) ◊ *a guerrilla movement* ⇒ compare FREEDOM FIGHTER
- *adj.* [only before noun] organized in an informal way and without official permission or approval: *Guerrilla actors took to the streets in army fatigues to protest against the war.* ◊ *guerrilla marketing* (= marketing that uses unusual methods in order to achieve the greatest effect for the smallest amount of money) ◊ *guerrilla gardening* (= growing plants on land that you do not own to make it more attractive)

**guess** /ɡes/ *verb, noun*
- *verb* **1** [I, T] to try and give an answer or make a judgement about sth without being sure of all the facts: *I don't really know. I'm just guessing.* ◊ ~ **at sth** *We can only guess at her reasons for leaving.* ◊ ~ + *adv.* *He guessed right/wrong.* ◊ ~ **(that)** … *I'd guess that she's about 30.* ◊ ~ **where, who, etc**… *Can you guess where I've been?* ◊ ~ **sth** *Can you guess his age?* ⇒ EXPRESS YOURSELF at SPECULATE **2** [T, I] to find the right answer to a question or the truth without knowing all the facts: ~ **sth** *She guessed the answer straight away.* ◊ ~ **what, where, etc**… *You'll never guess what she told me.* ◊ ~ **(that)** … *You would never guess (that) she had problems. She's always so cheerful.* ◊ *So it was Rob who broke the window? I might have guessed!* ◊ *If I had to guess, I'd say she was the one responsible for this.* ⇒ see also SECOND-GUESS **3** **I guess** …! [T] ~ **what, who, etc**… used to show that you are going to say sth surprising or exciting: *Guess what! He's asked me out! Guess who I've just seen!* **4** [T] (*informal*) to suppose that sth is true or likely: *I guess (that) you'll be looking for a new job now.* ◊ *He didn't see me, I guess.* ◊ *'Are you ready to go?' 'Yeah, I guess so.'* ◊ *'They aren't coming, then?' 'I guess not.'*

**IDM** **keep sb ˈguessing** (*informal*) to not tell sb about your plans or what is going to happen next: *It's the kind of book that keeps you guessing right to the end.*

- *noun* an attempt to give an answer or an opinion when you cannot be certain if you are right: (*BrE*) to **have/make a guess** ◊ (*NAmE*) to **take a guess**: *Go on! Have a guess!* ◊ *If I might* **hazard a guess***, I'd say she was about thirty.* ◊ *Who do you think I saw yesterday?* **I'll give you three guesses.** ◊ ~ **at sth** *But this is clearly just a* **wild guess** (= not sensible or accurate) *at what his motives could have been.* ◊ ~ **about sth** *The article is based on guesses about what might happen in the future.* ◊ ~ **as to sth** *the market's best guess as to the possible performance of the company* ◊ ~ **(that** …) *My guess is that we won't hear from him again.* ◊ **at a** ~ *At a guess, there were forty people at the party.*

**IDM** **ˈanybody's/ˈanyone's guess** (*informal*) something that nobody can be certain about: *What will happen next is anybody's guess.* **your ˈguess is as good as ˈmine** (*informal*) used to tell sb that you do not know any more about a subject than the person that you are talking to does: *'Who's going to win?' 'Your guess is as good as mine.'* ⇒ more at EDUCATED, MISS v.

**ˈguessing game** *noun* **1** a game in which you have to guess the answers to questions **2** a situation in which you do not know what is going to happen or what sb is going to do

**guess·ti·mate** (also **gues·ti·mate**) /ˈɡestɪmət/ *noun* (*informal*) an attempt to calculate sth that is based more on guessing than on information

**guess·work** /ˈɡeswɜːk; NAmE -wɜːrk/ *noun* [U] the process of trying to find an answer by guessing when you do not have enough information to be sure: *It was pure guesswork on our part.* ⇒ see also CONJECTURE *noun*

**guest** /ɡest/ *noun, verb*
- *noun* **1** a person that you have invited to your house or to a particular event that you are paying for: *They only use the dining room when they have guests.* ◊ *She had invited six guests to dinner.* ◊ **as a** ~ *I went to the theatre club as Helen's guest.* ◊ *He was the* **guest of honour** (= the

most important person invited to an event). ◊ *Liz was not on the guest list.* ⊃ see also HOUSE GUEST **2** A2 a person who is staying at a hotel, etc: *We have accommodation for 500 guests.* ◊ *Guests should vacate their rooms by 10.30 a. m.* ⊃ see also PAYING GUEST **3** (*especially NAmE*) a customer in a restaurant: *restaurant guests* **4** a famous person or performer who takes part in a television show, concert or other entertainment: *a guest star/artist* ◊ *Our special guest tonight is …* ◊ *He made a guest appearance on the show.* **5** a person who is invited to a particular place or organization, or to speak at a meeting: *a guest speaker* ◊ *as a~ The scientists are here as guests of our government.*
▶IDM **be my ˈguest** (*informal*) used to give sb permission to do sth that they have asked to do: '*Do you mind if I open the window?*' '*Be my guest.*'
■ *verb* [I] ~ (**on sth**) to take part in a television or radio show, a concert, a game, etc. as a visiting or temporary performer or player: *She guested on several chat shows while visiting Britain.*

ˈguest house *noun* **1** (*BrE*) a small hotel **2** (*NAmE*) a small house built near a large house, for guests to stay in

ˈgues·ti·mate = GUESSTIMATE

ˈguest room *noun* **1** a bedroom that is kept for guests to use **2** a bedroom in a hotel

ˈguest worker *noun* a person, usually from a poor country, who comes to another richer country in order to work there

**guff** /ɡʌf/ *noun* [U] (*informal*) ideas or talk that you think are stupid SYN **nonsense**

**guf·faw** /ɡəˈfɔː/ *verb* [I, T] (**+ speech**) to laugh noisily: *They all guffawed at his jokes.* ▶ **guf·faw** *noun*: *She let out a loud guffaw.*

**GUI** /ˈɡuː.i, ˌdʒiː juː ˈaɪ/ *noun* (*computing*) a way of giving instructions to a computer using things that can be seen on the screen such as symbols and menus (the abbreviation for 'graphical user interface')

**guid·ance** ?+ C1 W /ˈɡaɪdns/ *noun* [U] **1** ?+ C1 ~ (**on sth**) help or advice that is given to sb, especially by sb older or with more experience: *guidance for teachers on how to use video in the classroom* ◊ **under the ~of sb** *Activities all take place under the guidance of an experienced tutor.* ◊ (*NAmE*) *a guidance counselor* (= sb who advises students) **2** the process of controlling the direction of a ROCKET, etc., using electronic equipment: *a missile guidance system*

ˈguidance counselor *noun* (*NAmE*) a person who works in a school and is responsible for giving students advice about classes and helping them with personal problems

**guide** ❶ A2 /ɡaɪd/ *noun, verb*
■ *noun*
- PERSON **1** A2 a person who shows other people the way to a place, especially sb employed to show tourists around interesting places: *a tour guide* ◊ *We hired a local guide to get us across the mountains.* **2** a person who advises sb on how to live and behave: *a spiritual guide*
- BOOK/MAGAZINE **3** ?+ A2 a book, magazine, app, etc. that gives you information, help or instructions about sth: *Let's have a look at the TV guide and see what's on.* ◊ **~to sth** *a Guide to Family Health* ◊ **~for sb/sth** *study guides for mathematics and physics* **4** ?+ A2 (*also* **guide-book**) a book that gives information about a place for travellers or tourists: *travel guides* ◊ **~to sth** *a guide to Italy* ⊃ see also AUDIO GUIDE ⊃ WORDFINDER NOTE at TOURIST
- STH THAT HELPS YOU DECIDE **5** something that gives you enough information to be able to make a decision or form an opinion: *As a rough guide, allow half a cup of rice per person.* ◊ *I let my feelings be my guide.*
- GIRL **6 Guide** (*also old-fashioned* ˌGirl ˈGuide) (*both BrE*) (*US* ˌGirl ˈScout) a member of an organization (called **the Guides** *or* **the Girl Scouts**) that is similar to THE SCOUTS and that trains girls in practical skills and does a lot of activities with them, for example camping ⊃ compare BROWNIE
■ *verb*
- SHOW THE WAY **1** ?+ A2 ~ **sb (to/through/around sth)** to show sb the way to a place, often by going with them; to show sb a place that you know well: *She guided us through the busy streets.* ◊ *We were guided around the museums.*
⊃ SYNONYMS at TAKE

---

**705** | **guilty**

- INFLUENCE BEHAVIOUR/DEVELOPMENT **2** ~ **sb/sth** to direct or influence sb's behaviour or the development of sth: *He was always guided by his religious beliefs.* ◊ *The following principles guided the development of the project.*
- EXPLAIN **3** ~ **sb (through sth)** to explain sth to sb, especially sth complicated or difficult: *The health and safety officer will guide you through the safety procedures.*
- HELP SB/STH MOVE **4** ~ **sb/sth (+ adv./prep.)** to help sb/ sth to move in a particular direction; to move sth in a particular direction: *She took her arm and guided her across the busy road.* ◊ *The nurse guided the needle into position.* ⊃ see also GUIDING

**ˈguide-book** /ˈɡaɪdbʊk/ *noun* = GUIDE

**guid·ed** /ˈɡaɪdɪd/ *adj.* [usually before noun] that is led by sb who works as a guide: *a guided tour/walk*

ˌguided ˈmissile *noun* a MISSILE that can be controlled while in the air by electronic equipment

**ˈguide dog** (*NAmE also* ˈSeeing ˈEye dog™) *noun* a dog trained to guide a blind person

**ˈguide-line** ?+ B2 /ˈɡaɪdlaɪn/ *noun* **1** ?+ B2 **guidelines** [pl.] a set of rules or instructions that are given by an official organization telling you how to do sth, especially sth difficult: *The government has drawn up guidelines on the treatment of the mentally ill.* **2** ?+ B2 [C] something that can be used to help you make a decision or form an opinion: *The figures are a useful guideline when buying a house.*

**guid·ing** /ˈɡaɪdɪŋ/ *adj.* [only before noun] giving advice and help; having a strong influence on people: *She was inexperienced and needed a guiding hand.* ◊ *a guiding force*

**guild** /ɡɪld/ *noun* [C + sing./pl. v] **1** an organization of people who do the same job or who have the same interests or aims: *the Screen Actors' Guild* **2** an association of workers with special skills in the Middle Ages

**guild·hall** /ˈɡɪldhɔːl/ *noun* (*BrE*) a building in which the members of a GUILD used to meet, now often used for meetings and performances

**guile** /ɡaɪl/ *noun* [U] (*formal*) the use of clever but dishonest behaviour in order to trick people SYN **deceit**

**guile·less** /ˈɡaɪlləs/ *adj.* (*formal*) behaving in a very honest way; not knowing how to trick people ▶ **guile·less·ly** *adv.*

**guil·le·mot** /ˈɡɪlɪmɒt; *NAmE* -mɑːt/ *noun* a black and white bird with a long narrow BEAK that lives near the sea

**guil·lo·tine** /ˈɡɪlətiːn/ *noun, verb*
■ *noun* **1** a machine, originally from France, for cutting people's heads off. It has a heavy BLADE that slides down a wooden frame. **2** (*BrE*) [C] a device with a long blade for cutting paper or sheets of metal ⊃ compare PAPER CUTTER **3** [sing.] (*BrE*, *politics*) the setting of a time limit on a debate in Parliament
■ *verb* **1** ~ **sb** to kill sb by cutting off their head with a guillotine **2** ~ **sth** (*BrE*) to cut paper using a guillotine **3** ~ **sth** (*BrE*, *politics*) to limit the amount of time spent discussing a new law in Parliament: *to guillotine a bill*

**guilt** ?+ C1 /ɡɪlt/ *noun, verb*
■ *noun* [U] **1** ?+ C1 ~ (**about sth**) the unhappy feelings caused by knowing or thinking that you have done sth wrong: *She had feelings of guilt about leaving her children and going to work.* ◊ *Many survivors were left with a sense of guilt.* ◊ *a guilt complex* (= an exaggerated sense of guilt) **2** ?+ C1 the fact that sb has done sth illegal: *His guilt was proved beyond all doubt by the prosecution.* ◊ *an admission of guilt* OPP **innocence 3** ?+ C1 blame or responsibility for doing sth wrong or for sth bad that has happened: *The investigation will try to find out where the guilt for the disaster really lies.* ▶ **guilt·less** *adj.*
▶IDM **a ˈguilt trip** (*informal*) things you say to sb in order to make them feel guilty about sth: *Don't lay a guilt trip on your child about schoolwork.*
■ *verb*
▶PHRV **ˈguilt sb into sth/into doing sth** (*informal*) to make sb do sth by persuading them that it is wrong not to do it: *I only went because she guilted me into it.*

**guilty** ❶ B1 /ˈɡɪlti/ *adj.* (**guilt·ier, guilti·est**) HELP more guilty and most guilty are more common **1** ?+ B1 feeling ashamed because you have done sth that you know is

# guinea

wrong or have not done sth that you should have done: *John had a guilty look on his face.* ◊ *I had a guilty conscience and could not sleep.* ◊ **~ about (doing) sth** *I feel very guilty about leaving her.* **2** ? B1 having done sth illegal; being responsible for sth bad that has happened: *He pleaded guilty to murder.* ◊ **~ of sth** *The jury found the defendant not guilty of the offence.* ◊ *We've all been guilty of selfishness at some time in our lives.* ◊ **the guilty party** (= the person responsible for sth bad happening) OPP **innocent** ▶ **guilt·ily** /-tɪli/ *adv.*
IDM **a guilty ˈpleasure** something that you enjoy, even though you feel it is not really a good thing: *Daytime TV is one of my guilty pleasures.* **a ˌguilty ˈsecret** a secret that sb feels ashamed about

**guinea** /ˈɡɪni/ *noun* an old British gold coin or unit of money worth 21 SHILLINGS (= now £1.05). Prices are sometimes still given in guineas, for example when buying or selling horses.

**ˈguinea fowl** *noun* [C, U] (*pl.* **guinea fowl**) a bird of the PHEASANT family that has dark grey feathers with white spots, and is often used for food; the meat of this bird: *roast guinea fowl*

**ˈguinea pig** *noun* **1** a small animal with short ears and no tail, often kept as a pet **2** a person used in medical or other experiments: *Students in fifty schools are to act as guinea pigs for these new teaching methods.*

**Guin·ness™** /ˈɡɪnɪs/ *noun* [U, C] a type of very dark brown beer, with a white HEAD (= top) on it

**guise** /ɡaɪz/ *noun* a way in which sb/sth appears, often in a way that is different from usual or that hides the truth about them/it: **in a … ~** *The story appears in different guises in different cultures.* ◊ **under the ~ of sth** *His speech presented racist ideas under the guise of nationalism.*

**gui·tar** ? A1 /ɡɪˈtɑː(r)/ *noun* a musical instrument that usually has six strings and that you play with your fingers or with a PLECTRUM: *an acoustic/electric guitar* ◊ *a guitar player* ◊ *a guitar solo/riff* ◊ *Do you play the guitar?* ◊ *She plays guitar in a band.* ◊ **on ~** *The track features Anton on guitar and vocals.* ⊃ see also AIR GUITAR, BASS¹ *noun*, LEAD GUITAR, RHYTHM GUITAR

**gui·tar·ist** /ɡɪˈtɑːrɪst/ *noun* a person who plays the guitar

**Gu·ja·rati** (also **Gu·je·rati**) /ˌɡʊdʒəˈrɑːti/ *noun* **1** [C] a person from the state of Gujarat in western India **2** [U] the language of Gujarat ▶ **Gu·ja·rati** (also **Gu·je·rati**) *adj.*

**Gulag** /ˈɡuːlæɡ; NAmE -lɑːɡ/ *noun* **1** **the Gulag** [sing.] a system of prison labour camps in the Soviet Union from 1930 to 1955, where many people died **2 gulag** [C] any political labour camp: *Millions of innocent civilians were herded into gulags.*

**gulch** /ɡʌltʃ/ *noun* (*especially NAmE*) a narrow valley with steep sides that was formed by a fast stream flowing through it

**gulf** /ɡʌlf/ *noun* **1** [C] a large area of sea that is partly surrounded by land: *the Gulf of Mexico* **2 the Gulf** [sing.] *the Persian Gulf*, the area of sea between the Arabian PENINSULA and Iran: *the Gulf States* (= the countries with coasts on the Gulf) **3** [C, usually sing.] **~ (between A and B)** a large difference between two people or groups in the way that they think, live or feel: *The gulf between rich and poor is enormous.* **4** [C] a wide deep opening in the ground
IDM see BRIDGE *v.*

**the ˈGulf Stream** *noun* [sing.] a warm current of water flowing across the Atlantic Ocean from the Gulf of Mexico towards Europe

**gull** /ɡʌl/ (also **sea-gull**) *noun* a SEABIRD with long wings and usually white and grey or black feathers. There are several types of gull. ⊃ VISUAL VOCAB page V2 ⊃ see also HERRING GULL

**gul·let** /ˈɡʌlɪt/ *noun* the tube through which food passes from the mouth to the stomach SYN **oesophagus** ⊃ VISUAL VOCAB page V1

**gul·lible** /ˈɡʌləbl/ *adj.* too willing to believe or accept what other people tell you and therefore easily tricked SYN **naive** ▶ **gul·li·bil·ity** /ˌɡʌləˈbɪləti/ *noun* [U]

**gully** (also **gul·ley**) /ˈɡʌli/ *noun* (*pl.* **gul·lies, gul·leys**) **1** a small, narrow channel, usually formed by a stream or by rain **2** a deep DITCH

**gulp** /ɡʌlp/ *verb, noun*
■ *verb* **1** [T] **~ sth (down)** to SWALLOW large amounts of food or drink quickly: *He gulped down the rest of his tea and went out.* **2** [I] to SWALLOW, but without eating or drinking sth, especially because of a strong emotion such as fear or surprise: *She gulped nervously before trying to answer.* **3** [I, T] to breathe quickly and deeply, because you need more air: **~ (for sth)** *She came up gulping for air.* ◊ **~ sth (in)** *He leant against the car, gulping in the cold air.*
PHRV **ˌgulp sth↔ˈback** to stop yourself showing your emotions by SWALLOWING hard: *She gulped back her tears and forced a smile.*
■ *noun* **1 ~ (of sth)** an amount of sth that you SWALLOW or drink quickly: *He took a gulp of coffee.* **2** an act of breathing in or of SWALLOWING sth: *'Can you start on Monday?' Amy gave a gulp. 'Of course,' she said.* ◊ *He drank the glass of whisky in one gulp.*

**gum** /ɡʌm/ *noun, verb*
■ *noun* **1** [C, usually pl.] either of the areas of FLESH in the mouth to which the teeth are attached: *gum disease* **2** [U] a sticky substance produced by some types of tree **3** [U] a type of GLUE used for sticking light things together, such as paper **4** [U] = CHEWING GUM **5** [C] a fairly hard, coloured sweet that tastes of fruit and that you CHEW: *fruit gums*
IDM **by ˈgum!** (*old-fashioned, informal*) used to show surprise
■ *verb* (-mm-) **~ A to B** | **~ sth (down)** (*rather old-fashioned*) to spread GLUE on the surface of sth; to stick two things together with GLUE: *A large address label was gummed to the package.*
PHRV **ˌgum sth↔ˈup** [usually passive] (*informal*) to cover or fill sth with a sticky substance so that it stops moving or working as it should

**gum·ball** /ˈɡʌmbɔːl/ *noun* (*NAmE*) a small ball of CHEWING GUM that looks like a sweet

**gumbo** /ˈɡʌmbəʊ/ *noun* [U] **1** (*NAmE*) = OKRA **2** a thick chicken or SEAFOOD soup, usually made with the vegetable OKRA

**gum·boot** /ˈɡʌmbuːt/ *noun* (*BrE, old-fashioned*) = WELLINGTON

**gummy** /ˈɡʌmi/ *adj.* (*informal*) **1** sticky or covered in gum **2** a gummy smile shows your teeth and GUMS

**gump·tion** /ˈɡʌmpʃn/ *noun* [U] (*old-fashioned, informal*) **1** the intelligence needed to know what to do in a particular situation **2** courage and strength of mind

**gum·shoe** /ˈɡʌmʃuː/ *noun* (*NAmE, old-fashioned, informal*) a detective

**ˈgum tree** *noun* a EUCALYPTUS tree

**gun** ? A2 /ɡʌn/ *noun, verb*
■ *noun* **1** ? A2 [C] a weapon that is used for firing bullets or SHELLS: *I have never fired a gun in my life.* ◊ *He pointed a gun at her head.* ◊ *Should police officers carry guns?* ◊ *a toy/replica gun* ◊ *anti-aircraft guns* ◊ *A loaded gun was found in the vehicle.* ◊ *The guard drew his gun* (= took it out so it was ready to use). ◊ *She pulled a gun on me* (= took out a gun and aimed it at me). ◊ *The gun went off by accident.* ◊ *a gun battle between rival gangs* ◊ *high levels of gun crime/violence* ◊ *gun owners/ownership* ⊃ see also AIRGUN, HANDGUN, MACHINE GUN, RAY GUN, SHOTGUN, SIX-GUN, STUN GUN, SUB-MACHINE GUN, TOMMY GUN **2** [C] a tool that uses pressure to send out a substance or an object: *a staple gun* ⊃ see also SQUIRT GUN, WATER GUN **3 the gun** [sing.] the signal to begin a race, that is given by firing a special gun, called a STARTING PISTOL, into the air **4** [C] (*informal, especially NAmE*) a person who is paid to shoot sb: *a hired gun* ⊃ see also BIG GUN, FLASHGUN, LASER GUN, SON OF A GUN
IDM **(with) all/both guns ˈblazing** (*informal*) with a lot of energy and DETERMINATION: *The champions came out (with) all guns blazing.* **ˌhold / put a ˈgun to sb's ˈhead** to force sb to do sth that they do not want to do, by making threats **under the ˈgun** (*NAmE, informal*) experiencing a lot of pressure: *I'm really under the gun today.* ⊃ more at GREAT *adj.*, JUMP *v.*, SPIKE *v.*, STICK *v.*

**verb** (-nn-) **1** [I] (*NAmE*) (of an engine) to run very quickly: *a line of motorcycles with their engines gunning* **2** [T] ~ *sth* + *adv./prep.* (*NAmE*) to start driving a vehicle very fast: *He gunned the cab through the red light.*
**PHRV** be ˈgunning for sb (*informal*) to be looking for an opportunity to blame or attack sb be ˈgunning for sth to be competing for or trying hard to get sth: *She's gunning for the top job.* ˌgun sb↔ˈdown [usually passive] to shoot sb, especially killing or seriously injuring them

**gun·boat** /ˈgʌnbəʊt/ *noun* a small ship that is fitted with large guns

ˈgun carriage *noun* a support on wheels for a large heavy gun

ˈgun control *noun* [U] (especially in the US) laws that limit the sale and use of guns

ˈgun dog *noun* a dog trained to help in the sport of shooting, for example by finding birds that have been shot

**gun·fight** /ˈgʌnfaɪt/ *noun* a fight between people using guns ▸ **gun·fight·er** *noun*

**gun·fire** /ˈgʌnfaɪə(r)/ *noun* [U] the repeated firing of guns; the sound of guns firing: *an exchange of gunfire with the police* ◊ *I could hear gunfire.*

**gunge** /gʌndʒ/ (*BrE*) (also **gunk** *NAmE, BrE*) *noun* [U] (*informal*) any unpleasant, sticky or dirty substance ▸ **gungy** *adj.*

**gung-ho** /ˌgʌŋ ˈhəʊ/ *adj.* (*informal, disapproving*) too enthusiastic about sth, without thinking seriously about it, especially about fighting and war

**gunk** /gʌŋk/ (*especially NAmE*) (*BrE also* **gunge**) *noun* [U] (*informal*) any unpleasant, sticky or dirty substance ▸ **gunky** *adj.*

**gun·man** /ˈgʌnmən/ *noun* (*pl.* -men /-mən/) a man who uses a gun to steal from or kill people

**gun·metal** /ˈgʌnmetl/ *noun* [U] **1** a metal that is a mixture of COPPER, tin and ZINC **2** a blue-grey colour

**gun·nel** = GUNWALE

**gun·ner** /ˈgʌnə(r)/ *noun* **1** a member of the armed forces who is trained to use large guns **2** a soldier in the British ARTILLERY (= the part of the army that uses large guns)

**gun·nery** /ˈgʌnəri/ *noun* [U] (*specialist*) the design, production or operation of large military guns

**gunny** /ˈgʌni/ *noun* [U] a type of rough cloth used for making SACKS

**gun·point** /ˈgʌnpɔɪnt/ *noun*
**IDM** at ˈgunpoint while threatening sb or being threatened with a gun: *The driver was robbed at gunpoint.*

**gun·pow·der** /ˈgʌnpaʊdə(r)/ (*also* **pow·der**) *noun* [U] EXPLOSIVE powder used especially in bombs or FIREWORKS

**gun·run·ner** /ˈgʌnrʌnə(r)/ *noun* a person who secretly and illegally brings guns into a country ▸ **gun·run·ning** *noun* [U]

**gun·ship** /ˈgʌnʃɪp/ *noun* an armed military helicopter or other aircraft

**gun·shot** /ˈgʌnʃɒt; *NAmE* -ʃɑːt/ *noun* **1** [U] the bullets that are fired from a gun: *gunshot wounds* **2** [C] the firing of a gun; the sound of it being fired: *I heard the sound of gunshots out in the street.*

**gun·sight** /ˈgʌnsaɪt/ *noun* a part of a gun that you look through in order to aim it accurately ⊃ see also SIGHT *noun* (7)

**gun·sling·er** /ˈgʌnslɪŋə(r)/ *noun* (*NAmE*) (especially in the American Wild West) a person who was paid to kill people

**gun·smith** /ˈgʌnsmɪθ/ *noun* a person who makes and repairs guns

**gun·wale** (*also* **gun·nel**) /ˈgʌnl/ *noun* the upper edge of the side of a boat or small ship

**guppy** /ˈgʌpi/ *noun* (*pl.* -ies) a small FRESHWATER fish, commonly kept in AQUARIUMS

**gur·dwara** /gɜːˈdwɑːrə; *NAmE* gɜːrˈd-/ *noun* a building in which Sikhs WORSHIP

**gur·gle** /ˈgɜːgl; *NAmE* ˈgɜːrgl/ *verb, noun*
▪ *verb* **1** [I] to make a sound like water flowing quickly through a narrow space: *Water gurgled through the pipes.* ◊ *a gurgling stream* **2** [I] if a baby **gurgles**, it makes a noise in its throat when it is happy

▪ *noun* **1** a sound like water flowing quickly through a narrow space **2** the sound that babies make in the throat, especially when they are happy

**Gur·kha** /ˈgɜːkə; *NAmE* ˈgɜːrkə/ *noun* one of a group of people from Nepal who are known as good soldiers. Some Gurkhas are members of a REGIMENT in the British army.

**gurn** (*also* **girn**) /gɜːn/ *verb* [I] (*especially BrE*) to deliberately pull your face into a silly or unpleasant shape ▸ **gurn·er** *noun*

**gur·ney** /ˈgɜːni; *NAmE* ˈgɜːrni/ *noun* (*especially NAmE*) a type of TROLLEY that is used for moving patients in a hospital

**guru** /ˈguruː; *NAmE* ˈguːruː/ *noun* **1** a Hindu or Sikh religious teacher or leader **2** (*informal*) a person who is an expert on a particular subject or who is very good at doing sth: *a management/health/fashion etc. guru*

**gush** /gʌʃ/ *verb, noun*
▪ *verb* **1** [I] ~ **out of/from/into sth** | ~ **out/in** to flow or pour suddenly and quickly out of a hole in large amounts: *blood gushing from a wound* ◊ *Water gushed out of the pipe.* **2** [T] ~ **sth** (of a container/vehicle etc.) to suddenly let out large amounts of a liquid: *The tanker was gushing oil.* ◊ (*figurative*) *She absolutely gushed enthusiasm.* **3** [T, I] (+ **speech**) (*disapproving*) to express so much praise or emotion about sb/sth that it does not seem sincere: *'You are clever,' she gushed.*
▪ *noun* [usually sing.] **1** ~ **(of sth)** a large amount of liquid suddenly and quickly flowing or pouring out of sth: *a gush of blood* **2** ~ **(of sth)** a sudden strong expression of feeling: *a gush of emotion*

**gush·er** /ˈgʌʃə(r)/ *noun* **1** (*especially NAmE*) an OIL WELL where the oil comes out quickly and in large quantities **2** (*disapproving*) a person who expresses too much praise or emotion about sb/sth and does not seem sincere

**gush·ing** /ˈgʌʃɪŋ/ *adj.* (*disapproving*) expressing so much enthusiasm, praise or emotion that it does not seem sincere ▸ **gush·ing·ly** *adv.*

**gus·set** /ˈgʌsɪt/ *noun* an extra piece of cloth SEWN into a piece of clothing to make it wider, stronger or more comfortable

**gussy** /ˈgʌsi/ *verb* (**gus·sies, gussy·ing, gus·sied, gus·sied**)
**PHRV** ˌgussy ˈup | ˌgussy sb/sth ˈup (*NAmE, informal*) to dress yourself in an attractive way; to make sb/sth more attractive, especially in a SHOWY way **SYN** dress up: *Even the stars get tired of gussying up for the awards.*

**gust** /gʌst/ *noun, verb*
▪ *noun* **1** a sudden strong increase in the amount and speed of wind that is blowing: *A gust of wind blew his hat off.* ◊ *The wind was blowing in gusts.* ⊃ WORDFINDER NOTE at WIND¹ **2** a sudden strong expression of emotion: *a gust of laughter*
▪ *verb* [I] (of the wind) to suddenly blow very hard: *winds gusting up to 60 mph*

**gusto** /ˈgʌstəʊ/ *noun* [U] enthusiasm and energy in doing sth: *They sang with gusto.*

**gusty** /ˈgʌsti/ *adj.* [usually before noun] with the wind blowing in gusts: *a gusty morning* ◊ *gusty winds*

**gut** /gʌt/ *noun, verb, adj.*
▪ *noun* **1** [C] the tube in the body through which food passes when it leaves the stomach **SYN** intestine **2** [C] **guts** [pl.] the organs in and around the stomach, especially in an animal: *I'll only cook fish if the guts have been removed.* **3** [C] (*informal*) a person's stomach, especially when it is large **SYN** belly: *Have you seen the gut on him!* ◊ *a beer gut* (= caused by drinking a lot of beer regularly) **4** **guts** [pl.] (*informal*) the courage and strength of mind that it takes to do sth difficult or unpleasant: *He doesn't have the guts to walk away from a well-paid job.* **5** [C, usually pl.] the place where your natural feelings that make you react in a particular way are thought to be: **in your guts** *I had a feeling in my guts that something was wrong.* **6** **guts** [pl.] the most important part of sth: *the guts of the problem* **7** (*also* **catgut**) [U] thin strong string made from animals' INTESTINES and used in making musical instruments, tennis RACKETS and medical equipment

# gutless

**IDM** **go with your 'gut** to make a decision based on sth that you are certain about, even though you do not have any direct proof and cannot explain why you are certain: *I went with my gut and turned down the job.* **have sb's 'guts for 'garters** (*BrE, informal*) to be very angry with sb and punish them severely for sth they have done **slog/sweat/work your 'guts out** (*informal*) to work very hard to achieve sth: *I slogged my guts out for the exam.* ⊃ more at BUST v., GREEDY, HATE v., SPILL v.
- **verb** (**-tt-**) **1** [usually passive] to destroy the inside or contents of a building or room: **be gutted (by sth)** *The hotel was completely gutted by fire last year.* **2** ~ **sth** to remove the organs from inside a fish or an animal to prepare it for cooking
- **adj.** [only before noun] based on feelings and emotions rather than thought and reason: *a gut feeling/reaction ◇ You have to work on gut instinct.*

**gut·less** /ˈgʌtləs/ *adj.* not brave or determined enough to do sth

**gutsy** /ˈgʌtsi/ *adj.* (**guts·ier, gutsi·est**) (*informal*) **1** showing courage and the desire to succeed: *a gutsy fighter/win* **2** having strong and unusual qualities: *a gutsy red wine ◇ a gutsy song*

**gut·ted** /ˈgʌtɪd/ *adj.* [not before noun] (*BrE, informal*) extremely sad or disappointed: *Disappointed? I was gutted!*

**gut·ter** /ˈgʌtə(r)/ *noun, verb*
- **noun 1** [C] a long curved channel made of metal or plastic that is fixed under the edge of a roof to carry away the water when it rains: *a blocked/leaking gutter* **2** [C] a channel at the edge of a road where water collects and is carried away to DRAINS **3 the gutter** [sing.] the bad social conditions or low moral standards sometimes connected with the lowest level of society: *She rose from the gutter to become a great star. ◇ the language of the gutter* (= using swear words)
- **verb** [I] (*literary*) (of a flame or CANDLE) to burn in an unsteady way

**gut·ter·ing** /ˈgʌtərɪŋ/ *noun* [U] the system of gutters on a building; the material used to make gutters: *a length of guttering*

**the gutter 'press** *noun* [sing.] (*BrE, disapproving*) newspapers that print a lot of SHOCKING stories about people's private lives rather than serious news

**gut·tur·al** /ˈgʌtərəl/ *adj.* (of a sound) made or seeming to be made at the back of the throat: *guttural consonants ◇ a low guttural growl*

**'gut-wrenching** *adj.* (*informal*) very unpleasant; making you feel very upset

**guv** /gʌv/ *exclamation* (*BrE, informal*) used by a man to address another man who is a customer, etc., meaning 'sir'

**guv'nor** /ˈgʌvnə(r)/ *noun* (*BrE, informal*) (often used as a way of addressing sb) a man who is in a position of authority, for example your employer: *Do you want me to ask the guv'nor about it?* ⊃ see also GOVERNOR

**guy** ⓘ **A2** /gaɪ/ *noun* **1** ⓘ **A2** [C] (*informal*) a man: *a big/little guy ◇ a nice/smart/tough guy ◇ The poor guy must have been terrified. ◇ a Dutch guy ◇ At the end of the film the bad guy gets shot. ◇ While the cops should be the good guys, it's much more complex than that.* ⊃ see also FALL GUY, MR NICE GUY, WISE GUY **2 guys** [pl.] (*informal*) a group of people of either sex: *Come on, you guys, let's get going!* **3** [C] (in the UK) a model of a man dressed in old clothes that is burned on a BONFIRE on 5 November during the celebrations for Bonfire Night **4** (*also* **guy rope**) [C] a rope used to keep a POLE or tent in a secure position ⊃ picture at TENT

**Guy Fawkes night** /ˌgaɪ ˈfɔːks naɪt/ *noun* [U, C] Bonfire Night

**guz·zle** /ˈgʌzl/ *verb* [T, I] ~ **(sth)** (*informal, usually disapproving*) to drink sth quickly and in large amounts. In British English it also means to eat food quickly and in large amounts: *The kids seem to be guzzling soft drinks all day. ◇ (figurative) My car guzzles fuel.*

**guz·zler** /ˈgʌzlə(r)/ *noun* (*informal*) (especially in compounds) a person who drinks or eats sth quickly and in large amounts; sb/sth that uses a lot of fuel, power or another resource ⊃ see also GAS GUZZLER

**gweilo** /ˈgweɪləʊ/ *SEAsianE* /kwɪˈloʊ/ *noun* (*pl.* **-os**) (*SEAsianE*) a person who comes from a different country, especially from the western part of the world

**gybe** (*especially BrE*) (*NAmE usually* **jibe**) /dʒaɪb/ *verb, noun*
- **verb** [I] (*specialist*) to change direction when sailing with the wind behind you, by moving the sail from one side of the boat to the other ⊃ compare TACK (3)
- **noun** (*specialist*) an act of gybing

**gym** ⓘ **A1** /dʒɪm/ *noun* **1** ⓘ **A1** (*also formal* **gym·nasium**) [C] a room or hall with equipment for doing physical exercise, for example in a school: *The school has recently built a new gym. ◇* **in a**~ *to play basketball in the gym* **2** ⓘ **A1** [C] a private club where people go to do physical exercise in order to stay or become healthy and fit **SYN** health club: *I just joined a gym. ◇* **at a** ~ *I work out at the gym most days.* ⊃ WORDFINDER NOTE at FIT **3** [U] physical exercises done in a gym, especially at school: *I don't enjoy gym. ◇ gym shoes* ⊃ see also JUNGLE GYM

**gym·khana** /dʒɪmˈkɑːnə/ *noun* (*BrE*) **1** an event in which people riding horses take part in various competitions **2** (*IndE*) a public place with facilities for sports

**gym·na·sium** /dʒɪmˈneɪziəm/ *noun* (*pl.* **gym·na·siums** *or* **gym·na·sia** /-ziə/) (*formal*) a gym

**gym·nast** /ˈdʒɪmnæst/ *noun* a person who performs gymnastics, especially in a competition

**gym·nas·tics** /dʒɪmˈnæstɪks/ *noun* [U] physical exercises, often using special equipment, that develop and show the body's strength and ability to move and bend easily, often done as a sport in competitions: *a gymnastics competition ◇ (figurative) mental/verbal gymnastics* (= quick or clever thinking or use of words) ► **gym·nas·tic** *adj.* [only before noun]

**'gym shoe** *noun* **1** (*NAmE*) = SNEAKER **2** (*BrE, old-fashioned*) = PLIMSOLL

**gy·nae·colo·gist** (*BrE*) (*NAmE* **gyne·colo·gist**) /ˌgaɪnəˈkɒlədʒɪst/; *NAmE* -ˈkɑːl-/ *noun* a doctor who studies and treats the medical conditions and diseases of women, especially those connected with sexual REPRODUCTION ⊃ WORDFINDER NOTE at SPECIALIST

**gy·nae·col·ogy** (*BrE*) (*NAmE* **gyne·cology**) /ˌgaɪnəˈkɒlədʒi/; *NAmE* -ˈkɑːl-/ *noun* [U] the scientific study and treatment of the medical conditions and diseases of women, especially those connected with sexual REPRODUCTION ► **gy·nae·co·logic·al** (*BrE*) (*NAmE* **gyne-**) /ˌgaɪnəkəˈlɒdʒɪkl/; *NAmE* -ˈlɑːdʒ-/ *adj.*: *a gynaecological examination*

**gyp** /dʒɪp/ *noun, verb*
- **noun** [sing.] (*NAmE, informal*) an act of charging too much money for sth: *That meal was a real gyp.*
- **IDM** **give sb 'gyp** (*BrE, informal*) to cause sb a lot of pain: *My back's been giving me gyp lately.*
- **verb** (**-pp-**) ~ **sb** (*especially NAmE*) to cheat or trick sb, especially by taking their money

**gyp·sum** /ˈdʒɪpsəm/ *noun* [U] a soft white mineral like CHALK that is found naturally and is used in making PLASTER OF PARIS

**Gypsy** (*also* **Gipsy**) /ˈdʒɪpsi/ *noun* (*pl.* **-ies**) (*sometimes offensive*) **1** a member of a race of people, originally from Asia, who traditionally travel around and live in CARAVANS. Many people prefer to use the name Roma or Romani. **2** = TRAVELLER (2)

**gyr·ate** /dʒaɪˈreɪt; *NAmE* ˈdʒaɪreɪt/ *verb* [I, T] to move around in circles; to make sth, especially a part of your body, move around: *They began gyrating to the music. ◇ The leaves gyrated slowly to the ground. ◇* ~ **sth** *As the lead singer gyrated his hips, the crowd screamed wildly.* ► **gyr·ation** /dʒaɪˈreɪʃn/ *noun* [C, usually pl., U]

**gyro·scope** /ˈdʒaɪrəskəʊp/ (*also informal* **gyro** /ˈdʒaɪrəʊ/) *noun* a device consisting of a wheel that turns rapidly inside a frame and does not change position when the frame is moved. Gyroscopes are often used to keep ships and aircraft steady. ► **gyro·scop·ic** /ˌdʒaɪrəˈskɒpɪk/; *NAmE* -ˈskɑːp-/ *adj.*

**H** (also **h**) /eɪtʃ/ noun [C, U] (pl. **Hs**, **H's**, **h's** /ˈeɪtʃɪz/) the 8th letter of the English alphabet: *'Hat' begins with (an) H/'H'.* ⊃ compare AITCH ⊃ see also H-BOMB

**H2O** (also **H₂O**) /ˌeɪtʃ tuː ˈəʊ/ noun [U] (informal) water (the chemical symbol, used in non-scientific contexts): *A ten-minute shower uses 15 gallons of H2O.*

**ha¹** /hɑː/ exclamation **1** (also **hah**) the sound that people make when they are surprised or pleased, or when they have discovered sth: *Ha! It serves you right!* ◊ *Ha! I knew he was hiding something.* **2** (also **ha! ha!**) the word for the sound that people make when they laugh ◊ see also FUNNY HA-HA at FUNNY **3** (also **ha! ha!**) (informal, ironic) used to show that you do not think that sth is funny: *Ha! Ha! Very funny! Now give me back my shoes.* ⊃ see also HOO-HA

**ha²** abbr. (in writing) HECTARE

**ha·be·as cor·pus** /ˌheɪbiəs ˈkɔːpəs; NAmE ˈkɔːrp-/ noun [U] (from Latin, law) a law that states that a person who has been arrested should not be kept in prison longer than a particular period of time unless a judge in court has decided that it is right

**hab·er·dash·er** /ˈhæbədæʃə(r); NAmE -bərd-/ noun (old-fashioned) **1** (BrE) a person who owns or works in a shop selling small articles for SEWING, for example, needles, pins, cotton and buttons **2 hab·er·dash·er's** (pl. **hab·er·dash·ers**) (BrE) a shop that sells these things **3** (NAmE) a person who owns, manages or works in a shop that makes and sells men's clothes

**hab·er·dash·ery** /ˈhæbəˈdæʃəri; NAmE ˈhæbərdæʃəri/ noun (pl. **-ies**) (old-fashioned) **1** [U] (BrE) small articles for SEWING, for example needles, pins, cotton and buttons **2** [U] (NAmE) men's clothes **3** [C] a shop or part of a shop where haberdashery is sold

**habit** ❶ 🅰2 /ˈhæbɪt/ noun **1** ❷ 🅰2 [C] a thing that you do often and almost without thinking, especially sth that is hard to stop doing: *You need to change your eating habits.* ◊ *good/bad habits* ◊ *Most of us have some undesirable habits.* ◊ ~ **of doing sth** *The strategy is helping children develop the habit of reading for fun.* ◊ *It's all right to borrow money occasionally, but don't let it become a habit.* ◊ *I'd prefer you not to make a habit of it.* ◊ **in the ~ of doing sth** *I'm not in the habit of letting strangers into my apartment.* ◊ *I've got into the habit of turning on the TV as soon as I get home.* ⊃ WORDFINDER NOTE at BEHAVIOUR **2** ❓ 🅱1 [U] usual behaviour: **out of ~** *I only do it out of habit.* ◊ *I'm a creature of habit* (= I have a fixed and regular way of doing things). **3** [C] (informal) a strong need to keep using drugs, alcohol or cigarettes regularly: *He began to finance his habit through burglary.* ◊ *She's tried to give up smoking but just can't kick the habit.* ◊ *a 50-a-day habit* **4** [C] a long piece of clothing worn by a MONK or NUN ⒾⒹⓂ see FORCE n.

**hab·it·able** /ˈhæbɪtəbl/ (also less frequent **inhabitable**) adj. suitable for people to live in: *The house should be habitable by the new year.* 🆀🅿🅿 **uninhabitable**

**habi·tat** ❓+ 🅱2 /ˈhæbɪtæt/ noun the place where a particular type of animal or plant is normally found: *The panda's natural habitat is the bamboo forest.* ◊ *the destruction of wildlife habitat*

**habi·ta·tion** /ˌhæbɪˈteɪʃn/ noun **1** [U] the act of living in a place: *They looked around for any signs of habitation.* ◊ *The houses were unfit for human habitation* (= not clean or safe enough for people to live in). **2** [C] (formal) a place where people live: *The road serves the scattered habitations along the coast.*

**'habit-forming** adj. a **habit-forming** activity or drug is one that makes you want to continue doing it or taking it

**ha·bit·ual** /həˈbɪtʃuəl/ adj. **1** [only before noun] usual for or typical of sb/sth: *They waited for his habitual response.* ◊ (formal) *a person's place of habitual residence* **2** (of an action) done, often in a way that is annoying or difficult to stop: *habitual complaining* ◊ *the habitual use of heroin* **3** [only before noun] (of a person) doing sth that has become a habit and is therefore difficult to stop: *a habitual criminal/drinker/liar, etc.* 🅷🅴🅻🅿 Some speakers do not pronounce the 'h' at the beginning of **habitual** and use 'an' instead of 'a' before it. This now sounds old-fashioned. ▶ **ha·bit·ual·ly** /-əli/ adv.: *the dark glasses he habitually wore*

**ha·bitu·ated** /həˈbɪtʃueɪtɪd/ adj. ~ **(to sth)** (formal) familiar with sth because you have done it or experienced it often 🆂🆈🅽 **accustomed** ▶ **ha·bitu·ation** /həˌbɪtʃuˈeɪʃn/ noun [U] ~ **(of sb/sth) (to sth)**: *the habituation of animals to a new environment*

**ha·bi·tué** /həˈbɪtʃueɪ, æˈb-/ noun (from French, formal) a person who goes regularly to a particular place or event 🆂🆈🅽 **regular**: *a(n) habitué of upmarket clubs*

**ha·ci·enda** /ˌhæsiˈendə; NAmE ˌhɑːs-/ noun a large farm in a Spanish-speaking country

**hack** /hæk/ verb, noun

▪ verb **1** [T, I] to hit and cut sb/sth in a rough, heavy way: ~ **sb/sth + adv./prep.** *I hacked the dead branches off.* ◊ *They were hacked to death as they tried to escape.* ◊ *We had to hack our way through the jungle.* ◊ **+ adv./prep.** *We hacked away at the bushes.* **2** [T] ~ **sb/sth + adv./prep.** to kick sth roughly or without control: *He hacked the ball away.* **3** [I, T] (computing) to secretly find a way of looking at and/or changing information on sb else's computer system without permission: ~ **into sth** *He hacked into the bank's computer.* ◊ ~ **sth** *They had hacked secret data.* **4** [I] + **adv./prep.** (computing) to work together informally and often quickly with other people to create a program using different technologies: *We spent the morning hacking around with HTML and building web pages.* **5** [T] **can/can't hack it** (informal) to be able/not able to manage in a particular situation: *Lots of people leave this job because they can't hack it.* **6** [I] (usually **go hacking**) (especially BrE) to ride a horse for pleasure **7** [I] (NAmE, informal) to drive a taxi

▪ noun **1** (disapproving) a writer, especially of newspaper articles, who does a lot of low quality work and does not get paid much **2** (disapproving) a person who does the hard and often boring work for an organization, especially a politician: *a party hack* **3** an ordinary horse or one that can be hired **4** (NAmE, informal) a taxi **5** an act of hitting sth, especially with a cutting tool **6** a piece of computer CODE that provides a quick solution to a problem by adding to the official function of a program **7** (often in compounds) (informal) a strategy or technique that you use in order to manage an activity in a more efficient way: *Have you got any clever parenting hacks?* ◊ *Why not try these genius food hacks to save time?* ⊃ compare LIFEHACK

**hack·athon** /ˈhækəθɒn; NAmE -θɑːn/ noun (informal) an event at which a large number of people work together developing computer programs, usually over several days

**ˌhacked ˈoff** adj. [not before noun] (BrE, informal) extremely annoyed 🆂🆈🅽 **fed up**: *I'm really hacked off.*

**hack·er** /ˈhækə(r)/ noun a person who uses computers to get access to data in sb else's computer or phone system without permission ⊃ see also PHONE HACKER

**hack·ing** /ˈhækɪŋ/ noun [U] the activity of using computers to get access to data in sb else's computer or phone system without permission: *The government tax website is vulnerable to hacking, putting taxpayers' information at risk.* ⊃ see also PHONE HACKING

**ˈhacking ˈcough** noun [sing.] a dry painful COUGH that is repeated often

**hackles** /ˈhæklz/ noun [pl.] the hairs on the back of the neck of a dog, cat, etc. that rise when the animal is afraid or angry

ⒾⒹⓂ **make sb's ˈhackles rise | raise sb's ˈhackles** to make sb angry **sb's ˈhackles rise** to become angry: *Ben felt his hackles rise as the speaker continued.*

**ˈhack·ney ˈcar·riage** /ˈhækni kærɪdʒ/ (also **ˈhack·ney cab**) noun (BrE) a word used in official language for a taxi. In

---

s see | t tea | v van | w wet | z zoo | ʃ shoe | ʒ vision | tʃ chain | dʒ jam | θ thin | ð this | ŋ sing

# hackneyed

the past hackney carriages were carriages, pulled by horses, that were used as taxis.

**hack·neyed** /ˈhæknɪd/ *adj.* used too often and therefore boring **SYN** clichéd: *a hackneyed phrase/subject*

**hack·saw** /ˈhæksɔː/ *noun* a tool with a narrow BLADE (= cutting edge) in a frame, used for cutting metal ⇒ picture at SAW

**hack·tiv·ist** /ˈhæktɪvɪst/ *noun* a person who finds a way to look at other people's computer files without permission, in order to achieve or pursue particular political or social goals ⇒ compare ACTIVIST

**hacky** /ˈhæki/ *adj.* (*informal*) **1** not new or interesting; used too often and therefore boring: *a hacky joke* **2** (of a piece of computer code) that provides a quick but often badly designed solution to a problem, allowing the user to continue working until a better solution can be provided: *It's just a hacky workaround.*

**had** /həd, əd, *strong form* hæd/ ⇒ HAVE *verb*

**had·dock** /ˈhædək/ *noun* (*pl.* **had·dock**) [C, U] a sea fish like a COD but smaller that is white inside and used for food: *smoked haddock*

**Hades** /ˈheɪdiːz/ *noun* [U] (in ancient Greek stories) the land of the dead **SYN** hell

**Had·ith** /ˈhædɪθ/ *noun* (*pl.* **Had·ith** or **Had·iths**) **1** [sing.] a text containing things said by Muhammad and descriptions of his daily life, used by Muslims as a spiritual guide **2** [C] one of the things said by Muhammad, recorded in this text

**hadn't** /ˈhædnt/ *short form* had not

**haem·atite** (*BrE*) (*NAmE* **hema·tite**) /ˈhiːmətaɪt/ *noun* [U] (*geology*) a dark red rock from which iron is obtained

**haema·tol·ogy** (*BrE*) (*NAmE* **hema·tol·ogy**) /ˌhiːməˈtɒlədʒi/ *noun* [U] the scientific study of the blood and its diseases ▶ **haem·ato·logic·al** (*BrE*) (*NAmE* **hema-**) /ˌhiːmətəˈlɒdʒɪkl/ *NAmE* -ˈlɑːdʒ-/ *adj.* **haema·tolo·gist** (*NAmE* **hema-**) /ˌhiːməˈtɒlədʒɪst/ *NAmE* -ˈtɑːl-/ *noun*

**haema·toma** (*BrE*) (*NAmE* **hema·toma**) /ˌhiːməˈtəʊmə/ *NAmE* -ˈtoʊmə/ *noun* (*medical*) a SWELLING (= an area that is larger and rounder than normal) on the body consisting of blood that has become thick

**haemo-** /hiːmə, hiːmə; *BrE also* hiːˈmɒ; *NAmE also* hiːˈmɑː/ (*BrE*) (*NAmE* **hemo-**) *combining form* (in nouns and adjectives) connected with blood: *haemophilia*

**haemo·glo·bin** (*BrE*) (*NAmE* **hemo·glo·bin**) /ˌhiːməˈɡləʊbɪn/ *noun* [U] a red substance in the blood that carries OXYGEN and contains iron

**haemo·philia** (*BrE*) (*NAmE* **hemo·philia**) /ˌhiːməˈfɪliə/ *noun* [U] a medical condition that causes severe loss of blood from even a slight injury because the blood fails to CLOT normally. It usually affects only men although it can be passed on by women.

**haemo·phil·iac** (*BrE*) (*NAmE* **hemo·phil·iac**) /ˌhiːməˈfɪliæk/ *noun* a person who suffers from haemophilia

**haem·or·rhage** (*BrE*) (*NAmE* **hem·or·rhage**) /ˈhemərɪdʒ/ *noun, verb*

■ *noun* **1** [C, U] a medical condition in which there is severe loss of blood from a damaged BLOOD VESSEL inside a person's body: *a massive brain/cerebral haemorrhage* ◇ *He was checked for any signs of haemorrhage.* **2** [C, usually sing.] ~ (of sb/sth) a serious loss of people, money, etc. from a country, a group or an organization: *Poor working conditions have led to a steady haemorrhage of qualified teachers from our schools.*

■ *verb* **1** [I] to lose blood heavily, especially from a damaged BLOOD VESSEL inside the body; to have a haemorrhage **2** [T] ~sb/sth to lose money or people in large amounts at a fast rate

**haem·or·rhagic** (*BrE*) (*NAmE* **hem·or·rhagic**) /ˌheməˈrædʒɪk/ *adj.* (*medical*) happening with or caused by haemorrhage: *a haemorrhagic fever*

**haem·or·rhoids** (*BrE*) (*NAmE* **hem·or·rhoids**) /ˈhemərɔɪdz/ *noun* [*pl.*] (*medical*) VEINS at or near the ANUS

that have become painful and SWOLLEN (= larger than normal) **SYN** piles

**haft** /hɑːft; *NAmE* hæft/ *noun* the handle of a knife or weapon

**hag** /hæɡ/ *noun* (*offensive*) an ugly and/or unpleasant old woman

**hag·gard** /ˈhæɡəd; *NAmE* -ɡərd/ *adj.* looking very tired because of illness, worry or lack of sleep **SYN** drawn

**hag·gis** /ˈhæɡɪs/ *noun* [C, U] a Scottish dish that looks like a large round SAUSAGE made from the heart, lungs and LIVER of a sheep that are cut into small pieces, mixed with OATS, HERBS, etc. and boiled in a bag that is traditionally made from part of a sheep's stomach

**hag·gle** /ˈhæɡl/ *verb* [I, T] ~(with sb) (over/about sth) | ~sth (down) to argue with sb in order to reach an agreement, especially about the price of sth: *I left him in the market haggling over the price of a shirt.*

**hagi·og·raphy** /ˌhæɡiˈɒɡrəfi; *NAmE* -ˈɑːɡ-/ *noun* (*pl.* **-ies**) (*formal*) **1** [C, U] a book about the life of a person that praises them too much; this style of writing **2** [U] writing about the lives of SAINTS (= Christian holy people) ▶ **hagi·og·raph·er** *noun*

**hah** = HA¹

**haiku** /ˈhaɪkuː/ *noun* (*pl.* **haiku** or **haikus**) (*from Japanese*) a poem with three lines and usually 17 syllables, written in a style that is traditional in Japan

**hail** /heɪl/ *verb, noun*

■ *verb* **1** [T, usually passive] to describe sb/sth as being very good or special, especially in newspapers, etc.: *be hailed (as) sth The conference was hailed as a great success.* ◇ *Teenager Matt Brown is being hailed a hero for saving a young child from drowning.* **2** [T] ~sth to signal to a taxi or a bus, in order to get the driver to stop: *to hail a taxi/cab* **3** [T] ~sb (*literary*) to call to sb in order to say hello to them or attract their attention: *A voice hailed us from the other side of the street.* **4** [I] when **it hails**, small balls of ice fall like rain from the sky: *It's hailing!*

**PHRV** ˈhail from … (*formal*) to come from or have been born in a particular place: *His father hailed from Italy.*

■ *noun* **1** [U] small balls of ice that fall like rain: *We drove through hail and snow.* ⇒ WORDFINDER NOTE at SNOW **2** [sing.] **a ~ of sth** a large number or amount of sth that is aimed at sb in order to harm them: *a hail of arrows/bullets* ◇ *a hail of abuse*

**Hail Mary** /ˌheɪl ˈmeəri; *NAmE* ˈmeri/ *noun* (*pl.* **Hail Marys**) a Roman Catholic prayer to Mary, the mother of Jesus

**hail·stone** /ˈheɪlstəʊn/ *noun* [usually pl.] a small ball of ice that falls like rain

**hail·storm** /ˈheɪlstɔːm; *NAmE* -stɔːrm/ *noun* a storm during which hail falls from the sky

**hair** /heə(r); *NAmE* her/ *noun* **1** [U] the substance that looks like a mass of fine THREADS growing on a person's head: *She has long dark hair.* ◇ *brown/black/blonde/red/grey/white hair* ◇ *straight/curly/wavy hair* ◇ *comb/brush your hair* ◇ *to wash/dye your hair* ◇ *I'll be down in a minute. I'm doing* (= brushing, arranging, etc.) *my hair.* ◇ *I'm having my hair cut this afternoon.* ⇒ see also BIG HAIR ⇒ WORDFINDER NOTE at BLONDE **2** [C] hair growing on the body of a person or an animal: *body/facial/pubic hair* ⇒ see also CAMEL HAIR, HORSEHAIR **3** [C] a piece of hair from a person or an animal: *There's a hair in my soup.* ◇ *The rug was covered with cat hairs.* **4** **-haired** (in adjectives) having the type of hair mentioned: *dark-haired* ◇ *long-haired* **5** [C] a thing that looks like a fine THREAD growing on the leaves and STEMS of some plants ⇒ see also CROSS HAIRS

**IDM** **get in sb's ˈhair** (*informal*) to annoy sb by always being near them, asking them questions, etc. **a/the ˌhair of the ˈdog (that ˈbit you)** (*informal*) alcohol that you drink in order to make you feel better when you have drunk too much alcohol the night before **keep your ˈhair on** (*BrE, informal*) used to tell sb to stop shouting and become calm when they are angry **let your ˈhair down** (*informal*) to relax and enjoy yourself, especially in a lively way **make sb's ˈhair stand on end** (*informal*) to shock or frighten sb:

a chilling tale that will make your hair stand on end **not harm / touch a hair of sb's 'head** to not hurt sb physically in any way **not have a 'hair out of place** (of a person) to look extremely clean and neat **not turn a 'hair** to show no surprise, shock, etc. when sth unusual or unexpected happens ⇒ more at HANG v., HIDE n., SPLIT v., TEAR¹ v.

**hair·band** /ˈheəbænd; NAmE ˈherb-/ noun a narrow piece of cloth or curved plastic worn by women in their hair, that fits closely over the top of the head and behind the ears

**hair·brush** /ˈheəbrʌʃ; NAmE ˈherb-/ noun a brush for making the hair tidy or smooth

**hair·cut** /ˈheəkʌt; NAmE ˈherk-/ noun **1** the act of sb cutting your hair: *You need a haircut.* ◊ *I see you've had a haircut.* **2** the style in which sb's hair is cut: *What do you think of my new haircut?* ◊ *a trendy haircut* **3** a reduction in an amount of money or in the value of an ASSET: *The Prime Minister says he'd like to see banks take a bigger haircut from bad loans.*

**hair·do** /ˈheəduː; NAmE ˈherduː/ noun (pl. -os) (informal) the style in which a person's hair is arranged **SYN** **hairstyle**

**hair·dress·er** /ˈheədresə(r); NAmE ˈherd-/ noun **1** a person whose job is to cut, wash and shape hair **2** **hairdresser's** (pl. **hair·dress·ers**) a place where you can get your hair cut, washed and shaped ⇒ compare BARBER ▶ **hair·dress·ing** noun [U]

**hair·dryer** (also **hair·drier**) /ˈheədraɪə(r); NAmE ˈherd-/ noun a small machine used for drying your hair by blowing hot air over it

**ˈhair extension** (also **extension**) noun [usually pl.] pieces of artificial hair that are added to sb's own hair to make it longer

**hair·grip** /ˈheəɡrɪp; NAmE ˈherɡ-/ noun (also **grip**) (both BrE) (NAmE **bobby pin**) a small thin piece of metal or plastic folded in the middle, used by women for holding their hair in place ⇒ compare HAIRPIN

**hair·less** /ˈheələs; NAmE ˈherl-/ adj. without hair

**hair·line** /ˈheəlaɪn; NAmE ˈherl-/ noun **1** the edge of a person's hair, especially at the front: *a receding hairline* **2** (often used as an adjective) a very thin break or line: *a hairline crack/fracture*

**hair·net** /ˈheənet; NAmE ˈhern-/ noun a net worn over the hair to keep it in place

**hair·piece** /ˈheəpiːs; NAmE ˈherp-/ noun a piece of false hair worn to make your own hair look longer or thicker

**hair·pin** /ˈheəpɪn; NAmE ˈherp-/ noun **1** a small thin piece of wire that is folded in the middle, used by women for holding their hair in place ⇒ compare HAIRGRIP **2** = HAIRPIN BEND

**ˌhairpin ˈbend** (BrE) (NAmE **ˌhairpin ˈcurve**, **ˌhairpin ˈturn**) (also **hair·pin** BrE, NAmE) noun a sharp U-shaped bend in a road, especially a mountain road

**ˈhair-raising** adj. extremely frightening but often exciting: *a hair-raising adventure/story*

**ˈhair's breadth** noun [sing.] a very small amount or distance: *We won by a hair's breadth.* ◊ *They were within a hair's breadth of being killed.*

**ˌhair ˈshirt** noun a shirt made of rough cloth containing hair, worn in the past by people who wished to punish themselves for religious reasons

**hair·slide** /ˈheəslaɪd; NAmE ˈhers-/ (also **slide**) (both BrE) (NAmE **bar·rette**) noun a small attractive piece of metal or plastic used by women for holding their hair in place

**ˈhair-splitting** noun [U] (disapproving) the act of giving too much importance to small and unimportant differences in an argument **SYN** **quibble** **IDM** see SPLIT v.

**hair·spray** /ˈheəspreɪ; NAmE ˈhers-/ noun [U, C] a substance SPRAYED onto hair to hold it in a particular style

**ˈhair straighteners** (also **straighteners** /ˈstreɪtnəz; NAmE -nərz/) noun [pl.] an electrical tool with two metal or CERAMIC parts that you heat and use to make your hair straight

# half

**hair·style** /ˈheəstaɪl; NAmE ˈhers-/ noun the style in which sb's hair is cut or arranged

**hair·styl·ist** /ˈheəstaɪlɪst; NAmE ˈhers-/ noun = STYLIST (1)

**hairy** /ˈheəri; NAmE ˈheri/ adj. (**hair·ier**, **hairi·est**) **1** covered with a lot of hair: *a hairy chest/monster* ◊ *plants with hairy stems* **2** (informal) dangerous or frightening but often exciting: *Driving on icy roads can be pretty hairy.* ◊ *a hairy experience* ▶ **hairi·ness** noun [U]

**hajj** (also **haj**) /hædʒ/ noun (usually **the Hajj**) [sing.] the religious journey to Mecca that all Muslims try to make at least once in their lives

**haka** /ˈhɑːkə/ noun a traditional Maori war dance with singing. New Zealand rugby teams perform a version of it before games.

**hake** /heɪk/ noun [C, U] (pl. **hake**) a large sea fish that is used for food

**Hakka** /ˈhækə/ (also **Kejia**) noun [U] a form of Chinese spoken by a group of people in south-east China

**halal** /həˈlæl, -ˈlɑːl/ adj. **1** (of meat) from an animal that has been killed according to Muslim law: *halal meat* ◊ *a halal butcher* (= one who sells halal meat) **2** acceptable according to Muslim religious law ⇒ see also HARAM

**hal·cyon** /ˈhælsiən/ adj. [usually before noun] (literary) (of a period of time in the past) peaceful and happy: *the halcyon days of her youth*

**hale** /heɪl/ adj.
**IDM** **ˌhale and ˈhearty** (especially of an old person) strong and healthy

**half** ❶ **A1** /hɑːf; NAmE hæf/ noun, det., pron., adv.
■ noun (pl. **halves** /hɑːvz; NAmE hævz/) **1** ❷ **A1** either of two equal parts into which sth is or can be divided: *two and a half kilos* (= 2½) ◊ *One and a half hours are allowed for the exam.* ◊ *An hour and a half is allowed for the exam.* ◊ **~ of sth** *in the first half of the 20th century* ◊ *The two halves of the city were reunited in 1990.* ◊ **in ~** *I've divided the money in half.* ◊ **by ~** *We'll need to reduce the weight by half.* ⇒ see also HALVE **2** **A1** either of two periods of time into which a sports game, concert, etc. is divided: **in the …~** *No goals were scored in the first half.* **3** = HALF BACK ⇒ see also CENTRE HALF, FLY HALF, SCRUM HALF **4** (BrE, informal) half a PINT (= 0.568 of a LITRE in the UK and some other countries, and 0.473 of a LITRE in the US) of beer or a similar drink: *Two halves of bitter, please.*
**IDM** **and a ˈhalf** (informal) bigger, better, more important, etc. than usual: *That was a game and a half!* **ˌdo ˈnothing / not do ˈanything by ˈhalves** to do whatever you do completely and to the greatest possible degree: *You're expecting twins? Well, you never did do anything by halves.* **ˌgo half and ˈhalf | ˌgo ˈhalves (with sb)** to share the cost of sth equally with sb: *We go halves on all the bills.* **the ˈhalf of it** used in negative sentences to say that a situation is worse or more complicated than sb thinks: *'It sounds very difficult.' 'You don't know the half of it.'* **how the ˌother half ˈlives** the way of life of a different social group, especially one much richer than you **ˌtoo ˌclever, etc. by ˈhalf** (BrE, informal, disapproving) clever, etc. in a way that annoys you or makes you not trust sb/sth ⇒ more at MIND n., SIX, TIME n.
■ det., pron. **1** ❷ **A1** an amount equal to half of sth/sb: *I'll see you in half an hour.* ◊ *Half (of) the fruit was bad.* ◊ *Half of the money was mine.* ◊ *He has a half share in the company.* ◊ *Out of 36 candidates, half passed.* ⇒ **LANGUAGE BANK** at PROPORTION **2** **~ the time, fun, trouble, etc.** the largest part of sth: *Half the fun of gardening is never knowing exactly what's going to come up.* ◊ *Half the time you don't even listen to what I say.*
**IDM** **half a ˈloaf (is better than no ˈbread)** (saying) you should be grateful for sth, even if it is not as good, much, etc. as you really wanted; something is better than nothing **half a ˈminute, ˈsecond, etc.** (informal) a short time: *Hang on. I'll be ready in half a minute.* **ˌhalf past ˈone, ˈtwo, etc.** ❷ **A1** (also BrE, informal **half ˈone, ˈtwo, etc.**) 30 minutes after any hour on the clock

# half-and-half

- *adv.* **1** ⬢ A2 to the extent of half: *The glass was half full.* **2** ⬢ A2 partly: *The chicken was only half cooked.* ◊ *half-closed eyes* ◊ *I was still half asleep.* ◊ *I half expected them to follow us.*

**IDM** ˌhalf as ˈmany, ˈmuch, etc. aˈgain (*BrE*) (*US* ˌhalf aˈgain as ˌmuch) an increase of 50 per cent of the existing number or amount: *Spending on health is half as much again as it was in 2009.* ˌnot ˈhalf (*BrE, informal*) used to emphasize a statement or an opinion: *It wasn't half good* (= it was very good). ◊ *'Was she annoyed?' 'Not half!'* (= she was extremely annoyed) ˌnot ˈhalf as | ˌnot ˈhalf such a not nearly: *He is not half such a fool as they think.* ˌnot ˌhalf ˈbad (*informal*) (used to show surprise) not bad at all; good: *It really isn't half bad, is it?*

> ▼ **GRAMMAR POINT**
>
> **half / whole / quarter**
>
> - **Quarter, half** and **whole** can all be nouns: *Cut the apple into quarters.* ◊ *Two halves make a whole.*
> - **Whole** is also an adjective: *I've been waiting here for a whole hour.*
> - **Half** is also a determiner: *Half (of) the work is already finished.* ◊ *They spent half the time looking for a parking space.* ◊ *Her house is half a mile down the road.* Note that you do not put *a* or *the* in front of **half** when it is used in this way: *I waited for half an hour.* ◊ ~~I waited for a half an hour.~~
> - **Half** can also be used as an adverb: *This meal is only half cooked.*

ˌhalf-and-ˈhalf *adj., adv., noun*
- *adj.* being half one thing and half another: *I was in that half-and-half land where you are not completely asleep nor completely awake.* ▶ ˌhalf-and-ˈhalf *adv.*
- *noun* [U] (*NAmE*) a mixture of milk and cream that is used in tea and coffee

ˌhalf-ˈarsed (*BrE*) (*NAmE* ˌhalf-ˈassed) *adj.* (*slang*) **1** done without care or effort; not well planned **2** stupid

ˈhalf back (*also* half) (*NAmE also* halfback) *noun* **1** [C] one of the defending players in hockey or rugby whose position is between those who play at the front of a team and those who play at the back **2** (*also* tail·back) [C] one of the two attacking players in AMERICAN FOOTBALL whose position is behind the QUARTERBACK and next to the FULL BACKS **3** [U] the position a half back plays at (*also called* tailback in AMERICAN FOOTBALL)

ˌhalf-ˈbaked *adj.* [usually before noun] (*informal*) not well planned or considered: *a half-baked idea*

ˈhalf bath (*also* ˌhalf ˈbathroom) *noun* (*NAmE*) a small room in a house, containing a WASHBASIN and a toilet **SYN** pow·der room

ˈhalf board *noun* [U] (*BrE*) a type of accommodation at a hotel, etc. that includes breakfast and an evening meal ⇨ compare AMERICAN PLAN, BED AND BREAKFAST, FULL BOARD

ˈhalf-breed *noun* (*taboo, offensive*) a person whose parents are from different races, especially when one is white and the other is a Native American ▶ ˈhalf-breed *adj.* (*taboo, offensive*) **HELP** It is more acceptable to talk about 'a person of mixed race'.

ˈhalf-brother *noun* a person's **half-brother** is a boy or man with either the same mother or the same father as they have ⇨ compare STEPBROTHER

ˈhalf-caste *noun* (*taboo, offensive*) a person whose parents are from different races ▶ ˈhalf-caste *adj.* (*taboo, offensive*) **HELP** It is more acceptable to talk about 'a person of mixed race'.

ˌhalf-ˈcentury *noun* **1** a period of 50 years **2** (in CRICKET) a score of 50

ˌhalf-ˈcourt *noun* (in sport) the central line or area of a court, especially in basketball

ˌhalf-ˈday *noun* **1** a day on which people work only in the morning or in the afternoon: *Tuesday is her half-day.* **2** half a working day: *a half-day workshop*

ˌhalf ˈdollar *noun* a US coin worth 50 cents

ˌhalf-ˈhearted *adj.* done without enthusiasm or effort: *He made a half-hearted attempt to justify himself.* ▶ ˌhalf-ˈhearted·ly *adv.*

ˌhalf ˈhour (*also* ˌhalf an ˈhour) *noun* a period of 30 minutes: *He should arrive within the next half hour.* ◊ *a half-hour drive*

ˌhalf-ˈhourly *adj.* happening every 30 minutes: *a half-hourly bus service* ▶ ˌhalf-ˈhourly *adv.*: *The buses run half-hourly.*

ˈhalf-life *noun* [C] **1** (*physics*) the time taken for the RADIO-ACTIVITY of a substance to fall to half its original value **2** (*biology*) the time taken for the amount of a drug or other substance in the body to fall to half its original level

ˈhalf-light *noun* [sing., U] a light that is not clear or bright: *in the grey half-light of dawn*

ˌhalf ˈmast *noun* (*symb. NAmE also* ˌhalf-ˈstaff)
**IDM** at ˌhalf ˈmast (of a flag) flown at the middle of the MAST as a sign of respect for a person or people who have just died: *Flags were flown at half mast on the day of his funeral.*

ˌhalf ˈmeasures *noun* [pl.] a policy or plan of action that is weak and does not do enough: *There are no half measures with this company.*

ˌhalf-ˈmoon *noun* **1** the moon when only half of it can be seen from the earth; the time when this happens ⇨ compare FULL MOON, HARVEST MOON, NEW MOON **2** a thing that is like a half-moon in shape

ˈhalf note (*NAmE*) (*BrE* ˈminim) *noun* (*music*) a note that lasts twice as long as a CROTCHET/QUARTER NOTE ⇨ picture at MUSIC

ˈhalf pants *noun* [pl.] (*IndE, informal*) short trousers **SYN** shorts

ˈhalf·penny /ˈhɑːfpeni; *NAmE* ˈhæf-/ *noun* (*pl.* -ies) **1** (*also* ˈha'penny /ˈheɪpni/) a British coin in use until 1971, worth half a penny. There were 480 halfpennies in a pound. **2** (*also* ˈhalf·pence /ˈhɑːfpens; *NAmE* ˈhæf-/) a British coin in use between 1971 and 1984, worth half a penny. There were 200 halfpennies in a pound.

ˈhalf·pipe /ˈhɑːfpaɪp; *NAmE* ˈhæf-/ *noun* a structure or a channel cut into snow, in the shape of a U, used for performing complicated movements in SKATEBOARDING, IN-LINE SKATING and SNOWBOARDING

ˌhalf-ˈprice *adj.* costing half the usual price: *a half-price ticket* ▶ ˌhalf-ˈprice *adv.*: *Children aged under four go half-price.* ˌhalf ˈprice *noun* [U]: *Many items are at half price.*

ˈhalf-sister *noun* a person's **half-sister** is a girl or woman who has either the same mother or the same father as them ⇨ compare STEPSISTER

ˌhalf-ˈstaff *noun* (*NAmE*) = HALF MAST

ˈhalf step (*also* ˌhalf-ˈtone) (*both NAmE*) (*BrE* ˈsemi·tone) *noun* (*music*) half a TONE on a musical SCALE, for example the INTERVAL between C and C♯ or between E and F ⇨ compare STEP

ˈhalf-ˈterm *noun* (in British schools) a short holiday in the middle of each term: *the half-term break/holiday* ◊ *What are you doing at half-term?*

ˌhalf-ˈtimbered *adj.* [usually before noun] (of a building) having walls that are made from a wooden frame filled with stone, BRICKS, etc. so that the wooden FRAMEWORK can still be seen

ˌhalf-ˈtime *noun* [U] a short period between the two halves of a sports game during which the players rest: *The score at half-time was two all.* ◊ *the half-time score* ⇨ compare FULL TIME

ˈhalf·tone /ˈhɑːftəʊn; *NAmE* ˈhæf-/ *noun* **1** (*specialist*) a print of a black and white photograph in which the different shades of grey are produced from black DOTS (= small round marks) of different sizes **2** (*NAmE*) (*music*) = HALF STEP

**half-truth** noun a statement that gives only part of the truth, especially when it is intended to cheat sb: *The newspaper reports are a mixture of gossip, lies and half-truths.*

**half-volley** noun (in tennis and football (soccer)) a shot or kick immediately after the ball has BOUNCED

**half-way** /ˌhɑːfˈweɪ; *NAmE* ˈhæf-/ *adv.* **1** at an equal distance between two points; in the middle of a period of time: *It's about halfway between London and Bristol.* ◊ *He left halfway through the ceremony.* ◊ *I'm afraid we're not even halfway there yet.* **2** **~to/towards (doing) sth** part of the way towards doing or achieving sth: *This only goes halfway to explaining what really happened.* **3** **~decent** (*informal*) fairly, but not very, good: *Any halfway decent map will give you that information.* ▶ **half·way** *adj.*: *the halfway point/stage* **IDM** see MEET *v.*

**halfway house** noun **1 ~(towards sth)** the point in the middle of a process or the development of sth **2** [sing.] **~(between A and B)** (*BrE*) something that combines the features of two different things, as a COMPROMISE between them **3** [C] a place where prisoners, patients with mental health problems, etc. can stay for a short time after leaving a prison or hospital, before they start to live on their own again

**halfway line** noun a line across a sports field at an equal distance between the ends

**half-wit** /ˈhɑːfwɪt; *NAmE* ˈhæf-/ *noun* (*informal*) a stupid person SYN idiot ▶ **half-ˈwitted** *adj.*

**half-ˈyearly** *adj.* [only before noun] happening every six months; happening after the first six months of the year: *a half-yearly meeting* ◊ *the half-yearly sales figures* ▶ **half-yearly** *adv.*: *Interest will be paid half-yearly in June and December.*

**hali·but** /ˈhælɪbət/ *noun* [C, U] (*pl.* **hali·but**) a large flat sea fish that is used for food

**hali·tosis** /ˌhælɪˈtəʊsɪs/ *noun* [U] (*medical*) a condition in which the breath smells unpleasant SYN **bad breath**

**hall** /hɔːl/ *noun* **1** (*also* **hall·way** especially in *BrE*) (*NAmE also* **entry**) a space or passage inside the entrance or front door of a building: **in a~** *Her brother was standing in the front hall.* ⇨ see also ENTRANCE HALL **2** (*also* **hall·way**) (*NAmE*) a passage in a building with rooms down either side SYN **corridor**: **down the~** *I headed for Scott's office down the hall.* ◊ **across the~** *the room across the hall* **3** a building or large room for public meetings, meals, concerts, etc: *a concert/sports hall* ◊ *There are three dining halls on campus.* ◊ *the Royal Albert Hall* ◊ **in a~** *The next meeting is in the community hall on Tuesday.* ◊ **in a~** *A jumble sale will be held in the village hall on Saturday.* ⇨ see also CITY HALL, DANCE HALL, GUILDHALL, MEDICAL HALL, MUSIC HALL, STUDY HALL, TOWN HALL **4** (*also* (*NAmE*) **dorm**, **dormitory**, **residence hall**) = HALL OF RESIDENCE: **in hall(s)** *She's living in hall(s).* **5** (*BrE*) (often as part of a name) a large country house: *Haddon Hall*

**hal·le·lu·jah** /ˌhælɪˈluːjə/ (*also* **al·le·luia**) *noun* a song or shout of praise to God ▶ **hal·le·lu·jah** *exclamation*

**hall·mark** /ˈhɔːlmɑːk; *NAmE* -mɑːrk/ *noun*, *verb*
■ *noun* **1** a feature or quality that is typical of sb/sth: *Police said the explosion bore all the hallmarks of a terrorist attack.* **2** (in the UK) a mark put on gold, silver and PLATINUM objects that shows the quality of the metal and gives information about when and where the object was made
■ *verb* **~sth** to put a hallmark on metal goods

**hallo** (*BrE*) = HELLO

**Hall of ˈFame** noun (*pl.* **Halls of Fame**) (in the US) a list of people who have done a particular sport or activity particularly well. In many cases, this list is maintained in a museum for people to visit, also containing objects connected with famous people from the sport or activity: *the Country Music Hall of Fame*

**hall of ˈresidence** (*also* **hall**) *noun* (*pl.* **halls of residence**, **halls**) (*both BrE*) (*also* (*NAmE*) **dorm**, **dor·mi·tory**, **residence hall**) a building for university or college students to live in ⇨ WORDFINDER NOTE at UNIVERSITY

**hal·loumi**™ /həˈluːmi/ *noun* [U] a type of solid white cheese, originally from Cyprus, made from the milk of sheep or GOATS, used especially in cooked dishes

**hal·lowed** /ˈhæləʊd/ *adj.* [only before noun] **1** (especially of old things) respected and important SYN **sacred**: *one of the theatre's most hallowed traditions* **2** that has been made holy SYN **sacred**: *to be buried in hallowed ground*

**Hal·low·een** (*also* **Hal·low·e'en**) /ˌhæləʊˈiːn/ *noun* [C, U] the night of 31st October when it was believed in the past that dead people appeared from their GRAVES, and which is now celebrated in the US, Canada and the UK by children who dress as ghosts, WITCHES, etc. ⇨ see also TRICK OR TREAT at TRICK *noun*

**hal·lu·cin·ate** /həˈluːsɪneɪt/ *verb* [I, T] **~(sth) | ~that ...** to see or hear things that are not really there because of illness or drugs ⇨ WORDFINDER NOTE at DRUG

**hal·lu·cin·ation** /həˌluːsɪˈneɪʃn/ *noun* **1** [C, U] the fact of seeming to see or hear sb/sth that is not really there, especially because of illness or drugs: *to have hallucinations* ◊ *High temperatures can cause hallucination.* **2** [C] something that is seen or heard when it is not really there: *Was the figure real or just a hallucination?* **HELP** Some speakers do not pronounce the 'h' at the beginning of **hallucination** and use 'an' instead of 'a' before it. This now sounds old-fashioned.

**hal·lu·cin·atory** /həˈluːsɪnətri, həˌluːsɪˈneɪtəri; *NAmE* həˈluːsənətɔːri/ *adj.* [only before noun] connected with or causing hallucinations: *a hallucinatory experience* ◊ *hallucinatory drugs*

**hal·lu·cino·gen** /həˈluːsɪnədʒən/ *noun* a drug, such as LSD, that affects people's minds and makes them see and hear things that are not really there ▶ **hal·lu·cino·gen·ic** /həˌluːsɪnəˈdʒenɪk/ *adj.*: *hallucinogenic drugs/effects*

**hall·way** /ˈhɔːlweɪ/ *noun* **1** (especially *BrE*) = HALL (1) **2** (*NAmE*) = HALL (2)

**halo** /ˈheɪləʊ/ *noun* (*pl.* **-oes** *or* **-os**) **1** (in paintings, etc.) a circle of light shown around or above the head of a holy person: *She played the part of an angel, complete with wings and a halo.* ◊ (*figurative*) *a halo of white frizzy hair* **2** (*informal*) = CORONA

**halo·gen** /ˈhælədʒən/ *noun* (*chemistry*) any of a set of five chemical elements, including FLUORINE, CHLORINE and IODINE, that react with HYDROGEN to form ACIDS from which simple salts can be made. Halogens, in the form of gas, are used in lamps and cookers.

**halon** /ˈheɪlɒn; *NAmE* -lɑːn/ *noun* (*chemistry*) a gas that is made up of CARBON and one or more halogens, used especially to stop fires, but now known to damage the OZONE LAYER

**halt** /hɔːlt; *BrE also* hɒlt/ *verb*, *noun*
■ *verb* [I, T] to stop; to make sb/sth stop: *She walked towards him and then halted.* ◊ *'Halt!' the Major ordered* (= used as a command to soldiers). ◊ **~sb/sth** *The police were halting traffic on the parade route.* ◊ *The trial was halted after the first week.* **IDM** see TRACK *n.*
■ *noun* **1** [sing.] an act of stopping the movement or progress of sb/sth: *Work came to a halt when the machine broke down.* ◊ *The thought brought her to an abrupt halt.* ◊ *The car skidded to a halt.* ◊ *Strikes have led to a halt in production.* ◊ *They decided it was time to call a halt to the project* (= stop it officially). **2** [C] (*BrE*) a small train station in the country that has a platform but no buildings **IDM** see GRIND *v.*

**hal·ter** /ˈhɔːltə(r); *BrE also* ˈhɒl-/ *noun* **1** a rope or narrow piece of leather put around the head of a horse or other animal for leading it with **2** (usually used as an adjective) a narrow piece of cloth around the neck that holds a woman's dress or shirt in position, with the back and shoulders not covered: *She was dressed in a halter top and shorts.*

**halt·ing** /ˈhɔːltɪŋ; *BrE also* ˈhɒl-/ *adj.* [usually before noun] (especially of speech or movement) stopping and starting often, especially because you are not certain or are not very confident SYN **hesitant**: *a halting conversation* ◊ *a*

# halve

toddler's first few halting steps ▶ **halt·ing·ly** adv.: 'Well…' she began haltingly.

**halve** /hɑːv; NAmE hæv/ verb **1** [I, T] to reduce by a half; to make sth reduce by a half: *The shares have halved in value.* ◊ ~ **sth** *The company is halving its prices.* **2** [T] ~sth to divide sth into two equal parts **IDM** see TROUBLE n.

**halves** /hɑːvz; NAmE hævz/ pl. of HALF

**halwa** /ˈhælwɑː/ noun [U] a sweet food from South Asia, made from SEMOLINA or carrots, with ALMONDS and CARDAMOM

**hal·yard** /ˈhæljəd; NAmE -jərd/ noun (specialist) a rope used for raising or taking down a sail or flag

**ham** /hæm/ noun, verb
- noun **1** [U, C] meat from the top part of a pig's leg that has been CURED (= preserved using salt or smoke): *a slice of ham* ◊ *a ham sandwich* ◊ *The hams were cooked whole.* ⊃ compare BACON, GAMMON, PORK **2** [C] a person who sends and receives radio messages as a hobby rather than as a job: *a radio ham* **3** [C] (informal) (often used as an adjective) an actor who performs badly, especially by EXAGGERATING emotions: *a ham actor* **4** [C, usually pl.] (informal) the back part of a person's leg above the knee ⊃ see also HAMSTRING noun
- verb (-mm-)
**IDM** **ham it ˈup** (informal) (especially of actors) when people **ham it up**, they deliberately EXAGGERATE their emotions or movements

**ham·burg·er** /ˈhæmbɜːɡə(r); NAmE -bɜːrɡ-/ noun **1** (also **burg·er**) (BrE also **beef·burg·er**) [C] beef cut into small pieces and made into a flat round shape that is then fried, often served in a bread roll **2** (also **hamburger meat**, **ground ˈbeef**) (all NAmE) (BrE **mince**) [U] beef that has been cut very small in a special machine

**ham-ˈfisted** (NAmE also **ˈham-handed**) adj. (informal) not having much skill when using your hands or when dealing with people **SYN** clumsy: *his ham-fisted efforts to assist her*

**ham·let** /ˈhæmlət/ noun a very small village

**ham·mer** /ˈhæmə(r)/ noun, verb
- noun
- TOOL **1** [C] a tool with a handle and a heavy metal head, used for breaking things or hitting nails ⊃ see also CLAW HAMMER, JACK-HAMMER, SLEDGEHAMMER **2** [C] a tool with a handle and a wooden head, used by a person in charge of an AUCTION (= a sale at which things are sold to the person who offers the most money) in order to get people's attention when sth is just being sold **SYN** gavel: *to come/go under the hammer* (= to be sold at AUCTION)
- IN PIANO **3** [C] a small wooden part inside a piano, that hits the strings to produce a sound
- IN GUN **4** [C] a part inside a gun that makes the gun fire
- SPORT **5** [C] a metal ball attached to a wire, thrown as a sport **6** *often* **the hammer** [sing.] the event or sport of throwing the hammer

**IDM** ˌhammer and ˈtongs (informal) if two people are at it hammer and tongs or go at it hammer and tongs, they argue or fight with a lot of energy and noise
- verb
- HIT WITH TOOL **1** [I, T] to hit sth with a hammer: *I could hear somebody hammering next door.* ◊ ~ **sth (in/into/onto sth)** *She hammered the nail into the wall.* ◊ ~ **sth + adj.** *He was hammering the sheet of copper flat.*
- HIT MANY TIMES **2** [I, T] to hit sth hard many times, especially so that it makes a loud noise **SYN** pound: *Someone was hammering at the door.* ◊ *Hail was hammering down onto the roof.* ◊ (figurative) *I was so scared my heart was hammering (= beating very fast) in my chest.* ◊ ~ **sth** *He hammered the door with his fists.* ⊃ SYNONYMS AT BEAT

mallet    claw    hammer

- KICK/HIT BALL **3** [T] ~ **sth (+ adv./prep.)** (informal) to kick or hit a ball very hard: *He hammered the ball into the net.*
- DEFEAT EASILY **4** [T] ~ **sb** (informal) to defeat sb very easily: *Our team was hammered 5–1.*
- AFFECT BADLY **5** [T] ~ **sb/sth** (informal) to affect sb/sth very badly: *Eastern counties were brutally hammered by the weekend flooding.*

**PHRV** ˌhammer aˈway at sth to work hard in order to finish or achieve sth; to keep repeating sth in order to get the result that you want ˌhammer sth↔ˈhome **1** to emphasize a point, an idea, etc. so that people fully understand it **2** to kick a ball hard and score a goal ˌhammer sth ˈinto sb to make sb learn or remember sth by repeating it many times ˌhammer ˈout sth **1** to discuss a plan, an idea, etc. until everyone agrees or a decision is made: *to hammer out a compromise* **2** to play a tune, especially on a piano, loudly and not very well

ˌhammer and ˈsickle noun [sing.] symbols representing the people who work in industry and farming, used on the flag of the former Soviet Union and as a symbol of Communism

ˈhammer blow noun **1** a powerful hit with a hammer **2** (especially BrE) a sudden shock that harms sb/sth or is very disappointing: *The decision is a hammer blow for the steel industry.*

**ham·mered** /ˈhæməd; NAmE -mərd/ adj. [not before noun] (informal) very drunk

**ham·mer·head** /ˈhæməhed; NAmE -mərh-/ (also ˌham·merˈhead ˈshark) noun a SHARK with flat parts sticking out from either side of its head with eyes at the ends

**ham·mer·ing** /ˈhæmərɪŋ/ noun **1** [U, sing.] the sound of sb hitting sth with a HAMMER or with their FISTS: *the sound of hammering from the next room* **2** [C, usually sing.] (informal) an act of defeating or criticizing sb severely: *Our team took a real hammering in the first half.*

ˈhammer price noun the last and highest amount offered for sth at an AUCTION which is the price for which it is sold

**ham·mock** /ˈhæmək/ noun a type of bed made from a net or from a piece of strong material, with ropes at each end that are used to hang it between two trees, posts, etc.

**Hammond organ™** /ˈhæmənd ɔːɡən; NAmE ɔːrɡ-/ noun a type of electronic organ (= musical instrument)

**hammy** /ˈhæmi/ adj. (**ham·mier**, **ham·mi·est**) (informal) (of a style of acting) artificial or EXAGGERATED

**ham·per** /ˈhæmpə(r)/ verb, noun
- verb ~ **sb/sth** to prevent sb from easily doing or achieving sth **SYN** hinder
- noun **1** a large BASKET with a LID (= cover), especially one used to carry food in: *a picnic hamper* ⊃ picture at BASKET **2** (especially BrE) a box or package containing food, sent as a gift: *a Christmas hamper* **3** (NAmE) a large BASKET that you keep your dirty clothes in until they are washed ⊃ picture at BASKET

**ham·ster** /ˈhæmstə(r)/ noun an animal like a large mouse, with large CHEEKS (= sides of the face) for storing food. Hamsters are often kept as pets.

**ham·string** /ˈhæmstrɪŋ/ noun, verb
- noun **1** one of the five TENDONS behind the knee that connect the muscles of the upper leg to the bones of the lower leg: *a hamstring injury* ◊ *She's pulled a hamstring.* **2** a TENDON behind the HOCK (= middle JOINT) of the back leg of a horse and some other animals
- verb [often passive] (**ham·strung**, **ham·strung** /-strʌŋ/) ~ **sb/sth** to prevent sb/sth from working or taking action in the way that is needed

# hand

/hænd/ noun, verb
- noun
- PART OF BODY **1** [C] the part of the body at the end of the arm, including the fingers and THUMB: *Keep both hands on the steering wheel at all times.* ◊ *your right/left hand* ◊ *He was holding a large mug of coffee in his right hand.* ◊ *Put your hand up if you know the answer.* ◊ *She was on (her) hands and knees (= CRAWLING on the floor) looking for an earring.* ◊ *Couples strolled past holding hands.* ◊ *She introduced us and we shook hands.* ◊ *Give*

**hand** 715

*me your hand* (= hold my hand) *while we cross the road.* ◊ *He killed the snake **with his bare hands*** (= using only his hands). ◊ *a hand gesture/signal* ⇨ see also LEFT-HAND, RIGHT-HAND ⇨ **VISUAL VOCAB** page V1
- **-HANDED 2** (in adjectives) using the hand or number of hands mentioned: *a one-handed catch* ◊ *left-handed scissors* (= intended to be held in your left hand)
- **HELP 3** ⚡ B1 **a hand** [sing.] (*informal*) help in doing sth: *The neighbours are always willing to **lend a hand**.* ◊ **~ with sth** *Let me **give you a hand** with those bags* (= help you to carry them). ◊ *Do you **need a hand** with those invoices?*
- **ROLE IN SITUATION 4** [sing.] **~ in sth** the part or role that sb/sth plays in a particular situation; sb's influence in a situation: *Early reports suggest the hand of rebel forces in the bombings.* ◊ *Several of his colleagues **had a hand** in his downfall.* ◊ *This appointment was an attempt to **strengthen her hand** in policy discussions.*
- **ON CLOCK/WATCH 5** [C] (usually in compounds) a part of a clock or watch that points to the numbers ⇨ picture at CLOCK ⇨ see also HOUR HAND, MINUTE HAND, SECOND HAND
- **WORKER 6** [C] a person who does physical work on a farm or in a factory ⇨ see also FARMHAND, FIELD HAND, HIRED HAND, STAGEHAND
- **SAILOR 7** [C] a sailor on a ship: *All hands on deck!* ⇨ see also DECKHAND
- **HAND- 8** (in compounds) by a person rather than a machine: *hand-painted pottery* ◊ *hand-knitted* ◊ *This item should be hand-washed.* ⇨ see also HANDMADE
- **IN CARD GAMES 9** [C] a set of PLAYING CARDS given to one player in a game: *to be dealt a good/bad hand* **10** [C] one stage of a game of cards: *I'll have to leave after this hand.* ⇨ WORDFINDER NOTE at CARD
- **WRITING 11** [sing.] (*old use*) a particular style of writing ⇨ see also FREEHAND
- **MEASUREMENT FOR HORSE 12** [C] a unit for measuring the height of a horse, equal to 4 inches or 10.16 CENTIMETRES ⇨ see also DAB HAND, OLD HAND, SECOND-HAND, UNDERHAND

**IDM** **all hands on 'deck** (*also* **all hands to the 'pump**) (*saying, humorous*) everyone helps or must help, especially in a difficult situation: *There are 30 people coming to dinner tonight, so it's all hands on deck.* **(close/near) at 'hand** close to you in time or distance: *Help was at hand.* ◊ *The property is ideally located with all local amenities close at hand.* **at the hands of sb** | **at sb's hands** (*formal*) if you experience sth **at the hands of sb**, they are the cause of it **be good with your 'hands** to show skill at making or doing things with your hands **bind/tie sb hand and 'foot 1** to tie sb's hands and feet together so that they cannot move or escape **2** to prevent sb from doing what they want by creating rules, limits, etc. **by 'hand 1** by a person rather than a machine: *The fabric was painted by hand.* **2** if a letter is delivered **by hand**, it is delivered by the person who wrote it, or sb who is sent by them, rather than by post **fall into sb's 'hands/the 'hands of sb** (*formal*) to become controlled by sb: *The town fell into enemy hands.* ◊ *We don't want this document **falling into the wrong hands**.* **(at) first 'hand** by experiencing, seeing, etc. sth yourself rather than being told about it by sb else: *The President visited the area to see the devastation at first hand.* **get your 'hands dirty** to do physical work: *He's not frightened of getting his hands dirty.* **sb's 'hand (in marriage)** (*old-fashioned*) permission to marry sb, especially a woman: *He asked the general for his daughter's hand in marriage.* **'hand in 'glove (with sb)** working closely with sb, especially in a secret and/or illegal way **hand in 'hand 1** if two people are **hand in hand**, they are holding each other's hand **2** if two things **go hand in hand**, they are closely connected and one thing causes the other: *Poverty and poor health often go hand in hand.* **hands 'down** (*informal*) easily and without any doubt: *They won hands down.* ◊ *It is hands down the best movie this year.* ⇨ see also HANDS-DOWN **(get/take/keep your) hands 'off (sth/sb)** (*informal*) used to tell sb not to touch sth/sb: *Get your hands off my wife!* ◊ *Hey, hands off! That's my drink!* **hands 'up! 1** (*informal*) used to tell a group of people to raise one hand in the air if they know the answer to a question, etc: *Hands up all those who want to go swimming.* **2** used by sb who is threatening people with a gun to tell them to raise both hands in the air **have your 'hands full** to be very busy or too busy to do sth else: *She certainly has her hands full with four kids in the house.* **have your 'hands tied** to be unable to do what you want to do because of rules, promises, etc: *I really wish I could help but my hands are tied.* **hold sb's 'hand** to give sb support in a difficult situation: *Do you want me to come along and hold your hand?* **hold/put your 'hands up (to sth)** to admit that you have made a mistake or are responsible for sth bad: *I have to hold my hands up and admit that some of the problems have been all my own fault.* **in sb's capable, safe, etc. 'hands** being taken care of or dealt with by sb that you think you can rely on: *Can I leave these queries in your capable hands?* **in 'hand 1** if you have time or money **in hand**, it is left and available to be used **2** if you have a particular situation **in hand**, you are in control of it **3** the job, question, etc. **in hand** is the one that you are dealing with **4** if sb works a week, month, etc. **in hand**, they are paid for the work a week, etc. after they have completed it **in the hands of sb** | **in sb's 'hands** being taken care of or controlled by sb: *The matter is now in the hands of my lawyer.* ◊ *At that time, the castle was in enemy hands.* **keep your 'hand in** to occasionally do sth that you used to do a lot so that you do not lose your skill at it: *She retired last year but still teaches the odd class to keep her hand in.* **lay/get your 'hands on sb** to catch sb that you are annoyed with: *Wait till I get my hands on him!* **lay/get your 'hands on sth** to find or get sth: *I know their address is here somewhere, but I can't lay my hands on it right now.* **many hands make light 'work** (*saying*) used to say that a job is made easier if a lot of people help **off your 'hands** no longer your responsibility **on either/every 'hand** (*literary*) on both/all sides; in both/all directions **on 'hand** available, especially to help: *The emergency services were on hand with medical advice.* **on your 'hands** if you have sb/sth **on your hands**, you are responsible for or have to deal with them/it: *Let me take care of the invitations—you've enough on your hands with the caterers.* **(on the one hand ...) on the 'other (hand) ...** ⚡ B1 used to introduce different points of view, ideas, etc., especially when they are opposites: *On the one hand they'd love to have kids, but on the other, they don't want to give up their freedom.* ⇨ **LANGUAGE BANK** at CONTRAST **out of 'hand 1** difficult or impossible to control: *Unemployment is getting out of hand.* **2** if you reject, etc. sth **out of hand**, you do so immediately without thinking about it fully or listening to other people's arguments: *All our suggestions were dismissed out of hand.* **out of your 'hands** no longer your responsibility: *I'm afraid the matter is now out of my hands.* **play into sb's 'hands** to do exactly what an enemy, opponent, etc. wants so that they gain the advantage in a particular situation: *If we get the police involved, we'll be playing right into the protesters' hands.* **put your hand in your 'pocket** (*BrE*) to spend money or give it to sb: *I've heard he doesn't like putting his hand in his pocket.* **(at) second, third, etc. 'hand** by being told about sth by sb else who has seen it or heard about it, not by experiencing, seeing, etc. it yourself: *I'm fed up of hearing about these decisions third hand!* **take sb in 'hand** to deal with sb in a strict way in order to improve their behaviour **take sth into your own 'hands** to deal with a particular situation yourself because you are not happy with the way that others are dealing with it **throw your 'hand in** (*informal*) to stop doing sth or taking part in sth, especially because you are not successful **throw up your 'hands** to raise both hands in the air to show that you are feeling annoyed or upset about sth: *We threw up our hands in despair at the scale of the problem.* **to 'hand** that you can reach or get easily: *I'm afraid I don't have the latest figures to hand.* **turn your 'hand to sth** to start doing sth or be able to do sth, especially when you do it well: *Jim can turn his hand to most jobs around the house.* ⇨ more at BIG *adj.*, BIRD *n.*, BITE *v.*, BLOOD *n.*, CAP *n.*, CASH *n.*, CHANGE *v.*, CLOSE² *adv.*, COURAGE, DEAD *adj.*, EAT, FIRM *adj.*, FOLD *v.*, FREE *adj.*, HEAT, HEAVY *adj.*, HELP *v.*, IRON *adj.*, JOIN *v.*, KNOW *v.*, LAW, LIFE, LIFT *v.*, LIVE¹, MONEY, OFFER *v.*, OVERPLAY, PAIR *n.*, PALM *n.*, PUTTY, RAISE

# handbag

*v.*, SAFE *adj.*, SHOW *n.*, SHOW *v.*, STAY *v.*, TIME *n.*, TRY *v.*, UPPER *adj.*, WAIT *v.*, WASH *v.*, WHIP *v.*, WIN *v.*, WRING

■ *verb* **1** to pass or give sth to sb: ~ **sth to sb** *She handed the letter to me.* ◊ ~ **sb sth** *She handed me the letter.* **2** (*sometimes disapproving*) to allow sb to have sth, sometimes too easily: ~ **sth to sb** *Missed chances by United players handed a surprise victory to Stoke.* ◊ ~ **sb sth** *This decision effectively handed Burke control of the company.* **IDM** **hand sth to sb on a ˈplate** (*informal*) to give sth to sb without that person making any effort: *Nobody's going to hand you success on a plate.* **ˌhave (got) to ˈhand it to sb** (*informal*) used to say that sb deserves praise for sth: *You've got to hand it to her—she's a great cook.* **PHRV** ˌhand sth↔aˈround (*also* ˌhand sth↔ˈround *especially in BrE*) to offer or pass sth, especially food or drinks, to all the people in a group **ˌhand sth ˈback (to sb)** to give or return sth to the person who owns it or to where it belongs **ˌhand sth↔ˈdown (to sb) 1** [*usually passive*] to give or leave sth to sb who is younger than you: *These skills used to be handed down from father to son.* ⊃ related noun HAND-ME-DOWN **2** to officially give a decision/statement, etc. **SYN** announce: *The judge has handed down his verdict.* **ˌhand sth↔ˈin (to sb)** (*BrE also* ˌgive sth ˈin (to sb)) to give sth to a person in authority, especially a piece of work or sth that is lost: *You must all hand in your projects by the end of next week.* ◊ *I handed the watch in to the police.* ◊ *to hand in your notice/resignation* (= formally tell your employer that you want to stop working for them) **ˌhand sb↔ˈoff** (*BrE*) (*also* ˌstraight-ˈarm, ˌstiff-ˈarm *both NAmE*) (in sport) to push away a player who is trying to stop you, with your arm straight **ˌhand sth↔ˈon (to sb)** to give or leave sth for another person to use or deal with **ˌhand sth↔ˈout (to sb) 1** to give a number of things to the members of a group **SYN** distribute: *Could you hand these books out, please?* ⊃ related noun HANDOUT **2** (*informal*) to give advice, a punishment, etc: *He's always handing out advice to people.* **ˌhand ˈover (to sb)** | **ˌhand sth↔ˈover (to sb)** to give sb else your position of power or the responsibility for sth: *She resigned and handed over to one of her younger colleagues.* ◊ *He handed over his responsibility for the firm last year.* ⊃ related noun HANDOVER **ˌhand sb ˈover to sb** to let sb listen or speak to another person, especially on the phone or in a news broadcast: *I'll hand you over to my boss.* **ˌhand sth/sb↔ˈover (to sb)** to give sth/sb officially or formally to another person: *He handed over a cheque for $200000.* ◊ *They handed the weapons over to the police.* ⊃ related noun HANDOVER **ˌhand sth↔ˈround** (*especially BrE*) = HAND STH↔AROUND

▼ **VOCABULARY BUILDING**

**Using your hands**
Touch
These verbs describe different ways of touching things:

| | |
|---|---|
| feel | *I felt the bag to see what was in it.* |
| finger | *She fingered the silk delicately.* |
| handle | *Handle the fruit with care.* |
| rub | *She rubbed her eyes wearily.* |
| stroke | *The cat loves being stroked.* |
| pat | *He patted my arm and told me not to worry.* |
| tap | *Someone was tapping lightly at the door.* |
| squeeze | *I took his hand and squeezed it.* |

Hold
You can use these verbs to describe taking something quickly:

| | |
|---|---|
| grab | *I grabbed his arm to stop myself from falling.* |
| snatch | *She snatched the letter out of my hand.* |

These verbs describe holding things tightly:

| | |
|---|---|
| clasp | *Her hands were clasped behind her head.* |
| clutch | *The child was clutching a doll in her hand.* |
| grasp | *Grasp the rope with both hands and pull.* |
| grip | *He gripped his bag tightly and wouldn't let go.* |

**ˈhand·bag** /ˈhændbæg/ (*NAmE also* **purse**) *noun* a small bag for money, keys, etc., carried especially by women

**ˈhand baggage** *noun* [U] (*especially NAmE*) = HAND LUGGAGE

**hand·ball** /ˈhændbɔːl/ *noun* **1** [U] (*US also* ˌteam ˈhandball) a team game for two teams of seven players, usually played indoors, in which players try to score goals by throwing a ball with their hand **2** [U] (*NAmE*) a game in which players hit a small ball against a wall with their hand **3** /ˈhændbɔːl/ [C, U] (in football (soccer)) the offence of touching the ball with your hands: *a penalty for handball*

**ˈhand·basin** /ˈhændbeɪsn/ *noun* (*BrE*) a small bowl that has TAPS and is fixed to the wall, used for washing your hands in

**hand·bas·ket** /ˈhændbɑːskɪt; *NAmE* -bæs-/ *noun* **IDM** **ˌgo to hell in a ˈhandbasket** (*NAmE*) = GO TO THE DOGS at DOG *n.*

**hand·bell** /ˈhændbel/ *noun* a small bell with a handle, especially one of a set used by a group of people to play tunes

**hand·bill** /ˈhændbɪl/ *noun* a small printed advertisement that is given to people by hand

**hand·book** /ˈhændbʊk/ *noun* a book giving instructions on how to use sth or information about a particular subject ⊃ compare MANUAL

**hand·brake** /ˈhændbreɪk/ (*especially BrE*) (*NAmE usually* eˈmergency brake, ˈparking brake) *noun* a BRAKE in a vehicle that is operated by hand, designed to be used when the vehicle has already stopped: *to put the handbrake on* ◊ *to take the handbrake off* ◊ *Is the handbrake on?*

**hand·cart** /ˈhændkɑːt; *NAmE* -kɑːrt/ *noun* = CART (2)

**hand·craft** /ˈhændkrɑːft; *NAmE* -kræft/ *noun* (*NAmE*) = HANDICRAFT

**hand·craft·ed** /ˌhændˈkrɑːftɪd; *NAmE* -ˈkræf-/ *adj.* made with skill by hand, not by machine: *a handcrafted chair*

**ˈhand cream** *noun* [U] cream that you put on your hands to prevent dry skin

**hand·cuff** /ˈhændkʌf/ *verb* [*usually passive*] ~ **sb** to put handcuffs on sb or to fasten sb to sth/sb with handcuffs

**hand·cuffs** /ˈhændkʌfs/ (*also informal* cuffs) *noun* [pl.] a pair of metal rings joined by a chain, used for holding the WRISTS of a prisoner together: *a pair of handcuffs* ◊ *in handcuffs* *She was led away in handcuffs.*

**hand·ful** /ˈhændfʊl/ *noun* **1** [C] ~ (of sth) the amount of sth that can be held in one hand: *a handful of rice* **2** [sing.] ~ (of sb/sth) a small number of people or things: *Only a handful of people came.* **3** a ˈhandful [sing.] (*informal*) a person or an animal that is difficult to control: *Her children can be a real handful.*

**ˈhand grenade** *noun* a small bomb that is thrown by hand

**hand·gun** /ˈhændɡʌn/ *noun* a small gun that you can hold and fire with one hand

**hand-held** /ˈhændheld/ *adj.* [*usually before noun*] small enough to be held in the hand while being used: *a handheld camera/device* ▸ **hand-held** /ˈhændheld/ *noun*: *Versions of the game were released for consoles and handhelds.*

**hand·hold** /ˈhændhəʊld/ *noun* something on the surface of a steep slope, wall, etc. that a person can hold when climbing up it

**handi·cap** /ˈhændikæp/ *noun, verb*
■ *noun* **1** [C, U] (*old-fashioned, often offensive*) a permanent physical or mental condition that makes it difficult or impossible to use a particular part of your body or mind **SYN** disability: *Despite her handicap, Jane is able to hold down a full-time job.* ◊ *mental/physical/visual handicap* ⊃ note at DISABLED **2** [C] something that makes it difficult for sb to do sth **SYN** obstacle: *Not speaking the language proved to be a bigger handicap than I'd imagined.* **3** [C] (*sport*) a race or competition in which those who have most skill must run further, carry extra weight, etc. in order to give all those taking part an equal chance of winning; the

---

æ cat | ɑː father | e bed | ɜː fur | ə about | ɪ sit | iː see | i happy | ɒ got (*BrE*) | ɔː saw | ʌ cup | ʊ put | uː too

disadvantage that is given to sb you are competing against in such a race or competition **4** [C] (in golf) the number of STROKES (= hits) over PAR (= the expected number of strokes for a good player) that a player usually needs to complete a course. Handicaps are used to give an advantage to weaker players so that competition is more equal when they play against stronger players.

▪ **verb** (-pp-) [usually passive] to make sth more difficult for sb to do: **be handicapped (by sth)** *Smaller parties are seriously handicapped by the electoral system.*

**handi·capped** /ˈhændikæpt/ *adj.* (old-fashioned, often offensive) **1** suffering from a mental or physical handicap **SYN** **disabled**: *a visually handicapped child ◇ The accident left him physically handicapped.* ⊃ see also MENTALLY HANDICAPPED **2** **the handicapped** *noun* [pl.] people who are handicapped: *a school for the physically handicapped* ⊃ note at DISABLED

**han·di·craft** /ˈhændikrɑːft; *NAmE* -kræft/ (*NAmE also* **hand·craft**) *noun* [C, usually pl., U] **1** the activity of making attractive objects by hand: *to teach handicrafts ◇ Her hobbies are music, reading and handicraft.* **2** things made in this way: *traditional handicrafts bought by tourists*

**hand·ily** /ˈhændɪli/ *adv.* **1** in a way that is HANDY (= convenient): *We're handily placed for the train station.* **2** (especially *NAmE*) easily: *He handily defeated his challengers.*

**han·di·work** /ˈhændiwɜːk; *NAmE* -wɜːrk/ *noun* [U] **1** work that you do, or sth that you have made, especially using your artistic skill: *We admired her exquisite handiwork.* **2** a thing done by a particular person or group, especially sth bad: *This looks like the handiwork of an arsonist.*

**hand·job** /ˈhændʒɒb; *NAmE* -dʒɑːb/ *noun* (taboo, slang) the act of a person rubbing a man's PENIS with their hand to give sexual pleasure

**hand·ker·chief** /ˈhæŋkətʃɪf, -tʃiːf; *NAmE* -kərtʃ-/ *noun* (*pl.* **hand·ker·chiefs** or **hand·ker·chieves** /ˈhæŋkətʃiːvz; *NAmE* -kərtʃ-/) (*also informal* **hanky**, **han·kie**) a small piece of material or paper that you use for blowing your nose, etc.

### handles

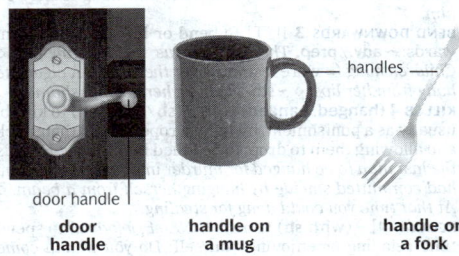

door handle | handle on a mug | handle on a fork

**han·dle** ⓘ B2 /ˈhændl/ *verb, noun*

▪ **verb**
• DEAL WITH **1** B2 [T] to deal with a situation, a person, an area of work or a strong emotion: *~ sth/sb A new man was appointed to handle the crisis. ◇ She's very good at handling her patients. ◇ to handle a situation/case ◇ He decided to handle things himself. ◇ This matter has been handled very badly. ◇ The sale was handled by Adams Commercial. ◇* (informal) *'Any problems?' 'Nothing I can't handle.' ◇* (informal) *I've got to go. I can't handle it any more* (= deal with a difficult situation).
• TOUCH WITH HANDS **2** B2 [T] *~ sth* to touch, hold or move sth with your hands: *Our cat hates being handled. ◇ The label on the box said: 'Fragile. Handle with care.'*
• CONTROL **3** [T] *~ sth* to control a vehicle, an animal, a tool, etc: *I wasn't sure if I could handle such a powerful car. ◇ She's a difficult horse to handle.* **4** [I] *~ well/badly* to be easy/difficult to drive or control: *The car handles well in any weather.*
• BUY/SELL **5** [T] *~ sth* to buy or sell sth **SYN** **deal in**: *They were arrested for handling stolen goods.*

▪ **noun**
• OF DOOR/WINDOW **1** B2 the part of a door, window, etc. that you use to open it: *She turned the handle and opened the door.* ◇ *a door handle*
• OF CUP/BAG/TOOL **2** B2 the part of an object, such as a cup, a bag or a tool, that you use to hold it or carry it: *the handle of a knife ◇ a broom handle* ⊃ see also LOVE HANDLES
• -HANDLED **3** (in adjectives) having the number or type of handle mentioned: *a long-handled spoon*
• NAME **4** a name or NICKNAME **5** a person's USERNAME on a social media site or online FORUM
**IDM** **get/have a 'handle on sb/sth** (informal) to understand or know about sb/sth, especially so that you can deal with it or them later: *I can't get a handle on these sales figures.* **give sb a 'handle (on sth)** (informal) to give sb enough facts or knowledge for them to be able to deal with sth ⊃ more at FLY *v.*

**handle·bar** /ˈhændlbɑː(r)/ *noun* [C] (usually **handlebars** [pl.]) a metal bar, with a handle at each end, that you use for controlling the direction in which a bicycle or motorcycle moves: *to hold onto the handlebars* ⊃ WORDFINDER NOTE at CYCLING ⊃ see also DROP HANDLEBARS

**handlebar mous·tache** (*US* **handlebar ˈmustache**) *noun* a MOUSTACHE that is curved upwards at each end

**hand·ler** /ˈhændlə(r)/ *noun* (especially in compounds) **1** a person who trains and controls animals, especially dogs **2** a person who carries or deals with sth as part of their job: *airport baggage handlers ◇ food handlers* **3** (especially *NAmE*) a person who organizes sth or advises sb: *the president's campaign handlers*

**hand·ling** B+ C1 /ˈhændlɪŋ/ *noun* [U] **1** B+ C1 the way that sb deals with or treats a situation, a person, an animal, etc: *I was impressed by his handling of the affair. ◇ This horse needs firm handling.* **2** B+ C1 the action of touching, feeling or holding sth with your hands: *toys that can stand up to rough handling* **3** the action of organizing or controlling sth: *data handling on computer* **4** the cost of dealing with an order, delivering goods, booking tickets, etc: *a small handling charge* **5** the way in which a vehicle can be controlled by the driver: *a car designed for easy handling* **6** (*BrE also* **car·riage**) (formal) the act or cost of transporting goods from one place to another

**hand·loom** /ˈhændluːm/ *noun* a machine for making cloth that is operated by hand

**ˈhand luggage** (especially *BrE*) (*also* **hand baggage**, **carry-on baggage** *both especially NAmE*) *noun* [U] small bags that you can keep with you on an aircraft

**hand·made** /ˌhændˈmeɪd/ *adj.* made by a person using their hands rather than by machines ⊃ compare MACHINE-MADE

**hand·maiden** /ˈhændmeɪdn/ (*also* **hand·maid** /ˈhændmeɪd/) *noun* **1** (old-fashioned) a female servant **2** (formal) something that supports and helps sth else: *Mathematics was once dubbed the handmaiden of the sciences.*

**ˈhand-me-down** *noun* [usually pl.] = CAST-OFF: *She hated having to wear her sister's hand-me-downs.* ▶ **ˈhand-me-down** = CAST-OFF

**hand·off** /ˈhændɒf; *NAmE* -ɔːf/ *noun* **1** (especially in rugby) an act of preventing an opponent from TACKLING you by blocking them with your hand while keeping your arm straight **2** (in AMERICAN FOOTBALL) an act of giving the ball to another player on your team

**hand·out** ⓢ /ˈhændaʊt/ *noun* **1** (sometimes disapproving) food, money or clothes that are given to a person who is poor ⊃ WORDFINDER NOTE at CHARITY **2** (often disapproving) money that is given to a person or an organization by the government, etc., for example to encourage commercial activity **3** a free document that gives information about an event or a matter of public interest, or that states the views of a political party, etc. ⊃ see also PRESS RELEASE **4** a document that is given to students in class or people attending a talk, etc. and that contains a summary of the lesson/talk, a set of exercises, etc.

# handover

**hand·over** /ˈhændəʊvə(r)/ *noun* [C, U] **1** the act of moving power or responsibility from one person or group to another; the period during which this is done: *the smooth handover of power from a military to a civilian government* **2** the act of giving a person or thing to sb in authority: *the handover of the hostages*

**hand·phone** /ˈhændfəʊn/ *noun* (SEAsianE) a mobile phone

**hand-picked** *adj.* carefully chosen for a special purpose

**hand·print** /ˈhændprɪnt/ *noun* a mark left by the flat part of someone's hand on a surface

**ˈhand puppet** (*especially NAmE*) (*BrE usually* **ˈglove puppet**) *noun* a type of PUPPET that you put over your hand and move using your fingers

**hand·rail** /ˈhændreɪl/ *noun* a long narrow bar that you can hold onto for support, for example when you are going up or down stairs ⊃ picture at STAIRCASE

**hand·saw** /ˈhændsɔː/ *noun* a SAW (= a tool with a long BLADE with sharp teeth along one edge) that is used with one hand only ⊃ picture at SAW

**hands-ˈdown** *adj.* [only before noun] **~winner/favourite/choice** (*informal*) easily the winner of a contest; definitely the one that people prefer: *These kits were hands-down favourites with our testers.* **IDM** see HAND *n.*

**hand·set** /ˈhændset/ *noun* **1** the part of a phone that you hold close to your mouth and ear to speak into and listen ⊃ compare RECEIVER **2** a mobile phone or smartphone, especially the main part of the phone not including the battery or SIM CARD: *mobile handsets* ◇ *handset manufacturers* **3** a device that you hold in your hand to operate a television, etc. ⊃ see also REMOTE CONTROL

**ˈhands-free** *adj.* (of a phone, etc.) able to be used without needing to be held in the hand

**hand·shake** /ˈhændʃeɪk/ *noun* an act of shaking sb's hand with your own, used especially to say hello or goodbye or when you have made an agreement ⊃ see also GOLDEN HANDSHAKE

**ˌhands-ˈoff** *adj.* [usually before noun] dealing with people or a situation by not becoming involved and by allowing people to do what they want to: *a hands-off approach to staff management* ⊃ compare HANDS-ON

**hand·some** /ˈhænsəm/ *adj.* (**hand·somer**, **hand·som·est**) **HELP** more handsome and most handsome are more common **1** (of men) attractive **SYN** good-looking: *a handsome face* ◇ *He's the most handsome man I've ever met.* ◇ *He was aptly described as 'tall, dark, and handsome'.* ⊃ SYNONYMS at BEAUTIFUL **2** (of women) attractive, with large strong features rather than small light ones: *a tall, handsome woman* ⊃ SYNONYMS at BEAUTIFUL **3** beautiful to look at: *a handsome horse/house/city* **4** large in amount or quantity: *a handsome profit* ◇ *He was elected by a handsome majority* (= a lot of people voted for him). **5** generous: *She paid him a handsome compliment.* ▸ **hand·some·ly** *adv.*: *a handsomely dressed man* ◇ *a handsomely produced book* ◇ *to be paid/rewarded handsomely* **hand·some·ness** *noun* [U]

**ˌhands-ˈon** *adj.* [usually before noun] doing sth rather than just talking about it: *hands-on computer training* ◇ *to gain hands-on experience of industry* ◇ *a hands-on style of management* ⊃ compare HANDS-OFF

**hand·spring** /ˈhændsprɪŋ/ *noun* a movement in gymnastics in which you jump through the air landing on your hands, then again landing on your feet

**hand·stand** /ˈhændstænd/ *noun* a movement in which you balance on your hands and put your legs straight up in the air

**ˌhand-to-ˈhand** *adj.* **hand-to-hand** fighting involves physical contact with your opponent

**ˌhand-to-ˈmouth** *adj.* [usually before noun] if you have a **hand-to-mouth** life, you spend all the money you earn on basic needs such as food and do not have anything left **IDM** see LIVE[1]

**ˈhand-wringing** *noun* [U] (*sometimes disapproving*) the behaviour that comes from being nervous or worried, especially when this seems EXCESSIVE (= more than seems reasonable or appropriate)

**hand·writ·ing** /ˈhændraɪtɪŋ/ *noun* [U] **1** writing that is done with a pen or pencil, not printed or typed **2** a person's particular style of writing in this way: *I can't read his handwriting.* **IDM** **the ˌhandwriting on the ˈwall** (NAmE) = THE WRITING IS ON THE WALL at WRITING: *It is amazing that not one of them saw the handwriting on the wall.*

**hand·writ·ten** /ˌhændˈrɪtn/ *adj.* written by hand, not printed or typed: *a handwritten note*

**handy** /ˈhændi/ *adj.* (**hand·ier**, **handi·est**) (*informal*) **1** easy to use or to do **SYN** useful: *a handy little tool* ◇ *handy hints/tips for removing stains* **2** [not before noun] located near to sb/sth; located or stored in a convenient place: *Always keep a first-aid kit handy.* ◇ *Have you got a pen handy?* ◇ **~for (doing) sth** (*BrE*) *Our house is very handy for the station.* **3** [not before noun] able to use your hands or tools to make or repair things well: *to be handy around the house* ⊃ see also HANDILY ▸ **handi·ness** *noun* [U] **IDM** **come in ˈhandy** (*informal*) to be useful: *The extra money came in very handy.* ◇ *Don't throw that away—it might come in handy.*

**handy·man** /ˈhændimæn/ *noun* (*pl.* **-men** /-men/) a man who is good at doing practical jobs inside and outside the house, either as a hobby or as a job

## hang ⓘ B1 /hæŋ/ *verb, noun*

■ *verb* (**hung**, **hung** /hʌŋ/) **HELP** In sense 4, **hanged** is used for the past tense and past participle.
- ATTACH FROM TOP **1** B1 [T, I] to attach sth, or to be attached, at the top so that the lower part is free or loose: **~sth + adv./prep.** *Hang your coat on the hook.* ◇ **~sth up** *Shall I hang your coat up?* ◇ **~sth (out)** (*BrE*) *Have you hung out the washing?* ◇ (*NAmE*) *Have you hung the wash?* ◇ **~adv./prep.** *There were several expensive suits hanging in the wardrobe.*
- FALL LOOSELY **2** [I] **~adv./prep.** when sth **hangs** in a particular way, it falls in that way: *Her hair hung down to her waist.* ◇ *He had lost weight and the suit hung loosely on him.*
- BEND DOWNWARDS **3** [I, T] to bend or let sth bend downwards: **~adv./prep.** *The dog's tongue was hanging out.* ◇ *Children hung* (= were leaning) *over the gate.* ◇ *A cigarette hung from her lips.* ◇ **~sth** *She hung her head in shame.*
- KILL SB **4** (**hanged, hanged**) [T, I] **~(sb/yourself)** to kill sb, usually as a punishment, by tying a rope around their neck and allowing them to drop; to be killed in this way: *He was the last man to be hanged for murder in this country.* ◇ *She had committed suicide by hanging herself from a beam.* ◇ *At that time you could hang for stealing.*
- RELAX **5** [I] **~(with sb)** (*especially NAmE, informal*) to spend time relaxing or enjoying yourself: *Do you wanna come hang with us?*
- PICTURES **6** [T, I] **~(sth)** to attach sth, especially a picture, to a HOOK (= a curved piece of metal) on a wall; to be attached in this way: *We hung her portrait above the fireplace.* ◇ *Several of his paintings hang in the Tate Gallery.* **7** [T, usually passive] to decorate a place by placing paintings, etc. on a wall: **be hung with sth** *The rooms were hung with tapestries.*
- WALLPAPER **8** [T] **~sth** to stick WALLPAPER to a wall
- DOOR/GATE **9** [T] **~sth** to attach a door or gate to a post so that it moves freely
- STAY IN THE AIR **10** [I] **+ adv./prep.** to stay in the air: *Smoke hung in the air above the city.*

**IDM** **ˈhang sth** (*BrE, informal*) used to say that you are not going to worry about sth: *Oh, let's get two and hang the expense!* **hang by a ˈhair/ˈthread** (of a person's life) to be in great danger **hang (on) ˈin there** (*informal*) to remain determined to succeed even when a situation is difficult **hang a ˈleft/ˈright** (*informal*) to take a left/right turn **hang on sb's ˈwords/on sb's every ˈword** to listen with great attention to sb you admire **hang ˈtough** (NAmE, *informal*) to be determined and refuse to change your attitude or ideas **let it all hang ˈout** (*informal*) to express your feelings freely ⇒ more at BALANCE n., FIRE n., GRIM, HEAVY adv., LOOSE adj., PEG n., WELL adv.

**PHRV** ,hang a'bout (*BrE, informal*) **1** to wait or stay near a place, not doing very much: *kids hanging about in the streets* **2** to be very slow doing sth: *I can't hang about—the boss wants to see me.* **3** (*informal*) used to tell sb to stop what they are doing or saying for a short time: *Hang about! There's something not quite right here.* ,hang a'round ( …) (*informal*) to wait or stay near a place, not doing very much: *You hang around here in case he comes, and I'll go on ahead.* ,hang a'round with sb (*informal*) to spend a lot of time with sb ,hang 'back to remain in a place after all the other people have left ,hang 'back (from sth) to hesitate because you are nervous about doing or saying sth: *I was sure she knew the answer but for some reason she hung back.* ,hang 'on **1** 🔊 **B2** (*informal*) used to ask sb to wait for a short time or to stop what they are doing: *Hang on—I'm not quite ready.* ◇ *Now hang on a minute—you can't really believe what you just said!* **2** to hold sth tightly: *Hang on tight—we're off!* ⇒ SYNONYMS at HOLD **3** to wait for sth to happen: *I haven't heard if I've got the job yet—they've kept me hanging on for days.* **4** (*informal*) used on the phone to ask sb who is calling to wait until they can talk to the person they want: *Hang on—I'll just see if he's here.* **5** to continue doing sth in difficult circumstances: *The team hung on for victory.* ,hang on sth to depend on sth: *A lot hangs on this decision.* ,hang 'on to sth **1** to hold sth tightly: *Hang on to that rope and don't let go.* **2** (*informal*) to keep sth, not sell it or give it away: *Let's hang on to those old photographs—they may be valuable.* ,hang 'out (*informal*) to spend a lot of time in a place: *The local kids hang out at the mall.* ⇒ related noun HANG-OUT ,hang sth↔'out (especially *BrE*) to attach things that you have washed to a piece of thin rope or wire, etc. outside so that they can dry; to attach sth such as a flag outside a window or in the street ,hang 'over sb if sth bad or unpleasant is **hanging over** you, you think about it and worry about it a lot because it is happening or might happen: *The possibility of a court case is still hanging over her.* ,hang to'gether **1** to fit together well; to be the same as or consistent with each other: *Their accounts of what happened don't hang together.* **2** (of people) to support or help one another ,hang 'up to end a phone conversation by putting down the phone RECEIVER or pressing the 'end call' button: *After I hung up I remembered what I'd wanted to say.* ,hang sth↔'up (*informal*) to finish using sth for the last time: *Ruth has hung up her dancing shoes.* ,hang 'up on sb (*informal*) to end a phone call by suddenly and unexpectedly putting the phone down or pressing the 'end call' button: *Don't hang up on me—we must talk!* ⇒ see also BE HUNG UP ON / ABOUT SB / STH at HUNG adj.

■ *noun* [sing.] the way in which a dress, piece of cloth, etc. falls or moves

**IDM** get the 'hang of sth (*informal*) to learn how to do or to use sth; to understand sth: *It's not difficult once you get the hang of it.*

**hangar** /ˈhæŋə(r)/ *noun* a large building in which aircraft are kept

**hang·dog** /ˈhæŋdɒg; *NAmE* -dɔːg/ *adj.* [only before noun] if a person has a **hangdog** look, they look sad or ashamed

**hanger** /ˈhæŋə(r)/ (also 'coat hanger, 'clothes hanger) *noun* a curved piece of wood, plastic or wire that you use to hang clothes up on

**hanger-'on** *noun* (*pl.* hangers-on) (*often disapproving*) a person who tries to be friendly with a famous person or who goes to important events, in order to get some advantage

**'hang-glider** *noun* **1** the frame used in hang-gliding **2** a person who goes hang-gliding

**'hang-gliding** *noun* [U] a sport in which you fly while hanging from a frame like a large KITE that you control with your body movements: *to go hang-gliding*

**hang·ing** /ˈhæŋɪŋ/ *noun* **1** [U, C] the practice of killing sb as a punishment by tying a rope around their neck and allowing them to drop from a high place; an occasion when this happens: *to sentence sb to death by hanging* ◇ *public*

**hangings 2** [C, usually pl.] a large piece of material that is hung on a wall or around a bed for decoration: *wall hangings*

**'hanging ,basket** *noun* a BASKET or similar container with flowers growing in it, that is hung from a building by a short chain or rope ⇒ picture at BASKET

**hang·man** /ˈhæŋmən/ *noun* (*pl.* -men /-mən/) **1** [C] a man whose job is to hang criminals **2** [U] /ˈhæŋmæn/ a game in which one player chooses a word and the other players try to guess it, letter by letter. Each time they guess wrongly, the first person draws one part of a person being hanged. The other players have to guess the word before the drawing is complete.

**'hang-out** *noun* (*informal*) a place where sb lives or likes to go often **SYN** haunt

**hang·over** /ˈhæŋəʊvə(r)/ *noun* **1** the headache and sick feeling that you have the day after drinking too much alcohol: *She woke up with a terrible hangover.* **2** [usually sing.] ~ (from sth) a feeling, custom, idea, etc. that remains from the past, although it is no longer practical or suitable: *the insecure feeling that was a hangover from her childhood* ◇ *hangover laws from the previous administration* ⇒ see also HOLDOVER

**han·gry** /ˈhæŋɡri/ *adj.* (han·grier, han·gri·est) (*informal*) angry or in a bad mood because you are hungry: *I get very hangry if I miss a meal.*

**the Hang Seng Index** /ðə ˌhæŋ ˈseŋ ˌɪndeks/ *noun* a figure that shows the relative price of shares on the Hong Kong Stock Exchange

**'hang-up** *noun* (*informal*) **1** ~ (about sth) an emotional problem about sth that makes you embarrassed or worried: *He's got a real hang-up about his height.* **2** (*NAmE*) a problem that delays sth being agreed or achieved

**hank** /hæŋk/ *noun* a long piece of wool, rope, hair, etc. that is wound into a large loose ball

**han·ker** /ˈhæŋkə(r)/ *verb* [I] to have a strong desire for sth: ~ after/for sth *He had hankered after fame all his life.* ◇ ~ to do sth *She hankered to go back to Australia.*

**han·ker·ing** /ˈhæŋkərɪŋ/ *noun* [usually sing.] ~ (for/after sth) | ~ (to do sth) a strong desire: *a hankering for a wealthy lifestyle*

**hanky** (also han·kie) /ˈhæŋki/ *noun* (*pl.* -ies) (*informal*) = HANDKERCHIEF

**hanky-panky** /ˌhæŋki ˈpæŋki/ *noun* [U] (*old-fashioned, informal, humorous*) sexual activity or slightly dishonest behaviour that is considered bad but not very seriously bad

**Han·sard** /ˈhænsɑːd; *NAmE* -sɑːrd/ *noun* [U] (in the British, Canadian, American, New Zealand or South African parliaments) the official written record of everything that is said in the parliament

**han·som** /ˈhænsəm/ (also 'hansom cab) *noun* a CARRIAGE with two wheels, pulled by one horse, used in the past to carry two passengers

**Ha·nuk·kah** (also Cha·nuk·ah) /ˈhænʊkə, ˈxæ-; *NAmE* ˈhɑːn-, ˈxɑː-/ *noun* an eight-day Jewish festival and holiday in December (or sometimes starting in late November) when Jews remember the occasion when the TEMPLE in Jerusalem was DEDICATED again in 165 BC

**ha'penny** /ˈheɪpni/ *noun* = HALFPENNY

**hap·haz·ard** /hæpˈhæzəd; *NAmE* -zərd/ *adj.* (*disapproving*) with no particular order or plan; not organized well: *The books had been piled on the shelves in a haphazard fashion.* ◇ *The government's approach to the problem was haphazard.* ▶ **hap·haz·ard·ly** *adv.*

**hap·less** /ˈhæpləs/ *adj.* [only before noun] (*formal*) not lucky; experiencing extreme bad luck: *the hapless victims of exploitation*

---

**O** Oxford Phrasal Academic Lexicon (OPAL) written and spoken word lists | **W** OPAL written word list | **S** OPAL spoken word list

# haploid

**hap·loid** /ˈhæplɔɪd/ adj. (biology) (of a cell) containing the set of CHROMOSOMES from one parent only ⊃ compare DIPLOID

**hap·pen** 🔊 A1 Ⓢ /ˈhæpən/ verb **1** ⚡ A1 [I] to take place, especially without being planned: *You'll never guess what's happened!* ◇ *Accidents like this happen all the time.* ◇ *You have to make things happen.* ◇ *I'll be there whatever happens.* ◇ *I don't know how this happened.* ◇ *I try to keep up with what is happening in the world.* **2** ⚡ A1 [I] to take place as the result of sth: *She pressed the button but nothing happened.* ◇ *What happens if nobody comes to the party?* ◇ *Just plug it in and see what happens.* **3** [T] **~ to be/do sth** to do or be sth by chance: *She happened to be out when we called.* ◇ *You don't happen to know his name, do you?* ◇ *it happens that …* *It happened that she was out when we called.* **4** [T] **~ to be/do sth** used to tell sb sth, especially when you are disagreeing with them or annoyed by what they have said: *That happens to be my mother you're talking about!*
**IDM** **anything can/might happen** used to say that it is not possible to know what the result of sth will be **as it happens/happened** used when you say sth that is surprising, or sth connected with what sb else has just said: *I agree with you, as it happens.* ◇ *As it happens, I have a spare set of keys in my office.* **it (just) so happens that …** by chance: *It just so happened they'd been invited too.* **these things 'happen** used to tell sb not to worry about sth they have done: *'Sorry—I've spilt some wine.' 'Never mind. These things happen.'* ⊃ more at ACCIDENT, EVENT, SHIT *n.*, WAIT *v.*
**PHRV** **'happen on sth** (*old-fashioned*) to find sth by chance **'happen to sb/sth** ⚡ A2 if sth **happens to** sb/sth, they experience it: *It's the best thing that has ever happened to me.* ◇ *What's happened to your car?* ◇ *I hope nothing (= nothing unpleasant) has happened to them.* ◇ *Do you know what happened to Gill Lovecy (= have you any news about her)?*

**hap·pen·ing** /ˈhæpənɪŋ/ *noun, adj.*
■ *noun* **1** [usually pl.] an event; something that happens, often sth unusual: *There have been strange happenings here lately.* **2** an artistic performance or event that is not planned
■ *adj.* [only before noun] (*informal*) where there is a lot of exciting activity; fashionable: *a happening place*

**hap·pen·stance** /ˈhæpənstæns/ *BrE also* -staːns/ *noun* [U, C] (*especially NAmE*) chance, especially when it results in sth good

**hap·pily** 🔊 A2 /ˈhæpɪli/ adv. **1** ⚡ A2 in a cheerful way; with feelings of pleasure: *children playing happily on the beach* ◇ *to be happily married* ◇ *And they all lived happily ever after* (= used as the end of a FAIRY TALE). **2** by good luck **SYN** **fortunately**: *Happily, the damage was only slight.* **3** willingly: *I'll happily help, if I can.* **4** (*formal*) in a way that is suitable or appropriate: *This suggestion did not fit very happily with our existing plans.*

**hap·pi·ness** 🔊 B1 /ˈhæpinəs/ *noun* [U] **1** ⚡ B1 the state of feeling or showing pleasure: *to find true happiness* ◇ *Her eyes shone with happiness.* **2** (*about/with sth*) the state of being satisfied that sth is good or right **SYN** **satisfaction**: *The meeting expressed happiness about the progress made.* ⊃ SYNONYMS at SATISFACTION

**happy** 🔊 A1 /ˈhæpi/
*adj.* (**hap·pier**, **hap·pi·est**)
• **FEELING/GIVING PLEASURE**
**1** ⚡ A1 feeling or showing pleasure; pleased: *a happy family* ◇ *a happy smile/face* ◇ *He always seemed happy enough.* ◇ *Money won't make you happy.* ◇ **~ to do sth** *We are happy to announce the engagement of our daughter.* ◇ **~ for sb** *I'm very happy for you.* ◇ **~ (that) …** *I'm happy (that) you could come.* ⊃ SYNONYMS at GLAD **2** ⚡ A1 giving or causing pleasure: *She had a very happy life.* ◇ *a happy marriage/childhood/*

WORD FAMILY
**happy** *adj.* (≠ unhappy)
**happily** *adv.* (≠ unhappily)
**happiness** *noun* (≠ unhappiness)

*occasion* ◇ *The story has a happy ending.* ◇ *Those were the happiest days of my life.*
• **AT CELEBRATION 3** ⚡ A1 if you wish sb a **Happy Birthday**, **Happy New Year**, etc. you mean that you hope they have a pleasant celebration
• **SATISFIED 4** ⚡ A2 satisfied that sth is good or right; not anxious: *I said I'd go just to keep him happy.* ◇ **~ with sb/sth** *Are you happy with that arrangement?* ◇ *She was happy enough with her performance.* ◇ **~ about sb/sth (doing sth)** *If there's anything you're not happy about, come and ask.*
• **WILLING 5** ⚡ A2 **~ to do sth** (*formal*) willing or pleased to do sth: *I'm perfectly happy to leave it till tomorrow.* ◇ *He will be more than happy to come with us.*
• **LUCKY 6** lucky; successful **SYN** **fortunate**: *By a happy coincidence, we arrived at exactly the same time.* ◇ *He is in the happy position of never having to worry about money.*
• **SUITABLE 7** (*formal*) (of words, ideas or behaviour) suitable and appropriate for a particular situation: *That wasn't the happiest choice of words.*
**IDM** **(not) a happy 'camper** (*BrE also* **(not) a happy 'bunny**) (*informal*) (not) pleased about a situation: *She wasn't a happy bunny at all.* **a happy e'vent** the birth of a baby **a/the happy 'medium** something that is in the middle between two choices or two ways of doing sth **many happy re'turns (of the 'day)** used to wish sb a happy and pleasant birthday ⊃ more at MEAN *n.*

▼ **SYNONYMS**
**happy**
satisfied • content • contented • joyful • blissful
These words all describe feeling, showing or giving pleasure.
**happy** feeling, showing or giving pleasure; satisfied with sth or not worried about it: *a happy marriage/memory/childhood* ◇ *I said I'd go, just to keep him happy.*
**satisfied** pleased because you have achieved sth or because sth has happened as you wanted it to; showing this: *She's never satisfied with what she's got.* ◇ *a satisfied smile*
**content** [not before noun] happy and satisfied with what you have: *I'm perfectly content just to lie in the sun.*
**contented** happy and comfortable with what you have; showing this: *a contented baby* ◇ *a long contented sigh*
**CONTENT OR CONTENTED?**
Being **contented** depends more on having a comfortable life; being **content** can depend more on your attitude to your life: you can *learn to be content with sth* by changing your attitude to it. People or animals can be **contented** but only people can be **content**.
**joyful** (*rather formal*) very happy; making people very happy
**blissful** making people very happy; showing this happiness: *three blissful weeks away*
**JOYFUL OR BLISSFUL?**
**Joy** is a livelier feeling; **bliss** is more peaceful.
**PATTERNS**
• happy/satisfied/content/contented **with** sth
• a happy/satisfied/contented/blissful **smile**
• a happy/joyful **occasion/celebration**
• to **feel** happy/satisfied/content/contented/joyful
• **very/perfectly/quite** happy/satisfied/content/contented

**happy-go-ˈlucky** *adj.* not caring or worrying about the future: *a happy-go-lucky attitude* ◇ *a happy-go-lucky sort of person*

**ˈhappy hour** *noun* [C, U] (*informal*) a time, usually in the early evening, when a pub or a bar sells alcoholic drinks at lower prices than usual

**hap·tic** /ˈhæptɪk/ *adj.* (*specialist*) relating to or involving the sense of touch: *Players use a haptic device such as a joystick to control the game.*

**hara-kiri** /ˌhærə ˈkɪri; *NAmE* ˌhɑːr-/ *noun* [U] (*from Japanese*) an act of killing yourself by cutting open your stomach with a SWORD, performed especially by the SAM-URAI in Japan in the past, to avoid losing honour

**har·am** /həˈræm, -ˈrɑːm/ *adj.* not permitted by Islamic law: *haram meat* **OPP** **halal**

**har·am·bee** /həˈræmbeɪ/ *EAfrE* [haˈrambeː] *noun* (*EAfrE*) **1** [C] a meeting that is held in order to collect money for sth, for example a community project: *They held a harambee meeting to raise funds for a new classroom.* **2** [U] the act of joining with other people to achieve a difficult task: *the spirit of harambee*

**har·angue** /həˈræŋ/ *verb, noun*
■ *verb* ~ sb (*disapproving*) to speak loudly and angrily in a way that criticizes sb/sth or tries to persuade people to do sth
■ *noun* (*disapproving*) a long loud angry speech that criticizes sb/sth or tries to persuade people to do sth

**har·ass** /ˈhærəs, həˈræs/ *NAmE* həˈræs, ˈhærəs/ *verb* **1** [often passive] to annoy or worry sb by putting pressure on them or saying or doing unpleasant things to them: *be harassed (by sb) He has complained of being harassed by the police.* ◊ *She claims she has been sexually harassed at work.* **2** ~ sb/sth to make repeated attacks on an enemy **SYN** **harry**

**har·assed** /ˈhærəst, həˈræst/ *NAmE* həˈræst, ˈhærəst/ *adj.* tired and anxious because you have too much to do: *a harassed-looking waiter* ◊ *harassed mothers with their children*

**har·ass·ment** ?+ **C1** /ˈhærəsmənt, həˈræsmənt/ *NAmE* həˈræsmənt, ˈhærəsmənt/ *noun* [U] **1** ?+ **C1** the act of annoying or worrying sb by putting pressure on them or saying or doing unpleasant things to them: *racial/sexual harassment* ◊ see also SEXUAL HARASSMENT **2** the act of making repeated attacks on an enemy: *guerrilla harassment of the enemy*

**har·bin·ger** /ˈhɑːbɪndʒə(r)/ *NAmE* ˈhɑːrb-/ *noun* ~ (of sth) (*formal* or *literary*) a sign that shows that sth is going to happen soon, often sth bad

**har·bour** ?+ **B2** (*US* **har·bor**) /ˈhɑːbə(r)/ *NAmE* ˈhɑːrb-/ *noun, verb*
■ *noun* ?+ **B2** [C, U] an area of water on the coast, protected from the open sea by strong walls, where ships can shelter: *Several boats lay at anchor in the harbour.* ◊ *to enter/leave harbour* ◊ WORDFINDER NOTE at SEA
■ *verb* **1** ~ sb to hide and protect sb who is hiding from the police: *Police believe someone must be harbouring the killer.* **2** ~ sth to keep feelings or thoughts, especially negative ones, in your mind for a long time: *The arsonist may harbour a grudge against the company.* ◊ *She began to harbour doubts about the decision.* **3** ~ sth to contain sth and allow it to develop: *Your dishcloth can harbour many germs.*

**'harbour master** (*US* **har·bor·mas·ter**) *noun* an official in charge of a harbour

**hard** ❶ **A1** /hɑːd/ *NAmE* hɑːrd/ *adj., adv.*
■ *adj.* (**hard·er, hard·est**)
• DIFFICULT **1** ?.**A1** difficult to do, understand or answer: *a hard choice/decision/question* ◊ **to do sth** *It is hard to believe that she's only nine.* ◊ *It's hard to see how they can lose.* ◊ *'When will the job be finished?' 'It's hard to say'* (= it is difficult to be certain).' ◊ *It's getting harder and harder to earn enough to pay the rent.* ◊ *Houses like this are extremely hard to find.* ◊ *I found it hard to believe what they told me.* ◊ **~ for sb** *It must be hard for her, bringing up four children on her own.* ◊ **~ for sb to do sth** *It's hard for old people to change their ways.* **OPP** **easy** **2** ?.**A1** full of difficulty and problems, especially because of a lack of money **SYN** **tough**: *Times were hard at the end of the war.* ◊ *She's had a hard life.* **OPP** **easy**
• NEEDING/USING EFFORT **3** **A1** needing or using a lot of physical strength or mental effort: *It's hard work shovelling snow.* ◊ *This is the hardest part of my job.* ◊ *I've had a long hard day.* ⊃ SYNONYMS at DIFFICULT **4** ?.**A1** (of people) putting a lot of effort or energy into an activity: *She's a very hard worker.* ◊ *He's hard at work on a new novel.* ◊ *When I left they were all still hard at it* (= working hard). **5** ?.**A2** done with a lot of strength or force: *He gave the door a good hard kick.* ◊ *a hard punch*

# hard

• SOLID/STIFF **6** ?.**A2** solid or stiff and difficult to bend or break: *Wait for the concrete to go hard.* ◊ *a hard mattress* ◊ *Diamonds are the hardest known mineral.* **OPP** **soft**
• WITHOUT SYMPATHY **7** ?.**B1** showing no kind feelings or sympathy: *My father was a hard man.* ◊ *She gave me a hard stare.* ◊ *He said some very hard things to me.*
• NOT AFRAID **8** (*informal*) (of people) showing no signs of fear or weakness; ready to fight or compete **SYN** **tough**: *Come and get me if you think you're hard enough.* ◊ *You think you're really hard, don't you?*
• FACTS/EVIDENCE **9** [only before noun] definitely true and based on information that can be proved: *Is there any hard evidence either way?* ◊ *The newspaper story is based on hard facts.*
• WEATHER **10** very cold and severe: *It had been a hard winter.* ◊ *There was a hard frost that night.* ⊃ compare MILD
• DRINK **11** [only before noun] strongly alcoholic: *hard liquor* ◊ (*informal*) *a drop of the hard stuff* (= a strong alcoholic drink) ⊃ compare SOFT DRINK
• WATER **12** containing CALCIUM and other mineral salts that make mixing with soap difficult: *a hard water area* ◊ *Our water is very hard.* **OPP** **soft**
• CONSONANTS **13** (*phonetics*) used to describe a letter *c* or *g* when pronounced as in 'cat' or 'go', rather than as in 'city' or 'giant' **OPP** **soft** ▶ **hard·ness** *noun* [U]: *water hardness* ◊ *hardness of heart*
**IDM** ▶ **be ˌhard on sb/sth 1** to treat or criticize sb in a very severe or strict way: *Don't be too hard on him—he's very young.* **2** to be difficult for or unfair to sb/sth: *It's hard on people who don't have a car.* **3** to be likely to hurt or damage sth: *Looking at a computer screen all day can be very hard on the eyes.* **drive / strike a hard ˈbargain** to argue in an aggressive way and force sb to agree on the best possible price or arrangement **give sb a hard ˈtime** to deliberately make a situation difficult and unpleasant for sb: *They really gave me a hard time at the interview.* **ˌhard and ˈfast** (especially after a negative) that cannot be changed in any circumstances: *There are no hard and fast rules about this.* **(as) ˌhard as ˈnails** showing no fear, sympathy or kind behaviour **ˌhard ˈcheese** (*BrE, informal*) used as a way of saying that you are sorry about sth, usually IRONICALLY (= you really mean the opposite) **ˌhard ˈgoing** difficult to understand or needing a lot of effort: *I'm finding his latest novel very hard going.* **ˌhard ˈluck** (*BrE*) used to tell sb that you feel sorry for them: *'Failed again, I'm afraid.' 'Oh, hard luck.'* **the hard ˈway** by having an unpleasant experience or by making mistakes: *She won't listen to my advice so she'll just have to learn the hard way.* **make hard ˈwork of sth** to use more time or energy on a task than is necessary **no hard ˈfeelings** used after you have been arguing with sb or have beaten them in a contest but you would still like to be friendly with them: *It looks like I'm the winner again. No hard feelings, Dave, eh?* **play hard to ˈget** (*informal*) to make yourself seem more attractive or interesting by not immediately accepting an invitation to do sth **too much like hard ˈwork** needing too much effort: *I can't be bothered making a hot meal—it's too much like hard work.* ⊃ more at ACT *n.*, JOB, LONG *adj.*, NUT *n.*, ROCK *n.*

■ *adv.* (**hard·er, hard·est**)
• WITH EFFORT **1** ?.**A1** with great effort; with difficulty: *to work hard* ◊ *You must try harder.* ◊ *She tried her hardest not to show how disappointed she was.* ◊ *He was still breathing hard after his run.* ◊ *Our victory was hard won* (= won with great difficulty).
• WITH FORCE **2** ?.**B1** with great force: *Don't hit it so hard!* ◊ (*figurative*) *Small businesses have been hit hard/hard hit by the recession.*
• CAREFULLY **3** ?.**B1** carefully and completely: *to think hard* ◊ *We thought long and hard before deciding to move house.*
• A LOT **4** heavily; a lot or for a long time: *It was raining hard when we set off.*
• LEFT/RIGHT **5** at a sharp angle to the left/right: *Turn hard right at the next junction.*
**IDM** ▶ **be / feel hard ˈdone by** (*informal*) to be or feel unfairly treated: *She has every right to feel hard done by—her parents have given her nothing.* **be ˌhard ˈpressed / ˈpushed to**

# hardback 722

do sth | **be hard 'put (to it) to do sth** to find it very difficult to do sth: *He was hard put to it to explain her disappearance.* **be hard 'up for sth** to have too few or too little of sth: *We're hard up for ideas.* ⊃ see also HARD UP ◊ **'hard on sth** (*literary*) very soon after: *His death followed hard on hers.* **take sth 'hard** to be very upset by sth: *He took his wife's death very hard.* ⊃ more at DIE v., HEEL n.

▼ **WHICH WORD?**

**hard / hardly**

- The adverb from the adjective **hard** is **hard**: *I have to work hard today.* ◊ *She has thought very hard about her future plans.* ◊ *It was raining hard outside.*
- **Hardly** is an adverb meaning 'almost not': *I hardly ever go to concerts.* ◊ *I can hardly wait for my birthday.* It cannot be used instead of **hard**: ~~*I've been working hardly today.*~~ ◊ ~~*She has thought very hardly about her future plans.*~~ ◊ ~~*It was raining hardly outside.*~~
- ⊃ note at HARDLY

**hard·back** /ˈhɑːdbæk; NAmE ˈhɑːrd-/ (*also* **hard·cover** *especially in NAmE*) *noun* [C, U] a book that has a stiff cover: *What's the price of the hardback?* ◊ **in ~** *It was published in hardback last year.* ◊ *hardback books/editions* ⊃ compare PAPERBACK

**hard·ball** /ˈhɑːdbɔːl; NAmE ˈhɑːrd-/ *noun* (*NAmE*) **1** the game of baseball (when contrasted with SOFTBALL) **2** used to refer to a way of behaving, especially in politics, that shows that a person is determined to get what they want: *I want us to play hardball on this issue.* ◊ *hardball politics*

**hard-'bitten** *adj.* not easily shocked and not showing emotion, because you have experienced many unpleasant things

**hard·board** /ˈhɑːdbɔːd; NAmE ˈhɑːrdbɔːrd/ *noun* [U] a type of stiff board made by pressing very small pieces of wood together into thin sheets

**hard-'boiled** *adj.* **1** (of an egg) boiled until the inside is hard ⊃ compare SOFT-BOILED **2** (of people) not showing much emotion

**hard 'by** *prep.* (*old-fashioned*) very near sth ▶ **hard 'by** *adv.*

**hard 'candy** *noun* [C, U] (*NAmE*) (*BrE* **boiled 'sweet**) [C] a hard CANDY (= sweet) made from boiled sugar, often tasting of fruit

**hard 'cash** (*BrE*) (*NAmE also* **cold 'cash**) *noun* [U] money, especially in the form of coins and notes, that you can spend

**hard-'charging** *adj.* [only before noun] (*especially NAmE*) working or performing with a lot of energy and skill: *He changed from a goofy kid to a hard-charging soldier.*

**hard 'cider** (*NAmE*) (*also* **cider** *especially in BrE*) *noun* [U, C] an alcoholic drink made from the juice of apples

**hard-'code** *verb* **~ sth** (*computing*) to write data so that it cannot easily be changed

**hard 'copy** *noun* [U, C] (*computing*) data from a computer that has been printed on paper

**hard 'core** *noun* [sing. + sing./pl. v.] the small central group in an organization, or in a particular group of people, who are the most active or who will not change their beliefs or behaviour: *It's really only the hard core that bother(s) to go to meetings.* ◊ *A hard core of drivers ignore(s) the law.*

**hard-'core** *adj.* **1** having a belief or a way of behaving that will not change: *hard-core party members* **2** showing or describing sexual activity in a detailed or violent way: *They sell hard-core pornography.* ⊃ compare SOFT-CORE

**hard 'court** *noun* an area with a hard surface for playing tennis on, not grass

**hard·cover** /ˈhɑːdkʌvə(r); NAmE ˈhɑːrd-/ *noun* (*especially NAmE*) = HARDBACK

**hard 'currency** *noun* [U, C] money that is easy to exchange for money from another country, because it is not likely to lose its value

**hard 'disk** (*also* **'hard drive**) *noun* a device that stores computer information on a SPINNING (= turning) disk, either internal or external to the computer

**hard-'drinking** *adj.* drinking a lot of alcohol

**hard 'drive** *noun* (*computing*) = HARD DISK

**hard 'drug** *noun* [usually pl.] a powerful illegal drug, such as HEROIN, that some people take for pleasure and can become ADDICTED to ⊃ compare SOFT DRUG

**hard-'earned** *adj.* that you get only after a lot of work and effort: *hard-earned cash* ◊ *We finally managed a hard-earned draw.*

**hard-'edged** *adj.* powerful, true to life and not affected by emotion: *the movie's hard-edged realism*

**hard·en** /ˈhɑːdn; NAmE ˈhɑːrdn/ *verb* **1** [I, T] to become or make sth become solid or stiff: *The varnish takes a few hours to harden.* ◊ **~ sth** *a method for hardening and preserving wood* **2** [I, T] if your voice, face, etc. **hardens**, or you **harden** it, it becomes more serious or severe: *Her face hardened into an expression of hatred.* ◊ **~ sth** *He hardened his voice when he saw she wasn't listening.* **3** [I, T] if sb's feelings or attitudes **harden** or sb/sth **hardens** them, they become more fixed and determined: *Public attitudes to the strike have hardened.* ◊ *Their suspicions hardened into certainty.* ◊ **~ sth** *The incident hardened her resolve to leave the company.* **4** [T] **~ sb/sth/yourself** to make sb less kind or less affected by extreme situations: *Joe sounded different, hardened by the war.* ◊ *They were hardened criminals* (= they showed no regret for their crimes). ◊ *In this job you have to harden your heart to pain and suffering.* ▶ **hard·en·ing** *noun* [U, sing.]: *hardening of the arteries* ◊ *a hardening of attitudes towards one-parent families*

**hard-'faced** *adj.* (*disapproving*) (of a person) showing no feeling or sympathy for other people

**hard-'fought** *adj.* that involves fighting very hard: *a hard-fought battle/win/victory*

**hard 'hat** *noun* a hat worn by building workers, etc. to protect their heads

**hard-'headed** *adj.* determined and not allowing your emotions to affect your decisions

**hard-'hearted** *adj.* giving no importance to the feelings or problems of other people ⊃ compare SOFT-HEARTED

**hard-'hitting** *adj.* not afraid to talk about or criticize sb/sth in an honest and very direct way: *a hard-hitting speech*

**hard 'labour** (*US* **hard 'labor**) *noun* [U] punishment in prison that involves a lot of very hard physical work

**hard 'left** *noun* [sing. + sing./pl. v.] (*especially BrE*) the members of a LEFT-WING political party who have the most extreme opinions: *hard-left policies*

**hard 'line** *noun* [sing.] a strict policy or attitude: *The judge's hard line against drug dealers* ◊ *The government took a hard line on the strike.*

**hard-'line** *adj.* [usually before noun] **1** (of a person) having very fixed beliefs and being unlikely or unwilling to change them: *a hard-line conservative* **2** (of ideas) very fixed and unlikely to change: *a hard-line attitude* ▶ **hard-liner** /ˌhɑːdˈlaɪnə(r); NAmE ˌhɑːrd-/ *noun*: *a Republican hardliner*

**hard-'luck story** *noun* a story about yourself that you tell sb in order to get their sympathy or help

**hard·ly** 🔊 B1 /ˈhɑːdli; NAmE ˈhɑːrd-/ *adv.* **1** 🔊 B1 almost no; almost not; almost none: *There's hardly any tea left.* ◊ *She hardly ever calls me* (= almost never). ◊ *We hardly know each other.* ◊ *It hardly seems fair to put all the blame on him.* ◊ *Hardly a day goes by without my thinking of her* (= I think of her almost every day). **2** 🔊 B2 used especially after 'can' or 'could' and before the main verb, to emphasize that it is difficult to do sth: *I can hardly keep my eyes open* (= I'm almost falling asleep). ◊ *I could hardly believe it when I read the letter.* **3** 🔊 B2 used to suggest that sth is unlikely or unreasonable or that sb is silly for saying or doing sth: *He is hardly likely to admit he was wrong.* ◊ *It's hardly surprising she was fired; she never did any work.* ◊ *It's hardly the time to discuss it now.* ◊ *You can hardly expect her to do it for free.* ⊃ note at HARD **4** used to say that sth has just begun, happened, etc: *We can't stop for coffee now, we've hardly started.* ◊ *We had hardly sat down to supper when the phone rang.* ◊ (*formal*) *Hardly had she spoken before she regretted it bitterly.*

> ▼ **GRAMMAR POINT**
>
> **hardly / scarcely / barely / no sooner**
>
> - **Hardly, scarcely** and **barely** can all be used to say that something is only just true or possible. They are used with words like *any* and *anyone*, with adjectives and verbs, and are often placed between *can, could, have, be,* etc. and the main part of the verb: *They have sold scarcely any copies of the book.* ◊ *I barely recognized her.* ◊ *His words were barely audible.* ◊ *I can hardly believe it.* ◊ I hardly can believe it.
> - **Hardly, scarcely** and **barely** are negative words and should not be used with *not* or other negatives: I can't hardly believe it.
> - You can also use **hardly, scarcely** and **barely** to say that one thing happens immediately after another: *We had hardly/scarcely/barely sat down at the table, when the doorbell rang.* In formal, written English, especially in a literary style, these words could be placed at the beginning of the sentence and then the subject and verb are turned around: *Hardly/Scarcely had we sat down at the table, when the doorbell rang.* Note that you usually use *when* in these sentences, not *than*. You can also use *before*: *I scarcely had time to ring the bell before the door opened.* **No sooner** can be used in the same way, but is always used with *than*: *No sooner had we sat down at the table than the doorbell rang.*
> - **Hardly** and **scarcely** can be used to mean 'almost never', but **barely** is not used in this way: *She hardly (ever) sees her parents these days.* ◊ She barely sees her parents these days.

**hard-ˈnosed** *adj.* not affected by feelings when trying to get what you want: *a hard-nosed journalist*

**hard of ˈhearing** *adj.* **1** unable to hear very well **2 the hard of hearing** *noun* [pl.] people who are unable to hear very well: *subtitles for the deaf and the hard of hearing*

**ˈhard-on** *noun* (*taboo, slang*) an ERECTION

**ˌhard ˈporn** *noun* [U] (*informal*) films, pictures, books, etc. that show sexual activity in a very detailed and sometimes violent way ⊃ compare SOFT PORN

**hard-ˈpressed** *adj.* **1** having a lot of problems, especially too much work, and too little time or money **2 ~ to do sth** finding sth very difficult to do: *You would be hard-pressed to find a better secretary.*

**ˌhard ˈright** *noun* [sing. + sing./pl. v.] (*especially BrE*) the members of a RIGHT-WING political party who have the most extreme opinions: *hard-right opinions*

**ˌhard ˈrock** *noun* [U] a type of loud rock music with a very strong beat, played on electric guitars

**ˌhard ˈscience** *noun* **1** [U] science that is based on measuring and observing physical facts or events and is not influenced by personal feelings or opinions **2** [C] a science that involves measuring and observing physical facts or events, such as physics and chemistry, and is not influenced by personal feelings or opinions

**hard-scrab-ble** /ˌhɑːdˈskræbl; NAmE ˌhɑːrd-/ *adj.* (*NAmE*) not having enough of the basic things you need to live: *a hardscrabble life/upbringing*

**ˌhard ˈsell** *noun* [sing.] a method of selling that puts a lot of pressure on the customer to buy ⊃ compare SOFT SELL

**hard-ship** /ˈhɑːdʃɪp; NAmE ˈhɑːrd-/ *noun* [U, C] a situation that is difficult and unpleasant because you do not have enough money, food, clothes, etc: *economic/financial, etc. hardship* ◊ *People suffered many hardships during that long winter.* ◊ *It was no hardship to walk home on such a lovely evening.*

**ˌhard ˈshoulder** (*BrE*) (*US* **ˈbreakdown lane**) *noun* [sing.] a narrow piece of ground with a hard surface next to a major road such as a MOTORWAY or INTERSTATE where vehicles can stop in an emergency: *to pull over onto the hard shoulder/into the breakdown lane* ⊃ WORDFINDER NOTE at ROAD

**ˈhard-top** /ˈhɑːdtɒp; NAmE ˈhɑːrdtɑːp/ *noun* a car with a metal roof

**ˌhard ˈup** *adj.* (*informal*) **1** having very little money, especially for a short period of time ⊃ note at POOR **2 ~ (for sth)** having nothing interesting to do, talk about, etc: '*You could always go out with Steve.*' '*I'm not that hard up!*'

**hard-ware** /ˈhɑːdweə(r); NAmE ˈhɑːrdwer/ *noun* [U] **1** (*computing*) the machines and electronic parts in a computer or other electronic system ⊃ compare SOFTWARE **2** (*BrE also, old-fashioned* **iron-mon-gery**) tools and equipment that are used in the house and garden: *a hardware shop/store* ⊃ WORDFINDER NOTE at STORE **3** the equipment, machines and vehicles used to do sth: *tanks and other military hardware*

**ˈhardware dealer** *noun* (*NAmE*) **1** (*BrE, old-fashioned* **iron-mon-ger**) a person who owns or works in a shop selling tools and equipment for the house and garden **2** (*BrE* **ˈhardware shop**, *BrE, old-fashioned* **ironmonger's**, **ˈhardware store** *BrE and NAmE*) a shop that sells tools and equipment for the house and garden

**hard-ˈwearing** *adj.* (*especially BrE*) that lasts a long time and remains in good condition: *a hard-wearing carpet*

**hard-ˈwired** /ˌhɑːdˈwaɪəd; NAmE ˌhɑːrdˈwaɪərd/ *adj.* **1** (*specialist*) (of computer functions) built into the permanent system and not provided by software **2** (of a skill, quality or type of behaviour) present as part of who you are and the way your brain is made, not learned from experience: *Many aspects of morality appear to be hardwired in the brain.*

**hard-ˈwon** *adj.* [usually before noun] that you only get after fighting or working hard for it: *She was not going to give up her hard-won freedom so easily.*

**hard-wood** /ˈhɑːdwʊd; NAmE ˈhɑːrd-/ *noun* [U, C] hard heavy wood from a BROADLEAVED tree ⊃ compare SOFTWOOD

**hard-ˈworking** *adj.* putting a lot of effort into a job and doing it well: *hard-working nurses*

**hardy** /ˈhɑːdi; NAmE ˈhɑːrdi/ *adj.* (**har-dier, har-di-est**) **1** strong and able to survive difficult conditions and bad weather: *a hardy breed of sheep* **2** (of a plant) that can live outside through the winter ▶ **hardi-ness** *noun* [U]

**hare** /heə(r); NAmE her/ *noun, verb*
■ *noun* an animal like a large RABBIT with very strong back legs, that can run very fast ⊃ picture at RABBIT IDM see MAD
■ *verb* [I] **+ adv./prep.** (*BrE*) to run or go somewhere very fast

**ˌhare-ˈbrained** *adj.* (*informal*) crazy and unlikely to succeed: *a hare-brained scheme/idea/theory*

**Hare Krishna** /ˌhɑːreɪ ˈkrɪʃnə, ˌhæri/ *noun* **1** [U] a religious group whose members wear orange ROBES and use the name of the Hindu god Krishna in their WORSHIP **2** [C] a member of this religious group

**harem** /ˈhɑːriːm, -rəm; NAmE ˈhærəm/ *noun* **1** the women or wives belonging to a rich man, especially in some Muslim societies in the past **2** the separate part of a traditional Muslim house where the women live **3** (*specialist*) a group of female animals that share the same male for producing young

**hari-cot** /ˈhærɪkəʊ/ (*also* **ˈharicot bean**) (*both BrE*) (*NAmE* **ˈnavy bean**) *noun* a type of small white bean that is usually dried before it is sold and then left in water before cooking

**hark** /hɑːk; NAmE hɑːrk/ *verb* [I] (*old use*) used only as an order to tell sb to listen

**PHRV ˈhark at sb** (*BrE, informal*) used only as an order to draw attention to sb who has just said sth stupid or who is showing that they are too proud: *Just hark at him! Who does he think he is?* **ˌhark ˈback (to sth) 1** to remember or talk about sth that happened in the past: *She's always harking back to how things used to be.* **2** to remind you of,

# harken

or to be like, sth in the past: *The newest styles hark back to the clothes of the Seventies.*

**har·ken** = HEARKEN

**Har·ley Street** /ˈhɑːli striːt; NAmE ˈhɑːrl-/ *noun* a street in central London in which many private doctors have their offices where they talk to and examine patients: *a Harley Street doctor*

**har·lot** /ˈhɑːlət; NAmE ˈhɑːrl-/ *noun* (*old use, disapproving*) a PROSTITUTE, or a woman who looks and behaves like one

**harm** 🅘 B2 🅦 /hɑːm; NAmE hɑːrm/ *noun, verb*
- *noun* 🅘 B2 [U] damage or injury that is caused by a person or an event: *He would never frighten anyone or cause them any harm.* ◊ *He may look fierce, but he means no harm.* ◊ *~ to sb/sth The court case will do serious harm to my business.* ◊ *The accident could have been much worse; luckily no harm was done.* ◊ *Don't worry, we'll see that the children come to no harm.* ◊ *I can't say I like Mark very much, but I don't wish him any harm.* ◊ *Hard work never did anyone any harm.* ◊ *Look, we're just going out for a few drinks, where's the harm in that?* ◊ *The treatment they gave him did him more harm than good.* ⊃ see also ACTUAL BODILY HARM, GRIEVOUS BODILY HARM, SELF-HARM
 ⓘⅮⅯ **it wouldn't do sb any harm (to do sth)** used to suggest that it would be a good idea for sb to do sth: *It wouldn't do you any harm to smarten yourself up.* **no ˈharm done** (*informal*) used to tell sb not to worry because they have caused no serious damage or injury **out of harm's ˈway** in a safe place where sb/sth cannot be hurt or injured or do any damage to sb/sth **there is no harm in (sb's) doing sth** | **it does no harm (for sb) to do sth** used to tell sb that sth is a good idea and will not cause any problems: *He may say no, but there's no harm in asking.* ◊ *It does no harm to ask.*
- *verb* 🅘 B2 ~ sb/sth to hurt or injure sb or to damage sth: *He would never harm anyone.* ◊ *Pollution can harm marine life.* ◊ *These revelations will harm her chances of winning the election.* ⊃ see also SELF-HARM ⓘⅮⅯ see FLY n., HAIR ⊃ SYNONYMS at DAMAGE

**harm·ful** 🅘 B2 🅦 /ˈhɑːmfl; NAmE ˈhɑːrm-/ *adj.* (*rather formal*) causing damage or injury to sb/sth, especially to a person's health or to the environment: *the harmful effects of alcohol* ◊ *harmful substances/chemicals/ bacteria* ◊ *Many household products are potentially harmful.* ◊ *~ to sb/sth Exercising in polluted air is harmful to your health.* ▶ **harm·fully** /-fəli/ *adv.* **harm·ful·ness** *noun* [U]

**harm·less** /ˈhɑːmləs; NAmE ˈhɑːrm-/ *adj.* **1** ~ (to sb/sth) unable or unlikely to cause damage or harm: *The bacteria is harmless to humans.* **2** unlikely to upset or offend anyone ⓢⓨⓝ **innocuous**: *It's just a bit of harmless fun.* ▶ **harm·less·ly** *adv.*: *The missile fell harmlessly into the sea.* **harm·less·ness** *noun* [U]

**har·mon·ic** /hɑːˈmɒnɪk; NAmE hɑːrˈmɑːn-/ *adj., noun*
- *adj.* [usually before noun] (*music*) relating to the way notes are played or sung together to make a pleasant sound
- *noun* [usually pl.] (*music*) **1** a note that sounds together with the main note being played and is higher and quieter than that note **2** a high quiet note that can be played on some instruments like the VIOLIN by touching the string very lightly

**har·mon·ica** /hɑːˈmɒnɪkə; NAmE hɑːrˈmɑːn-/ (*BrE* or *NAmE, old-fashioned* also **ˈmouth organ**) *noun* a small musical instrument that you hold against your lips and play by blowing or taking air in through it

**har·mo·ni·ous** /hɑːˈməʊniəs; NAmE hɑːrˈm-/ *adj.* (*approving*) **1** (of relationships, etc.) friendly, peaceful and without any arguments **2** arranged together in a way that is pleasant because each part goes well with the others ⓢⓨⓝ **pleasing**: *a harmonious combination of colours* **3** (of sounds) very pleasant when played or sung together ▶ **har·mo·ni·ous·ly** *adv.*: *They worked very harmoniously together.*

**har·mo·nium** /hɑːˈməʊniəm; NAmE hɑːrˈm-/ *noun* a musical instrument like a small organ. The player's feet operate the PEDALS to force air through metal pipes to produce the sound and the different notes are played on the keyboard.

**har·mon·ize** (*BrE also* **-ise**) /ˈhɑːmənaɪz; NAmE ˈhɑːrm-/ *verb* **1** [I] ~ (with sth) if two or more things **harmonize** with each other or one thing **harmonizes** with the other, the things go well together and produce an attractive result: *The new building does not harmonize with its surroundings.* **2** [T] ~ sth to make systems or rules similar in different countries or organizations: *the need to harmonize tax levels across the European Union* **3** [I] ~ (with sb/ sth) to play or sing music that combines with the main tune to make a pleasant sound ▶ **har·mon·iza·tion, -isa·tion** /ˌhɑːmənaɪˈzeɪʃn; NAmE ˌhɑːrmənəˈz-/ *noun* [U, C]

**har·mony** 🅘+ C1 /ˈhɑːməni; NAmE ˈhɑːrm-/ *noun* (*pl.* -ies) **1** 🅘+ C1 [U] (*approving*) a state of peaceful existence and agreement: *social/racial harmony* ◊ ~ *to live together in perfect harmony* ◊ **in** ~ **with sth** *the need to be in harmony with our environment* ⊃ compare DISCORD **2** 🅘+ C1 [U, C] (*music*) the way in which different notes that are played or sung together combine to make a pleasant sound: **in** ~ *to sing in harmony* ◊ *to study four-part harmony* ◊ *passionate lyrics and stunning vocal harmonies* ⊃ compare DISCORD ⊃ see also CLOSE HARMONY ⊃ WORDFINDER NOTE at SING **3** [C, U] (*approving*) an attractive combination of related things: *the harmony of colour in nature*

**har·ness** /ˈhɑːnɪs; NAmE ˈhɑːrn-/ *noun, verb*
- *noun* **1** a set of narrow pieces of leather and metal pieces that is put around the head and body of an animal, especially a horse, so that the animal can be controlled and fastened to a CARRIAGE, etc. ⊃ WORDFINDER NOTE at HORSE **2** a set of STRAPS (= long narrow pieces of a strong material) for fastening sth to a person's body or to keep them from moving off or falling: *a safety harness*
 ⓘⅮⅯ **in ˈharness** (*BrE*) doing your normal work, especially after a rest or a holiday **in harness (with sb)** (*BrE*) working closely with sb in order to achieve sth
- *verb* **1** to put a harness on a horse or other animal; to attach a horse or other animal to sth with a harness: ~ **sth to harness a horse** ◊ ~ **sth to sth** *We harnessed two ponies to the cart.* ◊ (*figurative*) *In some areas, the poor feel harnessed to their jobs.* **2** ~ sth to control and use the force or strength of sth to produce power or to achieve sth: *attempts to harness the sun's rays as a source of energy* ◊ *We must harness the skill and creativity of our workforce.*

**harp** /hɑːp; NAmE hɑːrp/ *noun, verb*
- *noun* a large musical instrument with strings stretched from top to bottom on a frame, played with the fingers
- *verb*
 ⓟⓗⓡⓥ **ˈharp on (about sth)** | **ˈharp on sth** (*informal, disapproving*) to keep talking about sth in a boring or annoying way

**harp·ist** /ˈhɑːpɪst; NAmE ˈhɑːrp-/ *noun* a person who plays the harp

**har·poon** /hɑːˈpuːn; NAmE hɑːrˈp-/ *noun, verb*
- *noun* a weapon like a SPEAR attached to a long rope that you can throw or fire from a gun and is used for catching large fish, WHALES, etc.
- *verb* ~ sth to hit sth with a harpoon

**harp·si·chord** /ˈhɑːpsɪkɔːd; NAmE ˈhɑːrpsɪkɔːrd/ *noun* an early type of musical instrument similar to a piano, but with strings that are PLUCKED (= pulled), not hit

**harp·si·chord·ist** /ˈhɑːpsɪkɔːdɪst; NAmE ˈhɑːrpsɪkɔːrd-/ *noun* a person who plays the harpsichord

**harpy** /ˈhɑːpi; NAmE ˈhɑːrpi/ *noun* (*pl.* -ies) **1** (in ancient Greek and Roman stories) a cruel creature with a woman's head and body and a bird's wings and feet **2** a cruel woman

**har·ri·dan** /ˈhærɪdən/ *noun* (*old-fashioned* or *literary*) an angry unpleasant old woman

**har·rier** /ˈhæriə(r)/ *noun* a BIRD OF PREY (= a bird that kills other creatures for food) of the HAWK family

**har·row** /ˈhærəʊ/ *noun* a piece of farming equipment that is pulled over land that has been PLOUGHED to break up the earth before planting ▶ **har·row** *verb* ~ sth

**har·row·ing** /ˈhærəʊɪŋ/ adj. making you feel very upset because you are very shocked or frightened

**har·rumph** /həˈrʌmf/ verb [I] (informal) to show that you disagree with or DISAPPROVE of sb/sth, especially by making a sound in your throat like a COUGH ▶ **har·rumph** noun [sing.]

**harry** /ˈhæri/ verb (har·ries, harry·ing, har·ried, har·ried) (formal) **1** ~ sb to annoy or upset sb by continuously asking them questions or for sth **SYN** harass: *She has been harried by the press all week.* **2** ~ sb/sth to make repeated attacks on an enemy **SYN** harass

**harsh** /hɑːʃ; NAmE hɑːrʃ/ adj. (harsh·er, harsh·est) **1** cruel, severe and unkind: *The punishment was harsh and unfair.* ◊ *The minister received some harsh criticism.* ◊ *the harsh treatment of slaves* ◊ *He regretted his harsh words.* ◊ *We had to face up to the harsh realities of life sooner or later.* **2** (of weather or living conditions) very difficult and unpleasant to live in: *a harsh winter/wind/climate* ◊ *the harsh conditions of poverty which existed for most people at that time* ⊃ WORDFINDER NOTE at CLIMATE **3** too strong and bright; ugly or unpleasant to look at: *harsh colours* ◊ *She was caught in the harsh glare of the headlights.* ◊ *the harsh lines of concrete buildings* **OPP** soft **4** unpleasant to listen to: *a harsh voice* **5** too strong and rough and likely to damage sth: *harsh detergents* ▶ **harsh·ly** adv.: *She was treated very harshly.* ◊ *Alec laughed harshly.* **harsh·ness** noun [U]

**hart** /hɑːt; NAmE hɑːrt/ noun a male DEER, especially a RED DEER; a STAG ⊃ compare BUCK, HIND

**har·tal** /hɑːˈtɑːl; NAmE hɑːrˈt-/ noun (especially IndE) (in South Asia) an occasion when all shops and businesses are closed as a protest; a GENERAL STRIKE

**har·vest** /ˈhɑːvɪst; NAmE ˈhɑːrv-/ noun, verb
▪ noun **1** [C, U] the time of year when the crops are gathered in on a farm, etc.; the act of cutting and gathering crops: *harvest time* ◊ *Farmers are extremely busy during the harvest.* **2** [C] the crops, or the amount of crops, cut and gathered: *the grain harvest* ◊ *a good/bad harvest* (= a lot of crops or few crops) ◊ *(figurative) The appeal produced a rich harvest of blankets, medicines and clothing.* ⊃ WORDFINDER NOTE at CROP **IDM** see REAP
▪ verb **1** ~ (sth) to cut and gather a crop; to catch a number of animals or fish to eat **2** [T] ~ sth (medical) to collect cells or TISSUE from sb's body for use in medical experiments or operations: *She had her eggs harvested and frozen for her own future use.*

**har·vest·er** /ˈhɑːvɪstə(r); NAmE ˈhɑːrv-/ noun **1** a machine that cuts and gathers grain ⊃ see also COMBINE noun **2** (old-fashioned) a person who helps to gather in the crops

**harvest ˈfestival** noun a celebration held in churches and schools to give thanks for crops that have been gathered, to which gifts of food are brought for the poor ⊃ compare THANKSGIVING

**harvest ˈmoon** noun [sing.] a full moon in the autumn nearest the time when day and night are of equal length ⊃ compare FULL MOON, HALF-MOON

**has** /həz, əz, strong form hæz/ ⊃ HAVE verb

**has-been** /ˈhæz biːn; NAmE bɪn/ noun (informal, disapproving) a person who is no longer as famous, successful or important as they used to be

**hash** /hæʃ/ noun, verb
▪ noun **1** [U, C] a hot dish of cooked meat and potatoes that are cut into small pieces and mixed together **2** [U] (informal) = HASHISH **3** (also ˈhash sign) (both BrE) (NAmE ˈpound sign) (also ˈhash-tag BrE and NAmE) [C] the symbol (#), especially one on a phone or computer keyboard
**IDM** make a ˈhash of sth (informal) to do sth badly: *I made a real hash of the interview.*
▪ verb
**PHRV** ˌhash sth↔ˈout (informal, especially NAmE) to discuss sth carefully and completely in order to reach an agreement or decide sth

**hash ˈbrowns** noun [pl.] potatoes and onions cut into small pieces, pressed into flat shapes and fried until they are brown

**hash·ish** /ˈhæʃiːʃ, hæˈʃiːʃ/ (also informal **hash**) noun [U] a drug made from the RESIN of the HEMP plant, which gives a feeling of being relaxed when it is smoked or put in the mouth and CHEWED. Use of the drug is illegal in many countries. **SYN** cannabis

**hash·tag** /ˈhæʃtæɡ/ noun **1** a word or phrase with the symbol '#' in front of it, used on social media websites and apps so that you can search for all messages with the same subject: *I often use hashtags to search for trending topics.* **2** = HASH (3)

**Has·id·ism** (also **Has·sid·ism**) /ˈhæsɪdɪzəm; NAmE ˈhɑːs-/ (also **Chas·id·ism**) noun [U] a form of the Jewish religion that has very strict beliefs ▶ **Hasid** (also **Has·sid**) /-sɪd/ (also **Chasid**) noun (pl. **-im**) **Has·id·ic** (also **Has·sid·ic**) /hæˈsɪdɪk; NAmE hɑːˈs-/ (also **Chas·id·ic**) adj.

**hasn't** /ˈhæznt/ short form has not

**Has·sid·ism** = HASIDISM

**has·sle** /ˈhæsl/ noun, verb
▪ noun [C, U] (informal) **1** a situation that is annoying because it involves doing sth difficult or complicated that needs a lot of effort: *Send them an email—it's a lot less hassle than phoning.* ◊ *legal hassles* **2** a situation in which people disagree, argue or annoy you: *Do as you're told and don't give me any hassle!*
▪ verb ~ sb (for sth/to do sth) (informal) to annoy sb or cause them trouble, especially by asking them to do sth many times **SYN** bother: *Don't keep hassling me! I'll do it later.*

**hast** /hæst/ thou hast (old use) a way of saying 'you have'

**haste** /heɪst/ noun [U] (formal) speed in doing sth, especially because you do not have enough time **SYN** hurry: *In her haste to complete the work on time, she made a number of mistakes.* ◊ **in** ~ *The letter had clearly been written in haste.* ◊ *After his first wife died, he married again with almost indecent haste.* ◊ *(old-fashioned) She* **made haste** *to open the door.*
**IDM** ˌmore ˈhaste, ˌless ˈspeed (BrE, saying) you will finish doing sth sooner if you do not try to do it too quickly because you will make fewer mistakes ⊃ more at MARRY

**has·ten** /ˈheɪsn/ verb **1** [I] ~ to do sth to say or do sth without delay: *She saw his frown and hastened to explain.* ◊ *He has been described as a 'charmless bore'—not by me, I* **hasten to add**. **2** [T] ~ sth (formal) to make sth happen sooner or more quickly: *The treatment she received may, in fact, have hastened her death.* ◊ *News of the scandal certainly hastened his departure from office.* **3** [I] + adv./prep. (literary) to go or move somewhere quickly **SYN** hurry

**hasty** /ˈheɪsti/ adj. (hasti·er, hasti·est) **1** said, made or done very quickly, especially when this has bad results **SYN** hurried: *a hasty departure/meal/farewell* ◊ *Let's not make any hasty decisions.* **2** ~ in doing sth (of a person) acting or deciding too quickly, without enough thought: *Perhaps I was too hasty in rejecting his offer.* **IDM** see BEAT v. ▶ **hasti·ly** /-stɪli/ adv.: *Perhaps I spoke too hastily.* ◊ *She hastily changed the subject.*

**hat** /hæt/ noun **1** a piece of clothing made to fit the head, often with a BRIM (= a flat edge that sticks out), usually worn out of doors: *a straw/woolly hat* ◊ *to wear a hat* ◊ *to* **put on/take off a hat** ◊ *to* **have a hat on** ⊃ see also BOWLER (2), BOBBLE HAT, COWBOY HAT, HARD HAT, HAT TIP, SUN HAT, TOP HAT **2** (informal) a position or role, especially as an official or professional role, when you have more than one such role: *I'm wearing two hats tonight—parent and teacher.* ◊ *I'm telling you this with my lawyer's hat on, you understand.* ⊃ see also COCKED HAT, HI-HAT, HIGH-HAT, OLD HAT
**IDM** ˌgo hat in ˈhand (to sb) (especially NAmE) (BrE usually ˌgo cap in ˈhand (to sb)) to ask sb for sth, especially money, in a very polite way that makes you seem less important | I take my ˈhat off to sb | ˌhats ˈoff to sb (both especially BrE) (NAmE usually I tip my ˈhat to sb) (informal) used to say that you admire sb very much for sth they have done ⊃ related noun HAT TIP ˌkeep sth under your

# hatch

**hat** (*informal*) to keep sth secret and not tell anyone else **my ˈhat** (*old-fashioned*) used to express surprise **out of a/the ˈhat** if sth such as a name is picked **out of a/the hat**, it is picked at RANDOM from a container into which all the names are put, so that each name has an equal chance of being picked, in a competition, etc. **throw your ˈhat into the ring** to announce officially that you are going to compete in an election, a competition, etc. ⇨ more at DROP *n.*, EAT, KNOCK *v.*, PASS *v.*, PULL *v.*, TALK *v.*

**hatch** /hætʃ/ *verb, noun*

■ *verb* **1** [I] ~ **(out)** (of a young bird, fish, insect, etc.) to come out of an egg: *Ten chicks hatched (out) this morning.* **2** [I] ~ **(out)** (of an egg) to break open so that a young bird, fish, insect, etc. can come out: *The eggs are about to hatch.* **3** [T] ~ **sth** to make a young bird, fish, insect, etc. come out of an egg: *The female must find a warm place to hatch her eggs.* **4** [T] ~ **sth (up)** to create a plan or an idea, especially in secret: *Have you been hatching up a deal with her?* IDM see COUNT *v.*

■ *noun* **1** (*also* **hatch·way**) an opening or a door in a ship, aircraft or SPACECRAFT **2** an opening in a wall between two rooms, especially a kitchen and a DINING ROOM, through which food can be passed: *a serving hatch* **3** an opening or a door in a floor or ceiling: *a hatch to the attic* IDM **down the ˈhatch** (*informal, saying*) used before drinking sth, especially to express good wishes before drinking alcohol ⇨ more at BATTEN *v.*

**hatch·back** /ˈhætʃbæk/ *noun* a car with a sloping door at the back that opens upwards

**hatch·ery** /ˈhætʃəri/ *noun* (*pl.* **-ies**) a place for hatching eggs as part of a business: *a trout hatchery*

**hatchet** /ˈhætʃɪt/ *noun* a small AXE (= a tool with a heavy metal BLADE for cutting things up) with a short handle ⇨ picture at AXE IDM see BURY

**ˈhatchet job** *noun* [usually sing.] ~ **(on sb/sth)** (*informal*) strong criticism that is often unfair and is intended to harm sb/sth: *The press did a very effective hatchet job on her last movie.*

**ˈhatchet man** *noun* (*informal*) a person employed by an organization to make changes that are not popular with the other people who work there

**hatch·ling** /ˈhætʃlɪŋ/ *noun* a baby bird or animal that has just come out of its shell

**hatch·way** /ˈhætʃweɪ/ *noun* = HATCH

**hate** 🅾 A1 /heɪt/ *verb, noun*

■ *verb* (not usually used in the progressive tenses) **1** ? A1 [T, I] to dislike sb/sth very much: ~ **sb/yourself** *The two boys hated each other.* ◊ ~ **sth** *I hate spinach.* ◊ *I really hate Monday mornings.* ◊ *I hate the way she always criticizes me.* ◊ ~ **it …** *He hated it in France* (= did not like the life there). ◊ *She's hating it at university.* ◊ ~ **it when …** *I hate it when people cry.* ◊ ~ **doing sth** *She hates making mistakes.* ◊ ~ **to do sth** *He hated to be away from his family.* ◊ *I hate to see him suffering like this.* ◊ *I hate to think what would have happened if you hadn't been there.* ◊ ~ **sb/sth doing sth** *He hates anyone parking in his space.* ◊ ~ **sb/sth to do sth** *I'd hate anything to happen to him.* ◊ ~ **for sb/sth to do sth** *I'd hate for all this to go to waste.* ◊ ~ **sb/yourself for (doing) sth** *I hated myself for feeling jealous.* ◊ *When children are taught to hate, the whole future of society is in danger.* ⇨ note at WANT **2** [no passive] ~ **to do sth** used when saying sth that you would prefer not to have to say, or when politely asking to do sth: *I hate to say it, but I don't think their marriage will last.* ◊ *I hate to trouble you, but could I use your phone?* IDM **hate sb's ˈguts** (*informal*) to dislike sb very much

■ *noun* **1** ? B1 [U] a very strong feeling of dislike for sb SYN **hatred**: *a look of hate* ◊ ~ **for sb/sth** *She was full of hate for the people who had betrayed her.* **2** [C] (*informal*) a person or thing that you hate: *Plastic flowers have always been a particular hate of mine.* IDM see PET *adj.*

▼ SYNONYMS

**hate**
dislike • can't stand • despise • can't bear • loathe • detest

These words all mean to have a strong feeling of dislike for sb/sth.

**hate** to have a strong feeling of dislike for sb/sth. NOTE Although **hate** is generally a very strong verb, it is also commonly used in spoken or informal English to talk about people or things that you dislike in a less important way, for example a particular type of food: *He hates violence in any form.* ◊ *I've always hated cabbage.*

**dislike** (*rather formal*) to not like sb/sth. NOTE **Dislike** is a rather formal word; it is less formal, and more usual, to say that you **don't like** sb/sth, especially in spoken English: *I don't like it when you phone me so late at night.*

**can't stand** (*rather informal*) used to emphasize that you really do not like sb/sth: *I can't stand his brother.* ◊ *She couldn't stand being kept waiting.*

**despise** to dislike and have no respect for sb/sth: *He despised himself for being so cowardly.*

**can't bear** used to say that you dislike sth so much that you cannot accept or deal with it: *I can't bear having cats in the house.*

CAN'T STAND OR CAN'T BEAR?
In many cases you can use either word, but **can't bear** is slightly stronger and slightly more formal than **can't stand**.

**loathe** to hate sb/sth very much: *They loathe each other.* NOTE **Loathe** is generally an even stronger verb than **hate**, but it can also be used more informally to talk about less important things, meaning 'really don't like': *Whether you love or loathe their music, you can't deny their talent.*

**detest** (*rather formal*) to hate sb/sth very much: *They absolutely detest each other.*

PATTERNS
- I hate / dislike / can't stand / can't bear / loathe / detest doing sth.
- I hate / can't bear **to do sth**.
- I hate / dislike / can't stand / can't bear **it when …**
- I **really** hate / dislike / can't stand / despise / can't bear / detest sb/sth.
- I **absolutely** hate / can't stand / loathe / detest sb/sth.

▼ WHICH WORD?

**hate / hatred**
- These two words have a similar meaning. **Hatred** is more often used to describe a very strong feeling of dislike for a particular person or thing: *Her deep hatred of her sister was obvious.* ◊ *a cat's hatred of water.* **Hate** is more often used when you are talking about this feeling in a general way: *a look of pure hate* ◊ *people filled with hate.*

**ˈhate crime** *noun* **1** [U] violent acts that are committed against people because they are of a different race, because they are GAY, etc. **2** [C] a single act of this type: *the victim of a hate crime*

**hate·ful** /ˈheɪtfl/ *adj.* very unkind or unpleasant: *a hateful person/place/face* ◊ ~ **to sb** *The idea of fighting against men of their own race was hateful to them.*

**hater** /ˈheɪtə(r)/ *noun* a person who hates sb/sth: *I'm not a woman hater, I just don't like Joan.* ◊ *He was a socialist and a hater of privilege.*

**ˈhate speech** *noun* [U] ~ **(against sb/sth)** speech or writing that attacks or threatens a particular group of people, especially on the basis of race, religion or sexual ORIENTATION: *She said they wouldn't tolerate hate speech against any religious community.*

**hath** /hæθ/ (*old use*) has

**hat·red** ? C1 /ˈheɪtrɪd/ *noun* [U, C] a very strong feeling of dislike for sb/sth: *He looked at me with intense hatred.* ◊ *There was fear and hatred in his voice.* ◊ ~ **for sb/sth** *She* felt nothing but hatred for her attacker. ◇ **~ of sb/sth** a profound hatred of war ◇ **~ towards sb** feelings of hatred towards the bombers ◇ **~ racial hatred** (= between people from different races) ◇ *The debate simply revived old hatreds.* ⮕ note at HATE

**hat·ter** /ˈhætə(r)/ *noun* (*old-fashioned*) a person who makes and sells hats IDM see MAD

**ˈhat tip** *noun* [usually sing.] (*especially NAmE*) **~ (to sb) (for sth)** used on the internet to acknowledge sb's part in sth, providing information or ideas for sth: *Hat tip to John Rowe for the link to this blog.*

**ˈhat-trick** *noun* three points, goals, etc. scored by the same player in a particular match or game; three successes achieved by one person: *to score a hat-trick*

**haughty** /ˈhɔːti/ *adj.* (**haught·ier**, **haught·iest**) behaving in an unfriendly way towards other people because you think that you are better than them SYN **arrogant**: *a haughty face/look/manner* ◇ *He replied with haughty disdain.* ▶ **haught·ily** /-tɪli/ *adv.* **haughti·ness** *noun* [U]

**haul** /hɔːl/ *verb, noun*
▪ *verb* **1** to pull sth/sb with a lot of effort: **~ sth/sb** *The wagons were hauled by horses.* ◇ **~ sth/sb + adv./prep.** *He reached down and hauled Liz up onto the wall.* ⮕ SYNONYMS at PULL **2** **~ yourself up/out of, etc.** to move yourself somewhere slowly and with a lot of effort: *She hauled herself out of bed.* **3** **~ sb + adv./prep.** to force sb to go somewhere they do not want to go: *A number of suspects have been hauled in for questioning.* **4** [usually passive] to make sb appear in court in order to be judged: **be hauled (up) before sb/sth** *He was hauled up before the local magistrates for dangerous driving.*
IDM **haul sb over the ˈcoals** (*BrE*) (*NAmE* **rake sb over the ˈcoals**) to criticize sb severely because they have done sth wrong
▪ *noun* **1** a large amount of sth that has been stolen or that is illegal: *a haul of weapons* ◇ *a drugs haul* **2** (*especially in sport*) a large number of points, goals, etc: *His haul of 40 goals in a season is a record.* **3** [usually sing.] the distance covered in a particular journey: *They began the long slow haul to the summit.* ◇ *Our camp is only a short haul from here.* ◇ *Take the coast road—it'll be less of a haul* (= an easier journey). ⮕ see also LONG HAUL, SHORT-HAUL **4** a quantity of fish caught at one time **5** [usually sing.] a hard pull: *When I shout, give a haul on the rope.*

**haul·age** /ˈhɔːlɪdʒ/ *noun* [U] (*BrE*) the business of transporting goods by road or railway; money charged for this: *the road haulage industry* ◇ *a haulage firm/contractor* ◇ *How much is haulage?*

**haul·ier** /ˈhɔːliə(r)/ (*BrE*) (*NAmE* **haul·er** /ˈhɔːlə(r)/) *noun* a person or company whose business is transporting goods by road or railway

**haunch** /hɔːntʃ/ *noun* **1 haunches** [pl.] the tops of the legs and BUTTOCKS; the similar parts at the back of the body of an animal that has four legs: **on your ~** *to crouch/squat on your haunches* (= with your haunches resting on the back of your heels) **2** [C] a back leg and LOIN of an animal that has four legs, eaten as food: *a haunch of venison*

**haunt** ⓘ⁺ ⒸⲈ /hɔːnt/ *verb, noun*
▪ *verb* ⓘ⁺ ⒸⲈ **~ sth/sb** if the ghost of a dead person **haunts** a place, people say that they have seen it there: *A headless rider haunts the country lanes.* **2** ⓘ⁺ ⒸⲈ **~ sb** if sth unpleasant **haunts** you, it keeps coming to your mind so that you cannot forget it: *The memory of that day still haunts me.* ◇ *For years she was haunted by guilt.* **3** ⓘ⁺ ⒸⲈ **~ sb** to continue to cause problems for sb for a long time: *That decision came back to haunt him.*
▪ *noun* a place that sb visits often or where they spend a lot of time: *The pub is a favourite haunt of artists.*

**haunt·ed** /ˈhɔːntɪd/ *adj.* **1** (of a building) believed to be visited by ghosts: *a haunted house* **2** (of an expression on sb's face) showing that sb is very worried: *There was a haunted look in his eyes.*

**haunt·ing** /ˈhɔːntɪŋ/ *adj.* beautiful, sad or frightening in a way that cannot be forgotten: *a haunting melody/experience/image* ▶ **haunt·ing·ly** *adv.*

727 **have**

**Hausa** /ˈhaʊsə, ˈhaʊzə/ *noun* [U] a language spoken by the Hausa people of West Africa, especially in Nigeria and Niger, and also used in other parts of West Africa as a language of communication between different peoples

**haute cou·ture** /ˌəʊt kuːˈtjʊə(r); *NAmE* -ˈtʊr/ *noun* [U] (*from French*) the business of making fashionable and expensive clothes; the clothes made in this business

**haute cuis·ine** /ˌəʊt kwɪˈziːn/ *noun* [U] (*from French*) cooking of a very high standard, following the style of traditional French cooking

**haut·eur** /əʊˈtɜː(r); *NAmE* hɔːˈt-/ *noun* [U] (*formal*) an unfriendly way of behaving towards other people that suggests that you think that you are better than they are

**ha·vala** /həˈvɑːlə/ *noun* = HAWALA

**have** ⓘ **A1** /həv, əv, *strong form* hæv/ *verb, auxiliary verb* ⮕ IRREGULAR VERBS on page R3
▪ *verb* (In some senses **have got** is also used, especially in British English.)
• **OWN/HOLD** **1** ⓘ **A1** (*also* **have got**) **~ sth** (not used in the progressive tenses) to own, hold or possess sth: *He had a new car and a boat.* ◇ *Have you got a job yet?* ◇ *I don't have that much money on me.* ◇ *She's got a BA in English.*
• **CONSIST OF** **2** ⓘ **A1** (*also* **have got**) **~ sth** (not used in the progressive tenses) be made up of: *In 2018 the party had 10000 members.*
• **QUALITY/FEATURE** **3** ⓘ **A1** (*also* **have got**) (not used in the progressive tenses) to show a quality or feature: **~ sth** *The ham had a smoky flavour.* ◇ *The house has gas-fired central heating.* ◇ *They have a lot of courage.* ◇ **~ sth + adj.** *He's got a front tooth missing.* **4** ⓘ **A1** (*also* **have got**) **~ sth to do sth** (not used in the progressive tenses) to show a particular quality by your actions: *Surely she didn't have the nerve to say that to him?*
• **RELATIONSHIP** **5** ⓘ **A1** (*also* **have got**) **~ sb/sth** (not used in the progressive tenses) used to show a particular relationship: *He's got three children.* ◇ *Do you have a client named Peters?*
• **STH AVAILABLE** **6** ⓘ **A1** (*also* **have got**) **~ sth** (not used in the progressive tenses) to be able to make use of sth because it is available: *Have you got time to call him?* ◇ *We have no choice in the matter.*

▼ **BRITISH/AMERICAN**

**have you got? / do you have?**

- **Have got** is the usual verb in *BrE* to show possession, etc. in positive statements in the present tense, in negative statements and in questions: *They've got a wonderful house.* ◇ *We haven't got a television.* ◇ *Have you got a meeting today?* Questions and negative statements formed with **do** are also common: *Do you have any brothers and sisters?* ◇ *We don't have a car.*
- **Have** is also used but is more formal: *I have no objection to your request.* ◇ *Have you an appointment?* Some expressions with **have** are common even in informal language: *I'm sorry, I haven't a clue.*
- In the past tense **had** is used in positive statements. In negatives and questions, forms with **did have** are usually used: *They had a wonderful house.* ◇ *We didn't have much time.* ◇ *Did she have her husband with her?*
- In *NAmE* **have** and forms with **do/does/did** are the usual way to show possession, etc. in positive statements, negatives and questions: *They have a wonderful house.* ◇ *We don't have a television.* ◇ *Do you have a meeting today?* **Have got** is not used in questions, but is used in positive statements, especially to emphasize that somebody has one thing rather than another: *'Does your brother have brown hair?' 'No, he's got blond hair.'*
- In both *BrE* and *NAmE* **have** and forms with **do/does** and **did** are used when you are referring to a habit or routine: *We don't often have time to talk.*

# have

- **SHOULD/MUST 7** 🔊 **A1** (also **have got**) ~ **sth** (not used in the progressive tenses) to be in a position where you ought to do sth: *We have a duty to care for the refugees.* **8** 🔊 **A1** (also **have got**) (not used in the progressive tenses) to be in a position of needing to do sth: ~ **sth** *I've got a lot of homework tonight.* ◇ ~ **sth to do** *I must go—I have a bus to catch.*
- **FEELING/THOUGHT 9** 🔊 **A1** (also **have got**) ~ **sth** (not used in the progressive tenses) to let a feeling or thought come into your mind: *He had the strong impression that someone was watching him.* ◇ *We've got a few ideas for the title.* ◇ (informal) *I've have it! We'll call it 'Word Magic'.*
- **ILLNESS 10** 🔊 **A1** (also **have got**) ~ **sth** (not used in the progressive tenses) to suffer from an illness or a disease: *I've got a headache.*
- **HOLD 11** 🔊 **A2** (also **have got**) ~ **sb/sth + adv./prep.** (not used in the progressive tenses) to hold sb/sth in the way mentioned: *She'd got him by the collar.* ◇ *He had his head in his hands.*
- **PUT/KEEP IN A POSITION 12** 🔊 **A2** (also **have got**) ~ **sth + adv./prep.** (not used in the progressive tenses) to place or keep sth in a particular position: *Mary had her back to me.* ◇ *I soon had the fish in a net.*
- **EXPERIENCE 13** 🔊 **A1** ~ **sth** to experience sth: *I went to a few parties and had a good time.* ◇ *I was having difficulty in staying awake.* ◇ *She'll have an accident one day.*
- **EVENT 14** 🔊 **A1** ~ **sth** to organize or hold an event: *Let's have a party.*
- **EAT/DRINK/SMOKE 15** 🔊 **A1** ~ **sth** to eat, drink or smoke sth: *to have breakfast/lunch/dinner* ◇ *I'll have the salmon* (= for example, in a restaurant) ◇ *I had a cigarette while I was waiting.*
- **DO STH 16** 🔊 **A1** ~ **sth** to perform a particular action: *I had a swim to cool down.* ◇ (BrE) *to have a wash/shower/bath*
- **GIVE BIRTH 17** 🔊 **A1** ~ **sb/sth** to give birth to sb/sth: *She's going to have a baby.*
- **EFFECT 18** 🔊 **A1** ~ **sth** to produce a particular effect: *His paintings had a strong influence on me as a student.* ◇ *The colour green has a restful effect.*
- **RECEIVE 19** 🔊 **A1** ~ **sth** (not usually used in the progressive tenses) to receive sth from sb: *I had a letter from my brother this morning.* ◇ *Can I have a Coke, please?* **HELP** For example, when ordering in a cafe or restaurant. In NAmE you can also say: *Can I get a Coke?* **20** 🔊 **A1** ~ **sth** to be given sth; to have sth done to you: *I'm having treatment for my back problem.* ◇ *How many driving lessons have you had so far?* **21** 🔊 **B1** (also **have got**) ~ **sth doing sth** (not used in the progressive tenses) to experience the effects of sb's actions: *We have orders coming in from all over the world.*
- **HAVE STH DONE 22** 🔊 **B1** ~ **sth done** (used with a past participle) to suffer the effects of what sb else does to you: *She had her bag stolen.* **23** 🔊 **B1** ~ **sth done** (used with a past participle) to cause sth to be done for you by sb else: *You've had your hair cut!* ◇ *We're having our car repaired.* **24** to tell or arrange for sb to do sth for you: ~ **sb do sth** *He had the bouncers throw them out of the club.* ◇ (informal) *I'll have you know* (= I'm telling you) *I'm a black belt in judo.* ◇ ~ **sb + adv./prep.** *She's always having the builders in to do something or other.*
- **PUT SB/STH IN A CONDITION 25** 🔊 **B1** to cause sb/sth to be in a particular state; to make sb react in a particular way: ~ **sb/sth + adj.** *I want to have everything ready in good time.* ◇ ~ **sb/sth doing sth** *He had his audience listening attentively.*
- **BE WITH 26** 🔊 **A2** (also **have got**) ~ **sb with you** (not used in the progressive tenses) to be with sb: *She had some friends with her.*
- **GUESTS 27** 🔊 **B1** [no passive] ~ **sb/sth** to take care of sb/sth in your home, especially for a limited period: *We're having the kids for the weekend.* **28** 🔊 **B1** [no passive] ~ **sb + adv./prep.** to entertain sb in your home: *We had some friends to dinner last night.*
- **ALLOW 29** (used in negative sentences, especially after *will not*, *cannot*, etc.) to allow sth; to accept sth without complaining: ~ **sth** *I'm sick of your rudeness—I won't have it any longer!* ◇ ~ **sb/sth doing sth** *We can't have people arriving late all the time.*
- **IN ARGUMENT 30** (also **have got**) ~ **sb** (informal) (not used in the progressive tenses) to put sb at a disadvantag in an argument: *You've got me there. I hadn't thought of that.*
- **SEX 31** ~ **sb** (slang) to have sex with sb: *He had her in his office.*
- **TRICK 32** [usually passive] (informal) to trick or cheat sb: **be had** *I'm afraid you've been had.*
- **FOR A JOB 33** [no passive] ~ **sb as sth** to take or accept sb for a particular role: *Who can we have as treasurer?*

**IDM** **HELP** Most idioms containing **have** are at the entries for the nouns and adjectives in the idioms, for example **have your eye on sb** is at **eye** *n*. **have (got) sth against sb** to dislike sb because of sth bad they have done to you in the past: *I don't have anything against her, we just don't get along.* **have ˈdone with sth** (especially *BrE*) to finish sth unpleasant so that it does not continue: *Let's have done with this silly argument.* **have ˈhad it** (informal) **1** to be in a very bad condition; to be unable to be repaired: *The car had had it.* **2** to be extremely tired: *I've had it! I'm going to bed.* **3** to have lost all chance of surviving sth: *When the truck smashed into me, I thought I'd had it.* **4** to be going to experience sth unpleasant: *Dad saw you scratch the car—you've had it now!* **5** to be unable to accept a situation any longer: *I've had it (up to here) with him—he's done it once too often.* **have it (that …)** to claim that it is a fact that …: *Rumour has it that we'll have a new manager soon.* **have (got) it/that ˈcoming (to you)** to be likely to suffer the unpleasant effects of your actions and to deserve to do so: *It was no surprise when she left him—everyone knew he had it coming to him.* **have it ˈin for sb** (informal) to not like sb and be unpleasant to them **have it ˈin you (to do sth)** (informal) to be capable of doing sth: *Everyone thinks he has it in him to produce a literary classic.* ◇ *You were great. I didn't know you had it in you.* **have it ˈoff/a ˈway (with sb)** (*BrE*, *slang*) to have sex with sb **have (got) ˈnothing on sb/sth** (informal) to be not nearly as good as sb/sth ⊃ see also HAVE (GOT) STH ON SB **not ˈhaving any** (informal) not willing to listen to or believe sth: *I tried to persuade her to wait but she wasn't having any.* **what ˈhave you** (informal) other things, people, etc. of the same kind: *There's room in the cellar to store old furniture and what have you.*

**PHRV** **have (got) sth aˈgainst sb/sth** (not used in the progressive tenses) to dislike sb/sth for a particular reason: *What have you got against Ruth? She's always been good to you.* **have sb ↔ ˈback** [no passive] to allow a husband, wife, partner, child, etc. to return after being apart from them; to allow a former employee to work for you again **have sth ˈback** [no passive] to receive sth that sb has borrowed or taken from you: *You can have your files back after we've checked them.* **have (got) sth ˈin** [no passive] (not used in the progressive tenses) to have a supply of sth in your home, etc: *Have we got enough food in?* **have sb ˈon** (informal) to try to make sb believe sth that is not true, usually as a joke: *You didn't really, did you? You're not having me on, are you?* **have (got) sth ˈon** [no passive] (not used in the progressive tenses) **1** to be wearing sth: *She had a red jacket on.* ◇ *He had nothing* (= no clothes) *on.* **2** to leave a piece of equipment working: *She has her TV on all day.* **3** to have arranged to do sth: *I can't see you this week—I've got a lot on.* **have (got) sth ˈon sb** [no passive] (informal) (not used in the progressive tenses) to know sth bad about sb, especially sth that connects them with a crime: *I'm not worried—they've got nothing on me.* **have sth ˈout** to cause sth, especially a part of your body, to be removed: *I had to have my appendix out.* **have sth ˈout (with sb)** [no passive] to try to settle an argument by discussing or arguing about it openly: *I need to have it out with her once and for all.* **have sb ˈup (for sth)** [usually passive] (*BrE*, informal) to cause sb to be accused of sth in court: *He was had up for manslaughter.*

■ **auxiliary verb** 🔊 **A2** used with the past participle to form perfect tenses: *I've finished my work.* ◇ *He's gone home, hasn't he?* ◇ *'Have you seen it?' 'Yes, I have/No, I haven't.'* ◇ *She'll have had the results by now.* ◇ *Had they left before you got there?* ◇ *If I hadn't seen it with my own eyes I wouldn't have believed it.* ◇ (formal) *Had I known that* (= if I had known that) *I would never have come.*

### GRAMMAR POINT

**could / should / would have**

A common mistake is to write 'could of' instead of *could have* or *could've*: *I could of told you that.* ◊ *I could've told you that.* The reason for the mistake is that the pronunciation of *'ve* is the same as that of *of* when it is not stressed. This is a common error but it is definitely considered wrong in standard English.

**haven** /'heɪvn/ *noun* a place that is safe and peaceful where people or animals are protected: *The hotel is a haven of peace and tranquillity.* ◊ *The river banks are a haven for wildlife.* ⇒ see also SAFE HAVEN, TAX HAVEN

**the 'have-nots** *noun* [pl.] people who do not have money and possessions ⇒ compare HAVES

**haven't** /'hævnt/ *short form* have not

**the 'haves** *noun* [pl.] people who have enough money and possessions: *the division between the haves and the have-nots* ⇒ compare HAVE-NOTS

**have to** ❶ A1 /'hæv tə, 'hæf tə/ *modal verb* ( **has to** /'hæz tə, 'hæs/, **had to, had to** /'hæd tə, 'hæt/) 1 ❷ A1 (*also* **have got to**) used to show that you must do sth: *Sorry, I've got to go.* ◊ *Did she have to pay a fine?* ◊ *You don't have to knock—just walk in.* ◊ *I haven't got to leave till seven.* ◊ *First, you have to think logically about your fears.* ◊ *I have to admit, the idea of marriage scares me.* ◊ *Do you have to go?* ◊ (*especially BrE*) *Have you got to go?* 2 ❷ A2 (*also* **have got to** *especially in BrE*) used to give advice or recommend sth: *You simply have to get a new job.* ◊ *You've got to try this recipe—it's delicious.* 3 ❷ B1 (*also* **have got to** *especially in BrE*) used to say that sth must be true or must happen: *There has to be a reason for his strange behaviour.* ◊ *This war has got to end soon.* 4 used to suggest that an annoying event happens in order to annoy you, or that sb does sth in order to annoy you: *Of course, it had to start raining as soon as we got to the beach.* ◊ *Do you have to hum so loudly?* (= it is annoying) ⇒ note at MODAL, MUST

### EXPRESS YOURSELF

**Asking about obligation**

When you are unsure about what is expected of you in a situation, you can ask about obligations:
- *What time **do we have to** be home?*
- *Are we **supposed to** show our ID cards?*
- *Is it **necessary to** apply for a visa?*
- *Is there a **legal obligation to** wear a bike helmet here?*

**havoc** /'hævək/ *noun* [U] a situation in which things are seriously damaged, destroyed or very confused: *The floods caused havoc throughout the area.* ◊ *Continuing strikes are beginning to **play havoc with** the national economy.* ◊ *These insects can **wreak havoc on** crops.*

**haw** /hɔː/ *verb* IDM see HUM *v.* ⇒ see also HEE-HAW

**Ha·wai·ian shirt** /həˌwaɪən ˈʃɜːt; *NAmE* ˈʃɜːrt/ *noun* a loose cotton shirt with a brightly coloured pattern and short SLEEVES

**ha·wala** /həˈwɑːlə/ (*also* **ha·vala**) *noun* [U] (in Arab countries and South Asia) a traditional system of transferring money to a person in another country or area, which involves paying money to an agent who then tells another agent in the relevant place to pay that person

**hawk** /hɔːk/ *noun, verb*
▪ *noun* 1 a strong fast BIRD OF PREY (= a bird that kills other creatures for food). There are several different types of hawks: *He waited, watching her like a hawk* (= watching her very closely). ⇒ see also SPARROWHAWK 2 a person, especially a politician, who supports the use of military force to solve problems OPP **dove**[1] IDM see EYE *n.*
▪ *verb* 1 [T] ~ sth to try to sell things by going from place to place asking people to buy them SYN **peddle** 2 [I, T] ~ (sth) to get PHLEGM (= a thick substance that forms in your nose and throat when you are ill) in your mouth when you COUGH

---

729

**hawk·er** /'hɔːkə(r)/ *noun* a person who makes money by selling goods, going from place to place and asking people to buy them

**hawk-'eyed** *adj.* (of a person) watching closely and carefully and noticing small details SYN **eagle-eyed**

**hawk·ish** /'hɔːkɪʃ/ *adj.* preferring to use military action rather than peaceful discussion in order to solve a political problem OPP **dovish**

**haw·thorn** /'hɔːθɔːn; *NAmE* -θɔːrn/ *noun* [U, C] a bush or small tree with THORNS, white or pink flowers and small dark red BERRIES

**hay** /heɪ/ *noun* [U] 1 grass that has been cut and dried and is used as food for animals: *a bale of hay* ⇒ compare STRAW 2 (*NAmE, informal*) a small amount of money IDM **make hay while the 'sun shines** (*saying*) to make good use of opportunities, good conditions, etc. while they last ⇒ more at HIT *v.*, ROLL *n.*

**'hay fever** *noun* [U] an illness that affects the nose, eyes and throat and is caused by POLLEN from plants that is breathed in from the air

**hay·loft** /'heɪlɒft; *NAmE* -lɔːft/ *noun* a place at the top of a farm building used for storing HAY

**hay·mak·ing** /'heɪmeɪkɪŋ/ *noun* [U] the process of cutting and drying grass to make HAY

**hay·ride** /'heɪraɪd/ *noun* (*NAmE*) a ride for pleasure on a CART filled with HAY, pulled by a horse or TRACTOR

**hay·stack** /'heɪstæk/ (*also less frequent* **hay·rick** /'heɪrɪk/) *noun* a large pile of HAY, used as a way of storing it until it is needed IDM see NEEDLE *n.*

**hay·wire** /'heɪwaɪə(r)/ *adj.* IDM **go 'haywire** (*informal*) to stop working correctly or become out of control: *After that, things started to go haywire.*

**haz·ard** ❷+ C1 /'hæzəd; *NAmE* -zərd/ *noun, verb*
▪ *noun* ❶+ C1 something that can be dangerous or cause damage: *a fire/safety hazard* ◊ *~ to sb/sth Growing levels of pollution represent a serious health hazard to the local population.* ◊ *~ of (doing) sth Everybody is aware of the hazards of smoking.* ⇒ see also MORAL HAZARD
▪ *verb* 1 to make a suggestion or guess that you know may be wrong: *~ sth Would you like to hazard a guess?* ◊ *+ speech 'Is it Tom you're going with?' she hazarded.* ◊ *~ that … I would hazard that she is the sole reason we are here.* 2 *~ sth* (*formal*) to risk sth or put it in danger SYN **endanger**: *Careless drivers hazard other people's lives as well as their own.*

**haz·ard·ous** /'hæzədəs; *NAmE* -zərd-/ *adj.* involving risk or danger, especially to sb's health or safety: *hazardous waste/materials/substances/chemicals* ◊ *a hazardous journey* ◊ *It would be hazardous to invest so much.* ◊ *~ to sb/sth a list of products that are potentially hazardous to health*

**'hazard pay** (*also* **'danger pay**) (*both US*) (*BrE* **'danger money**) *noun* [U] extra pay for doing work that is dangerous

**haze** /heɪz/ *noun, verb*
▪ *noun* 1 [C, U] air that is difficult to see through because it contains very small drops of water, especially caused by hot weather: *a heat haze* 2 [*sing.*] air containing sth that makes it difficult to see through it: *a haze of smoke/dust/steam* 3 [*sing.*] a mental state in which your thoughts, feelings, etc. are not clear: *an alcoholic haze*
▪ *verb* 1 [I, T] *~ (sth)* to become covered or to cover sth in a HAZE 2 [T] *~ sb* (*NAmE*) to play tricks on sb, especially a new student or sb who has just joined the army, or to give them very unpleasant things to do, sometimes as a condition for entering a FRATERNITY or SORORITY

**hazel** /'heɪzl/ *noun, adj.*
▪ *noun* [C, U] a small tree that produces small nuts (called hazelnuts) that can be eaten ⇒ compare FILBERT
▪ *adj.* (of eyes) between light brown and green or gold in colour

# hazelnut 730

**hazel·nut** /ˈheɪzlnʌt/ *noun* the small brown nut of the HAZEL tree ⊃ compare FILBERT ⊃ **VISUAL VOCAB** page V8

**hazy** /ˈheɪzi/ *adj.* (**hazi·er**, **hazi·est**) **1** not clear because of HAZE: *a hazy afternoon/sky* ◇ *hazy light/sunshine* ◇ *The mountains were hazy in the distance*. **2** not clear because of a lack of memory, understanding or detail SYN **vague**: *a hazy memory/idea* ◇ *What happened next is all very hazy.* **3** (of a person) uncertain or confused about sth: *I'm a little hazy about what to do next.* ▶ **haz·ily** /-zɪli/ *adv.*: *'Why now?' she wondered hazily.*

**H-bomb** *noun* = HYDROGEN BOMB

**HCF** /ˌeɪtʃ siː ˈef/ *abbr.* (*mathematics*) HIGHEST COMMON FACTOR

**HD** /ˌeɪtʃ ˈdiː/ *noun* [U] a system that gives television, film or video images that are extremely high quality, with very clear, sharp outlines and details (the abbreviation for 'high-definition'): **in ~** *The film was shot in HD.*

**HDMI** /ˌeɪtʃ diː em ˈaɪ/ *abbr.* high-definition multimedia interface (a system for connecting audio and video devices to electronic equipment such as a television or computer, in one cable): *Your DVDs will look better if connected through the HDMI socket.*

**HDTV** /ˌeɪtʃ diː tiː ˈviː/ *noun* [U] technology that produces extremely clear images on a television screen (the abbreviation for 'high definition television')

**HE** (*BrE*) (*also* **H.E.** *US, BrE*) *abbr.* **1** Her/His EXCELLENCY: *HE the Australian Ambassador* **2** /ˌeɪtʃ ˈiː/ HIGHER EDUCATION

**he** 🌐 **A1** /hi, iː, i, *strong form* hiː/ *pron., noun*
■ *pron.* (used as the subject of a verb) **1** a male person or animal that has already been mentioned or is easily identified: *Everyone liked my father—he was the perfect gentleman.* ◇ *He* (= the man we are watching) *went through that door.* **2** (*old-fashioned*) a person, male or female, whose sex is not stated or known, especially when referring to sb mentioned earlier or to a group in general: *Every child needs to know that he is loved.* ◇ (*saying*) *He who* (= anyone who) *hesitates is lost.* ◇ note at GENDER **3 He** used when referring to God ⊃ compare HIM
■ *noun* /hiː/ **1** [sing.] (*informal*) a male: *What a nice dog—is it a he or a she?* **2 he-** (in compound nouns) a male animal: *a he-goat*

**head** 🌐 **A1** /hed/ *noun, verb*
■ *noun*
• PART OF BODY **1** 🌐 **A1** [C] the part of the body on top of the neck containing the eyes, nose, mouth and brain: *She nodded her head in agreement.* ◇ *He shook his head in disbelief.* ◇ *The boys hung their heads in shame.* ◇ *She turned her head to look at him.* ◇ *to bow/tilt your head* ◇ *to raise/lift/lower your head* ◇ *The driver suffered head injuries.* ⊃ see also DEATH'S HEAD ⊃ **VISUAL VOCAB** page V1
• MIND **2** 🌐 **A2** [C] the mind or brain: *I sometimes wonder what goes on in that head of yours.* ◇ *I wish you'd use your head* (= think carefully before doing or saying sth). ◇ *The thought never entered my head.* ◇ **in sb's ~** *I can't work it out in my head—I need a calculator.* ◇ **into sb's ~** *Who's been putting such weird ideas into your head* (= making you believe that)? ◇ **out of sb's ~** *I can't get that tune out of my head.* ◇ *Try to put the exams out of your head* (= stop thinking about them). ⊃ see also BIG-HEAD, HOTHEAD
• MEASUREMENT **3 a head** [sing.] the size of a person's or animal's head, used as a measurement of distance or height: *She's a good head taller than her sister.* ◇ *The favourite won by a short head* (= a distance slightly less than the length of a horse's head).
• PAIN **4** [C, usually sing.] (*informal*) a continuous pain in your head SYN **headache**: *I woke up with a really bad head this morning.*
• OF GROUP/ORGANIZATION **5** 🌐 **A2** [C, U] the person in charge of a group of people or an organization: **~ of sth** *the heads of government/state* ◇ *She resigned as head of department.* ◇ *a former head of the Hong Kong Stock Exchange* ◇ *He is deputy head of the National Railway Museum.* ◇ *I was head coach of a Little League basketball team in Pittsburgh.* ◇ *the head gardener/chef/waiter*
• OF SCHOOL/COLLEGE **6** [C] (*often* **Head**) (*BrE*) the person in charge of a school or college SYN **headmaster**, **headmistress**, **head teacher**: *I've been called in to see the Head.* ◇ *the deputy head*
• SIDE OF COIN **7 heads** [U] the side of a coin that has a picture of the head of a person on it, used as one choice when a coin is TOSSED to decide sth ⊃ compare TAIL
• END OF OBJECT **8** [C, usually sing.] **~ (of sth)** the end of a long narrow object that is larger or wider than the rest of it: *the head of a nail* ⊃ see also BEDHEAD
• TOP **9** [sing.] **~ of sth** the top or highest part of sth: *at the head of the page* ◇ *They finished the season at the head of their league.*
• OF RIVER **10** [sing.] **the ~ of the river** the place where a river begins SYN **source**
• OF TABLE **11** [sing.] **the ~ of the table** the most important seat at a table: *The President sat at the head of the table.*
• OF LINE OF PEOPLE **12** [sing.] **the ~ of sth** the position at the front of a line of people: *The prince rode at the head of his regiment.*
• OF PLANT **13** [C] **~ (of sth)** the mass of leaves or flowers at the end of a STEM: *Remove the dead heads to encourage new growth.*
• ON BEER **14** [sing.] the mass of small bubbles on the top of a glass of beer
• OF SPOT **15** [C] the part of a spot on your skin that contains a thick yellow liquid (= PUS) ⊃ see also BLACKHEAD
• IN RECORDING SYSTEM **16** [C] the component of a sound or video recording system that converts data on the disk or tape into digital electronic data (and the other way round)
• NUMBER OF ANIMALS **17 ~ of sth** [pl.] used to say how many animals of a particular type are on a farm, in a HERD, etc: *200 head of sheep*
• PRESSURE **18 a ~ of steam** [sing.] the pressure produced by STEAM in a small space
• SEX **19** [U] (*taboo, slang*) ORAL sex (= using the mouth to give sb sexual pleasure): *to give head*

IDM **a/per ˈhead** for each person: *The meal worked out at $20 a head.* **bang/knock your/their ˈheads together** (*informal*) to force people to stop arguing and behave in a sensible way **be banging, etc. your head against a brick ˈwall** (*informal*) to keep trying to do sth that will never be successful: *Trying to reason with them was like banging my head against a brick wall.* **be/stand head and ˈshoulders above sb/sth** to be much better than other people or things **bite/snap sb's ˈhead off** (*informal*) to shout at sb in an angry way, especially without reason **bring sth to a ˈhead | come to a ˈhead** if you **bring** a situation **to a head** or if a situation **comes to a head**, you are forced to deal with it quickly because it suddenly becomes very bad **bury/hide your head in the ˈsand** to refuse to admit that a problem exists or refuse to deal with it **can't make head nor/or ˈtail of sth** to be unable to understand sth; *I couldn't make head nor tail of what he was saying.* **do sb's ˈhead in** (*BrE, informal*) to make sb feel confused, upset and/or annoyed: *Shut up! You're doing my head in.* **do sth standing on your ˈhead** (*informal*) to be able to do sth very easily and without having to think too much **from head to ˈfoot/ˈtoe** covering your whole body: *We were covered from head to foot in mud.* **get your ˈhead down** (*informal*) **1** (*BrE*) to sleep: *I managed to get my head down for an hour.* **2** = KEEP/GET YOUR HEAD DOWN *n.* **get your ˈhead round sth** (*BrE, informal*) to be able to understand or accept sth: *She's dead. I can't get my head round it yet.* **get it into your ˈhead (that …)** to start to understand or think sth: *When will you get it into your head that I don't want to discuss this any more! ◇ For some reason she's got it into her head that I don't like her.* **give sb their ˈhead** to allow sb to do what they want without trying to stop them **go head to ˈhead (with sb)** to deal with sb in a very direct and determined way **go to sb's ˈhead 1** (of alcohol) to make you feel drunk: *That glass of wine has gone straight to my head.* **2** (of success, praise, etc.) to make you feel too proud of yourself in a way that other people find annoying **have a good ˈhead on your ˈshoulders** to be a sensible person **have a head for sth 1** to be good at sth: *to have a head for figures/business* **2** if sb does not **have a head for heights**, they feel nervous and think they are going to fall when they look down from a high place **have your head in the ˈclouds 1** to be thinking about sth that is not connected with what you are doing **2** to have ideas, plans, etc. that are not realistic **have your ˈhead screwed on (the right way)** (*informal*) to be a sensible person **ˌhead ˈfirst 1** moving forwards or downwards with your head in front of the rest of your body: *He fell head first down the stairs.* **2** without thinking carefully about sth before acting ➡ **headlong:** *She got divorced and rushed head first into another marriage.* **your head is spinning | make your head spin** your head feels as though it is going round and round and you cannot balance, especially because you are ill or confused or have had a shock; to make you feel like this: *Her head was spinning from the pain.* **ˌhead over ˌheels in ˈlove** loving sb very much: *He's fallen head over heels in love with his boss.* **ˌheads or ˈtails?** used to ask sb which side of a coin they think will be facing upwards when it is TOSSED in order to decide sth by chance **ˈheads will roll (for sth)** (*informal*), *usually humorous*) used to say that some people will be punished because of sth that has happened **hold your ˈhead high | hold up your ˈhead** to be proud of or not feel ashamed about sth that you have done: *She managed to hold her head high and ignore what people were saying.* **in over your ˈhead** involved in sth that is too difficult for you to deal with: *After a week in the new job, I soon realized that I was in over my head.* **keep your ˈhead | keep a ˈclear/ˈcool ˈhead** to remain calm in a difficult situation **keep your ˈhead above water** to deal with a difficult situation, especially one in which you have financial problems, and just manage to survive **keep/get your ˈhead down** to avoid attracting attention to yourself **laugh, scream, etc. your ˈhead off** (*informal*) to laugh, etc. a lot and very loudly **lose your ˈhead** to become unable to act in a calm or sensible way **on your (own) head ˈbe it** used to tell sb that they will have to accept any unpleasant results of sth that they decide to do: *Tell him the truth if you want to, but on your own head be it!* **out of/off your ˈhead** (*BrE, informal*) **1** crazy **2** not knowing what you are saying or doing because of the effects of alcohol or drugs **over sb's ˈhead 1** too complicated or difficult for sb to understand: *A lot of the jokes went (= were) right over my head.* **2** to a higher position of authority than sb: *I couldn't help feeling jealous when she was promoted over my head.* **put our/your/their ˈheads together** to think about or discuss sth as a group **sth rears its (ugly) ˈhead** if sth unpleasant **rears its head** or **rears its ugly head**, it appears or happens **stand/turn sth on its ˈhead** to make people think about sth in a completely different way **take it into your head that…** to suddenly start thinking sth, especially sth that other people think is stupid **take it into your head to do sth** to suddenly decide to do sth, especially sth that other people think is stupid **turn sb's ˈhead** (of success, praise, etc.) to make a person feel too proud in a way that other people find annoying **two heads are better than ˈone** (*saying*) used to say that two people can achieve more than one person working alone ➡ more at BEAR *n*., BLOCK *n*., BOOK *n*., BOTHER *v*., DRUM *v*., EYE *n*., GUN *n*., HAIR, HEART *n*., HIT *v*., IDEA, KNOCK *v*., LAUGH *v*., NEED *v*., OLD, PRICE *n*., RING² *v*., ROOF *n*., SCRATCH *v*., STICK *v*., THICK *adj*., TOP *n*.

■ verb

- **MOVE TOWARDS 1** ⓘ B1 [I] (*also* **be headed**) + *adv.*/*prep.* to move in a particular direction: *Where are we heading?* ◇ *Where are you two headed?* ◇ *Let's head back home.* ◇ *She headed for the door.* ◇ (*figurative*) *Can you forecast where the economy is heading?*
- **GROUP/ORGANIZATION 2** ⓘ B1 [T] ~ **sth** (*also* **ˈhead sth↔ˈup**) to lead or be in charge of sth: *She has been appointed to head the research team.*
- **LIST/LINE OF PEOPLE 3** [T] ~ **sth** to be at the top of a list of names or at the front of a line of people: *Italy heads the table after two games.* ◇ *to head a march/procession*
- **BE AT TOP 4** [T, *usually passive*] to put a word or words at the top of a page or section of a book as a title: **be headed …** *The chapter was headed 'My Early Life'.*
- **FOOTBALL 5** [T] ~ **sth** to hit a football with your head: *Walsh headed the ball into an empty goal.*

**PHRV** **be ˈheading for sth** (*also* **be ˈheaded for sth**) to be likely to experience sth bad: *They look as though they're heading for divorce.* **ˌhead sb↔ˈoff** to get in front of sb in order to make them turn back or change direction

731

**SYN** intercept: *We'll head them off at the bridge!* **ˌhead sth↔ˈoff** to take action in order to prevent sth from happening: *He headed off efforts to replace him as leader.* **ˌhead sth↔ˈup** to lead or be in charge of a department, part of an organization, etc. ➡ *see also* HEAD *verb* (2)

**-head** /hed/ *suffix* (*informal*) (in nouns) a person who is very enthusiastic about a particular thing or is ADDICTED to a particular drug: *a gearhead* ◇ *a crackhead* ◇ *a smackhead* ◇ *a pothead*

**headˑache** ⓘ A2 /ˈhedeɪk/ *noun* **1** ⓘ A2 a continuous pain in the head: *He had a terrible headache.* ◇ *Red wine gives me a headache.* ◇ *I have* **a splitting headache** (= a very bad one). **2** (*informal*) a person or thing that causes worry or trouble: *The real headache will be getting the bank to lend you the money.*

**headˑband** /ˈhedbænd/ *noun* a narrow piece of cloth worn around the head, especially to keep hair or SWEAT out of your eyes when playing sports

**headˑbangˑer** /ˈhedbæŋə(r)/ *noun* (*informal*) **1** a person who likes to shake their head violently up and down while listening to rock music **2** a stupid or crazy person ▶ **headˑbanging** *noun* [U]

**headˑboard** /ˈhedbɔːd; *NAmE* -bɔːrd/ *noun* the board at the end of a bed where you rest your head when you are sitting up

**ˌhead ˈboy** *noun* (in some British schools) the boy who is chosen each year to represent his school

**headˑbutt** /ˈhedbʌt/ *verb* ~ **sb** (*especially BrE*) to deliberately hit sb hard with your head ▶ **headˑbutt** *noun*

**headˑcase** /ˈhedkeɪs/ *noun* (*BrE, informal*) a person who behaves in a strange way and who seems to be mentally ill

**headˑcount** /ˈhedkaʊnt/ *noun* an act of counting the number of people who are at an event, employed by an organization, etc.; the number of people that have been counted in this way: *to do a headcount* ◇ *What's the latest headcount?*

**headˑdress** /ˈhedˌdres/ *noun* a piece of clothing or a decoration worn on the head on special occasions

**headˑed** /ˈhedɪd/ *adj.* **1** (of writing paper) having the name and address of a person, an organization, etc. printed at the top: *headed notepaper* **2 -headed** (in adjectives) having the type of head or number of heads mentioned: *a bald-headed man* ◇ *a three-headed monster* ➡ *see also* BIG-HEADED, CLEAR-HEADED, COOL-HEADED, EMPTY-HEADED, HARD-HEADED, HOT-HEADED, LEVEL-HEADED, LIGHT-HEADED, MUDDLE-HEADED, PIG-HEADED, RED-HEADED, WRONG-HEADED

**headˑer** /ˈhedə(r)/ *noun* **1** (in football (soccer)) an act of hitting the ball with your head **2** a line or block of text that appears at the top of every page in a book or document ➡ *compare* FOOTER ➡ *see also* DOUBLE-HEADER

**headˑgear** /ˈhedɡɪə(r); *NAmE* -ɡɪr/ *noun* [U] anything worn on the head, for example a hat: *protective headgear*

**ˌhead ˈgirl** *noun* (in some British schools) the girl who is chosen each year to represent her school

**headˑhunt** /ˈhedhʌnt/ *verb* ~ **sb** to find sb who is suitable for a senior job and persuade them to leave their present job: *I was headhunted by a marketing agency.* ▶ **headˑhuntˑing** *noun* [U]

**headˑhuntˑer** /ˈhedhʌntə(r)/ *noun* **1** a person whose job is to find people with the necessary skills to work for particular companies and to persuade them to join those companies **2** a member of a people that collects the heads of the people they kill

**headˑing** /ˈhedɪŋ/ *noun* **1** a title printed at the top of a page or at the beginning of a section of a book: *chapter headings* **2** the subject of each section of a speech or piece of writing: *The company's aims can be grouped under three main headings.*

**headˑlamp** /ˈhedlæmp/ *noun especially BrE* = HEADLIGHT

# headland

**head·land** /ˈhedlənd, -lænd/ *noun* a narrow piece of high land that sticks out from the coast into the sea **SYN** **promontory**⇨ WORDFINDER NOTE at COAST

**head·less** /ˈhedləs/ *adj.* [usually before noun] without a head: *a headless body/corpse*
**IDM** **run around like a ˌheadless ˈchicken** to be very busy and active trying to do sth, but not very organized, with the result that you do not succeed

**head·light** /ˈhedlaɪt/ *noun* (*also* **head-lamp** *especially in BrE*) a large light, usually one of two, at the front of a vehicle; the BEAM from this light: *He dipped his headlights* (= directed the light downwards) *for the oncoming traffic.*

**head·line** 🔊 B1 /ˈhedlaɪn/ *noun, verb*
■ *noun* **1** 🔊 B1 [C] the title of a news article printed in large letters, especially at the top of the front page on a newspaper or the home page on a news website: *a newspaper headline* ⋄ **under a~** *They ran the story under the headline 'Home at last!'.* ⋄ **in the headlines** *The scandal was in the headlines for several days.* ⋄ **~about sb/sth** *an alarming headline about possible terrorist attacks* ⋄ *headline news* ⇨ see also BANNER HEADLINE ⬧ WORDFINDER NOTE at NEWSPAPER **2** **the headlines** [pl.] a short summary of the most important items of news, read at the beginning of a news programme on the radio or television
**IDM** **grab/hit/make the ˈheadlines** to be an important item of news in the media
■ *verb* **1** [T, usually passive] to give a story or article a particular headline: **be headlined …** *The story was headlined 'Back to the future'.* **2** [T, I] **~(sth)** to be the main performer in a concert or show: *The concert is to be headlined by Ed Sheeran.*

**head·liner** /ˈhedlaɪnə(r)/ *noun* the main performer or act in a show: *The band are among the headliners for the music festival next month.*

**head·lock** /ˈhedlɒk; NAmE -lɑːk/ *noun* (in WRESTLING) a way of holding an opponent's head so that they cannot move: *He had him in a headlock.*

**head·long** /ˈhedlɒŋ; NAmE -lɔːŋ/ *adv.* **1** with the head first and the rest of the body following **SYN** **head first**: *She fell headlong into the icy pool.* **2** without thinking carefully before doing sth: *The government is taking care not to rush headlong into another controversy.* **3** quickly and without looking where you are going: *He ran headlong into a police car.* ▶ **head·long** *adj.* [only before noun]: *a headlong dive/rush*

**head·man** /ˈhedmæn, -mən/ *noun* (*pl.* **-men** /ˈhedmen, -mən/) the leader of a traditional community or TRIBE **SYN** **chief**: *the village headman*

**head·mas·ter** /ˌhedˈmɑːstə(r); NAmE -ˈmæs-/, **head·mis·tress** /ˌhedˈmɪstrəs/ (*BrE, becoming old-fashioned*) (*BrE usually* **ˌhead ˈteacher**) (*NAmE usually* **prin·ci·pal**) *noun* a teacher who is in charge of a school, especially a private school

**ˌhead ˈoffice** *noun* [C, U + sing./pl. v.] the main office of a company; the managers who work there: *Their head office is in New York.* ⋄ *I don't know what head office will think about this proposal.*

**ˌhead of ˈstate** *noun* (*pl.* **heads of state**) the official leader of a country who is sometimes also the leader of the government

**ˌhead-ˈon** *adj.* [only before noun] **1** in which the front part of one vehicle hits the front part of another vehicle: *a head-on crash/collision* **2** in which people express strong views and deal with sth in a direct way: *There was a head-on confrontation between management and unions.* ▶ **ˌhead-ˈon** *adv.*: *The cars crashed head-on.* ⋄ *We hit the tree head-on.* ⋄ *to tackle a problem head-on* (= without trying to avoid it)

**head·phones** /ˈhedfəʊnz/ *noun* [pl.] a piece of equipment consisting of two EARPHONES joined by a band across the head that makes it possible to listen to music, the radio, etc. without other people hearing it: *a pair/set of headphones*

**head·quar·tered** /ˌhedˈkwɔːtəd; NAmE ˈhedkwɔːrtərd/ *adj.* [not before noun] having headquarters in a particular place: *News Corporation is headquartered in New York.*

**head·quar·ters** 🔊+ B2 /ˌhedˈkwɔːtəz; NAmE ˈhedkwɔːrtərz/ *noun* [U + sing./pl. v., C] (*pl.* **head·quar·ters**) (*abbr.* **HQ**) a place from which an organization or a military operation is controlled; the people who work there: *The firm's headquarters is/are in London.* ⋄ *Several companies have their headquarters in the area.* ⋄ *I'm now based at headquarters.* ⋄ *police headquarters* ⋄ *Headquarters in Dublin has/have agreed.* ⇨ see also GENERAL HEADQUARTERS

**head·rest** /ˈhedrest/ *noun* a support for the head, especially one attached to the back of a chair or seat, for example in a car

**head·room** /ˈhedruːm, -rʊm/ *noun* [U] **1** the amount of space between the top of a vehicle and an object it drives under **2** the amount of space between the top of your head and the roof of a vehicle: *There's a lot of headroom for such a small car.*

**head·scarf** /ˈhedskɑːf; NAmE -skɑːrf/ *noun* (*pl.* **head·scarves** /ˈhedskɑːvz; NAmE -skɑːrvz/) a square piece of cloth that covers the head, worn by women or girls

**head·set** /ˈhedset/ *noun* a pair of HEADPHONES, especially one with a MICROPHONE attached to it

**ˌhead ˈship** /ˈhedʃɪp/ *noun* **1 ~(of sth)** the position of being in charge of an organization: *the headship of the department* **2 ~(of sth)** (*BrE*) the position of being in charge of a school

**head·shot** /ˈhedʃɒt; NAmE -ʃɑːt/ *noun* **1** a photograph of a person's face or head and shoulders: *The casting director looks through hundreds of headshots before selecting actors for auditions.* **2** a bullet from a gun that is aimed at the head

**head·space** /ˈhedspeɪs/ *noun* [U] **1** the amount of air or empty space that is left above the contents of a container before it is SEALED (= tightly closed) **2** (*informal*) the way you think or feel about sth: *Whenever you read a book, you're entering the writer's headspace.* **3** (*informal*) time to think clearly without any pressure: *I could do with a bit of headspace just to think about what I'm doing.*

**head·stand** /ˈhedstænd/ *noun* a position in which a person has their head and hands on the ground and their feet straight up in the air

**ˌhead ˈstart** *noun* [sing.] **~(on/over sb)** an advantage that sb already has before they start doing sth: *Being able to speak French gave her a head start over the other candidates.*

**head·stone** /ˈhedstəʊn/ *noun* a piece of stone placed at one end of a GRAVE (= where a dead person is buried), showing the name, etc. of the person buried there **SYN** **gravestone**⇨ compare TOMBSTONE

**head·strong** /ˈhedstrɒŋ; NAmE -strɔːŋ/ *adj.* (*disapproving*) a **headstrong** person is determined to do things their own way and refuses to listen to advice

**ˌheads-ˈup** *noun* (*pl.* **heads-up** *or* **heads-ups**) **~(about sth)** (*especially NAmE*) a piece of information given in advance of sth or as advice: *Send everyone a heads-up about the changes well in advance.*

**ˌhead ˈtable** (*NAmE*) (*BrE* **ˌtop ˈtable**) *noun* the table at which the most important guests sit at a formal dinner

**ˌhead ˈteacher** (*also* **head·teacher**) (*also* **head**) (*both BrE*) (*NAmE* **prin·ci·pal**) *noun* a teacher who is in charge of a school

**ˌhead-to-ˈhead** (*also* **toe-to-toe**) *adj.* [only before noun] in which two people or groups face each other directly in order to decide the result of a competition or an argument: *a head-to-head battle/clash/contest* ▶ **ˌhead-to-ˈhead** (*also* **toe-to-toe**) *adv.*: *They are set to meet head-to-head in next week's final.* ⋄ *The product will go head-to-head* (= compete directly) *with the current brand leader.*

**head·waters** /ˈhedwɔːtəz; NAmE -tərz/ *noun* [pl.] streams forming the source of a river

---

b **b**ad | d **d**id | f **f**all | g **g**et | h **h**at | j **y**es | k **c**at | l **l**eg | m **m**an | n **n**ow | p **p**en | r **r**ed

**head·way** /ˈhedweɪ/ noun [U]
**IDM** **make ˈheadway (with/against/towards sth)** to make progress, especially when this is slow or difficult: *We are making little headway with the negotiations.* ◇ *The boat was unable to make much headway against the tide.*

**head·wind** /ˈhedwɪnd/ noun a wind that is blowing towards a person or vehicle, so that it is blowing from the direction in which the person or vehicle is moving ⊃ compare TAILWIND

**head·word** /ˈhedwɜːd; NAmE -wɜːrd/ noun (specialist) a word that forms a HEADING in a dictionary, under which its meaning is explained ⊃ WORDFINDER NOTE at DICTIONARY

**heady** /ˈhedi/ adj. (**head·ier**, **headi·est**) 1 [usually before noun] having a strong effect on your senses; making you feel excited and confident **SYN intoxicating**: *the heady days of youth* ◇ *the heady scent of hot spices* ◇ *a heady mixture of desire and fear* ⊃ SYNONYMS at EXCITING 2 [not before noun] (of a person) excited in a way that makes you do things without worrying about the possible results: *She felt heady with success.*

**heal** ℝ+ B2 /hiːl/ verb 1 ℝ+ B2 [I, T] to become healthy again; to make sth healthy again: *It took a long time for the wounds to heal.* ◇ *~ up The cut healed up without leaving a scar.* ◇ *~sth This will help to heal your cuts and scratches.* ◇ (figurative) *It was a chance to heal the wounds in the party* (= to repair the damage that had been done). ⊃ HOMOPHONES at HEEL 2 ℝ+ B2 [T] *~sb (of sth)* (old use or formal) to cure sb who is ill; to make sb feel happy again: *the story of Jesus healing ten lepers of their disease* ◇ *I felt healed by his love.* 3 ℝ+ B2 [T, I] *~(sth)* to put an end to sth or make sth easier to bear; to end or become easier to bear: *She was never able to heal the rift between herself and her father.* ◇ *The breach between them never really healed.*

**heal·er** /ˈhiːlə(r)/ noun 1 a person who treats sick people using natural powers rather than medicine: *a faith/spiritual healer* ⊃ see also FAITH HEALER 2 something that makes a bad situation easier to deal with: *Time is a great healer.*

**heal·ing** /ˈhiːlɪŋ/ noun [U] the process of becoming or making sb/sth healthy again; the process of getting better after an emotional shock: *the healing process* ◇ *emotional healing* ⊃ see also FAITH HEALING

**health** ① A1 /helθ/ noun [U] 1 A1 the condition of a person's body or mind: *to be good/bad for your health* ◇ *in ...~* ◇ *to be in poor/good health* ◇ *Here are some simple ways to improve your health and fitness.* ◇ *mental health* ◇ *a health problem/risk* ⊃ see also ILL HEALTH

**WORDFINDER** acute, condition, medicine, outbreak, pain, recover, relapse, terminal, treatment

2 A1 the state of being physically and mentally healthy: *He was nursed back to health by his wife.* ◇ *Rest and exercise restored her health.* ◇ *the role of diet in achieving and maintaining health* 3 A1 the work of providing medical services: *All parties are promising to increase spending on health.* ◇ *the Health Minister* ◇ **health professionals/workers** ◇ **health insurance** ◇ **health and safety regulations** (= laws that protect the health of people at work) 4 how successful sth is: *the health of the economy*
**IDM** **your (very) good ˈhealth!** said before drinking alcohol to express good wishes for sb's health and happiness ⊃ more at CLEAN adj., DRINK v., PROPOSE, RUDE

**ˈhealth·care** ℝ+ B2 (also **health care**) noun [U] the service of providing medical care: *the costs of healthcare for the elderly* ◇ **healthcare workers/professionals** ⊃ see also PRIMARY HEALTH CARE

**ˈhealth centre** (BrE) (US **ˈhealth center**) noun a building where a group of doctors see their patients and where some local medical services have their offices

**ˈhealth club** noun a private club where people go to do physical exercise in order to stay or become healthy and fit **SYN gym**

733 **hear**

**ˈhealth food** noun [U, C, usually pl.] food that does not contain any artificial substances and is therefore thought to be good for your health: *a health food store/shop*

**health·ful** /ˈhelθfl/ adj. [usually before noun] (formal or NAmE) good for your health ▸ **health·ful·ly** /ˈhelθfəli/ adv.

**ˈhealth service** noun a public service providing medical care ⊃ see also NATIONAL HEALTH SERVICE

**ˈhealth spa** noun = SPA (2) ⊃ WORDFINDER NOTE at FIT

**ˈhealth tourism** (especially BrE) (NAmE usually **ˈmedical ˈtourism**) noun [U] the practice of travelling abroad in order to have medical treatment

**ˈhealth visitor** noun (in the UK) a trained nurse whose job is to visit people in their homes, for example new parents, and give them advice on some areas of medical care

**healthy** ① A1 /ˈhelθi/ adj. (**health·ier**, **healthi·est**) 1 ℝ A1 having good health and not likely to become ill: *a healthy child/baby/adult* ◇ *a healthy animal/tree* ◇ *Stay healthy by eating well and exercising regularly.* **OPP unhealthy** ⊃ SYNONYMS at WELL 2 A1 [usually before noun] good for your health: *a healthy diet/lifestyle* ◇ *healthy eating/food/living* **OPP unhealthy** 3 ℝ A1 [usually before noun] showing that you are in good health: *to have a healthy appetite* 4 normal and sensible: *The child showed a healthy curiosity.* ◇ *She has a healthy respect for her rival's talents.* ◇ *It's not healthy the way she clings to the past.* **OPP unhealthy** 5 successful and working well: *a healthy economy* ◇ *Your car doesn't sound very healthy.* 6 [usually before noun] large and showing success: *a healthy bank balance* ◇ *a healthy profit* ▸ **health·ily** /-θɪli/ adv.: *to eat healthily* **healthi·ness** noun [U]

**heap** /hiːp/ noun, verb
▪ **noun** 1 an untidy pile of sth: *~(of sth) The building was reduced to a heap of rubble.* ◇ *a compost heap* ◇ **in a ~** *His clothes lay in a heap on the floor.* ◇ **in heaps** *Worn-out car tyres were stacked in heaps.* ⊃ see also COMPOST HEAP, SCRAPHEAP 2 [usually pl.] *~(of sth)* (informal) a lot of sth: *There's heaps of time before the plane leaves.* ◇ (NAmE) *I've got a heap of things to do.* 3 (informal, humorous) a car that is old and in bad condition
**IDM** **at the top/bottom of the ˈheap** high up/low down in the structure of an organization or a society: *These workers are at the bottom of the economic heap.* **collapse, fall, etc. in a ˈheap** to fall down heavily and not move **heaps ˈbetter, ˈmore, ˈolder, etc.** (BrE, informal) a lot better, etc: *Help yourself — there's heaps more.* ◇ *He looks heaps better than when I last saw him.*
▪ **verb** 1 *~sth (up)* to put things in an untidy pile: *Rocks were heaped up on the side of the road.* 2 to put a lot of sth in a pile on sth: *~A on B She heaped food on my plate.* ◇ *~B with A She heaped my plate with food.* 3 to give a lot of sth such as praise or criticism to sb: *~A on B He heaped praise on his team.* ◇ *~B with A He heaped his team with praise.* **IDM** see SCORN n.

**heap·ed** /hiːpt/ (especially BrE) (NAmE usually **heap·ing**) adj. (especially in recipes) used to describe a spoon, etc. that has as much in it or on it as it can hold: *a heaped teaspoon of sugar* ◇ *heaping plates of scrambled eggs* ⊃ compare LEVEL

**hear** ① A1 /hɪə(r); NAmE hɪr/ verb (**heard**, **heard** /hɜːd; NAmE hɜːrd/) 1 ℝ A1 [I, T] (not used in the progressive tenses) to be aware of sounds with your ears: *I can't hear very well.* ◇ *~sth/sb He heard a noise and went to investigate.* ◇ *~sb/sth doing sth He could hear a dog barking.* ◇ *~sb/sth do sth Did you hear him go out?* ◇ *~what ... Didn't you hear what I said?* ◇ *sb/sth is heard to do sth She has been heard to make threats to her former lover.* 2 ℝ A1 [T] (not used in the progressive tenses) to listen or pay attention to sb/sth: *~sth Did you hear that play on the radio last night?* ◇ *~sb/sth/yourself do sth Be quiet — I can't hear myself think!* (= it is so noisy that I can't think clearly) ◇ *~what ... We'd better hear what they have to say.* 3 ℝ A2 [I, T] (not usually used in the progressive tenses) to be told about sth: *Haven't you heard? She resigned.* ◇ *'I'm getting married.' 'So I've heard.'* ◇ *Things are going well from what I*

**hear.** ◇ ~ **about sb/sth** *I was sorry to hear about your accident.* ◇ *Come on! I want to hear all about it.* ◇ ~ **sth** *We had heard nothing for weeks.* ◇ *to hear a story/rumour/report* ◇ *When I heard the news, I was devastated.* ◇ ~ **(that)** ... *I was surprised to hear (that) he was married.* ◇ ~ **it said (that)** ... *I've heard it said (that) they met in Italy.* ◇ ~ **what, how, etc** ... *Did you hear what happened?* **4** [T] ~ **sth** to listen to and judge a case in court: *The appeal was heard in private.* ◇ *Today the jury began to hear the evidence.*

**IDM** ▶ **have you heard the one about ...?** used to ask sb if they have heard a particular joke before ▶ **hear! hear!** used to show that you agree with or approve of what sb has just said, especially during a speech ▶ **hear 'tell (of sth)** (*old-fashioned* or *formal*) to hear people talking about sth: *I've often heard tell of such things.* ▶ **I hear what you're 'saying** used to tell sb that you have listened to their opinion, especially when you are going to express a different opinion: *I hear what you're saying, but you're wrong.* ▶ **I've heard it all be'fore** (*informal*) used to say that you do not really believe sb's promises or excuses because they are the same ones you have heard before ▶ **let's hear it for ...** (*informal*) used to say that sb/sth deserves praise: *Let's hear it for the teachers, for a change.* ▶ **not/never hear the 'end of it** to keep being reminded of sth because sb is always talking to you about it: *If we don't get her a dog we'll never hear the end of it.* ▶ **you could hear a 'pin drop** it was extremely quiet: *The audience was so quiet you could have heard a pin drop.* ▶ **(do) you 'hear (me)?** (*informal*) used to tell sb in an angry way to pay attention and obey you: *You can't go—do you hear me?* ⊃ more at LAST¹ *n.*, THING, VOICE *n.*

**PHRV** ▶ **'hear from sb | 'hear sth from sb** to receive a letter, email, phone call, etc. from sb: *I look forward to hearing from you.* ◇ *I haven't heard anything from her for months.* ▶ **'hear of sb/sth** 🔒 B1 | **'hear sth of sth** 🔒 B1 to know about sb/sth because you have been told about them: *I've never heard of the place.* ◇ *She disappeared and was never heard of again.* ◇ *The last I heard of him he was living in Glasgow.* ◇ *This is the first I've heard of it!* ▶ **not 'hear of sth** to refuse to let sb do sth, especially because you want to help them: *She wanted to walk home but I wouldn't hear of it.* ◇ **not hear of sb doing sth** *He wouldn't hear of my walking home alone.* ⊃ see also UNHEARD-OF ▶ **hear sb 'out** to listen until sb has finished saying what they want to say

▼ **HOMOPHONES**

**hear** • **here** /hɪə(r); *NAmE* hɪr/

- **hear** *verb*: *I can't hear you—the signal is very bad.*
- **here** *adv*: *We don't need to move—we can see it all from here!*

**hear·er** /'hɪərə(r); *NAmE* 'hɪr-/ *noun* a person who hears sth or who is listening to sb **SYN** **listener**

**hear·ing** ❶ B2 /'hɪərɪŋ; *NAmE* 'hɪr-/ *noun* **1** 🔒 [U] the ability to hear: *Her hearing is poor.* ◇ *hearing loss* ⊃ see also HARD OF HEARING **2** [C] an official meeting at which the facts about a crime, complaint, etc. are presented to the person or group of people who will have to decide what action to take: *a court/disciplinary hearing* **3** [sing.] an opportunity to explain your actions, ideas or opinions: *to get/give sb a fair hearing* ◇ *His views may be unfashionable but he deserves a hearing.*

**IDM** ▶ **in/within (sb's) 'hearing** near enough to sb so that they can hear what is said **SYN** **earshot**: *She shouldn't have said such things in your hearing.* ◇ *I had no reason to believe there was anyone within hearing.* ▶ **out of 'hearing** too far away to hear sb/sth or to be heard: *She had moved out of hearing.*

**'hearing aid** *noun* a small device that fits inside the ear and makes sounds louder, used by people who cannot hear well: *to have/wear a hearing aid*

**'hearing dog** *noun* a dog trained to make a DEAF person (= a person who cannot hear well) aware of sounds such as the ringing of a phone or a DOORBELL

,**hearing-im'paired** *adj.* (*sometimes offensive*) not able to hear well; partly or completely DEAF **HELP** Many people prefer the term **hard of hearing**.

**heark·en** (*also* **hark·en**) /'hɑːkən; *NAmE* 'hɑːrk-/ *verb* [I] ~ **(to sb/sth)** (*old use*) to listen to sb/sth

**hear·say** /'hɪəseɪ; *NAmE* 'hɪrs-/ *noun* [U] things that you have heard from another person but do not (definitely) know to be true: *We can't make a decision based on hearsay and guesswork.* ◇ *hearsay evidence*

**hearse** /hɜːs; *NAmE* hɜːrs/ *noun* a long vehicle used for carrying the coffin (= the box for the dead body) at a FUNERAL ⊃ WORDFINDER NOTE at DIE

**heart** ❶ A2 /hɑːt; *NAmE* hɑːrt/ *noun, verb*

■ *noun*

- **PART OF BODY 1** 🔒 A2 [C] the organ in the chest that sends blood around the body, usually on the left in humans: *The patient's heart stopped beating for a few seconds.* ◇ *I could feel my heart pounding in my chest* (= because of excitement, etc.)*.* ◇ *to have a weak heart* ◇ *heart disease/problems* ◇ *heart patients/surgery* ⊃ see also CORONARY, OPEN-HEART SURGERY ⊃ VISUAL VOCAB page V1 **2** [C] (*literary*) the outside part of the chest where the heart is: *She clasped the photo to her heart.*
- **SHAPE 3** 🔒 B1 [C] a thing that is like a heart in shape, often red and used as a symbol of love; a symbol like a heart used to mean the verb 'love': *The words 'I love you' were written inside a big red heart.*
- **FEELINGS/EMOTIONS 4** 🔒 B1 [C] the place in a person where the feelings and emotions are thought to be, especially those connected with love: *She has a kind heart.* ◇ *He returned with a heavy heart* (= sad)*.* ◇ *Her novels tend to deal with affairs of the heart.* ◇ *The story captured the hearts and minds of a generation.* ◇ *His sad story touched her heart.* ◇ *the mysteries of the human heart* ⊃ see also BROKEN HEART
- **-HEARTED 5** 🔒 B2 (in adjectives) having the type of character or personality mentioned: *pure-hearted* ◇ *black-hearted* ⊃ see also BIG-HEARTED, BLEEDING HEART, COLD-HEARTED, FAINT-HEARTED, GOOD-HEARTED, HARD-HEARTED, KIND-HEARTED, LIGHT-HEARTED, SOFT-HEARTED, WARM-HEARTED
- **IMPORTANT PART 6** 🔒 B2 [sing.] the most important part of sth: ~ **of sth** *the heart of the matter/problem* ◇ *The committee's report went to the heart of the government's dilemma.* ◇ **at the ~ of sth** *The distinction between right and wrong lies at the heart of all questions of morality.* ◇ **at the/its ~** *The story, at its heart, is a simple tale of loss and rediscovery.*
- **CENTRE 7** 🔒 B2 [C, usually sing.] the part that is in the centre of sth: ~ **of sth** *a quiet hotel in the very heart of the city* ◇ **at the/its ~** *an open space with a small arena at the heart*
- **OF VEGETABLE 8** [C] the smaller leaves in the middle of a CABBAGE, LETTUCE, etc.
- **IN CARD GAMES 9** **hearts** [pl., U] one of the four SUITS (= sets) in a PACK of cards, with red heart symbols on them: *the queen of hearts* ◇ *Hearts is/are trumps.* **10** [C] one card from the suit called hearts: *Who played that heart?* ⊃ see also PURPLE HEART

**IDM** ▶ **at 'heart** used to say what sb is really like even though they may seem to be sth different: *He's still a socialist at heart.* ▶ **break sb's 'heart** to make sb feel very unhappy: *She broke his heart when she called off the engagement.* ◇ *It breaks my heart to see you like this.* ▶ **by 'heart** (*BrE also* **off by 'heart**) using only your memory: *I've seen the show so often I know all the songs by heart.* ◇ *She's learnt the whole speech off by heart.* ▶ **close/dear/near to sb's 'heart** having a lot of importance and interest for sb ▶ **from the (bottom of your) 'heart** in a way that is sincere: *I beg you, from the bottom of my heart, to spare his life.* ◇ *It was clearly an offer that came from the heart.* ▶ **give sb (fresh) 'heart** to make sb feel positive, especially when they thought that they had no chance of achieving sth ▶ **give your 'heart to sb** to give your love to one person ▶ **have a 'heart!** (*informal*) used to ask sb to be kind and/or reasonable ▶ **have a heart of 'gold** to be a very kind person ▶ **have a heart of 'stone** to be a person who does not show other people sympathy ▶ **heart and 'soul** with a lot of energy and enthusiasm: *They threw themselves heart and soul into the project.* ▶ **your heart goes 'out to sb** used to

say that you feel a lot of sympathy for sb: *Our hearts go out to the families of the victims.* **sb's heart is in their 'mouth** somebody feels nervous or frightened about sth: *My heart was in my mouth as I opened the envelope.* **sb's heart is in the right 'place** used to say that sb's intentions are kind and sincere even though they sometimes do the wrong thing **your 'heart is not in sth** used to say that you are not very interested in or enthusiastic about sth **sb's heart 'leaps** used to say that sb has a sudden feeling of happiness or excitement **sb's heart misses/skips a 'beat** used to say that sb has a sudden feeling of fear, excitement, etc. **sb's heart 'sinks** used to say that sb suddenly feels sad or depressed about sth: *My heart sank when I saw how much work there was left.* ◇ *She watched him go with a sinking heart.* **in good 'heart** (*BrE*) happy and cheerful **in your 'heart (of 'hearts)** if you know sth **in your heart**, you have a strong feeling that it is true: *She knew in her heart of hearts that she was making the wrong decision.* **it does sb's 'heart good (to do sth)** it makes sb feel happy when they see or hear sth: *It does my heart good to see the old place being taken care of so well.* **let your 'heart rule your 'head** to act according to what you feel rather than to what you think is sensible **lose 'heart** to stop hoping for sth or trying to do sth because you no longer feel confident **lose your 'heart (to sb/sth)** (*formal*) to fall in love with sb/sth **a man/woman after your own 'heart** a man/woman who likes the same things or has the same opinions as you **my heart 'bleeds (for sb)** (*ironic*) used to say that you do not feel sympathy for sb: '*I have to go to Brazil on business.' 'My heart bleeds for you!'* **not have the 'heart (to do sth)** to be unable to do sth because you know that it will make sb sad or upset **off by 'heart** (*BrE*) = BY HEART *n.* **pour out/open your 'heart to sb** to tell sb all your problems, feelings, etc. **set your 'heart on sth | have your heart 'set on sth** to want sth very much **take 'heart (from sth)** to feel more positive about sth, especially when you thought that you had no chance of achieving sth: *The government can take heart from the latest opinion polls.* **take sth to 'heart** to be very upset by sth that sb says or does **tear/rip the 'heart out of sth** to destroy the most important part or aspect of sth **to your heart's con'tent** as much as you want: *a supervised play area where children can run around to their heart's content* **with all your 'heart/your whole 'heart** completely: *I hope with all my heart that things work out for you.* ⊃ more at ABSENCE, CHANGE *n.*, CROSS *v.*, EAT, ETCH, EYE *n.*, FIND *v.*, GOODNESS, HOME *n.*, INTEREST *n.*, PLACE *n.*, SICK *adj.*, SOB *v.*, STEAL *v.*, STRIKE *v.*, TEAR¹ *v.*, WARM *v.*, WAY *n.*, WEAR *v.*, WIN *v.*, YOUNG *adj.*
- *verb* (*symb.* ♥) (*informal*) ~ **sb/sth** to like sb/sth very much; to love sb/sth: *She wore an 'I heart Dad' T-shirt.* ◇ *I ♥ New York.*

**heart·ache** /'hɑːteɪk; *NAmE* 'hɑːrt-/ *noun* [U, C] a feeling of being very sad or worried: *The relationship caused her a great deal of heartache.* ◇ *the heartaches of being a parent*

**'heart attack** *noun* [C, U] a sudden serious medical condition in which the flow of blood to the heart is blocked, sometimes causing death: *She died of a massive heart attack.* ⊃ compare CORONARY THROMBOSIS

**heart·beat** /'hɑːtbiːt; *NAmE* 'hɑːrt-/ *noun* **1** [C, U] the movement or sound of the heart as it sends blood around the body: *a rapid/regular heartbeat* **2** [sing.] **the ~ of sth** an important feature of sth, that is responsible for making it what it is: *The candidate said that he understood the heartbeat of the Hispanic community in California.* **IDM** **a 'heartbeat away (from sth)** very close to sth **in a 'heartbeat** very quickly, without thinking about it: *If I was offered another job, I'd leave in a heartbeat.*

**heart·break** /'hɑːtbreɪk; *NAmE* 'hɑːrt-/ *noun* [U, C] a feeling of being very sad: *They suffered the heartbreak of losing a child through cancer.* ▶ **heart·break·ing** *adj.*: *a heartbreaking story* ◇ *It's heartbreaking to see him wasting his life like this.*

**heart·broken** /'hɑːtbrəʊkən; *NAmE* 'hɑːrt-/ *adj.* extremely sad because of sth that has happened **SYN** **broken-hearted**

---

735 **hearty**

**heart·burn** /'hɑːtbɜːn; *NAmE* 'hɑːrtbɜːrn/ *noun* [U] a pain that feels like sth burning in your chest caused by ACID coming back up from your stomach

**heart·en** /'hɑːtn; *NAmE* 'hɑːrtn/ *verb* [usually passive] to give sb hope: **be heartened (by sth)** *I was heartened by all the support I received.* **OPP** **dishearten** ▶ **heart·en·ing** *adj.*: *It is heartening to see the determination of these young people.*

**'heart failure** *noun* [U] a serious medical condition in which the heart does not work correctly

**heart·felt** /'hɑːtfelt; *NAmE* 'hɑːrt-/ *adj.* [usually before noun] showing strong feelings that are sincere **SYN** **sincere**: *a heartfelt apology/plea/sigh* ◇ *heartfelt sympathy/thanks*

**hearth** /hɑːθ; *NAmE* hɑːrθ/ *noun* **1** the floor at the bottom of a FIREPLACE (= the space for a fire in the wall of a room); the area in front of this: *A log fire roared in the open hearth.* ◇ *The cat dozed in its favourite spot on the hearth.* **2** (*literary*) home and family life: *a longing for hearth and home*

**heart·ily** /'hɑːtɪli; *NAmE* 'hɑːrt-/ *adv.* **1** with obvious pleasure and enthusiasm: *to laugh/sing/eat heartily* **2** in a way that shows that you feel strongly about sth: *I heartily agree with her on this.* **3** extremely: *heartily glad/relieved*

**heart·land** /'hɑːtlænd; *NAmE* 'hɑːrt-/ *noun* (also **heartlands** [pl.]) **1** the central part of a country or an area: *the great Russian heartlands* **2** an area that is important for a particular activity or political party: *the industrial heartland of Germany* ◇ *the traditional Tory heartland of Britain's boardrooms*

**heart·less** /'hɑːtləs; *NAmE* 'hɑːrt-/ *adj.* feeling no sympathy for other people **SYN** **cruel**: *What a heartless thing to say!* ▶ **heart·less·ly** *adv.* **heart·less·ness** *noun* [U]

**'heart rate** *noun* how fast your heart is beating

**'heart-rending** *adj.* [usually before noun] causing very sad feelings **SYN** **heartbreaking**: *a heart-rending story*

**'heart-searching** *noun* [U] the process of examining carefully your feelings or reasons for doing sth, especially when this is difficult or painful

**heart·sick** /'hɑːtsɪk; *NAmE* 'hɑːrt-/ *adj.* [not usually before noun] (*literary*) extremely unhappy or disappointed

**'heart-stopping** *adj.* [usually before noun] causing feelings of great excitement or worry: *For one heart-stopping moment she thought they were too late.*

**heart·strings** /'hɑːtstrɪŋz; *NAmE* 'hɑːrt-/ *noun* [pl.] **IDM** **pull, tug, etc. at sb's heartstrings** to cause strong feelings of love or sympathy in sb: *It's a sad story that really tugs at your heartstrings.*

**'heart-throb** *noun* (*informal*) (used especially in newspapers) a famous man, usually an actor or a singer, that a lot of women find attractive

**'heart-to-'heart** *noun* [usually sing.] a conversation in which two people talk honestly about their feelings and personal problems: *to have a heart-to-heart with sb* ▶ **heart-to-'heart** *adj.*: *a heart-to-heart talk*

**'heart-warming** *adj.* causing feelings of happiness and pleasure

**heart·wood** /'hɑːtwʊd; *NAmE* 'hɑːrt-/ *noun* [U] the hard older inner layers of the wood of a tree ⊃ compare SAPWOOD

**'heart-wrenching** *adj.* causing very sad feelings **SYN** **heart-rending**: *Their stories are heart-wrenching.* ◇ *a heart-wrenching decision/experience/image*

**hearty** /'hɑːti; *NAmE* 'hɑːrti/ *adj.*, *noun*
- *adj.* (**heart·ier**, **hearti·est**) **1** [usually before noun] showing friendly feelings for sb: *a hearty welcome* **2** (*sometimes disapproving*) loud, cheerful and full of energy: *a hearty and boisterous fellow* ◇ *a hearty voice* **3** [only before noun] (of a meal) large; making you feel full: *a hearty breakfast* **4** [only before noun] (of your APPETITE) large; making you want to eat a lot: *to have a hearty appetite* **5** [usually before noun] showing that you feel strongly about sth: *He nodded*

# heat

*his head in hearty agreement.* ◊ *Hearty congratulations to everyone involved.* ◊ *a hearty dislike of sth* ▶ **hearti·ness** *noun* [U] **IDM** see HALE

- *noun* (*pl.* **-ies**) (*BrE, sometimes disapproving*) a person who is loud, cheerful and full of energy, especially one who plays a lot of sport

## heat ⓘ A2 /hiːt/ *noun, verb*

- *noun*
- **BEING HOT/TEMPERATURE 1** A2 [U, sing.] the quality of being hot: *Heat rises.* ◊ *He could feel the heat of the sun on his back.* ◊ *Computers generate heat of their own.* ◊ *The fire gave out a fierce heat.* ⊃ see also WHITE HEAT **2** A2 [U] (*physics*) heat seen as a form of energy that is transferred from one object or substance to another as a result of a difference in temperature: *Being a metal, aluminium readily conducts heat.* **3** A2 [U, C, usually sing.] the level of temperature: *Test the heat of the water before getting in.* ◊ *Set the oven to a low/high/moderate heat.* ◊ *Add the rice and reduce the heat.* ⊃ see also BLOOD HEAT **4** A2 [U] hot weather; the hot conditions in a building, vehicle, etc: *You should not go out in the heat of the day* (= at the hottest time). ◊ *to suffer from the heat* ◊ *the summer/afternoon/midday heat* ◊ **in the ~** *They worked all afternoon in the intense heat.* ⊃ see also PRICKLY HEAT
- **FOR COOKING 5** A2 [U] a source of heat, especially one that you cook food on: *Return the pan to the heat and stir.* ◊ *Simmer the soup for 10 minutes then remove from the heat.* ◊ **over a… ~** *Place the roasting tray over a medium heat on your cooker or hob.*
- **IN BUILDING/ROOM 6** A2 [U] (*especially NAmE*) = HEATING: *The heat wasn't on and the house was freezing.*
- **IN SPICY FOOD 7** a spicy quality in food that makes your mouth feel as if it is burning: *Chilli peppers add taste and heat to food.*
- **STRONG FEELINGS 8** [U] strong feelings, especially of anger or excitement: *'No, I won't,' he said with heat in his voice.* ◊ *The chairman tried to take the heat out of the situation* (= to make people calmer). ◊ **In the heat of the moment** *she forgot what she wanted to say* (= because she was so angry or excited). ◊ *In the heat of the argument he said a lot of things he regretted later.*
- **PRESSURE 9** [U] pressure on sb to do or achieve sth: *The heat is on now that the election is only a week away.* ◊ *United turned up the heat on their opponents with a second goal.* ◊ *Can she* **take the heat** *of this level of competition?*
- **RACE 10** [C] one of a series of races or competitions, the winners of which then compete against each other in the next part of the competition: *a qualifying heat* ◊ *She won her heat.* ◊ *He did well in the heats; hopefully he'll do as well in the final.* ⊃ see also DEAD HEAT

**IDM** **be on ˈheat** (*BrE*) (*NAmE* **be in ˈheat**) (of a female MAMMAL) to be ready to have sex and produce young **if you can't stand the ˈheat (get out of the ˈkitchen)** (*informal*) used to tell sb to stop trying to do sth if they find it too difficult, especially in order to suggest that they are less able than other people

- *verb* A2 [T, I] ~ (**sth**) to make sth hot or warm; to become hot or warm: *Heat the oil and add the onions.* ◊ *The system produced enough energy to heat several thousand homes.* ◊ *While the oven is heating, roll out the dough.*

**PHRV** **ˌheat ˈup 1** to become hot or warm **SYN** WARM: *The oven takes a while to heat up.* **2** (*BrE also* **hot ˈup**) to become more exciting or to show an increase in activity: *The election contest is heating up.* **ˌheat sth↔ˈup** to make sth hot or warm **SYN** WARM: *Just heat up the food in the microwave.*

**heat·ed** /ˈhiːtɪd/ *adj.* **1** (of a person or discussion) full of anger and excitement: *a heated argument/debate* ◊ *She became very heated.* **2** (of a room, building, etc.) made warmer using a heater: *a heated swimming pool* ◊ *centrally heated homes* **OPP** **unheated** ▶ **heat·ed·ly** *adv.*: *'You had no right!' she said heatedly.*

**heat·er** /ˈhiːtə(r)/ *noun* a machine used for making air or water warmer: *a gas heater* ◊ *a water heater* ⊃ see also IMMERSION HEATER, SPACE HEATER

**ˈheat exchanger** *noun* (*specialist*) a device for making heat pass between a solid object and a liquid or gas, or between two liquids/gases, without allowing the liquids/gases to mix

**heath** /hiːθ/ *noun* [C, U] a large area of open land that is not used for farming and is covered with rough grass and other small wild plants

**hea·then** /ˈhiːðn/ *noun, adj.*

- *noun* (*old-fashioned, offensive*) **1** used by people who have a strong religious belief as a way of referring to a person who has no religion or who believes in a religion that is not one of the world's main religions: *He set out to convert the heathen* (= people who are heathens). **2** used to refer to a person who shows lack of education
- *adj.* (*old-fashioned, offensive*) connected with heathens: *heathen gods*

**hea·ther** /ˈheðə(r)/ *noun* [U] a low wild plant with small purple, pink or white flowers, that grows on hills and areas of wild open land (= MOORLAND and HEATHLAND)

**heath·land** /ˈhiːθlənd/ *NAmE* -lænd/ *noun* [U] (*also* **heath·lands** [pl.]) a large area of heath

**Heath Rob·in·son** /ˌhiːθ ˈrɒbɪnsən/ *NAmE* ˈrɑːb-/ (*BrE*) (*NAmE* **Rube ˈGold·berg**) *adj.* [only before noun] (*humorous*) (of machines and devices) having a very complicated design, especially when used to perform a very simple task; not practical: *a Heath Robinson contraption*

**ˈheat index** *noun* [sing.] (*NAmE*) a measure of temperature and the effects of HUMIDITY combined. When the level of humidity is high, the air feels hotter and more uncomfortable.

**heat·ing** ⓘ B1 /ˈhiːtɪŋ/ (*especially BrE*) (*also* **heat** *especially in NAmE*) *noun* [U] the process of supplying heat to a room or building; a system used to do this: *to put/turn the heating on* ◊ *What type of heating do you have?* ◊ *a solar/gas-fired heating system* ⊃ see also CENTRAL HEATING

**ˈheat map** *noun* a diagram that uses different colours, or different shades of the same colour, to show different levels of activity: *This heat map of crime data shows where the crime hotspots are.*

**heat·proof** /ˈhiːtpruːf/ *adj.* that cannot be damaged by heat: *a heatproof dish*

**ˈheat-resistant** *adj.* not easily damaged by heat

**ˈheat-seeking** *adj.* [only before noun] (of a weapon) that moves towards the heat coming from the aircraft, etc. that it is intended to hit and destroy: *heat-seeking missiles*

**heat·stroke** /ˈhiːtstrəʊk/ *noun* [U] an illness with a high temperature and often loss of CONSCIOUSNESS, caused by being in too great a heat for too long ⊃ compare SUNSTROKE

**ˈheat·wave** /ˈhiːtweɪv/ *noun* a period of unusually hot weather

**heave** /hiːv/ *verb, noun*

- *verb* **1** [T, I] to lift, pull or throw sb/sth very heavy with one great effort: *~ sth/sb/yourself + adv./prep.* *I managed to heave the trunk down the stairs.* ◊ *They heaved the body overboard.* ◊ *+ adv./prep. We all heaved on the rope.* **2** [I] to rise up and down with strong, regular movements: *The boat heaved beneath them.* ◊ *~ with sth Her shoulders heaved with laughter.* **3** [T] *~ a sigh, etc.* to make a sound slowly and often with effort: *We all heaved a sigh of relief.* **4** [I] to experience the tight feeling in your stomach that you get before you VOMIT **SYN** RETCH: *The thought of it makes me heave.*

**IDM** **ˌheave into ˈsight/ˈview** (*formal*) (especially of ships) to appear, especially when moving gradually closer from a long way off: *A ship hove into sight.* **HELP** **Hove** is usually used for the past tense and past participle in this idiom.

**PHRV** **ˈheave to** (*specialist*) if a ship or its crew (= the people sailing it) **heave to**, the ship stops moving **HELP** **Hove** is usually used for the past tense and past participle in this phrasal verb.

- *noun* **1** [C] an act of lifting, pulling or throwing: *With a mighty heave he lifted the sack onto the truck.* **2** [U] (*especially literary*) a rising and falling movement: *the steady heave of the sea*

**heave-ho** /ˌhiːv ˈhəʊ/ noun [sing.]
- **IDM** **give sb the (old) heave-ho** (informal) to dismiss sb from their job; to end a relationship with sb

**heaven** ⓞ B2 /ˈhevn/ noun **1** B2 (also **Heaven**) [U] (used without *the*) (in some religions) the place believed to be the home of God where good people go when they die, sometimes imagined to be in the sky: *the kingdom of heaven* ◊ *I feel like I've died and gone to heaven.* ◊ **in~** *I told her Daddy was in heaven with God.* **2** B2 [U, C] (informal) a place or situation in which you are very happy: *This isn't exactly my idea of heaven!* ◊ **in~** *Shopping is my favourite pastime, so I was in heaven.* ◊ **it is~doing sth** *It was heaven being away from the office for a week.* ◊ *The island is truly a heaven on earth.* **3 the heavens** [pl.] (literary) the sky: *Four tall trees stretched up to the heavens.*
- **IDM** **(Good) ˈHeavens! | ˌHeavens aˈbove!** (informal) used to show that you are surprised or annoyed: *Good heavens, what are you doing?* **the heavens ˈopen** it begins to rain heavily **ˌmade in ˈheaven** (especially of a marriage or other relationship) seeming to be perfect ⊃ more at FOR-BID, GOD, HELP v., HIGH adj., KNOW v., MOVE v., NAME n., SEVENTH ordinal number, THANK

**heav·en·ly** /ˈhevnli/ adj. **1** [only before noun] connected with heaven: *our heavenly Father* (= God) ◊ *the heavenly kingdom* **2** [only before noun] connected with the sky: *heavenly bodies* (= the sun, moon, stars and planets) **3** (informal) very pleasant **SYN** wonderful: *a heavenly morning/feeling* ◊ *This place is heavenly.*

**ˈheaven-sent** adj. [usually before noun] happening unexpectedly and at exactly the right time

**heav·en·ward** /ˈhevnwəd/; NAmE -wərd/ (also **heav·en·wards**) adv. (literary) towards heaven or the sky: *to cast/raise your eyes heavenward* (= to show you are annoyed or impatient)

**heav·ily** ⓞ B1 /ˈhevɪli/ adv. **1** B1 to a great degree; in large amounts: *It was raining heavily.* ◊ *to drink heavily* ◊ *heavily armed police* (= carrying a lot of weapons) ◊ *a heavily pregnant woman* (= one whose baby is nearly ready to be born) ◊ *They are both heavily involved in politics.* ◊ *He relies heavily on his parents.* ◊ *She has been heavily criticized in the press.* **2** with a lot of force or effort: *She fell heavily to the ground.* **3 ~built** (of a person) with a large, solid and strong body **4** slowly and loudly: *She was now breathing heavily.* **5** in a slow way that sounds as though you are worried or sad: *He sighed heavily.* **6** in a way that makes you feel uncomfortable or anxious: *Silence hung heavily in the room.* ◊ *The burden of guilt weighed heavily on his mind.* **7 ~loaded/laden** full of or loaded with heavy things: *a heavily loaded van*

**heav·ing** /ˈhiːvɪŋ/ adj. [not before noun] **~(with sb/sth)** full of sb/sth: *The place was heaving with journalists.*

**heavy** ⓞ A2 /ˈhevi/ adj., noun, adv.
- adj. (**heav·ier**, **heavi·est**)
- • WEIGHING A LOT **1** A2 weighing a lot; difficult to lift or move: *a heavy weight/load* ◊ *She was struggling with a heavy suitcase.* ◊ *My brother is much heavier than me.* ◊ *He tried to push the heavy door open.* ◊ (especially NAmE) *Many young people today are too heavy* (= fat). ◊ (figurative) *Her father carried a heavy burden of responsibility.* **OPP** light ⊃ see also TOP-HEAVY
- • WORSE THAN USUAL **2** B1 more or worse than usual in amount, degree, etc: *the noise of heavy traffic* ◊ *heavy rain/rainfall/snow* ◊ *the effects of heavy drinking* ◊ *There was heavy fighting in the capital last night.* ◊ *She spoke with heavy irony.* **OPP** light
- • DRINKER/SMOKER/SLEEPER **3** B1 [only before noun] (of a person) doing the thing mentioned more, or more deeply, than usual: *a heavy drinker/smoker* ◊ *a heavy sleeper*
- • SOLID **4** (of sb/sth's appearance or structure) large and solid: *big, dark rooms full of heavy furniture* **OPP** delicate
- • MATERIAL **5** (of the material or substance that sth is made of) thick: *heavy curtains* ◊ *a heavy coat* **OPP** light
- • FULL OF STH **6 ~with sth** (literary) full of or loaded with sth: *trees heavy with apples* ◊ *The air was heavy with the scent of flowers.* ◊ *His voice was heavy with sarcasm.*
- • MACHINES **7** [usually before noun] (of machines, vehicles or weapons) large and powerful: *a wide range of engines and heavy machinery/equipment* ◊ *heavy lorries/trucks*
- • BUSY **8** [usually before noun] involving a lot of work or activity; very busy: *a heavy schedule* ◊ *She'd had a heavy day.*
- • WORK **9** hard, especially because it requires a lot of physical strength: *heavy lifting* ◊ *A gardener comes in to do the heavy work for me.*
- • FALL/HIT **10** falling or hitting sth with a lot of force: *a heavy fall/blow*
- • MEAL/FOOD **11** large in amount or very solid: *a heavy lunch/dinner/meal* **OPP** light
- • ARMY **12** [only before noun] (of soldiers) carrying heavy weapons: *the heavy infantry/cavalry* **OPP** light
- • SOUND **13** (of a sound that sb makes) loud and deep: *heavy breathing* ◊ *a heavy groan/sigh*
- • USING A LOT **14 ~on sth** (informal) using a lot of sth: *Older cars are heavy on gas.* ◊ *Don't go so heavy on the garlic.*
- • SERIOUS/DIFFICULT **15** (usually disapproving) (of a book, programme, style, etc.) serious; difficult to understand or enjoy: *We found the play very heavy.* ◊ *The discussion got a little heavy.*
- • SEA/OCEAN **16** dangerous because of big waves, etc: *strong winds and heavy seas*
- • AIR/WEATHER **17** hot and without enough fresh air, in a way that feels unpleasant: *It's very heavy—I think there'll be a storm.*
- • SOIL **18** wet, sticky and difficult to dig or to move over
- • STRICT **19** (of a person) very strict and severe: *Don't be so heavy on her—it wasn't her fault.* ▶ **heavi·ness** noun [U]
- **IDM** **get ˈheavy** (informal) to become very serious, because strong feelings are involved: *They started shouting at me. It got very heavy.* **heavy ˈgoing** used to describe sb/sth that is difficult to deal with or understand: *She's a bit heavy going.* ◊ *I found the course rather heavy going.* **heavy ˈhand** a way of doing sth or of treating people that is much stronger and less sensitive than it needs to be: *the heavy hand of management* **a heavy ˈheart** a very sad feeling: *She left her children behind with a heavy heart.* **the ˈheavy mob/brigade** (BrE, informal) a group of strong, often violent people employed to do sth such as protect sb **a heavy ˈsilence/ˈatmosphere** a situation when people do not say anything, but feel embarrassed or uncomfortable **make heavy ˈweather of sth** to seem to find sth more difficult or complicated than it needs to be ⊃ more at CROSS n., TOLL n.
- noun (pl. -**ies**) **1** [C] (informal) a large strong man whose job is to protect a person or place, often using violence **2** [U] (ScotE) strong beer, especially bitter: *a pint of heavy*
- adv.
- **IDM** **hang/lie ˈheavy 1 ~(on/in sth)** (of a feeling or sth in the air) to be very easy to notice in a particular place in a way that is unpleasant: *Smoke lay heavy on the far side of the water.* ◊ *Despair hangs heavy in the stifling air.* **2 ~on sb/sth** to cause sb/sth to feel uncomfortable or anxious: *The crime lay heavy on her conscience.*

**heavy ˈcream** (NAmE) (BrE **double cream**) noun [U] thick cream that contains a lot of fat and can be mixed so that it is no longer liquid ⊃ compare LIGHT CREAM

**heavy-ˈduty** adj. [only before noun] **1** not easily damaged and therefore suitable for hard physical work or to be used all the time: *a heavy-duty carpet* **2** (informal, especially NAmE) very serious or great in quantity: *I think you need some heavy-duty advice.*

**ˌheavy ˈgoods vehicle** noun (BrE) = HGV

**heavy-ˈhanded** adj. (disapproving) **1** not showing any understanding of the feelings of other people: *a heavy-handed approach* **2** using unnecessary force: *heavy-handed police methods* **3** (of a person) using too much of sth in a way that can cause damage: *Don't be too heavy-handed with the salt.*

**ˌheavy ˈhitter** (also **ˌbig ˈhitter**) noun (informal) a person who is successful and has a lot of influence: *Hollywood/industry/political heavy hitters*

# heavy industry

**heavy in'dustry** *noun* [U, C] industry that uses large machines to produce metal, vehicles, etc. ⊃ compare LIGHT INDUSTRY

**heavy 'lifting** *noun* [U] **1** the act of lifting heavy objects **2** hard or difficult work: *The film still has a lot of heavy lifting to do to make $40 million.* ◊ *Much of the heavy lifting in this report was done by the expert writers.*

**heavy 'metal** *noun* **1** [U] a type of rock music with a very strong beat played very loud on electric guitars, often using violent or strange language or ideas **2** [C] (*specialist*) a metal that has a very high DENSITY (= the relation of its weight to its volume), such as gold or LEAD

**heavy 'petting** *noun* [U] sexual activity that does not involve full SEXUAL INTERCOURSE

**heavy-set** /ˌhevɪˈset/ *adj.* having a broad heavy body **SYN** thickset

**heavy 'water** *noun* [U] (*chemistry*) water in which HYDROGEN is replaced by DEUTERIUM, making deuterium OXIDE. It is used in certain types of nuclear REACTORS.

**heavy·weight** /ˈheviweɪt/ *noun* **1** [U, C] a weight in BOXING and other sports, the heaviest class in normal use, in BOXING usually 81 KILOGRAMS or more; a BOXER or other competitor in this class: *a heavyweight champion* ⊃ see also LIGHT HEAVYWEIGHT **2** [C] a person or thing that weighs more than is usual **3** [C] a very important person, organization or thing that influences others: *a political heavyweight* ◊ *a heavyweight journal*

**He·bra·ic** /hɪˈbreɪɪk/ *adj.* of or connected with the Hebrew language or people: *Hebraic poetry*

**He·brew** /ˈhiːbruː/ *noun* **1** a member of an ancient race of people living in what is now Israel and Palestine. Their writings and traditions form the basis of the Jewish religion. **2** the language traditionally used by the Hebrew people **3** a modern form of the Hebrew language which is the official language of modern Israel ⊃ compare YIDDISH ▶ **He·brew** *adj.*

**heck** /hek/ *exclamation, noun* (*informal*) used to show that you are slightly annoyed or surprised; used to emphasize sth: *Oh heck, I'm going to be late!* ◊ **a ~ of a sth** *We had to wait a heck of a long time!* ◊ *It was a heck of a lot of fun.* ◊ *Who the heck are you?*
**IDM** **for the 'heck of it** (*informal*) just for pleasure rather than for a reason **what the 'heck!** (*informal*) used to say that you are going to do sth that you know you should not do: *It means I'll be late for work but what the heck!*

**heckle** /ˈhekl/ *verb* [T, I] **~ (sb)** to interrupt a speaker at a public meeting by shouting out questions or rude remarks **SYN** barrack: *He was booed and heckled throughout his speech.* ▶ **heck·ler** /-klə(r)/ *noun* **heck·ling** *noun* [U]

**hec·tare** /ˈhekteə(r), -tɑː(r); NAmE -ter/ *noun* (*abbr.* **ha**) a unit for measuring an area of land; 10 000 square metres or about 2.5 ACRES

**hec·tic** /ˈhektɪk/ *adj.* very busy; full of activity: *to lead a hectic life* ◊ *a hectic schedule*

**hec·to·litre** (*US* **hec·to·liter**) /ˈhektəliːtə(r)/ *noun* (*abbr.* **hl**) a unit for measuring volume; 100 LITRES

**hec·tor** /ˈhektə(r)/ *verb* **~ sb** (**+ speech**) (*formal*) to try to make sb do sth by talking or behaving in an aggressive way **SYN** bully ▶ **hec·tor·ing** *adj.*: *a hectoring tone of voice*

**he'd** /hiːd/ *short form* **1** he had **HELP** He'd is only used when *had* is an auxiliary verb: *He'd just left school.* When *had* is the main verb, use the full form: *I'm glad he had a good time.* ◊ *I'm glad he'd a good time.* **2** he would

**hedge** /hedʒ/ *noun, verb*
■ *noun* **1** a row of bushes or small trees growing close together, usually along the edge of a field, garden or road: *a privet hedge* **2 ~ against sth** a way of protecting yourself against the loss of sth, especially money: *to buy gold as a hedge against inflation*
■ *verb* **1** [I] to avoid giving a direct answer to a question or promising to support a particular idea, etc: *Just answer 'yes' or 'no'—and stop hedging.* **2** [T] **~ sth** to put a hedge around a field, etc. **3** [T, usually passive] (*formal*) to surround or limit sb/sth: **be hedged (with sth)** *His religious belief was always hedged with doubt.* ◊ **be hedged around (with sth)** *Their offer was hedged around with all sorts of conditions.*
**IDM** **hedge your 'bets** to reduce the risk of losing or making a mistake by supporting more than one side in a competition, an argument, etc., or by having several choices available to you
**PHRV** **'hedge against sth** to do sth to protect yourself against problems, especially against losing money: *a way of hedging against currency risks* **hedge sb/sth↔'in** to surround sb/sth with sth **SYN** **hem sb/sth in**: *The cathedral is now hedged in by other buildings.* ◊ (*figurative*) *Married life made him feel hedged in and restless.*

**'hedge fund** *noun* an investment fund involving a group of people who take high risks with their investments in order to try and make a lot of money

**hedge·hog** /ˈhedʒhɒɡ; NAmE -hɔːɡ/ *noun* a small brown animal with stiff parts like needles (called SPINES) covering its back. Hedgehogs are NOCTURNAL (= active mostly at night) and can roll into a ball to defend themselves when they are attacked.

**hedge·row** /ˈhedʒrəʊ/ *noun* (especially in the UK) a line of bushes and small trees planted along the edge of a field or road

**he·don·ism** /ˈhiːdənɪzəm, ˈhiːd-/ *noun* [U] the belief that pleasure is the most important thing in life ▶ **he·don·is·tic** /ˌhedəˈnɪstɪk, ˌhiːd-/ *adj.*

**he·don·ist** /ˈhiːdənɪst, ˈhiːd-/ *noun* a person who believes that pleasure is the most important thing in life

**the heebie-jeebies** /ðə ˌhiːbi ˈdʒiːbiz/ *noun* [pl.] (*old-fashioned, informal*) a feeling of nervous fear or worry

**heed** /hiːd/ *verb, noun*
■ *verb* **~ sb/sth** (*formal*) to pay careful attention to sb's advice or warning **SYN** notice
■ *noun* [U]
**IDM** **give/pay 'heed (to sb/sth)** | **take 'heed (of sb/sth)** (*formal*) to pay careful attention to sb/sth

**heed·less** /ˈhiːdləs/ *adj.* [not usually before noun] **~ (of sb/sth)** (*formal*) not paying careful attention to sb/sth ▶ **heed·less·ly** *adv.*

**hee-haw** /ˈhiː hɔː/ *noun* the way of writing the sound made by a DONKEY

**heel** /hiːl/ *noun, verb*
■ *noun*
- PART OF FOOT **1** [C] the back part of the foot below the ankle: *on your heels* *She took a potato from the fire and sat back on her heels.* ⊃ see also BACK-HEEL ▶ VISUAL VOCAB page V1
- PART OF SOCK/SHOE **2** [C] the part of a sock, etc. that covers the heel **3** [C] the raised part on the bottom of a shoe, boot, etc. that makes the shoe, etc. higher at the back: *shoes with a low/high heel* ◊ *a stiletto heel* ◊ *The sergeant clicked his heels and walked out.* ⊃ compare SOLE
- -HEELED **4** (in adjectives) having the type of heel mentioned: *high-heeled shoes* ⊃ see also WELL HEELED
- SHOES **5** **heels** [pl.] a pair of women's shoes that have high heels: *She doesn't often wear heels.* ⊃ see also KITTEN HEELS
- PART OF HAND **6** [C] **~ of your hand/palm** the raised part of the inside of the hand where it joins the WRIST
- UNPLEASANT MAN **7** [C] (*old-fashioned, informal*) a man who is unpleasant to other people and cannot be trusted ⊃ see also ACHILLES HEEL, DOWN AT HEEL
**IDM** **at/on sb's 'heels** following closely behind sb: *He fled from the stadium with the police at his heels.* **bring sb/sth to 'heel** **1** to force sb to obey you and accept discipline **2** to make a dog come close to you **come to 'heel** **1** (of a person) to agree to obey sb and accept their orders **2** (of a dog) to come close to the person who has called it **hard/hot on sb's/sth's 'heels** very close behind sb/sth; very soon after sth: *He turned and fled with Peter hot on his heels.* ◊ *News of rising unemployment followed hard on the heels of falling export figures.* **take to your 'heels** to run away from sb/sth **turn/spin on your 'heel** to turn

around suddenly so that you are facing in the opposite direction **under the ˈheel of sb** (*literary*) completely controlled by sb ⊃ more at COOL *v.*, DIG *v.*, DRAG *v.*, HEAD *n.*, KICK *v.*, TREAD *v.*
- *verb*
- REPAIR SHOE **1** [T] ~ **sth** to repair the heel of a shoe, etc.
- OF BOAT **2** [I] ~ **(over)** to lean over to one side: *The boat heeled over in the strong wind.*

▼ HOMOPHONES

**heal** • **heel** • **he'll** /hiːl/
- **heal** *verb*: *Salt can heal wounds.*
- **heel** *noun*: *Her heel caught in the stairs and she tumbled down.*
- **he'll** short form he will: *He'll arrive in a minute!*

**heft** /heft/ *verb*, *noun*
- *verb* **1** ~ **sth** (+ **adv./prep.**) to lift or carry sth heavy from one position to another: *The two men hefted the box into the car.* **2** ~ **sth** to lift or hold sth in order to estimate its weight: *Anna took the old sword and hefted it in her hands.*
- *noun* [U] (*especially NAmE*) **1** the weight of sb/sth: *She was surprised by the sheer heft of the package.* **2** ability or influence: *Her performance lacks emotional heft.*

**hefty** /ˈhefti/ *adj.* (**heft·i·er**, **hefti·est**) **1** (of a person or an object) big and heavy: *Her brothers were both hefty men in their forties.* **2** (*informal*) (of an amount of money) large; larger than usual or expected: *They sold it easily and made a hefty profit.* **3** using a lot of force: *He gave the door a hefty kick.* ▶ **heft·ily** /-tɪli/ *adv.*

**he·gem·ony** /hɪˈdʒeməni; *BrE also* ˈhedʒɪməni; *NAmE also* ˈhedʒɪməʊni/ *noun* [U, C] (*pl.* **-ies**) (*formal*) control by one country, organization, etc. over other countries, etc. with·in a particular group ▶ **hege·mon·ic** /ˌhedʒɪˈmɒnɪk; *NAmE* -ˈmɑːn-/ *adj.*: *hegemonic control*

**He·gira** (*also* **Hej·ira**) /ˈhedʒɪrə, hɪˈdʒaɪrə/ (*also* **Hijra**) *noun* [sing.] **1** (*usually* **the Hegira**) the occasion when Muhammad left Mecca to go to Medina in AD622 **2** the period that began at this time; the Muslim ERA

**heifer** /ˈhefə(r)/ *noun* a young female cow that has not yet had a CALF or has had only one calf

# **height** ⓘ A2 /haɪt/ *noun*
- MEASUREMENT **1** A2 [U, C] the measurement of how tall a person or thing is: *Height: 210 mm. Width: 57 mm. Length: 170 mm.* ◇ *Please state your height and weight.* ◇ *to be of medium/average height* ◇ **in** ~ *It is almost two metres in height.* ◇ **of sb/sth** *You can adjust the height of the chair.* ◇ *The plant can reach a height of over six feet.* ◇ *The table is available in several different heights.* ⊃ picture at DIMENSION
- BEING TALL **2** A2 [U] the quality of being tall or high: *The height of the mountain did not discourage them.* ◇ *His great height was rather a handicap.*
- DISTANCE ABOVE GROUND **3** A2 [C, U] a particular distance above the ground: *The aircraft was gaining height.* ◇ **at a** ~ **of sth** *The plane flew at a height of 3000 metres.* ◇ **at** ~ *to be at shoulder/chest/waist height* ◇ **from a …** ~ *The stone was dropped from a great height.*
- HIGH PLACE **4** B1 [C, usually pl.] (often used in names) a high place or position: *Brooklyn Heights* ◇ *He doesn't have a head for heights* (= is afraid of high places). ◇ *a fear of heights* ◇ **from a** ~ *The pattern of the ancient fields is clearly visible from a height.*
- STRONGEST POINT/LEVEL **5** B2 [sing.] the point when sth is at its strongest or best: *The fire reached its height around 2 a.m.* ◇ **at its** ~ *The crisis was at its height in May.* ◇ **at the** ~ **of sth** *She is still at the height of her powers.* ◇ **in the** ~ **of sth** *I wouldn't go there in the height of summer.* **6 heights** [pl.] a better or greater level of sth; a situation where sth is very good: *Their success had reached new heights.*
- EXTREME EXAMPLE **7** [sing.] ~ **of sth** an extreme example of a particular quality: *It would be the height of folly* (= very stupid) *to change course now.* ◇ *She was dressed in the height of fashion.*

IDM **draw yourself up/rise to your full ˈheight** to stand straight and tall in order to show that you are determined, powerful or important ⊃ more at DIZZY

**height·en** ⓘ + B1 /ˈhaɪtn/ *verb* [I, T] if a feeling or an effect **heightens**, or sth **heightens** it, it becomes stronger or increases SYN **intensify**: *Tension has heightened after the recent bomb attack.* ◇ ~ **sth** *The campaign is intended to heighten public awareness of the disease.*

**hein·ous** /ˈheɪnəs; *BrE also* ˈhiːn-/ *adj.* [usually before noun] (*formal*) morally very bad: *a heinous crime* ▶ **hein·ous·ly** *adv.* **hein·ous·ness** *noun* [U]

**heir** /eə(r); *NAmE* er/ *noun* HELP Use **an**, not **a**, before **heir**. **1** ~ **(to sth)** | ~ **(of sb)** a person who has the legal right to receive sb's property, money or title when that person dies: *to be heir to a large fortune* ◇ *the heir to the throne* (= the person who will be the next king or queen) ⊃ WORD-FINDER NOTE at FAMILY **2** a person who is thought to continue the work or a tradition started by sb else: *the president's political heirs*

▼ HOMOPHONES

**air** • **heir** /eə(r); *NAmE* er/
- **air** *noun*: *I kicked the ball high into the air.*
- **air** *verb*: *I opened the window to air the room.*
- **heir** *noun*: *He left most of his property to his eldest son and heir.*

ˈ**heir apˈparent** *noun* (*pl.* **heirs apparent**) **1** ~ **(to sth)** an HEIR whose legal right to receive sb's property, money or title cannot be taken away because it is impossible for sb with a stronger claim to be born ⊃ see also HEIR PRESUMPTIVE **2** a person who is expected to take the job of sb when that person leaves

**heir·ess** /ˈeəres, ˈeərəs; *NAmE* ˈerəs/ *noun* ~ **(to sth)** a female heir, especially one who has received or will receive a large amount of money HELP Use **an**, not **a**, before **heiress**.

**heir·loom** /ˈeəluːm; *NAmE* ˈerl-/ *noun*, *adj.*
- *noun* a valuable object that has belonged to the same family for many years: *a family heirloom* HELP Use **an**, not **a**, before **heirloom**.
- *adj.* [only before noun] (*especially NAmE*) **heirloom** plants are varieties that were commonly grown in the past but are no longer grown as commercial crops

ˈ**heir preˈsumptive** *noun* (*pl.* **heirs presumptive**) an HEIR who may lose his or her legal right to receive sb's property, money or title if sb with a stronger claim is born ⊃ see also HEIR APPARENT

**heist** /haɪst/ *noun*, *verb*
- *noun* (*informal*) an act of stealing sth valuable from a shop or bank SYN **robbery**: *a bank heist*
- *verb* ~ **sth** (*informal, especially NAmE*) to steal sth valuable from a shop or bank

**Hej·ira** = HEGIRA

**held** /held/ past tense, past part. of HOLD

**hel·ic·al** /ˈhelɪkl, ˈhiːl-/ *adj.* (*specialist*) like a HELIX

**hel·ices** /ˈhiːlɪsiːz/ *pl.* of HELIX

# **heli·cop·ter** ⓘ B1 /ˈhelɪkɒptə(r); *NAmE* -kɑːp-/ (*also informal* **cop·ter**, **chop·per**) *noun* an aircraft without wings that has large BLADES (= long flat parts) on top that go round. It can fly straight up from the ground and can also stay in one position in the air: *a police/rescue helicopter* ◇ **by** ~ *He was rushed to the hospital by helicopter.* ◇ *a helicopter pilot* ▶ WORDFINDER NOTE at AIRCRAFT

ˈ**helicopter parent** *noun* (*often disapproving*) a parent who pays extremely close attention to their child's education, problems, etc. and often makes decisions for the child

**he·lio·cen·tric** /ˌhiːliəˈsentrɪk/ *adj.* (*astronomy*) with the sun as the centre: *the heliocentric model of the solar system*

**he·lio·trope** /ˈhiːliətrəʊp/ *noun* **1** [C, U] a garden plant with pale purple flowers with a sweet smell **2** [U] a pale purple colour

# helipad

**heli·pad** /ˈhelɪpæd/ (*also* **ˈhelicopter pad**) *noun* a small area where helicopters can take off and land

**heli·port** /ˈhelɪpɔːt; *NAmE* -pɔːrt/ *noun* a place where helicopters take off and land

**heli-skiing** /ˈheli skiːɪŋ/ *noun* [U] the sport of flying in a helicopter to a place where there is a lot of snow on a mountain in order to ski there

**he·lium** /ˈhiːliəm/ *noun* [U] (*symb.* **He**) a chemical element. Helium is a very light gas that does not burn, often used to fill BALLOONS and to freeze food.

**helix** /ˈhiːlɪks/ *noun* (*pl.* **helices** /-lɪsiːz/) a shape like a SPIRAL or a line curved around a CYLINDER or CONE ⇨ see also DOUBLE HELIX

helices

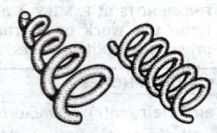

**hell** 🔤 **B2** /hel/ *noun*
**1** 🔤 **B2** [sing.] (*usually* **Hell**) (used without *a* or *the*) (in some religions) the place believed to be the home of DEVILS and where bad people go after death: *He was terrified of going to hell when he died.* ◇ *They were threatened with spending eternity in hell.* **2** 🔤 **B2** [U, sing.] a very unpleasant experience or situation in which people suffer very much: *The last three months have been hell.* ◇ *He went through hell during the trial.* ◇ *Her parents made her life hell.* ◇ *Being totally alone is my idea of hell on earth.* ◇ **in ~** *For the last few weeks my whole family has been in hell because of this.* ◇ **it is ~ doing sth** *It was hell getting through airport security.* ⇨ see also LIVING HELL **3** [U] a swear word that some people use when they are annoyed or surprised or to emphasize sth. Its use is offensive to some people: *Oh hell, I've burned the pan.* ◇ *What the hell do you think you are doing?* ◇ *Go to hell!* ◇ *I can't really afford it, but, what the hell* (= it doesn't matter)*, I'll get it anyway.* ◇ *He's as guilty as hell.* ◇ (*NAmE*) *'Do you understand?' 'Hell, no. I don't.'*
IDM **all ˈhell broke loose** (*informal*) suddenly there was a lot of noise, arguing, fighting, etc.: *There was a loud bang and then all hell broke loose.* **beat/kick (the) ˈhell out of sb/sth | knock ˈhell out of sb/sth** (*informal*) to hit sb/sth very hard: *He was a dirty player and loved to kick hell out of the opposition.* **(just) for the ˈhell of it** (*informal*) just for fun; for no real reason: *They stole the car just for the hell of it.* **from ˈhell** (*informal*) used to describe a very unpleasant person or thing; the worst that you can imagine: *They are the neighbours from hell.* **get the ˈhell out (of …)** (*informal*) to leave a place very quickly: *Let's get the hell out of here.* **give sb ˈhell** (*informal*) **1** to make life unpleasant for sb: *He used to give his mother hell when he was a teenager.* ◇ *My new shoes are giving me hell* (= are hurting me)*.* **2** to shout or speak angrily to sb: *Dad will give us hell when he sees that mess.* **go to hell in a ˈhandbasket** (*NAmE, informal*) = GO TO THE DOGS at DOG *n.* **hell for ˈleather** (*BrE, old-fashioned, informal*) as quickly as possible: *to ride hell for leather* **hell hath no ˈfury (like a woman ˈscorned)** used to refer to sb, usually a woman, who has reacted very angrily to sth, especially the fact that her husband or partner has been UNFAITHFUL **a/one hell of a … | a/one helluva …** /ˈheləvə/ (*slang*) used to give emphasis to what a person is saying: *The firm was in a hell of a mess when he took over.* ◇ *It must have been one hell of a party.* ◇ *That's one helluva big house you've got.* **(come) hell or high ˈwater** despite any difficulties: *I was determined to go, come hell or high water.* **Hell's ˈteeth** (*BrE, old-fashioned, informal*) used to express anger or surprise **like ˈhell 1** (*informal*) used for emphasis: *She worked like hell for her exams.* ◇ *My broken finger hurt like hell.* **2** (*informal*) used when you are refusing permission or saying that sth is not true: *'I'm coming with you.' 'Like hell you are* (= you certainly are not)*.'* **play (merry) ˈhell with sth/sb** (*BrE, informal*) to affect sth/sb badly **scare, annoy, etc. the ˈhell out of sb** (*informal*) to frighten, annoy, etc. sb very much **to ˈhell and back** (*informal*) used to say that sb has been through a difficult situation: *We'd been to hell and back together and we were still good friends.* **to ˈhell with sb/sth** (*informal*) used to express anger or dislike and to say that you no longer care about sb/sth and will take no notice of them: *'To hell with him,' she thought, 'I'm leaving.'* ⇨ more at BAT *n.*, BUG *v.*, CAT, GET, HOPE *n.*, PAY *v.*, RAISE *v.*, ROAD, SNOWBALL *n.*

**he'll** /hiːl/ short form he will ⇨ HOMOPHONES at HEEL

**hell-ˈbent** *adj.* **~ on sth/on doing sth** determined to do sth even though the results may be bad: *He seems hell-bent on drinking himself to death.*

**hel·le·bore** /ˈhelɪbɔː(r)/ *noun* a poisonous plant with divided leaves and large green, white or purple flowers

**Hel·len·ic** /heˈlenɪk, -ˈliːn-/ *adj.* of or connected with ancient or modern Greece

**Hel·len·is·tic** /ˌhelɪˈnɪstɪk/ *adj.* of or connected with the Greek history, language and culture of the 4th–1st centuries BC

**hell·fire** /ˈhelfaɪə(r)/ *noun* [U] the fires that are believed by some religious people to burn in hell, where bad people go to be punished after they die

**hell·hole** /ˈhelhəʊl/ *noun* (*informal*) a very unpleasant place

**hel·lion** /ˈheliən/ *noun* (*NAmE, informal*) a badly behaved child who annoys other people

**hell·ish** /ˈhelɪʃ/ *adj.* (*especially BrE, informal*) extremely unpleasant

**hello** 🔤 **A1** (*also* **hullo** *especially in BrE*) (*BrE also* **hallo**) /həˈləʊ/ *exclamation, noun* (*pl.* **-os**) **1** 🔤 **A1** used as a GREETING when you meet sb, in an email, when you answer the phone or when you want to attract sb's attention: *Hello John, how are you?* ◇ *Hello, is there anybody there?* ◇ *Say hello to Liz for me.* ◇ *They exchanged hellos* (= said hello to each other) *and forced smiles.* **2** (*BrE*) used to show that you are surprised by sth: *Hello, hello, what's going on here?* **3** (*informal*) used to show that you think sb has said sth stupid or is not paying attention: *Hello? You didn't really mean that, did you?* ◇ *I'm like, 'Hello! Did you even listen?'*

▼ MORE ABOUT …

### greetings

- **Hello** is used in all situations, including answering the phone.
- **Hi** is more informal and is very common.
- **Hey** is used in the same way as **hi**, especially in American English.
- **How are you?** or **How are you doing?** (*informal*) often follow **Hello** and **Hi**: *'Hello, Mark.' 'Oh, hi, Kathy! How are you?'*
- **Good morning** is often used by members of a family or people who work together when they see each other for the first time in the day. It can also be used in formal situations and on the phone. In informal speech, people may just say **Morning**.
- **Good afternoon** and **Good evening** are much less common. **Good night** is not used to greet somebody, but only to say goodbye late in the evening or when you are going to bed.
- If you are meeting someone for the first time, you can say **Pleased to meet you** or **Nice to meet you** (*less formal*). Some people use **How do you do?** in formal situations. The correct reply to this is **How do you do?**

**hell-ˈrais·er** /ˈhelreɪzə(r)/ *noun* a person who causes trouble by behaving loudly and often violently, especially when they have drunk too much alcohol

**Hells ˈAngel™** *noun* a member of a group of people, usually men, who ride powerful motorcycles, wear leather clothes and used to be known for their wild and violent behaviour

**hel·luva** /ˈheləvə/ ⇨ HELL

**helm** /helm/ *noun, verb*
■ *noun* a handle or wheel used for controlling the direction in which a boat or ship moves ⇨ compare TILLER
IDM **at the ˈhelm 1** in charge of an organization, project, etc. **2** controlling the direction in which a boat or ship

moves **take (over) the 'helm 1** to take charge of an organization, project, etc. **2** to begin controlling the direction in which a boat or ship moves
▪ *verb* **1** ~ **sth** to manage an organization: *He was called in to helm a bureau in charge of resources allocation at district level.* **2** ~ **sth** to direct a film or television programme: *She has already helmed a couple of fantastic short films.* **3** ~ **sth** to control the direction of a boat or ship

**hel·met** /ˈhelmɪt/ *noun* a type of hard hat that protects the head, worn, for example, by a police officer, a soldier or a person riding a bike or motorbike or playing some sports ⊃ see also BLUE HELMET, CRASH HELMET, PITH HELMET

**hel·met·ed** /ˈhelmɪtɪd/ *adj.* [only before noun] wearing a helmet

**helms·man** /ˈhelmzmən/ *noun* (*pl.* -**men** /-mən/) a person who controls the direction in which a boat or ship moves

**help** /help/ *verb, noun, exclamation*
▪ *verb*
• MAKE EASIER/BETTER **1** [I, T] to make it easier or possible for sb to do sth by doing sth for them or by giving them sth that they need: ~ **with sth** *He always helps with the housework.* ◇ ~ **sb** *They are trying their best to do a good job and help others.* ◇ ~ **sb with sth** *Jo will help us with some of the organization.* ◇ ~ **in doing sth** *Following these steps will help in protecting our environment.* ◇ ~ **sb (to) do sth** *Come and help me lift this box.* ◇ *This charity aims to help people to help themselves.* ◇ ~ **(to) do sth** *She helped organize the party.* **HELP** In verb patterns with a **to** infinitive, the 'to' is often left out, especially in informal or spoken English. ⊃ EXPRESS YOURSELF at SHALL **2** [I, T] to improve a situation; to make it easier for sth to happen: *The support of our families has helped enormously.* ◇ **it helps (doing sth)** *It helped being able to talk about it.* ◇ **it helps that...** *It certainly helped that her father is a duke!* ◇ ~ **towards sth** *The money raised will help towards (= partly pay for) the cost of organizing the championships.* ◇ ~ **sth** *It doesn't really help matters knowing that everyone is talking about us.* ◇ ~ **(to) do sth** *This should help to reduce the pain.* ◇ *We need new measures to help fight terrorism.*
• SB TO MOVE **3** [T] ~ **sb + adv./prep.** to help sb move or do some other action by letting them lean on you, guiding them, etc: *She helped him to his feet.* ◇ *We were helped ashore by local people.*
• GIVE FOOD/DRINK **4** [T] to give yourself/sb food, drinks, etc: ~ **yourself** *If you want another drink, just help yourself.* ◇ ~ **yourself/sb to sth** *Can I help you to some more salad?*
• STEAL **5** [T] ~ **yourself to sth** (*informal, disapproving*) to take sth without permission **SYN** steal: *He'd been helping himself to the money in the cash register.*
**IDM** **sb cannot 'help (doing) sth | sb cannot 'help but do sth** used to say that it is impossible to prevent or avoid sth: *I can't help thinking he knows more than he has told us.* ◇ *She couldn't help but wonder what he was thinking.* ◇ **It couldn't be helped** (= there was no way of avoiding it and we must accept it). ◇ *I always end up having an argument with her, I don't know why, I just can't help it.* ◇ *I couldn't help it if the bus was late* (= it wasn't my fault). ◇ *She burst out laughing—she couldn't help herself* (= couldn't stop herself). **give/lend a 'helping 'hand** to help sb **God/Heaven 'help sb** (*informal*) used to say that you are afraid sb will be in danger or that sth bad will happen to them: *God help us if this doesn't work.* **HELP** Some people find this use of **God** offensive. **so 'help me (God)** used to swear that what you are saying is true, especially in a court of law
**PHRV** **help sb 'off/'on with sth** to help sb take off/put on a piece of clothing: *Let me help you off with your coat.* **help 'out | help sb↔'out** to help sb, especially in a difficult situation: *He's always willing to help out.* ◇ *When I bought the house, my sister helped me out with a loan.*
▪ *noun*
• MAKING EASIER/BETTER **1** [U] the act of helping sb to do sth: *Thank you for all your help.* ◇ **to ask/call/appeal for help** ◇ ~ **with sth** *Do you need any help with that?* ◇ **of ~ (to sb)** *Can I be of any help to you?* ◇ **with the ~ of sb/sth** *She recovered with the help of her family and friends.* ◇ **without** **the ~ of sb/sth** *None of this would have been possible without their help.* ◇ *They have at last decided to enlist the help of experts.* ⊃ see also SELF-HELP
• FOR SB IN DANGER **2** [U] the act of helping sb who is in danger: *Quick, get help!* ◇ *She screamed for help.*
• ADVICE/MONEY **3** [U] advice, money, etc. that is given to sb in order to solve their problems: *professional/medical/financial help* ◇ *I decided to seek legal help.* ◇ ~ **in doing sth** *The organization offers practical help in dealing with paperwork.* ◇ ~ **with sth** *You should qualify for help with the costs of running a car.*
• ON A COMPUTER/PHONE, ETC. **4** [U] a function on a computer, phone, etc. that provides information on how to use the computer, phone, etc: *The online help is very good.* ◇ *a help file/page/menu/screen*
• BEING USEFUL **5** [U] the fact of being useful: *The map wasn't much help.* ◇ *Just shouting at him isn't going to be a lot of help.* ◇ **with the ~ of sth** *I managed to understand it with the help of a dictionary.*
• PERSON/THING **6** [sing.] **a ~ (to sb)** a person or thing that helps sb: *She was more of a hindrance than a help.* ◇ *Your advice was a big help.* ◇ (*ironic*) *You're a great help, I must say!*
• IN HOUSE **7** **the help** [U + sing./pl. v.] (*especially NAmE*) the person or people employed by sb to clean their house, etc. ⊃ see also HOME HELP
**IDM** **there is no 'help for it** (*especially BrE*) it is not possible to avoid doing sth that may harm sb in some way: *There's no help for it. We shall have to call the police.*
▪ *exclamation* used to call for help because you are in a dangerous situation: *Help, I'm stuck!*

▼ EXPRESS YOURSELF

**Asking for help**

If you need help, people are more likely to react favourably if you ask politely:
• *Could you possibly help me?*
• *I wonder if you could give me a hand?*
• *Would you mind opening the door for me?*
• *I wonder if you'd mind taking a picture of us?*
• *Could I ask you to keep an eye on my luggage for a moment?*

Responses:
• *Yes, of course.*
• *I'm sorry, I'm in a hurry.*
• *Sure.* (*informal or NAmE*)

**'help desk** *noun* a service, usually in a business company, that gives people information and help, especially if they are having problems with a computer

**help·er** /ˈhelpə(r)/ *noun* a person who helps sb to do sth: *a willing helper*

**help·ful** /ˈhelpfl/ *adj.* **1** able to improve a particular situation **SYN** useful: *helpful advice/information* ◇ *helpful hints/tips/suggestions/comments* ◇ *Sorry I can't be more helpful.* ◇ ~ **to do sth** *You may find it helpful to read this before making any decisions.* ◇ ~ **for sb (to do sth)** *It would be helpful for me to see the damage for myself.* ◇ ~ **in doing sth** *Role-play is helpful in developing communication skills.* ◇ ~ **to sb** *This final section will be particularly helpful to students.* **2** (*of a person*) willing to help sb: *I called the police but they weren't very helpful.* ◇ *The staff couldn't have been more helpful.* **OPP** unhelpful
▶ **help·ful·ly** /-fəli/ *adv.*: *She helpfully suggested that I try the local library.* **help·ful·ness** *noun* [U]

**help·ing** /ˈhelpɪŋ/ *noun* ~ **(of sth)** an amount of food given to sb at a meal **SYN** serving: *a small/generous helping* ◇ *We all had a second helping of pie.*

**help·less** /ˈhelpləs/ *adj.* **1** unable to take care of yourself or do things without the help of other people: *the helpless victims of war* ◇ *a helpless gesture/look* ◇ *He lay helpless on the floor.* ◇ *It's natural to feel helpless against such abuse.* ◇ *The worst part is being helpless to change anything.* **2** unable to control a strong feeling: *helpless panic/*

# helpline 742

**rage** ◇ ~ **with sth** *The audience was* ***helpless*** *with laughter.* ▶ **help·less·ly** *adv.*: *They watched* ***helplessly*** *as their home went up in flames.* **help·less·ness** *noun* [U] *a feeling/sense of helplessness*

**help·line** /ˈhelplaɪn/ *noun* a phone or online service that provides advice and information about particular problems

**help·mate** /ˈhelpmeɪt/ (*also less frequent* **help·meet** /ˈhelpmiːt/) *noun* (*formal or literary*) a helpful partner, especially a wife

**hel·ter-skel·ter** /ˌheltə ˈskeltə(r)/; *NAmE* ˌheltər-/ *noun, adj.*
■ *noun* (*BrE*) a tall tower at a FAIRGROUND that has a path winding around the outside of it from the top to the bottom for people to slide down
■ *adj.* [only before noun] done in a hurry and in a way that lacks organization: *a* ***helter-skelter*** *dash to meet the deadline* ▶ **hel·ter-skel·ter** *adv.*

**hem** /hem/ *noun, verb*
■ *noun* the edge of a piece of cloth that has been turned under and SEWN, especially on a piece of clothing: *to take up the* ***hem*** *of a dress* (= to make the dress shorter) ⇨ WORDFINDER NOTE at SEW
■ *verb* (**-mm-**) ~ **sth** to turn under and SEW the edge of a piece of cloth, especially on a piece of clothing: *to* ***hem*** *a skirt*
IDM **ˌhem and ˈhaw** (*NAmE*) (*BrE* **ˌhum and ˈhaw**) (*informal*) to take a long time to make a decision or before you say sth
PHRV **ˌhem sb/sthↃin** [often passive] to surround sb/ sth so that they cannot move or grow easily SYN **hedge sb/sth in**: *The village is* ***hemmed in*** *on all sides by mountains.* ◇ (*figurative*) *She felt* ***hemmed in*** *by all their petty rules and regulations.*

**ˈhe-man** *noun* (*pl.* **he-men**) (*often humorous*) a strong man with big muscles, especially one who likes to show other people how strong he is

**hema·tite** (*NAmE*) (*BrE* **haem·atite**) /ˈhiːmətaɪt/ *noun* (*geology*) a dark red rock from which iron is obtained

**hema·tol·ogy** (*NAmE*) (*BrE* **haema·tol·ogy**) /ˌhiːməˈtɒlədʒi; *NAmE* -ˈtɑːl-/ *noun* [U] the scientific study of the blood and its diseases ▶ **hema·to·logic·al** (*NAmE*) (*BrE* **haem-**) /ˌhiːmətəˈlɒdʒɪkl; *NAmE* -ˈlɑːdʒ-/ *adj.* **hema·tolo·gist** (*NAmE*) (*BrE* **haem-**) /ˌhiːməˈtɒlədʒɪst; *NAmE* -ˈtɑːl-/ *noun*

**hema·toma** (*NAmE*) (*BrE* **haem·atoma**) /ˌhiːməˈtəʊmə/ *noun* (*medical*) a SWELLING (= an area that is larger and rounder than normal) on the body consisting of blood that has become thick

**hemi·sphere** /ˈhemɪsfɪə(r); *NAmE* -sfɪr/ *noun* **1** one half of the earth, especially the half above or below the EQUATOR: *the* ***northern/southern hemisphere*** ⇨ WORDFINDER NOTE at EARTH **2** (*also* **cerebral hemisphere**) either half of the brain: *the* ***left/right hemisphere*** *of the brain* **3** one half of a SPHERE (= a round solid object)

**hemi·spher·ic·al** /ˌhemɪˈsferɪkl; *NAmE* -ˈsfɪr-, -ˈsfer-/ *adj.* having the shape of a hemisphere

**hem·line** /ˈhemlaɪn/ *noun* the bottom edge of a dress or skirt; the length of a dress or skirt: *Shorter* ***hemlines*** *are back in this season.*

**hem·lock** /ˈhemlɒk; *NAmE* -lɑːk/ *noun* **1** [U, C] a poisonous plant with a mass of small white flowers growing at the end of a STEM that is covered in spots **2** [U] poison made from hemlock

**hemo-** /ˈhiːməʊ, hiːmə; *BrE also* ˈhiːˈmɒ; *NAmE also* hiːˈmɑː/ (*NAmE*) (*BrE* **haemo-**) *combining form* (in nouns and adjectives) connected with blood: *hemophilia*

**hemo·philia** (*NAmE*) (*BrE* **haemo·philia**) /ˌhiːməˈfɪliə/ *noun* [U] a medical condition that causes severe loss of blood from even a slight injury because the blood fails to CLOT normally. It usually affects only men although it can be passed on by women.

**hemp** /hemp/ *noun* [U] a plant that is used for making rope and cloth, and also to make the drug CANNABIS

**hen** /hen/ *noun* **1** a female chicken, often kept for its eggs or meat: *a small flock of laying* ***hens*** ◇ ***battery hens*** **2** (especially in compounds) any female bird: *a hen pheasant* ⇨ compare COCK ⇨ see also MOORHEN ⇨ see also MOTHER HEN

**hence** /hens/ *adv.* (*formal*) for this reason: *We suspect they are trying to hide something,* ***hence*** *the need for an independent inquiry.* ⇨ LANGUAGE BANK at THEREFORE IDM **… days, weeks, etc. ˈhence** (*formal*) a number of days, etc. from now: *The true consequences will only be known several years* ***hence.***

**hence·forth** /ˌhensˈfɔːθ; *NAmE* -ˈfɔːrθ/ (*also* **hence·for·ward** /ˌhensˈfɔːwəd; *NAmE* -ˈfɔːrwərd/) *adv.* (*formal*) starting from a particular time and at all times in the future: *Friday 31 July 1925* ***henceforth*** *became known as 'Red Friday'.*

**hench·man** /ˈhentʃmən/ *noun* (*pl.* **-men** /-mən/) (*usually disapproving*) a helper or supporter of a powerful person, for example a political leader or criminal, who is prepared to use violence or become involved in illegal activities to help that person

**henge** /hendʒ/ *noun* a circle of large standing wooden or stone objects built in PREHISTORIC times

**henna** /ˈhenə/ *noun* [U] a red-brown DYE (= a substance used to change the colour of sth), used especially on the hair and skin

**ˈhen party** (*also* **ˈhen night**) (*both BrE*) (*NAmE* **bachelorette party**) *noun* a party that a woman has with her female friends just before she gets married ⇨ compare STAG NIGHT

**hen·pecked** /ˈhenpekt/ *adj.* (*informal*) a man who people say is ***henpecked*** has a wife or female partner who is always telling him what to do, and is too weak to disagree with her

**hep·at·ic** /hɪˈpætɪk/ *adj.* (*biology*) relating to the LIVER

**hepa·titis** /ˌhepəˈtaɪtɪs/ *noun* [U] a serious disease of the LIVER. There are three main forms: **hepatitis ˈA**, the least serious, caused by INFECTED food (= containing harmful bacteria), and **hepatitis ˈB** and **hepatitis ˈC**, both very serious and caused by INFECTED blood.

**hepta·gon** /ˈheptəgən; *NAmE* -gɑːn/ *noun* (*geometry*) a flat shape with seven straight sides and seven angles ▶ **hept·agon·al** /hepˈtægənl/ *adj.*

**hept·ath·lon** /hepˈtæθlən/ *noun* a sporting event, especially one for women, in which athletes compete in seven different events ⇨ compare BIATHLON, DECATHLON, PENTATHLON, TRIATHLON

**her** /hə(r), ɜː(r), ə(r), *strong form* hɜː(r)/ *pron., det.*
■ *pron.* used as the object of a verb, after the verb *be* or after a preposition to refer to a woman or girl who has already been mentioned or is easily identified: *We're going to call* ***her*** *Sophie.* ◇ *Please give* ***her*** *my regards.* ◇ *The manager will be free soon—you can wait for* ***her*** *here.* ◇ *That must be* ***her*** *now.* ⇨ compare SHE ⇨ note at GENDER
■ *det.* (the possessive form of *she*) of or belonging to a woman or girl who has already been mentioned or is easily identified: *Meg loves* ***her*** *job.* ◇ *She broke* ***her*** *leg skiing.* ⇨ see also HERS

**her·ald** /ˈherəld/ *verb, noun*
■ *verb* (*formal*) **1** ~ **sth** to be a sign that sth is going to happen: *These talks could* ***herald*** *a new era of peace.* **2** [often passive] to say in public that sb/sth is good or important: **be heralded (as sth)** *The report is being* ***heralded*** *as a blueprint for the future of transport.*
■ *noun* **1** something that shows that sth else is going to happen soon: *The government claims that the fall in unemployment is the* ***herald*** *of economic recovery.* **2** (in the past) a person who made announcements and carried messages from a ruler

**her·ald·ry** /ˈherəldri/ *noun* [U] the study of the COATS OF ARMS and the history of old families ▶ **her·al·dic** /heˈrældɪk/ *adj.*

**herb** /hɜːb; *NAmE* ɜːrb, hɜːrb/ *noun* a plant whose leaves, flowers or seeds are used to add taste to food, in medicines or for their pleasant smell. PARSLEY, MINT and OREGANO are all herbs: *a* ***herb*** *garden* ◇ (*NAmE*) an herb garden ⇒ VISUAL VOCAB page V8 **2** (specialist) a plant with a soft STEM that dies down after flowering

**herb·aceous** /hɜːˈbeɪʃəs; NAmE ɜːrˈb-, hɜːrˈ-/ adj. (specialist) connected with plants that have soft STEMS: *a herbaceous plant*

**herˌbaceous ˈborder** noun a piece of ground in a garden containing plants that produce flowers every year without being replaced

**herb·age** /ˈhɜːbɪdʒ; NAmE ˈɜːrb-, ˈhɜːr-/ noun [U] (specialist) plants in general, especially grass that is grown for cows, etc. to eat

**herb·al** /ˈhɜːbl; NAmE ˈɜːrbl, ˈhɜːr-/ adj., noun
■ *adj.* connected with or made from HERBS: *herbal medicine/remedies*
■ *noun* a book about HERBS, especially those used in medicines

**herb·al·ism** /ˈhɜːbəlɪzəm; NAmE ˈɜːrb-, ˈhɜːr-/ noun [U] the medical use of plants, especially as a form of ALTERNATIVE MEDICINE ⇒ WORDFINDER NOTE at TREATMENT

**herb·al·ist** /ˈhɜːbəlɪst; NAmE ˈɜːrb-, ˈhɜːr-/ noun a person who grows, sells or uses HERBS for medical purposes

**ˌherbal ˈtea** noun [U, C] a drink made from dried HERBS and hot water

**herbi·cide** /ˈhɜːbɪsaɪd; NAmE ˈɜːrb-, ˈhɜːr-/ noun [C, U] a chemical that is poisonous to plants, used to kill plants that are growing where they are not wanted ⇒ see also INSECTICIDE, PESTICIDE

**herbi·vore** /ˈhɜːbɪvɔː(r); NAmE ˈɜːrb-, ˈhɜːr-/ noun any animal that eats only plants ⇒ compare CARNIVORE, INSECTIVORE, OMNIVORE, VEGETARIAN ▶ **herb·iv·or·ous** /hɜːˈbɪvərəs; NAmE ɜːrˈb-, hɜːrˈ-/ adj.: *herbivorous dinosaurs*

**Her·cu·lean** /ˌhɜːkjuˈliːən; NAmE ˌhɜːrk-/ adj. [usually before noun] needing a lot of strength, DETERMINATION or effort: *a Herculean task* ORIGIN From the Greek myth in which **Hercules** proved his courage and strength by completing twelve very difficult tasks (called the Labours of Hercules).

**herd** /hɜːd; NAmE hɜːrd/ noun, verb
■ *noun* [C + sing. / pl. v.] **1** a group of animals of the same type that live and feed together: *a herd of cows/deer/elephants* ◊ *a beef/dairy herd* ⇒ compare FLOCK **2** (usually disapproving) a large group of people of the same type: *She pushed her way through a herd of lunchtime drinkers.* ◊ *the common herd* (= ordinary people) ◊ *Why follow the herd* (= do and think the same as everyone else)*?* IDM see RIDE v.
■ *verb* **1** [I, T] to move or make sb/sth move in a particular direction: **+ adv. /prep.** *We all herded on to the bus.* ◊ **~sb/sth + adv. /prep.** *They were herded together into trucks and driven away.* **2** [T] ~ sth to keep or look after a group of animals; to make animals move together as a group: *a shepherd herding his flock*
IDM **like herding ˈcats** (informal) used to describe a very difficult task, especially one that involves organizing people: *Managing a political party is a lot like herding cats.*

**herd·er** /ˈhɜːdə(r); NAmE ˈhɜːrd-/ noun a person whose job is to take care of a group of animals such as sheep or cows in the countryside

**ˈherd instinct** noun [sing.] the quality in people or animals of tending to behave or think like other people or animals

**herds·man** /ˈhɜːdzmən; NAmE ˈhɜːrdz-/ noun (pl. -men /-mən/) a person whose job is to take care of a group of animals such as sheep or cows in the countryside

**here** ❶ A1 S /hɪə(r); NAmE hɪr/ adv., exclamation
■ *adv.* **1** A1 used after a verb or preposition to mean 'in, at or to this position or place': *I live here.* ◊ *Put the box here.* ◊ *Click here for more details.* ◊ *Let's get out of here.* ◊ *Come over here.* ⓗ HOMOPHONES at HEAR **2** A1 used when you are giving or showing sth to sb: *Here's the money I promised you.* ◊ *Here's a dish that is simple and quick to make.* ◊ *Here is your opportunity.* ◊ *Here comes the bus.* ◊ *I can't find my keys. Oh, here they are.* ◊ *Here we are* (= we've arrived)*.* **3** A2 ~ to do sth used to show your role in a situation: *I'm here to help you.* **4** B1 now; at this point: *The countdown to Christmas starts here.* ◊ *Here the speaker*

743

paused to have a drink. **5** (used after a noun, for emphasis): *My friend here saw it happen.*
IDM **(the) ˌhere and ˈnow** the present time; at the present time: *our obsession with the here and now* ◊ *We're going to settle this here and now.* **ˌhere and ˈthere** in various places: *Papers were scattered here and there on the floor.* **ˌhere ˈgoes** (informal) used when you are telling people that you are just going to do sth exciting, dangerous, etc. **ˈhere's to sb/sth** used to wish sb health or success, as you lift a glass and drink a TOAST: *Here's to your future happiness!* **ˌhere, ˌthere and ˈeverywhere** in many different places; all around **ˌhere we ˈgo** (informal) said when sth is starting to happen: '*Here we go,*' *thought Fred,* '*she's sure to say something.*' **ˌhere we go aˈgain** (informal) said when sth is starting to happen again, especially with sth bad **ˌhere you ˈare** (informal) used when you are giving sth to sb: *Here you are. This is what you were asking for.* **ˌhere you ˈgo** (informal) used when you are giving sth to sb: *Here you go. Four copies, is that right?* **ˌneither ˌhere nor ˈthere** not important SYN **irrelevant**: *What might have happened is neither here nor there.* ⇒ more at OUT adv.
■ *exclamation* **1** (BrE) used to attract sb's attention: *Here, where are you going with that ladder?* **2** used when offering sth to sb: *Here, let me carry that for you.*

**here·abouts** /ˌhɪərəˈbaʊts; NAmE ˌhɪr-/ (NAmE also **hereabout**) adv. near this place: *There aren't many houses hereabouts.*

**here·after** /ˌhɪərˈɑːftə(r); NAmE ˌhɪrˈæf-/ adv., noun
■ *adv.* **1** (also **here·in·after**) (law) (in legal documents, etc.) in the rest of this document **2** (formal) from this time; in future ⇒ compare THEREAFTER **3** (formal) after death: *Do you believe in a life hereafter?*
■ *noun* **the hereafter** [sing.] a life believed to begin after death

**here·by** /ˌhɪəˈbaɪ; NAmE ˌhɪrˈb-/ adv. (in legal documents, etc.) as a result of this statement, and in a way that makes sth legal

**her·edi·tary** /həˈredɪtri; NAmE -teri/ adj. **1** (of a disease or characteristic) given to a child by its parents before it is born: *a hereditary disease/disorder* ◊ *hereditary physical traits, such as height and eye colour* **2** that is legally given to sb's child, when that person dies: *a hereditary title/monarchy* **3** holding a rank or title that is hereditary: *hereditary peers/rulers*

**her·ed·ity** /həˈredəti/ noun [U] the process by which mental and physical characteristics are passed by parents to their children; these characteristics in a particular person: *the debate over the effects of heredity and environment*

**here·in** /ˌhɪərˈɪn; NAmE ˌhɪr-/ adv. (formal or law) in this place, document, statement or fact: *Neither party is willing to compromise and herein lies the problem.*

**here·in·after** /ˌhɪərɪnˈɑːftə(r); NAmE ˌhɪrɪnˈæf-/ adv. (law) = HEREAFTER

**here·of** /ˌhɪərˈɒv; NAmE ˌhɪrˈʌv, -ˈɑːv/ adv. (law) of this: *a period of 12 months from the date hereof* (= the date of this document)

**her·esy** /ˈherəsi/ noun [U, C] (pl. **-ies**) **1** a belief or an opinion that is against the principles of a particular religion; the fact of holding such beliefs: *He was burned at the stake for heresy.* ◊ *the heresies of the early Protestants* **2** a belief or an opinion that disagrees strongly with what most people believe: *The idea is heresy to most employees of the firm.*

**her·et·ic** /ˈherətɪk/ noun a person who believes in or practises religious heresy ▶ **her·et·ical** /həˈretɪkl/ adj.: *heretical beliefs*

**here·to** /ˌhɪəˈtuː; NAmE ˌhɪrˈtuː/ adv. (law) to this

**here·to·fore** /ˌhɪətuˈfɔː(r); NAmE ˌhɪrt-/ adv. (law or formal) before this time

**here·upon** /ˌhɪərəˈpɒn; NAmE ˌhɪrəˈpɑːn/ adv. (literary) after this; as a direct result of this situation

**here·with** /ˌhɪəˈwɪð, -ˈwɪθ; NAmE ˌhɪrˈw-/ adv. (formal) with this letter, book or document: *I enclose herewith a copy of the policy.*

**her·it·able** /ˈherɪtəbl/ adj. (law) (of property) that can be passed from one member of a family to another

**heri·tage** 🔑 C1 /ˈherɪtɪdʒ/ noun [usually sing.] 1 🔑 C1 the history, traditions, buildings and objects that a country or society has had for many years and that are considered an important part of its character: *Spain's rich cultural heritage* ◇ *The building is part of our national heritage.* 2 (in compounds) used to describe a traditional product, brand, type of animal or plant variety, especially one that is old-fashioned, rare and of high quality: *a heritage breed/brand*

**ˈheritage centre** (US **ˈheritage center**) noun a place where there are exhibitions that people visit to learn about life in the past in a particular area

**herm·aph·ro·dite** /hɜːˈmæfrədaɪt; NAmE hɜːrˈm-/ noun (specialist) a person, an animal or a flower that has both male and female sexual organs or characteristics ▸ **hermaph·ro·dite** adj.

**her·men·eut·ic** /ˌhɜːməˈnjuːtɪk; NAmE ˌhɜːrməˈnuː-/ adj. (specialist) relating to the meaning of written texts

**her·men·eut·ics** /ˌhɜːməˈnjuːtɪks; NAmE ˌhɜːrməˈnuː-/ noun [pl.] (specialist) the area of study that analyses and explains written texts

**her·met·ic** /hɜːˈmetɪk; NAmE hɜːrˈm-/ adj. 1 (specialist) tightly closed so that no air can escape or enter SYN **airtight** 2 (formal, disapproving) closed and difficult to become a part of: *the strange, hermetic world of the theatre* ▸ **her·met·ic·al·ly** /-kli/ adv.: *a hermetically sealed container*

**her·mit** /ˈhɜːmɪt; NAmE ˈhɜːrm-/ noun a person who, usually for religious reasons, lives a very simple life alone and does not meet or talk to other people

**her·mit·age** /ˈhɜːmɪtɪdʒ; NAmE ˈhɜːrm-/ noun a place where a hermit lives or lived

**ˈhermit crab** noun a CRAB (= a sea creature with eight legs and, usually, a hard shell) that has no shell of its own and has to use the empty shells of other sea creatures

**her·nia** /ˈhɜːniə; NAmE ˈhɜːrn-/ noun [C, U] a medical condition in which part of an organ is pushed through a weak part in the muscle or TISSUE around it

**hero** 🔑 A2 /ˈhɪərəʊ; NAmE ˈhɪr-/ noun (pl. **-oes**) 1 🔑 A2 a person who is admired by many people for doing sth brave or good: *a war hero* (= sb who was very brave during a war) ◇ *a national/local hero* ◇ *The Olympic team were given a hero's welcome on their return home.* ◇ *he was hailed as a hero after the rescue.* ⮕ see also FOLK HERO 2 🔑 A2 the main male character in a story, novel, film, etc: *The hero of the novel is a ten-year old boy.* ◇ *action heroes like Bruce Willis* ⮕ see also ANTI-HERO, SUPERHERO ⮕ WORDFINDER NOTE at CHARACTER 3 🔑 A2 a person that you admire because of a particular quality or skill that they have: *my childhood hero* ◇ **~to sb** *He became a hero to millions for his decision to oppose the government's reforms.* 4 (NAmE) = SUBMARINE (2) ⮕ compare HEROINE

**hero·ic** /həˈrəʊɪk/ adj. 1 showing extreme courage and admired by many people SYN **courageous**: *a heroic figure* ◇ *Rescuers made heroic efforts to save the crew.* 2 showing a determined effort to succeed or to achieve sth, especially sth difficult: *We watched our team's heroic struggle to win back the cup.* 3 that is about or involves a hero: *a heroic story/poem* ◇ *heroic deeds/myths* 4 very large or great: *This was foolishness on a heroic scale.* ▸ **hero·ic·al·ly** /-kli/ adv.

**hero·ics** /həˈrəʊɪks/ noun [pl.] 1 (disapproving) talk or behaviour that is too brave or dramatic for a particular situation: *Remember, no heroics, we just go in there and do our job.* 2 actions that are brave and determined: *Thanks to Bateman's heroics in the second half, the team won 2–0.*

**her·oin** /ˈherəʊɪn/ noun [U] a powerful illegal drug made from MORPHINE, that some people take for pleasure and can become ADDICTED to: *a heroin addict*

**hero·ine** /ˈherəʊɪn/ noun 1 a girl or woman who is admired by many for doing sth brave or good: *the heroines of the revolution* 2 the main female character in a story, novel, film, etc: *The heroine is played by Demi Moore.* 3 a woman that you admire because of a particular quality or skill that she has: *Madonna was her teenage heroine.*

**hero·ism** /ˈherəʊɪzəm/ noun [U] very great courage

**heron** /ˈherən/ noun a large bird with a long neck and long legs, that lives near water

**ˈhero worship** noun [U] the feeling of admiring sb very much or too much because you think they are extremely beautiful, intelligent, etc.

**ˈhero-worship** verb (**-pp-**, NAmE also **-p-**) ~**sb** to admire sb very much or too much because you think they are extremely beautiful, intelligent, etc.

**her·pes** /ˈhɜːpiːz; NAmE ˈhɜːrp-/ noun [U] one of a group of diseases, caused by a virus, that cause painful spots on the skin, especially on the face and sexual organs

**her·ring** /ˈherɪŋ/ noun (pl. **her·ring** or **her·rings**) [U, C] a N Atlantic fish that swims in very large groups and is used for food: *shoals of herring* ◇ *fresh herring fillets* ◇ *pickled herrings* ⮕ see also RED HERRING

**herring·bone** /ˈherɪŋbəʊn/ noun [U] (often used before another noun) a pattern used, for example, in cloth consisting of lines of V-shapes that are PARALLEL to each other

herringbone pattern

**ˈherring gull** noun a large N Atlantic bird of the GULL family, with black tips to its wings

**hers** 🔑 A2 /hɜːz, ɜːz; NAmE hɜːrz, ɜːrz/ pron. of or belonging to her: *His eyes met hers.* ◇ *The choice was hers.* ◇ *a friend of hers* ⮕ note at GENDER

**her·self** 🔑 A2 /hɜːˈself, weak form həs-; NAmE hɜːrˈs-, weak form hər-/ pron. 1 🔑 A2 (the reflexive form of *she*) used when the woman or girl who performs an action is also affected by it: *She hurt herself.* ◇ *She must be very proud of herself.* 2 🔑 B1 used to emphasize the female subject or object of a sentence: *She told me the news herself.* ◇ *Jane herself was at the meeting.*

IDM **be, seem, etc. herˈself** 1 (of a woman or girl) to be in a normal state of health or happiness: *She didn't seem quite herself this morning.* 2 (of a woman or girl) not influenced by other people: *She needed space to be herself.* **(all) by herˈself** 1 alone; without anyone else: *She lives by herself.* 2 without help: *She runs the business by herself.* **(all) to herˈself** for only her to have or use; not shared: *She wants a room all to herself.*

**hertz** /hɜːts; NAmE hɜːrts/ noun (pl. **hertz**) (abbr. **Hz**) a unit for measuring the frequency of sound waves

**he's** short form 1 /hiːz/ his, IZ/ he is 2 /hiːz/ he has HELP *He's* is only used to mean 'he has' when *has* is an auxiliary verb: *He's just got here.* When *has* is the main verb, use the full form: *He has two children.* ◇ *He's two children.*

**hesi·tancy** /ˈhezɪtənsi/ noun [U, sing.] the state or quality of being slow or uncertain in doing or saying sth: *I noticed a certain hesitancy in his voice.*

**hesi·tant** /ˈhezɪtənt/ adj. slow to speak or act because you feel uncertain, embarrassed or unwilling: *a hesitant smile* ◇ *the baby's first few hesitant steps* ◇ ~**about sth** *She's hesitant about signing the contract.* ◇ ~**to do sth** *Doctors are hesitant to comment on the new treatment.* ▸ **hesi·tant·ly** adv.

**hesi·tate** 🔑 B2 /ˈhezɪteɪt/ verb 1 🔑 B2 [I, T] to be slow to speak or act because you feel uncertain or nervous: *She hesitated before replying.* ◇ ~**about/over (doing) sth** *I didn't hesitate for a moment about taking the job.* ◇ + speech 'I'm not sure,' she hesitated. 2 🔑 B2 [I] ~**to do sth** to be worried about doing sth, especially because you are not sure that it is right or appropriate: *Please do not*

**hesitate** to contact me if you have any queries. ▶ **hesi·ta·tion** /ˌhezɪˈteɪʃn/ noun [U, C]: *She agreed without the slightest hesitation.* ◇ *I have no hesitation in recommending her for the job.* ◇ *He spoke fluently and without unnecessary hesitations.*

**IDM** **he who ˈhesitates (is ˈlost)** (*saying*) if you delay in doing sth you may lose a good opportunity

**hes·sian** /ˈhesiən; *NAmE* ˈheʃn/ (*especially BrE*) (*NAmE usually* **burlap**) noun [U] a type of strong rough brown cloth, used especially for making SACKS

**hetero-** /ˈhetərəʊ, hetərə; *BrE also* hetəˈrɒ; *NAmE also* hetəˈrɑː/ *combining form* (in nouns, adjectives and adverbs) other; different: *heterogeneous* ◇ *heterosexual* ⊃ compare HOMO-

**het·ero·dox** /ˈhetərədɒks; *NAmE* -dɑːks/ *adj.* (*formal*) not following the usual or accepted beliefs and opinions ⊃ compare ORTHODOX, UNORTHODOX ▶ **het·ero·doxy** *noun* [U, C] (*pl.* **-ies**)

**het·ero·ge·neous** /ˌhetərəˈdʒiːniəs/ *adj.* (*formal*) consisting of many different kinds of people or things: *the heterogeneous population of the United States* **OPP** **homogeneous** ▶ **het·ero·gen·eity** /ˌhetərədʒəˈniːəti/ *noun* [U]

**het·ero·sex·ual** /ˌhetərəˈsekʃuəl/ *noun* a person who is sexually attracted to people of the opposite sex ⊃ compare BISEXUAL, HOMOSEXUAL ▶ **het·ero·sex·ual** *adj.*: *a heterosexual relationship* **het·ero·sexu·al·ity** /ˌhetərəˌsekʃuˈæləti/ *noun* [U]

**het·ero·zy·gote** /ˌhetərəˈzaɪɡəʊt/ *noun* (*biology*) a living thing that has two varying forms of a particular GENE, and whose young may therefore vary in a particular characteristic ▶ **het·ero·zy·gous** /-ɡəs/ *adj.*

**het up** /ˌhet ˈʌp/ *adj.* [not before noun] **~ (about/over sth)** (*informal*) anxious, excited or slightly angry: *What are you getting so het up about?*

**heur·is·tic** /hjʊəˈrɪstɪk; *NAmE* hjʊˈr-/ *adj.* (*formal*) **heuristic** teaching or education encourages you to learn by discovering things for yourself

**heur·is·tics** /hjʊəˈrɪstɪks; *NAmE* hjʊˈr-/ *noun* [U] (*formal*) a method of solving problems by finding practical ways of dealing with them, learning from past experience

**hew** /hjuː/ *verb* (**hewed**, **hewed** or **hewn** /hjuːn/) **1 ~ sth** (*old-fashioned*) to cut sth large with a tool: *to hew wood* **2 ~ sth (out of sth)** (*formal*) to make or shape sth large by cutting: *roughly hewn timber frames* ◇ *The statues were hewn out of solid rock.*

**hex** /heks/ *verb* **~ sb** to use magic powers in order to harm sb ▶ **hex** *noun*: *to put a hex on sb* ⊃ compare CURSE

**hexa-** /heksə, hekˈsæ/ (*also* **hex-** /heks/) *combining form* (in nouns, adjectives and adverbs) six; having six

**hexa·deci·mal** /ˌheksəˈdesɪml/ (*also* **hex** /heks/) *noun* (*computing*) a system for representing pieces of data using the numbers 0–9 and the letters A–F: *The number 107 is represented in hexadecimal as 6B.* ⊃ compare BINARY, DECIMAL (2) ▶ **hexa·deci·mal** *adj.*: *hexadecimal code/values*

**hexa·gon** /ˈheksəɡən; *NAmE* -ɡɑːn/ *noun* (*geometry*) a flat shape with six straight sides and six angles ⊃ picture at POLYGON ▶ **hex·agon·al** /hekˈsæɡənl/ *adj.*

**hexa·gram** /ˈheksəɡræm/ *noun* (*geometry*) a shape made by six straight lines, especially a star made from two TRIANGLES with equal sides

**hex·am·eter** /hekˈsæmɪtə(r)/ *noun* (*specialist*) a line of poetry with six stressed syllables

**hey** 🔊 **A1** /heɪ/ *exclamation* (*informal*) **1** 🔊 **A1** used to attract sb's attention or to express interest, surprise or anger: *Hey, can I just ask you something?* ◇ *Hey, leave my things alone!* **2** **A1** (*especially NAmE, informal*) used to say hello **SYN** **hi**: *Hey, Jake! How are you doing?* **3** used to show that you do not really care about sth or that you think it is not important: *That's the third time I've been late this week—but hey!—who's counting?* **4** (*SAfrE*) used at the end of a statement, to show that you have finished speaking, or to form a question or invite sb to reply: *Thanks for your help, hey.* ◇ *My new bike's nice, hey?*

**IDM** **what the ˈhey!** (*NAmE, informal*) used to say that sth does not matter or that you do not care about it: *This is probably a bad idea, but what the hey!*

**hey·day** /ˈheɪdeɪ/ *noun* [usually sing.] the time when sb/sth had most power or success, or was most popular **SYN** **prime**: *In its heyday, the company ran trains every fifteen minutes.* ◇ *a fine example from the heyday of Italian cinema* ◇ *a picture of Brigitte Bardot in her heyday*

**hey ˈpresto** *exclamation* (*BrE*) (*NAmE* **presto**) **1** something that people say when they have just done sth so quickly and easily that it seems to have been done by magic: *You just press the button and, hey presto, a perfect cup of coffee!* **2** something that people say just before they finish a magic trick

**HFC** /ˌeɪtʃ ef ˈsiː/ *noun* [C, U] a type of gas used especially in AEROSOLS (= types of container that release liquid in very small drops). HFCs are not harmful to the earth's OZONE LAYER. (the abbreviation for 'hydrofluorocarbon')

**HGV** /ˌeɪtʃ dʒiː ˈviː/ *noun* (*BrE*) a large vehicle such as a lorry (the abbreviation for 'heavy goods vehicle'): *You need an HGV licence for this job.*

**hi** 🔊 **A1** /haɪ/ *exclamation* (*informal*) used to say hello: *Hi guys!* ◇ *Hi, there! How're you doing?* ◇ *Say hi to her from me.*

**hia·tus** /haɪˈeɪtəs/ *noun* [sing.] (*formal*) **1** a break in activity when nothing happens **2** (*specialist*) a space, especially in a piece of writing or in a speech, where sth is missing

**hi·ber·nate** /ˈhaɪbəneɪt; *NAmE* -bərn-/ *verb* [I] (of animals) to spend the winter in a state like deep sleep ▶ **hi·ber·na·tion** /ˌhaɪbəˈneɪʃn; *NAmE* -bərˈn-/ *noun* [U]

**hi·bis·cus** /hɪˈbɪskəs, haɪ-/ *noun* [U, C] (*pl.* **hi·bis·cus**) a tropical plant or bush with large brightly coloured flowers

**hic·cup** (*also* **hic·cough**) /ˈhɪkʌp/ *noun, verb*

■ *noun* **1** [C] a sharp, usually repeated, sound made in the throat, that is caused by a sudden movement of the DIAPHRAGM and that you cannot control: *She gave a loud hiccup.* **2 (the) hiccups** [pl.] a series of hiccups: *I ate too quickly and got hiccups.* ◇ *He had the hiccups.* **3** [C] **~ (in sth)** (*informal*) a small problem or temporary delay: *There was a slight hiccup in the timetable.*

■ *verb* [I] to have (the) hiccups or a single hiccup

**hick** /hɪk/ *noun* (*informal, especially NAmE*) a person from the country who is considered to be stupid and to have little experience of life: *I was just a hick from Texas then.* ▶ **hick** *adj.*: *a hick town*

**hickey** /ˈhɪki/ (*NAmE*) (*BrE* **ˈlove bite**) *noun* a red mark on the skin that is caused by sb biting or SUCKING their partner's skin when they are kissing

**hick·ory** /ˈhɪkəri/ *noun* [U] the hard wood of the North American **ˈhickory tree**

**hid·den** 🔊+ **B2** /ˈhɪdn/ *adj.* **1** 🔊+ **B2** something that is **hidden** is kept or located in a place where it cannot be seen: *hidden dangers* ◇ *A reporter wearing a hidden camera got footage of the abuse.* **2** 🔊+ **B2** secret: *She felt sure the letter had some hidden meaning.*

**hidden aˈgenda** *noun* (*disapproving*) the secret intention behind what sb says or does: *There are fears of a hidden agenda behind this new proposal.*

**hide** 🔊 **A2** /haɪd/ *verb, noun*

■ *verb* ( **hid** /hɪd/, **hid·den** /ˈhɪdn/) **1** 🔊 **A2** [T] to put or keep sb/sth in a place where they/it cannot be seen or found **SYN** **conceal**: **~ sb/sth + adv./prep.** *He hid the letter in a drawer.* ◇ **~ sb/sth** *I keep my private papers hidden.* ◇ **~ sb/sth from sth (+ adv./prep.)** *They hid me from the police in their attic.* **2** 🔊 **A2** [I, T] to go somewhere where you hope you will not be seen or found: *Quick, hide!* ◇ **+ adv./prep.** *I hid under the bed.* ◇ **~ from sb (+ adv./prep.)** *We hid from our pursuers in an empty house.* ◇ **~ yourself + adv./prep.** *She hides herself away in her office all day.* **3** 🔊 **A2** [T] to cover sb/sth so that they/it cannot be seen **SYN** **conceal**: **~ sth + adv./prep.** *He hid his face in his hands.* ◇ **~ sth** *The house was hidden by trees.* ◇ *No amount of make-up could hide her age.* **4** 🔊+ **B1** [T] **~ sth** to keep sth

# hide-and-seek

secret, especially your feelings SYN **conceal**: *They didn't try to **hide** the fact that the film was a remake.* ◊ *I have never **tried to hide** the truth about my past.* ◊ *She struggled to hide her disappointment.* ◊ *They claim that they **have nothing to hide*** (= there was nothing wrong or illegal about what they did).

IDM **hide your light under a ˈbushel** to not let people know that you are good at sth **you can ˈrun but you ˈcan't ˈhide** used to say that whatever you do, you cannot escape the consequences of your actions ⇒ more at HEAD *n.*, MULTITUDE
PHRV **ˈhide behind sb/sth** (*disapproving*) to use sb/sth to protect yourself from criticism or punishment, especially in a way that people think is weak or shows a lack of courage: *She hides behind empty excuses and company policy.* **ˈhide behind sth** to use sth to keep secret your real identity, character or purpose: *He hid behind a false identity.*

■ *noun* **1** [C] (*BrE*) a place from which people can watch wild animals or birds, without being seen by them **2** [C, U] an animal's skin, especially when it is bought or sold or used for leather: *boots made from buffalo hide* **3** [sing.] (*especially NAmE, informal*) used to refer to sb's life or safety when they are in a difficult situation: *All he's worried about is his own hide* (= himself).
IDM **have/tan sb's ˈhide** (*old-fashioned, informal* or *humorous*) to punish sb severely **not see hide nor ˈhair of sb/sth** (*informal*) not to see sb/sth for some time: *I haven't seen hide nor hair of her for a month.* ⇒ more at SAVE *v.*

▼ SYNONYMS

### hide
**conceal • cover • disguise • mask • camouflage**

These words all mean to put or keep sb/sth in a place where they/it cannot be seen or found, or to keep the truth or your feelings secret.

**hide** to put or keep sb/sth in a place where they/it cannot be seen or found; to keep sth secret, especially your feelings: *He hid the letter in a drawer.* ◊ *She managed to hide her disappointment.*

**conceal** (*formal*) to hide sb/sth; to keep sth secret: *The paintings were concealed beneath a thick layer of plaster.* ◊ *Tim could barely conceal his disappointment.* NOTE When it is being used to talk about emotions, **conceal** is often used in negative statements.

**cover** to place sth over or in front of sth in order to hide it: *She covered her face with her hands.*

**disguise** to hide or change the nature of sth, so that it cannot be recognized: *He tried to disguise his accent.*

**mask** to hide a feeling, smell, fact, etc. so that it cannot be easily seen or noticed: *She masked her anger with a smile.*

**camouflage** to hide sb/sth by making them/it look like the things around, or like sth else: *The soldiers camouflaged themselves with leaves and twigs.*

PATTERNS
- to hide/conceal/disguise/mask sth **behind** sth
- to hide/conceal sth **under** sth
- to hide/conceal sth **from** sb
- to hide/conceal/disguise/mask **the truth/the fact that**...
- to hide/conceal/disguise/mask **your feelings**

**hide-and-seek** /ˌhaɪd ən ˈsiːk/ (*NAmE also* **hide-and-go-seek** /ˌhaɪd ən ɡəʊ ˈsiːk/) *noun* [U] a children's game in which one player covers his or her eyes while the other players hide, and then tries to find them

**hide·a·way** /ˈhaɪdəweɪ/ *noun* a place where you can go to hide or to be alone

**hide·bound** /ˈhaɪdbaʊnd/ *adj.* (*disapproving*) having old-fashioned ideas, rather than accepting new ways of thinking SYN **narrow-minded**

**hi-def** /ˌhaɪ ˈdef/ *adj.* [only before noun] (*informal*) = HIGH-DEFINITION

**hid·eous** /ˈhɪdiəs/ *adj.* very ugly or unpleasant SYN **revolting**: *a hideous face/building/dress* ◊ *Their new colour scheme is hideous!* ◊ *a hideous crime* ◊ *The whole experience had been like some hideous nightmare.* ▶ **hid·eous·ly** *adv.*: *His face was hideously deformed.*

**hide-out** /ˈhaɪdaʊt/ *noun* a place where sb goes when they do not want anyone to find them

**hidey-hole** (*also* **hidy-hole**) /ˈhaɪdi həʊl/ *noun* (*informal*) a place where sb hides, especially in order to avoid being with other people

**hid·ing** /ˈhaɪdɪŋ/ *noun* **1** [U] the state of being hidden: **in/into ~** *We spent months in hiding.* ◊ *After the trial, she had to* **go into hiding** *for several weeks.* **out of ~** *He only came out of hiding ten years after the war was over.* **2** [U] the act of hiding sth: *I could understand the hiding of certain military secrets.* **3** [C, usually sing.] (*especially BrE, informal*) a physical punishment, usually involving being hit hard many times SYN **beating**: *to give sb/get a (good) hiding* ◊ (*figurative*) *The team got a hiding in their last game.*
IDM **on a ˈhiding to ˈnothing** (*BrE, informal*) having no chance of success, or not getting much advantage even if you do succeed

**ˈhiding place** *noun* a place where sb/sth can be hidden

**hie** /haɪ/ *verb* [I] (**hies, hying, hied**) + *adv./prep.* (*old use*) to go quickly

**hier·arch·ic·al** W /ˌhaɪəˈrɑːkɪkl; *NAmE* -ˈrɑːrk-/ *adj.* arranged in a hierarchy: *a hierarchical society/structure/organization* ▶ **hier·arch·ic·al·ly** /ˌhaɪəˈrɑːkɪkli; *NAmE* -ˈrɑːrk-/ *adv.*

**hier·archy** W /ˈhaɪərɑːki; *NAmE* -ɑːrki/ *noun* (*pl.* **-ies**) **1** [C, U] a system, especially in a society or an organization, in which people are organized into different levels of importance from highest to lowest: *the social/political hierarchy* ◊ *She's quite high up in the management hierarchy.* **2** [C + sing./pl. v.] the group of people in control of a large organization or institution **3** [C] (*formal*) a system that ideas or beliefs can be arranged into according to their importance: *a hierarchy of needs*

**hiero·glyph** /ˈhaɪərəɡlɪf/ *noun* a picture or symbol of an object, representing a word, syllable or sound, especially as used in ancient Egyptian and other writing systems ▶ **hiero·glyph·ic** /ˌhaɪərəˈɡlɪfɪk/ *adj.*

**hiero·glyph·ics** /ˌhaɪərəˈɡlɪfɪks/ *noun* [pl.] writing that uses hieroglyphs

**hieroglyphics**

hieroglyph

**hi-fi** /ˈhaɪ faɪ/ *noun* [C, U] equipment for playing recorded music that produces high-quality STEREO sound ⇒ compare HIGH FIDELITY ▶ **hi-fi** *adj.* [usually before noun]: *a hi-fi system*

**higgledy-piggledy** /ˌhɪɡldi ˈpɪɡldi/ *adv.* (*informal*) in an untidy way that lacks any order: *Files were strewn higgledy-piggledy over the floor.* ▶ **higgledy-piggledy** *adj.*: *a higgledy-piggledy collection of houses*

**high** /haɪ/ *adj., adv., noun*

■ *adj.* (**higher, highest**)
• FROM BOTTOM TO TOP **1** measuring a long distance from the bottom to the top: *What's the highest mountain in the US?* ◊ *The house has a high wall all the way round it.* ◊ *shoes with high heels* ◊ *He has a round face with a high forehead.* OPP **low** **2** used to talk about the distance that sth measures from the bottom to the top: *How high is Everest?* ◊ *It's only a low wall—about a metre high.* ◊ *The grass was waist-high.*
• FAR ABOVE GROUND **3** at a level that is a long way above the ground or above the level of the sea: *a high*

WORD FAMILY
**high** *adj., noun, adv.*
**highly** *adv.*
**height** *noun*
**heighten** *verb*

branch/shelf/window ◊ The rooms had high ceilings. ◊ They were flying at high altitude. ◊ the grasslands of the high prairies **OPP** low
- **GREATER THAN NORMAL 4** ¶ **A2** greater or better than normal in quantity or quality, size or degree: *a high price/cost/speed/temperature* ◊ *a high rate of inflation* ◊ *high levels of pollution* ◊ *Demand is high at this time of year.* ◊ *high-quality goods* ◊ *a high risk of injury* ◊ *a high standard of craftsmanship* ◊ *a high proportion/percentage of sth* ◊ *A high degree of accuracy is needed.* ◊ **higher than...** *Sales were significantly higher than in previous years.* ◊ *The tree blew over in the high winds.* ◊ *We had high hopes for the business* (= we believed it would be successful). ⊃ HOMOPHONES at HIRE ⊃ compare LOW
- **CONTAINING A LOT 5** ¶ **B1** containing a lot of a particular substance: *a high potassium content* ◊ *a high-fat diet* ◊ **~in sth** *foods that are high in fat* **OPP** low
- **RANK/STATUS 6** [usually before noun] near the top in rank, status or importance: *She has held high office under three prime ministers.* ◊ **~ on sth** *Job security is high on his list of priorities.* **OPP** low ⊃ see also HIGH COURT
- **VALUABLE 7** of great value: *to play for high stakes* ◊ *My highest card is ten.* ◊ **~ against sth** *At the moment, the euro is high against the dollar, which makes for a good exchange rate.*
- **RIVER/SEA 8** when a river or the TIDE is **high**, the water reaches a long way up the river bank, beach, etc: *The river was very high and threatening to flood.* ⊃ see also HIGH TIDE
- **IDEALS/PRINCIPLES 9** [usually before noun] morally good: *a man of high ideals/principles*
- **APPROVING 10** [usually before noun] showing a lot of approval or respect for sb: *She is held in very high regard by her colleagues.* ◊ *You seem to have a high opinion of yourself!* **OPP** low
- **SOUND 11** at the upper end of the range of sounds that humans can hear; not deep or low: *She has a high voice.* ◊ *That note is definitely too high for me.* **OPP** low
- **OF PERIOD OF TIME 12** [only before noun] used to describe the middle or the most attractive part of a period of time: *high noon* ◊ *high summer*
- **FOOD 13** (of meat, cheese, etc.) beginning to go bad and having a strong smell
- **ON ALCOHOL/DRUGS 14** [not before noun] **~ (on sth)** (informal) behaving in an excited way because of the effects of alcohol or drugs
- **PHONETICS 15** (phonetics) = CLOSE²

**IDM** **be/get on your high ˈhorse** (informal) to behave in a way that shows you think you are better than other people **friends, people, etc. in high ˈplaces** friends, people, etc. in positions of power and influence: *He has friends in high places.* **have a ˈhigh old time** (old-fashioned, informal) to enjoy yourself very much **high and ˈdry 1** (of a boat, etc.) in a position out of the water: *Their yacht was left high and dry on a sandbank.* **2** in a difficult situation, without help or money **high and ˈmighty** (informal) behaving as though you think you are more important than other people **high as a ˈkite** (informal) behaving in a very excited way, especially because of being strongly affected by alcohol or drugs **in high ˈdudgeon** (old-fashioned, formal) in an angry or offended mood, and showing other people that you are angry: *He stomped out of the room in high dudgeon.* **smell, stink, etc. to high ˈheaven** (informal) **1** to have a strong unpleasant smell **2** to seem to be very dishonest or morally unacceptable ⊃ more at HELL, MORAL adj., ORDER n., PROFILE n., TIME n.

■ **adv.** (**highˈer, highˈest**)
- **FAR FROM GROUND/BOTTOM 1** ¶ **A2** at or to a position or level that is a long way up from the ground or from the bottom: *to climb/jump/leap high* ◊ *An eagle soared high overhead.* ◊ *His desk was piled high with papers.* ◊ **~ above (sth)** *The castle sits high above the wooded valley.*
- **VALUE/AMOUNT 2** ¶ **A2** at or to a large value, amount or price: *Prices are expected to rise even higher this year.* ◊ *Students who scored high on the test went on to do very well.*
- **IMPORTANT POSITION 3** ¶ **B1** to or at an important position: *She never rose very high in the company.* ◊ *She's aiming high* (= hoping to be very successful) *in her exams.*

- **SOUND 4** at a high pitch: *I can't sing that high.* **OPP** low

**IDM** **high and ˈlow** everywhere: *I've searched high and low for my purse.* **run ˈhigh** (especially of feelings) to be strong and angry or excited: *Feelings ran high as the election approached.* ⊃ more at FLY v., HEAD n., RIDE v.

■ **noun**
- **LEVEL/NUMBER 1** ¶ **B2** the highest level or number: *to hit/reach a high* ◊ *Exports are currently at record highs.* ◊ *Profits reached an all-time high last year.*
- **WEATHER 2** an area of high air pressure; an ANTICYCLONE: *A high over southern Europe is bringing fine, sunny weather to all parts.* **3** the highest temperature reached during a particular day, week, etc: *Highs today will be in the region of 25°C.*
- **FROM DRUGS 4** (informal) the feeling of extreme pleasure and excitement that sb gets after taking some types of drugs: *The high lasted all night.*
- **FROM SUCCESS/ENJOYMENT 5** (informal) the feeling of extreme pleasure and excitement that sb gets from doing sth fun or being successful at sth: *He was on a real high after winning the competition.* ◊ *the highs and lows of her acting career*
- **SCHOOL 6** used in the name of a high school: *He graduated from Little Rock High in 2012.* ⊃ see also JUNIOR HIGH SCHOOL

**IDM** **on ˈhigh 1** (formal) in a high place: *We gazed down into the valley from on high.* **2** (humorous) the people in senior positions in an organization: *An order came down from on high that lunchbreaks were to be half an hour and no longer.* **3** in heaven: *The disaster was seen as a judgement from on high.*

▼ **WHICH WORD?**

**high / tall**
- **High** is used to talk about the measurement from the bottom to the top of something: *The fence is over five metres high.* ◊ *He has climbed some of the world's highest mountains.* You also use **high** to describe the distance of something from the ground: *How high was the plane when the engine failed?*
- **Tall** is used instead of **high** to talk about people: *My brother's much taller than me.* **Tall** is also used for things that are high and narrow such as trees: *She ordered cold beer in a tall glass.* ◊ *tall factory chimneys* ◊ *Tall pine trees line the roadways.* Buildings can be **high** or **tall**.

**ˈhigh·ball** /ˈhaɪbɔːl/ *noun, verb*
■ *noun* (especially NAmE) a strong alcoholic drink, such as WHISKY or GIN, mixed with FIZZY water (= with bubbles) or GINGER ALE, etc. and served with ice
■ *verb* (NAmE, informal) **1** [I] + **adv./prep.** to go somewhere very quickly: *They highballed out of town.* **2** [T] **~ sth** to deliberately make an estimate of the cost, value, etc. of sth that is too high: *He thought she was highballing her salary requirements.* **OPP** lowball

**high-ˈborn** *adj.* (old-fashioned or formal) having parents who are members of the highest social class **SYN** aristocratic **OPP** low-born

**high·brow** /ˈhaɪbraʊ/ *adj.* (sometimes disapproving) interested in serious artistic or cultural ideas **SYN** intellectual: *highbrow newspapers* ◊ *highbrow readers* **OPP** lowbrow ⊃ compare MIDDLEBROW

**ˈhigh chair** *noun* a special chair with long legs and a little seat and table, for a small child to sit in when eating

**high-ˈclass** *adj.* **1** excellent; of good quality: *a high-class restaurant* ◊ *to stay in high-class accommodation* **2** connected with a high social class: *to come from a high-class background* **OPP** low-class

**ˌhigh comˈmand** *noun* [usually sing.] the senior leaders of the armed forces of a country

**ˌhigh comˈmission** *noun* **1** the office and the staff of an EMBASSY that represents the interests of one Commonwealth country in another **2** a group of people who are working for a government or an international

# High Commissioner

organization on an important project: *the United Nations High Commission for Refugees*

**High Com'missioner** *noun* **1** a person who is sent by one Commonwealth country to live in another, to protect the interests of their own country **2** a person who is head of an important international project: *the United Nations High Commissioner for Refugees*

**high-'concept** *adj.* (used about an idea in a film or television story) very interesting and unusual but simple to explain and likely to be popular with a wide audience: *'Honey, I Shrunk the Kids' is a high-concept comedy about a scientist who accidentally, well, shrinks his kids.*

**high 'court** *noun* **1** (*also* **High Court of 'Justice**) a court in England and Wales that deals with the most serious CIVIL cases (= not criminal cases) **2** [*sing.*] = SUPREME COURT

**'high day** *noun* (*BrE, old-fashioned*) the day of a religious festival
IDM **high days and 'holidays** festivals and special occasions

**high-defi'nition** *adj.* (*abbr.* **HD**) (*also informal* **high-'def**, *informal* **hi-def**) [only before noun] using or produced by a system that gives very clear detailed images: *high-definition television* ◊ *high-definition displays* ⇒ see also HDTV

**high-'end** *adj.* expensive and of high quality

**High·er** /ˈhaɪə(r)/ *noun* (in Scotland) an exam taken in a particular subject at a higher level than National 3, 4 and 5 qualifications. Highers are usually taken around the age of 17 to 18. ⇒ see also NQ

**high·er** /ˈhaɪə(r)/ *adj.* [only before noun] at a more advanced level; greater in rank or importance than others: *The case was referred to a higher court.* ◊ *higher mathematics* ◊ *My mind was on higher things.* **HOMOPHONES** at HIRE

**higher 'animals, higher 'plants** *noun* [*pl.*] (*specialist*) animals and plants that have reached an advanced stage of development, such as MAMMALS and FLOWERING plants

**higher de'gree** *noun* a degree taken after a first degree, at a more advanced level. Examples are an MA (Master of Arts), an MSc (Master of Science) or a PhD (Doctor of Philosophy)

**higher edu'cation** *noun* [U] (*abbr.* **HE**) education at university, especially to degree level ⇒ compare FURTHER EDUCATION, TERTIARY EDUCATION ⇒ WORDFINDER NOTE at STUDY

**higher-'up** *noun* (*informal*) a person who has a higher rank or who is more senior than you

**highest common 'factor** *noun* (*abbr.* **HCF**) (*mathematics*) the highest number that can be divided exactly into two or more numbers

**high ex'plosive** *noun* [C, U] a very powerful substance that is used in bombs and can damage a very large area

**high·fa·lu·tin** /ˌhaɪfəˈluːtɪn/ *adj.* (*informal*) trying to be serious or important, but in a way that often appears silly and unnecessary **SYN pretentious**

**high fi'delity** *noun* [U] very high quality recording and playing of sound by electronic equipment ⇒ compare HI-FI

**high 'five** *noun* an action to celebrate victory or to express happiness in which two people raise one arm each and hit their open hands together: *Way to go! High five!*

**high-'flown** *adj.* (*usually disapproving*) (of language and ideas) very grand and complicated **SYN bombastic**: *His high-flown style just sounds absurd today.*

**high-'flyer** (*also* **high-'flier**) *noun* a person who has the desire and the ability to be very successful in their job or their studies: *academic high-flyers*

**high-'flying** *adj.* [only before noun] **1** very successful: *a high-flying career woman* **2** that flies very high in the air

**high 'gear** *noun* [U] (*especially NAmE*) the highest GEAR in a vehicle that is used when you are driving fast
IDM **in/into high gear** in a state of intense activity: *Her career is back in high gear.* **kick/move/swing into high gear** to become more intense: *The campaign season for this year's elections doesn't really kick into high gear until June.*

**high-'grade** *adj.* [usually before noun] of very good quality: *high-grade petrol*

**high 'ground** *noun* **1** [U] land that is higher than the surrounding area, especially land that stays dry **2** (*usually* **the high ground**) [*sing.*] the advantage in a discussion or an argument, etc: *The government is claiming the high ground in the education debate.* IDM ⇒ see MORAL *adj.*

**high-'handed** *adj.* (of people or their behaviour) using authority in an unreasonable way, without considering the opinions of other people **SYN overbearing**

**'high-hat** *noun* = HI-HAT

**high 'heels** *noun* [*pl.*] shoes that have very high heels, usually worn by women ▸ **high-'heeled** *adj.* [only before noun]: *high-heeled shoes/boots*

**high 'jinks** (*NAmE also* **'hi-jinks**) *noun* [*pl.*] (*old-fashioned, informal*) lively and excited behaviour **SYN fun**

**high 'jump** *noun often* **the high jump** [*sing.*] a sporting event in which people try to jump over a high bar that is gradually raised higher and higher: *She won a silver medal in the high jump.*
IDM **be for the 'high jump** (*BrE, informal*) to be going to be severely punished

**high·land** /ˈhaɪlənd/ *adj., noun*
■ *adj.* [only before noun] **1** connected with an area of land that has hills or mountains: *highland regions* **2 Highland** connected with the Highlands of Scotland ⇒ compare LOWLAND
■ *noun* **1** [C, usually *pl.*] an area of land with hills or mountains **2 the Highlands** [*pl.*] the high mountain region of Scotland ⇒ compare LOWLAND

**Highland 'cattle** *noun* [*pl.*] cows of a type with long rough hair and large HORNS. An individual animal is a **Highland cow**.

**high·land·er** /ˈhaɪləndə(r)/ *noun* **1** a person who comes from an area where there are a lot of mountains **2 Highland·er** a person who comes from the Scottish Highlands ⇒ compare LOWLANDER

**Highland 'Games** *noun* [*pl.*] a Scottish event with traditional sports, dancing and music

**high-'level** *adj.* [usually before noun] **1** involving senior people: *high-level talks/negotiations* ◊ *high-level staff* **2** in a high position or place: *a high-level walk in the hills* **3** advanced: *a high-level course* **4** (*computing*) (of a computer language) similar to an existing language such as English, making it fairly simple to use **5** (of a description or summary) without a lot of detail: *That's the high-level description, but the details get more complicated.* **OPP low-level**

**'high life** *noun* (*also* **the high life**) [*sing.*, U] (*also* **high 'living** [U]) (*sometimes disapproving*) a way of life that involves going to parties and spending a lot of money on food, clothes, etc.

**high·life** /ˈhaɪlaɪf/ *noun* [U] a style of dance and music from West Africa influenced by rock and jazz and popular especially in the 1950s and 1960s

**high·light** /ˈhaɪlaɪt/ *verb, noun*
■ *verb* **1** ~ sth to emphasize sth, especially so that people give it more attention: *The report highlighted the importance of exercise to maintain a healthy body.* ◊ *Students highlighted the need for better communication between staff.* ◊ *to highlight the major problems/issues* ◊ *This study highlights the fact that couples are keen to assist others.* ⇒ LANGUAGE BANK at EMPHASIS **2** ~ sth to mark part of a text with a special coloured pen, or to mark an area on a computer screen, to emphasize it or make it easier to see: *I've highlighted the important passages in yellow.* **3** ~ sth to make some parts of your hair a lighter colour than the rest by using a chemical substance on them
■ *noun* **1** the best, most interesting or most exciting part of sth: *One of the highlights of the trip was seeing the Taj Mahal.* ◊ *The highlights of the match will be shown later*

this evening. **2 highlights** [pl.] areas of hair that are lighter than the rest, usually because a chemical substance has been put on them ⊃ compare LOWLIGHTS **3 highlights** [pl.] (*specialist*) the light or bright part of a picture or photograph

**high·light·er** /ˈhaɪlaɪtə(r)/ *noun* **1** (*also* **ˈhighlighter pen**) a special pen used for marking words in a text in bright colours **2** a coloured substance that you put above your eyes or on your CHEEKS to make yourself more attractive

**high·ly** ⓘ B1 ⦿ /ˈhaɪli/ *adv.* **1** B1 very: *It is highly unlikely that she'll be late.* ◇ *She had a highly successful career as a portrait painter.* ◇ *highly critical/sensitive* ◇ *a highly effective design* **2** B1 at or to a high standard, level or amount: *highly trained/educated* ◇ *a highly paid job* ◇ *The region boasts a highly skilled workforce.* **3** B2 with great respect or praise: *I highly recommend this book.* ◇ *His teachers think very highly of him* (= have a very good opinion of him). ◇ *She speaks highly of you.* ◇ *Her novels are very highly regarded.*

**ˌhighly ˈstrung** (*BrE*) (*NAmE* **highˈstrung**) *adj.* (of a person or an animal) nervous and easily upset: *a sensitive and highly-strung child* ◇ *Their new horse is very highly strung.* ⊃ compare NERVOUS

**highˈmaintenance** *adj.* needing a lot of attention or effort: *a high-maintenance garden* ◇ (*informal*) *a high-maintenance girlfriend* OPP **low-maintenance**

**highˈminded** *adj.* (of people or ideas) having strong moral principles ▶ **highˈminded·ness** *noun* [U]

**High·ness** /ˈhaɪnəs/ *noun* **His/Her/Your Highness** a title of respect used when talking to or about a member of the royal family ⊃ see also ROYAL HIGHNESS

**ˌhigh ˈnoon** *noun* **1** exactly twelve o'clock in the middle of the day **2** (*formal*) the most important stage of sth, when sth that will decide the future happens

**highˈoctane** *adj.* [only before noun] **1** (of fuel used in engines) of very good quality and very efficient **2** (*informal*) full of energy; powerful: *a high-octane athlete*

**highˈperformance** *adj.* [only before noun] that can go very fast or do complicated things: *a high-performance car/computer, etc.*

**highˈpitched** *adj.* (of sounds) very high: *a high-pitched voice/whistle* OPP **low-pitched**

**ˈhigh point** (*BrE also* **ˈhigh spot**) *noun* the best or most interesting part of sth: *It was the high point of the evening.* OPP **low point**

**highˈpowered** *adj.* **1** (of people) having a lot of power and influence; full of energy: *high-powered executives* **2** (of activities) important; with a lot of responsibility: *a high-powered job* **3** (*also* **highˈpower**) (of machines) very powerful: *a high-powered car/computer, etc.*

**ˌhigh ˈpressure** *noun* [U] **1** the condition of air, gas, or liquid that is kept in a small space by force: **at ~** *Water is forced through the pipes at high pressure.* **2** a condition of the air that affects the weather, when the PRESSURE is higher than average ⊃ compare LOW PRESSURE

**highˈpressure** *adj.* [only before noun] **1** that involves aggressive ways of persuading sb to do sth or to buy sth: *high-pressure sales techniques* **2** that involves a lot of worry and stress SYN **stressful**: *a high-pressure job* **3** using or containing a great force of a gas or a liquid: *a high-pressure water jet*

**highˈpriced** *adj.* [usually before noun] expensive: *high-priced housing/cars* OPP **low**

**ˌhigh ˈpriest** *noun* **1** the most important priest in the Jewish religion in the past **2** (*feminine* **ˌhigh ˈpriestess**) an important priest in some other non-Christian religions; (*figurative*) *Janis Joplin was known as the High Priestess of Rock.*

**highˈprofile** ⓘ+ C1 *adj.* [usually before noun] receiving or involving a lot of attention and discussion in the media: *a high-profile campaign* ⊃ see also PROFILE *noun*

**highˈranking** *adj.* senior; important: *a high-ranking officer/official* ◇ *a high-ranking post* OPP **low-ranking**

749 **high-tech**

**highˌresoˈlution** (*also informal* **hi-res**, **high-res**) *adj.* (of a photograph or an image on a computer or television screen) showing a lot of clear sharp detail: *a high-resolution scan* OPP **low-resolution**

**ˌhighˈrise** *adj.* [only before noun] (of a building) very tall and having a lot of floors: *high-rise housing* ⊃ WORDFINDER NOTE at CITY ▶ **ˈhigh-rise** *noun*: *to live in a high-rise* ⊃ compare LOW-RISE

**highˈrisk** *adj.* [usually before noun] involving a lot of danger and the risk of injury, death, damage, etc.: *a high-risk sport* ◇ *high-risk patients* (= who are very likely to get a particular illness) ⊃ compare LOW-RISK

**ˌhigh ˈroad** *noun* [usually sing.] **1** (*old-fashioned* except in road names) a main or important road: *Kilburn High Road* **2 ~ (to sth)** the most direct way: *This is the high road to democracy.*
IDM **take the ˈhigh road (in sth)** (*NAmE*) to take the most positive course of action: *He took the high road in his campaign.*

**ˈhigh ˌroller** *noun* (*especially NAmE*, *informal*) a person who spends a lot of money, especially on GAMBLING

**ˈhigh school** *noun* [C, U] **1** (in the US and some other countries) a school for young people between the ages of 14 and 18: *I went to high school in Ohio.* ⊃ see also JUNIOR HIGH SCHOOL, SENIOR HIGH SCHOOL **2** often used in England, Wales and Northern Ireland in the names of schools for young people between the ages of 11 and 18: *Worthing High School* ⊃ compare SECONDARY SCHOOL

**the ˌhigh ˈseas** *noun* [pl.] (*formal* or *literary*) the open ocean, especially areas that are not under the legal control of any one country

**ˌhigh ˈseason** *noun* [U, sing.] (*especially BrE*) the time of year when a hotel or tourist area receives most visitors ⊃ compare LOW SEASON

**highˈsecurity** *adj.* [only before noun] **1** (of buildings and places) very carefully locked and guarded: *a high-security prison* **2** (of prisoners) kept in a prison that is very carefully locked and guarded

**ˌHigh ˈSheriff** *noun* = SHERIFF (2)

**highˈsounding** *adj.* (*often disapproving*) (of language or ideas) complicated and intended to sound important SYN **pretentious**

**highˈspeed** *adj.* [only before noun] that travels, works or happens very fast: *a high-speed train* ◇ *a high-speed car chase*

**highˈspirited** *adj.* **1** (of people) very lively and active: *a high-spirited child* ◇ *high-spirited behaviour* **2** (of animals, especially horses) lively and difficult to control OPP **placid** ⊃ see also SPIRIT

**ˈhigh spot** *noun* (*BrE*) = HIGH POINT

**ˈhigh street** (*BrE*) (*NAmE* **ˈmain street**) *noun* **1** (especially in names) the main street of a town, where most shops, banks, etc. are: *Peckham High Street* ◇ *106 High Street, Peckham* ◇ *high-street banks/shops* **2** used to refer to shops and businesses that serve the general public: *high-street fashion* ◇ **on the ~** *Sales on the UK high street are in decline.*

**highˈstrung** (*NAmE*) (*BrE* **ˌhighly ˈstrung**) *adj.* (of a person or an animal) nervous and easily upset ⊃ SYNONYMS at NERVOUS

**ˌhigh ˈtable** *noun* [C, U] (*BrE*) a table on a raised platform, where the most important people at a formal dinner sit to eat

**highˈtail** /ˈhaɪteɪl/ *verb*
IDM **ˈhightail it** (*informal*, *especially NAmE*) to leave somewhere very quickly

**ˌhigh ˈtea** *noun* [C, U] (*BrE*) a meal consisting of cooked food, bread and butter and cakes, usually with tea to drink, eaten in the late afternoon or early evening instead of dinner ⊃ compare CREAM TEA

**highˈtech** (*also* **hi-tech**) *adj.* (*informal*) **1** using the most modern methods and machines, especially electronic

# high technology

ones: *high-tech industries* **2** (of designs, objects, etc.) very modern in appearance; using modern materials: *a high-tech table made of glass and steel* ⊃ compare LOW-TECH

**ˌhigh techˈnology** *noun* [U] the most modern methods and machines, especially electronic ones; the use of these in industry, etc.

**ˌhigh-ˈtension** *adj.* [only before noun] carrying a very powerful electric current: *high-tension wires/cables*

**ˌhigh ˈtide** (also ˌhigh ˈwater) *noun* [U, C] the time when the sea has risen to its highest level in a particular place; the sea at this time: *at* ~ *You can't walk along this beach at high tide.* OPP low tide ⊃ compare FLOOD TIDE, HIGH WATER

**ˈhigh-tops** *noun* [pl.] (*especially NAmE*) sports shoes that cover the ankle, worn especially for playing basketball ▶ **ˈhigh-top** *adj.* [usually before noun]: *high-top sneakers*

**ˌhigh ˈtreason** *noun* [U] = TREASON

**ˈhigh-up** *noun* (*BrE, informal*) an important person with a high rank

**ˌhigh-visiˈbility** *adj.* [usually before noun] (*also informal* ˌhigh-ˈvis, ˌhi-ˈvis) **1** used to describe clothing made of material that appears very bright and is very easy to see: *cyclists with high-visibility jackets* ◊ *Hard hats and high-vis vests must be worn on the building site.* **2** used to describe sth that is intended to attract a lot of attention: *a high-visibility ad campaign*

**ˌhigh ˈwater** *noun* [U] = HIGH TIDE IDM see HELL

**ˌhigh-ˈwater mark** *noun* a line or mark showing the highest point that the sea or FLOODWATER has reached: (*figurative*) *the high-water mark of Parisian fashion* (= the most successful time) ⊃ compare LOW-WATER MARK

**high-way** ʔ+ B2 /ˈhaɪweɪ/ *noun* **1** ʔ+ B2 (*especially NAmE*) a main road for travelling long distances, especially one connecting and going through cities and towns: *an interstate highway* ◊ *Highway patrol officers closed the road.* **2** (*BrE, formal*) a public road: *A parked car was obstructing the highway.*

IDM ˌhighway ˈrobbery (*informal, especially NAmE*) = DAYLIGHT ROBBERY at DAYLIGHT ▶ more at WAY *n.*

**the ˌHighway ˈCode** *noun* [sing.] (in the UK) the official rules for drivers and other users of public roads; the book that contains these rules

**ˈhigh-way-man** /ˈhaɪweɪmən/ *noun* (*pl.* -men /-mən/) a man, usually on a horse and carrying a gun, who stole from travellers on public roads in the past

**ˈhigh wire** *noun* [usually sing.] a rope or wire that is stretched high above the ground, and used by CIRCUS performers to walk and balance on SYN **tightrope**

**ˈhi-hat** (also **ˈhigh-hat**) *noun* a pair of CYMBALS on a set of drums, operated by the foot

**hi·jab** /ˈhɪdʒɑːb/ *noun* **1** [C, U] a piece of clothing that covers the head, worn in public by some Muslim women **2** [U] the religious system that controls the wearing of such clothing

**hi·jack** /ˈhaɪdʒæk/ *verb* **1** ~ **sth** to use violence or threats to take control of a vehicle, especially a plane, in order to force it to travel to a different place or to demand sth from a government: *The plane was hijacked by two armed men on a flight from London to Rome.* ◆ WORDFINDER NOTE at ATTACK **2** ~ **sth** (*disapproving*) to use or take control of sth, for example a meeting, in order to use it for your own aims and interests ▶ **hi·jack·ing** (also **hi-jack**) *noun* [C, U]: *There have been a series of hijackings recently in the area.* ◊ *an unsuccessful hijack* ⊃ compare CARJACKING

**hi·jack·er** /ˈhaɪdʒækə(r)/ *noun* a person who hijacks a plane or other vehicle

**hi-jinks** (*NAmE*) = HIGH JINKS

**Hijra** /ˈhɪdʒrə/ *noun* = HEGIRA

**hike** /haɪk/ *noun, verb*

■ *noun* **1** a long walk in the country: *They went on a ten-mile hike through the forest.* ◊ *We could go into town but it's a real hike* (= a long way) *from here.* **2** (*informal*) a large or sudden increase in prices, costs, etc: *a tax/price hike* ◊ ~ *in sth the latest hike in interest rates*

IDM **take a ˈhike** (*NAmE, informal*) a rude way of telling sb to go away

■ *verb* **1** [I, T] to go for a long walk in the country, especially for pleasure: *strong boots for hiking over rough country* ◊ ~ **sth** (*NAmE*) *I always wanted to hike the Rockies.* **2** [I] **go ˈhiking** to spend time hiking for pleasure: *If the weather's fine, we'll go hiking this weekend.* **3** [T] ~ **sth (up)** to increase prices, taxes, etc. suddenly by large amounts: *The government hiked up the price of milk by over 40%.*

PHRV **ˌhike sth**↔**ˈup** (*informal*) to pull or lift sth up, especially your clothing SYN **hitch**: *She hiked up her skirt and waded into the river.*

**hiker** /ˈhaɪkə(r)/ *noun* a person who goes for long walks in the country for pleasure ⊃ see also HITCHHIKER

**hik·ing** /ˈhaɪkɪŋ/ *noun* [U] the activity of going for long walks in the country for pleasure: *He loves hiking.* ◊ *hiking boots*

**hil·ari·ous** ʔ+ B2 /hɪˈleəriəs; *NAmE* -ˈler-/ *adj.* extremely funny: *a hilarious joke/story* ◊ *Lynn found the whole situation hilarious.* ◊ *Do you know Pete? He's hilarious.* ⊃ SYNONYMS at FUNNY ▶ **hil·ari·ous·ly** *adv.*: *hilariously funny*

**hil·ar·ity** /hɪˈlærəti/ *noun* [U] the state of finding sth very funny

**hill** ❶ A2 /hɪl/ *noun* **1** A2 [C] an area of land that is higher than the land around it, but not as high as a mountain: *a region of gently rolling hills* ◊ *a hill farm/town/fort* ◊ **in the hills** *I love walking in the hills* (= in the area where there are hills). ◊ *They stopped at the **top of the hill** to admire the view.* ⊃ see also ANTHILL, FOOTHILL, MOLEHILL **2** A2 [C] a slope on a road: *Always take care when driving down steep hills.* ◊ *a hill start* (= the act of starting a vehicle on a slope) ⊃ see also DOWNHILL *noun*, UPHILL **3 the Hill** [sing.] (*NAmE, informal*) = CAPITOL HILL

IDM **a ˌhill of ˈbeans** (*NAmE, old-fashioned, informal*) something that is not worth much **ˌover the ˈhill** (*informal*) (of a person) old and therefore no longer useful or attractive ▶ more at OLD

**hill·billy** /ˈhɪlbɪli/ *noun* (*pl.* -**ies**) (*NAmE*) (*offensive*) a person who lives in the country and is thought to be stupid by people who live in the towns

**hil·lock** /ˈhɪlək/ *noun* a small hill

**hill·side** /ˈhɪlsaɪd/ *noun* the side of a hill: *The crops will not grow on exposed hillsides.* ◊ *Our hotel was on the hillside overlooking the lake.*

**ˈhill station** *noun* a small town in the hills, especially in South Asia, where people go to find cooler weather in summer

**hill·top** /ˈhɪltɒp; *NAmE* -tɑːp/ *noun* the top of a hill: *the hilltop town of Urbino*

**hill·walk·ing** /ˈhɪlwɔːkɪŋ/ *noun* [U] the activity of walking on or up hills in the countryside for pleasure

**hilly** /ˈhɪli/ *adj.* (**hill·ier**, **hilli·est**) having a lot of hills: *a hilly area/region*

**hilt** /hɪlt/ *noun* the handle of a SWORD, knife, etc. ⊃ picture at SWORD

IDM **(up) to the ˈhilt** as much as possible: *We're mortgaged up to the hilt.* ◊ *They have promised to back us to the hilt.*

**him** ❶ A1 /hɪm, ɪm/ *pron.* **1** ʔ A1 used as the object of a verb, after the verb *be* or after a preposition to refer to a male person or animal that has already been mentioned or is easily identified: *When did you see him?* ◊ *He took the children with him.* ◊ *I'm taller than him.* ◊ *It's him.* ⊃ compare HE ⊃ note at GENDER **2 Him** used when referring to God

**him·self** ❶ A2 /hɪmˈself/ *pron.* **1** A2 (the reflexive form of *he*) used when the man or boy who performs an action is also affected by it: *He introduced himself.* ◊ *Peter ought to be ashamed of himself.* **2** ʔ B1 used to emphasize the male subject or object of a sentence: *The doctor said so himself.* ◊ *Did you see the manager himself?*

**IDM** **be, seem, etc. him'self 1** (of a man or boy) to be in a normal state of health or happiness: *He didn't seem quite himself this morning.* **2** (of a man or boy) not influenced by other people: *He needed space to be himself.* **(all) by him'self 1** alone; without anyone else: *He lives all by himself.* **2** without help: *He managed to repair the car by himself.* **(all) to him'self** for only him to have or use; not shared: *He has the house to himself during the week.*

**hind** /haɪnd/ *adj., noun*
- *adj.* [only before noun] the **hind** legs or feet of an animal with four legs are those at the back: *The horse reared up on its hind legs.* **OPP fore, front**
- *noun* a female DEER, especially a RED DEER; a DOE ⊃ compare HART

**hind-brain** /'haɪndbreɪn/ *noun* (*anatomy*) the part of the brain near the base of the head

**hin-der** /'hɪndə(r)/ *verb* to make it difficult for sb to do sth or for sth to happen **SYN** hamper: *~sb/sth a political situation that hinders economic growth ◊ Some teachers felt hindered by a lack of resources.* ◊ *~sb/sth from sth/from doing sth An injury was hindering him from playing his best.* ⊃ see also HINDRANCE

**Hindi** /'hɪndi/ *noun* [U] one of the official languages of India, spoken especially in northern India ▶ **Hindi** *adj.*

**hind-limb** /'haɪndlɪm/ *noun* one of the legs at the back of an animal's body

**hind-quar-ters** /ˌhaɪnd'kwɔːtəz; NAmE ˌhaɪndkwɔːrtərz/ *noun* [pl.] the back part of an animal that has four legs, including its two back legs

**hin-drance** /'hɪndrəns/ *noun* **1** [C, usually sing.] a person or thing that makes it more difficult for sb to do sth or for sth to happen: *To be honest, she was more of a hindrance than a help.* ◊ *~to sth/sb The high price is a major hindrance to potential buyers.* **2** [U] (*formal*) the act of making it more difficult for sb to do sth or for sth to happen: *(without …) ~ They were able to complete their journey without further hindrance.* ⊃ see also HINDER **IDM** see LET *n.*

**hind-sight** /'haɪndsaɪt/ *noun* [U] the understanding that you have of a situation only after it has happened and that means you would have done things in a different way: **with~** *With hindsight it is easy to say they should not have released him.* ◊ **in~** *What looks obvious in hindsight was not at all obvious at the time.* ◊ *It's easy to criticize with the benefit of hindsight.* ⊃ compare FORESIGHT

**Hindu** /'hɪnduː/ *noun* a person whose religion is Hinduism ▶ **Hindu** *adj.: a Hindu temple*

**Hin-du-ism** /'hɪnduːɪzəm/ *noun* [U] the main religion of India and Nepal which includes the WORSHIP of one or more gods and belief in REINCARNATION

**Hin-dutva** /hɪn'dʊtvə/ *noun* [U] the belief that Indian culture and the Indian way of life should be based mainly on Hindu values

**hinge** /hɪndʒ/ *noun, verb*
- *noun* a piece of metal, plastic, etc. on which a door, LID or gate moves freely as it opens or closes: *The door had been pulled off its hinges.*
- *verb* [usually passive] *~sth* to attach sth with a hinge ▶ **hinged** *adj.: a hinged door/lid*
**PHRV** **'hinge on/upon sth** (of an action, a result, etc.) to depend on sth completely: *Everything hinges on the outcome of these talks.* ◊ **hinge on/upon how, what, etc …** *His success hinges on how well he does at the interview.*

**Hing-lish** /'hɪŋɡlɪʃ/ *noun* [U] (*informal*) language that is a mixture of ENGLISH and HINDI, especially a type of English that includes many Hindi words

**hint** /hɪnt/ *noun, verb*
- *noun* **1** something that you say or do in an indirect way in order to show sb what you are thinking: *He gave a broad hint* (= one that was obvious) *that he was thinking of retiring.* ◊ *Should I drop a hint* (= give a hint) *to Matt?* **2** something that suggests what will happen in the future **SYN** sign: *At the first hint of trouble, they left.* **3** *~(of sth)* a small amount of sth **SYN** suggestion, trace: *a hint of a smile ◊ There was more than a hint of sadness in his voice. ◊ The walls were painted white with a hint of peach.* **4** *~(on sth)* (usually pl.) a small piece of practical information or advice **SYN** tip: *handy hints on saving money*
**IDM** **take a/the 'hint** to understand what sb wants you to do even though they tell you in an indirect way: *I thought they'd never go—some people just can't take a hint. ◊ Sarah hoped he'd take the hint and leave her alone.*
- *verb* [I, T] to suggest sth in an indirect way: *~at sth What are you hinting at? ◊ ~(that) … They hinted (that) there might be more job losses. ◊ +speech 'I might know something about it,' he hinted.*

**hin-ter-land** /'hɪntəlænd; NAmE -tərl-/ *noun* the areas of a country that are away from the coast, from the banks of a large river or from the main cities: *the rural/agricultural hinterland*

**hip** /hɪp/ *noun, adj., exclamation*
- *noun* **1** the area at either side of the body between the top of the leg and the middle part of the body; the JOINT at the top of the leg that connects it with the top part of the body: *She stood with her hands on her hips. ◊ These jeans are too tight around the hips. ◊ a hip replacement operation ◊ the hip bone ◊ She broke her hip in the fall.* ⊃ VISUAL VOCAB page V1 **2** *-hipped* (in adjectives) having hips of the size or shape mentioned: *large-hipped ◊ slim-hipped* **3** (also **'rose hip**) the red fruit that grows on some types of wild ROSE bush **IDM** see SHOOT *v.*
- *adj.* (**hip-per, hip-pest**) (*informal*) following or knowing what is fashionable in clothes, music, etc.
- *exclamation*
**IDM** **hip, hip, hoo'ray!** (also less frequent **hip, hip, hur'rah/hur'ray!**) used by a group of people to show their approval of sb. One person in the group says 'hip, hip' and the others then shout 'hooray': *'Three cheers for the bride and groom: Hip, hip …' 'Hooray!'*

**'hip flask** (NAmE also **flask**) *noun* a small flat bottle made of metal or glass and often covered with leather, used for carrying alcohol with you

**'hip-hop** *noun* [U] **1** a type of popular music with spoken words and a steady beat, originally played by young African Americans **2** the culture of the young African Americans and others who enjoy this type of music, including special styles of art, dancing, dress, etc.

**'hip-huggers** (NAmE) (BrE **hip-sters**) *noun* [pl.] trousers that fasten at the HIPS and do not reach as high as the WAIST (= the middle part of the body) ▶ **'hip-hugger** *adj.* [only before noun]

**'hip joint** *noun* the JOINT that connects the leg to the body, at the top of the THIGH bone

**'hip-pie** = HIPPY

**hippo** /'hɪpəʊ/ *noun* (*pl.* **-os**) (*informal*) = HIPPOPOTAMUS

**hippo-cam-pus** /ˌhɪpə'kæmpəs/ *noun* (*pl.* **hippo-campi** /ˌhɪpə'kæmpaɪ, -piː/) (*anatomy*) either of the two areas of the brain thought to be the centre of emotion and memory

**'hip pocket** *noun* a pocket at the back or the side of a pair of trousers or a skirt

**the Hippo-crat-ic oath** /ðə ˌhɪpəkrætɪk 'əʊθ/ *noun* [sing.] the promise that doctors make to keep to the principles of the medical profession

**hip-po-drome** /'hɪpədrəʊm/ *noun* **1** used in the names of some theatres and concert halls **2** (NAmE) an ARENA, especially one used for horse shows **3** a track in ancient Greece or Rome on which horse races or CHARIOT races took place

**hippo-pot-amus** /ˌhɪpə'pɒtəməs; NAmE -'pɑːt-/ (*also informal* **hippo**) *noun* (*pl.* **hippo-pot-amuses** /-məsɪz/ or **hip-po-pot-ami** /-maɪ/) a large heavy African animal with thick dark skin and short legs that lives in rivers and lakes

**hippy** (also **hippie**) /'hɪpi/ *noun* (*pl.* **-ies**) a person who rejects the way that most people live in Western society,

# hipster

often having long hair, wearing brightly coloured clothes and taking illegal drugs. The hippy movement was most popular in the 1960s.

**hip·ster** /ˈhɪpstə(r)/ noun a person who follows the latest trends and fashions in clothes, music, etc., especially those that are outside the cultural MAINSTREAM (= what is popular with most ordinary people) ▶ **hip·ster** adj. [only before noun]: *a hipster bar*

**hip·sters** /ˈhɪpstəz; NAmE -stərz/ (BrE) (NAmE **hip-hug·gers**) noun [pl.] trousers that fasten at the HIPS and do not reach as high as the middle part of the body: *a pair of hipsters* ▶ **hip·ster** adj. [only before noun]: *hipster jeans*

**hire** ⊕ B1 /ˈhaɪə(r)/ verb, noun
- verb 1 B1 [T, I] ~ (sb) to give sb a job: *She was hired three years ago.* ◊ *He does the hiring and firing in our company.* 2 B1 [T] ~ sb/sth to employ sb for a short time to do a particular job: *to hire a lawyer/detective* ◊ *They hired a firm of consultants to design the new system.* 3 B1 [T] (especially BrE) to pay money to borrow sth for a short time: ~sth *to hire a room/studio* ◊ ~sth from sb *We hired a car from a local firm.* ⊃ note at RENT
PHRV **hire sth ↔ ˈout** (especially BrE) to let sb use sth for a short time, in return for payment **hire yourself ˈout (to sb)** to arrange to work for sb: *He hired himself out to whoever needed his services.*
- noun 1 B2 [U] (especially BrE) the act of paying to use sth for a short time: *a hire car* ◊ *a car hire firm* ◊ *The price includes the hire of the hall.* ◊ **for** ~ *There are boats for hire on the lake.* ◊ **on** ~ **from sb/sth** *The costumes are on hire from the local theatre.* ⊃ note at RENT 2 [C] (especially NAmE) a person who has recently been given a job by a company IDM see PLY v.

▼ HOMOPHONES
higher • hire /ˈhaɪə(r)/
- higher (comparative of HIGH): *Asparagus grows faster at higher temperatures.*
- hire verb: *Can we hire a car here?*
- hire noun: *Look! There are rowing boats for hire on the lake!*

**hired ˈhand** noun (NAmE) a person who is paid to work for a short time on a farm or doing other MANUAL (1) work (= work using their hands or physical strength)

**hire·ling** /ˈhaɪəlɪŋ; NAmE -ərl-/ noun (disapproving) a person who is willing to do anything or work for anyone as long as they are paid

**ˈhire ˈpurchase** noun [U] (BrE) (abbr. **h.p.**, **HP**) (NAmE **inˈstallment plan**) a method of buying an article by making regular payments for it over several months or years. The article only belongs to the person who is buying it when all the payments have been made: **on** ~ *I bought my first car on hire purchase.* ◊ *a hire purchase agreement* ⊃ compare CREDIT

**hi-res** (also **high-res**) /ˌhaɪ ˈrez/ adj. (informal) = HIGH-RESOLUTION

**hir·sute** /ˈhɜːsjuːt; NAmE ˈhɜːrsuːt/ adj. (literary or humorous) (especially of a man) having a lot of hair on the face or body SYN hairy

**his** ⊕ A1 /hɪz, ɪz/ det., pron.
- det. (the possessive form of *he*) 1 A1 of or belonging to a man or boy who has already been mentioned or is easily identified: *James has sold his car.* ◊ *He broke his leg skiing.* 2 **His** of or belonging to God
- pron. A2 of or belonging to him: *He took my hand in his.* ◊ *The choice was his.* ◊ *a friend of his* ⊃ note at GENDER

**His·pan·ic** /hɪˈspænɪk/ adj., noun
- adj. of or connected with Spain or Spanish-speaking countries, especially those of Latin America
- noun a person whose first language is Spanish, especially one from a Latin American country living in the US or Canada HELP In the US **Hispanic** is the usual term used to talk about Spanish-speaking people living in the US. Other, more specific terms, such as LATINO and CHICANO are also sometimes used.

**His·pan·o-** /hɪˈspænəʊ/ combining form (in nouns and adjectives) Spanish: *the Hispano-French border* ◊ *Hispanophile*

**hiss** /hɪs/ verb, noun
- verb 1 [I] ~ (at sb/sth) to make a sound like a long 's': *The steam escaped with a loud hissing noise.* ◊ *The snake lifted its head and hissed.* 2 [T, I] ~ (sb/sth) | ~ (sb/sth + adv./prep.) to make a sound like a long 's' to show DISAPPROVAL of sb/sth, especially an actor or a speaker: *He was booed and hissed off the stage.* 3 [I, T] to say sth in a quiet angry voice: ~**at sb** *He hissed at them to be quiet.* ◊ + speech '*Leave me alone!' she hissed.*
- noun a sound like a long 's'; this sound used to show DISAPPROVAL of sb: *the hiss of the air brakes* ◊ *the snake's hiss* ◊ *The performance was met with boos and hisses.*

**ˈhissy fit** noun [C, usually sing.] (informal) a sudden short period of angry behaviour for no good reason SYN **tantrum**: *She threw a hissy fit because her dressing room wasn't painted blue.*

**his·ta·mine** /ˈhɪstəmiːn/ noun [U] (medical) a chemical substance that is given out in the body in response to an injury or an ALLERGY ⊃ see also ANTIHISTAMINE

**histo·gram** /ˈhɪstəɡræm/ noun (specialist) a diagram that uses RECTANGLES (= bars) of different heights (and sometimes different WIDTHS) to show different amounts, so that they can be compared ⊃ compare BAR CHART

**hist·ol·ogy** /hɪˈstɒlədʒi; NAmE -ˈstɑːl-/ noun [U] (biology) the scientific study of the extremely small structures that form living TISSUE ▶ **his·tolo·gist** noun

**histo·path·ology** /ˌhɪstəʊpəˈθɒlədʒi; NAmE -ˈθɑːl-/ noun [U] the study of changes in cells where disease is present

**his·tor·ian** ⊕+ B2 /hɪˈstɔːriən/ noun a person who studies or writes about history; an expert in history HELP Some speakers do not pronounce the 'h' at the beginning of **historian** and use 'an' instead of 'a' before it. This now sounds old-fashioned.

**his·tor·ic** ⊕ B1 /hɪˈstɒrɪk; NAmE -ˈstɔːr-/ adj. [usually before noun] 1 B1 important in history; likely to be thought of as important at some time in the future: *the restoration of historic buildings* ◊ *Take a tour of historic sites in the old city.* ◊ *It was a great fight, a historic moment in Irish sport.* ◊ *a historic event/occasion/victory* 2 of a period during which history was recorded: *in historic times* ⊃ compare PREHISTORIC 3 (of a crime or claim) that took place in the past but was not dealt with at the time: *There is still more to be done to right the historic injustice of slavery.* HELP Some speakers do not pronounce the 'h' at the beginning of **historic** and use 'an' instead of 'a' before it. This now sounds old-fashioned.

▼ WHICH WORD?
**historic / historical**
- **Historic** is usually used to describe something that is so important that it is likely to be remembered: *Today is a historic occasion for our country.* **Historical** usually describes something that is connected with the past or with the study of history, or something that really happened in the past: *I have been doing some historical research.* ◊ *Was Robin Hood a historical figure?*

**his·tor·ic·al** ⊕ B1 /hɪˈstɒrɪkl; NAmE -ˈstɔːr-/ adj. [usually before noun] 1 B1 connected with the past: *You must place these events in their historical context.* ◊ *stories based on historical fact* ◊ *This book provides a historical perspective.* ◊ *one of the greatest historical figures of all time, Alexander the Great* 2 B1 connected with the study of history: *historical documents/records/research* ◊ *historical evidence provided by scholars* ◊ *The building is of historical importance.* 3 B1 (of a book, film, etc.) about people and events in the past: *a historical novel/setting* ◊ *Good historical fiction sheds light on the past.* ⊃ WORDFINDER NOTE at STORY HELP Some speakers do not pronounce the 'h' at the beginning of **historical** and use 'an' instead of 'a' before it. This now sounds old-fashioned. ▶ **his·tor·ic·al·ly**

/-kli/ *adv.*: *The book is historically inaccurate.* ◊ *Historically, there has always been a great deal of rivalry between the two families.*

**his·tor·i·cism** /hɪˈstɒrɪsɪzəm; *NAmE* -ˈstɔːr-/ *noun* [U] the theory that cultural and social events and situations can be explained by history

**his·tor·i·og·raphy** /hɪˌstɒriˈɒɡrəfi; *NAmE* -ˌstɔːriˈɑːɡ-/ *noun* [U] the study of writing about history ▶ **his·tori·og·raph·ical** /hɪˌstɒriəˈɡræfɪkl; *NAmE* -ˌstɔːr-/ *adj.*

**his·tory** 🅐 **A1** 🔊 /ˈhɪstri/ *noun* (*pl.* **-ies**) **1** **A1** [U] all the events that happened in the past: *in~ a turning point in human history* ◊ *one of the worst disasters in recent history* ◊ *throughout~ Many people throughout history have dreamt of a world without war.* ◊ *The area was inhabited long before the dawn of recorded history* (= before people wrote about events). ◊ *These events changed the course of history.* **2** **A1** [sing., U] the past events connected with the development of a particular place, subject, etc: *the history of science/music/philosophy* ◊ *She is an expert in the history of the United States.* ◊ *The local history of the area is fascinating.* ◊ *The museum traces the history of the slave trade.* **3** **A1** [U] (*also* **History**) the study of past events, especially as a subject at school or university: *a history professor/teacher* ◊ *a degree in History* ◊ *cultural/social/ economic/political history* ◊ *modern/ancient history* ◊ *She's studying art history.* ⊃ see also NATURAL HISTORY **4** **A2** [C, U] a written or spoken account of real past events: *She's writing a new history of Europe.* ◊ *She went on to catalogue a long history of disasters.* ⊃ see also ORAL HISTORY **5** **B2** [C] the set of facts that are known about sb/sth's past: *I know nothing about his personal history.* ◊ *a patient's medical history* **6** **B2** [C, usually sing.] **a ~ of sth** a record of sth happening frequently in the past life of a person, family or place: *He has a history of violent crime.* ◊ *There is a history of heart disease in my family.* ⊃ see also CASE HISTORY, LIFE HISTORY **7** [U, sing.] **~ between A and B** a relationship between two people, groups, companies, etc. that started in the past and continued for a period of time, especially one involving bad or complicated feelings: *Sure there's history between Anna Mae and me, like you said.* **8** [C] a historical play: *Shakespeare's comedies, histories and tragedies*
**IDM** **be ˈhistory** (*informal*) to be dead or no longer important: *Another mistake like that and you're history.* ◊ *We won't talk about that—that's history.* ◊ *That's past history now.* **the ˈhistory books** the record of great achievements in history: *She has earned her place in the history books.* **history reˈpeats itself** used to say that things often happen later in the same way as before **make ˈhistory | go down in ˈhistory** to be or do sth so important that it will be recorded in history: *a discovery that made medical history* ⊃ more at REST *n.*

**ˈhistory-sheeter** *noun* (*IndE*) a person who has been found guilty of a crime in the past: *He was a history-sheeter who had served two years in jail for his crimes.*

**his·tri·on·ic** /ˌhɪstriˈɒnɪk; *NAmE* -ˈɑːn-/ *adj.* [usually before noun] (*formal, disapproving*) **histrionic** behaviour is very emotional and is intended to attract attention in a way that does not seem sincere ▶ **his·tri·on·ic·al·ly** /-kli/ *adv.* **his·tri·on·ics** *noun* [*pl.*]: *She was used to her mother's histrionics.*

**hit** 🅘 **A2** /hɪt/ *verb, noun*
■ *verb* (**hit·ting, hit, hit**)
• TOUCH SB/STH WITH FORCE **1** **A2** [T] to bring your hand, or an object you are holding, against sb/sth quickly and with force: **~ sb/sth** *I was afraid he was going to hit me.* ◊ **~ sb/ sth with sth** *She hit him with her umbrella.* ◊ **~ sb/sth (in/ on sth) (with sth)** *He hit the nail squarely on the head with the hammer.* ⊃ see also KING-HIT **2** **A2** [T, I] **~ (against) sth/sb** to come against sth/sb with force, especially causing damage or injury: *The bus hit the bridge.* ◊ *The boy was hit by a speeding car.* **3** **A2** [T] **~ sth** to knock a part of your body against sth: *I must have hit my knee.* ◊ **~ sth on/ against sth** *He hit his head on the low ceiling.* **4** **A2** [T, often passive] (of a bullet, bomb, etc. or a person using them) to reach and touch a person or thing suddenly and with force: **be ~ by sb/sth** *The town was hit by bombs again last night.* ◊ **~ sb/sth** *Not all the bullets hit their targets.* •

753

# hit

BALL **5** **A2** [T] **~ sth** to bring a BAT, etc. against a ball and push it away with force: *She hit the ball and ran to first base.* ◊ **~ sth + adv./prep.** *I hit the ball too hard and it went out of the court.* ⊃ see also PINCH-HIT **6** [T] **~ sth** (*sport*) to score points by hitting a ball: *to hit a home run*
• PRESS BUTTON **7** [T] **~ sth** (*informal*) to press sth such as a button to operate a machine, etc: *Hit the brakes!* ◊ *He picked up the phone and hit several buttons.*
• HAVE BAD EFFECT **8** **B1** [T, I] to have a bad effect on sb/sth: **~ (sb/sth)** *The tax increases will certainly hit the poor.* ◊ *A tornado hit on Tuesday night.* ◊ *Rural areas have been worst hit by the strike.* ◊ *Spain was one of the hardest hit countries.*
• ATTACK **9** [T, I] **~ (sb/sth)** to attack sb/sth: *We hit the enemy when they least expected it.*
• REACH **10** [T] **~ sth** (*informal*) to reach a place: *Follow this footpath and you'll eventually hit the road.* ◊ *The President hits town tomorrow.* **11** [T] **~ sth** to reach a particular level: *Temperatures hit 40° yesterday.* ◊ *The euro hit a record low in trading today.* ◊ *The film doesn't always hit its targets* (= succeed in what it is attempting to do).
• PROBLEM/DIFFICULTY **12** [T] **~ sth** (*informal*) to experience sth difficult or unpleasant: *We seem to have hit a problem.* ◊ *Everything was going well but then we hit trouble.*
• SUDDENLY REALIZE **13** [T] (*informal*) to come suddenly into your mind: **~ sb** *The idea hit me like a tornado.* ◊ **it hits sb** *I couldn't remember where I'd seen him before, and then it suddenly hit me.*
• BECOME AVAILABLE **14** [T] (*informal*) to become widely available for sale: *the latest board game to hit the market* ◊ *to hit the shops/stores/shelves* ◊ *Her shocking autobiography is about to hit the streets.*
**IDM** **hit (it) ˈbig** (*informal*) to be very successful: *The band has hit big in the US.* **hit the ˈbuffers** (*informal*) if a plan, sb's career, etc. **hits the buffers**, it suddenly stops being successful **hit the ˈdeck** (*informal*) to fall to the ground **ˌhit the ground ˈrunning** (*informal*) to start doing sth and continue very quickly and successfully **hit the ˈhay/ˈsack** (*informal*) to go to bed **hit sb (straight/right) in the ˈeye** to be very obvious to sb **ˈhit it** (*informal*) used to tell sb to start doing sth, such as playing music: *Hit it, Louis!* **hit it ˈoff (with sb)** (*informal*) to have a good friendly relationship with sb: *We hit it off straight away.* **hit the ˈjackpot** to make or win a lot of money quickly and unexpectedly **hit the nail on the ˈhead** to say sth that is exactly right **hit the ˈroad/ˈtrail** (*informal*) to start a journey **hit the ˈroof** = GO THROUGH THE ROOF at ROOF *n.* (2) **hit the ˈspot** (*informal*) if sth **hits the spot** it does exactly what it should do **hit a/the ˈwall** to reach a point when you cannot continue or make any more progress: *We hit a wall and we weren't scoring.* **hit sb when they're ˈdown** to continue to hurt sb when they are already defeated **hit sb where it ˈhurts** to affect sb where they will feel it most ⊃ more at HEADLINE *n.*, HOME *adv.*, KNOW *v.*, MARK *n.*, NERVE *n.*, NOTE *n.*, PAY DIRT, SHIT *n.*, SIX, STRIDE *n.*, WOODWORK
**PHRV** **ˌhit ˈback (at sb/sth)** to reply to attacks or criticism **SYN** **retaliate**: *In a TV interview she hit back at her critics.* **ˈhit on sb** (*NAmE, slang*) to start talking to sb to show them that you are sexually attracted to them **ˈhit on/upon sth** [no passive] (*rather informal*) to think of a good idea suddenly or by chance: *She hit on the perfect title for her new novel.* **ˌhit ˈout (at sb/sth)** to attack sb/ sth violently by fighting them or criticizing them: *I just hit out blindly in all directions.* ◊ *In a rousing speech the minister hit out at racism in the armed forces.* **ˌhit sb ˈup for sth | ˌhit sb for sth** (*NAmE, informal*) to ask sb for money: *Does he always hit you up for cash when he wants new clothes?* **ˈhit sb with sth** (*informal*) to tell sb sth, especially sth that surprises or shocks them: *How much is it going to cost, then? Come on, hit me with it!*
■ *noun*
• ACT OF HITTING **1** **A2** an act of hitting sb/sth with your hand or with an object held in your hand: *Give it a good hit.* ◊ *He made the winning hit.* ⊃ see also KING-HIT **2** **A2** an occasion when sth that has been thrown, fired, etc. at an object reaches that object; the fact of being hit by sth: *We finished the first round with a score of two hits and six*

# hit-and-miss 754

misses. ◊ One of the tanks *took a direct hit.* ◊ **~on sth** *Enemy planes scored a hit on a supply ship.*
- **STH POPULAR 3** A2 a person or thing that is very popular: *a hit show/comedy/musical* ◊ *a big/huge/smash hit* ◊ **~with sb** *The films have proved a hit with older audiences.*
- **POP MUSIC 4** A2 a successful pop song or record: *They are about to release an album of their greatest hits.* ◊ *She played all her old hits.* ◊ *a hit single/song*
- **COMPUTING 5** (*computing*) an occasion on which a web page is displayed or a file is downloaded from the internet: *Our website is getting a lot of hits from the USA.* ◊ *How many hits did you get?* **6** (*computing*) the fact of finding an item of data that matches a search: *The search generated 1848 hits.*
- **OF DRUG 7** (*slang*) an amount of an illegal drug that is taken at one time
- **MURDER 8** (*slang, especially NAmE*) a violent crime or murder ⊃ see also HITMAN
- IDM **be/make a 'hit (with sb)** to be liked very much by sb when they first meet you **take a 'hit** to be damaged or badly affected by sth: *The airline industry took a hit last year.*

▼ **SYNONYMS**

**hit**
**knock • bang • strike • bump • bash**

These words all mean to come against sth with a lot of force.

**hit** to come against sb/sth with force, especially causing damage or injury: *The boy was hit by a speeding car.*
**knock** to hit sth so that it moves or breaks; to put sb/sth into a particular state or position by hitting them/it: *Someone had knocked a hole in the wall.*
**bang** to hit sth in a way that makes a loud noise: *The baby was banging the table with his spoon.*
**strike** (*formal*) to hit sth hard: *The ship struck a rock.*
**bump** to hit sb/sth by accident: *In the darkness I bumped into a chair.*
**bash** (*informal*) to hit against sth very hard: *I braked too late, bashing into the car in front.*

PATTERNS
- to hit/knock/bang/bump/bash **against** sb/sth
- to knock/bang/bump/bash **into** sb/sth
- to hit/strike the **ground/floor/wall**

**hit-and-'miss** (*also* **hit-or-'miss**) *adj.* not done in a careful or planned way and therefore not likely to be successful

**hit-and-'run** *adj.* [only before noun] **1** (of a road accident) caused by a driver who does not stop to help: *a hit-and-run accident/death* ◊ *a hit-and-run driver* (= one who causes an accident but drives away without helping) **2** (of a military attack) happening suddenly and unexpectedly so that the people attacking can leave quickly without being hurt: *hit-and-run raids* ▶ **hit-and-'run** *noun*: *He was killed in a hit-and-run.*

**hitch** /hɪtʃ/ *verb, noun*
■ *verb* **1** [T, I] to get a free ride in a person's car; to travel around in this way, by standing at the side of the road and trying to get passing cars to stop: **~sth** *They hitched a ride in a truck.* ◊ (*BrE also*) *They hitched a lift.* **(+ adv./prep.)** *We spent the summer hitching around Europe.* ⊃ see also HITCHHIKE **2** [T] **~sth (up)** to pull up a piece of your clothing SYN **hike up**: *She hitched up her skirt and waded into the river.* **3** [T] **~yourself (up, etc.)** to lift yourself into a higher position, or the position mentioned: *She hitched herself up.* ◊ *He hitched himself onto the bar stool.* **4** [T] **~sth (to sth)** to tie or fasten sth to sth else with a rope, a HOOK, etc.: *She hitched the pony to the gate.*
IDM **get 'hitched** (*informal*) to get married
■ *noun* **1** a problem or difficulty that causes a short delay: **without a ~** *The ceremony went off without a hitch.* ⊃ see also TECHNICAL HITCH **2** a type of KNOT (= a join made by

tying together two pieces or ends of rope, etc.): *a clove hitch*

**hitch·hike** /'hɪtʃhaɪk/ *verb* [I] to travel by asking for free rides in other people's cars, by standing at the side of the road and trying to get passing cars to stop: *They hitch-hiked around Europe.* ⊃ see also HITCH *verb* ▶ **hitch·hiker** (*also* **hitch·er**) /'hɪtʃə(r)/ *noun*: *He picked up two hitchhikers on the road to Bristol.*

**hi-'tech** = HIGH-TECH

**hither** /'hɪðə(r)/ *adv.* (*old use*) to this place
IDM **hither and 'thither** | **hither and 'yon** (*especially literary*) in many different directions

**hith·er·to** /ˌhɪðə'tuː/ *NAmE* -ðər'tuː/ *adv.* (*formal*) until now; until the particular time you are talking about: *a hitherto unknown species of moth*

**'hit list** *noun* (*informal*) a list of people, organizations, etc. against whom some unpleasant action is being planned: *Which services are on the government's hit list?* ◊ *She was at the top of the terrorists' hit list for over two years.*

**hit·man** /'hɪtmæn/ *noun* (*pl.* **-men** /-men/) (*informal*) a criminal who is paid to kill sb

**hit-or-'miss** *adj.* = HIT-AND-MISS

**'hit-out** *noun* (in AUSTRALIAN RULES football) a hit of the ball towards a player from your team after it has been BOUNCED by the UMPIRE

**the 'hit parade** *noun* (*old-fashioned*) a list published every week that shows which pop records have sold the most copies

**'hit squad** *noun* a group of criminals or agents who are paid to kill a person

**hit·ter** /'hɪtə(r)/ *noun* (usually in compounds) **1** (in sports) a person who hits the ball in the way mentioned: *a big/long/hard hitter* ◊ *a left-handed/right-handed hitter* ⊃ see also DESIGNATED HITTER, NO-HITTER, SWITCH-HITTER **2** (in politics or business) a person who is powerful: *the heavy hitters of Japanese industry* ⊃ see also BIG HITTER

**HIV** /ˌeɪtʃ aɪ 'viː/ *noun* [U] the virus that can cause AIDS (the abbreviation for 'human immunodeficiency virus'): *to be infected with HIV* ◊ *to be HIV-positive/HIV-negative* (= to have had a medical test that shows that you are/are not infected with HIV)

**hive** /haɪv/ *noun, verb*
■ *noun* **1** (*also* **bee-hive**) [C] a structure made for bees to live in **2** [C] the bees living in a hive **3** [C, usually sing.] **a ~ of activity/industry** a place full of people who are busy **4 hives** [U, pl.] = URTICARIA
■ *verb*
PHRV **hive sth↔'off (to/into sth)** [often passive] (*especially BrE*) to separate one part of a group from the rest; to sell part of a business: *The IT department is being hived off into a new company.*

**hi-vis** /ˌhaɪ 'vɪz/ *adj.* = HIGH-VISIBILITY

**hiya** /'haɪjə/ *exclamation* (*informal*) used to say hello to sb in an informal way

**HI** *abbr.* HECTOLITRE

**HM** (*also* **H.M.**) *abbr.* HIS/HER MAJESTY('S): *HM the Queen* ◊ *HM Customs*

**HMG** *abbr.* (in writing) (*BrE*) Her Majesty's Government (a way of referring to the UK government in official contexts)

**hmm** (*also* **hm, h'm**) /m, hm/ *exclamation* used in writing to show the sound that you make to express doubt or when you are hesitating ⊃ compare MM

**HMRC** /ˌeɪtʃ em ɑː 'siː; *NAmE* ɑːr/ *abbr.* HM Revenue and Customs

**HM Revenue and 'Customs** *noun* [U] (*abbr.* **HMRC**) the government department in the UK that is responsible for collecting taxes ⊃ compare INTERNAL REVENUE SERVICE

**HMS** /ˌeɪtʃ em 'es/ *abbr.* Her/His Majesty's Ship (used before the name of a ship in the British NAVY): *HMS Apollo*

**HNC** /ˌeɪtʃ en 'siː/ *noun* a British university or college qualification, especially in a technical or scientific subject (the abbreviation for 'Higher National Certificate'): *to do an HNC in electrical engineering*

**HND** /ˌeɪtʃ en 'diː/ *noun* a British university or college qualification, especially in a technical or scientific subject (the abbreviation for 'Higher National Diploma'): *to do an HND in fashion design*

**ho** /həʊ/ *noun (pl.* **hos** *or* **hoes**) (*NAmE, taboo, slang*) **1** a female PROSTITUTE **2** an offensive word used about a woman, especially one who you think has sex with a lot of men ORIGIN Short form of *whore*. ⊃ see also HO HO

**hoagie** /'həʊgi/ *noun* (*NAmE*) **1** a long piece of bread filled with meat, cheese and salad **2** a piece of bread used to make a hoagie

**hoard** /hɔːd; *NAmE* hɔːrd/ *noun, verb*
- *noun* ~ (of sth) a collection of money, food, valuable objects, etc., especially one that sb keeps in a secret place so that other people will not find or steal it
- *verb* [I, T] ~ (sth) to collect and keep large amounts of food, money, etc., often secretly ▶ **hoard·er** *noun*

**hoard·ing** /'hɔːdɪŋ; *NAmE* 'hɔːrd-/ *noun* **1** (*BrE*) (*also* **bill-board** *NAmE, BrE*) [C] a large board on the outside of a building or at the side of the road, used for displaying advertisements **2** [C] (*BrE*) a temporary fence made of boards that is placed around an area of land until a building has been built **3** [U] the act of collecting and keeping large amounts of food, money, etc., often secretly

**hoar frost** /'hɔː frɒst; *NAmE* 'hɔːr frɔːst/ *noun* [U] a layer of small pieces of ice that look like white needles and that form on surfaces outside when temperatures are very low

**hoarse** /hɔːs; *NAmE* hɔːrs/ *adj.* if a person or their voice is **hoarse**, their voice sounds rough and unpleasant, especially because of a SORE throat (= a painful throat because of an infection): *He shouted himself hoarse.* ◊ *a hoarse cough/cry/scream* ▶ **hoarse·ly** *adv.* **hoarse·ness** *noun* [U]

**hoary** /'hɔːri/ *adj.* [usually before noun] **1** (*old-fashioned*) very old and well known and therefore no longer interesting: *a hoary old joke* **2** (*literary*) (especially of hair) grey or white because a person is old

**hoax** /həʊks/ *noun, verb*
- *noun* an act intended to make sb believe sth that is not true, especially sth unpleasant: *a bomb hoax* ◊ *hoax calls*
- *verb* ~ sb to trick sb by making them believe sth that is not true, especially sth unpleasant ▶ **hoax·er** *noun*

**hob** /hɒb; *NAmE* hɑːb/ *noun* **1** (*BrE*) (*NAmE* **stove·top** /'stəʊvtɒp; *NAmE* -tɑːp/) the top part of a cooker where food is cooked in pans; a similar surface that is built into a kitchen unit and is separate from the oven: *an electric/a gas hob* **2** a metal shelf at the side of a fire, used in the past for heating pans, etc. on

**hob·ble** /'hɒbl; *NAmE* 'hɑːbl/ *verb* **1** [I] (+ adv./prep.) to walk with difficulty, especially because your feet or legs hurt SYN limp: *The old man hobbled across the road.* **2** [T] ~ sth to tie together two legs of a horse or other animal in order to stop it from running away **3** [T] ~ sth to make it more difficult for sb to do sth or for sth to happen

**hobby** ⓘ A1 /'hɒbi; *NAmE* 'hɑːbi/ *noun* (*pl.* **-ies**) an activity that you do for pleasure when you are not working: *Her hobbies include swimming and gardening.* ◊ *as a ~ I only play jazz as a hobby.* ⊃ SYNONYMS at INTEREST ⊃ WORDFINDER NOTE at CLUB

**'hobby horse** *noun* **1** (*sometimes disapproving*) a subject that sb feels strongly about and likes to talk about: *to get on your hobby horse* (= talk about your favourite subject) **2** a toy made from a long stick that has a horse's head at one end. Children pretend to ride on it.

**hob·by·ist** /'hɒbiɪst; *NAmE* 'hɑːb-/ *noun* (*formal*) a person who is very interested in a particular hobby

**hob·gob·lin** /hɒb'gɒblɪn; ˌhɒbgɒblɪn; *NAmE* hɑːb'gɑːb-/ *noun* (in stories) a small ugly creature that likes to trick people or cause trouble

**hob·nob** /'hɒbnɒb; *NAmE* 'hɑːbnɑːb/ *verb* [I] (**-bb-**) ~ (with sb) (*informal*) to spend a lot of time with sb, especially sb who is rich and/or famous

**hobo** /'həʊbəʊ/ *noun (pl.* **-os** *or* **-oes**) (especially *NAmE, old-fashioned*) **1** a person who travels from place to place looking for work, especially on farms **2** = TRAMP

**Hob·son's choice** /ˌhɒbsnz 'tʃɔɪs; *NAmE* ˌhɑːbsnz/ *noun* [U] a situation in which sb has no choice because if they do not accept what is offered, they will get nothing ORIGIN From Tobias Hobson, a man who hired out horses in the 17th century. He gave his customers the choice of the horse nearest the stable door or none at all.

**hock** /hɒk; *NAmE* hɑːk/ *noun, verb*
- *noun* **1** [C] the middle JOINT of an animal's back leg **2** [U, C] (*BrE*) a German white wine **3** [U, C] = KNUCKLE **4** [U] (*informal*) that sth you own is in **hock**, you have exchanged it for money but hope to buy it back later
  IDM **be in 'hock (to sb)** to owe sb sth: *I'm in hock to the bank for £6000.*
- *verb* ~ sth (*informal*) to leave a valuable object with sb in exchange for money that you borrow SYN **pawn**

**hockey** ⓘ A2 /'hɒki; *NAmE* 'hɑːki/ *noun* [U] **1** ⓘ A2 (*BrE*) (*NAmE* **'field hockey**) a game played on a field by two teams of 11 players, with curved sticks and a small hard ball. Teams try to hit the ball into the other team's goal: *to play hockey* ◊ *a hockey stick/pitch/player/team* **2** ⓘ A2 (*NAmE*) (*BrE* **'ice hockey**) a game played on ice, in which players use long sticks to hit a hard rubber disc (called a PUCK) into the other team's goal: *She plays hockey in the winter.* ◊ *a hockey stick/puck/rink/player/team*

**hocus-pocus** /ˌhəʊkəs 'pəʊkəs/ *noun* [U] language or behaviour that makes no sense and is intended to hide the truth from people

**hodge-podge** /'hɒdʒpɒdʒ; *NAmE* 'hɑːdʒpɑːdʒ/ *noun* [sing.] (*NAmE*) = HOTCHPOTCH

**Hodg·kin lymphoma** /ˌhɒdʒkɪn lɪm'fəʊmə; *NAmE* ˌhɑːdʒ-/ (*also* **'Hodgkin's disease**) *noun* [U] a serious disease of the LYMPH NODES, LIVER and SPLEEN

**hoe** /həʊ/ *noun, verb*
- *noun* a garden tool with a long handle and a thin metal BLADE, used for breaking up soil and removing WEEDS (= plants growing where they are not wanted)
- *verb* [T, I] (**hoe·ing, hoed, hoed**) ~ (sth) to break up soil, remove plants, etc. with a hoe: *to hoe the flower beds*
  PHR V **hoe 'in** (*AustralE, NZE, informal*) to eat with enthusiasm

**hoe·down** /'həʊdaʊn/ *noun* (*NAmE*) **1** a social occasion when lively dances are performed **2** a lively dance

**hog** /hɒg; *NAmE* hɔːg/ *noun, verb*
- *noun* **1** (especially *NAmE*) a pig, especially one that is kept and made fat for eating **2** (*BrE*) a male pig that has been CASTRATED (= had part of its sex organs removed) and is kept for its meat ⊃ compare BOAR, SOW² ⊃ see also WARTHOG
  IDM **go the whole 'hog** (*informal*) to do sth completely or to the highest degree
- *verb* (**-gg-**) ~ sth (*informal*) to use or keep most of sth yourself and stop others from using or having it: *to hog the road* (= to drive so that other vehicles cannot pass) ◊ *to hog the bathroom* (= to spend a long time in it so that others cannot use it)

**Hog·ma·nay** /'hɒgmənei; ˌhɒgmə'nei; *NAmE* 'hɑːgmənei/ *noun* [U] (in Scotland) New Year's Eve (31 December) and the celebrations that happen on that day

**hog·wash** /'hɒgwɒʃ; *NAmE* 'hɔːgwɑːʃ/ *noun* [U] (*informal*) an idea, argument, etc. that you think is stupid

**ho ho** /ˌhəʊ 'həʊ/ *exclamation* **1** used to show the sound of a deep laugh **2** used to show surprise or TRIUMPH, especially at a discovery: *Ho, ho! What have we here?* ⊃ see also GUNG-HO, HEAVE-HO

**ho-hum** /ˌhəʊ 'hʌm/ *exclamation* used to show that you are bored

**the hoi pol·loi** /ðə ˌhɔɪ pə'lɔɪ/ *noun* [pl.] (*disapproving* or *humorous*) an offensive word for ordinary people

# hoist

**hoist** /hɔɪst/ *verb, noun*

■ *verb* to raise or pull sth up to a higher position, often using ropes or special equipment: ~ **sth/sb/yourself + adv./prep.** *He hoisted himself onto a high stool.* ◊ *The cargo was hoisted aboard by crane.* ◊ ~ **sth** *to hoist a flag/sail*
**IDM** **be hoist/hoisted by/with your own pe'tard** to be hurt or to have problems as a result of your own plans to hurt or trick others

■ *noun* a piece of equipment used for lifting heavy things, or for lifting people who cannot stand or walk

**hoity-toity** /ˌhɔɪti ˈtɔɪti/ *adj.* (*informal*) behaving in a way that suggests that you think you are more important than other people

**hokey** /ˈhəʊki/ *adj.* (*NAmE, informal*) expressing emotions in a way that seems EXAGGERATED or silly

**hoki** /ˈhəʊki/ *noun* (*pl.* **hoki**) a fish found in the seas off New Zealand

**hokum** /ˈhəʊkəm/ *noun* [U] (*informal, especially NAmE*) **1** a film, play, etc. that is not realistic and has no artistic qualities **2** an idea, argument, etc. that you think is stupid: *What a bunch of hokum!*

## hold 🔑 A2 /həʊld/ *verb, noun*

■ *verb* (**held, held** /held/)
- **IN HAND/ARMS 1** 🔑 A2 [T] to have sb/sth in your hand, arms, etc: ~ **sb/sth** *She was holding a large box.* ◊ *They were holding hands* (= the right hand of one person holding the left hand of the other). ◊ ~ **sb/sth + adv./prep.** *I held the mouse by its tail.* ◊ *The girl held her father's hand tightly.* ◊ *He was holding the baby in his arms.* ◊ *The winning captain held the trophy in the air.* ◊ *The lovers held each other close.* **2** 🔑 B1 [T] (**+ adv./prep.**) to put your hand on part of your body, usually because it hurts: *She groaned and held her head.*
- **IN POSITION 3** 🔑 B1 [T] to keep sb/sth in a particular position: ~ **sth + adv./prep.** *Hold your head up.* ◊ *Hold this position for a count of 10.* ◊ *The wood is held in position by a clamp.* ◊ *I had to hold my stomach in* (= pull the muscles flat) *to zip up my jeans.* ◊ ~ **sth + adj.** *I'll hold the door open for you.*
- **SUPPORT 4** 🔑 B1 [T] to support the weight of sb/sth: *I don't think that branch will hold your weight.*
- **CONTAIN 5** 🔑 B1 [T] ~ **sth/sb** to have enough space for sth/sb; to contain sth/sb: *This barrel holds 25 litres.* ◊ *The plane holds about 300 passengers.* **6** 🔑 B2 ~ **sth** to have or offer sth; to be going to bring sth: *I don't know what the future holds.* ◊ *This research holds the key to understanding life.*
- **MEETING 7** 🔑 B1 [T] ~ **sth** to have a meeting, competition, conversation, etc: *Each month she holds a meeting with her entire staff.* ◊ *to hold talks/discussions/a conversation* ◊ *The next conference will be held in Ohio.* ◊ *The country is holding its first free elections for 20 years.*
- **RECORD/TITLE 8** 🔑 B2 [T] ~ **sth** to have sth you have gained or achieved: *Who holds the world record for the long jump?* ◊ *She held the title of world champion for three years.*
- **JOB 9** 🔑 B2 [T] ~ **sth** to have a particular job or position: *How long has he held office?* ◊ *Men still hold most positions of power in this country.* ◊ *The professor will hold a seat on the advisory board.*
- **SB PRISONER 10** 🔑 B2 [T] to keep sb and not allow them to leave: ~ **sb** *Police are holding two men in connection with last Thursday's bank raid.* ◊ ~ **sb + noun** *He was held prisoner for two years.*
- **KEEP 11** 🔑 B2 [T] ~ **sth** to keep sb's attention or interest: *There wasn't much in the museum to hold my attention.* **12** [T, I] ~ **(sth) (at sth)** to keep sth at the same level, rate, speed, etc.; to stay at the same level, rate, etc: *Hold your speed at 70.* ◊ *In trading today the dollar held steady against the yen.* **13** [T] ~ **sth** to keep sth so that it can be used later: *records held on computer* ◊ *We can hold your reservation for three days.*
- **ON PHONE 14** [I, T] to wait until you can speak to the person you have phoned: *That extension is busy right now. Can you hold?* ◊ ~ **the line** *She asked me to hold the line.*
↪ **WORDFINDER NOTE** at **CALL**
- **OWN 15** [T] ~ **sth** (*rather formal*) to own or have sth: *Employees hold 30% of the shares.* ◊ *Applicants must hold a full driving licence.*
- **CONTROL 16** [T] ~ **sth** to defend sth against attack; to have control of sth: *The rebels held the radio station.*
- **REMAIN 17** [I] to remain strong and safe or in position: *They were afraid the dam wouldn't hold.* **18** [I] to remain the same: *How long will the fine weather hold?* ◊ *If their luck holds, they could still win the championship.*
- **OPINION 19** [T] to have a belief or an opinion about sb/sth: ~ **sth** *He holds strange views on education.* ◊ ~ **sb/sth + adv./prep./adj.** *She is held in high regard by her students* (= they have a high opinion of her). ◊ *firmly held beliefs* **20** [T] (*formal*) to consider that sth is true: ~ **that …** *I still hold that the government's economic policies are mistaken.* ◊ ~ **sb/sth + adj.** *Parents will be held responsible for their children's behaviour.* ◊ **be held to be sth** *These vases are held to be the finest examples of Greek art.*
- **ROAD/COURSE 21** [T] ~ **the road** (of a vehicle) to be in close contact with the road and easy to control, especially when driven fast **22** [T] ~ **a course** (of a ship or an aircraft) to continue to move in a particular direction
- **IN MUSIC 23** [T] ~ **sth** to make a note continue for a particular time
- **ALCOHOL 24** ~ **your drink** be able to drink a reasonable amount of alcohol without becoming drunk
- **IN SPORT 25** [T, I] ~ **(serve/your serve)** (in tennis, BADMINTON, etc.) to win a game in which you are SERVING
- **STOP 26** [T] ~ **sth** used to tell sb to stop doing sth or not to do sth: *Hold your fire!* (= don't shoot) ◊ *Hold the front page!* (= don't print it until a particular piece of news is available) ◊ (*NAmE, informal*) *Give me a hot dog, but hold the* (= don't give me any) *mustard.*

**IDM** **HELP** Most idioms containing **hold** are at the entries for the nouns and adjectives in the idioms, for example **hold the fort** is at **fort**. **hold 'good** to be true: *The same argument does not hold good in every case.* **'hold it** (*informal*) used to ask sb to wait, or not to move: *Hold it a second—I don't think everyone's arrived yet.* **there is no 'holding sb** a person cannot be prevented from doing sth: *Once she gets on to the subject of politics there's no holding her.*
**PHRV** **hold sth a'gainst sb** to allow sth that sb has done to make you have a lower opinion of them: *I admit I made a mistake—but don't hold it against me.*
**hold sb/sth↔'back 1** to prevent sb/sth from moving forward or crossing sth: *The police were unable to hold back the crowd.* **2** to prevent the progress or development of sb/sth: *Do you think that mixed-ability classes hold back the better students?* **hold sth↔'back 1** to not tell sb sth they want or need to know: *to hold back information* **2** to stop yourself from expressing how you really feel: *She just managed to hold back her anger.* ◊ *He bravely held back his tears.* **hold 'back (from doing sth)** | **hold sb 'back (from doing sth)** to hesitate or to make sb hesitate to act or speak: *She held back, not knowing how to break the terrible news.* ◊ *I wanted to tell him the truth, but something held me back.*
**hold sb↔'down 1** to prevent sb from moving, using force: *It took three men to hold him down.* **2** to prevent sb from having their freedom or rights: *The people are held down by a repressive regime.* **hold sth↔'down 1** to keep sth at a low level: *The rate of inflation must be held down.* **2** [no passive] to keep a job for some time: *He was unable to hold down a job after his breakdown.* **3** [no passive] (*NAmE, informal*) to limit sth, especially a noise: *Hold it down, will you? I'm trying to sleep!*
**hold 'forth** to speak for a long time about sth in a way that other people might find boring
**hold sth↔'in** to not express how you really feel: *to hold in your feelings/anger* **OPP** **let out**
**hold 'off 1** (of rain or a storm) to not start: *The rain held off just long enough for us to have our picnic.* **2** to not do sth immediately: *Many buyers are holding off until prices are lower.* **hold off doing sth** *Could you hold off making your decision for a few days?* **hold sb/sth↔'off** to stop sb/sth defeating you: *She held off all the last-minute challengers and won the race in a new record time.*
**hold 'on 1** (*informal*) used to tell sb to wait or stop **SYN** **wait**: *Hold on a minute while I get my breath back.* ◊

---

| b **b**ad | d **d**id | f **f**all | g **g**et | h **h**at | j **y**es | k **c**at | l **l**eg | m **m**an | n **n**ow | p **p**en | r **r**ed |

*Hold on! This isn't the right road.* **2** to survive in a difficult or dangerous situation: *They managed to hold on until help arrived.* **3** (*informal*) used on the phone to ask sb to wait until they can talk to the person they want: *Can you hold on? I'll see if he's here.* ˌhold sth↔ˈon to keep sth in position: *These nuts and bolts hold the wheels on.* ◊ *The knob is only held on by sticky tape.* ˌhold ˈon (to sth/sb) | ˌhold ˈon to sth/sb [no passive] to keep holding sth/sb: *Hold on and don't let go until I say so.* ◊ *He held on to the back of the chair to stop himself from falling.* ˌhold ˈon to sth | ˌhold ˈonto sth **1** to keep sth that is an advantage for you; to not give or sell sth to sb else: *You should hold on to your oil shares.* ◊ *She took an early lead in the race and held on to it for nine laps.* **2** to keep sth for sb else or for longer than usual: *I'll hold on to your mail for you until you get back.* ˌhold ˈout **1** to last, especially in a difficult situation: *We can stay here for as long as our supplies hold out.* **2** to resist or survive in a dangerous or difficult situation: *The rebels held out in the mountains for several years.* ˌhold ˈout sth to offer a chance, hope or possibility of sth: *Doctors hold out little hope of her recovering.* ˌhold sth↔ˈout to put your hand or arms, or sth in your hand, towards sb, especially to give or offer sth: *I held out my hand to steady her.* ◊ *He held out the keys and I took them.* ˌhold ˈout for sth [no passive] to cause a delay in reaching an agreement because you hope you will gain sth: *The union negotiators are holding out for a more generous pay settlement.* ˌhold ˈout on sb (*informal*) to refuse to tell or give sb sth ˌhold sth↔ˈover [usually passive] **1** to not deal with sth immediately; to leave sth to be dealt with later SYN postpone: *The matter was held over until the next meeting.* **2** to show a film, play, etc. for longer than planned: *The movie proved so popular it was held over for another week.* ˌhold sth ˈover sb to use knowledge that you have about sb to threaten them or make them do what you want ˌhold sb to sth **1** to make sb keep a promise **2** to stop the team that you are playing against scoring more points, etc. than you: *The league leaders were held to a 0–0 draw.* ˌhold toˈgether | ˌhold sth↔toˈgether **1** to remain, or to keep sth, united: *A political party should hold together.* ◊ *It's the mother who usually holds the family together.* **2** (of an argument, a theory or a story) to be logical or consistent: *Their case doesn't hold together when you look at the evidence.* ⊃ compare HANG TOGETHER **3** if a machine or an object **holds together** or sth **holds it together**, the different parts stay together so that it does not break ˌhold ˈup to remain strong and working effectively: *She's holding up well under the pressure.* ˌhold sb/sth↔ˈup [often passive] **1** to support sb/sth and stop them from falling **2** to delay or block the movement or progress of sb/sth: *An accident is holding up traffic.* ◊ *The project was held up by various legal problems.* ⊃ related noun HOLD-UP **3** to use or present sb/sth as an example: *She's always holding up her children as models of good behaviour.* ◊ *His ideas were held up to ridicule.* ˌhold ˈup ˈsth to steal from a bank, shop, etc. using a gun ⊃ related noun HOLD-UP ˈhold with sth [no passive] (used in negative sentences or in questions) to agree with sth SYN approve: *I don't hold with the use of force.* ◊ **hold with doing sth** *They don't hold with letting children watch as much TV as they want.*

■ noun
- **WITH HAND 1** [sing., U] the action of holding sth/sb; the way you are holding sb/sth SYN **grip**: *~ on sb/sth His hold on her arm tightened.* ◊ *She tried to keep hold of the child's hand.*
- **IN SPORT/A FIGHT 2** [C] a particular way of holding sb, especially in a fight or in a sport such as WRESTLING: *in a ~ He still had me in a tight hold.*
- **POWER/CONTROL 3** [sing.] influence, power or control over sb/sth: *He struggled to get a hold of his anger.* ◊ *~ on/over sb/sth What she knew about his past gave her a hold over him.* ⊃ see also STRANGLEHOLD
- **IN CLIMBING 4** [C] a place where you can put your hands or feet when climbing ⊃ see also FOOTHOLD, HANDHOLD, TOEHOLD
- **ON SHIP/PLANE 5** [C] the part of a ship or plane where the goods being carried are stored

757

IDM **ˌcatch, get, grab, take, etc.** (a) **ˈhold of sb/sth** to have or take sb/sth in your hands: *He caught hold of her wrists so she couldn't get away.* ◊ *Lee got hold of the dog by its collar.* ◊ *Quick, grab a hold of that rope.* ◊ *Gently, she took hold of the door handle and turned it.* **get ˈhold of sb** to contact or find sb: *Where have you been? I've been trying to get hold of you all day.* **get ˈhold of sth 1** to find sth that you want or need: *I need to get hold of Tom's address.* ◊ *It's almost impossible to get hold of tickets for the final.* **2** to learn or understand sth ˌno ˌholds ˈbarred with no rules or limits on what sb is allowed to do **on ˈhold 1** delayed until a later time or date: *She put her career on hold to have a baby.* ◊ *The project is on hold until more money is available.* **2** if a person on the phone is **put on hold**, they have to wait until the person they want to talk to becomes free or has found out the information that is needed **take (a) ˈhold** to begin to have complete control over sb/sth; to become very strong: *Panic took hold of him and he couldn't move.* ◊ *They got out of the house just before the flames took hold.* ◊ *It is best to treat the disease early before it takes a hold.* ⊃ more at WRONG *adj*

▼ **SYNONYMS**

**hold**

**hold on • cling • clutch • grip • grasp • clasp • hang on**

These words all mean to have sb/sth in your hands or arms.

**hold** to have sb/sth in your hand or arms: *She was holding a large box.* ◊ *I held the baby gently in my arms.*

**hold on (to sb/sth)** to continue to hold sb/sth; to put your hand on sb/sth and not take your hand away: *Hold on and don't let go until I say so.*

**cling** to hold on to sb/sth tightly, especially with your whole body: *Survivors clung to pieces of floating debris.*

**clutch** to hold sb/sth tightly, especially in your hand; to take hold of sth suddenly: *She stood there, the flowers still clutched in her hand.* ◊ *He felt himself slipping and clutched at a branch.*

**grip** to hold on to sth very tightly with your hand: *Grip the rope as tightly as you can.*

**grasp** to take a strong hold of sb/sth: *He grasped my hand and shook it warmly.* NOTE The object of **grasp** is often sb's hand or wrist.

**clasp** (*formal*) to hold sb/sth tightly in your hand or in your arms: *They clasped hands (= held each other's hands).* ◊ *She clasped the children in her arms.* NOTE The object of **clasp** is often your hands, sb else's hand or another person.

**hang on (to sth)** to hold on to sth very tightly, especially in order to support yourself or stop yourself from falling: *Hang on tight. We're off!*

**PATTERNS**
- to hold/clutch/grip/clasp sth **in your hand/hands**
- to hold/clutch/clasp sb/sth **in your arms**
- to hold/clutch/grip/grasp/clasp/hang **on to** sth
- to hold/cling/hang **on**
- to hold/clutch/clasp sth **to you**
- to hold/hold on to/cling to/clutch/grip/grasp/clasp/hang on to sb/sth **tightly**
- to hold/hold on to/cling to/clutch/grip/grasp/clasp sb/sth **firmly**
- to hold/hold on to/clutch/grip/clasp/hang on to sb/sth **tight**

**hold·all** /ˈhəʊldɔːl/ (*BrE*) (*NAmE* ˈduffel bag) *noun* a large bag made of strong cloth or soft leather, used when you are travelling for carrying clothes, etc.

**hold·er** /ˈhəʊldə(r)/ *noun* (often in compounds) **1** a person who has or owns the thing mentioned: *a licence holder* ◊ *a season ticket holder* ◊ *the current holder of the world record* ◊ *holders of high office* ◊ *the holder of a French passport* ⊃ see also OFFICE-HOLDER, RECORD HOLDER, TITLE-HOLDER **2** a thing that holds the object mentioned: *a pen holder* ⊃ see also CIGARETTE HOLDER

| s see | t tea | v van | w wet | z zoo | ʃ shoe | ʒ vision | tʃ chain | dʒ jam | θ thin | ð this | ŋ sing |

# holding

**hold·ing** /ˈhəʊldɪŋ/ *noun* **1** ~ **(in sth)** a number of shares that sb has in a company: *She has a 40% holding in the company.* **2** an amount of property that is owned by a person, museum, library, etc: *one of the most important private holdings of Indian art* **3** a piece of land that is rented by sb and used for farming ⇨ see also SMALLHOLDING

**ˈholding company** *noun* a company that is formed to buy shares in other companies, which it then controls

**ˈholding operation** *noun* a course of action that is taken so that a particular situation stays the same or does not become any worse

**ˈholding pattern** *noun* the route that a plane travels while it is flying above an airport waiting for permission to land

**hold·over** /ˈhəʊldəʊvə(r)/ *noun* (*NAmE*) a person or thing that survives from an earlier time, especially sb who keeps a position of power when the president or management of sth changes

**ˈhold-up** *noun* **1** a situation in which sth is prevented from happening for a short time **SYN** **delay**: *What's the hold-up?* ◇ *We should finish by tonight, barring hold-ups.* ◇ (*BrE*) *Sorry I'm late. There was a hold-up on the motorway.* **2** (*also informal* **ˈstick-up** *especially in NAmE*) an act of stealing from a bank, etc. using a gun **3** **hold-ups** [pl.] (*BrE*) STOCKINGS that are kept up by having a band of material that can stretch at the top

**hole** 🔑 **A2** /həʊl/ *noun, verb*
■ *noun*
- **HOLLOW SPACE 1** **A2** [C] a hollow space in sth solid or in the surface of sth: *He dug a deep hole in the garden.* ◇ ~ **in sth** *The bomb blew a huge hole in the ground.* ◇ *Water had collected in the holes in the road.* ⇨ see also SINKHOLE
- **OPENING 2** **B1** [C] a space or opening that goes all the way through sth: *a bullet hole* ◇ ~ **in sth** *There were holes in the knees of his trousers.* ◇ *a gaping hole in the ceiling* ◇ **to drill/bore/punch a hole** *in sth* ◇ **through a** ~ *The children climbed through a hole in the fence.* ⇨ see also BLACK HOLE, OZONE HOLE
- **ANIMAL'S HOME 3** [C] the home of a small animal: *a rabbit/mouse hole* ⇨ compare FOXHOLE, PIGEONHOLE
- **UNPLEASANT PLACE 4** [C, usually sing.] (*informal, disapproving*) an unpleasant place to live or be in **SYN** **dump**: *I am not going to bring up my child in this hole.* ⇨ see also HELLHOLE
- **IN GOLF 5** [C] a hollow in the ground that you must get the ball into; one of the sections of a golf course with the TEE at the beginning and the hole at the end: *an eighteen-hole golf course* ◇ *He liked to play a few holes after work.*
- **FAULT/WEAKNESS 6** [C, usually pl.] a fault or weakness in sth such as a plan, law or story: *I don't believe what she says—her story is full of holes.* ◇ *The movie has too many plot holes.* ◇ ~ **in sth** *He was found not guilty because of holes in the prosecution case.* ◇ *There are major security holes in the software.* ⇨ see also LOOPHOLE
- **EMPTY PLACE/POSITION 7** [sing.] ~ **(in sth)** a place or position that needs to be filled because sb/sth is no longer there: *After his wife left, there was a gaping hole in his life.* ◇ *Buying the new equipment left a big hole in the company's finances.* **HELP** There are many other compounds ending in **hole**. You will find them at their place in the alphabet.
- **IDM** **in a ˈhole** (*informal*) in a difficult situation: *He had got himself into a hole and it was going to be difficult to get out of it.* **in the ˈhole** (*NAmE, informal*) owing money: *We start the current fiscal year $30 million in the hole.* **make a ˈhole in sth** to use up a large amount of sth that you have, especially money: *School fees can make a big hole in your savings.* ⇨ more at ACE *n.*, BURN *v.*, DIG *v.*, PICK *v.*, SQUARE *adj.*

■ *verb*
- **MAKE A HOLE 1** [T, usually passive] to make a hole or holes in sth, especially a boat or ship: **be holed (by sth)** *The ship had been holed by a missile.*
- **IN GOLF 2** [T, I] to hit a golf ball into the hole: ~ **sth** *She holed a 25 foot putt.* ◇ ~ **(out)** *She holed out from 25 feet.*

**PHRV** **hole ˈup | be ˌholed ˈup** (*informal*) to hide in a place: *He'll hole up now and move again tomorrow, after dark.* ◇ *We believe the gang are holed up in the mountains.*

▼ **HOMOPHONES**

**hole • whole** /həʊl/
- **hole** *noun*: *She caught a fish through a hole in the ice.*
- **whole** *adj.*: *He hadn't told us the whole story.*
- **whole** *noun*: *The camera moves and you see the whole of the palace.*

**ˌhole-in-ˈone** *noun* (*pl.* **holes-in-one**) (in golf) an occasion when a player hits the ball from the TEE into the hole using only one shot

**ˌhole in the ˈheart** *noun* (*medical*) a condition in which a baby is born with a problem with the wall dividing the parts of its heart, so that it does not get enough OXYGEN in its blood

**ˌhole in the ˈwall** *noun* [sing.] (*informal*) **1** (*BrE*) = CASH MACHINE **2** (*NAmE*) a small dark shop or restaurant
▶ **hole-in-the-ˈwall** *adj.* [only before noun]: *hole-in-the-wall cash machines/restaurants*

**holey** /ˈhəʊli/ *adj.* a **holey** piece of clothing or material has a lot of holes in it

**holi·day** 🔑 ⓘ **A1** /ˈhɒlədeɪ, -di/ *NAmE* /ˈhɑːləˌdeɪ/ *noun, verb*

■ *noun* **1** **A1** [U] (*also* **holidays** [pl.]) (*both BrE*) (*NAmE* **vacation**) a period of time when you are not at work or school: *the school/summer/Christmas holidays* ◇ *She spent her holiday decorating the flat.* ◇ *I'm afraid Mr Walsh is away on holiday this week.* ◇ *The package includes 20 days' paid holiday a year.* ◇ **holiday pay** ⇨ compare LEAVE (1) **2** **A1** [C] (*BrE*) (*NAmE* **vacation**) a period of time spent travelling or resting away from home: *a camping/skiing/walking holiday* ◇ *a family holiday* ◇ **to have/take a holiday** ◇ **on** ~ *They met while on holiday in Greece.* ◇ *We went on holiday together last summer.* ◇ **for your holiday(s)** *Where are you going for your holidays this year?* ◇ *a holiday cottage/home* ◇ *a holiday destination/resort* ⇨ WORDFINDER NOTE at HOTEL ⇨ see also BUSMAN'S HOLIDAY

**WORDFINDER** break, camp, cruise, honeymoon, package tour, self-catering, tourist, travel, visa

**3** **A2** (*also* **ˌpublic ˈholiday**) [C] a day when most people do not go to work or school, especially because of a religious or national celebration: *a national holiday* ◇ *Today is a holiday in Wales.* ⇨ see also BANK HOLIDAY, LEGAL HOLIDAY, PUBLIC HOLIDAY, STATUTORY HOLIDAY **4** **holidays** [pl.] (*also* **ˈholiday season** [C]) (*NAmE*) the time from late November to early January that includes Thanksgiving, Christmas, Hanukkah and New Year: *Happy Holidays!*

■ *verb* (*BrE*) (*NAmE* **vacation**) [I] (+ *adv./prep.*) to spend a holiday somewhere: *She was holidaying with her family in Ireland.*

▼ **BRITISH/AMERICAN**

### holiday / vacation

- You use **holiday** (or **holidays**) in *BrE* and **vacation** in *NAmE* to describe the regular periods of time when you are not at work or school, or time that you spend travelling or resting away from home: *I get four weeks' holiday/vacation a year.* ◇ *He's on holiday/vacation this week.* ◇ *I like to take my holiday/vacation in the winter.* ◇ *the summer holidays/vacation.*
- In *NAmE* a **holiday** (or a **public holiday**) is a single day when government offices, schools, banks and businesses are closed: *The school will be closed Monday because it's a holiday.* This is called a **bank holiday** in *BrE*.
- The **holidays** is used in *NAmE* to refer to the time from late November to early January that includes Thanksgiving, Christmas, Hanukkah and the New Year.
- **Vacation** in *BrE* is used mainly to mean one of the periods when universities are officially closed for the students.

**holiday camp** noun (BrE) a place that provides accommodation and entertainment for large numbers of people who are on holiday

**holi·day·maker** /ˈhɒlədeɪmeɪkə(r), -dɪm-; NAmE ˈhɑːl-ədeɪm-/ noun (BrE) (NAmE **vacˈation·er**) a person who is visiting a place on holiday

**holier-than-thou** /ˌhəʊliə ðən ˈðaʊ; NAmE -ər-/ adj. (disapproving) showing that you think that you are morally better than other people **SYN self-righteous**: *I can't stand his holier-than-thou attitude.*

**holi·ness** /ˈhəʊlinəs/ noun **1** [U] the quality of being holy **2 His/Your Holiness** [C] a title of respect used when talking to or about the Pope and some other religious leaders: *His Holiness Pope Francis*

**hol·ism** /ˈhəʊlɪzəm/; BrE also /ˈhɒl-/; NAmE also /ˈhɑːl-/ noun [U] **1** (specialist) the idea that the whole of sth must be considered in order to understand its different parts ⊃ compare ATOMISM **2** (medical) the idea that the whole of a sick person, including their body, mind and way of life, should be considered when treating them, and not just the symptoms (= effects) of the disease

**hol·is·tic** /həʊˈlɪstɪk; NAmE həʊl-/ adj. **1** considering a whole thing or being to be more than a collection of parts: *a holistic approach to life* **2** (medical) treating the whole person rather than just the symptoms (= effects) of a disease: *holistic medicine* ⊃ WORDFINDER NOTE at TREATMENT ▶ **hol·is·tic·al·ly** /-kli/ adv.

**hol·land·aise sauce** /ˌhɒləndeɪz ˈsɔːs; NAmE ˌhɑːl-/ (also **hollandaise**) noun [U] a sauce made with butter, egg YOLKS (= yellow parts) and VINEGAR

**hol·ler** /ˈhɒlə(r); NAmE ˈhɑːl-/ verb [I, T] (informal, especially NAmE) to shout loudly **SYN yell**: ~ (at sb) *Don't holler at me!* ◇ + speech *'Look out!' I hollered.* ◇ ~ sth *He hollered something I couldn't understand.*

**hol·low** ❶ B2 /ˈhɒləʊ; NAmE ˈhɑːl-/ adj., noun, verb
■ adj. **1** having a hole or empty space inside: *a hollow ball/centre/tube/tree* ◇ *The tree trunk was hollow inside.* ◇ *Her stomach felt hollow with fear.* **2** (of parts of the face) sinking deeply into the face: *hollow eyes/cheeks* ◇ *hollow-eyed from lack of sleep* **3** [usually before noun] (of sounds) making a low sound like that made by an empty object when it is hit: *a hollow groan* **4** [usually before noun] not sincere: *hollow promises* ◇ *a hollow laugh* ◇ *Their appeals for an end to the violence had a hollow ring.* **5** [usually before noun] without real value: *to win a hollow victory* ▶ **hol·low·ly** adv.: *to laugh hollowly* **hol·low·ness** noun [U]: *the hollowness of the victory* IDM see RING² v.
■ noun **1** an area that is lower than the surface around it, especially on the ground: *muddy hollows* ◇ *The village lay secluded in a hollow of the hills* (= a small valley). ◇ *She noticed the slight hollows under her cheekbones.* **2** a hole or an empty space inside sth: *The squirrel disappeared into a hollow at the base of the tree.*
■ verb [usually passive] to make a flat surface go INWARD in a curve: **be hollowed (by sth)** *The stairs have been hollowed by centuries of use.*
PHR V **hollow sth↔out 1** to make a hole in sth by removing part of it: *Hollow out the cake and fill it with cream.* **2** to form sth by making a hole in sth else: *The cave has been hollowed out of the mountainside.*

**holly** /ˈhɒli; NAmE ˈhɑːli/ noun (pl. **-ies**) [U, C] a bush or small tree with hard shiny leaves with sharp points and bright red BERRIES in winter, often used as a decoration at Christmas: *a sprig of holly*

**hol·ly·hock** /ˈhɒlihɒk; NAmE ˈhɑːlihɑːk/ noun a tall garden plant with white, yellow, red or purple flowers growing up its STEM

**Hol·ly·wood** /ˈhɒliwʊd; NAmE ˈhɑːl-/ noun [U] the part of Los Angeles where the film industry is based (used to refer to the US film industry and the way of life that is associated with it)

**Hollywood ˈending** noun (usually disapproving) an ending in a film, novel, etc. that happens in the way you expect, is full of EXAGGERATED happiness or love, and may not be very realistic: *The film refuses to sell out and provide a Hollywood ending.*

---

**holo·caust** /ˈhɒləkɔːst; NAmE ˈhəʊl-, ˈhɑːl-/ noun **1** [C] a situation in which many things are destroyed and many people killed, especially because of a war or a fire: *a nuclear holocaust* **2 the Holocaust** [sing.] the killing of millions of Jews by the German Nazi government in the period 1941–5

**holo·gram** /ˈhɒləɡræm; NAmE ˈhəʊl-, ˈhɑːl-/ noun a special type of image that appears to be THREE-DIMENSIONAL (= solid rather than flat), especially one created using LASERS

**holo·graph** /ˈhɒləɡrɑːf; NAmE ˈhəʊləɡræf, ˈhɑːl-/ noun (specialist) a piece of writing that has been written by hand by its author

**holo·graph·ic** /ˌhɒləˈɡræfɪk; NAmE ˌhəʊl-, ˌhɑːl-/ adj. [usually before noun] produced using holograms; in the form of a HOLOGRAM: *a holographic picture*

**hols** /hɒlz; NAmE hɑːlz/ noun [pl.] (old-fashioned, BrE, informal) holidays

**Hol·stein** /ˈhɒlstaɪn, -stiːn; NAmE ˈhəʊl-/ noun a type of black and white cow that produces a lot of milk

**hol·ster** /ˈhəʊlstə(r)/ noun, verb
■ noun a leather case worn on a belt or on a narrow piece of leather under the arm, used for carrying a small gun
■ verb ~ sth to put a gun in a holster

**holy** ❶ B2 /ˈhəʊli/ adj. (**holi·er, holi·est**) **1** ❦ B2 [usually before noun] connected with God or a particular religion: *the Holy Bible* ◇ *holy books/scriptures* ◇ *the holy city of Mecca* ◇ *a holy day/month* ◇ *a holy war* (= one fought to defend the beliefs of a particular religion) **OPP unholy** **2** ❦ B2 good in a moral and religious way: *a holy life/man* **OPP unholy** **3** [only before noun] (informal) used to emphasize that you are surprised, afraid, etc: *Holy cow! What was that?* ⊃ see also HOLIER-THAN-THOU, HOLINESS

**Holy Comˈmunion** noun [U] = COMMUNION

**the ˌHoly ˈFather** noun [sing.] the POPE

**the ˌHoly ˈGhost** noun [sing.] = HOLY SPIRIT

**the ˌHoly ˈGrail** noun [usually sing.] = GRAIL

**the holy of holies** /ðə ˌhəʊli əv ˈhəʊliz/ noun [sing.] **1** the most holy part of a religious building **2** (humorous) a special room or building that can only be visited by important people

**ˌholy ˈorders** noun [pl.] the official position of being a priest: *to take holy orders* (= to become a priest)

**Holy·rood** /ˈhɒliruːd; NAmE ˈhɑːl-/ noun [U] the Scottish parliament and government: *elections to Holyrood* ORIGIN From the name of the part of Edinburgh where the parliament building is.

**the ˌHoly ˈSee** noun [sing.] **1** the job or authority of the Pope **2** the Roman Catholic court at the Vatican in Rome

**the ˌHoly ˈSpirit** (also **the ˌHoly ˈGhost**) noun [sing.] (in Christianity) God in the form of a spirit

**ˈholy water** noun [U] water that has been BLESSED by a priest

**ˌHoly ˈWeek** noun [U, C] in the Christian Church, the week before Easter Sunday

**ˌHoly ˈWrit** noun [U] (old-fashioned) the Bible: (figurative) *You shouldn't take what he says as Holy Writ* (= accept that it is true without questioning it).

**hom·age** /ˈhɒmɪdʒ, ˈɒmɑːʒ; NAmE ˈhɑːmɪdʒ, əʊˈmɑːʒ/ noun [U, C, usually sing.] ~ **(to sb/sth)** (formal) something that is said or done to show respect for sb: *The kings of France paid homage to no one.* ◇ *He describes his book as 'a homage to my father'.* ◇ *They stood in silent homage around the grave.*

**hom·bre** /ˈɒmbreɪ; NAmE ˈɑːm-/ noun (from Spanish, NAmE, informal) a man, especially one of a particular type: *Their quarterback is one tough hombre.*

**home** ❶ A1 /həʊm/ noun, adv., adj., verb
■ noun
• **HOUSE, ETC. 1** ❦ A1 [C, U] the house or flat that you live in, especially with your family: *Old people prefer to stay in*

# home base

*their own homes.* ◊ *the **family** home* ◊ *While travelling she missed the **comforts of home**.* ◊ *She leaves home at 7 every day.* ◊ *He **left** home* (= left his parents and began an independent life) *at sixteen.* ◊ **from~** *I'll call you from home later.* ◊ *Nowadays a lot of people **work from home*** (= do paid work at home). ◊ *stray dogs needing new homes* ⊃ see also AT-HOME, STAY-AT-HOME **2** [C] a house or flat, etc., when you think of it as property that can be bought and sold: *a **holiday/summer** home* ◊ *A lot of new **homes are being built** on the edge of town.* ◊ *He'd always dreamed of **owning his own** home.* ◊ *Private **home ownership** is increasing faster than ever.* ◊ *They applied for a **home improvement loan**.* ⊃ see also MOBILE HOME, SECOND HOME, STATELY HOME

**WORDFINDER** accommodation, deed, house, lease, let, location, mortgage, squat, tenant

- **TOWN/COUNTRY 3** [C, U] the town, district, country, etc. that you come from, or where you are living and that you feel you belong to: *I often think about my friends **back home**.* ◊ *Jane left England and made Greece her home.* ◊ **be ~ to sb** *Jamaica is home to over two million people.*
- **FAMILY 4** [C] used to refer to a family living together, and the way it behaves: *She came from a violent home.* ◊ *He had always wanted a real home with a wife and children.* ⊃ see also BROKEN HOME
- **FOR OLD PEOPLE/CHILDREN 5** [C] a place where people who cannot care for themselves live and are cared for by others: *a **children's** home* ◊ *an **old people's** home* ◊ *a **retirement** home* ◊ *a home for the mentally ill* ◊ **in a~** *She has lived in a home since she was six.* ⊃ see also CARE HOME, NURSING HOME, REST HOME
- **FOR PETS 6** [C] a place where pets with no owner are taken care of: *a dogs'/cats' home*
- **OF PLANT/ANIMAL 7** [sing., U] the place where a plant or animal usually lives; the place where sb/sth can be found: *This region is the home of many species of wild flower.* ◊ *The tiger's home is in the jungle.* ◊ **~ to sb/sth** *The Rockies are home to bears and mountain lions.*
- **WHERE STH IS KEPT 8** [C] (*informal*) a place where an object is kept: *We haven't **found a home** for all our books yet.*
- **WHERE STH FIRST DONE 9** [sing.] **the ~ of sth** the place where sth was first discovered, made or invented: *New Orleans, the home of jazz* ◊ *Greece, the home of democracy*

**IDM at 'home 1** in a person's own house, flat, etc.: *I called round last night, but you weren't at home.* ◊ *Oh no, I left my purse at home.* ◊ *He lived at home* (= with his parents) *until he was thirty.* **2** comfortable and relaxed: *Sit down and **make yourself at home**.* ◊ *Simon feels very at home on a horse.* **3** (used especially in JOURNALISM) in sb's own country, not in a foreign country: *The president is not as popular at home as he is abroad.* **4** if a sports team plays **at home**, it plays in the town, etc. that it comes from: *Leeds are playing at home this weekend.* ◊ *Is the match on Saturday at home or away?* **a͟way from ˈhome 1** away from a person's own house, flat, etc: *He works away from home during the week.* ◊ *I don't want to be away from home for too long.* **2** if a sports team plays **away from home**, it plays in the town, etc. that its opponent comes from : **a ˈhome from ˈhome** (*BrE*) (*NAmE* **a ˈhome away from ˈhome**) a place where you feel relaxed and comfortable as if you were in your own home , **ˈhome is where the ˈheart is** (*saying*) a home is where the people you love are , **home ˈsweet ˈhome** (*often ironic*) used to say how pleasant your home is (especially when you really mean that it is not pleasant at all) , **set up ˈhome** (*BrE*) (used especially about a couple) to start living in a new place: *They got married and set up home together in Hull.* , **when he's, it's, etc. at ˈhome** (*BrE*, *humorous*) used to emphasize a question about sb/sth: *Who's she when she's at home?* (= I don't know her) ⊃ more at CHARITY, CLOSE², *adj.*, EAT, MAN *n.*, SPIRITUAL *adj.*

■ *adv.*
- **WHERE YOU LIVE 1** to or at the place where you live: *Come on, it's time to **go home**.* ◊ *What time did you **get home** last night?* ◊ *She was so relieved that he had **come home***

*safely.* ◊ *He could not **return home** until 1989.* ◊ *After a month, they went **back home** to America.* ◊ *Anna will drive me home after work.* ◊ *Hello, you're **home early**.* ◊ (*NAmE*) *I like to **stay home** in the evenings.*
- **INTO CORRECT POSITION 2** into the correct position: *She leaned on the door and pushed the bolt home.* ◊ *He drove the ball home* (= scored a goal) *from 15 metres.* ◊ *The torpedo struck home on the hull of the ship.*

**IDM be home and ˈdry** (*BrE*) (*NAmE* **be home ˈfree**) to have done sth successfully, especially when it was difficult: *I could see the finish line and thought I was home and dry.* , **bring home the ˈbacon** (*informal*) to be successful at sth; to earn money for your family to live on , **bring sth ˈhome to sb** to make sb realize how important, difficult or serious sth is: *The television pictures brought home to us the full horror of the attack.* , **come ˈhome to sb** to become completely clear to sb, often in a way that is painful: *It suddenly came home to him that he was never going to see Julie again.* , **sth comes home to ˈroost** (*also* **the chickens come home to ˈroost**) used to say that if sb says or does sth bad or wrong, it will affect them badly in the future , **hit/strike ˈhome** if a remark, etc. **hits/strikes home**, it has a strong effect on sb, in a way that makes them realize what the true facts of a situation are: *Her face went pale as his words hit home.* ⊃ more at COW *n.*, DRIVE *v.*, LIGHT *n.*, PRESS *v.*, RAM *v.*, ROMP *v.*, WRITE

■ *adj.* [only before noun]
- **WHERE YOU LIVE 1** connected with the place where you live: *home **life*** (= with your family) ◊ *a person's **home address/country*** ◊ *We offer customers a free **home delivery service**.*
- **MADE/USED AT HOME 2** made or used at home: *home movies* ◊ *home cooking* ◊ *a **home computer***
- **OWN COUNTRY 3** (*especially BrE*) connected with your own country rather than foreign countries SYN **domestic**: *products for the home market* ◊ *the party's spokesman for **home affairs*** OPP **foreign**, **overseas**
- **IN SPORT 4** connected with a team's own sports ground: *a **home game/match/win*** ◊ *the **home team/side*** ◊ *Rangers were playing in front of their **home crowd**.* ⊃ compare AWAY

■ *verb*
**PHRV** ˈ**home ˈin on sth** (*also less frequent* **hone in on sth**) **1** to aim at sth and move straight towards it: *The missile homed in on the target.* **2** to direct your thoughts or attention towards sth: *I began to feel I was really homing in on the answer.*

**home ˈbase** *noun* [sing., U] **1** = HOME PLATE **2** the place where sb/sth usually lives, works or operates from

**home·body** /ˈhəʊmbɒdi; *NAmE* -bɑːdi/ *noun* (*pl.* **-ies**) (*informal*, *especially NAmE*) a person who enjoys spending time at home

**home·boy** /ˈhəʊmbɔɪ/ (*also* **homie**) *noun* (*NAmE*, *informal*) a male friend from the same town as you; a member of your gang (= a group of young people who go around together)

ˈ**home brew** *noun* [U] **1** beer that sb makes at home **2 home-brew** (*informal*) something that sb makes at home rather than buying it: *The security software he uses is homebrew.* ▸ ˌ**home ˈbrew** (*also* ˌ**home-ˈbrewed**) *adj.* [only before noun]

**home·buy·er** /ˈhəʊmbaɪə(r)/ *noun* a person who buys a house, flat, etc.

**home ˈcinema** (*BrE*) (*NAmE* **home ˈtheater**) *noun* [U, C] television and video equipment designed to give a similar experience to being in a cinema, with high-quality pictures and sound and a large screen

**home·com·ing** /ˈhəʊmkʌmɪŋ/ *noun* **1** [C, U] the act of returning to your home after being away for a long time **2** [C] (*NAmE*) a social event that takes place every year at a HIGH SCHOOL, college or university for people who used to be students there

**home conˈfinement** *noun* [U] (*NAmE*) = HOUSE ARREST

**the ˌHome ˈCounties** *noun* [pl.] the counties around London

**home ecoˈnomics** *noun* [U] cooking and other skills needed at home, taught as a subject in school

**home front** noun [sing.] the people who do not go to fight in a war but who stay in a country to work
IDM **on the home front** at home, or in your own country

**home·girl** /ˈhəʊmɡɜːl; NAmE -ɡɜːrl/ (also **homie**) noun (NAmE, informal) a female friend from the same town as you; a member of your gang (= a group of young people who go around together)

**home ground** noun 1 [C] (BrE) a sports ground that a team regularly plays on in their own area or town 2 [U] a place where sb lives or works and where they feel confident, rather than a place that is not familiar to them: *I'd rather meet him here on my own home ground.*

**home-grown** adj. 1 (of plants, fruit and vegetables) grown in a person's garden: *home-grown tomatoes* 2 made, born, trained or educated in your own country, town, etc.: *The team has a wealth of home-grown talent.*

**home help** noun (BrE, becoming old-fashioned) a person whose job is to help old or sick people with cooking, cleaning, etc.

**home improvement** noun [C, U] changes that are made to a house that increase its value; the activity of making these changes: *They've spent a lot of money on home improvements.* ◇ *home improvement products*

**home·land** /ˈhəʊmlænd/ noun 1 [usually sing.] the country where a person was born: *Many refugees have been forced to flee their homeland.* 2 (in the Republic of South Africa under the APARTHEID system in the past) one of the areas with some SELF-GOVERNMENT that were intended for a group of black African people to live in: *the Transkei homeland*

**homeland security** noun [U] (especially in the US) the activities and organizations whose aim is to prevent TERRORIST attacks: *the Department of Homeland Security*

**home·less** /ˈhəʊmləs/ adj. 1 having no home, and therefore typically living on the streets: *The scheme has been set up to help homeless people.* ⇨ WORDFINDER NOTE at POOR 2 **the homeless** noun [pl.] people who have no home: *helping the homeless* ▶ **home·less·ness** noun [U]

**home loan** noun (informal) = MORTGAGE

**home·ly** /ˈhəʊmli/ adj. (**home·lier**, **home·li·est**) 1 (BrE, approving) (of a place) making you feel comfortable, as if you were in your own home: *The hotel has a lovely homely feel to it.* 2 (approving, especially BrE) simple and good: *homely cooking* 3 (BrE, approving) (of a woman) warm and friendly and enjoying the pleasures of home and family: *His landlady was a kind, homely woman.* 4 (NAmE, disapproving) (of a person's appearance) not attractive SYN plain: *a homely child*

**home-made** adj. made at home, rather than produced in a factory and bought in a shop

**home·maker** /ˈhəʊmmeɪkə(r)/ noun (especially NAmE) a person, especially a woman, who manages a home and takes care of the house and family ▶ **home·making** noun [U]

**the Home Office** noun [sing. + sing./pl. v.] the British government department that deals with the law, the police and prisons in England and Wales, and with decisions about who can enter the country

**home office** noun 1 a room in sb's home that is used for work 2 (NAmE) the main office of a company SYN **head office**

**homeo·path** (BrE also **hom·oeo-**) /ˈhəʊmiəpæθ; BrE also ˈhɒm-/ noun a person who treats illness using homeopathic methods

**hom·eop·athy** (BrE also **hom·oeo-**) /ˌhəʊmiˈɒpəθi; ˌhɒm-; NAmE ˌhəʊmiˈɑːp-/ noun [U] a system of treating diseases or conditions using very small amounts of the substance that causes the disease or condition ⇨ WORDFINDER NOTE at TREATMENT ▶ **homeo·path·ic** (BrE also **hom·oeo-**) /ˌhəʊmiəˈpæθɪk; BrE also ˌhɒm-/ adj.: *homeopathic medicines/remedies/treatments*

**homeo·stasis** (BrE also **hom·oeo-**) /ˌhəʊmiəˈsteɪsɪs; BrE also ˌhɒm-/ noun [U] (biology) the process by which the body reacts to changes in order to keep conditions inside the body, for example temperature, the same

**home·own·er** /ˈhəʊməʊnə(r)/ noun a person who owns their house or flat

**home page** noun (computing) 1 the main page created by a company, an organization, etc. on the internet from which connections to other pages can be made 2 a page on the internet that you choose to appear first on your screen whenever you make a connection to the internet ⇨ WORDFINDER NOTE at WEBSITE

**home plate** (also **home base**) (NAmE also **plate**) noun (in baseball) the place where the person hitting the ball stands and where they must return to after running around all the bases

**homer** /ˈhəʊmə(r)/ noun (NAmE, informal) = HOME RUN: *He hit a homer.*

**home·room** /ˈhəʊmruːm, -rʊm/ noun [C, U] (NAmE) a room in a school where students go at the beginning of each school day, so that teachers can check who is in school; the time spent in this room

**home rule** noun [U] the right of a country or region to govern itself, especially after another country or region has governed it

**home run** (also NAmE, informal **homer**) noun (in baseball) a hit that allows the person hitting the ball to run around all the bases without stopping

**home·school·ing** /ˌhəʊmˈskuːlɪŋ/ noun [U] the practice of educating children at home, not in schools ▶ **home·school** /-ˈskuːl/ verb ~ **sb**: *They homeschooled their children.*

**home screen** noun the screen on a computer or phone from which you access all other functions: *You can customize the home screen with your favourites.* ⇨ compare DESKTOP (1)

**Home Secretary** noun the British government minister in charge of the Home Office

**home shopping** noun [U] the practice of ordering goods by phone or over the internet and having them delivered to your home

**home·sick** /ˈhəʊmsɪk/ adj. ~ **(for …)** sad because you are away from home and you miss your family and friends: *I felt homesick for Scotland.* ▶ **home·sick·ness** noun [U]

**home·spun** /ˈhəʊmspʌn/ adj. 1 (especially of ideas) simple and ordinary; not coming from an expert 2 (of cloth) made at home

**home·stay** /ˈhəʊmsteɪ/ noun [C, U] an arrangement that provides accommodation for students or tourists in the home of a family in exchange for payment: *The trip includes a homestay in a traditional village.* ◇ *Live with an American family in homestay and learn the language and customs.*

**home·stead** /ˈhəʊmsted/ noun, verb
▪ noun 1 a house with the land and buildings around it, especially a farm 2 (in the US in the past) a piece of land given to sb by the government on condition that they lived on it and grew crops on it
▪ verb [I] (NAmE, old-fashioned) to live and work on a homestead ▶ **home·stead·er** noun

**the home straight** (especially BrE) (also **the home stretch** especially in NAmE) noun [sing.] 1 the last part of a race 2 the last part of an activity, etc. when it is nearly completed

**home theater** (NAmE) (BrE **home cinema**) noun [U, C] television and video equipment designed to give a similar experience to being in a cinema, with high-quality pictures and sound and a large screen

**home town** (BrE) (NAmE **home·town**) noun the place where you were born or lived as a child

**home truth** noun [usually pl.] a true but unpleasant fact about a person, usually told to them by sb else: *It's time you told him a few home truths.*

**home·ward** /ˈhəʊmwəd; NAmE -wərd/ adj. going towards home: *the homeward journey* ▶ **home·ward** (also **home·wards** especially in BrE) adv.: *Commuters were heading*

**homework**

homeward at the end of the day. ◊ We drove homewards in silence. ◊ We were **homeward bound** at last. **HELP** In this phrase, always use **homeward**, not 'homewards': We were homewards bound.

**home·work** ❶ **A1** /ˈhəʊmwɜːk; NAmE -wɜːrk/ noun [U] **1** ❓ **A1** work that is given by teachers for students to do at home: *physics/geography/French, etc. homework* ◊ **for ~** *I have to write up the notes for homework.* ◊ *(especially NAmE) I have to finish this homework assignment.* **2** *(informal)* work that sb does to prepare for sth: *You could tell that he had really* **done his homework** *(= found out all he needed to know).*

**home·work·er** /ˈhəʊmwɜːkə(r); NAmE -wɜːrk-/ noun a person who works at home, often doing jobs that are not well paid such as making clothes for shops ▶ **home·work·ing** noun [U]

**homey** *(also* **homy***)* /ˈhəʊmi/ *adj., noun*
■ *adj. (especially NAmE, informal)* pleasant and comfortable, like home: *The hotel had a nice, homey atmosphere.*
■ *noun* = HOMIE

**homi·cidal** /ˌhɒmɪˈsaɪdl; NAmE ˌhɑːm-/ *adj.* likely to kill another person; making sb likely to kill another person: *a homicidal maniac* ◊ *He had clear homicidal tendencies.*

**homi·cide** /ˈhɒmɪsaɪd; NAmE ˈhɑːm-/ *noun* [C, U] *(especially NAmE, law)* the act of killing another person, especially when it is a crime: *the homicide bureau* (= the department of the US police that deals with murder) ⊃ compare CULPABLE HOMICIDE, JUSTIFIABLE HOMICIDE, MANSLAUGHTER, MURDER

**homie** *(also* **homey***)* /ˈhəʊmi/ *noun (NAmE, informal)* = HOMEBOY or HOMEGIRL

**hom·ily** /ˈhɒməli; NAmE ˈhɑːm-/ *(pl.* **-ies***) noun (formal, often disapproving)* a speech or piece of writing giving advice on the correct way to behave, etc: *She delivered a homily on the virtues of family life.*

**hom·ing** /ˈhəʊmɪŋ/ *adj.* [only before noun] **1** (of a bird or an animal) trained, or having a natural ability, to find the way home from a long distance away: *Many birds have a remarkable* **homing instinct**. **2** (of a MISSILE, etc.) fitted with an electronic device that enables it to find and hit the place or object it is aimed at: *a homing device*

**homing pigeon** *noun* a PIGEON (= a type of bird) that has been trained to find its way home from a long distance away, and that people race against other PIGEONS for sport

**hom·in·id** /ˈhɒmɪnɪd; NAmE ˈhɑːm-/ *noun (specialist)* any member of the family that includes modern humans and GREAT APES, as well as earlier creatures that no longer exist from which modern humans EVOLVED (= developed)

**hom·in·oid** /ˈhɒmɪnɔɪd; NAmE ˈhɑːm-/ *noun (specialist)* any member of a group that includes modern humans and ANTHROPOID APES (= that look similar to humans), as well as earlier creatures that no longer exist from which modern humans EVOLVED (= developed)

**hom·iny** /ˈhɒmɪni; NAmE ˈhɑːm-/ *noun* [U] dried CORN (MAIZE), boiled in water or milk, eaten especially in the southern states of the US

**Homo** /ˈhəʊməʊ/ *BrE also* ˈhɒm-/ *noun (from Latin, specialist)* the GENUS (= group) of PRIMATES that includes early and modern humans

**homo-** /ˈhəʊməʊ, həʊmə; BrE also* həˈmɒ; NAmE also* həˈmɑː/ *combining form* (in nouns, adjectives and adverbs) the same ⊃ compare HETERO-

**hom·oe·op·ath** *(BrE)* = HOMEOPATH

**hom·oe·op·athy** *(BrE)* = HOMEOPATHY

**hom·oeo·sta·sis** *(BrE)* = HOMEOSTASIS

**Homo erectus** /ˌhəʊməʊ ɪˈrektəs/ *noun* [U] *(from Latin, specialist)* an early form of human that was able to walk on two legs

**homo·erot·ic** /ˌhəʊməʊɪˈrɒtɪk, ˌhɒm-; NAmE ˌhəʊməʊ-ɪˈrɑːt-/ *adj.* relating to GAY sex and sexual desire

**homo·gen·eity** /ˌhəʊməʊdʒəˈniːəti; BrE also ˌhɒm-/ *noun* [U] *(formal)* the quality in a group of people or things of being all the same or all of the same type

**homo·ge·neous** /ˌhəʊməˈdʒiːniəs; NAmE ˌhəʊm-/ *(also* **homo·gen·ous** /həˈmɒdʒənəs; NAmE -ˈmɑːdʒ-/*) adj. (formal)* consisting of things or people that are all the same or all of the same type: *a homogeneous group/mixture/population* **OPP** heterogeneous

**hom·ogen·ized** *(BrE also* **-ised***)* /həˈmɒdʒənaɪzd; NAmE -ˈmɑːdʒ-/ *adj.* (of milk) treated so that the cream is mixed in with the rest

**homo·graph** /ˈhɒməɡrɑːf; NAmE ˈhɑːməɡræf/ *noun (grammar)* a word that is spelt like another word but has a different meaning from it, and may have a different pronunciation, for example *bow* /baʊ/, *bow* /bəʊ/

**hom·ologous** /həˈmɒləɡəs; NAmE həʊˈmɑːl-/ *adj.* **~ (with sth)** *(specialist)* similar in position, structure, etc. to sth else: *The seal's flipper is homologous with the human arm.*

**homo·nym** /ˈhɒmənɪm; NAmE ˈhɑːm-/ *noun (grammar)* a word that is spelt like another word (or pronounced like it) but that has a different meaning, for example *can* meaning 'be able' and *can* meaning 'put sth in a container' ⊃ WORDFINDER NOTE at WORD

**homo·pho·bia** /ˌhəʊməˈfəʊbiə; BrE also ˌhɒm-/ *noun* [U] a strong PREJUDICE (= unreasonable dislike) against GAY people ⊃ WORDFINDER NOTE at EQUAL ▶ **homo·pho·bic** /-bɪk/ *adj.*

**homo·phone** /ˈhɒməfəʊn; NAmE ˈhɑːm-, ˈhəʊm-/ *noun (grammar)* a word that is pronounced like another word but has a different spelling or meaning, for example *plain*, *plane* /pleɪn/

**Homo sapiens** /ˌhəʊməʊ ˈsæpienz; NAmE ˈseɪp-, ˈsæp-/ *noun* [U] *(from Latin, specialist)* the kind or species of human that exists now

**homo·sex·ual** /ˌhəʊməˈsekʃuəl; BrE also ˌhɒm-/ *noun* a person, usually a man, who is sexually attracted to people of the same sex: *a practising homosexual* ⊃ compare BISEXUAL, GAY, HETEROSEXUAL, LESBIAN ▶ **homo·sex·ual** *adj.*: *a homosexual act/relationship* **homo·sex·ual·ity** /ˌhəʊməˌsekʃuˈæləti; BrE also ˌhɒm-/ *noun* [U]

**homo·zy·gote** /ˌhɒməˈzaɪɡəʊt; NAmE ˌhəʊm-/ *noun (biology)* a living thing that has only one form of a particular GENE, and whose young are more likely to share a particular characteristic ▶ **homo·zy·gous** /-ɡəs/ *adj.*

**homy** = HOMEY

**Hon** *(also* **Hon.** *especially in NAmE)* /ɒn; NAmE ɑːn/ *abbr.* **1** HONORARY (used in official titles of jobs): *Hon Treasurer: D Shrimpton* **2** HONOURABLE: *the Hon Member for Bolsover* ⊃ see also RT HON

**hon·cho** /ˈhɒntʃəʊ; NAmE ˈhɑːn-/ *noun (pl. -os) (informal, especially NAmE)* the person who is in charge **SYN** boss: *Claude is the studio's* **head honcho**.

**hone** /həʊn/ *verb* **1** to develop and improve sth, especially a skill, over a period of time: **~ sth** *She honed her debating skills at college.* ◊ *It was a finely honed piece of writing.* ◊ **~ sth to sth** *His body was honed to perfection.* **2 ~ sth (to sth)** to make a knife or other tool sharp or sharper **SYN** sharpen

**PHRV** **hone ˈin on sth** = HOME IN ON STH

**hon·est** ❶ **B1** /ˈɒnɪst; NAmE ˈɑːn-/ *adj.* **1** ❓ **B1** always telling the truth, and never stealing or cheating: *an honest man/woman* **OPP** dishonest **2** ❓ **B1** not hiding the truth about sth: **~ about sth** *Are you being completely honest about your feelings?* ◊ **~ with sb** *Thank you for being so honest with me.* ◊ *Give me your honest opinion.* ◊ **To be honest** (= what I really think is), *it was one of the worst books I've ever read.* ◊ *The film has won accolades for being both* **brutally honest** *and very funny.* **3** showing an honest mind or attitude: *She's got an honest face.* ◊ *He made an* **honest mistake** *and deserves a second chance.* **4** (of work or wages) earned or resulting from hard work: *He hasn't done* **an honest day's work** *in his life.* ◊ *It's quite a struggle to make* **an honest living**. **HELP** Use **an**, not **a**, before **honest**.

**IDM** **honest!** (*informal*) used to emphasize that you are not lying: *I didn't mean it, honest!* **honest to ˈGod/ˈgoodness** used to emphasize that what you are saying is true: *Honest to God, Mary, I'm not joking.* **HELP** Some people find this use of **God** offensive. ⇒ see also HONEST-TO-GOODNESS **make an honest ˈwoman of sb** (*old-fashioned, humorous*) to marry a woman after having had a sexual relationship with her, especially if she is pregnant

▼ **SYNONYMS**

### honest
**frank • direct • open • outspoken • straight • blunt**

These words all describe people saying exactly what they mean without trying to hide feelings, opinions or facts.

**honest** not hiding the truth about sth: *Thank you for being so honest with me.*

**frank** honest in what you say, sometimes in a way that other people might not like: *To be frank with you, I think your son has little chance of passing the exam.*

**direct** saying exactly what you mean in a way that nobody can pretend not to understand: *You'll have to get used to his direct manner.* **NOTE** Being **direct** is sometimes considered positive but sometimes it is used as a 'polite' way of saying that sb is rude.

**open** (*approving*) (of a person) not keeping thoughts and feelings hidden: *He was quite open about his reasons for leaving.*

**outspoken** saying exactly what you think, even if this shocks or offends people: *She was outspoken in her criticism of the plan.*

**straight** honest and direct: *I don't think you're being straight with me.*

**blunt** saying exactly what you think without trying to be polite: *She has a reputation for blunt speaking.*

**WHICH WORD?**

- **Honest** and **frank** refer to *what* you say as much as *how* you say it: *a(n) honest/frank admission of guilt*. They are generally positive words, although it is possible to be *too* frank in a way that other people might not like. **Direct**, **outspoken** and **blunt** all describe sb's manner of saying what they think. **Outspoken** suggests that you are willing to shock people by saying what you believe to be right. **Blunt** and **direct** often suggest that you think honesty is more important than being polite. **Open** is positive and describes sb's character: *I'm a very open person.*

**PATTERNS**

- honest/frank/direct/open/outspoken/straight **about** sth
- honest/frank/direct/open/straight/blunt **with** sb
- a(n) honest/direct/straight/blunt **answer**
- a frank/direct/blunt **manner**

ˌhonest ˈbroker *noun* a person or country that tries to get other people or countries to reach an agreement or to solve a problem, without getting involved with either side

**hon·est·ly** /ˈɒnɪstli; *NAmE* ˈɑːn-/ *adv.* **1** in an honest way: *I can't believe he got that money honestly.* **OPP** **dishonestly** **2** used to emphasize that what you are saying is true, however surprising it may seem: *I didn't tell anyone, honestly!* ◊ *I honestly can't remember a thing about last night.* ◊ *You can't honestly expect me to believe that!* **3** (*informal*) used to show that you think sth is bad and are annoyed by it: *Honestly! Whatever will they think of next?*

ˌhonest-to-ˈgoodness *adj.* [only before noun] (*approving*) simple and good: *honest-to-goodness country food*

**hon·esty** ʔ+ B2 /ˈɒnəsti; *NAmE* ˈɑːn-/ *noun* [U] the quality of being honest: *She answered all my questions with her usual honesty.* ◊ *His honesty is not in question.* **IDM** **in (all) ˈhonesty** used to state a fact or an opinion that, though true, may seem disappointing: *The book isn't, in all honesty, as good as I expected.*

**honey** /ˈhʌni/ *noun* **1** [U] a sweet, sticky yellow-brown substance made by bees that is spread on bread, etc. like jam **2** [C] (*informal*) a way of addressing sb that you like or love: *Have you seen my keys, honey?* **3** [C] (*informal*) a person that you like or love and think is very kind: *He can be a real honey when he wants to be.* **IDM** see LAND *n.*

**ˈhoney-bee** /ˈhʌnibiː/ *noun* a bee that makes honey

**ˈhoney-comb** /ˈhʌnikəʊm/ (*also* **comb**) *noun* [C, U] a structure of cells with six sides, made by bees for holding their honey and their eggs

**ˈhoney-combed** /ˈhʌnikəʊmd/ *adj.* **~(with sth)** filled with holes, tunnels, etc.

**hon·eyed** /ˈhʌnid/ *adj.* (*literary*) **1** (of words) soft and intended to please, but often not sincere **2** tasting or smelling like honey, or having the colour of honey

**ˈhoney·moon** /ˈhʌnimuːn/ *noun, verb*

■ *noun* [usually sing.] **1** a holiday taken by a couple who have just got married: *We went to Venice for our honeymoon.* ◊ **on (your)~** *They're on their honeymoon.* ◊ *They go on honeymoon the day after the wedding.* ⇒ **WORDFINDER NOTE** at HOLIDAY **2** the period of time at the start of a new activity when nobody is criticized and people feel enthusiastic: *The honeymoon period for the government is now over.*

■ *verb* [I] **+ adv./prep.** to spend your honeymoon somewhere ▸ **ˈhoney·moon·er** *noun*

**ˈhoney-pot** /ˈhʌnipɒt; *NAmE* -pɑːt/ *noun* [usually sing.] (*BrE*) a place, thing or person that a lot of people are attracted to

**ˈhoney-suckle** /ˈhʌnisʌkl/ *noun* [U, C] a climbing plant with white, yellow or pink flowers with a sweet smell

**hongi** /ˈhɒŋi; *NAmE* ˈhɑːŋi/ *noun* (*NZE*) a traditional Maori GREETING in which people press their noses together

**honk** /hɒŋk; *NAmE* hɑːŋk/ *noun, verb*

■ *noun* **1** the noise made by a GOOSE **2** the noise made by a car HORN

■ *verb* **1** [I, T] if a car HORN **honks** or you **honk** or **honk the horn**, the horn makes a loud noise **SYN** **hoot**: *honking taxis* ◊ **~ at sb/sth** *Why did he honk at me?* ◊ **~ sth** *People honked their horns as they drove past.* **2** [I] when a GOOSE **honks**, it makes a loud noise

**honky** /ˈhɒŋki; *NAmE* ˈhɑːŋ-/ *noun* (*pl.* **-ies**) (*NAmE, slang*) an offensive word for a white person, used by black people

**ˌhonky-ˈtonk** /ˈhɒŋki tɒŋk; *NAmE* ˈhɑːŋki tɑːŋk/ *noun* **1** [C] (*NAmE*) a cheap, noisy bar or dance hall **2** [U] a type of lively jazz played on a piano

**honor, honˈor·able** (*US*) = HONOUR, HONOURABLE

**hon·or·arium** /ˌɒnəˈreəriəm; *NAmE* ˌɑːnəˈrer-/ *noun* (*pl.* **hon·or·aria** /-riə/) (*formal*) a payment made for sb's professional services **HELP** Use **an**, not **a**, before **honorarium**.

**hon·or·ary** /ˈɒnərəri; *NAmE* ˈɑːnəreri/ *adj.* (*abbr.* **Hon**) **1** (of a university degree, a rank, etc.) given as an honour, without the person having to have the usual qualifications: *an honorary doctorate/degree* **2** (of a position in an organization) not paid: *the honorary president* ◊ *The post of treasurer is a purely honorary position.* **3** treated like a member of a group without actually belonging to it: *She was treated as an honorary man.* **HELP** Use **an**, not **a**, before **honorary**.

**hon·or·ee** (*BrE also* **hon·our·ee**) /ˌɒnəˈriː; *NAmE* ˌɑːn-/ *noun* (*especially NAmE*) a person or thing that wins an award: *The author is a Pulitzer Prize honoree.* **HELP** Use **an**, not **a**, before **honoree**.

**hon·or·if·ic** /ˌɒnəˈrɪfɪk; *NAmE* ˌɑːn-/ *adj.* (*formal*) showing respect for the person you are speaking to: *an honorific title* **HELP** Use **an**, not **a**, before **honorific**.

**ˈhonor roll** *noun* (*US*) **1** (*BrE* **ˌroll of ˈhonour**) [usually sing.] a list of people who are being praised officially for sth they have done **2** a list of the best students in a college or HIGH SCHOOL

**ˈhonor society** *noun* (in the US) an organization for students with the best grades at school or college

**ˈhonor system** (*US*) (*BrE* **ˈhonour system**) *noun* [sing.] (*especially NAmE*) an agreement in which people are trusted to obey rules

# honour 764

**hon·our** ⓘ B2 (US **honor**) /ˈɒnə(r)/; NAmE /ˈɑːn-/ noun, verb

■ **noun** HELP Use **an**, not **a**, before **honour**.
- **RESPECT 1** B2 [U] great respect for sb: *the guest of honour* (= the most important one) ◊ *the seat/place of honour* (= given to the most important guest) ◊ *They stood in silence as a mark of honour to her.* ⊃ see also MAID OF HONOUR, MATRON OF HONOUR
- **PRIVILEGE 2** B2 [sing.] ~ **(to do sth)** something that you are very pleased or proud to do because people are showing you great respect SYN **privilege**: *It was a great honour to be invited here today.* ⊃ SYNONYMS at PLEASURE
- **MORAL BEHAVIOUR 3** B2 [U] the quality of knowing and doing what is morally right: *a man of honour*
- **REPUTATION 4** B2 [U] a good reputation; respect from other people: *upholding the honour of your country* ◊ *The family honour is at stake.* ⊃ compare DISHONOUR **5** [sing.] ~ **to sth/sb** a person or thing that causes others to respect and admire sth/sb: *She is an honour to the profession.*
- **AWARD 6** B2 [C] an award, official title, etc. given to sb as a reward for sth that they have done: *the New Year's Honours list* (= in Britain, a list of awards and titles given on January 1 each year) ◊ *to receive/win the highest honour* ◊ *to bestow an honour on sb* ⊃ see also ROLL OF HONOUR
- **AT UNIVERSITY/SCHOOL 7 honours, honors** [pl.] (*abbr.* **Hons**) (often used as an adjective) a university course that is of a higher level than a basic course (in the US also used to describe a class in school that is at a higher level than other classes): *an honours degree/course* ◊ *a First Class Honours degree* ◊ (*NAmE*) *I took an honors class in English.* **8 honours, honors** [pl.] if you pass an exam or graduate from a university or school **with honours**, you receive a special grade for having achieved a very high standard
- **JUDGE/MAYOR 9 His/Her/Your Honour** [C] a title of respect used when talking to or about a judge or a US MAYOR: *No more questions, Your Honour.*
- **IN CARD GAMES 10** [C, usually pl.] the cards that have the highest value

IDM **do sb an ˈhonour | do sb the ˈhonour (of doing sth)** (*formal*) to do sth to make sb feel very proud and pleased: *Would you do me the honour of dining with me?* **do the ˈhonours** to perform a social duty or ceremony, such as pouring drinks, making a speech, etc: *Would you do the honours and draw the winning ticket?* **have the ˈhonour of sth/of doing sth** (*formal*) to be given the opportunity to do sth that makes you feel proud and happy: *May I have the honour of the next dance?* **(there is) honour among ˈthieves** (*saying*) used to say that even criminals have standards of behaviour that they respect **(feel) honour-ˈbound to do sth** (*formal*) to feel that you must do sth because of your sense of moral duty: *She felt honour-bound to attend as she had promised to.* ⊃ compare DUTY-BOUND **the honours are ˈeven** no particular person, team, etc. is doing better than the others in a competition, an argument, etc. **in ˈhonour of sb/sth | in sb's/sth's ˈhonour** in order to show great respect for sb/sth: *a ceremony in honour of those killed in the explosion* ◊ *A banquet was held in her honour.* **on your ˈhonour** (*old-fashioned*) **1** used to promise very seriously that you will do sth or that sth is true: *I swear on my honour that I knew nothing about this.* **2** to be trusted to do sth: *You're on your honour not to go into my room.* ⊃ more at POINT *n.*

■ **verb**
- **SHOW RESPECT 1** B2 to do sth that shows great respect for sb/sth: ~**sb/sth** *our honoured guests* ◊ *Actors and musicians gathered to honour the memory of the late singer.* ◊ ~**sb with sth** *The President honoured us with a personal visit.*
- **GIVE AWARD 2** B2 [often passive] to give public praise, an award or a title to sb for sth they have done: **honour sb/sth (with sth) (for sth)** *He has been honoured with a knighthood for his scientific work.* ◊ ~**sb/sth as sth** *The exhibition was honored as best show in a public space.*
- **KEEP PROMISE 3** ~**sth** (*formal*) to do what you have agreed or promised to do: *I have every intention of honouring our contract.*

IDM **be/feel honoured (to do sth)** to feel proud and happy: *I was honoured to have been mentioned in his speech.*

**hon·our·able** (US **hon·or·able**) /ˈɒnərəbl/; NAmE /ˈɑːn-/ adj.
**1** deserving great respect: *a long and honourable career in government* ◊ *They managed an honourable 2–2 draw.* ◊ *With a few honourable exceptions, the staff were found to be incompetent.* **2** showing high moral standards: *an honourable man* **3** allowing sb to keep their good name and the respect of others: *an honourable compromise* ◊ *They urged her to do the honourable thing and resign.* ◊ *He received an honourable discharge from the army.* OPP **dishonourable 4** the **Honourable** (*abbr.* **Hon**) [only before noun] (in the UK) a title used by a child of some ranks of the NOBILITY **5 the/my Honourable …** (*abbr.* **Hon**) [only before noun] (in the UK) a title used by Members of Parliament when talking about or to another Member during a debate: *If my Honourable Friend would give me a chance to answer, …* **6** the **Honorable** (*abbr.* **Hon**) [only before noun] (in the US) a title of respect used for an official of high rank: *the Honorable Alan Simpson, US senator* ⊃ compare RIGHT HONOURABLE HELP Use **an**, not **a**, before **honourable**.
▸ **hon·our·ably** (US **hon·or·ably**) /-bli/ adv.: *to behave honourably*

**ˌhonourable ˈmention** (US **ˌhonorable ˈmention**) noun special praise given in a competition for work that is of a very high standard but does not win a prize: *Three other entries received honourable mentions.*

**hon·our·ee** = HONOREE

**ˈhonour killing** (US **ˈhonor killing**) noun [C, U] the murder of a relative, usually a girl or woman, because she has done sth that is thought to bring shame on the family: *She was the victim of a so-called 'honour killing'.*

**Hons** /ɒnz/; NAmE /ɑːnz/ *abbr.* (*BrE*) HONOURS (used after the name of a university degree): *Tim Smith BA (Hons)*

**hooch** /huːtʃ/ noun [U] (*especially NAmE, informal*) strong alcoholic drink, especially sth that has been made illegally

**hood** /hʊd/ noun **1** a part of a coat, etc. that you can pull up to cover the back and top of your head: *a jacket with a detachable hood* **2** a piece of cloth put over sb's face and head so that they cannot be recognized or so that they cannot see **3** a piece of coloured silk or fur worn over an academic GOWN to show the kind of degree held by the person wearing it **4** (*especially BrE*) a folding cover over a car, child's BUGGY, etc: *We drove all the way with the hood down.* **5** (*NAmE*) (*BrE* **bon·net**) the metal part over the front of a vehicle, usually covering the engine **6** a cover placed over a device or machine, for example, to protect it: *a lens hood* ◊ *an extractor hood* (= one that removes cooking smells from a kitchen) **7** (*especially NAmE, slang*) = HOODLUM (1) **8** (*also* **ˈhood**) (*especially NAmE, slang*) a neighbourhood, especially a person's own neighbourhood

IDM **under the ˈhood** at the fundamental level of how sth works rather than at the obvious surface level: *They are urging potential job seekers to take a look under the hood of industry.*

**-hood** /hʊd/ *suffix* (in nouns) **1** the state or quality of: *childhood* ◊ *falsehood* **2** a group of people of the type mentioned: *the priesthood*

**hood·ed** /ˈhʊdɪd/ adj. **1** having or wearing a hood: *a hooded jacket* ◊ *A hooded figure waited in the doorway.* **2** (of eyes) having large EYELIDS that always look as if they are partly closed

**hood·lum** /ˈhuːdləm; NAmE ˈhʊd-/ noun (*informal*) **1** (*also slang* **hood** *especially in NAmE*) a violent criminal, especially one who is part of a gang **2** a violent and noisy young man SYN **hooligan**

**hoo·doo** /ˈhuːduː/ noun (*pl.* **-oos**) (*especially US*) a person or thing that brings or causes bad luck

**hood·wink** /ˈhʊdwɪŋk/ verb ~**sb (into doing sth)** to trick sb: *She had been hoodwinked into buying a worthless necklace.*

**hoody** (*also* **hoodie**) /ˈhʊdi/ noun (*pl.* **-ies**) (*informal*) a jacket or a SWEATSHIRT with a hood

---

æ **cat** | ɑː **father** | e **bed** | ɜː **fur** | ə **about** | ɪ **sit** | iː **see** | i **happy** | ɒ **got** (*BrE*) | ɔː **saw** | ʌ **cup** | ʊ **put** | uː **too**

**hooey** /ˈhuːi/ noun [U] (especially NAmE, informal) ideas, statements or beliefs that you think are silly or not true; stupid talk SYN **nonsense**

**hoof** /huːf/ noun, verb
■ noun (pl. **hoofs** or **hooves** /huːvz/) the hard part of the foot of some animals, for example horses ⇒ see also CLOVEN HOOF ⇒ VISUAL VOCAB page V2
IDM **on the ˈhoof 1** meat that is sold, transported, etc. **on the hoof** is sold, etc. while the cow, sheep, etc. is still alive **2** (BrE, informal) if you do sth **on the hoof**, you do it quickly and without giving it your full attention because you are doing sth else at the same time
■ verb ~ sth (informal) to kick a ball very hard or a long way
IDM **ˈhoof it** (informal) to go somewhere on foot; to walk somewhere: *We hoofed it all the way to 42nd Street.*

**ˌhoof-and-ˈmouth disease** noun [U] (NAmE) = FOOT-AND-MOUTH DISEASE

**hoo-ha** /ˈhuː hɑː/ noun [U, sing.] (BrE, informal) noisy excitement, especially about sth unimportant SYN **fuss**

**hooks**

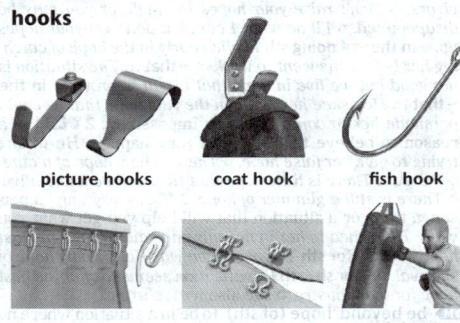

picture hooks    coat hook    fish hook

curtain hooks    hook and eye    left hook

**hook** /hʊk/ noun, verb
■ noun **1** a curved piece of metal, plastic or wire for hanging things on, catching fish with, etc: *a picture/curtain/coat hook* ◇ *a fish hook* ◇ *Hang your towel on the hook.* ⇒ see also BOATHOOK, FISH HOOK ⇒ WORDFINDER NOTE at FISHING **2** (in boxing) a short hard hit that is made with the ELBOW bent: *a left hook to the jaw* **3** (in CRICKET and golf) a way of hitting the ball so that it curves to the side instead of going straight ahead (usually by mistake in golf, but deliberately in CRICKET) **4** a thing that is used to make people interested in sth: *The images are used as a hook to get children interested in science.*
IDM **by ˌhook or by ˈcrook** using any method you can, even a dishonest one **hook, line and ˈsinker** completely: *What I said was not true, but he fell for it (= believed it) hook, line and sinker.* **off the ˈhook 1** having got free from a difficult situation or a punishment: *I lied to get him off the hook.* **2** (becoming old-fashioned) if you leave or take a LANDLINE phone **off the hook**, you take the RECEIVER (= the part that you pick up) off the place where it usually rests, so that nobody can call you ⇒ more at RING² v., SLING v.
■ verb **1** [T, I] to fasten or hang sth on sth else using a hook; to be fastened or hanging in this way: ~ sth + adv./prep. *We hooked the trailer to the back of the car.* ◇ + adv./prep. *a dress that hooks at the back* **2** [T, I] to put sth, especially your leg, arm or finger, around sth else so that you can hold onto it or move it; to go around sth else in this way: ~ sth + adv./prep. *He hooked his foot under the stool and dragged it over.* ◇ *Her thumbs were hooked into the pockets of her jeans.* ◇ + adv./prep. *Suddenly an arm hooked around my neck.* **3** [T] ~ sth to catch a fish with a hook: *It was the biggest pike I ever hooked.* ◇ (figurative) *She had managed to hook a wealthy husband.* **4** [T] ~ sth (especially in golf, CRICKET or football (soccer)) to hit or kick a ball so that it goes to one side instead of straight ahead (usually by mistake in golf but deliberately in other sports)
PHRV **ˌhook ˈup (to sth)** | **ˌhook sb/sth ˈup (to sth)** to connect sb/sth to a piece of electronic equipment, to a power supply or to the internet: *She was then hooked up to an IV drip.* ◇ *Check that the computer is hooked up to the printer.* ◇ *A large proportion of the nation's households are hooked up to the internet.* **ˌhook ˈup with sb** (informal) **1** to meet sb and spend time with them **2** to start working with sb: *They formed the band in 2018, hooking up with bass player Ed Burns.* **3** to form a temporary sexual relationship: *Hooking up with total strangers can be very dangerous.* **ˌhook sb ˈup with sb/sth** (informal) to put sb in contact with sb who can help them; to get sth for sb that they want: *Can you hook me up with someone with a car?*

**hoo·kah** /ˈhʊkə/ noun a long pipe for smoking that passes smoke through a container of water to cool it

**ˌhook and ˈeye** noun (pl. **hooks and eyes**) a device for fastening clothes, consisting of a small thin piece of metal curved round, and a HOOK that fits into it ⇒ picture at HOOK

**hooked** /hʊkt/ adj. **1** curved; like a hook in shape: *a hooked nose/beak/finger* **2** [not before noun] ~ (on sth) (informal) needing sth that is bad for you, especially a drug **3** [not before noun] ~ (on sth) (informal) enjoying sth very much, so that you want to do it, see it, etc. as much as possible **4** having one or more hooks

**hook·er** /ˈhʊkə(r)/ noun **1** the player in a rugby team, whose job is to pull the ball out of the SCRUM with his foot **2** (especially NAmE, informal) a PROSTITUTE

**hookey** = HOOKY

**ˈhook shot** noun **1** (in basketball) a shot in which a player starts with their back towards the BASKET and throws the ball towards the BASKET in a wide curve, by stretching their arm out to the side and throwing over their head **2** (in CRICKET) a shot in which a player hits the ball to the side by moving the BAT across their chest

**ˈhook-up** noun a connection between two pieces of equipment, especially electronic equipment used in broadcasting, or computers: *a satellite hook-up between the major European networks*

**hook·worm** /ˈhʊkwɜːm; NAmE -wɜːrm/ noun **1** [C] a WORM that lives in the INTESTINES of humans and animals **2** [U] a disease caused by hookworms

**hooky** (also **hookey**) /ˈhʊki/ (NAmE, old-fashioned)
IDM **play ˈhooky** (informal) (BrE **play ˈtruant**) to stay away from school without permission

**hoo·li·gan** /ˈhuːlɪɡən/ noun a young person who behaves in an extremely noisy and violent way in public, usually in a group: *English football hooligans* ▶ **hoo·li·gan·ism** noun [U]

**hoon** /huːn/ noun (AustralE, NZE, informal) a man who behaves in a rude and aggressive way, especially one who drives in a dangerous way ▶ **hoon** verb [I]

**hoop** /huːp/ noun **1** a large ring of plastic, wood or iron: *a barrel bound with iron hoops* **2** (also **ˌhoop ˈearring**) an EARRING in the shape of a ring: *a pair of plain gold hoops* **3** the ring that the players throw the ball through in the game of basketball in order to score points: *Let's shoot some hoops.* **4 hoops** [U] (NAmE, informal) the game of basketball: *He played junior college hoops in California.* **5** a large ring that was used as a children's toy in the past, or for animals or riders to jump through at a CIRCUS **6** = HULA HOOP **7** a small ARCH made of metal or plastic, put into the ground: *croquet hoops* (= in the game of CROQUET) ◇ *Grow lettuces under plastic stretched over wire hoops.* IDM see JUMP v.

**hooped** /huːpt/ adj. having the shape of a hoop: *hooped earrings*

**hoop·la** /ˈhuːplɑː/ noun **1** [U, sing.] (informal, especially NAmE) unnecessary excitement about sth that gets a lot of public attention **2** [U] (BrE) (NAmE **ˈring toss**) a game in which players try to throw rings over objects in order to win them as prizes

**hoo·poe** /ˈhuːpuː, -pəʊ/ noun an orange-pink bird with a long BEAK that curves downwards, black and white wings and a CREST on its head

**hoo·ray** /huˈreɪ/ exclamation **1** (also **hur·rah, hur·ray**) used to show that you are happy or that you approve of sth

# hooroo

**2** (also **hoo·roo**) (*AustralE*, *NZE*) goodbye [IDM] see HIP exclamation

**hoo·roo** /həˈruː/ *exclamation* (*AustralE*) = HOORAY (2)

**hoot** /huːt/ *verb*, *noun*
- *verb* **1** [I] to make a loud noise: *He had the audience hooting with laughter.* ◊ *Some people hooted in disgust.* **2** [I, T] (*BrE*) if a car HORN **hoots** or you **hoot** or **hoot the horn**, the horn makes a loud noise [SYN] **honk**: *hooting cars* ◊ *~ at sb/sth Why did he hoot at me?* ◊ *~ sth Passing motorists hooted their horns.* ◊ *The train hooted a warning* (= the driver sounded the horn to warn people). **3** [I] when an OWL **hoots**, it makes a long calling sound
- *noun* **1** [C] (*especially BrE*) a short loud laugh or shout: *The suggestion was greeted by hoots of laughter.* **2** [sing.] (*informal*) a situation or a person that you find very funny: *You ought to meet her—she's a hoot!* **3** [C] the loud sound made by the HORN of a vehicle **4** [C] the call of an OWL
- [IDM] **not ˈcare/give a ˈhoot** | **not ˈcare/give two ˈhoots** (*informal*) not to care at all

**hoote·nanny** /ˈhuːtnæni/ *noun* (*pl.* **-ies**) (*especially US*) an informal social event at which people play FOLK MUSIC, sing and sometimes dance

**hoot·er** /ˈhuːtə(r)/ *noun* **1** (*BrE*, rather old-fashioned) the device in a vehicle, or a factory, that makes a loud noise as a signal **2** (*BrE*, *slang*) a person's nose, especially a large one **3** [usually pl.] (*NAmE*, *slang*) a woman's breast

**Hoo·ver™** /ˈhuːvə(r)/ *noun* (*BrE*) = VACUUM CLEANER

**hoo·ver** /ˈhuːvə(r)/ *verb* [T, I] *~ (sth)* (*BrE*) to clean a carpet, floor, etc. with a vacuum cleaner [SYN] **vacuum**: *to hoover the carpet*
- [PHRV] **ˌhoover sth↔ˈup 1** to remove sth from a carpet, floor, etc. with a VACUUM CLEANER: *to hoover up all the dust* **2** (*informal*) to get or collect sth in large quantities: *The US and Canada usually hoover up most of the gold medals.*
▶ **hoo·ver·ing** *noun* [U]: *It's your turn to do the hoovering.*

**hooves** /huːvz/ *pl. of* HOOF

**hop** /hɒp/ *NAmE* haːp/ *verb*, *noun*
- *verb* (**-pp-**) **1** [I] (*+ adv./prep.*) (of a person) to move by jumping on one foot: *I couldn't put my weight on my ankle and had to hop everywhere.* ◊ *kids hopping over puddles* **2** [I] *+ adv./prep.* (of an animal or a bird) to move by jumping with all or both feet together: *A robin was hopping around on the path.* **3** [I] *+ adv./prep.* (*informal*) to go or move somewhere quickly and suddenly: *Hop in, I'll drive you home.* ◊ *to hop into/out of bed* ◊ *I hopped on the next train.* ◊ *We hopped over to Paris for the weekend.* **4** [T] *~ a plane, bus, train, etc.* (*NAmE*) to get on a plane, bus, etc. **5** [I] *~ (from sth to sth)* to change from one activity or subject to another: *I like to hop from channel to channel when I watch TV.* ⊃ see also BAR-HOP, CHANNEL-HOP
- [IDM] **ˈhop it** (*old-fashioned*, *BrE*, *informal*) usually used in orders to tell sb to go away [SYN] **go away**: *Go on, hop it!* **ˈhop to it** (*NAmE*, *informal*) = JUMP TO IT at JUMP v.
- *noun* **1** [C] a short jump by a person on one foot: *He crossed the hall with a hop, skip and a jump.* **2** [C] a short jump by an animal or a bird with all or both feet together **3** [C] a short journey, especially by plane **4** [C] a tall climbing plant with green female flowers that are like CONES in shape **5** **hops** [pl.] the green female flowers of the hop plant that have been dried, used for making beer **6** [C] (*old-fashioned*, *informal*) a social event at which people dance in an informal way ⊃ see also HIP-HOP [IDM] see CATCH v.

**hope** /həʊp/ *verb*, *noun*
- *verb* **1** [I, T] to want sth to happen and think that it is possible: *All we can do now is wait and hope.* ◊ *'Do you think it will rain?' 'I hope not.'* ◊ *Will you be back before dark?' 'I hope so, yes.'* ◊ *~ for sth We are hoping for good weather on Sunday.* ◊ *~ (that)… I hope (that) you're okay.* ◊ *I just hope we can find the right person.* ◊ *I can only hope there has been some mistake.* ◊ *Let's hope we can find a parking space.* ◊ *I hope and pray that he is released quickly.* ◊ *it is hoped (that) … It is hoped that over £10000 will be* raised. ◊ *~ to do sth She is hoping to win the gold medal.* [HELP] **Hope** can be used in the passive in the form **it is hoped that…** For must always be used with **hope** in other passive sentences: *The improvement that had been hoped for never came.* ◊ *The hoped-for improvement never came.* **2** *~ to do sth* to intend to do sth if possible: *We're hoping to address all these issues.*
- [IDM] **ˌhope against ˈhope (that…)** to continue to hope for sth although it is very unlikely to happen **ˌhope for the ˈbest** to hope that sth will happen successfully, especially where it seems likely that it will not **I should ˈhope so/not** | **so I should ˈhope** (*informal*) used to say that you feel very strongly that sth should/should not happen: *'Nobody blames you.' 'I should hope not!'* ⊃ more at CROSS v.
- *noun* **1** [U, C] a feeling of wanting and expecting a particular thing to happen; sth that you wish for: *Don't lose hope—we'll find her.* ◊ *She told me all her hopes and dreams.* ◊ *~ for sb/sth They have high hopes for their children.* ◊ *~ of sth There are hopes of a lasting peace.* ◊ *~ of doing sth They have given up hope of finding any more survivors.* ◊ *Don't raise your hopes too high, or you may be disappointed.* ◊ *I'll do what I can, but don't get your hopes up.* ◊ *in the ~ of doing sth I called early in the hope of catching her before she went to work.* ◊ *~ that… The situation is not good but we live in hope that it will improve.* ◊ *in the ~ that… He asked her again in the vain hope that he could persuade her to come* (= it was impossible). **2** [U] a reason to believe that sth good may happen: *He wasn't trying to give her false hope.* ◊ *There is now hope of a cure.* ◊ *~ that… There is little hope that they will be found alive.* ◊ *There is still a glimmer of hope.* **3** [C, usually sing.] a person, a thing or a situation that will help you get what you want: *He turned to her in despair and said, 'You're my last hope.'* ◊ *~ of/for sth The operation was Kelly's only hope of survival.* ◊ *~ for sth Privatization seems to offer the best hope for the industry.* ⊃ see also WHITE HOPE
- [IDM] **be beyond ˈhope (of sth)** to be in a situation where no improvement is possible **hold out ˈlittle, etc. ˈhope (of sth/that…)** | **not hold out any, much, etc. ˈhope (of sth/that…)** to offer little, etc. reason for believing that sth will happen: *The doctors did not hold out much hope for her recovery.* **hope springs eˈternal** (*saying*) people never stop hoping **not have a ˈhope (in ˈhell) (of doing sth)** (*informal*) to have no chance at all: *She doesn't have a hope of winning.* **ˌsome ˈhope!** (*BrE*, *informal*) used to say that there is no chance at all that sth will happen ⊃ more at DASH v., FAT v.

**ˈhoped-for** *adj.* [only before noun] wanted and thought possible: *The new policy did not bring the hoped-for economic recovery.*

**hope·ful** /ˈhəʊpfl/ *adj.*, *noun*
- *adj.* **1** *~ (that…)* [not usually before noun] (of a person) believing that sth you want will happen [SYN] **optimistic**: *~ (that…) I feel hopeful that we'll find a suitable house very soon.* ◊ *~ about sth He is not very hopeful about the outcome of the interview.* ◊ *~ of doing sth* (*BrE*) *She is hopeful of returning to work soon.* [OPP] **pessimistic** **2** [only before noun] (of a person's behaviour) showing hope: *a hopeful smile* **3** (of a thing) making you believe that sth you want will happen; bringing hope [SYN] **promising**: *The latest trade figures are a hopeful sign.* ◊ *The future did not seem very hopeful.* ▶ **hope·ful·ness** *noun* [U]
- *noun* a person who wants to succeed at sth: *50 young hopefuls are trying for a place in the England team.*

**hope·ful·ly** /ˈhəʊpfəli/ *adv.* **1** used to express what you hope will happen: *Hopefully, we'll arrive before dark.* [HELP] Although this is the most common use of **hopefully**, it is a fairly new use and some people think it is not correct. **2** showing hope: *'Are you free tonight?' she asked hopefully.*

**hope·less** /ˈhəʊpləs/ *adj.* **1** if sth is **hopeless**, there is no hope that it will get better or succeed: *a hopeless situation* ◊ *It's hopeless trying to convince her.* ◊ *Most of the students are making good progress, but Michael is a hopeless case.* ◊ *He felt that his life was a hopeless mess.* **2** (*BrE*, *informal*) extremely bad [SYN] **terrible**: *The buses are absolutely hopeless these days!* **3** (*especially BrE*) (of people) very bad (at sth); with no ability or skill [SYN] **terrible**: *a hopeless* driver ◊ ~ **at sth** *I'm hopeless at science.* ◊ **~ with sth** *I've always been hopeless with machinery.* **4** feeling or showing no hope: *She felt lonely and hopeless.* ▶ **hope·less·ly** *adv.*: *hopelessly outnumbered* ◊ *They were hopelessly lost.* ◊ *to be hopelessly in love* ◊ *'I'll never manage it,' he said hopelessly.* **hope·less·ness** *noun* [U]: *a sense/feeling of hopelessness*

**Hopi** /ˈhəʊpi/ *noun* (*pl.* **Hopi** or **Hopis**) a member of a Native American people, many of whom live in the US state of Arizona

**hop·per** /ˈhɒpə(r)/ *NAmE* ˈhɑːp-/ *noun* a container that is like a V in shape and holds grain, coal or food for animals, and lets it out through the bottom

**hop·ping** /ˈhɒpɪŋ/ *NAmE* ˈhɑːp-/ *adj., adv.*
■ *adj.* (*NAmE, informal*) very lively or busy: *The clubs in town are really hopping.*
■ *adv.*
IDM ˌhopping ˈmad (*informal*) very angry

**hop·scotch** /ˈhɒpskɒtʃ/ *NAmE* ˈhɑːpskɑːtʃ/ *noun* [U] a children's game played on a pattern of squares marked on the ground. Each child throws a stone into a square then HOPS (= jumps on one leg) and jumps along the empty squares to pick up the stone again.

**horde** /hɔːd/ *NAmE* hɔːrd/ *noun* (*sometimes disapproving*) a large crowd of people: *There are always hordes of tourists here in the summer.* ◊ **in** ~ *Football fans turned up in hordes.*

**hori·zon** ?+ C1 /həˈraɪzn/ *noun* **1** ?+ C1 **the horizon** [sing.] the furthest that you can see, where the sky seems to meet the land or the sea: *The sun sank below the horizon.* ◊ *A ship appeared on the horizon.* **2** ?+ C1 [C, usually pl.] the limit of your desires, knowledge or interests: *She wanted to travel to broaden her horizons.* ◊ *The company needs new horizons now.*
IDM **on the hoˈrizon** likely to happen soon: *There's trouble looming on the horizon.*

**hori·zon·tal** W /ˌhɒrɪˈzɒntl/ *NAmE* ˌhɔːrɪˈzɑːn-/ *adj., noun*
■ *adj.* flat and level; going across and PARALLEL to the ground rather than going up and down: *horizontal lines* ⊃ compare VERTICAL ⊃ picture at LINE ▶ **hori·zon·tal·ly** /-təli/ *adv.*: *Cut the cake in half horizontally and spread jam on one half.*
■ *noun* **1** **the hori·zon·tal** [U] a horizontal position: *He shifted his position from the horizontal.* **2** [C] a horizontal line or surface

**hor·mone** /ˈhɔːməʊn/ *NAmE* ˈhɔːrm-/ *noun* a chemical substance produced in the body or in a plant that encourages growth or influences how the cells and TISSUES function; an artificial substance that has similar effects: *growth hormones* ◊ *a hormone imbalance* ◊ *Oestrogen is a female sex hormone.* ▶ **hor·mo·nal** /hɔːˈməʊnl/ *NAmE* hɔːrˈm-/ *adj.* [usually before noun]: *the hormonal changes occurring during pregnancy*

ˌhormone reˈplacement therapy *noun* [U] = HRT

**horn** ?+ C1 /hɔːn/ *NAmE* hɔːrn/ *noun, verb*
■ *noun* **1** ?+ C1 [C] a hard pointed part that grows, usually in pairs, on the heads of some animals, such as sheep and cows. Horns are often curved. ⊃ VISUAL VOCAB page V2 **2** [U] the hard substance of which animal horns are made **3** ?+ C1 [C] a device in a vehicle for making a loud sound as a warning or signal: *to honk your car horn* (*BrE*) *to sound/toot your horn* ⊃ see also FOGHORN **4** [C] a simple musical instrument that consists of a curved metal tube that you blow into: *a hunting horn* **5** [C] (*especially BrE*) = FRENCH HORN: *a horn concerto* ⊃ see also ENGLISH HORN
IDM **blow / toot your own ˈhorn** (*NAmE, informal*) = BLOW YOUR OWN TRUMPET at BLOW *v.* **draw / pull your ˈhorns in** to start being more careful in your behaviour, especially by spending less money than before **on the horns of a diˈlemma** in a situation in which you have to make a choice between things that are equally unpleasant ⊃ more at BULL, LOCK *v.*
■ *verb*
PHR V ˌhorn ˈin (on sb / sth) (*NAmE, informal*) to involve yourself in a situation that does not really involve you: *I'm sure she doesn't want us horning in on her business.*

**horn·beam** /ˈhɔːnbiːm/ *NAmE* ˈhɔːrn-/ *noun* [C, U] a tree with smooth grey BARK and hard wood

**horn·bill** /ˈhɔːnbɪl/ *NAmE* ˈhɔːrn-/ *noun* a tropical bird with a very large curved BEAK

**horned** /hɔːnd/ *NAmE* hɔːrnd/ *adj.* having HORNS or having sth that looks like HORNS

**hor·net** /ˈhɔːnɪt/ *NAmE* ˈhɔːrn-/ *noun* a large WASP (= a black and yellow flying insect) that has a very powerful STING
IDM **a ˈhornets' nest** a difficult situation in which a lot of people get very angry: *His letter to the papers stirred up a real hornets' nest.*

**horn·pipe** /ˈhɔːnpaɪp/ *NAmE* ˈhɔːrn-/ *noun* a fast dance for one person, traditionally performed by sailors; the music for the dance

ˈhorn-rimmed *adj.* (of a pair of glasses) with frames made of material that looks like HORN

**horny** /ˈhɔːni/ *NAmE* ˈhɔːrni/ *adj.* (**horn·ier, horni·est**) **1** (*informal*) sexually excited: *to feel horny* **2** (*informal*) sexually attractive: *to look horny* **3** made of a hard substance like HORN: *the bird's horny beak* **4** (of skin, etc.) hard and rough: *horny hands*

**horo·scope** /ˈhɒrəskəʊp/ *NAmE* ˈhɔːr-/ *noun* a prediction of what is going to happen to sb in the future, based on the position of the stars and the planets when the person was born

**hor·ren·dous** /həˈrendəs/ *adj.* **1** terrible or extremely unpleasant SYN **horrific, horrifying**: *horrendous injuries* **2** (*informal*) extremely unpleasant and unacceptable SYN **terrible**: *horrendous traffic* HELP Some speakers do not pronounce the 'h' at the beginning of **horrendous** and use 'an' instead of 'a' before it. This now sounds old-fashioned. ⊃ SYNONYMS at TERRIBLE ▶ **hor·ren·dous·ly** *adv.*: *horrendously expensive*

**hor·rible** ❶ B1 /ˈhɒrəbl/ *NAmE* ˈhɔːr-/ *adj.* **1** ❶ B1 (*informal*) very bad or unpleasant; used to describe sth that you do not like: *What horrible weather!* ◊ *The coffee tasted absolutely horrible.* ◊ **it is ~ to do sth** *It was horrible to have to leave my family behind.* ⊃ SYNONYMS at TERRIBLE **2** ?+ B1 making you feel very shocked and frightened SYN **terrible**: *a pretty horrible experience* **3** ? B1 (*informal*) (of people or their behaviour) unfriendly, unpleasant or unkind SYN **nasty, obnoxious**: *What a horrible person* ◊ *What a horrible thing to say!* ◊ **~ to sb** *My sister was being horrible to me all day.* ▶ **hor·ribly** /-bli/ *adv.*: *It was horribly painful.* ◊ *The experiment went horribly wrong.*

**hor·rid** /ˈhɒrɪd/ *NAmE* ˈhɔːr-/ *adj.* (*old-fashioned or informal, especially BrE*) very unpleasant or unkind SYN **horrible**: *a horrid child* ◊ *a horrid smell* ◊ *Don't be so horrid to your brother.*

**hor·rif·ic** /həˈrɪfɪk/ *adj.* **1** extremely bad and making you feel shocked or frightened SYN **horrifying**: *a horrific murder/accident/attack, etc.* ◊ *Her injuries were horrific.* **2** (*informal*) very bad or unpleasant SYN **horrendous**: *We had a horrific trip.* HELP Some speakers do not pronounce the 'h' at the beginning of **horrific** and use 'an' instead of 'a' before it. This now sounds old-fashioned. ▶ **hor·rif·ic·al·ly** /-kli/ *adv.*

**hor·rify** /ˈhɒrɪfaɪ/ *NAmE* ˈhɔːr-/ *verb* (**hor·ri·fies, hor·ri·fy·ing, hor·ri·fied, hor·ri·fied**) to make sb feel extremely shocked or frightened SYN **appal**: **~ sb** *The whole country was horrified by the killings.* ◊ **it horrifies sb to do sth** *It horrified her to think that he had killed someone.* ◊ **it horrifies sb that …** *It horrified her that he had actually killed someone.* ▶ **hor·ri·fied** *adj.*: *He was horrified when he discovered the conditions in which they lived.* ◊ *She gazed at him in horrified disbelief.*

**hor·ri·fy·ing** /ˈhɒrɪfaɪɪŋ/ *NAmE* ˈhɔːr-/ *adj.* making you feel extremely shocked or frightened SYN **horrific**: *a horrifying sight/experience/story* ◊ *It's horrifying to see such poverty.* ▶ **hor·ri·fy·ing·ly** *adv.*

**hor·ror** ❶ B1 /ˈhɒrə(r)/ *NAmE* ˈhɔːr-/ *noun* **1** ? B1 [U] a feeling of great shock or fear: *The thought of being left alone filled her with horror.* ◊ **in ~** *People watched in horror*

# horror story

as the plane crashed to the ground. ◊ **with~** *She realized with horror that somebody had broken into her house.* ◊ **to sb's~** *To his horror, he realized that he couldn't escape* (= it upset him very much). ◊ **~at (doing) sth** *He expressed his horror at the idea that he was in some way to blame.* ◊ *She recoiled in horror at the sight of an enormous spider.* **2** [C, usually pl.] a very unpleasant or frightening experience: *an account of the horrors inflicted on the detainees* ◊ **the horrors of sth** *the horrors of war* **3** [U] **the ~ of sth** the very unpleasant nature of sth, especially when it shocks or frightens you: *The full horror of the accident was beginning to become clear.* ◊ *In his dreams he relives the horror of the attack.* **4** [sing.] a strong feeling of fear or of hating sth: **~ of sth** *a horror of deep water* ◊ **~of doing sth** *Most people have a horror of speaking in public.* **5** [U] a type of book, film, etc. that is designed to frighten people: *In this section you'll find horror and science fiction.* ◊ *fans of classic horror* ◊ *a horror film/movie/story* ➔ see also HORROR STORY **6** [C] (*BrE, informal*) a child who behaves badly: *Her son is a little horror.*
**IDM** **horror of 'horrors** (*also* **horrors!**) (*humorous or ironic*) used to emphasize how bad a situation is: *I stood up to speak and—horror of horrors—realized I had left my notes behind.* ➔ more at SHOCK *n.*

**'horror story** *noun* **1** a story about strange and frightening things that is designed to entertain people **2** (*informal*) a report that describes an experience of a situation as very unpleasant: *horror stories about visits to the dentist*

**'horror-struck** (*also* **'horror-stricken**) *adj.* suddenly feeling very shocked or frightened

**hors d'oeuvre** /ˌɔː ˈdɜːv/; *NAmE* ˌɔːr ˈdɜːrv/ *noun* [C, U] (*pl.* **hors d'oeuvres** /ˌɔː ˈdɜːv/; *NAmE* ˌɔːr ˈdɜːrv/) (*from French*) a small amount of food, usually cold, served before the main part of a meal ➔ compare STARTER

**horse** 🔑 **A1** /hɔːs; *NAmE* hɔːrs/ *noun, verb*
■ *noun* **1** **A1** a large animal with four legs, a MANE (= long thick hair on its neck) and a tail. Horses are used for riding on, pulling CARRIAGES, etc: *to ride a horse* ◊ *a ~ a rider on a white horse* ➔ see also COLT, FILLY, FOAL *n.*, GELDING, MARE, QUARTER HORSE, SHIRE HORSE, STALLION

**WORDFINDER** bridle, gallop, harness, paddock, rein, stable, stirrup, tack, thoroughbred

**2 the horses** [pl.] (*informal*) horse racing: *He lost a lot of money on the horses* (= by gambling on races). **3** a large object with legs, and sometimes handles, used in GYMNASTICS ➔ see also POMMEL HORSE, VAULTING HORSE ➔ see *also* CLOTHES HORSE, HOBBY HORSE, ROCKING HORSE, SEAHORSE, STALKING HORSE, TROJAN HORSE, WHITE HORSES
**IDM** **(straight) from the horse's 'mouth** (*informal*) (of information) given by sb who is directly involved and therefore likely to be accurate **hold your 'horses** (*informal*) used to tell sb that they should wait a moment and not be so excited that they take action without thinking about it first **horses for 'courses** (*BrE*) the act of matching people with suitable jobs or tasks **ORIGIN** This expression refers to the fact that horses race better on a track that suits them. **a one, two, three, etc. horse 'race** a competition or an election in which there are only one, two, etc. teams or candidates with a chance of winning **you can lead/take a horse to 'water, but you can't make it 'drink** (*saying*) you can give sb the opportunity to do sth, but you cannot force them to do it if they do not want to ➔ more at BACK *v.*, CART *n.*, CHANGE *v.*, DARK *adj.*, DEAD *adj.*, DRIVE *v.*, EAT, GIFT *n.*, HIGH *adj.*, STABLE *n.*, WILD *adj.*, WISH *n.*
■ *verb*
**PHRV** **horse a'round** (*BrE also* **horse a'bout**) (*informal*) to play in a way that is noisy and not very careful so that you could hurt sb or damage sth **SYN** fool

**horse-back** /ˈhɔːsbæk; *NAmE* ˈhɔːrs-/ *noun, adj.*
■ *noun*
**IDM** **on 'horseback** sitting on a horse; using horses: *a soldier on horseback*
■ *adj.* [only before noun] sitting on a horse: *a horseback tour* ► **horse-back** *adv.*: *to ride horseback*

**'horseback riding** *noun* [U] (*NAmE*) = RIDING

**horse-box** /ˈhɔːsbɒks; *NAmE* ˈhɔːrsbɑːks/ *noun* (*BrE*) a vehicle for transporting horses in, sometimes pulled behind another vehicle ➔ see also HORSE TRAILER

**horse 'chestnut** *noun* **1** a large tall tree with spreading branches, white or pink flowers and nuts that grow inside cases that are covered with short SPIKES ➔ VISUAL VOCAB page V6 ➔ see also CHESTNUT *noun* **2** the smooth brown nut of the horse chestnut tree **SYN** conker

**'horse-drawn** *adj.* [only before noun] (of a vehicle) pulled by a horse or horses

**'horse-flesh** /ˈhɔːsfleʃ; *NAmE* ˈhɔːrsfleʃ/ *noun* [U] **1** horses, especially when being bought or sold **2** the FLESH of a horse, especially when used as food

**'horse-fly** /ˈhɔːsflaɪ; *NAmE* ˈhɔːrsflaɪ/ *noun* (*pl.* **-ies**) a large fly that bites horses, cows and humans

**'horse-hair** /ˈhɔːsheə(r); *NAmE* ˈhɔːrsher/ *noun* [U] hair from the MANE or tail of a horse, used, in the past, for filling MATTRESSES, chairs, etc.

**'horse-man** /ˈhɔːsmən; *NAmE* ˈhɔːrs-/ *noun* (*pl.* **-men** /-mən/) a rider on a horse; a person who can ride horses well: *a good horseman* ➔ see also HORSEWOMAN

**'horse-man-ship** /ˈhɔːsmənʃɪp; *NAmE* ˈhɔːrs-/ *noun* [U] skill in riding horses

**'horse-play** /ˈhɔːspleɪ; *NAmE* ˈhɔːrs-/ *noun* [U] rough noisy play in which people push or hit each other for fun

**'horse-power** /ˈhɔːspaʊə(r); *NAmE* ˈhɔːrs-/ *noun* [C, U] (*pl.* horsepower) (*abbr.* **h.p.**) a unit for measuring the power of an engine: *a powerful car with a 170 horsepower engine*

**'horse race** *noun* a race between horses with riders

**'horse racing** (*also* **racing**) *noun* [U] a sport in which horses with riders race against each other

**horse-rad-ish** /ˈhɔːsrædɪʃ; *NAmE* ˈhɔːrs-/ *noun* [U] **1** a hard white root vegetable that has a taste like pepper **2** (*also* **horseradish 'sauce**) a sauce made from horseradish, that is eaten with meat: *roast beef and horseradish*

**'horse riding** *noun* [U] (*BrE*) = RIDING

**horse-shoe** /ˈhɔːsʃuː, ˈhɔːʃuː; *NAmE* ˈhɔːrsʃuː, ˈhɔːrʃuː/ *noun* **1** (*also* **shoe**) a piece of curved iron that is attached with nails to the bottom of a horse's foot. A horseshoe is often used as a symbol of good luck. **2** anything that is like a horseshoe in shape: *a horseshoe bend in the river*

**'horse-trading** *noun* [U] **1** the activity of buying and selling horses **2** the activity of discussing business with sb using clever or secret methods in order to reach an agreement that suits you

**'horse trailer** *noun* (*NAmE*) a vehicle for transporting horses in, pulled by another vehicle ➔ see also HORSEBOX

**horse-whip** /ˈhɔːswɪp; *NAmE* ˈhɔːrs-/ *noun, verb*
■ *noun* a long stick with a long piece of leather attached to the end that is used to control or train horses
■ *verb* (**-pp-**) **~ sb** to beat sb with a horsewhip

**horse-woman** /ˈhɔːswʊmən; *NAmE* ˈhɔːrs-/ *noun* (*pl.* **-women** /-wɪmɪn/) a woman rider on a horse; a woman who can ride horses well: *a good horsewoman*

**horsey** (*also* **horsy**) /ˈhɔːsi; *NAmE* ˈhɔːrsi/ *adj.* **1** interested in and involved with horses or horse racing **2** connected with horses; like a horse: *She had a long, horsey face.*

**horti-cul-ture** /ˈhɔːtɪkʌltʃə(r); *NAmE* ˈhɔːrt-/ *noun* [U] the study or practice of growing flowers, fruit and vegetables: *a college of agriculture and horticulture* ➔ compare GARDENING ► **horti-cul-tural** /ˌhɔːtɪˈkʌltʃərəl/; *NAmE* ˌhɔːrt-/ *adj.*: *a horticultural show* **horti-cul-tur-al-ist** *noun* **horti-cul-tur-ist** /-rɪst/ *noun*

**hos-anna** (*also* **hos-annah**) /həʊˈzænə/ *exclamation* used in WORSHIP to express praise, joy and love for God, especially in the Christian and Jewish religions ► **hos-anna** *noun*

**hose** /həʊz/ *noun, verb*
■ *noun* **1** (*also* **hose-pipe** /ˈhəʊzpaɪp/) [C, U] a long tube made of rubber, plastic, etc., used for putting water onto fires,

gardens, etc: *a garden hose* ◊ *a length of hose* ⮕ see also FIRE HOSE, PRESSURE HOSE **2** [pl.] = HOSIERY **3** [pl.] trousers that fit tightly over the legs, worn by men in the past: *doublet and hose*

■ **verb** to wash or pour water on sth using a hose: ~ **sth/sb** *Firemen hosed the burning car.*

**ho·siery** /ˈhəʊziəri; NAmE ˈhəʊʒə-/ noun [U] (*also* **hose** [pl.]) used especially in shops as a word for TIGHTS, STOCKINGS and socks: *the hosiery department*

**hos·pice** /ˈhɒspɪs; NAmE ˈhɑːs-/ noun a hospital for people who are dying: *an AIDS hospice*

**hos·pit·able** /hɒˈspɪtəbl, ˈhɒspɪtəbl; NAmE ˈhɑːspɪtəbl, hɑːˈspɪtəbl/ adj. **1** ~ **(to/towards sb)** (of a person) pleased to welcome guests; generous and friendly to visitors SYN **welcoming**: *The local people are very hospitable to strangers.* **2** having good conditions that allow things to grow; having a pleasant environment: *a hospitable climate* OPP **inhospitable** ▶ **hos·pit·ably** /-bli/ adv.

**hos·pital** ⓘ A1 /ˈhɒspɪtl; NAmE ˈhɑːs-/ noun a large building where people who are ill or injured are given medical treatment and care: **to/into (the)** ~ (BrE) *He had to go to/into hospital for treatment.* ◊ (NAmE) *He had to go to/into the hospital for treatment.* ◊ *to be admitted to/into (the) hospital* ◊ *to be taken/rushed to (the) hospital* ◊ *to leave (the) hospital* ◊ *in (the)* ~ *He died in hospital.* ◊ *in a* ~ *She works in a hospital in New York.* ◊ *out of (the)* ~ *She came out of the hospital this morning.* ◊ *at a* ~ *Doctors at the hospital decided to keep her in overnight.* ◊ *a private/local hospital* ◊ *The procedure requires a two-to-three-night hospital stay.* ⮕ see also COTTAGE HOSPITAL ⮕ WORDFINDER NOTE at ACCIDENT

WORDFINDER A & E, admit, consultant, doctor, ICU, inpatient, nurse, operation, ward

▼ BRITISH/AMERICAN
**hospital**
• In *BrE* you say **to hospital** or **in hospital** when you talk about somebody being there as a patient: *I had to go to hospital.* ◊ *She spent two weeks in hospital.*
• In *NAmE* you need to use **the**: *I had to go to the hospital.* ◊ *She spent two weeks in the hospital.*

**hos·pi·tal·ity** /ˌhɒspɪˈtæləti; NAmE ˌhɑːs-/ noun [U] **1** friendly and generous behaviour towards guests: *Thank you for your kind hospitality.* **2** food, drink or services that are provided by an organization for guests, customers, etc: *We were entertained in the company's hospitality suite.* ◊ *the hospitality industry* (= hotels, restaurants, etc.)

**hos·pi·tal·ize** (*BrE also* **-ise**) /ˈhɒspɪtəlaɪz; NAmE ˈhɑːs-/ verb [usually passive] ~ **sb** to send sb to a hospital for treatment ▶ **hos·pi·tal·iza·tion, -isa·tion** /ˌhɒspɪtəlaɪˈzeɪʃn; NAmE ˌhɑːspɪtələˈz-/ noun [U]: *a long period of hospitalization*

**host** ⓘ B1 /həʊst/ noun, verb
■ **noun 1** ⓘ B1 [C] a person who invites guests to a meal, a party, etc. or who has people staying at their house: *Ian, our host, introduced us to the other guests.* ⮕ see also HOSTESS **2** ⓘ B1 [C] a country, a city or an organization that holds and arranges a special event: *the host nation/country/city* ◊ ~ **to sb/sth** *The college is playing host to a group of visiting Russian scientists.* **3** ⓘ B1 [C] a person who introduces a television or radio show, and talks to guests SYN **compère**: *a radio/TV host* ⮕ see also ANNOUNCER, PRESENTER **4** [C] (*specialist*) an animal or a plant on which another animal or plant lives and feeds **5** [C] ~ **of sb/sth** a large number of people or things: *a host of possibilities* **6** (*also* **host computer**) [C] (*computing*) the main computer in a network that controls or supplies information to other computers that are connected to it: *transferring files from the host to your local computer* **7** **the Host** [sing.] the bread that is used in the Christian service of COMMUNION, after it has been BLESSED

IDM **be/play ˈhost to sth** to be a place where a particular plant, animal or feature is found: *Australia is host to some of the world's most dangerous animals.*

■ **verb 1** ⓘ B2 [T] ~ **sth** to organize an event to which others are invited and make all the arrangements for them: *to host an event/a conference/a meeting* **2** ⓘ B2 [T] ~ **sth** to introduce a television or radio programme, a show, etc: *Charlie Rose will host tonight's show.* SYN **compère 3** [T, I] ~ **(sth)** to organize a party that you have invited guests to: *to host a dinner* ◊ *Whose turn is it to host?* **4** [T] ~ **sth** (*computing*) to store a website on a computer connected to the internet, usually in return for payment: *a company that builds and hosts e-commerce sites*

**hos·tage** ⓘ+ C1 /ˈhɒstɪdʒ; NAmE ˈhɑːs-/ noun a person who is captured and held prisoner by a person or group, and who may be injured or killed if people do not do what the person or group is asking: *Three children were taken hostage during the bank robbery.* ◊ *He was held hostage for almost a year.* ◊ *The government is negotiating the release of the hostages.* ⮕ WORDFINDER NOTE at ATTACK

IDM **a ˌhostage to ˈfortune** something that you have, or have promised to do, that could cause trouble or worry in the future

**ˈhostage taker** noun a person, often one of a group, who captures sb and holds them prisoner, and who may injure or kill them if people do not do what the person or group is asking ▶ **ˈhostage-taking** noun [U]

**hos·tel** /ˈhɒstl; NAmE ˈhɑːs-/ noun **1** a building that provides cheap accommodation and sometimes meals to students, workers or travellers ⮕ see also YOUTH HOSTEL **2** (*BrE*) (*also* **shel·ter** NAmE, BrE) a building, usually run by a charity, where people who have no home can stay for a short time: *a hostel for the homeless* ⮕ WORDFINDER NOTE at POOR

**hos·tel·ry** /ˈhɒstəlri; NAmE ˈhɑːs-/ (pl. **-ies**) noun (*old use or humorous*) a pub or hotel

**host·ess** /ˈhəʊstəs; BrE also həʊˈstes/ noun **1** a woman who invites guests to a meal, a party, etc.; a woman who has people staying at her home: *Mary was always the perfect hostess.* **2** a woman who is employed to welcome and entertain men at a NIGHTCLUB **3** a woman who introduces and talks to guests on a television or radio show SYN **compère** ⮕ note at GENDER **4** (*NAmE*) a woman who welcomes the customers in a restaurant ⮕ see also AIR HOSTESS, HOST noun

**hos·tile** ⓘ+ C1 /ˈhɒstaɪl; NAmE ˈhɑːstl, ˈhɑːstaɪl/ adj. **1** ⓘ+ C1 aggressive or unfriendly and ready to argue or fight: *The speaker got a hostile reception from the audience.* ◊ ~ **to/towards sb/sth** *She was openly hostile towards her parents.* **2** ⓘ+ C1 ~ **(to sth)** strongly rejecting sth SYN **opposed**: *hostile to the idea of change* **3** making it difficult for sth to happen or to be achieved: *hostile conditions for plants to grow in* **4** belonging to a military enemy: *hostile territory* ⮕ WORDFINDER NOTE at CONFLICT **5** (*business*) (of an offer to buy a company, etc.) not wanted by the company that is to be bought: *a hostile takeover bid*

**hos·til·ity** ⓘ+ C1 /hɒˈstɪləti; NAmE hɑːˈs-/ noun **1** ⓘ+ C1 [U] aggressive or unfriendly feelings or behaviour: ~ **(to/towards sb/sth)** *feelings of hostility towards people from other backgrounds* ◊ ~ **between A and B** *There was open hostility between the two schools.* **2** ⓘ+ C1 [U] ~ **(to/towards sth)** strong and angry opposition towards an idea, a plan or a situation: *public hostility to nuclear power* **3** ⓘ+ C1 **hostilities** [pl.] (*formal*) acts of fighting in a war: *the start/outbreak of hostilities between the two sides* ◊ *a cessation of hostilities* (= an end to fighting)

**hot** ⓘ A1 /hɒt; NAmE hɑːt/ adj., verb
■ adj. (**hot·ter, hot·test**)
• TEMPERATURE **1** ⓘ A1 having a high temperature; producing heat: *It's hot today, isn't it?* ◊ *It was hot and getting hotter.* ◊ *Do you like this hot weather?* ◊ *a hot dry summer* ◊ *an unusually hot day* ◊ *Be careful—the plates are hot.* ◊ *All rooms have hot and cold water.* ◊ *a hot bath* ◊ *a hot meal* (= one that has been cooked) ◊ *When the weather gets hot, we often head to the beach.* ◊ *I couldn't live in a hot country* (=

# hot air

one which has high average temperatures. ◊ *Eat it while it's hot.* ◊ *I touched his forehead. He felt hot and feverish.* ⊃ see also BAKING *adj.*, BOILING HOT at BOILING, PIPING HOT, RED-HOT, WHITE-HOT **2** [A1] (of a person) feeling heat in an unpleasant or uncomfortable way: *Is anyone hot?* ◊ *I feel hot.* ◊ *Her cheeks were hot with embarrassment.* **3** [A1] making you feel hot: *London was hot and dusty.* ◊ *a long hot journey*
- FOOD WITH SPICES **4** [B1] containing pepper and SPICES that can produce a burning feeling in your mouth because they have a strong taste and smell: *hot spicy food* ◊ *You can make a curry hotter simply by adding chillies.* ◊ *hot mustard* OPP **mild** ⊃ WORDFINDER NOTE at TASTE
- CAUSING STRONG FEELINGS **5** involving a lot of activity, argument or strong feelings: *Today we enter the hottest phase of the election campaign.* ◊ *The environment has become a very hot issue.* ◊ *Competition is getting hotter day by day.*
- DIFFICULT/DANGEROUS **6** difficult or dangerous to deal with and making you feel worried or uncomfortable: *When things got too hot most journalists left the area.* ◊ *They're making life hot for her.*
- POPULAR **7** (*informal*) new, exciting and very popular: *This is one of the hottest clubs in town.* ◊ *They are one of this year's hot new bands.* ◊ *The couple are Hollywood's **hottest property**.*
- NEWS **8** fresh, very recent and usually exciting: *I've got some hot gossip for you!* ◊ *a story that is **hot off the press** (= has just appeared in the newspapers)*
- TIP/FAVOURITE **9** [only before noun] likely to be successful: *She seems to be the hot favourite for the job.* ◊ *Do you have any hot tips for today's race?*
- GOOD AT STH/KNOWING A LOT **10** [not before noun] ~ **at/on sth** (*informal*) very good at doing sth; knowing a lot about sth: *Don't ask me—I'm not too hot on British history.*
- ANGER **11** if sb has a **hot temper** they become angry very easily
- SEXUAL EXCITEMENT **12** feeling or causing sexual excitement: *You were as hot for me as I was for you.* ◊ *I've got a hot date tonight.*
- CAUSING SHOCK/ANGER **13** containing scenes, statements, etc. that are of an extreme nature and are likely to shock or anger people: *Some of the nude scenes were regarded as too hot for Broadway.* ◊ *The report was highly critical of senior members of the Cabinet and was considered too hot to publish.* ⊃ see also HOT STUFF
- STRICT **14** [not before noun] ~ **on sth** thinking that sth is very important and making sure that it always happens or is done: *They're very hot on punctuality at work.*
- MUSIC **15** (of music, especially jazz) having a strong and exciting rhythm
- GOODS **16** stolen and difficult to get rid of because they can easily be recognized: *I'd never have touched those phones if I'd known they were hot.*
- IN CHILDREN'S GAMES **17** [not before noun] used in children's games to say that the person playing is very close to finding a person or thing, or to guessing the correct answer: *You're getting hot!*

IDM **be ˌhot to ˈtrot** (*informal*) **1** to be very enthusiastic about starting an activity **2** to be excited in a sexual way **be in/get into hot ˈwater** (*informal*) to be in or get into trouble **go hot and ˈcold** to experience a sudden feeling of fear or worry: *When the phone rang I just went hot and cold.* **go/sell like hot ˈcakes** to be bought quickly or in great numbers **(all) hot and ˈbothered** (*informal*) in a state of worry or stress because you are under too much pressure, have a problem, are trying to hurry, etc. **hot on sb's/sth's ˈtracks/ˈtrail** (*informal*) close to catching or finding the person or thing that you have been running after or searching for **hot under the ˈcollar** (*informal*) angry or embarrassed: *He got very hot under the collar when I asked him where he'd been all day.* **in hot purˈsuit (of sb)** following sb closely and determined to catch them: *She sped away in her car with journalists in hot pursuit.* **not so/too ˈhot 1** not very good in quality: *Her spelling isn't too hot.* **2** not feeling well: *'How are you today?' 'Not so hot, I'm afraid.'* ⊃ more at BLOW *v.*, CAT, HEEL *n.*, STRIKE *v.*

■ *verb* (-tt-)
PHRV **ˌhot ˈup** (*BrE*) (*also* **ˌheat ˈup** *NAmE, BrE*) (*informal*) to become more exciting or to show an increase in activity: *Things are really hotting up in the election campaign.*

**ˌhot ˈair** *noun* [U] (*informal*) claims, promises or statements that sound impressive but have no real meaning or truth

**ˈhot-air balloon** *noun* = BALLOON

**ˈhot·bed** /ˈhɒtbed; *NAmE* ˈhɑːt-/ *noun* [usually sing.] ~ **of sth** a place where a lot of particular activity, especially sth bad or violent, is happening: *The area was a hotbed of crime.*

**ˌhot-ˈblooded** *adj.* (of a person) having strong emotions and easily becoming very excited or angry SYN **passionate** ⊃ compare WARM-BLOODED

**ˈhot button** *noun* (*NAmE, informal*) a subject or issue that people have strong feelings about and argue about a lot: *Race has always been a hot button in this country's history.* ◊ *the hot-button issue of nuclear waste disposal*

**ˌhot ˈchocolate** (*BrE also* **ˈchoc·olate**) *noun* [U, C] a drink made by mixing chocolate powder with hot water or milk; a cup of this drink: *Two coffees and a hot chocolate, please.*

**hotch·potch** /ˈhɒtʃpɒtʃ; *NAmE* ˈhɑːtʃpɑːtʃ/ (*especially BrE*) (*NAmE usually* **hodge·podge**) *noun* [sing.] (*informal*) a number of things mixed together without any particular order or reason

**ˌhot cross ˈbun** *noun* a small sweet bread roll that contains CURRANTS and has a pattern of a cross on top, traditionally eaten in the UK around Easter

**ˈhot dog** *noun* **1** a hot SAUSAGE served in a long bread roll **2** (*NAmE*) a person who performs clever or dangerous tricks while skiing, SNOWBOARDING or SURFING: *He's a real hot dog.*

**ˈhot-dog** *verb* (-gg-) [I] (*especially NAmE, informal*) to perform clever or dangerous tricks, especially while skiing, SNOWBOARDING or SURFING

**hotel** ❶ [A1] /həʊˈtel/ *noun* **1** [A1] a building where people stay, usually for a short time, paying for their rooms and meals: *a two-star/five-star, etc. hotel* ◊ *a luxury/ boutique hotel* ◊ *at/in a ~ We stayed in a friendly family-run hotel.* ◊ *hotel rooms/guests*

> WORDFINDER accommodation, book, full board, holiday, reception, reservation, room service, suite, vacancy

**2** (*AustralE, NZE*) a pub **3** (*IndE*) a restaurant HELP Some speakers do not pronounce the 'h' at the beginning of **hotel** and use 'an' instead of 'a' before it. This now sounds old-fashioned.

**ho·tel·ier** /həʊˈteliə(r), həʊˈteljer; *NAmE* ˌəʊtelˈjeɪ, həʊˈteljər/ *noun* a person who owns or manages a hotel

**hot·fix** /ˈhɒtfɪks; *NAmE* ˈhɑːt-/ *noun* (*computing*) a file that is used to correct a fault in a computer program

**ˌhot ˈflush** (*BrE*) (*NAmE* **ˌhot ˈflash**) *noun* a sudden hot and uncomfortable feeling in the skin, especially experienced by women during the MENOPAUSE

**hot·foot** /ˈhɒtfʊt; *NAmE* ˈhɑːt-/ *adv., verb*
■ *adv.* moving quickly and in a hurry: *He had just arrived hotfoot from London.*
■ *verb*
IDM **ˈhotfoot it** (*informal*) to walk or run somewhere quickly: *When the police arrived, they hotfooted it out of there.*

**hot·head** /ˈhɒthed; *NAmE* ˈhɑːt-/ *noun* a person who often acts too quickly, without thinking of what might happen ▶ **ˌhot-ˈheaded** *adj.*

**hot·house** /ˈhɒthaʊs; *NAmE* ˈhɑːt-/ *noun* **1** a heated building, usually made of glass, used for growing plants that need special conditions: *hothouse flowers* **2** a place or situation that encourages the rapid development of sb/sth, especially ideas and emotions

**ˈhot key** *noun* (*computing*) a key on a computer keyboard that you can press to perform a set of operations quickly, rather than having to press a number of different keys

**hot·line** /ˈhɒtlaɪn; NAmE ˈhɑːt-/ noun **1** a special phone line that people can use in order to get information or to talk about sth **2** a direct phone line between the heads of government in different countries

**hot·link** /ˈhɒtlɪŋk; NAmE ˈhɑːt-/ noun = LINK (4)

**hot·list** (also **hot list**) /ˈhɒtlɪst; NAmE ˈhɑːt-/ noun a list of popular, fashionable or important people or things

**hotly** /ˈhɒtli; NAmE ˈhɑːt-/ adv. **1** done in an angry or excited way or with a lot of strong feeling: *a hotly debated topic* ◊ *Recent reports in the press have been hotly denied.* ◊ *'Nonsense!' he said hotly.* ◊ *The results were hotly disputed.* **2** done with a lot of energy and DETERMINATION **SYN** **closely**: *hotly contested elections* ◊ *She ran out of the shop, hotly pursued by the store detective.*

**ˌhot ˈpants** noun [pl.] very short, tight women's SHORTS

**hot·plate** /ˈhɒtpleɪt; NAmE ˈhɑːt-/ noun a flat, heated metal surface, for example on a cooker, that is used for cooking food or for keeping it hot

**hot·pot** /ˈhɒtpɒt; NAmE ˈhɑːtpɑːt/ noun [C, U] (BrE) a hot dish of meat, potato, onion, etc. cooked slowly in liquid in the oven

**ˌhot poˈtato** noun [usually sing.] (informal) a problem, situation, etc. that is difficult and unpleasant to deal with

**ˈhot rod** noun a car that has been changed and improved to give it extra power and speed

**hots** /hɒts; NAmE hɑːts/ noun [pl.]
**IDM** **get/have the ˈhots for sb** (informal) to be sexually attracted to sb

**the ˈhot seat** noun [sing.] (informal) if sb is **in the hot seat**, they have to take responsibility for important or difficult decisions and actions

**hot·shot** /ˈhɒtʃɒt; NAmE ˈhɑːtʃɑːt/ noun (informal) a person who is extremely successful in their career or at a particular sport ▸ **hot·shot** adj. [only before noun]: *a hotshot lawyer*

**hot·spot** (also **hot spot**) /ˈhɒtspɒt; NAmE ˈhɑːtspɑːt/ noun (informal) **1** a place where fighting is common, especially for political reasons **2** a place with a particular kind of danger or problem: *They identified eight pollution hotspots at the mouth of the Thames.* **3** a place where there is a lot of activity or entertainment **4** a place that is very hot and dry, where a fire has been burning or is likely to start **5** (computing) an area on a computer screen that you can click on to start an operation such as loading a file **6** a place in a hotel, restaurant, airport, etc. that is fitted with a special device that enables you to connect a computer to the internet without using wires

**ˌhot ˈstuff** noun [U] (informal, especially BrE) **1** a person who is sexually attractive: *She's pretty hot stuff.* **2** a film, book, etc. that is exciting in a sexual way **3** ~ **(at sth)** a person who shows a lot of skill at sth: *She's really hot stuff at tennis.* **4** something that is likely to cause people to disagree or be angry: *These new proposals are proving to be hot stuff.*

**ˌhot-ˈtempered** adj. (especially BrE) tending to become very angry easily

**hot·tie** (also **hotty**) /ˈhɒti; NAmE ˈhɑːti/ noun (pl. -ies) (informal) a person who is very sexually attractive

**ˈhot tub** noun a heated bath, often outside, that several people can sit in together to relax

**ˌhot-ˈwater bottle** noun a rubber container that is filled with hot water and put in a bed to make it warm

**ˈhot-wire** verb ~ **sth** (informal) to start the engine of a vehicle by using a piece of wire instead of a key, usually in order to steal the vehicle

**Hou·dini** /huːˈdiːni/ noun a person or an animal that is very good at escaping **ORIGIN** From Harry Houdini, a famous performer in the US who escaped from ropes, chains, boxes, etc.

**hou·mous** = HUMMUS

**hound** /haʊnd/ noun, verb
■ noun a dog that can run fast and has a good sense of smell, used for hunting ⊃ see also BLOODHOUND, FOXHOUND, GREYHOUND, WOLFHOUND

■ verb ~ **sb** to keep following sb and not leave them alone, especially in order to get sth from them or ask them questions **SYN** **harass**: *They were hounded day and night by the press.*
**PHRV** **ˌhound sb ˈout (of sth)** | **ˌhound sb from sth** [usually passive] to force sb to leave a job or a place, especially by making their life difficult and unpleasant

**ˈhound dog** noun (NAmE) (especially in the southern US) a dog used in hunting

**hounds·tooth** /ˈhaʊndztuːθ/ noun [U] a type of large pattern with pointed shapes, often in black and white, used especially in cloth for jackets and suits

**hour** 🔊 **A1** /ˈaʊə(r)/ noun **HELP** Use **an**, not **a**, before **hour**. **1** 🔊 **A1** [C] (abbr. **hr**, **hr.**) 60 minutes; one of the 24 parts that a day is divided into: *I spent an hour on the phone.* ◊ *It will take about an hour to get there.* ◊ *The interview lasted half an hour.* ◊ *It was a three-hour exam.* ◊ *Most cats sleep 13–16 hours a day.* ◊ **for an**~ *I waited for a couple of hours and then I left.* ◊ **in an**~ *He'll be back in an hour.* ◊ **by the**~ *We're paid by the hour.* ◊ **per/an**~ *Top speed is 120 miles per hour.* ◊ *The rate of pay is £10.50 an hour.* ◊ **within the**~ *We hope to be there within the hour* (= in less than an hour). ◊ *Chicago is two hours away* (= it takes two hours to get there). ◊ *We're four hours ahead of New York* (= referring to the time difference). ⊃ see also HALF HOUR, KILOWATT-HOUR, MAN-HOUR **2** 🔊 **A2** [C, usually sing.] a period of about an hour, used for a particular purpose: *I spent my lunch hour shopping.* ⊃ see also HAPPY HOUR, LUNCH HOUR, RUSH HOUR **3** 🔊 **A2** **hours** [pl.] a fixed period of time during which people work, an office is open, etc: *Opening hours are from 10 to 6 each day.* ◊ *Most people in this kind of job tend to work long hours.* ◊ **during office, business, etc.** ~ *The library is open during normal working hours.* ◊ *a hospital's visiting hours* ◊ **after**~ *This is the only place to get a drink after hours* (= after the normal closing time for pubs). ◊ **out of**~ *You can contact me on this number out of hours* (= when the office is closed). ⊃ see also AFTER-HOURS, ZERO-HOURS **4** 🔊 **A2** **hours** [pl.] a long time: *It took hours getting there.* ◊ *'How long did it last?' 'Oh, hours and hours.'* ◊ **for**~ *I've been waiting for hours.* **5** [sing.] a particular point in time: *You can't turn him away at this hour of the night.* ⊃ see also WITCHING HOUR, ZERO HOUR **6** [C, usually sing.] the time when sth important happens: *This was often thought of as the country's finest hour.* ◊ *She thought her last hour had come.* ◊ *Don't desert me in my hour of need.* **7** **the hour** [sing.] the time when it is exactly 1 o'clock, 2 o'clock, etc: *The clock struck the hour.* ◊ **on the**~ *There's a bus every hour on the hour* **8** **hours** [pl.] used when giving the time according to the 24-hour clock, usually in military or other official language: *The first missile was launched at 2300 hours* (= at 11 p.m.). **HELP** This is pronounced '23 hundred hours'.
**IDM** **ˌall ˈhours** any time, especially a time that is not usual or suitable: *He's started staying out till all hours* (= until very late at night). ◊ *She thinks she can call me at all hours of the day and night.* **keep ... ˈhours** if you keep regular, strange, etc. **hours**, the times at which you do things (especially getting up or going to bed) are regular, strange, etc. **the ˌsmall/ˌearly ˈhours** (also especially ScotE **the wee ˌsmall ˈhours**, especially NAmE **the ˌwee ˈhours**) the period of time very early in the morning, soon after midnight: *We worked well into the small hours.* ◊ *The fighting began in the early hours of Saturday morning.* ⊃ more at ELEVEN, EVIL adj., KILL v., UNEARTHLY, UNGODLY

**hour·glass** /ˈaʊəɡlɑːs; NAmE -ɡlæs/ noun, adj. **HELP** Use **an**, not **a**, before **hourglass**.

■ noun a glass container holding sand that takes exactly an hour to pass through a small opening between the top and bottom sections

■ adj. [only before noun] a woman who has an **hourglass** figure, shape, etc. has large breasts and HIPS and a small WAIST

**ˈhour hand** noun the small hand on a clock or watch that points to the hour ⊃ picture at CLOCK

# hourly   772

**hour·ly** /ˈaʊəli; NAmE -ərli/ adj., adv. **HELP** Use **an**, not **a**, before **hourly**.
- adj. [only before noun] **1** done or happening every hour: *an hourly bus service* ◇ *Trains leave at hourly intervals.* ◆ see also HALF-HOURLY **2** an **hourly wage, fee, rate**, etc. is the amount that you earn every hour or pay for a service every hour: *an hourly rate of $30 an hour*
- adv. every hour: *Reapply sunscreen hourly and after swimming.* ◇ *Dressings are changed four hourly (= every four hours) to help prevent infection.* ◆ see also HALF-HOURLY

**house** ❶ **A1** *noun, verb*
- noun /haʊs/ (pl. **houses** /ˈhaʊzɪz/)
  - BUILDING **1** [C] a building for people to live in, usually for one family: *a two-bedroom house* ◇ **in the ~** *It was so hot outside we stayed in the house.* ◇ **inside/outside the ~** *A light was on inside the house.* ◇ **at sb's ~** *Let's have a party at my house.* ◇ *We need to build more houses.* ◇ *What time do you* **leave the house** *in the morning (= to go to work)?* ◇ *(BrE) We're* **moving house** *(= leaving our house and going to live in a different one).* ◇ **house prices** *(= prices of houses and flats)* ➔ WORDFINDER NOTE at HOME **2** [sing.] all the people living in a house **SYN** **household**: *Be quiet or you'll wake the whole house!* **3** [C] (in compounds) a building used for a particular purpose, for example for holding meetings in or keeping animals or goods in: *an opera house* ◇ *a henhouse* **4** **House** [sing.] *(BrE)* used in the names of office buildings: *Their offices are on the second floor of Chester House.*
  - COMPANY/INSTITUTION **5** [C] (in compounds) a company involved in a particular kind of business; an institution of a particular kind: *a fashion/banking/publishing house* ◇ *a religious house (= a CONVENT or a MONASTERY)* ➔ see also CLEARING HOUSE, IN-HOUSE
  - RESTAURANT **6** [C] (in compounds) a restaurant: *a steakhouse* ◇ *a coffee house* ◇ *a bottle of* **house wine** *(= the cheapest wine available in a particular restaurant, sometimes not listed by name)* ➔ see also FREE HOUSE, PUBLIC HOUSE, ROADHOUSE
  - PARLIAMENT **7** [C] (often **House**) a group of people who meet to discuss and make the laws of a country: *Legislation requires approval by both houses of parliament.* ➔ see also LOWER HOUSE, UPPER HOUSE **8** **the House** [sing.] the House of Commons or the House of Lords in the UK; the House of Representatives in the US
  - IN DEBATE **9 the house** [sing.] a group of people discussing sth in a formal debate: *I urge the house to vote against the motion.*
  - IN THEATRE **10** [C] the part of a theatre where the audience sits; the audience at a particular performance: *playing to a full/packed/empty house (= to a large/small audience)* ◇ *The spotlight faded and the house lights came up.* ➔ see also FRONT OF HOUSE, FULL HOUSE
  - IN SCHOOL **11** [C] (in some British schools) an organized group of students of different ages who compete against other groups in sports competitions, etc. and who may, in BOARDING SCHOOLS, live together in one building
  - FAMILY **12** [C] *(usually* **the House of …**) an old and famous family: *the House of Windsor (= the British royal family)*
  - MUSIC **13** [U] = HOUSE MUSIC ➔ see also ACID HOUSE, ART HOUSE, OPEN HOUSE, POWERHOUSE **HELP** There are many other compounds ending in **house**. You will find them at their place in the alphabet.
- **IDM** **bring the ˈhouse down** to make everyone laugh or CHEER, especially at a performance in the theatre **get on like a ˈhouse on fire** *(BrE)* (NAmE **get along like a ˈhouse on fire**) *(informal)* (of people) to become friends quickly and have a very friendly relationship **go all round the ˈhouses** *(BrE, informal)* to do sth or ask a question in a very complicated way instead of in a simple, direct way **keep ˈhouse** to cook, clean and do all the other jobs around the house **on the ˈhouse** drinks or meals that are **on the house** are provided free by the pub or restaurant and you do not have to pay **play ˈhouse** (of a child) to play at being a family in its home **put/set your (own) ˈhouse in order** to organize your own business or improve your own behaviour before you try to criticize sb else **set up**

**ˈhouse** to make a place your home: *They set up house together in a small flat in Brighton.* ➔ more at CLEAN v., DRY adj., EAT, PEOPLE n., SAFE adj.
- verb /haʊz/
  - PROVIDE HOME **1** ? **B2** ~ sb to provide a place for a person or an animal to live: *The government is committed to housing the refugees.*
  - KEEP STH **2** ? **B2** ~ sth to be the place where sth is kept or where sth operates from: *The library* **houses** *a collection of 15000 books.* ◇ *The building also* **houses** *the offices of the District Medical Officer.*

**ˈhouse arˈrest** *(NAmE also* **home conˈfinement**) *noun* [U] the state of being a prisoner in your own house rather than in a prison: **under ~** *She was* **placed under house arrest**.

**ˈhouse·boat** /ˈhaʊsbəʊt/ *noun* a boat that people can live in, usually kept at a particular place on a river or CANAL

**ˈhouse·bound** /ˈhaʊsbaʊnd/ *adj.* **1** unable to leave your house because you cannot walk very far as a result of being ill or old **2 the housebound** *noun* [pl.] people who are housebound

**ˈhouse·break·ing** /ˈhaʊsbreɪkɪŋ/ *noun* [U] *(especially BrE)* the crime of entering a house illegally by using force, in order to steal things from it **SYN** **burglary** ▶ **ˈhouse-breaker** *noun*

**ˈhouse-broken** *(NAmE) (BrE* **ˈhouse-trained**) *adj.* (of pet cats or dogs) trained to DEFECATE and URINATE outside the house or in a special box

**ˈhouse·coat** /ˈhaʊskəʊt/ *noun* a long loose piece of clothing, worn in the house by women

**ˈhouse dust mite** *noun* = DUST MITE

**ˈhouse·fly** /ˈhaʊsflaɪ/ *noun (pl.* **-ies**) a common fly that lives in houses

**house·ful** /ˈhaʊsfʊl/ *noun* [sing.] a large number of people in a house: *He grew up in a houseful of women.* ◇ *They had a houseful so we didn't stay.*

**ˈhouse guest** *noun* a person who is staying with you in your house for a short time

**house·hold** ❶ **B2** /ˈhaʊshəʊld/ *noun* all the people living together in a house or flat: *Most households now own at least one car.* ◇ *young people from low-income households* ◇ *families with a male/female* **head of household** ◇ **Household incomes** *have remained stagnant.* ◇ *Who does most of the* **household chores**? ◇ *Packaging makes up about a third of* **household waste**.

**house·hold·er** /ˈhaʊshəʊldə(r)/ *noun (formal)* a person who owns or rents the house that they live in

**ˌhousehold ˈname** *(also less frequent* **ˌhousehold ˈword**) *noun* a person, thing or name that has become very well known: *She became a household name in the 1960s.*

**ˈhouse-hunting** *noun* [U] the activity of looking for a house to buy ▶ **ˈhouse-hunter** *noun*

**ˈhouse husband** *noun* a man who stays at home to cook, clean, take care of the children, etc. while his wife or partner goes out to work ➔ compare HOUSEWIFE

**house·keep·er** /ˈhaʊskiːpə(r)/ *noun* **1** a person, usually a woman, whose job is to manage the shopping, cooking, cleaning, etc. in a house or an institution **2** a person whose job is to manage the cleaning of rooms in a hotel

**house·keep·ing** /ˈhaʊskiːpɪŋ/ *noun* [U] **1** the work involved in taking care of a house, especially shopping and managing money **2** the department in a hotel, a hospital, an office building, etc. that is responsible for cleaning the rooms, etc: *Call housekeeping and ask them to bring us some clean towels.* **3** *(also* **ˈhousekeeping money** *especially in BrE)* the money used to buy food, cleaning materials and other things needed for taking care of a house **4** jobs that are done to enable an organization or computer system to work well: *Most large companies now use computers for accounting and housekeeping operations.*

**house-maid** /ˈhaʊsmeɪd/ noun (old-fashioned) a female servant in a large house who cleans the rooms, etc. and often lives there

**house-mas-ter** /ˈhaʊsmɑːstə(r); NAmE -mæs-/, **house-mis-tress** /ˈhaʊsmɪstrəs/ noun (especially BrE) a teacher in charge of a group of children (called a HOUSE) in a school, especially a private school

**house-mate** /ˈhaʊsmeɪt/ noun a person that you share a house with, but who is not one of your family

**ˈhouse music** (also **house**) noun [U] a type of electronic dance music with a fast beat

**ˌhouse of ˈcards** noun [sing.] **1** a plan, an organization, etc. that is so badly arranged that it could easily fail **2** a structure built out of PLAYING CARDS

**the ˌHouse of ˈCommons** (also the **ˌCom·mons**) noun **1** [sing. + sing./pl. v.] (in the UK and Canada) the part of Parliament whose members are elected by the people of the country **2** [sing.] the building where the members of the House of Commons meet ⊃ compare HOUSE OF LORDS

**ˈhouse officer** noun (in the UK) a doctor who has finished medical school and who is working at a hospital to get further practical experience ⊃ compare INTERN

**ˌhouse of ˈGod** noun [sing.] (literary) a church or other religious building

**the ˌHouse of ˈLords** (also the **ˌLords**) noun **1** [sing. + sing./pl. v.] (in the UK) the part of Parliament whose members are not elected by the people of the country **2** [sing.] the building where members of the House of Lords meet ⊃ compare HOUSE OF COMMONS

**the ˌHouse of Repreˈsentatives** noun [sing. + sing./pl. v.] the larger part of Congress in the US, or of the Parliament in Australia, whose members are elected by the people of the country ⊃ compare SENATE (1) ⊃ WORDFINDER NOTE at CONGRESS

**ˈhouse party** noun a party held at which the guests stay at a house for a few days; the guests at this party

**house-plant** /ˈhaʊsplɑːnt; NAmE -plænt/ (BrE also **ˈpot plant**) noun a plant that you grow in a pot and keep indoors

**ˈhouse-proud** adj. spending a lot of time making your house look clean and attractive, and thinking that this is important

**house-room** /ˈhaʊsruːm, -rʊm/ noun [U] space in a house for sb/sth
IDM **not give sth ˈhouseroom** (BrE) to not like sth and not want it in your house

**ˈhouse-sit** verb (**house-sitting**, **house-sat**, **house-sat**) [I] to live in sb's house while they are away in order to take care of it for them

**the ˌHouses of ˈParliament** noun [pl.] (in the UK) the Parliament that consists of both the HOUSE OF COMMONS and the HOUSE OF LORDS; the buildings in London where the British Parliament meets

**ˈhouse style** noun [U, C] the way a company such as a PUBLISHER prefers its written materials to be expressed and arranged

**ˌhouse-to-ˈhouse** adj. [only before noun] visiting every house in a particular area: *a house-to-house collection/search* ◊ *The police are making house-to-house enquiries.*

**ˈhouse-trained** (BrE) (NAmE **ˈhouse-broken**) adj. (of pet cats or dogs) trained to DEFECATE and URINATE outside the house or in a special box

**house-wares** /ˈhaʊsweəz; NAmE -werz/ noun [pl.] (NAmE) (in shops/stores) small items used in the house, especially kitchen equipment

**ˈhouse-warming** (also **ˈhouse-warming party**) noun a party given by sb who has just moved into a new home

**house-wife** /ˈhaʊswaɪf/ noun (pl. **-wives** /-waɪvz/) a woman who stays at home to cook, clean, take care of the children, etc. while her husband or partner goes out to work ⊃ compare HOUSE HUSBAND

**house-work** /ˈhaʊswɜːk; NAmE -wɜːrk/ noun [U] the work involved in taking care of a home and family, for example cleaning and cooking: *to do the housework*

**hous-ing** ❶ B2 /ˈhaʊzɪŋ/ noun **1** B2 [U] houses, flats, etc. that people live in, especially when referring to their type, price or condition: *rental/student housing* ◊ *There is an urgent need to build more affordable housing.* ◊ *We must find a way to solve the city's housing crisis.* ◊ *the housing shortage* ◊ *the housing market* (= the activity of buying and selling houses, etc.) ⊃ see also AFFORDABLE HOUSING, PUBLIC HOUSING, SOCIAL HOUSING **2** B2 [U] the job of providing houses, flats, etc. for people to live in: *the housing department* ◊ *the council's housing policy* **3** [C] a hard cover that protects part of a machine: *a car's rear axle housing*

**ˈhousing association** noun (in the UK) an organization that owns houses, flats, etc. and helps people to rent or buy them at a low price

**ˈhousing benefit** noun [U, C] (in the UK) money given by the government to people who do not earn much, to help them pay for a place to live in

**ˈhousing estate** (BrE) (also **ˈhousing development** NAmE, BrE) noun an area in which a large number of houses or flats are planned and built together at the same time: *They live on a housing estate.*

**ˈhousing project** (also **proˈject**) noun (NAmE) a group of houses or apartments built for poor families, usually with government money ⊃ compare HOUSING SCHEME (2)

**ˈhousing scheme** noun (BrE) **1** a project, often funded by a local council or another organization, that provides homes for people to buy or rent at a low price: *The council has proposed plans for an affordable housing scheme.* **2** (ScotE, informal **scheme**) an area of SOCIAL HOUSING (= houses or flats for people to rent or buy at low prices): *Over 200 new properties have been built in the housing scheme.* ⊃ compare HOUSING PROJECT

**hove** /həʊv/ past tense, past part. of HEAVE

**hovel** /ˈhɒvl; NAmE ˈhʌvl/ noun (disapproving) a house or room that is not fit to live in because it is dirty or in very bad condition

**hover** /ˈhɒvə(r); NAmE ˈhʌv-/ verb **1** [I] (+ adv./prep.) (of birds, helicopters, etc.) to stay in the air in one place: *A hawk hovered over the hill.* **2** [I] (+ adv./prep.) (of a person) to wait somewhere, especially near sb, in a shy or uncertain manner: *He hovered nervously in the doorway.* **3** [I] + adv./prep. to stay close to sth, or to stay in an uncertain state: *Temperatures hovered around freezing.* ◊ *He hovered on the edge of consciousness.* ◊ *A smile hovered on her lips.*

**hover-board** /ˈhɒvəbɔːd; NAmE ˈhʌvərbɔːrd/ noun **1** (in SCIENCE FICTION stories) a short narrow board that travels above the surface of the ground, that you ride on in a standing position **2** (in real life) a type of electric SKATEBOARD

**hov·er·craft** /ˈhɒvəkrɑːft; NAmE ˈhʌvərkræft/ noun a vehicle that travels just above the surface of water or land, held up by air being forced downwards ⊃ compare HYDROFOIL

**HOV lane** /ˌeɪtʃ əʊ ˈviː leɪn/ noun (especially NAmE) high-occupancy vehicle lane (a part of the road that may only be used by vehicles that are carrying two or more people)

**how** ❶ A1 /haʊ/ adv. **1** A1 in what way or manner: *How does it work?* ◊ *He did not know how he ought to behave.* ◊ *I'll show you how to load the printer.* ◊ *'Her behaviour was very odd.' 'How so?'* ◊ *It's funny how* (= that) *people always remember him.* ◊ *Do you remember how* (= that) *the kids always loved going there?* ◊ *How ever did you get here so quickly?* ⊃ compare HOWEVER **2** A1 used to ask about sb's health or how well things are going for them: *How are you?* ◊ *How are you feeling now?* ◊ (informal) *Hey, how are you doing?* **3** A1 used to ask whether sth is successful or fun: *How was your trip?* ◊ *How did they play?* **4** A1 used before an adjective or adverb to ask about the amount, degree, etc. of sth, or about sb's age: *How often do you go swimming?* ◊ *I didn't know how much to bring.* ◊ *How much are those earrings* (= What do they cost?)*.* ◊ *How many people were there?* ◊ *How old is she?* **5** A1 used to express surprise, pleasure, etc: *How kind of you to help!* ◊ *How he wished he had been there!* **6** B1 in any

# howdy 774

way in which SYN **however**: *I'll dress how I like in my own house!*
IDM **how about …?** 1 used when asking for information about sb/sth: *I'm not going. How about you?* 2 used to make a suggestion: *How about a break?* ◇ *How about going for a meal?* ◇ (*especially NAmE*) *How about we go for a meal?* **how 'can/could you!** (*informal*) used to show that you think sb's behaviour is very bad or are very surprised by it: *Ben! How could you? After all they've done for us!* ◇ *Ugh! How can you eat that stuff?* **how do you 'do** (*old-fashioned*) used as a formal GREETING when you meet sb for the first time. The usual reply is also *How do you do?* **how's 'that?** (*informal*) 1 used to ask the reason for sth: *'I left work early today.' 'How's that (= Why)?'* 2 used when asking sb's opinion of sth: *I'll tuck your sheets in for you. How's that? Comfortable?* ◇ *Two o'clock on the dot! How's that for punctuality!* ⊃ more at COME v.

**howdy** /ˈhaʊdi/ *exclamation* (*NAmE*, *informal*, *often humorous*) used to say hello: *Howdy, partner.*

**how·ever** 🔑 🔊 /haʊˈevə(r)/ *adv.* 1 🔑 A1 used to introduce a statement that contrasts with sth that has just been said: *He was feeling bad. He went to work, however, and tried to concentrate.* ◇ *We thought the figures were correct. However, we have now discovered some errors.* 2 🔑 B2 used with an adjective or adverb to mean 'to whatever degree': *He wanted to take no risks, however small.* ◇ *She has the window open, however cold it is outside.* ◇ *However carefully I explained, she still didn't understand.* HELP When **ever** is used to emphasize **how**, meaning 'in what way or manner?', it is usually written as a separate word: *How ever did you get here so quickly?* 3 🔑 B2 in whatever way: *However you look at it, it's going to cost a lot.*

▼ **LANGUAGE BANK**

**however**
Ways of saying 'but'
- Politicians have promised to improve road safety. **So far, however,** little has been achieved.
- **Despite** clear evidence from road safety studies, no new measures have been introduced.
- Politicians have promised to improve road safety. **In spite of this/Despite this,** little has been achieved so far.
- **Although** politicians have promised to improve road safety, little has been achieved so far.
- Some politicians claim that the new transport policy has been a success. **In fact**, it has been a total disaster.
- Government campaigns have had a measure of success, **but the fact remains that** large numbers of accidents are still caused by careless drivers.

⊃ LANGUAGE BANK at NEVERTHELESS

**how·itz·er** /ˈhaʊtsə(r)/ *noun* a heavy gun that fires SHELLS high into the air for a short distance

**howl** /haʊl/ *verb, noun*
■ *verb* 1 [I] (of a dog, WOLF, etc.) to make a long, loud call 2 [I] ~ (in/with sth) to make a loud noise when you are angry, in pain, etc. or you find sth funny: *to howl in pain* ◇ *We howled with laughter.* ◇ *The baby was howling* (= crying loudly) *all the time I was there.* 3 [I] (of the wind) to blow hard and make a long loud noise: *The wind was howling around the house.* 4 [T] ~ **sth** | **+ speech** to say sth loudly and angrily: *The crowd howled its displeasure.*
PHR V **howl sb↔'down** to prevent a speaker from being heard by shouting angrily SYN **shout sb down**
■ *noun* 1 a long loud call made by a dog, WOLF, etc. 2 a loud noise showing that you are angry, in pain, etc. or you find sth funny: *to let out a howl of anguish* ◇ *The suggestion was greeted with howls of laughter.* 3 a long loud sound made when the wind is blowing strongly: *They listened to the howl of the wind through the trees.*

**howl·er** /ˈhaʊlə(r)/ *noun* (*informal*, *especially BrE*) a stupid mistake, especially in what sb says or writes SYN **error**: *The report is full of howlers.* ⊃ SYNONYMS at MISTAKE

**howl·ing** /ˈhaʊlɪŋ/ *adj.* [only before noun] 1 (of a storm, etc.) very violent, with strong winds: *a howling gale/storm/wind* 2 (*informal*) very great or extreme: *a howling success* ◇ *She flew into a howling rage.*

**how-'to** *adj.* [only before noun] providing detailed instructions or advice on how to do sth: *how-to books on computing* ▸ **how-'to** *noun* (*pl.* **-os**): *Visit our downloads page for free how-tos and tutorials.*

**how·zit** /ˈhaʊzɪt/ *SAfrE* [ˈhaʊzət] *exclamation* (*SAfrE*, *informal*) used to say hello when you meet sb: *Howzit Mandla, how's it going?* ◇ *Please say howzit to Nicki for me.*

**h.p.** *abbr.* 1 HORSEPOWER 2 /ˌeɪtʃ ˈpiː/ (*also* **HP**) (*BrE*) HIRE PURCHASE

**HQ** /ˌeɪtʃ ˈkjuː/ *abbr.* HEADQUARTERS: *See you back at HQ.* ◇ *police HQ*

**HR** /ˌeɪtʃ ˈɑː(r)/ *abbr.* HUMAN RESOURCES

**hr** (*also* **hr.** *especially in NAmE*) *abbr.* (*pl.* **hrs** *or* **hr**) (in writing) hour: *Cover and chill for 1 hr.*

**HRH** /ˌeɪtʃ ɑːr ˈeɪtʃ/ *abbr.* His/Her ROYAL HIGHNESS: *HRH the Duke of Sussex*

**HRT** /ˌeɪtʃ ɑːr ˈtiː/; *NAmE* ɑːr/ *noun* [U] medical treatment for women going through the MENOPAUSE in which HORMONES are added to the body (the abbreviation for 'hormone replacement therapy')

**Hsiang** = XIANG

**HTH** *abbr.* (especially in messages on social media) hope this helps: *You should be able to find information about courses on the institution's website. HTH*

**HTML** /ˌeɪtʃ tiː em ˈel/ *abbr.* (*computing*) Hypertext Markup Language (a system used to mark text for World Wide Web pages in order to obtain colours, style, pictures, etc.)

**HTTP** (*also* **http**) /ˌeɪtʃ tiː tiː ˈpiː/ *abbr.* (*computing*) Hypertext Transfer Protocol (the set of rules that control the way data is sent and received over the internet)

**hub** /hʌb/ *noun* 1 a central airport, station, etc. that operates many services: *The airport has become an international hub.* ◇ *a hub airport* 2 [usually sing.] ~ **(of sth)** the central and most important part of a particular place or activity: *the commercial hub of the city* ◇ *to be at the hub of things* (= where things happen and important decisions are made) 3 the central part of a wheel

**hub·bub** /ˈhʌbʌb/ *noun* [sing., U] 1 the loud sound made by a lot of people talking at the same time: *It was difficult to hear what he was saying over the hubbub.* 2 a situation in which there is a lot of noise, excitement and activity: *the hubbub of city life*

**hubby** /ˈhʌbi/ *noun* (*pl.* **-ies**) (*informal*) a husband

**hub·cap** /ˈhʌbkæp/ *noun* a round metal cover that fits over the HUB of a vehicle's wheel

**hu·bris** /ˈhjuːbrɪs/ *noun* [U] (*literary*) the fact of being too proud. In literature, a character with this quality ignores warnings and laws and this usually results in their DOWNFALL and death.

**huckle·berry** /ˈhʌklbəri/; *NAmE* -beri/ *noun* (*pl.* **-ies**) a small soft round purple North American fruit. The bush it grows on is also called a huckleberry.

**huck·ster** /ˈhʌkstə(r)/ *noun* (*old-fashioned*, *NAmE*) 1 (*disapproving*) a person who uses aggressive or annoying methods to sell sth 2 a person who sells things in the street or by visiting people's houses

**hud·dle** /ˈhʌdl/ *verb, noun*
■ *verb* 1 [I] ~ **(up/together) (+ adv./prep.)** (of people or animals) to gather closely together, usually because of cold or fear: *We huddled together for warmth.* ◇ *They all huddled around the fire.* 2 [I] ~ **(up) (+ adv./prep.)** to hold your arms and legs close to your body, usually because you are cold or frightened: *I huddled under a blanket on the floor.* ▸ **hud·dled** *adj.*: *People were huddled together around the fire.* ◇ *huddled figures in shop doorways* ◇ *We found him huddled on the floor.*
■ *noun* 1 a small group of people, objects or buildings that are close together, especially when they are not in any particular order: *People stood around in huddles.* ◇ *The*

| b **b**ad | d **d**id | f **f**all | g **g**et | h **h**at | j **y**es | k **c**at | l **l**eg | m **m**an | n **n**ow | p **p**en | r **r**ed |

*track led them to a huddle of outbuildings.* **2** (especially in AMERICAN FOOTBALL) a time when the players gather round to hear the plan for the next part of the game
**IDM** **get/go into a ˈhuddle (with sb)** to move close to sb so that you can talk about sth without other people hearing

**hue** /hjuː/ *noun* **1** (*literary or specialist*) a colour; a particular shade of a colour: *His face took on an unhealthy whitish hue.* ◊ *Her paintings capture the subtle hues of the countryside in autumn.* ⊃ SYNONYMS at COLOUR **2** (*formal*) a type of belief or opinion: *supporters of every political hue*
**IDM** **ˌhue and ˈcry** strong public protest about sth

**huff** /hʌf/ *verb, noun*
▪ *verb* [T, I] (+ *speech*) to say sth or make a noise in a way that shows you are offended or annoyed: *'Well, nobody asked you,' she huffed irritably.*
**IDM** **ˌhuff and ˈpuff** (*informal*) **1** to breathe in a noisy way because you are very tired: *Jack was huffing and puffing to keep up with her.* **2** to make it obvious that you are annoyed about sth without doing anything to change the situation: *After much huffing and puffing, she finally agreed to help.*
▪ *noun*
**IDM** **in a ˈhuff** (*informal*) in a bad mood, especially because sb has annoyed or upset you: *She went off in a huff.*

**huffy** /ˈhʌfi/ *adj.* (*informal*) in a bad mood, especially because sb has annoyed or upset you ▸ **huff·i·ly** /-fəli/ *adv.*

**hug** /hʌɡ/ *verb, noun*
▪ *verb* (-gg-) **1** [T, I] ~ (sb) (+ *adv./prep.*) to put your arms around sb and hold them tightly, especially to show that you like or love them **SYN** embrace: *They hugged each other.* ◊ *She hugged him tightly.* ◊ *They put their arms around each other and hugged.* **2** [T] ~ sth to put your arms around sth and hold it close to your body: *She sat in the chair, hugging her knees.* ◊ *He hugged the hot-water bottle to his chest.* **3** [T] ~ sth (of a path, vehicle, etc.) to keep close to sth for a distance: *The track hugs the coast for a mile.* **4** [T] ~ sth to fit tightly around sth, especially a person's body: *figure-hugging jeans*
▪ *noun* an act of putting your arms around sb and holding them tightly, especially to show that you like or love them: *She gave her mother a big hug.* ◊ *He stopped to receive hugs and kisses from the fans.* ◊ *They all got together for a group hug.* ⊃ see also BEAR HUG

**huge** ❶ **A2** **S** /hjuːdʒ/ *adj.* **1** ❷ **A2** extremely large in size or amount; great in degree **SYN** enormous, vast: *The sums of money involved are potentially huge.* ◊ *huge amounts of data* ◊ *I wasn't a huge fan of the movie.* ◊ *Becoming a mother made a huge difference to me.* ◊ *Anti-social behaviour affects a huge number of people daily.* ◊ *The party was a huge success.* ◊ *This is going to be a huge problem for us.* **2** (*informal*) very successful: *I think this band is going to be huge.*

**huge·ly** /ˈhjuːdʒli/ *adv.* **1** extremely: *hugely entertaining/important/popular/successful* **2** very much: *They intended to invest hugely in new technology.* ◊ *He turned around, grinning hugely.*

**huh** /hʌ/ *exclamation* **1** people use **Huh?** at the end of questions, suggestions, etc., especially when they want sb to agree with them: *So you won't be coming tonight, huh?* ◊ *Let's get out of here, huh?* **2** people say **Huh!** to show anger, surprise, DISAGREEMENT, etc. or to show that they are not impressed by sth: *Huh! Is that all you've done?* **3** (*NAmE*) (*BrE* **eh**) people say **Huh?** to show that they have not heard what sb has just said: *'Are you feeling OK?' 'Huh?'*
⊃ see also UH-HUH

**hula hoop** (*US* **Hula-Hoop**™) /ˈhuːlə huːp/ (*also* **hoop**) *noun* a large plastic ring that you move in a circle around the middle part of your body by moving your HIPS

**hula hoop**

**hulk** /hʌlk/ *noun* **1** the main part of an old vehicle or large structure that is no longer used: *the rusting hulks of cars* **2** a large heavy person: *a great hulk of a man* **3** a very large object, especially one that causes you to feel nervous or afraid

**hulk·ing** /ˈhʌlkɪŋ/ *adj.* [only before noun] very large or heavy, often in a way that causes you to feel nervous or afraid: *a hulking figure crouching in the darkness*

**hull** /hʌl/ *noun, verb*
▪ *noun* the main, bottom part of a ship, that goes in the water: *a wooden/steel hull* ◊ *They climbed onto the upturned hull and waited to be rescued.*
▪ *verb* ~ sth to remove the outer layer that covers PEAS, beans, grain, etc. or the ring of leaves attached to STRAWBERRIES

**hul·la·ba·loo** /ˌhʌləbəˈluː/ *noun* [sing.] (*informal*) a lot of loud noise, especially made by people who are annoyed or excited about sth **SYN** commotion, uproar

**hullo** (especially *BrE*) = HELLO

**hum** /hʌm/ *verb, noun*
▪ *verb* (-mm-) **1** [I, T] to sing a tune with your lips closed: *She was humming softly to herself.* ◊ ~ sth *What's that tune you're humming?* **2** [I] to make a low continuous sound: *The computers were humming away.* **3** [I] to be full of activity: *The streets were beginning to hum with life.*
**IDM** **ˌhum and ˈhaw** (*BrE*) (*NAmE* **ˌhem and ˈhaw**) (*informal*) to take a long time to make a decision or before you say sth
▪ *noun* [sing.] ~ (of sth) a low continuous sound: *the hum of bees/traffic/voices* ◊ *The room filled with the hum of conversation.*

**human** ❶ **A2** ❷ /ˈhjuːmən/ *adj., noun*
▪ *adj.* **1** ❷ **A2** [only before noun] of or connected with people rather than animals, machines or gods: *the human body/brain* ◊ *a terrible loss of human life* ◊ *human development/activity/behaviour* ◊ *Human remains* (= the body of a dead person) *were found inside the house.* ◊ *Contact with other people is a basic human need.* ◊ *This food is not fit for human consumption.* ◊ *one of the greatest leaders in human history* ◊ *He tried to use a bystander as a human shield.* ◊ *After washing her face, she felt almost human* (= like her normal self) *again.* **2** ❸ **B1** showing the weaknesses and desires that are typical of people, which means that other people should not criticize the person too much: *human weaknesses/failings* ◊ *It's only human to want the best for your children.* **3** ❹ **B1** having the same feelings and emotions as most ordinary people: *He's really very human when you get to know him.* ◊ *The public is always attracted to politicians who have the human touch* (= the ability to make ordinary people feel relaxed when they meet them).
⊃ compare INHUMAN, NON-HUMAN
**IDM** **the ˈhuman face of …** a person who is involved in a subject, issue, etc. and makes it easier for ordinary people to understand and have sympathy with it: *He is the human face of party politics.* **with a human ˈface** that considers the needs of ordinary people: *This was science with a human face.* ⊃ more at MILK *n.*
▪ *noun* ❷ **A2** (*also* **human ˈbeing**) a person rather than an animal or a machine: *Dogs can hear much better than humans.* ◊ *That is no way to treat another human being.*

**ˌhuman ˈcapital** *noun* [U] the skills, knowledge and experience of a person or group of people, seen as sth valuable that an organization or country can make use of: *The education system is central to the development of skills and human capital.*

**hu·mane** /hjuːˈmeɪn/ *adj.* (*approving*) being kind towards people and animals by making sure that they do not suffer more than is necessary: *a caring and humane society* ◊ *the humane treatment of refugees* ◊ *the humane killing of animals* **OPP** inhuman ▸ **hu·mane·ly** *adv.*: *to treat sb humanely* ◊ *meat that has been humanely produced* ◊ *The dog was humanely destroyed.*

**human error**

**human error** noun [U, C] **1** the fact of making mistakes as a natural result of being human; mistakes of this kind: *We must allow for human error.* **2** the fact that a mistake is made by a person, rather than as a result of technology failing to work correctly; mistakes of this kind: *The plane crash was caused by human error, not mechanical failure.*

**human geography** noun [U] the scientific study of how human activity affects or is affected by the surface of the earth

**human interest** noun [U] the part of a story in the media that people find interesting because it describes the experiences, feelings, etc. of the people involved

**hu·man·ism** /ˈhjuːmənɪzəm/ noun [U] a system of thought that considers that solving human problems with the help of reason is more important than religious beliefs. It emphasizes the fact that the basic nature of humans is good.

**hu·man·ist** /ˈhjuːmənɪst/ noun, adj.
▪ *noun* a person who believes in humanism
▪ *adj.* (also **hu·man·is·tic** /ˌhjuːməˈnɪstɪk/) believing in or based on HUMANISM: *humanist ideals*

**hu·mani·tar·ian** ʔ+ C1 /hjuːˌmænɪˈteəriən; NAmE -ˈter-/ adj. [usually before noun] **1** ʔ+ C1 connected with helping people who are suffering and improving the conditions that they are living in: *to provide humanitarian aid to the war zone* ◊ *humanitarian issues* ◊ *a humanitarian organization* ◊ *They are calling for the release of the hostages on humanitarian grounds.* **2** ʔ+ C1 (especially in journalism) describing an event or situation that causes or involves a lot of human suffering, especially one that requires aid to be provided to a large number of people: *a humanitarian crisis* ◊ *These floods are the worst humanitarian disaster the country has seen.* ▶ **hu·mani·tar·ian** noun **hu·mani·tar·ian·ism** noun [U]

**hu·man·ity** ʔ+ C1 /hjuːˈmænəti/ noun **1** ʔ+ C1 [U] people in general: *crimes against humanity* ⊃ note at GENDER **2** ʔ+ C1 [U] the state of being a person rather than a god, an animal or a machine: *The story was used to emphasize the humanity of Jesus.* ◊ *united by a sense of common humanity* **3** ʔ+ C1 [U] the quality of being kind to people and animals by making sure that they do not suffer more than is necessary; the quality of being HUMANE: *The judge was praised for his courage and humanity.* OPP **inhumanity 4** ʔ+ C1 **(the) humanities** [pl.] the subjects of study that are about the way people think and behave, for example literature, language, history and philosophy: *The college offers a wide range of courses in the arts and humanities.* ⊃ compare SCIENCE

**hu·man·ize** (*BrE also* **-ise**) /ˈhjuːmənaɪz/ verb ~ **sth** to make sth more pleasant or suitable for people; to make sth more HUMANE: *These measures are intended to humanize the prison system.*

**hu·man·kind** /ˌhjuːmənˈkaɪnd/ noun [U] people in general ⊃ see also MANKIND

**hu·man·ly** /ˈhjuːmənli/ adv. within human ability; in a way that is typical of human behaviour, thoughts and feelings: *The doctors did all that was humanly possible.* ◊ *He couldn't humanly refuse to help her.*

**human nature** noun [U] the ways of behaving, thinking and feeling that are shared by most people and are considered to be normal: *Her kindness has restored my faith in human nature* (= the belief that people are good). ◊ *It's only human nature to be worried about change.*

**hu·man·oid** /ˈhjuːmənɔɪd/ noun (especially in science fiction) a machine or creature that looks and behaves like a human ▶ **hu·man·oid** adj.

**the human race** noun [sing.] all people, considered together as a group

**human resources** noun **1** [pl.] people's skills and abilities, seen as sth a company, an organization, etc. can make use of ⊃ compare HUMAN CAPITAL **2** (*abbr.* **HR**) [U + sing./pl. v.] the department in a company that deals with employing and training people SYN **personnel**: *the human resources director*

**human right** noun [usually pl.] one of the basic rights that everyone has to be treated fairly and not in a cruel way, especially by their government: *The country has a poor record on human rights.* ◊ *The constitution guarantees basic human rights.* ◊ *A government that violates human rights cannot be tolerated.* ◊ *human rights abuses/violations* ◊ *human rights activists/campaigners* ⊃ WORDFINDER NOTE at EQUAL

**human shield** noun a person or group of people forced to stay near a possible target for attack, in order to prevent an attack: *The gunman used the hostages as a human shield.*

**human smuggling** noun [U] (*NAmE*) = **PEOPLE SMUGGLING**

**human trafficking** (*BrE also* **people trafficking**) noun [U] the crime of transporting or controlling people and forcing them to work in the sex trade or other forms of forced labour ▶ **human trafficker** (*BrE also* **people trafficker**) noun

**hum·ble** ʔ+ C1 /ˈhʌmbl/ adj., verb
▪ *adj.* (**hum·bler** /-blə(r)/, **hum·blest** /-blɪst/) **1** ʔ+ C1 showing you do not think that you are as important as other people SYN **modest**: *Be humble enough to learn from your mistakes.* ◊ *my humble tribute to this great man* ⊃ see also HUMILITY **2** ʔ+ C1 (*ironic* or *humorous*) used to suggest that you are not as important as other people, but in a way that is not sincere or not very serious: *In my humble opinion, you were in the wrong.* ◊ *My humble apologies. I did not understand.* **3** ʔ+ C1 having a low rank or social position: *a man of humble birth/origins* ◊ *a humble occupation* ◊ *the daughter of a humble shopkeeper* **4** (of a thing) not large or special in any way SYN **modest**: *a humble farmhouse* ◊ *The company has worked its way up from humble beginnings to become the market leader.* ▶ **hum·bly** /-bli/ adv.: *I would humbly suggest that there is something wrong here.* ◊ *'Sorry,' she said humbly.* IDM see EAT
▪ *verb* **1** ~ **sb** to make sb feel that they are not as good or important as they thought they were: *He was humbled by her generosity.* ◊ *a humbling experience* **2** [usually passive] to easily defeat an opponent, especially a strong or powerful one: **be humbled** *The world champion was humbled last night in three rounds.* **3** ~ **yourself** to show that you are not too proud to ask for sth, admit that you have been wrong, etc. ⊃ see also HUMILITY

**hum·bug** /ˈhʌmbʌɡ/ noun **1** [U] (*old-fashioned*) dishonest language or behaviour that is intended to trick people: *political humbug* **2** [C] (*old-fashioned*) a person who is not sincere or honest **3** [C] (*BrE*) a hard sweet made from boiled sugar, especially one that tastes of PEPPERMINT

**hum·ding·er** /ˌhʌmˈdɪŋə(r)/ noun [sing.] (*informal*) something that is very exciting or impressive: *It turned into a real humdinger of a game.*

**hum·drum** /ˈhʌmdrʌm/ adj. boring and always the same SYN **dull**, **tedious**: *a humdrum existence/job/life*

**hu·merus** /ˈhjuːmərəs/ noun (pl. **hu·meri** /-raɪ/) (*anatomy*) the large bone in the top part of the arm between the shoulder and the ELBOW ⊃ VISUAL VOCAB page V1

**humid** /ˈhjuːmɪd/ adj. (of the air or climate) warm and slightly wet: *These ferns will grow best in a humid atmosphere.* ◊ *The island is hot and humid in the summer.*

**humi·dex** /ˈhjuːmɪdeks/ noun [sing.] (*CanE*) a scale that measures how unpleasant hot and HUMID weather feels to people

**hu·midi·fier** /hjuːˈmɪdɪfaɪə(r)/ noun a machine used for making the air in a room less dry ⊃ see also DEHUMIDIFIER

**hu·mid·ity** /hjuːˈmɪdəti/ noun [U] **1** the amount of water in the air: *high/low humidity* ◊ *70% humidity* **2** conditions in which the air is wet and very warm: *These plants need heat and humidity to grow well.* ◊ *The humidity was becoming unbearable.* ⊃ WORDFINDER NOTE at CLIMATE

**hu·mili·ate** /hjuːˈmɪlieɪt/ verb ~ **sb**/**yourself**/**sth** to make sb feel ashamed or stupid and lose the respect of other people: *I didn't want to humiliate her in front of her colleagues.* ◊ *I've never felt so humiliated.* ◊ *The party was humiliated in the recent elections.* ▶ **hu·mili·at·ing** adj.: *a humiliating defeat* **hu·mili·ation** /hjuːˌmɪliˈeɪʃn/ noun [U, C]: *She suffered the humiliation of being criticized in public.*

æ cat | ɑː father | e bed | ɜː fur | ə about | ɪ sit | iː see | i happy | ɒ got (*BrE*) | ɔː saw | ʌ cup | ʊ put | uː too

**hu·mil·ity** /hjuːˈmɪləti/ *noun* [U] the quality of not thinking that you are better than other people; the quality of being humble: *Her first defeat was an early lesson in humility.* ◊ *an act of genuine humility*

**hum·ming·bird** /ˈhʌmɪŋbɜːd; *NAmE* -bɜːrd/ *noun* a small brightly coloured bird that lives in warm countries and that can stay in one place in the air by beating its wings very fast, making a continuous low sound (= a HUMMING sound)

**hum·mock** /ˈhʌmək/ *noun* (*BrE*) a small hill or pile of earth

**hum·mus** (*also* **hou·mous**) /ˈhʊməs, ˈhuːm-/ *noun* [U] a type of food, originally from the Middle East, that is a soft mixture of CHICKPEAS, SESAME seeds, oil, lemon juice and GARLIC

**hu·mon·gous** (*also* **hu·mun·gous**) /hjuːˈmʌŋɡəs/ *adj.* (*informal*) very big **SYN** enormous

**humor, hu·mor·less** (*US*) = HUMOUR, HUMOURLESS

**hu·mor·ist** /ˈhjuːmərɪst/ *noun* a person who is famous for writing or telling funny stories and jokes

**hu·mor·ous** 🔵 **B2** /ˈhjuːmərəs/ *adj.* funny; showing a sense of humour: *He gave a humorous account of their trip to Spain.* ◊ *a humorous look at the world of fashion* ◊ *The show offers a humorous take on family life.* ⊃ SYNONYMS at FUNNY ▶ **hu·mor·ous·ly** *adv.*: *The poem humorously describes local characters and traditions.*

**hu·mour** 🔵 **B2** (*US* **hu·mor**) /ˈhjuːmə(r)/ *noun, verb*
■ *noun* **1** 🔵 **B2** [U] the quality in sth that makes it funny; the ability to laugh at things that are funny: *a story full of gentle humour* ◊ *She ignored his feeble attempt at humour.* ◊ *They failed to see the humour of the situation.* ◊ *I can't stand people with no sense of humour.* ◊ *She has her very own brand of humour.* ◊ *The film is only funny if you appreciate French humour* (= things that cause French people to laugh). ⊃ see also GALLOWS HUMOUR, GSOH **2** [C, U] (*formal*) the state of your feelings or mind at a particular time: *to be in the best of humours* ◊ *The meeting dissolved in ill humour.* ◊ **out of ~** to be out of humour (= in a bad mood) ⊃ see also GOOD HUMOUR, GOOD-HUMOURED, ILL HUMOUR, ILL-HUMOURED **3** [C] (*old use*) one of the four liquids that were thought in the past to be in a person's body and to influence health and character ⊃ see also AQUEOUS HUMOUR, VITREOUS HUMOUR
■ *verb* **~ sb** to agree with sb's wishes, even if they seem unreasonable, in order to keep the person happy: *She thought it best to humour him rather than get into an argument.*

**hu·mour·less** (*US* **hu·mor·less**) /ˈhjuːmələs; *NAmE* -mərl-/ *adj.* not having or showing the ability to laugh at things that other people think are funny ▶ **hu·mour·less·ly** (*US* **hu·mor·less·ly**) *adv.*

**hump** /hʌmp/ *noun, verb*
■ *noun* **1** a large mass that sticks out above the surface of sth, especially the ground: *the dark hump of the mountain in the distance* ◊ (*BrE*) *a road/speed/traffic hump* (= a hump on a road that forces traffic to drive more slowly) ⊃ see also SPEED HUMP **2** a large curved part on the back of some animals, especially CAMELS **3** a round part that sticks out on the back of a person, caused by an unusual curve in the SPINE (= the row of bones in the middle of the back) **IDM** **be over the ˈhump** to have done the most difficult part of sth **get/take the ˈhump** | **give sb the ˈhump** (*BrE*, *informal*) to become annoyed or upset about sth; to make sb annoyed or upset about sth: *Fans get the hump when the team loses.* ⊃ more at BUST *v.*
■ *verb* **1** **~ sth** (**+ adv./prep.**) (*BrE*) to carry sth heavy: *I've been humping furniture around all day.* **2** **~ sb** (*taboo, slang*) to have sex with sb

**hump·back** /ˈhʌmpbæk/ *noun* **1** = HUMPBACK WHALE **2** = HUNCHBACK

**ˌhumpback ˈbridge** (*also* **ˌhumpbacked ˈbridge**) *noun* (*BrE*) a small bridge that slopes steeply on both sides

**ˈhumpback ˌwhale** (*also* **ˈhump-back**) *noun* a large WHALE (= a very large sea animal) with a back that is like a HUMP in shape

**humped** /hʌmpt/ *adj.* having a hump or humps; like a hump in shape: *a humped back* ◊ *He was tall and broad with humped shoulders.*

777 **hung**

**humph** /hʌmf/ *exclamation* the way of writing the sound that people use to show they do not believe sth or do not approve of it

**hu·mun·gous** = HUMONGOUS

**humus** /ˈhjuːməs/ *noun* [U] a substance formed from dead leaves and plants that helps plants grow

**Hun** /hʌn/ *noun* **1** a member of an aggressive NOMADIC people from Central Asia who INVADED Europe in the 4th and 5th centuries **2** (*taboo, offensive*) (*pl.* **Huns** *or* **the Hun**) an offensive word for a German person, used especially during the First and Second World Wars

**hunch** /hʌntʃ/ *verb, noun*
■ *verb* [I, T] to bend the top part of your body forward and raise your shoulders and back: (**+ adv./prep.**) *She leaned forward, hunching over the desk.* ◊ **~ sth** *He hunched his shoulders and thrust his hands deep into his pockets.*
▶ **hunched** *adj.*: *a hunched figure* ◊ *He sat hunched over his breakfast.*
■ *noun* a feeling that sth is true even though you do not have any evidence to prove it: *It seemed that the doctor's hunch had been right.* ◊ **~(that)** *I had a hunch (that) you'd be back.* ◊ *to follow/back your hunches*

**hunch·back** /ˈhʌntʃbæk/ (*also* **hump·back**) *noun* (*old-fashioned* or *offensive*) a HUMP on sb's back; a person who has a HUMP on their back ▶ **hunch·backed** *adj.*

**hun·dred** 🔵 **A1** /ˈhʌndrəd/ *number* **1** 🔵 **A1** 100: *One hundred (of the children) have already been placed with foster families.* ◊ *There were just a hundred of them there.* ◊ *This vase is worth several hundred dollars.* ◊ *She must be over a hundred* (= a hundred years old). ◊ *Hundreds of thousands of people are at risk.* ◊ *a hundred-year lease* **HELP** You say **a**, **one**, **two**, **several**, *etc.* **hundred** without a final 's' on 'hundred'. **Hundreds (of …)** can be used if there is no number or quantity before it. Always use a plural verb with **hundred** or **hundreds**, except when an amount of money is mentioned: *Four hundred (people) are expected to attend.* ◊ *Two hundred (pounds) was withdrawn from the account.* **2** 🔵 **A1** **a hundred** *or* **hundreds (of …)** (*usually informal*) a large amount: *hundreds of miles away* ◊ *for hundreds of years* ◊ *If I've said it once, I've said it a hundred times.* ◊ *I have **a hundred and one** things to do.* ◊ (*formal*) *Men died in their hundreds.* **3** **the hundreds** [pl.] the numbers from 100 to 999: *We're talking about a figure in the low hundreds.* **4** **the … hundreds** [pl.] the years of a particular century: *the early nineteen hundreds* (= written 'early 1900s') **5** **one**, **two**, **three**, *etc.* **~ hours** used to express whole hours in the 24-hour system: *twelve hundred hours* (= 12.00 midday) **IDM** **a/one ˌhundred per ˈcent 1** in every way **SYN** completely: *I'm not a hundred per cent sure.* ◊ *My family supports me one hundred per cent.* **2** completely fit and healthy: *I still don't feel a hundred per cent.* **give a ˌhundred (and ten) per ˈcent** to put as much effort into sth as you can; to give even more effort than could be expected: *Every player gave a hundred per cent tonight.* ⊃ more at NINETY

**ˌhundreds and ˈthousands** (*BrE*) (*also* **sprin·kles** especially in *NAmE*) *noun* [pl.] extremely small pieces of coloured sugar, used to decorate cakes, etc.

**hun·dredth** /ˈhʌndrədθ, -drətθ/ *ordinal number, noun*
■ *ordinal number* 100th: *her hundredth birthday*
■ *noun* each of one hundred equal parts of sth: *a/one hundredth of a second*

**hun·dred·weight** /ˈhʌndrədweɪt/ *noun* (*pl.* **hun·dred·weight**) (*abbr.* **cwt**) a unit for measuring weight equal to 112 pounds in the UK and 100 pounds in the US. There are 20 hundredweight in a TON.

**hung** /hʌŋ/ *adj., verb*
■ *adj.* [only before noun] **1** (*BrE*) (of a parliament or council) in which no political party has more elected members than all the other parties added together: *a hung parliament* **2** (of a JURY) unable to agree about whether sb is guilty of a crime
**IDM** **be hung up on/about sb/sth** (*informal, disapproving*) to be very worried about sb/sth; to be thinking about sb/

# hunger

sth too much: *You're not still hung up on that girl?* ◊ *He's too hung up about fitness.*
■ *verb* past tense, past part. of HANG

**hun·ger** /ˈhʌŋɡə(r)/ *noun, verb*
■ *noun* **1** [U] the state of not having enough food to eat, especially when this causes illness or death SYN **starvation**: *Around fifty people die of hunger every day in the camp.* ◊ *The organization works to alleviate world hunger and disease.* **2** [U] the feeling caused by a need to eat: *hunger pangs* ◊ *I felt faint with hunger.* **3** [sing.] ~ **(for sth)** (*formal*) a strong desire for sth: *a hunger for knowledge* ◊ *Nothing seemed to satisfy their hunger for truth.*
■ *verb*
PHRV ˈhunger for/after sth/sb (*literary*) to have a strong desire or need for sth/sb

**ˈhunger strike** *noun* [C, U] the act of refusing to eat for a long period of time in order to protest about sth: *to be on/go on hunger strike* ⊃ WORDFINDER NOTE at PROTEST ▶ **ˈhunger striker** *noun*

**hung·over** /ˌhʌŋˈəʊvə(r)/ *adj.* [not usually before noun] a person who is **hungover** is feeling ill because they drank too much alcohol the night before ⊃ see also HANGOVER

**hun·gry** /ˈhʌŋɡri/ *adj.* (**hun·grier**, **hun·gri·est**)
**1** feeling that you want to eat sth: *I'm really hungry.* ◊ *Is anyone getting hungry?* ◊ *All this talk of food is making me hungry.* ◊ *There were eight hungry mouths* (= hungry people) *to feed at home.* **2** not having enough food to eat: *Thousands are going hungry because of the failure of this year's harvest.* **3** **the hungry** *noun* [pl.] people who do not have enough food to eat **4** [only before noun] causing you to feel that you want to eat sth: *All this gardening is hungry work.* **5** having or showing a strong desire for sth: *power-hungry corporations* ◊ ~ **for sth** *Both parties are hungry for power.* ◊ ~ **to do sth** *Every day they come to school hungry to learn.* ◊ *His eyes had a wild hungry look in them.* ▶ **hun·grily** /-ɡrəli/ *adv.*: *They gazed hungrily at the display of food.* ◊ *He kissed her hungrily.*

**hunk** /hʌŋk/ *noun* **1** a large piece of sth, especially food, that has been cut or broken from a larger piece: *a hunk of bread/cheese/meat* **2** (*informal*) a man who is big, strong and sexually attractive: *He's a real hunk.*

**hun·ker** /ˈhʌŋkə(r)/ *verb*
PHRV ˌhunker ˈdown **1** (*especially NAmE*) to sit on your heels with your knees bent up in front of you SYN **squat**: *He hunkered down beside her.* **2** to prepare yourself to stay somewhere, keep an opinion, etc. for a long time **3** to refuse to change an opinion, way of behaving, etc.

**hun·kers** /ˈhʌŋkəz; *NAmE* -kərz/ *noun* [pl.]
IDM on your ˈhunkers sitting on your heels with your knees bent up in front of you SYN **haunch**

**hunky** /ˈhʌŋki/ *adj.* (**hunk·ier**, **hunk·iest**) (*informal*) (of a man) big, strong and sexually attractive

**hunky-dory** /ˌhʌŋki ˈdɔːri/ *adj.* [not before noun] (*informal*) if you say that **everything is hunky-dory**, you mean that there are no problems and that everyone is happy

**hunt** /hʌnt/ *verb, noun*
■ *verb* **1** [I, T] to go after wild animals in order to catch or kill them for food, sport or to make money: *Lions sometimes hunt alone.* ◊ ~ **sth** *Whales are still being hunted and killed in the Arctic.* ◊ ~ **(sth) for sth** *The animals are hunted for their fur.*

WORDFINDER chase, falconry, game, open season, pack, poach, prey, safari, trail

**2** [I] to look for sth that is difficult to find SYN **search**: ~ **for sth** *She is still hunting for a new job.* ◊ + *adv./prep.* *I've hunted everywhere but I can't find it.* ⊃ see also JOB-HUNT **3** [T, I] to look for sb in order to catch them or harm them: ~ **sb** *Police are hunting an escaped criminal.* ◊ ~ **for sb** *Detectives are hunting for thieves who broke into a warehouse yesterday.* **4** [I, T] ~ **(sth)** (in the UK) to go after and kill FOXES as a sport, riding horses and using dogs. FOX HUNTING with dogs has been illegal in England and Wales since 2005, but people still ride out with dogs following a SCENT TRAIL, without an actual FOX.
PHRV ˌhunt sb↔ˈdown to search for sb until you catch or find them, especially in order to punish or harm them ˌhunt sth↔ˈdown/ˈout to search for sth until you find it
■ *noun* **1** [C, usually sing.] an act of looking for sb/sth that is difficult to find: *The hunt is on for a suitable candidate.* ◊ ~ **for sb/sth** *Hundreds have joined a police hunt for the missing teenager.* ◊ **on the ~ for sb/sth** *They have been on the hunt for a new chief executive since July.* ◊ *a murder hunt* (= to find the person who has killed sb) ⊃ see also SCAVENGER HUNT, TREASURE HUNT, WITCH-HUNT **2** [C] (often in compounds) an act of going after wild animals to kill or capture them: *a tiger/seal hunt* **3** [C] (in the UK) an event at which people ride horses and hunt FOXES with dogs as a sport, illegal in England and Wales since 2005: *There was always a hunt on Boxing Day.* ◊ *a hunt meeting* ⊃ see also FOX HUNT **4** [C + sing./pl. v.] (in the UK) a group of people who regularly hunt FOXES as a sport. Since 2005, instead of a FOX, they follow a specially laid SCENT TRAIL.
IDM be in the ˈhunt to have a chance of winning: *The team are back in the hunt for the league title.*

**hunt·ed** /ˈhʌntɪd/ *adj.* (of an expression on sb's face) showing that sb is very worried or frightened, as if sb is following them and trying to catch them: *His eyes had a hunted look.*

**hunt·er** /ˈhʌntə(r)/ *noun* **1** a person who hunts wild animals for food or sport; an animal that hunts its food **2** (usually in compounds) a person who looks for and collects a particular kind of thing: *a treasure hunter* **3** (*BrE*) a fast strong horse used in hunting FOXES **4** (*NAmE*) a dog used in hunting ⊃ see also FORTUNE HUNTER, BARGAIN HUNTER, HEADHUNTER, HOUSE-HUNTER

**ˌhunter-ˈgather·er** *noun* a member of a group of people who do not live in one place but move around and live by hunting, fishing and gathering plants

**hunt·ing** /ˈhʌntɪŋ/ *noun* [U] **1** going after and killing wild animals as a sport or for food: *to go hunting* ◊ *Since 1977 otter hunting has been illegal.* **2** [U] (*BrE*) = FOX HUNTING **3** (in compounds) the process of looking for sth: *How's the job-hunting going?* ⊃ see also BARGAIN HUNTING, HOUSE-HUNTING

**ˈhunting ground** *noun* **1** ~ **(for sb)** a place where people with a particular interest can easily find what they want: *Crowded markets are a happy hunting ground for pickpockets.* **2** ~ **(for sb/sth)** a place where wild animals are hunted by people or other animals

**hunt·ress** /ˈhʌntrəs/ *noun* (*literary*) a woman who hunts wild animals

**hunts·man** /ˈhʌntsmən/ *noun* (*pl.* -men /-mən/) a man who hunts wild animals

**hur·dle** /ˈhɜːdl; *NAmE* ˈhɜːrdl/ *noun, verb*
■ *noun* **1** each of a series of VERTICAL frames that a person or horse jumps over in a race: *His horse fell at the final hurdle.* ◊ *to clear a hurdle* (= jump over it successfully) **2 hurdles** [pl.] a race in which runners or horses have to jump over hurdles: *the 300m hurdles* **3** a problem or difficulty that must be solved or dealt with before you can achieve sth SYN **obstacle**: *The next hurdle will be getting her parents' agreement.*
■ *verb* **1** [T, I] to jump over sth while you are running: ~ **sth** *He hurdled two barriers to avoid reporters.* ◊ ~ **over sth** *to hurdle over a fence* **2** [I] to run in a hurdles race

**hurd·ler** /ˈhɜːdlə(r)/ *noun* a person or horse that runs in races over hurdles

**hurd·ling** /ˈhɜːdlɪŋ/ *noun* [U] the sport of racing over hurdles

**hurl** /hɜːl/ *NAmE* hɜːrl/ *verb* **1** [T] ~ **sth/sb + adv./prep.** to throw sth/sb violently in a particular direction: *He hurled a brick through the window.* ⊃ SYNONYMS at THROW **2** [T] ~ **abuse, accusations, insults, etc. (at sb)** to shout offensive words, etc. at sb: *Rival fans hurled abuse at each other.* **3** [I] (*NAmE*, *slang*) to VOMIT

**hurl·ing** /ˈhɜːlɪŋ/ *NAmE* ˈhɜːrl-/ *noun* [U] an Irish ball game similar to hockey played by two teams of 15 boys or men

**hurly-burly** /ˈhɜːli ˈbɜːli/ NAmE /ˈhɜːrli ˈbɜːrli/ noun [U] a very noisy and busy activity or situation: *He enjoys the hurly-burly of political debate.*

**hur·rah** /həˈrɑː/ (*also* **hur·ray** /həˈreɪ/) *exclamation* = HOORAY

**hur·ri·cane** ❶ B1 /ˈhʌrɪkən; NAmE ˈhɜːrəkeɪn/ *noun* a violent storm with very strong winds, especially in the western Atlantic Ocean: *A powerful hurricane hit the Florida coast.* ◇ *Hurricane Sandy devastated the area.* ◇ *The hurricane season does not end until November.* ⊃ WORDFINDER NOTE at DISASTER ⊃ *compare* CYCLONE, TYPHOON

**hur·ried** /ˈhʌrid; NAmE ˈhɜːr-/ *adj.* [usually before noun] done too quickly because you do not have enough time SYN rushed: *I ate a hurried breakfast and left.* OPP **unhur·ried** ▸ **hur·ried·ly** /-rɪdli/ *adv.*: *I hurriedly got up and dressed.*

**hurry** ❶ B1 /ˈhʌri; NAmE ˈhɜːri/ *verb, noun*
■ *verb* (**hur·ries, hurry·ing, hur·ried, hur·ried**) **1** B1 [I] to move or act quickly because there is not much time SYN rush: *You'll have to hurry if you want to catch that train.* ◇ *~ to do sth The kids hurried to open their presents.* HELP In spoken English **hurry** can be used with **and** plus another verb, instead of with **to** and the infinitive, especially to tell sb to do sth quickly: *Hurry and eat before the soup gets cold.* **2** B1 [I] + *adv. / prep.* to move quickly in a particular direction SYN rush: *He picked up his bags and hurried across the courtyard.* ◇ *She hurried away without saying goodbye.* **3** B2 [T] to make sb do sth more quickly SYN rush: *~ sb I don't want to hurry you but we close in twenty minutes.* ◇ *~ sb into doing sth She was hurried into making an unwise choice.* **4** [T] *~ sth + adv. / prep.* to deal with sth quickly SYN rush: *Her application was hurried through.* **5** [T, usually passive] to do sth too quickly SYN rush: **be hurried** *A good meal should never be hurried.*
PHR V ˌhurry ˈon to continue speaking without giving anyone else time to say anything ˌhurry ˈup (with sth) to do sth more quickly because there is not much time: *I wish the bus would hurry up and come.* ◇ *Hurry up! We're going to be late.* ◇ *Hurry up with the scissors. I need them.* ˌhurry sb/sth↔up to make sb do sth more quickly; to make sth happen more quickly: *Can you do anything to hurry my order up?*
■ *noun* ❶ B1 [U, sing.] the need or wish to get sth done quickly: *Take your time—there's no hurry.* ◇ *What's the hurry? The train doesn't leave for an hour.* ◇ **in your ~ to do sth** *In my hurry to leave, I forgot my passport.*
IDM **in a ˈhurry 1** very quickly or more quickly than usual: *He had to leave in a hurry.* **2** not having enough time to do sth: *Sorry, I haven't got time to do it now—I'm in a hurry.* ◇ *Alice was in a tearing hurry as usual.* **in a ˈhurry to do sth** impatient to do sth: *My daughter is in such a hurry to grow up.* ◇ *Why are you in such a hurry to sell?* **in no ˈhurry (to do sth)** | **not in a / any ˈhurry (to do sth) 1** having plenty of time: *I don't mind waiting—I'm not in any particular hurry.* **2** not wanting or not willing to do sth: *We were in no hurry to get back to work after the holiday.* **sb will not do sth again in a ˈhurry** (*informal*) used to say that sb does not want to do sth again because it was not pleasant or fun: *I won't be going there again in a hurry—the food was terrible.*

**hurt** ❶ A2 /hɜːt; NAmE hɜːrt/ *verb, adj., noun*
■ *verb* (**hurt, hurt**) **1** ❶ A2 [T, I] to cause physical pain to sb / yourself; to injure sb / yourself: *~ sth He hurt his back playing squash.* ◇ *~ yourself Did you hurt yourself?* ◇ *~ (sb) Stop it. You're hurting me.* ◇ *No one was seriously hurt in the accident.* ◇ *My back is really hurting me today.* ◇ *My shoes hurt—they're too tight.* ⊃ SYNONYMS *at* INJURE

WORDFINDER bandage, bleed, bruise, fracture, plaster, sore, swell, wound

**2** ❶ A2 [I] to feel painful: *My feet hurt.* ◇ *Ouch! That hurt!* ◇ **it hurts when / if …** *It hurts when I bend my knee.* ◇ **it hurts to do sth** *It hurts to breathe.* **3** B1 [I, T] to make sb unhappy or upset: *What really hurt was that he never answered my letter.* ◇ *~ sb / sth I'm sorry, I didn't mean to*

779 **husband**

*hurt you.* ◇ *I didn't want to **hurt his feelings**.* ◇ **it hurts (sb) to do sth** *It hurt me to think that he would lie to me.* **4** [I] **be ˈhurting** (*informal*) to feel unhappy or upset: *I know you're hurting and I want to help you.* **5** [T] *~ sb / sth* to have a bad effect on sb / sth: *Many people on low incomes will be hurt by the government's plans.* ⊃ SYNONYMS *at* DAMAGE **6** [I] **be ˈhurting (for sth)** (*NAmE*) to be in a difficult situation because you need sth, especially money: *His campaign is already hurting for money.*
IDM ˌit ˌwon't / ˌwouldn't ˈhurt (sb / sth) (to do sth) used to say that sb should do a particular thing: *It wouldn't hurt you to help with the housework occasionally.* ⊃ *more at* FLY *n.*, HIT *v.*

■ *adj.* **1** ❶ A2 injured physically: *None of the passengers were badly hurt.* ◇ *Steve didn't look seriously hurt.* ◇ *Stop that or you'll get hurt!* OPP **unhurt 2** ❶ B1 upset and offended by sth that sb has said or done: *a hurt look / expression* ◇ *You have every right to feel hurt.* ◇ **that …** *She was deeply hurt that she had not been invited.*
■ *noun* ❶ B2 [U, C] (*rather informal*) a feeling of unhappiness because sb has been unkind or unfair to you: *There was hurt and real anger in her voice.* ◇ *It was a hurt that would take a long time to heal.*

▶ SYNONYMS
**hurt**
ache • burn • sting • tingle • itch • throb
These are all words that can be used when part of your body feels painful.
**hurt** (of part of your body) to feel painful; (of an action) to cause pain: *My feet hurt.* ◇ *Ouch! That hurt!*
**ache** to feel a continuous pain that is not severe: *I'm aching all over.*
**burn** (of part of your body) to feel very hot and painful: *Our eyes were burning from the chemicals in the air.*
**sting** to make sb feel a sharp burning pain or uncomfortable feeling in part of their body; (of part of your body) to feel this pain: *My eyes were stinging from the smoke.*
**tingle** (of part of your body) to feel as if a lot of small sharp points are pushing into the skin there: *The cold air made her face tingle.*
**itch** to have an uncomfortable feeling on your skin that makes you want to scratch; to make your skin feel like this: *I itch all over.* ◇ *Does the rash itch?*
**throb** (of part of your body) to feel pain as a series of regular beats: *His head throbbed painfully.*
PATTERNS
• your **eyes** hurt / ache / burn / sting / itch
• your **skin** hurts / burns / stings / tingles / itches
• your **flesh** hurts / burns / stings / tingles
• your **head** hurts / aches / throbs
• your **stomach** hurts / aches
• to **really** hurt / ache / burn / sting / tingle / itch / throb
• to hurt / ache / sting / itch **badly** / **a lot**
• It hurts / stings / tingles / itches.

**hurt·ful** /ˈhɜːtfl; NAmE ˈhɜːrt-/ *adj.* (of comments) making you feel upset and offended SYN **unkind**: *I cannot forget the hurtful things he said.* ◇ **~ to sb** *The bad reviews of her new book were very hurtful to her.* ▸ **hurt·ful·ly** /-fəli/ *adv.*: *He said, rather hurtfully, that he had better things to do than come and see me.*

**hur·tle** /ˈhɜːtl; NAmE ˈhɜːrtl/ *verb* [I] + *adv. / prep.* to move very fast in a particular direction: *A runaway car came hurtling towards us.*

**hus·band** ❶ A1 /ˈhʌzbənd/ *noun, verb*
■ *noun* ❶ A1 (*also informal* **hubby**) the man that sb is married to; a married man: *This is my husband, Steve.* ◇ *How did you meet your husband?* ◇ *She's finally decided to **leave her husband**.* ⊃ *see also* COMMON-LAW HUSBAND, HOUSE HUSBAND

---
**O** Oxford Phrasal Academic Lexicon (OPAL) written and spoken word lists | **W** OPAL written word list | **S** OPAL spoken word list

# husbandry

**IDM** **husband and 'wife** a man and woman who are married to each other: *They lived together as husband and wife* (= as if they were married) *for years.* ◊ *a husband-and-wife team*
- **verb** ~ **sth** (*formal*) to use sth very carefully and make sure that you do not waste it

**hus·band·ry** /ˈhʌzbəndri/ *noun* **1** farming, especially when done carefully and well: *animal/crop husbandry* **2** (*old-fashioned*) the careful use of food, money and supplies

**hush** /hʌʃ/ *verb, noun*
- **verb 1** [I] (used especially in orders) to be quiet; to stop talking or crying: *Hush now and try to sleep.* **2** [T] ~ **sb/sth** to make sb/sth become quieter; to make sb stop talking, crying, etc.
- **PHRV** **hush sth**↔**up** to hide information about a situation because you do not want people to know about it: *He claimed that the whole affair had been hushed up by the council.*
- **noun** [sing., U] a period of silence, especially following a lot of noise, or when people are expecting sth to happen: *There was a deathly hush in the theatre.* ◊ *A hush descended over the waiting crowd.* ◊ (*BrE, informal*) *Can we have a bit of hush?* (= please be quiet)

**hushed** /hʌʃt/ *adj.* **1** (of a place) quiet because nobody is talking; much quieter than usual: *A hushed courtroom listened as the boy gave evidence.* **2** [usually before noun] (of voices) speaking very quietly: *a hushed whisper*

**ˌhush-ˈhush** *adj.* (*informal*) secret and not known about by many people: *Their wedding was very hush-hush.*

**ˈhush money** *noun* [U] money that is paid to sb to prevent them from giving other people information that could be embarrassing or damaging

**ˈhush puppies** *noun* [pl.] small fried cakes made of CORNMEAL, eaten especially in the southern US

**husk** /hʌsk/ *noun, verb*
- **noun** the dry outer layer that covers nuts, fruits and seeds, especially grain
- **verb** ~ **sth** to remove the husks from grain, seeds, nuts, etc.

**husky** /ˈhʌski/ *adj., noun*
- **adj.** (**husk·ier, husk·iest**) **1** (of a person or their voice) sounding deep, quiet and rough, sometimes in an attractive way: *She spoke in a husky whisper.* **2** (*NAmE*) (of a man or boy) big and strong ▶ **husk·ily** /-skɪli/ *adv.* **huski·ness** *noun* [U]
- **noun** (*NAmE also* **huskie**) (*pl.* **-ies**) a large strong dog with thick hair, used for pulling SLEDGES across snow

**hus·sar** /həˈzɑː(r)/ *noun* (in the past) a CAVALRY soldier who carried light weapons

**hussy** /ˈhʌsi/ *noun* (*pl.* **-ies**) (*old-fashioned, disapproving*) a girl or woman who behaves in a way that is considered morally wrong

**hust·ings** /ˈhʌstɪŋz/ *noun* (*pl.* **hustings**) (*especially BrE*) **1** [C] a meeting before an election at which candidates speak to voters: *an election hustings* **2 the hustings** [pl.] the political meetings, speeches, etc. that take place in the period before an election: **on the ~** *Most candidates will be out on the hustings this week.*

**hus·tle** /ˈhʌsl/ *verb, noun*
- **verb 1** [T] ~ **sb** + **adv./prep.** to make sb move quickly by pushing them in a rough aggressive way: *He grabbed her arm and hustled her out of the room.* **2** [T] ~ **sb** (**into sth**) to force sb to make a decision before they are ready or sure **3** [T, I] ~ (**sth**) (*informal, especially NAmE*) to sell or obtain sth, often illegally: *to hustle dope* ◊ *They survive by hustling on the streets.* **4** [I] (*NAmE, informal*) to act in an aggressive way or with a lot of energy **5** [I] (*NAmE*) to work as a PROSTITUTE
- **noun** [U] busy noisy activity of a lot of people in one place: *We escaped from the hustle and bustle of the city for the weekend.*

**hust·ler** /ˈhʌslə(r)/ *noun* (*informal*) **1** (*especially NAmE*) a person who tries to trick sb into giving them money **2** (*NAmE*) a PROSTITUTE

**hut** /hʌt/ *noun* a small, simply built house or shelter: *a beach hut* ◊ *a wooden/mud hut*

**hutch** /hʌtʃ/ *noun* **1** a wooden box with a front made of wire, used for keeping RABBITS or other small animals in **2** (*NAmE*) a large piece of wooden furniture with shelves in the top part and cupboards below, used for displaying and storing cups, plates, etc.

**HVAC** /ˌeɪtʃviːˈæk/ *abbr.* (*especially US*) heating, ventilation and air conditioning (used to refer to a system that can heat or cool a building or allow fresh air to move around): *a new, efficient HVAC system*

**hya·cinth** /ˈhaɪəsɪnθ/ *noun* a plant with a mass of small blue, white or pink flowers with a sweet smell that grow closely together around a thick STEM

**hy·aena** = HYENA

**hy·brid** /ˈhaɪbrɪd/ *noun* **1** an animal or plant that has parents of different species or varieties: *A mule is a hybrid of a male donkey and a female horse.* ⇨ compare CROSSBREED ⇨ **WORDFINDER NOTE** at BREED **2** ~ (**between/of A and B**) something that is the product of mixing two or more different things **SYN** *mixture*: *The music was a hybrid of Western pop and traditional folk song.* **3** a vehicle that uses two different types of power, especially petrol or DIESEL and electricity **4** a bicycle that has been designed for use on the road or on rough ground ⇨ compare MOUNTAIN BIKE, ROAD BIKE ▶ **hy·brid** *adj.* [usually before noun]: *a hybrid car/vehicle*

**hy·brid·ize** (*BrE also* **-ise**) /ˈhaɪbrɪdaɪz/ *verb* [I, T] ~ (**sth**) (*specialist*) if an animal or a plant **hybridizes** or **is hybridized** with an animal or a plant of another species, they join together to produce a hybrid ▶ **hy·brid·iza·tion, -isa·tion** /ˌhaɪbrɪdaɪˈzeɪʃn; *NAmE* -dəˈz-/ *noun* [U]

**hydel** /ˈhaɪdel/ *abbr.* (*IndE*) HYDROELECTRIC

**hydr(o)-** /ˈhaɪdrəʊ, haɪdrə; *BrE also* haɪˈdrɒ; *NAmE also* haɪˈdrɑː/ *combining form* (in nouns, adjectives and adverbs) **1** relating to water **2** (*chemistry*) combined with HYDROGEN

**hydra** /ˈhaɪdrə/ *noun* **1 Hydra** (in ancient Greek stories) a snake with several heads. As one head was cut off, another one grew. In the end it was killed by Hercules. **2** (*formal*) a thing that is very difficult to deal with, because it continues for a long time or because it has many different aspects **3** (*biology*) an extremely small water creature with a body that is like a tube in shape and TENTACLES around its mouth

**hy·dran·gea** /haɪˈdreɪndʒə/ *noun* a bush with white, pink or blue flowers that grow closely together in the shape of a large ball

**hy·drant** /ˈhaɪdrənt/ *noun* = FIRE HYDRANT

**hy·drate** /haɪˈdreɪt; *NAmE* ˈhaɪdreɪt/ *verb* ~ **sth/sb** (*specialist*) to make sth/sb take in and hold water ⇨ see also DEHYDRATE ▶ **hy·dra·tion** /haɪˈdreɪʃn/ *noun* [U] ⇨ compare DEHYDRATE

**hy·draul·ic** /haɪˈdrɒlɪk; *NAmE* -ˈdrɔːl-/ *adj.* [usually before noun] **1** (of water, oil, etc.) moved through pipes, etc. under pressure: *hydraulic fluid* **2** (of a piece of machinery) operated by liquid moving under pressure: *hydraulic brakes* **3** connected with hydraulic systems: *hydraulic engineering* ▶ **hy·draul·ic·al·ly** /-kli/ *adv.*: *hydraulically operated doors*

**hyˌdraulic ˈfracturing** *noun* [U] (*formal or specialist*) = FRACKING

**hy·draul·ics** /haɪˈdrɒlɪks; *NAmE* -ˈdrɔːl-/ *noun* **1** [pl.] machines that work by the use of liquid moving under pressure **2** [U] the science of the use of liquids moving under pressure

**hydro** /ˈhaɪdrəʊ/ *noun* (*pl.* **-os**) **1** [U, C] electricity that is produced using the power of water (= HYDROELECTRICITY); a place where electricity is produced in this way (= a HYDROELECTRIC power plant) **2** [U] (*CanE*) electricity: *to pay your hydro bill*

**hydro·car·bon** /ˌhaɪdrəˈkɑːbən; *NAmE* -ˈkɑːrb-/ *noun* (*chemistry*) a chemical made up of HYDROGEN and CARBON only. There are many different hydrocarbons found in petrol, coal and natural gas.

**hy·dro·chlor·ic acid** /ˌhaɪdrəˈklɒrɪk ˈæsɪd; NAmE -ˌklɔːr-/ noun [U] (symb. **HCl**) (chemistry) an ACID containing HYDROGEN and CHLORINE

**hydro·cor·ti·sone** /ˌhaɪdrəʊˈkɔːtɪzəʊn; NAmE -ˈkɔːrt-/ noun [U] a HORMONE produced in the body that is used in drugs to help with diseases of the skin and muscles

**hydro·elec·tric** /ˌhaɪdrəʊɪˈlektrɪk/ adj. using the power of water to produce electricity; produced by the power of water: *a hydroelectric plant* ◇ *hydroelectric power* ⇒ WORDFINDER NOTE at ENERGY ▶ **hydro·elec·tri·city** /ˌhaɪdrəʊɪˌlekˈtrɪsəti/ noun [U]

**hydro·fluoro·car·bon** /ˌhaɪdrəʊˈflʊərəʊkɑːbən; NAmE -ˈflʊrəʊkɑːrb-/ noun (chemistry) = HFC

**hydro·foil** /ˈhaɪdrəfɔɪl/ noun a boat which rises above the surface of the water when it is travelling fast ⇒ compare HOVERCRAFT

**hydro·gen** ʟ+ 🅒🅘 /ˈhaɪdrədʒən/ noun [U] (symb. **H**) a chemical element. Hydrogen is a gas that is the lightest of all the elements. It combines with OXYGEN to form water.

**hy·dro·gen·ated** /haɪˈdrɒdʒəneɪtɪd; NAmE -ˈdrɑːdʒ-/ adj. (chemistry) **hydrogenated** oils have had hydrogen added to them

ˈhydrogen bomb (also **ˈH-bomb**) noun a very powerful nuclear bomb

ˈhydrogen perˈoxide noun [U] (symb. $H_2O_2$) (chemistry) = PEROXIDE

**hy·drol·ogy** /haɪˈdrɒlədʒi; NAmE -ˈdrɑːl-/ noun [U] (specialist) the scientific study of the earth's water, especially its movement in relation to land

**hy·droly·sis** /haɪˈdrɒlɪsɪs; NAmE -ˈdrɑːl-/ noun [U] (chemistry) a reaction with water that causes a COMPOUND to separate into its parts

**hydro·pho·bia** /ˌhaɪdrəˈfəʊbiə; NAmE -ˈfoʊbiə/ noun [U] extreme fear of water, which happens with RABIES infection in humans ▶ **hydro·pho·bic** /-bɪk/ adj.

**hydro·pon·ics** /ˌhaɪdrəˈpɒnɪks; NAmE -ˈpɑːn-/ noun [U] the process of growing plants in water or sand, rather than in soil

**hydro·ther·apy** /ˌhaɪdrəʊˈθerəpi/ noun [U] the treatment of disease or injury by doing physical exercises in water

**hy·drox·ide** /haɪˈdrɒksaɪd; NAmE -ˈdrɑːk-/ noun (chemistry) a chemical consisting of a metal and a combination of OXYGEN and HYDROGEN

**hyena** (also **hy·aena**) /haɪˈiːnə/ noun an African wild animal like a dog that hunts in groups or eats the meat of animals that are already dead and makes a sound like a human laugh

**hygge** /ˈhʊɡə/ (BrE also /ˈhjuːɡə/; NAmE also /ˈhuː-/) noun [U] (from Danish) the quality of being warm and comfortable that gives a feeling of happiness

**hy·giene** /ˈhaɪdʒiːn/ noun [U] the practice of keeping yourself and your living and working areas clean in order to prevent illness and disease: *food hygiene* ◇ *personal hygiene* ◇ *In the interests of hygiene, please wash your hands.*

**hy·gien·ic** /haɪˈdʒiːnɪk; NAmE -ˈdʒen-, -ˈdʒɪn-/ adj. clean and free of bacteria and therefore unlikely to spread disease: *Food must be prepared in hygienic conditions.* 🆗 **unhygienic** ▶ **hy·gien·ic·al·ly** /-kli/ adv.: *Medical supplies are disposed of hygienically.*

**hy·gien·ist** /haɪˈdʒiːnɪst/ (also **ˈdental hygienist**) noun a person who works with a dentist and whose job is to clean people's teeth and GUMS and give them advice about keeping them clean ⇒ WORDFINDER NOTE at DENTIST

**hymen** /ˈhaɪmən/ noun (anatomy) a piece of skin that partly covers the opening of the VAGINA in women who have never had sex

**hymn** /hɪm/ noun **1** a song of praise, especially one praising God and sung by Christians **2** [usually sing.] if a film, book, etc. is a **hymn to sth**, it praises it very strongly 🆔 see SING

ˈhymn book (also old-fashioned **hymˈnal** /ˈhɪmnəl/) noun a book of hymns

781

**hype** /haɪp/ noun, verb
■ noun [U] (informal, disapproving) advertisements and discussion in the media telling the public about a product and about how good or important it is: *marketing/media hype* ◇ *Don't believe all the hype—the book isn't that good.*
■ verb (informal, disapproving) to advertise sth a lot and make its good qualities seem better than they actually are, in order to get a lot of public attention for it: *his much hyped new movie opens in London.* ◇ *~ sth up This week the meeting was hyped up in the media as an important event.*

ˌhyped ˈup adj. (informal) (of a person) very worried or excited about sth that is going to happen

**hyper** /ˈhaɪpə(r)/ adj. (informal) excited and nervous; having too much nervous energy

**hyper-** /ˈhaɪpə(r)/ prefix (in adjectives and nouns) more than normal; too much: *hypercritical* ◇ *hypertension* ⇒ compare HYPO-

**hyper·active** /ˌhaɪpərˈæktɪv/ adj. (especially of children and their behaviour) too active and only able to keep quiet and still for short periods ▶ **hyper·activ·ity** /ˌhaɪpəræk-ˈtɪvəti/ noun [U]

**hyper·bar·ic** /ˌhaɪpəˈbærɪk; NAmE -pərˈb-/ adj. (physics) (of gas) at a higher pressure than normal

**hyper·bola** /haɪˈpɜːbələ; NAmE -ˈpɜːrb-/ noun (pl. **hyperbolas** or **hyper·bolae** /-liː/) a SYMMETRICAL open curve ⇒ picture at CONIC SECTION

**hyper·bole** /haɪˈpɜːbəli; NAmE -ˈpɜːrb-/ noun [U, C, usually sing.] a way of speaking or writing that makes sth sound better, more exciting, more dangerous, etc. than it really is 🆂🅈🅝 **exaggeration** ⇒ WORDFINDER NOTE at IMAGE

**hyper·bol·ic** /ˌhaɪpəˈbɒlɪk; NAmE -pərˈbɑːl-/ adj. **1** (mathematics) of or related to a hyperbola **2** (of language) deliberately EXAGGERATED; using hyperbole

**hyper·gly·caemia** (BrE) (NAmE **hyper·gly·cemia**) /ˌhaɪpəɡlaɪˈsiːmiə; NAmE -pərɡ-/ noun [U] (medical) the condition of having too high a level of BLOOD SUGAR

**hyper·in·fla·tion** /ˌhaɪpərɪnˈfleɪʃn/ noun [U] a situation in which prices rise very fast, causing damage to a country's economy

**hyper·link** /ˈhaɪpəlɪŋk; NAmE -pərl-/ noun = LINK (4): *Click on the hyperlink.* ⇒ WORDFINDER NOTE at WEBSITE

**hyper·mar·ket** /ˈhaɪpəmɑːkɪt; NAmE -pərmɑːrk-/ noun (BrE) a very large shop located outside a town, that sells a wide range of goods

**hyper·sen·si·tive** /ˌhaɪpəˈsensətɪv; NAmE -pərˈs-/ adj. **1** ~ (to sth) very easily offended: *He's hypersensitive to any kind of criticism.* **2** ~ (to sth) extremely physically sensitive to particular substances, medicines, light, etc: *Her skin is hypersensitive.* ▶ **hyper·sen·si·tiv·ity** /ˌhaɪpəˌsensəˈtɪvəti; NAmE -pərˌs-/ noun [U]

**hyper·space** /ˈhaɪpəspeɪs; NAmE -pərs-/ noun [U] **1** (specialist) space that consists of more than three DIMENSIONS **2** (in stories) a situation in which it is possible to travel faster than light

**hyper·ten·sion** /ˌhaɪpəˈtenʃn; NAmE -pərˈt-/ noun [U] (medical) blood pressure that is higher than is normal

**hyper·text** /ˈhaɪpətekst; NAmE -pərt-/ noun [U] text stored in a computer system that contains links that allow the user to move from one piece of text or document to another ⇒ see also HTML

**hyper·thy·roid·ism** /ˌhaɪpəˈθaɪrɔɪdɪzəm; NAmE -pərˈθ-/ noun [U] (medical) a condition in which the THYROID is too active, making the heart and other body systems function too fast

**hyper·trophy** /haɪˈpɜːtrəfi; NAmE -ˈpɜːrt-/ noun [U] (biology) an increase in the size of an organ or TISSUE because its cells grow in size

**hyper·ven·ti·late** /ˌhaɪpəˈventɪleɪt; NAmE -pərˈv-/ verb [I] (specialist) to breathe too quickly because you are very frightened or excited ▶ **hyper·ven·ti·la·tion** /ˌhaɪpəˌventɪ-ˈleɪʃn; NAmE -pərˌv-/ noun [U]

**hy·phen** /ˈhaɪfn/ noun the mark (-) used to join two words together to make a new one, as in *back-up*, to show that a word has been divided between the end of one line and the

| s see | t tea | v van | w wet | z zoo | ʃ shoe | ʒ vision | tʃ chain | dʒ jam | θ thin | ð this | ŋ sing |

# hyphenate

beginning of the next, or to show that sth is missing (as in *short-* and *long-term*) ⊃ compare DASH

**hy·phen·ate** /ˈhaɪfəneɪt/ *verb* ~ sth to join two words together using a hyphen; to divide a word between two lines of text using a hyphen: *Is your name hyphenated?* ▶ **hy·phen·ation** /ˌhaɪfəˈneɪʃn/ *noun* [U]: *hyphenation rules*

**hyp·no·sis** /hɪpˈnəʊsɪs/ *noun* [U] **1** an unconscious state in which sb can still see and hear and can be influenced to follow commands or answer questions: *under ~ She only remembered details of the accident under hypnosis.* **2** = HYPNOTISM: *He uses hypnosis as part of the treatment.* ◊ *Hypnosis helped me give up smoking.*

**hypno·ther·apy** /ˌhɪpnəʊˈθerəpi/ *noun* [U] a kind of treatment that uses HYPNOSIS to help with physical or emotional problems ▶ **hypno·ther·ap·ist** *noun*

**hyp·not·ic** /hɪpˈnɒtɪk/ *NAmE* /-ˈnɑːt-/ *adj.*, *noun*
■ *adj.* **1** making you feel as if you are going to fall asleep, especially because of a regular, repeated noise or movement SYN **mesmerizing**, **soporific**: *hypnotic music ◊ His voice had an almost hypnotic effect.* **2** [only before noun] connected with or produced by hypnosis: *a hypnotic trance/state* **3** (of a drug) making you sleep
■ *noun* (*specialist*) a drug that makes you sleep; a SLEEPING PILL

**hyp·no·tism** /ˈhɪpnətɪzəm/ (*also* **hyp·no·sis**) *noun* [U] the practice of hypnotizing a person (= putting them into an unconscious state)

**hyp·no·tist** /ˈhɪpnətɪst/ *noun* a person who hypnotizes people ▶ WORDFINDER NOTE at TREATMENT

**hyp·no·tize** (*BrE also* **-ise**) /ˈhɪpnətaɪz/ *verb* **1** ~ sb to produce a state of HYPNOSIS in sb **2** [usually passive] ~ sb (*formal*) to interest sb so much that they can think of nothing else SYN **mesmerize**

**hypo-** /ˈhaɪpəʊ, ˌhaɪpə; *BrE also* haɪˈpɒ; *NAmE also* haɪˈpɑː/ (*also* **hyp-** /haɪp/) *prefix* (in adjectives and nouns) under; below normal: *hypodermic ◊ hypothermia* ⊃ compare HYPER-

**hypo·allergen·ic** /ˌhaɪpəʊˌæləˈdʒenɪk/ *NAmE* /-lərˈdʒ-/ *adj.* (*specialist*) **hypoallergenic** substances and materials are unlikely to cause an ALLERGIC reaction in the person who uses them

**hypo·chon·dria** /ˌhaɪpəˈkɒndriə/ *NAmE* /-ˈkɑːn-/ *noun* [U] a state in which sb worries all the time about their health and believes that they are ill when there is nothing wrong with them

**hypo·chon·driac** /ˌhaɪpəˈkɒndriæk/ *NAmE* /-ˈkɑːn-/ *noun* a person who suffers from hypochondria: *Don't be such a hypochondriac!—there's nothing wrong with you.* ▶ **hypo·chon·driac** (*also* **hypo·chon·driacal** /ˌhaɪpəˌkɒnˈdraɪəkl/ *NAmE* /-ˌkɑːn-/) *adj.*

**hyp·oc·risy** /hɪˈpɒkrəsi/ *NAmE* /-ˈpɑːk-/ *noun* (*pl.* **-ies**) [U, C] (*disapproving*) behaviour that does not meet the moral standards or match the opinions that sb claims to have: *He condemned the hypocrisy of those politicians who do one thing and say another.*

**hypo·crite** /ˈhɪpəkrɪt/ *noun* (*disapproving*) a person whose behaviour does not meet the moral standards or match the opinions that they claim to have ▶ **hypo·crit·ical** /ˌhɪpəˈkrɪtɪkl/ *adj.*: *It would be hypocritical of me to have a church wedding when I don't believe in God.* **hypo·crit·ic·al·ly** /-kli/ *adv.*

**hypo·der·mic** /ˌhaɪpəˈdɜːmɪk/ *NAmE* /-ˈdɜːrm-/ (*also* **hypo·dermic ˈneedle**, **hypodermic sy'ringe**) *noun* a medical instrument with a long thin needle that is used to give sb an INJECTION under their skin ▶ **hypo·der·mic** *adj.*: *a hypodermic injection* (= one under the skin)

**hypo·gly·caemia** (*BrE*) (*NAmE* **hypo·gly·cemia**) /ˌhaɪpəʊɡlaɪˈsiːmiə/ *noun* [U] (*medical*) the condition of having too low a level of blood sugar

**hypot·en·use** /haɪˈpɒtənjuːz/ *NAmE* /-ˈpɑːtənuːs/ *noun* (*geometry*) the side opposite the RIGHT ANGLE of a RIGHT-ANGLED TRIANGLE ⊃ picture at TRIANGLE

**hypo·thal·amus** /ˌhaɪpəˈθæləməs/ *noun* (*anatomy*) an area in the central lower part of the brain that controls body temperature, HUNGER and the release of HORMONES

**hypo·ther·mia** /ˌhaɪpəˈθɜːmiə/ *NAmE* /-ˈθɜːrm-/ *noun* [U] a medical condition in which the body temperature is much lower than normal

**hy·poth·esis** /haɪˈpɒθəsɪs/ *NAmE* /-ˈpɑːθ-/ *noun* (*pl.* **hy·poth·eses** /-əsiːz/) **1** [C] an idea or explanation of sth that is based on a few known facts but that has not yet been proved to be true or correct SYN **theory**: *to formulate/confirm a hypothesis ◊ a hypothesis about the function of dreams* ⊃ see also NULL HYPOTHESIS ⊃ WORDFINDER NOTE at SCIENCE **2** [U] guesses and ideas that are not based on certain knowledge SYN **speculation**: *It would be pointless to engage in hypothesis before we have the facts.*

**hy·pothe·size** (*BrE also* **-ise**) /haɪˈpɒθəsaɪz/ *NAmE* /-ˈpɑːθ-/ *verb* [T, I] ~ (sth) | ~ that … (*formal*) to suggest a way of explaining sth when you do not definitely know about it; to form a hypothesis: *The causes can be hypothesized but not proved. ◊ We can only hypothesize that the cases we know about are typical.*

**hypo·thet·ic·al** /ˌhaɪpəˈθetɪkl/ *adj.* based on situations or ideas that are possible and imagined rather than real and true: *a hypothetical question/situation/example ◊ Let us take the hypothetical case of Sheila, a mother of two … ◊ I wasn't asking about anybody in particular—it was a purely hypothetical question.* ▶ **hypo·thet·ic·al·ly** /-kli/ *adv.*

**hypo·thy·roid·ism** /ˌhaɪpəʊˈθaɪrɔɪdɪzəm/ *noun* [U] (*medical*) a condition in which the THYROID is not active enough, making growth and mental development slower than normal

**hyp·ox·aemia** (*BrE*) (*NAmE* **hyp·ox·emia**) /ˌhaɪpɒkˈsiːmiə/ *NAmE* /-pɑːk-/ *noun* [U] (*medical*) a lower than normal amount of OXYGEN in the blood

**hyp·oxia** /haɪˈpɒksiə/ *NAmE* /-ˈpɑːk-/ *noun* [U] (*medical*) a condition in which not enough OXYGEN reaches the body's TISSUES

**hys·ter·ec·tomy** /ˌhɪstəˈrektəmi/ *noun* [C, U] (*pl.* **-ies**) a medical operation to remove a woman's WOMB

**hys·teria** /hɪˈstɪəriə/ *NAmE* /-ˈster-, -ˈstɪr-/ *noun* [U] **1** a state of extreme excitement, fear or anger in which a person, or a group of people, loses control of their emotions and starts to cry, laugh, etc: *There was mass hysteria when the band came on stage. ◊ A note of hysteria crept into her voice.* **2** (*disapproving*) an extremely excited and EXAGGERATED way of behaving or reacting to an event: *the usual media hysteria that surrounds royal visits ◊ public hysteria about AIDS* **3** (*medical*) a condition in which sb experiences violent or extreme emotions that they cannot control, especially as a result of shock

**hys·ter·ic·al** /hɪˈsterɪkl/ *adj.* **1** in a state of extreme excitement, and crying, laughing, etc. without any control: *hysterical screams ◊ a hysterical giggle ◊ He became almost hysterical when I told him. ◊ Let's not get hysterical. ◊ (disapproving) He thought I was being a hysterical female.* **2** (*informal*) extremely funny SYN **hilarious**: *She seemed to find my situation absolutely hysterical.* HELP Some speakers do not pronounce the 'h' at the beginning of **hysterical** and use 'an' instead of 'a' before it. This now sounds old-fashioned. ▶ **hys·ter·ic·al·ly** /-kli/ *adv.*: *to laugh/cry/scream/sob hysterically ◊ hysterically funny*

**hys·ter·ics** /hɪˈsterɪks/ *noun* [pl.] **1** an expression of extreme fear, excitement or anger that makes sb lose control of their emotions and cry, laugh, etc: *He went into hysterics when he heard the news.* **2** (*informal*) wild laughter: *She had the audience in hysterics.*
IDM **have hysterics** (*informal*) to be extremely upset and angry: *My mum'll have hysterics when she sees the colour of my hair.*

**Hz** *abbr.* (in writing) HERTZ

# Ii

**I** /aɪ/ *pron., noun, symbol, abbr.*

- **pron.** used as the subject of a verb when the speaker or writer is referring to himself/herself: *I think I'd better go now.* ◇ *When they asked me if I wanted the job, I said yes.* ◇ *I'm not going to fall, am I?* ◇ *I'm taller than her, aren't I?* ◇ *Jen and I went to London yesterday.* **HELP** In informal spoken English people sometimes say 'Jen and me went …', which is wrong because the subject pronoun **I** is needed in this position. This sometimes leads people to use 'and I' in the phrase 'between you and I', which is also wrong, because the object pronoun **me** is needed after the preposition **between**: *Between you and me …* ⊃ see also ME *pron.*
- **noun** (also **i**) [C, U] (*pl.* **Is, I's, i's** /aɪz/) the 9th letter of the English alphabet: *'Island' begins with (an) I/'I'.* **IDM** see DOT *v.*
- **symbol** (also **i**) the number 1 in ROMAN NUMERALS
- **abbr.** (also **I.**) (especially on maps) Island(s); ISLE

**i-** /aɪ/ *combining form* (*computing*) (in the names of products) INTERACTIVE (= allowing information to be passed continuously and in both directions between a device or piece of software and the person who uses it): *The Oxford iWriter teaches you how to plan and write essays.*

**-ial** /iəl, əl/ *suffix* (in adjectives) typical of: *dictatorial*
▶ **-ially** /iəli, əli/ (in adverbs): *officially*

**iam·bic** /aɪˈæmbɪk/ *adj.* (*specialist*) (of rhythm in poetry) in which one weak or short syllable is followed by one strong or long syllable: *a poem written in iambic pentameters* (= in lines of ten syllables, five short and five long)

**-ian** /iən/, **-an** /ən/ *suffix* **1** (in nouns and adjectives) from; typical of: *Bostonian* ◇ *Brazilian* ◇ *Shakespearian* ◇ *Libran* **2** (in nouns) a specialist in: *mathematician*

**-iana** /iɑːnə; *NAmE also* iænə/, **-ana** /ɑːnə; *NAmE also* ænə/ *suffix* (in nouns) a collection of objects, facts, stories, etc. connected with the person, place, period, etc. mentioned: *Mozartiana* ◇ *Americana* ◇ *Victoriana*

**IB** /ˌaɪ ˈbiː/ *abbr.* INTERNATIONAL BACCALAUREATE™: *to do the IB*

**IBAN** /ˈaɪbæn/ *noun* a bank account number that enables banks in other countries to identify your account so that money can be transferred between your account and accounts in those countries (the abbreviation for 'International Bank Account Number')

**Iber·ian** /aɪˈbɪəriən; *NAmE* -ˈbɪr-/ *adj.* relating to Spain and Portugal: *the Iberian peninsula*

**ibex** /ˈaɪbeks/ *noun* (*pl.* **ibex**) a mountain GOAT with long curved HORNS

**ibid.** /ˈɪbɪd/ (also **ib.**) *abbr.* (in writing) in the same book or piece of writing as the one that has just been mentioned (from Latin 'ibidem')

**-ibility** ⊃ -ABLE

**ibis** /ˈaɪbɪs/ *noun* (*pl.* **ibises**) a bird with a long neck, long legs and a long BEAK that curves downwards, that lives near water

**-ible, -ibly** ⊃ -ABLE

**Ibo** = IGBO

**IBS** /ˌaɪ biː ˈes/ *abbr.* IRRITABLE BOWEL SYNDROME

**ibu·profen** /ˌaɪbjuːˈprəʊfen/ *noun* [U] a drug used to reduce pain and INFLAMMATION

**-ic** /ɪk/ *suffix* **1** (in adjectives and nouns) connected with: *scenic* ◇ *economic* ◇ *Arabic* **2** (in adjectives) that performs the action mentioned: *horrific* ◇ *specific* ▶ **-ical** /ɪkl/ (in adjectives): *comical* **-ically** /ɪkli/ (in adverbs): *physically*

**ICE** /aɪs, ˌaɪ siː ˈiː/ *abbr.* (in a mobile phone contact list) in case of emergency (= the name and number of a person to contact if you are ill, you have an accident, etc.): *You should make sure that you have an ICE number stored in your phone.*

**ice** /aɪs/ *noun, verb*

- **noun 1** [U] water that has frozen and become solid: *The lake was covered with a sheet of ice.* ◇ *My hands are as cold as ice.* ◇ *substantial loss of sea ice in the Arctic Ocean* ⊃ see also ICY, BLACK ICE, DRY ICE **2** [sing.] (*usually* **the ice**) a frozen surface that people SKATE on: **on the ~** *Both teams are on the ice, waiting for the whistle.* ◇ *The dancers came out onto the ice.* **3** [U] a piece of ice used to keep food and drinks cold: *I'll have lemonade please—no ice.* **4** [C] (*old-fashioned, especially BrE*) an ice cream **5** [U] (*NAmE*) a type of sweet food that consists of ice that has been CRUSHED (= broken into very small pieces) and given a sweet taste

**IDM** **break the ˈice** to say or do sth that makes people feel more relaxed, especially at the beginning of a meeting, party, etc. ⊃ see also ICEBREAKER (2) **cut no ˈice (with sb)** to have no influence or effect on sb: *His excuses cut no ice with me.* **on ˈice 1** (of wine, etc.) kept cold by being surrounded by ice **2** (of a plan, etc.) not being dealt with now; waiting to be dealt with at a later time: *We've had to put our plans on ice for the time being.* **3** (of entertainment, etc.) performed by SKATERS on an ICE RINK: *Cinderella on ice* ⊃ more at THIN *adj.*

- **verb** ~ **sth** to cover a cake with ICING ⊃ see also DE-ICE

**PHRV** **ˌice ˈover/ˈup** | **ˌice sth↔ˈover/ˈup** to become covered with ice; to cover sth with ice

**ˈice age** (often **the Ice Age**) *noun* one of the long periods of time, thousands of years ago, when much of the earth's surface was covered in ice

**ˈice axe** (*US usually* **ˈice ax**) *noun* a tool used by people climbing mountains for getting a hold on ice and cutting steps into ice ⊃ picture at AXE

**ice·berg** /ˈaɪsbɜːɡ; *NAmE* -bɜːrɡ/ *noun* an extremely large mass of ice floating in the sea **IDM** see TIP *n.*

**ˌiceberg ˈlettuce** *noun* a type of LETTUCE (= a salad vegetable) with pale green leaves that form a tight ball

**ice·block** /ˈaɪsblɒk; *NAmE* -blɑːk/ *noun* (*AustralE, NZE*) a piece of ice with a sweet taste, served on a stick

**ˌice-ˈblue** *adj.* (especially of eyes) very pale blue in colour

**ˈice-bound** *adj.* surrounded by or covered in ice

**ice·box** /ˈaɪsbɒks; *NAmE* -bɑːks/ *noun* **1** (*BrE*) a separate section in a fridge for making and storing ice **2** (*US, old-fashioned*) a fridge

**ice·break·er** /ˈaɪsbreɪkə(r)/ *noun* **1** a strong ship designed to break a way through ice, for example in the Arctic or Antarctic **2** a thing that you do or say, such as a game or a joke, to make people feel more relaxed, especially at the beginning of a meeting, party, etc.

**ˈice bucket** *noun* a container filled with ice and used for keeping bottles of wine, etc. cold

**ˈice cap** *noun* a layer of ice permanently covering parts of the earth, especially around the North and South Poles

**ˈice chest** (*NAmE*) (*BrE* **ˈcool box**) *noun* a box with thick sides that you put ice in to keep things cold, especially food and drinks

**ˌice-ˈcold** *adj.* **1** as cold as ice; very cold: *ice-cold beer* ◇ *My hands were ice-cold.* **2** not having or showing any emotion: *His eyes had grown ice-cold.*

**ˈice cream** (also **ˌice ˈcream** especially in *BrE*) *noun* [U, C] a type of sweet frozen food made from milk fat, tasting of fruit, chocolate, etc. and often eaten as a DESSERT; a small amount of this food intended for one person, often served in a container made of biscuit that is like a CONE in shape: *Desserts are served with cream or ice cream.* ◇ *Who wants an ice cream?*

**ˈice cube** *noun* a small, usually square, piece of ice used for making drinks cold

**iced** /aɪst/ *adj.* **1** (of drinks) made very cold; containing ice: *iced coffee/tea* **2** (of a cake, etc.) covered with ICING: *an iced cake*

**ˈice dancing** (also **ˈice dance**) *noun* [U] the sport of dancing on ice ▶ **ˈice dancer** *noun*

# iced water

**iced ˈwater** (BrE) (NAmE ˈice water) noun water with ice in it for drinking

**ˈice field** noun a large area of ice, especially one near the North or South Pole

**ˈice floe** (also **floe**) noun a large area of ice, floating in the sea

**ˈice hockey** (BrE) (NAmE **hockey**) noun [U] a game played on ice, in which players use long sticks to hit a hard rubber disc (called a PUCK) into the other team's goal

**ˈice-house** /ˈaɪshaʊs/ noun a building for storing ice in, especially in the past, usually underground or partly underground

**ˈice lolly** (also informal **lolly**) (both BrE) (NAmE **Popˈsicle™**) noun a piece of ice with a sweet taste, served on a stick

**ˈice pack** noun a plastic container filled with ice that is used to cool parts of the body that are injured, etc.

**ˈice pick** noun a tool with a very sharp point for breaking ice with

**ˈice rink** (also **ˈskating rink, rink**) noun a specially prepared flat surface of ice, where you can ice-skate; a building where there is an ice rink

**ˈice sheet** noun (specialist) a layer of ice that covers a large area of land for a long period of time

**ˈice shelf** noun (specialist) a layer of ice that is attached to land and covers a large area of sea

**ˈice skate** (also **skate**) noun a boot with a thin metal BLADE (= sharp edge) on the bottom, that is used for SKATING on ice

**ˈice-skate** verb [I] to SKATE on ice ▶ **ˈice skater** noun

**ˈice skating** noun [U] = SKATING: to go ice skating

**ˈice water** (NAmE) (BrE ˌiced ˈwater) noun water with ice in it for drinking

**icicle** /ˈaɪsɪkl/ noun a pointed piece of ice that is formed when water freezes as it falls down from sth such as a roof ⊃ **WORDFINDER NOTE** AT SNOW

**icily** /ˈaɪsɪli/ adv. in an unfriendly way: 'I have nothing to say to you,' she said icily.

**icing** /ˈaɪsɪŋ/ (especially BrE) (NAmE usually **frosting**) noun [U] a sweet mixture of sugar and water, milk, butter or egg white that is used to cover and decorate cakes
**IDM** **the icing on the ˈcake** (NAmE also **the frosting on the ˈcake**) something extra and not essential that is added to an already good situation or experience and that makes it even better

**ˈicing sugar** (BrE) (US **conˈfectioner's sugar, ˈpowdered ˈsugar**) noun [U] sugar in the form of a fine white powder that is mixed with water to make icing

**icky** /ˈɪki/ adj. (**ickˈier, ickiˈest**) (informal) unpleasant (used especially about sth that is wet and sticky)

**icon** /ˈaɪkɒn; NAmE -kɑːn/ noun **1** a small symbol on a computer or smartphone screen that represents a program or a file: Click on the printer icon with the mouse. ◇ Tap the app icon on your phone to open it. ⊃ **WORDFINDER NOTE** AT FILE **2** a famous person or thing that people admire and see as a symbol of a particular idea, way of life, etc: Madonna and other pop icons of the 1980s ◇ a feminist/gay icon (= sb that feminists/gay people admire) **3** (also **ikon**) (in the Orthodox Church) a painting or statue of a holy person that is also thought of as a holy object

**iconˈic** /aɪˈkɒnɪk; NAmE -ˈkɑːn-/ adj. being a famous person or thing that people admire and see as a symbol of a particular idea, way of life, etc: Dover and the White Cliffs hold iconic status in British history. ◇ an iconic image/building/figure/brand

**iconoˈclast** /aɪˈkɒnəklæst; NAmE -ˈkɑːn-/ noun (formal) a person who criticizes popular beliefs or established customs and ideas

**iconoˈclasˈtic** /aɪˌkɒnəˈklæstɪk; NAmE -ˌkɑːn-/ adj. (formal) criticizing popular beliefs or established customs and ideas ▶ **iconoˈclasm** /aɪˈkɒnəklæzəm; NAmE -ˈkɑːn-/ noun [U]: the iconoclasm of the early Christians

**iconˈogˈraphy** /ˌaɪkəˈnɒɡrəfi; NAmE -ˈnɑːɡ-/ noun [U] the use or study of images or symbols in art

**-ics** /ɪks/ suffix (in nouns) the science, art or activity of: physics ◇ dramatics ◇ athletics

**ICT** /ˌaɪ siː ˈtiː/ noun [U] (BrE) the study of the use of computers, the internet, video, and other technology as a subject at school (the abbreviation for 'information and communications technology')

**ICU** /ˌaɪ siː ˈjuː/ noun intensive care unit (in a hospital) ⊃ **WORDFINDER NOTE** AT HOSPITAL

**icy** /ˈaɪsi/ adj. (**icier, iciest**) **1** very cold **SYN** **freezing**: icy winds/water ◇ My feet were icy cold. **2** covered with ice: icy roads **3** (of a person's voice, manner, etc.) not friendly or kind; showing feelings of dislike or anger: My eyes met his icy gaze. ⊃ see also ICILY ▶ **ˈiciˈness** noun [U]

**ICYMI** abbr. (informal) in case you missed it (used in emails, in text messages, on social media, etc. to bring sb's attention to sth of interest): ICYMI, here's a link to Sunday's podcast.

**ID** /ˌaɪ ˈdiː/ noun, verb
■ noun **1** [U, C] an official way of showing who you are, for example a document with your name, date of birth and often a photograph on it (the abbreviation for 'identity' or 'identification'): You must carry ID at all times. ◇ The police checked IDs at the gate. ◇ **an ID card**: You will need some form of photo ID. **2** [C] IDENTIFICATION: The police need a witness to make a positive ID. ⊃ see also CALLER ID
■ verb (**ID's, ID'ing, ID'd, ID'd**) (informal) **1** ~ sb to identify sb, usually a criminal or a dead body: The police haven't yet managed to ID the suspect. **2** ~ sb to ask sb to show a document that shows proof of their name, age, etc: The security guards ID'd everyone at the entrance to the festival.

**Id** = EID

**I'd** /aɪd/ short form **1** I had **HELP** I'd is only used when had is an auxiliary verb: I'd just missed the bus. When had is the main verb, use the full form: I had a good time at the party. ◇ I'd a good time at the party. **2** I would

**id** /ɪd/ noun (psychology) the part of the unconscious mind where many of a person's basic needs, feelings and desires are supposed to exist ⊃ compare EGO, SUPEREGO

**ˈID card** noun = IDENTITY CARD

**-ide** /aɪd/ suffix (chemistry) (in nouns) a COMPOUND of: chloride

# idea /aɪˈdɪə; NAmE -ˈdiːə/ noun
• PLAN/THOUGHT **1** [C] a plan, thought or suggestion, especially about what to do in a particular situation: It would be a good idea to call before we leave. ◇ That's a great idea! ◇ The surprise party was Jane's idea. ◇ ~for sth He already had an idea for his next novel. ◇ ~ of (doing) sth I like the idea of living on a boat. ◇ We've been toying with the idea of (= thinking about) getting a dog. ◇ Her family expected her to go to college, but she had other ideas. ◇ It might be an idea (= it would be sensible) to try again later. ◇ It seemed like a good idea at the time, and then it all went horribly wrong.
• IMPRESSION **2** [U, sing.] ~(of sth) a picture or an impression in your mind of what sb/sth is like: The brochure should give you a good idea of the hotel. ◇ I had some idea of what the job would be like. ◇ She doesn't seem to have any idea of what I'm talking about. ◇ An evening at home watching TV is not my idea of a good time. ◇ I don't want anyone getting the wrong idea (= getting the wrong impression of sth).
• OPINION **3** [C] an opinion or a belief about sth: ~(about/on sth) He has some very strange ideas about education. ◇ ~that … She rejects the idea that product quality has suffered.
• FEELING **4** [sing.] a feeling that sth is possible or is true: Where on earth did you get that idea? ◇ ~that … What gave you the idea that he'd be here? ◇ ~where, who, etc … I have a pretty good idea where I left it—I hope I'm right.

• AIM 5 B1 **the idea** [sing.] the aim or purpose of sth: *You'll soon get the idea* (= understand). ◊ **~ of (doing) sth** *What's the idea of the game?* ⊃ SYNONYMS at PURPOSE
IDM **give sb i'deas** | **put i'deas into sb's head** to give sb hopes about sth that may not be possible or likely; to make sb act or think in an unreasonable way: *Who's been putting ideas into his head?* **have no i'dea** ⓘ B1 | **not have the faintest, first, etc. idea** ⓘ B1 (*informal*) used to emphasize that you do not know sth: *'What's she talking about?' 'I've no idea.'* ◊ *He hasn't the faintest idea how to manage people.* **have the right i'dea** to have found a very good or successful way of living, doing sth, etc: *He's certainly got the right idea—retiring at 55.* **that's an idea!** (*informal*) used to reply in a positive way to a suggestion that sb has made: *Hey, that's an idea! And we could get a band, as well.* **'that's the idea!** (*informal*) used to encourage people and to tell them that they are doing sth right: *That's the idea! You're doing fine.* **you have no i'dea …** (*informal*) used to show that sth is hard for sb else to imagine: *You've no idea how much traffic there was tonight.* ⊃ more at BUCK *v.*

## ideal ⓘ A2 ⓦ /aɪˈdiːəl/ *adj.*, *noun*

■ *adj.* **1** ⓘ A2 perfect; most suitable: *an ideal location/place* ◊ **~ for sb/sth** *This beach is ideal for children.* ◊ *She's the ideal candidate for the job.* ◊ *The trip to Paris will be an ideal opportunity to practise my French.* ◊ *The prime minister admitted the current situation was 'not ideal'* (= was bad). **2** ⓘ A2 [only before noun] existing only in your imagination or as an idea; not likely to be real: *the search for ideal love* IDM see WORLD ▶ **ideal·ly** /-əli/ *adv.*: *She's ideally suited for this job.* ◊ *Ideally, I'd like to live in New York, but that's not possible.*

■ *noun* **1** ⓘ B2 [C] an idea or standard that seems perfect, and worth trying to achieve or obtain: *political ideals* ◊ *She found it hard to live up to his high ideals.* ◊ *advancing the ideals of freedom and democracy* **2** ⓘ B2 [C, usually sing.] **~ (of sth)** a person or thing that you think is perfect: *It's my ideal of what a family home should be.*

**ideal·ism** /aɪˈdiːəlɪzəm/ *noun* [U] **1** the belief that a perfect life, situation, etc. can be achieved, even when this is not very likely: *He was full of youthful idealism.* **2** (*philosophy*) the belief that our ideas are the only things that are real and that we can know about ⊃ compare MATERIALISM, REALISM ▶ **ideal·ist** *noun*: *He's too much of an idealist for this government.*

**ideal·is·tic** /ˌaɪdiəˈlɪstɪk/ *adj.* having a strong belief in perfect standards and trying to achieve them, even when this is not realistic: *She's still young and idealistic.* ▶ **ideal·is·tic·al·ly** /-kli/ *adv.*

**ideal·ize** (*BrE also* **-ise**) /aɪˈdiːəlaɪz/ *verb* **~ sb/sth** to consider or represent sb/sth as being perfect or better than they really are: *It is tempting to idealize the past.* ◊ *an idealized view of married life* ▶ **ideal·iza·tion**, **-isa·tion** /aɪˌdiːəlaɪˈzeɪʃn; *NAmE* -ləˈz-/ *noun* [U, C]

**idem** /ˈɪdem/ *adv.* (*from Latin*) from the same book, article, author, etc. as the one that has just been mentioned

**ident** /ˈaɪdent/ *noun* (*BrE*) a piece of music or a short film that is broadcast between programmes so that people can recognize a radio station or television channel

**iden·ti·cal** ⓘ+ B2 ⓦ /aɪˈdentɪkl/ *adj.* **1** ⓘ+ B2 similar in every detail: *a row of identical houses* ◊ *The two pictures are similar, although not identical.* ◊ **~ to sb/sth** *Her dress is almost identical to mine.* ◊ **~ with sb/sth** *The name on the ticket should be identical with the one in the passport.* ⊃ LANGUAGE BANK at SIMILARLY **2 the identical** [only before noun] the same: *This is the identical room we stayed in last year.* ▶ **iden·ti·cal·ly** /-kli/ *adv.*: *The children were dressed identically.*

**i,dentical 'twin** *noun* either of two children or animals born from the same mother at the same time who have developed from a single egg. Identical twins are of the same sex and look very similar. ⊃ compare FRATERNAL TWIN

**iden·ti·fi·able** /aɪˌdentɪˈfaɪəbl/ *adj.* that can be recognized: *identifiable characteristics* ◊ *The house is easily identifiable by the large tree outside.* OPP **unidentifiable**

---

785 **identify**

**iden·ti·fi·ca·tion** ⓘ+ C1 ⓦ /aɪˌdentɪfɪˈkeɪʃn/ *noun* **1** ⓘ+ C1 (*abbr.* **ID**) [U, C] the process of showing, proving or recognizing who or what sb/sth is: *The identification of the crash victims was a long and difficult task.* ◊ *Each product has a number for easy identification.* ◊ *an identification number* ◊ *Only one witness could make a positive identification.* ◊ *The hospital had mixed up the patients' identification tags.* ⊃ see also SELF-IDENTIFICATION **2** ⓘ+ C1 [U] the process of recognizing that sth exists, or is important: *The early identification of children with special educational needs is very important.* **3** ⓘ+ C1 (*abbr.* **ID**) [U] official papers or a document that can prove who you are: *Can I see some identification, please?* **4** ⓘ+ C1 [U, C] **~ (with sb/sth)** a strong feeling of sympathy, understanding or support for sb/sth: *her emotional identification with the play's heroine* ◊ *their increasing identification with the struggle for independence* **5** ⓘ+ C1 [U] **~ (of sb) (with sb/sth)** the process of making a close connection between one person or thing and another: *the voters' identification of the Democrats with high taxes*

**i,dentifi'cation card** *noun* (*NAmE*) = IDENTITY CARD

**i,dentifi'cation parade** *noun* (*also informal* **i'dentity parade**) (*both BrE*) (*also* **'line-up** *especially in NAmE*) a row of people, including one person who is suspected of a crime, who are shown to a witness to see if he or she can recognize the suspect

**iden·ti·fier** /aɪˈdentɪfaɪə(r)/ *noun* (*computing*) a series of characters used to refer to a program or set of data within a program

**iden·tify** ⓘ A2 ⓞ /aɪˈdentɪfaɪ/ *verb* (**iden·ti·fies, iden·ti·fy·ing, iden·ti·fied, iden·ti·fied**) **1** ⓘ A2 (*also informal* **ID**) to recognize sb/sth and be able to say who or what they are: **~ sb/sth** *She was able to identify her attacker.* ◊ **~ yourself** *Many of those arrested refused to identify themselves* (= would not say who they were). ◊ **~ sb/sth as sb/sth** *The bodies were identified as those of two suspected drug dealers.* ◊ **~ sb/sth by sth** *two species of waterbirds that can be identified by their distinctive beaks* **2** ⓘ B1 to find or discover sb/sth: **~ sb/sth** *First of all we must identify the problem areas.* ◊ *As yet they have not identified a buyer for the company.* ◊ **~ what, which, etc …** *They are*

▼ SYNONYMS

**identify**

know • recognize • name • make sb/sth out

These words all mean to be able to see or hear sb/sth and especially to be able to say who or what they are.

**identify** to be able to say who or what sb/sth is: *She was able to identify her attacker.*

**know** to be able to say who or what sth is when you see or hear it because you have seen or heard it before
NOTE **Know** is used especially to talk about sounds that seem familiar and when sb recognizes the quality or opportunity that sb/sth represents: *I couldn't see who was speaking, but I knew the voice.* ◊ *She knows a bargain when she sees one.*

**recognize** to know who sb is or what sth is when you see or hear them/it, because you have seen or heard them/it before: *I recognized him as soon as he came in the room.*

**name** to say the name of sb/sth in order to show that you know who/what they are: *The victim has not yet been named.*

**make sb/sth out** to manage to see or hear sb/sth that is not very clear: *I could just make out a figure in the darkness.*

PATTERNS
• to identify/know/recognize sb/sth **by** sth
• to identify/recognize/name sb/sth **as** sb/sth
• to identify/know/recognize/make out **who/what/how …**
• to **easily/barely/just** identify/recognize/make out sb/sth

# Identikit

trying to identify what is wrong with the present system. **3** ~ **sb/sth (as sb/sth)** to make it possible to recognize who or what sb/sth is: *In many cases, the clothes people wear identify them as belonging to a particular social class.* **PHRV** **i'dentify as sth** to recognize or decide that you belong to a particular category **SYN** **self-identify**: *young people who identify as transgender* **i'dentify with sb** to feel that you can understand and share the feelings of sb else **SYN** **sympathize**: *I didn't enjoy the book because I couldn't identify with any of the main characters.* **i'dentify sb with sth** to consider sb to be sth: *He was not the 'tough guy' the public identified him with.* **i'dentify sth with sth** to consider sth to be the same as sth else **SYN** **equate**: *You should not identify wealth with happiness.* **be i'dentified with sb/sth** to be closely connected with sb/sth: *The Church became increasingly identified with opposition to the regime.* **i'dentify yourself with sb/sth** to support sb/sth; to consider yourself to have a special connection with sb/sth: *He identified himself with the common people.*

**Iden·ti·kit™** /aɪˈdentɪkɪt/ (*BrE*) (*NAmE* **composite**) *noun* a picture of a person who is wanted by the police, made by putting together photographs of different features of faces from information that is given by sb who has seen the person

**iden·ti·kit** /aɪˈdentɪkɪt/ *adj.* [only before noun] (*especially BrE, disapproving*) very similar in a way that copies sth else rather than showing original thought: *This historic town will remain unspoilt by identikit coffee houses.* ◊ *Endless identikit Mariahs and Beyoncés were belting out the same old tunes.*

**iden·tity** ❶ **B1** ⓞ /aɪˈdentəti/ *noun* (*pl.* **-ies**) **1** **B1** [C, U] (*abbr.* **ID**) who or what sb/sth is: *The police are trying to discover the identity of the killer.* ◊ *to establish/reveal/confirm the identity of sb/sth* ◊ *Do you have any proof of identity?* ◊ *The thief used a false identity.* ◊ *Each object in the collection has a unique identity number.* ◊ *She went through an identity crisis in her teens* (= was not sure of who she was or of her place in society). ⊃ see also MISTAKEN IDENTITY **2** **B1** [C, U] the characteristics, feelings or beliefs that make people different from others: *national/cultural/personal identity* ◊ *ethnic/racial identity* ◊ *The region's sense of identity remained strong.* ◊ ~ **as sb/sth** *Scotland has never lost its identity as a separate nation.* ⊃ see also GENDER IDENTITY, SELF-IDENTITY **3** [sing., U] ~ **(with sb/sth)** | ~ **(between A and B)** the state or feeling of being very similar to and able to understand sb/sth: ~ **between A and B** *There's a close identity between fans and their team.*

**i'dentity card** (*also* **I'D card**) (*NAmE also* **i'dentifi·cation card**) *noun* a card with a person's name, date of birth, photograph, etc. on it that proves who they are

**i'dentity parade** *noun* (*BrE, informal*) = IDENTIFICATION PARADE

**i'dentity politics** *noun* [U + *sing./pl. v.*] political positions that are based on the social groups that people see themselves as belonging to, for example based on religion, race or social background, rather than on traditional political parties

**i'dentity theft** (*also* **i'dentity fraud**) *noun* [U, C] using sb else's name and personal information in order to obtain credit cards and other goods or to take money out of the person's bank accounts ▶ **i'dentity thief** *noun*

**ideo·gram** /ˈɪdiəɡræm/ (*also* **ideo·graph** /ˈɪdiəɡrɑːf; *NAmE* -ɡræf/) *noun* **1** a symbol that is used in a writing system, for example Chinese, to represent the idea of a thing, rather than the sounds of a word **2** (*specialist*) a sign or a symbol used to

**ideo·logic·al** **B2** /ˌaɪdiəˈlɒdʒɪkl; *NAmE* -ˈlɑːdʒ-/ *adj.* (*sometimes disapproving*) based on or connected with an IDEOLOGY: *ideological differences* ◊ *This was rejected for ideological reasons.* ◊ *His agenda has been purely ideological.* ▶ **ideo·logic·al·ly** /-kli/ *adv.*: *ideologically correct* ◊ *Particular films may be ideologically driven.*

# ideograms

Chinese character for 'soil'

Roman numeral representing three

wheelchair access sign

**ideo·logue** /ˈaɪdiəlɒɡ; *NAmE* -lɔːɡ/ (*also* **ideolo·gist** /ˌaɪdiˈɒlədʒɪst; *NAmE* -ˈɑːl-/) *noun* (*formal, sometimes disapproving*) a person whose actions are influenced by belief in a set of principles (= by an ideology)

**ideol·ogy** **C1** /ˌaɪdiˈɒlədʒi; *NAmE* -ˈɑːl-/ *noun* [C, U] (*pl.* **-ies**) (*sometimes disapproving*) **1** **C1** a set of ideas that an economic or political system is based on: *Marxist/capitalist ideology* **2** **C1** a set of beliefs, especially one held by a particular group, that influences the way people behave: *the ideology of gender roles* ◊ *alternative ideologies*

**ides** /aɪdz/ *noun* [pl.] the middle day of the month in the ancient Roman system, from which other days were calculated: *the ides of March*

**idi·ocy** /ˈɪdiəsi/ *noun* (*pl.* **-ies**) (*formal*) **1** [U] very stupid behaviour; the state of being very stupid **SYN** **stupidity** **2** [C] a very stupid act, remark, etc: *the idiocies of bureaucracy*

**idiom** /ˈɪdiəm/ *noun* **1** [C] a group of words whose meaning is different from the meanings of the individual words: *'Let the cat out of the bag' is an idiom meaning to tell a secret by mistake.* ⊃ SYNONYMS at WORD **2** [U, C] (*formal*) the kind of language and grammar used by particular people at a particular time or place **3** [U, C] (*formal*) the style of writing, music, art, etc. that is typical of a particular person, group, period or place: *the classical/contemporary/popular idiom*

**idiom·at·ic** /ˌɪdiəˈmætɪk/ *adj.* **1** containing expressions that are natural to a NATIVE SPEAKER of a language: *She speaks fluent and idiomatic English.* **2** containing an idiom: *an idiomatic expression* ▶ **idiom·at·ic·al·ly** /-kli/ *adv.*

**idio·syn·crasy** /ˌɪdiəˈsɪŋkrəsi/ *noun* (*pl.* **-ies**) a person's particular way of behaving, thinking, etc., especially when it is unusual; an unusual feature **SYN** **eccentricity**: *The car has its little idiosyncrasies.* ▶ **idio·syn·crat·ic** /ˌɪdiəsɪŋˈkrætɪk/ *adj.*: *His teaching methods are idiosyncratic but successful.*

**idiot** **C1** /ˈɪdiət/ *noun* **1** **C1** (*informal*) a very stupid person **SYN** **fool**: *When I lost my passport, I felt such an idiot.* ◊ *Not that switch, you idiot!* ⊃ see also VILLAGE IDIOT **2** (*old-fashioned, offensive*) a person with very low intelligence who cannot think or behave normally

**idi·ot·ic** /ˌɪdiˈɒtɪk; *NAmE* -ˈɑːt-/ *adj.* very stupid **SYN** **ridiculous**: *an idiotic question* ◊ *Don't be so idiotic!* ▶ **idi·ot·ic·al·ly** /-kli/ *adv.*

**idiot sav·ant** /ˌiːdiəʊ sæˈvɒ̃; *NAmE* -ˈvɑː/ *noun* (*pl.* **idiot sav·ants** *or* **idiots sav·ants** /ˌiːdiəʊ sæˈvɒ̃; *NAmE* -ˈvɑː/) (*from French*) a person who has severe LEARNING DIFFICULTIES, but who has an unusually high level of ability in a particular skill, for example in art or music, or in remembering things

**IDK** (*also* **idk**) /ˌaɪ diː ˈkeɪ/ *abbr.* (*informal*) (on SOCIAL MEDIA, in text messages, etc.) I don't know: *IDK what to do about it.*

**idle** /ˈaɪdl/ *adj., verb*
■ *adj.* **1** (*disapproving*) (of people) not working hard **SYN** **lazy**: *an idle student* **2** (of machines, factories, etc.) not in use: *to lie/stand/remain idle* **3** (of people) without work **SYN** **unemployed**: *Over ten per cent of the workforce is now idle.* **4** [usually before noun] with no particular purpose or effect: *idle chatter/curiosity* ◊ *It was just an idle threat* (= not serious). ◊ *It is idle to pretend that their marriage is a success.* **5** [usually before noun] (of time) not spent doing work or sth particular: *In idle moments, he carved wooden figures.* ▶ **idle·ness** *noun* [U]: *After a period of enforced idleness, she found a new job.*

■ **verb 1** [T, I] to spend time doing nothing important: ~ sth (+ adv./prep.) *They idled the days away, talking and watching television.* ◊ (+ adv./prep.) *They idled along by the river* (= walked slowly and with no particular purpose). **2** [I] (of an engine) to run slowly while the vehicle is not moving SYN **tick over:** *She left the car idling at the roadside.* **3** [T] ~ **sb/sth** (*NAmE*) to close a factory, etc. or stop providing work for the workers, especially temporarily: *The strikes have idled nearly 4000 workers.*

> ▼ **HOMOPHONES**
>
> **idle • idol** /ˈaɪdl/
> - **idle** *adj.*: *They haven't been idle since their first success—they still work hard.*
> - **idol** *noun*: *His bedroom is plastered with pictures of his screen idol Grace Kelly.*

**idler** /ˈaɪdlə(r)/ *noun* (*disapproving*) a person who is lazy and does not work SYN **loafer**

**idli** /ˈɪdli/ *noun* an Indian rice cake cooked using STEAM (= gas produced when water boils)

**idly** /ˈaɪdli/ *adv.* without any particular reason, purpose or effort; doing nothing: *She sat in the sun, sipping a cool drink.* ◊ *He wondered idly what would happen.* ◊ *We can't stand idly by* (= do nothing) *and let people starve.*

**idol** /ˈaɪdl/ *noun* **1** a person or thing that is loved and admired very much: *a pop/teen idol* ◊ *the idol of countless teenagers* ◊ *a fallen idol* (= sb who is no longer popular) ⊃ see also MATINEE IDOL ⊃ HOMOPHONES at IDLE **2** (*often disapproving*) a statue that is WORSHIPPED as a god

**idol·atry** /aɪˈdɒlətri; *NAmE* -ˈdɑːl-/ *noun* [U] (*often disapproving*) **1** the practice of WORSHIPPING statues as gods **2** (*formal*) too much love or praise for sb/sth: *football fans whose support for their team borders on idolatry* ▸ **idol·atrous** /-trəs/ *adj.*

**idol·ize** (*BrE also* **-ise**) /ˈaɪdəlaɪz/ *verb* (*sometimes disapproving*) ~ **sb** to admire or love sb very much, possibly too much SYN **worship**: *a pop star idolized by millions of fans* ◊ *They idolize their kids.* ▸ **idol·iza·tion, -isa·tion** /ˌaɪdəlaɪˈzeɪʃn; *NAmE* -ləˈz-/ *noun* [U]

**idyll** /ˈɪdɪl; *NAmE* ˈaɪdl/ *noun* **1** (*literary*) a happy and peaceful place, event or experience, especially one connected with the countryside **2** (*specialist*) a short poem or other piece of writing that describes a peaceful and happy scene

**idyl·lic** /ɪˈdɪlɪk; *NAmE* aɪ-/ *adj.* peaceful and beautiful; perfect, without problems: *a house set in idyllic surroundings* ◊ *to lead an idyllic existence* ◊ *The cottage sounds idyllic.* ▸ **idyl·lic·al·ly** /-kli/ *adv.*: *a house idyllically set in wooded grounds*

**i.e.** /ˌaɪ ˈiː/ *abbr.* used to explain exactly what the previous thing that you have mentioned means (from Latin 'id est'): *the basic essentials of life, i.e. housing, food and water*

> ▼ **LANGUAGE BANK**
>
> **i.e.**
> Explaining what you mean
> - Some poems are mnemonics, **i.e.** they are designed to help you remember something.
> - Some poems are mnemonics, **that is to say**, they are designed to help you remember something.
> - Mnemonic poems, **that is** poems designed to help you remember something, are an excellent way to learn lists.
> - A limerick's rhyme scheme is A–A–B–B–A. **In other words**, the first, second, and fifth lines all rhyme with one another, while the third and fourth lines have their own rhyme.
> - In this exercise the reader is encouraged to work out the meaning, **or rather** the range of meanings, of the poem.
> - This is a poem about death, **or, more precisely**, dying.
> - He says his poems deal with 'the big issues', **by which he means** love, loss, grief and death.
> ⊃ LANGUAGE BANK at ABOUT

**-ie** ⊃ -Y

---

**IED** /ˌaɪ iː ˈdiː/ *noun* a bomb made and used by people who are not members of the military forces of a country (the abbreviation for 'improvised explosive device')

**IELTS** /ˈaɪelts/ *abbr.* International English Language Testing System (a test that measures a person's ability to speak and write English at the level that is necessary to go to university in the UK, Ireland, Australia, Canada, South Africa and New Zealand)

**if** ❶ A1 /ɪf/ *conj., noun*

■ *conj.* **1** A1 used to say that one thing can, will or might happen or be true, depending on another thing happening or being true: *If you see him, give him this note.* ◊ *I'll only stay if you offer me more money.* ◊ *If necessary I can come at once.* ◊ *You can stay for the weekend if you like.* ◊ *If anyone calls, tell them I'm not at home.* ◊ *If he improved his IT skills, he'd* (= he would) *easily get a job.* ◊ *You would know what was going on if you'd* (= you had) *listened.* ◊ *They would have been here by now if they'd caught the early train.* ◊ *If I was in charge, I'd do things differently.* ◊ (*rather formal*) *If I were in charge …* **2** A1 when; whenever; every time: *If metal gets hot it expands.* ◊ *She glares at me if I go near her desk.* **3** A1 used after *ask, know, find out, wonder,* etc. to introduce one of two or more possibilities SYN **whether**: *Do you know if he's married?* ◊ *I wonder if I should wear a coat or not.* ◊ *He couldn't tell if she was laughing or crying.* ◊ *Listen to the tune and see if you can remember the words.* **4** A1 used after verbs or adjectives expressing feelings: *I am sorry if I disturbed you.* ◊ *I'd be grateful if you would keep it a secret.* ◊ *Do you mind if I turn the TV off?* **5** B1 used to admit that sth is possible, but to say that it is not very important: *If she has any weakness, it is her Italian.* ◊ *So what if he was late. Who cares?* **6** B1 used to ask sb to listen to your opinion: *If you ask me, she's too scared to do it.* ◊ *If you think about it, those children must be at school by now.* ◊ *If you remember, Mary was always fond of animals.* **7** used before an adjective to introduce a contrast: *He's a good player, if a little over-confident.* ◊ *We'll only do it once—if at all.* **8** (*formal*) used with *will* or *would* to ask sb politely to do sth: *If you will sit down for a few moments, I'll tell the manager you're here.* ◊ *If you would care to leave your name, we'll contact you as soon as possible.* **9** used before *could, may* or *might* to suggest sth or to interrupt sb politely: *If I may make a suggestion, perhaps we could begin a little earlier next week.*
IDM **if and ˈwhen** used to say sth about an event that may or may not happen: *If and when we ever meet again I hope he remembers what I did for him.* **if ˈanything** used to express an opinion about sth, or after a negative statement to suggest that the opposite is true: *I'd say he was more like his father, if anything.* ◊ *She's not thin—if anything she's on the plump side.* **if I were ˈyou** B1 used to give sb advice: *If I were you I'd start looking for another job.* **if ˈnot 1** used to introduce a different suggestion, after a sentence with *if*: *I'll go if you're going. If not* (= if you are not), *I'd rather stay at home.* **2** used after a *yes/no* question to say what will or should happen if the answer is 'no': *Are you ready? If not, I'm going without you.* ◊ *Do you want that cake? If not, I'll have it.* **3** used to suggest that sth may be even larger, more important, etc. than was first stated: *They cost thousands if not millions of pounds to build.* **if ˈonly** B2 used to say that you wish sth was true or that sth had happened: *If only I were rich.* ◊ *If only I knew her name.* ◊ *If only he'd remembered to send that letter.* ◊ *If only I had gone by taxi.* **if ˈso** if that is the case: *Do you do research in your studies? If so, what research methods do you use?* **it's not as ˈif** used to say that sth that is happening is surprising: *I'm surprised they've invited me to their wedding—it's not as if I know them well.* **ˈonly if** (*rather formal*) used to state the only situation in which sth can happen: *Only if a teacher has given permission is a student allowed to leave the room.* ◊ *Only if the red light comes on is there any danger to employees.* ⊃ more at EVEN *adv.*

■ *noun* (*informal*) a situation that is not certain: *If he wins—and it's a big if—he'll be the first Englishman to win for fifty* years. ◊ There are still a lot of **ifs and buts** before everything's settled.

> ▼ **GRAMMAR POINT**
>
> **if / whether**
>
> • Both **if** and **whether** are used in reporting questions which expect 'yes' or 'no' as the answer: *She asked if/ whether I wanted a drink.*, although **whether** sounds more natural with particular verbs such as **discuss**, **consider** and **decide**. When a choice is offered between alternatives, **if** or **whether** can be used: *We didn't know if/whether we should write or phone.* In this last type of sentence, **whether** is usually considered more formal and more suitable for written English.

**iff** /ɪf/ *conj.* (*mathematics*) an expression used in mathematics to mean 'if and only if'

**iffy** /ˈɪfi/ *adj.* (*informal*) **1** (*especially BrE*) not in perfect condition; bad in some way: *That meat smells a bit iffy to me.* **2** not certain: *The weather looks slightly iffy.*

**-ify** /faɪ/, **-fy** /faɪ/ *suffix* (in verbs) to make or become: *purify* ◊ *solidify*

**Igbo** (*also* **Ibo**) /ˈiːbəʊ/ *noun* [U] a language spoken by the Igbo people of West Africa, especially in south-east Nigeria

**igloo** /ˈɪɡluː/ *noun* (*pl.* **-oos**) a small round house or shelter built from blocks of hard snow by the Inuit people of northern North America and Greenland

**ig·ne·ous** /ˈɪɡniəs/ *adj.* (*geology*) (of rocks) formed when MAGMA (= melted or liquid material lying below the earth's surface) becomes solid, especially after it has poured out of a VOLCANO

**ig·nite** /ɪɡˈnaɪt/ *verb* [I, T] (*formal*) to start to burn; to make sth start to burn: *Gas ignites very easily.* ◊ (*figurative*) *Tempers ignited when the whole family spent Christmas together.* ◊ **~ sth** *Flames melted a lead pipe and ignited leaking gas.* ◊ (*figurative*) *His words ignited their anger.*

**ig·ni·tion** /ɪɡˈnɪʃn/ *noun* **1** [C, usually sing.] the electrical system of a vehicle that makes the fuel begin to burn to start the engine; the place in a vehicle where you start this system: *to turn the ignition on/off* ◊ *to put the key in the ignition* **2** [U] (*specialist*) the action of starting to burn or of making sth burn: *The flames spread to all parts of the house within minutes of ignition.*

**ig·noble** /ɪɡˈnəʊbl/ *adj.* (*formal*) not good or honest; that should make you feel shame SYN **base**: *ignoble thoughts* ◊ *an ignoble person* OPP **noble**

**ig·no·min·ious** /ˌɪɡnəˈmɪniəs/ *adj.* (*formal*) that makes, or should make, you feel ashamed SYN **disgraceful**, **humiliating**: *an ignominious defeat* ◊ *He made one mistake and his career came to an ignominious end.* ▶ **ig·no·min·ious·ly** *adv.*

**ig·no·miny** /ˈɪɡnəmɪni/ *noun* [U] (*formal*) public shame and loss of honour SYN **disgrace**: *They suffered the ignominy of defeat.*

**ig·nor·amus** /ˌɪɡnəˈreɪməs/ *noun* (*usually humorous*) a person who does not have much knowledge: *When it comes to music, I'm a complete ignoramus.*

**ig·nor·ance** /ˈɪɡnərəns/ *noun* [U] a lack of knowledge or information about sth: *They fought a long battle against prejudice and ignorance.* ◊ **~ of/about sth** *widespread ignorance about the disease* ◊ **in ~ of sth** *She was kept in ignorance of her husband's activities.* ◊ **out of/ through ~** *Children often behave badly out of ignorance.* ⊃ EXPRESS YOURSELF at KNOW
IDM **ignorance is ˈbliss** (*saying*) if you do not know about sth, you cannot worry about it: *Some doctors believe ignorance is bliss and don't give their patients all the facts.* ⊃ more at BLISSFUL

**ig·nor·ant** /ˈɪɡnərənt/ *adj.* **1** (*often disapproving*) not having or showing much knowledge or information about things; not educated: *an ignorant person/question* ◊ *Never make your students feel ignorant.* **2** not having any knowledge or information about a particular thing: **~ of sth** *At that time I was ignorant of events going on elsewhere.* ◊ **~ about sth** *He's ignorant about modern technology.* **3** (*informal, disapproving*) with very bad manners SYN **uncouth**: *a rude, ignorant person* ▶ **ig·nor·ant·ly** *adv.*

**ig·nore** /ɪɡˈnɔː(r)/ *verb* **1 ~ sth** to pay no attention to sth SYN **disregard**: *He ignored all the 'No Smoking' signs and lit up a cigarette.* ◊ *I made a suggestion but they chose to ignore it.* ◊ *We cannot afford to ignore their advice.* ◊ *We can't ignore the fact that there is a huge problem here.* **2 ~ sb** to pretend that you have not seen sb or that sb is not there: *She ignored him and carried on with her work.* OPP **acknowledge**

**iguana** /ɪˈɡwɑːnə/ *noun* a large tropical American LIZARD (= a type of REPTILE)

**ike·bana** /ˌɪkɪˈbɑːnə, ˌɪkeɪ-/ *noun* [U] (*from Japanese*) Japanese flower arranging, that has strict formal rules

**ikon** = ICON (3)

**il-** *prefix* ⊃ IN-

**ileum** /ˈɪliəm/ *noun* (*pl.* **ilea** /-liə/) (*anatomy*) the third part of the small INTESTINE ⊃ compare DUODENUM, JEJUNUM ▶ **ileal** /-əl/ *adj.*

**ilk** /ɪlk/ *noun* [usually sing.] (*sometimes disapproving*) type; kind: *the world of media people and their ilk* ◊ *I can't stand him, or any others of that ilk.*

**I'll** /aɪl/ *short form* **1** I shall **2** I will

**ill** /ɪl/ *adj., adv., noun*
■ *adj.* **1** (*especially BrE*) (*NAmE usually* **sick**) [not usually before noun] suffering from an illness or disease; not feeling well: *Her father is seriously ill in St Luke's hospital.* ◊ *chronically ill patients* ◊ *Uncle Harry is terminally ill with cancer* (= he will die from his illness). ◊ *the mentally ill* (= people with a mental illness). ◊ *She was taken ill suddenly.* ◊ *We both started to feel ill shortly after the meal.* ◊ (*formal*) *He fell ill and died soon after.* ⊃ see also ILLNESS ⊃ WORD-FINDER NOTE at MEDICINE **2** [only before noun] bad or harmful: *She suffered no ill effects from the experience.* ⊃ see also ILL HEALTH, ILL WILL **3** (*formal*) that brings, or is thought to bring, bad luck: *a bird of ill omen*
IDM **ill at ˈease** feeling uncomfortable and embarrassed: *I felt ill at ease in such formal clothes.* **it's an ˌill ˈwind (that blows nobody any good)** (*saying*) no problem is so bad that it does not bring some advantage to sb ⊃ more at FEELING
■ *adv.* **1** (especially in compounds) badly or in an unpleasant way: *The animals had been grossly ill-treated.* **2** (*formal*) badly; not in an acceptable way: *They live in an area ill served by public transport.* **3** (*formal*) only with difficulty: *We're wasting valuable time, time we can ill afford.*
IDM **speak/think ˈill of sb** (*formal*) to say or think bad things about sb: *Don't speak ill of the dead.* ⊃ more at BODE
■ *noun* **1** [pl.] people who are ill: *Even the seriously ill cannot get tests done immediately.* **2** [usually pl.] (*formal*) a problem or harmful thing; an illness: *social/economic ills* ◊ *the ills of the modern world* **3** [U] (*literary*) harm; bad luck: *I may not like him, but I wish him no ill.*

**ill-adˈvised** *adj.* not sensible; likely to cause difficulties in the future: *Her remarks were ill-advised, to say the least.* ◊ *You would be ill-advised to travel on your own.* ⊃ compare WELL ADVISED ▶ **ill-adˈvised·ly** *adv.*

**ill-asˈsort·ed** *adj.* (of a group of people or things) not seeming right or suitable for each other: *They seem an ill-assorted couple.*

**ill-ˈbred** *adj.* rude or badly behaved, especially because you have not been taught how to behave well OPP **well bred**

**ill-conˈcealed** *adj.* (*formal*) (of feelings or expressions of feeling) not hidden well from other people

**ill-conˈceived** *adj.* badly planned or designed

**ill-conˈsid·ered** *adj.* not carefully thought about or planned

**ill-deˈfined** *adj.* **1** not clearly described: *an ill-defined role* **2** not clearly marked or easy to see: *an ill-defined path* OPP **well defined**

**ill-dis·posed** adj. ~ **(towards sb)** (formal) not feeling friendly towards sb OPP **well disposed**

**il·legal** B1 /ɪˈliːgl/ adj., noun
- adj. B1 not allowed by the law: *illegal immigrants/aliens* ◊ *She promised to crack down on illegal immigration.* ◊ *dealing in illegal drugs* ◊ **it is ~ (for sb) to do sth** *It's illegal to drive through a red light.* OPP **legal** ▸ **il·legal·ly** /-gəli/ adv.: *an illegally parked car* ◊ *He entered the country illegally.*
- noun (especially NAmE) a person who lives or works in a country illegally

**il·legal·ity** /ˌɪliˈɡæləti/ noun (pl. -ies) **1** [U] the state of being illegal: *No illegality is suspected.* **2** [C] an illegal act ⊃ compare LEGALITY

**il·legible** /ɪˈledʒəbl/ (also **un·read·able**) adj. difficult or impossible to read: *an illegible signature* OPP **legible** ▸ **il·legibly** /-bli/ adv.

**il·legit·im·ate** /ˌɪləˈdʒɪtəmət/ adj. **1** born to parents who are not married to each other **2** (formal) not allowed by a particular set of rules or by law SYN **unauthorized**: *illegitimate use of company property* OPP **legitimate** ▸ **il·legit·im·acy** /-məsi/ noun [U] **il·legit·im·ate·ly** adv.

**ill-eˈquipped** adj. ~ **(for sth)** | ~ **(to do sth)** not having the necessary equipment or skills

**ill-ˈfated** (also less frequent **fated**) adj. (formal) not lucky and ending sadly, especially in death or failure: *an ill-fated expedition*

**ill-ˈfitting** adj. not the right size or shape: *ill-fitting clothes*

**ill-ˈfounded** adj. (formal) not based on fact or truth: *All our fears proved ill-founded.* OPP **well founded**

**ill-ˈgotten** adj. (old-fashioned or humorous) obtained dishonestly or unfairly: *ill-gotten gains* (= money that was not obtained fairly)

**ill ˈhealth** noun [U] the poor condition of a person's body or mind: *He retired early on grounds of ill health.* ⊃ SYNONYMS at ILLNESS

**ill ˈhumour** (US **ill ˈhumor**) noun [U, C] (literary) a bad mood OPP **good humour** ▸ **ill-ˈhumoured** (US **ill-ˈhumored**) adj.

**il·lib·eral** /ɪˈlɪbərəl/ adj. (formal) not allowing much freedom of opinion or action SYN **intolerant**: *illiberal policies*

**il·licit** /ɪˈlɪsɪt/ adj. **1** not allowed by the law SYN **illegal**: *illicit drugs* **2** not approved of by the normal rules of society: *an illicit love affair* ▸ **il·licit·ly** adv.

**ill-inˈformed** adj. having or showing little knowledge of sth OPP **well informed**

**il·lit·er·ate** /ɪˈlɪtərət/ adj., noun
- adj. **1** (of a person) not knowing how to read or write OPP **literate 2** (of a document or letter) badly written, as if by sb without much education **3** (usually after a noun or adverb) not knowing very much about a particular subject area: *computer illiterate* ◊ *musically illiterate* ▸ **il·lit·er·acy** /-rəsi/ noun [U]
- noun a person who is illiterate

**ill-ˈjudged** adj. (formal) that has not been carefully thought about; not appropriate in a particular situation

**ill-ˈmannered** adj. (formal) not behaving well or politely in social situations SYN **rude** OPP **well mannered**

**ill·ness** A2 /ˈɪlnəs/ noun **1** A2 [U] the state of being physically or mentally ill: *mental illness* ◊ *The virus can cause illness in humans.* ◊ *I missed a lot of school through illness last year.* **2** A2 [C] a type or period of illness: *serious/severe/chronic illnesses* ◊ *a terminal illness* ◊ *childhood illnesses* ◊ *He died after a long illness.* ◊ *She suffers from a debilitating illness.* ⊃ SYNONYMS at DISEASE ⊃ WORDFINDER NOTE at DISEASE

**il·logic·al** /ɪˈlɒdʒɪkl; NAmE ɪˈlɑːdʒ-/ adj. not sensible or thought out in a logical way: *illogical behaviour/arguments* ◊ *She has an illogical fear of insects.* OPP **logical** ▸ **il·logic·al·ity** /ˌɪlɒdʒɪˈkæləti; NAmE ɪˌlɑːdʒ-/ noun [U, C] (pl. -ies) **il·logic·al·ly** /ɪˈlɒdʒɪkli; NAmE ɪˈlɑːdʒ-/ adv.

**ill-ˈomened** /ˌɪl ˈəʊmənd/ adj. (formal) (of an event or activity) seeming likely to be unlucky or unsuccessful because there are a lot of unlucky signs relating to it

---

# illusion

▼ SYNONYMS

**illness**
sickness • ill health • trouble

These are all words for the state of being physically or mentally ill.

**illness** the state of being physically or mentally ill

**sickness** illness; bad health: *I recommend you get insurance against sickness and unemployment.*

**ILLNESS OR SICKNESS?**
**Sickness** is used especially in contexts concerning work and insurance. It is commonly found with words such as *pay*, *leave*, *absence* and *insurance*. **Illness** has a wider range of uses and is found in more general contexts.

**ill health** (rather formal) the state of being physically ill or having lots of health problems: *She resigned because of ill health.* NOTE **Ill health** often lasts a long period of time.

**trouble** illness or pain: *heart trouble.* NOTE When **trouble** is used with this meaning, it is necessary to say which part of the body is affected.

**PATTERNS**
- **chronic** illness/sickness/ill health
- to **suffer from** illness/sickness/ill health/heart, etc. trouble

---

**ill-preˈpared** adj. **1** ~ **(for sth)** not ready, especially because you were not expecting sth to happen: *The team was ill-prepared for a disaster on that scale.* **2** badly planned or organized: *an ill-prepared speech*

**ill-ˈstarred** adj. (formal) not lucky and likely to bring unhappiness or to end in failure: *an ill-starred marriage*

**ill-ˈtempered** adj. (formal) angry and rude or annoyed, especially when this seems unreasonable

**ill-ˈtimed** adj. done or happening at the wrong time: *an ill-timed visit* OPP **well timed**

**ill-ˈtreat** verb ~ **sb** to treat sb in a cruel or unkind way ▸ **ill-ˈtreatment** noun [U]: *the ill-treatment of prisoners*

**il·lu·min·ate** /ɪˈluːmɪneɪt/ verb **1** ~ **sth** (formal) to shine light on sth: *Floodlights illuminated the stadium.* ◊ *The earth is illuminated by the sun.* **2** ~ **sth** (formal) to make sth clearer or easier to understand SYN **clarify**: *This text illuminates the philosopher's early thinking.* **3** ~ **sth** to decorate a street, building, etc. with bright lights for a special occasion **4** ~ **sth** (literary) to make a person's face, etc. seem bright and excited SYN **light up**: *Her smile illuminated her entire being.*

**il·lu·min·ated** /ɪˈluːmɪneɪtɪd/ adj. [usually before noun] **1** lit with bright lights: *the illuminated city at night* **2** (of books, etc.) decorated with gold, silver and bright colours in a way that was done in the past, by hand: *illuminated manuscripts*

**il·lu·min·at·ing** /ɪˈluːmɪneɪtɪŋ/ adj. helping to make sth clear or easier to understand: *We didn't find the examples he used particularly illuminating.*

**il·lu·min·ation** /ɪˌluːmɪˈneɪʃn/ noun **1** [U, C] light or a place that light comes from: *The only illumination in the room came from the fire.* **2 illuminations** [pl.] (BrE) bright coloured lights used to decorate a town or building for a special occasion: *Christmas illuminations* **3** [C, usually pl.] a coloured decoration, usually painted by hand, in an old book **4** [U] (formal) understanding or explanation of sth: *spiritual illumination*

**ill-ˈused** adj. (old-fashioned or formal) badly treated; badly used

**il·lu·sion** B2 /ɪˈluːʒn/ noun **1** B2 [C, U] a false idea or belief, especially about sb or about a situation: **under the ~ that…** *She's under the illusion that* (= believes wrongly that) *she'll get the job.* ◊ **~ about sth** *The new president has no illusions about the difficulties facing her country* (= she knows that the country has serious problems). ◊ *He could*

# illusionist 790

*no longer distinguish between illusion and reality.* **2** [C] something that seems to exist but in fact does not, or seems to be sth that it is not: *Mirrors in a room often give an illusion of space.* ◇ *The idea of absolute personal freedom is an illusion.* ⊃ picture at OPTICAL ILLUSION

**il·lu·sion·ist** /ɪˈluːʒənɪst/ *noun* a person who performs tricks that seem strange or impossible to believe

**il·lu·sive** /ɪˈluːsɪv/ *adj. (literary)* not real although seeming to be **SYN** *illusory*: *There is an illusive sense of depth.* **HELP** *Illusive* is sometimes confused with *elusive*, which has a different meaning.

**il·lu·sory** /ɪˈluːsəri/ *adj. (formal)* not real, although seeming to be: *an illusory sense of freedom*

**il·lus·trate** /ˈɪləstreɪt/ *verb* **1** to use pictures, photographs, diagrams, etc. in a book, etc: *~sth She illustrated her own books.* ◇ *~sth with sth His lecture was illustrated with photos taken during the expedition.* **2** to make the meaning of sth clearer by using examples, pictures, etc: *~sth To illustrate my point, let me tell you a little story.* ◇ *~sth with sth Each topic is illustrated with concrete examples of economic practice.* ◇ *~how, what, etc… Here's an example to illustrate what I mean.* ⊃ LANGUAGE BANK at PROCESS¹ **3** *~sth | ~how, what, etc… | ~that…* to show that sth is true or that a situation exists **SYN** *demonstrate*: *The incident illustrates the need for better security measures.*

▼ **LANGUAGE BANK**

### illustrate

Referring to a chart, graph or table

- This bar chart **illustrates** how many journeys people made on public transport over a three-month period.
- This table **compares** bus, train, and taxi use between April and June.
- The results **are shown** in the chart below.
- In this pie chart, the survey results **are broken down** by age.
- This pie chart **breaks down** the survey results by age.
- **As can be seen from** these results, younger people use buses more than older people.
- **According to** these figures, bus travel accounts for 60% of public transport use.
- **From** the data in the above graph, **it is apparent that** buses are the most widely used form of public transport.

⊃ LANGUAGE BANK at EVIDENCE, FALL, INCREASE, PROPORTION, SURPRISING

**il·lus·trated** /ˈɪləstreɪtɪd/ *adj.* (of a book, newspaper, etc.) containing pictures: *an illustrated textbook* ◇ *a beautifully/lavishly illustrated work*

**il·lus·tra·tion** /ˌɪləˈstreɪʃn/ *noun* **1** [C] a drawing or picture in a book, magazine, for decoration or to explain sth: *50 full-colour illustrations* ◇ *~by sb a volume of Chaucer with illustrations by Edward Burne-Jones* **2** [U] the process of illustrating sth: *the art of book illustration* **3** [C, U] a story, an event or an example that clearly shows the truth about sth: *The statistics are a clear illustration of the point I am trying to make.* ◇ *Let me, by way of illustration, quote from one of her poems.* ⊃ SYNONYMS at EXAMPLE

**il·lus·tra·tive** /ˈɪləstrətɪv, -streɪt-; *NAmE* ɪˈlʌstrətɪv/ *adj. (formal)* helping to explain sth or show it more clearly **SYN** *explanatory*: *an illustrative example*

**il·lus·tra·tor** /ˈɪləstreɪtə(r)/ *noun* a person who draws or paints pictures for books, etc.

**il·lus·tri·ous** /ɪˈlʌstriəs/ *adj. (formal)* very famous and much admired, especially because of what you have achieved **SYN** *distinguished*: *The composer was one of many illustrious visitors to the town.* ◇ *a long and illustrious career*

**ill 'will** *noun* [U] bad and unkind feelings towards sb: *I bear Sue no ill will.*

**im-** ⊃ IN-

**IM** /ˌaɪ ˈem/ *noun, verb*
■ *noun (informal)* = INSTANT MESSAGE, INSTANT MESSAGING
■ *verb* [T, I] (IMs, IMing, IM'd, IM'd) *~(sb) | ~sb sth (informal)* = INSTANT-MESSAGE

**I'm** /aɪm/ *short form* I am

**image** /ˈɪmɪdʒ/ *noun* **1** [C] a picture, photograph or statue that represents sb/sth: *Most simple leaflets will include text and images.* ◇ *We already have more than 22 000 digital images on file.* ◇ *~of sb/sth Images of deer and hunters decorate the cave walls.* ◇ *a wooden image of the Hindu god Ganesh* ⊃ see also GRAVEN IMAGE **2** [C] a picture of sb/sth seen in a mirror, through a camera, or on a television, computer, phone, etc: *He stared at his own image reflected in the water.* ◇ *Slowly, an image began to appear on the screen.* ◇ *~from sth Police will study the images from CCTV cameras.* ◇ *~of sth The camera captured an image of the suspect and his car.* ⊃ see also MIRROR IMAGE **3** [C, U] the impression that a person, an organization, a product, etc. gives to the public: *His public image is very different from the real person.* ◇ *Image is very important in the music world.* ◇ *It was years before the country was able to project an image of stability again.* ◇ *The campaign aims to create a new image for the city.* ◇ *The company changed its name on the advice of an image consultant.* **4** [C] a mental picture that you have of what sb/sth is like or looks like: *images of the past* ◇ *I had a mental image of what she would look like.* ⊃ see also BODY IMAGE, SELF-IMAGE **5** [C] a word or phrase used with a different meaning from its normal one, in order to describe sth in a way that produces a strong picture in the mind: *poetic images of the countryside* ⊃ WORDFINDER NOTE at POETRY

**WORDFINDER** alliteration, euphemism, figure of speech, hyperbole, metaphor, metonymy, onomatopoeia, paradox

**IDM** **be the image of sb/sth** to look very like sb/sth else: *He's the image of his father.* ⊃ see also SPITTING IMAGE

**im·agery** /ˈɪmɪdʒəri/ *noun* [U] **1** language that produces pictures in the minds of people reading or listening: *poetic imagery* ⊃ see also METAPHOR **2** *(formal)* pictures, photographs, etc: *satellite imagery* (= for example, photographs of the earth taken from space)

**im·agin·able** /ɪˈmædʒɪnəbl/ *adj.* **1** used with superlatives, and with *all* and *every*, to emphasize that sth is the best, worst, etc. that you can imagine, or includes every possible example: *The house has the most spectacular views imaginable.* ◇ *They stock every imaginable type of pasta.* **2** possible to imagine: *These technological developments were hardly imaginable 30 years ago.*

**im·agin·ary** /ɪˈmædʒɪnəri; *NAmE* -neri/ *adj.* existing only in your mind or imagination: *The equator is an imaginary line around the middle of the earth.* ◇ *an imaginary friend* ◇ *We must listen to their problems, real or imaginary.*

**im·agin·ation** /ɪˌmædʒɪˈneɪʃn/ *noun* **1** [U, C] the ability to create pictures in your mind; the part of your mind that does this: *a vivid/fertile imagination* ◇ *He has no imagination.* ◇ *It doesn't take much imagination to guess what she meant.* ◇ *I won't tell you his reaction—I'll leave that to your imagination.* ◇ *Don't let your imagination run away with you* (= don't use too much imagination). ◇ *The new policies appear to have captured the imagination of the public* (= they find them interesting and exciting) ◇ *in your~ Nobody hates you—it's all in your imagination.* ◇ *(informal) Use your imagination!* (= used to tell sb that they will have to guess the answer to the question they have asked you, usually because it is obvious or embarrassing) **2** [U] something that you have imagined rather than sth that exists: *She was no longer able to distinguish between imagination and reality.* ◇ *Is it my imagination or have you lost a lot of weight?* **3** [U] *(approving)* the ability to have new and exciting ideas: *His writing lacks imagination.* ◇ *With a little imagination, you could turn this place into a palace.*

**IDM** **leave nothing/little to the imagiˈnation** (of clothes) to allow more of sb's body to be seen than usual: *Her tight-*

*fitting dress left nothing to the imagination.* ⇨ more at STRETCH *n.*

**im·agina·tive** /ɪˈmædʒɪnətɪv/ *adj.* (*approving*) having or showing new and exciting ideas **SYN** **inventive**: *an imaginative approach/idea/child* ◇ *recipes that make imaginative use of seasonal vegetables* **OPP** **unimaginative** ▶ **im·agina·tive·ly** *adv.*: *The stables have been imaginatively converted into offices.*

**im·agine** 🔑 **A1** /ɪˈmædʒɪn/ *verb* **1** **A1** [T, I] to form a picture in your mind of what sth might be like: *~ sth The house was just as she had imagined it.* ◇ *Imagine my surprise when I opened the door to find him standing there.* ◇ *It's hard to imagine a more cynical political strategy.* ◇ *~ (that) … Close your eyes and imagine (that) you are in a forest.* ◇ *~ what, how, etc … Can you imagine what it must be like to lose your job after 20 years?* ◇ *~ doing sth Imagine earning that much money!* ◇ *~ sb/sth doing sth I can just imagine him saying that!* ◇ *~ sb/sth to be/do sth I had imagined her to be older than that.* ◇ *~ sb/sth/yourself (as) sth He loved to imagine himself as the hero.* ◇ (*informal*) *'He was furious.' 'I can imagine.'* **2** 🔑 **A2** [T] to believe sth that is not true: *~ (that) … He's always imagining (that) we're talking about him behind his back.* ◇ *~ sth There's nobody there. You're imagining things.* **3** 🔑 **B1** [T] to think that sth is probably true **SYN** **suppose**, **assume** ⇨ EXPRESS YOURSELF at SPECULATE: *'Can we still buy tickets for the concert?' 'I imagine so.'* ◇ *~ (that) … I don't imagine (that) they'll refuse.*

▼ SYNONYMS

**imagine**
think • see • envisage • envision

These words all mean to form an idea in your mind of what sb/sth might be like.

**imagine** to form an idea in your mind of what sb/sth might be like: *The house was just as she had imagined it.*

**think** to imagine sth that might happen or might have happened: *We couldn't think where you'd gone.* ◇ *Just think —this time tomorrow we'll be lying on a beach.*

**see** to consider sth as a future possibility; to imagine sb as sth: *I can't see her changing her mind.* ◇ *His colleagues see him as a future director.*

**envisage** (*especially BrE*) to imagine what will happen in the future: *I don't envisage working with him again.* **NOTE** The usual word for this in American English is **envision** (see below).

**envision** to imagine what a situation will be like in the future, especially a situation that you intend to work towards: *They envision an equal society, free from poverty and disease.* **NOTE** **Envision** is used especially in business and political contexts. In North American English it is also used in the same way as **envisage**: *I don't envision working with him again.*

PATTERNS
- to imagine/see/envisage/envision sb/sth **as** sth
- to imagine/see/envisage/envision (sb) **doing** sth
- to imagine/think/see/envisage/envision **who/what/how** …
- to imagine/think/envisage/envision **that** …

**im·aging** /ˈɪmɪdʒɪŋ/ *noun* [U] (*computing*) the process of capturing, storing and showing an image on a computer screen: *imaging software* ⇨ see also THERMAL IMAGING

**im·agin·ings** /ɪˈmædʒɪnɪŋz/ *noun* [pl.] things that you imagine, that exist only in your mind

**imam** /ɪˈmɑːm/ *noun* (in Islam) **1** a religious man who leads the prayers in a MOSQUE **2** **Imam** the title of a religious leader

**IMAX™** /ˈaɪmæks/ *noun* **1** [U] technology that allows films to be shown on extremely large screens **2** [C] a cinema or screen that uses IMAX

**im·bal·ance** /ɪmˈbæləns/ *noun* [C, U] a situation in which two or more things are not the same size or are not treated the same, in a way that is unfair or causes problems: *~ (in/of sth) a global imbalance of/in power* ◇ *~ (between*

A and B) *Attempts are being made to redress* (= put right) *the imbalance between our import and export figures.*

**im·be·cile** /ˈɪmbəsiːl; *NAmE* -sl/ *noun* **1** a rude way to describe a person that you think is very stupid **SYN** **idiot**: *They behaved like imbeciles.* **2** (*old-fashioned, offensive*) a person who has a very low level of intelligence ▶ **im·be·cile** (*also* **im·be·cil·ic** /ˌɪmbəˈsɪlɪk/) *adj.* [usually before noun]: *imbecile remarks* **im·be·cil·ity** /-ləti/ *noun* [U, C]

**imbed** = EMBED

**im·bibe** /ɪmˈbaɪb/ *verb* **1** [I, T] ~ (sth) (*formal or humorous*) to drink sth, especially alcohol **2** [T] ~ sth (*formal*) to receive and understand ideas or information

**im·bizo** /ɪmˈbiːzəʊ; *SAfrE* [ɪmˈbiːzɔ] *noun* (*pl.* -os) (*SAfrE*) a meeting, especially one between politicians and members of the public, that is held in order to discuss general issues or a particular problem: *a government imbizo on poverty* ◇ *The minister of labour will be holding an imbizo with farmers in the area.*

**im·bongi** /ɪmˈbɒŋɡi; *NAmE* -ˈbɔːŋ-/ *SAfrE* [ɪmˈbɔːŋɡi] *noun* (*pl.* **iim·bongi** *or* **izim·bongi** /ˌɪzɪmˈbɒŋɡi/; *NAmE* -ˈbɔːŋ-/ *or* **im·bongis**) (*SAfrE*) (in traditional African society) a person who writes and performs poems praising an important figure

**im·bro·glio** /ɪmˈbrəʊliəʊ/ *noun* (*pl.* -os) (*formal*) a complicated, confused or embarrassing situation that causes many problems, especially in politics

**imbue** /ɪmˈbjuː/ *verb* [often passive] (*formal*) to fill sb/sth with strong feelings, opinions or values **SYN** **infuse**: *be imbued with sth Her voice was imbued with an unusual seriousness.* ◇ *He was imbued with a desire for social justice.*

**IMF** /ˌaɪ em ˈef/ *abbr.* International Monetary Fund (the organization within the United Nations that is concerned with trade and economic development)

**IMHO** (*also* **imho**) /ˌaɪ em eɪtʃ ˈəʊ/ *abbr.* (*often humorous*) in my humble opinion (used especially in emails, in text messages, on social media, etc. when you give your opinion about sth): *IMHO this film is a classic.* ⇨ compare IMO

**imi·tate** /ˈɪmɪteɪt/ *verb* **1** ~ sb/sth to copy sb/sth: *Her style of painting has been imitated by other artists.* ◇ *Art imitates Nature.* ◇ *Teachers provide a model for children to imitate.* ◇ *No computer can imitate the complex functions of the human brain.* **2** ~ sb to copy the way a person speaks or behaves, in order to make people laugh **SYN** **mimic**: *She knew that the girls used to imitate her and laugh at her behind her back.*

**imi·ta·tion** /ˌɪmɪˈteɪʃn/ *noun* **1** [C] a copy of sth, especially sth expensive: *a poor/cheap imitation of the real thing* ◇ *This latest production is a pale imitation of the original* (= it is not nearly as good). ◇ *imitation leather/pearls* ⇨ SYNONYMS at ARTIFICIAL **2** [U] the act of copying sb/sth: *A child learns to talk by imitation.* ◇ **in ~ of sb/sth** *Many corporate methods have been adopted by American managers in imitation of Japanese practice.* **3** [C] an act of copying the way sb talks and behaves, especially to make people laugh **SYN** **impersonation, impression**: *He does an imitation of Donald Trump.*

**imi·ta·tive** /ˈɪmɪtətɪv; *NAmE* -teɪt-/ *adj.* (*formal, sometimes disapproving*) that copies sb/sth: *movies that encourage imitative crime* ◇ *His work has been criticized for being imitative and shallow.*

**imi·ta·tor** /ˈɪmɪteɪtə(r)/ *noun* a person or thing that copies sb/sth else: *The band's success has inspired hundreds of would-be imitators.*

**im·macu·late** /ɪˈmækjələt/ *adj.* **1** perfectly clean and tidy, with no marks or FLAWS **SYN** **spotless**: *She always looks immaculate.* ◇ *an immaculate uniform/room* **2** containing no mistakes or faults **SYN** **perfect**: *an immaculate performance* ▶ **im·macu·late·ly** *adv.*: *immaculately dressed*

**the Im·maculate Con'ception** *noun* [sing.] (*religion*) the Roman Catholic belief that the Virgin Mary's soul was free from ORIGINAL SIN from the moment of her CONCEPTION

# immanent

**im·man·ent** /ˈɪmənənt/ *adj.* (*formal*) present as a natural part of sth; present everywhere

**im·ma·ter·ial** /ˌɪməˈtɪəriəl; *NAmE* -ˈtɪr-/ *adj.* **1** [not usually before noun] not important in a particular situation **SYN** **irrelevant**: *The cost is immaterial.* ◇ *~ to sb/sth It is immaterial to me whether he stays or goes.* **2** (*formal*) not having a physical form: *an immaterial God* **OPP** **material**

**im·ma·ture** /ˌɪməˈtjʊə(r); *NAmE* -ˈtʃʊr, -ˈtʊr/ *adj.* **1** behaving in a way that is not sensible and is typical of people who are much younger: *immature behaviour* ⊃ **WORDFINDER NOTE** at YOUNG **2** not fully developed or grown: *immature plants* **OPP** **mature** ▶ **im·ma·tur·ity** /ˌɪməˈtjʊərəti; *NAmE* -ˈtʃʊr-, -ˈtʊr-/ *noun* [U]

**im·meas·ur·able** /ɪˈmeʒərəbl/ *adj.* (*formal*) too large, great, etc. to be measured: *to cause immeasurable harm* ▶ **im·meas·ur·ably** /-bli/ *adv.*: *Housing standards improved immeasurably after the war.* ◇ *Stress has an immeasurably more serious effect on our lives than we realize.*

**im·me·di·acy** /ɪˈmiːdiəsi/ *noun* [U] (*formal*) **1** the quality in sth that makes it seem as if it is happening now, close to you, and is therefore important and requires attention quickly: *the immediacy of threat* ◇ *Email lacks the immediacy of online chat.* **2** lack of delay; speed: *Our aim is immediacy of response to emergency calls.*

**im·me·di·ate** ❶ **B1** ⓦ /ɪˈmiːdiət/ *adj.* **1** **B1** happening or done without delay **SYN** **instant**: *an immediate reaction/response* ◇ *to take immediate action* ◇ *RAM stores information for immediate access.* **2** **B2** [usually before noun] existing now and needing attention quickly: *Our immediate concern is to help the families of those who died.* ◇ *The report focuses on some of the more immediate problems facing us.* ◇ *The hospital says she's out of immediate danger.* **3** **B2** [only before noun] next to or very close to a particular place or time: *in the immediate vicinity* ◇ *in the immediate aftermath of the war* ◇ *The prospects for the immediate future are good.* ◇ *my immediate predecessor in the job* (= the person who had the job just before me) **4** [only before noun] nearest in relationship or rank: *The funeral was attended by her immediate family* (= her parents, children, brothers and sisters) *only.* ◇ *He is my immediate superior* (= the person directly above me) *in the company.* **5** [only before noun] having a direct effect: *The immediate cause of death is unknown.* **IDM** **with immediate effect** (*formal*) starting now: *She has resigned with immediate effect.*

**im·me·di·ate·ly** ❶ **A2** /ɪˈmiːdiətli/ *adv., conj.*
■ *adv.* **1** **A2** without delay **SYN** **at once**: *She answered almost immediately.* ◇ *They immediately began arguing.* ◇ *The point of my question may not be immediately apparent.* **2** **B2** (usually with prepositions) next to or very close to a particular place or time: *Turn right immediately after the church.* ◇ *the years immediately before the war* ◇ *the period immediately following her birth* **3** **B2** (usually with past participles) closely and directly: *Counselling is being given to those most immediately affected by the tragedy.*
■ *conj.* (*especially BrE*) as soon as: *Immediately she'd gone, I remembered her name.*

**im·me·mor·ial** /ˌɪməˈmɔːriəl/ *adj.* (*formal or literary*) that has existed for longer than people can remember: *an immemorial tradition* ◇ *My family has lived in this area from time immemorial* (= for a very long time).

**im·mense** **B2+** **C1** /ɪˈmens/ *adj.* extremely large or great **SYN** **enormous**: *There is still an immense amount of work to be done.* ◇ *The benefits are immense.* ◇ *a project of immense importance*

**im·mense·ly** /ɪˈmensli/ *adv.* extremely; very much **SYN** **enormously**: *immensely popular/difficult/grateful* ◇ *We enjoyed ourselves immensely.*

**im·mens·ity** /ɪˈmensəti/ *noun* [U] the large size of sth: *the immensity of the universe* ◇ *We were overwhelmed by the sheer immensity of the task.*

**im·merse** /ɪˈmɜːs; *NAmE* ɪˈmɜːrs/ *verb* **1** *~ sb/sth (in sth)* to put sb/sth into a liquid, especially so that they or it are completely covered* ⊃ **WORDFINDER NOTE** at LIQUID **2** *to become or make sb completely involved in sth: ~ yourself in sth She immersed herself in her work.* ◇ **be immersed in sth** *Clare and Phil were immersed in conversation in the corner.*

**im·mer·sion** /ɪˈmɜːʃn; *NAmE* ɪˈmɜːrʒn/ *noun* [U] **1** *~ (in sth)* the act of putting sb/sth into a liquid, especially so that they or it are completely covered; the state of being covered by a liquid: *Immersion in cold water resulted in rapid loss of heat.* ◇ *baptism by total immersion* (= putting the whole body underwater) **2** *~ (in sth)* the state of being completely involved in sth: *his long immersion in politics* ◇ *The course offers the opportunity for* **total immersion** *in the language and culture.* ◇ *a five-week French immersion program* (= in which the student will hear and use only French)

**imˈmersion heater** *noun* (*BrE*) a device that provides hot water for a house by heating water in a tank

**im·mer·sive** /ɪˈmɜːsɪv; *NAmE* ɪˈmɜːrs-/ *adj.* (of a game, performance, work of art, etc.) that seems to surround the player or viewer so they feel totally involved in the experience, often by using THREE-DIMENSIONAL computer images: *Immersive games can be used for training and education.*

**im·mi·grant** ❶ **B1** /ˈɪmɪɡrənt/ *noun* a person who has come to live permanently in a different country from the one they were born in: *illegal/undocumented immigrants* ◇ *~ from … immigrants from other European countries* ◇ *~ to … immigrants to the United States* ◇ *immigrant workers/communities/groups* ⊃ compare EMIGRANT, MIGRANT ⊃ see also LANDED IMMIGRANT

▼ **SYNONYMS**

**immigrant**
migrant • refugee • asylum seeker • expatriate

These words all describe people who have moved to a different country.

**immigrant** a person who has either chosen or been forced to leave their country and come to live permanently in a different country: *immigrants from other European countries*

**migrant** a person who moves from one place to another in order to find work or better living conditions: *The country has a large seasonal migrant population.*

**refugee** a person who has been forced to leave their country or home, because there is a war or for political, religious or social reasons: *There has been a steady flow of refugees from the war zone.*

**asylum seeker** a person who has been forced to leave their own country because they are in danger and who arrives in another country asking to be allowed to stay there: *to provide accommodation and support for asylum seekers*

**expatriate** a person living in a country that is not their own, usually by choice: *American expatriates in Paris*

**IMMIGRANT, MIGRANT, REFUGEE OR ASYLUM SEEKER?**
An **immigrant** has either chosen or been forced to leave their own country and move to another. A **refugee** has been forced to leave their own country. An **asylum seeker** has been forced to leave their own country and has arrived in another country asking to be allowed to stay. A **migrant** moves to another country, or within their own country, especially to find work or better living conditions.

**PATTERNS**
- **illegal/undocumented** immigrants/migrants
- **economic/skilled** migrants
- **political** refugees

**im·mi·grate** /ˈɪmɪɡreɪt/ *verb* [I] *~ (to …) (from …)* (*especially NAmE*) to come and live permanently in a country after leaving your own country ⊃ compare EMIGRATE

**im·mi·gra·tion** **B2+** **B2** /ˌɪmɪˈɡreɪʃn/ *noun* [U] **1** **B2** the process of coming to live permanently in a country that is not your own; the number of people who do this: *illegal/*

*legal immigration* ◇ *~from/into ... laws restricting immigration into the US* ◇ *immigration policy/reform* ⊃ compare EMIGRATION **2** ¶+ B2 (*also* **immi·gra·tion con'trol**) the place at a port, an airport, etc. where the passports and other documents of people coming into a country are checked: *to go through immigration* ◇ *immigration officers* ⊃ WORDFINDER NOTE at AIRPORT

**im·mi·nent** ¶+ C1 /'ɪmɪnənt/ *adj.* (especially of sth unpleasant) likely to happen very soon: *the imminent threat of invasion* ◇ *The system is in imminent danger of collapse.* ◇ *An announcement about his resignation is imminent.* ▶ **im·mi·nence** /-nəns/ *noun* [U]: *the imminence of death* **im·mi·nent·ly** *adv.*

**im·mo·bile** /ɪ'məʊbaɪl; NAmE -bl/ *adj.* **1** not moving SYN **motionless**: *She stood immobile by the window.* **2** unable to move: *His illness has left him completely immobile.* OPP **mobile** ▶ **im·mo·bil·ity** /ˌɪməʊ'bɪləti/ *noun* [U]

**im·mo·bil·ize** (*BrE also* **-ise**) /ɪ'məʊbəlaɪz/ *verb* ~ **sth/sb** to prevent sth/sb from moving or from working normally: *a device to immobilize the car engine in case of theft* ◇ *Always immobilize a broken leg immediately.* ▶ **im·mo·bil·iza·tion, -isa·tion** /ɪˌməʊbəlaɪ'zeɪʃn; NAmE -lə'z-/ *noun* [U]

**im·mo·bil·izer** (*BrE also* **-iser**) /ɪ'məʊbəlaɪzə(r)/ *noun* a device that is fitted to a car to stop it moving if sb tries to steal it

**im·mod·er·ate** /ɪ'mɒdərət/ NAmE ɪ'mɑːd-/ *adj.* [usually before noun] (*formal, disapproving*) extreme; not reasonable SYN **excessive**: *immoderate drinking* OPP **moderate** ▶ **im·mod·er·ate·ly** *adv.*

**im·mod·est** /ɪ'mɒdɪst; NAmE ɪ'mɑːd-/ *adj.* **1** (*disapproving*) having or showing a very high opinion of yourself and your abilities SYN **conceited 2** (of behaviour or clothing) that may shock people because it involves sex or attracts attention in a sexual way: *an immodest dress* OPP **modest**

**im·mo·late** /'ɪməleɪt/ *verb* ~ **sb/yourself** (*formal*) to kill sb/ yourself by burning them/yourself ▶ **im·mol·ation** /ˌɪmə'leɪʃn/ *noun* [U]

**im·moral** /ɪ'mɒrəl; NAmE ɪ'mɔːr-/ *adj.* **1** (of people and their behaviour) not considered to be good or honest by most people: *It's immoral to steal.* ◇ *There's nothing immoral about wanting to earn more money.* **2** not following accepted standards of sexual behaviour: *an immoral act/life/person* ◇ *They were charged with living off immoral earnings* (= money earned by working as a PROSTITUTE). ⊃ compare AMORAL, MORAL ▶ **im·mor·al·ity** /ˌɪmə'ræləti/ *noun* [U, C] (*pl.* **-ies**): *the immorality of war* ◇ *a life of immorality* **im·mor·al·ly** /ɪ'mɒrəli; NAmE ɪ'mɔːr-/ *adv.*

**im·mor·tal** /ɪ'mɔːtl; NAmE ɪ'mɔːrtl/ *adj., noun*
■ *adj.* **1** that lives or lasts forever: *The soul is immortal.* OPP **mortal 2** famous and likely to be remembered forever: *the immortal Goethe* ◇ *In the immortal words of Henry Ford, 'If it ain't broke, don't fix it'.*
■ *noun* **1** a person who is so famous that they will be remembered forever: *She is one of the Hollywood immortals.* **2** a god or other being who is believed to live forever

**im·mor·tal·ity** /ˌɪmɔː'tæləti; NAmE ˌɪmɔːr't-/ *noun* [U] the state of living or lasting forever: *belief in the immortality of the soul* ◇ *He is well on his way to showbusiness immortality.*

**im·mor·tal·ize** (*BrE also* **-ise**) /ɪ'mɔːtəlaɪz; NAmE ɪ'mɔːrt-/ *verb* ~ **sb/sth (in sth)** to prevent sb/sth from being forgotten in the future, especially by mentioning them in literature, making films about them, painting them, etc: *The poet fell in love with her and immortalized her in his verse.*

**im·mov·able** (*also less frequent* **im·move·able**) /ɪ'muːvəbl/ *adj.* **1** [usually before noun] that cannot be moved: *an immovable object* **2** (of a person or an opinion, etc.) impossible to change or persuade: *On this issue he is completely immovable.*

**im·mune** ¶+ B2 /ɪ'mjuːn/ *adj.* [not usually before noun] **1** ¶+ B2 ~ **(to sth)** that cannot catch or be affected by a particular disease or illness: *Adults are often immune to German measles.* **2** ¶+ C1 ~ **(to sth)** not affected by sth, especially sth that you might expect to be harmful: *You'll eventually become immune to criticism.* **3** ¶+ C1 ~ **(from sth)** protected from sth and therefore able to avoid it SYN **exempt**: *No one should be immune from prosecution.*

**im'mune response** *noun* (*biology*) the reaction of the body to the presence of an ANTIGEN (= a substance that can cause disease)

**im'mune system** *noun* the system in your body that produces substances to help it fight against infection and disease

**im·mun·ity** /ɪ'mjuːnəti/ *noun* (*pl.* **-ies**) **1** [U] the body's ability to avoid or not be affected by infection and disease: ~ **(to sth)** *immunity to infection* ◇ ~ **against sth** *The vaccine provides longer immunity against flu.* ⊃ WORDFINDER NOTE at DISEASE **2** [U] ~ **(to sth)** the state of not being affected by sth, especially sth that you might expect to be harmful: *the president's seeming immunity to criticism* **3** [U, C] ~ **(from sth)** the state of being protected from sth: *The spies were all granted immunity from prosecution.* ◇ *parliamentary/congressional immunity* (= protection against particular laws that is given to politicians) ◇ *Officials of all member states receive certain privileges and immunities.* ⊃ see also DIPLOMATIC IMMUNITY

**im·mun·ize** (*BrE also* **-ise**) /'ɪmjunaɪz/ *verb* ~ **sb/sth (against sth)** to protect a person or an animal from a disease, especially by giving them an INJECTION of a VACCINE ⊃ compare INOCULATE, VACCINATE ▶ **im·mun·iza·tion, -isa·tion** /ˌɪmjunaɪ'zeɪʃn; NAmE -nə'z-/ *noun* [U, C]: *an immunization programme to prevent epidemics*

**im·muno·defi·ciency** /ˌɪmjuːnəʊdɪ'fɪʃnsi/ (*also* **im·mune de'ficiency**) *noun* [U] a medical condition in which your body does not have the normal ability to resist infection: *human immunodeficiency virus or HIV*

**im·mun·ology** /ˌɪmju'nɒlədʒi/ NAmE -'nɑːl-/ *noun* [U] the scientific study of protection against disease ▶ **im·muno·logic·al** /ˌɪmjunə'lɒdʒɪkl; NAmE -'lɑːdʒ-/ *adj.*

**im·muno·sup·pres·sion** /ˌɪmjunəʊsə'preʃn/ *noun* [U] (*medical*) the act of stopping the body from reacting against ANTIGENS, for example in order to prevent the body from rejecting a new organ ▶ **im·muno·sup·pres·sant** /-'presnt/ *noun*

**im·mut·able** /ɪ'mjuːtəbl/ *adj.* (*formal*) that cannot be changed; that will never change SYN **unchangeable** ▶ **im·mut·abil·ity** /ɪˌmjuːtə'bɪləti/ *noun* [U]

**IMO** (*also* **imo**) /ˌaɪ em 'əʊ/ *abbr.* in my opinion (used especially in emails, in text messages, on social media, etc. when you give your opinion about sth): *It's a nice performance, not among his best, IMO.* ⊃ compare IMHO

**imp** /ɪmp/ *noun* **1** (in stories) a small creature like a little man, that has magic powers and behaves badly **2** a child who behaves badly, but not in a serious way

**im·pact** ⓘ B1 ⓞ *noun, verb*
■ *noun* /'ɪmpækt/ [C, usually sing., U] **1** ¶ B1 the powerful effect that sth has on sb/sth: *a positive/a negative/an adverse impact* ◇ *a significant/major/huge impact* ◇ *to have/make an impact* ◇ ~ **of sth** *to reduce/minimize the impact of sth* ◇ *the environmental impact of tourism* ◇ ~ **of doing sth** *the economic impact of leaving the European Union* ◇ ~ **on sb/sth** *Her speech made a profound impact on everyone.* ◇ ~ **of sth on sb/sth** *The report assesses the impact of the disease on mortality and population growth.* ⊃ see also LOW-IMPACT **2** ¶ B2 the act of one object hitting another; the force with which this happens: *craters made by meteorite impacts* ◇ *The impact of the blow knocked Jack off balance.* ◇ **on~** *The bomb explodes on impact* (= when it hits sth). ◇ *The car is fitted with side impact bars* (= to protect it from a blow from the side).
■ *verb* /ɪm'pækt/ **1** ¶ B1 [I, T] to have an effect on sb/sth SYN **affect**: ~ **on/upon sb/sth** *Her father's death impacted greatly on her childhood years.* ◇ ~ **sth** *environmental factors that may negatively impact children's development* **2** [I, T] ~ **(on/upon/with) sth** (*formal*) to hit sth with great force

**im·pact·ed** /ɪm'pæktɪd/ *adj.* (of a tooth) that cannot grow correctly because it is under another tooth

# impactful

**im·pact·ful** /ɪmˈpæktfl/ *adj.* having a major impact or effect: *It was a hugely impactful advertising campaign.*

**im·pair** /ɪmˈpeə(r); *NAmE* -ˈper/ *verb* ~ **sth** (*formal*) to damage sth or make sth worse ⊃ SYNONYMS at DAMAGE

**im·paired** /ɪmˈpeəd; *NAmE* -ˈperd/ *adj.* damaged or not functioning normally: *impaired vision/memory* ◇ *the problems faced by people who are visually impaired*

**im·pair·ment** /ɪmˈpeəmənt; *NAmE* -ˈperm-/ *noun* [U, C] (*specialist*) the state of having a physical or mental condition that means that part of your body or brain does not work correctly; a particular condition of this sort: *impairment of the functions of the kidney* ◇ *visual impairments*

**im·pala** /ɪmˈpɑːlə/ *noun* (*pl.* **im·pala** or **im·palas**) an African ANTELOPE with curly HORNS

**im·pale** /ɪmˈpeɪl/ *verb* **1** ~ **sth** (**on sth**) to push a sharp pointed object through sth SYN **spear**: *She impaled a lump of meat on her fork.* **2** ~ **sb / yourself on sth** if you **impale** yourself on sth, or **are impaled** on it, you have a sharp pointed object pushed into you and you may be caught somewhere by it: *He had fallen and been impaled on some iron railings.*

**im·panel** = EMPANEL

**im·part** /ɪmˈpɑːt; *NAmE* -ˈpɑːrt/ *verb* (*formal*) **1** ~ **sth** (**to sb**) to pass information, knowledge, etc. to other people SYN **convey 2** ~ **sth** (**to sth**) to give a particular quality to sth SYN **lend**: *The spice imparts an Eastern flavour to the dish.*

**im·par·tial** /ɪmˈpɑːʃl; *NAmE* -ˈpɑːrʃl/ *adj.* not supporting one person or group more than another SYN **neutral**, **unbiased**: *an impartial inquiry/observer* ◇ *to give impartial advice* ◇ *As chairman, I must remain impartial.* OPP **partial** ▸ **im·par·ti·al·ity** /ˌɪmˌpɑːʃiˈæləti; *NAmE* -ˌpɑːrʃ-/ *noun* [U] **im·par·tial·ly** /ɪmˈpɑːʃəli; *NAmE* -ˈpɑːrʃ-/ *adv.*

**im·pass·able** /ɪmˈpɑːsəbl; *NAmE* -ˈpæs-/ *adj.* (of a road, an area, etc.) impossible to travel on or through, especially because it is in bad condition or it has been blocked by sth OPP **passable**

**im·passe** /ˈæmpæs/ *noun* [usually sing.] a difficult situation in which no progress can be made because the people involved cannot agree what to do SYN **deadlock**: *to break/end the impasse* ◇ *Negotiations have reached an impasse.*

**im·pas·sioned** /ɪmˈpæʃnd/ *adj.* [usually before noun] (usually of speech) showing strong feelings about sth SYN **fervent**: *an impassioned plea/speech/defence*

**im·pas·sive** /ɪmˈpæsɪv/ *adj.* not showing any feeling or emotion SYN **emotionless**: *her impassive expression/face* ▸ **im·pas·sive·ly** *adv.*

**im·pa·tient** 🛈 B2 /ɪmˈpeɪʃnt/ *adj.* **1** 🛈 B2 annoyed by sb/sth, especially because you have to wait for a long time: *I'd been waiting for twenty minutes and I was getting impatient.* ◇ ~ **with sb/sth** *Try not to be too impatient with her.* ◇ ~ **at sth** *Sarah was becoming increasingly impatient at their lack of interest.* ◇ *He waved them away with an impatient gesture.* **2** 🛈 B2 wanting to do sth soon; wanting sth to happen soon: ~ **to do sth** *She was clearly impatient to leave.* ◇ ~ **for sth** *impatient for change* **3** ~ **of sb/sth** (*formal*) unable or unwilling to accept sth unpleasant: *impatient of criticism* ▸ **im·pa·tience** /-ʃns/ *noun* [U]: *She was bursting with impatience to tell me the news.* **im·pa·tient·ly** *adv.*: *We sat waiting impatiently for the movie to start.*

**im·peach** /ɪmˈpiːtʃ/ *verb* **1** ~ **sb** (**for sth**) (of a court or other official body, especially in the US) to charge an important public figure with a serious crime **2** ~ **sth** (*formal*) to raise doubts about sth SYN **question**: *to impeach sb's motives* ▸ **im·peach·ment** *noun* [U, C]

**im·peach·able** /ɪmˈpiːtʃəbl/ *adj.* (*especially US*) (of a crime) for which a politician or a person who works for the government can be impeached: *an impeachable offense*

**im·pec·cable** /ɪmˈpekəbl/ *adj.* without mistakes or faults SYN **perfect**: *impeccable manners/taste* ◇ *Her written English is impeccable.* ◇ *He was dressed in a suit and an impeccable white shirt.* ▸ **im·pec·cably** /-bli/ *adv.*: *to behave impeccably* ◇ *impeccably dressed*

**im·pe·cu·ni·ous** /ˌɪmpɪˈkjuːniəs/ *adj.* (*formal* or *humorous*) having little or no money SYN **penniless**, **poor**

**im·ped·ance** /ɪmˈpiːdns/ *noun* [U] (*physics*) a measurement of the total RESISTANCE of a piece of electrical equipment, etc. to the flow of an ALTERNATING CURRENT

**im·pede** /ɪmˈpiːd/ *verb* ~ **sth** (*formal*) to delay or stop the progress of sth SYN **hinder**, **hamper**: *Work on the building was impeded by severe weather.*

**im·pedi·ment** /ɪmˈpedɪmənt/ *noun* **1** ~ (**to sth**) (*formal*) something that delays or stops the progress of sth SYN **obstacle**: *The level of inflation is a serious impediment to economic recovery.* **2** a physical problem that makes it difficult to speak normally, hear easily, etc.: *a speech impediment*

**impel** /ɪmˈpel/ *verb* (**-ll-**) (*formal*) if an idea or feeling **impels** you to do sth, you feel as if you are forced to do it: ~ **sb to do sth** *He felt impelled to investigate further.* ◇ ~ **sb** (**to sth**) *There are various reasons that impel me to that conclusion.*

**im·pend·ing** /ɪmˈpendɪŋ/ *adj.* [only before noun] (usually of an unpleasant event) that is going to happen very soon SYN **imminent**: *his impending retirement* ◇ *warnings of impending danger/disaster*

**im·pene·trable** /ɪmˈpenɪtrəbl/ *adj.* **1** that cannot be entered, passed through or seen through: *an impenetrable jungle* ◇ *impenetrable darkness* OPP **penetrable 2** impossible to understand SYN **incomprehensible**: *an impenetrable mystery* ◇ ~ **to sb** *Their jargon is impenetrable to an outsider.* ▸ **im·pene·tra·bil·ity** /ɪmˌpenɪtrəˈbɪləti/ *noun* [U] **im·pene·trably** /ɪmˈpenɪtrəbli/ *adv.*

**im·pera·tive** /ɪmˈperətɪv/ *adj., noun*

▪ *adj.* **1** [not usually before noun] (*formal*) very important and needing immediate attention or action SYN **vital**: ~ (**that ...**) *It is absolutely imperative that we finish by next week.* ◇ ~ (**to do sth**) *It is imperative to continue the treatment for at least two months.* ⊃ LANGUAGE BANK at VITAL **2** (*formal*) expressing authority: *an imperative tone* **3** [only before noun] (*grammar*) expressing an order: *an imperative sentence*

▪ *noun* **1** (*formal*) a thing that is very important and needs immediate attention or action; a factor that makes sth necessary: *the economic imperative of quality education for all* **2** (*grammar*) the form of a verb that expresses an order; a verb in this form: *'Go away!' is an imperative.* ◇ **in the ~** *In 'Go away!' the verb is in the imperative.*

**im·per·cept·ible** /ˌɪmpəˈseptəbl; *NAmE* -pərˈs-/ *adj.* (*formal*) very small and therefore unable to be seen or felt;: *imperceptible changes in temperature* OPP **perceptible** ▸ **im·per·cept·ibly** /-bli/ *adv.*

**im·per·fect** /ɪmˈpɜːfɪkt; *NAmE* -ˈpɜːrf-/ *adj., noun*

▪ *adj.* containing faults or mistakes; not complete or perfect SYN **flawed**: *an imperfect world* ◇ *an imperfect understanding of English* ◇ *All our sale items are slightly imperfect.* ▸ **im·per·fect·ly** *adv.*

▪ *noun* **the imperfect** (*also* **the im·perfect 'tense**) [sing.] (*grammar*) the verb tense that expresses action in the past that is not complete. It is often called the past pro'gressive or past con'tinuous: *In 'while I was washing my hair', the verb is in the imperfect.*

**im·per·fec·tion** /ˌɪmpəˈfekʃn; *NAmE* -pərˈf-/ *noun* [C, U] a fault or weakness in sb/sth: *They learned to live with each other's imperfections.*

**im·per·ial** /ɪmˈpɪəriəl; *NAmE* -ˈpɪr-/ *adj.* [only before noun] **1** connected with an EMPIRE: *the imperial family/palace/army* ◇ *imperial power/expansion* **2** connected with the system for measuring length, weight and volume using pounds, inches, etc. ⊃ compare METRIC

**im·peri·al·ism** /ɪmˈpɪəriəlɪzəm; *NAmE* -ˈpɪr-/ *noun* [U] (*usually disapproving*) **1** a system in which one country controls other countries, often after defeating them in a war: *Roman imperialism* ⊃ WORDFINDER NOTE at CAPITALISM **2** the fact of a powerful country increasing its influence over other countries through business, culture, etc.: *cultural/economic imperialism*

**im·peri·al·ist** /ɪmˈpɪəriəlɪst; NAmE -ˈpɪr-/ noun (usually disapproving) a person, such as a politician, who supports imperialism ▶ **im·peri·al·ist** (also **im·peri·al·is·tic** /ɪmˌpɪəriəˈlɪstɪk; NAmE -ˌpɪr-/) adj.: an imperialist power ◊ imperialist ambitions

**im·peril** /ɪmˈperəl/ verb (-ll-, US -l-) ~ sth/sb (formal) to put sth/sb in danger SYN endanger

**im·peri·ous** /ɪmˈpɪəriəs; NAmE -ˈpɪr-/ adj. (formal, often disapproving) expecting people to obey you and treating them as if they are not as important as you: an imperious gesture/voice/command ▶ **im·peri·ous·ly** adv.: 'Get it now,' she demanded imperiously.

**im·per·ish·able** /ɪmˈperɪʃəbl/ adj. (formal or literary) that will last for a long time or forever SYN **enduring**

**im·per·man·ent** /ɪmˈpɜːmənənt; NAmE -ˈpɜːrm-/ adj. (formal) that will not last or stay the same forever OPP **permanent** ▶ **im·per·man·ence** /-mənəns/ noun [U]

**im·per·me·able** /ɪmˈpɜːmiəbl; NAmE -ˈpɜːrm-/ adj. ~ (to sth) (specialist) not allowing a liquid or gas to pass through OPP **permeable**

**im·per·mis·sible** /ˌɪmpɜːˈmɪsəbl; NAmE -pɜːrˈm-/ adj. that cannot be allowed: an impermissible invasion of privacy OPP **permissible**

**im·per·son·al** /ɪmˈpɜːsənl; NAmE -ˈpɜːrs-/ adj. **1** (usually disapproving) having no friendly human feelings or atmosphere; making you feel unimportant: a vast impersonal organization ◊ an impersonal hotel room ◊ Business letters need not be formal and impersonal. ◊ a cold impersonal stare **2** not referring to any particular person; not concerned with people as individuals: Let's keep the criticism general and impersonal. **3** (grammar) an **impersonal** verb or sentence has 'it' or 'there' as the subject ▶ **im·per·son·al·ity** /ɪmˌpɜːsəˈnæləti; NAmE -ˌpɜːrs-/ noun [U]: the cold impersonality of some modern cities **im·per·son·ally** /ɪmˈpɜːsənəli; NAmE -ˈpɜːrs-/ adv.

▼ **LANGUAGE BANK**

**impersonal**

Giving opinions using impersonal language

- **It is vital that** more is done to prevent the illegal trade in wild animals. ◊ (Compare: We have to do more to stop people trading wild animals illegally.)
- **It is clear that** more needs to be done to protect biodiversity. ◊ (Compare: We clearly need to do more to protect biodiversity.)
- **It is unfortunate that** the practice of keeping monkeys as pets still continues. ◊ (Compare: It's absolutely terrible that people still keep monkeys as pets.)
- **It is difficult** for many people to understand the reasons why certain individuals choose to hunt animals for sport. ◊ (Compare: I can't understand why anyone would want to kill animals for fun.)
- Unfortunately, **it would seem that** not enough is being done to support tiger conservation. ◊ (Compare: Governments aren't doing enough to help tiger conservation.)
- **There is no doubt that** the greatest threat to polar bears comes from global warming. ◊ (Compare: I believe that the greatest threat…)

⊃ LANGUAGE BANK at OPINION, PERHAPS, VITAL

**im·per·son·al 'pronoun** noun (grammar) a pronoun (in English, the pronoun 'it') that does not refer to a person or thing or to any other part of the sentence, for example in 'it was raining'

**im·per·son·ate** /ɪmˈpɜːsəneɪt; NAmE -ˈpɜːrs-/ verb ~ sb to pretend to be sb in order to trick people or to entertain them: He was caught trying to impersonate a security guard. ◊ They do a pretty good job of impersonating Laurel and Hardy. ▶ **im·per·son·ation** /ɪmˌpɜːsəˈneɪʃn; NAmE -ˌpɜːrs-/ noun [C, U] SYN **impression**: He did an extremely convincing impersonation of the singer.

**im·per·son·ator** /ɪmˈpɜːsəneɪtə(r); NAmE -ˈpɜːrs-/ noun a person who copies the way another person talks or behaves in order to entertain people: The show included a female impersonator (= a man dressed as a woman).

**im·per·tin·ent** /ɪmˈpɜːtɪnənt; NAmE -ˈpɜːrtn-/ adj. rude and not showing respect for sb who is older or more important SYN **impolite**: an impertinent question/child ◊ Would it be impertinent to ask why you're leaving? ⊃ SYNONYMS at RUDE ▶ **im·per·tin·ence** /ɪmˈpɜːtɪnəns; NAmE -ˈpɜːrtn-/ noun [U, C, usually sing.]: She had the impertinence to ask my age! **im·per·tin·ent·ly** adv.

**im·per·turb·able** /ˌɪmpəˈtɜːbəbl; NAmE -pərˈtɜːrb-/ adj. (formal) not easily upset or worried by a difficult situation; calm ▶ **im·per·turb·ability** /ˌɪmpəˌtɜːbəˈbɪləti; NAmE -pərˌtɜːrb-/ noun [U] **im·per·turb·ably** /ˌɪmpəˈtɜːbəbli; NAmE -pərˈtɜːrb-/ adv.

**im·per·vi·ous** /ɪmˈpɜːviəs; NAmE -ˈpɜːrv-/ adj. **1 ~ to sth** not affected or influenced by sth: impervious to criticism/pain **2** (specialist) not allowing a liquid or gas to pass through: an impervious rock/layer ◊ ~ **to sth** impervious to moisture

**im·pe·tigo** /ˌɪmpɪˈtaɪɡəʊ/ noun [U] a disease that causes painful areas on the skin

**im·petu·ous** /ɪmˈpetʃuəs/ adj. acting or done quickly and without thinking carefully about the results SYN **rash, impulsive**: an impetuous young woman ◊ an impetuous decision ▶ **im·petu·os·ity** /ɪmˌpetʃuˈɒsəti; NAmE -ˈɑːs-/ noun [U] **im·petu·ous·ly** /ɪmˈpetʃuəsli/ adv.

**im·petus** /ˈɪmpɪtəs/ noun **1** [U, sing.] something that encourages a process or activity to develop more quickly SYN **stimulus**: The debate seems to have lost much of its initial impetus. ◊ ~ **to sth/to do sth** to give (a) new/fresh impetus to sth ◊ ~ **for sth** His articles provided the main impetus for change. **2** [U] (specialist) the force or energy with which sth moves

**im·pinge** /ɪmˈpɪndʒ/ verb [I] ~ (on/upon sth/sb) (formal) to have a clear and definite effect on sth/sb, especially a bad one SYN **encroach**: He never allowed his work to impinge on his private life.

**im·pious** /ˈɪmpiəs, ˈɪmpaɪəs/ adj. (formal) showing a lack of respect for God and religion OPP **pious** ▶ **im·pi·ety** /ɪmˈpaɪəti/ noun [U]

**imp·ish** /ˈɪmpɪʃ/ adj. showing a lack of respect for sb/sth in a way that is funny rather than serious SYN **mischievous**: an impish grin/look ⊃ see also IMP ▶ **imp·ish·ly** adv.

**im·plac·able** /ɪmˈplækəbl/ adj. **1** (of strong negative opinions or feelings) that cannot be changed: implacable hatred **2** (of a person) unwilling to stop opposing sb/sth: an implacable enemy ▶ **im·plac·ably** /-bli/ adv.: to be implacably opposed to the plan

**im·plant** verb, noun
- **verb** /ɪmˈplɑːnt; NAmE -ˈplænt/ **1** [T] ~ **sth (in/into sth)** to fix an idea, attitude, etc. in sb's mind: Prejudices can easily become implanted in the mind. **2** [T] ~ **sth (in/into sth)** to put sth (usually sth artificial) into a part of the body, usually in a medical operation: an electrode implanted into the brain ⊃ compare TRANSPLANT **3** [I, T] ~ **(itself) (in/into sth)** (of an egg or an EMBRYO) to become fixed inside the body of a person or an animal so that it can start to develop ▶ **im·plant·ation** /ˌɪmplɑːnˈteɪʃn; NAmE -plæn-/ noun [U]
- **noun** /ˈɪmplɑːnt; NAmE -plænt/ something that is put into a part of the body, usually in a medical operation: silicone breast implants ⊃ compare TRANSPLANT

**im·plaus·ible** /ɪmˈplɔːzəbl/ adj. not seeming reasonable or likely to be true: an implausible claim/idea/theory ◊ It was all highly implausible. OPP **plausible** ▶ **im·plaus·ibility** /ɪmˌplɔːzəˈbɪləti/ noun [U, C] (pl. -ies) **im·plaus·ibly** /ɪmˈplɔːzəbli/ adv.

**im·ple·ment** verb, noun
- **verb** /ˈɪmplɪment/ ~ **sth** (formal) to make sth that has been officially decided start to happen or be used SYN **carry out**: to implement changes/decisions/policies/reforms
- **noun** /ˈɪmplɪmənt/ (formal) a tool or an instrument, often one that is quite simple and that is used outdoors: agricultural implements

# implementation

**im·ple·men·ta·tion** /ˌɪmplɪmenˈteɪʃn/ noun [U] (*formal*) the act of making sth that has been officially decided start to happen or be used: *the implementation of the new system*

**im·pli·cate** /ˈɪmplɪkeɪt/ verb **1** ~ sb (in sth) to show or suggest that sb is involved in sth bad or criminal: *He tried to avoid saying anything that would implicate him further.* **2** ~ sth (in/as sth) to show or suggest that sth is the cause of sth bad: *The results implicate poor hygiene as one cause of the outbreak.*
**IDM** **be implicated in sth** to be involved in a crime; to be responsible for sth bad: *Senior officials were implicated in the scandal.*

**im·pli·ca·tion** /ˌɪmplɪˈkeɪʃn/ noun **1** [C, usually pl.] a possible effect or result of an action or a decision: *They failed to consider the wider implications of their actions.* ◊ ~ (of sth) for sth *The development of the site will have implications for the surrounding countryside.* **2** [C, U] something that is suggested or indirectly stated (= sth that is implied): *The implication in his article is that being a housewife is greatly inferior to every other occupation.* ◊ **by** ~ *He criticized the Director and, by implication, the whole of the organization.* **3** [U] ~ (of sb) (in sth) the fact of being involved, or of involving sb, in sth, especially a crime **SYN** **involvement**: *He resigned after his implication in a sex scandal.*

**im·pli·cit** /ɪmˈplɪsɪt/ adj. **1** ~ (in sth) suggested without being directly expressed: *Implicit in his speech was the assumption that they were guilty.* ◊ *implicit criticism* **2** ~ (in sth) forming part of sth (although perhaps not directly expressed): *The ability to listen is implicit in the teacher's role.* **3** complete and not doubted **SYN** **absolute**: *She had the implicit trust of her staff.* ⇒ compare EXPLICIT
▸ **im·pli·cit·ly** adv.: *It reinforces, implicitly or explicitly, the idea that money is all-important.* ◊ *I trust John implicitly.*

**im·plied** /ɪmˈplaɪd/ adj. suggested without being directly expressed **SYN** **implicit**: *I disliked the implied criticism in his voice.*

**im·plode** /ɪmˈpləʊd/ verb **1** [I] to collapse into the centre **2** [I] (of an organization, a system, etc.) to fail suddenly and completely ▸ **im·plo·sion** /-ˈpləʊʒn/ noun [C, U]

**im·plore** /ɪmˈplɔː(r)/ verb (*formal* or *literary*) to ask sb to do sth in an anxious way because you want or need it very much **SYN** **beseech, beg**: ~ sb to do sth *She implored him to stay.* ◊ ~ (sb) + speech '*Help me,*' *he implored.* ◊ ~ sb *Tell me it's true. I implore you.* ▸ **im·plor·ing** adj.: *She gave him an imploring look.*

**imply** /ɪmˈplaɪ/ verb (im·plies, im·ply·ing, im·plied, im·plied) **1** to suggest that sth is true or that you feel or think sth, without saying so directly: ~ (that) ... *Are you implying (that) I am wrong?* ◊ *I disliked the implied criticism in his voice.* ◊ **it is implied that** ... *It was implied that we were at fault.* ⇒ note at INFER **2** to make it seem likely that sth is true or exists **SYN** **suggest**: ~ (that) ... *The survey implies (that) more people are moving house than was thought.* ◊ **it is implied that** ... *It was implied in the survey that* ... ◊ ~ sth *Popularity does not necessarily imply merit.* **3** ~ sth (of an idea, action, etc.) to make sth necessary in order to be successful **SYN** **mean**: *The project implies an enormous investment in training.*
⇒ see also IMPLICATION

**im·pol·ite** /ˌɪmpəˈlaɪt/ adj. not polite **SYN** **rude**: *Some people think it is impolite to ask someone's age.* ⇒ SYNONYMS at RUDE ▸ **im·pol·ite·ly** adv. **im·pol·ite·ness** noun [U]

**im·pol·it·ic** /ɪmˈpɒlətɪk; NAmE -ˈpɑːl-/ adj. (*formal*) not wise **SYN** **unwise**: *It would have been impolitic to refuse his offer.*

**im·pon·der·able** /ɪmˈpɒndərəbl; NAmE -ˈpɑːn-/ noun [usually pl.] (*formal*) something that is difficult to measure or estimate: *We can't predict the outcome. There are too many imponderables.* ▸ **im·pon·der·able** adj.

**im·port** noun, verb
- **noun** /ˈɪmpɔːt; NAmE -pɔːrt/ **1** [C, usually pl.] a product or service that is brought into one country from another: ~ from ... *food imports from abroad* ◊ ~ into/to ... *cheap imports into the United States* **OPP** **export 2** [U, pl.] the act of bringing a product or service into one country from another: *The report calls for a ban on the import of hazardous waste.* ◊ *imports of oil* ◊ **import duties/tariffs** ◊ *import controls/restrictions/quotas* ◊ *an import licence* **OPP** **export** ⇒ WORDFINDER NOTE at TRADE **3** [U] (*formal*) importance: *matters of great import* **4** [sing.] **the** ~ (**of sth**) (*formal*) the meaning of sth, especially when it is not immediately clear: *It is difficult to understand the full import of this statement.*
- **verb** /ɪmˈpɔːt; NAmE -ˈpɔːrt/ **1** to bring a product, a service, an idea, etc. into one country from another: ~ sth *The country has to import most of its raw materials.* ◊ ~ sth from ... into/to ... *goods imported from Japan into the US* ◊ *customs imported from the West* **2** ~ sth (from ...) (into ...) (*computing*) to get data from another program, changing its form so that the program you are using can read it **OPP** **export** ▸ **im·port·ation** /ˌɪmpɔːˈteɪʃn; NAmE -pɔːrt-/ noun [U, C] **SYN** **import**: *a ban on the importation of ivory*

**im·port·ance** /ɪmˈpɔːtns; NAmE -ˈpɔːrt-/ noun [U] the quality of being important: *She stressed the importance of careful preparation.* ◊ *to emphasize/highlight the importance of sth* ◊ *They attach great importance to the project.* ◊ *the relative importance of the two ideas* ◊ *of* ~ (**to sb**) *It's a matter of the utmost importance to me.* ◊ *He was very aware of his own importance* (= of his status). ⇒ see also SELF-IMPORTANCE

**im·port·ant** /ɪmˈpɔːtnt; NAmE -ˈpɔːrt-/ adj. **1** having a great effect on people or things; of great value: *an important issue/question/point/factor* ◊ *Money played an important role in his life.* ◊ *Listening is an important part of the job.* ◊ *The important thing is to keep trying.* ◊ ~ **to sb/sth** *The centre is extremely important to many local people.* ◊ ~ **for sb/sth** *Many chemicals are important for our health.* ◊ **it is** ~ **to do sth** *It is important to follow the manufacturer's instructions.* ◊ **It is important to note that** *total government funding has increased.* ◊ **it is** ~ **that** ... *It is important that he attend every day.* ◊ **it is** ~ **to sb that** ... (*BrE*) *It's very important to me that you should be there.* ◊ **it is** ~ **for sb/sth to do sth** *It is important for him to attend every day.* ⇒ see also ALL-IMPORTANT
⇒ LANGUAGE BANK at EMPHASIS **2** (of a person) having great influence or authority: *an important member of the team* ◊ *He likes to feel important.* ⇒ see also SELF-IMPORTANT ▸ **im·port·ant·ly** adv.: *More importantly, can he be trusted?* ◊ *She was sitting importantly behind a big desk.*
⇒ LANGUAGE BANK at EMPHASIS

**im·port·er** /ɪmˈpɔːtə(r); NAmE -ˈpɔːrt-/ noun a person, company, etc. that buys goods from another country in order to sell them in their own country: *a London-based importer of Italian food* ◊ *The US is a net importer of beef* (= imports more beef than it exports). ⇒ compare EXPORTER

**im·por·tun·ate** /ɪmˈpɔːtʃənət; NAmE -ˈpɔːrtʃ-/ adj. (*formal*) asking for things many times in a way that is annoying

**im·por·tune** /ˌɪmpɔːˈtjuːn; NAmE -pɔːrˈtuːn/ verb ~ sb (for sth) | ~ sb to do sth (*formal*) to ask sb for sth many times and in a way that is annoying **SYN** **pester**

**im·pose** /ɪmˈpəʊz/ verb **1** [T] to introduce a new law, rule, tax, etc.; to order that a rule, punishment, etc. be used: ~ sth *The UN Security Council imposed sanctions in 1992.* ◊ *to impose a penalty/fine/sentence/ban* ◊ ~ sth on/upon sth/sb *A new tax was imposed on fuel.* **2** [T] to force sb/sth to have to deal with sth that is difficult or unpleasant: ~ sth *He described the limitations imposed by his disease.* ◊ ~ sth on/upon sb/sth *This system imposes additional financial burdens on many people.* ◊ *to impose restrictions/constraints/obligations on sb/sth* **3** [T] ~ sth (on/upon sb) to make sb accept the same opinions, wishes, etc. as your own: *She didn't want to impose her values on her family.* ◊ *It was noticeable how a few people managed to impose their will on the others.* **4** [I] to expect sb to do sth for you or to spend time with you, when it may not be convenient for them: *You must stay for lunch.' 'Well, thanks, but I don't want to impose ...'* ◇ **~on/upon sb/sth** *Everyone imposes on Dave's good nature.* **5** [T] **~ yourself (on/upon sb/sth)** to make sb/ sth accept or be aware of your presence or ideas: *European civilization was the first to impose itself across the whole world.*

**im·pos·ing** /ɪmˈpəʊzɪŋ/ *adj.* impressive to look at; making a strong impression: *a grand and imposing building* ◇ *a tall imposing woman*

**im·pos·ition** /ˌɪmpəˈzɪʃn/ *noun* **1** [U] the act of introducing sth such as a new law or rule, or a new tax: *the imposition of martial law* ◇ *the imposition of tax on domestic fuel* **2** [C] an unfair or unreasonable thing that sb expects or asks you to do: *I'd like to stay if it's not too much of an imposition.*

**im·pos·sible** 🅞 **A2** /ɪmˈpɒsəbl; NAmE -ˈpɑːs-/ *adj.* **1** 🔑 **A2** that cannot exist or be done; not possible: *almost/virtually/nearly impossible* ◇ *Getting any kind of decent job was proving impossible.* ◇ *an impossible dream/goal* ◇ **~to do** *The outcome is impossible to predict.* ◇ **it is ~ to do sth** *It's impossible to say which is the best.* ◇ **it is ~ for sb to do sth** *It's impossible for me to be there before eight.* **OPP possible 2** very difficult to deal with: *I've been placed in an impossible position.* ◇ *Honestly, you're impossible at times!* **3 the impossible** *noun* [sing.] a thing that is or seems impossible: *to attempt the impossible* ▶ **im·pos·si·bil·ity** /ɪmˌpɒsəˈbɪləti; NAmE -ˌpɑːs-/ *noun* [U, C, usually sing.] (*pl.* **-ies**): *the sheer impossibility of providing enough food for everyone* ◇ *a virtual impossibility* **im·pos·sibly** /ɪmˈpɒsəbli; NAmE -ˈpɑːs-/ *adv.*: *an impossibly difficult problem* (= impossible to solve) ◇ *He was impossibly handsome* (= it was difficult to believe that he could be so HANDSOME). **IDM** see MISSION

**im·pos·tor** (*BrE also* **im·pos·ter**) /ɪmˈpɒstə(r); NAmE -ˈpɑːs-/ *noun* a person who pretends to be sb else in order to trick people

**im·pos·ture** /ɪmˈpɒstʃə(r); NAmE -ˈpɑːs-/ *noun* [U, C] (*formal*) an act of tricking people deliberately by pretending to be sb else

**im·po·tent** /ˈɪmpətənt/ *adj.* **1** having no power to change things or to influence a situation **SYN powerless**: *Without the chairman's support, the committee is impotent.* ◇ *She blazed with impotent rage.* **2** (of a man) unable to achieve an ERECTION and therefore unable to have full sex ▶ **im·po·tence** /-pətəns/ *noun* [U]: *a feeling of impotence in the face of an apparently insoluble problem* ◇ *male impotence* **im·po·tent·ly** *adv.*

**im·pound** /ɪmˈpaʊnd/ *verb* (*law*) **1 ~ sth** (of the police, courts of law, etc.) to take sth away from sb, so that they cannot use it **SYN confiscate**: *The car was impounded by the police after the accident.* **2 ~ sth** to shut up dogs, cats, etc. found on the streets in a POUND, until their owners collect them

**im·pov·er·ish** /ɪmˈpɒvərɪʃ; NAmE -ˈpɑːv-/ *verb* **1 ~ sb** to make sb poor: *These changes are likely to impoverish single-parent families even further.* **2 ~ sth** to make sth worse in quality: *Intensive cultivation has impoverished the soil.* ▶ **im·pov·er·ish·ment** *noun* [U]

**im·pov·er·ished** /ɪmˈpɒvərɪʃt; NAmE -ˈpɑːv-/ *adj.* **1** very poor; without money: *impoverished peasants* ◇ *the impoverished areas of the city* **SYNONYMS** at POOR **2** poor in quality, because sth is missing

**im·prac·tic·able** /ɪmˈpræktɪkəbl/ *adj.* impossible or very difficult to do; not practical in a particular situation: *It would be impracticable for each member to be consulted on every occasion.* **OPP practicable** ⊃ compare IMPRACTICAL ▶ **im·prac·tic·abil·ity** /ɪmˌpræktɪkəˈbɪləti/ *noun* [U]

**im·prac·ti·cal** /ɪmˈpræktɪkl/ *adj.* **1** not sensible or realistic: *It was totally impractical to think that we could finish the job in two months.* **2** (of people) not good at doing things that involve using the hands; not good at planning or organizing things **OPP practical** ⊃ compare IMPRACTICABLE ▶ **im·prac·ti·cal·ity** /ɪmˌpræktɪˈkæləti/ *noun* [U, C] (*pl.* **-ies**)

---

797

# impression

**im·pre·ca·tion** /ˌɪmprɪˈkeɪʃn/ *noun* (*formal*) a CURSE (= an offensive word that is used to express extreme anger)

**im·pre·cise** /ˌɪmprɪˈsaɪs/ *adj.* not giving exact details or making sth clear **SYN inaccurate**: *an imprecise definition* ◇ *imprecise information* ◇ *The witness's descriptions were too imprecise to be of any real value.* **OPP precise** ▶ **im·pre·cise·ly** *adv.*: *These terms are often used imprecisely and interchangeably.* **im·pre·ci·sion** /-ˈsɪʒn/ *noun* [U]: *There is considerable imprecision in the terminology used.*

**im·preg·nable** /ɪmˈpregnəbl/ *adj.* **1** an **impregnable** building is so strongly built that it cannot be entered by force: *an impregnable fortress* **2** strong and impossible to defeat or change **SYN invincible**: *The team built up an impregnable 5–1 lead.*

**im·preg·nate** /ˈɪmpregneɪt; NAmE ɪmˈpregneɪt/ *verb* **1** [usually passive] to make a substance spread through an area so that the area is full of the substance: **be impregnated (with sth)** *The pad is impregnated with insecticide.* **2 ~ sb/sth** (*formal*) to make a woman or female animal pregnant ▶ **im·preg·na·tion** /ˌɪmpregˈneɪʃn/ *noun* [U]

**im·pres·ario** /ˌɪmprəˈsɑːriəʊ/ *noun* (*pl.* **-os**) a person who organizes and often finances plays, concerts, etc.

**im·press** 🅞 **B2** /ɪmˈpres/ *verb* **1** 🔑 **B2** [T, I] if a person or thing **impresses** you, you admire them or it: **~(sb)** *We interviewed a number of candidates but none of them impressed us.* ◇ *The Grand Canyon never fails to impress.* ◇ *His sincerity impressed her.* ◇ **~sb with sth** *He impressed her with his sincerity.* ◇ **it impresses sb that ...** *It impressed me that she remembered my name.* ⊃ see also IMPRESSED, IMPRESSIVE **2** [T] **~ sth on/upon sb** (*formal*) to make sb understand how important, serious, etc. sth is by emphasizing it: *He impressed on us the need for immediate action.* **3** [T] **~ sth/itself on/upon sth** (*formal*) to have a great effect on sth, especially sb's mind, imagination, etc: *Her words impressed themselves on my memory.*

**im·pressed** 🅞 **B2** /ɪmˈprest/ *adj.* admiring sb/sth because you think they are particularly good, interesting, etc: *I must admit I am impressed.* ◇ **~ by/with/at sth** *She was suitably impressed* (= as impressed as sb had hoped) *with the painting.* ◇ **~ to see, hear, find, etc.** *We were impressed to see how well they'd done already.* ◇ **~ that ...** *I was impressed that she remembered my name.* ⊃ see also UNIMPRESSED

**im·pres·sion** 🅞 **B1** /ɪmˈpreʃn/ *noun*
- **IDEA/OPINION 1** 🔑 **B1** an idea, a feeling or an opinion that you get about sb/sth, or that sb/sth gives you: *My first impression of him was favourable.* ◇ *She gives the impression of being very busy.* ◇ **~ that ...** *I did not get the impression that they were unhappy about the situation.* ◇ *I had the impression that it was all done in a hurry.* ◇ *My impression is that there are still a lot of problems.* ◇ *Try and smile. You don't want to give people the wrong impression* (= that you are not friendly). ◇ *He does not want to give a false impression of progress.* ◇ *If you want to create the right impression, I suggest you wear a suit.*
- **EFFECT 2** 🔑 **B1** the effect that an experience or a person has on sb/sth: *You'll have to play better than that if you really want to* **make an impression** (= to make people admire you). ◇ **~ on sb** *His trip to India made a strong impression on him.* ◇ *My words made no impression on her.* ◇ *The whole business left a lasting impression on Margaret.*
- **DRAWING 3** a drawing showing what a person looks like or what a place or a building will look like in the future: *This is an artist's impression of the new stadium.*
- **COPY OF SB 4 ~ (of sb)** a clever or funny copy of the way a person acts or speaks **SYN impersonation**: *He did an impression of Tom Hanks.*
- **FALSE APPEARANCE 5** an appearance that may be false: *Clever lighting creates an impression of space in a room.*
- **MARK 6** a mark that is left when an object is pressed hard into a surface
- **BOOK 7** all the copies of a book that are printed at one time, with few or no changes to the contents since the last time the book was printed ⊃ compare EDITION

---

🅞 Oxford Phrasal Academic Lexicon (OPAL) written and spoken word lists | 🅦 OPAL written word list | 🅢 OPAL spoken word list

# impressionable

**IDM** **(be) under the im′pression that…** believing, usually wrongly, that sth is true or is happening: *I was under the impression that the work had already been completed.* ⇨ SYNONYMS at THINK

**im·pres·sion·able** /ɪmˈpreʃənəbl/ *adj.* (of a person, especially a young one) easily influenced or affected by sb/sth: *children at an impressionable age*

**Im·pres·sion·ism** (*also* **im·pres·sion·ism**) /ɪmˈpreʃənɪzəm/ *noun* [U] a style in painting developed in France in the late 19th century that uses colour to show the effects of light on things and to suggest atmosphere rather than showing exact details ▶ **Im·pres·sion·ist** (*also* **im·pres·sion·ist**) *adj.* [usually before noun]: *Impressionist landscapes*

**im·pres·sion·ist** /ɪmˈpreʃənɪst/ *noun* **1** (*usually* **Impressionist**) an artist who paints in the style of Impressionism: *Impressionists such as Monet and Pissarro* **2** a person who entertains people by copying the way a famous person speaks or behaves

**im·pres·sion·is·tic** /ɪmˌpreʃəˈnɪstɪk/ *adj.* giving a general idea rather than particular facts or details

**im·pres·sive** ❶ **B1** /ɪmˈpresɪv/ *adj.* (of things or people) making you admire them, because they are very large, good, SKILFUL, etc: *an impressive performance* ◊ *an impressive building with a huge tower* ◊ *one of the most impressive novels of recent years* ◊ *She was very impressive in the interview.* **OPP** **unimpressive** ▶ **im·pres·sive·ly** *adv.*: *impressively high* ◊ *impressively organized*

**im·pri·ma·tur** /ˌɪmprɪˈmɑːtə(r)/ *noun* [sing.] (*formal*) official approval of sth, given by a person in a position of authority

**im·print** *verb, noun*
■ *verb* [often passive] /ɪmˈprɪnt/ **1** ~ **A in/on B** | ~ **B with A** to have a great effect on sth so that it cannot be forgotten, changed, etc: *The terrible scenes were indelibly imprinted on his mind.* **2** ~ **A in/on B** | ~ **B with A** to print or press a mark or design onto a surface: ~ **B with A** *clothes imprinted with the logos of sports teams*
■ *noun* /ˈɪmprɪnt/ **1** ~ **(of sth) (in/on sth)** a mark made by pressing sth onto a surface: *the imprint of a foot in the sand* **2** [usually sing.] ~ **(of sth) (on sb/sth)** (*formal*) the lasting effect that a person or an experience has on a place or a situation **3** (*specialist*) the name of the PUBLISHER of a book, usually printed below the title on the first page; a brand name under which books are published

**im·prison** 🔊 + **C1** /ɪmˈprɪzn/ *verb* [often passive] to put sb in a prison or another place from which they cannot escape **SYN** **jail**: *be imprisoned (for sth)* *They were imprisoned for possession of drugs.* ◊ *be imprisoned (+ adv./prep.)* (*figurative*) *Some young mothers feel imprisoned in their own homes.*

**im·pris·on·ment** 🔊 + **C1** /ɪmˈprɪznmənt/ *noun* [U] ~ **(for sth)** the act of putting sb in a prison or another place from which they cannot escape; the state of being there: *to be sentenced to life imprisonment for murder* ⇨ see also FALSE IMPRISONMENT ⇨ WORDFINDER NOTE at FREEDOM

**im·prob·able** /ɪmˈprɒbəbl/ *NAmE* -ˈprɑː-/ *adj.* **1** not likely to be true or to happen **SYN** **unlikely**: *an improbable story* ◊ *It all sounded highly improbable.* ◊ ~ **that…** *It seems improbable that the current situation will continue.* **OPP** **probable** **2** seeming strange because it is not what you would expect **SYN** **unexpected**: *Her hair was an improbable shade of yellow.* ▶ **im·prob·abil·ity** /ɪmˌprɒbəˈbɪləti; *NAmE* -ˌprɑː-/ *noun* [U, C] (*pl.* **-ies**) *the improbability of finding them alive* ◊ *statistical improbability* **im·prob·ably** /ɪmˈprɒbəbli; *NAmE* -ˈprɑː-/ *adv.*: *He claimed, improbably, that he had never been there.* ◊ *an improbably happy ending*

**im·promp·tu** /ɪmˈprɒmptjuː; *NAmE* -ˈprɑːmptuː/ *adj.* done without preparation or planning **SYN** **improvised**: *an impromptu speech* ▶ **im·promp·tu** *adv.*: *Roy came up and just started speaking impromptu.*

**im·proper** /ɪmˈprɒpə(r); *NAmE* -ˈprɑːp-/ *adj.* (*formal*) **1** dishonest, or morally wrong: *improper business practices* ◊ *improper conduct* ◊ *There was nothing improper about our relationship* (= it did not involve sex). **OPP** **proper** **2** not right or appropriate for the situation **SYN** **inappropriate**: *It would be improper to comment at this stage.* **OPP** **proper** **3** wrong; not correct: *improper use of the drug* ▶ **im·prop·er·ly** *adv.*: *to behave improperly* ◊ *He was improperly dressed for the occasion.* ◊ *improperly cooked meat*

**im·pro·pri·ety** /ˌɪmprəˈpraɪəti/ *noun* [U, C] (*pl.* **-ies**) (*formal*) behaviour or actions that are dishonest, morally wrong or not appropriate for a person in a position of responsibility **OPP** **propriety**

**improv** /ˈɪmprɒv; *NAmE* -prɑːv/ *noun* [U] (*informal*) a type of performance, often involving comedy, that has not been SCRIPTED (= written) or REHEARSED (= practised) before the performance ⇨ compare IMPROVISATION

**im·prove** ❶ **A1** 🔊 /ɪmˈpruːv/ *verb, noun*
■ *verb* 🔊 **A1** [I, T] to become better than before; to make sth/sb better than before: *Overall the situation has improved dramatically.* ◊ *Things are improving every day.* ◊ *You should see your score improve significantly.* ◊ *Working conditions have greatly improved.* ◊ *The doctor says she should continue to improve* (= after an illness). ◊ ~ **sth** *This vital service helps to improve the quality of life for people with cancer.* ◊ *This was a much improved performance by the team.* ◊ ~ **yourself** *He's a guy who wants to improve himself, to be the best.*
**PHR V** **im′prove on/upon sth** to achieve or produce sth that is of a better quality than sth else: *We've certainly improved on last year's figures.*
■ *noun*
**IDM** **on the ′improve** (*AustralE, NZE, informal*) showing signs of improvement

**im·prove·ment** ❶ **B1** 🔊 /ɪmˈpruːvmənt/ *noun* **1** 🔊 **B1** [U] the act of making sth better; the process of sth becoming better: *The economy has shown significant improvement over the past 9 months.* ◊ *We expect to see further improvement over the coming year.* ◊ ~ **in sth** *There is a need for continuous improvement in performance.* ◊ *I think there is room for improvement in any organization.* ⇨ see also SELF-IMPROVEMENT **2** 🔊 **B1** [C] a change in sth that makes it better; sth that is better than it was before: *a significant/dramatic improvement* ◊ *a slight/steady improvement* ◊ ~ **in sth** *There has been a marked improvement in the quality of teaching.* ◊ ~ **to sth** *We have made some mechanical improvements to the car.* ◊ ~ **on/over sth** *This is a great improvement on your previous work.* ⇨ see also HOME IMPROVEMENT

**im·provi·dent** /ɪmˈprɒvɪdənt; *NAmE* -ˈprɑːv-/ *adj.* (*formal*) not thinking about or planning for the future; spending money in a careless way **OPP** **provident** ▶ **im·provi·dence** /-dəns/ *noun* [U]

**im·pro·visa·tion** /ˌɪmprəvaɪˈzeɪʃn; *NAmE* ɪmˌprɑːvəˈz-/ *noun* [U, C] the act of inventing music, the words in a play, a statement, etc. while you are playing or speaking, instead of planning it in advance; sth that is invented in this way: *jazz improvisation* ⇨ compare IMPROV

**im·pro·vise** /ˈɪmprəvaɪz/ *verb* **1** [I, T] to make or do sth using whatever is available, usually because you do not have what you really need: *There isn't much equipment. We're going to have to improvise.* ◊ ~ **sth** *We improvised some shelves out of planks of wood and bricks.* **2** [I, T] to invent music, the words in a play, a statement, etc. while you are playing or speaking, instead of planning it in advance: *'It'll be ready some time next week, I expect,' she said, improvising.* ◊ ~ **on sth** *He improvised on the melody.* ◊ ~ **sth** *an improvised speech*

**im·pru·dent** /ɪmˈpruːdnt/ *adj.* (*formal*) not wise or sensible **SYN** **unwise**: *It would be imprudent to invest all your money in one company.* **OPP** **prudent** ▶ **im·pru·dence** /-dns/ *noun* [U]; **im·pru·dent·ly** *adv.*

**im·pu·dent** /ˈɪmpjədənt/ *adj.* (*formal*) rude; not showing respect for other people **SYN** **impertinent**: *an impudent young fellow* ◊ *an impudent remark* ▶ **im·pu·dence** /-dəns/ *noun* [U]

**im·pugn** /ɪmˈpjuːn/ *verb* ~ **sth** (*formal*) to express doubts about whether sth is right, honest, etc. **SYN** **challenge**

**im·pulse** /ˈɪmpʌls/ noun **1** [C, usually sing., U] ~ **(to do sth)** a sudden strong wish or need to do sth, without stopping to think about the results: *He had a sudden impulse to stand up and sing.* ◇ *I resisted the impulse to laugh.* ◇ *Her first impulse was to run away.* ◇ **on (an)** ~ *The door was open and on (an) impulse she went inside.* ◇ *He tends to act on impulse.* **2** [C] (*specialist*) a force or movement of energy that causes sth else to react: *nerve/electrical impulses* **3** [C, usually sing., U] (*formal*) something that causes sb/sth to do sth or to develop and make progress: *to give an impulse to the struggling car industry*

**ˈimpulse buying** noun [U] buying goods without planning to do so in advance, and without thinking about it carefully ▶ **ˈimpulse buy** noun: *It was an impulse buy.*

**im·pul·sion** /ɪmˈpʌlʃn/ noun (*formal*) **1** [C] a strong desire to do sth **2** [U] a reason for doing sth: *Lack of food and water provided much of the impulsion for their speed.*

**im·pul·sive** /ɪmˈpʌlsɪv/ adj. (of people or their behaviour) acting suddenly without thinking carefully about what might happen because of what you are doing **SYN** **impetuous**, **rash**: *an impulsive decision/gesture* ◇ *You're so impulsive!* ◇ *He has an impulsive nature.* ▶ **im·pul·sive·ly** adv.: *Impulsively he reached out and took her hand.* **im·pul·sive·ness** noun [U]

**im·pun·ity** /ɪmˈpjuːnəti/ noun [U] (*formal, disapproving*) the fact of not getting punished for sth

**im·pure** /ɪmˈpjʊə(r); *NAmE* -ˈpjʊr/ adj. **1** not pure or clean; not consisting of only one substance but mixed with one or more substances often of poorer quality: *impure gold* **2** (*old-fashioned* or *formal*) (of thoughts or feelings) morally bad, especially because they are connected with sex **OPP** **pure**

**im·pur·ity** /ɪmˈpjʊərəti; *NAmE* -ˈpjʊr-/ noun (*pl.* **-ies**) **1** [C] a substance that is present in small amounts in another substance, making it dirty or of poor quality: *A filter will remove most impurities found in water.* **2** [U] the state of being dirty or not pure **OPP** **purity**

**im·pute** /ɪmˈpjuːt/ verb
**PHRV** **imˈpute sth to sb/sth** (*formal*) to say, often unfairly, that sb is responsible for sth or has a particular quality **SYN** **attribute**: *I denied the motives that my employer was imputing to me.* ▶ **im·put·ation** /ˌɪmpjuˈteɪʃn/ noun [C, U]

**in** 🔑 **A1** /ɪn/ prep., adv., adj., noun
■ *prep.* **HELP** For the special uses of **in** in phrasal verbs, look at the entries for the verbs. For example **deal in sth** is in the phrasal verb section at **deal**. **1** **A1** at a point within an area or a space: *a country in Africa* ◇ *The kids were playing in the street.* ◇ *It's in that drawer.* ◇ *I read about it in the paper.* **2** **A1** within the shape of sth; surrounded by sth: *She was lying in bed.* ◇ *sitting in an armchair* ◇ *Leave the key in the lock.* ◇ *Soak it in cold water.* **3** **A1** into sth: *He dipped his brush in the paint.* ◇ *She got in her car and drove off.* **4** **A1** forming the whole or part of sth/sb; contained within sth/sb: *There are 31 days in May.* ◇ *all the paintings in the collection* ◇ *I recognize his father in him* (= his character is similar to his father's). **5** **A1** during a period of time: *in 2021* ◇ *in the 18th century* ◇ *in spring/summer/autumn/winter* ◇ *in the fall* ◇ *in March* ◇ *in the morning/afternoon/evening* ◇ *I'm getting forgetful in my old age.* **6** **A1** after a particular length of time: *to return in a few minutes/hours/days/months.* ◇ *It will be ready in a week's time* (= one week from now). ◇ *She learnt to drive in three weeks* (= after three weeks she could drive). **7** **B1** (used in negative sentences or after *first, last*, etc.) for a particular period of time: *I haven't seen him in years.* ◇ *It's the first letter I've had in ten days.* **8** **A1** wearing sth: *dressed in their best clothes* ◇ *the man in the hat* ◇ *to be in uniform* ◇ *She was all in black.* **9** **A1** used to describe sth that is all around you: *We went out in the rain.* ◇ *He was sitting alone in the darkness.* **10** **A1** used to show the language, material, etc. used: *Say it in English.* ◇ *She wrote in pencil.* ◇ *Put it in writing.* ◇ *I paid in cash.* ◇ *He spoke in a loud voice.* **11** **A2** used to show a state or condition: *I'm in love!* ◇ *The house is in good repair.* ◇ *I must put my affairs in order.* ◇ *a man in his thirties* ◇ *The daffodils were in full bloom.* **12** **A2** involved in sth; taking part in sth: *to act in a play*

**13** **A2** used to show sb's job or profession: *He is in the army.* ◇ *She's in computers.* ◇ *in business* **14** **A2** used to show the form, shape, arrangement or quantity of sth: *a novel in three parts* ◇ *Roll it up in a ball.* ◇ *They sat in rows.* ◇ *People flocked in their thousands to see her.* **15** **B1** used to show the quality or thing that a judgement is being made about: *She was not lacking in courage.* ◇ *a country rich in minerals* ◇ *three metres in length* **16** while doing sth; while sth is happening: *In attempting to save the child from drowning, she nearly lost her own life.* ◇ *In all the commotion I forgot to tell him the news.* **17** used to introduce the name of a person who has a particular quality: *We're losing a first-rate editor in Jen.* **18** used to show a rate or relative amount: *a gradient of one in five* ◇ *a tax rate of 22 pence in the pound*

**IDM** **in that** /ˈɪn ðət/ (*formal*) for the reason that; because: *She was fortunate in that she had friends to help her.*

■ *adv.* **HELP** For the special uses of **in** in phrasal verbs, look at the entries for the verbs. For example **fill in (for sb)** is in the phrasal verb section at **fill**. **1** **A1** into an object, an area or a substance: *She opened the door and went in.* ◇ *The kids were playing by the river and one of them fell in.* **OPP** **out** **2** **A1** contained within an object, an area or a substance: *We were locked in.* ◇ *I can't drink coffee with milk in.* **3** **A1** (of people) at home or at a place of work: *Nobody was in when we called.* **OPP** **out** **4** **B1** (of trains, buses, etc.) at the place where people can get on or off, for example the station: *The bus is due in* (= it should arrive) *at six.* **5** **B1** (of letters, etc.) received: *Applications must be in by April 30.* **6** **B2** (of the TIDE) at or towards its highest point on land: *Is the tide coming in or going out?* **OPP** **out** **7** elected: *Several new councillors got in at the last election.* **8** (in CRICKET, baseball, etc.) if a team or team member is in, they are BATTING **OPP** **out** **9** (in tennis, etc.) if the ball is in, it has landed inside the line: *Her serve was just in.* **OPP** **out**

**IDM** **be in at sth** to be present when sth happens: *They were in at the start.* **be ˈin for sth** (*informal*) to be going to experience sth soon, especially sth unpleasant: *He's in for a shock!* ◇ *I'm afraid we're in for a storm.* **be / get ˈin on sth** (*informal*) to be/become involved in sth; to share or know about sth: *I'd like to be in on the plan.* ◇ *Is she in on the secret?* **be (ˈwell) ˈin with sb** (*informal*) to be (very) friendly with sb, and likely to get an advantage from the friendship **ˌin and ˈout (of sth)** going regularly to a place: *He was in and out of jail for most of his life.*

■ *adj.* [usually before noun] (*informal*) popular and fashionable: *Purple is the in colour this spring.* ◇ *Exotic pets are the in thing right now.* ◇ *Short skirts are in again.* ➔ see also IN-JOKE

■ *noun*
**IDM** **an ˈin to sth** = A WAY INTO STH at WAY *n*. **have an ˈin with sb** (*especially NAmE*) to have influence with sb **the ˌins and ˈouts (of sth)** all the details, especially the complicated or difficult ones: *the ins and outs of the problem* ◇ *He quickly learned the ins and outs of the job.*

**in.** abbr. (*pl.* **in.** or **ins.**) (in writing) INCH: *Height: 6ft 2in.*

**in-** prefix /ɪn/ **1** (also **il-** /ɪl/, **im-** /ɪm/, **ir-** /ɪr/) (in adjectives, adverbs and nouns) not; the opposite of: *infinite* ◇ *illogical* ◇ *immorally* ◇ *irrelevance* **2** (also **im-** /ɪm/) (in verbs) to put into the condition mentioned: *inflame* ◇ *imperil*

**-in** /ɪn/ combining form (in nouns) an activity in which many people take part: *a sit-in* ◇ *a teach-in*

**in·abil·ity** 🔑+ **C1** **W** /ˌɪnəˈbɪləti/ noun [U, sing.] ~ **(to do sth)** the fact of not being able to do sth: *the government's inability to provide basic services* ◇ *Some families go without medical treatment because of their inability to pay.* **OPP** **ability**

**in ab·sen·tia** /ˌɪn æbˈsenʃiə/ adv. (*from Latin*) while not present at the event being referred to: *Two foreign suspects will be tried in absentia.*

**in·ac·ces·sible** /ˌɪnækˈsesəbl/ adj. **1** difficult or impossible to reach, get or use: *They live in a remote area, inaccessible except by car.* ◇ ~ **to sb/sth** *The temple is now inaccessible to the public.* **OPP** **accessible 2** ~ **(to sb)**

# inaccurate

(of language or art) difficult to understand or appreciate: *The language of teenagers is often completely inaccessible to adults.* **OPP** **accessible** ▶ **in·ac·ces·si·bil·ity** /ˌɪnækˌsesəˈbɪləti/ *noun* [U]

**in·ac·cur·ate** /ɪnˈækjərət/ *adj.* not exact or accurate; with mistakes: *an inaccurate statement ◊ inaccurate information ◊ All the maps we had were wildly inaccurate.* **OPP** **accurate** ▶ **in·ac·cur·acy** /-rəsi/ *noun* [C, U] (*pl.* **-ies**): *The article is full of inaccuracies. ◊ The writer is guilty of bias and inaccuracy.* ⊃ SYNONYMS at MISTAKE **in·ac·cur·ate·ly** *adv.*

**in·ac·tion** /ɪnˈækʃn/ *noun* [U] (*usually disapproving*) lack of action; the state of doing nothing about a situation or a problem

**in·ac·ti·vate** /ɪnˈæktɪveɪt/ *verb* ~ **sth** (*specialist*) to make sth stop doing sth; to make sth no longer active

**in·act·ive** /ɪnˈæktɪv/ *adj.* **1** not doing anything; not active: *Some animals are inactive during the daytime. ◊ politically inactive ◊ The volcano has been inactive for 50 years.* **2** not in use; not working: *an inactive oil well* **3** having no effect: *an inactive drug/disease* **OPP** **active** ▶ **in·ac·tiv·ity** /ˌɪnækˈtɪvəti/ *noun* [U]: *periods of enforced inactivity and boredom ◊ The inactivity of the government was deplorable.*

**in·ad·equacy** /ɪnˈædɪkwəsi/ *noun* (*pl.* **-ies**) **1** [U] ~ **(of sth)** the state of not being enough or good enough: *the inadequacy of our resources* **OPP** **adequacy** **2** [U] a state of not being able or confident to deal with a situation: *a feeling/sense of inadequacy* **3** [C, usually pl.] ~ **(of/in sth)** a weakness; a lack of sth: *gross inadequacies in the data ◊ He had to face up to his own inadequacies as a father.*

**in·ad·equate** ?+ C1 W /ɪnˈædɪkwət/ *adj.* **1** ?+ C1 not enough; not good enough: *inadequate supplies ◊* ~ **for sth** *The system is inadequate for the tasks it has to perform. ◊* ~ **to do sth** *The food supplies are inadequate to meet the needs of the hungry.* **OPP** **adequate** **2** ?+ C1 (of people) not able, or not confident enough, to deal with a situation SYN **incompetent**: *I felt totally inadequate as a parent.* ▶ **in·ad·equate·ly** *adv.*: *to be inadequately prepared/insured/funded*

**in·ad·mis·sible** /ˌɪnədˈmɪsəbl/ *adj.* (*formal*) that cannot be allowed or accepted, especially in court: *inadmissible evidence* **OPP** **admissible**

**in·ad·vert·ent·ly** /ˌɪnədˈvɜːtntli; *NAmE* -ˈvɜːrt-/ *adv.* by accident; without intending to SYN **unintentionally**: *We had inadvertently left without paying the bill.* ▶ **in·ad·vert·ent** *adj.*: *an inadvertent omission* **in·ad·ver·tence** /ˌɪnədˈvɜːtns; *NAmE* -ˈvɜːrt-/ *noun* [U]

**in·ad·vis·able** /ˌɪnədˈvaɪzəbl/ *adj.* [not usually before noun] ~ **(for sb) (to do sth)** (*formal*) not sensible or wise; that you would advise against: *It is inadvisable to bring children on this trip.* **OPP** **advisable**

**in·ali·en·able** /ɪnˈeɪliənəbl/ *adj.* (*also less frequent* **un·ali·en·able**) [usually before noun] (*formal*) that cannot be taken away from you: *the inalienable right to decide your own future*

**inane** /ɪˈneɪn/ *adj.* stupid or silly; with no meaning: *an inane remark* ▶ **in·ane·ly** *adv.*: *to grin inanely* **in·an·ity** /ɪˈnænəti/ *noun* [U, C, usually pl.] (*pl.* **-ies**)

**in·ani·mate** /ɪnˈænɪmət/ *adj.* **1** not alive in the way that people, animals and plants are: *A rock is an inanimate object.* **OPP** **animate** **2** dead or appearing to be dead: *A man was lying inanimate on the floor.*

**in-ˈapp** *adj.* [only before noun] (*especially of a purchase*) made or available from within a particular app on a device such as a smartphone or tablet: *in-app purchases/ads* ▶ **in-ˈapp** *adv.*: *Extra features can be purchased in-app.*

**in·applic·able** /ɪnˈæplɪkəbl, ˌɪnəˈplɪkəbl/ *adj.* [not before noun] ~ **(to sb/sth)** that cannot be used, or that does not apply, in a particular situation: *These regulations are inapplicable to international students.* **OPP** **applicable**

**in·appro·pri·ate** ?+ C1 W /ˌɪnəˈprəʊpriət/ *adj.* not suitable or appropriate in a particular situation: *inappropriate behaviour/language ◊ it is* ~ **(for sb/sth) (to do sth)** *It would be inappropriate for me to comment. ◊* ~ **to/for sth** *clothes inappropriate to the occasion* **OPP** **appropriate** ▶ **in·appro·pri·acy** /-priəsi/ *noun* [U] **in·appro·pri·ate·ly** *adv.*: *She was inappropriately dressed for a funeral.* **in·appro·pri·ate·ness** *noun* [U]

**in·ar·ticu·late** /ˌɪnɑːˈtɪkjələt; *NAmE* ˌɪnɑːrˈt-/ *adj.* **1** (of people) not able to express ideas or feelings clearly or easily **2** (of speech) not using clear words; not expressed clearly: *an inarticulate reply* **OPP** **articulate** ▶ **in·ar·ticu·late·ly** *adv.*

**in·as·much as** /ˌɪnəzˈmʌtʃ əz/ *conj.* (*formal*) used to add a comment on sth that you have just said and to say in what way it is true: *He was a very unusual musician inasmuch as he was totally deaf.*

**in·at·ten·tion** /ˌɪnəˈtenʃn/ *noun* [U] (*usually disapproving*) lack of attention: *The accident was the result of a moment's inattention.*

**in·at·ten·tive** /ˌɪnəˈtentɪv/ *adj.* (*disapproving*) not paying attention to sth/sb: *an inattentive pupil ◊* ~ **to sth/sb** *inattentive to the needs of others* **OPP** **attentive** ▶ **in·at·ten·tive·ly** *adv.*

**in·aud·ible** /ɪnˈɔːdəbl/ *adj.* ~ **(to sb)** that you cannot hear: *The whistle was inaudible to the human ear.* **OPP** **audible** ▶ **in·audi·bil·ity** /ɪnˌɔːdəˈbɪləti/ *noun* [U] **in·aud·ibly** /ɪnˈɔːdəbli/ *adv.*

**in·aug·ural** /ɪˈnɔːɡjərəl/ *adj.* [only before noun] (of an official speech, meeting, etc.) first, and marking the beginning of sth important, for example the time when a new leader or parliament starts work, when a new organization is formed or when sth is used for the first time: *the President's inaugural address ◊ the inaugural meeting of the geographical society ◊ the inaugural flight of the space shuttle* ▶ **in·aug·ural** *noun* [usually sing.] (*especially NAmE*): *the presidential inaugural in January*

**in·aug·ur·ate** /ɪˈnɔːɡjəreɪt/ *verb* **1** ~ **sb (as sth)** to introduce a new public official or leader at a special ceremony: *He will be inaugurated (as) President in January.* **2** ~ **sth** to officially open a building or start an organization with a special ceremony: *The new theatre was inaugurated by the mayor.* **3** ~ **sth** (*formal*) to introduce a new development or an important change: *The moon landing inaugurated a new era in space exploration.* ▶ **in·aug·ur·ation** /ɪˌnɔːɡjəˈreɪʃn/ *noun* [U, C]: *the President's inauguration ◊ an inauguration speech*

**Inaugu'ration Day** *noun* (in the US) 20 January, officially the first day of a new President's period of office

**in·aus·pi·cious** /ˌɪnɔːˈspɪʃəs/ *adj.* (*formal*) showing signs that the future will not be good or successful: *an inauspicious start* **OPP** **auspicious** ▶ **in·aus·pi·cious·ly** *adv.*

**in·authen·tic** /ˌɪnɔːˈθentɪk/ *adj.* not what sb claims it is; that you cannot believe or rely on **OPP** **authentic** ▶ **in·authen·ti·city** /ˌɪnɔːθenˈtɪsəti/ *noun* [U]

**in·board** /ˈɪnbɔːd; *NAmE* -bɔːrd/ *adj.* (*specialist*) located on the inside of a boat, plane or car: *an inboard motor* **OPP** **outboard** ▶ **in·board** *adv.*

**in·born** /ˌɪnˈbɔːn; *NAmE* -ˈbɔːrn/ (*also less frequent* **in·bred**) *adj.* an **inborn** quality is one that you are born with SYN **innate**

**in·bound** /ˈɪnbaʊnd/ *adj.* travelling towards a place rather than leaving it: *inbound flights/passengers* **OPP** **outbound**

**in·bounds** /ˈɪnbaʊndz/ *adj.* (in basketball) relating to a throw that puts the ball into play again after it has gone out of play: *an inbounds pass*

**in·box** /ˈɪnbɒks; *NAmE* -bɑːks/ *noun* **1** the place on a computer or phone where new emails, text messages, etc. are shown: *I have a stack of emails in my inbox.* ⊃ WORDFINDER NOTE at MESSAGE **2** (*NAmE*) = IN TRAY

**in·bred** /ˌɪnˈbred/ *adj.* **1** produced by BREEDING (= producing young) among closely related members of a group of animals, people or plants: *an inbred racehorse* **2** = INBORN

**in·breed·ing** /ˈɪnbriːdɪŋ/ *noun* [U] BREEDING (= producing young) between closely related people or animals

**in·built** (*also* **in-built**) /ˈɪnbɪlt/ *adj.* [only before noun] **1** (*also less frequent* **built-in**) an **inbuilt** quality exists as an essential part of sth/sb: *His height gives him an inbuilt* advantage over his opponent. **2** (*also more frequent* **built-in**) included as part of a device and not separate from it: *a camera with inbuilt microphone*

**Inc.** /ɪŋk/ (*also* **inc.**) *abbr.* Incorporated (used after the name of a company in the US): *Texaco Inc.*

**inc.** *abbr.* (*BrE*) = INCL.

**in·cal·cul·able** /ɪnˈkælkjələbl/ *adj.* (*formal*) very large or very great; too great to calculate: *The oil spill has caused incalculable damage to the environment.* ⊃ compare CALCULABLE ▶ **in·cal·cul·ably** /-bli/ *adv.*

**in·can·des·cent** /ˌɪnkænˈdesnt; *NAmE* -kən-/ *adj.* **1** (*specialist*) giving out light when heated: *incandescent lamps* **2** (*formal*) very bright: *incandescent white* **3** (*formal*) full of strong emotion; extremely angry: *an incandescent musical performance* ◇ **~ with sth** *She was incandescent with rage.* ▶ **in·can·des·cence** /-sns/ *noun* [U]

**in·can·ta·tion** /ˌɪnkænˈteɪʃn/ *noun* [C, U] special words that are spoken or sung to have a magic effect; the act of speaking or singing these words

**in·cap·able** /ɪnˈkeɪpəbl/ *adj.* **1** not able to do sth: **~ of sth** *incapable of speech* ◇ **~ of doing sth** *The children seem to be totally incapable of working by themselves.* **2** not able to control yourself or your affairs; not able to do anything well: *He was found lying in the road, drunk and incapable.* ◇ *If people keep telling you you're incapable, you begin to lose confidence in yourself.* **OPP** capable

**in·cap·aci·tate** /ˌɪnkəˈpæsɪteɪt/ *verb* [usually passive] **~ sb/sth** (*formal*) to make sb/sth unable to live or work normally

**in·cap·acity** /ˌɪnkəˈpæsəti/ *noun* [U] (*formal*) **1 ~ (of sb/sth) (to do sth)** lack of ability or skill **SYN** **inability**: *their incapacity to govern effectively* **2** the state of being too ill to do your work or take care of yourself: *She returned to work after a long period of incapacity.*

**in-ˈcar** *adj.* [only before noun] relating to sth that you have or use inside a car, for example a radio: *in-car entertainment*

**in·car·cer·ate** /ɪnˈkɑːsəreɪt; *NAmE* -ˈkɑːrs-/ *verb* [usually passive] **~ sb (in sth)** (*formal*) to put sb in prison or in another place from which they cannot escape **SYN** **imprison** ▶ **in·car·cer·ation** /ɪnˌkɑːsəˈreɪʃn; *NAmE* -ˌkɑːrs-/ *noun* [U]

**in·car·nate** *adj., verb*
■ *adj.* /ɪnˈkɑːnət; *NAmE* -ˈkɑːrn-/ (usually after nouns) (*formal*) in human form: *The leader seemed the devil incarnate.*
■ *verb* /ɪnˈkɑːneɪt; *NAmE* -ˈkɑːrn-/ **~ sth** (*formal*) to give a definite or human form to a particular idea or quality **SYN** **embody**

**in·car·na·tion** /ˌɪnkɑːˈneɪʃn; *NAmE* -kɑːrˈn-/ *noun* **1** [C] a period of life in a particular form: *one of the incarnations of Vishnu* ◇ *He believed he had been a prince in a previous incarnation.* ◇ (*figurative*) *I worked for her in her earlier incarnation* (= her previous job) *as a lawyer.* **2** [C] a person who represents a particular quality, for example, in human form **SYN** **embodiment**: *the incarnation of evil* **3** [sing., U] (*also* **the Incarnation**) (in Christianity) the act of God coming to earth in human form as Jesus

**in·cau·tious** /ɪnˈkɔːʃəs/ *adj.* (*formal*) done without thinking carefully about the results; not thinking about what might happen ▶ **in·cau·tious·ly** *adv.*

**in·cen·di·ary** /ɪnˈsendiəri; *NAmE* -dieri/ *adj., noun*
■ *adj.* [only before noun] **1** designed to cause fires: *an incendiary device/bomb/attack* **2** (*formal*) causing strong feelings or violence **SYN** **inflammatory**: *incendiary remarks*
■ *noun* (*pl.* **-ies**) a bomb that is designed to make a fire start burning when it explodes **SYN** **firebomb**

**in·cense** *noun, verb*
■ *noun* /ˈɪnsens/ [U] a substance that produces a pleasant smell when you burn it, used particularly in religious ceremonies
■ *verb* /ɪnˈsens/ **~ sb** to make sb very angry: *The decision incensed the workforce.*

**in·censed** /ɪnˈsenst/ *adj.* very angry: *They were incensed at the decision.*

**in·cen·tive** /ɪnˈsentɪv/ *noun* **1** [C, U] **~ (for/to sb/sth) (to do sth)** something that encourages you to do sth: *There is no incentive for people to save fuel.* **OPP** **disincentive** **2** [C] a payment or CONCESSION (= a reduction in the amount of money that has to be paid) that encourages sb to do something: *tax incentives to encourage savings*

**in·cen·tiv·ize** (*BrE also* **-ise**) /ɪnˈsentɪvaɪz/ *verb* to encourage sb to behave in a particular way by offering them a reward: **~ sth** *ways to incentivize innovation* ◇ **~ sb to do sth** *You need to incentivize your existing customers to stay with you.*

**in·cep·tion** /ɪnˈsepʃn/ *noun* [sing.] (*formal*) the start of an institution, an organization, etc: *The club has grown rapidly since its inception in 2007.*

**in·ces·sant** /ɪnˈsesnt/ *adj.* (*usually disapproving*) never stopping **SYN** **constant**: *incessant noise/rain/chatter* ◇ *incessant meetings* ▶ **in·ces·sant·ly** *adv.*: *to talk incessantly*

**in·cest** /ˈɪnsest/ *noun* [U] sexual activity between two people who are very closely related in a family, for example, a brother and sister, or a father and daughter

**in·ces·tu·ous** /ɪnˈsestʃuəs/ *adj.* **1** involving sex between two people in a family who are very closely related: *an incestuous relationship* **2** (*disapproving*) involving a group of people who have a close relationship and do not want to include anyone outside the group: *The music industry is an incestuous business.* ▶ **in·ces·tu·ous·ly** *adv.*

**inch** /ɪntʃ/ *noun, verb*
■ *noun* **1** (*abbr.* **in.**) (in Britain and North America) a unit for measuring length or height, equal to 2.54 CENTIMETRES. There are 12 inches in a foot: *She's a few inches taller than me.* ◇ *a laptop with a 15-inch screen* ◇ *The snow is about one and a half inches deep.* ◇ *1.14 inches of rain fell last night.* ◇ *Every square inch of available land has been built on.* ◇ *a metal tube about three inches in diameter* **2** a small amount or distance: **by an~** *He escaped death by an inch.* ◇ **by inches** *The car missed us by inches.* ◇ **within an ~ of (doing) sth** *She was within an inch of being killed.* ◇ *They beat him (to) within an inch of his life* (= very severely). ◇ **inches (away) from (doing) sth** *He was just inches away from scoring.*
**IDM** **every inch 1** the whole of sth: *The doctor examined every inch of his body.* ◇ (*figurative*) *If they try to fire me I'll fight them every inch of the way.* **2** completely: *In his first game the young player already looked every inch a winner.* **give sb an ˈinch (and they'll take a ˈmile/ˈyard)** (*saying*) used to say that if you allow some people a small amount of freedom or power they will see you as weak and try to take a lot more **inch by ˈinch** very slowly and with great care or difficulty: *She crawled forward inch by inch.* **not budge/give/move an ˈinch** to refuse to change your position, decision, etc. even a little: *We tried to negotiate a lower price but they wouldn't budge an inch.* ⊃ more at TRUST *v.*
■ *verb* [I, T] to move or make sth move slowly and carefully in a particular direction: + *adv./prep. She moved forward, inching towards the rope.* ◇ **~ sth + adv./prep.** *I inched the car forward.* ◇ *He inched his way through the narrow passage.*

**in-charge** /ˈɪntʃɑːdʒ; *NAmE* -tʃɑːrdʒ/ *noun* (*IndE*) the person who is officially responsible for a department, etc: *the incharge of the district hospital*

**in·cho·ate** /ɪnˈkəʊət; *BrE also* ˈɪnkəʊeɪt/ *adj.* (*formal*) just beginning to form and therefore not clear or developed: *inchoate ideas*

**in·ci·dence** /ˈɪnsɪdəns/ *noun* **1** [C, usually sing.] **~ (of sth)** (*formal*) the extent to which sth happens or has an effect: *an area with a high incidence of crime* **2** [U] (*physics*) the way in which light meets a surface: *the angle of incidence*

**in·ci·dent** /ˈɪnsɪdənt/ *noun* **1** something that happens, especially sth unusual or unpleasant: *His bad behaviour was just an isolated incident.* ◇ *The most recent incident occurred last January.* ◇ **~ with sb/sth** *The*

# incidental

hot-headed tennis star became **involved in an incident** with the umpire. **2** [C, U] a serious or violent event, such as a crime, an accident or an attack: *a violent/serious incident* ◊ *She reported the incident to the police.* ◊ *He said that the authorities would investigate the incident.* ◊ **in an ~** *A 36-year-old man and a 25-year-old woman were stabbed in separate incidents.* ◊ **without ~** *The demonstration passed off without incident.* **3** [C] a DISAGREEMENT between two countries, often involving military forces: *a border/diplomatic incident*

**in·ci·den·tal** /ˌɪnsɪˈdentl/ *adj., noun*
■ *adj.* **1** ~ (to sth) happening in connection with sth else, but not as important as it, or not intended: *The discovery was incidental to their main research.* ◊ *incidental music* (= music used with a play or a film to give atmosphere) ◊ *You may be able to get help with incidental expenses* (= small costs that you have in connection with sth). **2** ~ **to sth** (*specialist*) happening as a natural result of sth: *These risks are incidental to the work of a firefighter.*
■ *noun* [usually pl.] something that happens in connection with sth else, but is less important: *You'll need money for incidentals such as tips and taxis.*

**in·ci·den·tal·ly** /ˌɪnsɪˈdentli/ *adv.* **1** used to introduce a new topic, or some extra information, or a question that you have just thought of **SYN** **by the way**: *Incidentally, have you heard the news about Sue?* **2** in a way that was not planned but that is connected with sth else: *The information was only discovered incidentally.*

**'incident room** *noun* (*BrE*) a room where the police work to collect evidence and information about a crime or accident that has taken place

**in·cin·er·ate** /ɪnˈsɪnəreɪt/ *verb* [often passive] ~ **sth** (*formal*) to burn sth, especially waste material, until it is completely destroyed ▸ **in·cin·er·ation** /ɪnˌsɪnəˈreɪʃn/ *noun* [U]: *high-temperature incineration plants*

**in·cin·er·ator** /ɪnˈsɪnəreɪtə(r)/ *noun* a container that is closed on all sides for burning waste at high temperatures ⊃ WORDFINDER NOTE at WASTE

**in·cipi·ent** /ɪnˈsɪpiənt/ *adj.* [usually before noun] (*formal*) just beginning: *signs of incipient unrest*

**in·cise** /ɪnˈsaɪz/ *verb* [often passive] ~ **A (in/on/onto B)** ◊ ~ **B (with A)** (*formal*) to cut words, designs, etc. into a surface ⊃ compare ENGRAVE

**in·ci·sion** /ɪnˈsɪʒn/ *noun* [C, U] a sharp cut made in sth, particularly during a medical operation; the act of making a cut in sth: *Make a small incision below the ribs.*

**in·ci·sive** /ɪnˈsaɪsɪv/ *adj.* (*approving*) **1** showing clear thought and good understanding of what is important, and the ability to express this: *incisive comments/criticism/analysis* ◊ *an incisive mind* **2** showing sb's ability to take decisions and act with force: *an incisive performance* ▸ **in·ci·sive·ly** *adv.* **in·ci·sive·ness** *noun* [U]

**in·ci·sor** /ɪnˈsaɪzə(r)/ *noun* one of the sharp teeth at the front of the mouth that are used for biting. Humans have eight incisors. ⊃ compare CANINE, MOLAR, PREMOLAR, WISDOM TOOTH

**in·cite** /ɪnˈsaɪt/ *verb* to encourage sb to do sth violent, illegal or unpleasant, especially by making them angry or excited: ~ **sth** *to incite crime/racial hatred/violence* ◊ ~ **sb (to do sth)** *They were accused of inciting the crowd to violence.* ◊ ~ **sb to do sth** *He incited the workforce to come out on strike.*

**in·cite·ment** /ɪnˈsaɪtmənt/ *noun* [U, C] ~ **(to sth)** the act of encouraging sb to do sth violent, illegal or unpleasant: *incitement to racial hatred*

**in·civil·ity** /ˌɪnsəˈvɪləti/ *noun* [U, C] (*pl.* **-ies**) (*formal*) rude behaviour; rude remarks ⊃ see also UNCIVIL

**incl.** (*BrE also* **inc.**) *abbr.* (in advertisements) including; included: *transport not incl.* ◊ *£29.53 inc. tax*

**in·clem·ent** /ɪnˈklemənt/ *adj.* (*formal*) (of the weather) not pleasant; cold, wet, etc. **OPP** **clement** ▸ **in·clem·ency** /-mənsi/ *noun* [U]

**in·clin·ation** /ˌɪnklɪˈneɪʃn/ *noun* **1** [U, C] a feeling that makes you want to do sth: ~ **(to do sth)** *He did not show the slightest inclination to leave.* ◊ *My natural inclination is to find a compromise.* ◊ *She had neither the time nor the inclination to help them.* ◊ ~ **(towards/for sth)** *She lacked any inclination for housework.* ◊ **by ~** *He was a loner by nature and by inclination.* ◊ *You must follow your own inclinations when choosing a career.* **2** [C] ~ **to do sth** a new way of doing sth that is starting to develop: *There is an inclination to treat geography as a less important subject.* **3** [C, usually sing., U] (*specialist*) a degree of sloping: *an inclination of 45°* ◊ *the angle of inclination* **4** [C] a small movement downwards, usually of the head

**in·cline** *verb, noun*
■ *verb* /ɪnˈklaɪn/ (*formal*) **1** [I, T] to tend to think or behave in a particular way; to make sb do this: ~ **to/towards sth** *I incline to the view that we should take no action at this stage.* ◊ ~ **to do sth** *The government is more effective than we incline to think.* ◊ ~ **sb to/towards sth** *Lack of money inclines many young people towards crime.* ◊ ~ **sb to do sth** *His obvious sincerity inclined me to trust him.* **2** [T] ~ **your head** to bend your head forward, especially as a sign of agreement, welcome, etc. **3** [I, T] ~ **(sth) (to/towards sth)** to lean or slope in a particular direction; to make sth lean or slope: *The land inclined gently towards the shore.*
■ *noun* /ˈɪnklaɪn/ (*formal*) a slope: *a steep/slight incline*

**in·clined** /ɪnˈklaɪnd/ *adj.* **1** [not before noun] ~ **(to do sth)** wanting to do sth: *She was inclined to trust him.* ◊ *He writes only when he feels inclined to.* ◊ *There'll be time for a swim if you feel so inclined.* **2** ~ **to do sth** tending to do sth; likely to do sth: *He's inclined to be lazy.* ◊ *They'll be more inclined to listen if you don't shout.* **3** ~ **to agree, believe, think, etc.** used when you are expressing an opinion but do not want to express it very strongly: *I'm inclined to agree with you.* **4** (used with particular adverbs) having a natural ability for sth; preferring to do sth: *musically/academically inclined children* **5** sloping; at an angle

**in·clude** /ɪnˈkluːd/ *verb* **1** (not used in the progressive tenses) if one thing **includes** another, it has the second thing as one of its parts: ~ **sth** *The tour included a visit to the Science Museum.* ◊ *Does the price include tax?* ◊ ~ **doing sth** *Your duties will include greeting visitors and directing them to the appropriate department.* **2** to make sb/sth part of sth: ~ **sb/sth in sth** *You should include some examples in your essay.* ◊ ~ **sb/sth as sth** *Representatives from the country were included as observers at the conference.* **OPP** **exclude**

**in·cluded** /ɪnˈkluːdɪd/ *adj.* [after noun] contained as part of sth: *all of Europe (Britain included)* ◊ *Is breakfast included?* ◊ *We all went, me included.* ◊ ~ **in/on sth** *Also included on the disc are English subtitles.*

**in·clud·ing** /ɪnˈkluːdɪŋ/ *prep.* (*abbr.* **incl.**, *BrE also* **inc.**) having sth as part of a group or set: *I've got three days' holiday including New Year's Day.* ◊ *Six people were killed in the riot, including a policeman.* ◊ *It's £7.50, not including tax.* **OPP** **excluding** ⊃ LANGUAGE BANK at E.G.

**in·clu·sion** /ɪnˈkluːʒn/ *noun* **1** [U] the fact of including sb/sth; the fact of being included: *His inclusion in the team is in doubt.* **2** [C] a person or thing that is included: *There were some surprising inclusions in the list.* **OPP** **exclusion**

**in·clu·sive** /ɪnˈkluːsɪv/ *adj.* **1** having the total cost, or the cost of sth that is mentioned, contained in the price: *The fully inclusive fare for the trip is £52.* ◊ ~ **of sth** *The rent is inclusive of water and heating.* **OPP** **exclusive** ⊃ see also ALL-INCLUSIVE **2** **(from) ... to ... inclusive** (*BrE*) including all the days, months, numbers, etc. mentioned: *We are offering free holidays for children aged two to eleven inclusive.* ◊ *The castle is open daily from May to October inclusive.* **3** deliberately including people, things, ideas, etc. from all sections of society, points of view, etc: *The party must adopt more inclusive strategies and a broader vision.* **OPP** **exclusive** ▸ **in·clu·sive·ly** *adv.*: *The word 'men' can be understood inclusively* (= including men and women). **in·clu·sive·ness** *noun* [U]

▼ BRITISH/AMERICAN
**inclusive / through**
- In *BrE*, **inclusive** is used to emphasize that you are including the days, months, numbers, etc. mentioned, especially in formal or official situations: *Answer questions 8 to 12 inclusive.* ◊ *The amusement park is open daily from May to October inclusive.*
- In *NAmE*, **through** is used: *Answer questions 8 through 12.* ◊ *The amusement park is open (from) May through October.*
- **To** can also be used with this meaning in *BrE* and *NAmE*: *The park is open from 1 May to 31 October.*

**in·cog·nito** /ˌɪnkɒɡˈniːtəʊ; *NAmE* -kɑːɡ-/ *adv.* in a way that prevents other people from finding out who you are: *Movie stars often prefer to travel incognito.* ▶ **in·cog·nito** *adj.*: *an incognito visit*

**in·co·her·ent** /ˌɪnkəʊˈhɪərənt; *NAmE* -ˈhɪr-, -ˈher-/ *adj.* **1** (of people) unable to express yourself clearly, often because of emotion: *She broke off, incoherent with anger.* **OPP** **coherent 2** (of sounds) not clear and hard to understand **SYN** **unintelligible**: *Rachel whispered something incoherent.* **3** not logical or well organized: *an incoherent policy* **OPP** **coherent** ▶ **in·co·her·ence** /-rəns/ *noun* [U] **in·co·her·ent·ly** *adv.*

**in·come** 🅾 **B2** /ˈɪnkʌm, -kəm/ *noun* [C, U] the money that a person, a region, a country, etc. earns from work, from investing money, from business, etc: *Average household income fell slightly.* ◊ *a weekly disposable income* (= the money that you have left to spend after tax, etc.) *of £200* ◊ *Net income for the year was $43m.* ◊ *Trying to earn an income as an artist can be hard.* ◊ *Tourism generates income for the local economy.* ◊ **on an ~** *These tax changes should help people on low incomes.* ◊ **~from sth** *They lived on the rental income from the property.* ◊ *Tourism is a major source of income for the area.* ◊ *higher/middle/lower income groups* ⊃ compare EXPENDITURE

▼ SYNONYMS
**income**
wage/wages • pay • salary • earnings
These are all words for money that a person earns or receives for their work.
**income** money that a person receives for their work, or from investments or business: *people on low incomes*
**wage/wages** money that employees get for doing their job, usually paid every week or every month: *a weekly wage of £180*
**pay** money that employees earn for doing their job: *The job offers good rates of pay.*
**salary** money that employees earn for doing their job, usually paid every month.
WAGE, PAY OR SALARY?
**Pay** is the most general of these three words. In the past, employees who worked in factories, shops etc. got their **wages** each week, often paid in cash. These days they are more likely to be paid each month, directly into their bank account, but the term **wage** is still used for these kinds of jobs. Employees who work in offices or professional people such as teachers or doctors receive a **salary** that is paid each month, but is usually expressed as an annual figure.
**earnings** money that a person earns from their work: *a rise in average earnings for factory workers*
PATTERNS
- (a) **high/low/basic** income / wage / pay / salary / earnings
- to **earn** an income / a wage / your pay / a salary
- to **be on** a(n) income / wage / salary of …

**in·comer** /ˈɪnkʌmə(r)/ *noun* (*BrE*) a person who comes to live in an area in which they have not grown up, especially in a rural community where most people have lived there all their lives

**income sup·port** *noun* [U] (in the UK and Canada) the money that the government pays to people who have no income or a very low income

# inconceivable

**income tax** *noun* [U, C] the amount of tax that you pay to the government according to how much you earn: *The standard rate of income tax was cut to 23p in the pound.*

**in·com·ing** /ˈɪnkʌmɪŋ/ *adj.* [only before noun] **1** recently elected or chosen: *the incoming government/president/administration* **OPP** **outgoing 2** arriving somewhere, or being received: *incoming flights* ◊ *the incoming tide* ◊ *incoming calls/mail* **OPP** **outgoing**

**in·com·men·sur·able** /ˌɪnkəˈmenʃərəbl/ *adj.* **~(with sth)** (*formal*) if two things are **incommensurable**, they are so completely different from each other that they cannot be compared

**in·com·men·sur·ate** /ˌɪnkəˈmenʃərət/ *adj.* **~(with sth)** (*formal*) not matching sth in size, importance, quality, etc. **OPP** **commensurate**

**in·com·mu·ni·cado** /ˌɪnkəˌmjuːnɪˈkɑːdəʊ/ *adj.* without communicating with other people, because you are not allowed to or because you do not want to: *The prisoner has been held incommunicado for more than a week.*

**in·com·par·able** /ɪnˈkɒmprəbl; *NAmE* -ˈkɑːm-/ *adj.* so good or impressive that nothing can be compared to it **SYN** **matchless**: *the incomparable beauty of Lake Garda* ▶ **in·com·par·abil·ity** /ɪnˌkɒmpərəˈbɪləti; *NAmE* -ˌkɑːm-/ *noun* [U] **in·com·par·ably** /ɪnˈkɒmprəbli; *NAmE* -ˈkɑːm-/ *adv.*

**in·com·pat·ible** /ˌɪnkəmˈpætəbl/ *adj.* **1 ~(with sth)** two actions, ideas, etc. that are **incompatible** are not acceptable or possible together because of basic differences: *The hours of the job are incompatible with family life.* ◊ *These two objectives are mutually incompatible.* **2** two people who are **incompatible** are very different from each other and so are not able to live or work happily together **3 ~(with sth)** two things that are **incompatible** are of different types so that they cannot be used or mixed together: *New computer software is often incompatible with older computers.* ◊ *Those two blood groups are incompatible.* **OPP** **compatible** ▶ **in·com·pati·bil·ity** /ˌɪnkəmˌpætəˈbɪləti/ *noun* [U, C] (*pl.* **-ies**)

**in·com·pe·tence** /ɪnˈkɒmpɪtəns; *NAmE* -ˈkɑːm-/ (*also less frequent* **in·com·pe·tency** /ɪnˈkɒmpɪtənsi; *NAmE* -ˈkɑːm-/) *noun* [U] the lack of skill or ability to do your job or a task as it should be done: *professional incompetence* ◊ *police incompetence* ◊ *He was dismissed for incompetence.*

**in·com·pe·tent** /ɪnˈkɒmpɪtənt; *NAmE* -ˈkɑːm-/ *adj., noun*
- *adj.* not having the skill or ability to do your job or a task as it should be done: *an incompetent teacher* ◊ *his incompetent handling of the affair* ◊ *The prime minister was attacked as incompetent to lead.* **OPP** **competent** ▶ **in·com·pe·tent·ly** *adv.*
- *noun* a person who does not have the skill or ability to do their job or a task as it should be done

**in·com·plete** /ˌɪnkəmˈpliːt/ *adj., noun*
- *adj.* not having everything that it should have; not finished or complete: *an incomplete set of figures* ◊ *Spoken language contains many incomplete sentences.* **OPP** **complete** ▶ **in·com·plete·ly** *adv.*: *The causes of the phenomenon are still incompletely understood.* **in·com·plete·ness** *noun* [U]
- *noun* (*NAmE*) the grade that a student gets for a course of education when they have not completed all the work for that course

**in·com·pre·hen·sible** /ɪnˌkɒmprɪˈhensəbl; *NAmE* -ˌkɑːm-/ *adj.* **~(to sb)** impossible to understand **SYN** **unintelligible**: *Some application forms can be incomprehensible to ordinary people.* ◊ *He found his son's actions totally incomprehensible.* **OPP** **comprehensible** ▶ **in·com·pre·hen·si·bil·ity** /ɪnˌkɒmprɪˌhensəˈbɪləti; *NAmE* -ˌkɑːm-/ *noun* [U] **in·com·pre·hen·sibly** /ɪnˌkɒmprɪˈhensəbli; *NAmE* -ˌkɑːm-/ *adv.*

**in·com·pre·hen·sion** /ɪnˌkɒmprɪˈhenʃn; *NAmE* -ˌkɑːm-/ *noun* [U] the state of not being able to understand sb/sth: *Anna read the letter with incomprehension.*

**in·con·ceiv·able** /ˌɪnkənˈsiːvəbl/ *adj.* impossible to imagine or believe **SYN** **unthinkable**: *It is inconceivable*

🅞 Oxford Phrasal Academic Lexicon (OPAL) written and spoken word lists | 🅦 OPAL written word list | 🅢 OPAL spoken word list

# inconclusive

that the minister was not aware of the problem. **OPP** conceivable ▶ **in·con·ceiv·ably** /-bli/ adv.

**in·con·clu·sive** /ˌɪnkənˈkluːsɪv/ adj. not leading to a definite decision or result: *inconclusive evidence/results/tests* ◊ *inconclusive discussions* **OPP** conclusive ▶ **in·con·clu·sive·ly** adv.: *The last meeting had ended inconclusively.*

**in·con·gru·ous** /ɪnˈkɒŋɡruəs; NAmE -ˈkɑːŋ-/ adj. strange, and not suitable in a particular situation **SYN** inappropriate: *Such traditional methods seem incongruous in our technical age.* ▶ **in·con·gru·ity** /ˌɪnkɒŋˈɡruːəti; NAmE -kɑːŋ-/ noun [U, C] (pl. **-ies**): *She was struck by the incongruity of the situation.* **in·con·gru·ous·ly** /ɪnˈkɒŋɡruəsli; NAmE -ˈkɑːŋ-/ adv.: *incongruously dressed*

**in·con·se·quen·tial** /ɪnˌkɒnsɪˈkwenʃl; NAmE -ˌkɑːn-/ adj. not important or worth considering **SYN** trivial: *inconsequential details* ◊ *inconsequential chatter* **OPP** consequential ▶ **in·con·se·quen·tial·ly** /-ʃəli/ adv.

**in·con·sid·er·able** /ˌɪnkənˈsɪdərəbl/ adj.
**IDM** **not incon'siderable** (formal) large; large enough to be considered important: *We have spent a not inconsiderable amount of money on the project already.*

**in·con·sid·er·ate** /ˌɪnkənˈsɪdərət/ adj. (disapproving) not giving enough thought to other people's feelings or needs **SYN** thoughtless: *inconsiderate behaviour* ◊ *It was inconsiderate of you not to call.* **OPP** considerate ▶ **in·con·sid·er·ate·ly** adv.

**in·con·sist·ent** **W** /ˌɪnkənˈsɪstənt/ adj. **1** [not usually before noun] ~ **(with sth)** if two statements, etc. are **inconsistent**, or one is **inconsistent with** the other, they cannot both be true because they give the facts in a different way: *The report is inconsistent with the financial statements.* ◊ *The witnesses' statements were inconsistent.* **2** ~ **with sth** not matching a set of standards, ideas, etc: *Her behaviour was clearly inconsistent with her beliefs.* **3** (disapproving) tending to change too often; not staying the same: *inconsistent results* ◊ *Children find it difficult if a parent is inconsistent.* **OPP** consistent ▶ **in·con·sist·ency** /-stənsi/ noun [U, C] (pl. **-ies**): *There is some inconsistency between the witnesses' evidence and their earlier statements.* ◊ *I noticed a few minor inconsistencies in her argument.* **in·con·sist·ent·ly** adv.

**in·con·sol·able** /ˌɪnkənˈsəʊləbl/ adj. very sad and unable to accept help or comfort: *They were inconsolable when their only child died.* ▶ **in·con·sol·ably** /-bli/ adv.: *to weep inconsolably*

**in·con·spicu·ous** /ˌɪnkənˈspɪkjuəs/ adj. not attracting attention; not easy to notice **OPP** conspicuous ▶ **in·con·spicu·ous·ly** adv.

**in·con·stant** /ɪnˈkɒnstənt; NAmE -ˈkɑːn-/ adj. (formal) **1** not FAITHFUL in love or friendship **SYN** fickle **2** that frequently changes **OPP** constant ▶ **in·con·stancy** /-stənsi/ noun [U]

**in·con·test·able** /ˌɪnkənˈtestəbl/ adj. (formal) that is true and cannot be disagreed with or denied **SYN** indisputable: *an incontestable right/fact* ▶ **in·con·test·ably** /-bli/ adv.

**in·con·tin·ence** /ɪnˈkɒntɪnəns; NAmE -ˈkɑːn-/ noun [U] the lack of ability to control the BLADDER and BOWELS **OPP** continence ▶ **in·con·tin·ent** /-tɪnənt/ adj.: *Many of our patients are incontinent.*

**in·con·tro·vert·ible** /ˌɪnkɒntrəˈvɜːtəbl; NAmE -kɑːntrəˈvɜːrt-/ adj. (formal) that is true and cannot be disagreed with or denied **SYN** indisputable: *incontrovertible evidence/proof* ▶ **in·con·tro·vert·ibly** /-bli/ adv.

**in·con·veni·ence** /ˌɪnkənˈviːniəns/ noun, verb
■ noun **1** [U] trouble or problems, especially in connection with what you need or would like yourself: *We apologize for the delay and regret any inconvenience it may have caused.* ◊ *I have already been put to considerable inconvenience.* **2** [C] a person or thing that causes problems or difficulties **SYN** nuisance: *I can put up with minor inconveniences.*
■ verb ~ **sb** (formal) to cause trouble or difficulty for sb: *I hope that we haven't inconvenienced you.*

**in·con·veni·ent** /ˌɪnkənˈviːniənt/ adj. causing trouble or problems, especially in connection with what you need or would like yourself: *an inconvenient time/place* **OPP** convenient ▶ **in·con·veni·ent·ly** adv.

**in·corp·or·ate** ?+ **B2 W** /ɪnˈkɔːpəreɪt; NAmE -ˈkɔːrp-/ verb **1** ?+ **B2** ~ **sth** to include sth so that it forms a part of sth: *The new car design incorporates all the latest safety features.* ◊ ~ **sth in/into/within sth** *We have incorporated all the latest safety features into the design.* ◊ *Many of your suggestions have been incorporated in the plan.* **2** [often passive] (business) to create a legally recognized company: *be incorporated The company was incorporated in 2008.* ▶ **in·corp·or·ation** /ɪnˌkɔːpəˈreɪʃn; NAmE -ˌkɔːrp-/ noun [U]: *the incorporation of foreign words into the language* ◊ *the articles of incorporation of the company*

**in·corp·or·ated** /ɪnˈkɔːpəreɪtɪd; NAmE -ˈkɔːrp-/ adj. (abbr. **Inc.** or **inc.**) (business) formed into a business company with legal status: *the Incorporated Society of British Advertisers* ◊ *Adobe Systems Incorporated*

**in·cor·por·eal** /ˌɪnkɔːˈpɔːriəl; NAmE -kɔːrˈp-/ adj. (formal) without a body or form

**in·cor·rect** ?+ **B2** /ˌɪnkəˈrekt/ adj. **1** ?+ **B2** not accurate or true: *incorrect information/spelling* ◊ *His version of what happened is incorrect.* **2** speaking or behaving in a way that does not follow the accepted standards or rules **OPP** correct ⊃ see also POLITICALLY CORRECT ▶ **in·cor·rect·ly** adv.: *an incorrectly addressed letter* **in·cor·rect·ness** noun [U]

**in·cor·ri·gible** /ɪnˈkɒrɪdʒəbl; NAmE -ˈkɔːr-/ adj. (disapproving or humorous) having bad habits that cannot be changed or improved **SYN** incurable: *Her husband is an incorrigible flirt.* ◊ *You're incorrigible!* ▶ **in·cor·ri·gibly** /-bli/ adv.

**in·cor·rupt·ible** /ˌɪnkəˈrʌptəbl/ adj. **1** (of people) not able to be persuaded to do sth wrong or dishonest, even if sb offers them money **2** that cannot DECAY or be destroyed **OPP** corruptible ▶ **in·cor·rupt·ibil·ity** /ˌɪnkəˌrʌptəˈbɪləti/ noun [U]

**in·crease** ? **A2** verb, noun
■ verb ? **A2** /ɪnˈkriːs/ [I, T] to become greater in amount, number, value, etc.; to make sth greater in amount, number, value, etc: *Costs have increased significantly.* ◊ *to increase dramatically/substantially* ◊ *The price of oil increased.* ◊ ~ **in sth** *Oil increased in price.* ◊ ~ **by sth** *The rate of inflation increased by 2 per cent.* ◊ ~ **from A to B** *The population has increased from 1.2 million to 1.8 million.* ◊ ~ **with sth** *Disability increases with age* (= the older sb is, the more likely they are to be disabled). ◊ ~ **sth** *Sun exposure may increase the risk of skin cancer.* ◊ *The company plans to significantly increase product availability over the next year.* ◊ ~ **sth by sth** *They've increased the price by 50 per cent.* ◊ ~ **sth from A to B** *Last month the reward was increased from $20000 to $40000.* ◊ *An increasing number of people live alone.* **OPP** decrease ▶ **in·creased** adj. [only before noun]: *increased demand* ◊ *an increased risk of heart attack or stroke*
■ noun ? **A2** /ˈɪnkriːs/ [C, U] a rise in the amount, number or value of sth: *price/tax/wage increases* ◊ *Profits show a steady increase.* ◊ ~ **in sth** *Last year the business saw a 3% increase in turnover.* ◊ *a significant/dramatic/substantial increase in sales* ◊ ~ **(of sth) (on sth)** *This is an increase of 12% on the previous year.* ◊ **on the** ~ *Homelessness is on the increase* (= increasing). **OPP** decrease

**in·creas·ing·ly** ? **B2** /ɪnˈkriːsɪŋli/ adv. more and more all the time: *increasingly difficult/important/popular* ◊ *It is becoming increasingly clear that this problem will not be easily solved.* ◊ *Increasingly, training is taking place in the office rather than outside it.*

**in·cred·ible** ? **A2** /ɪnˈkredəbl/ adj. **1** ? **A2** impossible or very difficult to believe **SYN** unbelievable: *an incredible story* ◊ **it is** ~ **(to sb) that** … *It's just incredible to me that only one person was hurt.* ◊ **it is** ~ **how** … *It really is incredible how she managed to get away with it.* ◊ **it is** ~ **to do sth** *It's incredible to think that the affair had been going on for years.* **2** ? **A2** extremely good **SYN** amazing: *The hotel was incredible.* ◊ **it is** ~ **to do sth** *It's just incredible to have him home again.* **3** **A2** (informal) extremely large:

▼ **LANGUAGE BANK**

**increase**
Describing an increase

- Student numbers in English language schools in this country **increased** from 66000 in 2018 to just over 84000 in 2019.
- The number of students **increased** by almost 30 per cent compared with the previous year.
- Student numbers **shot up** / **increased dramatically** in 2019.
- The proportion of Spanish students **rose sharply** from 5 per cent in 2018 to 14 per cent in 2019.
- There was a significant **rise** in student numbers in 2019.
- The 2019 figure was 84000, **an increase of** 28 per cent on the previous year.
- The 2019 figure was 84000, 28 per cent **up** on the previous year.
- As the chart shows, this can partly be explained by a **dramatic increase** in students from Spain.

⊃ LANGUAGE BANK at EXPECT, FALL, ILLUSTRATE, PROPORTION

an **incredible amount** of work ◊ *The prices they charge are absolutely incredible.*

**in·cred·ibly** /ɪnˈkredəbli/ *adv.* **1** **SYN** **unbelievably**: *It was all incredibly difficult.* ◊ *organizations doing incredibly important work* **2** in a way that is very difficult to believe: *Incredibly, she had no idea what was going on.*

**in·credu·lous** /ɪnˈkredʒələs/ *adj.* not willing or not able to believe sth; showing a lack of ability to believe sth: *'Here?' said Kate, incredulous.* ◊ *an incredulous look* ⊃ compare CREDULOUS ▶ **in·credu·lity** /ˌɪnkrəˈdjuːləti; *NAmE* -ˈduː-/ *noun* [U] **SYN** **disbelief**: *a look of surprise and incredulity* **in·credu·lous·ly** /ɪnˈkredʒələsli/ *adv.*: *He laughed incredulously.*

**in·cre·ment** /ˈɪŋkrəmənt/ *noun* **1** a regular increase in the amount of money that sb is paid for their job: *a salary of £25K with annual increments* **2** (*formal*) an increase in a number or an amount ▶ **in·cre·men·tal** /ˌɪŋkrəˈmentl/ *adj.*: *incremental costs* **in·cre·men·tal·ly** /-təli/ *adv.*

**in·crim·in·ate** /ɪnˈkrɪmɪneɪt/ *verb* ~ **sb** to make it seem as if sb has done sth wrong or illegal: *They were afraid of answering the questions and incriminating themselves.* ▶ **in·crim·in·at·ing** *adj.* [usually before noun]: *incriminating evidence* **in·crim·in·ation** /ɪnˌkrɪmɪˈneɪʃn/ *noun* [U]

**'in-crowd** *noun* [sing.] a small group of people within a larger group who seem to be the most popular or fashionable

**in·crust·ation** = ENCRUSTATION

**in·cu·bate** /ˈɪŋkjubeɪt/ *verb* **1** [T] ~ **sth** (of a bird) to sit on its eggs in order to keep them warm until they HATCH **2** [T] ~ **sth** (*biology*) to keep cells, bacteria, etc. at a suitable temperature so that they develop **3** [T] **be incubating sth** (*medical*) to have a disease developing inside you before symptoms appear **4** [I] (*medical*) (of a disease) to develop slowly without showing any signs

**in·cu·ba·tion** /ˌɪŋkjuˈbeɪʃn/ *noun* **1** [U] the HATCHING of eggs **2** [C] (*also* **incuˈbation period**) (*medical or biology*) the time between sb catching a disease and the appearance of the first symptoms **3** [U] (*biology*) the development and growth of bacteria, etc.

**in·cu·ba·tor** /ˈɪŋkjubeɪtə(r)/ *noun* **1** a piece of equipment in a hospital that new babies are placed in when they are weak or born too early, in order to help them survive ⊃ WORDFINDER NOTE at BABY **2** a machine like a box where eggs are kept warm until the young birds are born

**in·cu·bus** /ˈɪŋkjubəs/ *noun* (*pl.* **in·cu·buses** *or* **in·cubi** /-baɪ/) **1** (*literary*) a problem that makes you worry a lot **2** a male evil spirit, supposed in the past to have sex with a sleeping woman ⊃ compare SUCCUBUS

**in·cul·cate** /ˈɪnkʌlkeɪt; *NAmE* ɪnˈkʌlkeɪt/ *verb* (*formal*) to cause sb to learn and remember ideas, moral principles, etc., especially by repeating them often: ~ **sth (in / into sb)** *to inculcate a sense of responsibility in sb* ◊ ~ **sth with sth** *to*

---

805

*inculcate sb with a sense of responsibility* ▶ **in·cul·ca·tion** /ˌɪnkʌlˈkeɪʃn/ *noun* [U]

**in·cum·bency** /ɪnˈkʌmbənsi/ *noun* [U, C] (*pl.* **-ies**) (*formal*) an official position or the time during which sb holds it

**in·cum·bent** /ɪnˈkʌmbənt/ *noun, adj.*
■ *noun* a person who has an official position: *the present incumbent of the White House*
■ *adj.* **1** [only before noun] having an official position: *the incumbent president* **2** [not before noun] ~ **on / upon sb (to do sth)** (*formal*) necessary as part of sb's duties: *It was incumbent on them to attend.*

**incur** /ɪnˈkɜː(r)/ *verb* (**-rr-**) (*formal*) **1** ~ **sth** if you **incur** sth unpleasant, you are in a situation in which you have to deal with it: *She had incurred the wrath of her father by marrying without his consent.* **2** ~ **sth** if you **incur** costs, you have to pay them: *You risk incurring bank charges if you exceed your overdraft limit.*

**in·cur·able** /ɪnˈkjʊərəbl; *NAmE* -ˈkjʊr-/ *adj.* **1** that cannot be cured: *an incurable disease / illness* **OPP** **curable** **2** that cannot be changed **SYN** **incorrigible**: *She's an incurable optimist.* ▶ **in·cur·ably** /-bli/ *adv.*: *incurably ill / romantic*

**in·cur·ious** /ɪnˈkjʊəriəs; *NAmE* -ˈkjʊr-/ *adj.* (*formal*) having no interest in knowing or discovering things ▶ **in·cur·ious·ly** *adv.*

**in·cur·sion** /ɪnˈkɜːʃn; *NAmE* -ˈkɜːrʒn/ *noun* **1** ~ **(into sth)** (*formal*) a sudden attack on a place by foreign armies, etc. **2** ~ **(into sth)** (*formal*) the sudden appearance of sth in a particular area of activity that is either not expected or not wanted

**Ind.** *abbr.* (*BrE, politics*) INDEPENDENT: *G Green (Ind.)*

**in·daba** /ɪnˈdɑːbə/ *noun* (*SAfrE*) **1** a large meeting at which politicians, professional people, etc. have discussions about an important subject: *a national indaba on land reform* **2** (*informal*) a difficulty or matter that affects you: *I don't care what he does. That's his indaba!*

**in·debt·ed** /ɪnˈdetɪd/ *adj.* **1** ~ **(to sb) (for sth)** (*formal*) grateful to sb for helping you: *I am deeply indebted to my family for all their help.* **2** (of countries, governments, etc.) owing money to other countries or organizations: *a list of the fifteen most heavily indebted nations* ▶ **in·debt·ed·ness** *noun* [U]

**in·decency** /ɪnˈdiːsnsi/ *noun* (*pl.* **-ies**) **1** [U] behaviour that is thought to be morally or sexually offensive: *an act of gross indecency* (= in the past, a sexual act that was a criminal offence) **2** [C, usually sing.] an indecent act, expression, etc.

**in·decent** /ɪnˈdiːsnt/ *adj.* (*disapproving*) **1** (of behaviour, talk, etc.) thought to be morally offensive, especially because it involves sex or wearing no clothes: *indecent conduct / photos* ⊃ compare DECENT **2** (of clothes) showing parts of the body that are usually covered: *That skirt of hers is positively indecent.* **3** not appropriate or suitable: *They left the funeral with almost indecent haste* (= too quickly). ▶ **in·decent·ly** *adv.*: *He was charged with indecently assaulting five women.*

**inˌdecent asˈsault** *noun* [C, U] (*law*) a sexual attack on sb but one that does not include RAPE

**inˌdecent exˈposure** *noun* [U] (*law*) the crime of showing your sexual organs to other people in a public place

**in·de·cipher·able** /ˌɪndɪˈsaɪfrəbl/ *adj.* (of writing or speech) impossible to read or understand

**in·deci·sion** /ˌɪndɪˈsɪʒn/ *noun* (*also less frequent* **in·deci·sive·ness**) *noun* [U] the state of being unable to decide: *After a moment's indecision, he said yes.* ⊃ compare DECISION

**in·deci·sive** /ˌɪndɪˈsaɪsɪv/ *adj.* **1** (*disapproving*) (of a person) not able to make decisions quickly and effectively: *a weak and indecisive man* **2** not providing a clear and definite answer or result: *an indecisive battle* **OPP** **decisive** ▶ **in·deci·sive·ly** *adv.* **in·deci·sive·ness** *noun* [U] = INDECISION

**in·deed** /ɪnˈdiːd/ *adv.* **1** (*especially BrE*) used after *very* and an adjective or adverb to emphasize a statement, description, etc: *Thank you very much indeed!*

# indefatigable 806

◇ *I was very sad indeed to hear of your father's death.* **HELP** You can use this meaning without *very* but it is much more formal or literary: : *Rare indeed is the book that captivates adults and children alike.* **2** **B1** used to emphasize a positive statement or answer: *'Was he very angry?' 'Indeed he was.'* ◇ *'Do you agree?' 'Indeed I do/Yes, indeed.'* ◇ *'You said you'd help.' 'I did indeed—yes.'* ◇ *It is indeed a remarkable achievement.* **3** **B2** (*formal, especially BrE*) used to add information to a statement: *I don't mind at all. Indeed, I would be delighted to help.* **4** (*informal, especially BrE*) used to show that you are surprised at sth or that you find sth silly: *A ghost indeed! I've never heard anything so silly.* **5** (*informal*) used when you are repeating a question that sb has just asked and showing that you do not know the answer: *'Why did he do it?' 'Why indeed?'* **IDM** see FRIEND *n*.

**in·defat·ig·able** /ˌɪndɪˈfætɪɡəbl/ *adj.* (*formal, approving*) never giving up or getting tired of doing sth: *an indefatigable defender of human rights* ▶ **in·defat·ig·ably** /-bli/ *adv.*

**in·defens·ible** /ˌɪndɪˈfensəbl/ *adj.* **1** that cannot be defended or excused because it is morally unacceptable: *indefensible behaviour* ◇ *The Prime Minister was accused of defending the indefensible.* **2** (of a place or building) impossible to defend from military attack

**in·defin·able** /ˌɪndɪˈfaɪnəbl/ *adj.* difficult or impossible to define or explain: *She has that indefinable something that makes an actress a star.* ▶ **in·defin·ably** /-bli/ *adv.*

**in·def·in·ite** /ɪnˈdefɪnət/ *adj.* **1** lasting for a period of time that has no fixed end: *She will be away for the indefinite future.* **2** not clearly defined **SYN** *imprecise*: *an indefinite science*

**in·definite ˈarticle** *noun* (*grammar*) the word *a* or *an* in English, or a similar word in another language ⊃ compare DEFINITE ARTICLE

**in·def·in·ite·ly** /ɪnˈdefɪnətli/ *adv.* for a period of time with no fixed limit: *The trial was postponed indefinitely.*

**in·definite ˈpronoun** *noun* (*grammar*) a pronoun that does not refer to any person or thing in particular, for example 'anything' and 'everyone'

**in·del·ible** /ɪnˈdeləbl/ *adj.* **1** impossible to forget or remove **SYN** *permanent*: *The experience made an indelible impression on me.* ◇ *Her unhappy childhood left an indelible mark.* **2** (of ink, pens, etc.) leaving a mark that cannot be removed **SYN** *permanent*: *an indelible marker* ▶ **in·del·ibly** /-bli/ *adv.*: *That day is stamped indelibly on my memory.*

**in·deli·cate** /ɪnˈdelɪkət/ *adj.* (*formal*) likely to be thought rude or embarrassing: *an indelicate question* ▶ **in·deli·cacy** /-kəsi/ *noun* [U]

**in·dem·nify** /ɪnˈdemnɪfaɪ/ *verb* (**in·dem·ni·fies, in·dem·ni·fy·ing, in·dem·ni·fied, in·dem·ni·fied**) (*law*) **1** ~ **sb (against sth)** to promise to pay sb an amount of money if they suffer any damage or loss **2** ~ **sb (for sth)** to pay sb an amount of money because of the damage or loss that they have suffered ▶ **in·dem·ni·fi·ca·tion** /ɪnˌdemnɪfɪˈkeɪʃn/ *noun* [U]

**in·dem·nity** /ɪnˈdemnəti/ *noun* (*pl.* **-ies**) (*formal or law*) **1** [U] ~ **(against sth)** protection against damage or loss, especially in the form of a promise to pay for any damage or loss that happens: *an indemnity clause/fund/policy* ◇ *indemnity insurance* **2** [C] a sum of money that is given as payment for damage or loss

**in·dent** *verb, noun*
- *verb* /ɪnˈdent/ ~ **sth** to start a line of print or block of text further away from the edge of the page than the other lines: *The first line of each paragraph should be indented.*
- *noun* /ˈɪndent/ **1** ~ **(for sth)** (*business, especially BrE*) an official order for goods or equipment **2** = INDENTATION

**in·den·ta·tion** /ˌɪndenˈteɪʃn/ *noun* **1** [C] a cut, gap or mark in the edge or surface of sth: *The horse's hooves left deep indentations in the mud.* **2** (*also* **in·dent**) [C] a space left at the beginning of a line of print or writing **3** [U] the action of indenting sth or the process of being indented

**in·dent·ed** /ɪnˈdentɪd/ *adj.* (of an edge or a surface) an **indented** edge is not even, because parts of it are missing or have been cut away: *an indented coastline*

**in·den·ture** /ɪnˈdentʃə(r)/ *noun* a type of contract in the past that forced a servant or APPRENTICE to work for their employer for a particular period of time ▶ **in·den·tured** *adj.*

**in·de·pend·ence** **B2** **W** /ˌɪndɪˈpendəns/ *noun* [U] **1** **B2** ~ **(from sb/sth)** (of a country) freedom from political control by other countries: *Cuba gained independence from Spain in 1898.* **2** **B2** the time when a country gains freedom from political control by another country: *independence celebrations* ◇ *the first elections since independence* **3** **B2** the freedom to organize your own life, make your own decisions, etc. without needing help from other people: *He values his independence.* ◇ *a woman's financial independence* **OPP** *dependence* ⊃ WORDFINDER NOTE at FREEDOM

**Inde·pendence Day** *noun* 4 July, celebrated in the US as the anniversary of the day in 1776 when the Americans declared themselves independent of Britain ⊃ see also FOURTH OF JULY

**in·de·pend·ent** **A2** **W** /ˌɪndɪˈpendənt/ *adj., noun*
- *adj.*
- COUNTRY **1** **A2** (of a country) having its own government **SYN** *self-governing*: *an independent state/nation/country* ◇ *Mozambique became independent in 1975.*
- PERSON **2** **B1** confident and free to do things without needing help from other people: *Going away to college has made me much more independent.* ◇ *She's a very independent-minded young woman.* ◇ ~ **of sb/sth** *Students should aim to become more independent of their teachers.* **OPP** *dependent* **3** **B1** having or earning enough money so that you do not have to rely on sb else for help: ~ **of sb/sth** *It was important to me to be financially independent of my parents.* ◇ *a man of independent means* (= with an income that he does not earn by working) **OPP** *dependent*
- SEPARATE **4** **B2** done or given by sb who is not involved in a situation and so is able to judge it fairly: *an independent inquiry/review/investigation* ◇ *She went to a lawyer for some independent advice.* **5** **B2** not connected with or influenced by sth; not connected with each other: ~ **of sb/sth** *The police force should be independent of direct government control.* ◇ *Two independent research bodies reached the same conclusions.*
- ORGANIZATION/WORKER **6** **B2** supported by private money rather than government money: *independent television* ◇ *the independent sector* **7** **B2** not employed or controlled by a company; not created by a big company: *She was hired to do the work as an independent contractor.* ◇ *a low-budget independent film*
- POLITICIAN **8** not representing or belonging to a particular political party: *an independent candidate* ▶ **in·de·pend·ent·ly** *adv.*: ~ **(of sb/sth)** *The two departments work independently of each other.* ◇ *It was the first time that she had lived independently.*
- *noun* **1** (*abbr.* **Ind.**) a member of parliament, candidate, etc. who does not belong to a particular political party **2** a person who runs their own small business and is not employed or controlled by a company

**inde·pendent ˈschool** *noun* = PRIVATE SCHOOL

**inde·pendent ˈvariable** *noun* (*mathematics*) a VARIABLE whose value does not depend on another variable

**in-ˈdepth** *adj.* [usually before noun] very detailed, careful and complete: *an in-depth discussion/study* ⊃ see also DEPTH (5)

**in·des·crib·able** /ˌɪndɪˈskraɪbəbl/ *adj.* so extreme or unusual it is almost impossible to describe: *The pain was indescribable.* ▶ **in·des·crib·ably** /-skraɪbəbli/ *adv.*: *indescribably beautiful/boring*

**in·des·truct·ible** /ˌɪndɪˈstrʌktəbl/ *adj.* that is very strong and cannot easily be destroyed: *plastic containers that are virtually indestructible* ◇ *an indestructible bond of friendship*

**in·de·ter·min·ate** /ˌɪndɪˈtɜːmɪnət; *NAmE* -ˈtɜːrm-/ *adj.* that cannot be identified easily or exactly: *She was a tall woman of indeterminate age.* ▶ **in·de·ter·min·acy** /-nəsi/ *noun* [U]

**index** 🔑+ B2 W /ˈɪndeks/ *noun, verb*
■ *noun* **1** 🔑+ B2 (*pl.* **in·dexes**) a list of names or topics that are referred to in a book, etc., usually arranged at the end of a book in alphabetical order or listed in a separate file or book: *Look it up in the index.* ◊ *Author and subject indexes are available on a library database.* **2** (*BrE*) = CARD INDEX **3** 🔑+ C1 (*pl.* **in·dexes** or **in·dices** /-dɪsiːz/) a system that shows the level of prices and wages, etc. so that they can be compared with those of a previous date: *the cost-of-living index* ◊ *The Dow Jones index fell 15 points this morning.* ◊ *stock-market indices* ◊ *house price indexes* ⊃ see also CONSUMER PRICE INDEX, DOW JONES INDEX, FTSE INDEX™, HANG SENG INDEX, RETAIL PRICE INDEX, SHARE INDEX, STOCK INDEX **4** 🔑+ C1 (*pl.* **in·dices** /ˈɪndɪsiːz/) a sign or measure that sth else can be judged by: *The number of new houses being built is a good index of a country's prosperity.* **5** (*usually* **in·dices** [pl.]) (*mathematics*) the small number written above a larger number to show how many times that number must be multiplied by itself. In the EQUATION $4^2=16$, the number 2 is an **index**. ⊃ see also BODY MASS INDEX, GLYCAEMIC INDEX, HEAT INDEX, REFRACTIVE INDEX
■ *verb* **1** ~ **sth** to make an index of documents, the contents of a book, etc.; to add sth to a list of this type: *All publications are indexed by subject and title.* **2** [usually passive] ~ **sth (to sth)** to link wages, etc. to the level of prices of food, clothing, etc. so that they both increase at the same rate

**in·dex·ation** /ˌɪndekˈseɪʃn/ *noun* [U] the linking of increases in wages, etc. to increases in prices

**ˈindex card** *noun* a small card that you can write information on and keep with other cards in a box or file ⊃ see also CARD INDEX

**ˈindex finger** (*also* **first ˈfinger**, **forefinger**) *noun* the finger next to the THUMB

**index-ˈlinked** *adj.* (*BrE*) (of wages, etc.) rising in value according to increases in the cost of living ▶ **index-ˈlinking** *noun* [U]

**In·dian** /ˈɪndiən/ *noun* **1** a person from India or whose family comes from India **2** (*old-fashioned, offensive*) = NATIVE AMERICAN ⊃ see also AMERICAN INDIAN, RED INDIAN **3** (*CanE*) a Native Canadian who is not Inuit or Metis ⊃ see also WEST INDIAN ▶ **In·dian** *adj.* IDM see CHIEF *n.*, FILE *n.*

**Indian ˈink** (*NAmE also* **India ˈink**) *noun* [U] a very black INK used in drawing and technical drawing

**Indian ˈsummer** *noun* **1** a period of dry warm weather in the autumn **2** a pleasant period of success or improvement, especially later in sb's life

**in·di·cate** 🔑 B1 W /ˈɪndɪkeɪt/ *verb*
• SHOW **1** 🔑 B1 [T] to show that sth is true or exists: ~ **sth** *Initial tests indicate the presence of oxygen.* ◊ ~ **that**... *Research indicates that eating habits are changing fast.* ◊ *These findings clearly indicate that the scheme has improved pedestrian safety.* ◊ ~ **how, what etc**... *Our results indicate how misleading it could be to rely on this method.*
• SUGGEST **2** 🔑 B1 [T] to be a sign of sth; to show that sth is possible or likely: ~ **sth** *A red sky at night often indicates fine weather the next day.* ◊ ~ **that**... *Early results indicate that the government will be returned to power.*
• MENTION **3** [T] to mention sth, especially in an indirect way: ~ **(to sb) (that)**... *In his letter he indicated to us (that) he was willing to cooperate.* ◊ ~ **sth (to sb)** *He indicated his willingness to cooperate.* ◊ ~ **whether, when, etc**... *Has she indicated yet whether she would like to be involved?* ⊃ SYNONYMS at DECLARE
• POINT TO **4** [T] (*formal*) to make sb notice sth/sb, especially by pointing or moving your head: ~ **sb/sth (to sb)** | ~ **sth to sb** *She took out a map and indicated the quickest route to us.* ◊ ~ **where, which, etc**... *He indicated where the furniture was to go.* ◊ ~ **that**... *She indicated that I was to sit down.*
• GIVE INFORMATION **5** [T] ~ **sth** (*formal*) to represent information without using words: *Arrows indicate the direction*

807　　**indifference**

*of flow.* **6** [T] (*formal*) to give information in writing: ~ **sth** *You are allowed 20 kg of baggage unless indicated otherwise on your ticket.* ◊ ~ **which, where, etc**... *Please indicate clearly which colour you require.*
• SHOW MEASUREMENT **7** [T] ~ **sth** | ~ **how much, how many, etc**... (of an instrument for measuring things) to show a particular measurement: *When the temperature gauge indicates 90°F or more, turn off the engine.*
• IN VEHICLE **8** [I, T] (*BrE*) to show that your vehicle is going to change direction, by using lights or your arm SYN signal: *Always indicate before moving into another lane.* ◊ ~ **sth** *He indicated left and then turned right.* ◊ ~ **(that)**... *She indicated that she was turning right.*
• BE RECOMMENDED **9** [T, usually passive] (*formal*) to be necessary or recommended: **be indicated** *A course of chemotherapy was indicated.*

**in·di·ca·tion** 🔑+ B2 W /ˌɪndɪˈkeɪʃn/ *noun* **1** 🔑+ B2 [C, U] a remark or sign that shows that sth is happening or what sb is thinking or feeling: ~ **of sth** *They gave no indication of how the work should be done.* ◊ ~ **of doing sth** *He shows every indication* (= clear signs) *of wanting to accept the post.* ◊ ~ **that**... *There are clear indications that the economy is improving.* ◊ *All the indications are that the deal will go ahead as planned.* ⊃ SYNONYMS at SIGN **2** [C] ~ **(for sth)** (*medical*) a symptom that suggests that particular medical treatment is necessary

**in·di·ca·tive** /ɪnˈdɪkətɪv/ *adj., noun*
■ *adj.* **1** [not usually before noun] ~ **(of sth)** (*formal*) showing or suggesting sth: *Their failure to act is indicative of their lack of interest.* **2** [only before noun] (*grammar*) stating a fact
■ *noun* **the indicative** [sing.] (*grammar*) the form of a verb that states a fact: *In 'Ben likes school', the verb 'like' is in the indicative.*

**in·di·ca·tor** 🔑+ C1 W /ˈɪndɪkeɪtə(r)/ *noun* **1** 🔑+ C1 a sign that shows you what sth is like or how a situation is changing: *The economic indicators are better than expected.* ⊃ SYNONYMS at SIGN **2** a device on a machine that shows speed, pressure, etc: *a depth indicator* **3** (*BrE*) (*NAmE* **ˈturn signal**) (*also informal* **blink·er** *NAmE, BrE*) a light on a vehicle that flashes to show that the vehicle is going to turn left or right

**in·dices** /ˈɪndɪsiːz/ *pl.* of INDEX

**in·dict** /ɪnˈdaɪt/ *verb* [usually passive] (*especially NAmE, law*) to officially charge sb with a crime: **be indicted (for sth)** *The senator was indicted for murder.* ◊ **be indicted on charges/on a charge of sth** *She was indicted on charges of corruption.*

**in·dict·able** /ɪnˈdaɪtəbl/ *adj.* (*law*) **1** (of a crime) for which you can be charged as a serious crime that needs a trial by JURY: *an indictable offence* **2** (of a person) able to be charged with a crime

**in·dict·ment** 🔑+ C1 /ɪnˈdaɪtmənt/ *noun* **1** 🔑+ C1 [C, usually sing.] ~ **(of/on sb/sth)** a sign that a system, society, etc. is very bad or very wrong: *The poverty in our cities is a damning indictment of modern society.* **2** [C] (*especially NAmE*) an official statement accusing sb of a crime **3** [U] (*especially NAmE*) the act of officially accusing sb of a crime: *This led to his indictment on allegations of conspiracy.*

**indie** /ˈɪndi/ *adj., noun*
■ *adj.* (of a company, person or product) not belonging to, working for or produced by a large organization; independent: *an indie publisher/newspaper* ◊ *an indie band/record label*
■ *noun* **1** [C] a small independent company, or sth produced by such a company **2** (*also* **ˈindie music**) [U] pop or rock music produced by small, independent record companies

**in·dif·fer·ence** /ɪnˈdɪfrəns/ *noun* **1** [U, sing.] ~ **(to sb/sth)** a lack of interest, feeling or reaction towards sb/sth: *his total indifference to what people thought of him* ◊ *What she said is a matter of complete indifference to me.* ◊ *Their father treated them with indifference.* ◊ *an indifference to the needs of others* **2** [U] (*formal*) lack of importance: *This cannot be regarded as a matter of indifference.* **3** [U] the

# indifferent

fact of being average or not very good SYN **mediocrity**: *the indifference of the midfield players*

**in·dif·fer·ent** /ɪnˈdɪfrənt/ *adj.* **1** [not usually before noun] **~ (to sb/sth)** having or showing no interest in sb/sth: *The government cannot afford to be indifferent to public opinion.* **2** not very good SYN **mediocre**: *an indifferent meal* ◇ *The festival has the usual mixture of movies—good, bad and indifferent.* ▶ **in·dif·fer·ent·ly** *adv.*: *He shrugged indifferently.*

**in·di·gen·ous** /ɪnˈdɪdʒənəs/ *adj.* (*formal*) belonging to a particular place rather than coming to it from somewhere else SYN **native**: *the indigenous peoples/languages of the area* ◇ *~ to … The kangaroo is indigenous to Australia.*

**in·di·gent** /ˈɪndɪdʒənt/ *adj.* [usually before noun] (*formal*) very poor

**in·di·gest·ible** /ˌɪndɪˈdʒestəbl/ *adj.* **1** (of food) that cannot easily be DIGESTED in the stomach: *an indigestible meal* **2** (of facts, information, etc.) difficult to understand, and presented in a complicated way OPP **digestible**

**in·di·ges·tion** /ˌɪndɪˈdʒestʃən/ *noun* [U] pain caused by difficulty in DIGESTING food SYN **dyspepsia**

**in·dig·nant** /ɪnˈdɪɡnənt/ *adj.* feeling or showing anger and surprise because you think that you have been treated unfairly: *an indignant letter/look* ◇ **at/about** sth *She was very indignant at the way she had been treated.* ◇ **~ that …** *They were indignant that they hadn't been invited.* ⇨ SYNONYMS at ANGRY ▶ **in·dig·nant·ly** *adv.*: *'I'm certainly not asking him!' she retorted indignantly.*

**in·dig·na·tion** /ˌɪndɪɡˈneɪʃn/ *noun* [U] a feeling of anger and surprise caused by sth that you think is unfair or unreasonable: *The rise in train fares has aroused public indignation.* ◇ *~ at/about/over sth The government expressed its indignation over the way the incident had been handled.* ◇ *~ that … Joe quivered with indignation that Paul should speak to him like that.* ◇ **to the ~ of sb** *Some benefits apply only to men, much to the indignation of working women.* ◇ *to be full of righteous indignation* (= the belief that you are right to be angry even though other people do not agree)

**in·dig·nity** /ɪnˈdɪɡnəti/ *noun* [U, C] (*pl.* **-ies**) **~ (of sth/ of doing sth)** a situation that makes you feel embarrassed or ashamed because you are not treated with respect; an act that causes these feelings SYN **humiliation**: *The chairman suffered the indignity of being refused admission to the meeting.* ◇ *the daily indignities of imprisonment*

**in·digo** /ˈɪndɪɡəʊ/ *adj.* very dark blue in colour: *an indigo sky* ▶ **indigo** *noun* [U]

**in·dir·ect** /ˌɪndəˈrekt, -daɪˈr-/ *adj.* [usually before noun] **1** happening not as the main aim, cause or result of a particular action, but in addition to it: *the indirect effects of the war* ◇ *There would be some benefit, however indirect, to the state.* ◇ *indirect costs* (= costs that are not directly connected with making a product, for example training, heating, rent, etc.) **2** not done directly; done through sb/sth else: *territories under the indirect control of the British* **3** avoiding saying sth in a clear and obvious way: *The comment was an indirect attack on the prime minister.* **4** not going in a straight line: *an indirect route* ◇ *The plant prefers indirect sunlight.* OPP **direct** ▶ **in·dir·ect·ly** *adv.*: *The new law will affect us all, directly or indirectly.* **in·dir·ect·ness** *noun* [U]

**indirect ˈobject** *noun* (*grammar*) a noun, noun phrase or pronoun in a sentence, used after some verbs, that refers to the person or thing that an action is done to or for: *In 'Give him the money', 'him' is the indirect object and 'money' is the direct object.*

**indirect ˈquestion** (*also* reˌported ˈquestion) *noun* (*grammar*) a question in REPORTED SPEECH, for example *She asked where I was going.* HELP Do not put a question mark after an indirect question.

**indirect ˈspeech** *noun* [U] (*grammar*) = REPORTED SPEECH ⇨ compare DIRECT SPEECH

**indirect ˈtax** *noun* [C, U] a tax that is paid as an amount added to the price of goods and services and not paid directly to the government ⇨ compare DIRECT TAX ▶ **indirect taˈxation** *noun* [U]

**in·dis·cern·ible** /ˌɪndɪˈsɜːnəbl; *NAmE* -ˈsɜːrn-/ *adj.* that cannot be seen, heard or understood

**in·dis·cip·line** /ɪnˈdɪsɪplɪn/ *noun* [U] (*formal*) failure to obey rules and orders; a lack of control in the behaviour of a person or group of people OPP **discipline**

**in·dis·creet** /ˌɪndɪˈskriːt/ *adj.* (*disapproving*) not careful about what you say or do, especially when you reveal sth secret or sth that could be embarrassing or offensive: *an indiscreet comment* OPP **discreet** ▶ **in·dis·creet·ly** *adv.*

**in·dis·cre·tion** /ˌɪndɪˈskreʃn/ *noun* **1** [C] an act or remark that reveals sth secret or that could be embarrassing or offensive: *youthful indiscretions* **2** [U] the act of saying or doing sth without thinking about the effect it may have, especially when this reveals sth secret or sth that could be embarrassing or offensive: *He talked to the press in a moment of indiscretion.* ⇨ compare DISCRETION

**in·dis·crim·in·ate** /ˌɪndɪˈskrɪmɪnət/ *adj.* **1** an indiscriminate action is done without thought about what the result may be, especially when it causes people to be harmed: *indiscriminate attacks on motorists by youths throwing stones* ◇ *Doctors have been criticized for their indiscriminate use of antibiotics.* **2** acting without careful judgement: *She's always been indiscriminate in her choice of friends.* ▶ **in·dis·crim·in·ate·ly** *adv.*: *The soldiers fired indiscriminately into the crowd.*

**in·dis·pens·able** /ˌɪndɪˈspensəbl/ *adj.* too important to be without SYN **essential**: *Cars have become an indispensable part of our lives.* ◇ *~ to sb/sth She made herself indispensable to the department.* ◇ *~ for sth/for doing sth A good dictionary is indispensable for learning a foreign language.* OPP **dispensable** ⇨ SYNONYMS at ESSENTIAL ⇨ LANGUAGE BANK at VITAL

**in·dis·posed** /ˌɪndɪˈspəʊzd/ *adj.* (*formal*) **1** [not usually before noun] unable to do sth because you are ill, or for a reason you do not want to give SYN **unwell 2** [not before noun] **~ to do sth** not willing to do sth

**in·dis·pos·ition** /ˌɪndɪspəˈzɪʃn/ *noun* [C, U] (*formal*) a slight illness that makes you unable to do sth

**in·dis·put·able** /ˌɪndɪˈspjuːtəbl/ *adj.* that is true and cannot be disagreed with or denied SYN **undeniable**: *indisputable evidence* ◇ *an indisputable fact* ◇ *It is indisputable that the crime rate has been rising.* ⇨ compare DISPUTABLE ▶ **in·dis·put·ably** /-bli/ *adv.*: *This painting is indisputably one of his finest works.*

**in·dis·sol·uble** /ˌɪndɪˈsɒljəbl; *NAmE* -ˈsɑːl-/ *adj.* (*formal*) (of a relationship) that cannot be ended: *an indissoluble friendship* ▶ **in·dis·sol·ubly** /-bli/ *adv.*: *indissolubly linked*

**in·dis·tinct** /ˌɪndɪˈstɪŋkt/ *adj.* that cannot be seen, heard or remembered clearly SYN **vague, hazy** ▶ **in·dis·tinct·ly** *adv.*

**in·dis·tin·guish·able** /ˌɪndɪˈstɪŋɡwɪʃəbl/ *adj.* **1** **~ (from sth)** if two things are indistinguishable, or one is indistinguishable from the other, it is impossible to see any differences between them: *The male of the species is almost indistinguishable from the female.* **2** not clear; not able to be clearly identified: *His words were indistinguishable.*

**in·dium** /ˈɪndiəm/ *noun* [U] (*symb.* **In**) a chemical element. Indium is a soft silver-white metal.

**in·di·vid·ual** /ˌɪndɪˈvɪdʒuəl/ *noun, adj.*
■ *noun* **1** a person considered separately rather than as part of a group: *The competition is open to both teams and individuals.* ◇ *Treatment depends on the individual involved.* ◇ *donations from private individuals* (= ordinary people rather than companies, etc.) ◇ *as an ~ Every child is treated here as an individual.* **2** a single member of a class of things: *They live in a group or as individuals, depending on the species.* **3** a person who is original and very different from others: *She's grown into quite an individual.* **4** (*informal, usually disapproving*) a person of a particular type, especially a strange one: *an odd-looking individual* ◇ *So this individual came up and demanded money.*

■**adj. 1** [only before noun] (often used after *each*) considered separately rather than as part of a group: *We interviewed each **individual** member of the community.* ◊ *The minister refused to comment on **individual** cases.* **2** [only before noun] connected with one person; designed for one person: *respect for **individual** freedom* ◊ *A democracy must protect **individual** rights.* ◊ *an **individual** pizza* **3** (*usually approving*) typical of one particular person or thing in a way that is different from others SYN **distinctive**: *a highly **individual** style of dress*

**in·di·vidu·al·ism** /ˌɪndɪˈvɪdʒuəlɪzəm/ *noun* [U] **1** the quality of being different from other people and doing things in your own way **2** the belief that individual people in society should have the right to make their own decisions, etc., rather than be controlled by the government: *Capitalism stresses innovation, competition and individualism.* ▸ **in·di·vidu·al·ist** *noun*: *She's a complete individualist in her art.* **in·di·vidu·al·is·tic** /ˌɪndɪˌvɪdʒuəˈlɪstɪk/ (*also* **in·di·vidu·al·ist**) *adj.*: *an individualistic culture* ◊ *His music is highly individualistic and may not appeal to everyone.*

**in·di·vidu·al·ity** /ˌɪndɪˌvɪdʒuˈæləti/ *noun* [U, C] (*pl.* **-ies**) the qualities that make sb/sth different from other people or things: *She expresses her **individuality** through her clothes.*

**in·di·vidu·al·ize** (*BrE also* **-ise**) /ˌɪndɪˈvɪdʒuəlaɪz/ *verb* ~ **sth** to make sth different to suit the needs of a particular person, place, etc: *to **individualize** children's learning* ▸ **in·di·vidu·al·iza·tion**, **-isa·tion** /ˌɪndɪˌvɪdʒuəlaɪˈzeɪʃn/ *NAmE* -lə'z-/ *noun* [U]

**in·di·vidu·al·ized** (*BrE also* **-ised**) /ˌɪndɪˈvɪdʒuəlaɪzd/ *adj.* designed for a particular person or thing; connected with a particular person or thing: *individualized teaching* ◊ *a highly individualized approach to management*

**in·di·vidu·al·ly** W /ˌɪndɪˈvɪdʒuəli/ *adv.* separately, rather than as a group: *individually wrapped chocolates* ◊ *The manager spoke to them all individually.* ◊ *The hotel has 100 individually designed bedrooms.*

**in·di·vidu·ate** /ˌɪndɪˈvɪdʒueɪt/ *verb* [usually passive] ~ **sb/sth** (*formal*) to make sb/sth clearly different from other people or things of the same type

**in·di·vis·ible** /ˌɪndɪˈvɪzəbl/ *adj.* **1** that cannot be divided into separate parts OPP **divisible 2** ~ (**by sth**) (of a number) that cannot be divided by another number exactly ▸ **in·di·vis·ibil·ity** /ˌɪndɪˌvɪzəˈbɪləti/ *noun* [U] **in·di·vis·ibly** /ˌɪndɪˈvɪzəbli/ *adv.*

**Indo-** /ˈɪndəʊ/ *combining form* (in nouns and adjectives) Indian: *the Indo-Pakistan border*

**Indo-Ca·na·dian** *noun* [C] (*CanE*) a Canadian who was born in South Asia, especially India, or whose family originally came from South Asia

**in·doc·trin·ate** /ɪnˈdɒktrɪneɪt/ *NAmE* -ˈdɑːk-/ *verb* ~ **sb** (**with sth**) | ~ **sb** (**to do sth**) (*disapproving*) to force sb to accept a particular belief or set of beliefs and not allow them to consider any others: *They had been indoctrinated from an early age with their parents' beliefs.* ▸ **in·doc·trin·ation** /ɪnˌdɒktrɪˈneɪʃn/ *NAmE* -ˌdɑːk-/ *noun* [U]: *political/religious indoctrination*

**Indo-Euro·pean** *adj.* of or connected with the family of languages spoken in most of Europe and parts of western Asia (including English, French, Latin, Greek, Russian and Hindi)

**in·do·lent** /ˈɪndələnt/ *adj.* (*formal*) not wanting to work SYN **lazy** ▸ **in·do·lence** /-ləns/ *noun* [U]

**in·dom·it·able** /ɪnˈdɒmɪtəbl/ *NAmE* -ˈdɑːm-/ *adj.* (*formal, approving*) not willing to accept defeat, even in a difficult situation; very brave and determined

**in·door** /ˈɪndɔː(r)/ *adj.* [only before noun] **1** located, done or used inside a building: *an indoor swimming pool* ◊ *indoor games* OPP **outdoor 2** relating to sports played indoors: *the world indoor 200 metres champion*

**in·doors** /ˌɪnˈdɔːz/ *NAmE* -ˈdɔːrz/ *adv.* inside or into a building: *to stay indoors* ◊ *Many herbs can be grown indoors.* OPP **outdoors**

# indulgent

**in·dub·it·ably** /ɪnˈdjuːbɪtəbli/ *NAmE* -ˈduː-/ *adv.* (*formal*) in a way that cannot be doubted; without question SYN **undoubtedly**: *He was, indubitably, the most suitable candidate.* ▸ **in·dub·it·able** /-təbl/ *adj.*: *indubitable proof*

**in·duce** /ɪnˈdjuːs/ *NAmE* -ˈduːs/ *verb* **1** ~ **sb to do sth** (*formal*) to persuade or influence sb to do sth: *Nothing would induce me to take the job.* **2** ~ **sth** (*formal*) to cause sth: *drugs that induce sleep* ◊ *a drug-induced coma* **3** ~ **sb/sth** (*medical*) to make a woman start giving birth to her baby by giving her special drugs; to make a baby start being born by giving the mother special drugs: *an induced labour* ◊ *We'll have to induce her.* ⊃ WORDFINDER NOTE *at* BIRTH

**in·duce·ment** /ɪnˈdjuːsmənt/ *NAmE* -ˈduːs-/ *noun* [C, U] something that is given to sb to persuade them to do sth SYN **incentive**: ~ **to sb** (**to do sth**) *financial inducements to mothers to stay at home* ◊ ~ (**for sb**) (**to do sth**) *There is little inducement for them to work harder.* ◊ *Government officials have been accused of accepting inducements* (= BRIBES) *from local businessmen.*

**in·duct** /ɪnˈdʌkt/ *verb* [often passive] ~ **sb** (**into sth**) (**as sth**) (*formal*) **1** to formally give sb a job or position of authority, especially as part of a ceremony **2** to officially introduce sb into a group or an organization, especially the army **3** to introduce sb to a particular area of knowledge: *They were inducted into the skills of magic.*

**in·duct·ee** /ˌɪndʌkˈtiː/ *noun* (*especially NAmE*) a person who is being, or who has just been, introduced into a special group of people, especially sb who has just joined the army

**in·duc·tion** W /ɪnˈdʌkʃn/ *noun* **1** [U, C] ~ (**into sth**) the process of introducing sb to a new job, skill, organization, etc.; a ceremony at which this takes place **2** [U, C] the act of making a pregnant woman start to give birth, using artificial means such as a special drug **3** [U] (*specialist*) a method of discovering general rules and principles from particular facts and examples ⊃ compare DEDUCTION **4** [U] (*physics*) the process by which electricity or MAGNETISM passes from one object to another without them touching

**in·duc·tion course** *noun* (*BrE*) a training course for new employees, students, etc. that is designed to give them a general introduction to the business, school, etc.

**in·duct·ive** /ɪnˈdʌktɪv/ *adj.* **1** (*specialist*) using particular facts and examples to form general rules and principles: *an inductive argument* ◊ *inductive reasoning* ⊃ compare DEDUCTIVE **2** (*physics*) connected with the INDUCTION of electricity ▸ **in·duct·ive·ly** *adv.*: *a theory derived inductively from the data*

**in·dulge** /ɪnˈdʌldʒ/ *verb* **1** [I, T] to allow yourself to have or do sth that you like, especially sth that is considered bad for you: ~ **in sth** *They went into town to indulge in some serious shopping.* ◊ ~ **yourself** (**with sth**) *I indulged myself with a long hot bath.* **2** [T] ~ **sth** to satisfy a particular desire, interest, etc: *The inheritance enabled him to indulge his passion for art.* **3** [T] to be too generous in allowing sb to have or do whatever they like: ~ **sb** (**with sth**) *She did not believe in indulging the children with presents.* ◊ ~ **sth** *Her father had always indulged her every whim.* **4** [I] ~ **in sth** to take part in an activity, especially one that is illegal

**in·dul·gence** /ɪnˈdʌldʒəns/ *noun* **1** [U] (*usually disapproving*) the state or act of having or doing whatever you want; the state of allowing sb to have or do whatever they want: *to lead a life of indulgence* ◊ ~ **in sth** *Avoid excessive indulgence in sweets and canned drinks.* ◊ *There is no limit to the indulgence he shows to his grandchildren.* **2** [C] something that you allow yourself to have even though it is not essential: *The holiday was an extravagant indulgence.* ⊃ see also SELF-INDULGENCE **3** [U] (*formal*) the quality of being willing to ignore the weaknesses in sb/sth SYN **patience**: *They begged the audience's indulgence.*

**in·dul·gent** /ɪnˈdʌldʒənt/ *adj.* **1** (*usually disapproving*) tending to allow sb to have or do whatever they want: *indulgent parents* ◊ *an indulgent smile* ⊃ see also SELF-INDULGENT

**induna**

**2** willing or too willing to ignore the weaknesses in sb/sth SYN **patient**: *to take an indulgent view of sth* ▶ **in·dul·gent·ly** *adv.*: *to laugh indulgently*

**in·duna** /ɪnˈduːnə/ *noun* (*SAfrE*) a senior leader of a TRIBE

**in·dus·trial** ❶ B2 /ɪnˈdʌstriəl/ *adj.* [usually before noun] **1** ❓ B2 connected with industry: *an industrial dispute* ◊ *an industrial accident* ◊ **Industrial production** *fell in December by 1.4 per cent.* ◊ *policy with regard to future industrial development* ◊ *India has a large industrial sector.* **2** ❓ B2 used by industries: *industrial chemicals* **3** ❓ B2 having many industries: *an industrial city/town* ◊ *an industrial society* ◊ *the world's leading industrial nations* ➔ *see also* POST-INDUSTRIAL **4** very great in extent or amount: *They had made industrial quantities of food.* ◊ *They were guilty of fraud on an industrial scale.* ▶ **in·dus·tri·al·ly** /-əli/ *adv.*: *industrially advanced countries*

**in‚dustrial ˈaction** *noun* [U] (*especially BrE*) action that workers take, especially stopping work, to protest to their employers about sth ➔ WORDFINDER NOTE at UNION

**in‚dustrial archaeˈology** *noun* [U] the study of machines, factories, bridges, etc. used in the past in industry

**in‚dustrial ˈarts** (*also* ˈshop, ˈshop class) *noun* [U] (*NAmE*) a school subject in which students learn to make things from wood and metal using tools and machines

**inˈdustrial eˈstate** (*BrE*) (*NAmE* in‚dustrial ˈpark) *noun* an area especially for factories, on the edge of a town ➔ *compare* TRADING ESTATE

**in·dus·tri·al·ism** /ɪnˈdʌstriəlɪzəm/ *noun* [U] (*specialist*) an economic and social system based on industry

**in·dus·tri·al·ist** /ɪnˈdʌstriəlɪst/ *noun* a person who owns or runs a large factory or industrial company

**in·dus·tri·al·ize** (*BrE also* -ise) /ɪnˈdʌstriəlaɪz/ *verb* [T, I] ~ (sth) if a country or an area **is industrialized** or if it **industrializes**, industries are developed there: *The southern part of the country was slow to industrialize.* ▶ **in·dus·tri·al·iza·tion**, **-isa·tion** /ɪn‚dʌstriəlaɪˈzeɪʃn; *NAmE* -ləˈz-/ *noun* [U]: *the rapid industrialization of Japan* **in·dus·tri·al·ized**, **-ised** /ɪnˈdʌstriəlaɪzd/ *adj.*: *an industrialized country*

**inˈdustrial ˈpark** (*NAmE*) (*BrE* in‚dustrial eˈstate) *noun* an area especially for factories, on the edge of a town

**in‚dustrial reˈlations** *noun* [pl.] relations between employers and employees

**the In‚dustrial Revoˈlution** *noun* [sing.] the period in the 18th and 19th centuries in Europe and the US when machines began to be used to do work, and industry grew rapidly

**inˈdustrial-strength** *adj.* (*often humorous*) very strong or powerful: *industrial-strength coffee*

**in‚dustrial triˈbunal** *noun* (*BrE*) = EMPLOYMENT TRIBUNAL

**in·dus·tri·ous** /ɪnˈdʌstriəs/ *adj.* (*approving*) working hard; busy SYN **hard-working**: *an industrious student* ▶ **in·dus·tri·ous·ly** *adv.*

**in·dus·try** ❶ A2 /ˈɪndəstri/ *noun* (*pl.* -ies) **1** ❓ A2 [U] the production of goods from raw materials, especially in factories: *the needs of British industry* ◊ **in** ~ *She got a job in industry.* ➔ *see also* CAPTAIN OF INDUSTRY, HEAVY INDUSTRY, LIGHT INDUSTRY

WORDFINDER capacity, just-in-time, labour, lead time, output, raw material, shipping, supply chain, warehouse

**2** ❓ B2 [C] the people and activities involved in producing a particular thing, or in providing a particular service: *the steel/oil/auto industry* ◊ *the music/film/tourism industry* ◊ *We need to develop local industries.* ◊ **in an** ~ *She later worked in the banking industry.* ◊ *industry insiders/analysts/experts* ◊ (*figurative*) *the Kardashian industry* (= the large number of people involved in making the Kardashian family successful) ➔ *see also* CAPTAIN OF INDUSTRY,

COTTAGE INDUSTRY, PRIMARY INDUSTRY, SERVICE INDUSTRY **3** [U] (*formal*) the quality of working hard: *We were impressed by their industry.*

**Indy** /ˈɪndi/ (*also* ˈIndy racing, ˈIndy Car, ˈIndy car racing) *noun* [U] motor racing around a track that is raised at both sides

**Indy Car** /ˈɪndikɑː(r)/ *noun* **1** [U] = INDY **2** [C] a car used in Indy racing

**in·ebri·ated** /ɪˈniːbrieɪtɪd/ *adj.* (*formal or humorous*) drunk ▶ **in·ebri·ation** /ɪ‚niːbriˈeɪʃn/ *noun* [U]

**in·ed·ible** /ɪnˈedəbl/ *adj.* that you cannot eat because it is of poor quality, or poisonous OPP **edible**

**in·ef·fable** /ɪnˈefəbl/ *adj.* (*formal*) too great or beautiful to describe in words: *ineffable joy*

**in·ef·fect·ive** /‚ɪnɪˈfektɪv/ *adj.* not achieving what you want to achieve; not having any effect: *The new drug was ineffective.* ◊ *ineffective management* ◊ **~ in doing sth** *The law proved ineffective in dealing with the problem.* OPP **effective** ▶ **in·ef·fect·ive·ness** *noun* [U] **in·ef·fect·ive·ly** *adv.*

**in·ef·fec·tual** /‚ɪnɪˈfektʃuəl/ *adj.* (*formal*) without the ability to achieve much; weak; not achieving what you want to: *an ineffectual teacher* ◊ *an ineffectual attempt to reform the law* ▶ **in·ef·fec·tu·al·ly** /-əli/ *adv.*

**in·ef·fi·cient** /‚ɪnɪˈfɪʃnt/ *adj.* not doing a job well and not making the best use of time, money, energy, etc.: *an inefficient heating system* ◊ *inefficient government* ◊ *an extremely inefficient secretary* ◊ *inefficient use of time and energy* OPP **efficient** ▶ **in·ef·fi·ciency** /-ʃnsi/ *noun* [U, C] (*pl.* -ies): *waste and inefficiency in government* ◊ *inefficiencies in the system* **in·ef·fi·cient·ly** *adv.*

**in·el·eg·ant** /ɪnˈelɪɡənt/ *adj.* not attractive OPP **elegant** ▶ **in·el·eg·ant·ly** *adv.*

**in·eli·gible** /ɪnˈelɪdʒəbl/ *adj.* not having the necessary qualifications to have or to do sth: **~ (for sth)** *ineligible for financial assistance* ◊ **~ (to do sth)** *ineligible to vote* OPP **eligible** ▶ **in·eli·gi·bil·ity** /ɪn‚elɪdʒəˈbɪləti/ *noun* [U]

**in·eluct·able** /‚ɪnɪˈlʌktəbl/ *adj.* (*formal*) that you cannot avoid SYN **unavoidable** ▶ **in·eluct·ably** /-bli/ *adv.*

**inept** /ɪˈnept/ *adj.* acting or done with no skill: *He's intelligent but socially inept* (= not good at relating to people socially). ◊ *an inept remark* ▶ **in·ept·ly** *adv.*

**in·ep·ti·tude** /ɪˈneptɪtjuːd; *NAmE* -tuːd/ *noun* [U] lack of skill: *the ineptitude of the police in handling the situation*

**in·equal·ity** ❓+ C1 W /‚ɪnɪˈkwɒləti; *NAmE* -ˈkwɑːl-/ *noun* [U, C] (*pl.* -ies) the unfair difference between groups of people in society, when some have more wealth, status or opportunities than others: *inequality of opportunity* ◊ *economic inequalities between different areas* ◊ *racial inequality* OPP **equality** ➔ *see also* UNEQUAL

**in·equit·able** /ɪnˈekwɪtəbl/ *adj.* (*formal*) not fair; not the same for everyone SYN **unfair**: *inequitable distribution of wealth* OPP **equitable**

**in·equity** /ɪnˈekwəti/ *noun* [C, U] (*pl.* -ies) (*formal*) something that is unfair; the state of being unfair SYN **injustice**

**in·erad·ic·able** /‚ɪnɪˈrædɪkəbl/ *adj.* (*formal*) (of a quality or situation) that cannot be removed or changed

**inert** /ɪˈnɜːt; *NAmE* ɪˈnɜːrt/ *adj.* **1** (*formal*) without power to move or act: *He lay inert with half-closed eyes.* **2** (*chemistry*) without active chemical or other properties (= characteristics)

**iˌnert ˈgas** *noun* (*chemistry*) = NOBLE GAS

**in·er·tia** /ɪˈnɜːʃə; *NAmE* ɪˈnɜːrʃə/ *noun* [U] **1** (*usually disapproving*) lack of energy; lack of desire or ability to move or change: *I can't seem to throw off this feeling of inertia.* ◊ *the forces of institutional inertia in the school system* **2** (*physics*) a property (= characteristic) of MATTER (= a substance) by which it stays still or, if moving, continues moving in a straight line unless it is acted on by a force outside itself

**in·er·tial** /ɪˈnɜːʃl; *NAmE* ɪˈnɜːrʃl/ *adj.* (*specialist*) connected with or caused by inertia

**in·escap·able** /‚ɪnɪˈskeɪpəbl/ *adj.* (of a fact or a situation) that you cannot avoid or ignore SYN **unavoidable**: *an*

**inescapable** fact ◊ *This leads to the inescapable conclusion that the two things are connected.* ▶ **in·escap·ably** /-bli/ *adv.*

**in·es·sen·tial** /ˌɪnɪˈsenʃl/ *adj.* not necessary: *inessential luxuries* ▶ **in·es·sen·tial** *noun* [usually pl.]: *Few people had spare cash for inessentials.* ⊃ compare ESSENTIAL, NON-ESSENTIAL

**in·estim·able** /ɪnˈestɪməbl/ *adj.* (*formal*) too great to calculate: *The information he provided was of inestimable value.*

**in·ev·it·able** ʔ+ B2 /ɪnˈevɪtəbl/ *adj.* 1 ʔ+ B2 that you cannot avoid or prevent SYN **unavoidable**: *It was an inevitable consequence of the decision.* ◊ **it is ~that** *It was inevitable that there would be job losses.* ◊ *A rise in the interest rates seems inevitable.* 2 [only before noun] (*often humorous*) happening so often that you always expect it; *the English and their inevitable cups of tea* 3 **the inevitable** *noun* [sing.] something that is certain to happen: *You have to accept the inevitable.* ◊ *The inevitable happened—I forgot my passport.* ▶ **in·ev·it·abil·ity** /ɪnˌevɪtəˈbɪləti/ *noun* [U, C] (*pl.* **-ies**): *the inevitability of death* ◊ *There was an inevitability about their defeat.*

**in·ev·it·ably** ʔ+ B2 /ɪnˈevɪtəbli/ *adv.* 1 ʔ+ B2 as is certain to happen: *Inevitably, the press exaggerated the story.* 2 (*often humorous*) as you would expect: *Inevitably, it rained on the day of the wedding.*

**in·exact** /ˌɪnɪɡˈzækt/ *adj.* not accurate or exact: *an inexact description* ◊ *Economics is an inexact science.*

**in·ex·cus·able** /ˌɪnɪkˈskjuːzəbl/ *adj.* too bad to accept or forgive SYN **unjustifiable**: *inexcusable rudeness* OPP **excusable** ▶ **in·ex·cus·ably** /-bli/ *adv.*

**in·ex·haust·ible** /ˌɪnɪɡˈzɔːstəbl/ *adj.* that cannot be EXHAUSTED (= finished); very great: *an inexhaustible supply of good jokes* ◊ *Her energy is inexhaustible.*

**in·ex·or·able** /ɪnˈeksərəbl/ *adj.* (*formal*) (of a process) that cannot be stopped or changed SYN **relentless**: *the inexorable rise of crime* ▶ **in·ex·or·abil·ity** /ɪnˌeksərəˈbɪləti/ *noun* [U]: *the inexorability of progress* **in·ex·or·ably** /ɪnˈeksərəbli/ *adv.*: *events leading inexorably towards a crisis*

**in·ex·pe·di·ent** /ˌɪnɪkˈspiːdiənt/ *adj.* [not usually before noun] (*formal*) (of an action) not practical or suitable; that might have a bad effect: **it is ~to do sth** *It would be inexpedient to raise taxes further.* OPP **expedient**

**in·ex·pen·sive** /ˌɪnɪkˈspensɪv/ *adj.* not costing a lot of money: *a relatively inexpensive hotel* OPP **expensive** ⊃ SYNONYMS at CHEAP ▶ **in·ex·pen·sive·ly** *adv.*

**in·ex·peri·ence** /ˌɪnɪkˈspɪəriəns/; *NAmE* -ˈspɪr-/ *noun* [U] lack of knowledge and experience: *His mistake was due to youth and inexperience.*

**in·ex·peri·enced** /ˌɪnɪkˈspɪəriənst/; *NAmE* -ˈspɪr-/ *adj.* having little knowledge or experience of sth: *inexperienced drivers/staff* ◊ *a child too young and inexperienced to recognize danger* ◊ **~in sth** *inexperienced in modern methods* OPP **experienced**

**in·ex·pert** /ɪnˈekspɜːt/; *NAmE* -pɜːrt/ *adj.* without much skill ⊃ compare EXPERT ▶ **in·ex·pert·ly** *adv.*

**in·ex·plic·able** /ˌɪnɪkˈsplɪkəbl/ *adj.* that cannot be understood or explained SYN **incomprehensible**: *inexplicable behaviour* ◊ *For some inexplicable reason he gave up a fantastic job.* OPP **explicable** ▶ **in·ex·plic·ably** *adv.*: *inexplicably delayed/absent* ◊ *She inexplicably withdrew the offer.*

**in·ex·press·ible** /ˌɪnɪkˈspresəbl/ *adj.* (of feelings) too strong to be put into words: *inexpressible joy*

**in ex·tre·mis** /ˌɪn ɪkˈstriːmɪs/ *adv.* (*from Latin, formal*) 1 in a very difficult situation when very strong action is needed 2 at the moment of death

**in·ex·tric·able** /ˌɪnɪkˈstrɪkəbl, ɪnˈekstrɪkəbl/ *adj.* (*formal*) too closely linked to be separated: *an inextricable connection between the past and the present*

**in·ex·tric·ably** /ˌɪnɪkˈstrɪkəbli, ɪnˈekstrɪkəbli/ *adv.* if two things are **inextricably linked**, etc., it is impossible to separate them: *Europe's foreign policy is inextricably linked with that of the US.* ◊ *She had become inextricably involved in the campaign.*

# infect

**in·fal·lible** /ɪnˈfæləbl/ *adj.* 1 never wrong; never making mistakes: *infallible advice* ◊ *Doctors are not infallible.* OPP **fallible** 2 that never fails; always doing what it is supposed to do: *an infallible method of memorizing things* ▶ **in·fal·li·bil·ity** /ɪnˌfæləˈbɪləti/ *noun* [U]: *papal infallibility* **in·fal·libly** /ɪnˈfæləbli/ *adv.*

**in·fam·ous** ʔ+ C1 /ˈɪnfəməs/ *adj.* (*formal*) well known for being bad or evil SYN **notorious**: *a general who was infamous for his brutality* ◊ *the most infamous concentration camp* ◊ (*humorous*) *the infamous British sandwich* ⊃ compare FAMOUS

**in·famy** /ˈɪnfəmi/ *noun* (*pl.* **-ies**) (*formal*) 1 [U] the state of being well known for sth bad or evil: *a day that will live in infamy* 2 [U, C] evil behaviour; an evil act: *scenes of horror and infamy*

**in·fancy** /ˈɪnfənsi/ *noun* [U] 1 the time when a child is a baby or very young: **in ~** *to die in infancy* 2 the early development of sth: **in its ~** *a time when the cinema was still in its infancy*

**in·fant** ʔ+ C1 /ˈɪnfənt/ *noun, adj.*
■ *noun* 1 ʔ+ C1 (*formal* or *specialist*) a baby or very young child: *a nursery for infants under two* ◊ *their infant son* ◊ *She was seriously ill as an infant.* ◊ *Mozart was an infant prodigy* (= a young child with unusual ability). HELP In *NAmE* **infant** is only used for a baby, especially a very young one. 2 ʔ+ C1 (in England and Wales) a child at school between the ages of four and seven: *an infant school* ◊ *infant teachers* ◊ *I've known her since we were in the infants* (= at infant school). ⊃ WORDFINDER NOTE at AGE
■ *adj.* [only before noun] 1 designed to be used by infants: *infant formula* (= milk for babies) 2 new and not yet developed: *infant industries*

**in·fanti·cide** /ɪnˈfæntɪsaɪd/ *noun* (*formal*) 1 [U] the crime of a mother killing her child when it is less than one year old 2 [U] (in some cultures) the practice of killing babies that are not wanted, for example because they are girls and not boys 3 [C] a person who kills a baby, especially their own child

**in·fant·ile** /ˈɪnfəntaɪl/ *adj.* 1 (*disapproving*) typical of a small child (and therefore not suitable for adults or older children) SYN **childish** 2 [only before noun] (*formal* or *specialist*) connected with babies or very young children

**in·fanti·lize** (*BrE also* **-ise**) /ɪnˈfæntɪlaɪz/ *verb* **~ sb** (*formal*) to treat sb as though they are a child

**infant mor·tality** *noun* [U] the death of children under the age of one year

**in·fan·try** /ˈɪnfəntri/ *noun* [U + sing./pl. v.] soldiers who fight on foot: *infantry units* ◊ *The infantry was/were guarding the bridge.*

**in·fan·try·man** /ˈɪnfəntrimən/ *noun* (*pl.* **-men** /-mən/) a soldier who fights on foot

**in·farc·tion** /ɪnˈfɑːkʃn/; *NAmE* -ˈfɑːrk-/ *noun* [U, C] (*medical*) a condition in which the blood supply to an area of TISSUE is blocked and the tissue dies

**in·fatu·ated** /ɪnˈfætʃueɪtɪd/ *adj.* **~(with sb/sth)** having a very strong feeling of love or attraction for sb/sth so that you cannot think clearly and in a sensible way SYN **besotted**: *She was completely infatuated with him.*

**in·fatu·ation** /ɪnˌfætʃuˈeɪʃn/ *noun* [C, U] **~(with/for sb/sth)** very strong feelings of love or attraction for sb/sth, especially when these are unreasonable and do not last long: *It isn't love, it's just a passing infatuation.*

**in·fect** ʔ+ C1 /ɪnˈfekt/ *verb* 1 ʔ+ C1 to make a disease or an illness spread to a person, an animal or a plant: **~sb/sth (with sth)** *It is not possible to infect another person through kissing.* ◊ **be infected with sth** *people infected with HIV* 2 ʔ+ C1 [usually passive] to make a substance contain harmful bacteria that can spread disease SYN **contaminate**: **be infected (with sth)** *The eggs were infected with salmonella.* 3 **~sth (with sth)** to make a computer virus spread to another computer or program 4 **~sb (with sth)** to make sb share a particular feeling: *She infected the children with her enthusiasm for music.*

**in·fected** /ɪnˈfektɪd/ adj. **1** affected by harmful bacteria, a virus, etc: *The wound from the dog bite had become infected.* ◊ *an infected water supply* **2** (*computing*) affected by a computer virus: *an infected PC*

**in·fec·tion** ⓘ B2 /ɪnˈfekʃn/ noun **1** B2 [U] the act or process of causing or getting a disease: *to cause/prevent infection* ◊ *to be exposed to infection* ◊ *The drugs slow down the progression of HIV infection.* ◊ *to increase the risk of infection* ⊃ see also CROSS-INFECTION ⊃ compare CONTAGION **2** B2 [C] an illness that is caused by bacteria or a virus and that affects one part of the body: *an ear/a chest infection* ◊ *a viral/bacterial infection* ◊ *to cause an infection* ◊ *to spread an infection* ⊃ see also YEAST INFECTION ⊃ SYNONYMS at DISEASE ⊃ WORDFINDER NOTE at DISEASE

**in·fec·tious** /ɪnˈfekʃəs/ adj. **1** an **infectious** disease can be passed easily from one person to another, especially through air or water: *Flu is highly infectious.* ◊ (*figurative*) *infectious laughter* **2** [not usually before noun] if a person or an animal is **infectious**, they have a disease that can be spread to others: *I'm still infectious.* ⊃ compare CONTAGIOUS ▸ **in·fec·tious·ly** adv.: *to laugh infectiously* **in·fec·tious·ness** noun [U]

**in·fect·ive** /ɪnˈfektɪv/ adj. (*medical*) able to cause infection

**infer** ⓘ+ B2 Ⓦ /ɪnˈfɜː(r)/ verb (-rr-) **1** ⓘ+ B2 to reach an opinion or decide that sth is true on the basis of information that is available SYN **deduce**: *~ sth (from sth)* *Much of the meaning must be inferred from the context.* ◊ *~ that … It is reasonable to infer that the government knew about these deals.* **2** *~ (that) …* | *~ sth* (*non-standard*) to suggest indirectly that sth is true: *Are you inferring (that) I'm not capable of doing the job?*

▼ WHICH WORD?
**infer / imply**
- **Infer** and **imply** have opposite meanings. The two words can describe the same event, but from different points of view. If a speaker or writer **implies** something, they suggest it without saying it directly: *The article implied that the pilot was responsible for the accident.* If you **infer** something from what a speaker or writer says, you come to the conclusion that this is what he or she means: *I inferred from the article that the pilot was responsible for the accident.*
- **Infer** is now often used in informal speech with the same meaning as **imply**: *Are you inferring that I'm a liar?* However, this is still considered incorrect in standard English.

**in·fer·ence** Ⓦ /ˈɪnfərəns/ noun **1** [C] something that you can find out indirectly from what you already know SYN **deduction**: *to draw/make inferences from the data* ◊ *The clear inference is that the universe is expanding.* **2** [U] the act or process of forming an opinion, based on what you already know: *by ~* *If he is guilty then, by inference, so is his wife* (= it is logical to think so, from the same evidence).

**in·fer·ior** /ɪnˈfɪəriə(r); NAmE -ˈfɪr-/ adj., noun
- *adj.* **1** not good or not as good as sb/sth else: *of inferior quality* ◊ *inferior goods* ◊ *to make sb feel inferior* ◊ *~to sb/sth* *Modern music is often considered inferior to that of the past.* **2** [usually before noun] (*formal*) of lower rank; lower: *an inferior officer* OPP **superior**
- *noun* a person who is not as good as sb else; a person who is lower in rank or status

**in·fer·ior·ity** /ɪnˌfɪəriˈɒrəti; NAmE -ˌfɪriˈɔːr-/ noun [U] the state of not being as good as sb/sth else: *a sense of inferiority* ◊ *social inferiority* OPP **superiority**

**infeˌriority ˈcomplex** noun a feeling that you are not as good, as important or as intelligent as other people

**in·fer·nal** /ɪnˈfɜːnl/ noun /NAmE -ˈfɜːrnl/ adj. **1** [only before noun] (*old-fashioned*) extremely annoying: *Stop that infernal noise!* **2** (*literary*) connected with hell ▸ **in·fer·nal·ly** /-nəli/ adv.

**in·ferno** /ɪnˈfɜːnəʊ; NAmE -ˈfɜːrn-/ noun [usually sing.] (*pl. -os*) a very large dangerous fire that is out of control: *a blazing/raging inferno*

**in·fer·tile** /ɪnˈfɜːtaɪl; NAmE -ˈfɜːrtl/ adj. **1** (of people, animals and plants) not able to have babies or produce young: *an infertile couple* **2** (of land) not able to produce good crops OPP **fertile** ▸ **in·fer·til·ity** /ˌɪnfɜːˈtɪləti; NAmE -fɜːrt-/ noun [U]: *an infertility clinic* ◊ *infertility treatment for couples*

**in·fest** /ɪnˈfest/ verb [usually passive] (especially of insects or animals such as RATS) to exist in large numbers in a particular place, often causing damage or disease: **be infested (with sth)** *The kitchen was infested with ants.* ◊ *shark-infested waters* ▸ **in·fes·ta·tion** /ˌɪnfeˈsteɪʃn/ noun [C, U]: *an infestation of lice*

**in·fi·del** /ˈɪnfɪdəl, -del/ noun (*old use, offensive*) an offensive way of referring to sb who does not believe in what the speaker considers to be the true religion

**in·fi·del·ity** /ˌɪnfɪˈdeləti/ noun [U, C] (*pl. -ies*) the act of not being FAITHFUL to your wife, husband or partner, by having sex with sb else SYN **unfaithfulness**: *marital infidelity* ◊ *She could not forgive his infidelities.* OPP **fidelity**

**in·field** /ˈɪnfiːld/ noun, adv.
- *noun* [sing.] the inner part of the field in baseball, CRICKET and some other sports; the players in this part of the field ⊃ compare OUTFIELD
- *adv.* in or to the infield, especially in football (soccer) or rugby: *Mbappé came infield from the right to score.*

**in·fight·ing** /ˈɪnfaɪtɪŋ/ noun [U] arguments between people in the same group who are competing for power: *political infighting within the party*

**in·fill** /ˈɪnfɪl/ noun [U] **1** the filling in of a space with sth, especially the building of new houses in spaces between existing ones: *infill development* **2** the material used to fill in a space or a hole: *gravel infill* ▸ **in·fill** verb [I, T] *~ (sth)*

**in·fil·trate** /ˈɪnfɪltreɪt/ verb **1** [T, I] to enter or make sb enter a place or an organization secretly, especially in order to get information that can be used against it: *~ sth* *The headquarters had been infiltrated by enemy spies.* ◊ *~ sb into sth* *Rebel forces were infiltrated into the country.* ◊ *~ into sth* *The CIA agents successfully infiltrated into the terrorist organizations.* **2** [I, T] *~ (into) sth* (*specialist*) (especially of liquids or gases) to pass slowly into sth: *Only a small amount of the rainwater actually infiltrates into the soil.* ▸ **in·fil·tra·tion** /ˌɪnfɪlˈtreɪʃn/ noun [U, C]: *the infiltration of terrorists from across the border* ◊ *the infiltration of rain into the soil*

**in·fil·tra·tor** /ˈɪnfɪltreɪtə(r)/ noun a person who secretly becomes a member of a group or goes to a place, to get information or to influence the group

**in·fi·nite** /ˈɪnfɪnət/ adj., noun
- *adj.* **1** very great; impossible to measure SYN **boundless**: *an infinite variety of plants* ◊ *a teacher with infinite patience* ◊ (*ironic*) *The company in its infinite wisdom decided to close the staff restaurant* (= they thought it was a good thing to do, but nobody else agreed). **2** without end; without end: *an infinite universe* OPP **finite**
- *noun* [sing.] **1 the infinite** something that has no end **2 the Infinite** God

**in·fi·nite·ly** /ˈɪnfɪnətli/ adv. **1** (used especially in comparisons) very much: *Your English is infinitely better than my German.* **2** extremely; with no limit: *Human beings are infinitely adaptable.*

**in·fini·tesi·mal** /ˌɪnfɪnɪˈtesɪml/ adj. (*formal*) extremely small SYN **tiny**: *infinitesimal traces of poison* ◊ *an infinitesimal risk* ▸ **in·fini·tesi·mal·ly** /-məli/ adv.

**in·fini·tive** /ɪnˈfɪnətɪv/ noun (*grammar*) the basic form of a verb such as *be* or *run*. In English, an infinitive is used by itself, for example *swim* in *She can swim* (this use is sometimes called the **bare infinitive**), or with *to* (the **to-infinitive**) as in *She likes to swim.* ⊃ see also SPLIT INFINITIVE IDM see SPLIT v.

**in·fin·ity** /ɪnˈfɪnəti/ noun (*pl. -ies*) **1** [U] (*also* **in·fin·it·ies** [pl.]) the state of having no end or limit: *the infinity/infinities of space* **2** [U] a point far away that can never be reached: *The landscape seemed to stretch into infinity.* **3** (*symb.* ∞)

[U, C] (*mathematics*) a number larger than any other **4** [sing.] a large amount that is impossible to count: *an infinity of stars*

**in·finity pool** *noun* a swimming pool that is specially designed so that, when you are in it, the pool seems to stretch to the HORIZON (= where the sky seems to meet the land or sea)

**in·firm** /ɪnˈfɜːm; *NAmE* -ˈfɜːrm/ *adj.* **1** ill and weak, especially over a long period or as a result of being old **2 the infirm** *noun* [pl.] people who are weak and ill for a long period: *care for the elderly and infirm*

**in·firm·ary** /ɪnˈfɜːməri; *NAmE* -ˈfɜːrm-/ *noun* (*pl.* **-ies**) **1** (often used in names) a hospital **2** a special room in a school, prison, etc. for people who are ill

**in·firm·ity** /ɪnˈfɜːməti; *NAmE* -ˈfɜːrm-/ *noun* [U, C] (*pl.* **-ies**) weakness or illness over a long period: *We all fear disability or infirmity.* ◇ *the infirmities of old age*

**in·flame** /ɪnˈfleɪm/ *verb* (*formal*) **1** to cause very strong feelings, especially anger or excitement, in a person or in a group of people: ~ **sb/sth** *His comments have inflamed teachers all over the country.* ◇ *Her defiance inflamed his jealousy yet further.* ◇ **be inflamed with sth** *Her sister was inflamed with jealousy.* **2** ~ **sth** to make a situation worse or more difficult to deal with: *The situation was further inflamed by the arrival of the security forces.*

**in·flamed** /ɪnˈfleɪmd/ *adj.* **1** (of a part of the body) red, painful and hot because of infection or injury ⊃ SYNONYMS at PAINFUL **2** (of people, feelings, etc.) very angry or excited

**in·flam·mable** /ɪnˈflæməbl/ (*especially BrE*) *adj.* = FLAMMABLE: *inflammable material* **HELP** **Inflammable** looks like an opposite of **flammable** but in fact it has the same meaning. However, **flammable** is much more frequent than **inflammable** and carries less risk of the meaning being confused.

**in·flam·ma·tion** /ˌɪnfləˈmeɪʃn/ *noun* [U, C] a condition in which a part of the body becomes red, painful and SWOLLEN (= larger than normal) because of infection or injury

**in·flam·ma·tory** /ɪnˈflæmətri; *NAmE* -tɔːri/ *adj.* **1** (*disapproving*) intended to cause very strong feelings of anger: *inflammatory remarks* **2** (*medical*) causing or involving inflammation ⊃ see also ANTI-INFLAMMATORY

**in·flat·able** /ɪnˈfleɪtəbl/ *adj., noun*
■ *adj.* needing to be filled with air or gas before you use it: *an inflatable mattress*
■ *noun* **1** an inflatable boat **2** a large object made of plastic or rubber and filled with air or gas, used for children to play on, or as an advertisement for sth

**in·flate** /ɪnˈfleɪt/ *verb* **1** [T, I] ~ **(sth)** to fill sth or become filled with gas or air: *Inflate your life jacket by pulling sharply on the cord.* ◇ *The life jacket failed to inflate.* **2** [T] ~ **sth** to make sth appear to be more important or impressive than it really is **3** [T, I] ~ **(sth)** to increase the price of sth; to increase in price: *The principal effect of the demand for new houses was to inflate prices.* ◇ *Food prices are no longer inflating at the same rate as last year.* ⊃ compare DEFLATE, REFLATE

**in·flated** /ɪnˈfleɪtɪd/ *adj.* **1** (especially of prices) higher than is acceptable or reasonable: *inflated prices/salaries* **2** (of ideas, claims, etc.) believing or claiming that sb/sth is more important or impressive than they really are: *He has an inflated sense of his own importance.*

**in·fla·tion** /ɪnˈfleɪʃn/ *noun* [U] **1** a fall in the value of money and a general increase in prices; the rate at which this happens: *the fight against rising inflation* ◇ *to control/curb inflation* ◇ *to reduce/bring down inflation* ◇ *a high/low rate of inflation* ◇ *an inflation rate of 3%* ◇ *Wage increases must be in line with inflation.* ◇ *Inflation is currently running at 3%.* **2** (*disapproving*) a general rise in the level of sth that is awarded: *the gross inflation of executive salaries* **3** the act or process of filling sth with air or gas: *life jackets with an automatic inflation device* **OPP** **deflation**

**in·fla·tion·ary** /ɪnˈfleɪʃənri; *NAmE* -ʃəneri/ *adj.* [usually before noun] causing or connected with a general rise in the prices of services and goods: *the inflationary effects of price rises* ◇ *Our economy is in an inflationary spiral of wage and price increases* (= a continuing situation in which an increase in one causes an increase in the other).

**in·flect** /ɪnˈflekt/ *verb* (*grammar*) **1** [I] if a word **inflects**, its ending or spelling changes according to its GRAMMATICAL function in a sentence; if a language **inflects**, it has words that do this ⊃ WORDFINDER NOTE at GRAMMAR **2** [T, usually passive] ~ **sth (for sth)** to change the form of a word according to its GRAMMATICAL function ▶ **in·flect·ed** *adj.* [usually before noun]: *an inflected language/form/verb*

**in·flec·tion** (also **in·flex·ion** *especially in BrE*) /ɪnˈflekʃn/ *noun* [C, U] **1** a change in the form of a word, especially the ending, according to its GRAMMATICAL function in a sentence **2** a change in how high or low your voice is as you are speaking

**in·flex·ible** /ɪnˈfleksəbl/ *adj.* **1** (*disapproving*) that cannot be changed or made more suitable for a particular situation **SYN** **rigid**: *an inflexible attitude/routine/system* **2** (*disapproving*) (of people or organizations) unwilling to change their opinions, decisions, etc., or the way they do things: *He's completely inflexible on the subject.* **3** (of a material) difficult or impossible to bend **SYN** **stiff** **OPP** **flexible** ▶ **in·flex·ibil·ity** /ˌɪnfleksəˈbɪləti/ *noun* [U] **in·flex·ibly** /ɪnˈfleksəbli/ *adv.*

**in·flict** /ɪnˈflɪkt/ *verb* to make sb/sth suffer sth unpleasant: ~ **sth on/upon sb/sth** *They inflicted a humiliating defeat on the home team.* ◇ *Heavy casualties were inflicted on the enemy.* ◇ (*humorous*) *Do you have to inflict that music on us?* ◇ ~ **sth** *They surveyed the damage inflicted by the storm.* ▶ **in·flic·tion** /-ˈflɪkʃn/ *noun* [U]: *the infliction of pain*
**PHR** **inˈflict yourself/sb on sb** (*often humorous*) to force sb to spend time with you/sb, when they do not want to: *Sorry to inflict myself on you again like this!* ◇ *She inflicted her nephew on them for the weekend.*

**in-ˈflight** *adj.* [only before noun] provided or happening during a journey on a plane: *an in-flight meal/movie* ◇ *in-flight refuelling* ⊃ WORDFINDER NOTE at PLANE

**in·flow** /ˈɪnfləʊ/ *noun* **1** [C, U] the movement of a lot of money, people or things into a place from somewhere else **SYN** **influx** **2** [sing., U] the movement of a liquid or of air into a place from somewhere else: *an inflow pipe* **OPP** **outflow**

**in·flu·ence** /ˈɪnfluəns/ *noun, verb*
■ *noun* **1** [U, C] ~ **(of sb/sth) (on sb/sth)** the effect that sb/sth has on the way a person thinks or behaves or on the way that sth works or develops: *He had considerable influence on younger sculptors.* ◇ *Peer group members can exert a strong influence on each other's activities.* ◇ *the influence of the climate on agricultural production* [U] the power that sb/sth has to make sb/sth behave in a particular way: ~ **(over sb/sth)** *Her parents no longer have any real influence over her.* ◇ ~ **with sb** *She could probably exert her influence with the manager and get you a job.* ◇ **under the ~ of sb/sth** *He committed the crime under the influence of drugs.* **3** [C] a person or thing that affects the way a person behaves and thinks: *cultural influences* ◇ *His first music teacher was a major influence in his life.* ◇ ~ **on sb/sth** *Those friends are a bad influence on her.*
**IDM** **under the ˈinfluence** having had too much alcohol to drink: *She was charged with driving under the influence.*
■ *verb* **1** to have an effect on the way that sb behaves or thinks, especially by giving them an example to follow: ~ **sb/sth** *His writings have influenced the lives of millions.* ◇ *to be strongly/heavily/greatly influenced by sth* ◇ *Don't let me influence you either way.* ◇ ~ **how, whether, etc…** *The wording of questions can influence how people answer.* ◇ ~ **sb to do sth** *She was influenced to take up voluntary work by her teacher.* ◇ ~ **sb in sth** *Her parents tried to influence her in her choice of university.* **2** to have an effect on a particular situation and the way that it develops: ~ **sth** *A number of social factors influence life expectancy.* ◇ ~ **how, whether, etc…** *The speed at which you eat strongly influences how much you want to eat.*

**influence peddling** *noun* [U] (*especially NAmE*) the illegal activity of a politician doing sth for sb in return for payment SYN **corruption**

**in·flu·en·cer** /ˈɪnfluənsə(r)/ *noun* a person or thing that influences sb/sth, especially a person with the ability to influence potential buyers of a product or service by recommending it on SOCIAL MEDIA: *the social media feeds of fashion influencers*

**in·flu·en·tial** ʗ+ C1 /ˌɪnfluˈenʃl/ *adj.* having a lot of influence on sb/sth: *a highly influential book* ◊ **~ in sth** *She is one of the most influential figures in local politics.* ◊ **~ in doing sth** *The committee was influential in formulating government policy on employment.*

**in·flu·enza** /ˌɪnfluˈenzə/ *noun* [U] (*formal*) flu

**in·flux** /ˈɪnflʌks/ *noun* [usually sing.] the fact of a lot of people, money or things arriving somewhere: *a massive/sudden influx of visitors* ◊ **~ (of sb/sth) into …** *the influx of wealth into the region*

**info** ʗ+ B2 /ˈɪnfəʊ/ *noun* 1 ʗ+ B2 [U] (*informal*) information: *For more info, click here.* ◊ *I couldn't find any contact info for the company.* 2 **info-** (in nouns) connected with information: *an infosheet* ◊ *We send all potential clients an infopack.*

**info·graph·ic** /ˌɪnfəʊˈɡræfɪk/ *noun* information or data that is shown in a chart, diagram, etc. so that it is easy to understand: *The article contained some useful infographics.*

**info·mer·cial** /ˌɪnfəʊˈmɜːʃl; *NAmE* ˌɪnfəʊˈmɜːrʃl/ *noun* (*especially NAmE*) an advertising film that tries to give a lot of information about a subject, so that it does not appear to be an advertisement

**in·form** ❶ B2 W /ɪnˈfɔːm; *NAmE* -ˈfɔːrm/ *verb* 1 ʗ B2 to tell sb about sth, especially in an official way: **~ sb** *The government took this decision without consulting Parliament or informing the public.* ◊ **~ sb of/about sth** *Please inform us of any changes of address.* ◊ **~ sb that …** *I have been reliably informed* (= somebody I trust has told me) *that the couple will marry next year.* ◊ **~ sb + speech** *'He's already left,' she informed us.* ◊ **~ sb when, where, etc …** *I have not been informed when the ceremony will take place.* 2 **~ yourself (of/about sth)** to find out information about sth: *We need time to inform ourselves thoroughly of the problem.* 3 **~ sth** (*formal*) to have an influence on sth: *Religion informs every aspect of their lives.*
PHRV **inˌform on ˈsb** to give information to the police or sb in authority about sb's activities, especially illegal activities: *He informed on his own brother.*

**in·for·mal** ❶ A2 /ɪnˈfɔːml; *NAmE* -ˈfɔːrml/ *adj.* 1 ʗ A2 relaxed and friendly; not following strict rules of how to behave or do sth: *an informal meeting/gathering/visit* ◊ *informal discussions/talks* ◊ *Discussions are held on an informal basis within the department.* 2 ʗ A2 (of language) suitable for normal conversation and writing to friends rather than for serious speech and letters: *an informal expression* ⊃ compare FORMAL, SLANG 3 ʗ A2 (of clothes) suitable for wearing at home or when relaxing rather than for a special or an official occasion SYN **casual**: *I changed into more informal clothes.* OPP **formal** 4 (of work or business) done by individuals on a small scale, especially unofficially or illegally: *the informal economy/sector* ◊ *informal street traders* ▶ **in·for·mal·ity** /ˌɪnfɔːˈmæləti; *NAmE* -fɔːrˈm-/ *noun* [U] **in·for·mal·ly** /ɪnˈfɔːməli; *NAmE* -ˈfɔːrm-/ *adv.*: *They told me informally* (= not officially) *that I had got the job.* ◊ *to dress informally*

**inˌformal ˈsettlement** *noun* (*SAfrE*) a place where people decide to live and build temporary shelters, often followed by more permanent houses. Sometimes informal settlements are supplied with water, electricity, etc. and people can become owners of individual pieces of land.

**in·form·ant** /ɪnˈfɔːmənt; *NAmE* -ˈfɔːrm-/ *noun* 1 a person who gives secret information about sb/sth to the police or the media SYN **informer** 2 (*specialist*) a person who gives sb information about sth, for example to help them with their research: *His informants were middle-class professional women.*

**in·form·at·ics** /ˌɪnfəˈmætɪks; *NAmE* -fərˈm-/ *noun* [U] = INFORMATION SCIENCE

**in·for·ma·tion** ❶ A1 ⊙ /ˌɪnfəˈmeɪʃn; *NAmE* -fərˈm-/ (*also informal* **info**) *noun* [U] 1 ʗ A1 facts or details about sb/sth: *a piece of information* ◊ *a source of information* ◊ *More detailed information is not yet available.* ◊ *background information* ◊ *to collect/gather/obtain/receive information* ◊ *to provide/give/share/pass on information* ◊ **~ about sb/sth** *How can I get information about enrolling on the course?* ◊ **on sb/sth** *For further information on the diet, write to us at this address.* ◊ *Our information is that the police will shortly make an arrest.* ◊ **for the ~ of sb** *This leaflet is produced for the information of* (= to inform) *our customers.* ◊ *an information desk* ⊃ see also FREEDOM OF INFORMATION 2 (*NAmE, informal*) = DIRECTORY ENQUIRIES 3 data that is processed, stored or sent by a computer: *Algorithms are essential to the way computers process information.* 4 what is represented by a particular arrangement or sequence of things: *the transfer of genetic information from DNA to RNA* ▶ **in·for·ma·tion·al** /-ʃənl/ *adj.* [only before noun]: *the informational content of a book* ◊ *the informational role of the media*
IDM **for inforˈmation ˈonly** written on documents that are sent to sb who needs to know the information in them but does not need to deal with them **for your inforˈmation** 1 (*abbr.* **FYI** or **fyi**) = FOR INFORMATION ONLY 2 (*informal*) used to tell sb that they are wrong about sth: *For your information, I don't even have a car.* ⊃ more at MINE *n.*

▼ EXPRESS YOURSELF

**Asking for information**

When you want to find something out, it sounds more polite if you can phrase your questions in an indirect way:
- *Could you tell me* the best way to get to Paddington station, please?
- *Do you happen to know* whether Amy Brown works here?
- *I wonder whether/if you can help me. I'm trying to find out* which number to call for reservations.

**inforˈmation ˈscience** (*also* **in·form·at·ics**) *noun* [U] (*computing*) the study of processes for storing and obtaining information

**inforˈmation seˈcurity** (*also informal* **infosec**) *noun* [U] ways of protecting information, especially electronic data, from being used or seen without permission

**inforˈmation techˈnology** *noun* [U] (*abbr.* **IT**) the study or use of electronic equipment, especially computers, for storing, accessing, analysing and sending information

**inforˈmation ˈtheory** *noun* [U] (*mathematics*) a theory that is used to calculate the most efficient way to send information over distances in the form of signals or symbols

**in·forma·tive** /ɪnˈfɔːmətɪv; *NAmE* -ˈfɔːrm-/ *adj.* (*approving*) giving useful information: *The talk was both informative and entertaining.* OPP **uninformative**

**in·formed** W /ɪnˈfɔːmd; *NAmE* -ˈfɔːrmd/ *adj.* 1 having or showing a lot of knowledge about a particular subject or situation: *an informed critic* ◊ *They are not fully informed about the changes.* ◊ *Keep me informed of any developments.* OPP **uninformed** ⊃ see also ILL-INFORMED, WELL INFORMED 2 (of a decision or judgement) based on an understanding of the facts of a situation: *an informed choice/decision/opinion*

**in·form·er** /ɪnˈfɔːmə(r); *NAmE* -ˈfɔːrm-/ *noun* a person who gives information to the police or other authority

**info·sec** /ˈɪnfəʊsek/ *noun* [U] (*informal*) = INFORMATION SECURITY: *the infosec industry*

**info·tain·ment** /ˌɪnfəʊˈteɪnmənt/ *noun* [U] television programmes, etc. that present news and serious subjects in a way that entertains you

**infra-** /ˈɪnfrə/ *prefix* (in adjectives) below or beyond a particular limit: *infrared* ⊃ compare ULTRA-

**in·frac·tion** /ɪnˈfrækʃn/ noun [C, U] (formal) an act of breaking a rule or law SYN **infringement**: *minor infractions of EU regulations*

**in·fra·red** /ˌɪnfrəˈred/ adj. (physics) having or using ELECTROMAGNETIC waves that are longer than those of red light in the SPECTRUM, and that cannot be seen: *infrared radiation* ◊ *an infrared lamp* ⊃ compare ULTRAVIOLET

**in·fra·struc·ture** ⁀+ B2 /ˈɪnfrəstrʌktʃə(r)/ noun [C, U] the basic systems and services that are necessary for a country or an organization to run smoothly, for example buildings, transport and water and power supplies ▸ **in·fra·struc·tural** /ˌɪnfrəˈstrʌktʃərəl/ adj. [usually before noun]: *infrastructural development*

**in·fre·quent** /ɪnˈfriːkwənt/ adj. not happening often SYN **rare**: *her infrequent visits home* ◊ *Muggings are relatively infrequent in this area.* OPP **frequent** ▸ **in·fre·quent·ly** adv.: *This happens not infrequently* (= often).

**in·fringe** /ɪnˈfrɪndʒ/ verb (formal) **1** [T] ~ **sth** (of an action, a plan, etc.) to break a law or rule: *The material can be copied without infringing copyright.* **2** [T, I] to limit sb's legal rights: ~ **sth** *They said that compulsory identity cards would infringe civil liberties.* ◊ ~ **on/upon sth** *She refused to answer questions that infringed on her private affairs.* ▸ **in·fringe·ment** noun [U, C]: *copyright infringement* ◊ *an infringement of liberty*

**in·furi·ate** /ɪnˈfjʊərieɪt/ NAmE -ˈfjʊr-/ verb to make sb extremely angry SYN **enrage**: ~ **sb** *Her silence infuriated him even more.* ◊ **it infuriates sb that …/to do sth** *It infuriates me that she was not found guilty.*

**in·furi·at·ing** /ɪnˈfjʊərieɪtɪŋ/ NAmE -ˈfjʊr-/ adj. making you extremely angry: *an infuriating child/delay* ◊ *It is infuriating to talk to someone who just looks out of the window.* ▸ **in·furi·at·ing·ly** adv.: *to smile infuriatingly* ◊ *Infuriatingly, the shop had just closed.*

**in·fuse** /ɪnˈfjuːz/ verb **1** [T] ~ **A into B** | ~ **B with A** (formal) to make sb/sth have a particular quality: *Her novels are infused with sadness.* **2** [T] ~ **sth** (formal) to have an effect on all parts of sth: *Politics infuses all aspects of our lives.* **3** [T, I] ~ (**sth**) if you **infuse** HERBS, etc. or they **infuse**, you put them in hot water until the taste has passed into the water **4** [T] ~ **sth (into sth)** (medical) to slowly put a drug or other substance into a person's VEIN

**in·fu·sion** /ɪnˈfjuːʒn/ noun **1** [C, U] ~ **of sth (into sth)** (formal) the act of adding sth to sth else in order to make it stronger or more successful: *a cash infusion into the business* ◊ *an infusion of new talent into science education* ◊ *The company needs an infusion of new blood* (= new employees with new ideas). **2** [C] a drink or medicine made by leaving HERBS, etc. in hot water **3** [C, U] (medical) an act of slowly putting a drug or other substance into a person's VEIN; the drug that is used in this way

**-ing** /ɪŋ/ suffix used to make the present participle of regular verbs: *hating* ◊ *walking* ◊ *loving*

**in·geni·ous** /ɪnˈdʒiːniəs/ adj. **1** (of an object, a plan, an idea, etc.) very suitable for a particular purpose and resulting from clever new ideas: *an ingenious device/invention/experiment* ◊ *ingenious ways of saving energy* **2** (of a person) having a lot of clever new ideas and good at inventing things: *an ingenious cook* ◊ *She's very ingenious when it comes to finding excuses.* ▸ **in·geni·ous·ly** adv.: *ingeniously designed*

**in·génue** /ˈæʒənjuː; NAmE ˈændʒənuː/ noun (from French) an innocent young woman, especially in a film or play

**in·genu·ity** /ˌɪndʒəˈnjuːəti; NAmE -ˈnuː-/ noun [U] the ability to invent things or solve problems in clever new ways SYN **inventiveness**

**in·genu·ous** /ɪnˈdʒenjuəs/ adj. (formal, sometimes disapproving) honest, innocent and willing to trust people SYN **naive**: *You're too ingenuous.* ◊ *an ingenuous smile* ◊ *It is ingenuous to suppose that money did not play a part in his decision.* ⊃ compare DISINGENUOUS ▸ **in·genu·ous·ly** adv.

**in·gest** /ɪnˈdʒest/ verb ~ **sth** (specialist) to take food, drugs, etc. into your body, usually by SWALLOWING (= making them go down your throat) ▸ **in·ges·tion** /-ˈdʒestʃən/ noun [U]

**in·glori·ous** /ɪnˈɡlɔːriəs/ adj. [usually before noun] (literary) causing feelings of shame SYN **shameful**: *an inglorious chapter in the nation's history* ⊃ compare GLORIOUS ▸ **in·glori·ous·ly** adv.

**ingot** /ˈɪŋɡət/ noun a solid piece of metal, especially gold or silver, usually like a BRICK in shape

**in·grained** (also **en·grained**) /ɪnˈɡreɪnd/ adj. **1** ~ (**in sb/sth**) (of a habit, an attitude, etc.) that has existed for a long time and is therefore difficult to change SYN **deep-rooted**: *ingrained prejudices* **2** (of dirt) under the surface of sth and therefore difficult to get rid of

**in·grati·ate** /ɪnˈɡreɪʃieɪt/ verb [no passive] ~ **yourself (with sb)** (disapproving) to do things in order to make sb like you, especially sb who will be useful to you: *The first part of his plan was to ingratiate himself with the members of the committee.*

**in·grati·at·ing** /ɪnˈɡreɪʃieɪtɪŋ/ adj. (disapproving) trying too hard to please sb: *an ingratiating smile* ▸ **in·grati·at·ing·ly** adv.

**in·grati·tude** /ɪnˈɡrætɪtjuːd; NAmE -tuːd/ noun [U] the state of not feeling or showing that you are grateful for sth OPP **gratitude**

**in·gre·di·ent** ⓘ B1 /ɪnˈɡriːdiənt/ noun **1** ⁀ B1 one of the things from which sth is made, especially one of the foods that are used together to make a particular dish: *Our skin cream contains only natural ingredients.* ◊ *The only active ingredient in this medicine is aspirin.* **2** ⁀ B1 one of the things or qualities that are necessary to make sth successful: *It has all the ingredients of a good mystery story.* ◊ *An effective exercise programme has three key ingredients—intensity, frequency and duration.* ◊ ~ **for sth** *the essential ingredients for success*

**in·gress** /ˈɪŋɡres/ noun [U] (formal) the act of entering a place; the right to enter a place ⊃ compare EGRESS

**'in-group** noun (usually disapproving) a small group of people in an organization or a society whose members share the same interests, language, etc. and try to keep other people out SYN **clique**

**in·grow·ing** /ˈɪŋɡrəʊɪŋ/ (BrE) (also **in·grown** /ˈɪŋɡrəʊn; NAmE, BrE/) adj. [only before noun] (especially of a TOENAIL or a hair) growing into the skin

**in·habit** /ɪnˈhæbɪt/ verb ~ **sth** (formal) to live in a particular place: *some of the rare species that inhabit the area*

**in·hab·it·able** /ɪnˈhæbɪtəbl/ adj. = HABITABLE

**in·hab·it·ant** ⁀+ B2 /ɪnˈhæbɪtənt/ noun a person or an animal that lives in a particular place: *the oldest inhabitant of the village* ◊ *a town of 11 000 inhabitants*

**WORD FAMILY**
**inhabit** verb
**habitable** adj.
(≠ uninhabitable)
**inhabitable** adj.
(≠ uninhabitable)
**inhabited** adj.
(≠ uninhabited)
**inhabitant** noun
**habitation** noun

**in·hab·ited** /ɪnˈhæbɪtɪd/ adj. with people or animals living there: *The island is no longer inhabited.* ◊ *The building is now inhabited by birds.* OPP **uninhabited**

**in·hal·ant** /ɪnˈheɪlənt/ noun a drug or medicine that you breathe in

**in·hale** /ɪnˈheɪl/ verb [I, T] (rather formal) to take air, smoke, gas, etc. into your lungs as you breathe SYN **breathe in**: *She closed her eyes and inhaled deeply.* ◊ *He inhaled deeply on another cigarette.* ◊ ~ **sth** *Local residents needed hospital treatment after inhaling fumes from the fire.* OPP **exhale** ▸ **in·hal·ation** /ˌɪnhəˈleɪʃn/ noun [U, C]: *Hundreds of children were treated for smoke inhalation.*

**in·haler** /ɪnˈheɪlə(r)/ noun a small device containing medicine that you breathe in through your mouth, used by people who have problems with breathing ⊃ WORDFINDER NOTE at MEDICINE

**in·har·mo·ni·ous** /ˌɪnhɑːˈməʊniəs; NAmE -hɑːrˈm-/ adj. (formal) not combining well together or with sth else

# inhere

**in·here** /ɪnˈhɪə(r)/; *NAmE* -ˈhɪr/ *verb*
**PHR V** ▶ **in'here in sth** (*formal*) to be a natural part of sth: *the meaning which inheres in words*

**in·her·ent** /ɪnˈherənt; *BrE also* -ˈhɪər-; *NAmE also* -ˈhɪr-/ *adj.* ~ **(in sb/sth)** that is a basic or permanent part of sb/sth and that cannot be removed **SYN** **intrinsic**: *the difficulties inherent in a study of this type* ◇ *Violence is inherent in our society.* ◇ *an inherent weakness in the design of the machine* ▶ **in·her·ent·ly** *adv.*: *an inherently unworkable system*

**in·herit** /ɪnˈherɪt/ *verb* **1** ~ **(sth) (from sb)** to receive money, property, etc. from sb when they die: *She inherited a fortune from her father.* ⊃ compare DISINHERIT ⊃ WORDFINDER NOTE at RELATION **2** ~ **sth (from sb)** to have qualities, physical features, etc. that are similar to those of your parents, grandparents, etc: *He has inherited his mother's patience.* ◇ *an inherited disease* **3** [T] ~ **sth (from sb)** if you **inherit** a particular situation from sb, you are now responsible for dealing with it, especially because you have replaced that person in their job: *policies inherited from the previous administration*

**in·herit·able** /ɪnˈherɪtəbl/ *adj.* (*biology*) (of a feature or disease) capable of being passed from a parent to a child in the GENES: *inheritable characteristics*

**in·herit·ance** /ɪnˈherɪtəns/ *noun* **1** [C, U] the money, property, etc. that you receive from sb when they die; the fact of receiving sth when sb dies: *She spent all her inheritance in a year.* ◇ *The title passes by inheritance to the eldest son.* **2** [U, C, *usually sing.*] something from the past or from your family that affects the way you behave, look, etc: *our cultural inheritance* ◇ *Physical characteristics are determined by genetic inheritance.*

**in'heritance tax** *noun* [U] (especially in the UK) tax that you must pay on the money or property that you receive from sb when they die ⊃ compare ESTATE TAX

**in·heri·tor** /ɪnˈherɪtə(r)/ *noun* **1** [*usually pl.*] ~ **of sth** a person who is affected by the work, ideas, etc. of people who lived before them **SYN** **heir**: *We are the inheritors of a great cultural tradition.* **2** a person who receives money, property, etc. from sb when they die **SYN** **heir**

**in·hibit** /ɪnˈhɪbɪt/ *verb* **1** ~ **sth** (*formal*) to prevent sth from happening or make it happen more slowly or less frequently than normal: *A lack of oxygen may inhibit brain development in the unborn child.* **2** ~ **sb (from sth/from doing sth)** to make sb nervous or embarrassed so that they are unable to do sth: *The managing director's presence inhibited them from airing their problems.*

**in·hib·ited** /ɪnˈhɪbɪtɪd/ *adj.* unable to relax or express your feelings in a natural way: ~ **about (doing) sth** *Boys are often more inhibited than girls about discussing their problems.* ◇ **from doing sth** *No one should feel inhibited from taking part in the show.*

**in·hib·ition** /ˌɪnhɪˈbɪʃn, ˌɪnɪ-/ *noun* **1** [C, U] a shy or nervous feeling that stops you from expressing your real thoughts or feelings: *The children were shy at first, but soon lost their inhibitions.* ◇ *She had no inhibitions about making her opinions known.* **2** [U] the act of limiting or preventing a process or an action: *the inhibition of growth*

**in·hibi·tor** /ɪnˈhɪbɪtə(r)/ *noun* **1** (*chemistry*) a substance that delays or prevents a chemical reaction **2** (*biology*) a GENE that prevents another gene from being effective

**in·hos·pit·able** /ˌɪnhɒˈspɪtəbl; *NAmE* -hɑːˈs-/ *adj.* **1** (of a place) difficult to stay or live in, especially because there is no shelter from the weather **SYN** **unwelcoming**: *inhospitable terrain* ◇ *an inhospitable climate* **2** (of people) not giving a friendly or polite welcome to guests **OPP** **hospitable**

**in-'house** *adj.* [only before noun] existing or happening within a company or an organization: *an in-house magazine* ◇ *in-house language training* ▶ **in-'house** *adv.*: *This engine has been designed and produced in-house.* ◇ *I prefer working in-house than being at an agency.*

**in·human** /ɪnˈhjuːmən/ *adj.* **1** not showing sympathy or kind feelings for people who are suffering; very cruel: *inhuman and degrading treatment* **2** not human; not seeming to be produced by a human and therefore frightening: *There was a strange inhuman sound.* ⊃ compare HUMAN, NON-HUMAN, SUBHUMAN

**in·hu·mane** /ˌɪnhjuːˈmeɪn/ *adj.* not caring about the pain or problems of other people or animals; very cruel **SYN** **callous**: *inhumane treatment of animals/prisoners* **OPP** **humane** ▶ **in·hu·mane·ly** *adv.*

**in·hu·man·ity** /ˌɪnhjuːˈmænəti/ *noun* [U, C] (*pl.* **-ies**) cruel behaviour or treatment; the fact of not having the usual human qualities of showing sympathy and being kind: *man's inhumanity to man* ◇ *the inhumanities of the prison system* **OPP** **humanity**

**in·imi·cal** /ɪˈnɪmɪkl/ *adj.* (*formal*) **1** ~ **to sth** harmful to sth; not helping sth: *These policies are inimical to the interests of society.* **2** not friendly: *an inimical stare*

**in·im·it·able** /ɪˈnɪmɪtəbl/ *adj.* too good or individual for anyone else to copy with the same effect: *John related in his own inimitable way the story of his trip to Tibet.*

**ini·qui·tous** /ɪˈnɪkwɪtəs/ *adj.* (*formal*) very unfair or wrong **SYN** **wicked**: *an iniquitous system/practice*

**ini·quity** /ɪˈnɪkwəti/ *noun* [U, C] (*pl.* **-ies**) (*formal*) the fact of being very unfair or wrong; sth that is very unfair or wrong: *the iniquity of racial prejudice* ◇ *the iniquities of the criminal justice system*

**ini·tial** /ɪˈnɪʃl/ *adj., noun, verb*
■ *adj.* [only before noun] happening at the beginning; first: *an initial payment of £60 and ten instalments of £25* ◇ *in the initial stages* (= at the beginning) *of the campaign* ◇ *My initial reaction was to decline the offer.*
■ *noun* **1** [C] the first letter of a person's first name: *'What initial is it, Mrs Owen?' 'It's J, J for Jane.'* **2** **initials** [pl.] the first letters of all the names of a person or thing: *John Fitzgerald Kennedy was often known by his initials JFK.* ◇ *Just write your initials.*
■ *verb* (**-ll-**, *US* **-l-**) ~ **sth** to mark or sign sth with your initials: *Please initial each page and sign in the space provided.*

**ini·tial·ize** (*BrE also* **-ise**) /ɪˈnɪʃəlaɪz/ *verb* ~ **sth** (*computing*) to make a computer program or system ready for use or FORMAT a disk ▶ **ini·tial·iza·tion**, **-isa·tion** /ɪˌnɪʃəlaɪˈzeɪʃn; *NAmE* -ləˈz-/ *noun* [U]

**ini·tial·ly** /ɪˈnɪʃəli/ *adv.* at the beginning: *Initially, the system worked well.* ◇ *More people had been infected than was initially thought.* ◇ *He was initially reluctant to join the project.*

**ini·ti·ate** /ɪˈnɪʃieɪt/ *verb, noun*
■ *verb* /ɪˈnɪʃieɪt/ **1** ~ **sth** (*formal*) to make sth begin **SYN** **set/put in motion**: *to initiate legal proceedings against sb* ◇ *The government has initiated a programme of economic reform.* **2** ~ **sb (into sth)** to explain sth to sb and/or make them experience it for the first time: *Many of them had been initiated into drug use at an early age.* **3** ~ **sb (into sth)** to make sb a member of a particular group, especially as part of a secret ceremony: *Hundreds are initiated into the sect each year.*
■ *noun* /ɪˈnɪʃiət/ a person who has been allowed to join a particular group, organization, or religion and is learning its rules and secrets

**ini·ti·ation** /ɪˌnɪʃiˈeɪʃn/ *noun* [U] **1** the act of sb becoming a member of a group, often with a special ceremony; the act of introducing sb to an activity or skill: *an initiation ceremony* ◇ ~ **into sth** *her initiation into the world of marketing* **2** (*formal*) the act of starting sth: *the initiation of criminal proceedings*

**ini·tia·tive** /ɪˈnɪʃətɪv/ *noun* **1** [C] a new plan for dealing with a particular problem or for achieving a particular purpose: *a United Nations peace initiative* ◇ *Most policy initiatives come from the White House.* ◇ *to launch an initiative* ◇ ~ **to do sth** *new initiatives to improve animal welfare* ◇ ~ **by sb/sth** *a joint initiative by the Scottish and UK governments* **2** [U] the ability to decide and act on your own without waiting for sb to tell you what to do: *You won't get much help. You'll have to use* *your initiative.* ◊ *She did it on her own initiative* (= without anyone telling her to do it). **3** 🔑 **B2 the initiative** [sing.] the power or opportunity to act and gain an advantage before other people do: *to seize/regain the initiative* ◊ *It was up to the US to take the initiative in repairing relations.* **4** [C, U] (in some states of the US) a process by which ordinary people can suggest a new law by signing a PETITION: *a ballot initiative to establish a local minimum wage*

**ini·ti·ator** /ɪˈnɪʃieɪtə(r)/ *noun* (*formal*) the person who starts sth

**in·ject** 🔑+ **C1** /ɪnˈdʒekt/ *verb* **1** 🔑+ **C1** [T, I] to put a drug or other substance into a person's or an animal's body using a SYRINGE: *~ sth (into yourself/sb/sth) Adrenaline was injected into the muscle.* ◊ *~ (yourself/sb/sth) (with sth) She has been injecting herself with insulin since the age of 16.* **2** 🔑+ **C1** [T] to put a liquid or other substance into sth using a SYRINGE or similar instrument: *~ A (with B) The fruit is injected with chemicals to reduce decay.* ◊ *~ B (into A) Chemicals are injected into the fruit to reduce decay.* **3** [T] *~ sth (into sth)* to add a particular quality to sth: *His comments injected a note of humour into the proceedings.* **4** [T] *~ sth (into sth)* to give money to an organization, a project, etc. so that it can function: *They are refusing to inject any more capital into the industry.*

**in·jec·tion** 🔑+ **C1** /ɪnˈdʒekʃn/ *noun* **1** 🔑+ **C1** [C, U] an act of injecting sb with a drug or other substance: *to give sb an injection* ◊ *He was treated with penicillin injections.* ◊ *daily injections of insulin* ◊ *An anaesthetic was administered by injection.* ⊃ WORDFINDER NOTE at CURE **2** [C] a large sum of money that is spent to help improve a situation, business, etc: *The theatre faces closure unless it gets an urgent cash injection.* **3** [U, C] an act of forcing a liquid or other substance into sth: *a fuel injection system* ⊃ see also FUEL INJECTION

**in·jection ˈmoulding** (*BrE*) (*NAmE* **inˌjection ˈmolding**) *noun* [U] (*specialist*) a way of shaping plastic or rubber by heating it and pouring it into a MOULD ▸ **inˌjection-ˈmoulded** (*NAmE* **inˌjection-ˈmolded**) *adj.*

**ˈin-joke** (also **inside joke** especially in *NAmE*) *noun* a joke that is only understood by a particular group of people

**in·ju·di·cious** /ˌɪndʒuˈdɪʃəs/ *adj.* (*formal*) not sensible or wise; not appropriate in a particular situation **SYN** unwise: *an injudicious remark* **OPP** judicious ▸ **in·ju·di·cious·ly** *adv.*

**Injun** /ˈɪndʒən/ *noun* (*US*, *taboo*, *slang*) an offensive word for a Native American

**in·junc·tion** /ɪnˈdʒʌŋkʃn/ *noun* **1** an official order given by a court that demands that sth must or must not be done: *to seek/obtain an injunction* ◊ *~ against sb The court granted an injunction against the defendants.* ⊃ compare RESTRAINING ORDER **2** (*formal*) a warning or an order from sb in authority

**in·jure** 🛈 **B1** /ˈɪndʒə(r)/ *verb* **1** 🔑+ **B1** *~ sb/sth/yourself* to harm yourself or sb else physically, especially in an accident: *He injured his knee playing hockey.* ◊ *She was seriously injured in a riding accident.* ⊃ WORDFINDER NOTE at ACCIDENT **2** *~ sth* to damage sb's reputation, interests, feelings, etc: *This could seriously injure the company's reputation.*

**in·jured** 🛈 **B1** /ˈɪndʒəd; *NAmE* -dʒərd/ *adj.* **1** 🔑 **B1** physically hurt; having an injury: *an injured leg* ◊ *Luckily, she isn't injured.* ◊ *Carter is playing in place of the injured O'Reilly.* ◊ *seriously/critically/badly/severely injured* **OPP** uninjured **2 the injured** *noun* [pl.] the people injured in an accident, a battle, etc: *Ambulances took the injured to a nearby hospital.* **3** (of a person or their feelings) upset or offended because sth unfair has been done: *an injured look/tone* ◊ *injured pride*

**the ˌinjured ˈparty** *noun* [sing.] (*law*) the person who has been treated unfairly, or the person who claims in court to have been treated unfairly

**in·juri·ous** /ɪnˈdʒʊəriəs; *NAmE* -ˈdʒʊr-/ *adj.* *~ (to sb/sth)* (*formal*) causing or likely to cause harm or damage **SYN** damaging

817 **ink**

▼ SYNONYMS

**injure**
**wound · hurt · bruise · sprain · pull · strain**

These words all mean to harm yourself or sb else physically, especially in an accident.

**injure** to harm yourself or sb else physically, especially in an accident: *He injured his knee playing hockey.* ◊ *Three people were injured in the crash.*

**wound** [often passive] (*rather formal*) to injure part of the body, especially by making a hole in the skin using a weapon: *50 people were seriously wounded in the attack.*
**NOTE** **Wound** is often used to talk about people being hurt in war or in other attacks that affect a lot of people.

**hurt** to cause physical pain to sb/yourself; to injure sb/yourself: *Did you hurt yourself?*

INJURE OR HURT?
You can **hurt** or **injure** a part of the body in an accident. **Hurt** emphasizes the physical pain caused; **injure** emphasizes that the part of the body has been damaged in some way.

**bruise** to make a blue, brown or purple mark (= a bruise) appear on the skin after sb has fallen or been hit; to develop a bruise

**sprain** to injure part of your body, especially your ankle, wrist or knee, by suddenly twisting it, causing pain and swelling

**pull** to damage a muscle, etc, by using too much force

**strain** to injure yourself or part of your body by making it work too hard: *Don't strain your eyes by reading in poor light.*

PATTERNS
- to injure/hurt/strain **yourself**
- to injure/hurt/sprain/pull/strain a **muscle**
- to injure/hurt/sprain your **ankle/foot/knee/wrist/hand**
- to injure/hurt/strain your **back/shoulder/eyes**
- to injure/hurt your **spine/neck**
- to be **badly/severely/slightly** injured/wounded/hurt/bruised/sprained

**in·jury** 🛈 **A2** /ˈɪndʒəri/ *noun* (*pl.* **-ies**) **1** 🔑 **A2** [C, U] harm done to a person's or an animal's body, for example in an accident: *Two people sustained minor injuries.* ◊ *One of the girls suffered serious injuries.* ◊ *He was lucky to escape injury.* ◊ *a head injury* ◊ *~ to sb/sth One youth was treated for injuries to his arm.* ◊ *There were no injuries in the crash* (= no people injured). ◊ *because of ~ Two players are out of the team because of injury.* ◊ (*BrE*, *informal*) *Don't do that. You'll do yourself an injury* (= hurt yourself). ⊃ WORDFINDER NOTE at HURT ⊃ see also PERSONAL INJURY, RSI **2** [U] (*law*) damage to a person's feelings: *Damages may be awarded for emotional injury.* **IDM** see ADD

**ˈinjury time** *noun* [U] (*BrE*) time added at the end of a game of football, hockey, etc. because the game has been interrupted by injured players needing treatment

**in·just·ice** 🔑+ **C1** /ɪnˈdʒʌstɪs/ *noun* [U, C] the fact of a situation being unfair and of people not being treated equally; an unfair act or an example of unfair treatment: *fighting against poverty and injustice* ◊ *a burning sense of injustice* ◊ *social injustice* ◊ *She was enraged at the injustice of the remark.* ◊ *The report exposes the injustices of the system.* **OPP** justice

**IDM** **do yourself/sb an inˈjustice** to judge yourself/sb unfairly: *We may have been doing him an injustice. This work is good.*

**ink** 🔑+ **B2** /ɪŋk/ *noun*, *verb*
■ *noun* 🔑+ **B2** [U, C] coloured liquid for writing, drawing and printing: *in ~ written in ink* ◊ *different coloured inks* ◊ *a pen and ink drawing* ⊃ see also INDIAN INK, INKY, PEN-AND-INK

# inkjet printer

**verb 1** ~ sth to cover sth with ink so that it can be used for printing **2** ~ sth (*NAmE, informal*) to sign a document, especially a contract: *The group has just inked a $10 million deal.*

**PHRV** **ink sth↔'in** to write or draw in ink over sth that has already been written or drawn in pencil: (*figurative*) *The date for the presentation should have been inked in* (= made definite) *by now.*

**ink·jet printer** /ˈɪŋkdʒet ˌprɪntə(r)/ *noun* a printer that uses very small JETS to blow INK onto paper in order to form letters, numbers, etc.

**ink·ling** /ˈɪŋklɪŋ/ *noun* [usually sing.] a slight knowledge of sth that is happening or about to happen **SYN** suspicion: ~ (of sth) *He had no inkling of what was going on.* ◊ ~ (that …) *The first inkling I had that something was wrong was when I found the front door wide open.*

**'ink pad** *noun* a thick piece of soft material full of INK (= coloured liquid for writing, etc.), used with a rubber stamp

**ink·well** /ˈɪŋkwel/ *noun* a pot for holding INK (= coloured liquid for writing), especially one that fits into a hole in a desk (used in the past)

**inky** /ˈɪŋki/ *adj.* **1** black like ink: *the inky blackness of the cellar* **2** made dirty with ink: *inky fingers*

**in·laid** /ˌɪnˈleɪd/ *adj.* (of furniture, floors, etc.) decorated with designs of wood, metal, etc. that are set into the surface: *an inlaid wooden box* ◊ ~ with sth *a box inlaid with gold*

**in·land** *adv., adj.*
- *adv.* /ˌɪnˈlænd/ in or towards the middle of a country; away from the coast: *The town lies a few kilometres inland.* ◊ *We travelled further inland the next day.*
- *adj.* /ˈɪnlænd/ [usually before noun] **1** located in or near the middle of a country, not near the edge or on the coast: *inland areas* ◊ *inland lakes* ⊃ compare COASTAL **2** (*especially BrE*) taking place within one country, not between different countries **SYN** domestic: *inland trade*

**'in-laws** *noun* [pl.] (*informal*) your relatives by marriage, especially the parents of your husband or wife: *We're visiting my in-laws on Sunday.* ⊃ WORDFINDER NOTE at FAMILY

**inlay** *verb, noun*
- *verb* /ˌɪnˈleɪ/ [often passive] (in·lay·ing, in·laid, in·laid /-ˈleɪd/) to decorate the surface of sth by putting pieces of wood or metal into it in such a way that the surface remains smooth: **A is inlaid (with B)** *The lid of the box had been inlaid with silver.* ◊ **B is inlaid (into A)** *Gold and silver had been inlaid into the lid of the box.*
- *noun* /ˈɪnleɪ/ [C, U] a design or pattern on a surface made by setting wood or metal into it; the material that this design is made of: *The table was decorated with gold inlay.*

**inlet** /ˈɪnlet/ *noun* **1** a narrow area of water that stretches into the land from the sea or a lake, or between islands ⊃ WORDFINDER NOTE at COAST **2** (*specialist*) an opening through which liquid, air or gas can enter a machine: *a fuel inlet* **OPP** outlet

**in-line** (*also* inline) *adj.* (of a reference, link or image) placed within written text: *inline citations*

**'in-line skate** *noun* a type of boot with a line of small wheels attached to the bottom ⊃ compare ROLLERBLADE™, ROLLER SKATE ▸ **in-line 'skating** *noun* [U]

**in loco par·en·tis** /ɪn ˌləʊkəʊ pəˈrentɪs/ *adv.* (*from Latin, formal*) having the same responsibility for a child as a parent has

**in·mate** /ˈɪnmeɪt/ *noun* one of the people living in an institution such as a prison or a PSYCHIATRIC hospital: *The jail has 500 inmates.*

**in me·mor·iam** /ˌɪn məˈmɔːriəm/ *prep.* (*from Latin*) used to mean 'in memory of', for example on the stone over a GRAVE (= where a dead person is buried)

**in·most** /ˈɪnməʊst/ *adj.* [only before noun] = INNERMOST

**inn** /ɪn/ *noun* **1** (*BrE, old-fashioned*) a pub, usually in the country and often one where people can stay the night ⊃ see also COACHING INN **2** (*NAmE*) a small hotel, usually in the country **3 Inn** used in the names of many pubs, hotels and restaurants: *Holiday Inn*

**in·nards** /ˈɪnədz/ ; *NAmE* /ˈɪnərdz/ *noun* [pl.] (*informal*) **1** the organs inside the body of a person or an animal, especially the stomach **SYN** entrails, guts **2** the parts inside a machine

**in·nate** /ɪˈneɪt/ *adj.* (of a quality, feeling, etc.) that you have when you are born **SYN** inborn: *the innate ability to learn* ▸ **in·nate·ly** *adv.*: *He believes that humans are innately violent.*

**inner** /ˈɪnə(r)/ *adj.* [only before noun] **1** inside; towards or close to the centre of a place: *an inner courtyard* ◊ *inner London* **OPP** outer **2** (of feelings and thoughts) private and secret; not expressed or shown to other people: *She doesn't reveal much of her inner self.* ◊ *the inner workings of the mind*

**inner 'circle** *noun* the small group of people who have a lot of power in an organization, or who control it

**inner 'city** *noun* the part near the centre of a large city, which often has social problems: *There are huge problems in our inner cities.* ◊ *an inner-city area/school*

**inner 'ear** *noun* (*anatomy*) the parts of the ear that form the organs of balance and hearing, including the COCHLEA

**in·ner·most** /ˈɪnəməʊst/ ; *NAmE* /ˈɪnərm-/ *adj.* [only before noun] **1** (*also less frequent* in·most) most private, personal and secret: *I could not express my innermost feelings to anyone.* **2** nearest to the centre or inside of sth: *the innermost shrine of the temple* **OPP** outermost

**'inner tube** *noun* a rubber tube filled with air inside a tyre

**in·ning** /ˈɪnɪŋ/ *noun* (in baseball) one of the nine periods of a game in which each team has a turn at BATTING

**in·nings** /ˈɪnɪŋz/ *noun* (*pl.* in·nings) (in CRICKET) a period of time in a game during which a team or a single player is BATTING
**IDM** *sb had a good 'innings* (*BrE, informal*) used about sb who has died to say that they had a long life

**innit** /ˈɪnɪt/ *exclamation* (*BrE, non-standard*) **1** a way of saying 'isn't it': *Cold, innit?* **2** a way of saying any QUESTION TAG, such as 'don't you?' or 'haven't you?': *You got it, innit?*

**inn·keep·er** /ˈɪnkiːpə(r)/ *noun* (*old use*) a person who owns or manages an INN

**in·no·cence** /ˈɪnəsns/ *noun* [U] **1** the fact of not being guilty of a crime, etc: *She protested her innocence* (= said repeatedly that she was innocent). ◊ *This new evidence will prove their innocence.* **OPP** guilt **2** lack of knowledge and experience of the world, especially of evil or unpleasant things: *Children lose their innocence as they grow older.*
**IDM** *in all 'innocence* without knowing that sth is likely to offend or upset sb: *I asked if she was married in all innocence.*

**in·no·cent** /ˈɪnəsnt/ *adj., noun*
- *adj.* **1** not guilty of a crime, etc.; not having done sth wrong: *They have imprisoned an innocent man.* ◊ ~ (of (doing)) sth *She was found innocent of any crime.* ◊ *He was the innocent party* (= person) *in the breakdown of the marriage.* **OPP** guilty **2** [only before noun] suffering harm or being killed because of a crime, war, etc. although not directly involved in it: *an innocent bystander* ◊ *innocent victims of the bomb blast* ◊ *Thousands of innocent civilians have been killed in this conflict.* **3** having little experience of the world, especially of sexual matters, or of evil or unpleasant things **SYN** naive: *an innocent young child* **4** not intended to cause harm or upset sb **SYN** harmless: *It was all innocent fun.* ◊ *It was a perfectly innocent remark.* ▸ **in·no·cent·ly** *adv.*: *'Oh, Sue went too, did she?' I asked innocently* (= pretending I did not know that this was important).
- *noun* **1** an innocent person, especially a young child **2** a person involved by chance in a situation, especially a victim of crime or war

**in·nocu·ous** /ɪˈnɒkjuəs/ ; *NAmE* /ɪˈnɑːk-/ *adj.* (*formal*) **1** not intended or likely to offend or upset anyone **SYN** harmless: *It seemed a perfectly innocuous remark.* **2** not harmful or dangerous SYN harmless: *an innocuous substance* ▶ **in·noc·u·ous·ly** *adv.*

**in·nov·ate** /ˈɪnəveɪt/ *verb* [I, T] to introduce new things, ideas or ways of doing sth: *We must constantly adapt and innovate to ensure success in a growing market.* ◊ *~ sth to innovate new products* ▶ **in·nov·ator** /-veɪtə(r)/ *noun*

**in·nov·ation** 👤+ B2 /ˌɪnəˈveɪʃn/ *noun* 1 👤+ B2 [U] the introduction of new things, ideas or ways of doing sth: *an age of technological innovation* ◊ *~ in sth innovation in engineering* 2 👤+ B2 [C] a new idea, way of doing sth, etc. that has been introduced or discovered: *technological innovations designed to save energy* ◊ *~ in sth recent innovations in steel-making technology*

**in·nova·tive** 👤+ B2 /ˈɪnəveɪtɪv; BrE also -vət-/ (*also less frequent* **in·nov·atory** /ˌɪnəˈveɪtəri; NAmE also ˈɪnəvətɔːri/) *adj.* (*approving*) introducing or using new ideas, ways of doing sth, etc: *There will be a prize for the most innovative design.*

**in·nu·endo** /ˌɪnjuˈendəʊ/ *noun* [C, U] (*pl.* **-oes** *or* **-os**) (*disapproving*) an indirect remark about sb/sth, usually suggesting sth bad or rude; the use of remarks like this: *innuendoes about her private life* ◊ *The song is full of sexual innuendo.*

**in·nu·mer·able** /ɪˈnjuːmərəbl; NAmE ɪˈnuː-/ *adj.* too many to be counted; very many SYN **countless**: *Innumerable books have been written on the subject.*

**in·nu·mer·ate** /ɪˈnjuːmərət; NAmE ɪˈnuː-/ *adj.* unable to count or do simple mathematics OPP **numerate**

**in·ocu·late** /ɪˈnɒkjuleɪt; NAmE ɪˈnɑːk-/ *verb* ~ **sb (against sth)** to protect a person or an animal from catching a particular disease by INJECTING them with a mild form of the disease ◊ compare IMMUNIZE, VACCINATE ▶ **in·ocu·la·tion** /ɪˌnɒkjuˈleɪʃn; NAmE ɪˌnɑːk-/ *noun* [C, U]

**in·offen·sive** /ˌɪnəˈfensɪv/ *adj.* not likely to offend or upset anyone: *a shy, inoffensive young man* OPP **offensive**

**in·op·er·able** /ɪnˈɒpərəbl; NAmE -ˈɑːp-/ *adj.* 1 (of an illness, especially cancer) not able to be cured by a medical operation: *an inoperable brain tumour* 2 (*formal*) that cannot be used or made to work; not practical: *The policy was thought to be inoperable.* OPP **operable**

**in·op·era·tive** /ɪnˈɒpərətɪv; NAmE -ˈɑːp-/ *adj.* (*formal*) 1 (of a rule, system, etc.) that cannot be used because it is not legally or officially acceptable 2 (of a machine) not working; not functioning correctly OPP **operative**

**in·op·por·tune** /ɪnˈɒpətjuːn; NAmE ɪnˌɑːpərˈtuːn/ *adj.* (*formal*) happening at a bad time SYN **inappropriate, inconvenient**: *They arrived at an inopportune moment.* OPP **opportune**

**in·or·din·ate** /ɪnˈɔːdɪnət; NAmE -ˈɔːrd-/ *adj.* (*formal*) far more than is usual or expected SYN **excessive** ▶ **in·or·din·ate·ly** *adv.*: *inordinately high prices*

**in·or·gan·ic** /ˌɪnɔːˈɡænɪk; NAmE ˌɪnɔːrˈɡ-/ *adj.* 1 not consisting of or coming from any living substances: *inorganic fertilizers* OPP **organic** 2 (*chemistry*) relating to chemical COMPOUNDS that do not contain CARBON: *inorganic compounds* OPP **organic**

**inorganic ˈchemistry** *noun* [U] the branch of chemistry that deals with substances that do not contain CARBON ◊ compare ORGANIC CHEMISTRY

**in·pa·tient** /ˈɪnpeɪʃnt/ *noun* a person who stays in a hospital while receiving treatment ◊ compare OUTPATIENT ◊ WORDFINDER NOTE at HOSPITAL

**input** 👤+ B2 ◉ /ˈɪnpʊt/ *noun, verb*
■ *noun* 1 👤+ B2 [C, U] time, knowledge, ideas, etc. that you put into work, a project, etc. in order to make it succeed; the act of putting sth in: *I'd appreciate your input on this.* ◊ *~ into/to sth Her specialist input to the discussions has been very useful.* ◊ *~ of sth (into sth) There has been a big input of resources into the project from industry.* 2 👤+ B2 [U] (*computing*) the act of putting information into a computer; the information that you put in: *data input* ◊ WORDFINDER NOTE at PROGRAM 3 [C] (*specialist*) a place or means for electricity, data, etc. to enter a machine or system ◊ compare OUTPUT
■ *verb* (**in·put·ting, input, input** *or* **in·put·ting, in·put·ted, in·put·ted**) ~ **sth** to put information into a computer: *to input text/data/figures* ◊ compare OUTPUT

**in·quest** /ˈɪnkwest/ *noun* 1 an official investigation to find out the cause of sb's death, especially when it has not happened naturally: *An inquest was held to discover the cause of death.* ◊ *~ (on/into sth) a coroner's inquest into his death* 2 *~ (on/into sth)* a discussion about sth that has failed: *An inquest was held on the team's poor performance.*

**in·quire, in·quirer, in·quiring, in·quiry** = ENQUIRE, ENQUIRER, ENQUIRING, ENQUIRY

**in·qui·si·tion** /ˌɪnkwɪˈzɪʃn; NAmE ˌɪnk-/ *noun* 1 **the Inquisition** [sing.] the organization set up by the Roman Catholic Church to punish people who opposed its beliefs, especially from the fifteenth to the seventeenth century 2 [C] (*formal or humorous*) a series of questions that sb asks you, especially when they ask them in an unpleasant way

**in·quisi·tive** /ɪnˈkwɪzətɪv/ *adj.* 1 (*disapproving*) asking too many questions and trying to find out about what other people are doing, etc. SYN **curious**: *Don't be so inquisitive. It's none of your business!* 2 very interested in learning about many different things SYN **enquiring**: *a highly inquisitive mind* ▶ **in·quisi·tive·ly** *adv.* **in·quisi·tive·ness** *noun* [U]

**in·quisi·tor** /ɪnˈkwɪzɪtə(r)/ *noun* 1 a person who asks a lot of difficult questions, especially in a way that makes you feel threatened 2 an officer of the inquisition of the Roman Catholic Church ▶ **in·quisi·tor·ial** /ɪnˌkwɪzəˈtɔːriəl/ *adj.*: *He questioned her in a cold inquisitorial voice.*

**in·road** /ˈɪnrəʊd/ *noun* ~ **(into sth)** something that is achieved, especially by reducing the power or success of sth else: *This deal is their first major inroad into the American market.*
IDM **make inroads into/on sth** if one thing **makes inroads into** another, it has a clear and definite effect on the second thing, especially by reducing it, or influencing it: *Tax rises have made some inroads into the country's national debt.*

**in·sane** /ɪnˈseɪn/ *adj.* 1 (*informal*) very stupid, crazy or dangerous: *I must have been insane to agree to the idea.* ◊ see also INSANITY 2 (*informal*) extremely annoyed; angry: *This job is driving me insane.* 3 (*formal or old-fashioned*) seriously mentally ill and unable to live in normal society: *Doctors certified him as insane.* ◊ *The prisoners were slowly going insane.* OPP **sane** ◊ note at MENTAL HEALTH 4 **the insane** *noun* [pl.] (*old-fashioned*) people who are insane: *a hospital for the insane* ▶ **in·sane·ly** *adv.*: *He is insanely jealous.*

**in·sani·tary** /ɪnˈsænətri; NAmE -teri/ (*also* **un·sani·tary** *especially in NAmE*) *adj.* dirty and likely to spread disease OPP **sanitary**

**in·san·ity** /ɪnˈsænəti/ *noun* 1 [U] the state of being INSANE SYN **madness**: *He was found not guilty, by reason of insanity.* OPP **sanity** 2 [U] actions that are very stupid and possibly dangerous SYN **madness, lunacy**: *It would be sheer insanity to attempt the trip in such bad weather.*

**in·sati·able** /ɪnˈseɪʃəbl/ *adj.* always wanting more of sth; not able to be satisfied: *an insatiable appetite/curiosity/thirst* ◊ *There seems to be an insatiable demand for more powerful computers.* ▶ **in·sati·ably** /-bli/ *adv.*

**in·scribe** /ɪnˈskraɪb/ *verb* to write or cut words, your name, etc. onto sth: ~ **A (on/in B)** *His name was inscribed on the trophy.* ◊ ~ **B (with A)** *The trophy was inscribed with his name.* ◊ *She signed the book and inscribed the words 'with grateful thanks' on it.*

**in·scrip·tion** /ɪnˈskrɪpʃn/ *noun* words written in the front of a book or cut in stone or metal

**in·scrut·able** /ɪnˈskruːtəbl/ *adj.* (especially of a person's expression) impossible to understand or interpret ▶ **in·scrut·abil·ity** /ɪnˌskruːtəˈbɪləti/ *noun* [U] **in·scrut·ably** /ɪnˈskruːtəbli/ *adv.*

**inseam** /ˈɪnsiːm/ (NAmE) (BrE **inside ˈleg**) noun [sing.] a measurement of the length of the inside of sb's leg, used for making or choosing trousers of the correct size

**in·sect** /ˈɪnsekt/ noun any small creature with six legs and a body divided into three parts. Insects usually also have wings. ANTS, bees and flies are all insects: *insect species* ◊ *insect repellent* (= a chemical that keeps insects away) ◊ *an insect bite* ⊃ VISUAL VOCAB page V3 ⊃ see also STICK INSECT **HELP** **Insect** is often used to refer to other small creatures, for example spiders, although this is not correct scientific language.

**in·secti·cide** /ɪnˈsektɪsaɪd/ noun [C, U] a chemical used for killing insects ⊃ see also HERBICIDE, PESTICIDE ▶ **in·secti·cidal** /ɪnˌsektɪˈsaɪdl/ adj.

**in·sect·ivore** /ɪnˈsektɪvɔː(r)/ noun any animal that eats insects ⊃ compare CARNIVORE, HERBIVORE, OMNIVORE ▶ **in·sect·iv·or·ous** /ˌɪnsekˈtɪvərəs/ adj.

**in·se·cure** /ˌɪnsɪˈkjʊə(r); NAmE -ˈkjʊr/ adj. **1** not confident about yourself or your relationships with other people: *He's very insecure about his appearance.* ◊ *She felt nervous and insecure.* **2** not safe or protected: *Jobs nowadays are much more insecure than they were ten years ago.* ◊ *As an artist he was always financially insecure.* ◊ *an insecure password* ◊ *Insecure doors and windows* (= for example, without good locks) *make life easy for burglars.* **3** likely to move, fall down, etc. **SYN** unstable: *an insecure ladder/footbridge* **OPP** secure ▶ **in·se·cure·ly** adv.

**in·secur·ity** /ˌɪnsɪˈkjʊərəti; NAmE -ˈkjʊr-/ noun (pl. -ies) **1** [U, C] a lack of confidence about yourself or your relationships with other people; the thing that makes you feel like this: *feelings of insecurity* ◊ *We all have our fears and insecurities.* **2** [U] the state of not being safe or protected: *job insecurity* ◊ *the insecurity of wireless networks* ⊃ see also FOOD INSECURITY

**in·sem·in·ate** /ɪnˈsemɪneɪt/ verb ~ sb/sth (specialist) to put SPERM into a woman or female animal in order to make her pregnant: *The cows are artificially inseminated.* ▶ **in·sem·in·ation** /ɪnˌsemɪˈneɪʃn/ noun [U, C] ⊃ see also ARTIFICIAL INSEMINATION

**in·sens·ibil·ity** /ɪnˌsensəˈbɪləti/ noun [U] **1** (formal) the state of being unconscious **2** ~ (to sth) the fact of not being able to react to a particular thing: *insensibility to pain*

**in·sens·ible** /ɪnˈsensəbl/ adj. (formal) **1** [not before noun] ~ (to sth) unable to feel sth or react to it: *insensible to pain/cold* **2** [not before noun] ~ (of sth) not aware of a situation or of sth that might happen **SYN** unaware: *They were not insensible of the risks.* **3** [not before noun] unconscious as the result of injury, illness, etc: *He drank himself insensible.* ▶ **in·sens·ibly** /-bli/ adv.

**in·sensi·tive** /ɪnˈsensətɪv/ adj. **1** not realizing or caring how other people feel, and therefore likely to hurt or offend them **SYN** unsympathetic: *an insensitive remark* ◊ ~ **to sth** *She's completely insensitive to my feelings.* **2** ~ (to sth) not aware of changing situations, and therefore of the need to react to them: *The government seems totally insensitive to the mood of the country.* **3** ~ (to sth) not able to feel or react to sth: *insensitive to pain/cold* ◊ *He seems completely insensitive to criticism.* **OPP** sensitive ▶ **in·sensi·tive·ly** adv. **in·sensi·tiv·ity** /ɪnˌsensəˈtɪvəti/ noun [U]

**in·sep·ar·able** /ɪnˈseprəbl/ adj. **1** ~ (from sth) not able to be separated: *Our economic fortunes are inseparable from those of Europe.* **2** if people are **inseparable**, they spend most of their time together and are very good friends ▶ **in·sep·ar·abil·ity** /ɪnˌseprəˈbɪləti/ noun [U] **in·sep·ar·ably** /ɪnˈseprəbli/ adv.: *Our lives were inseparably linked.*

**in·sert** verb, noun
■ verb /ɪnˈsɜːt; NAmE -ˈsɜːrt/ **1** to put sth into sth else or between two things: ~ **sth (in/into sth)** *Insert coins into the slot and press for a ticket.* ◊ ~ **sth between A and B** *She picked up a knife and inserted it between the top of the drawer and the desk.* **2** to add sth to a piece of writing: ~ **sth** *Position the cursor where you want to insert a word.* ◊ ~ **sth into sth** *Later, he inserted another paragraph into his will.* ⊃ WORDFINDER NOTE at COMMAND
■ noun /ˈɪnsɜːt; NAmE -sɜːrt/ **1** ~ **(in sth)** an extra section added to a book, newspaper or magazine, especially to advertise sth: *an 8-page insert on the new car models* **2** ~ **(in sth)** something that is put inside sth else, or added to sth else: *These inserts fit inside any style of shoe.*

**in·ser·tion** /ɪnˈsɜːʃn; NAmE -ˈsɜːrʃn/ noun **1** [U, C] ~ **(in/into sth)** the act of putting sth inside sth else; a thing that is put inside sth else: *An examination is carried out before the insertion of the tube.* **2** [C, U] a thing that is added to a book, piece of writing, etc.; the act of adding sth: *the insertion of an extra paragraph*

**in-ˈservice** adj. [only before noun] (of training, courses of study, etc.) done while sb is working in a job, in order to learn new skills: *in-service training*

**inset** /ˈɪnset/ noun, verb
■ noun **1** a small picture, map, etc. inside a larger one: *For the Shetland Islands, see inset.* **2** something that is added on to sth else, or put inside sth else: *The windows have beautiful stained glass insets.*
■ verb (**in·set·ting, inset, inset**) **1** [usually passive] to fix sth into the surface of sth else, especially as a decoration: **A is inset (with B)** *The tables were inset with ceramic tiles.* ◊ **B is inset (into A)** *Ceramic tiles were inset into the tables.* **2** ~ **sth (into sth)** to put a small picture, map, etc. inside the borders of a bigger one

**in·shore** /ˌɪnˈʃɔː(r)/ adj. [usually before noun] in the sea but close to the SHORE: *an inshore breeze* ◊ *an inshore lifeboat* (= that stays close to the land) ▶ **inˈshore** adv.: *The boat came inshore* (= towards the land). ⊃ compare OFFSHORE

**in·side** /ɪnˈsaɪd/ prep., adv., noun, adj.
■ **prep.** (also **inˈside of** especially in NAmE) **1** on or to the inner part of sth/sb; within sth/sb: *Go inside the house.* ◊ *Inside the box was a gold watch.* ◊ *For years we had little knowledge of what life was like inside China.* ◊ *You'll feel better with a good meal inside you.* ◊ (figurative) *Inside most of us is a small child screaming for attention.* **OPP** outside **2** in less than the amount of time mentioned: *The job is unlikely to be finished inside (of) a year.* ⊃ compare OUTSIDE (4)
■ **adv. 1** on or to the inside: *She shook it to make sure there was nothing inside.* ◊ *He went inside* (= indoors) *to get his car keys.* ◊ (figurative) *I pretended not to care but I was screaming inside.* **OPP** outside **2** (informal) in prison: *He was sentenced to three years inside.*
■ **noun 1** [C, usually sing.] (usually **the inside**) the inner part, side or surface of sth: *The inside of the box was blue.* ◊ *the insides of the windows* ◊ **from the~** *The door was locked from the inside.* ◊ **on the~** *The shell is smooth on the inside.* **OPP** outside **2 the inside** [sing.] the part of a road nearest the edge, that is used by slower vehicles: **on the~** *He tried to overtake on the inside.* **OPP** outside **3 the inside** [sing.] the part of a curved road or track nearest to the middle or shortest side of the curve: **on the~** *The French runner is coming up fast on the inside.* **OPP** outside **4 insides** [pl.] (informal) a person's stomach and BOWELS: *She was so nervous, her insides were like jelly.*
**IDM** ˌinside ˈout with the part that is usually inside facing out: *You've got your sweater on inside out.* ◊ *Turn the bag inside out and let it dry.* ⊃ compare BACK TO FRONT **on the inˈside** belonging to a group or an organization and therefore able to get information that is not available to other people: *The thieves must have had someone on the inside helping them.* **turn sth ˌinside ˈout 1** to make a place very untidy when you are searching for sth: *The burglars had turned the house inside out.* **2** to cause large changes: *The new manager turned the old systems inside out.* ⊃ more at KNOW v.
■ **adj.** /ˈɪnsaɪd/ [only before noun] **1** forming the inner part of sth; not on the outside: *the inside pages of a newspaper* ◊ *an inside pocket* ◊ (BrE) *I was driving in the **inside lane*** (= the part nearest the edge, not the middle of the road). **2** known or done by sb in a group or an organization: *inside information* ◊ *Any newspaper would pay big money to get the **inside story** on her marriage.* ◊ *The robbery appeared to have been an **inside job**.*

**inside joke** noun (especially NAmE) = IN-JOKE

**inside leg** (BrE) (NAmE **inseam**) noun [sing.] a measurement of the length of the inside of sb's leg, used for making or choosing trousers of the correct size

**in·sider** ?+ C1 /ɪnˈsaɪdə(r)/ noun a person who knows a lot about a group or an organization, because they are part of it: *The situation was described by one insider as 'absolute chaos'.* ⊃ compare OUTSIDER

**insider trading** (also **insider dealing**) noun [U] the crime of buying or selling shares in a company with the help of information known only by those connected with the business, before this information is available to everybody

**inside track** noun [sing.] a position in which you have an advantage over sb else

**in·sidi·ous** /ɪnˈsɪdiəs/ adj. (formal, disapproving) spreading gradually or without being noticed, but causing serious harm: *the insidious effects of polluted water supplies* ▶ **in·sidi·ous·ly** adv.

**in·sight** ⓞ B2 Ⓦ /ˈɪnsaɪt/ noun 1 ？ B2 [C, U] an understanding of what sth is like: *There are many valuable insights in her book.* ◇ *to give sb/provide/offer insights* ◇ *~ into sth I hope you have gained some insight into the difficulties we face.* 2 ？ B2 [U] (approving) the ability to see and understand the truth about people or situations: *a writer of great insight* ◇ *With a flash of insight I realized what the dream meant.*

**in·sight·ful** /ɪnˈsaɪtfl/ adj. (approving) showing a clear understanding of a person or situation SYN perceptive

**in·sig·nia** /ɪnˈsɪɡniə/ noun (pl. **in·sig·nia** or **in·sig·nias**) the symbol, BADGE or sign that shows sb's rank or that they are a member of a group or an organization: *the royal insignia* ◇ *His uniform bore the insignia of a captain.*

**in·sig·nifi·cant** /ˌɪnsɪɡˈnɪfɪkənt/ adj. not big or valuable enough to be considered important: *an insignificant difference* ◇ *The levels of chemicals in the river are not insignificant.* ◇ *He made her feel insignificant and stupid.* OPP **significant** ▶ **in·sig·nifi·cance** /-kəns/ noun [U]: *Her own problems paled into insignificance beside this terrible news.* **in·sig·nifi·cant·ly** adv.

**in·sin·cere** /ˌɪnsɪnˈsɪə(r)/; NAmE -ˈsɪr/ adj. (disapproving) saying or doing sth that you do not really mean or believe: *an insincere smile* OPP **sincere** ▶ **in·sin·cere·ly** adv. **in·sin·cer·ity** /ˌɪnsɪnˈserəti/ noun [U]: *She accused him of insincerity.*

**in·sinu·ate** /ɪnˈsɪnjueɪt/ verb 1 (usually disapproving) to suggest indirectly that sth unpleasant is true SYN **imply**: *~ that … The article insinuated that he was having an affair with his friend's wife.* ◇ *~ sth What are you trying to insinuate?* ◇ *an insinuating smile* 2 *~ yourself into sth* (formal, disapproving) to succeed in gaining sb's respect, trust, etc. so that you can use the situation to your own advantage: *In the first act, the villain insinuates himself into the household of the man he intends to kill.* 3 *~ yourself/sth + adv./prep.* (formal) to slowly move yourself or a part of your body into a particular position or place: *She insinuated her right hand under his arm.*

**in·sinu·ation** /ɪnˌsɪnjuˈeɪʃn/ noun (usually disapproving) 1 [C] something that sb insinuates: *She resented the insinuation that she was too old for the job.* 2 [U] the act of insinuating sth

**in·sipid** /ɪnˈsɪpɪd/ adj. (disapproving) 1 having almost no taste SYN **flavourless**: *a cup of insipid coffee* 2 not interesting or exciting SYN **dull**: *After an hour of insipid conversation, I left.*

**in·sist** ⓞ B2 /ɪnˈsɪst/ verb 1 ？ B2 [I, T] to demand that sth happen or that sb agree to do sth: *I didn't really want to go but he insisted.* ◇ *'Please come with us.' 'Very well then, if you insist.'* ~ *on sb/sth doing sth She insisted on him wearing a suit* ◇ *~ that … He insists that she come.* ◇ (BrE also) *He insists that she should come.* ⊃ SYNONYMS at DEMAND 2 ？ B2 [I, T] to state clearly that sth is true, especially when other people do not believe you: *~ on sth He insisted on his innocence.* ◇ *~ (that) … He insisted (that) he was innocent.* ◇ *+ speech 'It's true,' she insisted.*

PHRV **insist on/upon sth** to demand sth and refuse to be persuaded to accept anything else: *We insisted on a refund of the full amount.* ◇ **insist on/upon doing sth** *They insisted upon being given every detail of the case.* **insist on doing sth** to continue doing sth even though other people think it is annoying: *They insist on playing their music late at night.*

**in·sist·ence** /ɪnˈsɪstəns/ noun [U] an act of demanding or saying sth clearly and refusing to accept any opposition or excuses: *at sb's ~ At her insistence, the matter was dropped.* ◇ *~ on/upon (doing) sth their insistence on strict standards of behaviour*

**in·sist·ent** /ɪnˈsɪstənt/ adj. 1 demanding sth and refusing to accept any opposition or excuses: *She didn't want to go but her brother was insistent.* ◇ *~ on (doing) sth They were insistent on having a contract for the work.* ◇ *~ that … Why are you so insistent that we leave tonight?* 2 continuing for a long period of time in a way that cannot be ignored: *insistent demands* ◇ *the insistent ringing of the telephone* ▶ **in·sist·ent·ly** adv.

**in situ** /ˌɪn ˈsɪtjuː; NAmE ˈsaɪtuː/ adv., adj. (from Latin) in the original or correct place

**in·so·bri·ety** /ˌɪnsəˈbraɪəti/ noun [U] (formal) the state of being drunk; wild and noisy behaviour that is typical of this state OPP **sobriety**

**in·so·far as** /ˌɪnsəˈfɑːr əz/ conj. = IN SO/AS FAR AS

**in·sole** /ˈɪnsəʊl/ noun a piece of material in the shape of your foot that is placed inside a shoe to make it more comfortable

**in·so·lent** /ˈɪnsələnt/ adj. extremely rude and showing a lack of respect: *an insolent child/smile* ⊃ SYNONYMS at RUDE ▶ **in·so·lence** /-ləns/ noun [U]: *Her insolence cost her her job.* **in·so·lent·ly** adv.

**in·sol·uble** /ɪnˈsɒljəbl; NAmE -ˈsɑːl-/ adj. 1 (of a problem, mystery, etc.) that cannot be solved or explained 2 *~ (in sth)* (of a substance) that does not DISSOLVE in a liquid OPP **soluble**

**in·solv·ent** /ɪnˈsɒlvənt; NAmE -ˈsɑːl-/ adj. not having enough money to pay what you owe SYN **bankrupt**: *The company has been declared insolvent.* OPP **solvent** ▶ **in·solv·ency** /-vənsi/ noun [U, C] (pl. -ies)

**in·som·nia** /ɪnˈsɒmniə; NAmE -ˈsɑːm-/ noun [U] the condition of being unable to sleep: *to suffer from insomnia* ⊃ see also SLEEPLESSNESS ⊃ WORDFINDER NOTE at SLEEP

**in·som·niac** /ɪnˈsɒmniæk; NAmE -ˈsɑːm-/ noun a person who regularly finds it difficult to sleep

**in·sou·ci·ance** /ɪnˈsuːsiəns/ noun [U] (formal) the state of not being worried about anything SYN **nonchalance**: *She hid her worries behind an air of insouciance.* ▶ **in·sou·ci·ant** /-ənt/ adj.

**Insp** abbr. INSPECTOR (especially in the British police force): *Chief Insp (Paul) King*

**in·spect** ?+ C1 /ɪnˈspekt/ verb 1 ？+ C1 to look closely at sth/sb, especially to check that everything is as it should be SYN **examine**: *~ sth/sb The teacher walked around inspecting their work.* ◇ *Make sure you inspect the goods before signing for them.* ◇ *~ sth/sb for sth The plants are regularly inspected for disease.* ⊃ SYNONYMS at CHECK 2 ？+ C1 *~ sth* to officially visit a school, factory, etc. in order to check that rules are being obeyed and that standards are acceptable: *Public health officials were called in to inspect the premises.* ⊃ SYNONYMS at CHECK

**in·spec·tion** ?+ C1 /ɪnˈspekʃn/ noun [U, C] 1 ？+ C1 an official visit to a school, factory, etc. in order to check that rules are being obeyed and that standards are acceptable: *Regular inspections are carried out at the prison.* ◇ *The head went on a tour of inspection of all the classrooms.* 2 ？+ C1 the act of looking closely at sth/sb, especially to check that everything is as it should be SYN **examination**: *The documents are available for inspection.* ◇ *Engineers carried out a thorough inspection of the track.* ◇ *on ~ On closer inspection, the notes proved to be forgeries.*

ⓞ Oxford Phrasal Academic Lexicon (OPAL) written and spoken word lists | Ⓦ OPAL written word list | Ⓢ OPAL spoken word list

# inspector

**in·spect·or** ◆+ B2 /ɪnˈspektə(r)/ noun 1 ◆+ (abbr. **Insp**) an officer of middle rank in the POLICE FORCE: *Inspector Maggie Forbes* ⊃ see also CHIEF INSPECTOR 2 ◆+ C1 a person whose job is to visit schools, factories, etc. to check that rules are being obeyed and that standards are acceptable: *a school/health/safety inspector* ⊃ see also TAX INSPECTOR 3 (in the UK) a person whose job is to check tickets on a bus or train

**in·spect·or·ate** /ɪnˈspektərət/ noun [C + sing. / pl. v.] (*especially BrE*) an official group of inspectors who work together on the same subject or at the same kind of institution: *The schools inspectorate has/have published a report on science teaching.*

**inˌspector of ˈtaxes** (*also* ˈtax inspector) noun (in the UK) a person who is responsible for collecting the tax that people must pay on the money they earn ⊃ see also TAX COLLECTOR, TAXMAN

**in·spir·ation** ◆+ C1 /ˌɪnspəˈreɪʃn/ noun 1 ◆+ C1 [U] ~ (for sth) | ~ (to do sth) the process that takes place when sb sees or hears sth that causes them to have exciting new ideas or makes them want to create sth, especially in art, music or literature: *Dreams can be a rich source of inspiration for an artist.* ◇ *Both poets drew their inspiration from the countryside.* ◇ *Looking for inspiration for a new dessert? Try this recipe.* 2 ◆+ C1 [C, usually sing.] a person or thing that is the reason why sb creates or does sth: *~ (for sth) He says my sister was the inspiration for his heroine.* ◇ *~ behind sth Clark was the inspiration behind Saturday's victory.* 3 ◆+ C1 [C, usually sing.] *~ (to/for sb)* a person or thing that makes you want to be better, more successful, etc: *Her charity work is an inspiration to us all.* 4 ◆+ C1 [C, usually sing., U] a sudden good idea: *He had an inspiration: he'd give her a dog for her birthday.* ◇ *It came to me in a flash of inspiration.*

**in·spir·ation·al** /ˌɪnspəˈreɪʃənl/ adj. providing inspiration: *an inspirational leader*

**in·spire** ❶ B2 /ɪnˈspaɪə(r)/ verb 1 ◆+ B2 to give sb the desire, confidence or enthusiasm to do sth well: *~ sb The actors' enthusiasm inspired the kids.* ◇ *~ sb with sth The actors inspired the kids with their enthusiasm.* ◇ *~ sb to sth His superb play inspired the team to a thrilling 5–0 win.* ◇ *~ sb to do sth By visiting schools, the actors hope to inspire children to put on their own productions.* 2 ◆+ *~ sth to give sb the idea for sth, especially sth artistic or that shows imagination*: *The choice of decor was inspired by a trip to India.* ◇ *His tragic story later inspired a Hollywood film.* 3 to make sb have a particular feeling or emotion: *Henry did not inspire confidence as a figure of authority.* ◇ *~ sb with sth Her work didn't exactly inspire me with confidence.* ◇ *~ sth in sb As a general, he inspired great loyalty in his troops.*

**in·spired** /ɪnˈspaɪəd/; *NAmE* -ərd/ adj. 1 having excellent qualities or abilities; produced with the help of INSPIRATION: *an inspired performance* ◇ *an inspired choice/guess* (= one that is right but based on feelings rather than knowledge) **OPP** **uninspired** 2 used with nouns, adjectives and adverbs to show how sth has been influenced: *politically inspired killings*

**in·spir·ing** /ɪnˈspaɪərɪŋ/ adj. exciting and encouraging you to do or feel sth: *an inspiring teacher* ◇ (*informal*) *The book is less than inspiring.* **OPP** **uninspiring** ⊃ see also AWE-INSPIRING

**in·sta·bil·ity** Ⓦ /ˌɪnstəˈbɪləti/ noun [U, C, usually pl.] (pl. **-ies**) 1 the quality or state of being likely to change or fail suddenly: *political and economic instability* 2 a mental condition in which sb's behaviour is likely to change suddenly: *mental/emotional instability* **OPP** **stability** ⊃ see also UNSTABLE

**Insta·gram**™ /ˈɪnstəɡræm/ (*also informal* **Insta**™ /ˈɪnstə/) noun [U] a SOCIAL MEDIA website where people can share photographs and short videos: *She shared photos on Instagram with her fans.*

**in·stall** ❶ B2 (*BrE also, less frequent* **in·stal**) /ɪnˈstɔːl/ verb 1 ◆+ B2 *~ sth* to fix equipment or furniture into position so that it can be used: *They're planning to install a new drainage system.* ◇ *Make sure the equipment is properly installed.* 2 ◆ *~ sth* to put a new program onto a computer: *to install software/an app* ◇ *~ sth on sth Be selective about the apps you install on your device.* ◇ **WORDFINDER NOTE** at SOFTWARE 3 *~ sb (as sth)* to put sb in a new position of authority, often with an official ceremony: *He was installed as President last May.* 4 *~ sb/yourself (+ adv./prep.)* to make sb/yourself comfortable in a particular place or position: *We installed ourselves in the front row.*

**in·stal·la·tion** ◆+ B2 /ˌɪnstəˈleɪʃn/ noun 1 ◆+ B2 [U, C] the act of fixing equipment or furniture in position so that it can be used: *installation costs* ◇ *Installation of the new system will take several days.* 2 ◆+ C1 [C] a piece of equipment or a machine that has been fixed in position so that it can be used: *a heating installation* 3 [U] the act of putting a new program onto a computer: *installation of the software* 4 [C] a place where specialist equipment is kept and used: *a military installation* 5 [U] the act of placing sb in a new position of authority, often with a ceremony: *the installation of the new chancellor* 6 [C] (*art*) a piece of modern sculpture that is made using sound, light, etc. as well as objects

**inˈstallment plan** (*NAmE*) (*BrE* **hire ˈpurchase**) noun [U, C] a method of buying an article by making regular payments for it over several months or years. The article only belongs to the person who is buying it when all the payments have been made. ⊃ compare CREDIT

**in·stal·ment** (*especially BrE*) (*NAmE usually* **in·stall·ment**) /ɪnˈstɔːlmənt/ noun 1 one of a number of payments that are made regularly over a period of time until sth has been paid for: *by/in instalments ~ We paid for the car in instalments.* ◇ *~ on sth The final instalment on the loan is due next week.* ◇ *They were unable to keep up* (= continue to pay regularly) *the instalments.* ⊃ SYNONYMS at PAYMENT 2 one of the parts of a story that appears regularly over a period of time in a newspaper, on television, etc. **SYN** **episode**

**in·stance** ❶ B2 ● /ˈɪnstəns/ noun, verb
- **noun** ◆ B2 a particular example or case of sth: *~ of sb/sth The report highlights a number of instances of injustice.* ◇ *~ of sb/sth doing sth There have been several instances of that happening.* ◇ *in an ~ In most instances, there will be no need for further treatment.* ◇ *I would normally suggest taking time off work, but in this instance I'm not sure that would do any good.* ⊃ SYNONYMS at EXAMPLE
  **IDM** **for ˈinstance** for example: *What would you do, for instance, if you found a member of staff stealing?* ⊃ LANGUAGE BANK at E.G. **in the ˈfirst instance** (*formal*) as the first part of a series of actions: *In the first instance, notify the police and then contact your insurance company.*
- **verb** *~ sth* (*formal*) to give sth as an example

**in·stant** ◆+ B2 /ˈɪnstənt/ adj., noun
- **adj.** 1 ◆+ B2 [usually before noun] happening immediately **SYN** **immediate**: *This account gives you instant access to your money.* ◇ *The show was an instant success.* ◇ *People today seem to want instant gratification.* 2 ◆+ B2 [only before noun] (of food) that can be made quickly and easily, usually by adding hot water: *instant coffee*
- **noun** [usually sing.] 1 a very short period of time **SYN** **moment**: *in an ~ I'll be back in an instant.* ◇ *for an ~ Just for an instant I thought he was going to refuse.* 2 a particular point in time: *at that ~ At that (very) instant, the door opened.* ◇ *the ~ (that) … I recognized her the instant (that) I saw her.* ◇ *this ~ Come here this instant* (= immediately)!

**in·stant·an·eous** /ˌɪnstənˈteɪniəs/ adj. happening immediately: *an instantaneous response* ◇ *Death was almost instantaneous.* ▶ **in·stant·an·eous·ly** adv.

**in·stant·ly** ◆+ B2 /ˈɪnstəntli/ adv. immediately: *Her voice is instantly recognizable.* ◇ *The driver was killed instantly.*

**ˌinstant ˈmessaging** noun [U] a system on the internet that allows people to exchange written messages with each other very quickly ▶ **ˌinstant ˈmessage** (*also* **IM**) noun [C, U]: *to send an instant message* ◇ *Word spreads by email and instant message.* **ˌinstant-ˈmessage** (*also* **IM**) *verb* [T, I]: *She spent most of the evening instant-messaging.* ◇ *~ sb He instant-messaged me last night.* ◇ *~ sb sth Can you instant-message me the news?*

**instant 'replay** (*BrE* also **action 'replay**) *noun* [C, U] part of sth, for example a sports game on television, that is immediately repeated, often more slowly, so that you can see a goal or another exciting or important moment again

**in·stead** /ɪnˈsted/ *adv.* in the place of sb/sth: *Lee was ill so I went instead.* ◇ *He didn't reply. Instead, he turned on his heel and left the room.* ◇ *She said nothing, preferring instead to save her comments till later.*

**in'stead of** *prep.* in the place of sb/sth: *We just had soup instead of a full meal.* ◇ *Now I can walk to work instead of going by car.*

**in·step** /ˈɪnstep/ *noun* **1** the top part of the foot between the ankle and toes ⇒ VISUAL VOCAB page V1 **2** the part of a shoe that covers the instep

**in·sti·gate** /ˈɪnstɪɡeɪt/ *verb* (*formal*) **1** ~ sth (especially *BrE*) to make sth start or happen, usually sth official **SYN bring sth about**: *The government has instigated a programme of economic reform.* **2** ~ sth to cause sth bad to happen: *They were accused of instigating racial violence.* ▸ **in·sti·ga·tion** /ˌɪnstɪˈɡeɪʃn/ *noun* [U] the act of causing sth to begin or happen: **at the ~ of** *An appeal fund was launched at the instigation of the President.* ◇ **at sb's ~** *It was done at his instigation.*

**in·sti·ga·tor** /ˈɪnstɪɡeɪtə(r)/ *noun* ~ (of sth) a person who causes sth to happen, especially sth bad: *the instigators of the riots*

**in·stil** (*BrE*) (*NAmE* **in·still**) /ɪnˈstɪl/ *verb* (-ll-) to gradually put an idea or attitude into sb's mind; to make sb feel, think or behave in a particular way over a period of time: *~ sth (in/into sb) to instil confidence/discipline/fear into sb* ◇ *~ sb with sth His father instilled him with a desire to fight injustice and corruption.*

**in·stinct** /ˈɪnstɪŋkt/ *noun* [U, C] **1** a natural quality that makes people and animals to behave in a particular way using the knowledge and abilities that they were born with rather than thought or training: *maternal instincts* ◇ **by ~** *Children do not know by instinct the difference between right and wrong.* ◇ *~ (is) to do sth His first instinct was to run away.* ◇ *~ for (doing) sth Horses have a well-developed instinct for fear.* ◇ *Even at school, he showed he had an instinct for* (= was naturally good at) *business.* ⇒ see also HERD INSTINCT, KILLER INSTINCT **2** a feeling that makes you do sth or believe that sth is true, even though it is not based on facts or reason **SYN intuition**: *I've always trusted my instincts in the past.* ◇ *~ about sb/sth Her instincts about him had been right.* ◇ *~ for … He had a gut instinct for when people were lying to him.* ◇ **on ~** *I acted purely on instinct.*

**in·stinct·ive** /ɪnˈstɪŋktɪv/ *adj.* based on instinct, not thought or training: *instinctive knowledge* ◇ *She's an instinctive player.* ◇ *My instinctive reaction was to deny everything.* ▸ **in·stinct·ive·ly** *adv.*: *He knew instinctively that something was wrong.*

**in·stinct·ual** /ɪnˈstɪŋktʃuəl/ *adj.* (*biology* or *psychology*) based on instinct; not learned

**in·sti·tute** /ˈɪnstɪtjuːt/; *NAmE* -tuːt/ *noun, verb*
■ *noun* an organization that has a particular purpose, especially one that is connected with education or a particular profession; the building used by this organization: *a research institute* ◇ *~ of sth institutes of higher education* ◇ *the Institute of Chartered Accountants* ◇ **at an ~** *She was a senior researcher at the institute.* ⇒ see also COLLEGIATE INSTITUTE
■ *verb* ~ sth (*formal*) to introduce a system, policy, etc. or start a process: *The new management intends to institute a number of changes.* ◇ *to institute criminal proceedings against sb*

**in·sti·tu·tion** /ˌɪnstɪˈtjuːʃn; *NAmE* -ˈtuː-/ *noun* **1** [C] a large important organization that has a particular purpose, for example a university or a bank: *a financial/an educational/an academic institution* ◇ *the Smithsonian Institution* ◇ *~ of sth The region boasts several*

823

# instruction

*institutions of higher education.* **2** [C] (*usually disapproving*) a building where people with special needs are taken care of, for example because they are old or mentally ill: *a mental institution* ◇ *We want this to be like a home, not an institution.* **3** [C] a custom or system that has existed for a long time among a particular group of people: *the institution of marriage* **4** [U] the act of starting or introducing sth such as a system or a law: *the institution of new safety procedures* **5** [C] (*informal, humorous*) a person who is well known because they have been in a particular place or job for a long time: *You must know him—he's an institution around here!*

**in·sti·tu·tion·al** /ˌɪnstɪˈtjuːʃənl; *NAmE* -ˈtuː-/ *adj.* [usually before noun] **1** connected with a large important organization, for example a university or bank: *institutional investors* **2** (*sometimes disapproving*) in or like a building where people with special needs are taken care of: *institutional care* ◇ *The rooms are rather drab and institutional.* **3** (*usually disapproving*) established as a normal part of an organization or culture: *institutional racism* ▸ **in·sti·tu·tion·al·ly** /-nəli/ *adv.*

**in·sti·tu·tion·al·ize** (*BrE* also **-ise**) /ˌɪnstɪˈtjuːʃənəlaɪz; *NAmE* -ˈtuː-/ *verb* **1** ~ sb to send sb who is not capable of living independently to live in a special building (= an institution) especially when it is for a long period of time **2** ~ sth to make sth become part of an organized system, society or culture, so that it is considered normal ▸ **in·sti·tu·tion·al·iza·tion, -isa·tion** /ˌɪnstɪˌtjuːʃənəlaɪˈzeɪʃn; *NAmE* -ˌtuːʃənəlɪˈz-/ *noun* [U]

**in·sti·tu·tion·al·ized** (*BrE* also **-ised**) /ˌɪnstɪˈtjuːʃənəlaɪzd; *NAmE* -ˈtuː-/ *adj.* **1** (*usually disapproving*) that has happened or been done for so long that it is considered normal: *institutionalized racism* **2** (of people) not able to live and think independently because they have spent so long in an institution: *institutionalized patients*

**in-'store** *adv., adj.* [only before noun] within a large shop: *The goods are promoted in-store.* ◇ *an in-store bakery*

**in·struct** /ɪnˈstrʌkt/ *verb* **1** (*formal*) to tell sb to do sth, especially in a formal or official way **SYN direct, order**: *~ sb to do sth The letter instructed him to report to headquarters immediately.* ◇ *~ sb where, what, etc … You will be instructed where to go as soon as the plane is ready.* ◇ *~ sb She arrived at 10 o'clock as instructed.* ◇ *~ that … He instructed that a wall be built around the city.* ◇ (*BrE* also) *He instructed that a wall should be built around the city.* ◇ *~ (sb) + speech 'Put it there,' she instructed (them).* ⇒ SYNONYMS at ORDER **2** ~ sb (in sth) (*formal*) to teach sb sth, especially a practical skill: *All our staff have been instructed in sign language.* **3** [usually passive] (*formal*) to give sb information about sth: *be instructed that … We have been instructed that a decision will not be made before the end of the week.* **4** ~ sb (to do sth) (*law*) to employ sb to represent you in a legal situation, especially as a lawyer

**in·struc·tion** /ɪnˈstrʌkʃn/ *noun, adj.*
■ *noun* **1 instructions** [pl.] detailed information on how to do or use sth **SYN direction**: *Follow the instructions on the packet carefully.* ◇ *~ on sth The plant comes with full instructions on how to care for it.* ◇ *~ for (doing) sth The website has easy instructions for making dozens of costumes for children.* **2** [C, usually pl.] something that sb tells you to do **SYN order**: *Climbers should always follow the instructions of their guide.* ◇ *~ on (doing) sth She gave him detailed instructions on the procedure to be followed.* ◇ *~ that … He left strict instructions that the box should only be opened after his death.* ◇ **to do sth** *I have explicit instructions to not let anyone else in.* ◇ **under instructions to do sth** *I'm under instructions to keep my speech short.* ◇ **on sb's instructions** *He phoned you on my instructions.* **3** [C] a piece of information that tells a computer to perform a particular operation **4** [U] (*formal*) the act of teaching sth to sb: *religious instruction* ◇ *the language/medium of instruction used in the school* ◇ *~ in sth She had no formal instruction in music.* ◇ *~ on (doing) sth basic instruction on using the internet*

# instructional

**adj.** [only before noun] giving detailed information on how to do or use sth (= giving instructions): *an instruction manual* ◊ *an instruction book/sheet*

**in·struc·tion·al** /ɪnˈstrʌkʃənl/ *adj.* [usually before noun] (*formal*) that teaches people sth: *instructional materials*

**in·struct·ive** /ɪnˈstrʌktɪv/ *adj.* giving a lot of useful information: *a most instructive experience* ◊ *It is instructive to see how other countries are tackling the problem.* ▸ **in·struct·ive·ly** *adv.*

**in·struct·or** 🔊 **A2** /ɪnˈstrʌktə(r)/ *noun* **1** **A2** a person whose job is to teach sb a practical skill or sport: *a fitness/driving/ski instructor* ◊ *a qualified/certified instructor* **2** (*NAmE*) a teacher below the rank of ASSISTANT PROFESSOR at a college or university

**in·stru·ment** 🔊 **A2** 🅦 /ˈɪnstrəmənt/ *noun* **1** **A2** = MUSICAL INSTRUMENT: *to play an instrument* ◊ *Is he learning an instrument?* ◊ *percussion/brass/string instruments* ⊃ see also STRINGED INSTRUMENT, WIND INSTRUMENT **2** **B2** a tool or device used for a particular task, especially for specialist or scientific work: *surgical/optical/scientific instruments* ◊ *a blunt/sharp instrument* ◊ *instruments of torture* ◊ **for (doing) sth** *the world's most powerful instrument for detecting gamma rays* **3** **B2** a device used for measuring speed, distance, temperature, etc. in a vehicle or on a machine: *the flight instruments* ◊ *the instrument panel* **4** (*formal*) something that is used by sb in order to achieve sth; a person or thing that makes sth happen: **~ for (doing) sth** *The law is not the best instrument for dealing with family matters.* ◊ **of sth** *an instrument of change* **5** **~ of sb/sth** (*formal*) a person who is used and controlled by sb/sth that is more powerful: *an instrument of fate* **6** (*law*) a formal legal document ⊃ see also STATUTORY INSTRUMENT

**in·stru·men·tal** 🔊 **C1** /ˌɪnstrəˈmentl/ *adj., noun*
■ *adj.* **1** **C1** **~ (in sth/in doing sth)** important in making sth happen: **~ in (doing) sth** *He was instrumental in bringing about an end to the conflict.* **2** **C1** made by or for musical instruments: *instrumental music* **3** (*grammar*) (in some languages) in the form that a noun, pronoun or adjective has when it refers to a thing that is used to do sth: *the instrumental case* ⊃ compare ACCUSATIVE, DATIVE, GENITIVE, NOMINATIVE, VOCATIVE ▸ **in·stru·men·tal·ly** /-təli/ *adv.*
■ *noun* **1** a piece of music (usually popular music) in which only musical instruments are used with no singing **2** (*grammar*) (in some languages) the form of a noun, pronoun or adjective when it refers to a thing that is used to do sth ⊃ compare ACCUSATIVE, DATIVE, GENITIVE, NOMINATIVE, VOCATIVE

**in·stru·men·tal·ist** /ˌɪnstrəˈmentəlɪst/ *noun* a person who plays a musical instrument ⊃ compare VOCALIST

**in·stru·men·ta·tion** /ˌɪnstrəmenˈteɪʃn/ *noun* [U] **1** a set of instruments used in operating a vehicle or a machine **2** the way in which a piece of music is written for a particular group of instruments

**in·sub·or·din·ation** /ˌɪnsəˌbɔːdɪˈneɪʃn/; *NAmE* -ˌbɔːrd-/ *noun* [U] (*formal*) the act of refusing to obey orders or show respect for sb who has a higher rank **SYN** disobedience ▸ **in·sub·or·din·ate** /ˌɪnsəˈbɔːdɪnət/; *NAmE* -ˈbɔːrd-/ *adj.*

**in·sub·stan·tial** /ˌɪnsəbˈstænʃl/ *adj.* **1** not very large, strong or important: *an insubstantial construction of wood and glue* ◊ *an insubstantial argument* **2** (*literary*) not real or solid: *as insubstantial as a shadow*

**in·suf·fer·able** /ɪnˈsʌfrəbl/ *adj.* extremely annoying, unpleasant and difficult to bear **SYN** unbearable ▸ **in·suf·fer·ably** /-bli/ *adv.*: *insufferably hot*

**in·suf·fi·cient** 🔊 **C1** 🅦 /ˌɪnsəˈfɪʃnt/ *adj.* **~ (to do sth)** | **~ (for sth)** (*formal*) not large, strong or important enough for a particular purpose **SYN** inadequate: *insufficient time* ◊ *His salary is insufficient to meet his needs.* **OPP** sufficient ▸ **in·suf·fi·cient·ly** *adv.* **in·suf·fi·ciency** /-ʃənsi/ *noun* [U, sing.] (*specialist*): *cardiac insufficiency*

824

**in·su·lar** /ˈɪnsjələ(r)/; *NAmE* -sə-/ *adj.* **1** (*disapproving*) only interested in your own country, ideas, etc. and not in those from outside: *The British are often accused of being insular.* **2** (*usually disapproving*) having little contact with other people: *people living restricted and sometimes insular existences* **3** (*specialist*) connected with an island or islands: *the coastal and insular areas* ▸ **in·su·lar·ity** /ˌɪnsjuˈlærəti/; *NAmE* -səˈl-/ *noun* [U]

**in·su·late** /ˈɪnsjuleɪt/; *NAmE* -səl-/ *verb* **1 ~ sth (from/against sth)** to protect sth with a material that prevents heat, sound, electricity, etc. from passing through: *Home owners are being encouraged to insulate their homes to save energy.* ⊃ WORDFINDER NOTE at ELECTRICITY **2 ~ sb/sth from/against sth** to protect sb/sth from unpleasant experiences or influences **SYN** shield

**in·su·lated** /ˈɪnsjuleɪtɪd/; *NAmE* -səl-/ *adj.* **1** protected with a material that prevents heat, sound, electricity, etc. from passing through: *insulated wires* ◊ *a well-insulated house* ◊ **~ against sth** *The laboratory was well insulated against outside noise.* **2** **~ against/from sth** protected from unpleasant influences or experiences: *Many financial institutions are now insulated against higher interest rates.* ◊ *The community was totally insulated from the outside world.*

**in·su·lat·ing** /ˈɪnsjuleɪtɪŋ/; *NAmE* -səl-/ *adj.* [only before noun] preventing heat, sound, electricity, etc. from passing through: *insulating materials*

**in·su·la·tion** /ˌɪnsjuˈleɪʃn/; *NAmE* -səˈl-/ *noun* [U] the act of protecting sth with a material that prevents heat, sound, electricity, etc. from passing through; the materials used for this: *Better insulation of your home will help to reduce heating bills.* ◊ *foam insulation*

**in·su·la·tor** /ˈɪnsjuleɪtə(r)/; *NAmE* -səl-/ *noun* a material or device used to prevent heat, electricity, or sound from escaping from sth

**in·su·lin** /ˈɪnsjəlɪn/; *NAmE* -sə-/ *noun* [U] a chemical substance produced in the body that controls the amount of sugar in the blood (by influencing the rate at which it is removed); a similar artificial substance given to people whose bodies do not produce enough naturally: *insulin-dependent diabetes*

**in·sult** 🔊 **C1** /ˈɪnsʌlt/ *noun, verb*
■ *noun* 🔊 **C1** /ˈɪnsʌlt/ a remark or an action that is said or done in order to offend sb: *The crowd were shouting insults at the police.* ◊ **~ to sb/sth** *His comments were seen as an insult to the president.* ◊ *The questions were an insult to our intelligence.* **IDM** see ADD
■ *verb* 🔊 **C1** /ɪnˈsʌlt/ **~ sb/sth** to say or do sth that offends sb: *I have never been so insulted in my life!* ◊ *She felt insulted by the low offer.*

**in·sult·ing** /ɪnˈsʌltɪŋ/ *adj.* causing or intending to cause sb to feel offended: *insulting remarks* ◊ **~ to sb/sth** *She was really insulting to me.*

**in·su·per·able** /ɪnˈsuːpərəbl/ *adj.* (*formal*) (of difficulties, problems, etc.) that cannot be dealt with successfully **SYN** insurmountable

**in·sup·port·able** /ˌɪnsəˈpɔːtəbl/; *NAmE* -ˈpɔːrt-/ *adj.* so bad or difficult that you cannot accept it or deal with it **SYN** intolerable

**in·sur·ance** 🔊 **B2** /ɪnˈʃʊərəns, -ˈʃɔːr-/; *NAmE* -ˈʃʊr-/ *noun* **1** **B2** [U, C] an arrangement with a company in which you pay them regular amounts of money and they agree to pay the costs, for example, if you die or are ill, or if you lose or damage sth: *health/medical insurance* ◊ *car/travel/unemployment insurance* ◊ *to have/buy insurance* ◊ **~ against sth** *to take out insurance against fire and theft* ◊ **on the/your ~** *Can you claim for the loss on your insurance?* ◊ *an insurance policy* ◊ *insurance premiums* (= the regular payments made for insurance) ⊃ see also LIFE INSURANCE, NATIONAL INSURANCE, THIRD-PARTY INSURANCE

**WORDFINDER** actuary, annuity, cover, excess, no-claims bonus, policy, premium, risk, underwrite

---

æ cat | ɑː father | e bed | ɜː fur | ə about | ɪ sit | iː see | i happy | ɒ got (*BrE*) | ɔː saw | ʌ cup | ʊ put | uː too

**2** [U] the business of providing people with insurance: *an insurance broker/company* ◊ *the insurance industry/business* ◊ **in ~** *He works in insurance.* **3** [U] money paid by or to an insurance company: *to pay insurance on your house* ◊ *When her husband died, she received £50000 in insurance.* **4** [U, C] **~ (against sth)** something you do to protect yourself against sth bad happening in the future: *At that time people had large families as an insurance against some children dying.*

**in·surance policy** *noun* a written contract between a person and an insurance company: *a travel insurance policy*

**in·sure** /ɪnˈʃʊə(r), -ˈʃɔː(r); *NAmE* -ˈʃʊr/ *verb* **1** [T, I] to buy insurance so that you will receive money if your property, car, etc. gets damaged or stolen, or if you get ill or die: **~ sth/yourself (for sth)** *The painting is insured for $1 million.* ◊ *Luckily he had insured himself against long-term illness.* ◊ (*figurative*) *Having a lot of children is a way of insuring themselves against loneliness in old age.* ◊ **~ against sth** *We strongly recommend insuring against sickness or injury.* **2** [T] **~ sb/sth** to sell insurance to sb for sth: *The company can refuse to insure a property that does not have window locks.* **3** (*especially NAmE*) = ENSURE

**in·sured** /ɪnˈʃʊəd, -ˈʃɔːd; *NAmE* -ˈʃʊrd/ *adj.* **1** having insurance: *Was the vehicle insured?* ◊ **~ to do sth** *You're not insured to drive our car.* ◊ **~ against sth** *It isn't insured against theft.* **2 the insured** *noun* (*pl.* **the insured**) (*law*) the person who has made an agreement with an insurance company and who receives money if, for example, they are ill or if they lose or damage sth

**in·surer** /ɪnˈʃʊərə(r), -ˈʃɔːr-; *NAmE* -ˈʃʊr-/ *noun* a person or company that provides people with insurance

**in·sur·gency** /ɪnˈsɜːdʒənsi; *NAmE* -ˈsɜːrdʒ-/ *noun* [U, C] (*pl.* **-ies**) an attempt to take control of a country by force **SYN** **rebellion** ⊃ see also COUNTER-INSURGENCY

**in·sur·gent** /ɪnˈsɜːdʒənt; *NAmE* -ˈsɜːrdʒ-/ *noun* [usually pl.] (*formal*) a person fighting against the government or armed forces of their own country **SYN** **rebel**: *an attack by armed insurgents* ▶ **in·sur·gent** *adj.* **SYN** **rebellious**: *insurgent groups/attacks*

**in·sur·mount·able** /ˌɪnsəˈmaʊntəbl; *NAmE* -sərˈm-/ *adj.* (*formal*) (of difficulties, problems, etc.) that cannot be dealt with successfully **SYN** **insuperable**

**in·sur·rec·tion** /ˌɪnsəˈrekʃn/ *noun* [C, U] **~ (against sb/sth)** a situation in which a large group of people try to take political control of their own country with violence **SYN** **uprising**: *an armed insurrection against the regime* ▶ **in·sur·rec·tion·ary** /ˌɪnsəˈrekʃənri; *NAmE* -ʃəneri/ *adj.*

**in·tact** /ɪnˈtækt/ *adj.* [not usually before noun] complete and not damaged **SYN** **undamaged**: *Most of the house remains intact even after two hundred years.* ◊ *He emerged from the trial with his reputation intact.*

**in·take** /ˈɪnteɪk/ *noun* **1** [U, C] the amount of food, drink, etc. that you take into your body: *high fluid intake* ◊ *to reduce your daily intake of salt* **2** [C + sing./pl. v., U] the number of people who are allowed to enter a school, college, profession, etc. during a particular period: *the annual student intake* **3** [C] a place where liquid, air, etc. enters a machine: *the air/fuel intake* **4** [C, usually sing.] an act of taking sth in, especially breath: *a sharp intake of breath*

**in·tan·gible** /ɪnˈtændʒəbl/ *adj.* **1** that exists but cannot be touched; difficult to describe, understand or measure: *The old building had an intangible air of sadness about it.* ◊ *The benefits are intangible.* **2** (*business*) that does not exist as a physical thing but is still valuable to a company: *intangible assets/property* **OPP** **tangible** ▶ **in·tan·gible** *noun* [usually pl.]: *intangibles such as staff morale and goodwill*

**in·te·ger** /ˈɪntɪdʒə(r)/ *noun* (*mathematics*) a whole number, such as 3 or 4 but not 3.5 ⊃ compare FRACTION

**in·te·gral** /ˈɪntɪɡrəl, ɪnˈteɡrəl/ *adj.* **1** being an essential part of sth: *Music is an integral part of the school's curriculum.* ◊ **~ to sth** *Practical experience is integral to the course.* **2** [usually before noun] included as part of sth, rather than supplied separately: *The unit comes complete with integral pump and heater.* **3** [usually

825 **intelligence**

before noun] having all the parts that are necessary for sth to be complete: *an integral system* ▶ **in·te·gral·ly** /-ɡrəli/ *adv.*

**in·te·grate** /ˈɪntɪɡreɪt/ *verb* **1** [I, T] to combine two or more things so that they work together; to combine with sth else in this way: **~ into/with sth** *These programs will integrate with your existing software.* ◊ **~ A (into/with B)** | **~ A and B** *These programs can be integrated with your existing software.* **2** [I, T] to become or make sb become accepted as a member of a social group, especially when they come from a different culture: **~ (into/with sth)** *They have not made any effort to integrate with the local community.* ◊ **~ sb (into/with sth)** *The policy is to integrate children with special needs into ordinary schools.* ⊃ compare SEGREGATE

**in·te·grated** /ˈɪntɪɡreɪtɪd/ *adj.* [usually before noun] **1** in which many different parts are closely connected and work successfully together: *an integrated transport system* (= including buses, trains, taxis, etc.) **2** including people from all groups, races, religions, etc: *an integrated school*

**integrated ˈcircuit** *noun* (*physics*) a small MICROCHIP that contains a large number of electrical connections and performs the same function as a larger CIRCUIT made from separate parts

**in·te·gra·tion** /ˌɪntɪˈɡreɪʃn/ *noun* **1** [U, C] the act or process of combining two or more things so that they work together: *The aim is to promote closer economic integration.* ◊ **~ of A and/with B** *His music is an integration of tradition and new technology.* ⊃ see also VERTICAL INTEGRATION **2** [U] the act or process of mixing people who have previously been separated, usually because of colour, race, religion, etc: *racial integration in schools* ◊ **~ (of sb) into sth** *the integration of disabled students into the general education system*

**in·teg·rity** /ɪnˈteɡrəti/ *noun* [U] **1** the quality of being honest and having strong moral principles: *personal/professional/artistic integrity* ◊ *to behave with integrity* **2** (*formal*) the state of being whole and not divided **SYN** **unity**: *to respect the territorial integrity of the nation*

**in·tel·lect** /ˈɪntəlekt/ *noun* **1** [U, C] the ability to think in a logical way and understand things, especially at an advanced level; your mind: *a man of considerable intellect* **2** [C] a very intelligent person: *She was one of the most formidable intellects of her time.*

**in·tel·lec·tual** /ˌɪntəˈlektʃuəl/ *adj., noun*
■ *adj.* **1** [usually before noun] connected with or using a person's ability to think in a logical way and understand things **SYN** **mental**: *intellectual curiosity* ◊ *an intellectual novel* **2** (of a person) well educated and enjoying activities in which you have to think seriously about things: *She's very intellectual.* ▶ **in·tel·lec·tual·ism** [U] (*usually disapproving*) **in·tel·lec·tu·al·ly** /-əli/ *adv.*: *intellectually challenging*
■ *noun* a person who is well educated and enjoys activities in which they have to think seriously about things

**ˌintelˈlectual ˈproperty** *noun* [U] (*law*) an idea, a design, etc. that sb has created and that the law prevents other people from copying: *intellectual property rights*

**in·tel·li·gence** /ɪnˈtelɪdʒəns/ *noun* [U] **1** the ability to learn, understand and think in a logical way about things; the ability to do this well: *a person of high/average/low intelligence* ◊ *He didn't even have the intelligence to call for an ambulance.* ⊃ see also ARTIFICIAL INTELLIGENCE, EMOTIONAL INTELLIGENCE **2** secret information that is collected, for example about a foreign country, especially one that is an enemy; the people that collect this information: *the head of military intelligence* ◊ **~ on/about sb/sth** *They hope to gather more intelligence on any further plots.* ▶ *intelligence agencies/services* ◊ *an intelligence officer/official/agent* ⊃ see also CENTRAL INTELLIGENCE AGENCY, COUNTER-INTELLIGENCE

# intelligence quotient

**in·telligence quotient** noun = IQ

**in·telligence test** noun a test to measure how well a person is able to understand and think in a logical way about things

**in·tel·li·gent** A2 /ɪnˈtelɪdʒənt/ adj. **1** A2 good at learning, understanding and thinking in a logical way about things; showing this ability: *a highly intelligent child* ◊ *She is clearly extremely intelligent.* ◊ *to have an intelligent conversation/discussion/debate* OPP **unintelligent 2** A2 (of an animal, a being, etc.) able to understand and learn things: *a search for intelligent life on other planets* **3** (*computing*) (of a computer, program, etc.) able to store information and use it in new situations: *intelligent robots/algorithms* ▶ **in·tel·li·gent·ly** adv.

> ### ▼ SYNONYMS
> **intelligent**
> smart • clever • brilliant • bright
> These words all describe people who are good at learning, understanding and thinking about things, and the actions that show this ability.
> **intelligent** good at learning, understanding and thinking in a logical way about things; showing this ability: *He's a highly intelligent man.* ◊ *She asked a lot of intelligent questions.*
> **smart** (*especially NAmE*) quick at learning and understanding things; showing the ability to make good business or personal decisions: *She's smarter than her brother.* ◊ *That was a smart career move.*
> **clever** (*sometimes disapproving, especially BrE*) quick at learning and understanding things; showing this ability: *How clever of you to work it out!* ◊ *He's too clever by half, if you ask me.* NOTE People use **clever** in the phrase: *Clever boy/girl!* to tell a young child that they have learnt or done sth well. When used to or about an adult **clever** can be disapproving.
> **brilliant** extremely intelligent or showing a lot of skill: *He's a brilliant young scientist.*
> **bright** intelligent; quick to learn: *She's probably the brightest student in the class.* NOTE **Bright** is used especially to talk about young people. Common collocations of **bright** include *girl, boy, kid, student, pupil.*
> PATTERNS
> • clever/brilliant **at** sth
> • a(n) intelligent/smart/clever/brilliant/bright **child/ boy/girl/man/woman**
> • a(n) intelligent/smart/clever/brilliant **thing to do**

**in·telligent deˈsign** noun [U] the belief that the universe and living things were created by an intelligent being: *the legal battle about the teaching of intelligent design as science* ⊃ compare CREATIONISM

**in·tel·li·gent·sia** /ɪnˌtelɪˈdʒentsiə/ (*usually* **the intelligentsia**) noun [sing. + sing./pl. v.] the people in a country or society who are well educated and are interested in culture, politics, literature, etc.

**in·tel·li·gible** /ɪnˈtelɪdʒəbl/ adj. ~ **(to sb)** that can be easily understood SYN **understandable**: *His lecture was readily intelligible to all the students.* OPP **unintelligible** ▶ **in·tel·li·gi·bil·ity** /ɪnˌtelɪdʒəˈbɪləti/ noun [U] **in·tel·li·gibly** /ɪnˈtelɪdʒəbli/ adv.

**in·tem·per·ate** /ɪnˈtempərət/ adj. (*formal*) **1** showing a lack of control over yourself: *intemperate language* OPP **temperate 2** (*old-fashioned*) regularly drinking too much alcohol ▶ **in·tem·per·ance** /-rəns/ noun [U]

**in·tend** B1 /ɪnˈtend/ verb **1** B1 [I, T] to have a plan, result or purpose in your mind when you do sth: *We finished later than we had intended.* ◊ **~to do sth** *I fully intended* (= definitely intended) *to pay for the damage.* ◊ **~sb/sth to do sth** *The writer clearly intends his readers to identify with the main character.* ◊ **~doing sth** (*BrE*) *I don't intend staying long.* ◊ **~sth** *The company intends a* slow-down in expansion. ◊ **~sb sth** *He intended her no harm* (= it was not his plan to harm her). ◊ *it is intended that … It is intended that production will start next month.* ◊ **~that …** *We intend that production will start next month.* **2** B2 [T] (*rather formal*) to plan that sth should have a particular meaning SYN **mean**: **~sth by sth** *What exactly did you intend by that remark?* ◊ **~sth as sth** *He intended it as a joke.*

**in·tend·ed** B2 /ɪnˈtendɪd/ adj. **1** B2 [only before noun] that you are trying to achieve or reach: *the intended purpose* ◊ *the intended audience* ◊ *The bullet missed its intended target.* **2** B2 planned or designed for sb/sth: **~for sb/sth** *The book is intended for children.* ◊ **~as sth** *The notes are intended as an introduction to the course.* ◊ **~to be/do sth** *This list is not intended to be a complete catalogue.* ⊃ see also UNINTENDED

**in·tense** B2 /ɪnˈtens/ adj. **1** B2 very great; very strong SYN **extreme**: *We were all suffering in the intense heat.* ◊ *They watched with intense interest.* ◊ *The President is under intense pressure to resign.* ◊ *the intense blue of her eyes* **2** B2 serious and often involving a lot of action in a short period of time: *intense competition* ◊ *It was a period of intense activity.* **3** (of a person) having or showing very strong feelings, opinions or thoughts about sb/sth: *an intense look* ◊ *He's very intense about everything.* ⊃ compare INTENSIVE ▶ **in·tense·ly** adv.: *She disliked him intensely.*

> ### ▼ WHICH WORD?
> **intense / intensive**
> Both these words can describe sth that involves a lot of action in a short period of time.
> • **intense** can often suggest sb's feelings about the thing being described: *The course was really intense—I found it difficult to wind down at the end of each day.*
> • **intensive** is a more objective description: *The five-day intensive course runs from 24 to 28 July.*

**in·ten·si·fier** /ɪnˈtensɪfaɪə(r)/ noun (*grammar*) a word, especially an adjective or an adverb, for example *so* or *very,* that makes the meaning of another word stronger

**in·ten·sify** C1 /ɪnˈtensɪfaɪ/ verb (**in·ten·si·fies, in·ten·si·fy·ing, in·ten·si·fied, in·ten·si·fied**) [I, T] to increase in degree or strength; to make sth increase in degree or strength SYN **heighten**: *Violence intensified during the night.* ◊ **~sth** *The opposition leader has intensified his attacks on the government.* ▶ **in·ten·si·fi·ca·tion** /ɪnˌtensɪfɪˈkeɪʃn/ noun [U, sing.]

**in·ten·sity** C1 /ɪnˈtensəti/ noun (pl. **-ies**) **1** C1 [U, sing.] the state or quality of being intense: *intensity of light/sound/colour* ◊ *intensity of feeling/concentration/relief* ◊ *He was watching her with an intensity that was unnerving.* ◊ *The storm resumed with even greater intensity.* **2** [U, C] (*specialist*) the strength of sth, for example light, that can be measured: *varying intensities of natural light*

**in·ten·sive** C1 /ɪnˈtensɪv/ adj. **1** C1 involving a lot of work or activity done in a short time: *an intensive language course* ◊ *two weeks of intensive training* ◊ *intensive diplomatic negotiations* ⊃ note at INTENSE **2** C1 complete and extremely detailed; done with a lot of care: *His disappearance has been the subject of intensive investigation.* **3** C1 (of methods of farming) aimed at producing as much food as possible using as little land or as little money as possible: *Traditionally reared animals grow more slowly than those reared under intensive farming conditions.* ◊ *intensive agriculture* ⊃ see also CAPITAL-INTENSIVE, LABOUR-INTENSIVE ▶ **in·ten·sive·ly** adv.: *This case has been intensively studied.* ◊ *intensively farmed land*

Oxford 3000 | Oxford 5000 | A1 A2 B1 B2 C1 CEFR level | PHRV phrasal verb(s) | IDM idiom(s)

**in·tensive 'care** (also **critical 'care**) noun [U] **1** continuous care and attention, often using special equipment, for people in hospital who are very seriously ill or injured: *She needed intensive care for several days.* ◇ *intensive care patients/beds* **2** (also **in,tensive 'care unit, ICU** [C]) the part of a hospital that provides intensive care: **in** ~ *The baby was in intensive care for 48 hours.*

**in·tent** ᵃ⁺ C1 /ɪnˈtent/ noun, adj.
■ noun ᵃ⁺ C1 [U] ~ **(to do sth)** (*formal or law*) what you intend to do SYN **intention**: *She denies possessing the drug with intent to supply.* ◇ *a letter/statement of intent* ◇ *His intent is clearly not to placate his critics.*
IDM **to all intents and 'purposes** (*NAmE usually* **for all intents and 'purposes**) in the effects that sth has, if not in reality; almost completely: *By 1981 the docks had, to all intents and purposes, closed.* ◇ *The two items are, for all intents and purposes, identical.*
■ adj. **1** showing strong interest and attention: *an intent gaze/look* ◇ *His eyes were suddenly intent.* **2** (*formal*) determined to do sth, especially sth that will harm other people: ~ **on/upon sth** *They were intent on murder.* ◇ ~ **on/upon doing sth** *Are you intent upon destroying my reputation?* **3** ~ **on/upon sth** giving all your attention to sth: *I was so intent on my work that I didn't notice the time.* ▶ **in·tent·ly** adv.: *She looked at him intently.*

**in·ten·tion** ᴼ B1 W /ɪnˈtenʃn/ noun [C, U] what you intend or plan to do; your aim: ~ **of doing sth** *I have no intention of going to the wedding.* ◇ *I have every intention of paying her back what I owe her.* ◇ **with the** ~ **of doing sth** *He left England with the intention of travelling in Africa.* ◇ ~ **to do sth** *He has announced his intention to retire.* ◇ ~ **in doing sth** *Her intentions in making this proposal are clear.* ◇ ~ **that** … *It was not my intention that she should suffer.* ◇ *She's full of good intentions but they rarely work out.* ◇ *I did it with the best (of) intentions* (= meaning to help), *but I only succeeded in annoying them.* ⸺ SYNONYMS at PURPOSE ⸺ see also WELL INTENTIONED IDM see ROAD

**in·ten·tion·al** /ɪnˈtenʃənl/ adj. done deliberately SYN **deliberate, intended**: *I'm sorry I left you off the list —it wasn't intentional.* OPP **unintentional** ▶ **in·ten·tion·al·ly** /-ʃənəli/ adv.: *She would never intentionally hurt anyone.* ◇ *I kept my statement intentionally vague.*

**inter** /ɪnˈtɜː(r)/ verb (-rr-) [usually passive] ~ **sb** (*formal*) to bury a dead person OPP **disinter** ⸺ see also INTERMENT

**inter-** /ɪntə(r)/ prefix (in verbs, nouns, adjectives and adverbs) between; from one to another: *interface* ◇ *interaction* ◇ *international* ⸺ compare INTRA-

**inter·act** ᵃ⁺ B2 ᴼ /ˌɪntərˈækt/ verb ᵃ⁺ B2 [I] ~ **(with sb)** to communicate with sb, especially while you work, play or spend time with them: *Teachers have a limited amount of time to interact with each child.* **2** ᵃ⁺ C1 [I] ~ **(with sth)** if one thing **interacts** with another, or if two things **interact**, the two things have an effect on each other: *Perfume interacts with the skin's natural chemicals.*

**inter·action** ᵃ⁺ B2 ᴼ /ˌɪntərˈækʃn/ noun [U, C] **1** ᵃ⁺ B2 ~ **(between A and B)** | ~ **(of A) (with B)** the act of communicating with sb, especially while you work, play or spend time with them: *the interaction between performers and their audience* **2** ᵃ⁺ C1 ~ **(between A and B)** | ~ **(of A) (with B)** if one thing has an **interaction** with another, or if there is an **interaction** between two things, the two things have an effect on each other: *the interaction of bacteria with the body's natural chemistry*

**inter·active** ᵃ⁺ C1 W /ˌɪntərˈæktɪv/ adj. **1** ᵃ⁺ C1 (*computing*) that allows information to be passed continuously and in both directions between a computer or other device and the person who uses it: *interactive displays/video* ◇ *using ICT to create an interactive learning experience* ◇ *an interactive online map that helps people find bicycle routes through the city* ⸺ WORDFINDER NOTE at SOFTWARE **2** ᵃ⁺ C1 that involves people working together and having an influence on each other: *The school believes in interactive teaching methods.* ▶ **inter·active·ly** adv. **inter·activ·ity** /ˌɪntəræktˈɪvəti/ noun [U]

**,interactive 'whiteboard** (abbr. **IWB**) noun a piece of classroom equipment using a computer connected to a large screen that you can write on or use to control the computer by touching it with your finger or a pen: *Nearly every classroom has an interactive whiteboard.*

**inter alia** /ˌɪntər ˈeɪliə/ adv. (*from Latin, formal*) among other things

**inter·breed** /ˌɪntəˈbriːd; *NAmE* -tərˈb-/ verb [I, T] (**interbred, interbred** /-ˈbred/) ~ **(sth) (with sth)** if animals from different species **interbreed**, or sb **interbreeds** them, they produce young together

**inter·cede** /ˌɪntəˈsiːd; *NAmE* -tərˈs-/ verb [I] ~ **(with sb) (for/on behalf of sb)** (*formal*) to speak to sb in order to persuade them to be kind to sb else or to help settle an argument SYN **intervene**: *They interceded with the authorities on behalf of the detainees.* ▶ **inter·ces·sion** /-ˈseʃn/ noun [U]: *the intercession of a priest*

**inter·cept** /ˌɪntəˈsept; *NAmE* -tərˈs-/ verb ~ **sb/sth** to stop sb/sth that is going from one place to another from arriving: *Reporters intercepted him as he tried to leave the hotel.* ◇ *The letter was intercepted.* ▶ **inter·cep·tion** /-ˈsepʃn/ noun [U, C]: *the interception of enemy radio signals*

**inter·cept·or** /ˌɪntəˈseptə(r); *NAmE* -tərˈs-/ noun a fast military plane that attacks enemy planes that are carrying bombs

**inter·change** noun, verb
■ noun /ˈɪntətʃeɪndʒ; *NAmE* -tərtʃ-/ **1** [C, U] the act of sharing or exchanging sth, especially ideas or information: *a continuous interchange of ideas* ◇ *electronic data interchange* **2** [C] a place where a road joins a major road such as a MOTORWAY or INTERSTATE, designed so that vehicles leaving or joining the road do not have to cross other lines of traffic
■ verb /ˌɪntəˈtʃeɪndʒ; *NAmE* -tərˈtʃ-/ **1** [T] ~ **sth (between A and B)** to share or exchange ideas, information, etc. **2** [T, I] to put each of two things or people in the other's place; to move or be moved from one place to another in this way: ~ **A and B** *to interchange the front and rear tyres of a car* ◇ ~ **(A) (with B)** *to interchange the front tyres with the rear ones* ◇ *The front and rear tyres interchange* (= can be exchanged).

**inter·change·able** /ˌɪntəˈtʃeɪndʒəbl; *NAmE* -tərˈtʃ-/ adj. that can be exchanged, especially without affecting the way in which sth works: *The two words are virtually interchangeable* (= have almost the same meaning). ◇ ~ **with sth** *The V8 engines are all interchangeable with each other.* ▶ **inter·change·abil·ity** /ˌɪntətʃeɪndʒəˈbɪləti; *NAmE* -tərtʃ-/ noun [U] **inter·change·ably** /ˌɪntəˈtʃeɪndʒəbli; *NAmE* -tərˈtʃ-/ adv.: *These terms are used interchangeably.*

**inter·city** /ˌɪntəˈsɪti; *NAmE* -tərˈs-/ adj. [usually before noun] (of transport) travelling between cities, usually with not many stops on the way: *an intercity rail service* ◇ *intercity travel*

**inter·col·le·gi·ate** /ˌɪntəkəˈliːdʒiət; *NAmE* -tərk-/ adj. (*especially NAmE*) involving competition between colleges: *intercollegiate football*

**inter·com** /ˈɪntəkɒm; *NAmE* -tərkɑːm/ noun a system of communication by phone or radio inside an office, plane, etc.; the device you press or switch on to start using this system: **over the** ~ *to announce sth over the intercom* ◇ *They called him on the intercom.*

**inter·com·mu·ni·ca·tion** /ˌɪntəkəˌmjuːnɪˈkeɪʃn; *NAmE* -tərk-/ noun [U] the process of communicating between people or groups

**inter·con·nect** /ˌɪntəkəˈnekt; *NAmE* -tərk-/ verb [T, I] to connect similar things; to be connected to or with similar things: ~ **A with B** *Bad housing is interconnected with debt and poverty.* ◇ ~ **A and B** *Bad housing, debt and poverty are interconnected.* ◇ ~ **(with sth)** *separate bedrooms that interconnect* ▶ **inter·con·nec·tion** /-ˈnekʃn/ noun [C, U]: *interconnections between different parts of the brain*

**inter·con·tin·en·tal** /ˌɪntəˌkɒntɪˈnentl; *NAmE* -tərˌkɑːn-/ adj. [usually before noun] between continents: *intercontinental flights/missiles/travel/trade*

# intercostal

**inter·cos·tal** /ˌɪntəˈkɒstl/ NAmE -tərˈkɑː-/ adj. (anatomy) located between the RIBS (= the curved bones that go around the chest): *intercostal muscles*

**inter·course** /ˈɪntəkɔːs; NAmE -tərkɔːrs/ noun [U] **1** (formal) = SEXUAL INTERCOURSE: *The prosecution stated that intercourse had occurred on several occasions.* ◊ *anal intercourse* **2** (old-fashioned) communication between people, countries, etc.: *the importance of social intercourse between different age groups*

**inter·cul·tural** /ˌɪntəˈkʌltʃərəl/ NAmE -tərˈk-/ adj. existing or happening between different cultures

**inter·cut** /ˌɪntəˈkʌt/ NAmE -tərˈk-/ verb (**inter·cut·ting**, **inter·cut**, **inter·cut**) ~ **sth (with sth)** (specialist) to put a film scene between two parts of a different scene: *Scenes of city life were intercut with interviews with local people.*

**inter·de·nom·in·ation·al** /ˌɪntədɪˌnɒmɪˈneɪʃənl/ NAmE -tərdɪˌnɑːm-/ adj. shared by different religious groups (= different DENOMINATIONS)

**inter·de·part·men·tal** /ˌɪntəˌdiːpɑːˈtmentl/ NAmE -tərˌdiːpɑːrt-/ adj. between departments; involving more than one department

**inter·de·pend·ent** /ˌɪntədɪˈpendənt/ NAmE -tərd-/ adj. that depend on each other; consisting of parts that depend on each other: *interdependent economies/organizations/relationships* ◊ *The world is becoming increasingly interdependent.* ▶ **inter·de·pend·ence** /-dəns/ (also less frequent **inter·de·pend·ency** pl. **-ies**) noun [U, C]

**inter·dict** /ˈɪntədɪkt; NAmE -tərd-/ noun **1** (law) an official order from a court that orders you not to do sth **2** (specialist) (in the Roman Catholic Church) an order banning sb from taking part in church services, etc.

**inter·dic·tion** /ˌɪntəˈdɪkʃn; NAmE -tərˈd-/ noun [U] (formal, especially NAmE) the act of stopping sth that is being transported from one place from reaching another place, especially by using force: *the Customs Service's drug interdiction programs*

**inter·dis·cip·lin·ary** /ˌɪntədɪsəˈplɪnəri; NAmE -tərˈdɪsəplɪneri/ adj. involving different areas of knowledge or study SYN **cross-disciplinary**: *interdisciplinary research* ◊ *an interdisciplinary approach*

**inter·est** 🅰1 /ˈɪntrəst, -trest/ noun, verb

■ noun
- **WANTING TO KNOW MORE 1** 🅰1 [U, sing.] the feeling that you have when you want to know or learn more about sb/sth: ~ **(in sth)** *Do your parents take an interest in your friends?* ◊ *By that time I had lost (all) interest in the idea.* ◊ *to show/express (an) interest in sth* ◊ ~ **in doing sth** *I have no interest in seeing the movie.* ◊ **with** ~ *I watched with interest.* ◊ **out of** ~ *Just out of interest, how much did it cost?* ◊ **As a matter of interest** (= I'd like to know), *what time did the party finish?* ⇨ compare DISINTEREST
- **ATTRACTION 2** 🅰1 [U] the quality that sth has when it attracts sb's attention or makes them want to know more about it: *There are many places of interest near the city.* ◊ **be of** ~ *These documents are of great historical interest.* ◊ **be of** ~ **to sb** *The subject is of no interest to me at all.* ◊ ~ **for sb** *This museum holds particular interest for geologists.* ⇨ see also HUMAN INTEREST, LOVE INTEREST
- **HOBBY 3** 🅰1 [C] an activity or a subject that you enjoy and that you spend time doing or studying: *Her main interests are music and tennis.* ◊ *He was a man of wide interests outside his work.* ◊ *My main research interest is herbal medicine.* ⇨ compare HOBBY
- **MONEY 4** 🅱1 [U] (finance) the extra money that you pay back when you borrow money or that you receive when you invest money: ~ **on sth** *to pay interest on a loan* ◊ **with** ~ *The money was repaid with interest.* ◊ *interest charges/payments* ◊ *Interest rates have risen by 1%.* ◊ *high rates of interest* ⇨ see also COMPOUND INTEREST, SIMPLE INTEREST ⇨ **WORDFINDER NOTE** at BANK
- **ADVANTAGE 5** 🅱2 [C, usually pl.] a good result or an advantage for sb/sth: *to promote/protect/defend sb's interests* ◊ *Tough talk doesn't always serve your interests.* ◊ **in sb's interest(s)** SYN *She was acting entirely in her own interests.* ◊ *These reforms were in the best interests of local government.* ◊ *It is in the public interest that these facts are made known.* ◊ **against sb's interests** *The policy is clearly working against the interests of consumers.* ⇨ see also SELF-INTEREST, VESTED INTEREST
- **SHARE IN BUSINESS 6** [C, usually pl.] ~ **(in sth)** a share in a business or company and its profits: *She has business interests in France.* ◊ *American interests in Europe* (= money invested in European countries) ⇨ see also CONTROLLING INTEREST
- **CONNECTION 7** [C, U] a connection with sth that affects your attitude to it, especially because you may benefit from it in some way: *I should, at this point, declare my interest.* ◊ ~ **in (doing) sth** *Organizations have an interest in ensuring that employee motivation is high.* ⇨ compare DISINTEREST ⇨ see also VESTED INTEREST
- **GROUP OF PEOPLE 8** [C, usually pl.] a group of people who are in the same business or who share the same aims that they want to protect: *powerful farming interests* ◊ *relationships between local government and business interests*

**IDM** **do sth (back) with interest** to do the same thing to sb as they have done to you, but with more force, enthusiasm, etc. **have sb's interests at ˈheart** to want sb to be happy and successful even though your actions may not show this **in the interest(s) of sth** in order to help or achieve sth: *New work practices were introduced in the interests of efficiency.* ⇨ more at CONFLICT n.

■ verb 🅰1 to attract your attention and make you feel interested; to make yourself give your attention to sth: ~ **sb** *Politics doesn't interest me.* ◊ ~ **sb/yourself in sth** *She has always interested herself in charity work.* ◊ **it interests sb to do sth** *It may interest you to know that Andy didn't accept the job.*

**PHRV** **ˈinterest sb in sth** to persuade sb to buy, do or eat sth: *Could I interest you in this model, Sir?*

▼ **SYNONYMS**

**interest**
hobby • game • pastime

These are all words for activities that you do for pleasure in your spare time.

**interest** an activity or a subject that you do or study for pleasure in your spare time: *Her main interests are music and gardening.*

**hobby** an activity that you do for pleasure in your spare time: *His hobbies include swimming and cooking.*

**game** a children's activity where they play with toys, pretend to be sb else, etc.; an activity that you do to have fun: *a game of cops and robbers* ◊ *He was playing games with the dog.*

**pastime** an activity that people do for pleasure in their spare time: *Eating out is the national pastime in France.*

**INTEREST, HOBBY OR PASTIME?**

- A **hobby** is often more active than an **interest**: *His main hobby is football* (= he plays football). ◊ *His main interest is football* (= he watches and reads about football, and may or may not play it). **Pastime** is used when talking about people in general; when you are talking about yourself or an individual person it is more usual to use **interest** or **hobby**: *Eating out is the national interest/hobby in France.* ◊ *Do you have any pastimes?*

**PATTERNS**

- a **popular** interest/hobby/pastime
- to **have/share** interests/hobbies
- to **take up/pursue** a(n) interest/hobby

**inter·est·ed** 🅰1 /ˈɪntrəstɪd, -tres-/ adj. **1** 🅰1 giving your attention to sth because you enjoy finding out about it or doing it; showing interest in sth and finding it exciting: *He sounded genuinely interested.* ◊ ~ **in sth/sb** *I'm very interested in history.* ◊ ~ **in doing sth** *Anyone interested in joining the club should contact us at the address below.* ◊ ~ **to do sth** *We would be interested to hear your views on this subject.* ◊ *an interested audience* ◊ *There's a talk on Italian art—are you interested* (= would you like to go)? **2** in a position to gain from a situation or be affected by it: *As an **interested** party, I was not allowed to vote.* ◊ ***Interested** groups will be given three months to give their views on the new development.*

▼ **WHICH WORD?**

**interested / interesting / uninterested / disinterested / uninteresting**

- The opposite of **interested** is **uninterested** or **not interested**: *He is completely uninterested in politics.* ◊ *I am not really interested in politics.*
- **Disinterested** means that you can be fair in judging a situation because you do not feel personally involved in it: *A solicitor can give you disinterested advice.* However, in speech it is sometimes used instead of **uninterested**, although this is thought to be incorrect.
- The opposite of **interesting** can be **uninteresting**: *The food was dull and uninteresting.* It is more common to use a different word such as **dull** or **boring**.

**ˌinterest-ˈfree** *adj.* with no interest charged on money borrowed: *an interest-free loan* ◊ *interest-free credit*

**ˈinterest group** *noun* a group of people who work together to achieve sth that they are particularly interested in, especially by putting pressure on the government, etc: *a special interest group of US lumber producers* ⊃ compare PRESSURE GROUP ⊃ see also SPECIAL INTEREST GROUP

**inter·est·ing** 🅘 🄐 Ⓢ /ˈɪntrəstɪŋ, -tres-/ *adj.* attracting your attention because it is/they are special, exciting or unusual: *an interesting question/point/idea* ◊ *She sounds like a really interesting person.* ◊ **it is ~ to do sth** *It will be interesting to see what happens.* ◊ **(it is) ~(that)…** | **~(that)…** *I find it interesting that she claims not to know him.* ◊ *Then things started to get interesting.* ◊ *She puts enough detail into the story to make it interesting.* ◊ *Her account makes interesting reading.* ▸ **inter·est·ing·ly** *adv.*: *Interestingly, there are very few recorded cases of such attacks.* ⊃ LANGUAGE BANK at SURPRISING

▼ **SYNONYMS**

**interesting**

fascinating • compelling • stimulating • gripping • absorbing

These words all describe sth that attracts or holds your attention because it is exciting, unusual or full of good ideas.

**interesting** attracting your attention because it is exciting, unusual or full of good ideas: *That's an interesting question, Daniel.*

**fascinating** extremely interesting or attractive: *The exhibition tells the fascinating story of the steam age.*

**compelling** (*rather formal*) so interesting or exciting that it holds your attention: *Her latest book makes compelling reading.*

**stimulating** full of interesting or exciting ideas; making people feel enthusiastic: *Thank you for a most stimulating discussion.*

**gripping** so exciting or interesting that it holds your attention completely: *His books are always so gripping.*

**absorbing** interesting and fun and holding your attention completely: *Chess can be an extremely absorbing game.*

PATTERNS

- interesting / fascinating / stimulating **for** sb
- interesting / fascinating **to** sb
- interesting / fascinating **that**…
- interesting / fascinating **to see / hear / find / learn / know**…
- a(n) interesting / fascinating / compelling / gripping **story / read / book**
- a(n) interesting / fascinating / stimulating **experience / discussion / idea**
- to **find** sth interesting / fascinating / compelling / stimulating / gripping / absorbing

**inter·face** ʕ+ 🄒 /ˈɪntəfeɪs; NAmE -tərf-/ *noun, verb*
■ *noun* **1** ʕ+ 🄒 (*computing*) the way a computer program presents information to a user or receives information from a user, in particular the LAYOUT of the screen and the menus: *the user interface* ⊃ WORDFINDER NOTE at PROGRAM ⊃ see also GUI, USER INTERFACE **2** (*computing*) an electrical CIRCUIT, connection or program that joins one device or system to another: *the interface between computer and printer* **3** **~ (between A and B)** the point where two subjects, systems, etc. meet and affect each other: *the interface between manufacturing and sales*
■ *verb* [I, T] **~ (sth) (with sth)** | **~ A and B** (*computing*) to be connected with sth using an interface; to connect sth in this way: *The new system interfaces with existing telephone equipment.*

**inter·faith** /ˈɪntəfeɪθ; NAmE -tərf-/ *adj.* [only before noun] between or connected with people of different religions: *an interfaith memorial service*

**inter·fere** ʕ+ 🄒 /ˌɪntəˈfɪə(r); NAmE -tərˈfɪr/ *verb* [I] to get involved in and try to influence a situation that should not really involve you, in a way that annoys other people: *I wish my mother would stop interfering and let me make my own decisions.* ◊ **~ in sth** *The police are very unwilling to interfere in family problems.*
PHRV **interˈfere with sb** **1** to illegally try to influence sb who is going to give evidence in court, for example by threatening them or offering them money **2** (*BrE*) to touch a child in a sexual way **interˈfere with sth** **1** to prevent sth from succeeding or from being done or happening as planned: *She never allows her personal feelings to interfere with her work.* **2** to touch, use or change sth, especially a piece of equipment, so that it is damaged or no longer works correctly: *I'd get fired if he found out I'd been interfering with his records.*

**inter·fer·ence** ʕ+ 🄒 /ˌɪntəˈfɪərəns; NAmE -tərˈfɪr-/ *noun* [U] **1** ʕ+ 🄒 the act of getting involved in and trying to influence a situation that should not really involve you, in a way that annoys other people: **~ (in sth)** *They resent foreign interference in the internal affairs of their country.* ◊ **~ with sth** *interference with proper medical procedures* **2** INTERRUPTION of a radio signal by another signal on a similar WAVELENGTH, causing extra noise that is not wanted
IDM **run interˈference** (*NAmE*) **1** (in AMERICAN FOOTBALL) to clear the way for the player with the ball by blocking players from the other team **2** (*informal*) to help sb by dealing with problems for them so that they do not need to deal with them

**inter·fer·ing** /ˌɪntəˈfɪərɪŋ; NAmE -tərˈfɪr-/ *adj.* [usually before noun] (*disapproving*) involving yourself in an annoying way in other people's private lives: *She's an interfering busybody!*

**inter·feron** /ˌɪntəˈfɪərɒn; NAmE -tərˈfɪrɑːn/ *noun* [U] (*biology*) a substance produced by the body to prevent harmful viruses from causing disease

**inter·gal·act·ic** /ˌɪntəɡəˈlæktɪk; NAmE -tərɡ-/ *adj.* [only before noun] existing or happening between GALAXIES of stars: *intergalactic space/travel*

**inter·gen·er·ation·al** /ˌɪntəˌdʒenəˈreɪʃənl; NAmE -tərˌdʒ-/ *adj.* [usually before noun] including or involving people of different generations or age groups: *intergenerational conflict*

**inter·gov·ern·men·tal** /ˌɪntəˌɡʌvnˈmentl; NAmE -tərˌɡʌvərn-/ *adj.* [only before noun] involving the governments of two or more countries: *an intergovernmental conference*

**in·terim** ʕ+ 🄒 /ˈɪntərɪm/ *adj., noun*
■ *adj.* [only before noun] **1** ʕ+ 🄒 intended to last for only a short time until sb/sth more permanent is found: *an interim government/measure/report* ◊ *The vice-president took power in **the interim period** before the election.* **2** (*finance*) calculated before the final results of sth are known SYN **provisional**: *interim figures/profits/results*
■ *noun*
IDM **in the ˈinterim** during the period of time between two events; until a particular event happens: *Despite everything that had happened in the interim, they had remained*

good friends. ◇ Her new job does not start until May and she will continue in the old job in the interim.

**in·te·ri·or** /ɪnˈtɪəriə(r); NAmE -ˈtɪr-/ noun, adj.
- noun 1 [C, usually sing.] the inside part of sth: *the interior of a building/a car* OPP **exterior** 2 **the interior** [sing.] the central part of a country or continent that is a long way from the coast: *an expedition into the interior of Australia* 3 **the Interior** [sing.] a country's own affairs rather than those that involve other countries: *the Department/Minister of the Interior*
- adj. 1 [only before noun] connected with the inside part of sth: *interior walls* OPP **exterior** 2 connected with the central part of a country or continent that is a long way from the coast: *the interior jungle regions* 3 connected with a country's own affairs rather than those that involve other countries: *the interior minister*

**inˌterior ˈangle** noun (*geometry*) an angle formed inside a shape where two sides of the shape meet ⇒ picture at ANGLE

**inˌterior ˈdecorator** noun a person whose job is to design and/or decorate a room or the inside of a house, etc. with paint, paper, carpets, etc. ▶ **inˌterior decoˈration** noun [U]: *an interior decoration scheme*

**inˌterior deˈsign** noun [U] the art or job of choosing the paint, carpets, furniture, etc. to decorate the inside of a house ▶ **inˌterior deˈsigner** noun

**inˌterior ˈmonologue** noun (in literature) a piece of writing that expresses a character's inner thoughts and feelings

**inter·ject** /ˌɪntəˈdʒekt; NAmE -tərˈdʒ-/ verb [T, I] + **speech** | ~ **(sth)** (*formal*) to interrupt what sb is saying with your opinion or a remark: *'You're wrong,' interjected Susan.*

**inter·jec·tion** /ˌɪntəˈdʒekʃn; NAmE -tərˈdʒ-/ noun (*grammar*) a short sound, word or phrase spoken suddenly to express an emotion. *Oh!*, *Look out!* and *Ow!* are interjections. SYN **exclamation**

**inter·lace** /ˌɪntəˈleɪs; NAmE -tərˈl-/ verb [T, I] ~ **(sth) (with sth)** (*formal*) to TWIST things together over and under each other; to be TWISTED together in this way: *Her hair was interlaced with ribbons and flowers.* ◇ *interlacing branches*

**inter·leave** /ˌɪntəˈliːv; NAmE -tərˈl-/ verb [often passive] ~ **sth (with sth)** to put sth, especially thin layers of sth, between things

**inter·link** /ˌɪntəˈlɪŋk; NAmE -tərˈl-/ verb [T, usually passive, I] to connect things; to be connected with other things: **be interlinked (with sth)** *The two processes are interlinked.* ◇ *a series of short interlinking stories*

**inter·lock** /ˌɪntəˈlɒk; NAmE -tərˈlɑːk/ verb [I, T] ~ **(sth) (with sth)** to fit or be fastened together securely: *Once the parts are interlocked, the structure stands firm.* ◇ *interlocking shapes/systems/pieces*

**inter·locu·tor** /ˌɪntəˈlɒkjətə(r); NAmE -tərˈlɑːk-/ noun (*formal*) 1 a person taking part in a conversation with you 2 a person or an organization that talks to another person or organization when acting for sb else

**inter·loper** /ˈɪntələʊpə(r); NAmE -tərl-/ noun a person who is present in a place or a situation where they do not belong or are not wanted SYN **intruder**

**inter·lude** /ˈɪntəluːd; NAmE -tərl-/ noun 1 a period of time between two events during which sth different happens: *a romantic interlude* (= a short romantic relationship) ◇ *Apart from a brief interlude of peace, the war lasted nine years.* 2 a short period of time between the parts of a play, film, etc: *There will now be a short interlude.* 3 a short piece of music or a talk, etc. played or given between the parts of a play or film or between other pieces of music: *a musical interlude*

**inter·marry** /ˌɪntəˈmæri; NAmE -tərˈm-/ verb (**inter·marries**, **inter·marry·ing**, **inter·married**, **inter·married**) 1 [I] to marry sb of a different race or from a different country or a different religious group: *Blacks and whites often intermarried* (= married each other). ◇ ~ **with sb** *They were not forbidden to intermarry with the local people.* 2 [I] to marry sb within your own family or group: *cousins who intermarry* ▶ **inter·mar·riage** /-rɪdʒ/ noun [U, C]: *intermarriage between blacks and whites*

**inter·medi·ary** /ˌɪntəˈmiːdiəri; NAmE -tərˈmiːdieri/ noun (pl. -ies) ~ **(between A and B)** a person or an organization that helps other people or organizations to make an agreement by being a means of communication between them SYN **mediator**, **go-between**: *Financial institutions act as intermediaries between lenders and borrowers.* ◇ *All talks have so far been conducted through an intermediary.* ▶ **inter·medi·ary** adj. [only before noun]: *to play an intermediary role in the dispute*

**inter·medi·ate** /ˌɪntəˈmiːdiət; NAmE -tərˈm-/ adj., noun
- adj. 1 [usually before noun] located between two places, things, states, etc: *an intermediate stage/step in a process* ◇ ~ **between A and B** *Liquid crystals are considered to be intermediate between liquid and solid.* 2 having more than a basic knowledge of sth but not yet advanced; suitable for sb who is at this level: *an intermediate skier/student* ◇ *an intermediate coursebook* ◇ *pre-/upper-intermediate classes*
- noun a person who is learning sth and who has more than a basic knowledge of it but is not yet advanced

**interˌmediate techˈnology** noun [U] technology that is suitable for use in developing countries as it is cheap and simple and can use local materials

**inter·ment** /ɪnˈtɜːmənt; NAmE -ˈtɜːrm-/ noun [C, U] (*formal*) the act of burying a dead person SYN **burial** ⇒ see also INTER

**inter·mezzo** /ˌɪntəˈmetsəʊ; NAmE -tərˈm-/ noun (pl. **inter·mezzi** /-siː/ or **inter·mezzos**) (*music, from Italian*) a short piece of music for the ORCHESTRA that is played between two parts in an OPERA or other musical performance

**inter·min·able** /ɪnˈtɜːmɪnəbl; NAmE -ˈtɜːrm-/ adj. lasting a very long time and therefore boring or annoying SYN **endless**: *an interminable speech/wait/discussion* ◇ *The drive seemed interminable.* ▶ **inter·min·ably** /-bli/ adv.: *The meeting dragged on interminably.*

**inter·min·gle** /ˌɪntəˈmɪŋgl; NAmE -tərˈm-/ verb [T, I] (*formal*) to mix people, ideas, colours, etc. together; to be mixed in this way: ~ **A with B** *The book intermingles fact with fiction.* ◇ ~ **A and B** *The book intermingles fact and fiction.* ◇ ~ **(with sb/sth)** *tourists and local people intermingling in the market square*

**inter·mis·sion** /ˌɪntəˈmɪʃn; NAmE -tərˈm-/ noun [C, U] 1 (*especially NAmE*) a short period of time between the parts of a play, film, etc: *Coffee was served during the intermission.* ◇ (*NAmE*) *After intermission, the second band played.* HELP This meaning is only [U] in NAmE. 2 a period of time during which sth stops before continuing again: *This state of affairs lasted without intermission for a hundred years.*

**inter·mit·tent** /ˌɪntəˈmɪtənt; NAmE -tərˈm-/ adj. stopping and starting often over a period of time, but not regularly SYN **sporadic**: *intermittent bursts of applause* ◇ *intermittent showers* ▶ **inter·mit·tent·ly** adv.: *Protests continued intermittently throughout November.*

**inter·mix** /ˌɪntəˈmɪks; NAmE -tərˈm-/ verb [T, I] ~ **(sth) (with sth)** to mix things together; to be mixed together: *Grass fields were intermixed with areas of woodland.*

**in·tern** verb, noun
- verb /ɪnˈtɜːn; NAmE -ˈtɜːrn/ [often passive] ~ **sb (in sth)** to put sb in prison during a war or for political reasons, although they have not been charged with a crime ⇒ see also INTERNEE ▶ **in·tern·ment** noun [U, C]: *the internment of suspected terrorists* ◇ *internment camps*
- noun /ˈɪntɜːn; NAmE -tɜːrn/ 1 a student or new graduate who is getting practical experience in a job, sometimes without pay, for example during the summer holiday: *a summer intern at a law firm* ⇒ WORDFINDER NOTE at TRAINING 2 (*NAmE*) an advanced student of medicine whose training is nearly finished and who is working in a hospital to get further practical experience ◇ compare HOUSE OFFICER ⇒ see also INTERNSHIP

**in·tern·al** /ɪnˈtɜːnl; NAmE -ˈtɜːrnl/ adj.
1 [only before noun] connected with the inside of sth:

the internal structure of a building ◇ internal doors **OPP** external 2 [B2] [only before noun] connected with the inside of your body: *internal organs* ◇ *internal bleeding/injuries* ◇ *The medicine is not for internal use.* **OPP** external ⇒ VISUAL VOCAB page V1 3 [B2] [usually before noun] involving or affecting only the people who are part of a particular organization rather than people from outside it: *The company has launched an internal investigation into the claims.* ◇ *an internal memo/document* ⇒ see also INTERNAL MARKET **OPP** external 4 [B2] [only before noun] connected with a country's own affairs rather than those that involve other countries **SYN** domestic: *internal affairs/security* ◇ *an internal flight* (= within a country) **OPP** external 5 coming from within a thing itself rather than from outside it: *a theory that lacks internal consistency* (= whose parts are not in agreement with each other) ◇ *Some photos contain internal evidence* (= fashions, transport, etc.) *that may help to date them.* 6 happening or existing in your mind **SYN** inner: *She struggled with her own internal conflicts.* ◇ *internal struggles/strife* ▶ **in·tern·al·ly** /-nəli/ *adv.*: *internally connected rooms* ◇ *The new posts were only advertised internally.*

**in·ternal com'bustion engine** *noun* a type of engine used in most cars that produces power by burning petrol or other fuel inside

**in·tern·al·ize** (*BrE also* -ise) /ɪnˈtɜːnəlaɪz/; *NAmE* -ˈtɜːrn-/ *verb* ~ **sth** (*specialist*) to make a feeling, an attitude, or a belief part of the way you think and behave ⇒ compare EXTERNALIZE ▶ **in·tern·al·iza·tion**, **-isa·tion** /ɪnˌtɜːnəl aɪˈzeɪʃn/; *NAmE* -ˌtɜːrnələˈz-/ *noun* [U]

**in·ternal 'market** *noun* (*business*) a situation in which different departments, countries, etc. in the same organization buy goods and services from each other

**in·ternal 'medicine** *noun* [U] (*NAmE*) the branch of medicine concerned with the treatment of diseases without doing medical operations

**the In·ternal 'Revenue Service** *noun* [sing.] (*abbr.* IRS) (in the US) the government department that is responsible for collecting most national taxes, for example income tax ⇒ compare HM REVENUE AND CUSTOMS

## inter·nation·al ❶ [A2] ○ /ˌɪntəˈnæʃnəl/; *NAmE* -tərˈn-/ *adj., noun*

■ *adj.* [usually before noun] 1 [A2] connected with or involving two or more countries: *international trade/law* ◇ *national and international affairs* ◇ *the international community* ◇ *an international organization/institution/agency* ◇ *an international airport/school/company* ◇ *He plays international rugby.* 2 [B1] used by people of many different countries: *large international hotels* ◇ *London is a truly international city.* ⇒ WORDFINDER NOTE at ALLY ▶ **inter·nation·al·ly** /-əli/ *adv.*: *internationally famous*

■ *noun* 1 (*BrE*) a sports competition involving teams from two countries: *the France-Scotland rugby international* 2 (*BrE*) a player who takes part in a sports competition against another country: *a former swimming international* 3 (*NAmE*) a person from a foreign country: *an English course for internationals*

**the Inter·national Bacca'laureate™** *noun* [sing.] (*abbr.* IB) an exam that is taken by students in many different countries in the world around the age of 18 or 19, and that includes up to six subjects

**the Inter·national 'Date Line** (*also* 'Date Line) *noun* [sing.] the imaginary line that goes from north to south of the earth through the Pacific Ocean. The date on the west side is different by one day from that on the east side. ⇒ WORDFINDER NOTE at EARTH

**inter·nation·al·ism** /ˌɪntəˈnæʃnəlɪzəm/; *NAmE* -tərˈn-/ *noun* [U] the belief that countries should work together in a friendly way

**inter·nation·al·ist** /ˌɪntəˈnæʃnəlɪst/; *NAmE* -tərˈn-/ *noun* 1 a person who believes that countries should work together in a friendly way 2 (*ScotE*) a player who takes part in a sports competition against another country: *a Scottish rugby internationalist* ▶ **inter·nation·al·ist** *adj.*

**inter·nation·al·ize** (*BrE also* -ise) /ˌɪntəˈnæʃnəlaɪz/; *NAmE* -tərˈn-/ *verb* ~ **sth** to bring sth under the control or protection of two or more nations; to make sth international ▶ **inter·nation·al·iza·tion**, **-isa·tion** /ˌɪntəˌnæʃnəlaɪˈzeɪʃn/; *NAmE* -tərˌnæʃnələˈz-/ *noun* [U]

**the Inter·national Pho'netic 'Alphabet** *noun* [sing.] (*abbr.* IPA) an alphabet that is used to show the pronunciation of words in any language

**inter·necine** /ˌɪntəˈniːsaɪn/; *NAmE* -tərˈniːsn/ *adj.* [only before noun] (*formal*) happening between members of the same group, country or organization: *internecine struggles/warfare/feuds*

**in·tern·ee** /ˌɪntɜːˈniː/; *NAmE* -tɜːrˈniː/ *noun* a person who is put in prison for political reasons, usually without a trial

## inter·net ❶ [A1] (*also* Inter·net) /ˈɪntənet/; *NAmE* -tərn-/ *noun* (*usually* the internet) (*also informal* the Net) [sing.] an international computer network connecting other networks and computers that allows people to share information around the world: *to surf/browse/access the internet* ◇ **on the** ~ *I looked it up on the internet.* ◇ **via the** ~ *We have kept in touch via the internet.* ◇ **over the** ~ *You can view the video feed over the internet.* ◇ *All the rooms have access to the internet/internet access.* ◇ *I couldn't get an internet connection.* ◇ *internet users* ◇ *The payment can be made through internet banking.* ⇒ see also INTRANET, WWW

**'internet dating** = ONLINE DATING

**in·tern·ist** /ɪnˈtɜːnɪst/; *NAmE* -ˈtɜːrn-/ *noun* (*NAmE*) a doctor who is a specialist in the treatment of diseases of the organs inside the body and who does not usually do medical operations

**in·tern·ment** /ɪnˈtɜːnmənt/; *NAmE* -ˈtɜːrn-/ ⇒ INTERN *verb*

**in·tern·ship** /ˈɪntɜːnʃɪp/; *NAmE* -tɜːrn-/ *noun* 1 a period of time during which a student or new graduate gets practical experience in a job, for example during the summer holiday: *an internship at a television station* ⇒ compare PLACEMENT (2), WORK EXPERIENCE 2 (*NAmE*) a job that an advanced student of medicine, whose training is nearly finished, does in a hospital to get further practical experience

**inter·oper·able** /ˌɪntərˈɒpərəbl/; *NAmE* -ˈɑːp-/ *adj.* (*specialist*) (of computer systems or programs) able to exchange information ▶ **inter·oper·abil·ity** /ˌɪntərˌɒpərəˈbɪləti/; *NAmE* -ˌɑːp-/ *noun* [U]: ~ **(between / with sth)** *interoperability between devices*

**inter·pene·trate** /ˌɪntəˈpenɪtreɪt/; *NAmE* -tərˈp-/ *verb* [I, T] ~ **(sth)** (*formal*) to spread completely through sth or from one thing to another in each direction ▶ **inter·pene·tra·tion** /ˌɪntəˌpenɪˈtreɪʃn/; *NAmE* -tərˌp-/ *noun* [U, C]

**inter·per·son·al** /ˌɪntəˈpɜːsənl/; *NAmE* -tərˈpɜːrs-/ *adj.* [only before noun] connected with relationships between people: *interpersonal skills*

**inter·plan·et·ary** /ˌɪntəˈplænɪtri/; *NAmE* -tərˈplænəteri/ *adj.* [only before noun] between planets: *interplanetary travel*

**inter·play** /ˈɪntəpleɪ/; *NAmE* -tərp-/ *noun* [U, sing.] ~ **(of / between A and B)** (*formal*) the way in which two or more things or people affect each other **SYN** interaction: *the interplay between politics and the environment* ◇ *the subtle interplay of colours*

**Inter·pol** /ˈɪntəpɒl/; *NAmE* -tərpɔːl/ *noun* [U + sing. / pl. v.] an international organization that enables the police forces of different countries to help each other to solve crimes

**in·ter·pol·ate** /ɪnˈtɜːpəleɪt/; *NAmE* -ˈtɜːrp-/ *verb* 1 + speech | ~ **sth** (*formal*) to make a remark that interrupts a conversation **SYN** interject: *'But why?' he interpolated.* 2 ~ **sth (into sth)** (*formal*) to add sth to a piece of writing **SYN** insert: *The lines were interpolated into the manuscript at a later date.* 3 ~ **sth** (*mathematics*) to add a value into a series by calculating it from surrounding known values ▶ **in·ter·pol·ation** /ɪnˌtɜːpəˈleɪʃn/; *NAmE* -ˌtɜːrp-/ *noun* [U, C]

# interpose

**in·ter·pose** /ˌɪntəˈpəʊz; NAmE -tərˈp-/ verb (formal) **1** + speech | ~ sth to add a question or remark into a conversation: *'Just a minute,' Charles interposed. 'How do you know?'* **2** ~ sb/sth (between A and B) to place sb/sth between two people or things: *He quickly interposed himself between Mel and the doorway.*

**in·ter·pret** /ɪnˈtɜːprət; NAmE -ˈtɜːrp-/ verb **1** [T] ~ sth to explain the meaning of sth: *The students were asked to interpret the poem.* ◊ *The data can be interpreted in many different ways.* **2** [T] to decide that sth has a particular meaning and to understand it in this way: ~ sth as sth *I didn't know whether to interpret her silence as acceptance or refusal.* ◊ ~ sth *The research focused on how parents interpret the behaviour of their toddlers.* ⊃ compare MISINTERPRET **3** [I, T] to translate one language into another as it is spoken: ~ (for sb) *She couldn't speak much English so her children had to interpret for her.* ◊ ~ sth *Interpreters must interpret everything that is said in the interaction.* **4** [T] ~ sth to perform a piece of music, a role in a play, etc. in a way that shows your feelings about its meaning: *He interpreted the role with a lot of humour.* ▶ **in·ter·pret·able** /-prətəbl/ adj.: *interpretable data*

**in·ter·pret·ation** /ɪnˌtɜːprəˈteɪʃn; NAmE -ˌtɜːrp-/ noun [C, U] **1** the particular way in which sth is understood or explained: *Her evidence suggests a different interpretation of the events.* ◊ *It is not possible for everyone to put their own interpretation on the law.* ◊ *Dreams are open to interpretation* (= they can be explained in different ways). **2** the particular way in which sb chooses to perform a piece of music, a role in a play, etc: *a modern interpretation of 'King Lear'*

**in·ter·pret·ative** /ɪnˈtɜːprətətɪv; NAmE -ˈtɜːrpəteɪt-/ (also **in·ter·pret·ive** /ɪnˈtɜːprətɪv; NAmE -ˈtɜːrp-/ especially in NAmE) adj. [usually before noun] (formal) connected with the particular way in which sth is understood, explained or performed; providing an interpretation: *an interpretative problem* ◊ *an interpretative exhibition*

**in·ter·pret·er** /ɪnˈtɜːprətə(r); NAmE -ˈtɜːrp-/ noun **1** a person whose job is to translate what sb is saying into another language: **through an ~** *Speaking through an interpreter, the President said that the talks were going well.* ◊ *a sign language interpreter* (= a person who translates what sb is saying into sign language for deaf people) ⊃ compare TRANSLATOR **2** a person who performs a piece of music or a role in a play in a way that clearly shows their ideas about its meaning: *She is one of the finest interpreters of Debussy's music.* **3** (computing) a computer program that changes the instructions of another program into a form that the computer can understand and use

**inter·racial** /ˌɪntəˈreɪʃl/ adj. [only before noun] involving people of different races: *interracial marriage*

**inter·reg·num** /ˌɪntəˈregnəm/ noun [usually sing.] (pl. **inter·reg·nums**) (formal) a period of time during which a country, an organization, etc. does not have a leader and is waiting for a new one

**inter·relate** /ˌɪntərɪˈleɪt/ verb [I, T] if two or more things **interrelate**, or if they are **interrelated**, they are closely connected and they affect each other: *a discussion of how the mind and body interrelate* ◊ ~ **with sth** *a discussion of how the mind interrelates with the body* ▶ **inter·related** adj.: *a number of interrelated problems*

**inter·rela·tion·ship** /ˌɪntərɪˈleɪʃnʃɪp/ (also **inter·rela·tion** /ˌɪntərɪˈleɪʃn/) noun [C, U] **~ (of/between A and B)** the way in which two or more things or people are connected and affect each other

**in·ter·ro·gate** /ɪnˈterəɡeɪt/ verb **1** ~ sb to ask sb a lot of questions over a long period of time, especially in an aggressive way: *He was interrogated by the police for over 12 hours.* ⊃ WORDFINDER NOTE at POLICE **2** ~ sth (specialist) to obtain information from a computer or other machine ▶ **in·ter·ro·ga·tion** /ɪnˌterəˈɡeɪʃn/ noun [U, C]: **under ~** *He confessed after four days under interrogation.* ◊ *She hated her parents' endless interrogations about where she'd been.*

⊃ SYNONYMS at INTERVIEW **in·ter·ro·ga·tor** /ɪnˈterəɡeɪtə(r)/ noun

**inter·roga·tive** /ˌɪntəˈrɒɡətɪv; NAmE -ˈrɑːɡ-/ adj., noun
■ adj. **1** (formal) asking a question; in the form of a question: *an interrogative gesture/remark/sentence* **2** (grammar) used in questions: *interrogative pronouns/determiners/adverbs* (= for example, *who*, *which* and *why*) ▶ **inter·roga·tive·ly** adv.
■ noun (grammar) a question word, especially a pronoun or a determiner such as *who* or *which*

**inter·roga·tory** /ˌɪntəˈrɒɡətri; NAmE -ˈrɑːɡ-/ adj., noun
■ adj. seeming to be asking a question or demanding an answer to sth: *an interrogatory stare*
■ noun (pl. **-ies**) (law) a written question, asked by one party in a legal case, that must be answered by the other party

**inter·rupt** /ˌɪntəˈrʌpt/ verb **1** [I, T] to say or do sth that makes sb stop what they are saying or doing: *Sorry to interrupt, but there's someone to see you.* ◊ ~ **with sth** *Would you mind not interrupting with questions all the time?* ◊ ~ **sb/sth (with sth)** *I hope I'm not interrupting you.* ◊ *They were interrupted by a knock at the door.* ◊ ~ **(sb) + speech** *'I have a question,' she interrupted.* **2** [T] ~ sth to stop sth for a short time: *The game was interrupted several times by rain.* ◊ *We interrupt this programme to bring you an important news bulletin.* **3** [T] ~ sth to stop a line, surface, view, etc. from being even or continuous: *There were no other buildings to interrupt the view of the valley.*

> **EXPRESS YOURSELF**
> 
> **Interrupting**
> 
> You may need to say something when somebody else is speaking, or you may be chairing a discussion where you have to stop one person talking too much. If you start talking at the same time as someone else, this will seem rude. To interrupt politely, you can say, for example:
> 
> • *Sorry to interrupt, but I have to disagree with that.*
> • *Could I just say something here?*
> • *If I could, let me stop you there for a moment and go back to your previous point.*
> • *Actually, we seem to have strayed a bit from the topic. Can we go back to the first point?*
> • *Just a moment, Sue. Can we hear what Jack has to say on this?*
> • *May I interrupt you there? I don't think that's true.* (formal)
> • *I'm sorry, but we're running short on time. Can you please summarize very quickly so we can finish up?* (formal)
> • *I appreciate your enthusiasm on this topic, but I'm afraid we have a couple more people to hear from.* (formal)
> • *Could you two please discuss that issue privately after the meeting? We have several more items to cover and need to move on at this point.* (formal)
> • *I'm sorry, I really have to stop you there. We've run out of time.* (formal)
> • *Let's save that conversation for another time.*

**inter·rup·tion** /ˌɪntəˈrʌpʃn/ noun [C, U] **1** something that temporarily stops an activity or a situation; a time when an activity is stopped: *The game continued after a short interruption because of rain.* ◊ **~ to sth** *The birth of her son was a minor interruption to her career.* ◊ **~ in sth** *an interruption in the power supply* ◊ **without ~** *I managed to work for two hours without interruption.* **2** the act of interrupting sb/sth and of stopping them from speaking: *He ignored her interruptions.* ◊ **without ~** *She spoke for 20 minutes without interruption.*

**inter·sect** /ˌɪntəˈsekt; NAmE -tərˈs-/ verb **1** [I, T] (of lines, roads, etc.) to meet or cross each other: **~ (sth)** *a pattern of intersecting streets* ◊ *The lines intersect at right angles.* ◊ **~ with sth** *The path intersected with a busy road.* **2** [T, usually passive] **~ sth (with sth)** to divide an area by crossing it: *The landscape is intersected with spectacular gorges.*

**inter·sec·tion** noun **1** /ˈɪntəsekʃn; NAmE -tərs-/ [C] (NAmE or formal, BrE) a place where two or more roads, lines, etc. meet or cross each other: *Traffic lights have been placed at all major intersections.* **2** /ˌɪntəˈsekʃn; NAmE -tərˈs-/ [U] the act of intersecting sth

**inter·sex** /ˈɪntəseks; NAmE -tərs-/ adj., noun
- **adj.** (medical) describing or relating to a person or animal that has both male and female sex organs or other sexual characteristics: *an intersex child* ◊ *to be born with intersex traits* ⊃ compare TRANSGENDER
- **noun** [U] (medical) the condition of having both male and female sex organs or other sexual characteristics

**inter·sperse** /ˌɪntəˈspɜːs; NAmE -tərˈspɜːrs/ verb **be interspersed with/in sth** to put sth in sth else or among or between other things: *Lectures will be interspersed with practical demonstrations.*

**inter·state** /ˈɪntəsteɪt; NAmE -tərs-/ adj., noun
- **adj.** [only before noun] between states, especially in the US: *interstate commerce*
- **noun** (also **interstate ˈhighway**) (in the US) a wide road, with at least two LANES in each direction, where traffic can travel fast for long distances across many states. You can only enter and leave interstates at special RAMPS. ⊃ compare MOTORWAY

**inter·stel·lar** /ˌɪntəˈstelə(r); NAmE -tərˈs-/ adj. [only before noun] between the stars in the sky ⊃ compare STELLAR

**in·ter·stice** /ɪnˈtɜːstɪs; NAmE -ˈtɜːrs-/ noun [usually pl.] (formal) a small break or space in sth

**inter·sti·tial** /ˌɪntəˈstɪʃl; NAmE -tərˈs-/ adj. (medical) in or related to small spaces between the parts of an organ or between groups of cells or TISSUES: *interstitial cells*

**inter·text·ual·ity** /ˌɪntətekstʃuˈæləti; NAmE -tərt-/ noun [U] (specialist) the relationship between texts, especially literary texts

**inter·twine** /ˌɪntəˈtwaɪn; NAmE -tərˈt-/ verb **1** [I, T, usually passive] if two or more things **intertwine** or are **intertwined**, they are TWISTED together so that they are very difficult to separate: *intertwining branches* ◊ **(be) intertwined (with sth)** *a necklace of rubies intertwined with pearls* **2** [T, usually passive, I] to be or become very closely connected with sth/sb else: **be intertwined** *Their political careers had become closely intertwined.*

**inter·val** ⓑ B2 Ⓦ /ˈɪntəvl; NAmE -tərvl/ noun **1** ⓑ B2 a period of time between two events: *The interval between major earthquakes might be 200 years.* **2** ⓑ B2 (BrE) (also **inter·mis·sion** NAmE, BrE) a short period of time separating parts of a play, film or concert: *There will be an interval of 20 minutes after the second act.* ⊃ WORDFINDER NOTE at CONCERT **3** [usually pl.] a short period during which sth different happens from what is happening the rest of the time: *She's delirious, but has lucid intervals.* ◊ (BrE) *The day should be mainly dry with sunny intervals.* **4** (music) a difference in PITCH (= how high or low a note sounds) between two notes: *an interval of one octave*
**IDM** **at (…) intervals 1** with time between: *Buses to the city leave at regular intervals.* ◊ *The runners started at 5-minute intervals.* **2** with spaces between: *Flaming torches were positioned at intervals along the terrace.*

**ˈinterval training** noun [U] sports training consisting of different activities that require different speeds or amounts of effort

**inter·vene** ⓑ C1 Ⓦ /ˌɪntəˈviːn; NAmE -tərˈv-/ verb **1** ⓑ C1 [I] to become involved in a situation in order to improve or help it: *She might have been killed if the neighbours hadn't intervened.* ◊ **~in sth** *The President intervened personally in the crisis.* ◊ **~to do sth** *They intervened to halt the attack.* **2** [T, I] (+ speech) to interrupt sb when they are speaking in order to say sth: *'But,' she intervened, 'what about the others?'* **3** [I] to happen in a way that delays sth or prevents it from happening: *They were planning to get married and then the war intervened.* **4** [I] (formal) to exist between two events or places: *I saw nothing of her during the years that intervened.*

**inter·ven·ing** /ˌɪntəˈviːnɪŋ; NAmE -tərˈv-/ adj. [only before noun] coming or existing between two events, dates, objects, etc: *Little had changed in the intervening years.*

**inter·ven·tion** ⓑ C1 Ⓦ /ˌɪntəˈvenʃn; NAmE -tərˈv-/ noun [U, C] **1** ⓑ C1 action taken to improve or help a situation: *calls for government intervention to save the steel industry* ◊ **~in sth** *In the second group of states, direct intervention in the economy was limited.* **2** ⓑ C1 action by a country to become involved in the affairs of another country when

833                                                                      **interview**

they have not been asked to do so: *armed/military intervention* ◊ **~in sth** *NATO intervention in the troubled region* ⊃ see also NON-INTERVENTION **3** ⓑ C1 action taken to improve a medical condition or illness: *a medical/surgical intervention* **4** **~(in sth)** the act of interrupting sb when they are speaking in order to say sth **5** an occasion when a group of people meet to take action with a friend or family member who has an ADDICTION to drugs or alcohol, in order to help them recover: *Her daughters staged an intervention.*

**inter·ven·tion·ism** /ˌɪntəˈvenʃənɪzəm; NAmE -tərˈv-/ noun [U] the policy or practice of a government influencing the economy of its own country, or of becoming involved in the affairs of other countries ⊃ see also NON-INTERVENTIONISM ▶ **inter·ven·tion·ist** /-ʃənɪst/ adj., noun: *interventionist policies*

**inter·view** ❶ A1 Ⓦ /ˈɪntəvjuː; NAmE -tərvjuː/ noun, verb
- **noun 1** ⓑ A1 a formal meeting at which sb is asked questions to see if they are suitable for a particular job, or for a course of study at a college, university, etc: *a job interview* ◊ **~(with sb/sth) (for sth)** *He has an interview next week for the manager's job.* ◊ **in/at an~** *In the interview they asked me about my future plans.* ⊃ WORDFINDER NOTE at APPLY ⊃ compare EXIT INTERVIEW **2** ⓑ A1 a meeting (often a public one) at which a journalist asks sb questions in order to find out their opinions: *a television/TV/radio/newspaper interview* ◊ *to do/give an interview* (= to agree to answer questions) ◊ *to conduct an interview* (= to ask sb questions in public) ◊ **in an~** *Yesterday, in an interview on German television, the minister denied the reports.* ◊ **~with sb** *an in-depth interview with the new governor* ◊ **~about sth** *an exclusive interview about her new book* **3** ⓑ A1 a private meeting between people when questions are asked and answered: *a telephone/phone interview* ◊ **~with sb** *an interview with the careers adviser*
- **verb 1** ⓑ A1 [T, I] **~(sb) (for sth)** to talk to sb and ask them questions at a formal meeting to find out if they are suitable for a job, course of study, etc: *Which post are you being interviewed for?* ◊ *We interviewed ten people for the job.* **2** [I] **~(for sth)** to talk to sb and answer questions at a formal meeting to get a job, a place on a course of study, etc: *The website gives you tips on interviewing for colleges.* ◊ *If you don't interview well you are unlikely to get the job.* **3** ⓑ A1 to ask sb questions about their life, opinions, etc, especially on the radio or television or for a newspaper or magazine: **~sb about sth** *Next week, I will be interviewing Spielberg about his latest movie.* ◊ **~sb** *The*

▼ **SYNONYMS**

**interview**
interrogation • audience • consultation

These are all words for a meeting or occasion when sb is asked for information, opinions or advice.

**interview** a formal meeting at which sb is asked questions, for example, to see if they are suitable for a particular job or course of study, or in order to find out their opinions about sth: *a job interview*

**interrogation** the process of asking sb a lot of questions, especially in an aggressive way, in order to get information; an occasion on which this is done: *He confessed after four days under interrogation.*

**audience** a formal meeting with an important person: *The Pope granted her a private audience.*

**consultation** a meeting with an expert, especially a doctor, to get advice or treatment.

PATTERNS
- an **in-depth** interview/consultation
- a **police** interview/interrogation
- to **have/request** a(n) interview/audience/consultation with sb
- to **give/grant** sb a(n) interview/audience/consultation
- to **carry out/conduct** an interview/interrogation

❶ Oxford Phrasal Academic Lexicon (OPAL) written and spoken word lists   |   Ⓦ OPAL written word list   |   ❺ OPAL spoken word list

**interviewee** 834

prime minister declined to be interviewed. ◊ **~sb on sth** I heard him being interviewed on the news earlier. **4** 🔑 A1 [T] **~sb (about sth)** to ask sb questions at a private meeting: *The police are waiting to interview the injured man.* ▶ **inter·view·ing** *noun* [U]: *The research involves in-depth interviewing.* ◊ *interviewing techniques*

**inter·view·ee** Ⓦ /ˌɪntəvjuːˈiː; *NAmE* -tərvjuː-/ *noun* the person who answers the questions in an interview

**inter·view·er** Ⓦ /ˈɪntəvjuːə(r); *NAmE* -tərvjuː-/ *noun* the person who asks the questions in an interview

**inter·war** /ˌɪntəˈwɔː(r); *NAmE* -tərˈwɔːr-/ *adj.* [only before noun] happening or existing between two wars, especially the First and the Second World Wars: *the interwar years/period*

**inter·weave** /ˌɪntəˈwiːv; *NAmE* -tərˈw-/ *verb* [T, usually passive, I] (**inter·wove** /-ˈwəʊv/, **inter·woven** /-ˈwəʊvn/) to TWIST together two or more pieces of THREAD, wool, etc: **be interwoven with sth** *The blue fabric was interwoven with red and gold thread.* ◊ **be interwoven** (*figurative*) *The problems are inextricably interwoven* (= very closely connected).

**in·tes·tate** /ɪnˈtesteɪt/ *adj.* (*law*) not having made a WILL (= a legal document that says what is to happen to a person's property when they die) ▶ **in·tes·tacy** /-stəsi/ *noun* [U]

**in·testinal forti·tude** *noun* (*NAmE, formal* or *humorous*) the courage and strength of mind necessary to do sth difficult or unpleasant (used when you want to avoid using the word *guts*): *He did not have the intestinal fortitude to implement the changes.*

**in·tes·tine** /ɪnˈtestɪn/ *noun* (*also* **intestines** [pl.]) a long tube in the body between the stomach and the ANUS. Food passes from the stomach to the **small in·testine** and from there to the **large in·testine**. ⇨ VISUAL VOCAB page V1 ▶ **in·tes·tinal** /ɪnˈtestɪnl, ˌɪntəˈstaɪnl/ *adj.* [usually before noun]

**in·tim·acy** /ˈɪntɪməsi/ *noun* (*pl.* **-ies**) **1** [U, sing.] the state of having a close personal relationship with sb: *She isn't capable of real intimacy.* ◊ **~between A and B** *The old intimacy between them had gone for ever.* ◊ **~with sb** *He enjoys an intimacy with the president.* **2** [U] a private and comfortable atmosphere: *The room had a peaceful sense of intimacy about it.* **3** [C, usually pl.] a thing that a person says or does to sb that they know very well **4** [U] (*formal* or *law*) sexual activity, especially an act of SEXUAL INTERCOURSE

**in·tim·ate**¹ 🔑+ C1 *adj., verb, noun*

■ *adj.* /ˈɪntɪmət/ **1** 🔑+ C1 (of people) having a close and friendly relationship: *intimate friends* ◊ *We're not **on intimate terms** with our neighbours.* **2** 🔑+ C1 private and personal, often in a sexual way: *The article revealed intimate details about his family life.* ◊ *the most intimate parts of her body* **3** (of a place or situation) encouraging close, friendly relationships, sometimes of a sexual nature: *an intimate restaurant* ◊ *He knew an intimate little bar where they would not be disturbed.* **4** (of knowledge) very detailed: *an intimate knowledge of the English countryside* **5** (of a link between things) very close: *an intimate connection between class and educational success* **6** **~(with sb)** (*formal* or *law*) having a sexual relationship with sb ▶ **in·tim·ate·ly** *adv.*: *intimately connected/linked/related* ◊ *an area of the country that he knew intimately* ◊ *She was intimately involved in the project.* ◊ *They touched each other intimately* (= in a sexual way).

■ *verb* /ˈɪntɪmeɪt/ (*formal*) to let sb know what you think or mean SYN **let it be known / make it known that …**: **~sth (to sb)** *He has already intimated to us his intention to retire.* ◊ **~(that)…** *He has already intimated (that) he intends to retire.*

■ *noun* /ˈɪntɪmət/ (*formal*) a close personal friend

**in·tim·ation** /ˌɪntɪˈmeɪʃn/ *noun* [C, U] (*formal*) the act of stating sth or of making it known, especially in an indirect way: *There was no intimation from his doctor that his condition was serious.*

**in·timi·date** /ɪnˈtɪmɪdeɪt/ *verb* **~sb (into sth / into doing sth)** to frighten or threaten sb so that they will do what you want: *They were accused of intimidating people into voting for them.* ◊ *She refused to be intimidated by their threats.* ▶ **in·timi·da·tion** /ɪnˌtɪmɪˈdeɪʃn/ *noun* [U]: *the intimidation of witnesses*

**in·timi·dated** /ɪnˈtɪmɪdeɪtɪd/ *adj.* [not usually before noun] feeling frightened and not confident in a particular situation: *We try to make sure children don't feel intimidated on their first day at school.*

**in·timi·dat·ing** /ɪnˈtɪmɪdeɪtɪŋ/ *adj.* frightening in a way that makes a person feel less confident: *an intimidating manner* ◊ **~for / to sb** *This kind of questioning can be very intimidating to children.*

**in·timi·da·tory** /ɪnˌtɪmɪˈdeɪtəri/ *adj.* (*formal*) intended to frighten or threaten sb

**into** 🔑 ❶ A1 /ˈɪntə, *before vowels* -tu, *strong form* -tuː/ *prep.*
HELP For the special uses of **into** in phrasal verbs, look at the entries for the verbs. For example **lay into sb / sth** is in the phrasal verb section at **lay**. **1** 🔑 A1 to a position in or inside sth: *Come into the house.* ◊ *She dived into the water.* ◊ *He threw the letter into the fire.* ◊ (*figurative*) *She turned and walked off into the night.* **2** 🔑 A1 in the direction of sth: *Speak clearly into the microphone.* ◊ *Driving into the sun, we had to shade our eyes.* **3** 🔑 A1 to a point at which you hit sb/sth: *The truck crashed into a parked car.* **4** to a point during a period of time: *She carried on working late into the night.* ◊ *He didn't get married until he was well into his forties.* **5** 🔑 A2 used to show a change in state: *The fruit can be made into jam.* ◊ *Can you translate this passage into German?* ◊ *They came into power in 2008.* ◊ *She was sliding into depression.* **6** used to show the result of an action: *He was shocked into a confession of guilt.* **7** 🔑 B1 about or in connection with sth: *an inquiry into safety procedures* **8** used when you are dividing numbers: *3 into 24 is 8.*
IDM **be 'into sb for sth** (*US, informal*) to owe sb money or be owed money by sb: *By the time he'd fixed the leak, I was into him for $500.* ◊ *The bank was into her for $100000.* **be 'into sth** (*informal*) to be interested in sth in an active way: *He's into surfing in a big way.*

**in·toler·able** /ɪnˈtɒlərəbl; *NAmE* -ˈtɑːl-/ *adj.* so bad or difficult that you cannot TOLERATE it; completely unacceptable SYN **unbearable**: *an intolerable burden/situation* ◊ *The heat was intolerable.* ▶ **in·toler·ably** /-bli/ *adv.*: *intolerably hot*

**in·toler·ant** /ɪnˈtɒlərənt; *NAmE* -ˈtɑːl-/ *adj.* **1 ~(of sb / sth)** (*disapproving*) not willing to accept ideas or ways of behaving that are different from your own OPP **tolerant 2** (*specialist*) not able to eat particular foods, use particular medicines, etc. without becoming ill: *recipes for people who are gluten intolerant* ▶ **in·toler·ance** /-rəns/ *noun* [U, C]: *religious intolerance* ◊ *food intolerances* ◊ *an intolerance to dairy products*

**in·ton·ation** /ˌɪntəˈneɪʃn/ *noun* **1** [U, C] (*phonetics*) the rise and fall of the voice in speaking, especially as this affects the meaning of what is being said: *intonation patterns* ◊ *In English, some questions have a rising intonation.* ⇨ compare **STRESS** ⇨ WORDFINDER NOTE at PRONUNCIATION **2** [U] (*music*) the quality of playing or singing exactly in tune

**in·tone** /ɪnˈtəʊn/ *verb* **~sth | + speech** (*formal*) to say sth in a slow and serious voice without much expression: *The priest intoned the final prayer.*

**in toto** /ɪn ˈtəʊtəʊ/ *adv.* (*from Latin, formal*) completely; including all parts

**in·toxi·cant** /ɪnˈtɒksɪkənt; *NAmE* -ˈtɑːk-/ *noun* (*specialist*) a substance such as alcohol that produces false feelings of pleasure and a lack of control

**in·toxi·cated** /ɪnˈtɒksɪkeɪtɪd; *NAmE* -ˈtɑːk-/ *adj.* (*formal*) **1** under the influence of alcohol or drugs ⇨ see also DRIVING WHILE INTOXICATED **2 ~(by / with sth)** very excited by sth, so that you cannot think clearly: *intoxicated with success* ▶ **in·toxi·cate** *verb* **~sb**

**in·toxi·cat·ing** /ɪnˈtɒksɪkeɪtɪŋ/ *adj.* (*NAmE* -ˈtɑːk-/ (*formal*) **1** (of alcoholic drink or a drug) that can cause sb to lose control of their behaviour or their physical and mental abilities **2** making you feel excited so that you cannot think clearly: *Power can be intoxicating.* ▶ **in·tox·i·ca·tion** /ɪnˌtɒksɪˈkeɪʃn; NAmE -ˌtɑːk-/ noun [U]

**intra-** /ɪntrə/ prefix (in adjectives and adverbs) inside; within: *intravenous* ◊ *intra-departmental* (= within a department) ⊃ compare INTER-

**in·tract·able** /ɪnˈtræktəbl/ adj. (formal) (of a problem or a person) very difficult to deal with OPP **tractable** ▶ **in·tract·abil·ity** /ɪnˌtræktəˈbɪləti/ noun [U]

**intra·mural** /ˌɪntrəˈmjʊərəl; NAmE -ˈmjʊr-/ adj. (especially NAmE) taking place within a single institution, especially a school or college: *Jeff played intramural basketball in high school.*

**intra·mus·cu·lar** /ˌɪntrəˈmʌskjələ(r)/ adj. (medical) happening inside a muscle or put into a muscle: *intramuscular pain* ◊ *an intramuscular injection*

**intra·net** /ˈɪntrənet/ noun (computing) a computer network that is private to a company, university, etc. often using the same software as the World Wide Web

**in·tran·si·gent** /ɪnˈtrænzɪdʒənt/ adj. (formal, disapproving) (of people) unwilling to change their opinions or behaviour in a way that would be helpful to others SYN **stubborn** ▶ **in·tran·si·gence** /-dʒəns/ noun [U]

**in·tran·si·tive** /ɪnˈtrænzətɪv/ adj. (grammar) (of verbs) used without a DIRECT OBJECT OPP **transitive**: *The verb 'die', as in 'He died suddenly', is intransitive.* ▶ **in·tran·si·tive·ly** adv.: *The verb is being used intransitively.*

**intra·op·era·tive** /ˌɪntrəˈɒpərətɪv; NAmE -ˈɑːp-/ adj. [only before noun] (medical) that happens or is done during a medical operation: *intraoperative nursing care* ⊃ compare POST-OPERATIVE, PREOPERATIVE

**intra·uter·ine** /ˌɪntrəˈjuːtəraɪn/ adj. (medical) within the UTERUS

**intrauterine deˈvice** noun = IUD

**intra·ven·ous** /ˌɪntrəˈviːnəs/ adj. (abbr. **IV**) (medical) (of drugs or food) going into a VEIN: *intravenous fluids* ◊ *an intravenous injection* ◊ *an intravenous drug user* ▶ **intra·ven·ous·ly** adv.

**ˈin tray** (especially BrE) (NAmE usually **inbox**) noun (in an office) a container on your desk for letters that are waiting to be read or answered ⊃ compare OUT TRAY

**in·trepid** /ɪnˈtrepɪd/ adj. (formal, often humorous) very brave; not afraid of danger or difficulties SYN **fearless**: *an intrepid explorer*

**in·tri·cacy** /ˈɪntrɪkəsi/ noun 1 **in·tri·ca·cies** [pl.] **the ~ of** the complicated parts or details of sth: *the intricacies of economic policy* 2 [U] the fact of having complicated parts, details or patterns: *the intricacy of the design*

**in·tri·cate** /ˈɪntrɪkət/ adj. having a lot of different parts and small details that fit together: *intricate patterns* ◊ *an intricate network of loyalties and relationships* ▶ **in·tri·cate·ly** adv.: *intricately carved*

**in·trigue** verb, noun
■ verb /ɪnˈtriːɡ/ 1 [T] ~ **sb** | **it intrigues sb that …** to make sb very interested and want to know more about sth: *You've really intrigued me—tell me more!* 2 [I] ~ **(with sb) (against sb)** (formal) to secretly plan with other people to harm sb
■ noun /ˈɪntriːɡ; ɪnˈtriːɡ/ 1 [U] the activity of making secret plans in order to achieve an aim, often by tricking people: *political intrigue* ◊ *The young heroine steps into a web of intrigue in the academic world.* 2 [C] a secret plan or relationship, especially one that involves sb else being tricked: *I soon learnt about all the intrigues and scandals that went on in the little town.* 3 [U] the atmosphere of interest and excitement that surrounds sth secret or important

**in·trigued** /ɪnˈtriːɡd/ adj. [not usually before noun] very interested in sth/sb and wanting to know more about it/them: *He was intrigued by her story.* ◊ ~ **to do sth** *I'm intrigued to know what you thought of the movie.*

**in·tri·guing** /ɪnˈtriːɡɪŋ/ adj. very interesting because of being unusual or not having an obvious answer: *These discoveries raise intriguing questions.* ◊ *an* 

835 **introduction**

*intriguing possibility* ◊ *He found her intriguing.* ▶ **in·tri·guing·ly** adv.

**in·trin·sic** /ɪnˈtrɪnzɪk/ adj. belonging to or part of the real nature of sth/sb: *the intrinsic value of education* ◊ *These tasks were repetitive, lengthy and lacking any intrinsic interest.* ◊ ~ **to sth** *Small local shops are intrinsic to the town's character.* ⊃ compare EXTRINSIC ▶ **in·trin·sic·al·ly** /-kli/ adv.: *There is nothing intrinsically wrong with the idea* (= it is good in itself but there may be outside circumstances which mean it is not suitable).

**intro** /ˈɪntrəʊ/ noun (pl. **-os**) (informal) an introduction to sth, especially to a piece of music or writing

**intro·duce** /ˌɪntrəˈdjuːs; NAmE -ˈduːs/ verb
• PEOPLE 1 to tell two or more people who have not met before what each other's names are; to tell sb what your name is: ~ **sb** *Allow me to introduce my mother.* ◊ ~ **A to B (as sth)** *He introduced me to a Greek girl at the party.* ◊ ~ **A and B** *Sue and Jo were introduced by a mutual friend.* ◊ *We have met before, but we haven't been formally introduced.* ◊ ~ **yourself (to sb)** *Can I introduce myself? I'm Helen Robins.*
• TV/RADIO SHOW 2 ~ **sb/sth** to be the main speaker in a television or radio show, who gives details about the show and who presents the people who are in it; to tell the audience the name of the person who is going to speak or perform: *The next programme will be introduced by Mary David.* ◊ *It is my pleasure to introduce my first guest on the show tonight…*
• IN A PIECE OF WRITING 3 to mention sth for the first time in a piece of writing: ~ **sth** *Introduce the topic and briefly state your own opinion.* ◊ *Each new idea should be introduced in a new paragraph.* ◊ ~ **sth to sb** *In Chapter 3 the author introduces the concept of the learner-centred classroom to readers.*
• NEW EXPERIENCE 4 to make sb learn about sth or do sth for the first time: ~ **sb to sth** *The first lecture introduces students to the main topics of the course.* ◊ ~ **sth to sb** *It was she who first introduced the pleasures of sailing to me.*
• NEW PRODUCT/LAW 5 to make sth available for use, discussion, etc. for the first time SYN **bring sb/sth in**: ~ **sth** *The company has recently introduced a new warehouse management system.* ◊ *Legislation will be introduced to ensure free bus travel for all pensioners.* ◊ ~ **sth into/to sth** *The government plans to gradually introduce the latest technology into all schools.*
• START 6 ~ **sth** to be the start of sth new: *Bands from London introduced the craze for this kind of music.* ◊ *A slow theme introduces the first movement.*
• PLANT/ANIMAL/DISEASE 7 to bring a plant, an animal or a disease to a place for the first time: ~ **sth (to sth) (from sth)** *Some new species were introduced accidentally to Australia from Europe.* ◊ ~ **sth into sth** *Diseases were inadvertently introduced into the environment by settlers.*
• IN PARLIAMENT 8 ~ **sth** (specialist) to formally present a new law so that it can be discussed: *to introduce a bill (before Parliament)*
• ADD 9 ~ **sth (into sth)** (formal) to put sth into sth: *Particles of glass had been introduced into the baby food.*
• ERRORS 10 to cause sth to contain errors: ~ **sth** *Measurement error could have been introduced by respondents' recall errors.* ◊ ~ **sth into sth** *The analyst's rankings rely on subjective information, which may introduce a bias into the rankings.*

**intro·duc·tion** /ˌɪntrəˈdʌkʃn/ noun
• OF BOOK/SPEECH 1 [C, U] the first part of a book or speech that gives a general idea of what is to follow: *a book with an excellent introduction and notes* ◊ ~ **to sth** *Can you write a brief introduction to the text?* ◊ *By way of introduction, let me give you the background to the story.* ⊃ compare PREFACE
• OF PEOPLE 2 [C] the act of making one person formally known to another or a group of others, in which you tell them the person's name: *Introductions were made and the conversation started to flow.* ◊ *Our speaker today needs no introduction* (= is already well known).

# introductory 836

▼ **EXPRESS YOURSELF**

**Making introductions**

There are different ways of introducing people to one another, depending on how formal the situation is:
- Amy, **do you know** my friend Simon?
- **Have you two met?** Jane, this is Matt.
- Ted, **this is Gwen**—she's Porter's mother.
- **Can I introduce you to** my colleague Professor Welsh? (formal)

Responses:
- **No, I don't think we've met. I'm** Harry.
- **Hello. Nice to meet you.**
- **Hi. I'm** Norman Miller.

- **BRINGING INTO USE/TO A PLACE** 3 [U] the act of bringing sth into use or existence for the first time, or of bringing sth to a place for the first time: **~ of sth** *the introduction of new manufacturing methods* ◊ *the introduction of compulsory military service* ◊ **~ of sth to/into** ... *the 1000th anniversary of the introduction of Christianity to Russia* 4 [C] a thing that is brought into use or introduced to a place for the first time: *The book lists plants suitable for the British flower garden, among them many new introductions.*
- **FIRST EXPERIENCE** 5 [sing.] **~ to sth** a person's first experience of sth: *This album was my first introduction to modern jazz.*
- **TO SUBJECT** 6 [C] a book or course for people beginning to study a subject: *'Global Politics: An Introduction'* ◊ **~ to sth** *It's a useful introduction to an extremely complex subject.*
- **IN MUSIC** 7 [C] (*music*) a short section at the beginning of a piece of music: *an eight-bar introduction*

**intro·duc·tory** /ˌɪntrəˈdʌktəri/ *adj.* **1** written or said at the beginning of sth as an introduction to what follows **SYN** **opening**: *introductory chapters/paragraphs/remarks* **2** intended as an introduction to a subject or an activity for people who have never done it before: *introductory courses/lectures* **3** offered for a short time only, when a product is first on sale: *a special introductory price of just $10* ◊ *This introductory offer is for these days only.*

**intro·spec·tion** /ˌɪntrəˈspekʃn/ *noun* [U] the careful examination of your own thoughts, feelings and reasons for behaving in a particular way

**intro·spect·ive** /ˌɪntrəˈspektɪv/ *adj.* tending to think a lot about your own thoughts, feelings, etc.

**intro·vert** /ˈɪntrəvɜːt; *NAmE* -vɜːrt/ *noun* a quiet person who is more interested in their own thoughts and feelings than in spending time with other people **OPP** **extrovert** ▶ **intro·ver·sion** /ˌɪntrəˈvɜːʃn; *NAmE* -ˈvɜːrʒn/ *noun* [U]

**intro·vert·ed** /ˈɪntrəvɜːtɪd; *NAmE* -vɜːrt-/ (*also* **intro·vert**) *adj.* more interested in your own thoughts and feelings than in spending time with other people **OPP** **extrovert**

**in·trude** /ɪnˈtruːd/ *verb* (*formal*) **1** [I] to go or be somewhere where you are not wanted or are not supposed to be: *I'm sorry to intrude, but I need to talk to someone.* ◊ **~ into/on/upon sb/sth** *legislation to stop newspapers from intruding on people's private lives* **2** [I] **~(on/into/upon sth)** to enter into sth in a way that is not wanted or to have an unpleasant effect on it: *The sound of the telephone intruded into his dreams.*

**in·truder** /ɪnˈtruːdə(r)/ *noun* **1** a person who enters a building or an area illegally **2** a person who is somewhere where they are not wanted: *The people in the room seemed to regard her as an unwelcome intruder.*

**in·tru·sion** /ɪnˈtruːʒn/ *noun* [U, C] **1** something that affects a situation or people's lives in a way that they do not want: **~(on/upon sth)** *They claim the noise from the new airport is an intrusion on their lives.* ◊ **~ (into sth)** *This was another example of press intrusion into the affairs of the royals.* **2** **~ (into/on/upon sth)** (*formal*) the act of entering a place that is private or where you may not be wanted: *She apologized for the intrusion but said she had an urgent message.*

**in·tru·sive** /ɪnˈtruːsɪv/ *adj.* **1** too direct, easy to notice, etc. in a way that is annoying or upsetting: *intrusive questions* ◊ *The constant presence of the media was very intrusive.* **2** (*phonetics*) (of a speech sound) produced in order to link two words together when speaking, for example the /r/ sound produced at the end of *law* by some English speakers in the phrase 'law and order'. Some people do not consider intrusive 'r' a feature of standard English.

**in·tub·ate** /ˈɪntjubeɪt; *NAmE* ˈɪntuː-/ *verb* [T, I] **~ (sb/sth)** to put a tube into a hollow space in the body, for example to allow a person to breathe: *They managed to intubate the victim inside the wrecked car.* ◊ *to intubate the trachea* ◊ *We made the decision not to intubate.*

**in·tuit** /ɪnˈtjuːɪt; *NAmE* -ˈtuː-/ *verb* **~ that ...** | **~ sth** | **~ what, why, etc ...** (*formal*) to know that sth is true based on your feelings rather than on facts, what sb tells you, etc: *She intuited that something was badly wrong.*

**in·tu·ition** /ˌɪntjuˈɪʃn; *NAmE* -tuː-/ *noun* **1** [U] the ability to know sth by using your feelings rather than considering the facts **2** [C] **~(that ...)** an idea or a strong feeling that sth is true although you cannot explain why: *I had an intuition that something awful was about to happen.*

**in·tui·tive** /ɪnˈtjuːɪtɪv; *NAmE* -ˈtuː-/ *adj.* **1** (of ideas) obtained by using your feelings rather than by considering the facts: *He had an intuitive sense of what the reader wanted.* ⇒ see also **COUNTER-INTUITIVE** **2** (of people) able to understand sth by using feelings rather than by considering the facts **3** (of computer software, etc.) easy to understand and to use ▶ **in·tui·tive·ly** *adv.*: *Intuitively, she knew that he was lying.*

**Inuit** /ˈɪnjuɪt; ˈɪnu-/ *noun* **1** [pl.] (*sing.* **Inuk** /ˈɪnʊk/) a race of people from northern Canada and parts of Greenland and Alaska. The name is sometimes also wrongly used to refer to people from Siberia and S and W Alaska. ⇒ compare **ESKIMO** **2** [U] = **INUKTITUT**

**Inuk·ti·tut** /ɪˈnʊktɪtʊt/ (*also* **Inuit**) *noun* [U] the language of the Inuit people

**in·un·date** /ˈɪnʌndeɪt/ *verb* **1** [often passive] to give or send sb so many things that they cannot deal with them all **SYN** **overwhelm, swamp: be inundated (with sth)** *We have been inundated with offers of help.* **2** **~ sth** (*formal*) to cover an area of land with a large amount of water **SYN** **flood** ▶ **in·un·da·tion** /ˌɪnʌnˈdeɪʃn/ *noun* [U, C]

**inure** /ɪˈnjʊə(r); *NAmE* ɪˈnjʊr/ *verb*
**PHRV** **iˈnure sb/yourself to sth** (*formal*) to make sb/yourself get used to sth unpleasant so that they/you are no longer strongly affected by it

**in·vade** /ɪnˈveɪd/ *verb* **1** [I, T] to enter a country, town, etc. using military force in order to take control of it: *Troops invaded on August 9th that year.* ◊ **~ sth** *When did the Romans invade Britain?* ⇒ WORDFINDER NOTE at ARMY **2** [T] **~ sth** to enter a place in large numbers, especially in a way that causes damage or problems: *Demonstrators invaded the government buildings.* ◊ *As the final whistle blew, fans began invading the field.* ◊ *The cancer cells may invade other parts of the body.* **3** [T] **~ sth** to affect sth in an unpleasant or annoying way: *Do the press have the right to invade her privacy in this way?* ⇒ see also **INVASION, INVASIVE**

**in·vader** /ɪnˈveɪdə(r)/ *noun* an army or a country that enters another country by force in order to take control of it; a soldier fighting in such an army: *a foreign invader* ◊ *They prepared to repel the invaders.* ◊ (*figurative*) *The white blood cells attack cells infected with an invader.*

**in·valid** *adj., noun, verb*

■ *adj.* /ɪnˈvælɪd/ **1** not legally or officially acceptable: *The treaty was declared invalid because it had not been ratified.* ◊ *People with invalid papers are deported to another country.* **2** not based on all the facts, and therefore not correct: *an invalid argument* **3** (*computing*) of a type that the computer cannot recognize: *An error code will be displayed if any invalid information has been entered.* ◊ *invalid characters* **OPP** **valid**

---

| æ cat | ɑː father | e bed | ɜː fur | ə about | ɪ sit | iː see | i happy | ɒ got (*BrE*) | ɔː saw | ʌ cup | ʊ put | uː too |

■ **noun** /ˈɪnvəlɪd/ a person who needs other people to take care of them, because of illness that they have had for a long time: *She had been a delicate child and her parents had treated her as an invalid.* ◇ *his invalid wife*
■ **verb** /ˈɪnvəlɪd/ ~ **sb (out)** | ~ **sb (out of sth)** (*BrE*) to force sb to leave the armed forces because of an illness or injury: *He was invalided out of the army in 1943.*

**in·vali·date** /ɪnˈvælɪdeɪt/ *verb* **1** ~ **sth** to prove that an idea, a story, an argument, etc. is wrong: *This new piece of evidence invalidates his version of events.* **2** ~ **sth** if you **invalidate** a document, a contract, an election, etc., you make it no longer legally or officially acceptable **OPP** **validate** ▶ **in·vali·da·tion** /ɪnˌvælɪˈdeɪʃn/ *noun* [U]

**in·val·id·ity** /ˌɪnvəˈlɪdəti/ *noun* [U] **1** (*BrE*, *specialist*) the state of being unable to take care of yourself because of illness or injury **2** (*formal*) the state of not being legally or officially acceptable ⊃ compare VALIDITY

**in·valu·able** /ɪnˈvæljuəbl/ *adj.* extremely useful **SYN** **valuable**: *invaluable information* ◇ ~ **to/for sb/sth** *The book will be invaluable for students in higher education.* ◇ ~ **in sth** *The research should prove invaluable in the study of children's language.* ⊃ compare VALUABLE **HELP** **Invaluable** means 'very valuable or useful'. The opposite of **valuable** is **valueless** or **worthless**.

**in·vari·able** /ɪnˈveəriəbl; *NAmE* -ˈver-/ *adj.* always the same; never changing **SYN** **unchanging**: *Her routine was invariable.* ◇ *his invariable courtesy and charm* ◇ *an invariable principle* ⊃ compare VARIABLE

**in·vari·ably** /ɪnˈveəriəbli; *NAmE* -ˈver-/ *adv.* always **SYN** **without fail**: *This acute infection of the brain is almost invariably fatal.* ◇ *This is not invariably the case.* ◇ *Invariably the reply came back, 'Not now!'*

**in·vari·ant** /ɪnˈveəriənt; *NAmE* -ˈver-/ *adj.* (*specialist*) always the same; never changing **SYN** **invariable**

**in·va·sion** **B2** /ɪnˈveɪʒn/ *noun* [C, U] **1** the act of an army entering another country by force in order to take control of it: *the German invasion of Poland in 1939* ◇ *the threat of invasion* ◇ *an invasion force/fleet* **2** **C1** the fact of a large number of people or things arriving somewhere, especially people or things that are unpleasant: *the annual tourist invasion* ◇ *Farmers are struggling to cope with an invasion of slugs.* ⊃ see also PITCH INVASION **3** **C1** an act or a process that affects sb/sth in a way that is not welcome: *The actress described the photographs of her as an invasion of privacy.* ⊃ see also INVADE

**in·va·sive** /ɪnˈveɪsɪv/ *adj.* (*formal*) **1** (especially of diseases within the body) spreading very quickly and difficult to stop: *invasive cancer* **2** (of medical treatment) involving cutting into the body: *invasive surgery* **OPP** **non-invasive** ⊃ see also INVADE

**in·vec·tive** /ɪnˈvektɪv/ *noun* [U] (*formal*) rude language and unpleasant remarks that sb shouts when they are very angry

**in·veigh** /ɪnˈveɪ/ *verb*
**PHRV** **inˈveigh against sb/sth** (*formal*) to criticize sb/sth strongly

**in·vei·gle** /ɪnˈveɪgl/ *verb* ~ **sb/yourself (into sth/into doing sth)** (*formal*) to achieve control over sb in a clever and dishonest way, especially so that they will do what you want: *He inveigled himself into her affections* (= dishonestly made her love him).

**in·vent** **A2** **S** /ɪnˈvent/ *verb* **1** **A2** ~ **sth** to produce or design sth that has not existed before: *Who invented the steam engine?* ⊃ see also REINVENT **2** **B1** ~ **sth** to say or describe sth that is not true, especially in order to trick people: *What excuse did he invent this time?* ◇ *Many children invent an imaginary friend.*

**in·ven·tion** **A2** /ɪnˈvenʃn/ *noun* **1** **A2** [C] a thing or an idea that has been invented: *Fax machines were a wonderful invention at the time.* **2** **A2** [U] the act of inventing sth: *Such changes have not been seen since the invention of the printing press.* **3** [C, U] the act of inventing a story or an idea and pretending that it is true; a story invented in this way: *This story is apparently a complete invention.* **4** [U] the ability to have new and inter-

837 **invest**

esting ideas: *John was full of invention—always making up new dance steps and sequences.* **IDM** see NECESSITY

**in·ven·tive** /ɪnˈventɪv/ *adj.* (*approving*) **1** (especially of people) able to think of new and interesting ideas **SYN** **imaginative**: *She has a highly inventive mind.* **2** (of ideas) new and interesting ▶ **in·ven·tive·ly** *adv.* **in·ven·tive·ness** /-tɪvnəs/ *noun* [U]

**in·ven·tor** /ɪnˈventə(r)/ *noun* a person who has invented sth or whose job is inventing things

**in·ven·tory** /ˈɪnvəntri; *NAmE* -tɔːri/ *noun*, *verb*
■ **noun** (*pl.* **-ies**) **1** [C] a written list of all the objects, furniture, etc. in a particular building: *an inventory of the museum's contents* **2** [U] (*NAmE*) all the goods in a store **SYN** **stock**: *The inventory will be disposed of over the next twelve weeks.* ◇ *inventory control* ⊃ compare STOCKTAKING
■ **verb** (**in·ven·tor·ies**, **in·ven·tory·ing**, **in·ven·tor·ied**, **in·ven·tor·ied**) ~ **sth** (*formal*) to make a complete list of sth; to include sth in a list: *I've inventoried my father's collection of prints.*

**in·verse** /ˌɪnˈvɜːs; *NAmE* -ˈvɜːrs/ *adj.* **1** [only before noun] opposite in amount or position to sth else: *A person's wealth is often in inverse proportion to their happiness* (= the more money they have, the less happy they are). ◇ *There is often an inverse relationship between the power of the tool and how easy it is to use.* **2** **the ˈinverse** *noun* [sing.] (*specialist*) the exact opposite of sth ▶ **in·verse·ly** *adv.*: *We regard health as inversely related to social class.*

**in·ver·sion** /ɪnˈvɜːʃn; *NAmE* -ˈvɜːrʒn/ *noun* [U, C] (*specialist*) the act of changing the position or order of sth to its opposite, or of turning sth into a position in which the top of it is where the bottom of it normally is: *the inversion of normal word order* ◇ *an inversion of the truth*

**in·vert** /ɪnˈvɜːt; *NAmE* -ˈvɜːrt/ *verb* ~ **sth** (*formal*) to change the normal position of sth, especially by turning it into a position in which the top of it is where the bottom of it normally is or by arranging it in the opposite order: *Place a plate over the cake tin and invert it.*

**in·ver·te·brate** /ɪnˈvɜːtɪbrət; *NAmE* -ˈvɜːrt-/ *noun* (*specialist*) any animal with no BACKBONE, for example a WORM ⊃ compare VERTEBRATE ▶ **in·ver·te·brate** *adj.*: *invertebrate pests*

**inˌverted ˈcommas** *noun* [pl.] (*BrE*) = QUOTATION MARKS
**IDM** **in inverted commas** (*informal*) used to show that you think a particular word, description, etc. is not true or appropriate: *The manager showed us to our 'luxury apartment', in inverted commas.*

**inˌverted ˈsnobbery** *noun* [U] (*BrE*, *disapproving*) the attitude that considers everything connected with high social status to be bad and that is proud of low social status

**in·vest** **B1** /ɪnˈvest/ *verb* **1** **B1** [I, T] to buy property, shares in a company, etc. in the hope of making a profit: *Now is a good time to invest.* ◇ ~ **in sth** *She advised us to invest in the property market.* ◇ ~ **sth (in sth)** *He invested his life savings in his daughter's business.* ⊃ WORD-FINDER NOTE at MONEY

**WORDFINDER** asset, bond, capital, dividend, equity, fund, interest, portfolio, share

**2** **B1** [I, T] (of an organization or government, etc.) to spend money on sth in order to make it better or more successful: ~ **(in/on sb/sth)** *The government has invested heavily in public transport.* ◇ ~ **sth (in/on sb/sth)** | ~ **sth in sb/sth** *The college is to invest $2 million in a new conference hall.* **3** [T] ~ **sth (in sth)** | ~ **sth (in) doing sth** to spend time, energy, effort, etc. on sth that you think is good or useful: ~ **sth in sth** *She had invested all her adult life in the relationship.* **4** [T] (*formal*) to give sb power or authority, especially as part of their job: ~ **sb with sth** *The new position invested her with a good deal of responsibility.* ◇ ~ **sb (as sth)** *The interview was broadcast on the same day he was invested as President.* ⊃ see also INVESTITURE

# investigate

**PHRV** **in vest in sth** (*informal, often humorous*) to buy sth that is expensive but useful: *Don't you think it's about time you invested in a new coat?* **in vest sb/sth with sth** (*formal*) to make sb/sth seem to have a particular quality: *Being a model invests her with a certain glamour.*

## in·ves·ti·gate ❶ B1 Ⓦ /ɪnˈvestɪɡeɪt/ *verb* 1 B1
[I, T] to carefully examine the facts of a situation, an event, a crime, etc. to find out the truth about it or how it happened: *The FBI has been called in to investigate.* ◊ (*informal*) *'What was that noise?' 'I'll go and investigate.'* ◊ ~ **sth** *Detectives are currently investigating possible links between the murders.* ◊ **to investigate a crime/a complaint/an incident** ◊ **what, how, etc…** *Police are investigating what happened.* 2 B1 [T] to try to find out information about sb's character, activities, etc: ~ **sb (for sth)** *This is not the first time he has been investigated by the police for fraud.* 3 B1 [T] to find out information and facts about a subject or problem by study or research: ~ **sth** *The study investigates the effects of feeding a high energy diet to cows.* ◊ ~ **how, what, etc…** *Researchers are investigating how foreign speakers gain fluency.*

## in·ves·ti·ga·tion ❶ B2 Ⓦ /ɪnˌvestɪˈɡeɪʃn/ *noun*
[C, U] 1 B2 an official examination of the facts about a situation, crime, etc: *a criminal/murder/police investigation* ◊ **under ~ (for sth/doing sth)** *She remains under investigation for fraud.* ◊ ~ **into sth** *The police are conducting ongoing investigations into the man's death.* ◊ **on ~** *On investigation, the noise turned out to be only a door banging.* 2 B2 a scientific or academic examination of the facts of a subject or problem **SYN** **enquiry**: *Further investigation revealed a flaw in this theory.* ◊ ~ **into sth** *the results of a preliminary investigation into stress at work*

**in·ves·ti·ga·tive** /ɪnˈvestɪɡətɪv; *NAmE* -ɡeɪt-/ (*also less frequent* **in·ves·ti·ga·tory** /ɪnˈvestɪɡətəri; *NAmE* -tɔːri/) *adj.* [usually before noun] involving examining an event or a situation to find out the truth: *The article was an excellent piece of investigative journalism.* ◊ *The police have full investigatory powers.*

**in·ves·ti·ga·tor** C1 Ⓦ /ɪnˈvestɪɡeɪtə(r)/ *noun* a person who examines a situation such as an accident or a crime to find out the truth: *air safety investigators* ◊ *a private investigator* (= a detective)

**in·ves·ti·ture** /ɪnˈvestɪtʃə(r)/ *noun* [U, C] the fact of sb formally receiving an official title or special powers; a ceremony at which this happens

## in·vest·ment ❶ B2 /ɪnˈvestmənt/ *noun* 1 B2
[U] the act of investing money in sth: *foreign/private investment* ◊ **to attract/encourage investment** ◊ **in sth** *This country needs investment in education.* ◊ *an investment trust/fund/firm* ⊃ see also INWARD INVESTMENT 2 B2 [C, U] the money that you invest, or the thing that you invest in: *a minimum investment of $10 000* ◊ *a substantial/significant/major investment* ◊ *Our investments are not doing well.* ◊ **as an ~** *We bought the house as an investment* (= to make money). ◊ *a high return on investment* 3 B1 [C] a thing that is worth buying because it will be useful or helpful: *A microwave is a good investment.* 4 [U, C] the act of giving time or effort to a particular task in order to make it successful: *The project has demanded considerable investment of time and effort.*

**in'vestment bank** (*BrE also* ˌmerchant ˈbank) *noun* a bank that deals mainly with buying and selling shares and other investments for businesses and private INVESTORS ⊃ compare COMMERCIAL BANK ▶ **in'vestment ˈbanker** *noun* **in'vestment 'banking** *noun* [U]

**in·ves·tor** B2 /ɪnˈvestə(r)/ *noun* a person or an organization that invests money in sth: *small investors* (= private people) ◊ *institutional investors* ⊃ see also ANGEL INVESTOR at ANGEL

**in·vet·er·ate** /ɪnˈvetərət/ *adj.* [usually before noun] (*formal, often disapproving*) 1 (of a person) always doing sth or enjoying sth, and unlikely to stop: *an inveterate liar* 2 (of a bad feeling or habit) done or felt for a long time and unlikely to change: *inveterate hostility*

**in·vidi·ous** /ɪnˈvɪdiəs/ *adj.* (*formal*) unpleasant and unfair; likely to offend sb or make them JEALOUS: *We were in the invidious position of having to choose whether to break the law or risk lives.* ◊ *It would be invidious to single out any one person to thank.*

**in·vigi·late** /ɪnˈvɪdʒɪleɪt/ (*BrE*) (*NAmE* ˈproc·tor) *verb* [T, I] ~ **(sth)** to watch people while they are taking an exam to make sure that they have everything they need, that they keep to the rules, etc: *to invigilate an exam* ⊃ **WORDFINDER NOTE** at EXAM ▶ **in·vigi·la·tion** /ɪnˌvɪdʒɪˈleɪʃn/ *noun* [U] **in·vigi·la·tor** /ɪnˈvɪdʒɪleɪtə(r)/ (*BrE*) (*NAmE* ˈproc·tor) *noun*: *If you have a problem, ask the invigilator.*

**in·vig·or·ate** /ɪnˈvɪɡəreɪt/ *verb* 1 ~ **sb** to make sb feel healthy and full of energy: *The cold water invigorated him.* ◊ *They felt refreshed and invigorated after the walk.* 2 ~ **sth** to make a situation, an organization, etc. efficient and successful: *They are looking into ways of invigorating the department.* ▶ **in·vig·or·at·ing** *adj.*: *an invigorating walk/shower*

**in·vin·cible** /ɪnˈvɪnsəbl/ *adj.* too strong to be defeated or changed **SYN** **unconquerable**: *The team seemed invincible.* ◊ *an invincible belief in his own ability* ▶ **in·vin·ci·bil·ity** /ɪnˌvɪnsəˈbɪləti/ *noun* [U]

**in·viol·able** /ɪnˈvaɪələbl/ *adj.* (*formal*) that must be respected and not attacked or destroyed: *the inviolable right to life* ◊ *inviolable territory* ◊ *an inviolable rule* ▶ **in·viol·abil·ity** /ɪnˌvaɪələˈbɪləti/ *noun* [U]

**in·viol·ate** /ɪnˈvaɪələt/ *adj.* (*formal*) that has been, or must be, respected and cannot be attacked or destroyed

**in·vis·ible** C1 /ɪnˈvɪzəbl/ *adj.* 1 C1 that cannot be seen: *a wizard who could make himself invisible* ◊ *She felt invisible in the crowd.* ◊ **to sb/sth** *stars invisible to the naked eye* **OPP** **visible** 2 (*economics*) connected with a service that a country provides, such as banks or tourism, rather than goods: *invisible earnings* ▶ **in·visi·bil·ity** /ɪnˌvɪzəˈbɪləti/ *noun* [U]: *The ink had faded to invisibility.* **in·vis·ibly** /ɪnˈvɪzəbli/ *adv.*: *He looked at me and nodded, almost invisibly.*

## in·vi·ta·tion ❶ A2 /ˌɪnvɪˈteɪʃn/ *noun* 1 A2 [C] a
spoken or written request to sb to do sth or to go somewhere: **to issue/extend an invitation** ◊ **to accept/turn down/decline an invitation** ◊ ~ **to sth** *I received an invitation to the party* ◊ ~ **to do sth** *I have an open invitation* (= not restricted to a particular date) *to visit my friend in Japan.* 2 B1 [U] the act of inviting sb or of being invited: *He produced an official letter of invitation.* ◊ *Admission is by invitation only.* ◊ **at the ~ of sb** *A concert was held at the invitation of the mayor.* 3 B1 [C] a card or piece of paper that you use to invite sb to sth: *We've already sent out the invitations.* ◊ *Have you ordered the wedding invitations yet?* 4 [C, usually sing.] ~ **to sb (to do sth)** | ~ **to sth** something that encourages sb to do sth or encourages sth to happen, usually sth bad: *Leaving the doors unlocked is an* **open invitation** *to burglars.*

**in·vi·ta·tion·al** /ˌɪnvɪˈteɪʃənl/ *noun* (*especially NAmE*) (often used in names) a competition, especially a sports event, that you can take part in only if you are invited ▶ **in·vi·ta·tion·al** *adj.*

## in·vite ❶ A2 /ɪnˈvaɪt/ *verb, noun*

■ *verb* 1 A2 to ask sb to come to a social event: ~ **sb to sth** *Have you been invited to their party?* ◊ ~ **sb** *I'd have liked to have gone but I wasn't invited.* ◊ ~ **sb for sth** *Let's invite them all for dinner.* ◊ ~ **sb to do sth** *They have invited me to go to Paris with them.* 2 B1 (*formal*) to ask sb formally to go somewhere or do sth; to make a formal or polite request for sth: ~ **sb (to/for sth)** *Successful candidates will be invited for interview next week.* ◊ ~ **sth (from sb)** *He invited questions from the audience.* ◊ ~ **sb to do sth** *Readers are invited to email their comments to us.* 3 ~ **sth** | ~ **sb/sth to do sth** to make sth, especially sth bad or unpleasant, likely to happen **SYN** **ask for**: *Such comments are just inviting trouble.* ⊃ see also UNINVITED

**PHRV** **in vite sb aˈlong** to ask sb to go somewhere with you and other people: *I got myself invited along.* **in vite**

**'back 1** to ask sb to come to your home after you have been somewhere together: *After the show, she invited me back for a drink.* **2** to ask sb to come to your home or another place for a second time: *They invited me back for a second interview.* **3** to ask sb to come to your home after you have been to theirs ⬥ in‚vite sb 'in to ask sb to come into your home, especially after you have been somewhere together ⬥ in‚vite sb 'over/a'round (*BrE also* in‚vite sb 'round) to ask sb to come to your home

■ *noun* /'ɪnvaɪt/ (*informal*) an invitation: *Thanks for your invite.*

▼ **EXPRESS YOURSELF**

**Inviting somebody to something**

Here are some ways of making and responding to invitations:
- **Would you like to** *come for a meal on Saturday?*
- *There's a presentation of our new product at the conference on Tuesday.* **Would you be interested in** *coming along?*
- *I'm going to the game on Saturday—***how about** *joining me?*
- *We're going to Boston—***do you want to come with us?** (*informal* or *NAmE*)

Responses:
- *That would be very nice, thank you.*
- *I'd love to, thanks very much.*
- *I'm sorry. I've already got something on* at the weekend.
- *I'm sorry. I already have plans on Saturday.*
- (*BrE*) **Thank you, I'll check** *my diary and let you know.*
- (*NAmE*) **Thank you, I'll check** *my calendar and let you know.*

**in·vit·ing** /ɪnˈvaɪtɪŋ/ *adj.* making you want to do, try, taste, etc. sth **SYN** **attractive**: *an inviting smell* ⋄ *The water looks really inviting.* ▶ **in·vit·ing·ly** *adv.*

**in vitro** /ɪn ˈviːtrəʊ/ *adj.* (*from Latin, biology*) (of processes) taking place outside a living body, in scientific APPARATUS: *in vitro experiments* ⋄ *the development of in vitro fertilization* ⊃ see also IVF ▶ **in vitro** *adv.*: *an egg fertilized in vitro*

**in vivo** /ɪn ˈviːvəʊ/ *adj.* (*from Latin, biology*) (of processes) taking place in a living body ▶ **in vivo** *adv.*

**in·vo·ca·tion** /ˌɪnvəˈkeɪʃn/ *noun* [U, C] **1** (*formal*) the act of asking for help, from a god or from a person in authority; the act of referring to sth or of calling for sth to appear ⊃ see also INVOKE **2** (*computing*) the act of making a particular function start

**in·voice** /'ɪnvɔɪs/ *noun, verb*

■ *noun* a list of goods that have been sold, work that has been done, etc., showing what you must pay **SYN** **bill**: *to send/issue/settle an invoice for the goods* ⋄ *an invoice for £250* ⊃ SYNONYMS at BILL

■ *verb* (*business*) to write or send sb a bill for work you have done or goods you have provided: **~sb (for sth)** *You will be invoiced for these items at the end of the month.* ⋄ **~sth (to sb/sth)** *Invoice the goods to my account.*

**in·voke** ꜛ+ 🄲🄸 /ɪnˈvəʊk/ *verb* **1** ꜛ+ 🄲🄸 **~sth (against sb)** to mention or use a law, rule, etc. as a reason for doing sth: *It is unlikely that libel laws will be invoked.* **2** ꜛ+ 🄲🄸 **~sth/sth** to mention a person, a theory, an example, etc. to support your opinions or ideas, or as a reason for sth: *She invoked several eminent scholars to back up her argument.* **3** **~sth** to mention sb's name to make people feel a particular thing or act in a particular way: *His name was invoked as a symbol of the revolution.* **4** **~sb** to make a request (for help) to sb, especially a god **5** **~sth** to make sb have a particular feeling or imagine a particular scene **SYN** **evoke**: *The opening paragraph invokes a vision of England in the early Middle Ages.* **HELP** Some people think this use is not correct and **evoke** should be used instead. **6** **~sth** (*computing*) to begin to run a program, etc: *This command will invoke the HELP system.* **7** **~sb/sth** to make evil appear by using magic

**in·vol·un·tary** /ɪnˈvɒləntri; *NAmE* -ˈvɑːlənteri/ *adj.* **1** *an* **involuntary** *movement, etc. is made suddenly, without you intending it or being able to control it*: *an involuntary cry of pain* **OPP** **voluntary** **2** happening without the person involved wanting it to: *the involuntary repatriation of immigrants* ⋄ *involuntary childlessness* ▶ **in·vol·un·tar·ily** /ɪnˈvɒləntrəli; *NAmE* ɪnˌvɑːlənˈterəli/ *adv.*

**in·volve** 🛈 🄰🄰2 🄾 /ɪnˈvɒlv; *NAmE* -ˈvɑːlv/ *verb* **1** ꜛ 🄰2 if a situation, an event or an activity **involves** sth, that thing is an important or necessary part or result of it **SYN** **entail**: **~sth** *Any investment involves an element of risk.* ⋄ **~doing sth** *The process involves using steam to sterilize the instruments.* ⋄ **~sb/sth doing sth** *The job involves me travelling all over the country.* **2** ꜛ 🄰2 **~sb/sth** if a situation, an event or an activity **involves** sb/sth, they take part in it or are affected by it: *There was a serious incident involving a group of youths.* **3** ꜛ 🄱1 to make sb take part in sth: **~sb (in sth/in doing sth)** *We want to involve as many people as possible in the celebrations.* ⋄ **~yourself (in sth)** *Parents should involve themselves in their child's education.* **4** **~sb (in sth)** to say or do sth to show that sb took part in sth, especially a crime **SYN** **implicate**: *His confession involved a number of other politicians in the affair.*

**PHRV** in'volve sb in sth to make sb experience sth, especially sth unpleasant: *You have involved me in a great deal of extra work.*

**in·volved** 🛈 🄱1 🅂 /ɪnˈvɒlvd; *NAmE* -ˈvɑːlvd/ *adj.*
**1** ꜛ 🄱1 [not before noun] taking part in sth; being part of sth or connected with sth: *Some people tried to stop the fight but I didn't want to get involved.* ⋄ *It can be helpful to talk about your worries to someone who is not directly involved.* ⋄ **~in sth** *He became actively involved in politics.* ⋄ **~with sth** *Several people have been involved with the project from the beginning.* **HELP** In this meaning, **involved** is often used directly after a noun: *We'll make our decision and contact the people involved.* **OPP** **uninvolved** **2** ꜛ 🄱2 [not usually before noun] giving a lot of time or attention to sb/sth: **~(with sth/sb)** *She was deeply involved with the local hospital.* ⋄ *You shouldn't allow yourself to become so heavily involved.* ⋄ *He's a very involved father (= he spends a lot of time with his children).* ⋄ **~in sth/sb** *I was so involved in my book I didn't hear you knock.* **OPP** **uninvolved** ⊃ see also SELF-INVOLVED **3** ꜛ 🄱2 [not usually before noun] having a close personal relationship with sb: *They're not romantically involved.* ⋄ **~with sb** *She became personally involved with her boss.* **OPP** **uninvolved** **4** complicated and difficult to understand **SYN** **complex**: *an involved plot*

**in·volve·ment** ꜛ+ 🄲🄸 🅆 /ɪnˈvɒlvmənt; *NAmE* -ˈvɑːlv-/ *noun* **1** ꜛ+ 🄲🄸 [U] **~(in/with sth/sb)** the act of taking part in sth or dealing with sb **SYN** **participation**: *US involvement in European wars* **2** ꜛ+ 🄲🄸 [U, C] **~(in/with sth)** the act of giving a lot of time and attention to sth you care about: *her growing involvement with contemporary music* **3** ꜛ+ 🄲🄸 [C, U] **~(with sth)** a close relationship with sb, especially a romantic or sexual relationship with sb that you are not married to: *He spoke openly about his involvement with the singer.* ⋄ *Nurses usually try to avoid emotional involvement with patients.*

**in·vul·ner·able** /ɪnˈvʌlnərəbl/ *adj.* that cannot be harmed or defeated: *to be in an invulnerable position* ⋄ **~to sth** *The submarine is invulnerable to attack while at sea.* **OPP** **vulnerable** ▶ **in·vul·ner·abil·ity** /ɪnˌvʌlnərəˈbɪləti/ *noun* [U]

**in·ward** /'ɪnwəd; *NAmE* -wərd/ *adj., adv.*

■ *adj.* **1** [only before noun] inside your mind and not shown to other people: *an inward smile* ⋄ *Her calm expression hid her inward panic.* **2** towards the inside or centre of sth: *an inward flow* ⋄ *an inward curve* **OPP** **outward**

■ *adv.* (*also* **in·wards** *especially in BrE*) **1** towards the inside or centre: *The door opens inwards.* **2** towards yourself and your interests: *Her thoughts turned inward.* ⋄ (*disapproving*) *an inward-looking person* (= one who is not interested in other people) **OPP** **outwards**

**inward in'vestment** *noun* [U, C] (*business*) money that is invested in a particular country from outside it; the act of investing in a particular country from outside it

**in·ward·ly** /'ɪnwədli; *NAmE* -wərd-/ *adv.* in your mind; secretly: *She groaned inwardly.* ⋄ *I was inwardly furious.* **OPP** **outwardly**

# inwardness

**in·ward·ness** /ˈɪnwədnəs; *NAmE* -wərd-/ *noun* [U] (*formal or literary*) interest in feelings and emotions rather than in the world around

**inwards** /ˈɪnwədz; *NAmE* -wərdz/ *adv.* (*especially BrE*) = INWARD

**in·yanga** /ɪnˈjɑːŋə/ *SAfrE* [ɪnˈjɛːŋɡɛ] *noun* (*pl.* **in·yangas** or **izin·yanga** /ˌɪzɪnˈjɑːŋə/) (*SAfrE*) a person who treats people who are ill using natural materials such as plants, etc. ⊃ compare SANGOMA

**ˌin-your-ˈface** *adj.* (*informal*) used to describe an attitude, a performance, etc. that is aggressive in style and deliberately designed to make people react strongly for or against it: *in-your-face action thrillers*

**iod·ide** /ˈaɪədaɪd/ *noun* [C] (*chemistry*) a chemical that contains iodine

**iod·ine** /ˈaɪədiːn; *NAmE* -daɪn/ *noun* [U] (*symb.* **I**) a chemical element. Iodine is a substance found in SEAWATER. A liquid containing iodine is sometimes used as an ANTISEPTIC (= a substance used on wounds to prevent infection).

**ion** /ˈaɪən; *BrE also* -ɒn; *NAmE also* -ɑːn/ *noun* (*physics or chemistry*) an ATOM or a MOLECULE with a positive or negative electric charge caused by its losing or gaining one or more ELECTRONS ⊃ **WORDFINDER NOTE** at ATOM

**-ion** (*also* **-ation, -ition, -sion, -tion, -xion**) *suffix* (in nouns) the action or state of: *hesitation ◇ competition ◇ confession*

**ionic** /aɪˈɒnɪk; *NAmE* -ˈɑːn-/ *adj.* **1** (*chemistry*) of or related to ions **2** (*chemistry*) (of a chemical BOND) using the electrical pull between positive and negative ions ⊃ compare COVALENT **3 Ionic** (*architecture*) used to describe a style of architecture in ancient Greece that uses a curved decoration in the shape of a SCROLL

**ion·ize** (*BrE also* **-ise**) /ˈaɪənaɪz/ *verb* [T, I] ~ (**sth**) (*specialist*) to change sth or be changed into ions ▸ **ion·iza·tion, -isa·tion** /ˌaɪənaɪˈzeɪʃn; *NAmE* -nəˈz-/ *noun* [U]

**the iono·sphere** /ɒɪ aɪˈɒnəsfɪə(r); *NAmE* -ˈɑːnəsfɪr/ *noun* [*sing.*] a layer of the earth's atmosphere between about 80 and 1000 kilometres above the surface of the earth that reflects radio waves around the earth ⊃ compare STRATOSPHERE

**iota** /aɪˈəʊtə/ *noun* **1** [*sing.*] (usually used in negative sentences) an extremely small amount: *There is not one iota of truth* (= no truth at all) *in the story.* ◇ *I don't think that would help one iota.* **2** the 9th letter of the Greek alphabet (I, ι)

**IOU** /ˌaɪ əʊ ˈjuː/ *noun* (*informal*) a written promise that you will pay sb the money you owe them (a way of writing 'I owe you'): *an IOU for £100*

**IPA** /ˌaɪ piː ˈeɪ/ *abbr.* International Phonetic Alphabet (an alphabet that is used to show the pronunciation of words in any language)

**iPad™** /ˈaɪpæd/ *noun* a brand of tablet computer: *I've downloaded a new camera app to my iPad.*

**IP address** /ˌaɪ ˈpiː ədres/ *noun* (*computing*) a series of numbers separated by DOTS (= round marks) that identifies a particular computer connected to the internet

**iPhone™** /ˈaɪfəʊn/ *noun* a brand of smartphone: *I use a dictionary app on my iPhone whenever I need to know a word in Spanish.*

**IPO** /ˌaɪ piː ˈəʊ/ *abbr.* (*business*) initial public offering (the act of selling shares in a company for the first time)

**iPod™** /ˈaɪpɒd; *NAmE* -pɑːd/ *noun* a brand of MP3 PLAYER that can store information taken from the internet and that you carry with you, for example so that you can listen to music

**ipso facto** /ˌɪpsəʊ ˈfæktəʊ/ *adv.* (*from Latin, formal*) because of the fact that has been mentioned: *You cannot assume that a speaker of English is ipso facto qualified to teach English.*

**IQ** /ˌaɪ ˈkjuː/ *noun* a measurement of a person's intelligence that is calculated from the results of special tests (the abbreviation for 'intelligence quotient'): *an IQ of 120 ◇ to have a high/low IQ ◇ IQ tests*

**ir-** ⊃ IN-

**IRA** /ˌaɪ ɑːr ˈeɪ/ *abbr.* the abbreviation for 'Irish Republican Army' (an organization that has fought for Northern Ireland to be united with the Republic of Ireland)

**iras·cible** /ɪˈræsəbl/ *adj.* (*formal*) becoming angry very easily SYN **irritable** ▸ **iras·ci·bil·ity** /ɪˌræsəˈbɪləti/ *noun* [U]

**irate** /aɪˈreɪt; *NAmE* also ˈaɪreɪt/ *adj.* very angry: *irate customers ◇ an irate phone call* ⊃ SYNONYMS at ANGRY

**IRC** /ˌaɪ ɑː ˈsiː; *NAmE* ɑːr/ *abbr.* Internet Relay Chat (an area of the internet where users can communicate directly with each other)

**ire** /ˈaɪə(r)/ *noun* [U] (*formal or literary*) anger SYN **wrath**: *to arouse/raise/provoke the ire of local residents ◇ (US) to draw the ire of local residents*

**iri·des·cent** /ˌɪrɪˈdesnt/ *adj.* (*formal*) showing many bright colours that seem to change in different lights: *a bird with iridescent blue feathers* ▸ **iri·des·cence** /-sns/ *noun* [U]

**irid·ium** /ɪˈrɪdiəm/ *noun* [U] (*symb.* **Ir**) a chemical element. Iridium is a very hard yellow-white metal, used especially in making ALLOYS.

**irio** /ˈɪəriəʊ/ *EAfrE* [ˈɪriəʊ] *noun* [U] (*EAfrE*) a type of food made from a mixture of some or all of the following: MAIZE, beans, green vegetables and PEAS

**iris** /ˈaɪrɪs/ *noun* **1** the round coloured part that surrounds the PUPIL of your eye **2** a tall plant with long pointed leaves and large purple or yellow flowers ⊃ VISUAL VOCAB page V7

**Irish** /ˈaɪrɪʃ/ *noun, adj.*
■ *noun* **1** (*also* **ˌIrish ˈGaelic, Gaelic**) the Celtic language of Ireland ⊃ compare ERSE **2 the Irish** [*pl.*] the people of Ireland
■ *adj.* of or connected with Ireland, its people or its language

**ˌIrish ˈcoffee** *noun* **1** [U] hot coffee mixed with WHISKEY and sugar, with thick cream on top **2** [C] a cup or glass of Irish coffee

**ˌIrish ˈstew** *noun* [U, C] a hot dish of MUTTON (= meat from a sheep) and vegetables boiled together

**irk** /ɜːk; *NAmE* ɜːrk/ *verb* ~ **sb** (**to do sth**) | **it irks sb that …** (*formal or literary*) to annoy sb: *Her flippant tone irked him.*

**irk·some** /ˈɜːksəm; *NAmE* ˈɜːrk-/ *adj.* (*formal*) annoying SYN **tiresome**: *I found the restrictions irksome.*

**IRL** /ˌaɪ ɑː ˈel; *NAmE* ɑːr/ *abbr.* in real life; not on the internet (used in chat on the internet): *If he did that IRL he'd have a bullet in his head.*

**iroko** /ɪˈrəʊkəʊ/ *noun* (*pl.* **-os**) **1** [C, U] a tall tree found in tropical West Africa that lives for many years. Some people believe that creatures with magic powers live in irokos. **2** [U] the wood from this tree, which is hard and used especially for outdoor building work

**iron** 🔊 **B1** /ˈaɪən; *NAmE* -ərn/ *noun, verb, adj.*
■ *noun*
- **METAL 1** 🔊 **B1** [U] (*symb.* **Fe**) a chemical element. Iron is a hard strong metal that is used to make steel and is also found in small quantities in blood and food: *iron gates/bars/railings ◇ the iron and steel industries ◇ iron ore* = rock containing iron) *◇ foods that are rich in iron ◇ patients with iron deficiency* (= not enough iron in their blood) ⊃ picture at CORRUGATED ⊃ see also CAST IRON, PIG IRON, WROUGHT IRON
- **TOOL 2** 🔊 **B1** [C] a tool with a flat metal base that can be heated and used to make clothes smooth: *a steam iron* ⊃ picture at IRONING BOARD **3** [C] (usually in compounds) a tool made of iron or another metal ⊃ see also GRAPPLING IRON, SOLDERING IRON, TIRE IRON
- **FOR PRISONERS 4 irons** [*pl.*] chains or other heavy objects made of iron, attached to the arms and legs of prisoners, especially in the past
- **IN GOLF 5** [C] one of the set of CLUBS (= sticks for hitting the ball with) that have a metal head ⊃ compare WOOD
**IDM** **have several, etc. irons in the ˈfire** to be involved in several activities or areas of business at the same time, hoping that at least one will be successful ⊃ more at PUMP v., RULE v., STRIKE v.

■ **verb** [B1] [T, I] to make clothes, etc. smooth by using an iron: *He was ironing when I arrived.* ◇ *~ sth I'll need to iron that dress before I can wear it.* ◦ see also IRONING
**PHR V** ˌiron sth↔ˈout **1** to remove the CREASES (= folds that you do not want) from clothes, etc. by using an iron **2** to get rid of any problems or difficulties that are affecting sth: *There are still a few details that need ironing out.*
■ **adj.** [only before noun] very strong and determined: *She was known as the 'Iron Lady'.* ◇ *a man of iron will*
**IDM** an iron ˈfist/ˈhand (in a velvet ˈglove) if you use the words **an iron fist/hand** when describing the way that sb behaves, you mean that they treat people severely. This treatment may be hidden behind a kind appearance (the **velvet glove**).
the ˈIron Age *noun* [sing.] the historical period about 3000 years ago when people first used iron tools
**iron-clad** /ˈaɪənklæd; *NAmE* -ərn-/ *adj.* so strong that it cannot be challenged or changed: *an ironclad alibi/contract/excuse/guarantee* ◇ *His memo is ironclad proof he was involved.* ◦ compare CAST-IRON (2)
the ˌIron ˈCurtain *noun* [sing.] the name that people used for the border that used to exist between Western Europe and the COMMUNIST countries of Central and Eastern Europe
**iron-ic** [C1] /aɪˈrɒnɪk; *NAmE* -ˈrɑːn-/ (*also less frequent* **iron-ic-al** /aɪˈrɒnɪkl; *NAmE* -ˈrɑːn-/) **1** [C1] showing that you really mean the opposite of what you are saying; expressing IRONY: *an ironic comment* **2** [C1] (of a situation) strange or funny because it is very different from what you expect: *it is ~ that… It's ironic that she became a teacher—she used to hate school.* ◦ see also IRONY
**iron-ic-al-ly** [C1] /aɪˈrɒnɪkli; *NAmE* -ˈrɑːn-/ *adv.* **1** [C1] in a way that shows that you really mean the opposite of what you are saying; in a way that expresses irony: *He smiled ironically.* **2** [C1] in a way that is strange or funny because it is very different from what you expect: *Ironically, the book she felt was her worst sold more copies than any of her others.*
**iron-ing** /ˈaɪənɪŋ; *NAmE* -ərn-/ *noun* [U] **1** the task of pressing clothes, etc. with an iron to make them smooth: *to do the ironing* **2** the clothes, etc. that you have just ironed or that need to be ironed: *a pile of ironing*
ˈironing board *noun* a long narrow board covered with cloth, and usually with folding legs, that you iron clothes on

ironing board
iron

**iron-mon-ger** /ˈaɪənmʌŋɡə(r); *NAmE* -ərnmɑːŋ-/ (*BrE*, old-fashioned) (*NAmE* ˈhardware dealer) *noun* **1** a person who owns or works in a shop selling tools and equipment for the house and garden **2** **ironmonger's** (*pl.* **iron-mon-gers**) (*BrE also* ˈhardware shop, *BrE and NAmE* ˈhardware store) a shop that sells tools and equipment for the house and garden ▸ **iron-mon-gery** /-ɡəri/ *noun* [U] (*BrE*) = HARDWARE
ˈiron rations *noun* [pl.] (*often humorous*) a small amount of food that soldiers and people walking or climbing carry to use in an emergency
**iron-stone** /ˈaɪənstəʊn; *NAmE* -ərn-/ *noun* [U] a type of rock that contains iron
**iron-work** /ˈaɪənwɜːk; *NAmE* -ərnwɜːrk/ *noun* [U] things made of iron, such as gates, parts of buildings, etc.
**iron-works** /ˈaɪənwɜːks; *NAmE* -ərnwɜːrks/ *noun* (*pl.* **iron-works**) [C + sing./pl. v.] a factory where iron is obtained from ORE (= rock containing metal), or where heavy iron goods are made
**irony** [C1] /ˈaɪrəni/ *noun* (*pl.* **-ies**) **1** [C1] [U, C] the funny or strange aspect of a situation that is very different from what you expect; a situation like this: *It was one of life's little ironies.* ◇ *the ~ (is) that… The irony is that when he finally got the job, he discovered he didn't like it.* **2** [C1] [U] the use of words that say the opposite of what you really mean, often as a joke and with a tone of voice that shows this: *'England is famous for its food,' she said with heavy irony.* ◇ *There was a note of irony in his voice.* ◇ *She said it without a hint/trace of irony.* ◦ see also DRAMATIC IRONY

**ir-radi-ance** /ɪˈreɪdiəns/ *noun* [U] (*physics*) a measurement of the amount of light that comes from sth
**ir-radi-ate** /ɪˈreɪdieɪt/ *verb* **1** ~ sb/sth to expose sb/sth to RADIATION **2** ~ sth (*specialist*) to treat food with GAMMA RADIATION in order to preserve it **3** ~ sth (with sth) (*literary*) to make sth look brighter and happier: *faces irradiated with joy* ▸ **ir-radi-ation** /ɪˌreɪdiˈeɪʃn/ *noun* [U]
**ir-ration-al** /ɪˈræʃənl/ *adj.* not based on, or not using, clear logical thought **SYN** **unreasonable**: *an irrational fear* ◇ *You're being irrational.* **OPP** **rational** ▸ **ir-ration-al-ity** /ɪˌræʃəˈnæləti/ *noun* [U, C, usually sing.] **ir-ration-al-ly** /ɪˈræʃnəli/ *adv.*: *to behave irrationally*
**ir-re-con-cil-able** /ɪˌrekənˈsaɪləbl, ɪˈrekənsaɪləbl/ *adj.* (*formal*) **1** if differences or DISAGREEMENTS are **irreconcilable**, they are so great that it is not possible to settle them **2** if an idea or opinion is **irreconcilable** with another, it is impossible for sb to have both of them together: *This view is irreconcilable with common sense.* **3** people who are **irreconcilable** cannot be made to agree: *irreconcilable enemies*
**ir-re-cov-er-able** /ˌɪrɪˈkʌvərəbl/ *adj.* (*formal*) that you cannot get back; lost: *irrecoverable costs* ◇ *irrecoverable loss of sight* **OPP** **recoverable** ▸ **ir-re-cov-er-ably** /-bli/ *adv.*
**ir-re-deem-able** /ˌɪrɪˈdiːməbl/ *adj.* (*formal*) too bad to be corrected, improved or saved **SYN** **hopeless** ▸ **ir-re-deem-ably** /-bli/ *adv.*: *irredeemably spoilt*
**ir-re-du-cible** /ˌɪrɪˈdjuːsəbl; *NAmE* -ˈduː-/ *adj.* (*formal*) that cannot be made smaller or simpler: *to cut staff to an irreducible minimum* ◇ *an irreducible fact* ▸ **ir-re-du-cibly** /-bli/ *adv.*
**ir-re-fut-able** /ˌɪrɪˈfjuːtəbl, ɪˈrefjətəbl/ *adj.* (*formal*) that cannot be proved wrong and that must therefore be accepted: *irrefutable evidence* ▸ **ir-re-fut-ably** /-bli/ *adv.*
**ir-regu-lar** /ɪˈreɡjələ(r)/ *adj., noun*
■ *adj.* **1** not arranged in an even way; not having an even, smooth pattern or shape **SYN** **uneven**: *irregular teeth* ◇ *an irregular outline* **2** not happening at times that are at an equal distance from each other; not happening regularly: *irregular meals* ◇ *an irregular heartbeat* ◇ *irregular attendance at school* ◇ *He visited his parents at irregular intervals.* **3** not normal; not according to the usual rules **SYN** **abnormal**: *an irregular practice* ◇ *His behaviour is highly irregular.* **4** (*grammar*) not formed in the normal way: *an irregular verb* **5** (of a soldier, etc.) not part of a country's official army **OPP** **regular** ▸ **ir-regu-lar-ly** *adv.*
■ *noun* a soldier who is not a member of a country's official army
**ir-regu-lar-ity** /ɪˌreɡjəˈlærəti/ *noun* (*pl.* **-ies**) **1** [C, U] an activity or a practice that is not according to the usual rules, or not normal: *alleged irregularities in the election campaign* ◇ *suspicion of financial irregularity* **2** [C, U] something that does not happen at regular INTERVALS: *a slight irregularity in his heartbeat* **3** [U, C] something that is not smooth or regular in shape or arrangement: *The paint will cover any irregularity in the surface of the walls.* ◦ compare REGULARITY
**ir-rele-vance** /ɪˈreləvəns/ (*also less frequent* **ir-rele-vancy** /ɪˈreləvənsi/ *pl.* **-ies**) *noun* **1** [U] lack of importance to or connection with a situation: *the irrelevance of the curriculum to children's daily life* **OPP** **relevance** **2** [C, usually sing.] something that is not important to or connected with a situation: *His idea was rejected as an irrelevance.*
**ir-rele-vant** [C1] [W] /ɪˈreləvənt/ *adj.* not important to or connected with a situation: *totally/completely/largely irrelevant* ◇ *irrelevant remarks* ◇ *Whether I believe you or not is irrelevant now.* ◇ *~ to sth/sb That evidence is*

# irreligious

irrelevant to the case. ◊ Many people consider politics irrelevant to their lives. **OPP** relevant ▶ **ir·rel·ev·ant·ly** adv.

**ir·re·li·gious** /ˌɪrɪˈlɪdʒəs/ adj. (formal) without any religious belief; showing no respect for religion

**ir·re·me·di·able** /ˌɪrɪˈmiːdiəbl/ adj. (formal) too bad to be corrected or cured: *an irremediable situation* ▶ **ir·re·me·di·ably** /-bli/ adv.

**ir·rep·ar·able** /ɪˈrepərəbl/ adj. (of a loss, injury, etc.) too bad or too serious to repair or put right: *to cause irreparable damage/harm to your health* ◊ *Her death is an irreparable loss.* **OPP** repairable ▶ **ir·rep·ar·ably** /-bli/ adv.: *irreparably damaged*

**ir·re·place·able** /ˌɪrɪˈpleɪsəbl/ adj. too valuable or special to be replaced ⊃ SYNONYMS at VALUABLE **OPP** replaceable

**ir·re·press·ible** /ˌɪrɪˈpresəbl/ adj. **1** (of a person) lively, happy and full of energy **SYN** ebullient: *The irrepressible Kane scored two goals.* **2** (of feelings, etc.) very strong; impossible to control or stop: *irrepressible confidence* ▶ **ir·re·press·ibly** /-bli/ adv.

**ir·re·proach·able** /ˌɪrɪˈprəʊtʃəbl/ adj. (of a person or their behaviour) free from fault and impossible to criticize **SYN** blameless

**ir·re·sist·ible** /ˌɪrɪˈzɪstəbl/ adj. **1** so strong that it cannot be stopped or resisted: *I felt an irresistible urge to laugh.* ◊ *His arguments were irresistible.* **2** so attractive that you feel you must have it: *an irresistible bargain* ◊ *On such a hot day, the water was irresistible* (= it made you want to swim in it). ◊ ~ **to sb** *The bright colours were irresistible to the baby.* ▶ **ir·re·sist·ibly** /-bli/ adv.: *They were irresistibly drawn to each other.*

**ir·res·ol·ute** /ɪˈrezəluːt/ adj. (formal) not able to decide what to do **OPP** resolute ▶ **ir·res·ol·ute·ly** adv. **ir·res·ol·u·tion** /ɪˌrezəˈluːʃn/ noun [U]

**ir·re·spect·ive of** /ˌɪrɪˈspektɪv əv/ prep. without considering sth or being influenced by it **SYN** regardless of: *Everyone is treated equally, irrespective of race.* ◊ *The weekly rent is the same irrespective of whether there are three or four occupants.*

**ir·re·spon·sible** /ˌɪrɪˈspɒnsəbl/ NAmE -ˈspɑːn-/ adj. (disapproving) (of a person) not thinking enough about the effects of what they do; not showing a feeling of responsibility: *an irresponsible teenager* ◊ *an irresponsible attitude* ◊ *It would be irresponsible to ignore the situation.* **OPP** responsible ▶ **ir·re·spon·si·bil·ity** /ˌɪrɪspɒnsəˈbɪləti; NAmE -spɑːn-/ noun [U] **ir·re·spon·sibly** /ˌɪrɪˈspɒnsəbli; NAmE -spɑːn-/ adv.

**ir·re·triev·able** /ˌɪrɪˈtriːvəbl/ adj. (formal) that you can never make right or get back: *an irretrievable situation* ◊ *the irretrievable breakdown of the marriage* ◊ *The money already paid is irretrievable.* ◊ *Some of the data is irretrievable.* **OPP** retrievable ▶ **ir·re·triev·ably** /-bli/ adv.: *Some of our old traditions are irretrievably lost.*

**ir·rev·er·ent** /ɪˈrevərənt/ adj. (usually approving) not showing respect to sb/sth that other people usually respect: *irreverent wit* ◊ *an irreverent attitude to tradition* ▶ **ir·rev·er·ence** /-rəns/ noun [U] **ir·rev·er·ent·ly** adv.

**ir·re·vers·ible** /ˌɪrɪˈvɜːsəbl; NAmE -ˈvɜːrs-/ adj. that cannot be changed back to what it was before: *an irreversible change/decline/decision* ◊ *irreversible brain damage* (= that will not improve) **OPP** reversible ▶ **ir·re·vers·ibly** /-bli/ adv.

**ir·re·voc·able** /ɪˈrevəkəbl/ adj. (formal) that cannot be changed **SYN** final: *an irrevocable decision/step* ▶ **ir·rev·oc·ably** /-bli/ adv.: *irrevocably committed*

**ir·ri·gate** /ˈɪrɪɡeɪt/ verb **1** ~ **sth** to supply water to an area of land, typically through pipes or channels, so that crops will grow: *irrigated land/crops* **2** ~ **sth** (medical) to wash out a wound or part of the body with a flow of water or liquid ▶ **ir·ri·ga·tion** /ˌɪrɪˈɡeɪʃn/ noun [U]: *irrigation channels*

**ir·rit·able** /ˈɪrɪtəbl/ adj. getting annoyed easily; showing your anger **SYN** bad-tempered: *to be tired and irritable* ◊ *an irritable gesture* ▶ **ir·rit·abil·ity** /ˌɪrɪtəˈbɪləti/ noun [U] **ir·rit·ably** /ˈɪrɪtəbli/ adv.

**irritable ˈbowel syndrome** noun [U] (abbr. **IBS**) a condition of the BOWELS that causes pain and DIARRHOEA or CONSTIPATION, often caused by stress or worry

**ir·ri·tant** /ˈɪrɪtənt/ noun **1** (specialist) a substance that makes part of your body painful **2** something that makes you annoyed or causes trouble ▶ **ir·ri·tant** adj. [usually before noun]: *irritant substances*

**ir·ri·tate** /ˈɪrɪteɪt/ verb **1** ~ **sb** to annoy sb, especially by sth you continuously do or by sth that continuously happens: *The way she puts on that accent really irritates me.* **2** ~ **sth** to make your skin or a part of your body painful: *Some drugs can irritate the lining of the stomach.* ▶ **ir·ri·tat·ing** adj.: *I found her extremely irritating.* ◊ *an irritating habit* ◊ *an irritating cough/rash* **ir·ri·tat·ing·ly** adv. **ir·ri·ta·tion** /ˌɪrɪˈteɪʃn/ noun [U, C]: *He noted, with some irritation, that the letter had not been sent.* ◊ *a skin irritation*

**ir·ri·tated** /ˈɪrɪteɪtɪd/ adj. ~ **(at/by/with sth)** annoyed or angry: *She was getting more and more irritated at his comments.*

**ir·rupt** /ɪˈrʌpt/ verb [I] + adv./prep. (formal) to enter or appear somewhere suddenly and with a lot of force: *Violence once again irrupted into their peaceful lives.* ▶ **ir·rup·tion** /ɪˈrʌpʃn/ noun [U, C]

**IRS** /ˌaɪ ɑː ˈes; NAmE ɑːr/ abbr. (in the US) the INTERNAL REVENUE SERVICE

**is** /ɪz/ ⊃ BE verb

**Is.** abbr. (especially on maps) Island(s); ISLE

**ISA**[1] /ˈaɪsə/ noun Individual Savings Account (a special account in the UK in which you can invest a limited amount each year without paying tax on the income)

**ISA**[2] /ˈaɪsə; ˌaɪ es ˈeɪ/ abbr. Industry Standard Architecture (the usual international system used for connecting computers and other devices)

**-isation, -isationally** ⊃ -IZATION

**ISBN** /ˌaɪ es biː ˈen/ noun a number that identifies an individual book and its PUBLISHER (the abbreviation for 'International Standard Book Number')

**is·chae·mia** (NAmE **is·che·mia**) /ɪˈskiːmiə/ noun [U] (medical) the situation when the supply of blood to an organ or part of the body, especially the heart muscles, is less than is needed

**ISDN** /ˌaɪ es diː ˈen/ abbr. integrated services digital network (a system for carrying sound signals, images, etc. along wires at high speed): *an ISDN internet connection*

**-ise** ⊃ -IZE

**ish** /ɪʃ/ adv. (BrE, informal) used after a statement to make it less definite: *I've finished. Ish. I still need to make the sauce.*

**-ish** /ɪʃ/ suffix (in adjectives) **1** from the country indicated: *Turkish* ◊ *Irish* **2** (sometimes disapproving) having the nature of; like: *childish* **3** fairly; approximately: *reddish* ◊ *thirtyish* ▶ **-ishly** /ɪʃli/ (in adverbs): *foolishly*

**isikuti** /ˌɪsiˈkuːti/ EAfrE [isiˈkuti] noun [U] (EAfrE) = ESIKUTI

**isi·Xhosa** /ˌɪsiˈkəʊsə, -ˈkɔːsə/ (also **Xhosa**) noun [U] the language spoken by the Xhosa people in South Africa

**isi·Zulu** /ˌɪsiˈzuːluː/ (also **Zulu**) noun [U] the language spoken by the Zulus and many other black South Africans

**Islam** /ˈɪzlɑːm, ɪzˈlɑːm/ noun [U] **1** the Muslim religion, based on belief in one God and revealed through Muhammad as the Prophet of Allah **2** all Muslims and Muslim countries in the world ▶ **Is·lam·ic** /ɪzˈlæmɪk, -ˈlɑːm-/ adj.: *Islamic law*

**Is·lam·ist** /ˈɪzləmɪst/ noun a person who believes strongly in the teachings of Islam ▶ **Is·lam·ism** /-mɪzəm/ noun [U] **Is·lam·ist** adj.

**is·land** ❶ **A1** /ˈaɪlənd/ noun **1** **A1** (abbr. **I., l., Is.**) a piece of land that is completely surrounded by water: *a small/tiny island* ◊ *a remote island off the coast of Scotland* ◊ *the Virgin Islands* ◊ **~ of ...** *the resort island of Bali* ◊ **on an ~** *We spent a week on the Greek island of Kos.* ◊ *an*

**island nation/state** ⇒ see also DESERT ISLAND **2** (*BrE*) = TRAFFIC ISLAND ⇒ see also SAFETY ISLAND

**is·land·er** /ˈaɪləndə(r)/ *noun* a person who lives on an island, especially a small one

**ˈisland-hopping** *noun* [U] the activity of travelling from one island to another in an area that has lots of islands, especially as a tourist

**isle** /aɪl/ *noun* (*abbr.* **I, I., Is.**) used especially in poetry and names to mean 'island': *the Isle of Skye* ◊ *the British Isles* ⇒ see also EMERALD ISLE

**islet** /ˈaɪlət/ *noun* a very small island

**ism** /ˈɪzəm/ *noun* (*usually disapproving*) used to refer to a set of ideas or system of beliefs or behaviour: *You're always talking in isms—sexism, ageism, racism.*

**-ism** /ɪzəm/ *suffix* (in nouns) **1** the action or result of: *criticism* **2** the state or quality of: *heroism* **3** the teaching, system or movement of: *Buddhism* **4** unfair treatment or feelings of hate for the reason mentioned: *racism* **5** a feature of language of the type mentioned: *an Americanism* ◊ *a colloquialism* **6** a medical condition or disease: *alcoholism*

**isn't** /ˈɪznt/ *short form* is not

**ISO** /ˌaɪ es ˈəʊ/ *abbr.* International Organization for Standardization (an organization established in 1946 to make the measurements used in science, industry and business standard throughout the world)

**iso-** /ˈaɪsəʊ, aɪsə; *BrE also* aɪˈsɒ; *NAmE also* aɪˈsɑː/ *combining form* (in nouns, adjectives and adverbs) equal: *isotope* ◊ *isometric*

**iso·bar** /ˈaɪsəbɑː(r)/ *noun* (*specialist*) a line on a weather map that joins places that have the same air pressure at a particular time

**isol·ate** ?+ B2 /ˈaɪsəleɪt/ *verb* **1** ?+ B2 to separate sb/sth physically or socially from other people or things: *~sb/yourself/sth Patients with the disease should be isolated.* ◊ *~sb/yourself/sth from sb/sth He was immediately isolated from the other prisoners.* ◊ *This decision will isolate the country from the rest of Europe.* **2** ?+ C1 ~sth (from sth) (*formal*) to separate a part of a situation, problem, idea, etc. so that you can see what it is and deal with it separately: *It is possible to isolate a number of factors that contributed to her downfall.* **3** ~sth (from sth) (*specialist*) to separate a single substance, cell, etc. from others so that you can study it: *Researchers are still trying to isolate the gene that causes this abnormality.*

**isol·ated** ?+ B2 W /ˈaɪsəleɪtɪd/ *adj.* **1** ?+ B2 (of buildings and places) far away from any others SYN **remote**: *isolated rural areas* ⇒ WORDFINDER NOTE at LOCATION **2** ?+ B2 without much contact with other people or other countries: *I felt very isolated in my new job.* ◊ *Elderly people easily become socially isolated.* ◊ *The decision left the country isolated from its allies.* **3** ?+ C1 single; happening once: *The police said the attack was an isolated incident.*

**isol·ation** ?+ C1 W /ˌaɪsəˈleɪʃn/ *noun* [U] **1** ?+ C1 the act of separating sb/sth; the state of being separate: *geographical isolation* ◊ *an isolation hospital/ward* (= for people with infectious diseases) ◊ *~(from sb/sth) The country has been threatened with complete isolation from the international community unless the atrocities stop.* ◊ *He lives in splendid isolation* (= far from, or in a superior position to, everyone else). **2** ?+ C1 ~(from sb/sth) the state of being alone or lonely: *Many unemployed people experience feelings of isolation and depression.*
**IDM** **in isolation (from sb/sth)** separately; alone: *To make sense, these figures should not be looked at in isolation.*

**isol·ation·ism** /ˌaɪsəˈleɪʃənɪzəm/ *noun* [U] the policy of not becoming involved in the affairs of other countries or groups ▸ **isol·ation·ist** /-nɪst/ *adj., noun: an isolationist foreign policy*

**iso·mer** /ˈaɪsəmə(r)/ *noun* **1** (*chemistry*) one of two or more COMPOUNDS that have the same ATOMS, but in different arrangements **2** (*physics*) one of two or more NUCLEI that have the same ATOMIC NUMBER, but different energy states ▸ **iso·mer·ic** /ˌaɪsəˈmerɪk/ *adj.* **iso·mer·ism** /aɪˈsɒmərɪzəm; *NAmE* -ˈsɑːm-/ *noun* [U]

---

843

---

# issue

**iso·met·ric** /ˌaɪsəˈmetrɪk/ *adj.* **1** (*specialist*) relating to a type of physical exercise in which muscles are made to work by CONTRACTING without any change that can be noticed in the length of muscle **2** (*geometry*) relating to a style of drawing in three DIMENSIONS without perspective

**iso·met·rics** /ˌaɪsəˈmetrɪks/ *noun* [pl.] physical exercises in which the muscles work against each other or against a fixed object

**isos·celes tri·angle** /aɪˌsɒsəliːz ˈtraɪæŋɡl; *NAmE* -ˌsɑːs-/ *noun* (*geometry*) a flat shape with two of its three straight sides the same length ⇒ picture at TRIANGLE

**iso·therm** /ˈaɪsəθɜːm; *NAmE* -θɜːrm/ *noun* (*specialist*) a line on a weather map that joins places that have the same temperature at a particular time

**iso·ton·ic** /ˌaɪsəʊˈtɒnɪk; *NAmE* -ˈtɑːn-/ *adj.* (of a drink) with added minerals and salts, intended to replace those lost during exercise

**iso·tope** /ˈaɪsətəʊp/ *noun* (*physics, chemistry*) one of two or more forms of a chemical element that have the same number of PROTONS but a different number of NEUTRONS in their ATOMS. They have different physical properties (= characteristics) but the same chemical ones: *radioactive isotopes* ◊ *the many isotopes of carbon*

**ISP** /ˌaɪ es ˈpiː/ *abbr.* internet service provider (a company that provides you with an internet connection and services such as email, etc.)

**I-spy** /ˌaɪ ˈspaɪ/ *noun* [U] a children's game in which one player gives the first letter of a thing that they can see and the others have to guess what it is

**Is·rael·ite** /ˈɪzrəlaɪt; *NAmE* -riə-/ *noun* a member of the ancient Hebrew nation described in the Bible

**issue** 🅘 B1 🅞 /ˈɪʃuː/ *noun, verb*
■ *noun*
• **TOPIC OF DISCUSSION 1** ? B1 [C] an important topic that people are discussing or arguing about: *a key/big/major issue* ◊ *Teacher education has become a political issue.* ◊ *They discussed a number of important environmental issues.* ◊ *Her work deals with issues of race and identity.* ◊ *The union plans to raise the issue of overtime.* ◊ *We really need to focus on the key issues and not get sidetracked.* ◊ *The meeting included discussion of a range of issues.* ⇒ see also SIDE ISSUE, WEDGE ISSUE
• **PROBLEM/WORRY 2** ? B2 [C] a problem or worry that sb has with sth: *The community is working together to address social issues and problems.* ◊ *All technical issues have now been resolved.* ◊ *Serious issues arose during the development of the new product.* ◊ *Money is not an issue.* ◊ *I'm not bothered about the cost—you're the one who's making it an issue.* ◊ *~about/around sb/sth She's always on a diet—she has issues about food.* ◊ *~with sb/sth He still has some issues with women* (= has some problems dealing with them). ⇒ see also NON-ISSUE
• **MAGAZINE/NEWSPAPER 3** [C] one of a regular series of magazines or newspapers: *the July issue of 'What Car?'* ◊ *The article appeared in issue 25.* ⇒ see also BACK ISSUE
• **OF STAMPS/COINS/SHARES 4** [C] a number or set of things that are supplied and made available at the same time: *The company is planning a new share issue.* ◊ *a special issue of stamps* ⇒ see also STANDARD ISSUE
• **MAKING AVAILABLE/KNOWN 5** [U] the act of supplying or making available things for people to buy or use: *I bought a set of the new stamps on the date of issue.* ◊ *~of sth to sb the issue of blankets to the refugees* ⇒ see also RIGHTS ISSUE **6** [U] the act of formally making sth known to people: *the issue of a joint statement by the French and German foreign ministers*
• **CHILDREN 7** [U] (*law*) children of your own: *He died without issue.*
**IDM** **be at ˈissue** to be the most important part of the subject that is being discussed: *What is at issue is whether she was responsible for her actions.* **take ˈissue with sb (about/on/over sth)** (*formal*) to start disagreeing or arguing with sb about sth: *I must take issue with you on that point.* ⇒ more at FORCE *v.*

---

| ʊ actual | aɪ my | aʊ now | eɪ say | əʊ go | ɔɪ boy | ɪə near | eə hair | ʊə pure |

# -ist

■ **verb**
- **MAKE KNOWN 1** ⓘ B2 to make sth known formally: ~ **sth** They **issued** a joint **statement** denying the charges. ◇ A warning was **issued** yesterday by the government, asking people to stay in their homes. ◇ ~ **sth to sb** The president has the authority to **issue orders** to the military.
- **GIVE 2** ⓘ B2 to give sth to sb, especially officially: ~ **sth** to issue a licence/certificate/permit/ticket ◇ ~ **sb sth** The authorities refused to issue him a visa. ◇ ~ **sb with sth** New members will be issued with a temporary identity card. ◇ ~ **sth to sb** Work permits were issued to only 5% of those who applied for them.
- **LAW 3** ~ **sth** to start a legal process against sb, especially by means of an official document: to issue a writ against sb ◇ A warrant has been issued for his arrest.
- **MAGAZINE 4** ~ **sth** to produce sth such as a magazine, article, etc: We issue a monthly newsletter.
- **STAMPS/COINS/SHARES 5** ~ **sth** to produce new stamps, coins, shares, etc. for sale to the public: They issued a special set of stamps to mark the occasion.

PHRV **ˈissue from sth** (formal) to come out of sth: A weak trembling sound issued from his lips. ▶ **is·su·er** noun: credit-card issuers

**-ist** /ɪst/ suffix (in nouns and some related adjectives) **1** a person who believes or practises sth: atheist **2** a member of a profession or business activity: dentist **3** a person who uses a thing: violinist **4** a person who does sth: plagiarist

**-ista** /ɪstə, iːstə/ suffix (often disapproving) (in nouns) a person who is very enthusiastic about sth: fashionistas who are slaves to the latest trends ⊃ see also BARISTA

**isth·mus** /ˈɪsməs/ noun a narrow piece of land, with water on each side, that joins two larger pieces of land

**IT** ⓘ B1 /ˌaɪ ˈtiː/ noun [U] the study and use of electronic processes and equipment to store and send information of all kinds, including words, pictures and numbers (the abbreviation for 'information technology'): the increasing use of IT in all aspects of today's society ◇ **in~** I've worked in IT for 30 years. ◇ the **IT industry/sector** ◇ an **IT company/department**

**it** ⓘ A1 /ɪt/ pron. (used as the subject or object of a verb or after a preposition) **1** ⓘ A1 used to refer to an animal or a thing that has already been mentioned or that is being talked about now: 'Where's your car?' 'It's in the garage.' ◇ Did you see it? ◇ The other room has two beds in it. ◇ Look! It's going up that tree. ◇ We have $500. Will it be enough for a deposit? **2** ⓘ A1 used to refer to a baby, especially one whose sex is not known: Her baby's due next month. She hopes it will be a boy. **3** ⓘ A1 used to identify a person: It's your mother on the phone. ◇ Hello, Peter, it's Mike here. ◇ Hi, it's me! ◇ Was it you who put these books on my desk? **4** ⓘ A1 used in the position of the subject of a verb when you are talking about time, the date, distance, the weather, etc: It's ten past twelve. ◇ It's our anniversary. ◇ It's two miles to the beach. ◇ It's a long time since they left. ◇ It was raining this morning. ◇ It's quite warm at the moment. **5** ⓘ A2 used to refer to a fact or situation that is already known or happening: When the factory closes, it will mean 500 people losing their jobs. ◇ Yes, I was at home on Sunday. What about it? (= Why do you ask?) ◇ Stop it, you're hurting me! **6** ⓘ A2 used in the position of the subject or object of a verb when the real subject or object is at the end of the sentence: Does it matter what colour it is? ◇ It's impossible to get there in time. ◇ It's no use shouting. ◇ She finds it boring at home. ◇ It appears that the two leaders are holding secret talks. ◇ I find it strange that she doesn't want to go. ⊃ **LANGUAGE BANK** at IMPERSONAL **7** ⓘ A2 used when you are talking about a situation: If it's convenient I can come tomorrow. ◇ It's good to talk. ◇ I like it here. **8** ⓘ A2 used to emphasize any part of a sentence: It's Jim who's the clever one. ◇ It's Spain that they're going to, not Portugal. ◇ It was three weeks later that he heard the news. **9** exactly what is needed: In this business, either you've got it or you haven't. ⊃ see also ITS

IDM **that is ˈit 1** this/that is the important point, reason, etc: That's just it—I can't work when you're making so much noise. **2** this/that is the end: I'm afraid that's it—we've lost. **ˈthis is ˈit 1** the expected event is just going to happen: Well, this is it! Wish me luck. **2** this is the main point: 'You're doing too much.' 'Well, this is it. I can't cope with any more work.'

**Ital·ian·ate** /ɪˈtæljəneɪt/ adj. in an Italian style: an Italianate villa

**ital·ic** /ɪˈtælɪk/ adj. (of letters that are printed, written or on screen) leaning to the right: The example sentences in this dictionary are printed in italic type. ◇ Use an italic font. ⊃ compare ROMAN

**itali·cize** (BrE also **-ise**) /ɪˈtælɪsaɪz/ verb [often passive] ~ **sth** to write, type or print sth in italics

**ital·ics** /ɪˈtælɪks/ noun [pl.] (also **italic** [sing.]) letters that lean to the right: Examples in this dictionary are in italics. ◇ Use italics for the names of books or plays. ⊃ compare ROMAN

**Italo-** /ɪtæləʊ/ combining form (with nouns and adjectives) Italian; Italian and something else: Italo-Americans ◇ Italophiles

**itch** /ɪtʃ/ verb, noun
■ **verb 1** [I] to have an uncomfortable feeling on your skin that makes you want to SCRATCH (= rub your skin with your nails); to make your skin feel like this: I itch all over. ◇ Does the rash itch? ◇ This sweater really itches. ⊃ SYNONYMS at HURT **2** [I] (informal) (often used in the progressive tenses) to want to do sth very much: ~ **for sth** The crowd was itching for a fight. ◇ ~ **to do sth** He's itching to get back to work.
■ **noun 1** [C, usually sing.] an uncomfortable feeling on your skin that makes you want to SCRATCH yourself (= rub your skin with your nails): to get/have an itch **2** [sing.] ~ **(to do sth)** (informal) a strong desire to do sth: She has an itch to travel. ◇ the creative itch IDM see SEVEN

**itchy** /ˈɪtʃi/ adj. having or producing an itch on the skin: an itchy nose/rash ◇ I feel itchy all over. ⊃ SYNONYMS at PAINFUL ▶ **itchi·ness** noun [U]

IDM **get/have itchy ˈfeet** (informal) to want to travel or move to a different place; to want to do sth different

**it'd** /ˈɪtəd/ short form **1** it had **2** it would

**-ite** /aɪt/ suffix (in nouns) (often disapproving) a person who follows or supports sb/sth: Blairite ◇ Trotskyite

**item** ⓘ A2 W /ˈaɪtəm/ noun **1** ⓘ A2 one thing on a list of things to buy, do, talk about, etc: What's the next item on the agenda? **2** ⓘ B1 a single object or thing: Can I pay for each item separately? ◇ **food/household items** ◇ ~ **of sth** A windproof jacket is an essential **item of clothing** for hillwalking. ⊃ see also COLLECTOR'S ITEM **3** ⓘ B1 a single piece of news in a newspaper, on television, online, etc: The following **news item** may be of interest to you.

IDM **be an ˈitem** (informal) to be involved in a romantic or sexual relationship: Are they an item?

**item·ize** (BrE also **-ise**) /ˈaɪtəmaɪz/ verb ~ **sth** to produce a detailed list of things: The report itemizes 23 different faults. ◇ an itemized phone bill (= each call is shown separately)

**it·er·ate** /ˈɪtəreɪt/ verb [I] to repeat a MATHEMATICAL or COMPUTING process or set of instructions again and again, each time applying it to the result of the previous stage

**it·er·ation** /ˌɪtəˈreɪʃn/ noun **1** [U, C] the process of repeating a MATHEMATICAL or COMPUTING process or set of instructions again and again, each time applying it to the result of the previous stage **2** [C] a new version of a piece of computer software

**it·era·tive** /ˈɪtərətɪv; NAmE -reɪt-, -rət-/ adj. (of a process) that involves repeating a process or set of instructions again and again, each time applying it to the result of the previous stage: We used an iterative process of refinement and modification.

**it·in·er·ant** /aɪˈtɪnərənt/ adj. [usually before noun] (formal) travelling from place to place, especially to find work: itinerant workers/musicians ◇ to lead an itinerant life ▶ **it·in·er·ant** noun: homeless itinerants

**it·in·er·ary** /aɪˈtɪnərəri; NAmE -reri/ noun (pl. -ies) a plan of a journey, including the route and the places that you visit ⊃ **WORDFINDER NOTE** at JOURNEY

**-ition** ⊃ -ION

**-itis** /aɪtɪs/ suffix (in nouns) **1** (medical) a disease of: tonsillitis **2** (informal, especially humorous) too much of; too much interest in: World Cup-itis

**it'll** /ˈɪtl/ short form it will

**its** ❶ **A1** /ɪts/ det. belonging to or connected with a thing, an animal or a baby: Turn the box on its side. ◊ Have you any idea of its value? ◊ The dog had hurt its paw. ◊ The baby threw its food on the floor.

**it's** /ɪts/ short form **1** it is **2** it has **HELP** It's is only used to mean 'it has' when has is an auxiliary verb: It's just stopped raining. When has is the main verb, use the full form: It has some great new features. ◊ It's some great new features.

**it·self** ❶ **A2** /ɪtˈself/ pron. **1** ❓ **A2** (the reflexive form of it) used when the animal or thing that does an action is also affected by it: The cat was washing itself. ◊ Does the computer turn itself off? ◊ The company has got itself into difficulties. ◊ There's no need for the team to feel proud of itself. **2** ❓ **B1** used to emphasize an animal, a thing, etc: The village itself is pretty, but the surrounding countryside is rather dull.
**IDM** be ˌpatience, ˌhonesty, simˌplicity, etc. itˈself to be an example of complete PATIENCE, etc: The manager of the hotel was courtesy itself. (all) by itˈself **1** AUTOMATICALLY; without anyone doing anything: The machine will start by itself in a few seconds. **2** alone: The house stands by itself in an acre of land. in itˈself considered separately from other things; in its true nature: In itself, it's not a difficult problem to solve. (all) to itˈself for only it to have or use; not shared with others: The company doesn't have the market to itself.

**itty-bitty** /ˌɪti ˈbɪti/ (also itsy-bitsy /ˌɪtsi ˈbɪtsi/) adj. [only before noun] (especially NAmE, informal) very small

**ITV** /ˌaɪ tiː ˈviː/ abbr. Independent Television (a group of British companies that produce programmes that are paid for by advertising)

**-ity** /əti/ suffix (in nouns) the quality or state of: purity ◊ oddity

**IUD** /ˌaɪ juː ˈdiː/ (also **coil**) noun a small plastic or metal object placed inside a woman's UTERUS (= where a baby grows before it is born) to stop her becoming pregnant (the abbreviation for 'intrauterine device')

**IV** /ˌaɪ ˈviː/ abbr., noun
■ abbr. INTRAVENOUS or INTRAVENOUSLY: an IV drip/infusion
■ noun (especially NAmE) = DRIP (3)

**I've** /aɪv/ short form I have **HELP** I've is usually only used when have is an auxiliary verb: I've just got here. When have is the main verb, use the full form: I have two children. ◊ I've two children.

**-ive** /ɪv/ suffix (in nouns and adjectives) tending to; having the nature of: explosive ◊ descriptive

**IVF** /ˌaɪ viː ˈef/ noun [U] (specialist) a process that FERTILIZES an egg from a woman outside her body. The egg is then put inside her UTERUS to develop. (the abbreviation for 'in vitro fertilization') ⊃ see also TEST-TUBE BABY

**ivory** /ˈaɪvəri/ (pl. -ies) noun **1** [U] a hard white substance like bone that forms the TUSKS (= long teeth) of elephants and some other animals: a ban on the ivory trade ◊ an ivory chess set **2** [C] an object made of ivory **3** [U] a pale colour between white and yellow

**ivory ˈtower** noun (disapproving) a place or situation where you are separated from the problems and practical aspects of normal life and therefore do not have to worry about or understand them: academics living in ivory towers

**ivy** /ˈaɪvi/ noun [U, C] (pl. -ies) a climbing plant, especially one with dark green shiny leaves with five points: stone walls covered in ivy ⊃ see also POISON IVY ⊃ **VISUAL VOCAB** page V7

**the ˌIvy ˈLeague** noun [sing.] a group of eight traditional universities in the eastern US with high academic standards and a high social status ⊃ compare OXBRIDGE ▶ **ˌIvy ˈLeague** adj.: Ivy League colleges

**IWB** abbr. = INTERACTIVE WHITEBOARD

**iwi** /ˈiːwi/ noun (pl. iwi) (NZE) a Maori community or people

**-ize** (BrE also -ise) /aɪz/ suffix (in verbs) **1** to become, make or make like: privatize ◊ fossilize ◊ Americanize **2** to speak, think, act, treat, etc. in the way mentioned: criticize ◊ theorize ◊ deputize ◊ pasteurize **3** to place in: hospitalize
▶ **-ization** /aɪzeɪʃn; NAmE əzeɪʃn/ (also **-isation**) (in nouns): immunization

---

Oxford Phrasal Academic Lexicon (OPAL) written and spoken word lists | Ⓦ OPAL written word list | Ⓢ OPAL spoken word list

# Jj

**J** (also **j**) /dʒeɪ/ noun [C, U] (pl. **Js**, **J's**, **j's** /dʒeɪz/) the 10th letter of the English alphabet: *'Jelly' begins with (a) J/'J'.*

**ja** /jɑː/ exclamation (SAfrE, informal) yes

**jab** /dʒæb/ verb, noun
- verb [T, I] (**-bb-**) to push a pointed object into sb/sth, or in the direction of sb/sth, with a sudden strong movement SYN prod: *~ sb/sth (in sth) (with sth) She jabbed him in the ribs with her finger.* ◊ *~ sth in sth She jabbed her finger in his ribs.* ◊ *~ (at sb/sth) (with sth) He jabbed at the picture with his finger.* ◊ *The boxer jabbed at his opponent.*
- noun **1** a sudden strong hit with sth pointed or with a FIST (= a tightly closed hand): *She gave him a jab in the stomach with her elbow.* ◊ *a boxer's left jab* **2** (BrE, informal) an INJECTION to help prevent you from catching a disease: *a flu jab*

**jab·ber** /ˈdʒæbə(r)/ verb [I, T] **~ (about sth) | + speech** (disapproving) to talk quickly and in an excited way so that it is difficult to understand what you are saying SYN **gabble**: *What is he jabbering about now?* ▶ **jab·ber** noun [U]

**jaca·randa** /ˌdʒækəˈrændə/ noun [C, U] a tropical tree with blue flowers and pleasant-smelling wood; the wood of this tree

**jack** /dʒæk/ noun, verb, adj.
- noun **1** [C] a device for raising heavy objects off the ground, especially vehicles so that a wheel can be changed **2** [C] an electronic connection between two pieces of electrical equipment **3** [C] (in a PACK of cards) a card with a picture of a young man on it, normally worth more than a ten and less than a queen: *the jack of clubs* ⇨ WORDFINDER NOTE at CARD **4** [C] (in the game of BOWLS) a small white ball towards which players roll larger balls **5** **jacks** [pl.] a children's game in which players BOUNCE a small ball and pick up small metal objects, also called jacks, before catching the ball **6** (also **jack ˈshit** taboo) [U] (NAmE, slang) (usually used in negative sentences) anything or nothing at all: *You don't know jack.* ⇨ see also BLACKJACK, FLAPJACK, UNION JACK
- IDM **a jack of ˈall trades** a person who can do many different types of work, but who perhaps does not do them very well ⇨ more at ALL RIGHT adj., WORK n.
- verb ~ **sth | ~ sb (for sth)** (NAmE, informal) to steal sth from sb, especially sth small or of low value: *Someone jacked my seat.*
- PHRV **ˌjack sb aˈround** (NAmE, informal) to treat sb in a way that is deliberately not helpful to them or wastes their time: *Let's go. We're being jacked around here.* **ˌjack ˈin/ ˈinto sth** (informal) to connect to a computer system: *I'm jacking into the internet now.* **ˌjack sth↔ˈin** (BrE, informal) to decide to stop doing sth, especially your job: *After five years, he decided to jack it all in.* **ˌjack ˈoff** (taboo, slang) (of a man) to MASTURBATE **ˌjack ˈup** (informal) to INJECT an illegal drug directly into your blood: *Drug users were jacking up in the stairwells.* **ˌjack sth↔ˈup** **1** to lift sth, especially a vehicle, off the ground using a jack **2** (informal) to increase sth, especially prices, by a large amount
- adj. [not before noun] **~ of sb/sth** (AustralE) tired of or bored with sb/sth

**jack·al** /ˈdʒækl, -kɔːl/ noun a wild animal like a dog, that eats the meat of animals that are already dead and lives in Africa and Asia

**jack·ass** /ˈdʒækæs/ noun (informal, especially NAmE) a stupid person: *Careful, you jackass!*

**jack·boot** /ˈdʒækbuːt/ noun **1** [C] a tall boot that reaches up to the knee, worn by soldiers, especially in the past **2 the jackboot** [sing.] used to refer to cruel military rule: *under the ~ to be under the jackboot of a dictatorial regime*

**ˌJack ˈcheese** noun [U] (NAmE) = MONTEREY JACK

**jack·daw** /ˈdʒækdɔː/ noun a black and grey bird of the CROW family

**jacked** /dʒækt/ (also ˌjacked ˈup) adj. (especially NAmE, informal) **1** feeling more active or having more energy because of the effects of a drug or a similar substance: *I think she was jacked on caffeine because she wouldn't stop talking.* **2** (of a person) having big muscles

**jacket** ⓘ A1 /ˈdʒækɪt/ noun **1** ⓘ A1 a piece of clothing worn on the top half of the body over a shirt, etc. that has arms and fastens down the front; a short, light coat: *a leather/denim/tweed jacket* ◊ *I have to wear a jacket and tie to work.* ⇨ see also BOMBER JACKET, DINNER JACKET, FLAK JACKET, FLIGHT JACKET, FLYING JACKET, LIFE JACKET, SMOKING JACKET, SPORTS JACKET, STRAITJACKET **2** (also ˈdust jacket) a loose paper cover for a book, usually with a design or picture on it **3** an outer cover around a hot water pipe, etc., for example to reduce loss of heat **4** (BrE) the skin of a baked potato: *potatoes baked in their jackets* **5** (especially NAmE) = SLEEVE (3)

**ˌjacket poˈtato** noun (BrE) = BAKED POTATO

**jack·fruit** /ˈdʒækfruːt/ noun **1** [C, U] a large tropical fruit **2** [C] the tree that jackfruits grow on

**jack·ham·mer** /ˈdʒækhæmə(r)/ noun (NAmE) (BrE pneuˈmatic ˈdrill) a large powerful tool, worked by air pressure, used especially for breaking up road surfaces

**ˈjack-in-the-box** noun a toy in the shape of a box with a figure inside on a spring that jumps up when you open the box

**jack·knife** /ˈdʒæknaɪf/ noun, verb
- noun (pl. **jack·knives** /-naɪvz/) a large knife with a BLADE (= cutting edge) that folds into the handle
- verb [I] to form a V-shape. For example if a lorry that is in two parts **jackknifes**, the driver loses control and the back part moves towards the front part.

**ˌjack-o'-ˈlantern** /ˌdʒæk əˈlæntən; NAmE ˌdʒæk əˈlæntərn/ noun a PUMPKIN (= a large orange vegetable) with a face cut into it and a CANDLE put inside to shine through the holes

**ˈjack plug** noun a type of PLUG used to make a connection between the parts of a SOUND SYSTEM, etc.

**jack·pot** /ˈdʒækpɒt; NAmE -pɑːt/ noun a large amount of money that is the most valuable prize in a game of chance: *to win the jackpot* ◊ *jackpot winners* ◊ (figurative) *United hit the jackpot (= were successful) with a 5–0 win over Liverpool.*

**jack·rab·bit** /ˈdʒækræbɪt/ noun a large North American HARE (= an animal like a large RABBIT) with very long ears

**ˌjack ˈshit** noun [U] (NAmE, taboo, slang) = JACK

**Jaco·bean** /ˌdʒækəˈbiːən/ adj. connected with the time when James I (1603–25) was King of England: *Jacobean drama*

**Ja·cuzzi**™ /dʒəˈkuːzi/ (also **spa** especially in NAmE) noun a large bath with a PUMP that moves the water around, giving a pleasant feeling to your body

**jade** /dʒeɪd/ noun [U] **1** a hard stone that is usually green and is used in making jewellery and beautiful objects: *a jade necklace* **2** objects made of jade: *a collection of Chinese jade* **3** (also ˌjade ˈgreen) a bright green colour

**jaded** /ˈdʒeɪdɪd/ adj. tired and bored, usually because you have had too much of sth: *I felt terribly jaded after working all weekend.* ◊ *It was a meal to tempt even the most jaded palate.*

**jag** /dʒæg/ noun (informal, especially NAmE) a short period of doing sth or of behaving in a particular way, especially in a way that you cannot control: *a crying jag*

**jagged** /ˈdʒægɪd/ adj. with rough, pointed, often sharp edges: *jagged rocks/peaks/edges*

**jag·uar** /ˈdʒægjuə(r); NAmE ˈdʒægwɑːr/ noun a large animal of the cat family, that has yellow-brown fur with black rings and spots. Jaguars live in parts of Central and South America.

**Jai** /dʒaɪ/ exclamation (IndE) used to show that you support or admire a leader, a nation, etc., or that you are pleased that they have been successful; an expression of WORSHIP to a god: *The whole crowd shouted 'Jai Mahatma!'*

**jail** ⚡+ B2 (BrE also, old-fashioned **gaol**) /dʒeɪl/ noun, verb
- noun ⚡+ B2 [U, C] a prison: *She spent a year in jail.* ◊ *He has been released from jail.* ◊ *a ten-year jail sentence* ◊ *Britain's overcrowded jails* ⇨ note at SCHOOL
- verb ⚡+ B2 [usually passive] to put sb in prison SYN **imprison**: **be jailed (for sth)** *He was jailed for life for murder.*

**jail·bait** /ˈdʒeɪlbeɪt/ noun [U] (informal) a girl or boy who is too young to have sex with legally

**jail·bird** /ˈdʒeɪlbɜːd; NAmE -bɜːrd/ noun (old-fashioned, informal) a person who has spent a lot of time in prison

**jail·break** /ˈdʒeɪlbreɪk/ noun (especially NAmE) an escape from prison, usually by several people

**jail·er** (BrE also **gaol·er**) /ˈdʒeɪlə(r)/ noun (old-fashioned) a person who guards prisoners in a prison

**jail·house** /ˈdʒeɪlhaʊs/ noun (NAmE) a prison

**Jain** /dʒeɪn/ noun a member of an Indian religion whose principles include not harming any living creature and a belief in REINCARNATION ▸ **Jain** adj. [only before noun] **Jain·ist** adj. **Jain·ism** noun [U]

**jala·peño** /ˌhæləˈpeɪnjəʊ; NAmE ˌhɑːlˈ-/ (also **jala peño ˈpepper**) noun (from Spanish) the small green fruit of a type of pepper plant, that has a very hot taste and is used in Mexican cooking

**jal·opy** /dʒəˈlɒpi; NAmE -ˈlɑːpi/ noun (pl. **-ies**) (old-fashioned, informal) an old car that is in bad condition

**jam** ❶ A2 /dʒæm/ noun, verb
- noun
- **SWEET FOOD** 1 ⚡ A2 [U, C] a thick sweet substance made by boiling fruit with sugar, often sold in JARS and spread on bread: *strawberry jam* ◊ *a jar/pot of jam* ◊ *recipes for jams and preserves* ◊ (BrE) *a jam doughnut* ⇨ compare JELLY, MARMALADE
- **MANY PEOPLE/VEHICLES** 2 [C] a situation in which it is difficult or impossible to move because there are so many people or vehicles in one particular place: *The bus was delayed in a five-mile jam.* ◊ *As fans rushed to leave, jams formed at all the exits.* ⇨ see also TRAFFIC JAM
- **MACHINE** 3 [C] a situation in which a machine does not work because sth is stuck in one position: *There's a paper jam in the photocopier.*
- IDM **be in a ˈjam** (informal) to be in a difficult situation **jam toˈmorrow** (BrE, informal) good things that are promised for the future but never happen: *They refused to settle for a promise of jam tomorrow.* ⇨ more at MONEY
- verb (-mm-)
- **PUSH WITH FORCE** 1 [T] ~ sth + adv./prep. to push sth somewhere with a lot of force: *He jammed his fingers in his ears.* ◊ *A stool had been jammed against the door.*
- **STOP MOVING/WORKING** 2 [I, T] to become unable to move or work; to make sth do this: ~ **(up)** *The photocopier keeps jamming up.* ◊ ~ **sth (up)** *There's a loose part that keeps jamming the mechanism.* ◊ + **adj.** *The valve has jammed shut.* ◊ ~ **sth + adj.** *He jammed the door open with a piece of wood.*
- **PUT INTO SMALL SPACE** 3 [T, usually passive, I] to put sb/sth into a small space where there is very little room to move SYN **squash, squeeze**: **be jammed + adv./prep.** *Six of us were jammed into one small car.* ◊ *We were jammed together like sardines in a can.* ◊ *The cupboards were jammed full of old newspapers.* ◊ + **adv./prep.** *Nearly 1000 students jammed into the hall.* ⇨ see also JAM-PACKED
- **FILL WITH PEOPLE/THINGS** 4 [T] ~ sth (up) (with sb/sth) to fill sth with a large number of people or things so that it is unable to function as it should SYN **block**: *Viewers jammed the switchboard with complaints.*
- **RADIO BROADCAST** 5 [T] ~ sth (specialist) to send out radio signals to prevent another radio broadcast from being heard
- **PLAY MUSIC** 6 [I, T] ~ (sth) to play music with other musicians in an informal way without preparing or practising first
- IDM **jam on the brake(s) | jam the brake(s) on** to operate the BRAKES on a vehicle suddenly and with force: *The car skidded as he jammed on the brakes.*

**jamb** /dʒæm/ noun a post at the side of a door or window

847 **jasmine**

**jam·ba·laya** /ˌdʒæmbəˈlaɪə/ noun [U] a spicy dish of rice, SEAFOOD, chicken, etc. from Louisiana in the southern US

**jam·bo·ree** /ˌdʒæmbəˈriː/ noun 1 a large party or celebration: *the movie industry's annual jamboree at Cannes* 2 a large meeting of SCOUTS or GUIDES

ˈ**jam jar** noun (BrE) a glass container for jam, etc.

**jammed** /dʒæmd/ adj. 1 [not before noun] not able to move SYN **stuck**: *I can't get the door open—it's completely jammed.* 2 (especially NAmE) very full; crowded SYN **jampacked**: *Hundreds more people were waiting outside the jammed stadium.*

**jammy** /ˈdʒæmi/ adj. 1 covered with jam: *jammy fingers* 2 (BrE, informal) lucky, especially because sth good has happened to you without you making any effort

**jam-ˈpacked** adj. [not usually before noun] ~ **(with sb/sth)** (informal) very full or crowded: *The train was jampacked with commuters.*

ˈ**jam session** noun an occasion when musicians perform in an informal way without practising first

**Jane Doe** /ˌdʒeɪn ˈdəʊ/ noun [usually sing.] (NAmE) 1 used to refer to a woman whose name is not known or is kept secret, especially in a court of law 2 an average woman ⇨ compare JOHN DOE

**jan·gle** /ˈdʒæŋɡl/ verb, noun
- verb 1 [I, T] to make an unpleasant sound, like two pieces of metal hitting each other; to make sth do this: *The shop bell jangled loudly.* ◊ ~ **sth** *He jangled the keys in his pocket.* 2 [I, T] ~ **(sth)** if your nerves **jangle**, or if sb/sth **jangles** them, you feel anxious or upset: *She was suddenly wide awake, her nerves jangling.*
- noun [usually sing.] a hard noise like that of metal hitting metal

**jani·tor** /ˈdʒænɪtə(r)/ noun (NAmE, ScotE) = CUSTODIAN (2)

**Janu·ary** ❶ A1 /ˈdʒænjuəri; NAmE -njueri/ noun [U, C] (abbr. **Jan.**) the 1st month of the year, between December and February HELP To see how **January** is used, look at the examples at **April**.

**Jap** /dʒæp/ noun (taboo, slang) an offensive word for a Japanese person

**jape** /dʒeɪp/ noun (BrE, old-fashioned) a trick or joke that is played on sb

**ja·pon·ica** /dʒəˈpɒnɪkə; NAmE -ˈpɑːn-/ noun [C, U] a Japanese bush that is often grown in gardens, and that has red flowers and pale yellow fruit

**jar** /dʒɑː(r)/ noun, verb
- noun 1 [C] a round glass container, with a LID (= cover), used for storing food, especially jam, HONEY, etc: *a storage jar* ⇨ see also JAM JAR, MASON JAR 2 [C] a jar and what it contains: *a jar of coffee* ⇨ see also COOKIE JAR 3 [C] a tall container with a wide mouth, with or without handles, used in the past for carrying water, etc: *a water jar* ⇨ see also BELL JAR 4 [C] (BrE, informal) a glass of beer: *Do you fancy a jar after work?* 5 [sing.] an unpleasant shock, especially from things being suddenly shaken or hit: *The fall gave him a nasty jar.*
- verb (-rr-) 1 [T, I] to give or receive a sudden sharp painful knock: ~ **sth** *The jolt seemed to jar every bone in her body.* ◊ ~ **(sth) (on sth)** *The spade jarred on something metal.* 2 [I, T] ~ **(on sb)** | ~ **(sth)** to have an unpleasant or annoying effect SYN **grate**: *His constant moaning was beginning to jar on her nerves.* ◊ *There was a jarring note of triumph in his voice.* 3 [I] ~ **(with sth)** to be different from sth in a strange or unpleasant way SYN **clash**: *Her brown shoes jarred with the rest of the outfit.*

**jar·gon** /ˈdʒɑːɡən; NAmE ˈdʒɑːrɡ-/ noun [U] (often disapproving) words or expressions that are used by a particular profession or group of people, and are difficult for others to understand: *medical/legal/computer, etc. jargon* ◊ *Try to avoid using too much technical jargon.*

**jas·mine** /ˈdʒæzmɪn/ noun [U, C] a plant with white or yellow flowers with a sweet smell, sometimes used to make PERFUME and also sometimes added to tea

# jaundice 848

**jaun·dice** /ˈdʒɔːndɪs/ noun [U] a medical condition in which the skin and the white parts of the eyes become yellow, caused by disease of the LIVER or blood

**jaun·diced** /ˈdʒɔːndɪst/ adj. **1** not expecting sb/sth to be good or useful, especially because of experiences that you have had in the past: *He had a jaundiced view of life.* ◇ *She looked on politicians with a jaundiced eye.* **2** suffering from jaundice: *a jaundiced patient/liver*

**jaunt** /dʒɔːnt/ noun (old-fashioned or humorous) a short journey that you make for pleasure SYN **excursion**

**jaun·ty** /ˈdʒɔːnti/ adj. **1** showing that you are feeling confident and pleased with yourself SYN **cheerful**: *a jaunty smile* **2** lively: *a jaunty tune* ▸ **jaunt·ily** /-tɪli/ adv.: *He set off jauntily, whistling to himself.* **jaunti·ness** noun [U]

**jav·elin** /ˈdʒævlɪn/ noun **1** [C] a light SPEAR (= a long stick with a pointed end) that is thrown in a sporting event **2** *often* **the javelin** [sing.] the event or sport of throwing a javelin as far as possible

**jaw** /dʒɔː/ noun, verb
■ noun **1** [C] either of the two bones at the bottom of the face that contain the teeth and move when you talk or eat: *the top/upper jaw* ◇ *the bottom/lower jaw* **2** [sing.] the lower part of the face; the lower jaw: *He has a strong square jaw.* ◇ *The punch broke my jaw.* ⊃ see also SLACK-JAWED **3** **jaws** [pl.] the mouth and teeth of a person or an animal: *The alligator's jaws snapped shut.* **4** **jaws** [pl.] the parts of a tool or machine that are used to hold things tightly: *the jaws of a vice*
IDM **sb's ˈjaw dropped/fell/sagged** used to say that sb suddenly looked surprised, shocked or disappointed **the jaws of ˈdeath, deˈfeat, etc.** (literary) used to describe an unpleasant situation that almost happens: *They narrowly escaped from the jaws of death.* **the jaws of a tunnel, etc.** the narrow entrance to a tunnel, etc., especially one that looks dangerous ⊃ more at SNATCH v.
■ verb [I] (informal, often disapproving) to talk, especially to talk a lot or for a long time

**jawan** /dʒəˈwɑːn/ noun (IndE) a soldier of low rank

**jaw·bone** /ˈdʒɔːbəʊn/ noun the bone that forms the lower jaw SYN **mandible** ⊃ VISUAL VOCAB page V1

**ˈjaw-dropping** adj. (informal) so large or good that it surprises you very much: *a jaw-dropping 5 million dollars* ◇ *The production is absolutely jaw-dropping.* ▸ **ˈjaw-droppingly** adv.: *jaw-droppingly beautiful*

**jaw·line** /ˈdʒɔːlaɪn/ noun the outline of the lower jaw

**jay** /dʒeɪ/ noun a European bird of the CROW family, with bright feathers and a noisy call ⊃ see also BLUEJAY

**jay·walk** /ˈdʒeɪwɔːk/ verb [I] (especially NAmE) to walk along or across a street illegally or without paying attention to the traffic ▸ **jay·walk·er** noun **jay·walk·ing** noun [U]

**jazz** ⓘ A2 /dʒæz/ noun, verb
■ noun ⓘ A2 [U] a type of music with strong rhythms, in which the players often IMPROVISE (= make up the music as they are playing), originally created by African American musicians at the beginning of the 20th century: *traditional/modern jazz* ◇ *a jazz band/club* ◇ *jazz musicians* ⊃ see also ACID JAZZ, TRAD JAZZ
IDM **and all that ˈjazz** (informal) and things like that: *How's it going? You know—love, life and all that jazz.*
■ verb
PHRV **jazz sth ↔ ˈup** (informal) **1** to make sth more interesting, exciting or attractive **2** to make a piece of music sound more modern, or more like popular music or jazz: *It's a jazzed up version of an old tune.*

**jazzed** /dʒæzd/ adj. [not before noun] (NAmE, informal) excited: *I was jazzed to meet someone so famous.*

**jazzy** /ˈdʒæzi/ adj. (informal) **1** in the style of jazz: *a jazzy melody/tune* **2** (sometimes disapproving) brightly coloured and likely to attract attention SYN **snazzy**: *That's a jazzy tie you're wearing.*

**JCB™** /ˌdʒeɪ siː ˈbiː/ noun (BrE) a powerful vehicle with a long arm for digging and moving earth

**J-cloth™** noun a type of light cloth used for cleaning

**jeal·ous** /ˈdʒeləs/ adj. **1** feeling angry or unhappy because sb you like or love is showing interest in sb else: *a jealous wife/husband* ◇ *He's only talking to her to make you jealous.* ⊃ WORDFINDER NOTE at LOVE **2** ~ (of sb/sth) feeling angry or unhappy because you wish you had sth that sb else has SYN **envious**: *She's jealous of my success.* ◇ *Children often feel jealous when a new baby arrives.* **3** ~ (of sth) wanting to keep or protect sth that you have because it makes you feel proud: *They are very jealous of their good reputation* (= they do not want to lose it). ▸ **jeal·ous·ly** adv.: *She eyed Natalia jealously.* ◇ *a jealously guarded secret*

**jeal·ousy** /ˈdʒeləsi/ noun (pl. **-ies**) **1** [U] a feeling of being jealous: *I felt sick with jealousy.* ◇ *sexual jealousy* **2** [C] an action or a remark that shows that a person is jealous: *I'm tired of her petty jealousies.*

**jeans** ⓘ A1 /dʒiːnz/ noun [pl.] trousers made of DENIM (= a type of strong cotton): *a pair of designer jeans* ◇ *skinny/baggy jeans* ◇ *ripped/faded jeans* ◇ **in ~** *a young man in jeans and a T-shirt* ⊃ see also BLUE JEANS, DENIM ORIGIN From **Janne**, the Old French name for Genoa, where the heavy cotton now used for jeans was first made.

**Jeep™** /dʒiːp/ noun a small strong vehicle used, especially by the army, for driving over rough ground

**jee·pers** /ˈdʒiːpəz/, NAmE -pərz/ (also **jeepers ˈcreepers**) exclamation (especially NAmE, informal) used to express surprise or shock: *Jeepers! That car nearly hit us!*

**jeer** /dʒɪə(r), NAmE dʒɪr/ verb, noun
■ verb [I, T] to laugh at sb or shout rude remarks at them to show that you do not respect them SYN **taunt**: *a jeering crowd* ◇ **~ at sb** *The police were jeered at by the waiting crowd.* ◇ **~ sb** *The players were jeered by disappointed fans.* ◇ **+ speech** *'Coward!' he jeered.*
■ noun [usually pl.] a rude remark that sb shouts at sb else to show that they do not respect or like them SYN **taunt**: *He walked on to the stage to be greeted with jeers and whistles.*

**jeez** /dʒiːz/ exclamation (especially NAmE, informal) used to express anger, surprise, etc.

**jeg·gings** /ˈdʒegɪŋz/ noun [pl.] trousers for women, made of cloth that stretches easily, that fit tightly over the legs and look like jeans

**jehad** = JIHAD

**Je·ho·vah** /dʒəˈhəʊvə/ (also **Yah·weh**) noun the name of God that is used in the Old Testament of the Bible

**Jeˌhovah's ˈWitness** noun a member of a religious organization based on Christianity, which believes that the end of the world is near and that only good people will come back to life and live peacefully forever

**je·junum** /dʒɪˈdʒuːnəm/ noun (anatomy) the second part of the small INTESTINE ⊃ compare DUODENUM, ILEUM ▸ **je·junal** /-nl/ adj.

**Jek·yll and Hyde** /ˌdʒekl ən ˈhaɪd/ noun [sing.] a person who is sometimes very pleasant (*Jekyll*) and sometimes very unpleasant (*Hyde*) or who leads two very separate lives ORIGIN From the story by Robert Louis Stevenson, *Dr Jekyll and Mr Hyde*, in which Dr Jekyll takes a drug which separates the good and bad sides of his personality into two characters. All the negative aspects go into the character of Mr Hyde.

**jell** (especially NAmE) (BrE usually **gel**) /dʒel/ verb **1** [I] (of two or more people) to work well together; to form a successful group: *We just didn't jell as a group.* **2** [I] (of an idea, a thought, a plan, etc.) to become clearer and more definite; to work well: *Ideas were beginning to jell in my mind.* ◇ *That day, everything jelled.* **3** [I] (specialist) (of a liquid) to become thicker and more solid; to form a GEL

**jel·lied** /ˈdʒelid/ adj. [only before noun] (especially BrE) prepared or cooked in JELLY: *jellied eels*

**jelly** /ˈdʒeli/ (pl. **-ies**) noun **1** [U, C] (BrE) (NAmE **jello**, **Jell-O™** [U]) a cold sweet TRANSPARENT food, made from GELATIN, sugar and fruit juice, that shakes when it is moved: *jelly and ice cream* ◇ *a raspberry jelly* **2** [U] a substance like jelly made from GELATIN and meat juices, served around meat, fish, etc. SYN aspic: *chicken in jelly* **3** [U, C] a type of jam that does not contain any pieces of fruit: *blackcurrant jelly* ⊃ compare JAM **4** [U] any thick sticky substance, especially a type of cream used on the skin ⊃ see also PETROLEUM JELLY **5** (also ˈjelly shoe) [C] a light plastic shoe designed for wearing on the beach and in the sea
IDM **be/feel like ˈjelly | turn to ˈjelly** (of legs or knees) to feel weak because you are nervous

**ˈjelly baby** noun (BrE) a small soft sweet in the shape of a baby, made from GELATIN and tasting of fruit

**ˈjelly bean** noun a small sweet that is like a bean in shape and has a hard outside and a centre like jelly

**jel·ly·fish** /ˈdʒelifɪʃ/ noun (pl. **jel·ly·fish**) a sea creature with a body like jelly and long thin parts called TENTACLES that can give a sharp STING (= a painful wound on the skin)

**ˈjelly roll** (NAmE) (BrE ˌSwiss ˈroll) noun a thin flat cake that is spread with jam, etc. and rolled up

**jembe** /ˈdʒembeɪ/ EAfrE [ˈdʒembe] noun (EAfrE) a farming tool with a long handle and a BLADE (= cutting edge) at one end, used for digging, breaking up soil or removing WEEDS (= plants growing where they are not wanted)

**jemmy** /ˈdʒemi/ (BrE) (NAmE **jimmy**) noun (pl. **-ies**) a short heavy metal bar used by thieves to force open doors and windows

**je ne sais quoi** /ʒə nə seɪ ˈkwɑː/ noun [U] (from French, often humorous) a good quality that is difficult to describe: *He has that je ne sais quoi that distinguishes a professional from an amateur.*

**jenny** /ˈdʒeni/ noun (pl. **-ies**) a female DONKEY or ASS

**jeop·ard·ize** (BrE also **-ise**) /ˈdʒepədaɪz/ NAmE **-pərd-**/ verb ~ **sth/sb** (formal) to risk harming or destroying sth/sb SYN **endanger**: *He would never do anything to jeopardize his career.*

**jeop·ardy** /ˈdʒepədi/ NAmE **-pərd-**/ noun
IDM **in ˈjeopardy** in a dangerous position or situation and likely to be lost or harmed ⊃ see also DOUBLE JEOPARDY

**jere·miad** /ˌdʒerɪˈmaɪæd/ noun (formal) a very long sad complaint or list of complaints

**jerk** /dʒɜːk; NAmE dʒɜːrk/ verb, noun
■ *verb* [T, I] to move or to make sth move with a sudden short sharp movement: *~ sth + adv./prep. She jerked her head up.* ◇ *He jerked the phone away from her.* ◇ *+ adv./prep. The bus jerked to a halt.* ◇ *He grabbed a handful of hair and jerked at it.* ◇ *~ sth + adj. She got to the door and jerked it open.*
PHRV ˌjerk sb aˈround (informal, especially NAmE) to make things difficult for sb, especially by not being honest with them: *Consumers are often jerked around by big companies.* ˌjerk ˈoff (taboo, slang) (of a man) to MASTURBATE ˌjerk ˈout | ˌjerk sth↔ˈout to say sth in a quick and sharp way because you are nervous
■ *noun* **1** [C] a sudden quick sharp movement SYN **jolt**: *with a ~ She sat up with a jerk.* **2** [C] (informal) a stupid person who often says or does the wrong thing **3** [U] meat that is MARINATED (= left in a mixture of oil and SPICES before being cooked) to give it a strong taste and then cooked over a wood fire: *jerk chicken*

**jer·kin** /ˈdʒɜːkɪn; NAmE ˈdʒɜːrk-/ noun a short jacket without arms, especially one worn by men in the past

**jerky** /ˈdʒɜːki; NAmE ˈdʒɜːrki/ adj., noun
■ *adj.* making sudden starts and stops and not moving smoothly ▸ **jerk·ily** /-kɪli/ adv.: *The car moved off jerkily.*
■ *noun* [U] meat that has been cut into long narrow pieces and smoked or dried: *beef jerky*

**Jerry** /ˈdʒeri/ noun (pl. **-ies**) (taboo, BrE, slang) an offensive word for a person from Germany, used especially during the First and Second World Wars

**ˈjerry·can** (also **ˈjerry can**) /ˈdʒerikæn/ noun (old-fashioned) a large metal or plastic container with flat sides, used for carrying petrol or water

**jer·sey** /ˈdʒɜːzi; NAmE ˈdʒɜːrzi/ noun **1** [C] a shirt worn by sb playing a sports game **2** [C] a KNITTED piece of clothing made of wool or cotton for the upper part of the body, with long SLEEVES and no buttons; a type of sweater **3** [U] a type of soft fine KNITTED cloth used for making clothes: *made from 100% cotton jersey* **4** **Jersey** [C] a type of light brown cow that produces high-quality milk

**Je·ru·sa·lem ar·ti·choke** /dʒəˌruːsələm ˈɑːtɪtʃəʊk; NAmE ˈɑːrt-/ noun (BrE also **ar·ti·choke**) a light-brown root vegetable that looks like a potato

**jes·sie** /ˈdʒesi/ (also **jessy**) noun (pl. **-ies**) (BrE, old-fashioned, offensive) a man or boy who is weak or who seems to behave too much like a woman

**jest** /dʒest/ noun, verb
■ *noun* (old-fashioned or formal) something said or done to make people laugh SYN **joke**
IDM **in ˈjest** as a joke: *The remark was made half in jest.* ◇ *'Many a true word is spoken in jest,' thought Rosie* = people often say things as a joke that are actually true).
■ *verb* [I, T] ~ **(about sth) | + speech** (formal or humorous) to say things that are not serious or true, especially in order to make sb laugh SYN **joke**: *Would I jest about such a thing?*

**jest·er** /ˈdʒestə(r)/ noun a man employed in the past at the COURT of a king or queen to entertain people by telling jokes and funny stories: *the court jester*

**Jes·uit** /ˈdʒezjuɪt; NAmE ˈdʒeʒəwət/ noun a member of the Society of Jesus, a Roman Catholic religious group: *a Jesuit priest*

**Jesus** /ˈdʒiːzəs/ (also **Jesus ˈChrist**) noun = CHRIST

**jet** /dʒet/ noun, verb
■ *noun* **1** [C] a plane driven by JET ENGINES: *a jet aircraft/fighter/airliner* ◇ *The accident happened as the jet was about to take off.* ⊃ see also JUMBO noun, JUMP JET ⊃ WORDFINDER NOTE at AIRCRAFT **2** [C] a strong narrow stream of gas, liquid or flame that comes very quickly out of a small opening. The opening is also called a jet: *The pipe burst and jets of water shot across the room.* ◇ *to clean the gas jets on the cooker* **3** [U] a hard black mineral that can be POLISHED and is used in jewellery
■ *verb* (-tt-) [I] + adv./prep. (informal) to fly somewhere in a plane

**ˌjet ˈblack** adj. deep shiny black in colour ⊃ WORDFINDER NOTE at BLONDE

**ˈjet engine** noun an engine that drives an aircraft forwards by pushing out a stream of gases behind it

**ˈjet lag** noun [U] the feeling of being tired and slightly confused after a long plane journey, especially when there is a big difference in the time at the place you leave and that at the place you arrive in ▸ **ˈjet-lagged** adj.

**jet·liner** /ˈdʒetlaɪnə(r)/ noun a large plane with a jet engine, that carries passengers

**ˈjet·pack** /ˈdʒetpæk/ noun (in SCIENCE FICTION stories) a device that sb wears on their shoulders like a BACKPACK that enables them to fly

**ˌjet-proˈpelled** adj. driven by JET ENGINES

**ˌjet proˈpulsion** noun [U] the use of JET ENGINES for power

**jet·sam** /ˈdʒetsəm/ noun things that are thrown away from a ship at sea and that float towards land ⊃ compare FLOTSAM

**the ˈjet set** noun [sing. + sing./pl. v.] rich and fashionable people who travel a lot

**ˈjet-setter** noun a rich, fashionable person who travels a lot ▸ **ˈjet-setting** adj. [usually before noun]: *her jet-setting millionaire boyfriend*

# Jet Ski™

**Jet Ski™** noun a vehicle with an engine, like a motorcycle, for riding across water ▶ **jet-skiing** noun [U]

**jet stream** noun 1 (usually **the jet stream**) [sing.] a strong wind that blows high above the earth and that has an effect on the weather 2 [C] the flow of gases from a plane's engine

**jet·ti·son** /ˈdʒetɪsn/ verb 1 ~ sth to throw sth out of a moving plane or ship to make it lighter: *to jettison fuel* 2 ~ sth/sb to get rid of sth/sb that you no longer need or want SYN discard: *He was jettisoned as team coach after the defeat.* 3 ~ sth to reject an idea, a belief, a plan, etc. that you no longer think is useful or likely to be successful SYN abandon

**jetty** /ˈdʒeti/ noun (pl. -ies) (NAmE also **dock**) a wall or platform built out into the sea, a river, etc., where boats can be tied and where people can get on and off boats

**Jew** /dʒuː/ noun a member of the people and cultural community whose traditional religion is Judaism and who come from the ancient Hebrew people of Israel; a person who believes in and practises Judaism

**jewel** /ˈdʒuːəl/ noun 1 a PRECIOUS STONE such as a diamond, RUBY, etc. SYN **gem** 2 [usually pl.] pieces of jewellery or beautiful objects that contain PRECIOUS STONES: *The family jewels are locked away in a safe.* ⇒ see also CROWN JEWELS 3 a small PRECIOUS STONE or piece of special glass that is used in the machine inside a watch 4 (*informal*) a person or thing that is very important or valuable ⇒ compare GEM IDM **the jewel in the ˈcrown** the most attractive or valuable part of sth

**jewel case** noun a plastic box for holding a CD or DVD

**jew·elled** (US **jew-eled**) /ˈdʒuːəld/ adj. decorated with jewels

**jew·el·ler** (US **jew·el·er**) /ˈdʒuːələ(r)/ noun 1 a person who makes, repairs or sells jewellery and watches 2 **jeweller's** (pl. **jew·el·lers**) a shop that sells jewellery and watches: *I bought it at the jeweller's near my office.*

**jew·el·lery** 🔵 A2 (US **jew·el·ry**) /ˈdʒuːəlri/ noun [U] objects such as rings and NECKLACES that people wear as decoration: *silver/gold jewellery* ⋄ *She has some lovely pieces of jewellery.* ⇒ see also COSTUME JEWELLERY

**Jew·ess** /ˈdʒuːəs/ noun (often offensive) an old-fashioned word for a Jewish woman

**Jew·ish** /ˈdʒuːɪʃ/ adj. connected with Jews or Judaism; believing in and practising Judaism: *We're Jewish.* ⋄ *the local Jewish community* ▶ **Jew·ish·ness** noun [U]

**Jewry** /ˈdʒuəri; NAmE ˈdʒuri, ˈdʒuːri/ noun [U] (formal) Jewish people as a group: *British Jewry*

**-ji** /dʒi/ combining form (IndE) used with people's names and titles to show respect: *Lalitaji* ⋄ *guruji*

**jib** /dʒɪb/ noun, verb
- *noun* 1 a small sail in front of the large sail on a boat 2 the arm of a CRANE that lifts things
- *verb* [I] (-bb-) ~ (at sth/at doing sth) (old-fashioned, informal) to be unwilling to do or accept sth: *She agreed to attend but jibbed at making a speech.*

**jibe** (also **gibe**) /dʒaɪb/ noun, verb
- *noun* 1 ~ (at sb/sth) an unkind or offensive remark about sb: *He made several cheap jibes at his opponent during the interview.* 2 (NAmE) = GYBE
- *verb* 1 [I, T] ~ (at sb) | ~ that… | + speech to say sth that is intended to make sb look silly or feel embarrassed: *He jibed repeatedly at the errors their team had made.* 2 [I] ~ (with sth) (NAmE, informal) to be the same as sth or to match it: *Your statement doesn't jibe with the facts.* 3 [I] (NAmE) (*specialist*) = GYBE ⇒ compare TACK (3)

**jiffy** /ˈdʒɪfi/ noun [usually sing.] (informal) (pl. -ies) a moment: **in a ~** *I'll be with you in a jiffy* (= very soon).

**Jiffy bag™** noun 1 (BrE) a thick soft ENVELOPE for sending things that might break or tear easily 2 (SAfrE) a clear plastic bag used for storing things in, especially food

**jig** /dʒɪɡ/ noun, verb
- *noun* 1 a quick lively dance; the music for this dance: *an Irish jig* 2 a device that holds sth in position and guides the tools that are working on it
- *verb* [I, T] (-gg-) ~ (sb/sth) (+ adv./prep.) to move or to make sb/sth move up and down with short quick movements: *He jigged up and down with excitement.*

**jig·ger** /ˈdʒɪɡə(r)/ noun = CHIGGER

**jig·gered** /ˈdʒɪɡəd; NAmE -ɡərd/ adj. [not before noun] IDM **I'll be ˈjiggered!** (old-fashioned, BrE, informal) used to show surprise

**jiggery-pokery** /ˌdʒɪɡəri ˈpəʊkəri/ noun [U] (informal, especially BrE) dishonest behaviour

**jig·gle** /ˈdʒɪɡl/ verb [I, T] (informal) to move or make sth move up and down or from side to side with short quick movements: (+ *adv./prep.*) *Stop jiggling around!* ⋄ *She jiggled with the lock.* ⋄ ~ **sth** (+ *adv./prep.*) *He stood jiggling his car keys in his hand.*

**jig·saw** /ˈdʒɪɡsɔː/ noun 1 (also **ˈjigsaw puzzle**) (also **puz·zle** especially in NAmE) a picture printed on CARDBOARD (= very thick, stiff card) or wood, that has been cut up into a lot of small pieces of different shapes that you have to fit together again: *to do a jigsaw* 2 a mysterious situation in which it is not easy to understand all the causes of what is happening; a complicated problem 3 a SAW (= a type of tool) with a narrow BLADE for cutting designs in thin pieces of wood or metal

**jihad** (also **jehad**) /dʒɪˈhɑːd/ noun [C, U] 1 (in Islam) a spiritual struggle within yourself to stop yourself breaking religious or moral laws 2 a holy war fought by Muslims to defend Islam

**jiko** /ˈdʒiːkəʊ; EAfrE [ˈdʒiko]/ noun (pl. -os) (EAfrE) a container made of metal or CLAY and used for burning CHARCOAL or small pieces of wood. It is used for cooking or to give heat.

**jil·bab** /ˈdʒɪlbæb/ noun a full-length piece of clothing worn over other clothes by some Muslim women

**jilt** /dʒɪlt/ verb [often passive] ~ **sb** to end a romantic relationship with sb in a sudden and unkind way: *He was jilted by his fiancée.* ⋄ *a jilted bride/lover*

**Jim Crow** /ˌdʒɪm ˈkrəʊ/ noun [U] the former practice in the US of using laws that allowed black people to be treated unfairly and kept separate from white people, for example in schools ORIGIN From the title of a song that was sung by white entertainers who tried to look and sound like African Americans.

**jimmy** /ˈdʒɪmi/ (NAmE) (BrE **jemmy**) noun (pl. -ies) a short heavy metal bar used by thieves to force open doors and windows

**jin·gle** /ˈdʒɪŋɡl/ noun, verb
- *noun* 1 [sing.] a sound like small bells ringing that is made when metal objects are shaken together: *the jingle of coins in his pocket* 2 [C] a short song or tune that is easy to remember and is used in advertising ⇒ WORDFINDER NOTE at RADIO
- *verb* [I, T] ~ (sth) to make a pleasant gentle sound like small bells ringing; to make sth do this: *The chimes jingled in the breeze.* ⋄ *She jingled the coins in her pocket.*

**jin·go·ism** /ˈdʒɪŋɡəʊɪzəm/ noun [U] (disapproving) a strong belief that your own country is best, especially when this is expressed in support of war with another country ▶ **jin·go·is·tic** /ˌdʒɪŋɡəʊˈɪstɪk/ adj.

**jink** /dʒɪŋk/ verb [I] ~ (+ adv./prep.) (BrE, informal) (especially in sport) to move quickly while changing direction suddenly and often, especially in order to avoid sb/sth

**jinks** /dʒɪŋks/ noun ⇒ HIGH JINKS

**jinx** /dʒɪŋks/ noun [sing.] ~ (on sb/sth) bad luck; sb/sth that is thought to bring bad luck in a mysterious way: *I'm convinced there's a jinx on this car.* ⇒ WORDFINDER NOTE at LUCK ▶ **jinx** verb ~ **sb/sth**

**jinxed** /dʒɪŋkst/ adj. (informal) having or bringing more bad luck than is normal: *The whole family seemed to be jinxed.*

**JIT** /dʒɪt/ abbr. JUST-IN-TIME

**jit·ter·bug** /ˈdʒɪtəbʌɡ/ NAmE -tərb-/ noun a fast dance that was popular in the 1940s

**jit·ters** /ˈdʒɪtəz/ NAmE -tərz/ (often **the jitters**) noun [pl.] (informal) feelings of being anxious and nervous, especially before an important event or before having to do sth difficult: *I always get the jitters before exams.*

**jit·tery** /ˈdʒɪtəri/ adj. (informal) anxious and nervous ⊃ SYNONYMS at NERVOUS

**jiu-jitsu** = JU-JITSU

**jive** /dʒaɪv/ noun, verb
■ noun **1** [U, sing.] a fast dance to music with a strong beat, especially popular in the 1950s **2** [U] (NAmE, old-fashioned, informal) ideas, statements or beliefs that you think are silly or not true SYN **nonsense**: *to talk jive*
■ verb **1** [I] to dance to jazz or ROCK AND ROLL music **2** [I, T] **~ (sb)** (NAmE, old-fashioned, informal) to try to make sb believe sth that is not true SYN **kid**

**Jnr** = JR

**job** ⓘ A1 /dʒɒb; NAmE dʒɑːb/ noun
• PAID WORK **1** ⓘ A1 work for which you receive regular payment: *I don't have a job at present.* ◇ *He's trying to get a job.* ◇ *I'm thinking of applying for a new job.* ◇ *to look for/find a job* ◇ *Did they offer you the job?* ◇ *~ as sth She took a job as a waitress.* ◇ *His brother's just lost his job.* ◇ *to leave/quit your job* ◇ *a temporary/permanent job* ◇ *a full-time/part-time job* ◇ *out of a ~ He's been out of a job (= unemployed) for six months now.* ◇ *The takeover of the company is bound to mean more job losses.* ◇ *There is so much competition in the job market currently.* ◇ *He certainly knows his job (= is very good at his job).* ◇ *I'm only doing my job (= I'm doing what I am paid to do).* ◇ *These projects will help create jobs in rural areas.* ⊃ see also DAY JOB, DESK JOB ⊃ WORDFINDER NOTE at EMPLOY
• TASK **2** A2 a particular task or piece of work that you have to do: *I've got various jobs around the house to do.* ◇ *Sorting these papers out is going to be a long job.* ◇ *The builder has a couple of jobs on at the moment.* ◇ *~ of doing sth She's taken on the job of organizing the Christmas party.* ⊃ see also BLOW JOB, NOSE JOB, PAINT JOB
• DUTY **3** A2 [usually sing.] (rather informal) a responsibility or duty: *He said he wouldn't do it because it wasn't his job.* ◇ *sb's ~ to do sth It's not my job to lock up!*
• CRIME **4** (informal) a crime, especially stealing: *a bank job* ◇ *an inside job (= done by sb in the organization where the crime happens)* ⊃ see also HATCHET JOB
• OBJECT **5** (informal) a particular kind of thing: *It's real wood —not one of those plastic jobs.*
• COMPUTING **6** an item of work that is done by a computer as a single unit
IDM **do a good, bad, etc. ˈjob (on sth) | make a good, bad, etc. job of sth** to do sth well, badly, etc: *They did a very professional job.* ◇ *You've certainly made an excellent job of the kitchen (= for example, painting it).* **do the ˈjob** (informal) to be effective or successful in doing what you want: *This extra strong glue should do the job.* **give sb/sth up as a bad ˈjob** (informal) to decide to stop trying to help sb or to do sth because there is no hope of success **good ˈjob!** (especially NAmE, informal) used to tell sb that they have done well at sth **a good ˈjob** (informal) used to say that you are pleased about a situation or that sb is lucky that sth happened: *It's a good job you were there to help.* **have a (hard/difficult) job doing/to do sth** to have difficulty doing sth: *You'll have a job convincing them that you're right.* ◇ *He had a hard job to make himself heard.* **a job of ˈwork** (BrE, old-fashioned or formal) work that you are paid to do or that must be done: *There was a job of work waiting for him that he was not looking forward to.* **jobs for the ˈboys** (BrE, informal, disapproving) people use the expression **jobs for the boys** when they are criticizing the fact that sb in power has given work to friends or relatives **just the ˈjob** (BrE) (also **just the ˈticket** NAmE, BrE) (informal, approving) exactly what is needed in a particular situation **more than your ˈjob's worth (to do sth)** (BrE, informal) not worth doing because it is against the rules or because it might cause you to lose your job: *It's more than my job's worth to let you in without a ticket.*

⊃ see also JOBSWORTH **on the ˈjob 1** while doing a particular job: *No sleeping on the job!* ◇ *on-the-job training* **2** (BrE, slang) having sex ⊃ more at ASLEEP, BEST n., DEVIL, WALK v.

▼ SYNONYMS

**job**
position • post • vacancy • appointment
These are all words for a position doing work for which you receive regular payment.
**job** work for which you receive regular payment: *He's trying to get a job in a bank.*
**position** (rather formal) a job: *a senior position in a large corporation*
JOB OR POSITION?
**Position** usually refers to a particular job within an organization, especially at a high level, and is not usually used about jobs generally. It is also often used in job applications, descriptions and advertisements.
**post** a job, especially an important one in a large organization: *a key post in the new government*
**vacancy** a job that is available for sb to do: *We have several vacancies for casual workers.*
**appointment** (rather formal, especially BrE) a job or position of responsibility: *This is a permanent appointment, requiring commitment and hard work.*
PATTERNS
• a **permanent/temporary** job/position/post/vacancy/appointment
• a **full-time/part-time** job/position/post/vacancy/appointment
• to **have/have got** a(n) job/position/post/vacancy/appointment
• to **apply for/fill** a job/position/post/vacancy
• to **resign from/leave/quit** a job/position/post

**job·bie** /ˈdʒɒbi; NAmE ˈdʒɑːbi/ noun (informal) used to refer to an object of a particular kind: *Her bikini was one of those expensive designer jobbies.*

**job·bing** /ˈdʒɒbɪŋ; NAmE ˈdʒɑːb-/ adj. [only before noun] (BrE) doing pieces of work for different people rather than a regular job: *a jobbing actor/builder*

**job·centre** /ˈdʒɒbsentə(r); NAmE ˈdʒɑːb-/ noun (BrE) a government office where people can get advice in finding work and where jobs are advertised

**ˈjob creation** noun [U] the process of providing opportunities for paid work, especially for people who are unemployed

**ˈjob description** noun a written description of the exact work and responsibilities of a job ⊃ WORDFINDER NOTE at APPLY

**ˈjob-hunt** verb [I] (usually used in the progressive tenses) to try to find a job: *At that time I had been job-hunting for six months.*

**job·less** /ˈdʒɒbləs; NAmE ˈdʒɑːb-/ adj. **1** without a job SYN **unemployed**: *The closure left 500 people jobless.* **2 the jobless** noun [pl.] people who are unemployed ▶ **job·less·ness** noun [U]

**ˈjob lot** noun (informal) a collection of different things, often of poor quality, especially when they are sold together

**ˈjob satisfaction** noun [U] the good feeling that you get when you have a job that you enjoy

**job·seeker** (also **job ˈseeker**) /ˈdʒɒbsiːkə(r); NAmE ˈdʒɑːbsiːkər/ noun often used in official language in the UK to describe a person without a job who is trying to find one

**ˈJobseeker's Alˈlowance** noun [U] (in the UK) money paid by the state to unemployed people who are looking for work ⊃ see also UNEMPLOYMENT BENEFIT

**ˈjob-sharing** noun [U] an arrangement for two people to share the hours of work and the pay of one job

**jobsworth** 852

▶ **ˈjob-share** noun: *The company encourages job-shares and part-time working.* **ˈjob-share** verb [I] ~ **(with sb)**

**jobs·worth** /ˈdʒɒbzwɜːθ; *NAmE* ˈdʒɑːbzwɜːrθ/ noun (*BrE, informal, disapproving*) a person who follows the rules of a job exactly, even when this causes problems for other people, or when the rules are not sensible

**Jock** /dʒɒk; *NAmE* dʒɑːk/ noun (*informal*) a way of describing a person from Scotland, that can be offensive

**jock** /dʒɒk; *NAmE* dʒɑːk/ noun **1** (*NAmE*) a man or boy who plays a lot of sport **2** (*NAmE*) a person who likes a particular activity: *a computer jock* **3** (*informal*) = DISC JOCKEY ⇨ compare SHOCK JOCK

**jockey** /ˈdʒɒki; *NAmE* ˈdʒɑːki/ noun, verb
■ noun a person who rides horses in races, especially as a job ⇨ see also DISC JOCKEY, RADIO JOCKEY
■ verb [I] ~ **(with sb) (for sth)** | ~ **(with sb) (to do sth)** to try all possible ways of gaining an advantage over other people: *The runners jockeyed for position at the start.* ◇ *The bands are constantly jockeying with each other for the number one spot.*

**jock·strap** /ˈdʒɒkstræp; *NAmE* ˈdʒɑːk-/ noun a piece of men's underwear worn to support or protect the sexual organs while playing sports

**jocu·lar** /ˈdʒɒkjələ(r); *NAmE* ˈdʒɑːk-/ adj. (*formal*) **1** humorous: *a jocular comment* **2** (of a person) enjoying making people laugh SYN jolly ⇨ see also JOKE ▶ **jocu·lar·ity** /ˌdʒɒkjəˈlærəti; *NAmE* ˌdʒɑːk-/ noun [U] **jocu·lar·ly** /ˈdʒɒkjələli; *NAmE* ˈdʒɑːkjələrli/ adv.

**jodh·purs** /ˈdʒɒdpəz; *NAmE* ˈdʒɑːdpərz/ noun [pl.] trousers that are loose above the knee and tight from the knee to the ankle, worn when riding a horse: *a pair of jodhpurs*

**joe** (*also* **Joe**) /dʒəʊ/ noun [usually sing.] (*NAmE, informal*) an ordinary working man: *a fitness program for the **average** joe*

**Joe Bloggs** /ˌdʒəʊ ˈblɒɡz; *NAmE* ˈblɑːɡz/ (*BrE*) (*NAmE* **Joe ˈBlow, John ˈDoe**) noun [sing.] (*informal*) a way of referring to a typical ordinary person

**Joe ˈPublic** (*BrE*) (*NAmE* **John Q. ˈPublic**) noun [U] (*informal*) people in general; the public

**Joe ˈSix-pack** /ˌdʒəʊ ˈsɪkspæk/ noun (*US, informal*) a man who is considered typical of a person who does MANUAL work: *Joe Sixpack doesn't care about that.*

**joey** /ˈdʒəʊi/ noun a young KANGAROO, WALLABY or POSSUM ⇨ VISUAL VOCAB page V2

**jog** /dʒɒɡ; *NAmE* dʒɑːɡ/ verb, noun
■ verb (-gg-) **1** (*also* **go jogging**) [I] to run slowly and steadily for a long time, especially for exercise: *I go jogging every evening.* **2** [T] ~ **sth/sb** to hit sth lightly and by accident SYN **nudge**: *Someone jogged her elbow, making her spill her coffee.*
IDM **jog sb's ˈmemory** to say or do sth that makes sb remember sth
PHRV **jog aˈlong** (*BrE, informal*) to continue as usual with little or no excitement, change or progress
**jog aˈlong** | **jog ˈon** (*BrE, informal*) used to tell sb rudely to go away or that you are not interested
■ noun [sing.] **1** a slow run, especially one done for physical exercise: *I like to go for a jog after work.* **2** a light push or knock SYN **nudge**

**jog·ger** /ˈdʒɒɡə(r); *NAmE* ˈdʒɑːɡ-/ noun **1** [C] a person who jogs regularly for exercise **2 joggers** [pl.] (*BrE*) soft loose trousers, with ELASTIC at the top, that you wear for doing exercise in

**jog·ging** /ˈdʒɒɡɪŋ; *NAmE* ˈdʒɑːɡ-/ noun [U] the activity of running slowly and steadily as a form of exercise: *to go jogging*

**ˈjogging suit** noun = TRACKSUIT

**jog·gle** /ˈdʒɒɡl; *NAmE* ˈdʒɑːɡl/ verb [I, T] ~ **(sb/sth)** (*informal*) to move or to make sb/sth move quickly up and down or from one side to another

**jog·trot** /ˈdʒɒɡtrɒt; *NAmE* ˈdʒɑːɡtrɑːt/ noun [sing.] a slow steady run

**john** /dʒɒn; *NAmE* dʒɑːn/ noun (*informal, especially NAmE*) a toilet

**John ˈBull** noun [U, C] (*old-fashioned*) used to refer to England or the English people, or to a typical Englishman

**John ˈDoe** noun (*usually sing.*) (*NAmE*) **1** a name used for a person whose name is not known or is kept secret, especially in a court of law **2** an average man ⇨ compare JANE DOE

**John ˈHan·cock** /ˌdʒɒn ˈhæŋkɒk; *NAmE* ˌdʒɑːn ˈhæŋkɑːk/ noun (*NAmE, informal*) a person's SIGNATURE (= their name written by them) ORIGIN John Hancock was an American politician who was the first person to sign the Declaration of Independence in 1776.

**Johnny-come-lately** /ˌdʒɒni kʌm ˈleɪtli; *NAmE* ˌdʒɑːn-/ noun [sing.] (*disapproving or humorous*) a person who has only recently arrived in a place or started an activity, especially sb who is more confident than they should be

**John Q. ˈPublic** (*NAmE*) (*BrE* **Joe ˈPublic**) noun [U] (*informal*) people in general; the public

**joie de vivre** /ˌʒwɑː də ˈviːvrə/ noun [U] (*from French*) a feeling of great happiness and pleasure in life

**join** 🔊 A1 /dʒɔɪn/ verb, noun
■ verb
• CONNECT **1** 🔊 A1 [T, I] to fix or connect two or more things together: ~ **A to/onto B** *Join one section of pipe to the next.* ◇ *The island is joined to the mainland by a bridge.* ◇ ~ **A and B together** *Join the two sections of pipe together.* ◇ ~ **(A and B) (up)** *Draw a line joining (up) all the crosses.* ◇ *How do these two pieces join?*
• BECOME ONE **2** 🔊 A1 [I, T] if two things or groups **join**, or if one thing or group **joins** another, they come together to form one thing or group: *the place where the two paths join* ◇ ~ **sth** *The path joins the road near the trees.* ◇ ~ **together** *Farmers can join together to get better prices.*
• CLUB/COMPANY **3** 🔊 A1 [T, I] ~ **(sth)** to become a member of an organization, a company, a club, etc: *to join a group/club/team/party* ◇ *He left school to join the army.* ◇ (*figurative*) *to join the ranks of the unemployed* ◇ *New members can join online.*
• DO STH WITH SB ELSE **4** 🔊 A1 [T] to take part in sth that sb else is doing or to go somewhere with them: ~ **sb** *Do you mind if I join you?* ◇ ~ **sb for sth** *Will you join us for lunch?* ◇ ~ **sb + adv./prep** *They've invited us to join them on their yacht.* ◇ ~ **sth** *Over 200 members of staff joined the strike.* ◇ ~ **sb in doing sth** *I'm sure you'll all join me in wishing Ted and Laura a very happy marriage.*
• TRAIN/PLANE **5** [T] ~ **sth** (*BrE*) if you **join** a train, plane, etc. you get on it
• ROAD/PATH/LINE **6** [T] ~ **sth** if you **join** a road or a line of people, you start to travel along it, or move into it
IDM **join ˈbattle (with sb)** (*formal*) to begin fighting sb: (*figurative*) *Local residents have joined battle with the council over the lack of parking facilities.* **join the ˈclub** (*informal*) used when sth bad that has happened to sb else has also happened to you: *So you didn't get a job either? Join the club!* **join ˈhands (with sb) 1** if two people **join hands**, they hold each other's hands **2** to work together in doing sth: *Education has been reluctant to join hands with business.* ⇨ more at BEAT v., FORCE n.
PHRV **join ˈin (sth/doing sth)** | **join ˈin (with sb/sth)** to take part in an activity with other people: *She listens but she never joins in.* ◇ *I wish he would join in with the other children.* **join ˈup** to become a member of the armed forces SYN **enlist**. **join ˈup (with sb)** to combine with sb else to do sth: *We'll join up with the other groups later.*
■ noun
• CONNECTION a place where two things are fixed together: *The two pieces were stuck together so well that you could hardly see the join.*

**joined-up** adj. [usually before noun] (*BrE*) **1 joined-up** writing is writing in which the letters in a word are joined to each other ⇨ compare PRINTING **2** intelligent and involving good communication between different parts so that they can work together effectively: *We need more joined-up thinking in our approach to the environment.*

**join·er** /ˈdʒɔɪnə(r)/ noun **1** (BrE) a person whose job is to make the wooden parts of a building, especially window frames, doors, etc. ⇒ compare CARPENTER **2** a person who joins an organization, club, etc: *All joiners will receive a welcome pack.*

**join·ery** /ˈdʒɔɪnəri/ noun [U] the work of a joiner or things made by a joiner

**joint** ⁀+ B2 /dʒɔɪnt/ adj., noun, verb

■ *adj.* ⁀+ B2 [only before noun] involving two or more people together: *a joint account* (= a bank account in the name of more than one person, for example a husband and wife) ◇ *The report was a joint effort* (= we worked on it together). ◇ *They finished in joint first place.* ◇ *They were joint owners of the house* (= they owned it together). ▶ **joint·ly** adv.: *The event was organized jointly by students and staff.*

■ *noun* **1** ⁀+ B2 a place where two bones are joined together in the body in a way that enables them to bend and move: *inflammation of the knee joint* ⇒ see also BALL-AND-SOCKET JOINT, HIP JOINT **2** ⁀+ C1 a place where two or more parts of an object are joined together, especially to form a corner **3** (BrE) a piece of ROAST meat: *a joint of beef* ◇ *the Sunday joint* (= one traditionally eaten on a Sunday) **4** (informal) a place where people meet to eat, drink, dance, etc., especially one that is cheap: *a fast-food joint* **5** (informal) a cigarette containing MARIJUANA (= an illegal drug)

IDM **out of ˈjoint 1** (of a bone) pushed out of its correct position **2** not working or behaving in the normal way ⇒ more at CASE v., NOSE n.

■ *verb* ~ **sth** to cut meat into large pieces, usually each containing a bone

**Joint ˈChiefs of ˈStaff** noun [pl.] (in the US) the leaders of the ARMED FORCES who advise the President on military matters

**ˌjoint deˈgree** noun (in the UK and some other countries) a university course in which you study two subjects to the same standard

**joint·ed** /ˈdʒɔɪntɪd/ adj. [usually before noun] having parts that fit together and can move: *a doll with jointed arms/legs* ⇒ see also DOUBLE-JOINTED

**ˈjoint family** noun (IndE) a family structure in which grandparents, uncles, aunts and cousins are considered as a single unit living in one house

**ˌjoint resoˈlution** noun (in the US) a decision that has been approved by the Senate and the House of Representatives

**ˌjoint-ˈstock company** noun (business) a company that is owned by all the people who have shares in it

**ˌjoint ˈventure** noun (business) a business project or activity that is begun by two or more companies, etc., which remain separate organizations

**joist** /dʒɔɪst/ noun a long thick piece of wood or metal that is used to support a floor or ceiling in a building ⇒ WORD-FINDER NOTE at CONSTRUCTION

**jo·joba** /həˈhəʊbə, həʊˈh-; NAmE həʊˈh-/ noun [U] oil from the seeds of an American plant, often used in COSMETICS **2** [U, C] the plant that produces these seeds

**joke** ⓘ A2 /dʒəʊk/ noun, verb

■ *noun* **1** ⁀ A2 something that you say or do to make people laugh, for example a funny story that you tell: *I can't tell jokes.* ◇ *She's always cracking jokes.* ◇ *They often make jokes at each other's expense.* ◇ *I didn't get the joke* (= understand it). ◇ *I wish he wouldn't tell dirty jokes* (= about sex). ◇ **as a**~ *I only did it as a joke* (= it was not meant seriously). ⇒ see also IN-JOKE, PRACTICAL JOKE ⇒ WORDFIND-ER NOTE at COMEDY **2** [sing.] (informal) a person, thing or situation that is silly or annoying and cannot be taken seriously: *This latest pay offer is a joke.* ⇒ see also JOCULAR

IDM **be/get beyond a ˈjoke** to become annoying and no longer acceptable **be no ˈjoke** to be difficult or unpleasant: *It's no joke trying to find a job these days.* **the ˈjoke's on sb** (informal) used to say that sb who tried to make another person look silly now looks silly instead **make a ˈjoke of sth** to laugh about sth that is serious or should be taken seriously **take a ˈjoke** to be able to laugh at a joke against yourself: *The trouble with her is she can't take a joke.*

■ *verb* **1** ⁀ A2 [I, T] to say sth to make people laugh; to tell a funny story: *She was laughing and joking with the children.* ◇ **~ about sth** *They often joked about all the things that could go wrong.* ◇ **+ speech** *'I cooked it myself, so be careful!' he joked.* **2** ⁀ A2 [I, T] to say sth that is not true because you think it is funny: *I didn't mean that—I was only joking.* ◇ **~ about (doing) sth** *She was only half joking about being president one day.* ◇ **~ that…** *She joked that she only loved him for his money.*

IDM **ˌjoking aˈpart** (BrE) | **ˌjoking aˈside** (BrE, NAmE) used to show that you are now being serious after you have said sth funny **you're ˈjoking** | **you must be ˈjoking** (informal) used to show that you are very surprised at what sb has just said: *She's going out with Dan? You're joking!* ◇ *No way am I doing that. You must be joking.*

**joker** /ˈdʒəʊkə(r)/ noun **1** a person who likes making jokes or doing silly things to make people laugh **2** (informal) a person that you think is stupid because they annoy you **3** an extra PLAYING CARD that is used in some card games, usually as a WILD CARD

IDM **the ˌjoker in the ˈpack** a person or thing that could change the way that things will happen in a way that cannot be predicted

**jokey** (also **joky**) /ˈdʒəʊki/ adj. (informal) funny; making people laugh

**jok·ing·ly** /ˈdʒəʊkɪŋli/ adv. in a way that is intended to be funny and not serious

**jol** /dʒɔl/ noun, verb (SAfrE, informal)

■ *noun* a time of having fun; a party: *Have a jol!* ◇ *a New Year's Eve jol*

■ *verb* [I] (-ll-) to have fun: *We jolled all night.*

**jol·lof rice** /ˌdʒɒləf ˈraɪs; NAmE ˌdʒɑːl-/ noun [U] a type of STEW eaten in West Africa made from rice, CHILLIES and meat or fish

**jolly** /ˈdʒɒli; NAmE ˈdʒɑːli/ adj., adv., verb, noun

■ *adj.* (**jol·lier**, **jol·li·est**) **1** happy and cheerful: *a jolly crowd/face/mood* **2** (old-fashioned) fun: *a jolly evening/party/time* ▶ **jol·lity** /-ləti/ noun [U] (old-fashioned): *scenes of high-spirits and jollity*

■ *adv.* (old-fashioned, BrE, informal) very: *That's a jolly good idea.*

IDM **ˌjolly ˈgood!** (old-fashioned, BrE, informal) used to show that you approve of sth that sb has just said **ˌjolly ˈwell** (old-fashioned, BrE, informal) used to emphasize a statement when you are annoyed about sth: *If you don't come now, you can jolly well walk home!*

■ *verb* (**jol·lies**, **jolly·ing**, **jol·lied**, **jol·lied**)

PHRV **ˌjolly sb aˈlong** to encourage sb in a cheerful way **ˌjolly sb ˈinto sth/into ˈdoing sth** to persuade or encourage sb to do sth by making them feel happy about it **ˌjolly sb/sth ˈup** to make sb/sth more cheerful

■ *noun* (pl. **-ies**) (BrE) a trip that you make for fun

IDM **get your ˈjollies** (informal) to get pleasure or have fun

**the ˌJolly ˈRoger** noun [sing.] a black flag with a white SKULL AND CROSSBONES on it, used in the past by PIRATES

**jolt** /dʒəʊlt/ verb, noun

■ *verb* **1** [I, T] to move or to make sb/sth move suddenly and roughly SYN jerk: (+ adv./prep.) *The truck jolted and rattled over the rough ground.* ◇ *The bus jolted to a halt.* ◇ (figurative) *Her heart jolted when she saw him.* ◇ **~ sb/sth (+ adv./prep.)** *He was jolted forwards as the bus moved off.* **2** [T] to give sb a sudden shock, especially so that they start to take action or deal with a situation: **~ sb/sth (into sth)** *His remark jolted her into action.* ◇ **~ sb/sth (out of sth)** *a method of jolting the economy out of recession* ◇ **~ sb/sth + adj.** *I was suddenly jolted awake.*

■ *noun* [usually sing.] **1** a sudden rough movement SYN jerk: *The plane landed with a jolt.* **2** a sudden strong feeling, especially of shock or surprise: *a jolt of dismay*

**Joneses** /ˈdʒəʊnzɪz/ noun [pl.]

IDM **keep up with the ˈJoneses** (informal, often disapproving) to try to have all the possessions and social achievements that your friends and neighbours have

# josh

**josh** /dʒɒʃ; NAmE dʒɑːʃ/ verb [I, T] ~ (sb) | + speech (informal) to gently make fun of sb or talk to them in a joking way SYN tease

**joss stick** /ˈdʒɒs stɪk; NAmE ˈdʒɑːs/ noun a thin wooden stick covered with a substance that burns slowly and produces a sweet smell

**jos·tle** /ˈdʒɒsl; NAmE ˈdʒɑːsl/ verb [T, I] ~ (sb) to push roughly against sb in a crowd: *The visiting president was jostled by angry demonstrators.* ◇ *People were jostling, arguing and complaining.* PHRV **ˈjostle for sth** to compete strongly and with force for sth: *People in the crowd were jostling for the best positions.*

**jot** /dʒɒt; NAmE dʒɑːt/ verb, noun
- verb (-tt-) PHRV **jot sth↔ˈdown** to write sth quickly: *I'll just jot down the address for you.*
- noun IDM **not a/one ˈjot** used to mean 'not even a small amount' when you are emphasizing a negative statement: *There's not a jot of truth in what he says* (= none at all).

**jot·ter** /ˈdʒɒtə(r); NAmE ˈdʒɑːt-/ noun (BrE) **1** a small book used for writing notes in **2** (ScotE) an exercise book

**jot·tings** /ˈdʒɒtɪŋz; NAmE ˈdʒɑːt-/ noun [pl.] short notes that are written down quickly

**joule** /dʒuːl/ noun (abbr. J) (physics) a unit of energy or work

**jour·nal** B1 /ˈdʒɜːnl; NAmE ˈdʒɜːrnl/ noun **1** a newspaper or magazine that deals with a particular subject or profession: *a scientific/an academic journal* ◇ *the British Medical Journal* ◇ *an online journal* ◇ *a journal article* **2** used in the title of some newspapers: *the Wall Street Journal* **3** B1 a written record of the things you do, see, etc. every day: *He kept a journal of his travels across Asia.* ⇒ compare DIARY

**jour·nal·ese** /ˌdʒɜːnəˈliːz; NAmE ˌdʒɜːrn-/ noun [U] (usually disapproving) a style of language that is thought to be typical of that used in newspapers

**jour·nal·ism** B2 /ˈdʒɜːnəlɪzəm; NAmE ˈdʒɜːrn-/ noun [U] the work of collecting and writing news stories for newspapers, magazines, radio, television or online news sites; the news stories that are written: *I'd like a career in journalism.* ◇ *This story was a good piece of investigative journalism.* ⇒ see also CITIZEN JOURNALISM, YELLOW JOURNALISM

**jour·nal·ist** A2 /ˈdʒɜːnəlɪst; NAmE ˈdʒɜːrn-/ noun a person whose job is to collect and write news stories for newspapers, magazines, radio, television or online news sites: *a freelance journalist* ◇ *She's an investigative journalist with a French newspaper.* ⇒ compare REPORTER ⇒ see also CITIZEN JOURNALIST ⇒ WORDFINDER NOTE at NEWSPAPER

**WORDFINDER** censorship, correspondent, coverage, editor, exclusive, news agency, newspaper, report, stringer

**jour·nal·is·tic** /ˌdʒɜːnəˈlɪstɪk; NAmE ˌdʒɜːrn-/ adj. [usually before noun] connected with the work of a journalist: *journalistic skills* ◇ *his journalistic background*

**jour·ney** A1 /ˈdʒɜːni; NAmE ˈdʒɜːrni/ noun, verb
- noun **1** A1 an act of travelling from one place to another, especially when they are far apart: *They went on a long train journey across India.* ◇ *Many refugees made the journey alone.* ◇ *Did you have a good journey?* ◇ *the outward/return journey* ◇ *It's a day's journey by car.* ◇ **on a ~** *She took her sister with her to keep her company on the journey.* ◇ **~ from …** *Devizes is a two-hour journey from London.* ◇ **~ to …** *It is unclear why he embarked on his final journey to Vienna.* ⇒ SYNONYMS at TRIP

**WORDFINDER** commute, departure, destination, excursion, expedition, itinerary, pilgrimage, safari, travel

**2** B2 ~ (from sth) (to sth) a long and often difficult process of personal change and development: *The book describes a spiritual journey from despair to happiness.*
- verb [I] (+ adv./prep.) (formal or literary) to travel, especially a long distance: *They journeyed for seven long months.*

**jour·ney·man** /ˈdʒɜːnimən; NAmE ˈdʒɜːrn-/ noun (pl. -men /-mən/) **1** (in the past) a person who was trained to do a particular job and who then worked for sb else **2** a person who has training and experience in a job and is a reliable but not a brilliant worker

**journo** /ˈdʒɜːnəʊ; NAmE ˈdʒɜːrn-/ (pl. -os) noun (BrE, informal) a journalist

**joust** /dʒaʊst/ verb **1** [I] to fight on horses using a long stick (= a LANCE) to try to knock the other person off their horse, especially as part of a formal contest in the past **2** [I] (formal) to argue with sb, especially as part of a formal or public debate ▶ **joust** noun

**jo·vial** /ˈdʒəʊviəl/ adj. very cheerful and friendly ▶ **jo·vi·al·ity** /ˌdʒəʊviˈæləti/ noun [U] **jo·vial·ly** /ˈdʒəʊviəli/ adv.

**jowl** /dʒaʊl/ noun [usually pl.] the lower part of sb's CHEEK (= part of the face below the eyes) when it is fat and hangs down below their CHIN (= part below the mouth): *a man with heavy jowls* IDM see CHEEK n.

**joy** B2 /dʒɔɪ/ noun **1** B2 [U] a feeling of great happiness SYN delight: *Her books have brought joy to millions.* ◇ **~ of (doing) sth** *the sheer joy of being with her again* ◇ **with ~** *I almost wept with joy.* ◇ **for ~** *I didn't expect them to jump for joy at the news* (= to be very pleased). ◇ *Tears of joy were running down her cheeks.* ◇ **to sb's ~** *To his great joy, she accepted.* ⇒ SYNONYMS at PLEASURE **2** [C] a person or thing that causes you to feel very happy: *the joys of fatherhood* ◇ *The game was a joy to watch.* **3** [U] (BrE, informal) (in questions and negative sentences) success or SATISFACTION: *We complained about our rooms but got no joy from the manager.* ◇ *'Any joy at the shops?' 'No, they didn't have what I wanted.'*
IDM **full of the joys of ˈspring** very cheerful ⇒ more at PRIDE n.

**joy·ful** /ˈdʒɔɪfl/ adj. very happy; causing people to be happy ⇒ SYNONYMS at HAPPY ▶ **joy·ful·ly** /-fəli/ adv. **joy·ful·ness** noun [U]

**joy·less** /ˈdʒɔɪləs/ adj. (formal) bringing no happiness; without joy: *a joyless childhood*

**joy·ous** /ˈdʒɔɪəs/ adj. (literary) very happy; causing people to be happy SYN joyful: *joyous laughter* ▶ **joy·ous·ly** adv.

**joy·rid·ing** /ˈdʒɔɪraɪdɪŋ/ noun [U] the crime of stealing a car and driving it for pleasure, usually in a fast and dangerous way ▶ **joy·ride** noun **joy·rider** noun

**joy·stick** /ˈdʒɔɪstɪk/ noun **1** a stick with a handle used with some computer games to move images on the screen **2** (informal) a stick with a handle in an aircraft that is used to control direction or height

**JP** /ˌdʒeɪ ˈpiː/ noun JUSTICE OF THE PEACE: *Helen Alvey JP*

**JPEG** /ˈdʒeɪpeg/ noun (computing) **1** [U] technology that reduces the size of files that contain images (the abbreviation for 'Joint Photographic Experts Group'): *JPEG files* **2** [C] an image created using this technology: *You can download the pictures as JPEGs.*

**Jr** (also **Jnr**) (both BrE) (also **Jr.** NAmE, BrE) abbr. JUNIOR ⇒ compare SR

**jua·kali** /dʒuːəˈkæli; NAmE -ˈkɑːli; EAfrE dʒuaˈkali/ noun [U] (EAfrE) (in Kenya) the informal jobs that people do to earn money, for example making useful things from metal and wood: *the juakali sector*

**ju·bi·lant** /ˈdʒuːbɪlənt/ adj. feeling or showing great happiness because of a success ▶ **ju·bi·lant·ly** adv.

**jubi·la·tion** /ˌdʒuːbɪˈleɪʃn/ noun [U] a feeling of great happiness because of a success

**ju·bi·lee** /ˈdʒuːbɪliː, ˌdʒuːbɪˈliː/ noun a special anniversary of an event, especially one that took place 25, 50 or 60 years ago; the celebrations connected with it ⇒ see also

DIAMOND JUBILEE, GOLDEN JUBILEE, SILVER JUBILEE
⇒ WORDFINDER NOTE at CELEBRATE

**Ju·da·ism** /ˈdʒuːdeɪɪzəm; *NAmE* -diɪz-, -deɪɪz-/ *noun* [U] the religion of the Jewish people, based mainly on the first five books of the Bible and the Talmud ▶ **Ju·da·ic** /dʒuːˈdeɪɪk/ *adj.* [only before noun]: *Judaic tradition*

**Judas** /ˈdʒuːdəs/ *noun* (*disapproving*) a person who treats a friend badly by lying to or about them or telling their secrets to other people **SYN** **traitor** **ORIGIN** According to the Bible, Judas Iscariot was a follower of Jesus Christ who betrayed him for thirty pieces of silver.

**jud·der** /ˈdʒʌdə(r)/ *verb* [I] to shake violently: *He slammed on the brakes and the car juddered to a halt.*

## judge ⓞ B1 /dʒʌdʒ/ *noun, verb*

■ *noun*
- **IN COURT 1** B1 a person in a court who has the authority to decide how criminals should be punished or to make legal decisions: *a High Court judge* ◊ *a federal/district judge* ◊ *the presiding trial judge* ◊ **before a~** *The case comes before Judge Cooper next week.* ◊ *The judge sentenced him to five years in prison.* ⇒ compare JUSTICE OF THE PEACE, MAGISTRATE
- **IN COMPETITION 2** B1 a person who decides who has won a competition: *The judges' decision is final.* ◊ *She has joined the panel of judges in the popular TV talent show.* ⇒ WORDFINDER NOTE at COMPETITION ⇒ see also TOUCH JUDGE
- **SB WHO GIVES OPINION 3** B1 [usually sing.] a person who has the necessary knowledge or skills to give their opinion about the value or quality of sb/sth: *She's a good judge of character.*

■ *verb*
- **FORM OPINION 1** B1 [I, T] to form an opinion about sb/sth, based on the information you have: *As far as I can judge, all of them are to blame.* ◊ **judging by sth** *Judging by her last email, they are having a wonderful time.* ◊ **to~from sth** *To judge from what he said, he was very disappointed.* ◊ **~sb/sth (on sth)** *Schools should not be judged only on exam results.* ◊ **~sb/sth + noun** *The tour was judged a great success.* ◊ **~sb/sth to be/do sth** *The concert was judged to have been a great success.* ◊ **~sb/sth + adj.** *They judged it wise to say nothing.* ◊ **~that ...** *He judged that the risk was too great.* ◊ **it is judged that ...** *It was judged that the risk was too great.* ◊ **~how, what, etc ...** *It was hard to judge how great the risk was.*
- **ESTIMATE 2** B1 [T] to guess the size, amount, etc. of sth: *~sth Young children are unable to judge the speed of traffic.* ◊ **~how, what, etc ...** *It's difficult to judge how long the journey will take.* ◊ **~sb/sth to be/do sth** *I judged him to be about 50.*
- **IN COMPETITION 3** B1 [T, I] to decide the result of a competition; to be the judge in a competition: *~sth She was asked to judge the essay competition.* ◊ **~sb/sth + noun/adj.** *The first team to cross the line will be judged the winner.*
- **GIVE OPINION 4** B2 [T, I] **~(sb)** to give your opinion about sb, especially when you think they are bad: *What gives you the right to judge other people?*
- **IN COURT 5** [T] to decide whether sb is guilty or innocent in a court: *~sth to judge a case* ◊ **~sb + adj.** *to judge sb guilty/not guilty*

**IDM** **don't judge a ˌbook by its ˈcover** (*saying*) used to say that you should not form an opinion about sb/sth from their appearance only

## judge·ment ⓞ B2 ⓞ (*also* judg·ment *especially in NAmE*) /ˈdʒʌdʒmənt/ *noun* **1** B2 [U] the ability to make sensible decisions after carefully considering the best thing to do: *good/poor/sound judgement* ◊ *She showed a lack of judgement when she gave Mark the job.* ◊ *It's not something I can give you rules for; you'll have to use your judgement.* ◊ *He achieved his aim **more by luck than judgement**.* ◊ *The accident was caused by an **error of judgement** on the part of the pilot.* **2** B2 [C, U] an opinion that you form about sth after thinking about it carefully; the act of making this opinion known to others: *In his portrait of the dictator he avoids any **moral judgements**.* ◊ **~about sth** *He refused to **make a judgement** about the situation.* ◊ **~on sth** *Who am I to **pass judgement** on her behaviour?* (= to criti-

cize it) ◊ **in sb's ~** *It was, in her judgement, the wrong thing to do.* ◊ *I did it **against my better judgement** (= although I thought it was perhaps the wrong thing to do).* ⇒ see also VALUE JUDGEMENT **3** (*usually* **judgment**) [C, U] the decision of a court or of a judge: *a judgment from the European Court of Justice* ◊ *The judgment will be given tomorrow.* ◊ *The court has yet to **pass judgment** (= say what its decision is) in this case.* **4** [C, usually sing.] **~(on sb)** (*formal*) something bad that happens to sb that is thought to be a punishment from God ⇒ see also DAY OF JUDGEMENT, LAST JUDGEMENT
**IDM** see RESERVE *v.*, SIT

**judge·men·tal** (*especially BrE*) (*also* **judg·men·tal** *especially in NAmE*) /dʒʌdʒˈmentl/ *adj.* **1** (*disapproving*) judging people and criticizing them too quickly ⇒ see also NON-JUDGEMENTAL **2** (*formal*) connected with the process of judging things: *the judgemental process*

**ˈjudgement call** (*also* **ˈjudgment call** *especially in NAmE*) *noun* (*informal*) a decision you have to make where there is no clear rule about what the right thing to do is, so that you have to use your own judgement

**ˈJudgement Day** (*also* **ˈJudgment Day** *especially in NAmE*) (*also* **the Day of ˈJudgement**, **the Last ˈJudgement**) *noun* [sing.] the day at the end of the world when, according to some religions, God will judge everyone who has ever lived

**ju·di·ca·ture** /ˈdʒuːdɪkətʃə(r)/ *noun* (*law*) **1** [U] the system by which courts, trials, etc. are organized in a country **2 the judicature** [sing. + sing./pl. v.] judges when they are considered as a group

**ju·di·cial** ⓞ C1 /dʒuˈdɪʃl/ *adj.* [usually before noun] connected with a court, a judge or legal judgement: *judicial powers* ◊ *the judicial process/system* ▶ **ju·di·cial·ly** /-ʃəli/ *adv.*

**juˌdicial ˈactivism** *noun* [U] (*law*) (in the US) the idea that it is not necessary to follow the exact words of the Constitution when new laws are made

**the juˈdicial branch** *noun* [sing.] (in the US) the part of the government consisting of judges and courts that interpret the laws ⇒ compare EXECUTIVE BRANCH, LEGISLATIVE BRANCH

**juˌdicial reˈstraint** *noun* [U] (*law*) (in the US) the idea that judges of the Supreme Court or other courts should not try to change a law that is allowed by the Constitution

**juˌdicial reˈview** *noun* (*law*) **1** [U] (in the US) the power of the Supreme Court to decide if sth is allowed by the Constitution **2** [C, U] (in the UK) a procedure in which a court examines an action or decision of a public body and decides whether it was right: *There is to be a judicial review of the visa changes.*

**ju·di·ciary** /dʒuˈdɪʃəri; *NAmE* -ʃieri/ *noun* (*usually* **the judiciary**) [C + sing./pl. v.] (*pl.* **-ies**) the judges of a country or a state, when they are considered as a group: *an independent judiciary* ⇒ compare EXECUTIVE, LEGISLATURE

**ju·di·cious** /dʒuˈdɪʃəs/ *adj.* (*formal, approving*) careful and sensible; showing good judgement **OPP** **injudicious** ▶ **ju·di·cious·ly** *adv.*: *a judiciously worded letter*

**judo** /ˈdʒuːdəʊ/ *noun* [U] (*from Japanese*) a sport in which two people fight and try to throw each other to the ground: *He does judo.* ◊ *She's a black belt in judo.*

**jug** (*BrE*) (*NAmE* **pitcher**)    **pitcher** (*BrE* **jug**)

**jug** /dʒʌɡ/ *noun* **1** (*BrE*) (*NAmE* **pitch·er**) a container with a handle and a LIP, for holding and pouring liquids: *a milk/water jug* **2** (*NAmE*) (*BrE* **pitch·er**) a large round container

# jugaad

with a small opening and a handle, and usually with a STOPPER or CAP, for holding liquids: *a five-gallon jug of beer* **3** the amount of liquid contained in a jug: *She spilled a jug of water.* **4 jugs** [pl.] (*taboo*, *slang*) an offensive word for a woman's breasts

**ju·gaad** /dʒʊˈɡɑːd/ *noun* (*IndE*) **1** [U] the use of skill and imagination to find an easy solution to a problem or to fix or make sth using cheap, basic items **2** [C] a vehicle made from different parts of other vehicles and used for carrying people, goods, etc., that is usually open at the front and the back and often not very safe to drive ▶ **ju·gaad** *adj.*: *jugaad innovation*

**jug·ful** /ˈdʒʌɡfʊl/ *noun* the amount of liquid contained in a jug

**jug·ger·naut** /ˈdʒʌɡənɔːt; NAmE -ɡərn-/ *noun* **1** (*BrE, often disapproving*) a very large lorry: *juggernauts roaring through country villages* **2** (*formal*) a large and powerful force or institution that cannot be controlled: *a bureaucratic juggernaut*

**jug·gle** /ˈdʒʌɡl/ *verb* **1** [I, T] to throw a set of three or more objects such as balls into the air and catch and throw them again quickly, one at a time, so as to keep at least one in the air at all times: *My uncle taught me to juggle.* ◇ **~ with sth** *to juggle with balls* ◇ **~ sth** (*figurative*) *I was juggling books, shopping bags and the baby* (= I was trying to hold them all without dropping them). **2** [T, I] **~(sth) (with sth)** to try to deal with two or more important jobs or activities at the same time so that you can fit all of them into your life: *Working mothers are used to juggling their jobs, their children's needs and their housework.* **3** [T] **~ sth** to organize information, figures, the money you spend, etc. in the most useful or effective way

**jug·gler** /ˈdʒʌɡlə(r)/ *noun* a person who juggles, especially in order to entertain people

**jugu·lar** /ˈdʒʌɡjələ(r)/ (*also* **ˈjugular vein**) *noun* any of the three large VEINS in the neck that carry blood from the head towards the heart
[IDM] **go for the ˈjugular** (*informal*) to attack sb's weakest point during a discussion, in an aggressive way

**juice** 🅾️ A1 /dʒuːs/ *noun*, *verb*
■ *noun* **1** 🅾️ A1 [U, C] the liquid that comes from fruit or vegetables; a drink made from this: *a glass of fruit juice* ◇ *a carton of apple juice* ◇ *Add the juice of two lemons.* ◇ *Two orange juices, please.* **2** [C, usually pl., U] the liquid that comes out of a piece of meat when it is cooked **3** [C, usually pl.] the liquid in the stomach that helps you to DIGEST food: *digestive/gastric juices* **4** [U] (*informal*) electricity: *My phone has run out of juice.* **5** [U] (*especially BrE, informal*) petrol [IDM] see STEW *v.*
■ *verb* **~ sth** to get the juice out of fruit or vegetables: *Juice two oranges.*
[PHRV] **ˌjuice sth↔ˈup** (*especially NAmE, informal*) to make sth more exciting or interesting

**ˈjuice bar** *noun* a cafe serving drinks made from fruit that has been freshly pressed

**ˈjuice box** *noun* (*NAmE*) a small box of juice for one person that usually has a STRAW attached to it

**juicer** /ˈdʒuːsə(r)/ *noun* **1** a piece of electrical equipment for getting the juice out of fruit or vegetables **2** (*NAmE*) (*BrE* **ˈlemon-squeezer**) a kitchen UTENSIL (= a tool) for pressing juice out of a fruit

**juicy** /ˈdʒuːsi/ *adj.* (**juici·er**, **juici·est**) **1** (*approving*) containing a lot of juice and good to eat: *soft juicy pears* ◇ *The meat was tender and juicy.* ⊃ WORDFINDER NOTE at CRISP **2** (*informal*) interesting because you find it exciting or it shocks you: *juicy gossip* **3** (*informal*) attractive because it will bring you a lot of money or happiness: *a juicy prize*

**ju-jitsu** (*also* **jiu-jitsu**) /dʒuː ˈdʒɪtsuː/ *noun* [U] a Japanese system of fighting from which the sport of JUDO was developed

**juju** /ˈdʒuːdʒuː/ *noun* **1** [U] a type of magic in West Africa **2** [C] an object used in West African magic **3** [U] a type of Nigerian music that uses guitars and drums

**juke-box** /ˈdʒuːkbɒks; NAmE -bɑːks/ *noun* a machine in a pub, bar, etc. that plays a song that you have chosen when you put coins into it (or, in modern machines, pay by card)

**julep** /ˈdʒuːlɪp/ *noun* [U, C] = MINT JULEP

**Ju·lian cal·en·dar** /ˌdʒuːliən ˈkælɪndə(r)/ *noun* [sing.] the system of arranging days and months in the year introduced by Julius Caesar, and used in Western countries until the GREGORIAN CALENDAR replaced it

**July** 🅾️ A1 /dʒuˈlaɪ/ *noun* [U, C] (*abbr.* **Jul.**) the 7th month of the year, between June and August [HELP] To see how **July** is used, look at the examples at **April**.

**jum·ble** /ˈdʒʌmbl/ *verb*, *noun*
■ *verb* (*often passive*) **~ sth (together/up)** to mix things together in a confused or untidy way: *Books, shoes and clothes were jumbled together on the floor.* ▶ **ˈjum·bled** *adj.*: *a jumbled collection of objects* ◇ *jumbled thoughts*
■ *noun* **1** [sing.] **~ (of sth)** an untidy or confused mixture of things: *a jumble of books and paper* ◇ *The essay was a meaningless jumble of ideas.* **2** [U] (*BrE*) a collection of old or used clothes, etc. that are no longer wanted and are going to be taken to a jumble sale

**ˈjumble sale** (*BrE*) (*also* **ˈrummage sale** *NAmE, BrE*) *noun* a sale of old or used clothes, etc. to make money for a church, school or other organization

**jumbo** /ˈdʒʌmbəʊ/ *noun*, *adj.*
■ *noun* (*pl.* **-os**) (*also* **ˈjumbo jet**) a large plane that can carry several hundred passengers, especially a Boeing 747
■ *adj.* [only before noun] (*informal*) very large; larger than usual: *a jumbo pack of cornflakes*

**jump** 🅾️ A2 /dʒʌmp/ *verb*, *noun*
■ *verb*
- **MOVE OFF/TO GROUND 1** 🅾️ A2 [I] to move quickly off the ground or away from a surface by pushing yourself with your legs and feet: *'Quick, jump!' he shouted.* ◇ **~ + adv./ prep.** *She jumped into the water to save them.* ◇ *She jumped down from the chair.* ◇ *The children were jumping up and down with excitement.* ◇ *The pilot jumped from the burning plane* (= with a PARACHUTE). ◇ **~ + noun** *She has jumped 2.2 metres.*
- **PASS OVER STH 2** 🅾️ A2 [I, T] to pass over sth by jumping [SYN] **leap**: **~ over sth** *He jumped over the wall to get away.* ◇ **~ sth** *Can you jump that gate?* ◇ **~ sth over sth** *I jumped my horse over all the fences.*
- **MOVE QUICKLY 3** 🅾️ A2 [I] **~ + adv./prep.** to move quickly and suddenly: *He jumped to his feet when they called his name.* ◇ *She jumped up and ran out of the room.* ◇ *Do you want a ride? Jump in.* **4** 🅾️ B1 [I] to make a sudden movement because of surprise, fear or excitement: *A loud bang made me jump.* ◇ *Her heart jumped when she heard the news.*
- **INCREASE 5** 🅾️ B2 [I] to rise suddenly by a large amount [SYN] **leap**: **~ by …** *Prices jumped by 60% last year.* ◇ **~ (from …) (to …)** *Sales jumped from $2.7 billion to $3.5 billion.*
- **CHANGE SUDDENLY 6** [I] **~ (about/around) (from sth to sth)** to change suddenly from one subject to another: *I couldn't follow the talk because he kept jumping about from one topic to another.* ◇ *The story then jumps from her childhood in New York to her first visit to London.*
- **LEAVE OUT 7** [T] **~ sth** to leave out sth and pass to a further point or stage: *You seem to have jumped several steps in the argument.*
- **OF MACHINE/DEVICE 8** [I] **(+ adv./prep.)** to move suddenly and unexpectedly, especially out of the correct position: *The needle jumped across the dial.*
- **ATTACK 9** [T, I] **~ (on) sb** (*informal*) to attack sb suddenly: *The thieves jumped him in a dark alleyway.*
- **VEHICLE 10** [T] **~ sth** (*NAmE*) to get on a vehicle very quickly, especially in a way that is dangerous or illegal: *to jump a bus* **11** (*NAmE*) = JUMP-START
- **BE LIVELY 12 be jumping** [I] (*informal*) to be very lively: *The bar's jumping tonight.*
[IDM] **be ˈjumping up and ˈdown** (*informal*) to be very angry or excited about sth **ˌjump down sb's ˈthroat** (*informal*) to

react very angrily to sb **jump the 'gun** to do sth too soon, before the right time **jump out of your 'skin** (*informal*) to move violently because of a sudden shock **jump the 'queue** (*BrE*) (*NAmE* **cut in 'line**, **jump the 'line**) to go to the front of a line of people without waiting for your turn: *She jumped the queue at the ticket counter.* **jump the 'rails** (of a train) to leave the track suddenly **jump the 'shark** (used especially about a television series, etc.) to include sth that is very hard to believe as an attempt to keep people watching, usually a sign that the show is not as good as it used to be: *Has the show finally jumped the shark?* **jump 'ship 1** to leave the ship on which you are serving, without permission **2** to leave an organization that you belong to, suddenly and unexpectedly **jump through 'hoops** to do sth difficult or complicated in order to achieve sth **jump 'to it** (*NAmE also* **hop 'to it**) (*informal*) used to tell sb to hurry and do something quickly ⇒ more at BAIL *n.*, BANDWAGON, CONCLUSION, DEEP END, LIGHT *n.*
**PHR V** ˈ**jump at sb** (*NAmE, informal*) = JUMP ON SB ˈ**jump at sth** to accept an opportunity, offer, etc. with enthusiasm **SYN** **leap at** ˌ**jump 'in 1** to interrupt a conversation: *Before she could reply Peter jumped in with an objection.* **2** to start to do sth very quickly without spending a long time thinking first ˈ**jump on sb** (*NAmE also* ˈ**jump at sb**) (*informal*) to criticize sb ˈ**jump 'out at sb** to be very obvious and easily noticed **SYN** **leap**: *The mistake in the figures jumped out at me.*
■ **noun**
• MOVEMENT **1** 🔊 an act of jumping: *to do a parachute jump* ◊ *~ of ... a jump of over six metres* ◊ *~ from sth Somehow he survived the jump from the third floor of the building.* ⇒ see also BROAD JUMP, BUNGEE JUMP, HIGH JUMP, LONG JUMP, SKI JUMP, TRIPLE JUMP
• BARRIER **2** a barrier like a narrow fence that a horse or a runner has to jump over in a race or competition: *The horse fell at the last jump.*
• INCREASE **3** 🔊 a sudden increase in amount, price or value: *unusually large price jumps* ◊ **in sth** *a 20 per cent jump in pre-tax profits*
• CHANGE **4** ~ **+ adv./prep.** a large or sudden change: *Is he good enough to* **make the jump** *into Formula One?* ◊ *The story takes a jump back in time.*
• SUDDEN MOVEMENT **5** a sudden movement caused by shock or surprise: *I sat up with a jump.*
**IDM** **to keep, etc. one jump ahead (of sb)** to keep your advantage over sb, especially your competitors, by taking action before they do or by making sure you know more than they do ⇒ more at HIGH JUMP, RUNNING *adj.*

ˈ**jump ball** *noun* (in basketball) a ball that the REFEREE throws up between two players to begin play

ˈ**jump cut** *noun* (*specialist*) (in films/movies) a sudden change from one scene to another

ˈ**jumped-up** *adj.* [only before noun] (*BrE, informal, disapproving*) thinking you are more important than you really are, particularly because you have risen in social status

**jump·er** /ˈdʒʌmpə(r)/ *noun* **1** (*BrE*) a piece of clothing for the upper part of the body, made of wool or cotton, with long SLEEVES (= arms) and no buttons **SYN** **sweater**: *a woolly jumper* **2** (*NAmE*) = PINAFORE (1) **3** a person, an animal or an insect that jumps: *He's a good jumper.*

ˈ**jumper cable** (*NAmE*) (*BrE* ˈ**jump lead**) *noun* [usually pl.] one of two cables that are used to start a car when it has no power in its battery. The jumper cables connect the battery to the battery of another car.

ˈ**jumping-ˈoff point** (*also* ˈ**jumping-ˈoff place**) *noun* a place from which to start a journey or new activity

ˈ**jump jet** *noun* an aircraft that can take off and land by going straight up or down, without needing a RUNWAY ⇒ WORDFINDER NOTE *at* AIRCRAFT

ˈ**jump lead** /ˈdʒʌmp liːd/ (*BrE*) (*NAmE* ˈ**jumper cable**) *noun* [usually pl.] one of two cables that are used to start a car when it has no power in its battery. The jump leads connect the battery to the battery of another car.

ˈ**jump-off** (*NAmE also* ˈ**ride-off**) *noun* (in the sport of SHOWJUMPING) an extra part of a competition in which

---

857　　　**junior**

horses that have the same score jump again to decide the winner

ˈ**jump rope** *noun*, **jump 'rope** *verb* (*NAmE*) ⇒ SKIPPING ROPE, SKIP *verb*

ˈ**jump shot** *noun* (in basketball) a shot made while jumping

ˈ**jump-start** (*NAmE also* **jump**) *verb* **1** ~ **sth** to start the engine of a car by connecting the battery to the battery of another car with JUMP LEADS **2** ~ **sth** to put a lot of energy into starting a process or an activity or into making it start more quickly

ˈ**jump·suit** /ˈdʒʌmpsuːt/ *noun* a piece of clothing that consists of trousers and a jacket or shirt SEWN together in one piece, worn as a fashion item or a uniform or to protect other clothes

**jumpy** /ˈdʒʌmpi/ *adj.* (*informal*) nervous and anxious, especially because you think that sth bad is going to happen

**junc·tion** 🔊+ 🄲 /ˈdʒʌŋkʃn/ *noun* **1** 🔊+ 🄲 (*especially BrE*) (*NAmE usually* **inter·sec·tion**) the place where two or more roads or railway lines meet: *It was near the junction of City Road and Green Street.* ◊ *Come off the motorway at junction 6.* ⇒ see also BOX JUNCTION, T-JUNCTION **2** a place where two or more cables, rivers or other things meet or are joined: *a telephone junction box*

**junc·ture** /ˈdʒʌŋktʃə(r)/ *noun* (*formal*) a particular point or stage in an activity or a series of events: *The battle had reached a crucial juncture.* ◊ **at this ~** *At this juncture, I would like to make an important announcement.*

**June** 🔊 🄰 /dʒuːn/ *noun* [U, C] (*abbr.* **Jun.**) the 6th month of the year, between May and July **HELP** To see how **June** is used, look at the examples at **April**.

**jun·gle** /ˈdʒʌŋɡl/ *noun* **1** [U, C] an area of tropical forest where trees and plants grow very thickly: *The area was covered in dense jungle.* ◊ *the jungles of South-East Asia* ◊ *jungle warfare* ◊ *Our garden is a complete jungle.* **2** [sing.] a dangerous or unfriendly place or situation, especially one where it is very difficult to be successful or to trust anyone: *It's a jungle out there — you've got to be strong to succeed.* ⇒ see also CONCRETE JUNGLE **IDM** see LAW

ˈ**jungle gym** (*NAmE*) (*BrE* ˈ**climbing frame**) *noun* a structure made of metal bars joined together for children to climb and play on ⇒ picture *at* FRAME

**jun·gli** /ˈdʒʌŋɡli/ *adj.* (*IndE*) wild; not educated

**jun·ior** 🔊 🄱 /ˈdʒuːniə(r)/ *adj., noun*
■ *adj.*
• OF LOW RANK **1** 🔊 🄱 [usually before noun] having a low rank in an organization or a profession: *a junior partner/minister/officer* ◊ **~ to sb** *She is junior to me.*
• IN SPORT **2** 🔊 🄱 [only before noun] connected with young people below a particular age, rather than with adults, especially in sports: *the world junior tennis championships*
• SON **3** **Junior** (*abbr.* **Jnr, Jr**) (especially in the US) used after the name of a man who has the same name as his father, to make it clear who is being referred to ⇒ compare THE YOUNGER
• SCHOOL/COLLEGE **4** [only before noun] (*BrE*) (of a school or part of a school) for children under the age of 11 or 13 **5** [only before noun] (*NAmE*) connected with the year before the last year in a HIGH SCHOOL or college: *I spent my junior year in France.* ⇒ compare SENIOR
■ *noun*
• IN SPORT **1** [C] a young person below a particular age, rather than an adult: *She has coached many of our leading juniors.*
• IN SCHOOL/COLLEGE **2** [C] (*BrE*) a child who goes to JUNIOR SCHOOL **3** [C] (*NAmE*) a student in the year before the last year in HIGH SCHOOL or college ⇒ compare SOPHOMORE
• LOW LEVEL JOB **4** [C] (*especially BrE*) a person who has a job at a low level within an organization: *office juniors*
• SON **5** [sing.] (*NAmE, informal*) a person's young son: *I leave junior with Mom when I'm at work.*

# junior college

**IDM** be ... years sb's 'junior | be sb's junior (by ...) to be younger than sb, by the number of years mentioned: *She's four years his junior.* ◊ *She's his junior by four years.*

**ˌjunior ˈcollege** *noun* (in the US) a college that offers programmes that are two years long. Some students go to a university or a college offering four-year programmes after they have finished studying at a junior college.

**ˌjunior ˈdoctor** *noun* (in the UK) a doctor who has finished medical school and who is working at a hospital to get further practical experience ⊃ compare HOUSE OFFICER, INTERN

**ˌjunior ˈhigh school** (also ˌjunior ˈhigh) *noun* [C, U] (in the US and Canada) a school for young people between the ages of 12 and 14 ⊃ compare MIDDLE SCHOOL (2), SENIOR HIGH SCHOOL

**ˈjunior school** *noun* [C, U] (in England and Wales) a school for children between the ages of 7 and 11

**ju·ni·per** /ˈdʒuːnɪpə(r)/ *noun* [U, C] a bush or small tree with purple BERRIES that are used in medicine and to add taste to GIN

**junk** /dʒʌŋk/ *noun, verb*
■ *noun* **1** [U] things that are considered to have no use or value **SYN** rubbish: *I've cleared out all that old junk in the attic.* ◊ *There's nothing but junk on the TV.* ◊ (*informal, disapproving*) *Is this all your junk* (= are these all your things)? ⊃ SYNONYMS at THING **2** [U] = JUNK FOOD **3** [C] a Chinese boat with a square sail and a flat bottom
■ *verb* ~ sth (*informal*) to get rid of sth because it is no longer valuable or useful

**ˈjunk bond** *noun* (*business*) a type of BOND that pays a high rate of interest because there is a lot of risk involved, often used to raise money quickly in order to buy the shares of another company

**jun·ket** /ˈdʒʌŋkɪt/ *noun* (*informal, disapproving*) a trip or celebration that organized for government officials or business people and paid for by sb else, especially using public money

**ˈjunk food** (also junk) *noun* [U] (also junk foods [pl.]) (*informal, disapproving*) food that is quick and easy to prepare and eat but that is thought to be bad for your health

**junkie** (also junky) /ˈdʒʌŋki/ *noun* (*informal*) a drug ADDICT (= a person who is unable to stop taking dangerous drugs)

**ˈjunk mail** *noun* [U] (*disapproving*) advertising material that is sent or emailed to people who have not asked for it ⊃ compare SPAM

**ˌjunk ˈscience** *noun* [U] (*disapproving*) used to refer to ideas and theories that seem to be well researched and scientific but in fact have little evidence to support them

**ˈjunk shop** *noun* (*especially BrE*) a shop that buys and sells old furniture and other objects, at cheap prices

**junky** /ˈdʒʌŋki/ *adj.* (*informal, especially NAmE*) of poor quality or of little value

**ˈjunk·yard** /ˈdʒʌŋkjɑːd; NAmE -jɑːrd/ (*especially NAmE*) (*especially BrE* scrap·yard) *noun* a place where old cars, machines, etc. are collected, so that parts of them, or the metal they are made of, can be sold to be used again

**junta** /ˈdʒʌntə; NAmE ˈhʊn-/ *noun* a military government that has taken power by force

**Ju·pi·ter** /ˈdʒuːpɪtə(r)/ *noun* the largest planet of the SOLAR SYSTEM, fifth in order of distance from the sun

**Jur·as·sic** /dʒuˈræsɪk/ *adj.* (*geology*) of the PERIOD between around 208 to 146 million years ago, when the largest known dinosaurs lived; of the rocks formed during this time ▶ **the Jur·as·sic** *noun* [sing.]

**jur·id·ic·al** /dʒʊəˈrɪdɪkl; NAmE dʒʊˈr-/ *adj.* [usually before noun] (*formal*) connected with the law, judges or legal matters

**jur·is·dic·tion** /ˌdʒʊərɪsˈdɪkʃn; NAmE ˌdʒʊr-/ *noun* (*formal*) **1** [U, C] ~ (over sb/sth) | ~ (of sb/sth) (to do sth) the authority that an official organization has to make legal decisions about sb/sth: *The English court had* no jurisdiction over the defendants. **2** [C] an area or a country in which a particular system of laws has authority ▶ **jur·is·dic·tion·al** /-ʃənl/ *adj.*

**jur·is·pru·dence** /ˌdʒʊərɪsˈpruːdns; NAmE ˌdʒʊr-/ *noun* [U] (*specialist*) the scientific study of law: *a professor of jurisprudence*

**jur·ist** /ˈdʒʊərɪst; NAmE ˈdʒʊr-/ *noun* (*formal*) a person who is an expert in law

**juror** /ˈdʒʊərə(r); NAmE ˈdʒʊr-/ *noun* a member of a jury

**jury** /ˈdʒʊəri; NAmE ˈdʒʊri/ *noun* [C + sing./pl. v.] (*pl. -ies*) **1** (also panel, 'jury panel *especially in NAmE*) a group of members of the public who listen to the facts of a case in a court and decide whether or not sb is guilty of a crime, or whether a claim has been proved: *members of the jury* ◊ *The jury has/have reached a verdict of guilty.* ◊ **on a ~** to be/sit/serve on a jury ◊ **by ~** the right to trial by jury ⊃ see also GRAND JURY **2** a group of people who decide who is the winner of a competition: **on a ~** *He was on the jury for this year's Booker Prize.*
**IDM** the jury is (still) 'out on sth used when you are saying that sth is still not certain

**ˈjury duty** (*BrE usually* 'jury service) *noun* [U] a period of time spent as a member of a jury in court

**jus** /ʒuː; NAmE also dʒuː/ *noun* [U] (*from French*) a thin sauce, especially one made from meat juices

**just** /dʒʌst/ *adv., adj.*
■ *adv.* **1** only: *There is just one method that might work.* ◊ ~ for sth *I decided to learn Japanese just for fun.* ◊ ~ to do sth *I waited an hour just to see you.* ◊ '*Can I help you?*' '*No thanks, I'm just looking.*' (= in a shop) **2** simply: *I just want to help.* ◊ *I'm just saying there are risks involved.* ◊ *I can't just drop all my commitments.* ◊ *This essay is just not good enough.* ◊ *I didn't mean to upset you. It's just that I had to tell somebody.* ◊ *This is not just another disaster movie—it's a masterpiece.* ◊ *Just because you're older than me doesn't mean you know everything.* **3** by a small amount: *You've just missed her.* ◊ *I only just caught the train.* ◊ ~ **over/under sth** *Inflation fell to just over 4 per cent.* ◊ ~ **after/before ...** *They must have got there just before I did.* **4** used to say that you/sb did sth or sth happened very recently: *I've just heard the news.* ◊ *When you arrived, he had only just left.* ◊ *She has just been telling us about her trip to Rome.* ◊ (*especially NAmE*) *I just saw him a moment ago.* ◊ *Just last week it was snowing and now it's 25 degrees.* ⊃ note at ALREADY **5** at this/that moment; now: *I'm just finishing my book.* ◊ *I was just beginning to enjoy myself when we had to leave.* ◊ *I'm just off* (= I am leaving now). **6** exactly: *This jacket is just my size.* ◊ *With him, everything always has to be just right.* ◊ *This gadget is just the thing for getting those nails out.* ◊ *Just my luck* (= the sort of bad luck I usually have). *My phone needs recharging.* ◊ *You're just in time.* ◊ ~ **like sb/sth** *She looks just like her mother.* ◊ ~ **what ...** *It's just what I wanted!* ◊ ~ **as ...** *It's just as I thought.* ◊ ~ **on sth** (*BrE*) *It's just on six* (= exactly six o'clock). **7** ~ **as ...** at the same moment as: *The clock struck six just as I arrived.* **8** ~ **as good, nice, easily, etc.** no less than; equally: *She's just as smart as her sister.* ◊ *You can get there just as cheaply by plane.* **9** going to do sth only a few moments from now or then: ~ **about to do sth** *The water's just about to boil.* ◊ ~ **going to do sth** *I was just going to tell you when you interrupted.* **10** (*informal*) really; completely: *The food was just wonderful!* ◊ *Relax—you're doing just fine.* ◊ *I can just imagine his reaction.* **11** used in orders to get sb's attention, give permission, etc: *Just listen to what I'm saying, will you?* ◊ *Just help yourselves.* **12** used to make a polite request, excuse, etc: *Could you just help me with this box, please?* ◊ *I've just got a few things to do first.* **13** could/might/may ~ used to show a slight possibility that sth is true or will happen: *Try asking Mike—he might just know the answer.* **14** used to agree with sb: '*He's very pompous.*' '*Isn't he just?*'
**IDM** could/might just as well ... used to say that you/sb would have been in the same position if you had done sth else, because you got little benefit or pleasure from what you did do: *The weather was so bad we might just as well have stayed at home.* | , **etc. would just as soon do sth**

used to say that you would equally well like to do sth as do sth else that has been suggested: *I'd just as soon stay at home as go out tonight.* **it is just as ˈwell (that …)** it is a good thing: *It is just as well that we didn't leave any later or we'd have missed him.* **just aˈbout** (*informal*) **1** almost; very nearly: *I've met just about everyone.* ◊ *'Did you reach your sales target?' 'Just about.'* **2** approximately: *She should be arriving just about now.* **just a ˈminute/ˈmoment/ˈsecond** (*informal*) used to ask sb to wait for a short time: *'Is Mr Burns available?' 'Just a second, please, I'll check.'* **just like ˈthat** suddenly, without warning or explanation **just ˈnow 1** at this moment: *Come and see me later—I'm busy just now.* **2** during this present period: *Business is good just now.* **3** only a short time ago: *I saw her just now.* **4** (*SAfrE*, *informal*) later; in a short period of time **just ˈso** done or arranged very accurately or carefully: *He liked polishing the furniture and making everything just so.* **just ˈthen** at that moment: *Just then, someone knocked at the front door.* **not just ˈyet** not now but probably quite soon: *I can't give you the money just yet.* ➜ more at CASE *n.*, LET *v.*, TICKET *n.*
- **adj.** [usually before noun] **1** that most people consider to be morally fair and reasonable **SYN** **fair**: *a just decision/law/society* **2** **the just** noun [pl.] people who are just **3** appropriate in a particular situation: *a just reward/punishment* ◊ *I think she got her just deserts* (= what she deserved). **OPP** **unjust** ▸ **ˈjustly** *adv.*: *to be treated justly* ◊ *to be justly proud of sth*

**justˑice** /ˈdʒʌstɪs/ *noun* **1** [U] the fair treatment of people: *She spent her life fighting for social justice and equality for women.* ◊ *He pledged to seek justice for the victims of the tragedy.* **OPP** **injustice** ➜ see also POETIC JUSTICE, ROUGH JUSTICE **2** [U] the quality of being fair or reasonable: *Who can deny the justice of their cause?* **OPP** **injustice** **3** [U] the legal system used to punish people who have committed crimes: *the criminal justice system* ◊ *the administration/obstruction of justice* ◊ (*BrE*) *They were accused of attempting to pervert the course of justice.* ◊ (*NAmE*) *They were accused of attempting to obstruct justice.* ➜ WORDFINDER NOTE at LAW ➜ see also MISCARRIAGE OF JUSTICE **4** (*also* **Justˑice**) [C] (*NAmE*) a judge in a court (also used before the name of a judge) ➜ see also CHIEF JUSTICE **5** **Justˑice** [C] (*BrE*, *CanE*) used before the name of a judge in a COURT OF APPEAL: *Mr Justice Davies* **IDM** ▸ **bring sb to ˈjustice** to arrest sb for a crime and put them on trial in court **do justice to ˈsb/ˈsth; do sb/sth ˈjustice 1** to treat or represent sb/sth fairly, especially in a way that shows how good, attractive, etc. they are: *That photo doesn't do you justice.* **2** to deal with sb/sth correctly and completely: *You cannot do justice to such a complex situation in just a few pages.* **do yourself ˈjustice** to do sth as well as you can in order to show other people how good you are: *She didn't do herself justice in the exam.* ➜ more at PERVERT *v.*

**Justice of the ˈPeace** *noun* (*pl.* **Justices of the Peace**) (*abbr.* **JP**) (*formal*) an official who acts as a judge in the lowest courts of law **SYN** **magistrate**

**justiˑciary** /dʒʌˈstɪʃəri; *NAmE* dʒəˈstɪʃieri/ *noun* (*pl.* **-ies**) **1** (*ScotE*) [C] a judge or similar officer **2** [U] the process by which justice is done

**justiˑfiˑable** /ˌdʒʌstɪˈfaɪəbl, ˈdʒʌstɪfaɪəbl/ *adj.* existing or done for a good reason, and therefore acceptable **SYN** **legitimate**: *justifiable pride* ▸ **justiˑfiˑably** /-bli/ *adv.*: *The university can be justifiably proud of its record.*

**justifiable ˈhomicide** *noun* [U] (*law*) in some countries, a killing that is not a criminal act, for example because you were trying to defend yourself ➜ compare CULPABLE HOMICIDE

**jusˑtiˑfiˑcaˑtion** /ˌdʒʌstɪfɪˈkeɪʃn/ *noun* [U, C] a good reason why sth exists or is done: *~ for (doing) sth I can see no possible justification for any further tax increases.* ◊ *with (some) ~ He was getting angry—and with some justification.* ➜ SYNONYMS at REASON **IDM** ▸ **in justifiˈcation (of sb/sth)** as an explanation of why sth exists or why sb has done sth: *All I can say in justification of her actions is that she was under a lot of pressure at work.*

**jusˑtiˑfied** /ˈdʒʌstɪfaɪd/ *adj.* **1** ~ (in doing sth) having a good reason for doing sth: *She felt fully justified in asking for her money back.* **2** existing or done for a good reason: *His fears proved justified.* **OPP** **unjustified**

**jusˑtify** /ˈdʒʌstɪfaɪ/ *verb* (**justˑiˑfies**, **justˑiˑfyˑing**, **justˑiˑfied**, **justˑiˑfied**) **1** to show that sb/sth is right or reasonable: *~ (sb/sth) doing sth How can they justify paying such huge salaries?* ◊ *~ sth Her success had justified the faith her teachers had put in her.* **2** to give an explanation or excuse for sth or for doing sth **SYN** **defend**: *~ sth/yourself The senator made an attempt to justify his actions.* ◊ *~ sth/yourself to sb You don't need to justify yourself to me.* ◊ *~ (sb/sth) doing sth The press release was intended to justify them sacking her.* **3** *~ sth* (*specialist*) to arrange lines of printed text so that one or both edges are straight **IDM** ➜ see END *n.*

**just-in-ˈtime** *adj.* (*abbr.* **JIT**) (*business*) used to describe a system in which parts or materials are only delivered to a factory just before they are needed ➜ WORDFINDER NOTE at INDUSTRY

**jut** /dʒʌt/ *verb* (**-tt-**) [I, T] to stick out further than the surrounding surface, objects, etc.; to make sth stick out **SYN** **protrude**, **project**: *~ (out) (from, into, over, etc. sth) A row of small windows jutted out from the roof.* ◊ *A rocky headland jutted into the sea.* ◊ *a jutting chin* ◊ *~ sth (out) She jutted her chin out stubbornly.*

**jute** /dʒuːt/ *noun* [U] thin THREADS from a plant, also called jute, used for making rope and rough cloth

**juˑvenˑile** /ˈdʒuːvənaɪl; *NAmE* -nl/ *adj.*, *noun*
- **adj.** **1** [only before noun] (*formal* or *law*) relating to young people who are not yet adults: *juvenile crime/employment* ◊ *juvenile offenders* ➜ WORDFINDER NOTE at AGE **2** (*disapproving*) silly and more typical of a child than an adult **SYN** **childish**: *juvenile behaviour* ◊ *Don't be so juvenile!*
- **noun** (*formal* or *law*) a young person who is not yet an adult

**juvenile ˈcourt** *noun* a court that deals with young people who are not yet adults

**juvenile deˈlinquent** *noun* a young person who is not yet an adult and who is guilty of committing a crime ▸ **juvenile deˈlinquency** *noun* [U]

**juˑvenˑilia** /ˌdʒuːvəˈnɪliə/ *noun* [pl.] (*formal*) writing, poetry, works of art, etc. produced by a writer or an artist when he/she was still young

**juxˑtaˑpose** /ˌdʒʌkstəˈpəʊz; *verb* [often passive] *~ A and/with B* (*formal*) to put people or things together, especially in order to show a contrast or a new relationship between them: *In the exhibition, abstract paintings are juxtaposed with shocking photographs.* ▸ **juxtaˑposˑition** /ˌdʒʌkstəpəˈzɪʃn/ *noun* [U, C]: *the juxtaposition of realistic and surreal situations in the novel*

**K** /keɪ/ noun, abbr., symbol
- **noun** (also **k**) [C, U] (pl. **Ks**, **K's**, **k's** /keɪz/) the 11th letter of the English alphabet: 'King' begins with (a) K/'K'.
- **abbr.** (pl. **K**) **1** (informal) one thousand: She earns 40K = £40000) a year. **2** (informal) kilometre(s): a 10K race **3** (computing) KILOBYTE(S) **4** KELVIN
- **symbol** the symbol for the chemical element POTASSIUM

**K-12** /ˌkeɪ ˈtwelv/ adj. (in the US) relating to education from KINDERGARTEN (= the class that prepares children for school) to 12th GRADE

**ka·bad·di** /kəˈbædi, -ˈbɑːdi/ noun [U] a South Asian sport played by teams of seven players on a RECTANGULAR sand court. A player from one team tries to capture a player from the other team and must hold his/her breath while running.

**Kab·ba·lah** (also **Ca·bala**, **Qa·ba·lah**) /kəˈbɑːlə, ˈkæbələ/ noun [U] (in Judaism) the ancient tradition of explaining holy texts through MYSTICAL means

**kabob** (NAmE) = KEBAB

**ka·buki** /kəˈbuːki/ noun [U] (from Japanese) traditional Japanese theatre, in which songs, dance and MIME are performed by men

**ka-ching** (BrE also **ker-ching**) /kəˈtʃɪŋ/ (NAmE also **cha-ching**) exclamation (informal) used to say that sb is getting a lot of money: The money was rolling in, ka-ching, ka-ching! ORIGIN A way of representing the noise made by a CASH REGISTER.

**Kaf·fir** /ˈkæfə(r)/ noun (taboo, slang, especially SAfrE) a very offensive word for a black African

**kaf·fi·yeh** = KEFFIYEH

**kafir** /ˈkæfɪə(r)/; NAmE -fər/ noun (offensive) an offensive word used by some Muslims to refer to a person who is not a Muslim

**Kaf·ka·esque** /ˌkæfkəˈesk/; NAmE ˌkɑːf-/ adj. used to describe a situation that is confusing and frightening, especially one involving complicated official rules and systems that do not seem to make any sense: My attempt to get a new passport turned into a Kafkaesque nightmare. ORIGIN From the name of the Czech writer Franz Kafka, whose novels often describe situations like this.

**kaf·tan** (also **caf·tan**) /ˈkæftæn/ noun **1** a long loose piece of clothing, usually with a belt at the WAIST, worn by men in Arab countries **2** a woman's long loose dress with long wide SLEEVES (= parts covering the arms)

**ka·goul** = CAGOULE

**ka·huna** /kəˈhuːnə/ noun
IDM **the big ka'huna** (NAmE, informal) the most important person, company, etc. in a particular area

**kai** /kaɪ/ noun (NZE, informal) food

**kai·ser** /ˈkaɪzə(r)/ noun (from German) **1 Kaiser** (in the past) a ruler of Germany, Austria or the Holy Roman Empire: Kaiser Wilhelm **2** (also **kaiser roll**) (NAmE) a round bread roll that is hard on the outside and soft inside

**kai·zen** /ˈkaɪzen/ noun [U] (from Japanese, business) the practice of continuously improving the way in which a company operates

**kajal** /ˈkʌdʒəl/ noun [U] a type of black MAKE-UP used by South Asian women, that is put around the edge of the eyes to make them more attractive

**Ka·lash·ni·kov** /kəˈlæʃnɪkɒf/; NAmE -ˈlɑːʃnɪkɑːf/ noun a type of RIFLE (= a long gun) that can fire bullets very quickly

**kale** /keɪl/ noun [U] a vegetable that is a type of CABBAGE with dark green or purple leaves

**kal·eido·scope** /kəˈlaɪdəskəʊp/ noun **1** [C] a toy consisting of a tube that you look through with loose pieces of coloured glass and mirrors at the end. When the tube is turned, the pieces of glass move and form different patterns **2** [sing.] a situation, pattern, etc. containing a lot of different parts that are always changing ▶ **kal·eido·scop·ic** /kəˌlaɪdəˈskɒpɪk/; NAmE -ˈskɑːp-/ adj.

**ka·meez** /kəˈmiːz/ noun (pl. **ka·meez** or **ka·meez·es**) a piece of clothing like a long shirt worn by many people from South Asia ⊃ see also SALWAR

**kami·kaze** /ˌkæmɪˈkɑːzi/ adj. [only before noun] (from Japanese) used to describe the way soldiers attack the enemy, knowing that they too will be killed SYN **suicidal**: a kamikaze pilot/attack ◊ (figurative) He made a kamikaze run across three lanes of traffic.

**kanga** (also **khanga**) /ˈkæŋɡə/ EAfrE /ˈkɑːŋɡə/ (also **leso**) noun (EAfrE) a large piece of light cloth with designs printed on it and worn by women around the lower body and legs or over the head and shoulders

**kan·ga·roo** /ˌkæŋɡəˈruː/ (also informal **roo**) noun (pl. **-oos**) a large Australian animal with a strong tail and back legs, that moves by jumping. The female carries its young in a pocket of skin (called a POUCH) on the front of its body. ⊃ VISUAL VOCAB page V2

**kanˈgaroo court** noun (disapproving) an illegal court that punishes people unfairly

**kanji** /ˈkændʒi, ˈkɑːn-/ noun [U, C] (pl. **kanji**) (from Japanese) a Japanese system of writing based on Chinese symbols, called characters; a symbol in this system

**Kan·nada** /ˈkɑːnədə/ (also **Kan·ar·ese** /ˌkænəˈriːz; NAmE ˌkɑːn-/) noun [U] a language spoken in Karnataka in south-west India

**kanzu** /ˈkænzuː/ EAfrE /ˈkɑːnzuː/ noun (in East Africa) a long loose piece of outer clothing made from white cloth and worn by men

**kao·lin** /ˈkeɪəlɪn/ noun [U] a type of fine white CLAY used in some medicines and in making PORCELAIN for cups, plates, etc.

**kapok** /ˈkeɪpɒk; NAmE -pɑːk/ noun [U] a soft white material used for filling CUSHIONS, soft toys, etc.

**kappa** /ˈkæpə/ noun the 10th letter of the Greek alphabet (K, κ) ⊃ see also PHI BETA KAPPA

**kaput** /kəˈpʊt/ adj. [not before noun] (informal) not working correctly; broken: The truck's kaput.

**kara·oke** /ˌkæriˈəʊki/ noun [U] (from Japanese) a type of entertainment in which a machine plays only the music of popular songs so that people can sing the words themselves: a karaoke machine/night/bar

**karat** (NAmE) = CARAT

**kar·ate** /kəˈrɑːti/ noun [U] a Japanese system of fighting in which you use your hands and feet as weapons: a karate chop (= a blow with the side of the hand)

**karma** /ˈkɑːmə; NAmE ˈkɑːrmə/ noun [U] **1** (in Buddhism and Hinduism) the sum of sb's good and bad actions in one of their lives, believed to decide what will happen to them in the next life **2 good/bad ~** (informal) the good/bad effect of doing a particular thing, being in a particular place, etc: Vegetarians believe that eating meat is bad karma.

**kar·mic** /ˈkɑːmɪk; NAmE ˈkɑːrm-/ adj. **1** (in Buddhism and Hinduism) connected with the idea of karma: the karmic wheel of life **2** (informal) showing good or bad luck that is considered to be a result of your actions: I must be paying back some karmic debt for missing my mother's birthday.

**kart** /kɑːt; NAmE kɑːrt/ noun a small motor vehicle used for racing ⊃ see also GO-KART

**kart·ing** /ˈkɑːtɪŋ; NAmE ˈkɑːrt-/ noun [U] the sport of racing in karts

**kas·bah** (also **cas·bah**) /ˈkæzbɑː/ noun a castle on high ground in a North African city or the area around it

**ka·tab·ol·ism** = CATABOLISM

**kayak** /ˈkaɪæk/ noun a light CANOE in which the part where you sit is covered over ▶ **kayak·ing** noun [U]: to go kayaking

**ka·yam·ba** /kaɪˈæmbə/ EAfrE /kɑːˈjɑːmbɑː/ noun (EAfrE) a flat musical instrument that you shake to make a noise

**kayo** /ˈkeɪəʊ/ noun (pl. **-os**) = KO

**kazoo** /kəˈzuː/ noun (pl. **-oos**) a small simple musical instrument consisting of a hollow pipe with a hole in it, that makes a BUZZING sound when you sing into it

**KB** (also **K**) abbr. (in writing) KILOBYTE

---

æ cat | ɑː father | e bed | ɜː fur | ə about | ɪ sit | iː see | i happy | ɒ got (BrE) | ɔː saw | ʌ cup | ʊ put | uː too

**Kb** (also **Kbit**) abbr. (in writing) KILOBIT

**Kbps** abbr. (in writing) kilobits per second (a unit for measuring the speed of a MODEM)

**KC** /ˌkeɪ ˈsiː/ noun, abbr. (in the UK) the highest level of BARRISTER, who can speak for the government in court. KC is the abbreviation for 'King's Counsel' and is used when there is a king in the UK. ⊃ compare QC

**kebab** (NAmE also **kabob**) /kɪˈbæb; NAmE -ˈbɑːb/ (also **ˈshish kebab** especially in NAmE) noun small pieces of meat and vegetables cooked on a wooden or metal stick ⊃ see also DONER KEBAB

**kedg·eree** /ˈkedʒəriː/ noun [U] a hot dish of rice, fish and eggs cooked together

**keel** /kiːl/ noun, verb
- noun the long piece of wood or steel along the bottom of a ship, on which the frame is built, and which sometimes sticks out below the bottom to help it to keep steady in the water and prevent it from falling on its side IDM see EVEN adj.
- verb [I, T] ~ **(sth) (over)** (of a ship or boat) to fall over to one side; to make sth fall over to one side SYN capsize
PHRV **ˌkeel ˈover** to fall over unexpectedly, especially because you feel ill: *Several of them keeled over in the heat.*

**keema** /ˈkiːmə/ noun [U] (IndE) meat that has been cut into very small pieces; a spicy dish made using this ingredient

**keen** ⊕ B1 /kiːn/ adj., verb
- adj. (**keen·er**, **keen·est**)
- EAGER/ENTHUSIASTIC 1 ⊕ B1 (*especially BrE*) wanting to do sth or wanting sth to happen very much SYN **eager**: ~ **to do sth** *John was very keen to help.* ◊ ~ **for sb/sth to do sth** *His father was keen for him to go to university.* ◊ **~ that…** *We are keen that our school should get involved too.* ◊ ~ **on doing sth** *I wasn't too keen on going to the party.* 2 ⊕ B1 [usually before noun] (*especially BrE*) enthusiastic about an activity or idea, etc: *a keen sportsman/gardener*
- LIKING SB/STH 3 ⊕ B1 (BrE, *informal*) liking sb/sth very much; very interested in sb/sth: ~ **on sb/sth** *Tom's very keen on Anna.* ◊ ~ **on doing sth** *She's not keen on being told what to do.* ⊃ SYNONYMS at LIKE
- CLEVER 4 [only before noun] quick to understand SYN **sharp, acute**: *a keen mind/intellect*
- IDEAS/FEELINGS 5 [usually before noun] strong or deep: *a keen sense of tradition* ◊ *He took a keen interest in his grandson's education.*
- SENSES 6 [only before noun] highly developed SYN **sharp**: *Dogs have a keen sense of smell.* ◊ *My friend has a keen eye for* (= is good at noticing) *a bargain.*
- COMPETITION 7 involving people competing very hard with each other for sth: *There is keen competition for places at the college.*
- PRICES 8 (*especially BrE*) kept low in order to compete with other prices SYN **competitive**
- WIND 9 (*literary*) extremely cold
- KNIFE 10 [usually before noun] (*literary*) having a sharp edge or point SYN **sharp** ▶ **keen·ly** adv.: *a keenly fought contest* ◊ *We were keenly aware of the danger.* **keen·ness** /ˈkiːnnəs/ noun [U]
IDM **(as) ˌkeen as ˈmustard** (BrE, *informal*) wanting very much to do well at sth; enthusiastic ⊃ more at MAD
- verb [I] (usually used in the progressive tenses) (*literary*) to make a loud, high sad sound, when sb has died

**keep** ⊕ A1 /kiːp/ verb, noun
- verb (**kept**, **kept** /kept/)
- NOT GIVE BACK 1 ⊕ A1 [T] ~ **sth** to continue to have sth and not give it back or throw it away: *He kept all her letters.* ◊ *She handed the waiter a hundred dollar bill and told him to keep the change.* ◊ *Always keep a backup of the file.*
- PUT/STORE 2 ⊕ A1 [T] ~ **sth + adv./prep.** to put or store sth in a particular place: *Keep your passport in a safe place.*
- SAVE FOR SB 3 ⊕ A1 [T] (*especially BrE*) to save sth for sb: ~ **sth for sb** *Please keep a seat for me.* ◊ ~ **sb sth** *Please keep me a seat.*
- STAY 4 ⊕ A1 [I, T] to stay in a particular condition or position; to make sb/sth do this: **~ + adj.** *We huddled together to keep warm.* ◊ **~ + adv./prep.** *The notice said 'Keep off* (= Do not walk on) *the grass'.* ◊ *Keep left along the wall.* ◊

861 **keep**

**~ sb/sth + adj.** *The doctors worked miracles to keep him alive.* ◊ **~ sb/sth + adv./prep.** *He kept his coat on.* ◊ *Don't keep us in suspense—what happened next?* ◊ **~ sth** *She had trouble keeping her balance.* ◊ **~ sb/sth doing sth** *I'm very sorry to keep you waiting.*
- CONTINUE 5 ⊕ A2 [I] to continue doing sth; to do sth repeatedly: **~ doing sth** *Keep smiling!* ◊ *Why does everyone keep saying that?* ◊ **~ on doing sth** *Don't keep on interrupting me!*
- SECRET 6 ⊕ B1 [T] **~ a secret | ~ sth secret (from sb)** to know sth and not tell it to anyone: *Can you keep a secret?* ◊ *She kept her past secret from us all.*
- PROMISE/APPOINTMENT 7 ⊕ B1 [T] **~ sth** to do what you have promised to do; to go where you have agreed to go: *She kept her promise to visit them.* ◊ *Mary kept her word and Henry was never informed.* ◊ *He failed to keep his appointment at the clinic.*
- DIARY/RECORD 8 ⊕ B1 [T] to write down sth as a record: *She kept a diary for over twenty years.* ◊ *We keep a record of all complaints that we receive.*
- ANIMALS 9 [T] **~ sth** to own and care for animals: *to keep bees/goats/hens*
- SHOP/RESTAURANT 10 [T] **~ sth** (*especially BrE*) to own and manage a shop or restaurant: *Her father kept a grocer's shop.*
- SUPPORT SB 11 [T] **~ sb/yourself** to provide what is necessary for sb to live; to support sb by paying for food, etc: *He scarcely earns enough to keep himself and his family.*
- DELAY 12 [T] **~ sb** to delay sb SYN **hold up**: *You're an hour late—what kept you?*
- ABOUT HEALTH 13 [I] **+ adv./prep.** (*informal*) used to ask or talk about sb's health: *How is your mother keeping?* ◊ *We're all keeping well.*
- OF FOOD 14 [I] to remain in good condition: *Finish off the pie—it won't keep.* ◊ (*informal, figurative*) *'I'd love to hear about it, but I'm late already.' 'That's OK—it'll keep* (= I can tell you about it later).'
- PROTECT 15 [T] (*formal*) to protect sb from sth: **~ sb** *May the Lord bless you and keep you* (= used in prayers in the Christian Church). ◊ **~ sb from sth** *His only thought was to keep the boy from harm.*
- IN SPORT 16 [T] **~ goal/wicket** (in football (soccer), hockey, CRICKET, etc.) to guard or protect the goal or WICKET ⊃ see also GOALKEEPER, WICKETKEEPER

IDM HELP Most idioms containing **keep** are at the entries for the nouns and adjectives in the idioms, for example **keep house** is at **house**. **ˌkeep ˈgoing 1** to make an effort to live normally when you are in a difficult situation or when you have experienced great pain and difficulty: *You just have to keep yourself busy and keep going.* **2** (*informal*) used to encourage sb to continue doing sth: *Keep going, Sarah, you're nearly there.* **ˌkeep sb ˈgoing** (*informal*) to be enough for sb until they get what they are waiting for: *Have an apple to keep you going till dinner time.*

PHRV **ˌkeep sb ˈafter** (NAmE) (BrE **ˌkeep sb⇿ˈback**) to make a student stay at school after normal hours as a punishment
**ˌkeep ˈat sth** to continue working at sth: *Come on, keep at it, you've nearly finished!* **ˌkeep sb ˈat sth** to make sb continue working at sth: *He kept us at it all day.*
**ˌkeep aˈway (from sb/sth)** to avoid going near sb/sth: *Keep away from the edge of the cliff.* **ˌkeep sb/sth aˈway (from sb/sth)** to prevent sb/sth from going somewhere: *Her illness kept her away from work for several weeks.*
**ˌkeep ˈback (from sb/sth)** to stay at a distance from sb/sth: *Keep well back from the road.* **ˌkeep sb⇿ˈback 1** (BrE) (NAmE **ˌkeep sb ˈafter**) to make a student stay at school after normal hours as a punishment **2** (NAmE) to make a student repeat a year at school because of poor grades **ˌkeep sb⇿ˈback (from sb/sth)** to make sb stay at a distance from sb/sth: *Barricades were erected to keep back the crowds.* **ˌkeep sth⇿ˈback 1** to prevent a feeling, etc. from being expressed SYN **restrain**: *She was unable to keep back her tears.* **2** to continue to have a part of sth: *He kept back half the money for himself.* **ˌkeep sth⇿ˈback (from sb)** to refuse to tell sb sth: *I'm sure she's keeping something back from us.*

# keeper

**,keep 'down** to hide yourself by not standing up straight: *Keep down! You mustn't let anyone see you.* **,keep sb↔'down** to prevent a person, group, etc. from expressing themselves freely ⓢⓨⓝ **oppress**: *The people have been kept down for years by a brutal regime.* **,keep sth↔'down 1** to make sth stay at a low level; to avoid increasing sth: *to keep down wages/prices/the cost of living* ◊ *Keep your voice down—I don't want anyone else to hear.* ◊ *Keep the noise down* (= be quiet). **2** to not bring sth back through the mouth from the stomach; to not VOMIT: *She's had some water but she can't keep any food down.* **,keep from sth** | **,keep yourself from sth** to prevent yourself from doing sth: *keep from doing sth She could hardly keep from laughing.* ◊ *I just managed to keep myself from falling.* **,keep sb from sth** to prevent sb from doing sth: *I hope I'm not keeping you from your work.* ◊ **keep sb from doing sth** *The church bells keep me from sleeping.* **,keep sth from sth** to avoid telling sb sth: *I think we ought to keep the truth from him until he's better.* **,keep sth from sth** to make sth stay out of sth: *She could not keep the dismay from her voice.* **,keep 'in with sb** (*BrE, informal*) to make sure that you stay friendly with sb, because you will get an advantage from doing so **,keep sth↔'in** to avoid expressing an emotion ⓢⓨⓝ **restrain**: *He could scarcely keep in his indignation.* **,keep sb 'in** to make sb stay indoors or in a particular place **,keep sb/yourself in sth** to provide sb/yourself with a regular supply of sth **,keep 'off** if rain, snow, etc. **keeps off**, it does not fall **,keep 'off sth 1** to avoid eating, drinking or smoking sth: *I'm trying to keep off fatty foods.* **2** to avoid mentioning a particular subject: *It's best to keep off politics when my father's around.* **,keep sb/sth↔'off** | **,keep sb/sth 'off sb/sth** to prevent sb/sth from coming near, touching, etc. sb/sth: *They lit a fire to keep off wild animals.* ◊ *Keep your hands off* (= do not touch) *me!* **,keep 'on** to continue: *Keep on until you get to the church.* **,keep sb↔'on** to continue to employ sb **,keep sth 'on** to continue to rent a house, flat, etc. **,keep 'on (at sb) (about sb/sth)** (*especially BrE*) to speak to sb often and in an annoying way about sb/sth ⓢⓨⓝ **go on, nag**: *He does keep on so!* ◊ *I'll do it—just don't keep on at me about it!* **,keep 'out (of sth)** to not enter a place; to stay outside: *The sign said 'Private Property—Keep Out!'* **,keep sb/sth↔'out (of sth)** to prevent sb/sth from entering a place: *Keep that dog out of my study!* **,keep 'out of sth** | **,keep sb 'out of sth** to avoid sth; to prevent sb from being involved in sth or affected by sth: *That child can't keep out of mischief.* ◊ *Keep the baby out of the sun.* **,keep to sth 1** to avoid leaving a path, road, etc. ⓢⓨⓝ **stick to sth**: *Keep to the track—the land is very boggy around here.* **2** to talk or write only about the subject that you are supposed to talk or write about: *Nothing is more irritating than people who do not **keep to the point**.* **3** to do what you have promised or agreed to do: *to keep to an agreement/an undertaking/a plan* **4** to stay in and not leave a particular place or position: *She's nearly 90 and mostly keeps to her room.* **,keep (yourself) to your'self** to avoid meeting people socially or becoming involved in their affairs: *Nobody knows much about him; he keeps himself very much to himself.* **,keep sth to your'self** to not tell other people about sth: *I'd be grateful if you kept this information to yourself.* **,keep sb 'under** to control or OPPRESS sb: *The local people are kept under by the army.* **,keep 'up** if particular weather **keeps up**, it continues without stopping: *The rain kept up all afternoon.* **,keep 'up (with sb/sth)** to move, make progress or increase at the same rate as sb/sth: *Slow down—I can't keep up!* ◊ *I can't keep up with all the changes.* ◊ *Wages are not keeping up with inflation.* **,keep 'up with sb** to continue to be in contact with sb: *How many of your old school friends do you keep up with?* **,keep 'up with sth 1** to learn about or be aware of the news, current events, etc: *She likes to keep up with the latest fashions.* **2** to continue to pay or do sth regularly: *If you do not keep up with the payments you could lose your home.* **,keep sb 'up** to prevent sb from going to bed: *I hope we're not keeping you up.* **,keep sth↔'up 1** to make sth stay at a high level: *The high cost of raw materials is keeping prices up.* **2** to continue sth at the same, usually high, level: *The enemy kept up the bombardment day and night.* ◊ *We're having difficulty keeping up our mortgage payments.* ◊ *Well done! **Keep up the good work/Keep it up!*** **3** to make sth remain at a high level: *They sang songs to keep their spirits up.* **4** to continue to use or practise sth: *to keep up old traditions* ◊ *Do you still keep up your Spanish?* **5** to take care of a house, garden, etc. so that it stays in good condition ⓢⓨⓝ **maintain** ⊃ related noun UPKEEP

▪ *noun* **1** [U] food, clothes and all the other things that a person needs to live; the cost of these things: *It's about time you got a job to **earn your keep**.* **2** [C] a large strong tower, built as part of an old castle
ⒾⒹⓂ **for 'keeps** (*informal*) forever: *Is it yours **for keeps** or does he want it back?* ⊃ more at EARN

**keep·er** /'kiːpə(r)/ *noun* **1** (especially in compounds) a person whose job is to take care of a building, its contents or sth valuable: *the keeper of geology at the museum* ⊃ see also SHOPKEEPER **2** a person whose job is to take care of animals, especially in a ZOO ⊃ see also GAMEKEEPER, ZOOKEEPER **3** (*BrE, informal*) = GOALKEEPER, WICKETKEEPER **4** (*informal*) a thing or person that is worth keeping ⒾⒹⓂ▶ see FINDER

**keep-'fit** *noun* [U] (*BrE*) physical exercises that you do, usually in a class with other people, in order to improve your strength and to stay healthy: *a keep-fit class*

**keep·ing** /'kiːpɪŋ/ *noun*
ⒾⒹⓂ **in sb's 'keeping** being taken care of by sb ⊃ see also SAFE KEEPING **in 'keeping (with sth)** appropriate or expected in a particular situation; in agreement with sth: *The latest results are in keeping with our earlier findings.* **out of 'keeping (with sth)** not appropriate or expected in a particular situation; not in agreement with sth: *The painting is out of keeping with the rest of the room.*

**keep·sake** /'kiːpseɪk/ *noun* a small object that sb gives you so that you will remember them ⓢⓨⓝ **memento**

**kef·fi·yeh** (*also* **kaf·fi·yeh**) /kəˈfiːjə/ *noun* a square of cloth worn on the head by some Arab men and fastened by a band

**keg** /keg/ *noun* **1** [C] a round wooden or metal container with a flat top and bottom, used especially for storing beer, like a BARREL but smaller ⊃ see also POWDER KEG **2** [U] (*BrE*) = KEG BEER

**'keg beer** (*BrE also* **keg**) *noun* [U, C] (in the UK) beer served from metal containers, using gas pressure

**Kejia** /keɪˈdʒɑː/ *noun* = HAKKA

**kelp** /kelp/ *noun* [U] a type of brown SEAWEED, sometimes used as a FERTILIZER to help plants grow

**kel·vin** /'kelvɪn/ *noun* (*abbr.* **K**) (*pl.* **kel·vin** *or* **kel·vins**) (The plural **kelvin** is preferred in scientific language.) a unit for measuring temperature. One kelvin is equal in size to one degree Celsius, but the **Kelvin scale** starts at ABSOLUTE ZERO and water freezes at 273.15 kelvin.

**ken** /ken/ *noun, verb*
▪ *noun*
ⒾⒹⓂ **beyond your 'ken** (*old-fashioned*) if sth is **beyond your ken**, you do not know enough about it to be able to understand it
▪ *verb* [I, T] (**-nn-**) ~ (sth) | ~ (that) ... | ~ what, where, etc ... (*ScotE, NEngE*) to know ⒽⒺⓁⓅ **Kent** is the usual form of the past tense used in Scotland.

**kendo** /'kendəʊ/ *noun* [U] (*from Japanese*) a Japanese form of the sport of FENCING, using light wooden weapons

**ken·nel** /'kenl/ *noun* **1** (*NAmE* **dog·house**) a small shelter for a dog to sleep in **2** (*usually* **kennels**) [C + sing./pl. v.] a place where people can leave their dogs to be taken care of when they go on holiday; a place where dogs are kept in order to produce young: **in kennels** *We put the dog in kennels when we go away.* ⊃ see also BOARDING KENNEL

**kept** /kept/ *past tense, past part.* OF KEEP

**,kept 'woman** *noun* (*old-fashioned*) a woman who is given money and a home by a man who visits her regularly to have sex

**ker·a·tin** /ˈkerətɪn/ noun [U] (biology) a PROTEIN that forms hair, feathers, HORNS, HOOFS, etc.

**kerb** (BrE) (NAmE **curb**) /kɜːb; NAmE kɜːrb/ noun the edge of the raised path at the side of a road, usually made of long pieces of stone: *The bus mounted the kerb* (= went onto the PAVEMENT) *and hit a tree.*

**ˈkerb-crawling** noun [U] (BrE) the crime of driving slowly along a road in order to find a PROSTITUTE ▶ **ˈkerb-crawler** noun

**kerb·side** (BrE) (NAmE **curb·side**) /ˈkɜːbsaɪd; NAmE ˈkɜːrb-/ noun [U] the side of the street or path near the kerb: *to stand at the kerbside* ◊ (BrE) *a kerbside recycling scheme* (= in which boxes of items for recycling are collected from outside people's houses) ◊ (NAmE) *a curbside recycling program*

**kerb·stone** (BrE) (NAmE **curb·stone**) /ˈkɜːbstəʊn; NAmE ˈkɜːrb-/ noun a block of stone or CONCRETE in a KERB

**ker·chief** /ˈkɜːtʃɪf; NAmE ˈkɜːrtʃ-/ noun (old-fashioned) a square piece of cloth worn on the head or around the neck ⊃ see also HANDKERCHIEF

**ker-ching** (BrE) = KA-CHING

**ker·fuf·fle** /kəˈfʌfl; NAmE kərˈf-/ noun [sing.] (BrE, informal) unnecessary excitement or activity SYN **commotion, fuss**

**ker·nel** /ˈkɜːnl; NAmE ˈkɜːrnl/ noun **1** the inner part of a nut or seed **2** the central, most important part of an idea or a subject

▼ **HOMOPHONES**
**colonel • kernel** /ˈkɜːnl; NAmE ˈkɜːrnl/
• **colonel** noun: *The colonel yelled out to his troops.*
• **kernel** noun: *The sun-dried tomato and pine kernel topping was delicious.*

**kero·sene** (also **kero·sine**) /ˈkerəsiːn/ noun [U] a type of fuel oil that is made from PETROLEUM and that is used in the engines of planes and for heat and light. In British English it is usually called PARAFFIN when it is used for heat and light: *a kerosene lamp*

**kes·trel** /ˈkestrəl/ noun a small BIRD OF PREY (= a bird that kills other creatures for food) of the FALCON family

**KET** /ket/ noun [U] a British test, now called 'A2 Key', that measures a person's ability to speak and write English as a foreign language at a basic level (the abbreviation for 'Key English Test')

**keta·mine** /ˈketəmiːn; BrE also -mɪn/ (also informal **ket** /ket/) noun [U] a substance that is used as an ANAESTHETIC, and also as a drug that is taken illegally for pleasure

**ketch** /ketʃ/ noun a sailing boat with two MASTS (= posts to support the sails)

**ketch·up** /ˈketʃəp/ (also **toˌmato ˈketchup**) (US also **catsup**) noun [U] a thick cold sauce made from tomatoes, usually sold in bottles

**ket·tle** /ˈketl/ noun, verb
■ noun a container with a LID, a handle and a SPOUT, used for boiling water: *an electric kettle* ◊ (BrE) *I'll put the kettle on* (= start boiling some water) *and make some tea.* IDM see DIFFERENT, POT n.
■ verb ~ sb (especially BrE) (of the police) to keep a group of people who are taking part in a DEMONSTRATION or protest held in an area with no easy way out, in order to make them behave in a peaceful way again: *Hundreds of protesters were kettled at the start of the demonstration.* ▶ **kettling** noun [U]: *Police used tactics such as kettling in an attempt to bring an end to the protest.*

**kettle·drum** /ˈketldrʌm/ noun a large metal drum with a round bottom and a thin plastic top that can be made looser or tighter to produce different musical notes. A set of kettledrums is usually called TIMPANI.

**Kev·lar™** /ˈkevlɑː(r)/ noun [U] an artificial substance used to give strength to tyres and other rubber products and clothing worn for protection such as HELMETS and BULLETPROOF VESTS

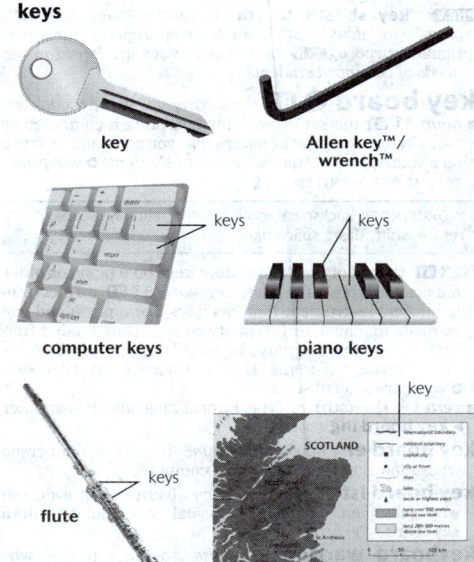

keys
key
Allen key™ / wrench™
computer keys
piano keys
flute
keys
key
SCOTLAND
map key

**key** /kiː/ noun, adj., verb
■ noun
• TOOL FOR LOCK **1** a piece of metal with a special shape used for locking a door, starting a car, etc: *to put/turn the key in the lock* ◊ *the car keys* ◊ *a set/bunch of keys* ◊ *~ to sth the spare key to the front door* ◊ *We'll have a duplicate key cut* (= made). ⊃ HOMOPHONES at QUAY ⊃ see also ALLEN KEY™, KEY CARD, MASTER KEY, PASS KEY
• MOST IMPORTANT THING **2** [usually sing.] a thing that makes you able to understand or achieve sth SYN **secret**: *~ to sth The key to success is preparation.* ◊ *~ to doing sth The driver of the car probably holds the key to solving the crime.* ◊ (especially NAmE) *The key is, how long can the federal government control the inflation rate?*
• ON COMPUTER **3** any of the buttons that you press to operate a computer, phone or TYPEWRITER: *Press the return key to enter the information.* ⊃ see also ALT KEY, HOT KEY, TAB KEY
• ON MUSICAL INSTRUMENT **4** any of the wooden or metal parts that you press to play a piano and some other musical instruments
• MUSIC **5** a set of related notes, based on a particular note. Pieces of music are usually written mainly using a particular key: *a sonata in the key of E flat major* ⊃ compare SCALE ⊃ see also OFF-KEY
• ANSWERS **6** a set of answers to exercises or problems: *Check your answers in the key at the back of the book.*
• ON MAP **7** an explanation of the symbols used on a map or plan ⊃ WORDFINDER NOTE at MAP ⊃ see also LOW-KEY IDM see LOCK n.

■ adj. [usually before noun] most important; essential SYN **critical, vital**: *the key issue/factor/point* ◊ *a key element/component/part/feature* ◊ *He was a key figure in the campaign.* ◊ *Both are key players in the peace process.* ◊ *She played a key role in the dispute.* ◊ *'Caution' is the key word in this situation.* ◊ *His contribution could be key.* ◊ *~ to (doing) sth Good communication is key to our success.* ⊃ HOMOPHONES at QUAY ⊃ SYNONYMS at MAIN

■ verb **1** to put information into a computer using a keyboard SYN **enter**: *~ sth I was busy keying data.* ◊ *~ in Key in your password.* ◊ *~ sth into sth The information is then keyed into a computer.* ⊃ HOMOPHONES at QUAY **2** to deliberately damage a car by SCRATCHING it with a key

**O** Oxford Phrasal Academic Lexicon (OPAL) written and spoken word lists | **W** OPAL written word list | **S** OPAL spoken word list

# keyboard 864

**PHRV** ˈkey sb/sth to sth [usually passive] (*especially NAmE*) to make sb/sth suitable or appropriate for a particular purpose **SYN** gear: *The classes are keyed to the needs of advanced students.*

**key·board** 🔊 **B1** /ˈkiːbɔːd/ *NAmE* -bɔːrd/ *noun, verb*
■ *noun* **1** **B1** the set of keys for operating a computer or TYPEWRITER, or the set of letters that you can touch to write on a smartphone or tablet: *keyboard shortcuts* ▶ WORDFINDER NOTE at COMPUTER

> **WORDFINDER** backspace, click, control, cursor, escape, return, shift, slash, space bar

**2** **B1** the set of black and white keys on a piano or other musical instrument: *a piano keyboard* **3** **B1** an electronic musical instrument that has keys like a piano and can be made to play in different styles or to sound like different instruments: *She plays keyboard and guitar.* ◇ **on (a)** ~ *The recording features Herbie Hancock on keyboard.*
⊃ compare SYNTHESIZER
■ *verb* [T, I] ~ **(sth)** to type information into a computer
▶ **key·board·ing** *noun* [U]

**key·board·er** /ˈkiːbɔːdə(r); *NAmE* -bɔːrd-/ *noun* a person whose job is to type data into a computer

**key·board·ist** /ˈkiːbɔːdɪst; *NAmE* -bɔːrd-/ *noun* a person who plays an electronic musical instrument with a keyboard

ˈ**keyboard warrior** *noun* (*disapproving*) a person who puts aggressive and offensive comments about people on the internet, especially one who hides their own identity

ˈ**key card** *noun* a special plastic card with information recorded on it that can be read by an electronic device, which can be used instead of a door key ⊃ compare SWIPE CARD

ˌ**keyed ˈup** *adj.* [not before noun] nervous and excited, especially before an important event

ˈ**key·hole** /ˈkiːhəʊl/ *noun* the hole in a lock that you put a key in

ˈ**keyhole ˈsurgery** (*BrE*) (*NAmE* ˌ**arthroˈscopic ˈsurgery**) *noun* [U] medical operations that involve only a very small cut being made in the patient's body

**key·log·ger** /ˈkiːlɒɡə(r); *NAmE* -lɔːɡ-/ *noun* (*computing*) a computer program that records all the keys that a user hits so that it is possible to discover secret information such as code words

**key·note** /ˈkiːnəʊt/ *noun* **1** [usually sing.] the central idea of a book, a speech, etc: *Choice is the keynote of the new education policy.* ◇ *a* **keynote speech/speaker** (= a very important one, introducing a meeting or its subject) **2** (*music*) the note on which the KEY is based ▶ ˈ**key·noter** *noun*: *For the first time, a woman will be the keynoter at the convention this year.*

**key·pad** /ˈkiːpæd/ *noun* a small set of buttons with numbers on used to operate a phone, a television or an electronic device

ˈ**key ring** *noun* a small ring that you put keys on to keep them together ⊃ picture at RING¹

ˈ**key signature** *noun* (*music*) the set of marks at the beginning of a printed piece of music to show what KEY the piece is in ⊃ picture at MUSIC

**key·stone** /ˈkiːstəʊn/ *noun* **1** (*architecture*) the central stone at the top of an ARCH that keeps all the other stones in position **2** [usually sing.] the most important part of a plan or argument that the other parts depend on

**key·stroke** /ˈkiːstrəʊk/ *noun* a single action of pressing a key on a computer or TYPEWRITER keyboard

**key·word** /ˈkiːwɜːd; *NAmE* -wɜːrd/ *noun* **1** a word or concept that is very important in a particular context: *When you're studying a language, the keyword is patience.* **2** a word or phrase that you type on a computer or phone to give an instruction or to search for information about sth: *Enter the keyword 'restaurants' and click on Search.*
⊃ **WORDFINDER NOTE** at PROGRAM

ˌ**key ˈworker** *noun* (*BrE*) a worker in one of the essential services such as health, education or the police: *The city council helps key workers find affordable housing.*

**kg** *abbr.* (*pl.* **kg** or **kgs**) (in writing) KILOGRAM(S): *10kg*

**khaki** /ˈkɑːki/ *noun* **1** [U] a strong yellow-brown cloth, used especially for making military uniforms **2** [U] a yellow-brown colour **3** **khakis** [pl.] (*NAmE*) trousers made from khaki cloth: *He wore a pair of baggy khakis.* ▶ **khaki** *adj.*: *khaki uniforms*

**khan** /kɑːn/ *noun* a title given to political leaders or officials in some countries of central Asia

**khanga** = KANGA

**kHz** *abbr.* (in writing) KILOHERTZ

ˌ**kia ˈora** /ˌkiː ˈɔːrə/ *exclamation* (*NZE*) a GREETING wishing good health

**KiB** *abbr.* (in writing) KIBIBYTE

**Kib** (*also* **Kibit**) *abbr.* (in writing) KIBIBIT

**kib·ble** /ˈkɪbl/ *noun* [U] grain and other ingredients, CRUSHED to produce a powder and then shaped into small hard balls and used for pet food

**kib·bled** /ˈkɪbld/ *adj.* [usually before noun] (of grain) pressed hard and broken to form rough pieces

**kib·butz** /kɪˈbʊts/ *noun* (*pl.* **kib·butz·im** /ˌkɪbʊtˈsiːm/) (in Israel) a type of farm or factory where a group of people live together and share all the work, decisions and income

**kibi·bit** /ˈkɪbibɪt/ *noun* (*abbr.* **Kib**) (*computing*) = KILOBIT (2)

**kibi·byte** /ˈkɪbibaɪt/ *noun* (*abbr.* **KiB**) (*computing*) = KILOBYTE (2)

**kib·lah** (*also* **kibla**) = QIBLAH

**ki·bosh** (*also* **ky·bosh**) /ˈkaɪbɒʃ; *NAmE* -bɑːʃ/ *noun* [sing.]
**IDM** **put the ˈkibosh on sth** (*informal*) to stop sth from happening; to cause sb's plans to fail

**kick** 🔊 **B1** /kɪk/ *verb, noun*
■ *verb* **1** **B1** [T, I] to hit sb/sth with your foot: *Stop kicking—it hurts!* ◇ ~ **sb/sth** *She was punched and kicked by her attackers.* ◇ ~ **sb/sth** + **adv./prep./adj.** *The boys were kicking a ball around in the yard.* ◇ *Vandals had kicked the door down.* ◇ ~ + **adv./prep.** *She kicked at the loose pebbles by the roadside.* **2** **B1** [T, I] to move your legs as if you were kicking sth: *The child was dragged away,* **kicking and screaming.** ◇ ~ **sth** *The dancers kicked their legs in the air.* **3** [T] ~ **yourself** (*informal*) to be annoyed with yourself because you have done sth stupid, missed an opportunity, etc: *He'll kick himself when he finds out he could have had the job.* **4** [T] ~ **sth** (in sports such as football (soccer) and rugby) to score points by kicking the ball: *to kick a penalty/goal* ⊃ see also DROP-KICK **5** [T] ~ **sth** (*informal*) to stop doing sth harmful that you have done for a long time: *He had been smoking for 15 years and wanted to* **kick the habit.**
**IDM** **kick (some) ˈass/ˈbutt** (*NAmE*, *taboo*, *slang*) **1** to act in a way that is aggressive or full of energy **2** to succeed or win in an impressive way **kick (some/sb's) ˈass** (*NAmE*, *taboo*, *slang*) to punish or defeat sb **kick the ˈbucket** (*informal or humorous*) to die **kick your ˈheels** (*BrE*) to have nothing to do while you are waiting for sb/sth: *We were kicking our heels, waiting for some customers.* **(drag sb) kicking and ˈscreaming** (*informal*) if you **drag sb kicking and screaming** to do sth, they only do it with great protests because they don't really want to do it at all: *The president had to be dragged kicking and screaming to the signing ceremony.* **kick sb in the ˈteeth** to treat sb badly or fail to give them help when they need it **kick sth into the long ˈgrass/into ˈtouch** (*BrE*) to reject sth or treat it as not important; to stop dealing with a problem: *He tends to deal with disputes by kicking them into the long grass.* **kick over the ˈtraces** (*BrE*, *old-fashioned*) to start to behave badly and refuse to accept any discipline or control **kick the ˈtyres** (*BrE*) (*NAmE* **kick the ˈtires**) (*especially NAmE*, *informal*) to test the quality of sth to see whether it is suitable for you before you buy it **kick up a ˈfuss, ˈstink, etc.** (*informal*) to complain loudly about sth **kick up your ˈheels** (*especially NAmE*, *informal*) to be relaxed and enjoy yourself **kick sb upˈstairs** (*informal*) to move sb to a job that seems to be more important but that actually has less

power or influence **kick sb when they're 'down** to continue to hurt sb when they are already defeated, etc. ➪ more at ALIVE, HELL

**PHRV** **'kick against sth** to protest about or resist sth: *Young people often kick against the rules.* **kick a'round** (*also* **kick a'bout** *especially in BrE*) (*informal*) **1** (usually used in the progressive tenses) to be lying somewhere not being used: *There's a pen kicking around on my desk somewhere.* **2** to go from one place to another with no particular purpose: *They spent the summer kicking around Europe.* **kick sb a'round** (*informal*) to treat sb in a rough or unfair way **kick sth a'round** (*also* **kick a'bout** *especially in BrE*) (*informal*) to discuss an idea, a plan, etc. in an informal way **kick 'back** (*especially NAmE*) to relax: *Kick back and enjoy the summer.* **kick 'in** (*informal*) **1** to begin to take effect: *Reforms will kick in later this year.* **2** (*also* **kick 'in sth**) (*both NAmE*) to give your share of money or help **kick 'off 1** when a football (soccer) game or a team, etc. **kicks off**, the game starts ➪ related noun KICK-OFF ➪ SYNONYMS at START **2** to suddenly become angry or violent **kick 'off (with sth)** (*informal*) to start: *What time shall we kick off?* ◊ *Tom will kick off with a few comments.* ➪ related noun KICK-OFF **kick sth↔'off** to remove sth by kicking: *to kick off your shoes* **kick 'off sth** (*informal*) to start a discussion, a meeting, an event, etc. **SYN** open: *Who is going to kick off the discussion?* **kick 'out (at sb/sth) 1** to try to hit sb/sth with your legs because you are angry or upset **2** to react violently to sb/sth that makes you angry or upset **kick sb 'out (of sth)** (*informal*) to make sb leave or go away (from somewhere) **kick 'up** (*especially NAmE*) (of wind or a storm) to become stronger **kick sth↔'up** to make sth, especially dust, rise from the ground

■ *noun* **1** 🗝 B1 a movement with the foot or the leg, usually to hit sth with the foot: *the first kick of the game* ◊ *She gave him a kick on the shin.* ◊ *If the door won't open, give it a kick.* ◊ *He aimed a kick at the dog.* ➪ see also CORNER KICK, DROP KICK, FREE KICK, GOAL KICK, PENALTY KICK, SPOT KICK **2** (*informal*) a strong feeling of excitement and pleasure **SYN** thrill: *I get a kick out of driving fast cars.* ◊ *He gets his kicks from hurting other people.* **for kicks** *What do you do for kicks?* ➪ WORDFINDER NOTE at ADVENTURE **3** [*usually sing.*] (*informal*) the strong effect that a drug or an alcoholic drink has: *This drink has quite a kick.* **4** [*usually pl.*] (*NAmE, informal*) a soft shoe that you wear for sports or as informal clothing: *The actor wore denim, a simple tee and a nice pair of kicks.* ➪ compare SNEAKER, TRAINER (1)

**IDM** **a kick in the 'pants/up the 'backside** (*informal*) if you think sb needs **a kick in the pants** or **a kick up the backside** you think they need to be strongly encouraged to do sth or behave better **a kick in the 'teeth** (*informal*) something that hurts sb/sth emotionally; a great DISAPPOINTMENT

**'kick-ass** (*also* **'ass-kicking**) *adj.* (*especially NAmE, slang*) **1** powerful and aggressive: *the movie's kick-ass heroine* ◊ *his reputation as a kick-ass coach* **2** extremely good and successful: *a kick-ass visual feast* ◊ *truly kick-ass quality*

**'kick-back** /'kɪkbæk/ *noun* (*informal*) money paid illegally to sb in return for work or help **SYN** bribe

**'kick-ball** /'kɪkbɔːl/ *noun* [U] a game that is based on baseball in which players kick the ball instead of hitting it with a BAT

**'kick-boxing** *noun* [U] a form of BOXING in which the people fighting each other can kick as well as hit with their FISTS (= closed hands)

**'kick drum** *noun* (*informal*) a large drum played using a PEDAL

**kick-er** /'kɪkə(r)/ *noun* **1** a person who kicks, especially the player in a sports team who kicks the ball to try to score points, for example in rugby **2** (*NAmE, informal*) a surprising end to a series of events

**'kick-ing** /'kɪkɪŋ/ *adj., noun*

■ *adj.* (*informal*) full of life and excitement: *The club was really kicking last night.*

■ *noun* [*sing.*] an act of kicking sb hard and repeatedly, especially when they are lying on the ground: *They gave him a good kicking.*

# kidney machine

**'kick-off** *noun* **1** [C, U] the start of a game of football (soccer): *The kick-off is at 3.* **2** [*sing.*] (*informal*) the start of an activity

**'kick-stand** /'kɪkstænd/ *noun* a long straight piece of metal fixed to a bicycle or a motorbike, used to make the bike stand UPRIGHT when the bike is not in use

**'kick-start** *verb, noun*

■ *verb* **1** ~ **sth** to start a motorcycle by pushing down a LEVER with your foot **2** ~ **sth** to do sth to help a process or project start more quickly or begin making progress again: *The government's attempt to kick-start the economy has failed.*

■ *noun* **1** (*also* **'kick-starter**) the part of a motorcycle that you push down with your foot in order to start it **2** a quick start that you give to sth by taking some action

**kid** 🗝 A2 /kɪd/ *noun, verb, adj.*

■ *noun* **1** 🗝 A2 [C] (*informal*) a child or young person: *Do you have any kids?* ◊ *How are the kids* (= your children)? ◊ *a bunch/gang/group of kids* ◊ *college/school kids* ◊ *You're acting like a little kid!* ◊ **as a~** *I remember reading with my grandmother as a young kid of 6.* **HELP** Kid is much more common than **child** in informal and spoken *NAmE*. ➪ see also BOOMERANG KID, WHIZZ-KID **2** [C] a young GOAT **3** [U] soft leather made from the skin of a young GOAT

**IDM** **handle/treat, etc. sb with kid 'gloves** to deal with sb in a very careful way so that you do not offend or upset them **'kids' stuff** (*BrE*) (*NAmE* **'kid stuff**) something that is so easy to do or understand that it is thought to be not very serious or only suitable for children ➪ more at NEW

■ *verb* (**-dd-**) (*informal*) **1** [I, T] (usually used in the progressive tenses) to tell sb sth that is not true, especially as a joke **SYN** joke: *I thought he was kidding when he said he was going out with a rock star.* ◊ *I didn't mean it. I was only kidding.* ◊ ~ **sb** *I'm not kidding you. It does work.* **2** [T] to allow sb/yourself to believe sth that is not true **SYN** deceive: ~ **sb/yourself** *They're kidding themselves if they think it's going to be easy.* ◊ ~ **sb/yourself (that)** ... *I tried to kid myself (that) everything was normal.*

**IDM** **no 'kidding** (*informal*) **1** used to emphasize that sth is true or that you agree with sth that sb has just said: *'It's cold!' 'No kidding!'* **2** used to show that you mean what you are saying: *I want the money back tomorrow. No kidding.* **you're 'kidding | you must be 'kidding** (*informal*) used to show that you are very surprised at sth that sb has just said

**PHRV** **kid a'round** (*especially NAmE*) to behave in a silly way

■ *adj.* ~ **sister/brother** (*especially NAmE, informal*) a person's younger sister/brother

**kid-die** (*also* **kid-dy**) /'kɪdi/ (*pl.* **-ies**) *noun* (*informal*) a young child: *a kiddies' party*

**kiddo** /'kɪdəʊ/ *noun* (*pl.* **kiddos**) (*informal*) used when speaking to a friend or a child: *Cheer up, kiddo—you'll be OK in a few days.*

**kid-nap** 🗝+ C1 /'kɪdnæp/ *verb* (**-pp-**, *US also* **-p-**) ~ **sb** to take sb away illegally and keep them as a prisoner, especially in order to get money or sth else for returning them **SYN** abduct, seize: *Two businessmen have been kidnapped by terrorists.* ➪ WORDFINDER NOTE at ATTACK ▶ **kidnapper** *noun*: *The kidnappers are demanding a ransom of $1 million.* **kid-nap-ping** (*also* **kid-nap**) *noun* [U, C]: *He admitted the charge of kidnap.* ◊ *the kidnapping of 12 US citizens*

**kid-ney** 🗝+ C1 /'kɪdni/ *noun* **1** 🗝+ C1 [C] either of the two organs in the body that remove waste products from the blood and produce URINE: *a kidney infection* ➪ VISUAL VOCAB page V1 **2** 🗝+ C1 [U, C] the kidneys of some animals that are cooked and eaten: *steak and kidney pie*

**'kidney bean** *noun* a type of red-brown bean like a kidney in shape that is usually sold in cans, or dried and then left in water before cooking ➪ VISUAL VOCAB page V9

**'kidney machine** *noun* a machine that does the work of a KIDNEY for sb whose kidneys are damaged or have been removed

# kikoi    866

**kikoi** /ˈkiːkɔɪ/ *EAfrE* [kiˈkoɪ] *noun* (*EAfrE*) a large piece of strong, coloured cloth used mainly as an item of clothing around the lower body and legs or over the shoulders

**kill** 🔊 **A2** /kɪl/ *verb, noun*
▪ *verb* **1** 🔊 **A2** [T, I] to make sb/sth die: ~ **(sb/sth)** *Cancer kills thousands of people every year.* ◊ *Tiredness while driving can kill.* ◊ *Dozens of civilians were killed or injured in the attack.* ◊ *She was nearly killed by a car bomb.* ◊ *Both members of the crew were killed instantly when the missile hit their aircraft.* ◊ *Three soldiers were killed in action* (= while fighting) *yesterday.* ◊ (*informal*) *My mother will kill me* (= be very angry with me) *when she finds out.* ◊ ~ **yourself** *He tried to kill himself with sleeping pills.* ◊ ~ **yourself doing sth** (*figurative*) *Don't kill yourself trying to get the work done by tomorrow. It can wait.* **2** [T] ~ **sth** to destroy sth or make it less good; to make sth stop: *to kill a rumour* ◊ *She claims that social media kills relationships.* ◊ *The defeat last night killed the team's chances of qualifying.* **3** [T] ~ **sth** (*informal*) to switch off a light or engine; to stop a computer program or process: *She killed the engine and climbed out.* **4** [T] ~ **sb** | **it kills sb to do sth** (*informal*) (usually used in the progressive tenses and not used in the passive) to cause sb pain: *My feet are killing me.* **5** [T] ~ **sb** (*especially NAmE*) to make sb laugh a lot: *Stop it! You're killing me!*
**IDM** **kill the goose that lays the golden ˈegg/ˈeggs** (*saying*) to destroy sth that would make you rich, successful, etc. **ˈkill or ˈcure** (*BrE*) used to say that what you are going to do will either be very successful or fail completely **ˈkill ˌtime** | **kill an ˈhour, a couple of ˈhours, etc.** to spend time doing sth that is not important while you are waiting for sth else to happen: *We killed time playing cards.* **kill ˌtwo birds with one ˈstone** to achieve two things at the same time with one action **kill sb/sth with ˈkindness** to be so kind to sb/sth that you in fact harm them **kill yourˌself ˈlaughing** (*BrE*) to laugh a lot: *He was killing himself laughing.* ➔ more at CURIOSITY, DRESSED, LOOK *n.*, TIME *n.*
**PHRV** **kill sb/sth↔ˈoff 1** to make a lot of plants, animals, etc. die: *Some drugs kill off useful bacteria in the user's body.* **2** to stop or get rid of sth: *He has effectively killed off any political opposition.*
▪ *noun* [usually sing.] **1** an act of killing, especially when an animal is hunted or killed: *A cat often plays with a mouse before the kill.* ◊ *The plane prepared to move in for the kill.* ◊ **in at the ~** *I was in at the kill when she finally lost her job* (= present at the end of an unpleasant process). **2** an animal that has been hunted and killed: *lions feeding on their kill*

**killˈer** /ˈkɪlə(r)/ *noun* **1** a person, an animal or a thing that kills: *Police are hunting his killer.* ◊ *Heart disease is the biggest killer in Scotland.* ◊ *an electric insect killer* ➔ see also GIANT-KILLER, KILLER INSTINCT, SERIAL KILLER **2** (*informal*) something that is very difficult, very exciting or shows a lot of skill: *The exam was a real killer.* ◊ *The new movie is a killer.*

**ˈkiller ˈapp** (*also* **ˌkiller appliˈcation**) *noun* (*informal*) a feature or function of a new technology or product that is so useful or popular that it becomes sth that everyone or all similar products have to have: *The barcode is one of the killer apps of the digital economy.*

**ˈkiller ˈbee** *noun* a type of bee that is very aggressive

**ˈkiller ˈcell** *noun* (*biology*) a white blood cell that destroys INFECTED cells or cancer cells

**ˈkiller ˈinstinct** *noun* [sing.] a quality that makes you determined to succeed or win at any cost: *The manager urged his players to find their killer instinct.*

**ˈkiller whale** *noun* = ORCA

**killˈing** 🔊 **B1** /ˈkɪlɪŋ/ *noun, adj.*
▪ *noun* 🔊 **B1** [C, U] an act of killing sb deliberately **SYN** murder: *Their leader condemned the torture and killing of innocent civilians.* ◊ *The mass killing* (= killing of a large number of people) *occurred when soldiers opened fire on protesters.* ◊ *a verdict of unlawful killing* ➔ see also HONOUR KILLING, MERCY KILLING, UNLAWFUL KILLING

**IDM** **make a ˈkilling** (*informal*) to make a lot of money quickly
▪ *adj.* making you very tired **SYN** exhausting: *a killing schedule*

**ˈkilling fields** *noun* [pl.] a place where very many people were killed, for example during a war

**ˈkill-joy** /ˈkɪldʒɔɪ/ *noun* (*disapproving*) a person who likes to stop other people from having fun

**ˈkill switch** *noun* a switch that can quickly stop a machine working, especially if sth goes wrong

**kiln** /kɪln/ *noun* a large oven for baking CLAY and BRICK, drying wood and grain, etc.

**kilo** /ˈkiːləʊ/ *noun* (*pl. -os*) = KILOGRAM

**kilo-** /ˈkɪləʊ, kɪlə; *BrE also* kɪˈlɒ; *NAmE also* kɪˈlɑː/ *combining form* (in nouns; used in units of measurement) **1** one thousand: *kilojoule* **2** $2^{10}$, or 1024

**ˈkilo-bit** /ˈkɪləbɪt/ *noun* (*abbr.* **Kb**) (*computing*) **1** a unit for measuring computer memory or data, equal to $10^3$, or 1000 BITS ➔ see also KBPS **2** (*also* **ˈkibi-bit**) a unit for measuring computer memory or data, equal to $2^{10}$, or 1024 BITS

**ˈkilo-byte** /ˈkɪləbaɪt/ *noun* (*abbr.* **K, KB**) (*computing*) **1** a unit for measuring computer memory or data, equal to $10^3$, or 1000 BYTES **2** (*also* **ˈkibi-byte**) a unit for measuring computer memory or data, equal to $2^{10}$, or 1024 BYTES

**ˈkilo-gram** (*BrE also* **ˈkilo-gramme**) /ˈkɪləɡræm/ (*also* **kilo**) *noun* (*abbr.* **kg**) a unit for measuring weight; 1000 GRAMS: *2 kilograms of rice* ◊ *Flour is sold by the kilogram.*

**ˈkilo-hertz** /ˈkɪləhɜːts; *NAmE* -hɜːrts/ *noun* (*abbr.* **kHz**) (*pl.* **ˈkilo-hertz**) a unit for measuring radio waves

**ˈkilo-joule** /ˈkɪlədʒuːl/ *noun* (*abbr.* **kJ**) a measurement of the energy that you get from food; 1000 JOULES

**kilo-metre** 🔊 **A1** (*US* **kiˈlo-meter**) /ˈkɪləmiːtə(r), kɪˈlɒmɪtə(r); *NAmE* kɪˈlɑːmɪtər/ *noun* (*abbr.* **km**, *informal* **k**) a unit for measuring distance; 1000 metres: *The industrial estate is 6 kilometres from the city centre.* ◊ *She had been driving at 110 kilometres per hour.* ◊ *Monaco is only two square kilometres in size.*

**ˈkilo-watt** /ˈkɪləwɒt; *NAmE* -wɑːt/ *noun* (*abbr.* **kW**) a unit for measuring electrical power; 1000 WATTS

**ˌkilowatt-ˈhour** *noun* (*abbr.* **kWh**) a unit for measuring electrical energy equal to the power provided by one kilowatt in one hour

**kilt** /kɪlt/ *noun* a skirt made of TARTAN cloth that reaches to the knees and is traditionally worn by Scottish men; a similar skirt worn by women

**kilt-ed** /ˈkɪltɪd/ *adj.* wearing a kilt

**kil-ter** /ˈkɪltə(r)/ *noun* [U]
**IDM** **out of ˈkilter 1** not agreeing with or the same as sth else: *His views are out of kilter with world opinion.* **2** no longer continuing or working in the normal way: *Long flights throw my sleeping pattern out of kilter for days.*

**kim-chi** (*also* **kim-chee**) /ˈkɪmtʃi/ *noun* [U] a spicy Korean dish made with PICKLED CABBAGE, onions, peppers, etc.

**ki-mono** /kɪˈməʊnəʊ/ *noun* (*pl. -os*) (*from Japanese*) a traditional Japanese piece of clothing like a long loose dress with wide SLEEVES (= parts covering the arms), worn on formal occasions; a DRESSING GOWN or ROBE in this style

**kin** /kɪn/ *noun* [pl.] (*old-fashioned* or *formal*) your family or your relatives ➔ compare KINDRED ➔ see also NEXT OF KIN
**IDM** see KITH

**kind** 🔊 **A1** 🔊 /kaɪnd/ *noun, adj.*
▪ *noun* 🔊 **B1** [C, U] a group of people or things that are the same in some way; a particular variety or type: ~ **of sb/sth** *three kinds of cakes/cake* ◊ *What kind of house do you live in?* ◊ *They sell all kinds of things.* ◊ *I need to buy paper and pencils, that kind of thing.* ◊ *We have the same kind of car.* ◊ **that ~ of sth** *I'll never have that kind of money* (= as much money as that). ◊ **this ~ of sth** *This kind of exercise is very popular.* ◊ **of a ~** *Exercises of this kind are very popular.* ◊ *music of all/various/different kinds* ◊ *The school is the first of its kind in Britain.* ◊ *Would you like a drink of some kind?* ◊ *The regions differ in size, but not in kind.*

---

| æ cat | ɑː father | e bed | ɜː fur | ə about | ɪ sit | iː see | i happy | ɒ got (*BrE*) | ɔː saw | ʌ cup | ʊ put | uː too |

**IDM** **in ˈkind 1** (of a payment) consisting of goods or services, not money: *As well as his salary, he gets benefits in kind.* **2** (*formal*) with the same thing: *She insulted him and he responded in kind.* **a ˈkind of** (*informal*) used to show that sth you are saying is not exact: *I had a kind of feeling this might happen.* **ˈkind of** (*also* **ˈkinda** /ˈkaɪndə/) (*informal*) slightly; in some ways: *That made me feel kind of stupid.* ◊ *I like him, kind of.* **nothing of the ˈkind/ˈsort** used to emphasize that the situation is very different from what has been said: *'I was terrible!' 'You were nothing of the kind.'* **of a ˈkind 1** (*disapproving*) not as good as it could be: *You're making progress of a kind.* **2** very similar: *They're two of a kind—both workaholics!* **one of a ˈkind** the only one like this **SYN** **unique**: *My father was one of a kind—I'll never be like him.* **something of the/that ˈkind** something like what has been said: *'He's resigning.' 'I'd suspected something of the kind.'*

■ *adj.* (**kind·er**, **kind·est**) **1** caring about others; gentle, friendly and generous: *a very kind and helpful person* ◊ *a kind heart/face* ◊ *a kind action/gesture/comment* ◊ *You've been very kind.* ◊ *~to sb/sth kind to animals* ◊ (*figurative*) *The weather was very kind to us.* ◊ *~to do sth Was it kind to let her find out this way?* ◊ *it is~of sb (to do sth) It was really kind of you to help me.* ◊ (*formal*) *Thank you for your kind words.* ◊ (*formal*) *'Do have another.' 'That's very kind of you* (= thank you).' **OPP unkind 2** (*formal*) used to make a polite request or give an order: *Would you be kind enough to close the window?* ⊃ see also KINDLY *adj.*, KINDNESS

▼ **GRAMMAR POINT**

**kind / sort**

- Use the singular (**kind / sort**) or plural (**kinds / sorts**) depending on the word you use before them: *each / one / every kind of animal* ◊ *all / many / other sorts of animals*.
- **Kind / sort of** is followed by a singular or uncountable noun: *This kind of question often appears in the exam.* ◊ *That sort of behaviour is not acceptable.*
- **Kinds / sorts of** is followed by a plural or uncountable noun: *These kinds of questions often appear in the exam.* ◊ *These sorts of behaviour are not acceptable.*
- Other variations are possible but less common: *These kinds of question often appear in the exam.* ◊ *These sort of things don't happen in real life.* (This example is very informal and is considered incorrect by some people.)
- Note also that these examples are possible, especially in spoken English: *The shelf was full of the sort of books I like to read.* ◊ *He faced the same kind of problems as his predecessor.* ◊ *There are many different sorts of animal on the island.* ◊ *What kind of camera is this?* ◊ *What kind / kinds of cameras do you sell?* ◊ *There were three kinds of cakes / cake on the plate.*

**kin·der** /ˈkɪndə(r)/ *noun* (*AustralE*, *informal*) = KINDERGARTEN

**kin·der·gar·ten** /ˈkɪndəɡɑːtn; *NAmE* -ɡɑːrtn/ *noun* (*from German*) **1** (*especially NAmE*) a school or class to prepare children aged five for school **2** (*BrE*, *AustralE*, *NZE*) = NURSERY SCHOOL

**kin·der·gar·ten·er** /ˈkɪndəɡɑːtənə(r)/; *NAmE* ˈkɪndərɡɑːrtənər/ (*US also* **kin·der·gart·ner** /ˈkɪndəɡɑːtnə(r)/; *NAmE* -ɡɑːrt-/) *noun* (*NAmE*) a child who is in kindergarten

**kind-ˈhearted** *adj.* kind and generous

**kin·dle** /ˈkɪndl/ *verb* **1** [I, T] to start burning; to make a fire start burning: *We watched as the fire slowly kindled.* ◊ *~sth to kindle a fire/flame* **2** [T, I] ~ (sth) to make sth such as an interest, emotion, etc. start to grow in sb; to start to be felt by sb: *It was her teacher who kindled her interest in music.* ◊ *Suspicion kindled within her.*

**kind·ling** /ˈkɪndlɪŋ/ *noun* [U] small dry pieces of wood, etc. used to start a fire

**kind·ly** /ˈkaɪndli/ *adv., adj.*

■ *adv.* **1** in a kind way: *She spoke kindly to them.* ◊ *He has kindly agreed to help.* **2** (*old-fashioned* or *formal*) used to ask or tell sb to do sth, sometimes when you are annoyed: *Kindly leave me alone!* ◊ *Visitors are kindly requested to sign the book.*

867

**IDM** **kindly adˈjust** (*IndE*) (mainly in writing) used to acknowledge and apologize for sth that causes problems or difficulties and ask people to accept and adapt to the situation **look ˈkindly on/upon sth/sb** (*formal*) to approve of sth/sb: *He hoped they would look kindly on his request.* **not take ˈkindly to sth/sb** to not like sth/sb: *She doesn't take kindly to sudden change.*

■ *adj.* [only before noun] (*especially old-fashioned* or *literary*) kind and caring ▶ **ˈkind·li·ness** *noun* [U]

**kind·ness** /ˈkaɪndnəs/ *noun* **1** [U] the quality of being kind: *to treat sb with kindness and consideration* **2** [C] a kind act: *I can never repay your many kindnesses to me.* **IDM** see KILL *v*., MILK *n*.

**kin·dred** /ˈkɪndrəd/ *noun, adj.*

■ *noun* (*old-fashioned* or *formal*) **1** [pl.] your family and relatives ⊃ compare KIN **2** [U] the fact of being related to another person: *ties of kindred*

■ *adj.* [only before noun] (*formal*) very similar; related: *food and kindred products* ◊ *I knew I'd found* **a kindred spirit** (= a person with similar ideas, opinions, etc.)

**kindy** /ˈkɪndi/ *noun* (*pl.* -**ies**) (*AustralE*, *NZE*, *informal*) = KINDERGARTEN

**kin·esis** /kɪˈniːsɪs, kaɪ-/ *noun* [U] (*specialist*) movement

**kin·et·ic** /kɪˈnetɪk, kaɪ-/ *adj.* [usually before noun] (*specialist*) of or produced by movement: *kinetic energy*

**king** /kɪŋ/ *noun* **1** the male ruler of an independent state that has a royal family: *the kings and queens of England* ◊ *the French king* ◊ *to* **be crowned king** ◊ *King George V*

**WORDFINDER** abdicate, accede, crown, government, monarch, reign, royal, succession, throne

**2** ~ (of sth) a person, an animal or a thing that is thought to be the best or most important of a particular type: *the king of comedy* ◊ *The lion is the king of the jungle.* **3** used in compounds with the names of animals or plants to describe a very large type of the thing mentioned: *a king penguin* **4** the most important piece used in the game of CHESS, that can move one square in any direction **5** a PLAYING CARD with the picture of a king on it

**IDM** **a ˈking's ˈransom** (*literary*) a very large amount of money **SYN** **fortune** ⊃ more at UNCROWNED

**king·dom** /ˈkɪŋdəm/ *noun* **1** a country that has a king or queen as HEAD OF STATE (= official leader of the country): *the United Kingdom* ◊ *the kingdom of God* (= heaven) **2** an area controlled by a particular person or where a particular thing or idea is important **3** one of the three traditional divisions of the natural world: *the animal, vegetable and mineral kingdoms* ⊃ **VISUAL VOCAB** pages V2, V3 **4** (*biology*) one of the five major groups into which all living things are organized ⊃ **WORDFINDER NOTE** at BREED

**IDM** **blow sb/sth to kingdom ˈcome** (*informal*) to completely destroy sb/sth with an explosion **till/until kingdom ˈcome** (*old-fashioned*) forever

**king·fish·er** /ˈkɪŋfɪʃə(r)/ *noun* a bird with a long BEAK that catches fish in rivers. The European kingfisher is small and brightly coloured and the American kingfisher is larger and blue-grey in colour.

**ˈking-hit** *noun* (*AustralE*, *NZE*, *informal*) a hard KNOCKOUT hit ▶ **ˈking-hit** *verb* (**king-hitting**, **king-hit**, **king-hit**) ~ sb

**king·ly** /ˈkɪŋli/ *adj.* (*literary*) like a king; connected with or good enough for a king **SYN** **regal**

**king·maker** /ˈkɪŋmeɪkə(r)/ *noun* a person who has a very strong political influence and is able to bring sb else to power as a leader

**king·pin** /ˈkɪŋpɪn/ *noun* the most important person in an organization or activity

**King's ˈBench** *noun* the word for QUEEN'S BENCH when the UK has a king

**King's ˈCounsel** *noun* = KC

# the King's English

**the ˈKing's ˈEnglish** noun [U] (old-fashioned) the word for the QUEEN'S ENGLISH when the UK has a king

**ˈKing's ˈevidence** noun [U] (law) the word for QUEEN'S EVIDENCE when the UK has a king

**king·ship** /ˈkɪŋʃɪp/ noun [U] the state of being a king; the official position of a king

**ˈking-size** (also **ˈking-sized**) adj. [usually before noun] very large; larger than normal when compared with a range of sizes: *a king-size bed* ◇ *a king-sized headache*

**the ˈKing's ˈSpeech** noun the word for the QUEEN'S SPEECH when the UK has a king

**kink** /kɪŋk/ noun, verb
- noun **1** a bend or TWIST in sth that is usually straight: *a dog with a kink in its tail* **2** a small problem in a plan, system, etc.: *We need to iron out the kinks in the new system.* **3** (informal, disapproving) an unusual feature in a person's character or mind, especially one that does not seem normal **4** [usually sing.] (NAmE) = CRICK
- verb [I, T] ~ **(sth)** to develop or make sth develop a bend or TWIST

**kinky** /ˈkɪŋki/ adj. (informal, usually disapproving) used to describe sexual behaviour that most people would consider strange or unusual

**kin·ship** /ˈkɪnʃɪp/ noun (formal) **1** [U] the fact of being related in a family: *the ties of kinship* **2** [U, sing.] a feeling of being close to sb because you have similar origins or attitudes **SYN** **affinity**

**kins·man** /ˈkɪnzmən/, **kins·woman** /ˈkɪnzwʊmən/ noun (pl. **-men** /-mən/, **-women** /-wɪmɪn/) (old-fashioned or literary) a relative

**kiondo** /kiˈɒndəʊ; NAmE -ˈɑːn-/ EAfrE [kiˈondo] noun (pl. **-os**) (EAfrE) a bag with one or two long handles and made from SISAL (= dried grass TWISTED together) or other materials

**kiosk** /ˈkiːɒsk; NAmE ˈkiːɑːsk/ noun **1** a small shop, open at the front, where newspapers, drinks, etc. are sold. In some countries kiosks also sell food and things used in the home. **SYN** **stand 2** a small structure in a public area used for providing information, showing advertisements or providing a service, typically via a computer screen: *a digital information kiosk* **SYN** **booth**

**kip** /kɪp/ noun, verb
- noun [U, C, usually sing.] (BrE, informal) sleep: *I must get some kip.* ◇ *Why don't you have a quick kip?*
- verb [I] (BrE, informal) (**-pp-**) to sleep: *You can kip on the sofa, if you like.*

**kip·pa** (also **kipa, kipah, kip·pah**) /kɪˈpɑː/ noun = YARMULKE

**kip·per** /ˈkɪpə(r)/ noun a HERRING (= a type of fish) that has been preserved using salt, then smoked

**kirk** /kɜːk; NAmE kɜːrk/ noun **1** [C] (ScotE) church: *the parish kirk* **2** the Kirk [sing.] a name often used for the national Church of Scotland

**kis·met** /ˈkɪzmet/ noun [U] (literary) the idea that everything that happens to you in your life is already decided and that you cannot do anything to change or control it **SYN** **destiny, fate**

**kiss** ⓘ B1 /kɪs/ verb, noun
- verb **1** B1 [I, T] to touch sb with your lips as a sign of love or sexual desire or when saying hello or goodbye: *They stood in a doorway kissing* (= kissing each other). ◇ *~ sb/sth Go and kiss your mother goodnight.* ◇ *She kissed him on both cheeks.* ◇ *He lifted the trophy up and kissed it.* ⇒ see also AIR-KISS **2** [T] ~ **sth** (literary) to gently move or touch sth: *The sunlight kissed the warm stones.*
- **IDM** **ˌkiss and ˈtell** a way of referring to sb talking publicly, usually for money, about a past sexual relationship with sb famous **kiss sb's ˈarse** (BrE) (NAmE **kiss sb's ˈass, kiss ˈass**) (taboo, slang) to be very nice to sb in order to persuade them to help you or to give you sth **HELP** A more polite way to express this is **lick sb's boots**. **ˌkiss sth ˈbetter** (informal) to take away the pain of an injury by kissing it: *Come here and let me kiss it better.* **ˌkiss sth goodˈbye**,

**ˌkiss goodˈbye to sth** (informal) to accept that you will lose sth or be unable to do sth: *Well, you can kiss goodbye to your chances of promotion.*
- **PHRV** **ˌkiss sth↔aˈway** to stop sb feeling sad or angry by kissing them: *He kissed away her tears.*
- noun ⓘ B1 the act of kissing sb/sth: *Come here and give me a kiss!* ◇ *a kiss on the cheek* ◇ *We were greeted with hugs and kisses.* ⇒ see also AIR KISS, FRENCH KISS
- **IDM** **the ˌkiss of ˈdeath** (informal, especially humorous) an event that seems good, but is certain to make sth else fail **the ˌkiss of ˈlife** (BrE) a method of helping sb who has stopped breathing to breathe again by placing your mouth on theirs and forcing air into their lungs **SYN** **mouth-to-mouth resuscitation** ⇒ more at STEAL v.

**kis·ser** /ˈkɪsə(r)/ noun **1** good, bad, etc. ~ a person who is very good, bad, etc. at kissing **2** (informal) a person's mouth

**kist** /kɪst/ noun (SAfrE) a large strong box, often made of wood, typically used for storing clothes, sheets, TABLECLOTHS, etc.

**Ki·swa·hili** /ˌkiːswəˈhiːli, ˌkɪswəˈh-/ (also **Swa·hili**) noun [U] a language widely used in East Africa, especially between people who speak different first languages

**kit** ⓘ+ B2 /kɪt/ noun, verb
- noun **1** ⓘ+ B2 [C, U] a set of tools or equipment that you use for a particular purpose: *a first-aid kit* ◇ *a drum kit* ⇒ SYNONYMS at EQUIPMENT ⇒ see also TOOLKIT **2** ⓘ+ B2 [C] a set of parts ready to be made into sth: *a kit for a model plane* **3** ⓘ+ B2 [U] (BrE) a set of clothes and equipment that you use for a particular activity: *sports kit*
- **IDM** **get your ˈkit off** (BrE, slang) to take your clothes off ⇒ more at CABOODLE
- verb (**-tt-**)
- **PHRV** **ˌkit sb ˈout/ˈup (in/with sth)** [usually passive] (BrE) to give sb the correct clothes and/or equipment for a particular activity: *They were all kitted out in brand-new ski outfits.*

**kit·bag** /ˈkɪtbæɡ/ noun (especially BrE) a long narrow bag, usually made of CANVAS in which soldiers, etc. carry their clothes and other possessions

**kitch·en** ⓘ A1 /ˈkɪtʃɪn/ noun a room in which meals are cooked or prepared: *We ate at the kitchen table.* ◇ (especially BrE) *The house has a fully fitted kitchen with custom-built units.* ⇒ see also SOUP KITCHEN
- **IDM** **ˌeverything but the kitchen ˈsink** (informal, humorous) a very large number of things, probably more than is necessary ⇒ more at HEAT n.

**kit·chen·ette** /ˌkɪtʃɪˈnet/ noun a small room or part of a room used as a kitchen, for example in a flat

**ˌkitchen ˈgarden** noun (BrE) a part of a garden where you grow vegetables and fruit for your own use

**ˈkitchen paper** (also **ˈkitchen roll, ˈkitchen towel**) (all BrE) (NAmE **paper ˈtowel**) noun [U] thick paper on a roll, used for cleaning up liquid, food, etc.

**kitchen-ˈsink** adj. [only before noun] (of plays, films, novels, etc.) dealing with ordinary life and ordinary people, especially when this involves describing the boring or difficult side of their lives: *a kitchen-sink drama*

**kit·chen·ware** /ˈkɪtʃɪnweə(r); NAmE -wer/ noun [U] used in shops to describe objects that you use in a kitchen, such as pans, bowls, etc.

**kite** /kaɪt/ noun **1** a toy made of a light frame covered with paper, cloth, etc., that you fly in the air at the end of one or more long strings: *to fly a kite* **2** a BIRD OF PREY (= a bird that kills other creatures for food) of the HAWK family
- **IDM** see FLY v., HIGH adj.

**kite·surf·ing** /ˈkaɪtsɜːfɪŋ; NAmE -sɜːrf-/ (also **kite·board·ing** /ˈkaɪtbɔːdɪŋ; NAmE -bɔːrd-/) noun [U] the sport of riding on water while standing on a short wide board and being pulled along by wind power, using a large kite

**kith** /kɪθ/ noun
- **IDM** **ˌkith and ˈkin** (old-fashioned) friends and relatives

**kitsch** /kɪtʃ/ noun [U] (disapproving) works of art or objects that are popular but that are considered to have no real artistic value or not to be in good taste, for example because they are SENTIMENTAL ▶ **kitsch** (also **kitschy**) adj.

**kit·ten** /ˈkɪtn/ noun **1** a young cat **2** the young of several other animals, such as RABBITS and BEAVERS
IDM ▶ **have 'kittens** (BrE, informal) to be very anxious, angry or upset about sth

**'kitten heels** noun [pl.] small, thin, curved heels on women's shoes

**kitty** /ˈkɪti/ noun (pl. **-ies**) **1** (informal) if money is put in a **kitty**, a group of people all give an amount and the money is spent on sth they all agree on: *We each put £50 in the kitty to cover the bills.* **2** (in card games, etc.) the sum of money that all the players bet, which is given to the winner **3** (informal) a way of referring to a cat

**'kitty party** noun (especially IndE) a regular social meeting of a group of women, held at either a member's house or a restaurant, where each person gives an amount of money and one is chosen to receive the whole sum

**kiwi** /ˈkiːwi/ noun **1 Kiwi** (informal) a person from New Zealand **2** a New Zealand bird with a long BEAK, short wings and no tail, that cannot fly **3** = KIWI FRUIT

**'kiwi fruit** noun (pl. **kiwi fruit**) (also **kiwi**) a small fruit with thin brown skin covered with small hairs, that is soft and green inside with black seeds ⊃ VISUAL VOCAB page V4

**kJ** abbr. (in writing) KILOJOULE

**KKK** /ˌkeɪ keɪ ˈkeɪ/ abbr. KU KLUX KLAN

**klap** /klʌp/ verb (**-pp-**) ~ **sb/sth** (SAfrE, informal) to hit sb/ sth: *I'll klap you!* ▶ **klap** noun: *to give sb a klap*

**Klaxon™** /ˈklæksn/ noun (BrE) a HORN, originally on a vehicle, that makes a loud sound as a warning

**Klee·nex™** /ˈkliːneks/ noun [U, C] (pl. **Klee·nex** or **Klee·nexes**) a paper HANDKERCHIEF; a TISSUE: *a box of Kleenex* ◇ *Here, have a Kleenex to dry your eyes.*

**klep·to·cracy** /klepˈtɒkrəsi; NAmE -ˈtɑːk-/ noun (pl. **-ies**) **1** [C, U] a form of government in which the leaders use their power to steal money and resources from the country that they rule: *The state apparatus has become a kleptocracy, with leaders using power for personal enrichment.* **2** [C] a society that is ruled by a kleptocracy ▶ **klep·to·crat** /ˈkleptəkræt/ noun **klep·to·crat·ic** /ˌkleptəˈkrætɪk/ adj.

**klep·to·mania** /ˌkleptəˈmeɪniə/ noun [U] a mental illness in which sb has a strong desire, which they cannot control, to steal things ▶ **klep·to·maniac** noun: *She's a kleptomaniac.*

**klick** (also **click**) /klɪk/ noun (NAmE, informal) a kilometre: *We're twenty klicks south of your position.*

**kloof** /kluːf/ SAfrE /kluəf/ noun (SAfrE) a valley or RAVINE with steep sides covered with woods or trees

**kludge** /kluːdʒ, klʌdʒ/ noun (computing) a solution to a problem that has been quickly and badly put together ▶ **kludge** verb [I, T] ~ **(sth)**

**klutz** /klʌts/ noun (especially NAmE, informal) a person who often drops things, is not good at sport(s), etc. ▶ **klutzy** /ˈklʌtsi/ adj.

**km** abbr. (pl. **km** or **kms**) (in writing) kilometre(s)

**kmph** /ˌkeɪ em piː ˈeɪtʃ/ abbr. = KPH

**knack** /næk/ noun [sing.] (informal) **1** a special skill or ability that you have naturally or can learn: *It's easy, once you've got the knack.* ◇ ~ **of/for (doing) sth** *He's got a real knack for making money.* **2** ~ **of doing sth** a habit of doing sth: *She has the unfortunate knack of always saying the wrong thing.*

**knacker** /ˈnækə(r)/ verb (BrE, slang) **1** ~ **sb** to make sb very tired SYN EXHAUST **2** ~ **sb/sth** to injure sb or damage sth ▶ **knacker·ing** adj. [not usually before noun] (BrE, informal): *I don't do aerobics any more—it's too knackering.*

**knack·ered** /ˈnækəd; NAmE -kərd/ adj. (BrE, slang) **1** [not usually before noun] extremely tired SYN EXHAUSTED, WORN OUT **2** too old or broken to use

869

# knickers

**'knacker's yard** (also **the 'knackers**) noun [usually sing.] (BrE, old-fashioned) a place where old and injured animals, especially horses, are taken to be killed

**knap·sack** /ˈnæpsæk/ noun (old-fashioned or NAmE) a small RUCKSACK

**knave** /neɪv/ noun **1** (old-fashioned) = JACK: *the knave of clubs* **2** (old use) a dishonest man or boy

**knead** /niːd/ verb **1** ~ **sth** to press and stretch DOUGH, wet CLAY, etc. with your hands to make it ready to use **2** ~ **sth** to rub and press muscles, etc. especially to relax them or to make them less painful

**knee** ⊙ A2 /niː/ noun, verb
■ noun **1** A2 the JOINT between the top and bottom parts of the leg where it bends in the middle: *a knee injury* ◇ *I had knee surgery three years ago.* ◇ *Bend your knees until you feel your thigh muscles working.* ◇ *He went down on one knee and asked her to marry him.* ◇ **on your knees** *She was on her knees scrubbing the kitchen floor.* ◇ *Everyone was down on (their) hands and knees* (= CRAWLING on the floor) *looking for the ring.* ◇ *He fell to his knees and begged for mercy.* ⊃ VISUAL VOCAB page V1 **2** A2 the part of a piece of clothing that covers the knee: **at the~** *These jeans are torn at the knee.* ◇ *a knee patch* **3** the top surface of the upper part of the legs when you are sitting down SYN LAP: *Come and sit on Daddy's knee.*
IDM ▶ **bring sb to their 'knees** to defeat sb, especially in a war ▶ **bring sth to its 'knees** to badly affect an organization, etc. so that it can no longer function: *The strikes brought the industry to its knees.* ▶ **put sb over your 'knee** to punish sb by making them lie on top of your knee and hitting their bottom ⊃ more at BEE, BEND v., MOTHER n., WEAK
■ verb (**kneed, kneed**) ~ **sb/sth** to hit or push sb/sth with your knee: *He kneed his attacker in the groin.*

**knee·cap** /ˈniːkæp/ noun, verb
■ noun the small bone that covers the front of the knee SYN PATELLA
■ verb (**-pp-**) ~ **sb** to shoot sb in the knee or break sb's kneecaps as a form of punishment that is not official and is illegal ▶ **knee·cap·ping** noun [C, U]

**knee-'deep** adj. up to your knees: *The snow was knee-deep in places.* ◇ (figurative) *I was knee-deep in work.* ▶ **knee-'deep** adv.: *I waded in knee-deep.*

**knee-'high** adj. high enough to reach your knees
IDM ▶ **knee-high to a 'grasshopper** (informal, humorous) very small; very young

**'knee-jerk** adj. [only before noun] (disapproving) produced in reaction to sth, without any serious thought: *It was a knee-jerk reaction on her part.*

**kneel** /niːl/ verb (**knelt, knelt** /nelt/) (**kneeled, kneeled** especially in NAmE) [I] to be in or move into a position where your body is supported on your knee or knees: *a kneeling figure* ◇ ~ **(down)** *We knelt (down) on the ground to examine the tracks.*

**'knee-length** adj. long enough to reach your knees: *knee-length shorts/socks*

**'knees-up** noun [usually sing.] (BrE, informal) a noisy party, with dancing

**knell** /nel/ noun [sing.] = DEATH KNELL

**knelt** /nelt/ past tense, past part. of KNEEL

**knew** /njuː; NAmE nuː/ past tense of KNOW ⊃ HOMOPHONES at NEW

**knick·er·bockers** /ˈnɪkəbɒkəz; NAmE -kərbɑːkərz/ (NAmE also **knick·ers**) noun [pl.] short, loose trousers that fit tightly just below the knee, worn especially in the past

**knick·ers** /ˈnɪkəz; NAmE -kərz/ noun [pl.] **1** (BrE) (also **panties** NAmE, BrE) a piece of women's underwear that covers the body from the middle part to the tops of the legs: *a pair of knickers* **2** (NAmE) = KNICKERBOCKERS ▶ **knick·er** adj. [only before noun]: *knicker elastic*

⊙ Oxford Phrasal Academic Lexicon (OPAL) written and spoken word lists | Ⓦ OPAL written word list | Ⓢ OPAL spoken word list

# knick-knack

**IDM** **get your ˈknickers in a twist** (*BrE*) (*NAmE* **get your ˈpanties in a bunch**) (*informal*) to become angry, confused or upset ⇒ more at WET *v.*

**knick-knack** /ˈnɪk næk/ *noun* [usually pl.] (*sometimes disapproving*) a small object of little worth that is used for decoration in a house **SYN** ornament

**knife** ❶ **A2** /naɪf/ *noun, verb*
■ *noun* ❶ **A2** (*pl.* **knives** /naɪvz/) a sharp BLADE (= metal edge) with a handle, used for cutting or as a weapon: *knives and forks* ◇ *a sharp knife* ◇ *a bread knife* (= one for cutting bread) ◇ *He had been stabbed repeatedly with a kitchen knife.* ◇ *a plan to tackle knife crime* ⇒ see also BUTTER KNIFE, CARVING KNIFE, FLICK KNIFE, JACKKNIFE *noun*, PALETTE KNIFE, PAPERKNIFE, PARING KNIFE, PENKNIFE, STANLEY KNIFE™, SWISS ARMY KNIFE™
**IDM** **the ˈknives are out (for sb)** the situation has become so bad that people are preparing to make one person take the blame, for example by taking away their job **like a knife through ˈbutter** (*informal*) easily; without meeting any difficulty **put/stick the ˈknife in | put/stick the ˈknife into sb** (*informal*) to behave towards sb in an unfriendly way and try to harm them **turn/twist the ˈknife (in the wound)** to say or do sth unkind deliberately; to make sb who is unhappy feel even more unhappy **under the ˈknife** (*informal*) having a medical operation
■ *verb* ~ **sb** to injure or kill sb with a knife **SYN** stab

**ˈknife-edge** *noun* [usually sing.] the sharp edge of a knife
**IDM** **on a ˈknife-edge 1** (of a situation, etc.) in a difficult or dangerous situation in which a very small change can cause sb/sth to succeed or fail: *The economy is balanced on a knife-edge.* **2** (of a person) very worried or anxious about the result of sth

**knife·point** /ˈnaɪfpɔɪnt/ *noun*
**IDM** **at ˈknifepoint** while being threatened, or threatening sb, with a knife: *She was robbed at knifepoint.*

**knight** /naɪt/ *noun, verb*
■ *noun* **1** (in the Middle Ages) a man of high social rank who had a duty to fight for his king. Knights are often shown in pictures riding horses and wearing ARMOUR. **2** (in the UK) a man who has been given a special honour by the king or queen and has the title *Sir* before his name ⇒ compare BARONET **3** a piece used in the game of CHESS that is like a horse's head in shape
**IDM** **a knight in shining ˈarmour** (*usually humorous*) a man who saves sb, especially a woman, from a dangerous situation
■ *verb* [usually passive] to give sb the rank and title of a knight: **be knighted (by sb)** *He was knighted by the Queen for his services to industry.*

▼ **HOMOPHONES**

**knight • night** /naɪt/
- **knight** *noun*: *The story tells of a knight who leaves the castle to fight a dragon.*
- **night** *noun*: *At night you can see thousands of stars.*

**knight·hood** /ˈnaɪthʊd/ *noun* (in the UK) the rank or title of a KNIGHT: *He received a knighthood in the New Year's Honours list.*

**knight·ly** /ˈnaɪtli/ *adj.* [usually before noun] (*literary*) consisting of knights; typical of a knight **SYN** chivalrous

**knit** /nɪt/ *verb, noun*
■ *verb* (**knit·ted, knit·ted**) **HELP** In senses 3 and 4 knit is usually used for the past tense and past participle. **1** [T, I] to make clothes, etc. from wool, cotton or other THREAD using two long thin KNITTING needles or a machine: ~ **(sth)** *I knitted this cardigan myself.* ◇ *Lucy was sitting on the sofa, knitting.* ◇ ~ **sb sth** *She's knitting the baby a shawl.* **2** [T, I] ~ **(sth)** to use a basic STITCH in knitting: *Knit one row, purl one row.* **3** [T, I] ~ **(sb/sth) (together)** to join people or things closely together or to be joined closely together: *a closely/tightly knit community* (= one in which relationships are very close) ◇ *Society is knit together by certain commonly held beliefs.* ⇒ see also CLOSE-KNIT, TIGHT-KNIT **4** [I, T] ~ **(sth)** (of broken bones) to grow together again to form one piece; to make broken bones grow together again **SYN** mend: *The bone failed to knit correctly.*
**IDM** **knit your ˈbrow(s)** to move your EYEBROWS together, to show that you are thinking hard, feeling angry, etc. **SYN** frown
■ *noun* [usually pl.] a piece of clothing that has been knitted: *winter knits*

**knit·ted** /ˈnɪtɪd/ (*also* **knit**) *adj.* made by knitting wool or another THREAD: *knitted gloves* ◇ *a white knit dress* ◇ *a hand-knitted sweater* ◇ *a cotton-knit shirt*

**knit·ter** /ˈnɪtə(r)/ *noun* a person who knits

**knit·ting** /ˈnɪtɪŋ/ *noun* [U] **1** an item that is being knitted: *Where's my knitting?* **2** the activity of knitting

**ˈknitting needle** *noun* a long thin piece of plastic or metal with a point at one end that you use for knitting. You usually use two together.

**knit·wear** /ˈnɪtweə(r)/; *NAmE* -wer/ *noun* [U] items of clothing that have been knitted

**knives** /naɪvz/ *pl.* of KNIFE

**knobs**

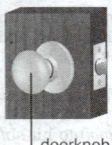
doorknob

knob on a drawer

knob on a radio

**knob** /nɒb; *NAmE* nɑːb/ *noun* **1** a round switch on a machine such as a radio that you use to turn it on and off, etc: *the volume control knob* **2** a round handle on a door or a DRAWER **3** a round shape like a ball on the surface or end of sth **4** (*especially BrE*) a small piece of sth such as butter **5** (*BrE, taboo, slang*) a PENIS
**IDM** **with ˈknobs on** (*BrE, slang*) used to say that sth is a more complicated version of what you mention: *It isn't art — it's just a horror movie with knobs on!*

**knob·bly** /ˈnɒbli/; *NAmE* ˈnɑːb-/ (*especially NAmE* **knobby** /ˈnɒbi/; *NAmE* ˈnɑːbi/) *adj.* having small, hard, raised areas on the surface: *knobbly knees*

**knock** ❶ **A2** /nɒk; *NAmE* nɑːk/ *verb, noun*
■ *verb*
- **AT DOOR/WINDOW 1** ❶ **B1** [I] to hit a door, etc. in order to attract attention **SYN** rap: *He knocked three times and waited.* ◇ ~ **at/on sth** *I knocked on the door and went straight in.*
- **HIT 2** ❶ **B1** [T, I] to hit sth hard, often by accident: ~ **sth (against/on sth)** *Be careful you don't knock your head on this low beam.* ◇ ~ **against/on sth** *Her hand knocked against the glass.* **3** ❶ **B1** [T] to hit sth so that it moves or breaks: ~ **sth + adv./prep.** *He'd knocked over a glass of water.* ◇ *I knocked the nail into the wall.* ◇ *They had to knock the door down to get in.* ◇ *The boys were knocking* (= kicking) *a ball around in the back yard.* ◇ ~ **sth** (*figurative*) *The criticism had knocked* (= damaged) *her self-esteem.* ⇒ SYNONYMS at HIT **4** [T] to put sb/sth into a particular state by hitting them/it: ~ **sb/sth + adj.** *The blow knocked me flat.* ◇ *He was knocked senseless by the blow.* ◇ ~ **sb/sth doing sth** *She knocked my drink flying.* ◇ ~ **sb/sth + adv./prep.** *The two rooms had been knocked into one* (= the wall between them had been knocked down). ⇒ SYNONYMS at HIT **5** [T] ~ **sth + adv./prep.** to make a hole in sth by hitting it hard: *They managed to knock a hole in the wall.*
- **OF HEART/KNEES 6** [I] if your heart **knocks**, it beats hard; if your knees **knock**, they shake, for example from fear: *My heart was knocking wildly.*
- **OF ENGINE/PIPES 7** [I] to make a regular sound of metal hitting metal, especially because there is sth wrong
- **CRITICIZE 8** [T] ~ **sb/sth** (*informal*) to criticize sb/sth, especially when it happens unfairly: *The newspapers are*

always knocking the England team. ◊ It may sound pretty childish, but **don't knock it** until you've tried it. **IDM** **I'll knock your 'block/'head off!** (informal) used to threaten sb that you will hit them **knock sb 'dead** (informal) to impress sb very much: *You look fabulous—you'll knock 'em dead tonight.* **knock sb/sth into a cocked 'hat** (BrE, old-fashioned) to be very much better than sb/sth **knock it 'off!** (informal) used to tell sb to stop making a noise, annoying you, etc. **knock sb off their 'pedestal/ 'perch** to make sb lose their position as sb/sth successful or admired **knock sth on the 'head** (BrE, informal) to stop sth from happening; to stop doing sth: *The recession knocked on the head any idea of expanding the company.* **knock on 'wood** (NAmE) (BrE **touch 'wood**) (saying) used when talking about your previous good luck or your hopes for the future, to avoid bringing bad luck **knock sb 'sideways** (informal) to surprise or shock sb so much that they are unable to react immediately **knock 'spots off sb/sth** (BrE, informal) to be very much better than sb/ sth **knock the 'stuffing out of sb** (informal) to make sb lose their confidence and enthusiasm **you could have knocked me down with a 'feather** (informal) used to express surprise ⊃ more at DAYLIGHTS, HEAD *n.*, HELL, SENSE *n.*, SHAPE *n.*, SIX, SOCK *n.*
**PHR V** **knock a'round …** (BrE also **knock a'bout …**) (informal) **1** to travel and live in various places: *He spent a few years knocking around Europe.* **2** used to say that sth is in a place but you do not know exactly where: *It must be knocking around here somewhere.* **knock a'round with sb/together** (BrE also **knock a'bout with sb/together**) (informal) to spend a lot of time with sb/together **knock sb/sth a'round** (BrE also **knock sb/sth a'bout**) (informal) to hit sb/sth repeatedly; to treat sb/sth roughly **knock sb 'back 1** (BrE) to prevent sb from achieving sth or making progress, especially by rejecting them or sth that they suggest or ask ⊃ related noun KNOCK-BACK **2** (BrE) to surprise or shock sb: *Hearing the news really knocked me back.* **knock sb 'back sth** (BrE, informal) to cost sb a lot of money: *That house must have knocked them back a bit.* **knock sth↔'back** (informal) to drink sth quickly, especially an alcoholic drink **knock sb 'down (from sth) (to sth)** (informal) to persuade sb to reduce the price of sth: *I managed to knock him down to $400.* **knock sb↔'down/'over** to hit sb and make them fall to the ground: *She was knocked down by a bus.* ◊ *He knocked his opponent down three times in the first round.* **knock sth↔'down** to destroy a building by breaking its walls **SYN** demolish: *These old houses are going to be knocked down.* **knock sth↔'down (from sth) (to sth)** (informal) to reduce the price of sth: *He knocked down the price from $80 to $50.* ⊃ see also KNOCK-DOWN **knock 'off | knock 'off sth** (informal) to stop doing sth, especially work: *Do you want to knock off early today?* ◊ *What time do you knock off work?* ◊ *Let's knock off for lunch.* **knock sb↔'off** (slang) to murder sb **knock sth↔'off 1** (informal) to complete sth quickly and without much effort: *He knocks off three novels a year.* **2** (BrE, slang) to steal sth; to steal from a place: *to knock off a load of recording equipment* ◊ *to knock off a bank* **knock sth↔'off | knock sth↔'off sth** (informal) to reduce the price or value of sth: *They knocked off $60 because of a scratch.* ◊ *The news knocked 13% off the company's shares.* **knock sb↔'out 1** to make sb go to sleep or become unconscious: *The blow knocked her out.* **2** (in boxing) to hit an opponent so that they cannot get up within a limited time and therefore lose the fight ⊃ related noun KNOCK-OUT **3** (informal) to surprise and impress sb very much: *The movie just knocked me out.* ⊃ related noun KNOCKOUT **knock sb/yourself 'out** to make sb/yourself very tired **SYN** wear out **knock sb↔'out (of sth)** to defeat sb so that they cannot continue competing **SYN** eliminate: *England had been knocked out of the World Cup.* ⊃ see also KNOCKOUT **knock sth↔'out** (informal) to produce sth, especially quickly and easily: *He knocks out five books a year.* **knock yourself 'out** (informal) to go ahead and do what you want: *You guys go and have fun. Knock yourselves out.* **knock sb↔'over** = KNOCK SB DOWN/OVER

**knock sth↔to'gether 1** (informal) to make or complete sth quickly and often not very well: *I knocked some bookshelves together from old planks.* **2** (BrE) to make two rooms or buildings into one by removing the wall between them: *The house consists of two cottages knocked together.* **knock 'up** (in tennis, etc.) to practise for a short time before the start of a match **knock sb↔'up 1** (BrE, informal) to wake sb by knocking on their door **2** (informal) to make a woman pregnant **knock sth↔'up** to prepare or make sth quickly and without much effort: *She knocked up a meal in ten minutes.*

■ **noun**
• AT DOOR/WINDOW **1** ⓘ **B1** the sound of sb hitting a door, window, etc. with their hand or with sth hard to attract attention: ~**on/at sth** *There was a knock at the door.*
• HIT **2** ⓘ **B1** a sharp hit from sth hard **SYN** bang: *He got a nasty knock on the head.*
• BAD EXPERIENCE **3** a bad experience that makes sb/sth less confident or successful

**knock·about** /'nɒkəbaʊt; NAmE 'nɑːk-/ adj. [usually before noun] (BrE) **knockabout** entertainment involves people acting in a deliberately silly way, for example falling over or hitting other people, in order to make the audience laugh **SYN** slapstick

**'knock-back** noun (informal) a difficulty or problem that makes you feel less confident that you will be successful in sth that you are doing, especially when sb rejects you or sth you suggest or ask

**'knock-down** adj., noun
■ **adj.** [only before noun] (informal) **1** (of prices, etc.) much lower than usual **SYN** rock-bottom **2** using a lot of force: *a knock-down punch*
■ **noun 1** (in boxing) an act of falling to the ground after being hit **2** (in football (soccer)) an act of hitting a high ball down to the ground or to another player

**knock·er** /'nɒkə(r); NAmE 'nɑːk-/ noun **1** (also **'door knock·er**) [C] a metal object attached to the outside of the door of a house, etc. that you hit against the door to attract attention **2** [C] (informal) a person who is always criticizing sb/ sth **3 knockers** [pl.] (taboo, slang) an offensive word for a woman's breasts

**'knock-'kneed** adj. having legs that turn towards each other at the knees

**'knock 'knees** noun [pl.] legs that turn towards each other at the knees

**'knock-on** adj. (especially BrE) causing other events to happen one after another in a series: *The increase in the price of oil had **a knock-on effect** on the cost of many other goods.*

**'knock-out** /'nɒkaʊt; NAmE 'nɑːk-/ noun, adj.
■ **noun 1** (abbr. KO) (in boxing) a hard hit that makes an opponent fall to the ground and be unable to get up, so that he or she loses the fight **2** (informal) a person or thing that is very attractive or impressive
■ **adj.** [only before noun] **1** (especially BrE) a **knockout** competition is one in which the winning player/team at each stage competes in the next stage and the losing one no longer takes part in the competition: *the knockout stages of the tournament* **2** a **knockout** blow is sth that hits sb so hard that they can no longer get up

**'knock-up** noun (BrE) a short practice before a game or match, especially of tennis

**knoll** /nəʊl/ noun a small round hill **SYN** mound

**knot** /nɒt; NAmE nɑːt/ noun, verb
■ **noun**
• IN STRING/ROPE **1** a join made by tying together two pieces or ends of string, rope, etc: *to tie a knot* ◊ *Tie the two ropes together with a knot.* ⊃ see also GORDIAN KNOT
• OF HAIR **2** a way of TWISTING hair into a small round shape at the back of the head: *She had her hair in a knot.* **3** a tight mass in sth such as hair or wool, where it has become TWISTED together: *hair full of knots and tangles*
• IN WOOD **4** a hard round spot in a piece of wood where there was once a branch

# knotty

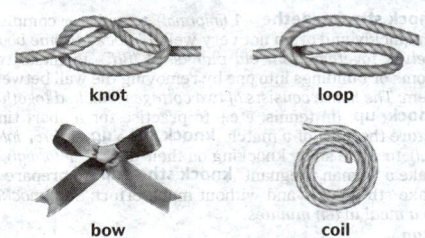

knot  loop  
bow  coil

- **GROUP OF PEOPLE 5** a small group of people standing close together
- **OF MUSCLES 6** a tight, hard feeling in the stomach, throat, etc. caused by nerves, anger, etc: *My stomach was in knots.* ◇ *I could feel a knot of fear in my throat.*
- **SPEED OF BOAT/PLANE 7** a unit for measuring the speed of boats and aircraft; one NAUTICAL MILE per hour **IDM** see RATE *n.*, TIE *v.*

■ *verb* (-tt-)
- **TIE WITH KNOT 1** [T] ~**sth** to fasten sth with a knot or knots: *He carefully knotted his tie.*
- **BEND INTO KNOT 2** [I] to become TWISTED into a knot **SYN** **tangle 3** [T] ~**sth** to TWIST hair into a particular shape: *She wore her hair loosely knotted on top of her head.*
- **MUSCLES 4** [I, T] ~**(sth)** if muscles, etc. knot or sth knots them, they become hard and painful because of fear, excitement, etc: *She felt her stomach knot with fear.*

**IDM** **get ˈknotted** (*BrE, informal, slang*) a rude way of telling sb to go away or of telling them that you are annoyed with them

**knotty** /ˈnɒti; *NAmE* ˈnɑːti/ *adj.* (**knot·tier, knot·ti·est**) **1** complicated and difficult to solve **SYN** **thorny**: *a knotty problem* **2** having parts that are hard and TWISTED together: *the knotty roots of the old oak tree*

# know **⓪ A1** /nəʊ/ *verb, noun*

■ *verb* (**knew** /njuː; *NAmE* nuː/, **known** /nəʊn/) (not used in the progressive tenses)
- **HAVE INFORMATION 1** ❓ **A1** [T, I] to have information in your mind as a result of experience or because you have learned or been told it: ~**sth** *No one knows the answer.* ◇ *I need to know your name.* ◇ *The truth about what happened is not yet known.* ◇ *All I know is that she used to work in a bank* (= I have no other information about her). ◇ **~(that) …** *People's handwriting changes as they get older.* ◇ *We know from experience that turning a hobby into a business is not easy.* ◇ *I know for a fact (that) he didn't go to the party.* ◇ *'There's no one in.' 'How do you know?'* ◇ *'You've got a flat tyre.' 'I know.'* ◇ *'Isn't that his car?' 'I wouldn't know./How should I know?'* (= I don't know and I am not the person you should ask.) ◇ **it is known that…** *It is widely known that CFCs can damage the ozone layer.* ◇ ~**where**, **who**, **etc…** *I knew where he was hiding.* ◇ *No one knows for sure who did it.* ◇ ~**about sth** *You know about Amanda's baby, don't you?* ◇ *I don't know about you, but I'm ready for something to eat.* ◇ ~**of sb/sth** *I know of someone who can help us.* ◇ *'Is anyone else coming?' 'Not that I know of.'* ◇ ~**to do sth** *Does he know to come here* (= that he should come here) *first?* ◇ ~**sb/sth to be/do sth** *We know her to be honest.* ◇ *Strobe lights are known to cause seizures.* ⇒ see also WELL KNOWN (2) ⇒ HOMOPHONES at NOSE ⇒ see also NEED-TO-KNOW ⇒ EXPRESS YOURSELF at INFORMATION
- **REALIZE 2** ❓ **A1** [T, I] to realize, understand or be aware of sth: **~(that)…** *As soon as I walked in the room I knew (that) something was wrong.* ◇ *She knew she was dying.* ◇ *'Martin was lying all the time.' 'I should have known.'* ◇ ~**what, how, etc…** *I knew perfectly well what she meant.* ◇ *I know exactly how you feel.* ◇ ~**sth** *This case is hopeless and he knows it* (= although he will not admit it).
- **FEEL CERTAIN 3** ❓ **A1** [T, I] to feel certain about sth: ~**(that) …** *He knew (that) he could trust her.* ◇ *I know it's here somewhere!* ◇ *I don't know that I can finish it by next week.* ◇ ~**(sth)** *'You were right—someone's been spreading rumours about you.' 'I knew it!'* ◇ *'She's the worst player in the team.' 'Oh, I don't know* (= I am not sure that I agree)— *she played well yesterday.'* ⇒ see also DON'T KNOW ⇒ HOMOPHONES at NEW
- **BE FAMILIAR 4** ❓ **A1** [T] ~**sb/sth** to be familiar with a person, place, thing, etc: *I've known David for 20 years.* ◇ *Do you two know each other* (= have you met before)? ◇ *She's very nice when you get to know her.* ◇ *Knowing Ben, we could be waiting a long time* (= it is typical of him to be late). ◇ *This man is known to the police* (= as a criminal). ◇ *I know Paris well.* ◇ *Do you know the play* (= have you seen or read it before)? ◇ *How many of your neighbours do you know by name?* ◇ *The new rules could mean the end of football as we know it* (= in the form that we are familiar with).
- **SKILL/LANGUAGE 5** ❓ **A1** [T] to have learned a skill or language and be able to use it: ~**sth** *Do you know any Japanese?* ◇ ~**how to do sth** *Do you know how to use spreadsheets?*
- **REPUTATION 6** ❓ **B1** [T, usually passive] to think that sb/sth is a particular type of person or thing or has particular characteristics: **be known as sth** *He has become widely known as an expert in child psychology.* ◇ **be known for sth** *She is best known for her work on the human brain.* ◇ **be known to be/do sth** *He's known to be an outstanding physicist.* ⇒ see also WELL KNOWN (1)
- **GIVE NAME 7** ❓ **B1** [T] [usually passive] to give sb/sth a particular name or title: **be known as sb/sth** *Iran was formerly known as Persia.* ◇ *Peter Wilson, also known as 'The Tiger'* ◇ **be known by sth** *The country was not yet known by the name of England.*
- **RECOGNIZE 8** ❓ **B1** [T] ~**sb/sth** to be able to recognize sb/sth: *I couldn't see who was speaking, but I knew the voice.* ◇ *She knows a bargain when she sees one.* ⇒ SYNONYMS at IDENTIFY
- **UNDERSTAND THE DIFFERENCE 9** [T] ~**sb/sth from sb/sth** to understand the difference between one person or thing and another **SYN** **distinguish, tell**: *I hope we have taught our children to know right from wrong.*
- **EXPERIENCE 10** [T] (only used in the perfect tenses) to have seen, heard or experienced sth: ~**sb/sth (to) do sth** *I've never known it (to) snow in July before.* ◇ **be known to do sth** *He has been known to spend all morning in the bathroom.* **11** [T] ~**sth** to have personal experience of sth: *He has known both poverty and wealth.* ◇ *She may be successful now, but she has known what it is like to be poor.*

**IDM** **beˌfore you know ˈwhere you are** very quickly or suddenly: *We were whisked off in a taxi before we knew where we were.* **be ˌnot to ˈknow** to have no way of realizing or being aware that you have done sth wrong: *'I'm sorry, I called when you were in bed.' 'Don't worry—you weren't to know.'* **for ˌall you, ˌI, they, etc. ˈknow** (*informal*) used to emphasize that you do not know sth and that it is not important to you: *She could be dead for all I know.* **ˌGod/ˈgoodness/ˈHeaven knows** (*informal*) **HELP** Some people may find this use of **God** offensive. **1** used to emphasize that you do not know sth: *God knows what else they might find.* ◇ *'Where are they?' 'Goodness knows.'* **2** used to emphasize the truth of what you are saying: *She ought to pass the exam—goodness knows she's been working hard enough.* **I ˌdon't know ˈhow, ˈwhy, etc…** (*informal*) used to criticize sb's behaviour: *I don't know how you can say things like that.* **I ˈknow** (*informal*) **1** /aɪ ˈnəʊ/ used to agree with sb or to show sympathy: *'What a ridiculous situation!' 'I know.'* **2** /ˌaɪ nəʊ/ used to introduce a new idea or suggestion: *I know, let's see what's on at the theatre.* **ˌknow sth as ˌwell as ˈI do** used to criticize sb by saying that they should realize or understand sth: *You know as well as I do that you're being unreasonable.* **ˌknow sb/sth ˈbackwards** (*especially BrE, informal*) to know sb/sth extremely well: *She must know the play backwards by now.* **ˌknow ˈbest** to know what should be done, etc. better than other people: *The doctor told you to stay in bed, and she knows best.* **ˌknow ˈbetter (than that/than to do sth)** to be sensible enough not to do sth: *He knows better than to judge by appearances.* **ˌknow sb by ˈsight** to recognize sb without knowing them well **ˌknow ˈdifferent/ˈotherwise** (*informal*) to have information or evidence that the opposite is true: *He says he doesn't care about what the critics write, but I know different.* **ˌknow full ˈwell** to be very aware of a fact and unable to deny or ignore it: *He knew full well what she thought of it.* **know sb/sth inside 'out | know sb/sth like the back of your 'hand** (*informal*) to be very familiar with sb/sth: *This is where I grew up. I know this area like the back of my hand.* **know your own 'mind** to have very clear and definite ideas about what you want to do **know your 'stuff** (*informal*) to know a lot about a particular subject or job **know your way a'round** to be familiar with a place, subject, etc. **know what you're 'talking about** (*informal*) to have knowledge about sth from your own experience **know which side your 'bread is buttered** (*informal*) to know where you can get an advantage for yourself **let it be known/make it known that …** (*formal*) to make sure that people are informed about sth, especially by getting sb else to tell them: *The President has let it be known that he does not intend to run for election again.* **let sb 'know** 🔑 A2 to tell sb about sth: *Let me know how I can help.* **make yourself 'known to sb** to introduce yourself to sb: *I made myself known to the hotel manager.* **not know any 'better** to behave badly, usually because you have not been taught the correct way to behave **not know your 'arse from your 'elbow** (*BrE, taboo, slang*) to be very stupid; to have absolutely no skill **not know 'beans about sth** (*NAmE, informal*) to know nothing about a subject **not know the first thing a'bout sb/sth** to know nothing at all about sb/sth **not know sb from 'Adam** (*informal*) to not know at all who sb is **not know what 'hit you** (*informal*) to be so surprised by sth that you do not know how to react **not know where to 'look** (*informal*) to feel very embarrassed and not know how to react **not know whether you're 'coming or 'going** (*informal*) to be so excited or confused that you cannot behave or think in a sensible way **not know you are 'born** (*BrE, informal*) to have an easy life without realizing how easy it is: *You people without kids don't know you're born.* **there's no 'knowing** used to say that it is impossible to say what might happen: *There's no knowing how he'll react.* **what does … know?** used to say that sb knows nothing about the subject you are talking about: *What does he know about football, anyway?* **what do you 'know?** (*informal*) used to express surprise: *Well, what do you know? Look who's here!* **you 'know** (*informal*) 1 used when you are thinking of what to say next: *Well, you know, it's difficult to explain.* 2 used to show that what you are referring to is known or understood by the person you are speaking to: *Guess who I've just seen? Maggie! You know—Jim's wife.* ◊ *You know that restaurant round the corner? It's closed down.* 3 used to emphasize sth that you are saying: *I'm not stupid, you know.* **you 'know something/'what?** (*informal*) used to introduce an interesting or surprising opinion, piece of news, etc: *You know something? I've never really enjoyed Christmas.* **you know 'who/'what** (*informal*) used to refer to sb/sth without mentioning a name **you never 'know** (*informal*) used to say that you can never be certain about what will happen in the future, especially when you are suggesting that sth good might happen ⇒ more at ANSWER *n.*, COST *n.*, DAY, DEVIL, FAR *adv.*, LORD *n.*, OLD, PAT *adv.*, ROPE *n.*, THING, TRUTH, WANT *v.*, WHAT

◼ *noun*

IDM ▶ **in the 'know** (*informal*) having more information about sth than most people: *Somebody in the know told me he's going to resign.*

▼ **EXPRESS YOURSELF**

**Saying that you don't know something or giving yourself time to think**

There are various ways of telling people that you haven't got the information they are asking for:
- *I really don't know.*
- *I'm afraid I don't have the faintest idea.*
- *Sorry, I have absolutely no idea.*
- *Has anyone left a message? No, not to my knowledge/not as far as I know.*
- *Well, that's a good question.*
- *Yes, that's an interesting point/idea.*
- *Well, let me see …*
- *Let me think about that for a moment.*

873 **knuckleduster**

**'know-all** (*BrE*) (also **'know-it-all** *NAmE, BrE*) *noun* (*informal, disapproving*) a person who behaves as if they know everything

**'know-how** *noun* [U] (*informal*) knowledge of how to do sth and experience in doing it: *We need skilled workers and technical know-how.*

**know·ing** /ˈnəʊɪŋ/ *adj.* [usually before noun] showing that you know or understand about sth that is supposed to be secret: *a knowing smile* ⇒ compare UNKNOWING

**know·ing·ly** /ˈnəʊɪŋli/ *adv.* 1 while knowing the truth or likely result of what you are doing SYN **deliberately**: *She was accused of knowingly making a false statement to the police.* 2 in a way that shows that you know or understand about sth that is supposed to be secret: *He glanced at her knowingly.*

**'know-it-all** (especially *NAmE*) (*BrE* also **'know-all**) *noun* (*informal, disapproving*) a person who behaves as if they know everything

**know·ledge** 🔑 A2 ◎ /ˈnɒlɪdʒ; *NAmE* ˈnɑːl-/ *noun* 1 🔑 A2 [U, sing.] the information, understanding and skills that you gain through education or experience: *scientific/technical knowledge and skills* ◊ *intimate/first-hand/basic knowledge* ◊ *It will be an opportunity to* **gain knowledge** *and experience.* ◊ ~ **of sth** *She has* **acquired** *a detailed knowledge of the subject.* ◊ *He had no* **prior knowledge** *of the language before visiting the country.* ◊ ~ **about sth** *There is a* **lack of knowledge** *about the tax system.* ⇒ see also CARNAL KNOWLEDGE, GENERAL KNOWLEDGE, SELF-KNOWLEDGE 2 🔑 B1 [U] the state of knowing about a particular fact or situation: ~ **(of sth)** *He denied all knowledge of the affair.* ◊ **without sb's** ~ *She sent the letter without my knowledge.* ◊ **with sb's** ~ *The film was made with the Prince's* **full knowledge** *and approval.* ◊ **in the ~ that …** *I went to sleep* **secure in the knowledge** *that I was not alone in the house.* ◊ *They could relax* **safe in the knowledge** *that they had the funding for the project.* 3 (used before another noun) information, considered as a resource to be used and supplied in industry, rather than producing goods: *the shift toward a* **knowledge economy** ◊ *Knowledge workers are driving our economy today.*

IDM **be common/public 'knowledge** to be sth that everyone knows, especially in a particular community or group **come to sb's 'knowledge** (*formal*) to become known by sb: *It has come to our knowledge that you have been taking time off without permission.* **to your 'knowledge** from the information you have, although you may not know everything: *'Are they divorced?' 'Not to my knowledge.'* ⇒ more at BEST *n.*

**know·ledge·able** /ˈnɒlɪdʒəbl; *NAmE* ˈnɑːl-/ *adj.* ~ **(about sth)** knowing a lot SYN **well informed**: *She is very knowledgeable about plants.* ▶ **know·ledge·ably** /-bli/ *adv.*

**known** /nəʊn/ *adj., verb*
◼ *adj.* [only before noun] known about, especially by a lot of people: *He's a known thief.* ◊ *The disease has no known cure.* ⇒ see also WELL KNOWN
◼ *verb* past part. of KNOW

**knuckle** /ˈnʌkl/ *noun, verb*
◼ *noun* 1 [C] any of the JOINTS in the fingers, especially those connecting the fingers to the rest of the hand ⇒ see also BARE-KNUCKLE 2 (*also* **hock**) [U, C] a piece of meat from the lower part of an animal's leg, especially a pig
IDM **near the 'knuckle** (*BrE, informal*) (of a remark, joke, etc.) connected with sex in a way that is likely to offend people or make them feel embarrassed ⇒ more at RAP *n.*, RAP *v.*

◼ *verb*
PHRV **knuckle 'down (to sth)** (*informal*) to begin to work hard at sth SYN **get down to**: *I'm going to have to knuckle down to some serious study.* **knuckle 'under (to sb/sth)** (*informal*) to accept sb else's authority

**knuckle·dust·er** (*also* **knuckle duster**) /ˈnʌkldʌstə(r)/ *noun* (*NAmE also* **brass 'knuckles** [pl.]) a metal cover that is put on the fingers and used as a weapon

# knucklehead 874

**knuckle·head** /ˈnʌklhed/ noun (especially NAmE, informal) a person who behaves in a stupid way

**KO** (also **kayo**) /ˌkeɪ ˈəʊ/ abbr. KNOCKOUT

**koala** /kəʊˈɑːlə/ (also **koˈala bear**) noun an Australian animal with thick grey fur, large ears and no tail. Koalas live in trees and eat leaves. HELP The form **koala bear** is still quite common but biologists do not consider it to be correct because koalas are not a type of bear. ⊃ VISUAL VOCAB page V2

**koek·sister** /ˈkʊksɪstə(r)/ noun (SAfrE) a South African sweet dish consisting of pieces of DOUGH with a special shape that are fried in oil and then covered in a sweet liquid, often eaten at the end of a meal: *The meal finishes with koeksisters, plaits of deep-fried dough dipped in syrup.*

**kofta** /ˈkɒftə; NAmE ˈkɔːf-/ noun [U, C] a Middle Eastern or South Asian dish of meat, fish or cheese mixed with SPICES and shaped into balls; one of these balls

**kohl** /kəʊl/ noun [U] a black powder that is used especially in Eastern countries. It is put around the eyes to make them more attractive.

**kohl·rabi** /ˌkəʊlˈrɑːbi/ noun [U] a vegetable of the CABBAGE family whose thick, round, white STEM is eaten

**koi** /kɔɪ/ (also **ˌkoi ˈcarp**) noun (pl. **koi** or **koi carp**) a large fish originally from Japan, often kept in fish PONDS

**ˈkola nut** = COLA NUT

**kombi** (also **combi**) /ˈkɒmbi; NAmE ˈkɑːm-/ SAfrE [ˈkɔmbi] noun (SAfrE) a vehicle that looks like a van, has windows at the sides and carries about ten people

**Ko·modo dragon** /kəˌməʊdəʊ ˈdræɡən/ noun a very large LIZARD from Indonesia

**kook** /kuːk/ noun (informal, especially NAmE) a person who acts in a strange or crazy way ▶ **kooky** adj.

**kooka·burra** /ˈkʊkəbʌrə; NAmE -bɜːrə/ noun an Australian bird that makes a strange laughing noise

**Koori** /ˈkʊəri; NAmE ˈkʊri/ noun (AustralE) an Aboriginal person from the south-east of Australia

**kop** /kɒp; NAmE kɑːp/ SAfrE [kɔp] noun 1 (SAfrE, informal) a head 2 (SAfrE) (especially in place names) a hill 3 (usually **the Kop**) (BrE) (especially in the past) an area of steps at a football (soccer) team's ground where that team's supporters stand to watch the game, especially at Liverpool Football Club

**kop·pie** /ˈkɒpi; NAmE ˈkɑːpi/ SAfrE [ˈkɔpi] noun (SAfrE) a small hill: *They went for a walk up the koppie.*

**kora** /ˈkɔːrə/ noun a West African musical instrument with 21 strings that pass over a body that has the shape of a bowl and are attached to a long wooden part

**Koran** (also **Qur'an**) /kəˈrɑːn/ noun **the Koran** [sing.] the holy book of the Islamic religion, written in Arabic, containing the word of Allah as revealed to the Prophet Muhammad ▶ **Kor·an·ic** /-ˈrænɪk/ adj.

**korma** /ˈkɔːmə; NAmE ˈkɔːrmə/ noun [U, C] a South Asian dish or sauce made with cream or YOGURT, and often ALMONDS: *chicken korma*

**ko·sher** /ˈkəʊʃə(r)/ adj. **1** (of food) prepared according to the rules of Jewish law **2** (informal) honest or legal: *Their business deals are not always completely kosher.*

**kow·tow** /ˌkaʊˈtaʊ/ verb [I] ~ **(to sb/sth)** (informal, disapproving) to show sb in authority too much respect and be too willing to obey them

**KP** /ˌkeɪ ˈpiː/ noun [U] (NAmE) work done by soldiers in the kitchen, usually as a punishment: *The sergeant assigned him to KP.* ORIGIN From 'kitchen police', a name for the soldiers.

**kph** /ˌkeɪ piː ˈeɪtʃ/ (also **kmph, km/h**) abbr. kilometres per hour HELP The forms **kph** and **kmph** are widely used, but the correct scientific form in the SI system is **km/h**.

**kraal** /krɑːl/ noun (SAfrE) **1** a traditional African village of HUTS surrounded by a fence **2** an area surrounded by a fence in which animals are kept: *a cattle kraal*

**kra·ken** /ˈkrɑːkən/ noun an extremely large imaginary creature that is said to appear in the sea near Norway

**Kraut** /kraʊt/ noun (taboo, slang) an offensive word for a person from Germany

**krill** /krɪl/ noun [pl.] very small SHELLFISH that live in the sea around the Antarctic and are eaten by WHALES

**kris** /kriːs/ noun a Malay or Indonesian knife with a BLADE with little curves on its edge

**krona** /ˈkrəʊnə/ noun (pl. **kro·nor** /ˈkrəʊnɔː(r), -nə(r)/) the unit of money in Sweden and Iceland

**krone** /ˈkrəʊnə/ noun (pl. **kro·ner** /-nə(r)/) the unit of money in Denmark and Norway

**kryp·ton** /ˈkrɪptɒn; NAmE -tɑːn/ noun [U] (symb. **Kr**) a chemical element. Krypton is a gas that does not react with anything, used in FLUORESCENT lights and LASERS.

**kryp·ton·ite** /ˈkrɪptənaɪt/ noun [U] a chemical element that exists only in stories about Superman, a character with special powers that he loses when he is near to kryptonite

**kudos** /ˈkjuːdɒs; NAmE ˈkuːdɑːs/ noun [U] **1** the praise and honour that goes with a particular achievement or position SYN prestige: *the kudos of playing for such a famous team* **2** ~ **(to sb) (for sth/doing sth)** (informal) special praise to sb for sth they have done: *Kudos to Bill for fixing that problem.*

**kudu** /ˈkuːduː/ noun (pl. **kudu** or **kudus**) a large grey or brown African ANTELOPE with white STRIPES (= narrow lines) on its sides. The male kudu has long, curly HORNS.

**kudzu** /ˈkʊdzuː/ noun [U] a climbing plant with purple flowers that grows very fast and is used as a food and in medicines

**Ku Klux Klan** /ˌkuː klʌks ˈklæn/ noun [sing. + sing./pl. v.] (abbr. **KKK**) a secret organization of white men in the southern states of the US who use violence to oppose social change and equal rights for black people

**kulfi** /ˈkʊlfi/ noun [C, U] a type of South Asian ice cream, usually served in the shape of a CONE

**kum·quat** /ˈkʌmkwɒt; NAmE -kwɑːt/ noun a fruit like a very small orange that has sweet skin that is eaten and an inner part that has a bitter sharp taste

**kung fu** /ˌkʌŋ ˈfuː/ noun [U] (from Chinese) a Chinese system of fighting without weapons, similar to KARATE

**kurta** /ˈkɜːtə; NAmE ˈkɜːrtə/ noun a loose shirt, worn by men or women in South Asia

**kvetch** /kvetʃ/ verb [I] (NAmE, informal) to complain about sth all the time SYN **moan, whine**

**kW** abbr. (pl. **kW**) (in writing) KILOWATT: *a 2kW electric fire*

**kwaai** /kwaɪ/ adj. (superlative **kwaai·est**, no comparative) (SAfrE) (informal) **1** very good: *a kwaai song* **2** angry or aggressive: *a kwaai dog*

**kwaito** /ˈkwaɪtəʊ/ noun [U] a type of South African dance music, often with words that are spoken or shouted rather than sung

**Kwan·zaa** /ˈkwɑːnzə/ noun [U] a cultural festival that is celebrated in the US by some African Americans from December 26 to January 1 ORIGIN From a phrase in Swahili that means 'first fruits'.

**kwashi·or·kor** /ˌkwɒʃiˈɔːkɔː(r); NAmE ˌkwɑːʃiˈɔːrkər/ noun [U] a dangerous health condition that is caused by not eating enough PROTEIN and mainly affects young children in tropical countries

**kwela** /ˈkweɪlə/ noun [U] a type of South African jazz music in which the main part is usually played on a PENNY WHISTLE (= a type of long WHISTLE with holes in it that you can cover with your fingers to produce different notes when you blow it)

**kWh** abbr. (pl. **kWh**) (in writing) KILOWATT-HOUR

**ky·bosh** = KIBOSH

**kylie** /ˈkaɪli/ noun (AustralE) a BOOMERANG

# Ll

**L** /el/ noun, abbr., symbol
- **noun** (also **l**) [C, U] (pl. **Ls**, **L's**, **l's** /elz/) the 12th letter of the English alphabet: *'Lion' begins with (an) L/'L'.* ⊃ see also L-PLATE
- **abbr.** **1 L.** (especially on maps) Lake: *L. Windermere* **2** (especially for sizes of clothes) large: *S, M and L* (= small, medium and large)
- **symbol** (also **l**) the number 50 in ROMAN NUMERALS

**l** abbr. (in writing) **1** (pl. **l**) LITRE(S) **2** (also **l.**) (pl. **ll**) line (on a page in a book) **3** left: *l to r: Thomas, Edward and Henry*

**LA** (also **L.A.**) /ˌel ˈeɪ/ abbr. the city of Los Angeles

**la** = LAH ⊃ see also À LA

**laa·ger** /ˈlɑːɡə(r)/ noun (SAfrE) (in the past) a group of WAGONS that were put into a circle in order to protect people in the middle: *They drew their wagons into a laager and set up camp.* ◇ *a laager mentality* (= one that is not willing to accept new ideas)

**Lab.** abbr. (in British politics) Labour

**lab** ⓘ A2 /læb/ noun (informal) a laboratory: *a computer/research lab* ◇ *in a~ She'd been working in the lab all day.* ◇ *a lab technician* ◇ *a lab coat* (= a white coat worn by scientists, etc. working in a laboratory) ⊃ see also CRIME LAB

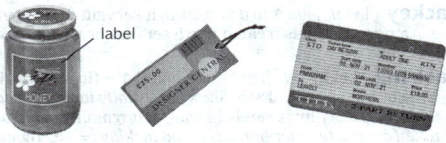

label on a jar    price tag    ticket

**label** ⓘ B1 ◉ /ˈleɪbl/ noun, verb
- **noun 1** ⓘ B1 a piece of paper, etc. that is attached to sth and that gives information about it SYN **tag, ticket**: *Always read the label carefully.* ◇ *price/address labels* ◇ *on a~ The washing instructions are on the label.* ⊃ see also OFF-LABEL, OWN-LABEL **2** (disapproving) a word or phrase that is used to describe sb/sth in a way that seems too general, unfair or not correct: *I hated the label 'housewife'.* **3** = DESIGNER LABEL: *today's major fashion labels* ◇ *He's really fashion-conscious and will only wear labels* (= clothes with a designer label). **4** a company that produces and sells music, CDs, etc: *the Virgin record label* ◇ *It's his first release for a major label.*
- **verb** (-ll-, US -l-) [often passive] **1** ⓘ B1 to fix a label on sth or write information on sth: *~sth (with sth) We carefully labelled each item with the contents and the date.* ◇ *~sth + adj. The file was labelled 'Private'.* **2** to describe sb/sth in a particular way, especially unfairly: *~sb/sth (as) sth He was labelled (as) a traitor by his former colleagues.* ◇ *~sb/sth + adj. It is unfair to label a small baby naughty.*

**labia** /ˈleɪbiə/ noun [pl.] the four folds of skin at the entrance to a woman's VAGINA

**labor** (US) = LABOUR

**la·bora·tory** ⓘ B1 /ləˈbɒrətri; NAmE ˈlæbrətɔːri/ noun (pl. **-ies**) (also informal **lab**) a room or building used for scientific research, experiments, testing, etc: *a clinical/research laboratory* ◇ *in a/the~ The effects of weathering can be simulated in the laboratory.* ◇ *laboratory experiments/tests* ◇ *The athletes' reflexes were tested under laboratory conditions.* ⊃ WORDFINDER NOTE at SCIENCE

**ˈLabor Day** noun a public holiday in the US and Canada on the first Monday of September, in honour of working people ⊃ compare MAY DAY

**la·bored, la·bor·er, la·bor·ing** (US) = LABOURED, LABOURER, LABOURING

**la·bori·ous** /ləˈbɔːriəs/ adj. taking a lot of time and effort: *a laborious task/process* ◇ *Checking all the information will be slow and laborious.* ▶ **la·bori·ous·ly** adv.

**ˈlabor union** noun (NAmE) = UNION (1)

**la·bour** ⓘ B2 (US **labor**) /ˈleɪbə(r)/ noun, verb
- **noun**
- WORK **1** ⓘ B2 [U] work, especially physical work: *manual labour* (= work using your hands) ◇ *The price will include the labour and materials.* ◇ *The company wants to keep down labour costs.* ◇ *The workers voted to withdraw their labour* (= to stop work as a means of protest). ◇ *a fair division of labour between men and women* ⊃ see also BONDED LABOUR, FORCED LABOUR, HARD LABOUR, SLAVE LABOUR **2** [C, usually pl.] (formal) a task or period of work: *He was so exhausted from the day's labours that he went straight to bed.*
- PEOPLE WHO WORK **3** ⓘ B2 [U] the people who work or are available for work in a country or company: *child/forced/slave labour* ◇ *Companies are making huge profits by exploiting cheap labour in poorer countries.* ◇ *There is a growing demand for skilled labour.* ◇ *New labour laws make it more difficult for employers to sack workers.* ⊃ WORDFINDER NOTE at INDUSTRY
- HAVING BABY **4** [U, C, usually sing.] the period of time or the process of giving birth to a baby: *in~ Jane was in labour for ten hours.* ◇ *She went into labour early.* ◇ *labour pains* ◇ *It was a difficult labour.* ⊃ WORDFINDER NOTE at BIRTH
- POLITICS **5 Labour** [U + sing./pl. v.] (abbr. **Lab.**) the British Labour Party: *He always votes Labour.* ◇ *Labour was/were in power for many years.*
- IDM **a ˌlabour of ˈlove** a hard task that you do because you want to, not because it is necessary
- **verb**
- STRUGGLE **1** [I] to try very hard to do sth difficult: *~(away) He was in his study labouring away over some old papers.* ◇ *~to do sth They laboured for years to clear their son's name.*
- WORK HARD **2** [I] to do hard physical work: *We laboured all day in the fields.* ◇ *(old-fashioned) the labouring classes* (= the working class)

> **SYNONYMS**
>
> **label**
> tag • sticker
>
> These are all words for a piece of paper, cloth or plastic that is attached to sth and gives information about it.
>
> **label** a small piece of paper, cloth or plastic that is attached to sth in order to show what it is or give information about it: *The washing instructions are on the label.* ◇ *address labels*
>
> **tag** (often used in compounds) a small piece of paper, cloth or plastic that is attached to sth, or that sb wears, in order to give information about it/them: *Everyone at the conference had to wear a name tag.*
>
> LABEL OR TAG?
>
> **Labels** in clothes are usually made of cloth and sewn in. **Tags** on clothes are usually made of card and cut off before you wear the clothes. A *name tag* can be stuck or tied onto sb to show who they are: *All babies in the hospital have name tags tied round their ankles.*
>
> *Price tag* is much more frequent than *price label* and is used for both literal and figurative meanings: *What does the price tag say?* ◇ *There is a £20 million price tag on the team's star player.* A **label** can also be a **sticker** that you put on an envelope.
>
> **sticker** a sticky label with a picture or message on it, that you stick on to sth.
>
> PATTERNS
> - a **price** label/tag/sticker
> - to **have** a label/tag/sticker
> - to **attach/put on/stick on** a label/tag/sticker
> - The label/tag/sticker **says**…

**labour camp**

• MOVE WITH DIFFICULTY **3** [I] (+ *adv.* / *prep.*) to move with difficulty and effort SYN **struggle**: *The horses laboured up the steep slope.*
IDM **labour the ˈpoint** to continue to repeat or explain sth that has already been said and understood
PHRV **ˈlabour under sth** (*formal*) to believe sth that is not true: *to labour under a misapprehension/delusion* ◊ *He's still labouring under the impression that he's written a great book.*

**ˈlabour camp** (*US* **ˈlabor camp**) *noun* a prison where people have to do hard work for long periods of time

**la·boured** (*US* **la·bored**) /ˈleɪbəd/; *NAmE* -bərd/ *adj.* **1** (of breathing) slow and taking a lot of effort **2** (of writing, speaking, etc.) not natural and seeming to take a lot of effort

**la·bour·er** (*US* **la·bor·er**) /ˈleɪbərə(r)/ *noun* a person whose job involves hard physical work that does not need special skills, especially work that is done outdoors ⊃ see also BONDED LABOURER

**ˈlabour force** (*US* **ˈlabor force**) *noun* [C + sing. / pl. v.] all the people who work for a company or in a country SYN **workforce**: *a skilled/an unskilled labour force*

**la·bour·ing** (*US* **la·bor·ing**) /ˈleɪbərɪŋ/ *noun* [U] hard physical work that does not need special skills: *a labouring job*

**ˈlabour-inˈtensive** (*US* **ˌlabor-inˈtensive**) *adj.* (of work) needing a lot of people to do it: *labour-intensive methods* ⊃ compare CAPITAL-INTENSIVE

**ˈlabour market** (*US* **ˈlabor market**) *noun* the number of people who are available for work in relation to the number of jobs available: *young people about to enter the labour market*

**the ˈLabour Party** (*also* **Laˑbour**) *noun* [sing. + sing. / pl. v.] one of the main British political parties, on the political left, that has traditionally represented the interests of working people: *the Labour Party leader*

**ˈlabour-saving** (*US* **ˈlabor-saving**) *adj.* [usually before noun] designed to reduce the amount of work or effort needed to do sth: *modern labour-saving devices such as washing machines and dishwashers*

**Lab·ra·dor** /ˈlæbrədɔː(r)/ *noun* a large dog that can be yellow, black or brown in colour, often used by blind people as a guide: *a golden/black/chocolate Labrador*

**la·bur·num** /ləˈbɜːnəm; *NAmE* -ˈbɜːrn-/ *noun* [C, U] a small tree with hanging bunches of yellow flowers

**laby·rinth** /ˈlæbərɪnθ/ *noun* (*formal*) a complicated series of paths, which it is difficult to find your way through: *We lost our way in the labyrinth of streets.* ◊ (*figurative*) *a labyrinth of rules and regulations* ⊃ compare MAZE ▸ **laby·rinˑthine** /ˌlæbəˈrɪnθaɪn; *NAmE* -θɪn, -θiːn/ *adj.*: (*formal*) *labyrinthine corridors* ◊ *labyrinthine legislation*

**lace** /leɪs/ *noun*, *verb*
■ *noun* **1** [U] a very thin material made from THREADS of cotton, silk, etc. that are made into a pattern with holes: *a lace handkerchief* ◊ *a tablecloth edged with lace* ◊ *lace curtains* ⊃ see also LACY **2** [C] = SHOELACE: *Your laces are undone.*
■ *verb* **1** [I, T] to be fastened with laces; to fasten sth with laces: **~ (up)** *She was wearing a dress that laced up at the side.* ◊ **~ sth (up)** *He was sitting on the bed lacing up his shoes.* ⊃ see also LACE-UP **2** [T] **~ sth** to put a lace through the holes in a shoe, a boot, etc. ⊃ related noun LACE-UP **3** [T] **~ sth (with sth)** to add a small amount of alcohol, a drug, poison, etc. to a drink SYN **spike**: *He had laced her milk with rum.* **4** [T] **~ sth (with sth)** to add a particular quality to a book, speech, etc: *Her conversation was laced with witty asides.* **5** [T] **~ sth** to TWIST sth together with another thing: *They sat with their fingers laced.*

**la·cer·ate** /ˈlæsəreɪt/ *verb* (*formal*) **1** **~ sth** to cut skin or part of the body with sth sharp: *His hand had been badly lacerated.* **2** **~ sb** to criticize sb very severely ▸ **la·cerˈation** /ˌlæsəˈreɪʃn/ *noun* [C, U]: *She suffered multiple lacerations to the face.*

**ˈlace-up** *noun* [usually pl.] (*especially BrE*) a shoe that is fastened with laces: *a pair of lace-ups* ◊ *lace-up boots* ⊃ compare OXFORD

**ˈlace-wing** /ˈleɪswɪŋ/ *noun* an insect that has large TRANSPARENT wings with lines on

**lach·ry·mose** /ˈlækrɪməʊs/ *adj.* (*formal*) tending to cry easily; making you cry SYN **tearful**

**lack** 🔊 B1 Ⓦ /læk/ *noun*, *verb*
■ *noun* 🔊 [U, sing.] the state of not having sth or not having enough of sth SYN **dearth, shortage**: **~ (of sth)** *a lack of understanding/knowledge/information/experience* ◊ *He was suffering from a complete lack of confidence.* ◊ **because of a ~ of sth** *The project was abandoned because of a total lack of support.* ◊ **due to (a) ~ of sth** *He was released due to lack of evidence.* ◊ **through ~ of sth** *The trip was cancelled through lack of interest.* IDM see TRY v.
■ *verb* 🔊 B1 [no passive] **~ sth** to have none or not enough of sth: *to lack confidence/experience/resources/power* ◊ *The team lacked the skill to compete at the highest level.* ◊ *She has the natural ability that her brother lacks.* ⊃ see also LACKING
IDM **ˌlack (for) ˈnothing** (*formal*) to have everything that you need ⊃ more at COURAGE

**lacka·dai·si·cal** /ˌlækəˈdeɪzɪkl/ *adj.* not showing enough care or enthusiasm

**lackey** /ˈlæki/ *noun* **1** (*old-fashioned*) a servant **2** (*disapproving*) a person who is treated like a servant or who behaves like one

**lack·ing** /ˈlækɪŋ/ *adj.* [not before noun] **1** **~ (in sth)** having none or not enough of sth: *She's not usually lacking in confidence.* ◊ *The film is sorely lacking in originality.* ◊ *He was taken on as a teacher but was found lacking* (= was thought not to be good enough). **2** not present or not available SYN **missing**: *I feel there is something lacking in my life.*

**lack·lustre** (*US* **lack·lus·ter**) /ˈlækˌlʌstə(r)/ *adj.* **1** not interesting or exciting; not bright: *a lacklustre performance* **2** (of the hair or eyes) not bright or shining; DULL

**la·con·ic** /ləˈkɒnɪk; *NAmE* -ˈkɑːn-/ *adj.* using only a few words to say sth ▸ **la·conˑic·al·ly** /-kli/ *adv.*

**lac·quer** /ˈlækə(r)/ *noun*, *verb*
■ *noun* [U] **1** a liquid that is used on wood or metal to give it a hard, shiny surface **2** (*old-fashioned*) a liquid that is SPRAYED on the hair so that it stays in place SYN **hairspray**
■ *verb* **1** **~ sth** to cover sth such as wood or metal with lacquer **2** **~ sth** (*BrE, old-fashioned*) to put lacquer on your hair

**la·crosse** /ləˈkrɒs; *NAmE* -ˈkrɔːs/ *noun* [U] a game played on a field by two teams of ten players who use sticks with curved nets on them to catch, carry and throw the ball

**lac·tate** /lækˈteɪt; *NAmE* ˈlækteɪt/ *verb* [I] (*specialist*) (of a woman or female animal) to produce milk to feed a baby or young animal ▸ **lacˈta·tion** /lækˈteɪʃn/ *noun* [U]: *the period of lactation*

**lac·tic acid** /ˌlæktɪk ˈæsɪd/ *noun* [U] a substance that forms in milk that is no longer fresh and is also produced in the muscles during hard exercise

**lacto·ba·cil·lus** /ˌlæktəʊbəˈsɪləs/ *noun* (*biology*) a type of bacteria that produces lactic acid

**lac·tose** /ˈlæktəʊs, -təʊz/ *noun* [U] (*chemistry*) a type of sugar found in milk

**la·cuna** /ləˈkjuːnə; *NAmE also* -ˈkuː-/ *noun* (*pl.* **-nae** /-niː/ *or* **la·cu·nas**) (*formal*) a place where sth is missing in a piece of writing or in an idea, a theory, etc. SYN **gap**

**lacy** /ˈleɪsi/ *adj.* made of or looking like LACE: *lacy underwear*

**lad** 🔊 C1 /læd/ *noun* **1** 🔊 [C] (*old-fashioned or informal*) a boy or young man: *Things have changed since I was a lad.* ◊ *He's a nice lad.* ⊃ compare LASS **2** **the ˈlads** [pl.] (*BrE, informal*) a group of friends that a man works with or spends free time with: *to go to the pub with the lads* ◊ *I tried to fit in and be one of the lads.* **3** [C, usually sing.] (*BrE, informal*) a lively young man, especially one who is very interested in women and having sex, drinks a lot of alcohol and enjoys sport: *Tony was a bit of a lad—always had an eye for the women.* ⊃ see also LADDISH **4** [C] (*BrE*) a person who works in a stable ⊃ see also STABLE BOY

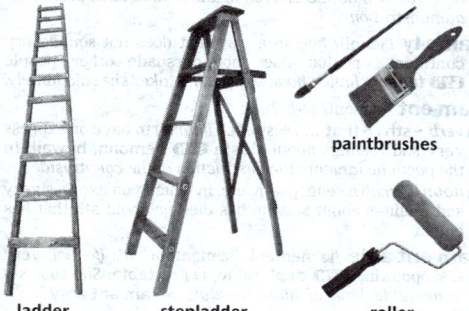

**ladder** **steppladder** **roller** **paintbrushes**

**lad·der** ⓘ+ B2 /ˈlædə(r)/ *noun, verb*
■ *noun* **1** ⓘ+ B2 a piece of equipment for climbing up and down a wall, the side of a building, etc., consisting of two lengths of wood or metal that are joined together by steps or RUNGS: *to climb up/fall off a ladder* ⊃ see also ROPE LADDER, STEPLADDER **2** ⓘ+ B2 [usually sing.] a series of stages by which you can make progress in your life or career: *to move up or down the social ladder* ◊ *the career ladder* (*BrE*) *to get onto the property ladder* (= buy your first home) **3** (*BrE*) (*NAmE* **run**) a long, thin hole in TIGHTS or STOCKINGS where some THREADS have broken **4** (*also* **'ladder tournament**) a competition in a particular sport or game in which teams or players are arranged in a list and they can move up the list by defeating one of the teams or players above
■ *verb* [I, T] **~ (sth)** (*BrE*) if TIGHTS or STOCKINGS **ladder** or you **ladder** them, a long, thin hole appears in them

**lad·die** /ˈlædi/ *noun* (*especially ScotE, informal*) a boy (often used as a way of speaking to a boy) ⊃ compare LASS

**lad·dish** /ˈlædɪʃ/ *adj.* (*informal*) behaving in a way that is supposed to be typical of a young man, especially one who is very interested in women and having sex, drinks a lot of alcohol and enjoys sport

**laden** /ˈleɪdn/ *adj.* **1 ~ (with sth)** heavily loaded with sth: *passengers laden with luggage* ◊ *The trees were laden with apples.* ◊ *a heavily/fully laden truck* ⊃ compare UNLADEN **2 ~ (with sth)** (*literary*) full of sth, especially sth unpleasant: *His voice was soft, yet laden with threat.* **3 -laden** used to form adjectives showing that sth is full of, or loaded with, the thing mentioned: *calorie-laden cream cakes*

**lad·ette** /lædˈet/ *noun* (*BrE, informal*) a young woman who enjoys drinking alcohol, sport or other activities usually considered to be typical of young men

**la-di-da** (*also* **lah-di-dah**) /ˌlɑː diː ˈdɑː/ *adj., exclamation*
■ *adj.* (*especially BrE, informal*) used to describe a way of speaking or behaving that is typical of upper-class people but that is not natural or sincere SYN **affected**
■ *exclamation* used when sb is annoying you, because they seem to think they are more important than they really are

**ladies' 'fingers** *noun* [pl.] (*BrE*) = OKRA

**ladies' man** (*also* **'lady's man**) *noun* a man who enjoys spending time with women and thinks he is attractive to them

**ladle** /ˈleɪdl/ *noun, verb*
■ *noun* a large, deep spoon with a long handle, used especially for serving soup
■ *verb* **1 ~ sth (+ adv./prep.)** to place food on a plate with a large spoon or in large quantities **2 ~ sth + adv./prep.** (*sometimes disapproving*) to give sb a lot of sth, especially money or advice SYN **dole sth out**

**lady** ⓘ A2 /ˈleɪdi/ (*pl.* **-ies**) *noun* **1** ⓘ A2 [C] a word used to mean 'woman' that some people, especially older people, consider is more polite: *There's a lady waiting to see you.* ◊ *an old/elderly lady* ◊ *He was with an attractive young lady.* ◊ *the ladies' golf championship* ◊ (*BrE*) *a tea lady* (= a woman who serves tea in an office) ◊ (*NAmE,*

877 **laid**

*approving*) *She's a tough lady.* ◊ *a lady doctor/golfer* HELP Some women object to the way **lady** is used in some of these examples and prefer it to be avoided if possible: *a doctor/a woman doctor* ◊ *There's someone waiting to see you.* ⊃ see also BAG LADY, CLEANING LADY, DINNER LADY, FIRST LADY, LEADING LADY (1), LUNCH LADY, OLD LADY **2** ⓘ A2 [C] a woman who is polite and well educated, has excellent manners and always behaves well: *His wife was a real lady.* ⊃ compare GENTLEMAN **3** ⓘ A2 [C, usually pl.] (*formal*) used when speaking to or about a girl or woman, especially sb you do not know: *Can I take your coats, ladies?* ◊ *Could I have your attention, **ladies and gentlemen**?* **4** [sing.] (*especially NAmE*) an informal way to talk to a woman, showing a lack of respect: *Listen, lady, don't shout at me.* **5** [C] (*old-fashioned*) (in the UK) a woman belonging to a high social class: *the lords and ladies of the court* ◊ *a lady's maid* **6 Lady** [C] (in the UK) a title used by a woman who is a member of the NOBILITY, or by sb who has been given the title 'lady' as an honour. The wives and daughters of some members of the NOBILITY and the wives of KNIGHTS are also called 'Lady': *Lady Howe* ◊ *Lady Jane Grey* ⊃ compare LORD, SIR **7 a/the ladies** [U] (*BrE*) (*NAmE* **'ladies' room**, **'women's room**) [C] a toilet for women in a public building or place: *Could you tell me where the ladies is?* **8 Our Lady** a title used to refer to Mary, the mother of Christ, especially in the Roman Catholic Church: *Our Lady of Lourdes*
IDM see FAT *adj.*, LEISURE

**lady·bird** /ˈleɪdibɜːd; *NAmE* -bɜːrd/ (*BrE*) (*NAmE* **lady·bug** /ˈleɪdibʌg/) *noun* a small flying insect, usually red with black spots ⊃ VISUAL VOCAB page V3

**lady-in-'waiting** *noun* (*pl.* **ladies-in-waiting**) a woman who goes to places with, and helps, a queen or princess

**lady·like** /ˈleɪdilaɪk/ *adj.* (*old-fashioned*) polite and quiet; typical of what is supposed to be socially acceptable for a woman SYN **refined**: *ladylike behaviour* ◊ *Her language was not very ladylike.*

**lady·ship** /ˈleɪdiʃɪp/ *noun* **1 Her/Your Ladyship** a title used when talking to or about a woman who is a member of the NOBILITY: *Does Your Ladyship require anything?* **2** (*BrE, informal*) a way of talking to or about a girl or woman that you think is behaving as if she thinks she is too important: *Perhaps her ladyship would like to hang up her own clothes today!* ⊃ compare LORDSHIP

**lady's man** = LADIES' MAN

**lag** /læg/ *verb, noun*
■ *verb* (**-gg-**) **1** [I] **~ (behind sb/sth) | ~ (behind)** to move or develop slowly or more slowly than other people, organizations, etc. SYN **trail**: *The little boy lagged behind his parents.* ◊ *We still lag far behind many of our competitors in using modern technology.* **2** [T] **~ sth (with sth)** (*BrE*) to cover pipes, etc. with a special material to stop the water in them from freezing, or to stop heat from escaping SYN **insulate**
■ *noun* = TIME LAG ⊃ see also JET LAG

**lager** /ˈlɑːgə(r)/ *noun* **1** [U, C] a type of light, pale beer that usually has a lot of bubbles: *a pint of lager* ◊ *German lagers* **2** [C] a glass, can or bottle of this

**'lager lout** *noun* (*BrE*) a young man who drinks too much alcohol and then behaves in a noisy and unpleasant way

**lag·gard** /ˈlægəd; *NAmE* -gərd/ *noun* (*old-fashioned*) a slow and lazy person, organization, etc.

**laggy** /ˈlægi/ *adj.* (**lag·gier, lag·gi·est**) (*informal*) (of a computer, computer game or internet connection) slow to respond: *The problem was a laggy internet connection.*

**la·goon** /ləˈguːn/ *noun* **1** a lake of salt water that is separated from the sea by a REEF or an area of rock or sand **2** (*NAmE*) a small area of fresh water near a lake or river **3** (*specialist*) an artificial area built to hold waste water before it is treated at a SEWAGE WORKS

**lah** (*also* **la**) /lɑː/ *noun* (*music*) the 6th note of a MAJOR SCALE

**lah-di-dah** = LA-DI-DA

**laid** /leɪd/ *past tense, past part.* of LAY

# laid-back

**laid-'back** *adj.* (*informal*) calm and relaxed; seeming not to worry about anything **SYN** **easy-going**: *a laid-back attitude to life*

**lain** /leɪn/ *past part.* of LIE¹

**lair** /leə(r); *NAmE* ler/ *noun* [usually sing.] **1** a place where a wild animal sleeps or hides **SYN** **den** **2** a place where sb goes to hide or to be alone **SYN** **den**, **hideout**

**laird** /leəd; *NAmE* lerd/ *noun* (in Scotland) a person who owns a large area of land

**lairy** /'leəri; *NAmE* 'leri/ *adj.* (*BrE*, *informal*) behaving in a way that seems too loud and confident

**laissez-faire** /ˌleseɪ 'feə(r); *NAmE* 'fer/ *noun* [U] (from French) the policy of allowing private businesses to develop without government control ▸ **laissez-faire** *adj.*: *a laissez-faire economy* ◇ *They have a laissez-faire approach to bringing up their children* (= they give them a lot of freedom).

**laity** /'leɪəti/ *noun* **the laity** [sing. + sing./pl. v.] all the members of a Church who are not CLERGY ⸺ see also LAYMAN

**lake** ⓘ **A2** /leɪk/ *noun* (*abbr.* **L.**) a large area of water that is surrounded by land: **in a** ~ *We swam in the lake.* ◇ **on a** ~ *There were a number of boats on the lake.* ◇ *Lake Ontario* ◇ (*figurative*) *a wine lake* (= a large supply of wine that is not being used)

**lake-side** /'leɪksaɪd/ *noun* [sing.] the area around the edge of a lake: *We went for a walk by the lakeside.* ◇ *a lakeside hotel*

**lakh** /læk/ *number* (plural verb) (*pl.* **lakh** or **lakhs**) (*IndE*) a hundred thousand

**'la-la land** *noun* [U] (*NAmE*, *informal*) **1** (*BrE* **cloud 'cuckoo land**) (*disapproving*) if you say that sb is living **in la-la land**, you mean that they do not understand what a situation is really like, but think it is much better than it is **2** Los Angeles or Hollywood, especially with regard to the film and television industry

**lam** /læm/ *noun*, *verb*
- *noun*
  **IDM** **on the 'lam** (*NAmE*, *informal*) escaping from sb, especially from the police
- *verb* (**-mm-**)
  **PHRV** **lam 'into sb** (*BrE*, *informal*) to attack sb violently with hard hits or words: *She really lammed into her opponent during the debate.*

**lama** /'lɑːmə/ *noun* **1** a title given to a spiritual leader in Tibetan Buddhism **2** a Buddhist MONK from Tibet or Mongolia

**lamb** /læm/ *noun*, *verb*
- *noun* **1** [C] a young sheep **2** [U] meat from a young sheep: *a leg of lamb* ◇ *lamb chops* ⸺ compare MUTTON **3** [C] (*informal*) used to describe or address sb with love or sympathy: *You poor lamb!*
  **IDM** **(like) a lamb/lambs to the 'slaughter** used to describe people who are going to do sth dangerous without realizing it ⸺ more at MUTTON, WELL *adv.*
- *verb* [I] (of a sheep) to give birth to a lamb

**lam-bada** /læm'bɑːdə/ *noun* a fast Brazilian dance performed by couples who hold each other closely

**lam-bast** (*also* **lam-baste**) /læm'bæst, -'beɪst/ *verb* ~ **sb/sth** (*formal*) to attack or criticize sb/sth very severely, especially in public **SYN** **lay into sb/sth**

**lambda** /'læmdə/ *noun* the 11th letter of the Greek alphabet (Λ, λ)

**lambs·wool** /'læmzwʊl/ *noun* [U] soft, fine wool from LAMBS, used for KNITTING clothes: *a lambswool sweater*

**lame** /leɪm/ *adj.* **1** (of people or animals) unable to walk well because of an injury to the leg or foot **2** (of an excuse, explanation, etc.) weak and difficult to believe **SYN** **feeble**, **unconvincing 3** not interesting or fun: *The humour is more lame than funny.* ▸ **lame·ness** *noun* [U]: *The disease has left her with permanent lameness.*

**lamé** /'lɑːmeɪ; *NAmE* lɑː'meɪ/ *noun* [U] a type of cloth into which gold- or silver-coloured THREAD has been TWISTED

**lame 'duck** *noun* **1** a person or an organization that is not very successful and that needs help **2** (*US*, *informal*) a politician or government whose period of office will soon end and who will not be elected again: *a lame-duck president/administration*

**lame·ly** /'leɪmli/ *adv.* in a way that does not sound very confident, or that does not persuade other people **SYN** **feebly**: '*I must have made a mistake,*' *she said lamely.*

**lam·ent** /lə'ment/ *verb*, *noun*
- *verb* ~ **sth** | ~ **that ...** | + **speech** (*formal*) to have or express very sad feelings about sb/sth **SYN** **bemoan**, **bewail**: *In the poem he laments the destruction of the countryside.*
- *noun* (*formal*) a song, poem, etc. in which you express very sad feelings about sb who has died or about sth that has ended

**lam·ent·able** /lə'mentəbl, 'læməntəbl/ *adj.* (*formal*) very disappointing **SYN** **deplorable**, **regrettable**: *She shows a lamentable lack of understanding.* ▸ **lam·ent·ably** /-bli/ *adv.*

**lam·en·ta·tion** /ˌlæmən'teɪʃn/ *noun* [C, U] (*formal*) an expression of feeling very sad or disappointed

**lam·ent·ed** /lə'mentɪd/ *adj.* (*formal or humorous*) (of sb/sth that has died or disappeared) missed very much: *her late lamented husband* ◇ *the last edition of the much lamented newspaper*

**lam·in·ate** /'læmɪnət/ *noun* [U, C] a material that is made by sticking several thin layers together

**lam·in·ated** /'læmɪneɪtɪd/ *adj.* **1** (of wood, plastic, etc.) made by sticking several thin layers together **2** covered with thin clear plastic for protection: *laminated membership cards*

**lam·ing·ton** /'læmɪŋtən/ *noun* (*AustralE, NZE*) a square piece of SPONGE cake that has been put in liquid chocolate and covered with small pieces of COCONUT

**lamp** ⓘ **A2** /læmp/ *noun* **1** ⓘ **A2** a device that uses electricity, oil or gas to produce light: *a desk/bedside lamp* ◇ *a street lamp* ◇ *an oil lamp* ◇ *to switch on/turn off a lamp* ⸺ see also ARC LAMP, FLOOR LAMP, FOG LAMP, GAS LAMP, LAVA LAMP, STANDARD LAMP, TABLE LAMP **2** an electrical device that produces RAYS of heat and that is used for medical or scientific purposes: *an infrared/ultraviolet lamp* ⸺ see also BLOWLAMP, SUNLAMP

**lamp·light** /'læmplaɪt/ *noun* [U] light from a lamp

**lam·poon** /læm'puːn/ *verb*, *noun*
- *verb* ~ **sb/sth** to criticize sb/sth publicly in a humorous way that makes them/it look silly **SYN** **satirize**: *His cartoons mercilessly lampooned the politicians of his time.*
- *noun* a piece of writing that criticizes sb/sth and makes them/it look silly

**'lamp post** *noun* (*especially BrE*) a tall post in the street with a lamp at the top: *The car skidded and hit a lamp post.* ⸺ compare STREET LIGHT

**lam·prey** /'læmpri/ *noun* a FRESHWATER fish with a round mouth that attaches itself to other fish and drinks their blood

**lamp·shade** /'læmpʃeɪd/ *noun* a cover for a lamp that is used to make the light softer or to direct it

**LAN** /læn/ *noun* (*computing*) a system for communicating by computer within a large building or group of buildings (the abbreviation for 'local area network') ⸺ compare WAN

**lance** /lɑːns; *NAmE* læns/ *noun*, *verb*
- *noun* a weapon with a long wooden handle and a pointed metal end that was used by people fighting on horses in the past
- *verb* **1** [T] ~ **sth** to cut open an INFECTED place on sb's body with a sharp knife in order to let out the PUS (= a yellow substance produced by infection): *to lance an abscess* **2** [I] + *adv./prep.* (of a pain) to move suddenly and quickly and be very sharp: *Pain lanced through his body.*

**ˌlance 'corporal** *noun* a member of one of the lower ranks in the British army: *Lance Corporal Alan Smith*

**lan·cer** /ˈlɑːnsə(r); NAmE ˈlæn-/ noun in the past, a member of a REGIMENT that used LANCES

**lan·cet** /ˈlɑːnsɪt; NAmE ˈlæn-/ noun a knife with a sharp point and two sharp edges, used by doctors for cutting skin, muscle, FLESH, etc.

**land** 🔊 **A1** /lænd/ noun, verb

■ noun
- **SURFACE OF EARTH 1** **A1** [U] the surface of the earth that is not sea: *The new project will reclaim the land from the sea.* ◊ ~ **on**~ *It was good to be back on land.* ◊ **by**~ *We travelled by land, though flying would have been cheaper.* ◊ *We can organize air transport, land transport and all accommodation for your trip.* ⮕ SYNONYMS at FLOOR, SOIL ⮕ see also DRY LAND
- **AREA OF GROUND 2** **A1** [U] (*also* **lands** [pl.]) an area of ground, especially of a particular type or used for a particular purpose **SYN** terrain: *agricultural/arable/fertile land* ◊ *Changes in land use can have significant effects on the local wildlife.* ◊ *a piece/plot of land* ◊ *They are not permitted to build on the surrounding green belt land* (= open land around a city). ◊ *The land rose to the east.* ◊ *Some of the country's richest grazing lands are in these valleys.* ⮕ see also COMMON LAND **3** [U] (*also formal* **lands** [pl.]) the area of ground that sb owns, especially when you think of it as property that can be bought or sold: *public/private land* ◊ *to own/buy/purchase/sell land* ◊ *He acquired a parcel of several acres of land.* ◊ *land ownership/acquisition* ◊ *During the war their lands were occupied by the enemy.* ⮕ see also NO MAN'S LAND
- **COUNTRYSIDE 4 the land** [U] used to refer to the countryside and the way people live in the country as opposed to in cities: *At the beginning of the 20th century almost a third of the population lived off the land* (= grew or produced their own food). ◊ *Many people leave the land to find work in towns and cities.* ⮕ SYNONYMS at COUNTRY
- **COUNTRY/REGION 5** [C] (*literary*) used to refer to a country or region in a way that involves the emotions or the imagination: *She longed to return to her native land.* ◊ *They dreamed of travelling to foreign lands.* ◊ *America is the land of freedom and opportunity.* **HELP** There are many other compounds ending in **land**. You will find them at their place in the alphabet.
- **IDM** **in the land of the ˈliving** (*often humorous*) alive; not sleeping; no longer ill **in the ˌland of ˈNod** (*old-fashioned, humorous*) sleeping: *Pete and Jo were still in the land of Nod, so I went out for a walk in the morning sunshine.* **the ˌland of ˌmilk and ˈhoney** a place where life is pleasant and easy and people are very happy **see, etc. how the ˈland lies** (*BrE*) to find out about a situation: *Let's wait and see how the land lies before we do anything.* ⮕ more at LIE¹ *n.*, LIVE¹, SPY *v.*

■ verb
- **OF BIRD/PLANE/INSECT 1** **A2** [I] to come down through the air onto the ground or another surface: *The plane landed safely.* ◊ *A fly landed on his nose.* **OPP** take off ⮕ see also CRASH-LAND ⮕ WORDFINDER NOTE at PLANE
- **OF PILOT 2** **A2** [T] ~ sth to control a plane and bring it down to the ground: *The pilot landed the plane safely.* ◊ *to land a helicopter/an aircraft*
- **ARRIVE IN PLANE/BOAT 3** **A2** [I] to arrive somewhere in a plane or a boat: *The flight is due to land at 3 o'clock.* ◊ *The troops landed at dawn.* ◊ *They were the first men to land on the moon.* **4** [T] ~ sb/sth to put sb/sth on land from an aircraft, a boat, etc: *The troops were landed by helicopter.*
- **FALL TO GROUND 5** **A2** [I] to come down somewhere after jumping, falling or being thrown: *She fell and landed heavily on her back.* ◊ *Several men were killed when rocket shells landed in the troop camp.* ◊ *The heavy ball landed with a thud.*
- **DIFFICULTIES 6** [I] + *adv./prep.* to arrive somewhere and cause difficulties that have to be dealt with: *Why do complaints always land on my desk* (= why do I always have to deal with them)?
- **JOB 7** [T] (*informal*) to succeed in getting a job, etc., especially one that a lot of other people want: *~ sth He's just landed a starring role in a Hollywood movie.* ◊ *~ sb/yourself sth She's just landed herself a company directorship.*
- **FISH 8** [T] ~ sth to catch a fish and bring it out of the water on to the land
- **IDM** **land a ˈblow, ˈpunch, etc.** to succeed in hitting sb/sth: *She landed a punch on his chin.* ⮕ more at FOOT *n.*
- **PHRV** **ˈland in sth** | **ˈland sb/yourself in sth** (*informal*) to get sb/yourself into a difficult situation: *She was arrested and landed in court.* ◊ *His hot temper has landed him in trouble before.* ◊ *Now you've really landed me in it!* (= got me into trouble) **ˌland ˈup in/at/on/with …** (*informal*) to reach a final position or situation, sometimes after other things have happened **SYN** end up: *We travelled around for a while and landed up in Seattle.* ◊ *He landed up in a ditch after he lost control of his car.* **ˈland sb/yourself with sth/sb** (*informal*) to give sb/yourself sth unpleasant to do, especially because nobody else wants to do it: *As usual, I got landed with all the boring jobs.*

▼ SYNONYMS

**land**
lot • ground • space • plot

These words all mean an area of land that is used for a particular purpose.

**land** an area of ground, especially one that is used for a particular purpose: *agricultural land*

**lot** (*NAmE*) a piece of land that is used or intended for a particular purpose: *building lots* ◊ *a parking lot*

**ground** an area of land that is used for a particular purpose: *The kids were playing on waste ground near the school.* ◊ *the site of an ancient burial ground*

LAND, LOT OR GROUND?

**Land** is used for large areas of open land in the country, especially when it is used for farming. A **lot** is often a smaller piece of land in a town or city, especially one intended for building or parking on. **Ground** is any area of open land; a **ground** is an area of land designed or used for a particular purpose or activity.

**space** a large area of land that has no buildings on it: *The city has plenty of open space.* ◊ *the wide open spaces of the Canadian prairies*

**plot** a small piece of land used or intended for a particular purpose: *She bought a small plot of land to build a house.* ◊ *a vegetable plot*

LOT OR PLOT?
- Either a **lot** or a **plot** can be used for building on. Only a **plot** can also be used for growing vegetables or burying people.

PATTERNS
- an **open** space
- **open/empty/vacant/waste/derelict** land/ground
- a/an **empty/vacant** lot/plot

**ˈland agent** *noun* (*especially BrE*) a person whose job is to manage land, farms, etc. for sb else

**lan·dau** /ˈlændɔː, -daʊ/ *noun* a CARRIAGE with four wheels and a roof that folds down in two sections, that is pulled by horses

**ˈland-based** *adj.* [usually before noun] located on or living on the land: *land-based missiles* ◊ *land-based animals*

**land·ed** /ˈlændɪd/ *adj.* [only before noun] **1** owning a lot of land: *the landed gentry* **2** including a large amount of land: *landed estates*

**ˌlanded ˈimmigrant** *noun* (*CanE*) a person from another country who has permission to live permanently in Canada

**ˈland·fall** /ˈlændfɔːl/ *noun* **1** [U, C] (*literary*) the act of arriving on land after a long journey by sea or by air, or the land that you first see or arrive at: *After three weeks they made landfall on the coast of Ireland.* **2** [C] = LANDSLIDE

**ˈland·fill** /ˈlændfɪl/ *noun* **1** [C, U] an area of land where large amounts of waste material are buried under the earth: *The map shows the position of the new landfills.* ◊ *a*

# landform

**landfill site** 2 [U] the process of burying large amounts of waste material: *the choice of landfill or incineration* 3 [U] waste material that will be buried ⇒ **WORDFINDER NOTE** at **WASTE**

**land·form** /'lændfɔːm; NAmE -fɔːrm/ *noun* (*geology*) a natural feature of the earth's surface

**'land grab** *noun* (*disapproving*) **1** an act of buying or taking land illegally or in a way that is considered morally wrong: *Residents fear a land grab by the wealthy elite.* **2** ~ (**for sth/sb**) an act of getting property or power in a way that is sudden, illegal or considered morally wrong: *The move was considered a land grab for younger TV viewers.* ▶ **'land grabber** *noun* **'land grabbing** *noun* [U]

**'land guard** *noun* (*WAfrE*) (mostly in Ghana) a member of an organized criminal group employed to protect land and property through the use of violence

**land·hold·ing** /'lændhəʊldɪŋ/ *noun* [C, U] (*specialist*) a piece of land that sb owns or rents; the fact of owning or renting land ▶ **'land-hold·er** *noun*: *farmers and landholders*

**land·ing** /'lændɪŋ/ *noun* **1** [C, U] an act of bringing an aircraft or a SPACECRAFT down to the ground after a journey: *a perfect/smooth/safe landing* ◇ *the first Apollo moon landing* ◇ *The pilot was forced to make an emergency landing.* ◇ *a landing site* OPP **take-off** ⇒ see also CRASH LANDING, FORCED LANDING **2** [C] the area at the top of a set of stairs where you arrive before you go up into an upstairs room or move onto another set of stairs ⇒ picture at STAIRCASE **3** [C] an act of bringing soldiers to land in an area that is controlled by the enemy **4** (*BrE also* **'landing stage**) [C] a flat wooden platform on the water where boats let people get on and off, and load and unload goods SYN **jetty**

**'landing craft** *noun* (*pl.* **'landing craft**) a boat with a flat bottom, carried on a ship. Landing craft open at one end so soldiers and equipment can be brought to land.

**'landing gear** *noun* [U] = **UNDERCARRIAGE**

**'landing lights** *noun* [*pl.*] **1** bright lamps on a plane that are switched on before it lands **2** lights that are arranged along the sides of a RUNWAY to guide a pilot when he or she is landing a plane

**'landing page** *noun* (*computing*) the part of a website that you reach first when you click on a link on the internet: *Have a different landing page for each advertising campaign.* ⇒ **WORDFINDER NOTE** at **WEBSITE**

**'landing stage** (*BrE*) (*also* **land·ing** *NAmE, BrE*) *noun* a flat wooden platform on the water where boats let people get on and off, and load and unload goods SYN **jetty**

**'landing strip** *noun* = **AIRSTRIP**

**land·lady** /'lændleɪdi/ *noun* (*pl.* **-ies**) **1** a woman from whom you rent a room, a house, etc. **2** (*BrE*) a woman who owns or manages a pub or a GUEST HOUSE ⇒ compare LANDLORD, PROPRIETOR

**land·less** /'lændləs/ *adj.* [usually before noun] not owning land for farming; not allowed to own land

**land·line** /'lændlaɪn/ *noun* a phone connection that uses wires carried on POLES or under the ground, in contrast to a mobile phone: *I'll call you later on the landline.*

**land·locked** /'lændlɒkt; NAmE -lɑːkt/ *adj.* almost or completely surrounded by land: *Switzerland is completely landlocked.*

**land·lord** /'lændlɔːd; NAmE -lɔːrd/ *noun* **1** a person or company from whom you rent a room, a house, an office, etc: *a buy-to-let landlord* (= who buys houses and flats in order to rent them out) ⇒ see also ABSENTEE LANDLORD **2** (*BrE*) a man who owns or manages a pub or a GUEST HOUSE ⇒ compare LANDLADY, PROPRIETOR

**land·lub·ber** /'lændlʌbə(r)/ *noun* (*informal*) a person with not much knowledge or experience of the sea or sailing

**land·mark** /'lændmɑːk; NAmE -mɑːrk/ *noun* **1** something, such as a large building, that you can see clearly from a distance and that will help you to know where you are: *The Empire State Building is a familiar landmark on the New York skyline.* **2** ~ (**in sth**) an event, a discovery, an invention, etc. that marks an important stage in sth SYN **milestone**: *The ceasefire was seen as a major landmark in the fight against terrorism.* ◇ *a landmark decision/ruling in the courts* **3** (*especially NAmE*) a building or a place that is very important because of its history, and that should be preserved SYN **monument** ⇒ see also LISTED BUILDING

**'land mass** *noun* (*specialist*) a large area of land, for example a continent

**land·mine** /'lændmaɪn/ *noun* a bomb placed on or under the ground, which explodes when vehicles or people move over it

**'land office** (*NAmE*) (*BrE* **'land registry**) *noun* a government office that keeps a record of areas of land and who owns them

**land·owner** /'lændəʊnə(r)/ *noun* a person who owns land, especially a large amount of land ▶ **'land-owner-ship** (*also* **'land-owning**) *noun* [U]: *private landownership* **'land-owning** *adj.* [only before noun]: *the great landowning families*

**'land reform** *noun* [U, C] the principle of dividing land for farming into smaller pieces so that more people can own some

**'land registry** (*BrE*) (*NAmE* **'land office**) *noun* a government office that keeps a record of areas of land and who owns them

**'Land Rover™** (*also* **'Land-Rover™**) *noun* a strong vehicle used for travelling over rough ground

**land·scape** /'lændskeɪp/ *noun, verb*
■ *noun* **1** [C, usually sing.] everything you can see when you look across a large area of land, especially in the country: *the woods and fields that are typical features of the English landscape* ◇ *an urban landscape* ◇ *the bleak/barren/rugged landscape of the area* ⇒ SYNONYMS at **COUNTRY**

**WORDFINDER** barren, fertile, lush, mountainous, rolling, rugged, undulating, volcanic, wooded

**2** [C, U] a painting of a view of the countryside; this style of painting: *an artist famous for his landscapes* ◇ *a landscape painter/painting* ⇒ compare TOWNSCAPE **3** [C, usually sing.] the characteristic features of an area of activity: *We can expect changes in the political landscape.* **4** [U] (used especially before another noun) the way of printing a document in which the top of the page is one of the longer sides: *Select the landscape option when printing the file.* ⇒ compare PORTRAIT (3) IDM see BLOT *n.*
■ *verb* ~ **sth** to improve the appearance of an area of land by changing the design and planting trees, flowers, etc. ▶ **'land-scap-ing** *noun* [U]: *The campus has attractive buildings and beautiful landscaping.*

**'landscape 'architect** *noun* a person whose job is planning and designing the environment, especially so that roads, buildings, etc. combine with the landscape in an attractive way ▶ **'landscape 'architecture** *noun* [U]

**'landscape 'gardener** *noun* a person whose job is designing and creating attractive parks and gardens ▶ **'landscape 'gardening** *noun* [U]

**land·slide** /'lændslaɪd/ *noun* **1** (*also* **'land-fall**) a mass of earth, rock, etc. that falls down the slope of a mountain or a CLIFF ⇒ see also LANDSLIP ⇒ **WORDFINDER NOTE** at **DISASTER 2** an election in which one person or party gets very many more votes than the other people or parties: *by a ~ She was expected to win by a landslide.* ◇ *a landslide victory*

**land·slip** /'lændslɪp/ *noun* a mass of rock and earth that falls down a slope, usually smaller than a landslide

**land·ward** /'lændwəd; NAmE -wərd/ *adj.* [only before noun] facing the land; away from the sea ▶ **'land-ward** (*also* **'land-wards**) *adv.*: *After an hour, the ship turned landward.*

**lane** /leɪn/ *noun* **1** a narrow road in the country: *winding country lanes* ◇ *We drove along a muddy lane* to reach the farmhouse. ⇒ see also MEMORY LANE **2** ⟨+ B2⟩ (often in place names) a city street: *Park Lane* ◊ *The quickest way is through the back lanes behind the bus station.* **3** ⟨+ B2⟩ a section of a wide road, that is marked by painted white lines, to keep lines of traffic separate: *the inside/middle lane* ◊ *the northbound/southbound lane* ◊ *to change lanes* ◊ *She signalled and pulled over into the slow lane.* ◊ *a four-lane highway* ⇒ see also BICYCLE LANE, BIKE LANE, BREAKDOWN LANE, BUS LANE, CYCLE LANE, FAST LANE, HOV LANE, OUTSIDE LANE, PASSING LANE, SLOW LANE ⇒ WORDFINDER NOTE at ROAD **4** ⟨+ C1⟩ a narrow marked section of a track or a swimming pool that is used by one person, for example when taking part in a race: *The Australian in lane four is coming up fast from behind.* **5** ⟨+ C1⟩ a route used by ships or aircraft on regular journeys: *one of the world's busiest shipping/sea lanes* ⇒ see also SEA LANE **6** (in TENPIN BOWLING) a narrow section of floor along which the ball is BOWLED: *a 20-lane bowling alley* [IDM] see FAST LANE

**lan·gous·tine** /ˌlɒŋɡuˈstiːn; NAmE læn-/ *noun* a SHELLFISH that is a type of small LOBSTER that may be prepared and eaten as SCAMPI

**lan·guage** 🔑 A1 🔊 /ˈlæŋɡwɪdʒ/ *noun*
- OF A COUNTRY **1** ⟨+ A1⟩ [C] the system of communication in speech and writing that is used by people of a particular country or area: *the English language* ◊ *It takes a long time to learn to speak a language well.* ◊ *All the children must learn a foreign language.* ◊ *German is my native language.* ◊ *Is English an official language in your country?* ◊ *The novel has been translated into over twenty languages.* ◊ *She has a good command of the Spanish language.* ◊ *Good language skills are essential in this job.* ◊ *They fell in love in spite of the language barrier* (= the difficulty of communicating when people speak different languages). ⇒ see also FIRST LANGUAGE, MODERN LANGUAGE, SECOND LANGUAGE, TARGET LANGUAGE, TONE LANGUAGE

◼ WORDFINDER accent, alphabet, dialect, grammar, literacy, literature, pronunciation, translate, word

- COMMUNICATION **2** ⟨+ A1⟩ [U] the use by humans of a system of sounds and words to communicate: *a qualification in language teaching* ◊ *a study of language acquisition in two-year-olds* ◊ *Language is constantly evolving.* ⇒ see also NATURAL LANGUAGE, WORLD LANGUAGE
- STYLE OF SPEAKING/WRITING **3** ⟨+ A2⟩ [U] a particular style of speaking or writing: *spoken/written language* ◊ *foul language* (= words that people may consider offensive) ◊ *The poem uses distinctly modern language.* ◊ *His strength is that he addresses his readers in plain language.* ◊ *the language of science* ⇒ see also BAD LANGUAGE
- MOVEMENTS/SYMBOLS/SOUND **4** ⟨+ A1⟩ [U, C] a way of expressing ideas and feelings using movements, symbols and sound: *the language of mime* ◊ *the language of dolphins/bees* ⇒ see also BODY LANGUAGE, SIGN LANGUAGE
- COMPUTING **5** ⟨+ A1⟩ [C, U] a system of symbols and rules that is used to operate a computer: *a programming language* ⇒ see also ASSEMBLY LANGUAGE, QUERY LANGUAGE

[IDM] **mind / watch your ˈlanguage** to be careful about what you say in order not to upset or offend sb: *Watch your language, young man!* **speak / talk the same ˈlanguage** to be able to communicate easily with another person because you share similar opinions and experience

**lan·guid** /ˈlæŋɡwɪd/ *adj.* moving slowly in an attractive way, not needing energy or effort: *a languid wave of the hand* ◊ *a languid afternoon in the sun* ▸ **lan·guid·ly** *adv.*: *He moved languidly across the room.*

**lan·guish** /ˈlæŋɡwɪʃ/ *verb* (*formal*) **1** [I] ~ **(in sth)** to be forced to stay somewhere or suffer sth unpleasant for a long time: *She continues to languish in a foreign prison.* **2** [I] to become weaker or fail to make progress: *The share price languished at 102p.*

**lan·guor** /ˈlæŋɡə(r)/ *noun* [U, sing.] (*literary*) the pleasant state of feeling lazy and without energy: *A delicious languor was stealing over him.* ▸ **lan·guor·ous** *adj.*: *a languorous pace of life* **lan·guor·ous·ly** *adv.*

881 **lap**

▼ SYNONYMS

**language**
vocabulary • terms • wording • terminology
These are all terms for the words and expressions people use when they speak or write, or for a particular style of speaking or writing.

**language** a particular style of speaking or writing: *Give your instructions in everyday language.* ◊ *the language of the legal profession*

**vocabulary** all the words that a person knows or uses, or all the words in a particular language; the words that people use when they are talking about a particular subject: *to have a wide / limited vocabulary* ◊ *The word has become part of advertising vocabulary.*

**terms** a way of expressing yourself or of saying sth: *I'll try to explain in simple terms.*

**wording** [usually sing.] the words that are used in a piece of writing or speech, especially when they have been carefully chosen: *It was the standard form of wording for a consent letter.*

**terminology** (*rather formal*) the set of technical words or expressions used in a particular subject: *medical terminology* ◊ *Scientists are constantly developing new terminologies.* [NOTE] *Literary / poetic terminology* is used for talking about literature or poetry. *Literary / poetic language* is used for writing in a literary or poetic style.

PATTERNS
- **formal / informal / everyday** language / vocabulary / terms
- **business / scientific / technical / specialized** language / vocabulary / terminology
- A word **enters** the language / the vocabulary.

**La Niña** /lɑː ˈniːnjə/ *noun* [U] the cooling of the water in the central and eastern Pacific Ocean that happens every few years and that affects the weather in many parts of the world ⇒ compare EL NIÑO (1)

**lank** /læŋk/ *adj.* **1** (of hair) straight, not bright and not attractive **2** (*SAfrE, informal*) large in number or amount: *I've got lank work to do.*

**lanky** /ˈlæŋki/ *adj.* (**lank·ier, lank·iest**) (of a person) having long, thin arms and legs and not moving in an easy way [SYN] **gangling**: *a tall, lanky teenager*

**lano·lin** /ˈlænəlɪn/ *noun* [U] an oil that comes from sheep's wool and is used to make skin creams

**lan·tern** /ˈlæntən; NAmE -tərn/ *noun* a lamp in a clear case, often a metal case with glass sides, and often with a handle, so that you can carry it outside ⇒ see also CHINESE LANTERN, MAGIC LANTERN

**lanth·anum** /ˈlænθənəm/ *noun* [U] (*symb.* **La**) a chemical element. Lanthanum is a silver-white metal.

**lan·yard** /ˈlænjɑːd, -jəd; NAmE -jərd/ *noun* **1** a string that you wear around your neck or WRIST for holding sth: *A lanyard is useful for carrying your ID card.* ◊ *a whistle lanyard* **2** a rope used to fasten sth, for example the sail of a ship

**lap** ⟨+ C1⟩ /læp/ *noun, verb*
- *noun* [C] **1** ⟨+ C1⟩ [usually sing.] the top part of your legs that forms a flat surface when you are sitting down: **on sb's ~** *There's only one seat so you'll have to sit on my lap.* ◊ **in sb's ~** *She sat with her hands in her lap.* **2** one journey from the beginning to the end of a track used for running, etc: *the fastest lap on record* ◊ *She has completed six laps.* ◊ *He was overtaken on the final lap.* ◊ **to do a lap of honour** (= go around the track again to celebrate winning) ◊ (*NAmE*) **to do a victory lap 3** a section of a journey, or of a piece of work, etc: **on the …~** *They're off on the first lap of their round-the-world tour.* ◊ *We've nearly finished. We're on the last lap.*

[IDM] **drop / dump sth in sb's ˈlap** (*informal*) to make sth the responsibility of another person: *They dropped the problem firmly back in my lap.* **sth drops / falls into sb's lap**

---

Oxford Phrasal Academic Lexicon (OPAL) written and spoken word lists | Ⓦ OPAL written word list | Ⓢ OPAL spoken word list

# lapa

somebody has the opportunity to do sth pleasant without having made any effort: *My dream job just fell into my lap.* **in the lap of the ˈgods** if the result of sth is **in the lap of the gods**, you do not know what will happen because it depends on luck or things you cannot control **in the lap of ˈluxury** in easy, comfortable conditions, and enjoying the advantages of being rich
- *verb* (**-pp-**) **1** [I] (of water) to touch sth gently and regularly, often making a soft sound: *The waves lapped around our feet.* ◇ *the sound of water lapping against the boat* **2** [T] ~ **sth** (of animals) to drink sth with quick movements of the tongue **3** [T] ~ **sb** (in a race) to pass another runner on a track who is one or more laps behind you

**PHRV** **lap sth↔ˈup 1** (*informal*) to accept or receive sth with great pleasure, without thinking about whether it is good, true or sincere: *It's a terrible movie but audiences everywhere are lapping it up.* ◇ *She simply lapped up all the compliments.* **2** to drink all of sth and to enjoy doing so: *The calf lapped up the bucket of milk.*

**lapa** /ˈlɑːpə/ *SAfrE* [ˈlɛːpɛ] *noun* (*SAfrE*) a shelter without walls on all sides, usually made of wooden POLES and covered with THATCH (= dry grass), especially used as a place for relaxing and eating meals

**laparˈos·copy** /ˌlæpəˈrɒskəpi/; *NAmE* -ˈrɑːs-/ *noun* (*pl.* **-ies**) (*medical*) a medical procedure using an instrument like a tube that is put through the wall of the ABDOMEN, in order to examine the inside of the body or perform surgery

**laparˈot·omy** /ˌlæpəˈrɒtəmi/; *NAmE* -ˈrɑːt-/ *noun* (*pl.* **-ies**) (*medical*) a cut in the ABDOMEN in order to perform an operation or an examination

**ˈlap belt** *noun* a type of SEAT BELT that goes across the middle part of your body

**ˈlap dancing** *noun* [U] sexually exciting dancing or STRIPTEASE that is performed close to, or sitting on, a customer in a bar or club

**lap-dog** /ˈlæpdɒg/; *NAmE* -dɔːg/ *noun* **1** a pet dog that is small enough to be carried **2** (*disapproving*) a person who is under the control of another person or group **SYN** poodle

**lapel** /ləˈpel/ *noun* one of the two front parts of the top of a coat or jacket that are joined to the COLLAR and are folded back

**lapi·dary** /ˈlæpɪdəri/; *NAmE* -deri/ *adj.* **1** (*formal*) (especially of written language) exact and showing good style **SYN** concise: *in lapidary style* **2** (*specialist*) connected with stones and the work of cutting and POLISHING them

**lapis lazˈuli** /ˌlæpɪs ˈlæzjuli/; *NAmE* -zəli/ *noun* [U] a bright blue stone, used in making jewellery

**lapse** /læps/ *noun*, *verb*
- *noun* **1** a small mistake, especially one that is caused by forgetting sth or by being careless: *a lapse of concentration/memory* ◇ *A momentary lapse in the final set cost her the match.* **2** a period of time between two things that happen **SYN** interval: *After a lapse of six months we met up again.* ◇ see also TIME-LAPSE **3** an example or period of bad behaviour from sb who normally behaves well
- *verb* **1** [I] (of a contract, an agreement, etc.) to no longer be legally recognized because the period of time that it lasts has come to an end: *She had allowed her membership to lapse.* **2** [I] to gradually become weaker or come to an end **SYN** expire: *His concentration lapsed after a few minutes.* **3** [I] ~ (**from sth**) to stop believing in or practising your religion: *He lapsed from Judaism when he was a student.*
  ▶ **lapsed** *adj.* [only before noun]: *a lapsed subscription* ◇ *lapsed faith* ◇ *a lapsed Catholic*

**PHRV** **ˈlapse into sth 1** to gradually pass into a worse or less active state or condition: *to lapse into unconsciousness/a coma* ◇ *She lapsed into silence again.* **2** to start speaking or behaving in a different way, often one that is less acceptable: *He soon lapsed back into his old ways.*

**lap·top** 🔊 **A2** /ˈlæptɒp/; *NAmE* -tɑːp/ (*also* **laptop comˈputer**) *noun* a small computer that can work with a battery and be easily carried: *I opened my laptop and started typing.* ◇ **on a ~** *She was still working on her laptop.* **SYN** notebook ⊃ compare DESKTOP COMPUTER, NETBOOK

**lap-wing** /ˈlæpwɪŋ/ *noun* a black and white bird of the PLOVER family

**lar·ceny** /ˈlɑːsəni/; *NAmE* ˈlɑːrs-/ *noun* [U, C] (*pl.* **-ies**) (*NAmE, law* or *BrE, old-fashioned*) the crime of stealing sth from sb; an occasion when this takes place **SYN** theft: *The couple were charged with grand/petty larceny* (= stealing things that are valuable/not very valuable).

**larch** /lɑːtʃ/; *NAmE* lɑːrtʃ/ *noun* [C, U] a tree with sharp, pointed leaves that fall in winter and hard, dry fruit called CONES

**lard** /lɑːd/; *NAmE* lɑːrd/ *noun*, *verb*
- *noun* [U] a solid white substance made from the melted fat of pigs that is used in cooking
- *verb* ~ **sth** to put small pieces of fat on or into sth before cooking it

**PHRV** **ˈlard sth with sth** [usually passive] (*often disapproving*) to include a lot of a particular kind of word or expressions in a speech or in a piece of writing: *His conversation was larded with Russian proverbs.*

**lar·der** /ˈlɑːdə(r)/; *NAmE* ˈlɑːrd-/ *noun* (*especially BrE*) a cupboard or small room in a house, used for storing food, especially in the past **SYN** pantry

**lar·don** /ˈlɑːdn/; *NAmE* ˈlɑːrdn/ *noun* [usually pl.] a small thick piece of BACON, often used to add fat to other meat in cooked dishes

**large** 🔊 **A1** 🔊 /lɑːdʒ/; *NAmE* lɑːrdʒ/ *adj.*, *verb*
- *adj.* (**larger**, **larg·est**) **1** **A1** big in size or quantity: *a large group/city/area/crowd/family* ◇ *a large number of people* ◇ *very large amounts of money* ◇ *Drought hit large parts of the country.* ◇ *The company has grown large enough to employ over 100 people.* ◇ *The kitchen is relatively large for a modern apartment.* ◇ *The population is slightly larger than that of Canada.* ◇ *Seoul is one of the world's largest cities.* ◇ *Who's the rather large* (= fat) *lady in the hat?* **2** 🔊 **A1** (*abbr.* **L**) used to describe one size in a range of sizes of clothes, food, products used in the house, etc: *small, medium, large* ◇ *Do you have these jeans in a larger size?* **3** 🔊 **A1** wide in range and involving many things: *a large and complex issue* ◇ *Some drugs are being used on a much larger scale than previously.* ◇ *The studies are often large in scope, with budgets to match.* ⊃ note at BIG ▶ **large·ness** *noun* [U]

**IDM** **at ˈlarge 1** (used after a noun) as a whole; in general: *the opinion of the public at large* **2** (of a dangerous person or animal) not captured; free: *Her killer is still at large.* **give/have it ˈlarge** (*BrE, slang*) to enjoy yourself, especially by dancing and drinking alcohol **in ˈlarge part | in large ˈmeasure** (*formal*) to a great extent: *Their success is due in large part to their determination.* **(as) large as ˈlife** (*humorous*) used to show surprise at seeing sb/sth: *I hadn't seen her for fifteen years and then there she was, (as) large as life.* **larger than ˈlife** looking or behaving in a way that is more interesting or exciting than other people, and so is likely to attract attention **SYN** flamboyant: *He's a larger than life character.* ⊃ more at BY *adv.*, LOOM *v.*, WRIT *v.*
- *verb*

**IDM** **ˈlarge it** | **ˈlarge it ˈup** (*BrE, slang*) to enjoy yourself, especially by dancing and drinking alcohol

**large·ly** 🔊 **B2** 🔊 /ˈlɑːdʒli/; *NAmE* ˈlɑːrdʒ-/ *adv.* to a great extent; mostly or mainly: *The manager was largely responsible for the team's victory.* ◇ *The popularity of the book is largely due to the fantastic illustrations.* ◇ *Women aged 35 to 50 are largely ignored by mainstream cinema.* ◇ *The decision was based largely on consumer feedback.* ◇ *He resigned largely because of the stories in the press.*

**ˌlarge-ˈscale** 🔊 **C1** *adj.* [usually before noun] **1** 🔊 **C1** involving many people or things, especially over a wide area: *large-scale development* ◇ *the large-scale employment of women* **2** (of a map, model, etc.) drawn or made to a scale that shows a small area of land or a building in great detail **OPP** small-scale

**lar·gesse** (*also* **lar·gess**) /lɑːˈdʒes/; *NAmE* lɑːrˈdʒ-/ *noun* [U] (*formal* or *humorous*) the act or quality of being generous with money; money that you give to people who have less than you: *She is not noted for her largesse* (= she is not generous). ◊ *to dispense largesse to the poor*

**lar·gish** /ˈlɑːdʒɪʃ; NAmE ˈlɑːrdʒ-/ adj. fairly large

**lar·go** /ˈlɑːɡəʊ; NAmE ˈlɑːrɡ-/ adv., adj., noun (from Italian, music)
- adv., adj. (used as an instruction) in a slow, serious way
- noun (pl. **-os**) a piece of music to be performed in a slow, serious way

**lark** /lɑːk; NAmE lɑːrk/ noun, verb
- noun **1** a small brown bird with a pleasant song ⇒ see also SKYLARK **2** [usually sing.] (*informal*) a thing that you do for fun or as a joke: **for a ~** *The boys didn't mean any harm—they just did it for a lark.* **3** (*BrE, informal*) (used after another noun) an activity that you think is a waste of time or that you do not take seriously: *Perhaps this riding lark would be more fun than she'd thought.*
- **IDM** **be/get up with the ˈlark** (*BrE, old-fashioned*) to get out of bed very early in the morning **blow ˈthat for a lark** (*also taboo* **sod ˈthat for a lark**) (*BrE, slang*) used by sb who does not want to do sth because it involves too much effort: *Sod that for a lark! I'm not doing any more tonight.*
- verb
- **PHRV** **lark aˈbout/aˈround** (*especially BrE, old-fashioned, informal*) to enjoy yourself by behaving in a silly way **SYN** **mess around**

**lar·ney** (*also* **lar·nie**) /ˈlɑːni; NAmE ˈlɑːrni/ adj. (SAfrE) very smart; expensive: *We were invited to a larney function.* ◊ *a larney hotel*

**lar·ri·kin** /ˈlærɪkɪn/ noun (*AustralE, NZE*) a person who ignores the normal rules of society or of an organization

**larva** /ˈlɑːvə; NAmE ˈlɑːrvə/ noun (pl. **lar·vae** /-viː/) an insect at the stage when it has just come out of an egg and looks like a short fat WORM ⇒ compare NYMPH (2) ⇒ **VISUAL VOCAB** page V3 ▶ **lar·val** /-vl/ adj. [only before noun]: *an insect in its larval stage*

**la·ryn·geal** /ləˈrɪndʒiəl/ adj. (*biology, phonetics*) related to or produced by the larynx

**laryn·gi·tis** /ˌlærɪnˈdʒaɪtɪs/ noun [U] a medical condition in which the larynx becomes SWOLLEN and painful, making speaking difficult

**lar·ynx** /ˈlærɪŋks/ noun (pl. **la·ryn·ges** /ləˈrɪndʒiːz/) (*anatomy*) the area at the top of the throat that contains the VOCAL CORDS **SYN** **voice box** ⇒ **VISUAL VOCAB** page V1

**la·sagne** (*also* **la·sagna**) /ləˈzænjə; NAmE -ˈzɑːn-/ noun **1** [U] large, flat pieces of PASTA **2** [U, C] an Italian dish made from layers of lasagne, meat and/or vegetables, and white sauce

**la·sciv·i·ous** /ləˈsɪviəs/ adj. (*formal, disapproving*) feeling or showing strong sexual desire: *a lascivious person* ◊ *lascivious thoughts* ▶ **la·sciv·i·ous·ly** adv. **la·sciv·i·ous·ness** noun [U]

**laser** ⁺ /ˈleɪzə(r)/ noun a device that gives out light in which all the waves OSCILLATE (= change direction and strength) together, typically producing a powerful BEAM of light that can be used for cutting metal, in medical operations, etc.: *a laser beam* ◊ *a laser navigation device* ◊ *The barcodes on the products are read by lasers.* ◊ *a laser show* (= lasers are used as entertainment) ◊ *She's had laser surgery on her eye.* ◊ *laser treatment/therapy*

**ˈlaser gun** noun **1** a piece of equipment that uses a laser to read a BARCODE or to find out how fast a vehicle or other object is moving **2** (in science fiction) a weapon that uses a powerful LASER

**ˈlaser printer** noun a printer that produces good-quality printed material by means of a laser

**lash** /læʃ/ verb, noun
- verb **1** [I, T] to hit sb/sth with great force **SYN** **pound**: + adv./prep. *The rain lashed at the windows.* ◊ *~ sth Huge waves lashed the shore.* ⇒ **SYNONYMS** at BEAT **2** [T] **~ sb/sth** to hit a person or an animal with a WHIP, rope, stick, etc. **SYN** **beat 3** [T] **~ sb/sth** to criticize sb/sth in a very angry way **SYN** **attack 4** [T] **~ sth + adv./prep.** to fasten sth tightly to sth else with ropes: *Several logs had been lashed together to make a raft.* ◊ *During the storm everything on deck had to be lashed down.* **5** [I, T] **~ (sth)** to move or to

883 **last**

move sth quickly and violently from side to side: *The crocodile's tail was lashing furiously from side to side.*
- **PHRV** **ˌlash ˈout (at sb/sth)** **1** to suddenly try to hit sb/sth: *She suddenly lashed out at the boy.* **2** to criticize sb in an angry way: *In a bitter article he lashed out at his critics.* **ˌlash ˈout on sth** (*BrE, informal*) to spend a lot of money on sth
- noun **1** = EYELASH: *her long dark lashes* **2** a hit with a WHIP, given as a form of punishment: *They each received 20 lashes for stealing.* ◊ (*figurative*) *to feel the lash of sb's tongue* (= to be spoken to in an angry and critical way) **3** the thin leather part at the end of a WHIP

**lash·ing** /ˈlæʃɪŋ/ noun **1 lash·ings** [pl.] (*BrE, informal*) a large amount of sth, especially of food and drink: *a bowl of strawberries with lashings of cream* **2** [C] an act of hitting sb with a WHIP as a punishment: (*figurative*) *He was given a severe tongue-lashing* (= angry criticism). **3** [C, usually pl.] a rope used to fasten sth tightly to sth else

**lass** /læs/ (*also* **las·sie** /ˈlæsi/) noun (*ScotE, NEngE*) a girl; a young woman ⇒ compare LAD, LADDIE

**ˌLassa ˈfever** /ˈlæsə fiːvə(r)/ noun [U] a serious disease, usually caught from RATS and found especially in West Africa

**lassi** /ˈlæsi/ noun [U, C] a South Asian drink made from YOGURT

**las·si·tude** /ˈlæsɪtjuːd; NAmE -tuːd/ noun [U] (*formal*) a state of feeling very tired in mind or body; lack of energy

**lasso** /læˈsuː, ˈlæsəʊ; NAmE ˈlæsəʊ/ noun, verb
- noun (pl. **-os** or **-oes**) a long rope with one end tied into a LOOP that is used for catching horses, cows, etc.
- verb **~ sth** to catch an animal using a lasso

**last¹** ⁺ /lɑːst; NAmE læst/ det., adv., noun, verb ⇒ see also LAST²
- det. **1** happening or coming after all other similar things or people: *We caught the last bus home.* ◊ *It's the last house on the left.* ◊ *She was last to arrive.* **2** [only before noun] most recent: *last night/Tuesday/month/summer/year* ◊ *her last book* ◊ *This last point is crucial.* ◊ *The last time I saw him was in May.* **3** [only before noun] that is the only one that remains **SYN** **final**: *This is our last bottle of water.* ◊ *He knew this was his last hope of winning.* **4** used to emphasize that sb/sth is the least likely or suitable: *The last thing she needed was more work.* ◊ *He's the last person I'd trust with a secret.*
- **IDM** **be on your/its last ˈlegs** to be going to die or stop functioning very soon; to be very weak or in bad condition **the day, week, month, etc. before ˈlast** the day, week, etc. just before the most recent one; two days, weeks, etc. ago: *I haven't seen him since the summer before last.* **ˌevery last ...** every person or thing in a group: *We spent every last penny we had on the house.* **ˌhave the last ˈlaugh** to be successful when you were not expected to be, making your opponents look stupid **in the last reˈsort** when there are no other possible courses of action **SYN** **at a pinch**: *In the last resort we can always walk home.* **your/the last ˈgasp** the point at which you/sth can no longer continue living, fighting, existing, etc. ⇒ see also LAST-GASP **the last ˈminute/ˈmoment** the latest possible time before an important event: *They changed the plans at the last minute.* ◊ *Don't leave your decision to the last moment.* **a/your last reˈsort** the person or thing you rely on when everything else has failed: *I've tried everyone else and now you're my last resort.* **the last ˈword (in sth)** the most recent, fashionable, advanced, etc. thing: *These apartments are the last word in luxury.* ⇒ more at ANALYSIS, BREATH, FAMOUS, LONG *adj.*, MAN *n.*, STRAW, THING, WEEK, WORD *n.*
- adv. **1** after anyone or anything else; at the end: *He came last in the race.* ◊ *They arrived last of all.* **2** most recently: *When did you see him last?* ◊ *I saw him last/I last saw him in New York two years ago.* ◊ *They last won the cup in 2006.*
- **IDM** **ˌlast but not ˈleast** used when mentioning the last person or thing of a group, in order to say that they are not less important than the others: *Last but not least, I'd*

# last

like to thank all the catering staff. **last in, first 'out** used, for example in a situation when people are losing their jobs, to say that the last people to be employed will be the first to go ⇨ more at FIRST *adv.*, LAUGH *v.*
- **noun the last** (*pl.* **the last**) **1** ⚫ ᴀ2 the person or thing that comes or happens after all other similar people or things: *Sorry I'm late—am I the last?* ◊ *They were the last to arrive.* **2** ⚫ ᴀ2 ~ *of sth* the only part or items that remain of sth: *These are the last of our apples.* **3 the last** [sing.] the latest: *That was the last I heard of him.* **4 the last** the least likely: *Known for their self-sufficiency, fishermen would be* **the last to admit** *to mental strain.*
  ▪ **IDM** **at (long) 'last** ⚫ B1 after much delay, effort, etc.; in the end **SYN** *finally*: *At last we're home!* ◊ *At long last the package arrived.* ⇨ note at LASTLY **hear/see the 'last of sb/sth** to hear/see sb/sth for the last time: *That was the last I ever saw of her.* ◊ *Unfortunately, I don't think we've heard the last of this affair.* **the last I 'heard** used to give the most recent news you have about sb/sth: *The last I heard he was still working at the garage.* **next/second to 'last** (*BrE also* **last but 'one**) the one before the last one: *She finished second to last.* **to/till the 'last** until the last possible moment, especially until death: *He died protesting his innocence to the last.* ⇨ more at BREATHE, FIRST *n.*
- **verb 1** ⚫ ᴀ2 [I] (not used in the progressive tenses) to continue for a particular period of time: *Each game lasts about an hour.* ◊ *How long does the play last?* ◊ *Nothing lasts forever.* ◊ *~ for sth The meeting only lasted for a few minutes.* **2** ⚫ ᴀ2 [I, T] to continue to exist or to function well: *This weather won't last.* ◊ *Our product looks better and lasts longer.* ◊ *while sth ~ It was fun while it lasted.* ◊ *~ sb These shoes should last you till next year.* **3** ⚫ [I, T] to survive sth or manage to stay in the same situation, despite difficulties: *She won't* **last long** *in that job.* ◊ *~ out Can you last out until I can get help?* ◊ *~ (out) sth Doctors say that she probably won't* **last out the night** (= she will probably die before the morning)*.* **4** ⚫ ᴀ2 [I, T] to be enough for sb to use, especially for a particular period of time: *~ (out) Will the coffee last out till next week?* ◊ *~ sb We've got enough food to last us (for) three days.*

> ▼ **WHICH WORD?**
> **last / take**
> Last and take are both used to talk about the length of time that something continues.
> - **Last** is used to talk about the length of time that an event continues: *How long do you think this storm will last?* ◊ *The movie lasted over two hours.* **Last** does not always need an expression of time: *His annoyance won't last.* **Last** is also used to say that you have enough of something: *The money she gave us should last until next week.*
> - **Take** is used to talk about the amount of time you need in order to go somewhere or do something. It must be used with an expression of time: *It takes (me) at least an hour to get home from work.* ◊ *How long will the flight take?* ◊ *The water took ages to boil.*

**last²** /lɑːst; *NAmE* læst/ *noun* a block of wood or metal in the shape of a foot, used in making and repairing shoes ⇨ see also LAST¹

**last 'call** *noun* **1** (*especially NAmE*) (*BrE usually* **last 'orders**) the last opportunity for people to buy drinks in a pub or a bar before it closes **2** the final request at an airport for passengers to get on their plane

**last-'ditch** *adj.* [only before noun] used to describe a final attempt to achieve sth, when there is not much hope of succeeding: *She underwent a heart transplant in a last-ditch attempt to save her.*

**last-'gasp** *adj.* [only before noun] done or achieved at the last possible moment: *a last-gasp 2–1 victory*

**last·ing** /ˈlɑːstɪŋ; *NAmE* ˈlæs-/ *adj.* [usually before noun] continuing to exist or to have an effect for a long time **SYN** *durable*: *Her words left a* **lasting impression** *on me.* ◊ *I formed several lasting friendships at college.* ◊ *The train-*ing was of no lasting value. ⇨ see also LONG-LASTING ▶ **last·ing·ly** *adv.*

**the ˌLast 'Judgement** (*also the* ˌLast 'Judgment *especially in NAmE*) *noun* [sing.] = JUDGEMENT DAY

**last·ly** /ˈlɑːstli; *NAmE* ˈlæst-/ *adv.* **1** used to introduce the final point that you want to make **SYN** *finally*: *Lastly, I'd like to ask you about your plans.* ⇨ LANGUAGE BANK at FIRST **2** at the end; after all the other things that you have mentioned: *Lastly, add the lemon juice.*

> ▼ **WHICH WORD?**
> **lastly / at last**
> - **Lastly** is used to introduce the last in a list of things or the final point you are making: *Lastly, I would like to thank my parents for all their support.*
> - **At last** is used when something happens after a long time, especially when there has been some difficulty or delay: *At last, after twenty hours on the boat, they arrived at their destination.* You can also use **finally, eventually** or **in the end** with this meaning, but not *lastly*.

**last-'minute** *adj.* [usually before noun] done, decided or organized just before sth happens or before it is too late: *a last-minute holiday*

**'last name** *noun* your family name ⇨ compare SURNAME

**ˌlast 'orders** *noun* [pl.] (*BrE*) (*also* ˌlast 'call *NAmE, BrE*) the last opportunity for people to buy drinks in a pub or a bar before it closes: *'Last orders, please!'*

**the ˌlast 'post** *noun* [sing.] (*BrE*) a tune played on a BUGLE at a military FUNERAL (= ceremony for a dead person) and at the end of the day in a military camp

**the ˌlast 'rites** *noun* [pl.] a Christian religious ceremony that a priest performs for, and in the presence of, a dying person: *to administer the last rites to sb* ◊ *to receive the last rites*

**lat.** *abbr.* (in writing) LATITUDE

**latch** /lætʃ/ *noun, verb*
- *noun* **1** a small metal bar that is used to fasten a door or a gate. You raise it to open the door and drop it to fasten it: *He lifted the latch and opened the door.* **2** (*especially BrE*) a type of lock on a door that needs a key to open it from the outside: *She listened for his key in the latch.*
  ▪ **IDM** **on the 'latch** (*BrE*) closed but not locked: *Can you leave the door on the latch so I can get in?*
- *verb* ~ *sth* to fasten sth with a latch
  ▪ **PHRV** **ˌlatch 'on (to sth)** | **ˌlatch 'onto sth** (*informal*) to understand an idea or what sb is saying: *It was a difficult concept to grasp, but I soon latched on.* **ˌlatch 'on (to sb/sth)** | **ˌlatch 'onto sb/sth** (*informal*) **1** to become attached to sb/sth: *antibodies that latch onto germs* **2** to join sb and stay in their company, especially when they would prefer you not to be with them **3** to develop a strong interest in sth: *She always latches on to the latest craze.*

**late** ⚫ ᴀ1 /leɪt/ *adj., adv.*
- *adj.* (**later, lat·est**) **1** ⚫ ᴀ1 [not usually before noun] arriving, happening or done after the expected, arranged or usual time: *I'm sorry I'm late.* ◊ *~ for sth She's late for work every day.* ◊ *My flight was an hour late.* ◊ *We apologize for the late arrival of this train.* ◊ *Interest will be charged for late payment.* ◊ *Because of the cold weather the crops are later this year.* **OPP** *early* **2** ⚫ [only before noun] near the end of a period of time, a person's life, etc: *in the late afternoon* ◊ *in late summer* ◊ *young people in their late teens* (= aged 18 or 19) ◊ *She married in her late twenties* (= when she was 28 or 29)*.* ◊ *The school was built in the late 1970s.* ◊ *The concert was cancelled at a very late stage.* **OPP** *early* **3** ⚫ ᴀ1 near the end of the day: *Let's go home—it's getting late.* ◊ *Look at the time—it's much later than I thought.* ◊ *What is the latest time I can have an appointment?* **OPP** *early* **4** [only before noun] (*formal*) (of a person) no longer alive: *her late husband* ◊ *the late Stephen Hawking* ▶ **late·ness** *noun* [U]: *They apologized for the lateness of the train.* ◊ *Despite the lateness of the hour, the children were not in bed.* ⇨ see also LATER *adj.*, LATEST *adj.*

**IDM** **be too ˈlate** happening after the time when it is possible to do sth: *It's too late to save her now.* ◊ *Buy now before it's too late.* ⊃ more at NIGHT
- *adv.* (comparative **later**, no *superlative*) **1** [A1] after the expected, arranged or usual time: *I got up late.* ◊ *Can I stay up late tonight?* ◊ *She has to work late tomorrow.* ◊ *The birthday card arrived three days late.* ◊ **~ for sth** *I'm running late for school.* **2** [A1] near the end of a period of time, a person's life, etc: *It happened late last year.* ◊ **~ in sth** *late in March/the afternoon* ◊ *He became an author late in life.* ◊ **as ~ as** *As late as* (= as recently as) *the 1990s, there was no effective treatment for this disease.* **3** [A1] near the end of the day: *There's a good film on late.* ◊ *I studied from early morning till late at night.* ◊ *They worked late into the night to finish the report.* **OPP** **early** ⊃ see also LATER *adv.*
**IDM** **ˌbetter late than ˈnever** (*saying*) used especially when you, or sb else, arrive/arrives late, or when sth such as success happens late, to say that this is better than not coming or happening at all **ˌlate in the ˈday** (*NAmE* also **ˌlate in the ˈgame**) (*disapproving*) after the time when an action could be successful: *He started working hard much too late in the day—he couldn't possibly catch up.* **ˌlate of …** (*formal*) until recently working or living in the place mentioned: *Professor Jones, late of Oxford University* of **ˈlate** (*formal*) recently: *I haven't seen him of late.* **too ˈlate** after the time when it is possible to do sth successfully: *She's left it too late to apply for the job.* ◊ *I realized the truth too late.*

▼ **GRAMMAR POINT**
### late / lately
- **Late** and **lately** are both adverbs, but **late** is used with similar meanings to the adjective **late**, whereas **lately** can only mean 'recently': *We arrived two hours late.* ◊ *I haven't heard from him lately.* **Lately** is usually used with a perfect tense of the verb.
- Look also at the idioms **be too late** (at the adjective) and **too late** (at the adverb).

**ˈlate·comer** /ˈleɪtkʌmə(r)/ *noun* a person who arrives late
**late·ly** [B2] /ˈleɪtli/ *adv.* recently; in the recent past: *Have you seen her lately?* ◊ *It's only lately that she's been well enough to go out.* ◊ (*BrE*) *I haven't been sleeping well just lately.* ◊ *She had lately returned from India.*
**ˌlate-ˈnight** *adj.* [only before noun] happening late at night; available after other things finish: *a late-night movie* ◊ *late-night shopping*
**la·tent** /ˈleɪtnt/ *adj.* [usually before noun] existing, but not yet clear, active or well developed: *latent disease* ◊ *These children have a huge reserve of latent talent.* ▶ **la·tency** /ˈleɪtənsi/ *noun* [U]

**later** 🔊 [A1] 🅢 /ˈleɪtə(r)/ *adv., adj.*
- *adv.* **1** [A1] at a time in the future; after the time you are talking about: *See you later.* ◊ *I met her again three years later.* ◊ *His father died later that year.* ◊ *We're going to Rome later in the year.* ◊ *She later became a doctor.* **OPP** **early** **2 Later!** (*BrE also* **Laters!**) (*informal*) a way of saying goodbye, used by young people: *Later, guys!*
**IDM** **later ˈon** (*informal*) at a time in the future; after the time you are talking about: *I'm going out later on.* ◊ *Much later on, she realized what he had meant.* **ˌnot/no later ˈthan …** by a particular time and not after it: *Please arrive no later than 8 o'clock.* ⊃ more at SOON
- *adj.* [only before noun] **1** [A2] coming after sth else or at a time in the future: *Rembrandt's later works* ◊ *This is discussed in more detail in a later chapter.* ◊ *The judge will give her ruling at a later date.* **2** [A2] near the end of a period of time, life, etc: *the later part of the seventeenth century* ◊ *In later life he started playing golf.* ◊ *She found happiness in her later years.* **OPP** **early**

**lat·eral** /ˈlætərəl/ *adj., noun*
- *adj.* [usually before noun] (*specialist*) relating to the side of sth or to movement to the side: *the lateral branches of a tree* ◊ *lateral eye movements* ▶ **lat·er·al·ly** /-rəli/ *adv.*
- *noun* **1** (*specialist*) a side part of sth, especially a SHOOT or branch that grows out from the side of a plant or tree **2** (in AMERICAN FOOTBALL) a pass thrown back or to the side: *Pryor threw a lateral to Palmer.*
**ˌlateral ˈthinking** *noun* [U] (*especially BrE*) a way of solving a problem by using your imagination to find new ways of looking at it

**lat·est** 🔊 [B1] /ˈleɪtɪst/ *adj., noun*
- *adj.* [B1] [only before noun] the most recent or newest: *the latest craze/fashion/trend* ◊ *his latest book/film/album* ◊ *Have you heard the latest news?* ◊ *the latest unemployment figures* ◊ *the latest version of the software*
- *noun* [B2] [U] *usually* **the latest** (*informal*) the most recent or the newest thing or piece of news: **the ~ (in sth)** *This is the latest in robot technology.* ◊ *Have you heard the latest?*
**IDM** **at the ˈlatest** no later than the time or the date mentioned: *Applications should be in by next Monday at the latest.*
**latex** /ˈleɪteks/ *noun* [U] **1** a thick white liquid that is produced by some plants and trees, especially rubber trees. Latex becomes solid when exposed to air, and is used to make medical products, clothes and MASKS: *latex gloves* **2** an artificial substance similar to this that is used to make paint, GLUE (= a sticky substance used for joining things together), etc.
**lath** /lɑːθ; *NAmE* læθ/ *noun* (*pl.* **laths** /lɑːðs; *NAmE* læðz/) a thin, narrow piece of wood that is used to support PLASTER (= material used for covering walls) on the inside walls and the ceilings of buildings
**lathe** /leɪð/ *noun* a machine that shapes pieces of wood or metal by holding and turning them against a fixed cutting tool

**la·ther** /ˈlɑːðə(r)/; *NAmE* ˈlæð-/ *noun, verb*
- *noun* [U, sing.] a white mass of small bubbles that is produced by mixing soap with water
**IDM** **get into a ˈlather | work yourself into a ˈlather** (*informal*) to get anxious or angry about sth, especially when it is not necessary **in a ˈlather** (*BrE, informal*) in a nervous, angry or excited state **SYN** **worked up**
- *verb* **1** [T] **~ sth** to cover sth with lather: *I lathered my face and started to shave.* **2** [I] to produce lather: *Soap does not lather well in hard water.*
**lathi** /ˈlɑːtiː/ *noun* (*IndE*) a long, thick stick, especially one used as a weapon by the police

**Latin** /ˈlætɪn; *NAmE* -tn/ *noun, adj.*
- *noun* **1** [U] the language of ancient Rome and the official language of its EMPIRE **2** [C] a person from countries where languages that have developed from Latin, such as Spanish, Portuguese, Italian or French, are spoken **3** [U] music of a kind that came originally from Latin America, typically with strong dance rhythms
- *adj.* **1** of or in the Latin language: *Latin poetry* **2** connected with or typical of the countries or peoples using languages developed from Latin, such as Spanish, Portuguese, Italian or French: *a Latin temperament* **3** connected with or typical of Latin American music: *music with a Latin beat*

**La·tina** /læˈtiːnə/ *noun* a woman or girl, especially one who is living in the US, who comes from Latin America, or whose family came from there ⊃ compare LATINO ▶ **La·tina** *adj.* [usually before noun]
**Latin Aˈmerica** /ˌlætɪn əˈmerɪkə; *NAmE* -tn/ *noun* [U] the parts of the Americas in which Spanish or Portuguese is the main language ⊃ note at AMERICAN
**Latin Aˈmerican** *adj., noun*
- *adj.* from or connected with Latin America
- *noun* a person from Latin America
**Lat·in·ate** /ˈlætɪneɪt/ *adj.* (of words or language) from Latin, or relating to Latin: *formal Latinate terms*
**La·tino** /læˈtiːnəʊ/ *noun* (*pl.* **-os**) a person, especially one who is living in the US, who comes from Latin America, or whose family came from there ⊃ compare CHICANO ▶ **La·tino** *adj.* [usually before noun]
**lati·tude** /ˈlætɪtjuːd; *NAmE* -tuːd/ *noun* **1** (*abbr.* **lat.**) [U] the distance of a place north or south of the EQUATOR (= the line around the world dividing north and south), measured

# latrine 886

in degrees ⊃ compare LONGITUDE ⊃ **WORDFINDER NOTE** at EARTH **2 latitudes** [pl.] a region of the world that is a particular distance from the EQUATOR: *the northern latitudes* **3** [U] (*formal*) freedom to choose what you do or the way that you do it **SYN** liberty ⊃ see also LEEWAY

**la·trine** /ləˈtriːn/ *noun* a toilet in a camp, etc., especially one made by digging a hole in the ground

**latte** /ˈlɑːteɪ; *BrE also* ˈlæt-/ (*also* **caffè latte** /ˌkæfeɪ ˈlɑːteɪ; *BrE also* ˈlæt-/) *noun* (*from Italian*) a drink made by adding a small amount of strong coffee to a glass or cup of hot FROTHY milk

**lat·ter** ?+ C1 W /ˈlætə(r)/ *adj., noun*
- *adj.* [only before noun] **1** ?+ C1 used to refer to the second of two things or people mentioned: *He chose the latter option.* ◇ *The latter point is the most important.* **2** ?+ C1 nearer to the end of a period of time than the beginning: *the latter half of the year* **3** recent: *In latter years, the population has grown a lot here.* ⊃ compare FORMER
- *noun* ?+ C1 **the latter** (*pl.* **the latter**) the second of two things or people mentioned: *He presented two solutions. The latter seems much better.* ◇ *The town has a concert hall and two theatres. The latter were both built in the 1950s.*

**ˈlatter-day** *adj.* [only before noun] being a modern version of a person or thing in the past: *a latter-day Robin Hood*

**lat·ter·ly** /ˈlætəli; *NAmE* -tərli/ *adv.* (*formal*) **1** most recently: *Latterly his painting has shown a new freedom of expression.* **2** towards the end of a period of time: *Her health declined rapidly and latterly she never left the house.*

**lattice**

lattice fence panel — lattice window — lattice pastry on a pie

**lat·tice** /ˈlætɪs/ *noun* [U, C] (*also* **lat·tice·work** /ˈlætɪswɜːk; *NAmE* -wɜːrk/ [U]) a structure that is made of thin, narrow pieces of wood or metal that cross over each other with spaces that are like diamonds in shape between them, used, for example, as a fence; any structure or pattern like this: *a low wall of stone latticework* ◇ *a lattice of branches* ▶ **lat·ticed** *adj.*

**ˈlattice ˈwindow** (*also* **ˌlatticed ˈwindow**) *noun* a window with small pieces of glass that are like diamonds in shape in a FRAMEWORK of narrow metal pieces ⊃ picture at LATTICE

**laud** /lɔːd/ *verb* ~ sb/sth (*formal*) to praise sb/sth

**laud·able** /ˈlɔːdəbl/ *adj.* (*formal*) deserving to be praised or admired, even if not really successful **SYN** commendable: *a laudable aim/attempt* ▶ **laud·ably** /-bli/ *adv.*

**laud·anum** /ˈlɔːdənəm/ *noun* [U] a drug made from OPIUM. In the past, people used to take laudanum to reduce pain and worry, and to help them sleep.

**laud·atory** /ˈlɔːdətəri; *NAmE* -tɔːri/ *adj.* (*formal*) expressing praise

**laugh** ?+ A1 /lɑːf; *NAmE* læf/ *verb, noun*
- *verb* **1** ?+ A1 [I, T] to make the sounds and movements of your face that show you think sth is funny or silly: *to laugh out loud* ◇ *I was laughing so hard that I had tears running down my cheeks.* ◇ *The show was hilarious—I couldn't stop laughing.* ◇ **~ at sth** *You never laugh at my jokes!* ◇ **~ about sth** *She was laughing hysterically about something he had said.* ◇ *She always makes me laugh.* ◇ *He burst out laughing* (= suddenly started laughing). ◇ **+ speech** *'You're crazy!' she laughed.* **2** [I] **be laughing** (*informal*) used to say that you are in a very good position, especially because you

have done sth successfully: *If we win the next game we'll be laughing.*
**IDM** ˌdon't make me ˈlaugh (*informal*) used to show that you think what sb has just said is impossible or stupid: *'Will your dad lend you the money?' 'Don't make me laugh!'* he who laughs ˌlast laughs ˈlongest (*saying*) used to tell sb not to be too proud of their present success; in the end another person may be more successful **laugh all the way to the ˈbank** (*informal*) to make a lot of money easily and feel very pleased about it **laugh in sb's ˈface** to show in a very obvious way that you have no respect for sb **laugh like a ˈdrain** (*BrE, informal*) to laugh very loudly **laugh on the other ˈside of your ˈface** (*BrE, informal*) to be forced to change from feeling pleased or satisfied to feeling disappointed or annoyed **laugh sb/sth out of ˈcourt** (*BrE, informal*) to completely reject an idea, a story, etc. that you think is not worth taking seriously at all **laugh till/until you ˈcry** to laugh so long and hard that there are tears in your eyes **laugh up your ˈsleeve (at sb/sth)** (*informal*) to secretly think that sth is funny **laugh your ˈhead off** (*informal*) to laugh very loudly and for a long time **not know whether to ˌlaugh or ˈcry** (*informal*) to be unable to decide how to react to a bad situation **you ˌhave/you've got to ˈlaugh** (*informal*) used to say that you think there is a funny side to a situation: *Well, I'm sorry you've lost your shoes, but you've got to laugh, haven't you?* ⊃ more at DIE v., KILL v., PISS v., SPLIT v.
**PHRV** ˈlaugh at sb/sth to make sb/sth seem stupid or not serious by making jokes about them/it **SYN** ridicule: *Everybody laughs at my accent.* ◇ *She is not afraid to laugh at herself* (= is not too serious about herself). **laugh sth↔off** (*informal*) to try to make people think that sth is not serious or important, especially by making a joke about it: *He laughed off suggestions that he was going to resign.*

- *noun* **1** ?+ A1 [C] the sound you make when you think that sth is funny or silly: *to give a laugh* ◇ *a short/nervous/hearty laugh* ◇ *His first joke got the biggest laugh of the night.* ◇ **with a ~** *'It was pretty crazy,' she said with a laugh.* ⊃ see also BELLY LAUGH **2 a laugh** [sing.] (*informal*) an occasion or thing that is good fun: *Come to the karaoke night—it should be a good laugh.* ◇ *And he didn't realize it was you? What a laugh!* **3 a laugh** [sing.] a person who is fun to be with: *Paula's a good laugh, isn't she?*
**IDM** do sth for a ˈlaugh/for ˈlaughs to do sth for fun or as a joke: *I just did it for a laugh, but it got out of hand.* **have a (good) ˈlaugh (about/over sth)** to find sth funny: *I was angry at the time but we had a good laugh about it afterwards.* ⊃ more at BARREL *n.*, LAST¹ *det.*

▼ **VOCABULARY BUILDING**

**Different ways of laughing**

- **cackle** to laugh in a loud, unpleasant way, especially in a high voice
- **chuckle** to laugh quietly, especially because you are thinking about something funny
- **giggle** to laugh in a silly way because you are embarrassed, nervous or you think sth is funny
- **guffaw** to laugh noisily
- **roar** to laugh very loudly
- **snigger/snicker** to laugh in a quiet, unpleasant way, especially at something rude or at someone's problems or mistakes
- **titter** to laugh quietly, especially in a nervous or embarrassed way

You can also **be convulsed with laughter** or **dissolve into laughter** when you find something very funny. In *BrE* people also **shriek with laughter** or **howl with laughter**.

**laugh·able** /ˈlɑːfəbl; *NAmE* ˈlæf-/ *adj.* silly and not worth taking seriously **SYN** absurd ▶ **laugh·ably** /-bli/ *adv.*

**laugh·ing** /ˈlɑːfɪŋ; *NAmE* ˈlæf-/ *adj.* showing that you think sth is funny; showing happiness: *his laughing blue eyes* ◇ *laughing faces*
**IDM** be no laughing ˈmatter to be sth serious that you should not joke about ⊃ more at DIE v., SPLIT v.

**ˈlaughing gas** *noun* [U] (*informal*) = NITROUS OXIDE

**laugh·ing·ly** /ˈlɑːfɪŋli; NAmE ˈlæf-/ adv. **1** in a way that shows you think sth is funny: *He laughingly agreed.* **2** used to show that you think a particular word is not at all a suitable way of describing something and therefore seems silly: *I finally reached what we laughingly call civilization.*

ˈ**laughing stock** noun [usually sing.] a person that everyone laughs at because they have done sth stupid: *I can't wear that! I'd be a laughing stock.*

ˌ**laugh-out-ˈloud** adj., adv. (abbr. LOL) [only before noun] (informal) extremely funny: *a laugh-out-loud moment* ◊ *The best scenes in the movie are laugh-out-loud funny.* **HELP** The abbreviation **LOL** is also used in text messages, social media, etc. to show that you think sth is funny or do not mean it seriously.

**laugh·ter** ❶ A2 /ˈlɑːftə(r); NAmE ˈlæf-/ noun [U] the act or sound of laughing: *to roar/howl with laughter* ◊ *tears/gales/peals of laughter* ◊ *Everyone* **burst into fits of laughter***.* ◊ *a house full of laughter* (= with a happy atmosphere) **IDM** see SPLIT v.

**launch** ❶ B2 /lɔːntʃ/ verb, noun
■ verb **1** ❓ B2 [T] ~ sth to start an activity, especially an organized one: *The government recently* **launched** *a national road safety* **campaign***.* ◊ *Police have* **launched** *an* **investigation** *into the incident.* ◊ *Government forces* **launched an attack** *against militants in the north of the country.* **2** ❓ B2 [T, I] ~ (sth) to make a product or service available to the public for the first time; to become available for the first time: *The company plans to* **launch the service** *to coincide with the World Cup this summer.* ◊ *The updated website will be* **officially launched** *at the conference in April.* ◊ *The new series launches in July.* **3** ❓ B2 [T] ~ sth to put a ship or boat into the water, especially one that has just been built: *The Navy is to launch a new warship today.* ◊ *The lifeboat was launched immediately.* **4** ❓ B2 [T] ~ sth to send sth such as a SPACECRAFT, weapon, etc. into space, into the sky or through water: *to launch a missile/rocket* ◊ *The satellite was successfully launched into orbit earlier this month.* ➔ **WORDFINDER NOTE** at SPACE **5** [T] ~ sth to criticize sb/sth or protest strongly: *He* **launched** *a biting* **attack** *on the senior management.* **6** [T] ~ yourself + adv./prep. to jump forwards with a lot of force: *Without warning he launched himself at me.* **7** [T, I] ~ sth (computing) to start a computer program; (of a computer program) to start: *You can launch programs and documents from your keyboard.* ◊ *I was impressed with how fast the app launches.*
**PHRV** ˈ**launch into sth** | ˈ**launch yourself into sth** to begin sth in an enthusiastic way, especially sth that will take a long time: *He launched into a lengthy account of his career.* ˌ**launch** ˈ**out** to do sth new in your career, especially sth more exciting: *It's time I launched out on my own.*
■ noun **1** ❓ B2 [usually sing.] the action of launching sth: *a missile/rocket* **launch** ◊ *the* **launch** *of the campaign/website/service* ◊ *The official* **launch date** *is in May.* **2** ❓ B2 an event at which sth is made available to the public for the first time: *a book/product* **launch** ◊ *About 50 artists attended the* **official launch** *of the exhibition.* ➔ compare SOFT LAUNCH **3** a large boat with a motor

**launch·er** /ˈlɔːntʃə(r)/ noun (often in compounds) a device that is used to send a ROCKET, a MISSILE, etc. into the sky: *a rocket launcher*

ˈ**launch pad** (also ˈ**launching pad**) noun a platform from which a SPACECRAFT, etc. is sent into the sky: *(figurative) She regards the job as a launch pad for her career in the media.*

**laun·der** /ˈlɔːndə(r)/ verb **1** ~ sth (formal) to wash, dry and iron clothes, etc: *freshly laundered sheets* **2** ~ sth to move money that has been obtained illegally into foreign bank accounts or legal businesses so that it is difficult for people to know where the money came from ➔ see also MONEY LAUNDERING

**laun·der·ette** /ˌlɔːndəˈret/ (also **laun·drette** /lɔːnˈdret/) (both BrE) (NAmE **Laun·dro·mat**™ /ˈlɔːndrəmæt/) noun a place where you can wash and dry your clothes in machines that you pay to use

**laun·dry** /ˈlɔːndri/ noun (pl. -ies) **1** [U] clothes, sheets, etc. that need washing, that are being washed, or that have been washed recently **SYN** washing: *a pile of clean/dirty* **laundry** ◊ *a laundry basket/room* **2** [U, sing.] the process or the job of washing clothes, sheets, etc: *to do the laundry* ◊ *The hotel has a laundry service.* **3** [C] a business or place where you send sheets, clothes, etc. to be washed **IDM** see DIRTY adj.

ˈ**laundry list** noun a long list of people or things: *a laundry list of problems*

**laure·ate** /ˈlɒriət; NAmE ˈlɔːr-/ noun a person who has been given an official honour or prize for sth important they have achieved: *a Nobel laureate* ➔ see also POET LAUREATE

**laurel** /ˈlɒrəl; NAmE ˈlɔːr-/ noun **1** [U, C] a bush or tree with dark, smooth, shiny leaves that remain on the bush and stay green through the year **2 laurels** [pl.] honour and praise given to sb because of sth that they have achieved **IDM** ˌ**look to your** ˈ**laurels** to be careful that you do not lose the success or advantage that you have over other people ˌ**rest/sit on your** ˈ**laurels** (usually disapproving) to feel so satisfied with what you have already achieved that you do not try to do any more

ˈ**laurel wreath** noun a ring of laurel leaves that was worn on the head in the past as a sign of victory

**lav** /læv/ noun (BrE, old-fashioned, informal) a toilet

**lava** /ˈlɑːvə/ noun [U] **1** hot liquid rock that comes out of a VOLCANO: *molten lava* ➔ picture at VOLCANO **2** this type of rock when it has cooled and become hard

ˈ**lava lamp** noun an electric lamp that contains a liquid in which a coloured substance like oil moves up and down in shapes that keep changing

**lava·tor·ial** /ˌlævəˈtɔːriəl/ adj. (especially BrE) **lavatorial** humour refers in a rude way to parts of the body, going to the toilet, etc.

**lav·atory** /ˈlævətri; NAmE -tɔːri/ noun (pl. -ies) (old-fashioned or formal) **1** (especially BrE) a toilet, or a room with a toilet in it: *There's a bathroom and a lavatory upstairs.* **2** (BrE) a public building or part of a building, with toilets in it: *The nearest public lavatory is at the station.*

**lav·en·der** /ˈlævəndə(r)/ noun [U] **1** a garden plant with bunches of purple flowers with a sweet smell **2** the flowers of the lavender plant that have been dried, used for making sheets, clothes, etc. smell nice: *lavender oil/water* **3** a pale purple colour

**lav·ish** /ˈlævɪʃ/ adj., verb
■ adj. **1** large in amount, or impressive, and usually costing a lot of money **SYN** extravagant, luxurious: *lavish gifts/costumes/celebrations* ◊ *They lived a very* **lavish lifestyle***.* ◊ *They rebuilt the house on an even more* **lavish scale** *than before.* **2** ~ (with/in sth) giving or doing sth generously: *He was lavish in his praise for her paintings.* ▶ **lav·ish·ly** adv.: *lavishly illustrated*
■ verb
**PHRV** ˈ**lavish sth on/upon sb/sth** to give a lot of sth, often too much, to sb/sth: *She lavishes most of her attention on her youngest son.*

**law** ❶ A2 ❷ /lɔː/ noun
• ONE RULE **1** ❓ A2 [C] a rule that deals with a particular crime, agreement, etc: *to* **pass a law** (= officially make it part of the system of laws) ◊ *~* **against (doing) sth** *Police don't have the resources to* **enforce the law** *against dumping waste.* ◊ *(informal) There ought to be a law against it!* ◊ *~* **on sth** *The company's actions* **violated the law** *on equal employment.* ◊ *The suspects were in clear* **violation of immigration laws***.* ➔ **WORDFINDER NOTE** at PARLIAMENT ➔ see also BLUE LAW, BY-LAW, LICENSING LAWS, MARTIAL LAW, NATURAL LAW
• SYSTEM OF RULES **2** ❓ A2 (also **the law**) [U] the whole system of rules that everyone in a country or society must obey: *If they entered the building they would be* **breaking the law***.* ◊ *The reforms have recently* **become law***.* ◊ **state/federal law** ◊ **against the** *~ In Sweden it is against the law to hit a child.* ◊ **within the** *~ Defence attorneys can use any means within*

# law-abiding

the law to get their client off. ◊ **outside the~** to operate outside the law ◊ **by~** *British schools are required by law to publish their exam results.* ◊ **under the (…)~ | under …~** *Under existing law, journalists cannot refuse to provide information to a jury.* ◊ **above the~** *Do not think you are above the law* (= that you cannot be punished by the law). ◊ **law enforcement** *agencies/officials*

**WORDFINDER** abide by sth, court, crime, justice, legal, police, prosecute, punish, trial

**3** [U] a particular branch of the law: *He specializes in international law.* ◊ *tax/employment law* ◊ **according to …~** *According to copyright law, the author is the owner of the material.* ⊃ see also CANON LAW, CASE LAW, CIVIL LAW, COMMON LAW, CRIMINAL LAW, PRIVATE LAW, STATUTE LAW
- **SUBJECT/PROFESSION 4** [U] the study of the law as a subject at university, etc.; the profession of being a lawyer: *a law student/professor* ◊ (NAmE) *He's in law school.* ◊ (BrE) *He's at law school.* ◊ *a law firm*
- **POLICE 5 the law** [sing.] used to refer to the police and the legal system: *Jim is always getting into trouble with the law.*
- **IN BUSINESS/NATURE/SCIENCE 6** [C] the fact that sth always happens in the same way in an activity or in nature **SYN principle**: *the laws of supply and demand* ◊ *the laws of nature/physics* **7** [C] a scientific rule that sb has stated to explain a natural process: *the first law of thermodynamics* ⊃ see also LEGAL, LEGALIZE, LEGISLATE, MURPHY'S LAW, PARKINSON'S LAW, SOD'S LAW
- **OF ORGANIZATION/ACTIVITY 8** [C] one of the rules that controls an organization or activity: *the laws of the Church* ◊ *The first law of kung fu is to defend yourself.* ◊ *the laws of cricket*
- **OF GOOD BEHAVIOUR 9** [C] a rule for good behaviour or how you should behave in a particular place or situation: *moral laws* ◊ *the unspoken laws of the street*

**IDM be a law unto your'self** to behave in an independent way and ignore rules or what other people want you to do **go to 'law** (BrE) to ask a court to settle a problem or DISAGREEMENT **law and order** a situation in which people obey the law and behave in a peaceful way: *The government struggled to maintain law and order.* ◊ *After the riots, the military was brought in to restore law and order.* ◊ *They claim to be the party of law and order.* **the law of 'averages** the principle that one thing will happen as often as another if you try enough times: *Keep applying and by the law of averages you'll get a job sooner or later.* **the law of the 'jungle** a situation in which people are prepared to harm other people in order to succeed **lay down the 'law** to tell sb with force what they should or should not do **take the 'law into your own 'hands** to do sth illegal in order to punish sb for doing sth wrong, instead of letting the police deal with them **there's no 'law against sth** (*informal*) used to tell sb who is criticizing you that you are not doing anything wrong: *I'll sing if I want to—there's no law against it.* ⊃ more at LETTER *n.*, POSSESSION, RULE *n.*, WRONG *adj.*

**law-abiding** *adj.* obeying and respecting the law: *law-abiding citizens*

**law-break-er** /'lɔːbreɪkə(r)/ *noun* a person who does not obey the law ▸ **law-break-ing** *noun* [U]

**'law court** *noun* = COURT OF LAW ⊃ note at COURT

**law-ful** /'lɔːfl/ *adj.* (*formal*) allowed or recognized by law; legal: *his lawful heir* **OPP** *unlawful* ▸ **law-ful-ly** /-fəli/ *adv.*: *a lawfully elected government* **law-ful-ness** *noun* [U]

**law-less** /'lɔːləs/ *adj.* **1** (of a country or an area) where laws do not exist or are not obeyed: *lawless streets* ◊ *the lawless days of the revolution* **2** (of people or their actions) without respect for the law **SYN anarchic, wild**: *lawless gangs* ▸ **law-less-ness** *noun* [U]

**law-maker** /'lɔːmeɪkə(r)/ *noun* a politician who helps make the laws of a country **SYN legislator**

**law-man** /'lɔːmæn/ *noun* (*pl.* **-men** /-men/) (*especially US*) an officer responsible for keeping law and order, especially a SHERIFF

**lawn** /lɔːn/ *noun* **1** [C] an area of ground covered in short grass in a garden or park, or used for playing a game on: *In summer we have to mow the lawn twice a week.* ◊ *a croquet lawn* **2** [U] a type of fine cotton or LINEN cloth used for making clothes

**'lawn bowling** *noun* [U] (*NAmE*) = BOWLS

**'lawn chair** *noun* (*especially NAmE*) a chair that can be folded and that people use when sitting outside

**lawn·mow·er** /'lɔːnməʊə(r)/ (*also* **mower**) *noun* a machine for cutting the grass on LAWNS

**'lawn sign** *noun* (*NAmE*) a board that people put outside their house in order to advertise sth or to show that they support a particular politician or political party

**lawn 'tennis** *noun* [U] (*old-fashioned* or *formal*) the usual form of tennis, played with a soft ball on an open court (originally a grass court)

**'law school** *noun* a US college at which people study to become lawyers. It is usually part of a university, and students enter it after they have their first degree: *She's at Harvard Law School* ⊃ see also LSAT

**law·suit** /'lɔːsuːt/ (*also* **suit**) *noun* **~ (against sb/sth)** a claim or complaint against sb that a person or an organization can make in court: *He filed a lawsuit against his record label.* ◊ *to bring/settle/dismiss a lawsuit*

**law·yer** /'lɔːjə(r)/ *noun* a person who is trained and qualified to advise people about the law and to represent them in court, and to write legal documents: *to hire a lawyer* ◊ *a defence lawyer* ◊ (*NAmE*) *a trial lawyer* ◊ *a human rights lawyer* ◊ *~ for sb lawyers for the defendants*

▼ MORE ABOUT …

**lawyers**

- **Lawyer** is a general term for a person who is qualified to advise people about the law, to prepare legal documents for them and/or to represent them in a court of law.
- In England and Wales, a **lawyer** who is qualified to speak in the higher courts of law is called a **barrister**. In Scotland a **barrister** is called an **advocate**.
- In NAmE **attorney** is a more formal word used for a lawyer and is used especially in job titles: *the District Attorney*
- **Counsel** is the formal legal word used for a lawyer who is representing someone in court: *counsel for the prosecution*
- **Solicitor** is the BrE term for a lawyer who gives legal advice and prepares documents, for example when you are buying a house, and sometimes has the right to speak in a court of law.
- In NAmE **solicitor** is only used in the titles of some lawyers who work for the government: *the Solicitor General*
- A **notary** is a person, often but not necessarily a lawyer, who has official authority to be a witness when sb signs a document and to make the document legally acceptable.

**lax** /læks/ *adj.* **1** (*disapproving*) not strict, severe or careful enough about work, rules or standards of behaviour **SYN slack, careless**: *lax security/discipline* ◊ *a lax attitude to health and safety regulations* **2** (of parts of the body) relaxed **OPP tense 3** (*phonetics*) (of a speech sound) produced with the muscles of the speech organs relaxed **OPP tense** ▸ **lax·ity** *noun* [U]

**laxa·tive** /'læksətɪv/ *noun* a medicine, food or drink that makes sb empty their BOWELS easily ▸ **laxa·tive** *adj.*

**lay** /leɪ/ *verb, adj., noun*
■ *verb* (**laid, laid** /leɪd/)
- **PUT DOWN/SPREAD 1** [T] to put sb/sth in a particular position, especially when it is done gently or carefully:

**~ sb/sth (+ adv./prep.)** *He laid a hand on my arm.* ◊ *Relatives laid wreaths on the grave.* ◊ *She laid the baby down gently on the bed.* ◊ *The horse laid back its ears.* ◊ **~ sth + adj.** *The cloth should be laid flat.* **2** [T] to spread sth on sth; to cover sth with a layer of sth: **~ A on/over B** *Before they started they laid newspaper on the floor.* ◊ *The grapes were laid to dry on racks.* ◊ **B is laid with A** *The floor was laid with newspaper.* **3** [T] **~ sth (down)** to put sth down, especially on the floor, ready to be used: *to lay a carpet/cable/pipe* ◊ *The first high-speed track was laid between Paris and Lyons.* ◊ *The foundations of the house are being laid today.* ◊ *(figurative) A series of short-term goals lays the foundation for long-term success.*
- **EGGS 4** [T, I] **~ (sth)** if a bird, an insect, a fish, etc. **lays eggs**, it produces them from its body: *The cuckoo lays its eggs in other birds' nests.* ◊ *new-laid eggs* ◊ *The hens are not laying well* (= not producing many eggs).
- **TABLE 5** [T] **~ sth** (*BrE*) to arrange knives, forks, plates, etc. on a table ready for a meal **SYN set**: *to lay the table*
- **PRESENT PROPOSAL 6** [T] **~ sth + adv./prep.** to present a proposal, some information, etc. to sb for them to think about and decide on: *The bill was laid before Parliament.*
- **DIFFICULT SITUATION 7** [T] **~ sb/sth + adv./prep.** (*formal*) to put sb/sth in a particular position or state, especially a difficult or unpleasant one **SYN place**: *to lay a responsibility/burden on sb* ◊ *to lay sb under an obligation to do sth*
- **WITH NOUNS 8** [T] **~ sth + adv./prep.** used with a noun to form a phrase that has the same meaning as the verb related to the noun: *to lay the blame on sb* (= to blame sb) ◊ *Our teacher lays great stress on good spelling* (= stresses it strongly).
- **PLAN/TRAP 9** [T] **~ sth** to prepare sth in detail: *to lay a trap for sb* ◊ *She began to lay her plans for her escape.* ◊ *Bad weather can upset even the best-laid plans.*
- **HAVE SEX 10** [T, usually passive] **~ sb** (*slang*) to have sex with sb: *He went out hoping to get laid that night.*
- **FIRE 11** [T] **~ sth** to prepare a fire by arranging wood, sticks or coal
- **BET 12** [T] to bet money on sth; to place a bet: **~ sth** *to lay a bet* ◊ **~ sth on sth** *She had laid $100 on the favourite.* ◊ **~ (sb) sth (that)...** *I'll lay you any money you like (that) he won't come.* **HELP** This pattern is not used in the passive. **13** past tense of **LIE**¹ **HELP** Idioms containing **lay** are at the entries for the nouns and adjectives in the idioms, for example **lay sth bare** is at **bare**.

**PHR V** **lay aˈbout sb (with sth)** (*BrE*) to attack sb violently: *The gang laid about him with sticks.* **lay aˈbout you/ yourself (with sth)** (*BrE*) to hit sb/sth without control or move your arms or legs violently in all directions: *She laid about herself with her stick to keep the dogs off.* **lay sth↔aˈside** (*formal*) **1** to put sth on one side and not use it or think about it **SYN set sth aside**: *He laid aside his book and stood up.* ◊ (*figurative*) *Doctors have to lay their personal feelings aside.* **2** (*also* **lay sth ˈby**) to keep sth to use, or deal with later **SYN put sth aside**: *They had laid money aside for their old age.* **lay sth↔ˈdown 1** to put sth down or stop using it **SYN put down**: *She laid the book down on the table.* ◊ *Both sides were urged to lay down their arms* (= stop fighting). **2** (*formal*) to stop doing a job, etc: *to lay down your duties* **3** if you **lay down** a rule or a principle, you state officially that people must obey it or use it: *You can't lay down hard and fast rules.* ◊ **it is laid down that...** *It is laid down that all candidates must submit three copies of their dissertation.* **4** [usually passive] to produce sth that is stored and gradually increases: *If you eat too much, the surplus is laid down as fat.* **lay sth↔ˈin/ˈup** to collect and store sth to use in the future: *to lay in food supplies* **lay ˈinto sb/sth** (*informal*) to attack sb violently with hard hits or words: *His parents really laid into him for wasting so much money.* **lay ˈoff** | **lay ˈoff sb/sth** (*informal*) used to tell sb to stop doing sth: *Lay off me will you—it's nothing to do with me.* ◊ **lay off doing sth** *Lay off bullying Jack.* **lay ˈoff sth** (*informal*) to stop using sth: *I think you'd better lay off fatty foods for a while.* **lay sb↔ˈoff** to stop employing sb because there is not enough work for them to do **SYN make sb redundant** ⊃ related noun LAY-OFF **lay ˈon sb/sth** (*BrE*, *informal*) to provide sth for sb, especially for food or entertainment: *to lay on food and drink* ◊ *A bus has been laid on to take guests to*

889 **layman**

*the airport.* **lay sth ˈon sb** (*informal*) to make sb have to deal with sth unpleasant or difficult: *Stop laying a guilt trip on me* (= making me feel guilty). **lay sb↔ˈout 1** to knock sb unconscious **2** to prepare a dead body to be buried **lay sth↔ˈout 1** to spread sth out so that it can be seen easily or is ready to use: *He laid the map out on the table.* ◊ **+ adj.** *Lay the material out flat.* **2** [often passive] to plan how sth should look and arrange it in this way: *The gardens were laid out with lawns and flower beds.* ◊ *a well-laid-out magazine* ⊃ related noun LAYOUT **3** to present a plan, an argument, etc. clearly and carefully **SYN set out**: *All the terms and conditions are laid out in the contract.* **4** (*informal*) to spend money **SYN fork out**: *I had to lay out a fortune on a new car.* ⊃ related noun OUTLAY **lay ˈover (at/in...)** (*NAmE*) to stay somewhere for a short time during a long journey ⊃ related noun LAYOVER ⊃ see also STOP OVER (AT/IN...) at STOP **lay sb ˈup** [usually passive] if sb is **laid up**, they are unable to work, etc. because of an illness or injury: *She's laid up with a broken leg.* **lay sth↔ˈup 1** = LAY STH IN/UP **2** if you **lay up** problems or trouble for yourself, you do sth that will cause you problems later **3** to stop using a ship or other vehicle while it is being repaired

■ *adj.* [only before noun] **1** not having expert knowledge or professional qualifications in a particular subject: *His book explains the theory for the lay public.* **2** not in an official position in the Church: *a lay preacher* ⊃ see also LAY-MAN, LAYPERSON, LAYWOMAN

■ *noun* **1** (*slang, offensive*) a partner in sex, especially a woman: *to be a great lay* **2** (*old use*) a poem that was written to be sung, usually telling a story

**IDM** **the ˌlay of the ˈland** (*NAmE*) (*BrE* **the ˌlie of the ˈland**) **1** the way the land in an area is formed and what physical characteristics it has **2** the way a situation is now and how it is likely to develop

▼ **WHICH WORD?**

**lay / lie**

- **lay** has an object and **lie** does not: *She was lying on the beach.* ◊ ~~*She was laying on the beach.*~~ ◊ *Why don't you lie on the bed?* ◊ ~~*Why don't you lay on the bed?*~~
- In the past tenses **laid** (from *lay*) is often wrongly used for **lay** or **lain** (from *lie*): *She had lain there all night.* ◊ ~~*She had laid there all night.*~~
- Some people use **lay** as a noun instead of **lie**, but this is not considered correct: *If you're tired, go and have a lie down.* ◊ ~~*Go and have a lay down.*~~

**lay·about** /ˈleɪəbaʊt/ *noun* (*BrE*, *old-fashioned*, *informal*, *disapproving*) a lazy person who does not do much work

**lay·away** /ˈleɪəweɪ/ *noun* [U] (*NAmE*) a system of buying goods in a store, where the customer pays a small amount of the price for an article and the store keeps the goods until the full price has been paid

**ˈlay-by** *noun* (*pl.* **-bys**) **1** [C] (*BrE*) an area at the side of a road where vehicles may stop for a short time ⊃ compare REST AREA ⊃ WORDFINDER NOTE at ROAD **2** [U, C] (*AustralE*, *NZE*, *SAfrE*) a system of paying some money for an article so that it is kept for you and you can pay the rest of the money later: **on ~** *You could secure it on lay-by.*

**layer** /ˈleɪə(r)/; *BrE also* /leə(r)/ *noun*, *verb*
■ *noun* **1** a quantity or sheet of sth that lies over a surface or between surfaces: **~(of sth)** *A thin layer of dust covered everything.* ◊ *How many layers of clothing are you wearing?* ◊ **in layers** *The paint is applied in layers.* **2** **~(of sth)** a level or part within a system or set of ideas: *There were too many layers of management in the company.* ◊ *the layers of meaning in the poem*
■ *verb* [often passive] **1 ~ sth** to arrange sth in layers: *Layer the potatoes and onions in a dish.* **2** to cut hair in layers of different lengths: **be layered** *Her hair had been layered.*

**lay·man** /ˈleɪmən/ *noun* (*pl.* **-men** /-mən/) (*also* **ˈlay·per·son**) **1** a person who does not have expert knowledge of a particular subject: *a book written for professionals and laymen alike* ◊ *to explain sth in layman's terms* (= in simple

# lay-off

language) **2** a person who is a member of a Church but is not a priest or member of the CLERGY ⇒ see also LAYWOMAN ⇒ note at GENDER

**'lay-off** *noun* **1** an act of making people unemployed because there is no more work left for them to do **2** a period of time when sb is not working or not doing sth that they normally do regularly: *an eight-week lay-off with a broken leg*

**lay·out** ⚬+ C1 /'leɪaʊt/ *noun* [usually sing.] the way in which the parts of sth such as the page of a book, a website, a garden or a building are arranged: *the layout of streets ◊ the magazine's attractive new page layout*

**lay·over** /'leɪəʊvə(r)/ (*NAmE*) (*BrE, NAmE* **stop-over**) *noun* a short stay somewhere between two parts of a journey

**lay·per·son** (*also* **'lay person**) /'leɪpɜːsn; *NAmE* -pɜːrsn/ *noun* (*pl.* **lay·people** *or* **lay·persons**) = LAYMAN: *The layperson cannot really understand mental illness.*

**lay·woman** /'leɪwʊmən/ *noun* (*pl.* **-women** /-wɪmɪn/) a woman who is a member of a Church but is not a priest or a member of the CLERGY ⇒ see also LAYMAN, LAYPERSON ⇒ note at GENDER

**laze** /leɪz/ *verb* [I] to relax and do very little: *We lazed by the pool all day.* ◊ **~about/around** *I've spent the afternoon just lazing around.*
**PHRV** **laze sth↔away** to spend time relaxing and doing very little **SYN** **lounge**: *They lazed away the long summer days.*

**lazy** ⚬ A2 /'leɪzi/ *adj.* (**lazi·er**, **lazi·est**) **1** ⚬ A2 (*disapproving*) unwilling to work or be active; doing as little as possible **SYN** **idle**: *He was not stupid, just lazy.* ◊ **too ~ to do sth** *I was feeling too lazy to go out.* **2** A2 not involving much energy or activity; slow and relaxed: *We spent a lazy day on the beach.* **3** (*disapproving*) showing a lack of effort or care: *a lazy piece of work* ◊ *We thought we were winning, so we got lazy.* **4** (*literary*) moving slowly **SYN** **torpid**: *the lazy river* ▸ **lazi·ly** /-zɪli/ *adv.*: *She woke up and stretched lazily.* **lazi·ness** *noun* [U]

**'lazy 'eye** *noun* an eye that does not see well because it is not used enough

**lb** (*BrE*) (*NAmE* **lb.**) *abbr.* (*pl.* **lb** *or* **lbs**) a pound in weight, equal to about 454 GRAMS (from Latin 'libra')

**lbw** /ˌel biː 'dʌblju:/ *abbr.* (in CRICKET) leg before wicket (When the ball hits a player's leg instead of hitting his or her BAT, and would have hit the WICKET if the leg had not stopped it, then that player is **out lbw** and has to stop BATTING.)

**l.c.** *abbr.* **1** (*specialist*) in the piece of text that has been quoted (from Latin 'loco citato') **2** (in writing) LETTER OF CREDIT **3** (in writing) LOWER CASE

**LCD** /ˌel siː 'diː/ *noun* **1** liquid crystal display (a way of showing information in electronic equipment. An electric current is passed through a special liquid and numbers and letters can be seen on a small screen.): *a pocket calculator with LCD* ◊ *an LCD screen* **2** LOWEST COMMON DENOMINATOR

**lea** /liː/ *noun* (*literary*) an open area of land covered in grass

**leach** /liːtʃ/ *verb* (*specialist*) **1** [I] **~ (from sth) (into sth)** | **~ out/away** (of chemicals, minerals, etc.) to be removed from soil, etc. by water passing through it: *Nitrates leach from the soil into rivers.* **2** [T] **~ sth (from sth) (into sth)** | **~ sth out/away** (of a liquid) to remove chemicals, minerals, etc. from soil: *The nutrient is quickly leached away.*

**lead¹** ⚬ A2 ⓢ /liːd/ *verb, noun* ⇒ see also LEAD²
■ *verb* (**led**, **led** /led/)
• SHOW THE WAY **1** ⚬ B1 [T, I] to go with or in front of a person or an animal to show the way or to make them go in the right direction **SYN** **guide**: *If you lead, I'll follow.* ◊ **~ sb/sth + adv./prep.** *He led us out into the grounds.* ◊ *The receptionist led the way to the boardroom.* ◊ *The robbers led police on a high-speed chase through the city.* ⇒ SYNONYMS at TAKE

• CONNECT TWO THINGS **2** ⚬ A2 [I] **~ from/to sth (to/from sth)** to connect one object or place to another: *steps leading from the kitchen to the cellar* ◊ *The wire led to a speaker.*
• OF ROAD/PATH/DOOR **3** ⚬ A2 [I, T] to go in a particular direction or to a particular place: **+ adv./prep.** *A path led down the hill.* ◊ *The road led away from the house directly to the lake.* ◊ *Which door leads to the yard?* ◊ **~ sb + adv./prep.** *The track led us through a wood.* ⇒ HOMOPHONES at LEAD²
• CAUSE **4** ⚬ A2 [I] **~ to sth** to have sth as a result **SYN** **result in**: *The carbon tax will inevitably lead to an increase in energy bills.* ◊ *the events that eventually led to war* ⇒ LANGUAGE BANK at CAUSE **5** ⚬ B1 [T] to be the reason why sb does or thinks sth: **~ sb (to sth)** *What led you to this conclusion?* ◊ *He's too easily led* (= easily persuaded to do or think sth). ◊ **~ sb to do sth** *Circumstances eventually led her to train as a doctor.* ◊ *The situation is far worse than we had been led to believe.*
• BE IN CONTROL **6** ⚬ A2 [T, I] **~ (sth)** to be in control of sth; to be the leader of sth: *to lead a team/group* ◊ *Inspector Sam Roland is leading the investigation.* ◊ *Who will lead the party in the next election?* ◊ *A good manager leads by example* (= shows people how to behave by behaving in that way themselves).
• BE BEST/FIRST **7** ⚬ B1 [T, I] to be the best at sth; to be in first place: **~ (sb/sth) (in sth)** *The department led the world in cancer research.* ◊ *We lead the way in space technology.* ◊ **~ (sb/sth) by sth** *The champion is leading (her nearest rival) by 18 seconds.*
• LIFE **8** ⚬ B2 [T] **~ sth** to have a particular type of life: *We lead a very quiet life.* ◊ *to lead a life of luxury/a miserable existence*
• PROCESS **9** [T] **~ sth** to cause a process to start: *The recent economic recovery was almost entirely led by exports.*
• IN CARD GAMES **10** [I, T] to play first; to play sth as your first card: *It's your turn to lead.* ◊ **~ sth** *to lead the ten of clubs*

**IDM** **lead sb a'stray** to make sb go in the wrong direction or do things they are wrong: *Jack's parents thought the other boys might lead him astray.* **lead sb by the 'nose** (*informal*) to make sb do everything you want; to control sb completely **lead the 'charge** to be the first to make the effort to do sth new **lead sb a (merry) 'dance** (*BrE, informal*) to cause sb a lot of trouble or worry **lead from the 'front** to take an active part in what you are telling or persuading others to do **lead (sb) 'nowhere** to have no successful result for sb: *This discussion is leading us nowhere.* **lead sb up/down the garden 'path** (*informal*) to make sb believe sth that is not true **SYN** **mislead** ⇒ more at BLIND *adj.*, HORSE *n.*, LIFE, THING

**PHRV** **lead 'off (from) sth** to start at a place and go away from it: *narrow streets leading off from the main square* **lead 'off** | **lead sth↔'off** to start sth: *Who would like to lead off the debate?* **lead sb 'on** (*informal*) to make sb believe sth that is not true, especially that you love them or find them attractive **lead 'up to sth** to be an introduction to or the cause of sth: *the weeks leading up to the exam* ◊ *the events leading up to the strike* **lead with sth 1** (of a newspaper) to have sth as the main item of news **2** (in boxing) to use a particular hand to begin an attack: *to lead with your right/left*

■ *noun*
• FIRST PLACE **1** ⚬ B1 **the lead** [sing.] the position ahead of everyone else in a race or competition: *She took the lead in the second lap.* ◊ *to hold (onto)/regain the lead* ◊ **in the ~** *The Democrats now appear to be in the lead.* ◊ **into the ~** *He has gone into the lead.* ◊ *The lead car is now three minutes ahead of the rest of the field.* **2** ⚬ B2 [sing.] **~ (over sb/sth)** the amount or distance that sb/sth is in front of sb/sth else **SYN** **advantage**: *a commanding/comfortable lead* ◊ *to extend/stretch/double/increase your lead* ◊ **~ of sth** *Labour have taken a lead of five points in the polls.* ◊ **~ (of sth) over sb/sth** *He managed to hold a lead of two seconds over his closest rival.*
• EXAMPLE **3** [sing.] an example or action for people to copy: *If one bank raises interest rates, all the others will follow their lead.* ◊ *If we take the lead in this* (= start to act), *others may follow.* ◊ *You go first, I'll take my lead from you.*

- INFORMATION **4** [C] a piece of information that may help to find out the truth or facts about a situation, especially a crime SYN **clue**: *The police will follow up all possible leads.*
- IN BUSINESS **5** [C] a person or thing that may be useful to you, especially a possible new customer or business opportunity: *The marketing campaign generated hundreds of new leads.*
- ACTOR/MUSICIAN **6** [C] the main part in a play, film, etc.; the person who plays this part: *Who is playing the lead?* ◊ *the male/female lead* ◊ *a lead role* ◊ *the lead singer in a band* ◊ *He played lead guitar on a number of tracks.*
- PERSON IN CHARGE **7** [C] the person in charge of a project, department, etc: *Sam is the lead on this project.* ◊ *Sarah Montague will become the lead presenter of the show from next month.*
- NEWS **8** [C] (*US*) = LEDE
- FOR DOG **9** (*BrE*) (*also* **leash** *especially in NAmE*) [C] a long piece of leather, chain or rope used for holding and controlling a dog: *on a~* *Dogs must be kept on a lead in the park.*
- FOR ELECTRICITY **10** [C] (*BrE*) a long piece of wire, usually covered in plastic, that is used to connect a piece of electrical equipment to a source of electricity ⇨ see also EXTENSION LEAD, JUMP LEAD IDM see BURY

**lead²** /led/ *noun* ⇨ see also LEAD¹ **1** [U] (*symb.* **Pb**) a chemical element. Lead is a heavy, soft grey metal, used especially in the past for water pipes or to cover roofs. **2** [C, U] the thin black part of a pencil that marks paper
IDM **go ˌdown like a ˌlead baˈlloon** (*informal*) to be very unsuccessful; to not be accepted by people ⇨ more at SWING *v.*

▼ HOMOPHONES

**lead • led** /led/
- **lead** *noun: Copper piping replaced the use of lead.*
- **led** *verb* (*past tense, past participle of* LEAD¹): *The staircase led to a secret passageway.*

**leadˑed** /ˈledɪd/ *adj.* [usually before noun] **1** (of petrol, metal, etc.) with lead added to it OPP **unleaded** **2** with a cover or a frame of lead: *a leaded roof*

**leadˑen** /ˈledn/ *adj.* (*literary*) **1** dark grey in colour like LEAD: *leaden skies* **2** heavy or slow: *a leaden heart* (= because you are sad)

**leadˑer** ❶ A2 W /ˈliːdə(r)/ *noun* **1** A2 a person who leads a group of people, especially the head of a country, an organization, etc: *party/world leaders* ◊ *a religious/political leader* ◊ *He was elected as leader of the Democratic Party.* ◊ *She became leader of the campaign group.* ◊ *Union leaders agreed to begin talks with the government.* ◊ *Tomorrow the President will meet with business leaders.* ⇨ see also MAJORITY LEADER, MINORITY LEADER, SQUADRON LEADER, THOUGHT LEADER **2** B1 a person or thing that is the best, or in first place in a race, business, etc: *She was among the leaders of the race from the start.* ◊ *The company has emerged as a world leader in the field of precision engineering.* ⇨ see also LOSS-LEADER, MARKET LEADER **3** (*BrE*) (*also* **conˑcertˑmaster** *especially in NAmE*) the most important VIOLIN player in an ORCHESTRA **4** (*BrE*) = EDITORIAL

**ˈleader ˌboard** *noun* a sign showing the names and current scores of the top players in a competition

**leadˑerˑless** /ˈliːdələs; *NAmE* -dərl-/ *adj.* without a leader: *Her sudden death left the party leaderless.*

**leadˑerˑship** ❶ B2 W /ˈliːdəʃɪp; *NAmE* -dərʃ-/ *noun* **1** B1 [U] the state or position of being a leader: *a leadership role/position* ◊ *a leadership contest* ◊ *the battle for the party leadership* ◊ *under sb's~* *The party thrived under his leadership.* **2** B2 [U] the ability to be a leader or the qualities a good leader should have: *Strong leadership is needed to captain the team.* ◊ *leadership qualities/skills* ⇨ see also THOUGHT LEADERSHIP **3** [C + sing./pl. v.] a group of leaders of a particular organization, etc: *The party leadership is/are divided.*

891

# leafy

**lead-free** /ˌled ˈfriː/ *adj.* (of petrol, paint, etc.) without any of the metal LEAD added to it

**ˌlead guˈitar** /ˌliːd ɡɪˈtɑː(r)/ *noun* [U] a guitar style that consists mainly of SOLOS and tunes rather than only CHORDS ⇨ compare RHYTHM GUITAR

**lead-in** /ˈliːd ɪn/ *noun* an introduction to a subject, story, show, etc.

**leadˑing** ❶ B1 /ˈliːdɪŋ/ *adj.* [only before noun] **1** B1 most important or most successful: *a leading expert/authority/figure/member* ◊ *She was offered the leading role in the new TV series.* ◊ *The leading causes of death are heart disease and cancer.* **2** B1 ahead of others in a race or contest: *She started the last lap just behind the leading group.* ◊ *These are the leading first-round scores.*

**ˌleading ˈarticle** (*also* **lead-er**) *noun* (*both BrE*) = EDITORIAL

**ˌleading ˈedge** *noun* **1** [sing.] the most important and advanced position in an area of activity, especially technology: *at the leading edge of scientific research* **2** [C] (*specialist*) the front or forward edge of sth moving, especially an aircraft wing ▸ **ˌleading-ˈedge** *adj.* [only before noun] SYN **cutting-edge**: *leading-edge technology*

**ˌleading ˈlady, ˌleading ˈman** *noun* the actor with the main female or male part in a play or film

**ˌleading ˈlight** *noun* an important, active or respected person in a particular area of activity: *She's one of the leading lights in the opera world.*

**ˌleading ˈquestion** *noun* a question that you ask in a particular way in order to get the answer you want

**lead-off** /ˈliːd ɒf; *NAmE* ɔːf/ *adj.* (*NAmE*) being the first of a series: *the lead-off track on the album*

**ˈlead shot** /ˌled ˈʃɒt; *NAmE* ˈʃɑːt/ *noun* = SHOT (8)

**ˈlead story** /ˌliːd ˈstɔːri/ *noun* the main or first item of news in a newspaper, magazine or news broadcast

**ˈlead time** /ˈliːd taɪm/ *noun* the time between starting and completing a production process; the time between placing an order and the item being delivered ⇨ WORDFINDER NOTE at INDUSTRY

**leaf** ❶ B1 /liːf/ *noun, verb*
■ *noun* (*pl.* **leaves** /liːvz/) **1** B1 [C] a flat green part of a plant, growing from a STEM or branch or from the root: *lettuce/cabbage/oak leaves* ◊ *the dead leaves of autumn/the fall* ◊ *Few trees are in leaf yet.* ◊ *The trees are just coming into leaf.* ⇨ see also BAY LEAF, CURRY LEAF, FIG LEAF, MAPLE LEAF, TEA LEAF ⇨ VISUAL VOCAB page V6 **2 -leaf, -leafed, -leaved** (in adjectives) having leaves of the type or number mentioned: *a four-leaf clover* ◊ *a broad-leaved plant* **3** [C] a sheet of paper, especially a page in a book ⇨ see also LOOSE-LEAF, OVERLEAF **4** [U] metal, especially gold or silver, in the form of very thin sheets: *gold leaf* **5** [C] a part of a table that can be lifted up, or an extra section that can be added into the table, in order to make the table bigger
IDM **take a ˈleaf from/out of sb's ˈbook** to copy sb's behaviour and do things in the same way that they do, because they are successful SYN **emulate** ⇨ more at NEW
■ *verb*
PHRV **ˈleaf through sth** to quickly turn over the pages of a book, etc. without reading them or looking at them carefully

**leaf-less** /ˈliːfləs/ *adj.* having no leaves SYN **bare**

**leaf-let** B1+ B2 /ˈliːflət/ *noun, verb*
■ *noun* B1+ B2 a printed sheet of paper or a few printed pages that are given free to advertise or give information about sth SYN **booklet, pamphlet**: *a leaflet on local places of interest* ⇨ WORDFINDER NOTE at ADVERTISE
■ *verb* [I, T] ~ **(sb/sth)** to give out leaflets to people: *We did a lot of leafleting in the area.*

**ˈleaf mould** (*BrE*) (*NAmE* **ˈleaf mold**) *noun* [U] soil consisting mostly of dead, DECAYING leaves

**leafy** /ˈliːfi/ *adj.* (**leaf·ier, leafi·est**) **1** having a lot of leaves: *Eat plenty of leafy green vegetables.* **2** (*approving*) (of a

# league

place) having a lot of trees and plants and therefore considered an attractive place to live: *leafy suburbs* **3** made by a lot of leaves or trees: *We sat in the leafy shade of an oak tree.*

**league** ⬤ B2 /liːɡ/ *noun* **1** ⬥ B2 a group of sports teams who all play each other to earn points and find which team is best: *Castleford have led the league for most of the season.* ◇ *a league match/game* ◇ **in a~** *the best team in the league* ⊃ see also BIG LEAGUE, LITTLE LEAGUE, MAJOR LEAGUE, MINOR LEAGUE, PREMIER LEAGUE, RUGBY LEAGUE **2** (*informal*) a level of quality, ability, etc: **in a~** *As a painter, he is in a league of his own* (= much better than others). ◇ *They're in a different league from us.* ◇ **not in sb's~** *When it comes to cooking, I'm not in her league* (= she is much better than me). ◇ **out of sb's~** *A house like that is out of our league* (= too expensive for us). ⊃ see also IVY LEAGUE **3** a group of people or nations who have combined for a particular purpose SYN **alliance**: *the League of Nations* ◇ *a meeting of the Women's League for Peace* **4** (*old use*) a unit for measuring distance, equal to about 3 miles or 4000 metres
IDM **in ˈleague (with sb)** making secret plans with sb

ˈleague table *noun* **1** (*BrE*) a table that shows the position of sports teams and how successfully they are performing in a competition SYN **standings 2** (*especially BrE*) a table that shows how well institutions such as schools or hospitals are performing in comparison with each other

**leak** ⬥ C1 /liːk/ *verb, noun*
▪ *verb* **1** ⬥ C1 [I, T] to allow liquid or gas to get in or out through a small hole: *a leaking pipe* ◇ *The roof was leaking.* ◇ **~sth** *The tank had leaked a small amount of water.* **2** ⬥ C1 [I] (of a liquid or gas) to get in or out through a small hole in sth: *Water had started to leak into the cellar.* **3** ⬥ C1 [T] **~sth (to sb)** to give secret information to the public, for example by telling a newspaper SYN **disclose**: *The contents of the report were leaked to the press.* ◇ *a leaked document*
PHRV **ˌleak ˈout** (of secret information) to become known to the public: *Details of the plan soon leaked out.*
▪ *noun* **1** ⬥ C1 a small hole that lets liquid or gas flow in or out of sth by accident: *a leak in the roof* ◇ *a leak in the gas pipe* **2** ⬥ C1 liquid or gas that escapes through a hole in sth: *a gas leak* ◇ *oil leaks/leaks of oil* **3** ⬥ C1 a deliberate act of giving secret information to the newspapers, etc: *a leak to the press about the government plans on tax* **4** (*slang*) an act of passing URINE from the body: **to have/take a leak** IDM see SPRING v.

**leak·age** /ˈliːkɪdʒ/ *noun* [C, U] an amount of liquid or gas escaping through a hole in sth; an occasion when there is a leak: *a leakage of toxic waste into the sea* ◇ *Check bottles for leakage before use.*

**leaky** /ˈliːki/ *adj.* having holes that allow liquid or gas to escape: *a leaky roof*

**lean** ⬤ B2 /liːn/ *verb, adj., noun*
▪ *verb* (**leaned, leaned**) (*BrE also* **leant, leant** /lent/) **1** ⬥ B2 [I] **~(+ adv./prep.)** to bend or move from a straight position to a sloping position: *I leaned back in my chair.* ◇ *A man was leaning out of the window.* ◇ *The tower is leaning dangerously.* **2** ⬥ B2 [I] to rest on or against sth for support: **~against sth** *A shovel was leaning against the wall.* ◇ **~on sth** *The old man was leaning heavily on a stick.* **3** ⬥ B2 [T] to make sth rest against sth in a sloping position: **~sth against sth** *Can I lean my bike against the wall?* ◇ **~sth on sth** *He leaned his elbows on the table and sighed.* IDM see BACKWARDS
PHRV **ˈlean on sb/sth 1** to depend on sb/sth for help and support SYN **rely**: *He leans heavily on his family.* **2** to try to influence sb by threatening them: *The government has been leaning on the TV company not to broadcast the show.*
**ˈlean to/towards/toward sth** to tend to prefer sth, especially a particular opinion or interest: *The UK leant towards the US proposal.*
▪ *adj.* (**lean·er, lean·est**) **1** (*usually approving*) (of people, especially men, or animals) without much fat; thin and fit: *a lean, muscular body* ◇ *He was tall, lean and hand-*

some. **2** (of meat) containing little or no fat **3** [*usually before noun*] (of a period of time) difficult and not producing much money, food, etc: *a lean period/spell* ◇ *The company recovered well after going through several lean years.* **4** (of organizations, etc.) strong and efficient because they avoid waste in their processes and do not have more employees than is necessary: *The changes made the company leaner and more competitive.* ▶ **lean·ness** /ˈliːnnəs/ *noun* [U]
▪ *noun* [U] the part of meat that has little or no fat

**lean·ing** /ˈliːnɪŋ/ *noun* [usually pl.] **~(toward(s) sth)** a feeling that makes you tend to prefer sth or to believe in particular ideas, opinions, etc. SYN **inclination, tendency**: *a leaning towards comedy rather than tragedy* ◇ *a person with socialist leanings*

**lean-to** /ˈliːn tuː/ *noun* (*pl.* **-tos**) a small building with its roof leaning against the side of a large building, wall or fence: *a lean-to garage*

**leap** ⬥ C1 /liːp/ *verb, noun*
▪ *verb* (**leapt, leapt** /lept/ *especially in BrE or* **leaped, leaped** *especially in NAmE*) **1** ⬥ C1 [I, T] to jump high or a long way: **+ adv./prep.** *A dolphin leapt out of the water.* ◇ *We leaped over the stream.* ◇ **~sth** *The horse leapt a five-foot wall.* **2** ⬥ C1 [I] **+ adv./prep.** to move or do sth suddenly and quickly: *She leapt out of bed.* ◇ *He leaped across the room to answer the door.* ◇ *I leapt to my feet* (= stood up quickly). ◇ *They leapt into action immediately.* ◇ (*figurative*) *She was quick to leap to my defence* (= speak in support of me). ◇ *The photo seemed to leap off the page* (= it got your attention immediately). ◇ *His name leapt out at me* (= I saw it immediately). **3** ⬥ C1 [I] **~(in sth) (from …) (to …)** to increase suddenly and by a large amount SYN **shoot up**: *The shares leapt in value from 476p to close at 536p.*
IDM **ˌlook before you ˈleap** (*saying*) used to advise sb to think about the possible results or dangers of sth before doing it ⊃ more at CONCLUSION, HEART *n.*
PHRV **ˈleap at sth** to accept a chance or an opportunity quickly and with enthusiasm SYN **jump at**: *I leapt at the chance to go to France.*
▪ *noun* **1** ⬥ C1 a long or high jump: *a leap of six metres* ◇ *She took a flying leap and landed on the other side of the stream.* ◇ (*figurative*) *His heart gave a sudden leap when he saw her.* **2** ⬥ C1 a sudden large increase in sth: *a leap in profits* **3** ⬥ C1 **~ + adv./prep.** a sudden change from one thing to another; very fast progress with sth: *Few people successfully make the leap from television to the movies.* ⊃ see also QUANTUM LEAP
IDM **by/in ˌleaps and ˈbounds** very quickly; in large amounts: *Her health has improved in leaps and bounds.* **a ˌleap in the ˈdark** an action or a risk that you take without knowing anything about the activity or what the result will be **a leap of ˈfaith** a belief in sth that is not known or has not been done before: *These reforms are totally untested and will require a leap of faith on the part of teachers.*

**leap·frog** /ˈliːpfrɒɡ; *NAmE* -frɔːɡ/ *noun, verb*

leapfrog

▪ *noun* [U] a children's game in which players take turns to jump over the backs of other players who are bending down
▪ *verb* (**-gg-**) [T, I] **~(sb/sth)** to get to a higher position or rank by going past sb else or by missing out some stages: *The win allowed them to leapfrog three teams to gain second place.*

ˈleap year *noun* one year in every four years when February has 29 days instead of 28

**learn** ⬤ A1 S /lɜːn; *NAmE* lɜːrn/ *verb* (**learned, learned** *or* **learnt, learnt** /lɜːnt; *NAmE* lɜːrnt/ *especially in BrE*) **1** ⬥ A1 [T, I] to gain knowledge or skill by studying, from experience, from being taught, etc: **~sth** *to learn a language/skill/trade* ◇ **~(sth) from sb/sth** *I learned a lot from* my father. ◊ **~ (sth) from doing sth** *You can learn a great deal just from watching other players.* ◊ **~ (about sth)** *She's very keen to learn about Japanese culture.* ◊ *The book is about how children learn.* ◊ **~ to do sth** *He's learning to play the trumpet.* ◊ **~ how to do sth** *Today we learnt how to use the new software.* ◊ **~ what, where, etc…** *Students need to learn what to do in an emergency.* **2** [T] **~ sth** to study and repeat sth in order to be able to remember it SYN **memorize**: *I learnt the poem by heart.* **3** [I, T] to gradually change your attitudes about sth so that you behave in a different way: **~ (from sth)** *I'm sure she'll learn from her mistakes.* ◊ **~ (that)…** *He'll just have to learn (that) he can't always have his own way.* ◊ **~ to do sth** *They soon learned to love living in the countryside.* **4** [I, T] to become aware of sth by hearing about it from sb else SYN **discover**: **~ of/about sth** *I first learnt of his death many years later.* ◊ **~ (that)…** *We were very surprised to learn (that) she had got married again.* ◊ **~ who, what, etc…** *We only learned who the new teacher was a few days ago.* ◊ **~ sth** *How did they react when they learned the news?* ◊ **it is learned that…** *It has been learned that 500 jobs are to be lost at the factory.*

IDM **learn (sth) the ˈhard way** to find out how to behave by learning from your mistakes or from unpleasant experiences, rather than from being told **learn your ˈlesson** to learn what to do or not to do in the future because you have had a bad experience in the past ⇒ more at COST n., LIVE¹, ROPE n.

▼ **VOCABULARY BUILDING**

**Learning**
- **learn**: *He's learning Spanish/to swim.*
- **study**: *She studied chemistry for three years.*
- **revise** (*BrE*) (*NAmE* **review**): *In this class we'll revise/review what we did last week.*
- **practise** (*BrE*) (*NAmE* **practice**): *If you practise speaking English, you'll soon improve.*
- **rehearse**: *We only had two weeks to rehearse the play.*

**learn·ed** /ˈlɜːnɪd; *NAmE* ˈlɜːrn-/ *adj.* [usually before noun] **1** (*formal*) having a lot of knowledge because you have studied and read a lot: *a learned professor* ◊ see also FRIEND noun (6) **2** (*formal*) connected with or for people who have a lot of knowledge; showing and expressing deep knowledge SYN **scholarly**: *a learned journal* **3** /lɜːnd; *NAmE* lɜːrnd/ developed by training or experience; not existing at birth: *a learned skill*

**learn·er** /ˈlɜːnə(r); *NAmE* ˈlɜːrn-/ *noun* **1** a person who is finding out about a subject or how to do sth: *a slow/quick learner* ◊ *a dictionary for learners of English* ◊ *learner-centred teaching methods* **2** (*BrE also* **learner ˈdriver**) a person who is learning to drive a car: *Learners are not allowed to drive without a licensed driver in the vehicle.*

**ˈlearner's permit** (*NAmE*) (*BrE* **proˈvisional ˈlicence**) *noun* an official document that you must have when you start to learn to drive

**learn·ing** /ˈlɜːnɪŋ; *NAmE* ˈlɜːrn-/ *noun* **1** [U] the process of learning sth: *lifelong/adult learning* ◊ *new methods to facilitate language learning* ◊ *a supportive learning environment* ◊ *Last season was a learning experience for the team.* ⇒ see also BLENDED LEARNING, DISTANCE LEARNING, E-LEARNING, MACHINE LEARNING, PROGRAMMED LEARNING **2** [U] knowledge that you get from reading and studying: *a woman of great learning* ⇒ see also BOOK LEARNING **3** [C] something that you learn, especially from your experience of working on sth: *We will be sharing key learnings from our project.*

**ˈlearning curve** *noun* the rate at which you learn a new subject or a new skill; the process of learning from the mistakes you make

**ˈlearning difficulties** *noun* [pl.] (*BrE*) mental problems that people may have from birth, or that may be caused by illness or injury, that affect their ability to learn things HELP The phrase **learning difficulties** is the standard term in British official contexts to talk about people who have difficulty learning because of a mental condition. The standard term in North America is **learning disability**.

893

**ˈlearning disability** *noun* [usually pl.] a mental problem that people may have from birth, or that may be caused by illness or injury, that affects their ability to learn things

**lease** /liːs/ *noun, verb*
■ *noun* a legal agreement that allows you to use a building, a piece of equipment or some land for a period of time, usually in return for rent: *to take out a lease on a house* ◊ *The lease expires/runs out next year.* ◊ *Under the terms of the lease, you have to pay maintenance charges.* ⇒ WORDFINDER NOTE at HOME
IDM **a (ˈnew) lease of ˈlife** (*BrE*) (*NAmE* **a (ˈnew) lease on ˈlife**) the chance to live or last longer, or with a better quality of life: *Since her hip operation she's had a new lease of life.*
■ *verb* to use or let sb use sth, especially property or equipment, in exchange for rent or a regular payment SYN **rent**: **~ sth** *We lease all our computer equipment.* ◊ **~ sth from sb** *They lease the land from a local farmer.* ◊ **~ sb sth** *A local farmer leased them the land.* ◊ **~ sth (out) (to sb)** *Parts of the building are leased out to tenants.*
▶ **leas·ing** *noun* [U]: *car leasing* ◊ *a leasing company*

**lease-back** /ˈliːsbæk/ *noun* [U] (*law*) the process of allowing the former owner of a property to continue to use it if they pay rent to the new owner; a legal agreement where this happens

**lease·hold** /ˈliːshəʊld/ *adj., noun*
■ *adj.* (*especially BrE*) (of property or land) that can be used for a limited period of time, according to the arrangements in a LEASE: *a leasehold property* ⇒ compare FREEHOLD ▶ **lease·hold** *adv.*: *to purchase land leasehold* ⇒ compare FREEHOLD
■ *noun* [U] (*especially BrE*) the right to use a building or a piece of land according to the arrangements in a LEASE: *to obtain/own the leasehold of a house* ⇒ compare FREEHOLD

**lease·hold·er** /ˈliːshəʊldə(r)/ *noun* (*especially BrE*) a person who is allowed to use a building or a piece of land according to the arrangements in a LEASE ⇒ compare FREEHOLDER

**leash** /liːʃ/ *noun, verb*
■ *noun* (*especially NAmE*) (*BrE usually* **lead**) a long piece of leather, chain or rope used for holding and controlling a dog: **on a ~** *All dogs must be kept on a leash in public places.* IDM see STRAIN v.
■ *verb* **~ sth** to control an animal, especially a dog, with a LEASH

**least** /liːst/ *det., pron., adv.*
■ *det., pron.* usually **the least** smallest in size, amount, degree, etc: *He's the best teacher, even though he has the least experience.* ◊ *She never had the least idea what to do about it.* ◊ *He gave (the) least of all towards the wedding present.* ◊ **the ~ of sth** *How others see me is the least of my worries* (= I have more important things to worry about). ◊ *It's the least I can do to help* (= I feel I should do more).
IDM **at the (very) ˈleast** used after amounts to show that the amount is the lowest possible: *It'll take a year, at the very least.* **ˌnot in the ˈleast** not at all: *Really, I'm not in the least tired.* ◊ *'Do you mind if I put the television on?' 'No, not in the least.'* ⇒ more at BIT, SAY v.
■ *adv.* to the smallest degree: *He always turns up just when you least expect him.* ◊ *She chose the least expensive of the hotels.* ◊ *I never hid the truth, least of all from you.* ◊ *We had to settle for the least worst option* (= the best of several options that were all bad).
IDM **at ˈleast 1** not less than: *It'll cost at least 500 dollars.* ◊ *She must be at least 40.* ◊ *Cut the grass at least once a week in summer.* ◊ *I've known her at least as long as you have.* **2** used to add a positive comment about a negative situation: *She may be slow but at least she's reliable.* **3** even if nothing else is true or you do nothing else: *You could at least listen to what he says.* ◊ *Well, at least they weren't bored.* **4** used to limit or make what you have just said less definite SYN **anyway**: *They seldom complained—officially at least.* ◊ *It works, at least I think it does.* **ˌnot ˈleast** especially: *The documentary caused a lot*

# leather

of bad feeling, not least among the workers whose lives it described. ⮕ more at LAST¹ adv., RESISTANCE, SAY v.

**least common de·nominator** noun (NAmE) = LOWEST COMMON DENOMINATOR

**least common multiple** noun (NAmE) = LOWEST COMMON MULTIPLE

**lea·ther** ⓘ B1 /ˈleðə(r)/ noun 1 B1 [U] material made by removing the hair or fur from animal skins and preserving the skins using special processes: *a leather jacket* ◊ *The soles are made of leather.* ◊ *a leather-bound book* ⮕ see also CHAMOIS (2), PATENT LEATHER, PLEATHER 2 **leathers** [pl.] clothes made from leather, especially those worn by people riding motorcycles IDM see HELL

**lea·ther·back** /ˈleðəbæk/ NAmE -ðərb-/ (also **leatherback 'turtle**, **leathery 'turtle**) noun a very large sea TURTLE with a shell that looks like leather

**lea·ther·ette** /ˌleðəˈret/ noun [U] an artificial material that looks and feels like leather

**lea·thery** /ˈleðəri/ adj. that looks or feels hard and tough like leather: *leathery skin*

**leave** ⓘ A1 /liːv/ verb, noun

■ verb (**left**, **left** /left/)
- **PLACE/PERSON 1** 🔊 A1 [I, T] to go away from a person or a place: *Come on, it's time we left* (= time for us to leave). ◊ ~ **for sth** *The plane leaves for Dallas at 12.35.* ◊ ~ **sth** *The plane leaves Heathrow at 12.35.* ◊ *I hate leaving home.*
- **HOME/JOB/SCHOOL 2** 🔊 A1 [I, T] to stop living at a place, belonging to a group, working for an employer, etc: *My assistant is threatening to leave.* ◊ ~ **sth** *He didn't leave home until he was 30.* ◊ ~ **sth** *People leave for better-paid jobs elsewhere.* ◊ ~ **sth for sth** *Many of her relatives had left Ireland for America.*
- **PARTNER 3** 🔊 A1 [I, T] to leave your wife, husband or partner permanently: *I was afraid you'd leave if you knew the truth.* ◊ ~ **sb** *I'll never leave you.* ◊ ~ **sb for sb** *She left him for a colleague.*
- **SB/STH IN PLACE/CONDITION 4** 🔊 A2 [T] to go away from a place without taking sth/sb with you: ~ **sth/sb** *I'll have to go back—I've left my jacket.* ◊ ~ **sth + adv./prep.** *I've left my bag on the bus.* ◊ ~ **sth/sb behind** *He wasn't well, so we had to leave him behind.* **5** 🔊 B1 [T] to make or allow sb/sth to remain in a particular condition, place, etc: ~ **sb/sth + adj.** *Leave the door open, please.* ◊ *The bomb blast left 25 people dead.* ◊ ~ **sb/sth doing sth** *Don't leave her waiting outside in the rain.* ◊ ~ **sth/sb to do sth** *Leave the rice to cook for 20 minutes.* ◊ ~ **sth** *He ate up his vegetables but left the chicken.* **6** 🔊 B1 **be left** [T] to remain to be used, sold, etc: *Is there any coffee left?* ◊ *You still have a few minutes left.* ◊ **be left to sb** *The only course of action left to me was to notify her employer.* **7** 🔊 B2 [T] to make sth happen or remain as a result: ~ **sth** *Red wine leaves a stain.* ◊ **to leave room/space for sth** ◊ ~ **sb with sth** *She left me with the impression that she was unhappy.* ◊ ~ **sb sth** *I'm afraid you leave me no choice.*
- **DELIVER 8** 🔊 B1 [T] to deliver, write or record sth to be seen or heard later: ~ **sth** *Lots of people had left comments under the post.* ◊ ~ **sth for sb** *Someone left this note for you.* ◊ ~ **sb sth** *Someone left you this note.*
- **STH TO DO LATER 9** 🔊 B1 [T] to not do sth or deal with sth immediately: ~ **sth** *Leave the dishes—I'll do them later.* ◊ ~ **sth until/till sth** *Why do you always leave everything until the last moment?* ◊ ~ **sth for sth** *Let's leave that topic for another day.*
- **RESPONSIBILITY TO SB 10** 🔊 B1 [T] to allow sb to take care of sth: ~ **sth to sb/sth** *You can leave the cooking to me.* ◊ *They didn't leave anything to chance* (= everything was planned carefully). ◊ ~ **it (up) to sb (to do sth)** *'Where shall we eat?' 'I'll leave it entirely (up) to you* (= you can decide).' ◊ ~ **sb + adv./prep.** *She left her assistant in charge.* ◊ ~ **sth with sb** *Leave it with me—I'm sure I can sort it out.* ◊ ~ **sb with sth** *They left me with all the clearing up.* ◊ ~ **sb/sth to do sth** *Can I leave you to lock up the shop?*
- **AFTER DEATH 11** 🔊 B2 [T] to give sth to sb when you die SYN **bequeath**: ~ **sth (to sb)** *She left £1 million to her daughter.* ◊ ~ **sb sth** *She left her daughter £1 million.* **12** [T] ~ **sb** to have family who continue to live after your death: *He leaves a wife and two children.*
- **MATHEMATICS 13** [T] ~ **sth** to have a particular amount left over: *Seven from ten leaves three.*

IDM HELP Most idioms containing **leave** are at the entries for the nouns and adjectives in the idioms, for example **leave sb in the lurch** is at **lurch**. **be left to yourself** 1 to be alone: *I didn't know anyone in New York, so I was left to myself to explore.* 2 to be allowed to do what you want: *Left to himself, the dog will eat anything and everything.* **leave sb 'be** (*informal*) to stop annoying sb or trying to get their attention SYN **leave/let sb alone**: *Why can't you stop texting me and just leave me be?* **leave 'go (of sth)** (*BrE, informal*) to stop holding on to sth SYN **let go**: *Let go of my arm—you're hurting me!* **leave it at 'that** (*informal*) to say or do nothing more about sth: *We'll never agree, so let's just leave it at that.* **leave it 'out** (*BrE, informal*) used to tell sb to stop doing sth ⮕ more at TAKE *v.*

PHR V **leave sth↔a'side** to not consider sth: *Leaving the expense aside, do we actually need a second car?* **leave sb/sth be'hind** 1 [*usually passive*] to make much better progress than sb: *Britain is being left behind in the race for new markets.* 2 to leave a person, place or state permanently: *She knew that she had left childhood behind.* ⮕ see also LEAVE *verb*, **leave 'off** (*informal*) to stop doing sth: *Start reading from where you left off last time.* ◊ **leave off doing sth** *He left off playing the piano to answer the door.* **leave sb/sth↔'off (sth)** to not include sb/sth on a list, etc: *You've left off a zero.* ◊ *We left him off the list.* **leave sb/sth 'out (of sth)** 🔊 B1 to not include or mention sb/sth in sth: *Leave me out of this quarrel, please.* ◊ *He hadn't been asked to the party and was feeling very left out.* ◊ *She left out an 'm' in 'accommodation'.* **be left 'over (from sth)** to remain when all that is needed has been used: *There was lots of food left over.* ⮕ related noun LEFTOVER

■ noun [U] 1 🔊 B2 a period of time when you are allowed to be away from work for a holiday or for a special reason: *to take a month's paid/unpaid leave* ◊ *How much annual leave do you get?* ◊ **on** ~ *soldiers home on leave* ⮕ see also COMPASSIONATE LEAVE, FAMILY LEAVE, MATERNITY LEAVE, PARENTAL LEAVE, PATERNITY LEAVE, SICK LEAVE 2 (*formal*) official permission to do sth: **without**~ *to be absent without leave* ◊ ~ **to do sth** *The court granted him leave to appeal against the sentence.* ◊ *She asked for leave of absence* (= permission to be away from work) *to attend a funeral.*

IDM **by/with your 'leave** (*formal*) with your permission **take (your) 'leave (of sb)** (*formal*) to say goodbye: *With a nod and a smile, she took leave of her friends.* **take leave of your 'senses** (*old-fashioned*) to start behaving as if you are crazy **without a by your 'leave; without so much as a by your 'leave** (*old-fashioned*) without asking permission; rudely ⮕ more at BEG

**-leaved** /liːvd/ ⮕ LEAF *noun*

**leaven** /ˈlevn/ noun, verb

■ noun [U] a substance, especially YEAST, that is added to bread before it is cooked to make it rise: (*figurative*) *A few jokes add leaven to a boring speech.*
■ verb [*often passive*] (*formal*) to make sth more interesting or cheerful by adding sth to it: **be leavened (with sth)** *Her speech was leavened with a touch of humour.*

**leav·er** /ˈliːvə(r)/ noun 1 (often in compounds) a person who is leaving a place: *school-leavers* 2 **Leaver** (*BrE*) a person believing that the UK should leave the European Union and so supporting BREXIT SYN **Brexiteer** OPP **Remainer**

**leaves** /liːvz/ pl. of LEAF

**'leave-taking** noun [U, C, *usually sing.*] (*formal*) the act of saying goodbye SYN **farewell**

**leav·ings** /ˈliːvɪŋz/ noun [pl.] something that you leave because you do not want it, especially food

**lech** /letʃ/ noun, verb (*BrE, informal, disapproving*)

■ noun a LECHER

■ *verb* [I] + *adv./prep.* to show an unpleasant sexual interest in sb: *to lech after/over sb*

**lech·er** /'letʃə(r)/ *noun* (*disapproving*) a man who shows an unpleasant sexual interest in sb ▶ **lech·ery** *noun* [U]

**lech·er·ous** /'letʃərəs/ *adj.* (*disapproving*) showing an unpleasant sexual interest in sb SYN **lascivious, lustful**

**leci·thin** /'lesɪθɪn/ *noun* [U] a natural substance found in animals, plants and in egg YOLKS. Lecithin is used as an ingredient in some foods.

**lec·tern** /'lektən; NAmE -tərn/ (*NAmE also* **po·dium**) *noun* a stand for holding a book, notes, computer, etc. when you are reading in church, giving a talk, etc. ⊃ picture at PODIUM

**lec·ture** 🅐 A2 S /'lektʃə(r)/ *noun, verb*

■ *noun* **1** A2 a talk that is given to a group of people to teach them about a particular subject, often as part of a university or college course: *to go to/attend a lecture* ◊ *to give/deliver a lecture* ◊ *~ on/about sth a series of lectures on Jane Austen* ◊ *~ to sb a book based on her lectures to students* ◊ *~ by sb a lecture by Professor Snow* ⊃ SYNONYMS at SPEECH ⊃ WORDFINDER NOTE at UNIVERSITY **2** a long, angry talk that sb gives to one person or a group of people because they have done sth wrong: *I know I should stop smoking—don't give me a lecture about it.*

■ *verb* **1** A2 [I] to give a talk or a series of talks to a group of people on a subject, especially as a way of teaching in a university or college: *He has taught and lectured at the University of Pretoria.* ◊ *~ on/in sth She lectures in Russian literature.* **2** [T] *~ sb (about/on sth)* | *~ sb (about doing sth)* to criticize sb or tell them how you think they should behave, especially when it is done in an annoying way: *He's always lecturing me about the way I dress.*

**lec·tur·er** S /'lektʃərə(r)/ *noun* **1** a person who gives a lecture: *She's a superb lecturer.* **2** (*especially in the UK*) a person who teaches at a university or college: *He's a lecturer in French at Oxford.*

**lec·ture·ship** /'lektʃəʃɪp; NAmE -tʃərʃ-/ *noun* the position of lecturer at a British university or college: *a lectureship in media studies*

**'lecture theatre** (*BrE*) (*also* **'lecture hall** *BrE and NAmE*) *noun* a large room with rows of seats on a slope, where lectures are given

**LED** /ˌel iː 'diː/ *noun* light-emitting diode (a device that produces a light on electrical and electronic equipment): *A single red LED shows that the power is switched on.* ⊃ compare OLED

**led** /led/ **1** *past tense, past part.* of LEAD¹ ⊃ HOMOPHONES at LEAD² **2 -led** (in adjectives) influenced or organized by: *a consumer-led society* ◊ *student-led activities*

**lede** (*also* **lead**) /liːd/ *noun* (*both US*) the first sentence or paragraph of a news story, giving the most important points of the story: *Check out this lede from Monday's front page story.* IDM see BURY

**ledge** /ledʒ/ *noun* **1** a narrow, flat piece of rock that sticks out from a CLIFF: *seabirds nesting on rocky ledges* **2** a narrow, flat shelf fixed to a wall, especially one below a window: *She put the vase of flowers on the window ledge.* ⊃ see also SILL, WINDOW LEDGE

**ledger** /'ledʒə(r)/ *noun* a book or electronic document in which a bank, a business, etc. records the money it has paid and received: *to enter figures in the purchase/sales ledger*

**lee** /liː/ *noun* **1** [sing.] the side or part of sth that provides shelter from the wind ⊃ compare LEEWARD, WINDWARD **2 lees** [pl.] the substance that is left at the bottom of a bottle of wine, a container of beer, etc. SYN **dregs**

**leech** /liːtʃ/ *noun* **1** a small WORM that usually lives in water and that attaches itself to other creatures and drinks their blood. Leeches were used in the past by doctors to remove blood from sick people. **2** (*disapproving*) a person who depends on sb else for money, or takes the profit from sb else's work

**leek** /liːk/ *noun* a vegetable like a long onion with many layers of wide leaves that are white at the bottom and green at the top. Leeks are eaten cooked. The leek is a national symbol of Wales. ⊃ VISUAL VOCAB page V5

**leer** /lɪə(r); NAmE lɪr/ *verb, noun*

■ *verb* [I] *~ (at sb)* to look or smile at sb in an unpleasant way that shows an evil or sexual interest in them ⊃ WORDFINDER NOTE at EXPRESSION

■ *noun* an unpleasant look or smile that shows sb is interested in a person in an evil or sexual way: *He looked at her with an evil leer.*

**leery** /'lɪəri; NAmE 'lɪri/ *adj.* (*informal*) *~ (of sth/sb)* | *~ (of doing sth)* careful about sth/sb because you suspect that there may be a danger or problem, and trying to avoid doing it or dealing with them SYN **wary**: *The government is leery of changing the current law.*

**leet** /liːt/ (*also* **leetspeak** /'liːtspiːk/) *noun* [U] an informal language or a code used on the internet, often in online GAMING, in which some letters are replaced by numbers, special symbols, etc.

**lee·ward** /'liːwəd; 'luːəd; NAmE 'liːwərd; 'luːərd/ *adj., noun*

■ *adj.* on the side of sth that is sheltered from the wind: *a harbour on the leeward side of the island* ▶ **lee·ward** *adv.* ⊃ compare WINDWARD

■ *noun* [U] the side or direction that is sheltered from the wind ⊃ compare WINDWARD

**lee·way** /'liːweɪ/ *noun* [U] the amount of freedom that you have to change sth or to do sth in the way you want to SYN **latitude**: *How much leeway should parents give their children?*

IDM **make up 'leeway** (*BrE*) to get out of a bad position that you are in, especially because you have lost a lot of time

**left** 🅐 A1 /left/ *adj., adv., noun, verb*

■ *adj.* A1 [only before noun] on the side of your body that is towards the west when you are facing north: *Fewer people write with their left hand than with their right.* ◊ *your left knee/leg/foot/arm* ◊ *The university is on the left bank of the river.* ◊ *Take a left turn at the intersection.* ◊ (*sport*) *a left back/wing* OPP **right**

IDM **have two left 'feet** (*informal*) to be very AWKWARD in your movements, especially when you are dancing or playing a sport

■ *adv.* A1 on or to the left side: *Turn left at the intersection.* ◊ *Look left and right before you cross the road.* OPP **right**

IDM **left, right and 'centre** (*also* **right, left and 'centre**, **right and 'left**) (*informal*) in all directions; everywhere: *He's giving away money left, right and centre.*

■ *noun* **1** A1 **the/sb's left** [sing.] the left side or direction: *on the ~ (of sb/sth) Take the next road on the left.* ◊ *to the ~ (of sb/sth) Twist your body to the left, then to the right.* ◊ *on/to sb's ~ She was sitting on my left.* ◊ *from the ~ the figures in the second column from the left* ◊ *Arabic script is read from right to left.* ◊ *the top/bottom/far left* **2** 🅐 [sing.] **the first, second, etc. left** the first, second. road on the left side: *Take the first left.* **3 a left** [sing.] a turn to the left: *Take a left onto Route 130.* ◊ (*NAmE also*) *to make a left* ◊ (*informal*) *to hang a left* **4** 🅐 B1 **the left, the Left** [sing. + sing./pl. v.] political groups who support the ideas and beliefs of SOCIALISM; the part of a political party whose members are most in favour of social change: *The Left only has/have a small chance of winning power.* ◊ *parties of the left* ◊ *on the ~ (of sth) She is on the far left of the party.* ◊ *a left-leaning newspaper* ⊃ see also HARD LEFT **5** [C] (in boxing) a hard hit that is made with your left hand: *He hit him with two sharp lefts.* OPP **right**

■ *verb past tense, past part.* of LEAVE

**left 'brain** *noun* [U, sing.] the left side of the human brain, that is thought to be used for analysing and for processing language ⊃ compare RIGHT BRAIN

**'left-field** *adj.* (*informal*) not following what is usually done; different, surprising and interesting: *a left-field comedy drama*

**left 'field** *noun* [U] **1** (in baseball) the left part of the field, or the position played by the person who is there **2** (*informal*) an opinion or a position that is strange or unusual and a long way from the normal position: *The governor is way out/over in left field.*

**ˈleft-hand** *adj.* [only before noun] **1** on the left side of sth: *the left-hand side of the street* ◊ *the top left-hand corner of the page* **2** relating to a person's left hand: *a tennis player with a left-hand grip* ◊ *a left-hand glove* **OPP** right-hand

**ˌleft-hand ˈdrive** *adj.* (of a vehicle) with the STEERING WHEEL on the left side **OPP** right-hand drive

**ˌleft-ˈhanded** *adj.* **1** (of a person) finding it easier to use the left hand to write, hit a ball, etc. than the right: *a left-handed golfer* ◊ *I'm left-handed.* **2** (of tools, etc.) designed to be used by sb who finds it easier to use their left hand: *left-handed scissors* **3** (of actions, etc.) done with your left hand: *a left-handed serve* **OPP** right-handed ▶ **ˌleft-ˈhanded** *adv.*: *She writes left-handed.* **ˌleft-ˈhanded·ness** *noun* [U] **IDM** see BACKHANDED

**ˌleft-ˈhander** *noun* a person who finds it easier to use their left hand to write, etc. with than their right **OPP** right-hander

**leftie** = LEFTY

**left·ist** /ˈleftɪst/ *noun* a person who supports LEFT-WING political parties and their ideas **OPP** right-wing ▶ **left·ism** /ˈleftɪzəm/ *noun* [U] **left·ist** *adj.*: *leftist groups*

**left·most** /ˈleftməʊst/ *adj.* [only before noun] furthest to the left

**ˌleft-of-ˈcentre** *adj.* = CENTRE-LEFT

**left·over** /ˈleftəʊvə(r)/ *noun* **1** [usually pl.] food that has not been eaten at the end of a meal **2** an object, a custom or a way of behaving that remains from an earlier time **SYN** relic: *He's a leftover from the hippies in the 1960s.* ▶ **left·over** *adj.* [only before noun] **SYN** surplus: *Use any leftover meat to make a curry.*

**left·ward** /ˈleftwəd/; *NAmE* -wərd/ (*BrE also* **left·wards**) *adj.* [only before noun] **1** towards the left: *to move your eyes in a leftward direction* **2** towards more LEFT-WING political ideas: *a leftward swing in public opinion* **OPP** rightward ▶ **left·ward** (*BrE also* **left·wards**) *adv.*

**ˌleft-ˈwing** *adj.* strongly supporting the ideas of SOCIALISM: *left-wing groups*

**ˌleft ˈwing** *noun* **1** [sing. + sing./pl. v.] the part of a political party whose members are most in favour of social change: *on the left wing of the party* **2** [C, U] an attacking player or position on the left side of the field in a sports game

**ˌleft-ˈwinger** *noun* **1** a person on the LEFT WING of a political party: *a Labour left-winger* **2** a person who plays on the left side of the field in a sports game **OPP** right-winger

**lefty** (*also* **leftie**) /ˈlefti/ *noun* (*pl. -ies*) (*informal*) **1** (*especially BrE, sometimes disapproving*) a person who has SOCIALIST views **2** (*especially NAmE*) a person who uses their left hand to write, hit a ball, etc. ▶ **lefty** *adj.*: *a lefty feminist lecturer* ◊ *a lefty pitcher*

**leg** 🔊 **A1** /leɡ/ *noun, verb*
■ *noun*
- **PART OF BODY 1** **A1** [C] one of the long parts that connect the feet to the rest of the body: *your left/right leg* ◊ *I broke my leg playing football.* ◊ *She has a broken leg.* ◊ *The bear rose up on its hind legs.* ◊ *a wooden leg* ◊ *a leg injury* ⊃ see also BOW LEGS, DADDY-LONG-LEGS, FORELEG, INSIDE LEG, LEGGY, LEGROOM, SEA LEGS ⊃ VISUAL VOCAB page V1
- **MEAT 2** **B1** [C, U] the leg of an animal, especially the top part, cooked and eaten: *frogs' legs* ◊ *chicken legs* ◊ *~ of sth roast leg of lamb*
- **OF TROUSERS/PANTS 3** **B1** [C] the part of a pair of trousers that covers the leg: *a trouser/pant leg* ◊ *in the ~ These jeans are too long in the leg.*
- **OF TABLE/CHAIR 4** **B1** [C] one of the long thin parts on the bottom of a table, chair, etc. that support it: *a table/chair leg*
- **-LEGGED 5** /leɡd, leɡɪd/ (in adjectives) having the number or type of legs mentioned: *a three-legged stool* ◊ *a long-legged insect* **HELP** When -legged is used with numbers, it is

nearly always pronounced /leɡd/; in other adjectives it can be pronounced /leɡɪd/ or /leɡd/. ⊃ see also CROSS-LEGGED
- **OF JOURNEY/RACE 6** [C] ~ (of sth) one part of a journey or race **SYN** section, stage ⊃ see also DOG-LEG
- **SPORTS GAME 7** [C] (*BrE*) one of a pair of matches played between the same opponents in a sports competition, which together form a single round (= stage) of the competition

**IDM** **break a ˈleg!** (*informal*) used to wish sb good luck, especially to an actor before they go on stage **get your ˈleg over** (*BrE, informal*) (of a man) to have sex **have ˈlegs** (*informal*) if you say that a news story, etc. **has legs**, you mean that people will continue to be interested in it for a long time **not have a ˈleg to ˈstand on** (*informal*) to be in a position where you are unable to prove sth or explain why sth is reasonable: *Without written evidence, we don't have a leg to stand on.* ⊃ more at ARM *n.*, FAST *adv.*, LAST¹ *det.*, PULL *v.*, SHAKE *v.*, STRETCH *v.*, TAIL *n.* ⊃ see also LEG-UP

■ *verb* (-gg-)
**IDM** **ˈleg it** (*especially BrE, informal*) to run, especially in order to escape from sb: *We saw the police coming and legged it down the road.*

**leg·acy** 🔊 /ˈleɡəsi/ *noun, adj.*
■ *noun* (*pl. -ies*) **1** ⊕ **C1** money or property that is given to you by sb when they die **SYN** inheritance: *They each received a legacy of $5000.* **2** ⊕ **C1** a situation that exists now because of events, actions, etc. that took place in the past: *Future generations will be left with a legacy of pollution and destruction.*
■ *adj.* [only before noun] used to describe a computer system or product that is no longer available to buy but is still used because it would be too difficult or expensive to replace it: *How can we integrate new technology with our legacy systems?* ◊ *legacy hardware/software*

**legal** 🔊 **B1** 🆆 /ˈliːɡl/ **1** **B1** [only before noun] connected with the law: *the legal profession/system* ◊ *to take/seek legal advice* ◊ *a legal adviser/expert/team* ◊ *legal fees/costs* ◊ *They are currently facing a long legal battle in the US courts.* **2** 🔊 **B1** allowed or required by law: *legal rights/obligations* ◊ *The driver was more than three times over the legal limit* (= the amount of alcohol you are allowed to have in your body when you are driving). ◊ *Should euthanasia be made legal?* ◊ *it is ~ (for sb) to do sth It is now perfectly legal to gamble online in Nevada.* **OPP** illegal ▶ **WORDFINDER NOTE** at LAW ▶ **le·gal·ly** /-ɡəli/ *adv.*: *a legally binding agreement* ◊ *to be legally responsible for sb/sth*

**ˌlegal ˈaction** *noun* [U] (*also* **ˌlegal proˈceedings**) the act of using the legal system to settle an argument, etc: *to take/begin legal action against sb* ◊ *They have threatened us with legal action.*

**ˌlegal ˈage** *noun* [sing., U] the age when sb has the legal rights and responsibilities of an adult: *~ to do sth/for (doing) sth What's the legal age to vote in the UK?* ◊ *of ~ Both witnesses must be of legal age.*

**ˌlegal ˈaid** *noun* [U] money that is given by the government or another organization to sb who needs help to pay for legal advice or a lawyer

**ˌlegal ˈeagle** (*also* **ˌlegal ˈbeagle**) *noun* (*humorous*) a lawyer, especially one who is very clever

**le·gal·ese** /ˌliːɡəˈliːz/ *noun* [U] (*informal, often disapproving*) the sort of language used in legal documents that is difficult to understand

**ˌlegal ˈhigh** *noun* a substance that people smoke, INJECT, etc. for the physical and mental effects it has, and that, until 2016, was not banned by the law

**ˌlegal ˈholiday** *noun* (in the US) a public holiday that is fixed by law ⊃ compare BANK HOLIDAY

**le·gal·is·tic** /ˌliːɡəˈlɪstɪk/ *adj.* (*disapproving*) obeying the law too strictly: *a legalistic approach to family disputes*

**le·gal·ity** /lɪˈɡæləti/ *noun* (*pl. -ies*) **1** [U] the fact of being legal: *They intended to challenge the legality of his claim in the courts.* ◊ *The arrangement is of doubtful legality.* ◊ *The government does not recognize the legality of this court.* **2** [C, usually pl.] the legal aspect of an action or a situation:

You need a lawyer to explain all the legalities of the contracts. ⊃ compare ILLEGALITY

**le·gal·ize** (BrE also **-ise**) /ˈliːɡəlaɪz/ verb ~ **sth** to make sth legal ▶ **le·gal·iza·tion**, **-isa·tion** /ˌliːɡəlaɪˈzeɪʃn; NAmE -ləˈz-/ noun [U]

**'legal pad** noun (NAmE) a number of sheets of paper with lines on them, fastened together at one end

**'legal proceedings** noun [pl.] = LEGAL ACTION

**'legal-size** (also **legal**) adj. (NAmE) (of paper) 8½ inches (215.9 mm) wide and 14 inches (355.6 mm) long

**,legal 'tender** noun [U] money that can be legally used to pay for things in a particular country

**leg·ate** /ˈleɡət/ noun the official representative of the Pope in a foreign country: *a papal legate*

**lega·tee** /ˌleɡəˈtiː/ noun (law) a person who receives money or property (= a LEGACY) when sb dies

**le·ga·tion** /lɪˈɡeɪʃn/ noun **1** a group of DIPLOMATS representing their government in a foreign country in an office that is below the rank of an EMBASSY **2** the building where these people work

**le·gato** /lɪˈɡɑːtəʊ/ adj. (from Italian, music) to be played or sung in a smooth, even manner ▶ **le·gato** adv. OPP staccato

**le·gend** ?+ B2 /ˈledʒənd/ noun **1** ?+ B2 [C, U] a story from ancient times about people and events, that may or may not be true; this type of story SYN **myth**: *the legend of Robin Hood* ◊ *the heroes of Greek legend* ◊ *Legend has it that the lake was formed by the tears of a god.* ⊃ compare URBAN MYTH **2** ?+ C1 [C] a very famous person, especially in a particular field, who is admired by other people: *a jazz/screen/sporting legend* ◊ *She was a legend in her own lifetime.* ◊ *Many of golf's living legends were playing.* **3** [C] (specialist) the explanation of a map or a diagram in a book SYN **key 4** [C] (formal) a piece of writing on a sign, a label, a coin, etc.

**le·gend·ary** ?+ C1 /ˈledʒəndri; NAmE -deri/ adj. **1** ?+ C1 very famous and talked about a lot by people: *a legendary figure* ◊ *the legendary Bob Dylan* ◊ *Her patience and tact are legendary.* **2** ?+ C1 [only before noun] mentioned in stories from ancient times: *legendary heroes* ⊃ compare FABLED

**le·ger·de·main** /ˌledʒədəˈmeɪn; NAmE -dʒərd-/ noun [U] (from French, formal) = SLEIGHT OF HAND

**leg·gings** /ˈleɡɪŋz/ noun [pl.] trousers for women that fit tightly over the legs, made of cloth that stretches easily: *a pair of leggings*

**leggy** /ˈleɡi/ adj. (informal) (especially of girls and women) having long legs: *a tall, leggy schoolgirl*

**le·gible** /ˈledʒəbl/ adj. (of written or printed words) clear enough to read: *legible handwriting* ◊ *The signature was still legible.* OPP **illegible** ▶ **le·gi·bil·ity** /ˌledʒəˈbɪləti/ noun [U] **le·gibly** /ˈledʒəbli/ adv.

**le·gion** /ˈliːdʒən/ noun, adj.
■ noun **1** a large group of soldiers that forms part of an army, especially the one that existed in ancient Rome: *the French Foreign Legion* ◊ *Caesar's legions* **2** (formal) a large number of people of one particular type: *legions of photographers*
■ adj. [not before noun] (formal) very many SYN **numerous**: *The medical uses of herbs are legion.*

**le·gion·ary** /ˈliːdʒənəri; NAmE -neri/ noun (pl. **-ies**) a soldier who is part of a legion ▶ **le·gion·ary** adj. [only before noun]

**le·gion·naire** /ˌliːdʒəˈneə(r); NAmE -ˈner/ noun a member of a LEGION, especially the French Foreign Legion

**legion'naires' disease** noun [U] a serious lung disease caused by bacteria, especially spread by AIR CONDITIONING and similar systems

**le·gis·late** /ˈledʒɪsleɪt/ verb [I] ~ **(for/against/on sth)** (formal) to make a law affecting sth: *The King restricted Parliament's power to legislate.* ◊ *The government will legislate against discrimination in the workplace.* ◊ (figurative) *You can't legislate against bad luck!*

---

897 | **leisure**

**le·gis·la·tion** ?+ C1 /ˌledʒɪsˈleɪʃn/ noun [U] **1** ?+ C1 a law or a set of laws passed by a parliament: *an important piece of legislation* ◊ *New legislation on the sale of drugs will be introduced next year.* **2** ?+ C1 the process of making and passing laws: *Legislation will be difficult and will take time.* ⊃ WORDFINDER NOTE at PARLIAMENT

**le·gis·la·tive** ?+ C1 /ˈledʒɪslətɪv; NAmE -leɪt-/ adj. [only before noun] (formal) connected with the act of making and passing laws: *a legislative assembly/body/council* ◊ *legislative powers*

**the ,legislative 'branch** noun [sing.] (in the US) the part of the government, consisting of the House of Representatives and the Senate, that has the power to make laws ⊃ compare EXECUTIVE BRANCH, JUDICIAL BRANCH

**le·gis·la·tor** /ˈledʒɪsleɪtə(r)/ noun (formal) a member of a group of people that has the power to make laws

**le·gis·la·ture** ?+ C1 /ˈledʒɪslətʃə(r); NAmE -leɪtʃ-/ noun (formal) a group of people who have the power to make and change laws: *a democratically elected legislature* ◊ *the national/state legislature* ⊃ compare EXECUTIVE, JUDICIARY

**legit** /lɪˈdʒɪt/ adj. (informal) legal, or acting according to the law or the rules: *The business seems legit.*

**le·git·im·ate** ?+ C1 /lɪˈdʒɪtɪmət/ adj. **1** ?+ C1 for which there is a fair and acceptable reason SYN **valid, justifiable**: *a legitimate grievance* ◊ *It seemed a perfectly legitimate question.* ◊ *Politicians are legitimate targets for satire.* **2** ?+ C1 allowed and acceptable according to the law SYN **legal**: *the legitimate government of the country* ◊ *Is his business strictly legitimate?* OPP **illegitimate 3** (of a child) born when its parents are legally married to each other **illegitimate** ▶ **le·git·im·acy** /-məsi/ noun [U]: *the dubious legitimacy of her argument* ◊ *I intend to challenge the legitimacy of his claim.* **le·git·im·ate·ly** adv.: *She can now legitimately claim to be the best in the world.*

**le·git·im·ize** (BrE also **-ise**) /lɪˈdʒɪtɪmaɪz/ verb (formal) **1** ~ **sth** to make sth that is wrong or unfair seem acceptable: *The movie has been criticized for apparently legitimizing violence.* **2** ~ **sth** to make sth legal SYN **legalize 3** ~ **sb** to give a child whose parents are not married to each other the same rights as those whose parents are

**leg·less** /ˈleɡləs/ adj. **1** without legs **2** (BrE, informal) very drunk

**Lego™** /ˈleɡəʊ/ noun [U] a children's toy that consists of small coloured bricks that fit together

**'leg-room** /ˈleɡruːm; ˈleɡrʊm/ noun [U] the amount of space available for your legs when you are sitting in a car, plane, theatre, etc.

**leg·ume** /ˈleɡjuːm; lɪˈɡjuːm/ noun (specialist) any plant that has seeds in long PODS. PEAS and beans are legumes.

**le·gum·in·ous** /lɪˈɡjuːmɪnəs/ adj. [usually before noun] (specialist) relating to plants of the legume family

**'leg-up** noun (informal) **1** (especially BrE) an act of helping sb to get on a horse, over a wall, etc. by allowing them to put their foot in your hands and lifting them up **2** (especially BrE) an act of helping sb to improve their situation: *The loan from his father gave him a leg-up when he needed it.*
IDM **have/get a leg-up on sb** (NAmE, informal) to have/get an advantage over sb: *They are trying to get a leg-up on the competition.*

**'leg warmer** noun [usually pl.] a kind of sock without a foot that covers the leg from the ankle to the knee, often worn when doing exercise

**leg·work** /ˈleɡwɜːk; NAmE -wɜːrk/ noun [U] (informal) difficult or boring work that takes a lot of time and effort but is necessary

**leis·ure** ❶ B1 /ˈleʒə(r); NAmE ˈliːʒ-/ noun [U] **1** ? B1 time when you are not working or studying; free time: *These days we have more money and more leisure to enjoy it.* ◊ *Make the most of your leisure time!* **2** B1 activities that you enjoy in your free time: *These days we have increased opportunities for leisure.* ◊ *leisure activities/pursuits* ◊ *public parks and leisure facilities*

# leisure centre

**IDM** **at ˈleisure** **1** with no particular activities; free: *Spend the afternoon at leisure in the town centre.* **2** without hurrying: *Let's have lunch so we can talk at leisure.* **at your ˈleisure** *(formal)* when you have the time to do sth without hurrying: *I suggest you take the forms away and read them at your leisure.* **a ˌgentleman/ˌlady of ˈleisure** *(humorous)* a man/woman who does not have to work

**ˈleisure centre** *noun* (*BrE*) a public building where people can go to do sports and other activities in their free time

**leis·ured** /ˈleʒəd; *NAmE* ˈliːʒərd/ *adj.* **1** [only before noun] not having to work and therefore having a lot of time to do what you enjoy: *the leisured classes* **2** *(infrequent)* = LEISURELY

**leis·ure·ly** /ˈleʒəli; *NAmE* ˈliːʒərli/ *(also less frequent* **leis·ured)** *adj.* [usually before noun] done without hurrying: *a leisurely meal* ◇ *They set off at a leisurely pace.* ▶ **leis·ure·ly** *adv.*: *Couples strolled leisurely along the beach.*

**ˈleisure suit** *noun* (*NAmE*) an informal suit consisting of a shirt and trousers made of the same cloth, popular in the 1970s

**leis·ure·wear** /ˈleʒəweə(r); *NAmE* ˈliːʒərwer/ *noun* [U] (used especially by shops/stores and clothes companies) informal clothes worn for relaxing or playing sports in

**leit·motif** *(also* **leit·motiv)** /ˈlaɪtməʊtiːf/ *noun (from German)* **1** *(music)* a short tune in a piece of music that is often repeated and is connected with a particular person, thing or idea **2** an idea or a phrase that is repeated often in a book or work of art, or is typical of a particular person or group

**lek·got·la** /leˈxɒtlə; *NAmE* -ˈxɑːt-/ *SAfrE* [leˈxɔtli] *noun* (*SAfrE*) an important meeting of politicians or government officials

**lek·ker** /ˈlekə(r)/ *adj., adv.* (*SAfrE, informal*)
■ *adj.* good or nice; tasting good: *It was lekker to see you again.* ◇ *a lekker meal*
■ *adv.* very: *I'm lekker full.*

**lemma** /ˈlemə/ *noun (pl.* **lem·mas** *or* **lem·mata** /-tə/) **1** *(specialist)* a statement that is assumed to be true in order to test the truth of another statement **2** *(linguistics)* the basic form of a word, for example the singular form of a noun or the infinitive form of a verb, as it is shown at the beginning of a dictionary entry

**lem·ming** /ˈlemɪŋ/ *noun* a small animal like a mouse, that lives in cold northern countries. Sometimes large groups of lemmings MIGRATE (= move from one place to another) in search of food. Many of them die on these journeys and there is a popular belief that lemmings kill themselves by jumping off CLIFFS: *Lemming-like we rushed into certain disaster.*

**lemon** **❶** **A2** /ˈlemən/ *noun, adj.*
■ *noun* **1** [C, U] a yellow CITRUS fruit with juice that has a bitter, sharp taste. Slices of lemon and lemon juice are used in cooking and drinks: *Add a squeeze of* **lemon juice**. ◇ *Squeeze the juice of half a lemon over the fish.* ◇ *a gin and tonic with ice and lemon* ⊃ VISUAL VOCAB page V4 **2** [U, C] lemon juice or a drink made from lemon ⊃ see also BITTER LEMON **3** *(also* **lemon ˈyellow)** [U] a pale yellow colour **4** [C] *(especially NAmE, informal)* a thing that cannot be used because it does not work as it should **SYN** **dud 5** [C] (*BrE*) a stupid person **SYN** **idiot**
■ *adj. (also* **lemon ˈyellow)** pale yellow in colour

**lem·on·ade** /ˌleməˈneɪd/ *noun* **1** [U, C] (*BrE*) a sweet FIZZY drink (= with bubbles) that tastes of lemon **2** [U, C] a drink made from lemon juice, sugar and water **3** [C] a glass or bottle of lemonade

**ˈlemon balm** *noun* [U] a HERB with leaves that taste of lemon

**ˈlemon ˈcurd** *noun* [U] a thick, sweet, yellow substance made from lemon, sugar, eggs and butter, spread on bread, etc. or used to fill cakes

**ˈlemon·grass** /ˈleməngrɑːs; *NAmE* -græs/ *noun* [U] a type of grass with a lemon taste that grows in hot countries and is used especially in south-east Asian cooking

**ˈlemon-squeezer** (*BrE*) (*NAmE* **ˈjuicer**) *noun* a kitchen UTENSIL (= a tool) for pressing juice out of a fruit

**lem·ony** /ˈleməni/ *adj.* tasting or smelling of lemon: *a lemony flavour*

**lemur** /ˈliːmə(r)/ *noun* an animal like a monkey, with thick fur and a long tail, that lives in trees in Madagascar

**lend** **❶** **A2** /lend/ *verb* (**lent, lent** /lent/) **1** **❷** **A2** [T] to give sth to sb or allow them to use sth that belongs to you, which they have to return to you later **SYN** **loan**: **~(out) sth (to sb)** *I've lent the car to a friend.* ◇ **~sb sth** *Can you lend me £10?* ◇ *Has he returned that book you lent him?* ⊃ note at BORROW **2** **❷** **A2** [T, I] (of a bank or financial institution) to give money to sb on condition that they pay it back over a period of time and pay interest on it **SYN** **loan**: **~sb sth** *They refused to lend us the money.* ◇ **~(sth) (to sb)** *The bank refused to lend the money to us.* ◇ *Banks are less willing to lend in these uncertain times.* ⊃ compare BORROW ⊃ WORDFINDER NOTE at LOAN **3** [T] *(formal)* to give a particular quality to a person or a situation: **~sth (to sb/sth)** *The setting sun lent an air of melancholy to the scene.* ◇ **~sb/sth sth** *Her presence lent the occasion a certain dignity.* **4** [T] to give or provide help, support, etc: **~sth (to sb/sth)** *I was more than happy to lend my support to such a good cause.* ◇ **~sb/sth sth** *He came along to lend me moral support.*

**IDM** **ˌlend an ˈear (to sb/sth)** to listen in a patient and kind way to sb **ˌlend (sb) a (helping) ˈhand (with sth)** *(informal)* to help sb with sth: *I went over to see if I could lend a hand.* **ˌlend your ˈname to sth** *(formal)* **1** to let it be known in public that you support or agree with sth: *I am more than happy to lend my name to this campaign.* **2** to have a place named after you **ˌlend supˈport, ˈweight, ˈcredence, etc. to sth** to make sth seem more likely to be true or real: *This latest evidence lends support to her theory.* ⊃ more at HELP *v.*
**PHRV** **ˈlend itself to sth** to be suitable for sth: *Her voice doesn't really lend itself well to blues singing.*

**lend·er** /ˈlendə(r)/ *noun (finance)* a person or an organization that lends money ⊃ compare BORROWER ⊃ see also MONEYLENDER, PAYDAY LENDER

**lend·ing** /ˈlendɪŋ/ *noun* [U] *(finance)* the act of lending money: *Lending by banks rose to $10 billion last year.* ⊃ compare BORROWING ⊃ see also PAYDAY LENDING, PREDATORY LENDING

**ˈlending library** *noun* a public library from which you can borrow books and take them away to read at home ⊃ compare REFERENCE LIBRARY

**ˈlending rate** *noun (finance)* the rate of interest that you must pay when you borrow money from a bank or another financial organization

**length** **❶** **B1** /leŋθ/ *noun*
• SIZE/MEASUREMENT **1** **❷** **B1** [U, C] the size or measurement of sth from one end to the other: *Measure the length of the line from A to B.* ◇ **in ~** *The river is 300 miles in length.* ◇ *The snake usually reaches a length of 100cm.* ◇ *Safety barriers will be installed* **along the full length** *of the road.* ◇ *Look at the length of that queue!* ⊃ compare BREADTH, WIDTH ⊃ picture at DIMENSION ⊃ see also FOCAL LENGTH **2** **❷** **B1** [U] the quality of being long: *Did you see the length of his hair?*
• TIME **3** **❷** **B1** [U, C] the amount of time that sth lasts: *The average length of each song on the album is six minutes.* ◇ *These changes will shorten the* **length of time** *spent waiting for test results.* ◇ *She got a headache if she had to read for* **any length of time** *(= for a long time).* ◇ *Size of pension depends partly on length of service with the company.* ◇ *~ Each class is 45 minutes in length.*
• OF BOOK/FILM **4** **❷** **B1** [C, U] the amount of writing in a book, or a document, etc.; the amount of time that a film lasts: *There is a maximum length of 2500 words.* ◇ **in ~** *The document is over 800 pages in length.* ⊃ see also FEATURE-LENGTH
• -LENGTH **5** (in adjectives) having the length mentioned: *shoulder-length hair* ⊃ see also FULL-LENGTH, KNEE-LENGTH, SHOULDER-LENGTH

- **OF SWIMMING POOL 6** [C] the distance from one end of a swimming pool to the other: *He swims 50 lengths a day.* ⇒ compare WIDTH ⇒ **WORDFINDER NOTE** at SWIMMING
- **IN RACE 7** [C] the size of a horse or boat from one end to the other, when it is used to measure the distance between two horses or boats taking part in a race: *The horse won by two clear lengths.*
- **LONG THIN PIECE 8** [C] a long, thin piece of sth: *a length of rope/string/wire* ◊ *timber sold in lengths of 2, 5 or 10 metres* ⇒ see also LONG

**IDM** at ˈlength | at … length 1 for a long time and in detail: *He quoted at length from the report.* ◊ *We have already discussed this matter at great length.* 2 (*literary*) after a long time: *'I'm still not sure,' he said at length.* **go to any, some, great, etc. ˈlengths (to do sth)** to put a lot of effort into doing sth, especially when this seems extreme: *She goes to extraordinary lengths to keep her private life private.* **the length and ˈbreadth of …** in or to all parts of a place: *They have travelled the length and breadth of Europe giving concerts.* ⇒ more at ARM *n.*

**length·en** /ˈleŋθən/ *verb* [I, T] to become longer; to make sth longer: *The afternoon shadows lengthened.* ◊ *~ sth I need to lengthen this skirt.* **OPP** shorten

**length·ways** /ˈleŋθweɪz/ (*BrE*) (*also* **length·wise** /ˈleŋθwaɪz/ *especially in NAmE*) *adv.* in the same direction as the longest side of sth: *Cut the banana in half lengthways.*

**lengthy** ?+ C1 /ˈleŋθi/ *adj.* (**length·ier, length·iest**) very long, and often too long, in time or size: *lengthy delays* ◊ *the lengthy process of obtaining a visa* ◊ *a lengthy explanation*

**le·ni·ent** /ˈliːniənt/ *adj.* not as strict as expected when punishing sb or when making sure that rules are obeyed: *a lenient sentence/fine* ◊ *The judge was far too lenient with him.* ▶ **le·ni·ency** /-ənsi/ (*also less frequent* **le·ni·ence**) *noun* [U]: *She appealed to the judge for leniency.* **le·ni·ent·ly** *adv.*: *to treat sb leniently*

**lens** ?+ B2 /lenz/ *noun* 1 ?+ B2 a curved piece of glass or plastic that makes things look larger, smaller or clearer when you look through it: *a pair of glasses with tinted lenses* ⇒ picture at BINOCULARS, FRAME 2 ? B2 a piece of equipment that is part of a camera, containing one or more lenses: *a camera with an adjustable lens* ◊ *a lens cap/cover* ⇒ see also FISHEYE, TELEPHOTO LENS, WIDE-ANGLE LENS, ZOOM LENS 3 ?+ B2 (*informal*) = CONTACT LENS: *Have you got your lenses in?* 4 (*anatomy*) the clear part of the eye, behind the PUPIL, that focuses light so that you can see clearly

**lens·man** /ˈlenzmən/ *noun* (*pl.* **-men** /-mən/) a professional photographer or CAMERAMAN

**Lent** /lent/ *noun* [U] in the Christian Church, the period of 40 days from Ash Wednesday to the day before Easter, during which some Christians give up some type of food or activity that they enjoy in memory of what Christ suffered

**lent** /lent/ *past tense, past part.* of LEND

**len·til** /ˈlentl/ *noun* a small green, orange or brown seed that is usually dried and used in cooking, for example in soup or STEW

**Leo** /ˈliːəʊ/ *noun* 1 [U] the fifth sign of the ZODIAC, the Lion 2 [C] (*pl.* **-os**) a person born when the sun is in this sign, that is between 23 July and 22 August, approximately

**leo·nine** /ˈliːənaɪn/ *adj.* (*literary*) like a lion

**leop·ard** /ˈlepəd; *NAmE* -pərd/ *noun* a large animal of the cat family, usually with yellow-brown fur with black spots. Leopards live in Africa and southern Asia. ⇒ compare PANTHER

**IDM** **a ˌleopard cannot change its ˈspots** (*saying*) people cannot change their character, especially if they have a bad character

**ˈleopard-crawl** *verb* [I] + *adv./prep.* (*SAfrE*) (often used about soldiers) to move with your body as close to the ground as possible, using your ELBOWS and knees to push you forward

899  **lessen**

**leo·tard** /ˈliːətɑːd; *NAmE* -tɑːrd/ *noun* a piece of clothing that fits tightly over the body from the neck down to the tops of the legs, usually covering the arms, worn by dancers, women doing physical exercises, etc.

**LEP** /ˌel iː ˈpiː/ *abbr.* [only before noun] (*NAmE, specialist*) Limited English Proficient or Limited English Proficiency (used to describe students who cannot speak English very well): *schools with large numbers of LEP children*

**leper** /ˈlepə(r)/ *noun* 1 a person suffering from LEPROSY 2 a person that other people avoid because they have done sth that these people do not approve of

**lep·re·chaun** /ˈleprəkɔːn/ *noun* (in Irish stories) a creature like a little man, with magic powers

**lep·rosy** /ˈleprəsi/ *noun* [U] a disease that causes painful white areas on the skin and can destroy nerves, muscles, etc. ⇒ see also LEPER

**les·bian** ?+ C1 /ˈlezbiən/ *adj., noun*
- *adj.* ?+ C1 (of a woman) sexually attracted to other women; connected with LESBIANS: *the lesbian and gay community* ◊ *a lesbian relationship*
- *noun* a woman who is sexually attracted to other women: *lesbians and gays* ⇒ compare GAY, HOMOSEXUAL ⇒ see also LGBT, LIPSTICK LESBIAN ▶ **les·bian·ism** *noun* [U]

**le·sion** /ˈliːʒn/ *noun* (*medical*) an area of damage to the skin or part of the body caused by injury or by illness: *skin/brain lesions*

**leso** /ˈlesəʊ/ *EAfrE* [ˈleso] *noun* (*pl.* **-os**) = KANGA

**less** ❶ A2 ⓞ /les/ *det., pron., adv., prep.*
- *det., pron.* ? A2 used with uncountable nouns to mean 'a smaller amount of': *~ sth less butter/time/importance* ◊ *He was advised to smoke fewer cigarettes and drink less beer.* ◊ *~ to do We have less to worry about now.* ◊ *~ of sth They say we should exercise and eat less of some kinds of fat.* ◊ *~ than … We'll be there in less than no time* (= very soon). ◊ *The victory was nothing less than a miracle.* ◊ *~ of sth than … It is less of a problem than I'd expected.* **HELP** People often use **less** with countable nouns: *There were less cars on the road then.* This is not considered correct in standard English, and **fewer** should be used instead.
**IDM** **ˌless and ˈless** smaller and smaller amounts; at a rate that is decreasing: *As time passed, she saw less and less of all her old friends at home.* **ˌless is ˈmore** (*saying*) including only what is essential can create a more effective product or result: *His simple, elegant paintings reflect his principle that less is more.* **no ˈless** (*often ironic*) used to suggest that sth is surprising or impressive: *She's having lunch with the Director, no less.* **no ˌless than …** used to emphasize a large amount: *The guide contains details of no less than 115 hiking routes.*
- *adv.* ? A2 to a smaller degree; not so much: *less expensive/likely/intelligent* ◊ *less often/enthusiastically* ◊ *~ than … I read much less now than I used to.* ◊ *The receptionist was less than* (= not at all) *helpful.* ◊ *She wasn't any the less happy for* (= she was perfectly happy) *being on her own.* ◊ *That this is a positive stereotype makes it no less a stereotype, and therefore unacceptable.*
**IDM** **ˌless and ˈless** continuing to become smaller in amount: *She found the job less and less attractive.* **much / still ˈless** and certainly not: *No explanation was offered, still less an apology.* ⇒ more at MORE *adv.*
- *prep.* used before a particular amount that must be taken away from the amount just mentioned **SYN** minus: *a monthly salary of $2000 less tax and insurance*

**-less** /ləs/ *suffix* (in adjectives) 1 without: *treeless* ◊ *meaningless* 2 not doing; not affected by: *tireless* ◊ *selfless* ▶ **-less·ly** /ləsli/ (in adverbs): *hopelessly* **-less·ness** /ləsnəs/ (in nouns): *helplessness*

**les·see** /leˈsiː/ *noun* (*law*) a person who has use of a building, an area of land, etc. on a LEASE ⇒ compare LESSOR, TENANT

**less·en** /ˈlesn/ *verb* [I, T] to become or make sth become smaller, weaker, less important, etc. **SYN** diminish: *The noise began to lessen.* ◊ *~ sth to lessen the risk/impact/*

# lesser

effect of sth ▶ **less·en·ing** noun [sing., U]: *a lessening of tension*

▼ HOMOPHONES

lessen • lesson /ˈlesn/
- **lessen** verb: *The aim is to lessen the impact of farming practices on the environment.*
- **lesson** noun: *I have a guitar lesson after school today.*

**less·er** /ˈlesə(r)/ adj. [only before noun] **1** not as great in size, amount or importance as sth/sb else: *people of lesser importance* ◊ *They were all involved to a greater or lesser degree* (= some were more involved than others). ◊ *The law was designed to protect wives, and, to a lesser extent, children.* ◊ *He was encouraged to plead guilty to the lesser offence.* **2** (*specialist*) used in the names of some types of animals, birds and plants that are smaller than similar kinds **OPP** greater ▶ **less·er** adv.: *one of the lesser-known Caribbean islands*
**IDM** the ˌlesser of two ˈevils | the ˌlesser ˈevil the less unpleasant of two unpleasant choices

**les·son** /ˈlesn/ noun **1** a period of time in which sb is taught sth: *She gives piano lessons.* ◊ *I'm having driving lessons.* ◊ **~ in sth** *He took lessons in Thai cookery.* ◊ **~ on sth** *a history lesson on the Roman Empire* ◊ (*especially BrE*) *Our first lesson on Tuesdays is French.* ◊ (*especially BrE*) *What did we do last lesson?* ⊃ compare CLASS ⊃ HOMOPHONES at LESSEN **2** something that is intended to be learned: *The coursebook is divided into 30 lessons.* ◊ **~ on sth** *Other countries can teach us a lesson or two on industrial policy.* **3** an experience, especially an unpleasant one, that sb can learn from so that it does not happen again in the future: *The accident taught me a lesson I'll never forget.* ◊ *There are lessons to be learned from this mistake.* ◊ **~ to sb** *Let that be a lesson to you* (= so that you do not make the same mistake again). ◊ **~ on/about (doing) sth** *The film offers an important lesson on the value of friendship.* ⊃ see also OBJECT LESSON **4** (*old-fashioned*) a passage from the Bible that is read to people during a church service in the Church of England **SYN** reading
**IDM** see LEARN

**les·sor** /leˈsɔː(r)/ noun (*law*) a person who gives sb the use of a building, an area of land, etc. on a LEASE **SYN** landlord ⊃ compare LESSEE

**lest** /lest/ conj. (*formal* or *literary*) **1** in order to prevent sth from happening: *He gripped his brother's arm lest he be trampled by the mob.* **HELP** Lest usually takes a verb in the subjunctive: *Lest anyone doubt my story …* ◊ *Lest anyone doubts my story …* ◊ *Lest anyone doubted my story …* It is also acceptable to use *should*: *Lest anyone should doubt my story …* **2** used to introduce the reason for the particular emotion mentioned: *She was afraid lest she had revealed too much.*

**let** /let/ verb, noun

■ verb (**let·ting, let, let**)
- **MAKING SUGGESTIONS 1 let's** [no passive] used for making suggestions or as a polite way of telling people what you want them to do: *'Shall we check it again?' 'Yes, let's.'* ◊ **let's do sth** *Let's go to the beach.* ◊ *Right, let's begin.* ◊ *Let's not tell her what we did.* ◊ *Now let's not be silly about this.*
- **OFFERING HELP 2** [no passive] **~sb/sth do sth** used for offering help to sb: *Let me help you with that.* ◊ *Here, let me do it.* ◊ *Let us get those boxes down for you.*
- **MAKING REQUESTS 3** [no passive] **~sb/sth do sth** used for making requests or giving instructions: *Let me have your report by Friday.* ◊ *Let me know* (= tell me) *how I can help.*
- **ALLOW 4** [no passive] to allow sb to do sth or sth to happen without trying to stop it: **~sb/sth do sth** *Let them splash around in the pool for a while.* ◊ *Don't let her upset you.* ◊ *Let your body relax.* ◊ **~sb/sth** *He'd eat chocolate all day long if I let him.* **5** to give sb permission to do sth: **~sb/sth do sth** *They won't let him leave the country.* ◊ **~sb/sth** *I wanted to go but my parents wouldn't let me.*
- **6 ~sb/sth + adv./prep.** to allow sb/sth to go somewhere: *to let sb into the house* ◊ *I'll give you a key so that you can let yourself in.* ◊ *Please let me past.* ◊ *The cat wants to be let out.*
- **CHALLENGING 7** [no passive] **~sb/sth do sth** used to show that you are not afraid or worried about sb doing sth: *If he thinks he can cheat me, just let him try!*
- **WISHING 8** [no passive] **~sb/sth do sth** (*literary*) used to express a strong wish for sth to happen: *Let her come home safely!*
- **INTRODUCING STH 9** [no passive] **~sb/sth do sth** used to introduce what you are going to say or do: *Let me give you an answer.* ◊ *Let me just finish this and then I'll come.*
- **IN CALCULATING 10** [no passive] **~sb/sth do sth** (*specialist*) used to say that you are supposing sth to be true when you calculate sth: *Let line AB be equal to line CD.*
- **HOUSE/ROOM 11 ~sth (out) (to sb)** (*especially BrE*) to allow sb to use a house, room, etc. in return for regular payments: *I let the spare room.* ◊ *They decided to let out the smaller offices at low rents.* ⊃ see also BUY-TO-LET ⊃ WORD-FINDER NOTE at HOME ⊃ note at RENT

**IDM HELP** Most idioms containing **let** are at the entries for the nouns and adjectives in the idioms, for example *let alone* is at **alone**. ˌlet sb/sth ˈbe to stop trying to change the behaviour or state of sb/sth: *I know I'm being grumpy, but I'm really tired so just let me be.* ˌlet ˈfall sth to mention sth in a conversation, by accident or as if by accident **SYN** drop: *She let fall a further heavy hint.* ˌlet sb ˈgo **1** to allow sb to be free **SYN** free: *Will they let the hostages go?* **2** to make sb have to leave their job: *They're having to let 100 employees go because of falling profits.* ˌlet sb/sth ˈgo | ˌlet ˈgo (of sb/sth) **1** to stop holding sb/sth: *Don't let the rope go.* ◊ *Don't let go of the rope.* ◊ *Let go! You're hurting me!* **2** to give up an idea or an attitude, or control of sth: *It's time to let the past go.* ◊ *It's time to let go of the past.* ˌlet sth ˈgo to stop taking care of a house, garden, etc: *I'm afraid I've let the garden go this year.* ˌlet yourself ˈgo **1** to behave in a relaxed way without worrying about what people think of your behaviour: *Come on, enjoy yourself, let yourself go!* **2** to stop being careful about how you look and dress, etc: *He has let himself go since he lost his job.* ˌlet sb ˈhave it (*informal*) to attack sb physically or with words ˌlet it ˈgo (at ˈthat) to say or do no more about sth: *I don't entirely agree, but I'll let it go at that.* ◊ *I thought she was hinting at something, but I let it go.* ˌlet me ˈsee/ˈthink | ˌlet's ˈsee used when you are thinking or trying to remember sth: *Now let me see—where did he say he lived?* ˌlet's just ˈsay used when commenting on a situation to suggest that you could say sth more or worse but prefer not to: *Let's just say he wasn't very happy about the decision* (= he was very unhappy or angry about it). ˌlet us ˈsay used when making a suggestion or giving an example: *I can let you have it for, well let's say £100.* ˌto ˈlet (of a room, flat or house) available for rent: *The website advertises flats to let in the local area.*

**PHRV** ˌlet sb↔ˈdown to fail to help or support sb as they had hoped or expected: *I'm afraid she let us down badly.* ◊ *This machine won't let you down.* ◊ *He trudged home feeling lonely and let down.* ⊃ related noun LET-DOWN ˌlet sb/sth↔ˈdown to make sb/sth less successful than they it should be: *She speaks French very fluently, but her pronunciation lets her down.* ˌlet sth↔ˈdown **1** to let or make sth go down: *We let the bucket down by a rope.* **2** to make a dress, skirt, coat, etc. longer, by reducing the amount of material that is folded over at the bottom **OPP** take sth up **3** (*BrE*) to allow the air to escape from sth deliberately: *Some kids had let my tyres down.* ˌlet sb/yourself ˈin for sth (*informal*) to involve sb/yourself in sth that is likely to be unpleasant or difficult: *I volunteered to help, and then I thought 'Oh no, what have I let myself in for!'* ˌlet sb ˈin on sth | ˌlet sb ˈinto sth (*informal*) to allow sb to share a secret: *Are you going to let them in on your plans?* ˌlet sth ˈinto sth to put sth into the surface of sth so that it does not stick out from it: *a window let into a wall* ˌlet sb ˈoff (with sth) to not punish sb for sth they have done wrong, or to give them only a light punishment: *They let us off lightly.* ◊ *She was let off with a warning.* ˌlet sb ˈoff sth (*BrE*) to allow sb not to do sth or not to go somewhere: *He let us off homework today.* let

**sth 'off** to fire a gun or make a bomb, etc. explode: *The boys were letting off fireworks.* **let 'on (to sb)** *(informal)* to tell a secret: *I'm getting married next week, but please don't let on to anyone.* ◇ **let on (to sb) that ...** *She let on that she was leaving.* **let 'out** *(NAmE)* (of school classes, films/movies, meetings, etc.) to come to an end, so that it is time for people to leave: *The movie has just let out.* **let sb 'out** to make sb stop feeling that they are involved in sth or have to do sth: *They think the attacker was very tall—so that lets you out.* ⊃ related noun LET-OUT **let sth 'out 1** to give a shout, etc: *to let out a scream of terror* ◇ *Everyone let out a huge sigh of relief.* **2** to make a shirt, coat, etc. looser or larger **let 'up** *(informal)* **1** to become less strong: *The pain finally let up.* **2** to make less effort: *We mustn't let up now.* ⊃ related noun LET-UP
■ **noun**
• IN TENNIS **1** a SERVE that lands in the correct part of the COURT but must be taken again because it has touched the top of the net
• HOUSE/ROOM **2** *(BrE)* an act of renting a house, flat, room, etc.; a house, flat, room etc. that is available to rent: *a long-term/short-term let* ◇ *Similar barns had been converted to holiday lets.*
**IDM** **without ,let or 'hindrance** *(formal* or *law)* without being prevented from doing sth; freely

**-let** /lət/ *suffix* (in nouns) small; not very important: *booklet* ◇ *piglet* ◇ *starlet*

**'let-down** *noun* [C, usually sing., U] *(informal)* something that is disappointing because it is not as good as you expected it to be **SYN** **disappointment, anticlimax**

**le·thal** ⓘ **C1** /'li:θl/ *adj.* **1** ⓘ **C1** causing or able to cause death **SYN** **deadly, fatal**: *a lethal dose of poison* ◇ *a lethal weapon* ◇ *(figurative) The closure of the factory dealt a lethal blow to the town.* **2** ⓘ **C1** *(informal)* causing or able to cause a lot of harm or damage: *You and that car—it's a lethal combination!* ▶ **le·thal·ly** /-θəli/ *adv.*

**leth·argy** /'leθədʒi; *NAmE* -θərdʒi/ *noun* [U] the state of not having any energy or enthusiasm for doing things **SYN** **listlessness, inertia** ▶ **leth·ar·gic** /lə'θɑ:dʒɪk; *NAmE* -'θɑ:rdʒ-/ *adj.*: *The weather made her lethargic.*

**'let-out** *noun* [sing.] *(BrE)* an event or a statement that allows sb to avoid having to do sth: *Good—we have a let-out now.* ◇ *a let-out clause* (= in a contract)

**let's** /lets/ *short form* let us: *Let's break for lunch.*

**let·ter** ⓘ **A1** /'letə(r)/ *noun, verb*
■ **noun 1** ⓘ **A1** a written, typed or printed message that is put in an ENVELOPE or attached to an email and sent to sb: *to write/send (sb) a letter* ◇ *(BrE) to post a letter* ◇ *(NAmE) to mail a letter* ◇ *a thank-you/resignation/rejection letter* ◇ *~to/from sb In a letter to members, the Chairman explained the changes.* ◇ **a~of sth** *a letter of recommendation/complaint/apology* ◇ **by~** *You will be notified by letter.* **HELP** You will find compounds ending in **letter** at their place in the alphabet. **2** ⓘ **A1** a written or printed sign representing a sound used in speech: *'B' is the second letter of the alphabet.* ◇ **in ... letters** *She typed the word 'HISTORY' in capital letters.* ⊃ see also CAPITAL LETTER **3** *(NAmE)* a sign in the shape of a letter that is SEWN onto clothes to show that a person plays in a school or college sports team
**IDM** **the ,letter of the 'law** *(often disapproving)* the exact words of a law or rule rather than its general meaning: *They insist on sticking to the letter of the law.* **to the 'letter** doing/following exactly what sb/sth says, paying attention to every detail: *I followed your instructions to the letter.*
■ **verb 1** [T, usually passive] to give a letter to sth as part of a series or list: **lettered (+ noun)** *the stars lettered Alpha and Beta* **2** [T, usually passive] to print, paint, SEW, etc. letters onto sth: **lettered (in sth)** *a black banner lettered in white* **3** [I] *(NAmE)* to receive a letter made of cloth that you SEW onto your clothes for playing in a school or college sports team

**'letter bomb** *noun* a small bomb that is sent to sb hidden in a letter that explodes when the ENVELOPE is opened ⊃ see also PARCEL BOMB

**'let·ter·box** /'letəbɒks; *NAmE* -tərbɑ:ks/ *noun, verb*
■ **noun** [U] = WIDESCREEN

■ *verb* ~ *sth* to present a film on television with the image a lot wider than it is high, and with a black band at the top and bottom: *a letterboxed edition*

**'letter box** *noun* *(BrE)* **1** *(NAmE* **'mail slot)** a narrow opening in a door or wall through which mail is delivered ⊃ picture at POSTBOX **2** *(NAmE* **'mail·box)** a small box near the main door of a building or by the road, which mail is delivered to ⊃ compare PILLAR BOX, POSTBOX

**'letter carrier** *noun (NAmE)* = MAIL CARRIER

**let·ter·head** /'letəhed; *NAmE* -tərh-/ *noun* the name and address of a person, a company or an organization printed at the top of their writing paper or at the top of an official email

**let·ter·ing** /'letərɪŋ/ *noun* [U] **1** letters or words that are written or printed in a particular style: *Gothic lettering* **2** the process of writing, drawing or printing letters or words

**'letter of 'credit** *noun (pl.* **letters of credit)** *(finance)* a letter from a bank that allows you to get a particular amount of money from another bank

**'letter opener** *noun (especially NAmE)* = PAPERKNIFE

**let·ting** /'letɪŋ/ *noun (BrE)* an act of renting out a house or other property to sb else; a house or property that you rent out: *holiday lettings*

**let·tuce** /'letɪs/ *noun* [U, C] a plant with large green leaves that are eaten raw, especially in salad. There are many types of lettuce: *a bacon, lettuce and tomato sandwich* ◇ *Buy a lettuce and some tomatoes.* ⊃ see also COS LETTUCE, ICEBERG LETTUCE ⊃ VISUAL VOCAB page V5

**'let-up** *noun* [U, sing.] ~ **(in sth)** a period of time during which sth stops or becomes less strong, difficult, etc.; a reduction in the strength of sth **SYN** **lull**: *There is no sign of a let-up in the recession.*

**leuco·cyte** (also **leuko-cyte**) /'lu:kəsaɪt/ *noun* (*biology*) = WHITE BLOOD CELL

**leu·kae·mia** *(BrE)* *(NAmE* **leu·ke·mia)** /lu:'ki:miə/ *noun* [U] a serious disease in which too many white blood cells are produced, causing weakness and sometimes death

**levee** /'levi/ *noun (NAmE)* **1** a low wall built at the side of a river to prevent it from flooding **2** a place on a river where boats can let passengers on or off

**level** ⓘ **A2** ⓘ /'levl/ *noun, adj., verb*
■ **noun**
• HEIGHT **1** ⓘ **A2** [C, U] the height of sth in relation to the ground or to what it used to be: *The cables are buried one metre below ground level.* ◇ *The floodwater nearly reached roof level.* ◇ *The river has fallen to its lowest level since 2012.* ◇ *the level rose/dropped/decreased/increased* ◇ **on a~(with sth)** *On the second floor you are on a level with* (= at the same height as) *the treetops.* ⊃ see also EYE LEVEL, SEA LEVEL, WATER LEVEL
• FLOOR/LAYER **2** ⓘ **A2** [C] a floor of a building; a layer of ground: *a multi-level parking lot* ◇ **on a~** *The restaurant is on the level below this one.* ◇ *The library is all on one level.* ⊃ see also SPLIT-LEVEL
• AMOUNT **3** ⓘ **B1** [C] the amount of sth that exists in a particular situation at a particular time: *a low level of support for the proposed changes* ◇ *Increase your level of activity to burn more calories.* ◇ *to raise/reduce the level of sth* ◇ *low/high/elevated blood cholesterol levels* ◇ *a reduction/a rise/a decrease/an increase/a change in energy levels* ◇ **at a/the ...~** *Profits were at the same level as the year before.*
• STANDARD **4** ⓘ **B1** [C, U] a particular standard or quality: *The hotel's level of service is consistently high.* ◇ *The participants had different levels of education.* ◇ *What is the level of this course?* ◇ **at a ...~** *She has played tennis at a high level.* ◇ **on a~** *Both players are on a level* (= of the same standard). ◇ *I refuse to sink to their level* (= behave as badly as them). ⊃ see also A LEVEL, ENTRY-LEVEL, O LEVEL
• RANK IN SCALE **5** ⓘ **B2** [U, C] a position or rank in a scale of size or importance: *the upper levels of government* ◇ **at (a) ...~** *Discussions are currently being held at national*

**level crossing**

**level.** ◇ **at local/international level** ⇨ see also HIGH-LEVEL, TOP-LEVEL
- **POINT OF VIEW 6** ⦿ B2 [C] a particular way of looking at, reacting to or understanding sth: **on a …~** *Fables can be understood on various levels.* ◇ **at a …~** *At a conscious level, I was quite satisfied with my life.*
- **IN COMPUTER GAMES 7** [C] one of a series of stages in a computer game. Players progress from easy to more advanced levels within the game: *a computer game with 15 levels*
- **TOOL 8** [C] = SPIRIT LEVEL

IDM **on the ˈlevel** (*NAmE also* **on the ˌup and ˈup**) (*informal*) honest; legal SYN **above ˈboard**: *I'm not convinced he's on the level.* ◇ *Are you sure this deal is on the level?* ⇨ more at PAR

■ *adj.*
- **FLAT 1** ⦿ B1 having a flat surface that does not slope: *Pitch the tent on level ground.* ◇ *Add a level tablespoon of flour (= enough to fill the spoon but not so much that it goes above the level of the edge of the spoon).* ⇨ compare HEAPED
- **EQUAL 2** ⦿ B2 having the same height, position, value, etc. as sth: *Are these pictures level?* ◇ **~ with sth** *This latest rise is intended to keep wages level with inflation.* ◇ *He bent down so that his eyes were nearly level with hers.* ◇ *She drew level with (= came beside) the police car.* **3 ~ (with sb)** (*especially BrE, sport*) having the same score as sb: *A good second round brought him level with the tournament leader.* ◇ *England fought well to stay on level terms.* ◇ *France took an early lead but Wales soon drew level (= scored the same number of points).*
- **VOICE/LOOK 4** not showing any emotion; steady SYN **even**: *a level gaze* ⇨ see also LEVELLY

IDM **be level ˈpegging** (*BrE*) to have an equal or even score: *The contestants were level pegging after round 3.* **do/try your level ˈbest (to do sth)** to do as much as you can to try to achieve sth **a ˌlevel ˈplaying field** a situation in which everyone has the same opportunities

■ *verb* (**-ll-**, *US* **-l-**)
- **MAKE FLAT 1** ⦿ B2 [T] **~ sth (off/out)** to make sth flat or smooth: *The first coat of plaster levels out the surface of the wall.*
- **MAKE EQUAL 2** ⦿ B2 [T, I] **~ (sth)** to make sth, especially a score in sport, equal or similar: *Davies levelled the score at 2 all.* ◇ *to level the match/game*
- **DESTROY 3** [T] **~ sth** to destroy a building or a group of trees completely by knocking it down SYN **raze**: *The blast levelled several buildings in the area.*
- **POINT 4** [T] **~ sth (at sb)** to point sth, especially a gun, at sb: *I had a gun levelled at my head.*

IDM **ˌlevel the ˈplaying field** to create a situation where everyone has the same opportunities

PHRV **ˌlevel sth aˈgainst/ˈat sb** to say publicly that sb is to blame for sth, especially a crime or a mistake: *The speech was intended to answer the charges levelled against him by his opponents.* **ˌlevel sth↔ˈdown** to make standards, amounts, etc. be of the same low or lower level: *Teachers are accused of levelling standards down to suit the needs of less able students.* **ˌlevel ˈoff/ˈout 1** to stop rising or falling and remain level: *The plane levelled off at 1500 feet.* ◇ *After the long hill, the road levelled out.* **2** to stay at a steady level of development or progress after a period of sharp rises or falls: *Sales have levelled off after a period of rapid growth.* ⇨ WORDFINDER NOTE at TREND **ˌlevel ˈup / ˌlevel sth↔ˈup** (in computer games) to win points and get new skills, weapons, etc. for your character **ˌlevel sth↔ˈup** to make standards, amounts, etc. be of the same high or higher level **ˌlevel with sb** (*informal*) to tell sb the truth and not hide any unpleasant facts from them

**ˌlevel ˈcrossing** (*BrE*) (*NAmE* **ˌgrade ˈcrossing**, **ˈrailroad crossing**) *noun* a place where a road crosses a railway line at the same level (not on a bridge)

**ˌlevel-ˈheaded** *adj.* (*approving*) calm and sensible; able to make good decisions even in difficult situations

**lev·el·ler** (*US* **lev·el·er**) /ˈlevələ(r)/ *noun* [usually sing.] an event or a situation that makes everyone equal whatever their age, importance, etc: *death, the great leveller*

**lev·el·ly** /ˈlevəli/ *adv.* in a calm and steady way: *She looked at him levelly.*

**lever** /ˈliːvə(r); *NAmE* ˈlev-/ *noun, verb*
■ *noun* **1** a handle used to operate a vehicle or a machine: *Pull the lever towards you to adjust the speed.* ⇨ see also GEAR LEVER **2** a long piece of wood, metal, etc. used for lifting or opening sth by sb placing one end of it under an object and pushing down on the other end **3 ~ (for/against sth)** an action that is used to put pressure on sb to do sth they do not want to do: *The threat of sanctions is our most powerful lever for peace.*
■ *verb* to move sth with a lever SYN **prise**: **~ sth + adv./prep.** *I levered the lid off the pot with a knife.* ◇ **~ sth + adj.** *They managed to lever the door open.*

**lever·age** /ˈliːvərɪdʒ; *NAmE* ˈlev-/ *noun, verb*
■ *noun* [U] **1** (*formal*) the ability to influence what people do: *diplomatic leverage* **2** (*specialist*) the act of using a lever to open or lift sth; the force used to do this **3** (*BrE also* **gearing**) (*finance*) the relationship between the amount of money that a company owes and the value of its shares
■ *verb* **~ sth** (*business*) to get as much advantage or profit as possible from sth that you have: *The company needs to leverage its resources.*

**ˌleveraged ˈbuyout** *noun* (*business*) the act of buying a company using money that is borrowed based on the value of the company being bought

**le·via·than** /ləˈvaɪəθən/ *noun* **1** (in the Bible) a very large sea MONSTER **2** (*literary*) a very large and powerful thing: *the leviathan of government bureaucracy*

**Levi's™** /ˈliːvaɪz/ *noun* [pl.] a US make of jeans

**levi·tate** /ˈlevɪteɪt/ *verb* [I, T] **~ (sth)** to rise and float in the air with no physical support, apparently by means of magic or by using special mental powers; to make sth rise in this way ▶ **levi·ta·tion** /ˌlevɪˈteɪʃn/ *noun* [U, C]

**lev·ity** /ˈlevəti/ *noun* [U] (*formal*) behaviour that shows a lack of respect for sth serious and that treats it with humour SYN **frivolity**

**levy** /ˈlevi/ *noun, verb*
■ *noun* (*pl.* **-ies**) **~ (on sth)** an extra amount of money that has to be paid, especially as a tax to the government: *to put/impose a levy on oil imports*
■ *verb* (**levies, levy·ing, lev·ied, lev·ied**) **~ sth (on sb/sth)** to use official authority to demand and collect a payment, tax, etc: *a tax levied by the government on excess company profits*

**lewd** /luːd; *BrE also* ljuːd/ *adj.* referring to or involving sex in a rude and offensive way SYN **obscene**: *lewd behaviour/jokes/suggestions* ▶ **ˈlewd·ly** *adv.* **ˈlewd·ness** *noun* [U]

**lex·eme** /ˈleksiːm/ (*also* **ˌlexical ˈunit**) *noun* (*linguistics*) a word or several words that have a meaning that is not expressed by any of its separate parts

**lex·ic·al** /ˈleksɪkl/ *adj.* [usually before noun] (*linguistics*) connected with the words of a language: *lexical items (= words and phrases)* ▶ **lex·ic·al·ly** /-kli/ *adv.*

**ˌlexical ˈunit** *noun* = LEXEME

**lexi·cog·raph·er** /ˌleksɪˈkɒɡrəfə(r); *NAmE* -ˈkɑːɡ-/ *noun* a person who writes and edits dictionaries

**lexi·cog·raphy** /ˌleksɪˈkɒɡrəfi; *NAmE* -ˈkɑːɡ-/ *noun* [U] the theory and practice of writing dictionaries

**lexi·col·ogy** /ˌleksɪˈkɒlədʒi; *NAmE* -ˈkɑːl-/ *noun* [U] the study of the form, meaning and behaviour of words

**lexi·con** /ˈleksɪkən; *NAmE* -kɑːn/ *noun* **1 the lexicon** [sing.] (*linguistics*) all the words and phrases used in a particular language or subject; all the words and phrases used and known by a particular person or group of people: *the lexicon of finance and economics* **2** [C] a list of words on a particular subject or in a language in alphabetical order: *a lexicon of technical scientific terms* **3** [C] a dictionary, especially one of an ancient language, such as Greek or Hebrew

**lexis** /ˈleksɪs/ *noun* [U] (*linguistics*) all the words and phrases of a particular language SYN **vocabulary**

**ley** /leɪ/ *noun* **1** (*also* **ˈley line**) an imaginary line that is believed to follow the route of an ancient track and to have special powers **2** (*specialist*) an area of land where grass is grown temporarily instead of crops

**Ley·land cy·press** /ˌleɪlənd ˈsaɪprəs/ (*also* **ley·landii** /leɪˈlændiaɪ/) *noun* a tree (a type of CONIFER) that grows very quickly, often used to divide gardens

**lezzy** (*also* **lezzie**) /ˈlezi/ *noun, adj.* (*pl.* **-ies**) (*especially BrE, informal, offensive*) (a woman who is) sexually attracted to other women SYN **lesbian**

**LGBT** /ˌel dʒiː biː ˈtiː/ *abbr.* lesbian, gay, bisexual and transgender

**LGBTI** /ˌel dʒiː biː tiː ˈaɪ/ *abbr.* lesbian, gay, bisexual, transgender and intersex: *LGBTI rights*

**LGBTQ** /ˌel dʒiː biː tiː ˈkjuː/ *abbr.* lesbian, gay, bisexual, transgender and queer (or questioning): *the LGBTQ community*

**l.h.** *abbr.* (in writing) LEFT HAND

**li·abil·ity** /ˌlaɪəˈbɪləti/ *noun* (*pl.* **-ies**) **1** [U] the state of being legally responsible for sth: **~ (for sth)** *The company cannot accept liability for any damage caused by natural disasters.* ⬥ **~ to sb** *The company has liabilities to its employees.* ⊃ see also LIMITED LIABILITY **2** [C, usually sing.] (*informal*) a person or thing that causes you a lot of problems: *Since his injury, Jones has become more of a liability than an asset to the team.* **3** [C, usually pl.] the amount of money that a person or company owes: *The company is reported to have liabilities of nearly $90000.* ⊃ compare ASSET

**li·able** ℞+ C1 /ˈlaɪəbl/ *adj.* [not before noun] **1** ℞+ C1 **~ (for sth)** legally responsible for paying the cost of sth: *You will be liable for any damage caused.* ⬥ *The court ruled he could not be held personally liable for his wife's debts.* **2** ℞+ C1 **~ to do sth** likely to do sth: *We're all liable to make mistakes when we're tired.* ⬥ *The bridge is liable to collapse at any moment.* **3** **~ to sth** likely to be affected by sth SYN **prone**: *You are more liable to injury if you exercise infrequently.* **4** **~ to sth** likely to be punished by law for sth: *Offenders are liable to fines of up to $500.* **5** **~ for/to sth | ~ to do sth** having to do sth by law: *People who earn under a certain amount are not liable to pay tax.*

**li·aise** /liˈeɪz/ *verb* **1** [I] **~ (with sb)** (*especially BrE*) to work closely with sb and exchange information with them: *He had to liaise directly with the police while writing the report.* **2** [I] **~ (between A and B)** to act as a link between two or more people or groups: *Her job is to liaise between students and teachers.*

**li·aison** /liˈeɪzn; *NAmE* ˈliːəzɑːn, liˈeɪzɑːn/ *noun* **1** [U, sing.] a relationship between two organizations or different departments in an organization, involving the exchange of information or ideas: *We are hoping to establish better customer liaison.* ⬥ **~ between A and B** *Our role is to ensure liaison between schools and parents.* ⬥ **~ with sb** *We work in close liaison with the police.* **2** [C] **~ (to/with sb/sth)** a person whose job is to make sure there is a good relationship between two groups or organizations: *the White House liaison to organized labor* **3** [C] **~ (with sb)** a secret sexual relationship, especially if one or both partners are already in a relationship with sb else SYN **affair**

**li·aison officer** *noun* a person whose job is to make sure that there is a good relationship between two groups of people, organizations, etc. ⊃ see also LIAISON (2)

**liar** /ˈlaɪə(r)/ *noun* a person who tells lies

**lib** /lɪb/ *noun* (*informal*) used in the names of organizations demanding greater freedom, equal rights, etc. (the abbreviation for 'liberation'): *women's lib* ⊃ see also AD LIB, AD-LIB

**li·ba·tion** /laɪˈbeɪʃn/ *noun* (*formal*) (in the past) a gift of wine to a god

**Lib Dem** /ˌlɪb ˈdem/ *abbr.* (in British Politics) LIBERAL DEMOCRAT: *I voted Lib Dem.*

**libel** /ˈlaɪbl/ *noun, verb*
■ *noun* [U, C] the act of printing a statement about sb that is not true and that gives people a bad opinion of them; the statement that is printed: *He sued the newspaper for libel.* ⬥ *a libel action* (= a case in a court of law) ⊃ compare SLANDER

■ *verb* (**-ll-**, *US* **-l-**) **~ sb** to publish a written statement about sb that is not true: *He claimed he had been libelled in an article the magazine had published.* ⊃ compare SLANDER

**li·bel·lous** (*US* **li·bel·ous**) /ˈlaɪbələs/ *adj.* containing a LIBEL about sb: *a libellous statement*

**lib·eral** ℞+ C1 /ˈlɪbərəl/ *adj., noun*
■ *adj.*
• RESPECTING OTHER OPINIONS **1** ℞+ C1 willing to understand and respect other people's behaviour, opinions, etc., especially when they are different from your own; believing people should be able to choose how they behave: *liberal attitudes/views/opinions*
• POLITICS **2** ℞+ C1 wanting or allowing a lot of political and economic freedom and supporting steady social, political or religious change: *Some politicians want more liberal trade relations with Europe.* ⬥ *liberal democracy* ⬥ *liberal theories* ⬥ *a liberal politician* ⊃ WORDFINDER NOTE at CAPITALISM ⊃ see also NEOLIBERAL **3** *Liberal* connected with the British Liberal Party in the past, or a Liberal Party in another country
• GENEROUS **4** **~ (with sth)** generous; given in large amounts SYN **lavish**: *She is very liberal with her money.* ⬥ *I think Sam is too liberal with his criticism* (= he criticizes people too much).
• EDUCATION **5** a liberal education is about increasing sb's general knowledge and experience rather than particular skills: *a liberal education*
• NOT EXACT **6** not completely accurate or exact SYN **free**: *a liberal translation of the text* ⬥ *a liberal interpretation of the law* ▶ **lib·er·al·ly** /-rəli/ *adv.*: *Apply the cream liberally.* ⬥ *The word 'original' is liberally interpreted in copyright law.*
■ *noun*
• SB WHO RESPECTS OTHERS **1** ℞+ C1 a person who understands and respects other people's opinions and behaviour, especially when they are different from their own: *He liked to think of himself as a liberal.*
• POLITICS **2** ℞+ C1 a person who supports political, social and religious change: *Reform is popular with middle-class liberals.* ⊃ see also NEOLIBERAL **3** *Liberal* (*politics*) a member of the British Liberal Party in the past, or of a Liberal Party in another country

**liberal 'arts** *noun* [pl.] (*especially NAmE*) subjects of study that develop students' general knowledge and ability to think, rather than their technical skills

**Liberal 'Democrat** *noun* (*abbr.* **Lib Dem**) a member or supporter of the Liberal Democrats

**the Liberal 'Democrats** *noun* [pl.] (*abbr.* **Lib Dems**) one of the main British political parties, in favour of some political and social change, but not extreme ⊃ compare CONSERVATIVE PARTY, LABOUR PARTY

**lib·er·al·ism** /ˈlɪbərəlɪzəm/ *noun* [U] liberal opinions and beliefs, especially in politics ⊃ compare NEOLIBERALISM

**lib·er·al·ity** /ˌlɪbəˈræləti/ *noun* [U] (*formal*) **1** respect for political, religious or moral views, even if you do not agree with them **2** the quality of being generous

**lib·er·al·ize** (*BrE also* **-ise**) /ˈlɪbərəlaɪz/ *verb* **~ sth** to make sth such as a law or a political or religious system less strict ▶ **lib·er·al·iza·tion, -isa·tion** /ˌlɪbərəlaɪˈzeɪʃn; *NAmE* -ləˈz-/ *noun* [U]

**lib·er·ate** /ˈlɪbəreɪt/ *verb* **1** **~ sb/sth (from sb/sth)** to free a country or a person from the control of sb else: *The city was liberated by the advancing army.* **2** **~ sb (from sth)** to free sb from sth that limits their control over and pleasure in their own life: *Writing poetry liberated her from the routine of everyday life.* ▶ **lib·er·ator** *noun*

**lib·er·ated** /ˈlɪbəreɪtɪd/ *adj.* free from the limits of traditional ideas about social and sexual behaviour

**lib·er·ation** ℞+ C1 /ˌlɪbəˈreɪʃn/ *noun* [U, sing.] **1** ℞+ C1 **~ (from sth)** the act or process of freeing a country or a person from the control of sb else: *a war of liberation* **2** ℞+ C1 the act or process of freeing sb from sth that limits their control over or pleasure in their own life: *the struggle for women's liberation in the 1970s* ⬥ **~ from sth** *liberation from poverty*

# liberation theology

**libe‚ration the'ology** *noun* [U] a Christian movement, developed mainly by Latin American Catholics, that deals with social justice and the problems of people who are poor, as well as with spiritual matters

**lib·er·tar·ian** /ˌlɪbəˈteəriən; NAmE -ˈter-/ *noun* a person who strongly believes that people should have the freedom to do and think as they like

**lib·er·tine** /ˈlɪbətiːn; NAmE -bərt-/ *noun* (*formal*, *disapproving*) a person, usually a man, who leads a life that is not moral and who is interested in pleasure, especially sexual pleasure

**lib·erty** C1 /ˈlɪbəti; NAmE -bərti/ *noun* (*pl.* **-ies**) **1** [U] freedom to live as you choose without too many limits from government or authority: *the fight for justice and liberty* ➲ WORDFINDER NOTE at FREEDOM **2** [U] the state of not being a prisoner or a slave: *He had to endure six months' loss of liberty.* **3** [C] the legal right and freedom to do sth: *The right to vote should be a liberty enjoyed by all.* ◊ *People fear that security cameras could infringe personal liberties.* ➲ see also CIVIL LIBERTY **4** [sing.] an act or a statement that may offend or annoy sb, especially because it is done without permission or does not show respect: *He took the liberty of reading my files while I was away.* IDM **at 'liberty** (*formal*) (of a prisoner or an animal) no longer in prison or in a CAGE SYN **free** **at liberty to do sth** (*formal*) having the right or freedom to do sth SYN **free**: *You are at liberty to say what you like.* **take 'liberties with sb/sth 1** to make important and unreasonable changes to sth, especially a book: *The movie takes considerable liberties with the novel that it is based on.* **2** (*old-fashioned*) to be too friendly with sb, especially in a sexual way

**li·bid·in·ous** /lɪˈbɪdɪnəs/ *adj.* (*formal*) having or expressing strong sexual feelings

**li·bido** /lɪˈbiːdəʊ/ *noun* (*pl.* **-os**) [U, C, usually sing.] (*specialist*) sexual desire: *loss of libido*

**Libra** /ˈliːbrə/ *noun* **1** [U] the 7th sign of the ZODIAC, the SCALES **2** [C] a person born when the sun is in this sign, that is between 23 September and 22 October, approximately ▶ **Li·bran** /-brən/ *noun*, *adj.*

**li·brar·ian** /laɪˈbreəriən; NAmE -ˈbrer-/ *noun* a person who is in charge of or works in a library ▶ **li·brar·ian·ship** *noun* [U]: *a degree in librarianship*

**li·brary** A1 /ˈlaɪbrəri, -bri; NAmE -breri/ *noun* (*pl.* **-ies**) **1** A1 a building in which collections of books, newspapers, etc. and sometimes films and recorded music are kept for people to read, study or borrow: *a public/university/school library* ◊ *a library book* ◊ *a toy library* (= for borrowing toys from) ◊ *How often do you go to the library?* ➲ see also LENDING LIBRARY, MOBILE LIBRARY, REFERENCE LIBRARY **2** B1 a collection of books, newspapers, films, recorded music, etc. held in a library or stored in digital form: *a music/photo library* ◊ *The Media Centre houses a digital library of radio and television programmes.* **3** a room in a large house where most of the books are kept **4** (*formal*) a personal collection of books, music recordings, etc: *a new edition to add to your library* **5** a series of books, recordings, etc. produced by the same company and similar in appearance: *a library of children's classics*

**the ˌLibrary of ˈCongress** *noun* [sing.] the US national library

**li·bret·tist** /lɪˈbretɪst/ *noun* a person who writes the words for an OPERA or a musical play

**li·bretto** /lɪˈbretəʊ/ *noun* (*pl.* **-os** or **li·bretti** /-tiː/) (*music, from Italian*) the words that are sung or spoken in an OPERA or a musical play ➲ WORDFINDER NOTE at OPERA

**lice** /laɪs/ *pl.* of LOUSE

**li·cence** B2 (*US* **li·cense**) /ˈlaɪsns/ *noun* **1** [C] an official document that shows that permission has been given to do, own or use sth: *Applicants must hold a valid driving licence.* ◊ *to grant/issue a licence* ◊ *James lost his licence for six months* (= had his licence taken away by the police as a punishment). ◊ *~ for sth a licence for the software* ◊ *~ to do sth You need a licence to fish in this river.* ◊ *without a ~ He was caught driving a car without a licence.* ◊ *Is there a licence fee?* ➲ see also DRIVING LICENCE, MARRIAGE LICENCE, OFF-LICENCE, PROVISIONAL LICENCE, SPECIAL LICENCE ➲ WORDFINDER NOTE at CAR **2** [U, sing.] **~(to do sth)** (*formal*) freedom to do or say whatever you want, often sth bad or unacceptable: *Lack of punishment seems to give youngsters licence to break the law.* **3** [U] (*formal*) freedom to behave in a way that is not considered sexually moral IDM **artistic/poetic ˈlicence** the freedom of artists or writers to change facts in order to make a story, painting, etc. more interesting or beautiful **a licence to print ˈmoney** (*disapproving*) used to describe a business that makes a lot of money with little effort **under ˈlicence** (of a product) made with the permission of a company or an organization

**li·cense** C1 /ˈlaɪsns/ *verb*, *noun*
■ *verb* C1 (*BrE also, less frequent* **li·cence**) to give sb official permission to do, own, or use sth: **~sth** *The new drug has not yet been licensed in the US.* ◊ (*BrE*) *licensing hours* (= the times when alcohol can be sold at a pub, etc.) ◊ **~sb/sth to do sth** *They had licensed the firm to produce the drug.*
■ *noun* (*NAmE*) = LICENCE: *a driver's license* ◊ *a license for the software* ◊ *a license holder* (= a person who has been given a license) ➲ see also DRIVER'S LICENSE

**li·censed** /ˈlaɪsnst/ *adj.* **1** (*BrE*) having official permission to sell alcoholic drinks: *a licensed restaurant* **2** that you have official permission to own: *Is that gun licensed?* **3** **~to do sth** having official permission to do sth: *She is licensed to fly solo.*

**li·cen·see** /ˌlaɪsənˈsiː/ *noun* **1** (*BrE*) a person who has a licence to sell alcoholic drinks **2** a person or company that has a licence to make sth or to use sth

**ˈlicense number** (*NAmE*) (*BrE* **regiˈstration number, regisˈtration**) *noun* the series of letters and numbers that are shown on a LICENSE PLATE at the front and back of a vehicle to identify it

**ˈlicense plate** (*NAmE*) (*BrE* **ˈnumber plate, regisˈtration plate**) *noun* a metal or plastic plate on the front and back of a vehicle that shows its LICENSE NUMBER

**ˈlicensing laws** *noun* [pl.] British laws that state where and when alcoholic drinks can be sold

**li·cen·tious** /laɪˈsenʃəs/ *adj.* (*formal*, *disapproving*) behaving in a way that is not considered sexually moral ▶ **li·cen·tious·ness** *noun* [U]

**li·chee** = LYCHEE

**li·chen** /ˈlaɪkən, ˈlɪtʃən/ *noun* [U, C] a very small grey or yellow plant that spreads over the surface of rocks, walls and trees and does not have any flowers ➲ VISUAL VOCAB page V7 ➲ compare MOSS

**licit** /ˈlɪsɪt/ *adj.* (*formal*) allowed or legal OPP illicit ▶ **licit·ly** *adv.*

**lick** /lɪk/ *verb*, *noun*
■ *verb* **1** [T] to move your tongue over the surface of sth in order to eat it, make it wet or clean it: **~sth** *He licked his fingers.* ◊ *I'm tired of licking envelopes.* ◊ *The cat sat licking its paws.* ◊ **~sth + adj.** *She licked the spoon clean.* **2** [T] **~sth + adv./prep.** to eat or drink sth by licking it: *The cat licked up the milk.* ◊ *She licked the honey off the spoon.* **3** [T, I] (of flames) to touch sth lightly: **~sth** *Flames were soon licking the curtains.* ◊ **~at sth** *The flames were now licking at their feet.* **4** [T] **~sb/sth** (*informal*) to easily defeat sb or deal with sth: *We thought we had them licked.* ◊ *It was a tricky problem but I think we've licked it.* IDM **lick sb's ˈboots** (*BrE*, *taboo*, *slang* **lick sb's ˈarse**) (*disapproving*) to show too much respect for sb in authority because you want to please them SYN **crawl lick your ˈwounds** to spend time trying to get your strength or confidence back after a defeat or a disappointing experience ➲ more at LIP, SHAPE *n.*
■ *noun* **1** [C] an act of licking sth with the tongue: *Can I have a lick of your ice cream?* **2** [sing.] **a ~of paint** (*informal*) a small amount of paint, used to make a place look better: *What this room needs is a lick of paint.* **3** [C] (*informal*) a

short piece of music played on a guitar in jazz or pop music: *a guitar/blues lick*
**IDM** **at a (fair) ˈlick** (*informal*) fast; at a high speed **a lick and a ˈpromise** (*informal*) the act of performing a task quickly and carelessly, especially of washing or cleaning sth quickly

**lickety-split** /ˌlɪkəti ˈsplɪt/ *adv.* (*NAmE, old-fashioned, informal*) very quickly; immediately

**lick·ing** /ˈlɪkɪŋ/ *noun* [*sing.*] (*informal*) a severe defeat in a battle, game, etc. **SYN** **thrashing**

**lic·orice** (*especially NAmE*) = LIQUORICE

**lid** /lɪd/ *noun* **1** a cover over a container that can be removed or opened by turning it or lifting it: *a dustbin lid* ◊ *I can't get the lid off this jar.* **2** = EYELID
**IDM** **keep a/the ˈlid on sth** **1** to keep sth secret or hidden **2** to keep sth under control: *The government is keeping the lid on inflation.* **lift the ˈlid on sth** | **take/blow the ˈlid off sth** to tell people unpleasant facts about sth: *Her article lifts the lid on bullying in the workplace.* **put the (tin) ˈlid on sth/things** (*BrE, informal*) to be the final act or event that causes your plans or hopes to fail ⊃ more at FLIP *v.*

▼ SYNONYMS

**lid**

top • cork • cap • plug

These are all words for a cover for a container.

**lid** a cover over a container that can be removed or opened by turning or lifting it: *a jar with a tight-fitting lid*

**top** a thing that you put over the end of sth such as a pen or bottle in order to close it

**cork** a small, round object made of cork or plastic that is used for closing bottles, especially wine bottles

**cap** (*often in compounds*) a top for a pen or a cover for protecting sth such as the lens of a camera

**plug** a round piece of material that you put into a hole in order to block it; a flat, round rubber or plastic thing that you put into the hole of a sink in order to stop the water from flowing out: *a bath plug*

PATTERNS
- a **tight-fitting** lid/top/cap
- a **screw** top/cap
- a **pen** lid/top
- to **put on/screw on/take off/unscrew** the lid/top/cap
- to **pull out** the cork/plug

**lid·ded** /ˈlɪdɪd/ *adj.* [*usually before noun*] **1** (*of containers*) having a lid **2** (*literary*) used to describe a person's expression when their EYELIDS appear large or their eyes are almost closed: *heavily lidded eyes* ◊ *his lidded gaze*

**lido** /ˈliːdəʊ; *BrE also* ˈlaɪd-/ *noun* (*pl.* **-os**) (*BrE*) a public outdoor swimming pool or part of a beach used by the public for swimming, water sports, etc.

**lido·caine** /ˈlaɪdəkeɪn/ (*also* **lig·no·caine** /ˈlɪɡnəkeɪn/) *noun* [U] a substance used as a LOCAL ANAESTHETIC, for example to stop people feeling pain when teeth are removed

**lie¹** 🔊 **A1** /laɪ/ *verb, noun* ⊃ see also LIE²
■ *verb* (**lies, lying, lay** /leɪ/, **lain** /leɪn/) **1** **A1** [I] (of a person or an animal) to be or put yourself in a flat position so that you are not standing or sitting: ~ + *adv./prep.* *to lie on your back/side/front* ◊ *She lay in bed listening to music.* ◊ *~ + adj.* *I lay awake all night worrying about it.* ⊃ note at LAY² **2** **B2** [I] (of a thing) to be or remain in a flat position on a surface: ~ + *adv./prep.* *Clothes were lying all over the floor.* ◊ ~ + *adj.* *The book lay open on the desk.* **3** **B2** [I] to be, remain or be kept in a particular state: ~ + *adj.* *Houses lie empty while people are homeless.* ◊ *These machines have lain idle since the factory closed.* ◊ ~ + *adv./prep.* *Much of the city now lay in ruins.* **4** **B2** [I] (of ideas, qualities, problems, etc.) to exist or be found: *~ in sth* *The problem lies in deciding when to intervene.* ◊ *~ with sb* *The fault lies with you.* ◊ ~ + *adv./prep.* *The answer seems to lie elsewhere.* **5** **B2** [I] ~ + *adv./prep.* (of a town, natural feature, etc.) to be located in a particular place: *The town lies on the coast.* **6** [I] + *adv./prep.* to be spread out in a

905

**Lieut.**

particular place: *The valley lay below us.* **7** [I] (*BrE*) to be in a particular position during a competition: + *adv./prep.* *Thompson is lying in fourth place.* ◊ + *adj.* *After five games the German team are lying second.* ⊃ compare LAY
**IDM** **lie aˈhead/in ˈstore** to be going to happen to sb in the future: *You are young and your whole life lies ahead of you.* **lie in ˈstate** (of the dead body of an important person) to be placed on view in a public place before being buried **lie in ˈwait (for sb)** to hide, waiting to surprise, attack or catch sb: *He was surrounded by reporters who had been lying in wait for him.* **lie ˈlow** (*informal*) to try not to attract attention to yourself **take sth lying ˈdown** to accept an offensive remark or act without protesting or reacting ⊃ more at BED *n.*, BOTTOM *n.*, HEAVY *adv.*, LAND *n.*, SLEEP *v.*
**PHRV** **lie aˈround** (*BrE also* **lie aˈbout**) **1** to be left somewhere in an untidy or careless way, not put away in the correct place: *Don't leave toys lying around—someone might trip over them.* **2** (of a person) to spend time doing nothing and being lazy ⊃ related noun LAYABOUT **lie ˈback** to do nothing except relax: *You don't have to do anything—just lie back and enjoy the ride.* **lie beˈhind sth** to be the real reason for sth, often hidden: *What lay behind this strange outburst?* **lie ˈdown** to be or get into a flat position, especially in bed, in order to sleep or rest: *Go and lie down for a while.* ◊ *He lay down on the sofa and soon fell asleep.* ⊃ related noun LIE-DOWN **lie ˈin** (*also* **ˌsleep ˈin** *NAmE, BrE*) to stay in bed after the time you usually get up: *It's a holiday tomorrow, so you can lie in.* ⊃ related noun LIE-IN **ˈlie with sb (to do sth)** (*formal*) to be sb's duty or responsibility: *It lies with you to accept or reject the proposals.*

■ *noun*
**IDM** **the ˌlie of the ˈland** (*BrE*) (*NAmE* **the ˌlay of the ˈland**) **1** the way the land in an area is formed and what physical characteristics it has **2** the way a situation is now and how it is likely to develop: *Check out the lie of the land before you make a decision.*

**lie²** 🔊 **B1** /laɪ/ *verb, noun* ⊃ see also LIE¹
■ *verb* 🔊 **B1** [I] (**lies, lying, lied, lied**) to say or write sth that you know is not true: *You could see from his face that he was lying.* ◊ *~ to sb* *Don't lie to me!* ◊ *~ about (doing) sth* *She lies about her age.* ◊ *The camera cannot lie* (= give a false impression). ⊃ see also LIAR
**IDM** **lie through your ˈteeth** (*informal*) to say sth that is not true at all: *The witness was clearly lying through his teeth.* **ˌlie your ˈway into/out of sth** to get yourself into or out of a situation by lying
■ *noun* 🔊 **B1** a statement made by sb knowing that it is not true: *to tell a lie* ◊ *The whole story is nothing but a pack of lies.* ◊ *That's an outright lie!* ◊ *~ about sb/sth* *How dare you spread such vicious lies about other people?* ⊃ see also WHITE LIE
**IDM** **give the ˈlie to sth** (*formal*) to show that sth is not true ⊃ more at LIVE¹, TELL, TISSUE

**lied** /liːd/ *noun* (*pl.* **lieder** /ˈliːdə(r)/) (*from German*) a German song for one singer and piano

**ˈlie detector** (*also specialist* **poly·graph**) *noun* a piece of equipment that is used to find out if sb is telling the truth

**ˌlie-ˈdown** *noun* [*sing.*] (*BrE, informal*) a short rest, especially on a bed

**liege** /liːdʒ/ (*also* **ˌliege ˈlord**) *noun* (*old use*) a king or lord

**ˈlie-in** *noun* (*BrE*) a time when you stay in bed longer than normal in the morning

**lien** /ˈliːən/ *noun* [U] ~ (in/over sth) (*law*) the right to keep sb's property until a debt is paid

**lieu** /luː/ *noun* (*formal*)
**IDM** **in lieu (of sth)** instead of: *They took cash in lieu of the prize they had won.* ◊ *We work on Saturdays and have a day off in lieu during the week.*

**Lieut.** (*also* **Lt**) (*both BrE*) (*NAmE* **Lt.**) *abbr.* (in writing) LIEUTENANT

🅞 Oxford Phrasal Academic Lexicon (OPAL) written and spoken word lists | 🅦 OPAL written word list | 🅢 OPAL spoken word list

# lieutenant

**lieu·ten·ant** /lefˈtenənt; NAmE luːˈt-/ noun (abbr. **Lieut.**, **Lt**) **1** an officer of middle rank in the army, NAVY, or AIR FORCE: *Lieutenant Paul Fisher* ⇨ see also FIRST LIEUTENANT, FLIGHT LIEUTENANT, SECOND LIEUTENANT **2** (in compounds) an officer just below the rank mentioned: *a lieutenant colonel* **3** (in the US) a police officer of fairly high rank **4** a person who helps sb who is above them in rank or who performs their duties when that person is unable to ⇨ see also LORD LIEUTENANT

**lieuˌtenant ˈcolonel** noun an officer of middle rank in the US army, US AIR FORCE or British army

**lieuˌtenant comˈmander** noun an officer of middle rank in the NAVY

**lieuˌtenant ˈgeneral** noun an officer of very high rank in the army

**lieuˌtenant ˈgovernor** noun **1** (in Canada) an official who represents the head of state in a PROVINCE **2** (in the US) a state official with a rank just below the GOVERNOR

**life** 🔊 A1 /laɪf/ noun (pl. **lives** /laɪvz/)

- **STATE OF LIVING 1** 🔊 A1 [U] the ability to breathe, grow, produce young, etc. that people, animals and plants have before they die and that objects do not have: *life and death* ◇ *The body was cold and showed no signs of life.* ◇ *I wish we could bring dinosaurs back to life.* ◇ *In spring the countryside bursts into life.* ⇨ see also PRO-LIFE **2** 🔊 A1 [U, C] the state of being alive as a human; an individual person's existence: *The floods caused a massive loss of life* (= many people were killed). ◇ *He risked his life to save his daughter from the fire.* ◇ *The operation saved her life.* ◇ *My grandfather lost his life* (= was killed) *in the war.* ◇ *The bombing claimed the lives of* (= killed) *thousands of people.* ◇ *Attempts have been made on his life* (= people have tried to kill him).

- **LIVING THINGS 3** 🔊 A1 [U] living things: *plant/animal/insect life* ◇ *Plastic is a threat to marine life.* ◇ *Nuclear war could mean the end of life on earth.*

- **PERIOD OF TIME 4** 🔊 A1 [C, U] the period between sb's birth and their death; a part of this period: *He's lived here all his life.* ◇ *sb's whole/entire life* ◇ *He will spend the rest of his life* (= until he dies) *in a wheelchair.* ◇ *to have a long/short life* ◇ **in sb's ~** *She's had some interesting experiences in her life.* ◇ *in early/later life* ◇ *Brenda took up tennis late in life.* ◇ **for ~** *There's no such thing as a job for life any longer.* ◇ *She stayed there until the end of her life.* ◇ *He was sentenced to life imprisonment.* ⇨ see also CHANGE OF LIFE **5** 🔊 A1 [C] a period of sb's life when they are in a particular situation or job: *She has been an accountant all her working life.* ◇ **throughout sb's ~** *They were very happy throughout their married life.* ◇ **~ as sth** *He met a lot of interesting people during his life as a student.* **6** 🔊 B1 [C] the period of time when sth exists or functions: *In Italy the average life of a government is eleven months.* ◇ *These machines have a limited life* (= they do not function well for very long). ◇ *These smaller, lighter phones tend to have a shorter battery life.* ◇ **~ as sth** *The International Stock Exchange started life as a coffee shop.* ⇨ see also HALF-LIFE, LONG-LIFE, SHELF LIFE

- **EXPERIENCE/ACTIVITIES 7** 🔊 A1 [U] the experience and activities that are typical of all people's existences: *the worries of everyday life* ◇ *Commuting is part of daily life for many people.* ◇ *Trees and green spaces enhance our quality of life.* ◇ *We have no time just to enjoy life.* ◇ *Life can be hard.* ◇ *We bought a dishwasher to make life easier.* ◇ **in ~** *In real life* (= when she met him) *he wasn't how she had imagined him at all.* ◇ *a life event/experience* ⇨ see also REAL-LIFE, TRUE-LIFE **8** 🔊 A1 [U, C] the activities and experiences that are typical of a particular way of living: *We just want a normal family life.* ◇ *She enjoyed political life.* ◇ *His fame was so sudden that he was unprepared for public life.* ◇ *country/city/island life* ◇ *How do you find life in Japan?* ⇨ see also HIGH LIFE, LOW LIFE, LOW-LIFE **9** 🔊 A1 [C] a person's experiences during their life; the activities that form a particular part of a person's life: *to have/live/lead a … life* ◇ *He has had a good life.* ◇ *a hard/an easy life* ◇ *Her daily life involved meeting lots of people.* ◇ *Meeting Penny changed my life.* ◇ *They emigrated to start a new life in Canada.* ◇ *He doesn't like to talk about his private life.* ◇ *She has a full social life.* ◇ **a ~ of sth** *They lead a life of luxury.* ⇨ see also LOVE LIFE, SEX LIFE

- **ENERGY/EXCITEMENT 10** 🔊 B1 [U] the quality of being active and exciting **SYN** **vitality**: *This is a great holiday resort that is full of life.*

- **PUNISHMENT 11** [U] the punishment of being sent to prison for life or a very long period of time; life IMPRISONMENT: *The judge gave him life.*

- **IN ART 12** [U] a living model or a real object or scene that people draw or paint: *She had lessons in drawing from life.* ◇ *a life class* (= one in which art students draw a naked man or woman) ⇨ see also STILL LIFE

- **STORY OF LIFE 13** [C] a story of sb's life **SYN** **biography**: *She wrote a life of Mozart.*

- **IN GAMES 14** [C] (in children's games or computer games) one of a set number of chances before a player is out of a game: *He's lost two lives, so he's only got one left.*

**IDM** **be sb's ˈlife** be the most important person or thing to sb: *My children are my life.* ◇ *Writing is his life.* **bring sb/sth to ˈlife** to make sb/sth more interesting or exciting: *The new teacher really brought French to life for us.* ◇ *Flowers can bring a dull room back to life.* **come to ˈlife 1** to become more interesting, exciting or full of activity: *The match finally came to life in the second half.* **2** to start to act or move as if alive: *In my dream all my toys came to life.* **for dear ˈlife | for your ˈlife** as hard or as fast as possible: *She was holding on to the rope for dear life.* ◇ *Run for your life!* **for the ˈlife of you** (informal) however hard you try: *I cannot for the life of me imagine why they want to leave.* **frighten/scare the ˈlife out of sb** (informal) to frighten sb very much **full of ˈbeans/ˈlife** having a lot of energy **get a ˈlife** (informal) used to tell sb to stop being boring and to do sth more interesting **lay down your ˈlife (for sb/sth)** (literary) to die in order to save sb/sth **SYN** **sacrifice lead/live the ˈlife of ˈRiley** (old-fashioned, informal, often disapproving) to live a happy and comfortable life with no problems or responsibilities **life after ˈdeath** the possibility or belief that people continue to exist in some form after they die **the life and ˈsoul of the party, etc.** (BrE) the liveliest and funniest person at a party, etc. **life is ˈcheap** (disapproving) used to say that there is a situation in which it is not thought to be important if people somewhere die or are treated badly **(have) a life of its ˈown** (of an object) seeming to move or function by itself without a person touching or working it **life's too ˈshort** (informal) used to say that it is not worth wasting time doing sth that you dislike or that is not important **make life ˈdifficult (for sb)** to cause problems for sb **the ˈman/ˈwoman in your life** (informal) the man or woman that you are having a sexual or romantic relationship with **not on your ˈlife** (informal) used to say that you will definitely not do sth **take sb's ˈlife** to kill sb **take your (own) ˈlife** to kill yourself **take your life in your ˈhands** to risk being killed: *You take your life in your hands just crossing the road here.* **that's ˈlife** (informal) used when you are disappointed about sth but know that you must accept it **where there's ˈlife (, there's ˈhope)** (saying) in a bad situation you must not give up hope because there is always a chance that it will improve ⇨ more at BET v., BREATH, BREATHE, DEPART, DOG n., END v., FACT, FEAR n., FIGHT v., KISS n., LARGE adj., LEASE n., LIGHT n., MATTER n., MISERY, NINE, RISK v., SAVE v., SLICE n., SPRING v., STAFF n., STORY, TIME n., TRUE adj., VARIETY, WALK n., WAY n.

**ˈlife-affirming** adj. making you believe that life and people are good; offering hope for a better future: *Meeting them all was a positive and life-affirming experience.*

**ˌlife-and-ˈdeath** (also ˌlife-or-ˈdeath) adj. [only before noun] extremely serious, especially when there is a situation in which people might die: *a life-and-death decision/struggle*

**ˈlife assurance** noun [U] (BrE) = LIFE INSURANCE

**ˈlife-belt** /ˈlaɪfbelt/ noun **1** (BrE) a large ring made of material that floats well, that is used to rescue sb who has fallen into water, to prevent them from DROWNING **2** (NAmE) a special belt worn to help sb float in water ⇨ see also LIFE JACKET, LIFE PRESERVER

**life·blood** /ˈlaɪfblʌd/ noun [U] **1** ~ (of sth) the thing that keeps sth strong and healthy and is necessary for successful development: *Tourism is the lifeblood of the city.* **2** (*literary*) a person's blood, when it is thought of as the thing that is necessary for life

**life·boat** /ˈlaɪfbəʊt/ noun **1** a special boat that is sent out to rescue people who are in danger at sea: *a lifeboat crew/station* **2** a small boat carried on a ship in order to save the people on board if the ship sinks or gets into difficulties at sea

**life·buoy** /ˈlaɪfbɔɪ; NAmE -buːi, -bɔɪ/ noun a piece of material that floats well, often in the shape of a ring, used to rescue sb who has fallen into water, by keeping them above water

**life coach** (also **coach**) noun a person who is employed by sb to give them advice about how to achieve the things they want in their life and work ▶ **life coaching** (also **coach·ing**) noun [U]

**life cover** (also **life assurance**) noun (*BrE*) = LIFE INSURANCE

**life cycle** noun **1** (*biology*) the series of forms into which a living thing changes as it develops: *the life cycle of the butterfly* **2** the period of time during which sth, for example a product, is developed and used

**life drawing** noun **1** [U] the activity or skill of drawing pictures of people who are present in front of you, usually when they have no clothes on: *a life drawing class* **2** [C] a picture of a person, usually with no clothes on, who was present in front of the artist who drew them

**life-enhancing** adj. (*approving*) making you feel happier and making life more fun

**life expectancy** (also less frequent **life expectation**) noun [U, C] (NAmE also **expectation of life**) the number of years that a person is likely to live; the length of time that sth is likely to exist or continue for

**life force** noun [U] **1** the force that gives sb/sth their strength or energy: *He looked very ill—his life force seemed to have drained away.* **2** the force that keeps all life in existence: *In Hindi philosophy the life force is known as prana.*

**life form** noun (*specialist*) a living thing such as a plant or an animal

**life-giving** adj. [usually before noun] (*literary*) that gives life or keeps sth alive

**life·guard** /ˈlaɪfɡɑːd; NAmE -ɡɑːrd/ (AustralE, NZE **life-saver, surf ˈlifesaver**) noun a person who is employed at a beach or a swimming pool to rescue people who are in danger in the water

**life·hack** (also **life hack**) /ˈlaɪfhæk/ noun (*informal*) a strategy or technique that you use in order to manage your time and daily activities in a more efficient way: *This useful website offers good lifehacks for better use of your time and your technology.* ⊃ compare HACK (7)

**life ˈhistory** noun all the events that happen in the life of a person, an animal or a plant

**life insurance** (BrE also **life assurance, life cover**) noun [U] a type of insurance in which you make regular payments so that you receive a sum of money when you are a particular age, or so that your family will receive a sum of money when you die: *a life insurance policy*

**life jacket** (also **life vest** especially in NAmE) noun a jacket without arms that can be filled with air, designed to help you float if you fall in water

**life·less** /ˈlaɪfləs/ adj. **1** (*formal*) dead or appearing to be dead ⟨SYN⟩ inanimate **2** not living; not having living things growing on or in it: *lifeless machines* ◊ *a lifeless planet* **3** not bright or exciting; not having the qualities that make sth/sb interesting and full of life ⟨SYN⟩ lacklustre: *his lifeless performance on stage*

**life-like** /ˈlaɪflaɪk/ adj. exactly like a real person or thing ⟨SYN⟩ realistic: *a lifelike statue/drawing/toy*

**life-line** /ˈlaɪflaɪn/ noun **1** a line or rope thrown to rescue sb who is in difficulty in the water **2** a line attached to sb who goes deep under the sea, for sending signals to the surface **3** something that is very important for sb and that they depend on: *The extra payments are a lifeline for most single mothers.*

**life-long** /ˈlaɪflɒŋ; NAmE -lɔːŋ/ adj. [only before noun] lasting or existing all through your life: *Paul became his lifelong friend.*

**life-or-ˈdeath** adj. = LIFE-AND-DEATH

**life ˈpeer** noun (in the UK) a person who is given the title of PEER (= 'Lord' or 'Lady') but who cannot pass it on to their son or daughter

**life preserver** noun (NAmE) a piece of material that floats well, often in the shape of a ring, or a jacket made of such material, used to rescue a person who has fallen into water, by keeping them above water

**lifer** /ˈlaɪfə(r)/ noun (*informal*) a person who has been sent to prison for their whole life

**life raft** noun an open boat made of plastic or rubber that is filled with air, used for rescuing people from sinking ships or planes

**life-saver** /ˈlaɪfseɪvə(r)/ noun **1** a thing that helps sb in a difficult situation; sth that saves sb's life: *The new drug is a potential lifesaver.* **2** (also **surf ˈlifesaver**) (AustralE, NZE) = LIFEGUARD

**life-saving** adj., noun
- adj. [usually before noun] that is going to save sb's life: *a life-saving heart operation*
- noun [U] the skills needed to save sb who is in water and is DROWNING: *a life-saving qualification*

**life science** noun [pl.] any of the sciences that involve the study of humans, animals or plants ⊃ compare EARTH SCIENCE, NATURAL SCIENCE, PHYSICAL SCIENCE

**life ˈsentence** noun the punishment by which sb spends the rest of their life or a very long period of time in prison

**life-size** (also **life-sized**) adj. the same size as a person or thing really is: *a life-size statue*

**life skill** noun [usually pl.] a skill that is necessary or extremely useful to manage well in daily life

**life·span** /ˈlaɪfspæn/ noun the length of time that sth is likely to live, continue or function: *Worms have a lifespan of a few months.*

**life story** noun the story that sb tells you about their whole life

**life·style** /ˈlaɪfstaɪl/ noun [C, U] the way in which a person or a group of people lives and works: *a healthy lifestyle* ◊ *It was a big change in lifestyle when we moved to the country.* ◊ *lifestyle choices/changes*

**life supˈport** noun [U] the fact of sb being on a life support machine: *Families want the right to refuse life support.* ◊ **on ~** *She's critically ill, on life support.*

**life supˈport machine** (also **life supˈport system**) noun a piece of equipment that keeps sb alive when they are extremely ill and cannot breathe without help: *He was put on a life support machine in intensive care.*

**life's ˈwork** (BrE) (NAmE **life-work** /ˈlaɪfwɜːk; NAmE -ˈwɜːrk/) noun [sing.] the main purpose or activity in a person's life, or their greatest achievement

**life-threaten·ing** adj. that is likely to kill sb: *His heart condition is not life-threatening.*

**life·time** /ˈlaɪftaɪm/ noun the length of time that sb lives or that sth lasts: *a lifetime of experience* ◊ **in/during sb's ~** *His diary was not published during his lifetime.* ◊ **in the ~ of sth** *in the lifetime of the present government* ◊ *Memories can last a lifetime.* ◊ *The veteran actor was honoured with a lifetime achievement award.*
**IDM** **the chance, etc. of a ˈlifetime** a wonderful opportunity, etc. that you are not likely to get again **once in a ˈlifetime** used to describe sth special that is not likely to happen to you again: *An opportunity like this comes once in a lifetime.* ◊ *a once-in-a-lifetime experience*

**life vest** noun (NAmE) = LIFE JACKET

# lift

**lift** ⓘ [A2] /lɪft/ verb, noun

■ **verb**

- **RAISE 1** [A2] [T, I] to raise sb/sth or be raised to a higher position or level: ~ **sb/sth (up)** *I lifted the lid of the box and peered in.* ◇ ~ **sb/sth (up) + adv./prep.** *He stood there with his arms lifted above his head.* ◇ *(figurative) John lifted his eyes* (= looked up) *from his book.* ◇ *Her eyebrows lifted. 'Apologize? Why?'*
- **MOVE SB/STH 2** [A2] [T] ~ **sb/sth + adv./prep.** to take hold of sb/sth and move them/it to a different position: *I lifted the baby out of the chair.* ◇ *He lifted the suitcase down from the rack.* **3** [T] ~ **sb/sth (+ adv./prep.)** to transport people or things by air: *The survivors were lifted to safety by helicopter.* ⇨ see also AIRLIFT
- **REMOVE LAW/RULE 4** [B2] [T] ~ **sth** to remove or end controls or limits: *to lift a ban* ◇ *to lift sanctions/restrictions* ◇ *The US remained opposed to lifting the embargo.*
- **HEART/SPIRITS 5** [I, T] to become or make sb more cheerful: *His heart lifted at the sight of her.* ◇ ~ **sth** *The news lifted our spirits.*
- **OF MIST/CLOUDS 6** [I] to rise and disappear **SYN** **disperse**: *The fog began to lift.* ◇ *(figurative) Gradually my depression started to lift.*
- **STEAL 7** [T] ~ **sth (from sb/sth)** *(informal)* to steal sth: *He had been lifting electrical goods from the store where he worked.* ⇨ see also SHOPLIFTING
- **COPY IDEAS/WORDS 8** [T] ~ **sth (from sth)** to use sb's ideas or words without asking permission or without saying where they come from: *She lifted most of the ideas from a book she had been reading.* ⇨ compare PLAGIARIZE
- **VEGETABLES 9** [T] ~ **sth** to dig up vegetables or plants from the ground: *to lift potatoes*
- **INCREASE 10** [T, I] ~ **(sth)** to make the amount or level of sth greater; to become greater in amount or level: *Interest rates were lifted yesterday.*

**IDM** **not lift/raise a finger/hand (to do sth)** *(informal)* to do nothing to help sb: *The children never lift a finger to help around the house.*

**PHRV** **lift ˈoff** (of a ROCKET or helicopter) to leave the ground and rise into the air ⇨ related noun LIFT-OFF

■ **noun**

- **MACHINE 1** [A2] *(BrE)* *(NAmE* **ˈele·va·tor**) [C] a machine that carries people or goods up and down to different levels in a building or a mine: *It's on the sixth floor—let's take the lift.* ⇨ see also CHAIRLIFT, FORKLIFT TRUCK, SKI LIFT
- **FREE RIDE 2** [B1] *(NAmE also* **ride**) [C] a free ride in a car, etc. to a place you want to get to: *I'm going your way—do you want a lift?* ◇ ~ **+ adv./prep.** *I'll give you a lift to the station.* ◇ *She hitched a lift on a truck.*
- **HAPPIER FEELING 3** [sing.] a feeling of being happier or more confident than before **SYN** **boost**: *Passing the exam gave him a real lift.*
- **RISING MOVEMENT 4** [sing.] a movement in which sth rises or is lifted up: *the puzzled lift of his eyebrows*
- **ON AIRCRAFT 5** [U] the pressure of air moving upwards on an aircraft when flying ⇨ compare DRAG

**ˈlift-off** *noun* [C, U] the act of a ROCKET or helicopter leaving the ground and rising into the air: *Ten minutes to lift-off.* ⇨ compare BLAST-OFF

**liga·ment** /ˈlɪgəmənt/ *noun* a strong band of TISSUE in the body that connects bones and supports muscles and keeps them in position: *I've torn a ligament.*

**li·gate** /ˈlaɪgeɪt/ *verb* ~ **sth** *(medical)* to tie up an ARTERY or other BLOOD VESSEL or tube in the body, with a LIGATURE
▸ **li·ga·tion** /laɪˈgeɪʃn/ *noun* [U]

**liga·ture** /ˈlɪɡətʃə(r)/ *noun (specialist)* something that is used for tying sth very tightly, for example to stop the loss of blood from a wound

**light** ⓘ [A1] /laɪt/ *noun, adj., verb, adv.*

■ **noun**

- **FROM SUN/LAMPS 1** [A1] [U] the energy from the sun, a lamp, etc. that makes it possible to see things: *bright/dim light* ◇ *a room with good natural light* ◇ *White paint reflects the light.* ◇ *The knife gleamed as it caught the light* (= as the light shone on it). ◇ **by the ~ of sth** *She could just see by the light of the candle.* ◇ **into the ~** *Bring it into the light so I can see it.* ◇ **a beam/ray of light** ⇨ see also FIRST LIGHT, HALF-LIGHT **2** [A1] [C, usually sing.] a particular type of light with its own colour or qualities: *A cold, grey light crept under the curtains.* ⇨ see also BLACK LIGHT, NORTHERN LIGHTS
- **LAMP 3** [A1] [C] a thing that produces light, especially an electric light: *to turn/switch the lights on/off* ◇ *to turn out the light(s)* ◇ *Suddenly all the lights went out.* ◇ *It was an hour before the lights came on again.* ◇ *A light flashed in the distance.* ◇ *A bright light shone in his eyes.* ◇ *ceiling/wall lights* ◇ *Keep going—the lights* (= traffic lights) *are green.* ◇ *Check your car before you drive to make sure that your lights are working.* ◇ *She felt along the wall and found the light switch.* ⇨ see also BACKUP LIGHT, BRAKE LIGHT, FAIRY LIGHTS, GREEN LIGHT, HEADLIGHT, LEADING LIGHT, RED LIGHT, STOP LIGHT, STREET LIGHT, TAIL LIGHT, TRAFFIC LIGHT, TUBE LIGHT
- **EXPRESSION IN EYES 4** [sing.] an expression in sb's eyes that shows what they are thinking or feeling: *There was a soft light in her eyes as she looked at him.*
- **IN PICTURE 5** [U] light colours in a picture, which contrast with darker ones: *the artist's use of light and shade*
- **FOR CIGARETTE 6** [sing.] a match or device with which you can light a cigarette: *(BrE) Have you got a light?* ◇ *(NAmE, BrE) Do you have a light?*
- **WINDOW 7** [C] *(architecture)* a window or an opening to allow light in: *leaded lights* ⇨ see also SKYLIGHT

**IDM** **according to sb's/sth's ˈlights** *(formal)* according to the standards that sb sets for himself or herself **be in sb's ˈlight** to be between sb and a source of light: *Could you move—you're in my light.* **be/go out like a ˈlight** *(informal)* to go to sleep very quickly **bring sth to ˈlight** to make new information known to people: *These facts have only just been brought to light.* **cast/shed/throw ˈlight on sth** to make a problem, etc. easier to understand: *Recent research has thrown new light on the causes of the disease.* **come to ˈlight** to become known to people: *New evidence has recently come to light.* **in a good, bad, favourable, etc. ˈlight** if you see sth or put sth **in a good, bad, etc. light**, it seems good, bad, etc: *You must not view what happened in a negative light.* ◇ *They want to present their policies in the best possible light.* **in the light of sth** *(BrE)* *(NAmE* **in light of sth**) after considering sth: *He rewrote the book in the light of further research.* **jump the ˈlights** *(BrE)* (*also* **run a (red) ˈlight, run the ˈlights** *especially in NAmE*) *(informal)* to fail to stop at a red traffic light **the lights are on but nobody's ˈhome** *(saying, humorous)* used to describe sb who is stupid, not thinking clearly or not paying attention **light at the end of the ˈtunnel** something that shows you are nearly at the end of a long and difficult time or situation **(the) light ˈdawned (on sb)** somebody suddenly understood or began to understand sth: *I puzzled over the problem for ages before the light suddenly dawned.* **the light of sb's ˈlife** the person sb loves more than any other **see the ˈlight 1** to finally understand or accept sth, especially sth obvious **2** to begin to believe in a religion **see the ˈlight (of ˈday)** to begin to exist or to become publicly known about: *He's written a lot of good material that has never seen the light of day.* **set ˈlight to sth** *(especially BrE)* to make sth start burning **SYN** **ignite**: *A spark from the fire had set light to a rug.* ⇨ more at BRIGHT *adj.*, COLD *adj.*, HIDE *v.*, SWEETNESS

■ **adj.** (**light·er, light·est**)

- **COLOURS 1** [A1] pale in colour: *light blue eyes* ◇ *Lighter shades suit you best.* ◇ *People with pale complexions should avoid wearing light colours.* **OPP** **dark**
- **WITH NATURAL LIGHT 2** [A2] full of light; having the natural light of day: *We'll leave in the morning as soon as it's light.* ◇ *It gets light at about 5 o'clock.* ◇ *It was a light spacious apartment at the top of the building.* **OPP** **dark**
- **WEIGHT 3** [A2] easy to lift or move; not weighing very much: *The device is light and portable.* ◇ *Carry this bag—it's the lightest.* ◇ *Hydrogen gas is lighter than air.* ◇ *The little girl was as light as a feather.* **OPP** **heavy 4** [A2] [usually before noun] of less than average or usual weight: *light summer clothes* ◇ *Only light vehicles are allowed over the old bridge.* **OPP** **heavy 5** used with a unit of weight to say that sth weighs less than it should do: *The delivery of potatoes was several kilos light.*

- GENTLE **6** [usually before noun] gentle and without weight; not using much force: *She felt a light tap on her shoulder.* ◊ *the sound of quick light footsteps* ◊ *You only need to apply light pressure.* ◊ *As a boxer, he was always light on his feet* (= quick and elegant in the way he moved). **OPP** heavy
- WORK/EXERCISE **7** [usually before noun] easy to do; not making you tired: *After his accident he was moved to lighter work.* ◊ *Her duties are relatively light.* ◊ *You are probably well enough to take a little light exercise.*
- NOT GREAT **8** not great in amount, degree, etc: *Traffic was light.* ◊ *Light rain is forecast.* ◊ *Civilian casualties were comparatively light.* **OPP** heavy
- NOT SERIOUS/SEVERE **9** fun rather than serious and not needing much mental effort: *light reading for the beach* ◊ *light entertainment* ◊ *We all needed a little light relief at the end of a long day* (= sth funny or fun that comes after sth serious or boring). **10** not serious: *She kept her tone light.* ◊ *This programme looks at the lighter side of politics.* ◊ *On a lighter note, we end the news today with a story about a duck called Quackers.* **11** not severe: *He was convicted of assaulting a police officer but he got off with a light sentence.*
- FOOD **12** (of a meal) small in quantity: *a light meal/supper/snack/breakfast* ◊ *Light refreshments will be provided.* **OPP** heavy **13** not containing much fat, sugar or other rich ingredients and therefore easy to DIGEST: *Stick to a light diet.* ⊃ see also LITE **14** containing a lot of air: *This pastry is so light.*
- DRINK **15** low in alcohol: *a light beer* **16** (IndE) (of tea or coffee) containing a lot of water **SYN** weak: *I don't like my coffee too light.* **OPP** strong
- ARMY **17** [only before noun] (of soldiers) carrying only light weapons: *the light infantry/cavalry* **OPP** heavy
- SLEEP **18** [only before noun] a person in a light sleep is easy to wake: *She drifted into a light sleep.* ◊ *I've always been a light sleeper.* **OPP** deep
- CHEERFUL **19** [usually before noun] free from worry; cheerful: *I left the island with a light heart.* ▶ **light·ness** noun [U] ⊃ see also LIGHTLY

**IDM** **be light on sth** (BrE) to not have enough of sth: *We seem to be light on fuel.* **a light touch** the ability to deal with sth in a sensitive and relaxed way: *She handles this difficult subject with a light touch.* **make 'light of sth** to treat sth as not being important and not serious **make light 'work of sth** to do sth quickly and with little effort ⊃ more at HAND *n*.

■ *verb* (**lit**, **lit** /lɪt/) **HELP** Lighted is also used for the past tense and past participle, especially in front of nouns.
- START TO BURN **1** [T] ~sth to make sth start to burn: *She lit a candle.* ◊ *Come in, I'll light a fire and you can get warmed up.* ◊ *The gas lamps were lit.* ◊ *a lighted match* ◊ *a lit cigarette* **2** [I] (used especially in negative sentences) to start to burn: *The fire wouldn't light.*
- GIVE LIGHT **3** [T, usually passive] to give light to sth or to a place: **be lit (by sth)** *At night the hall was lit by candles.* ◊ *a dimly lit street* ◊ *a brightly lit room* **4** [T] ~sth (*literary*) to guide sb with a light: *Our way was lit by a full moon.*

**PHRV** **light on/upon sth** (*literary*) to see or find sth by accident: *His eye lit upon a small boat on the horizon.* **light ˈup** | **light sth↔ˈup 1** to become or to make sth become bright with light or colour: *There was an explosion and the whole sky lit up.* **2** if sb's eyes or face **light up**, or sth **lights them up**, they show happiness or excitement: *His eyes lit up when she walked into the room.* ◊ *A smile lit up her face.* **3** (*informal*) to begin to smoke a cigarette: *They all lit up as soon as he left the room.* ◊ *He sat back and lit up a cigarette.*

■ *adv.* **IDM** see TRAVEL *v*.

▼ **WHICH WORD?**
**light / lighting**
- The noun **light** has several different meanings and is used in many phrases. **Lighting** can only be used to talk about the type of light in a place or how lights are used to achieve a particular effect: *the lighting system* ◊ *the movie's interesting lighting effects* ◊ *The lighting at the disco was fantastic.*

---

909 **light meter**

**light ˈaircraft** *noun* (*pl.* **light aircraft**) a small plane with seats for no more than about six passengers

**ˈlight bulb** (*also* **bulb**) *noun* the glass part that fits into an electric lamp, etc. to give light when it is switched on

**light-ˈcoloured** (US **light-ˈcolored**) *adj.* pale in colour; not dark

**light ˈcream** (NAmE) (BrE **single ˈcream**) *noun* [U] thin cream that is used in cooking and for pouring over food ⊃ compare HEAVY CREAM

**light·ed** /ˈlaɪtɪd/ *adj.* **1** a lighted CANDLE, cigarette, match, etc. is burning **2** a lighted window is bright because there are lights on inside the room **OPP** unlit

**light·en** /ˈlaɪtn/ *verb* **1** [T] ~sth to reduce the amount of work, debt, worry, etc. that sb has **SYN** lessen: *equipment to lighten the load of domestic work* ◊ *The measures will lighten the tax burden on small businesses.* **2** [I, T] to become or make sth become brighter or lighter in colour: *The sky began to lighten in the east.* ◊ ~sth *Use bleach to lighten the wood.* **3** [I, T] to feel or make sb feel less sad, worried or serious **SYN** cheer: ~(up) *My mood gradually lightened.* ◊ ~sth (up) *She told a joke to lighten the atmosphere.* **4** [T] ~sth to make sth lighter in weight

**PHRV** **lighten ˈup** (*informal*) used to tell sb to become less serious or worried about sth: *Come on, John. Lighten up!*

**light·er** /ˈlaɪtə(r)/ *noun* **1** (*also* **ciga'rette lighter**) a small device that produces a flame for lighting cigarettes, etc. **2** a boat with a flat bottom used for carrying goods to and from ships in HARBOUR

**light-ˈfingered** *adj.* (*informal*) likely to steal things

**light-ˈfooted** *adj.* moving quickly and easily, in an attractive way

**light-ˈheaded** *adj.* not completely in control of your thoughts or movements; slightly FAINT: *After two glasses of wine he began to feel light-headed.*

**light-ˈhearted** *adj.* **1** intended to be fun rather than too serious: *a light-hearted speech* **2** cheerful and without problems: *She felt light-hearted and optimistic.* ▶ **light-ˈheartedly** *adv.*

**light ˈheavyweight** (*also* **cruiserweight**) *noun* [U, C] a weight in BOXING and other sports, between MIDDLEWEIGHT and HEAVYWEIGHT, in BOXING usually between 75 and 81 KILOGRAMS; a BOXER or other competitor in this class

**light·house** /ˈlaɪthaʊs/ *noun* a tower or other building that contains a strong light to warn and guide ships near the coast

**light ˈindustry** *noun* [U, C] industry that produces small or light objects such as things used in the house ⊃ compare HEAVY INDUSTRY

**light·ing** /ˈlaɪtɪŋ/ *noun* [U] **1** the arrangement or type of light in a place: *electric/natural lighting* ◊ *good/poor lighting* ◊ *The play had excellent sound and lighting effects.* **2** the use of electric lights in a place: *the cost of heating and lighting* ◊ *street lighting* ⊃ note at LIGHT

**ˈlighting engineer** *noun* a person who works in television, the theatre, etc. and whose job is to control and take care of the lights

**light·ly** /ˈlaɪtli/ *adv.* **1** gently; with very little force or effort: *He kissed her lightly on the cheek.* **2** to a small degree; not much: *It began to snow lightly.* ◊ *She tended to sleep lightly nowadays* (= it was easy to disturb her). ◊ *I try to eat lightly* (= not to eat heavy or GREASY food). **3** in a way that sounds as though you are not particularly worried or interested **SYN** nonchalantly: '*I'll be all right,*' *he said lightly.* **4** without being seriously considered: *This is not a problem we should take lightly.*

**IDM** **get off/be let off lightly** (*informal*) to be punished or treated in a way that is less severe than you deserve or may have expected

**ˈlight meter** *noun* a device used to measure how bright the light is before taking a photograph

# lightning 910

**light·ning** /ˈlaɪtnɪŋ/ noun, adj.
- **noun** [U] a flash, or several flashes, of very bright light in the sky caused by electricity: *a flash of lightning* ◊ *a violent storm with thunder and lightning* ◊ *He was struck by lightning and killed.* ◊ *Lightning strikes caused scores of fires across the state.* ⊃ see also FORKED LIGHTNING, SHEET LIGHTNING
- **IDM** **lightning never strikes (in the same place) twice** (saying) an unusual or unpleasant event is not likely to happen in the same place or to the same people twice **like (greased) ˈlightning** very fast
- **adj.** [only before noun] very fast or sudden

**ˈlightning bug** noun (NAmE) = FIREFLY

**ˈlightning conductor** (BrE) (also **ˈlightning rod** especially in NAmE) noun **1** a long straight piece of metal or wire leading from the highest part of a building to the ground, put there to prevent lightning damaging the building **2** a person or thing that attracts criticism, especially if the criticism is then not directed at sb/sth else

**ˈlightning strike** noun an incident in which LIGHTNING hits sb/sth

**ˈlight pen** noun **1** a piece of equipment, like a pen in shape, that is sensitive to light and that can be used to pass information to a computer when it touches the screen **2** a similar piece of equipment that is used for reading BARCODES

**ˈlight pollution** noun [U] the existence of too much artificial light in the environment, for example from street lights, which makes it difficult to see the stars

**light·ship** /ˈlaɪtʃɪp/ noun a small ship that stays at a particular place at sea and that has a powerful light on it to warn and guide other ships

**ˈlight show** noun a display of changing coloured lights, for example at a pop concert

**ˈlight stick** noun = GLOW STICK

**light·weight** /ˈlaɪtweɪt/ adj., noun
- **adj. 1** made of thinner material and less heavy than usual: *a lightweight jacket* **2** (disapproving) not very serious or impressive: *a lightweight book* ◊ *He was considered too lightweight for the job.*
- **noun 1** [U, C] a weight in BOXING and other sports, between FEATHERWEIGHT and WELTERWEIGHT, in BOXING usually between 57 and 60 KILOGRAMS; a BOXER or other competitor in this class: *a lightweight champion* **2** [C] a person or thing that weighs less than is usual **3** [C] (informal, disapproving) a person or thing of little importance or influence: *a political lightweight* ◊ *He's an intellectual lightweight* (= he does not think very deeply or seriously)

**ˈlight year** noun **1** (astronomy) the distance that light travels in one year, $9.4607 \times 10^{12}$ kilometres: *The nearest star to earth is about 4 light years away.* **2 light years** [pl.] a very long time: *Full employment still seems light years away.*

**lig·nite** /ˈlɪɡnaɪt/ noun [U] a soft brown type of coal

**lig·no·caine** /ˈlɪɡnəkeɪn/ noun [U] = LIDOCAINE

**lik·able** (especially NAmE) = LIKEABLE

**like** /laɪk/ prep., verb, conj., noun, adj., adv.
- **prep. 1** similar to sb/sth: *She's wearing a dress like mine.* ◊ *He's very like his father.* ◊ *She looks nothing like* (= not at all like) *her mother.* ◊ *That sounds like* (= I think I can hear) *him coming now.* **2** used to ask sb's opinion of sb/sth: *What's it like studying in Spain?* ◊ *This new girlfriend of his—what's she like?* **3** in the same way as/ sth: *Students were angry at being treated like children.* ◊ *He ran like the wind* (= very fast). ◊ *You do it like this.* ◊ *I, like everyone else, had read these stories in the press.* ◊ *Don't look at me like that.* ◊ (informal) *The candles are arranged like so* (= in this way). ⊃ LANGUAGE BANK at SIMILARLY **4** for example: *anti-utopian novels like 'Animal Farm' and '1984'* ⊃ note at AS **5** used to show what is usual or typical for sb: *It's just like her to tell everyone about it.*
- **IDM** **more like …** used to give a number or an amount that is more accurate than one previously mentioned: *He believes the figure should be more like $10 million.* **more ˈlike (it)** (informal) **1** better; more acceptable: *This is more like it! Real food—not that canned muck.* **2** used to give what you think is a better description of sth: *Just talking? Arguing more like it.* **what is sb ˈlike?** (BrE, informal) used to say that sb has done sth annoying, silly, etc: *Oh, what am I like? I just completely forgot it.*
- **verb** (not usually used in the progressive tenses) **1** [T] to find sb/sth pleasant, attractive or of a good enough standard; to enjoy sth: **~sb/sth** *She's nice. I like her.* ◊ *I really like him.* ◊ *Do you like their new house?* ◊ *Which tie do you like best?* ◊ *How did you like Japan* (= did you find it pleasant)? ◊ *I don't like the way he's looking at me.* ◊ *You've got to go to school, whether you like it or not.* ◊ **~doing sth** *We like having people to stay.* ◊ **~sb/sth doing sth** *I didn't like him taking all the credit.* ◊ **~to do sth** *I like to see them enjoying themselves.* ◊ **~it when …** *I like it when you do that.* **HELP** Like is not usually used in the progressive tenses. However, in informal English, it is becoming more common to say *I'm liking* sth when you mean that you are currently enjoying it: (informal) **be liking (doing) sth** *I'm liking this song.* ⊃ note at WANT ⊃ SYNONYMS at LOVE **2** [T] used with *would* or *should* as a polite way to say what you want or to ask what sb wants: **~sth** *Would you like a drink?* ◊ **~to do sth** *I'd like to think it over.* ◊ *I would like to thank you all for coming tonight.* ◊ *How can they afford it? That's what I'd like to know.* ◊ **~sb/sth to do sth** *We'd like you to come and visit us.* ◊ **~for sb to do sth** (NAmE) *I'd like for us to work together.* ⊃ note at WANT ⊃ EXPRESS YOURSELF at PLEASE **3** [T, no passive] to prefer to do sth; to prefer sth to be made or to happen in a particular way: **~to do sth** *At weekends I like to sleep late.* ◊ **~sth + adj.** *I like my coffee strong.* **4** [T] used in negative sentences to mean 'to be unwilling to do sth': **not~to do sth** *I didn't like to disturb you.* ◊ **not~doing sth** *He doesn't like asking his parents for help.* **5** [T, no passive] **what/whatever sb likes** to want: *Do what you like—I don't care.* ◊ *You can dye your hair whatever colour you like.* **6 ~sth** if you like sth on SOCIAL MEDIA, a news website, a blog, etc. you show that you agree with it or that you think it is good by clicking a special button: *By the next morning, over twenty of my friends had liked my new profile picture.*
- **IDM** **how would you like it?** used to emphasize that sth bad has happened to you and you want some sympathy: *How would you like it if someone called you a liar?* **if you ˈlike** (informal) **1** used to politely agree to sth or to suggest sth: *'Shall we stop now?' 'If you like.'* ◊ *If you like, we could go out this evening.* **2** used when you express sth in a new way or when you are not confident about sth: *It was, if you like, the dawn of a new era.* **I like ˈthat!** (old-fashioned, informal) used to protest that sth that has been said is not true or fair: *'She called you a cheat.' 'Well, I like that!'* **I/I'd like to think** used to say that you hope or believe that sth is true: *I like to think I'm broad-minded.* **what's not to ˈlike?** (informal, humorous) used to say that sth is very good or you enjoy it: *You get paid to eat chocolate. So what's not to like?*
- **noun 1** **likes** [pl.] the things that you like: *We all have different likes and dislikes.* **2** [sing.] a person or thing that is similar to another: *jazz, rock and the like* (= similar types of music) ◊ *a man whose like we shall not see again* ◊ *You're not comparing yourself with like.* **3** [C] if something on SOCIAL MEDIA, a news website, a blog, etc. receives a like, it means that somebody has shown that they agree with it or think it is good by clicking a special button: *The band now has thousands of likes.*
- **IDM** **the likes of sb/sth** (informal) used to refer to sb/sth that is considered as a type, especially one that is considered as good as sb/sth else: *She didn't want to associate with the likes of me.*
- **conj.** (informal) **1** in the same way as: *No one sings the blues like she did.* ◊ *It didn't turn out like I intended.* ◊ **Like I said** (= as I said before), *you're always welcome to stay.* **2** as if: *She acts like she owns the place.* **HELP** You will find more information about this use of *like* at the entries for the verbs **act, behave, feel, look** and **sound** and in the note at **as**.
- **adj.** [only before noun] (formal) having similar qualities to another person or thing: *a chance to meet people of like*

Oxford 3000 | Oxford 5000 | CEFR level | PHRV phrasal verb(s) | IDM idiom(s)

mind (= with similar interests and opinions) ◊ *She responded in like manner.*
■ **adv. 1** used in very informal speech, for example when you are thinking what to say next, explaining sth, or giving an example of sth: *It was, like, weird.* ◊ *It was kind of scary, like.* ◊ *It's really hard. Like I have no time for my own work.* **2** used in very informal speech to show that what you are saying may not be exactly right but is nearly so: *I'm leaving in like twenty minutes.* ◊ *It's going to cost like a hundred dollars.* **3 I'm, he's, she's, etc. ~** used in very informal speech, to mean 'I say', 'he/she says', etc: *And then I'm like 'No Way!'* **4** used in informal speech instead of *as* to say that sth happens in the same way: *There was silence, but not like before.* ⊃ note at AS
**IDM** **(as) like as 'not** | **like e'nough** | **most/very 'like** (*old-fashioned*) quite probably: *She would be in bed by now, as like as not.*

▼ **SYNONYMS**

**like**

love • be fond of • be keen on sth • adore

These words all mean to find sth pleasant, attractive or of a good enough standard, or to enjoy sth.

**like** to find sth pleasant, attractive or of a good enough standard; to enjoy sth: *Do you like their new house?* ◊ *I like to see them enjoying themselves.*

**love** to like or enjoy sth very much: *He loved the way she smiled.*

**be fond of sth** to like or enjoy sth, especially sth you have liked or enjoyed for a long time: *We were fond of the house and didn't want to leave.*

**be keen on sth** (*BrE informal*) (often used in negative statements) to like or enjoy sth: *I'm not keen on spicy food.* ◊ *She's not keen on being told what to do.*

**adore** (*informal*) to like or enjoy sth very much: *She adores working with children.*

LOVE OR ADORE?
- **Adore** is more informal than **love**, and is used to express a stronger feeling.

PATTERNS
- to like/love/be fond of/be keen on/adore doing sth
- to like/love **to do sth**
- to like/love sth **very much**
- I like/love/adore **it** here/there/when ...
- to like/love/adore **the way** sb does sth
- to **really** like/love/adore sb/sth
- to be **really** fond of/keen on sth

**-like** /laɪk/ *combining form* (in adjectives) similar to; typical of: *childlike* ◊ *shell-like*

**like·able** (*especially BrE*) (*also* **lik·able** *especially in NAmE*) /ˈlaɪkəbl/ *adj.* pleasant and easy to like: *a very likeable man* **OPP** **unlikeable**

**like·li·hood** ¿+ **C1** /ˈlaɪklihʊd/ *noun* [U, sing.] the chance of sth happening; how likely sth is to happen **SYN** **probability**: *There is very little likelihood of that happening.* ◊ *In all likelihood* (= very probably) *the meeting will be cancelled.* ◊ *The likelihood is that* (= it is likely that) *unemployment figures will continue to fall.*

**like·ly** ❶ **A2** ⊙ /ˈlaɪkli/ *adj., adv.*
■ **adj.** (**like·lier**, **like·li·est**) **1** ¿ having a good chance of happening or being sth; PROBABLE or expected: *the most likely explanation/outcome/scenario* ◊ *A threat level of 'Severe' means a terrorist attack is highly likely.* ◊ *~ to do sth Tickets are likely to be expensive.* ◊ *~ (that) ... It's hardly likely (that) they'll refuse.* ⊃ LANGUAGE BANK at EXPECT **2** seeming suitable for a purpose **SYN** **promising**: *She seems the most likely candidate for the job.*
**IDM** **a 'likely story** (*informal, ironic*) used to show that you do not believe what sb has said
■ **adv.**
**IDM** **as likely as 'not** | **most/very 'likely** very probably: *As likely as not she's forgotten all about it.* **not 'likely!** (*informal, especially BrE*) used to disagree strongly with a statement or suggestion: *Me? Join the army? Not likely!*

911

▼ **EXPRESS YOURSELF**

**Expressing likelihood**

When you are talking about possible situations, you can express how likely you think they are:
- **It's pretty much inevitable** that prices will go up this year.
- **I think** it's likely to rain this afternoon.
- I'm **probably** going to be away then.
- **I guess there's a fifty per cent chance that** they'll say no.
- **It's unlikely, but not totally impossible, I suppose.**
- **They can't possibly/really be** serious about buying a boat!
- Let's start without them. **They're bound to be** late.

▼ **GRAMMAR POINT**

**likely**
- In standard *BrE* the adverb **likely** is often used with a word such as *most, more* or *very*: *We will most likely see him later.* In journalism and less formal language, however, **likely** is used on its own: *The deal will likely result in more cuts to services.* In informal *NAmE* **likely** is often used on its own, and this is not considered incorrect: *We will likely see him later.* ◊ *He said that he would likely run for President.*

**like-'minded** *adj.* having similar ideas and interests

**liken** /ˈlaɪkən/ *verb*
**PHRV** **'liken sth/sb to sth/sb** (*formal*) to compare one thing or person to another and say they are similar: *Life is often likened to a journey.*

**like·ness** /ˈlaɪknəs/ *noun* **1** [C, U] the fact of being similar to another person or thing, especially in appearance; an example of this **SYN** **resemblance**: *Joanna bears a strong likeness to her father.* ◊ *Do you notice any family likeness between them?* **2** [C, usually sing.] a painting, drawing, etc. of a person, especially one that looks very like them: *The drawing is said to be a good likeness of the girl's attacker.*

**likes** /laɪks/ *noun* ⊃ LIKE *noun*

**like·wise** ¿+ **B2** /ˈlaɪkwaɪz/ *adv.* **1** ¿+ **B2** (*formal*) the same; in a similar way: *He voted for the change and he expected his colleagues to do likewise.* **2** (*formal*) also: *Her second marriage was likewise unhappy.* **3** (*informal*) used to show that you feel the same towards sb or about sth: *'Let me know if you ever need any help.' 'Likewise.'*

**lik·ing** /ˈlaɪkɪŋ/ *noun* [sing.] **~ (for sb/sth)** the feeling that you like sb/sth; the pleasure in sth **SYN** **fondness**: *He had a liking for fast cars.* ◊ *She had taken a liking to him on their first meeting.*
**IDM** **for your 'liking** if you say, for example, that sth is too hot **for your liking**, you mean that you would prefer it to be less hot: *The town was too crowded for my liking.* **to your 'liking** (*formal*) suitable, and how you like sth: *The coffee was just to his liking.*

**lilac** /ˈlaɪlək/ *noun* **1** [U, C] a bush or small tree with purple or white flowers with a sweet smell that grow closely together in the shape of a CONE **2** [U] a pale purple colour ▸ **lilac** *adj.*: *a lilac dress*

**Lil·li·pu·tian** /ˌlɪlɪˈpjuːʃn/ *adj.* (*formal*) extremely small **SYN** **diminutive, tiny** **ORIGIN** From the land of **Lilliput**, in Jonathan Swift's *Gulliver's Travels*, where the people are only 15cm high.

**lilo** /ˈlaɪləʊ/ (*also* **Li-Lo**™) *noun* (*pl.* **-os**) (*BrE*) a plastic or rubber bed that is filled with air and used when camping or for floating on water

**lilt** /lɪlt/ *noun* [sing.] **1** the pleasant way in which a person's voice rises and falls: *Her voice had a soft Welsh lilt to it.* **2** a regular rising and falling pattern in music, with a strong rhythm ▸ **lilt·ing** *adj.*

**lily** /ˈlɪli/ *noun* (*pl.* **-ies**) a large white or brightly coloured flower with PETALS that CURL back from the centre. There are many types of lily. ⊃ see also WATER LILY ⊃ VISUAL VOCAB page V7 **IDM** see GILD

**lily**

⊙ Oxford Phrasal Academic Lexicon (OPAL) written and spoken word lists | **W** OPAL written word list | **S** OPAL spoken word list

**lily-livered** /ˈlɪli lɪvəd; NAmE -vərd/ adj. (old-fashioned) not having any courage; not brave SYN **cowardly**

**lily of the ˈvalley** noun [C, U] (pl. **lilies of the valley**) a plant with small white flowers that are like bells in shape

**ˈlily pad** noun a round floating leaf of a WATER LILY

**lily-ˈwhite** adj. **1** almost pure white in colour: *lily-white skin* **2** morally perfect: *They want me to conform, to be lily-white.*

**lima bean** /ˈliːmə biːn, ˈlaɪm-; NAmE ˈlaɪm-/ noun (NAmE) a type of round, pale green bean. Several lima beans grow together inside a flat POD.

**limb** /lɪm/ noun **1** an arm or a leg; a similar part of an animal, such as a wing: *an artificial limb* ◇ *For a while, she lost the use of her limbs.* **2 -limbed** (in adjectives) having the type of limbs mentioned: *long-limbed* ◇ *loose-limbed* **3** a large branch of a tree ⇒ VISUAL VOCAB page V6
**IDM** **out on a ˈlimb** (informal) not supported by other people: *Are you prepared to go out on a limb (= risk doing sth that other people are not prepared to do) and make your suspicions public?* **tear/rip sb ˈlimb from ˈlimb** (often humorous) to attack sb very violently ⇒ more at RISK v.

**limba** /ˈlɪmbə/ noun = AFARA

**lim·ber** /ˈlɪmbə(r)/ verb
**PHRV** **ˌlimber ˈup** to do physical exercises in order to stretch and prepare your muscles before taking part in a race, sporting activity, etc. SYN **warm up**

**lim·bic sys·tem** /ˈlɪmbɪk sɪstəm/ noun (biology) a system of nerves in the brain involving several different areas, connected with basic emotions such as fear and anger and basic needs such as the need to eat and have sex

**limbo** /ˈlɪmbəʊ/ noun (pl. **-os**) **1** [C] a West Indian dance in which you lean backwards and go under a bar that is made lower each time you go under it **2** [U, sing.] a situation in which you are not certain what to do next, cannot take action, etc., especially because you are waiting for sb else to make a decision: *the limbo of the stateless person* ◇ **in ~** *His life seemed stuck in limbo; he could not go forward and he could not go back.*

**lime** /laɪm/ noun, verb
■ noun **1** (also **quick·lime**) [U] a white substance obtained by heating LIMESTONE, used in building materials and to help plants grow **2** [C, U] a small green fruit, like a lemon, with juice that has a bitter, sharp taste, used in cooking and in drinks; the juice of this fruit: *lime juice* ◇ *slices of lime* ⇒ VISUAL VOCAB page V4 **3** (also **ˈlime tree**) [C] a tree on which limes grow **4** (also **ˈlime tree**, **ˈlinden tree**, **lin·den**) [C] a large tree with light-green, heart-shaped leaves and yellow flowers: *an avenue of limes* **5** [U] = LIME GREEN
■ verb ~ sth to add the substance lime to soil, especially in order to control the ACID in it

**lime-ˈgreen** adj. (also **lime**) bright yellow-green in colour ▶ **lime ˈgreen** (also **lime**) noun [U]

**lime·light** /ˈlaɪmlaɪt/ noun [U] (usually **the limelight**) the centre of public attention: **in the ~** *to be in the limelight* ◇ **out of the ~** *to stay out of the limelight* ◇ *to steal/hog the limelight* (= take attention away from other people)

**lim·er·ick** /ˈlɪmərɪk/ noun a humorous short poem, with two long lines that RHYME with each other, followed by two short lines that rhyme with each other and ending with a long line that rhymes with the first two

**lime·scale** /ˈlaɪmskeɪl/ noun [U] (BrE) the hard white substance, mainly consisting of CALCIUM CARBONATE, that is left by water on the inside of pipes, etc.

**lime·stone** /ˈlaɪmstəʊn/ noun [U] a type of white rock that contains CALCIUM, used in building and in making CEMENT

**ˈlime water** noun [U] (chemistry) a liquid containing CALCIUM HYDROXIDE that shows the presence of CARBON DIOXIDE by turning white

**Limey** /ˈlaɪmi/ noun (NAmE, AustralE, old-fashioned, informal) a slightly offensive word for a British person

**limit** /ˈlɪmɪt/ noun, verb
■ noun **1** the greatest or smallest amount of sth that is allowed SYN **restriction**: *They imposed a strict spending limit.* ◇ *Do not exceed the recommended limit of 6g of salt per day.* ◇ **~ on sth** *The EU has set strict limits on levels of pollution.* ◇ **within limits** *to keep government spending within acceptable limits* ◇ **over the ~** *You can't drive—you're over the limit (= you have drunk more alcohol than is legal when driving).* ⇒ see also AGE LIMIT, SPEED LIMIT, TIME LIMIT **2** a point at which sth stops being possible or existing: *She knew the limits of her power.* ◇ *to push/test the limits of sth* ◇ *His arrogance knew (= had) no limits.* ◇ **~ to sth** *There is a limit to the amount of pain we can bear.* ◇ **to the ~** *The team performed to the limit of its capabilities.* **3** [pl.] the furthest edge of an area or a place: *We were reaching the limits of civilization.* ◇ *the city limits (= the imaginary line which officially divides the city from the area outside)* ⇒ see also OFF-LIMITS
**IDM** **be the ˈlimit** (old-fashioned, informal) to be extremely annoying **within ˈlimits** to some extent: *I'm willing to help, within limits.* ⇒ more at PUSH v., SKY n.
■ verb **1** ~ **sth** to stop sth from increasing beyond a particular amount or level SYN **restrict**: *measures to limit carbon dioxide emissions* ◇ *The amount of money you have to spend will limit your choice.* ◇ *Try to limit the number of trips you make.* ◇ *to limit sb's ability/freedom/power to do sth* **2** ~ **sb/yourself (to sth)** to stop yourself or sb from having, using or doing more than a particular amount or number of sth: *I've limited myself to 1000 calories a day to try and lose weight.* ◇ *Families are limited to four free tickets each.*
**PHRV** **ˈlimit sth to sb/sth** [usually passive] to make sth exist or happen only in a particular place or within a particular group: *Violent crime is not limited to big cities.* ◇ *The teaching of history should not be limited to dates and figures.*

**lim·i·ta·tion** /ˌlɪmɪˈteɪʃn/ noun **1** [U] the act or process of limiting or controlling sb/sth SYN **restriction**: *They would resist any limitation of their powers.* ⇒ SYNONYMS at LIMIT ⇒ see also DAMAGE LIMITATION **2** [C] ~ **(on sth)** a rule, fact or condition that limits sth SYN **curb, restraint**: *to impose limitations on imports* ◇ *Disability is a physical limitation on your life.* ⇒ see also STATUTE OF LIMITATIONS **3** [C, usually pl.] a limit on what sb/sth can do or how good they or it can be: *This technique is useful but it has its limitations.*

**lim·it·ed** /ˈlɪmɪtɪd/ adj. **1** not very great in amount or extent: *We are doing our best with the limited resources available.* **2** having a particular limit of time, numbers, etc: *There are only a limited number of jobs available.* ◇ **~ to sth** *Entry is limited to 150 people.* ⇒ see also LTD

**ˌlimited ˈcompany** (also **ˌlimited liaˈbility ˈcompany**) noun (in the UK) a private company whose owners only have to pay its debts up to the amount they invested in the company ⇒ see also LTD, PUBLIC LIMITED COMPANY

**ˌlimited eˈdition** noun a fixed, usually small, number of copies of a book, picture, etc. produced at one time

**ˌlimited liaˈbility** noun [U] (law) (in the UK) the legal position by which the SHAREHOLDERS of a company only have to pay its debts up to the value of their shares

**lim·it·ing** /ˈlɪmɪtɪŋ/ adj. **1** putting limits on what is possible: *Lack of cash is a limiting factor.* **2 -limiting** putting a limit on the thing mentioned: *people with life-limiting illnesses*

**lim·it·less** /ˈlɪmɪtləs/ adj. without a limit; very great SYN **infinite**: *the limitless variety of consumer products* ◇ *The possibilities were almost limitless.*

**limo** /ˈlɪməʊ/ noun (pl. **-os**) (informal) = LIMOUSINE ⇒ see also STRETCH LIMO

**lim·ou·sine** /ˈlɪməziːn, ˌlɪməˈziːn/ (also informal **limo**) noun **1** a large, expensive, comfortable car: *a long black chauffeur-driven limousine* ⇒ see also STRETCH LIMO **2** (especially NAmE) a large vehicle that takes people to and from an airport **3** (especially NAmE) a kind of luxury taxi that you can hire for a few hours, especially for a special event with a group of people

## ▼ SYNONYMS

### limit
restriction • control • constraint • restraint • limitation

These are all words for sth that limits what you can do or what can happen.

**limit** the greatest or smallest amount of sth that is allowed: *The EU has set strict limits on pollution levels.* ◇ *the speed limit*

**restriction** (*rather formal*) a rule or law that limits what you can do: *There are no restrictions on the amount of money you can withdraw.*

**control** (often in compounds) the act of limiting or managing sth; a method of doing this: *arms control*

**constraint** (*rather formal*) a fact or decision that limits what you can do: *We have to work within severe constraints of time and money.*

**restraint** (*rather formal*) a decision, a rule, an idea, etc. that limits what you can do; the act of limiting sth because it is necessary or sensible to do so: *The government has imposed export restraints on some products.* ◇ *The unions are unlikely to accept any sort of wage restraint.*

**limitation** the act or process of limiting sth; a rule, fact or condition that limits sth: *They would resist any limitation of their powers.*

RESTRICTION, CONSTRAINT, RESTRAINT OR LIMITATION?
- These are all things that limit what you can do. A **restriction** is rule or law that is made by sb in authority. A **constraint** is sth that exists rather than sth that is made, although it may exist as a result of sb's decision. A **restraint** is also sth that exists: it can exist outside yourself, as the result of sb else's decision; but it can also exist inside you, as a fear of what other people may think or as your own feeling about what is acceptable: *moral/social/cultural restraints*. A **limitation** is more general and can be a rule that sb makes or a fact or condition that exists.

PATTERNS
- limits/restrictions/controls/constraints/restraints/limitations **on** sth
- limits/limitations **to** sth
- **severe** limits/restrictions/controls/constraints/restraints/limitations
- **tight** limits/restrictions/controls/constraints
- to **impose/remove** limits/restrictions/controls/constraints/restraints/limitations
- to **lift** restrictions/controls/constraints/restraints

**limp** /lɪmp/ *adj., verb, noun*
- *adj.* **1** having no strength or energy: *His hand went limp and the knife clattered to the ground.* ◇ *She felt limp and exhausted.* **2** not stiff or strong: *The hat had become limp and shapeless.* ▶ **limp·ly** *adv.*: *Her hair hung limply over her forehead.*
- *verb* **1** [I] to walk slowly or with difficulty because one leg is injured: *She had twisted her ankle and was limping.* + *adv./prep.*: *Matt limped painfully off the field.* **2** [I] + *adv./prep.* to move slowly or with difficulty after being damaged: *The plane limped back to the airport.* ◇ (*figurative*) *The government was limping along in its usual way.*
- *noun* [usually sing.] a way of walking in which one leg is used less than normal because it is injured or stiff: *to walk with a slight/pronounced limp*

**lim·pet** /ˈlɪmpɪt/ *noun* a small SHELLFISH that sticks very tightly to rocks: *The Prime Minister clung to his job like a limpet, despite calls for him to resign.*

**lim·pid** /ˈlɪmpɪd/ *adj.* (*literary*) (of liquids, etc.) clear **SYN** transparent: *limpid eyes/water*

**limp-ˈwristed** *adj.* (*informal, offensive*) an offensive way of describing a man who is EFFEMINATE (= looks or behaves like a woman)

**LINC** /lɪŋk/ *abbr.* Language Instruction for Newcomers to Canada (free language classes provided by the govern-ment to people from other countries who come to live in Canada)

**linch·pin** (*also* **lynch-pin**) /ˈlɪntʃpɪn/ *noun* a person or thing that is the most important part of an organization, a plan, etc., because everything else depends on them or it

**Lin·coln's Birth·day** /ˌlɪŋkənz ˈbɜːθdeɪ; *NAmE* ˈbɜːrθ-/ *noun* [U] (in some US states) a legal holiday on 12 February in memory of the birthday of Abraham Lincoln

**linc·tus** /ˈlɪŋktəs/ *noun* [U] (*BrE*) thick liquid medicine that you take for a SORE throat (= a painful throat because of an infection) or a COUGH: *cough linctus*

**lin·den** /ˈlɪndən/ (*also* **linden tree**) *noun* = LIME (4)

**lines**

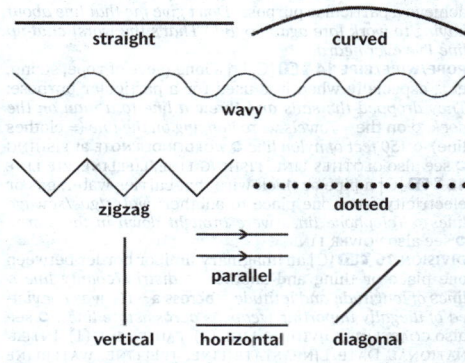

**line 🛈 A1 🔊** /laɪn/ *noun, verb*
- *noun*
- LONG THIN MARK **1** A1 [C] a long, thin mark on a surface: *a straight/solid/dotted/dashed line* ◇ *a vertical/horizontal line* ◇ *parallel lines* ◇ *Draw a thick black line across the page.* ⇒ see also BAR LINE, DOTTED LINE, IN-LINE **2** A1 [C] a long, thin mark on the ground to show the limit or border of sth, especially of a playing area in some sports: *The first to cross the line wins the race.* ◇ *They were all waiting on the starting line.* ◇ **over/across the ~** *The ball was over the line.* ◇ **behind the ~** *Your feet must be behind the line when you serve* (= in tennis). ⇒ see also FINISHING LINE, FIRE LINE, FOUL LINE, GOAL LINE, SIDELINE *noun*, TOUCHLINE **3** A2 [C] a mark like a line on sb's skin that people usually get as they get older **SYN** wrinkle: *He has fine lines around his eyes.*
- ROW OF PEOPLE/THINGS **4** A2 [C] a row of people or things next to each other or behind each other: **in a ~** *The children all stood in a line.* ◇ **~ of sth** *They were stuck in a line of traffic.* ◇ *a straight/long line of trees* ⇒ see also PICKET LINE **5** A2 [C] (*NAmE*) a queue of people: *A line formed at each teller window.* ◇ **in ~** *to stand/wait in line* ◇ *If you want a ticket, get in line.* ◇ **~ for sth** *There's a line for the women's bathroom.*
- PHONE **6** A2 [C] a phone connection; a particular phone number: *The phone lines were jammed* (= very busy) *with people calling to complain.* ◇ *I was talking to John when the line suddenly went dead.* ◇ *If you hold the line* (= stay on the phone and wait), *I'll see if she is available.* ◇ **on the ~** *It's your mother on the line.* ◇ *Your bill includes line rental.* ⇒ see also FIXED-LINE, HELPLINE, HOTLINE, LANDLINE, OFF-LINE, ONLINE, OPEN LINE ⇒ WORDFINDER NOTE at CALL
- RAILWAY/BUS **7** A2 [C] a railway track or other transport route; a section of a transport system or route: *The train was delayed because a tree had fallen across the line.* ◇ *a rail line* ◇ (*BrE also*) *a railway line* ◇ *the East Coast line* ◇ *We got off the bus near the end of the line at San Gerardo.* ⇒ see also MAIN LINE
- ROUTE/DIRECTION **8** B1 [C, usually sing.] the direction that sb/sth is moving or located in: **in a ~** *Just keep going in a straight line.* ◇ **~ of sth** *Be careful to stay out of the line of fire* (= the direction sb is shooting in). ◇ *They followed the*

# line

*line of the river for three miles.* **9** [C] a route from one place to another especially when it is used for a particular purpose: *Their aim was to block guerrilla* **supply lines***.*
- **WORDS 10** [A1] [C] *(abbr.* **l***)* a row of words on a page or the empty space where they can be written; the words of a song or poem or other piece of writing: *Look at line 5 of the text.* ◇ *Write the title of your essay on the top line.* ◇ *I can only remember the first two lines of that song.* ◇ *A team of programmers wrote 200 000* **lines of code** (= computer programming language). ➔ WORDFINDER NOTE at PLAY ➔ see also BOTTOM LINE, SUBJECT LINE, TOP LINE **11** [B1] [C] the words spoken by an actor in a play or film: *to learn your lines* ◇ **~ from sth** *a line from the film 'Casablanca'* **12 lines** [pl.] *(BrE)* (in some schools) a punishment in which a child has to write out a particular sentence a number of times **13** [C] *(informal)* a remark, especially when sb says it to achieve a particular purpose: *Don't give me that line about having to work late again.* ◇ *(BrE) That's the worst* **chat-up line** *I've ever heard.*
- **ROPE/WIRE/PIPE 14** [B1] [C, U] a long piece of rope, string, etc., especially when it is used for a particular purpose: *They dropped the sails and threw a line to a man on the dock.* ◇ **on the ~** *Towels were hanging on the line* (= clothes line). ◇ *150 feet of nylon line* ➔ WORDFINDER NOTE at FISHING ➔ see also CLOTHES LINE, FISHING LINE, LIFELINE, ZIP LINE **15** [B1] [C] a pipe or thick wire that carries water, gas or electricity from one place to another: *water/gas/sewage lines* ◇ *Telephone lines were brought down in the storm.* ➔ see also POWER LINE
- **DIVISION 16** [B1] [C] an imaginary limit or border between one place or thing and another: *a district/county line* ◇ *lines of longitude and latitude* ◇ **across a ~** *He was convicted of illegally importing weapons across state lines.* ➔ see also COASTLINE, DIVIDING LINE (2), FAULT LINE (1), INTERNATIONAL DATE LINE, STATE LINE, TREELINE, WATERLINE **17** [B1] [C] the division between one area of thought or behaviour and another or between one group of people and another: *Mass consumption* **blurred the lines** *of class distinction.* ◇ **~ between A and B** *There is a* **fine line** *between informing the public and alarming them.* ➔ see also DIVIDING LINE (1), FAULT LINE (2), POVERTY LINE, RED LINE
- **ATTITUDE/ARGUMENT 18** [B2] [C, usually sing.] an attitude or a belief, especially one that sb states publicly: **~ on sth** *He supported the official line on education.* ◇ *The government is taking a firm line on terrorism.* ➔ see also HARD LINE, HARD-LINE, PARTY LINE **19** [B2] [C] a method or way of doing or thinking about sth: **~ of sth** *I don't follow your line of reasoning.* ◇ *She decided to try a different* **line of argument** (= way of persuading sb of sth). ◇ *sb's first line of attack/defence* ◇ *The police are pursuing a new* **line of inquiry** (= way of finding out information). ➔ see also FIRST-LINE
- **SERIES 20** [B2] [C, usually sing.] a series of people, things or events that follow one another in time: *to pass sth down through the male/female line* ◇ **~ of sth** *She came from a* **long line of** *doctors.* ◇ *This novel is the latest in a long line of thrillers that he has written.* **21** [B2] [C, usually sing.] a series of people in order of importance: **~ of sth** *a line of command* ◇ **down the ~** *(from sb/sth) Orders came down the line from the very top.* ◇ **in ~ (to sb/sth)** *He is second in line to the chairman.* ◇ *to be* **next in line** *to the throne* ➔ see also LINE MANAGER
- **SHAPE 22** [C] the edge, outline or shape of sb/sth: *He traced the line of her jaw with his finger.* ◇ *a beautiful sports car with sleek lines* ➔ see also A-LINE, BIKINI LINE
- **IN FACTORY 23** [C] a system of making sth, in which the product moves from one worker to the next until it is finished ➔ see also PRODUCTION LINE
- **ACTIVITY 24** [sing.] a type or area of business, activity or interest: **~ of sth** *My line of work pays pretty well.* ◇ **in the … ~** *You can't do much in the art line without training.* ➔ see also SIDELINE *noun*
- **PRODUCT 25** [C] a type of product: *Some lines sell better than others.* ◇ *new product lines* ◇ **~ in sth** *We are starting a new line in casual clothes.*
- **TRANSPORT 26** [C] (often used in names) a company that provides transport for people or goods: *a shipping/bus line* ➔ see also AIRLINE
- **SOLDIERS 27** [C] a row or series of military defences where the soldiers are fighting during a war: *They were trapped* **behind enemy lines** (= in the area controlled by the enemy). ➔ see also FRONT LINE
- **DRUGS 28** [C] *(slang)* an amount of COCAINE that is spread out in a thin line, ready to take

**IDM** **a'bove the line 1** *(finance)* connected with the income that a company receives and the costs it has to pay in its daily business, which affect the profit it makes: *All these costs are above the line and directly hit profits.* ➔ compare BELOW THE LINE (1) **2** *(business)* connected with advertising in the MASS MEDIA: *They planned an advertising campaign with both above-the-line and social media components.* ➔ compare BELOW THE LINE (2) **along/down the 'line** *(informal)* at some point during an activity or a process: *Somewhere along the line a large amount of money went missing.* ◇ *We'll make a decision on that further down the line.* **along/on (the) … 'lines 1** *(informal)* in the way that is mentioned: *The new system will operate* **along the same lines** *as the old one.* ◇ *They voted along class lines.* **2** *(informal)* similar to the way or thing that is mentioned: *Those aren't his exact words, but he said something along those lines.* **be, come, etc. on 'line** to be working or functioning: *The new working methods will come on line in June.* ➔ see also ONLINE **be'low the line 1** *(finance)* connected with unusual costs or income that a company pays or receives, that are not part of its daily business and are taken away or added after calculating profits: *There was a £4 million extraordinary charge below the line.* ➔ compare ABOVE THE LINE (1) **2** *(business)* connected with advertising by means of direct mail, email, SOCIAL MEDIA, events, etc: *We are planning social networking, digital marketing and below-the-line activities across the country.* ➔ compare ABOVE THE LINE (2) **3** connected with a section at the end of an online article or BLOG POST where readers can put comments **bring sb/sth, come, get, fall, etc. into 'line (with sb/sth)** to behave or make sb/sth behave in the same way as other people or how they should behave: *The other members of the board must be brought into line.* **cut in 'line** *(also* **jump the 'line)** *(NAmE)* = JUMP THE QUEUE at JUMP *v.* **in (a) 'line (with sth)** in a position that forms a straight line with sth: *An eclipse happens when the earth and moon are in line with the sun.* **in 'line for sth** likely to get sth: *She is in line for promotion.* **in the line of 'duty** while doing a job: *A policeman was injured in the line of duty yesterday.* **in 'line with sth** similar to sth or so that one thing is closely connected with another: *Annual pay increases will be in line with inflation.* **lay it on the 'line** *(informal)* to tell sb clearly what you think, especially when they will not like what you say: *The manager laid it on the line—some people would have to lose their jobs.* **(put sth) on the 'line** *(informal)* at risk: *If we don't make a profit, my job is on the line.* **out of 'line (with sb/sth) 1** not forming a straight line **2** different from sth: *London prices are way out of line with the rest of the country.* **3** *(BrE also* **out of 'order)** *(informal)* behaving in a way that is not acceptable or right **walk/tread a fine/thin line (between A and B)** to be in a difficult or dangerous situation where you could easily make a mistake: *He was walking a fine line between being funny and being rude.* ➔ more at BATTLE *n.*, CROSS *v.*, DRAW *v.*, END *n.*, FIRING LINE, FIRM *adj.*, HOOK *n.*, OVERSTEP, PITCH *v.*, READ *v.*, RESISTANCE, SIGN *v.*, STEP *v.*, TOE *v.*

■ **verb**
- **COVER INSIDE 1** [B2] **~ sth** to cover the inside of sth with a layer of another material, especially to keep it clean or make it stronger: **~ sth with sth** *Line the pan with greaseproof paper.* **2** [B2] **~ sth** to form a layer on the inside of sth: *the membranes that line the nose*
- **FORM ROWS 3** [B2] to form lines or rows along sth: **~ sth** *Crowds lined the streets to watch the race.* ◇ **be lined with sth** *The walls were lined with books.* ➔ see also LINED

**IDM** **line your (own)/sb's 'pockets** to get richer or make sb richer, especially by taking unfair advantage of a situation or by being dishonest

**PHR V** **line ˈup** to stand in a line or row; to form a queue: *Line up, children!* ◇ *Cars lined up waiting to board the ship.* **ˌline sb/sth↔ˈup** **1** to arrange people or things in a straight line or row: *The suspects were lined up against the wall.* ◇ *He lined the bottles up along the shelf.* **2** to arrange for an event or activity to happen, or arrange for sb to be available to do sth: *Mark had a job lined up when he left college.* ◇ *I've got a lot lined up this week* (= I'm very busy). ◇ *She's lined up a live band for the party.* **ˌline sth↔ˈup (with sth)** to move one thing into a correct position in relation to another thing

**lin·eage** /ˈlɪniɪdʒ/ *noun* [U, C] (*formal*) the series of families that sb comes from originally **SYN** **ancestry**

**lin·eal** /ˈlɪniəl/ *adj.* [only before noun] (*formal*) coming in a direct line from an earlier or later generation of the same family as sb: *a lineal descendant of the company's founder*

**lin·ea·ments** /ˈlɪniəmənts/ *noun* [pl.] (*formal*) the typical features of sth

**lin·ear** ⁊+ **C1** /ˈlɪniə(r)/ *adj.* **1** ⁊+ **C1** of or in lines: *In his art he broke the laws of scientific linear perspective.* **2** ⁊+ **C1** going from one thing to another in a single series of stages: *Students do not always progress in a linear fashion.* **OPP** **non-linear** **3** of length: *linear measurement* (= for example metres, feet, etc.) **4** (*mathematics*) able to be represented by a straight line on a GRAPH: *linear equations* **5** (of television) broadcast and watched at regular times according to a schedule: *People are watching linear TV much less these days, preferring on-demand platforms like Netflix.* ⇨ compare ON-DEMAND ▶ **lin·ear·ity** /ˌlɪniˈærəti/ *noun* [U]: *She abandoned the linearity of the conventional novel.* **lin·ear·ly** /ˈlɪniəli/ *NAmE* -ərli/ *adv.*

**line·back·er** /ˈlaɪnbækə(r)/ *noun* (in AMERICAN FOOTBALL) a DEFENSIVE player who tries to TACKLE members of the other team

**ˈline-caught** *adj.* (of fish) caught with a line and HOOK (= a curved piece of metal), not in a net: *We sell only line-caught wild fish.*

**lined** /laɪnd/ *adj.* **1** (of skin, especially on the face) having folds or lines because of age, worry, etc. **SYN** **wrinkled**: *a deeply lined face* **2** (of paper) having lines printed or drawn across it: *Lined paper helps keep handwriting neat.* **3** (of clothes) having a LINING inside them: *a lined skirt* **4** **-lined** having the object mentioned along an edge or edges, or as a LINING: *a tree-lined road*

**ˈline dancing** *noun* [U] a type of dancing originally from the US, in which people dance in lines without partners, all doing a complicated series of steps at the same time

**ˈline drawing** *noun* a drawing that consists only of lines

**ˈline drive** *noun* (in baseball) a powerful hit in a straight line near to the ground

**ˈline graph** *noun* a diagram that shows the relationship between the measurements of two things as points that are joined together by lines: *The line graph shows changes in individual patients over time.*

**line·man** /ˈlaɪnmən/ *noun* (*pl.* **-men** /-mən/) (*NAmE*) **1** a player in the front line of an AMERICAN FOOTBALL team **2** = LINESMAN (2)

**ˈline management** *noun* [U] (*BrE*) the system of organizing a company, etc. in which information and instructions are passed from each manager to the person one rank below them ▶ **ˈline manager** *noun*: *Review your training needs with your line manager.*

**linen** /ˈlɪnɪn/ *noun* [U] **1** a type of cloth made from FLAX, used to make high-quality clothes, sheets, etc: *a linen tablecloth* **2** sheets, TABLECLOTHS, PILLOWCASES, etc: (*BrE*) *a linen cupboard* ◇ (*NAmE*) *a linen closet* ⇨ see also BED LINEN, TABLE LINEN ⇨ WORDFINDER NOTE at STORE **IDM** see DIRTY *adj.*

**ˌline of ˈcredit** (*also* **ˈcredit line**) *noun* an amount of money that a financial organization such as a bank is willing to lend to a person or organization

**ˌline of ˈsight** (*also* ˌline of ˈvision, ˈsight-line) *noun* an imaginary line that goes from sb's eye to sth that they are looking at: *There was a column directly in my line of sight, so I could only see half the stage.*

915 **linguist**

**line-out** *noun* (in rugby) a situation that happens when the ball goes out of play, when players from each team stand in opposite lines and jump to try to catch the ball when it is thrown back in

**liner** /ˈlaɪnə(r)/ *noun* **1** a large ship that carries passengers: *an ocean liner* ◇ *a luxury cruise liner* **2** (especially in compounds) a piece of material used to cover the inside surface of sth: *nappy liners* ⇨ see also BIN LINER **3** MAKE-UP that is put around the edge of the eyes or lips ⇨ see also EYELINER, LIP LINER

**ˈliner note** (*BrE also*, *becoming old-fashioned* ˈsleeve note) *noun* [usually pl.] information about the music or the performers that comes with a CD or DVD or is printed on the cover of a record

**lines·man** /ˈlaɪnzmən/ *noun* (*pl.* **-men** /-mən/) **1** an official who helps the REFEREE in some games that are played on a field or court, especially in deciding whether or where a ball crosses one of the lines. Linesmen are now officially called **referee's assistants** in football (soccer). **2** (*BrE*) (*NAmE* **line·man**) a person whose job is to repair phone or electricity power lines

**ˈline-up** ⁊+ **C1** *noun* [usually sing.] **1** ⁊+ **C1** the people who are going to take part in a particular event: *an impressive line-up of speakers* ◇ *the starting line-up* (= the players who will begin the game) **2** ⁊+ **C1** a set of items, events etc. arranged to follow one another **SYN** **programme**: *A horror movie completes this evening's TV line-up.* **3** (*especially NAmE*) (*BrE also* iˌdentifiˈcation parade, *informal* iˈdentity parade) a row of people, including one person who is suspected of a crime, who are shown to a witness to see if he or she can recognize the criminal

**ling** /lɪŋ/ *noun* [U] a low-growing plant that is a type of HEATHER and that grows on areas of wild open land (= MOORLAND)

**-ling** /lɪŋ/ *suffix* (in nouns) (*sometimes disapproving*) small; not important: *duckling* ◇ *princeling*

**lin·ger** ⁊+ **C1** /ˈlɪŋɡə(r)/ *verb* **1** ⁊+ **C1** [I] to continue to exist for longer than expected: *The faint smell of her perfume lingered in the room.* ◇ **~ on** *The civil war lingered on well into the 1930s.* **2** ⁊+ **C1** [I] (+ *adv./prep.*) to stay somewhere for longer because you do not want to leave; to spend a long time doing sth: *She lingered for a few minutes to talk to Nick.* ◇ *We lingered over breakfast on the terrace.* **3** [I] **~ (on sb/sth)** to continue to look at sb/sth or think about sth for longer than usual: *His eyes lingered on the diamond ring on her finger.* **4** [I] **~ (on)** to stay alive but become weaker: *He lingered on for several months after the heart attack.*

**lin·ge·rie** /ˈlɒnʒəri; *NAmE* ˌlɑːndʒəˈreɪ/ *noun* [U] (used especially by shops/stores) women's underwear ⇨ WORDFINDER NOTE at STORE

**lin·ger·ing** /ˈlɪŋɡərɪŋ/ *adj.* slow to end or disappear: *a painful and lingering death* ◇ *a last lingering look* ◇ *lingering doubts* ◇ *a lingering smell of machine oil* ▶ **lin·ger·ing·ly** *adv.*

**lingo** /ˈlɪŋɡəʊ/ *noun* [sing.] (*informal*) **1** a language, especially a foreign language: *He doesn't speak the lingo.* **2** (*especially NAmE*) expressions used by a particular group of people **SYN** **jargon**: *baseball lingo*

**ˌlingua ˈfranca** /ˌlɪŋɡwə ˈfræŋkə/ *noun* (*pl.* **lingua francas**) [usually sing.] (*linguistics*) a shared language of communication used between people whose main languages are different: *English has become a lingua franca in many parts of the world.*

**lin·gual** /ˈlɪŋɡwəl/ *adj.* **1** (*anatomy*) related to the tongue **2** (*specialist*) related to speech or language **3** (*phonetics*) of a speech sound) produced using the tongue ▶ **ˈlin·gual·ly** /-ɡwəli/ *adv.*

**lin·guist** /ˈlɪŋɡwɪst/ *noun* **1** a person who knows several foreign languages well: *She's an excellent linguist.* ◇ *I'm afraid I'm no linguist* (= I find foreign languages difficult). **2** a person who studies languages or LINGUISTICS

# linguistic

**lin·guis·tic** /lɪŋˈgwɪstɪk/ *adj.* connected with language or the scientific study of language: *linguistic and cultural barriers* ◊ *a child's innate linguistic ability* ◊ *new developments in linguistic theory* ▶ **lin·guis·tic·al·ly** /-kli/ *adv.*

**lin·guis·tics** /lɪŋˈgwɪstɪks/ *noun* [U] (*linguistics*) the scientific study of language or of particular languages ⊃ see also APPLIED LINGUISTICS

**lini·ment** /ˈlɪnəmənt/ *noun* [C, U] a liquid, especially one made with oil, that you rub on a painful part of your body to reduce the pain

**lin·ing** /ˈlaɪnɪŋ/ *noun* **1** [C] a layer of material used to cover the inside surface of sth: *a pair of leather gloves with fur linings* ⊃ WORDFINDER NOTE at SEW **2** [U] the layer that covers the inner surface of a part of the body: *the stomach lining* IDM see CLOUD *n.*

**link** 🔑 A2 👁 /lɪŋk/ *noun, verb*
■ *noun* **1** 🔑 A2 a connection between two or more people or things: *~ between A and B Police suspect there may be a link between the two murders.* ◊ *There is evidence for a strong* **causal** *link between exposure to sun and skin cancer.* ◊ *to establish/find a link* ◊ *~ to/with sb/sth These photographs are a* **direct** *link with the past.* ⊃ see also MISSING LINK **2** 🔑 A2 a relationship between two or more people, countries or organizations: *~ with sb/sth to establish trade links with Asia* ◊ *Producers are forging direct links with consumers.* ◊ *The department tries to maintain close links with industry.* ◊ *~ between A and B Social workers provide a vital link between hospital and community.* **3** 🔑 A2 a means of travelling or communicating between two places: *a high-speed rail link* ◊ *a video link* ◊ *~ between A and B The canal was an important transport link between England and Wales.* ◊ *~ via sth We're trying to establish a link via satellite.* ◊ *via a ~ The speech was broadcast via a satellite link.* **4** 🔑 A2 (*also* **hot·link, hyper·link**) (*computing*) a place in an electronic document that is connected to another electronic document or to another part of the same document: *You can find all the details by* **clicking this** *link.* ◊ *Follow the links to watch our exclusive trailer.* ◊ *~ to sth I've posted a link to the article, for those who are interested.* **5** each ring of a chain ⊃ see also CUFFLINK
IDM **a link in the chain** one of the stages in a process or a line of argument ⊃ more at WEAK
■ *verb* **1** 🔑 A2 [T] to make a physical or electronic connection between one object, machine, place, etc. and another SYN CONNECT: *~ A to B The video cameras are linked to a powerful computer.* ◊ *~ A with B The Channel Tunnel links Britain with the rest of Europe.* ◊ *~ A and B A pedestrian bridge links the two buildings.* ◊ *~ A and B together When computers are networked, they are linked together so that information can be transferred between them.* **2** 🔑 A2 [T, often passive] if sth **links** two things, facts or situations, or they **are linked**, they are connected in some way: **be linked** *The two factors are directly linked.* ◊ *The personal and social development of the child are inextricably linked* (= they depend on each other). ◊ **be linked to/with sth** *Exposure to ultraviolet light is closely linked to skin cancer.* ◊ *~ A to/with B There was no evidence linking the men to the crime.* ◊ *~ A and B What links Jane Austen and Oscar Wilde* (= what is the connection between them)? **3** 🔑 A2 [T, I] (*computing*) to create a link between web pages or electronic documents: *~ sth I only link posts that are food-related.* ◊ *~ (A) to B Thanks for linking to my article.* **4** to state or suggest that there is a connection or relationship between two things or people SYN ASSOCIATE: *~ A to B Detectives have linked the break-in to a similar crime in the area last year.* ◊ *~ A with B Newspapers have linked his name with the singer.* **5** *~ A and B* to join two things by putting one through the other: *The two girls linked arms as they strolled down the street.*
PHRV **ˌlink ˈup (with sb/sth)** to join or become joined with sb/sth: *The two spacecraft will link up in orbit.* ◊ *The bands have linked up for a charity concert.* ⊃ related noun LINK-UP

**link·age** /ˈlɪŋkɪdʒ/ *noun* **1** [U, C] *~ (between A and B)* the act of linking things; a link or system of links SYN CONNEC-tion: *This chapter explores the linkage between economic development and the environment.* **2** [C] a device that links two or more things

**ˈlinking verb** (*also* **cop·ula**) *noun* (*grammar*) a verb such as *be* or *become* that connects a subject with the adjective or noun (called the COMPLEMENT) that describes it: *In 'She became angry', the verb 'became' is a linking verb.*

**links** /lɪŋks/ *noun* = GOLF LINKS

**ˈlink-up** *noun* a connection formed between two things, for example two companies or two broadcasting systems: *a live satellite link-up with the conference*

**lino** /ˈlaɪnəʊ/ *noun* [U] (*BrE, informal*) = LINOLEUM

**lino·cut** /ˈlaɪnəʊkʌt/ *noun* a design or shape cut in a piece of LINO, used to make a print; a print made in this way

**li·no·leum** /lɪˈnəʊliəm/ (*also BrE, informal* **lino**) *noun* [U] a type of strong material with a hard shiny surface, used for covering floors

**lin·seed** /ˈlɪnsiːd/ *noun* = FLAXSEED

**ˈlinseed oil** (*also* **ˈflaxseed oil**) *noun* [U] an oil made from FLAXSEEDS, used in paint or to protect wood, etc.

**lint** /lɪnt/ *noun* [U] **1** (*especially BrE*) a type of soft cotton cloth used for covering and protecting wounds **2** (*specialist*) short fine FIBRES that come off the surface of cloth when it is being made **3** (*especially NAmE*) (*BrE usually* **fluff**) small soft pieces of wool, cotton, etc. that stick on the surface of cloth

**lin·tel** /ˈlɪntl/ *noun* (*architecture*) a piece of wood, stone, metal or CONCRETE over a door or window that forms part of the frame

**Linux™** /ˈlɪnəks, ˈlaɪ-/ *noun* [U] (*computing*) an OPERATING SYSTEM based on UNIX that is available free in the basic version

**lion** 🔑 A1 /ˈlaɪən/ *noun* a large, powerful animal of the cat family that hunts in groups and lives in parts of Africa and southern Asia. Lions have yellow-brown fur and the male has a MANE (= long, thick hair round its neck): *The lion shook its mane and roared.* ⊃ compare LIONESS ⊃ see also MOUNTAIN LION, SEA LION ⊃ VISUAL VOCAB page V2
IDM **the ˈlion's den** a difficult situation in which you have to face a person or people who are unfriendly or aggressive towards you **the ˈlion's share (of sth)** the largest or best part of sth when it is divided ⊃ more at BEARD *v.*

**lion·ess** /ˈlaɪənəs/ *noun* a female lion

**lion·ize** (*BrE also* **-ise**) /ˈlaɪənaɪz/ *verb* *~ sb* (*formal*) to treat sb as a famous or important person

**lip** 🔑 B1 /lɪp/ *noun* **1** 🔑 B1 [C] either of the two soft edges at the opening to the mouth: *The assistant pursed her lips.* ◊ *your upper/lower/top/bottom lip* ◊ **on the lips** *She kissed him on the lips.* ⊃ see also CLEFT LIP **2** **-lipped** (in adjectives) having the type of lips mentioned: *thin-lipped* ◊ *thick-lipped* ⊃ see also TIGHT-LIPPED **3** [C] *~ (of sth)* the edge of a container or a hollow place in the ground SYN RIM: *He ran his finger around the lip of the cup.* ◊ *Lava bubbled a few feet below the lip of the crater.* ⊃ picture at JUG **4** [U] (*informal*) words spoken to sb that are rude and show a lack of respect for that person SYN CHEEK: *Don't let him give you any lip!*
IDM **lick/smack your ˈlips 1** to move your tongue over your lips, especially before eating sth good **2** (*informal*) to show that you are excited about sth and want it to happen soon: *They were licking their lips at the thought of clinching the deal.* **my lips are ˈsealed** used to say that you will not repeat sb's secret to other people **on ˈeveryone's ˈlips** if sth is **on everyone's lips**, they are all talking about it ⊃ more at BITE *v.*, PASS *v.*, READ *v.*, SLIP *n.*, STIFF *adj.*

**lip·ase** /ˈlaɪpeɪs, ˈlɪ-/ *NAmE* -peɪs/ *noun* [U] (*chemistry*) an ENZYME (= a chemical substance in the body) that makes fats change into ACIDS and alcohol

**ˈlip gloss** *noun* [U, C] a substance that is put on the lips to make them look shiny

**lipid** /ˈlɪpɪd/ *noun* (*chemistry*) any of a group of natural substances that do not DISSOLVE in water, including plant oils and STEROIDS

**lip liner** noun [U] a substance that is put on the outline of the lips, to prevent LIPSTICK from spreading

**lipo·pro·tein** /ˈlɪpəprəʊtiːn, ˈlaɪ-/ noun (biology) a PROTEIN that combines with a lipid and carries it to another part of the body in the blood

**lipo·some** /ˈlɪpəsəʊm, ˈlaɪ-/ noun (chemistry) a very small SAC (= part shaped like a bag) formed of lipid MOLECULES, used to carry a drug to a particular part of the body

**lipo·suc·tion** /ˈlɪpəʊsʌkʃn, ˈlaɪ-/ noun [U] a way of removing fat from sb's body by using SUCTION

**lippy** /ˈlɪpi/ adj., noun
- adj. (BrE, informal) showing a lack of respect in the way that you speak to sb SYN **cheeky**
- noun (also **lippie**) [U, C] (pl. **-ies**) (BrE, informal) = LIPSTICK

**lip-read** /ˈlɪp riːd/ verb [I, T] ~ (sb/sth) to understand what sb is saying by watching the way their lips move ▶ **lip-reading** noun [U]

**lip service** noun [U] if sb pays **lip service** to sth, they say that they approve of it or support it, without proving their support by what they actually do: *All the parties pay lip service to environmental issues.*

**lip·stick** /ˈlɪpstɪk/ noun [U, C] a substance made into a small stick, used for colouring the lips; a small stick of this substance: *She was wearing bright red lipstick.*
⊃ WORDFINDER NOTE at MAKE-UP ⊃ picture at STICK

**lipstick lesbian** noun (informal) a LESBIAN who dresses in a style that is fashionable and FEMININE (= typical of a woman): *the lipstick lesbian stereotype*

**lip-sync** (also **lip-synch**) verb [I, T] to move your mouth, without speaking or singing, so that its movements match the sound on a recorded song, etc: ~ (to sth) *She lip-synced to a Beatles song.* ◊ ~ sth *He lip-synced 'Return to Sender'.*

**li·quefy** /ˈlɪkwɪfaɪ/ verb [I, T] (**li·que·fies**, **li·que·fy·ing**, **li·que·fied**, **li·que·fied**) ~ (sth) (formal) to become liquid; to make sth liquid

**li·queur** /lɪˈkjʊə(r); NAmE -ˈkɜːr/ (NAmE also **cor·dial**) noun **1** [U, C] a strong, sweet, alcoholic drink, sometimes tasting of fruit. It is usually drunk in very small glasses after a meal. **2** [C] a glass of liqueur

**li·quid** ⊙ B1 /ˈlɪkwɪd/ noun, adj.
- noun ⊙ B1 [C, U] a substance that flows freely and is not a solid or a gas, for example water or oil: *She poured the dark brown liquid down the sink.* ◊ *the transition from liquid to vapour* ⊃ see also WASHING-UP LIQUID

WORDFINDER absorb, condense, dilute, dissolve, evaporate, filter, immerse, rinse, saturated

- adj. **1** ⊙ B1 in the form of a liquid; not a solid or a gas: *liquid nitrogen* ◊ *liquid soap* ◊ *The detergent comes in powder or liquid form.* ◊ *a bar selling snacks and liquid refreshment* (= drinks) **2** (finance) in cash, or that can easily be changed into cash: *liquid assets* **3** (literary) clear, like water SYN **limpid**: *liquid blue eyes* **4** (literary) (of sounds) clear, pure and flowing: *the liquid song of a blackbird*

**li·quid·ate** /ˈlɪkwɪdeɪt/ verb **1** [I, T] ~ (sth) to close a business and sell everything it owns in order to pay debts **2** [T] ~ sth (finance) to sell sth in order to get money: *to liquidate assets* **3** [T] ~ sth (finance) to pay a debt **4** [T] ~ sb/sth (informal) to destroy or remove sb/sth that causes problems; to kill sb SYN **annihilate**: *The government tried to liquidate the rebel movement and failed.*

**li·quid·ation** /ˌlɪkwɪˈdeɪʃn/ noun [U] **1** (BrE, AustralE, law) the process of closing a company, selling what it owns and paying its debts: *The company has gone into liquidation.* ⊃ compare CHAPTER 11 **2** (finance) the action of selling sth to get money or to avoid losing money: *Falling prices may lead to further liquidation of stocks.*

**li·quid·ator** /ˈlɪkwɪdeɪtə(r)/ noun a person or organization responsible for closing down a business and using any profits from the sale to pay its debts

**liquid crystal dis·play** noun = LCD

**li·quid·ity** /lɪˈkwɪdəti/ noun [U] (finance) the state of owning things of value that can easily be exchanged for cash

**li·quid·ize** (BrE also **-ise**) /ˈlɪkwɪdaɪz/ verb ~ sth (especially BrE) to press fruit, vegetables, etc. into a thick liquid SYN **purée**

**li·quid·izer** (BrE also **-iser**) /ˈlɪkwɪdaɪzə(r)/ noun (BrE) = BLENDER

**liquid paraffin** (BrE) (NAmE **mineral oil**) noun [U] a liquid with no colour and no smell that comes from PETROLEUM and is used in medicines and COSMETICS

**li·quor** /ˈlɪkə(r); NAmE/ noun [U] **1** (especially NAmE) strong alcoholic drink SYN **spirit**: *hard liquor* ◊ *She drinks wine and beer but no liquor.* **2** (BrE, specialist) any alcoholic drink: *intoxicating liquor*

**li·quor·ice** (especially BrE) (also **lic·or·ice** especially in NAmE) /ˈlɪkərɪʃ, -rɪs/ noun [U, C] a black substance with a strong taste, obtained from the root of a plant, used in medicine and to make sweets; a sweet made from this substance

**liquor store** (also **package store**) (both US) (BrE **off-licence**) noun a shop that sells alcoholic drinks in bottles and cans to take away

**lira** /ˈlɪərə; NAmE ˈlɪrə/ noun (pl. **lire** /ˈlɪəreɪ; NAmE ˈlɪreɪ/) (abbr. **l.**) the unit of money in Malta, Syria and Turkey, and in the past in Italy (replaced there in 2002 by the euro)

**lisle** /laɪl/ noun [U] a fine, smooth cotton THREAD used especially for making TIGHTS and STOCKINGS

**lisp** /lɪsp/ noun, verb
- noun [usually sing.] a speech fault in which the sound 's' is pronounced 'th': *She spoke with a slight lisp.*
- verb [I, T] (+ **speech**) to speak with a lisp

**list** ⊙ A1 ⊙ /lɪst/ noun, verb
- noun **1** ⊙ A1 [C] a series of names, items, figures, etc., especially when they are written or printed: *The guest list includes numerous celebrities.* ◊ **on the ~** *Is your name on the list?* ◊ *Her novel shot to the top of the bestseller list.* ◊ *He plays drums, guitar, piano, flute, the list goes on.* ◊ **~ of sth** *a list of names/candidates/questions* ◊ *I made a list of things to do.* ◊ *Having to wait hours came high on the list of complaints.* ⊃ see also A-LIST, B-LIST, BUCKET LIST, DEAN'S LIST, HIT LIST, LAUNDRY LIST, MAILING LIST, READING LIST, SHOPPING LIST, SHORTLIST noun, TO-DO LIST, WAITING LIST, WAIT LIST, WINE LIST, WORD LIST **2** [sing.] the fact of a ship leaning to one side IDM see DANGER
- verb **1** ⊙ A1 [T] ~ sth to write a list of things in a particular order: *We were asked to list our ten favourite songs.* ◊ *The key items are listed below.* **2** [T, often passive] to mention or include sb/sth in a list: **be listed in sth** *Key benefits are listed in Table 1.* ◊ **be listed among sb/sth** *The koala is listed among Australia's endangered animals.* ◊ **be listed as sth** *soldiers listed as missing* ◊ **be listed under sth** *Articles may be listed under more than one heading.* **3** [I, T] ~ (at sth) | ~ sth (especially NAmE) to be put or put sth in a list of things for sale: *This laptop lists at $500.* **4** [I] (of a ship) to lean to one side

**listed building** noun (BrE) a building that is officially protected because it has artistic or historical value ⊃ see also LANDMARK

**lis·ten** ⊙ A1 /ˈlɪsn/ verb, noun
- verb **1** ⊙ A1 [I] to pay attention to sb/sth that you can hear: *Listen! What's that noise? Can you hear it?* ◊ *Sorry, I wasn't really listening.* ◊ **~ to sb/sth** *to listen to music/the radio* ◊ *I listened carefully to her story.* HELP *You cannot 'listen sth' (without 'to'): I'm fond of listening to classical music. ◊ I'm fond of listening classical music.* **2** A1 [I] (informal) used to tell sb to take notice of what you are going to say: *Listen, there's something I have to tell you.* **3** ⊙ B1 [I] to take notice of what sb says to you so that you follow their advice or believe them: *I tried to warn her, but she wouldn't listen.* ◊ **~ to sb/sth** *None of this would have happened if you'd listened to me.* ◊ *The government is willing to listen to any concerns that people have.*

PHRV **listen for sth**| **listen out for sth** to be prepared to hear a particular sound: *Can you listen out for the doorbell?* **listen in (on/to sth) 1** to listen to a conversation that you are not supposed to hear: *You shouldn't listen in on*

# listenable 918

*other people's conversations.* **2** to listen to a radio broadcast **listen ˈup** *(especially NAmE, informal)* used to tell people to listen carefully because you are going to say sth important
- **noun** [usually sing.] an act of listening: *Have a listen to this.*

**lis·ten·able** /ˈlɪsnəbl/ *adj. (informal)* pleasant to listen to

**lis·ten·er** 🛈 A2 /ˈlɪsənə(r)/ *noun* **1** A2 a person who listens: *a good listener* (= sb who you can rely on to listen with attention or sympathy) **2** A2 a person listening to a radio programme or PODCAST: **~to sth** *Listeners to Radio 4 have plenty to look forward to this week.*

**ˈlistening post** *noun* a place where people who are part of an army listen to enemy communications to try to get information that will give them an advantage

**lis·teria** /lɪˈstɪəriə; *NAmE* -ˈstɪr-/ *noun* [U] a type of bacteria that makes people ill if they eat food that contains it

**list·ing** ✝+ C1 /ˈlɪstɪŋ/ *noun* **1** ✝+ C1 [C] a list, especially an official or published list of people or things, often arranged in alphabetical order: *a comprehensive listing of all airlines* **2 listings** [pl.] information online or in a newspaper or magazine about what films, plays, etc. are being shown in a particular town or city: *a listings website/magazine* **3** [C] a position or an item on a list: *(business) The company is seeking a stock exchange listing* (= for trading shares).

**list·less** /ˈlɪstləs/ *adj.* having no energy or enthusiasm **SYN** lethargic: *The illness left her feeling listless and depressed.* ▶ **list·less·ly** *adv.* **list·less·ness** *noun* [U]

**ˈlist price** *noun* [usually sing.] *(business)* the price at which goods are advertised for sale, for example in a CATALOGUE

**lit** /lɪt/ *past tense, past part.* of LIGHT

**lit·any** /ˈlɪtəni/ *noun (pl. -ies)* **1** a series of prayers to God for use in church services, spoken by a priest, etc., with set responses by the people **2 ~ (of sth)** *(formal)* a long boring account of a series of events, reasons, etc: *a litany of complaints*

**lit·chi** *(especially NAmE)* = LYCHEE

**lite** /laɪt/ *adj. (informal)* **1** (of food or drink) containing fewer CALORIES than other versions of the same type of food, and therefore less likely to make you fat (a way of spelling 'light'): *lite ice cream* **2** (used after a noun) *(disapproving)* used to say that a thing is similar to sth else but lacks many of its serious or important qualities: *I would describe this movie as 'Hitchcock lite'.*

**liter** *(US)* = LITRE

**lit·er·acy** ✝+ C1 /ˈlɪtərəsi/ *noun* [U] **1** ✝+ C1 the ability to read and write: *a campaign to promote adult literacy ◇ basic literacy skills* **OPP** illiteracy ⊃ WORDFINDER NOTE at LANGUAGE **2** ✝+ C1 (in compounds) knowledge or skills in a specific area: *digital/financial literacy* ⊃ see also COMPUTER LITERACY

**lit·eral** /ˈlɪtərəl/ *adj.* **1** [usually before noun] being the most basic meaning of a word or phrase, rather than an extended or POETIC meaning: *I am not referring to 'small' people in the literal sense of the word. ◇ The literal meaning of 'petrify' is 'turn to stone'.* ⊃ compare FIGURATIVE, METAPHORICAL **2** [usually before noun] that follows the original words exactly: *a literal translation* ⊃ compare FREE **3** *(disapproving)* not having or showing any imagination: *Her interpretation of the music was too literal.* ▶ **lit·er·al·ness** *noun* [U]

**lit·er·al·ly** ✝+ B2 /ˈlɪtərəli/ *adv.* **1** ✝+ B2 in a literal way **SYN** exactly: *The word 'planet' literally means 'wandering body'. ◇ When I told you to 'get lost' I didn't expect to be taken literally.* **2** ✝+ C1 used to emphasize the truth of sth that may seem surprising: *There are literally hundreds of prizes to win.* **3** ✝+ C1 *(informal)* used to emphasize a word or phrase, even if it is not actually true in a literal sense: *I literally jumped out of my skin.*

**lit·er·ary** ✝+ B2 /ˈlɪtərəri; *NAmE* -reri/ *adj.* **1** ✝+ B2 connected with literature: *literary criticism/theory* **2** ✝+ C1 (of a language or style of writing) suitable for or typical of a work of literature: *It was Chaucer who really turned English into a literary language.* **3** ✝+ B1 liking literature very much; studying or writing literature: *a literary man*

**lit·er·ate** /ˈlɪtərət/ *adj.* **1** able to read and write **OPP** illiterate ⊃ see also NUMERATE **2** (in compounds) having skills or knowledge in a specific area: *to be scientifically/financially literate* ⊃ see also COMPUTER-LITERATE

**lit·er·ati** /ˌlɪtəˈrɑːti/ **the literati** *noun* [pl.] *(formal)* educated and intelligent people who enjoy literature

**lit·era·ture** 🛈 B1 ⊙ /ˈlɪtrətʃə; *NAmE also* -tʃʊr/ *noun* [U] **1** B1 pieces of writing that are valued as works of art, especially novels, plays and poems (in contrast to technical books and newspapers, magazines, etc.): *English/American/French literature ◇ great works of literature* ⊃ WORDFINDER NOTE at WRITE **2** pieces of writing or printed information on a particular subject: *sales literature ◇ ~ on sth a review of the scientific literature on the topic* ⊃ WORDFINDER NOTE at LANGUAGE

**lithe** /laɪð/ *adj.* (of a person or their body) moving or bending easily, in a way that is attractive ▶ **lithe·ly** *adv.*

**lith·ium** /ˈlɪθiəm/ *noun* [U] *(symb.* **Li***)* a chemical element. Lithium is a soft, very light, silver-white metal used in batteries and ALLOYS.

**litho·graph** /ˈlɪθəɡrɑːf; *NAmE* -ɡræf/ *noun* a picture printed by lithography

**lith·og·raphy** /lɪˈθɒɡrəfi; *NAmE* -ˈθɑːɡ-/ *noun (also informal* **litho** /ˈlaɪðəʊ/*)* [U] the process of printing from a smooth surface, for example a metal plate, that has been specially prepared so that INK (= coloured liquid) only sticks to the design to be printed ▶ **litho·graph·ic** /ˌlɪθəˈɡræfɪk/ *adj.*

**lith·ology** /lɪˈθɒlədʒi; *NAmE* -ˈθɑːl-/ *noun* **1** the study of the general physical characteristics of rocks ⊃ compare PETROLOGY **2** the general physical characteristics of a rock or the rocks in a particular area

**litho·sphere** /ˈlɪθəsfɪə(r); *NAmE* -sfɪr/ *noun* [sing.] *(geology)* the layer of rock that forms the outer part of the earth

**liti·gant** /ˈlɪtɪɡənt/ *noun (law)* a person who is making or defending a claim in court

**liti·gate** /ˈlɪtɪɡeɪt/ *verb* [I, T] **~ (sth)** *(law)* to take a claim or disagreement to court ▶ **liti·ga·tor** *noun*

**liti·ga·tion** /ˌlɪtɪˈɡeɪʃn/ *noun* [U] *(law)* the process of making or defending a claim in court: *The company has been in litigation with its previous auditors for a full year.*

**li·ti·gious** /lɪˈtɪdʒəs/ *adj. (formal, disapproving)* too ready to take arguments to court ▶ **li·ti·gious·ness** *noun* [U]

**lit·mus** /ˈlɪtməs/ *noun* [U] a substance that turns red when it touches an ACID and blue when it touches an ALKALI: *litmus paper*

**ˈlitmus test** *noun* **1** = ACID TEST: *The outcome will be seen as a litmus test of government concern for conservation issues.* **2** a test using litmus

**litre** ✝+ B2 *(US* **liter***)* /ˈliːtə(r)/ *noun (abbr.* **l***)* a unit for measuring volume, equal to 1.76 British PINTS or 2.11 American PINTS: *3 litres of water ◇ a litre bottle of wine ◇ a car with a 3.5 litre engine*

**lit·ter** ✝+ B2 /ˈlɪtə(r)/ *noun, verb*
- **noun 1** ✝+ B2 [U] small pieces of rubbish such as paper, cans and bottles, that people have left lying in a public place: *There will be fines for people who drop litter.* **2** [sing.] **~ of sth** a number of things that are lying in an untidy way: *The floor was covered with a litter of newspapers, clothes and empty cups.* **3** [U] a dry substance that is put in a shallow open box for pets, especially cats, to use as a toilet when they are indoors: *cat litter ◇ (BrE) a litter tray ◇ (NAmE) a litter box* **4** [C] a number of baby animals that one mother gives birth to at the same time: *a litter of puppies ◇ the runt* (= the smallest and weakest baby) *of the litter* **5** [U] the substance, especially STRAW, that is used for farm animals to sleep on **6** [C] a kind of chair or bed that was used in the past for carrying important people
- **verb 1** [T] **~ sth** to be spread around a place, making it look untidy: *Piles of books and papers littered the floor. ◇ Broken glass littered the streets.* **2** [T, usually passive, I] to leave things in a place, making it look untidy: **be littered**

**with sth** *The floor was littered with papers.* ◊ *He was arrested for littering.* **3** [T] **be littered with sth** to contain or involve a lot of a particular type of thing, usually sth bad: *Your essay is littered with spelling mistakes.*

**'litter bin** (*BrE*) (*NAmE* **'trash can**) *noun* a container for people to put rubbish in, in the street or in a public building

**'litter lout** (*BrE*) (also **lit·ter·bug** /'lɪtəbʌɡ; *NAmE* -tərb-/ *NAmE*, *BrE*) *noun* (*informal*, *disapproving*) a person who leaves LITTER in public places

**lit·tle** ⓘ 🅰🅹 /'lɪtl/ *adj., det., pron., adv.*
■ *adj.* [usually before noun] **HELP** The forms **littler** /'lɪtlə(r)/ and **littlest** /'lɪtlɪst/ are rare. It is more common to use **smaller** and **smallest**. **1** 🅰🅹 not big; small; smaller than others: *a little house* ◊ *a little old lady* ◊ *We passed through several nice little towns.* ◊ *It was a tiny little room.* ◊ *'Which do you want?' 'I'll take the little one.'* ◊ *She gave a little laugh.* ◊ (*BrE*) *We should manage, with a little bit of luck.* ◊ *Here's a little something* (= a small present) *for your birthday.* **2** 🅰🅹 young: *a little boy/girl* ◊ *He's just a little kid.* ◊ *my little brother/sister* (= younger brother/sister) ◊ *The little ones were already in bed.* ◊ *I lived in America when I was little.* **3** 🅰🅹 (of distance or time) short: *A little while later the phone rang.* ◊ *Shall we walk a little way?* **4** 🅱🅹 used after an adjective to show approval, sympathy or dislike, especially in a PATRONIZING way (= one that suggests that you think you are better than sb): *The poor little thing! It's lost its mother.* ◊ *What a nasty little man!* ◊ *She's a good little worker.* ◊ *He'd become quite the little gentleman.* **5** 🅱🅹 not important; not serious: *I can't remember every little detail.* ◊ *Sometimes it's the little things that count.* ▸ **little·ness** *noun* [U]
**IDM** **a little 'bird told me** (*informal*) used to say that sb told you sth but you do not want to say who it was ⊃ more at WONDER *n.*
■ *det., pron.* **1** 🅰🅹 **a little** used with uncountable nouns to mean 'a small amount', 'some': *a little milk/sugar/tea* ◊ *If you have any spare milk, could you give me a little?* ◊ *I've only read a little of the book so far.* ◊ (*formal*) *It caused not a little/no little* (= a lot of) *confusion.* ◊ *After a little* (= a short time) *he got up and left.* **2** 🅰🅹 used with uncountable nouns to mean 'not much': *There was little doubt in my mind.* ◊ *Students have little or no choice in the matter.* ◊ *I understood little of what he said.* ◊ *She said little or nothing* (= hardly anything) *about her experience.* ◊ *Tell him as little as possible.*
**IDM** **little by 'little** slowly; gradually: *Little by little the snow disappeared.* ◊ *His English is improving little by little.*
■ *adv.* (**less, least**) **1** 🅰🅹 **a little (bit)** to a small degree: *She seemed a little afraid of going inside.* ◊ *These shoes are a little (bit) too big for me.* ◊ *These days I'm a little more relaxed.* ◊ (*informal*) *Everything has become just that little bit harder.* ⊃ note at BIT **2** 🅱🅹 not much; only slightly: *He is little known as an artist.* ◊ *I slept very little last night.* ◊ *Little did I know that this spelled the end of my career.*

**little 'finger** *noun* the smallest finger of the hand **SYN** pinky
**IDM** **twist/wrap/wind sb around your little 'finger** (*informal*) to persuade sb to do anything that you want

**'Little League** *noun* [sing., U] (in the US) a baseball league for children

**'little people** *noun* [pl.] **1** all the people in a country who have no power ⊃ see also LITTLE PERSON **2** **the little people** small imaginary people with magic powers **SYN** fairies

**'little person** (also **Little Person**) *noun* (*pl.* **little people**, **Little People**) a person who will never grow to a normal height because of a physical condition

**lit·toral** /'lɪtərəl/ *noun* (*specialist*) the part of a country that is near the coast ▸ **lit·toral** *adj.* [only before noun]: *littoral states*

**lit·urgy** /'lɪtədʒi; *NAmE* -tərdʒi/ *noun* [C, U] (*pl.* **-ies**) a fixed form of prayers and actions used in public WORSHIP in some religions, especially Christianity ▸ **li·tur·gic·al** /lɪ'tɜːdʒɪkl; *NAmE* -'tɜːrdʒ-/ *adj.* **li·tur·gic·al·ly** /-kli/ *adv.*

**liv·able** (especially *NAmE*) = LIVEABLE

# live

**live¹** ⓘ 🅰🅹 /lɪv/ *verb* ⊃ see also LIVE²
• IN A PLACE **1** 🅰🅹 [I] ~ + *adv./prep.* to have your home in a particular place: *to live in a house/a flat/an apartment* ◊ *We used to live in London.* ◊ *people living in rural areas* ◊ *Where do you live?* ◊ *She needs to find somewhere to live.* ◊ *It's a great place to live.* ◊ *Both her children still live at home.* ◊ (*informal*) *Where do these plates live* (= where are they usually kept)?
• BE ALIVE **2** 🅰🅹 [I] to remain alive: *The doctors said he only had six months to live.* ◊ *Women live longer than men in general.* ◊ ~ **to do sth** *She lived to see her first grandchild.* **3** 🅰🅹 [I] to be alive, especially at a particular time: *When did Handel live?* ◊ *He's the greatest player who ever lived.*
• TYPE OF LIFE **4** 🅰🅹 [I, T] to spend your life in a particular way: ~ + *adv./prep. He lived in poverty most of his life.* ◊ *Most of the people live well, with nice houses and plenty to eat.* ◊ ~ **sth** *She lived a very peaceful life.* ◊ ~ + *noun She lived and died a single woman.*
• BE REMEMBERED **5** 🅰🅸 [I] ~ + *adv./prep.* to continue to exist or be remembered **SYN** remain: *This moment will live in our memory for many years to come.*
• HAVE EXCITEMENT **6** [I] to have a full and exciting life: *I don't want to be stuck in an office all my life—I want to live!*
**IDM** **live and 'breathe sth** to be very enthusiastic about sth: *He just lives and breathes football.* **live and 'let live** (*saying*) used to say that you should accept other people's opinions and behaviour even though they are different from your own **live by your 'wits** to earn money by clever or sometimes dishonest means **live the 'dream** to have a way of life that seems perfect: *With her own TV show and a flat in Paris, she is living the dream.* **live (from) hand to 'mouth** to spend all the money you earn on basic needs such as food without being able to save any money ⊃ see also HAND-TO-MOUTH **live in the 'past** to behave as though society, etc. has not changed, when in fact it has **live in 'sin** (*old-fashioned* or *humorous*) to live together and have a sexual relationship without being married **live it 'up** (*informal*) to enjoy yourself in an exciting way, usually spending a lot of money **live a 'lie** to keep sth important about yourself a secret from other people, so that they do not know what you really think, what you are really like, etc. **live off the fat of the 'land** to have enough money to be able to afford expensive things, food, drink, etc. **live off the 'land** to eat whatever food you can grow, kill or find yourself **live to fight another 'day** (*saying*) used to say that although you have failed or had a bad experience, you will continue **live under a 'rock** (*informal*) to be unaware of popular culture and important events that are happening in the world: *Unless you've been living under a rock for the last few decades, you'll be aware that Arctic sea ice is melting.* **you haven't 'lived** used to tell sb that if they have not had a particular experience their life is not complete: *You've never been to New York? You haven't lived!* **you live and 'learn** used to express surprise at sth new or unexpected you have been told ⊃ more at BORROW, CLOVER, HALF *n.*, LIFE, LONG *adv.*, PEOPLE *n.*, POCKET *n.*, ROUGH *adv.*, TELL
**PHR V** **'live by sth** to follow a particular belief or set of principles: *That's a philosophy I could live by.* **'live by doing sth** to earn money or to get the things you need by doing a particular thing: *a community that lives by fishing* **live sth↔'down** to be able to make people forget about sth embarrassing you have done: *She felt so stupid. She'd never be able to live it down.* **'live for sb/sth** to think that sb/sth is the main purpose of or the most important thing in your life: *She lives for her work.* ◊ *After his wife died, he had nothing to live for.* **'live 'in** to live at the place where you work or study: *They have an au pair living in.* ⊃ see also LIVE-IN **'live off sb/sth** (often *disapproving*) to receive the money you need to live from sb/sth because you do not have any yourself: *She's still living off her parents.* ◊ *to live off welfare* **'live off sth** to have one particular type of food as the main thing you eat in order to live: *He seems to live off junk food.* **'live 'on** to continue to live or exist: *She died ten years ago but her memory lives on.* **'live on sth 1** to eat a particular type of food to live: *Small birds live mainly on insects.* **2** (often *disapproving*) to

# live

eat only or a lot of a particular type of food: *She lives on burgers.* **3** to have enough money for the basic things you need to live: *You can't live on forty pounds a week.* **ˌlive ˈout** to live away from the place where you work or study: *Some college students will have to live out.* **ˌlive ˈout sth 1** to actually do what you have only thought about doing before: *to live out your fantasies* **2** to spend the rest of your life in a particular way: *He lived out his days alone.* **ˌlive ˈthrough sth** to experience a disaster or other unpleasant situation and survive it: *He has lived through two world wars.* **ˌlive toˈgether** = LIVE WITH SB **ˌlive ˈup to sth** to do as well as or be as good as other people expect you to: *He failed to live up to his parents' expectations.* The team called 'The No-Hopers' certainly lived up to its name. **ˌlive ˈwith sb** (also **ˌlive toˈgether**) **1** [A1] to live in the same house **2** [A1] to share a home and have a sexual relationship without being married SYN **cohabit ˌlive ˈwith sth** to accept sth unpleasant: *I just had to learn to live with the pain.*

**live²** [B1] /laɪv/ *adj., adv.* ⇒ see also LIVE¹

■ *adj.* [usually before noun]
- **NOT DEAD 1** [B1] living; not dead: *live animals* ◇ *the number of live births* (= babies born alive) ◇ *We saw a real live rattlesnake!*
- **NOT RECORDED 2** [B1] (of a broadcast) sent out while the event is actually happening, not recorded first and broadcast later: *a live broadcast* ◇ *live coverage of the World Cup* ◇ *on live television/TV* **3** [B1] (of a performance) given or made when people are watching, not recorded: *The club has live music most nights.* ◇ *the magic of a live performance* ◇ *It was the first interview I'd done in front of a live audience* (= with people watching). **4** [B1] (of a recording) made at a live performance, not in a recording studio: *a live recording made at Wembley Arena*
- **ELECTRICITY 5** (of a wire or device) connected to a source of electrical power: *That terminal is live.*
- **BULLETS/MATCHES 6** still able to explode or light; ready for use: *live ammunition*
- **COALS 7** live coals are burning or are still hot and red
- **YOGURT 8** live YOGURT still contains the bacteria needed to turn milk into yogurt
- **QUESTION/SUBJECT 9** of interest or importance at the present time: *Pollution is still very much a live issue.*
- **INTERNET 10** (of an electronic link) functioning correctly, so that it is connected to another document or page on the internet: *Here are some live links to other aviation-related web pages.*

IDM **a live ˈwire** a person who is lively and full of energy

■ *adv.* [B1] broadcast at the time of an actual event; played or recorded at an actual performance: *The show is going out live.* ◇ *We'll be reporting live from Beijing.* ◇ *Three great local bands will be playing live.*

IDM **go ˈlive** (of a project, website, computer system, etc.) to start; to become OPERATIONAL (= ready to be used)

**live·able** (especially BrE) (also **liv·able** especially in NAmE) /ˈlɪvəbl/ *adj.* **1** (BrE also **live·able in** [not before noun]) (of a house, etc.) fit to live in SYN **habitable**: *safer and more liveable residential areas* ◇ *The place looks liveable in.* **2** (of life) worth living SYN **endurable 3** [not before noun] **~ with** that can be dealt with: *The problem is paying the mortgage—everything else is liveable with.* **4** [only before noun] (of a wage, etc.) enough to live on: *a liveable salary*

**ˈlive action** /ˌlaɪv ˈækʃn/ *noun* [U] part of a film that is made using real people or animals, rather than using drawings, models or computers ▸ **live-ˈaction** *adj.* [only before noun]: *a live-action movie*

**ˈlive blog** /ˈlaɪv blɒg; NAmE blɑːg/ *noun* a blog or a MICRO-BLOG on which a description of an event is given as it takes place ▸ **ˈlive-blog** *verb* [T, I]: *He live-blogged from the top of the mountain.* ◇ *~ sth to live-blog an event/an election/a debate*

**ˈlived-in** *adj.* (of a place) that has been used continuously for so long that it does not look new: (approving) *The room had a comfortable, lived-in feel about it.*

**ˈlive feed** /ˌlaɪv ˈfiːd/ *noun* the broadcast of sound or video over the internet from a live (not recorded) source, for example a concert or sports event: *We watched live feeds from the International Space Station.*

**ˈlive-in** /ˈlɪv ɪn/ *adj.* **1** (of an employee) living in the house where they work: *a live-in nanny* **2 ~ lover, boyfriend, girlfriend, etc.** a person who lives with their sexual partner but is not married to them

**live·li·hood** /ˈlaɪvlihʊd/ *noun* [C, usually sing., U] a means of earning money in order to live SYN **living**: *Communities on the island depended on whaling for their livelihood.* ◇ *a means/source of livelihood*

**live·long** /ˈlɪvlɒŋ; NAmE -lɔːŋ/ *adj.*
IDM **the livelong ˈday** (*literary*) the whole length of the day

**live·ly** [B2] /ˈlaɪvli/ *adj.* (live·li·er, live·li·est) **1** [B2] full of life and energy; active and enthusiastic SYN **animated, vivacious**: *an intelligent and lively young woman* ◇ *a lively and enquiring mind* ◇ *He showed a lively interest in politics.* **2** [B2] (of a place, an event, etc.) full of interest or excitement: *a lively bar* ◇ *a lively debate/discussion* **3** (of colours) strong and definite: *a lively shade of pink* **4** (especially BrE) busy and active: *They do a lively trade in souvenirs and gifts.* ▸ **live·li·ness** *noun* [U]

**liven** /ˈlaɪvn/ *verb*
PHRV **ˌliven ˈup** | **ˌliven sb/sth ˈup** to become or to make sb/sth more interesting or exciting: *The game didn't liven up till the second half.* ◇ *Let's put some music on to liven things up.*

**liver** [C1] /ˈlɪvə(r)/ *noun* **1** [C] a large organ in the body that cleans the blood and produces BILE: *liver disease* ◇ *He had a liver transplant at the age of 12.* ⇒ VISUAL VOCAB page V1 **2** [U, C] the liver of some animals that is cooked and eaten: *liver and onions* ◇ *chicken livers*

**liv·er·ied** /ˈlɪvərid/ *adj.* **1** (BrE) painted in a LIVERY: *liveried aircraft* **2** wearing LIVERY: *liveried servants*

**Liv·er·pud·lian** /ˌlɪvəˈpʌdliən; NAmE -vərˈp-/ *noun* a person from Liverpool in north-west England ⇒ compare SCOUSE ▸ **Liv·er·pud·lian** *adj.*

**ˈliver sausage** (BrE) (NAmE **liv·er·wurst** /ˈlɪvəwɜːst; NAmE -vərwɜːrst/) *noun* [U] a type of soft SAUSAGE made from LIVER, usually spread cold on bread

**liv·ery** /ˈlɪvəri/ *noun* [U, C] (*pl.* **-ies**) **1** (BrE) the colours in which the vehicles, aircraft or products of a particular company are painted **2** a special uniform worn by servants or officials, especially in the past

**ˈlivery stable** (also **ˈlivery yard**) *noun* a place where people can pay to keep their horses or can hire a horse

**lives** /laɪvz/ *pl.* of LIFE

**live·stock** /ˈlaɪvstɒk; NAmE -stɑːk/ *noun* [U, pl.] the animals kept on a farm, for example cows or sheep ⇒ WORD-FINDER NOTE at FARM

**ˈlive stream** /ˈlaɪv striːm/ *noun* a live broadcast of an event over the internet

**live-stream** /ˈlaɪv striːm/ *verb* [often passive] **~ sth** to broadcast or receive live video and sound of an event over the internet

**livid** /ˈlɪvɪd/ *adj.* **1** extremely angry SYN **furious 2** dark blue-grey in colour: *a livid bruise*

**liv·ing** [B1] /ˈlɪvɪŋ/ *adj., noun*

■ *adj.* **1** [B1] alive now: *all living things* ◇ *living organisms* ◇ *the finest living pianist* **2** [only before noun] (of a place) used for living rather than working in: *The workers' living quarters were cramped and uncomfortable.* ◇ *a separate living space/area* **3** [only before noun] used or practised now: *living languages* (= those still spoken) ◇ *a living faith*
IDM **be ˌliving ˈproof of sth/that…** to show by your actions or qualities that a particular fact is true: *He is living proof that age is no barrier to new challenges.* **with-in/in ˌliving ˈmemory** at a time, or during the time, that is remembered by people still alive: *the coldest winter in living memory*

■ *noun* **1** [B1] [C, usually sing.] money to buy the things that you need in life: *She earns her living as a freelance journalist.* ◇ *to make a decent/good/meagre living* ◇ **for a ~** *What* do you **do for a living**? ◊ to **scrape a living** from part-time tutoring **2** 🔑 **B1** [U] a way or style of life: *the pressures of daily living* ◊ *The aim was to educate children and parents on tooth care and* **healthy living**. ◊ *Their* **standard of living** *is very low.* ◊ *The* **cost of living** *has risen sharply.* ◊ **poor living conditions/standards 3 the living** [pl.] people who are alive now: *the living and the dead* **IDM** see LAND *n.* **4** [C] (*BrE*) (especially in the past) a position in the Church as a priest and the income and house that go with this **SYN** benefice

**the living 'dead** noun [pl.] (in stories) dead bodies that have been made partly alive again, so they can move and kill but not think for themselves **SYN** zombies ⊃ compare UNDEAD

,**living 'death** noun [sing.] a life that is worse than being dead

,**living 'hell** noun [sing.] a very unpleasant situation that causes a lot of pain and difficulty and lasts a long time

,**living 'roof** noun = GREEN ROOF

,**living 'room** (*BrE also* ,**sitting room**) noun a room in a house where people sit together, watch television, etc. **SYN** lounge

,**living 'wage** noun [sing.] a wage that is high enough for sb to buy the things they need in order to live

,**living 'will** noun a document stating your wishes about medical treatment in the case that you become so ill that you can no longer make decisions about it, in particular asking doctors to stop treating you and let you die

**liz·ard** /ˈlɪzəd; *NAmE* -zərd/ noun a REPTILE with a long body and tail, four short legs and a rough skin. There are many different types of lizard. ⊃ see also LOUNGE LIZARD

**ll** *abbr.* (in writing) lines (the plural form of 'l')

**llama** /ˈlɑːmə/ noun a South American animal kept for its soft wool or for carrying loads

**LLB** (*BrE*) (*NAmE* **LL.B.**) /ˌel el ˈbiː/ noun a first university degree in law (the abbreviation for 'Bachelor of Laws')

**LLD** (*BrE*) (*NAmE* **LL.D.**) /ˌel el ˈdiː/ noun the highest university degree in law (the abbreviation for 'Doctor of Laws')

**LLM** (*BrE*) (*NAmE* **LL.M.**) /ˌel el ˈem/ noun a second university degree in law (the abbreviation for 'Master of Laws')

**lm** *abbr.* LUMEN

**LMS** /ˌel em ˈes/ noun a software system for managing training and education using the internet (the abbreviation for 'learning management system')

**lo** /ləʊ/ exclamation (*old use* or *humorous*) used for calling attention to a surprising thing

**IDM** ,**lo and be'hold** (*humorous*) used for calling attention to a surprising or annoying thing

**load** 🔑 **B2** /ləʊd/ noun, verb

■ noun

- **STH CARRIED 1** 🔑 **B2** [C] something that is being carried (usually in large amounts) by a person, vehicle, etc: *The trucks waited at the warehouse to pick up their loads.* ◊ **~of sth** *The women came down the hill with their loads of firewood.* ◊ *These backpacks are designed to* **carry a heavy load**. ◊ *A lorry* **shed its load** (= accidentally dropped its load) *on the motorway.* **2** 🔑 **B2** [C] (often in compounds) the total amount of sth that sth can carry or contain: *a busload of tourists* ◊ *They ordered three truckloads of sand.* ◊ *He put half a load of washing in the machine.* ◊ *The plane took off with a* **full load**.
- **WEIGHT 3** [C, usually sing.] the amount of weight that is pressing down on sth: *a load-bearing wall* ◊ *Modern backpacks spread the load over a wider area.*
- **LARGE AMOUNT 4** 🔑 **B2** [sing.] (*also* **loads** [pl.]) (*informal*) a large number or amount of people or things; plenty: *a load/loads of sb/sth* ◊ *She's got loads of friends.* ◊ *He wrote loads and loads of letters to people.* ◊ *Uncle Jim brought a whole load of presents for the kids.* ◊ **a load/loads to do** *There's loads to do today.*
- **RUBBISH/NONSENSE 5** [sing.] ~ **of rubbish, garbage, nonsense, etc.** (*especially BrE, informal*) used to emphasize that sth is wrong, stupid, bad, etc: *You're talking a load of rubbish.*

- **WORK 6** [C] an amount of work that a person or machine has to do: *Teaching loads have increased in all types of school.* ⊃ see also CASELOAD, WORKLOAD
- **RESPONSIBILITY/WORRY 7** [C, usually sing.] a feeling of responsibility or worry that is difficult to deal with **SYN** burden: *She thought she would not be able to* **bear the load** *of bringing up her family alone.* ◊ *Knowing that they had arrived safely* **took a load off** *my mind.*
- **ELECTRICAL POWER 8** [C] the amount of electrical power that is being supplied at a particular time

**IDM** ,**get a 'load of sb/sth** (*informal*) used to tell sb to look at or listen to sb/sth: *Get a load of that dress!*

■ verb

- **GIVE/RECEIVE LOAD 1** 🔑 **B2** [T, I] to put a large quantity of things or people onto or into sth: **~sth** *We loaded the car in ten minutes.* ◊ *Can you help me load the dishwasher?* ◊ **~sth (up) (with sth)** *Men were loading up a truck with timber.* ◊ **~sth/sb into/onto sth** *Sacks were being loaded onto the truck.* ◊ **~(up)** *We finished loading and set off.* **OPP** unload ⊃ see also FRONT-LOAD **2** [I] to receive a load: *The ship was still loading.* **OPP** unload **3** [T] **~sb with sth** to give sb a lot of things, especially things they have to carry: *They loaded her with gifts.*
- **GUN/CAMERA 4** [T, I] to put sth into a weapon, camera or other piece of equipment so that it can be used: **~sth (into sth)** *She loaded a new cartridge into the printer.* ◊ **~sth (with sth)** *She loaded the printer with a new cartridge.* ◊ **~(sth)** *Is the gun loaded?* **OPP** unload
- **COMPUTING 5** [T, I] **~(sth)** to put data or a program into the memory of a computer, usually from local disk STORAGE: *The program automatically loads the file.* ◊ *This page won't load on my laptop.* ⊃ compare DOWNLOAD

**IDM** ,**load the 'dice (against/in favour of sb)** to put sb at an unfair disadvantage/advantage: *He has always felt that the dice were loaded against him in life.*

**PHRV** ,**load sb/sth 'down (with sth)** [usually passive] to give sb/sth a lot of heavy things to carry **SYN** weigh sb/sth down: *She was loaded down with bags of groceries.*

,**load 'up on sth** (*informal*) to take, buy, eat or drink a large amount of sth: *I went down to the store and loaded up on drinks.*

**load·ed** /ˈləʊdɪd/ adj.

- **FULL 1** carrying a load; full and heavy **SYN** laden: *a fully loaded truck* ◊ **~(with sth)** *a truck loaded with supplies* ◊ *She came into the room carrying a loaded tray.* **2 ~with sth** (*informal*) full of a particular thing, quality or meaning: *cakes loaded with calories*
- **RICH 3** [not before noun] (*informal*) very rich: *Let her pay— she's loaded.*
- **ADVANTAGE/DISADVANTAGE 4** ~**in favour of sb/sth | ~against sb/sth** acting either as an advantage or a disadvantage to sb/sth in a way that is unfair: *a system that is loaded in favour of the young* (= gives them an advantage)
- **WORD/STATEMENT 5** having more meaning than you realize at first and intended to make you think in a particular way: *It was a* **loaded question** *and I preferred not to comment.*
- **GUN/CAMERA 6** containing bullets, film, etc: *a loaded shotgun*
- **DRUNK 7** (*especially NAmE, informal*) very drunk

**load·ing** /ˈləʊdɪŋ/ noun [U, C] **1** (*AustralE, NZE*) extra money that sb is paid for their job because they have special skills or qualifications **2** an extra amount of money that you must pay in addition to the usual price: *The 2% loading for using the card abroad has been removed.*

**'load-shedding** noun [U] the practice of stopping the supply of electricity for a period of time because the demand is greater than the supply

**loaf** /ləʊf/ noun, verb

■ noun (*pl.* **loaves** /ləʊvz/) an amount of bread that has been shaped and baked in one piece: *a loaf of bread* ◊ *Two white loaves, please.* ◊ *a sliced loaf* ⊃ see also FRENCH LOAF, MEAT LOAF **IDM** see HALF *det.*, USE *v.*

■ verb [I] **~(about/around)** (*informal*) to spend your time not doing anything, especially when you should be

# loafer

working SYN **hang about**: *A group of kids were loafing around outside.*

**loaf·er** /ˈləʊfə(r)/ *noun* **1** a person who wastes their time rather than working **2** a flat leather shoe that you can put on your foot without fastening it

**loam** /ləʊm/ *noun* [U] (*specialist*) good quality soil containing sand, CLAY and DECAYED vegetable matter ▶ **loamy** *adj.*

**loan** 🔑 B2 /ləʊn/ *noun*, *verb*
- *noun* **1** 🔑 B2 [C] money that an organization such as a bank lends and sb borrows: *to take out/repay a loan* (= to borrow money/pay it back) ◇ *She took out an $8000 personal loan.* ◇ *bank loans with low interest rates* ◇ *It took three years to repay my student loan* (= money lent to a student). ◇ *a car/ home loan* (= a loan to buy a car/house) ⊃ WORDFINDER NOTE at BANK

  **WORDFINDER** credit, debt, deposit, interest, lend, money, mortgage, overdraft, risk

  **2** 🔑 B2 [sing.] the act of lending sth; the state of being lent: *~ of sth I even gave her the loan of my car.* ◇ *on ~ (from sb/sth) an exhibition of paintings on loan* (= borrowed) *from private collections* ◇ *on ~ from sb/sth The striker, on loan from United, scored his first goal for City today* (= he is playing for City for a fixed period by agreement with his own team, United).
- *verb* ~ **sth (to sb)** (especially *NAmE*) to lend sth to sb, especially money: *The bank is happy to loan money to small businesses.* ◇ *~ sb sth A friend loaned me $1000.* **2** (especially *BrE*) to lend a valuable object to a museum, etc: *~ sth This exhibit was kindly loaned by the artist's family.* ◇ *~ sth (out) to sb/sth The painting has been loaned to the Walker Art Gallery.* ◇ *~ sb sth He loaned the museum his entire collection.*

**ˈloan shark** *noun* (*disapproving*) a person who lends money at very high rates of interest

**loan·word** /ˈləʊnwɜːd; *NAmE* -wɜːrd/ *noun* (*linguistics*) a word from another language used in its original form: *'Latte' is a loanword from Italian.*

**loath** (also less frequent **loth**) /ləʊθ/ *adj.* **~ to do sth** (*formal*) not willing to do sth: *He was loath to admit his mistake.*

**loathe** /ləʊð/ *verb* (not used in the progressive tenses) **~ sb/sth** | **~ doing sth** to dislike sb/sth very much SYN **detest**: *I loathe modern art.* ◇ *They loathe each other.* ⊃ SYNONYMS at HATE

**loath·ing** /ˈləʊðɪŋ/ *noun* [sing., U] (*formal*) **~ (for/of sb/sth)** a strong feeling of hating sb/sth: *She looked at her attacker with fear and loathing.* ◇ *Many soldiers returned with a deep loathing of war.* ⊃ see also SELF-LOATHING

**loath·some** /ˈləʊðsəm/ *adj.* (*formal*) extremely unpleasant; DISGUSTING SYN **repulsive**

**loaves** /ləʊvz/ *pl.* of LOAF

**lob** /lɒb; *NAmE* lɑːb/ *verb* (**-bb-**) **1 ~ sth + adv./prep.** (*informal*) to throw sth so that it goes quite high through the air: *Stones were lobbed over the wall.* ⊃ SYNONYMS at THROW **2** (*sport*) to hit or kick a ball in a high curve through the air, especially so that it lands behind the person you are playing against: *~ sth (+ adv./prep.) He lobbed the ball over the defender's head.* ◇ *~ sb She managed to lob the keeper.*
▶ **lob** *noun*: *to play a lob*

**lobby** 🔑+ C1 /ˈlɒbi; *NAmE* ˈlɑːbi/ *noun*, *verb*
- *noun* (*pl.* **-ies**) **1** 🔑+ C1 [C] a large area inside the entrance of a public building where people can meet and wait SYN **foyer**: *a hotel lobby* **2** [C] (in the British Parliament) a large hall that is open to the public and used for people to meet and talk to Members of Parliament **3** 🔑+ C1 [C + sing./pl. v.] a group of people who try to influence politicians on a particular issue SYN **pressure group**: *The gun lobby is/are against any change in the law.* **4** [C, sing.] (*BrE*) an organized attempt by a group of people to influence politicians on a particular issue: *a recent lobby of Parliament by pensioners*
- *verb* 🔑+ C1 (**lob·bies**, **lobby·ing**, **lob·bied**, **lob·bied**) [T, I] ~ **(sb) (for/against sth)** to try to influence a politician or

the government and, for example, persuade them to support or oppose a change in the law: *Farmers will lobby Congress for higher subsidies.* ◇ *Women's groups are lobbying to get more public money for children.* ▶ **lobby·ist** *noun*: *political lobbyists*

**lobe** /ləʊb/ *noun* **1** = EARLOBE **2** a part of an organ in the body, especially the lungs or brain ⊃ see also FRONTAL LOBE

**lo·belia** /ləʊˈbiːliə/ *noun* [C, U] a small garden plant with small blue, red or white flowers

**lob·ola** /ləˈbəʊlə, -ˈbɔːlə/ *SAfrE* [lɔˈbɔːle] *noun* [U] (*SAfrE*) in traditional African culture, a sum of money or number of CATTLE that a man's family pays to a woman's family in order that he can marry her: *to pay lobola*

**lob·ot·om·ize** (*BrE* also **-ise**) /ləˈbɒtəmaɪz; *NAmE* -ˈbɑːt-/ *verb* **1 ~ sb** to perform a LOBOTOMY on sb **2 ~ sb** to make sb less intelligent or less mentally active

**lob·ot·omy** /ləˈbɒtəmi; *NAmE* -ˈbɑːt-/ *noun* (*pl.* **-ies**) a rare medical operation that cuts into part of a person's brain in order to treat mental illness

**lob·ster** /ˈlɒbstə(r); *NAmE* ˈlɑːb-/ *noun* **1** [C] a sea creature with a hard shell, a long body divided into sections, eight legs and two large CLAWS (= curved and pointed arms for catching and holding things). Its shell is black but turns bright red when it is boiled. ⊃ picture at SHELLFISH **2** [U] meat from a lobster, used for food

**ˈlobster pot** *noun* a piece of equipment for catching lobsters that is like a BASKET in shape

**local** 🔑 A1 🄌 /ˈləʊkl/ *adj.*, *noun*
- *adj.* [usually before noun] **1** 🔑 A1 belonging to or connected with the particular place or area that you are talking about or with the place where you live: *local people/residents/ businesses* ◇ *members of the local community* ◇ *the local police* ◇ *local elections* ◇ *A local man was accused of the murder.* ◇ *Our children go to the local school.* ◇ *a local newspaper* (= one that gives local news) ◇ *local radio* (= a radio station that broadcasts to one area only) **2** affecting only one part of the body: *Her tooth was extracted under local anaesthetic.* ▶ **lo·cal·ly** /-kəli/ *adv.*: *to work locally* ◇ *Do you live locally?* (= in this area) ◇ *locally grown fruit*
- *noun* **1** 🔑 B1 [usually pl.] a person who lives in a particular place or district: *The locals are very friendly.* **2** (*BrE, informal*) a pub near where you live: *I called in at my local on the way home.* **3** (*NAmE*) a branch of a labor union **4** (*NAmE*) a bus or train that stops at all places on the route

**lo·cal** *adj.* = LOW-CAL

**ˌlocal ˈarea ˈnetwork** *noun* (*computing*) = LAN

**ˌlocal auˈthority** *noun* (*BrE*) the organization that is responsible for the government of an area in the UK

**ˈlocal call** *noun* a phone call to a place that is near

**ˌlocal ˈcolour** (*US* **ˌlocal ˈcolor**) *noun* [U] the typical things, customs, etc. in a place that make it interesting, and that are used in a picture, story or film to make it seem real

**lo·cale** /ləʊˈkɑːl; *NAmE* -ˈkæl/ *noun* (*specialist* or *formal*) a place where sth happens

**ˌlocal ˈgovernment** *noun* **1** [U] (*especially BrE*) the system of government of a town or an area by elected representatives of the people who live there **2** [C] (*NAmE*) the organization that is responsible for the government of a local area and for providing services, etc: *state and local governments*

**lo·cal·ity** /ləʊˈkæləti/ *noun* (*pl.* **-ies**) (*formal*) **1** the area that surrounds the place you are in or are talking about SYN **vicinity**: *people living in the locality of the power station* ◇ *in the ~ There is no airport in the locality.* **2** the place where sb/sth exists: *We talk of the brain as the locality of thought.* ◇ *The birds are found in over 70 different localities.*

**lo·cal·ize** (*BrE* also **-ise**) /ˈləʊkəlaɪz/ *verb* **1 ~ sth** to limit sth or its effects to a particular area SYN **confine** **2 ~ sth** (*formal*) to find out where sth is: *animals' ability to localize sounds* **3** to make sth suitable for a particular place, area or market: *We will localize the app into French, Japanese, and two written forms of Chinese.* ▶ **lo·cal·iza·tion**, **-isa·tion** /ˌləʊkəlaɪˈzeɪʃn; *NAmE* -ləˈz-/ *noun* [U]

**lo·cal·ized** (*BrE also* **-ised**) /ˈləʊkəlaɪzd/ *adj.* (*formal*) happening within one small area: *a localized infection* (= in one part of the body) ◊ *localized fighting*

**ˈlocal time** *noun* [U] the time of day in the particular part of the world that you are talking about: *We reach Delhi at 2 o'clock local time.*

**lo·cate** /ləʊˈkeɪt; *NAmE* ˈləʊkeɪt/ *verb* **1** [T] **~ sb/sth** to find the exact position of sb/sth: *The mechanic located the fault immediately.* ◊ *Rescue planes are trying to locate the missing sailors.* **2** [T] **~ sth + adv./prep.** to put or build sth in a particular place SYN **site**: *They located their headquarters in Swindon.* ⊃ compare RELOCATE **3** [I] **+ adv./prep.** (*especially NAmE*) to start a business in a particular place: *There are tax breaks for businesses that locate in rural areas.*

**lo·cated** /ləʊˈkeɪtɪd; *NAmE* ˈləʊkeɪtɪd/ *adj.* [not usually before noun] **~ + adv./prep.** if sth is **located** in a particular place, it exists there or has been put there SYN **situated**: *a small town located 30 miles south of Chicago* ◊ *The offices are conveniently located just a few minutes from the main station.*

**lo·ca·tion** /ləʊˈkeɪʃn/ *noun* **1** [C] a place where sth happens or exists; the position of sth: *a honeymoon in a secret location* ◊ *Mobile phones can determine our exact location and relay it to the police in an emergency.* ⊃ SYNONYMS at PLACE ⊃ WORDFINDER NOTE at HOME

> **WORDFINDER** isolated, neighbourhood, outskirts, provincial, residential, rough, rural, suburban, urban

**2** [C, U] a place outside a film studio where scenes of a film are made: **~ for sth** *A mountain in the Rockies became the location for a film about Everest.* ◊ **on ~** *The movie was shot entirely on location in Italy.* ⊃ WORDFINDER NOTE at FILM **3** [U] the act of finding the position of sb/sth **4** [C] (*computing*) a position or an address in computer memory

**loca·tive** /ˈlɒkətɪv; *NAmE* ˈlɑːk-/ *noun* (*grammar*) (in some languages) the form of a noun, pronoun or adjective when it expresses the idea of place ⊃ see also ACCUSATIVE, DATIVE, GENITIVE, INSTRUMENTAL *noun* (2), NOMINATIVE, VOCATIVE ▶ **loca·tive** *adj.*

**lo·ca·tor** /ləʊˈkeɪtə(r); *NAmE* ˈləʊkeɪtər/ *noun* a device or system for finding sth: *The company lists 5000 stores on the store locator part of its website.*

**loc. cit.** /ˌlɒk ˈsɪt; *NAmE* ˈlɑːk-/ *abbr.* in the piece of text quoted (from Latin 'loco citato')

**loch** /lɒk, lɒx; *NAmE* lɑːk, lɑːx/ *noun* (in Scotland) a lake or a narrow area of sea almost surrounded by land ⊃ see also LOUGH

**loci** /ˈləʊkaɪ, ˈləʊsaɪ/ *pl.* of LOCUS

**lock** /lɒk; *NAmE* lɑːk/ *verb, noun*
■ *verb*
• FASTEN **1** [T, I] **~ (sth)** to fasten sth with a lock; to be fastened with a lock: *Did you lock the door?* ◊ *This suitcase doesn't lock.* OPP **unlock**
• KEEP SAFE **2** [T] **~ sth + adv./prep.** to put sth in a safe place and lock it: *She locked her passport and money in the safe.*
• BECOME FIXED **3** [I, T] **~ (sth) (in/into/around, etc. sth) | ~ (sth) (together)** to become or make sth become fixed in one position and unable to move: *The brakes locked and the car skidded.* ◊ *He locked his helmet into position with a click.*
• IN DIFFICULT SITUATION **4** [T] **be locked in/into sth** to be involved in a difficult situation, an argument, etc: *The two sides are locked into a bitter dispute.* ◊ *She felt locked in a loveless marriage.*
• BE HELD TIGHTLY **5** [T] **be locked together/in sth** to be held very tightly by sb: *They were locked in a passionate embrace.*
• COMPUTING **6** [T] **~ sth** (*computing*) to use a code or PASSWORD to prevent data on a phone or computer from being changed or looked at by sb without permission: *These files are locked to protect confidentiality.* ◊ *My phone is locked and I've forgotten the password.*
IDM **ˌlock ˈhorns (with sb) (over sth)** to get involved in an argument with sb: *The company has locked horns with the unions over proposed pay cuts.*
PHRV **ˌlock sb aˈway** = LOCK SB UP/AWAY **ˌlock sth aˈway** = LOCK STH UP/AWAY **ˌlock sb/yourˈself ˈin (...)** to prevent sb from leaving a place by locking the door: *At 9 p.m. the prisoners are locked in for the night.* **ˌlock ˈonto sth** (of a MISSILE, etc.) to find the thing that is being attacked and follow it **ˌlock sb/yourˈself ˈout (of sth)** to prevent sb from entering a place by locking the door: *I'd locked myself out of the house and had to break a window to get in.* **ˌlock sb ˈout 1** (of an employer) to refuse to allow workers into their place of work until they agree to particular conditions ⊃ related noun LOCKOUT **2** to prevent sb from taking part in sth: *people who are locked out of the job market because they have a criminal record* **ˌlock ˈup | ˌlock sth↔ˈup** to make a building safe by locking the doors and windows: *Don't forget to lock up at night.* ◊ *He locked up the shop and went home.* **ˌlock sb↔ˈup/aˈway** (*informal*) to put sb in prison ⊃ related noun LOCK-UP **ˌlock sth↔ˈup/aˈway 1** to put sth in a safe place that can be locked **2** to put money into an investment that you cannot easily turn into cash: *Their capital is all locked up in property.*

■ *noun*
• FOR DOOR, WINDOW, ETC. **1** [C] a device that keeps a door, window, box, etc. shut, usually needing a key to open it: *She turned the key in the lock.* ⊃ see also COMBINATION LOCK, MORTISE LOCK
• FOR VEHICLE/EQUIPMENT **2** [C] a device that prevents a vehicle, machine or piece of equipment from being used: *a bicycle lock* ◊ *a steering lock* ⊃ see also D-LOCK, TIME LOCK
• ON COMPUTER/PHONE **3** [C] a feature on a computer or mobile phone that prevents sb from accessing it without a code: *There's a security lock on the phone.*
• BEING FIXED IN POSITION **4** [U] a state in which the parts of a machine, etc. do not move **5** [U, sing.] (*BrE*) (on a car, etc.) the amount that the front wheels can be turned in one direction or the other in order to turn the vehicle: *I had the steering wheel on full lock* (= I had turned it as far as it would turn). ⊃ see also ANTI-LOCK
• ON CANAL OR RIVER **6** [C] a section of CANAL or river with a gate at either end, in which the water level can be changed so that boats can move from one level of the canal or river to another
• HAIR **7** [C] a few hairs that hang or lie together on your head: *John brushed a lock of hair from his eyes.* **8 locks** [pl.] (*literary*) a person's hair: *She shook her long, flowing locks.*
• IN RUGBY **9** [C] a player in the second row of the SCRUM
• TOTAL CONTROL **10** [sing.] **a ~ (on sth)** (*NAmE*) total control of sth: *One company had a virtual lock on all orange juice sales in the state.* ⊃ see also ARMLOCK, HEADLOCK
IDM **ˌlock, stock and ˈbarrel** including everything: *He sold the business lock, stock and barrel.* **(keep sth/put sth/be) under ˌlock and ˈkey** locked up safely somewhere; in prison: *We keep our valuables under lock and key.* ◊ *I will not rest until the murderer is under lock and key.* ⊃ more at PICK *v.*

**lock·able** /ˈlɒkəbl; *NAmE* ˈlɑːk-/ *adj.* that you can lock

**lock·down** /ˈlɒkdaʊn; *NAmE* ˈlɑːk-/ *noun* [C, U] an official order to control the movement of people or vehicles because of a dangerous situation: *a three-day lockdown of American airspace* ◊ *Prisoners have been placed on lockdown to prevent further violence at the jail.*

**ˌlocked-ˈin syndrome** *noun* [U] a medical condition, usually resulting from a STROKE, in which the person is conscious but unable to feel or move the body and most of the muscles in the face

**lock·er** /ˈlɒkə(r); *NAmE* ˈlɑːk-/ *noun* a small cupboard that can be locked, where you can leave your clothes, bags, etc. while you play a sport or go somewhere

**locker room** noun a room with lockers in it, at a school, gym, etc., where people can change their clothes ⇨ compare CHANGING ROOM

**locket** /ˈlɒkɪt; NAmE ˈlɑːk-/ noun a piece of jewellery in the form of a small case that you wear on a chain around your neck and in which you can put a picture, piece of hair, etc.

**lock-in** noun (BrE) an occasion when customers are locked in a bar or club after it has closed so that they can continue drinking privately

**lock-out** /ˈlɒkaʊt; NAmE ˈlɑːk-/ noun a situation when an employer refuses to allow workers into their place of work until they agree to various conditions

**lock-smith** /ˈlɒksmɪθ; NAmE ˈlɑːk-/ noun a person whose job is making, fitting and repairing locks

**lock-step** /ˈlɒkstep; NAmE ˈlɑːk-/ noun [U] (especially NAmE) **1** a way of walking together where people move their feet at the same time: **in ~ (with sb)** *The coffin was carried by six soldiers walking in lockstep.* ◊ (figurative) *Politicians and the media are marching in lockstep on this issue* (= they agree). **2** a situation where things happen at the same time or change at the same rate: *a lockstep approach to teaching* ◊ **in ~ (with sth)** *Cases of breathing difficulties increase in lockstep with air pollution.*

**lock-up** noun **1** a small prison where prisoners are kept for a short time **2** (BrE) a small shop that the owner does not live in; a garage that is usually separate from other buildings and that is rented to sb ▶ **lock-up** adj. [only before noun]: *a lock-up garage*

**loco** /ˈləʊkəʊ; NAmE -koʊ/ noun, adj.
▪ noun (pl. **-os**) (informal) = LOCOMOTIVE ⇨ see also IN LOCO PARENTIS
▪ adj. [not before noun] (especially NAmE, informal) crazy

**loco·motion** /ˌləʊkəˈməʊʃn; NAmE ˌloʊkəˈmoʊʃn/ noun [U] (formal) movement or the ability to move

**loco·motive** /ˌləʊkəˈməʊtɪv; NAmE ˌloʊkəˈmoʊtɪv/ noun, adj.
▪ noun (also informal **loco**) a railway engine that pulls a train: *steam/diesel/electric locomotives* ⇨ WORDFINDER NOTE at TRAIN
▪ adj. (formal) connected with movement

**locum** /ˈləʊkəm; NAmE ˈloʊkəm/ (BrE) (NAmE **locum tenens** /ˌləʊkəm ˈtenenz; NAmE -nenz/) noun a doctor or priest who does the work of another doctor or priest while they are sick, on holiday, etc.; the position of such a doctor or priest

**locus** /ˈləʊkəs; NAmE ˈloʊkəs/ noun (pl. **loci** /ˈləʊkaɪ; ˈləʊsaɪ/) (specialist or formal) the exact place where sth happens or that is thought to be the centre of sth

**lo-cust** /ˈləʊkəst; NAmE ˈloʊkəst/ noun a large insect that lives in hot countries and sometimes flies in large groups, destroying all the plants and crops of an area: *a swarm of locusts*

**lo·cu·tion** /ləˈkjuːʃn/ noun (specialist) **1** [U] a style of speaking **2** [C] a particular phrase, especially one used by a particular group of people

**lode** /ləʊd; NAmE loʊd/ noun a line of ORE (= metal in the ground or in rocks)

**lode·star** /ˈləʊdstɑː(r); NAmE ˈloʊd-/ noun **1** the POLE STAR (= a star that is used by sailors to guide a ship) **2** (formal) a person or principle that guides sb's behaviour or actions

**lode·stone** /ˈləʊdstəʊn; NAmE ˈloʊdstoʊn/ noun a piece of iron that acts as a MAGNET

**lodge** /lɒdʒ; NAmE lɑːdʒ/ noun, verb
▪ noun **1** [C] a small house in the country where people stay when they want to take part in some types of outdoor sport: *a hunting lodge* **2** [C] a small house at the gates of a park or in the land belonging to a large house **3** [C] a room at the main entrance to a building for the person whose job is to see who enters and leaves the building: *All visitors should report to the porter's lodge.* **4** [C + sing./pl. v.] the members of a branch of a society such as the Freemasons; the building where they meet: *a masonic lodge* **5** [C] the home of a BEAVER or an OTTER **6** [C] a Native American's tent or home built of LOGS **7** [C] a small house, often made from wood, where people stay on holiday, especially in a small village that has been built for this purpose: *a holiday lodge*
▪ verb **1** [T] **~ sth (with sb) (against sb/sth)** (formal) to make a formal statement about sth to a public organization or authority SYN **register, submit**: *They lodged a compensation claim against the factory.* ◊ *Portugal has lodged a complaint with the International Court of Justice.* **2** [I] **+ adv./prep.** (old-fashioned) to pay to live in a room in sb's house SYN **board**: *He lodged with Mrs Brown when he arrived in the city.* **3** [T] **~ sb (+ adv./prep.)** to provide sb with a place to sleep or live SYN **accommodate**: *The refugees are being lodged at an old army base.* **4** [I, T] to become fixed or stuck somewhere; to make sth become fixed or stuck somewhere: **~ in sth** *One of the bullets lodged in his chest.* ◊ **~ sth in sth** *She lodged the number firmly in her mind.* **5** [T] **~ sth with sb/in sth** to leave money or sth valuable in a safe place SYN **deposit**: *Your will should be lodged with your lawyer.*

**lodg·er** /ˈlɒdʒə(r); NAmE ˈlɑːdʒər/ noun (especially BrE) a person who pays rent to live in sb's house

**lodg·ing** /ˈlɒdʒɪŋ; NAmE ˈlɑːdʒ-/ noun (especially BrE) **1** [U] temporary accommodation: *full board and lodging* (= a room to stay in and all meals provided) **2** [C, usually pl.] (old-fashioned) a room or rooms in sb else's house that you rent to live in: *It was cheaper to live in lodgings than in a hotel.*

**lodging house** noun (BrE, old-fashioned) a house in which lodgings can be rented

**loft** /lɒft; NAmE lɔːft/ noun, verb
▪ noun **1** (especially BrE) a space just below the roof of a house, often used for storing things and sometimes made into a room: *a loft conversion* (= one that has been made into a room or rooms for living in) ⇨ compare ATTIC, GARRET **2** an upper level in a church, or a farm or factory building: *the organ loft* **3** a flat in a former factory, etc., that has been made suitable for living in: *They lived in a SoHo loft.* **4** (NAmE) a part of a room that is on a higher level than the rest: *The children slept in a loft in the upstairs bedroom.*
▪ verb **~ sth** (sport) to hit, kick or throw a ball very high into the air

**lofty** /ˈlɒfti; NAmE ˈlɔːf-/ adj. (**loft·ier, lofti·est**) (formal) **1** (of buildings, mountains, etc.) very high and impressive: *lofty ceilings/rooms/towers* **2** [usually before noun] (approving) (of a thought, an aim, etc.) deserving praise because of its high moral quality: *lofty ambitions/ideals/principles* **3** (disapproving) showing a belief that you are worth more than other people SYN **haughty**: *her lofty disdain for other people* ▶ **loft·ily** /-tɪli/ adv. **lofti·ness** noun [U]

**log** /lɒɡ; NAmE lɔːɡ/ noun, verb
▪ noun **1** a thick piece of wood that is cut from or has fallen from a tree: *logs for the fire* ⇨ see also YULE LOG ⇨ VISUAL VOCAB page V6 **2** (also **log·book**) an official record of events during a particular period of time, especially a journey on a ship or plane: *The captain keeps a log.* **3** a written or digital record of activity on a computer or phone line: *I checked the server's error logs.* **4** (informal, mathematics) = LOGARITHM IDM see EASY adj., SLEEP v.
▪ verb (**-gg-**) **1** **~ sth** to put information in an official record or write a record of events SYN **record**: *The police log all phone calls.* **2** **~ sth** to travel a particular distance or for a particular length of time SYN **clock up**: *The pilot has logged 1 000 hours in the air.* **3** **~ sth** to cut down trees in a forest for their wood
PHRV **log ˈin/ˈon (to sth)** (computing) to perform the actions that allow you to begin using a computer system, application or online account: *You need a password to log on.* ◊ *I logged in to my Twitter account.* HELP **Log on** is used more frequently to talk about starting a computer and **log in** to talk about entering a particular website or application. However, you can use either form in either case. **ˌlog sb ˈin/ˈon (to sth)** (computing) to allow sb to begin using a computer system, application or online account: *The system is unable to log you on.* **ˌlog ˈoff/ˈout (of sth)** (computing) to perform the actions that allow you to finish using a computer system, application or online account: *Log off before switching the computer off.* ◊ *Make sure you*

log out of your account on public computers. **HELP** **Log off** is used more frequently to talk about finishing your session on a computer and **log out** to talk about leaving a particular website or application. However, you can use either form in either case. ◇ **log sb ↔ 'off/'out (of sth)** (*computing*) to cause sb to finish using a computer system, application or online account

**-log** (*NAmE*) = -LOGUE

**loga·rithm** /ˈlɒɡərɪðəm; *NAmE* ˈlɔːɡ-/ (*also informal* **log**) *noun* (*mathematics*) any of a series of numbers set out in lists that make it possible to work out problems by adding and SUBTRACTING instead of multiplying and dividing ⊃ WORDFINDER NOTE at MATHS ▶ **loga·rith·mic** /ˌlɒɡəˈrɪðmɪk; *NAmE* ˌlɔːɡ-/ *adj.*

**log·book** /ˈlɒɡbʊk; *NAmE* ˈlɔːɡ-/ *noun* **1** (*BrE, becoming old-fashioned*) a document that records official details about a vehicle, especially a car, and its owner ⊃ compare REGISTRATION **2** = LOG (2)

**log 'cabin** *noun* a small house built of logs

**log·ger** /ˈlɒɡə(r); *NAmE* ˈlɔːɡ-/ *noun* a person whose job is cutting down trees for their wood, especially on a large scale for industry ⊃ compare LUMBERJACK

**log·ger·heads** /ˈlɒɡəhedz; *NAmE* ˈlɔːɡərh-/ *noun*
**IDM** **at loggerheads (with sb) (over sth)** in strong DISAGREEMENT: *The two governments are still at loggerheads over the island.*

**log·gia** /ˈləʊdʒə; *BrE also* ˈlɒdʒiə; *NAmE* ˈlɑːdʒiə/ *noun* a room or gallery with one or more open sides, especially one that forms part of a house and has one side open to the garden

**log·ging** /ˈlɒɡɪŋ; *NAmE* ˈlɔːɡ-/ *noun* [U] the work or business of cutting down trees for their wood

**logic** ʕ+ **C1 W** /ˈlɒdʒɪk; *NAmE* ˈlɑːdʒ-/ *noun* **1** ʕ+ **C1** [U] a way of thinking or explaining sth: *I fail to see the logic behind his argument.* ◇ *The two parts of the plan were governed by the same logic.* **2** ʕ+ **C1** [U, sing.] sensible reasons for doing sth: *Linking the proposals in a single package did have a certain logic.* ◇ *a strategy based on sound commercial logic* ◇ **~ to/in sth** *There is no logic in any of their claims.* **3** ʕ+ **C1** [U] (*philosophy*) the science of thinking about or explaining the reason for sth using formal methods: *the rules of logic* **4** [U] (*computing*) a system or set of principles used in preparing a computer or electronic device to perform a particular task

**lo·gic·al** ❶ **B2 W** /ˈlɒdʒɪkl; *NAmE* ˈlɑːdʒ-/ *adj.* **1** ʕ **B2** (of an action, event, etc.) seeming natural, reasonable or sensible: *It was a logical conclusion from the child's point of view.* **2** ʕ **B2** following or able to follow the rules of logic in which ideas or facts are based on other true ideas or facts: *a logical argument* ◇ *Computer programming needs someone with a logical mind.* **OPP** **illogical** ▶ **logic·al·ly** /-kli/ *adv.*: *to argue logically*

**-logical, -logic** ⊃ -OLOGY

**logical 'positivism** *noun* [U] (*philosophy*) the belief that the only problems that have meaning are those that can be solved using logical thinking

**'logic circuit** *noun* (*computing*) a series of logic gates that performs operations on data that is put into a computer

**'logic gate** (*also* **gate**) *noun* (*computing*) an electronic switch that reacts in one of two ways to data that is put into it. A computer performs operations by passing data through a very large number of logic gates.

**lo·gi·cian** /ləˈdʒɪʃn/ *noun* a person who studies or has a lot of skill in logic

**login** /ˈlɒɡɪn; *NAmE* ˈlɔːɡ-/ (*also* **logon**) *noun* **1** [U] the act of starting to use a computer system or online account, usually by typing a name or word that you choose to use: *If you've forgotten your login ID, click this link.* **2** [C] the name that you use to enter a computer system or online account: *Enter your login and password and press 'go'.*

**-logist** ⊃ -OLOGY

**lo·gis·tics** /ləˈdʒɪstɪks/ *noun* **1** [U + sing./pl. v.] **~(of sth)** the practical organization that is needed to make a complicated plan successful when a lot of people and equipment are involved: *the logistics of moving the company to a new building* **2** [U] (*business*) the business of transporting and delivering goods **3** [U] the activity of moving equipment, supplies and people for military operations: *a revolution in military logistics* ▶ **lo·gis·tic** (*also* **lo·gis·tic·al** /-ˈdʒɪstɪkl/) *adj.*: *logistic support* ◇ *Organizing famine relief presents huge logistical problems.* **lo·gis·tic·al·ly** /-kli/ *adv.*

**log·jam** /ˈlɒɡdʒæm; *NAmE* ˈlɔːɡ-/ *noun* **1** a difficult situation in which you cannot make progress easily, especially because people cannot agree ⊃ compare BOTTLENECK (2) **2** a mass of LOGS floating on a river and blocking it

**logo** ʕ+ **B2** /ˈləʊɡəʊ/ *noun* (*pl.* **-os**) a printed design or symbol that a company or an organization uses as its special sign

**log·off** /ˈlɒɡɒf; *NAmE* ˈlɔːɡɔːf/ (*also* **log-out**) *noun* [U] the act of finishing using a computer system or online account

**logon** /ˈlɒɡɒn; *NAmE* ˈlɔːɡɑːn/ *noun* = LOGIN

**log·out** /ˈlɒɡaʊt; *NAmE* ˈlɔːɡ-/ *noun* = LOGOFF

**-logue** (*US also* **-log**) /lɒɡ; *NAmE* lɔːɡ/ *combining form* (in nouns) talk or speech: *a monologue*

**-logy** ⊃ -OLOGY

**loin** /lɔɪn/ *noun* **1** [U, C] a piece of meat from the back or sides of an animal, near the tail: *loin of pork* **2** **loins** [pl.] (*old-fashioned*) the part of the body between the middle part and the tops of the legs **3** **loins** [pl.] (*literary*) a person's sex organs **IDM** see GIRD

**loin·cloth** /ˈlɔɪnklɒθ; *NAmE* -klɔːθ/ *noun* a piece of cloth worn around the body at the HIPS by men in some hot countries, sometimes as the only piece of clothing worn

**loi·ter** /ˈlɔɪtə(r)/ *verb* [I] to stand or wait somewhere especially with no obvious reason **SYN** **hang around**: *Teenagers were loitering in the street outside.*

**LOL** (*also* **lol**) /ˌel əʊ ˈel; *BrE also* lɒl; *NAmE also* lɑːl/ *abbr.* = LOLZ

**loll** /lɒl; *NAmE* lɑːl/ *verb* **1** [I] **+ adv./prep.** to lie, sit or stand in a lazy, relaxed way: *He lolled back in his chair by the fire.* **2** [I] **+ adv./prep.** (of your head, tongue, etc.) to move or hang in a relaxed way: *My head lolled against his shoulder.*

**lol·li·pop** /ˈlɒlipɒp; *NAmE* ˈlɑːlipɑːp/ (*also* **lolly**) (*also NAmE, informal* **suck·er**) *noun* a hard round or flat sweet made of boiled sugar on a small stick

**'lollipop man, 'lollipop lady** *noun* (*BrE, informal*) a person whose job is to help children cross a busy road on their way to and from school by holding up a sign on a stick telling traffic to stop

**lol·lop** /ˈlɒləp; *NAmE* ˈlɑːl-/ *verb* [I] **(+ adv./prep.)** (*especially BrE, informal*) to walk or run with long steps in a way that is not smooth or easy: *The dog came lolloping towards them.*

**lolly** /ˈlɒli; *NAmE* ˈlɑːli/ *noun* (*pl.* **-ies**) (*informal*) **1** [C] (*BrE*) = LOLLIPOP **2** [C] (*BrE*) = ICE LOLLY **3** [U] (*BrE, old-fashioned*) money **4** [C] (*AustralE, NZE*) a sweet

**lolz** (*also* **lols** /lɒlz; *NAmE* lɑːlz/) (*also* **LOL, lol** /ˌel əʊ ˈel; *BrE also* lɒl; *NAmE also* lɑːl/) *exclamation* (*informal*) (in emails, social media, etc. from the abbreviation for 'laugh out loud') used to express fun, laughter or the feeling that sth makes you smile: *The dog kept running around chasing its tail. Lolz.* ⊃ compare LULZ ▶ **lolz** *noun* [pl.]: *This is no time for lolz—we're dealing with a serious matter!* ◇ *He went to the supermarket in his pyjamas, just for lolz.*

**Lon·don·er** /ˈlʌndənə(r)/ *noun* a person from London in England, or living in London

**lone** /ləʊn/ *adj.* [only before noun] **1** without any other people or things **SYN** **solitary**: *a lone sailor crossing the Atlantic* **2** (*especially BrE*) without a husband, wife or partner to share the care of children **SYN** **single**: *a lone mother/parent/father* ⊃ note at ALONE
**IDM** **a ˌlone 'wolf** a person who prefers to be alone

# lonely

**lone·ly** ❶ **B1** /ˈləʊnli/ *adj.* (**lone·lier**, **lone·li·est**) **1** ❷ **B1** unhappy because you have no friends or people to talk to: *She lives alone and often feels lonely.* **2** ❷ **B1** (of a situation or period of time) sad and spent alone: *all those lonely nights at home watching TV* **3** ❷ **B1** [only before noun] (of places) where only a few people ever come or visit **SYN** **isolated**: *a lonely beach* ⊃ note at ALONE ▶ **lone·li·ness** *noun* [U]: *a period of loneliness in his life*

**lonely ˈheart** *noun* a person looking for a romantic partner by advertising in a newspaper or online: *This is a story about two lonely hearts who manage to find love.* ◊ *the lonely hearts column in the newspaper*

**lone ˈparent** (*BrE*) (*also* **single ˈparent** *BrE and NAmE*) *noun* a person who takes care of their child or children without a husband, wife or partner

**loner** /ˈləʊnə(r)/ *noun* a person who is often alone or who prefers to be alone, rather than with other people

**lone·some** /ˈləʊnsəm/ *adj.*, *noun*
■ *adj.* (*especially NAmE*) **1** unhappy because you are alone and do not want to be or because you have no friends: *I felt so lonesome after he left.* **2** (of a place) where not many people go; a long way from where people live: *a lonesome road* ⊃ note at ALONE
■ *noun*
**IDM** (**all**) **by/on your lonesome** (*informal*) alone: *Are you here all by your lonesome?*

**long** ❶ **A1** /lɒŋ/; *NAmE* lɔːŋ/ *adj.*, *adv.*, *verb*
■ *adj.* (**long·er** /ˈlɒŋɡə(r)/; *NAmE* ˈlɔːŋ-/, **long·est** /-ɡɪst/)

| | WORD FAMILY |
|---|---|
| | **long** *adj.*, *adv.* |
| | **length** *noun* |
| | **lengthy** *adj.* |
| | **lengthen** *verb* |

• DISTANCE **1** ❷ **A1** measuring or covering a great length or distance, or a greater length or distance than usual: *She had long dark hair.* ◊ *He walked down the long corridor.* ◊ *It was the world's longest bridge.* ◊ *a long journey/walk/drive/flight* ◊ *We're a long way from anywhere here.* ◊ *It's a long way away.* **OPP** **short 2** ❷ **A1** used for asking or talking about particular lengths or distances: *How long is the River Nile?* ◊ *The table is six feet long.* ◊ *The report is only three pages long.*
• TIME **3** ❷ **A1** lasting or taking a great amount of time or more time than usual: *He's been ill (for) a long time.* ◊ *There was a long silence before she spoke.* ◊ *I like it now the days are getting longer* (= it stays light for more time each day). ◊ *a long book/film/list* (= taking a lot of time to read/watch/deal with) ◊ *Nurses have to work long hours* (= for more hours in the day than is usual). ◊ (*NAmE*) *He stared at them for the longest time* (= for a very long time) *before answering.* ◊ *Chicago has a long history of country music.* **OPP** **short 4** ❷ **A1** used for asking or talking about particular periods of time: *How long is the course?* ◊ *I think it's only three weeks long.* ◊ *How long a stay did you have in mind?* ⊃ see also WEEK-LONG, YEAR-LONG **5** ❷ **A1** seeming to last or take more time than it really does because, for example, you are very busy or not happy: *I'm tired. It's been a long day.* ◊ *We were married for ten long years.* **OPP** **short**
• CLOTHES **6** ❷ **A1** covering all or most of your legs or arms: *She usually wears long skirts.* ◊ *a long-sleeved shirt* **OPP** **short**
• HAVING A LOT OF STH **7** ~ **on sth** (*informal*) having a lot of a particular quality: *The government is long on ideas but short on performance.*
• VOWEL SOUNDS **8** (*phonetics*) a **long** vowel is pronounced for a longer time than other vowels: *Compare the long vowel in 'beat' and the short vowel in 'bit'.* **OPP** **short**
**IDM** **as long as your ˈarm** (*informal*) very long: *There's a list of repairs as long as your arm.* **at long ˈlast** after a long time **SYN** **finally**: *At long last his prayers had been answered.* **at the ˈlongest** not longer than the particular time given: *It will take an hour at the longest.* **by a ˈlong way** by a great amount **go back a long ˈway** (of two or more people) to have known each other for a long time: *We go back a long way, he and I.* **go a long ˈway** (of money, food, etc.) to last a long time: *She seems to make her money go a long way.* ◊ *A small amount of this paint goes a long way* (= covers a large area). ◊ (*ironic*) *I find that a little of Jerry's company can go a long way* (= I quickly get tired of being with him). **have come a long ˈway** to have made a lot of progress: *We've come a long way since the early days of the project.* **have a long way to ˈgo** to need to make a lot of progress before you can achieve sth: *She still has a long way to go before she's fully fit.* **how long is a piece of ˈstring?** (*BrE*, *informal*) used to say that there is no definite answer to a question: *'How long will it take?' 'How long's a piece of string?'* **in the long ˈrun** relating to a longer period in the future: *This measure inevitably means higher taxes in the long run.* **It's a ˌlong ˈstory.** (*informal*) used to say that the reasons for sth are complicated and you would prefer not to give all the details **the long and (the) ˈshort of it** used when you are telling sb the essential facts about sth or what effect it will have, without explaining all the details **the long arm of sth** the power and/or authority of sth: *There is no escape from the long arm of the law.* **(pull, wear, etc.) a long ˈface** (to have) an unhappy or disappointed expression **long in the ˈtooth** (*humorous, especially BrE*) old or too old **ORIGIN** This originally referred to the fact that a horse's teeth appear to be longer as it grows older, because its gums shrink. **a ˈlong shot** an attempt or a guess that is not likely to be successful but is worth trying: *It's a long shot, but it just might work.* **(to cut a) long story ˈshort** (*BrE*) (*NAmE* **(to make a) long story ˈshort**) (*informal*) used when you are saying that you will get to the point of what you are saying quickly, without including all the details **long time no ˈsee** (*informal*) used to say hello to sb you have not seen for a long time **not by a ˈlong chalk** (*BrE*) (*also* **not by a ˈlong shot**, *NAmE, BrE*) not nearly; not at all: *It's not over yet—not by a long chalk.* **take a long (cool/hard) look at sth** to consider a problem or possibility very carefully and without hurrying: *We need to take a long, hard look at all the options.* **take the ˈlong view (of sth)** to consider what is likely to happen or be important over a long period of time rather than only considering the present situation ⊃ more at BROAD *adj.*, KICK *v.*, TERM *n.*, WAY *n.*

■ *adv.* (**long·er** /ˈlɒŋɡə(r)/; *NAmE* ˈlɔːŋ-/, **long·est** /-ɡɪst/) **1** ❷ **A1** for a long time: *Have you been here long?* ◊ *Stay as long as you like.* ◊ *This may take longer than we thought.* ◊ *Shows don't usually last this long.* ◊ *I won't be long* (= I'll return, be ready, etc. soon). ◊ *How long have you been waiting?* ◊ *Those carefree college years are long gone.* **2** ❷ **A1** a long time before or after a particular time or event: *He retired long before the war.* ◊ *It wasn't long before she had persuaded him* (= it only took a short time). ◊ **before** ~ *We'll be home before long* (= soon). ◊ ~ **ago** *The house was pulled down long ago.* ◊ *Not long ago* (= quite recently) *phones were only used for speaking to people or maybe sending texts.* ◊ ~ **past sth** *It was long past midnight.* ◊ ~ **since** *Long since* (= a long time before the present time) *moved away.* **3** ❷ **A2** used after a noun to emphasize that sth happens for the whole of a particular period of time: *We had to wait all day long.* ◊ *The baby was crying all night long.* ◊ *They stayed up the whole night long.*
**IDM** **as/so ˈlong as 1** ❷ **B2** only if: *We'll go as long as the weather is good.* **2** ❷ **B2** since; to the extent that: *So long as there is a demand for these drugs, the financial incentive for drug dealers will be there.* **for (so) ˈlong** ❷ **B1** for (such) a long time: *Will you be away for long?* ◊ *I'm sorry I haven't written to you for so long.* **how long have you ˈgot?** (*BrE*) (*NAmE* **how long do you ˈhave?**) (*informal*) used to say that sth is going to take a long time to explain: *What do I think about it? How long have you got?* **long live sb/sth** used to say that you hope sb/sth will live or last for a long time: *Long live the King!* ◊ *Long live public libraries!* **no/any ˈlonger** ❷ **B1** used to say that sth that was possible or true before, is not now: *I can't wait any longer.* ◊ *He no longer lives here.* **so ˈlong** (*informal*) goodbye ⊃ more at LAUGH *v.*

■ *verb* [I] to want sth very much especially if it does not seem likely to happen soon **SYN** **yearn**: ~ **for sb/sth** *Lucy had always longed for a brother.* ◊ ~ **for sb to do sth** *He* longed for Pat to phone. ◊ **~ to do sth** *I'm longing to see you again.* ⊃ see also LONGED-FOR

▼ **WHICH WORD?**

**(for) long / (for) a long time**

- Both **(for) long** and **(for) a long time** are used as expressions of time. In positive sentences **(for) a long time** is used: *We've been friends a long time.* **(For) long** is not used in positive sentences unless it is used with *too*, *enough*, *as*, *so*, *seldom*, etc: *I stayed out in the sun for too long.* ◊ *You've been waiting long enough.* Both **(for) long** and **(for) a long time** can be used in questions, but **(for) long** is usually preferred: *Have you been waiting long?*
- In negative sentences **(for) a long time** sometimes has a different meaning from **(for) long**. Compare: *I haven't been here for a long time* (= It is a long time since the last time I was here) and *I haven't been here long* (= I arrived here only a short time ago).

**long.** *abbr.* (in writing) LONGITUDE

**long-a`waited** *adj.* that people have been waiting for for a long time: *her long-awaited new novel*

**'long ball** *noun* (in baseball) a HOME RUN (= a hit that allows the person hitting the ball to run around all the bases without stopping)

**'long·board** /'lɒŋbɔːd; *NAmE* 'lɔːŋbɔːrd/ *noun* a long board used in SURFING

**'long·boat** /'lɒŋbəʊt; *NAmE* 'lɔːŋ-/ *noun* **1** a large ROWING BOAT, used especially for travelling on the sea **2** = LONGSHIP

**'long·bow** /'lɒŋbəʊ; *NAmE* 'lɔːŋ-/ *noun* a large BOW made of a long, thin, curved piece of wood that was used in the past for shooting ARROWS

**long-'distance** *adj.* [only before noun] **1** travelling or involving travel between places that are far apart: *a long-distance commuter* ◊ *long-distance flights* **2** operating between or involving people and places that are far apart: *a long-distance phone call* ◊ *The pair embarked on a **long-distance relationship**, while he was in London and she stayed in New York.* **3** relating to a race distance of 6 miles or 10 000 metres or longer: *a long-distance runner* ▸ **long 'distance** *adv.*: *It's a relaxing car to drive long distance.* ◊ *to call long distance*

**long di'vision** *noun* [U] (*mathematics*) a method of dividing one number by another in which all the stages involved are written down

**long-drawn-'out** *adj.* = DRAWN-OUT SYN protracted: *long-drawn-out negotiations*

**'long `drink** *noun* a cold drink that fills a tall glass, such as LEMONADE or beer

**'longed-for** *adj.* [only before noun] that sb has been wanting or hoping for very much: *the birth of a longed-for baby*

**lon·gev·ity** /lɒn'dʒevəti; *NAmE* lɔːn-/ *noun* [U] (*formal*) long life; the fact of lasting a long time: *We wish you both health and longevity.* ◊ *He prides himself on the longevity of the company.*

**'long·hair** /'lɒŋheə(r); *NAmE* 'lɔːŋher/ *noun* a type of cat with long hair ⊃ compare SHORTHAIR

**'long·hand** /'lɒŋhænd; *NAmE* 'lɔːŋ-/ *noun* [U] ordinary writing, not typed or written in SHORTHAND

**'long `haul** *noun* **1** [U] (in the context of passenger flights or transporting goods) a long distance: *I have never enjoyed flying long haul.* **2** [C, usually sing.] a difficult task that takes a long time and a lot of effort to complete: *She knows that becoming world champion is going to be a long haul.* IDM **be in sth for the long `haul** to be willing to continue doing a task until it is finished: *I promise I am in this for the long haul.* **over the long `haul** (especially *NAmE*) over a long period of time

**'long-haul** *adj.* [only before noun] involving the transport of goods or passengers over long distances: *long-haul flights/routes* OPP short-haul ⊃ WORDFINDER NOTE at PLANE

**'long `horn** /'lɒŋhɔːn; *NAmE* 'lɔːŋhɔːrn/ *noun* a type of cow with long HORNS

**'long·house** /'lɒŋhaʊs; *NAmE* 'lɔːŋ-/ *noun* **1** (in parts of Malaysia and Indonesia) a large house in a village where several families live together **2** (in North America in the past) a traditional house used by some Native Americans **3** (in Europe in the past) an old type of house in which people and animals lived together

**long·ing** /'lɒŋɪŋ; *NAmE* 'lɔːŋ-/ *noun*, *adj.*
- *noun* [C, U] a strong feeling of wanting sth/sb: **~ (for sb/sth)** *a longing for home* ◊ **~ (to do sth)** *She was filled with longing to hear his voice again.* ◊ *romantic longings* ◊ *His voice was husky with longing* (= sexual desire).
- *adj.* [only before noun] feeling or showing that you want sth very much: *He gave a longing look at the ice cream.*
▸ **long·ing·ly** *adv.*: *We looked longingly towards the hills.*

**long·ish** /'lɒŋɪʃ; *NAmE* 'lɔːŋ-/ *adj.* [only before noun] fairly long: *longish hair* ◊ *There was a longish pause.*

**lon·gi·tude** /'lɒŋɡɪtjuːd, 'lɒndʒɪ-; *NAmE* 'lɑːndʒɪtuːd/ *noun* [U] (*abbr.* **long.**) the distance of a place east or west of the Greenwich MERIDIAN, measured in degrees: *the longitude of the island* ⊃ compare LATITUDE

**lon·gi·tu·din·al** /ˌlɒŋɡɪ'tjuːdənl, ˌlɒndʒɪ-; *NAmE* ˌlɑːndʒə'tuː-/ *adj.* (*specialist*) **1** going downwards rather than across: *The plant's stem is marked with thin, green, longitudinal stripes.* **2** relating to the development of sth over a period of time: *a longitudinal study of ageing* **3** connected with longitude: *the town's longitudinal position* ▸ **lon·gi·tu·din·al·ly** /-nəli/ *adv.*

**'long `johns** *noun* [pl.] (*informal*) warm UNDERPANTS with long legs down to the ankles: *a pair of long johns*

**'long `jump** (*NAmE* also **broad jump**) *noun* often **the long jump** [sing.] a sporting event in which people try to jump as far forward as possible after running up to a line

**long-'lasting** *adj.* that can or does last for a long time: *long-lasting effects* ◊ *a long-lasting agreement* ⊃ compare DURABLE

**long-'life** *adj.* **1** made to last longer than the ordinary type: *long-life batteries* **2** (*BrE*) made to remain fresh longer than the ordinary type: *long-life milk*

**long-'lived** /ˌlɒŋ 'lɪvd; *NAmE* ˌlɔːŋ 'lɪvd, 'laɪvd/ *adj.* having a long life; lasting for a long time ⊃ SYNONYMS at OLD

**long-'lost** *adj.* [only before noun] that you have not seen or received any news of for a long time: *a long-lost friend*

**long-'range** *adj.* [only before noun] **1** travelling a long distance: *long-range missiles* **2** made for a period of time that will last a long way into the future: *a long-range weather forecast* ◊ *long-range plans* ⊃ compare SHORT-RANGE

**'long-running** *adj.* [only before noun] that has been continuing for a long time: *a long-running dispute* ◊ *a long-running TV series*

**'long-serving** *adj.* [only before noun] having had the job or position mentioned for a long time: *long-serving employees*

**'long·ship** /'lɒŋʃɪp; *NAmE* 'lɔːŋ-/ (also **long·boat**) *noun* a long narrow ship used by the Vikings

**'long·shore·man** /'lɒŋʃɔːmən; *NAmE* 'lɔːŋʃɔːrm-/ *noun* (*pl.* -men /-mən/) (*NAmE*) (also **dock·er** especially in *BrE*) a man whose job is moving goods on and off ships ⊃ compare STEVEDORE

**long-'sighted** (*BrE*) (*NAmE* ˌfar-'sighted) *adj.* [not usually before noun] not able to see things that are close to you clearly OPP short-sighted ▸ **long-'sighted·ness** (also **'long `sight**) *noun* [U]

**long-'standing** ?+ C1 *adj.* [usually before noun] that has existed or lasted for a long time: *a long-standing relationship*

**'long-stay** *adj.* [usually before noun] **1** likely to need treatment or care for a long time: *long-stay patients* ◊ *long-stay hospitals/institutions/wards* (= for long-stay patients) **2** for people who wish to park their cars for a long period: *long-stay parking*

---

| ʊ actual | aɪ my | aʊ now | eɪ say | əʊ go | ɔɪ boy | ɪə near | eə hair | ʊə pure |

**long-suffer·ing** *adj.* [usually before noun] dealing with problems or another person's unpleasant behaviour patiently: *his long-suffering wife*

**long-term** ⬤ B2 *adj., adv.*
- *adj.* B2 [usually before noun] lasting or having an effect over a long period of time: *a long-term goal* ◇ *the long-term future* ◇ *the long-term effects/consequences/impact of sth* ◇ *a long-term commitment/relationship* ◇ *The long-term trend is for prices to rise.* ◇ *the long-term unemployed* ➔ compare SHORT-TERM
- *adv.* B2 over a long period of time: *to benefit/affect sb long-term* ◇ *It is unclear if this shift will continue long-term.* ◇ *We need to think long-term* (= think about what will happen over a long period of time) *if we want to get any serious results.*

**long-time** ⬤+ C1 *adj.* [only before noun] having been the particular thing mentioned for a long time: *his long-time colleague*

**long wave** *noun* [U, C] (*abbr.* **LW**) a radio wave with a length of more than 1000 metres; the band of radio waves at this length, used for broadcasting: **on ~** *to broadcast on long wave* ➔ compare SHORT WAVE

**long·ways** /ˈlɒŋweɪz/ *NAmE* /ˈlɔːŋ-/ (*also* **long·wise** /ˈlɒŋwaɪz/ *NAmE* /ˈlɔːŋ-/) *adv.* in the same direction as the longest side of sth ⓢⓨⓝ **lengthways**

**long weekˈend** *noun* a holiday of three or four days from Friday or Saturday to Sunday or Monday

**long-winded** *adj.* (*disapproving*) (especially of talking or writing) continuing for too long and therefore boring ⓢⓨⓝ **tedious**

**loo** /luː/ *noun* (*pl.* **loos**) (*BrE, informal*) a toilet: *She's gone to the loo.* ◇ *Can I use your loo, please?*

**loo·fah** /ˈluːfə/ *noun* a long, rough bath SPONGE made from the dried fruit of a tropical plant

**look** ⬤ A1 Ⓢ /lʊk/ *verb, noun, exclamation*
- *verb*
- **USE EYES** **1** A1 [I] to turn your eyes in a particular direction: *Look closely and tell me what you see.* ◇ *If you look carefully you can just see our house from here.* ◇ *Look! I'm sure that's Jennifer Lawrence!* ◇ **at sb/sth** *She looked at me and smiled.* ◇ **~ + adv./prep.** *I got up and looked out of the window.* ◇ *She looked across to the other side of the room.* ◇ see also FORWARD-LOOKING
- **SEARCH** **2** A1 [I] to try to find sb/sth: **~ for sb/sth** *Where have you been? We've been looking for you.* ◇ *Are you still looking for a job?* ◇ *They are always looking for ways to save money.* ◇ **~ + adv./prep.** *I can't find my book—I've looked everywhere.*
- **PAY ATTENTION** **3** A1 [I, T] to pay attention to sth: **~ at sth** *Look at the time! We're going to be late.* ◇ **~ where, what, etc** … *Can't you look where you're going?*
- **APPEAR/SEEM** **4** A1 linking verb to seem; to appear: **+ adj.** *You look great!* ◇ *The garden looks nice.* ◇ *That book looks interesting.* ◇ **~ like sb/sth** *That looks like an interesting book.* ◇ **~ like sb/sth to sb** *It doesn't look like fun to me.* ◇ **+ noun** *You made me look a complete fool!* ➔ see also GOOD-LOOKING **5** A1 [I] (not usually used in the progressive tenses) to have a particular appearance: **~ like sb/sth** *That photograph doesn't look like her at all.* ◇ *'What does your cousin look like?' 'He's tall and thin with brown hair.'* ◇ **~ as if … /as though …** *You look as though you slept badly.* ⒽⒺⓁⓅ In spoken English people often use **like** instead of **as if** or **as though** in this meaning, especially in *NAmE*: *You look like you slept badly.* This is quite informal and not always considered correct in written *BrE*. **6** B1 [I] to seem likely to happen or be true: *It looks like rain* (= it looks as if it's going to rain). ◇ **~(to sb) as if …/as though …** *It doesn't look as if we'll be moving after all.* ◇ **~(to sb) like …** (*informal*) *It looks to me like they have a plan.* ⒽⒺⓁⓅ This use of **like** instead of **as if** or **as though** is quite informal and is not always considered correct in written *BrE*.
- **FACE** **7** [I] **+ adv./prep.** to face a particular direction: *The house looks east.* ◇ *The hotel looks out over the harbour.*

ⒾⒹⓂ ⒽⒺⓁⓅ Most idioms containing **look** are at the entries for the nouns and adjectives in the idioms, for example **look daggers at sb** is at **dagger**. **be just ˈlooking** used in a shop to say that you are not ready to buy sth: *'Can I help you?' 'I'm just looking, thank you.'* **be ˈlooking to do sth** to try to find ways of doing sth: *The government is looking to reduce inflation.* **look ˈbad | not look ˈgood** to be considered bad behaviour or bad manners: *It looks bad not going to your own brother's wedding.* **look ˈbad (for sb)** to show that sth bad might happen: *He's had another heart attack; things are looking bad for him, I'm afraid.* **look ˈgood** to show success or that sth good might happen: *This year's sales figures are looking good.* **look ˈhere** (*old-fashioned*) used to protest about sth: *Now look here, it wasn't my fault.* **look how/what/who …** used to give an example that proves what you are saying or makes it clearer: *Look how lazy we've become.* ◇ *Be careful climbing that ladder. Look what happened last time.* **look no ˈfurther** used to say that sth is exactly what sb needs and so they do not need to consider any other options: *Those looking for an enjoyable evening need look no further than the hotel's nightclub.* **look sb ˌup and ˈdown** to look at sb in a careful or critical way **(not) look yourˈself** to (not) have your normal healthy appearance: *You're not looking yourself today* (= you look tired or ill/sick). **never/not look ˈback** (*informal*) to become more and more successful: *Her first novel was published in 2007 and since then she hasn't looked back.* **not much to ˈlook at** (*informal*) not attractive **to ˈlook at sb/sth** judging by the appearance of sb/sth: *To look at him you'd never think he was nearly fifty.*

ⓅⒽⓇⓋ **ˌlook ˈafter sb/sth/yourself** (*especially BrE*) **1** A2 to be responsible for or to take care of sb/sth/yourself: *Who's going to look after the children while you're away?* ◇ *I'm looking after his affairs while he's in hospital.* ◇ *Don't worry about me—I can look after myself* (= I don't need any help). ➔ note at CARE **2** to make sure that things happen to sb's advantage: *He's good at looking after his own interests.* **ˌlook aˈhead (to sth)** to think about what is going to happen in the future
**ˌlook aˈround** (*also* **ˌlook ˈround** *especially in BrE*) to turn your head so that you can see sth: *People came out of their houses and looked around.* **ˌlook aˈround (sth)** (*also* **ˌlook ˈround (sth)** *especially in BrE*) to visit a place or building, walking around it to see what is there: *Let's look around the town this afternoon.* **ˌlook aˈround for sth** (*also* **ˌlook ˈround for sth** *especially in BrE*) to search for sth in a number of different places: *We're looking around for a house in this area.*
**ˌlook at sth 1** to examine sth closely: *Your ankle's swollen—I think the doctor ought to look at it.* ◇ *I haven't had time to look at* (= read) *the papers yet.* **2** to think about, consider or study sth: *The company is looking at ways to reduce waste.* ◇ *The implications of the new law will need to be looked at.* **3** to view or consider sth in a particular way: *Looked at from that point of view, his decision was easier to understand.*
**ˌlook ˈback (at sth)** A2 to look again at sth that you read or wrote earlier, in order to remind yourself what it said: *Look back at your notes and summarize what you have learned.* **ˌlook ˈback (at/on sth)** to think about sth in the past ⓢⓨⓝ **reflect**: *to look back on your childhood*
**ˌlook ˈdown on sb** to think that you are better than sb: *She looks down on people who haven't been to college.*
**ˈlook for sth** to hope for sth; to expect sth: *We shall be looking for an improvement in your work this term.*
**ˌlook ˈforward to sth** B1 to be thinking with pleasure about sth that is going to happen (because you expect to enjoy it): *I'm looking forward to the weekend.* ◇ **look forward to doing sth** *We're really looking forward to seeing you again.*
**ˌlook ˈin (on sb)** to make a short visit to a place, especially sb's house when they are ill or need help: *She looks in on her elderly neighbour every evening.* ◇ *Why don't you look in on me next time you're in town?*
**ˌlook ˈinto sth** to examine sth: *A working party has been set up to look into the problem.*
**ˌlook ˈon** to watch sth without becoming involved in it yourself: *Passers-by simply looked on as he was attacked.*

⊃ related noun ONLOOKER **look on sb/sth as sb/sth** to consider sb/sth to be sb/sth: *She's looked on as the leading authority on the subject.* **look on sb/sth with sth** to consider sb/sth in a particular way SYN *regard: They looked on his behaviour with contempt.*
**look 'out** ? B1 used to warn sb to be careful, especially when there is danger SYN *watch out: Look out! There's a car coming.* **look 'out for sb** to take care of sb and make sure nothing bad happens to them **look 'out for sb/sth** ? B1 **1** ? B1 to try to avoid sth bad happening or doing sth bad SYN *watch out: You should look out for pickpockets.* ◊ *Do look out for spelling mistakes in your work.* **2** to keep trying to find sth or meet sb: *I'll look out for you at the conference.* ⊃ related noun LOOKOUT **look 'out for sb/ yourself** to think only of sb's/your own advantage, without worrying about other people: *You should look out for yourself from now on.* **look sth⇿ 'out (for sb/ sth)** (*BrE*) to search for sth from among your possessions: *I'll look out those old photographs you wanted to see.*
**look sth⇿ 'over** to examine sth to see how good, big, etc. it is: *We looked over the house again before we decided we would rent it.*
**look 'round (sth)** = LOOK AROUND (STH)
**look 'round for sth** = LOOK AROUND FOR STH
**look 'through sb** [no passive] to ignore sb by pretending not to see them: *She just looked straight through me.* **look through sth** [no passive] to examine or read sth quickly: *She looked through her notes before the exam.*
**look to sb for sth** | **look to sb to do sth** (*formal*) to rely on or expect sb to provide sth or do sth: *We are looking to you for help.* **look to sth** (*formal*) to consider sth and think about how to make it better: *We need to look to ways of improving our marketing.*
**look 'up** (*informal*) (of business, sb's situation, etc.) to become better SYN *improve: At last things were beginning to look up.* **look 'up (from sth)** to raise your eyes when you are looking down at sth: *She looked up from her book as I entered the room.* **look sb⇿ 'up** [no passive] (*informal*) to visit or make contact with sb, especially when you have not seen them for a long time: *Do look me up the next time you're in London.* **look sth⇿ 'up** ? A2 to look for information in a dictionary or REFERENCE BOOK, or by using a computer: *Can you look up the opening times on the website?* ◊ *I looked it up in the dictionary.* **look 'up to sb** to admire or respect sb

■ **noun**
• USING EYES **1** ? A2 [C, usually sing.] an act of looking at sb/ sth: *~ at sb/sth Here, have a look at this.* ◊ *Take a look at these figures!* ◊ *Make sure you get a good look at their faces.* ◊ *One look at his face and Jenny stopped laughing.* ◊ *Alex and Michael exchanged looks* (= they looked at each other). ◊ *~ around It's an interesting place. Do you want to take a look around?*
• SEARCH **2** ? A2 [C, usually sing.] an act of trying to find sth/ sb: *~ for sth/sb I've had a good look for it, but I can't find it.* ◊ *~ + adv./prep. I had a furtive look in her bag when her back was turned.*
• EXAMINE A PROBLEM/SITUATION **3** ? B1 [C, usually sing.] an act of examining a problem or situation carefully: *I gave the figures a quick look.* ◊ *a brief/an in-depth look* ◊ *~ at sth We'll be taking a close look at these proposals* (= examining them carefully).
• EXPRESSION **4** ? B1 [C] an expression in your eyes or face: *He didn't like the look in her eyes.* ◊ *She had a worried look on her face.* ◊ *He gave me a funny look.* ◊ *~ of sth a look of disgust/horror/shock/surprise*
• APPEARANCE **5** ? B1 [C] the way sb/sth looks; the appearance of sb/sth: *a fabric with the look of silk* ◊ *I don't like the look of that guy* (= I don't trust him, judging by his appearance). ◊ *by/from the ~(s) of sth/sb It's going to rain today by the look of it* (= judging by appearances). **6** ? B1 **looks** [pl.] a person's appearance, especially when the person is attractive: *She has her father's good looks.* ◊ *He lost his looks* (= became less attractive) *in later life.* ⊃ see also GOOD-LOOKING
• FASHION **7** ? B1 [sing.] a fashion; a style: *They've given the place a completely new look.* ◊ *Wear the top with jeans for a more casual look.* ⊃ see also WET LOOK

929

# lookalike

IDM **if looks could 'kill …** used to describe the very angry or unpleasant way sb is/was looking at you: *I don't know what I've done to upset him, but if looks could kill …* ⊃ more at DIRTY *adj.*, LONG *adj.*
■ **exclamation** used to make sb pay attention to what you are going to say, often when you are annoyed: *Look, I think we should go now.* ◊ *Look, that's not fair.*

▼ SYNONYMS

**look**
watch • see • view • observe

These words all mean to turn your eyes in a particular direction.

**look** to turn your eyes in a particular direction: *If you look carefully you can just see our house from here.* ◊ *She looked at me and smiled.*
**watch** to look at sb/sth for a time, paying attention to what happens: *to watch television* ◊ *Watch what I do, then you try.*
**see** to watch a game, television programme, performance, etc: *In the evening we went to see a movie.*
**view** (*formal*) to look at sth, especially when you look carefully; to watch television, a film, etc: *People came from all over the world to view her work.*
WATCH, SEE OR VIEW?
You can *see/view a film/programme* but you cannot: *see/ view television.* **View** is more formal than **see** and is used especially in business contexts.
**observe** (*formal*) to watch sb/sth carefully, especially to learn more about them or it: *The patients were observed over a period of several months.*
PATTERNS
• to look/watch **for** sb/sth
• to watch/observe **what/who/how …**
• to look/watch/view/observe (sb/sth) **with** amazement/surprise/disapproval, etc.
• to watch/see/view a **film/show/programme**
• to watch/see a **match/game/fight**
• to look (at sb/sth)/watch (sb/sth)/observe sb/sth **carefully/closely**

▼ SYNONYMS

**look**
glance • gaze • stare • glimpse • glare

These are all words for an act of looking, when you turn your eyes in a particular direction.

**look** an act of looking at sb/sth: *Here, have a look at this.*
**glance** a quick look: *She stole a glance at her watch.*
**gaze** a long, steady look at sb/sth: *She felt embarrassed under his steady gaze.*
**stare** a long look at sb/sth, especially in a way that is unfriendly or that shows surprise: *She gave the officer a blank stare and shrugged her shoulders.*
**glimpse** a look at sb/sth for a very short time, when you do not see the person or thing completely: *He caught a glimpse of her in the crowd.*
**glare** a long, angry look at sb/sth: *She fixed her questioner with a hostile glare.*
PATTERNS
• a look/glance **at** sb/sth
• a **penetrating/piercing** look/glance/gaze/stare
• a **long** look/glance/stare
• a **brief** look/glance/glimpse
• to **have/get/take** a look/glance/glimpse
• to **avoid** sb's glance/gaze/stare

**look·alike** /'lʊkəlaɪk/ *noun* (often used after a person's name) a person who looks very similar to the person mentioned: *an Elvis lookalike*

# looker

**look·er** /ˈlʊkə(r)/ noun (informal) a way of describing an attractive person, usually a woman: *She's a real looker!*

**ˈlook-in** noun
**IDM** **(not) get/have a ˈlook-in** (BrE, informal) (not) to get a chance to take part or succeed in sth: *She talks so much that nobody else can get a look-in.*

**ˈlooking glass** noun (old-fashioned) a mirror

**look·out** /ˈlʊkaʊt/ noun **1** a place for watching from, especially for danger or an enemy coming towards you: *a lookout point/tower* **2** a person who has the responsibility of watching for sth, especially danger, etc.: *One of the men stood at the door to act as a lookout.*
**IDM** **be ˈsb's lookout** (BrE, informal) used to say that you do not think sb's actions are sensible, but that it is their own problem or responsibility: *If he wants to waste his money, that's his lookout.* **be on the ˈlookout (for sb/sth) | keep a ˈlookout (for sb/sth)** (informal) to watch carefully for sb/sth in order to avoid danger, etc. or in order to find sth you want: *The public should be on the lookout for symptoms of the disease.*

**ˈlook-see** noun [sing.] (informal) a quick look at sth: *Come and have a look-see.*

**look·up** /ˈlʊkʌp/ noun [U] the act of searching for and finding electronic information: *Our new database allows for fast, intelligent lookup.*

**loom** ⓘ+ **C1** /luːm/ verb, noun
■ verb **1** ⓘ+ **C1** [I] (+ adv./prep.) to appear as a large shape that is not clear, especially in a frightening way: *A dark shape loomed up ahead of us.* **2** ⓘ+ **C1** [I] (of sth bad) to appear serious and likely to happen soon: *There was a crisis looming.*
**IDM** **ˌloom ˈlarge** to be frightening and make you worried because sth seems hard to avoid: *The prospect of war loomed large.*
■ noun a machine for making cloth by crossing THREADS over and under other threads that go in a different direction

**loon** /luːn/ noun **1** a large North American bird that eats fish and makes a noise like a laugh **2** = LOONY

**loonie** /ˈluːni/ noun (CanE) the Canadian dollar or a Canadian one-dollar coin

**loony** /ˈluːni/ adj., noun
■ adj. (informal, sometimes offensive) crazy or strange
■ noun (pl. -ies) (also **loon**) (informal, offensive) a person who has strange ideas or who behaves in a strange way

**ˈloony bin** noun (old-fashioned, informal, offensive) a humorous and offensive way of referring to a hospital for people who are mentally ill

**loop** ⓘ+ **C1** /luːp/ noun, verb
■ noun **1** ⓘ+ **C1** a shape like a curve or circle made by a line curving right round: *The road went in a huge loop around the lake.* **2** ⓘ+ **C1** a piece of rope, wire, etc. in the shape of a curve or circle: *He tied a loop of rope around his arm.* ◊ *Make a loop in the string.* ◊ *a belt loop (= on trousers, etc. for holding a belt in place)* ⊃ picture at KNOT **3** a long, narrow piece of film or tape on which the pictures and sound are repeated continuously: *The film is on a loop.* ◊ (figurative) *His mind kept turning in an endless loop.* **4** (computing) a set of instructions that is repeated again and again until a particular condition is satisfied **5** a complete CIRCUIT for electrical current **6** (BrE) a railway line or road that leaves the main track or road and then joins it again **7** **the Loop** (US, informal) the business centre of the US city of Chicago
**IDM** **in the ˈloop | out of the ˈloop** (informal) part of a group of people that is dealing with sth important; not part of this group **knock/throw sb for a ˈloop** (NAmE, informal) to shock or surprise sb
■ verb **1** [T] ~sth + adv./prep. to form or bend sth into a loop: *He looped the strap over his shoulder.* **2** [I] + adv./prep. to move in a way that makes the shape of a loop: *The river loops around the valley.* ◊ *The ball looped high up in the air.*

**IDM** **ˌloop the ˈloop** to fly or make a plane fly in a circle going up and down

**loop·hole** /ˈluːphəʊl/ noun ~(in sth) a mistake in the way a law, contract, etc. has been written that enables people to legally avoid doing sth that the law, contract, etc. had intended them to do: *a legal/tax loophole* ◊ *to close existing loopholes*

**loopy** /ˈluːpi/ adj. (informal) **1** not sensible; strange **SYN** **crazy 2** (BrE) very angry **SYN** **furious**: *He'll go loopy when he hears!*

**loose** ⓘ **B2** /luːs/ adj., verb, noun
■ adj. (loos·er, loos·est)
• **NOT FIXED/TIED 1** ⓘ **B2** not securely fixed where it should be; able to become separated from sth: *a loose button/tooth* ◊ *Check that the plug has not come loose.* **2** ⓘ **B2** not tied together; not held in position by anything or contained in anything: *She usually wears her hair loose.* ◊ *The potatoes were sold loose, not in bags.* **3** ⓘ **B2** [not usually before noun] free to move around without control; not tied up or shut in somewhere: *The sheep had got out and were loose on the road.* ◊ *The horse had broken loose (= escaped) from its tether.* ◊ *During the night, somebody had cut the boat loose from its moorings.*
• **CLOTHES 4** ⓘ **B2** not fitting closely: *On long flights, wear loose clothing and comfortable shoes.* **OPP** **tight**
• **NOT SOLID/HARD 5** not tightly packed together; not solid or hard: *loose soil* ◊ *a fabric with a loose weave*
• **NOT STRICT/EXACT 6** not strictly organized or managed: *a loose alliance/coalition/federation* **7** not exact; not very careful: *a loose translation* ◊ *loose thinking*
• **NOT MORAL 8** [usually before noun] (old-fashioned) having or involving an attitude to sexual relationships that people consider to be morally wrong: *a young man of loose morals*
• **BALL 9** (sport) not in any player's control: *He pounced on a loose ball.*
• **BODY WASTE 10** having too much liquid in it: *a baby with loose bowel movements* ▶ **loose·ness** noun [U]
**IDM** **break/cut (sb/sth) ˈloose from sb/sth** to separate yourself or sb/sth from a group of people or their influence, etc.: *The organization broke loose from its sponsors.* ◊ *He cut himself loose from his family.* **hang/stay ˈloose** (especially NAmE, informal) to remain calm; to not worry: *It's OK—hang loose and stay cool.* **have a loose ˈtongue** to talk too much, especially about things that are private **let ˈloose** (BrE) (NAmE **cut ˈloose**) (informal) to do sth or to happen in a way that no one controls: *Teenagers need a place to let loose.* **let ˈloose sth** to make a noise or remark, especially in a loud or sudden way: *She let loose a stream of abuse.* **let sb/sth ˈloose 1** to free sb/sth from whatever holds them/it in place: *She let her hair loose and it fell around her shoulders.* ◊ *Who's let the dog loose?* **2** to give sb complete freedom to do what they want in a place or situation: *He was at last let loose in the kitchen.* ◊ *A team of professionals were let loose on the project.* ⊃ more at **FAST** adv., **HELL**, **SCREW** n.
■ verb (formal)
• **RELEASE 1** ~sth (on/upon sb/sth) to release sth or let it happen or be expressed in a completely free way: *His speech loosed a tide of nationalist sentiment.*
• **MAKE STH LOOSE 2** ~sth to make sth loose, especially sth that is tied or held tightly **SYN** **loosen**: *I loosed the reins and allowed the horse to gallop.*
• **FIRE BULLETS 3** ~sth (off) (at sb/sth) to fire bullets, ARROWS, etc. **HELP** Do not confuse this verb with **to lose** (= to be unable to find sth).
■ noun
**IDM** **on the ˈloose** (of a person or an animal) having escaped from somewhere; free **SYN** **at large**: *Three prisoners are still on the loose.*

**ˌloose ˈcannon** noun a person, usually a public figure, who often behaves in a way that nobody can predict

**ˌloose ˈchange** noun [U] coins that you have in a pocket or a bag

**ˌloose ˈcover** (BrE) (NAmE **slip-cover**) noun [usually pl.] a cover for a chair, etc. that you can take off, for example to wash it

**loose 'end** noun [usually pl.] a part of sth such as a story that has not been completely finished or explained: *The play has too many loose ends.* ◊ *There are still a few ends to tie up* (= a few things to finish).
IDM **at a loose 'end** (BrE) (NAmE usually **at loose 'ends**) (informal) having nothing to do and not knowing what you want to do: *Come and see us, if you're at a loose end.*

**loose-'fitting** adj. (of clothes) not fitting the body tightly
OPP **tight-fitting**

**loose-'leaf** adj. [usually before noun] (of a book, file, etc.) having pages that can be put in and taken out separately: *a loose-leaf binder*

**loose-'limbed** adj. (literary) (of a person) moving in an easy, not stiff, way

**loose·ly** /ˈluːsli/ adv. **1** in a way that is not strong or tight: *She fastened the belt loosely around her waist.* **2** in a way that is not exact: *to use a term loosely* ◊ *The play is loosely based on his childhood in Russia.*

**loos·en** /ˈluːsn/ verb **1** [T, I] ~ (sth) to make sth less tight or strongly fixed; to become less tight or strongly fixed SYN **slacken**: *First loosen the nuts, then take off the wheel.* ◊ *The rope holding the boat loosened.* **2** [T] ~ sth to make a piece of clothing, hair, etc. loose, when it has been tied or fastened **3** [T] ~ your hands, hold, etc. to hold sb/sth less tightly: *He loosened his grip and let her go.* ◊ (figurative) *The military regime has not loosened its hold on power.* **4** [T] ~ sth to make sth weaker or less carefully managed than before SYN **relax**: *The party has loosened its links with big business.* OPP **tighten**
IDM **loosen sb's 'tongue** to make sb talk more freely than usual: *A bottle of wine had loosened Harry's tongue.*
PHRV **loosen 'up** to relax and stop worrying: *Come on, Jo. Loosen up.* **loosen 'up** | **loosen sb/sth ⇌ 'up** to relax your muscles or parts of the body or to make them relax, before taking exercise, etc.

**loot** /luːt/ verb, noun
■ verb **1** [T, I] ~ (sth) to steal things from shops or buildings after a RIOT, fire, etc: *More than 20 shops were looted.* **2** (IndE) ~ sth (from sb/sth) to steal sth (from sb/sth): *A gang went through the train and looted money from passengers.* ◊ *Clothes and jewellery were looted from her house.* **3** (IndE) ~ sb/sth to steal money or property from a person or a place: (figurative) *The Government is looting the public.* ◊ *He was stopped by the police while trying to loot a bank.*
▶ **loot·er** noun **loot·ing** noun [U]
■ noun [U] **1** money and valuable objects taken by soldiers from the enemy during a battle SYN **booty 2** (informal) money and valuable objects that have been stolen by thieves **3** (informal) money

**lop** /lɒp; NAmE lɑːp/ verb (-pp-) ~ sth to cut down a tree, or cut some large branches off it
PHRV **lop sth ⇌ 'off (sth) 1** to remove part of sth by cutting it, especially to remove branches from a tree SYN **chop 2** to make sth smaller or less by a particular amount: *They lopped 20p off the price.*

**lope** /ləʊp/ verb [I] + adv./prep. to run taking long relaxed steps: *The dog loped along beside her.* ◊ *He set off with a loping stride.* ▶ **lope** noun [usually sing.]

**lop-sided** /ˌlɒpˈsaɪdɪd; NAmE ˌlɑːp-/ adj. **1** having one side lower, smaller, etc. than the other: *a lopsided grin/mouth* **2** lacking balance; with a lot more attention, points, votes, etc. on one side than the other: *The article presents a somewhat lopsided view of events.* ◊ *a lopsided victory/win/defeat/loss* ▶ **lop-sided-ly** adv.

**lo·qua·cious** /ləˈkweɪʃəs/ adj. (formal) talking a lot SYN **talkative** ▶ **lo·qua·city** /-ˈkwæsəti/ (also **lo·qua·cious·ness**) noun [U]

**lord** 🔊 **B2** /lɔːd; NAmE lɔːrd/ noun, verb
■ noun **1** 🔊 **B2** [C] (in the UK) a man of high rank in the NOBILITY (= people of high social class), or sb who has been given the title 'lord' as an honour ⇒ compare LADY **2** 🔊 **B2** **Lord** (in the UK) the title used by a lord: *Lord Beaverbrook* **3 Lord** a title used for some high official positions in the UK: *the Lord Chancellor* ◊ *the Lord Mayor* **4 My Lord** (in the UK) a title of respect used when speaking to a judge, BISHOP or some male members of the NOBILITY (= people of high social class) ⇒ compare LADY **5** a powerful man in MEDIEVAL Europe, who owned a lot of land and property: *a feudal lord* ◊ *the lord of the manor* ⇒ see also OVERLORD, WARLORD **6** (usually **the Lord**) [sing.] a title used to refer to God or Christ: *Love the Lord with all your heart.* **7 Our Lord** [sing.] a title used to refer to Christ **8 the Lords** [sing. + sing./pl. v.] = HOUSE OF LORDS: *The Lords has/have not yet reached a decision.* ⇒ compare COMMONS
IDM **(good) 'Lord!** | **oh 'Lord!** exclamation used to show that you are surprised, annoyed or worried about sth: *Good Lord, what have you done to your hair!* **'Lord knows …** used to emphasize what you are saying: *Lord knows, I tried to teach her.* **'Lord ('only) knows (what, where, why, etc.) …** (informal) used to say that you do not know the answer to sth: *'Why did she say that?' 'Lord knows!'* HELP Some people may find the use of **Lord** in these expressions offensive. ⇒ more at DRUNK adj., YEAR
■ verb
IDM **'lord it over sb** (disapproving) to act as if you are better or more important than sb

**Lord Lieu'tenant** noun an official who represents the Queen or King in each county of the UK: *the Lord Lieutenant of Oxfordshire*

**lord·ly** /ˈlɔːdli; NAmE ˈlɔːrd-/ adj. **1** behaving in a way that suggests that you think you are better than other people SYN **haughty 2** large and impressive; suitable for a lord SYN **imposing**: *a lordly mansion*

**Lord 'Mayor** noun the title of the MAYOR of the City of London and some other cities in the UK, Ireland, Australia and Canada

**lord·ship** /ˈlɔːdʃɪp; NAmE ˈlɔːrd-/ noun **1 His/Your Lordship** a title of respect used when speaking to or about a judge, a BISHOP or a NOBLEMAN: *His Lordship is away on business.* ⇒ compare LADYSHIP **2** (BrE, informal) a humorous way of talking to or about a boy or man that you think is trying to be too important: *Can his lordship manage to switch off the TV?* **3** [U] the power or position of a LORD

**the Lord's 'Prayer** noun [sing.] the prayer that Jesus Christ taught the people who followed him, that begins 'Our Father …'

**lore** /lɔː(r)/ noun [U] knowledge and information related to a particular subject, especially when this is not written down; the stories and traditions of a particular group of people: *weather lore* ◊ *Celtic lore* ⇒ see also FOLKLORE

**lo-'res** (also **low-'res**) adj. (informal) = LOW-RESOLUTION

**lorry** 🔊 **A2** /ˈlɒri; NAmE ˈlɔːri/ (BrE) noun (pl. -ies) (also **truck** especially in NAmE) a large vehicle for carrying heavy loads by road: *a lorry driver* ◊ *a lorry load of frozen fish* ◊ **by ~** *Emergency food supplies were brought in by lorry.* IDM see BACK n.

**lose** 🔊 **A1** /luːz/ verb (lost, lost /lɒst; NAmE lɔːst/)
• NOT FIND **1** 🔊 **A1** [T] ~ sth/sb to be unable to find sth/sb SYN **mislay**: *I've lost my keys.* ◊ *The tickets seem to have got lost.* ◊ *She lost her husband in the crowd.*
• HAVE STH/SB TAKEN AWAY **2** 🔊 **A1** [T] ~ sth/sb to have sth/sb taken away from you, especially as a result of an accident, dying, etc: *She lost a leg in a car crash.* ◊ *Some families lost everything* (= all they owned) *in the flood.* ◊ *She lost her baby* (= had a MISCARRIAGE) *three months into the pregnancy.* ◊ *They lost both their sons* (= they were killed) *in the war.* ◊ *The ship was lost at sea* (= it sank). ◊ *Many people lost their lives* (= were killed). **3** 🔊 **A1** [T] ~ sth/sb to have to give up sth; to fail to keep sth/sb: *He's lost his job.* ◊ *You will lose your deposit if you cancel the order.* ◊ *Sit down or you'll lose your seat.* ◊ *The government has lost control of the city.* ◊ **~ sth to sb/sth** *The company has lost a lot of business to its competitors.*
• HAVE LESS **4** 🔊 **A1** [T] ~ sth to no longer have sth, or have less of sth than you had before, especially as a result of getting older: *to lose your hair/teeth* ◊ *to lose your sight/eyesight/hearing/memory* ◊ *There's new hope for people*

# loser

*trying to lose weight.* ◊ *I've lost ten pounds since I started this diet.* **5** [A1] [T] ~ **sth** to have less and less of a quality or ability, especially until you no longer have any of it: *She seemed to have lost interest in food.* ◊ *to lose faith/confidence* ◊ *He lost his nerve at the last minute.* ◊ *At that moment he lost his balance and fell.* ◊ *The train was losing speed.*
- **NOT WIN 6** [A1] [T, I] to be defeated; to fail to win a competition, a court case, an argument, etc.; to cause sb to be defeated: ~ **sth** *So far they haven't lost a game.* ◊ *to lose a race/an election/a battle/a war* ◊ ~ **to sb** *We lost to a stronger team.* ◊ ~ **(sth) by sth** *He lost by less than 100 votes.* ◊ ~ **sb sth** *Many believe the incident lost them the election.*
- **NOT KEEP 7** [A1] [T, I] to fail to keep sth you want or need, especially money; to cause sb to fail to keep sth: ~ **sth** *The business is losing money.* ◊ *Poetry always loses something in translation.* ◊ ~ **sth by doing sth** *You have nothing to lose by telling the truth.* ◊ ~ **on sth** *We lost on that deal.* ◊ ~ **sth** *His carelessness lost him the job.*
- **NOT UNDERSTAND/HEAR 8** [T] ~ **sth** to fail to get, hear or understand sth: *His words were lost* (= could not be heard) *in the applause.* ◊ ~ **sb** (*informal*) to be no longer understood by sb: *I'm afraid you've lost me there.*
- **ESCAPE 10** [T] ~ **sb/sth** to escape from sb/sth **SYN** **evade**, **shake off**: *We managed to lose our pursuers in the darkness.*
- **TIME 11** [T] ~ **sth** to waste time or an opportunity: *We lost twenty minutes changing a tyre.* ◊ *Hurry—there's no time to lose!* ◊ *We lost no time in setting out for London.* **12** [T, I] ~ **(sth)** if a watch or clock **loses** or **loses time**, it goes too slowly or becomes a particular amount of time behind the correct time: *This clock loses two minutes a day.* **OPP** **gain**

**IDM** **HELP** Most idioms containing **lose** are at the entries for the nouns and adjectives in the idioms, for example **lose your bearings** is at **bearing**. **'lose it** (*informal*) to be unable to stop yourself from crying, laughing, etc.; to become crazy: *Then she just lost it and started screaming.*

**PHRV** **lose your'self in sth** to become so interested in sth that it takes all your attention **lose 'out (on sth)** (*informal*) to not get sth you wanted or feel you should have: *While the stores make big profits, it's the customer who loses out.* **lose 'out to sb/sth** (*informal*) to not get business, etc. that you expected or used to get because sb/sth else has taken it: *Small businesses are losing out to the large chains.*

**los·er** /ˈluːzə(r)/ *noun* **1** a person who is defeated in a competition: *winners and losers* ◊ *He's **a good/bad loser*** (= he accepts defeat well/badly). **2** (*rather informal*) a person who is regularly unsuccessful, especially when you have a low opinion of them: *She's one of life's losers.* ◊ *He's **a born loser**.* **3** a person who suffers because of a particular action, decision, etc: *The real losers in all of this are the students.*

**loss** [B1] ⦿ /lɒs; NAmE lɔːs/ *noun* **1** [B1] [U, C, usually sing.] the state of no longer having sth or as much of sth; the process that leads to this: *I want to report the loss of a package.* ◊ *weight loss* ◊ *hearing/memory loss* ◊ *The closure of the factory will lead to a number of job losses.* ◊ *When she died I was filled with a sense of loss.* ◊ ~ **of sth** *He suffered a loss of confidence.* ◊ *loss of earnings/income* (= the money you do not earn because you are prevented from working) **2** [B2] [C] money that has been lost by a business or an organization: *The company has announced net losses of $1.5 million.* ◊ ~ **on sth** *We made a loss on* (= lost money on) *the deal.* **OPP** **profit 3** [C, U] the death of a person: *He is mourning the loss of his wife.* ◊ *the tragic loss of a child* ◊ *Enemy troops suffered heavy losses.* ◊ *The drought caused widespread loss of life.* **4** [B2] [sing.] the disadvantage that is caused when sb leaves, or when a useful or valuable object is taken away; a person who causes a disadvantage by leaving: **a ~ to sb/sth** *Her departure is a big loss to the school.* ◊ *She will be a great loss to the company.* ⦿ see also **DEAD LOSS 5** [C] a failure to win a contest: *Brazil's 2–1 loss to Argentina*

**IDM** **at a 'loss 1** not knowing what to say or do: *His comments left me at a loss for words.* ◊ *I'm at a loss what to do next.* **2** in a way that loses you money: *We are now operating at a loss.* **be sb's 'loss** used to say that if sb chooses not to do sth, they will not obtain a benefit they could have had: *If people can't appreciate how great this film is, it's their loss.* **cut your 'losses** to stop doing sth that is not successful before the situation becomes even worse **loss of 'face** the state of being less respected by other people or looking stupid because of sth you have done

**'loss-leader** *noun* an item that a shop sells at a very low price, so that they lose money on it, in order to attract customers

**'loss·less** /ˈlɒsləs; NAmE ˈlɔːs-/ *adj.* (*specialist*) involving no loss of data or electrical energy **OPP** **lossy**

**'loss-making** *adj.* (of a company or business) not making a profit; losing money

**lossy** /ˈlɒsi; NAmE ˈlɔːsi/ *adj.* (*specialist*) involving the loss of data or electrical energy **OPP** **lossless**

**lost** ⦿ [A2] /lɒst; NAmE lɔːst/ *adj., verb*
- *adj.* **1** [A2] unable to find your way; not knowing where you are: *We always **get lost** in London.* ◊ *We're completely lost.* **2** [A2] that cannot be found or brought back: *I'm still looking for that lost file.* ◊ *a lost cat/dog/pet* ◊ *Your invitation must have **got lost** in the post.* ⦿ see also **LONG-LOST 3** [usually before noun] that cannot be obtained; that cannot be found or created again: *Piracy is costing film studios millions in lost revenues.* ◊ *She's trying to recapture her lost youth.* ◊ *He regretted the lost* (= wasted) *opportunity to apologize to her.* **4** [B2] [not usually before noun] unable to deal successfully with a particular situation: *I felt so lost after my mother died.* ◊ ~ **without sb/sth** *We would be lost without your help.* ◊ *He's a **lost soul*** (= a person who does not seem to know what to do, and seems unhappy). **5** [B2] [not usually before noun] unable to understand sth because it is too complicated: *They spoke so quickly I just got lost.* ◊ *Hang on a minute—I'm lost.*

**IDM** **all is not 'lost** there is still some hope of making a bad situation better **be lost for 'words** to be so surprised, confused, etc. that you do not know what to say **be 'lost in sth** to be giving all your attention to sth so that you do not notice what is happening around you: *to be lost in thought* **be 'lost on sb** to be not understood or noticed by sb: *His jokes were completely lost on most of the students.* **be lost to the 'world** to be giving all your attention to sth so that you do not notice what is happening around you **get 'lost** (*informal*) a rude way of telling sb to go away, or of refusing sth **give sb up for 'lost** (*formal*) to stop expecting to find sb alive **make up for lost 'time** to do sth quickly or very often because you wish you had started doing it sooner ⦿ more at **LOVE** *n.*
- *verb* past tense, past part. of **LOSE**

**lost and 'found** (*NAmE*) (*BrE* **lost 'property**) *noun* [U] the place where items that have been found are kept until they are collected

**lost 'cause** *noun* something that has failed or that cannot succeed

**lost 'property** *noun* [U] (*BrE*) **1** items that have been found in public places and are waiting to be collected by the people who lost them: *a lost-property office* **2** (*NAmE* **lost and 'found**) the place where items that have been found are kept until they are collected

**lot** ⦿ [A1] /lɒt; NAmE lɑːt/ *pron., det., adv., noun*
- *pron.* [A1] **a lot** (also *informal* **lots**) a large number or amount: *'How many do you need?' 'A lot.'* ◊ *Have some more cake. There's lots left.* ◊ *He has invited nearly a hundred people but a lot aren't able to come.* ◊ **a ~ to do** *I have a lot to do today.* ◊ *She still has an awful lot* (= a very large amount) *to learn.* ⦿ note at **MANY**, **MUCH**
- *det.* [A1] **a lot of** (also *informal* **lots of**) a large number or amount of sb/sth: *What a lot of presents!* ◊ *A lot of people are coming to the meeting.* ◊ *black coffee with lots of sugar* ◊ *I saw a lot of her* (= I saw her often) *last summer.* ⦿ note at **MANY**, **MUCH**
- *adv.* (*informal*) **1** [A1] **a lot** used with verbs to mean 'a great amount': *I care a lot about you.* ◊ *Thanks a lot for your help.*

◇ *I play tennis quite a lot* (= often) *in the summer.* **2** ⚹ A2 **a lot** (*also informal* **lots**) used with adjectives and adverbs to mean 'much': *I'm feeling a lot better today.* ◇ *I spend a lot more time with my family now.* ◇ *I eat lots less than I used to.* ⊃ note at MUCH
■ *noun*
• WHOLE AMOUNT/NUMBER **1 the lot, the whole lot** [sing. + sing./pl. v.] (*informal*) the whole number or amount of people or things: *He's bought a new laptop, microphone, printer—the lot.* ◇ *Get out of my house, **the lot of you**!* ◇ ***That's the lot!*** (= that includes everything) ◇ ***That's your lot!*** (= that's all you're getting)
• GROUP/SET **2** [C + sing./pl. v.] (*especially BrE*) a group or set of people or things: *The first lot of visitors has/have arrived.* ◇ *I have several lots of essays to mark this weekend.* ◇ (*informal*) *What do **you** lot want?*
• ITEMS TO BE SOLD **3** [C] an item or a number of items to be sold, especially at an AUCTION: *Lot 46: six chairs* ⊃ see also JOB LOT
• AREA OF LAND **4** [C] an area of land used for a particular purpose: *a parking lot* ◇ *a vacant lot* (= one available to be built on or used for sth) ◇ (*especially NAmE*) *We're going to build a house on this lot.* ⊃ SYNONYMS at LAND ⊃ see also PARKING LOT
• LUCK/SITUATION **5** [sing.] a person's luck or situation in life **SYN** *destiny*: *She was feeling dissatisfied with her lot.*
**IDM** **all ˈover the lot** (*NAmE*) = ALL OVER THE PLACE at PLACE *n*. **a bad ˈlot** (*BrE*, *old-fashioned*) a person who is dishonest **by ˈlot** using a method of choosing sb to do sth in which each person takes a piece of paper, etc. from a container and the one whose paper has a special mark is chosen **draw/cast ˈlots (for sth/to do sth)** to use a method of choosing sb/sth that involves putting a number folded pieces of paper in a bag, one of them with a mark on it. People then take it in turns to take a piece of paper from the bag and the one who takes the paper with the mark on it is chosen: *They drew lots for the right to go first.* **fall to sb's ˈlot (to do sth)** (*formal*) to become sb's task or responsibility **throw in your ˈlot with sb** to decide to join sb and share their successes and problems ⊃ more at BEST *n*.

**lo-ˈtech** = LOW-TECH

**loth** = LOATH

**Lothˑario** /ləˈθɑːriəʊ; *BrE also* -ˈθeər-; *NAmE also* -ˈθer-/ *noun* (*pl.* **-os**) a man who has sex with a lot of women: *He has a reputation as the office Lothario.* **ORIGIN** From the name of a character in an 18th century play by Nicholas Rowe.

**loˑtion** /ˈləʊʃn/ *noun* [C, U] a liquid used for cleaning, protecting or treating the skin: (*a*) *body/hand lotion* ◇ *suntan lotion*

**lotta** /ˈlɒtə; *NAmE* ˈlɑːtə/ (*also* **lotsa** /ˈlɒtsə; *NAmE* ˈlɑːt-/) (*informal*, *non-standard*) a written form of 'lot of' or 'lots of' that shows how it sounds in informal speech: *We're gonna have a lotta fun.* **HELP** You should not write this form unless you are copying somebody's speech.

**lotˑtery** ⚹+ B2 /ˈlɒtəri; *NAmE* ˈlɑːt-/ *noun* (*pl.* **-ies**) **1** ⚹+ B2 [C] a way of raising money for a government, charity, etc. by selling tickets that have different numbers on them that people have chosen. Numbers are then chosen by chance and the people who have those numbers on their tickets win prizes: *the national/state lottery* ◇ *a lottery ticket* ⊃ compare DRAW, RAFFLE ⊃ WORDFINDER NOTE at GAMBLING **2** ⚹+ B2 [sing.] (*often disapproving*) a situation whose result or success is based on luck rather than on effort or careful organization **SYN** *gamble*: *Some people think that marriage is a lottery.* ⊃ see also POSTCODE LOTTERY

**lotto** /ˈlɒtəʊ; *NAmE* ˈlɑːt-/ *noun* (*pl.* **lottos**) **1** [U] a game of chance similar to BINGO but with the numbers drawn from a container by the players instead of being called out **2** [C] a lottery

**lotus** /ˈləʊtəs/ *noun* **1** a tropical plant with white or pink flowers that grows on the surface of lakes in Africa and Asia: *a lotus flower* ⊃ VISUAL VOCAB page V7 **2** a picture in the shape of the lotus plant, used in art and architecture, especially in ancient Egypt **3** (in ancient Greek stories) a

---

# lounge bar

fruit that is supposed to make you feel happy and relaxed when you have eaten it, as if in a dream

**ˈlotus position** *noun* [sing.] a way of sitting with your legs crossed, used especially when people MEDITATE or do YOGA

**louche** /luːʃ/ *adj.* (*especially BrE*, *formal*) not socially acceptable, but often still attractive despite this

**loud** ⚹ A2 /laʊd/ *adj.*, *adv.*
■ *adj.* (**loudˑer**, **loudˑest**) **1** ⚹ A2 making a lot of noise: *loud laughter* ◇ *a **deafeningly** loud bang* ◇ *She spoke in a very loud voice.* ◇ *That music's too loud—please turn it down.* **2** strongly expressed: *There were loud protests from the food and drink industry.* **3** (of a person or their behaviour) talking very loudly, too much and in a way that is annoying **4** (of colours, patterns, etc.) too bright and not showing good taste **SYN** *gaudy*, *garish* ▸ **loudˑness** *noun* [U]
■ *adv.* ⚹ A2 (**loudˑer**, **loudˑest**) (*informal*) in a way that makes a lot of noise or can be easily heard **SYN** *loudly*: *Do you have to play that music so loud?* ◇ *You'll have to speak louder—I can't hear you.*
**IDM** **ˌloud and ˈclear** in a way that is very easy to understand: *The message is coming through loud and clear.* **out ˈloud** in a voice that can be heard by other people: *I laughed out loud.* ◇ *Please read the letter out loud.* ⊃ compare ALOUD ⊃ more at ACTION *n*., CRY *v*., THINK *v*.

▼ **WHICH WORD?**
**loud / loudly / aloud**
• **Loudly** is the usual adverb from the adjective **loud**: *The audience laughed loudly at the joke.*
• **Loud** is very common as an adverb in informal language. It is nearly always used in phrases such as **loud enough**, **as loud as** or with **too**, **very**, **so**, etc: *Don't play your music too loud.* ◇ *I shouted as loud as I could.*
• **Louder** is also used in informal styles to mean 'more loudly': *Can you speak louder?*
• **Out loud** is a common adverb meaning 'so that people can hear': *Can you read the letter out loud?* ◇ *He laughed out loud at his own joke.* **Aloud** has the same meaning but is fairly formal. It can also mean 'in a loud voice'.

**loudˑhailˑer** /ˌlaʊdˈheɪlə(r)/ *noun* (*BrE*) = MEGAPHONE

**loudˑly** ⚹ A2 /ˈlaʊdli/ *adv.* in a way that makes a lot of noise: *She screamed as loudly as she could.*

**loudˑmouth** /ˈlaʊdmaʊθ/ *noun* (*informal*) a person who is annoying because they talk too loudly or too much in an offensive or stupid way ▸ **loudˑmouthed** *adj.*

**loudˑspeakˑer** /ˌlaʊdˈspiːkə(r)/ *noun* **1** [C] a piece of equipment that changes electrical signals into sound, used in public places for announcing things, playing music, etc: *over a/the ~* *Their names were called over the loudspeaker.* ⊃ see also PUBLIC ADDRESS SYSTEM, TANNOY™ **2** [C, U] a function on a phone that allows you to hear without holding the phone to your ear: *She used her phone's loudspeaker to let everyone listen.* ◇ *on ~* *The phone was on loudspeaker so I could hear both sides of the conversation.*

**lough** /lɒk, lɒx; *NAmE* lɑːk, lɑːx/ *noun* (in Ireland) a lake or a narrow area of sea that is almost surrounded by land: *Lough Corrib* ⊃ see also LOCH

**lounge** /laʊndʒ/ *noun*, *verb*
■ *noun* **1** a room for waiting in at an airport, etc: *the departure lounge* ◇ *the VIP/business lounge* ⊃ WORDFINDER NOTE at AIRPORT **2** a public room in a hotel, club, etc. for waiting or relaxing in: *the television lounge* **3** (*BrE*) a room in a private house for sitting and relaxing in **SYN** *living room*, *sitting room* ⊃ see also SUN LOUNGE **4** (*BrE*) = LOUNGE BAR
■ *verb* [I] (+ *adv./prep.*) to stand, sit or lie in a lazy way **SYN** *laze*: *Several students were lounging around, reading newspapers.*

**ˈlounge bar** (*also* **salˑoon**) (*both BrE*) *noun* a bar in a pub, hotel, etc. that is more comfortable than the other bars and where the drinks are usually more expensive ⊃ compare PUBLIC BAR

# lounge chair

**ˈlounge chair** noun (NAmE) = CHAISE LONGUE (2)

**ˈlounge lizard** noun (old-fashioned, informal) a person who does no work and who likes to be with rich, fashionable people

**loun·ger** /ˈlaʊndʒə(r)/ noun (especially BrE) a long comfortable chair that supports your legs, used for sitting or lying on, especially outdoors ⊃ compare SUNLOUNGER

**ˈlounge suit** noun (BrE) a man's suit of matching jacket and trousers, worn especially in offices and on fairly formal occasions

**louse** /laʊs/ noun, verb
■ noun **1** (pl. **lice** /laɪs/) a small insect that lives on the bodies of humans and animals: *head lice* ⊃ see also NIT, WOODLOUSE **2** (pl. **louses**) (informal, disapproving) a very unpleasant person
■ verb
**PHRV** **ˌlouse sth↔ˈup** (informal) to do sth very badly or cause it to fail

**lousy** /ˈlaʊzi/ adj. (**lous·ier**, **lousi·est**) (informal) **1** very bad **SYN** awful, terrible: *What lousy weather!* ◊ *She felt lousy* (= ill). **2** [only before noun] used to show that you feel annoyed or offended because you do not think that sth is worth very much: *All she bought me was this lousy T-shirt.* **3** ~ **with sth/sb** (NAmE) having too much of sth or too many people: *This place is lousy with tourists in August.*

**lout** /laʊt/ noun a man or boy who behaves in a rude and aggressive way **SYN** yob ⊃ see also LAGER LOUT, LITTER LOUT ▶ **lout·ish** adj.: *loutish behaviour*

**lou·vre** (US **lou·ver**) /ˈluːvə(r)/ noun one of a set of narrow pieces of wood, plastic, etc. in a door or a window that are designed to let air and some light in, but to keep out strong light or rain; a door or a window that has these narrow pieces across it ▶ **louvred** (US **lou·vered**) adj.

**lov·able** (also **love·able**) /ˈlʌvəbl/ adj. having qualities that people find attractive and easy to love, often despite any faults **SYN** endearing: *a lovable child* ◊ *a lovable rogue*

**love** ⓘ A1 /lʌv/ noun, verb
■ noun
- LIKING AND CARING **1** ⓘ A1 [U] a very strong feeling of liking and caring for sb/sth, especially a member of your family or a friend: *She has earned the love and respect of many people.* ◊ ~ **for sb/sth** *a mother's unconditional love for her children* ◊ ~ **of sb/sth** *love of your country* ⊃ see also SELF-LOVE, TOUGH LOVE
- ROMANTIC **2** ⓘ A1 [U] a strong feeling of romantic attraction for sb: *I'm sure you will find true love.* ◊ **in** ~ *We're in love!* ◊ *They're madly in love.* ◊ **in** ~ **with sb** *She was in love with him.* ◊ *They fell in love with each other.* ◊ ~ **for sb** *They finally expressed their love for each other.* ◊ *It was love at first sight* (= they were attracted to each other the first time they met). ◊ *a love song/story* ⊃ see also COURTLY LOVE, FREE LOVE, PUPPY LOVE

> **WORDFINDER** affair, date, go out with sb, jealous, partner, passionate, relationship, romantic

- PLEASURE **3** ⓘ A1 [U, sing.] the strong feeling of pleasure that sth gives you: ~ **of sth** *They shared a love of learning.* ◊ ~ **for sth** *her love for her garden* ◊ **in** ~ **with sth** *He's in love with his work.* ◊ *I fell in love with the house.*
- SB/STH YOU LIKE **4** ⓘ A2 [C] a person, a thing or an activity that you like very much: *Take care, my love.* ◊ *He was the love of my life* (= the person I loved most). ◊ *I like most sports but tennis is my first love.*
- FRIENDLY NAME **5** [C] (BrE, informal) a word used as a friendly way of addressing sb: *Can I help you, love?* ⊃ compare DUCK
- IN TENNIS **6** [U] a score of zero (points or games): *40–love!* ◊ *She won the first set six-love/six games to love.*

**IDM** **(just) for ˈlove** | **(just) for the ˈlove of sth** without receiving payment or any other reward: *They're all volunteers, working for the love of it.* **for the love of ˈGod** (old-fashioned, informal) used when you are expressing anger and the fact that you are impatient: *For the love of God, tell me what he said!* **HELP** Some people find this use of **God** offensive. **ˌgive/send my ˈlove to sb** (informal) used to send good wishes to sb: *Give my love to Mary when you see her.* ◊ *Bob sends his love.* **ˈlove from** | **(lots of) ˈlove (from)** (informal) used at the end of a letter to a friend or to sb you love, followed by your name: *Lots of love, Jenny* **love is ˈblind** (saying) when you love sb, you cannot see their faults **make ˈlove (to sb)** to have sex: *It was the first time they had made love.* **not for love or/nor ˈmoney** if you say you cannot do sth **for love nor money**, you mean it is completely impossible to do it: *We couldn't find a taxi for love nor money.* **ˌthere's little/no love ˌlost between A and B** they do not like each other: *There's no love lost between her and her in-laws.* ⊃ more at FAIR adj., HEAD n., LABOUR n.

■ verb
- LIKING AND CARING **1** ⓘ A1 ~ **sb/sth** (not used in the progressive tenses) to have very strong feelings of liking and caring for sb: *I love you.* ◊ *If you love each other, why not get married?* ◊ *Her much-loved brother lay dying of AIDS.* ◊ *He had become a well-loved member of staff.* ◊ *Relatives need time to grieve over loved ones they have lost.* ◊ *to love your country*
- LIKE/ENJOY **2** ⓘ A1 (not usually used in the progressive tenses) to like or enjoy sth very much **SYN** adore: ~ **sth** *I absolutely love your shoes.* ◊ ~ **it when sb does sth** *I just love it when you bring me presents!* ◊ ~ **it** *They love it in Spain* (= they like the life there). ◊ *He loved the way she smiled.* ◊ *It was one of his best-loved songs.* ◊ (ironic) *You're going to love this. They've changed their minds again.* ◊ ~ **doing sth** (especially BrE) *My dad loves watching football.* ◊ ~ **to do sth** (especially NAmE) *I love to go out dancing.* ◊ ~ **sb/sth to do sth** *He loved her to sing to him.* ◊ (informal) **be loving (doing) sth** *I'm loving my new leather jacket.* ⊃ note at WANT ⊃ SYNONYMS at LIKE **3** ⓘ A2 **would love** used to say that you would very much like sth: ~ **to do sth** *Come on Rory, the kids would love to hear you sing.* ◊ *I haven't been to Brazil, but I'd love to go.* ◊ ~ **sb/sth to do sth** *I'd love her to come and live with us.* ◊ ~ **sth** *'Coffee?' 'I'd love one, thanks.'*

**IDM** **ˌlove you and ˈleave you** (informal, humorous) used to say that you must go, although you would like to stay longer: *Well, time to love you and leave you.*

> ▼ **SYNONYMS**
> 
> **love**
> 
> like • be fond of sb • adore • be devoted to sb • care for sb • dote on sb
> 
> These words all mean to have feelings of liking or caring for sb.
> 
> **love** to have strong feelings of caring for sb: *I love you.*
> 
> **like** to find sb pleasant and enjoy being with them: *She's nice. I like her.*
> 
> **be fond of sb** to have warm or loving feelings for sb, especially sb you have known for a long time: *I've always been very fond of your mother.*
> 
> **adore** to love sb very much: *It's obvious that she adores him.*
> 
> **be devoted to sb** to love sb very much and support them in everything: *They are devoted to their children.*
> 
> **care for sb** to love sb, especially in a way that is based on a feeling of liking them very much or wanting to protect them, rather than sex: *He cared for her more than she realized.* **NOTE** Care for sb is often used when sb has not told anyone about their feelings or is just starting to be aware of them. It is also used when sb wishes that sb loved them, or doubts that sb does: *If he really cared for you, he wouldn't behave like that.*
> 
> **dote on sb** to feel and show great love for sb, ignoring their faults: *He dotes on his children.*
> 
> **PATTERNS**
> - to **really** love/like/adore/care for/dote on sb
> - to be **really/genuinely** fond of/devoted to sb
> - to love/like/care for sb **very much**

**ˈlove affair** noun **1** a romantic and/or sexual relationship between two people who are in love and not married to each other **2** ~ **(with sth)** great enthusiasm for sth **SYN** **passion**: *the English love affair with gardening*

**love-bird** /ˈlʌvbɜːd; *NAmE* -bɜːrd/ *noun* **1** [C] a small African PARROT (= a bird with brightly coloured feathers) **2 lovebirds** [pl.] (*humorous*) two people who love each other very much and show this in their behaviour

**love bite** (*BrE*) (*NAmE* **hickey**) *noun* a red mark on the skin that is caused by sb biting or SUCKING their partner's skin as a sexual act

**love child** *noun* (used especially in newspapers, etc.) a child born to parents who are not married to each other

**loved-up** *adj.* (*informal*) **1** happy and excited because of the effects of the illegal drug ECSTASY **2** full of romantic love for sb

**love handles** *noun* [pl.] (*informal, humorous*) extra fat at the sides of a person's WAIST (= middle part of the body)

**love-'hate relationship** *noun* [usually sing.] a relationship in which your feelings for sb/sth are a mixture of love and hate

**love-in** *noun* (*informal*) **1** (*old-fashioned*) a party at which people freely show their love and sexual attraction for each other, associated with HIPPIES in the 1960s **2** (*disapproving*) an occasion when people are being especially pleasant to each other, in a way that you believe is not sincere

**love interest** *noun* **1** [C, usually sing.] a character in a film or story who has a romantic role, often as the main character's partner ⊃ WORDFINDER NOTE at CHARACTER **2** [U] a theme or part of the plot in a story or film that is mainly about love between two characters: *The film is all action and violence and completely without love interest.*

**love-less** /ˈlʌvləs/ *adj.* without love: *a loveless marriage*

**love letter** *noun* a letter that you write to sb telling them that you love them

**love life** *noun* the part of your life that involves your romantic and sexual relationships

**love-li-ness** /ˈlʌvlinəs/ *noun* [U] (*formal*) the state of being very attractive **SYN** **beauty**

**love-lorn** /ˈlʌvlɔːn; *NAmE* -lɔːrn/ *adj.* (*literary*) unhappy because the person you love does not love you

**love·ly** ⊙ **A2** /ˈlʌvli/ *adj., noun*

■ *adj.* (**love·lier**, **love·li·est**) **HELP** You can also use **more lovely** and **most lovely**. (*especially BrE*) **1** **A2** beautiful; attractive: *lovely countryside/eyes/flowers* ◊ *She looked particularly lovely that night.* ◊ *He has a lovely voice.* ⊃ SYNONYMS at BEAUTIFUL **2** **A2** (*informal*) very pleasant; wonderful: *'Can I get you anything?' 'A cup of tea would be lovely.'* ◊ *What a lovely surprise!* ◊ *How lovely to see you!* ◊ *Isn't it a lovely day?* ◊ *We've had a lovely time.* ◊ *It's a lovely old farm.* ◊ *It's been lovely having you here.* ◊ (*ironic*) *You've got yourself into a lovely mess, haven't you?* ⊃ SYNONYMS at WONDERFUL **3** **A2** (*informal*) (of a person) very kind, generous and friendly: *Her mother was a lovely woman.*
**IDM** **lovely and 'warm, 'cold, 'quiet, etc.** (*BrE, informal*) used when you are emphasizing that sth is good because of the quality mentioned: *It's lovely and warm in here.*
■ *noun* (*pl.* **-ies**) (*old-fashioned*) a beautiful woman

**love-mak·ing** /ˈlʌvmeɪkɪŋ/ *noun* [U] sexual activity between two people, especially the act of having sex

**love match** *noun* a marriage of two people who are in love with each other

**love nest** *noun* [usually sing.] (*informal*) a house or an apartment where two people who are not married but are having a sexual relationship can meet, especially in secret

**lover** /ˈlʌvə(r)/ *noun* **1** a partner in a sexual relationship outside marriage: *He denied that he was her lover.* ◊ *We were lovers for several years.* ◊ *The park was full of young lovers holding hands.* **2** (often in compounds) a person who likes or enjoys a particular thing: *a lover of music* ◊ *an art lover* ◊ *a nature lover*

**love seat** *noun* a comfortable seat with a back and arms, for two people to sit on

**love·sick** /ˈlʌvsɪk/ *adj.* unable to think clearly or behave in a sensible way because you are in love with sb, especially sb who is not in love with you

**love triangle** *noun* [usually sing.] a situation that involves three people, each of whom loves at least one of the others, for example a married woman, her husband, and another man that she loves

**lovey-dovey** /ˌlʌvi ˈdʌvi/ *adj.* (*informal*) expressing romantic love in a way that is slightly silly

**lov·ing** /ˈlʌvɪŋ/ *adj.* **1** feeling or showing love and care for sb/sth **SYN** **affectionate, tender**: *a warm and loving family* ◊ *She chose the present with loving care.* **2 -loving** (in adjectives) enjoying the object or activity mentioned: *fun-loving young people* ⊃ see also FUN-LOVING, PEACE-LOVING
▶ **lov·ing·ly** *adv.*: *He gazed lovingly at his children.* ◊ *The house has been lovingly restored.*

**low** ⊙ **A2** ⊙ /ləʊ/ *adj., adv., noun, verb*

■ *adj.* (**lower, low·est**)
• **NOT HIGH/TALL 1** ⚑ **A2** not high or tall; not far above the ground: *a low wall/building/table* ◊ *a low range of hills* ◊ *low clouds* ◊ *flying at low altitude* ◊ *The sun was low in the sky.* **OPP** **high**
• **NEAR BOTTOM 2** ⚑ **A2** at or near the bottom of sth: *low back pain* ◊ *the lower slopes of the mountain* ◊ **in the ~ 20s, 30s, etc.** *temperatures in the low 20s* (= no higher than 21–23°) **OPP** **high**
• **CLOTHING 3** not high at the neck: *a dress with a low neckline* ⊃ see also LOW-CUT
• **LEVEL/VALUE 4** ⚑ **B1** (*also* **low-**) (often in compounds) below the usual or average amount, level or value: *a low level of unemployment* ◊ **lower prices/costs** ◊ *the lowest rates of interest for 40 years* ◊ *the lowest temperature ever recorded* ◊ **low-income** *families* ◊ *a* **low-cost** *airline* ◊ *There is a* **low** *risk of failure.* ◊ *Incomes are significantly lower than in other parts of the country.* ◊ **~ in sth** *This yogurt is very low in fat.* **OPP** **high 5** ⚑ **B1** (of a river or lake) below the usual water level: *The reservoir was low after the long drought.* **6** ⚑ **B1** having a reduced amount or not enough of sth: *Our supplies are running low* (= we only have a little left). ◊ **~ on sth** *They were low on fuel.*
• **STANDARD 7** ⚑ **B1** below the usual or expected standard: *Students with the lowest scores retook the test.* ◊ *low marks/grades* ◊ *a low standard of living* **OPP** **high**
• **STATUS 8** ⚑ **B1** below other people or things in importance or status: *lower forms of life* (= creatures with a very simple structure) ◊ *jobs with low status* ◊ *Training was given a very low priority.* ◊ *the* **lower classes** *of society* **OPP** **high**
• **OPINION 9** ⚑ **B1** [usually before noun] not very good **SYN** **poor**: *She has a very low opinion of her own abilities.* **OPP** **high**
• **SOUND 10** ⚑ **B1** not high; not loud: *The cello is lower than the violin.* ◊ *They were speaking in low voices.* **OPP** **high**
• **DEPRESSED 11** weak or depressed; with very little energy **SYN** **down**: *I'm feeling really low.* ◊ *They were in low spirits.*
• **NOT HONEST 12** (of a person) not honest **SYN** **disreputable**: *He mixes with some pretty low types.*
• **LIGHT 13** not bright **SYN** **dim**: *The lights were low and romance was in the air.*
• **IN VEHICLE 14** if a vehicle is in **low gear**, it travels at a slower speed in relation to the speed of the engine
• **PHONETICS 15** = OPEN
**IDM** **at a low 'ebb** in a poor state; worse than usual: *Morale among teachers is at a low ebb.* **be brought 'low** (*old-fashioned*) to lose your wealth or your high position in society **lay sb 'low** if sb is **laid low** by/with an injury or illness, they feel very weak and are unable to do much **the lowest of the 'low** people who are not respected at all because they are not honest, moral or important at all ⊃ more at PROFILE *n.*

■ *adv.* (**lower, low·est**)
• **NOT HIGH 1** ⚑ **A2** in or into a low position, not far above the ground: *to crouch/bend low* ◊ *a plane flying low over the town* ◊ *low-flying aircraft* ◊ *The sun sank lower towards the horizon.*

# lowball

- **NEAR BOTTOM** 2 A2 in or into a position near the bottom of sth: *a window set low in the wall* ◊ *The candles were burning low.*
- **LEVEL** 3 A2 (especially in compounds) at a level below what is usual or expected: *low-priced goods* ◊ *a low-powered PC* ◊ *a very low-scoring game*
- **SOUND** 4 B1 not high; not loudly: *He's singing an octave lower than the rest of us.* ◊ *Can you turn the music lower—you'll wake the baby.* IDM see HIGH *adv.*, LIE¹ *v.*, SINK *v.*, STOOP *v.*

■ *noun*

- **LEVEL/VALUE** 1 B2 a low level or point; a low figure: *The temperature reached a record low in London last night.* ◊ *The government's popularity has hit a new low.* ◊ *at a ~ The yen is at an all-time low against the dollar.* ◊ *to a ~ to sink/plunge/plummet to a new low*
- **DIFFICULT TIME** 2 a very difficult time in sb's life or career: *The break-up of her marriage marked an all-time low in her life.* ◊ *We all experience highs and lows in life.*
- **WEATHER** 3 an area of low pressure in the atmosphere: *Another low is moving in from the Atlantic.* OPP **high**

IDM **sink / stoop to a new / an all-time 'low** to behave in a worse way than ever before: *The government has stooped to an all-time low with this policy.*

- *verb* [I] (*literary*) when a cow **lows**, it makes a deep sound SYN **moo**

**low-ball** /ˈləʊbɔːl/ *verb* ~ **sth** (*NAmE, informal*) to deliberately make an estimate of the cost, value, etc. of sth that is too low: *He lowballed the cost of the project in order to obtain federal funding.* OPP **highball**

**low-'born** *adj.* (*old-fashioned* or *formal*) having parents who are members of a low social class OPP **high-born**

**low-brow** /ˈləʊbraʊ/ *adj.* (*usually disapproving*) having no connection with or interest in serious cultural or cultural ideas OPP **highbrow** ⊃ compare MIDDLEBROW

**low-'budget** *adj.* [only before noun] involving spending only a small amount of money: *a low-budget film* OPP **big-budget**

**low-cal** (*also* **lo-cal**) /ˌləʊ ˈkæl/ *adj.* (*informal*) (of food and drink) containing very few CALORIES

**low-'carb** *adj.* [usually before noun] (*informal*) used to describe food or a diet that is low in CARBOHYDRATES: *a low-carb diet*

**low-'class** *adj.* 1 of poor quality 2 connected with a low social class OPP **high-class**

**low-'cost** *adj.* [usually before noun] 1 below the usual cost; cheap: *low-cost housing/transport/food* 2 producing or supplying sth that is cheap or costs less than usual to buy: *a low-cost airline* ◊ *They can now successfully compete against low-cost foreign producers.*

**the 'Low Countries** *noun* [pl.] the region of Europe that consists of the Netherlands, Belgium and Luxembourg (used especially in the past)

**low-'cut** *adj.* (of dresses etc.) with the top very low so that you can see the neck and the top of the chest

**'low-down** *adj., noun*

■ *adj.* [only before noun] (*informal*) not fair or honest SYN **mean**: *What a dirty, low-down trick!*

■ *noun* **the low-down** [sing.] **the ~ on (sb/sth)** (*informal*) the true facts about sb/sth, especially those considered most important to know: *Jane gave me the low-down on the other guests at the party.*

**'low-end** *adj.* [usually before noun] at the cheaper end of a range of similar products

## lower¹ S /ˈləʊə(r)/ *verb, adj.*

■ *verb* 1 B2 [T, I] to reduce sth or to become less in value, quality, etc.: ~ **sth** *He lowered his voice to a whisper.* ◊ *This drug is used to lower blood pressure.* ◊ **to lower the rate/cost/price/level** of sth ◊ *Her voice lowered as she spoke.* OPP **raise** 2 B2 [T] to let or make sth/sb go down: ~ **sth** *He had to lower his head to get through the door.* ◊ *She lowered her newspaper and looked around.* ◊ ~ **sth/sb**

+ *adv./prep.* *They lowered him down the cliff on a rope.* OPP **raise**

IDM **lower the 'bar** to set a new, lower standard of quality or performance: *In the current economic climate we may need to lower the bar on quotas.* OPP **raise the bar** ⊃ compare SET THE BAR **lower your'self (by doing sth)** (usually used in negative sentences) to behave in a way that makes other people respect you less SYN **demean**: *I wouldn't lower myself by working for him.* ⊃ more at SIGHT *n.*, TEMPERATURE

■ *adj.* [only before noun] 1 located below sth else, especially sth of the same type, or the other of a pair: *the lower deck of a ship* ◊ *His lower lip trembled.* 2 at or near the bottom of sth: *the mountain's lower slopes* ◊ *I have problems with my lower back.* 3 (of a place) located towards the coast, on low ground or towards the south of an area: *the lower reaches of the Nile* OPP **upper**

**lower 'case** *noun* [U] (*specialist*) (in printing and writing) the small form of letters, for example a, b, c rather than A, B, C: **in ~** *The text is all in lower case.* ◊ *lower-case letters* ⊃ compare CAPITAL, UPPER CASE

**lower 'chamber** *noun* = LOWER HOUSE

**the lower 'classes** *noun* [pl.] (*also* **the lower 'class** [sing.]) the groups of people who are considered to have the lowest social status and who have less money and/or power than other people in society ▶ **lower 'class** *adj.*: *The new bosses were condemned as 'too lower class'.* ◊ *a lower-class accent* ⊃ compare UPPER CLASS

**lower 'house** (*also* **lower 'chamber**) *noun* [sing.] the larger group of people who make laws in a country, usually consisting of elected representatives, such as the House of Commons in the UK or the House of Representatives in the US ⊃ compare UPPER HOUSE

**the lower middle 'class** *noun* [sing. + sing. / pl. v.] (*also* **the lower middle classes** [pl.]) the class of people in society, especially in the past, between the working class and the middle class, such as office workers or SHOPKEEPERS, but not professional people

**the lower 'orders** *noun* [pl.] (*old-fashioned, offensive*) people who are considered to be less important because they belong to groups with a lower social status

**'lower school** *noun* a school, or the classes in a school, for younger students, usually between the ages of 11 and 14 ⊃ compare UPPER SCHOOL

**lowest common de'nominator** *noun* 1 (*NAmE usually* **least common de'nominator**) (*mathematics*) the smallest number that the bottom numbers of a group of FRACTIONS can be divided into exactly 2 (*NAmE also* **least common de'nominator**) (*disapproving*) something that is simple enough to seem interesting to, or to be understood by, the highest number of people in a particular group; the sort of people who are least intelligent or accept sth that is of low quality: *The school syllabus seems aimed at the lowest common denominator.*

**lowest common 'multiple** (*especially BrE*) (*NAmE usually* **least common 'multiple**) *noun* (*mathematics*) the smallest number that a group of numbers can be divided into exactly: *18 is the lowest common multiple of 6 and 9.*

**low-'fat** *adj.* [usually before noun] containing only a small amount of fat, or less fat than the usual full-fat version: *low-fat cheese* ◊ *a low-fat diet*

**low-'grade** *adj.* [usually before noun] 1 of low quality 2 (*medical*) of a less serious type: *a low-grade infection*

**low-hanging 'fruit** *noun* (*informal*) the things that are easiest to achieve out of a set of tasks or goals: *This type of pollution is a low-hanging fruit that can be tackled easily.*

**low-'impact** *adj.* [usually before noun] 1 involving movements that do not put a lot of stress on the body: *low-impact aerobics* 2 not causing very many problems or changes, especially in the environment: *low-impact tourism*

**low-'key** *adj.* not intended to attract a lot of attention: *Their wedding was a very low-key affair.*

**low·land** /ˈləʊlənd/ *adj., noun*
- *adj.* [only before noun] connected with an area of land that is fairly flat and not very high above sea level ⇨ compare HIGHLAND
- *noun* **1** [pl., U] an area of land that is fairly flat and not very high above sea level: *the lowlands of Scotland* ◊ *Much of the region is lowland.* ⇨ compare HIGHLAND **2 the Lowlands** [pl.] the region of Scotland south and east of the Highlands, which has flatter countryside.

**low·land·er** /ˈləʊləndə(r)/ *noun* a person who comes from an area that is flat and low ⇨ compare HIGHLANDER

**low-ˈlevel** *adj.* [usually before noun] **1** close to the ground: *low-level bombing attacks* **2** of low rank; involving people of junior rank: *a low-level job* ◊ *low-level negotiations* **3** not containing much of a particular substance especially RADIOACTIVITY: *low-level radioactive waste* **4** (*computing*) (of a computer language) similar to MACHINE CODE in form **OPP** high-level

**ˈlow life** *noun* **1** [U] the life and behaviour of people who are outside normal society, especially criminals **2** ˈlow-life (*pl. -lifes*) (*informal*) a person who is outside normal society, especially a criminal ▸ **ˈlow-life** *adj.*: *a low-life bar*

**low·lights** /ˈləʊlaɪts/ *noun* [pl.] areas of a person's hair that have been made darker than the rest, with the use of a chemical substance ⇨ compare HIGHLIGHT

**lowly** /ˈləʊli/ *adj.* (**low·lier, low·li·est**) (*often humorous*) low in status or importance **SYN** humble, obscure

**low-ˈlying** *adj.* (of land) not high, and usually fairly flat

**low-ˈmaintenance** *adj.* not needing much attention or effort: *a low-maintenance garden* **OPP** high-maintenance

**low-ˈpaid** *adj.* earning or providing very little money: *low-paid workers* ◊ *It is one of the lowest-paid jobs.*

**low-ˈpitched** *adj.* (of sounds) deep; low: *a low-pitched voice* **OPP** high-pitched

**ˈlow point** *noun* the least interesting, least pleasant or worst part of sth **OPP** high point

**low ˈpressure** *noun* [U] **1** the condition of air, gas or liquid that is kept in a container with little force: *at ~ Water supplies to the house are at low pressure.* **2** a condition of the air that affects the weather when the pressure is lower than average ⇨ compare HIGH PRESSURE

**low-ˈprofile** *adj.* receiving or involving very little attention: *a low-profile campaign* ⇨ see also A HIGH/LOW PROFILE at PROFILE *noun*

**low-ˈranking** *adj.* junior; not very important: *a low-ranking officer/official* **OPP** high-ranking

**low-ˈrent** *adj.* [usually before noun] **1** not costing much to rent: *a low-rent apartment* **2** (*especially NAmE*) of poor quality or low social status: *her low-rent boyfriend*

**low-resoˈlution** (*also informal* **ˈlo-res, ˈlow-res**) *adj.* (of a photograph or an image on a computer or television screen) not showing a lot of clear detail: *a low-resolution scan* **OPP** high-resolution

**ˈlow-rise** *adj., noun*
- *adj.* [only before noun] **1** (of a building) low, with only a few floors: *low-rise housing* ⇨ compare HIGH-RISE **2** (of a pair of jeans, etc.) cut so that the top is much lower than the level of the WAIST
- *noun* a low building with only a few floors

**low-ˈrisk** *adj.* [usually before noun] involving only a small amount of danger and little risk of injury, death, damage, etc. **SYN** safe: *a low-risk investment* ◊ *low-risk patients* (= who are very unlikely to get a particular illness) **OPP** high-risk

**ˈlow season** (*also* **ˈoff season**) *noun* [U, sing.] (*especially BrE*) the time of year when a hotel or tourist area receives fewest visitors **OPP** high season

**low-ˈslung** *adj.* **1** (of trousers) cut to fit low on the HIPS: *a pair of low-slung jeans* **2** (*especially NAmE*) low and close to the ground: *a low-slung building*

**low-ˈtech** (*also* **ˈlo-tech**) *adj.* (*informal*) not involving the most modern technology or methods **OPP** high-tech

**ˈlow tide** (*also* **ˈlow ˈwater**) *noun* (U, C] the time when the sea is at its lowest level in a particular place; the sea at

this time: **at ~** *The island can only be reached at low tide.* **OPP** high tide

**low-ˈwater mark** *noun* a line or mark showing the lowest point that the sea reaches at low tide **OPP** high-water mark

**lox** /lɒks; *NAmE* lɑːks/ *noun* [U] (*NAmE*) smoked SALMON (= a type of fish)

**loyal** /ˈlɔɪəl/ *adj.* remaining constant in your support of sb/sth **SYN** true: *a loyal friend/supporter* ◊ ~**to sb/sth** *She has always remained loyal to her political principles.* **OPP** disloyal ▸ **loy·al·ly** /-əli/ *adv.*

**loyal·ist** /ˈlɔɪəlɪst/ *noun* **1** a person who promises support and commitment to the leader or government, or to a political party, especially during a time of change **2 Loyalist** a person who supports the union between Great Britain and Northern Ireland ⇨ compare REPUBLICAN

**loy·alty** /ˈlɔɪəlti/ *noun* (*pl.* **-ies**) **1** [U] the quality of being constant in your support of sb/sth: *Can I count on your loyalty?* ◊ ~**to/towards sb/sth** *They swore their loyalty to the king.* ◊ *Companies are eager to build brand loyalty in their customers* (= to keep them buying the same brand). **2** [C, usually pl.] a strong feeling that you want to support and be loyal to sb/sth: *a case of divided loyalties* (= with strong feelings of support for two different causes, people, etc.)

**ˈloyalty card** *noun* (*BrE*) a card given to customers by a shop to encourage them to shop there regularly. Each time they buy sth they collect points that will allow them to have an amount of money taken off goods they buy in the future. ⇨ WORDFINDER NOTE at BUY

**loz·enge** /ˈlɒzɪndʒ; *NAmE* ˈlɑːz-/ *noun* **1** (*geometry*) a figure with four sides in the shape of a diamond that has two opposite angles more than 90° and the other two less than 90° **2** a small sweet, often in a lozenge shape, especially one that contains medicine and that you DISSOLVE (= turn to liquid) in your mouth: *throat/cough lozenges*

**LP** /ˌel ˈpiː/ *noun* a record that plays for about 25 minutes each side and turns 33 times per minute (the abbreviation for 'long-playing record')

**LPG** /ˌel piː ˈdʒiː/ *noun* [U] a fuel that is a mixture of gases kept in a liquid form by the pressure in a container (the abbreviation for 'liquefied petroleum gas')

**ˈL-plate** *noun* (in the UK and some other countries) a white sign with a large red letter L on it, that you put on a car when you are learning to drive

**LPN** /ˌel piː ˈen/ *noun* (in the US) licensed practical nurse

**LSAT** /ˌel es eɪ ˈtiː, ˈelsæt/ *noun* Law School Admission Test (a test taken by students who want to study law in the US)

**LSD** /ˌel es ˈdiː/ (*also slang* **acid**) *noun* [U] a powerful illegal drug that affects people's minds and makes them see and hear things that are not really there

**Lt** (*BrE*) (*NAmE* **Lt.**) *abbr.* (in writing) LIEUTENANT: *Lt (Helen) Brown*

**Ltd** *abbr.* Limited (used after the name of a British company or business): *Pearce and Co. Ltd*

**LTE** /ˌel tiː ˈiː/ *noun* [U] an international system for digital communication using mobile phones on which the internet can be accessed at high speeds (the abbreviation for 'long-term evolution')

**lu·bri·cant** /ˈluːbrɪkənt/ (*also informal* **lube** /luːb/) *noun* [U, C] a substance, for example oil, that you put on surfaces or parts of a machine so that they move easily and smoothly

**lu·bri·cate** /ˈluːbrɪkeɪt/ *verb* ~**sth** to put a lubricant on sth such as the parts of a machine, to help them move smoothly **SYN** grease, oil ▸ **lu·bri·ca·tion** /ˌluːbrɪˈkeɪʃn/ *noun* [U]

**lu·bri·cious** /luːˈbrɪʃəs/ *adj.* (*formal*) showing a great interest in sex in a way that is considered unpleasant or unacceptable **SYN** lewd

**lucid** /ˈluːsɪd/ *adj.* **1** clearly expressed; easy to understand **SYN** clear: *a lucid style/explanation* **2** able to think clearly, especially during or after a period of mental illness: *In a*

# Lucifer

*rare lucid moment, she looked at me and smiled.* ▶ **lu·cid·ity** /luːˈsɪdəti/ *noun* [U] **lu·cid·ly** /ˈluːsɪdli/ *adv.*

**Lu·ci·fer** /ˈluːsɪfə(r)/ *noun* [sing.] the DEVIL SYN **Satan**

**luck** ⓘ A2 /lʌk/ *noun, verb*
■ *noun* [U] **1** A2 good things that happen to you by chance, not because of your own efforts or abilities: **with (any) ~** *With any luck, we'll be home before dark.* ◇ **a bit of luck,** *we'll finish on time.* ◇ **with (doing) sth** *So far I have had no luck with finding a job.* ◇ *I could hardly believe my luck when he said yes.* ◇ *It was* **a stroke of luck** *that we found you.* ◇ **by~** *By sheer luck nobody was hurt in the explosion.* ◇ *We* **wish her luck** *in her new career.* ◇ **in~** *You're in luck* (= lucky)—*there's one ticket left.* ◇ **out of~** *You're out of luck. She's not here.* ◇ *What* **a piece of luck!** ⇒ see also BEGINNER'S LUCK **2** A2 chance; the force that causes good or bad things to happen to people SYN **fortune**: *to have good/bad luck* ◇ **~ with sth** *We had horrible luck with the weather.* ⇒ see also HARD-LUCK STORY

**WORDFINDER** amulet, charm, coincidence, fate, fortune, jinx, mascot, superstition, talisman

IDM **any 'luck?** (*informal*) used to ask sb if they have been successful with sth: *'Any luck?' 'No, they're all too busy to help.'* **as luck would 'have it** in the way that chance decides what will happen: *As luck would have it, the train was late.* **bad, hard, etc. luck (on sb)** used to express sympathy for sb: *Bad luck, Helen, you played very well.* ◇ *It's hard luck on him that he wasn't chosen.* **be down on your 'luck** (*informal*) to have no money because of a period of bad luck **the best of 'luck (with sth)** | **good 'luck (with sth)** (*informal*) used to wish sb success with sth: *The best of luck with your exams.* ◇ *Good luck! I hope it goes well.* **better luck 'next time** (*informal*) used to encourage sb who has not been successful at sth **for 'luck 1** because you believe it will bring you good luck, or because this is a traditional belief: *Take something blue. It's for luck.* **2** (*informal*) for no particular reason: *I gave the mixture one more stir for luck.* **good 'luck to sb** (*informal*) used to say that you do not mind what sb does as it does not affect you, but you hope they will be successful: *It's not something I would care to try myself but if she wants to, good luck to her.* **just my/sb's 'luck** (*informal*) used to show you are not surprised sth bad has happened to you, because you are not often lucky: *Just my luck to arrive after they had left.* **your/sb's 'luck is in** used to say that sb has been lucky or successful **the luck of the 'draw** the fact that chance decides sth, in a way that you cannot control **no such 'luck** used to show that you are disappointed because sth you were hoping for did not happen ⇒ more at HARD *adj.*, POT *n.*, PUSH *v.*, TOUGH *adj.*, TRY *v.*, WORSE *adj.*
■ *verb*
PHRV **luck 'out** (NAmE, *informal*) to be lucky: *I guess I really lucked out when I met her.*

**luck·less** /ˈlʌkləs/ *adj.* having bad luck SYN **unlucky**: *the luckless victim of the attack*

**lucky** ⓘ A2 /ˈlʌki/ *adj.* (**luck·ier, lucki·est**) **1** A2 having good luck SYN **fortunate**: **~ to do sth** *His friend was killed and he knows he is lucky to be alive.* ◇ *She was lucky enough to be chosen for the team.* ◇ **~ (that)** *You were lucky (that) you spotted the danger in time.* ◇ *You can* **think yourself lucky** *you didn't get mugged.* ◇ *Mark is* **one of the lucky ones**—*he at least has somewhere to sleep.* ◇ *the lucky winners* **2** A2 being the result of good luck: **~ (for sb) (that …)** *It was lucky for us that we were able to go.* ◇ *That was the luckiest escape of my life.* ◇ *a lucky guess* **3** A2 bringing good luck: *a lucky charm* ⇒ see also HAPPY-GO-LUCKY ▶ **luck·ily** /-kɪli/ *adv.*: **~ (for sb)** *Luckily for us, the train was late.* ◇ *Luckily, I am a good swimmer.*
IDM **get 'lucky** (*informal*) **1** to have good luck: *She hopes that some day she'll get lucky and win the jackpot.* **2** to meet sb new and have sex with them: *Mike's hoping to get lucky tonight.* **lucky 'you, 'me, etc.** (*informal*) used to show that you think sb is lucky to have sth, be able to do sth, etc.: *'I'm off to Paris.' 'Lucky you!'* **you'll be 'lucky** (*informal*) used to tell sb that sth that they are expecting probably will not happen: *'I was hoping to get a ticket for Saturday.' 'You'll be lucky.'* **you, etc. should be so 'lucky** (*informal*) used to tell sb that they will probably not get what they are hoping for, and may not deserve it ⇒ more at STRIKE *v.*, THANK, THIRD *ordinal number*

**lucky 'dip** (*BrE*) (*NAmE* **'grab bag**) *noun* [usually sing.] a game in which people choose a present from a container of presents without being able to see what it is going to be

**lu·cra·tive** /ˈluːkrətɪv/ *adj.* producing a large amount of money; making a large profit: *a lucrative business/contract/market* ⇒ SYNONYMS at SUCCESSFUL ▶ **lu·cra·tive·ly** *adv.*

**lucre** /ˈluːkə(r)/ *noun* [U] (*disapproving*) money, especially when it has been obtained in a way that is not honest or moral: *the lure of filthy lucre*

**Lud·dite** /ˈlʌdaɪt/ *noun* (*disapproving*) a person who is opposed to new technology or working methods ORIGIN Named after Ned Lud, one of the workers who destroyed machinery in factories in the early 19th century, because they believed it would take away their jobs.

---

▼ **SYNONYMS**

**luck**

chance • coincidence • accident • fate • destiny

These are all words for things that happen or the force that causes them to happen.

**luck** the force that causes good or bad things to happen to people: *This ring has always brought me good luck.*

**chance** the way that some things happen without any cause that you can see or understand: *The results could simply be due to chance.*

**coincidence** the fact of two things happening at the same time by chance, in a surprising way: *They met through a series of strange coincidences.*

**accident** something that happens unexpectedly and is not planned in advance: *Their early arrival was just an accident.*

**fate** the power that is believed to control everything that happens and that cannot be stopped or changed: *Fate decreed that she would never reach America.*

**destiny** the power that is believed to control events: *I believe there's some force guiding us—call it God, destiny or fate.*

**FATE OR DESTINY?**
- **Fate** can be kind, but this is an unexpected gift; just as often, **fate** is cruel and makes people feel helpless. **Destiny** is more likely to give people a sense of power: people who have *a strong sense of destiny* usually believe that they are meant to be great or do great things.

**PATTERNS**
- **by …** luck / chance / coincidence / accident
- **It's no** coincidence / accident **that …**
- **pure / sheer** luck / chance / coincidence / accident
- **to believe in** luck / coincidences / fate / destiny

---

▼ **EXPRESS YOURSELF**

**Wishing somebody luck**

If someone is going to do something difficult, you can wish them luck:
- *Good luck!*
- *The best of luck for the exam!* (*BrE*)
- *I hope it goes well! We'll be thinking about you.*
- *All the best! I'll keep my fingers crossed for you.*

Responses:
- *Thanks.*
- *I'll do my best.*

**ludic** /ˈluːdɪk/ adj. (formal) tending to play and have fun, make jokes, etc., especially when there is no particular reason for doing this

**ludi·crous** /ˈluːdɪkrəs/ adj. unreasonable; that you cannot take seriously SYN **absurd, ridiculous**: *a ludicrous suggestion* ◇ *It was ludicrous to think that the plan could succeed.* ▸ **ludi·crous·ly** adv.: *ludicrously expensive* **ludi·crous·ness** noun [U]

**lug** /lʌɡ/ verb, noun
■ verb (-gg-) ~ sth + adv./prep. (informal) to carry or drag sth heavy with a lot of effort: *I had to lug my bags up to the fourth floor.*
■ noun (specialist) a part of sth that sticks out, used as a handle or support

**luge** /luːʒ, luːdʒ/ noun **1** [C] a type of SLEDGE (= a vehicle for sliding over ice) for racing, used by one or two people lying on their backs with their feet pointing forwards **2 the luge** [sing.] the event or sport of racing down a track of ice on a luge

**Luger™** /ˈluːɡə(r)/ noun a type of small gun that was made in Germany

**lug·gage** /ˈlʌɡɪdʒ/ noun [U] **1** (especially BrE) bags, cases, etc. that contain sb's clothes and things when they are travelling SYN **baggage**: *There's room for one more piece of luggage.* ◇ *You stay there with the luggage while I find a cab.* ⊃ note at BAGGAGE ⊃ see also HAND LUGGAGE **2** (especially NAmE) empty bags, cases, etc. for putting your clothes and things in when you are travelling: *a new set of luggage*

**'luggage rack** noun **1** a shelf for bags above the seats in a train, bus, etc. ⊃ WORDFINDER NOTE at TRAIN ⊃ picture at RACK **2** (especially NAmE) = ROOF RACK

**lu·gu·bri·ous** /ləˈɡuːbriəs/ adj. sad and serious SYN **doleful**: *a lugubrious expression* ▸ **lu·gu·bri·ous·ly** adv.

**luke·warm** /ˌluːkˈwɔːm; NAmE -ˈwɔːrm/ adj. (often disapproving) **1** slightly warm SYN **tepid**: *Our food was only lukewarm.* ⊃ SYNONYMS at COLD **2** not interested or enthusiastic: *a lukewarm response* ◇ *~ about sb/sth She was lukewarm about the plan.*

**lull** /lʌl/ noun, verb
■ noun [usually sing.] ~ (in sth) a quiet period between times of activity: *a lull in the conversation/fighting* ◇ *Just before an attack everything would go quiet but we knew it was just the lull before the storm* (= before a time of noise or trouble).
■ verb **1** [T] ~ sb to make sb relaxed and calm SYN **soothe**: *The vibration of the engine lulled the children to sleep.* **2** [T, I] ~ (sth) to make sth, or to become, less strong: *His father's arrival lulled the boy's anxiety.*
PHRV **lull sb 'into sth** to make sb feel confident and relaxed, especially so that they do not expect it when he does sth bad or dishonest: *His friendly manner lulled her into a false sense of security* (= made her feel safe with him when she should not have).

**lul·laby** /ˈlʌləbaɪ/ noun (pl. **-ies**) a soft, gentle song sung to make a child go to sleep

**lulz** (also **luls**) /lʌlz/ exclamation (informal) (in emails, comments on SOCIAL MEDIA, etc.) used to express the feeling that sth makes you laugh, especially because sb has done sth that makes them look silly: *She didn't realize that there was ice cream all over the back of her dress! Lulz.* ⊃ compare LOLZ ▸ **lulz** noun [pl.]: *They posted embarrassing photos of him on the internet, just for the lulz.*

**lum·bago** /lʌmˈbeɪɡəʊ/ noun [U] pain in the muscles and JOINTS of the lower back

**lum·bar** /ˈlʌmbə(r)/ adj. [only before noun] (medical) relating to the lower part of the back

**'lumbar puncture** noun [C, U] (NAmE also **'spinal tap** [C]) (medical) a medical procedure in which liquid is removed from the lower part of the SPINE with a hollow needle, usually in order to DIAGNOSE a medical problem (= identify what it is)

**lum·ber** /ˈlʌmbə(r)/ noun, verb
■ noun [U] (especially NAmE) = TIMBER

■ verb **1** [I] + adv./prep. to move in a slow and heavy way: *A family of elephants lumbered by.* **2** [T, usually passive] (informal) to give sb a responsibility, etc., that they do not want and that they cannot get rid of: **be/get lumbered (with sb/sth)** *When our parents went out, my sister got lumbered with me for the evening.*

**lum·ber·ing** /ˈlʌmbərɪŋ/ adj. moving in a slow and heavy way: *a lumbering dinosaur*

**lum·ber·jack** /ˈlʌmbədʒæk; NAmE -bərdʒ-/ noun (especially in the US and Canada in the past) a person whose job is cutting down trees or cutting or transporting wood ⊃ compare LOGGER

**lum·ber·yard** /ˈlʌmbəjɑːd; NAmE -bərjɑːrd/ (NAmE) ('timber yard) noun a place where wood for building, etc. is stored and sold

**lu·men** /ˈluːmɪn/ noun (abbr. **lm**) (physics) a unit for measuring the rate of flow of light

**lu·mi·nance** /ˈluːmɪnəns/ noun [U] (physics) the amount of light given out in a particular direction from a particular area

**lu·mi·nary** /ˈluːmɪnəri; NAmE -neri/ noun (pl. **-ies**) a person who is an expert or a great influence in a special area or activity

**lu·mi·nes·cence** /ˌluːmɪˈnesns/ noun [U] (specialist or literary) a quality in sth that produces light ▸ **lu·mi·nes·cent** /-ˈnesnt/ adj.

**lu·mi·nous** /ˈluːmɪnəs/ adj. **1** shining in the dark; giving out light: *luminous paint* ◇ *luminous hands on a clock* ◇ *staring with huge luminous eyes* ◇ (figurative) *the luminous quality of the music* **2** very bright in colour: *They painted the door a luminous green.* ▸ **lu·mi·nos·ity** /ˌluːmɪˈnɒsəti; NAmE -ˈnɑːs-/ noun [sing., U] (formal or literary) **lu·mi·nous·ly** adv. (formal or literary)

**lump** /lʌmp/ noun, verb
■ noun **1** a piece of sth hard or solid, usually without a particular shape: *a lump of coal/cheese/wood* ◇ *This sauce has lumps in it.* **2** (informal, BrE) = SUGAR LUMP: *One lump or two?* **3** a SWELLING (= an area that is larger and rounder than normal) under the skin, sometimes a sign of serious illness: *He was unhurt apart from a lump on his head.* ◇ *Check your breasts for lumps every month.* **4** (especially BrE, informal) a heavy, lazy or stupid person
IDM **have, etc. a 'lump in your throat** to feel pressure in the throat because you are very angry or emotional **take your 'lumps** (NAmE, informal) to accept bad things that happen to you without complaining
■ verb ~ **A and B together** | ~ **A (in) with B** to put or consider different things together in the same group, even when they are actually quite different: *You can't lump all Asian languages together.*
IDM **'lump it** (informal) to accept sth unpleasant because there's no other choice: *I'm sorry you're not happy about it but you'll just have to lump it.* ◇ *That's the situation—like it or lump it!*

**lump·ec·tomy** /lʌmˈpektəmi/ noun (pl. **-ies**) an operation to remove a TUMOUR from sb's body, especially from a woman's breast

**lump·en** /ˈlʌmpən/ adj. (BrE, literary) looking heavy and ugly or stupid

**'lump sum** (also **'lump sum 'payment**) noun an amount of money that is paid at one time and not on separate occasions

**lumpy** /ˈlʌmpi/ adj. full of lumps; covered in lumps: *lumpy sauce* ◇ *a lumpy mattress*

**lu·nacy** /ˈluːnəsi/ noun [U] **1** behaviour that is stupid or crazy SYN **madness**: *It's sheer lunacy driving in such weather.* **2** (old-fashioned) mental illness SYN **madness**

**lunar** /ˈluːnə(r)/ adj. [usually before noun] connected with the moon: *a lunar eclipse/landscape*

**'lunar 'cycle** noun (astronomy) a period of 19 years, after which the new moon and full moon return to the same day of the year

**lunar month** *noun* the average time between one new moon and the next (about 29½ days) ᴐ compare CALENDAR MONTH

**ˈlunar ˈyear** *noun* a period of twelve lunar months (about 354 days)

**lu·na·tic** /ˈluːnətɪk/ *noun, adj.*
- *noun* **1** a person who does crazy things that are often dangerous SYN **maniac**: *This lunatic in a white van pulled out right in front of me!* **2** (*old-fashioned*) a person who is severely mentally ill (the use of this word is now offensive) ORIGIN Originally from the Latin *lunaticus* (*luna* = moon), because people believed that the changes in the moon made people go mad temporarily.
- *adj.* crazy, silly or extremely stupid: *lunatic ideas* ◊ *a lunatic smile*
- IDM **the ˈlunatic ˈfringe** *noun* [sing. + sing./pl. v.] (*disapproving*) those members of a political or other group whose views are considered to be very extreme and crazy

**ˈlunatic aˈsylum** *noun* (*old-fashioned, especially BrE*) an institution where mentally ill people live

**lunch** 🔑 A1 /lʌntʃ/ *noun, verb*
- *noun* 🔑 A1 [U, C] a meal eaten in the middle of the day: *She's gone to lunch.* ◊ *I'm ready for some lunch.* ◊ *I always eat/have lunch at my desk.* ◊ **for ~** *What shall we have for lunch?* ◊ *We serve hot and cold lunches.* ◊ *a one-hour lunch break* ◊ ***Let's do lunch*** (= have lunch together). ᐅ note at MEAL ᐅ see also BAG LUNCH, BOX LUNCH, PACKED LUNCH, PLOUGHMAN'S LUNCH
- IDM **ˌout to ˈlunch** (*especially NAmE, informal*) behaving in a strange or confused way ᐅ more at FREE *adj.*
- *verb* [I] (*formal*) to have lunch, especially at a restaurant: *He lunched with a client at the Ritz.*

**ˈlunch box** *noun* a container to hold a meal that you take away from home to eat

**lunch·eon** /ˈlʌntʃən/ *noun* [C, U] a formal lunch or a formal word for lunch: *a charity luncheon* ◊ *Luncheon will be served at one, Madam.*

**ˈlunch home** *noun* (*IndE*) a restaurant

**ˈlunch hour** *noun* the time around the middle of the day when you stop work or school to eat lunch: *I usually go to the gym during my lunch hour.*

**ˈlunch lady** (*US*) (*BrE* **ˈdinner lady**) *noun* a woman whose job is to serve meals to children in schools

**lunch·room** /ˈlʌntʃruːm, -rʊm/ *noun* (*NAmE*) a large room in a school or office where people eat lunch

**lunch·time** /ˈlʌntʃtaɪm/ *noun* [U, C] the time around the middle of the day when people usually eat lunch: *The package still hadn't arrived by lunchtime.* ◊ *a lunchtime concert* ◊ *The sandwich bar is generally packed at lunchtimes.*

**lung** 🔑 B2 /lʌŋ/ *noun* either of the two organs in the chest that you use for breathing: *lung cancer* ◊ *Obesity can raise the risk of lung disease.* ᐅ see also BLACK LUNG ᐅ VISUAL VOCAB page V1

**ˈlung-busting** *adj.* [only before noun] needing so much effort and energy that you have difficulty breathing SYN **exhausting**: *a lung-busting climb/hill* ◊ *She won a bronze medal for her lung-busting efforts in the 1500 metres final.*

**lunge** /lʌndʒ/ *verb, noun*
- *verb* [I] **~ (at/towards/for sb/sth)** | **~ (forward)** to make a powerful forward movement, especially in order to attack sb or take hold of sth
- *noun* [usually sing.] **1 ~ (at sb)** | **~ (for sb/sth)** a powerful forward movement of the body and arm that a person makes towards another person or thing, especially when attacking or trying to take hold of them: *He made a lunge for the phone.* **2** (in the sport of FENCING) a THRUST made by putting one foot forward and making the back leg straight

**lung·fish** /ˈlʌŋfɪʃ/ *noun* (*pl.* **lungfish**) a long fish that can breathe air and survive for a period of time out of water

**lung·ful** /ˈlʌŋfʊl/ *noun* the amount of sth such as air or smoke that is breathed in at one time

**lungi** /ˈlʊŋɡi/ *noun* a piece of clothing worn in South and south-east Asia consisting of a piece of cloth, usually worn wrapped around the HIPS and reaching the ankles

**Luo** /ˈluːəʊ/ *noun, adj.*
- *noun* (*pl.* **Luo** or **Luos**) **1** [C] a member of an ETHNIC group living in Kenya and the upper Nile valley **2** [U] the language of the Luo
- *adj.* [usually before noun] belonging to or connected with the Luo or their language

**lupin** (*BrE*) (*NAmE* **lu·pine**) /ˈluːpɪn/ *noun* a tall garden plant with many small flowers growing up its thick STEM

**lu·pine** /ˈluːpaɪn/ *adj.* (*formal*) like a WOLF; connected with a wolf or wolves

**lupus** /ˈluːpəs/ *noun* [U] a disease that affects the skin or sometimes the JOINTS

**lurch** /lɜːtʃ; *NAmE* lɜːrtʃ/ *verb, noun*
- *verb* **1** [I] (+ *adv./prep.*) to make a sudden, unsteady movement forward or to one side SYN **stagger, sway**: *Suddenly the horse lurched to one side and the child fell off.* ◊ *The man lurched drunkenly out of the pub.* ◊ (*figurative*) *Their relationship seems to lurch from one crisis to the next.* **2** [I] if your heart or stomach **lurches**, you have a sudden feeling of fear or excitement
- *noun* [usually sing.] a sudden, unsteady movement that moves you forward or to the side and nearly makes you lose your balance: *The train gave a violent lurch.* ◊ *His heart gave a lurch when he saw her.*
- IDM **leave sb in the ˈlurch** (*informal*) to fail to help sb when they are relying on you to do so

**lurch·er** /ˈlɜːtʃə(r); *NAmE* ˈlɜːrtʃər/ *noun* (*BrE*) a dog that is a mixture of two different types of dog, one of which is a GREYHOUND

**lure** /lʊə(r); *NAmE* lʊr/ *verb, noun*
- *verb* **~ sb** (+ *adv./prep.*) (*disapproving*) to persuade or trick sb to go somewhere or to do sth by promising them a reward SYN **entice**: *The child was lured into a car but managed to escape.* ◊ *Young people are lured to the city by the prospect of a job and money.*
- *noun* **1** [usually sing.] **the ~ of sth** the attractive qualities of sth: *Few can resist the lure of adventure.* **2** a thing that is used to attract fish or animals, so that they can be caught

**Lurex™** /ˈljʊəreks; *NAmE* ˈlʊr-/ *noun* [U] a type of thin metal THREAD; a cloth containing this THREAD, used for making clothes

**lurid** /ˈlʊərɪd; *NAmE* ˈlʊr-/ *adj.* (*disapproving*) **1** too bright in colour, in a way that is not attractive **2** (especially of a story or piece of writing) presented in a way that is intended to shock: *lurid headlines* ◊ *The paper gave all the lurid details of the murder.* ▶ **lur·id·ly** *adv.*

**lurk** /lɜːk; *NAmE* lɜːrk/ *verb, noun*
- *verb* **1** [I] (+ *adv./prep.*) to wait somewhere secretly, especially because you are going to do sth bad or illegal SYN **skulk**: *Why are you lurking around outside my house?* ◊ *A crocodile was lurking just below the surface.* **2** [I] (+ *adv./prep.*) when sth unpleasant or dangerous **lurks**, it is present but not in an obvious way: *At night, danger lurks in these streets.* **3** [I] (*computing*) to read a discussion in a CHAT ROOM, etc. on the internet, without taking part in it yourself
- *noun* (*AustralE, NZE, informal*) a clever trick that is used in order to get sth

**lurve** /lɜːv; *NAmE* lɜːrv/ *noun* [U] (*BrE, informal, humorous*) a non-standard spelling of 'love', used especially to refer to romantic love: *It's Valentine's Day and lurve is in the air.*

**lus·cious** /ˈlʌʃəs/ *adj.* **1** having a strong, pleasant taste SYN **delicious**: *luscious fruit* **2** (of cloth, colours or music) soft and deep or heavy in a way that gives you pleasure to feel, look at or hear SYN **rich**: *luscious silks and velvets* **3** (especially of a woman) sexually attractive

**lush** /lʌʃ/ *adj., noun*
- *adj.* **1** (of plants, gardens, etc.) growing thickly and strongly in a way that is attractive; covered in healthy grass and plants SYN **luxuriant**: *lush vegetation* ◊ *the lush green countryside* ᐅ WORDFINDER NOTE at LANDSCAPE **2** beautiful and making you feel pleasure: *The colours are lush, rich*

and warm. **3** (*informal*) attractive or pleasant: *This shampoo smells lush.*
- **noun** (*especially NAmE, informal*) = ALCOHOLIC

**lust** /lʌst/
- **noun** (*often disapproving*) [U, C] **1** ~ **(for sb)** very strong sexual desire, especially when love is not involved: *Their affair was driven by pure lust.* **2** ~ **(for sth)** very strong desire for sth or pleasure in sth: *to satisfy his lust for power* ◊ *She has a real lust for life* (= she really enjoys life). ⊃ see also BLOODLUST
- **verb**
- **PHRV** ˈlust after/for sb/sth (*often disapproving*) to feel an extremely strong, especially sexual, desire for sb/sth

**lust·ful** /ˈlʌstfl/ *adj.* (*often disapproving*) feeling or showing strong sexual desire **SYN** lascivious

**lus·tre** (*US* **lus·ter**) /ˈlʌstə(r)/ *noun* [U] **1** the shining quality of a surface **SYN** sheen: *Her hair had lost its lustre.* **2** the quality of being special in a way that is exciting: *The presence of the prince added lustre to the occasion.* ⊃ compare LACKLUSTRE

**lus·trous** /ˈlʌstrəs/ *adj.* (*formal*) soft and shining **SYN** glossy: *thick, lustrous hair*

**lusty** /ˈlʌsti/ *adj.* healthy and strong **SYN** vigorous: *a lusty young man* ◊ *lusty singing* ▸ **lust·ily** /-stɪli/ *adv.*: *singing lustily*

**lute** /luːt/ *noun* an early type of musical instrument with strings, played like a guitar

**lu·ten·ist** (*also* **lu·tan·ist**) /ˈluːtənɪst/ *noun* a person who plays the lute

**Lu·ther·an** /ˈluːθərən/ *noun* a member of a Christian Protestant Church that follows the teaching of the 16th century German religious leader Martin Luther ▸ **Lu·ther·an** *adj.*

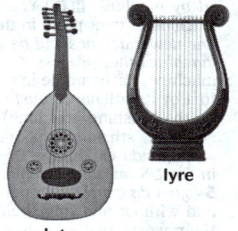
lyre
lute

**luv** /lʌv/ *noun* **1** (*BrE*) a way of spelling 'love', when used as an informal way of addressing sb: *Never mind, luv.* **2** an informal way of spelling 'love', for example when ending a letter: *See you soon, lots of luv, Sue.*

**luv·vie** (*also* **luvvy**) /ˈlʌvi/ *noun* (*BrE, informal, disapproving*) an actor, especially when he or she behaves in a way that seems EXAGGERATED and not sincere

**lux·uri·ant** /lʌɡˈʒʊəriənt; *NAmE* -ˈʒʊr-/ *adj.* **1** (of plants or hair) growing thickly and strongly in a way that is attractive: *luxuriant vegetation* ◊ *thick, luxuriant hair* **2** (especially of art or the atmosphere of a place) rich in sth that is pleasant or beautiful: *the poet's luxuriant imagery* ▸ **lux·uri·ance** /-riəns/ *noun* [U]: *the luxuriance of the tropical forest*

**lux·uri·ant·ly** /lʌɡˈʒʊəriəntli; *NAmE* -ˈʒʊr-/ *adv.* **1** in a way that is thick and attractive: *a tall, luxuriantly bearded man* **2** (especially of a way of moving your body) in a way that is comfortable and gives pleasure: *She turned luxuriantly on her side, yawning.*

**lux·uri·ate** /lʌɡˈʒʊərieɪt; *NAmE* -ˈʒʊr-/ *verb*
- **PHRV** luˈxuriate in sth to relax while enjoying sth very pleasant: *She luxuriated in all the attention she received.*

**lux·uri·ous** /lʌɡˈʒʊəriəs; *NAmE* -ˈʒʊr-/ *adj.* very comfortable; containing expensive things that give pleasure **SYN** sumptuous: *a luxurious hotel* ◊ *luxurious surroundings* **OPP** spartan ▸ **lux·uri·ous·ly** *adv.*: *luxuriously comfortable* ◊ *a luxuriously furnished apartment* ◊ *She stretched luxuriously on the bed.*

**lux·ury** 🔊 **B1** /ˈlʌkʃəri/ *noun, adj.*
- **noun** (*pl.* **-ies**) **1** 🔊 **B1** [U] the fact of enjoying special and expensive things, particularly food and drink, clothes and places: *a life of unimaginable luxury* ◊ **in**~ *Now we'll be able to live in luxury for the rest of our lives.* **2** [C] a thing that is expensive and pleasant but not essential **SYN** extravagance: *small luxuries like chocolate and flowers* ◊ *I love having a long, hot bath—it's one of life's little luxuries.* ◊ *It was a luxury if you had a washing* machine in those days. **3** [U, sing.] a pleasure or an advantage that you do not often have: *We had the luxury of being able to choose from four good candidates for the job.* **IDM** see LAP *n.*
- **adj.** 🔊 **B1** [only before noun] expensive and of very high quality: *a luxury hotel/car/apartment* ◊ *luxury goods*

**LW** *abbr.* (*especially BrE*) LONG WAVE: *1500m LW*

**-ly** /li/ *suffix* **1** (in adverbs) in the way mentioned: *happily* ◊ *stupidly* **2** (in adjectives) having the qualities of: *cowardly* ◊ *scholarly* **3** (in adjectives and adverbs) after INTERVALS of: *hourly* ◊ *daily*

**ly·chee** (*also* **li·chee**) (*also* **lit·chi** *especially in NAmE*) /ˈlaɪtʃi; *NAmE* ˈliːtʃi, ˈlaɪtʃi/ *noun* a small Chinese fruit with thick, rough red skin and that is white inside with a large seed ⊃ VISUAL VOCAB page V4

**Lycra**™ /ˈlaɪkrə/ (*also* **span·dex**) *noun* [U] an artificial material that stretches, used for making clothes that fit close to the body, especially sports clothes

**lye** /laɪ/ *noun* [U] a strongly ALKALINE chemical used in various industrial processes, including washing

**lying** /ˈlaɪɪŋ/ *pres. part.* of LIE¹, LIE² ⊃ see also LOW-LYING

**lying-ˈin** *noun* [sing.] (*old-fashioned*) the period of time during which a woman in the past stayed in bed before and after giving birth to a child

**Lyme disease** /ˈlaɪm dɪziːz/ *noun* [U] a serious disease that causes a high temperature and pain in the JOINTS of the body, caused by bacteria carried by TICKS (= small insects)

**lymph** /lɪmf/ *noun* [U] a clear liquid containing white blood cells that helps to clean the TISSUES of the body and helps to prevent infections from spreading ▸ **lymph·at·ic** /lɪmˈfætɪk/ *adj.* [only before noun]: *the lymphatic system*

**ˈlymph node** (*also* **ˈlymph gland**) *noun* one of the small round parts of the LYMPHATIC system that forms LYMPHOCYTES and helps fight infection

**lympho·cyte** /ˈlɪmfəsaɪt/ *noun* (*biology*) a type of small white blood cell with one round NUCLEUS, found especially in the LYMPHATIC system

**lymph·oma** /lɪmˈfəʊmə/ *noun* [U, C] cancer of the LYMPH NODES

**lynch** /lɪntʃ/ *verb* ~ **sb** if a crowd of people **lynch** sb whom they consider guilty of a crime, they capture them, do not allow them to have a trial in court, and kill them illegally, usually by hanging ▸ **lynch·ing** *noun* [C, U]

**ˈlynch mob** *noun* a crowd of people who gather to lynch sb

**lynch·pin** = LINCHPIN

**lynx** /lɪŋks/ *noun* (*pl.* **lynx** or **lynxes**) a wild animal of the cat family, with yellow-brown fur (sometimes with spots on it) and a very short tail

**lyre** /ˈlaɪə(r)/ *noun* an ancient musical instrument with strings fastened in a frame that is like a U in shape. It was played with the fingers. ⊃ picture at LUTE

**lyric** 🔊 **B2** /ˈlɪrɪk/ *noun, adj.*
- **noun 1** 🔊 **B2** **lyrics** [pl.] the words of a popular song: *music and lyrics by Rodgers and Hart* **2** [C] a lyric poem ⊃ compare EPIC
- **adj. 1** (of poetry) expressing a person's personal feelings and thoughts ⊃ compare EPIC ⊃ WORDFINDER NOTE at POETRY **2** connected with, or written for, singing

**lyr·ical** /ˈlɪrɪkl/ *adj.* expressing strong emotion in a way that is beautiful and shows imagination **SYN** expressive: *a lyrical melody* ◊ *He began to wax lyrical* (= talk in an enthusiastic way) *about his new car.*

**lyr·ic·al·ly** /ˈlɪrɪkli/ *adv.* **1** in a way that expresses strong emotion **2** connected with the words of a song: *Both musically and lyrically it is very effective.*

**lyr·icism** /ˈlɪrɪsɪzəm/ *noun* [U] the expression of strong emotion in poetry, art, music, etc.

**lyr·icist** /ˈlɪrɪsɪst/ *noun* a person who writes the words of popular songs

# M m

**M** /em/ *noun, abbr., symbol*
- *noun* (also **m**) [C, U] (*pl.* **Ms, M's, m's** /emz/) the 13th letter of the English alphabet: *'Milk' begins with (an) M/'M'.*
- *abbr.* **1** (also **med.**) (especially for sizes of clothes) medium: *S, M and L* (= small, medium and large) **2** (used with a number to show the name of a British MOTORWAY): *heavy traffic on the M25*
- *symbol* (also **m**) the number 1000 in ROMAN NUMERALS

**m** (also **m.**) *abbr.* (in writing) **1** male **2** married **3** metre(s): *800m medium wave* **4** mile(s) **5** million(s): *population: 10m*

**MA** (*BrE*) (*NAmE* **M.A.**) /ˌem ˈeɪ/ *noun* a second university degree in an ARTS subject, or, in Scotland, a first university degree in an arts subject (the abbreviation for 'Master of Arts'): *to be/have/do an MA* ◊ (*BrE*) *Julie Bell MA*

**ma** /mɑː/ *noun* (*informal*) mother: *I'm going now, Ma.* ◊ *'I want my ma,' sobbed the little girl.*

**ma'am** /mæm; *BrE also* mɑːm/ *noun* [*sing.*] **1** (*NAmE*) used as a polite way of addressing a woman: *'Can I help you, ma'am?'* ⊃ compare SIR **2** (*BrE*) used when addressing the Queen or senior women officers in the police or army ⊃ see also MADAM

**maas** /mɑːs/ *noun* (*SAfrE*) = AMASI

**Maasai** (also **Masai**) /ˈmɑːsaɪ; *BrE also* ˈmæs-/
- *noun* (*pl.* **Maasai** or **Maasais**) a member of an ETHNIC group living in Tanzania and Kenya
- *adj.* (usually before noun) belonging to or connected with the Maasai

**Mac** /mæk/ *noun* [*sing.*] (*NAmE, informal*) used to address a man whose name you do not know

**mac** (also **mack**) /mæk/ (also *old-fashioned* **mack·in·tosh**) *noun* (all *BrE*) a coat made of material that keeps you dry in the rain

**ma·cabre** /məˈkɑːbrə/ *adj.* unpleasant and strange because connected with death and frightening things SYN **ghoulish, grisly**: *a macabre tale/joke/ritual*

**mac·adam** /məˈkædəm/ *noun* [U] a road surface made of layers of broken stones, mixed with TAR

**maca·da·mia** /ˌmækəˈdeɪmiə/ (also **maca·damia nut**) *noun* the round nut of an Australian tree ⊃ VISUAL VOCAB page V8

**ma·caque** /məˈkæk, -ˈkɑːk/ *noun* a type of monkey that lives in Africa and Asia

**maca·roni** /ˌmækəˈrəʊni/ *noun* [U] PASTA in the shape of hollow tubes

**macaroni ˈcheese** (*BrE*) (*NAmE* ˌmacaroni and ˈcheese, *informal* ˌmac and ˈcheese, ˌmac n ˈcheese) *noun* [U] a hot dish of macaroni in a cheese sauce

**maca·roon** /ˌmækəˈruːn/ *noun* a soft, round, sweet biscuit made with ALMONDS or COCONUT

**macaw** /məˈkɔː/ *noun* a large Central and South American tropical bird of the PARROT family, with bright feathers and a long tail

**mac·chi·ato** /ˌmækiˈɑːtəʊ; *NAmE* mɑːk-/ *noun* (*from Italian*) a drink made with ESPRESSO coffee and a small amount of hot milk

**Mace**™ /meɪs/ *noun* [U] a chemical that makes your eyes and skin STING (= feel a sharp pain), that some people, including police officers, carry in SPRAY cans so that they can defend themselves against people attacking them

**mace** /meɪs/ *noun* **1** [C] a large decorated stick, carried as a sign of authority by an official such as a MAYOR ⊃ compare SCEPTRE **2** [C] a large heavy stick that has a head with metal points on it, used in the past as a weapon **3** [U] the dried outer layer that covers NUTMEGS (= the hard nuts of a tropical tree), used in cooking as a SPICE

**ma·cer·ate** /ˈmæsəreɪt/ *verb* [T, I] **~ (sth)** (*specialist*) to make sth (especially food) soft by leaving it in a liquid; to become soft in this way

**Mach** /mɑːk, mæk/ *noun* [U] (often followed by a number) a measurement of speed, used especially for aircraft. Mach 1 is the speed of sound: *a fighter plane with a top speed of Mach 3* (= 3 times the speed of sound)

**ma·chete** /məˈʃeti/ *noun* a broad, heavy knife used as a cutting tool and as a weapon

**Ma·chia·vel·lian** /ˌmækiəˈveliən/ *adj.* (*formal, disapproving*) using clever plans to achieve what you want, without people realizing what you are doing SYN **cunning, unscrupulous** ORIGIN From the name of Niccolò Machiavelli, an Italian politician (1469–1527), who explained in his book *The Prince* that it was often necessary for rulers to use immoral methods in order to achieve power and success.

**ma·chin·ation** /ˌmæʃɪˈneɪʃn/ *noun* [*usually pl.*] (*disapproving*) a secret and complicated plan SYN **plot, intrigue**

**ma·chine** ❶ A1 /məˈʃiːn/ *noun, verb*
- *noun* **1** A1 (often in compounds) a piece of equipment with many parts that work together to do a particular task. The power used to work a machine may be electricity, STEAM, gas, etc. or human power: *Machines have replaced human labour in many industries.* ◊ *to operate/run a machine* ◊ *How does this machine work?* ◊ *a washing/sewing machine* ◊ *a machine for making plastic toys* ◊ *They have installed a new coffee machine in the staff room.* ◊ *to invent/design a machine* ◊ **by ~** *The potatoes are planted by machine.* HELP You will find compounds ending in **machine** at their place in the alphabet. **2** A1 a computer: *The new machines will be shipped next month.* ◊ *We build machines that process data.* **3** A1 (*informal*) a particular machine, for example in the home, when you do not refer to it by its full name: *Just put those clothes in the machine* (= the washing machine). **4** an organized system for achieving sth and the people who control it: *the president's propaganda machine* ◊ *These years saw a massive growth in the US military machine.* ⊃ see also WAR MACHINE (1) **5** (*often disapproving*) a person who acts without thinking and without allowing their feelings to show or to affect their work: *In this movie he plays a lean, mean killing machine.* ⊃ see also MECHANICAL IDM see COG
- *verb* [T, I] **~ (sth)** (*specialist*) to make or shape sth with a machine: *This material can be cut and machined easily.*

**ma·chine code** (also **ma·chine language**) *noun* [C, U] (*computing*) a code in which instructions are written in the form of numbers so that a computer can understand and act on them

**ma·chine gun** *noun* a gun that fires many bullets one after the other very quickly: *a burst/hail of machine-gun fire* ⊃ see also SUB-MACHINE GUN

**ma·chine-gun** *verb* (**-nn-**) **~ sb/sth** to shoot sb/sth with a machine gun

**ma·chine ˈlearning** *noun* [U] a type of ARTIFICIAL INTELLIGENCE in which computers use huge amounts of data to learn how to do tasks rather than being programmed to do them: *machine learning technologies/algorithms*

**ma·chine-ˈmade** *adj.* made by a machine ⊃ compare HANDMADE

**ma·chine-ˈreadable** *adj.* (of data) in a form that a computer can understand

**ma·chin·ery** ❶ C1 /məˈʃiːnəri/ *noun* **1** ❶ C1 [U] machines as a group, especially large ones: *agricultural/industrial machinery* ◊ *a piece of machinery* **2** [U] the parts of a machine that make it work **3** [U, *sing.*] the organization or structure of sth; the system for doing sth: *the machinery of government* ◊ **~ for doing sth** *There is no machinery for resolving disputes.*

**ma·chine shop** *noun* **1** a place where machines, engines and similar items are made or repaired **2** a small company that uses machines to make or repair things

**ma·chine tool** *noun* a tool for cutting or shaping metal, wood, etc., driven by a machine

**ma·chine trans·lation** *noun* [U] the process of translating language by computer

**ma·chin·ist** /məˈʃiːnɪst/ *noun* **1** a person whose job is operating a machine, especially machines used in industry for cutting and shaping things, or a SEWING machine **2** a person whose job is to make or repair machines

**mach·ismo** /məˈtʃɪzməʊ, -ˈkɪz-; NAmE mɑːˈtʃiːz-, -ˈkiːz-/ noun [U] (from Spanish, usually disapproving) aggressive male behaviour that emphasizes the importance of being strong rather than being intelligent and sensitive

**macho** /ˈmætʃəʊ; NAmE ˈmɑːtʃ-/ adj. (usually disapproving) male in an aggressive way: *He's too macho to ever admit he was wrong.* ◊ *macho pride/posturing*

**mack** = MAC

**mack·erel** /ˈmækrəl/ noun [C, U] (pl. **mack·erel**) a sea fish with blue-green bands on its body, that is used for food: *smoked mackerel*

**mack·in·tosh** /ˈmækɪntɒʃ; NAmE -tɑːʃ/ noun (old-fashioned) = MAC

**mac·ramé** /məˈkrɑːmi; NAmE ˈmækrəmeɪ/ noun [U] the art of tying KNOTS in string in an attractive pattern, to make items for decoration

**macro** /ˈmækrəʊ/ noun (pl. -**os**) (computing) a single instruction in a computer program that causes a complete series of instructions to be carried out, in order to perform a particular task

**macro-** /ˈmækrəʊ/ combining form (in nouns, adjectives and adverbs) large; on a large scale: *macroeconomics* **OPP** micro-

**macro·bi·ot·ic** /ˌmækrəʊbaɪˈɒtɪk; NAmE -ˈɑːt-/ adj. a **macrobiotic** diet consists of whole grains and vegetables grown without chemical treatment and is based on the principles of the balance of YIN and YANG

**macro·cosm** /ˈmækrəʊkɒzəm; NAmE -kɑːz-/ noun any large, complete structure that contains smaller structures, for example the universe ⊃ compare MICROCOSM

**macro·eco·nom·ics** /ˌmækrəʊˌiːkəˈnɒmɪks, -ˌek-/; NAmE -ˈnɑːm-/ noun [U] the study of large economic systems, such as those of whole countries or areas of the world
▶ **macro·eco·nom·ic** adj.: *macroeconomic policy*

**macro·phage** /ˈmækrəfeɪdʒ/ noun (biology) a large cell that is able to remove harmful substances from the body, and is found in blood and TISSUE

**mad** 🔑 **B1** /mæd/ adj. (**mad·der**, **mad·dest**) **1** **B1** (especially BrE) having a mind that does not work normally; mentally ill: *They realized that he had gone mad.* ◊ *Inventors are not mad scientists.* ◊ *I'll go mad if I have to wait much longer.* ◊ *She seemed to have gone stark raving mad.* ⊃ see also BARKING MAD **2** **B1** (especially BrE, informal) very stupid; not at all sensible: *You must be mad to risk it.* ◊ *It was a mad idea.* ◊ *'I'm going to buy some new clothes.' 'Well, don't go mad* (= spend more than is sensible).*' **3** **B1** [not before noun] (especially NAmE, informal) very angry: *He got mad and walked out.* ◊ *~at/with sb (for doing sth) She's mad at me for being late.* ◊ *~about sth They're pretty mad about being lied to.* ◊ (BrE) *That noise is driving me mad.* ◊ (BrE) *He'll go mad when he sees the damage.* ⊃ SYNONYMS at ANGRY **4** **B1** [not usually before noun] (BrE, informal) liking sth/sb very much; very interested in sth: ~**about sth/sb** *He's always been mad about kids.* ◊ ~**on sth** *He's mad to be mad on tennis* ◊ ~**for sth/sb** *Scott's mad for peanuts.* ◊ *football-mad boys* ◊ *She's completely power-mad.* **5** **B1** done without thought or control; wild and excited: *The crowd made a mad rush for the exit.* ◊ *Only a mad dash got them to the meeting on time.* ◊ (BrE) *The team won and the fans went mad.* ◊ ~**with sth** *to be mad with anger/excitement/grief/jealousy/love/power* **6** (of a dog) suffering from RABIES **SYN** rabid **7** (NAmE, informal) great: *Love him or hate him, the man's got mad skills.* ◊ *I have to give mad props* (= proper respect) *to the camera team.* ⊃ compare CRAZY
**IDM** **like ˈcrazy / ˈmad** (informal) very fast, hard, much, etc.: *I had to run like mad to catch the bus.* **(as) mad as a ˈhatter / a March ˈhare** (informal) (of a person) mentally ill; crazy **ORIGIN** Because of the chemicals used in hat-making, workers often suffered from mercury poisoning, which can cause loss of memory and damage to the nervous system. Lewis Carroll was probably thinking of this when he created the eccentric character of the Hatter in *Alice's Adventures in Wonderland*. A **March hare** was called mad because of the strange behaviour of hares during the mating season. **mad ˈkeen (on sth/sb)** (BrE, informal) liking sth/sb very much; very interested in sth: *He's mad keen on planes.* ⊃ more at HOPPING adv., RAVING adv.

▼ **SYNONYMS**

**mad**
crazy • nuts • batty • out of your mind • (not) in your right mind

These are all informal words that describe sb who has a mind that does not work normally.

**mad** (especially BrE, informal) having a mind that does not work normally: *I thought I'd go mad if I stayed any longer.* **NOTE** **Mad** is an informal word used to suggest that sb's behaviour is very strange, often because of extreme emotional pressure. It is offensive if used to describe sb suffering from a real mental illness; say instead that sb is *mentally ill* or has *mental health issues*. **Mad** is not usually used in this meaning in North American English; use **crazy** instead.

**crazy** (informal) having a mind that does not work normally: *A crazy old woman rented the upstairs room.* **NOTE** Like **mad**, **crazy** is offensive if used to describe sb suffering from a real mental illness.

**nuts** [not before noun] (informal) mad: *That noise is driving me nuts!* ◊ *You guys are nuts!*

**batty** (especially BrE, informal) slightly mad, in a harmless way: *Her mum's completely batty.*

**out of your mind** (informal) unable to think or behave normally, especially because of extreme shock or worry: *She was out of her mind with grief.*

**(not) in your right mind** (informal) (not) mentally normal: *No one in their right mind would choose to work there.*

PATTERNS
• to be mad / crazy / nuts / out of your mind / not in your right mind **to do sth**
• to go mad / crazy / nuts / batty
• to **drive sb** mad / crazy / nuts / batty / out of their mind
• **completely** mad / crazy / nuts / batty / out of your mind

**madam** /ˈmædəm/ noun **1** [sing.] (formal) used when speaking or writing to a woman in a formal or business situation: *Can I help you, madam?* ◊ *Dear Madam* (= used like *Dear Sir* in a letter) ⊃ see also MA'AM **2** [C] (especially BrE, informal, disapproving) a girl or young woman who expects other people to do what she wants: *She's a proper little madam.* **3** [C] a woman who is in charge of the PROSTITUTES in a BROTHEL

**mad·cap** /ˈmædkæp/ adj. [usually before noun] (informal) (of people, plans, etc.) crazy and not caring about danger; not sensible **SYN** reckless: *madcap schemes/escapades*

**mad ˈcow disease** noun [U] (informal) = BSE

**mad·den** /ˈmædn/ verb [usually passive] ~**sb/sth** to make a person or an animal very angry or crazy **SYN** infuriate
▶ **mad·den·ing** adj.: *maddening delays* **mad·den·ing·ly** adv.: *Progress is maddeningly slow.*

**mad·ding** /ˈmædɪŋ/ adj. (literary) behaving in a crazy way; making you feel angry or crazy
**IDM** **far from the madding ˈcrowd** in a quiet and private place

**made** /meɪd/ **1** past tense, past part. of MAKE **2** -**made** (in adjectives) made in the way, place, etc. mentioned: *well-made* ◊ *home-made* ⊃ see also CUSTOM-MADE, MACHINE-MADE, READY-MADE, SELF-MADE, TAILOR-MADE
**IDM** **have (got) it ˈmade** (informal) to be sure of success; to have everything that you want **(be) ˈmade for sb / each other** to be completely suitable for sb/each other: *Peter and Judy seem made for each other, don't they?* **what sb is ˈmade of** (informal) how sb reacts in a difficult situation: *Don't give up now, Sam—show us what you're made of.*

**Ma·deira** /məˈdɪərə; NAmE -ˈdɪrə/ (also **Maˌdeira ˈwine**) noun **1** [U, C] a strong wine, often sweet, from the island of Madeira **2** [C] a glass of Madeira

**mad·eleine** /ˈmædlɪn, -leɪn/ noun a type of small cake

**made to ˈmeasure** adj. (of clothes, curtains, etc.) made specially to fit a particular person, window, etc.

**made to order**

**made to ˈorder** *adj.* (of clothes, furniture, etc.) made specially for a particular customer

**ˈmade-up** *adj.* **1** wearing MAKE-UP: *a heavily **made-up** face/woman* **2** not true or real; invented: *a **made-up** story/word/name*

**mad·house** /ˈmædhaʊs/ *noun* **1** [usually sing.] (*informal*) a place where there is noise and a lack of order: *Don't work in that department; it's a madhouse.* **2** (*old use*) a hospital for people who are mentally ill

**Madi·son Av·enue** /ˌmædɪsn ˈævənjuː; *NAmE* -nuː/ *noun* [U] the US advertising industry ORIGIN From the name of the street in New York where many advertising companies have their offices.

**madly** /ˈmædli/ *adv.* **1** (only used *after* a verb) in a way that shows a lack of control: *She was rushing around madly trying to put out the fire.* ◇ *His heart thudded madly against his ribs.* **2** (*informal*) very, extremely: *madly excited/jealous* ◇ *She's **madly in love** with him.*

**mad·man** /ˈmædmən/ *noun* (*pl.* **-men** /-mən/) a man who has a serious mental illness: *The killing was the act of a madman.* ◇ *He drove **like a madman**.* ◇ *Some madman* (= stupid person) *deleted all the files.* ➔ see also MADWOMAN

**mad·ness** /ˈmædnəs/ *noun* [U] **1** (*old-fashioned*) the state of having a serious mental illness SYN **insanity**: *There may be a link between madness and creativity.* **2** crazy or stupid behaviour that could be dangerous: *It would be sheer madness to trust a man like that.* ◇ *In a **moment of madness** she had agreed to go out with him.* IDM see METHOD

**ma·donna** /məˈdɒnə; *NAmE* -ˈdɑːnə/ *noun* **1 the Madonna** [sing.] the Virgin Mary, mother of Jesus Christ **2** [C] a statue or picture of the Virgin Mary

**ma·dras** /məˈdræs, -ˈdrɑːs; *NAmE also* ˈmædrəs/ *noun* [U, C] a spicy Indian dish, usually containing meat: *chicken madras*

**ma·dra·sa** (*also* **ma·dra·sah**) /məˈdræsə/ *noun* a college where the Islamic faith is taught

**mad·ri·gal** /ˈmædrɪɡl/ *noun* a song for several singers, usually without musical instruments, popular in the 16th century

**mad·woman** /ˈmædwʊmən/ *noun* (*pl.* **-women** /-wɪmɪn/) a woman who has a serious mental illness ➔ see also MADMAN

**mael·strom** /ˈmeɪlstrɒm; *NAmE* -strəm/ *noun* [usually sing.] **1** (*literary*) a situation full of strong emotions or confusing events, that is hard to control and makes you feel frightened **2** a very strong current of water that moves in circles SYN **whirlpool**

**maes·tro** /ˈmaɪstrəʊ/ *noun* (*pl.* **-os**) (often used as a way of addressing sb, showing respect) a great performer, especially a musician: *Maestro Giulini* ◇ *The winning goal was scored by the maestro himself.*

**Mafia** /ˈmæfiə; *NAmE* ˈmɑːf-/ *noun* **1 the Mafia** [sing. + sing./pl. v.] a secret organization of criminals, that is active especially in Sicily, Italy and the US **2 mafia** [C + sing./pl. v.] an organized group of criminals similar to the Mafia in the way it operates: *the rise of criminal mafias in various parts of Europe* **3 mafia** [C + sing./pl. v.] a group of people within an organization or a community who use their power to get advantages for themselves: *a member of the local mafia* ◇ *Politics is still dominated by the middle-class mafia.*

**Mafi·oso** /ˌmæfiˈəʊsəʊ; *NAmE* ˌmɑːfiˈoʊsoʊ/ *noun* (*pl.* **Mafi·osi** /-siː/) a member of the Mafia or a similar criminal organization

**maga·zine** 🔊 A1 /ˌmæɡəˈziːn; *NAmE* ˈmæɡəziːn/ *noun* **1** A1 (*also informal* **mag** /mæɡ/) a type of large thin book with a paper cover that you can buy every week or month, containing articles, photographs, etc., often on a particular topic; a similar collection of articles, etc. that appears regularly online: *a weekly/monthly magazine* ◇ *a magazine article/interview/story/feature/piece* ◇ *an online magazine* ◇ *a literary/news magazine* ◇ *to read/edit/publish a magazine* ◇ *a magazine editor/publisher/journalist/reporter* ◇ *Her designer clothes were from the pages of a glossy fashion magazine.* **2** a radio or television programme that is about a particular topic: *a regional news magazine on TV* ◇ *a **magazine** programme/program* **3** the part of a gun that holds the bullets before they are fired **4** a room or building where weapons, EXPLOSIVES and bullets are stored

**ma·genta** /məˈdʒentə/ *adj.* between red and purple in colour ▸ **ma·genta** *noun* [U]

**mag·got** /ˈmæɡət/ *noun* a creature like a small, short WORM that is the young form of a fly and is found in meat and other food that is going bad. Maggots are often used as BAIT to catch fish.

**Magi** /ˈmeɪdʒaɪ/ **the Magi** *noun* [pl.] (in the Bible) the three wise men from the East who are said to have brought presents to the baby Jesus

**magic** 🔊 B1 /ˈmædʒɪk/ *noun, adj., verb*
■ *noun* [U] **1** 🔊 B1 the secret power of appearing to make impossible things happen by saying special words or doing special things: *Do you believe in magic?* ◇ *He sensed the presence of powerful **dark magic*** (= evil magic). ◇ ***as if by**~ *He suddenly appeared as if by magic.* ◇ ***like**~ *A passage was cleared through the crowd like magic.* ➔ see also BLACK MAGIC **2** 🔊 B1 the art of doing tricks that seem impossible in order to entertain people: *He earns extra money doing magic at children's parties.* ◇ *a magic show/trick* SYN **conjuring** **3** 🔊 B1 a special quality or ability that sb/sth has, that seems too wonderful to be real SYN **enchantment**: *dance and music which capture the magic of India* ◇ *Like all truly charismatic people, he can **work his magic** on both men and women.* ◇ *The show is three hours of pure magic.* ◇ *His goal on New Year's Day was **a moment of magic**.* IDM see WEAVE v.
■ *adj.* **1** 🔊 B1 having or using special powers to make impossible things happen or seem to happen: *a magic spell/charm/potion* ◇ *There is no magic formula for passing exams—only hard work.* **2** 🔊 B1 (*informal*) having a special quality that makes sth seem wonderful: *It was a magic moment when the two sisters were reunited after 30 years.* ◇ *Then he said the **magic words**: 'I can help you with that.'* ◇ *She has a **magic touch** with the children and they do everything she asks.* **3** [not before noun] (*BrE, informal*) very good or a lot of fun: *'What was the trip like?' 'Magic!'*
■ *verb* (**-ck-**) ~ **sb/sth** + **adv./prep.** to make sb/sth appear somewhere, disappear or turn into sth, by magic, or as if by magic

**magic·al** 🔊+ C1 /ˈmædʒɪkl/ *adj.* **1** 🔊+ C1 containing magic; used in magic: *magical powers* ◇ *Her words had a magical effect on us.* **2** 🔊+ C1 (*informal*) wonderful; extremely pleasant SYN **enchanting**: *a truly magical feeling* ◇ *We spent a magical week in Paris.* ▸ **ma·gic·al·ly** /-kli/ *adv.*

**ˌmagical ˈrealism** *noun* [U] = MAGIC REALISM

**ˈmagic ˈbullet** *noun* [usually sing.] **1** (*medical*) a medical treatment that works very quickly and effectively against a particular illness **2** = SILVER BULLET

**ˈmagic ˈcarpet** *noun* (in stories) a carpet that can fly and carry people

**ma·gi·cian** /məˈdʒɪʃn/ *noun* **1** a person who can do magic tricks SYN **conjuror** **2** (in stories) a person who has magic powers SYN **sorcerer**

**ˈmagic ˈlantern** *noun* a piece of equipment used in the past to make pictures appear on a white wall or screen

**ˈmagic ˈmushroom** (*BrE or becoming old-fashioned*, *NAmE*) (*NAmE usually, informal* **shroom** /ʃruːm, ʃrʊm/) *noun* a type of MUSHROOM that has an effect like some drugs and that may make people who eat it HALLUCINATE (= see things that are not there)

**ˈmagic ˈnumber** *noun* a figure that has a special meaning: *She needs to reach the magic number of 270 votes to win the White House.*

**ˈmagic ˈrealism** (*also* **ˌmagical ˈrealism**) *noun* [U] a style of writing that mixes realistic events with FANTASY

**ˈmagic ˈwand** *noun* = WAND: *I wish I could **wave a magic wand** and make everything all right again.*

**magis·ter·ial** /ˌmædʒɪˈstɪəriəl; *NAmE* -ˈstɪr-/ *adj.* (*formal*) **1** (especially of a person or their behaviour) having or showing power or authority: *He talked with the magisterial authority of the head of the family.* **2** (of a book or piece of writing) showing great knowledge or understanding **SYN** **authoritative**: *his magisterial work 'The Roman Wall in Scotland'* **3** [only before noun] connected with a magistrate ▶ **magis·teri·al·ly** /-riəli/ *adv.*

**the magis·tracy** /ðə ˈmædʒɪstrəsi/ *noun* [sing. + sing./pl. v.] magistrates as a group

**magis·trate** 🔑+ **C1** /ˈmædʒɪstreɪt/ *noun* an official who acts as a judge in the lowest courts of law **SYN** **Justice of the Peace**: *to come up before the magistrates*

**magma** /ˈmæɡmə/ *noun* [U] (*specialist*) very hot liquid rock found below the earth's surface ⊃ picture at VOLCANO

**Magna Carta** /ˌmæɡnə ˈkɑːtə; *NAmE* ˈkɑːrtə/ *noun* a document officially stating the political and legal rights of the English people, that King John was forced to sign in 1215 (often referred to as the basis for modern English law)

**magna cum laude** /ˌmæɡnə kʊm ˈlɔːdi, ˈlaʊdeɪ/ *adv., adj.* (*from Latin*) (in the US) at the second of the three highest levels of achievement that students can reach when they finish their studies at college: *She graduated magna cum laude from UCLA.* ⊃ compare CUM LAUDE, SUMMA CUM LAUDE

**mag·nani·mous** /mæɡˈnænɪməs/ *adj.* (*formal*) kind, generous and forgiving, especially towards an enemy or competitor: *a magnanimous gesture* ◊ *He was magnanimous in defeat and praised his opponent's skill.* ▶ **mag·na·nim·ity** /ˌmæɡnəˈnɪməti/ *noun* [U]: *She accepted the criticism with magnanimity.* **mag·nani·mous·ly** /mæɡˈnænɪməsli/ *adv.*

**mag·nate** /ˈmæɡneɪt/ *noun* a person who is rich, powerful and successful, especially in business: *a media/property/ shipping magnate*

**mag·ne·sium** /mæɡˈniːziəm/ *noun* [U] (*symb.* **Mg**) a chemical element. Magnesium is a light, silver-white metal that burns with a bright, white flame.

**mag·net** /ˈmæɡnət/ *noun* **1** a piece of iron that attracts objects made of iron towards it, either naturally or because of an electric current that is passed through it **2** [usually sing.] ~ (**for sb/sth**) a person, place or thing that sb/sth is attracted to: *In the 1990s the area became a magnet for new investment.* **3** an object with a magnetic surface that you can stick onto a metal surface: *fridge magnets of your favourite cartoon characters*

**mag·net·ic** 🔑+ **C1** /mæɡˈnetɪk/ *adj.* [usually before noun] **1** 🔑+ **C1** behaving like a magnet; that can be attracted by a magnet: *magnetic materials* ◊ *Steel is magnetic.* ◊ *The block becomes magnetic when the current is switched on.* **2** 🔑+ **C1** connected with or produced by magnetism: *magnetic properties/forces* ◊ *a magnetic disk* (= one containing magnetic material that stores information to be used by a computer) **3** that people find very powerful and attractive: *a magnetic personality* ▶ **mag·net·ic·al·ly** /-kli/ *adv.*

**magˌnetic ˈcompass** *noun* = COMPASS (1)

**magˌnetic ˈfield** *noun* an area around a MAGNET or MAGNETIC object, where there is a force that will attract some metals towards it

**magˌnetic ˈnorth** *noun* [U] the direction that is approximately north as it is shown on a magnetic compass ⊃ compare TRUE NORTH

**magˌnetic ˈstrip** *noun* a line of MAGNETIC material on a plastic card, containing information

**magˌnetic ˈtape** *noun* [U] a type of plastic tape that is used for recording sound, pictures or computer information

**mag·net·ism** /ˈmæɡnətɪzəm/ *noun* [U] **1** a physical property (= characteristic) of some metals such as iron, produced by electric currents, that causes forces between objects, either pulling them towards each other or pushing them apart **2** the qualities of sth, especially a person's character, that people find powerful and attractive: *She exudes sexual magnetism.*

**mag·net·ize** (*BrE also* -**ise**) /ˈmæɡnətaɪz/ *verb* **1** [usually passive] ~ **sth** (*specialist*) to make sth metal behave like a MAGNET **2** ~ **sb** to strongly attract sb: *Cities have a powerful magnetizing effect on young people.*

**ˈmagnet school** *noun* (in the US) a school in a large city that offers extra courses in some subjects in order to attract students from other areas of the city

**mag·ni·fi·ca·tion** /ˌmæɡnɪfɪˈkeɪʃn/ *noun* **1** [U] the act of making sth look larger: *The insects were examined under magnification.* **2** [C, U] the degree to which sth is made to look larger; the degree to which sth is able to make things look larger: *a magnification of 10 times the actual size* ◊ *high/low magnification* ◊ *The telescope has a magnification of 50.*

**mag·nifi·cent** 🔑+ **B2** /mæɡˈnɪfɪsnt/ *adj.* extremely attractive and impressive; deserving praise **SYN** **splendid**: *The Taj Mahal is a magnificent building.* ◊ *She looked magnificent in her wedding dress.* ◊ *You've all done a magnificent job.* ▶ **mag·nifi·cence** /-sns/ *noun* [U]: *the magnificence of the scenery* **mag·nifi·cent·ly** *adv.*: *The public have responded magnificently to our appeal.*

**mag·ni·fier** /ˈmæɡnɪfaɪə(r)/ *noun* a piece of equipment that is used to make things look larger

**mag·nify** /ˈmæɡnɪfaɪ/ *verb* (**mag·ni·fies**, **mag·ni·fy·ing**, **mag·ni·fied**, **mag·ni·fied**) **1** ~ **sth** (**to/by sth**) to make sth look bigger than it really is, for example by using a LENS or MICROSCOPE **SYN** **enlarge**: *bacteria magnified to 1000 times their actual size* ◊ *an image magnified by a factor of 4* **2** ~ **sth** to make sth bigger, louder or stronger: *The sound was magnified by the high roof.* ◊ *The dry summer has magnified the problem of water shortages.* **3** ~ **sth** to make sth seem more important or serious than it really is **SYN** **exaggerate**

**ˈmagnifying glass** *noun* a LENS (= a curved piece of glass), usually with a handle, that you look through and that makes things look bigger than they really are

**mag·ni·tude** 🔑+ **C1** /ˈmæɡnɪtjuːd; *NAmE* -tuːd/ *noun* **1** 🔑+ **C1** [U] (*formal*) the great size or importance of sth; the degree to which sth is large or important: *We did not realize the magnitude of the problem.* ◊ *a discovery of the first magnitude* ⊃ see also ORDER OF MAGNITUDE **2** [C, U] (*astronomy*) the degree to which a star is bright: *The star varies in brightness by about three magnitudes.* **3** [C, U] (*geology*) the size of an earthquake

**mag·no·lia** /mæɡˈnəʊliə/ *noun* **1** [C] a tree with large white, pink or purple flowers that smell sweet **2** [U] (*BrE*) a very pale cream colour

**mag·num** /ˈmæɡnəm/ *noun* a bottle containing 1.5 LITRES of wine, etc.

**ˌmagnum ˈopus** *noun* [sing.] (*from Latin*) a large and important work of art, literature or music, especially one that people think is the best work ever produced by that artist, writer, etc.

**mag·pie** /ˈmæɡpaɪ/ *noun* a black and white bird with a long tail and a noisy call. There is a popular belief that magpies like to steal small bright objects.

**magus** /ˈmeɪɡəs/ *noun* (*pl.* **magi** /ˈmeɪdʒaɪ/) **1** a member of the group to which priests in ancient Persia belonged **2** a man with magic powers

**ma·hala** /məˈhɑːlə/ *SAfrE* [məˈhɛːlɛ] *adj., adv.* (*SAfrE*) (*informal*) free of charge

**maha·raja** (*also* **maha·rajah**) /ˌmɑːhəˈrɑːdʒə/ *noun* an Indian prince, especially one who ruled over one of the states of India in the past

**maha·rani** (*also* **maha·ranee**) /ˌmɑːhəˈrɑːni/ *noun* the wife of a maharaja

**maha·rishi** /ˌmɑːhəˈrɪʃi, -ˈriːʃi/ *noun* a Hindu spiritual leader or wise man

**ma·hatma** /məˈhætmə, -ˈhɑːt-/ *noun* **1** a holy person in South Asia who is respected by many people **2** **the Mahatma** Mahatma Gandhi, the Indian spiritual leader who opposed British rule in India

**mah·jong** (*also* **mah·jongg** *especially in NAmE*) /ˌmɑːˈdʒɒŋ; *NAmE* -ˈʒɑːŋ/ *noun* [U] (*from Chinese*) a Chinese game played with small pieces of wood with symbols on them

**ma·hog·any** /məˈhɒɡəni; *NAmE* -ˈhɑːɡ-/ *noun* [U] **1** the hard red-brown wood of a tropical tree, used for making

# mahout

furniture: *a mahogany table* **2** a red-brown colour: *skin tanned to a deep mahogany*

**ma·hout** /məˈhaʊt/ *noun* a person who works with, rides and cares for an elephant

**maid** /meɪd/ *noun* **1** (often in compounds) a female servant in a house or hotel: *There is a maid to do the housework.* ⇒ see also BARMAID, CHAMBERMAID, HOUSEMAID, MILKMAID, NURSEMAID **2** (*old use*) a young woman who is not married ⇒ see also OLD MAID

**mai·dan** /maɪˈdɑːn/ *noun* an open space in or near a town in South Asia, usually covered with grass

**maid·en** /ˈmeɪdn/ *noun*, *adj.*
■ *noun* **1** (*literary*) a young girl or woman who is not married: *stories of knights and fair maidens* **2** (*also* **maiden 'over**) (in CRICKET) an OVER in which no points are scored
■ *adj.* [only before noun] being the first of its kind: *a maiden flight/voyage* (= the first journey made by a plane/ship) ◊ *a maiden speech* (= the first speech made by an MP in the parliaments of some countries)

**maiden 'aunt** *noun* (*old-fashioned*) an aunt who has not married

**maid·en·head** /ˈmeɪdnhed/ *noun* (*old use*) **1** the state of being a VIRGIN **2** (*anatomy*) = HYMEN

**'maiden name** *noun* a woman's family name before marriage: *Kate kept her maiden name when she got married* (= did not change her surname to that of her husband).

**maid of 'honour** (*US* **maid of 'honor**) *noun* (*pl.* **maids of honour / honor**) (especially in the US) a young woman or girl who is not married and who is the main BRIDESMAID at a wedding ⇒ compare MATRON OF HONOUR

**maid·ser·vant** /ˈmeɪdsɜːvənt; *NAmE* -sɜːrv-/ *noun* (*old-fashioned*) a female servant in a house ⇒ compare MANSERVANT

**mail** ⓘ A2 /meɪl/ *noun*, *verb*
■ *noun* **1** A2 (*BrE also* **post**) [U] the official system used for sending and delivering letters, packages, etc.: *a mail service/train/van* ◊ *the Royal Mail* ◊ (*especially NAmE*) *regular/postal mail* (= rather than email) ◊ **in the ~** *Hard copies of the documents are in the mail to you.* ◊ **by ~** *We do our business by mail.* ◊ (*especially NAmE*) **via ~** *We did not get any message via mail or email.* ⇒ see also AIRMAIL, CERTIFIED MAIL, SNAIL MAIL, V-MAIL™, VOICEMAIL **2** A2 (*BrE also* **post**) [U] letters, packages, etc. that are sent and delivered: *There isn't much mail today.* ◊ *I sat down to open the mail.* ◊ *to send/receive/deliver mail* ◊ **in the ~** *Is there a letter from them in the mail?* ◊ **hate mail** (= letters containing insults and threats) ◊ note at POST ⇒ see also DIRECT MAIL, JUNK MAIL, SURFACE MAIL **3** A2 [U, C] messages/a message sent or received on a computer: *Check regularly for new mail.* ◊ *You've got mail.* ◊ *incoming/outgoing mail* ◊ *The company's mail server was down.* ◊ *You can delete your mails with a single swipe.* ⇒ see also ELECTRONIC MAIL, EMAIL *noun* **4** used in the title of some newspapers: *the Mail on Sunday* **5** [U] = CHAIN MAIL: *a coat of mail*
■ *verb* **1** A2 (*especially NAmE*) to send sth to sb using the POSTAL system: **~ sth (to sb/sth)** *Don't forget to mail that letter to your mother.* ◊ **~ sb sth** *Don't forget to mail your mother that letter.* ◊ **~ sb/sth** *The company intends to mail 50 000 households in the area.* ◊ note at POST **2** A2 to send a message to sb by email: **~ sb** *Please mail us at the following email address.* ◊ **~ sth (to sb/sth)** *The virus mails itself forward to everyone in your address book.* ◊ **~ sb sth** *Can you mail me that document you mentioned?*
PHRV **mail sth ↔ 'out** to send out a large number of letters, emails, etc. at the same time: *The brochures were mailed out last week.*

**mail·bag** /ˈmeɪlbæɡ/ (*BrE also* **post·bag**) *noun* **1** a large, strong bag that is used for carrying letters and packages **2** [usually sing.] all the letters, emails, etc. received by a newspaper, a TV station, a website, or an important person at a particular time or about a particular subject

**mail·box** /ˈmeɪlbɒks; *NAmE* -bɑːks/ *noun* **1** the area of a computer's memory where email messages are stored **2** (*NAmE*) **letter box**) a small box near the main door

▼ **HOMOPHONES**

**mail • male** /meɪl/
- **mail** *noun*: I think the card got lost in the mail.
- **mail** *verb*: I'll mail you a formal invitation.
- **male** *adj.*: The male characters in the book are all well drawn.
- **male** *noun*: The strongest male will become the leader of the pack.

of a building or by the road, which mail is delivered to ⇒ picture at POSTBOX **3** (*NAmE*) (*BrE* **post·box**) a public box, for example in the street, that you put letters into when you send them ⇒ picture at POSTBOX

**'mail carrier** (*also* **'letter carrier**) (*both NAmE*) *noun* = MAILMAN

**'mail drop** *noun* **1** (*especially NAmE*) an address where sb's mail is delivered, when it is not where they live or work **2** (*NAmE*) a box in a building where sb's mail is kept for them to collect **3** (*BrE*) an occasion when mail is delivered

**mail·er** /ˈmeɪlə(r)/ *noun* **1** (*especially NAmE*) = MAILING (2) **2** (*NAmE*) an ENVELOPE, box, etc. for sending small things by mail

**mail·ing** /ˈmeɪlɪŋ/ *noun* **1** [U] the act of sending items by mail or email: *The strike has delayed the mailing of tax reminders.* ◊ *a mailing address* **2** (*also* **mailer** *especially in NAmE*) [C] an item that is sent by mail or email, especially one that is sent to a large number of people: *An order form is included in the mailing.* ◊ *to send out a mass mailing* ⇒ WORDFINDER NOTE at ADVERTISE

**'mailing list** *noun* **1** a list of the names and addresses of people who are regularly sent information, advertising material, etc. by an organization: *I am already on your mailing list.* **2** a list of names and email addresses kept on a computer so that you can send a message to a number of people at the same time

**mail·man** /ˈmeɪlmæn/ *noun* (*pl.* **-men** /-men/) (*also* **'mail carrier**, **'letter carrier**) (*all NAmE*) (*BrE* **postman**, **postwoman**) a person whose job is to collect and deliver letters, etc. ⇒ note at GENDER

**'mail merge** *noun* [U] a computer program that enables the same letter, email, etc. to be sent to a large number of people by AUTOMATICALLY adding names and addresses from an address list

**'mail order** *noun* [U] a system of buying and selling goods through the mail: *All our products are available by mail order.* ◊ *a mail-order company* ◊ *a mail-order catalogue*

**mail·room** /ˈmeɪlruːm, -rʊm/ (*especially NAmE*) (*BrE usually* **'post room**) *noun* the department of a company that deals with sending and receiving mail

**'mail shot** /ˈmeɪlʃɒt; *NAmE* -ʃɑːt/ *noun* advertising or information that is sent to a large number of people at the same time by mail or email ⇒ WORDFINDER NOTE at ADVERTISE

**'mail slot** (*NAmE*) (*BrE* **'letter box**) *noun* a narrow opening in a door or wall through which mail is delivered ⇒ picture at POSTBOX

**maim** /meɪm/ *verb* **~ sb** to injure sb seriously, causing permanent damage to their body SYN **incapacitate**: *Hundreds of people are killed or maimed in car accidents every week.*

**main** ⓘ A1 ⓞ /meɪn/ *adj.*, *noun*
■ *adj.* A1 [only before noun] being the largest or most important of its kind: *Be careful crossing the main road.* ◊ *the main course* (= of a meal) ◊ *We have our main meal at lunchtime.* ◊ *Reception is in the main building.* ◊ *Loss of habitat is the main reason for the bird's decline.* ◊ *The main thing is to stay calm.* IDM see EYE *n.*
■ *noun* **1** [C] a large pipe that carries water or gas to a building; a large cable that carries electricity to a building: *a leaking gas main* ⇒ see also WATER MAIN **2** a large pipe that carries waste water and SEWAGE (= human waste, etc.) away from a building **3 the mains** [U, pl.] (*BrE*) the place where the supply of water, gas or electricity to a building or an area starts; the system of providing gas, water and electricity to a building or of carrying it away

from a building: *The house is not yet connected to the mains.* ◇ **at the ~** *The electricity supply has been cut off at the mains.* ◇ *Plug the transformer into the mains* (= the place on a wall where electricity is brought into a room). ◇ **mains gas/water/electricity** ◇ *The shaver will run off batteries or mains.* ◇ **mains drainage**

**IDM** **in the 'main** used to say that a statement is true in most cases: *The service here is, in the main, reliable.*

▼ **SYNONYMS**

**main**
major • key • central • principal • chief • prime

These words all describe sb/sth that is the largest or most important of its kind.

**main** [only before noun] largest or most important: *Be careful crossing the main road.* ◇ *The main thing is to remain calm.*

**major** [usually before noun] very large or important: *He played a major role in setting up the system.* **NOTE** When **major** is used with *the* or *my/your/his/her/our/their* it means 'the largest or most important': *Our major concern here is combating poverty.* In this meaning it is only used to talk about ideas or worries that people have, not physical things, and it is also more formal than **main**: *Be careful crossing the major road.* ◇ *The major thing is to remain calm.*

**key** [usually before noun] most important; essential: *He was a key figure in the campaign.* **NOTE** **Key** is used most frequently in business and political contexts. It can be used to talk about ideas, or the part that sb plays in a situation, but not physical things. It is slightly more informal than **major**, especially when used after a noun and linking verb: *Speed is key at this point.*

**central** (*rather formal*) most important: *The central issue is that of widespread racism.* **NOTE** **Central** is used in a similar way to **key**, but is more formal. It is most frequently used in the phrase *sth is central to sth else.*

**principal** [only before noun] (*rather formal*) most important: *The principal reason for this omission is lack of time.* **NOTE** **Principal** is mostly used for statements of fact about which there can be no argument. To state an opinion, or to try to persuade sb of the facts as you see them, it is more usual to use **key** or **central**: *The key/central issue here is …*

**chief** [only before noun] (*rather formal*) most important: *Unemployment was the chief cause of poverty.*

**prime** [only before noun] (*rather formal*) most important; to be considered first: *My prime concern is to protect my property.*

**PATTERNS**
- a/the main/major/key/central/principal/chief/prime **aim/concern**
- a/the main/major/principal **road/town/city**
- the main/key **thing** is to …
- to be **of** major/key/central/prime **importance**

**main 'clause** *noun* (*grammar*) a group of words that includes a subject and a verb and can form a sentence ⊃ compare SUBORDINATE CLAUSE

**the ,main 'drag** *noun* [sing.] (*especially NAmE, informal*) the most important or the busiest street in a town

**main·frame** /ˈmeɪnfreɪm/ (*also* **mainframe com'puter**) *noun* a large, powerful computer, usually the centre of a network and shared by many users ⊃ compare PERSONAL COMPUTER

**the 'main·land** ʕ+ **C1** /ðə ˈmeɪnlənd, -lænd/ *noun* [sing.] the main area of land of a country or region, not including any islands near to it: **to/from ~** *a boat to/from the mainland* ◇ *The Hebrides are to the west of the Scottish mainland.* ▶ **main·land** *adj.* [only before noun]: *mainland Greece/Europe*

**main·line** /ˈmeɪnlaɪn/ *adj., verb*
■ *adj.* (*especially NAmE*) belonging to the system, or connected with the ideas that most people accept or believe in **SYN** mainstream: *mainline churches/faiths*
■ *verb* [T, I] **~ (sth)** (*slang*) to take an illegal drug by INJECTING it into a VEIN: *At 18 he was mainlining heroin.*

947 **maintenance**

**main 'line** *noun* an important railway line between two cities ▶ **main-'line** *adj.: a main-line station*

**main·ly** **O** **B1** /ˈmeɪnli/ *adv.* **1** ʕ **B1** more than anything else; also used to talk about the most important reason for sth **SYN** chiefly, primarily: *They eat mainly fruit and nuts.* ◇ *'Where do you export to?' 'France, mainly.'* ◇ **~ because of sth** *The population almost doubles in summer, mainly because of the jazz festival.* ◇ **~ due to sth** *The rise in inflation is mainly due to higher food prices.* **2** ʕ **B1** in most cases; used to talk about the largest part of a group of people or things: *Anorexia is an illness that occurs mainly in adolescents.* ◇ *The people in the hotel were mainly foreign tourists.* ⊃ LANGUAGE BANK at GENERALLY

**,main 'man** *noun* [sing.] (*informal*) a man who is important to you because he is a trusted friend or employee; the most important man in a situation: *Of course I trust you—you're my main man!*

**main·sail** /ˈmeɪnseɪl, -sl/ *noun* the largest and most important sail on a boat or ship

**main·spring** /ˈmeɪnsprɪŋ/ *noun* **1** [usually sing.] **~ (of sth)** (*formal*) the most important part of sth; the most important influence on sth **2** the most important spring in a watch, clock, etc.

**main·stay** /ˈmeɪnsteɪ/ *noun* [usually sing.] **~ (of sth)** a person or thing that is the most important part of sth and enables it to exist or be successful: *Cocoa is the country's economic mainstay.*

**main·stream** ʕ+ **C1** /ˈmeɪnstriːm/ *noun, adj., verb*
■ *noun* ʕ+ **C1** **the mainstream** [sing.] the ideas and opinions that are thought to be normal because they are shared by most people; the people whose ideas and opinions are most accepted: *His radical views place him outside the mainstream of American politics.*
■ *adj.* **1** ʕ+ **C1** considered normal because it reflects what is done or accepted by most people: *mainstream culture/politics* ◇ *mainstream economists/journalists* ◇ *the mainstream press/media* **2** **mainstream** education is for children who do not have any special needs or difficulties
■ *verb* **1** **~ sth** to make a particular idea or opinion accepted by most people: *Vegetarianism has been mainstreamed.* **2** **~ sb** (*especially NAmE*) to include children with mental or physical problems in ordinary school classes

**mainstream 'media** (*abbr.* **MSM**) *noun* [U + sing./pl. v.] traditional media such as newspapers and broadcasting: *The mainstream media was/were not covering the story.*

**'main street** *noun* (*NAmE*) **1** (*BrE* **'high street**) [C] (*especially in names*) the main street of a town, where most shops, banks, etc. are **2** **Main Street** [U] typical middle-class Americans: *Main Street won't be happy with this new program.*

**main·tain** **O** **B2** **O** /meɪnˈteɪn/ *verb* **1** ʕ **B2** **~ sth** to make sth continue at the same level, standard, etc. **SYN** preserve: *to maintain law and order/standards/a balance/control* ◇ *ANU has maintained its position as Australia's top university.* ◇ *The two countries have always maintained close relations.* ◇ (*formal*) *She maintained a dignified silence.* ◇ *to maintain prices* (= prevent them from falling or rising) **2** ʕ **B2** **~ sth** to keep a building, a machine, etc. in good condition by checking or repairing it regularly: *The house is large and difficult to maintain.* **3** ʕ **B2** **~ sb/sth** to support sb/sth over a long period of time by giving money, paying for food, etc. **SYN** keep: *Her income was barely enough to maintain one child, let alone three.* **4** ʕ **B2** to keep stating that sth is true, even though other people do not agree or do not believe it **SYN** insist: **~ (that)** … *The men maintained (that) they were out of the country when the crime was committed.* ◇ **~ sth** *She has always maintained her innocence.* ◇ **+ speech** *'But I'm innocent!' she maintained.* ⊃ LANGUAGE BANK at ARGUE

**main·ten·ance** ʕ+ **C1** /ˈmeɪntənəns/ *noun* [U] **1** ʕ+ **C1** the act of keeping sth in good condition by checking or repairing it regularly: *The school pays for heating and the maintenance of the buildings.* ◇ *car maintenance* ⊃ see also HIGH-MAINTENANCE, LOW-MAINTENANCE **2** ʕ+ **C1** the act of making a state or situation continue: *the maintenance*

**main verb**   948

*of international peace* **3** the money needed for sb's living expenses; the act of providing this money: *Most students need to take out loans for maintenance as well as tuition fees.* **4** (*BrE, law*) money that sb must pay regularly to their former wife, husband or partner, especially when they have had children together: *He has to pay maintenance to his ex-wife.* ◊ **child maintenance** ◊ **a maintenance order** (= given by a court of law) ⇨ see also ALIMONY

**ˌmain ˈverb** *noun* [usually sing.] (*grammar*) the verb in a MAIN CLAUSE

**mai·son·ette** /ˌmeɪzəˈnet/ *noun* (*BrE*) a flat with rooms on two floors within a building, usually with a separate entrance

**maître d'** /ˌmeɪtrə ˈdiː/ *NAmE also* -tər/ *noun* (*pl.* **maître d's** /-ˈdiːz/ *or formal* **maître d'hôtel** /ˌmeɪtrə dəʊˈtel; *NAmE also* -tər/ *pl.* **maîtres d'hôtel** /ˌmeɪtrə dəʊˈtel; *NAmE also* -tər/) (*from French, informal*) **1** a head waiter **2** a man who manages a hotel

**maize** /meɪz/ (*BrE*) (*NAmE* **corn**) *noun* [U] a tall plant grown for its large yellow grains that are used for making flour or eaten as a vegetable; the grains of this plant ⇨ VISUAL VOCAB page V8 ⇨ see also CORN ON THE COB, SWEETCORN

**Maj.** *abbr.* (in writing) MAJOR: *Maj. (Tony) Davies* ◊ *Maj. Gen.* (= Major General)

**ma·jes·tic** /məˈdʒestɪk/ *adj.* impressive because of size or beauty SYN **awe-inspiring**, **splendid**: *a majestic castle/river/view* ▸ **ma·jes·tic·al·ly** /-kli/ *adv.*

**maj·esty** /ˈmædʒəsti/ *noun* (*pl.* **-ies**) **1** [U] the impressive and attractive quality that sth has: *the sheer majesty of St Peter's in Rome* ◊ *the majesty of the music* **2** [C] **His/Her Majesty**, **Your Majesty** a title of respect used when speaking about or to a king or queen **3** [U] royal power

**ma·jim·bo** /məˈdʒɪmbəʊ; *EAfrE* /maˈdʒɪmbo/ *noun* (*EAfrE*) a system of government in a country with several smaller states, each of which has some power

**major** 🔊 A2 🔊 /ˈmeɪdʒə(r)/ *adj., noun, verb*

■ *adj.* **1** A2 [usually before noun] very large or important: *a major road* ◊ *major international companies* ◊ *to play a major role in sth* ◊ *major sporting events* ◊ *a major issue/factor/project/challenge* ◊ *We have encountered major problems.* ◊ *Four major cities will remove diesel cars by 2025.* ◊ *There were calls for major changes to the welfare system.* OPP **minor** ⇨ SYNONYMS at MAIN **2** [not before noun] serious: *Never mind—it's not major.* **3** (*music*) based on a SCALE (= a series of eight notes) in which the third note is two whole TONES/STEPS higher than the first note: *the key of D major* compare MINOR **4** (*NAmE*) related to sb's main subject of study in college

■ *noun* **1** [C] (*abbr.* **Maj.**) an officer of fairly high rank in the army or the US AIR FORCE: *Major Smith* ◊ *He's a major in the US army.* ⇨ see also DRUM MAJOR, SERGEANT MAJOR **2** [C] (*NAmE*) the main subject or course of a student at college or university: *Her major is French.* **4** compare MINOR ⇨ WORDFINDER NOTE at UNIVERSITY **3** [C] (*NAmE*) a student studying a particular subject as the main part of their course: *She's a French major.* **4** a major organization or competition: *The output of the big five oil majors has fallen in recent years.* **5** **the majors** [pl.] (*NAmE, sport*) the MAJOR LEAGUES

■ *verb*

**PHRV** ˈ**major in sth** (*NAmE, AustralE, NZE*) to study sth as your main subject at a university or college: *She majored in history at Stanford.* ˈ**major on sth** (*BrE*) to pay particular attention to one subject, issue, etc.

**ma·jor·ette** /ˌmeɪdʒəˈret/ *noun* (*especially NAmE*) = DRUM MAJORETTE

**ˌmajor ˈgeneral** *noun* an officer of very high rank in the army or the US AIR FORCE: *Major General William Hunt*

**ma·jor·ity** 🔊 B2 🔊 /məˈdʒɒrəti; *NAmE* -ˈdʒɔːr-/ *noun* (*pl.* **-ies**) **1** B2 [sing. + sing./pl. v.] the largest part of a group of people or things: *~ (of sb/sth) The majority of people interviewed prefer TV to radio.* ◊ *The majority was/were in favour of banning smoking.* ◊ *This treatment is not available in the vast majority of hospitals.* ◊ *to represent/form/constitute/comprise the majority of sb/sth* ◊ *in a/the ~ (of sth) In the nursing profession, women are in the majority.* ◊ *a majority decision* (= one that is decided by what most people want) ◊ *We make decisions by majority vote.* ◊ *the majority opinion/view* OPP **minority** ⇨ see also MORAL MAJORITY, SILENT MAJORITY **2** B2 [C] the number of votes by which one political party wins an election; the number of votes by which one side in a discussion, etc. wins: *by/with a ~ of sth She was elected by a majority of 749.* ◊ *The resolution was carried by a huge majority.* ◊ *~ over sb They had a large majority over their nearest rivals.* ◊ *They have a clear majority* (= large majority) *in Parliament.* ◊ *to win/get/gain/secure a majority* HELP In British politics, a **majority** is the difference between the number of votes for the winning candidate and the number of votes for the second-placed candidate. In American politics, a **majority** is the difference between the number of votes for the winning candidate and the combined number of votes for all the other candidates. In American politics, if the winning candidate has less than half of all the votes, this is not called a majority, but a **plurality**. ⇨ see also ABSOLUTE MAJORITY, OVERALL MAJORITY ⇨ WORDFINDER NOTE at DEMOCRACY **3** [C] (*NAmE*) the difference between the number of votes given to the candidate who wins the election and the total number of votes of all the other candidates: *Without this shift, Kerry would have had a popular majority of a million votes.* ⇨ see also PLURALITY **4** [U] (*law*) the age at which you are legally considered to be an adult

**maˈjority leader** *noun* the leader of the political party that has the majority in either the House of Representatives or the Senate in the US

**maˌjority ˈrule** *noun* [U] a system in which power is held by the group that has the largest number of members

**maˌjority ˈverdict** *noun* (*law*) a decision made by a JURY in a court case that most members, but not all, agree with

**ˈmajor league** (*also* **ˈMajor league**) *noun* (*NAmE*) a league of professional sports teams, especially in baseball, that play at the highest level

**ˈmajor-league** *adj.* [only before noun] (*NAmE*) **1** (*sport*) connected with teams that play in the major leagues, especially in baseball: *a major-league team* **2** very important and having a lot of influence: *a major-league business*

**ˈmajor·ly** /ˈmeɪdʒəli; *NAmE* -dʒərli/ *adv.* (used before an adjective) (*especially NAmE, informal*) very; extremely: *majorly disappointed*

**make** 🔊 A1 🔊 /meɪk/ *verb, noun* ⇨ see also MADE

■ *verb* (**made**, **made** /meɪd/)

• CREATE **1** A1 to create or prepare sth by combining materials or putting parts together: *~ sth to make a table/dress/cake* ◊ *to make bread/cement/paper* ◊ *She makes her own clothes.* ◊ *made in France* (= on a label) ◊ **be made (out) of sth** *What's your shirt made of?* ◊ *What's your shirt made out of?* ◊ **be made from sth** *Wine is made from grapes.* ◊ *~ sth into sth The grapes are made into wine.* ◊ *~ sth for sb She made coffee for us all.* ◊ *~ sb sth She made us all coffee.* ⇨ note at DO¹ **2** A1 *~ sth* to write, create or prepare sth: *These regulations were made to protect children.* ◊ *My lawyer has been urging me to make a will.* ◊ *She has made* (= directed or acted in) *several movies.*

• CAUSE TO APPEAR/HAPPEN/BECOME/DO **3** A1 to cause sth to appear as a result of breaking, tearing, hitting or removing material: *~ sth + adv./prep. The stone made a dent in the roof of the car.* ◊ *~ sth The holes in the cloth were made by moths.* **4** A1 *~ sth* to cause sth to exist, happen or be done: *to make a noise/mess/fuss* ◊ *She tried to make a good impression on the interviewer.* ◊ *I keep making the same mistakes.* **5** A1 *~ sb/sth/yourself + adj.* to cause sb/sth to feel, show or have a particular quality; to cause sb/sth to be or become sth: *The news made him very happy.* ◊ *She made her objections clear.* ◊ *He made it clear that he objected.* ◊ *The full story was never made public.* ◊ *Can you make yourself understood in Russian?* ◊ *She couldn't make herself heard above the noise of the traffic.* ◊ *The terrorists made it known that tourists would be targeted.* **6** A1 *~ sb/sth do sth* to cause sb/sth to do sth: *She always makes me laugh.* ◊ *This dress makes me look fat.* ◊ *What makes you say that* (= why do you think so)*?* ◊ *Nothing will make me change my mind.* **7** B1 to cause sb/sth to be or become a particular kind of thing or person: *~ sth of sb/sth This isn't very important—I don't want to make an*

issue of it. ◊ Don't **make a habit of it**. ◊ You've **made a terrible mess** of this job. ◊ It's important to try and **make something of** (= achieve sth in) your life. ◊ We'll make a tennis player of you yet. ◊ ~**sth + noun** I made painting the house my project for the summer. ◊ She **made it her business** to find out who was responsible.
- **A BED** 8 [A2] ~**a bed** to arrange a bed so that it is neat and ready for use
- **A DECISION/GUESS/COMMENT, ETC.** 9 [A2] ~**a decision, guess, comment, etc.** to decide, guess, etc. sth: *Come on! It's time we made a start.* **HELP** Make can be used in this way with a number of different nouns. These expressions are included at the entry for each noun.
- **FORCE** 10 [A2] to force sb to do sth: ~**sb do sth** *They made me repeat the whole story.* ◊ **be made to do sth** *She must be made to comply with the rules.* ◊ ~**sb** *He never cleans his room and his mother never tries to make him.*
- **REPRESENT** 11 [A2] to represent sb/sth as being or doing sth: ~**sb/sth + adj.** *You've made my nose too big* (= for example in a drawing). ◊ ~**sb/sth + noun** *He makes King Lear a truly tragic figure.*
- **APPOINT** 12 [A2] ~**sb + noun** to elect or choose sb as sth: *She made him her assistant.*
- **BE SUITABLE** 13 [A2] linking verb + **noun** to become or develop into sth; to be suitable for sth: *She would have made an excellent teacher.* ◊ *This room would make a nice office.*
- **EQUAL** 14 [A2] linking verb + **noun** to add up to or equal sth: *5 and 7 make 12.* ◊ *A hundred cents make one euro.* **15** linking verb + **noun** to be a total of sth: *That makes the third time he's failed his driving test!*
- **MONEY** 16 [A2] ~**sth** to earn or gain money: *She makes $100000 a year.* ◊ **to make a profit/loss** ◊ *We need to think of ways to make money.* ◊ *He made a fortune on the stock market.* ◊ *He makes a living as a stand-up comic.*
- **CALCULATE** 17 [no passive] ~**sth + noun** to think or calculate sth to be sth: *What time do you make it?* ◊ *I make that exactly $50.*
- **REACH** 18 [no passive] ~**sth** to manage to reach or go to a place or position: *Do you think we'll make Dover by 12?* ◊ *I'm sorry I couldn't make your party last night.* ◊ *He'll never make* (= get a place in) *the team.* ◊ *The story made* (= appeared on) *the front pages of the national newspapers.* ◊ *We just managed to make the deadline* (= to finish sth in time).
- **STH SUCCESSFUL** 19 ~**sth** to cause sth to be a success: *Good wine can make a meal.* ◊ *The news really made my day.*

**IDM** **HELP** Most idioms containing **make** are at the entries for the nouns and adjectives in the idioms, for example **make merry** is at **merry**. **make as if to do sth** to make a movement that makes it seem as if you are just going to do sth: *He made as if to speak.* **make 'do (with sth)** to manage with sth that is not really good enough: *We were in a hurry so we had to make do with a quick snack.* **make 'good** to become rich and successful **make sth 'good** 1 to pay for, replace or repair sth that has been lost or damaged: *She promised to make good the damage.* 2 to do sth that you have promised, threatened, etc. to do **SYN** **fulfil** **make it** 1 to be successful in your career: *He never really made it as an actor.* 2 to succeed in reaching a place in time, especially when this is difficult: *The flight leaves in twenty minutes—we'll never make it.* 3 to be able to be present at a place: *I'm sorry I won't be able to make it* (= for example, to a party) *on Saturday.* 4 to survive after a serious illness or accident; to deal successfully with a difficult experience: *The doctors think he's going to make it.* ◊ ~**through sth** *I don't know how I made it through the week.* **make it with sb** (*NAmE, slang*) to have sex with sb **make like ...** (*NAmE, informal*) to pretend to be, know or have sth in order to impress people: *He makes like he's the greatest actor of all time.* **make the 'most of sth/sb/yourself** to gain as much advantage, pleasure, etc. as you can from sb/sth: *It's my first trip abroad so I'm going to make the most of it.* ◊ *She doesn't know how to make the most of herself* (= make herself appear in the best possible way). **make 'much of sth/sb** to treat sth/sb as very important: *He always makes much of his humble origins.* **make or 'break sb/sth** to be the thing that makes sb/sth either a success or a failure: *This movie will make or break him as a director.* ◊ *It's make-or-break time for the company.* **make something of yourself** to be successful in

949 **make**

your life: *I wanted to study hard and really make something of myself.*

**PHR V** **make for sth** 1 to move towards sth 2 to help to make sth possible: *Constant arguing doesn't make for a happy marriage.* ⇒ see also (BE) MADE FOR SB/EACH OTHER at MADE
**make sb/sth into sb/sth** to change sb/sth into sth/sth **SYN** **turn into**: *We're making our attic into an extra bedroom.*
**make sth of sb/sth** to understand the meaning or character of sb/sth: *What do you make of it all?* ◊ *I can't make anything of this note.* ◊ *I don't know what to make of* (= think of) *the new manager.*
**make 'off** to hurry away, especially in order to escape **make 'off with sth** to steal sth and hurry away with it: *Thieves made off with $30000 worth of computer equipment.*
**make 'out** 1 (*informal*) used to ask if sb managed well or was successful in a particular situation: *How did he make out while his wife was away?* 2 **make out (with sb)** (*NAmE, informal*) to kiss and touch sb in a sexual way; to have sex with sb **make sb 'out** to understand sb's character **make sb/sth↔'out** 1 to manage to see sb/sth or read or hear sth **SYN** **distinguish**: *I could just make out a figure in the darkness.* ◊ **make out what, who, etc ...** *I could hear voices but I couldn't make out what they were saying.* ⇒ SYNONYMS at IDENTIFY 2 to say that sth is true when it may not be **SYN** **claim**: *She's not as rich as people make out.* ◊ **make out that ...** *He made out that he had been robbed.* ◊ **make sb/sth out to be/do sth** *She makes herself out to be smarter than she really is.* **make sth↔'out** 1 to write out or complete a form or document: *He made out a cheque for €100.* ◊ *The doctor made out a prescription for me.* 2 (used in negative sentences and questions) to understand sth; to see the reasons for sth: *How do you make that out* (= what are your reasons for thinking that)? ◊ **make out what, why, etc ...** *I can't make out what she wants.*
**make sth↔'over (to sb/sth)** 1 to legally give sth to sb: *He made over the property to his eldest son.* 2 to change sth in order to make it look different or use it for a different purpose; to give sb a different appearance by changing their clothes, hair, etc. **SYN** **transform** ⇒ related noun MAKEOVER
**make towards sth** to start moving towards sth: *He made towards the door.*
**make 'up | make yourself/sb↔'up** to put powder, LIPSTICK, etc. on sb's/sb's face to make it more attractive or to prepare for an appearance in the theatre, on television, etc. ⇒ related noun MAKE-UP (1) **make sth↔'up** 1 [B1] to form sth **SYN** **constitute**: *Women make up 56 per cent of the student numbers.* ◊ **be made up of sth** *The course is made up of 12 two-hour sessions.* ⇒ related noun MAKE-UP ⇒ LANGUAGE BANK at PROPORTION 2 to put sth together from several different things ⇒ related noun MAKE-UP 3 [B1] to invent a story, etc., especially in order to trick or entertain sb: *He made up some excuse about his daughter being sick.* ◊ *I told the kids a story, making it up as I went along.* ◊ *You made that up!* 4 to complete a number or an amount required: *We need one more person to make up a team.* 5 to replace sth that has been lost; to COMPENSATE for sth: *Can I leave early this afternoon and make up the time tomorrow?* 6 to prepare a medicine by mixing different things together 7 to prepare a bed for use; to create a temporary bed: *We made up the bed in the spare room.* ◊ *They made up a bed for me on the sofa.* 8 (*especially NAmE*) to clean a hotel room and make the bed: *The maid asked if she could make up the room.* **make 'up for sth** to do sth that corrects a bad situation **SYN** **compensate**: *Nothing can make up for the loss of a child.* ◊ *After all the delays, we were anxious to make up for lost time.* ◊ *Her enthusiasm makes up for her lack of experience.* **make 'up (to sb) for sth** to do sth for sb or give them sth because you have disappointed them or caused them trouble and wish to show that you are sorry **SYN** **compensate**: *How can I make up for the way I've treated you?* ◊ (*informal*) *I'll make it up to you, I promise.* **make 'up to sb** (*BrE, informal, disapproving*) to be pleasant to sb, praise them, etc., especially in order to get an advantage for

# make-believe

yourself **make 'up (with sb)** (*BrE also* **make it 'up**) to end an argument with sb and become friends again: *Why don't you two kiss and make up?* ◇ *Has he made it up with her yet?* ◇ *Have they made it up yet?*

■ *noun* ⓘ B2 the name or type of a machine, piece of equipment, etc. that is made by a particular company: *~ of sth What make of car does he drive?* ◇ *a Swiss make of watch* ◇ *There are so many different makes to choose from.*

**IDM** **on the 'make** (*informal, disapproving*) trying to get money or an advantage for yourself

▼ **SYNONYMS**

### make

do • create • develop • produce • generate • form

These words all mean to make sth from parts or materials, or to cause sth to exist or happen.

**make** to create or prepare sth by combining materials or putting parts together; to cause sth to exist or happen: *She makes her own clothes.* ◇ *She **made a good impression** on the interviewer.*

**do** (*rather informal*) to make or prepare sth, especially sth artistic or sth to eat: *He did a beautiful drawing of a house.* ◇ *Who's doing the food for the party?*

**create** to make sth exist or happen, especially sth new that did not exist before: *Scientists disagree about how the universe was created.*

**MAKE OR CREATE?**
Make is a more general word and is more often used for physical things: you would usually *make a table/dress/cake* but *create for jobs/wealth*. You can use **create** for sth physical in order to emphasize how original or unusual the object is: *Try this new dish, created by our head chef.*

**develop** (used especially in business contexts) to think of and produce a new product: *to develop new software*

**produce** to make things to be sold; to create sth using skill: *a factory that produces microchips*

**generate** to produce or create sth, especially power, money or ideas: *to generate electricity* ◇ *Brainstorming is a good way of generating ideas.*

**form** [often passive] to make sth from sth else; to make sth into sth else: *Rearrange the letters to form a new word.* ◇ *The chain is formed from 136 links.*

**PATTERNS**
- to make/create/develop/produce/generate/form sth **from/out of** sth
- to make/form sth **into** sth
- to make/produce **wine**
- to create/develop **a new product**
- to create/produce/generate **income/profits/wealth**
- to produce/generate **electricity/heat/power**

**'make-believe** *noun* [U] **1** (*disapproving*) imagining or pretending things to be different or more exciting than they really are ⓢ **fantasy**: *They live in a world of make-believe.* **2** imagining that sth is real, or that you are sb else, for example in a child's game: *'Let's play make-believe,'* said Sam.

**make·over** /ˈmeɪkəʊvə(r)/ *noun* [C, U] the process of improving the appearance of a person or a place, or of changing the impression that sth gives

**maker** /ˈmeɪkə(r)/ *noun* **1** [C] ~ **(of sth)** (often in compounds) a person, company or piece of equipment that makes or produces sth: *a decision/law/policy maker* ◇ *programme makers* ◇ *a new film/movie from the makers of 'Terminator'* ◇ *If it doesn't work, send it back to the maker.* ◇ *an electric coffee-maker* ◇ *one of the best winemakers in France* ⊃ see also COFFEE MAKER, DECISION-MAKER, FILM-MAKER, HOLIDAYMAKER, PEACEMAKER, TROUBLEMAKER **2 the, his, your, etc. Maker** [sing.] God **IDM** see MEET *v.*

**make·shift** /ˈmeɪkʃɪft/ *adj.* [usually before noun] used temporarily for a particular purpose because the real thing is not available ⓢ **provisional, improvised**: *A few cushions formed a makeshift bed.*

**'make-up** ⓘ B2 *noun* **1** ⓘ B2 [U] substances used especially by women to make their faces look more attractive, or used by actors to change their appearance: *eye make-up* ◇ *to put on your make-up* ◇ *She never wears make-up.* ◇ *a make-up artist* (= a person whose job is to put make-up on the faces of actors and models)

**WORDFINDER** blusher, cleanser, eyeliner, eyeshadow, foundation, lipstick, mascara, moisturizer, nail polish

**2** ⓘ C1 [sing.] the different qualities that combine to form sb's character or being: *Jealousy is not part of his make-up.* ◇ *a person's genetic make-up* **3** ⓘ C1 [sing.] ~ **(of sth)** the different things, people, etc. that combine to form sth; the way in which they combine: *the make-up of a TV audience* ◇ (*specialist*) *the page make-up of a text* (= the way in which the words and pictures are arranged on a page) **4** [C] (*NAmE*) a special exam taken by students who missed or failed an earlier one

**make·weight** /ˈmeɪkweɪt/ *noun* an unimportant person or thing that is only added or included in sth in order to make it the correct number, quantity, size, etc.

**'make-work** *noun* [U] (*NAmE*) work that has little value but is given to people to keep them busy: *In some departments there is too much make-work.* ◇ *These are simply make-work schemes for accountants.*

**mak·ing** ⓘ B2 /ˈmeɪkɪŋ/ *noun* [U] (often in compounds) the act or process of making or producing sth: *strategic decision-making* ◇ *film-making* ◇ *dressmaking* ◇ *tea- and coffee-making facilities* ◇ ~ **of sth** *the making of social policy* ⊃ see also DECISION-MAKING, EPOCH-MAKING, FILM-MAKING, HAYMAKING, LOSS-MAKING, MISCHIEF-MAKING, NON-PROFIT, PROFIT-MAKING

**IDM** **be the 'making of sb** to make sb become a better or more successful person: *University was the making of Joe.* **have the 'makings of sth** to have the qualities that are necessary to become sth: *Her first novel has all the makings of a classic.* **in the 'making** in the process of becoming sth or of being made: *This model was two years in the making.* ◇ *These events are history in the making.* **of your own 'making** (of a problem, difficulty, etc.) created by you rather than by sb/sth else

**ma·kuti** /mæˈkuːti/ *EAfrE* [maˈkuti] *noun* [pl.] (*EAfrE*) the leaves of a PALM tree, used as a material to make fences, BASKETS, etc. and roofs, especially on the coast of East Africa: *a makuti roof*

**mal-** /mæl/ *combining form* (in nouns, verbs and adjectives) bad or badly; not correct or correctly: *malpractice* ◇ *malodorous* ◇ *malfunction*

**mal·ach·ite** /ˈmæləkaɪt/ *noun* [U] a green mineral that can be POLISHED (= made smooth and shiny by rubbing), used to make beautiful objects

**mal·ad·just·ed** /ˌmæləˈdʒʌstɪd/ *adj.* having mental and emotional problems that lead to unacceptable behaviour ⊃ compare WELL ADJUSTED ▶ **mal·ad·just·ment** /-ˈdʒʌstmənt/ *noun* [U]

**mal·ad·min·is·tra·tion** /ˌmælədˌmɪnɪˈstreɪʃn/ *noun* [U] (*formal*) the fact of managing a business or an organization in a bad or dishonest way

**mal·ad·roit** /ˌmæləˈdrɔɪt/ *adj.* (*formal*) done without skill, especially in a way that annoys or offends people ⓢ **clumsy**

**mal·ady** /ˈmælədi/ *noun* (*pl.* **-ies**) **1** (*formal*) a serious problem ⓢ **ill**: *Violent crime is only one of the maladies afflicting modern society.* **2** (*old use*) an illness

**mal·aise** /məˈleɪz/ *noun* [U, sing.] (*formal*) a general feeling of being ill, unhappy or not satisfied, or that sth is wrong in society, without being able to explain or identify what is wrong ⓢ **unease**: *economic/financial/social malaise* ◇ *a serious malaise among the staff*

**mala·prop·ism** /ˈmæləprɒpɪzəm; *NAmE* -prɑːp-/ *noun* a mistake sb makes when they use a word that sounds similar to the word they wanted to use, but means sth different and sounds funny **ORIGIN** From Mrs Malaprop, a character in Richard Brinsley Sheridan's play *The Rivals*, who confuses words like this all the time.

**mal·aria** /məˈleəriə; *NAmE* -ˈler-/ *noun* [U] a serious disease that causes a high temperature and SHIVERING (=

shaking of the body) caused by the bite of some types of MOSQUITO ▶ **mal·ar·ial** /-riəl/ *adj.*: *malarial insects/ patients/regions*

**ma·lar·key** /mə'lɑːki; NAmE -'lɑːrki/ *noun* [U] (*informal, disapproving*) behaviour or an idea that you think is silly and makes no sense or has no meaning

**Ma·lay·alam** /ˌmʌlə'jɑːləm, ˌmɑː-l-/ *noun* [U] a language spoken in Kerala in south-west India

**mal·con·tent** /'mælkəntent; NAmE ˌmælkən'tent/ *noun* [usually pl.] (*formal, disapproving*) a person who is not satisfied with a situation and who complains about it, or causes trouble in order to change it

**male** ⓘ A2 ⓞ /meɪl/ *adj., noun*

■ *adj.* 1 A2 being a man or boy: *a male friend/colleague/ partner* ◇ *a male nurse/model/dancer* ◇ *All the attackers were male, aged between 25 and 30.* ◇ *The workforce is predominantly male.* ⊃ HOMOPHONES at MAIL 2 A2 (*abbr.* **m**) belonging to the sex that does not lay eggs or give birth to babies: *a male bird* ◇ *male hormones/fertility/sexuality* 3 A2 of men; typical of men; affecting men: *male attitudes to women* ◇ *traditionally male interests* ◇ (BrE) *a male voice choir* ⊃ compare MASCULINE 4 (*biology*) (of a plant or flower) producing POLLEN: *Live oaks produce male flowers called catkins.* 5 (*specialist*) (of electrical PLUGS, parts of tools, etc.) having a part that sticks out that is designed to fit into a hole, SOCKET, etc: *male connectors/adapters* ⊃ compare FEMALE ▶ **male·ness** *noun* [U]: *the chromosome that determines maleness*

■ *noun* A2 a male person, animal or plant: *The male of the species has a white tail.* ◇ *a male-dominated profession* ◇ *an adult/adolescent male* ◇ (*formal*) *The body is that of a white male aged about 40.* ⊃ compare FEMALE ⊃ HOMOPHONES at MAIL ⊃ see also ALPHA MALE, SHE-MALE

**ˌmale ˈbonding** *noun* [U] the act of forming close friendships between men

**ˌmale ˈchauvinism** (*also* ˌchauˈvin·ism) *noun* [U] (*disapproving*) the belief held by some men that men are more important, intelligent, etc. than women

**ˌmale ˈchauvinist** (*also* ˌchauˈvin·ist) *noun* (*disapproving*) a man who believes men are more important, intelligent, etc. than women: *She denounced him as a male chauvinist pig.*

**mal·efac·tor** /'mælɪfæktə(r)/ *noun* (*formal*) a person who does wicked, illegal or very bad things

**ma·levo·lent** /mə'levələnt/ *adj.* [usually before noun] (*formal*) having or showing a desire to harm other people SYN **malicious, wicked** OPP **benevolent** ▶ **ma·levo·lence** /-ləns/ *noun* [U]: *an act of pure malevolence* **ma·levo·lent·ly** *adv.*

**mal·for·ma·tion** /ˌmælfɔː'meɪʃn; NAmE -fɔːr'm-/ *noun* 1 [C] a part of the body that is not formed correctly: *Some fetal malformations cannot be diagnosed until late in pregnancy.* 2 [U] the state of not being correctly formed

**mal·formed** /ˌmæl'fɔːmd; NAmE -'fɔːrmd/ *adj.* (*specialist*) badly formed or shaped

**mal·func·tion** /ˌmæl'fʌŋkʃn/ *verb* [I] (of a machine, etc.) to fail to work correctly ▶ **mal·func·tion** *noun* [C, U]

**mal·ice** /'mælɪs/ *noun* [U] a desire to harm sb caused by a feeling of hate: *She is entirely without malice.* ◇ *out of ~ He sent the letter out of malice.* ◇ *He certainly bears you no malice* (= does not want to harm you).
IDM **with ˌmalice aˈforethought** (*law*) with the deliberate intention of committing a crime or harming sb

**ma·li·cious** /mə'lɪʃəs/ *adj.* 1 having or showing a desire to harm sb or hurt their feelings, caused by a feeling of hate SYN **malevolent, spiteful**: *malicious gossip/lies/rumours* ◇ *He took malicious pleasure in telling me what she had said.* 2 (*computing*) (of software or computer code) intended to damage sb's computer or data files ▶ **ma·li·cious·ly** *adv.*

**ma·lign** /mə'laɪn/ *verb, adj.*

■ *verb* ~ sb/sth (*formal*) to say bad things about sb/sth publicly SYN **slander**: *She feels she has been much maligned by the press.*

■ *adj.* [usually before noun] (*formal*) causing harm: *a malign force/influence/effect* ⊃ compare BENIGN

**ma·lig·nancy** /mə'lɪɡnənsi/ *noun* (*pl.* **-ies**) (*formal*) 1 [C] a malignant mass of TISSUE in the body SYN **tumour** 2 [U] the state of being malignant

**ma·lig·nant** /mə'lɪɡnənt/ *adj.* 1 (of a TUMOUR or disease) that cannot be controlled and is likely to cause death: *malignant cells* OPP **non-malignant** ⊃ compare BENIGN 2 (*formal*) having or showing a strong desire to harm sb SYN **malevolent**

**ma·lin·ger** /mə'lɪŋɡə(r)/ *verb* (*usually* **be malingering**) [I] (*disapproving*) to pretend to be ill, especially in order to avoid work ▶ **ma·lin·ger·er** *noun*

**mall** ⓘ B1 /mɔːl; BrE also mæl/ (*also* **ˈshopping mall**) (*both especially NAmE*) *noun* a large building or covered area that has many shops, restaurants, etc. inside it: *Let's go to the mall.* ◇ *Teenagers would go hang at the mall after school.* ◇ *Check out outlet malls* (= ones which sell goods at reduced prices) *and discount stores for good deals.* ⊃ compare ARCADE (3), SHOPPING CENTRE ⊃ see also STRIP MALL

**mal·lam** (*also* **Mal·lam**) /'mɑːləm/ WAfrE [maːlàm] *noun* (WAfrE) a Muslim religious teacher; sometimes used as a title of respect for anybody who is seen as wise or highly educated, for example a university teacher

**mal·lard** /'mælɑːd; NAmE -lərd/ *noun* (*pl.* **mal·lards** *or* **mal·lard**) a common wild DUCK

**mal·le·able** /'mæliəbl/ *adj.* 1 (*specialist*) (of metal, etc.) that can be hit or pressed into different shapes easily without breaking or CRACKING (= starting to split) 2 (of people, ideas, etc.) easily influenced or changed ▶ **mal·le·abil·ity** /ˌmæliə'bɪləti/ *noun* [U]

**mal·let** /'mælɪt/ *noun* 1 a wooden tool with a long handle and a large head, used for hitting things ⊃ picture at HAMMER, TENT 2 a piece of equipment with a long handle and a wooden head, used for hitting the ball in the games of CROQUET and POLO

**mal·low** /'mæləʊ/ *noun* [C, U] a plant with STEMS covered with small hairs, and pink, purple or white flowers. There are many types of mallow.

**mal·nour·ished** /ˌmæl'nʌrɪʃt; NAmE -'nɜːr-/ *adj.* in bad health because of a lack of food or a lack of the right type of food

**mal·nu·tri·tion** /ˌmælnju'trɪʃn; NAmE -nuː-/ *noun* [U] a poor condition of health caused by a lack of food or a lack of the right type of food ⊃ compare NUTRITION

**mal·odor·ous** /ˌmæl'əʊdərəs/ *adj.* (*formal or literary*) having an unpleasant smell

**mal·prac·tice** /ˌmæl'præktɪs/ *noun* [U, C] (*law*) careless, wrong or illegal behaviour while in a professional job: *medical malpractice* ◇ *a malpractice suit* ◇ *He is currently standing trial for alleged malpractices.*

**malt** /mɔːlt; BrE also mɒlt/ *noun* 1 [U] grain, usually BARLEY, that has been left in water for a period of time and then dried, used for making beer, WHISKY, etc. 2 [U, C] = MALT WHISKY

**malt·ed** /'mɔːltɪd/ *adj.* [only before noun] 1 having been made into malt: *malted barley* 2 having had malt added to it

**Mal·tese** /ˌmɔːl'tiːz/ *adj., noun* (*pl.* **Mal·tese**)
■ *adj.* from or connected with Malta
■ *noun* 1 [C] a person from Malta 2 [U] the language of Malta

**Mal·thusian** /mæl'θjuːziən; NAmE -'θuːʒn/ *adj.* related to the theory of Thomas Malthus that, since populations naturally grow faster than the supply of food, failure to control their growth leads to disaster

**mal·tose** /'mɔːltəʊz, -təʊs/ *noun* [U] (*biology*) a type of sugar that is produced in the body by the action of ENZYMES on STARCH (= a food substance found in flour, rice, potatoes, etc.)

**mal·treat** /ˌmæl'triːt/ *verb* ~ sb/sth to be very cruel to a person or an animal SYN **ill-treat** ▶ **mal·treat·ment** *noun* [U]

**ˌmalt ˈvinegar** *noun* [U] VINEGAR which is made from grain rather than from wine

# malt whisky 952

**malt ˈwhisky** (also **malt**) noun [U, C] high-quality WHISKY made only from MALT, not from ordinary grain; a glass of this

**malˈware** /ˈmælweə(r); NAmE -wer/ noun [U] software such as a virus specifically designed to damage or gain access to a computer system without the user knowing ORIGIN A combination of *malicious* and *software*.

**mam** /mæm/ noun (BrE, dialect, informal) mother

**mama** (also **mamma**) noun **1** /ˈmæmə; BrE also məˈmɑː/ (NAmE or BrE, old-fashioned) mother ⊃ see also MUMMY **2** /ˈmæmə/ in some places in Africa, a mother or older woman (often used as a title that shows respect): *Leave this work to us, mama.* ◊ *Miriam Makeba became known as Mama Africa.* ◊ *Mama Ngina Kenyatta*

**ˈmama's boy** (NAmE) (BrE **ˈmummy's boy**) noun (disapproving) a boy or man who depends too much on his mother

**mamba** /ˈmæmbə/ noun a black or green poisonous African snake

**mambo** /ˈmæmbəʊ/ noun (pl. **-os**) **1** a lively Latin American dance **2** a female VOODOO priest

**mamˑmal** /ˈmæml/ noun any animal that gives birth to live young, not eggs, and feeds its young on milk. Cows, humans and WHALES are all mammals. ⊃ VISUAL VOCAB page V2 ▶ **mamˑmaˑlian** /məˈmeɪliən/ adj.

**mamˑmary** /ˈmæməri/ adj. [only before noun] (biology) relating to the breasts: *mammary glands* (= parts of the breast that produce milk)

**mamˑmoˑgram** /ˈmæməgræm/ noun an examination of a breast using X-RAYS to check for cancer

**mamˑmogˑraphy** /mæˈmɒɡrəfi; NAmE -ˈmɑːɡ-/ noun [U] the use of X-RAYS to check for cancer in a breast

**Mamˑmon** /ˈmæmən/ noun [U] (formal, disapproving) a way of talking about money and wealth when it has become the most important thing in sb's life and as important as a god

**mamˑmoth** /ˈmæməθ/ noun, adj.
■ noun an animal like a large elephant covered with hair, that lived thousands of years ago and is now EXTINCT
■ adj. [usually before noun] extremely large SYN **huge**: *a mammoth task* ◊ *a financial crisis of mammoth proportions*

**mammy** /ˈmæmi/ noun (pl. **-ies**) **1** (dialect, informal) mother **2** (offensive) an offensive word used in the past in the southern states of the US for a black woman who cared for a white family's children

**ˈmammy-wagon** noun (WAfrE, old-fashioned) a lorry with a roof and seats for people to travel in

**mamˑpara** noun (SAfrE) = MOMPARA

**man** A1 /mæn/ noun, verb, exclamation
■ noun /mæn/
• MALE PERSON **1** A1 [C] an adult male human: *a good-looking young man* ◊ *the relationships between men and women* ◊ *the men's team/game/race/doubles/singles/event* ◊ *The board of directors is dominated by middle-aged white men.* ◊ *He was one of the great men of history.* ⊃ see also BEST MAN, DIRTY OLD MAN, LADIES' MAN, MEN'S ROOM, NEW MAN, STRAW MAN
• HUMANS **2** B1 also **Man** [U] humans as a group, both male and female: *the damage caused by man to the environment* ◊ *The common man* (= ordinary people) *is losing faith in democratic institutions.* ⊃ note at GENDER **3** [C] (literary or old-fashioned) a person, either male or female: *All men must die.* **4** [U] humans from a particular period of history: *early/modern/Prehistoric man*
• PARTICULAR TYPE OF MAN **5** [C] (in compounds) a man who comes from the place mentioned or whose job or interest is connected with the thing mentioned: *a Frenchman* ◊ *a businessman* ◊ *a medical man* ◊ *a sportsman* ⊃ note at GENDER **6** [C] a man who likes or who does the thing mentioned: *a betting/fighting/drinking man* ⊃ see also FAMILY MAN, GOD-MAN, ONE-MAN **7** [C] a man who works for or supports a particular organization, comes from a particular town, etc: *the BBC's man in Moscow* (= the man who reports on news from Moscow) ◊ *a loyal Republican Party man* ⊃ see also RIGHT-HAND MAN, YES-MAN
• SOLDIER/WORKER **8** [C, usually pl.] a soldier or a male worker who obeys the instructions of a person of higher rank: *The officer refused to let his men take part in the operation.* **9** [C] a man who comes to your house to do a job: *the gas man* ◊ *The man's coming to repair the TV today.*
• FORM OF ADDRESS **10** [sing.] (especially NAmE, informal) used for addressing a male person: *Nice shirt, man!* ◊ *Hey man. Back off!* **11** [sing.] (old-fashioned) used for addressing a male person in an angry or impatient way: *Don't just stand there, man—get a doctor!*
• HUSBAND/BOYFRIEND **12** [C] a person's husband, boyfriend or male partner: *What's her new man like?* ◊ *I now pronounce you man and wife* (= you are now officially married). ⊃ see also FANCY MAN, OLD MAN
• STRONG/BRAVE PERSON **13** [C] a person who is strong and brave or has other qualities that some people think are particularly male: *Come on, now—be a man.* ◊ *She's more of a man than he is.* ⊃ see also HE-MAN, MAIN MAN, MUSCLEMAN, SUPERMAN
• PEOPLE IN AUTHORITY **14** the **Man** [sing.] (NAmE, informal) a group or person that is thought to be in authority or control, especially the police or white people in government: *Activists marched to the police station to voice their displeasure with the Man.*
• SERVANT **15** [sing.] (old-fashioned, formal) a male servant: *My man will drive you home.*
• IN CHESS, ETC **16** [C] one of the figures or objects that you play with in a game such as CHESS ⊃ see also CHESSMAN
IDM **as one ˈman** with everyone doing or thinking the same thing at the same time; in agreement **be sb's ˈman** to be the best or most suitable person to do a particular job, etc: *For a superb haircut, David's your man.* **be ˈman enough (to do sth/for sth)** to be strong or brave enough: *He was not man enough to face up to his responsibility.* **be your own ˈman/ˈwoman** to act or think independently, not following others or being ordered **every man for himˈself** (saying) people must take care of themselves and not give or expect any help: *In business, it's every man for himself.* **make a ˈman (out) of sb** to make a young man develop and become more adult **a/the ˌman about ˈtown** (old-fashioned) a man who frequently goes to fashionable parties, clubs, theatres, etc. ˌman and ˈboy from when sb was young to when they were old or older: *He's been doing the same job for 50 years—man and boy.* **the ˌman (and/ or woman) in the ˈstreet** an average or ordinary person, either male or female: *Politicians often don't understand the views of the man in the street.* **a ˌman of ˈGod/the ˈcloth** (old-fashioned, formal) a religious man, especially a priest or a CLERGYMAN **(the) ˌman of the ˈmatch** (BrE, sport) a man who is chosen as having given the best performance in a game of football (soccer), CRICKET, etc: *Pogba was named man of the match.* ⊃ compare MVP (1) **the ˌman of the ˈmoment** the man who is the best at a particular point in time: *Man of the moment Tom Ford greets the crowd at the end of his show.* **man's best ˈfriend** a way of describing a dog **a ˌman's ˌhome is his ˈcastle** (US) (BrE **an ˌEnglishman's ˌhome is his ˈcastle**) (saying) a person's home is a place where they can be private and safe and do as they like **a ˈman's man** a man who is more popular with men than with women **ˌman to ˈman** between two men who are treating each other honestly and equally: *I'm telling you all this man to man.* ◊ *a man-to-man talk* **one man's ˈmeat is another man's ˈpoison** (saying) used to say that different people like different things; what one person likes very much, another person does not like at all **separate/sort out the ˌmen from the ˈboys** to show or prove who is brave, SKILFUL, etc. and who is not **to a ˈman | to the last ˈman** used to emphasize that sth is true of all the people being described: *They answered 'Yes,' to a man.* ◊ *They were all destroyed, to the last man.* **you can't keep a good man ˈdown** (saying) a person who is determined or wants sth very much will succeed ⊃ more at GRAND adj., HEART n., MARKED, NEXT adj., ODD, PART n., PEOPLE n., POOR, POSSESSED, SUBSTANCE, THING, WORLD
■ verb (-nn-) ~ sth to work at a place or be in charge of a place or a machine SYN **crew**, **staff**: *Soldiers manned barricades around the city.* ◊ *The telephones are manned 24 hours a day by volunteers.*
PHRV ˌman ˈup (informal) to start being brave or strong in order to deal with a difficult situation: *He should man up and tell his boss what he really thinks.*

■ **exclamation** (*especially NAmE, informal*) used to express surprise, anger, etc: *Man, that was great!*

**mana** /ˈmɑːnə, ˈmænə/ *noun* [U] (in Maori and some other belief systems) a spiritual power, authority or energy within people, places or things

**man·acle** /ˈmænəkl/ *noun, verb*
■ *noun* [usually pl.] one of two metal bands joined by a chain, used for fastening a prisoner's ankles or WRISTS together
■ *verb* [usually passive] *~ sb/sth* to put manacles on sb's WRISTS or ankles, to stop them from escaping

**man·age** 🔑 A2 /ˈmænɪdʒ/ *verb*
• BUSINESS/TEAM **1** ⓘ A2 [T, I] *~(sth)* to control or be in charge of a business, a team, an organization, land, etc: *to manage a business/factory/bank/hotel/soccer team* ◇ *to manage a department/project* ◇ *I think that Forestry Tasmania manages the forest.* ◇ *We need people who are good at managing.* ➔ see also STAGE-MANAGE
• DO STH DIFFICULT **2** ⓘ B1 [T, I] to succeed in doing sth, especially sth difficult: *I don't know exactly how we'll manage it, but we will, somehow.* ◇ *Can you manage another piece of cake?* (= eat one) ◇ *~ to do sth We managed to get to the airport in time.* ◇ *How did you manage to persuade him?* ◇ *She somehow managed to escape through the window.* ◇ (*humorous*) *He always manages to say the wrong thing.* ◇ *We couldn't have managed without you.* ◇ *'Need any help?' 'No, thanks. I can manage.'* ➔ note at CAN¹ **3** [T] *~ sth* to succeed in achieving or producing sth: *In spite of his disappointment, he managed a weak smile.* ◇ *Davies manages light humour without seeming silly.*
• DEAL WITH PROBLEMS **4** ⓘ B1 [I] to be able to solve your problems, deal with a difficult situation, etc. SYN **cope**: *She's 82 and can't manage on her own any more.* ◇ *~ with/without sb/sth How do you manage without a car?*
• MONEY/TIME/INFORMATION **5** ⓘ B1 [I] to be able to live or survive without having much money, support, sleep, etc: *young families who are just about managing* ◇ *~ on sth He has to manage on less than £100 a week.* ◇ *He generally managed on five hours' sleep a night.* ◇ *~ with sth Everyone will just have to manage with less.* **6** ⓘ B1 [T] *~ sth* to use money, time, information, etc. in a sensible way: *Don't tell me how to manage my affairs.* ◇ *a computer program that helps you manage data efficiently* ◇ *This enables pension funds to manage risk.* **7** ⓘ B1 [T] *~ sth* to be able to do sth at a particular time: *Let's meet up again—can you manage next week sometime?*
• CONTROL **8** ⓘ B1 [T] *~sb/sth* to keep sb/sth under control; to be able to deal with sb/sth: *It's like trying to manage an unruly child.* ◇ *Can you manage that suitcase?* ◇ *She manages horses better than anyone I know.*
• LAND **9** [T] *~ sth* to control how land is used, so that it is used in a sensible way: *The landowners manage their land to provide habitat for the desired species.* ◇ *All the timber comes from sustainably managed forests.*

**man·age·able** /ˈmænɪdʒəbl/ *adj.* possible to deal with or control: *Use conditioner regularly to make your hair soft and manageable.* ◇ *The debt has been reduced to a more manageable level.* OPP **unmanageable**

**man·aged** /ˈmænɪdʒd/ *adj.* [only before noun] done or arranged with care and control: *The money will be invested in managed funds.* ◇ *Only wood from managed forests is used in our furniture.* ➔ WORDFINDER NOTE at GREEN

**managed ˈcare** *noun* [U] (*NAmE*) a HEALTHCARE system that controls medical costs by offering a limited choice of doctors and hospitals or charging extra for those not on the list

**man·age·ment** 🔑 B1 /ˈmænɪdʒmənt/ *noun*
**1** ⓘ B1 [U] the activity of running and controlling a business or similar organization: *a career in management* ◇ *hotel/project management* ◇ *a management training course* ◇ *The report blames bad management.* ◇ *Effective financial management is essential.* **2** ⓘ B1 [C + sing./pl. v., U] the people who run and control a business or similar organization: *The management is/are considering closing the factory.* ◇ *under … ~ The shop is now under new management.* ◇ *junior/middle/senior management* ◇ *the bank's/airline's/hospital's management* ◇ *a management decision/job* ◇ *A new board and management team took over.* ◇ *My role is to act as a mediator between employees and management.* ◇ *Most managements are keen to avoid strikes.*

**953** | **mandate**

**3** ⓘ B1 [U] the act or skill of dealing with people or situations in a successful way: *classroom management* ◇ *time management* (= the way in which you organize how you spend your time) ◇ *Security is all about risk management.* ◇ *a waste management system/company/plan* ◇ *management of staff/patients/resources* ◇ *Diet plays an important role in the management of heart disease.* ➔ see also SELF-MANAGEMENT

**ˌmanagement conˈsultant** *noun* a person whose job is to give professional advice about how to run a company or an organization more effectively

**man·ager** 🔑 A2 /ˈmænɪdʒə(r)/ *noun* **1** ⓘ A2 a person who is in charge of running a business, a shop or a similar organization or part of one: *a bank/hotel manager* ◇ *the sales/marketing/human resources manager* ◇ *a fund/portfolio/asset manager* ◇ *The company always needs project managers.* ◇ *I'm a senior manager in a multinational company.* ◇ *a meeting of area managers* ◇ *If you have any questions, speak to your manager.* ➔ see also ACTOR-MANAGER, FLOOR MANAGER, LINE MANAGER, MIDDLE MANAGER, STAGE MANAGER ➔ WORDFINDER NOTE at BUSINESSMAN **2** a person who deals with the business affairs of an actor, a musician, etc: *The comedian is unavailable for comment, according to her manager.* ◇ *The band's manager said that the gig sold out in hours.* **3** a person who trains and organizes a sports team: *the new manager of Italy* **4** a person who is good at managing resources: *She's a good manager who never throws any food away.* ◇ *TV ads depicted the candidate as a would-be efficient manager of the US economy.*

**man·ager·ess** /ˌmænɪdʒəˈres/ *noun* (*BrE, old-fashioned*) a woman who is in charge of a small business, for example, a shop, restaurant or hotel ➔ note at GENDER

**man·ager·ial** /ˌmænəˈdʒɪəriəl; *NAmE* -ˈdʒɪr-/ *adj.* [usually before noun] connected with the work of a manager: *Does she have any managerial experience?* ➔ WORDFINDER NOTE at WORK

**ˌmanaging diˈrector** *noun* (*abbr.* **MD**) (*especially BrE*) the person who is in charge of a business

**ma·ñana** /mæˈnjɑːnə/ *adv.* (*from Spanish*) at some time in the future (used when a person cannot or will not say exactly when)

**mana·tee** /ˈmænəti/ *noun* a large water animal with front legs and a strong tail but no back legs that lives along the Atlantic coasts of West Africa and North and South America

**Man·cu·nian** /mænˈkjuːniən/ *noun* a person from Manchester in north-west England ▶ **Man·cu·nian** *adj.*

**man·dala** /ˈmændələ/ *noun* a round picture that represents the universe in some Eastern religions

**man·da·rin** /ˈmændərɪn/ *noun* **1** [C] a powerful official of high rank, especially in the CIVIL SERVICE SYN **bureaucrat** **2** [C] a government official of high rank in China in the past **3** **Mandarin** [U] the standard form of Chinese, which is the official language of China **4** (*also* ˌmandarin ˈorange) [C] a type of small orange with loose skin that comes off easily

**man·date** ⓘ+ C1 *noun, verb*
■ *noun* /ˈmændeɪt/ **1** ⓘ+ C1 the authority to do sth, given to a government or other organization by the people who vote for it in an election: *~ (to do sth) The election victory gave the party a clear mandate to continue its programme of reform.* ◇ *~ for sth a mandate for an end to the civil war* **2** the period of time for which a government is given power: *The presidential mandate is limited to two terms of four years each.* **3** *~ (to do sth)* (*formal*) an official order given to sb to perform a particular task: *The bank had no mandate to honour the cheque.* **4** the power given to a country to govern another country or region, especially in the past
■ *verb* /ˈmændeɪt; *BrE also* ˌmænˈdeɪt/ (*formal*) **1** *~ that …* | *~ sb to do sth* | *~ sth* (*especially NAmE*) to order sb to behave, do sth or vote in a particular way; to order sth to be done: *The law mandates that imported goods be identified as such.* **2** (*often passive*) to give sb, especially a government or a committee, the authority to do sth: **be mandated to do sth** *The assembly was mandated to draft a constitution.*

**man·dated** /ˈmændeɪtɪd/ adj. [only before noun] (formal) **1** (of a country or state) placed under the rule of another country: *mandated territories* **2** required by law: *a mandated curriculum* **3** having a mandate to do sth: *a mandated government*

**man·da·tory** /ˈmændətəri, mænˈdeɪtəri; NAmE ˈmændətɔːri/ adj. (formal) required by law SYN **compulsory**: *The offence carries a mandatory life sentence.* ◊ *~ (for sb) (to do sth) It is mandatory for blood banks to test all donated blood for the virus.*

**man·dazi** /mænˈdɑːzi/ EAfrE [maˈndazi] noun (pl. **man·dazi**) (EAfrE) a small cake made of fried DOUGH

**man·dible** /ˈmændɪbl/ noun (anatomy) **1** the JAWBONE ⇨ VISUAL VOCAB page V1 **2** the upper or lower part of a bird's BEAK **3** either of the two parts that are at the front and on either side of an insect's mouth, used especially for biting and CRUSHING food ⇨ VISUAL VOCAB page V3

**man·dir** /ˈmændɪə(r); NAmE -dɪr/ noun (IndE) a TEMPLE

**man·do·lin** /ˌmændəˈlɪn, ˈmændəlɪn/ noun a musical instrument with metal strings (usually eight) arranged in pairs, and a curved back, played with a PLECTRUM

**man·drake** /ˈmændreɪk/ noun [C, U] a poisonous plant used to make drugs, especially ones to make people sleep, thought in the past to have magic powers

**mane** /meɪn/ noun **1** the long hair on the neck of a horse or a lion ⇨ VISUAL VOCAB page V2 **2** (informal or literary) a person's long or thick hair

**man-eater** noun **1** a wild animal that attacks and eats humans **2** (informal, humorous) a woman who has many sexual partners ▶ **man-eating** adj. [only before noun]: *a man-eating tiger*

**man·eu·ver, man·eu·ver·able, man·eu·ver·ing** (US) = MANOEUVRE, MANOEUVRABLE, MANOEUVRING

**man·ful·ly** /ˈmænfəli/ adv. using a lot of effort in a brave and determined way ▶ **man·ful** /-fl/ adj. [only before noun]

**manga** /ˈmæŋɡə; NAmE ˈmɑːŋ-/ noun [C, U] (pl. **manga**) (from Japanese) a Japanese style of COMIC STRIP, which may be aimed at either adults or children

**man·ga·nese** /ˈmæŋɡəniːz/ noun [U] (symb. **Mn**) a chemical element. Manganese is a grey-white metal that breaks easily, used in making glass and steel.

**mange** /meɪndʒ/ noun [U] a skin disease that affects MAMMALS, caused by a PARASITE ⇨ see also MANGY

**man·ger** /ˈmeɪndʒə(r)/ noun a long open box that horses and cows can eat from IDM see DOG n.

**mange·tout** /ˌmɒnʒˈtuː/ (BrE) (NAmE **snow pea**) noun (pl. **mange·tout** or **mange·touts** /-ˈtuːz/) [usually pl.] a type of very small PEA that grows in long, flat green PODS that are cooked and eaten whole

**man·gle** /ˈmæŋɡl/ verb, noun
■ verb **1** [usually passive] to tear or TWIST sth so that it is badly damaged: **be mangled** *His hand was mangled in the machine.* **2** *~ sth* to change sth good into sth bad, for example a language or a piece of music, by saying it wrongly or playing it badly SYN **ruin** ▶ **man·gled** adj.: *mangled bodies/remains*
■ noun (also **wring·er**) a machine with two ROLLERS used especially in the past for pressing the water out of clothes that had been washed

**mango** /ˈmæŋɡəʊ/ noun [C, U] (pl. **-oes** or **-os**) a tropical fruit with smooth yellow or red skin, that is soft and orange inside with a large seed ⇨ VISUAL VOCAB page V4

**man·go·steen** /ˈmæŋɡəstiːn/ noun a tropical fruit, with a thick red-brown skin, that is sweet and white inside with a lot of juice ⇨ VISUAL VOCAB page V4

**man·grove** /ˈmæŋɡrəʊv; NAmE ˈmæŋɡ-/ noun a tropical tree that grows in mud or at the edge of rivers and has roots that are above ground: *mangrove swamps*

**mangy** /ˈmeɪndʒi/ adj. [usually before noun] **1** (of an animal) suffering from MANGE: *a mangy dog* **2** (informal) dirty and in bad condition SYN **moth-eaten**: *a mangy old coat*

**man·handle** /ˈmænhændl/ verb **1** *~ sb* to push, pull or handle sb roughly: *Bystanders claim they were manhandled by security guards.* **2** *~ sth + adv./prep.* to move or lift a heavy object using a lot of effort SYN **haul**: *They were trying to manhandle an old sofa across the road.*

**man·hat·tan** /mænˈhætn/ noun an alcoholic drink made by mixing WHISKY with VERMOUTH

**man·hole** /ˈmænhəʊl/ noun a hole in the street that has a cover over it, used when sb needs to go down to examine the pipes or SEWERS below the street

**man·hood** /ˈmænhʊd/ noun **1** [U] the state or time of being an adult man rather than a boy **2** [U] the qualities that a man is supposed to have, for example courage, strength and sexual power: *Her new-found power was a threat to his manhood.* **3** [sing.] (literary or humorous) a man's PENIS. People use 'manhood' to avoid saying 'penis'. **4** [U] (literary) all the men of a country: *The nation's manhood died on the battlefields of World War I.* ⇨ compare WOMANHOOD

**ˈman-hour** noun [usually pl.] an hour, regarded in terms of the amount of work that can be done by one person in one hour

**man·hunt** /ˈmænhʌnt/ noun an organized search by a lot of people for a criminal or a prisoner who has escaped

**mania** /ˈmeɪniə/ noun **1** [C, usually sing., U] ~ (**for sth/for doing sth**) an extremely strong desire or enthusiasm for sth, often shared by a lot of people at the same time SYN **craze**: *He had a mania for fast cars.* ◊ *Football mania is sweeping the country.* **2** [U] (psychology) a mental illness in which sb has an OBSESSION about sth that makes them extremely anxious, violent or confused

**-mania** /ˈmeɪniə/ combining form (in nouns) mental illness of a particular type: *kleptomania* ▶ **-maniac** /ˈmeɪniæk/ (in nouns): *a pyromaniac*

**ma·niac** /ˈmeɪniæk/ noun **1** (informal) a person who behaves in an extremely dangerous, wild or stupid way SYN **madman**: *He was driving like a maniac.* **2** a person who has an extremely strong desire or enthusiasm for sth, to an extent that other people think is not normal SYN **fanatic** ⇨ see also SEX MANIAC **3** (old use, psychology) a person suffering from mania: *a homicidal maniac* ▶ **ma·niac** adj. [only before noun]: *a maniac driver/killer*

**ma·ni·acal** /məˈnaɪəkl/ adj. wild or violent: *maniacal laughter* ▶ **ma·ni·acal·ly** /-kli/ adv.

**manic** /ˈmænɪk/ adj. **1** (informal) full of activity, excitement and stress; behaving in a busy, excited, anxious way SYN **hectic**: *Things are manic in the office at the moment.* ◊ *The performers had a manic energy and enthusiasm.* **2** (psychology) connected with MANIA: *manic mood swings* ▶ **man·ic·al·ly** /-kli/ adv.: *I rushed around manically, trying to finish the housework.*

**ˌmanic deˈpression** noun [U] (old-fashioned) = BIPOLAR DISORDER

**ˌmanic-deˈpres·sive** adj., noun (old-fashioned) = BIPOLAR

**Mani·chae·an** (also **Mani·che·an**) /ˌmænɪˈkiːən/ adj. (religion, philosophy) based on the belief that there are two opposites in everything, for example good and evil or light and dark

**mani·cure** /ˈmænɪkjʊə(r); NAmE -kjʊr/ noun, verb
■ noun [C, U] the care and treatment of a person's hands and nails: *to have a manicure* ⇨ compare PEDICURE
■ verb *~ sth* to care for and treat your hands and nails

**mani·cured** /ˈmænɪkjʊəd; NAmE -kjʊrd/ adj. **1** (of hands or fingers) with nails that are neatly cut and POLISHED **2** (of gardens, a LAWN, etc.) very neat and well cared for

**mani·cur·ist** /ˈmænɪkjʊərɪst; NAmE -kjʊr-/ noun a person whose job is the care and treatment of the hands and nails

**mani·fest** /ˈmænɪfest/ verb, adj., noun
■ verb (formal) **1** ~ **sth (in sth)** to show sth clearly, especially a feeling, an attitude or a quality SYN **demonstrate**: *Social tensions were manifested in the recent political crisis.* **2** ~ **itself (in sth)** to appear or become easy to notice SYN **appear**: *The symptoms of the disease manifested themselves ten days later.*
■ adj. ~ **(to sb) (in sth)** (formal) easy to see or understand SYN **clear**: *His nervousness was manifest to all those present.* ◊ *The anger he felt is manifest in his paintings.*

▶ **mani·fest·ly** *adv.*: *manifestly unfair* ◊ *The party has manifestly failed to achieve its goal.*
■ *noun* (*specialist*) a list of goods or passengers on a ship or an aircraft

**mani·fest·ation** /ˌmænɪfeˈsteɪʃn/ *noun* (*formal*) **1** [C, U] ~ (of sth) an event, action or thing that is a sign that sth exists or is happening; the act of appearing as a sign that sth exists or is happening: *The riots are a clear manifestation of the people's discontent.* ◊ *Some manifestation of your concern would have been appreciated.* **2** [C] an appearance of a ghost or spirit: *The church is the site of a number of supernatural manifestations.*

**mani·festo** /ˌmænɪˈfestəʊ/ *noun* (*pl.* **-os**) a written statement in which a group of people explain their beliefs and aims, especially one published by a political party to say what they will do if they win an election: *an election manifesto* ◊ *the party manifesto* ⇨ WORDFINDER NOTE at DEMOCRACY

**mani·fold** /ˈmænɪfəʊld/ *adj.*, *noun*
■ *adj.* (*formal*) many; of many different types: *The possibilities were manifold.*
■ *noun* (*specialist*) a pipe or CHAMBER with several openings, especially one for taking gases in and out of a car engine: *the exhaust manifold*

**mani·kin** (*also* **man·ni·kin**) /ˈmænɪkɪn/ *noun* **1** a model of the human body that is used for teaching art or medicine ⇨ compare MANNEQUIN **2** (*old-fashioned*) a very small man SYN **dwarf**

**Ma·nila** (*also* **ma·nila**, **Ma·nilla**, **ma·nilla**) /məˈnɪlə/ *noun* [U] strong brown paper, used especially for making ENVELOPES

**man·ioc** /ˈmænɪɒk; *NAmE* -ɑːk/ *noun* [U] = CASSAVA

**ma·nipu·late** /məˈnɪpjuleɪt/ *verb* **1** (*disapproving*) to control or influence sb/sth, often in a dishonest way so that they do not realize it: *~sb/sth She uses her charm to manipulate people.* ◊ *As a politician, he knows how to manipulate public opinion.* ◊ *~sb into sth/into doing sth They managed to manipulate us into agreeing to help.* **2** ~ sth (*formal*) to control, use or change sth with skill: *to manipulate the gears and levers of a machine* ◊ *Computers are very efficient at manipulating information.* ◊ *genetically manipulated organisms* **3** ~ sth (*specialist*) to move a person's bones or JOINTS into the correct position

**ma·nipu·la·tion** /məˌnɪpjuˈleɪʃn/ *noun* **1** [U, C] (*disapproving*) behaviour that controls or influences sb/sth, often in a dishonest way so that they do not realize it: *Advertising like this is a cynical manipulation of the elderly.* **2** [U] (*formal*) the control or use of sth in a way that shows skill: *data manipulation* ◊ *manipulation of images* **3** [U, C] (*specialist*) the skill or act of moving a person's bones or JOINTS into the correct position: *manipulation of the bones of the back*

**ma·nipu·la·tive** /məˈnɪpjələtɪv; *NAmE* -leɪt-/ *adj.* **1** (*disapproving*) showing skill at influencing sb or forcing sb to do what you want, often in an unfair way **2** (*formal*) connected with the ability to handle objects with skill: *manipulative skills such as typing and knitting*

**ma·nipu·la·tor** /məˈnɪpjuleɪtə(r)/ *noun* (*often disapproving*) a person who shows skill at influencing people or situations in order to get what they want

**man·kind** /mænˈkaɪnd/ *noun* [U] all humans, thought about as one large group; the human race: *the history of mankind* ◊ *an invention for the good of all mankind* ⇨ note at GENDER ⇨ compare WOMANKIND ⇨ see also HUMANKIND

**manky** /ˈmæŋki/ *adj.* (*BrE*, *informal*) dirty and unpleasant

**manly** /ˈmænli/ *adj.* (*often approving*) (**man·lier**, **man·li·est**) having the qualities or physical features that are admired or expected in a man ▶ **man·li·ness** *noun* [U]

**man-ˈmade** *adj.* made by people; not natural SYN **artificial**: *a man-made lake* ◊ *man-made fibres such as nylon and polyester* ⇨ SYNONYMS at ARTIFICIAL

**manna** /ˈmænə/ *noun* [U] (in the Bible) the food that God provided for the people of Israel during their 40 years in the desert: (*figurative*) *To the refugees, the food shipments were manna from heaven* (= an unexpected and very welcome gift).

**manned** /mænd/ *adj.* if a machine, a vehicle, a place or an activity is **manned**, it has or needs a person to control or operate it: *manned space flight* OPP **unmanned**

**man·ne·quin** /ˈmænɪkɪn/ *noun* **1** a model of a human body, used for displaying clothes in shops ⇨ compare MANIKIN **2** (*old-fashioned*) a person whose job is to wear and display new styles of clothes SYN **model**

**man·ner** A2 /ˈmænə(r)/ *noun* **1** **manners** [pl.] behaviour that is considered to be polite in a particular society or culture: *to have good/bad manners* ◊ *It is bad manners to talk with your mouth full.* ◊ *He has no manners* (= behaves very badly). ⇨ see also TABLE MANNERS ⇨ WORDFINDER NOTE at BEHAVIOUR **2** [sing.] (*formal*) the way that sth is done or happens: *in a ... She answered in a businesslike manner.* ◊ *The manner in which the decision was announced was extremely regrettable.* **3** [sing.] the way that sb behaves towards other people: *to have an aggressive/a friendly/a relaxed manner* ◊ *His manner was polite but cool.* ◊ *in a ... (towards sb) She behaved in a threatening manner towards her mother.* ⇨ see also BEDSIDE MANNER, COMEDY OF MANNERS **4 manners** [pl.] (*formal*) the habits and customs of a particular group of people: *the social morals and manners of the seventeenth century*
IDM **all ˈmanner of sb/sth** many different types of people or things: *The problem can be solved in all manner of ways.* **in a ˈmanner of ˈspeaking** if you think about it in a particular way; true in some but not all ways: *All these points of view are related, in a manner of speaking.* **in the ˈmanner of sb/sth** (*formal*) in a style that is typical of sb/sth: *a painting in the manner of Raphael* **(as/as if) to the ˈmanner ˈborn** (*formal*) as if sth is natural for you and you have done it many times in the past **what ˈmanner of ...** (*formal* or *literary*) what kind of ...: *What manner of man could do such a terrible thing?*

**man·nered** /ˈmænəd; *NAmE* -nərd/ *adj.* **1** (*disapproving*) (of behaviour, art, writing, etc.) trying to impress people by being formal and not natural SYN **affected** ⇨ WORDFINDER NOTE at STORY **2** -**mannered** (in compounds) having the type of manners mentioned: *a bad-mannered child* ⇨ see also ILL-MANNERED, MILD-MANNERED, WELL MANNERED

**man·ner·ism** /ˈmænərɪzəm/ *noun* **1** [C] a particular habit or way of speaking or behaving that sb has but is not aware of: *nervous/odd/irritating mannerisms* **2** [U] too much use of a particular style in painting or writing **3 Mannerism** [U] a style in 16th century Italian art that did not show things in a natural way but made them look strange or out of their usual shape

**man·ner·ist** /ˈmænərɪst/ (*usually* **Man·ner·ist**) *adj.* (of painting or writing) in the style of Mannerism

**man·ni·kin** = MANIKIN

**man·nish** /ˈmænɪʃ/ *adj.* (*usually disapproving*) (of a woman or of sth belonging to a woman) having qualities that are thought of as typical of or suitable for a man

**mano a mano** /ˌmɑːnəʊ ɑː ˈmɑːnəʊ/ *adv.* (*especially NAmE*, from Spanish, *informal*) with two people facing each other directly in order to decide an argument or a competition: *It's time to settle this mano a mano.*

**mano-a-mano** /ˌmɑːnəʊ ɑː ˈmɑːnəʊ/ *adj.*, *noun* (*especially NAmE*, from Spanish, *informal*)
■ *adj.* with two people facing each other directly in order to decide an argument or a competition: *a mano-a-mano battle*
■ *noun* (*pl.* **mano-a-manos**) a fight or contest, especially one between two people

**man·oeuv·rable** (*US* **man·euv·er·able**) /məˈnuːvərəbl/ *adj.* that can easily be moved into different positions: *a highly manoeuvrable vehicle* ▶ **man·oeuv·ra·bil·ity** /məˌnuːvərəˈbɪləti/ (*US* **man·eu·ver·abil·ity**) *noun* [U]

**man·oeuvre** (*US* **man·eu·ver**) /məˈnuːvə(r)/ *noun*, *verb*
■ *noun* **1** [C] a movement performed with care and skill: *a complicated/skilful manoeuvre* ◊ *You will be asked to perform some standard manoeuvres during your driving test.* **2** [C, U] a clever plan, action or movement that is used to give sb an advantage SYN **move**: *diplomatic manoeuvres* ◊ *a complex manoeuvre in a game of chess* **3 manoeuvres**

# manoeuvring

[pl.] military exercises involving a large number of soldiers, ships, etc: **on ~** *The army is on manoeuvres in the desert.*

**IDM** **freedom of/room for ma'noeuvre** the chance to change the way that sth happens and influence decisions that are made

- **verb 1** [I, T] to move or turn with skill or care; to move or turn sth with skill or care: **~ (for sth)** *The yachts manoeuvred for position.* ◇ *There was very little room to manoeuvre.* ◇ **~ sth (+ adv./prep.)** *She manoeuvred the car carefully into the garage.* **2** [I, T] to control or influence a situation in a way that shows skill but is sometimes dishonest: *The new laws have left us little room to manoeuvre* (= not much opportunity to change or influence a situation). ◇ **~ sth + adv./prep.** *She manoeuvred her way to the top of the company.*

**man·oeuv·ring** (*US* **man·eu·ver·ing**) /məˈnuːvərɪŋ/ *noun* [U, C] ways of achieving your aims that are clever, show skill and are often dishonest

**ˌman of ˈletters** *noun* (*pl.* **men of letters**) (*old-fashioned*) a man who is a writer, or who writes about literature

**ˌman-of-ˈwar** *noun* (*pl.* **men-of-war**) a sailing ship used in the past for fighting

**manor** /ˈmænə(r)/ *noun* (*BrE*) **1** (*also* **ˈmanor house**) a large country house surrounded by land that belongs to it **2** an area of land with a manor house on it **3** (*BrE, slang*) an area in which sb works or for which they are responsible, especially officers at a police station

**man·orial** /məˈnɔːriəl/ *adj.* typical of or connected with a manor, especially in the past

**man·power** /ˈmænpaʊə(r)/ *noun* [U] the number of workers needed or available to do a particular job: *a need for trained/skilled manpower* ◇ *a manpower shortage*

**man·qué** /ˈmɒŋkeɪ; NAmE mɑːŋˈkeɪ/ *adj.* (following nouns) (*from French, formal or humorous*) used to describe a person who hoped to follow a particular career but who failed in it or never tried it: *He's really an artist manqué.*

**manse** /mæns/ *noun* the house of a Christian minister, especially in Scotland

**man·ser·vant** /ˈmænsɜːvənt; NAmE -sɜːrv-/ *noun* (*pl.* **men·ser·vants**) (*old-fashioned*) a male servant, especially a man's personal servant ➔ compare MAIDSERVANT

**man·sion** /ˈmænʃn/ *noun* **1** [C] a large, impressive house: *an 18th century country mansion* **2** **Mansions** [pl.] (*BrE*) used in the names of blocks of flats: *2 Moscow Mansions, Cromwell Road*

**ˈman-sized** (*also* **ˈman-size**) *adj.* [only before noun] suitable or large enough for a man: *a man-sized breakfast*

**man·slaugh·ter** /ˈmænslɔːtə(r)/ *noun* [U, C] (*law*) the crime of killing sb illegally but not deliberately ➔ compare CULPABLE HOMICIDE, HOMICIDE, MURDER

**man·splain** /ˈmænspleɪn/ *verb* **~ sth (to sb)** (*informal, disapproving*) (of a man) to explain sth to a woman in a way that shows he thinks he knows and understands more than she does: *I don't really need economics mansplained to me.* ▶ **man·splain·ing** *noun* [U]

**manta** /ˈmæntə/ (*also* **ˌmanta ˈray**) *noun* a large fish that lives in tropical seas and swims by moving two parts like large flat wings

**man·tel·piece** (*also* **man·tle·piece**) /ˈmæntlpiːs/ (*also* **man·tel**, **man·tle** /ˈmæntl/ (*especially in NAmE*)) *noun* a shelf above a FIREPLACE

**man·tis** /ˈmæntɪs/ *noun* (*pl.* **man·tis** or **man·tises**) = PRAYING MANTIS

**man·tle** /ˈmæntl/ *noun, verb*

- *noun* **1** [sing.] **the ~ of sb/sth** (*literary*) the role and responsibilities of an important person or job, especially when they are passed on from one person to another: *The vice-president must now take on the mantle of supreme power.* **2** [C] (*literary*) a layer of sth that covers a surface: *hills with a mantle of snow* **3** [C] a loose piece of clothing without SLEEVES (= parts covering the arms), worn over other clothes, especially in the past **SYN** **cloak**, **covering** **4** [sing.]

(*geology*) the part of the earth below the CRUST and surrounding the core **5** [C] = MANTELPIECE

- *verb* **~ sth** (*literary*) to cover the surface of sth

**man·tra** /ˈmæntrə; NAmE ˈmɑː-, ˈmæn-/ *noun* **1** a word, phrase or sound that is repeated again and again, especially during prayer or MEDITATION: *a Buddhist mantra* **2** a statement or SLOGAN that is often repeated: *the environmental mantra of 'reduce, reuse, recycle'*

**man·trap** /ˈmæntræp/ *noun* **1** a piece of equipment used in the past for catching people, especially people who tried to steal things from sb's land **2** any electronic device that is used to catch people who are doing sth dishonest

**man·ual** /ˈmænjuəl/ *adj., noun*

- *adj.* **1** (of work, etc.) involving using the hands or physical strength: *manual labour/jobs/skills* ◇ *manual and non-manual workers* ➔ WORDFINDER NOTE at WORK **2** operated or controlled by hand rather than by machine or using electricity, etc: *a manual gearbox* ◇ *My camera has manual and automatic functions.* **3** connected with using the hands: *manual dexterity* ▶ **manu·al·ly** /-əli/ *adv.*: *manually operated*
- *noun* **1** a book that tells you how to do or operate sth, especially one that comes with a machine, etc. when you buy it: *a computer/car/instruction manual* ➔ compare HANDBOOK **2** (*BrE*) (*NAmE, informal* **ˈstick shift**) a vehicle with a system of GEARS operated by the driver using a GEAR LEVER ➔ compare AUTOMATIC (2)

**IDM** **on ˈmanual** not being operated by a machine, etc. but by hand: *Leave the controls on manual.*

**manu·fac·ture** /ˌmænjuˈfæktʃə(r)/ *verb, noun*

- *verb* **1** **~ sth** to make goods in large quantities, using machines **SYN** **mass-produce**: *manufactured goods* **2** **~ sth** to invent a story, an excuse, etc: *a news story manufactured by an unscrupulous journalist* **3** **~ sth** (*specialist*) to produce a substance: *Vitamins cannot be manufactured by our bodies.*
- *noun* **1** [U] the process of producing goods in large quantities **SYN** **mass production**: *the manufacture of cars* **2** **manufactures** [pl.] (*specialist*) manufactured goods: *a major importer of cotton manufactures*

**manu·fac·tur·er** /ˌmænjuˈfæktʃərə(r)/ *noun* a person or company that produces goods in large quantities **SYN** **maker**: *a car/computer manufacturer* ◇ *Always follow the manufacturer's instructions.* ◇ *Faulty goods should be returned to the manufacturers.*

**manu·fac·tur·ing** /ˌmænjuˈfæktʃərɪŋ/ *noun* [U] the business or industry of producing goods in large quantities in factories, etc: *Many jobs in manufacturing were lost during the recession.* ◇ *manufacturing industry*

**ma·nure** /məˈnjʊə(r); NAmE -ˈnʊr/ *noun, verb*

- *noun* [U] the waste matter from animals that is spread over or mixed with the soil to help plants and crops grow **SYN** **dung**
- *verb* **~ sth** to put manure on or in soil to help plants grow

**manu·script** /ˈmænjuskrɪpt/ *noun* (*abbr.* **MS**) **1** a copy of a book, piece of music, etc. before it has been printed: *an unpublished/original manuscript* ◇ *in ~ I read her poems in manuscript.* **2** a very old book or document that was written by hand before printing was invented: *medieval illuminated manuscripts*

**ˈmanuscript paper** *noun* [U] paper printed with STAVES for writing music on

**Manx** /mæŋks/ *adj.* of or connected with the Isle of Man, its people or the language once spoken there

**many** /ˈmeni/ *det., pron.* **1** used with plural nouns and verbs, especially in negative sentences or in more formal English, to mean 'a large number of'. Also used in questions to ask about the size of a number, and with 'as', 'so' and 'too': *We don't have very many copies left.* ◇ *You can't have one each. We haven't got many.* ◇ *Many people feel that the law should be changed.* ◇ *Many of those present disagreed.* ◇ *How many children do you have?* ◇ *There are too many mistakes in this essay.* ◇ *He made ten mistakes in as many* (= ten) *lines.* ◇ *New drivers have twice as many accidents as experienced drivers.* ◇ *Don't take so many.* ◇ *I've known her for a great many* (= very many) *years.* ◇ *Even if one person is hurt that is one too many.* ◇ *It was one of my many mistakes.* ◇ *a*

**many-headed monster 2 the many** used with a plural verb to mean 'most people': *a government which improves conditions for the many* **3 many a** *(formal)* used with a singular noun and verb to mean 'a large number of': *Many a good man has been destroyed by drink.*

**IDM as many as …** used to show surprise that the number of people or things involved is so large: *There were as many as 200 people at the lecture.* **have had one too many** *(informal)* to be slightly drunk **many's the …** *(formal)* used to show that sth happens often: *Many's the time I heard her use those words.*

---

▼ **GRAMMAR POINT**

**many / a lot (of) / lots (of)**

- **Many** is used only with countable nuns. It is used mainly in questions and negative sentences: *Do you go to many concerts? ◊ How many people came to the meeting? ◊ I don't go to many concerts.* Although it is not common in statements, it is used after **so**, **as** and **too**: *You made too many mistakes.*
- In statements **a lot (of)** or **lots (of)** *(informal)* are much more common: *I go to a lot of concerts. ◊ How many shows did you see?' 'Lots!'* However, they are not used with measurements of time or distance: *I stayed in England for many / quite a few / ten weeks. ◊ I stayed in England a lot of weeks.* When **a lot (of) / lots (of)** means 'many', it takes a plural verb: *Lots of people like Italian food.* You can also use **plenty of** *(informal)*: *Plenty of stores stay open late.* These phrases can also be used in questions and negative sentences.
- **A lot of / lots of** is still felt to be informal, especially in *BrE*, so in formal writing it is better to use **many** or **a large number of** in statements.

⊃ note at MUCH

---

**man·yatta** /mænˈjætə/ *EAfrE* [maˈnata] *noun* (*EAfrE*) (among the MAASAI and some other African peoples) a group of small houses with a fence around them

**Mao·ism** /ˈmaʊɪzəm/ *noun* [U] the ideas of the 20th century Chinese COMMUNIST leader Mao Zedong ▶ **Mao·ist** /-ɪst/ *noun, adj.*

**Maori** /ˈmaʊri/ *noun* **1** [C] a member of a race of people who were the original people living in New Zealand **2** [U] the language of the Maori people ▶ **Maori** *adj.*

**map** ❶ A1 /mæp/ *noun, verb*

■ *noun* **1** A1 a drawing or plan of the earth's surface or part of it, showing countries, towns, rivers, etc.: *a map of France ◊ a street map of Miami ◊ a map of the area/region/world/route ◊ to read a/the map* (= understand the information on a map) ◊ *large-scale maps ◊ a / the ~ Can you find Black Hill on the map? ◊ I'll draw you a map of how to get to my house. ◊ Click here to download a map. ◊ an interactive map* ⊃ WORDFINDER NOTE at EARTH ⊃ see also ROAD MAP

| WORDFINDER compass, globe, GPS, grid, key, latitude, navigate, reference, scale |

**2** a diagram to show the positions of things over an area: *an electron density map* ⊃ see also HEAT MAP, MIND MAP **IDM all over the map** (*NAmE*, *informal*) lacking organization; in a confused state **off the map** (of a place) very far away or remote: *Although the town was completely off the map, I was glad that I made the effort to visit.* **put sb / sth on the map** to make sb/sth famous or important: *This chicken dish put the chef firmly on the map. ◊ The exhibition has helped put the city on the map.* ⊃ more at WIPE *v.*

■ *verb* (-pp-) **1** B2 ~ **sth** to make a map of an area **SYN** **chart**: *an unexplored region that has not yet been mapped* **2 ~ sth** to discover or give information about sth, especially the way it is arranged or organized: *It is now possible to map the different functions of the brain.* ▶ **map·ping** *noun* [U]: *the mapping of the Indian subcontinent ◊ gene mapping*

**PHRV 'map sth on/onto sth** to link a group of qualities, items, etc. with their source, cause, position on a scale, etc.: *Grammar information enables students to map the structure of a foreign language onto their own.* **map**

---

957                                                                                                                       **march**

**sth↔'out** to plan or arrange sth in a careful or detailed way: *He has his career path clearly mapped out.*

**maple** /ˈmeɪpl/ *noun* **1** (*also* **'maple tree**) [C, U] a tall tree with leaves that have five points and turn bright red or yellow in the autumn. Maples grow in northern countries. **2** (*also* **'maple wood**) [U] the wood of the maple tree

**'maple leaf** *noun* **1** [C] the leaf of the maple tree, used as a symbol of Canada **2 the Maple Leaf** [sing.] the flag of Canada

**'maple syrup** *noun* [U] a sweet, sticky sauce made with liquid obtained from some types of maple tree, often eaten with PANCAKES

*maple leaf*

**mar** /mɑː(r)/ *verb* (**-rr-**) **~ sth** to damage sth or make sth less good or successful **SYN** **blight, ruin**: *The game was marred by the behaviour of drunken fans.*

**ma·racas** /məˈrækəz/; *NAmE* -ˈrɑːk-/ *noun* [pl.] a pair of simple musical instruments consisting of hollow balls containing BEADS or beans that are shaken to produce a sound

**mar·as·chino** /ˌmærəˈʃiːnəʊ, -ˈskiː-/ *noun* (*pl.* **-os**) **1** [U, C] a strong, sweet alcoholic drink made from black CHERRIES **2** (*also* **maraschino 'cherry**) [C] a CHERRY preserved in maraschino used to decorate alcoholic drinks

**Ma·ra·thi** /məˈrɑːti, -ˈræti/ *noun* [U] a language spoken in Maharashtra in western India

**mara·thon** ❶ B2 /ˈmærəθən; *NAmE* -θɑːn/ *noun* **1** ❶ B2 a long running race of about 42 kilometres or 26 miles: *the London marathon ◊ to run a marathon ◊ a marathon runner* **2** ❶ C1 an activity or a piece of work that lasts a long time and requires a lot of effort, concentration, etc: *The interview was a real marathon.* **ORIGIN** From the story that in ancient Greece a messenger ran from Marathon to Athens (22 miles) with the news of a victory over the Persians. ▶ **mara·thon** *adj.* [only before noun]: *a marathon journey lasting 56 hours ◊ a marathon legal battle*

**ma·raud·ing** /məˈrɔːdɪŋ/ *adj.* [only before noun] (of people or animals) going around a place in search of things to steal or people to attack: *marauding wolves* ▶ **ma·raud·er** *noun*

**mar·ble** /ˈmɑːbl; *NAmE* ˈmɑːrbl/ *noun* **1** [U] a type of hard stone that is usually white and often has coloured lines in it. It can be POLISHED (= made smooth and shiny by rubbing) and is used in building and for making statues, etc: *a slab/block of marble ◊ a marble floor/sculpture* **2** [C] a small ball of coloured glass that children roll along the ground in a game **3 marbles** [U] a game played with marbles: *Three boys were playing marbles.* **4 marbles** [pl.] (*informal*) a way of referring to sb's intelligence or mental ability: *He's losing his marbles* (= he's not behaving in a sensible way).

**mar·bled** /ˈmɑːbld; *NAmE* ˈmɑːrb-/ *adj.* having the colours and/or patterns of marble: *marbled wallpaper*

**marb·ling** /ˈmɑːblɪŋ; *NAmE* ˈmɑːrb-/ *noun* [U] the method of decorating sth with a pattern that looks like marble

**March** ❶ A1 /mɑːtʃ; *NAmE* mɑːrtʃ/ *noun* [U, C] (*abbr.* **Mar.**) the 3rd month of the year, between February and April **HELP** To see how **March** is used, look at the examples at **April**. **IDM** see MAD

**march** ❶+ C1 /mɑːtʃ; *NAmE* mɑːrtʃ/ *verb, noun*

■ *verb* **1** ❶+ C1 [I] to walk with stiff regular steps like a soldier: *Quick march!* (= the order to start marching) *◊ + adv. / prep. Soldiers were marching up and down outside the government buildings. ◊ + noun They marched 20 miles to reach the capital.* **2** ❶+ B2 [I] + adv. / prep. to walk somewhere quickly in a determined way: *She marched over to me and demanded an apology.* **3** ❶+ C1 [I] to walk through the streets in a large group in order to protest about sth **SYN** **demonstrate** ⊃ WORDFINDER NOTE at PROTEST **4** ❶+ C1 [T] **~ sb + adv. / prep.** to force sb to walk somewhere with you: *The guards marched the prisoner away.*

**IDM get your 'marching orders** (*informal*) to be ordered to leave a place, a job, etc. **give sb their 'marching orders**

---

| u **actual** | aɪ **my** | aʊ **now** | eɪ **say** | əʊ **go** | ɔɪ **boy** | ɪə **near** | eə **hair** | ʊə **pure** |

# marcher

(*informal*) to order sb to leave a place, their job, etc. **march to (the beat of a different ˈdrummer/ˈdrum | march to a different ˈbeat/ˈtune** to behave in a different way from other people; to have different attitudes or ideas: *She was a gifted and original artist who marched to a different drummer.*

**PHRV** ˌmarch ˈon to move on or pass quickly: *Time marches on and we still have not made a decision.* ˈmarch on … to march to a place to protest about sth or to attack it: *Several thousand people marched on City Hall.*

- **noun 1** [C] an organized walk by many people from one place to another, in order to protest about sth, or to express their opinions: *protest marches* ◊ *to go on a march* ⊃ compare DEMONSTRATION **2** [C] an act of marching; a journey made by marching: *The army began their long march to the coast.* ⊃ see also FORCED MARCH **3** [sing.] **the ~ of sth** the steady development or forward movement of sth: *the march of progress/technology/time* **4** [C] a piece of music written for marching to: *a funeral march*

**IDM** **on the ˈmarch** marching somewhere: *The enemy are on the march.* ⊃ more at STEAL *v.*

**march·er** /ˈmɑːtʃə(r)/ *NAmE* ˈmɑːrtʃ-/ *noun* a person who is taking part in a march as a protest **SYN** **demonstrator**

**ˈmarching band** *noun* [C + sing./pl. v.] a group of musicians who play while they are marching

**ˈmarching season** *noun* (in Northern Ireland) the time in July and August when PROTESTANT groups MARCH (= walk) through the streets in memory of victories over CATHOLICS in the 17th century

**mar·chion·ess** /ˌmɑːʃəˈnes/ *NAmE* ˌmɑːrʃ-/ *noun* **1** a woman who has the rank of a MARQUESS **2** the wife of a MARQUESS ⊃ compare MARQUISE

**Mardi Gras** /ˌmɑːdi ˈɡrɑː/ *NAmE* ˈmɑːrdi ɡrɑː/ *noun* [U] (*from French*) the day before the beginning of Lent, celebrated as a holiday in some countries, with music and dancing in the streets ⊃ compare SHROVE TUESDAY

**mare** /meə(r)/ *NAmE* mer/ *noun* **1** a female horse or DONKEY ⊃ compare FILLY, STALLION **2** (*BrE, informal*) = NIGHTMARE (2): *I had a complete mare booking tickets for the concert.*

**IDM** **a ˈmare's nest 1** a discovery that seems interesting but is found to have no value **2** a very complicated situation

**marg** /mɑːɡ/ *NAmE* mɑːrɡ/ *noun* (*IndE*) a road, street or path: *Mahatma Gandhi Marg* ◊ (*figurative*) *The Bhakti marg* (*the path of devotion*) *teaches followers to forget the physical self in pursuit of the Lord.*

**mar·gar·ine** /ˌmɑːdʒəˈriːn/ *NAmE* ˈmɑːrdʒərən/ (*also BrE, informal* **marge** /mɑːdʒ/ *NAmE* mɑːrdʒ/) *noun* [U] a yellow substance like butter made from animal or vegetable fats, used in cooking or spread on bread, etc.

**mar·ga·rita** /ˌmɑːɡəˈriːtə/ *NAmE* ˌmɑːrɡ-/ *noun* an alcoholic drink made by mixing fruit juice with TEQUILA

**mar·gin** /ˈmɑːdʒɪn/ *NAmE* ˈmɑːrdʒ-/ *noun* [C] **1** the empty space at the side of a written or printed page: *the left-hand/right-hand margin* ◊ *a narrow/wide margin* ◊ *in the ~ notes scribbled in the margin* **2** [usually sing.] the amount of time, or number of votes, etc. by which sb wins sth: *He won by a narrow margin.* ◊ *by a ~ of sth She beat the other runners by a margin of ten seconds.* **3** (*business*) = PROFIT MARGIN: *What are your average operating margins?* ◊ *a gross margin of 45 per cent* **4** [usually sing.] an extra amount of sth such as time, space, money, etc. that you include in order to make sure that sth is successful: *a safety margin* ◊ *The narrow gateway left me little margin for error as I reversed the car.* ⊃ see also MARGIN OF ERROR **5** (*formal*) the extreme edge or limit of a place: *the eastern margin of the Indian Ocean* **6** [usually pl.] the part not included in the main part of a group or situation **SYN** **fringe**: **on the margins of sth** *people living on the margins of society* **7** (*AustralE, NZE*) an amount that is added to a basic wage, paid for special skill or responsibility

**mar·gin·al** /ˈmɑːdʒɪnl/ *NAmE* ˈmɑːrdʒ-/ *adj., noun*
- *adj.* **1** small and not important **SYN** **slight**: *a marginal improvement in weather conditions* ◊ *The story will only be of marginal interest to our readers.* **2** not part of a main or important group or situation: *marginal groups in society* **3** (*especially BrE, politics*) won or lost by a very small number of votes and therefore very important or interesting as evidence of public opinion: *a marginal seat/constituency* **4** [only before noun] written in the margin of a page: *marginal notes/comments* **5** (of land) that cannot produce enough good crops to make a profit
- *noun* (*BrE*) a seat in a parliament, on a local council, etc. that was won by a very small number of votes: *a Labour marginal*

**mar·gi·na·lia** /ˌmɑːdʒɪˈneɪliə/ *NAmE* ˌmɑːrdʒ-/ *noun* [pl.] **1** notes written in the margins of a book, etc. **2** facts or details that are not very important

**mar·gin·al·ize** (*BrE also* **-ise**) /ˈmɑːdʒɪnəlaɪz/ *NAmE* ˈmɑːrdʒ-/ *verb* ~sb to make sb feel as if they are not important and cannot influence decisions or events; to put sb in a position in which they have no power ⊃ WORD-FINDER NOTE at EQUAL ▸ **mar·gin·al·iza·tion, -isa·tion** /ˌmɑːdʒɪnəlaɪˈzeɪʃn/ *NAmE* ˌmɑːrdʒɪnələˈz-/ *noun* [U]: *the marginalization of the elderly*

**mar·gin·al·ly** /ˈmɑːdʒɪnəli/ *NAmE* ˈmɑːrdʒ-/ *adv.* very slightly; not very much: *They now cost marginally more than they did last year.*

**margin of ˈerror** *noun* [usually sing.] an amount that you allow when you calculate sth, for the possibility that a number is not completely accurate: *The survey has a margin of error of 2.5 per cent.*

**mar·guer·ite** /ˌmɑːɡəˈriːt/ *NAmE* ˌmɑːrɡ-/ *noun* a small white garden flower with a yellow centre

**mari·achi** /ˌmæriˈɑːtʃi/ *NAmE* ˌmɑːr-/ *noun* [C, U] a musician who plays traditional Mexican music, usually as part of a small group that travels from place to place; the type of music played by these musicians: *a mariachi band*

**Marie Celeste** /ˌmæri səˈlest, ˌmɑːr-/ *noun* [sing.] = MARY CELESTE

**mari·gold** /ˈmærɪɡəʊld/ *noun* an orange or yellow garden flower. There are several types of marigold.

**ma·ri·juana** (*also* **ma·ri·huana**) /ˌmærəˈwɑːnə/ (*also informal* **pot**) *noun* [U] a drug (illegal in many countries) made from the dried leaves and flowers of the HEMP plant, which gives the person smoking it a feeling of being relaxed **SYN** **cannabis**

**ma·rimba** /məˈrɪmbə/ *noun* a musical instrument like a XYLOPHONE

**mar·ina** /məˈriːnə/ *noun* a specially designed HARBOUR for small boats and YACHTS

**mar·in·ade** /ˌmærɪˈneɪd/ *noun* [C, U] a mixture of oil, wine, SPICES, etc., in which meat, fish or other food is left before it is cooked in order to make it softer or to give it a particular taste

**marin·ate** /ˈmærɪneɪt/ (*also* **mar·in·ade**) *verb* [T, I] ~ (sth) if you **marinate** food or it **marinates**, you leave it in a marinade before cooking it

**mar·ine** /məˈriːn/ *adj., noun*
- *adj.* [only before noun] **1** connected with the sea and the creatures and plants that live there: *marine life* ◊ *a marine biologist* (= a scientist who studies life in the sea) **2** connected with ships or trade at sea
- *noun* a soldier who is trained to serve on land or at sea, especially one in the US Marine Corps or the British Royal Marines

**mari·ner** /ˈmærɪnə(r)/ *noun* (*old-fashioned* or *literary*) a sailor

**mar·io·nette** /ˌmæriəˈnet/ *noun* a PUPPET whose arms, legs and head are moved by strings

**mari·tal** /ˈmærɪtl/ *adj.* [only before noun] connected with marriage or with the relationship between a married couple: *marital difficulties/breakdown*

**marital ˈstatus** *noun* [U] (*formal*) (used especially on official forms) the fact of whether you are single, married, divorced, etc: *questions about age, sex and marital status*

**mari·time** /ˈmærɪtaɪm/ *adj.* [only before noun] **1** connected with the sea or ships: *a maritime museum* **2** (*formal*) near the sea: *maritime Antarctica*

**mar·joram** /ˈmɑːdʒərəm; NAmE ˈmɑːrdʒ-/ noun [U] a plant with leaves that smell sweet and are used in cooking as a HERB, often when dried

**mark** ⓘ A2 /mɑːk; NAmE mɑːrk/ verb, noun

■ verb
- **WRITE/DRAW 1** A2 [T] to write or draw a symbol, line, etc. on sth in order to give information about it: *~sth The flood level is marked by a white line on the wall.* ◊ *~A with B Items marked with an asterisk can be omitted.* ◊ *~B on A Prices are marked on the goods.* ◊ *~sb/sth + adj. The teacher marked her absent* (= made a mark by her name to show that she was absent). ◊ *Why have you marked this wrong?* ◊ *Do not open any mail marked 'Confidential'.*
- **GIVE MARK/GRADE 2** B1 [T, I] ~(sth) (*especially BrE*) to give marks to students' work: *I hate marking exam papers.* ◊ *I spend at least six hours a week marking.* ⊃ compare GRADE
- **DAMAGE 3** B2 [T, I] ~(sth) to make a mark on sth in a way that damages it or makes it look less good; to become damaged or be made to look less good in this way: *A large purple scar marked his cheek.* ◊ *The surfaces are made from a material that doesn't mark.*
- **SHOW POSITION 4** B2 [T] to show the position of sth **SYN** indicate: *~sth Yellow arrows mark the way.* ◊ *The cross marks the spot where the body was found.* ◊ *be marked in/with sth The route has been marked in red.*
- **CELEBRATE 5** [T] ~sth to celebrate or officially remember an event that you consider to be important: *a ceremony to mark the 50th anniversary of the end of the war* ◊ *The event marked a milestone in the hotel's success story.*
- **SHOW CHANGE 6** [T] ~sth to be a sign that sth new is going to happen: *This agreement marks the start of a new phase in international relations.* ◊ *This speech may mark a change in government policy.*
- **GIVE PARTICULAR QUALITY 7** [T, usually passive] (*formal*) to give sb/sth a particular quality or character **SYN** characterize: (be) marked by sth *a life marked by suffering* ◊ be marked as sth *He was marked as an enemy of the poor.*
- **PAY ATTENTION 8** [T] (*old-fashioned*) used to tell sb to pay careful attention to sth: ~sth *There'll be trouble over this, mark my words.* ◊ *~what, how, etc… You mark what I say, John.*
- **IN SPORT 9** [T] ~sb (*BrE*) (in a team game) to stay close to an opponent in order to prevent them from getting the ball: *Hughes was marking Taylor.* ◊ *Our defence had him closely marked.* ⊃ see also MARKING

IDM **mark time 1** to pass the time while you wait for sth more interesting: *I'm just marking time in this job—I'm hoping to get into journalism.* **2** (of soldiers) to make MARCHING movements without moving forwards **mark ˈyou** (*especially BrE, old-fashioned, informal*) used to remind sb of sth they should consider in a particular case: *She hasn't had much success yet. Mark you, she tries hard.*

PHRV **mark sb ˈdown** (*BrE*) to reduce the mark given to sb in an exam, etc: *She was marked down because of poor grammar.* **mark sb ˈdown as sth** (*especially BrE*) to recognize sb as a particular type: *I hadn't got him marked down as a liberal.* **mark sth↔ˈdown 1** to reduce the price of sth: *All goods have been marked down by 15 per cent.* OPP **mark up** ⊃ related noun MARKDOWN **2** to make a note of sth for future use or action: *The factory is already marked down for demolition.* **mark sth↔ˈoff (from sb/sth)** to make sb/sth seem different from other people or things: *Each of London's districts had a distinct character that marked it off from its neighbours.* **mark sth↔ˈoff 1** to separate sth by marking a line between it and sth else: *The playing area was marked off with a white line.* **2** to put a mark by or through sth written or printed to show that it has been dealt with: *He marked off their names on the list.* **mark sb ˈout as/for sth** to make people recognize sb as special in some way: *She was marked out for early promotion.* **mark sth↔ˈout** to draw lines to show the edges of sth: *They marked out a tennis court on the lawn.* **mark sth↔ˈup 1** to increase the price of sth: *Share prices were marked up as soon as trading started.* OPP **mark down** ⊃ related noun MARKUP **2** (*specialist*) to mark or correct a text, etc., for example for printing: *to mark up a manuscript*

■ noun
- **SYMBOL 1** A2 a written or printed symbol that is used as a sign of sth, for example the quality of sth or who made or owns it: *punctuation marks* ◊ *Any piece of silver bearing his mark is extremely valuable.* ◊ *I put a mark in the margin to remind me to check the figure.* ⊃ see also EXCLAMATION MARK, PUNCTUATION MARK, QUESTION MARK, QUOTATION MARKS, STRESS MARK, TRADEMARK
- **STANDARD/GRADE 2** B1 (*especially BrE*) a number or letter that is given to show the standard of sb's work or performance or is given to sb for answering sth correctly: *to get a good/poor mark in English* ◊ *to give sb a high/low mark* ◊ *What's the pass mark* (= the mark you need in order to pass)? ⊃ see also BLACK MARK, GRADE noun ⊃ WORDFINDER NOTE at EXAM **3** B1 (*especially BrE*) a point given for a correct answer in an exam or competition: *You get two marks for each correct answer.* ◊ *You will lose marks for bad grammar.* ◊ *I got full marks* (= all the possible points) *in the spelling test.* ◊ (*ironic*) *'You're wearing a tie!' 'Full marks for observation.'*
- **SPOT/DIRT 4** B2 a small area of dirt, a spot or a cut on a surface that makes it look less good: *The children left dirty marks all over the kitchen floor.* ◊ *There was a red mark on his arm.* ◊ *a burn/scratch mark* ◊ *Detectives found no marks on the body.* **5** a spot or area of colour on the body of a person or an animal that helps you to recognize them: *a horse with a white mark on its head* ◊ *He was about six feet tall, with no distinguishing marks.* ⊃ SYNONYMS at PATCH ⊃ see also BEAUTY MARK, BIRTHMARK, MARKING
- **SIGN 6** a sign that a quality or feeling exists: *On the day of the funeral businesses remained closed as a mark of respect.* ◊ *Such coolness under pressure is the mark of a champion.*
- **LEVEL 7** a level or point that sth reaches that is thought to be important: *Unemployment has passed the four million mark.* ◊ *She was leading at the half-way mark.* ⊃ see also LOW-WATER MARK
- **MACHINE/VEHICLE 8 Mark** (followed by a number) a particular type or model of a machine or vehicle: *the Mark II engine*
- **IN GAS OVEN 9 Mark** (*BrE*) (followed by a number) a particular level of temperature in a gas oven: *Preheat the oven to gas Mark 6.*
- **FOR SIGNING DOCUMENT 10** a cross made on a document instead of a SIGNATURE by sb who is not able to write their name

▼ SYNONYMS

**mark**
stain • fingerprint • streak • speck • blot • smear • spot

These are all words for a small area of dirt or another substance on a surface.

**mark** a small area of dirt, a spot or a cut on a surface that makes it look less good: *The kids left dirty marks all over the kitchen floor.*

**stain** a dirty mark on sth that is difficult to remove, especially one made by a liquid: *blood stains*

**fingerprint** a mark on a surface made by the pattern of lines on the end of a person's finger, often used by the police to identify criminals: *Her fingerprints were all over the gun.*

**streak** a long, thin mark or line that is a different colour from the surface it is on: *She had streaks of grey in her hair.*

**speck** a very small mark, spot or piece of a substance on sth: *There isn't a speck of dust anywhere in the house.*

**blot** a spot or dirty mark left on sth by a substance such as ink or paint being dropped on a surface

**smear** a mark made by sth such as oil or paint being spread or rubbed on a surface

**spot** a small dirty mark on sth: *There were grease spots all over the walls.*

PATTERNS
- a streak/speck/blot/smear/spot of sth
- a greasy mark/stain/smear
- an ink mark/stain/blot/spot
- a grease mark/stain/spot
- to leave a mark/stain/fingerprint/streak/speck/blot/smear

---

Ⓞ Oxford Phrasal Academic Lexicon (OPAL) written and spoken word lists  |  Ⓦ OPAL written word list  |  Ⓢ OPAL spoken word list

# markdown

• **TARGET** **11** (*formal*) a target: *Of the blows delivered, barely half found their mark.* ◊ *to hit/miss the mark*

**IDM** ▶ **be close to/near the ˈmark** to be fairly accurate in a guess, statement, etc. **be off the ˈmark** not to be accurate in a guess, statement, etc: *No, you're way off the mark.* **be on the ˈmark** to be accurate or correct: *That estimate was right on the mark.* **get off the ˈmark** to start scoring in a game or sport: *Stewart got off the mark with a four.* **hit/miss the ˈmark** to succeed/fail in achieving or guessing sth: *He blushed furiously and Robyn knew she had hit the mark.* **leave your/its/a ˈmark (on sth/sb)** to have an effect on sth/sb, especially a bad one, that lasts for a long time: *Such a traumatic experience was bound to leave its mark on the children.* **make your/a ˈmark (on sth)** to become famous and successful in a particular area **not be/feel up to the ˈmark** (*BrE*, *old-fashioned*) not to feel as well or lively as usual **on your ˌmarks, get ˈset, ˈgo!** used to tell runners in a race to get ready and then to start **quick/slow off the ˈmark** fast/slow in reacting to a situation **up to the ˈmark** (*BrE*) (*NAmE* **up to ˈsnuff**) as good as it/they should be **SYN** **up to scratch**: *Your work isn't really up to the mark.* ⊃ more at OVERSTEP, SHORT *adv.*, TOE *v.*, WIDE *adj.*

**mark·down** /ˈmɑːkdaʊn; *NAmE* ˈmɑːrk-/ *noun* [usually sing.] a reduction in price

**marked** /mɑːkt; *NAmE* mɑːrkt/ *adj.* **1** easy to see **SYN** **noticeable, distinct**: *a marked difference/improvement* ◊ *a marked increase in profits* ◊ *She is quiet and studious,* **in marked contrast** *to her sister.* **2** (*linguistics*) (of a word or form of a word) showing a particular feature or style, such as being formal or informal **OPP** **unmarked** ▶ **mark·ed·ly** /ˈmɑːkɪdli; *NAmE* ˈmɑːrk-/ *adv.*: *Her background is markedly different from her husband's.* ◊ *This year's sales have risen markedly.*

**IDM** **a marked ˈman/ˈwoman** a person who is in danger because their enemies want to harm them

**mark·er** ℹ️+ **B2** /ˈmɑːkə(r); *NAmE* ˈmɑːrk-/ *noun* **1** ℹ️+ **B2** [C] an object or a sign that shows the position of sth: *a boundary marker* ◊ *He placed a marker where the ball had landed.* **2** ℹ️+ **B2** [sing.] **a ~ (of/for sth)** a sign that sth exists or that shows what it is like: *Price is not always an accurate marker of quality.* **3** (*BrE also* **ˈmarker pen**) a pen with a thick FELT tip **4** (*BrE*) (*NAmE* **grader**) a person who marks students' work or exam papers **5** (*BrE*) (in team games, especially football (soccer)) a player who stays close to a player on the other team in order to stop them getting the ball

**IDM** **lay/put/set down a marker (for sth)** to do sth that sets a standard for your competitors or shows what you intend to do or achieve in the future: *The reigning champions laid down a marker with a 36–0 defeat of their opponents.*

**mar·ket** 🅾️ **A1** /ˈmɑːkɪt; *NAmE* ˈmɑːrk-/ *noun, verb*

■ *noun* **1** **A1** [C] an occasion when people buy and sell goods; the open area or building where they meet to do this: *a fruit/flower/fish market* ◊ *an antiques market* ◊ *an indoor/a street market* ◊ *market stalls/traders* ◊ *at the ~ We buy our fruit and vegetables at the market.* ◊ *Thursday is* **market day**. ◊ *a* **market town** (= a town in Britain where a regular market is or was held) ◊ *see also* FARMERS' MARKET, FLEA MARKET **2** ℹ️ **B1** [sing.] business or trade, or the amount of trade in a particular type of goods: *the world market in coffee* ◊ *They have increased their* **share of the market** *by 10 per cent.* ◊ *The firm will expand its size to claim more* **market share**. ◊ *the property/housing/job market* (= the number and type of houses, jobs, etc. that are available) ◊ *They have* **cornered the market in** *sportswear* (= sell the most). ◊ *New companies have* **entered the market**. ◊ *The big players still* **dominate the market**. ⊃ WORDFINDER NOTE *at* TRADE ⊃ *see also* LABOUR MARKET **3** ℹ️ **B1** [C] a particular area, country or section of the population that might buy goods: *the Japanese market* ◊ *the global/domestic market* ◊ *The young, health-conscious female consumer is our* **target market**. ⊃ *see also* COMMON MARKET **4** ℹ️ [sing.] **~ (for sth)** the number of people who want to buy sth **SYN** **demand**: *a growing/declining market for second-hand cars* ◊ *There's not much of a market for tourist art on the island.* ⊃ *see also* MARKET RESEARCH, MASS-MARKET **5** ℹ️ **B2** (*often* **the market**) [sing.] people who buy and sell goods in competition with each other: *The market will decide if the TV station has any future.* ◊ *a market-based/market-led/market-driven economy* **6** [C] = STOCK MARKET: *the futures market* ◊ *a market crash* **HELP** There are many other compounds ending in **market**. You will find them at their place in the alphabet.

**IDM** **in the ˈmarket for sth** interested in buying sth: *I'm not in the market for a new car at the moment.* **on the ˈmarket** available for people to buy: *to put your house on the market* ◊ *The house came on the market last year.* ◊ *There are hundreds of different brands on the market.* **on the open ˈmarket** available to buy without any limits **play the ˈmarket** to buy and sell STOCKS and shares in order to make a profit **take sth off the ˈmarket/ˈshelves** to stop sth from being sold: *The slimming pills were taken off the market.* ⊃ more at BUYER, PRICE *v.*, SELLER

■ *verb* **1** ℹ️ **B1** to advertise a product in a particular way in order to make people want it **SYN** **promote**: *~sth The company utilizes every media tool available to market its products.* ◊ *The drug had been successfully marketed in Germany.* ◊ *~sth as sth It is marketed as a low-alcohol wine.* ◊ *~sth to sb School meals need to be marketed to children in the same way as other food.* ⊃ *see also* MARKETING **2** to offer a product for sale **SYN** **sell**: *Many farmers have taken steps to directly market their meat to consumers.* ◊ *All her products are marketed online on her website.*

**mar·ket·able** /ˈmɑːkɪtəbl; *NAmE* ˈmɑːrk-/ *adj.* easy to sell; attractive to customers or employers: *marketable products/skills/qualifications* ▶ **mar·ket·abil·ity** /ˌmɑːkɪtəˈbɪləti; *NAmE* ˌmɑːrk-/ *noun* [U]

**ˌmarket capitaliˈzation** (*also* **ˌmarket ˈcap**) *noun* [U, C] the value of a company that is bought and sold on the STOCK MARKET, calculated by multiplying the total number of shares by the present share price ⊃ *see also* CAPITALIZE (2)

**ˌmarket eˈconomy** *noun* an economic system in which salaries and the prices of goods are determined by SUPPLY AND DEMAND rather than by the state

**mar·ket·eer** /ˌmɑːkɪˈtɪə(r); *NAmE* ˌmɑːrkɪˈtɪr/ *noun* (usually in compounds) a person who is in favour of a particular system of buying and selling: *a free marketeer* (= a person who believes in a FREE MARKET system of trade) ⊃ *see also* BLACK MARKETEER

**ˌmarket ˈforces** *noun* [pl.] the economic factors that affect the price of, demand for and supply of a product or service

**ˌmarket ˈgarden** (*BrE*) (*US* **ˈtruck farm**) *noun* a type of farm where vegetables and fruit are grown for sale ▶ **ˌmarket ˈgardener** *noun* **ˌmarket ˈgardening** *noun* [U]

**mar·ket·ing** 🅾️ **B1** /ˈmɑːkɪtɪŋ; *NAmE* ˈmɑːrk-/ *noun* [U] the activity of presenting, advertising and selling a company's products or services in the best possible way: *a marketing campaign/strategy* ◊ *a marketing manager/director/department* ◊ *digital/internet/online marketing* ◊ *Direct marketing already provides a number of ways to target specific individuals.* ◊ *She works in* **sales and marketing**. ◊ *~ of sth The marketing of produce by village women has brought economic benefits.* ◊ *A printed newsletter is still an excellent marketing tool.* ⊃ WORDFINDER NOTE *at* ADVERTISE ⊃ *see also* DIRECT MARKETING, VIRAL MARKETING ▶ **mar·ket·er** *noun*: *a company that is a developer and marketer of software*

**ˈmarketing mix** *noun* [usually sing.] (*business*) the combination of the features of a product, its price, the way it is advertised and where it is sold, each of which a company can change to persuade people to buy the product

**ˌmarket ˈleader** *noun* **1** the company that sells the largest quantity of a particular kind of product **2** a product that is the most successful of its kind

**mar·ket·place** ℹ️+ **C1** /ˈmɑːkɪtpleɪs; *NAmE* ˈmɑːrk-/ *noun* **1** ℹ️+ **C1** **the marketplace** [sing.] the activity of competing with other companies to buy and sell goods, services, etc: *Companies must be able to survive in the marketplace.* ◊

the education marketplace **2** (also ˌmarket ˈsquare) [C] an open area in a town where a market is held

ˌmarket ˈprice noun the price that people are willing to pay for sth at a particular time

ˌmarket reˈsearch (also ˌmarket ˈresearch) noun [U] the work of collecting information about what people buy and why

ˌmarket ˈshare noun [U, C] (business) the amount that a company sells of its products or services compared with other companies selling the same things: *They claim to have a 40 per cent worldwide market share.* ⊃ compare MINDSHARE

ˌmarket ˈvalue noun [U, C] what sth would be worth if it were sold

**mark·ing** /ˈmɑːkɪŋ; NAmE ˈmɑːrk-/ noun **1** [C, usually pl.] a pattern of colours or marks on animals, birds or wood **2** [C, usually pl.] lines, colours or shapes painted on roads, vehicles, etc: *Road markings indicate where you can stop.* **3** [U] (*especially BrE*) (*NAmE usually* ˈgrad·ing) the activity of checking and correcting the written work or exam papers of students: *She does her marking in the evenings.* **4** [U] (in team games, especially football (soccer)) the practice of staying close to a player on the other team in order to stop them getting the ball

**marks·man** /ˈmɑːksmən; NAmE ˈmɑːrks-/, **marks·woman** /ˈmɑːkswʊmən; NAmE ˈmɑːrks-/ noun (pl. -men /-mən/, -women /-wɪmɪn/) a person who shows skill in accurate shooting

**marks·man·ship** /ˈmɑːksmənʃɪp; NAmE ˈmɑːrks-/ noun [U] skill in shooting

**mark·up** /ˈmɑːkʌp; NAmE ˈmɑːrk-/ noun **1** [usually sing.] an increase in the price of sth based on the difference between the cost of producing it and the price it is sold at: *an average markup of 10 per cent* ◇ *The markup on food in a restaurant is at least 100 per cent.* **2** [U] (*computing*) the symbols used in computer documents that give information about the structure of the document and tell the computer how it is to appear on the computer screen, or how it is to appear when printed: *a markup language* **3** [U, C] the process or result of marking or correcting a text, etc., for example for printing

**marl** /mɑːl; NAmE mɑːrl/ noun **1** [U, C] soil consisting of CLAY and LIME **2** [U] a type of cloth with THREADS in it that are not of an even colour: *blue marl leggings*

**mar·lin** /ˈmɑːlɪn; NAmE ˈmɑːrl-/ noun (pl. mar·lin) a large sea fish with a long, sharp nose, that people catch for sport

**mar·ma·lade** /ˈmɑːməleɪd; NAmE ˈmɑːrm-/ noun [U] JAM made from oranges, lemons, etc., eaten on bread, especially at breakfast ⊃ compare JAM

**Mar·mite™** /ˈmɑːmaɪt; NAmE ˈmɑːrm-/ noun [U] (in the UK) a dark substance with a strong taste made from YEAST and spread on bread, etc. SYN yeast extract: *Marmite sandwiches* ⊃ compare VEGEMITE™ HELP Because it is thought that people either love or hate Marmite, it is used to refer to things that create strong reactions: *a marmite issue* ◇ *They're a marmite band.*

**mar·mo·set** /ˈmɑːməset, -məzet; NAmE ˈmɑːrm-/ noun a small monkey with a long, thick tail that lives in Central and South America

**mar·mot** /ˈmɑːmət; NAmE ˈmɑːrm-/ noun a small European or American animal that lives in holes in the ground

**ma·roon** /məˈruːn/ adj., noun, verb
- adj. dark red-brown in colour
- noun **1** [U] a dark red-brown colour **2** [C] a large FIREWORK that shoots into the air and makes a loud noise, used to attract attention, especially at sea
- verb [usually passive] ~ **sb** to leave sb in a place that they cannot escape from, for example an island SYN strand: *'Lord of the Flies' is a novel about English schoolboys marooned on a desert island.*

**marque** /mɑːk; NAmE mɑːrk/ noun (*formal*) a well-known make of a product, especially a car, that is expensive and fashionable: *the Porsche marque*

**mar·quee** /mɑːˈkiː; NAmE mɑːrˈkiː/ noun, adj.
- noun **1** (*especially BrE*) a large tent used at social events **2** (*NAmE*) a covered entrance to a theatre, hotel, etc., often with a sign on or above it
- adj. [only before noun] (*especially NAmE*) (especially in sport) most important or most popular: *He is one of the marquee names in men's tennis.*

**mar·quess** (also **mar·quis**) /ˈmɑːkwɪs; NAmE ˈmɑːrkwɪs/ noun (in the UK) a NOBLEMAN of high rank between an EARL and a DUKE: *the Marquess of Bath* ⊃ compare MARCHIONESS

**mar·quet·ry** /ˈmɑːkɪtri; NAmE ˈmɑːrk-/ noun [U] patterns or pictures made of small pieces of wood fitted together on the surface of furniture, etc.; the art of making these patterns

**mar·quis** /ˈmɑːkwɪs; NAmE ˈmɑːrkwɪs/ noun **1** (in some European countries but not the UK) a NOBLEMAN of high rank between a COUNT and a DUKE **2** = MARQUESS

**mar·quise** /mɑːˈkiːz; NAmE mɑːrˈk-/ noun **1** the wife of a marquis **2** a woman who has the rank of a marquis ⊃ compare MARCHIONESS

**mar·riage** ᴼᴷ B1 /ˈmærɪdʒ/ noun **1** B1 [C] the legal relationship between two people who are married to each other: *a happy/an unhappy marriage* ◇ *All of her children's marriages ended in divorce.* ◇ *She has two children by a previous marriage.* ◇ *Same-sex marriages are now recognized in many countries.* ⊃ see also ARRANGED MARRIAGE, CIVIL MARRIAGE, EQUAL MARRIAGE, MIXED ⊃ WORDFINDER NOTE at LOVE **2** B1 [U] the state of being married: *They don't believe in marriage.* ◇ *My parents are celebrating 30 years of marriage.* ◇ **before/outside ~** *They strongly disapprove of sex outside marriage.* **3** [C] the ceremony in which two people marry each other: *Their marriage took place in a local church.* HELP **Wedding** is more common in this meaning. ⊃ WORDFINDER NOTE at WEDDING **4** a combination of two things: **~of A and B** *The new collection is a marriage of fashion and technology.* ◇ **~between A and B** *the marriage between a young team and an experienced coach*
IDM ▸ **by ˈmarriage** when sb is related to you **by marriage**, they are married to sb in your family, or you are married to sb in their family ⊃ more at HAND *n.*

**mar·riage·able** /ˈmærɪdʒəbl/ adj. (*old-fashioned*) suitable for marriage: *She had reached marriageable age.*

ˈmarriage broker noun a person who is paid to arrange for two people to meet and marry

ˈmarriage bureau noun (*BrE, old-fashioned*) an organization that introduces people who are looking for sb to marry

ˈmarriage certificate (US ˈmarriage license) noun a legal document that proves two people are married

ˈmarriage eˈquality noun [U] = EQUAL MARRIAGE

ˈmarriage licence (*BrE*) (*NAmE* ˈmarriage license) noun a document that allows two people to get married

ˈmarriage of conˈvenience noun a marriage that is made for practical, financial or political reasons and not because the two people love each other

**mar·ried** ᴼᴷ A1 /ˈmærid/ adj. **1** A1 having a husband or wife: *a married man/woman* ◇ *Is he married?* ◇ *a happily/an unhappily married couple* ◇ **~to sb** *She's married to John.* ◇ *Sam and Chris are getting married on Saturday.* ◇ *How long have you been married?* OPP unmarried **2** B1 [only before noun] connected with marriage: *Are you enjoying married life?* ◇ *Her married name* (= the family name of her husband) *is Jones.* **3 ~ to sth** very involved in sth so that you have no time for other activities or interests: *My brother is married to his job.*

**mar·row** /ˈmærəʊ/ noun **1** [U] = BONE MARROW **2** (*BrE*) [U, C] a large, long vegetable that grows on the ground. Marrows have dark green skin and are white inside. ⊃ VISUAL VOCAB page V5

**marry** ᴼᴷ A2 /ˈmæri/ verb (mar·ries, marry·ing, mar·ried, mar·ried) **1** A2 [T, I] to become the

**WORD FAMILY**
**marry** verb
**marriage** noun
**married** adj.
   (≠ unmarried)

# Mars

husband or wife of sb; to get married to sb: **~(sb)** *She married a German.* ◊ *We* **got married** *in a small village church.* ◊ *He never married.* ◊ *I guess I'm* **not the marrying kind** (= the kind of person who wants to get married). ◊ **+ adj.** *They married young.* HELP It is more common to say: They're getting married next month. than: They're marrying next month. **2** [T] **~ sb** to perform a ceremony in which two people get married: *They were married by the local priest.* **3** [T] **~ sb (to sb)** to find a husband or wife for sb, especially your daughter or son **4** [T] **~ A and/to/with B** *(formal)* to combine two different things, ideas, etc. successfully SYN **unite**: *The music business marries art and commerce.* IDM **marry in ˈhaste (, repent at ˈleisure)** *(saying)* people who marry quickly, without really getting to know each other, may discover later that they have made a mistake **marry ˈmoney** to marry a rich person PHRV **ˌmarry ˈinto sth** to become part of a family or group because you have married sb who belongs to it: *She married into the aristocracy.* **ˌmarry sb↔ˈoff (to sb)** *(disapproving)* to find a husband or wife for sb, especially your daughter or son **ˌmarry sth↔ˈup (with sth)** to combine two things, people or parts of sth successfully

**Mars** /mɑːz; *NAmE* mɑːrz/ *noun* the planet in the SOLAR SYSTEM that is fourth in order of distance from the sun, between the Earth and Jupiter

**Marˈsala** /mɑːˈsɑːlə; *NAmE* mɑːrˈs-/ *noun* [U] a dark, strong, sweet wine from Sicily. It is usually drunk with the sweet course of a meal.

**marsh** /mɑːʃ; *NAmE* mɑːrʃ/ *noun* [C, U] an area of low land that is always soft and wet because there is nowhere for the water to flow away to: *Cows were grazing on the marshes.* ⇒ see also SALT MARSH ▶ **marshy** *adj.*: *marshy ground/land*

**marˈshal** /ˈmɑːʃl; *NAmE* ˈmɑːrʃl/ *noun, verb*
■ *noun* **1** (usually in compounds) an officer of the highest rank in the armed forces of some countries: *Field Marshal Lord Haig* ◊ *Marshal of the Royal Air Force* ⇒ see also AIR CHIEF MARSHAL, AIR MARSHAL, AIR VICE-MARSHAL, FIELD MARSHAL **2** a person responsible for making sure that public events, especially sports events, take place without any problems, and for controlling crowds SYN **steward 3** (in the US) an officer whose job is to put court orders into effect: *a federal marshal* **4** (in some US cities) an officer of high rank in a police or fire department
■ *verb* (-ll-, *US* -l-) *(formal)* **1 ~ sth** to gather together and organize the people, things, ideas, etc. that you need for a particular purpose SYN **muster**: *They have begun marshalling forces to send relief to the hurricane victims.* ◊ *to marshal your arguments/thoughts/facts* **2 ~ sb** to control or organize a large group of people, especially soldiers: *The general marshalled his troops.*

**ˈmarshalling yard** *noun* *(BrE)* a place where railway WAGONS are connected, prepared, etc. to form trains

**ˌMarshal of the ˌRoyal ˈAir Force** *noun* the highest rank of officer in the British AIR FORCE

**marshˈland** /ˈmɑːʃlænd; *NAmE* ˈmɑːrʃ-/ *noun* [U, C] an area of soft, wet land

**marshˈmalˈlow** /ˌmɑːʃˈmæləʊ; *NAmE* ˈmɑːrʃmeləʊ/ *noun* [C, U] a pink or white sweet that feels soft and ELASTIC when you bite it

**marˈsuˈpial** /mɑːˈsuːpiəl; *NAmE* mɑːrˈs-/ *noun* any animal that carries its young in a pocket of skin (called a POUCH) on the mother's stomach. KANGAROOS and KOALAS are marsupials. ⇒ VISUAL VOCAB page V2 ▶ **marˈsuˈpial** *adj.* [only before noun]

**mart** /mɑːt; *NAmE* mɑːrt/ *noun* *(especially NAmE)* a place where things are bought and sold: *a used car mart*

**marˈten** /ˈmɑːtɪn; *NAmE* ˈmɑːrtn/ *noun* a small wild animal with a long body, short legs and sharp teeth. Martens live in forests and eat smaller animals: *a pine marten*

**marˈtial** /ˈmɑːʃl; *NAmE* ˈmɑːrʃl/ *adj.* *(formal)* [only before noun] connected with fighting or war

**ˌmartial ˈart** *noun* [usually pl.] any of the fighting sports that include JUDO and KARATE

**ˌmartial ˈlaw** *noun* [U] a situation where the army of a country controls an area instead of the police during a time of trouble: *to declare/impose/lift martial law* ◊ *under ~ The city remains firmly under martial law.*

**Marˈtian** /ˈmɑːʃn; *NAmE* ˈmɑːrʃn/ *adj., noun*
■ *adj.* *(astronomy)* related to or coming from the planet Mars
■ *noun* an imaginary creature from the planet Mars

**marˈtinet** /ˌmɑːtɪˈnet; *NAmE* ˌmɑːrtnˈet/ *noun* *(formal)* a very strict person who demands that other people obey orders or rules completely

**marˈtini** /mɑːˈtiːni; *NAmE* mɑːrˈt-/ *noun* **1** **Martini™** [U] a type of VERMOUTH **2** [U, C] an alcoholic drink made with GIN and VERMOUTH **3** [C] a glass of martini: *a dry martini*

**ˌMartin ˌLuther ˌKing ˌJr. ˈDay** /ˌmɑːtɪn ˌluːθə ˌkɪŋ ˈdʒuːniə ˌdeɪ; *NAmE* ˌmɑːrtn ˌluːθər ˌkɪŋ ˌdʒuːˈnɪər/ *noun* a national holiday in the US on the third Monday in January to celebrate the birthday of Martin Luther King, Jr., who was active in the struggle to win more rights for African Americans

**marˈtyr** /ˈmɑːtə(r); *NAmE* ˈmɑːrt-/ *noun, verb*
■ *noun* **1** a person who is killed because of their religious or political beliefs: *the early Christian martyrs* ◊ **~ to sth** *a martyr to the cause of freedom* **2** *(usually disapproving)* a person who tries to get sympathy from other people by telling them how much he or she is suffering **3 ~ to sth** *(informal)* a person who suffers very much because of an illness, problem or situation: *She's a martyr to her nerves.*
■ *verb* [usually passive] **~ sb** to kill sb because of their religious or political beliefs

**marˈtyrˈdom** /ˈmɑːtədəm; *NAmE* ˈmɑːrtərd-/ *noun* [U] the painful experiences or death of a martyr

**marˈtyred** /ˈmɑːtəd; *NAmE* ˈmɑːrtərd/ *adj.* [usually before noun] *(disapproving)* showing that you are in pain or are suffering so that people will be kind to you: *She wore a perpetually martyred expression.*

**marˈvel** /ˈmɑːvl; *NAmE* ˈmɑːrvl/ *noun, verb*
■ *noun* **1** a wonderful and surprising person or thing SYN **wonder**: *the marvels of nature/technology* **2** **marvels** [pl.] wonderful results or things that have been achieved SYN **wonders**: *The doctors have done marvels for her.*
■ *verb* [I, T] (-ll-, *US* -l-) **~ (at sth) | ~ that … | + speech** to be very surprised or impressed by sth: *Everyone marvelled at his courage.*

**marˈvelˈlous** *(US* **marˈvelˈous***)* /ˈmɑːvələs; *NAmE* ˈmɑːrv-/ *adj.* extremely good; wonderful SYN **fantastic**, **splendid**: *This will be a marvellous opportunity for her.* ◊ *The weather was marvellous.* ◊ **It is ~ what, how, etc …** *It's marvellous what modern technology can do.* ▶ **marˈvelˈlousˈly** *(US* **marˈvelˈousˈly***)* *adv.*

**Marxˈism** /ˈmɑːksɪzəm; *NAmE* ˈmɑːrk-/ *noun* [U] the political and economic theories of Karl Marx (1818–83) which explain the changes and developments in society as the result of opposition between the social classes ▶ **Marxˈist** /-sɪst/ *noun* **Marxˈist** *adj.*: *Marxist theory/doctrine/ideology*

**ˌMary Celesˈte** /ˌmeəri səˈlest; *NAmE* ˌmer-/ *noun* [sing.] *(also* **Marie Celesˈte***) noun* used to talk about a place where all the people who should be there have disappeared in a mysterious way: *Where is everyone? It's like the Mary Celeste here today.* ORIGIN From the name of the US ship *Mary Celeste*, which in 1872 was found at sea with nobody on board.

**marˈziˈpan** /ˈmɑːzɪpæn; *NAmE* ˈmɑːrzɪ-/ *noun* [U] a sweet substance, sometimes with yellow colour added, made from ALMONDS, sugar and eggs and used to make sweets and to cover cakes

**Masai** = MAASAI

**maˈsala** /məˈsɑːlə/ *noun* [U] **1** a mixture of SPICES used in South Asian cooking ⇒ see also GARAM MASALA **2** a dish made with masala: *chicken masala*

**masˈcara** /mæˈskɑːrə; *NAmE* -ˈskærə/ *noun* [U, C] a type of MAKE-UP that is put on EYELASHES to make them look dark and thick ⇒ WORDFINDER NOTE at MAKE-UP

**masˈcarˈpone** /ˌmæskəˈpəʊneɪ; *NAmE* ˌmɑːskɑːrˈp-/ *noun* [U] *(from Italian)* a type of soft Italian cheese that looks like cream

**masˈcot** /ˈmæskət; *NAmE* -skɑːt/ *noun* a person, animal or thing that people believe will bring them good luck, or that represents an organization or event: *The team's mascot is* *a giant swan.* ◊ *Miraitowa—the official mascot of the Tokyo 2020 Olympics* ⊃ WORDFINDER NOTE at LUCK

**mas·cu·line** /ˈmæskjəlɪn/ *adj., noun*
- *adj.* **1** having the qualities or appearance considered to be typical of men; connected with or like men: *He was handsome and strong, and very masculine.* ◊ *That suit makes her look very masculine.* ⊃ compare FEMININE, MALE **2** (*grammar*) belonging to a class of words that refer to male people or animals and often have a special form: *'He' and 'him' are masculine pronouns.* **3** (*grammar*) (in some languages) belonging to a class of nouns, pronouns or adjectives that have masculine GENDER, not FEMININE or NEUTER: *The French word for 'sun' is masculine.*
- *noun* **1** the masculine [sing.] the masculine GENDER (= form of nouns, adjectives and pronouns) **2** [C] a masculine word or word form ⊃ compare FEMININE, NEUTER

**mas·cu·lin·i·ty** /ˌmæskjəˈlɪnəti/ *noun* [U] the fact of being a man; the qualities that are considered to be typical of men: *He felt it was a threat to his masculinity.*

**mas·cu·lin·ize** (*BrE also* **-ise**) /ˈmæskjəlɪnaɪz/ *verb* ~ sth/sb (*formal*) to make sth or sb more like a man

**mash** /mæʃ/ *noun, verb*
- *noun* **1** (*especially BrE*) = MASHED POTATO **2** [U] grain cooked in water until soft, used to feed farm animals **3** [U] a mixture of MALT grains and hot water, used for making beer, etc. **4** [sing.] **a ~ (of sth)** any food that has been pressed hard so that it becomes a soft mass: *The soup was a mash of grain and vegetables.* ⊃ see also MISHMASH
- *verb* ~ sth (up) to make food into a soft mass: *Mash the fruit up with a fork.* ▶ **mashed** *adj.*: *mashed banana*

**mashed po·ta·to** *noun* (*also* **mash**) [U] (*both especially BrE*) (*also* **mashed po·ta·toes** [pl.] *BrE and NAmE*) potatoes that have been boiled and made into a soft mass, often mixed with butter and milk

**mash-up** *noun* a combination of elements from different sources used to create a new song, video, computer file, program, etc: *a video mash-up* ◊ *Most mash-ups are simple remixes that DJs have been doing for decades.* ◊ *It's a web service that allows people to create mash-ups of movies, combining scenes from various films.*

**mask** /mɑːsk; *NAmE* mæsk/ *noun, verb*
- *noun* **1** something that you wear over your face to hide it, or to frighten or entertain other people: *The robbers wore stocking masks.* ◊ *The kids were all wearing animal masks.* **2** something that you wear over part or all of your face in order to protect it: *a surgical/gas mask* ◊ *a fencing mask* ⊃ see also GAS MASK, OXYGEN MASK **3** a thick cream made of various substances that you put on your face and neck in order to improve the quality of your skin: *a face mask* **4** [usually sing.] a manner or an expression that hides your true character or feelings: *He longed to throw off the mask of respectability.* ◊ *Her face was a cold, blank mask.* ⊃ see also DEATH MASK
- *verb* ~ sth to hide a feeling, smell, fact, etc. so that it cannot be easily seen or noticed SYN **disguise, veil**: *She masked her anger with a smile.* ⊃ SYNONYMS at HIDE

surgical mask    Halloween mask

**masked** /mɑːskt; *NAmE* mæskt/ *adj.* wearing a mask: *a masked gunman*

**masked 'ball** *noun* a formal party at which guests wear masks

**masking tape** *noun* [U] sticky tape that you use to keep an area clean or protected when you are painting around or near it

**maso·chism** /ˈmæsəkɪzəm/ *noun* **1** the practice of getting sexual pleasure from being hurt or controlled by sb else ⊃ compare SADISM **2** (*informal*) pleasure in sth that most people would find unpleasant or painful: *You spent the whole weekend in a tent in the rain? That's masochism!* ▶ **maso·chist** /-kɪst/ *noun* **maso·chis·tic** /ˌmæsəˈkɪstɪk/ *adj.*: *masochistic behaviour/tendencies*

---

**mason** /ˈmeɪsn/ *noun* **1** a person who builds using stone, or works with stone **2 Mason** = FREEMASON

**the Mason-Dixon Line** /ðə ˌmeɪsn ˈdɪksn laɪn/ *noun* [sing.] the border between the US states of Maryland and Pennsylvania that is thought of as the dividing line between the south of the US and the north. In the past it formed the northern border of the states where slaves were owned.

**Ma·son·ic** /məˈsɒnɪk; *NAmE* -ˈsɑːn-/ *adj.* connected with FREEMASONS

**Mason jar** *noun* (*NAmE*) a glass container with a wide opening and a metal top that SCREWS on tightly, used for preserving fruit and vegetables, especially in the home

**ma·son·ry** /ˈmeɪsənri/ *noun* [U] **1** the parts of a building that are made of stone: *She was injured by falling masonry.* ⊃ WORDFINDER NOTE at CONSTRUCTION **2** the work of building with stone

**masque** /mɑːsk; *NAmE* mæsk/ *noun* a play written in VERSE, often with music and dancing, popular in England in the 16th and 17th centuries

**mas·quer·ade** /ˌmæskəˈreɪd; *BrE also* ˌmɑːs-/ *noun, verb*
- *noun* **1** (*formal*) a way of behaving that hides the truth or a person's true feelings **2** (*especially NAmE*) a type of party where people wear special costumes and MASKS over their faces, to hide their identities
- *verb* [I] ~ as sth to pretend to be sth that you are not: *commercial advertisers masquerading as private individuals*

**Mass** /mæs/ *noun* **1** (*sometimes* **mass**) [U, C] (especially in the Roman Catholic Church) a ceremony held in memory of the last meal that Christ had with his DISCIPLES: *to go to Mass* ◊ *a priest celebrating/saying Mass* ⊃ see also BLACK MASS, COMMUNION, EUCHARIST **2** [C] a piece of music that is written for the prayers, etc. of this ceremony: *Bach's Mass in B minor*

**mass** /mæs/ *noun, adj., verb*
- *noun* **1** [C] a large amount of a substance that does not have a definite shape or form: *The hill appeared as a black mass in the distance.* ◊ ~ **of sth** *a mass of snow and rocks falling down the mountain* **2** [C, usually sing.] ~ **of sth** a large amount or quantity of sth: *a mass of blonde hair* ◊ *I began sifting through the mass of evidence.* **3** [sing.] ~ **of sth** a large number of people or things grouped together, often in a confused way: *I struggled through the mass of people to the exit.* ◊ *The page was covered with a mass of figures.* **4** **masses (of sth)** [pl.] (*informal*) a large number or amount of sth SYN **lots**: *There were masses of people in the shops yesterday.* ◊ *I've got masses of work to do.* ◊ *Don't give me any more. I've eaten masses!* **5** the masses [pl.] the ordinary people in society who are not leaders or who are considered to be not very well educated: *government attempts to suppress dissatisfaction among the masses* ◊ *a TV programme that brings science to the masses* **6** the mass of sth [sing.] the most; the majority: *The reforms are unpopular with the mass of teachers and parents.* **7** [U, C] (*specialist*) the quantity of material that sth contains: *calculating the mass of a planet* ◊ *a mass of 46.3 kg* HELP **Weight** is used in non-technical language for this meaning. ⊃ see also BIOMASS, BODY MASS INDEX, CRITICAL MASS, LAND MASS, RELATIVE ATOMIC MASS
- IDM **be a 'mass of sth** to be full of or covered with sth: *The rose bushes are a mass of flowers in June.* ◊ *Her arm was a mass of bruises.*
- *adj.* [only before noun] affecting or involving a large number of people or things: *mass unemployment/production* ◊ *victims of a mass shooting* ◊ *Their latest product is aimed at the mass market.* ⊃ see also MASS-MARKET, MASS MEDIA, WEAPON OF MASS DESTRUCTION
- *verb* [I, T] to come together in large numbers; to gather people or things together in large numbers: (+ *adv./prep.*) *Demonstrators had massed outside the embassy.* ◊ *Dark clouds massed on the horizon.* ◊ ~ **sb/sth** *The general massed his troops for a final attack.* ▶ **massed** *adj.*: *the massed ranks of his political opponents*

## massacre

**mas·sa·cre** ⚑+ `C1` /ˈmæsəkə(r)/ *noun, verb*
- *noun* [C, U] **1** ⚑+ `C1` the killing of a large number of people especially in a cruel way: *the bloody massacre of innocent civilians* ◊ *Nobody survived the massacre.* **2** (*informal*) a very big defeat in a game or competition: *The game was a 10–0 massacre for our team.*
- *verb* **1** ~ **sb** to kill a large number of people, especially in a cruel way **2** ~ **sb** (*informal*) to defeat sb in a game or competition by a high score

**mas·sage** /ˈmæsɑːʒ; *NAmE* məˈsɑːʒ/ *noun, verb*
- *noun* [U, C] the action of rubbing and pressing a person's body with the hands, especially to reduce pain in the muscles and JOINTS: *Massage will help the pain.* ◊ *a back massage* ◊ *to give sb a massage* ◊ *massage oils* ➠ WORDFINDER NOTE at TREATMENT
- *verb* **1** ~ **sth** to rub and press a person's body with the hands, especially to reduce pain in the muscles and JOINTS: *He massaged the aching muscles in her feet.* **2** ~ **sth into sth** to rub a substance into the skin, hair, etc: *Massage the cream into your skin.* **3** ~ **sth** (*disapproving*) to change facts, figures, etc. in order to make them seem better than they really are: *The government was accused of massaging the unemployment figures.*
- IDM **ˈmassage sbˈs ˈego** to say nice things about sb, often in a way that is not sincere, in order to make them feel better, more confident, more attractive, etc.

**ˈmassage parlour** (*US* **ˈmassage parlor**) *noun* **1** a place where you can pay to have a massage **2** a place that is supposed to offer the service of massage, but is also where men go to pay for sex with PROSTITUTES

**masse** /mæs/ ➠ EN MASSE

**mas·seur** /mæˈsɜː(r)/ *noun* a person whose job is giving people MASSAGES

**mas·seuse** /mæˈsɜːz; *NAmE* məˈsuːs/ *noun* a woman whose job is giving people MASSAGES

**mas·sif** /ˈmæsiːf/ *noun* (*specialist*) a group of mountains that form a large mass

**mas·sive** ⚑ `B2` /ˈmæsɪv/ *adj.* **1** ⚑ `B2` very large, heavy and solid: *a massive rock* ◊ *the massive walls of the castle* **2** ⚑+ `B2` extremely large or serious: *massive amounts of money* ◊ *a massive increase in spending* ◊ *These farmers grow crops on a massive scale.* ◊ *He suffered a massive heart attack.* ◊ (*BrE, informal*) *Their house is massive.* ◊ *They have a massive great house.* **3** (*informal*) very successful or important: *This band is going to be massive.*
▶ **mas·sive·ly** *adv.*

**ˌmass-ˈmarket** *adj.* [only before noun] (of goods etc.) produced for very large numbers of people

**the ˌmass ˈmedia** *noun* [pl.] sources of information and news such as newspapers, television, radio and the internet, that reach and influence large numbers of people

**ˈmass noun** *noun* (*grammar*) **1** an uncountable noun **2** a noun that is usually uncountable but can be made plural or used with *a* or *an* when you are talking about different types of sth. For example, *bread* is used as a mass noun in *the shop sells several different breads.*

**ˈmass number** *noun* (*physics*) the total number of PROTONS and NEUTRONS in an ATOM

**ˌmass-proˈduce** *verb* ~ **sth** to produce goods in large quantities, using machines ▶ **ˌmass-proˈduced** *adj.*: *mass-produced goods* **ˌmass proˈduction** *noun* [U]: *the mass production of consumer goods*

**ˌmass ˈtransit** (*also* **ˌpublic ˈtransit**) *noun* [U] (*NAmE*) the system of public transport in cities, including the SUBWAY, buses, etc. ➠ compare RAPID TRANSIT

**mast** /mɑːst; *NAmE* mæst/ *noun* **1** a tall POLE on a boat or ship that supports the sails **2** a tall metal tower with an AERIAL that sends and receives radio, television or phone signals: *people who worry about the health risks of mobile phone masts* **3** a tall POLE that is used for holding a flag
- IDM see NAIL *v.* ➠ see also HALF MAST

**mast·ec·tomy** /mæˈstektəmi/ *noun* [C, U] (*pl.* **-ies**) a medical operation to remove a person's breast

**mas·ter** ⚑ `B2` /ˈmɑːstə(r)/; *NAmE* ˈmæs-/ *noun, verb, adj.*
- *noun*
  - • OF SERVANTS **1** ⚑ `B2` (especially in the past) a man who has people working for him, often as servants in his home: *They lived in fear of their master.* ◊ *the exploitation of slaves by their former masters*
  - • PERSON IN CONTROL **2** ⚑+ `B2` a person who is in charge of an organization or group: *His political masters are all old right-wing politicians.* ◊ *the country's former colonial masters* ➠ see also HARBOUR MASTER **3** ~ **of sth** a person who is able to control sth: *She was no longer master of her own future.*
  - • PERSON WITH SKILL **4** a person who shows a lot of skill at sth: ~ **of sth** *a master of disguise* ◊ *a master of her craft* ◊ ~ **at doing sth** *a master at managing money* ➠ see also GRANDMASTER, PAST MASTER
  - • FAMOUS PAINTER **5** a famous painter who lived in the past: *an exhibition of work by the French master, Monet* ➠ see also OLD MASTER
  - • UNIVERSITY DEGREE **6** **master's** (*also* **ˈmaster's degree**) a second university degree, or, in Scotland, a first university degree, such as an MA: *He has a Master's in Business Administration.* ◊ *She holds a master's degree in journalism.* ➠ see also MA, MB, MBA, MSc **7** (*usually* **Master**) a person who has a master's degree: *a Master of Arts/Science*
  - • ANIMAL OWNER **8** the owner of an animal, especially a dog or horse: *The dog saved its master's life.* ➠ compare MISTRESS
  - • TEACHER **9** (*BrE, old-fashioned*) a male teacher at a school, especially a private school: *the physics master* ➠ compare HEADMASTER, MISTRESS, SCHOOLMASTER
  - • CAPTAIN OF SHIP **10** the captain of a ship that transports goods
  - • ORIGINAL RECORD/TAPE/MOVIE **11** (often used as an adjective) a version of a recording from which copies are made: *the master copy*
  - • TITLE **12** **Master** (*old-fashioned*) a title used when speaking to or about a boy who is too young to be called *Mr* (also used in front of the name on an ENVELOPE, etc.) **13** **Master** (in the UK) the title of the head of some schools and university colleges: *the Master of Wolfson College* **14** **Master** a title used for speaking to or about some religious teachers or leaders
  - IDM **be your own ˈmaster/ˈmistress** to be free to make your own decisions rather than being told what to do by sb else ➠ more at SERVE *v.*
- *verb*
  - • LEARN/UNDERSTAND **1** ⚑ `B2` ~ **sth** to learn or understand sth completely: *She never completely mastered the art of lip-reading.* ◊ *to master new skills/techniques* ◊ *French was a language he had never mastered.*
  - • CONTROL **2** ~ **sth** to manage to control an emotion: *She struggled hard to master her temper.* ◊ *Simon was unable to master his impatience.* **3** ~ **sth/sb** to gain control of an animal or a person
- *adj.* [only before noun]
  - • SHOWING SKILL **1** ~ **baker/chef/mason, etc.** used to describe a person who shows a lot of skill at the job mentioned, especially one who is able to teach the skills to others: *the skills of a master craftsman*
  - • MOST IMPORTANT **2** the largest and/or most important: *the master bedroom* ◊ *a master file/switch*

**ˈmaster·class** /ˈmɑːstəklɑːs; *NAmE* ˈmæstərklæs/ *noun* a lesson, especially in music, given by a famous expert to students with a lot of skill: *The opera star gave a masterclass to a group of young singers.*

**ˈmaster·ful** /ˈmɑːstəfl; *NAmE* ˈmæstərfl/ *adj.* **1** (of a person, especially a man) able to control people or situations in a way that shows confidence as a leader **2** = MASTERLY: *a masterful performance* ▶ **ˈmaster·ful·ly** /-fəli/ *adv.*: *He took her arm masterfully and led her away.*

**ˈmaster key** (*also* **ˈpass key**) *noun* a key that can be used to open many different locks in a building

**mas·ter·ly** /ˈmɑːstəli; *NAmE* ˈmæstərli/ (*also* **ˈmas·ter·ful**) *adj.* showing great skill or understanding: *a masterly performance* ◊ *Her handling of the situation was masterly.*

**master·mind** /ˈmɑːstəmaɪnd; NAmE ˈmæstərm-/ noun, verb
- noun [usually sing.] an intelligent person who plans and directs a complicated project or activity (often one that involves a crime)
- verb ~ sth to plan and direct a complicated project or activity

**ˌmaster of ˈceremonies** noun (abbr. **MC**) a person who introduces guests or people who provide entertainment at a formal occasion

**master·piece** /ˈmɑːstəpiːs; NAmE ˈmæstərp-/ (also **master·work**) noun a work of art such as a painting, film, book, etc. that is an excellent, or the best, example of the artist's work: *The museum houses several of his Cubist masterpieces.* ◊ *Her work is a masterpiece of* (= an excellent example of) *simplicity.*

**ˈmaster plan** noun a detailed plan that is designed to make a complicated project successful

**ˈmaster's degree** (also **master's**) noun a further university degree that you study for after a first degree

**master·stroke** /ˈmɑːstəstrəʊk; NAmE ˈmæstərs-/ noun [usually sing.] something clever that you do that gives a successful result

**master·work** /ˈmɑːstəwɜːk; NAmE ˈmæstərwɜːrk/ noun = MASTERPIECE: *a literary/musical/cinematic masterwork*

**mas·tery** /ˈmɑːstəri; NAmE ˈmæs-/ noun **1** [U, sing.] ~ (of sth) great knowledge about or understanding of a particular thing SYN command: *She has mastery of several languages.* **2** [U] ~ (of/over sb/sth) control or power: *human mastery of the natural world*

**mast·head** /ˈmɑːsthed; NAmE ˈmæst-/ noun **1** the top of a MAST on a ship **2** the name of a newspaper at the top of the front page or website **3** (NAmE) the part of a newspaper or a news website that gives details of the people who work on it and other information about it

**mas·tic** /ˈmæstɪk/ noun [U] **1** a substance that comes from the BARK of a tree and is used in making VARNISH **2** a substance that is used in building to fill holes and keep out water

**mas·ti·cate** /ˈmæstɪkeɪt/ verb [I] (*specialist*) to bite food many times as you eat it SYN chew ▶ **mas·ti·ca·tion** /ˌmæstɪˈkeɪʃn/ noun [U]

**mas·tiff** /ˈmæstɪf/ noun a large, strong dog with short hair

**mas·titis** /mæˈstaɪtɪs/ noun [U] (*medical*) painful SWELLING (= the condition of being larger or rounder than normal) of the breast or UDDER usually because of infection

**mas·tur·bate** /ˈmæstəbeɪt; NAmE -stərb-/ verb **1** [I, T] ~(yourself) to give yourself sexual pleasure by rubbing your sexual organs **2** [T] ~ sb to give sb sexual pleasure by rubbing their sexual organs ▶ **mas·tur·ba·tion** /ˌmæstəˈbeɪʃn; NAmE -stərˈb-/ noun [U] **mas·tur·ba·tory** /ˌmæstəˈbeɪtəri; NAmE ˈmæstərbətɔːri/ adj.

**mat** /mæt/ noun, adj.
- noun **1** a small piece of thick carpet or strong material that is used to cover part of a floor: *Wipe your feet on the mat before you come in, please.* ⊃ see also BATH MAT, DOORMAT, MOUSE MAT, PRAYER MAT at PRAYER RUG, WELCOME MAT **2** a piece of thick material such as rubber or plastic used especially in some sports for people to lie on or fall onto: *a judo/an exercise mat* **3** a small piece of plastic, wood or cloth used on a table for decoration or to protect the surface from heat or damage: *a table mat* ⊃ see also BEER MAT, PLACE MAT **4** a thick mass of sth that is stuck together: *a mat of hair* ⊃ see also MATTED
  IDM **go to the ˈmat (with sb) (for sb/sth)** (NAmE, informal) to support or defend sb/sth in an argument with sb **take sb/sth to the ˈmat** (US, informal) to get involved in an argument with sb/sth
- adj. (US) = MATT

**mata·dor** /ˈmætədɔː(r)/ noun (*from Spanish*) a person who fights and kills the BULL in a BULLFIGHT

**ma·tatu** /mæˈtætuː/ EAfrE [maˈtatu] noun (EAfrE) (in Kenya) a small, privately owned bus, often decorated with pictures, words or phrases, that carries passengers and has a driver that you pay to take you somewhere, usually along a fixed route with other stops for people to get on and off

# matchbook

**match** ❶ **A1** /mætʃ/ noun, verb
- noun
- **IN SPORT 1** **A1** [C] (*especially BrE*) a sports event where people or teams compete against each other: (*BrE*) *a football match* ◊ (*NAmE, BrE*) *a tennis match* ◊ *a league match* ◊ *They are playing an important match against Liverpool on Saturday.* ◊ *to win/lose a match* ◊ *I'll probably watch the match on TV.* ⊃ see also RETURN MATCH, SHOUTING MATCH, SHOUTING MATCH, SLANGING MATCH, TEST MATCH ⊃ WORDFINDER NOTE at SPORT
- **AN EQUAL 2** [sing.] a person who is equal to sb else in strength, skill, intelligence, etc.: **a/no~for sb (at sth)** *I was no match for him at tennis.* ◊ **sb's match (at sth)** *I was his match at tennis.*
- **SB/STH THAT COMBINES WELL 3** [sing.] a person or thing that combines well with sb/sth else: *The curtains and carpet are a good match.* ◊ **a...~for sb** *Jo and Ian are a perfect match for each other.*
- **STH THE SAME 4** [C] a thing that is or looks exactly the same as or very similar to sth else: *I've found a vase that is an exact match of the one I broke.*
- **FOR LIGHTING FIRES 5** [C] a small stick made of wood or CARDBOARD that is used for lighting a fire, cigarette, etc.: *a box of matches* ◊ *to strike a match* (= to make it burn) ◊ *to put a match to sth* (= set fire to sth)
- **MARRIAGE 6** [C] (*old-fashioned*) a marriage or a marriage partner ⊃ see also LOVE MATCH
  IDM **find/meet your ˈmatch (in sb)** to meet sb who is equal to or even better than you in strength, skill or intelligence ⊃ more at MAN n.

- verb
- **FIND STH SIMILAR/CONNECTED 1** **A1** [T] to find sb/sth that goes together with or is connected with another person or thing: ~ A and B *Match the words and pictures.* ◊ **~ A to/with B** *The aim of the competition is to match the quote to the person who said it.*
- **BE THE SAME 2** **A2** [T, I] ~(sth) if two things **match** or if one thing **matches** another, they are the same or very similar: *Her fingerprints match those found at the scene of the crime.* ◊ *A man matching his description was seen running from a car.* ◊ *As a couple they are not very well matched* (= they are not very suitable for each other). ◊ *The two sets of figures don't match.*
- **COMBINE WELL 3** **B2** [T, I] if two things **match**, or if one thing **matches** another, they have the same colour, pattern, or style and therefore look attractive together: **~(sth)** *Her dark hair matched the colour of her eyes.* ◊ *None of these glasses match* (= they are all different). ◊ **to~(sth)** *The doors were painted blue to match the walls.* ◊ *a scarf with gloves to match* ⊃ see also MATCHING
- **BE EQUAL/BETTER 4** [T] ~ sb/sth to be as good, interesting, successful, etc. as sb/sth else SYN **equal**: *The profits made in the first year have never been matched.* ◊ *Job opportunities in the industry do not match the level of interest.* ◊ *The teams were evenly matched.* **5** [T] ~ sth to make sth the same as or better than sth else: *The company was unable to match his current salary.*
- **PROVIDE STH SUITABLE 6** [T] ~ sth to provide sth that is suitable for or enough for a particular situation: *Investment in hospitals is needed now to match the future needs of the country.* IDM see DESCRIPTION, MIX v.
  PHRV **ˈmatch sth against sth** to compare sth with sth else in order to find things that are the same or similar: *New information is matched against existing data in the computer.* **ˈmatch sb/sth against/with sb/sth** to arrange for sb to compete in a game or competition against sb else: *We are matched against last year's champions in the first round.* **ˌmatch ˈup (to sb/sth)** (usually used in negative sentences) to be as good, interesting, successful as sb/sth SYN **measure up (to sth/sb)**: *The trip failed to match up to her expectations.* **ˌmatch ˈup (with sth)** to be the same or similar SYN **tally, agree**: *The suspects' stories just don't match up.* **ˌmatch sth ˈup (with sth)** to find things that belong together or that look attractive together: *She spent the morning matching up orders with invoices.*

**match·book** /ˈmætʃbʊk/ noun (NAmE) a piece of folded card containing matches and a surface to light them on

# matchbox

**match·box** /'mætʃbɒks; NAmE -bɑːks/ noun a small box for holding matches

**'match-fixing** noun [U] (in sport) the act of deciding in a way that is not honest what the result of a particular game will be before it is played: *Several countries have suffered soccer match-fixing scandals.* ⊃ compare SPOT-FIXING

**match·ing** ❶ B2 /'mætʃɪŋ/ adj. [only before noun] **1** B2 (of clothing, material, objects, etc.) having the same colour, pattern, style, etc. and therefore looking attractive together: *The two sisters wore matching outfits.* ◊ *a pine table with four matching chairs* **2** equal in number or amount; having the same qualities, etc: *The college will provide matching funds (= equal to the amount already raised) to complete the project.* ◊ *Stem cells from a matching donor were injected into the patient.*

**match·less** /'mætʃləs/ adj. (formal) so good that nothing can be compared with it SYN incomparable: *matchless beauty/skill*

**match·maker** /'mætʃmeɪkə(r)/ noun a person who tries to arrange marriages or relationships between others ▶ **match·mak·ing** noun [U]

**'match play** noun [U] a way of playing golf in which your score depends on the number of holes that you win rather than the number of times you hit the ball in the whole game ⊃ compare STROKE PLAY

**match 'point** noun [U, C] (especially in tennis) a point that, if won by a player, will also win them the match

**match·stick** /'mætʃstɪk/ noun a single wooden match: *starving children with legs like matchsticks*

**match-up** /'mætʃʌp/ noun (NAmE) a sports event where two players or teams compete against each other: *This may be the most exciting matchup of the season.*

**match·wood** /'mætʃwʊd/ noun [U] very small pieces of wood

**mate** B2 /meɪt/ noun, verb
■ noun
• FRIEND **1** B2 [C] (BrE, AustralE, informal) a friend: *They've been best mates since school.* ◊ *I was with a mate.* ⊃ WORDFINDER NOTE at FRIEND
• FRIENDLY NAME **2** B2 [C] (BrE, AustralE, informal) used as a friendly way of addressing sb, especially between men: *Sorry mate, you'll have to wait.* ◊ *All right, mate?*
• SB YOU SHARE WITH **3** B2 [C] (in compounds) a person you share an activity or accommodation with: *workmates/teammates/playmates/classmates* ◊ *my room-mate/flatmate* ⊃ see also AGE-MATE, RUNNING MATE, SOULMATE
• BIRD/ANIMAL **4** B2 [C] the sexual partner of a bird or animal: *A male bird sings to attract a mate.*
• SEXUAL PARTNER **5** [C] (informal) a husband, wife or other sexual partner
• JOB **6** [C] (BrE) a person whose job is to help a worker who has had training in a skill: *a builder's/plumber's mate*
• ON SHIP **7** [C] an officer in a commercial ship below the rank of captain or MASTER ⊃ see also FIRST MATE
• IN CHESS **8** [U] = CHECKMATE
■ verb
• ANIMALS/BIRDS **1** B2 [I] ~ (with sth) (of two animals or birds) to have sex in order to produce young: *Do foxes ever mate with dogs?* ⊃ see also MATING **2** [T] ~ sth (to/with sth) to put animals or birds together so that they will have sex and produce young
• IN CHESS **3** [T] = CHECKMATE

**ma·ter·ial** ❶ A2 ❶ /məˈtɪəriəl; NAmE -ˈtɪr-/ noun, adj.
■ noun **1** A2 [C, U] a substance that things can be made from: *building materials (= bricks, sand, glass, etc.)* ◊ *Every item we sell is made out of recycled material.* ◊ *All the furniture is crafted from natural materials.* ◊ *synthetic/man-made materials* ⊃ see also RAW MATERIAL **2** B1 [C, usually pl., U] things that are needed in order to do a particular activity: *teaching materials* ◊ *They publish a range of educational materials.* ◊ *The company produces its own training material.* ⊃ SYNONYMS at EQUIPMENT **3** B1 [C, U] information or ideas used in books, etc: *She's collecting material for her latest novel.* ◊ *This is not suitable reading material for a child.* ◊ *The letters were used as source material in this new biography.* **4** B1 [U, C] cloth used for making clothes, curtains, etc. SYN fabric: *a piece of material* ◊ *'What material is this dress made of?' 'Cotton.'* ⊃ note at FABRIC **5** [U] items used in a performance: *The band played all new material at the gig.* **6** a person with particular qualities or suitable for a particular opportunity: *The teacher saw her as good university material (= good enough to go to university).*
■ adj. **1** B2 [only before noun] connected with money, possessions, etc. rather than with the needs of the mind or spirit: *material possessions/wealth* ◊ *The early pioneers had few material resources at their disposal.* OPP spiritual **2** B2 [only before noun] connected with the physical world rather than with the mind or spirit: *the material world* OPP immaterial **3** (formal or law) important and needing to be considered: *material evidence/facts* ◊ ~ to sth *She omitted information that was material to the case.* ⊃ see also IMMATERIAL ▶ **ma·teri·al·ly** /-riəli/ adv.: *Materially they are no better off.* ◊ *Their comments have not materially affected our plans (= in a clear and definite or important way).*

**ma·teri·al·ism** /məˈtɪəriəlɪzəm; NAmE -ˈtɪr-/ noun [U] **1** (usually disapproving) the belief that money, possessions and physical comforts are more important than spiritual values **2** (philosophy) the belief that only material things exist ⊃ compare IDEALISM ⊃ see also DIALECTICAL MATERIALISM

**ma·teri·al·ist** /məˈtɪəriəlɪst; NAmE -ˈtɪr-/ noun, adj.
■ noun **1** a person who believes that money, possessions and physical comforts are more important than spiritual values in life **2** a person who believes in the philosophy of materialism
■ adj. **1** (disapproving) = MATERIALISTIC **2** relating to the belief that only material things exist: *Some atheists have a materialist philosophy.*

**ma·teri·al·is·tic** /məˌtɪəriəˈlɪstɪk; NAmE -ˌtɪr-/ (also **materialist**) adj. (disapproving) caring more about money and possessions than anything else: *We're living in a highly materialistic society.*

**ma·teri·al·ize** (BrE also **-ise**) /məˈtɪəriəlaɪz; NAmE -ˈtɪr-/ verb **1** [I] (usually used in negative sentences) to take place or start to exist as expected or planned: *The promotion he had been promised failed to materialize.* **2** [I] to appear suddenly and/or in a way that cannot be explained: *A tall figure suddenly materialized at her side.* ◊ (informal) *The train failed to materialize (= it did not come).* ▶ **ma·teri·al·iza·tion, -isa·tion** /məˌtɪəriəlaɪˈzeɪʃn; NAmE -ˌtɪriələˈz-/ noun [U, C]

**ma·ter·iel** /məˌtɪəriˈel; NAmE -ˌtɪr-/ noun [U] (specialist) military weapons and equipment

**ma·ter·nal** /məˈtɜːnl; NAmE -ˈtɜːrnl/ adj. **1** having feelings that are typical of a caring mother towards a child: *maternal love* ◊ *I'm not very maternal.* ◊ *She didn't have any maternal instincts.* **2** connected with being a mother: *Maternal age affects the baby's survival rate.* **3** [only before noun] related through the mother's side of the family: *my maternal grandfather (= my mother's father)* ▶ **mater·nal·ly** /-nəli/ adv.: *She behaved maternally towards her students.* ⊃ compare PATERNAL

**ma·ter·nity** /məˈtɜːnəti; NAmE -ˈtɜːrn-/ noun [U] the state of being or becoming a mother: *maternity clothes (= clothes for women who are pregnant)* ◊ *a maternity ward/hospital (= one where women go to give birth to their babies)*

**ma'ternity leave** noun [U] a period of time when a woman is allowed to be away from work before and after having a baby: **on ~** *Ellie is currently on maternity leave.* ⊃ WORDFINDER NOTE at PREGNANT ⊃ see also FAMILY LEAVE, PARENTAL LEAVE, PATERNITY LEAVE

**mate·ship** /'meɪtʃɪp/ noun [U] (AustralE, NZE, informal) friendship, especially between men

**matey** /'meɪti/ adj., noun
■ adj. ~ (with sb) (BrE, informal) friendly, sometimes in a way that is not completely sincere: *She started off being quite matey with everyone.*
■ noun (BrE) used by men as an informal way of addressing another man

**math** /mæθ/ (*NAmE*) (*BrE* **maths** /mæθs/) *noun* [U] **1** mathematics, especially as a subject in school: *a math teacher* **2** the process of calculating using numbers: *Is your math correct?*

**IDM** **do the ˈmath** to think carefully about sth before doing it so that you know all the relevant facts or figures: *If only someone had done the math!*

**math·emat·ic·al** ⓘ+ **C1** /ˌmæθəˈmætɪkl/ *adj.* connected with or involving mathematics: *mathematical calculations/problems/models* ◊ *to assess children's mathematical ability* ▶ **math·emat·ic·al·ly** /-kli/ *adv.*: *It's mathematically impossible.*

**math·em·at·ician** /ˌmæθəməˈtɪʃn/ *noun* a person who is an expert in mathematics

**math·emat·ics** ⓘ **A2** /ˌmæθəˈmætɪks/ (*formal*) (*BrE also* **maths** /mæθs/) (*NAmE also* **math** /mæθ/) *noun* **1** **A2** [U] the science of numbers and shapes. Branches of mathematics include ARITHMETIC, ALGEBRA, GEOMETRY and TRIGONOMETRY: *the school mathematics curriculum* ◊ *applied/pure mathematics* **2** [U + sing./pl. v.] the process of calculating using numbers: *He worked out the very difficult mathematics in great detail.* ◊ *Her proof is a remarkable piece of mathematics.*

**maths** ⓘ **A2** /mæθs/ (*BrE*) (*NAmE* **math** /mæθ/) *noun* **1** **A2** [U] mathematics, especially as a subject in school: *The core subjects are English, maths and science.* ◊ *a maths teacher* **2** [U + sing./pl. v.] the process of calculating using numbers: *If my maths is/are right, the answer is 142.*

**WORDFINDER** algebra, arithmetic, calculus, equation, geometry, logarithm, numeracy, problem, trigonometry

**IDM** **do the ˈmaths** to think carefully about sth before doing it so that you know all the relevant facts or figures: *Do the maths before you take on more debt.*

**mat·inee** (*also* **mat·inée**) /ˈmætɪneɪ; *NAmE* ˌmætnˈeɪ/ *noun* an afternoon performance of a play, etc.; an afternoon showing of a film ⇒ **WORDFINDER NOTE** at PERFORMANCE

**ˈmatinee idol** (*also* **matinée idol**) *noun* (*old-fashioned*) an actor who is popular with women

**mat·ing** /ˈmeɪtɪŋ/ *noun* [U, C] sex between animals: *the mating season*

**mat·ins** (*also* **mat·tins**) /ˈmætɪnz; *NAmE* -tnz/ *noun* [U] the service of morning prayer, especially in the Anglican Church ⇒ compare EVENSONG, VESPERS

**ma·toke** /mæˈtəʊkeɪ; *NAmE* -ˈtoʊk-/ *EAfrE* [maˈtoke] *noun* [U] (*EAfrE*) a type of green banana grown in Uganda and other places in East Africa and used for cooking; the cooked food made from this type of banana and eaten with STEW

**ma·tri·arch** /ˈmeɪtriɑːk; *NAmE* -ɑːrk/ *noun* a woman who is the head of a family or social group ⇒ compare PATRIARCH

**ma·tri·arch·al** /ˌmeɪtriˈɑːkl; *NAmE* -ˈɑːrkl/ *adj.* (of a society or system) controlled by women rather than men; passing power, property, etc. from mother to daughter rather than from father to son: *The animals live in matriarchal groups.* ⇒ compare PATRIARCHAL

**ma·tri·archy** /ˈmeɪtriɑːki; *NAmE* -ɑːrki/ *noun* [C, U] (*pl.* **-ies**) a social system that gives power and authority to women rather than men ⇒ compare PATRIARCHY

**ma·tric** /məˈtrɪk/ *noun* [U] (*SAfrE*) **1** the final year of school: *We studied that book in matric.* **2** the work and examinations in the final year of school: *He passed matric with four distinctions.* ◊ *She's preparing to write matric.*

**matri·ces** /ˈmeɪtrɪsiːz/ *pl.* of MATRIX

**ma·tric eˈxemption** *noun* [U] (*SAfrE*) the fact of successfully completing the final year of school and being able to study at university or college: *A senior certificate with matric exemption is required for entry to university.*

**matri·cide** /ˈmætrɪsaɪd/ *noun* [U, C] (*formal*) the crime of killing your mother; a person who is guilty of this crime ⇒ compare FRATRICIDE, PARRICIDE, PATRICIDE

**ma·tricu·lant** /məˈtrɪkjulənt/ *noun* (*SAfrE*) a student who has passed the last exam in the final year of school (matric)

**ma·tricu·late** /məˈtrɪkjuleɪt/ *verb* [I] (*formal*) to officially become a student at a university: *She matriculated in 1995.* **2** [I] (*SAfrE*) to successfully complete the final year of school ▶ **ma·tricu·la·tion** /məˌtrɪkjuˈleɪʃn/ *noun* [U]

**matri·lin·eal** /ˌmætrɪˈlɪniəl/ *adj.* (*specialist*) used to describe the relationship between mother and children that continues in a family with each generation, or sth that is based on this relationship: *She traced her family history by matrilineal descent* (= starting with her mother, her mother's mother, etc.). ⇒ compare PATRILINEAL

**matri·mo·nial** /ˌmætrɪˈməʊniəl; *NAmE* -ˈmoʊ-/ *adj.* [usually before noun] (*formal or specialist*) connected with marriage or with being married: *matrimonial problems* ◊ *the matrimonial home*

**matri·mony** /ˈmætrɪməni; *NAmE* -məʊni/ *noun* [U] (*formal or specialist*) marriage; the state of being married: *holy matrimony*

**mat·rix** /ˈmeɪtrɪks/ *noun* (*pl.* **matri·ces** /-trɪsiːz/) **1** (*mathematics*) an arrangement of numbers, symbols, etc. in rows and columns, treated as a single quantity **2** (*formal*) the formal social, political, etc. situation from which a society or person grows and develops: *the European cultural matrix* **3** (*formal or literary*) a system of lines, roads, etc. that cross each other, forming a series of squares or shapes in between **SYN** network: *a matrix of paths* **4** (*specialist*) a MOULD in which sth is shaped **5** (*computing*) a group of electronic CIRCUIT elements arranged in rows and columns like a GRID **6** (*geology*) a mass of rock in which minerals, PRECIOUS STONES, etc. are found in the ground

**ma·tron** /ˈmeɪtrən/ *noun* **1** (*BrE*) a woman who works as a nurse in a school **2** (*BrE*) a senior female nurse in charge of the other nurses in a hospital **3** (*becoming old-fashioned*) an older married woman

**ma·tron·ly** /ˈmeɪtrənli/ *adj.* (*disapproving*) (of a woman) no longer young, and rather fat

**matron of ˈhonour** (*US* **matron of ˈhonor**) *noun* [sing.] a married woman who is the most important BRIDESMAID at a wedding ⇒ compare MAID OF HONOUR

**matt** (*BrE*) (*US* **mat**) (*also* **matte** *NAmE, BrE*) /mæt/ *adj.* (of a colour, surface, or photograph) not shiny: *a matt finish* ◊ *matt white paint* ◊ *Prints are available on matt or glossy paper.*

**mat·ted** /ˈmætɪd/ *adj.* (of hair, etc.) forming a thick mass, especially because it is wet and dirty

**mat·ter** ⓘ **A2** Ⓦ /ˈmætə(r)/ *noun, verb*

■ *noun*

• **PROBLEM 1** ⓘ **A2** **the matter** [sing.] used (to ask) if sb is upset, unhappy, etc. or if there is a problem: *What's the matter? Is there something wrong?* ◊ *Is anything the matter?* ◊ *~ with sb/sth Is something the matter with Bob? He seems very down.* ◊ *There's something the matter with my eyes.* ◊ *'We've bought a new TV.' 'What was the matter with the old one?'* ◊ *What's the matter with you today* (= why are you behaving like this)?

• **SUBJECT/SITUATION 2** ⓘ **B1** [C] a subject or situation that you must consider or deal with **SYN** affair: *It's a private matter.* ◊ *They had important matters to discuss.* ◊ *She may need your help with some business matters.* ◊ *financial/legal/political matters* ◊ *Do I have any choice in the matter?* ◊ *I always consulted him on matters of policy.* ◊ *~ for sb It's a matter for the police* (= for them to deal with). ◊ *~ of sth (formal) It was a matter of some concern to most of those present* (= sth they were worried about). ◊ *It should have been a simple matter to check.* ◊ *Let's get on with the matter in hand* (= what we need to deal with now). ◊ *I wasn't prepared to let the matter drop* (= stop discussing it). ◊ *I did not feel that we had got to the heart of the matter* (= the most important part). ◊ *And that is the crux of the matter* (= the most important thing about the matter). **3** ⓘ **B1** **matters** [pl.] the present situation, or the situation that you are talking about **SYN** things: *Unfortunately, there is nothing we can do to improve matters.* ◊ *I'd forgotten the keys, which didn't help matters.* ◊ *And then, to make matters worse, his parents turned up.* ◊ *I decided to take matters into my own hands* (= deal with the situation myself). ◊ *Matters came to a head* (= the situation became very difficult) *with his resignation.*

# matter-of-fact

- **A MATTER OF (DOING) STH 4** [sing.] a situation that involves sth or depends on sth **SYN question**: ~ **of sth** *Learning to drive is all a matter of coordination.* ◇ *Some people prefer the older version to the new one. It's* ***a matter of taste.*** ◇ *She resigned over* ***a matter of principle.*** ◇ *The government must deal with this* ***as a matter of urgency.*** ◇ *Just as a matter of interest* (= because it is interesting, not because it is important), *how much did you pay for it?* ◇ *'I think this is the best so far.' 'Well, that's* ***a matter of opinion*** (= other people may think differently).' ◇ *It's not pure fantasy! It's a plain* ***matter of fact.*** ◇ **~ of doing sth** *That's not a problem. It's* ***simply a matter of letting people know in time.*** ⇨ see also MATTER-OF-FACT
- **SUBSTANCE 5** [U] (*physics*) physical substance that everything in the world is made of; not mind or spirit: *to study the properties of matter* ⇨ see also DARK MATTER **6** [U] (*formal*) a substance or things of a particular sort: *Add plenty of organic matter to improve the soil.* ◇ *elimination of waste matter from the body* ◇ *She didn't approve of their choice of* ***reading matter.*** ⇨ see also GREY MATTER, SUBJECT MATTER

**IDM as a matter of 'fact 1** used to add a comment on sth that you have just said, usually adding sth that you think the other person will be interested in: *It's a nice place. We've stayed there ourselves, as a matter of fact.* **2** used to disagree with sth that sb has just said **SYN actually**: *'I suppose you'll be leaving soon, then?' 'No, as a matter of fact I'll be staying for another two years.'* ⇨ see also MATTER-OF-FACT **be another / a different 'matter** to be very different: *I know which area they live in, but whether I can find their house is a different matter.* **for 'that matter** used to add a comment on sth that you have just said: *I didn't like it much. Nor did the kids, for that matter.* **it's just / only a matter of 'time (before …)** used to say that sth will definitely happen, although you are not sure when: *It's only a matter of time before they bring out their own version of the software.* **(as) a matter of 'course** (as) the usual and correct thing to do: *We always check people's addresses as a matter of course.* **a matter of 'hours, 'minutes, etc. | a matter of 'inches, 'metres, etc.** only a few hours, minutes, etc.: *It was all over in a matter of minutes.* ◇ *The bullet missed her by a matter of inches.* **a ˌmatter of 'life and / or 'death** used to describe a situation that is very important or serious **a matter of 'record** (*formal*) something that has been recorded as being true **no matter** used to say that sth is not important: *If that doesn't work out, no matter, I'll rent for another year or two.* **no matter who, what, where, etc.** used to say that sth is always true, whatever the situation is, or that sb should certainly do sth: *They don't last long no matter how careful you are.* ◇ *Call me when you get there, no matter what the time is.* ⇨ more at FACT, LAUGHING

- ■ **verb** [I, T] (not used in the progressive tenses) to be important or have an important effect on sb/sth: *'I'm afraid I forgot that book again.'* ***'It doesn't matter*** (= it is not important enough to worry about).' ◇ *After his death, nothing seemed to matter any more.* ◇ **~ to sb** *The children matter more to her than anything else in the world.* ◇ **~ who, what, etc …** *Does it really matter who did it?* ◇ **~ to sb who, what, etc …** *It doesn't matter to me what you do.* ◇ **~ (to sb) that …** *It didn't matter that the weather was bad.* ◇ *What does it matter if I spent $100 on it—it's my money!* ◇ *As long as you're happy, that's* ***all that matters.*** ◇ *He's been in prison, you know—* ***not that it matters*** (= that information does not affect my opinion of him).

ˌmatter-of-'fact *adj.* without showing any emotion, especially in a situation in which you would expect sb to express their feelings **SYN unemotional**: *She told us the news of his death in a very matter-of-fact way.* ▶ ˌmatter-of-'factly *adv.*

**matting** /ˈmætɪŋ/ *noun* rough WOVEN material for making MATS: *coconut matting*

**mattins** = MATINS

**mattress** /ˈmætrəs/ *noun* the soft part of a bed, that you lie on: *a soft/hard mattress* ⇨ see also AIR MATTRESS

**maturation** /ˌmætʃuˈreɪʃn/ *noun* [U] (*formal*) **1** the process of becoming or being made mature (= ready to eat or drink after being left for a period of time) **2** the process of becoming adult ▶ **matuˈrational** /-ʃənl/ *adj.*

**mature** /məˈtʃʊə(r), -ˈtjʊə(r); NAmE -ˈtʃʊr, -ˈtʊr/ *adj., verb*

- ■ *adj.* **HELP maturer** is occasionally used instead of **more mature**
- **SENSIBLE 1** (of a child or young person) behaving in a sensible way, like an adult: *Jane is very mature for her age.* ◇ *a mature and sensible attitude* **OPP immature**
- **FULLY GROWN 2** (of a person, a tree, a bird or an animal) fully grown and developed: *sexually mature* ◇ *a mature oak/eagle/elephant* **OPP immature** ⇨ **SYNONYMS** at OLD
- **WINE / CHEESE 3** developed over a period of time to produce a strong, rich taste
- **NO LONGER YOUNG 4** used as a polite or humorous way of saying that sb is no longer young: *clothes for the mature woman* ◇ *a man of mature years*
- **WORK OF ART 5** created late in an artist's life and showing great understanding and skill
- **INSURANCE POLICY 6** (*business*) ready to be paid ▶ **maˈturely** *adv.*

**IDM on mature reˈflection / consideˈration** (*formal*) after thinking about sth carefully and for a long time

- ■ *verb*
- **BECOME FULLY GROWN 1** [I] to become fully grown or developed: *This particular breed of cattle matures early.* ◇ *Technology in this field has matured considerably over the last decade.*
- **BECOME SENSIBLE 2** [I] to develop emotionally and start to behave like a sensible adult: *He has matured a great deal over the past year.*
- **DEVELOP SKILL 3** [I] **~ (into sth)** to fully develop a particular skill or quality: *She has matured into one of the country's finest actresses.*
- **WINE / CHEESE 4** [I, T] **~ (sth)** if wine, cheese, etc. **matures** or is **matured**, it develops over a period of time to produce a strong, rich taste
- **INSURANCE POLICY 5** [I] (*business*) to reach the date when it must be paid

**maˌture 'student** *noun* (*BrE*) an adult student who goes to college or university some years after leaving school

**maturity** /məˈtʃʊərəti, -ˈtjʊə-; NAmE -ˈtʃʊr-, -ˈtʊ-/ *noun* [U] **1** the quality of thinking and behaving in a sensible, adult manner: *He has maturity beyond his years.* ◇ *Her poems show great maturity.* ⇨ compare IMMATURITY **2** (of a person, an animal, or a plant) the state of being fully grown or developed: *The forest will take 100 years to* ***reach maturity.*** ⇨ compare IMMATURITY **3** understanding and skill that an artist develops over a period of time **4** (*business*) (of an insurance policy, etc.) the time when money you have invested is ready to be paid

**matzo** (*also* **matzoh, matzah**) /ˈmætsəʊ; NAmE ˈmɑːt-/ *noun* [U, C] (*pl.* **-os** *or* **-ohs**) a type of bread in the form of a large, flat biscuit, traditionally eaten by Jews during Passover; one of these biscuits

**maudlin** /ˈmɔːdlɪn/ *adj.* **1** talking in a silly, emotional way, often feeling sorry for yourself **SYN sentimental 2** (of a book, film or song) expressing or causing EXAGGERATED emotions, especially in way that is not sincere **SYN sentimental**

**maul** /mɔːl/ *verb* **1 ~ sb** (of an animal) to attack and injure sb by tearing their body **SYN savage 2 ~ sb/sth** to touch sb/sth in an unpleasant and/or violent way **3 ~ sth/sb** to criticize sth/sb severely and publicly **SYN savage 4 ~ sb** (*informal*) to defeat sb easily **SYN thrash** ▶ **mauling** *noun* [usually sing.]: *The play received a mauling from the critics.* ◇ *They face a mauling by last year's winners.*

**Maundy Thursday** /ˌmɔːndi ˈθɜːzdeɪ, -di; NAmE ˈθɜːrz-/ *noun* [U, C] (in the Christian Church) the Thursday before Easter

**mausoleum** /ˌmɔːzəˈliːəm/ *noun* a special building made to hold the dead body of an important person or the dead bodies of a family: *the royal mausoleum*

**mauve** /məʊv/ *adj.* pale purple in colour ▶ **mauve** *noun* [U]

**maven** /ˈmeɪvn/ *noun* (*NAmE*) an expert on sth

**mav·er·ick** /ˈmævərɪk/ noun a person who does not behave or think like everyone else, but who has independent, unusual opinions ▶ **mav·er·ick** adj. [only before noun]: *a maverick film director*

**maw** /mɔː/ noun **1** (literary) something that seems like a big mouth that SWALLOWS sth up completely **2** (old-fashioned) an animal's stomach or throat

**mawk·ish** /ˈmɔːkɪʃ/ adj. (disapproving) expressing or sharing emotion in a way that is EXAGGERATED or embarrassing SYN **sentimental**: *a mawkish poem* ▶ **mawk·ish·ness** noun [U]

**max** /mæks/ abbr., verb
- abbr. **1** (also **max.** especially in NAmE) maximum: *max temperature 18°C* **2** (informal) at the most: *It'll cost $50 max.* OPP **min.**
- IDM **to the ˈmax** to the highest level or greatest amount possible: *She believes in living life to the max.*
- verb
- PHRV **max ˈout** | **max sth↔ˈout** (informal) to reach, or make sth reach, the limit at which nothing more is possible: *I maxed out all my credit cards* (= reached the spending limit on each one).

**maxi** /ˈmæksi/ noun a long coat, dress or skirt that reaches to the ankles

**max·illa** /mækˈsɪlə/ noun (pl. **max·il·lae** /-liː/) (anatomy) the JAW ▶ **max·il·lary** /mækˈsɪləri; NAmE ˈmæksɪleri/ adj. [only before noun]: *a maxillary fracture*

**maxim** /ˈmæksɪm/ noun a well-known phrase that expresses sth that is usually true or that people think is a rule for sensible behaviour

**max·imal** /ˈmæksɪml/ adj. [usually before noun] (specialist) as great or as large as possible ▶ **max·imal·ly** adv.

**max·im·ize** ʔ+ C1 W (BrE also **-ise**) /ˈmæksɪmaɪz/ verb **1** ʔ+ C1 ~ sth to increase sth as much as possible: *to maximize efficiency/fitness/profits* ◊ (computing) *Maximize the window to full screen.* **2** ʔ+ C1 ~ sth to make the best use of sth: *to maximize opportunities/resources* OPP **minimize** ▶ **max·im·iza·tion, -isa·tion** /ˌmæksɪmaɪˈzeɪʃn; NAmE -məˈz-/ noun

**max·imum** ⓘ B2 ⚬ /ˈmæksɪməm/ adj., noun
- adj. ʔ B2 [only before noun] (abbr. **max**) as large, fast, etc. as is possible, or the most that is possible or allowed: *the maximum amount/number of sth* ◊ *the maximum speed/temperature/volume* ◊ *For maximum effect do the exercises every day.* ◊ *a maximum security prison* OPP **minimum** ▶ **max·imum** adv.: *The table has a length of four feet maximum.*
- noun ʔ B2 [usually sing.] (pl. **max·ima** /ˈmæksɪmə/) (abbr. **max**) the greatest amount, size, speed, etc. that is possible, recorded or allowed: *a maximum of 30 children in a class* ◊ *The July maximum* (= the highest temperature recorded in July) *was 30°C.* ◊ *What is the absolute maximum you can afford to pay?* ◊ **to the ~** *The job will require you to use all your skills to the maximum.* ⊃ compare MINIMUM

**May** ⓘ A1 /meɪ/ noun [U, C] the fifth month of the year, between April and June HELP To see how **May** is used, look at the examples at **April**.

**may** ⓘ A2 ⚬ /meɪ/ modal verb, noun
- modal verb (negative **may not** /meɪ nɒt; NAmE nɑːt/, rare short form **mayn't** /ˈmeɪənt/, pt **might** /maɪt/, negative **might not** /ˈmaɪt nɒt; NAmE nɑːt/, rare short form **mightn't** /ˈmaɪtnt/) **1** ʔ A2 used to say that sth is possible: *That may or may not be true.* ◊ *He may have* (= perhaps he has) *missed his train.* ◊ *They may well win.* ◊ *There is a range of programs on the market which may be described as design aids.* **2** ʔ B1 (formal) used to ask for or give permission: *May I come in?* ◊ *You may come in if you wish.* ⊃ note at CAN¹ **3** ʔ B2 used when admitting that sth is true before introducing another point, argument, etc: *He may be a good father but he's a terrible husband.* **4** (formal) used as a polite way of making a comment, asking a question, etc: *You look lovely, if I may say so.* ◊ *May I ask why you took that decision?* ◊ *If I may just add one thing …* **5** (formal) used to express wishes and hopes: *May she rest in peace.* ◊ *Business has been thriving in the past year. Long may it continue to do so.* **6** (formal) used to say what the purpose of

sth is: *There is a need for more resources so that all children may have a decent education.* ⊃ note at MODAL
- IDM **be that as it ˈmay** (formal) despite that SYN **nevertheless**: *I know that he has tried hard; be that as it may, his work is just not good enough.* ⊃ more at WELL adv.
- noun [U] the white or pink flowers of the HAWTHORN

**maybe** ⓘ A1 /ˈmeɪbi/ adv., noun
- adv. **1** ʔ A1 used when you are not certain that sth will happen or that sth is true or is a correct number SYN **perhaps**: *Maybe he'll come, maybe he won't.* ◊ *'Are you going to sell your house?' 'Maybe.'* ◊ *Is she right? Maybe, maybe not.* ◊ *Maybe it will do me some good to go for a run.* ◊ *It will cost two, maybe three hundred pounds.* ◊ *We go there maybe once or twice a month.* **2** ʔ A1 used when making a suggestion SYN **perhaps**: *I thought maybe we could go together.* ◊ *Maybe you should tell her.* **3** ʔ A1 used when replying to a question or an idea, especially when you are not sure whether to agree or disagree SYN **perhaps**: *'I think he should resign.' 'Maybe.'* ◊ *'Am I nervous? Well, maybe just a little.'* ◊ *'You should stop work when you have the baby.' 'Maybe, but I can't afford to.'*
- noun something that is only a possibility and is not certain to happen or succeed: *These are all maybes—there is no certainty.*

**ˈMay bug** noun = COCKCHAFER

**May·day** /ˈmeɪdeɪ/ noun [U] an international radio signal used by ships and aircraft needing help when they are in danger ORIGIN From the French *venez m'aider* 'come and help me'.

**ˈMay Day** noun the first day of May, celebrated as a spring festival and, in some countries, as a holiday in honour of working people ⊃ compare LABOR DAY

**may·fly** /ˈmeɪflaɪ/ noun (pl. **-ies**) a small insect that lives near water and only lives for a very short time

**may·hem** /ˈmeɪhem/ noun [U] fear and a great lack of order, usually caused by violent behaviour or by some sudden terrible event: *There was absolute mayhem when everyone tried to get out at once.*

**may·on·naise** /ˌmeɪəˈneɪz; NAmE ˈmeɪəneɪz/ (also informal **mayo** /ˈmeɪəʊ/) noun [U] a thick, cold white sauce made from eggs, oil and VINEGAR, added to sandwiches, salads, etc: *egg mayonnaise* (= a dish made with hard-boiled eggs and mayonnaise)

**mayor** ʔ+ B2 /meə(r); NAmE ˈmeɪər/ noun **1** ʔ+ B2 the head of the government of a town or city, etc., elected by the public: *the Mayor of New York* ◊ *Mayor Bob Anderson* **2** ʔ+ B2 (in England, Wales and Northern Ireland) the head of a town, BOROUGH or county council, chosen by other members of the council to represent them at official ceremonies, etc. ⊃ compare PROVOST ▶ **may·oral** /ˈmeərəl; NAmE ˈmeɪə-/ adj. [only before noun]: *mayoral robes/duties*

**may·or·alty** /ˈmeərəlti; NAmE ˈmeɪə-/ noun (pl. **-ies**) (formal) **1** the title or position of a mayor **2** the period of time during which a person is a mayor

**may·or·ess** /meəˈres; NAmE ˈmeɪərəs/ noun **1** a woman who has been elected mayor ⊃ note at GENDER **2** (in England, Wales and Northern Ireland) the wife of a mayor or a woman who helps a mayor at official ceremonies

**may·pole** /ˈmeɪpəʊl/ noun a coloured POLE decorated with flowers that people dance round in celebrations on MAY DAY

**maz·door** /mʌzˈdʊə(r), -ˈdɔː(r); NAmE -ˈdʊr/ noun (IndE) a person whose job involves hard physical work that does not need special skills

**maze** /meɪz/ noun **1** a system of paths separated by walls or HEDGES built in a park or garden, that is designed so that it is difficult to find your way through: *We got lost in the maze.* ⊃ compare LABYRINTH **2** a complicated network of paths and passages: *The building is a maze of corridors.* **3** [usually sing.] a large number of complicated rules or details that are difficult to understand: *a maze of regulations* **4** (NAmE) a printed PUZZLE in which you have to draw a line that shows a way through a complicated pattern of lines

# mazurka

**ma·zur·ka** /məˈzɜːkə; NAmE -ˈzɜːrkə/ noun a fast Polish dance for four or eight couples, or a piece of music for this dance

**MB** abbr. **1** /ˌem ˈbiː/ (in the UK) Bachelor of Medicine (a university degree in medicine): *Philip Watt MB* **2** (in writing) MEGABYTE: *512MB of memory*

**Mb** (also **Mbit**) abbr. (in writing) MEGABIT

**MBA** /ˌem biː ˈeɪ/ noun a second university degree in business (the abbreviation for 'Master of Business Administration'): *to do an MBA*

**MBE** /ˌem biː ˈiː/ noun an award given to some people in the UK for a special achievement; a person who has received this award (the abbreviation for 'Member (of the Order) of the British Empire'): *She was made an MBE in 2007. ◇ Jim Cronin MBE*

**mbira** /əmˈbɪərə/ NAmE -ˈbɪrə/ SAfrE [mˈbirə] noun (pl. **mbira** or **mbiras** /əmˈbɪərəz/ NAmE -ˈbɪr-/) (SAfrE) = THUMB PIANO

**MC** /ˌem ˈsiː/ noun **1** a person who introduces guests or people who provide entertainment at a formal occasion (the abbreviation for 'master of ceremonies' **2 M.C.** the abbreviation for 'Member of Congress' **3** a person who provides entertainment at a club or party by giving instructions to the DJ and performing RAP music

**MCAT** /ˈemkæt/ noun a test that students must pass in order to study medicine in the US (the abbreviation for 'Medical College Admission Test')

**McCoy** /məˈkɔɪ/ noun

**IDM the real Mcˈ Coy** (*informal*) something that is what sb claims it is and that has value, not a copy: *It's an American flying jacket, the real McCoy.*

**ˈm-commerce** noun [U] (*BrE, business*) the business of buying and selling products on the internet by using mobile phones and other similar technology: *m-tickets and other m-commerce products*

**MD** /ˌem ˈdiː/ noun **1** the abbreviation for 'Doctor of Medicine': *Paul Clark MD* **2** (*BrE*) the person who is in charge of a business (the abbreviation for 'managing director'): *Where's the MD's office?*

**MDF** /ˌem diː ˈef/ noun [U] a building material made of wood or other plant FIBRES pressed together to form boards (the abbreviation for 'medium density fibreboard')

**MDT** /ˌem diː ˈtiː/ abbr. MOUNTAIN DAYLIGHT TIME

**ME** /ˌem ˈiː/ noun **1** (*BrE*) (also **chronic faˈtigue syndrome** NAmE, BrE) [U] an illness that makes people feel extremely weak and tired and that can last a long time (the abbreviation for 'myalgic encephalomyelitis') **2** (*NAmE*) MEDICAL EXAMINER

**me** ⓘ A1 pron., noun

■ **pron.** ⓘ A1 /mi, *strong form* miː/ the form of *I* that is used when the speaker or writer is the object of a verb or preposition, or after the verb *be*: *Don't hit me. ◇ Excuse me! ◇ Give it to me. ◇ You're taller than me. ◇ Hello, it's me. ◇ 'Who's there?' 'Only me.'* HELP The use of *me* in the last three examples is correct in modern standard English. In these sentences would be considered much too formal for almost all contexts, especially in *BrE*.

■ **noun** (*BrE*) (*NAmE* **mi**) /miː/ (*music*) the third note of a MAJOR SCALE

**mea culpa** /ˌmeɪə ˈkʊlpə/ exclamation (*from Latin, often humorous*) used when you are admitting that sth is your fault

**mead** /miːd/ noun [U] a sweet alcoholic drink made from HONEY and water, drunk especially in the past

**meadow** /ˈmedəʊ/ noun a field covered in grass, used especially for HAY: *water meadows* (= near a river) ⊃ see also SALT MARSH

**meadow·lark** /ˈmedəʊlɑːk; NAmE -lɑːrk/ noun an American singing bird that lives on the ground

**meagre** (*US* **mea·ger**) /ˈmiːɡə(r)/ adj. small in quantity and poor in quality SYN **paltry**: *a meagre diet of bread and water ◇ She supplements her meagre income by cleaning at night.*

**meal** ⓘ A1 /miːl/ noun **1** A1 [C] an occasion when people eat food, especially breakfast, lunch or dinner: *Try not to eat between meals. ◇ Lunch is his main meal of the day. ◇* (*especially BrE*) *to go out for a meal* (= to go to a restaurant to have a meal) *◇ What time would you like your evening meal?* ⊃ WORDFINDER NOTE at EAT **2** A1 [C] the food that is eaten at a meal: *Enjoy your meal. ◇ a three-course meal* ⊃ see also READY MEAL **3** [U] (often in compounds) grain that has been made into a powder, used as food for animals and for making flour ⊃ see also BARIUM MEAL, BONEMEAL, MEALIE MEAL, OATMEAL, WHOLEMEAL

**IDM make a ˈmeal of sth** (*informal*) to spend a lot of time, energy, etc. doing sth in a way that other people think is unnecessary and/or annoying ⊃ more at SQUARE adj.

▽ **MORE ABOUT ...**

**meals**

- People use the words **dinner**, **lunch**, **supper** and **tea** in different ways depending on which English-speaking country they come from. In Britain it may also depend on which part of the country or which social class a person comes from.
- A meal eaten in the middle of the day is usually called **lunch**. If it is the main meal of the day it may also be called **dinner** in *BrE*, especially in the north of the country and in schools: *I make sure my kids have a hot school dinner, not just a packed lunch.*
- A main meal eaten in the evening is usually called **dinner**, especially if it is a formal meal. **Supper** is also an evening meal, but more informal than **dinner** and usually eaten at home. It can also be a late meal or something to eat and drink before going to bed.
- In *BrE*, **tea** is a light meal in the afternoon with sandwiches, cakes, etc. and a cup of tea: *a cream tea.* It can also be a main meal eaten early in the evening, especially by children: *What time do the kids have their tea?*
- As a general rule, if **dinner** is the word someone uses for the meal in the middle of the day, they probably call the meal in the evening **tea** or **supper**. If they call the meal in the middle of the day **lunch**, they probably call the meal in the evening **dinner**.
- **Brunch**, a combination of breakfast and lunch, is becoming more common, especially as a meal where your guests serve themselves.

**meal·ie** /ˈmiːli/ noun [C, usually pl., U] (*SAfrE*) **1** = MAIZE **2** = CORN ON THE COB

**ˈmealie meal** noun [U] (*SAfrE*) MAIZE that has been made into a powder, used especially for PORRIDGE

**meals on ˈwheels** noun [pl.] a service that takes meals to old or sick people in their homes

**ˈmeal ticket** noun **1** (*informal*) a person or thing that you see only as a source of money and food: *He suspected that he was just a meal ticket for her.* **2** (*NAmE*) a card or ticket that gives you the right to have a cheap or free meal, for example at school

**meal·time** /ˈmiːltaɪm/ noun a time in the day when you eat a meal

**meal·worm** /ˈmiːlwɜːm; NAmE -wɜːrm/ noun a LARVA which is used to feed pet birds

**mealy** /ˈmiːli/ adj. (especially of vegetables or fruit) soft and dry when you eat them

**mealy-ˈmouthed** adj. (*disapproving*) not willing or honest enough to speak in a direct or open way about what you really think: *mealy-mouthed politicians*

**mean** ⓘ A1 /miːn/ verb, adj., noun

■ **verb** (**meant, meant** /ment/)

• HAVE AS MEANING **1** A1 (not used in the progressive tenses) (of a word) to have sth as a meaning in the same or another language: *~sth What does this sentence mean? ◇ What does 'lark' mean? ◇ The word 'Kuching' means 'cat' in Malay. ◇ What is meant by 'batch processing'?* **2** A1 (not used in the progressive tenses) to have sth as a meaning; to represent sth: *~sth by sth What do we mean by democracy? ◇ ~sth to sb Does the name 'Jos Vos' mean anything to you* (= do you know who he is)? *◇ (that) ... The flashing*

light means (that) you must stop. ◇ ~sth The Olympics have come to mean a wide variety of things.
• **INTEND AS MEANING 3** 🔊 **A2** (not used in the progressive tenses) to intend to say sth on a particular occasion: ~sth by sth What did he mean by that remark? ◇ ~sth 'Perhaps we should try another approach.' 'What do you mean?' (= I don't understand what you are suggesting.) ◇ 'What's that supposed to mean?' demanded John. ◇ What do you mean, you thought I wouldn't mind? (= of course I mind and I am very angry) ◇ What she means is that there's no point in waiting here. ◇ I always found him a little strange, if you know what I mean (= if you understand what I mean by 'strange'). ◇ I know what you mean (= I understand and feel sympathy). I hated learning to drive too. ◇ (informal) It was like—weird. Know what I mean? ◇ I see what you mean (= I understand although I may not agree), but I still think it's worth trying. ◇ I know what I mean (= I was right and this proves it, doesn't it)? She never agrees to anything I suggest. ◇ 'But Pete doesn't know we're here!' 'That's what I mean! (= that's what I have been trying to tell you.)' ◇ Do you mean Ann Smith or Mary Smith? ◇ ~ (that) … Did he mean (that) he was dissatisfied with our service? ◇ You mean (= are you telling me) we have to start all over again?
⊃ LANGUAGE BANK at I.E. ⊃ EXPRESS YOURSELF at CORRECT
• **HAVE AS PURPOSE 4** 🔊 **B1** to have sth as a purpose or intention **SYN** intend: ~sth What did she mean by leaving so early (= why did she do it)? ◇ Don't laugh! I mean it (= I am serious). ◇ He means trouble (= to cause trouble). ◇ ~sth as sth Don't be upset—I'm sure she meant it as a compliment. ◇ ~ what … He means what he says (= is not joking, exaggerating, etc.). ◇ ~sth for sb/sth The chair was clearly meant for a child. ◇ Don't be angry. I'm sure she meant it for the best (= intended to be helpful). ◇ ~to do sth She means to succeed. ◇ I'm sorry I hurt you. I didn't mean to. ◇ I'm feeling very guilty—I've been meaning to call my parents for days, but still haven't got around to it. ◇ ~sb/sth to do sth I didn't mean you to read the letter. ◇ You're meant to (= you are supposed to) pay before you go in. ◇ ~(that) … (formal) I never meant (that) you should come alone.
• **HAVE AS RESULT 5** 🔊 **B1** to have sth as a result or a likely result **SYN** entail: ~sth Spending too much now will mean a shortage of cash next year. ◇ Being frugal doesn't necessarily mean doing without. ◇ Lower energy consumption means less pollution. ◇ Touching the wires means instant death. ◇ ~to be/do sth Do you have any idea what it means to be poor? ◇ ~(that) … We'll have to be careful with money but that doesn't mean (that) we can't enjoy ourselves. ◇ ~doing sth This new order will mean working overtime. ◇ ~sb/sth doing sth The injury could mean him missing next week's game. ◇ High unemployment means people are spending less.
• **BE IMPORTANT 6** 🔊 **B1** [no passive] ~sth to sb to be of value or importance to sb: Your friendship means a great deal to me. ◇ $20 means a lot (= represents a lot of money) when you live on $100 a week. ◇ Money means nothing to him. ◇ Her children mean the world to her.
• **INTEND SB TO BE/DO STH 7** 🔊 **B2** [often passive] to intend sb to be or do sth: be meant for sth/sb I was never meant for the army (= did not have the qualities needed to become a soldier). ◇ Duncan and Makiko were meant for each other (= are very suitable as partners). ◇ ~sb/sth to be sth His father meant him to be an engineer. ◇ She did everything to get the two of them together, but I guess it just wasn't meant to be.
**IDM** **be meant to be sth** to be generally considered to be sth: This restaurant is meant to be excellent. **I mean** 🔊 **A2** (informal) used to explain or correct what you have just said: It was so boring—I mean, nothing happened for the first hour! ◇ She's English—Scottish, I mean. **mean ˈbusiness** (informal) to be serious in your intentions: He has the look of a man who means business. **mean (sb) no ˈharm** | **not mean (sb) any ˈharm** to not have any intention of hurting sb **mean to ˈsay** used to emphasize what you are saying or to ask sb if they really mean what they say: I mean to say, you should have known how he would react! ◇ Do you mean to say you've lost it? **ˈmean well** to have good intentions, although their effect may not be good

▪ **adj. (ˈmean·er, ˈmean·est)**
• **NOT GENEROUS 1** (BrE) (NAmE cheap) not willing to give or share things, especially money: She's always been mean with money. **OPP** generous ⊃ see also STINGY

971 | **meaning**

• **UNKIND 2** ~(to sb) (of people or their behaviour) unkind, for example by not letting sb have or do sth: Don't be so mean to your little brother!
• **ANGRY/VIOLENT 3** (especially NAmE) likely to become angry or violent: That's a mean-looking dog.
• **SHOWING SKILL 4** (informal) very good and showing skill: He's a mean tennis player. ◇ She plays a mean game of chess.
• **AVERAGE 5** [only before noun] (specialist) average; between the highest and the lowest, etc: the mean temperature
• **INTELLIGENCE 6** (formal) (of a person's understanding or ability) not very great: This should be clear even to the meanest intelligence.
• **POOR 7** (literary) poor and dirty in appearance: mean houses/streets **8** (old-fashioned) born into or coming from a low social class ▶ **ˈmean·ly** adv. **ˈmean·ness** /ˈmiːnnəs/ noun [U]
**IDM** **be no mean …** (approving) used to say that sb is very good at doing sth: His mother was a painter, and he's no mean artist himself.

▪ **noun** ⊃ see also MEANS
• **MIDDLE WAY 1** ~(between A and B) a quality, condition, or way of doing sth that is in the middle of two extremes and better than either of them: He needed to find a mean between frankness and rudeness.
• **AVERAGE 2** (also arithˈmetic ˈmean) (mathematics) the value found by adding together all the numbers in a group, and dividing the total by the number of numbers ⊃ see also GEOMETRIC MEAN
**IDM** **the happy/golden ˈmean** (approving) a course of action that is not extreme

**me·an·der** /miˈændə(r)/ verb **1** [I] (+ adv./prep.) (of a river, road, etc.) to bend with curves rather than being in a straight line: The stream meanders slowly down to the sea. **2** [I] (+ adv./prep.) to walk slowly and change direction often, especially without a particular aim **SYN** wander **3** [I] (+ adv./prep.) (of a conversation, discussion, etc.) to develop slowly and change subject often, in a way that makes it boring or difficult to understand ▶ **me·ander** noun: the meanders of a river

**me·an·der·ings** /miˈændrɪŋz/ noun [pl.] **1** a course that does not follow a straight line: the meanderings of a river/path **2** walking or talking without any particular aim: his philosophical meanderings

**meanie** (also **meany**) /ˈmiːni/ noun (pl. **-ies**) (informal) used especially by children to describe an unkind person who will not give them what they want

**mean·ing** 🔊 **A1** 🌐 /ˈmiːnɪŋ/ noun, adj.

▪ **noun**
• **OF SOUND/WORD/SIGN 1** 🔊 **A1** [U, C] ~(of sth) the thing or idea that a sound, word, sign, etc. represents: What's the meaning of this word? ◇ Words often have several meanings. ◇ I am using the word with its original meaning. ◇ 'Honesty'? He doesn't know the meaning of the word!
⊃ WORDFINDER NOTE at DICTIONARY
• **OF WHAT SB SAYS/DOES 2** 🔊 **A2** [U, C] the things or ideas that sb wishes to communicate to you by what they say or do: It is important to make your meaning clear. ◇ I don't quite get your meaning (= understand what you mean to say). ◇ What's the meaning of this? I explicitly told you not to leave the room.
• **OF FEELING/EXPERIENCE 3** 🔊 **B1** [U] the real importance of a feeling or an experience: With Anna he learned the meaning of love. ◇ The story explores the true meaning of freedom. ◇ It is difficult to grasp the meaning of these events.
• **OF BOOK/PAINTING 4** 🔊 **B1** [U, C] the ideas that a writer, artist, etc. wishes to communicate through a book, painting, etc: several layers of meaning ◇ There are, of course, deeper meanings in the poem.
• **SENSE OF PURPOSE 5** 🔊 **B1** [U] the quality or sense of purpose that makes you feel that your life is valuable: Her life seemed to have lost all meaning. ◇ Having a child gave new meaning to their lives.

▪ **adj.** [usually before noun] = MEANINGFUL (3) ⊃ see also WELL MEANING

○ Oxford Phrasal Academic Lexicon (OPAL) written and spoken word lists | Ⓦ OPAL written word list | Ⓢ OPAL spoken word list

# meaningful

**mean·ing·ful** C1 W /ˈmiːnɪŋfl/ *adj.* **1** C1 serious and important: *a meaningful relationship/discussion/experience* **2** having a meaning that is easy to understand: *These statistics are not very meaningful.* **3** (*also less frequent* **mean·ing**) intended to communicate or express sth to sb, without any words being spoken: *She gave me a meaningful look.* ▶ **mean·ing·ful·ly** /-fəli/ *adv.* **mean·ing·ful·ness** *noun* [U]

**mean·ing·less** /ˈmiːnɪŋləs/ *adj.* **1** without any purpose or reason and therefore not worth doing or having SYN **pointless**: *a meaningless existence* ◇ *We fill up our lives with meaningless tasks.* **2** not considered important SYN **irrelevant**: *Fines are meaningless to a huge company like that.* **3** not having a meaning that is easy to understand: *To me that painting is completely meaningless.* ▶ **mean·ing·less·ly** *adv.* **mean·ing·less·ness** *noun* [U]

**means** T B2 O /miːnz/ *noun* (*pl.* **means**) **1** T B2 [C] an action, an object or a system by which a result is achieved; a way of achieving or doing sth: ~ **of sth** *Email is a highly effective means of communication.* ◇ *The state is in control of the means of production.* ◇ *We needed to get to London but we had no means of transport.* ◇ ~ **of doing sth** *Is there any means of contacting him?* ◇ **as a ~ of (doing) sth** *Interest rates are used as a means of controlling borrowing.* ◇ ~ **to do sth** *They are using peaceful means to achieve their aims.* ◇ ~ **to sth** *Equality is an end in itself, not just a means to a goal.* ◇ **by … ~** *This weed can be controlled by various means.* **2** [pl.] the money that a person has: *a man of means* (= a rich man) ◇ **according to sb's ~** *People should pay according to their means.* ◇ **within sb's ~** *Are the monthly repayments within your means* (= can you afford them)*?* ◇ *Try to **live within your means** (= not spend more money than you have).* ◇ **beyond sb's ~** *Private school fees are beyond the means of most people* (= more than they can afford)*.* ◇ ~ **to do sth** *He doesn't have the means to support a wife and child.* IDM **by ˈall means** used to say that you are very willing for sb to have sth or do sth: '*Do you mind if I have a look?' 'By all means.'* **by means of sth** (*formal*) with the help of sth: *The load was lifted by means of a crane.* **by ˈno means | not by ˈany (manner of) means** not at all: *She is by no means an inexperienced teacher.* ◇ *We haven't won yet, not by any means.* **a ˌmeans to an ˈend** a thing or an action that is not interesting or important in itself but is a way of achieving sth else: *He doesn't particularly like the work but he sees it as a means to an end.* ⇒ more at END *n.*, FAIR *adj.*, WAY *n.*

**ˈmeans test** *noun* an official check of sb's wealth or income in order to decide if they are poor enough to receive money from the government, etc. for a particular purpose ▶ **ˈmeans-test** *verb* [usually passive] ~ **sb/sth**

**ˈmeans-tested** *adj.* paid to sb according to the results of a means test: *means-tested benefits*

**meant** /ment/ *past tense, past part.* of MEAN

**mean·time** T B1 /ˈmiːntaɪm/ *noun, adv.*
■ *noun* (*also* **meanwhile**)
IDM **for the ˈmeantime/ˈmeanwhile** (*BrE*) for a short period of time but not permanently: *I'm changing my email address but for the meantime you can use the old one.* **in the ˈmeantime/ˈmeanwhile** T C1 in the period of time between two times or two events: *My first novel was rejected by six publishers. In the meantime I had written a play.*
■ *adv.* (*informal*) = MEANWHILE: *I'll contact them soon. Meantime don't tell them I'm back.*

**mean·while** T B1 /ˈmiːnwaɪl/ *adv., noun*
■ *adv.* **1** B1 (*also meaning* **mean·time**) while sth else is happening: *Bob spent fifteen months alone on his yacht. Ann, meanwhile, took care of the children on her own.* **2** B1 (*also informal* **mean·time**) in the period of time between two times or two events: *The doctor will see you again next week. Meanwhile, you must rest as much as possible.* **3** B1 used to compare two aspects of a situation: *Stress can be extremely damaging to your health. Exercise, meanwhile, can reduce its effects.*
■ *noun*
IDM **for the ˈmeanwhile/ˈmeantime** (*BrE*) for a short period of time but not permanently: *We need some new curtains, but these will do for the meanwhile.* **in the ˈmeanwhile/ˈmeantime** in the period of time between two times or two events: *I hope to go to medical school eventually. In the meanwhile, I am going to study chemistry.*

**meany** = MEANIE

**mea·sles** /ˈmiːzlz/ *noun* [U] a disease, especially of children, that causes a high temperature and small red spots that cover the whole body ⇒ see also GERMAN MEASLES

**measly** /ˈmiːzli/ *adj.* (*informal, disapproving*) very small in size or quantity; not enough: *I get a measly £4 an hour.*

**meas·ur·able** /ˈmeʒərəbl/ *adj.* **1** that can be measured **2** [usually before noun] large enough to be noticed or to have a clear and definite effect: *measurable improvements* ▶ **meas·ur·ably** /-bli/ *adv.*: *Working conditions have changed measurably in the last ten years.*

**meas·ure** T B1 O /ˈmeʒə(r)/ *verb, noun*
■ *verb*
• SIZE/QUANTITY **1** B1 to find the size, quantity, etc. of sth in standard units: ~ **sth/sb** *a device that measures the level of radiation in the atmosphere* ◇ *measuring equipment/instruments* ◇ ~ **sth in sth** *A ship's speed is measured in knots.* ◇ ~ **sb/sth for sth** *He's gone to be measured for a new suit.* ◇ ~ **how much, how long, etc. …** *A dipstick is used to measure how much oil is left in an engine.* **2** B2 **linking verb** (not used in the progressive tenses) + **noun** to be a particular size, length, amount, etc: *The main bedroom measures 12ft by 15ft.* ◇ *The pond measures about 2 metres across.*
• JUDGE **3** B1 ~ **sth | ~ how, what, etc. …** to judge the importance, value or effect of sth SYN **assess**: *It is difficult to measure the success of the campaign at this stage.*
PHRV **ˌmeasure sb/sth aˈgainst sb/sth** to compare sb/sth with sb/sth: *The figures are not very good when measured against those of our competitors.* **ˌmeasure sth↔ˈout** to take the amount of sth that you need from a larger amount: *He measured out a cup of milk and added it to the mixture.* **ˌmeasure ˈup | ˌmeasure sb/sth↔ˈup (for sth)** to measure sb/sth: *We spent the morning measuring up and deciding where the furniture would go.* **ˌmeasure ˈup (to sth/sb)** (usually used in negative sentences and questions) to be as good, successful, etc. as expected or needed SYN **match up**: *Last year's intake just didn't measure up.* ◇ *The job failed to measure up to her expectations.* **ˌmeasure sb ˈup** to look at sb carefully in order to assess them: *The two shook hands and silently measured each other up.* ◇ *He glanced at her out of the corner of his eye, measuring her up.*
■ *noun*
• OFFICIAL ACTION **1** B1 [C] an official action that is done in order to achieve a particular aim: *safety/security/austerity measures* ◇ *a temporary/emergency measure* ◇ *a series/number/package/range of measures* ◇ **as a … ~** *Police in riot gear were in attendance as a precautionary measure.* ◇ ~ **to do sth** *We must take preventive measures to reduce crime in the area.* ◇ *The government is introducing tougher measures to combat crime.* ◇ ~ **against sth** *measures against racism* ⇒ SYNONYMS at ACTION ⇒ see also HALF MEASURES, SAFETY MEASURE
• UNIT OF SIZE/QUANTITY **2** B2 [C, U] a unit used for stating the size, quantity or degree of sth; a system or a scale of these units: *weights and measures* ◇ *The Richter Scale is a measure of ground motion.* ◇ *Which measure of weight do pharmacists use?* ◇ *liquid/dry measure* **3** [C] (especially of alcohol) a standard quantity: *a generous measure of whisky*
• WAY OF SHOWING/JUDGING **4** B2 [C] a way of judging or measuring sth: ~ **of sth** *an accurate measure of ability* ◇ *Exam results are only one measure of a school's success.* ◇ **as a … ~** *Companies can use their stock price as a performance measure.* ◇ ~ **of sth** *a sign of the size or the strength of sth: Sending flowers is a measure of how much you care.*
• AMOUNT **6** [sing.] ~ **of sth** a particular amount of sth, especially a fairly large amount SYN **degree**: *A measure of technical knowledge is desirable in this job.* ◇ *She achieved some measure of success with her first book.*
• INSTRUMENT FOR MEASURING **7** [C] an instrument such as a stick, a long tape or a container that is marked with

standard units and is used for measuring ⊃ see also TAPE MEASURE
- **SUGGESTED NEW LAW** **8** [C] (*NAmE*) a written suggestion, especially one for a new law made by the LAWMAKERS of a state: *a motion to refer the measure to another committee* ◊ *a ballot measure* (= a change in the law that voters decide on)
- **IN MUSIC** **9** (*BrE usually* **bar**) [C] one of the short sections of equal length that a piece of music is divided into, and the notes that are in it ⊃ picture at MUSIC

**IDM** **beyond ˈmeasure** (*formal*) very much: *He irritated me beyond measure.* **for good ˈmeasure** as an extra amount of sth in addition to what has already been done or given: *Use 50g of rice per person and an extra spoonful for good measure.* **full/short ˈmeasure** the whole of sth or less of sth than you expect or should have: *We experienced the full measure of their hospitality.* ◊ *The concert only lasted an hour, so we felt we were getting short measure.* **get/take/have the ˈmeasure of sb/sth | get/have/take sb's ˈmeasure** (*formal*) to form an opinion about sth, especially sb's character or abilities, so that you can deal with them: *After only one game, the chess champion had the measure of his young opponent.* **in full ˈmeasure** (*formal*) to the greatest possible degree **in no small ˈmeasure | in some, equal, etc. ˈmeasure** (*formal*) to a large extent or degree; to some, etc. extent or degree: *The introduction of a new tax accounted in no small measure for the downfall of the government.* ◊ *Our thanks are due in equal measure to every member of the team.* **made to ˈmeasure** (*BrE*) made especially for one person according to particular measurements **SYN** **bespoke**: *You'll need to get a suit made to measure.* ◊ *a made-to-measure suit* ⊃ more at LARGE *adj*.

**meas·ured** /ˈmeʒəd; *NAmE* -ʒərd/ *adj.* slow and careful; showing control: *She replied in a measured tone to his threat.* ◊ *He walked down the corridor with measured steps.*

**meas·ure·less** /ˈmeʒələs; *NAmE* -ʒərl-/ *adj.* (*literary*) very great or without limits: *the measureless oceans*

**meas·ure·ment** 🔊 **B2** /ˈmeʒəmənt; *NAmE* -ʒərm-/ *noun* **1** 🔊 **B2** [U, C] the act or the process of finding the size, quantity or degree of sth: *the metric system of measurement* ◊ *Accurate measurement is very important in science.* ◊ *The research is based on the measurement of body fat in schoolchildren.* ◊ *It is important to take precise measurements of the structure.* **2** 🔊 **B2** [C, usually pl.] the size, length or amount of sth: *to take sb's **chest/waist measurement*** ◊ *Do you know your measurements* (= the size of parts of your body)? ◊ *The exact measurements of the room are 3 metres 20 by 2 metres 84.* **3** [C] a unit or system of measuring: *A hand is a measurement used for measuring horses.*

**ˈmeasuring cup** *noun* a metal or plastic container used especially in the US for measuring quantities when cooking

**ˈmeasuring jug** *noun* (*BrE*) a glass or plastic container for measuring liquids when cooking

**ˈmeasuring spoon** *noun* a metal or plastic spoon used especially in the US for measuring quantities when cooking

**ˈmeasuring tape** *noun* = TAPE MEASURE

**meat** 🔊 **A1** /miːt/ *noun* **1** 🔊 **A1** [U, C] the soft part of an animal or a bird that can be eaten as food; a particular type of this: *a piece/slice of meat* ◊ *horse meat* (= from a horse) ◊ *dog meat* (= either for a dog or from a dog) ◊ *meat-eating animals* ◊ *Store raw meat on the bottom shelf of the refrigerator.* ◊ *cooked/processed meats* ◊ *meat products* ◊ *There's not much meat on this chop.* ◊ (*figurative, humorous*) *There's not much meat on her* (= she is very thin). ⊃ see also BUSHMEAT, DARK MEAT, HAMBURGER, MINCEMEAT, RED MEAT, SAUSAGE MEAT, WHITE MEAT **2** [U] **~ (of sth)** the important or interesting part of sth **SYN** **substance**: *This chapter contains the real meat of the writer's argument.* ◊ *Let's get right to **the meat of the matter** and address the problem.* **IDM** see DEAD *adj.*, EASY *adj.*, MAN *n*.

# mechanism

▼ **HOMOPHONES**

**meat • meet** /miːt/
- **meat** *noun*: *I won't have any meat, thank you—I'm a vegetarian.*
- **meet** *verb*: *I'll meet you at the station when your train gets in.*

**ˌmeat and poˈtatoes** *noun* [U] (*NAmE*) the most basic and important aspects or parts of sth: *Issues like this are the newspaper's meat and potatoes.*

**ˌmeat-and-poˈtatoes** *adj.* [only before noun] (*NAmE*) **1** dealing with the most basic and important aspects of sth: *a meat-and-potatoes argument* **2** liking plain, simple things: *He's a real meat-and-potatoes guy.*

**ˌmeat and two ˈveg** *noun* [U] (*BrE, informal*) a dish of meat with potatoes and another vegetable, considered as typical, traditional British food

**ˈmeat·ball** /ˈmiːtbɔːl/ *noun* meat cut into very small pieces and made into a ball, usually eaten hot with a sauce

**ˈmeat grinder** *noun* (*NAmE*) = MINCER

**ˈmeat loaf** *noun* [C, U] meat, onions, etc. that are cut into very small pieces, mixed together and shaped like a LOAF of bread and then baked

**ˈmeat packing** *noun* [U] (*NAmE*) the process of killing animals and preparing the meat for sale

**meaty** /ˈmiːti/ *adj.* (**meat·ier, meati·est**) **1** containing a lot of meat **2** smelling or tasting like meat: *a meaty taste* **3** (*approving*) containing a lot of important or interesting ideas **SYN** **substantial**: *a meaty discussion* **4** (*informal*) large and fat; with a lot of FLESH **SYN** **fleshy**: *a meaty hand* ◊ *big, meaty tomatoes*

**mebi·bit** /ˈmebɪbɪt/ *noun* (*abbr.* Mib) (*computing*) = MEGABIT (2)

**mebi·byte** /ˈmebɪbaɪt/ *noun* (*abbr.* MiB) (*computing*) = MEGABYTE (2)

**Mecca** /ˈmekə/ *noun* **1** a city in Saudi Arabia that is the holiest city of Islam, being the place where the Prophet Muhammad was born **2** (*usually* **mecca**) a place that many people like to visit, especially for a particular reason: *The coast is a mecca for tourists.*

**mecha** /ˈmekə/ *noun* (*pl.* **mecha** *or* **mechas**) (*from Japanese*) (in Japanese films, games and COMICS) a large fighting machine in the shape of an animal or a person, usually controlled by a person who rides inside it

**mech·an·ic** 🔊+ **B2** /məˈkænɪk/ *noun* **1** 🔊+ **B2** [C] a person whose job is repairing machines, especially the engines of vehicles: *a car/motor mechanic* **2** **mechanics** [U] the science of movement and force ⊃ see also QUANTUM MECHANICS **3** **mechanics** [U] the practical study of machines: *the school's car maintenance department where students learn basic mechanics* **4** **mechanics** the working parts of a machine: *He looks at the mechanics of a car before the bodywork.* **5** **the mechanics** [pl.] the way sth works or is done: *The exact mechanics of how payment will be made will be decided later.*

**mech·an·ic·al** 🔊+ **B2** /məˈkænɪkl/ *adj.* **1** 🔊+ **B2** operated by power from an engine: *a mechanical device/toy/clock* ◊ *mechanical parts* **2** 🔊+ **B2** relating to machines and engines: *mechanical problems/defects* ◊ *The breakdown was due to a mechanical failure.* **3** (*often disapproving*) (of people's behaviour and actions) done without thinking, like a machine **SYN** **routine**: *a mechanical gesture/response* **4** connected with the physical laws of movement and cause and effect (= with MECHANICS): *mechanical processes* **5** (of a person) good at understanding how machines work ▶ **mech·an·ic·al·ly** /-kli/ *adv.*: *a mechanically powered vehicle* ◊ *She spoke mechanically, as if thinking of something else.* ◊ *He's always been mechanically minded.*

**meˌchanical engiˈneering** *noun* [U] the study of how machines are designed, built and repaired ▶ **meˌchanical engiˈneer** *noun*

**mech·an·ism** 🔊+ **B2** 🔊 /ˈmekənɪzəm/ *noun* **1** 🔊+ **B2** a set of moving parts in a machine that performs a task: *a*

# mechanistic 974

delicate watch mechanism **2** [?]+ C1 a method or a system for achieving sth: *mechanisms for dealing with complaints from the general public* **3** [?]+ C1 a system of parts in a living thing that together perform a particular function: *the balance mechanism in the ears* ◊ *Pain acts as a natural defence mechanism.*

**mech·an·is·tic** /ˌmekəˈnɪstɪk/ *adj.* (*often disapproving*) connected with the belief that all things in the universe can be explained as if they were machines: *the mechanistic philosophy that compares the brain to a computer* ▶ **mech·an·is·tic·al·ly** /-kli/ *adv.*

**mech·an·ize** (*BrE also* **-ise**) /ˈmekənaɪz/ *verb* [usually passive] to change a process, so that the work is done by machines rather than people SYN **automate**: *be mechanized* ◊ *The production process is now highly mechanized.* ▶ **mech·an·iza·tion, -isa·tion** /ˌmekənaɪˈzeɪʃn; *NAmE* -nəˈz-/ *noun* [U]: *the increasing mechanization of farm work*

**mecha·tron·ics** /ˌmekəˈtrɒnɪks; *NAmE* -ˈtrɑːn-/ *noun* [U] technology that combines ELECTRONICS and MECHANICAL ENGINEERING

**the Med** /ðə ˈmed/ *noun* [sing.] (*informal*) the Mediterranean Sea

**med** /med/ *adj.* (*especially NAmE, informal*) medical: *a med student* ◊ *She's in med school.* ⊃ see also MEDS, PRE-MED

medals   shield
trophy   rosette   cup

**medal** [?]+ B2 /ˈmedl/ *noun, verb*
■ *noun* [?]+ B2 a flat piece of metal, usually like a coin in shape, that is given to the winner of a competition or to sb who has been brave, for example in war: *to win a gold medal in the Olympics* ◊ *to award a medal for bravery* ⊃ see also BRONZE MEDAL, GOLD MEDAL, SILVER MEDAL IDM ⊃ see DESERVE
■ *verb* [I] (**-ll-**, *US* **-l-**) to win a medal in a competition: *Evans has medalled at several international events.*

**med·al·lion** /məˈdæliən/ *noun* a piece of jewellery in the shape of a large, flat coin worn on a chain around the neck

**med·al·list** (*BrE*) (*US* **med·al·ist**) /ˈmedəlɪst/ *noun* a person who has received a medal, usually for winning a competition in a sport: *an Olympic medallist* ◊ *a gold/silver/bronze medallist* ⊃ see also BRONZE MEDALLIST, GOLD MEDALLIST, SILVER MEDALLIST

**ˈMedal of ˈHonor** *noun* the highest award that the US gives to a member of the armed forces who has shown very great courage in a war

**ˈmedal play** *noun* [U] = STROKE PLAY

**med·dle** /ˈmedl/ *verb* (*disapproving*) **1** [I] ~ (**in** / **with sth**) to involve yourself in sth that should not really involve you SYN **interfere**: *He had no right to meddle in her affairs.* **2** [I] ~ (**with sth**) to touch sth in a careless way, especially when it is not yours or when you do not know how to use it correctly: *Somebody had been meddling with her computer.* ▶ **med·dling** *noun* [U]

**med·dler** /ˈmedlə(r)/ *noun* (*disapproving*) a person who tries to get involved in sth that should not really involve them SYN **busybody**

**meddle·some** /ˈmedlsəm/ *adj.* (*disapproving*) (of people) enjoying getting involved in situations that have nothing to do with them SYN **interfering**

**mede·vac** (*also* **medi·vac**) /ˈmedɪvæk/ *noun* [U] (*especially NAmE*) the movement of injured soldiers or other people to hospital in a helicopter or other aircraft ⊃ compare AIR AMBULANCE

**media** [1] A2 W /ˈmiːdiə/ *noun* **1** [?] **the media** [C + sing./pl. v.] the main ways that large numbers of people receive information and entertainment, that is television, radio, newspapers and the internet: *the national/international media* ◊ *The news media reported extensively on the story.* ◊ *The media was/were accused of influencing the final decision.* ◊ *Digital media change so quickly.* ◊ *print/ electronic/broadcast media* ◊ *This is a story that the mainstream media refuses to cover.* ◊ **in the ~** *The trial was fully reported in the media.* ◊ *Any event attended by the actor received widespread media coverage.* HELP The word **media** comes from the Latin plural of **medium**. In modern English it can be treated as either a singular or plural noun: *The media has/have followed the story closely.* A new plural form, **medias**, is also increasingly being used: *The medias of several countries have been following the story.* ⊃ see also MAINSTREAM MEDIA, MASS MEDIA, NEW MEDIA, SOCIAL MEDIA **2** *pl.* of MEDIUM

**medi·aeval** = MEDIEVAL

**medi·al** /ˈmiːdiəl/ *adj.* (*specialist*) located in the middle, especially of the body or of an organ

**me·dian** /ˈmiːdiən/ *adj., noun*
■ *adj.* [only before noun] (*specialist*) **1** having a value in the middle of a series of values: *the median age/price* **2** located in or passing through the middle: *a median point/line*
■ *noun* **1** (*mathematics*) the middle value of a series of numbers arranged in order of size **2** (*geometry*) a straight line passing from a point of a TRIANGLE to the centre of the opposite side **3** (*also* **ˈmedian strip**) (*both NAmE*) (*BrE* **ˌcentral reserˈvation**) a narrow piece of land that separates the two sides of a major road such as a MOTORWAY or INTERSTATE

**ˌmedia-ˈsavvy** *adj.* having a good understanding of the influence of the internet, newspapers, television, etc. and how to use it effectively

**ˈmedia studies** *noun* [U + sing./pl. v.] the study of newspapers, television, radio, the internet, etc. as a subject at school, etc.

**me·di·ate** W /ˈmiːdieɪt/ *verb* **1** [I, T] to try to end a situation between two or more people or groups who disagree by talking to them and trying to find things that everyone can agree on: **~ (in sth)** *The Secretary-General was asked to mediate in the dispute.* ◊ **~ between A and B** *An independent body was brought in to mediate between staff and management.* ◊ **~ sth** *to mediate differences/disputes/problems* **2** [T] **~ sth** to succeed in finding a solution to a problem between people or groups who disagree SYN **negotiate**: *They mediated a settlement.* **3** [T, usually passive] (*formal or specialist*) to influence sth and/or make it possible for it to happen: *be mediated (by sth)* *Educational success is mediated by economic factors.* ▶ **me·di·ation** /ˌmiːdiˈeɪʃn/ *noun* [U, C]

**me·di·ator** /ˈmiːdieɪtə(r)/ *noun* a person or an organization that tries to get agreement between people or groups who disagree with each other

**medic** /ˈmedɪk/ *noun* **1** (*especially BrE, informal*) a medical student or doctor **2** (*NAmE*) a person who is trained to give medical treatment, especially sb in the armed forces

**Medic·aid** /ˈmedɪkeɪd/ *noun* [U] (in the US) the insurance system that provides medical care for poor people

**med·ic·al** [1] A2 W /ˈmedɪkl/ *adj., noun*
■ *adj.* [usually before noun] connected with illness and injury and their treatment: *medical care/treatment* ◊ *the medical profession* ◊ *medical research/advances* ◊ *her medical condition/history/records* ◊ *a medical student/ school* ◊ *medical staff* ◊ *a medical certificate (= a*

statement by a doctor that gives details of your state of health) ⇒ see also MED **2** connected with ways of treating illness that do not involve cutting the body: *medical or surgical treatment* ▸ **med·ic·al·ly** /-kli/ *adv.*: *medically fit/unfit*
- *noun* (*also* **medical exami'nation**) a careful and complete examination of your body that a doctor does, for example before you start a particular job ⇒ see also EXAM

**medical e'xaminer** *noun* (*abbr.* **ME**) (*NAmE*) an official whose job is to investigate deaths that occur in unusual circumstances, including examination of the body in order to find out the cause of death ⇒ compare PATHOLOGIST

**'medical hall** *noun* (*IndE*, *informal*) a CHEMIST'S

**'medical officer** *noun* (*abbr.* **MO**) a doctor employed in an organization to deal with medical and health matters

**'medical school** (*NAmE also* **med school** *informal*) *noun* a college or a department of a university where students study to obtain a degree in medicine

**'medical 'tourism** *noun* [U] (*especially NAmE*) = HEALTH TOURISM

**Medi·care** /'medɪkeə(r)/; *NAmE* -ker/ *noun* [U] **1** (in the US) the government insurance system that provides medical care for people over 65 **2** (in Australia and Canada) the national medical care system for all people that is paid for by taxes (spelt 'medicare' in Canada)

**medi·cate** /'medɪkeɪt/ *verb* **1** ~ **sb (with sth) (for sth)** to give sb medicine, especially a drug that affects their behaviour ⇒ see also SELF-MEDICATE **2** ~**sth** to treat a health problem using medicine or a drug: *Sometimes we medicate the symptoms without fixing the underlying problem.*

**medi·cated** /'medɪkeɪtɪd/ *adj.* **1** [not before noun] (of a person) being given medicine, especially a drug that affects their behaviour: *All the patients are heavily medicated.* **2** [usually before noun] containing a substance for preventing or curing infections of your skin or hair: *medicated soap/shampoo*

**medi·ca·tion** /ˌmedɪˈkeɪʃn/ *noun* [U, C] a drug or another form of medicine that you take to prevent or to treat an illness; treatment involving drugs: ~ **(for sth)** *Are you currently taking any medication?* ◇ **on** ~ **(for sth)** *She is on medication for depression.* ◇ *Many flu medications are available without a prescription.* ⇒ WORDFINDER NOTE at CURE

**me·di·cin·al** /məˈdɪsɪnl/ *adj.* helpful in the process of curing illness or infection: *medicinal herbs/plants* ◇ *medicinal properties/use* ◇ (*humorous*) *He claims he keeps a bottle of brandy only for medicinal purposes.*

**medi·cine** /'medsn, 'medɪsn/; *NAmE* 'medɪsn/ *noun* **1** [U] the study and treatment of diseases and injuries: *advances in modern medicine* ◇ *to study/practise medicine* ◇ *a professor of medicine* ◇ *conventional/orthodox medicine* ◇ *alternative/complementary medicine* ◇ *Acupuncture has long been a part of traditional Chinese medicine.* ◇ *a rapidly developing field of medicine* ⇒ see also ALTERNATIVE MEDICINE, AYURVEDIC MEDICINE, COMPLEMENTARY MEDICINE, DEFENSIVE MEDICINE, FAMILY MEDICINE, INTERNAL MEDICINE, SOCIALIZED MEDICINE, SPORTS MEDICINE, TRADITIONAL MEDICINE **2** [U, C] a substance that you take in order to cure an illness, especially a liquid that you drink or SWALLOW: *Did you take your medicine?* ◇ *Your doctor can prescribe medicine to ease your symptoms.* ◇ *cough medicine* ◇ *Chinese herbal medicines* ⇒ see also COUGH MEDICINE at COUGH MIXTURE ⇒ WORDFINDER NOTE at DOCTOR

WORDFINDER administer, capsule, dispense, dose, inhaler, medication, pharmacy, placebo

IDM **the best 'medicine** the best way of improving a situation, especially of making you feel happier: *Laughter is the best medicine.* **a taste/dose of your own 'medicine** the same bad treatment that you have given to others: *Let the bully have a taste of his own medicine.*

**'medicine ball** *noun* a large, heavy ball that you throw, catch, hold and roll as a form of exercise

975

**'medicine man** *noun* (especially among Native Americans) a person who is believed to have special magic powers that can be used to make sick people well again ⇒ compare WITCH DOCTOR

**med·ico** /'medɪkəʊ/ *noun* (*pl.* **-os**) (*informal*) a doctor

**medi·eval** (*also* **medi·aeval**) /ˌmediˈiːvl; *NAmE also* ˌmiːdiˈiː-/ *adj.* [usually before noun] connected with the Middle Ages (about AD1000 to AD1450): *medieval architecture/castles/manuscripts* ◇ *the literature of the late medieval period*

**me·di·ocre** /ˌmiːdiˈəʊkə(r)/ *adj.* (*disapproving*) not very good; of only average standard: *a mediocre musician/talent/performance* ◇ *I thought the play was only mediocre.*

**me·di·oc·rity** /ˌmiːdiˈɒkrəti; *NAmE* -ˈɑːk-/ *noun* (*pl.* **-ies**) (*disapproving*) **1** [U] the fact of being average or not very good: *His acting career started brilliantly, then sank into mediocrity.* **2** [C] a person who is not very good at sth: *a brilliant leader, surrounded by mediocrities*

**medi·tate** /'medɪteɪt/ *verb* **1** [I] to focus your mind, usually in silence, especially for religious reasons or in order to make your mind calm **2** [I] ~ **(on/upon sth)** (*formal*) to think deeply about sth: *He went off to meditate on the new idea.* **3** [T] ~**sth** (*formal*) to plan sth in your mind; to consider doing sth SYN contemplate: *They were meditating revenge.*

**medi·ta·tion** /ˌmedɪˈteɪʃn/ *noun* **1** [U] the practice of focusing your mind in silence, especially for religious reasons or in order to make your mind calm: *She found peace through yoga and meditation.* ⇒ see also TRANSCENDENTAL MEDITATION **2** [U] the activity of thinking deeply about sth, especially so that you do not notice the people or things around you: **in**~ *He was deep in meditation and didn't see me come in.* **3** [C, usually pl.] ~ **(on sth)** (*formal*) serious thoughts on a particular subject that sb writes down or speaks: *his meditations on life and art*

**medi·ta·tive** /'medɪtətɪv; *NAmE* -teɪt-/ *adj.* (*formal*) thinking very deeply; involving deep thought SYN **thoughtful**: *She found him in a meditative mood.* ◇ *a meditative poem*

**Medi·ter·ra·nean** /ˌmedɪtəˈreɪniən/ *adj.*, *noun*
- *adj.* [only before noun] relating to the Mediterranean Sea or the countries that surround it; typical of this area: *a Mediterranean country* ◇ *a Mediterranean climate*
- *noun* **the Mediterranean** [sing.] the Mediterranean Sea or the countries that surround it: *The hotel boasts spectacular views of the Mediterranean.*

**me·dium** /'miːdiəm/ *adj.*, *noun*
- *adj.* [usually before noun] (*abbr.* **M**) in the middle between a larger and smaller size, amount, length, temperature, etc. SYN **average**: *There are three sizes—small, medium and large.* ◇ *a man of medium height/build* ◇ *Cook over a medium heat for 15 minutes.* ◇ *a medium dry white wine* ◇ *Choose medium to large tomatoes.* IDM see TERM *n.*
- *noun* (*pl.* **media** /-diə/ *or* **me·diums**) **1** a way of communicating information, etc. to people: *the medium of radio/television* ◇ *electronic/audiovisual media* ◇ ~ **of sth** *The internet is the modern medium of communication.* ◇ ~ **for doing sth** *A T-shirt can be an excellent medium for getting your message across.* HELP The plural in this meaning is usually **media**. ⇒ see also MEDIA, MASS MEDIA **2** something that is used for a particular purpose: ~ **of sth** *English is the medium of instruction* (= the language used to teach other subjects). ◇ ~ **for doing sth** *Video is a good medium for learning a foreign language.* **3** (*computing*) the material used for storing computer files, such as on MAGNETIC TAPE or discs **4** the material or the form that an artist, a writer or a musician uses: *the medium of paint/poetry/drama* ◇ *Watercolour is his favourite medium.* ◇ *The portrait is mixed media on wood.* **5** (*biology*) a substance that sth exists or grows in or that it travels through: *The bacteria were growing in a sugar medium.* **6** (*pl.* **me·diums**) a person who claims to be able to communicate with the spirits of dead people IDM see HAPPY

**'medium-sized** (*also* **'medium-size**) *adj.* of average size: *a medium-sized saucepan* ◇ *a medium-size car/business/town*

# medium-term

**'medium-term** *adj.* used to describe a period of time into the future that is neither very long nor very short, for example a few weeks or months: *the government's medium-term financial strategy*

**'medium wave** *(abbr.* **MW)** *noun* [U] *(also* **the medium wave** [sing.]) a band of radio waves with a length of between 100 and 1000 metres, used for broadcasting: **on (the)** ~ *648m on (the) medium wave* ⊃ compare SHORT WAVE

**me·di·vac** = MEDEVAC

**med·ley** /ˈmedli/ *noun* **1** a piece of music consisting of several songs or tunes played or sung one after the other: *a medley of Beatles hits* **2** a mixture of people or things of different kinds: *a medley of flavours/smells* **3** a swimming race in which swimmers use a different STROKE (= style of swimming) for each section of the race, either individually or in teams: *the 4×100 metres medley*

**meds** /medz/ *noun* [pl.] (*informal*) medicine; MEDICATION: *He'd forgotten to take his meds.*

**'med school** *noun* (*NAmE, informal*) = MEDICAL SCHOOL

**meek** /miːk/ *adj.* (**meek·er, meek·est**) **1** quiet, gentle, and always ready to do what other people want without expressing your own opinion **SYN** **compliant, self-effacing**: *They called her Miss Mouse because she was so meek and mild.* **2 the meek** *noun* [pl.] people who are meek ▶ **meek·ly** *adv.*: *He meekly did as he was told.* **meek·ness** *noun* [U]

**meer·kat** /ˈmɪəkæt; *NAmE* ˈmɪrk-/ *noun* a small southern African animal with a long tail, which often stands up on its back legs. Meerkats are a type of MONGOOSE.

**meet** ⓘ A1 /miːt/ *verb, noun*

■ *verb* (**met, met** /met/)
- BY CHANCE **1** A1 [I, T, no passive] to be in the same place as sb by chance and talk to them: *Maybe we'll meet again some time.* ◇ *~sb Did you meet anyone in town?* ◇ *I've never met anyone like her.*
- BY ARRANGEMENT **2** A1 [I, T, no passive] to come together formally in order to discuss sth: *The committee meets on Fridays.* ◇ *~sb The Prime Minister met other European leaders for talks.* ◇ *~with sb The President met with senior White House aides.* ◇ *~to do sth They met to discuss the project while both were in Paris.* **3** A1 [I, T, no passive] to come together socially after you have arranged it: *~(for sth) Let's meet for a drink after work.* ◇ *~sb (for sth) We're meeting them outside the theatre at 7.* **4** A1 [T] to go to a place and wait there for a particular person or thing to arrive: *~sb/sth Will you meet me at the airport?* ◇ *The hotel bus meets all incoming flights.* ◇ *~sb off sth I met him off the train.* ⊃ HOMOPHONES at MEAT
- FOR THE FIRST TIME **5** A1 [I, T, no passive] to see and know sb for the first time; to be introduced to sb: *I don't think we've met.* ◇ *~sb Where did you first meet your husband?* ◇ (*especially BrE*) **Pleased to meet you** (= when you first meet sb). ◇ **Nice meeting you** (= when you leave sb after meeting them for the first time). ◇ *There's someone I want you to meet.* ◇ *Have you met Miranda?* ◇ *I love meeting people.*
- SATISFY **6** B2 [T] *~sth* to do or satisfy what is needed or what sb asks for **SYN** **fulfil**: *How can we best meet the needs of all the different groups?* ◇ *The airport must be expanded to meet demand.* ◇ *to meet a target/challenge/goal* ◇ *to meet the requirements/criteria/standards*
- IN CONTEST **7** [I, T, no passive] to play, fight, etc. together as opponents in a competition: *Smith and Jones met in last year's final.* ◇ *~sb Smith met Jones in last year's final.*
- EXPERIENCE STH **8** [T] *~sth* to experience sth, often sth unpleasant **SYN** **come across, encounter**: *Others have met similar problems.* ◇ *How she met her death will probably never be known.*
- TOUCH/JOIN **9** [I, T] to touch sth; to join: *The curtains don't meet in the middle.* ◇ *~sth That's where the river meets the sea.* ◇ *His hand met hers.*
- PAY **10** [T] *~sth* to pay sth: *The cost will be met by the company.*

**IDM** **meet sb's 'eye(s)** | **meet sb's 'gaze, 'look, etc.** | **people's 'eyes meet 1** [T, I] if you **meet sb's eye(s)**, you look directly at them as they look at you; if two people's eyes meet, they look directly at each other: *She was afraid to met my eye.* ◇ *Their eyes met across the crowded room.* ◇ *She met his gaze without flinching.* **2** [T] **~your eyes** if a sight **meets your eyes**, you see it: *A terrible sight met their eyes.* **meet sb half'way** to reach an agreement with sb by giving them part of what they want **meet your 'Maker** (*especially humorous*) to die **there is more to sb/sth than meets the 'eye** a person or thing is more complicated or interesting than you might think at first ⊃ more at END *n.*, MATCH *n.*, RUBBER *n.*, TWAIN

**PHRV** **meet 'up (with sb)** (*rather informal*) to meet sb, especially by arrangement: *They met up again later for a drink.* **'meet with sb** to meet sb, especially for discussions: *The President met with senior White House aides.* **'meet with sth 1** to be received or treated by sb in a particular way: *Her proposal met with resistance from the Left.* ◇ *to meet with success/failure* **2** to experience sth unpleasant: *She was worried that he might have met with an accident.* **'meet sth with sth** to react to sth in a particular way **SYN** **receive**: *His suggestion was met with howls of protest.*

■ *noun* **1** (*especially NAmE*) a sports competition: *a track meet* ⊃ compare MEETING (4) **2** (*BrE*) an event at which horse riders and dogs meet to go hunting. FOX HUNTING with dogs is now illegal in the UK but people still ride out with dogs following a SCENT TRAIL, without an actual FOX. ⊃ see also SWAP MEET

**meet-and-'greet** *adj.* [only before noun] (of an event) arranged so that sb, especially a famous person, can meet and talk to people ▶ **'meet and greet** *noun*

**meet·ing** ⓘ A1 /ˈmiːtɪŋ/ *noun* **1** A1 [C] an occasion when people come together to discuss or decide sth: *to attend/hold a meeting* ◇ *to schedule/convene/arrange/organize/call a meeting* ◇ *a board/council/committee/public meeting* ◇ *in/at a ~ I'll be in a meeting all morning—can you take my calls?* ◇ *~with sb She is due to have a meeting with senior government officials.* ◇ *~about sth A public meeting about the proposal takes place on Monday.* ◇ *Facilities include nine meeting rooms.* ⊃ see also ANNUAL GENERAL MEETING, TOWN MEETING

**WORDFINDER** agenda, AGM, apology, brainstorming, breakout, chair, committee, convene, the minutes

**2 the meeting** [sing.] the people at a meeting: *The meeting will discuss how to resolve the ongoing crisis in this region.* **3** A1 [C] a situation in which two or more people meet together, because they have arranged it or by chance **SYN** **encounter**: **at a ~** *At our first meeting I was nervous.* ◇ *It was a chance meeting that would change my life.* ◇ *~with sb This was only my second meeting with him.* **4** [C] (*BrE*) a sports event or set of races, especially for horses: *an athletics meeting* ◇ *a race meeting* ⊃ compare MEET (1) ⊃ see also RACE MEETING **5** an occasion when people, especially Quakers, come together for WORSHIP ⊃ see also PRAYER MEETING

**IDM** **a meeting of 'minds** a close understanding between people with similar ideas, especially when they meet to do sth or meet for the first time

**'meeting house** *noun* a place where Quakers meet for WORSHIP

**'meeting place** *noun* a place where people often meet: *The cafe is a popular meeting place for students.*

**meet-up** /ˈmiːtʌp/ *noun* (*US*) an informal meeting or social event: *You are welcome to attend the meetup on Sunday.*

**meg** /meg/ *noun* (*informal*) = MEGABYTE: *more than 512 megs of memory* ◇ *24-meg broadband*

**mega** /ˈmegə/ *adj.* [usually before noun] (*informal*) very large or impressive **SYN** **huge, great**: *The song was a mega hit last year.* ▶ **mega** *adv.*: *They're mega rich.*

**mega-** /ˈmegə/ *combining form* (in nouns) **1** very large or great: *a megastore* **2** (in units of measurement) one million: *a megawatt* **3** (*computing*) (in units of measurement) $2^{20}$, or 1048576

**mega·bit** /ˈmegəbɪt/ *noun* (*abbr.* **Mb**) (*computing*) **1** a unit of computer memory or data, equal to $10^6$, or $1000^2$, (= 1000000) BITS **2** (*also* **mebi·bit**) a unit of computer memory or data, equal to $2^{20}$, or $1024^2$, (= 1048576) BITS

**mega·bucks** /ˈmegəbʌks/ noun [pl.] (informal) a very large amount of money: *He earns megabucks.*

**mega·byte** /ˈmegəbaɪt/ (also informal **meg**) noun (abbr. **MB**) (computing) **1** a unit of computer memory or data, equal to 10⁶, or 1000², (= 1000000) BYTES: *a 512-megabyte flash drive* **2** (also **mebi·byte**) a unit of computer memory or data, equal to 2²⁰, or 1024², (= 1048576) BYTES

**mega·city** /ˈmegəsɪti/ noun (pl. **-ies**) a very large city, usually one with a population of over 10 million people

**mega·hertz** /ˈmegəhɜːts; NAmE -hɜːrts/ noun (pl. **mega·hertz**) (abbr. **MHz**) a unit for measuring radio waves and the speed at which a computer operates; 1000000 HERTZ

**mega·lith** /ˈmegəlɪθ/ noun a very large stone, especially one put in a place that was used for ceremonies in ancient times ▸ **mega·lith·ic** /ˌmegəˈlɪθɪk/ adj.

**meg·alo·mania** /ˌmegələˈmeɪniə/ noun [U] **1** (specialist) a mental illness or condition in which sb has a much greater belief in their own importance or power than is reasonable **2** a strong feeling that you want to have more and more power

**meg·alo·maniac** /ˌmegələˈmeɪniæk/ noun a person suffering from or showing megalomania ▸ **meg·alo·maniac** adj.

**meg·alop·olis** /ˌmegəˈlɒpəlɪs; NAmE -ˈlɑːp-/ noun (formal) a very large city or group of cities where a great number of people live

**mega·phone** /ˈmegəfəʊn/ (BrE also **loudhailer**, NAmE also **bullhorn**) noun a device for making your voice sound louder, that is wider at one end, like a CONE, and is often used at outside events ⊃ compare LOUDHAILER, MICROPHONE

**mega·pixel** /ˈmegəpɪksl/ noun a million PIXELS (= very small individual areas on a computer screen), used to measure the quality of a digital screen or image: *a 12 megapixel digital camera*

**mega·star** /ˈmegəstɑː(r)/ noun (informal) a very famous singer, actor, musician, etc.

**mega·store** /ˈmegəstɔː(r)/ noun a very large shop, especially one that sells one type of product, for example computers or furniture

**mega·ton** (also **mega·tonne**) /ˈmegətʌn/ noun a unit for measuring the power of an EXPLOSIVE, equal to one million TONS of TNT: *a one megaton nuclear bomb*

**mega·watt** /ˈmegəwɒt; NAmE -wɑːt/ noun (abbr. **MW**) a unit for measuring electrical power; one million WATTS

**meh** /me/ exclamation, adj. (informal) used to show that you are not at all interested in or impressed by sth: *'So how was the movie?' 'Meh. The action scenes aren't awful, but there's nothing great about it.'* ◊ *She does an OK job on a meh song.*

**mehndi** (also **mehendi**) /ˈmendi/ noun (IndE) **1** [U, C] the art of applying a temporary design to a person's skin using a red-brown DYE (= a substance used to change the colour of sth), especially for their wedding day; this type of decoration: *She wore traditional dress and mehndi at the event.* **2** [U] a type of red-brown DYE made from HENNA that is used to create mehndis

**mei·osis** /maɪˈəʊsɪs/ noun [U, C] (pl. **meioses** /-ˈəʊsiːz/) (biology) a special type of cell division that happens in two stages and produces four cells, each with half the number of CHROMOSOMES of the original cell, for the purpose of sexual REPRODUCTION

**-meister** /ˈmaɪstə(r)/ combining form (in nouns) (informal) a person thought of as important in a particular field or having a lot of skill at a particular activity: *a horror-meister*

**mela** /ˈmeɪlə/ noun (IndE) a type of entertainment event, usually held outdoors, or a religious festival

**mela·mine** /ˈmeləmiːn/ noun [U] a strong, hard plastic material, used especially for covering surfaces such as the tops of tables, and for making cups, etc.

**mel·an·cho·lia** /ˌmelənˈkəʊliə/ noun (old-fashioned) a mental illness in which the patient is depressed and worried by unnecessary fears

977 **melodramatics**

**mel·an·chol·ic** /ˌmelənˈkɒlɪk; NAmE -ˈkɑːl-/ adj. (old-fashioned or literary) having or expressing the feeling of being sad, especially when that feeling is like an illness

**mel·an·choly** /ˈmelənkəli, -kɒli; NAmE -kɑːli/ noun, adj.
- noun [U] (literary) a feeling of being very sad that lasts for a long time and often cannot be explained: *A mood of melancholy descended on us.*
- adj. (literary) very sad or making you feel very sad SYN **mournful**, **sombre**: *melancholy thoughts/memories* ◊ *The melancholy song died away.*

**me·lange** /meɪˈlɑːnʒ/ noun (from French, formal) a mixture or variety of different things: *a melange of different cultures*

**mel·anin** /ˈmelənɪn/ noun [U] (specialist) a dark substance in the skin and hair that causes the skin to change colour in the sun's light

**mela·noma** /ˌmeləˈnəʊmə/ noun [C, U] (medical) a type of cancer that appears as a dark spot or TUMOUR on the skin

**mela·to·nin** /ˌmeləˈtəʊnɪn/ noun [U] (biology) a HORMONE that helps REGULATE (= control) waking and sleeping in humans and animals, and which is sometimes used to treat INSOMNIA (= the condition of being unable to sleep)

**meld** /meld/ verb [I, T] ~ (A) with B / ~ (A and B) (together) (formal) to combine with sth else; to make sth combine with sth else SYN **blend**

**melee** /ˈmeleɪ; NAmE ˈmeɪl-/ noun [sing.] (from French) a situation in which a crowd of people are rushing or pushing each other in a confused way

**mel·lif·lu·ous** /meˈlɪfluəs/ adj. (formal) (of music or of sb's voice) sounding sweet and smooth; very pleasant to listen to

**mel·low** /ˈmeləʊ/ adj., verb
- adj. (**mel·low·er**, **mel·low·est**) **1** (of colour or sound) soft, rich and pleasant: *mellow autumn colours* ◊ *Mellow music and lighting helped to create the right atmosphere.* **2** (of a taste or flavour) smooth and pleasant: *a mellow, fruity wine* **3** (of people) calm, gentle and reasonable because of age or experience: *Dad's certainly grown mellower with age.* **4** (informal) (of people) relaxed, calm and happy, especially after drinking alcohol: *After two glasses of wine, I was feeling mellow.*
- verb **1** [I, T] to become or make sb become less extreme in behaviour, etc., especially as a result of growing older: *She had mellowed a great deal since their days at college.* ◊ ~ sb *A period spent working abroad had done nothing to mellow him.* **2** [I, T] to become or to make a colour become less bright, especially over a period of time **3** [I, T] ~ (sth) to develop or make wine develop a pleasant and less bitter taste over a period of time

PHRV **mellow 'out** (especially NAmE, informal) to enjoy yourself by relaxing and not doing much

**me·lod·ic** /məˈlɒdɪk; NAmE -ˈlɑːd-/ adj. **1** [only before noun] connected with the main tune in a piece of music: *The melodic line is carried by the two clarinets.* **2** = MELODIOUS

**me·lod·ica** /məˈlɒdɪkə; NAmE -ˈlɑːd-/ noun a musical instrument that has a keyboard and a part that you blow into

**me·lo·di·ous** /məˈləʊdiəs/ (also **me·lod·ic**) adj. pleasant to listen to, like music: *a rich, melodious voice* ▸ **me·lo·di·ous·ly** adv.

**melo·drama** /ˈmelədrɑːmə/ noun [U, C] **1** a story, play or novel that is full of exciting events and in which the characters and emotions seem too EXAGGERATED to be real: *a gripping Victorian melodrama* ◊ *Instead of tragedy, we got melodrama.* **2** events, behaviour, etc. that are EXAGGERATED or extreme: *Her love of melodrama meant that any small problem became a crisis.*

**melo·dra·mat·ic** /ˌmelədrəˈmætɪk/ adj. (often disapproving) full of exciting and extreme emotions or events; behaving or reacting to sth in an EXAGGERATED way: *a melodramatic plot full of deceit and murder* ▸ **melo·dra·mat·ic·al·ly** /-kli/ adv.

**melo·dra·mat·ics** /ˌmelədrəˈmætɪks/ noun [pl.] behaviour or events that are melodramatic: *Let's have no more melodramatics, if you don't mind.*

---

**O** Oxford Phrasal Academic Lexicon (OPAL) written and spoken word lists | **W** OPAL written word list | **S** OPAL spoken word list

**mel·ody** 🔑+ C1 /ˈmelədi/ *noun* (*pl.* **-ies**) **1** 🔑+ C1 [C] a tune, especially the main tune in a piece of music written for several instruments or voices: *a haunting melody* ◇ *The melody is then taken up by the flutes.* **2** 🔑+ C1 [C] a piece of music or a song with a clear or simple tune: *old Irish melodies* **3** [U] the arrangement of musical notes in a tune: *a few bars of melody drifted towards us* ➲ WORDFINDER NOTE at SING

**melon** /ˈmelən/ *noun* [C, U] a large fruit with hard green, yellow or orange skin, that is sweet inside with juice and a lot of seeds: *a slice of melon* ➲ see also WATERMELON

**melt** ⓘ B2 /melt/ *verb* **1** 🔑 B2 [I, T] to become or make sth become liquid as a result of heating: *The snow showed no sign of melting.* ◇ *melting ice* ◇ **~ sth** *The sun had melted the snow.* ◇ *boiled potatoes with melted butter* ➲ compare DEFROST, DE-ICE, MELTING POINT **2** [I, T] to become or to make a feeling, an emotion, etc. become gentler and less strong: *The tension in the room began to melt.* ◇ **~ sth** *Her trusting smile melted his heart.* **3** (of a person) to become extremely hot: *Today the temperature got up to 36 degrees and it felt like I was melting.*
IDM **ˌmelt in your ˈmouth** (of food) to be soft and very good to eat ➲ more at BUTTER *n.*
PHR V **ˌmelt aˈway** | **ˌmelt sth↔aˈway** to disappear or make sth disappear gradually: *At the first sign of trouble, the crowd melted away.* **ˌmelt sth↔ˈdown** to heat a metal or WAX object until it is liquid, especially so that the metal or wax can be used to make sth else ➲ related noun MELTDOWN **ˈmelt into sth** to gradually become part of sth and therefore become difficult to see

**melt·down** /ˈmeltdaʊn/ *noun* [U, C] **1** a serious accident in which the central part of a nuclear REACTOR melts, causing harmful RADIATION to escape **2** (*economics*) a situation where sth fails or becomes weaker in a sudden or dramatic way: **in ~** *The country is in economic meltdown.* ◇ *a meltdown on the New York Stock Exchange*

**melt·ing** /ˈmeltɪŋ/ *adj.* [usually before noun] (*literary*) persuading you to feel love or sympathy: *his melting eyes* ▶ **melt·ing·ly** *adv.*

**ˈmelting point** (*also* **ˈmelting temperature**) *noun* [U, C] the temperature at which a solid substance will melt

**ˈmelting pot** *noun* [usually sing.] a place or situation in which large numbers of different people, ideas, etc. are mixed together: *the vast melting pot of American society*
IDM **in the ˈmelting pot** (*especially BrE*) likely to change; in the process of changing

**mem·ber** ⓘ A1 Ⓦ /ˈmembə(r)/ *noun* **1** 🔑 A1 **~ (of sth)** a person, an animal or a plant that belongs to a particular group: *a **member of the family/community*** ◇ *He is an important **member of our team**.* ◇ ***Members of the public** are invited to come and view the work* ◇ *characteristics common to all members of the species* ◇ ***family/staff members*** **2** 🔑 A1 a person, a country or an organization that has joined a particular group, club or team: ***party/union members*** ◇ *a meeting of **member states/countries*** ◇ *How much does it cost to **become a member**?* ◇ **~ of sth** *an active member of the local church* ➲ WORDFINDER NOTE at CLUB ➲ see also CHARTER MEMBER, FOUNDER MEMBER, SERVICE MEMBER **3 Member** (in the UK) a Member of Parliament: *the Hon. Member for Brent North* ➲ see also PRIVATE MEMBER **4** (used in a title) a person who has been given an honour: *Murray was made a Member of the Order of Australia for his services to Association Football.* **5** (*old use* or *literary*) a part of the body, especially an arm or a leg **6** (*formal*) a PENIS. People say 'member' to avoid saying 'penis'.

**ˌMember of ˈParliament** *noun* = MP

**mem·ber·ship** 🔑+ B2 /ˈmembəʃɪp; *NAmE* -bərʃ-/ *noun* **1** 🔑+ B2 [U, C] the state of being a member of a group, a club, an organization, etc: **~ of sth** (*BrE*) *Who is eligible to apply for membership of the association?* ◇ **~ in sth** (*NAmE*) *membership in the association* ◇ *Memberships are available on a monthly or yearly basis.* ◇ *a **membership card/fee*** **2** 🔑+ C1 [C + sing./pl. v.] the members, or the number of members, of a group, a club, an organization, etc: *The membership has/have not yet voted.* ◇ *The club has a membership of more than 500.*

**mem·brane** /ˈmembreɪn/ *noun* [C, U] **1** a thin layer of skin or TISSUE that connects or covers parts inside the body ➲ see also MUCOUS MEMBRANE **2** a very thin layer found in the structure of cells in plants **3** a thin layer of material used to prevent air, liquid, etc. from entering a particular part of sth: *a waterproof membrane* ▶ **mem·bran·ous** /-brənəs/ *adj.* (*specialist*)

**meme** /miːm/ *noun* **1** an idea that is passed from one member of society to another, not in the GENES but often by people copying it: *Other cultures have similar versions of this meme.* ◇ *the political and cultural memes of the 21st century* **2** an image, a video, a piece of text, etc. that is passed very quickly from one internet user to another, often with slight changes that make it humorous: *an internet meme/a blog meme*

**me·mento** /məˈmentəʊ/ *noun* (*pl.* **-oes** or **-os**) a thing that you keep or give to sb to remind you or them of a person or place SYN **souvenir**: *a memento of our trip to Italy*

**me·mento mori** /məˌmentəʊ ˈmɔːri/ *noun* (*pl.* **me·mento mori**) an object or symbol that reminds or warns you of death

**memo** 🔑+ C1 /ˈmeməʊ/ *noun* (*pl.* **-os**) (*also formal* **memo·ran·dum**) an official note from one person to another in the same organization: *to **write/send a memo*** ◇ **~ to sb** *She circulated a memo to the staff.*

**mem·oir** 🔑+ C1 /ˈmemwɑː(r)/ *noun* **1** 🔑+ C1 **memoirs** [pl.] an account written by sb, especially sb famous, about their life and experiences **2** 🔑+ C1 [C] (*formal*) a written account of sb's life, a place, or an event, written by sb who knows it well

**mem·ora·bilia** /ˌmemərəˈbɪliə/ *noun* [pl.] things that people collect because they once belonged to a famous person, or because they are connected with a particular interesting place, event or activity: *football/Beatles memorabilia*

**mem·or·able** 🔑+ B2 /ˈmemərəbl/ *adj.* worth remembering or easy to remember, especially because of being special or unusual SYN **unforgettable**: *The holiday provided many memorable moments.* ◇ *a truly memorable occasion/event* ◇ *memorable lines/lyrics/phrases* ◇ **~ for sth** *The city is memorable for its fantastic beaches.* ▶ **mem·or·ably** /-bli/ *adv.*

**memo·ran·dum** /ˌmeməˈrændəm/ *noun* (*pl.* **memo·randa** /-də/) **1** (*formal*) = MEMO: *an internal memorandum* **2** (*law*) a record of a legal agreement that has not yet been formally prepared and signed **3** a proposal or report on a particular subject for a person, an organization, a committee, etc: *a detailed memorandum to the commission on employment policy*

**me·mor·ial** 🔑+ C1 /məˈmɔːriəl/ *noun, adj.*
■ ***noun*** **1** 🔑+ C1 [C] a statue, stone, etc. that is built in order to remind people of an important past event or of a famous person who has died: ***a war memorial*** (= in memory of soldiers who died in a war) ◇ **~ to sb/sth** *a memorial to victims of the Holocaust* **2** 🔑+ C1 [sing.] **~ to sb/sth** a thing that will continue to remind people of sb/sth: *The painting will be a lasting memorial to a remarkable woman.* **3** [C] a ceremony that is held to remember sb who has died or an important past event
■ ***adj.*** [only before noun] created or done in order to remember sb who has died: *a **memorial statue/plaque/prize*** ◇ *The **memorial service** will be held at a local church.* ◇ *the John F Kennedy Memorial Hospital*

**Meˈmorial Day** *noun* a holiday in the US, usually the last Monday in May, in honour of members of the armed forces who have died in war ➲ see also REMEMBRANCE SUNDAY, VETERANS DAY

**me·mor·ial·ize** (*BrE also* **-ise**) /məˈmɔːriəlaɪz/ *verb* **~ sb/sth** (*formal*) to produce sth that will continue to exist and remind people of sb who has died or sth that has gone SYN **commemorate**

**me·mor·iam** ➲ IN MEMORIAM

**mem·or·ize** (*BrE also* **-ise**) /ˈmeməraɪz/ *verb* **~ sth** to learn sth carefully so that you can remember it exactly: *to memorize a poem*

**mem·ory** 🔊 **A2** **S** /ˈmeməri/ (pl. **-ies**) noun
- **ABILITY TO REMEMBER 1** 🔊 **A2** [C, U] your ability to remember things: **for sth** *I have a bad memory for names.* ◊ *People have short memories* (= they soon forget). ◊ *He had a great memory for detail.* ◊ **from~** *She can recite the whole poem from memory.* ◊ *He suffered memory loss for weeks after the accident.* ◊ *Are you sure? Memory can play tricks on you.* ➲ see also PHOTOGRAPHIC MEMORY **2** 🔊 **A2** [U] the period of time that a person or group of people is able to remember events: **in …~** *There hasn't been peace in the country in my memory.* ◊ *It was the worst storm in recent memory.* ◊ **within …~** *This hasn't happened within living memory* (= nobody alive now can remember it). ➲ see also FOLK MEMORY
- **STH YOU REMEMBER 3** 🔊 **A2** [C] a thought of sth that you remember from the past **SYN** **recollection**: *Her poems are often based on childhood memories.* ◊ **~of sth** *I have vivid memories of my grandparents.* ◊ **~of doing sth** *I have many happy memories of working there.* ◊ *The photos bring back lots of good memories.* ➲ see also FALSE MEMORY **4** [U] (*formal*) what is remembered about sb after they have died: *Her memory lives on* (= we still remember her). ◊ *They held a feast to honour the memory of Patroclus, his slain comrade.*
- **COMPUTING 5** 🔊 **A2** [C, U] the part of a computer where information is stored; the amount of space in a computer for storing information: *32 gigabytes of memory* ➲ **WORD-FINDER NOTE** at COMPUTER ➲ see also FLASH MEMORY, RAM, RANDOM-ACCESS MEMORY, READ-ONLY MEMORY, VIRTUAL MEMORY

**IDM** **if (my) memory serves me well, correctly, etc.** if I remember correctly | **in memory of sb | to the memory of sb** intended to show respect and remind people of sb who has died: *He founded the charity in memory of his late wife.* ➲ more at ETCH, JOG v., SIEVE n.

ˈ**memory bank** noun the memory of a device such as a computer

ˈ**memory card** noun an electronic device that can be used to store data, used especially with digital cameras, mobile phones, music players, etc. ➲ compare SD CARD

ˈ**memory ˈlane** noun
**IDM** **a trip/walk down ˌmemory ˈlane** time that you spend thinking about and remembering the past or going to a place again in order to remind yourself of past experiences

ˈ**Memory Stick**™ noun (*especially BrE*) a small memory device that can be used to store data from a computer and to move it from one computer to another **SYN** **flash drive**

**mem·sahib** /ˈmemsɑːb, -sɑːhɪb; *NAmE* -sɑːhɪb, -sɑːb/ noun used in India, especially in the past, to address a married woman with high social status, often a European woman

**men** /men/ pl. of MAN

**men·ace** /ˈmenəs/ noun, verb
- noun **1** [C, usually sing.] **~(to sb/sth)** a person or thing that causes, or may cause, serious damage, harm or danger **SYN** **threat**: *a new initiative aimed at beating the menace of illegal drugs* **2** [U] an atmosphere that makes you feel threatened or frightened: *a sense/an air/a hint of menace in his voice* **3** [C, usually sing.] (*informal*) a person or thing that is annoying or causes trouble **SYN** **nuisance** **4 menaces** [pl.] (*BrE, law*) threats that sb will cause harm if they do not get what they are asking for: **with ~ to** demand money with menaces
- verb **~sth/sb** (*formal*) to be a possible danger to sth/sb **SYN** **threaten**: *The forests are being menaced by major development projects.*

**men·acing** /ˈmenəsɪŋ/ adj. seeming likely to cause you harm or danger **SYN** **threatening**: *a menacing face/tone* ◊ *At night, the dark streets become menacing.* ▸ **men·acing·ly** adv.: *The thunder growled menacingly.*

**mé·nage** /meɪˈnɑːʒ/ noun [usually sing.] (*from French, formal or humorous*) all the people who live together in one house **SYN** **household**

**ménage à trois** /ˌmeɪnɑːʒ ɑː ˈtwɑː/ noun (pl. **ménages à trois** /ˌmeɪnɑːʒ ɑː ˈtwɑː/) [usually sing.] (*from French*) a situation where three people, especially a husband, wife and LOVER, live together and have sexual relationships with each other

**men·agerie** /məˈnædʒəri/ noun a collection of wild animals kept in CAGES, etc. for people to see

**mend** /mend/ verb, noun
- verb **1** [T] **~sth** (*BrE*) to repair sth that has been damaged or broken so that it can be used again: *Could you mend my bike for me?* ➲ see also FENCE-MENDING **2** [T] **~sth** to repair a hole in a piece of clothing, etc: *He mended shoes for a living.* **3** [T] **~sth** to find a solution to a problem or DISAGREEMENT: *They tried to mend their differences.* **4** [I] (*old-fashioned*) (of a person) to improve in health after being ill **SYN** **recover**: *He's mending slowly after the operation.* **5** [I] (of a broken bone) to join up and return to normal
**IDM** **mend (your) ˈfences (with sb)** to find a solution when you disagree with sb ➲ related noun FENCE-MENDING | **mend your ˈways** to stop behaving badly ➲ more at SAY v.
- noun
**IDM** **on the ˈmend** (*informal*) getting better after an illness or injury; improving after a difficult situation: *My leg is definitely on the mend now.* ◊ *Does he believe the economy's really on the mend?*

**men·da·cious** /menˈdeɪʃəs/ adj. (*formal*) not telling the truth **SYN** **lying**

**men·da·city** /menˈdæsəti/ noun [U] (*formal*) the act of not telling the truth **SYN** **lying**

**mend·er** /ˈmendə(r)/ noun (*BrE*) (usually in compounds) a person who repairs sth: *road menders*

**men·di·cant** /ˈmendɪkənt/ adj. (*formal*) (especially of members of religious groups) living by asking people for money and food ▸ **men·di·cant** noun

**men·folk** /ˈmenfəʊk/ noun [pl.] (*old-fashioned*) men of a particular family or community: *a society sending its menfolk off to war* ➲ compare WOMENFOLK

**me·nial** /ˈmiːniəl/ adj., noun
- adj. (*usually disapproving*) (of work) not considered important; not needing special skills and often boring or badly paid: *menial jobs/work* ◊ *menial tasks like cleaning the floor*
- noun (*old-fashioned*) a person with a menial job

**men·in·ges** /məˈnɪndʒiːz/ noun [pl.] (*anatomy*) the three MEMBRANES (= thin layers of material) that surround the brain and SPINAL CORD

**men·in·gi·tis** /ˌmenɪnˈdʒaɪtɪs/ noun [U] a serious disease in which the MEMBRANES surrounding the brain and SPINAL CORD develop an infection and become SWOLLEN (= larger than normal), causing severe headache, a high temperature and sometimes death

**me·nis·cus** /məˈnɪskəs/ noun (pl. **me·nisci** /-ˈnɪsaɪ/) **1** (*physics*) the curved surface of a liquid in a tube **2** (*anatomy*) a thin layer of CARTILAGE between the surfaces of some JOINTS, for example the knee

**Men·non·ite** /ˈmenənaɪt/ noun a member of a Protestant religious group that lives in the US and Canada. Mennonites live a simple life and do not work as public officials or soldiers.

**meno·pause** /ˈmenəpɔːz/ (*also informal* **the ˈchange (of life)**) noun [U] (*often* **the menopause**) [sing.] the time during which a woman gradually stops MENSTRUATING, usually at around the age of 50: *to reach (the) menopause* ▸ **meno·pausal** /ˌmenəˈpɔːzl/ adj.: *menopausal symptoms/women*

**me·norah** /mɪˈnɔːrə/ noun a traditional Jewish object to hold seven or nine CANDLES

**mensch** /menʃ/ noun (*NAmE, informal*) a good person, especially sb who does sth kind or helpful

**men·ses** /ˈmensiːz/ noun (*often* **the menses**) [pl.] (*specialist*) the flow of blood each month from a woman's body

ˈ**men's room** noun (*NAmE*) a public toilet for men

**men·strual** /ˈmenstruəl/ adj. [usually before noun] connected with the time when a woman menstruates each month: *The average length of a woman's menstrual cycle is 28 days.* ◊ *menstrual blood* ◊ (*formal*) *a menstrual period* ➲ compare PREMENSTRUAL

**men·stru·ate** /ˈmenstrueɪt/ verb [I] (*formal*) when a woman **menstruates**, there is a flow of blood from her womb, usually once a month

# menstruation

**men·stru·ation** /ˌmenstruˈeɪʃn/ noun [U] (formal) the process or time of menstruating ⊃ compare PERIOD

**mens·wear** /ˈmenzweə(r); NAmE -wer/ noun [U] (used especially in shops/stores) clothes for men: *the menswear department* ⊃ WORDFINDER NOTE at STORE

**-ment** /mənt/ suffix (in nouns) the action or result of: *bombardment* ◇ *development* ▶ **-mental** /mentl/ (in adjectives): *governmental* ◇ *judgemental*

**men·tal** ❶ B1 O /ˈmentl/ adj. **1** B1 [usually before noun] connected with or happening in the mind; involving the process of thinking: *the mental process of remembering* ◇ *Do you have a mental picture of what it will look like?* ◇ *I made a mental note to talk to her about it.* ◇ *He has a complete mental block* (= difficulty in understanding or remembering) *when it comes to physics.* **2** B1 [usually before noun] connected with the state of health of the mind or with the treatment of illnesses of the mind: *a mental disorder/illness* ◇ *She was suffering from physical and mental exhaustion.* ◇ (old-fashioned) *a mental hospital/patient* HELP The use of **mental** in these compounds is now considered old-fashioned, sometimes even offensive. The preferred terms now are *psychiatric hospital/patient.* ⊃ compare PSYCHIATRIC **3** [not usually before noun] (*BrE, slang*) crazy: *Watch him. He's mental.* ◇ *My dad will go mental* (= be very angry) *when he finds out.* ◇ *We were just losing so much money—it was mental.*

**ˌmental ˈage** noun [C, usually sing.] **~ (of sth)** the level of sb's ability to think, understand, etc. that is judged by comparison with the average ability for children of a particular age: *She is 16 but has a mental age of 5.* ⊃ compare CHRONOLOGICAL AGE

**ˌmental aˈrithmetic** noun [U] adding, multiplying, etc. numbers in your mind without writing anything down or using a CALCULATOR

**ˌmental ˈhealth** noun [U] **1** the state of health of sb's mind: *Volunteering can also improve your mental health and help you live longer.* ◇ *to have mental health issues/problems* **2** the system for treating people with mental health problems: *The government has announced £600 million extra funding for mental health.* ◇ *pressure on mental health services*

▼ **WHICH WORD?**

**Talking about mental health**

- Do not use the words **mad** or **crazy** to describe sb who is suffering from a real mental illness. Say instead that sb has **mental health issues/problems** or is **mentally ill**: *I have experienced mental health issues since the age of 14.* ◇ *a charity that helps mentally ill people live independently*
- **Disturbed** can be used to describe sb who has mental health issues because of very unhappy or unpleasant experiences: *He works with emotionally disturbed children.*
- **Insane** is a formal or old-fashioned term used to describe sb suffering from a serious mental illness and unable to live in normal society: *The question is, was the man insane when he committed the crime?* However, **insane** is more often used in informal English to describe sb who is not suffering from a mental illness, but whose mind does not work normally, especially because they are under pressure. This meaning is used in the phrases *go insane* and *drive sb insane.*

**men·tal·ity** /menˈtæləti/ noun [usually sing.] (*pl.* **-ies**) the particular attitude or way of thinking of a person or group SYN **mindset**: *I can't understand the mentality of people who are unkind to their pets.* ◇ *a criminal/ghetto mentality* ⊃ see also SIEGE MENTALITY

**men·tal·ly** /ˈmentəli/ adv. connected with or happening in the mind: *mentally ill* ◇ *The baby is very mentally alert.* ◇ *Mentally, I began making a list of things I had to do.*

**ˌmentally ˈhandicapped** adj. (*old-fashioned, offensive*) (of a person) slow to learn or to understand things because of a problem with the brain HELP It is now more usual to say that people with this kind of problem **have learning difficulties.**

**men·tee** /menˈtiː/ noun a person who is advised and helped by a more experienced person over a period of time, especially within a formal MENTORING programme in a company, a university, etc.: *the mentor/mentee relationship* ⊃ compare MENTOR

**men·thol** /ˈmenθɒl; NAmE -θɔːl/ noun [U] a substance that tastes and smells of MINT, that is used in some medicines for colds and to give a strong, cool taste to cigarettes, TOOTHPASTE, etc.

**men·tion** ❶ A2 S /ˈmenʃn/ verb, noun

■ verb **1** A2 to write or speak about sth/sb, especially without giving much information: **~ sth/sb** *Sorry, I won't mention it again.* ◇ *Now that you mention it, she did seem to be in a strange mood.* ◇ **~ sth/sb to sb** *Nobody mentioned anything to me about it.* ◇ **~ where, why, etc …** *Did she mention where she was going?* ◇ **~ that …** *You mentioned in your letter that you might be moving abroad.* ◇ **~ doing sth** *Did I mention going to see Vicky on Sunday?* ◇ **~ sth/sb to sb** *The cruise visits most places mentioned in the article.* ⊃ see also ABOVE-MENTIONED, AFOREMENTIONED **2 ~ sth/sb (as sth/sb)** to refer to sb/sth as being interesting, especially as a possible candidate for a job or position: *His name has been mentioned as a future MP.*

IDM **ˌdon't ˈmention it** (*informal*) used as a polite answer when sb has thanked you for sth SYN **you're welcome**: *'Thanks for all your help.' 'Don't mention it.'* **not to ˈmention** used to introduce extra information and emphasize what you are saying: *He has two big houses in this country, not to mention his villa in France.* ◇ *I admired her confidence, not to mention the fact that she was intelligent and well spoken.*

■ noun [U, C, usually sing.] **1** B1 an act of referring to sb/sth in speech or writing: *He made no mention of her work.* ◇ *The concert didn't even get a mention in the newspapers.* ◇ **at the ~ of sth/sb** *I went white at the mention of her name.* **2** an act of acknowledging sb/sth as deserving praise: *Phil deserves (a) special mention for all the help he gave us.*

▼ **SYNONYMS**

**mention**

refer to sb/sth • speak • cite • quote

These words all mean to write or speak about sb/sth, often in order to give an example or prove sth.

**mention** to write or speak about sth/sb, especially without giving much information: *Nobody mentioned anything to me about it.*

**refer to sb/sth** (*rather formal*) to mention or speak about sb/sth: *I promised not to refer to the matter again.*

**speak** to mention or describe sth/sb: *Witnesses spoke of a great ball of flame.*

**cite** (*formal*) to mention sth as a reason or an example, or in order to support what you are saying: *He cited his heavy workload as the reason for his breakdown.*

**quote** to mention an example of sth to support what you are saying: *Can you quote me an instance of when this happened?*

CITE OR QUOTE?

- You can **cite** reasons or examples, but you can only **quote** examples: *He quoted his heavy workload as the reason for his breakdown.* **Cite** is a more formal word than **quote** and is often used in more formal situations, for example in descriptions of legal cases.

PATTERNS

- to mention/refer to/speak of/cite/quote sb/sth **as** sb/sth
- to mention/refer to/cite/quote a(n) **example/instance/case** of sth
- **frequently/often** mentioned/referred to/spoken of/cited/quoted
- the example mentioned/referred to/cited/quoted **above/earlier/previously**

**men·tor** ❷+ C1 /ˈmentɔː(r)/ noun **1** ❷+ C1 an experienced person who advises and helps sb with less experience over a period of time ⊃ compare MENTEE **2** an experienced person in a company, university, etc. who trains and advises new employees or students: *The company runs a mentor programme.* ▶ **men·tor·ing** /-tərɪŋ/ *noun* [U]: *a mentoring programme*

**men·tor·ship** /ˈmentəʃɪp; *NAmE* -tərʃ-/ *noun* **1** [U] the advice and help provided by a mentor to a less experienced person over a period of time, especially as part of a formal programme in a company, university, etc: *under the ~ of sb Young researchers participate in the project under the mentorship of senior colleagues.* **2** [C] a period of time during which sb receives advice and help from a mentor

**menu** 🔊 **A1** /ˈmenjuː/ *noun* **1** 🔊 **A1** a list of the food that is available at a restaurant or to be served at a meal: *May we have the menu?* ◇ *to ask for/look at the menu* ◇ *the lunch/dinner menu* ◇ **on the~** *What's on the menu (= for dinner) tonight?* ⇨ **WORDFINDER NOTE** at **RESTAURANT 2** 🔊 **A1** (*computing*) a list of possible choices that are shown on a computer screen: *a pull-down/pop-up menu* ◇ *When highlighted information is clicked, a pop-up menu appears.* ◇ *I clicked on a menu item called 'connect to server'.* ◇ *a menu option/button* ⇨ **WORDFINDER NOTE** at **FILE** ⇨ see also **DROP-DOWN MENU**

**ˈmenu bar** *noun* (*computing*) a bar at the top of a computer screen that contains DROP-DOWN MENUS such as 'File', 'Edit' and 'Help'

**meow** /miˈaʊ/ (*BrE also* **miaow**) *noun* the crying sound made by a cat ⇨ see also **MEW** ▶ **meow** (*BrE also* **miaow**) *verb* [I]

**MEP** /ˌem iː ˈpiː/ *noun* a person elected as the representative at the European Parliament of any of the CONSTITUENCIES of countries that are members of the European Union (the abbreviation for 'Member of the European Parliament')

**meph·e·drone** /ˈmefədrəʊn/ (*also informal* **miaow miaow**, **meow meow**) *noun* [U] a drug, made from chemical substances, that affects people's moods and makes them feel more active. Use of the drug is illegal in some countries.

**mer·can·tile** /ˈmɜːkəntaɪl; *NAmE* ˈmɜːrkəntiːl, -taɪl/ *adj.* (*formal*) connected with trade and commercial affairs

**mer·can·ti·lism** /ˈmɜːkæntɪlɪzəm; *NAmE* mɜːrˈkæntiːˈk-/ *noun* [U] (*specialist*) the economic theory that trade increases wealth ▶ **mer·can·ti·list** /-lɪst/ *adj.* **mer·can·ti·list** *noun*

**mer·cen·ary** /ˈmɜːsənəri; *NAmE* ˈmɜːrsəneri/ *noun, adj.*
■ *noun* (*pl.* -ies) a soldier who will fight for any country or group that offers payment: *foreign mercenaries* ◇ *mercenary soldiers*
■ *adj.* (*disapproving*) only interested in making or getting money: *a mercenary society/attitude* ◇ *She's interested in him for purely mercenary reasons.*

**merch** /mɜːtʃ; *NAmE* mɜːrtʃ/ *noun* [U] (*informal*) = MERCHANDISE

**mer·chan·dise** *noun, verb*
■ *noun* /ˈmɜːtʃəndaɪs, -daɪz; *NAmE* ˈmɜːrtʃ-/ (*also* **merch** *informal*) [U] **1** (*formal*) goods that are bought or sold; goods that are for sale in a shop: *a wide selection of merchandise* ⇨ **SYNONYMS** at **PRODUCT** **2** things you can buy that are connected with or that advertise a particular event or organization: *official Olympic merchandise*
■ *verb* /ˈmɜːtʃəndaɪz; *NAmE* ˈmɜːrtʃ-/ *~ sth* to sell sth using advertising, etc.

**mer·chan·dis·ing** /ˈmɜːtʃəndaɪzɪŋ; *NAmE* ˈmɜːrtʃ-/ *noun* [U] **1** the activity of selling goods, or of trying to sell them, by advertising or displaying them **2** products connected with a popular film, person or event; the process of selling these goods: *millions of pounds' worth of Batman merchandising*

**mer·chant** 🔊+ **C1** /ˈmɜːtʃənt; *NAmE* ˈmɜːrtʃ-/ *noun, adj.*
■ *noun* **1** 🔊+ **C1** a person who buys and sells goods in large quantities, especially one who imports and exports goods: *a coal/wine merchant* ◇ *Venice was once a city of rich merchants.* ⇨ see also **BUILDERS' MERCHANT** **2** (*NAmE*) a person who sells goods to the public, especially through a store: *The credit cards are accepted by 10 million merchants worldwide.* **3** (*BrE, informal, disapproving*) a person who likes a particular activity: *a speed merchant* (= sb who likes to

981

# mere

drive fast) ◇ *noise merchants* (= for example, a band who make a lot of noise) **IDM** see **DOOM** *n.*
■ *adj.* [only before noun] connected with the transport of goods by sea: *merchant seamen*

**mer·chant·able** /ˈmɜːtʃəntəbl; *NAmE* ˈmɜːrtʃ-/ *adj.* (*formal or law*) in a good enough condition to be sold: *Goods must be of merchantable quality.*

**ˈmerchant ˈbank** *noun* (*BrE*) = INVESTMENT BANK ▶ **ˈmerchant ˈbanker** *noun* **ˈmerchant ˈbanking** *noun* [U]

**ˈmer·chant·man** /ˈmɜːtʃəntmən; *NAmE* ˈmɜːrtʃ-/ *adj.* **-men** /-mən/) (*also* **ˈmerchant ˈship**) *noun* a ship used for carrying goods for trade rather than a military ship

**ˈmerchant ˈnavy** (*BrE*) (*NAmE* **ˈmerchant maˈrine**) *noun* [C + sing./pl. v.] a country's commercial ships and the people who work on them

**mer·ci·ful** /ˈmɜːsɪfl; *NAmE* ˈmɜːrs-/ *adj.* **1** ready to forgive people and be kind to them **SYN** *humane*: *a merciful God* ◇ *They asked her to be merciful to the prisoners.* **2** (of an event) seeming to be lucky, especially because it brings an end to sb's problems or pain: *Death came as a merciful release.* ⇨ see also **MERCY**

**mer·ci·ful·ly** /ˈmɜːsɪfəli; *NAmE* ˈmɜːrs-/ *adv.* **1** used to show that you feel sb/sth is lucky because a situation could have been much worse **SYN** *thankfully*: *Deaths from the disease are mercifully rare.* ◇ *Mercifully, everyone arrived on time.* **2** in a kind way: *He was treated mercifully.*

**mer·ci·less** /ˈmɜːsɪləs; *NAmE* ˈmɜːrs-/ *adj.* showing no sympathy or kind treatment **SYN** *cruel*: *a merciless killer/attack* ◇ *the merciless heat of the sun* ▶ **mer·ci·less·ly** *adv.* ⇨ see also **MERCY**

**mer·cur·ial** /mɜːˈkjʊəriəl; *NAmE* mɜːrˈkjʊr-/ *adj.* **1** (*literary*) often changing or reacting in a way that is unexpected **SYN** *volatile*: *Emily's mercurial temperament made her difficult to live with.* **2** (*literary*) lively and quick: *a brilliant, mercurial mind* **3** (*specialist*) containing MERCURY

**Mer·cury** /ˈmɜːkjəri; *NAmE* ˈmɜːrk-/ *noun* the smallest planet in the SOLAR SYSTEM, nearest to the sun

**mer·cury** /ˈmɜːkjəri; *NAmE* ˈmɜːrk-/ *noun* [U] (*symb.* Hg) a chemical element. Mercury is a poisonous silver liquid metal, used in THERMOMETERS.

**mercy** 🔊+ **C1** /ˈmɜːsi; *NAmE* ˈmɜːrsi/ *noun* (*pl.* -ies) **1** 🔊+ **C1** [U] a kind or forgiving attitude towards sb that you have the power to harm or have a right to punish **SYN** *humanity*: *to ask/beg/plead for mercy* ◇ *They showed no mercy to their hostages.* ◇ *God have mercy on us.* ◇ *The troops are on a mercy mission* (= a journey to help people) *in the war zone.* **2** [C, usually sing.] (*informal*) an event or a situation to be grateful for, usually because it stops sth unpleasant: *It is a ~ (that)… It's a mercy she wasn't seriously hurt.* ⇨ see also **MERCIFUL**, **MERCILESS**
**IDM** **at the mercy of sb/sth** not able to stop sb/sth harming you because they have power or control over you: *I'm not going to put myself at the mercy of the bank.* ◇ *We were at the mercy of the weather.* **leave sb/sth to the mercy/mercies of sb/sth** to leave sb/sth in a situation that may cause them to suffer or to be treated badly **throw yourself on sb's mercy** (*formal*) to put yourself in a situation where you must rely on sb to be kind to you and not harm or punish you ⇨ more at **SMALL** *adj.*

**ˈmercy killing** *noun* [C, U] the act of killing sb because you do not want them to suffer, for example because they are in severe pain **SYN** *euthanasia*

**mere** 🔊+ **C1** /mɪə(r); *NAmE* mɪr/ *adj., noun*
■ *adj.* [only before noun] (*superlative* **mer·est**, no *comparative*) **1** 🔊+ **C1** used when you want to emphasize how small, unimportant, etc. sb/sth is: *It took her a mere 20 minutes to win.* ◇ *A mere 2 per cent of their budget has been spent on publicity.* ◇ *He seemed so young, a mere boy.* ◇ *You've got the job. The interview will be a mere formality.* **2** 🔊+ **C1** used when you are saying that the fact that a particular thing is present in a situation is enough to have an influence on that situation: *His mere presence* (= just the fact that he was there) *made her feel afraid.* ◇ *The mere fact that they were prepared to talk was encouraging.* ◇ *The*

# merely

*mere thought of* eating made him feel sick. ◊ *The merest* (= the slightest) *hint of smoke is enough to make her feel ill.*
- *noun* (*BrE*, *literary*) (also used in names) a small lake

**mere·ly** /ˈmɪəli/; *NAmE* ˈmɪrli/ *adv.* used meaning 'only' or 'simply' to emphasize a fact or sth that you are saying: *It is not merely a job, but a way of life.* ◊ *He said nothing, merely smiled and watched her.* ◊ *They agreed to go merely because they were getting paid for it.* ◊ *I'm merely stating what everybody knows anyway.*

**me·tri·cious** /məˈtrɪʃəs/ *adj.* (*formal*) seeming attractive, but in fact having no real value

**merge** /mɜːdʒ/; *NAmE* mɜːrdʒ/ *verb* **1** [I, T] to combine or make two or more things combine to form a single thing: *The banks are set to merge next year.* ◊ *The two groups have merged to form a new party.* ◊ ~ **with sth** *His department will merge with mine.* ◊ ~ **into sth** *The villages expanded and merged into one large town.* ◊ ~ **(A and B) (together)** *Fact and fiction merge together in his latest thriller.* ◊ ~ **A with B** *His department will be merged with mine.* ◊ ~ **sth** *The company was formed by merging three smaller firms.* ◊ ~ **sth into sth** *Merge multiple text files into one master file.* **2** [I] ~ **(into sth)** if two things **merge**, or if one thing **merges into** another, the differences between them gradually disappear so that it is impossible to separate them: *The hills merged into the dark sky behind them.*
**IDM** **merge into the ˈbackground** (of a person) to behave quietly when you are with a group of people so that they do not notice you

**mer·ger** /ˈmɜːdʒə(r)/; *NAmE* ˈmɜːrdʒ-/ *noun* [C, U] the act of joining two or more organizations or businesses into one: ~ **between/of A and B** *a merger between the two banks* ◊ ~ **with sth** *our proposed merger with the university* ◊ *There are local companies ripe for merger or acquisition.*
→ **WORDFINDER NOTE** at **DEAL**

**me·rid·ian** /məˈrɪdiən/ *noun* one of the lines that is drawn from the North Pole to the South Pole on a map of the world

**me·ringue** /məˈræŋ/ *noun* [U, C] a sweet white mixture made from egg whites and sugar, usually baked until hard and dry and used to make cakes; a small cake made from this mixture: *a lemon meringue pie*

**me·rino** /məˈriːnəʊ/ *noun* (*pl.* **-os**) **1** [C] a type of sheep with long, fine wool **2** [U] the wool of the merino sheep or a type of cloth made from this wool, used for making clothes

**merit** /ˈmerɪt/ *noun*, *verb*
- *noun* **1** [U] (*formal*) the quality of being good and of deserving praise or reward **SYN worth**: *a work of outstanding artistic merit* ◊ *without* ~ *The plan is entirely without merit.* ◊ **on** ~ *I want to get the job on merit.* **2** [C, usually pl.] a good feature that deserves praise or reward **SYN strength**: *We will consider each case on its (own) merits* (= without considering any other issues, feelings, etc.). ◊ *They weighed up the relative merits of the four candidates.* **3** [C] (*BrE*) a grade in an exam or for a piece of work at school or university that is very good → compare **DISTINCTION** (5) **4** [C] (*BrE*) a special mark or award given as a reward for good behaviour at school
- *verb* (not used in the progressive tenses) ~ **(doing) sth** (*formal*) to deserve praise, attention, etc. **SYN deserve**: *He claims that their success was not merited.* ◊ *The case does not merit further investigation.*

**mer·it·oc·racy** /ˌmerɪˈtɒkrəsi/; *NAmE* -ˈtɑːk-/ *noun* (*pl.* **-ies**) **1** [C, U] a country or social system where people get power or money on the basis of their ability **2** *the* **meritocracy** [sing.] the group of people with power in this kind of social system ▶ **mer·ito·crat·ic** /ˌmerɪtəˈkrætɪk/ *adj.*

**meri·tori·ous** /ˌmerɪˈtɔːriəs/ *adj.* (*formal*) deserving praise **SYN praiseworthy**

**mer·lin** /ˈmɜːlɪn/; *NAmE* ˈmɜːrl-/ *noun* a small BIRD OF PREY (= a bird that kills other creatures for food) of the FALCON family

**mer·maid** /ˈmɜːmeɪd/; *NAmE* ˈmɜːrm-/ *noun* (in stories) a creature with a woman's head and body, and a fish's tail instead of legs

**mer·man** /ˈmɜːmæn/; *NAmE* ˈmɜːrm-/ *noun* (*pl.* **-men** /-men/) (in stories) a creature with a man's head and body and a fish's tail instead of legs, like a male MERMAID

**mer·rily** /ˈmerəli/ *adv.* **1** in a happy, cheerful way: *They chatted merrily.* **2** without thinking about the problems that your actions might cause **SYN gaily**: *She carried on merrily, not realizing the offence she was causing.*

**mer·ri·ment** /ˈmerɪmənt/ *noun* [U] (*formal*) happy talk, fun and the sound of people laughing **SYN jollity**, **mirth**

**merry** /ˈmeri/ *adj.* (**mer·rier**, **mer·ri·est**) **1** happy and cheerful **SYN cheery**: *a merry grin* **2 Merry Christmas** used at Christmas to say that you hope that sb has a pleasant holiday **3** (*especially BrE*, *informal*) slightly drunk **SYN tipsy**
**IDM** **make ˈmerry** (*old-fashioned*) to enjoy yourself by singing, laughing, drinking, etc. **the more the ˈmerrier** (*saying*) the more people or things there are, the better the situation will be or the more fun people will have: *'Can I bring a friend to your party?' 'Sure—the more the merrier!'* → more at **EAT**, **HELL**, **LEAD**[1] *v.*

merry-go-round/ carousel         roundabout/ merry-go-round

**ˈmerry-go-round** *noun* **1** (also **car·ou·sel** especially in *NAmE*) (*BrE* also **round·about**) a round platform with model horses, cars, etc. that turns around and around and that children ride on at a FAIRGROUND **2** (*NAmE*) (*BrE* **round·about**) a round platform for children to play on in a park, etc. that is pushed round while the children are sitting on it **3** continuous busy activity or a continuous series of changing events: *He was tired of the merry-go-round of romance and longed to settle down.*

**merry·mak·ing** /ˈmerimeɪkɪŋ/ *noun* [U] (*literary*) fun and pleasure with singing, laughing, drinking, etc. **SYN revelry**

**mesa** /ˈmeɪsə/ *noun* (*pl.* **mesas**) a hill with a flat top and steep sides that is common in the south-west of the US

**mes·cal** /ˈmeskæl, meˈskæl/ *noun* = **PEYOTE**

**mes·ca·line** (also **mes·ca·lin**) /ˈmeskəlɪn/ *noun* [U] a drug obtained from a type of CACTUS, that affects people's minds and makes them see and hear things that are not really there

**mesh** /meʃ/ *noun*, *verb*
- *noun* **1** [U, C] material made of a network of wire or plastic THREADS: *wire mesh over the door of the cage* **2** [C, usually sing.] the spaces between the individual wires or THREADS that form a mesh: *If the mesh is too big, small rabbits can squeeze through.* **3** [C, usually sing.] a complicated situation or system that it is difficult to escape from **SYN web**
- *verb* (*formal*) **1** [I, T] to fit together or match closely, especially in a way that works well; to make things fit together successfully: ~ **(sth) (with sth)** *This evidence meshes with earlier reports of an organized riot.* ◊ ~ **(sth) (together)** *His theories mesh together various political and religious beliefs.* **2** [I] (*specialist*) (of parts of a machine) to fit together as they move: *If the cogs don't mesh correctly, the gears will keep slipping.*

**mes·mer·ic** /mezˈmerɪk/ *adj.* [usually before noun] (*formal*) having such a strong effect on people that they cannot give their attention to anything else **SYN hypnotic**

**mes·mer·ize** (*BrE* also **-ise**) /ˈmezməraɪz/ *verb* [usually passive] ~ **sb** to have such a strong effect on you that you cannot give your attention to anything else **SYN fascinate** ▶ **mes·mer·iz·ing** (*BrE* also **-is·ing**) *adj.*: *Her performance was mesmerizing.*

**meso·phyll** /ˈmezəfɪl, ˈmiːz-/ *noun* [U] (*biology*) the material that the inside of a leaf is made of

**mes·quite** /meˈskiːt/ (also **meˈsquite tree**) noun a North American tree that grows in the south-western US and Mexico, often used for making CHARCOAL for GRILLING food: *mesquite-grilled chicken*

**mess** 🔊 **B1** /mes/ noun, verb
■ noun
• UNTIDY STATE **1** 🔊 **B1** [C, usually sing.] a dirty or untidy state: **in a~** *The room was in a mess.* ◇ *The kids made a mess in the bathroom.* ◇ *'What a mess!' she said, surveying the scene after the party.* ◇ *My hair's a real mess*
• DIFFICULT SITUATION **2** 🔊 [C, usually sing.] a situation that is full of problems, usually because of a lack of organization or because of mistakes that sb has made: **in a~** *The economy is in a mess.* ◇ *a financial mess* ◇ *I feel I've made a mess of things.* ◇ *How did this whole mess start?* ◇ *Let's try to sort out the mess.* ◇ *How do we get out of this mess?* ◇ *The biggest question is how they got into this mess in the first place.*
• PERSON **3** [sing.] a person who is dirty or whose clothes and hair are not tidy: *You're a mess!* **4** [sing.] (*informal*) a person who has serious problems and is in a bad mental condition
• ANIMAL WASTE **5** [U, C] (*informal*) the EXCREMENT (= solid waste matter) of an animal, usually a dog or cat
• A LOT **6** [sing.] **a ~ of sth** (*NAmE, informal*) a lot of sth: *There's a mess of fish down there, so get your lines in the water.*
• ARMED FORCES **7** [C] (also **ˈmess hall** especially in NAmE) a building or room in which members of the armed forces have their meals: *the officers' mess*
■ verb
• MAKE UNTIDY **1** [T] **~ sth** (*especially NAmE, informal*) to make sth dirty or untidy: *Careful—you're messing my hair.*
• OF AN ANIMAL **2** [I] to empty its BOWELS somewhere that it should not
IDM **no ˈmessing** (*informal*) used to say that sth has been done easily: *We finished in time, no messing.* **not mess aˈround** (*BrE also* **not mess aˈbout**) (*informal*) to do sth quickly, efficiently or in the right way: *When they decide to have a party they don't mess around.*
PHR V **mess aˈround** (*BrE also* **mess aˈbout**) **1** to behave in a silly and annoying way, especially instead of doing sth useful SYN **fool around**: *Will you stop messing around and get on with some work?* **2** to spend time doing sth for pleasure in a relaxed way: *We spent the day messing around on the river.* **mess aˈround (with sb)** (*BrE also* **mess aˈbout (with sb)**) to have a sexual relationship with sb, especially when you should not **mess aˈround with sth** (*BrE also* **mess aˈbout with sth**) **1** to touch or use sth in a careless and/or annoying way: *Who's been messing around with my computer?* **2** to spend time playing with sth, repairing sth, etc. **mess sb aˈround** (*BrE also* **mess sb aˈbout**) (*BrE*) to treat sb in an unfair and annoying way, especially by changing your mind a lot or not doing what you said you would **mess ˈup** | **mess sth↔ˈup** to fail at sth or do it badly: *I've really messed up this time.* ◇ *If you cancel now you'll mess up all my arrangements.* **mess sb↔ˈup 1** (*informal*) to cause sb to have serious emotional or mental problems **2** (*NAmE, informal*) to physically hurt sb, especially by hitting them: *He was messed up pretty bad by the other guy.* **mess sth↔ˈup** to make sth dirty or untidy: *I don't want you messing up my nice clean kitchen.* **ˈmess with sb/sth** (usually used in negative sentences) to get involved with sb/sth that may be harmful: *I wouldn't mess with him if I were you.*

**mes·sage** 🔊 **A1** /ˈmesɪdʒ/ noun, verb
■ noun **1** 🔊 **A1** a written or spoken piece of information, etc. that you send to sb or leave for sb when you cannot speak to them yourself: *There were no messages for me at the hotel.* ◇ *I never got your message.* ◇ *We've had an urgent message saying that your father's ill.* ◇ *Jenny's not here at the moment. Can I take a message?* ◇ *I left a message on her voicemail.* ◇ *I've been trying to get you all day—don't you ever listen to your messages?* ◇ **~ (from sb) (to sb)** *Messages of support have been arriving from all over the country.* ◇ *a televised message from the president to the American people* ⮕ WORDFINDER NOTE AT CALL ⮕ see also ERROR MESSAGE **2** 🔊 **A1** a piece of information sent in electronic form, for example by email or mobile phone: *an email/a text/an SMS message* ◇ *There were four messages in my inbox.* ◇ *He sent me a message.* ◇ *I turned on my cell phone to check my messages.* ◇ *Fans post messages on her website.* ◇ *I keep getting an error message when I try to connect to the internet.* ⮕ see also DIRECT MESSAGE, INSTANT MESSAGE, TEXT MESSAGE

WORDFINDER address, attachment, compose, draft, email, emoticon, forward, inbox, re

**3** 🔊 **B1** [usually sing.] an important moral, social or political idea that a book, speech, etc. is trying to communicate: *a film with a strong religious message* ◇ *The campaign is trying to get the message across to young people that drugs are dangerous.* ◇ *I think this movie sends the wrong message to her young fans.* ⮕ see also MIXED MESSAGE **4** a piece of information that is sent from the brain to a part of the body, or from a part of the body to the brain: *The message arrives in your brain in a fraction of a second.* **5 messages** [pl.] (*ScotE, IrishE*) shopping: *to do the messages* ◇ *to go for the messages* ◇ *You can leave your messages* (= the things that you have bought) *here*.
IDM **get the ˈmessage** (*informal*) to understand what sb is trying to tell you indirectly: *When he started looking at his watch, I got the message and left.* **on/off ˈmessage** stating/not stating the official view of the political party or organization you represent
■ verb to send a text message, or a message through an INSTANT MESSAGING service, etc. to sb: **~ sb** *Fiona just messaged me.* **~ sb sth** *Brian messaged me the news.* ⮕ see also DM *verb*, TEXT-MESSAGE ⮕ **mesˈsaging** *noun* [U]: *the popular mobile messaging service WhatsApp* ⮕ see also INSTANT MESSAGING, TEXT-MESSAGING

▼ EXPRESS YOURSELF
**Leaving a phone message**
If you phone someone who is not able to take your call, you may need to leave a message:
• Could I speak to Jay Black, please?
• Could you give him a message?
• Is there a time that might be good for me to try him again?
• Can you let him know I'll call back?
• Could you ask him to call me back? My number is…

**ˈmessage board** (also **disˈcussion board**, **disˈcussion forum**) noun a place on the internet where people can exchange ideas and opinions about a topic: *I posted a question on the message board.*

**mes·sen·ger** /ˈmesɪndʒə(r)/ noun a person who gives a message to sb or who delivers messages to people as a job: *He sent the order by messenger.* ◇ *a bike/bicycle messenger* IDM see SHOOT v.

**Mes·siah** /məˈsaɪə/ noun **1 the Messiah** [sing.] (in Christianity) Jesus Christ, who was sent by God into the world to save people from evil and SIN **2 the Messiah** [sing.] (in Judaism) a king who will be sent by God to save the Jewish people **3 messiah** a leader who people believe will solve the problems of a country or the world SYN **saviour**: *He's seen by many as a political messiah.*

**mes·si·an·ic** /ˌmesiˈænɪk/ adj. (*formal*) **1** relating to a messiah **2** attempting to make big changes in society or to a political system in an extremely determined and enthusiastic way: *The reforms were carried out with an almost messianic zeal.*

**Messrs** (*BrE*) (*NAmE* **Messrs.**) /ˈmesəz; *NAmE* -sərz/ *abbr.* (used as the plural of 'Mr' before a list of names and before names of business companies): *Messrs Smith, Brown and Jones* ◇ *Messrs T Brown and Co*

**messy** /ˈmesi/ adj. (**messˈier**, **messˈiest**) **1** dirty and/or untidy SYN **chaotic**: *The house was always messy.* ◇ (*NAmE*) *Her long black hair was messy and dirty.* **2** making sb/sth dirty and/or untidy: *It was a messy job.* **3** (of a situation) unpleasant, confused or difficult to deal with: *The divorce was painful and messy.*

**mes·tiza** /meˈstiːzə/ noun a Latin American woman who has both Spanish and Native American ANCESTORS

**mes·tizo** /meˈstiːzəʊ/ noun (*pl.* **-os**) a Latin American who has both Spanish and Native American ANCESTORS

# the Met

**the Met** /ðə ˈmet/ noun **1** [sing. + sing./pl. v.] the police force in London (the abbreviation for 'the Metropolitan Police') **2** [sing.] the abbreviation for 'the Metropolitan Opera House' in New York

**Met** /met/ abbr. (informal) METEOROLOGICAL: *the Met Office weather forecast service*

**met** /met/ past tense, past part. of MEET

**meta-** /ˌmetə, məˈtæ/ combining form (in nouns, adjectives and verbs) **1** connected with a change of position or state: *metamorphosis* ◊ *metabolism* **2** higher; beyond: *metaphysics* ◊ *metalanguage*

**ˈmeta-analysis** noun [C, U] (pl. **meta-analyses**) research that combines the results of a number of related studies: *The meta-analysis included data from nine cohort studies with 1280 children.*

**me·tab·ol·ism** /məˈtæbəlɪzəm/ noun [U, C] (biology) the chemical processes in living things that change food, etc. into energy and materials for growth: *The body's metabolism is slowed down by extreme cold.* ▶ **meta·bol·ic** /ˌmetəˈbɒlɪk; NAmE -ˈbɑːl-/ adj. [usually before noun]: *a metabolic process/disorder* ◊ *a high/low metabolic rate*

**me·tab·ol·ize** (BrE also **-ise**) /məˈtæbəlaɪz/ verb (biology) **1** [T] ~**sth** to turn food, minerals, etc. in the body into new cells, energy and waste products by means of chemical processes **2** [I] (of food, minerals, etc.) to be turned into new cells, energy and waste products by means of chemical processes in the body

**meta·car·pal** /ˌmetəˈkɑːpl; NAmE -ˈkɑːrpl/ noun (anatomy) any of the five bones in the hand between the WRIST and the fingers ⊃ VISUAL VOCAB page V1

**meta·data** /ˈmetədeɪtə; BrE also -dɑːtə; NAmE also -dætə/ noun [U] information that describes other information in order to help you understand or use it: *In the metadata she found the author and location of the file.*

**meta·fic·tion** /ˈmetəfɪkʃn/ noun [U] a type of play, novel, etc. in which the author deliberately reminds the audience, reader, etc. that it is fiction and not real life

**metal** /ˈmetl/ noun [C, U] a type of solid mineral substance that is usually hard and shiny and that heat and electricity can travel through, for example tin, iron and gold: *a piece/sheet of metal* ◊ *a metal pipe/bar/box/plate* ◊ *a heap of scrap metal* ◊ *a roof of sheet metal* ◊ *The frame is made of metal.* ⊃ see also BASE METAL, HEAVY METAL, PRECIOUS METAL, TRANSITION METAL IDM see PEDAL n.

**meta·lan·guage** /ˈmetəlæŋɡwɪdʒ/ noun [C, U] (linguistics) the words and phrases that people use to talk about or describe language or a particular language

**ˈmetal detector** noun **1** an electronic device that you use to look for metal objects that are buried under the ground **2** an electronic machine that is used, for example at an airport, to see if people are hiding metal objects such as weapons

**ˈmetal fatigue** noun [U] weakness in metal that is frequently put under pressure that makes it likely to break

**met·alled** /ˈmetld/ adj. (of a road or track) made or repaired with small pieces of broken stone

**me·tal·lic** /məˈtælɪk/ adj. [usually before noun] **1** that looks, tastes or sounds like metal: *metallic paint/colours/blue* ◊ *a metallic taste* ◊ *a metallic sound/click* **2** made of or containing metal: *a metallic object* ◊ *metallic compounds*

**me·tal·lur·gist** /məˈtælədʒɪst; NAmE ˈmetələːrdʒɪst/ noun a scientist who studies metals and their uses

**me·tal·lurgy** /məˈtælədʒi; NAmE ˈmetələːrdʒi/ noun [U] the scientific study of metals and their uses ▶ **me·tal·lur·gical** /ˌmetəˈlɜːdʒɪkl; NAmE ˌmetlˈɜːrdʒ-/ adj.

**met·al·work** /ˈmetlwɜːk; NAmE -wɜːrk/ noun [U] **1** the activity of making objects out of metal; objects that are made out of metal **2** the metal parts of sth: *cracks in the metalwork* ▶ **met·al·work·er** noun

**meta·morph·ic** /ˌmetəˈmɔːfɪk; NAmE -ˈmɔːrf-/ adj. (geology) (of rocks) formed by the action of heat and pressure

**meta·morph·ose** /ˌmetəˈmɔːfəʊz; NAmE -ˈmɔːrf-/ verb **1** [I] ~**(from sth) (into sth)** (biology) (of an insect or an AMPHIBIAN, such as a frog) to change from its young form to its adult form in two or more separate stages; to experience metamorphosis: *The caterpillar will eventually metamorphose into a butterfly.* **2** [I] ~**(from sth) (into sth)** (formal) to change into sth completely different, especially over a period of time SYN transform

**meta·mor·phosis** /ˌmetəˈmɔːfəsɪs; NAmE -ˈmɔːrf-/ noun (pl. **meta·mor·phoses** /-fəsiːz/) [C, U] **1** ~**(of sth) (into sth)** (biology) the process in which an insect or an AMPHIBIAN (such as a frog) changes from its young form to its adult form in two or more separate stages: *the metamorphosis of a caterpillar into a butterfly* **2** ~**(from sth) (into sth)** (formal) a process in which sb/sth changes completely into sth different SYN transformation: *She had undergone an amazing metamorphosis from awkward schoolgirl to beautiful woman.*

**meta·phor** /ˈmetəfə(r), -fɔː(r)/ noun [C, U] a word or phrase used to describe sb/sth else, in a way that is different from its normal use, in order to show that the two things have the same qualities and to make the description more powerful, for example *She has a heart of stone*; the use of such words and phrases: *a game of football used as a metaphor for the competitive struggle of life* ◊ *the writer's striking use of metaphor* ⊃ compare SIMILE ⊃ WORDFINDER NOTE at IMAGE

**meta·phor·ical** /ˌmetəˈfɒrɪkl; NAmE -ˈfɔːr-/ adj. connected with or containing metaphors: *metaphorical language* ⊃ compare FIGURATIVE, LITERAL ▶ **meta·phor·ic·al·ly** /-kli/ adv.: *I'll leave you in Robin's capable hands—metaphorically speaking, of course!*

**meta·phys·ics** /ˌmetəˈfɪzɪks/ noun [U] the branch of philosophy that deals with the nature of existence, truth and knowledge ▶ **meta·phys·ic·al** /-zɪkl/ adj.: *metaphysical problems/speculation*

**me·tas·ta·sis** /məˈtæstəsɪs/ noun [U, C] (pl. **me·tas·ta·ses** /-təsiːz/) (medical) the development of TUMOURS in different parts of the body resulting from cancer that has started in another part of the body; one of these tumours ▶ **me·tas·tat·ic** /ˌmetəˈstætɪk/ adj.

**meta·tar·sal** /ˌmetəˈtɑːsl; NAmE -ˈtɑːrsl/ noun (anatomy) any of the bones in the part of the foot between the ankle and the toes ⊃ VISUAL VOCAB page V1

**mete** /miːt/ verb
PHRV **ˌmete sth↔ˈout (to sb)** (formal) to give sb a punishment; to make sb suffer bad treatment: *Severe penalties were meted out by the court.* ◊ *the violence meted out to the prisoners*

**me·teor** /ˈmiːtiə(r), -tiɔː(r)/ noun a piece of rock from outer space that makes a bright line across the night sky as it burns up while falling through the earth's atmosphere: *a meteor shower* ⊃ see also SHOOTING STAR

**me·teor·ic** /ˌmiːtiˈɒrɪk; NAmE -ˈɔːr-/ adj. **1** achieving success very quickly: *a meteoric rise to fame* ◊ *a meteoric career* **2** relating to meteors: *meteoric craters*

**me·teor·ite** /ˈmiːtiəraɪt/ noun a piece of rock from outer space that hits the earth's surface ⊃ WORDFINDER NOTE at UNIVERSE

**me·teor·olo·gist** /ˌmiːtiəˈrɒlədʒɪst; NAmE -ˈrɑːl-/ noun a scientist who studies meteorology

**me·teor·ology** /ˌmiːtiəˈrɒlədʒi; NAmE -ˈrɑːl-/ noun [U] the scientific study of the earth's atmosphere and its changes, used especially in predicting what the weather will be like ▶ **me·teoro·logic·al** /ˌmiːtiərəˈlɒdʒɪkl; NAmE -ˈlɑːdʒ-/ adj.

**meter** /ˈmiːtə(r)/ noun, verb
■ noun **1** (especially in compounds) a device that measures and records the amount of electricity, gas, water, etc. that you have used or the time and distance you have travelled, etc: *A man came to read the gas meter.* ◊ *The cab driver left the meter running while he waited for us.* ◊ *Installing a smart meter will allow you to see how much water you are using in real time.* ⊃ see also LIGHT METER **2** = PARKING METER **3** **-meter** (in compounds) a device for measuring the thing mentioned: *speedometer* ◊ *altimeter* ◊ *calorimeter* **4** (US) = METRE: *Who holds the record in the 100 meters?*

■ **verb** ~ **sth** to measure sth (for example how much gas, electricity, etc. has been used) using a meter

**meth** /meθ/ (also **crystal 'meth**, **crys·tal**) noun [U] (informal) a powerful illegal drug, METHAMPHETAMINE, that looks like small pieces of glass: *the growing meth problem in our rural communities*

**metha·done** /'meθədəʊn/ noun [U] a drug that is used to treat people who are trying to stop taking the illegal drug HEROIN

**meth·am·pheta·mine** /ˌmeθæm'fetəmiːn/ (also informal **meth**, **crystal 'meth**) noun [U] a powerful illegal drug

**me·thane** /'miːθeɪn; NAmE 'meθ-/ noun [U] (symb. CH₄) a gas without colour or smell, that burns easily and is used as fuel. Natural gas consists mainly of methane.

**metha·nol** /'meθənɒl; NAmE -nɔːl, -nəʊl/ noun [U] (symb. CH₃OH) a poisonous form of alcohol formed when METHANE reacts with OXYGEN

**methi·cil·lin** /ˌmeθɪ'sɪlɪn/ noun [U] a drug that can be used against infections where PENICILLIN is not effective

**me·thinks** /mɪ'θɪŋks/ verb [I, T] (**me·thought**) (only used in the forms **methinks** and **methought**) ~ **(that)** ... (old use or humorous) I think; it seems to me

**method** ⓘ A2 ⊙ /'meθəd/ noun 1 ⓘ A2 [C] a particular way of doing sth: *Which method is the most effective?* ⬥ **traditional/alternative methods** ⬥ ~ **of sth** *a scientific method of data analysis* ⬥ ~ **of doing sth** *a reliable method of measuring blood pressure* ⬥ ~ **for (doing) sth** *the best method for arriving at an accurate prediction of the costs* ⬥ ~ **to do sth** *Developing new methods to keep insects out of food packages is critical.* ⬥ *to use/employ/apply a method* ⬥ *to devise/propose/adopt a method* ⊃ see also BARRIER METHOD 2 [U] the quality of being well planned and organized
IDM **there's (a) method in sb's madness** there is a reason for sb's behaviour and it is not as strange or as stupid as it seems

**'method acting** noun [U] a method of preparing for a role in which an actor tries to experience the life and feelings of the character he or she will play ▶ **'method actor** noun

**meth·od·ical** /mə'θɒdɪkl; NAmE -'θɑːd-/ adj. 1 done in a careful and logical way: *a methodical approach/study* 2 (of a person) doing things in a careful and logical way SYN **disciplined**, **precise**: *to have a methodical mind* ▶ **meth·od·ic·al·ly** /-kli/ adv.: *They sorted slowly and methodically through the papers.*

**Meth·od·ist** /'meθədɪst/ noun a member of a Christian Protestant Church that broke away from the Church of England in the 18th century ▶ **Meth·od·ism** /-dɪzəm/ noun [U] **Meth·od·ist** adj.: *a Methodist church/preacher*

**meth·od·ology** ⓘ+ C1 Ⓦ /ˌmeθə'dɒlədʒi; NAmE -'dɑːl-/ noun (pl. -ies) [C, U] (formal) a set of methods and principles used to perform a particular activity: *recent changes in the methodology of language teaching* ▶ **meth·odo·logic·al** /ˌmeθədə'lɒdʒɪkl; NAmE -'lɑːdʒ-/ adj. [usually before noun]: *methodological problems* **meth·odo·logic·al·ly** /-kli/ adv.

**methought** /mɪ'θɔːt/ past tense of METHINKS

**meths** /meθs/ noun [U] (especially BrE, informal) = METHYLATED SPIRIT

**Me·thu·selah** /mə'θjuːzələ; NAmE -'θuː-/ noun used to describe a very old person: *I'm feeling older than Methuselah.* ORIGIN From Methuselah, a man in the Bible who is supposed to have lived for 969 years.

**methy·lated 'spirit** /ˌmeθəleɪtɪd 'spɪrɪt/ (also **methy·lated spirits**) (also informal **meths** especially in BrE) noun [U] a type of alcohol that is not fit for drinking, used as a fuel for lighting and heating and for cleaning off dirty marks

**me·ticu·lous** /mə'tɪkjələs/ adj. (approving) paying careful attention to every detail SYN **fastidious**, **thorough**: *meticulous planning/records/research* ⬥ ~ **in (doing) sth** *He's always meticulous in keeping the records up to date.* ⬥ ~ **about sth** *My father was meticulous about his appearance.* ▶ **me·ticu·lous·ly** adv.: *a meticulously planned schedule* ⬥ *meticulously clean* **me·ticu·lous·ness** noun [U]

**mé·tier** /'metieɪ; NAmE meɪ'tjeɪ/ noun [usually sing.] (from French, formal) a person's work, especially when they have a natural skill or ability for it

**'me-time** noun [U] (informal) time when a person who is normally very busy relaxes or does sth they enjoy: *The spa is popular with women who want a bit of me-time.*

**Metis** /meɪ'tiː; NAmE pl. **Metis** /meɪ'tiː, -'tiːz/) (CanE) (especially in Canada) a person with one Aboriginal parent and one European parent, or a person whose family comes from both Aboriginal and European backgrounds

**me·ton·ymy** /mə'tɒnəmi; NAmE -'tɑːn-/ noun [U] (linguistics) the act of referring to sth by the name of sth else that is closely connected with it, for example using *the White House* for *the US president* ⊃ WORDFINDER NOTE at IMAGE

**'me-too** adj. [only before noun] (informal) done or produced because of sth successful that sb else has done: *The magazine 'Hello!' gave rise to a number of me-too publications.*

**metre** ⓘ A1 (US **meter**) /'miːtə(r)/ noun 1 ⓘ A1 [C] (abbr. **m**) a unit for measuring length; a hundred CENTIMETRES: *a 50-metre swimming pool* ⬥ *Every few metres the cat stopped and turned to look at me.* ⬥ *Over 3700 square metres of office space is available.* ⬥ *The huge sculpture is made of 500 cubic metres of ice.* ⬥ *an athlete running at 10 metres per second* 2 [C, U] (abbr. **m**) used in the name of races: *She came second in the 200 metres.* ⬥ *the 4×100 metre(s) relay* 3 [U, C] the arrangement of strong and weak stresses in lines of poetry that produces the rhythm; a particular example of this: *the hexameter, the epic metre of Homer*

**met·ric** /'metrɪk/ adj., noun
■ adj. 1 based on the metric system: *metric units/measurements/sizes* ⬥ *British currency went metric in 1971.* 2 made or measured using the metric system: *These screws are metric.* ⊃ compare IMPERIAL 3 = METRICAL
■ noun 1 **metrics** [pl.] a set of numbers or statistics used for measuring sth, especially results that show how well a business, school, computer program, etc. is doing: *There are a lot of different metrics on which to gauge success.* 2 [U] (informal) the METRIC SYSTEM: **in** ~ *It's easier to work in metric.* 3 **metrics** [pl.] the use or study of METRE in poetry

**met·ric·al** /'metrɪkl/ (also **met·ric**) adj. connected with the rhythm of a poem, produced by the arrangement of stress on the syllables in each line

**the 'metric system** noun [sing.] the system of measurement that uses the metre, the KILOGRAM and the LITRE as basic units

**metric 'ton** noun = TONNE

**metro** /'metrəʊ/ noun, adj.
■ noun (pl. **-os**) 1 (also **the Metro**) [sing.] an underground train system, especially the one in Paris: **on the** ~ *to travel on the metro* ⬥ **by** ~ *I get to work by metro.* ⬥ *the Paris Metro* ⬥ *a metro station* ⊃ note at UNDERGROUND 2 (IndE) a large or capital city, especially Delhi, Kolkata, Mumbai or Chennai: *Here are the temperatures recorded at the four metros at 5 o'clock this morning.*
■ adj. [only before noun] (NAmE, informal) = METROPOLITAN: *the New York metro areas*

**me·trol·ogy** /mə'trɒlədʒi; NAmE -'trɑːl-/ noun [U] the scientific study of measurement ▶ **me·tro·logic·al** /ˌmetrə'lɒdʒɪkl; NAmE -'lɑːdʒ-/ adj.

**me·tro·nome** /'metrənəʊm/ noun a device that makes a regular sound like a clock and is used by musicians to help them keep the correct rhythm when playing a piece of music ▶ **met·ro·nom·ic** /ˌmetrə'nɒmɪk; NAmE -'nɑːm-/ adj.: *His financial problems hit the headlines with almost metronomic regularity.*

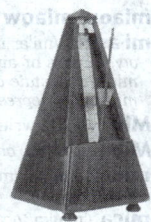

metronome

**me·trop·olis** /mə'trɒpəlɪs; NAmE -'trɑːp-/ noun a large, important city (often the capital city of a country or region)

**met·ro·pol·itan** /ˌmetrə'pɒlɪtən; NAmE -'pɑːl-/ adj. [only before noun] 1 (also NAmE, informal

# metrosexual

**metro**) connected with a large or capital city: *the New York metropolitan area* ◊ *metropolitan districts/regions* ⊃ WORDFINDER NOTE at CITY **2** connected with a particular country rather than with the other regions of the world that the country controls: *metropolitan France/Spain*

**met·ro·sex·ual** /ˌmetrəˈsekʃuəl/ noun (informal) a HETEROSEXUAL man who lives in a city and is interested in things like fashion and shopping ▶ **met·ro·sex·ual** adj.

**met·tle** /ˈmetl/ noun [U] the ability and DETERMINATION to do sth successfully despite difficult conditions: *The next game will be a real test of their mettle.*
IDM **on your ˈmettle** prepared to use all your skills, knowledge, etc. because you are being tested

**mew** /mjuː/ noun the soft, high noise that a cat makes ▶ **mew** verb [I]: *The kitten mewed pitifully.*

**mewl** /mjuːl/ verb [I] to make a weak crying sound ▶ **mewl·ing** noun [U] **mewl·ing** adj.: *mewling babies*

**mews** /mjuːz/ noun (pl. **mews**) (BrE) a short, narrow street with a row of STABLES (= buildings used to keep horses in) that have been made into small houses

**ˈmews house** (BrE) (US **ˈcarriage house**) noun a house in a mews

**Mex·ican** /ˈmeksɪkən/ adj., noun
■ adj. from or connected with Mexico
■ noun a person from Mexico

**Mexican ˈwave** noun [C] (BrE) (NAmE **the ˈwave** [sing.]) a continuous movement that looks like a wave on the sea, made by a large group of people, especially people watching a sports game, when one person after another stands up, raises their arms, and then sits down again

**mez·za·nine** /ˈmezəniːn/ noun **1** a floor that is built between two floors of a building and is smaller than the other floors: *a bedroom on the mezzanine* ◊ *a mezzanine floor* **2** (NAmE) the first area of seats above the ground floor in a theatre; the first few rows of these seats ⊃ see also DRESS CIRCLE

**mezzo-soprano** /ˌmetsəʊ səˈprɑːnəʊ; NAmE -ˈpræn-, -ˈprɑːn-/ (also **mezzo**) noun (pl. **mezzo-sopranos, mezzos**) (from Italian) a singing voice with a range between SOPRANO and ALTO; a woman with a mezzo-soprano voice

**mg** abbr. (in writing) MILLIGRAM(S)

**Mgr** abbr. (in writing) MONSIGNOR

**MHA** /ˌem eɪtʃ ˈeɪ/ noun (in Canada) Member of the House of Assembly (the parliament in Newfoundland and Labrador)

**MHz** abbr. (in writing) MEGAHERTZ

**mi** = ME noun

**MI5** /ˌem aɪ ˈfaɪv/ noun [U] the British government organization that deals with national security within the UK. Its official name is 'the Security Service'.

**MI6** /ˌem aɪ ˈsɪks/ noun [U] the British government organization that deals with information from outside the UK that concerns British national security. Its official name is 'the Secret Intelligence Service'.

**MIA** /ˌem aɪ ˈeɪ/ abbr. (especially NAmE) (of a soldier) missing in action (missing after a battle)

**miaow** (BrE) (also **meow** NAmE, BrE) /miˈaʊ/ noun the crying sound made by a cat ⊃ see also MEW ▶ **miaow** (BrE) (also **meow** NAmE, BrE) verb [I]

**ˈmiaow miaow** noun [U] (informal) = MEPHEDRONE

**mi·asma** /miˈæzmə, maɪˈæ-/ noun [C, usually sing., U] (literary) a mass of air that is dirty and smells unpleasant: *A miasma of stale alcohol hung around him.* ◊ (figurative) *the miasma of depression*

**MiB** abbr. (in writing) MEBIBYTE

**Mib** (also **Mibit**) abbr. (in writing) MEBIBIT

**mic** (also **mike**) /maɪk/ noun (informal) = MICROPHONE ⊃ see also OPEN MIC

**mica** /ˈmaɪkə/ noun [U] a clear mineral that splits easily into thin flat layers and is used to make electrical equipment

**ˈmic drop** noun (especially NAmE, informal) **1** the act of deliberately dropping your MICROPHONE at the end of a performance or speech that you think you did particularly well **2** used to say that a performance, speech or point made in a discussion is so impressive that nobody can reply or follow it up: *Wow! Boom! Mic drop!*

**mice** /maɪs/ pl. of MOUSE

**Mich·ael·mas** /ˈmɪklməs/ noun [U] (in the Christian Church) the holy day in honour of St Michael, 29 September

**Michelin man** /ˈmɪtʃəlɪn mæn, ˈmɪʃə-/ noun
IDM **like the/a ˈMichelin man** having a wide, round body because of being very fat or wearing a lot of thick, heavy clothes ORIGIN From the fat cartoon character made of tyres used as a symbol of the Michelin™ tyre company.

**Mick** /mɪk/ noun (taboo, slang) an offensive word for a person from Ireland

**mickey** /ˈmɪki/ noun
IDM **take the ˈmickey/ˈmick (out of sb)** (BrE, informal) to make sb look or feel silly by copying the way they talk, behave, etc. or by making them believe sth that is not true, often in a way that is not intended to be unkind SYN **tease, mock**

**Mickey ˈMouse** adj. (disapproving) not of high quality; too easy: *It's only a Mickey Mouse job.*

**micro-** /ˈmaɪkrəʊ, ˈmaɪkrə; BrE also ˈmaɪˈkrɒ; NAmE also ˈmaɪˈkrɑː/ combining form **1** (in nouns, adjectives and adverbs) small; on a small scale: *microchip* ◊ *microorganism* OPP **macro- 2** (in nouns; used in units of measurement) one millionth: *a microlitre*

**mi·crobe** /ˈmaɪkrəʊb/ noun an extremely small living thing that you can only see under a MICROSCOPE and that may cause disease

**micro·beads** /ˈmaɪkrəʊbiːdz/ noun [pl.] extremely small pieces of plastic, used in products such as soap, face cream and TOOTHPASTE

**micro·bio·lo·gist** /ˌmaɪkrəʊbaɪˈɒlədʒɪst; NAmE -ˈɑːl-/ noun a scientist who studies microbiology

**micro·bi·ol·ogy** /ˌmaɪkrəʊbaɪˈɒlədʒi; NAmE -ˈɑːl-/ noun [U] the scientific study of very small living things, such as bacteria ▶ **micro·bio·logic·al** /ˌmaɪkrəʊˌbaɪəˈlɒdʒɪkl; NAmE -ˈlɑːdʒ-/ adj.

**micro·blog·ging** /ˈmaɪkrəʊblɒɡɪŋ; NAmE -blɑːɡ-/ noun [U] the activity of sending regular short messages, photos or videos over the internet, either to a selected group of people, or so that they can be viewed by anyone, as a means of keeping people informed about your activities and thoughts ⊃ compare TWITTER ▶ **micro·blog** noun **micro·blog** verb (-gg-) [I]

**micro·brew·ery** /ˈmaɪkrəʊbruːəri/ noun (pl. -ies) a small BREWERY (= a factory where beer is made), that often sells its beer to visitors or only sells it locally

**micro·chip** /ˈmaɪkrəʊtʃɪp/ noun, verb
■ noun (also **chip**) a very small piece of a material that is a SEMICONDUCTOR, used to carry a complicated electronic CIRCUIT
■ verb (-pp-) ~ sth to put a microchip under the skin of an animal as a way of identifying it

**micro·cli·mate** /ˈmaɪkrəʊklaɪmət/ noun (specialist) the weather in a particular small area, especially when this is different from the weather in the surrounding area

**micro·cosm** /ˈmaɪkrəʊkɒzəm; NAmE -kɑːz-/ noun a thing, a place or a group that has all the features and qualities of sth much larger: *The family is a microcosm of society.* ⊃ compare MACROCOSM
IDM **in ˈmicrocosm** on a small scale: *The developments in this town represent in microcosm what is happening in the country as a whole.*

**micro·elec·tron·ics** /ˌmaɪkrəʊɪˌlekˈtrɒnɪks; NAmE -ˈtrɑːn-/ noun [U] the design, production and use of very small electronic CIRCUITS ▶ **micro·elec·tron·ic** adj. [only before noun]

**micro·fibre** (US **micro·fiber**) /ˈmaɪkrəʊfaɪbə(r)/ noun [U] a very light artificial material with very fine THREADS

**micro·fiche** /ˈmaɪkrəʊfiːʃ/ noun [U, C] a piece of film with written information on it in print of very small size.

Microfiches can only be read with a special machine: **on** ~ *The directory is available on microfiche.*

**micro·film** /ˈmaɪkrəʊfɪlm/ *noun* [U, C] film used for storing written information on in print of very small size

**micro·fi·nance** /ˈmaɪkrəʊfaɪnæns/ *noun* [U] a system of providing services such as lending money and saving for people who are too poor to use banks

**micro·gram** /ˈmaɪkrəʊɡræm/ *noun* (*symb.* μg) a unit for measuring weight; a millionth of a GRAM

**micro·light** /ˈmaɪkrəʊlaɪt/ (*BrE*) (*NAmE* **ultra·light**) *noun* a very small light aircraft for one or two people

**micro·man·age** /ˈmaɪkrəʊmænɪdʒ/ *verb* [T, I] ~ **(sth)** (*disapproving*) to control every detail of an activity or project, especially your employees' work: *The problem may be that you are micromanaging your team.* ◇ *bosses who micromanage* ▸ **micro·man·age·ment** *noun* [U] ▸ **micro·man·ager** *noun*

**micro·meter** *noun* **1** (*US*) = MICROMETRE **2** /maɪˈkrɒmɪtə(r); *NAmE* -ˈkrɑːm-/ a device used for measuring very small distances or spaces

**micro·metre** (*US* **micro·meter**) /ˈmaɪkrəʊmiːtə(r)/ *noun* (*symb.* μm) a unit for measuring length, equal to one millionth of a metre

**mi·cron** /ˈmaɪkrɒn; *NAmE* -krɑːn/ *noun* = MICROMETRE **HELP** The term **micron** is still in common use, but **micrometre** is now preferred in scientific contexts.

**micro·organ·ism** /ˌmaɪkrəʊˈɔːɡənɪzəm; *NAmE* -ˈɔːrɡ-/ *noun* (*specialist*) a very small living thing that you can only see under a MICROSCOPE

**micro·pay·ment** /ˈmaɪkrəʊpeɪmənt/ *noun* a very small payment that you make online, for example each time you use a particular page or service on the internet

**micro·phone** /ˈmaɪkrəfəʊn/ (*also informal* **mic**, **mike**) *noun* a device that is used for recording sounds or for making your voice louder when you are speaking or singing to an audience: *to speak into the microphone* ◇ *Their remarks were picked up by the hidden microphones.* ᑐ WORDFINDER NOTE at CONCERT

**micro·plas·tic** /ˈmaɪkrəʊplæstɪk/ *noun* (*also* **micro·plas·tics** [pl.]) extremely small pieces of plastic in the environment that come from consumer products and industrial waste: *microplastic particles/pollution*

**micro·pro·ces·sor** /ˌmaɪkrəʊˈprəʊsesə(r); *NAmE* -ˈprɑːs-/ *noun* (*computing*) a small unit of a computer that contains all the functions of the CENTRAL PROCESSING UNIT

**micro·scope** /ˈmaɪkrəskəʊp/ *noun* an instrument used in scientific study for making very small things look larger so that you can examine them carefully: *a microscope slide* ◇ **under a/the ~** *The bacteria were then examined under the microscope.* ᑐ *see also* ELECTRON MICROSCOPE **IDM** **under the ˈmicroscope** if you put sth **under the microscope** you examine or analyse it in great detail: *In the play, love and marriage are put under the microscope.*

**micro·scop·ic** /ˌmaɪkrəˈskɒpɪk; *NAmE* -ˈskɑːp-/ *adj.* **1** (*usually before noun*) extremely small and difficult or impossible to see without a microscope: *a microscopic creature/particle* ◇ (*humorous*) *The sandwiches were microscopic!* **2** [only before noun] using a microscope: *a microscopic analysis/examination* ▸ **micro·scop·ic·al·ly** /-kli/ *adv.*: *microscopically small creatures* ◇ *All samples are examined microscopically.*

**micro·scopy** /maɪˈkrɒskəpi; *NAmE* -ˈkrɑːs-/ *noun* [U] (*specialist*) the use of MICROSCOPES to look at very small creatures, objects, etc.

**micro·sec·ond** /ˈmaɪkrəʊsekənd/ *noun* (*symb.* μs) one millionth of a second

**micro·site** /ˈmaɪkrəʊsaɪt/ *noun* a small website containing more detailed information that can be accessed from a larger website: *The museum has a microsite to accompany the exhibition.*

**micro·sur·gery** /ˌmaɪkrəʊˈsɜːdʒəri; *NAmE* -ˈsɜːrdʒ-/ *noun* [U] the use of extremely small instruments and MICRO-SCOPES in order to perform very detailed and complicated medical operations

**micro·wave** /ˈmaɪkrəweɪv/ *noun, verb*
▪ *noun* **1** (*also formal* **microwave ˈoven**) a type of oven that cooks or heats food very quickly using ELECTROMAGNETIC waves rather than heat: *Reheat the soup in the microwave.* ◇ *microwave cookery/meals* ᑐ *compare* OVEN **2** (*specialist*) an ELECTROMAGNETIC wave that is shorter than a radio wave but longer than a light wave
▪ *verb* **~ sth** to cook or heat sth in a microwave ▸ **micro·wave·able** (*also* **micro·wav·able**) *adj.*: *microwaveable meals*

**mid-** /mɪd/ *combining form* (in nouns and adjectives) in the middle of: *mid-morning coffee* ◇ *mid-century furniture* ◇ *She's in her mid-thirties.* ◇ *The coach was fired midseason.*

**mid** /mɪd/ *prep.* (*literary*) = AMID

**ˌmid-ˈair** *noun* [U] a place in the air or the sky, not on the ground: **in ~** *The bird caught the insects in mid-air.* ▸ **ˌmid-ˈair** *adj.*: *a mid-air collision*

**Midas touch** /ˈmaɪdəs tʌtʃ/ *noun* (*usually* **the Midas touch**) [sing.] the ability to make a financial success of everything you do **ORIGIN** From the Greek myth in which King Midas was given the power to turn everything he touched into gold.

**ˌmid-Atˈlantic** *adj.* [only before noun] **1** connected with the area on the east coast of the US, that is near New York and immediately to the south of it: *the mid-Atlantic states/coast* **2** in the middle of the Atlantic ocean: (*figurative*) *a mid-Atlantic accent* (= a form of English that uses a mixture of British and American sounds)

**mid·brain** /ˈmɪdbreɪn/ *noun* (*anatomy*) a small central part of the brain

**mid·day** /ˌmɪdˈdeɪ/ *noun* [U] 12 o'clock in the middle of the day; the period around this time **SYN** noon: *The train arrives at midday.* ◇ *a midday meal* ◇ *the heat of the midday sun*

**mid·den** /ˈmɪdn/ *noun* (in the past) a pile of waste near a house, especially animal waste **SYN** dungheap

**mid·dle** 🅰 /ˈmɪdl/ *noun, adj.*
▪ *noun* **1** **the middle** [sing.] the part of sth that is at an equal distance from all its edges or sides; a point or a period of time between the beginning and the end of sth: **in the ~** *a lake with an island in the middle* ◇ *This chicken isn't cooked in the middle.* ◇ **in the ~ of sth** *Her car was stuck in the middle of the road.* ◇ *The phone rang in the middle of the night.* ◇ *His picture was right/bang* (= exactly) *in the middle of the front page.* ◇ **down the ~** *Take a sheet of paper and draw a line down the middle.* ◇ **by the ~ of sth** *I should have finished by the middle of the week.* ◇ *I like a story with a beginning, a middle and an end.* ᑐ *see also* MONKEY IN THE MIDDLE, PIGGY IN THE MIDDLE **2** [C, *usually sing.*] (*informal*) a person's WAIST: *He grabbed her around the middle.* ᑐ *see also* MIDDLE-OF-THE-ROAD
**IDM** **be in the middle of sth/of doing sth** to be busy doing sth: *They were in the middle of dinner when I called.* ◇ *I'm in the middle of writing a difficult letter.* **the middle of ˈnowhere** (*informal*) a place that is a long way from other buildings, towns, etc: *She lives on a small farm in the middle of nowhere.* ˌsplit/diˈvide (sth) down the ˈmiddle to divide sth into two equal parts; to divide into two equal parts: *The country was split down the middle over the strike* (= half supported it, half did not). ᑐ *more at* CATCH v.
▪ *adj.* [only before noun] in a position in the middle of an object, group of objects, people, etc.; between the beginning and the end of sth: *Pens are kept in the middle drawer.* ◇ *She's the middle child of three.* ◇ *He was very successful in his middle forties.* ◇ *a middle-sized room* ◇ *the middle-income groups in society*
**IDM** **(steer, take, etc.) a middle ˈcourse | (find, etc.) a/the middle ˈway** (to take/find) an acceptable course of action that avoids two extreme positions

**ˌmiddle ˈage** *noun* [U] the period of your life when you are neither young nor old, between the ages of about 45 and 60: *a pleasant woman in early/late middle age*

# middle-aged

**middle-ّaged** adj. **1** (of a person) neither young nor old ⊃ WORDFINDER NOTE at AGE **2 the middle aged** noun [pl.] people who are middle-aged **3** (disapproving) (of a person's attitudes or behaviour) rather boring and old-fashioned

**the Middle ّAges** noun [pl.] in European history, the period from about AD1000 to AD1450

**ˌmiddle-age ّspread** (also **ˌmiddle-aged ّspread**) noun [U] (humorous) the fat around the stomach that some people develop in middle age

**Middle America** /ˌmɪdl əˈmerɪkə/ noun [U] the middle class in the US, especially those people who represent traditional social and political values, and who come from small towns and SUBURBS rather than cities

**middle-brow** /ˈmɪdlbraʊ/ adj. [usually before noun] (usually disapproving) (of books, music, art, etc.) of good quality but not needing a lot of thought to understand ⊃ compare HIGHBROW, LOWBROW

**middle ّC** noun [U] the musical note C near the middle of the piano keyboard

**ˌmiddle-class** adj. **1** connected with the middle social class: *a middle-class background/family/suburb* **2** (disapproving) typical of people from the middle social class, for example having traditional views: *a middle-class attitude* ◊ *The magazine is very middle-class.*

**middle ّclass** noun [C + sing./pl. v.] the social class whose members are neither very rich nor very poor and that includes professional and business people: *the upper/lower middle class* ◊ *the growth of the middle classes* ⊃ compare UPPER CLASS, WORKING CLASS ⊃ see also THE LOWER MIDDLE CLASS

**the ˌmiddle ّdistance** noun [sing.] the part of a painting or a view that is neither very close nor very far away: *His eyes were fixed on a small house in the middle distance.*

**ˌmiddle-ّdistance** adj. [only before noun] (sport) connected with running a race over a distance that is neither very short nor very long: *a middle-distance runner* (= for example, somebody who runs 800 or 1500 metre races)

**ˌmiddle ّear** noun [sing.] the part of the ear behind the EARDRUM, containing the little bones that transfer sound VIBRATIONS

**the ˌMiddle ّEast** noun [sing.] an area that covers southwest Asia and north-east Africa, stretching from the Mediterranean to Pakistan and including the Arabian PENINSULA ⊃ compare FAR EAST ▶ **Middle ّEastern** adj.

**Middle England** /ˌmɪdl ˈɪŋɡlənd/ noun [U] the middle classes in England, especially people who have traditional social and political ideas and do not live in London

**Middle ّEnglish** noun [U] an old form of English that was used between about AD1150 and AD1500 ⊃ compare OLD ENGLISH

**Middle-Euroّpean** adj. of or related to central Europe or its people

**ˌmiddle ّfinger** noun the longest finger in the middle of each hand

**ˌmiddle ground** noun [U] a set of opinions, decisions, etc. that two or more groups who oppose each other can agree on; a position that is not extreme: *Negotiations have failed to establish any middle ground.* ◊ *~ between A and B The ballet company now occupies the middle ground between classical ballet and modern dance.*

**middle-man** /ˈmɪdlmæn/ noun (pl. -men /-men/) **1** a person or company that buys goods from the company that makes them and sells them to sb else: *Buy direct from the manufacturer and cut out the middleman.* **2** a person who helps to arrange things between people who do not want to talk directly to each other SYN **intermediary**, go-between

**ˌmiddle ّmanagement** noun [U + sing./pl. v.] the people who are in charge of small groups of people and departments within a business organization but who are not involved in making important decisions that will affect the whole organization ▶ **ˌmiddle ّmanager** noun

**ˌmiddle ّname** noun a name that comes between your first name and your family name
IDM **be sb's middle ّname** (informal) used to say that sb has a lot of a particular quality: *'Patience' is my middle name!*

**ˌmiddle-of-the-ّroad** adj. **1** (of people, policies, etc.) not extreme; acceptable to most people SYN **moderate**: *a middle-of-the-road newspaper* **2** (of music) pleasant to listen to but not very exciting

**ˌmiddle-ّranking** adj. [only before noun] having a responsible job or position, but not one of the most important

**ˌmiddle school** noun **1** (in the UK) a school for children between the ages of about 9 and 13 **2** (in the US and Canada) a school for children between the ages of about 11 and 14 ⊃ compare JUNIOR HIGH SCHOOL, UPPER SCHOOL

**middle-ware** /ˈmɪdlweə(r); NAmE -wer/ noun [U] (computing) a layer of software in a computer between the operating system and applications that provides additional facilities not provided by the operating system

**ˌmiddle-ّweight** /ˈmɪdlweɪt/ noun [U, C] a weight in BOXING and other sports, between WELTERWEIGHT and LIGHT HEAVYWEIGHT, in BOXING usually between 67 and 75 KILOGRAMS; a BOXER or other competitor in this class: *a middleweight champion*

**the ˌMiddle ّWest** noun [sing.] = MIDWEST

**mid-dling** /ˈmɪdlɪŋ/ adj. [usually before noun] of average size, quality, status, etc. SYN **moderate, unremarkable**: *a golfer of middling talent* IDM see FAIR adj.

**mid-field** /ˈmɪdfiːld, ˌmɪdˈfiːld/ noun [U, C, sing.] the central part of a sports field; the group of players in this position: **(in)~** *He plays (in) midfield.* ◊ *The team's midfield looks strong.* ◊ *a midfield player* ▶ **mid-field-er** /ˌmɪdˈfiːldə(r)/ noun

**midge** /mɪdʒ/ noun a small flying insect that lives especially in wet places and that bites humans and animals

**midget** /ˈmɪdʒɪt/ noun, adj.
■ noun **1** (taboo, offensive) an offensive word for a person who is very short because of the medical condition DWARFISM **2** (informal) a very small person or animal
■ adj. [only before noun] very small

**MIDI** /ˈmɪdi/ noun [U] a connection or program that connects electronic musical instruments and computers

**Mid-lands** /ˈmɪdləndz/ noun **the Midlands** [sing. + sing./pl. v.] the central part of a country, especially the central counties of England ▶ **Mid-land** adj. [only before noun]

**mid-life** /ˈmɪdlaɪf/ noun [U] the middle part of your life when you are neither young nor old: *It is not difficult to take up a new career in midlife.* ◊ *midlife stresses*

**ˌmidlife ّcrisis** noun [usually sing.] the worried and disappointed feelings or lack of confidence that a person may feel in the middle part of their life

**mid-night** /ˈmɪdnaɪt/ noun [U] **1** 12 o'clock at night: *She heard the clock strike midnight.* ◊ *~ They had to leave at midnight.* ◊ *At/on the stroke of midnight fireworks lit up the sky.* ◊ *We have to catch the midnight train.* **2** (especially NAmE) = MIDNIGHT BLUE IDM see BURN v., FLIT n.

**ˌmidnight ّblue** (also **ˌmid-night** especially in NAmE) noun [U] a very dark blue colour ▶ **ˌmidnight ّblue** adj.

**the ˌmidnight ّsun** noun [sing.] the sun that you can see at midnight in the middle of the summer near the North and South Poles

**mid-point** /ˈmɪdpɔɪnt/ noun [usually sing.] the point that is at an equal distance between the beginning and the end of sth; the point that is at an equal distance between two things: *the midpoint of the decade* ◊ *At its midpoint, the race had no clear winner.* ◊ *~ between A and B the midpoint between the first number and the last*

**ˌmid-ّrange** adj. [only before noun] (especially of a product for sale) neither the best nor the worst that is available: *a mid-range computer*

**mid-riff** /ˈmɪdrɪf/ noun the part of the body between the chest and the WAIST: *a bare midriff*

**mid·ship·man** /ˈmɪdʃɪpmən/ noun (pl. **-men** /-mən/) an officer of the lowest rank in the NAVY: *Midshipman Paul Brooks*

**mid-'sized** (also **mid·size**) /ˈmɪdsaɪz/ adj. (especially NAmE) of average size, neither large nor small

**midst** ?+ C1 /mɪdst/ noun [sing.] (used after a preposition) (formal) the middle part of sth SYN **middle: in the ~ of sth** *Such beauty was unexpected in the midst of the city.* IDM **in the midst of (doing) sth** while sth is happening or being done; while you are doing sth: *a country in the midst of a recession* ◊ *She discovered it in the midst of sorting out her father's things.* **in their/our/its/your midst** (formal) among or with them/us/it/you: *There is a traitor in our midst.*

**mid·stream** /ˌmɪdˈstriːm/ noun [U] the middle part of a river, stream, etc: *We anchored in midstream.* IDM **(in) midstream** in the middle of doing sth; while sth is still happening: *Their conversation was interrupted in midstream by the baby crying.* ⊃ more at CHANGE v.

**mid·sum·mer** /ˌmɪdˈsʌmə(r)/ noun [U] the middle of summer, especially the period in June in northern parts of the world, in December in southern parts: *a midsummer evening*

**Midsummer's 'Day** (BrE) (also **Midsummer 'Day** NAmE, BrE) noun 24 June, in northern parts of the world

**mid·term** /ˌmɪdˈtɜːm; NAmE ˌmɪdˈtɜːrm/ adj., noun
■ adj. [only before noun] **1** in the middle of the period that a government, a council, etc. is elected for: *midterm elections* **2** for or connected with a period of time that is neither long nor short; in the middle of a particular period: *a midterm solution* ◊ *midterm losses* ⊃ see also LONG-TERM, SHORT-TERM **3** in the middle of one of the main periods of the academic year: *a midterm examination/break* ⊃ see also HALF-TERM
■ noun **1** the middle of a government's time in power, an academic term, or a period of PREGNANCY: *Nixon resigned in midterm.* ◊ **midterm elections 2** (NAmE) an exam in the middle of an academic term: *I've been studying hard for my midterms.*

**mid·town** /ˈmɪdtaʊn/ noun [U] (NAmE) the part of a city that is between the central business area and the outer parts: *a house in midtown* ◊ *midtown Manhattan* ⊃ compare DOWNTOWN, UPTOWN

**mid·way** /ˌmɪdˈweɪ/ adv. **1** in the middle of a period of time; between two places SYN **halfway**: *The goal was scored midway through the first half.* **2** with some of the characteristics of one thing and some of another: *The expression on her face was midway between shock and relief.* ▶ **mid·way** adj.: *to reach the midway point* ◊ *a midway path between the two factions*

**mid·week** /ˌmɪdˈwiːk/ noun [U] the middle of the week (from Tuesday to Thursday): **in~** *to play a match in midweek* ◊ *By midweek he was too tired to go out.* ◊ *a midweek defeat for the team* ▶ **mid·week** adv.: *It's cheaper to travel midweek.*

**the Mid·west** /ðə ˌmɪdˈwest/ (also **the Middle 'West**) noun [sing.] the northern central part of the US ▶ **Mid·west·ern** /ˌmɪdˈwestən; NAmE -stərn/ adj.

**mid·wife** /ˈmɪdwaɪf/ noun (pl. **mid·wives** /-waɪvz/) a person, especially a woman, who is trained to help women give birth to babies ⊃ compare DOULA ⊃ WORDFINDER NOTE at BIRTH

**mid·wif·ery** /ˈmɪdwɪfəri; NAmE also -ˈwaɪ-/ noun [U] the profession and work of a midwife

**mid·win·ter** /ˌmɪdˈwɪntə(r)/ noun [U] the middle of winter, around December in northern parts of the world, June in southern parts: *midwinter weather*

**mid·year** /ˈmɪdjɪə, -jɜː; NAmE -jɪr/ noun (NAmE) **1** [U] the middle of the year: *Our annual reviews will take place at midyear.* **2** [C] an exam taken in the middle of the year at school or college ▶ **mid·year** adj.: *midyear elections*

**mien** /miːn/ noun [sing.] (formal or literary) a person's appearance or manner that shows how they are feeling

**miffed** /mɪft/ adj. [not usually before noun] (informal) slightly angry or upset SYN **annoyed**

---

989 **migration**

**might** ? A2 ⓢ /maɪt/ modal verb, noun
■ modal verb (negative **might not**, short form **mightn't** /ˈmaɪtnt/) **1** A2 used when showing that sth is or was possible: *He might get there in time, but I can't be sure.* ◊ *It might not be too late to save the building.* ◊ *The pills might have helped him, if only he'd taken them regularly.* ◊ *He might say that now* (= it is true that he does), *but he can soon change his mind.* **2** used as the past tense of *may* when reporting what sb has said: *He said he might come tomorrow.* **3** used to make a polite suggestion: *You might try calling the help desk.* ◊ *I thought we might go to the zoo on Saturday.* **4** (BrE) used to ask permission politely: *Might I use your phone?* **5** (formal) used to ask for information: *How might the plans be improved upon?* ◊ *And who might she be?* **6** used to show that you are annoyed about sth that sb could do or could have done: *I think you might at least offer to help!* ◊ *Honestly, you might have told me!* **7** used to say that you are not surprised by sth: *I might have guessed it was you!* ◊ *Her film was full of magical effects, as you might expect.* **8** used to emphasize that an important point has been made: *'And where is the money coming from?' 'You might well ask!'* ⊃ note at MODAL IDM see WELL adv.
■ noun [U] (formal or literary) great strength, energy or power: *America's military might* ◊ *I pushed the rock with all my might.* IDM **might is 'right** (saying) having the power to do sth gives you the right to do it: *Their foreign policy is based on the principle that 'might is right'.*

**'might-have-been** noun [usually pl.] (informal) an event or situation that could have happened or that you wish had happened, but that did not

**might·ily** /ˈmaɪtɪli/ adv. (old-fashioned) **1** very; very much: *mightily impressed/relieved* **2** (formal) with great strength or effort: *We have struggled mightily to win back lost trade.*

**mighty** /ˈmaɪti/ adj., adv.
■ adj. (**might·ier**, **mighti·est**) **1** (especially literary) very strong and powerful: *a mighty warrior* ◊ *He struck him with a mighty blow across his shoulder.* **2** large and impressive SYN **great**: *the mighty Mississippi River* IDM see HIGH adj., PEN n.
■ adv. (informal, especially NAmE) (with adjectives and adverbs) very SYN **really**: *mighty difficult* ◊ *driving mighty fast*

**mi·graine** /ˈmaɪɡreɪn; BrE also ˈmiːɡ-/ noun [U, C] a very severe type of headache that often makes a person feel sick and have difficulty in seeing: *severe migraine* ◊ *I'm getting a migraine.*

**mi·grant** /ˈmaɪɡrənt/ noun, adj.
■ noun **1** a person who moves from one place to another in order to find work or better living conditions: *undocumented/illegal migrants* ◊ *an increase in the number of refugees and migrants* ⊃ compare EMIGRANT, IMMIGRANT ⊃ SYNONYMS at IMMIGRANT ⊃ see also ECONOMIC MIGRANT **2** a bird or an animal that moves from one place to another according to the season
■ adj. [only before noun] **1** (of a person) moving from one place to another in order to find work or better living conditions: *These industries relied on migrant workers from poorer rural areas.* **2** (of a bird or an animal) moving from one place to another according to the season: *Migrant birds bring new viruses when they fly into the country.*

**mi·grate** ⓦ /maɪˈɡreɪt; NAmE ˈmaɪɡreɪt/ verb **1** [I] (of birds, animals, etc.) to move from one part of the world to another according to the season: *Swallows migrate south in winter.* **2** [I] (of a lot of people) to move from one town, country, etc. to go and live and/or work in another SYN **emigrate**: *Thousands were forced to migrate from rural to urban areas in search of work.* **3** [I] (specialist) to move from one place to another: *The infected cells then migrate to other areas of the body.* **4** [I, T] **~(sb)** (computing) to change, or cause sb to change, from one computer system to another **5** [T] **~sth** (computing) to move programs or HARDWARE from one computer system to another

**mi·gra·tion** ?+ C1 ⓦ /maɪˈɡreɪʃn/ noun [U, C] **1** ?+ C1 the movement every year of large numbers of birds or

---

ⓞ Oxford Phrasal Academic Lexicon (OPAL) written and spoken word lists | ⓦ OPAL written word list | ⓢ OPAL spoken word list

# migratory

animals from one place to another: *the seasonal migration of blue whales* **2** ~ (from ...) (to ...) the movement of people to a new country or area in order to find work or better living conditions: *migration from rural to urban areas* ◊ *It was one of the largest mass migrations in US history.* **3** the act of moving programs, etc. from one computer system to another; the fact of changing from one computer system to another

**mi·gra·tory** /ˈmaɪɡrətri, məˈɡreɪtəri; NAmE ˈmaɪɡrətɔːri/ *adj.* (*specialist*) connected with, or having the habit of, regular migration: *migratory flights/birds*

**mi·kado** /mɪˈkɑːdəʊ/ *noun* (*pl.* **-os**) (*from Japanese*) a title given in the past to the EMPEROR of Japan

**mike** /maɪk/ *noun, verb*
- **noun** (*informal*) = MICROPHONE
- **verb** [usually passive] to connect sb/sth to a MICROPHONE: **be miked (up)** *The minister was already miked up for the interview.*

**mi·lady** /mɪˈleɪdi/ *noun* (*pl.* **-ies**) (*old use or humorous*) used when talking to or about a woman who is a member of the British NOBILITY or of high class ⸺ compare MILORD

**mil·age** = MILEAGE

## mild B1 /maɪld/ *adj., noun*

- *adj.* (**milder, mildest**) **1** B1 not severe or strong: *a mild form of the disease* ◊ *a mild case of flu* ◊ *The symptoms were mild.* ◊ *a mild punishment/criticism* ◊ *It's safe to take a mild sedative.* ◊ *Use a soap that is mild on the skin.* **2** B1 (of weather) not very cold, and therefore pleasant: *the mildest winter since records began* ◊ *a mild climate* ⸺ compare HARD **3** B1 (of feelings) not great or extreme SYN **slight**: *mild irritation/amusement/disapproval* ◊ *She looked at him in mild surprise.* **4** B1 (of a taste) not strong, spicy or bitter: *a fairly mild flavour* ◊ *mild cheese* ◊ *a mild curry* OPP **strong, hot 5** (of people or their behaviour) gentle and kind; not usually getting angry or violent SYN **equable**: *a mild woman, who never shouted* ▸ **mild·ness** *noun* [U]: *the mildness of a sunny spring day* ◊ *her mildness of manner*
- *noun* [U] (*BrE*) a type of dark beer with a mild taste: *Two pints of mild, please.* ⸺ compare BITTER

**mil·dew** /ˈmɪldjuː; NAmE -duː/ *noun* [U] a very small white FUNGUS that grows on walls, plants, food, etc. in warm wet conditions

**mil·dewed** /ˈmɪldjuːd; NAmE -duːd/ *adj.* with MILDEW growing on it

**mild·ly** /ˈmaɪldli/ *adv.* **1** slightly; not very much: *mildly surprised/irritated/interested* **2** in a gentle manner: *'I didn't mean to upset you,' he said mildly.* IDM **to put it mildly** used to show that what you are talking about is much more extreme, etc. than your words suggest: *The result was unfortunate, to put it mildly* (= it was extremely unfortunate).

**mild-'mannered** *adj.* (of a person) gentle and not usually getting angry or violent

**mild 'steel** *noun* [U] a type of steel containing very little CARBON that is easy to shape but cannot be made stronger and harder through heating and cooling

## mile A1 /maɪl/ *noun*

**1** A1 [C] (*abbr.* **m**) (in Britain and North America) a unit for measuring distance equal to 1 609 metres or 1 760 yards: *a 20-mile drive to work* ◊ *an area of four square miles* ◊ *a mile-long procession* ◊ *The nearest bank is about half a mile down the road.* ◊ *The boys were left stranded two miles from home.* ◊ *He runs 10 miles every morning.* ◊ *We did about 30 miles a day on our cycling trip.* ◊ *The car must have been doing at least 100 miles an hour.* ◊ (*BrE*) *My car does 35 miles to the gallon.* ◊ (*NAmE*) *My car gets 35 miles to the gallon.* ⸺ see also AIR MILES™, COUNTRY MILE, FOOD MILE, MPH, NAUTICAL MILE, SEA MILE **2** A2 [usually pl.] a large area or a long distance: *miles and miles of desert* ◊ *There isn't a house for miles around here.* ◊ *I'm not walking—it's miles away.* ◊ (*informal*) *She's taller than you by a mile.* **3 the mile** [sing.] a race over one mile: *He ran the mile in less than four minutes.* ◊ *a four-minute mile* IDM **be ˌmiles aˈway** (*informal*) to be thinking deeply about sth and not aware of what is happening around you **go the ˌextra ˈmile (for sb/sth)** to make a special effort to achieve sth, help sb, etc. **ˌmiles from ˈanywhere** (*informal*) in a place that is a long way from a town and surrounded only by a lot of open country, sea, etc: *We broke down miles from anywhere.* **run a ˈmile (from sb/sth)** (*informal*) to show that you are very frightened of doing sth **see, spot, tell, smell, etc. sth a ˈmile off** (*informal*) to see or realize sth very easily and quickly: *He's wearing a wig—you can see it a mile off.* **stand/stick out a ˈmile** to be very obvious or easy to notice ⸺ more at INCH *n.*, MISS *n.*

**mile·age** (*also* **mil·age**) /ˈmaɪlɪdʒ/ *noun* **1** [U, C, usually sing.] the distance that a vehicle has travelled, measured in miles: *My annual mileage is about 10000.* ◊ *a used car with one owner and a low mileage* ◊ *The car rental included unlimited mileage, but not fuel.* ◊ *I get a mileage allowance if I use my car for work* (= an amount of money paid for each mile I travel). **2** (*NAmE* **gas mileage**) [U, C] the number of miles that a vehicle can travel using a particular amount of fuel: *If you drive carefully you can get better mileage from your car.* **3** [U] (*informal*) the amount of advantage or use that you can get from a particular event or situation: *I don't think the press can get any more mileage out of that story.* IDM **your ˌmileage may ˈvary** (*abbr.* **YMMV**) (*informal*) used to say that people may experience a particular thing in different ways

**mile·om·eter** = MILOMETER

**mile·post** /ˈmaɪlpəʊst/ *noun* (*especially NAmE*) **1** a post by the side of the road that shows how far it is to the next town, and to other places **2** = MILESTONE (1)

**miles** /maɪlz/ *adv.* (*informal*) very much SYN **far**: *I'm feeling miles better today, thanks.* ◊ *I'm miles behind with my work.*

**mile·stone** /ˈmaɪlstəʊn/ *noun* **1** (*also* **mile·post** *especially in NAmE*) a very important stage or event in the development of sth SYN **landmark 2** a stone by the side of a road that shows how far it is to the next town and to other places

**mi·lieu** /ˈmiːljɜː; NAmE -ˈjuː/ *noun* [C, usually sing.] (*pl.* **mi·lieux** *or* **mi·lieus** /ˈmiːljɜːz; NAmE -ˈjuːz/) (*from French, formal*) the social environment that you live or work in SYN **background**

**mili·tant** ?+ C1 /ˈmɪlɪtənt/ *noun, adj.*
- *noun* ?+ C1 a person who uses, or is willing to use, force or strong pressure to achieve their aims, especially to achieve social or political change: *Student militants were fighting with the police.*
- *adj.* ?+ C1 using, or willing to use, force or strong pressure to achieve your aims, especially to achieve social or political change: *militant groups/leaders* ▸ **mili·tancy** /-tənsi/ *noun* [U]: *a growing militancy amongst the unemployed* **mili·tant·ly** *adv.*

**mili·tar·ism** /ˈmɪlɪtərɪzəm/ *noun* [U] (*usually disapproving*) the belief that a country should have great military strength in order to be powerful ▸ **mili·tar·ist** /-rɪst/ *noun*: *Militarists ran the country.* **mili·tar·is·tic** /ˌmɪlɪtəˈrɪstɪk/ *adj.*: *militaristic government*

**mili·tar·ize** (*BrE also* **-ise**) /ˈmɪlɪtəraɪz/ *verb* [usually passive] **1** ~ sth to send armed forces to an area: *a militarized zone* OPP **demilitarize 2** ~ sth to make sth similar to an army: *a militarized police force* ▸ **mili·tar·iza·tion, -isa·tion** /ˌmɪlɪtəraɪˈzeɪʃn; NAmE -rəˈz-/ *noun* [U]

## mili·tary B2 /ˈmɪlətri; NAmE -teri/ *adj., noun*

- *adj.* B2 [usually before noun] connected with soldiers or the armed forces: *We may have to take military action.* ◊ *military training/intelligence* ◊ *military force/operations* ◊ *military uniform/service/personnel* ◊ *a military coup* ⸺ compare CIVILIAN ▸ **mili·tar·ily** /ˈmɪlətrəli; NAmE ˌmɪləˈterəli/ *adv.*: *a militarily superior country* ◊ *We may have to intervene militarily in the area.*
- *noun* B2 **usually the military** (*pl.* **-ies**) [C + sing. / pl. v.] soldiers; the armed forces: *The military was/were called in to deal with the riot.* ◊ *members/branches of the military* ◊ **in the ~** *He served in the military.* ◊ *foreign militaries*

**military band** *noun* a large group of soldiers who play wind instruments and drums, sometimes while MARCHING ⇨ compare CONCERT BAND

**military po'lice** *noun* (*abbr.* **MP**) (*often* **the military police**) [pl.] the police force that is responsible for the army, NAVY, etc.

**military service** *noun* [U] **1** a period during which young people serve in the armed forces: *to be called up* ◊ *She has to do her military service.* **2** the time sb spends in the armed forces: *He's completed 30 years of active military service.*

**mili·tate** /ˈmɪlɪteɪt/ *verb*
**PHRV** **ˈmilitate against sth** (*formal*) to prevent sth; to make it difficult for sth to happen or exist **SYN** hinder: *The supervisor's presence militated against a relaxed atmosphere.*

**mili·tia** /məˈlɪʃə/ *noun* [sing. + sing. / pl. v.] a group of people who are not professional soldiers but who have had military training and can act as an army

**mili·tia·man** /məˈlɪʃəmən/ *noun* (*pl.* **-men** /-mən/) a member of a militia

**milk** /mɪlk/ *noun*, *verb*
▪ *noun* [U] **1** the white liquid produced by cows, GOATS and some other animals as food for their young and used as a drink by humans: *a pint/litre of milk* ◊ *a glass/bottle/carton of milk* ◊ *fresh/dried/powdered milk* ◊ *Do you take milk in your tea?* ◊ *milk products* (= butter, cheese, etc.) ◊ *milk production/prices* ◊ *I am allergic to cow's milk.* ◊ (*BrE*) *full-fat/semi-skimmed/skimmed milk* (= milk with none/some/most of the fat removed) ◊ (*NAmE*) *Shall I get skim milk or 2%?* ⇨ see also BUTTERMILK, CONDENSED MILK, DRY MILK, EVAPORATED MILK, MOOSE MILK, POWDERED MILK, SKIMMED MILK **2** the white liquid that is produced by women and female MAMMALS for feeding their babies: *breast milk* **3** (in compounds) a white liquid produced by or made from plants: *coconut/almond milk* ⇨ see also SOYA MILK
**IDM** **the milk of human ˈkindness** (*literary*) kind behaviour, considered to be natural to humans ⇨ more at CRY *v.*, LAND *n.*
▪ *verb* **1** ~ **sth** to take milk from a cow, GOAT, etc. **2** (*disapproving*) to obtain as much money, advantage, etc. for yourself as you can from a particular situation, especially in a dishonest way: ~ **A (from B)** *She's milked a small fortune from the company over the years.* ◊ ~ **B (of A)** *She's milked the company of a small fortune.* ◊ *I know he's had a hard time lately, but he's certainly milking it for all it's worth* (= using it as an excuse to do things that people would normally object to). **IDM** see DRY *adj.*

**milk ˈchocolate** *noun* [U] light-brown chocolate made with milk ⇨ compare DARK CHOCOLATE, WHITE CHOCOLATE

**milk·ing** /ˈmɪlkɪŋ/ *noun* [U] the process of taking milk from a cow, etc: *milking machines/sheds*

**milk·maid** /ˈmɪlkmeɪd/ *noun* (in the past) a woman whose job was to take milk from cows and make butter and cheese

**milk·man** /ˈmɪlkmən/ *noun* (*pl.* **-men** /-mən/) (especially in the UK) a person whose job is to deliver milk to customers each morning

**milk ˈpowder** (*also* **ˌpowdered ˈmilk**) (*both BrE*) (*US* **ˈdry milk**) *noun* [U] dried milk in the form of a powder

**milk·shake** /ˈmɪlkʃeɪk/ (*also* **shake**) *noun* a drink made of milk, and sometimes ice cream, with the added taste of fruit or chocolate, which is mixed or shaken until it is full of bubbles: *a banana milkshake* ⇨ compare PROTEIN SHAKE

**ˈmilk tooth** (*BrE*) (*also* **ˈbaby tooth** *NAmE*, *BrE*) *noun* any of the first set of teeth in young children that drop out and are replaced by others

**milk·weed** /ˈmɪlkwiːd/ *noun* [C, U] a North American plant that produces a white juice like milk

**milky** /ˈmɪlki/ *adj.* **1** made of milk; containing a lot of milk: *a hot milky drink* ◊ *milky tea/coffee* **2** like milk: *milky* (= not clear) *blue eyes* ◊ *milky* (= white) *skin*

**the ˌMilky ˈWay** *noun* [sing.] a band of light across the night sky made up of a huge number of stars that form a large part of the GALAXY that includes our sun and its planets

**mill** /mɪl/ *noun*, *verb*
▪ *noun* **1** a building fitted with equipment for GRINDING grain into flour; a machine for GRINDING grain ⇨ see also WATERMILL, WINDMILL **2** (often in compounds) a factory that produces a particular type of material: *a cotton/cloth/steel/paper mill* ◊ *mill owners/workers* ⇨ SYNONYMS at FACTORY ⇨ see also ROLLING MILL, RUMOUR MILL, SAWMILL **3** (often in compounds) a small machine for GRINDING a solid substance into powder: *a pepper mill* ⇨ see also RUN-OF-THE-MILL, TREADMILL
**IDM** **go through the ˈmill** | **put sb through the ˈmill** to have or make sb have a difficult time ⇨ more at GRIST
▪ *verb* [often passive] ~ **sth** to GRIND sth (= break or press it into very small pieces) in a mill
**PHRV** **ˌmill aˈround** (*also* **ˌmill aˈbout**) (especially of a large group of people) to move around an area without seeming to be going anywhere in particular: *Fans were milling around outside the hotel.* ⇨ see also MILLING

**mil·len·nial** /mɪˈleniəl/ *adj.*, *noun*
▪ *adj.* **1** connected with a period of a thousand years: *millennial timescales* **2** connected with the anniversary of a thousand years: *the millennial celebrations in New York's Times Square* **3** connected with the generation of people who were born between the early 1980s and the late 1990s: *the millennial generation*
▪ *noun* [usually pl.] a person who was born between the early 1980s and the late 1990s; a member of GENERATION Y: *Millennials are willing to take risks and see career change as normal.*

**mil·len·nium** /mɪˈleniəm/ *noun* (*pl.* **mil·len·nia** /-niə/ *or* **mil·len·niums**) **1** a period of 1000 years, especially as calculated before or after the birth of Christ: *the second millennium AD* **2** **the millennium** the time when one period of 1000 years ends and another begins: *How did you celebrate the millennium?*

**mill·er** /ˈmɪlə(r)/ *noun* a person who owns or works in a MILL for making flour

**mil·let** /ˈmɪlɪt/ *noun* [U] a type of plant that grows in hot countries and produces very small seeds. The seeds are used as food, mainly to make flour, and also to feed to birds and animals. ⇨ VISUAL VOCAB page V8

**milli-** /ˈmɪli/ *combining form* (in nouns; used in units of measurement) one thousandth: *milligram*

**milli·bar** /ˈmɪlibɑː(r)/ *noun* a unit for measuring the pressure of the atmosphere. One thousand millibars are equal to one BAR.

**milli·gram** (*BrE also* **milli·gramme**) /ˈmɪlɪɡræm/ *noun* (*abbr.* **mg**) a unit for measuring weight; a thousandth of a GRAM

**milli·litre** (*US* **milli·liter**) /ˈmɪliliːtə(r)/ *noun* (*abbr.* **ml** /mɪl/) a unit for measuring the volume of liquids and gases; a 1000th of a LITRE

**milli·metre** (*US* **milli·meter**) /ˈmɪlimiːtə(r)/ *noun* (*abbr.* **mm**) a unit for measuring length; a 1000th of a metre

**mill·iner** /ˈmɪlɪnə(r)/ *noun* a person whose job is making and/or selling women's hats

**mill·in·ery** /ˈmɪlɪnəri; *NAmE* -neri/ *noun* [U] **1** the work of a milliner **2** hats sold in shops

**mill·ing** /ˈmɪlɪŋ/ *adj.* [only before noun] (of people) moving around in a large mass: *I had to fight my way through the milling crowd.*

**mil·lion** /ˈmɪljən/ *number* **1** (*abbr.* **m**) 1000000: *a population of half a million* ◊ *tens of millions of dollars* ◊ *It must be worth a million* (= pounds, dollars, etc.)*.* ◊ *millions of years old* **HELP** You say *a*, *one*, *two*, *several*, etc. **million** without a final 's' on 'million'. **Millions (of …)** can be used if there is no number or quantity before it. Always use a plural verb with **million** or **millions**, except when an amount of money is mentioned: *Four million (people) were affected.* ◊ *Two million (pounds) was withdrawn from the account.* **2** **a million** or **millions (of …)** (*informal*) a very large amount: *I still have a million things to do.* ◊ *There were millions of people there.* ◊ *He made his millions* (= all his money) *on currency deals.* **HELP** There are more examples of how to use numbers at the entry for **hundred**.

# millionaire

**IDM** **look/feel like a million ˈdollars/ˈbucks** (*informal*) to look/feel extremely good **ˈone, etc. in a ˈmillion** a person or thing that is very unusual or special: *He's a man in a million.*

**mil·lion·aire** /ˌmɪljəˈneə(r)/; *NAmE* -ˈner/ *noun* a person who has a million pounds, dollars, etc.; a very rich person: *an oil millionaire* ◊ *She's a millionaire several times over.* ◊ *a millionaire businessman* ⊃ see also MULTIMILLIONAIRE

**mil·lion·air·ess** /ˌmɪljəˈneərəs; *NAmE* -ˈner-/ *noun* (*old-fashioned*) a woman who is a millionaire

**mil·lionth** /ˈmɪljənθ/ *ordinal number, noun*
- *ordinal number* 1 000 000th
- *noun* each of one million equal parts of sth: *a/one millionth of a second*

**milli·pede** /ˈmɪlɪpiːd/ *noun* a small creature like an insect, with a long thin body divided into many sections, each with two pairs of legs

**milli·sec·ond** /ˈmɪlɪsekənd/ *noun* (*specialist*) a 1 000th of a second: (*figurative*) *I hesitated a millisecond too long.*

**mil·li·volt** /ˈmɪlivəʊlt; *BrE also* -vɒlt/ *noun* (*physics*) a unit for measuring the force of an electric current; a 1 000th of a VOLT

**mill·stone** /ˈmɪlstəʊn/ *noun* one of two flat round stones used, especially in the past, to GRIND (= press hard and break) grain to make flour
**IDM** **a millstone around/round your ˈneck** a difficult problem or responsibility that it seems impossible to solve or get rid of: *My debts are a millstone around my neck.*

**ˈmill wheel** *noun* a large wheel that is turned by water and that makes the machines in a MILL work

**mil·om·eter** (*also* **mile·ometer**) /maɪˈlɒmɪtə(r); *NAmE* -ˈlɑːm-/ (*both BrE*) (*NAmE* **odom·eter**) (*also informal* **the clock** *BrE and NAmE*) *noun* an instrument in a vehicle that measures the number of miles it has travelled

**mi·lord** /mɪˈlɔːd; *NAmE* -ˈlɔːrd/ *noun* (*old use or humorous*) used when talking to or about a man who is a member of the British NOBILITY ⊃ compare MILADY

**mime** /maɪm/ *noun, verb*
- *noun* [U, C] (especially in the theatre) the use of movements of your hands or body and the expressions on your face to tell a story or to act sth without speaking; a performance using this method of acting: *The performance consisted of dance, music and mime.* ◊ *a mime artist* ◊ *She performed a brief mime.*
- *verb* 1 [T, I] to act, tell a story, etc. by moving your body and face but without speaking: **~ (sth)** *Each player has to mime the title of a movie, play or book.* ◊ **~ doing sth** *He mimed climbing a mountain.* 2 [I, T] **~ (to sth)** | **~ (sth)** to pretend to sing a song that is actually being sung by sb else on a recording: *The band was miming to a backing track.*

**mi·mesis** /mɪˈmiːsɪs, maɪ-/ *noun* [U] 1 (*specialist*) the way in which the real world and human behaviour is represented in art or literature 2 (*specialist*) the fact of a particular social group changing their behaviour by copying the behaviour of another social group 3 (*biology*) the fact of a plant or animal developing a similar appearance to another plant or animal 4 (*medical*) the fact of a set of symptoms suggesting that sb has a particular disease, when in fact that person has a different disease or none

**mi·met·ic** /mɪˈmetɪk/ *adj.* (*specialist or formal*) copying the behaviour or appearance of sb/sth else

**mimic** /ˈmɪmɪk/ *verb, noun*
- *verb* (**-ck-**) 1 **~ sb/sth** | **+ speech** to copy the way sb speaks, moves, behaves, etc., especially in order to make other people laugh: *She's always mimicking the teachers.* ◊ *He mimicked her southern accent.* 2 **~ sth** (*specialist or formal*) to look or behave like sth else **SYN imitate**: *The robot was programmed to mimic a series of human movements.*
- *noun* a person or an animal that can copy the voice, movements, etc. of others

**mim·ic·ry** /ˈmɪmɪkri/ *noun* [U] the action of copying or the skill of being able to copy the voice, movements, etc. of others: *a talent for mimicry*

**mi·mosa** /mɪˈməʊzə, -ˈməʊsə/ *noun* 1 [C, U] a plant with leaves that are sensitive to touch and light 2 [C, U] an Australian tree with balls of yellow flowers 3 (*NAmE*) (*BrE* **Buck's ˈFizz**) [C] an alcoholic drink made by mixing SPARKLING white wine (= has bubbles) with orange juice

**Min** /mɪn/ *noun* [U] a form of Chinese spoken mainly in south-east China

**min.** *abbr.* 1 (in writing) minute(s): *Cook for 8–10 min. until tender.* 2 (in writing) minimum: *min. charge £4.50* **OPP** max

**min·aret** /ˌmɪnəˈret/ *noun* a tall thin tower, usually forming part of a MOSQUE, from which Muslims are called to prayer

**min·atory** /ˈmɪnətəri; *NAmE* -tɔːri/ *adj.* (*formal*) expressing a threat of harm or violence **SYN threatening**: *minatory words*

**mince** /mɪns/ *verb, noun*
- *verb* 1 (*NAmE also* **grind**) [T] **~ sth** to cut food, especially meat, into very small pieces using a special machine (called a MINCER): *minced beef* 2 [I] **+ adv./prep.** (*disapproving*) to walk with quick short steps, in a way that is not natural: *He minced over to serve us.*
**IDM** **not mince (your) ˈwords** to say sth in a direct way even though it might offend other people
- *noun* [U] (*BrE*) meat, especially beef, that has been cut into very small pieces in a special machine: *a pound of mince* ⊃ compare HAMBURGER (2)

**mince·meat** /ˈmɪnsmiːt/ *noun* [U] (*especially BrE*) a mixture of dried fruit, SPICES, etc. used especially for making PIES
**IDM** **make ˈmincemeat of sb** (*informal*) to defeat sb completely in a fight, an argument or a competition

**ˌmince ˈpie** *noun* a small round PIE filled with mincemeat, traditionally eaten at Christmas, especially in the UK

**min·cer** /ˈmɪnsə(r)/ *noun* (*especially BrE*) (*NAmE usually* **ˈmeat grinder**) *noun* a machine for cutting food, especially meat, into very small pieces

**min·cing** /ˈmɪnsɪŋ/ *adj.* (*disapproving*) (of a way of walking or speaking) very light and careful; not natural: *short mincing steps*

**mind** ❶ **A2** /maɪnd/ *noun, verb*
- *noun*
- **ABILITY TO THINK** 1 **A2** [C, U] the part of a person that makes them able to be aware of things, to think and to feel: *the conscious/subconscious mind* ◊ *There were all kinds of thoughts running through my mind.* ◊ *There was no doubt in his mind that he'd get the job.* ◊ *'Drugs' are associated in most people's minds with drug abuse.* ◊ *She was in a disturbed state of mind.* ◊ *I could not have complete peace of mind before they returned.* ◊ *The campaign to win the hearts and minds of the public continues.* ◊ *I felt refreshed in mind and body.* ⊃ see also FRAME OF MIND, PRESENCE OF MIND 2 **A2** [C] your ability to think and reason; your intelligence; the particular way that sb thinks **SYN intellect**: *to have a brilliant/good/keen mind* ◊ *a creative/evil/suspicious mind* ◊ *She had a lively and enquiring mind.* ◊ *His mind is as sharp as ever.* ◊ *I've no idea how her mind works!* ◊ *He had the body of a man and the mind of a child.* ◊ *insights into the criminal mind* ⊃ see also ONE-TRACK MIND
- **INTELLIGENT PERSON** 3 [C] a person who is very intelligent **SYN brain**: *She was one of the greatest minds of her generation.* ◊ *Larry is one of the best trained minds in the industry.* ⊃ see also MASTERMIND *noun*
- **THOUGHTS** 4 **A2** [C] your thoughts, interest, etc: *Keep your mind on your work!* ◊ *Her mind is completely occupied by the new baby.* ◊ *The lecture dragged on and my mind*

wandered. ◇ *He gave his mind to the arrangements for the next day.* ◇ *As for avoiding you, nothing could be further from my mind* (= I was not thinking of it at all).
- **MEMORY 5** [C, usually sing.] your ability to remember things: *When I saw the exam questions my mind just went blank* (= I couldn't remember anything). ◇ *Sorry—your name has gone right out of my mind.*

**IDM** **be all in sb's/the 'mind** to be sth that only exists in sb's imagination: *These problems are all in your mind, you know.* **bear/keep sb/sth in 'mind | bear/keep in 'mind that…** to remember sb/sth; to remember or consider that… **be bored, frightened, pissed, stoned, etc. out of your 'mind** (*informal*) to be extremely bored, etc. **be in two 'minds about sth/about doing sth** (*BrE*) (*NAmE* **be of two 'minds about sth/about doing sth**) to be unable to decide what you think about sb/sth, or whether to do sth or not: *I was in two minds about the book* (= I didn't know if I liked it or not). ◇ *She's in two minds about accepting his invitation.* **be of one/the same 'mind (about sb/sth)** to have the same opinion about sb/sth **be/go out of your 'mind** to be unable to think or behave in a normal way; to become crazy: (*informal*) *You're lending them money? You must be out of your tiny mind!* ⇒ SYNONYMS at MAD **be out of your 'mind with worry, etc.** to be extremely worried, etc. **bring/call sb/sth to 'mind** (*formal*) **1** to remember sb/sth **SYN** recall: *She couldn't call to mind where she had seen him before.* **2** to remind you of sb/sth **SYN** recall: *The painting brings to mind some of Picasso's early works.* **come/spring to 'mind** if sth **comes/springs to mind**, you suddenly remember or think of it: *When discussing influential modern artists, three names immediately come to mind.* **have a good mind to do sth | have half a mind to do sth** **1** used to say that you think you will do sth, although you are not sure: *I've half a mind to come with you tomorrow.* **2** used to say that you think that what sb has done is bad and should do sth about it, although you probably will not: *I've a good mind to write and tell your parents about it.* **have sb/sth in 'mind (for sth)** to be thinking of sb/sth, especially for a particular job, etc: *Do you have anyone in mind for this job?* ◇ *Watching TV all evening wasn't exactly what I had in mind!* **have it in mind to do sth** (*formal*) to intend to do sth **have a mind of your 'own** to have your own opinion and make your own decisions without being influenced by other people: *She has a mind of her own and isn't afraid to say what she thinks.* ◇ (*humorous*) *My computer seems to have a mind of its own!* **lose your 'mind** to become mentally ill **make up your 'mind | make your 'mind up** to decide sth: *They're both beautiful—I can't make up my mind.* ◇ *Have you made up your minds where to go for your honeymoon?* ◇ *You'll never persuade him to stay—his mind's made up* (= he has definitely decided to go). ◇ *Come on—it's make your mind up time!* **mind over 'matter** the use of the power of your mind to deal with physical problems **your mind's 'eye** your imagination: *He pictured the scene in his mind's eye.* **on your 'mind** if sb/sth is **on your mind**, you are thinking and worrying about them/it a lot: *You've been on my mind all day.* ◇ *Don't bother your father tonight—he's got a lot on his mind.* **put sb in mind of sb/sth** (*old-fashioned*) to make sb think of sb/sth; to remind sb of sb/sth **put/set sb's 'mind at ease/rest** to do or say sth to make sb stop worrying about sth **SYN** reassure **put/set/turn your 'mind to sth | set your 'mind on sth** to decide you want to achieve sth and give this all your attention: *She could have been a brilliant pianist if she'd put her mind to it.* **put/get sth out of your 'mind** to stop thinking about sb/sth; to deliberately forget sb/sth: *I just can't get her out of my mind.* **take your mind off sth** to make you forget about sth unpleasant for a short time **SYN** distract **to 'my mind** in my opinion: *It was a ridiculous thing to do, to my mind.* ⇒ more at BACK *n.*, BEND *v.*, BLOW *v.*, BOGGLE, CAST *v.*, CHANGE *v.*, CHANGE *n.*, CLOSE¹ *v.*, CROSS *v.*, ETCH, GREAT *adj.*, KNOW *v.*, MEETING, OPEN *adj.*, OPEN *v.*, PAY *v.*, PIECE *n.*, PREY *v.*, PUSH *v.*, RIGHT *adj.*, SIEVE *n.*, SIGHT *n.*, SLIP *v.*, SPEAK, STICK *v.*, TURN *n.*, UNSOUND

■ *verb*
- **BE UPSET/ANNOYED 1** [T, I] (used especially in questions or with negatives; not used in the passive) to be upset, annoyed or worried by sth: ~**(sth)** *I don't mind the cold—it's the rain I don't like.* ◇ *I hope you don't mind the noise.* ◇ *He wouldn't have minded so much if she'd told him* 

# mind

*the truth.* ◇ ~**about sth** *Did she mind about not getting the job?* ◇ ~ **doing sth** *Did she mind not getting the job?* ◇ ~**sb/sth doing sth** *Do your parents mind you leaving home?* ◇ (*formal*) *Do your parents mind your leaving home?* ◇ ~**how, what, etc…** *She never minded how hot it was.* ◇ ~**that…** *He minded that he hadn't been asked.*
- **ASKING PERMISSION 2** [I, T] used to ask for permission to do sth, or to ask sb in a polite way to do sth: *Do you mind if I open the window?* ◇ ~**sb doing sth** *Are you married, if you don't mind me asking?* ◇ (*formal*) *Are you married, if you don't mind my asking?* ◇ ~**doing sth** *Would you mind explaining that again, please?* ◇ *Do you mind driving? I'm feeling pretty tired.* ⇒ EXPRESS YOURSELF at POLITE, PERMISSION
- **NOT CARE/WORRY 3** **not mind** [I, T, no passive] to not care or not be concerned about sth: *'Would you like tea or coffee?' 'I don't mind—either's fine.'* ◇ ~**sb** *Don't mind her—she didn't mean what she said.* ◇ *Don't mind me* (= don't let me disturb you)*—I'll just sit here quietly.*
- **BE WILLING 4** **not mind doing sth** [T] to be willing to do sth: *I don't mind helping if you can't find anyone else.*
- **WARNING 5** (*BrE*) (*also* **watch** *NAmE, BrE*) [T] used to tell sb to be careful about sth or warn them about a danger: ~**sth** *Mind* (= Don't fall on) *that step!* ◇ *Mind your head!* (= for example, be careful you don't hit it on a low ceiling) ◇ *Mind your language!* (= don't speak in a rude or offensive way) ◇ ~**how, where, etc…** *Mind how you go!* (= often used when you say goodbye to sb) ◇ *Mind where you're treading!* ◇ ~**(that)…** *Mind you don't cut yourself—that knife's very sharp.* ◇ *You must be home for dinner, mind.* **HELP** *'That'* is nearly always left out in this pattern.
- **OBEY 6** [T] ~**sb** (*NAmE*, *IrishE*) to pay attention to what sb says, and obey them: *And the moral of the story is: always mind your mother!*
- **TAKE CARE OF 7** (*especially BrE*) (*NAmE usually* **watch**) [T] ~**sb/sth** to take care of sth **SYN** look after: *Who's minding the children this evening?* ◇ *Could you mind my bags for a moment?*

**IDM** **do you 'mind?** (*ironic*) used to show that you are annoyed about sth that sb has just said or done: *Do you mind? I was here before you.* **I don't mind ad'mitting, 'telling you…, etc.** used to emphasize what you are saying, especially when you are talking about sth that may be embarrassing for you: *I was scared, I don't mind telling you!* **I don't mind if I 'do** (*informal*) used to say politely that you would like sth you have been offered: *'Cup of tea, Brian?' 'I don't mind if I do.'* **if you don't 'mind | if you 'wouldn't 'mind** **1** used to check that sb does not object to sth you want to do, or to ask sb politely to do sth: *I'd like to ask you a few questions, if you don't mind.* ◇ *Can you read that form carefully, if you wouldn't mind, and then sign it.* **2** (*often ironic*) used to show that you object to sth that sb has said or done: *I give the orders around here, if you don't mind.* **3** used to refuse an offer politely: *'Will you come with us tonight?' 'I won't, if you don't mind—I've got a lot of work to do.'* **if you 'don't mind me/my 'saying so…** used when you are going to criticize sb or say sth that might upset them: *That colour doesn't really suit you, if you don't mind my saying so.* **I wouldn't mind sth/doing sth** used to say politely that you would very much like to do sth: *I wouldn't mind a cup of coffee, if it's no trouble.* ◇ *I wouldn't mind having his money!* **mind your own 'business** (*informal*) to think about your own affairs and not ask questions about or try to get involved in other people's lives: *'What are you reading?' 'Mind your own business!'* ◇ *I was just sitting there, minding my own business, when a man started shouting at me.* **mind the 'shop** (*BrE*) (*NAmE* **mind the 'store**) to be in charge of sth for a short time while sb is away: *Who's minding the shop while the boss is abroad?* **'mind you** (*informal*) used to add sth to what you have just said, especially sth that makes it less strong: *I've heard they're getting divorced. Mind you, I'm not surprised—they were always arguing.* **mind your Ps and Qs** (*informal*) to behave in the most polite way you can **never 'mind** **1** (*especially BrE*) used to tell sb not to worry or be upset: *Have you broken it? Never mind, we can buy another one.* **2** used to suggest that sth is not important: *This isn't where I intended to take you—but never mind, it's just as good.* **3** used to emphasize that what is true about the first thing you have said is even more true about the second **SYN** let

# mind-bending

**alone**: *I never thought she'd win once, never mind twice!* **never mind (about) (doing) sth** used to tell sb they shouldn't think about sth or do sth because it is not as important as sth else, or because you will do it: *Never mind your car—what about the damage to my fence?* ◇ *Never mind washing the dishes—I'll do them later.* **never mind the fact that** used to say that one thing is a surprising contrast to another: *The big house is a status symbol—never mind the fact that most of the rooms will be empty.* **never you mind** (*informal*) used to tell sb not to ask about sth because you are not going to tell them: *'Who told you about it?' 'Never you mind!'* ◇ *Never you mind how I found out—it's true, isn't it?* ⊃ more at LANGUAGE, STEP *n*.
**PHRV** **mind out** (*BrE*, *informal*) used to tell sb to move so that you can pass: *Mind out—you're in the way there!* **mind out (for sb/sth)** (*BrE*) used to warn sb of danger **SYN** **watch out**: *Have some of my plum jam—but mind out for the stones.*

'**mind-bending** *adj.* (*informal*) having a strong effect on your mind, like a drug: *a mind-bending experience/concept/drug*

'**mind-blowing** *adj.* (*informal*) very exciting, impressive or surprising: *Watching your baby being born is a mind-blowing experience.*

'**mind-boggling** *adj.* (*informal*) very difficult to imagine or to understand; extremely surprising: *a problem of mind-boggling complexity* ⊃ compare BOGGLE

**mind·ed** /ˈmaɪndɪd/ *adj.* **1** (used with adjectives to form compound adjectives) having the way of thinking, the attitude or the type of character mentioned: *a fair-minded employer* ◇ *high-minded principles* ◇ *I appeal to all like-minded people to support me.* ⊃ see also ABSENT-MINDED, BLOODY-MINDED, BROAD-MINDED, FAIR-MINDED, FEEBLE-MINDED, HIGH-MINDED, LIKE-MINDED, NARROW-MINDED, OPEN-MINDED, RIGHT-MINDED, SINGLE-MINDED, SMALL-MINDED, STRONG-MINDED, TOUGH-MINDED **2** (used with adverbs to form compound adjectives) having the type of mind that is interested in or able to understand the areas mentioned: *I'm not very politically minded.* **3** (used with nouns to form compound adjectives) interested in or enthusiastic about the thing mentioned: *a reform-minded government* **4** [not before noun] *~ (to do sth)* (*formal*) wishing or intending to do sth **SYN** **inclined**: *She was minded to accept their offer.*

**mind·er** /ˈmaɪndə(r)/ *noun* (*especially BrE*) a person whose job is to take care of and protect another person: *a star surrounded by her minders* ⊃ see also CHILDMINDER

**mind·ful** /ˈmaɪndfl/ *adj.* *~ of sb/sth* | *~ that …* (*formal*) remembering sb/sth and considering them or it when you do sth **SYN** **conscious**: *mindful of our responsibilities* ◇ *Mindful of the danger of tropical storms, I decided not to go out.*

**mind·ful·ness** /ˈmaɪndflnəs/ *noun* [U] (*formal*) **1** *~ (of sth)* the fact of remembering sb/sth and considering them/it when you do sth **SYN** **consciousness**: *their mindfulness of the wider cinematic tradition* **2** a mental state achieved by concentrating on the present moment, while calmly accepting the feelings and thoughts that come to you, used as a technique to help you relax

'**mind game** *noun* something that you do or say in order to make sb feel less confident, especially to gain an advantage for yourself

**mind·less** /ˈmaɪndləs/ *adj.* **1** (*disapproving*) done or acting without thought and for no particular reason or purpose **SYN** **senseless**: *mindless violence* ◇ *mindless vandals* **2** (*disapproving*) not needing thought or intelligence **SYN** **dull**: *a mindless and repetitive task* **3** *~ of sb/sth* (*formal*) not remembering sb/sth and not considering them or it when you do sth: *We explored the whole town, mindless of the cold and rain.* ▶ **mind·less·ly** *adv.*

'**mind map** *noun* a diagram that presents information with a central idea in the middle and connected ideas arranged around it

'**mind-numbing** *adj.* very boring: *mind-numbing conversation* ▶ '**mind-numbing·ly** *adv.*: *The lecture was mind-numbingly tedious.*

'**mind reader** *noun* (*often humorous*) a person who knows what sb else is thinking without being told

**mind·set** /ˈmaɪndset/ *noun* a set of attitudes or fixed ideas that sb has and that are often difficult to change **SYN** **mentality**: *a conservative mindset* ◇ *the mindset of the current generation*

**mind·share** /ˈmaɪndʃeə(r); NAmE -ʃer/ *noun* [U] (*business*) the extent of knowledge of a company or product among consumers, compared with their knowledge of others of the same type ⊃ compare MARKET SHARE

**mine** ⊕ A2 /maɪn/ *pron.*, *noun*, *verb*
■ *pron.* (the possessive form of *I*) **1** A2 of or belonging to the person writing or speaking: *That's mine.* ◇ *of~ He's a friend of mine* (= one of my friends). ◇ *She wanted one like mine* (= like I have). **2** (*BrE*, *informal*) my home: *Let's go back to mine after the show.*
■ *noun* **1** B1 a deep hole or holes under the ground where minerals such as coal, gold, etc. are dug: *a copper/diamond mine* ◇ *mine owners/workers* ◇ *They were appalled at the poor working conditions in the mines.* ⊃ compare PIT, QUARRY ⊃ see also COAL MINE, GOLD MINE, MINING **2** B2 a type of bomb that is hidden under the ground or in the sea and that explodes when sb/sth touches it: *Soldiers laid anti-personnel mines in the fields.* ⊃ see also LANDMINE
**IDM** **a mine of infor′mation/′data (about/on sb/sth)** a person, book, etc. that can give you a lot of information on a particular subject ⊃ more at CANARY
■ *verb* **1** [T, I] to dig holes in the ground in order to find and obtain coal, diamonds, etc.: *~A (for B) The area has been mined for slate for centuries.* ◇ *~B Uranium is mined from deep underground.* ◇ *~(for B) They were mining for gold.* **2** [T] *~ sth* to place mines below the surface of an area of land or water; to destroy a vehicle with mines: *The coastal route had been mined.* ◇ *The UN convoy was mined on its way to the border.*

'**mine dump** *noun* (*SAfrE*) = DUMP (2)

**mine·field** /ˈmaɪnfiːld/ *noun* **1** an area of land or water where MINES (= bombs that explode when they are touched) have been hidden **2** a situation that contains hidden dangers or difficulties: *a legal minefield* ◇ *Tax can be a minefield for the unwary.*

**mine·hunt·er** /ˈmaɪnhʌntə(r)/ *noun* (*BrE*) a military ship for finding and destroying MINES (= bombs that explode when they are touched)

**miner** ⊕+ B2 /ˈmaɪnə(r)/ *noun* a person who works in a mine taking out coal, gold, diamonds, etc.: *Rescuers are trying to save miners trapped underground after a gas explosion.* ⊃ see also COAL MINER ■ HOMOPHONES at MINOR

**min·eral** ⊕ B2 /ˈmɪnərəl/ *noun* **1** B2 [C, U] a substance that is naturally present in the earth and is not formed from animal or vegetable matter, for example gold and salt. Some minerals are also present in food and drink and in the human body and are essential for good health: *a country rich in mineral resources* ◇ *mineral deposits/extraction* ◇ *the recommended intake of vitamins and minerals* ⊃ compare VEGETABLE **2** [C, usually pl.] (*BrE*, *formal*) (*NAmE* **soda**) a sweet drink with various different tastes that has bubbles of gas in it and does not contain alcohol: *Soft drinks and minerals sold here.*

**min·er·al·ogist** /ˌmɪnəˈrælədʒɪst/ *noun* a scientist who studies mineralogy

**min·er·al·ogy** /ˌmɪnəˈrælədʒi/ *noun* [U] the scientific study of minerals ▶ **min·er·al·ogic·al** /ˌmɪnərəˈlɒdʒɪkl; NAmE -ˈlɑːdʒ-/ *adj.*

'**mineral oil** *noun* [U] **1** (*BrE*) = PETROLEUM **2** (*NAmE*) (*BrE* **liquid 'paraffin**) a liquid with no colour and no smell that comes from PETROLEUM and is used in medicines and COSMETICS

'**mineral water** *noun* **1** [U, C] water from a SPRING in the ground that contains mineral salts or gases: *A glass of mineral water, please.* **2** [C] a glass or bottle of mineral water

**mine·shaft** /ˈmaɪnʃɑːft; NAmE -ʃæft/ *noun* a deep narrow hole that goes down to a mine

**min·es·trone** /ˌmɪnəˈstrəʊni/ *noun* [U] an Italian soup containing small pieces of vegetables and PASTA

**mine·sweep·er** /ˈmaɪnswiːpə(r)/ noun a ship used for finding and clearing away MINES (= bombs that explode when they are touched)

**mine·work·er** /ˈmaɪnwɜːkə(r); NAmE -wɜːrk-/ noun a person who works in a mine

**min·gle** /ˈmɪŋɡl/ verb 1 [I, T] to combine or make one thing combine with another: *The sounds of laughter and singing mingled in the evening air.* ◇ **~ (A) (with B)** *Her tears mingled with the blood on her face.* ◇ *He felt a kind of happiness mingled with regret.* ◇ **~ (A and B) (together)** *The flowers mingle together to form a blaze of colour.* ⊃ SYNONYMS at MIX 2 [I] to move among people and talk to them, especially at a social event SYN circulate: *The princess was not recognized and mingled freely with the crowds.* ◇ *If you'll excuse me, I must go and mingle (= talk to other guests).*

**mini** /ˈmɪni/ noun = MINISKIRT

**mini-** /ˈmɪni/ combining form (in nouns) small: *mini-break (= a short holiday)* ◇ *minigolf*

**min·i·a·ture** /ˈmɪnətʃə(r); NAmE also -tʃʊr/ adj., noun
■ adj. [only before noun] very small; much smaller than usual: *miniature roses* ◇ *a rare breed of miniature horses* ◇ *It looks like a miniature version of James Bond's car.*
■ noun 1 a very small detailed painting, often of a person 2 a very small copy or model of sth; a very small version of sth: *brandy miniatures (= very small bottles)*
IDM **in miniature** on a very small scale: *a doll's house with everything in miniature* ◇ *Through play, children act out in miniature the dramas of adult life.*

**'miniature golf** noun [U] (NAmE) = MINIGOLF

**min·i·a·tur·ist** /ˈmɪnɪtʃərɪst/ noun a painter who paints small works of art

**min·i·a·tur·ize** (BrE also **-ise**) /ˈmɪnətʃəraɪz/ verb ~ sth to make a much smaller version of sth ▶ **min·i·a·tur·iza·tion, -isa·tion** /ˌmɪnətʃərarˈzeɪʃn; NAmE -rəˈz-/ noun [U] **min·i·a·tur·ized, -ised** /ˈmɪnətʃəraɪzd/ adj. [only before noun]: *a miniaturized listening device*

**mini·bar** /ˈmɪnibɑː(r)/ noun a small fridge in a hotel room, with drinks in it, which are added to the guests' hotel bill if they drink them

**mini·bus** /ˈmɪnibʌs/ noun a small vehicle with seats for about twelve people

**mini·cab** /ˈmɪnikæb/ noun (BrE) a taxi that you have to order by phone and cannot stop in the street

**mini·dress** /ˈmɪnidres/ noun a very short dress

**mini·golf** /ˈmɪniɡɒlf; NAmE -ɡɑːlf/ (also **'miniature golf**) noun [U] a type of golf played on a small course that mainly involves PUTTING the ball over short distances. Sometimes you also have to hit the ball through or over little tunnels, hills, bridges and other objects. ⊃ compare CRAZY GOLF

**minim** /ˈmɪnɪm/ (BrE) (NAmE **'half note**) noun (*music*) a note that lasts twice as long as a CROTCHET ⊃ picture at MUSIC

**min·imal** ♪+ C1 Ⓦ /ˈmɪnɪml/ adj. very small in size or amount; as small as possible: *The work was carried out at minimal cost.* ◇ *There's only a minimal amount of risk involved.* ◇ *The damage to the car was minimal.* ⊃ compare MAXIMAL ▶ **min·im·al·ly** /-məli/ adv.: *minimally invasive surgery* ◇ *The episode was reported minimally in the press.*

**min·im·al·ist** /ˈmɪnɪməlɪst/ noun an artist, a musician or a designer who uses very simple ideas or a very small number of simple elements in their work ▶ **min·im·al·ism** /-lɪzəm/ noun [U] **min·im·al·ist** adj.

**min·im·ize** ♪+ C1 Ⓦ /ˈmɪnɪmaɪz/ (BrE also **-ise**) verb 1 ♪+ C1 ~ sth to reduce sth, especially sth bad, to the lowest possible level: *Good hygiene helps to minimize the risk of infection.* 2 ♪+ C1 ~ sth to try to make sth seem less important than it really is SYN **play down**: *He always tried to minimize his own faults, while exaggerating those of others.* 3 ~ sth to make sth small, especially on a computer screen: *Minimize any windows you have open.* OPP **maximize** ▶ **min·im·iza·tion, -isa·tion** /ˌmɪnɪmarˈzeɪʃn; NAmE -məˈz-/ noun [U]

**min·imum** ❶ B2 Ⓦ /ˈmɪnɪməm/ adj., noun
■ adj. ♪+ C1 [usually before noun] (*abbr.* **min.**) the smallest that is possible or allowed; extremely small: *a minimum charge/price* ◇ *the minimum number/level* ◇ *the minimum age for retirement* ◇ *The trust failed to meet the minimum standards expected.* ◇ *The work was done with the minimum amount of effort.* OPP **maximum** ▶ **min·imum** adv.: *You'll need £200 minimum for your holiday expenses.*
■ noun (*pl.* **min·ima** /-nɪmə/) [C, usually sing.] 1 ♪+ B2 (*abbr.* **min.**) the smallest or lowest amount that is possible, required or recorded: *The class needs a minimum of six students to continue.* ◇ **to a~** *Costs should be kept to a minimum.* ◇ *Temperatures will fall to a minimum of 10 degrees.* ◇ **as a ~** *As an absolute minimum, you should spend two hours in the evening studying.* ◇ **at a ~** *Candidates must have a degree at a minimum.* 2 ♪+ B2 [sing.] an extremely small amount: *He passed the exams with the minimum of effort.* ◇ *They had military experience, but a bare minimum of police training.* OPP **maximum**

**minimum se'curity 'prison** (NAmE) (BrE **open 'prison**) noun a prison in which prisoners have more freedom than in ordinary prisons

**minimum 'wage** noun [sing., U] the lowest wage that an employer is allowed to pay by law: *to introduce a national minimum wage* ◇ **on ~** *workers on minimum wage*

**min·ing** ♪+ C1 /ˈmaɪnɪŋ/ noun [U] the process of getting coal and other minerals from under the ground; the industry involved in this: *coal/diamond/gold/tin mining* ◇ *a mining company/community/engineer* ⊃ see also DATA MINING, MINE noun

**min·ion** /ˈmɪnjən/ noun (*disapproving* or *humorous*) an unimportant person in an organization who has to obey orders; a servant

**mini-'roundabout** noun (BrE) a white circle painted on a road at a place where two or more roads meet, that all traffic must go around in the same direction

**mini·ser·ies** /ˈmɪnisɪəriːz; NAmE -sɪr-/ noun (*pl.* **mini·ser·ies**) a television play that is divided into a number of parts and shown on different days

**mini·skirt** /ˈmɪniskɜːt; NAmE -skɜːrt/ (also **mini**) noun a very short skirt

**min·is·ter** ❶ B2 /ˈmɪnɪstə(r)/ noun, verb
■ noun 1 ♪+ B2 (often **Minister**) (in the UK and many other countries) a senior member of the government who is in charge of a government department or a branch of one: *the Minister of Education* ◇ *a meeting of EU Foreign Ministers* ◇ *senior ministers in the Cabinet* ◇ *cabinet/government ministers* ◇ *the finance/defence/interior/justice minister* ⊃ see also FIRST MINISTER, PRIME MINISTER ⊃ **WORDFINDER NOTE** at GOVERNMENT 2 ♪+ B2 (in some Protestant Christian Churches) a trained religious leader: *a Methodist minister* ⊃ compare PASTOR, PRIEST, VICAR 3 a person, lower in rank than an AMBASSADOR, whose job is to represent their government in a foreign country
■ verb
PHRV **'minister to sb/sth** (*formal*) to care for sb, especially sb who is sick or old, and make sure that they have everything they need SYN **tend**

**min·is·ter·ial** /ˌmɪnɪˈstɪəriəl; NAmE -ˈstɪr-/ adj. connected with a government minister or ministers: *decisions taken at ministerial level* ◇ *to hold ministerial office (= to have the job of a government minister)*

**min·is·ter·ing** /ˈmɪnɪstərɪŋ/ adj. [only before noun] (*formal*) caring for people: *She could not see herself in the role of ministering angel.*

**Minister of 'State** noun a British government minister but not one who is in charge of a department ⊃ compare SECRETARY OF STATE

**min·is·tra·tions** /ˌmɪnɪˈstreɪʃnz/ noun [pl.] (*formal* or *humorous*) the act of helping or caring for sb especially when they are ill or in trouble

**min·is·try** ♪+ C1 /ˈmɪnɪstri/ noun (*pl.* **-ies**) 1 ♪+ B2 [C] a government department that has a particular area of responsibility: *the Ministry of Defence* ◇ *a ministry spokesperson* 2 **the Ministry** [sing. – sing. / pl. v.] ministers of religion, especially Protestant ministers, when they are mentioned as a group 3 [C, usually sing.] the spiritual work

# minivan

or service of a Christian or group of Christians; the period of time spent serving the Church

**mini·van** /ˈmɪnivæn/ (*especially NAmE*) (*BrE usually* **people carrier**) *noun* a large car, like a van, designed to carry up to eight people

**mink** /mɪŋk/ *noun* (*pl.* **mink** or **minks**) **1** [C] a small wild animal with thick shiny fur, a long body and short legs. Mink are often kept on farms for their fur: *a mink farm* **2** [U] the skin and shiny brown fur of the mink, used for making expensive coats, etc: *a mink jacket* **3** [C] a coat or jacket made of mink

**minke** /ˈmɪŋkə; *BrE also* -ki/ (*also* **minke whale**) *noun* a small WHALE that is dark grey on top and white below

**min·now** /ˈmɪnəʊ/ *noun* **1** a very small FRESHWATER fish **2** a company or sports team that is small or unimportant

**minor** 🔑 B2 Ⓦ /ˈmaɪnə(r)/ *adj., noun, verb*

- *adj.* **1** 🔑 B2 [usually before noun] not very large, important or serious: *a minor road* ◇ *to suffer minor injuries* ◇ *to undergo minor surgery* ◇ *youths imprisoned for minor offences* ◇ *minor modifications/adjustments* ◇ *There may be some minor changes to the schedule.* ◇ *Women played a relatively minor role in the organization.* ◇ *The minor characters in the story are all well drawn.* OPP **major 2** (*music*) based on a SCALE in which the third note is a SEMITONE/ HALF STEP higher than the second note: *the key of C minor* ⇒ *compare* MAJOR
- *noun* **1** (*law*) a person who is under the age at which you legally become an adult and are responsible for your actions: *It is an offence to serve alcohol to minors.* ⇒ WORD-FINDER NOTE at AGE **2** (*especially NAmE*) a subject that you study at university in addition to your MAJOR
- *verb*

PHR V **minor in sth** (*NAmE*) to study sth at college, but not as your main subject ⇒ *compare* MAJOR

▼ **HOMOPHONES**
miner • minor /ˈmaɪnə(r)/
- **miner** *noun*: *He started work as a coal miner at 14.*
- **minor** *adj.*: *The novel is now regarded as a minor classic.*
- **minor** *noun*: *She arrived in the country as an unaccompanied minor.*

**mi·nor·ity** 🔑 B2 Ⓦ /maɪˈnɒrəti; *NAmE* -ˈnɔːr-/ *noun* (*pl.* **-ies**) **1** 🔑 B2 [sing. + sing./pl. v.] the smaller part of a group; less than half of the people or things in a large group: *Only a small minority of students is/are interested in politics these days.* ◇ *Only a tiny minority of products is/ are affected.* ◇ *That's very much a minority view.* ◇ *Minority interest groups have gained disproportionate influence.* ◇ **among a/the~** *You are definitely among the minority.* ◇ *minority shareholders in the bank* OPP **majority 2** 🔑 B2 [C] a small group within a community or country that is different because of race, religion, language, etc: *the rights of ethnic/racial minorities* ◇ *There is a large German-speaking minority in the east of the country.* ◇ *persecuted/ oppressed minorities* ◇ *minority languages* ◇ (*NAmE*) *The school is 95 per cent minority* (= 95 per cent of children are not white Americans but from different groups). ◇ (*NAmE*) *minority neighborhoods* (= where no or few white people live) ◇ *minority groups/populations/leaders* ⇒ *see also* BAME, BME, ETHNIC MINORITY, VISIBLE MINORITY **3** [U] (*law*) the state of being under the age at which you are legally an adult ⇒ *compare* MAJORITY (4)

IDM **be in a/the minority** to form less than half of a large group **be in a minority of 'one** (*often humorous*) to be the only person to have a particular opinion or to vote a particular way

**mi·nority ˈgovernment** *noun* [C, U] a government that has fewer seats in parliament than the total number held by all the other parties

**mi·nority ˈleader** *noun* (in the US Senate or House of Representatives) a leader of a political party that does not have a majority

**ˈminor league** (*also* **Minor league**) *noun* (*NAmE*) a league of professional sports teams, especially in baseball, that play at a lower level than the major leagues

**ˈminor-league** *adj.* [only before noun] (*NAmE*) **1** (*sport*) connected with teams in the minor leagues in baseball: *a minor-league team* **2** not very important and having little influence: *a minor-league business*

**Mi·no·taur** /ˈmaɪnətɔː(r), ˈmɪ-/ *noun* (in ancient Greek stories) an imaginary creature who was half man and half BULL

**min·ster** /ˈmɪnstə(r)/ *noun* (*BrE*) a large or important church: *York Minster*

**min·strel** /ˈmɪnstrəl/ *noun* a musician or singer in the Middle Ages

**mint** /mɪnt/ *noun, verb*

- *noun* **1** [U] a plant whose leaves have a fresh smell and taste that are added to food and drinks and used in cooking as a HERB. There are many types of mint: *mint-flavoured toothpaste* ◇ *I decorated the fruit salad with a sprig of mint.* ◇ *roast lamb with mint sauce* ⇒ VISUAL VOCAB page V8 **2** [C] a sweet that tastes of a type of mint called PEPPERMINT: *after-dinner mints* **3** [C] a place where coins and BANKNOTES are made: *the Royal Mint* (= the one where British coins and notes are made) **4 a mint** [sing.] (*informal*) a large amount of money: *to make/cost a mint*

IDM **in mint conˈdition** new or as good as new; in perfect condition

- *verb* **~sth** to make a coin from metal

**mint·ed** /ˈmɪntɪd/ *adj.* **1** freshly/newly ~ recently produced, invented, etc: *a newly minted expression* **2** (of food) tasting of mint **3** (*BrE, informal*) very rich

**ˈmint ˈjulep** (*also* **julep**) *noun* [U, C] an alcoholic drink made by mixing BOURBON with MINT, sugar and CRUSHED ice (= that has been broken into very small pieces)

**minty** /ˈmɪnti/ *adj.* tasting or smelling of MINT: *a minty flavour/smell*

**min·uet** /ˌmɪnjuˈet/ *noun* a slow formal dance that was popular in the 17th and 18th centuries; a piece of music for this dance

**minus** /ˈmaɪnəs/ *prep., noun, adj.*

- *prep.* **1** used when you SUBTRACT (= take away) one number or thing from another one: *Seven minus three is four* (7−3=4). ◇ *the former Soviet Union, minus the Baltic republics and Georgia* **2** used to express temperature below zero degrees: *It was minus ten.* ◇ *The temperature dropped to minus 28 degrees centigrade (−28°C).* **3** (*informal*) without sth that was there before: *We're going to be minus a car for a while.* OPP **plus**[1] IDM *see* PLUS[1] *prep.*
- *noun* **1** (*also* **ˈminus sign**) The symbol (−), used in mathematics **2** (*informal*) a negative quality; a disadvantage: *Let's consider the pluses and minuses of changing the system.* OPP **plus**[1]
- *adj.* **1** [only before noun] (*mathematics*) lower than zero: *a minus figure/number* **2** [only before noun] making sth seem negative and less attractive or good: *What are the car's minus points* (= the disadvantages)? ◇ *On the minus side, rented property is expensive and difficult to find.* **3** [after noun] (used in a system of grades) slightly lower than the grade A, B, etc: *I got (a) B minus (B−) in the test.* OPP **plus**[1]

**min·us·cule** /ˈmɪnəskjuːl/ *adj.* extremely small

**min·ute**[1] 🔑 A1 /ˈmɪnɪt/ *noun, verb* ⇒ *see also* MINUTE[2]

- *noun*
- PART OF HOUR **1** 🔑 A1 [C] (*abbr.* **min.**) each of the 60 parts of an hour, that are equal to 60 seconds: **minutes to …** *It's four minutes to six.* ◇ **minutes past …** *four minutes past two* ◇ **minutes after/before …** *five minutes after/before midnight* ◇ **in …** *minutes I'll be back in a few minutes.* ◇ **for … minutes** *Boil the rice for 20 minutes.* ◇ **within minutes** *The ship sank within minutes.* ◇ **per~** *The pump delivers seven gallons per minute.* ◇ *a ten-minute bus ride* ◇ *Two minutes later the phone rang.* ◇ *I enjoyed every minute of the party.*
- VERY SHORT TIME **2** 🔑 A1 [sing.] (*informal*) a very short time: *It only takes a minute to make a salad.* ◇ *Could you* **wait a minute**, *please?* ◇ **Hang on a minute**—*I'll just get my coat.* ◇ *I just have to finish this—I won't be a minute.* ◇ **for a~** *Could I see you for a minute?* ◇ **in a~** *I'll be with you in a*

# misapprehension

*minute, Jo.* ◊ *Typical English weather—one minute it's raining and the next minute the sun is shining.*
- **EXACT MOMENT 3** [sing.] an exact moment in time: **at that/the ~** *At that very minute, Tom walked in.* ◊ *I've got things on my mind at the minute.* ⇒ see also LAST-MINUTE
- **ANGLES 4** [C] each of the 60 equal parts of a degree, used in measuring angles: *37 degrees 30 minutes (37° 30')*
- **RECORD OF MEETING 5 the minutes** [pl.] a summary or record of what is said or decided at a formal meeting: *We read through the minutes of the last meeting.* ◊ *Who is going to take the minutes (= write them)?* ⇒ WORDFINDER NOTE at MEETING
- **SHORT NOTE 6** [C] a short note on a subject, especially one that recommends a course of action

**IDM** **(at) any 'minute ('now)** very soon: *Hurry up! He'll be back any minute now.* **by the 'minute** very fast: *Matters grew worse by the minute.* **fifteen minutes of 'fame** a short period of being famous: *Everybody wants their fifteen minutes of fame.* **the minute (that) ...** as soon as ...: *I want to see him the minute he arrives.* **not for a/one 'minute** certainly not; not at all: *I don't think for a minute that she'll accept but you can ask her.* **this minute** immediately; now: *Come down this minute!* ◊ *I don't know what I'm going to do yet—I've just this minute found out.* **to the 'minute** exactly: *The train arrived at 9.05 to the minute.* **up to the 'minute** (*informal*) **1** fashionable and modern: *Her styles are always up to the minute.* **2** having the latest information: *The traffic reports are up to the minute.* ⇒ see also UP-TO-THE-MINUTE ⇒ more at BORN *v.*, JUST *adv.*, LAST¹ *det.*, WAIT *v.*
- **verb** [often passive] **~ sth | ~ that ...** to write down sth that is said at a meeting in the official record (= the minutes): *I'd like that last remark to be minuted.*

**mi·nute²** /maɪˈnjuːt; *NAmE* -ˈnuːt/ *adj.* ⇒ see also MINUTE¹ (**mi·nut·er, mi·nut·est**) **1** extremely small **SYN** tiny: *minute amounts of chemicals in the water* ◊ *The kitchen on the boat is minute.* **2** very detailed, careful and complete: *a minute examination/inspection* ◊ *She remembered everything in minute detail/in the minutest detail(s).* ▶ **mi·nute·ly** *adv.*: *The agreement has been examined minutely.*

**minute hand** /ˈmɪnɪt hænd/ *noun* [usually sing.] the hand on a watch or clock that points to the minutes ⇒ picture at CLOCK

**mi·nu·tiae** /maɪˈnjuːʃiː, -ʃiaɪ; *NAmE* mɪˈnuː-/ *noun* [pl.] very small details: *the minutiae of the contract*

**minx** /mɪŋks/ *noun* [sing.] (*old-fashioned* or *humorous*) a girl or young woman who is clever at getting what she wants, and does not show respect

**MIPS** /mɪps/ *abbr.* (*computing*) million instructions per second (a unit for measuring computer speed)

**mir·acle** /ˈmɪrəkl/ *noun* **1** [C] an act or event that does not follow the laws of nature and is believed to be caused by God **SYN** wonder: *the miracle of rising from the grave* **2** [sing.] (*informal*) a lucky thing that happens that you did not expect or think was possible **SYN** wonder: *an economic miracle* ◊ *a miracle cure/drug* ◊ *it is a ~(that) ... It's a miracle (that) nobody was killed in the crash.* ◊ *It would take a miracle to make this business profitable.* **3** [C] **~ of sth** a very good example or product of sth **SYN** wonder: *The car is a miracle of engineering.*
**IDM** **work/perform 'miracles** to achieve very good results: *Her exercise programme has worked miracles for her.*

**mi·racu·lous** /mɪˈrækjələs/ *adj.* like a miracle; completely unexpected and very lucky **SYN** extraordinary, phenomenal: *miraculous powers of healing* ◊ *She's made a miraculous recovery.* ▶ **mi·racu·lous·ly** *adv.*: *They miraculously survived the plane crash.*

**mir·age** /ˈmɪrɑːʒ, mɪˈrɑːʒ; *NAmE* məˈrɑːʒ/ *noun* **1** an effect caused by hot air in deserts or on roads, that makes you think you can see sth, such as water, which is not there **2** a hope or wish that you cannot make happen because it is not realistic **SYN** illusion: *His idea of love was a mirage.*

**Mi·randa** /məˈrændə/ *adj.* (in the US) relating to the fact that the police must tell sb who has been arrested about their rights, including the right not to answer questions, and warn them that anything they say may be used as evidence against them: *The police read him his Miranda rights.* **ORIGIN** From the decision of the Supreme Court on the case of Miranda v the State of Arizona in 1966.

**mire** /ˈmaɪə(r)/ *noun* [U] an area of deep mud **SYN** bog: *The wheels sank deeper into the mire.* ◊ (*figurative*) *My name had been dragged through the mire* (= my reputation was ruined). ◊ (*figurative*) *The government was sinking deeper and deeper into the mire* (= getting further into a difficult situation).

**mired** /ˈmaɪəd; *NAmE* -ərd/ *adj.* [not before noun] **1 ~ in sth** (*literary*) in a difficult or unpleasant situation that you cannot escape from: *The country was mired in recession.* **2** stuck in deep mud

**mir·ror** /ˈmɪrə(r)/ *noun, verb*
- *noun* **1** [C] a piece of special flat glass that reflects images, so that you can see yourself when you look in it: **in the ~** *He looked at himself in the mirror.* ◊ *Remember to look in the mirror* (= in a car, when driving) *before signalling.* ◊ *the bathroom mirror* ⇒ see also REAR-VIEW MIRROR, TWO-WAY MIRROR, WING MIRROR **2 a ~ of sth** [sing.] something that shows what sth else is like: *The face is the mirror of the soul.* **3 =** MIRROR SITE **IDM** see SMOKE *n.*
- *verb* **1 ~ sb/sth** to have features that are similar to sth/sth else and that show what it is like **SYN** reflect: *The music of the time mirrored the feeling of optimism in the country.* **2 ~ sb/sth** to show the image of sb/sth on the surface of water, glass, etc. **SYN** reflect: *She saw herself mirrored in the window.*

**mir·ror·ball** /ˈmɪrəbɔːl; *NAmE* -rərb-/ *noun* a decoration consisting of a large ball covered in small mirrors that hangs from the ceiling and turns to produce lighting effects

**mir·rored** /ˈmɪrəd; *NAmE* -rərd/ *adj.* [only before noun] having a mirror or mirrors or behaving like a mirror: *mirrored doors/sunglasses*

**mirror 'image** *noun* an image of sth that is like a REFLECTION of it, either because it is exactly the same or because the right side of the original object appears on the left and the left side appears on the right

**'mirror site** (also **mir·ror**) *noun* (*computing*) a website that is a copy of another website but that has a different address on the internet

**mirth** /mɜːθ; *NAmE* mɜːrθ/ *noun* [U] happiness, fun and the sound of people laughing **SYN** merriment: *The performance produced much mirth among the audience.*

**mirth·less** /ˈmɜːθləs; *NAmE* ˈmɜːrθ-/ *adj.* (*formal*) (especially of a laugh) not really showing that you enjoy sth or think it is funny: *a mirthless laugh/smile* ▶ **mirth·less·ly** *adv.*

**MIS** /ˌem aɪ ˈes/ *abbr.* (*computing*) management information system (a system that stores information for use by business managers)

**mis-** /mɪs/ *prefix* (in verbs and nouns) bad or wrong; badly or wrongly: *misbehaviour* ◊ *misinterpret*

**mis·ad·ven·ture** /ˌmɪsədˈventʃə(r)/ *noun* **1** [U] (*BrE, law*) death caused by accident, rather than as a result of a crime: *a verdict of death by misadventure* **2** [C, U] (*formal*) bad luck or a small accident **SYN** mishap

**mis·aligned** /ˌmɪsəˈlaɪnd/ *adj.* not in the correct position in relation to sth else: *a misaligned vertebra* ▶ **mis·align·ment** /-ˈlaɪnmənt/ *noun* [U, C]: *The tests revealed a slight misalignment of the eyes.*

**mis·an·thrope** /ˈmɪsənθrəʊp/ *noun* (*formal*) a person who hates and avoids other people

**mis·an·throp·ic** /ˌmɪsənˈθrɒpɪk; *NAmE* -ˈθrɑːp-/ *adj.* (*formal*) hating and avoiding other people ▶ **mis·an·thropy** /mɪˈsænθrəpi/ *noun* [U]

**mis·ap·pli·ca·tion** /ˌmɪsæplɪˈkeɪʃn/ *noun* [U, C] (*formal*) the use of sth for the wrong purpose or in the wrong way

**mis·ap·ply** /ˌmɪsəˈplaɪ/ *verb* [usually passive] (**mis·ap·plies, mis·ap·ply·ing, mis·ap·plied, mis·ap·plied**) **~ sth** (*formal*) to use sth for the wrong purpose or in the wrong way

**mis·ap·pre·hen·sion** /ˌmɪsæprɪˈhenʃn/ *noun* [U, C] (*formal*) a wrong idea about sth, or sth you believe to be true

# misappropriate

that is not true: *I was under the misapprehension that the course was for complete beginners.*

**mis·ap·pro·pri·ate** /ˌmɪsəˈprəʊprieɪt/ *verb* ~ *sth* (*formal*) to take sb else's money or property for yourself, especially when they have trusted you to take care of it **SYN** embezzle ⊃ compare APPROPRIATE ▶ **mis·ap·pro·pri·ation** /ˌmɪsəˌprəʊpriˈeɪʃn/ *noun* [U]

**mis·be·got·ten** /ˌmɪsbɪˈɡɒtn; *NAmE* -ˈɡɑːtn/ *adj.* [usually before noun] (*formal*) badly designed or planned

**mis·be·have** /ˌmɪsbɪˈheɪv/ *verb* [I, T] to behave badly: *Any child caught misbehaving was made to stand at the front of the class.* ◊ ~**yourself** *I see the dog has been misbehaving itself again.* **OPP** behave ▶ **mis·be·hav·iour** (*BrE*) (*NAmE* **mis·be·hav·ior**) /-jə(r)/ *noun* [U]

**mis·cal·cu·late** /ˌmɪsˈkælkjuleɪt/ *verb* **1** [T, I] to estimate an amount, a figure, a measurement, etc. wrongly: ~**(sth)** *They had seriously miscalculated the effect of inflation.* ◊ ~ **how long, how much, etc …** *He had miscalculated how long the trip would take.* **2** [T, I] ~**(sth)** | ~ **how, what, etc …** to judge a situation wrongly **SYN** misjudge: *She miscalculated the level of opposition to her proposals.* ▶ **mis·cal·cu·la·tion** /ˌmɪskælkjuˈleɪʃn/ *noun* [C, U]: *to make a miscalculation*

**mis·car·riage** /ˈmɪskærɪdʒ; *BrE also* ˌmɪsˈkærɪdʒ/ *noun* [C, U] the process of giving birth to a baby before it is fully developed and able to survive; an occasion when this happens: *to have a miscarriage* ◊ *The pregnancy ended in miscarriage at 11 weeks.* ⊃ compare ABORTION ⊃ WORDFINDER NOTE at PREGNANT

**mis·carriage of ˈjustice** *noun* [U, C] (*law*) a situation in which a court makes a wrong decision, especially when sb is punished when they are innocent

**mis·carry** /ˌmɪsˈkæri/ *verb* (**mis·car·ries, mis·carry·ing, mis·car·ried, mis·car·ried**) **1** [I, T] ~**(sth)** to give birth to a baby before it is fully developed and able to live: *The shock caused her to miscarry.* **2** [I] (*formal*) (of a plan) to fail **SYN** come to nothing

**mis·cast** /ˌmɪsˈkɑːst; *NAmE* -ˈkæst/ *verb* [usually passive] (**mis·cast, mis·cast**) ~ *sb* **(as** *sb***/***sth***)** | ~ *sth* to choose an actor to play a role for which they are not suitable; to give the roles in a play or film to unsuitable actors

**mis·ce·gen·ation** /ˌmɪsɪdʒəˈneɪʃn/ *noun* [U] (*formal*) the fact of children being produced by parents who are considered to be of different races, especially when one parent is white

**mis·cel·lan·eous** /ˌmɪsəˈleɪniəs/ *adj.* [usually before noun] consisting of many different kinds of things that are not connected and do not easily form a group **SYN** diverse, various: *a sale of miscellaneous household items* ◊ *She gave me some money to cover any miscellaneous expenses.*

**mis·cel·lany** /mɪˈseləni; *NAmE* ˈmɪsəleɪni/ *noun* [sing.] (*formal*) a group or collection of different kinds of things **SYN** assortment

**mis·chance** /ˌmɪsˈtʃɑːns; *NAmE* -ˈtʃæns/ *noun* [U, C] (*formal*) bad luck

**mis·chief** /ˈmɪstʃɪf/ *noun* [U] **1** bad behaviour (especially of children) that is annoying but does not cause any serious damage or harm: *Those children are always getting into mischief.* ◊ *I try to keep out of mischief.* ◊ *It's very quiet upstairs; they must be up to some mischief!* **2** the wish or TENDENCY to behave or play in a way that causes trouble: *Her eyes were full of mischief.* **3** (*formal*) harm or injury that is done to sb or to their reputation: *The incident caused a great deal of political mischief.* **IDM** **do yourself a ˈmischief** (*BrE, informal*) to hurt yourself physically: *Watch how you use those scissors—you could do yourself a mischief!* **make ˈmischief** to do or say sth deliberately to upset other people, or cause trouble between them

**ˈmischief-making** *noun* [U] the act of deliberately causing trouble for people, such as harming their reputation

**mis·chiev·ous** /ˈmɪstʃɪvəs/ *adj.* **1** enjoying playing tricks and annoying people **SYN** naughty: *a mischievous boy* ◊ *a mischievous grin/smile/look* **2** (*formal*) (of an action or a statement) causing trouble, such as damaging sb's reputation: *mischievous lies/gossip* ▶ **mis·chiev·ous·ly** *adv.*

**mis·cible** /ˈmɪsəbl/ *adj.* (*specialist*) (of liquids) that can be mixed together

**mis·com·mu·ni·ca·tion** /ˌmɪskəˌmjuːnɪˈkeɪʃn/ *noun* [U, C] failure to make information or your ideas and feelings clear to sb, or to understand what sb says to you

**mis·con·ceive** /ˌmɪskənˈsiːv/ *verb* ~ *sth* (*formal*) to understand sth in the wrong way **SYN** misunderstand

**mis·con·ceived** /ˌmɪskənˈsiːvd/ *adj.* badly planned or judged; not carefully thought about: *a misconceived education policy* ◊ *their misconceived expectations of country life*

**mis·con·cep·tion** /ˌmɪskənˈsepʃn/ *noun* [C, U] ~ **(about** *sth***)** a belief or an idea that is not based on correct information, or that is not understood by people: *frequently held misconceptions about the disease* ◊ *a popular misconception* (= one that a lot of people have) ◊ *Let me deal with some common misconceptions.* ◊ *views based on misconception and prejudice* ⊃ compare PRECONCEPTION

**mis·con·duct** /ˌmɪsˈkɒndʌkt; *NAmE* -ˈkɑːn-/ *noun* [U] (*formal*) **1** unacceptable behaviour, especially by a professional person: *a doctor accused of gross misconduct* (= very serious misconduct) ◊ *professional misconduct* **2** bad management of a company, etc: *misconduct of the company's financial affairs*

**mis·con·struc·tion** /ˌmɪskənˈstrʌkʃn/ *noun* [U, C] (*formal*) a completely wrong understanding of sth

**mis·con·strue** /ˌmɪskənˈstruː/ *verb* ~ *sth* (**as** *sth*) (*formal*) to understand sb's words or actions wrongly **SYN** misinterpret: *It is easy to misconstrue confidence as arrogance.*

**mis·count** /ˌmɪsˈkaʊnt/ *verb* [T, I] ~ **(sth)** to count sth wrongly: *The votes had been miscounted.*

**mis·cre·ant** /ˈmɪskriənt/ *noun* (*IndE or literary*) a person who has done sth wrong or illegal

**mis·deed** /ˌmɪsˈdiːd/ *noun* [usually pl.] (*formal*) a bad or evil act **SYN** wrongdoing

**mis·de·mean·our** (*US* **mis·de·meanor**) /ˌmɪsdɪˈmiːnə(r)/ *noun* **1** (*formal*) an action that is bad or unacceptable, but not very serious: *youthful misdemeanours* **2** (*US, law*) a crime that is considered to be less serious than a FELONY

**mis·diag·nose** /ˌmɪsdaɪəɡˈnəʊz, ˌmɪsˈdaɪəɡnəʊz/ *verb* to give an explanation of the nature of an illness or a problem that is not correct: ~ **sth (as sth)** *Her depression was misdiagnosed as stress.* ◊ ~ **sb (with sth)** *He was misdiagnosed with cancer.* ▶ **mis·diag·nosis** /ˌmɪsdaɪəɡˈnəʊsɪs/ *noun* [C, U] (*pl.* **mis·diag·noses** /-ˈnəʊsiːz/)

**mis·dial** /ˌmɪsˈdaɪəl/ *verb* [I, T] (-**ll**-, *NAmE* -**l**-) ~ **(sth)** to call the wrong phone number by mistake

**mis·dir·ect** /ˌmɪsdəˈrekt, -daɪˈr-/ *verb* **1** [usually passive] to use sth in a way that is not appropriate to a particular situation: **be misdirected** *Their efforts over the past years have been largely misdirected.* **2** ~ *sb***/***sth* (**to** *sth*) to send sb/sth in the wrong direction or to the wrong place **3** ~ *sb***/***sth* (*law*) (of a judge) to give a JURY (= the group of people who decide if sb is guilty of a crime) wrong information about the law ▶ **mis·dir·ec·tion** /-ˈrekʃn/ *noun* [U]

**mise en scène** /ˌmiːz ɒn ˈsen; *NAmE* ɑːn/ *noun* [sing.] (*from French*) **1** (*specialist*) the arrangement of furniture, SCENERY, LIGHTING, etc. used on the stage for a play in the theatre, or in front of the camera in a film **2** (*formal*) the place or scene where an event takes place: *Venice provided the mise en scène for the conference.*

**miser** /ˈmaɪzə(r)/ *noun* (*disapproving*) a person who loves money and hates spending it

**mis·er·able** /ˈmɪzrəbl/ *adj.* **1** very unhappy or uncomfortable: *We were cold, wet and thoroughly miserable.* ◊ *Don't look so miserable!* ◊ *She knows how to make life miserable for her employees.* **2** making you feel very unhappy or uncomfortable **SYN** depressing: *miserable housing conditions* ◊ *I spent a miserable weekend alone at home.* ◊ *What a miserable day!* (= cold and wet) ◊ *The play was a miserable failure.* **3** [only before noun] (*disapproving*) (of a person) always unhappy, unfriendly and in a bad mood **SYN** grumpy: *He was a miserable old devil.* **4** too small in quantity or

How can anyone live on such a miserable wage? ▶ **mis·er·ably** /-bli/ adv.: *They wandered around miserably.* ◊ *a miserably cold day* ◊ *He failed miserably as an actor.* **IDM** see SIN n.

**mi·ser·ly** /ˈmaɪzəli; NAmE -zərli/ adj. (disapproving) **1** (of a person) hating to spend money **SYN** **mean 2** (of a quantity or amount) too small **SYN** **paltry**

**mis·ery** /ˈmɪzəri/ noun (pl. **-ies**) **1** [U] great physical or mental pain: *Fame brought her nothing but misery.* **2** [U] very poor living conditions **SYN** **poverty**: *The vast majority of the population lives in utter misery.* **3** [C] something that causes great physical or mental pain: *the miseries of unemployment* **4** [C] (BrE, informal) a person who is always unhappy and complaining: *Don't be such an old misery!* **IDM** **make sb's life a ˈmisery** to behave in a way that makes sb else feel very unhappy **put an animal, a bird, etc. out of its ˈmisery** to kill a creature because it has an illness or injury that cannot be treated **put sb out of their ˈmisery** (informal) to stop sb worrying by telling them sth that they are anxious to know: *Put me out of my misery—did I pass or didn't I?*

**mis·fire** /ˌmɪsˈfaɪə(r)/ verb **1** [I] (of a plan or joke) to fail to have the effect that you had intended **SYN** **go wrong 2** (also **miss**) [I] (of an engine) to not work correctly because the petrol does not burn at the right time **3** [I] (of a gun, etc.) to fail to send out a bullet, etc. when fired ⊃ compare BACKFIRE

**mis·fit** /ˈmɪsfɪt/ noun a person who is not accepted by a particular group of people, especially because their behaviour or their ideas are very different: *a social misfit*

**mis·for·tune** /ˌmɪsˈfɔːtʃuːn; NAmE -ˈfɔːrtʃən/ noun **1** [U] bad luck: *He has known great misfortune in his life.* ◊ *We had the misfortune to run into a violent storm.* **2** [C] an accident, condition or event caused by bad luck **SYN** **blow**, **disaster**: *She bore her misfortunes bravely.*

**mis·giv·ing** /ˌmɪsˈɡɪvɪŋ/ noun [C, usually pl., U] feelings of doubt or worry about what might happen, or about whether or not sth is the right thing to do: *I read the letter with a sense of misgiving.* ◊ *~ about (doing) sth I had grave misgivings about making the trip.*

**mis·guided** /ˌmɪsˈɡaɪdɪd/ adj. wrong because you have misunderstood or judged a situation badly **SYN** **inappropriate**: *She only did it in a misguided attempt to help.* ▶ **mis·guided·ly** adv.

**mis·handle** /ˌmɪsˈhændl/ verb **1** *~ sth* to deal badly with a problem or situation **SYN** **mismanage**: *The entire campaign had been badly mishandled.* **2** *~ sb/sth* to touch or treat sb/sth in a rough and careless way: *The equipment could be dangerous if mishandled.* ▶ **mis·hand·ling** noun [U]: *the government's mishandling of the economy*

**mis·hap** /ˈmɪshæp/ noun [C, U] a small accident or piece of bad luck that does not have serious results: *a slight mishap* ◊ *a series of mishaps* ◊ *I managed to get home without (further) mishap.*

**mis·hear** /ˌmɪsˈhɪə(r); NAmE -ˈhɪr/ verb [T, I] (**mis·heard**, **mis·heard** /-ˈhɜːd; NAmE -ˈhɜːrd/) *~ (sb/sth) | ~ what …* to fail to hear correctly what sb says, so that you think they said sth else: *You may have misheard her—I'm sure she didn't mean that.* ◊ *I thought he said he was coming today, but I must have misheard.*

**mis·hit** /ˌmɪsˈhɪt/ verb (**mis·hit·ting**, **mis·hit**, **mis·hit**) *~ sth* (in a game) to hit the ball badly so that it does not go where you had intended ▶ **mis·hit** /ˈmɪshɪt/ noun

**mish·mash** /ˈmɪʃmæʃ/ noun [sing.] (informal, usually disapproving) a confused mixture of different kinds of things, styles, etc.

**mis·in·form** /ˌmɪsɪnˈfɔːm; NAmE -ˈfɔːrm/ verb [often passive] to give sb wrong information about sth: **be misinformed (about sth)** *They were deliberately misinformed about their rights.* ◊ *a misinformed belief* (= based on wrong information) ▶ **mis·in·for·ma·tion** /ˌmɪsɪnfəˈmeɪʃn; NAmE -fər-/ noun [U]: *a campaign of misinformation*

**mis·in·ter·pret** /ˌmɪsɪnˈtɜːprət; NAmE -ˈtɜːrp-/ verb *~ sth (as sth/doing sth)* to understand sth/sb wrongly **SYN** **misconstrue**, **misread**: *His comments were misinterpreted as a criticism of the project.* ⊃ compare INTERPRET

▶ **mis·in·ter·pret·ation** /ˌmɪsɪntɜːprəˈteɪʃn; NAmE -tɜːrp-/ noun [U, C]: *A number of these statements could be open to misinterpretation* (= could be understood wrongly).

**mis·judge** /ˌmɪsˈdʒʌdʒ/ verb [T, I] **1** *~ sb/sth | ~ how, what, etc …* to form a wrong opinion about a person or situation, especially in a way that makes you deal with them or it unfairly: *She now realizes that she misjudged him.* **2** *~ sth | ~ how long, how far, etc …* to estimate sth such as time or distance wrongly: *He misjudged the distance and his ball ended in the lake.* ▶ **mis·judge·ment** (also **mis·judg·ment**) noun [C, U]

**mis·lay** /ˌmɪsˈleɪ/ verb (**mis·laid**, **mis·laid** /-ˈleɪd/) *~ sth* (formal, especially BrE) to put sth somewhere and then be unable to find it again, especially for only a short time **SYN** **lose**: *I seem to have mislaid my keys.*

**mis·lead** /ˌmɪsˈliːd/ verb [T, I] (**mis·led**, **mis·led** /-ˈled/) to give sb the wrong idea or impression and make them believe sth that is not true **SYN** **deceive**: *~ (sb) (about sth) He deliberately misled us about the nature of their relationship.* ◊ *Statistics taken on their own are liable to mislead.* ◊ *~ sb into doing sth The company misled hundreds of people into investing their money unwisely.*

**mis·lead·ing** /ˌmɪsˈliːdɪŋ/ adj. giving the wrong idea or impression and making you believe sth that is not true **SYN** **deceptive**: *misleading information/advertisements* ▶ **mis·lead·ing·ly** adv.: *These bats are sometimes misleadingly referred to as 'flying foxes'.*

**mis·man·age** /ˌmɪsˈmænɪdʒ/ verb *~ sth* to deal with or manage sth badly **SYN** **mishandle** ▶ **mis·man·age·ment** noun [U]: *accusations of corruption and financial mismanagement*

**mis·match** /ˈmɪsmætʃ/ noun *~ (between A and B)* a combination of things or people that do not go together well or are not suitable for each other: *a mismatch between people's real needs and the available facilities* ▶ **mis·match** /ˌmɪsˈmætʃ/ verb [often passive]: *~ sb/sth They made a mismatched couple.*

**mis·name** /ˌmɪsˈneɪm/ verb [usually passive] *~ sb/sth* to give sb/sth a name that is wrong or not appropriate

**mis·nomer** /ˌmɪsˈnəʊmə(r)/ noun a name or a word that is not appropriate or accurate: *'Villa' was something of a misnomer—the place was no more than an old farmhouse.*

**miso** /ˈmiːsəʊ/ noun [U] a substance made from beans, used in Japanese cooking

**mis·ogyn·ist** /mɪˈsɒdʒɪnɪst; NAmE -ˈsɑːdʒ-/ noun (formal) a person who hates women ▶ **mis·ogyn·is·tic** /mɪˌsɒdʒɪˈnɪstɪk; NAmE -ˌsɑːdʒ-/ (also **mis·ogyn·ist**) adj.: *misogynistic attitudes* **mis·ogyny** /mɪˈsɒdʒɪni; NAmE -ˈsɑːdʒ-/ noun [U]

**mis·place** /ˌmɪsˈpleɪs/ verb *~ sth* to put sth somewhere and then be unable to find it again, especially for a short time **SYN** **mislay**

**mis·placed** /ˌmɪsˈpleɪst/ adj. **1** not appropriate or correct in the situation: *misplaced confidence/optimism/fear* **2** (of love, trust, etc.) given to a person who does not deserve or return those feelings: *misplaced loyalty*

**mis·print** /ˈmɪsprɪnt/ noun a mistake such as a spelling mistake that is made when a book, etc. is printed ⊃ SYNONYMS at MISTAKE

**mis·pro·nounce** /ˌmɪsprəˈnaʊns/ verb *~ sth* to pronounce a word wrongly ▶ **mis·pro·nun·ci·ation** /ˌmɪsprənʌnsiˈeɪʃn/ noun [C, U]

**mis·quote** /ˌmɪsˈkwəʊt/ verb *~ sb/sth* to repeat what sb has said or written in a way that is not correct: *The senator claims to have been misquoted in the article.* ▶ **mis·quo·ta·tion** /ˌmɪskwəʊˈteɪʃn/ noun [C, U]

**mis·read** /ˌmɪsˈriːd/ verb (**mis·read**, **mis·read** /-ˈred/) **1** to understand sb/sth wrongly **SYN** **misinterpret**: *~ sth I'm afraid I completely misread the situation.* ◊ *~ sth as sth His confidence was misread as arrogance.* **2** *~ sth (as sth)* to read sth wrongly: *I misread the 1 as a 7.*

**mis·re·mem·ber** /ˌmɪsrɪˈmembə(r)/ verb [T, I] to remember sth in a way that is not accurate or true: *~ sth People often misremember their vacations as more idyllic than they actually were.*

# misreport

**mis·re·port** /ˌmɪsrɪˈpɔːt; NAmE -ˈpɔːrt/ verb ~ sth | ~ what, how, etc ... to give a report of an event, etc. that is not correct: *The newspapers misreported the facts of the case.*

**mis·rep·re·sent** /ˌmɪsˌreprɪˈzent/ verb [often passive] (formal) to give information about sb/sth that is not true or complete so that other people have the wrong impression about them/it: ~ sb/sth *He felt that the book misrepresented his opinions.* ◇ ~ sb/sth as sth *In the article she was misrepresented as an uncaring mother.* ◇ ~ what, how, etc ... *The report misrepresented what the group believes.*
▶ **mis·rep·re·sen·ta·tion** /ˌmɪsˌreprɪzenˈteɪʃn/ noun [C, U]: *a deliberate misrepresentation of the facts*

**mis·rule** /ˌmɪsˈruːl/ noun [U] (formal) bad government: *The regime finally collapsed after 25 years of misrule.*

## miss 🅞 A1 /mɪs/ verb, noun

■ verb
- **BE LATE** 1 A1 [T] ~ sth/sb to be or arrive too late for sth: *If I don't leave now I'll miss my plane.* ◇ *Sorry I'm late—have I missed anything?* ◇ *'Is Ann there?' 'You've just missed her (= she has just left).'* ◇ *If you miss the deadline, you'll have to pay a fine.*
- **NOT BE/GO SOMEWHERE** 2 A2 [T] ~ sth to fail to be or go somewhere: *She hasn't missed a game all year.* ◇ *You missed a good party last night (= because you did not go).* ◇ *'Are you coming to the school play?' 'I wouldn't miss it for the world.'*
- **NOT DO STH** 3 A2 [T] ~ sth to fail to do sth: *You can't afford to miss meals (= not eat meals) when you're in training.* ◇ *You have to miss a turn (= to not play when it is your turn in a game).* 4 A2 [T] ~ sth to not take the opportunity to do sth: *The sale prices were too good to miss.* ◇ *It was an opportunity not to be missed.* ◇ *She missed the opportunity to take part.* ◇ *Jackson never missed a chance to serve as teacher and mentor.*
- **NOT HIT, CATCH, ETC.** 5 B1 [T, I] to fail to hit, catch, reach, etc. sth: ~ (sb/sth) *How many goals has he missed this season?* ◇ *The bullet missed her by about six inches.* ◇ *It was a joke that missed its target.* ◇ *The company has missed all its targets this year.* ◇ *She threw a plate at him and only narrowly missed.* ◇ ~ doing sth *She narrowly missed hitting him.*
- **NOT HEAR/SEE** 6 B1 [T] ~ sth to fail to hear, see or notice sth: *The hotel is the only white building on the road—you can't miss it.* ◇ *Don't miss next week's issue!* ◇ *I missed her name.* ◇ *No one will want to miss this film.* ◇ *Your mother will know who's moved in—she doesn't miss much.*
- **NOT UNDERSTAND** 7 B1 [T] ~ sth to fail to understand sth: *He completely missed the joke.* ◇ *You're missing the point (= failing to understand the main part) of what I'm saying.*
- **FEEL SAD** 8 A2 [T] to feel sad because you can no longer see sb or do sth that you like: ~ sb/sth *I still miss her a lot.* ◇ *Anne, who died on 22 July, will be sadly missed by all who knew her.* ◇ *What did you miss most when you were in France?* ◇ *I'm really going to miss Cheri's cooking.* ◇ ~ (sb/sth) doing sth *I don't miss getting up at six every morning!*
⊃ HOMOPHONES at MIST
- **NOTICE STH NOT THERE** 9 [T] ~ sb/sth to notice that sb/sth is not where they/it should be: *When did you first miss the necklace?* ◇ *We seem to be missing some students this morning.*
- **AVOID STH BAD** 10 [T] to avoid sth unpleasant SYN escape: ~ sth *If you go now you should miss the crowds.* ◇ ~ doing sth *He fell and just missed knocking the whole display over.*
- **OF ENGINE** 11 = MISFIRE

IDM **he, she, etc. doesn't miss a ˈtrick** (*informal*) used to say that sb notices every opportunity to gain an advantage **ˌmiss the ˈboat** (*informal*) to be unable to take advantage of sth because you are too late: *If you don't buy now, you may find that you've missed the boat.* **ˌmiss your ˈguess** (*NAmE, informal*) to make a mistake: *Unless I miss my guess, your computer needs a new hard drive.* ⊃ more at HEART n., MARK n.

PHRV **ˌmiss sb/sth↔ˈout** (*BrE*) to fail to include sb/sth in sth SYN omit: *I'll just read through the form again to make sure I haven't missed anything out.* **ˌmiss ˈout (on sth)** to fail to benefit from sth useful or fun by not taking part in it: *Of course I'm coming—I don't want to miss out on all the fun!*

■ noun
- **TITLE/FORM OF ADDRESS** 1 **Miss** used before the family name, or the first and family names, of a woman who is not married, in order to speak or write to her politely: *That's all, thank you, Miss Lipman.* HELP The title **Miss** can also be used by a married woman who keeps her own family name for professional purposes. ⊃ compare MRS, MS 2 **Miss** a title given to the winner of a beauty contest in a particular country, town, etc: *Miss Brighton* ◇ *the Miss World contest* 3 **Miss** (*informal*) used especially by men to address a young woman when they do not know her name: *Will that be all, Miss?* 4 **Miss** (*BrE, informal*) used as a form of address by children in some schools to a woman teacher, whether she is married or not: *Good morning, Miss!* ⊃ compare SIR 5 (*old-fashioned*) a girl or young woman
- **NOT HIT, CATCH, ETC.** 6 a failure to hit, catch or reach sth: *The penalty miss cost us the game.* ⊃ see also NEAR MISS

IDM **give sth a ˈmiss** (*informal, especially BrE*) to decide not to do sth, eat sth, etc: *I think I'll give badminton a miss tonight.* **a ˌmiss is as ˌgood as a ˈmile** (*saying*) there is no real difference between only just failing in sth and failing in it badly because the result is still the same

**mis·sal** /ˈmɪsl/ noun a book that contains the prayers, etc. that are used at MASS in the Roman Catholic Church

**mis-ˈsell** verb (**mis-sold, mis-sold**) to sell sb sth that is not suitable for their needs, for example by not giving them all the information they need: ~ sth *If the policy was mis-sold, the insurance company must be responsible.* ◇ ~ sb sth | ~ sth to sb *The bank had mis-sold them a £200 000 loan.*
▶ **ˌmis-ˈselling** noun [U]: *the mis-selling of financial products* ◇ *mis-selling complaints*

**mis·shap·en** /ˌmɪsˈʃeɪpən/ adj. with a shape that is not normal or natural: *misshapen feet*

**mis·sile** 🅟 C1 /ˈmɪsaɪl; NAmE -sl/ noun 1 🅟 C1 a weapon that is sent through the air and that explodes when it hits the thing that it is aimed at: *nuclear missiles* ◇ *a missile base/site* ⊃ see also BALLISTIC MISSILE, CRUISE MISSILE, GUIDED MISSILE 2 an object that is thrown at sb to hurt them SYN projectile

## miss·ing 🅞 A2 /ˈmɪsɪŋ/ adj. 1 A2 that cannot be found or that is not in its usual place; that has been removed, lost or destroyed SYN lost: *I never found the missing piece.* ◇ *missing data* ◇ *My gloves have been missing for ages.* ◇ *Two files have gone missing.* ◇ (*especially BrE*) *Our cat's gone missing again.* ◇ *The book has two pages missing.* ◇ *The book has two missing pages.* ◇ ~ from sth *He didn't notice there was anything missing from his room until later on.* 2 A2 (of a person) not at home; not found: *a missing four-year-old girl* ◇ *They still hoped to find their missing son.* ◇ *a woman who went missing three months ago* ◇ *Posters of missing persons lined the walls.* 3 A2 (of a person) not present after an accident, battle, etc. but not known to have been killed: *He was reported missing, presumed dead.* ◇ *Many soldiers were listed as missing in action.* ⊃ see also MIA 4 A2 not included, often when it should have been: *Fill in the missing words in this text.* ◇ ~ from sth *There were several candidates missing from the list.*

**ˌmissing ˈlink** noun 1 [C] something, such as a piece of information, that is necessary for sb to be able to understand a problem or in order to make sth complete 2 **the missing link** [sing.] an animal similar to humans that was once thought to exist at the time that APES were developing into humans

**ˌmissing ˈperson** noun (*pl.* **missing persons**) a person who has disappeared from their home and whose family are trying to find them with the help of the police

## mis·sion 🅞 B2 /ˈmɪʃn/ noun

- **OFFICIAL JOB/GROUP** 1 🅟 B2 [C] an important official job that a person or group of people is given to do, especially when they are sent to another country: *a trade mission to China* ◇ *a diplomatic mission* ◇ *a rescue mission* ◇ *a fact-finding mission* ◇ *a mercy mission to aid homeless refugees* 2 [C] a group of people doing such a job; the place where they work: *He is the head of the British mission in Berlin.*
- **TEACHING CHRISTIANITY** 3 [U, C] the work of teaching people about Christianity, especially in a foreign country; a group of people doing such work: *Gandhi's attitude to*

*mission and conversion* ◊ *a Catholic mission in Africa* **4** [C] a building or group of buildings used by a Christian mission
- **YOUR DUTY 5** [C] particular work that you feel it is your duty to do SYN **vocation**: *Her mission in life was to work with the homeless.* ◊ *a man with a mission*
- **OF ARMED FORCES 6** [C] an important job that is done by a soldier, group of soldiers, etc: *The squadron flew on a reconnaissance mission.* ◊ *The military are fulfilling an important peacekeeping mission.*
- **SPACE FLIGHT 7** [C] a flight into space: *a US space mission* ⇒ WORDFINDER NOTE at SPACE

IDM **mission ac'complished** used when you have successfully completed what you have had to do  **mission im'possible** a difficult or impossible task

**mis·sion·ary** /ˈmɪʃənri; NAmE -ʃəneri/ *noun* (*pl.* -**ies**) a person who is sent to a foreign country to teach people about religion, especially Christianity: *Baptist missionaries* ◊ *missionary work* ◊ (*figurative*) *She spoke about her new project with missionary zeal* (= with great enthusiasm).

**the ˌmissionary poˈsition** *noun* [sing.] a position for having sex in which a man and a woman face each other, with the man lying on top of the woman

**ˌMission Conˈtrol** *noun* [sing. + sing. / pl. v.] the people on earth who control and communicate with the people on a flight into space: *This is Mission Control calling the space shuttle Discovery.*

**ˌmission-ˈcritical** *adj.* essential for an organization to function successfully: *mission-critical employees/software/applications*

**ˈmission statement** *noun* an official statement of the aims of a company or an organization

**mis·sis** /ˈmɪsɪz/ *noun* = MISSUS

**mis·sive** /ˈmɪsɪv/ *noun* (*formal or humorous*) a letter, especially a long or an official one

**mis·speak** /ˌmɪsˈspiːk/ *verb* [I, T] (*especially NAmE*) (**mis·spoke** /-ˈspəʊk/, **mis·spoken** /-ˈspəʊkən/) to say sth in a way that is not clear or not accurate: **~(to sb)** *He was confused and may have misspoken to reporters.* ◊ **~ yourself** *Let me rephrase, I think I misspoke myself.* ◊ **~ sth** *a misspoken word*

**mis·spell** /ˌmɪsˈspel/ *verb* (**mis·spelled, mis·spelled** or **mis·spelt, mis·spelt** /-ˈspelt/) **~ sth** to spell a word wrongly
▶ **mis·spell·ing** *noun* [C, U]

**mis·spent** /ˌmɪsˈspent/ *adj.* [usually before noun] (of time or money) spent in a careless rather than a useful way: *He joked that being good at cards was the sign of **a misspent youth** (= having wasted his time when he was young).*

**mis·step** /ˌmɪsˈstep/ *noun* (*especially NAmE*) a mistake; a wrong action

**mis·sus** /ˈmɪsɪz/ *noun* [usually sing.] (*BrE*) **1** (*also* **mis·sis**) (*informal, becoming old-fashioned*) (used after 'the', 'my', 'your', 'his') a man's wife: *How's the missus* (= your wife)? **2** (*informal*) (used especially by young people) girlfriend: *My missus doesn't like computer games.* ◊ *my current missus* **3** (*also* **mis·sis**) (*slang, becoming old-fashioned*) used by some people as a form of address to a woman whose name they do not know: *Is this your bag, missus?*

**missy** /ˈmɪsi/ *noun* (*especially NAmE, informal*) used when talking to a young girl, especially to express anger: *Don't you speak to me like that, missy!*

**mist** /mɪst/ *noun, verb*
■ *noun* **1** [U, C] a cloud of very small drops of water in the air just above the ground, that make it difficult to see HELP *Mist is less thick than* fog.: *The hills were shrouded in mist.* ◊ *Early morning mist patches will soon clear.* ◊ *The origins of the story are **lost in the mists of time*** (= forgotten because it happened such a long time ago). ◊ (*figurative*) *She gazed at the scene through a mist of tears.* ⇒ compare FOG ⇒ see also MISTY **2** [sing.] a fine SPRAY of liquid, for example from an AEROSOL can
■ *verb* **1** [T, I] **~ (sth) (up)** ~ **(over)** when sth such as glass **mists** or **is misted**, it becomes covered with very small drops of water, so that it is impossible to see through it: *The windows were misted up with condensation.* ◊ *As he came in from the cold, his glasses misted up.* **2** [I, T] if your eyes **mist** or sth **mists** them, they fill with tears: **~ (over /**

1001

**mistake**

**up)** *Her eyes misted over as she listened to the speech.* ◊ **~ sth (up)** *Tears misted his eyes.* **3** [T] **~ sth** to SPRAY sth, for example the leaves of a plant, with very small drops of liquid

▼ **HOMOPHONES**

**missed • mist** /mɪst/
- **missed** *verb* (*past tense, past participle of* **MISS**): *He missed his daughter when she left home.*
- **mist** *noun*: *They could barely see each other through the thick mist.*
- **mist** *verb*: *My glasses mist up every time I open the oven door!*

**mis·take** OPAL A1 /mɪˈsteɪk/ *noun, verb*
■ *noun* **1** OPAL A1 an action or an opinion that is not correct, or that produces a result that you did not want: *It's easy to **make a mistake**.* ◊ *Don't worry, we all **make mistakes**.* ◊ *You are making **a big mistake**.* ◊ *a terrible/serious/huge mistake* ◊ *It's **a common mistake*** (= one that a lot of people make). ◊ *You must try to **learn from your mistakes**.* ◊ *He is determined not to repeat the mistakes of his predecessors.* ◊ *This letter is addressed to someone else—there must be some mistake.* ◊ **the ~ of doing sth** *I made the mistake of giving him my address.* ◊ **it is a ~ to do sth** *It would be a mistake to ignore his opinion.* **2** OPAL B1 a word, figure, etc. that is not said or written down correctly SYN **error**: *It's a common mistake among learners of English.* ◊ *Her essay is full of spelling mistakes.* ◊ *If students correct their own mistakes, learning improves.* ◊ **~ (in) doing sth** *The waiter made a mistake (in) adding up the bill.*
IDM **and ˈno mistake** (*old-fashioned, especially BrE*) used to show that you are sure about the truth of what you have just said: *This is a strange business and no mistake.* **by miˈstake** by accident; without intending to: *I took your bag instead of mine by mistake.* **in miˈstake for sth** thinking that sth is sth else: *Children may eat pills in mistake for sweets.* **ˌmake no miˈstake (about sth)** used to emphasize what you are saying, especially when you want to warn sb about sth: *Make no mistake (about it), this is one crisis that won't just go away.*
■ *verb* OPAL B2 (**mis·took** /-ˈstʊk/, **mis·taken** /-ˈsteɪkən/) to not understand or judge sb/sth correctly SYN **misconstrue**: **~ sb/sth** *I admit that I mistook his intentions.* ◊ *There was no mistaking* (= it was impossible to mistake) *the bitterness in her voice.* ◊ **~ sb/sth as sb/sth** *I mistook her offer as*

▼ **SYNONYMS**

**mistake**
error • inaccuracy • slip • howler • misprint
These are all words for a word, figure or fact that is not said, written down or typed correctly.
**mistake** a word or figure that is not said or written down correctly: *It's a common mistake among learners of English.* ◊ *spelling mistakes*
**error** (*rather formal*) a word, figure, etc. that is not said or written down correctly: *There are too many errors in your work.* NOTE **Error** is a more formal way of saying **mistake**.
**inaccuracy** (*rather formal*) a piece of information that is not exactly correct: *The article is full of inaccuracies.*
**slip** a small mistake, usually made by being careless or not paying attention
**howler** (*informal, especially BrE*) a stupid mistake, especially in what sb says or writes: *The report is full of howlers.* NOTE A **howler** is usually an embarrassing mistake that shows that the person who made it does not know sth that they really should know.
**misprint** a small mistake in a printed text
PATTERNS
- a(n) mistake / error / inaccuracy / slip / howler / misprint in sth
- to **make** a(n) mistake / error / slip / howler
- to **contain / be full of** mistakes / errors / inaccuracies / howlers / misprints

# mistaken

*a threat.* ◊ **~ what …** *Sorry—I mistook what you said.* ◊ *My cab driver thought I must be mistaken about the new restaurant.*

**PHR V** **mi'stake sb/sth for sb/sth** to think wrongly that sb/sth is sb/sth else **SYN** **confuse with**: *I think you must be mistaking me for someone else.*

**mis·taken** /mɪˈsteɪkən/ *adj.* **1** [not usually before noun] **~(about sb/sth)** wrong in your opinion or judgement: *You are completely mistaken about Jane.* ◊ *Unless I'm very much mistaken, that's Paul's wife over there.* **2** based on a wrong opinion or bad judgement **SYN** **misguided**: *mistaken views/ideas* ◊ *I told her my secret in the mistaken belief that I could trust her.* ▸ **mis·taken·ly** *adv.*: *He mistakenly believed that his family would stand by him.*

**mi‚staken i'dentity** *noun* [U, C] a situation in which you think wrongly that you recognize sb or have found the person you are looking for: *He was shot in what seems to have been a case of mistaken identity.*

**mis·ter** /ˈmɪstə(r)/ *noun* **1** **Mister** the full form, not often used in writing, of the abbreviation *Mr* **2** (*informal*) used, especially by children, to address a man whose name they do not know: *Please, mister, can we have our ball back?*

**mis·time** /ˌmɪsˈtaɪm/ *verb* **~ sth** to do sth at the wrong time, especially when this makes sth bad or unpleasant happen: *The horse completely mistimed the jump and threw its rider.* ▸ **mis·tim·ing** *noun* [U]: *The failure of the talks was mainly due to insensitivity and mistiming.*

**mistle·toe** /ˈmɪsltəʊ, ˈmɪzl-/ *noun* [U] a plant with small shiny white BERRIES that grows on other trees and is often used as a decoration at Christmas: *the tradition of kissing under the mistletoe*

**mis·took** /mɪˈstʊk/ *past tense of* MISTAKE

**mis·treat** /ˌmɪsˈtriːt/ *verb* **~ sb/sth** to treat a person or an animal in a cruel, unkind or unfair way **SYN** **ill-treat**, **mal-treat** ▸ **mis·treat·ment** *noun* [U]

**mis·tress** /ˈmɪstrəs/ *noun* **1** a man's (usually a married man's) **mistress** is a woman that he is having a regular sexual relationship with and who is not his wife **2** (*BrE, old-fashioned*) a female teacher in a school, especially a private school: *the Biology mistress* **3** (in the past) the female head of a house, especially one who employed servants: *the mistress of the house* **4** (*old-fashioned*) the female owner of a dog or other animal **5** (*old-fashioned*) a woman who is in a position of authority or control, or who has a lot of skill in sth: *She wants to be mistress of her own affairs* (= to organize her own life). ⊃ compare MASTER

**mis·trial** /ˈmɪstraɪəl/ *noun* (*law*) **1** a trial that is not considered legally VALID because of a mistake in the way it has been conducted **2** (*NAmE*) a trial in which the JURY cannot reach a decision

**mis·trust** /ˌmɪsˈtrʌst/ *verb, noun*
▪ *verb* **~ sb/sth** to have no confidence in sb/sth because you think they may be harmful; to not trust sb/sth **SYN** **distrust** ⊃ note at DISTRUST
▪ *noun* [U, sing.] a feeling that you cannot trust sb/sth **SYN** **suspicion**: *a climate of mistrust and fear* ◊ *She has a deep mistrust of strangers.* ▸ **mis·trust·ful** /-fl/ *adj.*: **~ (of sb/sth)** *Some people are very mistrustful of computers.* **mis·trust·ful·ly** /-fəli/ *adv.*

**misty** /ˈmɪsti/ *adj.* **1** with a lot of MIST: *a misty morning* **2** not clear or bright **SYN** **blurred**: *misty memories* ◊ (*literary*) *His eyes grew misty* (= full of tears) *as he talked.*

**misty-'eyed** *adj.* feeling full of emotion and having tears in your eyes

**mis·un·der·stand** /ˌmɪsʌndəˈstænd; *NAmE* -dərˈs-/ *verb* [T, I] (**mis·un·der·stood, mis·un·der·stood** /-ˈstʊd/) to fail to understand sb/sth correctly: **~ (sb/sth)** *I completely misunderstood her intentions.* ◊ *Don't misunderstand me —I am grateful for all you've done.* ◊ *I thought he was her husband—I must have misunderstood.* ◊ **~ what, how, etc …** *She must have misunderstood what I was trying to say.*

**mis·un·der·stand·ing** /ˌmɪsʌndəˈstændɪŋ; *NAmE* -dərˈs-/ *noun* **1** [U, C] a situation in which a comment, an instruction, etc. is not understood correctly: *There must be some misunderstanding—I thought I ordered the smaller model.* ◊ **~ of/about sth** *There is still a fundamental misunderstanding about the real purpose of this work.* ◊ **~ between A and B** *All contracts are translated to avoid any misunderstanding between the companies.* **2** [C] a slight DISAGREEMENT or argument: *We had a little misunderstanding over the bill.*

**mis·un·der·stood** /ˌmɪsʌndəˈstʊd; *NAmE* -dərˈs-/ *adj.* having qualities that people do not see or fully understand: *a much misunderstood illness* ◊ *She felt very alone and misunderstood.*

**mis·use** *noun, verb*
▪ *noun* /ˌmɪsˈjuːs/ [U, C, usually sing.] (*formal*) the act of using sth in a dishonest way or for the wrong purpose **SYN** **abuse**: *alcohol/drug misuse* ◊ *the misuse of power/authority* ◊ *a misuse of public funds*
▪ *verb* /ˌmɪsˈjuːz/ (*formal*) **1 ~ sth** to use sth in the wrong way or for the wrong purpose **SYN** **abuse**, **ill-treat**: *individuals who misuse power for their own ends* **2 ~ sb** to treat sb badly and/or unfairly

**mite** /maɪt/ *noun* **1** [C] a very small creature like a spider that lives in soil, on plants or animals, or inside houses in carpets, etc: *house dust mites* ⊃ see also DUST MITE **2** [C] a small child or animal, especially one that you feel sorry for: *Poor little mite!* **3** **a mite** [sing.] (*old-fashioned*) (used as an adverb) a little; rather: *The place looked a mite expensive.*

**miter** (*US*) = MITRE

**miti·gate** /ˈmɪtɪɡeɪt/ *verb* **~ sth** (*formal*) to make sth less harmful, serious, etc. **SYN** **alleviate**: *action to mitigate poverty* ◊ *Soil erosion was mitigated by the planting of trees.*

**miti·gat·ing** /ˈmɪtɪɡeɪtɪŋ/ *adj.* [only before noun] **~ circumstances/factors** (*law or formal*) circumstances or factors that provide a reason that explains sb's actions or a crime, and make them easier to understand so that the punishment may be less severe

**miti·ga·tion** /ˌmɪtɪˈɡeɪʃn/ *noun* [U] (*formal*) a reduction in how unpleasant, serious, etc. sth is
**IDM** **in miti'gation** (*law*) with the aim of making a crime seem less serious or easier to forgive: *In mitigation, the defence lawyer said his client was seriously depressed at the time of the assault.*

**mi·to·chon·drion** /ˌmaɪtəʊˈkɒndriən; *NAmE* -ˈkɑːn-/ *noun* (*pl.* **mitochondria** /-driə/) (*biology*) a small part found in most cells, in which the energy in food is released ▸ **mito·chon·drial** /-əl/ *adj.*: *mitochondrial DNA*

**mi·tosis** /maɪˈtəʊsɪs/ *noun* [U] (*biology*) the usual process by which cells divide, producing two cells each with the same number of CHROMOSOMES as the original cell

**mitre** (*US* **miter**) /ˈmaɪtə(r)/ *noun, verb*
▪ *noun* **1** a tall pointed hat worn by BISHOPS at special ceremonies as a symbol of their position and authority **2** (*also* **'mitre joint**) a corner JOINT, formed by two pieces of wood each cut at an angle, as in a picture frame ⊃ picture at DOVETAIL
▪ *verb* **~ sth** (*specialist*) to join two pieces of wood together with a mitre JOINT

**mitt** /mɪt/ *noun* **1** = MITTEN **2** (in baseball) a large thick leather glove worn for catching the ball **3** [usually pl.] (*slang*) a hand: *I'd love to get my mitts on one of those.*

**mit·ten** /ˈmɪtn/ (*also* **mitt**) *noun* a type of glove that covers the four fingers together and the THUMB separately: *a pair of mittens*

**Mitty** ⊃ WALTER MITTY

**mix** /mɪks/ *verb, noun*
▪ *verb*
• COMBINE **1** [I, T] if two or more substances or things **mix** or you **mix** them, they combine, usually in a way that means they cannot easily be separated: *Oil and water do not mix.* ◊ **~ with sth** *Oil does not mix with water.* ◊ **~ A and B (together)** *Mix all the ingredients together in a bowl.* ◊ *If you mix blue and yellow, you get green.* ◊ **~ A with B** *I don't like to mix business with pleasure* (= combine social events

## ▼ SYNONYMS

### mix
**stir • mingle • blend**

These words all refer to substances, qualities, ideas or feelings combining or being combined.

**mix** to combine two or more substances, qualities, ideas or feelings, usually in a way that means they cannot easily be separated; to be combined in this way: *Mix all the ingredients together in a bowl.* ◊ *Oil and water do not mix.*

**stir** to move a liquid or substance around, using a spoon or sth similar, in order to mix it completely: *She stirred her tea.*

**mingle** to combine or be combined. NOTE **Mingle** can be used to talk about sounds, colours, feelings, ideas, qualities or substances. It is used in written English to talk about how a scene or event appears to sb or how they experience it: *The sounds of laughter and singing mingled in the evening air.* ◊ *He felt a kind of happiness mingled with regret.*

**blend** to mix two or more substances or flavours together; to be mixed together: *Blend the flour with the milk to make a smooth paste.*

**MIX OR BLEND?**
- If you **blend** things when you are cooking you usually combine them more completely than if you just **mix** them. **Mix** can be used to talk about colours, feelings or qualities as well as food and substances. In this meaning **blend** is mostly used in the context of cooking. It is also used to talk about art, music, fashion, etc. with the meaning of 'combine in an attractive way'.

**PATTERNS**
- to mix/mingle/blend (sth) **with** sth
- to mix/stir/mingle/blend sth **into** sth
- to mix/stir/mingle/blend sth **together**
- to mix/stir/blend **ingredients**
- to mix/mingle/blend **flavours**
- to mix/blend **colours**
- **mixed/mingled feelings**
- to mix/stir/blend sth **thoroughly/well/gently**

---

with doing business). ◊ ~ **A into B** *Smith often mixed sand into her paint to create a textured surface.* **2** B1 [T] to prepare sth by combining two or more different substances: ~*sth* *With this range of paints, you can mix your own colours.* ◊ *Be sure to mix the solution properly.* ◊ ~*sth* **for sb** *Why don't you mix a cocktail for our guests?* ◊ ~*sth* *Why don't you mix our guests a cocktail?* **3** [I] if two or more things, people or activities **do not mix**, they are likely to cause problems or danger if they are combined: *Children and fireworks don't mix.*
- MEET PEOPLE **4** B2 [I] ~ **(with sb)** to meet and talk to different people, especially at social events SYN **socialize**: *They don't mix much with the neighbours.*
- MUSIC/SOUNDS **5** [T] ~*sth* (*specialist*) to combine different recordings of voices and/or instruments to produce a single piece of music

IDM **be/get mixed 'up in sth** to be/become involved in sth, especially sth illegal or dishonest **be/get mixed 'up with sb** to be/become friendly with or involved with sb that other people do not approve of ˌmix and 'match to combine things in different ways for different purposes: *You can mix and match courses to suit your requirements.* ˌmix it (with sb) (*BrE*) (*NAmE* ˌmix it 'up (with sb)) (*informal*) to argue with sb or cause trouble ˌmix it 'up to do sth differently from the way it is usually done: *The show has been the same for ten years, so it's time to mix it up.*

PHRV ˌmix sth↔'in (with sth) to add one substance to others, especially in cooking: *Mix the remaining cream in with the sauce.* ˌmix sth 'into sth to combine one substance with others, especially in cooking: *Mix the fruit into the rest of the mixture.* ˌmix sth 'into/to sth to produce sth by combining two or more substances, especially in cooking SYN **blend**: *Add the milk and mix to a smooth dough.* ˌmix sth↔'up to change the order or arrangement of a group of things, especially by mistake or in a way that you do not want SYN **muddle**: *Someone has mixed up all the application forms.* ➔ related noun MIX-UP

---

1003      **mixed up**

ˌmix sb/sth 'up (with sb/sth) to think wrongly that sb/sth is sb/sth else SYN **confuse**: *I think you must be mixing me up with someone else.* ➔ see also MIXED UP

■ noun
- COMBINATION **1** B1 [C, usually sing.] a combination of different people or things SYN **blend**: *a school with a good social mix of children* ◊ *The town offers a fascinating mix of old and new.* ◊ *a pair of wool mix socks* (= made of wool and other materials) **2** B2 [C, U] a combination of things that you need to make sth, often sold as a powder to which you add water, etc: *a cake mix* ◊ *cement mix*
- IN POPULAR MUSIC **3** [C] = REMIX **4** [sing.] the particular way that instruments and voices are arranged in a piece of music **5** [C] an arrangement of several songs or pieces of music into one continuous piece, especially for dancing

IDM **throw, etc. sth in/into the mix** (*informal*) to add sth that has an effect on a situation: *When you throw into the mix the passion and energy of a young artist, you have a recipe for success.*

**mixed** 🔊 B2 /mɪkst/ *adj.* **1** B2 consisting of different qualities or elements: *a mixed diet* **2** B2 having both good and bad qualities or feelings: *I still have mixed feelings about going to Brazil* (= I am not sure what to think). ◊ *The results were decidedly mixed.* ◊ *The weather has been very mixed recently.* ◊ *Having a famous father can be a mixed blessing.* ◊ *The play was given a mixed reception by the critics* (= some liked it, some did not). ◊ *British athletes had mixed fortunes in yesterday's competition.* **3** B2 [only before noun] consisting of different kinds of people, for example, people from different races and cultures: *an ethnically mixed community* ◊ *people of mixed race* ◊ *a mixed marriage* (= between two people of different races or religions) **4** B2 [only before noun] consisting of different types of the same thing: *a mixed salad* ◊ *a mixed woodland of ash, oak and birch* ◊ (*BrE*) *The students in the class are of mixed ability* (= different levels of ability). **5** B2 [usually before noun] of or for both males and females: *a mixed school* ◊ *I'd rather not talk about it in mixed company.*

ˌmixed 'bag *noun* [sing.] (*informal*) a collection of things or people of very different types

ˌmixed 'blessing *noun* [usually sing.] something that has advantages and disadvantages

ˌmixed 'doubles *noun* [U + sing./pl. v.] (in tennis, etc.) a game in which a man and a woman play together against another man and woman

ˌmixed e'conomy *noun* an economic system in a country in which some companies are owned by the state and some are private

ˌmixed 'farming *noun* [U] a system of farming in which farmers both grow crops and keep animals

ˌmixed 'grill *noun* (*BrE*) a hot dish of different types of meat and vegetables that have been GRILLED: *a mixed grill of bacon, sausages, tomatoes and mushrooms*

ˌmixed martial 'arts *noun* [U] (*abbr.* MMA) an extreme sport in which two people fight each other using the techniques of BOXING, WRESTLING and MARTIAL ARTS

ˌmixed 'message *noun* a message that gives information in a way that is confusing and not consistent: *The candidate has sent mixed messages about his views on worker visas.*

ˌmixed 'metaphor *noun* a combination of two or more METAPHORS or idioms that produces a silly effect, for example, 'He put his foot down with a firm hand.'

ˌmixed 'number *noun* (*mathematics*) a number consisting of a whole number and a PROPER FRACTION, for example 3¼

ˌmixed-'race *adj.* (*also* bi-racial *especially in NAmE*) in connection with or containing people of two different races: *a mixed-race child* (= with parents of different races). HELP You can also say *a child of mixed race.* ➔ see also RACE *noun* (4)

ˌmixed 'up *adj.* (*informal*) confused because of mental, emotional or social problems: *a mixed-up kid/teenager* ➔ WORDFINDER NOTE at YOUNG

---

s see | t tea | v van | w wet | z zoo | ʃ shoe | ʒ vision | tʃ chain | dʒ jam | θ thin | ð this | ŋ sing

# mixer

**mixer** /ˈmɪksə(r)/ noun **1** a machine or device used for mixing things: *a food mixer* ◇ (*BrE*) *a mixer tap* (= one in which hot and cold water can be mixed together before it comes out of the pipe) ⊃ see also CEMENT MIXER **2** a drink such as fruit juice that is not alcoholic and that can be mixed with alcohol: *low-calorie mixers* **3** (*specialist*) a device used for mixing together different sound or picture signals in order to produce a single sound or picture; a person whose job is to operate this device
**IDM a good/bad ˈmixer** a person who finds it easy/difficult to talk to people they do not know, for example at a party

**mixie** /ˈmɪksi/ noun (*IndE*) an electric machine used for mixing food or liquid

**ˈmixing bowl** noun a large bowl for mixing food in

**ˈmixing desk** noun a piece of electronic equipment for mixing sounds, used especially when recording or broadcasting music

**mix·ture** ⓘ B1 /ˈmɪkstʃə(r)/ noun **1** B1 [C, usually sing.] a combination of different things: *~ of A and B The city is a mixture of old and new buildings.* ◇ *We listened to the news with a mixture of surprise and horror.* **2** B1 [C, U] a substance made by mixing other substances together: *cake mixture* ◇ *Add the eggs to the mixture and beat well.* ⊃ see also COUGH MIXTURE **3** [C] (*specialist*) a combination of two or more substances that mix together without any chemical reaction taking place: *Exposures to chemical mixtures have produced unexpected effects.* ⊃ compare COMPOUND **4** [U] the act of mixing different substances together

**ˈmix-up** noun (*informal*) a situation in which things go wrong, especially because sb has made a mistake SYN muddle: *There has been a mix-up over the dates.*

**ml** /mɪl/ abbr. (*pl.* **ml** or **mls**) (in writing) MILLILITRE: *25 ml water*

**MLA** /ˌem el ˈeɪ/ noun (in Canada and Northern Ireland) Member of the Legislative Assembly

**M'lud** /məˈlʌd/ noun (*BrE*) used when speaking to the judge in court: *My client pleads guilty, M'lud.*

**mm** abbr., exclamation
- **abbr.** (in writing) MILLIMETRE: *rainfall 6 mm* ◇ *a 35 mm camera*
- **exclamation** (*also* **mmm**) /m/ the way of writing the sound that people make to show that they are listening to sb or that they agree, they are thinking, they like sth, they are not sure, etc.: *Mm, I know what you mean.* ◇ *Mm, what lovely cake!* ◇ *Mmm, I'm not so sure that's a good idea.* ⊃ compare HMM

**MMA** /ˌem em ˈeɪ/ abbr. = MIXED MARTIAL ARTS

**MMO** /ˌem em ˈəʊ/ noun (*pl.* **MMOs**) (*also* **MMOG** /ˌem em əʊ ˈdʒiː/, **MMORPG** /ˌem em əʊ ˌɑː piː ˈdʒiː/; *NAmE* ˌɑːr/) an online video game in which thousands of people can play at the same time: *MMO games/players* ORIGIN The full form of the abbreviation **MMORPG** is *massively multiplayer online role-playing game.* ⊃ see also ROLE-PLAYING GAME

**MMR** /ˌem em ˈɑː(r)/ abbr. MEASLES, MUMPS, RUBELLA (= a VACCINATION given to small children to prevent these three diseases): *the MMR vaccine*

**MNA** /ˌem en ˈeɪ/ noun (*CanE*) Member of the National Assembly

**MNC** /ˌem en ˈsiː/ noun a large business company that does business in several different countries (the abbreviation for 'multinational corporation')

**mne·mon·ic** /nɪˈmɒnɪk; *NAmE* -ˈmɑːn-/ noun a word, sentence, poem, etc. that helps you to remember sth ▶ **mne·mon·ic** adj. [only before noun]: *a mnemonic device*

**MO** /ˌem ˈəʊ/ noun **1** (*BrE*) MEDICAL OFFICER **2** (*also* **M.O.**) MODUS OPERANDI

**mo** /məʊ/ noun [sing.] (*BrE, informal*) a very short period of time SYN moment: *See you in a mo!* ⊃ see also SLO-MO

**moa** /ˈməʊə/ noun a large bird that could not fly, that was found in New Zealand but is now EXTINCT (= no longer exists)

**moan** /məʊn/ verb, noun
- **verb 1** [I, T] (of a person) to make a long deep sound, usually because you are unhappy or suffering or are experiencing sexual pleasure SYN groan: *The injured man was lying on the ground, moaning.* ◇ *~ in/with sth to moan in/with pain* ◇ *+ speech 'I might never see you again,' she moaned.* **2** [I, T] *~ (at sb)* (*informal*) to complain about sth in a way that other people find annoying SYN grumble, whine: *~ (on) (about sth) (to sb) What are you moaning on about now?* ◇ *~ (at sb) (about sth) They're always moaning and groaning about how much they have to do.* ◇ *~ that … Bella moaned that her feet were cold.* ⓢ SYNONYMS at COMPLAIN **3** [I] (*literary*) (especially of the wind) to make a long deep sound ▶ **moan·er** noun
- **noun 1** [C] a long deep sound, usually made because you are unhappy or suffering or are experiencing sexual pleasure SYN groan: *a low moan of despair/anguish* **2** [C] (*informal*) a complaint about sth: *We had a good moan about work.* ◇ *His letters are full of the usual moans and groans.* **3** [sing.] (*literary*) a long deep sound, especially the sound that is made by the wind

**moat** /məʊt/ noun a deep wide channel that was dug around a castle, etc. and filled with water to make it more difficult for enemies to attack ▶ **moat·ed** adj. [usually before noun]: *a moated manor house*

**mob** ⓘ C1 /mɒb; *NAmE* mɑːb/ noun, verb
- **noun 1** ⓘ C1 [C, sing. + sing./pl. v.] a large crowd of people, especially one that may become violent or cause trouble: *an angry/unruly mob* ◇ *The mob was/were preparing to storm the building.* ◇ *an excited mob of fans* ◇ *mob rule* (= a situation in which a mob has control, rather than people in authority) ⊃ see also LYNCH MOB **2** [C, usually sing.] (*informal*) a group of people who are similar in some way SYN gang: *All the usual mob were there.* **3 the Mob** [sing.] (*informal*) the people involved in organized crime; the MAFIA **4** [C] (*AustralE, NZE*) a group of animals SYN flock, herd: *a mob of cattle* IDM see HEAVY adj.
- **verb** (-bb-) **1** *~ sth* if a crowd of birds or animals mob another bird or animal, they gather round it and attack it **2** [usually passive] if a person is mobbed by a crowd of people, the crowd gathers round them in order to see them and try and get their attention, sometimes in a slightly aggressive way SYN besiege: *be mobbed (by sb) The star was mobbed by eager fans.*

**mo·bile** ⓘ A2 W /ˈməʊbaɪl; *NAmE* -bl/ adj., noun
- **adj. 1** A2 [usually before noun] connected with mobile phones, tablets, etc: *What's your mobile number?* ◇ *Mobile users spent 35 per cent more time on their devices this year.* ◇ *mobile apps aimed at children* ◇ *mobile networks/operators* (= companies that provide mobile phone services) ◇ *mobile platforms/operating systems* **2** B1 [usually before noun] that is not fixed in one place and can be moved easily and quickly: *mobile equipment* ◇ *a mobile clinic/shop/library* (= one inside a vehicle) ⊃ compare STATIONARY **3** [not usually before noun] (of a person) able to move or travel around easily: *a kitchen especially designed for the elderly or people who are less mobile* ◇ *You really need to be mobile* (= have a car) *if you live in the country.* ⊃ compare IMMOBILE **4** (of people) able to change your social class, your job or the place where you live easily: *a highly mobile workforce* (= people who can move easily from place to place) ◇ *We have become an increasingly mobile society.* ⊃ see also UPWARDLY MOBILE **5** (of a face or its features) changing shape or expression easily and often
- **noun 1** A2 [C] (*BrE*) a mobile phone: *Call me on my mobile.* **2** B1 [U] (*BrE*) the internet when it is accessed on mobile phones: *the rise/importance/growth of mobile* ◇ *the growing use of mobile for banking services* ◇ *on~ The site works on both desktop and mobile.* **3** a decoration made from wire, etc. that is hung from the ceiling and that has small objects hanging from it which move when the air around them moves: *A colourful mobile moved gently above the baby's cot.*

**ˈmobile deˈvice** noun any small COMPUTING device, such as a smartphone or tablet

**ˈmobile ˈhome** noun **1** (*especially NAmE*) (*also* **trailer** *NAmE*) a small building for people to live in that is made in a factory and moved to a permanent place **2** (*BrE*) (*NAmE* **trailer**) a large CARAVAN that can be moved, sometimes with wheels, that is usually parked in one place and used for living in

**mobile library** (*BrE*) (*NAmE* **bookmobile**) *noun* a van that contains a library and travels from place to place so that people in different places can borrow books

**mobile phone** (*also* **mobile**) (*both BrE*) (*also* **cell phone, cellular phone**, *informal* **cell** *all especially NAmE*) *noun* a phone that does not have wires and works by radio, that you can carry with you and use anywhere: *Please make sure all mobile phones are switched off during the performance.*

**mobility** /məʊˈbɪləti/ *noun* [U] **1** the ability to move easily from one place, social class or job to another: *social/geographical/career mobility* ⇒ see also UPWARD MOBILITY **2** the ability to move or travel around easily: *An electric wheelchair has given her greater mobility.* ⇒ WORDFINDER NOTE at OLD

**mobility scooter** *noun* a type of light electric vehicle with a seat, a bar for controlling the direction in which it moves and three or more wheels, designed for people who are unable to move easily from one place to another because they are elderly, DISABLED, etc.

**mobilize** (*BrE also* **-ise**) /ˈməʊbəlaɪz/ *verb* **1** [T, I] ~ (sb) to work together in order to achieve a particular aim; to organize a group of people to do this **SYN rally**: *The unions mobilized thousands of workers in a protest against the cuts.* **2** [T] ~ sth to find and start to use sth that is needed for a particular purpose **SYN marshal**: *They were unable to mobilize the resources they needed.* **3** [T, I] ~ (sb/sth) if a country mobilizes its army, or if a country or army mobilizes, it makes itself ready to fight in a war: *The troops were ordered to mobilize.* ⇒ compare DEMOBILIZE ▶ **mobilization, -isation** /ˌməʊbɪləˈzeɪʃn; *NAmE* -ləˈz-/ *noun* [U, C]

**Möbius strip** (*also* **Moebius strip**) /ˈmɜːbiəs strɪp/ *noun* a surface with one continuous side, formed by joining the ends of a narrow piece of material after TWISTING one end through 180 degrees

Möbius strip

**mobster** /ˈmɒbstə(r); *NAmE* ˈmɑːb-/ *noun* a member of a group of people who are involved in organized crime

**moccasin** /ˈmɒkəsɪn; *NAmE* ˈmɑːk-/ *noun* a flat shoe that is made from soft leather and has large STITCHES around the front, of a type originally worn by Native Americans ⇒ see also WATER MOCCASIN

**mocha** /ˈmɒkə; *NAmE* ˈməʊkə/ *noun* **1** [U] a type of coffee of very good quality **2** [C, U] a drink made with this type of coffee, often with chocolate added

**mock** /mɒk; *NAmE* mɑːk/ *verb, adj., noun*
■ *verb* **1** [T, I] ~ (sb/sth) | ~ (sb) + speech to laugh at sb/sth in an unkind way, especially by copying what they say or do **SYN make fun of**: *He's always mocking my French accent.* ◊ *The other children mocked her, laughing behind their hands.* ◊ *You can mock, but at least I'm willing to have a try!* **2** [T] ~ sth (*formal*) to show no respect for sth: *The new exam mocked the needs of the majority of children.* ▶ **mocker** *noun*
**PHRV mock sth↔up** to create a copy or sample of sth: *We've mocked up a couple of sample designs.*
■ *adj.* [only before noun] **1** not sincere **SYN sham**: *mock horror/surprise* **2** that is a copy of sth; not real: *a mock election* ◊ *a mock interview/examination* (= used to practise for the real one)
■ *noun* (in the UK) a practice exam that you do before the official one: *The mocks are in November.* ◊ *What did you get in the mock?*

**mockers** /ˈmɒkəz; *NAmE* ˈmɑːkərz/ *noun* [pl.]
**IDM put the mockers on sth/sb** (*BrE, informal*) to stop sth from happening; to bring bad luck to sth/sb: *We were going to have a barbecue but the rain put the mockers on that idea.*

**mockery** /ˈmɒkəri; *NAmE* ˈmɑːk-/ *noun* (*pl.* **-ies**) **1** [U, C] comments or actions that are intended to make sb/sth seem silly **SYN ridicule, scorn**: *She couldn't stand any more of their mockery.* **2** [C, *usually sing.*] (*disapproving*) an

---

action, a decision, etc. that is a failure and that is not as it is supposed to be **SYN travesty**: *It was a mockery of a trial.*
**IDM make a mockery of sth** to make sth seem silly or without effect: *The trial made a mockery of justice.*

**mocking** /ˈmɒkɪŋ; *NAmE* ˈmɑːk-/ *adj.* (of behaviour, an expression, etc.) showing that you think sb/sth is silly **SYN contemptuous**: *a mocking smile* ◊ *Her voice was faintly mocking.* ▶ **mockingly** *adv.*

**mockingbird** /ˈmɒkɪŋbɜːd; *NAmE* ˈmɑːkɪŋbɜːrd/ *noun* a grey and white American bird that can copy the songs of other birds

**mock-up** *noun* a model or a copy of sth, often the same size as it, that is used for testing, or for showing people what the real thing will look like

**MOD** /ˌem əʊ ˈdiː/ *abbr.* Ministry of Defence (the government department in the UK that is responsible for defence)

**mod** /mɒd; *NAmE* mɑːd/ *noun, verb*
■ *noun* (*informal, computing*) a piece of equipment or a computer program that has been changed so that it works in a way that was not intended by the producer: *The mod in question allows players to zoom right in to the action.*
■ *verb* (-**dd**-) (*informal, computing*) ~ sth to change a piece of equipment or a computer program so that it works in a way that was not intended by the producer: *a specially modded system*

**modal** /ˈməʊdl/ (*also* **modal verb**, **modal auxiliary**, **modal auxiliary verb**) *noun* (*grammar*) a verb such as *can*, *may* or *will* that is used with another verb (not a modal) to express possibility, permission, intention, etc. ▶ **modal** *adj.* ⇒ compare AUXILIARY

▼ **GRAMMAR POINT**

**modal verbs**

- The **modal verbs** are **can**, **could**, **may**, **might**, **must**, **ought to**, **shall**, **should**, **will** and **would**. **Dare**, **need**, **have to** and **used to** also share some of the features of modal verbs.
- Modal verbs have only one form. They have no *-ing* or *-ed* forms and do not add *-s* to the 3rd person singular form: *He can speak three languages.* ◊ *She will try and visit tomorrow.*
- Modal verbs are followed by the infinitive of another verb without **to**. The exceptions are **ought to**, **have to** and **used to**: *You must find a job.* ◊ *You ought to stop smoking.* ◊ *I used to smoke but I gave up two years ago.*
- Questions are formed without **do/does** in the present, or **did** in the past: *Can I invite Mary?* ◊ *Should I have invited Mary?*
- Negative sentences are formed with **not** or the short form **-n't** and do not use **do/does** or **did**.

You will find more help with how to use modal verbs at the dictionary entries for each verb.

**modality** /məʊˈdæləti/ *noun* (*pl.* **-ies**) **1** [C] (*formal*) the particular way in which sth exists, is experienced or is done: *They are researching a different modality of treatment for the disease.* **2** [U] (*linguistics*) the idea expressed by modals **3** [C] (*biology*) the kind of senses that the body uses to experience things: *the visual and auditory modalities*

**mod con** /ˌmɒd ˈkɒn; *NAmE* ˌmɑːd ˈkɑːn/ *noun* [usually pl.] (*BrE, informal*) (especially in advertisements) any of the things in a house or flat that make living there easier and more comfortable

**modding** /ˈmɒdɪŋ; *NAmE* ˈmɑːd-/ *noun* [U] (*informal, computing*) the activity of changing a piece of equipment or a computer program so that it works in a way that was not intended by the producer: *There are stiff penalties for illegal modding.*

**mode** /məʊd/ *noun* **1** [C] a particular way of doing sth; a particular type of sth: *a mode of communication* ◊ *a mode of behaviour* ◊ *environment-friendly modes of transport* **2** [C, U] the way in which a piece of equipment is set to perform a particular task: *Switch the*

# model

camera into the automatic *mode*. ⇒ see also SAFE MODE **3** [U, C] a particular way of feeling or behaving: *to be in holiday mode* **4** [C, usually sing.] a particular style or fashion in clothes, art, etc: *a pop video made by a director who really understands the mode* ⇒ see also MODISH **5** [sing.] (*specialist*) a set of notes in music that form a SCALE: *major/minor mode* **6** [sing.] (*mathematics*) the value that appears most frequently in a series of numbers

## model /mɒdl; NAmE ˈmɑːdl/ noun, verb

■ noun
- SMALL COPY **1** a copy of sth, usually smaller than the original object: *a working model* (= one in which the parts move) *of a fire engine* ◊ *a model aeroplane* ◊ *The architect had produced a scale model of the proposed shopping complex.*
- EXAMPLE TO COPY **2** something such as a text or a system that can be used as an example for other people to copy: *Look at the writing model on page 58.* ◊ *a model text/essay* ◊ *The nation's constitution provided a model that other countries followed.* ◊ *Different funding models are used in schools.* **3** (*approving*) a person or thing that is considered an excellent example of sth: *It was a model of clarity.* ◊ *a model student* ◊ *a model farm* (= one that has been specially designed to work well) ⇒ see also ROLE MODEL
- FASHION **4** a person whose job is to wear and show new styles of clothes and be photographed wearing them: *a fashion model* ◊ *a male model* ⇒ see also GLAMOUR MODEL
- FOR ARTIST **5** a person who is employed to be painted, drawn, photographed, etc. by an artist or photographer
- DESIGN **6** a particular design or type of product: *The latest models will be on display at the motor show.*
- IN BUSINESS **7** (usually in compounds) a way of running a business, based on a particular way of getting the money you need and identifying and reaching your customers; a type of BUSINESS MODEL: *They may abandon the traditional cooperative model.* ◊ **under a ... ~** *Under a subscription model, consumers will typically pay a monthly fee to access the online library.*
- DESCRIPTION OF SYSTEM **8** a simple description of a system, used for explaining how sth works or calculating what might happen, etc: *the standard economic model of supply and demand* ◊ *to propose/construct/test a model* ◊ *She developed a computer model to help farmers with pest control.* ◊ **according to a ~** *According to this model, by the middle of the century temperatures will rise by 1–3°.*

■ verb (-ll-, US -l-)
- CREATE COPY **1** [T] ~ **sth** to create a copy or description of an activity, a situation, etc. so that you can study it before dealing with the real thing SYN simulate: *The program can model a typical home page for you.* ◊ *We can accurately model the development process.* **2** ~ **sth** to represent sth, especially in a diagram: *This finite set of data can be modelled by a growth curve.*
- CLAY, ETC. **3** [T] ~ **sth** to shape CLAY, etc. in order to make sth: *a statue modelled in bronze*
- CLOTHES **4** [T] ~ **sth (for sb)** to wear clothes in order to show them to people who might want to buy them: *The wedding gown is being modelled for us by the designer's daughter.*
- WORK AS MODEL **5** [I] to work as a model for an artist or in the fashion industry: *Ralph's been modelling since he was 16.*
- SET AN EXAMPLE **6** [T] ~ **sth** to set an example of behaviour that you want other people to copy: *Managers must model behaviour that is open and vulnerable.*

**PHRV** **ˈmodel yourself on sb** to copy the behaviour, style, etc. of sb you like and respect in order to be like them: *As a politician, he modelled himself on Churchill.* **ˈmodel sth on/upon/after sth** to make sth so that it looks, works, etc. like sth else: *The country's parliament is modelled on the British system.* ◊ *This system is closely modelled upon one used in French hospitals.* ◊ *A new town centre is modelled after Italian hill towns.*

**ˈmodel home** (*NAmE*) (*BrE* **ˈshow house**, **ˈshow home**) *noun* a house in a group of new houses that has been painted and filled with furniture, so that people who might want to buy one of the houses can see what they will be like

**modˈelˈler** (*US* **modˈelˈer**) /ˈmɒdələ(r); NAmE ˈmɑːd-/ *noun* **1** a person who makes models of objects **2** a person who makes a simple description of a system or a process that can be used to explain it, etc.

**modˈelˈling** (*US* **modˈelˈing**) /ˈmɒdəlɪŋ; NAmE ˈmɑːd-/ *noun* [U] **1** the work of a fashion model: *a career in modelling* ◊ *a modelling agency* **2** the activity of making models of objects: *clay modelling* **3** the work of making a simple description of a system or a process that can be used to explain it, etc: *mathematical/statistical/computer modelling* ◊ *macroeconomic modelling and policy analysis*

**ˈmodel ˈvillage** *noun* **1** a small model of a village, or a collection of small models of famous buildings arranged like a village **2** (*old use*) a village with good-quality houses, especially one built in the past by an employer for workers to live in

**modem** /ˈməʊdem; NAmE -dəm, -dem/ *noun* a device that is used at both ends of a connection between two computers to allow data to be sent over phone lines

**modˈerˈate** *adj., verb, noun*

■ *adj.* /ˈmɒdərət; NAmE ˈmɑːd-/ **1** that is neither very good, large, hot, etc. nor very bad, small, cold, etc: *students of moderate ability* ◊ *Even moderate amounts of the drug can be fatal.* ◊ *The team enjoyed only moderate success last season.* ◊ *Cook over a moderate heat.* **2** having or showing opinions, especially about politics, that are not extreme: *moderate views/policies* ◊ *a moderate socialist* **3** staying within limits that are considered to be reasonable by most people: *a moderate drinker* ◊ *moderate wage demands* **OPP** extreme, immoderate

■ *verb* /ˈmɒdəreɪt; NAmE ˈmɑːd-/ **1** [I, T] (*formal*) to become or make sth become less extreme, severe, etc: *By evening the wind had moderated slightly.* ◊ ~ **sth** *We agreed to moderate our original demands.* **2** [T, I] ~ **(sth)** (*BrE*) to check that an exam has been marked fairly and in the same way by different people **3** [T, I] ~ **(sth)** to be in charge of a discussion or debate and make sure it is fair: *The television debate was moderated by a law professor.* **4** [T] ~ **sth** to be responsible for preventing offensive material from being published on a website; to remove offensive material from a website: *to moderate an internet forum* ◊ *Comments on this article will be moderated.*

■ *noun* /ˈmɒdərət; NAmE ˈmɑːd-/ a person who has opinions, especially about politics, that are not extreme ⇒ compare EXTREMIST

**modˈerˈateˈly** /ˈmɒdərətli; NAmE ˈmɑːd-/ *adv.* **1** to an average extent; fairly but not very SYN **reasonably**: *a moderately successful career* ◊ *She only did moderately well in the exam.* ◊ *Cook in a moderately hot oven.* **2** within reasonable limits: *He only drinks (alcohol) moderately.*

**modˈerˈaˈtion** /ˌmɒdəˈreɪʃn; NAmE ˌmɑːd-/ *noun* [U] **1** the quality of being reasonable and not being extreme: *There was a call for moderation on the part of the trade unions.* ◊ **in ~** *Alcohol should only ever be taken in moderation* (= in small quantities). **2** (*BrE*) (*in education*) the process of making sure that the same standards are used by different people in marking exams, etc. **3** the process of checking content that is added to a website and removing any material that is offensive: *Comment moderation makes people think twice before posting.*

**modˈerˈaˈtor** /ˈmɒdəreɪtə(r); NAmE ˈmɑːd-/ *noun* **1** a person whose job is to help people or groups who disagree to reach an agreement ⇒ see also MEDIATOR **2** (*especially NAmE*) a person whose job is to make sure that a discussion or a debate is fair **3** (*BrE*) a person whose job is to make sure that an exam is marked fairly **4** a person who is responsible for preventing offensive material from being published on a website: *moderators of online discussion groups* **5** **Moderator** a religious leader in the Presbyterian Church who is in charge of the Church council

**modˈern** /ˈmɒdn; NAmE ˈmɑːdərn/ *adj.* **1** [only before noun] of the present time or recent times SYN **contemporary**: *the modern industrial world* ◊ *the wonders of modern science* ◊ *modern society* ◊ *in modern times* ◊ *They are modern day heroes, battling for change.* ◊ *Modern European history* ◊ *modern Greek*

Stress is a major problem of modern life. **2** [only before noun] (of styles in art, music, fashion, etc.) new and intended to be different from traditional styles SYN **contemporary**: *The gallery has regular exhibitions of modern art.* ◊ *modern architecture/dance/drama/jazz* ◊ *modern American cinema* ◊ *modern and contemporary sculpture* **3** (*usually approving*) using the latest technology, designs, materials, ideas, etc. SYN **up to date**: *a modern computer system* ◊ *modern methods of farming* ◊ *the most modern, well-equipped hospital in London* ◊ **modern** *aircraft technology* ◊ *The school is thoroughly modern in its approach.* **4** (of ways of behaving, thinking, etc.) new and not always accepted by most members of society: *She has very modern ideas about educating her children.*

**modern 'dance** *noun* [U] a form of dance that was developed in the early 20th century by people who did not like the limits of traditional BALLET

**modern-'day** *adj.* [only before noun] **1** of the present time SYN **contemporary**: *modern-day America* **2** used to describe a modern form of sb/sth, usually sb/sth bad or unpleasant, that existed in the past: *It has been called modern-day slavery.*

**modern 'English** *noun* [U] the English language in the form it has been in since about 1500

**mod·ern·ism** /ˈmɒdənɪzəm/; *NAmE* ˈmɑːdərn-/ *noun* [U] **1** modern ideas or methods **2** a style and movement in art, architecture and literature popular in the early 20th century in which modern ideas, methods and materials were used rather than traditional ones ⊃ compare POST-MODERNISM ▶ **mod·ern·ist** /-nɪst/ *adj.* [only before noun]: *modernist art* **mod·ern·ist** *noun*

**mod·ern·is·tic** /ˌmɒdəˈnɪstɪk; *NAmE* ˌmɑːdərˈn-/ *adj.* (of a painting, building, piece of furniture, etc.) painted, designed, etc. in a very modern style

**mod·ern·ity** /məˈdɜːnəti; *NAmE* -ˈdɜːrn-/ *noun* [U] the condition of being new and modern

**mod·ern·ize** (*BrE also* **-ise**) /ˈmɒdənaɪz; *NAmE* ˈmɑːdərn-/ *verb* **1** [T] ~ **sth** to make a system, methods, etc. more modern and more suitable for use at the present time SYN **update**: *The company is investing $9 million to modernize its factories.* **2** [I] to start using modern equipment, ideas, etc: *Unfortunately we lack the resources to modernize.* ▶ **mod·ern·iza·tion**, **-isa·tion** /ˌmɒdənaɪˈzeɪʃn; *NAmE* ˌmɑːdərnəˈz-/ *noun* [U]

**modern 'language** *noun* (*especially BrE*) a language that is spoken or written now, especially a European language, such as French or Spanish, that you study at school, university or college: *the department of modern languages* ◊ *a degree in modern languages*

**mod·est** /ˈmɒdɪst; *NAmE* ˈmɑːd-/ *adj.* **1** not very large, expensive, important, etc: *modest improvements/reforms* ◊ *He charged a relatively modest fee.* ◊ *a modest little house* ◊ *The research was carried out on a modest scale.* **2** (*approving*) not talking much about your own abilities or possessions: *She's very modest about her success.* ◊ *You're too modest!* OPP **immodest** **3** (of people, especially women, or their clothes) shy about showing much of the body; not intended to attract attention, especially in a sexual way SYN **demure**: *a modest dress* OPP **immodest** ▶ **mod·est·ly** *adv.*

**mod·esty** /ˈmɒdəsti; *NAmE* ˈmɑːd-/ *noun* [U] **1** the fact of not talking much about your abilities or possessions: *He accepted the award with characteristic modesty.* ◊ *I hate false* (= pretended) *modesty.* **2** the action of behaving or dressing so that you do not show your body or attract sexual attention **3** the state of being not very large, expensive, important, etc: *They tried to disguise the modesty of their achievements.*

**modi·cum** /ˈmɒdɪkəm/; *NAmE* ˈmɑːd-/ *noun* [sing.] (*formal*) a fairly small amount, especially of sth good or pleasant: *They should win, given a modicum of luck.*

**modi·fi·ca·tion** /ˌmɒdɪfɪˈkeɪʃn/; *NAmE* ˌmɑːd-/ *noun* [U, C] ~ **(of/to/in sth)** the act or process of changing sth in order to improve it or make it more acceptable; a change that is made SYN **adaptation**: *Considerable modification of the existing system is needed.* ◊ *It might be necessary to make a few slight modifications to the design.*

1007

**modi·fier** /ˈmɒdɪfaɪə(r)/; *NAmE* ˈmɑːd-/ *noun* (*grammar*) a word or group of words that describes a noun phrase or limits its meaning in some way

**mod·ify** /ˈmɒdɪfaɪ/; *NAmE* ˈmɑːd-/ *verb* (**modi·fies, modi·fy·ing, modi·fied, modi·fied**) **1** ~ **sth** to change sth slightly, especially in order to make it more suitable for a particular purpose SYN **adapt**: *Patients are taught how to modify their diet.* ◊ *The software we use has been modified for us.* ◊ *The law has been significantly modified since that ruling.* ◊ *heavily/highly modified* ◊ *A modified version of my article was published in the newspaper.* ⊃ see also GENETICALLY MODIFIED **2** ~ **sth** to make sth less extreme SYN **adjust**: *She refused to modify her behaviour.* ◊ *He later modified his view of the party.* **3** ~ **sth** (*grammar*) a word, such as an adjective or adverb, that **modifies** another word or group of words describes it or limits its meaning in some way: *In 'walk slowly', the adverb 'slowly' modifies the verb 'walk'.*

**mod·ish** /ˈməʊdɪʃ/ *adj.* (*sometimes disapproving*) fashionable

**modu·lar** /ˈmɒdjələ(r)/; *NAmE* ˈmɑːdʒə-/ *adj.* **1** (of a course of study, especially at a British university or college) consisting of separate units from which students may choose several: *a modular course* **2** (of machines, buildings, etc.) consisting of separate parts or units that can be joined together

**modu·late** /ˈmɒdjəleɪt/; *NAmE* ˈmɑːdʒə-/ *verb* **1** [T] ~ **sth** (*formal*) to change the quality of your voice in order to create a particular effect by making it louder, softer, lower, etc. **2** [I] ~ **(from sth) (to/into sth)** (*music*) to change from one musical KEY (= set of notes) to another **3** [T] ~ **sth** (*specialist*) to affect sth so that it becomes more regular, slower, etc: *drugs that effectively modulate the disease process* **4** [T] ~ **sth** (*specialist*) to change the rate at which a sound wave or radio signal VIBRATES (= the frequency) so that it is clearer ▶ **modu·la·tion** /ˌmɒdjəˈleɪʃn/; *NAmE* ˌmɑːdʒə-/ *noun* [U, C] ⊃ see also AM *abbr.*, FREQUENCY MODULATION at FM

**mod·ule** /ˈmɒdjuːl/; *NAmE* ˈmɑːdʒuːl/ *noun* **1** a unit that can form part of a course of study, especially at a college or university in the UK: *The course consists of ten core modules and five optional modules.* **2** (*computing*) a unit of a computer system or program that has a particular function **3** one of a set of separate parts or units that can be joined together to make a machine, a piece of furniture, a building, etc. **4** a unit of a SPACECRAFT that can function independently of the main part: *the lunar module*

**modus op·er·andi** /ˌməʊdəs ˌɒpəˈrændiː/; *NAmE* ˌɑːp-/ *noun* [sing.] (*from Latin, formal*) (*abbr.* **MO**) a particular method of working

**modus vi·vendi** /ˌməʊdəs vɪˈvendiː/ *noun* [sing.] (*from Latin, formal*) an arrangement that is made between people, institutions or countries who have very different opinions or ideas, so that they can live or work together without arguing

**Moe·bius strip** = MÖBIUS STRIP

**mog·gie** (*also* **moggy**) /ˈmɒgi/; *NAmE* ˈmɑːgi/ *noun* (*pl.* **-ies**) (*BrE, informal*) a cat, especially an ordinary one of no particular BREED

**mogul** /ˈməʊgl/ *noun* **1** a very rich, important and powerful person SYN **magnate**: *a movie mogul* **2** *Mogul* (*also* **Moghul, Mughal**) /ˈmuːgɑːl/) a member of the Muslim DYNASTY (= ruling family) that ruled much of India from the 16th to the 19th century **3** a raised area of hard snow that you jump over when you are skiing. Moguls are either formed naturally by skiers turning, or artificially, for use in skiing competitions.

**mo·hair** /ˈməʊheə(r)/; *NAmE* -her/ *noun* [U] soft wool or cloth made from the fine hair of the ANGORA GOAT, used for making clothes: *a mohair sweater*

**Mo·ham·med** = MUHAMMAD

**Mo·hawk** /ˈməʊhɔːk/ *noun* (*pl.* **Mohawk** *or* **Mohawks**) a member of a Native American people, many of whom live in New York State and Canada

**Mo·hi·can** /məʊˈhiːkən/ (*especially BrE*) (*also* **Mo·hawk** /ˈməʊhɔːk/ *especially in NAmE*) *noun* a way of cutting the

# moi

hair in which it is removed from the head by SHAVING except for a narrow area of hair in the middle that is sometimes made to stick up

**moi** /mwɑː/ *exclamation* (*humorous, from French*) me: *'Did you eat all the biscuits?' 'Who? Moi?'*

**moire** /mwɑː(r)/ (*also* **moiré** /ˈmwɑːreɪ; *NAmE* mwɑːˈreɪ/) *noun* [U] a type of silk cloth with a pattern on its surface like small waves

**moist** /mɔɪst/ *adj.* slightly wet: *warm moist air* ◊ *a rich moist cake* ◊ *Water the plants regularly to keep the soil moist.* ◊ *Her eyes were moist* (= with tears). ⊃ SYNONYMS at WET ▶ **moist·ness** *noun* [U]

**moisten** /ˈmɔɪsn/ *verb* [T, I] ~ (sth) to become or make sth slightly wet: *He moistened his lips before he spoke.*

**moisture** /ˈmɔɪstʃə(r)/ *noun* [U] very small drops of water or other liquid that are present in the air, on a surface or in a substance: *the skin's natural moisture* ◊ *a material that is designed to absorb/retain moisture*

**mois·tur·ize** (*BrE also* **-ise**) /ˈmɔɪstʃəraɪz/ *verb* [T, I] ~ (sth) to put a special cream on your skin to make it less dry: *a moisturizing cream/lotion* ◊ *a product that soothes and moisturizes*

**mois·tur·izer** (*BrE also* **-iser**) /ˈmɔɪstʃəraɪzə(r)/ *noun* [C, U] a cream that is used to make the skin less dry ⊃ WORDFINDER NOTE at MAKE-UP

**mojo** /ˈməʊdʒəʊ/ *noun* (*pl.* **mojos**) **1** [U] magic power **2** [C] a small object, or a collection of small objects in a bag, that is believed to have magic powers **3** [U] the power of sb's attractive personality

**molar** /ˈməʊlə(r)/ *noun* any of the large, flat teeth at the back of the mouth used for CRUSHING and CHEWING food ⊃ compare CANINE, INCISOR, PREMOLAR, WISDOM TOOTH

**mo·las·ses** /məˈlæsɪz/ *noun* [U] **1** a thick black sweet sticky liquid produced when sugar is REFINED (= made pure) **2** (*NAmE*) (*BrE* **trea·cle**) this thick black sticky liquid when it is used in cooking

**mold, mold·er, mold·ing, moldy** (*US*) = MOULD, MOULDER, MOULDING, MOULDY

**mole** /məʊl/ *noun* **1** a small animal with dark grey fur, that is almost blind and digs tunnels under the ground to live in ⊃ see also MOLEHILL **2** a small dark brown mark on the skin, sometimes slightly higher than the skin around it ⊃ compare FRECKLE **3** a person who works within an organization and secretly passes important information to another organization or country **4** (*chemistry*) a unit for measuring the amount of substance

**mol·ecule** /ˈmɒlɪkjuːl; *NAmE* ˈmɑːl-/ *noun* (*chemistry*) a group of ATOMS that forms the smallest unit that a substance can be divided into without a change in its chemical nature: *A molecule of water consists of two atoms of hydrogen and one atom of oxygen.* ⊃ WORDFINDER NOTE at CHEMISTRY ▶ **mo·lec·ular** /məˈlekjələ(r)/ *adj.* [only before noun]: *molecular structure/biology*

**mole·hill** /ˈməʊlhɪl/ *noun* a small pile of earth that a MOLE leaves on the surface of the ground when it digs underground IDM see MOUNTAIN

**mole·skin** /ˈməʊlskɪn/ *noun* [U] a type of strong cotton cloth with a soft surface, used for making clothes

**mo·lest** /məˈlest/ *verb* **1** ~ sb to attack sb, especially a child, sexually SYN **abuse 2** ~ sb (*old-fashioned*) to attack sb physically ▶ **mo·lest·ation** /ˌmɒleˈsteɪʃn; *NAmE* ˌməʊl-/ *noun* [U, C] **mo·lest·er** /məˈlestə(r)/ *noun: a child molester*

**moll** /mɒl; *NAmE* mɑːl/ *noun* (*old-fashioned, slang*) the female friend of a criminal

**mol·lify** /ˈmɒlɪfaɪ; *NAmE* ˈmɑːl-/ *verb* (**mol·li·fies, mol·li·fy·ing, mol·li·fied, mol·li·fied**) ~ sb (*formal*) to make sb feel less angry or upset SYN **placate**

**mol·lusc** (*BrE*) (*US* **mol·lusk**) /ˈmɒləsk; *NAmE* ˈmɑːl-/ *noun* (*specialist*) any creature with a soft body that is not divided into different sections, and usually a hard outer shell. SNAILS and SLUGS are molluscs. ⊃ compare BIVALVE, SHELLFISH

**molly·cod·dle** /ˈmɒlikɒdl; *NAmE* ˈmɑːlikɑːdl/ *verb* (*disapproving, becoming old-fashioned*) ~ sb to protect sb too much and make their life too comfortable and safe ⊃ compare CODDLE

**Molo·tov cock·tail** /ˌmɒlətɒf ˈkɒkteɪl; *NAmE* ˌmɑːlətɔːf ˈkɑːk-/ (*BrE also* **petrol bomb**) *noun* a simple bomb that consists of a bottle filled with petrol and a piece of cloth in the end that is made to burn just before the bomb is thrown

**molt** (*US*) = MOULT

**mol·ten** /ˈməʊltən/ *adj.* (of metal, rock or glass) heated to a very high temperature so that it becomes liquid

**mo·lyb·denum** /məˈlɪbdənəm/ *noun* [U] (*symb.* **Mo**) a chemical element. Molybdenum is a silver-grey metal that breaks easily and is used in some ALLOY steels.

**mom** /mɒm; *NAmE* mɑːm/ *noun* (*NAmE*) (*BrE* **mum**) (*informal*) a mother: *Where's my mom?* ◊ *Mom and Dad* ◊ *Are you listening, Mom?* ⊃ see also SOCCER MOM

**mom-and-pop** *adj.* [only before noun] (*NAmE*) (of a shop/store or business) owned and run by a husband and wife, or by a family

**mo·ment** /ˈməʊmənt/ *noun* **1** a very short period of time: *Could you wait a moment, please?* ◊ *One moment, please* (= Please wait a short time). ◊ **for a ~** *He thought for a moment before replying.* ◊ **in a ~** *I'll be back in a moment.* ◊ *Have you got a moment?* ◊ *This won't take a moment.* ◊ *We arrived* **not a moment too soon** (= almost too late). ◊ *Moments later* (= a very short time later), *I heard a terrible crash.* **2** [sing.] an exact point in time: **at the ~** *We're busy at the moment* (= now). ◊ *At that very moment, the phone rang.* ◊ **in a ~ of sth** *I agreed in a moment of weakness.* ◊ **From that ~ on** *From that moment on, she never felt really well again.* ⊃ see also EUREKA MOMENT **3** [C] a good time for doing sth; an opportunity: *I'm waiting for* **the right moment** *to tell him the bad news.* ◊ *Have I caught you at a bad moment?* **4** [C] a particular time in sb's life, or in the course of an event or the development of sth: *That was one of the happiest moments of my life.* ◊ *The film has many memorable moments.* ◊ *This referendum is a* **defining moment** *for our nation.* ◊ *I managed to* **capture the moment** *on film.* IDM **(at) any moment (now)** very soon: *Hurry up! He'll be back any moment now.* **at this moment in time** (*informal*) now, at the present time: *At this moment in time, I don't know what my decision will be.* **be having a moment** (*informal*) **1** to be popular for a short time (used about something that is not usually popular): *Classic '70s hairstyles are having a moment once more.* **2** (of a person) to not act normally for a short time, for example when you forget where you are or what you are doing: *Sorry, I was just having a moment. What time is it?* **3** (of two people) to have a short argument or romantic exchange: *Oh, sorry—were you two having a moment?* **for the moment/present** for now; for a short time: *This house is big enough for the moment, but we'll have to move if we have children.* **have its/your moments** to have short times that are better, more interesting, etc. than others: *The job isn't exciting all the time, but it has its moments.* **in the moment** completely mentally involved in what you are doing or experiencing: *The time goes so quickly—you just have to remember to stay in the moment.* **the (very) moment (that)...** as soon as...: *I want to see him the moment he arrives.* **the moment of truth** a time when sb/sth is tested, or when important decisions are made **not for a/one moment** certainly not; not at all: *I don't think for a moment that she'll accept but you can ask her.* **of moment** very important: *matters of great moment* **of the moment** (of a person, a job, an issue, etc.) famous, important and talked about a lot now: *She's the fashion designer of the moment.* ⊃ more at JUST *adv.*, LAST[1] *det.*, NOTICE *n.*, PSYCHOLOGICAL, SPUR *n.*, WAIT *v.*

**mo·ment·ar·ily** /ˈməʊməntrəli; *NAmE* ˌməʊmənˈterəli/ *adv.* **1** for a very short time SYN **briefly**: *He paused momentarily.* **2** (*NAmE*) very soon; in a moment: *I'll be with you momentarily.*

**mo·ment·ary** /ˈməʊməntri; *NAmE* -teri/ *adj.* lasting for a very short time SYN **brief**: *a momentary lapse of concentration* ◊ *momentary confusion*

**mo·men·tous** /məˈmentəs/; *NAmE* moʊˈm-/ *adj.* very important or serious, especially because there may be important results **SYN** **historic**: *a momentous decision/event/occasion*

**mo·men·tum** /məˈmentəm/; *NAmE* moʊˈm-/ *noun* [U] **1** the ability to keep increasing or developing: *The fight for his release gathers momentum each day.* ◇ *They began to lose momentum in the second half of the game.* **2** a force that is gained by movement: *The vehicle gained momentum as the road dipped.* **3** (*specialist*) the quantity of movement of a moving object, measured as its mass multiplied by its speed

**mommy** /ˈmɒmi; *NAmE* ˈmɑːmi/ *noun* (*pl.* **-ies**) (*also* **momma** /ˈmɒmə; *NAmE* ˈmɑːmə/) (*both NAmE*) (*BrE* **mummy**) (*informal*) a child's word for a mother

**mom·para** /ˈmɒmˈpɑːrə/ *SAfrE* [mɛmˈpɑːrə] (*also* **mampara**) *noun* (*SAfrE*) an offensive name for a person that you think is stupid

**Mon.** *abbr.* (in writing) Monday

**mon-** ➔ MONO-

**monad** /ˈmoʊnæd; *BrE also* ˈmɒn-; *NAmE also* ˈmɑːn-/ *noun* (*philosophy*) a single simple thing that cannot be divided, for example an ATOM or a person

**mon·arch** /ˈmɒnək; *NAmE* ˈmɑːnərk, -rk/ *noun* a person who rules a country, for example a king or a queen ➔ WORDFINDER NOTE at KING

**mo·nar·chic·al** /məˈnɑːkɪkl; *NAmE* -ˈnɑːrk-/ *adj.* [usually before noun] (*formal*) connected with a leader such as a king or a queen or with the system of government by a king or queen

**mon·arch·ist** /ˈmɒnəkɪst; *NAmE* ˈmɑːnərk-, -nɑːrk-/ *noun* a person who believes that a country should be ruled by a king or queen ▶ **mon·arch·ist** *adj.*

**mon·archy** /ˈmɒnəki; *NAmE* ˈmɑːnərki, -nɑːr-/ *noun* (*pl.* **-ies**) **1** *usually* **the monarchy** [sing., U] a system of government by a king or a queen: *plans to abolish the monarchy* **2** [C] a country that is ruled by a king or queen: *There are several constitutional monarchies in Europe.* ➔ compare REPUBLIC **3 the monarchy** [sing.] the king or queen of a country and their family

**mon·as·tery** /ˈmɒnəstri; *NAmE* ˈmɑːnəsteri/ *noun* (*pl.* **-ies**) a building in which MONKS (= members of a male religious community) live together

**mo·nas·tic** /məˈnæstɪk/ *adj.* **1** connected with MONKS or monasteries **2** (of a way of life) simple and quiet and possibly CELIBATE **SYN** **ascetic**

**mo·nas·ti·cism** /məˈnæstɪsɪzəm/ *noun* [U] the way of life of MONKS in monasteries

**Mon·day** /ˈmʌndeɪ, -di/ *noun* [C, U] (*abbr.* **Mon.**) the day of the week after Sunday and before Tuesday, the first day of the working week: *It's Monday today, isn't it?* ◇ *She started work last Monday.* ◇ *Are you busy next Monday?* ◇ *Monday morning/afternoon/evening* ◇ *We'll discuss this at Monday's meeting.* ◇ *I work Monday to Friday.* ◇ *I work Mondays to Fridays.* ◇ **on~** *We'll meet on Monday* (= next Monday). ◇ *We met on Monday* (= last Monday). ◇ (*informal or NAmE*) *We'll meet Monday.* ◇ **on Mondays** *The museum is closed on Mondays* (= every Monday). ◇ (*especially NAmE*) *The museum is closed Mondays.* ◇ **on a~** *He was born on a Monday.* ◇ *I went to Paris on Thursday, and came back the following Monday.* ◇ (*BrE*) *'When did the accident happen?' 'It was the Monday* (= the Monday of the week we are talking about).' ◇ (*BrE*) *Come back Monday week* (= a week after next Monday). **ORIGIN** From the Old English for 'day of the moon', translated from Latin *lunae dies*.

**mon·et·ar·ism** /ˈmʌnɪtərɪzəm; *NAmE* ˈmɑːn-/ *noun* [U] the policy of controlling the amount of money available in a country as a way of keeping the economy strong

**mon·et·ar·ist** /ˈmʌnɪtərɪst; *NAmE* ˈmɑːn-/ *noun* a person who supports monetarism ▶ **mon·et·ar·ist** *adj.*: *a monetarist economic policy*

**mon·et·ary** /ˈmʌnɪtri; *NAmE* ˈmɑːnɪteri/ *adj.* [only before noun] connected with money, especially all the money in a country: *monetary policy/growth* ◇ *an item of little mon-*

# money

*etary value* ◇ *closer European political, monetary and economic union* ➔ SYNONYMS at ECONOMIC

**mon·et·ize** (*BrE also* **-ise**) /ˈmʌnɪtaɪz/; *NAmE* ˈmɑːn-/ *verb* ~ **sth** to earn money from sth, especially a business or an ASSET (= sth that a business owns): *Newspapers try to monetize their online content in several ways.* ▶ **mon·et·iza·tion** (*BrE also* **-isa·tion**) /ˌmʌnɪtaɪˈzeɪʃn/; *NAmE* ˌmɑːnɪtəˈz-/ *noun* [U]: *The monetization of the website is expected to increase the company's profits.*

credit card    debit card

coin

cash            note/bill

**money** /ˈmʌni/ *noun* **1** [U] what you earn by working or selling things, and use to buy things: *to borrow/save/spend/earn money* ◇ *How much money is there in my account?* ◇ *The money is much better in my new job.* ◇ *If the item is not satisfactory, you will get your money back.* ◇ *We'll need to raise more money* (= collect or borrow it) *next year.* ◇ *Can you lend me some money until tomorrow?* ◇ *Be careful with that—it cost a lot of money.* ◇ *This is a great product, well worth the money.* ◇ *To hold another election is a waste of time and money.* ➔ WORDFINDER NOTE at LOAN

**WORDFINDER** afford, bank, bankrupt, capital, economy, expense, finance, invest, profit

**2** [U] coins or paper notes: *I counted the money carefully.* ◇ *Where can I change my money into dollars?* ➔ see also FUNNY MONEY, PAPER MONEY, READY MONEY **HELP** You will find other compounds ending in **money** at their place in the alphabet. **3** [U] a person's wealth including their property: *He lost all his money.* ◇ *The family made their money in the 18th century.* ➔ see also NEW MONEY, OLD MONEY **4 moneys** or **monies** [pl.] (*law or old use*) sums of money: *a statement of all monies paid into your account*

**IDM** **be in the ˈmoney** (*informal*) to have a lot of money to spend **for ˈmy money** (*informal*) in my opinion: *For my money, he's one of the greatest comedians of all time.* **get your ˈmoney's worth** to get enough value or pleasure out of sth, considering the amount of money, time, etc. that you are spending on it **good ˈmoney** a lot of money; money that you earn with hard work: *Thousands of people paid good money to watch the band perform.* ◇ *Don't waste good money on that!* **have money to ˈburn** to have so much money that you do not have to be careful with it **ˌmade of ˈmoney** (*informal*) very rich **make ˈmoney** to earn a lot of money; to make a profit: *The movie should make money.* ◇ *There's money to be made from tourism.* **make/lose money hand over ˈfist** to make/lose money very fast and in large quantities **money for ˈjam/old ˈrope** (*BrE, informal*) money that is earned very easily, for sth that needs little effort **money is no ˈobject** money is not sth that needs to be considered, because there is plenty of it available: *She travels around the world as if money is no object.* **ˌmoney ˈtalks** (*saying*) people who have a lot of money have more power and influence than others **on the ˈmoney** (*informal*) correct; accurate: *His prediction was right on the money.* **put ˈmoney into sth** to invest money in a business or a particular project: *We would welcome interest from anyone prepared to put money into the club.* **put your ˈmoney on sb/sth** **1** to bet that a particular horse, dog, etc. will win a race **2** to feel very sure that sth is true or that sb will succeed: *He'll be there* tonight. I'd put money on it. **put your money where your 'mouth is** (*informal*) to support what you say by doing sth practical; to show by your actions that you really mean sth **throw good money after 'bad** (*disapproving*) to spend more money on sth, when you have wasted a lot on it already **throw your 'money about/around** (*informal*) to spend money in a careless and obvious way **throw 'money at sth** (*disapproving*) to try to deal with a problem or improve a situation by spending money on it, when it would be better to deal with it in other ways: *It is inappropriate simply to throw money at these problems.* ⇒ more at BEST *n.*, CAREFUL, COIN *v.*, EASY *adj.*, GROW, LICENCE, LOVE *n.*, MARRY, OLD MONEY, PAY *v.*, POT *n.*, ROLL *v.*, RUN *n.*, TIME *n.*

▼ SYNONYMS

**money**
cash • change

These are all words for money in the form of coins or paper notes.

**money** money in the form of coins or paper notes: *I counted the money carefully.* ◊ *Where can I change my money into dollars?* ◊ **paper money** (= money that is made of paper, not coins)

**cash** money in the form of coins or paper notes: *How much cash do you have on you?* ◊ *Payments can be made by cheque or in cash.*

MONEY OR CASH?

If it is important to contrast money in the form of coins and notes and money in other forms, use **cash**: *How much money/cash do you have on you?* ◊ *Payments can be made by cheque or in money.* ◊ *Customers are offered a discount if they pay money.*

**change** the money that you get back when you have paid for sth giving more money than the amount it costs; coins rather than paper money: *The ticket machine doesn't give change.* ◊ *I don't have any **small change** (= coins of low value).*

PATTERNS

- to **draw out/get out/take out/withdraw** money/cash
- **ready** money/cash (= money that you have available to spend immediately)

'**money-back guaran'tee** *noun* an official promise by a shop, etc. to return the money you have paid for sth if it is not of an acceptable standard

'**money bags** *noun* (*informal*, *humorous*) **1** [pl.] money; wealth: *He could not convince those who held the money bags that his idea was viable.* **2 moneybags** [C] (*pl.* **moneybags**) a very rich person

'**money box** *noun* (*especially BrE*) a small closed box with a narrow opening and sometimes with a lock and key, into which children put coins as a way of saving money ⇒ compare PIGGY BANK

**mon·eyed** (*also* **mon·ied**) /'mʌnid/ *adj.* [only before noun] (*formal*) having a lot of money SYN rich: *the moneyed classes*

'**money-grubbing** (*also* '**money-grabbing**) *adj.* [only before noun] (*informal*, *disapproving*) trying to get a lot of money ▶ '**money-grubber** (*also* '**money-grabber**) *noun*

'**money laundering** *noun* [U] the crime of moving money that has been obtained illegally into foreign bank accounts or legal businesses so that it is difficult for people to know where the money came from ▶ '**money launderer** *noun*: *Money launderers hide billions each year.*

'**money-lend·er** /'mʌnilendə(r)/ *noun* (*old-fashioned*) a person whose business is lending money, usually at a very high rate of interest

'**money-maker** /'mʌnimeɪkə(r)/ *noun* a product, business, etc. that produces a large profit ▶ '**money-mak·ing** *adj.*: *a moneymaking movie* '**money-mak·ing** *noun* [U]

'**money market** *noun* the trade in SHORT-TERM loans between banks and other financial institutions

'**money order** (*especially NAmE*) (*BrE also* '**postal order**) *noun* an official document that you can buy at a bank or a post office and send to sb so that they can exchange it for money

'**money-saving** *adj.* [only before noun] that helps you spend less money: *money-saving offers/tips*

'**money-spinner** *noun* (*BrE*, *informal*) something that earns a lot of money

'**money supply** *noun* [sing., U] (*economics*) the total amount of money that exists in the economy of a country at a particular time

'**money transfer** (*also* '**cash transfer**) *noun* [C, U] the act of moving money from one bank or place to another; the money moved in this way

**mon·goose** /'mɒŋguːs; *NAmE* 'mɑːŋ-/ *noun* (*pl.* **mongooses** /-guːsɪz/) a small tropical animal with fur, that kills snakes, RATS, etc.

**mon·grel** /'mʌŋɡrəl/ (*especially BrE*) (*also* **mutt** *especially in NAmE*) *noun* a dog that is a mixture of different types

**mon·ied** = MONEYED

**moni·ker** /'mɒnɪkə(r); *NAmE* 'mɑːn-/ *noun* (*humorous*) a name

**mon·ism** /'məʊnɪzəm; *BrE also* 'mɒn-; *NAmE also* 'mɑːn-/ *noun* (*religion*) the belief that there is only one god

**moni·tor** 🔊 **B2** 🅦 /'mɒnɪtə(r); *NAmE* 'mɑːn-/ *noun*, *verb*

■ *noun* **1** 🔊 **B2** a screen that shows information from a computer; a television screen used to show particular kinds of information: *The details of today's flights are displayed on the monitor.* ◊ *The pages are designed to be viewed on a computer monitor.* ◊ *We included the costs of monitor, keyboard, mouse and speakers.* **2** a piece of equipment used to check or record sth: *He was lying there hooked up to a heart monitor.* ◊ *a baby/child monitor* **3** a person whose job is to check that sth is done fairly and honestly, especially in a foreign country: *UN monitors declared the referendum fair.* **4** a student in a school who performs special duties, such as helping the teacher: *He was a star pupil and the class monitor.* **5** a large tropical LIZARD (= a type of REPTILE)

■ *verb* **1** 🔊 **B2** to watch and check sth over a period of time in order to see how it develops, so that you can make any necessary changes SYN **track**: *~sth Each student's progress is closely monitored.* ◊ *~sb The patient is carefully monitored.* ◊ *~what, how, etc… We need to monitor how the situation develops.* **2** *~sth* to use technology to watch sb/sth, especially for reasons of security: *A police helicopter will be used to monitor crime hotspots.* **3** *~sth* to listen to phone calls, foreign radio broadcasts, etc. in order to find out information that might be useful: *a police state where every activity is monitored* ◊ *The company routinely monitors all its employees' emails.*

**monk** 🔊+ **C1** /mʌŋk/ *noun* a member of a religious group of men who often live apart from other people in a MONASTERY and who do not marry or have personal possessions: *Benedictine/Buddhist monks* ⇒ compare FRIAR, NUN

**mon·key** 🔊 **A2** /'mʌŋki/ *noun* **1** 🔊 **A2** an animal with a long tail, that climbs trees and lives in hot countries. There are several types of monkey and they are related to APES and humans: *Like humans, apes and monkeys live in complex social groupings.* HELP In non-scientific language, people sometimes use the word **monkey** for animals like CHIMPANZEES, which have no tails and are in fact APES. ⇒ see also RHESUS MONKEY, SPIDER MONKEY **2** (*informal*) a child who is active and likes playing tricks on people: *Come here, you cheeky little monkey!* **3** (*BrE*, *slang*) £500 IDM **get a monkey off your 'back** (*informal*) to free yourself of sth that causes you worry or difficulty: *The team have never beaten Germany and they'll be desperate to get that monkey off their backs.* **I don't/couldn't give a 'monkey's** (*BrE*, *slang*) used to say, in a way that is not very polite, that you do not care about sth, or are not at all interested in it **make a 'monkey (out) of sb** (*informal*) to make sb seem stupid ⇒ more at BRASS

'**monkey business** *noun* [U] (*informal*) dishonest or silly behaviour

**monkey in the middle** (NAmE) (BrE **piggy in the middle, pig in the middle**) noun **1** a children's game where two people throw a ball to each other over the head of another person who tries to catch it **2** a person who is caught between two people or groups who are fighting or arguing

**monkey nut** noun (BrE) a PEANUT with its shell still on

**monkey's wedding** noun (SAfrE, informal) used to describe a period of time when it is raining while the sun is shining: *Look! It's a monkey's wedding!*

**monkey wrench** (BrE also **adjustable spanner**, NAmE also **adjustable wrench**) noun a tool with a part that can be moved to hold and turn things of different WIDTHS ⇒ compare SPANNER, WRENCH ⇒ picture at SPANNER
**IDM** **(throw) a ('monkey) 'wrench in/into sth** (NAmE) (BrE **(throw) a 'spanner in the works**) (to cause) a delay or problem with sth that sb is planning or doing

**mono** /ˈmɒnəʊ; NAmE ˈmɑːn-/ adj., noun
■ adj. (also **mono·phon·ic**) (music) recording or producing sound that comes from only one direction: *a mono recording* ⇒ compare STEREO
■ noun [U] **1** a system of recording or producing sound that comes from only one direction: *recorded in mono* ⇒ compare STEREO **2** (NAmE, informal) = MONONUCLEOSIS

**mono-** /ˈmɒnəʊ, ˈmɒnə, məˈnɒ; NAmE ˈmɑːnəʊ, ˈmɑːnə, məˈnɑː/ (also **mon-** /ˈmɒn; NAmE ˈmɑːn/) combining form (in nouns and adjectives) one; single: *monorail ◇ monogamy*

**mono·chro·mat·ic** /ˌmɒnəkrəˈmætɪk; NAmE ˌmɑːnəkroʊ-/ adj. **1** containing or using only one colour: *monochromatic light* **2** (physics) (of light or other RADIATION) of a single WAVELENGTH or FREQUENCY: *monochromatic radiation*

**mono·chrome** /ˈmɒnəkrəʊm; NAmE ˈmɑːn-/ adj. **1** (of photographs, etc.) using only black, white and shades of grey: *monochrome illustrations/images* ◇ (figurative) *a dull monochrome life* **2** using different shades of one colour
▶ **mono·chrome** noun [U]: *an artist who works in monochrome*

**mon·ocle** /ˈmɒnəkl; NAmE ˈmɑːn-/ noun a single glass LENS for one eye, held in place by the muscles around the eye and used by people in the past to help them see clearly

**mono·cul·ture** /ˈmɒnəkʌltʃə(r); NAmE ˈmɑːn-/ noun **1** [U] the practice of growing only one type of crop on a certain area of land ⇒ WORDFINDER NOTE at CROP **2** [C, U] a society consisting of people who are all the same race, all share the same beliefs, etc.: *a global economic monoculture*

**mono·cyte** /ˈmɒnəsaɪt; NAmE ˈmɑːn-/ noun (biology) a type of large white blood cell with a simple OVAL NUCLEUS that can remove harmful substances from the body

**mon·og·amy** /məˈnɒɡəmi; NAmE -ˈnɑːɡ-/ noun **1** the fact or custom of being married to only one person at a particular time ⇒ compare BIGAMY, POLYGAMY **2** the practice or custom of having a sexual relationship with only one partner at a particular time ▶ **mon·og·am·ous** /-məs/ adj.: *a monogamous marriage* ◇ *Most birds are monogamous.*

**mono·gram** /ˈmɒnəɡræm; NAmE ˈmɑːn-/ noun two or more letters, usually the first letters of sb's names, that are combined in a design and marked on items of clothing, etc. that they own ▶ **mono·grammed** adj.: *a monogrammed handkerchief*

**mono·graph** /ˈmɒnəɡrɑːf; NAmE ˈmɑːnəɡræf/ noun (specialist) a detailed written study of a single subject, usually in the form of a short book

**mono·lin·gual** /ˌmɒnəˈlɪŋɡwəl; NAmE ˌmɑːn-/ adj. speaking or using only one language: *a monolingual dictionary* ⇒ compare BILINGUAL, MULTILINGUAL

**mono·lith** /ˈmɒnəlɪθ; NAmE ˈmɑːn-/ noun **1** a large single VERTICAL block of stone, especially one that was shaped into a column by people living in ancient times, and that may have had some religious meaning **2** (often disapproving) a single, very large organization that is very slow to change and not interested in individual people ▶ **mono·lith·ic** /ˌmɒnəˈlɪθɪk; NAmE ˌmɑːn-/ adj.: *a monolithic block* ◇ *the monolithic structure of the state*

**mono·logue** (US also **mono·log**) /ˈmɒnəlɒɡ; NAmE ˈmɑːnəlɔːɡ/ noun **1** [C] a long speech by one person during a conversation that stops other people from speaking or expressing an opinion: *He went into a long monologue about life in America.* **2** [U, C] a long speech in a play, film, etc. spoken by one actor, especially when alone **3** [C, U] a dramatic story, especially in VERSE, told or performed by one person: *a dramatic monologue* ⇒ compare DIALOGUE, SOLILOQUY ⇒ see also INTERIOR MONOLOGUE

**mono·nu·cle·osis** /ˌmɒnəʊˌnjuːkliˈəʊsɪs; NAmE ˌmɑːnoʊˌnuː-/ (also informal **mono**) (both NAmE) (BrE **glandular fever**) noun [U] a disease that causes the LYMPH GLANDS to SWELL (= become large, round and painful) and makes the person feel very weak for a long time

**mono·phon·ic** /ˌmɒnəˈfɒnɪk; NAmE ˌmɑːnəˈfɑːn-/ adj. (music) = MONO

**mono·plane** /ˈmɒnəpleɪn; NAmE ˈmɑːn-/ noun an early type of plane with one set of wings ⇒ compare BIPLANE

**mon·op·ol·ist** /məˈnɒpəlɪst; NAmE -ˈnɑːp-/ noun (specialist) a person or company that has a MONOPOLY

**mon·op·ol·is·tic** /məˌnɒpəˈlɪstɪk; NAmE -ˌnɑːp-/ adj. (formal) controlling or trying to get complete control over sth, especially an industry or a company

**mon·op·ol·ize** (BrE also **-ise**) /məˈnɒpəlaɪz; NAmE -ˈnɑːp-/ verb **1** ~ sth to have or take control of the largest part of sth so that other people are prevented from sharing it: *Men traditionally monopolized jobs in the printing industry.* ◇ *As usual, she completely monopolized the conversation.* **2** ~ sb to have or take a large part of sb's attention or time so that they are unable to speak to or deal with other people ▶ **mon·op·ol·iza·tion, -isa·tion** /məˌnɒpəlaɪˈzeɪʃn; NAmE -ˌnɑːpələˈz-/ noun [U]

**mon·op·oly** /məˈnɒpəli; NAmE -ˈnɑːp-/ noun (pl. -ies) **1** ~ (in/of/on sth) (business) the complete control of trade in particular goods or the supply of a particular service; a type of goods or a service that is controlled in this way: *In the past central government had a monopoly on television broadcasting.* ◇ *Electricity, gas and water were considered to be natural monopolies.* ⇒ compare DUOPOLY, OLIGOPOLY ⇒ WORDFINDER NOTE at TRADE **2** [usually sing.] ~ in/of/on sth the complete control, possession or use of sth; a thing that belongs only to one person or group and that other people cannot share: *Managers do not have a monopoly on stress.* ◇ *A good education should not be the monopoly of the rich.* **3 Monopoly™** a BOARD GAME in which players have to pretend to buy and sell land and houses, using pieces of paper that look like money

**Mo'nopoly money** noun [U] money that does not really exist or has no real value: *Inflation was so high that the notes were like Monopoly money.* **ORIGIN** From the toy money used in the board game *Monopoly™*.

**mono·rail** /ˈmɒnəʊreɪl; NAmE ˈmɑːn-/ noun **1** [U] a railway system in which trains travel along a track consisting of a single metal bar, usually one placed high above the ground **2** [C] a train used in a monorail system

**mono·so·dium glu·ta·mate** /ˌmɒnəˌsəʊdiəm ˈɡluːtəmeɪt; NAmE ˌmɑːn-/ noun [U] (abbr. **MSG**) a chemical that is sometimes added to food to improve its taste

**mono·syl·lab·ic** /ˌmɒnəsɪˈlæbɪk; NAmE ˌmɑːn-/ adj. **1** having only one syllable: *a monosyllabic word* **2** (of a person or their way of speaking) saying very little, in a way that appears rude to other people

**mono·syl·lable** /ˈmɒnəsɪləbl; NAmE ˈmɑːn-/ noun a word with only one syllable, for example, 'it' or 'no'

**mono·the·ism** /ˈmɒnəʊθiːɪzəm; NAmE ˈmɑːn-/ noun [U] the belief that there is only one God ⇒ compare POLYTHEISM ▶ **mono·the·ist** /-ɪst/ noun **mono·the·is·tic** /ˌmɒnəʊθiˈɪstɪk; NAmE ˌmɑːn-/ adj.

**mono·tone** /ˈmɒnətəʊn; NAmE ˈmɑːn-/ noun, adj.
■ noun [usually sing.] a sound or way of speaking in which the tone and volume remain the same and therefore seem boring: *He spoke in a flat monotone.*
■ adj. [only before noun] without any changes or differences in sound or colour: *He spoke in a monotone drawl.* ◇ *monotone engravings*

**mon·ot·on·ous** /məˈnɒtənəs; NAmE -ˈnɑːt-/ adj. never changing and therefore boring **SYN** **dull, repetitious**: *a*

# monotony 1012

*monotonous voice/diet/routine* ◇ *monotonous work* ◇ *New secretaries came and went with monotonous regularity.*
▶ **mon·ot·on·ous·ly** *adv.*

**mon·ot·ony** /məˈnɒtəni; *NAmE* -ˈnɑːt-/ *noun* [U] boring lack of variety: *She watches television to relieve the monotony of everyday life.*

**mono·treme** /ˈmɒnətriːm; *NAmE* ˈmɑːn-/ *noun* (*specialist*) a class of animal including the ECHIDNA and the PLATYPUS, that lays eggs, but also gives milk to its babies

**mono·un·sat·ur·ated fat** /ˌmɒnəʊˌsætʃəreɪtɪd ˈfæt; *NAmE* ˌmɑːn-/ *noun* [C, U] a type of fat found, for example, in OLIVES and nuts, that does not encourage the harmful development of CHOLESTEROL ⮕ see also POLYUNSATURATED FAT, SATURATED FAT, TRANS-FATTY ACID, UNSATURATED FAT

**Mon·si·gnor** /mɒnˈsiːnjə(r); *NAmE* mɑːn-/ *noun* (*abbr.* **Mgr**) used as a title when speaking to or about a priest of high rank in the Roman Catholic Church

**mon·soon** /ˌmɒnˈsuːn; *NAmE* ˌmɑːn-/ *noun* **1** a period of heavy rain in summer in South Asia; the rain that falls during this period **2** a wind in South Asia that blows from the south-west in summer, bringing rain, and the north-east in winter ⮕ WORDFINDER NOTE at RAIN

**mon·ster** /ˈmɒnstə(r); *NAmE* ˈmɑːn-/ *noun, adj.*
■ *noun* **1** (in stories) an imaginary creature that is very large, ugly and frightening: *a monster with three heads* ◇ *prehistoric monsters* ⮕ see also GREEN-EYED MONSTER **2** an animal or a thing that is very large or ugly: *Their dog's an absolute monster!* **3** a person who is very cruel and evil **4** (*humorous*) a child who behaves badly
■ *adj.* [only before noun] (*informal*) unusually large SYN **giant**: *monster mushrooms*

**monster ˈtruck** *noun* an extremely large PICKUP with very large wheels, often used for racing

**mon·stros·ity** /mɒnˈstrɒsəti; *NAmE* mɑːnˈstrɑːs-/ *noun* (*pl.* -ies) something that is very large and very ugly, especially a building SYN **eyesore**: *a concrete monstrosity*

**mon·strous** /ˈmɒnstrəs; *NAmE* ˈmɑːn-/ *adj.* **1** considered to be SHOCKING and unacceptable because it is morally wrong or unfair SYN **outrageous**: *a monstrous lie/injustice* **2** very large SYN **gigantic**: *a monstrous wave* **3** very large, ugly and frightening SYN **horrifying**: *a monstrous figure/creature* ▶ **mon·strous·ly** *adv.*: *monstrously unfair* ◇ *a monstrously fat man*

**mon·tage** /ˈmɒntɑːʒ; ˈmɒntɑːʒ; *NAmE* mɑːnˈtɑːʒ/ *noun* **1** [C] a picture, film or piece of music or writing that consists of many separate items put together, especially in an interesting or unusual combination: *a photographic montage* **2** [U] the process of making a montage

**mon·tane** /ˈmɒnteɪn; *NAmE* ˈmɑːn-/ *adj.* [only before noun] (*specialist*) connected with mountains

**Mon·terey Jack** /ˌmɒntəreɪ ˈdʒæk; *NAmE* ˌmɑːn-/ (*NAmE also* ˈJack cheese) *noun* [U] a type of white American cheese with a mild taste

**month** /mʌnθ/ *noun* **1** [C] any of the twelve periods of time into which the year is divided, for example May or June: *the month of August* ◇ *the wettest months of the year* ◇ *We're moving house next month.* ◇ *Last month I went on a school trip to Germany.* ◇ *We got married two months ago.* ◇ **a/per ~** *She earns $2000 a month.* ◇ *The rent is £800 per month.* ◇ *Have you read this month's 'Physics World'?* ◇ *Prices continue to rise* **month after month** (= over a period of several months). ◇ *Her anxiety mounted* **month by month** (= as each month passed). ⮕ see also CALENDAR MONTH **2** [C] a period of about 30 days, for example, 3 June to 3 July: *The baby is three months old.* ◇ *a three-month-old baby* ◇ *They lived in Toronto during their first few months of marriage.* ◇ *The past few months have been hectic.* ◇ *several months later* ◇ *a six-month contract* ◇ *a month-long strike* ◇ *He visits Paris once or twice a month.* ◇ *In recent months the company has launched three new products.* ⮕ see also LUNAR MONTH **3** **months** [pl.] a long time, especially a period of several months: *He had to wait for months for the visas to come through.* ◇ *It took months to find another job.* ◇ **for months** *It hasn't rained for months.*
IDM **(in) a month of ˈSundays** (*informal*) used to emphasize that sth will never happen or will take a very long time: *You won't find it, not in a month of Sundays.* ⮕ more at FLAVOUR *n.*

**month·ly** /ˈmʌnθli/ *adj., adv., noun*
■ *adj.* **1** happening once a month or every month: *a monthly meeting/visit/magazine* **2** paid, calculated or legally acceptable for one month: *a monthly salary of £1000* ◇ *a monthly season ticket* ◇ *Summers are hot, with monthly averages above 22°C.*
■ *adv.* every month or once a month: *She gets paid monthly.*
■ *noun* (*pl.* -ies) a magazine published once a month: *the fashion monthlies*

**monty** /ˈmɒnti; *NAmE* ˈmɑːn-/ *noun*
IDM **the full ˈmonty** the full amount that people expect or want: *They'll do the full monty* (= take off all their clothes) *if you pay them enough.*

**monu·ment** /ˈmɒnjumənt; *NAmE* ˈmɑːn-/ *noun* **1** **~ (to sb/sth)** a building, column, statue, etc. built to remind people of a famous person or event: *A monument to him was erected in St Paul's Cathedral.* **2** a building that has special historical importance: *an ancient monument* **3** **~ to sth** a thing that remains as a good example of sb's qualities or of what they did: *These recordings are a monument to his talent as a pianist.*

**monu·men·tal** /ˌmɒnjuˈmentl; *NAmE* ˌmɑːn-/ *adj.* **1** [usually before noun] very important and having a great influence, especially as the result of years of work SYN **historic**: *Gibbon's monumental work 'The Decline and Fall of the Roman Empire'* **2** [only before noun] very large, good, bad, stupid, etc. SYN **major**: *We have a monumental task ahead of us.* ◇ *a monumental error/disaster/cock-up* **3** [only before noun] appearing in or serving as a monument: *a monumental inscription/tomb*

**monu·men·tal·ly** /ˌmɒnjuˈmentəli; *NAmE* ˌmɑːn-/ *adv.* (used to describe negative qualities) extremely: *monumentally stupid*

**moo** /muː/ *noun* (*pl.* **moos**) the long deep sound made by a cow ▶ **moo** *verb* [I]

**MOOC** /muːk/ *noun* a course of study that is made available over the internet, usually without charge, to a very large number of people (the abbreviation for 'massive open online course')

**mooch** /muːtʃ/ *verb* (*informal*) **1** [I] **+ adv./prep.** (*BrE*) to walk slowly with no particular purpose; to be somewhere not doing very much SYN **potter**: *He's happy to mooch around the house all day.* **2** [I, T] **~ (sth) (off sb)** (*NAmE*) to get money, food, etc. from sb else instead of paying for it yourself SYN **cadge**: *He's always mooching off his friends.*

**mood** /muːd/ *noun* **1** [C] the way you are feeling at a particular time: **in a … ~** *She's* **in a good mood** *today* (= happy and friendly). ◇ *He's always* **in a bad mood** (= unhappy, or angry and impatient). ◇ *to be in a* **foul/festive mood** ◇ **in the ~ for (doing) sth** *I'm just not in the mood for a party tonight.* ◇ *He was* **in no mood for** *being polite to visitors.* ◇ **in the ~ (to do sth)** *I'm not really in the mood to go out tonight.* ◇ *Some addicts suffer violent* **mood swings** (= changes of mood) *if deprived of the drug.* HELP *In scientific contexts* **mood** *can be uncountable:* Serotonin is a brain chemical that regulates mood. **2** [C] a period of being angry or impatient: **in a ~** *I wonder why he's in such a mood today.* ◇ *She was* **in one of her moods** (= one of her regular periods of being angry or impatient). **3** [sing.] the way a group of people feel about sth; the atmosphere in a place or among a group of people: *The mood of the meeting was distinctly pessimistic.* ◇ *The movie* **captures the mood** *of the interwar years perfectly.* ◇ *He threw in some jokes to* **lighten the mood.** **4** [C] (*grammar*) one of the sets of verb forms or categories of verb use that expresses facts, orders, questions, wishes or conditions: *the indicative/imperative/subjunctive mood*

**ˈmood-altering** *adj.* (of drugs) having an effect on your mood: *mood-altering substances*

**ˈmood music** *noun* [U] music intended to create a particular atmosphere, especially a relaxed or romantic one

**moody** /ˈmuːdi/ adj. (**mood·ier**, **moodi·est**) **1** having moods that change quickly and often: *Moody people are very difficult to deal with.* **2** angry or upset, often for no particular reason SYN **grumpy**: *Why are you so moody today?* **3** (of a film, piece of music or place) suggesting particular emotions, especially sad ones ▶ **mood·ily** /-dɪli/ adv.: *He stared moodily into the fire.* **moodi·ness** noun [U]

**mooli** /ˈmuːli/ (also **dai·kon**) noun [U, C] a long white root vegetable that you can eat ⇨ VISUAL VOCAB page V5

**moon** ❶ A2 /muːn/ noun, verb
■ noun **1** A2 (usually **the moon**) (also **the Moon**) [sing.] the round object that moves around the earth once every 27½ days and shines at night by light reflected from the sun: *the surface of the moon* ◊ *the first man to walk on the moon* ◊ *a moon landing* **2** A2 [sing.] the moon as it appears in the sky at a particular time: *a crescent moon* ◊ *There's no moon tonight* (= no moon can be seen). ◊ *By the light of the moon I could just make out shapes and outlines.* ⇨ see also FULL MOON, HALF-MOON, HARVEST MOON, NEW MOON **3** [C] a natural satellite that moves around a planet other than the earth: *How many moons does Jupiter have?*
IDM ▶ **ask, cry, etc. for the ˈmoon** (*informal*) to ask for sth that is difficult or impossible to get or achieve • **many ˈmoons ago** (*literary*) a very long time ago • **over the ˈmoon** (*informal, especially BrE*) extremely happy and excited ⇨ more at ONCE adv., PROMISE v.
■ verb [I, T] ~ (**sb**) (*informal*) to show your bottom to people in a public place as a joke or a way to cause offence
PHRV ▶ **moon aˈbout/aˈround** (*especially BrE, informal*) to spend time doing nothing or walking around with no particular purpose, especially because you are unhappy • **ˈmoon over sb** (*informal*) to spend time thinking about sb that you love, especially when other people think this is silly or annoying SYN **pine for**

**moon·beam** /ˈmuːnbiːm/ noun a stream of light from the moon

**ˈMoon Boot**™ noun a thick warm boot with an outer surface of cloth or plastic, worn in snow or cold weather

**moong** /muːŋ/ noun = MUNG

**Moonie** /ˈmuːni/ noun an offensive word for a member of the Unification Church

**moonie** /ˈmuːni/ noun
IDM ▶ **do a ˈmoonie** (*BrE, informal*) to show your bottom in public

**moon·less** /ˈmuːnləs/ adj. without a moon that can be seen: *a moonless night/sky*

**moon·light** /ˈmuːnlaɪt/ noun, verb
■ noun [U] the light of the moon: *to go for a walk by moonlight/in the moonlight* IDM see FLIT n.
■ verb [I] (**moon·lighted**, **moon·lighted**) (*informal*) to have a second job that you do secretly, without telling your main employer

**moon·lit** /ˈmuːnlɪt/ adj. lit by the moon: *a moonlit night/beach*

**moon·scape** /ˈmuːnskeɪp/ noun **1** a view of the surface of the moon **2** an area of land that is empty, with no trees, water, etc., and looks like the surface of the moon

**moon·shine** /ˈmuːnʃaɪn/ noun [U] **1** (*old-fashioned, NAmE*) WHISKY or other strong alcoholic drinks made and sold illegally **2** (*informal*) silly talk SYN **nonsense**

**moon·stone** /ˈmuːnstəʊn/ noun [C, U] a smooth white shiny SEMI-PRECIOUS stone

**moon·struck** /ˈmuːnstrʌk/ adj. slightly crazy, especially because you are in love

**moon·walk** /ˈmuːnwɔːk/ verb **1** [I] to walk on the moon **2** [I] to do a dance movement that consists of walking backwards, sliding the feet smoothly over the floor ▶ **moon·walk** noun

**Moor** /mɔː(r), mʊə(r)/; NAmE /mʊr/ noun a member of a Muslim people of north-west Africa who ruled part of Spain until the 15th century ▶ **Moor·ish** adj.: *the Moorish architecture of Córdoba*

**moor** /mɔː(r), mʊə(r)/; NAmE /mʊr/ noun, verb
■ noun (*especially BrE*) **1** [C, usually pl.] a high open area of land that is not used for farming, especially an area covered with rough grass and HEATHER: *the North York moors* ◊ *to go for a walk on the moors* **2** [U] = MOORLAND: *moor and rough grassland*
■ verb [I, T] to attach a boat, ship, etc. to a fixed object or to the land with a rope, or ANCHOR it SYN **tie up**: *We moored off the north coast of the island.* ◊ ~ **sth (to sth)** *A number of fishing boats were moored to the quay.*

**moor·hen** /ˈmɔːhen, ˈmʊə-/; NAmE /ˈmʊrh-/ noun a small black bird with a short, red and yellow BEAK that lives on or near water

**moor·ing** /ˈmɔːrɪŋ, ˈmʊər-/; NAmE /ˈmʊr-/ noun **1 moorings** [pl.] the ropes, chains, etc. by which a ship or boat is MOORED: *The boat slipped its moorings and drifted out to sea.* **2** [C] the place where a ship or boat is MOORED: *private moorings* ◊ *to find a mooring* ◊ *mooring ropes*

**moor·land** /ˈmɔːlənd, ˈmʊəl-/; NAmE /ˈmʊrl-/ (also **moor**) noun [U, C, usually pl.] (*especially BrE*) land that consists of MOORS: *walking across open moorland*

**moose** /muːs/ noun (*pl.* **moose**) a large DEER that lives in North America. In Europe and Asia it is called an ELK. ⇨ picture at ELK

**ˈmoose milk** noun (*CanE*) **1** [U, C] an alcoholic drink made by mixing RUM with milk **2** [U] any strong alcoholic drink that is made at home

**moot** /muːt/ adj., verb
■ adj. (*NAmE*) unlikely to happen and therefore not worth considering: *He argued that the issue had become moot since the board had changed its policy.*
IDM ▶ **a moot ˈpoint/ˈquestion** (*BrE, NAmE*) a matter about which there may be difference of opinion or a lack of understanding
■ verb [usually passive] (*formal*) to suggest an idea for people to discuss SYN **propose, put forward**: **be mooted** *The plan was first mooted at last week's meeting.*

**ˈmoot court** noun (*especially NAmE*) a MOCK court in which law students practise trials

mop    squeegee    rubber gloves
squeegee
bucket

**mop** /mɒp; NAmE mɑːp/ noun, verb
■ noun **1** a tool for washing floors that has a long handle with soft material or a bunch of thick strings at the end: *a mop and bucket* ⇨ see also SQUEEGEE (2) **2** a kitchen UTENSIL (= a tool) for washing dishes, that has a short handle with soft material at one end **3** a mass of thick, often untidy, hair: *a mop of curly red hair*
■ verb (**-pp-**) ~ **sth** to clean sth with a mop: *She wiped all the surfaces and mopped the floor.* **2** ~ **sth (from sth)** to remove liquid from the surface of sth using a cloth: *He took out a handkerchief to mop his brow* (= to remove the sweat). IDM see FLOOR n.
PHRV ▶ **mop sth⇔up 1** to remove the liquid from a surface: *Do you want some bread to mop up that sauce?* **2** to complete or end sth by dealing with the final parts: *There are a few things that need mopping up before I can leave.*

**3** to use up what is left of sth: *Buying new equipment mopped up what was left of this year's budget.* **4** to get rid of the last few people who continue to oppose you, especially by capturing or killing them: *Troops combed the area to mop up any remaining resistance.* **5** to ABSORB (= take in) sth and make it part of sth larger: *A number of smaller companies were mopped up by the American multinational.*

**mope** /məʊp/ *verb* [I] to spend your time doing nothing and feeling sorry for yourself SYN **brood**: *Moping won't do any good!*
PHRV **mope a'round/a'bout ( ...)** (*disapproving*) to spend time walking around a place with no particular purpose, especially because you feel sorry for yourself: *Instead of moping around the house all day, you should be out there looking for a job.*

**moped** /ˈməʊped/ *noun* a motorcycle with a small engine and also PEDALS

**mop·pet** /ˈmɒpɪt; *NAmE* ˈmɑːp-/ *noun* (*informal*) an attractive small child, especially a girl

**MOR** /ˌem əʊ ˈɑː(r)/ *noun* [U] music that is pleasant to listen to, but is not exciting or original (the abbreviation for 'middle-of-the-road')

**mo·raine** /məˈreɪn; *BrE also* mɒˈr-/ *noun* [U, C] (*specialist*) a mass of earth, stones, etc., carried along by a GLACIER and left when it melts

**moral** B2 /ˈmɒrəl; *NAmE* ˈmɔːr-/ *adj., noun*
■ *adj.* **1** B2 [only before noun] connected with principles of right and wrong behaviour: *a moral issue/dilemma* ◊ *traditional moral values* ◊ *a decline in moral standards* ◊ *moral and ethical questions* ◊ *moral philosophy* ◊ *The newspapers were full of moral outrage at the weakness of other countries.* **2** B2 [only before noun] based on your own sense of what is right and fair, not on legal rights or duties SYN **ethical**: *moral responsibility/duty/authority* ◊ *a moral imperative* ◊ *I make no moral judgement on this decision.* ◊ *Governments have at least a moral obligation to answer these questions.* ◊ *The job was to call on all her diplomatic skills and moral courage* (= the courage to do what you think is right). **3** B2 following the standards of behaviour considered acceptable and right by most people SYN **good, honourable**: *He led a very moral life.* ◊ *a very moral person* ➔ compare AMORAL, IMMORAL **4** [only before noun] able to understand the difference between right and wrong: *Children are not naturally moral beings.*
IDM **take, claim, seize, etc. the moral 'high ground** to claim that your side of an argument is morally better than your opponents' side; to argue in a way that makes your side seem morally better
■ *noun* **1** B2 **morals** [pl.] standards or principles of good behaviour, especially in matters of sexual relationships: *Young people these days have no morals.* ◊ *The play was considered an affront to public morals.* ◊ (*old-fashioned*) *a woman of loose morals* (= with a low standard of sexual behaviour) **2** [C] a practical lesson that a story, an event or an experience teaches you: *The moral of the story is always stick to what you do best.* ◊ *And the moral is that crime doesn't pay.*

**moral 'compass** *noun* the ability to judge what is right and wrong and to behave in an appropriate way: *He is not the only politician who has lost his moral compass.*

**mor·ale** /məˈrɑːl; *NAmE* -ˈræl/ *noun* [U] the amount of confidence and enthusiasm, etc. that a person or a group has at a particular time: *to boost/raise/improve morale* ◊ *Morale amongst the players is very high at the moment.* ◊ *Staff are suffering from low morale.*

**moral 'fibre** (*US* **moral 'fiber**) *noun* [U] the inner strength to do what you believe to be right in difficult situations

**moral 'hazard** *noun* [U, sing.] (*economics*) lack of reason to try to avoid risk when protected from its consequences, for example by insurance

**mor·al·ist** /ˈmɒrəlɪst; *NAmE* ˈmɔːr-/ *noun* **1** (*often disapproving*) a person who has strong ideas about moral principles, especially one who tries to tell other people how they should behave **2** a person who teaches or writes about moral principles

**mor·al·is·tic** /ˌmɒrəˈlɪstɪk; *NAmE* ˌmɔːr-/ *adj.* (*usually disapproving*) having or showing very fixed ideas about what is right and wrong, especially when this causes you to judge other people's behaviour

**mor·al·ity** C1 /məˈræləti/ *noun* (*pl.* **-ies**) **1** C1 [U] principles relating to right and wrong or good and bad behaviour: *matters of public/private morality* ◊ *Standards of morality seem to be dropping.* **2** C1 [U] the degree to which sth is right or wrong, good or bad, etc. according to moral principles: *a debate on the morality of abortion* **3** [U, C] a system of moral principles followed by a particular group of people SYN **ethics** ➔ compare IMMORALITY ➔ WORDFINDER NOTE at BEHAVIOUR

**mo'rality play** *noun* a type of play that was popular in the 15th and 16th centuries and was intended to teach a moral lesson, using characters to represent good and bad qualities

**mor·al·ize** (*BrE also* **-ise**) /ˈmɒrəlaɪz; *NAmE* ˈmɔːr-/ *verb* [I] (*usually disapproving*) to tell other people what is right and wrong especially in order to emphasize that your opinions are correct SYN **preach**

**mor·al·ly** /ˈmɒrəli; *NAmE* ˈmɔːr-/ *adv.* according to principles of good behaviour and what is considered to be right or wrong: *to act morally* ◊ *morally right/wrong/justified/unacceptable* ◊ *He felt morally responsible for the accident.*

**the moral ma'jority** *noun* [sing. + sing./pl. v.] the largest group of people in a society, considered as having very traditional ideas about moral matters, religion, sexual behaviour, etc.

**moral sup'port** *noun* [U] the act of helping sb by showing your approval and interest, rather than by giving financial or practical support: *My sister came along just to give me some moral support.*

**moral 'victory** *noun* a situation in which your ideas or principles are proved to be right and fair, even though you may not have succeeded where practical results are considered

**mor·ass** /məˈræs/ *noun* [usually sing.] (*formal*) **1** an unpleasant and complicated situation that is difficult to escape from SYN **web 2** a dangerous area of low soft, wet land SYN **bog, quagmire**

**mora·tor·ium** /ˌmɒrəˈtɔːriəm; *NAmE* ˌmɔːr-/ *noun* (*pl.* **-riums** or **-toria** /-riə/) ~ **(on sth)** a temporary stopping of an activity, especially by official agreement: *The convention called for a two-year moratorium on commercial whaling.*

**moray** /ˈmɒreɪ; *NAmE* ˈmɔːr-/ (*also* **moray 'eel**) *noun* a type of EEL that hides among rocks in warm seas

**mor·bid** /ˈmɔːbɪd; *NAmE* ˈmɔːrb-/ *adj.* **1** having or expressing a strong interest in sad or unpleasant things, especially disease or death: *He had a morbid fascination with blood.* ◊ *'He might even die.' 'Don't be so morbid.'* **2** (*medical*) connected with disease ▶ **mor·bid·ity** /mɔːˈbɪdəti; *NAmE* mɔːrˈb-/ *noun* [U] **mor·bid·ly** /ˈmɔːbɪdli; *NAmE* ˈmɔːrb-/ *adv.*

**morcha** /ˈmɔːtʃə; *NAmE* ˈmɔːrtʃə/ *noun* (*IndE*) a large public meeting or MARCH (= organized walk by many people), organized to support a particular idea or political party: *They're planning on taking out a morcha at the minister's house.*

**mor·dant** /ˈmɔːdnt; *NAmE* ˈmɔːrd-/ *adj.* (*formal*) critical and unkind, but funny SYN **caustic**: *His mordant wit appealed to students.* ▶ **mor·dant·ly** *adv.*

**more** A1 /mɔː(r)/ *det., pron., adv.*
■ *det., pron.* A1 (used as the comparative of 'much', 'a lot of', 'many') a larger number or amount of: *I want some more!* ◊ *sth more bread/cars* ◊ *people with more money than sense* ◊ *~ of sth/sb I can't stand much more of this.* ◊ *I hope we'll see more of you* (= see you again or more often). ◊ *~ than ... She earns a lot more than I do.* ◊ *There is room for no more than three cars.*
IDM **more and 'more** B1 continuing to become larger in number or amount: *More and more people are banking on-line.* ◊ *She spends more and more time alone in her room.*

*adv.* **1** ~ (than ...) used to form the comparative of most adjectives and adverbs with two or more syllables: *She was far more intelligent than her sister.* ◊ *He read the letter more carefully the second time.* **2** ~ (than ...) to a greater degree than sth else; to a greater degree than usual: *I like her more than her husband.* ◊ *a course for more advanced students* ◊ *It had more the appearance of a deliberate crime than of an accident.* ◊ *I had no complaints and* **no more** (= neither) *did Tom.* ◊ *Signing the forms is* **little more than** (= only) *a formality.* ◊ *I'm* **more than** *happy* (= extremely happy) *to take you there in my car.* ◊ *She was* **more than a little** *shaken* (= extremely shaken) *by the experience.* ◊ (*formal*) *I will torment you* **no more** (= no longer). ⊃ see also ANY MORE **3** again: *Could you repeat that* **once more** (= one more time)?
**IDM** **more and 'more** at a rate that keeps increasing **SYN** increasingly: *I was becoming more and more irritated by his behaviour.* **more or 'less 1** almost: *I've more or less finished the book.* **2** approximately: *She could earn $200 a night, more or less.* **the more, less, etc ..., the more, less, etc ...** used to show that two things change to the same degree: *The more she thought about it, the more depressed she became.* ◊ *The less said about the whole thing, the happier I'll be.* **what is 'more** used to add a point that is even more important: *You're wrong, and what's more you know it!* ⊃ LANGUAGE BANK at ADDITION

**more·ish** /ˈmɔːrɪʃ/ *adj.* (*BrE, informal*) if food or drink is **moreish**, it tastes so good that you want to have more of it

**morel** /məˈrel/ (*also* **mo·rel 'mushroom**) *noun* a type of MUSHROOM that you can eat, with a top that is full of holes

**more·over** /mɔːrˈəʊvə(r)/ *adv.* (*formal*) used to introduce some new information that adds to or supports what you have said previously **SYN** **in addition (to sb/sth)**: *A talented artist, he was, moreover, a writer of some note.* ⊃ LANGUAGE BANK at ADDITION

**mores** /ˈmɔːreɪz/ *noun* [pl.] (*formal*) the customs and behaviour that are considered typical of a particular social group or community **SYN** **conventions**

**morgue** /mɔːɡ/; *NAmE* mɔːrɡ/ *noun* **1** a building in which dead bodies are kept before they are buried or CREMATED (= burned) ⊃ compare MORTUARY ⊃ WORDFINDER NOTE at DIE **2** a place where dead bodies that have been found are kept until they can be identified

**mori·bund** /ˈmɒrɪbʌnd; *NAmE* ˈmɔːr-/ *adj.* (*formal*) **1** (of an industry, an institution, a custom, etc.) no longer effective and about to come to an end completely **2** in a very bad condition; dying: *a moribund patient/tree*

**Mor·mon** /ˈmɔːmən; *NAmE* ˈmɔːrm-/ *noun* a member of a religion formed by Joseph Smith in the US in 1830, officially called 'the Church of Jesus Christ of Latter-day Saints': *a Mormon church/chapel*

**morn** /mɔːn; *NAmE* mɔːrn/ *noun* [usually sing.] (*literary*) morning

**morn·ing** /ˈmɔːnɪŋ; *NAmE* ˈmɔːrn-/ *noun*
■ *noun* **1** the early part of the day from the time when people wake up until 12 o'clock in the middle of the day or before lunch: *They left for Spain early this morning.* ◊ *See you tomorrow morning.* ◊ *She drove to Bristol yesterday morning.* ◊ *She still felt unwell the following morning.* ◊ **in the ~** *I prefer coffee in the morning.* ◊ **first thing in the morning** ◊ *She woke every morning at the same time.* ◊ *I walk to work most mornings.* ◊ *He's been in a meeting all morning.* ◊ *Our group meets on Friday mornings.* ◊ **on the ~of sth** *We got the news on the morning of the wedding.* ◊ *the morning papers* ⊃ see also COFFEE MORNING, GOOD MORNING **2** the part of the day from midnight to MIDDAY: **in the ~** *I didn't get home until two in the morning!* ◊ *He died in the early hours of Sunday morning.* **3 mornings** *adv.* in the morning of each day: *I only work mornings.*
**IDM** **in the 'morning 1** between midnight and MIDDAY: *It must have happened at about five o'clock in the morning.* **2** during the morning of the next day; tomorrow morning: *I'll give you a call in the morning.* **the morning after (the night before)** (*humorous*) the morning after an evening of drinking **morning, noon and 'night** at all times of the day and night (used to emphasize that sth happens very often or that it happens continuously): *She*

1015 **morsel**

talks about him morning, noon and night. ◊ *The work continues morning, noon and night.* ⊃ more at OTHER
■ *exclamation* (*informal*) = GOOD MORNING

**morning-'after** *adj.* [only before noun] **1** happening the next day, after an exciting or important event: *After his election victory, the president held a morning-after news conference.* **2** used to describe how sb feels the next morning, after an occasion when they have drunk too much alcohol: *a morning-after headache*

**morning-'after pill** *noun* a drug that a woman can take some hours after having sex in order to avoid becoming pregnant

**morning coat** (*BrE*) (*NAmE* **cut·away**) *noun* a black or grey jacket for men, short at the front and very long at the back, worn as part of morning dress ⊃ compare TAILS

**morning dress** *noun* [U] clothes worn by a man on very formal occasions, for example a wedding, including a morning coat and dark trousers

**morning glory** *noun* [C, U] a climbing plant with flowers like TRUMPETS in shape that open in the morning and close in late afternoon

**morning sickness** *noun* [U] the need to VOMIT that some women feel, often only in the morning, when they are pregnant, especially in the first months ⊃ WORDFINDER NOTE at PREGNANT

**the morning 'star** *noun* [sing.] the planet Venus, when it shines in the east before the sun rises

**morning suit** *noun* (*BrE*) a suit worn by a man on very formal occasions, for example a wedding, including a MORNING COAT and dark trousers

**moron** /ˈmɔːrɒn; *NAmE* -rɑːn/ *noun* (*informal*) an offensive way of referring to sb that you think is very stupid: *They're a bunch of morons.* ◊ *You moron—now look what you've done!* ▸ **mor·on·ic** /məˈrɒnɪk; *NAmE* -ˈrɑːn-/ *adj.*: *a moronic stare* ◊ *a moronic TV programme*

**mor·ose** /məˈrəʊs/ *adj.* unhappy, in a bad mood and not talking very much **SYN** **gloomy**: *She just sat there looking morose.* ▸ **mor·ose·ly** *adv.*

**morph** /mɔːf; *NAmE* mɔːrf/ *verb* **1** [I, T] ~ (sth) (into sth) to change smoothly from one image to another using computer ANIMATION; to make an image change in this way **2** [I, T] ~ (sb/sth) (into sb/sth) to change, or make sb/sth change, into sth different

**mor·pheme** /ˈmɔːfiːm; *NAmE* ˈmɔːrf-/ *noun* (*grammar*) the smallest unit of meaning that a word can be divided into: *The word 'like' contains one morpheme but 'un-like-ly' contains three.*

**mor·phine** /ˈmɔːfiːn; *NAmE* ˈmɔːrf-/ (*also old-fashioned* **mor·phia** /ˈmɔːfiə; *NAmE* ˈmɔːrf-/) *noun* [U] a powerful drug that is made from OPIUM and used to reduce pain

**morph·ology** /mɔːˈfɒlədʒi; *NAmE* mɔːrˈfɑːl-/ *noun* [U] **1** (*biology*) the form and structure of animals and plants, studied as a science **2** (*linguistics*) the forms of words, studied as a branch of linguistics ⊃ compare GRAMMAR, SYNTAX ▸ **mor·pho·logic·al** /ˌmɔːfəˈlɒdʒɪkl; *NAmE* ˌmɔːrfəˈlɑːdʒ-/ *adj.*

**morris dance** /ˈmɒrɪs dɑːns; *NAmE* ˈmɔːrɪs dæns/ *noun* a traditional English dance that is performed by a group of people wearing special clothes decorated with bells and carrying sticks that they hit together ▸ **'morris dancer** *noun* **'morris dancing** *noun* [U]

**mor·row** /ˈmɒrəʊ; *NAmE* ˈmɔːr-/ *noun* **the morrow** [sing.] (*old-fashioned, literary*) the next day; tomorrow: *We had to leave on the morrow.* ◊ *Who knows what the morrow* (= the future) *will bring?*

**Morse code** /ˌmɔːs ˈkəʊd; *NAmE* ˌmɔːrs/ *noun* [U] a system for sending messages, using combinations of long and short sounds or flashes of light to represent letters of the alphabet and numbers

**mor·sel** /ˈmɔːsl; *NAmE* ˈmɔːrsl/ *noun* a small amount or a piece of sth, especially food: *a tasty morsel of food* ◊ *He ate it all, down to the last morsel.*

# mortal

**mor·tal** /ˈmɔːtl; NAmE ˈmɔːrtl/ *adj., noun*

- *adj.* **1** that cannot live forever and must die: *We are all mortal.* **OPP** IMMORTAL **2** (*literary*) causing death or likely to cause death; very serious: *a mortal blow/wound* ◊ *to be in mortal danger* ◊ (*figurative*) *Her reputation suffered a mortal blow as a result of the scandal.* ⇒ compare FATAL **3** [only before noun] (*formal*) lasting until death **SYN** **deadly**: *mortal enemies* ◊ *They were locked in mortal combat* (= a fight that will only end with the death of one of them). **4** [only before noun] (*formal*) (of fear, etc.) extreme: *We lived in mortal dread of him discovering our secret.*
- *noun* (*often humorous*) a human, especially an ordinary person with little power or influence **SYN** **human being**: *old stories about gods and mortals* ◊ (*humorous*) *Such things are not for mere mortals like ourselves.* ◊ (*humorous*) *She can deal with complicated numbers in her head, but we lesser mortals need calculators!*

**mor·tal·ity** /mɔːˈtæləti; NAmE mɔːrˈt-/ *noun* (*pl.* **-ies**) **1** [U] the state of being human and not living forever: *After her mother's death, she became acutely aware of her own mortality.* **2** [U] the number of deaths in a particular situation or period of time: *Mortality from lung cancer is still increasing.* ⇒ see also INFANT MORTALITY **3** [C] (*specialist*) a death: *hospital mortalities* (= deaths in hospital)

**mor·tal·ly** /ˈmɔːtəli; NAmE ˈmɔːrt-/ *adv.* (*literary*) **1** causing or resulting in death **SYN** **fatally**: *mortally wounded/ill* **2** extremely: *mortally afraid/offended*

**mortal ˈsin** *noun* [C, U] (in the Roman Catholic Church) a very serious SIN for which you can be sent to HELL unless you CONFESS and are forgiven

**mor·tar** /ˈmɔːtə(r); NAmE ˈmɔːrt-/ *noun, verb*
- *noun* **1** [U] a mixture of sand, water, LIME and CEMENT used in building for holding BRICKS and stones together **2** [C] a heavy gun that fires bombs and SHELLS high into the air; the bombs that are fired by this gun: *to come under mortar fire/attack* **3** [C] a small hard bowl in which you can CRUSH substances such as seeds and grains to make them into powder with a special object (called a PESTLE) ⇒ see also BRICKS AND MORTAR
- *verb* [I, T] ~ **(sb/sth)** to attack sb/sth using a mortar

**ˈmortar board** *noun* a black hat with a stiff square top, worn by some university teachers and students at special ceremonies ⇒ compare CAP

**mort·gage** /ˈmɔːɡɪdʒ; NAmE ˈmɔːrɡ-/ *noun, verb*
- *noun* (*also informal* **home ˈloan**) a legal agreement by which a bank or similar organization lends you money to buy a house, etc., and you pay the money back over a particular number of years; the sum of money that you borrow: *to apply for/take out/pay off a mortgage* ◊ *mortgage rates* (= of interest) ◊ *a mortgage on the house* ◊ *a mortgage of £60000* ◊ *monthly mortgage payments* ⇒ WORDFINDER NOTE at HOME ⇒ see also ENDOWMENT MORTGAGE, REPAYMENT MORTGAGE
- *verb* ~ **sth** to give a bank, etc. the legal right to own your house, land, etc. if you do not pay the money back that you have borrowed from the bank to buy the house or land: *He had to mortgage his house to pay his legal costs.*

**ˈmortgage bond** *noun* (*SAfrE*) = BOND

**mort·ga·gee** /ˌmɔːɡɪˈdʒiː; NAmE ˌmɔːrɡ-/ *noun* (*specialist*) a person or an organization that lends money to people to buy houses, etc.

**mort·ga·gor** /ˈmɔːɡɪdʒɔː(r); NAmE ˈmɔːrɡ-/ *noun* (*specialist*) a person who borrows money from a bank or a similar organization to buy a house, etc.

**mor·ti·cian** /mɔːˈtɪʃn; NAmE mɔːrˈt-/ *noun* (*NAmE*) = UNDERTAKER

**mor·tify** /ˈmɔːtɪfaɪ; NAmE ˈmɔːrt-/ *verb* [usually passive] (**mor·ti·fies**, **mor·ti·fy·ing**, **mor·ti·fied**, **mor·ti·fied**) to make sb feel very ashamed or embarrassed **SYN** **humiliate**: *be mortified (to do sth)* *She was mortified to realize he had heard every word she said.* ▶ **mor·ti·fi·ca·tion** /ˌmɔːtɪfɪˈkeɪʃn; NAmE ˌmɔːrt-/ *noun* [U] **mor·ti·fy·ing** /ˈmɔːtɪfaɪɪŋ; NAmE ˈmɔːrt-/ *adj.*: *How mortifying to have to apologize to him!*

**mor·tise** (*also* **mor·tice**) /ˈmɔːtɪs; NAmE ˈmɔːrt-/ *noun* (*specialist*) a hole cut in a piece of wood, etc. to receive the end of another piece of wood, so that the two are held together ⇒ see also TENON

**ˈmortise lock** *noun* a lock that is fitted inside a hole cut into the edge of a door, not one that is fitted on the surface of one side

**mor·tu·ary** /ˈmɔːtʃəri; NAmE ˈmɔːrtʃueri/ *noun* (*pl.* **-ies**) **1** a room or building, for example part of a hospital, in which dead bodies are kept before they are buried or CREMATED (= burned) **2** (*NAmE*) = FUNERAL PARLOUR ⇒ compare MORGUE

**mo·saic** /məʊˈzeɪɪk/ *noun* [C, U] a picture or pattern made by placing together small pieces of glass, stone, etc. of different colours: *a Roman mosaic* ◊ *a design in mosaic* ◊ *mosaic tiles* ◊ (*figurative*) *A mosaic of fields, rivers and woods lay below us.*

**mosey** /ˈməʊzi/ *verb* [I] + **adv./prep.** (*informal*) to go in a particular direction slowly and with no definite purpose: *He moseyed on over to the bar.*

**mosh** /mɒʃ; NAmE mɑːʃ/ *verb* [I] to dance and jump up and down violently or without control at a concert where rock music is played

**ˈmosh pit** *noun* the place, just in front of the stage, where the audience at a concert of rock music dances and jumps up and down

**Mos·lem** /ˈmɒzləm; NAmE ˈmɑːz-/ *noun* = MUSLIM **HELP** The form **Moslem** is sometimes considered old-fashioned. Use **Muslim**. ▶ **Mos·lem** *adj.* = MUSLIM

**mosque** /mɒsk; NAmE mɑːsk/ *noun* a building where Muslims go to WORSHIP (= praise God)

**mos·quito** /məˈskiːtəʊ; *BrE also* mɒˈs-/ *noun* (*pl.* **-oes** *or* **-os**) a flying insect that bites humans and animals and drinks their blood. One type of mosquito can spread the disease MALARIA: *a mosquito bite* ⇒ VISUAL VOCAB page V3

**moˈsquito net** *noun* a net that you hang over a bed, etc. to keep mosquitoes away from you

**moss** /mɒs; NAmE mɔːs/ *noun* [U, C] a very small green or yellow plant without flowers that spreads over wet surfaces, rocks, trees, etc: *moss-covered walls* ⇒ compare LICHEN ⇒ see also SPANISH MOSS ⇒ VISUAL VOCAB page V7 **IDM** see ROLL *v.*

**mossy** /ˈmɒsi; NAmE ˈmɔːsi/ *adj.* covered with moss

**most** /məʊst/ *det., pron., adv.*
- *det., pron.* (used as the superlative of 'much', 'a lot of', 'many') **1** the largest in number or amount: *Who do you think will get (the) most votes?* ◊ *She had the most money of all of them.* ◊ *I spent most time on the first question.* ◊ *Who ate the most?* ◊ *The director has the most to lose.* **HELP** *The* can be left out in informal *BrE*. **2** more than half of sb/sth; almost all of sb/sth: *I like most vegetables.* ◊ *Most classical music sends me to sleep.* ◊ *As most of you know, I've decided to resign.* ◊ *Most of the people I had invited turned up.* ◊ *There are thousands of verbs in English and most (of them) are regular.* **HELP** *The* is not used with **most** in this meaning.
- **IDM** **at (the) ˈmost** not more than: *As a news item it merits a short paragraph at most.* ◊ *There were 50 people there, at the very most.* ⇒ more at MAKE *v.*, PART *n.*
- *adv.* **1** used to form the superlative of most adjectives and adverbs of two or more syllables: *the most boring/beautiful part* ◊ *It was the people with the least money who gave most generously.* **HELP** When **most** is followed only by an adverb, *the* is not used: *This reason is mentioned most frequently*, but: *This is the most frequently mentioned reason.* **2** to the greatest degree: *What did you enjoy (the) most?* ◊ *It was what she wanted most of all.* **HELP** *The* is often left out in informal English. **3** (*formal*) very; extremely; completely: *It was most kind of you to meet me.* ◊ *We shall most probably never meet again.* ◊ *This technique looks easy, but it most certainly is not.* **4** (*NAmE, informal*) almost: *I go to the store most every day.*

**-most** /məʊst/ *suffix* (in adjectives) the furthest: *inmost* (= the furthest in) ◊ *southernmost* ◊ *topmost* (= the furthest up/nearest to the top)

**most favoured ˈnation** (*US* **most favored nation**) *noun* a country to which another country allows the most advantages in trade, because they have a good relationship

**most·ly** 🔑 **A2** /ˈməʊstli/ *adv.* mainly; generally: *The sauce is mostly cream.* ◇ *We're mostly out on Sundays.* ◇ *Revenue grew by 18 per cent, **mostly due to** the opening of 33 new stores.*

**MOT** /ˌem əʊ ˈtiː/ (*also* **MOT test**) *noun* a test that any vehicle in the UK over three years old must take in order to make sure that it is safe and in good condition (the abbreviation for 'Ministry of Transport'): *I've got to take the car in for its MOT.* ◇ *to **pass/fail the MOT***

**mote** /məʊt/ *noun* (*old-fashioned*) a very small piece of dust **SYN** **speck**

**motel** /məʊˈtel/ (*also* **motor lodge**) (*NAmE also* **motor inn**) *noun* a hotel for people who are travelling by car, with space for parking cars near the rooms

**motet** /məʊˈtet/ *noun* a short piece of church music, usually for voices only ◇ *compare* CANTATA

**moth** /mɒθ; *NAmE* mɔːθ/ *noun* a flying insect with a long thin body and four large wings, like a BUTTERFLY, but less brightly coloured. Moths fly mainly at night and are attracted to bright lights. ◇ VISUAL VOCAB page V3

**moth·ball** /ˈmɒθbɔːl; *NAmE* ˈmɔːθ-/ *noun, verb*
- *noun* a small white ball made of a chemical with a strong smell, used for keeping moths away from clothes
**IDM** **in ˈmothballs** stored and not in use, often for a long time
- *verb* [usually passive] **1** to stop using a piece of equipment but keep it in good condition so that it can easily be used again: ***be mothballed*** *Coal-fired power plants are being shut down or mothballed.* **2** to decide not to develop sth such as a plan for a period of time **SYN** **shelve**: ***be mothballed*** *The original proposal had been mothballed years ago.*

**moth-eaten** *adj.* **1** (of clothes, etc.) damaged or destroyed by moths **2** (*informal, disapproving*) very old and in bad condition **SYN** **shabby**

**mother** 🔑 **A1** /ˈmʌðə(r)/ *noun, verb*
- *noun* **1** ❓ **A1** a female parent of a child or animal; a person who is acting as a mother to a child: *I want to buy a present for my mother and father.* ◇ *the relationship between mother and baby* ◇ *She's the mother of twins.* ◇ *a mother of three* (= with three children) ◇ *a young/new/single mother* ◇ *an **expectant*** (= pregnant) ***mother*** ◇ *working/stay-at-home mothers* ◇ *the mother chimpanzee caring for her young* ◇ see also BIRTH MOTHER, EARTH MOTHER, QUEEN MOTHER, SURROGATE MOTHER **2** the title of a woman who is head of a CONVENT (= a community of NUNS) ◇ see also MOTHER SUPERIOR
**IDM** **at your ˈmother's ˈknee** when you were very young: *I learnt these songs at my mother's knee.* **the ˈmother of (all) sth** (*informal*) used to emphasize that sth is very large, unpleasant, important, etc.: *I got stuck in the mother of all traffic jams.* ◇ more at NECESSITY, OLD
- *verb* ~ **sb/sth** to care for sb/sth because you are their mother, or as if you were their mother: *He was a disturbed child who needed mothering.* ◇ *Stop mothering me!*

**mother·board** /ˈmʌðəbɔːd; *NAmE* -ðərbɔːrd/ *noun* (*computing*) the main board of a computer, containing all the CIRCUITS

**ˈmother country** *noun* [sing.] **1** the country where you or your family were born and that you feel a strong emotional connection with **2** the country that controls or used to control the government of another country

**ˈmother figure** *noun* an older woman that you go to for advice, support, help, etc., as you would to a mother ◇ see also FATHER FIGURE

**mother·fuck·er** /ˈmʌðəfʌkə(r); *NAmE* -ðərf-/ *noun* (*taboo, slang, especially NAmE*) a very offensive word used to show great anger or dislike towards sb, especially a man

**ˈmother ˈhen** *noun* (*sometimes disapproving*) a woman who likes to care for and protect people and who worries about them a lot

**mother·hood** /ˈmʌðəhʊd; *NAmE* -ðərh-/ *noun* [U] the state of being a mother: *Motherhood suits her.*

**mother·ing** /ˈmʌðərɪŋ/ *noun* [U] the act of caring for and protecting children or other people: *an example of good/poor mothering*

---

1017 **motion picture**

**Mothering ˈSunday** *noun* [U, C] (*BrE, becoming old-fashioned*) = MOTHER'S DAY

**mother-in-law** *noun* (*pl.* **mothers-in-law**) the mother of your husband or wife ◇ *compare* FATHER-IN-LAW

**mother·land** /ˈmʌðəlænd; *NAmE* -ðərl-/ *noun* (*formal*) the country that you were born in and that you feel a strong emotional connection with ◇ see also FATHERLAND

**mother·less** /ˈmʌðələs; *NAmE* -ðərl-/ *adj.* having no mother because she has died or does not live with you

**ˈmother lode** *noun* [usually sing.] a very rich source of gold, silver, etc. in a mine: (*especially NAmE, figurative*) *Her own experiences have provided her with a mother lode of material for her songs.*

**mother·ly** /ˈmʌðəli; *NAmE* -ðərli/ *adj.* having the qualities of a good mother; typical of a mother **SYN** **maternal**: *motherly love* ◇ *She was a kind, motherly woman.*

**Mother ˈNature** *noun* [U] the natural world, when you consider it as a force that affects the world and humans

**mother-of-ˈpearl** (*also* **pearl**) *noun* [U] the hard smooth shiny substance in various colours that forms a layer inside the shells of some types of SHELLFISH and is used in making buttons and for decoration

**ˈMother's Day** *noun* a day on which mothers traditionally receive cards and gifts from their children, celebrated in the UK on the fourth Sunday in Lent and in the US on the second Sunday in May

**mother·ship** /ˈmʌðəʃɪp; *NAmE* -ðərʃ-/ (*also* **ˈmother ship**) *noun* a large ship or SPACECRAFT that smaller ones go out from **2** a place or an organization that is the base of sth: *The company is breaking away from the mothership and rebranding itself.*

**Mother Suˈperior** *noun* a woman who is the head of a female religious community, especially a CONVENT (= a community of NUNS)

**mother-to-ˈbe** *noun* (*pl.* **mothers-to-be**) a woman who is pregnant

**mother ˈtongue** *noun* the language that you first learn to speak when you are a child **SYN** **first language**

**motif** /məʊˈtiːf/ *noun* **1** a design or a pattern used as a decoration: *wallpaper with a flower motif* **2** a subject, an idea or a phrase that is repeated and developed in a work of literature or a piece of music ◇ see also LEITMOTIF **SYN** **theme**

**mo·tion** ❓+ **B2** /ˈməʊʃn/ *noun, verb*
- *noun* **1** ❓+ **B2** [U, sing.] the act or process of moving or the way sth moves: *Newton's laws of motion* ◇ *The swaying motion of the ship was making me feel seasick.* ◇ *Rub the cream in with a circular motion.* ◇ ***in ~*** (*formal*) *Do not alight while the train is still in motion* (= moving). ◇ see also BROWNIAN MOTION, PERPETUAL MOTION, SLOW MOTION **2** ❓+ **C1** [C] a particular movement made usually with your hand or your head, especially to communicate sth **SYN** **gesture**: *At a single motion of his hand, the room fell silent.* **3** ❓+ **C1** [C] a formal proposal that is discussed and voted on at a meeting: *to **table/put forward a motion*** ◇ *to **propose a motion*** (= to be the main speaker in favour of a motion) ◇ *The **motion was adopted/carried** by six votes to one.* ◇ WORDFINDER NOTE at DEBATE **4** [C] (*BrE, formal*) an act of emptying the BOWELS; the waste matter that is emptied from the bowels
**IDM** **go through the ˈmotions (of doing sth)** to do or say sth because you have to, not because you really want to **set/put sth in ˈmotion** to start sth moving: *They set the machinery in motion.* ◇ (*figurative*) *The wheels of change have been set in motion.*
- *verb* [I, T] to make a movement, usually with your hand or head, to show sb what you want them to do: ***~ to sb (to do sth)*** *I motioned to the waiter.* ◇ ***~ (for) sb to do sth*** *He motioned for us to follow him.* ◇ ***~ sb + adv./prep.*** *She motioned him into her office.*

**mo·tion·less** /ˈməʊʃnləs/ *adj.* not moving; still: *She stood absolutely motionless.*

**motion ˈpicture** *noun* (*especially NAmE*) a film that is made for the cinema

# motion sickness

**'motion sickness** *noun* [U] the unpleasant feeling that you are going to VOMIT, that some people have when they are moving, especially in a vehicle

**mo·tiv·ate** /'məʊtɪveɪt/ *verb* **1** [often passive] ~ **sb (to do sth)** to be the reason why sb does sth or behaves in a particular way: *He is motivated entirely by self-interest.* **2** to make sb want to do sth, especially sth that involves hard work and effort: ~ **sb** *She's very good at motivating her students.* ◇ ~ **sb to do sth** *The plan is designed to motivate employees to work more efficiently.* **3** ~ **sth** (*SAfrE, formal*) to give reasons for sth that you have stated: *Please motivate your answer to question 5.* ▶ **mo·tiv·ated** *adj.: a racially motivated attack* ◇ *a highly motivated student* (= one who is very interested and works hard) **OPP unmotivated** ⇒ see also SELF-MOTIVATED **mo·tiv·ator** *noun*: *Desire for status can be a powerful motivator.*

**mo·tiv·ation** /ˌməʊtɪ'veɪʃn/ *noun* **1** [C, U] the reason why sb does sth or behaves in a particular way: ~ **(behind sth)** *What is the motivation behind this sudden change?* ◇ ~ **for (doing) sth** *Most people said that pay was their main motivation for working.* **2** [U] the feeling of wanting to do sth, especially sth that involves hard work and effort: *He's intelligent enough but he lacks motivation.* **3** [C] (*SAfrE*) a statement or piece of writing in which you give reasons for sth: *All research proposals must be accompanied by a full motivation.* ▶ **mo·tiv·ation·al** /-ʃənl/ *adj.* (*formal*): *an important motivational factor* ◇ *a motivational speaker/speech*

**mo·tive** /'məʊtɪv/ *noun, adj.*
- *noun* ~ **(for sth)** a reason for doing sth: *There seemed to be no motive for the murder.* ◇ *I'm suspicious of his motives.* ◇ *the profit motive* (= the desire to make a profit) ◇ *I have an ulterior motive in offering to help you.* ⇒ SYNONYMS at REASON ▶ **mo·tive·less** *adj.: an apparently motiveless murder/attack*
- *adj.* [only before noun] (*specialist*) causing movement or action: *motive power/force* (= for example electricity to operate machinery)

**mot·ley** /'mɒtli; *NAmE* 'mɑːt-/ *adj.* (*disapproving*) consisting of many different types of people or things that do not seem to belong together: *The room was filled with a motley collection of furniture and paintings.* ◇ *The audience was a motley crew of students and tourists.*

**moto·cross** /'məʊtəʊkrɒs; *NAmE* -krɔːs/ (*BrE also* **scram·bling**) *noun* [U] the sport of racing motorcycles over rough ground

**moto·neur·on** /ˌməʊtəʊ'njʊərɒn; *NAmE* -'nʊrɑːn/ *noun* = MOTOR NEURON

**motor** /'məʊtə(r)/ *noun, adj., verb*
- *noun* **1** a device that uses electricity, petrol, etc. to produce movement and makes a machine, a vehicle, a boat, etc. work: *an electric motor* ◇ *Batteries power the motor.* ◇ *He started the motor.* ⇒ see also OUTBOARD MOTOR **2** a source of power, energy or movement: *Consumer spending has been the motor of economic growth.* **3** (*BrE, old-fashioned or humorous*) a car: *He uses the motor for local shopping trips.* ◇ *I'm so rich now I can buy a shiny new motor!*
- *adj.* [only before noun] **1** having an engine; using the power of an engine: *motor vehicles* **2** (*especially BrE*) connected with vehicles that have engines: *the motor industry* ◇ *I like all forms of motor sports.* ◇ *a motor accident* ◇ *motor insurance* ◇ *motor fuel* **3** (*specialist*) connected with movement of the body that is produced by muscles; connected with the nerves that control movement: *uncoordinated motor activity* ◇ *Both motor and sensory functions are affected.*
- *verb* [I] + *adv./prep.* (*BrE, old-fashioned*) to travel by car, especially for pleasure ▶ **motor·ing** *noun* [U]: *They're planning a motoring holiday to France this year.*

**motor·bike** /'məʊtəbaɪk; *NAmE* -tərb-/ *noun* **1** (*especially BrE*) = MOTORCYCLE: *Ben drove off on his motorbike.* **2** (*NAmE*) a bicycle that has a small engine ⇒ compare E-BIKE

**motor·boat** /'məʊtəbəʊt; *NAmE* -tərb-/ *noun* a small fast boat driven by an engine

**motor·cade** /'məʊtəkeɪd; *NAmE* -tərk-/ *noun* a line of vehicles including one or more that famous or important people are travelling in: *The President's motorcade glided by.*

**'motor car** *noun* (*BrE, formal*) (*NAmE, old-fashioned*) a car

**motor·cycle** /'məʊtəsaɪkl; *NAmE* -tərs-/ (*also* **motor·bike** *especially in BrE*) *noun* a road vehicle with two wheels, driven by an engine, with one seat for the driver and often a seat for a passenger behind the driver: *to ride a motorcycle* ◇ **on a** ~ *She rode round Italy on a motorcycle.* ◇ *motorcycle racing* ◇ *a motorcycle accident*

**motor·cyc·ling** /'məʊtəsaɪklɪŋ; *NAmE* -tərs-/ *noun* [U] the activity or sport of riding motorcycles

**motor·cyc·list** /'məʊtəsaɪklɪst; *NAmE* -tərs-/ *noun* a person riding a motorcycle: *a police motorcyclist* ◇ *leather-clad motorcyclists* ⇒ compare BIKER (1)

**motor·home** /'məʊtəhəʊm; *NAmE* -tərh-/ (*NAmE also* **motor home**, **RV**, **recreational vehicle**) (*BrE also* **camp·er**, **'camper van**) *noun* a large vehicle designed for people to live and sleep in when they are travelling

**motor·ing** /'məʊtərɪŋ/ *adj.* [only before noun] connected with driving a car: *a motoring offence*

**motor·ist** /'məʊtərɪst/ *noun* a person driving a car ⇒ WORDFINDER NOTE at CAR ⇒ compare PEDESTRIAN

**motor·ized** (*BrE also* **-ised**) /'məʊtəraɪzd/ *adj.* [only before noun] **1** having an engine: *motorized vehicles* ◇ *a motorized wheelchair* **2** (of groups of soldiers, etc.) using vehicles with engines: *motorized forces/divisions*

**'motor lodge** (*NAmE also* **'motor inn**) *noun* = MOTEL

**motor·mouth** /'məʊtəmaʊθ; *NAmE* -tərm-/ *noun* (*pl.* **motor·mouths** /-maʊðz/) (*informal, disapproving*) a person who talks too fast and too much

**motor 'neuron** (*also* **moto·neur·on**) *noun* (*biology*) a nerve cell that sends signals to a muscle or GLAND

**motor 'neurone disease** (*also* **motor neuron disease**) *noun* [U] a disease in which the nerves and muscles become gradually weaker until the person dies

**'motor park** *noun* (*WAfrE*) a station for passengers to get on or off buses or taxis: *Passengers are set down at Molete Motor Park.*

**'motor racing** (*especially BrE*) (*NAmE usually* **'auto racing**) *noun* [U] the sport of racing fast cars on a special track

**'motor scooter** (*especially NAmE*) (*BrE usually* **scoot·er**) *noun* a light motorcycle, usually with small wheels and a curved metal cover at the front to protect the rider's legs

**motor·sport** /'məʊtəspɔːt; *NAmE* -tərspɔːrt/ *noun* [U] (*especially BrE*) (*NAmE usually* **motorsports** [pl.]) the sport of racing fast cars or motorcycles on a special track

**'motor vehicle** *noun* any road vehicle driven by an engine

**motor·way** /'məʊtəweɪ; *NAmE* -tərw-/ *noun* [C, U] (in the UK) a wide road, with at least two LANES in each direction, where traffic can travel fast for long distances between large towns. You can only enter and leave motorways at special JUNCTIONS: *busy/congested motorways* ◇ *Join the motorway at Junction 19.* ◇ *Leave the motorway at the next exit.* ◇ *A nine-mile stretch of motorway has been closed.* ◇ *a motorway service area/service station* ⇒ compare INTERSTATE ⇒ WORDFINDER NOTE at ROAD

**Mo·town**™ /'məʊtaʊn/ *noun* [U] a style of music popular in the 1960s and 1970s, produced by an African American music company based in Detroit **ORIGIN** From the informal name for the city of Detroit, known for its motor industry.

**motte** /mɒt; *NAmE* mɑːt/ *noun* the small hill on which the FORT is built in a motte-and-bailey castle

**motte-and-'bailey 'castle** *noun* an old type of castle that consists of a FORT on a small hill surrounded by an outer wall

**mot·tled** /'mɒtld; *NAmE* 'mɑːt-/ *adj.* marked with shapes of different colours without a regular pattern

**motto** /'mɒtəʊ; *NAmE* 'mɑːt-/ *noun* (*pl.* **-oes** *or* **-os**) a short sentence or phrase that expresses the aims and beliefs of a person, a group, an institution, etc. and is used as a rule of behaviour: *The school's motto is: 'Duty, Honour, Country'.* ◊ *'Live and let live.' That's my motto.*

**mould** (*US* **mold**) /məʊld/ *noun, verb*
- *noun* **1** [C] a container that you pour a liquid or soft substance into, which then becomes solid in the same shape as the container, for example when it is cooled or cooked: *A clay mould is used for casting bronze statues.* ◊ *Pour the chocolate into a heart-shaped mould.* **2** [C, usually sing.] a particular style showing the characteristics, attitudes or behaviour that are typical of sb/sth: *a hero in the 'Superman' mould* ◊ *He is cast in a different mould from his predecessor.* **3** *She doesn't fit (into) the traditional mould of an academic.* **3** [U, C] a fine soft green, grey or black substance like fur that is a type of FUNGUS and that grows on old food or on objects that are left in warm wet air: *There's mould on the cheese.* ◊ *moulds and fungi* ◊ *mould growth*
⊃ see also LEAF MOULD
**IDM** **break the ˈmould (of sth)** to change what people expect from a situation, especially by acting in a dramatic and original way
- *verb* **1** [T] to shape a soft substance into a particular form or object by pressing it or by putting it into a mould: **~A (into B)** *First, mould the clay into the desired shape.* ◊ **~B (from/out of/in A)** *The figure had been moulded in clay.* **2** [T] to strongly influence the way sb's character, opinions, etc. develop: **~sb/sth** *The experience had moulded and coloured her whole life.* ◊ **~sb/sth into sb/sth** *He moulded them into a superb team.* **3** [I, T] **~(sth) to sth** to fit or make sth fit tightly around the shape of sth: *The fabric moulds to the body.*

**mould·er** (*US* **mol·der**) /ˈməʊldə(r)/ *verb* [I] to DECAY (= become destroyed by natural processes) slowly and steadily: *The room smelt of disuse and mouldering books.*

**mould·ing** (*US* **mold·ing**) /ˈməʊldɪŋ/ *noun* [C, U] a narrow piece of plastic, stone, wood, etc. around the top edge of a wall, on a door, etc., usually for decoration ⊃ see also INJECTION MOULDING

**mouldy** (*US* **moldy**) /ˈməʊldi/ *adj.* **1** covered with or containing MOULD: *mouldy bread/cheese* ◊ *Strawberries go mouldy very quickly.* **2** old and not in good condition

**moult** (*US* **molt**) /məʊlt/ *verb, noun*
- *verb* **1** [I, T] **~(sth)** (of a bird or an animal) to lose feathers or hair before new feathers or hair grow **2** [I] (of feathers or hair) to fall out before new feathers or hair grow
- *noun* a loss of feathers or hair, especially as a regular feature of the life cycle of a bird or an animal

**mound** /maʊnd/ *noun* **1** a large pile of earth or stones; a small hill: *a Bronze Age burial mound* ◊ *The castle was built on top of a natural grassy mound.* **2** a pile SYN **heap**: *a small mound of rice/sand* **3** **~of sth** (*informal*) a large amount of sth SYN **heap**: *I've got a mound of paperwork to do.* **4** (in baseball) the small raised area where the player who throws the ball (called the PITCHER) stands

**mount** ❶ B2 /maʊnt/ *verb, noun*
- *verb*
- • ORGANIZE **1** B2 [T] **~sth** to organize and begin sth SYN **arrange**: *Residents mounted a campaign to fight the plans.* ◊ *MPs will mount a fresh challenge to this new policy.* ◊ *an attack mounted by terrorists* ◊ *The National Gallery mounted a major exhibition of her work.*
- • INCREASE **2** B2 [I] to increase gradually: *Pressure is mounting on the government to change the law.* ◊ *The death toll continues to mount.* ⊃ see also MOUNTING
- • BICYCLE/HORSE **3** B2 [T, I] **~(sth)** (*rather formal*) to get on a bicycle, horse, etc. in order to ride it: *He mounted his horse and rode away.* OPP **dismount** ⊃ see also MOUNTED
- • GO UP STH **4** [T] **~sth** (*formal*) to go up sth, or up on to sth that is raised SYN **ascend**: *She slowly mounted the steps.* ◊ *He mounted the platform and addressed the crowd.*
- • CAMERA/PICTURE/JEWEL, ETC. **5** [T] **~sth (on/onto/in sth)** to fix sth into position on sth, so that you can use it, look at it or study it: *Cameras are mounted around the city.* ◊ *The diamond is mounted in gold.*
- • OF MALE ANIMAL **6** [T] **~sth** to get onto the back of a female animal in order to have sex **IDM** see GUARD *n.*
**PHRV** **ˌmount ˈup** to increase gradually in size and quantity SYN **build up**: *Meanwhile, my debts were mounting up.*

**1019** **mounting**

- *noun*
- • MOUNTAIN **1** **Mount** (*abbr.* **Mt**) (used in modern English only in place names) a mountain or a hill: *Mt Kilimanjaro* ◊ *St Michael's Mount*
- • HORSE **2** (*formal* or *literary*) a horse that you ride on
- • FOR DISPLAYING/SUPPORTING STH **3** something such as a piece of card or glass that you put sth on or attach sth to, to display it **4** (*also* **mount·ing**) something that an object stands on or is attached to for support: *an engine/gun mount*

**moun·tain** ❶ A1 /ˈmaʊntən; *NAmE* -tn/ *noun*
**1** ❶ A1 a very high hill, often with rocks near the top: *the mountains of Andalusia* ◊ *snow-capped mountains* ◊ *to climb a mountain* ◊ **in the mountains** *We spent a week walking in the mountains.* ◊ *to enjoy the mountain air/scenery* ◊ *the world's longest mountain range* ◊ *a mountain rescue team*

**WORDFINDER** altitude, foothill, peak, precipice, ridge, slope, summit, valley, volcano

**2** **~(of sth/sb)** (*informal*) a very large amount or number of sth; the very large size of sth/sb: *a mountain of work* ◊ *We made mountains of sandwiches.*
**IDM** **make a ˌmountain out of a ˈmolehill** (*disapproving*) to make an unimportant matter seem important ⊃ more at MOVE *v.*

**ˌmountain ˈash** *noun* = ROWAN

**ˈmountain bike** *noun* a bicycle with a strong frame, wide tyres and many GEARS, designed for riding on rough ground ⊃ see also HYBRID (4), ROAD BIKE ▸ **ˈmountain biking** *noun* [U]

**ˌMountain ˈDaylight Time** *noun* [U] (*abbr.* **MDT**) the time used in summer in parts of the US and Canada near the Rocky Mountains that is six hours earlier than UTC

**moun·tain·eer** /ˌmaʊntəˈnɪə(r); *NAmE* -tnˈɪr/ *noun* a person who climbs mountains as a sport

**moun·tain·eer·ing** /ˌmaʊntəˈnɪərɪŋ; *NAmE* -tnˈɪr-/ *noun* [U] the sport or activity of climbing mountains: *to go mountaineering* ◊ *a mountaineering expedition*

**ˈmountain lion** *noun* (*NAmE*) = PUMA

**ˈmountain man** *noun* (*NAmE*) a man who lives in the mountains, especially one who catches and kills animals for their fur

**moun·tain·ous** /ˈmaʊntənəs/ *adj.* **1** having many mountains: *a mountainous region/terrain* ⊃ WORDFINDER NOTE at LANDSCAPE **2** very large in size or amount; like a mountain SYN **huge**: *mountainous waves*

**moun·tain·side** /ˈmaʊntənsaɪd; *NAmE* -tn-/ *noun* the side or slope of a mountain: *Tracks led up the mountainside.*

**ˌMountain ˈStandard Time** *noun* [U] (*abbr.* **MST**) the time used in winter in parts of the US and Canada near the Rocky Mountains that is seven hours earlier than UTC

**ˈMountain time** *noun* [U] the standard time in the parts of the US and Canada that are near the Rocky Mountains

**moun·tain·top** /ˈmaʊntəntɒp; *NAmE* -tnta:p/ *noun* the top of a mountain ▸ **ˈmoun·tain·top** *adj.* [only before noun]: *a mountaintop ranch*

**mount·ed** /ˈmaʊntɪd/ *adj.* [only before noun] **1** (of a person, especially a soldier or a police officer) riding a horse: *mounted policemen* **2** placed on sth or attached to sth for display or support: *a mounted photograph* **3** **-mounted** (in compounds) attached to the thing mentioned for support: *a ceiling-mounted fan* ⊃ see also WALL-MOUNTED

**Moun·tie** /ˈmaʊnti/ *noun* (*informal*) a member of the Royal Canadian Mounted Police

**mount·ing** /ˈmaʊntɪŋ/ *adj., noun*
- *adj.* [only before noun] increasing, often in a manner that causes or expresses worry SYN **growing**: *mounting excitement/concern/tension* ◊ *There is mounting evidence of serious effects on people's health.*
- *noun* = MOUNT (4): *The engine came loose from its mountings.*

# mourn

**mourn** /mɔːn; NAmE mɔːrn/ verb [T, I] to feel and show that you are sad because sb has died; to feel sad because sth no longer exists or is no longer the same **SYN** grieve: ~ sth *He was still mourning his brother's death.* ◊ *They mourn the passing of a simpler way of life.* ◊ ~ (for sb/sth) *Today we mourn for all those who died in two world wars.* ◊ *She mourned for her lost childhood.* ⊃ WORDFINDER NOTE at DIE

**mourn·er** /'mɔːnə(r); NAmE 'mɔːrn-/ noun a person who attends a FUNERAL, especially a friend or a relative of the dead person

**mourn·ful** /'mɔːnfl; NAmE 'mɔːrn-/ adj. very sad **SYN** melancholy: *mournful eyes* ◊ *mournful music* ◊ *I couldn't bear the mournful look on her face.* ▶ **mourn·ful·ly** /-fəli/ adv.: *The dog looked mournfully after its owner.*

**mourn·ing** /'mɔːnɪŋ; NAmE 'mɔːrn-/ noun [U] **1** the feeling of being sad that you have and show because sb has died **SYN** grief: *The government announced a day of national mourning for the victims.* ◊ *She was still in mourning for her husband.* **2** clothes that people wear to show that they are sad at sb's death

**mouse** ⓣ **A1** /maʊs/ noun, verb
■ noun **1** 🗝 **A1** (*pl.* **mice** /maɪs/) a small animal that is covered in fur and has a long thin tail. Mice live in fields, in people's houses or where food is stored: *a field mouse* ◊ *a house mouse* ◊ *The stores were overrun with rats and mice.* ◊ *She crept upstairs, quiet as a mouse.* ◊ (*figurative*) *He was a weak little mouse of a man.* ⊃ see also DORMOUSE **2** 🗝 **A1** (*pl.* **mice** or **mouses**) (*computing*) a small device that is moved by hand across a surface to control the movement of the CURSOR on a computer screen: *Use the mouse to drag the icon to a new position.* ◊ *Click the left mouse button twice to highlight the program.* ◊ *With simple mouse clicks, the viewer can navigate the room.* **IDM** see CAT
■ verb **PHRV** **'mouse over sth** (*computing*) to use the mouse to move over sth on a computer screen: *Mouse over the link in the original message.* ▶ **mouse-over** /'maʊsəʊvə(r); NAmE -oʊvər/ noun [C, U]: *the use of mouseovers in web design*

**'mouse mat** (*BrE*) (*especially NAmE* **'mouse pad**) noun a small square of material that is the best kind of surface on which to use a computer mouse

**mous·er** /'maʊsə(r)/ noun a cat that catches mice

**mouse·trap** /'maʊstræp/ noun a piece of equipment for catching mice, especially one with a powerful spring that SNAPS down onto the mouse when it touches a piece of cheese or other food attached to the mousetrap

**mous·ey** = MOUSY

**mous·saka** /muːˈsɑːkə/ noun [U, C] a Greek dish made from layers of AUBERGINE and meat with cheese on top

**mousse** /muːs/ noun [C, U] **1** a cold DESSERT (= a sweet dish) made with cream and egg whites and with fruit, chocolate, etc. to give it a sweet taste; a similar dish made with fish, vegetables, etc: *a chocolate/strawberry mousse* ◊ *salmon/mushroom mousse* **2** a substance that is sold in AEROSOLS, for example the light white substance that is used on hair to give it a particular style or to improve its condition

**mous·tache** (*US* **mus·tache**) /məˈstɑːʃ; *BrE also* məˈstɑːʃ; *NAmE also* məˈstæʃ/ noun **1** a line of hair that a man allows to grow on his upper lip ⊃ see also HANDLEBAR MOUSTACHE **2 moustaches** [pl.] a very long moustache ⊃ compare BEARD

**mous·tached** (*US* **mus·tached**) /məˈstɑːʃt; *BrE also* məˈstɑːʃt; *NAmE also* məˈstæʃt/ adj. [usually before noun] having a moustache ⊃ compare MUSTACHIOED

**mousy** (*also* **mousey**) /'maʊsi/ adj. (*disapproving*) **1** (of hair) of a light brown colour ⊃ WORDFINDER NOTE at BLONDE **2** (*usually disapproving*) (of people) shy and quiet; without a strong personality

**mouth** ⓣ **A1** /maʊθ/ noun, verb
■ noun /maʊθ/ (*pl.* **mouths** /maʊðz/)
• PART OF FACE **1** 🗝 **A1** the opening in the face used for speaking, eating, etc.; the area inside the head behind this opening: *She opened her mouth to say something.* ◊ *His mouth twisted into a wry smile.* ◊ *Their mouths fell open* (= they were surprised). ◊ *Don't talk with your mouth full* (= when eating). ◊ *The creature was foaming/frothing at the mouth.* ⊃ see also FOOT-AND-MOUTH DISEASE
• PERSON NEEDING FOOD **2** a person considered only as sb who needs to be provided with food: *Now there would be another mouth to feed.* ◊ *The world will not be able to support all these extra hungry mouths.*
• OF RIVER **3** 🗝 **B2** the place where a river joins the sea: *the mouth of the Hudson River*
• ENTRANCE/OPENING **4** ~ (of sth) the entrance or opening of sth: *the mouth of a cave/pit* ⊃ see also GOALMOUTH
• WAY OF SPEAKING **5** a particular way of speaking: *He has a foul mouth on him!* ◊ *Watch your mouth!* (= stop saying things that are rude and/or offensive) ⊃ see also LOUDMOUTH
• -MOUTHED **6** (in adjectives) having the type or shape of mouth mentioned: *a wide-mouthed old woman* ◊ *a narrow-mouthed cave* ⊃ see also OPEN-MOUTHED **7** (in adjectives) having a particular way of speaking: *a rather crude-mouthed individual* ⊃ see also FOUL-MOUTHED, MEALY-MOUTHED, POTTY-MOUTHED

**IDM** **be all 'mouth** (*informal*) if you say sb **is all mouth**, you mean that they talk a lot about doing sth, but are, in fact, not brave enough to do it **down in the 'mouth** unhappy and depressed **keep your 'mouth shut** (*informal*) to not talk about sth to sb because it is a secret or because it will upset or annoy them: *I've warned them to keep their mouths shut about this.* ◊ *Now she's upset—why couldn't you keep your mouth shut?* **out of the mouths of 'babes (and 'sucklings)** (*saying*) used when a small child has just said sth that seems very wise or clever **run off at the 'mouth** (*NAmE, informal*) to talk too much, in a way that is not sensible ⊃ more at BIG *adj.*, BORN *v.*, BREAD, BUTTER *n.*, FOAM *v.*, FOOT *n.*, GIFT *n.*, HEART *n.*, HORSE *n.*, LIVE¹, MELT, MONEY, SHOOT *v.*, SHUT *v.*, TASTE *n.*, WATCH *v.*, WORD *n.*

■ verb /maʊð/ **1** ~ sth | + speech to move your lips as if you were saying sth, but without making a sound: *He mouthed a few obscenities at us and then moved off.* **2** ~ sth | + speech (*disapproving*) to say sth that you do not really feel, believe or understand: *They're just mouthing empty slogans.*

**PHRV** **mouth 'off (at/about sth)** (*informal*) to talk or complain loudly about sth

**mouth·feel** /'maʊθfiːl/ noun [C, U] the way an item of food or drink feels in the mouth: *The drink has a creamy mouthfeel.*

**mouth·ful** /'maʊθfʊl/ noun **1** [C] an amount of food or drink that you put in your mouth at one time: *She took a mouthful of water.* **2** [sing.] (*informal*) a word or a phrase that is long and complicated or difficult to pronounce **IDM** **give sb a 'mouthful** (*informal, especially BrE*) to speak angrily to sb, perhaps swearing at them

**'mouth organ** noun = HARMONICA

**mouth·piece** /'maʊθpiːs/ noun **1** the part of a phone or radio device that is next to your mouth when you speak **2** the part of a musical instrument that you place between your lips **3** ~ (of/for sb) (*often disapproving*) a person, newspaper, etc. that speaks to represent another person or group of people: *The media is controlled by the state and acts as a mouthpiece for the ruling party.*

**mouth-to-mouth re·susciˈtation** (*also* **mouth-to-ˈmouth**) noun [U] the act of breathing into the mouth of an unconscious person in order to fill their lungs with air **SYN** the kiss of life

**mouth·wash** /'maʊθwɒʃ; NAmE -wɔːʃ/ noun [C, U] a liquid used to make the mouth fresh and healthy

**'mouth-watering** adj. (*approving*) **mouth-watering** food looks or smells so good that you want to eat it immediately **SYN** tempting: *a mouth-watering display of cakes* ◊ (*figurative*) *mouth-watering travel brochures*

**mouthy** /'maʊθi; 'maʊði/ adj. (*informal, disapproving*) used to describe a person who talks a lot, sometimes expressing their opinions strongly and in a rude way

**mov·able** (*also* **move·able**) /ˈmuːvəbl/ *adj., noun*
- *adj.* **1** that can be moved from one place or position to another: *movable partitions* ◇ *a doll with a movable head* **2** (*law*) (of property) able to be taken from one house, etc. to another
- *noun* [C, usually pl.] (*law*) a thing that can be moved from one house, etc. to another; a personal possession

## move ❶ A1 Ⓢ /muːv/ *verb, noun*
- *verb*
- **CHANGE POSITION 1** A1 [I, T] to change position or make sb/sth change position in a way that can be seen, heard or felt: *Don't move—stay perfectly still.* ◇ *The bus was already moving when I jumped onto it.* ◇ **+ adv./prep.** *He could hear someone moving around in the room above.* ◇ *Phil moved towards the window.* ◇ *You can hardly move in this pub on Saturdays* (= because it is so crowded). ◇ *You can't move for books in her room.* ◇ **~sth** *I can't move my fingers.* ◇ **~sth + adv./prep.** *We moved our chairs a little nearer.*
- **CHANGE HOUSE/JOB 2** A2 [I, T] to change the place where you live, have your work, etc: *We don't like it here so we've decided to move.* ◇ **~(from …) (to …)** *The company's moving to Scotland.* ◇ **~away** *She's been all on her own since her daughter moved away.* ◇ **~house** (*BrE*) *We moved house last week.* **3** A2 [T] **~sb (from …) (to …)** to make sb change from one job, class, etc. to another SYN **transfer**: *I'm being moved to the New York office.*
- **IN BOARD GAMES 4** A2 [I, T] (in CHESS and other board games) to change the position of a piece: *It's your turn to move.* ◇ **~sth** *She moved her queen.*
- **LEAVE/BEGIN 5** [I] (*informal*) to leave, begin sth, etc. quickly: *Let's move—it's time we went shopping.*
- **CHANGE IDEAS/TIME 6** B2 [I, T] to change; to change sth SYN **shift**: **(+ adv./prep.)** *The government has not moved on this issue.* ◇ *Things have moved on a lot.* ◇ **~sth (+ adv./prep.)** *Let's move the meeting to Wednesday.*
- **MAKE PROGRESS 7** B2 [I] to make progress in the way or direction mentioned SYN **progress**: **~on** *Time is moving on.* ◇ **~ahead** *Share prices moved ahead today.* ◇ **+ adv./prep.** *Things are not moving as fast as we hoped.*
- **TAKE ACTION 8** [I] to take action; to do sth SYN **act**: *The police moved quickly to dispel the rumours.* ◇ *The firm moved to reassure customers.* ⊃ SYNONYMS at ACTION
- **CAUSE STRONG FEELINGS 9** B2 [T] to cause sb to have strong feelings, especially of sympathy or of being sad: **~sb** *We were **deeply** moved by her plight.* ◇ **~sb to sth** *Grown men were **moved to tears** at the horrific scenes.* ⊃ see also MOVING
- **MAKE SB DO STH 10** [T] (*formal*) to cause sb to do sth SYN **prompt**: **~sb to do sth** *She felt moved to address the crowd.* ◇ **~sb** *He works **when the spirit moves him*** (= when he wants to).
- **SELL 11** [T, I] **~(sth)** to sell goods; to be sold: *How quickly can we move this stock?*
- **SUGGEST FORMALLY 12** [T] (*formal*) to suggest sth formally so that it can be discussed and decided SYN **put forward**: **~sth** *The Opposition moved an amendment to the Bill.* ◇ **~that …** *I move that a vote be taken on this.*

**IDM** **get ˈmoving** (*informal*) to begin, leave, etc. quickly: *It's late—we'd better get moving.* **get sth ˈmoving** (*informal*) to cause sth to make progress: *The new director has really got things moving.* **move heaven and ˈearth** to do everything you possibly can in order to achieve sth **ˈmove it** (especially in orders) (*informal*) to do sth more quickly because there is not much time: *Move it! We're going to be late!* **move ˈmountains** to make a great effort to do sth: *The director moved mountains to remake this classic film.* ⊃ more at ASS, FORWARD *adv.*, TIME *n.*

**PHRV** **move aˈlong** to go to a new position, especially in order to make room for other people: *The bus driver asked them to move along.* **move ˈin** | **move ˈinto sth** to start to live in your new home: *Our new neighbours moved in yesterday.* OPP **move out** **ˈmove in sth** to live, spend your time, etc. in a particular social group: *She only moves in the best circles.* **move ˈin (on sb/sth)** to move towards sb/sth from all directions, especially in a THREATENING way: *The police moved in on the terrorists.* **move ˈin with sb** to start living with sb in the house or flat where they already live **move ˈoff** (especially of a vehicle) to start moving; to leave **move ˈon** to move away from the scene of an accident, etc. **move ˈon (to sth)** B1 to start doing or discussing sth new: *I've been in this job long enough—it's time I moved on.* ◇ *Can we move on to the next item on the agenda?* **move sb ˈon** (of police, etc.) to order sb to move away from the scene of an accident, etc. **move ˈout** to leave your old home OPP **move in** **move ˈover** (*also* **move ˈup**) to change your position in order to make room for sb: *There's room for another one if you move up a bit.*

- *noun*
- **CHANGE OF POSITION 1** B1 [usually sing.] a change of place or position: *Don't **make a move**!* ◇ *Every move was painful.* ◇ *She felt he was watching her **every move**.* ◇ *He performed some energetic **dance moves**.* ⊃ see also MOVEMENT
- **CHANGE OF HOUSE/JOB 2** B1 an act of changing the place where you live or work: *What's the date of your move?* ◇ *Her new job is just a sideways move.* ◇ **~(from …) (to …)** *Their move from Italy to the US has not been a success.*
- **IN GAMES/SPORTS 3** B1 an act of changing the position of a piece in CHESS or other games that are played on a board: *The game was over in only six moves.* ◇ *It's your move.* **4** B2 an action in a sport or game: *In probably the best move of the game, Moseley scored the important try.*
- **ACTION 5** B2 an action that you do or need to do to achieve sth: *Getting a job in marketing was a good **career move**.* ◇ *'I'll give you 30 per cent of the price.' **Good move**, I thought.* ◇ **~by sb/sth** *This latest move by the government has aroused fierce opposition.* ◇ **~to do sth** *The management have made no move to settle the strike.* ⊃ see also FALSE MOVE
- **CHANGE OF IDEAS/BEHAVIOUR 6** B2 a change in ideas, attitudes or behaviour SYN **shift**, **trend**: **~away from sth** *There has been a move away from nuclear energy.* ◇ **~to/towards sth** *There are moves towards greater trade liberalization.*

**IDM** **be on the ˈmove 1** to be travelling from place to place **2** to be moving; to be going somewhere: *The car was already on the move.* ◇ *The firm is on the move to larger offices.* **3** = BE ON THE GO at GO *n.* **get a ˈmove on** (*informal*) you tell sb to **get a move on** when you want them to hurry **make the first ˈmove** to do sth before sb else, for example in order to end an argument or to begin sth: *If he wants to see me, he should make the first move.* **make a ˈmove** (*BrE*, *informal*) to begin a journey or a task: *It's getting late—we'd better make a move.* **make a ˈmove on sb** (*informal*) **1** to try to start a sexual relationship with sb **2** (*sport*) to try to pass sb who is in front of you in a race **make a, your, etc. ˈmove** to do the action that you intend to do or need to do in order to achieve sth: *The rebels waited until nightfall before they made their move.* ⊃ more at BUST *v.*

**move·able** = MOVABLE

## move·ment ❶ A2 ● /ˈmuːvmənt/ *noun*
- **CHANGING POSITION 1** A2 [C, U] an act of moving the body or part of the body: *hand/eye movements* ◇ *She observed the gentle movement of his chest as he breathed.* ◇ *Loose clothing gives you greater freedom of movement.* ◇ *There was a sudden movement in the undergrowth.* ◇ *The dance combined colour, movement and music.* **2** B1 [C, U] an act of moving from one place to another or of moving sth from one place to another: *enemy troop movements* ◇ *laws to allow free movement of goods and services* ◇ *Fences restricted the movement of people and animals.* ⊃ see also PINCER MOVEMENT
- **GROUP OF PEOPLE 3** B1 [C + sing./pl. v.] a group of people who share the same ideas or aims: *the trade union movement* ◇ *the labour movement* ◇ *the civil rights movement* ◇ *the Romantic movement* (= for example in literature) ◇ **~to build/join/support a movement** ◇ **~for sth** *She led a movement for women's rights.* ◇ *a mass movement for change* ⊃ see also CIVIL RIGHTS MOVEMENT
- **PERSON'S ACTIVITIES 4** **movements** [pl.] a person's activities over a period of time, especially as watched by sb else: *The police are keeping a close watch on the suspect's movements.* ◇ *to track/monitor sb's movements*
- **CHANGE OF IDEAS/BEHAVIOUR 5** [sing.] a slow steady change in what people in society do or think SYN **trend**: **~away from sth** *We see a big movement away from cash.* ◇ **~towards sth** *a movement towards greater sexual equality*

**mover**

- **PROGRESS 6** [U] ~ (in sth) progress, especially in a particular task: *It needs cooperation from all the countries to get any movement in arms control.*
- **CHANGE IN AMOUNT 7** [U, C] ~ (in sth) a change in amount: *There has been no movement in oil prices.*
- **MUSIC 8** [C] any of the main parts that a long piece of music is divided into: *the slow movement of the First Concerto*
- **OF BOWELS 9** [C] (*medical*) = BOWEL MOVEMENT

**mover** /ˈmuːvə(r)/ *noun* **1** a person or thing that moves in a particular way: *a great mover on the dance floor* ⇒ see also PRIME MOVER **2** a person whose job is to move furniture from one house to another: *professional furniture movers* ⇒ compare REMOVER ⇒ see also EARTH MOVER
**IDM** **ˌmovers and ˈshakers** people with power in important organizations

**movie** ⓘ **A1** /ˈmuːvi/ *noun* (*especially NAmE*) **1** **A1** [C] a series of moving pictures recorded with sound that tells a story, watched at a movie theater or on a television or other device **SYN** film: *You'll love this movie.* ◊ *Let's watch a movie tonight.* ◊ *Have you seen the latest Miyazaki movie?* ◊ *to rent/download a movie* ◊ *to make a horror movie* ◊ *a movie starring Jennifer Lawrence* ◊ *a famous movie director* ◊ *the Hollywood movie industry* ◊ *a movie studio* ⇒ see also ACTION MOVIE, B-MOVIE, BUDDY MOVIE, ROAD MOVIE, SNUFF MOVIE **2** **A1** **the movies** [pl.] when you go to **the movies**, you go to a movie theater to see a movie: *Let's go to the movies.* **3** **A1** **the movies** [pl.] movies as an art or an industry: *I've always wanted to work in the movies.* ◊ *Is it glamorous like in the movies?*

**movie-goer** /ˈmuːviɡəʊə(r)/ *noun* (*especially NAmE*) = FILMGOER

**ˈmovie star** *noun* (*especially NAmE*) = FILM STAR

**ˈmovie theater** (*also* ˈtheater, ˈmovie house) *noun* (*NAmE*) = CINEMA (1): *The documentary opens tomorrow in movie theaters nationwide.*

**mov·ing** **B2** /ˈmuːvɪŋ/ *adj.* **1 B2** causing strong, often sad, feelings about sb/sth: *a deeply moving experience* ⇒ WORDFINDER NOTE at STORY **2** [only before noun] (of things) changing from one place or position to another: *the moving parts of a machine* ◊ *fast-moving water* ◊ *a moving target* ▶ **mov·ing·ly** *adv.*: *She described her experiences in Africa very movingly.*

**ˈmoving van** (*NAmE*) (*BrE* re·ˈmoval van, ˈfurniture van) *noun* a large van used for moving furniture and other goods from one home or business to another

**mow** /məʊ/ *verb* [T, I] (mowed, mown /məʊn/ *or* mowed) ~ (sth) to cut grass, etc. using a machine or tool with a special BLADE (= sharp cutting edge) or BLADES: *I mow the lawn every week in summer.* ◊ *the smell of new-mown hay*
**PHRV** **mow sb**↔**down** to kill sb using a machine or a gun, especially when several people are all killed at the same time

**mower** /ˈməʊə(r)/ *noun* (*especially in compounds*) a machine that cuts grass: *a lawnmower* ◊ *a motor/rotary mower*

**moxie** /ˈmɒksi/ *NAmE* /ˈmɑːk-/ *noun* [U] (*NAmE, informal*) courage, energy and DETERMINATION

**moz·za·rella** /ˌmɒtsəˈrelə/ *NAmE* /ˌmɑːt-/ *noun* [U] a type of soft white Italian cheese with a mild taste

**moz·zie** /ˈmɒzi/ *NAmE* /ˈmɑːzi/ *noun* (*pl.* -ies) (*informal*) = MOSQUITO

**MP** /ˌem ˈpiː/ *noun* **1** a person who has been elected to represent the people of a particular area in a parliament (the abbreviation for 'Member of Parliament'): *Michael Phillips MP* ◊ *Write to your local MP to protest.* ◊ *Conservative/Labour MPs* ◊ *the MP for Oxford East* **2** a member of the MILITARY POLICE

**MP3** /ˌem piː ˈθriː/ *noun* [U, C] a method of reducing the size of a computer file containing sound; a file that is reduced in size in this way

**MP3 player** *noun* a small piece of equipment that can store information taken from the internet and that you can carry with you, for example so that you can listen to music

**MP4** /ˌem piː ˈfɔː(r)/ *noun* [U, C] a method of reducing the size of a computer file containing sound and images; a file that is reduced in size in this way

**MPEG** /ˈempeɡ/ *noun* (*computing*) **1** [U] technology that reduces the size of files that contain video images or sounds: *an MPEG file* **2** [C] a file produced using this technology

**mpg** /ˌem piː ˈdʒiː/ *abbr.* miles per gallon (used for saying how much petrol a vehicle uses): *It does 40 mpg.* ◊ (*NAmE*) *It gets 40 mpg.*

**mph** /ˌem piː ˈeɪtʃ/ *abbr.* miles per hour: *a 60 mph speed limit*

**MPV** /ˌem piː ˈviː/ *noun* a large car like a van (the abbreviation for 'multipurpose vehicle') **SYN** people carrier

**Mr** (*BrE*) (*also* Mr. *NAmE, BrE*) /ˈmɪstə(r)/ *abbr.* **1** a title that comes before a man's family name, or before his first and family names together: *Mr Brown* ◊ *Mr John Brown* ◊ *Mr and Mrs Brown* **2** a title used to address a man in some official positions: *Thank you, Mr Chairman.* ◊ *Mr. President* ⇒ see also MISTER

**Mr. ˈClean** *noun* (*especially NAmE, informal*) a man, especially a politician, who is considered to be very honest and good: *The scandal destroyed his image as Mr. Clean.*

**MRI** /ˌem ɑːr ˈaɪ/ *noun* [U, C] (*medical*) a method of using a strong MAGNETIC FIELD to produce an image of the inside of a person's body (the abbreviation for 'magnetic resonance imaging'): *an MRI scan*

**Mr ˈNice Guy** *noun* (*informal*) a way of describing a man who is very honest and thinks about the wishes and feelings of other people: *I was tired of helping other people. From now on it was no more Mr Nice Guy* (= I would stop being pleasant and kind).

**Mr ˈRight** *noun* (*informal*) the man who would be the right husband for a particular woman: *I'm not getting married in a hurry—I'm waiting for Mr Right to come along.*

**Mrs** (*BrE*) (*also* Mrs. *NAmE, BrE*) /ˈmɪsɪz/ *abbr.* a title that comes before a married woman's family name or before her first and family names together: *Mrs Hill* ◊ *Mrs Susan Hill* ◊ *Mr and Mrs Hill* ⇒ compare MISS, MS

**MRSA** /ˌem ɑːr es ˈeɪ/ *noun* [U] a type of bacteria that cannot be killed by standard ANTIBIOTICS (the abbreviation for 'methicillin-resistant Staphylococcus aureus'): *rising rates of MRSA infections in hospitals* ⇒ see also SUPERBUG

**MS** (*NAmE also* M.S.) /ˌem ˈes/ *abbr.* **1** = MULTIPLE SCLEROSIS **2** = MANUSCRIPT **3** = MSC

**Ms** (*BrE*) (*also* Ms. *NAmE, BrE*) /mɪz, məz/ *abbr.* a title that comes before a woman's family name or before her first and family names together, and that can be used when you do not want to state whether she is married or not: *Ms Murphy* ◊ *Ms Jean Murphy* ⇒ compare MISS, MRS

**MSc** /ˌem es ˈsiː/ (*BrE*) (*NAmE* M.S., MS) *noun* a second university degree in science (the abbreviation for 'Master of Science'): (*BrE*) *to be/have/do an MSc* ◊ (*BrE*) *J Stevens MSc*

**MSG** /ˌem es ˈdʒiː/ *abbr.* MONOSODIUM GLUTAMATE

**MSM** /ˌem es ˈem/ *noun* [U + sing./pl. v.] (*computing*) = MAINSTREAM MEDIA: *The line is beginning to blur between influential blogs and MSM.*

**MSP** /ˌem es ˈpiː/ *noun* the abbreviation for 'Member of the Scottish Parliament': *Alex Neil MSP* ◊ *Write to your local MSP to protest.* ◊ *Labour MSPs*

**MST** /ˌem es ˈtiː/ *abbr.* MOUNTAIN STANDARD TIME

**Mt** (*also* Mt. *especially in NAmE*) *abbr.* (*especially on maps*) MOUNT: *Mt Kenya*

**mu** /mjuː/ *noun* the 12th letter of the Greek alphabet (M, μ)

**much** ⓘ **A1** /mʌtʃ/ *det., pron., adv.*
■ **det., pron.** **A1** used with uncountable nouns, especially in negative sentences to mean 'a large amount of sth', or after 'how' to ask about the amount of sth. It is also used with 'as', 'so' and 'too': *I don't have much money with me.* ◊ '*Got any money?' 'Not much.'* ◊ *How much water do you need?* ◊ *How much is it* (= What does it cost)? ◊ *Take as much time as you like.* ◊ *There was so much traffic that we were an hour late.* ◊ *I've got far too much to do.* ◊ (*formal*) *I*

lay awake for much of the night. ◊ (formal) There was much discussion about the reasons for the failure. **IDM** **as ˈmuch** the same: *Please help me get this job—you know I would do as much for you.* ◊ *'Roger stole the money.' 'I thought as much.'* **as much as sb can do** used to say that sth is difficult to do: *No dessert for me, thanks. It was as much as I could do to finish the main course.* **ˌnot much ˈin it** used to say that there is little difference between two things: *I won, but there wasn't much in it* (= our scores were nearly the same). **ˌnot much of a …** not a good …: *He's not much of a tennis player.* **ˈthis much** used to introduce sth positive or definite: *I'll say this much for him—he never leaves a piece of work unfinished.* **ˌtoo ˈmuch** a situation or experience that is too difficult to deal with: *It all proved too much for him.* ◊ more at BIT, MAKE v.

■ *adv.* **A1** (**more**, **most**) to a great degree: *Thank you very much for the flowers.* ◊ *I would very much like to see you again.* ◊ *He isn't in the office much* (= often). ◊ *You worry too much.* ◊ *My new job is much the same as the old one.* ◊ *Much to her surprise he came back the next day.* ◊ *She's much better today.* ◊ *The other one was much too expensive.* ◊ *Nikolai's English was much the worst.* ◊ *We are very much aware of the lack of food supplies.* ◊ *I'm not much good at tennis.* ◊ *He was much loved by all who knew him.* ◊ *an appeal to raise much-needed cash* **IDM** **ˈmuch as** although: *Much as I would like to stay, I really must go home.* ◆ more at BETTER *n.*, LESS *adv.*

> ### GRAMMAR POINT
> #### much / a lot of / lots of
> - **Much** is used only with uncountable nouns. It is used mainly in questions and negative sentences: *Do you have much free time?* ◊ *How much experience have you had?* ◊ *I don't have much free time.*
> - In statements **a lot of** or **lots of** (*informal*) is much more common: *How much (money) does she earn?* ◊ *She earns a lot of money.* You can also use **plenty (of)**. These phrases can also be used in questions and negative sentences.
> - **A lot of / lots of** is still felt to be informal, especially in BrE, so in formal writing it is better to use **much**, **a great deal of** or **a large amount of**.
> - **Very much** and **a lot** can be used as adverbs: *I miss my family very much.* ◊ *I miss very much my family.* ◊ *I miss my family a lot.* ◊ *Thanks a lot.* In negative sentences you can use **much**: *I didn't enjoy the film (very) much.*
> ◆ note at MANY

**much·ness** /'mʌtʃnəs/ *noun*
**IDM** **ˌmuch of a ˈmuchness** very similar; almost the same: *The two candidates are much of a muchness—it's hard to choose between them.*

**muck** /mʌk/ *noun, verb*
■ *noun* **1** waste matter from farm animals **SYN** manure: *to spread muck on the fields* **2** (*informal*, *especially BrE*) dirt or mud: *Can you wipe the muck off the windows?* **3** (*informal*, *especially BrE*) something very unpleasant: *I can't eat this muck!* **IDM** **where there's ˌmuck there's ˈbrass** (*BrE*, *saying*) used to say that a business activity that is unpleasant or dirty can bring in a lot of money
■ *verb*
**PHRV** **ˌmuck aˈbout/aˈround** (*BrE*, *informal*) to behave in a silly way, especially when you should be working or doing sth else **SYN** **mess around** **ˌmuck aˈbout/aˈround with sth** (*BrE*, *informal*, *disapproving*) to do sth, especially to a machine, so that it does not work correctly **SYN** **mess around with sth**: *Who's been mucking around with my radio?* **ˌmuck sb aˈbout/aˈround** (*BrE*, *informal*) to treat sb badly, especially by changing your mind a lot, or by not being honest **SYN** **mess sb around**: *They've really mucked us about over our car insurance.* **ˌmuck ˈin** (*BrE*, *informal*) **1** to work with other people in order to complete a task: *If we all muck in, we could have the job finished by the end of the week.* **2** to share food, accommodation, etc. with other people: *We didn't have much money, but everyone just mucked in together.* **ˌmuck ˈout** | **ˌmuck sth ⇔ ˈout** to clean out the place where an animal lives **ˌmuck sth ⇔ ˈup** (*informal*, *especially BrE*) **1** to do sth badly so that you fail to achieve what you wanted or hoped to achieve **SYN** **mess up**: *He completely mucked up his English exam.* **2** to cause

---

1023 muddy

a plan or an arrangement to fail **SYN** **mess up** **3** to make sth dirty: *I don't want you mucking up my nice clean floor.*

**muck·rak·ing** /'mʌkreɪkɪŋ/ *noun* [U] (*informal*, *disapproving*) the activity of looking for information about people's private lives that they do not wish to make public ▶ **muck·raker** *noun*: *Not every reporter needs to be a muckraker.*

**mucky** /'mʌki/ *adj.* (*informal*, *especially BrE*) **1** dirty: *mucky hands* **2** sexually offensive **SYN** **obscene**: *mucky books/jokes*

**ˌmucous ˈmembrane** *noun* (*anatomy*) a thin layer of skin that covers the inside of the nose and mouth and the outside of other organs in the body, producing mucus to prevent these parts from becoming dry

**mucus** /'mjuːkəs/ *noun* [U] a thick liquid that is produced in parts of the body, such as the nose, by a mucous membrane ▶ **mu·cous** /'mjuːkəs/ *adj.*: *mucous glands*

**mud** **⊙** **B1** /mʌd/ *noun* [U] wet earth that is soft and sticky: *The car wheels got stuck in the mud.* ◊ *Your boots are covered in mud.* ◊ *mud bricks/huts* (= made of dried mud) ◆ SYNONYMS at SOIL **IDM** **fling, sling, etc. ˈmud (at sb)** to criticize sb or accuse sb of bad things in order to damage their reputation, especially in politics ◆ see also MUD-SLINGING **ˌmud ˈsticks** (*saying*) people remember and believe the bad things they hear about other people, even if they are later shown to be false ◆ more at CLEAR *adj.*, DRAG *v.*, NAME *n.* ◆ see also MUDFLAT

**ˈmud bath** *noun* **1** a bath in hot mud that contains a lot of minerals, which is taken, for example, to help with RHEUMATISM **2** *usually* **mud·bath** a place where there is a lot of mud: *Heavy rain turned the campsite into a mudbath.*

**mud·dle** /'mʌdl/ *verb, noun*
■ *verb* (*especially BrE*) **1** to put things in the wrong order or mix them up: *~ sth Don't do that—you're muddling my papers.* ◊ *~ sth up Their letters were all muddled up together in a drawer.* **2** *~ sb (up)* to confuse sb: *Slow down a little—you're muddling me.* **3** *~ sb/sth (up)* | *~ A (up) with B* to confuse one person or thing with another **SYN** **mix up**: *I muddled the dates and arrived a week early.* ◊ *He got all muddled up about what went where.* ◊ *They look so alike, I always get them muddled up.*
**PHRV** **ˌmuddle aˈlong** (*especially BrE*, *informal*) to continue doing sth without any clear plan or purpose: *We can't just keep muddling along like this.* **ˌmuddle ˈthrough** (*informal*) to achieve your aims even though you do not know exactly what you are doing and do not have the correct equipment, knowledge, etc: *We'll muddle through somehow.*
■ *noun* (*especially BrE*) **1** [C, usually sing.] a state in which it is difficult to think clearly: **in a ~**: *Can you start from the beginning again—I'm in a muddle.* **2** [C, usually sing., U] *~ (about/over sth)* a situation in which there is a lack of understanding about arrangements, etc. and things are done wrong: *There was a muddle over the theatre tickets.* ◊ *There followed a long period of confusion and muddle.* **3** [C, usually sing., U] a state in which things are untidy and not in order **SYN** **mess**: **in a ~**: *My papers are all in a muddle.*

**mud·dled** /'mʌdld/ *adj.* (*especially BrE*) confused: *He gets muddled when the teacher starts shouting.* ◊ *muddled thinking*

**ˌmuddle-ˈheaded** *adj.* confused or with confused ideas: *muddle-headed thinkers*

**mud·dling** /'mʌdlɪŋ/ *adj.* (*especially BrE*) confusing and difficult to understand; not clear

**muddy** /'mʌdi/ *adj., verb*
■ *adj.* (**mud·di·er**, **mud·di·est**) **1** full of or covered in mud: *a muddy field/track* ◊ *muddy boots/knees* ◆ SYNONYMS at DIRTY **2** (of a liquid) containing mud; not clear: *muddy water* ◊ *a muddy pond* **3** (of colours) not clear or bright: *muddy green/brown*
■ *verb* (**mud·dies**, **muddy·ing**, **mud·died**, **mud·died**) *~ sth* to make sth muddy
**IDM** **muddy the ˈwaters, ˈissue, etc.** (*disapproving*) to make a simple situation confused and more complicated than it really is

# mudflap

**mud·flap** /ˈmʌdflæp/ noun one of a set of pieces of flexible material that are fixed behind the wheels of a car, motorcycle, etc. to prevent them from throwing up mud, stones or water

**mud·flat** /ˈmʌdflæt/ noun [usually pl.] an area of flat muddy land that is covered by the sea when it comes in at HIGH TIDE

**mud·guard** /ˈmʌdgɑːd; NAmE -gɑːrd/ (BrE) (NAmE **fender**) noun a curved cover over a wheel of a bicycle or motorcycle

**ˈmud pack** noun a substance containing CLAY that you put on your face and take off after a short period of time, used to improve the condition of your skin

**ˈmud ˌpie** noun wet earth that is made into the shape of a PIE as part of a game played by children

**mud·slide** /ˈmʌdslaɪd/ noun a large amount of mud sliding down a mountain, often destroying buildings and injuring or killing people below

**ˈmud-slinging** noun [U] (*disapproving*) the act of criticizing sb and accusing them of sth in order to damage their reputation

**muesli** /ˈmjuːzli/ noun [U] a mixture of grains, nuts, dried fruit, etc. served with milk and eaten for breakfast

**muez·zin** /muːˈezɪn, mjuː-/ noun a man who calls Muslims to prayer, usually from the tower of a MOSQUE

**muff** /mʌf/ noun, verb
- noun a short tube of fur or other warm material that you put your hands into to keep them warm in cold weather ⊃ see also EARMUFFS
- verb ~ sth (*informal*, *disapproving*) to miss an opportunity to do sth well: *He muffed his lines* (= he forgot them or said them wrongly). ◇ *It was a really simple shot, and I muffed it.*

**muf·fin** /ˈmʌfɪn/ noun 1 (BrE) (NAmE ˈEnglish ˈmuffin) a type of round flat bread roll, usually TOASTED and eaten hot with butter 2 a small cake in the shape of a cup, often containing small pieces of fruit, etc: *a blueberry muffin*

**muf·fle** /ˈmʌfl/ verb 1 ~ sth to make a sound quieter or less clear: *He tried to muffle the alarm clock by putting it under his pillow.* 2 ~ sb/sth (up) in sth to wrap or cover sb/sth in order to keep them/it warm: *She muffled the child up in a blanket.*

**muf·fled** /ˈmʌfld/ adj. (of sounds) not heard clearly because sth is in the way that stops the sound from travelling easily: *muffled voices from the next room*

**muf·fler** /ˈmʌflə(r)/ noun 1 (NAmE) (BrE **si·len·cer**) a device that is fixed to the EXHAUST of a vehicle in order to reduce the amount of noise that the engine makes 2 a device that is fitted to an instrument in order to reduce the amount of noise that it makes, or to a camera, a MICROPHONE, etc. to reduce the amount of noise coming from things that you do not want to record 3 (*old-fashioned*) a thick piece of cloth worn around the neck to keep you warm SYN **scarf**

**mufti** /ˈmʌfti/ noun 1 [C] (also **Mufti**) a Muslim who is an expert in legal matters connected with Islam 2 [U] (*old-fashioned*) ordinary clothes worn by people such as soldiers who wear uniform in their job: *officers in mufti*

**mug** /mʌɡ/ noun, verb
- noun 1 a tall cup for drinking from, usually with straight sides and a handle, used without a SAUCER: *a coffee mug* ◇ *a beer mug* (= a large glass with a handle) 2 a mug and what it contains: *a mug of coffee* 3 (*slang*) a person's face: *I never want to see his ugly mug again.* 4 (*informal*) a person who is stupid and easy to trick: *They made me look a complete mug.* ◇ *He's no mug.*
- IDM **a ˈmug's game** (*disapproving*, *especially BrE*) an activity that is unlikely to be successful or make a profit
- verb (-gg-) 1 [T] ~ sb to attack sb violently in order to steal their money, jewellery, etc., especially in a public place: *She had been mugged in the street in broad daylight.* 2 [I] ~ (for sb/sth) (*informal*) to make silly expressions with your face or behave in a silly, EXAGGERATED way, especially on the stage or before a camera: *to mug for the cameras*

PHRV **ˌmug sth↔ˈup** | **ˌmug ˈup on sth** (BrE, *informal*) to learn sth, especially in a short time for a particular purpose, for example an exam

**mug·ger** /ˈmʌɡə(r)/ noun a person who threatens or attacks sb in order to steal their money, jewellery, etc., especially in a public place

**mug·ging** /ˈmʌɡɪŋ/ noun 1 [U, C] the crime of attacking sb violently, or threatening to do so, in order to steal their money, especially in a public place: *Mugging is on the increase.* ◇ *There have been several muggings here recently.* 2 [U] (*IndE*) learning sth by repeating it until you remember it rather than by understanding the meaning of it

**muggy** /ˈmʌɡi/ adj. (of weather) warm and slightly wet in an unpleasant way SYN **close²**: *a muggy August day*

**Mug·hal** /ˈmuːɡɑːl/ = MOGUL

**mug·shot** /ˈmʌɡʃɒt; NAmE -ʃɑːt/ noun (*informal*) a photograph of sb's face kept by the police in their records to identify criminals

**Mu·ham·mad** (also **Mo·ham·med**) /məˈhæmɪd; NAmE məʊˈhɑːm-/ noun the Arab PROPHET through whom the Koran was REVEALED and the religion of Islam established and completed

**mu·ja·hi·deen** (also **mu·ja·he·deen, mu·ja·he·din, mu·ja·hi·din**) /ˌmuːdʒəhɪˈdiːn/ noun [pl.] (in some Muslim countries) soldiers fighting in support of their strong Muslim beliefs

**mu·kene** /muːˈkeɪneɪ/ EAfrE [muːˈkene] noun [C, U] (pl. **mu·kene**) (EAfrE) small fish that are dried to preserve them, and often fried and then cooked with tomatoes and milk to make a STEW

**mu·latto** /mjuˈlætəʊ; NAmE məˈlɑːt-/ noun (pl. **-os** or **-oes**) (*offensive*) a person with one black parent and one white parent

**mul·berry** /ˈmʌlbəri; NAmE -beri/ noun (pl. **-ies**) 1 (also **ˈmulberry tree**) [C] a tree with broad dark green leaves and BERRIES that can be eaten. SILKWORMS (that make silk) eat the leaves of the white mulberry. 2 [C] the small purple or white BERRY of the mulberry tree 3 [U] a deep red-purple colour

**mulch** /mʌltʃ/ noun, verb
- noun [C, U] material, for example, DECAYING leaves, that you put around a plant to protect its base and its roots, to improve the quality of the soil or to stop WEEDS growing
- verb ~ sth to cover the soil or the roots of a plant with a mulch

**mule** /mjuːl/ noun 1 an animal that has a female horse and a male DONKEY as parents, used especially for carrying loads: *He's as stubborn as a mule.* 2 (*slang*) a person who is paid to take drugs illegally from one country to another: *a drug/drugs mule* 3 a SLIPPER (= a soft shoe for wearing indoors) or a woman's shoe that is open around the heel

**mull** /mʌl/ verb
PHRV **ˌmull sth↔ˈover** to spend time thinking carefully about a plan or proposal SYN **consider**: *I need some time to mull it over before making a decision.*

**mul·lah** /ˈmʌlə, ˈmʊlə/ noun a Muslim teacher of religion and holy law

**mulled** /mʌld/ adj. [only before noun] **mulled** wine has been mixed with sugar and SPICES and heated

**mul·let** /ˈmʌlɪt/ noun 1 (pl. **mul·let**) [C, U] a sea fish that is used for food. The two main types are **ˌred ˈmullet** and **ˌgrey ˈmullet**. 2 [C] (*informal*) a HAIRSTYLE for men in which the hair is short at the front and sides and long at the back

**mul·lion** /ˈmʌliən/ noun (*architecture*) a solid VERTICAL piece of stone, wood or metal between two parts of a window
▸ **mul·lioned** adj. [only before noun]: *mullioned windows*

**multi-** /ˈmʌlti; NAmE also mʌltaɪ/ *combining form* (in nouns and adjectives) more than one; many: *multicoloured* ◇ *a multipack* ◇ *a multimillion-dollar business* ◇ *a multi-ethnic society*

**ˌmulti-ˈaccess** adj. (*computing*) allowing several people to use the same system at the same time

**multi·cel·lu·lar** /ˌmʌltiˈseljələ(r)/; *NAmE* -tar's-/ *adj.* (*biology*) having many cells: *Plants and animals are multicellular organisms.*

**multi·chan·nel** /ˌmʌltiˈtʃænl/; *NAmE also* -taɪtʃ-/ *adj.* having or using many different television or communication channels

**multi·col·oured** (*US* **multi·col·ored**) /ˌmʌltiˈkʌləd/; *NAmE* ˌmʌltiˈkʌlərd, -tar'k-/ (*BrE also* **multi·col·our**) (*US also* **multi·col·or**) *adj.* consisting of or decorated with many colours, especially bright ones: *a multicoloured dress*

**multi·cul·tural** /ˌmʌltiˈkʌltʃərəl/; *NAmE also* -tar'k-/ *adj.* for or including people of several different races, religions, languages and traditions: *We live in a multicultural society.* ◇ *a multicultural approach to education*

**multi·cul·tural·ism** /ˌmʌltiˈkʌltʃərəlɪzəm/; *NAmE also* -tar'k-/ *noun* [U] the practice of giving importance to all cultures in a society: *an organization that promotes multiculturalism* ◇ *critics of multiculturalism*

**multi·di·men·sion·al** /ˌmʌltidaɪˈmenʃənl, -dɪ-/; *NAmE also* -taɪdɪ-/ *adj.* having several DIMENSIONS (= measurements in space): *multidimensional space*

**multi·dis·cip·lin·ary** /ˌmʌltidɪsɪˈplɪnəri/; *NAmE* ˌmʌltiˈdɪsəplɪneri, -taɪ'd-/ *adj.* involving several different subjects of study: *a multidisciplinary course*

**multi-ethnic** (*also* **multiethnic**) *adj.* consisting of people from many different races or cultures: *New York City is one of the country's most multi-ethnic cities.*

**multi·fa·cet·ed** /ˌmʌltiˈfæsɪtɪd/; *NAmE also* -tar'f-/ *adj.* (*formal*) having many different aspects to be considered: *a complex and multifaceted problem*

**multi·fari·ous** /ˌmʌltiˈfeəriəs/; *NAmE* -ˈfer-/ *adj.* (*formal*) of many different kinds; having great variety: *the multifarious life forms in the coral reef* ◇ *a vast and multifarious organization*

**multi·func·tion·al** /ˌmʌltiˈfʌŋkʃənl/ *adj.* having several different functions: *a multifunctional device*

**multi·grain** /ˈmʌltigreɪn/; *NAmE also* -taɪg-/ *adj.* containing several different types of grain: *multigrain bread*

**multi·lat·eral** /ˌmʌltiˈlætərəl/; *NAmE also* -tar'l-/ *adj.* **1** in which three or more groups, nations, etc. take part: *multilateral negotiations* **2** having many sides or parts ⊃ compare BILATERAL, TRILATERAL, UNILATERAL

**multi·lat·eral·ism** /ˌmʌltiˈlætərəlɪzəm/; *NAmE also* -tar'l-/ *noun* [U] (*politics*) the policy of trying to make multilateral agreements in order to achieve nuclear DISARMAMENT

**multi·lin·gual** /ˌmʌltiˈlɪŋɡwəl/; *NAmE also* -tar'l-/ *adj.* **1** speaking or using several different languages: *multilingual translators/communities/societies* ◇ *a multilingual classroom* **2** written or printed in several different languages: *a multilingual phrase book* ⊃ compare BILINGUAL, MONOLINGUAL

**multi·media** /ˌmʌltiˈmiːdiə/; *NAmE also* -tar'm-/ *adj.* [only before noun] **1** (in computing) using sound, pictures and film in addition to text on a screen: *multimedia systems/products* ◇ *the multimedia industry* (= producing CD-ROMs etc.) **2** (in teaching and art) using several different ways of giving information or several different materials: *a multimedia approach to learning* ▶ **multi·media** *noun* [U]: *the use of multimedia in museums*

**multi·mill·ion·aire** /ˌmʌltimɪljəˈneə(r)/; *NAmE* ˌmʌltimɪljəˈner, -taɪm-/ *noun* a person who has money and possessions worth several million pounds, dollars, etc.

**multi·nation·al** /ˌmʌltiˈnæʃnəl/; *NAmE also* -tar'n-/ *adj.*, *noun*
- *adj.* existing in or involving many countries: *multinational companies/corporations* ◇ *A multinational force is being sent to the trouble spot.*
- *noun* a company that operates in several different countries, especially a large and powerful company

**multi·pack** /ˈmʌltipæk/ *noun* a package containing a number of products that are similar or the same, often costing less than the cost of buying each item separately: *The ice creams are sold either individually or in multipacks of four.*

**multi·party** /ˌmʌltiˈpɑːti/; *NAmE* -ˈpɑːrti/ *adj.* [only before noun] involving several different political parties

# multitasking

**multi·play·er** /ˈmʌltipleɪə(r)/ *adj.* [usually before noun] used to describe a computer game that can be played by more than one person at the same time: *The game will support up to four players in multiplayer mode.*

**mul·tiple** ❶ B2 Ⓦ /ˈmʌltɪpl/ *adj.*, *noun*
- *adj.* [only before noun] **1** B2 many in number; involving many different people or things: *The shape appears multiple times within each painting.* ◇ *research based on multiple sources* ◇ *multiple copies of documents* ◇ *a story that works on multiple levels* ◇ *a multiple entry visa* ◇ *a multiple birth* (= several babies born to a mother at one time) **2** (of a disease or injury) complex in its nature or effects; affecting several parts of the body: *She suffered multiple injuries in the crash.*
- *noun* (*mathematics*) a quantity that contains another quantity an exact number of times: *14, 21 and 28 are all multiples of 7.* ⊃ see also LEAST COMMON MULTIPLE, LOWEST COMMON MULTIPLE

**ˌmultiple-ˈchoice** *adj.* (of questions in a test, QUIZ, etc.) showing several possible answers from which you must choose the correct one

**ˌmultiple scleˈrosis** *noun* [U] (*abbr.* MS) a disease of the nervous system that gets worse over a period of time with loss of feeling in the body and loss of control of movement and speech

**multi·plex** /ˈmʌltɪpleks/ (*BrE also* **multiplex ˈcinema**) *noun* a large cinema with several separate rooms with screens

**multi·pli·ca·tion** /ˌmʌltɪplɪˈkeɪʃn/ *noun* [U] **1** the act or process of multiplying numbers: *the multiplication sign* (×) ⊃ compare DIVISION **2** the act or process of increasing very much in number or amount: *Multiplication of cells leads to rapid growth of the organism.*

**multipliˈcation table** (*also* **table**, *informal* **times ˈtable**) *noun* a list showing the results when a number is multiplied by a set of other numbers, especially 1 to 12, in turn

**multi·pli·city** /ˌmʌltɪˈplɪsəti/ *noun* [sing., U] (*formal*) a great number and variety of sth: *This situation can be influenced by a multiplicity of different factors.*

**multi·plier** /ˈmʌltɪplaɪə(r)/ *noun* (*mathematics*) a number by which another number is multiplied

**multi·ply** ❶ B2 /ˈmʌltɪplaɪ/ *verb* (**multi·plies**, **multi·ply·ing**, **multi·plied**, **multi·plied**) **1** B2 [I, T] to add a number to itself a particular number of times: *The children are already learning to multiply and divide.* ◇ *~ A by B* **2** multiplied by 4 is/equals/makes 8 (= 2×4=8). ◇ *Multiply the length by the width.* ◇ *~ A and B (together)* *Multiply 2 and 6 together and you get 12.* **2** B2 [I, T] to increase or make sth increase very much in number or amount: *Our problems have multiplied since last year.* ◇ *~ sth Cigarette smoking multiplies the risk of cancer.* **3** [I, T] (*biology*) to produce young animals, bacteria, etc. in large numbers: *Rabbits multiply rapidly.* ◇ *~ sth It is possible to multiply these bacteria in the laboratory.*

**multi·pro·ces·sor** /ˌmʌltiˈprəʊsesə(r)/; *NAmE* ˌmʌltiˈprɑːs-, -tar'p-/ *noun* a computer with more than one CENTRAL PROCESSING UNIT

**multipurpose** /ˌmʌltiˈpɜːpəs/; *NAmE* ˌmʌltiˈpɜːrp-, -tar'p-/ *adj.* able to be used for several different purposes: *a multipurpose tool/machine* ⊃ see also MPV

**multi·racial** /ˌmʌltiˈreɪʃl/; *NAmE also* -tar'r-/ *adj.* including or involving several different races of people: *a multiracial society*

**ˌmulti-storey ˈcar park** (*also* **multi-storey**) (*both BrE*) (*NAmE* **ˈparking garage**) *noun* a large building with several floors for parking cars in

**multi·task** /ˌmʌltiˈtɑːsk/; *NAmE* -ˈtæsk/ *verb* **1** [I] (of a computer) to operate several programs at the same time **2** [I] to do several things at the same time: *Women seem to be able to multitask better than men.*

**multi·tasking** /ˌmʌltiˈtɑːskɪŋ/; *NAmE* -ˈtæs-/ *noun* [U] **1** (*computing*) the ability of a computer to operate several programs at the same time **2** the ability to do several things at the same time

**Multi-touch™** *noun* [U] a range of functions that enables you to give instructions on a TOUCH SCREEN, keyboard, etc. by touching different areas or keys at the same time: *a Multi-touch screen/display/keyboard* ◇ *Multi-touch capability/technology*

**multi·track** /ˈmʌltitræk/ *adj.* (*specialist*) relating to the mixing of several different pieces of music

**mul·ti·tude** /ˈmʌltɪtjuːd; *NAmE* -tuːd/ *noun* (*formal*) **1** [C] ~ (of sth/sb) an extremely large number of things or people: *a multitude of possibilities* ◇ *a multitude of birds* ◇ *These elements can be combined in a multitude of different ways.* ◇ *The region attracts tourists in their multitudes.* **2 the multitude** [sing. + sing./pl. v.] (*also* **the multi·tudes** [pl.]) (*sometimes disapproving*) the mass of ordinary people: *It was an elite that believed its task was to enlighten the multitude.* ◇ *to feed the starving multitudes* **3** [C] (*literary*) a large crowd of people SYN **throng**: *He preached to the assembled multitude.* IDM **cover/hide a multitude of sins** (*often humorous*) to hide the real situation or facts when these are not good or pleasant

**multi·tu·di·nous** /ˌmʌltɪˈtjuːdɪnəs; *NAmE* -ˈtuː-/ *adj.* (*formal*) extremely large in number

**multi-ˈuser** *adj.* (*computing*) able to be used by more than one person at the same time: *a multi-user software licence*

**multi·vita·min** /ˌmʌltiˈvɪtəmɪn; *NAmE* -ˈvaɪt-, -ˈtaɪv-/ *noun* a tablet or medicine containing several vitamins

**multi-ˈword** *adj.* [only before noun] (*linguistics*) consisting of more than one word: *multi-word units such as 'fall in love'*

**mum** A1 /mʌm/ *noun, adj.*
■ *noun* A1 (*BrE*) (*NAmE* **mom**) (*informal*) a mother: *My mum says I can't go.* ◇ *Happy Birthday, Mum.* ◇ *A lot of mums and dads have the same worries.* ◇ *She's a single mum with two kids.* ◇ *expectant/new/young/teenage mums* ◇ *stay-at-home/working mums*
■ *adj.* IDM **keep mum** (*informal*) to say nothing about sth; to stay quiet: *He kept mum about what he'd seen.* **mum's the ˈword** (*informal*) used to tell sb to say nothing about sth and keep it secret

**mum·ble** /ˈmʌmbl/ *verb, noun*
■ *verb* [I, T] to speak or say sth in a quiet voice in a way that is not clear SYN **mutter**: ~ (to sb/yourself) *I could hear him mumbling to himself.* ◇ **~sth (to sb/yourself)** *She mumbled an apology and left.* ◇ + speech *'Sorry,' she mumbled.* ◇ **~ that …** *She mumbled that she was sorry.*
■ *noun* [usually sing.] (*also* **mum·bling** [C, usually pl., U]) speech or words that are spoken in a quiet voice in a way that is not clear: *He spoke in a low mumble, as if to himself.* ◇ *They tried to make sense of her mumblings.*

**mumbo jumbo** /ˌmʌmbəʊ ˈdʒʌmbəʊ/ *noun* [U] (*informal, disapproving*) language or a ceremony that seems complicated and important but is actually without real sense or meaning SYN **nonsense**

**mum·mer** /ˈmʌmə(r)/ *noun* an actor in an old form of drama without words

**mum·mify** /ˈmʌmɪfaɪ/ *verb* [usually passive] (**mum·mi·fies**, **mum·mi·fy·ing**, **mum·mi·fied**, **mum·mi·fied**) ~sth to preserve a dead body by treating it with special oils and wrapping it in cloth SYN **embalm**

**mummy** /ˈmʌmi/ *noun* (*pl.* **-ies**) **1** (*BrE*) (*NAmE* **mommy**, **momma**) (*informal*) a child's word for a mother: *'I want my mummy!' he wailed.* ◇ *It hurts, Mummy!* ◇ *Mummy and Daddy will be back soon.* ➔ see also YUMMY MUMMY **2** a body of a human or an animal that has been mummified: *an Egyptian mummy*

**mummy's boy** (*BrE*) (*NAmE* **mama's boy**) *noun* (*disapproving*) a boy or man who depends too much on his mother

**mumps** /mʌmps/ *noun* [U] a disease, especially of children, that causes painful SWELLINGS at the sides of the face and under the ears

**munch** /mʌntʃ/ *verb* [I, T] to eat sth steadily and often noisily, especially sth hard and/or dry SYN **chomp**: ~on/**at sth** *She munched on an apple.* ◇ **~sth** *He sat in a chair munching his toast.* ◇ *I munched my way through a huge bowl of cereal.*

**munch·ies** /ˈmʌntʃiz/ *noun* [pl.] (*informal*) **1** small items of food **2 the munchies** a sudden strong desire for food: *to get/have the munchies*

**munch·kin** /ˈmʌntʃkɪn/ *noun* (*NAmE*, *informal*) a small person or a child: *Who's this adorable munchkin?*

**mun·dane** /mʌnˈdeɪn/ *adj.* (*often disapproving*) not interesting or exciting SYN **dull**, **ordinary**: *a mundane task/job* ◇ *I lead a pretty mundane existence.* ◇ *On a more mundane level, can we talk about the timetable for next week?*

**mung** /mʌŋ; *BrE also* muːŋ/ (*also* **moong**) *noun* **1** (*also* **ˈmung bean**) a small round green bean **2** the tropical plant that produces these beans

**mu·ni·ci·pal** B1+ C1 /mjuːˈnɪsɪpl/ *adj.* [usually before noun] connected with or belonging to a town, city or district that has its own local government: *municipal elections/councils* ◇ *municipal workers* ◇ *the Los Angeles Municipal Art Gallery*

**mu·ni·ci·pal·ity** /mjuːˌnɪsɪˈpæləti/ *noun* (*pl.* **-ies**) (*formal*) a town, city or district with its own local government; the group of officials who govern it

**mu·nifi·cent** /mjuːˈnɪfɪsnt/ *adj.* (*formal*) extremely generous: *a munificent patron/gift/gesture* ▶ **mu·nifi·cence** /-sns/ *noun* [U]

**mu·ni·tions** /mjuːˈnɪʃnz/ *noun* [pl.] military weapons, AMMUNITION and equipment: *a shortage of munitions* ◇ *a munitions factory* ▶ **mu·ni·tion** *adj.* [only before noun]: *a munition store*

**munt·jac** (*also* **munt·jak**) /ˈmʌntdʒæk/ *noun* a type of small DEER, originally from south-east Asia

**mup·pet** /ˈmʌpɪt/ *noun* (*BrE*, *informal*) a stupid person

**mural** /ˈmjʊərəl; *NAmE* ˈmjʊr-/ *noun* a painting, usually a large one, done on a wall, sometimes on an outside wall of a building ▶ **mural** *adj.* [only before noun]: *mural paintings*

**mur·der** B1 /ˈmɜːdə(r); *NAmE* ˈmɜːrd-/ *noun, verb*
■ *noun* **1** B1 [U, C] the crime of killing sb deliberately SYN **homicide**: *He was found guilty of murder.* ◇ *She has been charged with the attempted murder of her husband.* ◇ *to commit (a) murder* ◇ *a murder case/investigation/charge/trial* ◇ *The rebels were responsible for the mass murder of 400 civilians.* ◇ *the families of the murder victims* ◇ *What was the murder weapon?* ◇ *The play is a murder mystery.* ➔ compare MANSLAUGHTER **2** [U] (*informal*) used to describe sth that is difficult or unpleasant: *It's murder trying to get to the airport at this time of day.* ◇ *It was murder (= very busy and unpleasant) in the office today.* IDM **get away with ˈmurder** (*informal, often humorous*) to do whatever you want without being stopped or punished ➔ more at SCREAM *v.*
■ *verb* **1** B1 ~sb to kill sb deliberately and illegally: *He denies murdering his wife's lover.* ◇ *The boy was brutally murdered.* **2** ~sth to change sth good into sth bad because you do not do it very well SYN **butcher**: *Critics accused him of murdering the English language (= writing or speaking it very badly).* **3** ~sb (*informal*) to defeat sb completely, especially in a team sport SYN **thrash** IDM **I could ˈmurder a …** (*informal, especially BrE*) used to say that you very much want to eat or drink sth: *I could murder a beer.* **sb will/is going to ˈmurder you, me, etc.** (*informal*) used to warn or predict that another person will be very angry with sb/you: *She's going to murder me if I don't get this finished on time.*

**mur·der·er** /ˈmɜːdərə(r); *NAmE* ˈmɜːrd-/ *noun* a person who has killed sb deliberately and illegally SYN **killer**: *a convicted murderer* ◇ *a mass murderer (= who has killed a lot of people)*

**mur·der·ess** /ˈmɜːdərəs; *NAmE* ˈmɜːrd-/ *noun* (*old-fashioned*) a woman who has killed sb deliberately and illegally; a female murderer

**mur·der·ous** /ˈmɜːdərəs; *NAmE* ˈmɜːrd-/ *adj.* intending or likely to murder SYN **savage**: *a murderous villain/tyrant* ◇ *a murderous attack* ◇ *She gave him a murderous look (= a very angry one).* ▶ **mur·der·ous·ly** *adv.*

**murk** /mɜːk; *NAmE* mɜːrk/ *noun* (*usually* **the murk**) [U] DARKNESS caused by smoke, FOG, etc. SYN **gloom**

**murky** /ˈmɜːki; NAmE ˈmɜːrki/ adj. (**murk·ier, murki·est**) **1** (of a liquid) not clear; dark or dirty with mud or another substance SYN **cloudy**: *She gazed into the murky depths of the water.* **2** (of air, light, etc.) dark and unpleasant because of smoke, FOG, etc: *a murky night* **3** (*disapproving or humorous*) (of people's actions or character) not clearly known and suspected of not being honest: *He had a somewhat murky past.* ◊ *the murky world of arms dealing*

**mur·mur** /ˈmɜːmə(r); NAmE ˈmɜːrm-/ verb, noun
■ verb **1** [T, I] ~ **(sth)** | + **speech** | ~ **that …** to say sth in a soft quiet voice that is difficult to hear or understand: *She murmured her agreement.* ◊ *He murmured something in his sleep.* ◊ *She was murmuring in her ear.* **2** [I] to make a quiet continuous sound: *The wind murmured in the trees.* **3** [I] ~ **(against sb/sth)** (*literary*) to complain about sb/sth, but not openly
■ noun **1** [C] a quietly spoken word or words: *She answered in a faint murmur.* ◊ *Murmurs of 'Praise God' went around the circle.* **2** [C] (*also* **mur·mur·ings** [pl.]) a quiet expression of feeling: *a murmur of agreement/approval/complaint* ◊ *He paid the extra cost without a murmur* (= without complaining at all). ◊ *polite murmurings of gratitude* **3** (*also* **mur·mur·ing** [sing.]) a low continuous sound in the background: *the distant murmur of traffic* **4** [C] (*medical*) a very quiet sound in the chest, usually a sign of damage or disease in the heart: *a heart murmur*

**Murphy's Law** /ˌmɜːfiz ˈlɔː; NAmE ˌmɜːrf-/ noun (*humorous*) a statement of the fact that, if anything can possibly go wrong, it will go wrong

**mur·ram** /ˈmʌrəm; NAmE ˈmɜːr-/ noun [U] a type of red soil that is often used to make roads in Africa

**muscle** 🔊 B1 /ˈmʌsl/ noun, verb
■ noun **1** 🔊 B1 [C, U] a piece of body TISSUE that you make tight and relax in order to move a particular part of the body; the TISSUE that forms the muscles of the body: *a calf/neck/thigh muscle* ◊ *to pull/tear/strain a muscle* ◊ *He poses and flexes his muscles in the mirror.* ◊ *Contract and relax the muscles in your fingers a few times.* ◊ *He didn't move a muscle* (= stood completely still). ◊ *Lift weights to build muscle.* ◊ *muscle fibre/tissue/mass* ⊃ see also ABDUCTOR (2), ADDUCTOR, CILIARY MUSCLE, EXTENSOR, FLEXOR, GLUTEUS, SKELETAL MUSCLE, SMOOTH MUSCLE ⊃ HOMOPHONES at MUSSEL **2** [U] physical strength: *He's an intelligent player but lacks the muscle of older competitors.* **3** [U] the power and influence to make others do what you want: *to exercise political/industrial/financial muscle* ◊ *The countries tried to flex their collective muscle.*
▶ **muscled** adj.: *heavily muscled shoulders* IDM see FLEX v.
■ verb [I, T] (*especially NAmE, informal*) to move or move sth in a particular direction by using your physical strength: + **adv./prep.** *He tried to muscle to the front of the line.* ◊ ~ **sb/sth** + **adv./prep.** *He muscled the ball up between two defenders.*
PHRV **muscle ˈin (on sb/sth)** (*informal, disapproving*) to involve yourself in a situation when you have no right to do so, in order to get sth for yourself ⊃ HOMOPHONES at MUSSEL

**ˈmuscle-bound** adj. (*often disapproving*) having large stiff muscles

**ˈmuscle·man** /ˈmʌslmæn/ noun (*pl.* **-men** /-men/) a big strong man, especially one employed to protect sb/sth

**mus·cu·lar** /ˈmʌskjələ(r)/ adj. **1** relating to the muscles: *muscular tension/power/tissue* **2** (*also informal* **muscly** /ˈmʌsli/) having strong large muscles: *a muscular body/build/chest* ◊ *He was tall, lean and muscular.*

**muscular ˈdystrophy** /ˌmʌskjələ ˈdɪstrəfi; NAmE -lər-/ noun [U] a medical condition that some people are born with in which the muscles gradually become weaker

**mus·cu·lat·ure** /ˈmʌskjələtʃə(r)/ noun [U, sing.] (*biology*) the system of muscles in the body or part of the body

**muse** /mjuːz/ noun, verb
■ noun **1** a person or spirit that gives a writer, painter, etc. ideas and the desire to create things SYN **inspiration**: *He felt that his muse had deserted him* (= that he could no longer write, paint, etc.). **2 Muse** (in ancient Greek and Roman stories) one of the nine GODDESSES who encouraged poetry, music and other branches of art and literature

---

1027 musical

---

■ verb (*formal*) **1** [I] ~ **(about/on/over/upon sth)** to think carefully about sth for a time, ignoring what is happening around you SYN **ponder**: *I sat quietly, musing on the events of the day.* ⊃ see also MUSING **2** [T] + **speech** | ~ **that …** to say sth to yourself in a way that shows you are thinking carefully about it: *'I wonder why?' she mused.*

**mu·seum** 🔊 A1 /mjuˈziːəm/ noun a building in which objects of artistic, cultural, historical or scientific interest are kept and shown to the public: *a museum of modern art* ◊ *a science museum* ◊ *to visit a museum* ◊ *at/in a ~ The items will go on display at the museum next year.* ◊ *a museum director/curator*

**muˈseum piece** noun **1** an object that is of enough historical or artistic value to have in a museum **2** (*humorous*) a thing or person that is old-fashioned, or old and no longer useful

**mush** /mʌʃ/ noun **1** [U, sing.] (*usually disapproving*) a soft thick mass or mixture: *The vegetables had turned to mush.* ◊ *His insides suddenly felt like mush.* **2** [U] (*NAmE*) a type of thick PORRIDGE made from CORN (MAIZE)

**musher** /ˈmʌʃə(r)/ noun (*NAmE*) a person who drives a dog SLED

**mush·room** /ˈmʌʃrʊm, -ruːm/ noun, verb
■ noun a FUNGUS with a round flat head and short STEM. Many mushrooms can be eaten: *a field mushroom* (= the most common type that is eaten, often just called a 'mushroom', and often grown to be sold) ◊ *fried mushrooms* ◊ *cream of mushroom soup* ⊃ VISUAL VOCAB page V5 ⊃ see also BUTTON MUSHROOM, MAGIC MUSHROOM, OYSTER MUSHROOM, TOADSTOOL
■ verb **1** [I] to rapidly grow or increase in number: *We expect the market to mushroom in the next two years.* **2** (*usually* **go ˈmushrooming**) [I] to gather mushrooms in a field or wood

**ˈmushroom cloud** noun a large cloud, like a mushroom in shape, that forms in the air after a nuclear explosion

**mushy** /ˈmʌʃi/ adj. (**mush·ier, mushi·est**) **1** soft and thick, like mush: *Cook until the fruit is soft but not mushy.* ⊃ WORDFINDER NOTE at CRISP **2** (*informal, disapproving*) too emotional in a way that is embarrassing SYN **sentimental**: *mushy romantic novels*

**ˌmushy ˈpeas** noun [pl.] (*BrE*) cooked PEAS that are made into a soft mixture

**music** 🔊 A1 /ˈmjuːzɪk/ noun [U] **1** 🔊 A1 sounds that are arranged in a way that is pleasant or exciting to listen to. People sing music or play it on instruments: *pop/dance/rock music* ◊ *Do you like classical music?* ◊ *He plays traditional Asian music.* ◊ *to listen to music* ◊ *She could hear music playing somewhere.* ◊ *to stream/share/download music* ◊ *to write/compose music* ◊ *to perform/record music* ◊ *Every week they get together to make music* (= to play music or sing). ◊ *the popularity of Mozart's music* ◊ *It was a charming piece of music.* ◊ *The poem has been set to music* (= music has been written for it) ◊ *Birmingham's live music scene* ◊ *music lovers/fans* ◊ *Every summer he runs a three-day music festival.* ◊ *The band released a music video on YouTube today.* HELP There are many compounds ending in **music**. You will find them at their place in the alphabet. ⊃ WORDFINDER NOTE at DANCE **2** 🔊 A1 the art of writing or playing music: *He studied music in Moscow.* ◊ *a career in music* ◊ *a music teacher* ◊ *music lessons* ◊ *the music business/industry* **3** 🔊 A1 the written or printed signs that represent the sounds to be played or sung in a piece of music: *Can you read music* (= understand the signs in order to play or sing a piece of music)? ◊ *I had to play it without the music.* ◊ *The paper or book with the musical notes on it) was still open on the piano.* ⊃ see also SHEET MUSIC
IDM **music to your ˈears** news or information that you are very pleased to hear ⊃ more at FACE v.

**mu·sic·al** 🔊 A2 /ˈmjuːzɪkl/ adj., noun
■ adj. **1** 🔊 A2 [only before noun] connected with music; containing music: *musical styles/tastes* ◊ *to have exceptional musical talent* ◊ *a first-rate musical performance* ◊ *a diverse range of musical genres* ◊ *She had a brilliant career*

# musical box

### musical notation

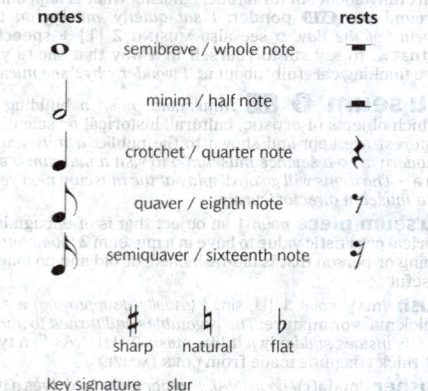

in **musical theatre**. ◇ *A jazz band provided the musical accompaniment to the meal.* **2** (of a person) with a natural skill or interest in music: *She's very musical.* **OPP unmusical 3** (of a sound) pleasant to listen to, like music: *a musical voice* ◇ *The language often sounds musical.* **OPP unmusical**

■ *noun* a play or film in which part or all of the story is told using songs and often dancing: *the star of the hit West End musical*

**'musical box** *noun* (*especially BrE*) = MUSIC BOX

**musical 'chairs** *noun* [U] **1** a children's game in which players run round a row of chairs while music is playing. Each time the music stops, players try to sit down on one of the chairs, but there are always more players than chairs. **2** (*often disapproving*) a situation in which people frequently exchange jobs or positions

**musical 'comedy** *noun* [C, U] a play or film with a humorous or romantic story, songs and dancing; this style of play or film; a musical

**musical di'rector** *noun* the person who is in charge of the music in a show in the theatre

**musical 'instrument** (*also* in·stru·ment) *noun* an object used for producing musical sounds, for example a piano or a drum: *Most pupils learn (to play) a musical instrument.* ◇ *the instruments of the orchestra*

**mu·sic·al·ity** /ˌmjuːzɪˈkæləti/ *noun* [U] (*formal*) skill and understanding in performing music

**music·al·ly** /ˈmjuːzɪkli/ *adv.* **1** in a way that is connected with music: *musically gifted* ◇ *Musically speaking, their latest album is nothing special.* **2** with musical skill: *He plays really musically.* **3** in a way that is pleasant to listen to, like music: *to laugh/speak musically*

**'music box** (*also* **'musical box** *especially in BrE*) *noun* a box containing a device that plays a tune when the box is opened

**'music hall** *noun* (*BrE*) **1** (*also* **vaude·ville** *NAmE, BrE*) [U] a type of entertainment popular in the late 19th and early 20th centuries, including singing, dancing and comedy **2** (*NAmE* **'vaudeville theater**) [C] a theatre used for popular entertainment in the late 19th and early 20th centuries

**mu·si·cian** /mjuˈzɪʃn/ *noun* a person who plays a musical instrument or writes music, especially as a job: *a jazz/rock/classical musician* ◇ *She has been a professional musician for over 25 years.* ◇ *The competition recognizes talented young musicians.*

**mu·si·cian·ship** /mjuˈzɪʃnʃɪp/ *noun* [U] skill in performing or writing music

**mu·sic·ology** /ˌmjuːzɪˈkɒlədʒi/; *NAmE* -ˈkɑːl-/ *noun* [U] the study of the history and theory of music ▶ **mu·sic·olo·gist** *noun*

**'music stand** *noun* a frame, especially one that you can fold, that is used for holding sheets of music while you play a musical instrument

**'music video** *noun* = VIDEO (3)

**mus·ing** /ˈmjuːzɪŋ/ *noun* [U, C, usually pl.] a period of thinking carefully about sth or telling people your thoughts about it: *We had to sit and listen to his musings on life.*

**musk** /mʌsk/ *noun* [U] a substance with a strong smell that is used in making some PERFUMES. It is produced naturally by a type of male DEER. ▶ **musky** *adj.*: *a musky perfume* (= smelling of or like musk)

**mus·ket** /ˈmʌskɪt/ *noun* an early type of long gun that was used by soldiers in the past

**mus·ket·eer** /ˌmʌskəˈtɪə(r)/; *NAmE* -ˈtɪr/ *noun* **1** (in the past) a soldier who used a musket **2** (in France in the 17th and 18th centuries) a soldier of the king's household, employed to guard the king

**musk·rat** /ˈmʌskræt/ *noun* a North American water animal that has a strong smell and is hunted for its fur

**Mus·lim** /ˈmʊzlɪm, ˈmʌz-, ˈmʊslɪm/ *noun* a person whose religion is Islam ➔ see also BLACK MUSLIM ▶ **Mus·lim** *adj.* ➔ see also MOSLEM

**mus·lin** /ˈmʌzlɪn/ *noun* [U] a type of fine cotton cloth that you can almost see through, used, especially in the past, for making clothes and curtains

**muso** /ˈmjuːzəʊ/ *noun* (*pl.* **-os**) (*BrE, informal*) a person who plays, or is very interested in, music and knows a lot about it

**muss** /mʌs/ *verb* ~ **sth (up)** (*NAmE*) to make sb's clothes or hair untidy: *Hey, don't muss up my hair!*

**mus·sel** /ˈmʌsl/ *noun* a small SHELLFISH that can be eaten, with a black shell in two parts ➔ picture at SHELLFISH

▼ **HOMOPHONES**

**muscle • mussel** /ˈmʌsl/

- **muscle** *noun*: *You should stretch before exercise to avoid muscle injuries.*
- **muscle** *verb*: *Don't let that bully muscle in on your success!*
- **mussel** *noun*: *Grandad's mussel linguine recipe was absolutely mouth-watering.*

**must** *modal verb, noun*

■ *modal verb* /məst, *strong form* mʌst/ (*negative* **must not**, *short form* **mustn't** /ˈmʌsnt/) **1** used to say that sth is necessary or very important (sometimes involving a rule or a law): *All visitors must report to reception.* ◇ *Cars must not be parked in front of the entrance* (= it is not allowed). ◇ (*formal*) *I must ask you not to do that again.* ◇ *You mustn't say things like that.* ◇ *I must go and get the kids from school.* ◇ *I must admit* (= I feel that I should admit) *I was surprised it cost so little.* ◇ (*especially BrE*) *Must you always question everything I say?* (= it is annoying) ◇ *'Do we have to finish this today?' 'Yes, you must.'* **HELP** Note that the negative for the last example is: 'No, you don't have to.' ➔ **EXPRESS YOURSELF** at HAVE TO **2** used to say that sth is likely or logical: *You must be hungry after all that walking.* ◇ *He must have known* (= surely he knew) *what she wanted.* ◇ *I'm sorry, she's not here. She must have left already* (= that must be the explanation). **3** (*especially BrE*) used to recommend that sb does sth because you think it is a good idea: *You simply must read this book.* ◇ *We must get together soon for lunch.* ➔ note at MODAL
**IDM** **if you 'must (do sth)** used to say that sb may do sth but you do not really want them to: *'Can I smoke?' 'If you must.'* ◇ *It's from my boyfriend, if you must know.* ▪ **must-see/must-read/must-have, etc.** used to tell people that

sth is so good or interesting that they should see, read, get it, etc: *Sydney is one of the world's must-see cities.* ◊ *The magazine is a must-read in the show business world.*
⇒ more at NEEDS
- **noun** /mʌst/ [usually sing.] (*informal*) something that you must do, see, buy, etc: *His new novel is a must for all lovers of crime fiction.*

▼ **GRAMMAR POINT**

**must / have (got) to / must not / don't have to**

Necessity and Obligation

- **Must** and **have (got) to** are used in the present to say that something is necessary or should be done. **Have to** is more common in NAmE, especially in speech: *You must be home by 11 o'clock.* ◊ *I must wash the car tomorrow.* ◊ *I have to collect the children from school at 3 o'clock.* ◊ *Nurses have to wear a uniform.*
- In *BrE* there is a difference between them. **Must** is used to talk about what the speaker or listener wants, and **have (got) to** about rules, laws and other people's wishes: *I must finish this essay today. I'm going out tomorrow.* ◊ *I have to finish this essay today. We have to hand them in tomorrow.*
- There are no past or future forms of **must**. To talk about the past you use **had to** and **has had to**: *I had to wait half an hour for a bus.* **Will have to** is used to talk about the future, or **have to** if an arrangement has already been made: *We'll have to borrow the money we need.* ◊ *I have to go to the dentist tomorrow.*
- Questions with **have to** are formed using **do**: *Do the children have to wear a uniform?* In negative sentences both **must not** and **don't have to** are used, but with different meanings. **Must not** is used to tell somebody not to do something: *Passengers must not undo their seat belts until the signs have been switched off.* The short form **mustn't** is used especially in *BrE*: *You mustn't leave the gate open.* **Don't have to** is used when it is not necessary to do something: *You don't have to pay for the tickets in advance.* ◊ *She doesn't have to work at weekends.*
⇒ note at NEED

Certainty

- Both **must** and **have to** are used to say that you are certain about something. **Have to** is the usual verb used in *NAmE* and this is becoming more frequent in *BrE* in this meaning: *He has (got) to be the worst actor on TV!* ◊ (*BrE*) *This must be the most boring party I've ever been to.* If you are talking about the past, use **must have**: *Your trip must have been fun!*

**mus·tache** (*US*) (*BrE* **mous·tache**) /ˈmʌstæʃ; *BrE* also məˈstɑːʃ; *NAmE also* məˈstæʃ/ *noun* **1** a line of hair that a man allows to grow on his upper lip **2 mustaches** [pl.] a very long mustache ⇒ compare BEARD

**mus·tached** (*US*) (*BrE* **mous·tached**) /ˈmʌstæʃt; *BrE* also məˈstɑːʃt; *NAmE also* məˈstæʃt/ *adj.* [usually before noun] having a mustache ⇒ compare MUSTACHIOED

**mus·tachi·oed** /məˈstɑːʃiəʊd; *NAmE* -ˈstæʃ-/ *adj.* (*literary*) having a large moustache that is curly at the ends

**mus·tang** /ˈmʌstæŋ/ *noun* a small American wild horse

**mus·tard** /ˈmʌstəd; *NAmE* -tərd/ *noun* [U] **1** a thick cold yellow or brown sauce, made from the seeds of some mustard plants, that tastes hot and spicy and is usually eaten with meat: *a jar of mustard* ◊ *mustard powder* ◊ **French/English mustard 2** a small plant with yellow flowers, grown for its seeds that are used to make mustard **3** (*BrE*) the leaves of the mustard plant that are eaten raw in salads: *mustard and cress* (= leaves of white mustard grown with CRESS) **4** a colour between yellow and brown
▶ **mus·tard** *adj.*: *a mustard sweater*
**IDM (not) cut the ˈmustard** to (not) be as good as expected or required: *I didn't cut the mustard as a hockey player.* ⇒ more at KEEN *adj.*

**ˈmustard gas** *noun* [U] a poisonous gas that burns the skin, used in chemical weapons, for example during the First World War

**ˈmustard greens** *noun* [pl.] the dark green leaves of a type of MUSTARD plant, that are cooked or eaten raw in salads, especially in the Southern US

**mus·ter** /ˈmʌstə(r)/ *verb, noun*
- **verb 1** [T] ~ **sth (up)** to find as much support, courage, etc. as you can SYN **summon**: *We mustered what support we could for the plan.* ◊ *She left the room with all the dignity she could muster.* **2** [I, T] to come together or to bring people, especially soldiers, together, for example for military action SYN **gather**: *The troops mustered.* ◊ ~ **sb/sth** *to muster an army* **3** [T] ~ **sth** (*AustralE, NZE*) to gather together sheep or cows
- **noun** a group of people, especially soldiers, that have been brought together IDM see PASS *v.*

**musty** /ˈmʌsti/ *adj.* (**mus·ti·er**, **musti·est**) smelling wet and unpleasant because of a lack of fresh air SYN **dank**: *a musty room*

**mut·able** /ˈmjuːtəbl/ *adj.* (*formal*) that can change; likely to change ▶ **mut·abil·ity** /ˌmjuːtəˈbɪləti/ *noun* [U]

**mu·tant** /ˈmjuːtənt/ *adj., noun*
- **adj.** (*biology*) (of a living thing) different in some way from others of the same kind because of a change in its GENETIC structure: *a mutant gene*
- **noun 1** (*biology*) a living thing with qualities that are different from its parents' qualities because of a change in its GENETIC structure **2** (*informal*) (in stories about space, the future, etc.) a living thing with an unusual and frightening appearance because of a change in its GENETIC structure

**mu·tate** /mjuːˈteɪt; *NAmE* ˈmjuːteɪt/ *verb* **1** [I, T] (*biology*) to develop or make sth develop a new form or structure, because of a GENETIC change: ~ **(into sth)** *the ability of the virus to mutate into new forms* ◊ **sth** *mutated genes* **2** [I] ~ **(into sth)** to change into a new form: *Rhythm and blues mutated into rock and roll.* ⇒ see also MUTATION

**mu·ta·tion** /mjuːˈteɪʃn/ *noun* **1** [U, C] (*biology*) a process in which the GENETIC material of a person, a plant or an animal changes in structure when it is passed on to children, etc., causing different physical characteristics to develop; a change of this kind: *cells affected by mutation* ◊ *genetic mutations* ⇒ WORDFINDER NOTE at BIOLOGY **2** [U, C] a change in the form or structure of sth: (*linguistics*) *vowel mutation*

**mute** /mjuːt/ *adj., noun, verb*
- **adj. 1** not speaking; not expressed in speech SYN **silent**: *The child sat mute in the corner of the room.* ◊ *a look of mute appeal* **2** (*old-fashioned, offensive*) (of a person) unable to speak SYN **dumb**
- **noun 1** [U] = MUTE BUTTON: *During a phone call, press mute to turn off the microphone.* **2** [C] (*music*) a device made of metal, rubber or plastic that you use to make the sound of a musical instrument softer **3** [C] (*old-fashioned, offensive*) a person who is not able to speak ⇒ see also DEAF MUTE
- **verb 1** ~ **sth** to turn off the sound on a phone, television, etc: *A button on the speaker mutes the microphone.* **2** ~ **sth** to make the sound of sth, especially a musical instrument, quieter or softer, sometimes using a mute: *He muted the strings with his palm.* **3** ~ **sth** to make sth weaker or less severe SYN **tone down**: *She thought it better to mute her criticism.*

**ˈmute button** *noun* [C] (*also* **mute** [U]) **1** a button on a phone that you press in order to stop yourself from being heard by the person at the other end of the line (while you speak to sb else) **2** a button that you press in order to turn off the sound on a television, computer, etc.

**muted** /ˈmjuːtɪd/ *adj.* **1** (of sounds) quiet; not as loud as usual: *They spoke in muted voices.* **2** (of emotions, opinions, etc.) not strongly expressed: *The proposals received only a muted response.* **3** (of colours, light, etc.) not bright: *a dress in muted shades of blue* **4** (of musical instruments) used with a mute: *muted trumpets* **5** (of a television, computer, etc.) with the sound turned off

**mute·ly** /ˈmjuːtli/ *adv.* without speaking SYN **silently**

**muti** /ˈmuːti/ *noun* [U] (*SAfrE*) **1** African medicines or magic CHARMS that are prepared from plants, animals, etc. **2** any kind of medicine

# mutilate

**mu·ti·late** /ˈmjuːtɪleɪt/ verb 1 ~ sb/sth to damage sb's body very severely, especially by cutting or tearing off part of it: *The body had been badly mutilated.* 2 ~ sth to damage sth very badly SYN **vandalize**: *Intruders slashed and mutilated several paintings.* ▶ **mu·ti·la·tion** /ˌmjuːtɪˈleɪʃn/ noun [U, C]: *Thousands suffered death or mutilation in the bomb blast.* ⇨ see also FGM, SELF-MUTILATION

**mu·tin·eer** /ˌmjuːtɪˈnɪə(r); NAmE -ˈnɪr/ noun a person who takes part in a MUTINY

**mu·tin·ous** /ˈmjuːtənəs/ adj. 1 refusing to obey the orders of sb in authority; wanting to do this SYN **rebellious**: *mutinous workers* ◇ *a mutinous expression* 2 taking part in a mutiny ▶ **mu·tin·ous·ly** adv.

**mu·tiny** /ˈmjuːtəni/ noun, verb
■ noun (pl. -ies) [U, C] the act of refusing to obey the orders of sb in authority, especially by soldiers or sailors: *Discontent among the ship's crew finally led to the outbreak of mutiny.* ◇ *the famous movie 'Mutiny on the Bounty'* ◇ *We have a family mutiny on our hands!*
■ verb [I] (mu·tin·ies, mu·tiny·ing, mu·tin·ied, mu·tin·ied) (especially of soldiers or sailors) to refuse to obey the orders of sb in authority

**mut·ism** /ˈmjuːtɪzəm/ noun [U] (*medical*) a medical condition in which a person is unable to speak or chooses not to speak

**mutt** /mʌt/ noun (*especially NAmE, informal*) a dog, especially one that is not of a particular BREED SYN **mongrel**

**mut·ter** /ˈmʌtə(r)/ verb, noun
■ verb 1 [T, I] to speak or say sth in a quiet voice that is difficult to hear, especially because you are annoyed about sth: + *speech* '*How dare she,*' *he muttered under his breath.* ◇ ~(sth) (to sb/yourself) (about sth) *She just sat there muttering to herself.* ◇ *I muttered something about needing to get back to work.* ◇ ~ that ... *He muttered that he was sorry.* 2 [I, T] ~(about sth) | ~ that ... to complain about sth, without saying publicly what you think SYN **grumble**: *Workers continued to mutter about the management.*
■ noun [usually sing.] a quiet sound or words that are difficult to hear: *the soft mutter of voices*

**mut·ter·ing** /ˈmʌtərɪŋ/ noun 1 (also **mutterings** [pl.]) complaints that you express privately rather than openly: *There have been mutterings about his leadership.* 2 words that you speak very quietly to yourself

**mut·ton** /ˈmʌtn/ noun [U] meat from a fully grown sheep ⇨ compare LAMB
**IDM** **mutton dressed as ˈlamb** (*BrE, informal, disapproving*) used to describe a woman who is trying to look younger than she really is, especially by wearing clothes that are designed for young people

**mu·tual** /ˈmjuːtʃuəl/ adj. 1 used to describe feelings that two or more people have for each other equally, or actions that affect two or more people equally: *mutual respect/understanding* ◇ *mutual support/aid* ◇ *I don't like her, and I think the feeling is mutual* (= she doesn't like me either). 2 [only before noun] shared by two or more people: *We met at the home of a mutual friend.* ◇ *They soon discovered a mutual interest in music.* ▶ **mu·tu·al·ity** /ˌmjuːtʃuˈæləti/ noun [U, C] (*formal*)

**ˈmutual fund** (NAmE) (BrE **unit ˈtrust**) noun a company that offers a service to people by investing their money in various different businesses

**mu·tu·al·ly** /ˈmjuːtʃuəli/ adv. felt or done equally by two or more people: *a mutually beneficial/supportive relationship* ◇ *Can we find a mutually convenient time to meet?*
**IDM** ˌmutually exˈclusive (of two possibilities or ideas) that cannot both exist, be chosen or be true at the same time: *The two views are not mutually exclusive.*

**Muzak™** /ˈmjuːzæk/ noun [U] (*often disapproving*) continuous recorded music that is played in shops, restaurants, airports, etc. SYN **piped music**

**muz·zle** /ˈmʌzl/ noun, verb
■ noun 1 the nose and mouth of an animal, especially a dog or a horse ⇨ VISUAL VOCAB page V2 ⇨ compare SNOUT 2 a device made of leather or plastic that you put over the nose and mouth of an animal, especially a dog, to prevent it from biting people 3 the open end of a gun, where the bullets come out
■ verb 1 [usually passive] ~ sth to put a muzzle over the head of an animal, especially a dog, to prevent it from biting people 2 ~ sb/sth to prevent sb from expressing their opinions in public as they want to SYN **gag**: *They accused the government of muzzling the press.*

**muzzy** /ˈmʌzi/ adj. (*BrE, informal*) 1 unable to think in a clear way: *a muzzy head* ◇ *Those drugs made me feel muzzy.* 2 not clear: *a muzzy voice* ◇ *muzzy plans*

**MV** /ˌem ˈviː/ abbr. (*BrE*) (used before the name of a ship) motor vessel: *the MV Puma*

**MVP** /ˌem viː ˈpiː/ noun 1 (*especially NAmE*) most valuable player (the best player in a team): *He has just earned his fourth MVP award this season.* ⇨ compare (THE) MAN OF THE MATCH 2 minimum viable product (a basic version of a digital product that is developed first in order to test the product idea and get reactions from users before developing a more advanced version): *Build an MVP quickly and get feedback on it.*

**MW** abbr. 1 MEDIUM WAVE 2 (pl. **MW**) MEGAWATT

**MWA** /ˌem dʌblju: ˈeɪ/ noun the abbreviation for 'Member of the Welsh Assembly'

**mwah** (also **mwa**) /mwɑː/ exclamation used to represent the sound that some people make when they kiss sb on the side of the face

**mwa·limu** /mwɑːˈliːmuː; EAfrE [mwɑˈlimu] noun (*EAfrE*) 1 a teacher 2 **Mwalimu** a title or form of address for sb who is respected as a teacher: *Mwalimu Julius Nyerere*

**mwa·nan·chi** /mwəˈnæntʃi/ EAfrE [mwanaˈntʃi] noun (pl. **wa·nan·chi** /wəˈnæntʃi/ EAfrE [wanaˈntʃi]) (*EAfrE*) an ordinary citizen; a member of the public: *The common mwananchi is demanding change.* ⇨ see also WANANCHI

**my** ❶ A1 /maɪ/ det. (the possessive form of I) 1 A1 of or belonging to the speaker or writer: *Where's my passport?* ◇ *My feet are cold.* 2 used in exclamations to express surprise, etc: *My goodness! Look at the time.* ◇ (*especially NAmE*) *Oh my! What are we going to do?* 3 used when speaking to sb, to show love: *my dear/darling/love* 4 used when speaking to sb that you consider to have a lower status than you: *My dear girl, you're wrong.*

**my·al·gia** /maɪˈældʒə/ noun [U] (*medical*) pain in a muscle ▶ **my·al·gic** /-dʒɪk/ adj. ⇨ see also ME

**my·al·gic en·ceph·alo·my·eli·tis** /ˌmaɪˌældʒɪk enˌsefələʊmaɪəˈlaɪtɪs; BrE also -ke-/ noun [U] = ME

**my·col·ogy** /maɪˈkɒlədʒi; NAmE -ˈkɑː-/ noun [U] the scientific study of FUNGI ⇨ see also FUNGUS

**mye·lin** /ˈmaɪəlɪn/ noun [U] (*biology*) a mixture of PROTEINS and fats that surrounds many nerve cells, increasing the speed at which they send signals

**mye·loma** /ˌmaɪəˈləʊmə; C, U/ (pl. **mye·lo·mas** or **mye·lo·mata** /-tə/) noun (*medical*) a type of cancer found as a TUMOUR inside the bone

**mynah** /ˈmaɪnə/ (also **ˈmynah bird**) noun a south-east Asian bird with dark feathers, that can copy human speech

**MYOB** /ˌem waɪ əʊ ˈbiː/ abbr. (*informal*) (especially in emails, comments on SOCIAL MEDIA, etc.) mind your own business (think about your own affairs and do not ask questions about or try to get involved in other people's lives)

**myo·car·dial** /ˌmaɪəʊˈkɑːdiəl; NAmE -ˈkɑːrd-/ adj. [only before noun] (*medical*) relating to the TISSUE (= cells) that forms the heart muscle

**my·opia** /maɪˈəʊpiə/ noun [U] 1 (*specialist*) the condition of being unable to see things clearly when they are far away SYN **short sight** 2 (*formal, disapproving*) the state of being unable to see what the results of a particular action or decision will be; the failure to think about anything outside your own situation ▶ **my·opic** /maɪˈɒpɪk; NAmE -ˈɑːp-/ adj.: (*specialist*) *a myopic child/eye* ◇ (*disapproving*) *a myopic strategy* ◇ *myopic voters* SYN **short-sighted** **my·opic·al·ly** /-kli/ adv.

**myr·iad** /ˈmɪriəd/ BrE also -riæd/ noun (*literary*) an extremely large number of sth: *Designs are available in a myriad of colours.* ▶ **myr·iad** adj.: *the myriad problems of modern life*

**myrrh** /mɜː(r)/ noun [U] a sticky substance with a sweet smell that comes from trees and is used to make PERFUME and INCENSE

**myr·tle** /ˈmɜːtl/; NAmE /ˈmɜːrtl/ noun [U, C] a bush with shiny leaves, pink or white flowers and blue-black BERRIES

**my·self** 🔑 A2 /maɪˈself/ pron. **1** ? A2 (the reflexive form of *I*) used when the speaker or writer is also the person affected by an action: *I cut myself on a knife.* ◊ *I wrote a message to myself.* ◊ *I found myself unable to speak.* ◊ *I haven't been feeling myself recently* (= I have not felt well). ◊ *I needed space to be myself* (= not influenced by other people). **2** ? B1 used to emphasize the fact that the speaker is doing sth: *I'll speak to her myself.* ◊ *I myself do not agree.*
**IDM** **(all) by my·self 1** alone; without anyone else: *I live by myself.* **2** without help: *I painted the room all by myself.* **(all) to my·self** for the speaker or writer alone to have or use; not shared: *I had a whole pizza to myself.*

**mys·teri·ous** 🔑 B2 /mɪˈstɪəriəs/; NAmE -ˈstɪr-/ adj. **1** ? B2 difficult to understand or explain; strange: *He died in mysterious circumstances.* ◊ *the mysterious disappearance of his wife* ◊ *The whole thing was very mysterious.* **2** ? B2 (of a place) seeming strange or secret: *The gardens looked dark and mysterious in the twilight.* **3** ? B2 (especially of people) strange and interesting because you do not know much about them SYN **enigmatic**: *She meets a mysterious stranger who offers to help her.* **4** (of people) not saying much about sth, especially when other people want to know more: *He was being very mysterious about where he was going.* ▶ **mys·teri·ous·ly** adv.: *My watch had mysteriously disappeared.* ◊ *Mysteriously, the streets were deserted.* ◊ *She was silent, smiling mysteriously.* **mys·teri·ous·ness** noun [U]

**mys·tery** 🔑 B1 /ˈmɪstri/; NAmE -stəri/ noun (pl. -ies) **1** ? B1 [C] something that is difficult to understand or explain: *It is one of the great unsolved mysteries of this century.* ◊ *Their motives remain a mystery.* ◊ *She tried to solve the mystery of the boy's sudden death.* ◊ **It is a ~ to sb why, how, etc…** *It's a complete mystery to me why they chose him.* **2** ? B1 [C] (often used as an adjective) a person or thing that is strange and interesting because you do not know much about them or it: *He's a bit of a mystery.* ◊ *There was a mystery guest on the programme.* ◊ (*BrE*) *a mystery tour* (= when you do not know where you are going) ◊ **~ to sb** *My sister is a complete mystery to me.* **3** ? [U] the quality of being difficult to understand or to explain, especially when this makes sb/sth seem interesting and exciting: *Mystery surrounds her disappearance.* ◊ *His past is shrouded in mystery* (= not much is known about it). ◊ *The dark glasses give her an air of mystery.* **4** ? B1 [C] a story, a film or a play in which crimes and strange events are only explained at the end: *He is the author of several murder mysteries.* **5** **mysteries** [pl.] secret religious ceremonies; secret knowledge: (*figurative*) *the teacher who initiated me into the mysteries of mathematics* **6** [C] a religious belief that cannot be explained or proved in a scientific way: *the mystery of creation*

**ˌmystery ˈshopper** noun a person whose job is to visit or phone a shop or other business, or use their website, pretending to be a customer, in order to get information on the quality of the service, the facilities, etc. ▶ **ˈmystery ˈshopping** noun [U]

**mys·tic** /ˈmɪstɪk/ noun a person who uses prayer and MEDITATION to try to become united with God or to understand important things that are beyond normal human understanding ▶ **mys·tic** adj. = MYSTICAL

**mys·tic·al** /ˈmɪstɪkl/ (also less frequent **mys·tic**) adj. **1** having spiritual powers or qualities that are difficult to understand or to explain: *mystical forces/powers* ◊ *mystic beauty* ◊ *Watching the sun rise over the mountain was an almost mystical experience.* **2** connected with mysticism: *the mystical life* ▶ **mys·tic·al·ly** /-kli/ adv.

**mys·ti·cism** /ˈmɪstɪsɪzəm/ noun [U] the belief that knowledge of God or of real truth can be found through prayer and MEDITATION rather than through reason and the senses: *Eastern mysticism*

**mys·tify** /ˈmɪstɪfaɪ/ verb [often passive] (**mys·ti·fies, mys·ti·fy·ing, mys·ti·fied, mys·ti·fied**) to make sb confused because they do not understand sth SYN **baffle**: *be mystified (by sth)* *They were totally mystified by the girl's disappearance.* ▶ **mys·ti·fi·ca·tion** /ˌmɪstɪfɪˈkeɪʃn/ noun [U]: *He looked at her in mystification.* **mys·ti·fy·ing** /ˈmɪstɪfaɪɪŋ/ adj.

**mys·tique** /mɪˈstiːk/ noun [U, sing.] the quality of being mysterious or secret that makes sb/sth seem interesting or attractive: *The mystique surrounding the monarchy has gone for ever.*

**myth** ?+ B2 /mɪθ/ noun [C, U] **1** ?+ B2 a story from ancient times, especially one that was told to explain natural events or to describe the early history of a people; this type of story SYN **legend**: *ancient Greek myths* ◊ *a creation myth* (= that explains how the world began) ◊ *the heroes of myth and legend* **2** ?+ B2 something that many people believe but that does not exist or is false SYN **fallacy**: *It is time to dispel the myth of a classless society* (= to show that it does not exist). ◊ *Contrary to popular myth, women are not worse drivers than men.* ⊃ see also URBAN MYTH

**myth·ic** /ˈmɪθɪk/ adj. **1** (also **myth·ic·al**) that has become very famous, like sb/sth in a myth SYN **legendary**: *Scott of the Antarctic was a national hero of mythic proportions.* **2** = MYTHICAL (1)

**myth·ic·al** /ˈmɪθɪkl/ adj. [usually before noun] **1** (also less frequent **myth·ic**) existing only in ancient myths SYN **legendary**: *mythical beasts/heroes* **2** (also less frequent **myth·ic**) that does not exist or is not true SYN **fictitious**: *the mythical 'rich uncle' that he boasts about* **3** = MYTHIC (1)

**mytho·logic·al** /ˌmɪθəˈlɒdʒɪkl/; NAmE -ˈlɑːdʒ-/ adj. [usually before noun] connected with ancient MYTHS: *mythological subjects/figures/stories*

**myth·ology** /mɪˈθɒlədʒi/; NAmE -ˈθɑːl-/ noun (pl. -ies) [U, C] **1** ancient MYTHS in general; the ancient MYTHS of a particular culture, society, etc: *Greek mythology* ◊ *a study of the religions and mythologies of ancient Rome* **2** ideas that many people think are true but that do not exist or are false: *the popular mythology that life begins at forty*

**myxo·ma·tosis** /ˌmɪksəməˈtəʊsɪs/ noun [U] a disease of RABBITS that usually causes death

**mzee** /əmˈzeɪ/ *EAfrE* [ˈmzeː] noun (*EAfrE*) **1** a person who is respected because of their age, experience or authority; an ELDER **2** **Mzee** a title for a man that shows respect: *Mzee Kenyatta*

**mzungu** /əmˈzʊŋɡu/ *EAfrE* [mˈzuŋɡu] noun, adj. (*EAfrE*)
■ **noun** (pl. **wazungu** /wəˈzʊŋɡuː/ [waˈzuŋɡu]) a white person with European family origins: *He was the only mzungu there.*
■ **adj.** connected with white European family origins

# N n

**N** /en/ *noun, abbr., symbol*
- *noun* (also **n**) (*pl.* **Ns, N's, n's** /enz/) **1** [C, U] the 14th letter of the English alphabet: *'Night' begins with (an) N/'N'.* **2** [U] (*mathematics*) used to represent a number whose value is not mentioned: *The equation is impossible for any value of n greater than 2.* ⊃ see also NTH
- *abbr.* (in writing) **1** (*NAmE* also **No.**) north; northern: *N Ireland* **2** NEWTON
- *symbol* (in writing) the symbol for the chemical element NITROGEN

**n.** *abbr.* (in writing) noun

**n/a** *abbr.* (in writing) **1** not applicable (used on a form as an answer to a question that does not apply to you) **2** not available

**NAACP** /ˌen ˌdʌbəl ˌeɪ siː ˈpiː/ *abbr.* National Association for the Advancement of Colored People (an organization in the US that works for the rights of African Americans)

**NAAFI** /ˈnæfi/ *noun* [sing.] an organization which provides shops and places to eat for British soldiers (the abbreviation for 'Navy, Army and Air Force Institutes')

**naan** = NAN²

**naar·tjie** /ˈnɑːtʃi; *NAmE* ˈnɑːrtʃi/ *SAfrE* [ˈnɑːrki] *noun* (*SAfrE*) a type of small orange with a loose skin that you can remove easily

**nab** /næb/ *verb* (**-bb-**) (*informal*) **1** ~ **sb** to catch or arrest sb who is doing sth wrong SYN **collar**: *He was nabbed by the police for speeding.* **2** ~ **sth** to take or get sth: *Who's nabbed my drink?*

**nabob** /ˈneɪbɒb; *NAmE* -bɑːb/ *noun* **1** a Muslim ruler or officer in the Mogul Empire **2** a rich or important person

**nachos** /ˈnætʃəʊz; *NAmE* ˈnɑːtʃ-/ *noun* [pl.] (*from Spanish*) a dish of TORTILLA CHIPS served with beans, cheese, SPICES, etc.

**nada** /ˈnɑːdə/ *noun* [U] (*from Spanish, informal, especially NAmE*) nothing: *What is it worth? Zero, zilch, nada!*

**nadir** /ˈneɪdɪə(r); *NAmE* -dɪr/ *noun* [sing.] (*formal*) the worst moment of a particular situation: *the nadir of his career ◊ Company losses reached their nadir in 2009.* OPP **zenith**

**nae** /neɪ/ *det.* (*ScotE*) no: *We have nae money.* ▸ **nae** *adv.*: *It's nae* (= not) *bad.*

**naff** /næf/ *adj.* (*BrE, informal*) not having or showing style, taste, quality, etc: *There was this really naff music playing in the background.*

**nag** /næɡ/ *verb, noun*
- *verb* (**-gg-**) **1** [I, T] to keep complaining to sb about their behaviour or keep asking them to do sth SYN **pester**: ~ (**at sb**) *Stop nagging—I'll do it as soon as I can.* ◊ ~ **sb** (**to do sth**) *She had been nagging him to paint the fence.* ◊ ~ **sb about sth** *She constantly nagged her daughter about getting married.* **2** [I, T] to worry you or cause you pain continuously: ~ **at sb** *A feeling of unease nagged at her.* ◊ ~ **sb** *Doubts nagged me all evening.*
- *noun* **1** a person who keeps asking sb to do sth in an annoying way **2** (*old-fashioned, informal*) a horse

**na·gana** /nəˈɡɑːnə/ *EAfrE* [nɑˈɡɑnɑ] *noun* [U] (*EAfrE*) a serious illness that cows can get from a type of fly (= a TSETSE FLY)

**nagar** /ˈnʌɡə(r); *NAmE* ˈnɑːɡ-/ *noun* (*IndE*) a town, a city, an area in a city, or a SUBURB (= an area where people live that is outside the centre of a city)

**nag·ging** /ˈnæɡɪŋ/ *adj.* [only before noun] **1** continuing for a long time and difficult to cure or remove: *a nagging pain/doubt* **2** complaining: *a nagging voice*

**nah** /næ/ *exclamation* (*informal*) no

**naiad** /ˈnaɪæd/ *noun* (*pl.* **naiads** or **nai·ades** /ˈnaɪədiːz/) (in ancient stories) a water spirit

**nail** 🔊 B1 /neɪl/ *noun, verb*
- *noun* **1** 🔊 B1 the thin hard layer covering the outer tip of the fingers or toes: *Stop biting your nails! ◊ nail clippers* ⊃ see also FINGERNAIL, TOENAIL **2** 🔊 B1 a small thin pointed piece of metal with a flat head, used for joining pieces of wood together or hanging things on a wall: *She hammered the nail in.* ⊃ compare SCREW, TACK IDM **a nail in sb's/sth's 'coffin** something that makes the end or failure of an organization, sb's plans, etc. more likely to happen **on the 'nail** (*BrE, informal*) (of payment) without delay: *They're good customers who always pay on the nail.* ⊃ more at FIGHT *v.*, HARD *adj.*, HIT *v.*, TOUGH *adj.*
- *verb* **1** ~ **sth** (+ *adv./prep./adj.*) to fasten sth to sth with a nail or nails: *I nailed the sign to a tree.* **2** ~ **sb** (*informal*) to catch sb and prove they are guilty of a crime or of doing sth bad: *The police haven't been able to nail the killer.* **3** ~ **a lie, myth, etc.** (*informal*) to prove that sth is not true: *We must nail this lie.* **4** ~ **sth** (*informal*) to achieve sth or do sth right, especially in sport: *He nailed a victory in the semi-finals.* ◊ *She nailed it on her second jump.* IDM **nail your colours to the 'mast** (*especially BrE*) to say publicly and clearly what you believe or who you support PHRV **nail sth↔down 1** to fasten sth in place with a nail or nails **2** to reach an agreement or a decision, usually after a lot of discussion: *All the parties seem anxious to nail down a ceasefire.* **nail sb↔down (to sth)** to force sb to agree to a definite promise or tell you exactly what they intend to do: *She says she'll come, but I can't nail her down to a specific time.* **nail sth↔up 1** to fasten sth to a wall, post, etc. with a nail or nails **2** to put nails into a door or window so that it cannot be opened

**'nail bar** *noun* a place where you can pay to have the nails on your fingers and toes shaped, coloured and made more attractive

**'nail-biter** *noun* a situation that makes you feel excited or anxious because you do not know what is going to happen: *The final game of the competition was a real nail-biter.*

**'nail-biting** *adj.* [usually before noun] making you feel very excited or anxious because you do not know what is going to happen: *a nail-biting finish ◊ It's been a nail-biting couple of weeks waiting for my results.*

**'nail brush** *noun* a small stiff brush for cleaning your nails

**'nail clippers** *noun* [pl.] a small tool for cutting the nails on your fingers and toes

**ˌnailed 'on** *adj.* (*BrE, informal*) **1** certain or definite: *The referee refused to award a nailed-on penalty.* **2** (in BETTING) believed to be very likely to succeed: *a nailed-on bet*

**'nail file** *noun* a small metal tool with a rough surface for shaping the nails on your fingers and toes

**'nail polish** (*BrE also* **'nail varnish**) *noun* [U] clear or coloured liquid that you paint on the nails on your fingers or toes to make them look attractive: *nail polish/varnish remover* ⊃ WORDFINDER NOTE at MAKE-UP

**'nail scissors** *noun* [pl.] small SCISSORS that are usually curved, used for cutting the nails on your fingers and toes: *a pair of nail scissors*

**naive** (also **naïve**) /naɪˈiːv/ *adj.* **1** (*disapproving*) not having enough knowledge, good judgement or experience of life and too willing to believe that people always tell you the truth: *to be politically naive ◊ I can't believe you were so naive as to trust him! ◊ a naive question* ⊃ WORDFINDER NOTE at YOUNG **2** (*approving*) (of people and their behaviour) innocent and simple SYN **artless**: *Their approach to life is refreshingly naive.* ⊃ compare SOPHISTICATED **3** (*specialist*) (of art) in a style which is deliberately very simple, often uses bright colours and is similar to that produced by a child ▸ **naive·ly** (also **naïve·ly**) *adv.*: *I naively assumed that I would be paid for the work.* **naiv·ety** (also **naïv·ety, naiv·eté**) /-ˈiːvəti/ *noun* [U]: *They laughed at the naivety of his suggestion. ◊ She has lost none of her naivety.*

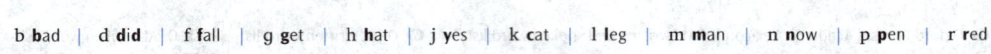

**naked** /ˈneɪkɪd/ adj. **1** not wearing any clothes **SYN** **bare**: *a naked body* ◊ *naked shoulders* ◊ *He was naked from the waist up.* ◊ *They often wandered around the house stark naked* (= completely naked). ◊ *They found him half naked and bleeding to death.* ◊ *The prisoners were stripped naked.* ⇒ see also BUCK NAKED **2** [usually before noun] with nothing to cover it **SYN** **bare**: *a naked light* ◊ *a naked sword* ◊ *Mice are born naked* (= without fur). ◊ (*BrE*) *a naked flame* **HELP** In American English this is called an *open flame*. **3** [only before noun] (of emotions, attitudes, etc.) expressed strongly and not hidden: *naked aggression* ◊ *the naked truth* **4** [not usually before noun] unable to protect yourself from being harmed, criticized, etc. **SYN** **helpless**: *He still felt weak and drained after his ordeal.* ▸ **naked·ly** *adv.*: *nakedly aggressive* **naked·ness** *noun* [U]
**IDM** **the naked ˈeye** the normal power of your eyes without the help of an instrument: *The planet should be visible with/to the naked eye.*

▼ **WHICH WORD?**
**naked / bare**
Both these words can be used to mean 'not covered with clothes' and are frequently used with the following nouns:

| naked ~ | bare ~ |
| --- | --- |
| body | feet |
| man | arms |
| fear | walls |
| aggression | branches |
| flame | essentials |

- **Naked** is more often used to describe a person or their body and **bare** usually describes a part of the body.
- **Bare** can also describe other things with nothing on them: *bare walls* ◊ *a bare hillside*. **Naked** can mean 'without a protective covering': *a naked sword*.
- **Bare** can also mean 'just enough': *the bare minimum*. **Naked** can be used to talk about strong feelings that are not hidden: *naked fear*. Note also the idiom: (visible) to/with **the naked eye**.

**na·mas·kar** /ˈnʌməˌskɑː(r)/ *noun* [U] (*IndE*) a way of GREETING sb in which the hands are placed together as in prayer and the head is bent forwards

**namby-pamby** /ˌnæmbi ˈpæmbi/ *adj.* (*informal, disapproving*) weak and too emotional

**name** /neɪm/ *noun, verb*
■ *noun* **1** a word or words that a particular person, animal, place or thing is known by: *What's your name?* ◊ *What is/was the name, please?* (= a polite way of asking sb's name) ◊ *Please write your full name and address below.* ◊ *Leave your name and number* (= phone number) *and we'll call you later.* ◊ *Are you changing your name when you get married?* ◊ *Do you know the name of this flower?* ◊ *~ for sth Rubella is just another name for German measles.* ◊ *under a …~ The company reopened under a new name.* **HELP** There are many compounds ending in **name**. You will find them at their place in the alphabet. **2** [usually sing.] a reputation that sb/sth has; the opinion that people have about sb/sth: *She first made her name as a writer of children's books.* ◊ *He's made quite a name for himself* (= become famous). ◊ *The college has a good name for languages.* ◊ *This kind of behaviour gives students a bad name.* ⇒ see also GOOD NAME **3** (in compound adjectives) having a name or a reputation of the kind mentioned, especially one that is known by a lot of people: *a big-name company* ◊ *brand-name goods* ⇒ see also HOUSEHOLD NAME, NO-NAME (2) **4** a famous person: *He is a big name in the world of rock music.* ⇒ see also NO-NAME (1)
**IDM** **by ˈname** using the name of sb/sth: *She asked for you by name.* ◊ *The principal knows all the students by name.* ◊ *I only know her by name* (= I have heard about her but I have not met her). **by the ˈname of …** (*formal*) who is called: *a young actor by the name of Tom Rees* **enter sb's/your ˈname (for sth)** (*also* **put sb's/your ˈname down (for sth)**) to apply for a place at a school, in a competition, etc. for sb or yourself: *Have you entered your name for the quiz yet?* **give your ˈname to sth** to discover or invent sth

which then becomes known by your name: *Henry Hudson gave his name to New York's Hudson River.* **ˌgo by the ˈname of …** to use a name that may not be your real one **have your/sb's ˈname on it** | **with your/sb's ˈname on it** (*informal*) if sth **has your name on it**, or there is sth **with your name on it**, it is intended for you: *He took my place and got killed. It should have been me—that bullet had my name on it.* ◊ *Are you coming for dinner this evening? I've got a steak here with your name on it!* **in ˌall but ˈname** used to describe a situation which exists in reality but that is not officially recognized: *He runs the company in all but name.* **in ˈGod's/ˈHeaven's name** | **in the name of ˈGod/ˈHeaven** used especially in questions to show that you are angry, surprised or shocked: *What in God's name was that noise?* ◊ *Where in the name of Heaven have you been?* **HELP** Some people find this use of **God** offensive. **in the name of ˈsb/ˈsth** | **in sb's/sth's ˈname** **1** for sb; showing that sth officially belongs to sb: *We reserved two tickets in the name of Brown.* ◊ *The car is registered in my name.* **2** using the authority of sb/sth; as a representative of sb/sth: *I arrest you in the name of the law.* **3** used to give a reason or an excuse for doing sth, often when what you are doing is wrong: *crimes committed in the name of religion* **in ˈname only** officially recognized but not existing in reality: *He's party leader in name only.* **sb's name is ˈmud** (*informal, usually humorous*) used to say that sb is not liked or popular because of sth they have done **the name of the ˈgame** (*informal*) the most important aspect of an activity; the most important quality needed for an activity: *Hard work is the name of the game if you want to succeed in business.* **a name to ˈconjure with** (*BrE*) **1** (*NAmE* **a name to ˈreckon with**) a person or thing that is well known and respected in a particular field: *Miyazaki is still a name to conjure with among anime fans.* **2** (*humorous*) used when you mention a name that you think is difficult to remember or pronounce: *He comes from Tighnabruaich —now there's a name to conjure with!* **put a ˈname to sb/sth** to know or remember what sb/sth is called: *I*

▼ **MORE ABOUT…**
**names and titles**
Names
- Your **name** is either your whole name or one part of your name: *My name is Maria.* ◊ *His name is Tom Smith.*
- Your **last name** or **family name** (also called **surname** in *BrE*) is the name that all members of your family share.
- Your **first name/names** (*formal* **forename**) is/are the name(s) your parents gave you when you were born. In *BrE* some people use the expression **Christian name(s)** to refer to a person's first name(s).
- Your **middle name(s)** is/are any name(s) your parents gave you other than the one that is placed first. The initial of this name is often used as part of your name, especially in America: *John T. Harvey*
- Your **full name** is all your names, usually in the order: first + middle + last name
- A woman's **maiden name** is the family name she had before she got married. Some women keep this name after they are married and do not use their husband's name. In North America, married women often use their maiden name followed by their husband's family name: *Hillary Rodham Clinton.*

Titles
- **Mr** (for both married and unmarried men)
- **Mrs** (for married women)
- **Miss** (for unmarried women)
- **Ms** (a title that some women prefer to use as it does not distinguish between married and unmarried women)
- **Doctor, Professor, President, Vice-President, Reverend** (or **Rev**), etc.

The correct way to talk to someone is:
- first name, if you know them well: *Hello, Maria.*
- or title + name: *Hello, Mr Brown.*
- or **Doctor** (medical), **Professor**, etc. on its own: *Thank you, Doctor.* This is only used for a very limited number of titles.

# name-calling

recognize the tune but I can't put a name to it. **take sb's name in ˈvain** to show a lack of respect when using sb's name or when talking about them: (humorous) *Have you been taking my name in vain again?* **(have sth) to your ˈname** to have or own sth: *an Olympic athlete with five gold medals to his name* ◊ *She doesn't have a penny/cent to her name* (= she is very poor). **under the name (of) …** using a name that may not be your real name ⊃ more at ANSWER v., BIG adj., CALL v., DOG n., DRAG v., DROP v., LEND, MIDDLE NAME, NAME v., REJOICE, ROSE n.

- **verb 1** [often passive] to give a name to sb/sth SYN **call**: *~ sb/sth (after/for sb) He was named after his father* (= given his father's first name). ◊ *~ sb/sth + noun They named their son John.* ◊ *adv. + named He plays the evil scientist, the aptly named Dr Weird.* **2** to say the name of sb/sth SYN **identify**: *~ sb/sth The victim has not yet been named.* ◊ *He refused to name his accomplice.* ◊ *Can you name all the American states?* ◊ *~ sb/sth as sb/sth The missing man has been named as James Kelly.* ⊃ SYNONYMS at IDENTIFY **3** *~ sth* to state sth exactly SYN **specify**: *Name your price.* ◊ *They're engaged, but they haven't yet named the day* (= chosen the date for their wedding). ◊ *Activities available include squash, archery and swimming, to name but a few.* ◊ *Chairs, tables, cabinets—you name it, she makes it* (= she makes anything you can imagine). **4** to choose sb for a job or position SYN **nominate**: *~ sb as sth I had no hesitation in naming him (as) captain.* ◊ *~ sb (to sth) When she resigned, he was named to the committee in her place.* ◊ *~ sb to do sth Mr Shah has been named to run the new research unit.*
 IDM **ˌname and ˈshame** (BrE) to publish the names of people or organizations who have done sth wrong or illegal: *Businesses which fail in their duty to protect the environment should be named and shamed.* **ˌname ˈnames** to give the names of the people involved in sth, especially sth wrong or illegal

**ˈname-calling** *noun* [U] the act of using rude or offensive words about sb

**ˈname-check** /ˈneɪmtʃek/ *noun, verb*
- *noun* an occasion when the name of a person or thing is publicly mentioned or included in a list, especially as a way of thanking or praising them: *She started her speech by giving a namecheck to all the people who had helped her.*
- *verb* *~ sb/sth* to publicly mention or include sb/sth in a list, especially as a way of thanking or praising them: *The songs namecheck other artists and bands.* ◊ *The book was namechecked in today's paper.*

**ˈname day** *noun* a day which is special for a Christian with a particular name because it is the day which celebrates a SAINT with the same name

**ˈname-dropping** *noun* [U] (*disapproving*) the act of mentioning the names of famous people you know or have met in order to impress other people ▸ **ˈname-drop** *verb* [I] ⊃ see also DROP NAMES at DROP *verb*

**name·less** /ˈneɪmləs/ *adj.* **1** [usually before noun] having no name; whose name you do not know: *a nameless grave* ◊ *thousands of nameless and faceless workers* **2** whose name is kept secret SYN **anonymous**: *a nameless source in the government* ◊ *a well-known public figure who shall remain nameless* **3** [usually before noun] (*literary*) difficult or too unpleasant to describe: *nameless horrors* ◊ *a nameless longing*

**name·ly** /ˈneɪmli/ *adv.* used to introduce more exact and detailed information about sth that you have just mentioned: *We need to concentrate on our target audience, namely women aged between 20 and 30.*

**name·plate** /ˈneɪmpleɪt/ *noun* **1** a sign on the door or the wall of a building showing the name of a company or the name of a person who is living or working there **2** a piece of metal or plastic on an object showing the name of the person who owns it, made it or presented it

**name·sake** /ˈneɪmseɪk/ *noun* a person or thing that has the same name as sb/sth else: *Unlike his more famous namesake, this Gordon Brown has little interest in politics.*

**ˈname tag** *noun* a small piece of plastic, paper or metal that you wear, with your name on it ⊃ WORDFINDER NOTE at CONFERENCE

**nan**[1] /næn/ *noun* (*BrE*) = NANNY (2)

**nan**[2] (also **naan**) /nɑːn/ (also **ˈnan bread**, **ˈnaan bread**) *noun* [U] a type of soft flat South Asian bread

**nana**[1] (*BrE also* **nanna**) /ˈnænə/ *noun* (*informal*) = NANNY (2)

**nana**[2] /ˈnɑːnə/ *noun* (*old-fashioned, BrE, informal*) a stupid person SYN **idiot**: *I felt a right nana.*

**nanny** /ˈnæni/ *noun* (*pl.* **-ies**) **1** a person whose job is to take care of young children in the children's own home **2** (*also* **nan**) (*both BrE*) (used by children, especially as a form of address) a grandmother: *When is Nanny coming to stay?* ◊ *my nan and grandad* ⊃ see also GRANNY
 IDM **the ˈnanny state** (*disapproving*) a way of talking about government which shows that you do not approve of it and suggests that it is too involved in controlling and protecting people in a way that limits their freedom

**ˈnanny goat** *noun* a female GOAT ⊃ compare BILLY GOAT

**nanny·ing** /ˈnæniɪŋ/ *noun* [U] **1** the job of being a child's NANNY **2** (*BrE, disapproving*) the fact of helping and protecting sb too much

**nano-** /ˈnænəʊ/ *combining form* (in nouns and adjectives; used especially in units of measurement) one billionth: *nanosecond*

**nano·metre** (*US* **nano·meter**) /ˈnænəʊmiːtə(r)/ *noun* (*abbr.* **nm**) one thousand millionth of a metre

**nano·par·ticle** /ˈnænəʊpɑːtɪkl; NAmE -pɑːrt-/ *noun* a piece of matter less than 100 nanometres long

**nano·scale** /ˈnænəʊskeɪl/ *adj.* [usually before noun] a size that can be measured in nanometres: *nanoscale particles/devices/electronics*

**nano·sec·ond** /ˈnænəʊsekənd/ *noun* (*abbr.* **ns**) one thousand millionth of a second

**nano·tech·nol·ogy** /ˌnænəʊtekˈnɒlədʒi; NAmE -ˈnɑːl-/ *noun* [U] the branch of technology that deals with structures that are less than 100 NANOMETRES long. Scientists often build these structures using individual MOLECULES of substances. ▸ **nano·tech·nolo·gist** *noun* **nano·tech·no·logic·al** /ˌnænəʊˌteknəˈlɒdʒɪkl; NAmE -ˈlɑːdʒ-/ *adj.*: *nanotechnological research*

**nap** /næp/ *noun, verb*
- *noun* **1** [C] a short sleep, especially during the day SYN **snooze**: *to take/have a nap* ⊃ SYNONYMS at SLEEP ⊃ compare SIESTA ⊃ see also CATNAP, POWER NAP **2** [sing.] the short fine THREADS on the surface of some types of cloth, usually lying in the same direction **3** [C] (*BrE*) advice given by an expert on which horse is most likely to win a race
- *verb* [I] (**-pp-**) to sleep for a short time, especially during the day ⊃ see also POWER-NAP IDM see CATCH *v.*

**napa** = NAPPA

**na·palm** /ˈneɪpɑːm/ *noun* [U] a sticky substance like JELLY, made from petrol, that burns easily and is used in making bombs

**nape** /neɪp/ *noun* [sing.] *~ (of sb's neck)* the back of the neck: *Her hair was cut short at the nape of her neck.*

**naph·tha** /ˈnæfθə, ˈnæpθə/ *noun* [U] a type of oil that starts burning very easily, used as fuel or in making chemicals

**naph·tha·lene** /ˈnæfθəliːn, ˈnæpθ-/ *noun* [U] (*chemistry*) a substance used in MOTHBALLS (= used for keeping MOTHS away from clothes) and in industrial processes

**nap·kin** /ˈnæpkɪn/ *noun* **1** (*also* **ˈtable napkin**) a piece of cloth or paper used at meals for protecting your clothes and cleaning your lips and fingers SYN **serviette**: *a napkin ring* (= for holding a napkin when it is not in use) *made of silver* **2** (*NAmE*) = SANITARY NAPKIN **3** (*BrE, old-fashioned or formal*) = NAPPY

**nappa** (*also* **napa**) /ˈnæpə/ *noun* [U] a type of soft leather made from the skin of sheep or GOATS

**nappe** /næp/ *noun* (*geology*) a thin layer of rock that lies on top of a different type of rock

**nap·py** /ˈnæpi/ noun (pl. **-ies**) (BrE) (NAmE **di·a·per**) a piece of soft cloth or other thick material that is folded around a baby's bottom and between its legs to take in and hold its body waste: *I'll change her nappy.* ◇ *a dirty nappy* ◇ *a disposable nappy* (= one that is made to be used once only) ◇ *nappy rash* ⇒ WORDFINDER NOTE at BABY

**narc** /nɑːk; NAmE nɑːrk/ noun (NAmE, informal) a police officer whose job is to stop people selling or using drugs illegally

**nar·cis·sism** /ˈnɑːsɪsɪzəm; NAmE ˈnɑːrs-/ noun [U] (formal, disapproving) the habit of admiring yourself too much, especially your appearance ▸ **nar·cis·sist** /ˈnɑːsɪsɪst; NAmE ˈnɑːrs-/ noun **nar·cis·sis·tic** /ˌnɑːsɪˈsɪstɪk; NAmE ˌnɑːrs-/ adj. ORIGIN From the Greek myth in which Narcissus, a beautiful young man, fell in love with his own reflection in a pool. He died and was changed into the flower which bears his name.

**nar·cis·sus** /nɑːˈsɪsəs; NAmE nɑːrˈs-/ noun (pl. **nar·cissi** /-ˈsɪsaɪ/) a plant with white or yellow flowers that appear in spring. There are many types of narcissus, including the DAFFODIL.

**nar·co·lepsy** /ˈnɑːkəʊlepsi; NAmE ˈnɑːrk-/ noun [U] (medical) a condition in which sb falls into a deep sleep when they are in a relaxing environment

**nar·co·sis** /nɑːˈkəʊsɪs; NAmE nɑːrˈk-/ noun [U] (medical) a state caused by drugs in which sb is unconscious or keeps going to sleep

**nar·cot·ic** /nɑːˈkɒtɪk; NAmE nɑːrˈkɑːt-/ noun, adj.
■ noun **1** (formal) a powerful illegal drug that affects the mind in a harmful way. HEROIN and COCAINE are narcotics: *a narcotics agent* (= a police officer investigating the illegal trade in drugs) **2** (medical) a substance that relaxes you, reduces pain or makes you sleep: *a mild narcotic*
■ adj. **1** (of a drug) that affects your mind in a harmful way **2** (of a substance) making you sleep: *a mild narcotic effect*

**narked** /nɑːkt; NAmE nɑːrkt/ adj. [not usually before noun] (old-fashioned, BrE, informal) annoyed

**narky** /ˈnɑːki; NAmE ˈnɑːrki/ adj. (**nark·ier**, **narki·est**) (BrE, informal) becoming angry or annoyed very easily

**nar·rate** /nəˈreɪt; NAmE ˈnæreɪt/ verb **1** ~ sth (formal) to tell a story SYN **relate**: *She entertained them by narrating her adventures in Africa.* ⇒ WORDFINDER NOTE at PLOT **2** ~ sth to speak the words that form the text of a DOCUMENTARY film or programme: *The film was narrated by Andrew Sachs.*

**nar·ra·tion** /nəˈreɪʃn, næˈr-/ noun (formal) **1** [U, C] the act or process of telling a story, especially in a novel, a film or a play **2** [C] a description of events that is spoken during a film, a play, etc. or with music: *He has recorded the narration for the production.*

**nar·ra·tive** ⓘ B1 /ˈnærətɪv/ noun, adj.
■ noun (formal) **1** ⓘ B1 [C] a description of events SYN **story**: *a gripping narrative of their journey up the Amazon* ◇ *a collection of personal narratives* ◇ *a historical narrative of the United States* **2** ⓘ B1 [U] the part of a novel that tells the story, rather than the dialogue: *The novel contains too much dialogue and not enough narrative.* **3** [C, U] a way of explaining events to illustrate a set of aims or values: *a new narrative about economic globalization*
■ adj. ⓘ B1 [only before noun] (formal) describing events or telling a story: *narrative fiction* ◇ *a straightforward narrative structure* ◇ *a narrative poem*

**nar·ra·tor** /nəˈreɪtə(r); NAmE ˈnæreɪtər/ noun a person who tells a story, especially in a book, play or film; the person who speaks the words in a television programme but who does not appear in it: *a first-person narrator* ⇒ WORDFINDER NOTE at BOOK

**nar·row** ⓘ A2 /ˈnærəʊ/ adj., verb
■ adj. (**nar·row·er**, **nar·row·est**) **1** ⓘ A2 measuring a short distance from one side to the other, especially in relation to length: *narrow streets* ◇ *a narrow bed/doorway/shelf* ◇ *narrow shoulders/hips* ◇ *There was only a narrow gap between the bed and the wall.* ◇ (figurative) *the narrow confines of prison life* OPP **broad**, **wide** **2** ⓘ B2 [usually before noun] only just achieved or avoided: *a narrow victory* ◇ *She was elected by a narrow majority.* ◇ *He had a narrow escape when his car skidded on the ice.* ◇ *He lost the race by the narrowest of margins.* **3** ⓘ B2 limited in variety or numbers SYN **restricted**: *The shop sells only a narrow range of goods.* ◇ *a narrow circle of friends* OPP **wide** **4** ⓘ B2 limited in a way that ignores important issues or the opinions of other people: *narrow interests* ◇ *She has a very narrow view of the world.* OPP **broad** **5** limited in meaning; exact: *I am using the word 'education' in the narrower sense.* OPP **broad** ▸ **nar·row·ness** noun [U, sing.]: *The narrowness of the streets caused many traffic problems.* ◇ *We were surprised by the narrowness of our victory.* ◇ *His attitudes show a certain narrowness of mind.* IDM see STRAIGHT adj.
■ verb [I, T] **1** ⓘ B2 to become or make sth less wide: *This is where the river narrows.* ◇ *Her eyes narrowed* (= almost closed) *menacingly.* ◇ ~ sth *His eyes narrowed to slits.* ◇ ~ sth *He narrowed his eyes at her.* **2** ⓘ B2 to become or make sth more limited in range or extent: *The company has narrowed the gap between premium and discount brands.* ◇ ~ sth *The gap between the two teams has narrowed to three points.*
PHR V **narrow sth↔down (to sth)** to reduce the number of possibilities or choices: *We narrowed the choices down to five categories.* ◇ *We have narrowed down the list to four candidates.*

▼ WHICH WORD?

**narrow / thin**

These adjectives are frequently used with the following nouns:

| narrow ~ | thin ~ |
|---|---|
| road | man |
| entrance | legs |
| bed | ice |
| stairs | line |
| majority | layer |
| victory | material |
| range | cream |

● **Narrow** describes something that is a short distance from side to side. **Thin** describes people, or something that has a short distance through it from one side to the other.
● **Thin** is also used of things that are not as thick as you expect. **Narrow** can be used with the meanings 'only just achieved' and 'limited'.

**nar·row·band** /ˈnærəʊbænd/ noun [U] (specialist) signals that use a narrow range of frequencies ⇒ compare BROADBAND

**nar·row·boat** /ˈnærəʊbəʊt/ noun (BrE) a long narrow boat, used on CANALS

**ˈnarrow gauge** noun [U] a size of railway track that is not as wide as the standard track that is used in the UK and the US: *a narrow-gauge railway*

**nar·row·ly** /ˈnærəʊli/ adv. **1** only by a small amount: *The car narrowly missed a cyclist.* ◇ *She narrowly escaped injury.* ◇ *The team lost narrowly.* **2** (sometimes disapproving) in a way that is limited: *a narrowly defined task* ◇ *a narrowly specialized education* **3** closely; carefully: *She looked at him narrowly.*

**ˌnarrow-ˈminded** adj. (disapproving) not willing to listen to new ideas or to the opinions of others SYN **bigoted**, **intolerant**: *a narrow-minded attitude* ◇ *a narrow-minded nationalist* OPP **broad-minded**, **open-minded** ▸ **ˌnarrow-ˈminded·ness** noun [U]

**nar·rows** /ˈnærəʊz/ noun [pl.] a narrow channel that connects two larger areas of water

**nar·whal** /ˈnɑːwəl; NAmE ˈnɑːrwɑːl/ noun a small white WHALE from the Arctic region. The male narwhal has a long TUSK (= outer tooth).

**nary** /ˈneəri; NAmE ˈneri/ adj. (old use or dialect) not a; no

**NASA** /ˈnæsə/ abbr. National Aeronautics and Space Administration (a US government organization that does research into space and organizes space travel)

**nasal** /ˈneɪzl/ adj. **1** connected with the nose: *the nasal passages* ◇ *a nasal spray* **2** (of sb's voice) sounding as if it is produced partly through the nose: *a nasal accent/twang*

# nascent

**3** (phonetics) (of a speech sound) produced by allowing air to flow through the nose but not the mouth. The nasal consonants in English are /m/, /n/ and /ŋ/, as in *sum*, *sun* and *sung*.

**nas·cent** /ˈneɪsnt; BrE also ˈnæs-/ adj. (formal) beginning to exist; not yet fully developed

**the NASDAQ** /ðə ˈnæzdæk/ noun [sing.] National Association of Securities Dealers Automated Quotations (a computer system in the US that supplies the current price of shares to the people who sell them)

**na·stur·tium** /nəˈstɜːʃəm; NAmE -ˈstɜːrʃ-/ noun a garden plant with round flat leaves and red, orange or yellow flowers that are sometimes eaten in salads

**nasty** /ˈnɑːsti; NAmE ˈnæs-/ adj. (**nas·tier**, **nas·ti·est**)
**1** very bad or unpleasant: *a nasty accident* ◇ *The news gave me a nasty shock.* ◇ *I got a nasty surprise when I opened the door and saw who was there.* ◇ *This coffee has a nasty taste.* ◇ *Don't buy that coat—it looks cheap and nasty.* **2** unkind; unpleasant **SYN mean**: *to make nasty remarks about sb* ◇ *the nastier side of her character* ◇ *to have a nasty temper* ◇ *Life has a nasty habit of repeating itself.* ◇ *That was a nasty little trick.* ◇ *~ to sb Don't be so nasty to your brother.* **3** dangerous or serious: *a nasty bend* (= dangerous for cars going fast) ◇ *a nasty injury* **4** offensive; in bad taste: *to have a nasty mind* ◇ *nasty jokes* ▸ **nas·tily** /-stɪli/ adv.: *'I hate you,' she said nastily.* **nas·ti·ness** noun [U]
**IDM get/turn ˈnasty 1** to start making threats or become violent: *You'd better do what he says or he'll turn nasty.* **2** to become bad or unpleasant: *It looks as though the weather is going to turn nasty again.* **a nasty piece of ˈwork** (BrE, informal) a person who is unpleasant, unkind or dishonest ⇒ more at TASTE *n.*

**natal** /ˈneɪtl/ adj. [only before noun] (formal) relating to the place where or the time when sb was born: *her natal home* ⇒ see also ANTENATAL, PERINATAL, POSTNATAL, PRENATAL

**na·tal·ity** /neɪˈtæləti/ noun [U] (specialist) the number of births every year for every 1000 people in the population **SYN birth rate**

**natch** /nætʃ/ adv. (informal) used to say that sth is obvious or exactly as you would expect **SYN naturally**: *He was wearing the latest T-shirt, natch.*

**na·tion** /ˈneɪʃn/ noun **1** [C] a country considered as a group of people with the same language, culture and history, who live in a particular area under one government: *European/Arab/Asian nations* ◇ *the African nations* ◇ *developing nations* ◇ *industrialized nations* ◇ *Leaders of the nations signed a declaration of support.* ◇ *This is an important moment in our nation's history.* ⇒ see also RAINBOW NATION, MOST FAVOURED NATION **2** [sing.] all the people in a country **SYN population**: *The entire nation, it seemed, was watching TV.* ◇ *They are a nation of food lovers.* ▸ **na·tion·hood** /-hʊd/ noun [U]: *Citizenship is about the sense of nationhood.*

**na·tion·al** /ˈnæʃnəl/ adj., noun
■ adj. [usually before noun] **1** connected with a particular nation; shared by a whole nation: *national and local newspapers* ◇ *national and international news* ◇ *national and regional politics* ◇ *a national election* ◇ *a matter of national security* ◇ *It is in the national interest to have a public enquiry.* ◇ *The national average is just over two children per family.* ◇ *They are afraid of losing their national identity.* **2** owned, controlled or paid for by the government: *a national airline/museum/theatre*
■ noun (specialist) a citizen of a particular country: *foreign nationals* ◇ *Polish nationals living in Germany*

**national ˈanthem** noun the official song of a nation that is sung on special occasions

**the National Assembly for Wales** /ðə ˌnæʃnəl əˌsembli fə ˈweɪlz; NAmE fər/ noun = WELSH ASSEMBLY

**national conˈvention** noun a meeting held by a political party, especially in the US, to choose a candidate to take part in the election for President

**national ˈcostume** noun [C, U] (also **national ˈdress** [U]) the clothes traditionally worn by people from a particular country, especially on special occasions or for formal ceremonies

**the ˌnational ˈcurriculum** noun [sing.] (in England and Wales) a programme of study in all the main subjects that children aged 5 to 16 in state schools must follow

**ˌnational ˈdebt** noun [usually sing.] the total amount of money that the government of a country owes

**the ˌNational ˈFront** noun [sing. + sing./pl. v.] (in the UK) a small political party with extreme views, especially on issues connected with race

**ˌnational ˈgrid** noun [sing.] (BrE) the system of power lines that joins the places where electricity is produced, and takes electricity to all parts of the country

**the ˌNational ˈGuard** noun [sing.] **1** a small army, often used to protect a political leader **2** the army in each state of the US that can be used by the national government if needed

**the ˌNational ˈHealth Service** noun [sing.] (abbr. **NHS**) the public health service in the UK that provides medical care and is paid for by taxes: *I got my glasses on the National Health (Service).*

**ˌNational Inˈsurance** noun [U] (abbr. **NI**) (in the UK) a system of payments that have to be made by employers and employees to provide help for people who are sick, old or unemployed

**na·tion·al·ism** /ˈnæʃnəlɪzəm/ noun **1** the desire by a group of people who share the same race, culture, language, etc. to form an independent country: *Scottish nationalism* **2** (sometimes disapproving) a feeling of loving your country very much and being very proud of it; a feeling that your country is better than any other

**na·tion·al·ist** /ˈnæʃnəlɪst/ noun **1** a person who wants their country to become independent: *Scottish nationalists* **2** (sometimes disapproving) a person who loves their country very much and is very proud of it; a person who feels that their country is better than any other ▸ **na·tion·al·ist** adj.: *nationalist sentiments*

**na·tion·al·is·tic** /ˌnæʃnəˈlɪstɪk/ adj. (usually disapproving) loving your country very much and being very proud of it, so that you think that it is better than any other

**na·tion·al·ity** /ˌnæʃəˈnæləti/ noun (pl. **-ies**) **1** [U, C] the legal status of belonging to a particular nation: *to take/have/hold French nationality* ◇ *All applicants will be considered regardless of age, sex, religion or nationality.* ◇ *The college attracts students of all nationalities.* ◇ *She has dual nationality* (= is a citizen of two countries). **2** [C] a group of people with the same language, culture and history who form part of a political nation: *Kazakhstan alone contains more than a hundred nationalities.*

**na·tion·al·ize** (BrE also **-ise**) /ˈnæʃnəlaɪz/ verb ~ sth to put an industry or a company under the control of the government, which becomes its owner: *nationalized industries* **OPP denationalize, privatize** ▸ **na·tion·al·iza·tion**, **-isa·tion** /ˌnæʃnəlaɪˈzeɪʃn; NAmE -ləˈz-/ noun [U, C]

**the ˌNational ˈLeague** noun (in the US) one of the two organizations for professional baseball ⇒ see also AMERICAN LEAGUE

**na·tion·al·ly** /ˈnæʃnəli/ adv. relating to a country as a whole; relating to a particular country: *The programme was broadcast nationally.* ◇ *Meetings were held locally and nationally.* ◇ *He's a talented athlete who competes nationally and internationally.*

**the ˌNational ˈMotto** noun [sing.] the official US motto 'In God we trust'

**ˌnational ˈpark** noun an area of land that is protected by the government for people to visit because of its natural beauty and historical or scientific interest

**ˌnational ˈservice** noun [U] the system in some countries in which young people have to do military training for a period of time **SYN military service**: *to do your national service*

**ˌNational ˈSocialism** noun [U] (politics) the policies of the German Nazi party ▸ **ˌNational ˈSocialist** noun, adj.

**ˌnational ˈtrail** noun a long route through beautiful country where people can walk or ride

**the ˌNational ˈTrust** *noun* an organization that owns and takes care of places of historical interest or natural beauty in England, Wales and Northern Ireland, so that people can go and visit them

**ˌnation ˈstate** *noun* a group of people with the same culture, language, etc. who have formed an independent country

**na·tion·wide** 🔑+ **C1** /ˌneɪʃnˈwaɪd/ *adj., adv.* happening or existing in all parts of a particular country: *a nationwide campaign* ◊ *The company has over 500 stores nationwide.*

**na·tive** 🔑 **B1** /ˈneɪtɪv/ *adj., noun*
■ *adj.* **1** 🔑 **B1** [only before noun] connected with the place where you were born and lived for the first years of your life: *your native land/country/city* ◊ *Her native language is Korean.* ◊ *It is a long time since he has visited his native Chile.* ⊃ see also NATIVE SPEAKER **2** 🔑 [only before noun] connected with the place where you have always lived or have lived for a long time: *native Berliners* **3** [only before noun] (*sometimes offensive*) connected with the people who originally lived in a country before other people, especially white people, came there: *native peoples* ◊ *native art* ◊ *a record of Native American life* **4** (of animals and plants) existing naturally in a place **SYN** **indigenous** ⊃ see also NON-NATIVE: *the native plants of America* ◊ *native species* ◊ *~ to …The tiger is native to India.* **5** [only before noun] that you have naturally without having to learn it **SYN** **innate**: *native cunning* **6** (of a metal or another mineral) found in a pure state: *native gold/silver/copper* **7** (*computing*) designed for or built into a particular system, especially using the language or computer code associated with a particular computer or PROCESSOR: *native apps*
**IDM** **go ˈnative** (*often humorous*) (of a person staying in another country) to try to live and behave like the local people
■ *noun* **1** 🔑 **B1** a person who was born in a particular country or area: *a native of New York* **2** 🔑 **B1** a person who lives in a particular place, especially sb who has lived there a long time **SYN** **local**: *You can always tell the difference between the tourists and the natives.* ◊ *She speaks Italian like a native.* **3** (*old-fashioned, offensive*) a word used in the past by Europeans to describe a person who lived in a place originally, before white people arrived there: *disputes between early settlers and natives* **4** an animal or a plant that lives or grows naturally in a particular area: *The kangaroo is a native of Australia.*

**ˌNative Aˈmerican** (*also* **Aˌmerican ˈIndian**) *noun* a member of any of the races of people who were the original people living in America ▶ **Native Aˈmerican** *adj.*: *Native American languages*

**ˌNa·tive Caˈn·ad·ian** *noun* (*CanE*) a member of any of the races of people who were the original people living in what is now Canada; a Canadian Indian, Inuit or Metis ⊃ compare FIRST NATIONS

**ˌnative ˈspeaker** *noun* a person who speaks a language as their first language and has not learned it as a foreign language

**na·tiv·ity** /nəˈtɪvəti/ *noun* **1 the Nativity** [sing.] the birth of Jesus Christ, celebrated by Christians at Christmas **2** a picture or a model of the baby Jesus Christ and the place where he was born

**naˈtivity play** *noun* a play about the birth of Jesus Christ, usually performed by children at Christmas

**NATO** /ˈneɪtəʊ/ (*also* **Nato**) *abbr.* North Atlantic Treaty Organization. NATO is an organization to which many European countries and the US and Canada belong. They agree to give each other military help if necessary.

**nat·ter** /ˈnætə(r)/ *verb* [I] **~ (away / on) (about sth)** (*informal*) to talk for a long time, especially about unimportant things **SYN** **chat** ▶ **nat·ter** *noun* [sing.] (*BrE, informal*): *to have a good natter*

**natty** /ˈnæti/ *adj.* (*old-fashioned, informal*) **1** neat and fashionable: *a natty suit* **2** well designed; clever: *a natty little briefcase* ▶ **nat·tily** /-təli/ *adv.*

**nat·ural** 🔑 **A1** ⊕ /ˈnætʃrəl/ *adj., noun*
■ *adj.*
• IN NATURE **1** 🔑 **A1** [only before noun] existing in nature; not made or caused by humans: *the natural world* (= of trees,

1037 **naturalize**

rivers, animals and birds) ◊ *a country's natural resources* (= its coal, oil, forests, etc.) ◊ *wildlife in its natural habitat* ◊ *the natural beauty of flowers* ◊ *My hair soon grew back to its natural colour* (= after being DYED). ◊ *The clothes are available in warm natural colours.* ⊃ compare SUPERNATURAL **2** 🔑 (especially of food) having little or no processing: *natural yogurt* (= with no flavour added) ◊ *I try to eat a sugar-free, natural food diet.*
• EXPECTED **3** 🔑 **B1** normal; as you would expect: *to die of natural causes* (= not by violence, but normally, of old age) ◊ *Singing for her was as natural as breathing.* ◊ *He thought social inequality was all part of the natural order of things.* ◊ *She was the natural choice for the job.* ◊ **it is ~ (for sb) to do sth** *It's only natural to worry about your children.* ◊ **it is ~ that …** *It's natural that he would want to see his own son.* ⊃ compare UNNATURAL
• BEHAVIOUR/ABILITY **4** 🔑 **B1** used to describe behaviour or abilities that are part of the character that a person or an animal was born with: *the natural agility of a cat* ◊ *the natural processes of language learning* ◊ *She has a natural ability with children.* **5** 🔑 **B1** [only before noun] having an ability that you were born with: *He's a natural leader.*
• RELAXED **6** relaxed and not pretending to be sb/sth different: *It's difficult to look natural when you're feeling nervous.*
• PARENTS / CHILDREN **7** [only before noun] (of parents or their children) related by blood: *His natural mother was unable to care for him so he was raised by an aunt.* **8** [only before noun] (*old use* or *formal*) (of a son or daughter) born to parents who are not married **SYN** **illegitimate**: *She was a natural daughter of King James II.*
• BASED ON HUMAN REASON **9** [only before noun] based on human reason alone: *natural justice/law*
• IN MUSIC **10** used after the name of a note to show that the note is neither SHARP nor FLAT. The written symbol is (♮): *B natural* ⊃ picture at MUSIC
■ *noun*
• PERSON **1** **~ (for sth)** a person who is very good at sth without having to learn how to do it, or who has all the right qualities for a particular job: *She took to flying like a natural.* ◊ *He's a natural for the role.*
• IN MUSIC **2** a normal musical note, not its SHARP or FLAT form. The written symbol is (♮).

**ˌnatural-ˈborn** *adj.* [only before noun] having a natural ability or skill that you have not had to learn

**ˌnatural ˈchildbirth** *noun* [U] a method of giving birth to a baby in which a woman chooses not to take drugs and does special exercises to make her relaxed

**ˌnatural diˈsaster** *noun* a sudden and violent event in nature (such as an earthquake, hurricane or flood) that kills or injures a lot of people or causes a lot of damage

**ˌnatural ˈgas** *noun* [U] gas that is found under the ground or the sea and that is used as a fuel

**ˌnatural ˈhistory** *noun* [U, C] the study of plants and animals; an account of the plant and animal life of a particular place: *the Natural History Museum* ◊ *He has written a natural history of Scotland.*

**nat·ur·al·ism** /ˈnætʃrəlɪzəm/ *noun* [U] **1** a style of art or writing that shows people, things and experiences as they really are **2** (*philosophy*) the theory that everything in the world and life is based on natural causes and laws, and not on spiritual or SUPERNATURAL ones

**nat·ur·al·ist** /ˈnætʃrəlɪst/ *noun* a person who studies animals, plants, birds and other living things

**nat·ur·al·is·tic** /ˌnætʃrəˈlɪstɪk/ *adj.* **1** (of artists, writers, etc. or their work) showing things as they appear in the natural world **2** copying the way things are in the natural world: *to study behaviour in laboratory and naturalistic settings*

**nat·ur·al·ize** (*BrE also* **-ise**) /ˈnætʃrəlaɪz/ *verb* [usually passive] **1** [T] **~ sb** to make sb who was not born in a particular country a citizen of that country **2** [T] **~ sth** to introduce a plant or an animal to a country where it is not NATIVE **3** [I] (of a plant or an animal) to start growing or living naturally in a country where it is not NATIVE ▶ **nat·ur·al·iza·tion**, **-isa·tion** /ˌnætʃrəlaɪˈzeɪʃn; *NAmE* -lə'z-/ *noun* [U]

---

Ⓞ Oxford Phrasal Academic Lexicon (OPAL) written and spoken word lists | Ⓦ OPAL written word list | Ⓢ OPAL spoken word list

**natural language** noun [C, U] a language that has developed in a natural way by people using it to communicate, rather than an invented language or computer code

**natural language processing** noun [U] (abbr. **NLP**) the use of computers to process natural languages, for example for translating

**natural law** noun [U] a set of moral principles on which human behaviour is based

**nat·ur·al·ly** ⓘ B1 Ⓦ /ˈnætʃrəli/ adv. **1** B1 in a way that you would expect SYN **of course**: *Naturally, I get upset when things go wrong.* ◇ *After a while, we naturally started talking about the children.* ◇ *'Did you complain about the noise?' 'Naturally.'* **2** B1 without special help, treatment or action by sb: *naturally occurring chemicals* ◇ *plants that grow naturally in poor soils* **3** B1 as a normal, logical result of sth: *This leads naturally to my next point.* **4** B1 in a way that shows or uses abilities or qualities that a person or an animal is born with: *to be naturally artistic* ◇ *a naturally gifted athlete* **5** in a relaxed and normal way: *Just act naturally.*
IDM **come ˈnaturally (to sb/sth)** if sth **comes naturally** to you, you are able to do it very easily and very well: *Making money came naturally to him.*

**nat·ur·al·ness** /ˈnætʃrəlnəs/ noun [U] **1** the state or quality of being like real life: *The naturalness of the dialogue made the book so true to life.* **2** the quality of behaving in a normal, relaxed or innocent way: *Teenagers lose their childhood simplicity and naturalness.* **3** the style or quality of happening in a normal way that you would expect: *the naturalness of her reaction*

**natural number** noun (*mathematics*) a positive whole number such as 1, 2 or 3, and sometimes also zero

**natural phiˈlosophy** noun [U] (*old use*) the study of the physical world, which developed into the natural sciences

**natural ˈscience** noun [C, usually pl., U] the sciences that involve studying the physical world. Chemistry, biology and physics are all natural sciences. ⊃ compare EARTH SCIENCE, LIFE SCIENCE

**natural seˈlection** noun [U] the process by which plants, animals, etc. that can adapt to their environment survive and produce young, while the others disappear

**natural ˈwastage** (*BrE*) (*also* at·tri·tion *especially in NAmE*) noun [U] the process of reducing the number of people who are employed by an organization by, for example, not replacing people who leave their jobs

**na·ture** ⓘ A2 ⓞ /ˈneɪtʃə(r)/ noun
• PLANTS, ANIMALS **1** A2 (*often* **Nature**) [U] all the plants, animals and things that exist in the universe that are not made by people: *the beauties of nature* ◇ *man-made substances not found in nature* ◇ *nature conservation* HELP You cannot use 'the nature' in this meaning: *the beauties of the nature*. It is often better to use another appropriate word, for example **the countryside**, **the scenery** or **wildlife**: *We stopped to admire the scenery.* ◇ *We stopped to admire the nature.* **2** A2 (*often* **Nature**) [U] the way that things happen in the physical world when it is not controlled by people: *the forces/laws of nature* ◇ *Her illness was Nature's way of telling her to do less.* ⊃ see also MOTHER NATURE
• CHARACTER **3** B1 [C, U] the usual way that a person or an animal behaves that is part of their character: *by ~ She is very sensitive by nature.* ◇ *it is not in sb's ~ to do sth It's not in his nature to be unkind.* ◇ *We appealed to his better nature* (= his kindness). ⊃ see also GOOD NATURE, HUMAN NATURE, SECOND NATURE
• BASIC QUALITIES **4** B2 [sing.] the basic qualities of a thing: *the changing nature of society* ◇ *It's difficult to define the exact nature of the problem.* ◇ *in ~ My work is very specialized in nature.*

WORD FAMILY
**nature** noun
**natural** adj. (≠ unnatural)
**naturally** adv. (≠ unnaturally)

• TYPE/KIND **5** [sing.] a type or kind of sth: *of a … ~ books of a scientific nature* ◇ *Don't worry about things of that nature.*
• -NATURED **6** (in adjectives) having the type of character or quality mentioned: *a good-natured man*
IDM **aˈgainst ˈnature** not natural; not moral: *Murder is a crime against nature.* **(get, go, etc.) back to ˈnature** (to return to) a simple kind of life in the country, away from cities **in the ˈnature of ˈsth** similar to sth; a type of sth; in the style of sth: *His speech was in the nature of an apology.* **in the ˈnature of things** in the way that things usually happen: *In the nature of things, young people often rebel against their parents.* **let nature take its ˈcourse** to allow natural processes to happen, without trying to stop or change them (used especially in the context of illness) ⊃ more at CALL n., FORCE n.

**ˈnature reserve** noun an area of land where the animals and plants are protected

**ˈnature strip** noun (*AustralE*) a piece of public land between the edge of a house, or other building, and the street, usually planted with grass

**ˈnature trail** noun a path through countryside which you can follow in order to see the interesting plants and animals that are found there

**na·tur·ism** /ˈneɪtʃərɪzəm/ noun [U] (*especially BrE*) = NUDISM

**na·tur·ist** /ˈneɪtʃərɪst/ noun (*especially BrE*) = NUDIST

**na·tur·op·athy** /ˌneɪtʃəˈrɒpəθi/ NAmE -ˈrɑːp-/ noun [U] a system for treating diseases or conditions using natural foods and HERBS and various other techniques, rather than artificial drugs ► **na·turo·path** /ˈneɪtʃərəpæθ/ noun: *A medical herbalist or naturopath will be able to advise on individual treatment plans.* **na·turo·path·ic** /ˌneɪtʃərəˈpæθɪk/ adj. [only before noun]: *naturopathic medicine* ◇ *a naturopathic physician*

**naught** = NOUGHT (2)

**naughty** /ˈnɔːti/ adj. (naugh·tier, naugh·ti·est) **1** (especially of children) behaving badly; not willing to obey: *a naughty boy/girl* ◇ (*humorous*) *I'm being very naughty—I've ordered champagne!* **2** (*informal, often humorous*) slightly rude; connected with sex SYN **risqué**: *a naughty joke/word* ► **naugh·tily** /-təli/ adv. **naugh·ti·ness** noun [U]

**ˈnaughty step** noun [sing.] (*BrE*) a quiet place, for example a step, where a child has to stay for a short period of time as a punishment for behaving badly: *He wouldn't stop shouting so she made him sit on the naughty step until he had calmed down.* ◇ (*figurative*) *The MP is now on the naughty step for leaking confidential information to the press.*

**nau·sea** /ˈnɔːziə/ noun [U] the feeling that you have when you want to VOMIT, for example because you are sick or are shocked or frightened by sth: *A wave of nausea swept over her.* ◇ *Nausea and vomiting are common symptoms.* ⊃ see also AD NAUSEAM

**nau·se·ate** /ˈnɔːzieɪt/ verb **1** ~ sb to make sb feel that they want to VOMIT **2** ~ sb to make sb feel full of horror SYN **revolt, sicken**: *I was nauseated by the violence in the movie.* ► **nau·se·at·ing** adj.: *a nauseating smell* ◇ *his nauseating behaviour* **nau·se·at·ing·ly** adv.

**nau·se·ous** /ˈnɔːziəs; NAmE ˈnɔːʃəs/ adj. **1** feeling as if you want to VOMIT: *She felt dizzy and nauseous.* **2** making you feel as if you want to VOMIT: *a nauseous smell*

**naut·ical** /ˈnɔːtɪkl/ adj. connected with ships, sailors and sailing: *nautical terms*

**nautical ˈmile** (*also* **ˈsea mile**) noun a unit for measuring distance at sea; 1852 metres

**naut·ilus** /ˈnɔːtɪləs/ noun a creature with a shell that lives in the sea. It has TENTACLES around its mouth and its shell fills with gas to help it float.

**Nav·ajo** (*also* **Nava·ho**) /ˈnævəhəʊ/ noun (*pl.* **Nav·ajo** *or* **Nav·ajos**) a member of the largest group of Native American people, most of whom live in the US states of Arizona, New Mexico and Utah

**naval** B1 /ˈneɪvl/ adj. connected with the NAVY of a country: *a naval base/officer/battle*

**Nava·rat·ri** /ˌnævəˈrætri; NAmE ˌnɑːvəˈrɑːt-/ (*also* **Navarat·ra** /ˌnævəˈrætrə; NAmE ˌnɑːvəˈrɑːt-/) noun a Hindu festival lasting for nine nights, which takes place in the autumn

**nave** /neɪv/ *noun* the long central part of a church where most of the seats are ⊃ compare TRANSEPT

**navel** /ˈneɪvl/ (*also informal* **belly button**) (*BrE, informal* **tummy button**) *noun* the small round part in the middle of the stomach, on the front of sb's body, where the UMBILICAL CORD was cut at birth ⊃ VISUAL VOCAB page V1

**navel-gazing** *noun* [U] (*disapproving*) the fact of thinking too much about a single issue and how it could affect you, without thinking about other things that could also affect the situation

**navel orange** *noun* a large orange without seeds that has a part at the top that looks like a navel

**nav·ig·able** /ˈnævɪɡəbl/ *adj.* **1** (of rivers, lakes, etc.) wide and deep enough for ships and boats to sail on **2** (of a website, app, etc.) on which it is easy to find the information, section, etc. that you want ▶ **nav·ig·abil·ity** /ˌnævɪɡəˈbɪləti/ *noun* [U]

**navi·gate** /ˈnævɪɡeɪt/ *verb* **1** [I, T] to plan and direct the course of ship, plane, car etc., for example by using a map: *to navigate by the stars* ◊ *I'll drive, and you can navigate.* ◊ ~ **through sth** *There's nothing worse than navigating through heavy traffic.* ⊃ WORDFINDER NOTE at MAP **2** [T] ~ **sth** to sail along, over or through a sea, river etc: *The river became too narrow and shallow to navigate.* **3** [T] ~ **sth** to find the right way to deal with a difficult or complicated situation: *We next had to navigate a complex network of committees.* **4** [I, T] (*computing*) to find your way around on the internet or on a particular website: ~ **(through) sth** *Lots of these sites are hard to navigate through.* ⊃ WORDFINDER NOTE at WEB

**navi·ga·tion** 🔑 B2 /ˌnævɪˈɡeɪʃn/ *noun* [U] **1** 🔑 B2 the skill or the process of planning a route for a ship or other vehicle and taking it there: *navigation systems* ◊ *an expert in navigation* **2** 🔑 C1 the movement of ships or aircraft: *the right of navigation through international waters* **3** 🔑 C1 the way that you move around a website or the internet when you are looking for information: *The site was redesigned to improve navigation.* ▶ **nav·iga·tion·al** /-ʃənl/ *adj.*: *navigational aids*

**navi'gation bar** *noun* a long narrow area near the top or side of a page on a website that contains links to other pages ⊃ compare ADDRESS BAR

**navi·ga·tor** /ˈnævɪɡeɪtə(r)/ *noun* a person who navigates, for example on a ship or an aircraft

**navvy** /ˈnævi/ *noun* (*pl.* **-ies**) (*BrE*) (in the past) a person employed to do hard physical work, especially building roads, railways or CANALS

**navy** /ˈneɪvi/ *noun* (*pl.* **-ies**) **1** [C + sing. / pl. v.] the part of a country's armed forces that fights at sea, and the ships that it uses: *the British and German navies* ◊ *He's joined the navy/the Navy.* ◊ *an officer in the navy/the Navy* ◊ *The navy is/are considering buying six new warships.* ⊃ see also MERCHANT NAVY, NAVAL

> WORDFINDER admiral, aircraft carrier, base, captain, command, fleet, submarine, torpedo, warship

**2** [U] = NAVY BLUE

**navy bean** (*NAmE*) (*BrE* **hari·cot**, **haricot bean**) *noun* a type of small white bean that is usually dried before it is sold and then left in water before cooking

**navy blue** (*also* **navy**) *adj.* very dark blue in colour: *a navy blue suit* ▶ **navy blue** (*also* **navy**) *noun* [U]: *She was dressed in navy blue.*

**naw** /nɔː/ *exclamation* (*ScotE, NEngE, NAmE, informal*) no, used when answering a question: '*Want some toast?*' '*Naw.*'

**nawab** /nəˈwɑːb/ *noun* **1** an Indian ruler during the Mogul Empire **2** (*IndE*) a Muslim with high social status or rank

**Naxa·lite** /ˈnæksəlaɪt/ *noun* (in India) a member of a group which believes in political revolution in order to change the system of how land is owned. It took its name from Naxalbari in West Bengal, where it started.

**nay** /neɪ/ *adv.* **1** (*old-fashioned*) used to emphasize sth you have just said by introducing a stronger word or phrase: *Such a policy is difficult, nay impossible.* **2** (*old use* or *dialect*) no ⊃ compare YEA

**nay·say·er** /ˈneɪseɪə(r)/ *noun* a person who opposes or expresses doubts about sth: *There are always naysayers who claim the plan won't work.*

**Nazi** /ˈnɑːtsi/ *noun* **1** a member of the National Socialist party which controlled Germany from 1933 to 1945 **2** (*disapproving*) a person who uses their power in a cruel way; a person with extreme and unreasonable views about race ▶ **Nazi** *adj.* **Nazism** /-sɪzəm/ *noun* [U]

**NB** (*also* **N.B.**) /ˌen ˈbiː/ *abbr.* used in writing to make sb take notice of a particular piece of information that is important (from Latin '*nota bene*'): *NB The office will be closed from 1 July.*

**NBA** /ˌen biː ˈeɪ/ *abbr.* National Basketball Association (the US organization responsible for professional basketball)

**NBC** /ˌen biː ˈsiː/ *abbr.* National Broadcasting Company (a US company that produces and broadcasts television and radio programmes): *NBC News*

**NC-17** /ˌen siː ˌsevnˈtiːn/ *abbr.* no children under 17. If a movie has the label NC-17, no one aged 17 or under is allowed to see it in a movie theater in the US. ⊃ compare G (1), PG-13, R (5)

**NCO** /ˌen siː ˈəʊ/ *noun* non-commissioned officer (a soldier who has a rank such as CORPORAL or SERGEANT)

**NCT** /ˌen siː ˈtiː/ *noun* **1** (in England) a test taken by children at the ages of 7 and 11, also called SAT (the abbreviation for 'National Curriculum Test') **2** (in Ireland) a test that all cars over 4 years old must have to check whether they are safe to drive (the abbreviation for 'National Car Test')

**NDE** /ˌen diː ˈiː/ *abbr.* = NEAR-DEATH EXPERIENCE

**ndugu** /ənˈduːɡuː/ *EAfrE* [ˈnduɡu] *noun* (*EAfrE*) (*usually* **Ndugu**) (in Tanzania) a title for a man or woman that shows respect

**NE** *abbr.* north-east; north-eastern: *NE England*

**Ne·an·der·thal** /niˈændətɑːl; *NAmE* -dərθɔːl/ (*also* **nean·derthal**) *adj.* **1** used to describe a type of human being who used stone tools and lived in Europe during the early period of human history **2** (*disapproving*) very old-fashioned and not wanting any change: *neanderthal attitudes* **3** (*disapproving*) (of a man) unpleasant, rude and not behaving in a socially acceptable way ▶ **Ne·an·der·thal** *noun*

**neap tide** /ˈniːp taɪd/ (*also* **neap**) *noun* a TIDE in the sea in which there is only a very small difference between the level of the water at HIGH TIDE and that at LOW TIDE

**near** 🔑 A1 /nɪə(r); *NAmE* nɪr/ *prep., adj., adv., verb*

■ *prep.* (*also* **near to, near·er (to), near·est (to)**) HELP **Near to** is not usually used before the name of a place, person, festival, etc. **1** 🔑 A1 at a short distance away from sb/sth: *Do you live near here?* ◊ *Go and sit nearer (to) the fire.* ⊃ note at NEXT **2** 🔑 B1 a short period of time from sth: *My birthday is very near Christmas.* ◊ *I'll think about it nearer (to) the time* (= when it is just going to happen). **3** 🔑 B1 used before a number to mean 'approximately', 'just below or above': *Share prices are near their record high of last year.* ◊ *Profits fell from $11 million to nearer $8 million.* **4** 🔑 B1 similar to sb/sth in quality, size, etc: *Nobody else comes near her in intellect.* ◊ *He's nearer 70 than 60.* ◊ *This colour is nearest (to) the original.* **5** 🔑 B1 ~ **(doing) sth** close to a particular state: *a state near (to) death* ◊ *She was near to tears* (= almost crying). ◊ *We came near to being killed.* IDM see HAND *n.*, HEART *n.*, MARK *n.*

■ *adj.* (**near·er, near·est**) HELP In senses 1 to 4 **near** and **nearer** do not usually go before a noun; **nearest** can go either before or after a noun. **1** 🔑 A1 a short distance away SYN **close**[2]: *His house is very near.* ◊ *Where's the nearest bank?* ⊃ note at NEXT **2** 🔑 B1 a short time away in the future: *The conflict is unlikely to be resolved in the near future* (= very soon). **3** 🔑 B1 coming next after sb/sth: *She has a 12-point lead over her nearest rival.* **4** 🔑 B1 (*usually* **nearest**) similar; most similar: *He was the nearest thing to* (= the person most like) *a father she had ever had.* ⊃ see also O.N.O. **5** 🔑 B2 [only before noun] (no comparative or

# nearby

superlative) close to being sb/sth: *The election proved to be a near disaster for the party.* ◊ *a near impossibility* **6** B2 [only before noun] **~relative/relation** used to describe a close family connection: *Only the nearest relatives were present at the funeral.* ▶ **near·ness** *noun* [U]: *the nearness of death*
**IDM** **your ˌnearest and ˈdearest** (*informal*) your close family and friends **a ˌnear ˈthing** a situation in which you are successful, but which could also have ended badly: *Phew! That was a near thing! It could have been a disaster.* ◊ *We won in the end but it was a near thing.* **to the nearest…** followed by a number when counting or measuring approximately: *We calculated the cost to the nearest 50 dollars.*
■ *adv.* (near·er, near·est) **1** A1 at a short distance away: *A bomb exploded somewhere near.* ◊ *She took a step nearer.* ◊ *Visitors came from near and far.* **2** B1 a short time away in the future: *The exams are drawing near.* **3** (especially in compounds) almost: *a near-perfect performance* ◊ *I'm as near certain as can be.*
**IDM** **as ˌnear as** as accurately as: *There were about 3000 people there, as near as I could judge.* **as ˌnear as ˈdamn it/ˈdammit** (*BrE*, *informal*) used to say that an amount is so nearly correct that the difference does not matter: *It will cost £350, or as near as dammit.* **near eˈnough** (*BrE*, *informal*) used to say that sth is so nearly true that the difference does not matter: *We've been here twenty years, near enough.* **not at all**: *The job doesn't pay anywhere near enough for me.* **so ˌnear and ˌyet so ˈfar** used to comment on sth that was almost successful but in fact failed ⊃ more at PRETTY *adv.*
■ *verb* [T, I] **~ (sth)** (*rather formal*) to come close to sth in time or space SYN **approach**: *The project is nearing completion.* ◊ *She was nearing the end of her life.* ◊ *We neared the top of the hill.* ◊ *As Christmas neared, the children became more and more excited.*

▼ **WHICH WORD?**

**near / close**
- The adjectives **near** and **close** are often the same in meaning, but in some phrases only one of them may be used: *the near future* ◊ *a near neighbour* ◊ *a near miss* ◊ *a close contest* ◊ *a close encounter* ◊ *a close call*. **Close** is more often used to describe a relationship between people: *a close friend* ◊ *close family* ◊ *close links*. You do not usually use **near** in this way.

**near·by** ?+ B2 /ˌnɪəˈbaɪ; *NAmE* ˌnɪrˈb-/ *adj.*, *adv.*
■ *adj.* ?+ [usually before noun] near in position; not far away: *Her mother lived in a nearby town.* ◊ *There were complaints from nearby residents.*
■ *adv.* ?+ B2 a short distance from sb/sth; not far away: *They live nearby.* ◊ *The car is parked nearby.*

**ˌnear-death exˈperience** *noun* (*abbr.* **NDE**) an occasion when sb almost dies, which they often remember as leaving their body or going down a tunnel

**the ˌNear ˈEast** *noun* [sing.] a term sometimes used for the MIDDLE EAST, especially in historical contexts

**near·ly** ? A2 /ˈnɪəli; *NAmE* ˈnɪrli/ *adv.* almost; not quite; not completely: *The bottle's nearly empty.* ◊ *I've worked here for nearly two years.* ◊ *It's nearly time to leave.* ◊ *The audience was nearly all men.* ◊ *He's nearly as tall as you are.* ◊ *They're nearly always late.* ◊ *She very nearly died.* ⊃ note at ALMOST
**IDM** **not ˈnearly** much less than; not at all: *It's not nearly as hot as last year.* ◊ *There isn't nearly enough time to get there now.* ⊃ more at PRETTY *adv.*

**ˌnear ˈmiss** *noun* **1** a situation when a serious accident or a disaster very nearly happens: *The two planes were involved in a near miss.* **2** a bomb or a shot that nearly hits what it is aimed at but misses it: (*figurative*) *He should have won the match—it was a near miss.* ⊃ see also A NEAR THING at NEAR *adj.*

**near·side** /ˈnɪəsaɪd; *NAmE* ˈnɪrs-/ *adj.* [only before noun] (*BrE*) (for a driver) on the side that is nearest the edge of the road: *the car's nearside doors* ◊ *Keep to the nearside lane.* OPP **offside** ▶ **the ˈnear·side** *noun* [sing.]: *The driver lost control and veered to the nearside.* OPP **offside**

**ˌnear-ˈsight·ed** /ˌnɪəˈsaɪtɪd; *NAmE* ˌnɪrˈs-/ *adj.* (*especially NAmE*) = SHORT-SIGHTED OPP **far-sighted** ▶ **ˌnear-ˈsight·ed·ness** *noun* [U]

**neat** ? B2 /niːt/ *adj.* (neat·er, neat·est) **1** ? B2 tidy and in order; carefully done or arranged: *a neat desk* ◊ *neat handwriting* ◊ *neat rows of books* ◊ *She was wearing a neat black suit.* ◊ *They sat in her neat and tidy kitchen.* **2** ? B2 (of people) liking to keep things tidy and in order; looking tidy or doing things in a tidy way: *Try and be neater!* ◊ *By nature he was clean and neat.* **3** small, with an attractive shape or appearance SYN **trim**: *her neat figure* **4** simple but clever: *a neat explanation* ◊ *a neat solution to the problem* **5** (*NAmE*, *informal*) good; excellent: *It's a really neat movie.* ◊ *We had a great time—it was pretty neat.* **6** (*BrE*) (*also* **straight** *BrE and NAmE*) (especially of alcoholic drinks) not mixed with water or anything else: *neat whisky* ▶ **neat·ly** *adv.*: *neatly folded clothes* ◊ *The box fitted neatly into the drawer.* ◊ *She summarized her plan very neatly.* **neat·ness** *noun* [U]

**neat·en** /ˈniːtn/ *verb* **~ sth** to make sth tidy

**neb·ula** /ˈnebjələ/ *noun* (*pl.* **nebu·lae** /-liː/) (*astronomy*) a mass of dust or gas that can be seen in the night sky, often appearing very bright; a bright area in the night sky caused by a large cloud of stars that are far away

**nebu·lizer** (*BrE also* **-iser**) /ˈnebjəlaɪzə(r)/ *noun* a device for producing a fine SPRAY of liquid, used especially for taking particular medicines: *I get short of breath and I have to use a nebulizer in the mornings.*

**nebu·lous** /ˈnebjələs/ *adj.* (*formal*) not clear SYN **vague**: *a nebulous concept*

**ne·ces·sar·ies** /ˈnesəsəriz; *NAmE* -ser-/ *noun* [pl.] (*old-fashioned*) the things that you need, especially in order to live

**ne·ces·sar·ily** ? B1 ○ /ˌnesəˈserəli; *BrE also* ˈnesəsərəli/ *adv.* used to say that sth cannot be avoided: *The number of places available is necessarily limited.*
**IDM** **not ˌneces·ˈsarily** ? B1 used to say that sth is possibly true but not definitely or always true: *Biggest doesn't necessarily mean best.* ◊ *It isn't necessarily true that sugar is bad for you.* ◊ *'We're going to lose.' 'Not necessarily.'*

**ne·ces·sary** ? A2 W /ˈnesəsəri; *NAmE* -seri/ *adj.* **1** ? A2 that is needed for a purpose or a reason SYN **essential**: *~ to do sth It may be necessary to buy a new one.* ◊ *~ for sb to do sth It doesn't seem necessary for us to meet.* ◊ *~ for sth Food is necessary for survival.* ◊ *I'll make the necessary arrangements.* ◊ *Radical change was a necessary step for reform.* ◊ *if~ If necessary, you can contact me at home.* ◊ *when~ Only use your car when absolutely necessary.* ◊ *where~ Changes can easily be made where necessary.* ◊ *He has the expertise necessary to make it work.* **2** B2 [only before noun] that must exist or happen and cannot be avoided SYN **inevitable**: *This is a necessary consequence of progress.*
**IDM** **a ˌnecessary ˈevil** a thing that is bad or that you do not like but that you must accept for a particular reason

**ne·ces·si·tate** /nəˈsesɪteɪt/ *verb* (*formal*) to make sth necessary: *~ sth Recent financial scandals have necessitated changes in parliamentary procedures.* ◊ *~ doing sth Increased traffic necessitated widening the road.* ◊ *~ sb/sth doing sth His new job necessitated him/his getting up at six.*

**ne·ces·sity** ?+ B2 W /nəˈsesəti/ *noun* **1** ?+ B2 [U] the fact that sth must happen or be done; the need for sth: *~ for sth We recognize the necessity for a written agreement.* ◊ *~ of (doing) sth We were discussing the necessity of employing more staff.* ◊ *~ (for sb) to do sth There had never been any necessity for her to go out to work.* ◊ *of ~ This is, of necessity, a brief and incomplete account.* **2** ?+ B2 [C] a thing that you must have and cannot manage without: *Many people cannot even afford basic necessities such as food and clothing.* ◊ *Air-conditioning is an absolute necessity in this climate.* **3** ?+ C1 [C, usually sing.] a situation that must happen and that cannot be avoided: *Living in London, he felt, was an unfortunate necessity.*

**IDM** ne,cessity is the ,mother of in'vention (saying) a difficult new problem forces people to think of a solution to it ⇒ more at VIRTUE

### necks

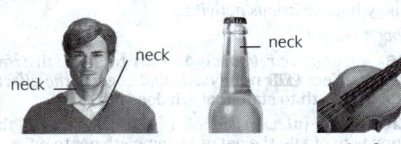

neck    neck of a bottle    neck of a violin

**neck** 🔊 **A2** /nek/ noun, verb
- **noun 1** **A2** [C] the part of the body between the head and the shoulders: *He tied a scarf around his neck.* ◇ *Giraffes have very long necks.* ◇ *She craned* (= stretched) *her neck to get a better view.* ◇ *He broke his neck in the fall.* ◇ *Somebody's going to* **break their neck** (= injure themselves) *on these steps.* ⇒ VISUAL VOCAB page V1 **2** [C] the part of a piece of clothing that fits around the neck: *He wore a casual shirt with an open neck.* ⇒ see also CREW NECK, POLO NECK, TURTLENECK, V-NECK **3 -necked** (in adjectives) having the type of neck mentioned: *a round-necked sweater* ⇒ see also OPEN-NECKED **4** [C] ~(of sth) a long narrow part of sth: *the neck of a bottle* ◇ *a neck of land* ◇ *the neck of a guitar* **5** [U] ~(of sth) the neck of an animal, cooked and eaten: *neck of lamb* ⇒ see also BOTTLENECK, REDNECK, ROUGHNECK
**IDM** **be up to your neck in sth** to have a lot of sth to deal with: *We're up to our neck in debt.* ◇ *He's in it* (= trouble) *up to his neck.* **by a 'neck** if a person or an animal wins a race **by a neck**, they win it by a short distance ,**get it in the 'neck** (BrE, informal) to be shouted at or punished because of sth that you have done ,**neck and 'neck (with sb/sth)** level with sb in a race or competition ⇒ compare NIP AND TUCK ,**neck of the 'woods** (informal) a particular place or area: *He's from your neck of the woods* (= the area where you live)*.* ⇒ more at BLOCK *n.*, BRASS, BREATHE, MILLSTONE, PAIN *n.*, RISK *v.*, SAVE *v.*, SCRUFF, STICK *v.*, WRING
- **verb** (*usually* **be necking**) [I] (*old-fashioned, informal*) when two people **are necking**, they are kissing each other in a sexual way

**neck·er·chief** /'nekətʃɪf; *NAmE* -kərtʃ-/ *noun* a square of cloth that you wear around your neck

**neck·lace** /'nekləs/ *noun, verb*
- **noun** a piece of jewellery consisting of a chain, string of BEADS, etc. worn around the neck: *a diamond necklace*
- **verb** ~sb to kill sb by putting a burning car tyre around their neck ▸ **neck·lacing** *noun* [U]

**neck·line** /'neklaɪn/ *noun* the edge of a piece of clothing, especially a woman's, which fits around or below the neck: *a dress with a low/round/plunging neckline*

**neck·tie** /'nektaɪ/ *noun* (*old-fashioned or NAmE*) = TIE (1)

**necro·man·cer** /'nekrəʊmænsə(r)/ *noun* a person who claims to communicate by magic with people who are dead

**necro·mancy** /'nekrəʊmænsi/ *noun* [U] **1** the practice of claiming to communicate by magic with the dead in order to learn about the future **2** the use of magic powers, especially evil ones

**necro·philia** /,nekrə'fɪliə/ *noun* [U] sexual interest in dead bodies ▸ **necro·phil·iac** /-liæk/ *noun*

**ne·crop·olis** /nə'krɒpəlɪs; *NAmE* -'krɑːp-/ *noun* (*pl.* **ne·crop·olises** /-lɪsɪz/) a CEMETERY (= place where dead people are buried), especially a large one in an ancient city

**nec·ropsy** /'nekrɒpsi; *NAmE* -krɑːp-/ *noun* (*pl. -ies*) (*NAmE*) an official examination of a dead body (especially that of an animal) in order to discover the cause of death **SYN** AUTOPSY

**ne·cro·sis** /ne'krəʊsɪs/ *noun* [U] (*medical*) the death of most or all of the cells in an organ or TISSUE caused by injury, disease or a loss of blood supply

**nec·tar** /'nektə(r)/ *noun* [U] **1** a sweet liquid that is produced by flowers and collected by bees for making HONEY **2** a delicious drink: *On such a hot day, even water was nectar.* **ORIGIN** In ancient Greek and Roman stories, **nectar** was the drink of the gods. **3** the thick juice of some fruits as a drink: *peach nectar*

**nec·tar·ine** /'nektəriːn/ *noun* a round red and yellow fruit, like a PEACH with smooth skin

**née** /neɪ/ *adj.* (*from French*) a word used after a married woman's name to introduce the family name that she had when she was born: *Jane Smith, née Brown*

**need** 🔊 **A1** 🔊 /niːd/ *verb, noun, modal verb*
- **verb 1** **A1** to require sth/sb because they are essential or very important, not just because you would like to have them: ~**sth/sb** *Do you need any help?* ◇ *Don't go—I might need you.* ◇ *They badly needed a change.* ◇ *We desperately need hard facts on this disease.* ◇ *Food aid is urgently needed.* ◇ *What do you need your own computer for? You can use ours.* ◇ *She needs more time to recover.* ◇ *I don't need your comments, thank you.* ◇ ~**to do sth** *I need to get some sleep.* ◇ *You don't need to leave yet, do you?* ◇ *You need to know how toxic the product is.* ◇ *This shirt needs to be washed.* ◇ **sth needs doing** *This shirt needs washing.* **2** **A1** ~**to do sth** used to show what you should or have to do: *All you need to do is complete this form.* ◇ *I didn't need to go to the bank after all—Mary lent me the money.*
**IDM** **need (to have) your 'head examined** (*informal*) to be crazy

▼ **GRAMMAR POINT**

**need**
- There are two separate verbs **need**.
- **Need** as a main verb has the question form **do you need?**, the negative **you don't need** and the past forms **needed, did you need?** and **didn't need**. It has two meanings: 1. to require something or to think that something is necessary: *Do you need any help?* ◇ *I needed to get some sleep.* 2. to have to or to be obliged to do sth: *Will we need to show our passports?*
- **Need** as a modal verb has **need** for all forms of the present tense, **need you?** as the question form and **need not (needn't)** as the negative. To talk about the past, use the perfect forms **need have** and **needn't have** with the past participle. It is used to say that something is or is not necessary: *Need I pay the whole amount now?*

- **noun 1** **A2** [sing., U] a situation when sth is necessary or must be done: *to satisfy/meet/fulfil a need* ◇ ~ **for sth** *There is an urgent need for qualified teachers.* ◇ *They identified a need for further training.* ◇ ~**for sb/sth to do sth** *There is no need for you to get up early tomorrow.* ◇ ~**to do sth** *There's no need to cry* (= stop crying)*.* ◇ *I had no need to open the letter—I knew what it would say.* ◇ **in ~ of sth** *The house is in need of a thorough clean.* ◇ *We will contact you again if the need arises.* **2** **A2** [C, U] a strong feeling that you want sb/sth or must have sth: *to fulfil an emotional need* ◇ ~**to do sth** *She felt the need to talk to someone.* ◇ **in ~ of sb/sth** *I'm in need of some fresh air.* ◇ *She had no more need of me.* **3** **A2** [C, usually pl.] the things that sb requires in order to live in a comfortable way or achieve what they want: *financial needs* ◇ *Food, clothing and shelter are basic human needs.* ◇ *We will devise a programme to suit your individual needs.* ◇ *children with special educational needs* ⇒ see also SPECIAL NEEDS **4** **A2** [U] the state of not having enough food, money or support **SYN** hardship: **in~** *The charity aims to provide assistance to people in need.* ◇ *These children are in dire need.* ◇ *He helped me in my hour of need* (= at the time when I really needed help)*.* ⇒ see also NEEDY
**IDM** **if need 'be** if necessary: *There's always food in the freezer if need be.* ⇒ more at CRYING *adj.*, FRIEND *n.*
- **modal verb** **B1** (*negative* **need not**, *short form* **needn't** /'niːdnt/) (*rather formal*) used to state that sth is/was not necessary or that only very little is/was necessary; used to ask if sth is/was necessary: ~**(not) do sth** *You needn't bother asking Rick—I know he's too busy.* ◇ *I need hardly tell you* (= you must already know) *that the work is dangerous.* ◇ *If she wants anything, she need only ask.* ◇ *All you*

# needful

*need bring are sheets.* ◊ **~(not) have done sth** *You needn't have worried* (= it was not necessary for you to worry, but you did)—*it all turned out fine.* ◊ **Need you have paid so much?** **HELP** Except in the negative (**needn't**), the use of **need** as a modal verb is rather formal; it is more usual to use **need to**, especially in positive statements and questions: *If you want anything, you only need to ask.* ◊ *Did you need to pay so much?* ⊃ note at MODAL

**need·ful** /ˈniːdfl/ *adj., noun*
■ *adj.* (*formal*) **1** necessary **2** ~(of sth) needing sth: *She thought we were needful of advice.*
■ *noun*
**IDM** **do the ˈneedful** (*especially IndE*) to do what is necessary: *We will do the needful to get these projects through as quickly as possible.*

**nee·dle** ⓘ **B1** /ˈniːdl/ *noun, verb*
■ *noun* [C]
• FOR SEWING **1** **B1** a small thin piece of steel that you use for SEWING, with a point at one end and a hole for the THREAD at the other: *a needle and thread* ◊ *the eye* (= hole) *of a needle* ◊ *Can you thread this needle?* ⊃ see also PINS AND NEEDLES
• FOR KNITTING **2** = KNITTING NEEDLE
• FOR DRUGS **3** **B1** a very thin, pointed piece of steel used on the end of a SYRINGE for putting a drug into sb's body, or for taking blood out of it: *a hypodermic needle*
• ON INSTRUMENT **4** **B2** a thin piece of metal on a scientific instrument that moves to point to the correct measurement or direction: *The compass needle was pointing north.*
• ON PINE TREE **5** [usually pl.] the thin, hard, pointed leaf of a PINE tree: *pine needles on the forest floor* ⊃ VISUAL VOCAB page V6
• ON RECORD PLAYER **6** the very small pointed piece of metal that touches a record that is being played in order to produce the sound **SYN** stylus
**IDM** **a needle in a ˈhaystack** a thing that is almost impossible to find: *Searching for one man in this city is like looking for a needle in a haystack.*
■ *verb* ~sb (*informal*) to deliberately annoy sb, especially by criticizing them continuously **SYN** antagonize: *Don't let her needle you.*

**needle·point** /ˈniːdlpɔɪnt/ *noun* [U] a type of SEWING in which you use very small STITCHES to make a picture on strong cloth

**need·less** /ˈniːdləs/ *adj.* (of sth bad) not necessary; that could be avoided **SYN** unnecessary: *needless suffering* ◊ *Banning smoking would save needless deaths.* ▶ **need·less·ly** *adv.*: *Many soldiers died needlessly.* ◊ *The process was needlessly slow.*
**IDM** **needless to ˈsay** used to emphasize that the information you are giving is obvious: *The problem, needless to say, is the cost involved.*

**needle·work** /ˈniːdlwɜːk/; *NAmE* -wɜːrk/ *noun* [U] things that are SEWN by hand, especially for decoration; the activity of making things by SEWING

**needn't** /ˈniːdnt/ *short form* need not

**needs** /niːdz/ *adv.* (*old use*) in a way that cannot be avoided: *We must needs depart.*
**IDM** **needs ˈmust (when the Devil drives)** (*saying*) in certain situations it is necessary for you to do sth that you do not like or enjoy

**need-to-ˈknow** *adj.*
**IDM** **on a ˌneed-to-ˈknow basis** with people being told only the things they need to know when they need to know them, and no more than that: *Information will be released strictly on a need-to-know basis.*

**needy** /ˈniːdi/ *adj.* (**need·ier**, **needi·est**) **1** (of people) not having enough money, food, clothes, etc. ⊃ SYNONYMS at POOR **2** **the needy** *noun* [pl.] people who do not have enough money, food, etc. **3** (of people) not confident, and needing a lot of love and emotional support from other people

**neep** /niːp/ *noun* (*ScotE, informal*) a SWEDE (= a large round yellow root vegetable): *neeps and tatties*

**ne'er** /neə(r)/; *NAmE* ner/ *adv.* (*literary*) never

**ˈne'er-do-well** *noun* (*old-fashioned*) a lazy person who is not helpful or useful

**ne·far·i·ous** /nɪˈfeəriəs; *NAmE* -ˈfer-/ *adj.* (*formal*) criminal; extremely bad: *nefarious activities*

**neg.** *abbr.* NEGATIVE

**neg·ate** /nɪˈɡeɪt/ *verb* (*formal*) **1** ~sth to stop sth from having any effect **SYN** nullify: *Alcohol negates the effects of the drug.* **2** ~sth to state that sth does not exist

**neg·ation** /nɪˈɡeɪʃn/ *noun* (*formal*) **1** [C, usually sing., U] the exact opposite of sth; the act of causing sth not to exist or to become its opposite: *This political system was the negation of democracy.* **2** [U] the act of disagreeing with sb/sth or refusing to do sth: *She shook her head in negation.*

**nega·tive** ⓘ **A1** ⓞ /ˈneɡətɪv/ *adj., noun, verb*
■ *adj.*
• BAD **1** **B1** bad or harmful: *The crisis had a negative effect on trade.* ◊ *a negative impact on public services* ◊ *The whole experience was definitely more positive than negative.* **OPP** positive
• GRAMMAR **2** **A1** containing a word such as 'no', 'not', 'never', etc.: *a negative form/sentence* **OPP** affirmative, positive ⊃ see also DOUBLE NEGATIVE
• NO **3** **B1** expressing the answer 'no': *His response was negative.* ◊ *They received a negative reply.* **OPP** affirmative
• NOT HOPEFUL **4** **B1** considering only the bad side of sth/sb; having no enthusiasm or hope: *negative feedback/comments* ◊ *Scientists have a fairly negative attitude to the theory.* ◊ '*He probably won't show up.' 'Don't be so negative.*' ◊ ~about sth *She's been rather negative about the idea.* ◊ ~in sth *He was too negative in his thinking.* **OPP** positive
• SCIENTIFIC TEST **5** **B1** (*abbr.* neg.) not showing any evidence of a particular substance or medical condition: *Her pregnancy test was negative.* ◊ *negative results* ◊ *He tested negative for HIV infection.* **OPP** positive
• ELECTRICITY **6** (*specialist*) containing or producing the type of electricity that is carried by an ELECTRON: *a negative charge/current* ◊ *the negative terminal of a battery* **OPP** positive
• NUMBER/QUANTITY **7** less than zero: *a negative trade balance* ◊ *The industry suffered negative growth* (= a decline) *throughout the decade.* **OPP** positive
• IMAGE **8** (of a photograph or an image) showing light and shade, or colours, in the opposite way to the original: *In a negative image of the photograph, dark is light and right is left.* ▶ **nega·tive·ly** *adv.*: *to react negatively to stress* ◊ *to respond negatively* ◊ *negatively charged electrons*
■ *noun*
• NO **1** **B2** a word or statement that means 'no'; an act of refusing to do sth or of denying sth (*formal*): **in the ~** *She answered in the negative* (= said 'no'). **OPP** affirmative
• BAD QUALITY **2** **B2** **the negative** a bad quality or aspect of a situation: *Try not to focus on the negative.* ◊ *The positives outweigh the negatives.*
• IN SCIENTIFIC TEST **3** **B2** the result of a test or an experiment that shows that a substance or condition is not present: *a high proportion of false negatives* **OPP** positive
• GRAMMAR **4** a word such as 'no', 'not', 'never', etc. ⊃ see also DOUBLE NEGATIVE
• IN PHOTOGRAPHY **5** a developed film showing the dark areas of an actual scene as light and the light areas as dark ⊃ compare POSITIVE
■ *verb* (*formal*) **1** ~sth to refuse to agree to a proposal or a request **2** ~sth to prove that sth is not true

**negative ˈequity** *noun* [U] the situation in which the value of sb's house is less than the amount of money that is still owed to a MORTGAGE company, such as a bank

**nega·tiv·ity** /ˌneɡəˈtɪvəti/ (*also* **nega·tiv·ism** /ˈneɡətɪvɪzəm/) *noun* [U] (*formal*) the fact of tending to consider only the bad side of sth/sb; a lack of enthusiasm or hope

**neg·lect** **C1** /nɪˈɡlekt/ *verb, noun*
■ *verb* **1** **C1** ~sb/sth to fail to take care of sb/sth: *She denies neglecting her baby.* ◊ *The buildings had been neglected for years.* **2** **C1** ~sth to not give enough attention to sth: *Dance has been neglected by television.* ◊ *She has*

neglected her studies. ◊ They are **neglecting their duty** as elected representatives. **3** **~ to do sth** (formal) to fail or forget to do sth that you ought to do **SYN** omit: *You neglected to mention the name of your previous employer.* ⊃ see also NEGLIGENCE

■ **noun** [U] the fact of not giving enough care or attention to sth/sb; the state of not receiving enough care or attention: *The buildings are crumbling from* **years of neglect**. ◊ *The place smelled of decay and neglect.* ◊ **~ of sth/sb** *The law imposes penalties for the neglect of children.*

**neg·lect·ed** /nɪˈɡlektɪd/ *adj.* not receiving enough care or attention: *neglected children* ◊ *a neglected area of research*

**neg·lect·ful** /nɪˈɡlektfl/ *adj.* (formal) not giving enough care or attention to sb/sth: *neglectful parents* ◊ **~ of sth/sb** *She became neglectful of her appearance.*

**neg·li·gee** (also **neg·ligée**) /ˈneɡlɪʒeɪ; NAmE ˌneɡlɪˈʒeɪ/ *noun* a woman's DRESSING GOWN made of very thin cloth

**neg·li·gence** /ˈneɡlɪdʒəns/ *noun* [U] (law or formal) the failure to give sb/sth enough care or attention: *The accident was caused by negligence on the part of the driver.* ◊ *The doctor was sued for medical negligence.*

**neg·li·gent** /ˈneɡlɪdʒənt/ *adj.* **1** **~ (in sth / not doing sth)** (law or formal) failing to give sb/sth enough care or attention, especially when this has serious results: *grossly negligent* ◊ *The school had been negligent in not informing the child's parents about the incident.* **2** (literary) (of a person or their manner) relaxed; not formal **SYN** nonchalant: *He waved his hand in a negligent gesture.* ▶ **neg·li·gent·ly** *adv.*: *The defendant drove negligently and hit a lamp post.* ◊ *She was leaning negligently against the wall.*

**neg·li·gible** /ˈneɡlɪdʒəbl/ *adj.* of very little importance or size and not worth considering **SYN** insignificant: *The cost was negligible.* ◊ *a negligible effect/impact/amount*

**ne·go·ti·able** /nɪˈɡəʊʃiəbl/ *adj.* **1** that you can discuss or change before you make an agreement or a decision: *The terms of employment are negotiable.* ◊ *The price was not negotiable.* **2** (business) that you can exchange for money or give to another person in exchange for money **OPP** non-negotiable

**ne·go·ti·ate** /nɪˈɡəʊʃieɪt/ *verb* **1** [I] to try to reach an agreement by formal discussion: **~ (with sb) (for sth)** *The government will not negotiate with terrorists.* ◊ *We have been negotiating for more pay.* ◊ **~ (with sb) about/on sth** *They have refused to negotiate on this issue.* ◊ *a strong negotiating position* ◊ *negotiating skills* ⊃ WORDFINDER NOTE at PEACE **2** [T] **~ sth** to arrange or agree sth by formal discussion: *to negotiate a deal/contract/treaty/settlement* ◊ *We successfully negotiated the release of the hostages.* **3** [T] **~ sth** (formal) to successfully get over or past a difficult part on a path or route: *The climbers had to negotiate a steep rock face.*

**the neˈgotiating table** *noun* [sing.] (used mainly in newspapers) a formal discussion to try and reach an agreement: *We want to get all the parties back to the negotiating table.*

**ne·go·ti·ation** /nɪˌɡəʊʃiˈeɪʃn/ *noun* [C, usually pl., U] formal discussion between people who are trying to reach an agreement: *peace/trade/contract negotiations* ◊ *They begin another* **round of negotiations** *today.* ◊ *to enter into/open/begin negotiations* ◊ *to continue/resume/conclude negotiations* ◊ **~ with sb** *They were conducting secret negotiations with Spain.* ◊ **~ between A and B** *The rent is a matter for negotiation between the landlord and the tenant.* ◊ **in ~ with sb** *A contract is prepared in negotiation with our clients.* ◊ **under ~** *The issue is still under negotiation.* ◊ *The price is generally* **open to negotiation**. ⊃ WORDFINDER NOTE at DEAL

**ne·go·ti·ator** /nɪˈɡəʊʃieɪtə(r)/ *noun* a person who is involved in formal discussions between people who are trying to reach an agreement, especially as part of their job

**Negro** /ˈniːɡrəʊ/ *noun* (pl. **-oes**) (old-fashioned, often offensive) a member of a race of people with dark skin who originally came from Africa

**Negro ˈspiritual** *noun* = SPIRITUAL

**neigh** /neɪ/ *verb* [I] when a horse **neighs** it makes a long high sound ▶ **neigh** *noun*

**neigh·bour** (US **neigh·bor**) /ˈneɪbə(r)/ *noun, verb*

■ **noun 1** a person who lives next to you or near you: *We've had a lot of support from all our* **friends and neighbours**. ◊ *Our* **next-door neighbours** *are very noisy.* ◊ **~ to sb** *She's been a very good neighbour to me.* ⊃ WORDFINDER NOTE at FRIEND **2** a country that is next to or near another country: *What is Britain's nearest neighbour?* **3** a person or thing that is standing or located next to another person or thing: *Stand quietly, children, and try not to talk to your neighbour.* ◊ *The tree fell slowly, its branches caught in those of its neighbours.* **4** (literary) any other human: *We should all love our neighbours.*

■ **verb** **~ sth** to be located next to or near to: *The farm neighbours the holiday village.*

**neigh·bour·hood** (US **neigh·bor·hood**) /ˈneɪbəhʊd; NAmE -bərh-/ *noun* **1** a district or an area of a town; the people who live there: *We grew up in the same neighbourhood.* ◊ *a poor/quiet/residential neighbourhood* ◊ *an old working-class neighbourhood* ◊ *Manhattan is divided into distinct neighborhoods.* ◊ *the neighbourhood police* ◊ *He shouted so loudly that the whole neighbourhood could hear him.* **2** the area that you are in or the area near a particular place **SYN** vicinity: *We searched the surrounding neighbourhood for the missing boy.* ◊ **in the ~ of …** *Houses in the neighbourhood of Paris are extremely expensive.* ⊃ WORDFINDER NOTE at LOCATION
**IDM** **in the neighbourhood of** (of a number or an amount) approximately; not exactly: *It cost in the neighbourhood of $500.*

**ˌneighbourhood ˈwatch** (US **ˌneighborhood ˈwatch**) *noun* [U] an arrangement by which a group of people in an area watch each other's houses regularly as a way of preventing crime

**neigh·bour·ing** (US **neigh·bor·ing**) /ˈneɪbərɪŋ/ *adj.* [only before noun] located or living near or next to a place or person: *a neighbouring house* ◊ *neighbouring towns* ◊ *a neighbouring farmer*

**neigh·bour·ly** (US **neigh·bor·ly**) /ˈneɪbəli; NAmE -bərli/ *adj.* **1** involving people, countries, etc. that live or are located near each other: *the importance of good neighbourly relations between the two states* ◊ *neighbourly help* ◊ *a neighbourly dispute* **2** friendly and helpful **SYN** kind: *It was a neighbourly gesture of theirs.* ▶ **neigh·bour·li·ness** (US **neighbor·li·ness**) *noun* [U]: *good neighbourliness* ◊ *a sense of community and neighbourliness*

▼ **GRAMMAR POINT**

**neither / either**
- After **neither** and **either** you use a singular verb: *Neither candidate was selected for the job.*
- **Neither of** and **either of** are followed by a plural noun or pronoun and a singular or plural verb. A plural verb is more informal: *Neither of my parents speaks/speak a foreign language.*
- When **neither … nor …** or **either … or …** are used with two singular nouns, the verb can be singular or plural. A plural verb is more informal.

**nei·ther** /ˈnaɪðə(r), ˈniːð-; NAmE ˈniːð-, ˈnaɪð-/ *det., pron., adv.*

■ **det., pron.** not one nor the other of two things or people: *Neither answer is correct.* ◊ *Neither of them has/have a car.* ◊ *They produced two reports,* **neither of which** *contained any useful suggestions.* ◊ *'Which do you like?' 'Neither. I think they're both ugly.'*

■ **adv. 1** used to show that a negative statement is also true of sb/sth else: *He didn't remember and* **neither did I**. ◊ *I hadn't been to New York before and* **neither had Jane**. ◊ *'I can't understand a word of it.'* ***'Neither can I.'*** ◊ (informal) *'I don't know.'* ***'Me neither.'*** **2** **neither … nor …** used to show that a negative statement is true of two things: *I neither knew nor cared what had happened to him.* ◊ *Their house is neither big nor small.* ◊ *Neither the TV nor the DVD player actually work/works.*

# nematode

**nema·tode** /ˈnemətəʊd/ (also **nematode ˈworm**) noun a WORM with a thin body that is shaped like a tube and not divided into sections

**nem·esis** /ˈneməsɪs/ noun (pl. **nem·eses** /-məsiːz/) (formal) **1** [C] the person or thing that causes somebody to lose their power, position, etc. and that cannot be avoided: *Has she finally met her nemesis?* **2** [C] a person or thing that has competed with somebody or been an enemy for a long time: *He strode out to face his old nemesis.* **3** [U, sing.] punishment or defeat that is deserved and cannot be avoided

**neo-** /niːəʊ, niːə; BrE also niːɒ; NAmE also niːɑː/ combining form (in adjectives and nouns) new; in a later form: *neo-Georgian* ◊ *neo-fascist*

**neo·clas·sic·al** /ˌniːəʊˈklæsɪkl/ adj. [usually before noun] used to describe art and architecture that is based on the style of ancient Greece or Rome

**neo·co·lo·ni·al·ism** /ˌniːəʊkəˈləʊniəlɪzəm/ noun [U] (disapproving) the use of economic or political pressure by powerful countries to control or influence other countries

**neo·con·ser·va·tive** /ˌniːəʊkənˈsɜːvətɪv; NAmE -ˈsɜːrv-/ adj. (politics) relating to political, economic, religious, etc. beliefs that return to traditional conservative views in a slightly changed form ▶ **neo·con·ser·va·tive** (also **neo·con** /ˈniːəʊkɒn; NAmE -kɑːn/) noun

**neo·cor·tex** /ˌniːəʊˈkɔːteks; NAmE -ˈkɔːrt-/ noun (anatomy) the part of the brain that controls sight and hearing

**neo·dym·ium** /ˌniːəʊˈdɪmiəm/ noun [U] (symb. **Nd**) a chemical element. Neodymium is a silver-white metal.

**neo·liberal** /ˌniːəʊˈlɪbərəl/ adj. [usually before noun] (politics) relating to a type of LIBERALISM that believes in a global free market, without government regulation, with businesses and industry controlled and run for profit by private owners ▶ **neo·liberal·ism** noun [U]

**Neo·lith·ic** /ˌniːəˈlɪθɪk/ adj. of the later part of the STONE AGE: *Neolithic stone axes* ◊ *Neolithic settlements*

**neo·lo·gism** /niˈɒlədʒɪzəm; NAmE -ˈɑːl-/ noun (formal) a new word or expression or a new meaning of a word

**neon** /ˈniːɒn; NAmE ˈniːɑːn/ noun [U] (symb. **Ne**) a chemical element. Neon is a gas that does not react with anything and that shines with a bright light when electricity is passed through it: *neon lights/signs*

**neo·natal** /ˌniːəʊˈneɪtl/ adj. (specialist) connected with a child that has just been born: *the hospital's neonatal unit* ◊ *neonatal care*

**neo·nate** /ˈniːəʊneɪt/ noun (medical) a baby that has recently been born, especially within the last four weeks

**neo·phyte** /ˈniːəfaɪt/ noun (formal) **1** a person who has recently started an activity: *The site gives neophytes the chance to learn from experts.* **2** a person who has recently changed to a new religion **3** a person who has recently become a priest or recently entered a religious order

**neo·prene** /ˈniːəpriːn/ noun [U] an artificial material which looks like rubber, used for making WETSUITS

**NEPAD** /ˈnepæd/ abbr. (SAfrE) New Partnership for Africa's Development (= a plan decided by governments in Africa to help the continent's economy)

**nephew** /ˈnefjuː; ˈnevjuː/ noun the son of your brother or sister; the son of your husband's or wife's brother or sister ⇒ compare NIECE

**nepo·tism** /ˈnepətɪzəm/ noun [U] (disapproving) giving unfair advantages to your own family if you are in a position of power, especially by giving them jobs

**Nep·tune** /ˈneptjuːn; NAmE -tuːn/ noun a planet in the SOLAR SYSTEM that is 8th in order of distance from the sun

**nerd** /nɜːd; NAmE nɜːrd/ noun (informal, disapproving) **1** a person who is boring, stupid and not fashionable SYN **geek** **2** a person who is very interested in computers SYN **geek** ▶ **nerdy** adj.

---

**nerve** ❶ B2 /nɜːv; NAmE nɜːrv/ noun, verb

■ noun **1** B2 [C] any of the long FIBRES that carry messages between the brain and parts of the body, enabling you to move, feel pain, etc: *the optic nerve* ◊ *nerve cells/fibres/endings* ◊ *Every nerve in her body was tense.* ◊ *The disease can also cause nerve damage.* **2** B2 **nerves** [pl.] feelings of worry or stress: *Even after years as a singer, he still suffers from nerves before a performance.* ◊ *I need something to calm my nerves.* ◊ *to settle/soothe/steady your nerves* ◊ *Everyone's nerves were on edge* (= everyone felt TENSE). ◊ *He lives on his nerves* (= is always worried). **3** [U] **nerves** [pl.] the courage to do sth difficult or dangerous SYN **guts**: *It took a lot of nerve to take the company to court.* ◊ *I was going to have a go at parachuting but lost my nerve at the last minute.* ◊ *to hold/keep your nerve* **4** [sing., U] (informal) a way of behaving that other people think is rude or not appropriate SYN **cheek**: *I don't know how you have the nerve to show your face after what you said!* ◊ *He's got a nerve asking us for money!* ◊ *'Then she demanded to see the manager!' 'What a nerve!'* IDM **be a bag/bundle of ˈnerves** (informal) to be very nervous **get on sb's ˈnerves** (informal) to annoy sb: *It really gets on my nerves when people talk loudly on the phone in public.* **have nerves of ˈsteel** to be able to remain calm in a difficult or dangerous situation **hit/touch/strike a (raw/sensitive) ˈnerve** to mention a subject that makes sb feel angry, upset, embarrassed, etc: *You touched a raw nerve when you mentioned his first wife.* ◊ *The article struck a raw nerve as it revived unpleasant memories.* ⇒ more at STRAIN v., STRIKE v., WAR

■ verb **~ yourself for sth/to do sth** to give yourself the courage or strength to do sth difficult or unpleasant: *He nerved himself to ask her out.*

**ˈnerve agent** noun a substance that damages the NERVOUS SYSTEM, especially one used as a weapon: *chemical weapons, including nerve agents and mustard gas*

**ˈnerve centre** (BrE) (especially US **nerve center**) noun the place from which an activity or organization is controlled and instructions are sent out

**ˈnerve gas** noun a poisonous gas used in war that attacks your CENTRAL NERVOUS SYSTEM

**nerve·less** /ˈnɜːvləs; NAmE ˈnɜːrvləs/ adj. **1** having no strength or feeling: *The knife fell from her nerveless fingers.* **2** having no fear: *She is a nerveless rider.* OPP **nervous**

**ˈnerve-racking** (also **ˈnerve-wracking**) adj. making you feel very nervous and worried

**ner·vous** ❶ A2 /ˈnɜːvəs; NAmE ˈnɜːrv-/ adj. **1** A2 anxious about sth or afraid of sth: *I felt really nervous before the interview.* ◊ *~ about sth Consumers are very nervous about the future.* ◊ *~ of sb/sth The horse may be nervous of cars.* ◊ *~ about/of doing sth He had been nervous about inviting us.* ◊ *a nervous laugh/glance/smile* (= one that shows that you feel anxious) ◊ *By the time the police arrived, I was a nervous wreck.* OPP **confident** ⇒ SYNONYMS at WORRIED **2** B1 easily worried or frightened: *She was a thin, nervous girl.* ◊ *He's not the nervous type.* ◊ *She was of a nervous disposition.* **3** B2 connected with the body's nerves and often affecting you mentally or emotionally: *a nervous condition/disorder/disease* ◊ *She was in a state of nervous exhaustion.* IDM see SHADOW n. ▶ **ner·vous·ly** adv.: *She smiled nervously.* **ner·vous·ness** noun [U]: *He tried to hide his nervousness.*

**nervous ˈbreakdown** (also **ˈbreak·down**) noun a period of mental illness in which sb becomes very depressed, anxious and tired, and cannot deal with normal life: *to have/suffer a nervous breakdown*

**ˈnervous system** noun the system of all the nerves in the body that carries messages between the brain and the rest of the body ⇒ see also CENTRAL NERVOUS SYSTEM

**nervy** /ˈnɜːvi; NAmE ˈnɜːrvi/ adj. (informal) **1** (BrE) anxious and nervous **2** (NAmE) brave and confident in a way that might offend other people, or show a lack of respect

**-ness** /nəs/ suffix (in nouns) the quality, state or character of: *dryness* ◊ *blindness* ◊ *silliness*

## ▼ SYNONYMS
**nervous**
neurotic • on edge • jittery

These words all describe people who are easily frightened or are behaving in a frightened way.

**nervous** easily worried or frightened: *He was of a nervous disposition.* NOTE See also the entry for **worried**.

**neurotic** not behaving in a reasonable, calm way, because you are worried about sth: *She became neurotic about keeping the house clean.*

**on edge** nervous or easily made angry: *She was always on edge before an interview.*

**jittery** (*informal*) anxious and nervous: *All this talk of job losses was making him jittery.*

**PATTERNS**
- a nervous/neurotic **man/woman/girl**
- to **feel** nervous/on edge/jittery
- a **bit** nervous/on edge/jittery

---

**nest** /nest/ *noun, verb*
- *noun* **1** [C] a hollow place or structure that a bird makes or chooses for laying its eggs in and sheltering its young ⇒ VISUAL VOCAB page V2 **2** [C] a place where insects or other small creatures live and produce their young **3** [sing.] a secret place which is full of bad people and their activities: *a nest of thieves* **4** [sing.] the home, thought of as the safe place where parents bring up their children: *to leave the nest* (= leave your parents' home) ⇒ see also EMPTY NEST **5** [C, usually sing.] a group or set of similar things that are made to fit inside each other: *a nest of tables* IDM SEE FEATHER *v.*, FLY *v.*, HORNET, MARE
- *verb* **1** [I] to make and use a nest: *Thousands of seabirds are nesting on the cliffs.* **2** [T] ~ **sth** (*specialist*) to put types of information together, or inside each other, so that they form a single unit

**'nest box** (*also* **'nesting box**) *noun* a box provided for a bird to make its NEST in

**'nest egg** *noun* (*informal*) a sum of money that you save to use in the future

**nes·tle** /ˈnesl/ *verb* **1** [I] + *adv./prep.* to sit or lie down in a warm or soft place: *He hugged her and she nestled against his chest.* **2** [T] ~ **sb/sth** + *adv./prep.* to put or hold sb/sth in a comfortable position in a warm or soft place: *He nestled the baby in his arms.* **3** [I] + *adv./prep.* to be located in a position that is protected, sheltered or partly hidden: *The little town nestles snugly at the foot of the hill.*

**nest·ling** /ˈnestlɪŋ/ *noun* a bird that is too young to leave the NEST

**net** /net/ *noun, adj., verb*
- *noun* **1** [C, U] material that is made of string, THREAD or wire TWISTED or tied together, with small spaces in between; a piece of this material used for a particular purpose: *fishing nets ◊ net curtains* ⇒ see also DRIFT NET, FISHNET, HAIRNET, MOSQUITO NET, NETTING, SAFETY NET ⇒ WORDFINDER NOTE at FISHING **2** **the net** [sing.] (in sports) the frame covered in net that forms the goal: *to kick the ball into the back of the net* **3** **the net** [sing.] (in tennis, etc.) the piece of net between the two players that the ball goes over **4** [C, usually pl.] (in CRICKET) a piece of ground with a net around it, used for practising BATTING and BOWLING **5 the net** (*also* **the Net**) [sing.] (*informal*) the internet: *to surf the net* **6** [C] a network of radios or computers that are connected to each other
  IDM SEE CAST *v.*, SLIP *v.*, SPREAD *v.*, WIDEN
- *adj.* (*BrE also* **nett**) **1** [usually before noun] a **net** amount of money is the amount that remains when nothing more is to be taken away: *a net profit of £500 ◊ net income/earnings* (= after tax has been paid) ⇒ compare GROSS **2** [only before noun] the **net** weight of sth is the weight without its container or the material it is wrapped in: *450gms net weight* ⇒ compare GROSS **3** [only before noun] final, after all the important facts have been included: *The net result is that small shopkeepers are being forced out of business. ◊ Canada is now a substantial net importer of medicines* (= it imports more than it exports). *◊ a net gain* ▶ **net** *adv.*: *a salary of $50 000 net ◊ Interest on the investment will be paid net* (= tax will already have been taken away). ⇒ compare GROSS
- *verb* (-tt-) **1** ~ **sth** to earn an amount of money as a profit after you have paid tax on it: *The sale of paintings netted £17 000.* **2** ~ **sth** to catch sth, especially fish, in a net **3** ~ **sb/sth** to catch sb or obtain sth with skill: *A swoop by customs officers netted a large quantity of drugs.* **4** ~ **sth** (*especially BrE*) to kick or hit a ball into the goal SYN score: *He has netted 21 goals so far this season.* **5** ~ **sth** to cover sth with a net or nets

**net·ball** /ˈnetbɔːl/ *noun* [U] a game played by two teams of seven players, especially women or girls. Players score by throwing a ball through a high net hanging from a ring on a post.

**net·book** /ˈnetbʊk/ *noun* a small laptop computer, designed especially for using the internet and email ⇒ compare NOTEBOOK

**net 'curtain** (*BrE*) (*NAmE* **cur·tain**) *noun* a very thin curtain that you hang at a window, which allows light to enter but stops people outside from being able to see inside

**nether** /ˈneðə(r)/ *adj.* [only before noun] (*literary or humorous*) lower: *a person's nether regions* (= their GENITALS)

**the neth·er·world** /ðə ˈneðəwɜːld; *NAmE* -ðərwɜːrld/ *noun* [sing.] (*literary*) the world of the dead SYN **hell**

**neti·zen** /ˈnetɪzn/ *noun* (*informal, humorous*) a person who uses the internet a lot

**net neu'trality** (*also* **network neutrality**) *noun* [U] the principle that internet service providers should allow access to all websites and programs without trying to block or promote particular sites or products

**nett** (*BrE*) = NET

**net·ting** /ˈnetɪŋ/ *noun* [U] material that is made of string, THREAD or wire TWISTED or tied together, with spaces in between: *wire netting*

**net·tle** /ˈnetl/ *noun, verb*
- *noun* (*also* **'stinging nettle**) a wild plant with leaves that have pointed edges, are covered in fine hairs and STING (= cause you pain) if you touch them ⇒ VISUAL VOCAB page V7 IDM SEE GRASP *v.*
- *verb* ~ **sb** (*informal, especially BrE*) to make sb slightly angry SYN **annoy**: *My remarks clearly nettled her.*

**net·work** /ˈnetwɜːk; *NAmE* -wɜːrk/ *noun, verb*
- *noun* **1** a complicated system of roads, lines, tubes, nerves, etc. that are connected to each other and operate together: *a rail/road/canal network ◊ a mobile phone network ◊ ~ of sth a network of veins* **2** a closely connected group of people, companies, etc. that exchange information, etc: *a communications/distribution network ◊ to build/create/develop a network ◊ ~ of sb/sth a network of friends* ⇒ see also SOCIAL NETWORK (2) **3** (*computing*) a number of computers and other devices that are connected together so that equipment and information can be shared: *The office network allows users to share files and software, and to use a central printer. ◊ across/over/via a ~ Users can access data across a network. ◊ You can print and scan from your device via a wireless network.* ⇒ see also LAN, LOCAL AREA NETWORK, NEURAL NETWORK, SOCIAL NETWORK (1), WAN **4** a group of radio or television stations in different places that are connected and that broadcast the same programmes at the same time: *the four big US television networks ◊ The show was first aired on the cable network Showtime. ◊ ~ of sth He's chairman of a network of radio stations.* IDM SEE OLD BOY
- *verb* **1** [T, usually passive] ~ **sth** (*computing*) to connect a number of computers and other devices together so that equipment and information can be shared **2** [T, usually passive] ~ **sth** to broadcast a television or radio programme on stations in several different areas at the same time **3** [I] to try to meet and talk to people who may be useful to you in your work: *Conferences are a good place to network.*

# network effect

**'network effect** *noun* (*economics*) the effect that happens when a product or service gains value as more people use it

**net·work·ing** /ˈnetwɜːkɪŋ; *NAmE* -wɜːrk-/ *noun* [U] a system of trying to meet and talk to other people who may be useful to you in your work ▶ **net·work·er** *noun*: *To be an effective networker, you need to find good contacts and develop relationships.*

**network neu'trality** *noun* [U] = NET NEUTRALITY

**neur·al** /ˈnjʊərəl; *NAmE* ˈnʊr-/ *adj.* (*specialist*) connected with a nerve or the NERVOUS SYSTEM: *neural processes*

**neur·al·gia** /njʊəˈrældʒə; *NAmE* nʊˈr-/ *noun* [U] (*medical*) a sharp pain felt along a nerve, especially in the head or face ▶ **neur·al·gic** /-dʒɪk/ *adj.*

**neural 'network** (*also* **neural 'net**) *noun* (*computing*) a computer system which is designed to work in a similar way to the human brain and nervous system

**neuro-** /ˈnjʊərəʊ, njʊərə, njʊəˈrɒ; *NAmE* nʊrəʊ, nʊrə, nʊˈrɑː/ *combining form* (in nouns, adjectives and adverbs) connected with the nerves: *neuroscience* ◊ *a neurosurgeon*

**neuro·biol·ogy** /ˌnjʊərəʊbaɪˈɒlədʒi; *NAmE* ˌnʊrəʊbaɪˈɑːl-/ *noun* [U] the scientific study of the biology of the NERVOUS SYSTEM, especially in connection with behaviour ▶ **neuro·bio·logic·al** /ˌnjʊərəʊˌbaɪəˈlɒdʒɪkl; *NAmE* ˌnʊrəʊˌbaɪəˈlɑːdʒ-/ *adj.*

**neuro·lin·guis·tics** /ˌnjʊərəʊlɪŋˈɡwɪstɪks; *NAmE* ˌnʊr-/ *noun* [U] (*psychology*) the study of the way the human brain processes language

**neuro·logic·al** /ˌnjʊərəˈlɒdʒɪkl; *NAmE* ˌnʊrəˈlɑːdʒ-/ *adj.* relating to nerves or to the science of NEUROLOGY: *neurological damage*

**neurolo·gist** /njʊəˈrɒlədʒɪst; *NAmE* nʊˈrɑːl-/ *noun* a doctor who studies and treats diseases of the nerves ⇒ WORDFINDER NOTE at SPECIALIST

**neurol·ogy** /njʊəˈrɒlədʒi; *NAmE* nʊˈrɑːl-/ *noun* [U] the scientific study of nerves and their diseases

**neuron** /ˈnjʊərɒn; *NAmE* ˈnʊrɑːn; (*also* **neur·one** /ˈnjʊərəʊn; *NAmE* ˈnʊr-/ *especially in BrE*) *noun* (*biology*) a cell that carries information within the brain and between the brain and other parts of the body; a nerve cell ⇒ see also MOTOR NEURONE DISEASE

**neuro·science** /ˈnjʊərəʊsaɪəns; *NAmE* ˈnʊr-/ *noun* [U] the science that deals with the structure and function of the brain and the NERVOUS SYSTEM ▶ **neuro·scientist** /-rəʊsaɪəntɪst/ *noun*

**neur·osis** /njʊəˈrəʊsɪs; *NAmE* nʊˈr-/ *noun* [C, U] (*pl.* **neur·oses** /-ˈrəʊsiːz/) **1** (*medical*) a mental illness in which a person suffers strong feelings of fear and worry **2** any strong fear or worry SYN anxiety

**neuro·sur·gery** /ˈnjʊərəʊsɜːdʒəri; *NAmE* ˈnʊrəʊsɜːrdʒ-/ *noun* [U] medical operations performed on the nervous system, especially the brain ▶ **neuro·sur·geon** /-dʒən/ *noun*

**neur·ot·ic** /njʊəˈrɒtɪk; *NAmE* nʊˈrɑːt-/ *adj.*, *noun*
- *adj.* **1** caused by or suffering from neurosis: *neurotic obsessions* **2** not behaving in a reasonable, calm way, because you are worried about sth: *She became neurotic about keeping the house clean.* ◊ *a brilliant but neurotic actor* ▶ SYNONYMS at NERVOUS ▶ **neur·ot·ic·al·ly** /-kli/ *adv.*
- *noun* a neurotic person

**neuro·toxin** /ˈnjʊərəʊtɒksɪn; *NAmE* ˈnʊrəʊtɑːk-/ *noun* (*specialist*) a poison that affects the NERVOUS SYSTEM

**neuro·trans·mit·ter** /ˈnjʊərəʊtrænzmɪtə(r); *NAmE* ˈnʊr-/ *noun* (*biology*) a chemical that carries messages from nerve cells to other nerve cells or muscles

**neu·ter** /ˈnjuːtə(r); *NAmE* ˈnuː-/ *adj.*, *verb*
- *adj.* (*grammar*) (in some languages) belonging to a class of nouns, pronouns, adjectives or verbs whose GENDER is not FEMININE or MASCULINE: *The Polish word for 'window' is neuter.*
- *verb* **1** ~ sth to remove part of the sex organs of an animal so that it cannot produce young: *Has your cat been neutered?* **2** ~ sth (*disapproving*) to prevent sth from having the effect that it ought to have

**neu·tral** /ˈnjuːtrəl; *NAmE* ˈnuː-/ *adj.*, *noun*
- *adj.*
- IN DISAGREEMENT/CONTEST **1** not supporting or helping either side in a DISAGREEMENT, competition, etc. SYN **impartial**, **unbiased**: *Journalists are supposed to be politically neutral.* ◊ *I didn't take my father's or my mother's side; I tried to remain neutral.*
- IN WAR **2** not belonging to any of the countries that are involved in a war; not supporting any of the countries involved in a war: *neutral territory/waters* ◊ *Switzerland was neutral during the war.*
- WITHOUT STRONG FEELING/INFLUENCE **3** deliberately not expressing any strong feeling: *'So you told her?' he said in a neutral tone of voice.* **4** not affected by sth: *He believes that technology is morally neutral until it is applied.* ⇒ see also GENDER-NEUTRAL
- COLOUR **5** not very bright or strong, such as grey or light brown: *a neutral colour scheme* ◊ *neutral tones*
- CHEMISTRY **6** neither ACID nor ALKALINE
- ELECTRICAL **7** (*abbr.* **N**) having neither a positive nor a negative electrical charge: *the neutral wire in a plug* ▶ **neu·tral·ly** /-trəli/ *adv.*
- IDM **on neutral 'ground/'territory** in a place that has no connection with either of the people or sides who are meeting and so does not give an advantage to either of them: *We decided to meet on neutral ground.*
- *noun*
- IN VEHICLE **1** [U] the position of the GEARS of a vehicle in which no power is carried from the engine to the wheels: *in ~ to leave the car in neutral*
- IN DISAGREEMENT/WAR **2** [C] a person or country that does not support either side in a DISAGREEMENT, competition or war
- COLOUR **3** [C] a colour that is not bright or strong, such as grey or light brown: *The room was decorated in neutrals.*

**neu·tral·ity** /njuːˈtræləti; *NAmE* nuː-/ *noun* [U] the state of not supporting either side in a DISAGREEMENT, competition or war ⇒ see also NET NEUTRALITY

**neu·tral·ize** (*BrE also* -**ise**) /ˈnjuːtrəlaɪz; *NAmE* ˈnuː-/ *verb* **1** ~ sth to stop sth from having any effect: *The latest figures should neutralize the fears of inflation.* **2** ~ sth (*chemistry*) to make a substance NEUTRAL **3** ~ sth to make a country or an area NEUTRAL ▶ **neu·tral·iza·tion**, **-isa·tion** /ˌnjuːtrəlaɪˈzeɪʃn; *NAmE* ˌnuːtrələˈz-/ *noun* [U]

**'neutral zone** *noun* **1** (in ICE HOCKEY) an area that covers the central part of the RINK, between two blue lines **2** (in AMERICAN FOOTBALL) an imaginary area between the teams where no player except the CENTRE is allowed to step until play has started

**neu·trino** /njuːˈtriːnəʊ; *NAmE* nuː-/ *noun* (*pl.* **-os**) (*physics*) an extremely small PARTICLE that has no electrical charge, and which rarely reacts with other matter

**neu·tron** /ˈnjuːtrɒn; *NAmE* ˈnuːtrɑːn/ *noun* (*physics*) a very small piece of matter (= a substance) that carries no electric charge and that forms part of the NUCLEUS (= central part) of an ATOM ⇒ see also ELECTRON, PROTON ⇒ WORDFINDER NOTE at ATOM

**never** /ˈnevə(r)/ *adv.*, *exclamation*
- *adv.* **1** not at any time; on any occasion: *You never help me.* ◊ *He'll never forget her.* ◊ *He has never been abroad.* ◊ *She had never seen so much snow.* ◊ *He vowed never to return.* ◊ *'Would you vote for him?' 'Never.'* ◊ *'I work for a company called Orion Technology.' 'Never heard of them.'* ◊ *Never in all my life have I seen such a horrible thing.* ◊ *Never ever tell anyone your password.* ◊ *Never before has English cuisine been so stylish.* **2** used to emphasize a negative statement instead of 'not': *I never knew* (= didn't know until now) *you had a twin sister.* ◊ (*especially BrE*) *Someone might find out, and that would never do* (= that is not acceptable). ◊ *He never so much as smiled* (= did not smile even once). ◊ *Most people have never even heard of Iggy.* ◊ (*BrE, slang*) *'You took my bike.' 'No, I never.'* ◊ (*old-fashioned or humorous*) *Never fear* (= Do not worry), *everything will be all right.*
- IDM **never say 'never** used to say that nothing is impossible: *Many thought the book could not become a movie, but with Hollywood never say never.* **on the ˌnever-'never** (*old-fashioned, BrE, informal*) on HIRE PURCHASE (= by making payments over a long period): *to buy a new car on the*

**never-never** **Well, I never (did)!** (*old-fashioned*) used to express surprise or DISAPPROVAL
- **exclamation** (*informal*) used to show that you are very surprised about sth because you do not believe it is possible: '*I got the job.*' '*Never!*' IDM see MIND v.

**never-ending** *adj.* seeming to last forever SYN **endless**, **interminable**: *Housework is a never-ending task.*

**nev·er·the·less** ❶ B2 ○ /ˌnevəˈðeles; NAmE -vərð-/ *adv.* despite sth that you have just mentioned SYN **nonetheless**: *There is little chance that we will succeed in changing the law. Nevertheless, it is important that we try.* ◇ *Our defeat was expected but it is disappointing nevertheless.*

▼ **LANGUAGE BANK**
**nevertheless**
Conceding a point and making a counterargument
- **While** *the film is undoubtedly too long, it is* **nevertheless** *an intriguing piece of cinema.*
- **It can be argued that** *the movie is too long. It is* **nonetheless** *an intriguing piece of cinema.*
- *The film is undoubtedly too long.* **Still***, it is an intriguing piece of cinema.*
- **Of course***, huge chunks of the book have been sacrificed in order to make a two-hour movie,* **but** *it is* **nevertheless** *a successful piece of storytelling.*
- *Critics are wrong to argue that the film's plot is too complicated.* **Certainly** *there are a couple of major twists,* **but** *audiences will have no difficulty following them.*
- **It is true that** *you cannot make a good movie without a good script,* **but it is equally true** *that a talented director can make a good script into an excellent film.*
- **It remains to be seen whether** *these two movies herald a new era of westerns,* **but there is no doubt that** *they represent welcome additions to the genre.*

⊃ LANGUAGE BANK at ARGUE, HOWEVER, IMPERSONAL, OPINION

**new** ❶ A1 ○ /njuː; NAmE nuː/ *adj.* (**newer, new·est**)
- NOT EXISTING BEFORE **1** A1 not existing before; recently made, invented, introduced, etc: *Have you read her new novel?* ◇ *new technology* ◇ *a new baby* ◇ *a new addition to the family* (= a baby) ◇ *new ways of doing things* ◇ *This idea isn't new.* ◇ *The latest model has over 100 new features.* ⊃ see also BRAND NEW OPP **old 2 the new** *noun* [U] something that is new: *It was a good mix of the old and the new.*
- RECENTLY BOUGHT **3** A1 recently bought: *Let me show you my new dress.*
- NOT USED BEFORE **4** A1 not used or owned by anyone before: *A second-hand car costs a fraction of a new one.*
- DIFFERENT **5** A1 different from the previous one: *I like your new hairstyle.* ◇ *When do you start your new job?* ◇ *He's made a lot of new friends.* OPP **old**
- NOT FAMILIAR **6** A1 already existing but not seen, experienced, etc. before; not familiar: *This is a new experience for me.* ◇ *I'd like to learn a new language.* ◇ *the discovery of a new star* ◇ *Manga is drawing in a* **whole** *new generation of readers.* ◇ *to try/learn/do something new* ◇ **~ to sb** *Our system is probably new to you.* ◇ *Hard work is nothing new to Bill.*
- RECENTLY ARRIVED **7** A1 not yet familiar with sth because you have only just started, arrived, etc: *a new arrival/recruit* ◇ *You're new here, aren't you?* ◇ **~ to sth** *I should tell you, I'm completely new to this kind of work.* ◇ *I am new to the town.*
- JUST BEGINNING **8** A1 [usually before noun] just beginning or beginning again: *a new day* ◇ *It was a new era in the history of our country.* ◇ *She went to Australia to start a new life.*
- NEW- **9** used in compounds to describe sth that has recently happened: *He was enjoying his new-found freedom.*
- MODERN **10** (usually with *the*) modern; of the latest type: *the new morality* ◇ *They called themselves the New Romantics.*
- WITH FRESH ENERGY **11** having fresh energy, courage or health: *Since he changed jobs he's looked like a new man.*
- RECENTLY PRODUCED **12** only recently produced or developed: *The new buds are appearing on the trees now.*

◇ *new potatoes* (= ones dug from the soil early in the season) ▶ **new·ness** *noun* [U] ⊃ see also NEWLY

IDM **break new ˈground** to make a new discovery or do sth that has not been done before ⊃ see also GROUNDBREAKING **(as) ˌgood as ˈnew** | **like ˈnew** in very good condition, as it was when it was new: *I've had your coat cleaned—it's as good as new now.* **… is the new …** (*informal*) used to say that sth has become very fashionable and can be thought of as replacing sth else: *Brown is the new black.* ◇ *Comedy is the new rock and roll.* ◇ *Fifty is the new forty.* **a ˌnew ˈbroom** (*BrE, often disapproving*) a person who has just started to work for an organization, department, etc., especially in a senior job, and who is likely to make a lot of changes: *Well, you know what they say—a new broom sweeps clean.* **a/the ˌnew kid on the ˈblock** (*informal*) a person who is new to a place, an organization, etc: *Despite his six years in politics, he was still regarded by many as the new kid on the block.* **the ˌnew ˈnormal** a situation that used to be unusual but is now what you should expect: *Scientists say these weather patterns could be the new normal for Florida.* **a ˌnew one on ˈme** (*informal*) used to say that you have not heard a particular idea, piece of information, joke, etc. before: *'Have you come across this before?' 'No, it's a new one on me.'* **ˌturn over a new ˈleaf** to change your way of life to become a better, more responsible person **ˌwhat's ˈnew?** (*informal*) used as a friendly GREETING: *Hi! What's new?* ⊃ more at BLOOD *n.*, BRAVE *adj.*, BREATHE, COMPLEXION, EMPEROR, LOW *n.*, TEACH

▼ **HOMOPHONES**
**knew • new** /njuː; NAmE nuː/
- **knew** *verb* (past tense of KNOW): *I knew you would say that!*
- **new** *adj.*: *This new piece is less traditional than her early work.*

**ˌNew ˈAge** *adj.* connected with a way of life that rejects modern Western values and is based on spiritual ideas and beliefs, ASTROLOGY, etc: *a New Age festival* ◇ *New Age travellers* (= people in Britain who reject the values of modern society and travel from place to place, living in their vehicles) ▶ **ˌNew ˈAge** *noun* [U]

**new·bie** /ˈnjuːbi; NAmE ˈnuː-/ (*also* **newb** /njuːb; NAmE nuːb/ *especially in NAmE*) *noun* (*informal*) a person who is new to a particular environment or activity and has little experience, especially in using computers SYN **novice** ⊃ see also NOOB

**new·born** /ˈnjuːbɔːn; NAmE ˈnuːbɔːrn/ *adj.* [only before noun] recently born: *a newborn baby*

**ˈnew build** *noun* [C, U] (*BrE*) a building, ship or aircraft that has been built very recently or that is to be built soon; buildings, etc. of this type: *400 new builds are planned for the village.* ◇ *We wanted the modern convenience of new build.* ◇ *new-build properties/apartments*

**new·comer** /ˈnjuːkʌmə(r); NAmE ˈnuː-/ *noun* **~ (to sth)** a person who has only recently arrived in a place or started an activity

**New ˈEngland** /ˌnjuː ˈɪŋglənd; NAmE ˌnuː-/ *noun* an area in the north-eastern US that includes the states of Maine, New Hampshire, Vermont, Massachusetts, Rhode Island and Connecticut

**new·fan·gled** /ˌnjuːˈfæŋgld; NAmE ˌnuː-/ *adj.* (usually before noun) (*disapproving*) used to describe sth that has recently been invented or introduced, but that you do not like because it is not what you are used to, or is too complicated

**ˌnew-ˈfound** *adj.* [only before noun] recently discovered or achieved: *How is she handling her new-found fame?* ◇ *his new-found freedom/confidence/enthusiasm*

**newly** ❶+ B2 /ˈnjuːli; NAmE ˈnuː-/ *adv.* (usually before a past participle) recently: *a newly qualified doctor* ◇ *a newly created job* ◇ *a newly independent republic*

**ˈnewly-wed** *noun* [usually pl.] a person who has recently got married ▶ **ˈnewly-wed** *adj.*

# new man

**ˌnew ˈman** *noun* (*BrE*) a man who shares the work in the home that is traditionally done by women, such as cleaning, cooking and taking care of children. New men are considered sensitive and not aggressive.

**ˌnew ˈmedia** *noun* [pl.] new information and entertainment products and services that use digital technologies such as the internet

**ˌnew ˈmoney** *noun* [U] wealth that has been made or acquired recently; people who have become wealthy recently ⇨ compare NOUVEAU RICHE, OLD MONEY

**ˌnew ˈmoon** *noun* **1** the moon when it looks like a thin curved shape (= a CRESCENT) **2** the time of the month when the moon has this shape ⇨ compare FULL MOON, HALF-MOON

**news** /njuːz; *NAmE* nuːz/ *noun* [U] **1** new information about sth that has happened recently: *What's the latest news?* ◊ *Have you* **heard the news**? *Pat's leaving!* ◊ *That's great news.* ◊ *Tell me all your news.* ◊ *Do you want the good news or the bad news first?* ◊ *a piece/bit of news* ◊ *~ of sb/sth Have you had any news of Patrick?* ◊ *~ on sth Any news on the deal?* ◊ *~ about sb/sth He gave me some news about the office move.* ◊ *~ that … Messengers brought news that the battle had been lost.* ◊ (*informal*) *It's news to me* (= I haven't heard it before). **2** reports of recent events that appear in newspapers or on television, radio or the internet: *national/international/local news* ◊ *a news story/item/report* ◊ *a TV/radio news bulletin* ◊ *news media/coverage* ◊ *You can catch all the latest news on our website.* ◊ *breaking news* (= news that is arriving about events that have just happened) ◊ *The wedding was front-page news.* ◊ *~ of sth News of a serious road accident is just coming in.* ◊ *~ on sth Is there any news on the car bomb attack?* ◊ *~ about sb/sth I'm not interested in news about celebrities.* ◊ *in the ~ She is always in the news.* ⇨ see also FAKE NEWS ⇨ WORDFINDER NOTE at PROGRAMME **3** **the news** a regular television or radio broadcast of the latest news: *to listen to/watch the news* ◊ *Can you put the news on?* ◊ *the nine o'clock news* ◊ *on the ~ I saw it on the news.* **4** a person, thing or event that is considered to be interesting enough to be reported as news: *Pop stars are always news.* ⇨ see also NEWSY

**IDM** **be bad ˈnews (for sb/sth)** to be likely to cause problems: *Central heating is bad news for indoor plants.* **be good ˈnews (for sb/sth)** to be likely to be helpful or give an advantage: *The cut in interest rates is good news for homeowners.* **break the ˈnews (to sb)** to be the first to tell sb some bad news: *There's no easy way to break the news.* **no news is ˈgood news** (*saying*) if there were bad news we would hear it, so as we have heard nothing, it is likely that nothing bad has happened: *I still haven't heard anything about the job, but no news is good news.*

**ˈnews agency** (*also* **ˈpress agency**) *noun* an organization that collects news and supplies it to newspapers and television and radio companies ⇨ WORDFINDER NOTE at JOURNALIST

**ˈnews·agent** /ˈnjuːzeɪdʒənt; *NAmE* ˈnuːz-/ (*BrE*) *noun* **1** (*US* **ˈnews·deal·er**) a person who owns or works in a shop selling newspapers and magazines, and often sweets and cigarettes **2** **newsagent's** (*pl.* **news·agents**) (*also* **ˈpaper shop**) a shop that sells newspapers, magazines, sweets, etc: *I'll go to the newsagent's on my way home.*

**ˈnews·cast** /ˈnjuːzkɑːst; *NAmE* ˈnuːzkæst/ *noun* (*especially NAmE*) a news programme on radio or television

**ˈnews·cast·er** /ˈnjuːzkɑːstə(r); *NAmE* ˈnuːzkæs-/ (*BrE* **ˈnews·read·er**) *noun* a person who reads the news on television or radio

**ˈnews conference** *noun* (*especially NAmE*) = PRESS CONFERENCE

**ˈnews·deal·er** /ˈnjuːzdiːlə(r); *NAmE* ˈnuːz-/ (*US*) (*BrE* **ˈnews·agent**) *noun* **1** a person who owns or works in a shop selling newspapers and magazines, and often sweets and cigarettes **2** (*BrE also* **ˈpaper shop**) a shop that sells newspapers, magazines, sweets, etc. ⇨ see also NEWS STAND

**ˈnews desk** *noun* the department of a newspaper office or a radio or television station where news is received and prepared for printing or broadcasting: *She works on the news desk.*

**ˈnews·feed** /ˈnjuːzfiːd; *NAmE* ˈnuːz-/ *noun* **1** a service that provides regular news to be broadcast or distributed on the internet: *Get the latest tips and stories straight to your newsfeed.* **2** an item of information provided by this service: *I glanced through my newsfeeds.*

**ˈnews·flash** /ˈnjuːzflæʃ; *NAmE* ˈnuːz-/ (*also* **flash**) *noun* (*especially BrE*) a short item of important news that is broadcast on radio or television, often interrupting a programme

**ˈnews·gath·er·ing** /ˈnjuːzgæðərɪŋ; *NAmE* ˈnuːz-/ *noun* [U] the process of doing research on news items, especially ones that will be broadcast on television or printed in a newspaper ▸ **ˈnews·gath·er·er** /ˈnjuːzgæðərə(r); *NAmE* ˈnuːz-/ *noun*

**ˈnews·group** /ˈnjuːzgruːp; *NAmE* ˈnuːz-/ *noun* a site on a computer network, especially the internet, where people can discuss a particular subject and exchange information about it

**ˈnews·let·ter** /ˈnjuːzletə(r); *NAmE* ˈnuːz-/ *noun* a report containing news of the activities of a club or organization that is sent regularly to all its members ⇨ WORDFINDER NOTE at CLUB

**ˈnews·man** /ˈnjuːzmæn; *NAmE* ˈnuːz-/, **ˈnews·woman** /ˈnjuːzwʊmən; *NAmE* ˈnuːz-/ *noun* (*pl.* **-men** /-men/, **-women** /-wɪmɪn/) a journalist who works for a newspaper or a television or radio station: *a crowd of reporters and TV newsmen*

**ˈnews·paper** /ˈnjuːzpeɪpə(r); *NAmE* ˈnuːz-/ *noun* **1** [C] a set of large printed sheets of paper, or a website, containing news, articles, advertisements, etc. and published every day or every week; the organization responsible for producing this: *a daily/weekly newspaper* ◊ *a local/national newspaper* ◊ *an online newspaper* ◊ *a newspaper article/report/headline* ◊ *newspapers and news websites* ◊ *Which newspaper do you read?* ◊ *to publish/own/print a newspaper* ◊ *The newspaper reported on Friday that the boy had been found.* ◊ *in the ~ I read about it in the newspaper.* ◊ *She works for the local newspaper* (= the company that produces it). ⇨ see also PAPER *noun*, QUALITY NEWSPAPER ⇨ WORDFINDER NOTE at JOURNALIST

**WORDFINDER** article, columnist, editorial, feature, headline, journalist, obituary, review, supplement

**2** [U] paper taken from old newspapers: *Wrap all your glasses in newspaper.*

**ˈnews·paper·man** /ˈnjuːzpeɪpəmæn; *NAmE* ˈnuːzpeɪpərm-/, **ˈnews·paper·woman** /ˈnjuːzpeɪpəwʊmən; *NAmE* ˈnuːzpeɪpərwʊ-/ *noun* (*pl.* **-men** /-men/, **-women** /-wɪmɪn/) a journalist who works for a newspaper

**ˈnew·speak** /ˈnjuːspiːk; *NAmE* ˈnuː-/ *noun* [U] language that is not clear or honest, for example the language that is used in political PROPAGANDA

**ˈnews·print** /ˈnjuːzprɪnt; *NAmE* ˈnuːz-/ *noun* [U] the cheap paper that newspapers are printed on

**ˈnews·read·er** /ˈnjuːzriːdə(r); *NAmE* ˈnuːz-/ *noun* (*BrE*) = NEWSCASTER

**ˈnews·reel** /ˈnjuːzriːl; *NAmE* ˈnuːz-/ *noun* a short film of news that was shown in the past in cinemas

**ˈnews·room** /ˈnjuːzruːm; -rʊm; *NAmE* ˈnuːz-/ *noun* the room at a newspaper office or a radio or television station where news is received and prepared for printing or broadcasting

**ˈnews stand** (*NAmE* **news·stand**) /ˈnjuːzstænd; *NAmE* ˈnuːz-/ *noun* a place on the street, at a station, etc. where you can buy newspapers and magazines

**ˈnews ticker** (*also* **ticker**) *noun* a line of text containing news which passes across the screen of a computer or television

**ˈnews·wire** /ˈnjuːzwaɪə(r); *NAmE* ˈnuːz-/ *noun* a service that provides the latest news, for example using the internet

**ˈnews·worthy** /ˈnjuːzwɜːði; *NAmE* ˈnuːzwɜːrði/ *adj.* interesting and important enough to be reported as news

**newsy** /ˈnjuːzi; *NAmE* ˈnuː-/ *adj.* (*informal*) full of news that is interesting and fun to hear or read: *a newsy letter*

**newt** /njuːt; *NAmE* nuːt/ *noun* a small animal with short legs, a long tail and cold blood, that lives both in water and on land (= is an AMPHIBIAN)

**the ˌNew ˈTestament** *noun* [sing.] the second part of the Bible, that describes the life and teachings of Jesus Christ ⇨ compare OLD TESTAMENT

**newˈton** /ˈnjuːtən; *NAmE* ˈnuː-/ *noun* (*abbr.* **N**) (*physics*) a unit of force. One newton is equal to the force that would give a MASS of one KILOGRAM an ACCELERATION (= an increase in speed) of one metre per second per second.

**ˌnew ˈtown** *noun* one of the complete towns that were planned and built in the UK after 1946

**ˌnew ˈwave** *noun* [U, sing.] **1** a group of people who together introduce new styles and ideas in art, music, cinema, etc: *one of the most exciting directors of the Australian new wave* ◇ *new wave films* **2** a style of rock music popular in the 1970s

**the ˌNew ˈWorld** *noun* [sing.] a way of referring to North, Central and South America, used especially in the past ⇨ compare OLD WORLD

**ˌnew ˈyear** (*also* ˌNew ˈYear) *noun* [U, sing.] the beginning of the year: *Happy New Year!* ◇ *We're going to Germany for Christmas and New Year.* ◇ *I'll see you in the new year.* ⇨ see also RESOLUTION
**IDM** **see in the ˌNew ˈYear** | **see the ˌNew ˈYear in** to stay up until midnight on 31 December to celebrate the start of the new year

**ˌNew Year's ˈDay** (*NAmE also* ˌNew ˈYear's) *noun* [U] 1 January

**ˌNew Year's ˈEve** (*NAmE also* ˌNew ˈYear's) *noun* [U] 31 December, especially the evening of that day

**next** ⓞ A1 /nekst/ *adj.*, *adv.*, *noun*
■ *adj.* [only before noun] **1** ⓘ A1 (usually with *the*) coming straight after sb/sth in time, order or space: *The next train to Baltimore is at ten.* ◇ *The next six months will be the hardest.* ◇ *the next chapter* ◇ *Who's next?* ◇ *the woman in the next room* ◇ *I fainted and the next thing I knew I was in the hospital.* ◇ (*informal*) *Round here, you leave school and next thing you know you're married with three kids.* **2** ⓘ A1 (used without *the*) ~ **Monday, week, summer, year,** etc. the Monday, week, etc. immediately following: *Next Thursday is 12 April.* ◇ *Next time I'll bring a book.* ◇ *next month's rent* **HELP** With days of the week, you can also put the day first: *On Friday next, we're going to France.* This is less frequent and sounds more formal.
**IDM** **the ˌnext ˈman, woman, person,** etc. the average person: *I can enjoy a joke as well as the next man, but this is going too far.* ⇨ more at DAY, LUCK *n.*
■ *adv.* **1** ⓘ A1 after sth else; then; afterwards: *What happened next?* ◇ *Next, I heard the sound of voices.* ◇ *What came next was a real shock.* ⇨ LANGUAGE BANK at FIRST, PROCESS¹ **2** ⓘ B1 ~ **best, biggest, most important,** etc … **(after/to sb/sth)** following in the order mentioned: *Jo was the next oldest after Martin.* ◇ *The next best thing to flying is gliding.* **3** used in questions to express surprise: *You're going bungee jumping? Whatever next?*
■ *noun* ⓘ B1 (*also* **the next**) [sing.] a person or thing that is next: *One moment he wasn't there, the next he was.* ◇ *the week after next* ◇ *The next to appear was his wife.*

▼ **WHICH WORD?**

**next / nearest**

- (The) next means 'after this / that one' in time or in a series of events, places or people: *When is your next appointment?* ◇ *Turn left at the next traffic lights.* ◇ *Who's next?* (The) nearest means 'closest' in space: *Where's the nearest supermarket?*
- Notice the difference between the prepositions **nearest to** and **next to**: *Janet's sitting nearest to the window* (= of all the people in the room). ◇ *Sarah's sitting next to the window* (= right beside it). In informal *BrE* **nearest** can be used instead of **nearest to**: *Who's sitting nearest the door?*

---

1049

**nice**

**ˌnext ˈdoor** *adv.*, *adj.*, *noun*
■ *adv.* in the next room, house or building: *The cat is from the house next door.* ◇ *The manager's office is just next door.* ◇ *We live next door to the bank.* ▶ **ˌnext-ˈdoor** *adj.* [only before noun]: *our next-door neighbours* ◇ *the next-door house*
■ *noun* [U + sing. / pl. v.] (*BrE, informal*) the people who live in the house or flat next to yours: *Is that next door's dog?*

**ˌnext of ˈkin** *noun* [C, U] (*pl.* **next of kin**) your closest living relative or relatives: *I'm her next of kin.* ◇ *Her next of kin have been informed.* ◇ *The form must be signed by next of kin.*

**ˈnext to** ⓞ A1 *prep.* **1** ⓘ A1 in or into a position right by sb/sth **SYN** beside: *We sat next to each other.* ⇨ note at NEXT **2** following in order or importance after sb/sth: *Next to skiing my favourite sport is skating.* **3** almost: *Charles knew next to nothing about farming.* ◇ *The horse came next to last* (= the one before the last one) *in the race.* **4** in comparison with sb/sth: *Next to her I felt like a fraud.*

**ˌnext toˈmorrow** *adv.* (*WAfrE*) the day after tomorrow

**nexus** /ˈneksəs/ *noun* [sing.] (*formal*) a complicated series of connections between different things

**Nez Percé** /ˌnez ˈpɜːs; *NAmE* ˈpɜːrs/ *noun* (*pl.* **Nez Percé** or **Nez Percés**) a member of a Native American people, many of whom now live in the US state of Idaho **ORIGIN** From the French for 'pierced nose'.

**NFC** /ˌen ef ˈsiː/ *abbr.* **1 the NFC** (in the US) the National Football Conference (one of the two groups of teams in the National Football League) **2** near field communication (a type of technology that allows communication over short distances between mobile phones and other electronic devices in order to make payments, etc.): *an NFC device / payment*

**NFL** /ˌen ef ˈel/ *abbr.* (in the US) National Football League (the US organization for professional AMERICAN FOOTBALL)

**NGO** /ˌen dʒiː ˈəʊ/ *noun* non-governmental organization (a charity, association, etc. that is independent of government and business)

**ngoma** /əŋˈɡəʊmə/ *EAfrE* [ˈŋɡoma] *noun* **1** [C] a traditional drum from southern or eastern Africa **2** [C, U] (*EAfrE*) a celebration or performance that involves dancing, singing and playing drums

**NHS** /ˌen eɪtʃ ˈes/ *abbr.* National Health Service (the public health service in Britain that provides medical treatment and is paid for by taxes): *an NHS hospital* ◇ *I had the operation done on the NHS* (= paid for by the NHS).

**NI** /ˌen ˈaɪ/ *abbr.* (in the UK) NATIONAL INSURANCE

**niaˈcin** /ˈnaɪəsɪn/ (*also* ˌnicoˈtinˌic ˈacid) *noun* [U] a vitamin of the B group that is found in foods such as milk and meat

**nib** /nɪb/ *noun* the metal point of a pen

**nibˈble** /ˈnɪbl/ *verb*, *noun*
■ *verb* **1** [T, I] to bite sth with small bites, especially food: *~ sth We sat drinking wine and nibbling olives.* ◇ *He nibbled her ear playfully.* ◇ *~ (at / on sth) She took some cake from the tray and nibbled at it.* **2** [I] ~ **(at sth)** to show a slight interest in an offer, idea, etc: *He nibbled at the idea, but would not make a definite decision.*
**PHRV** **nibble aˈway at sth** to take away small amounts of sth, so that the total amount is gradually reduced **SYN** erode: *Inflation is nibbling away at spending power.*
■ *noun* **1** [C] a small bite of sth, especially food **2** **nibbles** [pl.] small things to eat with a drink before a meal or at a party

**nice** ⓞ A1 /naɪs/ *adj.* ( **nicer**, **nicest**)
• PLEASANT / ATTRACTIVE **1** ⓘ A1 pleasant or attractive: *a nice day / smile / place* ◇ *nice weather* ◇ *Did you have a nice time?* ◇ *You look very nice.* ◇ *We all had the flu last week—it wasn't very nice.* ◇ *'Do you want to come, too?' 'Yes, that would be nice.'* ◇ *The nicest thing about her is that she never criticizes us.* ◇ *It was a nice touch to end the film as it started.* ◇ **it is ~ to do sth** *It's nice to know that somebody appreciates what I do.* ◇ *Nice to meet you!* (= a friendly GREETING when you meet sb for the first time) ◇ *It is*

# nice-looking  1050

~ doing sth *It's been nice meeting you.* ◊ *it is ~ that ... It's nice that you can come with us.* ◊ *it would be ~ if ... It would be nice if he moved to London.* **2** used before adjectives or adverbs to emphasize how pleasant sth is: *a nice hot bath* ◊ *a nice long walk* ◊ *It's a **nice** little place you have here.* ◊ *~ and ... He seemed nice and friendly.* ◊ *It was nice and warm yesterday.* ◊ *Everyone arrived nice and early.* **HELP** **Nice and** with another adjective cannot be used before a noun: *a nice and quiet place*.
- **KIND/FRIENDLY 3** kind; friendly: *Our new neighbours are very nice.* ◊ *He's a really nice guy.* ◊ *She's one of the nicest people you'll ever meet.* ◊ *~ to sb Be nice to me. I'm not feeling well.* ◊ *~ of sb (to do sth) It was nice of them to invite us.* ◊ *~ about sth I complained to the manager and he was very nice about it.* ◊ *I asked him **in the nicest possible way** to put his cigarette out.* **OPP** nasty ⊃ see also MR NICE GUY
- **NOT NICE 4** *(ironic)* bad or unpleasant: *That's a nice thing to say!* ◊ *That's a nice way to speak to your mother!*
- **SMALL DETAILS 5** *(formal)* involving a very small detail or difference **SYN** **subtle**: *a nice point of law (= one that is difficult to decide)* ▶ **nice·ness** *noun* [U]: *In some professions, niceness does not get you very far.*
**IDM** **as nice as ˈpie** *(informal)* very kind and friendly, especially when you are not expecting it **have a nice ˈday!** *(informal, especially NAmE)* a friendly way of saying goodbye, especially to customers **make ˈnice (with sb)** *(NAmE, informal)* to be pleasant or polite to sb, especially when you do not really want to: *Cole and his opponent made nice for the cameras at the press event.* **nice ˈone!** *(BrE, informal)* used to show you are pleased when sth good has happened or sb has said sth funny: *You got the job? Nice one!* **nice ˈwork!** *(informal, especially BrE)* used to show you are pleased when sb has done sth well: *You did a good job today. Nice work, James!* **nice work if you can ˈget it** *(informal)* used when you wish that you had sb's success or good luck and think they have achieved it with little effort

▼ **VOCABULARY BUILDING**

### Nice and very nice

Instead of saying that something is **nice** or **very nice**, try to use more precise and interesting adjectives to describe things:
- **pleasant**/**perfect**/**beautiful** weather
- a **cosy**/a **comfortable**/an **attractive** room
- a **pleasant**/an **interesting**/an **enjoyable** experience
- **expensive**/**fashionable**/**smart** clothes
- a **kind**/a **charming**/an **interesting** man
- The party was **fun**.

In conversation you can also use **great**, **wonderful**, **lovely** and (in BrE) **brilliant**: *The party was great.* ◊ *We had a brilliant weekend.*
⊃ note at GOOD

**ˈnice-looking** *adj.* attractive: *What a nice-looking man!*

**nice·ly** /ˈnaɪsli/ *adv.* **1** in an attractive or acceptable way; well: *The room was nicely furnished.* ◊ *The plants are coming along nicely (= growing well).* **2** in a kind, friendly or polite way: *If you ask her nicely she might say yes.* **3** *(formal)* carefully; exactly: *His novels nicely describe life in Britain between the wars.*
**IDM** **do ˈnicely 1** to be making good progress: *Her new business is doing very nicely.* **2** to be acceptable: *Tomorrow at ten will do nicely (= will be a good time).*

**ni·cety** /ˈnaɪsəti/ *noun (pl. -ies) (formal)* **1** [C, usually pl.] the small details or points of difference, especially relating to the correct way of behaving or of doing things **2** [U] *(formal)* the quality of being very detailed or careful about sth **SYN** **precision**: *the nicety of his argument*

**niche** /niːʃ, nɪtʃ/ *noun, adj.*
- *noun* **1** a comfortable or suitable role, job, way of life, etc: *He eventually found his niche in sports journalism.* **2** *(business)* a small section of the market for a particular kind of product or service: *They spotted a niche in the market, with no serious competition.* **3** a small hollow place, especially in a wall to contain a statue, etc., or in the side of a hill **SYN** **nook** **4** *(biology)* a position or role taken by a kind of living thing within its community. Different living things may have the same niche in different places, for example ANTELOPES in Africa and KANGAROOS in Australia.
- *adj.* *(business)* (of products, services or interests) appealing to only a small section of the population: *a niche market/product* ◊ *the development of niche marketing (= aiming products at particular groups)*

**nick** /nɪk/ *noun, verb*
- *noun* **1** **the nick** [sing.] *(BrE, slang)* a prison or a police station: *He'll end up in the nick.* **2** a small cut in the edge or surface of sth
**IDM** **in good, bad, etc. ˈnick** *(BrE, informal)* in good, bad, etc. condition or health **in the nick of ˈtime** *(informal)* at the very last moment; just before sth bad happens, so that you manage to avoid it, but only just
- *verb* **1** [T] *~ sth/yourself* to make a small cut in sth: *He nicked himself while shaving.* **2** [T] *~ sth (from sb/sth)* *(BrE, informal)* to steal sth **SYN** **pinch**: *Who nicked my pen?* **3** [T] *(BrE, informal)* to arrest sb for committing a crime: *You're nicked!* ◊ **be nicked for sth** *I was nicked for speeding.* **4** [I] + **adv./prep.** *(AustralE, NZE, informal)* to go somewhere quickly

**nickel** /ˈnɪkl/ *noun* **1** [U] *(symb. Ni)* a chemical element. Nickel is a hard silver-white metal used in making some types of steel and other ALLOYS. **2** [C] a coin of the US and Canada worth 5 cents

**nick·name** /ˈnɪkneɪm/ *noun, verb*
- *noun* an informal, often humorous, name for a person that is connected with their real name, their personality or appearance, or with sth they have done
- *verb* [often passive] *~ sb/sth + noun* to give a nickname to sb/sth: *She was nicknamed 'The Ice Queen'.*

**nico·tine** /ˈnɪkətiːn/ *noun* [U] a poisonous substance in TOBACCO that people become ADDICTED to, so that it is difficult to stop smoking

**nico·tin·ic acid** /ˌnɪkətɪnɪk ˈæsɪd/ *noun* [U] = NIACIN

**niece** /niːs/ *noun* the daughter of your brother or sister; the daughter of your husband's or wife's brother or sister ⊃ compare NEPHEW

**nifty** /ˈnɪfti/ *adj.* *(informal)* **1** accurate and showing skill: *There's some nifty guitar work on his latest album.* **2** practical; working well **SYN** **handy**: *a nifty little gadget for slicing cucumbers*

**nig·gard·ly** /ˈnɪɡədli; NAmE -ɡərd-/ *adj.* *(formal, disapproving)* **1** unwilling to be generous with money, time, etc. **SYN** **mean** **2** (of a gift or an amount of money) not worth much and given unwillingly **SYN** **miserly**

**nig·ger** /ˈnɪɡə(r)/ *noun* *(taboo, slang)* a very offensive word for a black person

**nig·gle** /ˈnɪɡl/ *noun, verb*
- *noun* **1** *(BrE)* a small criticism or complaint **2** a slight feeling, such as worry, doubt, etc. that does not go away: *a niggle of doubt* **3** a slight pain: *He gets the occasional niggle in his right shoulder.*
- *verb* **1** [I, T] to annoy sb slightly; to make sb slightly worried **SYN** **bother**: *~ at sb A doubt niggled at her.* **it niggles sb that...** *(BrE): It niggled him that she had not phoned back.* | *~ sb (BrE): Something was niggling her.* **2** [I] *~ (about/over sth)* to argue about sth unimportant; to criticize sb for sth that is unimportant **SYN** **quibble**

**nig·gling** /ˈnɪɡlɪŋ/ *(also less frequent nig·gly /ˈnɪɡli/) adj.* **1** used to describe a slight feeling of worry or pain that does not go away: *She had niggling doubts about their relationship.* **2** not important **SYN** **petty**: *niggling details*

**nigh** /naɪ/ *adv.* **1** *~ on (old-fashioned)* almost; nearly: *They've lived in that house for nigh on 30 years.* ⊃ see also WELL-NIGH **2** *(old use or literary)* near: *Winter was drawing nigh.*

**night** /naɪt/ *noun* [U, C] **1** the time between one day and the next when it is dark, when people usually sleep: **at~** *These animals only come out at night.* ◊ **by~** *They sleep by day and hunt by night.* ◊ *in the~ Does your baby still wake in the night?* ◊ *She woke up in the middle of the night.* ◊ *The accident happened on Friday night.* ◊ **on the~of...** *on the night of 10 January/January 10* ◊ *Did you*

hear the storm **last night**? ◊ *I lay awake **all night**.* ◊ *Where did you spend the night?* ◊ *You're welcome to **stay the night** here.* ◊ *What is he doing calling **at this time of night**?* ◊ *You'll feel better after you've had **a good night's sleep**.* ◊ *a sleepless night* ◊ *The trip was for ten nights.* ◊ **per~** *The hotel costs €95 per person per night.* ◊ *the night train/boat/flight* ◊ *the night sky* ◊ **Night fell** (= it became dark). ⊃ see also NIGHTS ⊃ HOMOPHONES *at* KNIGHT **2** 🅰 *the evening until you go to bed: Let's go out **on Saturday night**.* ◊ *Bill's parents came for dinner **last night**.* ◊ *She doesn't like to walk home **late at night**.* ◊ *I saw her in town **the other night** (= a few nights ago).* ◊ *He came round **tomorrow night**.* ◊ *He had plans to spend **a quiet night at home**.* ⊃ see also GOODNIGHT **3** *an evening when a special event happens: the **first/opening night** (= of a play, film, etc.).* ◊ *We'll be up late **on election night**.* ◊ *a karaoke night* ◊ *an Irish/Scottish, etc. night (= with Irish/Scottish music, entertainment, etc.).* ⊃ see also STAG NIGHT ▸ **nights** *adv.: He can't get used to working nights (= at night).*
🄸🄳🄼 ▸ **have an early / a late 'night** *to go to bed earlier or later than usual: I've had a lot of late nights recently.* **have a good / bad 'night** *to sleep well/badly during the night* **have a night on the 'tiles** (*BrE, informal*) *to stay out late enjoying yourself* **,night and 'day** (*also* **,day and 'night**) *all the time; continuously: The machines are kept running night and day.* **,night 'night** *used especially by children or to children, to mean 'goodnight': Night night, sleep tight!* **a night 'out** *an evening that you spend enjoying yourself away from home: They enjoy a night out occasionally.* ⊃ more at ALL RIGHT *adj.*, DANCE *v.*, DAY, DEAD *n.*, MORNING *n.*, SPEND *v.*, STILL *adj.*, THING

**night·cap** /ˈnaɪtkæp/ *noun* **1** *a drink, usually containing alcohol, taken before going to bed* **2** *(in the past) a soft cap worn in bed*

**night·clothes** /ˈnaɪtkləʊðz/ *noun* [pl.] *clothes that you wear in bed*

**night·club** /ˈnaɪtklʌb/ *noun a place that is open late in the evening where people can go to dance, drink, etc.*

**night·dress** /ˈnaɪtdres/ (*BrE*) (*NAmE or old-fashioned* **nightgown**) (*also informal* **nightie** *BrE, NAmE*) *noun a long loose piece of clothing like a thin dress, worn by a woman or girl in bed*

**'night duty** *noun* [U] *work that people have to do at night, for example in a hospital: to be on night duty*

**night·fall** /ˈnaɪtfɔːl/ *noun* [U] (*formal or literary*) *the time in the evening when it becomes dark* 🆂🆈🅽 **dusk**

**night·gown** /ˈnaɪtɡaʊn/ *noun* (*NAmE or old-fashioned*) = NIGHTDRESS

**nightie** /ˈnaɪti/ *noun* (*informal*) = NIGHTDRESS

**night·in·gale** /ˈnaɪtɪŋɡeɪl/ *noun a small brown bird, the male of which has a beautiful song*

**night·life** /ˈnaɪtlaɪf/ *noun* [U] *entertainment that is available in the evening and at night*

**'night light** *noun a light or CANDLE that is left on at night*

**night·ly** /ˈnaɪtli/ *adj. happening every night: a nightly news bulletin* ▸ **night·ly** *adv.*

**night·mare** 🛈 🅱🟰 /ˈnaɪtmeə(r); *NAmE* -mer/ *noun* **1** 🅱🟰 *a dream that is very frightening or unpleasant: He still has nightmares about the accident.* **2** 🅱🟰 *an experience that is very frightening and unpleasant, or very difficult to deal with: The trip turned into a nightmare when they both got sick.* ◊ (*informal*) *Nobody knows what's going on—it's a nightmare!* ◊ (*informal*) *Filling in all those forms was a nightmare.* ◊ *Losing a child is most people's **worst nightmare**.* ◊ *If it goes ahead, it will be the **nightmare scenario** (= the worst thing that could happen).* ◊ *~ **for sb** What a nightmare for you!* ▸ **night·mar·ish** /ˈnaɪtmeərɪʃ; *NAmE* -mer-/ *adj.: nightmarish living conditions*

**'night owl** *noun* (*informal*) *a person who enjoys staying up late at night*

**'night school** *noun* [U, C] (*old-fashioned*) *classes for adults, held in the evening*

**night·shirt** /ˈnaɪtʃɜːt; *NAmE* -ʃɜːrt/ *noun a long loose shirt worn in bed*

**night·spot** /ˈnaɪtspɒt; *NAmE* -spɑːt/ *noun* (*informal*) *a place people go to for entertainment at night* 🆂🆈🅽 **nightclub**

1051 **ninth**

**night·stand** /ˈnaɪtstænd/ (*also* **'night table**) (*both NAmE*) *noun* = BEDSIDE TABLE

**night·stick** /ˈnaɪtstɪk/ *noun* (*NAmE*) = BATON (1)

**'night-time** *noun* [U] *the time when it is dark: This area can be very noisy at night-time.*

**night·watch·man** /ˌnaɪtˈwɒtʃmən; *NAmE* -ˈwɑːtʃ-/ *noun* (*pl.* **-men** /-mən/) *a man whose job is to guard a building such as a factory at night*

**night·wear** /ˈnaɪtweə(r); *NAmE* -wer/ *noun* [U] (*used especially in shops/stores*) *clothes that are worn in bed*

**ni·hil·ism** /ˈnaɪɪlɪzəm/ *noun* [U] (*philosophy*) *the belief that life has no meaning or purpose and that religious and moral principles have no value* ▸ **ni·hil·is·tic** /ˌnaɪɪˈlɪstɪk/ *adj.: Her latest play is a nihilistic vision of the world of the future.*

**ni·hil·ist** /ˈnaɪɪlɪst/ *noun a person who believes in nihilism*

**nil** /nɪl/ *noun, adj.*
■ *noun* [U] (*especially BrE*) *the number 0, especially as the score in some games* 🆂🆈🅽 **zero**: *Newcastle beat Leeds four nil/by four goals to nil.*
■ *adj.* [not before noun] *not existing: The doctors rated her chances as nil (= there was no chance).*

**nim·ble** /ˈnɪmbl/ *adj.* (**nim·bler** /-blə(r)/, **nim·blest** /-blɪst/) **1** *able to move quickly and easily* 🆂🆈🅽 **agile**: *You need nimble fingers for that job.* ◊ *She was extremely nimble on her feet.* **2** *able to think, react and adapt quickly: a nimble mind* ▸ **nim·bly** /-bli/ *adv.*

**nim·bus** /ˈnɪmbəs/ *noun* (*specialist*) **1** [C, usually sing., U] *a large grey rain cloud* **2** [C, usually sing.] *a circle of light*

**nimby** /ˈnɪmbi/ *noun* (*pl.* **-ies**) (*disapproving, humorous*) *a person who claims to be in favour of a new development or project, but objects if it is too near their home and will affect them in some way* 🄾🅁🄸🄶🄸🄽 *Formed from the first letters of 'not in my back yard'.*

**nin·com·poop** /ˈnɪŋkəmpuːp/ *noun* (*old-fashioned, informal*) *a stupid person*

**nine** 🛈 🅰 /naɪn/ *number* **9** 🄷🄴🄻🄿 *There are examples of how to use numbers at the entry for **five**.*
🄸🄳🄼 ▸ **have nine 'lives** (*especially of a cat*) *to be very lucky in dangerous situations* **a ,nine days' 'wonder** *a person or thing that makes people excited for a short time but does not last very long* **,nine times out of 'ten** *almost every time: I'm always emailing her, but nine times out of ten she doesn't reply.* **,nine to 'five** *the normal working hours in an office: I work nine to five.* ◊ *a nine-to-five job* **the ,whole ,nine 'yards** (*informal, especially NAmE*) *everything, or a situation which includes everything: When Dan cooks dinner he always goes the whole nine yards, with three courses and a choice of dessert.* ⊃ more at CLOUD *n.*, DRESSED, POSSESSION

**nine·teen** 🛈 🅰 /ˌnaɪnˈtiːn/ *number* **19** ▸ **nineteenth** /-ˈtiːnθ/ *ordinal number, noun*
🄸🄳🄼 ▸ **talk, etc. nineteen to the 'dozen** (*BrE, informal*) *to talk, etc. without stopping: She was chatting away, nineteen to the dozen.*

**ninety** 🛈 🅰 /ˈnaɪnti/ **1** 🛈 🅰 *number* **90** **2** *noun the* **nineties** [pl.] *numbers, years or temperatures from 90 to 99: The temperature must be in the nineties today.* ▸ **nineti·eth** /-əθ/ *ordinal number, noun* 🄷🄴🄻🄿 *There are examples of how to use ordinal numbers at the entry for **fifth**.*
🄸🄳🄼 ▸ **in your nineties** *between the ages of 90 and 99* **,ninety-nine ,times out of a 'hundred** *almost always*

**ninja** /ˈnɪndʒə/ *noun* (*pl.* **ninjas** *or* **ninja**) (*from Japanese*) *a person trained in traditional Japanese skills of fighting and moving quietly*

**ninny** /ˈnɪni/ *noun* (*pl.* **-ies**) (*old-fashioned, informal*) *a stupid person*

**ninth** /naɪnθ/ *ordinal number, noun*
■ *ordinal number* 9th 🄷🄴🄻🄿 *There are examples of how to use ordinal numbers at the entry for **fifth**.*
■ *noun each of nine equal parts of sth*

# niobium

**nio·bium** /naɪˈəʊbiəm/ *noun* [U] (*symb.* **Nb**) a chemical element. Niobium is a silver-grey metal used in steel ALLOYS.

**nip** /nɪp/ *verb*, *noun*
- *verb* (**-pp-**) **1** [T, I] to give sb/sth a quick painful bite or pressing their skin together hard with your finger and THUMB: *~sth He winced as the dog nipped his ankle.* ◊ *~ at sth She nipped at my arm.* **2** [I, T] (of cold, wind, etc.) to harm or damage sth: *~at sth The icy wind nipped at our faces.* ◊ *~sth The new leaves had been nipped by a late frost.* **3** [I] + *adv./prep.* (*BrE*, *informal*) to go somewhere quickly and/or for only a short time SYN **pop**: *He's just nipped out to the bank.* ◊ *A car nipped in (= got in quickly) ahead of me.*
- **IDM** **nip sth in the 'bud** to stop sth when it has just begun because you can see that problems will come from it
- **PHRV** **nip sth↔off** to remove a part of sth with your finger or with a tool
- *noun* **1** the act of giving sb a small bite or pressing their skin together hard with your finger and THUMB **2** (*informal*) a feeling of cold: *There was a real nip in the air.* ⊃ see also NIPPY **3** (*informal*) a small drink of strong alcohol

**nip and 'tuck** *adj.*, *adv.*, *noun*
- *adj.*, *adv.* if a race or competition is **nip and tuck**, it is a very close contest with the competitors almost level with each other: *The presidential contest is nip and tuck.* ⊃ compare NECK AND NECK (WITH SB/STH)
- *noun* (*informal*) a medical operation in which skin is removed or made tighter to make sb look younger or more attractive, especially a FACELIFT

**nip·per** /ˈnɪpə(r)/ *noun* (*informal*) a small child

**nip·ple** /ˈnɪpl/ *noun* **1** either of the two small round dark parts on a person's chest. Babies can drink milk from their mother's breasts through the nipples. ⊃ VISUAL VOCAB page V1 **2** (*NAmE*) (*BrE* **teat**) the rubber part at the end of a baby's bottle that the baby SUCKS on with its lips and tongue in order to get milk, etc. from the bottle **3** a small metal, plastic or rubber object that is like a nipple in shape with a small hole in the end, especially one that is used as part of a machine to direct oil, etc. into a particular place: *a grease nipple*

**nippy** /ˈnɪpi/ *adj.* **1** (*BrE*) able to move quickly and easily: *a nippy little sports car* **2** (*informal*) (of the weather) cold

**niqab** /nɪˈkɑːb/ *noun* a piece of cloth that covers the face but not usually the eyes, worn in public by some Muslim women

**nir·vana** /nɪəˈvɑːnə; *NAmE* nɪrˈvɑː-/ *noun* [U] (in the religion of Buddhism) the state of peace and happiness that a person achieves after giving up all personal desires

**nit** /nɪt/ *noun* **1** the egg or young form of a LOUSE (= a small insect that lives in human hair) **2** (*BrE*, *informal*) a stupid person

**nite** /naɪt/ *noun* (*informal*) non-standard spelling of 'night': *It's Movie Nite every Monday.*

**nit·pick·ing** /ˈnɪtpɪkɪŋ/ *noun* [U] (*informal*, *disapproving*) the habit of finding small mistakes in sb's work or paying too much attention to small details that are not important
▶ **nit·picker** *noun* **nit·pick·ing** *adj.* [only before noun]

**ni·trate** /ˈnaɪtreɪt/ *noun* [U, C] (*chemistry*) a COMPOUND containing NITROGEN and OXYGEN. There are several different nitrates and they are used especially to make soil better for growing crops: *We need to cut nitrate levels in water.*

**ni·tric acid** /ˌnaɪtrɪk ˈæsɪd/ *noun* [U] (*chemistry*) (*symb.* HNO₃) a powerful clear substance that can destroy most substances and is used to make EXPLOSIVES and other chemical products

**ni·trite** /ˈnaɪtraɪt/ *noun* [U, C] (*chemistry*) a COMPOUND containing NITROGEN and OXYGEN. There are several different nitrites.

**ni·tro·gen** /ˈnaɪtrədʒən/ *noun* [U] (*symb.* **N**) a chemical element. Nitrogen is a gas that is found in large quantities in the earth's atmosphere. ▶ **ni·tro·gen·ous** /naɪˈtrɒdʒənəs; *NAmE* -ˈtrɑːdʒ-/ *adj.*

**nitrogen di'oxide** *noun* [U] (*chemistry*) a brown poisonous gas. Nitrogen dioxide is formed when some metals are DISSOLVED in NITRIC ACID.

**nitro·gly·cer·ine** /ˌnaɪtrəʊˈglɪsərɪn; *BrE also* -riːn/ (*especially BrE*) (*US usually* **nitro·gly·cerin** /ˌnaɪtrəʊˈglɪsərɪn/) *noun* [U] a powerful liquid EXPLOSIVE

**ni·trous oxide** /ˌnaɪtrəs ˈɒksaɪd; *NAmE* ˈɑːk-/ (*also informal* **'laughing gas**) *noun* [U] a gas used especially in the past by dentists to prevent you from feeling pain

**the nitty-gritty** /ðə ˌnɪti ˈɡrɪti/ *noun* [sing.] (*informal*) the basic or most important details of an issue or a situation: *Time ran out before we could get down to the real nitty-gritty.*

**nit·wit** /ˈnɪtwɪt/ *noun* (*informal*) a stupid person

**nivas** /ˈnɪvɑːs/ *noun* (*pl.* **nivases**) (*IndE*) a building where people live or stay, such as a house, a block of flats/apartment building, a hotel, etc.

**nix** /nɪks/ *verb*, *noun*
- *verb* *~sth* (*NAmE*, *informal*) to prevent sth from happening by saying 'no' to it
- *noun* [U] (*NAmE*, *informal*) nothing

**NLP** /ˌen el ˈpiː/ *abbr.* NATURAL LANGUAGE PROCESSING

**no** 0̸ A1 /nəʊ/ *exclamation*, *det.*, *adv.*, *noun*
- *exclamation* **1** A1 used to give a negative reply or statement: *Just say yes or no.* ◊ *'Are you ready?' 'No, I'm not.'* ◊ *Sorry, the answer's no.* ◊ *'Another drink?' 'No, thanks.'* ◊ *It's about 70—no, I'm wrong—80 kilometres from Rome.* ◊ *No! Don't touch it! It's hot.* ◊ *'It was Tony.' 'No, you're wrong. It was Ted.'* ◊ *'It's not very good, is it?' 'No, you're right, it isn't (= I agree).'* **2** A1 used to express shock or surprise at what sb has said: *'She's had an accident.' 'Oh no!'* ◊ *'I'm leaving!' 'No!'*
- **IDM** **not take no for an answer** to refuse to accept that sb does not want sth, will not do sth, etc: *You're coming and I won't take no for an answer!* ⊃ more at YES exclamation
- *det.* **1** A1 not one; not any; not a: *No student is to leave the room.* ◊ *I have no meetings this morning.* ◊ *There's no bread left.* ◊ *No two days are the same.* ⊃ see also NO ONE **2** A1 used, for example on notices, to say that sth is not allowed: *No smoking!* **3** used to express the opposite of what is mentioned: *She's no fool (= she's intelligent).* ◊ *It was no easy matter (= it was difficult).* **4** *there's ~ doing sth* used to say that it is impossible to do sth: *There's no telling what will happen next.*
- *adv.* used before adjectives and adverbs to mean 'not': *She's feeling no better this morning.* ◊ *Reply by no later than 21 July.*
- *noun* (*pl.* **noes** /nəʊz/) **1** an answer that shows you do not agree with an idea, a statement, etc.; a person who says 'no': *Can't you give me a straight yes or no?* ◊ *When we took a vote there were nine yesses and three noes.* ◊ *I'll put you down as a no.* **2 the noes** [pl.] the total number of people voting 'no' in a formal debate, for example in a parliament: *The noes have it (= more people have voted against sth than for it).* OPP **ayes**

**No.** *abbr.* **1** (*also* **no.**) (*BrE also* **No** , **no**) (*pl.* **Nos**, **nos**) number: *Room No. 145* **2** (*NAmE*) north; northern

**Noah's ark** /ˌnəʊəz ˈɑːk; *NAmE* ˈɑːrk/ *noun* = ARK

**no-'ball** *noun* (in CRICKET) a ball that is BOWLED (= thrown) in a way that is not allowed and which means that a RUN (= a point) is given to the other team

**Nobel Prize** /ˌnəʊbel ˈpraɪz/ *noun* one of six international prizes given each year for excellent work in physics, chemistry, medicine, literature, ECONOMICS and work towards world peace

**no·bil·ity** /nəʊˈbɪləti/ *noun* **1 the nobility** [sing. + sing./pl. v.] people of high social position who have titles such as that of DUKE or DUCHESS SYN **aristocracy 2** [U] (*formal*) the quality of being noble in character

**noble** B2 C1 /ˈnəʊbl/ *adj.*, *noun*
- *adj.* (**no·bler** /-blə(r)/, **no·blest** /-blɪst/) **1** C1 having or showing fine personal qualities that people admire, such as courage, HONESTY and care for others: *a noble leader* ◊ *noble ideals* ◊ *He died for a noble cause.* OPP **ignoble** **2** C1 belonging to a family of high social rank (= belonging to the nobility) SYN **aristocratic**: *a man of noble birth* **3** very impressive in size or quality SYN **splendid**: *a noble*

building ▶ **nobly** /-bli/ adv.: *She bore the disappointment nobly.* ◇ *to be nobly born*
- **noun** a person who comes from a family of high social rank; a member of the nobility **SYN** aristocrat

**noble 'gas** (*also* **inert 'gas, rare 'gas**) *noun* (*chemistry*) any of a group of gases that do not react with other chemicals. ARGON, HELIUM, KRYPTON and NEON are noble gases.

**noble·man** /ˈnəʊblmən/, **noble·woman** /ˈnəʊblwʊmən/ *noun* (*pl.* **-men** /-mən/, **-women** /-wɪmɪn/) a person from a family of high social rank; a member of the NOBILITY **SYN** aristocrat

**no·blesse ob·lige** /nəʊˌbles əˈbliːʒ/ *noun* [U] (*from French*) the idea that people who have special advantages of wealth, etc. should help other people who do not have these advantages

**no·body** ❶ **A1** /ˈnəʊbədi/ *pron., noun*
- **pron.** **A1** = NO ONE: *Nobody knew what to say.* **HELP** **Nobody** is more common than **no one** in spoken English. ⊃ compare ANYBODY, EVERYBODY, SOMEBODY
- **noun** (*pl.* **-ies**) a person who has no importance or influence **SYN** nonentity: *She rose from being a nobody to being a superstar.* ⊃ compare SOMEONE

**no-'brain·er** *noun* (*informal*) a decision or a problem that you do not need to think about much because it is obvious what you should do

**no-'claims bonus** (*also* **no-'claim bonus, no-'claim(s) discount**) *noun* (*all BrE*) a reduction in the cost of your insurance because you made no claims in the previous year ⊃ WORDFINDER NOTE at INSURANCE

**noc·tur·nal** /nɒkˈtɜːnl; *NAmE* nɑːkˈtɜːrnl/ *adj.* **1** (of animals) active at night **OPP** diurnal **2** (*formal*) happening during the night: *a nocturnal visit*

**noc·turne** /ˈnɒktɜːn; *NAmE* ˈnɑːktɜːrn/ *noun* a short piece of music in a romantic style, especially for the piano

**Nod** /nɒd; *NAmE* nɑːd/ *noun* [U] **IDM** see LAND *n.*

**nod** ❷ **C1** /nɒd; *NAmE* nɑːd/ *verb, noun*
- **verb** (**-dd-**) **1** ❷ **C1** [I, T] if you **nod, nod** your head or your head **nods**, you move your head up and down to show agreement, understanding, etc: *I asked him if he would help me and he nodded.* ◇ *Her head nodded in agreement.* ◇ **~ sth** *He nodded his head sympathetically.* ◇ *She nodded approval.* **2** ❷ **C1** [I, T] to move your head down and up once to say hello or goodbye to sb or to give them a sign to do sth: **~ (to/at sb)** *The president nodded to the crowd as he passed in the motorcade.* ◇ **~ to/at sb to do sth** *She nodded at him to begin speaking* ◇ **~ sth (to/at sb)** *to nod a greeting* **3** ❷ **C1** [I] **+ adv./prep.** to move your head in the direction of sb/sth to show that you are talking about them/it: *I asked where Steve was and she nodded in the direction of the kitchen.* **4** [I] to let your head fall forward when you are sleeping in a chair: *He sat nodding in front of the fire.*
**PHR V** **nod 'off** (*informal*) to fall asleep for a short time while you are sitting in a chair
- **noun** a small quick movement of the head down and up again: *to give a nod of approval/agreement/encouragement* **IDM** **get the 'nod** (*informal*) to be chosen for sth; to be given permission or approval to do sth: *He got the nod from the team manager* (= he was chosen for the team). **give sb/sth the 'nod** (*informal*) **1** to give permission for sth; to agree to sth: *We've been given the nod to expand the business.* ◇ *I hope he'll give the nod to the plan.* **2** to choose sb for sth **a ˌnod and a 'wink** | **a ˌnod is as good as a 'wink** used to say that a suggestion or a HINT will be understood, without anything more being said: *Everything could be done by a nod and a wink.* **a (passing) nod to sth** something that you do or say to acknowledge the importance or influence of sth: *The house is white, in a passing nod to Greek tradition.* **on the 'nod** (*BrE, informal*) if a proposal is accepted **on the nod**, it is accepted without any discussion

**node** /nəʊd/ *noun* **1** (*biology*) a place on the STEM of a plant from which a branch or leaf grows **2** (*biology*) a small SWELLING (= an area that is larger and rounder than normal) on a root or branch **3** a point at which two lines or systems meet or cross: *a network node* **4** (*computing*) a piece of equipment such as a computer, that is attached to a network **5** (*anatomy*) a small hard mass of TISSUE,

---

1053  **noisy**

especially near a JOINT in the human body: *a lymph node* ▶ **nodal** /ˈnəʊdl/ *adj.*

**nod·ule** /ˈnɒdjuːl; *NAmE* ˈnɑːdʒuːl/ *noun* a small round mass of cells or SWELLING, especially on a plant

**Noel** /nəʊˈel/ *noun* [C, U] a word for 'Christmas' used especially in songs or on cards: *Joyful Noel*

**noes** /nəʊz/ *pl.* of NO

**no-'fault** *adj.* [only before noun] (*law, especially NAmE*) not involving a decision as to who is to blame for sth: *no-fault insurance* (= in which the insurance company pays for damage, etc. without asking whose fault it was)

**no-'fly zone** *noun* an area above a country where planes from other countries are not allowed to fly, especially during a war

**no-'frills** *adj.* [only before noun] (especially of a service or product) including only the basic features, without anything that is unnecessary, especially things added to make sth more attractive or comfortable: *a no-frills airline*

**no-'go area** *noun* (especially *BrE*) an area, especially in a city, which is dangerous for people to enter, or that the police or army do not enter, often because it is controlled by a violent group: *Some clubs are no-go areas for people over 30.* ◇ (*figurative*) *This subject is definitely a no-go area* (= we must not discuss it).

**no-'good** *adj.* [only before noun] (*slang*) (of a person) bad; not helpful or useful

**no-'hitter** *noun* (*NAmE*) a baseball game in which the PITCHER (= the player who throws the ball) does not allow the players on the opposing team to get any hits

**no-'hoper** *noun* (*informal*) a person or an animal that is considered very unlikely to be successful

**noir** /nwɑː(r)/ *noun* [U, C] a type of film, fiction or drama in which there are strong feelings of fear or evil; a film, etc. made in this way: *The scene was classic noir, with a unique mix of shocking violence and twisted humour.* ⊃ see also FILM NOIR

**noise** ❶ **A2** /nɔɪz/ *noun* **1** ❷ **A2** [C, U] a sound, especially when it is loud, unpleasant or frightening: *a rattling noise* ◇ *What's that noise?* ◇ *I heard a loud noise and turned around.* ◇ *Don't make a noise.* ◇ *They were making too much noise.* ◇ *I was woken by the noise of a car starting up.* ◇ *to reduce noise levels* ◇ **above the** ~ *We had to shout above the noise of the traffic.* ⊃ see also WHITE NOISE **2** [U] (*specialist*) extra electrical or electronic signals that are not part of the signal that is being broadcast or TRANSMITTED and which may damage it **3** [U] information that is not wanted and that can make it difficult for the important or useful information to be seen clearly: *There is some noise in the data which needs to be reduced.*
**IDM** **make a 'noise (about sth)** (*informal*) to complain loudly **make 'noises (about sth)** (*informal*) **1** to talk in an indirect way about sth that you think you might do: *The company has been making noises about closing several factories.* **2** to complain about sth **make soothing, encouraging, reassuring, etc. noises** to make remarks of the kind mentioned, even when that is not what you really think: *He made all the right noises at the meeting yesterday* (= said what people wanted to hear). ⊃ more at BIG *adj.*

▼ **WHICH WORD?**

**noise / sound**
- **Noise** is usually loud and unpleasant. It can be countable or uncountable: *Try not to make so much noise.* ◇ *What a terrible noise!*
- **Sound** is a countable noun and means something that you hear: *All she could hear was the sound of the waves.* You do not use words like *much* or *a lot of* with **sound**.

**noise·less** /ˈnɔɪzləs/ *adj.* (*formal*) making little or no noise **SYN** silent: *He moved with noiseless steps.* ▶ **noise·less·ly** *adv.*

**noisy** ❶ **A2** /ˈnɔɪzi/ *adj.* (**nois·ier, nois·iest**) **1** ❷ **A2** making a lot of noise: *noisy children/traffic/crowds* ◇ *He*

# Nollywood

was kept awake by noisy neighbours. ◊ *a noisy protest* (= when people shout) ◊ *The kids were even noisier than the dogs.* ◊ *The engine is very noisy at high speed.* ◊ *They are a small but noisy pressure group* (= they attract attention to their ideas by frequent discussion and argument in public and in the media). **2** full of noise: *a noisy classroom/office* ◊ *The party was getting a bit noisy.* ▶ **nois·ily** /-zɪli/ *adv.*: *The children were playing noisily upstairs.*

**Nolly·wood** /ˈnɒliwʊd; *NAmE* ˈnɑː-/ *noun* [U] (*informal*) used to refer to the Nigerian film industry, mainly based in Lagos ⊃ compare BOLLYWOOD, HOLLYWOOD

**nomad** /ˈnəʊmæd/ *noun* a member of a community that moves with its animals from place to place ▶ **no·mad·ic** /nəʊˈmædɪk/ *adj.*: *nomadic tribes* ◊ *the nomadic life of a foreign correspondent*

**ˈno man's land** *noun* [U, sing.] an area of land between the borders of two countries or between two armies, that is not controlled by either

**nom de guerre** /ˌnɒm də ˈɡeə(r); *NAmE* ˌnɑːm də ˈɡer/ *noun* (*pl.* **noms de guerre** /ˌnɒm də ˈɡeə(r); *NAmE* ˌnɑːm də ˈɡer/) (*from French*, *formal*) a false name that is used, for example, by sb who belongs to a military organization that is not official

**nom de plume** /ˌnɒm də ˈpluːm; *NAmE* ˌnɑːm/ *noun* (*pl.* **noms de plume** /ˌnɒm də ˈpluːm; *NAmE* ˌnɑːm/) (*from French*) a name used by a writer instead of their real name **SYN** pen name, pseudonym

**no·men·clat·ure** /nəˈmeŋklətʃə(r); *NAmE* ˈnəʊmənˌkleɪtʃər/ *noun* [U, C] (*formal*) a system of naming things, especially in a branch of science

**nom·in·al** /ˈnɒmɪnl; *NAmE* ˈnɑːm-/ *adj.* **1** being sth in name only, and not in reality: *the nominal leader of the party* ◊ *He remained in nominal control of the business for another ten years.* **2** (of a sum of money) very small and much less than the normal cost or charge **SYN** token: *We only pay a nominal rent.* **3** (*grammar*) connected with a noun or nouns ▶ **nom·in·al·ly** /-nəli/ *adv.*: *He was nominally in charge of the company.*

**nom·in·ate** /ˈnɒmɪneɪt; *NAmE* ˈnɑːm-/ *verb* **1** to formally suggest that sb/sth should be chosen for an important role, prize, position, etc. **SYN** propose: ~ *sb/sth* (*for sth*) *She has been nominated for the presidency.* ◊ ~ *sb/sth (as) sth* | ~ *sb/sth* + *noun He was nominated (as) best actor.* ◊ ~ *sb/sth to do sth I nominated Paul to take on the role of treasurer.* **2** ~ *sb/sth* to choose sb to do a particular job **SYN** appoint: ~ *sb (to/as sth) I have been nominated to the committee.* ◊ ~ *sb to do sth She was nominated to speak on our behalf.* **3** ~ *sth (as sth)* to choose a time, date or title for sth **SYN** select: *1 December has been nominated as the day of the election.*

**nom·in·ation** /ˌnɒmɪˈneɪʃn; *NAmE* ˌnɑːm-/ *noun* [U, C] the act of suggesting or choosing sb as a candidate in an election, or for a job or an award; the fact of being suggested for this: *Membership of the club is by nomination only.* ◊ *He won the nomination as Democratic candidate for the presidency.* ◊ *They opposed her nomination to the post of Deputy Director.* ◊ *He has had nine Oscar nominations.* ⊃ WORDFINDER NOTE at CONGRESS

**nom·ina·tive** /ˈnɒmɪnətɪv; *NAmE* ˈnɑːm-/ (*also* **sub·ject·ive**) *noun* (*grammar*) (in some languages) the form of a noun, a pronoun or an adjective when it is the subject of a verb ⊃ compare ACCUSATIVE, DATIVE, GENITIVE, INSTRUMENTAL (2), LOCATIVE, VOCATIVE ▶ **nom·ina·tive** *adj.*: *nominative pronouns*

**nom·inee** /ˌnɒmɪˈniː; *NAmE* ˌnɑːm-/ *noun* **1** a person who has been formally suggested for a job, a prize, etc: *a presidential nominee* ◊ *an Oscar nominee* **2** (*business*) a person in whose name money is invested in a company, etc.

**non-** /nɒn; *NAmE* nɑːn/ *prefix* (in nouns, adjectives and adverbs) not: *nonsense* ◊ *non-fiction* ◊ *non-alcoholic* ◊ *non-profit-making* ◊ *non-committally* **HELP** Most compounds with **non** are written with a hyphen in *BrE* but are written as one word with no hyphen in *NAmE*.

**nona·gen·ar·ian** /ˌnɒnədʒəˈneəriən, ˌnəʊn-; *NAmE* ˌnəʊnədʒəˈner-, ˌnɑːn-/ *noun* a person who is between 90 and 99 years old ▶ **nona·gen·ar·ian** *adj.*

**non-ag·gres·sion** *noun* [U] (often used as an adjective) a relationship between two countries that have agreed not to attack each other: *a policy of non-aggression* ◊ *a non-aggression pact/treaty*

**non-alco·hol·ic** *adj.* (of a drink) not containing any alcohol: *a non-alcoholic drink* ◊ *Can I have something non-alcoholic?*

**non-a·ligned** *adj.* not providing support for or receiving support from any of the powerful countries in the world ▶ **non-a·lignment** *noun* [U]: *a policy of non-alignment*

**ˈno-name** *adj.* [only before noun] (*NAmE*) **1** not famous: *a no-name comedian* **2** not having a BRAND NAME (= a name under which a product is sold): *cheap, no-name soda*

**non-ap·pear·ance** *noun* [U] (*formal*) failure to be in a place where people expect to see you

**non-at·tend·ance** *noun* [U] failure to go to a place at a time or for an event where you are expected

**non-be·liever** (*also* **nonbeliever** *especially in NAmE*) *noun* a person who has no religious faith or does not believe in a particular philosophy: *an effort to convert non-believers* **OPP** believer ⊃ compare UNBELIEVER

**non-ˈbinary** *adj.* (of a person) choosing not to be identified as either male or female: *The novelist identifies as non-binary.* ⊃ compare GENDER IDENTITY

**non-ˈbinding** (*also* **nonbinding** *especially in NAmE*) *adj.* that does not have to be obeyed according to the law: *The result of the referendum is non-binding.* ◊ *He proposed a non-binding contract.* **OPP** binding

**non-biode·grad·able** *adj.* a substance or chemical that is **non-biodegradable** cannot be changed by the action of bacteria to a natural state that does not harm the environment **OPP** biodegradable

**non·cha·lant** /ˈnɒnʃələnt; *NAmE* ˌnɑːnʃəˈlɑːnt/ *adj.* behaving in a calm and relaxed way; giving the impression that you are not feeling worried **SYN** casual: *to appear/look/sound nonchalant* ◊ *'It'll be fine,' she replied, with a nonchalant shrug.* ▶ **non·cha·lance** /ˈnɒnʃələns; *NAmE* ˌnɑːnʃəˈlɑːns/ *noun* [U]: *an air of nonchalance* **non·cha·lant·ly** /ˈnɒnʃələntli; *NAmE* ˌnɑːnʃəˈlɑːntli/ *adv.*: *He was leaning nonchalantly against the wall.*

**non-ˈcitizen** *noun* (*NAmE*) = ALIEN

**non-ˈcombat·ant** *noun* **1** a member of the armed forces who does not actually fight in a war, for example an army doctor **2** in a war, a person who is not a member of the armed forces **SYN** civilian ⊃ compare COMBATANT

**non-com·mis·sioned ˈofficer** *noun* (*abbr.* NCO) a soldier in the army, etc. who has a rank such as SERGEANT or CORPORAL, but not a high rank ⊃ compare COMMISSIONED OFFICER

**non-com·mit·tal** *adj.* not giving an opinion; not showing which side of an argument you agree with: *a non-committal reply/tone* ◊ *The doctor was non-committal about when I could drive again.* ⊃ see also COMMIT (4) ▶ **non-com·mit·tal·ly** *adv.*

**non-com·pli·ance** *noun* [U] ~ (*with sth*) the fact of failing or refusing to obey a rule: *There are penalties for non-compliance with the fire regulations.* **OPP** compliance

**non-con·form·ist** /ˌnɒnkənˈfɔːmɪst; *NAmE* ˌnɑːnkənˈfɔːrm-/ *noun* **1 Nonconformist** (in England and Wales) a member of a Protestant Church that is not part of the Church of England **2** a person who does not follow normal ways of thinking or behaving ▶ **non-con·form·ist**, **Non·con·form·ist** *adj.*

**non-con·form·ity** /ˌnɒnkənˈfɔːməti; *NAmE* ˌnɑːnkənˈfɔːrm-/ (*also* **non-con·form·ism** /ˌnɒnkənˈfɔːmɪzəm; *NAmE* ˌnɑːnkənˈfɔːrm-/) *noun* [U] **1** the fact of not following normal ways of thinking and behaving **2 Nonconformity** the beliefs and practices of Nonconformist Churches

**non-con·tribu·tory** *adj.* (of an insurance or pension plan) paid for by the employer and not the employee **OPP** contributory

**non-contro·ver·sial** *adj.* not causing, or not likely to cause, people to disagree **OPP controversial HELP** This is not as strong as **uncontroversial**, which is more common.

**non-co·ope·r·ation** *noun* [U] the act of refusing to help a person in authority by doing what they have asked you to do, especially as a form of protest: *A strike is unlikely, but some forms of non-cooperation are being considered.* ⊃ compare COOPERATION (2)

**non-'count** *adj.* (*grammar*) = UNCOUNTABLE

**non-cu'stod·ial** *adj.* [only before noun] (*law*) **1** (of a punishment) that does not involve a period of time in prison: *a non-custodial sentence/penalty* **2** (of a parent) not having CUSTODY of a child **OPP custodial**

**non-'dairy** *adj.* [only before noun] not made with milk or cream: *a non-dairy whipped topping*

**non-denomi'national** (*also* **nondenominational** *especially in NAmE*) *adj.* open or acceptable to people of any religious group, especially any branch of the Christian Church: *a non-denominational memorial service* **OPP denominational**

**non·de·script** /ˈnɒndɪskrɪpt; *NAmE* ˈnɑːn-/ *adj.* (*disapproving*) having no interesting or unusual features or qualities **SYN dull**

**none** ⓘ A2 /nʌn/ *pron., adv.*
■ *pron.* A2 ~ (of sb/sth) not one of a group of people or things; not any: *None of these pens works/work.* ◇ *We have three sons but none of them lives/live nearby.* ◇ *We saw several houses but none we really liked.* ◇ *Tickets for Friday? Sorry we've got none left.* ◇ *He told me all the news but none of it was very exciting.* ◇ *'Is there any more milk?' 'No, none at all.'* ◇ (*formal*) *Everybody liked him but none* (= nobody) *more than I.*
**IDM** **have/want none of sth** to refuse to accept sth: *I offered to pay but he was having none of it.* **none but** (*literary*) only: *None but he knew the truth.* **none the 'less** = NONETHELESS **none 'other than** used to emphasize who or what sb/sth is, when this is surprising: *Her first customer was none other than Mrs Obama.*
■ *adv.* **1** used with *the* and a comparative to mean 'not at all': *She told me what it meant at great length but I'm afraid I'm none the wiser.* ◇ *He seems none the worse for the experience.* **2** used with *too* and an adjective or adverb to mean 'not at all' or 'not very': *She was looking none too pleased.*

▼ **GRAMMAR POINT**

**none of**
- When you use **none of** with an uncountable noun, the verb is in the singular: *None of the work was done.*
- When you use **none of** with a plural noun or pronoun, or a singular noun referring to a group of people or things, you can use either a singular or a plural verb. The singular form is used in a formal style in *BrE*: *None of the trains is/are going to London.* ◇ *None of her family has/have been to college.*

**non·en·tity** /nɒnˈentəti; *NAmE* nɑːn-/ *noun* (*pl.* -ies) (*disapproving*) a person without any special qualities, who has not achieved anything important **SYN nobody**

**non-es'sential** *adj.* [usually before noun] not completely necessary ⊃ compare ESSENTIAL **HELP** This is not as strong as **inessential**, and is more common. **Inessential** can suggest disapproval. ▶ **non-es'sential** *noun* [usually pl.]: *I have no money for non-essentials.*

**none·the·less** ⓘ C1 /ˌnʌnðəˈles/ (*also* **none the 'less**) *adv.* (*formal*) despite this fact **SYN nevertheless**: *The book is too long but, nonetheless, informative and entertaining.* ◇ *The problems are not serious. Nonetheless, we shall need to tackle them soon.* ⊃ LANGUAGE BANK at NEVERTHELESS

**non-e'vent** *noun* (*informal*) an event that was expected to be interesting, exciting and popular but is in fact very disappointing **SYN anticlimax**

**non-ex'ecutive** *adj.* [only before noun] (*BrE, business*) a **non-executive** director of a company can give advice at a high level but does not have the power to make decisions about the company

**non-e'xistent** *adj.* not existing; not real: *a non-existent problem* ◇ *'How's your social life?' 'Non-existent, I'm afraid.'* ◇ *Hospital beds were scarce and medicines were practically non-existent.* ⊃ compare EXISTENT ▶ **non-e'xistence** *noun* [U]

**non-'fat** (*also* **non-fat**) /ˌnɒnˈfæt; *NAmE* ˌnɑːn-/ *adj.* [usually before noun] containing no fat **SYN fat-free**: *nonfat yogurt* ⊃ compare LOW-FAT

**non-'fiction** *noun* [U] books, articles or texts about real facts, events and people: *I prefer reading non-fiction.* ◇ *the non-fiction section of the library* **OPP fiction**

**non-'finite** *adj.* (*grammar*) a **non-finite** verb form or clause does not show a particular tense, PERSON or NUMBER **OPP finite**

**non-govern'mental** (*also* **nongovernmental** *especially in NAmE*) *adj.* [only before noun] (especially of an organization) not part of or associated with any government: *non-governmental aid organizations* ⊃ compare GOVERNMENTAL, NGO

**non-'human** *adj.* not human: *similarities between human and non-human animals* ⊃ compare HUMAN (1), INHUMAN

**non-inter'vention** (*also* **non-inter'ference**) *noun* [U] the policy or practice of not becoming involved in other people's DISAGREEMENTS, especially those of foreign countries ▶ **non-inter'ventionism** *noun* [U] **non-inter'ventionist** *adj.*

**non-in'vasive** *adj.* (of medical treatment) not involving cutting into the body **OPP invasive**

**non-'issue** *noun* a subject of little or no importance

**non-'judgemental** (*BrE*) (*NAmE* usually **nonjudgmental**, **non-judgmental** *BrE and NAmE*) *adj.* avoiding moral judgements; not quick to judge people and criticize them **OPP judgemental**

**non-'linear** *adj.* (*specialist*) that does not develop from one thing to another in a single smooth series of stages **OPP linear**

**non-ma'lignant** *adj.* (of a TUMOUR) not caused by cancer and not likely to be dangerous **SYN benign** **OPP malignant**

**non-'native** *adj.* **1** (of animals, plants, etc.) not existing naturally in a place but coming from somewhere else **2** a **non-native** speaker of a language is one who has not spoken it from the time they first learnt to talk **OPP native**

**non-ne'gotiable** *adj.* **1** that cannot be discussed or changed **2** (of a cheque, etc.) that cannot be changed for money by anyone except the person whose name is on it **OPP negotiable**

**'no-no** *noun* [sing.] (*informal*) a thing or a way of behaving that is not acceptable in a particular situation

**no-'nonsense** *adj.* [only before noun] simple and direct; only paying attention to important and necessary things

**non-'partisan** *adj.* [usually before noun] not supporting the ideas of one particular political party or group of people strongly **OPP partisan**

**non-'payment** *noun* [U] (*formal*) failure to pay a debt, a tax, rent, etc.

**non-'person** *noun* (*pl.* **non-persons**) a person who is thought not to be important, or who is ignored

**non'plussed** (*US also* **non·plused**) /ˌnɒnˈplʌst; *NAmE* ˌnɑːn-/ *adj.* surprised and confused so that you do not know what to do or say

**non-pre'scription** *adj.* (of drugs) that you can buy directly without a special form from a doctor

**non-pro'fessional** *adj.* **1** having a job that does not need a high level of education or special training; connected with a job of this kind: *non-professional staff such as porters and maintenance workers* **2** doing sth as a hobby rather than as a paid job: *non-professional actors* ⊃ compare PROFESSIONAL, UNPROFESSIONAL ⊃ see also AMATEUR *adj.*

**non-'profit** ⓘ C1 (*also* **non-'profit-making**) *adj.* (*BrE*) (of an organization) without the aim of making a profit: *an independent non-profit organization* ◇ *The centre is run on a non-profit basis.* ◇ *The charity is non-profit-making.*

# nonprofit

**non·profit** /ˌnɒnˈprɒfɪt; *NAmE* nɑːnˈprɑːf-/ *adj., noun* (*NAmE*) = NOT-FOR-PROFIT

**ˌnon-proˈlifeˌrˈation** *noun* [U] a limit to the increase in the number of nuclear and chemical weapons that are produced

**ˌnon-proˈpriˌetary** *adj.* not made by or belonging to a particular company: *non-proprietary medicines* **OPP** proprietary

**ˌnon-reˈfundˌable** (*also* **ˌnon-reˈturnable**) *adj.* (of a sum of money) that cannot be returned: *a non-refundable deposit* ◊ *a non-refundable ticket* (= you cannot return it and get your money back)

**ˌnon-reˈnewable** *adj.* **1** (of natural resources such as gas or oil) that cannot be replaced after use **2** that cannot be continued or repeated for a further period of time after it has ended: *a non-renewable contract* **OPP** renewable

**ˌnon-ˈresident** *adj., noun*
- *adj.* (*formal*) **1** (of a person or company) not living or located permanently in a particular place or country **2** not living in the place where you work or in a house that you own **3** not staying at a particular hotel: *Non-resident guests are welcome to use the hotel swimming pool.*
- *noun* **1** a person who does not live permanently in a particular country **2** a person not staying at a particular hotel

**ˌnon-resiˈdentˌial** *adj.* **1** that is not used for people to live in **2** that does not require you to live in the place where you work or study: *a non-residential course*

**ˌnon-reˈturnˌable** *adj.* **1** = NON-REFUNDABLE **2** that you cannot give back, for example to a shop, to be used again; that will not be given back to you: *non-returnable bottles* ◊ *a non-returnable deposit* **OPP** returnable

**ˌnon-scienˈtifˌic** *adj.* not involving or connected with science or scientific methods ⊃ compare SCIENTIFIC, UNSCIENTIFIC

**non·sense** ?+ **C1** /ˈnɒnsns; *NAmE* ˈnɑːnsens, -sns/ *noun* **1** ?+ **C1** [U, C] ideas, statements or beliefs that you think are silly or not true **SYN** rubbish: *Reports that he has resigned are nonsense.* ◊ *You're talking nonsense! ◊ 'I won't go.' 'Nonsense! You must go!'* ◊ *It's nonsense to say they don't care.* ◊ *The idea is an economic nonsense.* **2** ?+ **C1** [U] spoken or written words that have no meaning or make no sense: *a book of children's nonsense poems* ◊ *Most of the translation he did for me was complete nonsense.* **3** [U] silly or unacceptable behaviour: *The new teacher won't stand for any nonsense.* ⊃ see also NO-NONSENSE
- **IDM** **make (a) ˈnonsense of sth** to reduce the value of sth by a lot; to make sth seem silly: *If people can bribe police officers, it makes a complete nonsense of the legal system.* ⊃ more at STUFF *n.*

**ˈnonsense word** *noun* a word with no meaning

**non·sensˌical** /ˌnɒnˈsensɪkl; *NAmE* ˌnɑːn-/ *adj.* silly; with no meaning **SYN** absurd

**non sequiˌtur** /ˌnɒn ˈsekwɪtə(r); *NAmE* ˌnɑːn/ *noun* (*from Latin, formal*) a statement that does not seem to follow what has just been said in any natural or logical way

**ˌnon-ˈslip** *adj.* that helps to prevent sb/sth from slipping; that does not slip: *a non-slip bath mat*

**ˌnon-ˈsmoker** *noun* a person who does not smoke **OPP** smoker

**ˌnon-ˈsmoking** *adj.* [usually before noun] **1** (*also* **ˌnoˈsmoking**) (of a place) where people are not allowed to smoke: *This is a non-smoking area.* **2** (of a person) who does not smoke: *She's a non-smoking, non-drinking fitness fanatic.* ▸ **ˌnon-ˈsmoking** (*also* **ˌnoˈsmoking**) *noun* [U]: *Non-smoking is now the norm in most workplaces.*

**ˌnon-speˈcifˌic** *adj.* [usually before noun] **1** not definite or clearly defined; general: *The candidate's speech was non-specific.* **2** (*medical*) (of pain, a disease, etc.) with more than one possible cause

**ˌnon-ˈstandard** *adj.* **1** (of language) not considered correct by most educated people: *non-standard dialects* ◊ *non-standard English* ⊃ compare STANDARD (4) **2** not the usual size, type, etc: *The paper was of non-standard size.*

**ˌnon-ˈstarter** *noun* (*informal*) a thing or a person that has no chance of success: *As a business proposition, it's a non-starter.*

**ˌnon-ˈstick** *adj.* [usually before noun] (of cooking equipment) covered with a substance that prevents food from sticking to it: *a non-stick frying pan*

**ˌnon-ˈstop** *adj.* **1** (of a train, a journey, etc.) without any stops **SYN** direct: *a non-stop flight to Tokyo* ◊ *a non-stop train/service* **2** without any breaks or stops **SYN** continuous: *non-stop entertainment/work* ▸ **ˌnon-ˈstop** *adv.*: *We flew non-stop from Paris to Chicago.* ◊ *It rained non-stop all week.*

**ˌnon-ˈtoxic** (*NAmE also* **nontoxic**) *adj.* not poisonous or not harmful to your health: *a non-toxic paint* **OPP** toxic

**ˌnon-traˈditional** *adj.* not following the usual methods, practices, etc. in a particular area of activity: *students from non-traditional backgrounds* **OPP** traditional

**ˌnon-ˈunion** (*also less frequent* **ˌnon-ˈunionized**, **-ised**) *adj.* [usually before noun] **1** not belonging to a trade union: *non-union labour/workers* **2** (of a business, company, etc.) not accepting trade unions or employing trade union members

**ˌnon-ˈveg** (*informal*) (*also* **ˌnon-vegeˈtarian**) *adj.* (*IndE, SEAsianE*) **1** not suitable for a person who does not eat meat or fish; containing or serving meat and/or fish: *The buffet contained both veg and non-veg options.* ◊ *a non-veg restaurant* **2** (of a person) having a diet that includes meat and/or fish **OPP** veg

**ˌnon-vegeˈtarian** *noun* (*IndE, SEAsianE*) a person who eats meat, fish, eggs, etc. ▸ **ˌnon-vegeˈtarian** *adj.* = NON-VEG

**ˌnon-ˈverbal** *adj.* [usually before noun] not involving words or speech: *non-verbal communication*

**ˌnon-ˈviolence** *noun* [U] the policy of using peaceful methods, not force, to bring about political or social change

**ˌnon-ˈviolent** *adj.* **1** using peaceful methods, not force, to bring about political or social change: *non-violent resistance* ◊ *a non-violent protest* **2** not involving force, or injury to sb: *non-violent crimes*

**ˌnon-ˈwhite** *noun* a person who is not a member of a race of people who have white skin ▸ **ˌnon-ˈwhite** *adj.*

**noob** /nuːb/ *noun* (*informal*) a person who takes part in an activity, usually an online video game, but lacks relevant knowledge and therefore performs badly ⊃ see also NEWBIE

**noo·dle** /ˈnuːdl/ *noun* [usually pl.] a long thin piece of PASTA, used especially in Chinese and Italian cooking: *chicken noodle soup* ◊ *Would you prefer rice or noodles?*

**nook** /nʊk/ *noun* a small quiet place or corner that is sheltered or hidden from other people: *a shady nook in the garden* ◊ *dark woods full of secret nooks and crannies*
- **IDM** **every ˌnook and ˈcranny** (*also IndE* **every ˌnook and ˈcorner**) (*informal*) every part of a place; every aspect of a situation

**nooky** (*also* **nookie**) /ˈnʊki/ *noun* [U] (*slang*) sexual activity

**noon** ?+ **C1** /nuːn/ *noun* [U] 12 o'clock in the middle of the day **SYN** midday: *We should be there by noon.* ◊ *The conference opens at 12 noon on Saturday.* ◊ *the noon deadline for the end of hostilities* ◊ *I'm leaving on the noon train.* ⊃ see also HIGH NOON **IDM** see MORNING *n.*

**noon·day** /ˈnuːndeɪ/ *adj.* [only before noun] (*old-fashioned or literary*) happening or appearing at noon: *the noonday sun*

**no one** ? **A1** (*also* **noˈbody**) *pron.* not anyone; no person: *No one was at home.* ◊ *There was no one else around.* ◊ *We were told to speak to no one.* **HELP** **No one** is much more common than **nobody** in written English.

**noose** /nuːs/ *noun* a circle that is tied on one end of a rope, with a KNOT that allows the circle to get smaller as the other end of the rope is pulled, that can be used to kill sb by hanging them by the neck: *a hangman's noose* ◊ (*figurative*) *His debts were a noose around his neck.*

**nope** /nəʊp/ *exclamation* (*informal*) used to say 'no': *'Have you seen my pen?' 'Nope.'*

**'no place** adv. (informal, especially NAmE) = NOWHERE: *I have no place else to go.*

**nor** 0️⃣ **B1** /nɔː(r)/ conj., adv. **1** **B1** neither ... nor ... | not ... nor ... and not: *She seemed neither surprised nor worried.* ◊ *He wasn't there on Monday. Nor on Tuesday, for that matter.* ◊ (formal) *Not a building nor a tree was left standing.* **2** **B1** used before a positive verb to agree with sth negative that has just been said: *She doesn't like them and nor does Jeff.* ◊ *'I'm not going.' 'Nor am I.'*

**Nor·dic** /ˈnɔːdɪk; NAmE ˈnɔːrd-/ adj. **1** of or connected with the countries of Scandinavia, Finland and Iceland **2** typical of a member of a European race of people who are tall and have blue eyes and blonde hair

**nor'easter** /ˌnɔːrˈiːstə(r)/ (also **northeaster** /ˌnɔːθˈiːstə(r); NAmE ˌnɔːrθ-/) noun (especially NAmE) a strong wind or storm that comes from the north-east, especially in New England in the United States

**norm** ⓡ+ **B2** Ⓦ /nɔːm; NAmE nɔːrm/ noun, verb
- **noun 1** ⓡ+ **B2** (often **the norm**) [sing.] a situation or a pattern of behaviour that is usual or expected **SYN** **rule**: *a departure from the norm* ◊ *Older parents seem to be the norm rather than the exception nowadays.* **2** ⓡ+ **C1** **norms** [pl.] standards of behaviour that are typical of or accepted within a particular group or society: *social/cultural norms* **3** ⓡ+ **C1** [C] a required or agreed standard, amount, etc.: *detailed education norms for children of particular ages*
- **verb** ~ sth to change sth so that it is of the required standard; to establish a required or agreed standard for sth: *You can use the information to norm the test.*

**nor·mal** ⓡ **A2** ⓞ /ˈnɔːml; NAmE ˈnɔːrml/ adj., noun
- **adj. 1** ⓡ **A2** typical, usual or ordinary; what you would expect: *quite/perfectly normal* ◊ *Her temperature is normal.* ◊ *They are just quiet, normal people.* ◊ **it is ~ (for sb) to do sth** *It's normal to feel tired after such a long trip.* ◊ *He should be able to lead a perfectly normal life.* ◊ *Divorce is complicated enough in normal circumstances, but this situation is even worse.* ◊ **Under normal circumstances,** *I would say 'yes'.* ◊ **In the normal course of events** *I wouldn't go to that part of town.* ◊ *The unemployment rate was above normal levels.* ◊ *We are open during normal office hours.* **2** ⓡ **B1** not suffering from any mental or physical DISORDER: *People who commit such crimes aren't normal.* ◊ *Rebecca was born a normal, healthy baby.* **OPP** **abnormal** **IDM** see PER
- **noun 1** ⓡ **B1** [U] the usual or average state, level or standard: **above/below ~** *The rainfall has been above normal for the time of year.* ◊ **(back) to ~** *Things soon returned to normal.* ◊ **as ~** *Life continued as normal.* **2** [C] (informal) a person who is ordinary or healthy **IDM** see NEW

**normal distri'bution** noun (statistics) the usual way in which a particular feature varies among a large number of things or people, represented on a GRAPH by a line that rises to a high round curve in the middle ⊃ compare BELL CURVE

**nor·mal·ity** /nɔːˈmæləti; NAmE nɔːrˈm-/ (also **nor·malcy** /ˈnɔːmlsi; NAmE ˈnɔːrm-/ especially in NAmE) noun [U] a situation where everything is normal or as you would expect it to be: *They are hoping for a return to normality now that the war is over.*

**nor·mal·ize** (BrE also **-ise**) /ˈnɔːməlaɪz; NAmE ˈnɔːrm-/ verb [T, I] ~ (sth) (formal) to fit or make sth fit a normal pattern or condition: *a lotion to normalize oily skin* ◊ *The two countries agreed to normalize relations* (= return to a normal, friendly relationship, for example after a disagreement or war). ◊ *It took time until the political situation had normalized.* ▶ **nor·mal·iza·tion, -isa·tion** /ˌnɔːməlaɪˈzeɪʃn; NAmE ˌnɔːrmələˈz-/ noun [U]: *the normalization of relations*

**nor·mal·ly** ⓡ **A2** Ⓦ /ˈnɔːməli; NAmE ˈnɔːrm-/ adv. **1** ⓡ **A2** usually; in normal circumstances: *I would never normally discuss this.* ◊ *He didn't eat as much as he normally does.* ◊ *It normally takes 20 minutes to get there.* ◊ *They played at venues not normally associated with classical music.* ◊ **to function/operate/develop normally 2** ⓡ **A2** in the usual or ordinary way: *Her heart is beating normally.* ◊ *Just try to behave normally.*

**Nor·man** /ˈnɔːmən; NAmE ˈnɔːrm-/ adj. **1** used to describe the style of architecture in Britain in the 11th and 12th centuries that developed from the ROMANESQUE style: *a Norman church/castle* **2** connected with the Normans (= the people from northern Europe who defeated the English in 1066 and then ruled the country): *the Norman Conquest*

**nor·ma·tive** /ˈnɔːmətɪv; NAmE ˈnɔːrm-/ adj. (formal) describing or setting standards or rules of behaviour: *a normative approach*

**noro·virus** /ˈnɒrəʊvaɪrəs; NAmE ˈnɔːr-/ noun [U, sing.] (BrE also **winter 'vomiting bug/virus**) [C] a disease, caused by a virus, that makes people VOMIT and have DIARRHOEA very badly for a few days

**Norse** /nɔːs; NAmE nɔːrs/ noun [U] the Norwegian language, especially in an ancient form, or the Scandinavian language group

**north** 0️⃣ **A1** /nɔːθ; NAmE nɔːrθ/ noun, adj., adv.
- **noun** [U, sing.] (abbr. **N**, **No.**) **1** ⓡ **A1** usually **the north** the direction that is on your left when you watch the sun rise; one of the four main points of the COMPASS: *Which way is north?* ◊ *cold winds coming from the north* ◊ **to the ~ (of ...)** *Mount Kenya is to the north of* (= further north than) *Nairobi.* ⊃ picture at COMPASS ⊃ compare EAST, SOUTH, WEST ⊃ see also MAGNETIC NORTH, TRUE NORTH **2** ⓡ **A1** **the north**, **the North** the northern part of a country, a region or the world: *birds migrating from the north* ◊ **in the ~** *Houses are less expensive in the North* (= of England) *than in the South.* ◊ *The main road ran across the north of the island.* **3** **the North** the north-east states of the US which fought against the South in the American Civil War **4** **the North** the richer and more developed countries of the world, especially in Europe and North America
- **adj.** [only before noun] **1** ⓡ **A1** (abbr. **N**, **No.**) in or towards the north: *North London* ◊ *the north bank of the river* **2** **a north wind** blows from the north: *A cold north wind blew in from the sea.* ⊃ compare NORTHERLY
- **adv. 1** ⓡ **A1** towards the north: *The house faces north.* ◊ *a train heading north* **2** ⓡ **A1** ~ **of sth** nearer to the north than sth: *They live ten miles north of Boston.* **3** ~ **of sth** (finance or NAmE, informal) more or higher than sth: *The estimated value is north of $5.4 billion.* **OPP** **south**
**IDM** **up 'north** (informal) to or in the north of a country, especially England: *They've gone to live up north.*

**north·bound** /ˈnɔːθbaʊnd; NAmE ˈnɔːrθ-/ adj. travelling or leading towards the north: *northbound traffic* ◊ *the northbound carriageway of the motorway*

**'north-country** adj. [only before noun] connected with the northern part of a country or region: *a north-country accent*

**north-'east** noun (usually **the north-east**) [sing.] (abbr. **NE**) the direction or region at an equal distance between north and east ⊃ picture at COMPASS ▶ **north-'east** adv., adj.

**north-'easter·ly** adj. **1** [only before noun] in or towards the north-east: *travelling in a north-easterly direction* **2** [usually before noun] (of winds) blowing from the north-east

**north-'eastern** adj. [only before noun] (abbr. **NE**) connected with the north-east

**north-'eastwards** (especially BrE) (also **north-'eastward** especially in NAmE) adv. towards the north-east ▶ **north-'eastward** adj.

**north·er·ly** /ˈnɔːðəli; NAmE ˈnɔːrðərli/ adj., noun
- **adj. 1** [only before noun] in or towards the north: *travelling in a northerly direction* **2** [usually before noun] (of winds) blowing from the north: *a northerly breeze* ⊃ compare NORTH
- **noun** (pl. **-ies**) a wind that blows from the north

**north·ern** 0️⃣ **B1** (also **Northern**) /ˈnɔːðən; NAmE ˈnɔːrðərn/ adj. [usually before noun] (abbr. **N**, **No.**) located in the north or facing north; connected with or typical of

# northerner

the north part of the world or a region: *the northern slopes of the mountains* ◊ *the northern part of Syria* ◊ *northern Scotland* ◊ *a northern accent*

**north·ern·er** /ˈnɔːðənə(r); NAmE ˈnɔːrðərn-/ *noun* a person who comes from or lives in the northern part of a country

**the Northern Ireland Assembly** /ðə ˌnɔːðən ˈaɪələnd əˈsembli; NAmE ˌnɔːrðərn ˈaɪərl-/ *noun* [sing.] **1** the regional government of Northern Ireland from 1973 to 1986 **2** the parliament of Northern Ireland that was first elected in 1998

**the Northern ˈLights** *noun* [pl.] (*also* **au·ro·ra bor·ealis** [sing.]) bands of coloured light, mainly green and red, that are sometimes seen in the sky at night in the most northern countries of the world

**north·ern·most** /ˈnɔːðənməʊst; NAmE ˈnɔːrðərn-/ *adj.* [usually before noun] furthest north: *the northernmost city in the world*

**north-north-ˈeast** *noun* [sing.] (*abbr.* **NNE**) the direction at an equal distance between north and north-east ▶ **north-north-ˈeast** *adv.*

**north-north-ˈwest** *noun* [sing.] (*abbr.* **NNW**) the direction at an equal distance between north and north-west ▶ **north-north-ˈwest** *adv.*

**the North ˈPole** *noun* [sing.] the point on the surface of the earth that is furthest north

**the North ˈSea** *noun* [sing.] the part of the Atlantic Ocean that is next to the east coast of Britain

**the North-South Diˈvide** *noun* [sing.] (*BrE*) the economic and social differences between the north and south of a country, especially when one half of the country is richer than the other

**north·wards** /ˈnɔːθwədz; NAmE ˈnɔːrθwərdz/ (*especially BrE*) (*also* **north·ward** *especially in NAmE*) *adv.* towards the north: *to go/look/turn northwards* ▶ **north·ward** *adj.*: *in a northward direction*

**north-ˈwest** *noun* (*usually* **the north-west**) [sing.] (*abbr.* **NW**) the direction or region at an equal distance between north and west ⇒ picture at COMPASS ▶ **north-ˈwest** *adv., adj.*

**north-ˈwester·ly** *adj.* **1** [only before noun] in or towards the north-west **2** (of winds) blowing from the north-west

**north-ˈwestern** *adj.* [only before noun] (*abbr.* **NW**) connected with the north-west

**north-ˈwestwards** (*especially BrE*) (*also* **north-ˈwestward** *especially in NAmE*) *adv.* towards the north-west ▶ **north-ˈwestward** *adj.*

**Norway rat** /ˌnɔːweɪ ˈræt; NAmE ˌnɔːrw-/ *noun* = BROWN RAT

**nose** 🔊 A1 /nəʊz/ *noun, verb*
■ *noun* **1** 🔊 A1 [C] the part of the face that sticks out above the mouth, used for breathing and smelling things: *He broke his nose in the fight.* ◊ *She wrinkled her nose in disgust.* ◊ *to breathe through your ~* Try to breathe through your nose. ◊ *He blew his nose* (= cleared it by blowing strongly into a HANDKERCHIEF). ◊ *a blocked/runny nose* ◊ *Stop picking your nose!* (= removing dirt from it with your finger) ◊ *He held his nose as he passed the stinking dustbins.* ◊ *He pushed his glasses up the bridge of his nose* (= the hard part near the top). ⇒ see also NASAL **2** -**nosed** (in adjectives) having the type of nose mentioned: *red-nosed* ◊ *large-nosed* ⇒ see also HARD-NOSED **3** [C] the front part of a plane, SPACECRAFT, etc. **4** [sing.] **a ~ for sth** a special ability for finding or recognizing sth SYN **instinct**: *As a journalist, she has always had a nose for a good story.* **5** [sing.] a sense of smell: *a dog with a good nose* **6** [sing.] a smell that is characteristic of a particular wine SYN **bouquet**
IDM **cut off your nose to spite your ˈface** (*informal*) to do sth when you are angry that is meant to harm sb else but that also harms you **get up sb's ˈnose** (*BrE, informal*) to annoy sb **give sb a bloody ˈnose** to defeat sb: *We have to give him a bloody nose in the election.* **have your nose in ˈsth** (*informal*) to be reading sth and giving it all your attention **have a nose ˈround** (*BrE, informal*) to look around a place; to look for sth in a place **keep your ˈnose clean** (*informal*) to avoid doing anything wrong or illegal: *Since leaving prison, he's managed to keep his nose clean.* **keep your nose out of ˈsth** to try not to become involved in things that should not really involve you **keep your nose to the ˈgrindstone** (*informal*) to work hard for a long period of time without stopping **look down your ˈnose at sb/sth** (*informal, especially BrE*) to behave in a way that suggests that you think that you are better than sb or that sth is not good enough for you SYN **look down on sb** **nose to ˈtail** (*BrE*) if cars, etc. are nose to tail, they are moving slowly in a long line with little space between them **on the ˈnose** (*informal, especially NAmE*) exactly: *The budget should hit the $136 billion target on the nose.* **poke/stick your nose into ˈsth** (*informal*) to try to become involved in sth that should not involve you **put sb's ˈnose out of joint** (*informal*) to upset or annoy sb, especially by not giving them enough attention **turn your ˈnose up at sth** (*informal*) to refuse sth, especially because you do not think that it is good enough for you **under sb's ˈnose** (*informal*) **1** if sth is **under sb's nose**, it is very close to them but they cannot see it: *I searched everywhere for the letter and it was under my nose all the time!* **2** if sth happens **under sb's nose**, they do not notice it even though it is not being done secretly: *The police didn't know the drugs ring was operating right under their noses.* **with your nose in the ˈair** (*informal*) in a way that is not friendly and suggests that you think that you are better than other people ⇒ more at BOOK *n.*, FOLLOW, LEAD[1] *v.*, PAY *v.*, PLAIN *adj.*, POWDER *v.*, RUB *v.*, SKIN *n.*, THUMB *v.*, TROUGH
■ *verb* **1** [I, T] to move forward slowly and carefully: + *adv./prep. The plane nosed down through the thick clouds.* ◊ *~ your way + adv./prep. The taxi nosed its way back into the traffic.* **2** [I] + *adv./prep.* (of an animal) to search for sth or push sth with its nose: *Dogs nosed around in piles of refuse.*
PHRV **nose aˈround (for sth)** (*also* **nose aˈbout (for sth)** *especially in BrE*) to look for sth, especially information about sb SYN **poke around**: *We found a man nosing around in our backyard.* **nose sth↔ˈout** (*informal*) to discover information about sb/sth by searching for it: *Reporters nosed out all the details of the affair.*

▼ HOMOPHONES

**knows • nose** /nəʊz/

• **knows** *verb* (*third person of* KNOW): *Who knows what the future will bring?*
• **nose** *noun*: *Breathe in through your nose and out through your mouth.*

**nose·bleed** /ˈnəʊzbliːd/ *noun* a flow of blood that comes from the nose

**ˈnose cone** *noun* the pointed front end of a ROCKET, an aircraft, etc.

**nose·dive** /ˈnəʊzdaɪv/ *noun, verb*
■ *noun* [sing.] **1** a sudden steep fall or drop; a situation where sth suddenly becomes worse or begins to fail: *Oil prices took a nosedive in the crisis.* ◊ *These policies have sent the construction industry into an abrupt nosedive.* **2** the sudden sharp fall of an aircraft towards the ground with its front part pointing down
■ *verb* **1** [I] (of prices, costs, etc.) to fall suddenly SYN **plummet**: *Building costs have nosedived.* **2** [I] (of an aircraft) to fall suddenly with the front part pointing towards the ground

**ˈnose job** *noun* (*informal*) a medical operation on the nose to improve its shape

**ˈnose ring** *noun* **1** a ring that is put in an animal's nose for leading it **2** a ring worn in the nose as a piece of jewellery

**nosey** = NOSY

**nosh** /nɒʃ; NAmE nɑːʃ/ *noun, verb*
■ *noun* (*informal*) **1** [U, sing.] (*old-fashioned, BrE*) food; a meal: *She likes her nosh.* ◊ *Did you have a good nosh?* **2** [C] (*especially NAmE*) a small meal that you eat quickly between main meals
■ *verb* [I, T] ~ (sth) (*informal*) to eat

**no-ˈshow** noun (informal) a person who is expected to be somewhere and does not come; a situation where this happens

**no-ˈsmoking** adj. = NON-SMOKING

**nos·tal·gia** /nɒˈstældʒə; NAmE nəˈs-, nɑːˈs-/ noun [U] a sad feeling mixed with pleasure when you think of happy times in the past: *a sense/wave/pang of nostalgia* ◊ *She is filled with nostalgia for her own college days.* ▶ **nos·tal·gic** /-dʒɪk/ adj.: *nostalgic memories* ◊ *I feel quite nostalgic for the place where I grew up.* **nos·tal·gic·al·ly** /-kli/ adv.: *to look back nostalgically to your childhood*

**nos·tril** /ˈnɒstrəl; NAmE ˈnɑːs-/ noun either of the two openings at the end of the nose that you breathe through

**nos·trum** /ˈnɒstrəm; NAmE ˈnɑːs-/ noun (disapproving) **1** (formal) an idea that is intended to solve a problem but that will probably not succeed **2** (old-fashioned) a medicine that is not made in a scientific way, and that is not effective

**nosy** (also **nosey**) /ˈnəʊzi/ adj. (informal, disapproving) too interested in things that do not involve you, especially other people's affairs SYN **inquisitive**: *nosy neighbours* ◊ *Don't be so nosy—it's none of your business.* ▶ **nosi·ly** /-zɪli/ adv. **nosi·ness** noun [U]

**not** 🅞 🅐🅘 /nɒt; NAmE nɑːt/ adv. **1** 🅐🅘 (often reduced to **n't**) used with *be, do* or *have* to form the negative of verbs; used to form the negative of modal verbs like *can* or *must*: *She did not/didn't see him.* ◊ *It's not/It isn't raining.* ◊ *It's cold, isn't it?* ◊ *Don't you eat meat?* ◊ *I can't see from here.* ◊ *He must not go.* **2** 🅐🅘 used to give the following word or phrase a negative meaning, or to reply in the negative: *He warned me not to be late.* ◊ *I was sorry not to have seen them.* ◊ *Not everybody agrees.* ◊ *They had still not decided.* ◊ *'Who's next?' 'Not me.'* ◊ *'What did you do at school?' 'Not a lot.'* ◊ *It's not easy being a parent* (= it's difficult). **3** 🅐🅘 used after *hope, expect, believe,* etc. to give a negative reply: *'Will she be there?' 'I hope not.'* ◊ *'Is it ready?' 'I'm afraid not.'* ◊ (formal) *'Does he know?' 'I believe not.'* **4** 🅐🅘 **or ~** used to show a negative possibility: *I don't know if he's telling the truth or not.* ◊ *Whether you succeed or not depends on the how skilled you are.* **5** 🅐🅘 used to say that you do not want sth or will not allow sth: *'Some more?' 'Not for me, thanks.'* ◊ *'Can I throw this out?' 'Certainly not.'* **6** even less than: *She was standing not three feet in front of me.* **7** used to suggest that the opposite of the following word or phrase is true: *This could all happen in the **not too distant future*** (= soon). ◊ *His view on the matter was **not a million miles away** from* (= close to) *mine.* **8** (humorous, informal) used to emphasize the opposite of a statement: *Well, that sounds like a fun evening—not!* IDM **ˌnot a … | ˌnot one …** used for emphasis to mean 'no thing or person': *He didn't speak to me—not one word.* **ˌnot at ˈall** used to politely accept thanks or to agree to sth: *'Thanks a lot.' 'Not at all.'* ◊ *'Will it bother you if I smoke?' 'Not at all.'* **ˈnot that** used to state that you are not suggesting sth: *She hasn't written—not that she said she would.* ⇨ more at ONLY adv.

**not·able** 📖+ 🅒🅘 /ˈnəʊtəbl/ adj., noun
▪ adj. 📖+ 🅒🅘 (rather formal) deserving to be noticed or to receive attention; important SYN **striking**: *a notable success/achievement/example* ◊ *His eyes are his most notable feature.* ◊ *~ (for sth)* *The town is notable for its ancient harbour.* ◊ *With a few notable exceptions, everyone gave something.*
▪ noun [usually pl.] (formal) a famous or important person: *All the usual local notables were there.*

**not·ably** 📖+ 🅒🅘 /ˈnəʊtəbli/ adv. **1** 📖+ 🅒🅘 used for giving a good or the most important example of sth SYN **especially**: *The house had many drawbacks, most notably its price.* **2** to a great degree SYN **remarkably**: *This has not been a notably successful project.*

**no·tar·ize** (BrE also **-ise**) /ˈnəʊtəraɪz/ verb *~ sth* (law) if a document is **notarized**, it is given legal status by a NOTARY

**no·tary** /ˈnəʊtəri/ noun (pl. -ies) (also **ˌnotary ˈpublic** pl. **ˌnotaries ˈpublic**) (law) a person, especially a lawyer, with official authority to be a witness when sb signs a document and to make this document legally acceptable

1059 **note**

**no·ta·tion** /nəʊˈteɪʃn/ noun [U, C] a system of signs or symbols used to represent information, especially in mathematics, science and music ⇨ picture at MUSIC

**notch** /nɒtʃ; NAmE nɑːtʃ/ noun, verb
▪ noun **1** a level on a scale, often marking quality or achievement: *The quality of the food here has dropped a notch recently.* ⇨ see also TOP-NOTCH **2** a V-shape or a circle cut in an edge or a surface, sometimes used to keep a record of sth: *For each day he spent on the island, he cut a new notch in his stick.* **3** each of a series of holes, for example in a belt: *She tightened her belt an extra notch.*
▪ verb **1** *~ sth (up)* (informal) to achieve sth such as a win or a high score: *The team has notched up 20 goals already this season.* **2** *~ sth* to make a small cut in the shape of a V in an edge or a surface

**note** 🅞 🅐🅘 🅞 /nəʊt/ noun, verb
▪ noun
• **TO REMIND YOU 1** 🅐🅘 [C] a short piece of writing to help you remember sth: *Please **make a note** of the dates.* ◊ *She made a **mental note*** (= decided that she must remember) *to ask Alan about it.* ◊ ***Note to self*** (= a mental instruction): *book more holidays.*
• **SHORT LETTER 2** 🅐🅘 [C] a short informal letter: *Just a quick note to say thank you for a wonderful evening.* ◊ *She left a note for Ben on the kitchen table.* ◊ *He wrote a note to his parents saying he was leaving.* ◊ *a **suicide note***
• **INFORMATION 3** 🅐🅘 **notes** [pl.] information that you write down when sb is speaking, or when you are reading a book, etc: *He sat **taking notes** of everything that was said.* ◊ *Can I borrow your **lecture notes**?* **4** 🅐🅘 **notes** [pl.] detailed information that is kept about a particular person, topic or situation: *Patients' **medical notes** have gone missing.* ◊ ***notes on sth*** *He kept notes on the birds, mammals, reptiles and plants he saw on walks.* **5** 🅑🅘 [C, usually pl.] information about a performance, an actor's career, a piece of music, etc. printed in a special book or on a record cover, etc: *The booklet has full notes on each artist.* ⇨ see also LINER NOTE
• **IN BOOK 6** 🅑🅘 [C] a short comment on a word or passage in a book: *a new edition of 'Hamlet', with explanatory notes* ◊ *See note 3, page 259.* ⇨ see also FOOTNOTE, SIDE NOTE
• **MONEY 7** 🅑🅘 (BrE) (also **ˈbank-note** especially in BrE) (NAmE usually **bill**) [C] a piece of paper money: *a £5 note* ◊ *We only exchange notes and traveller's cheques.* ⇨ picture at MONEY
• **IN MUSIC 8** 🅑🅘 [C] a single sound of a particular length and PITCH (= how high or low a sound is), made by the voice or a musical instrument; the written or printed sign for a musical note: *He played the first few notes of the tune.* ◊ ***high/low notes*** ◊ *I played a lot of **wrong notes** because I was so nervous.* ⇨ WORDFINDER NOTE at SING ⇨ picture at MUSIC ⇨ see also HALF NOTE, WHOLE NOTE
• **QUALITY 9** [sing.] a particular quality in sth, for example in sb's voice or the atmosphere at an event; a comment on sth with a particular quality SYN **air**: *~ of sth* *There was a note of amusement in his voice.* ◊ ***on a …~*** *It's good to finish on a positive note.* ◊ *On a more serious note* (= speaking more seriously) … ◊ *On a slightly different note* (= changing the subject slightly), *let's talk about …* ◊ *As a side note, the entire festival is free.*
• **OFFICIAL DOCUMENT 10** [C] an official document with a particular purpose: *a sick note from your doctor* ◊ *The buyer has to sign a delivery note as proof of receipt.* ⇨ see also CREDIT NOTE, PROMISSORY NOTE **11** [C] (specialist) an official letter from the representative of one government to another: *an exchange of diplomatic notes*
IDM **ˌhit/ˌstrike the ˌright/ˌwrong ˈnote** (especially BrE) to do, say or write sth that is suitable/not suitable for a particular occasion **of ˈnote** of importance or of great interest: *a scientist of note* ◊ *The museum contains nothing of great note.* **ˌsound/ˌstrike a ˈnote (of sth)** to express feelings or opinions of a particular kind: *She sounded a note of warning in her speech.* **ˌtake ˈnote (of sth)** to pay attention to sth and be sure to remember it: *Take note of what he says.* ⇨ more at COMPARE v.
▪ verb (rather formal) **1** 🅑🅘 to notice or pay careful attention to sth: *~ sth* *Note the fine early Baroque altar inside the chapel.* ◊ *~ (that) …* *Please note (that) the office will be*

# notebook

closed on Monday. ◊ **~ how, where,** etc... *Note how these animals sometimes walk with their tails up in the air.* ◊ **it is noted that...** *It should be noted that dissertations submitted late will not be accepted.* ◊ **be noted for sth** *We are also noted for our delicious home-made patisserie.* ⊃ SYNONYMS at NOTICE ⊃ LANGUAGE BANK at EMPHASIS **2** to mention sth because it is important or interesting: *There are a few points here that are worth noting.* ◊ **~ that...** *The report noted that deaths on the roads had fallen by 2 per cent in 2017.* ◊ **~ how, where,** etc... *The author notes how journalists must, inevitably, simplify complex issues.* ◊ **it is noted that...** *It is noted that the available treatments for this condition remain expensive.* ◊ **Unless otherwise noted**, *the translations are mine.* ◊ *These policies,* **as noted above**, *are not always successful.* ⊃ SYNONYMS at COMMENT ⊃ LANGUAGE BANK at ARGUE **3** to record sth in writing **SYN** **note down**: *As he noted in his diary on 19 November...* **PHRV** **note sth ↔ down** to write down sth important so that you will not forget it **SYN** jot

**note·book** /ˈnəʊtbʊk/ *noun* **1** a small book of plain paper for writing notes in **2** (*NAmE*) (*BrE* **exercise book**) a small book for students to write their work in **3** (also **notebook computer**) a small computer that can work with a battery and be easily carried **SYN** **laptop** ⊃ compare DESKTOP COMPUTER, NETBOOK

**noted** /ˈnəʊtɪd/ *adj.* well known because of a special skill or feature **SYN** **famous**: *a noted dancer* ◊ **for sth** *He is not noted for his sense of humour.* ◊ **~ as sth** *The lake is noted as a home to many birds.*

**No. 10** = NUMBER TEN

**note·pad** /ˈnəʊtpæd/ *noun* sheets of paper that are held together at the top and used for writing notes on: *a notepad by the phone for messages*

**note·paper** /ˈnəʊtpeɪpə(r)/ (also **writing paper**) *noun* [U] paper for writing letters on

**note·worthy** /ˈnəʊtwɜːði; *NAmE* -wɜːrði/ *adj.* deserving to be noticed or to receive attention because it is unusual, important or interesting **SYN** **significant**

**not-for-ˈprofit** (*NAmE* **non-profit**) *adj., noun*
- *adj.* without the aim of making a profit: *a not-for-profit organization*
- *noun* an organization that does not aim to make a profit

**'nother** /ˈnʌðə(r)/ *adj.* (*non-standard*) another: *'nother thing just occurred to me.* **IDM** see WHOLE *adj.*

**noth·ing** /ˈnʌθɪŋ/ *pron.* **1** not anything; no single thing: *There was nothing in her bag.* ◊ *There's nothing you can do to help.* ◊ *The doctor said there was nothing wrong with me.* ◊ *Nothing else matters to him apart from his job.* ◊ *It cost us nothing to go in.* ◊ (*BrE*) *He's five foot nothing* (= exactly five feet tall). **2** very little; something that is not at all important or interesting: *We did nothing at the weekend.* ◊ *'What's that in your pocket?' 'Oh, nothing.'* ◊ *I know* **next to nothing** (= almost nothing) *about art.* **IDM** **be ˈnothing to sb** to be a person for whom sb has no feelings: *I used to love her but she's nothing to me any more.* **be/have ˈnothing to ˈdo with sb/sth** to have no connection with sb/sth: *Get out! It's nothing to do with you* (= you have no right to know about it). ◊ *That has nothing to do with what we're discussing.* **for ˈnothing 1** without payment **SYN** **free**: *She's always trying to get something for nothing.* **2** with no reward or result: *All that preparation was for nothing because the visit was cancelled.* **have ˈnothing on sb** (*informal*) **1** to have much less of a particular quality than sb/sth: *I'm quite a fast worker, but I've got nothing on her!* **2** (of the police, etc.) to have no information that could show sb to be guilty of sth **it is/was ˈnothing** used as a polite way of replying when sb thanks you for doing sth, to show that you were happy to do it **not for ˈnothing** for a very good reason: *Not for nothing was he called the king of rock and roll.* **ˈnothing but** **B2** only; no more/less than: *Nothing but a miracle can save her now.* ◊ *I want nothing but the best for my children.* **ˈnothing if not** extremely; very: *The trip was nothing if not varied.* **ˈnothing less than** used to emphasize how great or extreme sth is: *It was nothing less than a disaster.* **ˈnothing ˈlike** (*informal*) **1** not at all like: *It looks nothing like a horse.* **2** not nearly; not at all: *I had nothing like enough time to answer all the questions.* **ˌnothing ˈmuch** not a great amount of sth; nothing of great value or importance: *There's nothing much in the fridge.* ◊ *I got up late and did nothing much all day.* **(there's) nothing ˈto it** (it's) very easy: *You'll soon learn. There's nothing to it really.* **there is/was ˈnothing (else) ˈfor it (but to do sth)** there is no other action to take except the one mentioned: *There was nothing else for it but to resign.* **there is/was ˈnothing in sth** something is/was not true: *There was a rumour she was going to resign, but there was nothing in it.* **there's ˈnothing like sth** used to say that you enjoy sth very much: *There's nothing like a brisk walk on a cold day!* ⊃ more at STOP *v.*, SWEET *adj.*

**noth·ing·ness** /ˈnʌθɪŋnəs/ *noun* [U] a situation where nothing exists; the state of not existing

**no·tice** /ˈnəʊtɪs/ *verb, noun*
- *verb* (not usually used in the progressive tenses)
  - SEE/HEAR **1** [I, T] to see or hear sb/sth; to become aware of sb/sth: *People were making fun of him but he didn't seem to notice.* ◊ **~ sb/sth** *The first thing I noticed about the room was the smell.* ◊ *You can't* **fail to notice** *the poverty of the region.* ◊ **to barely/hardly/scarcely notice** sth ◊ **~ (that)...** *I couldn't help noticing (that) she was wearing a wig.* ◊ *He* **won't even notice** *I'm gone.* ◊ **~ how, what,** etc... *Did you notice how Rachel kept looking at her watch?* ◊ **~ sb/sth do sth** *I noticed them come in.* ◊ **~ sb/sth doing sth** *I didn't notice him leaving.*
  - PAY/GET ATTENTION **2** [T] **~ sb/sth** to pay attention to sb/sth: *Notice the way the bridge is supported by its suspension cables.* **3** [T] **get (yourself) noticed** to get attention from other people: *She wears those strange clothes just to get herself noticed.*
- *noun*
  - GIVING INFORMATION **1** [C] a sheet of paper giving written or printed information, usually put in a public place: *There was a notice on the board saying the class had been cancelled.* **2** [C] a board or sign giving information, an instruction or a warning: *a notice saying 'Keep off the Grass'*
  - ANNOUNCING STH **3** [C] a small advertisement or announcement in a newspaper or magazine: *notices of births, marriages and deaths* **4** [C] a short announcement made at the beginning or end of a meeting, a church service, etc: *There are just two notices this week.*
  - PAYING ATTENTION **5** [U] the fact of sb paying attention to sb/sth or knowing about sth: *Don't* **take any notice of** *what you read in the papers.* ◊ **Take no notice of** *what he says.* ◊ *These protests have really made the government* **sit up and take notice** (= realize the importance of the situation). ◊ *It was Susan who* **brought the problem to my notice** (= told me about it). ◊ *Normally, the letter would not have* **come to my notice** (= I would not have known about it). ◊ *The work received little notice in the national media.* ◊ (*formal*) *It will not have* **escaped your notice** *that there have been some major changes in the company.*
  - WARNING **6** [U] information or a warning given in advance of sth that is going to happen: *You are welcome to come and stay as long as you give us* **plenty of notice**. ◊ *I'm sorry it's such* **short notice** — *we didn't know ourselves until today.* **without ~** *Prices may be altered without notice.* ◊ *The bar is closed* **until further notice** (= until you are told that it is open again). ◊ *Councils can issue* **fixed penalty notices** (= sums of money that must be paid) *for litter and graffiti.* ◊ **~ that...** *This new law* **serves notice** *that criminals will not go unpunished.*
  - WHEN LEAVING JOB/HOUSE **7** [U, C] a formal letter or statement saying that you will or must leave your job or house at the end of a particular period of time: *He has* **handed in his notice**. ◊ *They gave her two weeks'* **notice**. ◊ *We received an eviction notice today.*
  - REVIEW OF BOOK/PLAY **8** [C] a short article in a newspaper or magazine, giving an opinion about a book, play, etc. **SYN** review

**IDM** **at short ˈnotice** | **at a moment's ˈnotice** (*NAmE* also **on short ˈnotice**) not long in advance; without warning or time for preparation: *This was the best room we could get*

## SYNONYMS

### notice
note • detect • observe • witness

These words all mean to see sth, especially when you pay careful attention to it.

**notice** to see, hear or become aware of sb/sth; to pay attention to sb/sth: *The first thing I noticed about the room was the smell.*

**note** (*rather formal*) to notice or pay careful attention to sth: *Please note (that) the office will be closed on Monday.* NOTE This word is very common in business English: *Note that the prices are inclusive of VAT.*

**detect** to discover or notice sth, especially sth that is not easy to see, hear, etc: *The tests are designed to detect the disease early.*

**observe** (*formal*) to see or notice sb/sth: *Have you observed any changes lately?* ◊ *The police observed a man enter the bank.*

**witness** (*rather formal*) to see sth happen: *Police have appealed for anyone who witnessed the incident to contact them.*

### PATTERNS
- to notice/note/detect/observe **that/how/what/where/who…**
- to notice/observe/witness **sth happen/sb do sth**

---

at such short notice. ◊ *You must be ready to leave at a moment's notice.*

**no·tice·able** /ˈnəʊtɪsəbl/ *adj.* easy to see or notice; clear or definite: *a noticeable improvement* ◊ *There is a noticeable difference between the two brands.* ◊ **~ in sb/sth** *This effect is particularly noticeable in younger patients.* ◊ **it is ~ that…** *It was noticeable that none of the family were present.* ▶ **no·tice·ably** /-bli/ *adv.*: *Her hand was shaking noticeably.* ◊ *Marks were noticeably higher for girls than for boys.* ◊ *The question of childcare was noticeably absent from the discussion.*

**no·tice·board** /ˈnəʊtɪsbɔːd; *NAmE* -bɔːrd/ (*BrE*) (*NAmE* **bulletin board**) (also **board** *BrE*, *NAmE*) *noun* a board for putting notices on

**no·ti·fi·able** /ˈnəʊtɪfaɪəbl/ *adj.* [usually before noun] (*formal*) (of a disease or a crime) so dangerous or serious that it must by law be reported officially to the authorities

**no·ti·fi·ca·tion** /ˌnəʊtɪfɪˈkeɪʃn/ *noun* [U, C] (*formal*) official information of sth; the act of giving or receiving this information: *advance/prior notification* (= telling sb in advance about sth) ◊ *written notification* ◊ *You should receive (a) notification of our decision in the next week.*

**no·tify** /ˈnəʊtɪfaɪ/ *verb* [often passive] (**no·ti·fies, no·ti·fy·ing, no·ti·fied, no·ti·fied**) (*formal*) to formally or officially tell sb about sth **SYN** **inform**: **~sb** *Competition winners will be notified by post.* ◊ **~sb of sth** *The police must be notified of the date of the demonstration.* ◊ **~sth to sb** *The date of the demonstration must be notified to the police.* ◊ **~sb that…** *Members have been notified that there will be a small increase in the fee.*

**no·tion** /ˈnəʊʃn/ *noun* an idea, a belief or an understanding of sth: **~of sth** *a political system based on the notions of equality and liberty* ◊ *She had only a vague notion of what might happen.* ◊ *The author challenges preconceived notions of storytelling.* ◊ **~that…** *I have to reject the notion that greed can be a good thing.* ◊ **~how, what, why, etc…** *I haven't the faintest notion how to get there.* ◊ **~about sth** *I don't have any romantic notions about rural living.*

**no·tion·al** /ˈnəʊʃənl/ *adj.* (*formal*) based on a guess, estimate or theory; not existing in reality ▶ **no·tion·al·ly** /-nəli/ *adv.*

**no·tori·ety** /ˌnəʊtəˈraɪəti/ *noun* [U, sing.] the state of being famous for being bad in some way: **~ (for sth)** *She achieved notoriety for her affair with the senator.* ◊ **as sth** *He gained a certain notoriety as a gambler.*

---

1061 **novel**

**no·tori·ous** /nəʊˈtɔːriəs/ *adj.* well known for being bad: *a notorious criminal* ◊ **~ for sth/for doing sth** *The country is notorious for its appalling prison conditions.* ◊ **~ as sth** *The bar has become notorious as a meeting-place for drug dealers.* ▶ **no·tori·ous·ly** *adv.*: *Mountain weather is notoriously difficult to predict.*

**not·with·stand·ing** /ˌnɒtwɪθˈstændɪŋ, -wɪð-/; *NAmE* ˈnɑːt-/ *prep., adv., conj.*
■ *prep.* (*formal*) (also used following the noun it refers to) without being affected by sth; despite sth: *Notwithstanding some major financial problems, the school has had a successful year.* ◊ *The bad weather notwithstanding, the event was a great success.*
■ *adv.* (*formal*) despite this **SYN** **however, nevertheless**: *Notwithstanding, the problem is a significant one.*
■ *conj.* (*formal*) although; despite the fact that

**nou·gat** /ˈnuːgɑː; *NAmE* -gət/ *noun* [U] a hard sweet that has to be CHEWED a lot, often containing nuts, CHERRIES, etc. and pink or white in colour

**nought** /nɔːt/ *noun* **1** [C, U] (*BrE*) (also **zero** *NAmE, BrE*) the figure 0: *A million is written with six noughts.* ◊ *nought point one* (= written 0.1) ◊ *I give the programme nought out of ten for humour.* **2** (*also* **naught**) [U] (*literary*) used in particular phrases to mean 'nothing': *All our efforts have come to nought* (= have not been successful).

**the nought·ies** (*also* **the Noughties**) /ðə ˈnɔːtiz/ *noun* [pl.] (*BrE*) the years from 2000 to 2009

**ˌnoughts and ˈcrosses** (*BrE*) (*NAmE* **tic-tac-toe**) *noun* [U] a simple game in which two players take turns to write Os or Xs in a set of nine squares. The first player to complete a row of three Os or three Xs is the winner.

**noun** /naʊn/ *noun* (*grammar*) (*abbr.* **n.**) a word that refers to a person (such as *Ann* or *doctor*), a place (such as *Paris* or *city*) or a thing, a quality or an activity (such as *plant, joy* or *tennis*) ⊃ see also ABSTRACT NOUN, COLLECTIVE NOUN, COMMON NOUN, COUNT NOUN, MASS NOUN, PROPER NOUN, UNCOUNT NOUN ⊃ WORDFINDER NOTE at GRAMMAR

**ˈnoun phrase** *noun* (*grammar*) a word or group of words in a sentence that behaves in the same way as a noun, that is as a subject, an object, a COMPLEMENT, or as the object of a preposition: *In the sentence 'I spoke to the driver of the car', 'the driver of the car' is a noun phrase.*

**nour·ish** /ˈnʌrɪʃ; *NAmE* ˈnɜːr-/ *verb* **1** **~sb/sth** to keep a person, an animal or a plant alive and healthy with food, etc: *All the children were well nourished and in good physical condition.* **2** **~sth** (*formal*) to allow a feeling, an idea, etc. to develop or grow stronger: *By investing in education, we nourish the talents of our children.* ▶ **nour·ish·ing** *adj.*: *nourishing food*

**nour·ish·ment** /ˈnʌrɪʃmənt; *NAmE* ˈnɜːr-/ *noun* [U] (*formal* or *specialist*) food that is needed to stay alive, grow and stay healthy **SYN** **nutrition**: *Can plants obtain adequate nourishment from such poor soil?* ◊ (*figurative*) *As a child, she was starved of intellectual nourishment.*

**nous** /naʊs/ *noun* [U] (*BrE, informal*) intelligence and the ability to think and act in a practical way **SYN** **common sense**

**nou·veau riche** /ˌnuːvəʊ ˈriːʃ/ *noun* (*pl.* **nou·veaux riches** /ˌnuːvəʊ ˈriːʃ/ *or* **the nou·veau riche**) (*from French, disapproving*) a person who has recently become rich and likes to show how rich they are in a very obvious way ▶ **nou·veau riche** *adj.*

**nou·velle cuis·ine** /ˌnuːvel kwɪˈziːn/ *noun* [U] (*from French*) a modern style of cooking that avoids heavy foods and serves small amounts of different dishes arranged in an attractive way on the plate

**nova** /ˈnəʊvə/ *noun* (*pl.* **novae** /-viː/ *or* **novas**) (*astronomy*) a star that suddenly becomes much brighter for a short period ⊃ compare SUPERNOVA

**novel** /ˈnɒvl; *NAmE* ˈnɑːvl/ *noun, adj.*
■ *noun* **1** [C] a story long enough to fill a complete book, in which the characters and events are usually imaginary: *to write/publish/read a novel* ◊ *detective/historical/romantic novels* ◊ *the novels of Jane Austen* ◊ *Her latest novel is set in Cornwall.* ◊ *a best-selling novel* ⊃ see also GRAPHIC

# novelette

**NOVEL** ⇒ **WORDFINDER NOTE** at BOOK **2 the novel** [sing.] the type of literature that novels represent: *The novel is the most adaptable of all literary forms.*
- **adj.** (*often approving*) different from anything known before; new, interesting and often seeming slightly strange: *a novel feature*

**nov·el·ette** /ˌnɒvlˈet; NAmE ˌnɑːvˈl-/ *noun* a short novel, especially a romantic novel that is considered to be badly written

**nov·el·ist** /ˈnɒvəlɪst; NAmE ˈnɑːv-/ *noun* a person who writes novels: *a romantic/historical novelist*

**nov·el·is·tic** /ˌnɒvəˈlɪstɪk; NAmE ˌnɑːv-/ *adj.* (*formal*) typical of or used in novels

**nov·ella** /nəˈvelə/ *noun* a short novel

**nov·elty** /ˈnɒvlti; NAmE ˈnɑːv-/ *noun*,
- *noun* (*pl.* **-ies**) **1** [U] the quality of being new, different and interesting: *It was fun working there at first but* ***the novelty soon wore off*** (= it became boring). ◊ *There's a certain novelty value in this approach.* **2** [C] a thing, person or situation that is interesting because it is new, unusual or has not been known before: *Electric cars are still something of a novelty.* **3** [C] a small cheap object sold as a toy or a decoration
- *adj.* [only before noun] different and unusual; intended to be humorous and to catch people's attention: *a novelty teapot*

**No·vem·ber** /nəʊˈvembə(r)/ *noun* [U, C] (*abbr.* **Nov.**) the 11th month of the year, between October and December **HELP** To see how **November** is used, look at the examples at **April**.

**nov·ice** /ˈnɒvɪs; NAmE ˈnɑːv-/ *noun* **1** a person who is new and has little experience in a skill, job or situation: *I'm a complete novice at skiing.* ◊ *computer software for novices/the novice user* **2** a person who has joined a religious group and is preparing to become a MONK or a NUN **3** a horse that has not yet won an important race

**no·vi·ti·ate** (*also* **no·vi·ci·ate**) /nəʊˈvɪʃiət/ *noun* (*formal*) a period of being a novice

**now** /naʊ/ *adv., conj.*
- *adv.* **1** (at) the present time: *Where are you living now?* ◊ *It's too late now.* ◊ *It's been two weeks now since she called.* ◊ *I can tell you right now that you're wrong.* **from ~ on** *From now on I'll be more careful.* **by ~** *He should be home by now.* **up till ~** *I've lived at home up till now.* **for ~** *That's all for now.* **2** at or from this moment, but not before: *Start writing now.* ◊ *I am now ready to answer your questions.* **3** (*informal*) used to show that you are annoyed about sth: *Now they want to tax food!* ◊ *What do you want now?* **4** used to get sb's attention before changing the subject or asking them to do sth: *Now, listen to what she's saying.* ◊ *Now, the next point is quite complex.* ◊ *Now come and sit down.* ◊ *Now let me think…*
- **IDM** **(every) now and aˈgain/ˈthen** from time to time; occasionally: *Every now and again she checked to see if he was still asleep.* **now for ˈsb/ˈsth** used when turning to a fresh activity or subject: *And now for some travel news.* **ˌnow, ˈnow** (*also* **ˌnow ˈthen**) used to show in a mild way that you do not approve of sth: *Now now, that's enough noise.* **now … now …** at one time … at another time …: *Her moods kept changing—now happy, now sad.* **(it's) ˌnow or ˈnever** this is the only opportunity sb will have to do sth **ˈnow then 1** = NOW, NOW *adv.* **2** used when making a suggestion or an offer: *Now then, who wants to come for a walk?* **ˈnow what?** (*informal*) **1** (*also* **what is it ˈnow?**) used when you are annoyed because sb is always asking questions or interrupting you: *'Yes, but Dad…' 'Now what?'* **2** used to say that you do not know what to do next in a particular situation
- *conj.* **~ (that) …** because the thing mentioned is happening or has just happened: *Now that the kids have left home we've got a lot of extra space.*

**now·adays** /ˈnaʊədeɪz/ *adv.* at the present time, in contrast with the past: *Nowadays most kids prefer going online to reading books.*

**no·where** /ˈnəʊweə(r); NAmE -wer/ (*also informal* **ˈno place** especially in NAmE) *adv.* not in or to any place: *I had nowhere to live, so I was sleeping on my sister's couch.* ◊ *There was nowhere for me to sit.* ◊ *'Where are you going this weekend?' 'Nowhere special.'* ◊ *She doesn't want to stay there but she has nowhere else to go.* ◊ *Nowhere do plants flourish with such vigour as they do in tropical rainforests.*
- **IDM** **from/out of nowhere** in a sudden and surprising way: *A huge flock of sheep seemed to appear from nowhere.* ◊ *The attack came from nowhere.* **get/go ˈnowhere | get sb ˈnowhere** to make no progress or have no success; to not enable sb to make progress or have success: *We discussed it all morning but got nowhere.* ◊ *Talking to him will get you nowhere.* ◊ *His career was going nowhere fast.* ◊ *The campaign over pay and conditions was getting nowhere.* **nowhere to be ˈfound/ˈseen | nowhere in ˈsight** impossible for anyone to find or see: *The children were nowhere to be seen.* ◊ *A peace settlement is nowhere in sight* (= is not likely in the near future). ⇒ more at LEAD[1] *v.*, MIDDLE *n.*, NEAR *adv.*

**ˌno-ˈwin** *adj.* [only before noun] (of a situation, policy, etc.) that will end badly whatever you decide to do: *We are considering the options available to us in this no-win situation.*

**ˈnow-now** *adv.* (*SAfrE, informal*) **1** within a short period of time: *I'll be with you now-now.* **2** a short time ago: *She left now-now.*

**nowt** /naʊt/ *pron.* (*BrE, dialect, informal*) nothing: *There's nowt wrong with it.*

**nox·ious** /ˈnɒkʃəs; NAmE ˈnɑːk-/ *adj.* (*formal*) poisonous or harmful: *noxious fumes*

**noz·zle** /ˈnɒzl; NAmE ˈnɑːzl/ *noun* a narrow piece that is attached to the end of a pipe or tube to direct the stream of liquid, air or gas passing through

**NQ** /ˌen ˈkjuː/ *noun* (in Scotland) one of a range of courses and exams that are taken in a number of different subjects and at different levels between the ages of approximately 15 and 18. These include National 3, 4 and 5 (replacing STANDARD GRADE exams). (the abbreviation for 'National Qualification')

**nr** *abbr.* (*BrE*) near (used, for example, in the address of a small village): *Howden, nr Goole*

**NRA** /ˌen ɑːr ˈeɪ/ *abbr.* National Rifle Association (a US organization that supports the right of citizens to own a gun)

**NRI** /ˌen ɑːr ˈaɪ/ *noun* (*IndE*) Non-Resident Indian (a person of Indian origin who is working somewhere else but who keeps links with India)

**ns** *abbr.* (in writing) NANOSECOND

**NSFW** *abbr.* not safe (or suitable) for work (used in emails, on internet FORUMS, etc. to show a link to a website or WEB PAGE that contains images, text or video that people may find offensive)

**nth** /enθ/ *adj.* [only before noun] (*informal*) used when you are stating that sth is the last in a long series and emphasizing how often sth has happened: *It's the nth time I've explained it to you.*
- **IDM** **to the nth deˈgree** extremely; to an extreme degree

**NTSC** /ˌen tiː es ˈsiː/ *noun* [U] (*specialist*) a television broadcasting system that is used in North America and Japan ⇒ compare PAL

**nu** /njuː/ *noun* the 13th letter of the Greek alphabet (N, ν)

**nu·ance** /ˈnjuːɑːns; NAmE ˈnuː-/ *noun* [C, U] a very slight difference in meaning, sound, colour or sb's feelings that is not usually very obvious: *He watched her face intently to catch every nuance of expression.*

**nub** /nʌb/ *noun* [sing.] **the ~ (of sth)** the central or essential point of a situation, problem, etc: *The nub of the matter is that business is declining.*

**nu·bile** /ˈnjuːbaɪl; NAmE ˈnuːbl, -baɪl/ *adj.* (of a girl or young woman) sexually attractive

**nu·clear** /ˈnjuːkliə(r); NAmE ˈnuː-/ *adj.* [usually before noun] **1** using, producing or resulting from nuclear energy: *a nuclear power plant/station* ◊ *nuclear-powered submarines* ◊ *a nuclear reactor* ◊ *nuclear waste/*

**fuel** ⇒ WORDFINDER NOTE at ENERGY 2 ⟨B1⟩ connected with weapons that use nuclear energy: *nuclear weapons/arms* ◊ *a nuclear bomb/missile/warhead* ◊ *a nuclear explosion/attack/war* ◊ *the country's nuclear capability* (= the fact that it has nuclear weapons) ◊ *The country is developing a nuclear weapons program.* **3** (*physics*) of the NUCLEUS (= central part) of an ATOM: *nuclear particles* ◊ *a nuclear reaction* ⇒ WORDFINDER NOTE at PHYSICS

**nuclear de'terrent** *noun* a nuclear weapon or weapons system that is intended to stop an enemy from attacking: *the country's nuclear deterrents*

**nuclear 'energy** (*also* **nuclear 'power**, **a,tomic 'energy**, **a,tomic 'power**) *noun* [U] a powerful form of energy produced by changing matter into energy by splitting the NUCLEI (= central parts) of ATOMS. It is used to produce electricity.

**nuclear 'family** *noun* (*specialist*) a family that consists of father, mother and children, when it is thought of as a unit in society ⇒ compare EXTENDED FAMILY

**nuclear 'fission** *noun* [U] = FISSION

**nuclear-'free** *adj.* [usually before noun] (of a country or a region) not having or allowing nuclear energy, weapons or materials: *a nuclear-free zone*

**nuclear 'fuel** *noun* [U] a substance that can be used as a source of NUCLEAR ENERGY because it is capable of NUCLEAR FISSION

**nuclear 'fusion** *noun* [U] = FUSION

**nuclear 'option** *noun* (*politics*) the most extreme possible response to a particular situation: *Currency controls would be the nuclear option.*

**nuclear 'physics** *noun* [U] the area of physics which deals with the NUCLEUS of ATOMS and with nuclear energy ▶ **nuclear 'physicist** *noun*

**nuclear 'power** *noun* [U] = NUCLEAR ENERGY

**nuclear re'actor** *noun* = REACTOR

**nuclear 'waste** *noun* [U] waste material which is RADIOACTIVE, especially used fuel from nuclear power stations

**nuclear 'winter** *noun* a period of great cold and DARKNESS which scientists believe would follow a nuclear war, caused by smoke and dust in the atmosphere blocking heat and light from the sun

**nu·cle·ic acid** /ˌnjuːˈkliːɪk ˈæsɪd, -ˈkleɪɪk/ *NAmE* ˌnuː-/ *noun* [U, C] (*chemistry*) either of two substances, DNA and RNA, that are present in all living cells

**nu·cleo·tide** /ˈnjuːkliətaɪd; *NAmE* ˈnuː-/ *noun* (*chemistry*) one of the many small MOLECULES that combine to form DNA and RNA

**nu·cleus** /ˈnjuːkliəs; *NAmE* ˈnuː-/ *noun* (*pl.* **nu·clei** /-kliaɪ/) **1** (*physics*) the part of an ATOM that contains most of its mass and that carries a positive electric charge ⇒ see also NEUTRON, PROTON ⇒ WORDFINDER NOTE at ATOM **2** (*biology*) the central part of some cells, containing the GENETIC material **3** the central part of sth around which other parts are located or collected: *These paintings will form the nucleus of a new collection.*

**nude** /njuːd; *NAmE* nuːd/ *adj., noun*
■ *adj.* **1** (especially of a human figure in art) not wearing any clothes ⟨SYN⟩ naked: *a nude model* ◊ *he asked me to pose nude for him.* **2** involving people who are not wearing any clothes: *a nude photograph* ◊ *Are there any nude scenes in the movie?* **3** (*NAmE*) (of PANTYHOSE, etc.) skin-coloured
■ *noun* a work of art consisting of a NAKED human figure; a NAKED human figure in art: *a bronze nude by Rodin* ◊ *a reclining nude*
⟨IDM⟩ **in the 'nude** not wearing any clothes ⟨SYN⟩ naked: *She refuses to be photographed in the nude.*

**nudge** /nʌdʒ/ *verb, noun*
■ *verb* **1** [T] ~ **sb/sth** to push sb gently, especially with your ELBOW, in order to get their attention: *He nudged me and whispered, 'Look who's just come in.'* **2** [T] ~ **sb/sth + adv./prep.** to push sb/sth gently or gradually in a particular direction: *He nudged the ball past the goalie and into the net.* ◊ *She nudged me out of the way.* ◊ (*figurative*) *He nudged the conversation towards the subject of money.* ◊ (*figurative*) *She tried to nudge him into changing his mind* (= persuade him to do it). **3** [T, I] ~ **(sth) + adv./prep.** to move forward by pushing with your ELBOW: *He nudged his way through the crowd.* **4** [T] ~ **sth (+ adv./prep.)** to reach or make sth reach a particular level: *Inflation was nudging 20 per cent.* ◊ *This afternoon's sunshine could nudge the temperature above freezing.*
■ *noun* a slight push, usually with the ELBOW: *She gave me a gentle nudge in the ribs to tell me to shut up.* ◊ (*figurative*) *He can work hard but he needs a nudge now and then.*
⟨IDM⟩ **,nudge ,nudge, wink 'wink | a ,nudge and a 'wink** used to suggest sth to do with sex without actually saying it: *They've been spending a lot of time together, nudge nudge, wink wink.*

**nudie** /ˈnjuːdi; *NAmE* ˈnuː-/ *adj.* (*informal*) showing or including people wearing no clothes: *nudie photographs*

**nud·ism** /ˈnjuːdɪzəm; *NAmE* ˈnuː-/ (*also* **na·tur·ism** *especially in BrE*) *noun* [U] the practice of not wearing any clothes because you believe this is more natural and healthy

**nud·ist** /ˈnjuːdɪst; *NAmE* ˈnuː-/ (*also* **na·tur·ist** *especially in BrE*) *noun* a person who does not wear any clothes because they believe this is more natural and healthy: *a nudist beach/camp*

**nud·ity** /ˈnjuːdəti; *NAmE* ˈnuː-/ *noun* [U] the state of wearing no clothes: *The committee claimed that there was too much nudity on television.*

**nu·ga·tory** /ˈnjuːɡətəri; *NAmE* ˈnuːɡətɔːri/ *adj.* (*formal*) having no purpose or value ⟨SYN⟩ worthless

**nug·get** /ˈnʌɡɪt/ *noun* **1** a small piece of a valuable metal or mineral, especially gold, that is found in the earth **2** a small round piece of some types of food: *chicken nuggets* **3** a small thing such as an idea or a fact that people think of as valuable ⟨SYN⟩ snippet: *a useful nugget of information*

**nuis·ance** /ˈnjuːsns; *NAmE* ˈnuː-/ *noun* **1** [C, usually sing.] a thing, person or situation that is annoying or causes trouble or problems: *I don't want to be a nuisance so tell me if you want to be alone.* ◊ *I hope you're not making a nuisance of yourself.* ◊ *It's a nuisance having to go back tomorrow.* ◊ *What a nuisance!* **2** [C, U] (*law*) behaviour by sb that annoys other people and that a court can order the person to stop: *He was charged with causing a public nuisance.*

**'nuisance call** *noun* a phone call made by a person who wants to annoy sb, sometimes by making comments about sex, or to threaten them

**nuke** /njuːk; *NAmE* nuːk, njuːk/ *verb, noun* (*informal*)
■ *verb* ~ **sth** to attack a place with nuclear weapons
■ *noun* a nuclear weapon

**null** /nʌl/ *adj.* (*specialist*) having the value zero: *a null result*
⟨IDM⟩ **,null and 'void** (*law*) (of an election, agreement, etc.) having no legal force; not VALID: *The contract was declared null and void.*

**'null hypothesis** *noun* (*statistics*) the idea that an experiment that is done using two groups of people will show the same results for each group

**nul·lify** /ˈnʌlɪfaɪ/ *verb* (**nul·li·fies, nul·li·fy·ing, nul·li·fied, nul·li·fied**) **1** ~ **sth** (*formal or law*) to make sth such as an agreement or order lose its legal force ⟨SYN⟩ invalidate: *Judges were unwilling to nullify government decisions.* **2** ~ **sth** (*formal*) to make sth lose its effect or power ⟨SYN⟩ negate: *An unhealthy diet will nullify the effects of training.*

**nul·lity** /ˈnʌləti/ *noun* [sing.] (*formal or law*) the fact of sth, for example a marriage, having no legal force or no longer being officially recognized; something which is no longer officially recognized

**numb** /nʌm/ *adj., verb*
■ *adj.* **1** if a part of your body is **numb**, you cannot feel anything in it, for example because of cold: *to be/go numb* ◊ *numb with cold* ◊ *I've just been to the dentist and my face is still numb.* **2** unable to feel, think or react in the normal way: *He felt numb with shock.* ⇒ see also NUMBING
▶ **numb·ly** *adv.*: *Her life would never be the same again, she realized numbly.* **numb·ness** *noun* [U]: *pain and numbness in my fingers* ◊ *He was still in a state of numbness and shock from the accident.*

# number

- **verb 1** ~ sth to make a part of your body unable to feel anything, for example because of cold: *His fingers were numbed with the cold.* **2** ~ sb to make sb unable to feel, think or react in a normal way, for example because of an emotional shock SYN **stun**: *We sat there in silence, numbed by the shock of her death.*

## num·ber ⓘ A1 ⊙ /ˈnʌmbə(r)/ noun, verb

■ **noun**
- **WORD/SYMBOL 1** A1 [C] a word or symbol that represents an amount or a quantity SYN **figure**: *Think of a number and multiply it by two.* ◇ *a high/low number* ◇ *even numbers* (= 2, 4, 6, etc.) ◇ *odd numbers* (= 1, 3, 5, etc.) ◇ *You owe me 27 dollars? Make it 30, that's a good round number.* ⊃ see also ATOMIC NUMBER, CARDINAL *noun* (2), MAGIC NUMBER, MASS NUMBER, ORDINAL, PRIME NUMBER, REGISTRATION NUMBER, SERIAL NUMBER, WHOLE NUMBER
- **POSITION IN SERIES 2** A1 [C] (*abbr.* **No.**, *BrE also* **No**) (*symb.* #) used before a figure to show the position of sth in a series: *They live at number 26.* ◇ *The song reached number 5 in the charts.*
- **TELEPHONE, ETC. 3** A1 [C] (often in compounds) a set of figures that is used to identify sth or communicate by phone, etc: *Ask for the customer's name and phone number.* ◇ *I'm sorry, I think you have the wrong number* (= wrong phone number). ◇ *Call this number and ask to speak to John.* ◇ *What is your account number, please?* ⊃ see also BOX NUMBER, E-NUMBER, PHONE NUMBER, PIN, REGISTRATION NUMBER, SERIAL NUMBER
- **QUANTITY 4** A1 [C] a quantity of people or things: ~ **of sb/sth** *A large number of people have applied for the job.* ◇ *In a small number of cases the illness is fatal.* ◇ *The number of homeless people has increased dramatically.* ◇ *Huge numbers of* (= very many) *animals have died.* ◇ *A number of* (= some) *problems have arisen.* ◇ *I could give you any number of* (= a lot of) *reasons for not going.* ◇ **in**~ *We were eight in number* (= there were eight of us). ◇ *Nurses are leaving the profession in increasing numbers.* ◇ *staff/student numbers* HELP *A plural verb is needed after* **a/an (large, small, etc.) number of …**
- **GROUP OF PEOPLE 5** [sing.] (*formal*) a group or quantity of people: *one of our number* (= one of us) ◇ *The prime minister is elected by MPs from among their number.*
- **MAGAZINE 6** [C] (*BrE*) the version of a magazine, etc. published on a particular day, in a particular month, etc. SYN **issue**: *the October number of 'Vogue'*
- **SONG/DANCE 7** [C] a song or dance, especially one of several in a performance: *They sang a slow romantic number.*
- **THING ADMIRED 8** [sing.] (*informal*) (following one or more adjectives) a thing, such as a dress or a car, that is admired: *She was wearing a black velvet number.*
- **GRAMMAR 9** [U] the form of a word, showing whether one or more than one person or thing is being talked about: *The word 'men' is plural in number.* ◇ *The subject of a sentence and its verb must agree in number.*

IDM **by numbers** following a set of simple instructions identified by numbers: *painting by numbers* ◇ **by the 'numbers** (*NAmE*) following closely the accepted rules for doing sth ◇ **have (got) sb's 'number** (*informal*) to know what sb is really like and what they plan to do: *He thinks he can fool me but I've got his number.* ◇ **your 'number is up** (*informal*) the time has come when you will die or lose everything ◇ **'numbers game** a way of considering an activity, etc. that considers only the number of people doing sth, things achieved, etc., not with who or what they are: *MPs were playing the numbers game as the crucial vote drew closer.* ⊃ more at CUSHY, OPPOSITE *adj.*, SAFETY, STRENGTH, WEIGHT *n.*

■ **verb**
- **MAKE A SERIES 1** A2 [T] to give a number to sth as part of a series or list: ~ **sth** *All the seats in the stadium are numbered.* ◇ *I couldn't work out the numbering system for the hotel rooms.* ◇ ~ **sth from … to …** *Number the car's features from 1 to 10 according to importance.* ◇ ~ **sth** + **noun** *The doors were numbered 2, 4, 6 and 8.*
- **MAKE STH AS TOTAL 2** [I] + **noun** to make a particular number when added together SYN **add up to**: *The crowd numbered more than a thousand.* ◇ *We numbered 20* (= there were 20 of us in the group).
- **INCLUDE 3** [T, I] (*formal*) to include sb/sth in a particular group; to be included in a particular group: ~ **sb/sth among sth** *I number her among my closest friends.* ◇ ~ **among sth** *He numbers among the best classical actors in Britain.* IDM see DAY

**'number crunching** *noun* [U] (*informal*) the process of calculating numbers, especially when a large amount of data is involved and the data is processed in a short space of time

**numbered** /ˈnʌmbəd; *NAmE* -bərd/ *adj.* having a number to show that it is part of a series or list: *The players all wear numbered shirts.* IDM see DAY

**num·ber·less** /ˈnʌmbələs; *NAmE* -bərl-/ *adj.* (*literary*) too many to be counted SYN **innumerable**

**number 'one** *noun, adj.* (*informal*)
■ **noun 1** [U] the most important or best person or thing: *We're number one in the used car business.* **2** [U, C] the pop song or recording that has sold the most copies/had the most downloads in a particular week: *The new album went straight to number one.* ◇ *She's had three number ones.* **3** [U] yourself: *Looking after number one is all she thinks about.* **4** [sing.] (*informal*) an expression used especially by children or when speaking to children to talk about passing liquid waste from the body: *It's only a number one.* ⊃ compare NUMBER TWO
■ **adj.** [only before noun] most important or best: *the world's number one athlete* ◇ *the number one priority*

**'number plate** (*also* **regi'stration plate**) (*both BrE*) (*NAmE* **'license plate**) *noun* a metal or plastic plate on the front and back of a vehicle that shows its REGISTRATION NUMBER

**Number 'Ten** (*also* **No. 10**) *noun* [U + sing./pl. v.] 10 Downing Street, London, the official home of the British prime minister, often used to refer to the government: *Number Ten had nothing to say on the matter.*

**number 'two** *noun* [sing.] (*informal*) an expression used especially by children or when speaking to children to talk about passing solid waste from the body: *Mum, I need a number two.* ⊃ compare NUMBER ONE

**numb·ing** /ˈnʌmɪŋ/ *adj.* (of an experience or a situation) making you unable to feel anything: *numbing cold/fear* ◇ *Watching television had a numbing effect on his mind.*

**numb·skull** (*also* **num·skull**) /ˈnʌmskʌl/ *noun* (*informal*) a stupid person

**nu·mer·acy** /ˈnjuːmərəsi; *NAmE* ˈnuː-/ *noun* [U] a good basic knowledge of mathematics; the ability to understand and work with numbers: *standards of literacy and numeracy* ⊃ WORDFINDER NOTE at MATHS ▶ **nu·mer·ate** /-rət/ *adj.*: *All students should be numerate and literate when they leave school.* OPP **innumerate**

**nu·meral** /ˈnjuːmərəl; *NAmE* ˈnuː-/ *noun* a sign or symbol that represents a number ⊃ see also ARABIC NUMERAL, ROMAN NUMERAL

**nu·mer·ator** /ˈnjuːməreɪtə(r); *NAmE* ˈnuː-/ *noun* (*mathematics*) the number above the line in a FRACTION, for example 3 in the FRACTION ¾ ⊃ compare DENOMINATOR

**nu·mer·ic·al** /njuːˈmerɪkl; *NAmE* nuː-/ (*also less frequent* **nu·mer·ic** /njuːˈmerɪk; *NAmE* nuː-/) *adj.* relating to numbers; expressed in numbers: *numerical data* ◇ *The results are expressed in descending numerical order.* ▶ **nu·mer·ic·al·ly** /-kli/ *adv.*: *to express the results numerically*

**nu·mer·ology** /ˌnjuːməˈrɒlədʒi; *NAmE* ˌnuːməˈrɑː-/ *noun* [U] the use of numbers to try to tell sb what will happen in the future ▶ **nu·mero·logic·al** /ˌnjuːmərəˈlɒdʒɪkl; *NAmE* ˌnuːmərəˈlɑː-/ *adj.*

**nu·mer·ous** ⓘ B2 /ˈnjuːmərəs; *NAmE* ˈnuː-/ *adj.* (*formal*) existing in large numbers SYN **many**: *He has been late on numerous occasions.* ◇ *The advantages of this system are too numerous to mention.* ◇ *I tried numerous times to talk to Chris.* ◇ *Dr Malcolm has won numerous awards.*

**nu·min·ous** /ˈnjuːmɪnəs; *NAmE* ˈnuː-/ *adj.* (*formal*) having a strong religious and spiritual quality that makes you feel that God is present

**nu·mis·mat·ics** /ˌnjuːmɪzˈmætɪks; *NAmE* ˌnuː-/ *noun* [U] the study of coins and MEDALS ▶ **nu·mis·mat·ic** *adj.*

**nu·mis·ma·tist** /njuːˈmɪzmətɪst; *NAmE* nuː-/ *noun* a person who collects or studies coins or MEDALS

**numpty** /ˈnʌmpti/ (pl. **-ies**) noun (BrE, informal) a stupid person

**num·skull** = NUMBSKULL

**nun** /nʌn/ noun a member of a religious community of women who promise to serve God all their lives and often live together in a CONVENT ⊃ compare MONK

**nun·cio** /ˈnʌnsiəʊ/ noun (pl. **-os**) a representative of the POPE (= the leader of the Roman Catholic Church) in a foreign country: *a papal nuncio*

**nun·nery** /ˈnʌnəri/ noun (pl. **-ies**) (old-fashioned or literary) = CONVENT

**nup·tial** /ˈnʌpʃl/ adj. [only before noun] (formal) connected with marriage or a wedding: *nuptial bliss* ◇ *a nuptial mass*

**nup·tials** /ˈnʌpʃlz/ noun [pl.] (old-fashioned) a wedding

**nurse** ⓘ A1 /nɜːs; NAmE nɜːrs/ noun, verb
- **noun 1** A1 a person whose job is to take care of sick or injured people, usually in a hospital: *a registered nurse* ◇ *a qualified/trained nurse* ◇ *student nurses* ◇ *a male nurse* ◇ *a dental nurse* (= one who helps a dentist) ◇ *a psychiatric nurse* (= one who works in a hospital for people with mental illnesses) ◇ *a nurses' station* (= an office for nurses in a hospital) ◇ *Nurse Bennett* ◇ *Nurse, come quickly!* ⊃ see also CHARGE NURSE, DISTRICT NURSE, PRACTICAL NURSE, REGISTERED NURSE, STAFF NURSE ⊃ WORDFINDER NOTE at HOSPITAL ⊃ note at GENDER **2** (*also* **nurse-maid** (old-fashioned)) (in the past) a woman or girl whose job was to take care of babies or small children in their own homes ⊃ see also NURSERY NURSE, WET NURSE
- **verb 1** [T] ~ **sb** to care for sb who is ill or injured: *He worked in a hospital for ten years nursing cancer patients.* ◇ *She nursed her daughter back to health.* **2** [T] ~ **sth** to take care of an injury or illness, especially by resting and not trying to do too much: *Several weeks after the match, he was still nursing a shoulder injury.* ◇ *You'd better go to bed and nurse that cold.* ◇ (*figurative*) *She was nursing her hurt pride.* ◇ (*figurative*) *European markets were still nursing their wounds after Monday's losses.* **3** [T] ~ **sth** (formal) to have a strong feeling or idea in your mind for a long time SYN harbour: *to nurse an ambition/a grievance/a grudge* ◇ *She had been nursing a secret desire to see him again.* **4** [T] ~ **sth** to give special care or attention to sb/sth: *to nurse tender young plants* **5** [T] ~ **sth** to hold a drink for a long time, drinking it slowly: *He sat nursing his cup of coffee.* **6** [I, T] (of a woman or female animal) to feed a baby with milk from the breast SYN **suckle**: *a nursing mother* ◇ ~ **sb/sth** *The lioness is still nursing her cubs.* ⊃ compare BREASTFEED **7** [I] (of a baby) to drink milk from its mother's breast SYN **suckle**

**nurse·maid** /ˈnɜːsmeɪd; NAmE ˈnɜːrs-/ noun (old-fashioned) = NURSE (2)

**ˌnurse pracˈtitioner** noun a nurse who is trained to do many of the tasks usually done by a doctor

**nur·sery** /ˈnɜːsəri; NAmE ˈnɜːrs-/ noun, adj.
- **noun** (pl. **-ies**) **1** (BrE) a place where young children are cared for while their parents are at work; a DAY NURSERY or nursery school: **at** ~ *Her youngest child is at nursery now.* ⊃ compare DAY CARE CENTER, PRESCHOOL **2** (NAmE or old-fashioned) a room in a house where a baby sleeps **3** (old-fashioned) a room in a house where young children can play **4** a place where young plants and trees are grown for sale or for planting somewhere else
- **adj.** [only before noun] (BrE) connected with the education of children from 2 to 5 years old: *nursery education* ◇ *a nursery teacher*

**nur·sery·man** /ˈnɜːsərimən; NAmE ˈnɜːrs-/ noun (pl. **-men** /-mən/) a person who owns or works in a nursery

**ˈnursery nurse** noun (BrE) a person whose job involves taking care of small children in a DAY NURSERY

**ˈnursery rhyme** noun a simple traditional poem or song for children

**ˈnursery school** noun a school for children between the ages of about two and five SYN **preschool** ⊃ compare KINDERGARTEN, PLAYGROUP

**nurs·ing** ⓘ B2 /ˈnɜːsɪŋ; NAmE ˈnɜːrs-/ noun [U] the job or skill of caring for people who are sick or injured: *a career in nursing* ◇ *nursing care* ◇ *the nursing profession*

**ˈnursing home** noun a small private hospital, especially one where old people live and are cared for

**nur·ture** /ˈnɜːtʃə(r); NAmE ˈnɜːrtʃ-/ verb, noun
- **verb** (formal) **1** ~ **sb/sth** to care for and protect sb/sth while they are growing and developing: *These delicate plants need careful nurturing.* ◇ *children nurtured by loving parents* **2** ~ **sth** to help sb/sth to develop and be successful SYN **foster**: *It's important to nurture a good working relationship.* **3** ~ **sth** to have a feeling, an idea, a plan, etc. for a long time and encourage it to develop: *She secretly nurtured a hope of becoming famous.*
- **noun** [U] (formal) care and support given to sb/sth while they are growing

**nut** ⓘ A2 /nʌt/ noun, verb
- **noun 1** A2 (often in compounds) a small hard fruit with a very hard shell that grows on some trees: *to crack a nut* (= open it) ◇ *a cashew* ◇ *a hazelnut* ◇ *nuts and raisins* ◇ *She has a severe nut allergy.* ⊃ see also BETEL NUT, COLA NUT, MONKEY NUT, PINE NUT ⊃ VISUAL VOCAB pages V6, V8 **2** a small piece of metal with a hole through the centre that is SCREWED onto a BOLT to hold pieces of wood, parts of machines, etc. together: *to tighten a nut* ◇ *a wheel nut* ⊃ picture at BOLT ⊃ see also WING NUT **3** (BrE, slang) a person's head or brain **4** (BrE *also* **ˈnut·ter**) (informal) a strange or crazy person: *He's a complete nut, if you ask me.* ⊃ see also NUTS, NUTTY **5** (informal) (in compounds) a person who is extremely interested in a particular subject, activity, etc.: *a fitness/tennis/computer nut* **6 nuts** [pl.] (slang) a man's TESTICLES
- IDM **do your ˈnut** (BrE, informal) to become very angry **a hard/tough ˈnut** (informal) a person who is difficult to deal with or to influence **a hard/tough ˈnut (to ˈcrack)** a difficult problem or situation to deal with **the ˌnuts and ˈbolts (of sth)** (informal) the basic practical details of a subject or an activity **off your ˈnut** (BrE, informal) crazy ⊃ more at SLEDGEHAMMER
- **verb** (**-tt-**) ~ **sb** (BrE, informal) to deliberately hit sb hard with your head
- PHR V **ˌnut sth ˈout** (AustralE, NZE, informal) to calculate sth or find the answer to sth: *I'm going to have to nut it out on a piece of paper.*

**nut·case** /ˈnʌtkeɪs/ noun (informal) a crazy person

**nut·crack·er** /ˈnʌtkrækə(r)/ noun (BrE *also* **nut·crack·ers** [pl.]) a tool for breaking open the shells of nuts

**nut·meg** /ˈnʌtmeg/ noun [U, C] the hard seed of a tropical tree originally from south-east Asia, used in cooking as a SPICE, especially to give extra taste to cakes and sauces: *freshly grated nutmeg* ⊃ VISUAL VOCAB page V8

**nutra·ceut·ical** /ˌnjuːtrəˈsuːtɪkl, -ˈsjuː-; NAmE ˌnuːtrəˈsuː-/ noun = FUNCTIONAL FOOD

**nu·tri·ent** /ˈnjuːtriənt; NAmE ˈnuː-/ noun (specialist) a substance that is needed to keep a living thing alive and to help it to grow: *a lack of essential nutrients* ◇ *Plants draw minerals and other nutrients from the soil.* ◇ *children suffering from a serious nutrient deficiency*

**nu·tri·tion** ⓘ B2 /njuˈtrɪʃn; NAmE nuː-/ noun [U] **1** ⓘ B2 the process by which living things receive the food necessary for them to grow and be healthy: *advice on diet and nutrition* ◇ *to study food science and nutrition* ⊃ WORDFINDER NOTE at FIT ⊃ compare MALNUTRITION **2** ⓘ C1 food that is needed to grow and be healthy SYN **nourishment**: *A feeding tube gives her nutrition and water.* ▸ **nu·tri·tion·al** /-ʃənl/ (*also less frequent* **nu·tri·tive** /ˈnjuːtrətɪv; NAmE ˈnuː-/) adj.: *the nutritional value of milk* **nu·tri·tion·al·ly** /ˈnjuːtrɪʃənəli; NAmE nuː-/ adv.: *a nutritionally balanced menu*

**nu·tri·tion·ist** /njuˈtrɪʃənɪst; NAmE nuː-/ noun a person who is an expert on the relationship between food and health ⊃ see also DIETICIAN

**nu·tri·tious** /njuˈtrɪʃəs; NAmE nuː-/ adj. (of food) very good for you; containing many of the substances which help the body to grow SYN **nourishing**: *tasty and nutritious meals*

**nuts** /nʌts/ adj. [not before noun] (informal) **1** crazy: *My friends think I'm nuts for saying yes.* ◇ *That phone ringing all the time is driving me nuts!* ⊃ SYNONYMS at MAD **2** ~ **about sb/sth** very much in love with sb; very

# nutshell

enthusiastic about sth: *He's absolutely nuts about her.* **IDM** see SOUP *n.*

**nut·shell** /ˈnʌtʃel/ *noun*
**IDM** **(put sth) in a nutshell** (to say or express sth) in a very clear way, using few words: *To put it in a nutshell, we're bankrupt.*

**nut·ter** /ˈnʌtə(r)/ *noun* (*BrE, informal*) = NUT (4)

**nutty** /ˈnʌti/ *adj.* (**nut·tier**, **nut·ti·est**) **1** tasting of or containing nuts: *a nutty taste* **2** (*informal*) slightly crazy: *She's got some nutty friends.* ◇ *He's as nutty as a fruitcake* (= completely crazy). **3** (*informal*) liking sb/sth very much

**nuz·zle** /ˈnʌzl/ *verb* [T, I] to touch or rub sb/sth with the nose or face, especially to show love: ~ **sb/sth** *She nuzzled his ear.* ◇ + **adv./prep.** *The child nuzzled up against his mother.*

**NVQ** /ˌen viː ˈkjuː/ *noun* a British qualification that shows that you have reached a particular standard in the work that you do (the abbreviation for 'National Vocational Qualification'): *NVQ Level 3 in Catering*

**NW** *abbr.* north-west; north-western: *NW Australia*

**NY** *abbr.* New York

**nyama choma** /ˌnjæmə ˈtʃəʊmə; *NAmE* ˈtʃoʊmə/ *EAfrE* [ˈnjama ˈtʃoma] *noun* [U] (*EAfrE*) meat that is cooked over a fire

**nyatiti** /njæˈtiːti; *EAfrE* [njaˈtiti] *noun* (*EAfrE*) a musical instrument with eight strings, played with the fingers

**NYC** *abbr.* New York City

**nylon** /ˈnaɪlɒn; *NAmE* -lɑːn/ *noun* **1** [U] a very strong artificial material, used for making clothes, rope, brushes, etc: *a nylon fishing line* ◇ *This material is 45 per cent nylon.* **2 nylons** [pl.] (*old-fashioned*) women's STOCKINGS or TIGHTS made of nylon

**nymph** /nɪmf/ *noun* **1** (in ancient Greek and Roman stories) a spirit of nature in the form of a young woman, that lives in rivers, woods, etc. **2** (*biology*) a young insect that has a body form that does not change very much as it grows: *a dragonfly nymph* ⊃ compare LARVA

**nym·pho·maniac** /ˌnɪmfəˈmeɪniæk/ (*also informal* **nympho** /ˈnɪmfəʊ/ *pl.* **-os**) *noun* (*disapproving*) a woman who has, or wants to have, sex very often ▸ **nym·pho·mania** /ˌnɪmfəˈmeɪniə/ *noun* [U]

**NZ** (*also* **N.Z.**) *abbr.* New Zealand

**O** /əʊ/ noun, exclamation, symbol
- **noun** (also **o**) (pl. **Os**, **O's**, **o's** /əʊz/) **1** [C, U] the 15th letter of the English alphabet: *'Orange' begins with (an) O/'O'.* **2** used to mean 'zero' when saying phone numbers, etc.: *My number is six o double three (= 6033).* ⊃ see also **O LEVEL**
- **exclamation** (*old use* or *literary*) = OH
- **symbol** the symbol for the chemical element OXYGEN

**o'** /ə/ *prep.* used in written English to represent an informal way of saying *of*: *a couple o' times*

**oaf** /əʊf/ *noun* a stupid, unpleasant or rough person, especially a man: *Mind that cup, you clumsy oaf!* ▶ **oaf·ish** *adj.*

**oak** /əʊk/ *noun* **1** [C, U] (also **oak tree** [C]) a large tree that produces small nuts called ACORNS. Oaks are common in northern countries and can live to be hundreds of years old: *an ancient oak tree* ◊ *forests of oak and pine* ⊃ VISUAL VOCAB page V6 **2** [U] the hard wood of the oak tree: *oak beams* ◊ *This table is made of solid oak.*

**oak·en** /ˈəʊkən/ *adj.* [only before noun] (*literary*) made of oak

**OAP** /ˌəʊ eɪ ˈpiː/ *noun* (*BrE, becoming old-fashioned*) a person who receives an old-age pension (the abbreviation for 'old-age pensioner')

**oar** /ɔː(r)/ *noun* a long POLE with a flat part at one end that is used for ROWING a boat: *He pulled as hard as he could on the oars.* ⊃ compare PADDLE
**IDM** **put/stick your 'oar in** (*BrE, informal*) to give your opinion, advice, etc. without being asked and when it is probably not wanted **SYN** **interfere**

▸ **HOMOPHONES**
**oar • or • ore** /ɔː(r)/
- **oar** noun: *We took one oar each and started rowing.*
- **or** conj.: *Do you want cheese or jam in your sandwich?*
- **ore** noun: *The country has rich deposits of iron ore.*

**oars·man** /ˈɔːzmən/ *NAmE* /ˈɔːrz-/, **oars·woman** /ˈɔːzwʊmən/ *NAmE* /ˈɔːrz-/ *noun* (*pl.* **-men** /-mən/, **-women** /-wɪmɪn/) a person who ROWS a boat, especially as a member of a crew (= team)

**oasis** /əʊˈeɪsɪs/ *noun* (*pl.* **oases** /-ˈeɪsiːz/) **1** an area in the desert where there is water and where plants grow **2** a pleasant place or period of time in the middle of sth unpleasant or difficult **SYN** **haven**: *an oasis of calm* ◊ *a green oasis in the heart of the city*

**oat** /əʊt/ *adj.* [only before noun] made from or containing OATS: *oat cakes* ◊ *oat bran* ⊃ see also OATCAKE, OATMEAL

**oat·cake** /ˈəʊtkeɪk/ *noun* a Scottish biscuit made with oats, which is not sweet

**oath** /əʊθ/ *noun* (*pl.* **oaths** /əʊðz/) **1** a formal promise to do sth or a formal statement that sth is true: *to take/swear an oath of allegiance* ◊ *Before giving evidence, witnesses in court have to take the oath* (= promise to tell the truth). **2** (*old-fashioned*) an offensive word or phrase used to express anger, surprise, etc.; a swear word: *She heard the sound of breaking glass, followed by a muttered oath.*
**IDM** **on/under 'oath** (*law*) having made a formal promise to tell the truth in court: *Is she prepared to give evidence on oath?* ◊ *The judge reminded the witness that he was still under oath.*

**oat·meal** /ˈəʊtmiːl/ *noun* [U] **1** flour made from oats, used to make biscuits, PORRIDGE, etc. **2** (*NAmE*) = PORRIDGE **3** a pale brown colour ▶ **oat·meal** *adj.*: *an oatmeal carpet*

**oats** /əʊts/ *noun* [pl.] grain grown in cool countries as food for animals and for making flour, PORRIDGE, etc. ⊃ VISUAL VOCAB page V8 ⊃ see also OAT **IDM** see SOW¹

**ob·du·rate** /ˈɒbdjərət/ *NAmE* /ˈɑːbdə-/ *adj.* (*formal, usually disapproving*) refusing to change your mind or your actions in any way **SYN** **stubborn** ▶ **ob·du·racy** /-rəsi/ *noun* [U] **ob·du·rate·ly** *adv.*

**OBE** /ˌəʊ biː ˈiː/ *noun* an award given in the UK for a special achievement; a person who has received this award (the abbreviation for 'Officer of the Order of the British Empire'): *She was made an OBE.* ◊ *Matthew Silk OBE*

**obedi·ent** /əˈbiːdiənt/ *adj.* doing what you are told to do; willing to obey: *an obedient child* ◊ ~ **to sb/sth** *He was always obedient to his father's wishes.* **OPP** **disobedient**
▸ **obedi·ence** /-əns/ *noun* [U]: *blind/complete/unquestioning/total obedience* ◊ ~ **to sb/sth** *He has acted in obedience to the law.* **obedi·ent·ly** *adv.*
**IDM** **your obedient servant** (*old use*) used to end a formal letter

**obei·sance** /əʊˈbeɪsns/ *NAmE* /-ˈbiːs-/ *noun* (*formal*) **1** [U] respect for sb/sth; the quality of being willing to obey sb **2** [C] the act of bending your head or the upper part of your body in order to show respect for sb/sth

**ob·el·isk** /ˈɒbəlɪsk/ *NAmE* /ˈɑːb-, ˈəʊb-/ *noun* a tall pointed stone column with four sides, put up in memory of a person or an event

**obese** /əʊˈbiːs/ *adj.* (*formal* or *medical*) (of people) very fat, in a way that is not healthy ⊃ compare OVERWEIGHT (1) ⊃ note at FAT

**obes·ity** /əʊˈbiːsəti/ *noun* [U] (*formal* or *medical*) the quality or fact of being very fat, in a way that is not healthy: *Obesity can increase the risk of heart disease.*

**obey** /əˈbeɪ/ *verb* [T, I] to do what you are told or expected to do: ~ **sth** *to obey a command/an order/rules/the law* ◊ ~ **sb** *He had always obeyed his parents without question.* ◊ *'Sit down!' Meekly, she obeyed.* **OPP** **disobey**

**ob·fus·cate** /ˈɒbfəskeɪt/ *NAmE* /ˈɑːb-/ *verb* [I, T] ~ **(sth)** (*formal*) to make sth less clear and more difficult to understand, usually deliberately **SYN** **obscure** ▶ **ob·fus·ca·tion** /ˌɒbfəˈskeɪʃn/ *NAmE* /ˌɑːb-/ *noun* [U, C]

**ob-gyn** /ˌɒb ˈɡaɪn/ *NAmE* /ˌɑːb/ *noun* (*NAmE, informal*) **1** [U] the branches of medicine that deal with the birth of children (= OBSTETRICS) and the diseases of women (= GYNAECOLOGY) **2** [C] a doctor who is trained in this type of medicine

**obi** /ˈəʊbi/ *noun* (*from Japanese*) a wide piece of cloth worn around the WAIST (= middle part) of a Japanese KIMONO

**ob·itu·ary** /əˈbɪtʃuəri/ *NAmE* /əʊˈbɪtʃueri/ *noun* (*pl.* **-ies**) an article about sb's life and achievements, that is printed in a newspaper soon after they have died ⊃ WORDFINDER NOTE at NEWSPAPER

**ob·ject** *noun, verb*
- **noun** /ˈɒbdʒɪkt, -dʒekt/ *NAmE* /ˈɑːb-/ **1** a thing that can be seen and touched, but is not alive: *everyday objects such as cups and saucers* ◊ *inanimate objects* (= things that are not alive) ◊ *a physical/material object* (= that you can see and touch) ◊ *The scanner detected a metal object.* ⊃ see also UFO **2** ~ **of desire, study, attention, etc.** a person or thing that sb DESIRES, studies, pays attention to, etc. ⊃ see also SEX OBJECT **3** an aim or a purpose: *Her sole object in life is to become a travel writer.* ◊ *The object is to educate people about road safety.* ◊ *If you're late, you'll defeat the whole object of the exercise.* ⊃ SYNONYMS at TARGET **4** (*grammar*) a noun, noun phrase or pronoun that refers to a person or thing that is affected by the action of the verb (called the DIRECT OBJECT), or that the action is done to or for (called the INDIRECT OBJECT) ⊃ compare SUBJECT
**IDM** see MONEY
- **verb** /əbˈdʒekt/ **1** [I] to say that you disagree with or oppose sth: *If nobody objects, we'll postpone the meeting till next week.* ◊ ~ **to sb/sth** *Members of the council strongly objected to plans to sell off the land.* ◊ ~ **to doing sth** *I really object to being charged for parking.* ◊ ~ **to sb doing sth** *Who could object to people having fun?* **2** [T] ~ **that…** + **speech** to give sth as a reason for opposing sth **SYN** **protest**: *He objected that the police had arrested him without sufficient evidence.* ⊃ SYNONYMS at COMPLAIN

**ob·jec·ti·fi·ca·tion** /əbˌdʒektɪfɪˈkeɪʃn/ *noun* [U] (*formal*) the act of treating people as if they are objects, without rights or feelings of their own

**ob·jec·tify** /əbˈdʒektɪfaɪ/ *verb* (**ob·jec·ti·fies, ob·jec·ti·fy·ing, ob·jec·ti·fied, ob·jec·ti·fied**) ~ **sb/sth** (*formal*) to treat sb/sth as an object, without rights or feelings of their own: *magazines that objectify women*

# objection 1068

> **VOCABULARY BUILDING**
>
> **Objects you can use**
>
> It is useful to know some general words to help you describe objects, especially if you do not know the name of a particular object.
>
> - A **device** is something that has been designed to do a particular job: *There is a new device for cars that warns drivers of traffic jams ahead.*
> - A **gadget** is a small object that does something useful, but is not really necessary: *His kitchen is full of gadgets he never uses.*
> - An **instrument** is used especially for careful or scientific work: *'What do you call the instrument that measures temperature?' 'A thermometer.'*
> - A **tool** is something that you use for making and repairing things: *'Have you got one of those tools for turning screws?' 'Do you mean a screwdriver?'*
> - A **machine** has moving parts and is used for a particular job. It usually stands on its own: *'What's a blender?' 'It's an electric machine for mixing soft food or liquid.'*
> - An **appliance** is a large machine that you use in the house, such as a washing machine.
> - **Equipment** means all the things you need for a particular activity: *climbing equipment.*
> - **Apparatus** means all the tools, machines or equipment that you need for something: *firefighters wearing breathing apparatus.*

**ob·jec·tion** /əbˈdʒekʃn/ *noun* [C, U] a reason why you do not like or are opposed to sth; a statement about this: *I'd like to come too, if you have no objection.* ◊ *They raised no objections at the time.* ◊ *~ to sth The main objection to the plan was that it would cost too much.* ◊ *There was widespread objection to the proposals.* ◊ *~ to (sb) doing sth I have no objection to him coming to stay.* ◊ *~ from sb The proposal will go ahead despite strong objections from the public.* ◊ *~ that ... He dismissed the objection that the plan was too expensive.*

**ob·jec·tion·able** /əbˈdʒekʃənəbl/ *adj.* (*formal*) unpleasant or offensive: *objectionable people/odours* ◊ *Why are you being so objectionable today?*

**ob·ject·ive** /əbˈdʒektɪv/ *noun, adj.*

- *noun* **1** something that you are trying to achieve **SYN** goal: *the primary/principal/key objective* ◊ *The main objective of this meeting is to give more information on our plans.* ◊ *to achieve/meet/accomplish your objectives* ◊ *You must set realistic aims and objectives for yourself.* ⇒ SYNONYMS at TARGET **2** (*also* **objective ˈlens**) (*specialist*) the LENS in a TELESCOPE or MICROSCOPE that is nearest to the object being looked at

- *adj.* **1** not influenced by personal feelings or opinions; considering only facts **SYN** unbiased: *an objective assessment of the situation* ◊ *objective truth/facts/reality* ◊ *objective criteria/measures/measurements* ◊ *He doesn't even pretend to be impartial and objective.* **OPP** subjective **2** (*philosophy*) existing outside the mind; based on facts that can be proved: *objective reality* **OPP** subjective **3** [only before *noun*] (*grammar*) the **objective** CASE is the one which is used for the object of a sentence ▶ **ob·ject·ive·ly** *adv.*: *Looked at objectively, the situation is not too bad.* ◊ *Can these effects be objectively measured?* **ob·ject·iv·ity** /ˌɒbdʒekˈtɪvəti/ *NAmE* ˌɑːb-/ *noun* [U]: *There was a lack of objectivity in the way the candidates were judged.* ◊ *scientific objectivity* **OPP** subjectivity

ˈ**object lesson** *noun* [usually sing.] a practical example of what you should or should not do in a particular situation

**ob·ject·or** /əbˈdʒektə(r)/ *noun* ~ (**to sth**) a person who objects to sth: *There were no objectors to the plan.* ⇒ see also CONSCIENTIOUS OBJECTOR

**objet d'art** /ˌɒbʒeɪ ˈdɑː; *NAmE* ˌɑːbʒeɪ ˈdɑːr/ *noun* (*pl.* **objets d'art** /ˌɒbʒeɪ ˈdɑː; *NAmE* ˌɑːbʒeɪ ˈdɑːr/) (*from French*) a small artistic object, used for decoration

**ob·li·gated** /ˈɒblɪɡeɪtɪd; *NAmE* ˈɑːb-/ *adj.* ~ (**to do sth**) (*NAmE or formal, BrE*) having a moral or legal duty to do sth **SYN** obliged: *He felt obligated to help.*

**ob·li·ga·tion** /ˌɒblɪˈɡeɪʃn; *NAmE* ˌɑːb-/ *noun* **1** [U] the state of being forced to do sth because it is your duty, or because of a law, etc.: *~ to do sth You are under no obligation to buy anything.* ◊ *under any/no ~ She did not feel under any obligation to tell him the truth.* ◊ *I don't want people coming to see me out of a sense of obligation.* ◊ **without ~** *We will send you an estimate for the work without obligation* (= you do not have to accept it). **2** [C] something which you must do because you have promised, because of a law, etc. **SYN** commitment: *legal/professional/financial obligations* ◊ *~ to do sth We have a moral obligation to protect the environment.* ◊ *~ on sb I felt that there was a moral obligation on me to tell the story.* ◊ *to fulfil/meet your obligations* ◊ *~ to/toward sb We have an obligation to our consumers.* ⇒ EXPRESS YOURSELF at HAVE TO

**ob·liga·tory** /əˈblɪɡətri; *NAmE* -tɔːri/ *adj.* **1** ~ (**for sb**) (**to do sth**) (*formal*) that you must do because of the law, rules, etc. **SYN** compulsory: *~ for sb to do sth It is obligatory for all employees to wear protective clothing.* **OPP** optional **2** (*often humorous*) that you do because you always do it, or other people in the same situation always do it: *In the mid-60s he took the almost obligatory trip to India.*

**ob·lige** /əˈblaɪdʒ/ *verb* (*formal*) **1** [T, usually passive] ~ **sb to do sth** to force sb to do sth, by law, because it is a duty, etc.: *Parents are obliged by law to send their children to school.* ◊ *I felt obliged to ask them to dinner.* ◊ *He suffered a serious injury that obliged him to give up work.* **2** [I, T] to help sb by doing what they ask or what you know they want: *Call me if you need any help—I'd be happy to oblige.* ◊ **~ sb (with sth)** *Would you oblige me with some information?* ◊ **~ sb (by doing sth)** *Oblige me by keeping your suspicions to yourself.*

**ob·liged** /əˈblaɪdʒd/ *adj.* [not before *noun*] (*formal*) used when you are expressing thanks or asking politely for sth, to show that you are grateful to sb: *I'd be obliged if you would keep this to yourself.* ◊ **~ to sb (for sth/for doing sth)** *I'm much obliged to you for helping us.*

**ob·li·ging** /əˈblaɪdʒɪŋ/ *adj.* (*formal*) very willing to help **SYN** accommodating, helpful: *They were very obliging and offered to wait for us.* ▶ **ob·li·ging·ly** *adv.*

**ob·lique** /əˈbliːk/ *adj., noun*

- *adj.* **1** not expressed or done in a direct way **SYN** indirect: *an oblique reference/approach/comment* **2** (*of a line*) sloping at an angle **3** [usually before *noun*] (*geometry*) (of an angle) greater or less than 90° ▶ **ob·lique·ly** *adv.*: *He referred only obliquely to their recent problems.* ◊ *Always cut stems obliquely to enable flowers to absorb more water.*
- *noun* (*BrE*) = SLASH (3)

**ob·lit·er·ate** /əˈblɪtəreɪt/ *verb* [often passive] ~ **sth** to remove all signs of sth, either by destroying or covering it completely: *The building was completely obliterated by the bomb.* ◊ *The snow had obliterated their footprints.* ◊ *Everything that happened that night was obliterated from his memory.* ▶ **ob·lit·er·ation** /əˌblɪtəˈreɪʃn/ *noun* [U]

**ob·liv·ion** /əˈblɪviən/ *noun* [U] **1** a state in which you are not aware of what is happening around you, usually because you are unconscious or asleep: *He often drinks himself into oblivion.* ◊ *Sam longed for the oblivion of sleep.* **2** the state in which sb/sth has been forgotten and is no longer famous or important **SYN** obscurity: *An unexpected victory saved him from political oblivion.* ◊ *Most of his inventions have been consigned to oblivion.* **3** a state in which sth has been completely destroyed: *Hundreds of homes had been bombed into oblivion during the first weeks of the war.*

**ob·liv·ious** /əˈblɪviəs/ *adj.* [not usually before *noun*] not aware of sth: **~ (of sth)** *He drove off, oblivious of the damage he had caused.* ◊ **~ (to sth)** *You eventually become oblivious to the noise.* ▶ **ob·liv·ious·ly** *adv.*

**ob·long** /ˈɒblɒŋ; *NAmE* ˈɑːblɔːŋ/ *adj.* **1** an **oblong** shape has four straight sides, two of which are longer than the other two, and four angles of 90° **2** (*NAmE*) used to describe any shape that is longer than it is wide: *an oblong melon* ▶ **oblong** *noun*: *a tiny oblong of glass in the roof* ⇒ see also RECTANGLE

**ob·nox·ious** /əbˈnɒkʃəs; NAmE -ˈnɑːk-/ adj. extremely unpleasant, especially in a way that offends people SYN offensive: *obnoxious behaviour* ◇ *a thoroughly obnoxious little man* ◇ *obnoxious odours* ▶ **ob·nox·ious·ly** adv.

**obo** (also **o.b.o.**) abbr. (NAmE) or best offer (used in small advertisements to show that sth may be sold at a lower price than the price that has been asked): *$800 obo* ⇒ compare O.N.O.

**oboe** /ˈəʊbəʊ/ noun a musical instrument of the WOODWIND group. It is like a pipe in shape and has a double REED at the top that you blow into.

**obo·ist** /ˈəʊbəʊɪst/ noun a person who plays the oboe

**ob·scene** /əbˈsiːn/ adj. **1** connected with sex in a way that most people find offensive: *obscene gestures/language/books* ◇ *an obscene phone call* (= in which sb says obscene things) **2** extremely large in size or amount in a way that most people find unacceptable and offensive SYN outrageous: *He earns an obscene amount of money.* ◇ *It's obscene to spend so much on food when millions are starving.* ▶ **ob·scene·ly** adv.: *to behave obscenely* ◇ *obscenely rich*

**ob·scen·ity** /əbˈsenəti/ noun (pl. **-ies**) **1** [U] obscene language or behaviour: *The editors are being prosecuted for obscenity.* ◇ *the laws on obscenity* **2** [C, usually pl.] an obscene word or act: *She screamed a string of obscenities at the judge.*

**ob·scur·ant·ism** /ˌɒbskjuˈræntɪzəm; NAmE ɑːbˈskjʊərəntɪzəm/ noun [U] (formal) the practice of deliberately preventing sb from understanding or discovering sth ▶ **ob·scur·ant·ist** /-tɪst/ adj.

**ob·scure** /əbˈskjʊə(r); NAmE -ˈskjʊr/ adj., verb

■ adj. **1** not well known SYN unknown: *an obscure German poet* ◇ *He was born around 1650 but his origins remain obscure.* **2** difficult to understand: *I found her lecture very obscure.* ◇ *For some obscure reason, he failed to turn up.* ▶ **ob·scure·ly** adv.: *They were making her feel obscurely worried* (= for reasons that were difficult to understand).
■ verb ~ sth to make it difficult to see, hear or understand sth: *The view was obscured by fog.* ◇ *We mustn't let these minor details obscure the main issue.*

**ob·scur·ity** /əbˈskjʊərəti; NAmE -ˈskjʊr-/ noun (pl. **-ies**) **1** [U] the state in which sb/sth is not well known or has been forgotten: *The actress was only 17 when she was plucked from obscurity and made a star.* ◇ *He spent most of his life working in obscurity.* **2** [U, C, usually pl.] the fact of being difficult to understand; something that is difficult to understand: *The course teaches students to avoid ambiguity and obscurity of expression.* ◇ *a speech full of obscurities* **3** [U] (literary) the state of being dark SYN darkness

**ob·se·quies** /ˈɒbsəkwiz; NAmE ˈɑːb-/ noun [pl.] (formal) ceremonies at a FUNERAL: *state obsequies*

**ob·se·qui·ous** /əbˈsiːkwiəs/ adj. (formal, disapproving) trying too hard to please sb, especially sb who is important SYN servile: *an obsequious manner* ▶ **ob·se·qui·ous·ly** adv.: *smiling obsequiously* **ob·se·qui·ous·ness** noun [U]

**ob·serv·able** /əbˈzɜːvəbl; NAmE -ˈzɜːrv-/ adj. that can be seen or noticed: *observable differences* ◇ *Similar trends are observable in mainland Europe.* ▶ **ob·serv·ably** /-bli/ adv.

**ob·serv·ance** /əbˈzɜːvəns; NAmE -ˈzɜːrv-/ noun **1** [U, sing.] the practice of obeying a law, celebrating a festival or behaving according to a particular custom: *~(of sth) observance of the law* ◇ *a strict observance of the Sabbath* **2** [C, usually pl.] an act performed as part of a religious or traditional ceremony: *religious observances*

**ob·serv·ant** /əbˈzɜːvənt; NAmE -ˈzɜːrv-/ adj. **1** good at noticing things around you SYN sharp-eyed: *Observant walkers may see red deer along this stretch of the road.* ◇ *How very observant of you!* **2** (formal) careful to obey religious laws and customs

**ob·ser·va·tion** ⓣ B2 ⓞ /ˌɒbzəˈveɪʃn; NAmE ˌɑːbzərˈv-/ noun **1** ⓣ B2 [U, C] the act of watching sb/sth carefully for a period of time, especially to learn sth: *Most information was collected by direct observation of the animals' behaviour.* ◇ *results based on scientific observations* ◇ *We managed to escape observation* (= we were not seen). ◇ **under~** *The suspect is being kept under observation* (= watched closely by the police). ◇ *She has outstanding powers of observation* (= the ability to notice things around her). ◇ *an observation post/tower* (= a place from where sb, especially an enemy, can be watched) **2** ⓣ B2 [C] (formal) a comment, especially based on sth you have seen, heard or read SYN remark: *~about/on sth He began by making a few general observations about the report.* ⇒ SYNONYMS at STATEMENT ▶ **ob·ser·va·tion·al** /-ʃənl/ adj.

**ob·serv·a·tory** /əbˈzɜːvətri; NAmE -ˈzɜːrvətɔːri/ noun (pl. **-ies**) a special building with a TELESCOPE or other equipment that scientists use to watch the stars, the weather, etc.

**ob·serve** ⓣ B2 ⓞ /əbˈzɜːv; NAmE -ˈzɜːrv/ verb **1** ⓣ B2 [T] (formal) to see or notice sb/sth: *Have you observed any changes lately?* ◇ *All the characters in the novel are closely observed* (= seem like people in real life). ◇ *~sb/sth do sth The police observed a man enter the bank.* ◇ *~sb/sth doing sth They observed him entering the bank.* ◇ *~that ... She observed that all the chairs were already occupied.* ◇ **be observed to do sth** *He was observed to follow her closely.* HELP This pattern is only used in the passive. ⇒ SYNONYMS at COMMENT, NOTICE **2** ⓣ B2 [T, I] (formal) to watch sb/sth carefully, especially to learn more about them SYN monitor: *He observes keenly, but says little.* ◇ *~sb/sth I felt he was observing everything I did.* ◇ *~how, what, etc. ... They observed how the parts of the machine fitted together.* ⇒ SYNONYMS at LOOK **3** [T] *~that ...* | *+ speech* (formal) to make a remark SYN comment: *She observed that it was getting late.* **4** [T] *~sth* to obey rules, laws, etc: *Will the rebels observe the ceasefire?* ◇ *The crowd observed a minute's silence* (= were silent for one minute) *in memory of those who had died.* **5** [T] *~sth* (formal) to celebrate festivals, birthdays, etc: *Do they observe Christmas?*

**ob·ser·ver** ⓣ+ B2 Ⓦ /əbˈzɜːvə(r); NAmE -ˈzɜːrv-/ noun **1** ⓣ+ B2 a person who watches sb/sth: *According to observers, the plane exploded shortly after take-off.* ◇ *To the casual observer* (= somebody who does not pay much attention), *the system appears confusing.* ⇒ SYNONYMS at WITNESS **2** ⓣ+ C1 a person who attends a meeting, lesson, etc. to listen and watch but not to take part: *A team of British officials were sent as observers to the conference.* **3** a person who watches and studies particular events, situations, etc. and is therefore considered to be an expert on them: *a royal observer*

**ob·sess** ⓣ+ C1 /əbˈses/ verb **1** ⓣ+ C1 [T, usually passive] to completely fill your mind so that you cannot think of anything else, in a way that is not normal: **be obsessed by sb/sth** *He's obsessed by computers.* ◇ **be obsessed with sb/sth** *She's completely obsessed with him.* ◇ *~sb The need to produce the most exciting newspaper story obsesses most journalists.* **2** [I] *~(about sth)* to be always talking or worrying about a particular thing, especially when this annoys other people: *I think you should try to stop obsessing about food.* ⇒ see also SELF-OBSESSED

**ob·ses·sion** ⓣ+ C1 /əbˈseʃn/ noun **1** ⓣ+ C1 [U, C] the state in which a person's mind is completely filled with thoughts of one particular thing or person in a way that is not normal: *Her fear of flying is bordering on obsession.* ◇ *~with sb/sth There's a national obsession with celebrity in England.* **2** ⓣ+ C1 [C] *~(with sb)* a person or thing that sb thinks about too much: *Fitness has become an obsession with him.*

**ob·ses·sion·al** /əbˈseʃənl/ adj. thinking too much about one particular person or thing, in a way that is not normal: *She is obsessional about cleanliness.* ◇ *obsessional behaviour* ▶ **ob·ses·sion·al·ly** /-ʃənəli/ adv.

**ob·ses·sive** /əbˈsesɪv/ adj., noun

■ adj. thinking too much about one particular person or thing, in a way that is not normal: *He's becoming more and more obsessive about punctuality.* ◇ *an obsessive attention to detail* ▶ **ob·ses·sive·ly** adv.: *obsessively jealous* ◇ *He worries obsessively about his appearance.*
■ noun (psychology) a person whose mind is filled with thoughts of one particular thing or person so that they cannot think of anything else

# obsidian

**ob,sessive com'pulsive di'sorder** noun [U] = OCD

**ob·sid·ian** /əbˈsɪdiən/ noun [U] a type of dark rock that looks like glass and comes from VOLCANOES

**ob·so·les·cence** /ˌɒbsəˈlesns; NAmE ˌɑːb-/ noun [U] (formal) the state of becoming old-fashioned and no longer useful: *products with built-in/planned obsolescence* (= designed not to last long so that people will have to buy new ones) ▶ **ob·so·les·cent** /-ˈlesnt/ adj.

**ob·so·lete** /ˈɒbsəliːt; NAmE ˌɑːbsəˈliːt/ adj. no longer used because sth new has been invented SYN **out of date**: *obsolete technology* ◊ *With technological changes many traditional skills have become obsolete.*

**obs·tacle** /ˈɒbstəkl; NAmE ˈɑːb-/ noun **1** ~ a situation, an event, etc. that makes it difficult for you to do or achieve sth SYN **hindrance**: *So far, we have managed to overcome all the obstacles that have been placed in our path.* ◊ ~ **to sth/to (sb) doing sth** *A lack of qualifications can be a major obstacle to finding a job.* **2** an object that is in your way and that makes it difficult for you to move forward: *The area was full of streams and bogs and other natural obstacles.* **3** (in SHOWJUMPING) a fence, etc. for a horse to jump over

**'obstacle course** noun **1** a series of objects that people taking part in a race have to climb over, under, through, etc. **2** a series of difficulties that people have to deal with in order to achieve a particular aim **3** (NAmE) (BrE **as'sault course**) an area of land with many objects that are difficult to climb, jump over or go through, which is used, especially by soldiers, for improving physical skills and strength

**'obstacle race** noun a race in which the people taking part have to climb over, under, through, etc. various objects

**ob·stet·ri·cian** /ˌɒbstəˈtrɪʃn; NAmE ˌɑːb-/ noun a doctor who is trained in obstetrics ⇒ WORDFINDER NOTE at SPECIALIST

**ob·stet·rics** /əbˈstetrɪks/ noun [U] the branch of medicine that deals with the birth of children ⇒ WORDFINDER NOTE at BIRTH ▶ **ob·stet·ric** /-ˈstetrɪk/ adj.: *obstetric medicine*

**ob·stin·ate** /ˈɒbstɪnət; NAmE ˈɑːb-/ adj. **1** (often disapproving) refusing to change your opinions, way of behaving, etc. when other people try to persuade you to; showing this SYN **stubborn**: *He can be very obstinate when he wants to be!* ◊ *her obstinate refusal to comply with their request* **2** [usually before noun] difficult to get rid of or deal with SYN **stubborn**: *the obstinate problem of unemployment* ◊ *an obstinate stain* ▶ **ob·stin·acy** /-nəsi/ noun [U]: *an act of sheer obstinacy* **ob·stin·ate·ly** adv.: *He obstinately refused to consider the future.*

**ob·strep·er·ous** /əbˈstrepərəs/ adj. (formal or humorous) noisy and difficult to control

**ob·struct** /əbˈstrʌkt/ verb (formal) **1** ~ **sth** to block a road, an entrance, a passage, etc. so that sb/sth cannot get through, see past, etc: *You can't park here, you're obstructing my driveway.* ◊ *First check that the accident victim doesn't have an obstructed airway.* ◊ *The pillar obstructed our view of the stage.* **2** ~ **sb/sth** to prevent sb/sth from doing sth or making progress, especially when this is done deliberately SYN **hinder**: *They were charged with obstructing the police in the course of their duty.* ◊ *terrorists attempting to obstruct the peace process*
IDM **ob,struct 'justice** (NAmE) (BrE **per,vert the course of 'justice**) (law) to tell a lie or to do sth in order to prevent the police, etc. from finding out the truth about a crime

**ob·struc·tion** /əbˈstrʌkʃn/ noun **1** [U, C] the fact of trying to prevent sth/sb from making progress: *the obstruction of justice* ◊ *He was arrested for obstruction of a police officer in the execution of his duty.* **2** [U, C] the fact of blocking a road, an entrance, a passage, etc: *obstruction of the factory gates* ◊ *The abandoned car was causing an obstruction.* **3** [C] something that blocks a road, an entrance, etc: *It is my job to make sure that all pathways are clear of obstructions.* **4** [C, U] (medical) something that blocks a passage or tube in your body; a medical condition resulting from this SYN **blockage**: *He had an operation to remove an obstruction in his throat.* ◊ *bowel/intestinal*

*obstruction* **5** [U] (sport) the offence of unfairly putting your body in front of a player of the other team so they cannot move to get the ball

**ob·struc·tion·ism** /əbˈstrʌkʃənɪzəm/ noun [U] (formal) the practice of trying to prevent a parliament or committee from making progress, passing laws, etc. ▶ **ob·struction·ist** /-ɪst/ noun, adj.

**ob·struct·ive** /əbˈstrʌktɪv/ adj. **1** trying to prevent sb/sth from making progress: *Of course she can do it. She's just being deliberately obstructive.* ⇒ compare CONSTRUCTIVE **2** [only before noun] (medical) connected with a passage, tube, etc. in your body that has become blocked: *obstructive lung disease*

**ob·tain** /əbˈteɪn/ verb (formal) **1** [T] ~ **sth** to get sth, especially by making an effort: *to obtain information/data/results* ◊ *I've been trying to obtain permission to publish this material.* ◊ *I finally managed to obtain a copy of the report.* ◊ *To obtain the overall score, add up the totals in each column.* **2** [I] (not used in the progressive tenses) (of rules, systems, customs, etc.) to exist SYN **apply**: *These conditions no longer obtain.*

**ob·tain·able** /əbˈteɪnəbl/ adj. [not usually before noun] that can be obtained SYN **available**: *Full details are obtainable from any post office.*

**ob·trude** /əbˈtruːd/ verb [I, T] ~ **(sth/yourself) (on/upon sb)** (formal) to become or make sth/yourself noticed, especially in a way that is not wanted: *Music from the next room obtruded upon his thoughts.*

**ob·tru·sive** /əbˈtruːsɪv/ adj. easy to notice in an unpleasant way: *The sofa would be less obtrusive in a paler colour.* ◊ *They tried to ensure that their presence was not too obtrusive.* ▶ **ob·tru·sive·ly** adv.

**ob·tuse** /əbˈtjuːs; NAmE -ˈtuːs/ adj. **1** (formal, disapproving) slow or unwilling to understand sth: *Are you being deliberately obtuse?* **2** [usually before noun] (geometry) (of an angle) between 90° and 180° ⇒ compare ACUTE (6) ▶ **ob·tuse·ness** noun [U].

**ob,tuse 'angle** noun an angle between 90° and 180° ⇒ picture at ANGLE ⇒ compare ACUTE ANGLE, ADJACENT ANGLE, EXTERIOR ANGLE, INTERIOR ANGLE, REFLEX ANGLE, RIGHT ANGLE

**obv** adv. (informal) = OBVS

**ob·verse** /ˈɒbvɜːs; NAmE ˈɑːbvɜːrs/ noun (usually **the obverse**) [sing.] **1** (formal) the opposite of sth: *The obverse of love is hate.* **2** (specialist) the side of a coin or MEDAL that has the head or main design on it ⇒ compare THE REVERSE

**ob·vi·ate** /ˈɒbvieɪt; NAmE ˈɑːb-/ verb ~ **sth** (formal) to remove a problem or the need for sth SYN **preclude**: *This new evidence obviates the need for any further enquiries.*

**ob·vi·ous** /ˈɒbviəs; NAmE ˈɑːb-/ adj. **1** easy to see or understand SYN **clear**: *I know you don't like her but try not to make it so obvious.* ◊ *He agreed with obvious pleasure.* ◊ ~ **(to sb) (that ...)** *It was obvious to everyone that the child had been badly treated.* ◊ ~ **from sth that ...** *It's obvious from what she said that something is wrong.* ◊ *For obvious reasons, I'd prefer not to give my name.* ◊ *The reasons for this decision were not immediately obvious.* ⇒ SYNONYMS at CLEAR **2** that most people would think of or agree to: *She was the obvious choice for the job.* ◊ *There's no obvious solution to the problem.* ◊ *This seemed the most obvious thing to do.* **3** (disapproving) not interesting, new or showing imagination; unnecessary because it is clear to everyone: *The ending was pretty obvious.* ◊ *I may be stating the obvious but without more money the project cannot survive.* ▶ **ob·vi·ous·ness** noun [U]

**ob·vi·ous·ly** /ˈɒbviəsli; NAmE ˈɑːb-/ adv. **1** used when giving information that you expect other people to know already or agree with SYN **clearly**: *Obviously, we don't want to spend too much money.* ◊ *Diet and exercise are obviously important.* **2** used to say that a particular situation or fact is easy to see or understand: *He was obviously drunk.* ◊ *They're obviously not coming.* ◊ *'I didn't realise it was a formal occasion.' 'Obviously!'* (= I can see by the way you are dressed)

---

æ cat | ɑː father | e bed | ɜː fur | ə about | ɪ sit | iː see | i happy | ɒ got (BrE) | ɔː saw | ʌ cup | ʊ put | uː too

**obvs** /ɒvz/ NAmE /ɑːvz/ (also **obv**) adv. (informal) (in text messages, on SOCIAL MEDIA, etc.) obviously

**oca·ri·na** /ˌɒkəˈriːnə/ NAmE /ˌɑːk-/ noun a small musical instrument like an egg in shape that you blow into, with holes for the fingers

ocarina

**oc·ca·sion** ⬤ B1 /əˈkeɪʒn/ noun, verb
▪ noun 1 B1 [C] a particular time when sth happens: **on an ~ on this/that occasion** ◇ I've met him on several occasions. ◇ They have been seen together on two **separate occasions**. ◇ On one occasion, she called me in the middle of the night. ◇ Only on **rare occasions** do I go out socially. ◇ **~when …** I can remember very few occasions when he had to cancel because of ill health. ◇ He used the occasion to announce further tax cuts. **2** B1 [C] a special event, ceremony or celebration: a great/memorable/happy/momentous occasion ◇ Turn every meal into **a special occasion**. ◇ They **marked the occasion** (= celebrated it) with an open-air concert. ◇ Their wedding turned out to be quite an occasion. ◇ **on the ~ of sth** He was presented with the watch on the occasion of his retirement. ➔ WORDFINDER NOTE at CELEBRATE **3** B2 [sing.] a suitable time for sth: **~for (doing) sth** It should have been an occasion for rejoicing, but she could not feel any real joy. ◇ I'll speak to him about it **if the occasion arises** (= if I get a chance). **4** [U, sing.] (formal) a reason or cause: **~to do sth** I've had no occasion to visit him recently. ◇ **~of/for sth** Her death was the occasion of mass riots. ◇ I'm willing to go to court over this **if the occasion arises** (= if it becomes necessary).
IDM **on oc·ca·sion(s)** sometimes but not often: He has been known on occasion to lose his temper. ➔ more at SENSE n.
▪ verb (formal) to cause sth: **~sth** The flight delay was occasioned by the need for a further security check. ◇ **~sb sth** The decision occasioned us much anxiety.

**oc·ca·sion·al** ⬤+ C1 /əˈkeɪʒənl/ adj. [only before noun] happening or done sometimes but not often: He works for us on an occasional basis. ◇ I enjoy the occasional glass of wine. ◇ He spent five years in Paris, with occasional visits to Italy. ◇ **an occasional smoker** (= a person who smokes, but not often)

**oc·ca·sion·al·ly** ⬤ B2 /əˈkeɪʒnəli/ adv. sometimes but not often: We occasionally meet for a drink after work. ◇ This type of allergy can very occasionally be fatal.

**oc·casional table** noun a small light table that is easy to move, used for different things at different times

**the Oc·ci·dent** /ˈɒksɪdənt/ NAmE /ˈɑːk-/ noun [sing.] (formal) the western part of the world, especially Europe and America ➔ compare ORIENT ▸ **oc·ci·den·tal** /ˌɒksɪˈdentl/ NAmE /ˌɑːk-/ adj.

**oc·clude** /əˈkluːd/ verb **~sth** (specialist) to cover or block sth: an occluded artery ▸ **oc·clu·sion** /əˈkluːʒn/ noun [U]

**oc·cult** /ˈɒkʌlt, ɒˈkʌlt/ NAmE /əˈkʌlt/ adj. **1** [only before noun] connected with magic powers and things that cannot be explained by reason or science SYN **supernatural**: occult practices **2** **the occult** noun [sing.] everything connected with occult practices, etc: He's interested in witchcraft and the occult.

**oc·cult·ist** /ˈɒkʌltɪst, əˈkʌltɪst/ NAmE /əˈkʌltɪst/ noun a person who is involved in the occult

**oc·cu·pancy** /ˈɒkjəpənsi/ NAmE /ˈɑːk-/ noun [U] (formal) the act of living in or using a building, room, piece of land, etc: Prices are based on **full occupancy** of an apartment. ◇ to be in **sole occupancy**

**oc·cu·pant** /ˈɒkjəpənt/ NAmE /ˈɑːk-/ noun **1** a person who lives or works in a particular house, room, building, etc: All outstanding bills will be paid by the previous occupants. **2** a person who is in a vehicle, seat, etc. at a particular time: The car was badly damaged but the occupants were unhurt.

**oc·cu·pa·tion** ⬤+ B2 W /ˌɒkjuˈpeɪʃn/ NAmE /ˌɑːk-/ noun **1** ⬤+ B2 [C] a job or profession: Please state your name, age and occupation below. ➔ SYNONYMS at WORK **2** ⬤+ C1 [C] the way in which you spend your time, especially when you are not working: Her main occupation seems to be shopping. **3** ⬤+ C1 [U] the act of moving into a country, town, etc. and taking control of it using military force; the period of time during which a country, town, etc. is controlled in this way: the Roman occupation of Britain ◇ **under ~** The zones under occupation contained major industrial areas. ◇ occupation forces **4** ⬤+ C1 [U] (formal) the act of living in or using a building, room, piece of land, etc: The offices will be ready for occupation in June. ◇ **in ~** The following applies only to tenants in occupation after January 1, 2010. ◇ The level of **owner occupation** (= people owning their homes) has increased rapidly in the last 30 years.

**oc·cu·pa·tion·al** /ˌɒkjuˈpeɪʃənl/ NAmE /ˌɑːk-/ adj. [only before noun] connected with a person's job or profession: occupational health ◇ an **occupational risk/hazard** ◇ an occupational pension scheme ▸ **oc·cu·pa·tion·al·ly** adv.: occupationally induced disease

**occu·pational ˈtherapist** noun a person whose job is to help people get better after illness or injury by giving them special activities to do

**occu·pational ˈtherapy** noun [U] the work of an occupational therapist

**oc·cu·pied** /ˈɒkjupaɪd/ NAmE /ˈɑːk-/ adj. **1** [not before noun] being used by sb: Only half of the rooms are occupied at the moment. ➔ see also OWNER-OCCUPIED **2** [not before noun] busy: The most important thing is to **keep yourself occupied**. ◇ **~doing sth/in doing sth** He's fully occupied looking after three small children. ◇ **~with (doing) sth** Only half her time is occupied with politics. **3** (of a country, etc.) controlled by people from another country, etc., using military force: He spent his childhood in occupied Europe.
OPP **unoccupied**

**oc·cu·pier** /ˈɒkjupaɪə(r)/ NAmE /ˈɑːk-/ noun **1 ~(of sth)** (formal) a person who lives in or uses a building, room, piece of land, etc. SYN **occupant**: The letter was addressed to the occupier of the house. ➔ see also OWNER-OCCUPIER **2** [usually pl.] a member of an army that has entered and taken control of a foreign country, etc.

**oc·cupy** ⬤+ B2 W /ˈɒkjupaɪ/ NAmE /ˈɑːk-/ verb (oc·cu·pies, oc·cu·py·ing, oc·cu·pied, oc·cu·pied) **1** ⬤+ B2 **~sth** to fill or use a space, an area or an amount of time SYN **take up**: The bed seemed to occupy most of the room. ◇ Administrative work occupies half of my time. **2** ⬤+ C1 **~sth** (formal) to live or work in a room, house or building: He occupies an office on the 12th floor. **3** ⬤+ C1 **~sth** to enter a place in a large group and take control of it, especially by military force: The capital has been occupied by the rebel group. ◇ Protesting students occupied the TV station. ➔ WORDFINDER NOTE at PROTEST **4** ⬤+ C1 to fill your time or keep you busy doing sth: **~sb/sth/yourself** a game that will occupy the kids for hours ◇ Problems at work continued **to occupy his mind** for some time. ◇ **~sb/sth/yourself with sb/sth** She occupied herself with routine office tasks. ◇ **~sb/sth/yourself (in) doing sth** She occupied herself doing routine office tasks. **5** ⬤+ C1 **~sth** to have an official job or position SYN **hold**: The president occupies the position for four years.

**occur** ⬤ B1 ⬤ /əˈkɜː(r)/ verb (-rr-) (formal) **1** B1 [I] to happen: When exactly did the **incident occur**? ◇ Something unexpected occurred. ◇ Three major **events occurred** in my life that year. **2** B2 [I] + adv./prep. to exist or be found somewhere: Sugar occurs naturally in fruit. ◇ **naturally occurring** chemicals in the brain
PHRV **oc·cur to sb** (of an idea or a thought) to come into your mind: The idea occurred to him in a dream. ◇ **occur to sb that …** It didn't occur to him that his wife was having an affair. ◇ **~to do sth** It didn't occur to her to ask for help.

**oc·cur·rence** ⬤+ C1 ⬤ /əˈkʌrəns/ NAmE /əˈkɜːrəns/ noun (formal) **1** ⬤+ C1 [C] something that happens or exists: a **common/everyday/frequent/regular occurrence** ◇ Vandalism used to be a **rare occurrence** here. ◇ The program counts the number of occurrences of any word within the text. **2** ⬤+ C1 [U] **~(of sth)** the fact of sth happening or existing: a link between the occurrence of skin cancer and the use of computer monitors

# OCD

**OCD** /ˌəʊ siː ˈdiː/ noun [U] a mental DISORDER in which sb feels they have to repeat certain actions or activities to get rid of fears or unpleasant thoughts (the abbreviation for 'obsessive compulsive disorder'): *to suffer from OCD*

**ocean** /ˈəʊʃn/ noun **1** (usually **the ocean**) [sing.] (especially NAmE) the mass of salt water that covers most of the earth's surface: *the depths of the ocean* ◇ *People were swimming in the ocean despite the hurricane warning.* ◇ *The plane hit the ocean several miles offshore.* ◇ *Our beach house is just a couple of miles from the ocean.* ◇ *an ocean liner* ◇ *Ocean levels are rising.* **2** (usually **Ocean**) [C] one of the five large areas that the ocean is divided into: *the Antarctic/Arctic/Atlantic/Indian/Pacific Ocean* ⇒ note at SEA
**IDM** **an ocean of sth** (also **oceans of sth**) (informal) a large amount of sth ⇒ more at DROP n.

**ocean-front** /ˈəʊʃnfrʌnt/ often **the oceanfront** (NAmE) (BrE **seafront**) noun [sing.] the part of a town facing the ocean: *the hotels lining the oceanfront* ◇ *an oceanfront hotel* ⇒ compare BEACHFRONT

**'ocean-going** adj. [only before noun] (of ships) made for crossing the sea or ocean, not for journeys along the coast or up rivers

**Ocea·nia** /ˌəʊsiˈɑːniə, ˌəʊʃi-; NAmE ˌəʊʃiˈæn-/ noun [U] a large region of the world consisting of the Pacific islands and the seas around them

**ocean·ic** /ˌəʊʃiˈænɪk/ adj. [usually before noun] (specialist) living in or connected with the ocean: *oceanic fish*

**ocean·og·raphy** /ˌəʊʃəˈnɒɡrəfi; NAmE -ˈnɑːɡ-/ noun [U] the scientific study of the ocean ▸ **ocean·og·raph·er** noun

**ocean 'trench** noun = TRENCH (3)

**oce·lot** /ˈɒsəlɒt; NAmE ˈɑːsəlɑːt, ˈəʊs-/ noun a wild animal of the cat family, that has yellow fur with black lines and spots, found in Central and South America

**och** /ɒk, ɒx; NAmE ɑːk, ɑːx/ exclamation (ScotE, IrishE) used to express the fact that you are surprised, sorry, etc: *Och, aye* (= Oh, yes).

**ochre** (US also **ocher**) /ˈəʊkə(r)/ noun [U] **1** a type of red or yellow earth used in some paints and DYES **2** the red or yellow colour of ochre

**ocker** /ˈɒkə(r); NAmE ˈɑːk-/ noun (AustralE, informal) a rude or aggressive Australian man ▸ **ocker** adj.

**o'clock** /əˈklɒk; NAmE əˈklɑːk/ adv. used with the numbers 1 to 12 when telling the time, to mean an exact hour: *He left between five and six o'clock.* ◇ *at/after/before eleven o'clock*

**OCR** /ˌəʊ siː ˈɑː(r)/ abbr. (computing) OPTICAL CHARACTER RECOGNITION

**octa·gon** /ˈɒktəɡən; NAmE ˈɑːktəɡɑːn/ noun (geometry) a flat shape with eight straight sides and eight angles ⇒ picture at POLYGON ▸ **oc·tag·on·al** /ɒkˈtæɡənl; NAmE ɑːk-/ adj.: *an octagonal coin*

**octa·he·dron** /ˌɒktəˈhiːdrən; NAmE ˌɑːk-/ noun (geometry) a solid figure with eight flat sides, especially one whose sides are eight equal TRIANGLES ⇒ picture at SOLID

**oc·tane** /ˈɒkteɪn; NAmE ˈɑːk-/ noun a chemical substance in petrol, used as a way of measuring its quality: *high-octane fuel*

**oct·ave** /ˈɒktɪv; NAmE ˈɑːk-/ noun (music) the difference (the INTERVAL) between the first and last notes in a series of eight notes on a SCALE: *to play an octave higher* ◇ *Orbison's vocal range spanned three octaves.*

**oc·tavo** /ɒkˈteɪvəʊ, -ˈtɑːv-; NAmE ɑːk-/ noun (pl. **-os**) (specialist) a size of a book page that is made by folding each sheet of paper into eight LEAVES (= 16 pages)

**octet** /ɒkˈtet; NAmE ɑːk-/ noun **1** [C + sing./pl. v.] a group of eight singers or musicians **2** [C] a piece of music for eight singers or musicians

**octo-** /ˈɒktəʊ, ɒktə; NAmE ɑːktəʊ, ɑːktə/ (also **oct-** /ɒkt; NAmE ɑːkt/) combining form (in nouns, adjectives and adverbs) eight; having eight: *octagon*

**Oc·to·ber** /ɒkˈtəʊbə(r); NAmE ɑːk-/ noun [U, C] (abbr. **Oct.**) the 10th month of the year, between September and November **HELP** To see how **October** is used, look at the examples at **April**.

**oc·to·gen·ar·ian** /ˌɒktədʒəˈneəriən; NAmE ˌɑːktədʒəˈner-/ noun a person between 80 and 89 years old

**octo·pus** /ˈɒktəpəs; NAmE ˈɑːktəpəs/ noun [C, U] (pl. **octo·puses**) a sea creature with a soft round body and eight long arms, that is sometimes used for food ⇒ VISUAL VOCAB page V3

**ocu·lar** /ˈɒkjələ(r); NAmE ˈɑːk-/ adj. [only before noun] **1** (specialist) connected with the eyes: *ocular muscles* **2** (formal) that can be seen: *ocular proof*

**OD** /ˌəʊ ˈdiː/ verb [I] (**OD's**, **OD'ing**, **OD'd**) ~ (**on sth**) (informal) = OVERDOSE

**odd** /ɒd; NAmE ɑːd/ adj. (**odder**, **oddest**)
• STRANGE **1** strange or unusual: *They're very odd people.* ◇ *There's something odd about that man.* ◇ *That painting looks very odd.* ◇ *it is/seems~that…* *It seems odd that nobody noticed anything wrong.* ◇ *It's most odd that* (= very odd that) *she hasn't written.* ◇ *The odd thing was that he didn't recognize me.* ⇒ compare PECULIAR
• ODD- **2** (in compounds) strange or unusual in the way mentioned: *an odd-looking house* ◇ *an odd-sounding name*
• NUMBERS **3** (no comparative or superlative) (of numbers) that cannot be divided exactly by the number two: *1, 3, 5 and 7 are odd numbers.* **OPP** **even**
• NOT REGULAR/OFTEN **4 the odd** [only before noun] (no comparative or superlative) happening or appearing occasionally; not happening often **SYN** **occasional**: *He makes the odd mistake—nothing too serious.*
• VARIOUS **5** [only before noun] (no comparative or superlative) of no particular type or size; various: *decorations made of odd scraps of paper*
• NOT MATCHING **6** [usually before noun] (no comparative or superlative) not with the pair or set that it belongs to; not matching: *You're wearing odd socks!*
• AVAILABLE **7** [only before noun] available; that sb can use **SYN** **spare**: *Could I see you when you've got an odd moment?*
• APPROXIMATELY **8** (no comparative or superlative; usually placed immediately after a number) approximately or a little more than the number mentioned: *How old is she—seventy odd?* ◇ *He's worked there for twenty-odd years.*
▸ **odd·ness** noun [U]: *the oddness of her appearance* ◇ *His oddness frightened her.*
**IDM** **the odd man/one 'out** a person or thing that is different from others or does not fit easily into a group or set: *At school he was always the odd man out.* ◇ *Dog, cat, horse, shoe—which is the odd one out?* ⇒ more at FISH n.

**odd·ball** /ˈɒdbɔːl; NAmE ˈɑːd-/ noun (informal) a person who behaves in a strange or unusual way ▸ **odd·ball** adj.: *oddball characters*

**odd·ity** /ˈɒdəti; NAmE ˈɑːd-/ noun (pl. **-ies**) **1** [C] a person or thing that is strange or unusual: *The book deals with some of the oddities of grammar and spelling.* **2** [U] the fact of being strange or unusual: *She suddenly realized the oddity of her remark and blushed.*

**odd 'jobs** noun [pl.] small jobs of various types: *to do odd jobs around the house*

**odd·ly** /ˈɒdli; NAmE ˈɑːd-/ adv. **1** in a strange or unusual way **SYN** **strangely**: *She's been behaving very oddly lately.* ◇ *The creature had an oddly shaped head.* ◇ *The name sounded oddly familiar.* **2** used to show that sth is surprising **SYN** **surprisingly**: *She felt, oddly, that they had been happier when they had no money.* ◇ *Oddly enough, the most expensive tickets sold fastest.*

**odd·ments** /ˈɒdmənts; NAmE ˈɑːd-/ noun [pl.] (especially BrE) **1** small pieces of cloth, wood, etc. that are left after a larger piece has been used to make sth **SYN** **remnant** **2** small items that are not valuable or are not part of a larger set **SYN** **bits and pieces/bobs**

**odds** /ɒdz; NAmE ɑːdz/ noun [pl.] **1** (usually **the odds**) the degree to which sth is likely to happen: *The odds are very much in our favour* (= we are likely to succeed). ◇ *The odds are heavily against him* (= he is not likely to succeed). ◇ *The odds are that* (= it is likely that) *she'll win.* ◇ *What are the odds* (= how likely is it) *he won't turn up?*

**2** [C1] something that makes it seem impossible to do or achieve sth: *They secured a victory in the face of overwhelming odds.* ◊ *She* **defied the odds** *to beat the clear favourite.* ◊ *to beat/overcome the odds* ◊ **against the ~** *The film is a heart-warming tale of triumph against the odds.* ◊ *Against all (the) odds, he made a full recovery.* ◊ **~ against (doing) sth** *The odds against making a profit in this business are huge.* **3** [C1] (in betting) the connection between two numbers that shows how much money sb will receive if they win a bet: *odds of ten to one* (= ten times the amount of money that has been bet by sb will be paid to them if they win) ◊ **on sb/sth** *They are offering long/short odds* (= the prize money will be high/low because there is a high/low risk of losing) *on the defending champion.* ◊ (*figurative*) *I'll* **lay odds** *on him getting the job* (= I'm sure he will get it).
⇒ WORDFINDER NOTE at GAMBLING
IDM **be at ˈodds (with sb) (over/on sth)** to disagree with sb about sth: *He's always at odds with his father over politics.* **be at ˈodds (with sth)** to be different from sth, when the two things should be the same SYN **conflict**: *These findings are at odds with what is going on in the rest of the country.* **it makes no ˈodds** (*informal, especially BrE*) used to say that sth is not important: *It makes no odds to me whether you go or stay.* **over the ˈodds** (*BrE, informal*) more money than you would normally expect: *Many collectors are willing to pay over the odds for early examples of his work.* ⇒ more at STACKED

**ˌodds and ˈends** (*BrE also* **ˌodds and ˈsods**) *noun* [pl.] (*informal*) small items that are not valuable or are not part of a larger set: *She spent the day sorting through a box full of odds and ends.* ◊ *I've got a few odds and ends* (= small jobs) *to do before leaving.*

**ˌodds-ˈon** *adj.* very likely to happen, win, etc: *the* **odds-on favourite** (= the person, horse, etc. that is most likely to succeed, to win a race, etc.) ◊ *It's odds-on that he'll be late.* ◊ *Arazi is odds-on to win the Kentucky Derby.*

**ode** /əʊd/ *noun* a poem that speaks to a person or thing or celebrates a special event: *Keats's 'Ode to a Nightingale'*

**odi·ous** /ˈəʊdiəs/ *adj.* (*formal*) extremely unpleasant SYN **horrible**: *What an odious man!*

**odium** /ˈəʊdiəm/ *noun* [U] (*formal*) a feeling of hate or dislike that a lot of people have towards sb, because of sth they have done

**odom·eter** /əʊˈdɒmɪtə(r)/, *NAmE* -ˈdɑːm-/ (*NAmE*) (*BrE* **mil·om·eter, mile·ometer**) (*also informal* **the clock** *US, BrE*) *noun* an instrument in a vehicle that measures the number of miles it has travelled

**odor·ous** /ˈəʊdərəs/ *adj.* (*literary* or *specialist*) having a smell: *odorous gases*

**odour** (*US* **odor**) /ˈəʊdə(r)/ *noun* [C, U] (*formal*) a smell, especially one that is unpleasant: *a* **foul/musty/pungent**, *etc.* **odour** ◊ *the stale odour of cigarette smoke* ◊ (*figurative*) *the odour of suspicion* ⇒ see also BODY ODOUR
IDM **be in good/bad ˈodour (with sb)** (*formal*) to have/not have sb's approval and support

**odour·less** (*US* **odor·less**) /ˈəʊdələs/; *NAmE* -dərl-/ *adj.* without a smell: *an odourless liquid*

**odys·sey** /ˈɒdəsi/; *NAmE* ˈɑːd-/ *noun* [sing.] (*literary*) a long journey during which sb has a lot of interesting and exciting experiences ORIGIN From the **Odyssey**, a Greek poem that is said to have been written by Homer, about the adventures of **Odysseus**. After a battle in Troy, Odysseus had to spend ten years travelling before he could return home.

**OECD** /ˌəʊ iː siː ˈdiː/ *abbr.* Organization for Economic Cooperation and Development (an organization of industrial countries that encourages trade and economic growth)

**oe·dema** (*BrE*) (*NAmE* **edema**) /ɪˈdiːmə/ *noun* [U] (*medical*) a condition in which liquid collects in the spaces inside the body and makes it SWELL (= become larger or rounder than normal)

**Oedi·pal** /ˈiːdɪpl/; *NAmE* ˈed-, ˈiːd-/ *adj.* [usually before noun] connected with an Oedipus complex

**ˈOedi·pus com·plex** /ˈiːdɪpəs kɒmpleks/; *NAmE* ˈedɪpəs kɑːm-, ˈiːd-/ *noun* [sing.] (*psychology*) feelings of sexual desire that a boy has for his mother and the JEALOUS feelings towards his father that this causes ORIGIN From the Greek story of **Oedipus**, whose father Laius had been told by the oracle that his son would kill him. Laius left Oedipus on a mountain to die, but a shepherd rescued him. Oedipus returned home many years later but did not recognize his parents. He killed his father and married his mother, Jocasta.

**o'er** /ɔː(r), ˈəʊə(r)/ *adv., prep.* (*old use*) over

**oe·sopha·gus** (*BrE*) (*NAmE* **esopha·gus**) /iˈsɒfəgəs/; *NAmE* iˈsɑːf-/ *noun* (*pl.* **-pha·guses, -ph·agi** /-gaɪ/) (*anatomy*) the tube through which food passes from the mouth to the stomach SYN **gullet** ⇒ VISUAL VOCAB page V1

**oes·tro·gen** (*BrE*) (*NAmE* **es·tro·gen**) /ˈiːstrədʒən/; *NAmE* ˈes-/ *noun* [U] a HORMONE produced in women's OVARIES that causes them to develop the physical and sexual features that are typical of females and that causes them to prepare their body to have babies ⇒ compare PROGESTERONE, TESTOSTERONE

**oes·trus** (*BrE*) (*NAmE* **es·trus**) /ˈiːstrəs/; *NAmE* ˈes-/ *noun* [U] (*specialist*) a period of time in which a female animal is FERTILE and ready to have sex ⇒ compare BE ON HEAT

**oeuvre** /ˈɜːvrə/ *noun* [sing.] (*from French, formal*) all the works of a writer, artist, etc: *Picasso's oeuvre*

**of** ❶ [A1] /əv; *BrE strong form* ɒv; *NAmE strong form* ʌv/ *prep.* **1** [C1] belonging to sb; relating to sb: *a friend of mine* ◊ *the love of a mother for her child* ◊ *the role of the teacher* ◊ *Can't you throw out that old bike of Tommy's?* ◊ *the paintings of Monet* HELP When you are talking about everything someone has painted, written, etc., use **of**. When you are referring to one or more examples of somebody's work, use **by**: *a painting by Monet* **2** [A1] belonging to sth; being part of sth; relating to sth: *the lid of the box* ◊ *the director of the company* ◊ *a member of the team* ◊ *the result of the debate* **3** [A1] coming from a particular background or living in a place: *a woman of Italian descent* ◊ *the people of Wales* **4** [A1] relating to or showing sb/sth: *a story of passion* ◊ *a photo of my dog* ◊ *a map of India* **5** [A1] used to say what sb/sth is, consists of or contains: *the city of Dublin* ◊ *the issue of housing* ◊ *a crowd of people* ◊ *a glass of milk* **6** [A1] used with measurements and expressions of time, age, etc: *2 kilos of potatoes* ◊ *an increase of 2 per cent* ◊ *a girl of 12* ◊ *the fourth of July* ◊ *the year of his birth* ◊ (*old-fashioned*) *We would often have a walk of an evening.* **7** [A1] used to show sb/sth belongs to a group, often after *some, a few*, etc: *some of his friends* ◊ *a few of the problems* ◊ *the most famous of all the stars* **8** [A1] used to show the position of sth/sb in space or time: *just north of Detroit* ◊ *at the time of the revolution* ◊ (*NAmE*) *at a quarter of eleven tonight* (= 10.45 p.m.) **9** [A1] used after nouns formed from verbs. The noun after 'of' can be either the object or the subject of the action: *the arrival of the police* (= they arrive) ◊ *criticism of the police* (= they are criticized) ◊ *fear of the dark* ◊ *the howling of the wind* **10** [A1] used after some verbs before mentioning sb/sth involved in the action: *to deprive sb of sth* ◊ *He was cleared of all blame.* ◊ *Think of a number, any number.* **11** [A1] used after some adjectives before mentioning sb/sth that a feeling relates to: *to be proud of sth* **12** [A1] used to give your opinion of sb's behaviour: *It was kind of you to offer.* **13** used when one noun describes a second one: *Where's that idiot of a boy* (= the boy that you think is stupid)?
IDM **of ˈall** used before a noun to say that sth is very surprising: *I'm surprised that you of all people should say that.* **of all the ...** used to express anger: *Of all the nerve!*

**off** ❶ [A1] /ɒf; *NAmE* ɔːf/ *adv., prep., adj., noun, verb*
■ *adv.* HELP For the special uses of **off** in phrasal verbs, look at the entries for the verbs. For example **come off** is in the phrasal verb section at **come**. **1** [A1] used to say that sth has been removed or become separated: *He's had his beard shaved off.* ◊ *Take your coat off.* ◊ *The label must have fallen off.* ◊ *Don't leave the toothpaste with the top off.* **2** [A1] not connected or functioning: *The water is off.* ◊ *Make sure the TV is off.* **3** [A2] away from a place; at a distance in time or space: *I called him but he ran off.* ◊ *Sarah's off in India somewhere.* ◊ *I must be off* (= I must leave) *soon.* ◊ *Summer's not far off now.* ◊ *A solution is still some way off.* ◊ *Off you go! Enjoy yourselves!* HELP **Off you go!** is a friendly way of telling sb to go away, or giving them

# off-

permission to go away, when this is what they want to do anyway. It is different from **Go away!**, which is a rude way of telling sb you do not want them to stay. **4** away from work or duty: *She's off today.* ◇ *I've got three days off next week.* ◇ *How many days did you take off?* ◇ *I need some time off.* **5** starting a race: *They're off* (= the race has begun). **6** taken from the price: *shoes with $20 off* ◇ *All shirts have/are 10 per cent off.* **7** no longer going to happen; cancelled: *The wedding is off.* **8** (*especially BrE*) (of an item on a menu) no longer available or being served: *Sorry, the duck is off.* **9** behind or at the sides of the stage in a theatre SYN **offstage**

**IDM** **be better/worse off (doing sth)** to be in a better or worse situation: *She's better off without him.* ◇ *The weather was so bad we'd have been better off staying at home.* ◇ *We can't be any worse off than we are already.* **be ˌoff for ˈsth** (*informal*) to have a particular amount of sth: *How are we off for coffee* (= how much do we have?) ⊃ see also BADLY OFF **be well/better/badly, etc. ˈoff** used to say how much money sb has: *Families will be better off under the new law* (= will have more money). ◇ *They are both comfortably off* (= have enough money to be able to buy what they want without worrying too much about the cost). **ˌoff and ˈon/ˌon and ˈoff** from time to time; now and again: *It rained on and off all day.*

- **prep.** **HELP** For the special uses of **off** in phrasal verbs, look at the entries for the verbs. For example **take sth off sth** is in the phrasal verb section at **take**. **1** down or away from a place or at a distance in space or time: *I fell off the ladder.* ◇ *Keep off the grass!* ◇ *an island off the coast of Spain* ◇ *They were still 100 metres off the summit.* ◇ *Scientists are still a long way off finding a cure.* ◇ *We're getting right off the subject.* **2** used to say that sth has been removed: *You need to take the top off the bottle first!* ◇ *I want about an inch off the back of my hair.* **3** away from work or duty: *He's had ten days off school.* **4** away from a price: *They knocked £500 off the car.* **5** leading away from sth, for example a road or room: *We live off Main Street.* ◇ *There's a bathroom off the main bedroom.* **6** (*informal*) from a person or place: *I got this off a website somewhere.* **7** off (*non-standard or NAmE, informal*) off; from: *She jumped off of the wall.* ◇ *I got it off of my brother.* **8** not wanting or liking sth that you usually eat or use: *I'm off* (= not drinking) *alcohol for a week.* ◇ *He's finally off drugs* (= he no longer takes them).

- **adj.** [not before noun] **1** (*BrE*) (of food) no longer fresh enough to eat or drink: *This fish has gone off.* ◇ *The milk smells off.* ◇ *It's off.* **2 ~(with sb)** (*informal, especially BrE*) not polite or friendly: *He was a bit off with me this morning.* **3** (*informal, especially BrE*) not acceptable: *It's a bit off expecting us to work on Sunday.*

- **noun** [sing.] **the off** the start of a race: *They're ready for the off.*

- **verb** ~ **sb** (*informal, especially NAmE*) to kill sb

**off-** /ɒf; NAmE ɔːf/ *prefix* (in nouns, adjectives, verbs and adverbs) not on; away from: *offstage* ◇ *offload*

**ˌoff-ˈair** *adj.* (in radio and television) not being broadcast: *off-air recording* OPP **on-air** ▶ **ˌoff-ˈair** *adv.*: *to record off-air*

**offal** /ˈɒfl; NAmE ˈɔːfl/ *noun* [U] (*US also* **vaˈriety meats** [pl.]) the inside parts of an animal, such as the heart and LIVER, cooked and eaten as food

**ˈoff-beat** /ˌɒfˈbiːt; NAmE ˌɔːf-/ *adj.* [usually before noun] (*informal*) different from what most people expect SYN **unconventional**: *offbeat humour* ◇ *an offbeat approach to interviewing*

**ˌoff-ˈBroadway** *adj.* (*NAmE*) **1** (of a theatre) not on Broadway, New York's main theatre district **2** (of a play) unusual in some way and often by a new writer ⊃ compare FRINGE THEATRE

**ˌoff-ˈcentre** (*US* **ˌoff-ˈcenter**) *adv., adj.* not exactly in the centre of sth

**ˌoff ˈcolour** (*US* **ˌoff ˈcolor**) *adj.* **1** [not before noun] (*BrE, informal*) not in good health; looking or feeling ill **2** [usually before noun] (*especially NAmE*) an **off-colour** joke is one that people think is rude, usually because it is about sex

**ˈoff-cut** /ˈɒfkʌt; NAmE ˈɔːf-/ *noun* (*especially BrE*) a piece of wood, paper, etc. that remains after the main piece has been cut

**ˈoff day** *noun* (*informal*) a day when you do not do things as well as usual

**ˌoff-ˈduty** *adj.* (especially of police, military and medical staff) not at work: *an off-duty policeman*

**of·fence** (*US* **of·fense**) /əˈfens/ *noun* **1** [C] an illegal act SYN **crime**: *a criminal/serious/minor/sexual offence* ◇ *a capital offence* (= one for which sb may be punished by death) ◇ *He was not aware that he had committed an offence.* ◇ *New legislation makes it an offence to carry guns.* ◇ *~ against sb/sth* *an offence against society/humanity/the state* ⊃ WORDFINDER NOTE at TRIAL **2** [U] the feeling of being upset or angry at sth that sb has said or done: *The photo may cause offence to some people.* ◇ *No one will take offence* (= feel upset or insulted) *if you leave early.* ◇ *Many readers took offence at the article.* ◇ *I'm sure he meant no offence when he said that.*

**IDM** **no offence** (*informal*) used to say that you do not mean to upset or show a lack of respect for sb by sth you say or do: *No offence, but I'd really like to be on my own.*

**of·fend** /əˈfend/ *verb* **1** [T, often passive, I] ~(sb) to make sb feel upset because of sth you say or do that is rude or embarrassing: *They'll be offended if you don't go to their wedding.* ◇ *Neil did not mean to offend anybody with his joke.* ◇ *A TV interviewer must be careful not to offend.* **2** [T] ~**sb/sth** to seem unpleasant to sb: *The smell from the farm offended some people.* ◇ *an ugly building that offends the eye* **3** [I] (*formal*) to commit a crime or crimes: *He started offending at the age of 16.* **4** [I] ~**(against sb/sth)** (*formal*) to be against what people believe is morally right: *comments that offend against people's religious beliefs* ▶ **of·fend·ed** *adj.*: *Alice looked rather offended.*

**of·fend·er** /əˈfendə(r)/ *noun* **1** (*rather formal*) a person who commits a crime: *a persistent/serious/violent, etc. offender* ◇ *a young offender institution* ⊃ see also FIRST OFFENDER, SEX OFFENDER, YOUNG OFFENDER **2** a person or thing that does sth wrong: *When it comes to pollution, the chemical industry is a major offender.*

**of·fend·ing** /əˈfendɪŋ/ *adj.* [only before noun] **1** causing you to feel annoyed or upset; causing problems: *The offending paragraph was deleted.* ◇ *The traffic jam soon cleared once the offending vehicle had been removed.* **2** guilty of a crime: *The offending driver received a large fine.*

**of·fense** *noun* (*US*) **1** /əˈfens/ [C] = OFFENCE: *to commit an offense* ◇ *The new law makes it a criminal offense to drink alcohol in public places.* ◇ *a minor/serious offense* ◇ *She pleaded guilty to five traffic offenses.* **2** /ˈɒfens; NAmE ˈɑːf-/ [sing. + sing./pl. v.] (*BrE* **atˈtack** [sing.]) (*sport*) the members of a team whose main aim is to score points against the other team; a method of attack: *The team's offense is stronger than their defense.* ◇ *He played offense for the Chicago Bulls.* ⊃ compare DEFENCE

**of·fen·sive** /əˈfensɪv/ *adj., noun*

- **adj.** **1** rude in a way that causes sb to feel upset or annoyed because it shows a lack of respect: *offensive remarks* ◇ *The programme contains language which some viewers may find offensive.* ◇ *~ to sb* *His comments were deeply offensive to a large number of single mothers.* OPP **inoffensive** **2** (*formal*) extremely unpleasant SYN **obnoxious**: *an offensive smell* ⊃ SYNONYMS at DISGUSTING **3** [only before noun] connected with the act of attacking sb/sth: *an offensive war* ◇ *offensive action* ◇ *He was charged with carrying an offensive weapon.* ⊃ compare DEFENSIVE **4** (*NAmE, sport*) connected with the team that has control of the ball; connected with the act of scoring points: *offensive play* ◇ *an offensive player/lineman/tackle* ⊃ compare DEFENSIVE ▶ **of·fen·sive·ly** *adv.* **of·fen·sive·ness** *noun* [U]

- **noun** **1** a military operation in which large numbers of soldiers, etc. attack another country SYN **strike**: *an air offensive* ◇ *They launched the offensive on January 10.* **2** a series of actions aimed at achieving sth in a way that attracts a lot of attention SYN **campaign**: *The government has launched a new offensive against crime.* ◇ *a sales offensive* ◇ *The public seems unconvinced by their latest charm offensive* (= their attempt to make people like them).

**IDM** ▶ **be on the of·fensive** to be attacking sb/sth rather than waiting for them to attack you ▶ **go on (to) the offensive** | **take the offensive** to start attacking sb/sth before they start attacking you

**of·fer** ❶ **A2** **W** /ˈɒfə(r); NAmE ˈɔːf-/ *verb, noun*

■ *verb* **1** **A2** [T, I] to say that you are willing to give sth to sb: ~ **(sth)** *Josie had offered her services as a guide.* ◇ *He offered some useful advice.* ◇ *to offer support/protection/help* ◇ *I don't think they need help, but I think I should offer anyway.* ◇ ~ **sth for sth** *He offered $4000 for the car.* ◇ ~ **sth to sb** *They decided to offer the job to Jo.* ◇ ~ **sb sth** *They decided to offer Jo the job.* ◇ *I gratefully took the cup of coffee she offered me.* ◇ ~ **sb sth to do sth** *Taylor offered him 500 dollars to do the work.* ➔ **EXPRESS YOURSELF** at **SHALL** **2** **A2** [T, I] to say that you are willing to do sth for sb: ~ **to do sth** *The kids offered to do the dishes.* ◇ + **speech** *'I'll do it,' she offered.* **3** **A2** [T] to make sth available for sale or use: ~ **sth** *The hotel offers excellent facilities for families.* ◇ *Both companies offer a range of software.* ◇ ~ **sth for sth** *The property will be offered for sale by auction on May 24.* **4** **A2** [T] to provide the opportunity for sth; to provide access to sth: ~ **sth** *The job didn't offer any prospects for promotion.* ◇ *He did not offer any explanation for his behaviour.* ◇ ~ **sb sth** *The program has offered her many opportunities for travel.* **5** [T] ~ **sth (to sb/sth)** to show that you are ready to resist or attack sb/sth: *Universities offered little resistance to these changes.* ◇ *He never lost his temper or offered violence to anyone.* **6** [T] ~ **sth/sb (up) (to sb)** (*formal*) to give sth to God: *We offered up our prayers for the men's safe return.*
**IDM** ▶ **have sth to offer** to have sth available that sb wants: *Oxford has a lot to offer visitors in the way of entertainment.* ◇ *a young man with a great deal to offer* (= who is intelligent, has many skills, etc.) ▶ **offer your ˈhand** (*formal*) to hold out your hand for sb to shake

■ *noun* **1** **A2** an act of saying that you are willing to do sth for sb or give sth to sb: *to receive a job offer* ◇ *to accept/reject/decline an offer* ◇ ~ **of sth** *Thank you for your kind offer of help.* ◇ *I took him up on his offer of a loan.* ◇ *You can't just turn down offers of work like that.* ◇ *an offer of marriage* ◇ ~ **to do sth** *I accepted her offer to pay.* **2** **A2** an amount of money that sb is willing to pay for sth: ~ **for sth** *I've had an offer of $2500 for the car.* ◇ *They've decided to accept our original offer.* ◇ *The offer has been withdrawn.* ◇ ~ **(that)…** *(they) made me an offer I couldn't refuse.* ◇ *The original price was £3000, but I'm open to offers* (= willing to consider offers that are less than that). ➔ **WORDFINDER NOTE** at **DEAL** ➔ see also **O.N.O.** **3** **A2** a reduction in the normal price of sth, usually for a short period of time: *This special offer is valid until the end of the month.* ◇ ~ **on sth** *We have an offer on beer at the moment.*
**IDM** ▶ **on ˈoffer 1** that can be bought, used, etc: *The following is a list of courses currently on offer.* ◇ *Prizes worth more than £20000 are on offer.* **2** (*especially BrE*) on sale at a lower price than normal for a short period of time: *Italian wines are on (special) offer this week.* ▶ **under ˈoffer** (*BrE*) if a house or other building is **under offer**, sb has agreed to buy it at a particular price

▼ **EXPRESS YOURSELF**

**Offering somebody something**

Particularly when you are the host, you may want to make polite offers to your guests:
• **Would you like** *a magazine to read?*
• **Can I get you** *a coffee?*
• **Can I offer you** *something to drink?*
• **How about** *something to eat? I could make some sandwiches.*
• **If you'd like to use / If you need** *the bathroom, it's the second door on the right.*
• **Feel free to** *go upstairs and have a rest if you'd like to.*

Responses:
• *That would be nice. I'd like a cup of tea, please.*
• *Yes, please. A glass of orange juice would be lovely.*
• *If you're sure it's no trouble, I'd love a coffee.*
• *No, thank you. I'm fine for now.*
• *Not for me, thanks.*
• *I'm fine, thanks. Maybe later.*

1075 **officer**

**of·fer·ing** **C1** /ˈɒfərɪŋ; NAmE ˈɔːf-/ *noun* **1** **C1** something that is produced for other people to use, watch, enjoy, etc: *the latest offering from the Canadian-born writer* **2** something that is given to a god as part of a religious ceremony ➔ see also **BURNT OFFERING**, **PEACE OFFERING**

**of·fer·tory** /ˈɒfətri; NAmE ˈɔːfərtɔːri/ *noun* (*pl.* **-ies**) **1** the offering of bread and wine to God at a church service **2** an offering or a collection of money during a church service

**off-ˈgrid** *adj.* = **OFF-THE-GRID**

**off·hand** /ˌɒfˈhænd; NAmE ˌɔːf-/ *adj., adv.*
■ *adj.* (*disapproving*) not showing much interest in sb/sth in a way that is rude or upsets sb: *an offhand manner* ◇ *He was very offhand with me.* ▶ **off·hand·ed·ly** /-ˈhændɪdli/ *adv.*: *He spoke offhandedly, making it clear I had no say in the matter.*
■ *adv.* without being able to check sth or think about it: *I don't know offhand how much we made last year.*

**of·fice** ❶ **A1** /ˈɒfɪs; NAmE ˈɑːf-/ *noun*
• **ROOM/BUILDING 1** **A1** [C] a room, set of rooms or building where people work, usually sitting at desks: *Are you going to the office today?* ◇ **in / at the ~** *I'm sorry, Mr Anders is not in the office today.* ◇ *office workers* ◇ *an office building* ◇ *office space* ➔ see also **BACK OFFICE**, **HEAD OFFICE** **2** **A1** [C] a room in which a particular person works, usually at a desk: *Some people have to share an office.* ◇ *Come into my office.* ➔ see also **HOME OFFICE 3** [C] (*NAmE*) (*BrE* **surˈgery**) a place where a doctor, dentist or vet sees patients: *a doctor's/dentist's office* **4** **A1** [C] (often in compounds) a room or building used for a particular purpose, especially to provide information or a service: *a ticket office* ➔ see also **BOOKING OFFICE**, **BOX OFFICE**, **FRONT OFFICE**, **POST OFFICE**, **PRESS OFFICE**, **REGISTRY OFFICE**, **SORTING OFFICE**
• **GOVERNMENT DEPARTMENT 5** **A2** **Office** [C] used in the names of some British government departments: *the Home Office* ◇ ~ **of sth** *the Office of Fair Trading* ➔ see also **LAND OFFICE**
• **IMPORTANT POSITION 6** **B2** [U, C] an important position of authority, especially in government; the work and duties connected with this: *She held office as a cabinet minister for ten years.* ◇ **in ~** *How long has he been in office?* ◇ *The scandal cast a shadow over his time in office.* ◇ *The present government took office in 2017.* ◇ *She has announced she will not run for office again.* ◇ **the ~ of sth** *She held the office of treasurer for five years.*
**IDM** ▶ **through sb's good ˈoffices** (*formal*) with sb's help

**ˈoffice block** (*BrE*) (*also* **ˈoffice building** *NAmE, BrE*) *noun* a large building that contains offices, usually belonging to more than one company

**ˈoffice boy**, **ˈoffice girl** *noun* (*old-fashioned*) a young person employed to do simple tasks in an office

**ˈoffice-holder** (*also* **ˈoffice-bearer**) *noun* a person who is in a position of authority, especially in the government or a government organization

**ˈoffice hours** *noun* [pl.] the time when people in offices are normally working: *Our telephone lines are open during normal office hours.*

**of·fi·cer** ❶ **A2** /ˈɒfɪsə(r); NAmE ˈɑːf-/ *noun* **1** **A2** a person who is in a position of authority in the armed forces: *army/military/naval officers* ◇ *senior officers in the Royal Air Force* ◇ *The matter was passed on to me, as your commanding officer.* ➔ **WORDFINDER NOTE** at **ARMY** ➔ see also **COMMISSIONED OFFICER**, **DUTY OFFICER**, **FIRST OFFICER**, **FLYING OFFICER**, **PETTY OFFICER**, **PILOT OFFICER**, **STAFF OFFICER**, **WARRANT OFFICER 2** **A2** [C] (often used as a form of address) = **POLICE OFFICER**: *the officer in charge of the case* ◇ *the investigating officer* ◇ *Yes, officer, I saw what happened.* ➔ see also **PEACE OFFICER 3** (*NAmE*) a title for a police officer: *Officer Dibble* **4** **A2** (often in compounds) a person who is in a position of authority in the government or a large organization: *an environmental health officer* ◇ *a customs/prison/welfare officer* ◇ *He was a former officer in the Secret Service.* ➔ see also **CHIEF EXECUTIVE OFFICER**, **CHIEF FINANCIAL OFFICER**, **FIELD OFFICER**, **HOUSE OFFICER**, **LIAISON OFFICER**, **MEDICAL OFFICER**, **PRESS OFFICER**, **PROBATION OFFICER**, **RETURNING OFFICER**

**office worker** *noun* a person who works in the offices of a business or company

**of·fi·cial** ⓘ B1 /əˈfɪʃl/ *adj., noun*

■ *adj.* **1** B1 [usually before noun] agreed to, said, done, etc. by sb who is in a position of authority: *an official announcement/decision/statement* ◇ *according to* **official** *figures/statistics* ◇ *The news is not yet official.* ◇ *An official inquiry has been launched into the cause of the accident.* ◇ *The country's* **official** *language is Spanish.* ◇ *The film's* **official website** *is also very informative.* **2** B1 [only before noun] connected with the job of sb who is in a position of authority: *official duties/responsibilities* ◇ *the Prime Minister's* **official residence** ◇ *He attended in his official capacity as mayor.* ◇ *This was her first official engagement.* ◇ *He made an* **official** *visit to Tokyo in March.* **3** B1 [only before noun] formal and attended by people in authority: *an official function/reception* ◇ *The* **official opening** *is planned for October.* **4** B2 [only before noun] that is told to the public but may not be true: *I only knew the official version of events.* ◇ *The* **official line** *is that the date for the election has not yet been decided.* OPP **unofficial**

■ *noun* B2 (often in compounds) a person who is in a position of authority in a large organization: *She is the government official in charge of the project.* ◇ *a senior official in the State Department* ◇ *a bank/company/court official*
⊃ see also FOURTH OFFICIAL

**of·fi·cial·dom** /əˈfɪʃldəm/ *noun* [U] (*disapproving*) people who are in positions of authority in large organizations when they seem to be more interested in following rules than in being helpful

**of·fi·cial·ese** /əˌfɪʃəˈliːz/ *noun* [U] (*disapproving*) language used in official documents that is thought by many people to be too complicated and difficult to understand

**of·fi·cial·ly** /əˈfɪʃəli/ *adv.* **1** publicly and by sb who is in a position of authority: *The library will be officially opened by the local MP.* ◇ *We haven't yet been told officially about the closure.* ◇ *The college is not an officially recognized English language school.* **2** according to a particular set of rules, laws, etc: *Many of those living on the streets are not officially homeless.* ◇ *I'm not officially supposed to be here.* **3** according to information that has been told to the public but that may not be true: *Officially, he resigned because of bad health.* OPP **unofficially**

**of·fi·cial re·ceiv·er** *noun* (*law, BrE*) = RECEIVER (3)

**of·fi·cial 'secret** *noun* (in the UK) a piece of information known only to the government and some of its employees, which it is illegal for them to tell anyone under the Official Secrets Act

**the Of·fi·cial 'Secrets Act** *noun* (in the UK) a law that prevents people giving information if the government wants it to remain secret

**of·fi·ci·ate** /əˈfɪʃieɪt/ *verb* **1** [I, T] **~ (at) sth** to act as an official in charge of sth, especially a sports event: *A referee from a neutral country will officiate (at) the game.* **2** [I] **~ (at sth)** (*formal*) to do the official duties at a public or religious ceremony

**of·fi·cious** /əˈfɪʃəs/ *adj.* (*disapproving*) too ready to tell people what to do or to use the power you have to give orders SYN **self-important**: *a nasty officious little man*
▶ **of·fi·cious·ly** *adv.*: *'You can't park here,' he said officiously.* **of·fi·cious·ness** *noun* [U]

**off·ing** /ˈɒfɪŋ; *NAmE* ˈɔːf-/ *noun*
IDM **in the offing** (*informal*) likely to appear or happen soon: *I hear there are more staff changes in the offing.*

**off-'key** *adj.* **1** (of a voice or of a musical instrument) not in tune **2** not suitable or correct in a particular situation SYN **inappropriate**: *Some of his remarks were very off-key.* ▶ **off-'key** *adv.*: *to sing off key*

**off-'kilter** *adj.* **1** not perfectly straight or balanced; not in line with sth else: *a slightly off-kilter, hand-drawn circle* **2** slightly strange or unusual: *an off-kilter comedy*

**off-'label** *adj.* relating to the use of a drug for sth other than what it was originally created for: *A number of people suffered reactions due to off-label prescriptions.* ▶ **off-**

**label** *adv.*: *The antidepressant was prescribed off-label to treat an eating disorder.*

**off-'licence** (*BrE*) (*US* **'liquor store**, **'package store**) *noun* a shop that sells alcoholic drinks in bottles and cans to take away

**off-'limits** *adj.* **1 ~ (to sb)** (of a place) where people are not allowed to go: *The site is off-limits to the general public.* **2** not allowed to be discussed: *The subject was ruled off-limits.*

**off·line** /ˌɒfˈlaɪn; *NAmE* ˌɔːf-/ *adj.* (*computing*) not directly controlled by or connected to a computer or to the internet: *For offline orders, call this number.* ▶ **off·line** *adv.*: *How do I write an email offline?* ⊃ see also ONLINE
IDM **take sth offline** to talk about sth on a later occasion, perhaps because it does not interest the other people who are present at a meeting: *Could you two take that offline so we can move onto the other items on the agenda?*

**off·load** /ˌɒfˈləʊd; *NAmE* ˌɔːfˈloʊd/ *verb* **1** to take a load of goods off a ship, train or truck SYN **unload**: **~ sth** *The goods were offloaded at the dock.* ◇ *They will be offloading the truck tomorrow morning.* ◇ **~ sth from sth** *The cargo containers were offloaded from the ships.* **2 ~ sth/sb (onto sb)** to get rid of sth/sb that you do not need or want by passing it/them to sb else: *He managed to offload the unwanted shares onto a client.* **3 ~ sth/sb (on/onto sb)** to make a problem or worry less severe by talking to sb else: *It's nice to have someone you can offload your problems onto.*

**off-'peak** *adj.* [only before noun] happening or used at a time that is less popular or busy, and therefore cheaper: *off-peak electricity/travel* ▶ **off-'peak** *adv.*: *Phone calls cost 20c per unit off-peak.* ⊃ compare PEAK

**off-'piste** *adj.* away from the tracks of hard snow that have been prepared for skiing on: *off-piste skiing* ▶ **off-'piste** *adv.*: *We enjoy skiing off-piste.*

**off-'putting** *adj.* (*informal, especially BrE*) not pleasant, in a way that prevents you from liking sb/sth: *I find his manner very off-putting.*

**off-ramp** *noun* (*NAmE, SAfrE*) a road used for driving off a major road such as an INTERSTATE ⊃ compare ON-RAMP, SLIP ROAD

**off-road** *adv., adj.* [usually before noun] not on the public road; on rough ground: *Many 4x4 owners have never driven off-road.* ◇ *an off-road vehicle*

**off-'roader** *noun* **1** a vehicle which is driven across rough ground as a sport **2** a person who drives a vehicle across rough ground as a sport ▶ **off-'roading** *noun* [U]

**off-'screen** *adj.* [only before noun] happening to an actor in real life, not in a film: *They were off-screen lovers.* ▶ **off-'screen** *adv.*: *She looks totally different off-screen.* ⊃ compare ON-SCREEN

**'off season** *noun* [sing.] **1** the time of the year that is less busy in business and travel SYN **low season 2** (*NAmE*) (*BrE* **close season**) (*sport*) a time of year when teams do not play games in a particular sport ▶ **off-'season** *adj.* [only before noun]: *off-season prices* **off-'season** *adv.*: *We prefer to travel off-season.*

**off·set** /ˈɒfset; *NAmE* ˈɔːf-/ *verb, adj.*

■ *verb* (**off·set·ting**, **off·set**, **off·set**) to use one cost, payment or situation in order to cancel or reduce the effect of another: **~ sth** *Prices have risen in order to offset the increased cost of materials.* **~ sth against sth** (*BrE*): *What expenses can you offset against tax?*

■ *adj.* [only before noun] used to describe a method of printing in which INK (= coloured liquid) is put onto a metal plate, then onto a rubber surface and only then onto the paper ⊃ see also CARBON OFFSET

**off·shoot** /ˈɒfʃuːt; *NAmE* ˈɔːf-/ *noun* **1** a thing that develops from sth, especially a small organization that develops from a larger one **2** (*specialist*) a new STEM that grows on a plant

**off·shore** /ˌɒfˈʃɔː(r); *NAmE* ˌɔːf-/ *adj.* [usually before noun] **1** happening or existing in the sea, not far from the coast: *offshore drilling* ◇ *an offshore island* ⊃ compare ONSHORE (1) **2** (of winds) blowing from the land towards the sea: *offshore breezes* ⊃ compare ONSHORE (2) **3** (*business*) (of money, companies, etc.) kept or located in a foreign country that has more generous tax laws than the home country: *offshore investments* ▶ **off·shore** *adv.*: *a ship anchored offshore* ◊ *profits earned offshore* ⊃ compare INSHORE, ONSHORE

**off·shor·ing** /ˈɒfʃɔːrɪŋ; NAmE ˈɔːf-/ *noun* [U] the practice of a company in one country arranging for people in another country to do work for it: *the offshoring of call-centre jobs to India* ▶ **off·shore** *verb* ~ *sth*

**off·side** /ˌɒfˈsaɪd; NAmE ˌɔːf-/ *adj., noun, adv.*
■ *adj.* **1** (*US also* **off·sides**) in some sports, for example football (soccer) and ice hockey, a player is **offside** if he or she is in a position, usually ahead of the ball, that is not allowed: *He was offside when he scored.* ◊ *the offside rule* **OPP** **onside 2** (*BrE*) on the side of a vehicle that is furthest from the edge of the road: *the offside mirror* **OPP** **nearside**
■ *noun* [U] **1** (*US also* **off·sides**) the fact of being offside in a game such as football (soccer) or ice hockey: *The goal was disallowed for offside.* **2** /ˌɒfˈsaɪd; NAmE ˌɔːf-/ **the offside** (*BrE*) the side of a vehicle that is furthest from the edge of the road: *The offside was damaged.* **OPP** **the nearside**
■ *adv.* (in some sports, for example football (soccer) and ice hockey) in a position, usually ahead of the ball, that is not allowed

**off·sider** /ˈɒfsaɪdə(r); NAmE ˈɔːf-/ *noun* (*AustralE, NZE, informal*) a person who works with or helps sb else

**off·spring** ?+ **C1** /ˈɒfsprɪŋ; NAmE ˈɔːf-/ *noun* (*pl.* **off·spring**) (*formal or humorous*) **1** ?+ **C1** a child of a particular person or couple: *the problems parents have with their teenage offspring* ◊ *to produce/raise offspring* **2** ?+ **C1** the young of an animal or plant: *Female badgers may give birth to as many as five offspring.*

**off·stage** /ˌɒfˈsteɪdʒ; NAmE ˌɔːf-/ *adj.* **1** not on the stage in a theatre; not where the audience can see: *offstage sound effects* **2** happening to an actor in real life, not on the stage: *The stars were having an offstage relationship.* ▶ **off·stage** *adv.*: *The hero dies offstage.* **OPP** **onstage**

**off-street** *adj.* [usually before noun] not on the public road: *an apartment with off-street parking* **OPP** **on-street**

**off-the-ˈcuff** ⊃ CUFF *noun* **HELP** You will also find other compounds beginning **off-the-** at the entry for the last word in the compound.

**off-the-ˈgrid** (*also* **off-ˈgrid**) *adj.* (*especially NAmE*) not using the public supplies of electricity, gas, water, etc: *an off-the-grid house, independent of traditional utility services* ⊃ see also GRID

**off-the-ˈshelf** *adj.* [only before noun] (of a product) that can be bought immediately and does not have to be specially designed or ordered: *off-the-shelf software packages* ⊃ see also SHELF

**off-ˈwhite** *adj.* white, but not pure white in colour ▶ **off-ˈwhite** *noun* [U]

**ˈoff year** *noun* (*US*) a year in which there are no important elections, especially no election for president ▶ **ˈoff-year** *adj.*

**OFSTED** /ˈɒfsted; NAmE ˈɔːf-/ *abbr.* the Office for Standards in Education (a British government department that is responsible for checking that standards in schools are acceptable)

**oft** /ɒft; NAmE ɔːft/ *adv.* (*old use*) often

**oft-** /ɒft; NAmE ɔːft/ *prefix* (in adjectives) often: *an oft-repeated claim*

**often** ❶ **A1** ⊘ /ˈɒfn, ˈɒftən; NAmE ˈɔːfn, ˈɔːftən/ *adv.* **1** **A1** many times **SYN** **frequently**: *We often go there.* ◊ *I've often wondered what happened to him.* ◊ *How often do you go to the theatre?* ◊ *I see her quite often.* ◊ *Try to exercise as often as possible.* ◊ *We should meet for lunch more often.* ◊ *It is not often that you get such an opportunity.* **2** **A1** in many cases **SYN** **commonly**: *Old houses are often damp.* ◊ *People are often afraid of things they don't understand.* ◊ *All too often the animals die through neglect.* **IDM** **as often as ˈnot** | **more often than ˈnot** usually; in a way that is typical of sb/sth: *As often as not, he's late for work.* **every so ˈoften** occasionally; sometimes ⊃ more at ONCE *adv.*

**often·times** /ˈɒfntaɪmz, ˈɒftən-; NAmE ˈɔːfn-, ˈɔːftən-/ *adv.* (*old use* or *NAmE*) often

1077 **oilman**

**ogle** /ˈəʊɡl; NAmE also ˈɑːɡl/ *verb* [T, I] ~ (**sb**) to look hard at sb in an offensive way, usually showing sexual interest: *He was not in the habit of ogling women.*

**ogre** /ˈəʊɡə(r)/ *noun* **1** (in stories) a cruel and frightening giant who eats people **2** a very frightening person: *My boss is a real ogre.*

**OH** *abbr.* (*BrE, informal*) (especially in text messages, on SOCIAL MEDIA, etc.) other half (a person's wife, husband or partner)

**oh** ❶ **A1** /əʊ/ *exclamation* **1** ?+ **A1** used when you are reacting to sth that has been said, especially if you did not know it before: *'I saw Ben yesterday.' 'Oh yes, how is he?'* ◊ *'Emma has a new job.' 'Oh, has she?'* **2** **A1** used to express surprise, fear, joy, etc: *Oh, how wonderful!* ◊ *Oh no, I've broken it!* **3** ?+ **A1** used to attract sb's attention: *Oh, Sue! Could you help me a moment?* **4** used when you are thinking of what to say next: *I've been in this job for, oh, about six years.* ⊃ compare O

**ohm** /əʊm/ *noun* (*physics*) a unit for measuring electrical RESISTANCE

**ohmi·god** (*also* **ohmy·god**) = OMIGOD

**oho** /əʊˈhəʊ/ *exclamation* used for showing that you are surprised in a happy way, or that you recognize sb/sth

**ˈoh-oh** *exclamation* = UH-OH

**oh-ˈso** *adv.* (*informal*) extremely: *their oh-so ordinary lives*

**oi** (*also* **oy**) /ɔɪ/ *exclamation* (*BrE, informal*) used to attract sb's attention, especially in an angry way: *Oi, you! What do you think you're doing?*

**-oid** /ɔɪd/ *suffix* (in adjectives and nouns) similar to: *humanoid* ◊ *rhomboid*

**oik** /ɔɪk/ *noun* (*BrE, slang*) an offensive way of referring to a person that you consider rude or stupid, especially a person of a lower social class

**oil** ❶ **A2** /ɔɪl/ *noun, verb*
■ *noun* **1** ?+ **A2** [U] a thick liquid that is found in rock underground **SYN** **petroleum**: *drilling for oil* ◊ *crude oil* ◊ *rising world oil prices* ◊ *an oil spill* ◊ *The country is rich in oil reserves.* ◊ *oil companies* ◊ *the oil industry* ⊃ see also PEAK OIL ⊃ **WORDFINDER NOTE** at ENERGY **2** ?+ **A1** [U] a form of PETROLEUM that is used as fuel and to make parts of machines move smoothly: *fuel oil* ◊ *engine oil* ◊ *an oil lamp/heater* ◊ *Put some oil in the car.* ⊃ see also GAS OIL **3** ?+ **A1** [U, C] a smooth thick liquid that is made from plants or animals and is used in cooking: *Fry the potato in a little sunflower oil.* ◊ *vegetable oils* ⊃ see also FLAXSEED OIL, OLIVE OIL, PALM OIL **4** [U] a smooth thick liquid that is made from plants, minerals, etc. and is used on the skin or hair: *lavender bath oil* ◊ *suntan oil* ⊃ see also ESSENTIAL OIL **5** [U] (*also* **oils** [*pl.*]) coloured paint containing oil used by artists: *in* ~ *a painting done in oils* ◊ *landscapes in oil* ⊃ see also OIL PAINT **6** [C] = OIL PAINTING: *Among the more important Turner oils was 'Venus and Adonis'.* ⊃ see also OILY, CASTOR OIL, COD LIVER OIL, LINSEED OIL, SNAKE OIL **IDM** see BURN *v.*, POUR
■ *verb* ~ **sth** to put oil onto or into sth, for example a machine, in order to protect it or make it work smoothly: *He oiled his bike and pumped up the tyres.* **IDM** **oil the ˈwheels** (*BrE*) (*NAmE* **grease the ˈwheels**) to help sth to happen easily and without problems, especially in business or politics

**ˈoil-bearing** *adj.* [only before noun] producing or containing oil

**ˈoil·can** /ˈɔɪlkæn/ *noun* a metal container for oil, especially one with a long thin SPOUT, used for putting oil onto machine parts

**ˈoil colour** (*US* **ˈoil color**) *noun* [C, U] = OIL PAINT

**oiled** /ɔɪld/ *adj.* **well** ~ (*BrE, informal*) drunk

**ˈoil·field** /ˈɔɪlfiːld/ *noun* an area where oil is found in the ground or under the sea

**ˈoil-fired** *adj.* [usually before noun] (of a heating system, etc.) burning oil as fuel

**ˈoil·man** /ˈɔɪlmæn/ *noun* (*pl.* **-men** /-men/) a man who owns an oil company or works in the oil industry

**oil paint** (also **oil colour**) noun [C, U] a type of paint that contains oil

**oil painting** noun **1** (also **oil**) [C] a picture painted in OIL PAINT **2** [U] the art of painting in OIL PAINT
IDM **be no oil painting** (BrE, humorous) used when you are saying that a person is not attractive to look at

**oil pan** noun (NAmE) = SUMP (2)

**oil rig** (also **oil platform**) noun a large structure with equipment for getting oil from under the ground or under the sea

**oilseed rape** noun [U] = RAPE (3)

**oil slick** noun = SLICK (1)

**oil tanker** noun a large ship with containers for carrying oil

**oil well** (also **well**) noun a hole made in the ground to obtain oil

**oily** /ˈɔɪli/ adj. (**oil·i·er**, **oili·est**) **1** containing or covered with oil: *oily fish* ◇ *an oily rag* **2** feeling, tasting, smelling or looking like oil: *an oily substance* **3** (disapproving) (of a person or their behaviour) trying to be too polite, in a way that is annoying SYN **obsequious**: *an oily smile* ▶ **oili·ness** noun [U]

**oink** /ɔɪŋk/ exclamation, noun used to represent the sound a pig makes

**oint·ment** /ˈɔɪntmənt/ noun [U, C] a smooth substance that you rub on your skin to make a wound or painful place get better or stop hurting SYN **cream**: *antiseptic ointment*
IDM see FLY n.

**OJ** /ˌəʊ ˈdʒeɪ/ noun [U] (NAmE, informal) orange juice

**Ojibwa** /əʊˈdʒɪbwɑː/ (pl. **Ojibwa** or **Ojib·was**) noun a member of a Native American people, many of whom live in the US states of Michigan, Wisconsin and Minnesota and in Ontario in Canada

**OK** A1 S (also **okay**) /ˌəʊˈkeɪ/ exclamation, adj., adv., noun, verb
- **exclamation** (informal) **1** A1 yes; all right: '*Shall we go for a walk?' 'OK.'* **2** A1 used to attract sb's attention or to introduce a comment: *Okay, let's go.* **3** A1 used to check that sb agrees with you or understands you: *The meeting's at 2, OK?* ◇ *I'll do it my way, OK?* **4** A1 used to stop people arguing with you or criticizing you: *OK, so I was wrong. I'm sorry.*
- **adj., adv.** (informal) **1** A1 safe and well; in a calm or happy state: *Are you OK?* ⇒ SYNONYMS at WELL **2** A1 ~ (for sb) (to do sth) all right; acceptable; in an acceptable way: *Is it OK if I leave now?* ◇ *Is it OK for me to come too?* ◇ *Does my hair look okay?* ◇ *I think I did OK in the exam.* ◇ *Whatever you decide, it's okay by me.* ◇ *an okay movie* ⇒ EXPRESS YOURSELF at PERMISSION
- **noun the OK** [sing.] (informal) permission SYN **go-ahead**: *I'm still waiting for the boss to give me the OK.*
- **verb** (**OK's, OK'ing, OK'd, OK'd**) ~ sth (informal) to officially agree to sth or allow it to happen SYN **approve**: *She filled in an expenses claim and her manager OK'd it.*

**okada** /ɒˈkɑːdə; NAmE ɔːˈkɑː-/ WAfrE /ɔkada/ noun (WAfrE) a motorcycle that is used as a taxi

**okapi** /əʊˈkɑːpi/ noun an African animal that belongs to the same family as the GIRAFFE, but is smaller with a dark body and white lines across its legs

**oke** /əʊk/ (also **ou**) noun (SAfrE, informal) a man or a boy: *He's quite a big oke.*

**okey-doke** /ˌəʊki ˈdəʊk/ (also **okey-dokey** /ˌəʊki ˈdəʊki/) exclamation (informal) used to express agreement SYN **OK**

**okra** /ˈəʊkrə; BrE also ˈɒk-/ noun [U] a plant of the MALLOW family, with long green seed cases that are eaten as a vegetable. The vegetable is also known as LADIES' FINGERS, GUMBO or BHINDI in different parts of the world. ⇒ VISUAL VOCAB page V5

**old** A1 /əʊld/ adj. (**old·er**, **old·est**)
- **AGE 1** A1 of a particular age: **be … years, months, etc.** ~ *The baby was only a few hours old.* ◇ *In those days most people left school when they were only fifteen years old.* ◇ *At thirty years old, he was already earning £40 000 a year.* ◇ *two fourteen-year-old boys* ◇ *a class for five-year-olds* (= children who are five) ◇ *I didn't think she was old enough for the responsibility.* ◇ *How old is this building?* ◇ *He's the oldest player in the team.* ◇ *She's much older than me.*
- **NOT YOUNG 2** A1 having lived for a long time; no longer young: **to get/grow old** ◇ *The old man lay propped up on cushions.* ◇ *a little old lady* ◇ *She was a woman grown old before her time* (= who looked older than she was). OPP **young 3 the old** noun [pl.] old people: *The old feel the cold more than the young.*

WORDFINDER care home, dementia, frail, geriatric, mobility, pensioner, retire, sprightly, widow

- **NOT NEW 4** A1 having existed or been used for a long time: *old habits* ◇ *He always gives the same old excuses.* ◇ *This carpet's getting pretty old now.* OPP **new 5** A1 [only before noun] former; belonging to past times or a past time in your life: *Things were different in the old days.* ◇ *I went back to visit my old school.* ◇ *Old and Middle English* **6** A1 [only before noun] used to refer to sth that has been replaced by sth else: *We had more room in our old house.* OPP **new 7** A1 [only before noun] known for a long time: *She's an old friend of mine* (= I have known her for a long time). ◇ *We're old rivals.* ⇒ compare RECENT
- **GOOD OLD/POOR OLD 8** [only before noun] (informal) used to show kind feelings or a lack of respect: *Good old Dad!* ◇ *You poor old thing!* ◇ *I hate her, the silly old cow!*
IDM **any old …** (informal) any item of the type mentioned (used when it is not important which particular item is chosen): *Any old room would have done.* **any old how** (informal) in a careless or untidy way: *The books were piled up all over the floor any old how.* **as old as the 'hills** very old; ancient **for 'old times' sake** if you do sth **for old times' sake**, you do it because it is connected with sth good that happened to you in the past **the ˈgood/ˈbad old days** an earlier period of time in your life or in history that is seen as better/worse than the present: *That was in the bad old days of rampant inflation.* **of 'old** (formal or literary) in or since past times: *in days of old* ◇ *We know him of old* (= we have known him for a long time). **old 'boy, 'chap, 'man, etc.** (old-fashioned, BrE, informal) used by older men of the middle and upper classes as a friendly way of addressing another man **old enough to be sb's 'father/'mother** (disapproving) very much older than sb (especially used to suggest that a romantic or sexual relationship between the two people is not appropriate) **old enough to know 'better** old enough to behave in a more sensible way than you actually did **(have) an old head on young 'shoulders** used to describe a young person who acts in a more sensible way than you would expect for a person of their age **the (same) old 'story** what usually happens: *It's the same old story of a badly managed project with inadequate funding.* **an old 'wives' tale** (disapproving) an old idea or belief that people now know is not correct **one of the 'old school** an old-fashioned person who likes to do things as they were done in the past ⇒ see also OLD SCHOOL ⇒ more at CHIP n., FOOL n., GRAND adj., HEAVE-HO, HIGH adj., MONEY, OLD MONEY, RIPE, SETTLE v., TEACH, TOUGH adj., TRICK n.

**old age** noun [U, sing.] the time of your life when you are old: *Old age can bring many problems.* ◇ **in your ~** *He lived alone in his old age.*

**old-age 'pension** noun (BrE, CanE) a regular income paid by the state to people above a particular age

**old-age 'pensioner** noun (abbr. **OAP**) (BrE, CanE, becoming old-fashioned) a person who receives an old-age pension ⇒ see also SENIOR CITIZEN

**old age se'curity** noun [U] (abbr. **OAS**) (CanE) a regular income paid by the government to people above the age of 65

**the Old Bai·ley** /ðiˌəʊld ˈbeɪli/ noun [sing.] the main criminal court in London

**old 'bat** noun (BrE, informal, disapproving) a silly or annoying old person

**old boy** noun **1 'old boy** (BrE) a man who used to be a student at a particular school, usually a private one **2 old 'boy** (informal, especially BrE) an old man: *The old boy next door has died.* ⇒ see also GOOD OLD BOY, OLD GIRL

## SYNONYMS

**old**

elderly • aged • long-lived • mature

These words all describe sb/sth that has lived for a long time or that usually lives for a long time.

**old** having lived for a long time; no longer young: *She's getting old—she's 75 next year.*

**elderly** (*rather formal*) used as a polite word for 'old': *She is very busy caring for two elderly relatives.*

**aged** (*formal*) very old: *Having aged relatives to stay in your house can be quite stressful.*

**long-lived** having a long life; lasting for a long time: *Everyone in my family is exceptionally long-lived.*

**mature** used as a polite or humorous way of saying that sb is no longer young: *clothes for the mature woman*

PATTERNS
- a(n) old / elderly / aged / long-lived / mature **man/woman**
- a(n) old / elderly / aged / mature **gentleman/lady/couple**

## WHICH WORD?

**older / elder**

- The usual comparative and superlative forms of **old** are **older** and **oldest**: *My brother is older than me.* ◊ *The palace is the oldest building in the city.* In *BrE* you can also use **elder** and **eldest** when comparing the ages of people, especially members of the same family, although these words are not common in speech now. As adjectives they are only used before a noun and you cannot say 'elder than': *my older/elder sister* ◊ *the elder/older of their two children* ◊ *I'm the eldest/oldest in the family.*

IDM **the ,old 'boy network** (*BrE, informal, often disapproving*) (especially in the past) the situation in many British companies, government departments and branches of the armed forces where people give jobs to former students of the school or university that they went to: *Most of the managers were chosen by the old boy network and many of them turned out to be incompetent.*

,old 'buffer *noun* (*BrE, old-fashioned*) = BUFFER

the ,old 'country *noun* [sing.] the country where you were born, especially when you have left it to live somewhere else

,old 'dear *noun* (*BrE, informal*) an old woman

olde /əʊld, 'əʊldi/ *adj.* [only before noun] (*old use*) a way of spelling 'old' that was used in the past and is now sometimes used in names and advertisements to give the impression that sth is traditional: *a pub that tries to recreate the flavour of olde England*

olden /'əʊldən/ *adj.*
IDM **in the ,olden 'days** (*also* **in ,olden 'times**) a long time ago in the past: *What was life like in the olden days, Gran?*

,Old 'English (*also* ,Anglo-'Saxon) *noun* [U] the English language before about 1150, which is very different from modern English

,olde 'worlde /ˌəʊldi 'wɜːldi; *NAmE* 'wɜːrldi/ *adj.* [usually before noun] (*BrE, humorous*) (of a place or its atmosphere) trying deliberately to seem old-fashioned: *the olde worlde atmosphere of the tea room with its log fire*

**old-'fashioned** 🔑 B1 *adj.* 1 B1 (*sometimes disapproving*) not modern; no longer fashionable SYN dated: *old-fashioned clothes/styles/methods/equipment* ◊ *These sweets are still made in the old-fashioned way.* ◊ *Critics regarded her films as hopelessly old-fashioned.* ⇒ compare FASHIONABLE 2 B1 (*sometimes disapproving*) (of a person) believing in old or traditional ways; having traditional ideas: *My parents are old-fashioned about relationships and marriage.* 3 *good~...* (*approving*) simple, traditional and good quality: *At heart, it's just a good old-fashioned detective story.*

,old 'flame *noun* a former sexual partner: *She met an old flame at the party.*

1079  **oligarch**

,old 'girl *noun* 1 ,old 'girl (*BrE*) a woman who used to be a student at a particular school, usually a private one 2 ,old 'girl (*informal, especially BrE*) an old woman: *The old girl next door has died.*

,Old 'Glory *noun* (*NAmE*) a name for the flag of the US

the ,old 'guard *noun* [sing. + sing./pl. v.] the original members of a group or an organization, who are often against change

,old 'hand *noun* ~ (at sth/at doing sth) a person with a lot of experience and skill in a particular activity: *She's an old hand at dealing with the press.*

,old 'hat *noun* [U] something that is old-fashioned and no longer interesting: *Today's hits rapidly become old hat.*

oldie /'əʊldi/ *noun* (*informal*) an old person or thing ⇒ see also GOLDEN OLDIE

,old 'lady *noun* (*informal*) a person's wife or mother

,old 'maid *noun* (*old-fashioned, disapproving*) a woman who has never married and is now no longer young

,old 'man *noun* (*informal*) a person's husband or father

,old 'master *noun* 1 a famous painter, especially of the 13th–17th centuries in Europe 2 a picture painted by an old master

,old 'money *noun* [U] wealth that has been in a family for many generations; people whose families have been wealthy for many generations ⇒ compare NEW MONEY

,old 'people's home (*BrE*) (*also* re'tirement home *NAmE, BrE*) *noun* a place where old people live and are cared for

,old 'school *adj.* old-fashioned or traditional

old·ster /'əʊldstə(r)/ *noun* (*informal*) an old person

'old-style *adj.* [only before noun] typical of past fashions or times: *an old-style dress shop* ◊ *old-style politics*

the ,Old 'Testament *noun* [sing.] the first part of the Bible, that tells the history of the Jews, their beliefs and their relationship with God before the birth of Christ ⇒ compare NEW TESTAMENT

'old-time *adj.* [only before noun] typical of the past: *old-time dancing*

'old-,timer *noun* 1 a person who has been connected with a club or an organization, or who has lived in a place, for a long time SYN veteran 2 (*NAmE*) an old man

,old 'woman *noun* 1 (*informal, especially BrE*) a person's wife or mother 2 (*BrE, disapproving*) a man who worries too much about things that are not important

the ,Old 'World *noun* [sing.] Europe, Asia and Africa ⇒ compare NEW WORLD

'old-world *adj.* [only before noun] (*approving*) belonging to past times; not modern: *an old-world hotel with character and charm*

ole /əʊl/ *adj.* used in written English to represent how some people say the word 'old': *My ole man used to work there.*

olé /əʊ'leɪ/ *exclamation* (*from Spanish, informal*) used for showing approval or happiness

ole·an·der /ˌəʊli'ændə(r)/ *noun* [C, U] a Mediterranean bush or tree with white, pink or red flowers and long pointed thick leaves

OLED /ˈəʊled, ˌəʊ iː 'diː/ *noun* organic light-emitting diode (a device made with light-producing ORGANIC material that is used in visual displays like televisions and mobile phones): *This television has an OLED screen.* ⇒ compare LED

'O level (*also* ,ordinary 'level) *noun* [C, U] (in England and Wales in the past) an exam in a particular subject, at a lower level than A LEVEL, usually taken at the age of 16. In 1988 it was replaced by the GCSE: *O level French* ◊ *She took six subjects at O level.* ◊ *He's got an O level in Russian.* ⇒ compare GCE

ol·fac·tory /ɒl'fæktəri; *NAmE* ɑːl-, əʊl-/ *adj.* [only before noun] (*specialist*) connected with the sense of smell: *olfactory cells/organs*

oli·garch /'ɒlɪɡɑːk; *NAmE* 'ɑːləɡɑːrk, əʊl-/ *noun* 1 a member of an oligarchy 2 an extremely rich and powerful

---

🅞 Oxford Phrasal Academic Lexicon (OPAL) written and spoken word lists | 🅦 OPAL written word list | 🅢 OPAL spoken word list

# oligarchy

**oli·garchy** /ˈɒlɪɡɑːki; NAmE ˈɑːləɡɑːrki, ˈəʊl-/ noun (pl. -ies) **1** [U] a form of government in which only a small group of people hold all the power **2** [C + sing. / pl. v.] the people who hold power in an oligarchy **3** [C] a country governed by an oligarchy

**oli·gop·oly** /ˌɒlɪˈɡɒpəli; NAmE ˌɑːlɪˈɡɑːp-, ˌəʊl-/ noun (pl. -ies) (business) a market in which there are only a few companies producing or selling a product or service. This can result in less competition and higher prices for customers. ⊃ compare DUOPOLY, MONOPOLY (1)

**olive** /ˈɒlɪv; NAmE ˈɑː-l-/ noun, adj.
■ noun **1** [C] a small green or black fruit with a strong taste, which is eaten or used for its oil **2** (also **olive tree**) [C] a tree on which olives grow: *olive groves* **3** (also **olive ˈgreen**) [U] a grey-green colour
■ adj. **1** (also **olive-ˈgreen**) grey-green in colour **2** (of skin) yellow-brown in colour: *an olive complexion*

**ˈolive branch** noun [usually sing.] a symbol of peace; sth you say or do to show that you wish to make peace with sb: *Management is **holding out an olive branch** to the strikers.*

**olive ˈoil** noun [U] oil produced from OLIVES, used in cooking and on salad ⊃ see also EXTRA VIRGIN

**-ology** /ˈɒlədʒi; NAmE ˈɑːlədʒi/, **-logy** /lədʒi/ combining form (in nouns) **1** a subject of study: *sociology ⋄ genealogy* **2** a characteristic of speech or writing: *phraseology* ▶ **-ological** /əˈlɒdʒɪkl; NAmE əˈlɑːdʒɪkl/, **-logical** /lɒdʒɪkl; NAmE lɑːdʒɪkl/ (also **-ologic** /əˈlɒdʒɪk; NAmE əˈlɑːdʒɪk/, **-logic** /lɒdʒɪk; NAmE lɑːdʒɪk/) (in adjectives): *pathological* **-ologist** /ˈɒlədʒɪst; NAmE ˈɑːlədʒɪst/: *biologist*

**Olym·piad** /əˈlɪmpiæd/ noun **1** an occasion when the modern Olympic games are held: *The 31st Olympiad took place in Rio de Janeiro.* **2** an international competition in a particular subject, especially a science: *the 50th International Physics Olympiad*

**Olym·pian** /əˈlɪmpiən/ noun, adj. (formal)
■ noun a person who takes part or has taken part in the Olympic Games: *the greatest Olympian of all time*
■ adj. **1** [only before noun] relating to the ancient or modern Olympic games: *Olympian gymnasts* **2** like a god; powerful and impressive

**Olym·pic** /əˈlɪmpɪk/ adj. [only before noun] connected with the Olympic Games: *an Olympic athlete/medallist*

**the Oˌlympic ˈGames** (also **the Olym·pics**) noun [pl.] an international sports festival held every four years in a different country: *the London Olympics, held in 2012*

**om·buds·man** /ˈɒmbʊdzmən; NAmE ˈɑːmbʌdz-/ noun (pl. -men /-mən/) an official whose job is to examine and report on complaints made by ordinary people about companies, the government or public authorities

**omega** /ˈəʊmɪɡə; NAmE əʊˈmeɡə/ noun the last letter of the Greek alphabet (Ω, ω)

**ˌOmega-ˈ3** (also **ˌOmega-3 fatty ˈacid**) noun any of a group of ACIDS, found mainly in fish oils, that many people think are important for human health

**om·elette** (NAmE also **om·elet**) /ˈɒmlət; NAmE ˈɑːm-/ noun a hot dish of eggs mixed together and fried, often with cheese, meat, vegetables, etc. added: *a cheese and mushroom omelette*
IDM **you canˈt make an ˌomelette without breaking ˈeggs** (saying) you cannot achieve sth important without causing a few small problems

**omen** /ˈəʊmən/ noun a sign of what is going to happen in the future SYN **portent**: *a good/bad omen ⋄ an omen of death/disaster ⋄ ~ for sth The omens for their future success are not good.*

**omena** /əˈmeɪnə/ EAfrE /ɒˈmeɪnə/ noun [C, U] (pl. **omena**) (EAfrE) small fish that are dried to preserve them, and often fried and then cooked with tomatoes and milk to make a STEW

**OMG** /ˌəʊ em ˈdʒiː/ abbr. oh my God (used to express surprise, excitement, etc., especially in TEXT MESSAGES, on SOCIAL MEDIA, etc.): *OMG—I can't believe your parents are letting you go to Thailand on your own!*

**omi·cron** /əʊˈmaɪkrɒn; NAmE ˈɑːməkrɑːn/ noun the 15th letter of the Greek alphabet (Ο, ο)

**omi·god** (also **ohmigod**, **ohmygod**) /ˌəʊmaɪˈɡɒd; NAmE -ˈɡɑːd/ (also **omigosh** /ˌəʊmaɪˈɡɒʃ; NAmE -ˈɡɑːʃ/) exclamation (informal) used to show that you are shocked or cannot believe sth: *Omigod, we're going out of business! ⋄ Omigod, is that really his wife?*

**om·in·ous** /ˈɒmɪnəs; NAmE ˈɑːm-/ adj. suggesting that sth bad is going to happen in the future SYN **foreboding**: *There were ominous dark clouds gathering overhead. ⋄ She picked up the phone but there was an ominous silence at the other end.* ▶ **om·in·ous·ly** adv.

**omis·sion** /əˈmɪʃn/ noun (formal) **1** [U] ~ (from sth) the act of not including sb/sth or not doing sth; the fact of not being included or done: *Everyone was surprised at her omission from the squad. ⋄ The play was shortened by the omission of two scenes. ⋄ sins of omission (= not doing things that should be done)* **2** [C] a thing that has not been included or done: *There were a number of errors and omissions in the article.*

**omit** /əˈmɪt/ verb (-tt-) (formal) **1** to not include sth/sb, either deliberately or because you have forgotten it/them SYN **leave sb/sth out**: ~ sth/sb *If you are a student, you can omit questions 16–18.* ⋄ ~ sth/sb from sth *People were surprised that Smith was omitted from the team.* **2** ~ **to do sth** to not do or fail to do sth: *She omitted to mention that they were staying the night.*

**omni-** /ˈɒmni; NAmE ˈɑːmni/ combining form (in nouns, adjectives and adverbs) of all things; in all ways or places: *omnivore ⋄ omnipresent*

**omni·bus** /ˈɒmnɪbəs; NAmE ˈɑːm-/ noun, adj.
■ noun **1** (BrE) a television or radio programme that combines several recent programmes in a series: *the 90-minute Sunday omnibus edition* **2** a large book that contains a number of books, for example novels by the same author **3** (old-fashioned) a bus
■ adj. (NAmE) including many things or different types of thing: *an omnibus law*

**omni·dir·ec·tion·al** /ˌɒmnɪdəˈrekʃənl, -ˈdaɪr-; NAmE ˌɑːm-/ adj. (specialist) receiving or sending signals in all directions: *an omnidirectional microphone*

**om·nipo·tent** /ɒmˈnɪpətənt; NAmE ɑːm-/ adj. (formal) having total power; able to do anything: *an omnipotent God* ▶ **om·nipo·tence** /-pətəns/ noun [U]: *the omnipotence of God*

**omni·pres·ent** /ˌɒmnɪˈpreznt; NAmE ˌɑːm-/ adj. (formal) present everywhere: *These days the media are omnipresent.* ▶ **omni·pres·ence** /-zns/ noun [U]

**om·nis·ci·ent** /ɒmˈnɪsiənt; NAmE ɑːmˈnɪʃənt/ adj. (formal) knowing everything: *The novel has an omniscient narrator.* ▶ **om·nis·ci·ence** /ɒmˈnɪsiəns; NAmE ɑːmˈnɪʃəns/ noun [U]

**omni·vore** /ˈɒmnɪvɔː(r); NAmE ˈɑːm-/ noun an animal or a person that eats all types of food, especially both plants and meat ⊃ compare CARNIVORE, HERBIVORE, INSECTIVORE

**om·niv·or·ous** /ɒmˈnɪvərəs; NAmE ɑːm-/ adj. **1** eating all types of food, especially both plants and meat ⊃ compare CARNIVOROUS, HERBIVOROUS **2** having wide interests in a particular area or activity: *She has always been an omnivorous reader.*

**on** /ɒn; NAmE ɑːn/ prep., adv.
■ prep. HELP For the special uses of **on** in phrasal verbs, look at the entries for the verbs. For example **turn on sb** is in the phrasal verb section at **turn**. **1** in or into a position covering, touching or forming part of a surface: *a picture on a wall ⋄ There's a mark on your skirt. ⋄ the diagram on page 5 ⋄ Put it down on the table. ⋄ He had been hit on the head. ⋄ She climbed on to the bed.* HELP This could also be written: *onto the bed* **2** supported by sb/sth: *She was standing on one foot. ⋄ Try lying on your back. ⋄ Hang your coat on that hook.* **3** used to show a means of transport: *He was on the plane from New York. ⋄ to travel on the bus/tube/coach ⋄ I came on my bike. ⋄ a woman on horseback* **4** by means of sth; using sth: *She played a tune on her guitar. ⋄ The information is available on the internet. ⋄ We spoke on the phone. ⋄ What's on TV? ⋄ The programme's on Channel 4.* **5** used to show a day or date:

*He came on Sunday.* ◊ *We meet on Tuesdays.* ◊ *on May the first/the first of May* ◊ *on the evening of May the first* ◊ *on one occasion* ◊ *on your birthday* **6** [A1] used to describe an activity or a state: *to be on business/holiday/vacation* ◊ *The book is currently on loan.* **7** [A1] used to show direction: *on the left/right* ◊ *He turned his back on us.* **8** [A2] at or near a place: *a town on the coast* ◊ *a house on the Thames* ◊ *We lived on an estate.* **9** [A2] used to show the basis or reason for sth: *a story based on fact* ◊ *On their advice I applied for the job.* **10** [B1] immediately after sth: *On arriving home I discovered they had gone.* ◊ *Please report to reception on arrival.* ◊ *There was a letter waiting for him on his return.* **11** [B1] about sth/sb: *a book on South Africa* ◊ *She tested us on irregular verbs.* **12** [B1] used to show that sb belongs to a group or an organization: *to be on the committee/staff/jury/panel* ◊ *Whose side are you on* (= which of two or more different views do you support)? **13** [B1] eating or drinking sth; using a drug or a medicine regularly: *He lived on a diet of junk food.* ◊ *The doctor put me on antibiotics.* **14** [B1] paid for by sth: *to live on a pension/a student grant* ◊ *to be on a low wage* ◊ *You can't feed a family on £50 a week.* ◊ *Drinks are on me* (= I am paying). **15** [B1] used when giving a phone number: *You can get me on 020 7946 0887.* ◊ *She's on extension 2401.* **16** [B2] used with some nouns or adjectives to say who or what is affected by sth: *a ban on smoking* ◊ *He's hard on his kids.* ◊ *Go easy on the mayo!* (= do not take/give me too much) **17** being carried by sb; in the possession of sb: *Have you got any money on you?* **18** compared with sb/sth: *Sales are up on last year.*
- **adv.** [HELP] For the special uses of **on** in phrasal verbs, look at the entries for the verbs. For example **get on** is in the phrasal verb section at **get**. **1** [A1] on sb's body; being worn: *Put your coat on.* ◊ *I didn't have my glasses on.* ◊ *What did she have on* (= what was she wearing)? **2** [A1] covering, touching or forming part of sth: *Make sure the lid is on.* **3** [A1] in or into a vehicle: *The bus stopped and four people got on.* ◊ *They hurried on to the plane.* ⇒ see also ONTO **4** [A1] connected or operating; being used: *The lights were all on.* ◊ *The TV is always on in their house.* ◊ *We were without electricity for three hours but it's on again now.* **5** [A1] used to show that sb/sth moves or is sent forward: *She stopped for a moment, then walked on.* ◊ *Keep straight on for the beach.* ◊ *From then on he never trusted her again.* ◊ *Please send the letter on to my new address.* **6** [A2] used to show that sth continues: *He worked on without a break.* ◊ *If you like a good story, read on.* **7** [B2] happening: *There was a war on at the time.* ◊ *What's on at the movies?* ◊ *The band are on* (= performing) *in ten minutes.* **8** [B2] planned to take place in the future: *The game is still on* (= it has not been cancelled). ◊ *I don't think we've got anything on this weekend.* ◊ *I'm sorry we can't come—we've got a lot on.* **9** [B2] on duty; working: *I'm on now till 8 tomorrow morning.*
[IDM] **be ˈon about sth** (*informal*) to talk about sth; to mean sth: *I didn't know what he was on about. It didn't make sense.* **be/go/keep ˈon about sth** (*informal*, *disapproving*) to talk in a boring or complaining way about sth: *Stop keeping on about it!* **be/go/keep ˈon at sb (to do sth)** (*informal*, *disapproving*) to keep asking or telling sb sth so that they become annoyed or tired: *He was on at me again to lend him money.* **be ˈon for sth** (*informal*) to want to do sth: *Is anyone on for a drink after work?* **it isnˈt ˈon** (also **it's not ˈon**) (*informal*) used to say that sth is not acceptable. **ˌon and ˈon** without stopping; continuously: *She went on and on about her trip.* **ˌwhat are you, etc. ˈon?** (*informal*) used when you are very surprised at sb's behaviour and are suggesting that they are acting in a similar way to sb using drugs **you're ˈon** (*informal*) used when you are accepting a bet ⇒ more at OFF *adv.*

**ˌon-ˈair** *adj.* (in radio and television) being broadcast: *She explains how she deals with on-air technical problems.* [OPP] **off-air** [IDM] see AIR *n.*

**ˈonan·ism** /ˈəʊnənɪzəm/ *noun* [U] (*formal*) = MASTURBATION

**on·board** /ˈɒnbɔːd; *NAmE* ˈɑːnbɔːrd/ *verb* (*business*) **1** [T] ~ **sb** to ensure a new employee or customer becomes familiar with an organization or its products or services: *The goal is to get new clients onboarded quickly.* **2** [I, T] ~ **(sth)** to become familiar with how sth works, especially a piece of technology or software ▶ **onˈboard·ing** *noun* [U]: *We offer a full training and onboarding programme.*

---

1081 **one**

**ˌon-ˈboard** *adj.* [only before noun] **1** on a ship, aircraft or vehicle: *an on-board motor* **2** (*also* **onboard**) (*computing*) relating to, or controlled by, part of the main CIRCUIT BOARD: *a PC with onboard sound*

**ˌon-ˈcall** [only before noun] (*especially NAmE*) (of a doctor, police officer, etc.) available for work if necessary, especially in an emergency: *on-call doctors* ⇒ see also CALL *noun*

**once** 🔊 [A1] /wʌns/ *adv.*, *conj.*
- **adv. 1** [A1] on one occasion only; one time: *I've only been there once.* ◊ *He cleans his car once a week.* ◊ *She only sees her parents once every six months.* ◊ (*informal*) *He only did it the once.* **2** [A1] at some time in the past: *I once met your mother.* ◊ *He once lived in Zambia.* ◊ *This book was famous once, but nobody reads it today.* **3** used in negative sentences and questions, and after *if* to mean 'ever' or 'at all': *He never once offered to help.* ◊ *If she once decides to do something, you won't change her mind.* **4** used with a preposition or another adverb to mean 'as soon as/sth is/was': *Once inside the gate, Sam hurried up the path.*
[IDM] **ˌall at ˈonce 1** suddenly: *All at once she lost her temper.* **2** all together; at the same time [SYN] **simultaneously**: *I can't do everything all at once—you'll have to be patient.* **at ˈonce 1** [B2] immediately; without delay: *Come here at once!* **2** at the same time [SYN] **simultaneously**: *Don't all speak at once!* ◊ *I can't do two things at once.* **(just) for ˈonce** | **just this ˈonce** (*informal*) on this occasion (which is in contrast to what happens usually): *Just for once he arrived on time.* ◊ *Can't you be nice to each other just this once?* **ˌgoing ˈonce, ˌgoing ˈtwice, ˈsold** (*especially NAmE*) (*BrE also* **ˌgoing, ˌgoing, ˈgone**) said by an AUCTIONEER to show that an item has been sold **once aˈgain** [B2] | **once ˈmore** one more time; another time: *Once again the train was late.* ◊ *Let me hear it just once more.* **once a …, always a …** used to say that sb cannot change: *Once an actor, always an actor.* **once (and) for ˈall** now and for the last time; finally or completely: *We need to settle this once and for all.* **ˌonce ˈbitten, ˌtwice ˈshy** (*saying*) after an unpleasant experience you are careful to avoid sth similar **once in a ˌblue ˈmoon** (*informal*) very rarely **(every) once in a ˈwhile** occasionally **once or ˈtwice** a few times: *I don't know her well, I've only met her once or twice.* **ˌonce too ˈoften** used to say that sb has done sth wrong or stupid again, and this time they will suffer because of it: *You've tried that trick once too often.* **once upon a ˈtime** used, especially at the beginning of stories, to mean 'a long time ago in the past': *Once upon a time there was a beautiful princess.*
- **conj.** [B1] as soon as; when: *We didn't know how we would cope once the money had gone.* ◊ *The water is fine once you're in!*

**ˈonce-over** *noun*
[IDM] **ˌgive sb/sth a/the ˈonce-over** (*informal*) **1** to look at sb/sth quickly to see what they are/it is like **2** to clean sth quickly: *She gave the room a quick once-over before the guests arrived.*

**on·col·ogy** /ɒŋˈkɒlədʒi; *NAmE* ɑːŋˈkɑːl-/ *noun* [U] the scientific study of and treatment of TUMOURS in the body ▶ **on·col·ogist** *noun*

**on·com·ing** /ˈɒnkʌmɪŋ; *NAmE* ˈɑːn-/ *adj.* [only before noun] coming towards you [SYN] **approaching**: *Always walk facing the oncoming traffic.*

**ˌon-deˈmand** *adj.* [only before noun] done or happening whenever sb asks: *The new network promises lightning-fast access to on-demand video.* ⇒ compare LINEAR (5) ⇒ see also DEMAND *noun*, PRINT ON DEMAND

**one** 🔊 [A1] /wʌn/ *number, det., pron.*
- **number, det. 1** [A1] the number 1: *Do you want one or two?* ◊ *There's only room for one person.* ◊ *One more, please!* ◊ *a one-bedroomed apartment* ◊ *I'll see you at one* (= one o'clock). **2** [A1] used in formal language or for emphasis before *hundred*, *thousand*, etc., or before a unit of measurement: *It cost one hundred and fifty pounds.* ◊ *He lost by less than one second.* **3** [A1] used for emphasis to mean 'a single' or 'just one': *There's only one thing we can do.* **4** [A1] a person or thing, especially when they are part of a

# one another

group: *One of my friends lives in Brighton.* ◊ *One place I'd really like to visit is Bali.* **5** 🔑 A1 used for emphasis to mean 'the only one' or 'the most important one': *He's the one person I can trust.* ◊ *Her one concern was for the health of her baby.* ◊ *It's the one thing I can't stand about him.* **6** 🔑 used when you are talking about a time in the past or the future, without actually saying which one: *I saw her one afternoon last week.* ◊ *One day* (= at some time in the future) *you'll understand.* **7** 🔑 A1 the same: *They all went off in one direction.* **8** (*informal, especially NAmE*) used for emphasis instead of *a* or *an*: *That was one hell of a game!* ◊ *She's one snappy dresser.* **9** (*formal* or *old-fashioned*) used with a person's name to show that the speaker does not know the person SYN **certain**: *He worked as an assistant to one Mr Ming.*

IDM **as ˈone** (*formal*) in agreement; all together: *We spoke as one on this matter.* **(be) at ˈone (with sb/sth)** (*formal*) to feel that you completely agree with sb/sth, or that you are part of sth: *a place where you can feel at one with nature* **for ˈone** used to emphasize that a particular person does sth and that you believe other people do too: *I, for one, would prefer to postpone the meeting.* **get sth in ˈone** to understand or guess sth immediately **get one ˈover (on) sb/sth** (*informal*) to get an advantage over sb/sth: *I'm not going to let them get one over on me!* **go one ˈbetter (than sb/sth)** to do sth better than sb else or than you have done before SYN **outdo**: *She did well this year and next year she hopes to go one better.* **(all) in ˈone** used to say that sb/sth has different roles, contains different things or is used for different purposes: *She's a mother and company director in one.* ◊ *It's a public relations office, a press office and a private office all in one.* ⊃ see also ALL-IN-ONE **ˌone after aˈnother/the ˈother** first one person or thing, and then another, and then another, up to any number or amount: *The bills kept coming in, one after another.* **ˌone and ˈall** (*old-fashioned, informal*) everyone: *Happy New Year to one and all!* **ˌone and ˈonly** used to emphasize that sb is famous: *Here she is, the one and only Rihanna!* **ˌone and the ˈsame** used for emphasis to mean 'the same': *I never realized Ruth Rendell and Barbara Vine were one and the same* (= the same person using two different names). **ˌone by ˈone** separately and in order: *I went through the items on the list one by one.* **ˌone or ˈtwo** 🔑 A2 a few: *We've had one or two problems—nothing serious.* **ˌone ˈup (on sb)** having an advantage over sb **when you've ˈseen, ˈheard, etc. ˈone, you've ˈseen, ˈheard, etc. them ˈall** (*saying*) used to say that all types of the things mentioned are very similar: *I don't like science fiction novels much. When you've read one, you've read them all.* ⊃ more at MINORITY, SQUARE *n.*

■ *pron.* **1** 🔑 A1 used to avoid repeating a noun, when you are referring to sb/sth that has already been mentioned, or that the person you are speaking to knows about: *I'd like an ice cream. Are you having one, too?* ◊ *Our car's always breaking down. But we're getting a new one soon.* ◊ *She was wearing her new dress, the red one.* ◊ *Steve's the one with the blue jacket.* ◊ *My favourite band? Oh, that's a hard one* (= a hard question). ◊ *What made you choose the one rather than the other?* ◊ (*BrE*) *How about those ones over there?* ⊃ HOMOPHONES at ONE **2** 🔑 A1 used when you are identifying the person or thing you are talking about: *Our house is the one next to the school.* ◊ *The students who are most successful are usually the ones who come to all the classes.* **3** 🔑 A1 ~ of a person or thing belonging to a particular group: *It's a present for one of my children.* ◊ *We think of you as one of the family.* **4** 🔑 B1 a person of the type mentioned: *10 o'clock is too late for the little ones.* ◊ *He ached to be home with his loved ones.* ◊ *~ to do sth She was never one to criticize.* **5** 🔑 B2 (*formal*) used to mean 'people in general' or 'I', when the speaker is referring to himself or herself: *One should never criticize if one is not sure of one's facts.* ◊ *One gets the impression that they disapprove.* HELP This use of **one** is very formal and now sounds old-fashioned. It is much more usual to use **you** for 'people in general' and **I** when you are talking about yourself. **6** **a ˈone** (*old-fashioned, especially BrE*) a person whose behaviour is funny or surprising: *Oh, you are a one!* **7** **the ~ about sth** the joke: *Have you heard the one about the Englishman, the Irishman and the Scotsman?*

▶ **HOMOPHONES**

**one • won** /wʌn/
- **one** *number*: *There can only be one winner.*
- **one** *pron.*: *Which do you prefer? The flowery one or the stripy one?*
- **won** *verb* (*past tense, past participle of* WIN): *He's just won his 19th singles title.*

▶ **GRAMMAR POINT**

**one / ones**

**One/ones** is used to avoid repeating a countable noun, but there are some times when you should not use it, especially in formal speech or writing:

- After a possessive (*my, your, Mary's*, etc.), *some, any, both* or a number, unless it is used with an adjective: '*Did you get any postcards?' 'Yes, I bought four nice ones.*' ◊ *I bought four ones.*
- It can be left out after superlatives, *this, that, these, those, either, neither, another, which*, etc: '*Here are the designs. Which (one) do you prefer?' 'I think that (one) looks the most original.'*
- **These ones** and **those ones** are not used in *NAmE*, and are unusual in *BrE*: *Do you prefer these designs or those?*
- It is never used to replace uncountable nouns and is unusual with abstract countable nouns: *The Scottish legal system is not the same as the English system*, is better than *…as the English one.*

IDM **be (a) one for (doing) sth** to be a person who enjoys sth, or who does sth often or well: *I've never been a great one for fish and chips.*

**ˌone aˈnother** *pron.* **one another** is used when you are saying that each member of a group does sth to or for the other people in the group SYN **each other**: *We all try and help one another.* ◊ *I think we've learned a lot about one another in this session.*

**ˌone-armed ˈbandit** *noun* = SLOT MACHINE (2)

**ˌone-diˈmensional** *adj.* **1** having only one of the following: height, length or WIDTH: *These are one-dimensional structures in which the electrons can move in only one spatial direction.* **2** (*disapproving*) without depth or variety and so not interesting: *He is something of a dull and one-dimensional villain.*

**ˌone-horse ˈtown** *noun* (*informal*) a small town with not many interesting things to do or places to go to

**ˈone-liner** *noun* (*informal*) a short joke or funny remark: *He came out with some good one-liners.*

**ˌone-ˈman** *adj.* [only before noun] done or controlled by one person only; suitable for one person: *a one-man show/business* ◊ *a one-man tent* ⊃ see also ONE-WOMAN

**ˌone-man ˈband** *noun* a street musician who plays several instruments at the same time; (*figurative*) *He runs the business as a one-man band* (= one person does everything).

**ˈoneness** /ˈwʌnnəs/ *noun* [U] (*formal*) the state of being completely united with sb/sth, or of being in complete agreement with sb: *a sense of oneness with the natural world*

**ˌone-night ˈstand** *noun* (*informal*) a sexual relationship that lasts for a single night; a person that sb has this relationship with: *I wanted it to be more than a one-night stand.* ◊ *For her I was just a one-night stand.*

**ˈone-off** *adj., noun*
■ *adj.* (*BrE*) (*NAmE* **ˈone-shot**) [only before noun] made or happening only once and not regularly: *a one-off payment*
■ *noun* (*BrE*) a thing that is made or that happens only once and not regularly: *It was just a one-off; it won't happen again.*

**ˌone-on-ˈone** *adj.* [usually before noun] (*NAmE*) = ONE-TO-ONE

**ˈone-piece** *adj.* [only before noun] (especially of clothes) consisting of one piece, not separate parts: *a one-piece swimsuit*

**oner·ous** /'əʊnərəs; NAmE 'ɑːn-/ adj. (formal) needing great effort; causing trouble or worry SYN **taxing**: *an onerous duty/task/responsibility*

**one's** /wʌnz/ det. the possessive form of *one*: *One tries one's best.*

**one·self** /wʌn'self/ pron. (formal) **1** (the reflexive form of *one*) used as the object of a verb or preposition when 'one' is the subject of the verb or is understood as the subject: *One has to ask oneself what the purpose of the exercise is.* ◊ *One cannot choose freedom for oneself without choosing it for others.* ◊ *It is difficult to make oneself concentrate for long periods.* **2** used to emphasize *one*: *One likes to do it oneself.* HELP **One** and **oneself** are very formal words and now sound old-fashioned. It is much more usual to use **you** and **yourself** for referring to people in general and **I** and **myself** when the speaker is referring to himself or herself. IDM **be oneself** to be in a normal state of body and mind, not influenced by other people: *One needs space to be oneself.* **(all) by one'self 1** alone; without anyone else **2** without help **(all) to one'self** not shared with anyone

**'one-shot** (NAmE) (BrE **,one-'off**) adj. [only before noun] made or happening only once and not regularly

**,one-'sided** adj. **1** (disapproving) (of an argument, opinion, etc.) showing only one side of the situation; not balanced SYN **biased**: *The press were accused of presenting a very one-sided picture of the issue.* **2** (of a competition or a relationship) involving people who have different abilities; involving one person more than another: *a totally one-sided match* ◊ *a one-sided conversation* (= in which one person talks most of the time)

**'one·sie** /'wʌnzi/ noun a piece of clothing that covers the top half of the body and the legs

**Onesies**™ /'wʌnziz/ noun (NAmE) a piece of clothing for babies that covers the top half of the body and sometimes also the legs. It fastens between the legs.

**,one-size-fits-'all** adj. [only before noun] designed to be suitable for a wide range of situations or needs: *a one-size-fits-all monetary policy*

**'one-,star** adj. [usually before noun] **1** having one star in a system that measures quality. The highest standard is usually represented by four or five stars: *a one-star hotel* **2** (in the US) having the fifth-highest military rank, and wearing uniform which has one star on it: *a one-star general*

**'one-stop** adj. [only before noun] in which you can buy or do everything you want in one place: *Our agency is a one-stop shop for all your travel needs.*

**'one-time** adj. [only before noun] **1** former: *her one-time best friend, Anna* **2** not to be repeated SYN **one-off**: *a one-time fee of $500*

**,one-to-'one** (especially BrE) (NAmE usually **,one-on-'one**) adj. [usually before noun] **1** between two people only: *a one-to-one meeting* **2** matching sth else in an exact way: *There is no one-to-one correspondence between sounds and letters.* ► **,one-to-'one** adv.: *He teaches one-to-one.*

**,one-track 'mind** noun [usually sing.] if sb has a **one-track mind**, they can only think about one subject (often used to refer to sb thinking about sex)

**,one-trick 'pony** noun (becoming old-fashioned, disapproving) a performer who is only famous for one song, etc.; a person or business that is only good at doing one thing: *This comedian is no one-trick pony.*

**one-upmanship** /wʌn'ʌpmənʃɪp/ noun [U] (disapproving) the skill of getting an advantage over other people

**,one-'way** adj. [usually before noun] **1** moving or allowing movement in only one direction: *one-way traffic* ◊ *a one-way valve* **2** (especially NAmE) (BrE also **sin·gle**) a **one-way** ticket, etc. can be used for travelling to a place but not back again ⊃ compare RETURN (7) **3** operating in only one direction: *Theirs was a one-way relationship* (= one person made all the effort).

**,one-way 'mirror** noun = TWO-WAY MIRROR

**,one-'woman** adj. [only before noun] done or controlled by one woman only: *a one-woman show*

**,on-'field** adj. at or on a sports field: *on-field medical treatment*

**on·going** /ˈɒŋɡəʊɪŋ; NAmE 'ɑːn-/ adj. [usually before noun] continuing to exist or develop: *an ongoing debate/discussion/process* ◊ *The police investigation is ongoing.*

**onion** /'ʌnjən/ noun [C, U] a round vegetable with many layers inside each other and a brown, red or white skin. Onions have a strong smell and taste: *Chop the onions finely.* ◊ *French onion soup* ⊃ see also SPRING ONION ⊃ VISUAL VOCAB page V5

**on·line** /ˌɒn'laɪn; NAmE ˌɑːn-/ adj., adv.
■ adj. **1** (of an activity or service) available on or done using the internet or other computer network: *Online shopping is both cheap and convenient.* ◊ *online stores/services/retailers* ◊ *online dating/gaming/banking* ◊ *He spends hours playing online games.* ◊ *All this information is now online.* OPP **offline 2** (of a person) connected to the internet; able to connect to the internet: *You can see which of your friends are online and send them messages.* ◊ *It's estimated that five billion users are now online.*
■ adv. **1** onto the internet; using the internet or other computer network: *Many children would rather go online than watch television.* ◊ *Many people now do their banking online.* OPP **offline** ⊃ see also OFFLINE, BE, COME, ETC. ON LINE at LINE noun **2** WORDFINDER NOTE at WEBSITE **2** in or into operation or existence: *The new system will go online this month.* ◊ *More renewable energy is coming online.*

**,online 'dating** (also **'internet dating**) noun [U] using the internet to arrange to meet sb and possibly begin a romantic relationship with them: *an online dating service/site*

**on·look·er** /'ɒnlʊkə(r); NAmE 'ɑːn-/ noun a person who watches sth that is happening but is not involved in it SYN **bystander**: *A crowd of onlookers gathered at the scene of the crash.* ⊃ SYNONYMS at WITNESS

**only** /'əʊnli/ adj., adv., conj.
■ adj. [only before noun] **1** used to say that no other or others of the same group exist or are there: *She's their only daughter.* ◊ *We were the only people there.* ◊ *I was not the only one with moist eyes at the end of the film.* ◊ *The only real difference between them is their packaging.* **2** used to say that sb/sth is the best and you would not choose any other: *She's the only person for the job.* IDM **the only thing is …** (informal) used before mentioning a worry or problem you have with sth: *I'd love to come —the only thing is I might be late.* ⊃ more at NAME n., ONE number
■ adv. **1** nobody or nothing except: *There are only a limited number of tickets available.* ◊ *The bar is for members only.* ◊ *You only have to look at her to see she doesn't eat enough.* ◊ *Only five people turned up.* **2** in no other situation, place, etc: *I agreed, but only because I was frightened.* ◊ *Children are admitted only if accompanied by an adult.* HELP In formal written English **only** (or **only if and its clause**) can be placed first in the sentence. In the second part of the sentence, be, do, have, etc. come before the subject and the main part of the verb: *Only in Paris do you find bars like this.* ◊ *Only if these conditions are fulfilled can the application proceed to the next stage.* **3** no more important, interesting, serious, etc. than: *It was only a suggestion.* ◊ *Don't blame me, I'm only the messenger!* ◊ *He was only teasing you.* **4** no more than; no longer than: *She's only 21 and she runs her own business.* ◊ *I've only ever seen her once.* ◊ *Only about 20 per cent of the crop is exported.* **5** not until: *We only got here yesterday.* ◊ (formal) *Only then did she realize the stress he was under.* HELP When only begins a sentence be, do, have, etc. come before the subject and the main part of the verb. **6** used to say that sb can do no more than what is mentioned, although this is probably not enough: *We can only guess what happened.* ◊ *He could only watch helplessly as the car plunged into the ravine.* ◊ *I only hope that she never finds out.* ⊃ see also READ-ONLY **7** used to say that sth will have a bad effect: *If you do that, it will only make matters worse.* ◊ *Trying to reason with him only enrages him even more.* **8** **~ to do sth** used to mention sth that happens immediately afterwards, especially sth that is

# only child

surprising, disappointing, etc: *She turned up the driveway, only to find her way blocked.*
**IDM** **not only … (but) (also) …** **B1** used to emphasize that sth else is also true: *She not only wrote the text but also selected the illustrations.* ⊃ LANGUAGE BANK at ADDITION **only ˈjust 1** not long ago/before: *We've only just arrived.* **2** almost not: *He only just caught the train.* ◊ *I can afford it, but only just.* **only too …** very: *I was only too pleased to help.* ◊ *Children can be difficult as we know only too well.* **you're only young ˈonce** (*saying*) young people should enjoy themselves as much as possible, because they will have to work and worry later in their lives ⊃ more at EYE *n.*, IF *conj.*, TIME *n.*
■ *conj.* (*informal*) except that; but: *I'd love to come, only I have to work.* ◊ *It tastes like chicken, only stronger.*

**ˌonly ˈchild** *noun* a child who has no brothers or sisters: *I'm an only child.*

**o.n.o.** (also **ono**) *abbr.* (*BrE*) or near/nearest offer (used in small advertisements to show that sth may be sold at a lower price than the price that has been asked): *Guitar £200 o.n.o.* ⊃ compare OBO

**on-ˈoff** *adj.* [only before noun] **1** (of a switch) having the positions 'on' and 'off': *an on-off switch* **2** (of a relationship) interrupted by periods when the relationship is not continuing

**ono·mato·poeia** /ˌɒnəˌmætəˈpiːə; *NAmE* ˌɑːn-/ *noun* [U] (*specialist*) the fact of words containing sounds similar to the noises they describe, for example *hiss*; the use of words like this in a piece of writing ⊃ WORDFINDER NOTE at IMAGE ▶ **ono·mato·poe·ic** /-ˈpiːɪk/ *adj.*: *Bang and pop are onomatopoeic words.*

**ˈon-ramp** *noun* (*NAmE*, *SAfrE*) a road used for driving onto a major road such as an INTERSTATE ⊃ compare OFF-RAMP, SLIP ROAD

**on·rush** /ˈɒnrʌʃ; *NAmE* ˈɑːn-/ *noun* [sing.] a strong movement forward; the sudden development of sth

**on-ˈscreen** *adj.* [only before noun] **1** appearing or written on the screen of a computer, television or cinema: *on-screen courtroom dramas* ◊ *on-screen messages* **2** connected with the imaginary story of a film and not with real life: *His on-screen father is also his father in real life.* ⊃ compare OFF-SCREEN ▶ **on-ˈscreen** *adv.*

**on·set** /ˈɒnset; *NAmE* ˈɑːn-/ *noun* [sing.] the beginning of sth, especially sth unpleasant: *the onset of disease/old age/winter*

**on·shore** /ˈɒnʃɔː(r); *NAmE* ˈɑːn-/ *adj.* [usually before noun] **1** on or towards land: *an onshore oil field* ◊ compare OFFSHORE (1) **2** (of wind) blowing from the sea towards the land ⊃ compare OFFSHORE (2) ▶ **on·shore** *adv.* ⊃ compare OFFSHORE

**on·side** /ˌɒnˈsaɪd; *NAmE* ˌɑːn-/ *adj.* in some sports, for example football (soccer) and ice hockey, a player who is **onside** is in a position where playing the ball or PUCK is allowed ▶ **on·side** *adv.* **OPP** **offside**
**IDM** **get/keep sb onˈside** (*BrE*) to get/keep sb's support: *The party needs to keep the major national newspapers onside if it's going to win the next election.*

**on·slaught** /ˈɒnslɔːt; *NAmE* ˈɑːn-/ *noun* [C, usually sing.] a strong or violent attack: **~ against/on sb/sth** *the enemy onslaught on our military forces* ◊ **~ of sth/sb** *an onslaught of abuse* ◊ (*figurative*) *The town survives the onslaught of tourists every summer.*

**on·stage** /ˌɒnˈsteɪdʒ; *NAmE* ˌɑːn-/ *adj.* on the stage in a theatre; in front of an audience: *onstage fights* ▶ **on·stage** *adv.* **OPP** **offstage**

**on-ˈstreet** *adj.* [only before noun] (of parking facilities) located at the side of a public road rather than in a garage, a drive, etc. **OPP** **off-street**

**onto** **1** **A2** /ˈɒntə, *before vowels* -tu; *NAmE* ˈɑːn-/ (also **on to**) *prep.* **1** **A2** used with verbs to express movement on or to a particular place or position: *Move the books onto the second shelf.* ◊ *She stepped down from the train onto the platform.* **2** **A2** used to show that sth faces in a particular direction: *The window looked out onto the terrace.*

---

**PHRV** **be ˈonto sb 1** (*informal*) to know about what sb has done wrong: *She knew the police would be onto them.* **2** to be talking to sb, usually in order to ask or tell them sth: *They've been onto me for ages to get a job.* **be ˈonto sth** to know about or be in a situation that could lead to a good result for you: *Scientists believe they are onto something big.* ◊ *She's onto a good thing with that new job.*

**ontol·ogy** /ɒnˈtɒlədʒi; *NAmE* ɑːnˈtɑːl-/ *noun* **1** [U] a branch of philosophy that deals with the nature of existence **2** [C] a list of concepts and categories in a subject area that shows the relationships between them: *a guide to creating a marketing ontology* ▶ **onto·logic·al** /ˌɒntəˈlɒdʒɪkl; *NAmE* ˌɑːntəˈlɑːdʒ-/ *adj.*

**on-ˈtrend** *adj.* very fashionable: *That jacket is bang on-trend.* ◊ *an on-trend haircut*

**onus** /ˈəʊnəs; *NAmE* ˈoʊ-/ *noun* (usually **the onus**) [sing.] (*formal*) the responsibility for sth: *The onus is on employers to follow health and safety laws.*

**on·ward** /ˈɒnwəd; *NAmE* ˈɑːnwərd/ *adj.* [only before noun] (*formal*) continuing or moving forward: *Ticket prices include your flight and onward rail journey.*

**on·wards** /ˈɒnwədz; *NAmE* ˈɑːnwərdz/ (*especially BrE*) (*NAmE usually* **on·ward**) *adv.* **1** **from … onwards** continuing from a particular time: *They lived there from the 1980s onwards.* ◊ *The pool is open from 7 a.m. onwards.* **2** (*formal*) forward: *We drove onwards towards the coast.*

**onyx** /ˈɒnɪks; *NAmE* ˈɑːn-/ *noun* [U] a type of stone that has layers of different colours in it, usually used to make or decorate objects

**oo·dles** /ˈuːdlz/ *noun* [pl.] **~ (of sth)** (*old-fashioned*, *informal*) a large amount of sth **SYN** **load**

**ooh** /uː/ *exclamation* used for expressing surprise, happiness or pain

**oom·pah** /ˈʊmpɑː, ˈuːm-/ (also **oompah-pah**) *noun* (*informal*) used to refer to the sound produced by a group of BRASS instruments: *an oompah band*

**oomph** /ʊmf/ *noun* [U] (*informal*) energy; a special good quality: *a styling product to give your hair more oomph*

**oops** /ʊps, uːps/ *exclamation* **1** used when sb has almost had an accident, broken sth, etc: *Oops! I almost spilled the wine.* **2** used when you have done sth embarrassing, said sth rude by accident, told a secret, etc: *Oops, I shouldn't have said that.*

**oops-a-daisy** /ˈʊps ə ˌdeɪzi, ˈʌps/ *exclamation* = UPSY-DAISY

**ooze** /uːz/ *verb*, *noun*
■ *verb* **1** [I, T] if a thick liquid **oozes** from a place, or if sth **oozes** a thick liquid, the liquid flows from the place slowly: **~ from/out of/through sth** | **~ out** *Blood oozed out of the wound.* ◊ **~ with sth** *an ugly swelling oozing with pus* ◊ **~ sth** *The wound was oozing blood.* ◊ *a plate of toast oozing butter* **2** [T, I] to show a particular quality or feeling strongly; (of a particular quality or feeling) to be shown strongly **SYN** **exude**: **~ sth** *She walked into the party oozing confidence.* ◊ **~ with sth** *His voice oozed with sex appeal.* ◊ **~ from sth** *She shook her head, disgust oozing from every pore.*
■ *noun* **1** [U] very soft mud, especially at the bottom of a lake or river **2** [sing.] the very slow flow of a thick liquid ▶ **oozy** *adj.*

**op** /ɒp; *NAmE* ɑːp/ *noun* **1** (*BrE*, *informal*) = OPERATION (1): *I'm going in for my op on Monday.* **2 ops** [pl.] (*informal*): *She works in Sales Ops.* **3** (usually pl.] = OPERATION (8): **on ops** *to go out on ops* ◊ *special ops* ◊ *black ops* (= secret military activities, especially illegal ones) ◊ *He was in charge of a covert ops team.*

**Op.** (also **op.**) *abbr.* OPUS: *Webern's Five Pieces, Op. 10*

**opa·city** /əʊˈpæsəti; *NAmE* oʊ-/ *noun* [U] **1** (*specialist*) the fact of being difficult to see through; the fact of being OPAQUE **2** (*formal*) the fact of being difficult to understand; the fact of being OPAQUE **OPP** **transparency**

**opal** /ˈəʊpl; *NAmE* ˈoʊpl/ *noun* [C, U] a white or almost clear SEMI-PRECIOUS stone in which changes of colour are seen, used in jewellery: *an opal ring*

**opal·es·cent** /ˌəʊpəˈlesnt; *NAmE* ˌoʊp-/ *adj.* (*formal* or *literary*) changing colour like an opal

**opaque** /əʊˈpeɪk/ *adj.* **1** (of glass, liquid, etc.) not clear enough to see through or allow light through: *opaque glass* ◊ *opaque tights* **2** (of speech or writing) difficult to understand; not clear SYN **impenetrable**: *The jargon in his talk was opaque to me.* OPP **transparent**

**ˈop art** *noun* [U] a style of modern art that uses patterns and colours in a way that makes the images seem to move as you look at them

**op. cit.** /ˌɒp ˈsɪt; *NAmE* ˌɑːp/ *abbr.* used in formal writing to refer to a book or an article that has already been mentioned

**ˈop-code** /ˈɒpkəʊd; *NAmE* ˈɑːp-/ *noun* = OPERATION CODE

**OPEC** /ˈəʊpek/ *abbr.* Organization of Petroleum Exporting Countries (an organization of countries that produce and sell oil)

**ˌop-ˈed** (*also* **ˌop-ˈed page**) *noun* (*NAmE*) the page in a newspaper opposite the EDITORIAL page that contains comment on the news and articles on particular subjects

**open** ⓘ A1 /ˈəʊpən/ *adj., verb, noun*
■ *adj.*
- NOT CLOSED **1** ⓘ A1 allowing things or people to go through; not closed or blocked: *A wasp flew in the open window.* ◊ *She had left the door wide open.* ◊ *The castle gates swung open.* ◊ *The mountain pass is kept open all year.* ◊ *open borders* ◊ *Taylor headed the ball into the open goal.* OPP **closed 2** ⓘ A1 (of sb's eyes, mouth, etc.) with EYELIDS or lips apart: *She had difficulty keeping her eyes open* (= because she was very tired). ◊ *He was breathing through his open mouth.* OPP **closed 3** ⓘ A1 spread out; with the edges apart: *The flowers are all open now.* ◊ *The book lay open on the table.* OPP **closed**
- NOT FASTENED **4** ⓘ A1 not fastened or covered, so that things can easily come out or be put in: *Leave the envelope open.* ◊ *The bag burst open and everything fell out.* **5** ⓘ A1 (of clothes) not fastened: *Her coat was open.*
- NOT ENCLOSED **6** ⓘ A2 not surrounded by anything; not closed in: *open country/countryside* (= without forests, buildings, etc.) ◊ *a city with a lot of parks and wide open spaces* ◊ *driving along the open road* (= part of a road in the country, where you can drive fast) ◊ *We left port and headed for the open sea.*
- NOT COVERED **7** ⓘ A2 with no cover or roof on: *an open drain* ◊ *people working in the open air* (= not in a building) ◊ **~ to sth** *The hall of the old house was open to the sky.* ◊ *an open wound* (= with no skin covering it) ◊ *an open fire* ◊ (*NAmE*) *an open flame* HELP In British English this is called a *naked flame*.
- FOR CUSTOMERS/VISITORS **8** ⓘ A1 [not usually before noun] if a shop, bank, business, etc. is **open**, it is ready for business and will allow customers or visitors to come in: *Is the museum open on Sundays?* ◊ *I declare this festival open.* ◊ *The bank is open for business again.* OPP **closed**
- OF COMPETITION/BUILDING **9** if a competition, meeting, etc. is **open**, anyone can enter, attend it, etc.: *an open debate/championship/scholarship* ◊ *She was tried in open court* (= the public could go and listen to the trial). ◊ *The debate was thrown open to the audience.* **10** ⓘ B1 [not before noun] **~ to sb** if a competition, building, etc. is **open** to particular people, those people can enter it: *The competition is open to young people under the age of 18.* ◊ *The house is not open to the public.* OPP **closed**
- AVAILABLE **11** ⓘ B2 [not before noun] to be available and ready to use: *Is the offer still open?* ◊ *I want to keep my Swiss bank account open.* ◊ **~ to sb** *What options are open to us?* OPP **closed 12** ⓘ B2 [not before noun] if a phone line or other channel of communication is **open**, it is ready to take calls, receive requests, etc: *Lines are open 8 am to 7 pm weekdays.* ◊ *It is important to keep communication channels open.* OPP **closed**
- NOT PROTECTED **13** ⓘ B2 likely to suffer sth such as criticism, injury, etc. SYN **vulnerable**: **~ to sth** *The system is open to abuse.* ◊ *He has laid himself wide open to political attack.*
- NOT HIDDEN **14** ⓘ B2 known to everyone; not kept hidden: *an open quarrel* ◊ *open government* ◊ *their open display of affection* ◊ *His eyes showed open admiration as he looked at her.*
- HONEST **15** ⓘ B2 honest; not keeping thoughts and feelings hidden SYN **frank**: *a frank and open discussion* ◊ **~ with sb** *She was always open with her parents.* ◊ **~ about sth** *He was quite open about his reasons for leaving.* ⊃ SYNONYMS at HONEST **16** ⓘ B2 willing to listen to and think about new ideas: *He was in an open frame of mind.* ◊ **~ to sth** *They are very open to new ideas.*
- NOT YET DECIDED **17** ⓘ B2 not yet finally decided or settled: *The race is still wide open* (= anyone could win). ◊ *Which route is better remains an open question* (= it is not decided). ◊ *In an interview try to ask open questions* (= to which the answer is not just 'yes' or 'no').
- MAKING STH POSSIBLE **18** ⓘ B2 **~ to sth** allowing sth; making sth possible: *The price is not open to negotiation.* ◊ *Some phrases in the contract are open to interpretation.*
- TICKET **19** that does not have to be used on a particular day: *I have an open ticket, so I can travel any day I like.*
- CLOTH **20** with wide spaces between the THREADS: *an open weave*
- PHONETICS **21** (*also* **low**) (of a vowel) produced with the tongue in the lowest possible position ⊃ compare CLOSE[2] (16)

IDM **be an ˌopen ˈsecret** if sth is **an open secret**, many people know about it, although it is supposed to be a secret **have/keep an ˌopen ˈmind (about/on sth)** to be willing to listen to or accept new ideas or suggestions **keep your ˈears/ˈeyes open (for sb/sth)** to listen or look out for sb/sth that you might hear or see **an ˌopen ˈbook** if you describe sb or their life as **an open book**, you mean that you can easily understand them and know everything about them **an ˌopen inviˈtation (to sb)** **1** an invitation to sb to visit you at any time **2** if sth is **an open invitation** to criminals, etc., it encourages them to commit a crime by making it easier: *Leaving your camera on the seat in the car is an open invitation to thieves.* **with ˌopen ˈarms** if you welcome sb **with open arms**, you are extremely happy and pleased to see them ⊃ more at BURST *v.*, DOOR, EYE *n.*, MARKET *n.*, OPTION *n.*

■ *verb*
- DOOR/WINDOW/LID **1** ⓘ A1 [T, I] **~(sth)** to move a door, window, LID, etc. into a position that is no longer closed; to get into this position: *Mr Chen opened the car door for his wife.* ◊ *The door opened and Alan walked in.* OPP **close**[1]
- CONTAINER/PACKAGE **2** ⓘ A1 [T] **~ sth** to remove or UNDO the top, cover, etc. of a container or package in order to see or get what is inside: *Shall I open another bottle?* ◊ *He opened the letter and read it.*
- EYES **3** ⓘ A1 [T, I] **~(sth)** if you **open** your eyes or your eyes **open**, you move your EYELIDS upwards so that you can see OPP **close**[1]
- MOUTH **4** ⓘ A1 [T, I] **~(sth)** if you **open** your mouth or your mouth **opens**, you move your lips, for example in order to speak: *He hardly ever opens his mouth* (= speaks).
- BOOK **5** ⓘ A1 [T] **~ sth** to turn the cover or the pages of a book, newspaper, etc. so that it is no longer closed: *Open your books at page 25.* OPP **close**[1]
- COMPUTING **6** ⓘ A1 [T, I] **~(sth)** to start a computer program or file so that you can use it on the screen; to become available on a computer screen: *Open the camera app and tap 'Options'.* ◊ *to open a file/page/window/tab* ◊ *The page opens in a new tab.* ⊃ WORDFINDER NOTE at FILE
- SPREAD OUT **7** ⓘ A1 [I, T] to spread out or UNFOLD; to spread sth out or UNFOLD it: *What if the parachute doesn't open?* ◊ *The flowers are starting to open.* ◊ **~ sth** *Open the map on the table.* ◊ *He opened his arms wide to embrace her.*
- BORDER/ROAD **8** ⓘ A1 [T] to make it possible for people, cars, goods, etc. to pass through a place: **~ sth** *When did the country open its borders?* ◊ *The road will be opened again in a few hours after police have cleared it.* ◊ **~ sth to sth** *The bridge was opened to traffic in March 2017.* OPP **close**[1]
- FOR CUSTOMERS/VISITORS **9** ⓘ A1 [I, T] (of a shop, business, etc.) to start business for the day; to start business for the first time: *What time does the bank open?* ◊ *The store opens for business on Friday.* ◊ **~ sth** *The company opened its doors for business a month ago.* OPP **close**[1] **10** ⓘ A1 [I] to be ready for people to go to: *The new hospital opens on July 1st.* ◊ *When does the play open?* ◊ *The building opened to the public in 2019.* OPP **close**[1]
- START STH **11** ⓘ A2 [T] **~ sth** to start an activity or event; to begin using or doing sth: *You need just one pound to open*

# open access

an account with us. ◊ *The police have **opened an investigation** into the death.* ◊ *Troops **opened fire on** (= started shooting at) the crowd.* ◊ **~ sth with sth** *They will **open** the new season with a performance of 'Carmen'.* ⊃ SYNONYMS at START **12** [I, T] ~ (sth) (with sth) (of a story, film, etc.) to start in a particular way; to make sth start in a particular way: *The story opens with a murder.* • WITH CEREMONY **13** [T] ~ sth to perform a ceremony showing that a building can start being used: *The Queen officially **opened** the bridge in March.* • MAKE STH POSSIBLE **14** to make it possible to reach, have, use or do sth: *This decision **opens** the possibility of a fresh election.* ◊ **~ sth for sb/sth** *The bus route has opened a new world for me.* ◊ **~ sth to sb/sth** *The country opened its markets to the rest of the world for the first time.*

**IDM** **open 'doors for sb** to provide opportunities for sb to do sth and be successful **open your/sb's 'eyes (to sth)** to realize or make sb realize the truth about sth: *Travelling really opens your eyes to other cultures.* **open your/sb's 'mind to sth** to become or make sb aware of new ideas or experiences **open the 'way for sb/sth (to do sth)** to make it possible for sb to do sth or for sth to happen ⊃ more at HEART n., HEAVEN

**PHRV** **open 'into/onto sth** to lead to another room, area or place **open 'out** to become bigger or wider: *The street opened out into a small square.* **open 'out (to sb)** (BrE) = OPEN UP (TO SB) **open 'up 1** to begin shooting: *Anti-aircraft guns opened up.* **2** (often used in orders) to open a door, container, etc: *Open up or we'll break the door down!* **open 'up (to sb)** (BrE also **open 'out (to sb)**) to talk about what you feel and think; to become less shy and more willing to communicate: *It helps to discuss your problems but I find it hard to open up.* **open sth↔'up** | **open 'up 1** to become or make sth possible, available or able to be reached: *The railway opened up the east of the country.* ◊ *Exciting possibilities were opening up for her in the new job.* **2** to begin business for the day: *I open up the store for the day at around 8.30.* **OPP** close up **3** to start a new business: *There's a new Thai restaurant opening up in town.* **OPP** close down **4** to develop or start to happen or exist; to develop or start sth: *A division has opened up between the two ministers over the issue.* ◊ *Scott opened up a 3-point lead in the first game.* **5** to appear and become wider; to make sth wider when it is narrow or closed: *The wound opened up and started bleeding.* ◊ *The operation will open up the blocked passages around his heart.* **OPP** close up **open sth↔'up** to make sth open that is shut, locked, etc: *She laid the book flat and opened it up.*

■ *noun* **the open** [sing.]
• OUTDOORS **1** outdoors; the countryside: **in the ~** *Children need to play out in the open.*
• NOT HIDDEN **2 in/into the ~** not hidden or secret: *Government officials do not want these comments in the open.* ◊ *They intend to **bring** their complaints **out into the open.***

▼ EXPRESS YOURSELF
**Conversation openers**
What can you say when you have to speak to someone for the first time or when you have to open a meeting? Here are some possible ways of starting a conversation or getting the audience's attention before a talk or speech:
• *Do you mind if I sit here?*
• *Hello, is this seat taken?*
• *May I join you? Can I get you a coffee?*
• *Lovely weather we're having!/Can you believe this rain/wind/cold/sunshine?*
• *Excuse me, could I ask you a question?*
• *Shall we make a start? I think it's almost three o'clock.* (BrE)
• *Shall we get started? I'd like to introduce our speaker.* (especially NAmE)
• *I think everyone's here, so I'd like to welcome you to this conference.*

**open 'access** *noun* [U] ~ (to sth) the fact of sth being available to anyone who wants it: *Technology, she stressed, provides open access to education.*

**the open 'air** *noun* [sing.] a place outside rather than in a building: *He likes to cook in the open air.*

**open-'air** *adj.* [only before noun] happening or existing outside rather than inside a building: *an open-air swimming pool*

**open 'bar** *noun* [U, C] an occasion when all the drinks at a party or other event have been paid for by sb else or are included in the ticket price

**open 'carry** *noun* [U] (NAmE) the practice of openly carrying a gun in public ⊃ compare CONCEALED CARRY

**open·cast** /ˈəʊpənkɑːst; NAmE -kæst/ (BrE) (NAmE **open-'pit**) *adj.* [usually before noun] in **opencast** mines coal is taken directly out of the ground near the surface, without digging tunnels

**'open day** (BrE) (NAmE **open 'house**) *noun* a day when people can visit a school, an organization, etc. and see the work that is done there

**open 'door** *noun, adj.*
■ *noun* [sing.] ~ (to sth/sb) a situation that allows sth to happen, or that allows people to go to a place or get information without controls or limits: *The government's policy is an open door to disaster.* ◊ *An insecure computer system is an open door to criminals.*
■ *adj.* **open-'door** [only before noun] **1** (of a policy, system, principle, etc.) allowing people or goods freedom to come into a country; allowing people to go to a place or get information without controls or limits: *the country's **open-door** policy for refugees* **2** a policy within a company or other organization designed to allow people to freely communicate with the people in charge: *We operate an **open-door** policy here, and are always willing to listen to our students' suggestions.*

**open-'ended** *adj.* without any limits, aims or dates fixed in advance: *an open-ended discussion* ◊ *The contract is open-ended.*

**open·er** /ˈəʊpənə(r)/ *noun* **1** (usually in compounds) a tool that is used to open things: *a can opener* ◊ *a bottle-opener* ⊃ see also EYE-OPENER, TIN OPENER **2** the first in a series of things such as sports games; the first action in an event, a game, etc: *They won the opener 4–2.* ◊ *Jones scored the opener.* ◊ *a good conversation opener* **3** (in CRICKET) either of the two BATSMEN who start play
**IDM** **for 'openers** (*informal, especially* NAmE) as a beginning or first part of a process **SYN** for starters

**open-faced 'sandwich** (*also* **open-face 'sandwich**) (*both* NAmE) (BrE **open 'sandwich**) *noun* a slice of bread with meat, cheese, etc. on top but without a second slice of bread to cover this

**open-'handed** *adj.* **1** generous and giving willingly: *an open-handed host* **2** using the flat part of the hand: *an open-handed blow*

**open-'hearted** *adj.* kind and friendly

**open-heart 'surgery** *noun* [U] a medical operation on the heart, during which the patient's blood is kept flowing by a machine

**open 'house** *noun* **1** [U, sing.] a place or a time at which visitors are welcome: *It's always open house at their place.* **2** (NAmE) (BrE **open day**) [C] a day when people can visit a school, an organization, etc. and see the work that is done there **3** [C] a time when people who are interested in buying a particular house or apartment can look around it

**open·ing** /ˈəʊpənɪŋ/ *noun, adj.*
■ *noun* **1** [C] a space or hole that sb/sth can pass through: *We could see the stars through an opening in the roof.* ◊ **~ to sth** *It looks like the opening to a small cave.* **2** [C, usually sing.] the beginning or first part of sth: *The movie has an exciting opening.* ◊ **~ to sth** *It's such a brave opening to a book.* **OPP** ending **3** [C, usually sing.] a ceremony to celebrate the start of a public event or the first time a new building, road, etc. is used: **~ of sth** *the official opening of the new hospital* ◊ *tickets for the opening ceremony* ◊ *The gallery has scheduled a **grand opening** for June 29.* **4** [C, U] the act or process of making sth open or of becoming open: **~ of sth** *the opening of a flower* ◊ *the opening of the new play* ◊ *Late opening of supermarkets is common in Britain now.* ⊃ compare CLOSING **5** [C] a job that is available **SYN** vacancy: *There are several openings in the sales department.* **6** [C] a good opportunity for sb: *Winning the competition was the*

*opening* she needed for her career. **7** [C] part of a piece of clothing that is made to open and close so that it can be put on easily: *The skirt has a side opening.*
- *adj.* [only before noun] first; beginning: *his opening remarks* ◊ *the opening chapter of the book* **OPP** **closing**

**ˈopening hours** *noun* [pl.] the time during which a shop, bank, etc. is open for business

**ˌopening ˈnight** *noun* [usually sing.] the first night that, for example, a play is performed or a film is shown to the public ⇒ **WORDFINDER NOTE** at PERFORMANCE

**ˈopening time** *noun* [U] (*BrE*) the time when pubs can legally open and begin to serve drinks **OPP** **closing time**

**ˌopening ˈup** *noun* [sing.] **1** the process of removing controls or limits and making sth such as land or jobs available to more people: *the opening up of new opportunities for women in business* **2** the process of making sth ready for use: *the opening up of a new stretch of highway*

**ˌopen ˈletter** *noun* a letter of complaint or protest to an important person or group that is printed in a newspaper so that the public can read it

**ˈopen line** *noun, adj.*
- *noun* a phone communication in which conversations can be heard or recorded by others
- *adj.* **open-line** [only before noun] relating to a radio or television programme that the public can take part in by phone: *an open-line radio show*

**openˈly** /ˈəʊpənli/ *adv.* without hiding any feelings, opinions or information: *Can you talk openly about sex with your parents?* ◊ *The men in prison would never cry openly* (= so that other people could see).

**ˌopen ˈmarket** *noun* [sing.] a situation in which companies can trade without limits, and prices depend on the amount of goods and the number of people buying them: *on the ~ to buy/sell/trade on the open market*

**ˌopen ˈmic** (*also* **ˌopen ˈmike**) *noun* [U] an occasion in a club when anyone can sing, play music or tell jokes: *open-mic night*

**ˌopen-ˈminded** *adj.* willing to listen to, think about or accept different ideas **OPP** **narrow-minded** ▶ **ˌopen-ˈminded·ness** *noun* [U]

**ˌopen-ˈmouthed** *adj.* with your mouth open because you are surprised or shocked

**ˌopen-ˈnecked** (*also* **ˌopen-ˈneck**) *adj.* (of a shirt) worn without a tie and with the top button undone

**open·ness** /ˈəʊpənnəs/ *noun* [U] **1** the quality of being honest and not hiding information or feelings **2** ~ (**to sth**) the quality of being able to think about, accept or listen to different ideas or people **3** the quality of not being limited or covered

**ˌopen-ˈpit** (*NAmE*) (*BrE* **ˌopen-ˈcast**) *adj.* [usually before noun] in **open-pit** mines coal is taken directly out of the ground near the surface, without digging tunnels

**ˌopen-ˈplan** *adj.* an **open-plan** building or area does not have inside walls dividing it up into rooms: *an open-plan office*

**ˌopen ˈprison** (*BrE*) (*NAmE* **ˌminimum seˈcurity ˈprison**) *noun* a prison in which prisoners have more freedom than in ordinary prisons

**ˌopen ˈsandwich** (*BrE*) (*NAmE* **ˌopen-faced ˈsandwich**) *noun* a slice of bread with meat, cheese, etc. on top but without a second slice of bread to cover this

**ˌopen ˈseason** *noun* [sing.] **1** ~ (**for sth**) the time in the year when it is legal to hunt and kill particular animals or birds, or to catch fish, for sport **OPP** **close season** ⇒ **WORDFINDER NOTE** at HUNT **2** ~ **for/on sb/sth** a time when criticizing a particular group of people becomes very popular, as if it is no longer important to be polite or fair: *It seems to be open season on teachers now.*

**ˌopen ˈslather** *noun* [U] (*AustralE, disapproving*) freedom to act without controls or limits: *The changes will give developers open slather.*

**ˌopen-ˈsource** *adj.* (*computing*) used to describe software for which the original SOURCE CODE is made available to anyone

**ˌopen-ˈtoed** *adj.* (of shoes) not covering the toes: *open-toed sandals*

---

1087 **operation**

**ˌopen-ˈtop** (*also* **ˌopen-ˈtopped**) *adj.* (*BrE*) (of a vehicle) having no roof

**ˌopen ˈverdict** *noun* an official decision in a British court stating that the exact cause of a person's death is not known

**op·era** B2 /ˈɒprə; *NAmE* ˈɑːp-/ *noun* **1** [C, U] a dramatic work in which all or most of the words are sung to music; works of this type as an art form or entertainment: *Puccini's operas* ◊ *to go to the opera* ◊ *an opera singer* ◊ *light/grand opera* ⇒ see also SOAP OPERA

> **WORDFINDER** aria, chorus, coloratura, diva, libretto, orchestra pit, recitative, score, surtitles

**2** C1 [C] a company that performs opera; a building in which operas are performed: *the Vienna State Opera* ▶ **op·er·at·ic** /ˌɒpəˈrætɪk; *NAmE* ˌɑːp-/ *adj.*: *operatic arias/composers*

**op·er·able** /ˈɒpərəbl; *NAmE* ˈɑːp-/ *adj.* **1** that functions; that can be used: *Less than half the rail network was operable.* **2** (of a medical condition) that can be treated by an operation **OPP** **inoperable**

**ˈopera house** *noun* a theatre where operas are performed

**op·er·and** /ˈɒpərænd; *NAmE* ˈɑːp-/ *noun* (*mathematics*) the number on which an operation is to be done

**op·er·ate** B2 /ˈɒpəreɪt; *NAmE* ˈɑːp-/ *verb*
- MACHINE **1** B2 [I] + *adv./prep.* to work in a particular way **SYN** **function**: *Most domestic freezers operate at below −18°C.* ◊ *Solar panels can only operate in sunlight.* ◊ (*figurative*) *Some people can only operate well under pressure.* **2** B2 [T] ~ **sth** to use or control a machine or make it work: *What skills are needed to operate this machinery?*
- BUSINESS/ORGANIZATION/SERVICE **3** B2 [T] ~ **sth** to manage a business, organization or service: *The airline currently operates flights to 25 countries.* ◊ *He started and operated a successful technology business.* **4** B2 [I] + *adv./prep.* (of a business, organization or service) to work, especially in a particular way or from a particular place: *A new late-night service is now operating.* ◊ *They plan to operate from a new office in Edinburgh.* ◊ *Retailers operate in a fast-paced environment.*
- SYSTEM/PROCESS **5** B2 [I, T] to be used or working; to use sth or make it work: *The regulation operates in favour of married couples.* ◊ ~ **sth** *France operates a system of subsidized loans to dairy farmers.*
- MEDICAL **6** B2 [I] to cut open sb's body in order to remove a part that has a disease or to repair a part that is damaged: *Surgeons operated last night.* ◊ ~ **on sb/sth** *We will have to operate on his eyes.* ◊ *She was operated on the next day.*
- OF SOLDIERS **7** [I] (+ *adv./prep.*) to be involved in military activities in a place: *Troops are operating from bases in the north.*

**ˈoperating system** *noun* (*abbr.* **OS**) a set of programs that controls the way a computer works and runs other programs ⇒ **WORDFINDER NOTE** at PROGRAM

**ˈoperating table** *noun* a special table that you lie on to have a medical operation in a hospital: **on the ~** *The patient died on the operating table* (= during an operation).

**ˈoperating theatre** (*also* **theatre**) (*both BrE*) (*NAmE* **ˈoperating room**) *noun* a room in a hospital used for medical operations

**op·er·ation** B1 /ˌɒpəˈreɪʃn; *NAmE* ˌɑːp-/ *noun*
- MEDICAL **1** B1 (*also* *BrE, informal* **op**) [C] the process of cutting open a part of a person's body in order to remove or repair a damaged part: *Will I need to* **have an operation**? ◊ *He underwent a three-hour heart operation.* ◊ ~ (**on sb/sth**) (**to do sth**) *an operation on her lung to remove a tumour* ◊ ~ **for sth** *Doctors performed an emergency operation for appendicitis last night.* ⇒ **WORDFINDER NOTE** at HOSPITAL

> **WORDFINDER** amputate, anaesthetic, graft, procedure, scalpel, scrubs, stitch, surgery, transplant

# operational

- **ORGANIZED ACTIVITY 2** [C] an organized activity that involves several people: *a rescue/security operation* ◊ *~against sb/sth The police have launched a major operation against drug suppliers.* ◊ *the UN peacekeeping operations* ⊃ see also HOLDING OPERATION
- **BUSINESS 3** [C] a business or company, usually one that involves many parts: *a huge multinational operation* ◊ *He runs a successful dairy operation.* **4** [C, usually pl.] the activity or work done in a company, or in an area of business or industry: *The firm is looking to expand its operations overseas.* ◊ *The directors are not involved in day-to-day operations of the business.*
- **COMPUTER 5** [C, U] an act performed by a machine, especially a computer: *The whole operation is performed in less than three seconds.*
- **MACHINE/SYSTEM 6** [U] the way that parts of a machine or a system work; the process of making sth work: *Regular servicing guarantees the smooth operation of the engine.* ◊ *Operation of the device is extremely simple.* **7** [U] the action of functioning; the fact of being used or active or having an effect: *The factory will cease operation at the end of the year.* ◊ *in~ The system has been in operation for six months.* ◊ *into~ The new rules come into operation from next week.* ◊ *It's time to put our plan into operation.*
- **MILITARY ACTIVITY 8** (*also* **op**) [C, usually pl.] military activity: *joint military/combat operations* ◊ *US forces conducted ground and air operations.* ⊃ see also SPECIAL OPERATION
- **MATHEMATICS 9** [C] a process in which a number or quantity is changed by adding, multiplying, etc.

**op·er·ation·al** /ˌɒpəˈreɪʃənl; NAmE ˌɑːp-/ adj. **1** [usually before noun] connected with the way in which a business, machine, system, etc. works: *operational activities/costs/difficulties* **2** [not usually before noun] ready or available to be used: *The new airport is now fully operational.* **3** [only before noun] connected with a military operation: *operational headquarters* ▶ **op·er·ation·al·ly** /-nəli/ adv.

**operational ˈresearch** (*also* **operations reˈsearch**) noun [U] (*specialist*) the study of how businesses are organized, in order to make them more efficient

**opeˈration code** (*also* **op-code**) noun [U, C] (*computing*) an instruction written in MACHINE CODE which relates to a particular task

**opeˈrations room** noun a room from which military or police activities are controlled

**op·era·tive** /ˈɒpərətɪv; NAmE ˈɑːp-/ noun, adj.
■ noun **1** (*specialist*) a worker, especially one who works with their hands: *a factory operative* ◊ *skilled/unskilled operatives* **2** (*especially NAmE*) a person who does secret work, especially for a government organization: *an intelligence operative*
■ adj. **1** [not usually before noun] ready to be used; in use SYN functional: *This law becomes operative immediately.* ◊ *The station will be fully operative again in January.* **2** [only before noun] (*medical*) connected with a medical operation: *operative treatment* ⊃ see also POST-OPERATIVE
**IDM** **the operative word** used to emphasize that a particular word or phrase is the most important one in a sentence: *I was in love with her—'was' being the operative word.*

**op·er·ator** /ˈɒpəreɪtə(r); NAmE ˈɑːp-/ noun **1** (often in compounds) a person who operates equipment or a machine: *a computer/machine operator* ⊃ see also CAMERA OPERATOR, SYSTEM OPERATOR **2** (often in compounds) a person or company that runs a particular business: *a tour operator* ◊ *a bus operator* **3** (*BrE, old-fashioned* **tel·eph·on·ist**) a person who works on the phone SWITCHBOARD of a large company or organization, especially at a TELEPHONE EXCHANGE: *Dial 100 and ask for the operator.* **4** (*informal, especially disapproving*) a person who shows skill at getting what they want, especially when this involves behaving in a dishonest way: *a smooth/slick/shrewd operator* **5** (*mathematics*) a symbol or function which represents an operation in mathematics ⊃ see also BOOLEAN OPERATOR

**op·er·etta** /ˌɒpəˈretə; NAmE ˌɑːp-/ noun a short OPERA, usually with a humorous subject

**oph·thal·mic** /ɒfˈθælmɪk, ɒpˈθ-; NAmE ɑːfˈθælmɪk, ɑːpˈθ-/ adj. (*medical*) connected with the eye: *ophthalmic surgery*

**ophˌthalmic opˈtician** noun (*BrE*) = OPTICIAN (1)

**oph·thal·molo·gist** /ˌɒfθælˈmɒlədʒɪst, ˌɒpθ-; NAmE ˌɑːfθəˈmɑːl-, ˌɑːpθ-/ noun a doctor who studies and treats the diseases of the eye ⊃ WORDFINDER NOTE at SPECIALIST

**oph·thal·mol·ogy** /ˌɒfθælˈmɒlədʒi, ˌɒpθ-; NAmE ˌɑːfθəˈmɑːl-, ˌɑːpθ-/ noun [U] the scientific study of the eye and its diseases

**opi·ate** /ˈəʊpiət/ noun (*formal*) a drug made from OPIUM. Opiates are used in medicine to reduce severe pain.

**opine** /əʊˈpaɪn/ verb *~ that …* (*formal*) to express a particular opinion: *He opined that Prague was the most beautiful city in Europe.*

**opin·ion** /əˈpɪnjən/ noun **1** [C] your feelings or thoughts about sb/sth, rather than a fact SYN view: *He has very strong political opinions.* ◊ *~about sth/sb We were invited to give our opinions about how the work should be done.* ◊ *~of sb/sth I've recently changed my opinion of her.* ◊ *~on sth You will have the chance to voice your opinions on the matter.* ◊ *~that … The chairman expressed the opinion that job losses were inevitable.* ◊ *in my~ In my personal opinion, it's a very sound investment.* ◊ *If you want my opinion, I think you'd be crazy not to accept.* ⊃ LANGUAGE BANK at ACCORDING TO ⊃ EXPRESS YOURSELF at THINK **2** [U] the beliefs or views of a group of people: *legal/medical/political opinion* (= the beliefs of people working in the legal, etc. profession) ◊ *There is a difference of opinion* (= people disagree) *as to the merits of the plan.* ◊ *Opinion is divided* (= people disagree) *on the issue.* ◊ *Popular opinion is shifting in favour of change.* ◊ *Which is the better is a matter of opinion* (= people have different opinions about it). ◊ *~among sb Opinion among fans is mixed, but most approve the new direction.* ⊃ see also PUBLIC OPINION **3** [C] advice from a professional person: *The couple sought the opinions of other doctors who confirmed the diagnosis.* ◊ *Get an expert opinion before you invest.* ◊ *I'd like a second opinion* (= advice from another person) *before I make a decision.*
**IDM** **be of the opinion that …** (*formal*) to believe or think that … **have a good, bad, high, low, etc. opinion of sb/sth** to think that sb/sth is good, bad, etc: *The boss has a very high opinion of her.* ⊃ more at CONSIDER

▼ **LANGUAGE BANK**

### opinion

Giving your personal opinion

- *In my opinion*, everyone should have some understanding of science.
- Everyone should, *in my opinion*, have some understanding of science.
- *It seems to me that* many people in this country have a poor understanding of science.
- This is, *in my view*, the result of a failure of the scientific community to get its message across.
- Another reason why so many people have such a poor understanding of science is, *I believe*, the lack of adequate funding for science in schools.
- Smith argues that science is separate from culture. *My own view is that* science belongs with literature, art, philosophy and religion as an integral part of our culture.
- *In this writer's opinion*, the more the public know about science, the less they will fear and distrust it.

⊃ SYNONYMS at THINK
⊃ LANGUAGE BANK at ACCORDING TO, ARGUE, IMPERSONAL, NEVERTHELESS, PERHAPS

**opin·ion·ated** /əˈpɪnjəneɪtɪd/ (*also* **ˌself-oˈpinion·ated**) adj. (*disapproving*) having very strong opinions that you are not willing to change

**oˈpinion poll** noun = POLL

**opium** /ˈəʊpiəm/ noun [U] a powerful drug made from the juice of a type of POPPY (= a kind of flower), used in the past in medicines to reduce pain and help people sleep.

Some people take opium illegally for pleasure and can become ADDICTED to it.

**opos·sum** /əˈpɒsəm/; *NAmE* əˈpɑːs-/ (*AustralE, NZE* or *NAmE, informal* **pos·sum**) *noun* a small American or Australian animal that lives in trees and carries its young in a POUCH (= a pocket of skin on the front of the mother's body)

**op·pon·ent** ⬤ B2 /əˈpəʊnənt/ *noun* **1** ? B2 a person that you are playing or fighting against in a game, competition, argument, etc. SYN **adversary**: *a political opponent* ◊ *a worthy/formidable/fierce/tough/staunch opponent* ◊ *The team's opponents are unbeaten so far this season.* **2** ? B2 a person who is against sth and tries to change or stop it: ~ **of sth** *Opponents of abortion* ◊ *Opponents argue that the scheme would be prohibitively expensive.*

**op·por·tune** /ˈɒpətjuːn/; *NAmE* ˌɑːpərˈtuːn/ *adj.* (*formal*) **1** (of a time) suitable for doing a particular thing, so that it is likely to be successful SYN **favourable**: *The offer could not have come at a more opportune moment.* **2** (of an action or event) done or happening at the right time to be successful: *an opportune remark* OPP **inopportune**
▸ **op·por·tune·ly** *adv.*

**op·por·tun·ism** /ˈɒpətjuːnɪzəm/; *NAmE* ˌɑːpərˈtuː-/ *noun* [U] (*disapproving*) the practice of using situations unfairly to gain advantage for yourself without thinking about how your actions will affect other people: *political opportunism*

**op·por·tun·ist** /ˌɒpəˈtjuːnɪst/; *NAmE* ˌɑːpərˈtuː-/ (*also* **op·por·tun·is·tic**) *adj.* (*usually before noun*) (*often disapproving*) making use of an opportunity, especially to get an advantage for yourself; not done in a planned way: *an opportunist crime* ▸ **op·por·tun·ist** *noun*: *80 per cent of burglaries are committed by casual opportunists.*

**op·por·tun·is·tic** /ˌɒpətjuːˈnɪstɪk/; *NAmE* ˌɑːpərtuː-/ *adj.* **1** (*disapproving*) = OPPORTUNIST **2** [only before noun] (*medical*) harmful to people whose IMMUNE SYSTEM has been made weak by disease or drugs: *an opportunistic infection*

**op·por·tun·ity** ⬤ A2 W /ˌɒpəˈtjuːnəti/; *NAmE* ˌɑːpərˈtuː-/ *noun* [C, U] (*pl.* **-ies**) a time when a particular situation makes it possible to do or achieve sth SYN **chance**: *Don't miss this opportunity!* ◊ ~ **to do sth** *You'll have the opportunity to ask any questions at the end.* ◊ *I'd like to take this opportunity to thank my colleagues for their support.* ◊ ~ **for sb to do sth** *The conference offers a unique opportunity for professionals to meet each other.* ◊ ~ **for (doing) sth** *There was no opportunity for further discussion.* ◊ ~ **of doing sth** *At least give him the opportunity of explaining what happened.* ◊ *career/employment/job opportunities* ◊ *He is rude to me at every opportunity* (= whenever possible). ◊ *They intend to close the school at the earliest opportunity* (= as soon as possible). ◊ *I would definitely go if the opportunity arose.* ◊ *a window of opportunity* (= a period of time when the circumstances are right for doing sth) ⊃ see also EQUAL OPPORTUNITIES, PHOTO OPPORTUNITY

**oppor'tunity cost** *noun* [C, U] the fact that when you choose one option, you lose the potential benefits of the other options: *There may be an opportunity cost to not having your money invested elsewhere.*

**oppor'tunity shop** (*also* **'op shop**) *noun* (*AustralE, NZE*) a shop that sells clothes and other goods given by people to raise money for a charity SYN **charity shop**, **thrift shop**

**op·pose** ⬤ B2 /əˈpəʊz/ *verb* **1** ? B2 to disagree strongly with sb's plan, policy, etc. and try to change it or prevent it from succeeding: ~ **sb/sth** *This party would bitterly oppose the re-introduction of the death penalty.* ◊ *He threw all those that opposed him into prison.* ◊ ~ **(sb/sth) doing sth** *I would oppose changing the law.* ◊ *compare* PROPOSE **2** ~ **sb** to compete with sb in a contest: *He intends to oppose the prime minister in the leadership election.*

**op·posed** ⬤ B2 /əˈpəʊzd/ *adj.* [not usually before noun] **1** ? B2 (of a person) disagreeing strongly with sth and trying to stop it: ~ **(to sth)** *He was strongly opposed to modernism in art.* ◊ *She remained bitterly opposed to the idea of moving abroad.* ◊ *They are totally opposed to abortion.* **2** ? B2 (of ideas, opinions, etc.) very different from sth: *Our views are diametrically opposed on this issue.* ◊

~ **to sth** *His actions seemed directly opposed to the values of the company.*
IDM **as op'posed to** (*formal*) used to make a contrast between two things: *200 attended, as opposed to 300 the previous year.* ◊ *This exercise develops suppleness as opposed to* (= rather than) *strength.*

**op·pos·ing** /əˈpəʊzɪŋ/ *adj.* [only before noun] **1** (of teams, armies, forces, etc.) playing, fighting, working, etc. against each other: *a player from the opposing side* ◊ *It is time for opposing factions to unite and work towards a common goal.* **2** (of attitudes, views, etc.) very different from each other

**op·pos·ite** ⬤ A1 /ˈɒpəzɪt/; *NAmE* ˈɑːp-/ *adj., noun, prep., adv.*
■ *adj.* **1** ? A1 [only before noun] on the other side of a particular area from sb/sth and usually facing them: *Answers are given on the opposite page.* ◊ *We live further down on the opposite side of the road.* ◊ *It's not easy having a relationship when you live at opposite ends of the country.* **2** ? A1 (used after the noun) facing the speaker or sb/sth that has been mentioned: *I could see smoke coming from the windows of the house directly opposite.* ◊ *He sat down in the chair opposite.* **3** ? A1 [usually before noun] as different as possible from sth: *I watched them leave and then drove off in the opposite direction.* ◊ *She tried calming him down but it seemed to be having the opposite effect.* ◊ *students at opposite ends of the ability range* ◊ ~ **to sb/sth** *She took a view opposite to that of Fraser.*
IDM **your ˌopposite ˈnumber** (*informal*) a person who does the same job as you in another organization: *The Foreign Secretary is currently having talks with his opposite number in the White House.* **the ˌopposite ˈsex** the other sex: *He found it difficult to talk to members of the opposite sex.* ⊃ more at PULL *v.*
■ *noun* ? A1 a person or thing that is as different as possible from sb/sth else: *Hot and cold are opposites.* ◊ **the ~ of sth** *What is the opposite of heavy?* ◊ *She says the exact opposite of what she means—it's confusing.* ◊ **the ~ to sth** *The effect was exactly the opposite to what he intended.* ◊ *I thought she would be small and blonde but she's the complete opposite.* ◊ *'Is it better now?' 'Quite the opposite, I'm afraid.'* ◊ *I ask you to do something and you go and do the opposite —why?*
IDM **ˌopposites at'tract** used to say that people who are very different are often attracted to each other
■ *prep.* **1** ? A1 on the other side of a particular area from sb/sth, and usually facing them: *I sat opposite him during the meal* (= on the other side of the table). ◊ *The bank is opposite the supermarket* (= on the other side of the road). ◊ *Write your address opposite* (= next to) *your name.* **2** acting in a film or play as the partner of sb: *She starred opposite Tom Hanks.*
■ *adv.* ? A1 on the other side of a particular area from sb/sth and usually facing them: *There's a newly married couple living opposite* (= on the other side of the road). ◊ *See opposite* (= on the opposite page) *for further details.*

**op·pos·ition** ⬤ B2 /ˌɒpəˈzɪʃn/; *NAmE* ˌɑːp-/ *noun* **1** ? B2 [U, sing.] the act of strongly disagreeing with sb/sth, especially with the aim of preventing sth from happening: *Opposition came primarily from students.* ◊ ~ **to sb/sth** *Delegates expressed strong opposition to the plans.* ◊ *He spent five years in prison for his opposition to the regime.* ◊ *The army met with fierce opposition in every town.* ◊ *The proposal faced stiff opposition.* ◊ *opposition forces* (= people who are arguing, fighting, etc. with another group) **2** ? B2 [U] the act of competing against sb in a contest: *She won against determined opposition from last year's champion.* **3** ? B2 **the opposition** [sing. + sing. / pl. v.] the people you are competing against in business, a competition, a game, etc: *He's gone to work for the opposition.* ◊ *The opposition is/are mounting a strong challenge to our business.* ◊ *Liverpool couldn't match the opposition in the final and lost 2–0.* **4** ? B2 **the Opposition** (*NAmE* **the opposition**) [sing. + sing. / pl. v.] the main political party that is opposed to the government; the political parties that are in a parliament but are not part of the government: *the leader of the Opposition* ◊ *Opposition MPs/*

# oppress

politicians/parties ◊ *the Opposition spokesman on education* ⇒ **WORDFINDER NOTE** at GOVERNMENT **5** [U, C] (*formal*) the state of being as different as possible; two things that are as different as possible: *the opposition between good and evil* ◊ *His poetry is full of oppositions and contrasts.*
▶ **op·pos·ition·al** /-ʃənl/ *adj.* [usually before noun] (*formal*): *oppositional groups/tactics*
**IDM** **in oppo'sition** (of a political party) forming part of a parliament but not of the government **in oppo'sition to sb/sth 1** disagreeing strongly with sb/sth, especially with the aim of preventing sth from happening: *Protest marches were held in opposition to the proposed law.* **2** contrasting two people or things that are very different: *Leisure is often defined in opposition to work.*

**op·press** /əˈpres/ *verb* **1** ~ **sb** to treat sb in a cruel and unfair way, especially by not giving them the same freedom, rights, etc. as other people: *The regime is accused of oppressing religious minorities.* ⇒ **WORDFINDER NOTE** at FREEDOM **2** ~ **sb** to make sb only able to think about things that make them sad or worried **SYN** **weigh down**: *The gloomy atmosphere in the office oppressed her.* ▶ **op·pres·sion** /əˈpreʃn/ *noun* [U]: *victims of oppression*

**op·pressed** /əˈprest/ *adj.* **1** treated in a cruel and unfair way and not given the same freedom, rights, etc. as other people: *oppressed minorities* **2 the oppressed** *noun* [pl.] people who are oppressed

**op·pres·sive** /əˈpresɪv/ *adj.* **1** treating people in a cruel and unfair way and not giving them the same freedom, rights, etc. as other people: *oppressive laws* ◊ *an oppressive regime* **2** (of the weather) extremely hot and unpleasant and not having enough fresh air **SYN** **stifling**: *oppressive heat* **3** making you feel unhappy and anxious **SYN** **stifling**: *an oppressive relationship* ▶ **op·pres·sive·ly** *adv.*: *to behave oppressively* ◊ *oppressively hot* ◊ *He suffered from an oppressively dominant mother.* **op·pres·sive·ness** *noun* [U]

**op·pres·sor** /əˈpresə(r)/ *noun* a person or group of people that treats sb in a cruel and unfair way, especially by not giving them the same rights, etc. as other people

**op·pro·brium** /əˈprəʊbriəm/ *noun* [U] (*formal*) severe criticism of a person, country, etc. by a large group of people ▶ **op·pro·bri·ous** /-briəs/ *adj.*: *an opprobrious remark*

**'op shop** *noun* (AustralE, NZE) = OPPORTUNITY SHOP

**opt** /ɒpt; *NAmE* ɑːpt/ *verb* [I, T] to choose to take or not to take a particular course of action: ~ **for/against sth** *After graduating she opted for a career in music.* ◊ ~ **to do sth** *Many workers opted to leave their jobs rather than take a pay cut.* ⇒ SYNONYMS at CHOOSE
**PHRV** **opt 'in (to sth)** to choose to be part of a system or an agreement **opt 'out (of sth) 1** to choose not to take part in sth: *Employees may opt out of the company's pension plan.* **2** (of a school or hospital in England) to choose not to be under the control of the local authority ⇒ related noun OPT-OUT

**optic** /ˈɒptɪk; *NAmE* ˈɑːp-/ *adj., noun*
■ *adj.* [usually before noun] (*specialist*) connected with the eye or the sense of sight: *the optic nerve* (= from the eye to the brain)
■ *noun* a device for measuring out exact amounts of strong alcoholic drinks in a bar

**op·tic·al** /ˈɒptɪkl; *NAmE* ˈɑːp-/ *adj.* [usually before noun] **1** connected with the sense of sight or the relationship between light and sight: *optical effects* **2** used to help you see sth more clearly: *optical aids* ◊ *optical instruments such as microscopes and telescopes* **3** (*computing*) using light for reading or storing information: *optical storage* ◊ *an optical disk/drive/mouse* ▶ **op·tic·al·ly** /-kli/ *adv.*

**optical 'character recognition** *noun* [U] (*abbr.* OCR) (*computing*) the process of reading printed documents by machine so that the information can be processed by a computer or sent over a network

**optical 'fibre** (*US* **optical 'fiber**) *noun* [C, U] a thin glass string through which light can be TRANSMITTED (= sent)

## optical illusions

Are there two prongs or three?

Horizontal line A and horizontal line B are of equal length, but horizontal line A appears to be longer.

**optical il'lusion** *noun* something that tricks your eyes and makes you think that you can see sth that is not there, or makes you see sth as different from what it really is

**op·tic·als** /ˈɒptɪklz; *NAmE* ˈɑːp-/ *noun* [pl.] (*IndE*) a pair of glasses

**op·ti·cian** /ɒpˈtɪʃn; *NAmE* ɑːp-/ *noun* **1** (*also* **oph'thalmic op'tician**) (*both BrE*) (*especially NAmE* **op'tom·etrist**) a person whose job is to examine people's eyes and to recommend and sell glasses **2** (*especially NAmE*) (*BrE usually* **dispensing optician**) a person whose job is to make and supply glasses, but who does not test people's eyes **3** **op'tician's** (*pl.* **op'ticians**) the shop where an optician works: *to go to the optician's* **4** a person who makes LENSES, glasses, etc.

**op·tics** /ˈɒptɪks; *NAmE* ˈɑːp-/ *noun* [U] the scientific study of sight and light ⇒ see also FIBRE OPTICS

**op·ti·mal** /ˈɒptɪməl; *NAmE* ˈɑːp-/ *adj.* = OPTIMUM ⇒ compare SUBOPTIMAL ▶ **op·ti·mal·ly** /-məli/ *adv.*

**op·ti·mism** /ˈɒptɪmɪzəm; *NAmE* ˈɑːp-/ *noun* [U] a feeling that good things will happen and that sth will be successful: *a mood of cautious optimism* ◊ *There are very real grounds for optimism.* ◊ **with** ~ *We may now look forward with optimism.* ◊ ~ **about/for sth** *optimism about/for the future* **OPP** **pessimism**

**op·ti·mist** /ˈɒptɪmɪst; *NAmE* ˈɑːp-/ *noun* a person who always expects good things to happen or things to be successful: *I'm an eternal optimist—I'm sure things will get better.* **OPP** **pessimist**

**op·ti·mis·tic** /ˌɒptɪˈmɪstɪk; *NAmE* ˌɑːp-/ *adj.* expecting good things to happen or sth to be successful; showing this feeling **SYN** **positive**: *We are now taking a more optimistic view.* ◊ *in an optimistic mood* ◊ ~ **about sth** *She's not very optimistic about the outcome of the talks.* ◊ ~ **that...** *They are cautiously optimistic that the reforms will take place.* ◊ *I think you're being a little over-optimistic.* **OPP** **pessimistic** ▶ **op·ti·mis·tic·al·ly** /-kli/ *adv.*

**op·ti·mize** (*BrE also* **-ise**) /ˈɒptɪmaɪz; *NAmE* ˈɑːp-/ *verb* **1** ~ **sth** to make sth as good as it can be; to use sth in the best possible way: *to optimize the use of resources* **2** (*computing*) to change data, software, etc. in order to make it work more efficiently or to make it suitable for a particular purpose: *It is important that websites are optimized for mobile devices.*

**op·ti·mum** /ˈɒptɪməm; *NAmE* ˈɑːp-/ *adj.* [only before noun] **1** (*also* **op·ti·mal**) the best possible; producing the best possible results: *the optimum use of resources* ◊ *the optimum conditions for effective learning* **2 the optimum** *noun* [sing.] the best possible result, set of conditions, etc. **SYN** **ideal**

**op·tion** /ˈɒpʃn; *NAmE* ˈɑːp-/ *noun, verb*
■ *noun* **1** [C, U] something that you can choose to have or do; the freedom to choose what you do: *As I see it, we have two options...* ◊ *There are various options open to you.* ◊ **to explore/consider/look at all your options** *Going to college was not an option for me.* ◊ *Selling the house was our only option.* ◊ *Waiting a year may be your best option.* ◊ *We felt this was the most viable option.* ◊ *I had no option but to* (= I had to) *ask him to leave.* ◊ ~ **of (doing) sth** *Students have the option of studying abroad in their second year.* ◊ ~ **to do sth** *A savings plan that gives you the option to vary your monthly payments.* ◊ *This particular model comes with a wide range of options* (= things you can choose to have with when buying sth but which you will have to pay extra for)*.* ⇒ see also NUCLEAR OPTION **2** [C] a subject that a student can choose to study, but that they do not have to do: *The course offers options in design and computing.* **3** [C] the right to buy or sell sth at some time in the future: *share options* (= the right to buy shares in a company) ◊ ~ **on sth** *We have an option on the house.* ◊ *He has promised me first option on his car* (= the opportunity to buy it

before anyone else). ◊ **~to do sth** *The property is for rent with an option to buy at any time.* ⊃ see also SHARE OPTION, STOCK OPTION **4** [C] (*computing*) one of the choices you can make when using a computer program: *Choose the 'Cut' option from the Edit menu.*
**IDM** **keep/leave your ˈoptions open** to avoid making a decision now so that you still have a choice in the future **a/an/the ˌsoft/ˌeasy ˈoption** (*often disapproving*) a choice that is thought to be easier because it involves less effort, difficulty, etc: *They are anxious that the new course should not be seen as a soft option.* ◊ *He decided to* **take the easy option** *and give them what they wanted.*
■ *verb* ~ **sth** to buy or sell the right to own or use sth at some time in the future: *The novel has been optioned for the screen by his production company.*

### SYNONYMS
**option**
choice • alternative • possibility
These are all words for sth that you choose to do in a particular situation.
**option** something that you can choose to have or do; the freedom to choose what you do: *As I see it, we have two options…* ◊ *Students have the option of studying abroad in their second year.* **NOTE** **Option** is also the word used in computing for one of the choices you can make when using a computer program: *Choose the 'Cut' option from the Edit menu.*
**choice** the freedom to choose what you do; something that you can choose to have or do: *If I had the choice, I would stop working tomorrow.* ◊ *There is a wide range of choices open to you.*
**alternative** something that you can choose to have or do out of two or more possibilities: *You can be paid in cash weekly or by cheque monthly: those are the two alternatives.*
**OPTION, CHOICE OR ALTERNATIVE?**
**Choice** is slightly less formal than **option** and **alternative** is slightly more formal. **Choice** is most often used for 'the freedom to choose', although you can sometimes also use **option** (but not usually **alternative**): *If I had the choice/option, I would…* ◊ *If I had the alternative, I would…* ◊ *parental choice in education* ◊ *parental option/alternative in education*. Things that you can choose are **options**, **choices** or **alternatives**. However, **alternative** is more frequently used to talk about choosing between two things rather than several.
**possibility** one of the different things that you can do in a particular situation: *We need to explore a wide range of possibilities.* ◊ *The possibilities are endless.* **NOTE** **Possibility** can be used in a similar way to **option**, **choice** and **alternative**, but the emphasis here is less on the need to make a choice, and more on what is available.
**PATTERNS**
- **with/without** the option/choice/possibility of sth
- a(n) **good/acceptable/reasonable/possible** option/choice/alternative
- the **only** option/choice/alternative/possibility **open to** sb
- to **have** a/an/the option/choice **of doing sth**
- to **have no** option/choice/alternative **but to** do sth
- a **number/range** of options/choices/alternatives/possibilities

**opˑtionˑal** /ˈɒpʃənl; *NAmE* ˈɑːp-/ *adj.* that you can choose to do or have if you want to: *Certain courses are compulsory; others are optional.* ◊ *This model comes with a number of* ***optional extras*** (= things you can choose to have but which you will have to pay extra for).
**opˑtomˑetrist** /ɒpˈtɒmətrɪst; *NAmE* ɑːpˈtɑːm-/ (*BrE also* **opˌtician**, **ophˌthalmic opˈtician**) *noun* a person whose job is to examine people's eyes and to recommend and sell glasses
**opˑtomˑetry** /ɒpˈtɒmətri; *NAmE* ɑːpˈtɑːm-/ *noun* [U] the job of measuring how well people can see and checking their eyes for disease
**ˈopt-out** *noun* (often used as an adjective) **1** (in Britain) the action of a school or hospital that decides to manage its

1091

# orange

own money and is therefore no longer controlled by a LOCAL AUTHORITY or similar organization **2** the act of choosing not to be involved in an agreement: *an opt-out clause* ◊ *MPs hoped to reverse Britain's opt-out from the treaty.*
**opuˑlent** /ˈɒpjələnt; *NAmE* ˈɑːp-/ *adj.* (*formal*) **1** made or decorated using expensive materials **SYN** **luxurious 2** (of people) extremely rich **SYN** **wealthy** ▸ **opuˑlence** /-ləns/ *noun* [U] **opuˑlentˑly** *adv.*
**opus** /ˈəʊpəs; *NAmE* ˈoʊ-/ *noun* (*pl.* **opera** /ˈɒpərə; *NAmE* ˈɑːp-/) [*usually sing.*] **1** (*abbr.* **op.**) a piece of music written by a famous COMPOSER and usually followed by a number that shows when it was written: *Beethoven's Opus 18* **2** (*formal*) an important piece of literature, etc., especially one that is on a large scale **SYN** **work** ⊃ see also MAGNUM OPUS

**or** 🛈 **A1** /ɔː(r)/ *conj.* **1** 🛈 **A1** used to introduce another possibility: *Is your sister older or younger than you?* ◊ *Are you coming or not?* ◊ *Is it a boy or a girl?* **HELP** In a list, **or** is usually only used before the last item: *It can be black, white or grey.* ⊃ compare EITHER … OR … ⊃ HOMOPHONES at OAR **2** 🛈 **A1** used in negative sentences when mentioning two or more things: *He can't read or write.* ◊ *There are people without homes, jobs or family.* ⊃ compare NEITHER … NOR … **3** 🛈 **A1** (*also* **or else**) used to warn or advise sb that sth bad could happen; OTHERWISE: *Turn the heat down or it'll burn.* **4** 🛈 **A1** used between two numbers to show approximately how many: *There were six or seven of us there.* **5** 🛈 **A1** used to introduce a word or phrase that explains or means the same as another: *geology, or the science of the earth's crust* ◊ *It weighs a kilo, or just over two pounds.* **6** 🛈 **A1** used to say why sth must be true: *He must like her, or he wouldn't keep calling her.* **7** 🛈 **A1** used to introduce a different or opposite idea: *He was lying—or was he?*
**IDM** **or so** 🛈 **B2** about; approximately: *It'll cost €100 or so.* **or ˌsomebody/ˌsomething/ˌsomewhere** 🛈 **B1** | **ˌsomebody/ˌsomething/ˌsomewhere or ˈother** 🛈 **B1** (*informal*) used when you are not exactly sure about a person, thing or place: *He's a factory supervisor or something.* ◊ *'Who said so?' 'Oh, somebody or other. I can't remember who it was.'*

**-or** /ə(r)/ *suffix* (in nouns) a person or thing that performs the action: *actor* ⊃ compare -EE, -ER
**orˑacle** /ˈɒrəkl; *NAmE* ˈɔːr-/ *noun* **1** (in ancient Greece) a place where people could go to ask the gods for advice or information about the future; the priest or PRIESTESS through whom the gods were thought to give their message: *They consulted the oracle at Delphi.* **2** (in ancient Greece) the advice or information that the gods gave, which often had a hidden meaning **3** [*usually sing.*] (*often humorous*) a person or book that gives valuable advice or information: *My sister's the oracle on investment matters.*
**orˑacuˑlar** /əˈrækjələ(r)/ *adj.* (*formal or humorous*) of or like an oracle; with a hidden meaning
**oral** 🛈+ **C1** /ˈɔːrəl/ *adj., noun*
■ *adj.* **1** 🛈+ **C1** [*usually before noun*] spoken rather than written: *a test of both oral and written French* ◊ *oral evidence* ⊃ SYNONYMS at SPOKEN ⊃ compare VERBAL **2** [*only before noun*] connected with the mouth: *oral hygiene* ◊ *oral sex* (= using the mouth to STIMULATE sb's sex organs) **3** (*phonetics*) (of a speech sound) produced by allowing air to flow through the mouth but not the nose ⊃ compare NASAL ▸ **orˑalˑly** /-rəli/ *adv.*: *Answers can be written or presented orally on tape.* ◊ *Not to be taken orally* (= a warning on some medicines to show that they must not be swallowed).
■ *noun* **1** (*especially BrE*) a spoken exam, especially in a foreign language: *a French oral* ◊ *He failed the oral.* **2** (*NAmE*) a spoken exam in a university ⊃ WORDFINDER NOTE at EXAM
**ˌoral ˈhistory** *noun* [U] the collection and study of historical information using sound recordings of interviews with people who remember past events
**orˑange** 🛈 **A1** /ˈɒrɪndʒ; *NAmE* ˈɔːr-/ *noun, adj.*
■ *noun* [C, U] **1** 🛈 **A1** a round CITRUS fruit with thick skin of a colour between red and yellow and a lot of sweet juice: *orange peel/zest/rind* ◊ *an orange tree* ◊ *freshly squeezed orange juice* ◊ *orange groves* (= groups of orange trees) ◊ *orange blossom* ⊃ VISUAL VOCAB page V4 ⊃ see also BLOOD ORANGE, NAVEL ORANGE **2** 🛈 **A1** (*BrE*) orange juice, or a

# Orangeman

drink made from or tasting of oranges: *Would you like some orange?* ◊ *A vodka and orange, please.* **3** a bright colour between red and yellow IDM see APPLE
- **adj. 1** between red and yellow in colour: *yellow and orange flames* ◊ *Tom was wearing a bright orange jacket.* **2 Orange** related to or belonging to a Protestant political group which believes that Northern Ireland should remain part of the UK: *an Orange march*

**Or·ange·man** /ˈɒrɪndʒmən; *NAmE* ˈɔːr-/ *noun* (pl. **-men** /-mən/) a member of the Orange Order, a Protestant political organization that wants Northern Ireland to remain part of the United Kingdom

**or·an·gery** /ˈɒrɪndʒəri; *NAmE* ˈɔːr-/ *noun* (pl. **-ies**) a glass building where orange trees are grown

**orang·utan** /əˈræŋətæn/ *noun* a large APE (= an animal like a large monkey with no tail) with long arms and red-brown hair, that lives in Borneo and Sumatra ORIGIN From Malay *orang utan / hutan*, meaning 'person of the forest'.

**ora·tion** /ɔːˈreɪʃn/ *noun* (*formal*) a formal speech made on a public occasion, especially as part of a ceremony

**ora·tor** /ˈɒrətə(r); *NAmE* ˈɔːr-/ *noun* (*formal*) a person who makes formal speeches in public or is good at public speaking: *a fine political orator*

**ora·tor·ical** /ˌɒrəˈtɒrɪkl; *NAmE* ˌɔːrəˈtɔːr-/ *adj.* (*formal, sometimes disapproving*) connected with the art of public speaking: *oratorical skills*

**ora·torio** /ˌɒrəˈtɔːriəʊ; *NAmE* ˌɔːr-/ *noun* (pl. **-os**) a long piece of music for singers and an ORCHESTRA, usually based on a story from the Bible ⊃ compare CANTATA

**ora·tory** /ˈɒrətri; *NAmE* ˈɔːrətɔːri/ *noun* (pl. **-ies**) **1** [U] the skill of making powerful and effective speeches in public SYN **rhetoric 2** [C] a room or small building that is used for private prayer or WORSHIP

**orb** /ɔːb; *NAmE* ɔːrb/ *noun* **1** (*literary*) an object like a ball in shape, especially the sun or moon **2** a gold ball with a cross on top, carried by a king or queen at formal ceremonies as a symbol of power ⊃ compare SCEPTRE

**orbit**

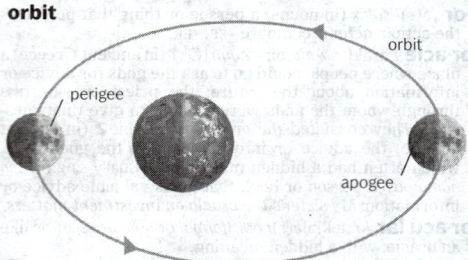

**orbit** /ˈɔːbɪt; *NAmE* ˈɔːrb-/ *noun, verb*
- *noun* **1** [C, U] a curved path followed by a planet or an object as it moves around another planet, star, moon, etc.: *the earth's orbit around the sun* ◊ *in~ a space station in orbit around the moon* ◊ *into~ A new satellite has been put into orbit around the earth.* ⊃ WORDFINDER NOTE at SPACE **2** [sing.] an area that a particular person, organization, etc. deals with or is able to influence: **within sb's~** *to come/fall/be within sb's orbit*
- *verb* [T, I] to move in an orbit (= a curved path) around a much larger object, especially a planet, star, etc.: *Stars near the edge of the galaxy orbit more slowly.* ◊ *~ (around) sth The earth takes a year to orbit the sun.*

**or·bit·al** /ˈɔːbɪtl; *NAmE* ˈɔːrb-/ *adj., noun*
- *adj.* [only before noun] **1** connected with the orbit of a planet or object in space **2** (*BrE*) (of a road) built around the edge of a town or city to reduce the amount of traffic travelling through the centre
- *noun* (*BrE*) a very large RING ROAD, especially if it is a MOTORWAY: *the M25 London orbital*

**or·bit·er** /ˈɔːbɪtə(r); *NAmE* ˈɔːrb-/ *noun* a SPACECRAFT designed to move around a planet or moon rather than to land on it

**orca** /ˈɔːkə; *NAmE* ˈɔːrkə/ (also **killer whale**) *noun* a black and white WHALE that eats meat

**Or·ca·dian** /ɔːˈkeɪdiən; *NAmE* ɔːrˈk-/ *noun* a person from the islands of Orkney in Scotland ▶ **Or·ca·dian** *adj.*

**orch·ard** /ˈɔːtʃəd; *NAmE* ˈɔːrtʃərd/ *noun* a piece of land, normally separated from the surrounding area, in which fruit trees are grown

**or·ches·tra** /ˈɔːkɪstrə; *NAmE* ˈɔːrk-/ *noun* **1** [C + sing./pl. v.] a large group of people who play various musical instruments together, led by a CONDUCTOR: *She plays the flute in the school orchestra.* ◊ *the Scottish Symphony Orchestra* ⊃ see also CHAMBER ORCHESTRA, SYMPHONY ORCHESTRA **2 the orchestra** [sing.] (*NAmE*) (*BrE* **the ˈorchestra stalls, the stalls**) the seats that are nearest to the stage in a theatre

**or·ches·tral** /ɔːˈkestrəl; *NAmE* ɔːrˈk-/ *adj.* connected with an orchestra: *orchestral music*

**ˈorchestra pit** (also **pit**) *noun* the place in a theatre just in front of the stage where the orchestra sits and plays for an OPERA, a BALLET, etc. ⊃ WORDFINDER NOTE at OPERA

**or·ches·trate** /ˈɔːkɪstreɪt; *NAmE* ˈɔːrk-/ *verb* **1 ~ sth** to arrange a piece of music in parts so that it can be played by an orchestra **2 ~ sth** to organize a complicated plan or event very carefully or secretly SYN **stage-manage**: *a carefully orchestrated publicity campaign* ▶ **or·ches·tra·tion** /ˌɔːkɪˈstreɪʃn; *NAmE* ˌɔːrk-/ *noun* [C, U]

**or·chid** /ˈɔːkɪd; *NAmE* ˈɔːrk-/ *noun* a plant with brightly coloured flowers of unusual shapes. There are many different types of orchid and some of them are very rare. ⊃ VISUAL VOCAB page V7

**or·dain** /ɔːˈdeɪn; *NAmE* ɔːrˈd-/ *verb* **1 ~ sb | ~ sb (as) sth** to make sb a priest, minister or RABBI: *He was ordained (as) a priest last year.* ⊃ see also ORDINATION **2 ~ sth | ~ that …** (*formal*) (of God, the law or FATE) to order or command sth; to decide sth in advance: *Fate had ordained that they would never meet again.*

**or·deal** /ɔːˈdiːl; ˈɔːdiːl; *NAmE* ɔːrˈdiːl/ *noun* [usually sing.] a difficult or unpleasant experience: *They had survived a terrifying ordeal.* ◊ *The interview was less of an ordeal than she'd expected.* ◊ *~ of (doing) sth They are to be spared the ordeal of giving evidence in court.*

**order** /ˈɔːdə(r); *NAmE* ˈɔːrd-/ *noun, verb*
- *noun*
• ARRANGEMENT **1** [U, C] the way in which people or things are placed or arranged in relation to each other: **in …~** *The names are listed in alphabetical order.* ◊ *The winning scores, in reverse order, are as follows.* ◊ **in the/a …~** *Put the words in the correct order.* ◊ *Let's take the problems in a different order.* ◊ **in~ of sth** *arranged in order of preference/importance/priority* ◊ **out of~** *Scenes in films are often shot out of order.* ◊ *Make sure you get the chronological order right.* ⊃ see also RUNNING ORDER **2** [U] the state of being carefully and neatly arranged: **in / into~** *It was time she put her life in order.* ◊ *The house had been kept in good order.* ◊ *Get your ideas into some sort of order before beginning to write.* ◊ *It is one of the functions of art to bring order out of chaos.* OPP **disorder**
• CONTROLLED STATE **3** [U] the state that exists when people obey laws, rules or authority: *to maintain/restore order* ◊ **in~** *Some teachers find it difficult to keep their classes in order.* ◊ *The film was banned as a potential threat to public order.* ⊃ compare DISORDER ⊃ see also LAW AND ORDER at LAW, POINT OF ORDER
• FOOD/DRINKS **4** [C] a request for food or drinks in a restaurant, bar, etc.: *The waiter came to take their orders.* ◊ *a food/drink(s) order* ◊ **~ for sth** *an order for steak and fries* ⊃ see also LAST ORDERS, SIDE ORDER ⊃ WORDFINDER NOTE at RESTAURANT **5** [C] food or drinks that you ask for in a restaurant, bar, etc.: *The waiter brought my order.*
• GOODS **6** [C, U] a request to make or supply goods: **~ for sth** *I would like to place an order for ten copies of this book.* ◊ *an order form* ◊ **on~** *The machine parts are still on order* (= they have been ordered but have not yet been received). ◊ **to~** *These items can be made to order* (= produced especially for a particular customer). ⊃ see also MAIL ORDER, ORDER BOOK, PRE-ORDER *noun* **7** [C] goods supplied in response to a particular order that sb has placed: *The stationery order has arrived.*

- **INSTRUCTIONS** **8** [C] something that sb is told to do by sb in authority: *Dogs can be trained to* **obey orders**. ◇ *to* **follow/disobey/defy orders** ◇ **~from sb** *She takes orders only from the president.* ◇ **~ to do sth** *The general gave the order to advance.* ◇ **~ for sb/sth to do sth** *He issued orders for the work to begin.* ◇ **under orders (to do sth)** *I'm under orders not to let anyone in.* ◇ **by (the) ~ of sb/sth** *Interest rates can be controlled by order of the central bank.* ◇ (*informal*) *No sugar for me—doctor's orders.* ⇒ see also COMMUNITY ORDER, COURT ORDER, EXCLUSION ORDER, EXECUTIVE ORDER, GAGGING ORDER, PRESERVATION ORDER, PROTECTION ORDER, RESTRAINING ORDER, SUPERVISION ORDER
- **MONEY** **9** [C] a formal written instruction for sb to be paid money or to do sth ⇒ see also BANKER'S ORDER, COURT ORDER, MONEY ORDER, POSTAL ORDER, STANDING ORDER
- **SYSTEM** **10** [C, usually sing.] (*formal*) the way that a society, the world, etc. is arranged, with its system of rules and customs: *a change in the political and* **social order** ◇ *the natural order of things* ◇ *He was seen as a threat to the* **established order**. ◇ *A new* **world order** *seems to be emerging.*
- **SOCIAL CLASS** **11** [C, usually pl.] (*disapproving or humorous*) a social class: *the lower orders*
- **BIOLOGY** **12** [C] a group into which animals, plants, etc. that have similar characteristics are divided, smaller than a CLASS and larger than a FAMILY: *the order of primates* ⇒ compare GENUS ⇒ WORDFINDER NOTE at BREED ⇒ VISUAL VOCAB page V3
- **RELIGIOUS COMMUNITY** **13** [C + sing./pl. v.] a group of people living in a religious community, especially MONKS or NUNS: *religious orders* ◇ *the Benedictine order*
- **SPECIAL HONOUR** **14** [C + sing./pl. v.] a group of people who have been given a special honour by a queen, king, president, etc: *The Order of the Garter is an ancient order of chivalry.* **15** [C] a BADGE or RIBBON worn by members of an order who have been given a special honour
- **SECRET SOCIETY** **16** [C + sing./pl. v.] a secret society whose members meet for special ceremonies: *the Ancient Order of Druids*

**IDM** **be in/take (holy) 'orders** to be/become a priest **call/bring sb/sth to 'order** to order sb to obey the formal rules of a meeting, to start a formal meeting **in 'order 1** (of an official document) that can be used because it is all correct and legal **SYN** **valid**: *Is your work permit in order?* **2** (*formal*) as it should be: *Is everything in order, sir?* **3** if sth is **in order**, it is a suitable thing to do or say on a particular occasion: *I think a drink would be in order.* **in 'order (to do sth)** (*formal*) allowed according to the rules of a meeting, etc: *Is it in order to speak now?* **in order that** (*formal*) so that sth can happen: *All those concerned must work together in order that agreement can be reached on this issue.* **in order to do sth** [B1] with the purpose or intention of doing or achieving sth: *She arrived early in order to get a good seat.* ◇ *In order to get a complete picture, further information is needed.* ⇒ LANGUAGE BANK at PROCESS¹ **in running/working 'order** (especially of machines) working well: *The engine is now in perfect working order.* **of a high order | of the highest/first order** of a high quality or degree; of the highest quality or greatest degree: *The job requires diplomatic skills of a high order.* ◇ *She was a snob of the first order.* **of/in the order of sth** (*BrE*) (*NAmE* **on the order of**) (*formal*) about sth; approximately sth: *She earns something in the order of £80 000 a year.* **the order of the 'day** common, popular or suitable at a particular time or for a particular occasion: *Pessimism seems to be the order of the day.* **Order! Order!** used by the person in charge of a formal meeting or debate to remind people to obey the rules of the meeting **out of 'order 1** (of a machine, etc.) not working correctly: *The phone is out of order.* **2** not arranged correctly or neatly: *I checked the files and some of the papers were out of order.* **3** (*BrE*) (*also* **out of 'line** *BrE and NAmE*) (*informal*) behaving in a way that is not acceptable or right: *You were well out of order taking it without asking.* **4** (*formal*) not allowed by the rules of a formal meeting or debate: *His objection was ruled out of order.* ⇒ more at CALL v., HOUSE n., LAW, MARCH v., PECK v., SHORT adj., STARTER, TALL

■ *verb*
- **FOOD/DRINK** **1** [B1] [T, I] to ask for sth to eat or drink in a restaurant, bar, etc: *~(sth) I ordered a beer and a sandwich.* ◇ *Have you ordered yet?* ◇ *~sb/yourself sth He ordered himself a double whisky.* ◇ *~(sth) for sb Will you order for me while I make a phone call?*
- **GOODS/SERVICE** **2** [A2] [T, I] to ask for goods to be made or supplied; to ask for a service to be provided: *~(sth) To order a copy of the report, visit our website.* ◇ *You will be given a reference number when you order.* ◇ *~(sth) from sb/sth | ~sth from sb/sth These boots can be ordered direct from the manufacturer.* ◇ *~sb/yourself sth Shall I order you a taxi?* ⇒ see also PRE-ORDER *verb*
- **GIVE INSTRUCTIONS** **3** [T] to use your position of authority to tell sb to do sth or say that sth must happen: *~sb to do sth The officer ordered them to fire.* ◇ *The company was ordered to pay compensation to its former employees.* ◇ *~sb + adv./prep. They were ordered out of the class for fighting.* ◇ *~sth The government has ordered an investigation into the accident.* ◇ *Your doctor may order an MRI scan.* ◇ *~that ... The court ordered that a psychological report be prepared.* ◇ *~(sb) + speech 'Sit down and be quiet,' she ordered.* ⇒ EXPRESS YOURSELF at TELL
- **ORGANIZE/ARRANGE** **4** [T] *~sth* to organize or arrange sth: *The list is ordered alphabetically.* ◇ *I need time to order my thoughts.* ⇒ see also ORDERED, DISORDERED **IDM** see DOCTOR *n*.

**PHR V** **order sb a'round** (*also* **order sb a'bout** especially in *BrE*) (*disapproving*) to keep telling sb what to do in a way that is annoying or unpleasant

> ▼ **SYNONYMS**
>
> **order**
>
> tell • instruct • direct • command
>
> These words all mean to use your position of authority to say to sb that they must do sth.
>
> **order** to use your position of authority to tell sb to do sth: *The company was ordered to pay compensation to its former employee.* ◇ *'Come here at once!' she ordered.*
>
> **tell** to say to sb that they must or should do sth: *He was told to sit down and wait.* ◇ *Don't tell me what to do!*
>
> **instruct** (*rather formal*) to tell sb to do sth, especially in a formal or official way: *The letter instructed him to report to headquarters immediately.*
>
> **direct** (*formal*) to give an official order: *The judge directed the jury to return a verdict of not guilty.*
>
> **command** to use your position of authority to tell sb to do sth: *He commanded his men to retreat.*
>
> ORDER OR COMMAND?
> - **Order** is a more general word than **command** and can be used about anyone in a position of authority, such as a parent, teacher or government telling sb to do sth. **Command** is slightly stronger than **order** and is the normal word to use about an army officer giving orders, or in any context where it is normal to give orders without any discussion about them. It is less likely to be used about a parent or teacher.
>
> PATTERNS
> - to order/tell/instruct/direct/command sb **to do sth**
> - to order/instruct/direct/command **that ...**
> - to **do** sth as ordered/told/instructed/directed/commanded

**'order book** *noun* a record kept by a business of the products it has agreed to supply to its customers, often used to show how well the business is doing: *We have a full order book for the coming year.*

**or·dered** /ˈɔːdəd; *NAmE* ˈɔːrdərd/ *adj.* [usually before noun] carefully arranged or organized **SYN** **orderly**: *an ordered existence* ◇ *a well-ordered society* **OPP** **disordered**

**'order form** *noun* a document filled in by customers when ordering goods

**or·der·ing** /ˈɔːdərɪŋ; *NAmE* ˈɔːrd-/ *noun* [C, U] the way in which sth is ordered or arranged; the act of putting sth into an order **SYN** **arrangement**: *Many possible orderings may exist.* ◇ *the successful ordering of complex data*

# orderly

**or·der·ly** /ˈɔːdəli; NAmE ˈɔːrdərli/ adj., noun
- *adj.* **1** arranged or organized in a neat, careful and logical way SYN **tidy**: *a calm and orderly life* ◇ *vegetables planted in orderly rows* **2** behaving well; peaceful: *an orderly demonstration* OPP **disorderly** ▸ **or·der·li·ness** *noun* [U]
- *noun* (pl. **-ies**) **1** a person who works in a hospital, usually doing jobs that do not need any special training **2** a soldier who does jobs that do not need any special training

**ˌorder of ˈmagnitude** *noun* (*mathematics*) a level in a system of ordering things by size or amount, where each level is higher by a FACTOR of ten: *The actual measurement is two orders of magnitude (= a hundred times) greater than we expected.* ◇ (*figurative*) *The problem is of the same order of magnitude for all concerned.*

**ˈOrder Paper** *noun* (*BrE*) a list of the subjects to be discussed by Parliament on a particular day

**or·din·al** /ˈɔːdɪnl; NAmE ˈɔːrdnəl/ (*also* **ˌordinal ˈnumber**) *noun* a number that refers to the position of sth in a series, for example 'first', 'second', etc. ⊃ compare CARDINAL ▸ **or·din·al** *adj.*

**or·din·ance** /ˈɔːdɪnəns; NAmE ˈɔːrd-/ *noun* [C, U] (*formal*) an order or a rule made by a government or sb in a position of authority

**or·din·and** /ˈɔːdɪnænd; NAmE ˈɔːrd-/ *noun* a person who is preparing to become a priest, minister or RABBI

**or·din·ar·ily** /ˈɔːdnrəli; NAmE ˌɔːrdnˈerəli/ *adv.* **1** in a normal way SYN **normally**: *To the untrained eye, the children were behaving ordinarily.* **2** used to say what normally happens in a particular situation, especially because sth different is happening this time SYN **usually**: *Ordinarily, she wouldn't have bothered arguing with him.* ◇ *We do not ordinarily carry out this type of work.*

**or·din·ary** /ˈɔːdnri; NAmE ˈɔːrdneri/ *adj.*
**1** [usually before noun] not unusual or different in any way: *an ordinary sort of day* ◇ *in the ordinary course of events* ◇ *ordinary people like you and me* ◇ *This was no ordinary meeting.* **2** (*disapproving*) having no unusual or interesting features: *The meal was very ordinary.* ⊃ compare EXTRAORDINARY ▸ **or·din·ari·ness** *noun* [U]
**IDM** **in the ordinary way** (*BrE*) used to say what normally happens in a particular situation: *In the ordinary way, she's not a nervous person.* **out of the ˈordinary** unusual or different: *I'm looking for something a little more out of the ordinary.*

**ˈordinary level** *noun* = O LEVEL

**ˌordinary ˈseaman** *noun* (*abbr.* **OS**) a sailor of the lowest rank in the British NAVY

**ˌordinary ˈshare** *noun* a fixed unit of a company's capital. People who own ordinary shares have voting rights in the company.

**or·din·ate** /ˈɔːdɪnət; NAmE ˈɔːrd-/ *noun* (*mathematics*) the COORDINATE that gives the distance along the VERTICAL AXIS

**or·din·ation** /ˌɔːdɪˈneɪʃn; NAmE ˌɔːrdnˈeɪ-/ *noun* [U, C] the act or ceremony of making sb a priest, minister or RABBI ⊃ see also ORDAIN

**ord·nance** /ˈɔːdnəns; NAmE ˈɔːrd-/ *noun* [U] **1** large guns on wheels SYN **artillery** **2** military supplies and materials: *an ordnance depot*

**ˌOrdnance ˈSurvey map** *noun* a very detailed map of an area of Britain or Ireland, prepared by an organization called the **Ordnance Survey**, which is supported by the government

**ore** /ɔː(r)/ *noun* [U, C] rock, earth, etc. from which metal can be obtained: *iron ore* ⊃ HOMOPHONES at OAR

**ore·gano** /ˌɒrɪˈɡɑːnəʊ; NAmE əˈreɡənəʊ/ *noun* [U] a plant with leaves that have a sweet smell and are used in cooking as a HERB ⊃ VISUAL VOCAB page V8

**organ** /ˈɔːɡən; NAmE ˈɔːrɡ-/ *noun* **1** a part of the body that has a particular purpose, such as the heart or the brain; part of a plant with a particular purpose: *the internal organs* ◇ *the sense organs (= the eyes, ears, nose, etc.)* ◇ *the sexual/reproductive organs* ◇ *an organ transplant/donor* ◇ *the vital organs (= the brain, heart, lungs, etc.)* ⊃ VISUAL VOCAB page V1 **2** (*especially humorous*) a PENIS: *the male organ* **3** (*also* **ˈpipe organ**) a large musical instrument with keys like a piano. Sounds are produced by air forced through pipes: *She plays the organ in church.* ◇ *organ music* ◇ compare HARMONIUM ⊃ see also HAMMOND ORGAN **4** a musical instrument similar to a pipe organ, but without pipes: *an electric organ* ⊃ see also BARREL ORGAN **5** (*formal*) an official organization that is part of a larger organization and has a special purpose: *the organs of government* **6** (*formal*) a newspaper or magazine that gives information about a particular group or organization; a means of communicating the views of a particular group: *The People's Daily is the official organ of the Chinese Communist Party.*

**ˈorgan grinder** *noun* a person who plays a BARREL ORGAN (= a large musical instrument played by turning a handle): (*humorous*) *He's only the organ grinder's monkey (= an unimportant person who does what he is told to do).*

**or·gan·ic** /ɔːˈɡænɪk; NAmE ɔːrˈɡ-/ *adj.* [usually before noun] **1** (of food, farming methods, etc.) produced or practised without using artificial chemicals: *organic cheese/vegetables/wine, etc.* ◇ *an organic farmer/gardener* ◇ *organic farming/horticulture* ⊃ WORDFINDER NOTE at CROP **2** produced by or from living things: *Improve the soil by adding organic matter.* OPP **inorganic** **3** (*chemistry*) relating to chemical COMPOUNDS that contain CARBON and mainly or ultimately come from living things: *organic compounds* OPP **inorganic** **4** (*specialist*) connected with the organs of the body: *organic disease* **5** (*formal*) consisting of different parts that are all connected to each other: *the view of society as an organic whole* **6** (*formal*) happening in a slow and natural way, rather than suddenly: *the organic growth of foreign markets* ▸ **or·gan·ic·al·ly** /-kli/ *adv.*: *organically grown fruit* ◇ *The cardboard disintegrates organically.* ◇ *Doctors could find nothing organically wrong with her.* ◇ *The organization should be allowed to develop organically.*

**orˌganic ˈchemistry** *noun* [U] the branch of chemistry that deals with substances that contain CARBON ⊃ compare INORGANIC CHEMISTRY

**or·gan·ism** /ˈɔːɡənɪzəm; NAmE ˈɔːrɡ-/ *noun* **1** (*biology or formal*) a living thing, especially one that is extremely small ⊃ see also MICROORGANISM ⊃ WORDFINDER NOTE at BIOLOGY **2** (*formal*) a system consisting of parts that depend on each other: *the social organism (= society)*

**or·gan·ist** /ˈɔːɡənɪst; NAmE ˈɔːrɡ-/ *noun* a person who plays the organ

**or·gan·iza·tion** /ˌɔːɡənaɪˈzeɪʃn; NAmE ˌɔːrɡənəˈz-/ *noun* **1** [C] a group of people who form a business, club, etc. together in order to achieve a particular aim: *He's the president of a large international organization.* ◇ *a voluntary/non-profit/non-governmental organization* ◇ *Sarah joined a student organization.* ◇ *to found/form/establish an organization* ◇ *the World Health Organization* **2** [U] the act of making arrangements or preparations for sth SYN **planning**: *I leave most of the organization of these conferences to my assistant.* **3** [U] the way in which the different parts of sth are arranged SYN **structure**: *The report studies the organization of labour within the company.* ◇ *They experimented with new forms of social organization.* **4** [U] the quality of being arranged in a neat, careful and logical way: *She is highly intelligent but her work lacks organization.*

**or·gan·iza·tion·al** /ˌɔːɡənaɪˈzeɪʃənl; NAmE ˌɔːrɡənəˈz-/ *adj.* (*BrE also* **-isa·tion·al**) **1** connected with the way in which the different parts of sth are arranged; connected with an organization SYN **structural**: *organizational changes within the party* **2** having or showing the ability to arrange or organize things well: *Candidates will require good organizational skills.* ◇ *The occasion was an organizational triumph.* ▸ **or·gan·iza·tion·al·ly** /-nəli/ (*BrE also* **-isa·tion·al·ly**) *adv.*

**or·gan·ize** /ˈɔːɡənaɪz; NAmE ˈɔːrɡ-/ *verb* **1** [T] ~ sth to make all the arrangements for sth to happen or be provided: *He helped to organize various events.* ◇ *to organize a conference/meeting* ◇ *I'll invite people if you can organize food and drinks.*

[T] ~ sth to arrange sth or the parts of sth into a particular order or structure: *Modern computers can organize large amounts of data very quickly.* ◊ *You should try and organize your time better.* ◊ ~ **sth + adv./prep.** *The complex is organized around a central courtyard.* **3** [T] ~ **yourself/sb** to plan your/sb's work and activities in an efficient way: *I'm sure you don't need me to organize you.* **4** [T, I] ~ **(sb/yourself) (into sth)** to form a group of people with a shared aim, especially a union or political party: *the right of workers to organize themselves into unions* ⊃ see also DISORGANIZED

**or·gan·ized** ❶ B1 (*BrE also* **-ised**) /ˈɔːɡənaɪzd; *NAmE* ˈɔːrɡ-/ *adj.* **1** B1 [only before noun] involving large numbers of people who work together to do sth in a way that has been carefully planned: *an organized body of workers* ◊ *organized religion* (= traditional religion followed by large numbers of people who obey a fixed set of rules) ◊ *organized crime* (= committed by professional criminals working in large groups) ⊃ compare UNORGANIZED **2** B1 arranged or planned well or in the way mentioned: *a carefully organized campaign* ◊ *a well-organized office* ⊃ compare DISORGANIZED **3** B1 (of a person) able to plan your work, life, etc. well and in an efficient way: *a very organized person* ◊ *Isn't it time you started to get organized?* ⊃ compare DISORGANIZED

**or·gan·iz·er** ❶ B1 (*BrE also* **-iser**) /ˈɔːɡənaɪzə(r); *NAmE* ˈɔːrɡ-/ *noun* a person who makes the arrangements for sth: *the organizers of the festival* ◊ *an event organizer* ⊃ see also COMMUNITY ORGANIZER

**or·gano·phos·phate** /ˌɔːɡænəʊˈfɒsfeɪt; *NAmE* ˌɔːrɡænoʊˈfɑːs-/ *noun* a chemical containing CARBON and PHOSPHORUS, used for example in farming to kill insects

**or·ganza** /ɔːˈɡænzə; *NAmE* ɔːrˈɡ-/ *noun* [U] a type of thin stiff cloth that you can see through, used for making formal dresses

**or·gasm** /ˈɔːɡæzəm; *NAmE* ˈɔːrɡ-/ *noun* [U, C] the moment during sexual activity when feelings of sexual pleasure are at their strongest: *to achieve/reach orgasm* ◊ *to have an orgasm*

**or·gas·mic** /ɔːˈɡæzmɪk; *NAmE* ɔːrˈɡ-/ *adj.* [only before noun] connected with or like an orgasm

**or·gi·as·tic** /ˌɔːdʒiˈæstɪk; *NAmE* ˌɔːrdʒ-/ *adj.* [usually before noun] (*formal*) typical of an orgy

**orgy** /ˈɔːdʒi; *NAmE* ˈɔːrdʒi/ *noun* (*pl.* **-ies**) **1** a party at which there is a lot of eating, drinking and sexual activity: *a drunken orgy* **2** ~ **(of sth)** (*disapproving*) an extreme amount of a particular activity: *The rebels went on an orgy of killing.*

**Ori·ent** /ˈɔːriənt/ **the Orient** *noun* [sing.] (*old-fashioned, literary*) the eastern part of the world, especially China and Japan ⊃ compare OCCIDENT

**ori·ent** ❿ /ˈɔːriənt/ (*also* **orien·tate**) *verb* **1** [usually passive] ~ **sb/sth (to/towards sb/sth)** to direct sb/sth towards sth; to make or adapt sb/sth for a particular purpose: *Our students are oriented towards science subjects.* ◊ *policies oriented to the needs of working mothers* ◊ *We run a commercially oriented operation.* ◊ *Neither of them is politically oriented* (= interested in politics). **2** ~ **yourself** to find your position in relation to everything that is around or near you: *The mountaineers found it hard to orient themselves in the fog.* **3** ~ **yourself** to make yourself familiar with a new situation: *It took him some time to orient himself in his new school.* ⊃ compare DISORIENTATE

**orien·tal** /ˌɔːriˈentl/ *adj.* connected with or typical of the eastern part of the world, especially China and Japan, and the people who live there: *oriental languages*

**Orien·tal** /ˌɔːriˈentl/ *noun* (*old-fashioned, often offensive*) a person from China, Japan or other countries in East Asia

**orien·tal·ist** /ˌɔːriˈentəlɪst/ *noun* a person who studies the languages, arts, etc. of ORIENTAL countries

**orien·tate** /ˈɔːriəntent/ *verb* = ORIENT

**orien·ta·tion** ❶ /ˌɔːriənˈteɪʃn/ *noun* **1** ❿ [U, C] a person's basic beliefs or feelings about a particular subject: *religious/political orientation* ◊ *a person's sexual orientation* (= whether they are attracted to men, women or both) **2** ❿ [U, C] the type of aims or interests that a person or an organization has; the act of directing your aims towards a particular thing: *The course is essentially theoretical in orientation.* ◊ ~ **to/towards sth** *Companies have been forced into a greater orientation to the market.* **3** ❿ [U] training or information that you are given before starting a new job, course, etc: *an orientation session/program/course* **4** [C] (*specialist*) the direction in which an object faces: *The orientation of the planet's orbit is changing continuously.*

**-oriented** /ˈɔːrientɪd/ (*also* **-orientated** /ˈɔːrienteɪtɪd/) *combining form* directed towards sth or made or adapted for a particular purpose: *long-term oriented organizations* ◊ *family-orientated events*

**orien·teer·ing** /ˌɔːriənˈtɪərɪŋ; *NAmE* -ˈtɪr-/ *noun* [U] the sport of following a route across country on foot, as quickly as possible, using a map and COMPASS

**ori·fice** /ˈɒrɪfɪs; *NAmE* ˈɔːr-/ *noun* (*formal or humorous*) a hole or opening, especially one in the body: *the nasal orifice*

**ori·gami** /ˌɒrɪˈɡɑːmi; *NAmE* ˌɔːr-/ *noun* [U] the Japanese art of folding paper into attractive shapes

**ori·gin** ❶ B2 ⓞ /ˈɒrɪdʒɪn; *NAmE* ˈɔːr-/ *noun* [C, U] (*also* **origins** [pl.]) **1** ❿ B2 the point from which sth starts; the cause of sth: ~ **of sth** *the origins of life on earth* ◊ **in** ~ *Most coughs are viral in origin* (= caused by a virus). ◊ **of** ... *a letter of doubtful origin* ◊ *This particular custom has its origins in Wales.* **2** ❿ B2 a person's social and family background: *She has risen from humble origins to immense wealth.* ◊ **of** ... *people of German origin* ◊ *children of various ethnic origins* ◊ **of** ~ *a person's country of origin* (= where they were born) ◊ **by** ~ *He is a Londoner by origin.*

**ori·gin·al** ❶ A2 Ⓦ /əˈrɪdʒənl/ *adj., noun*

■ *adj.* **1** A2 [only before noun] existing at the beginning of a particular period, process or activity: *The room still has many of its original features.* ◊ *I think you should go back to your original plan.* **2** B1 new and interesting in a way that is different from anything that has existed before; able to produce new and interesting ideas: *an original idea* ◊ *That's not a very original suggestion.* ◊ *an original thinker* **3** B1 [usually before noun] painted, written, etc. by the artist rather than copied: *an original painting by local artist Graham Tovey* ◊ *The original manuscript has been lost.* ◊ *Only original documents* (= not photocopies) *will be accepted as proof of status.*

■ *noun* **1** B1 a document, work of art, etc. produced for the first time, from which copies are later made: *This painting is a copy; the original is in Madrid.* ◊ *Send out the photocopies and keep the original.* **2** (*formal*) a person who thinks, behaves, dresses, etc. in an unusual way
IDM **in the oˈriginal** in the language in which a book, etc. was first written, before being translated: *I studied Italian so that I would be able to read Dante in the original.*

**ori·gin·al·ity** /əˌrɪdʒəˈnæləti/ *noun* [U] the quality of being new and interesting in a way that is different from anything that has existed before: *This latest collection lacks style and originality.*

**ori·gin·al·ly** ❶ B1 Ⓦ /əˈrɪdʒənəli/ *adv.* used to describe the situation that existed at the beginning of a particular period or activity, especially before sth was changed: *The school was originally very small.* ◊ *Originally, we had intended to go to Italy, but then we won the trip to Greece.* ◊ *Laib originally planned to be a doctor.*

**oˌriginal ˈsin** *noun* [U] (in Christianity) the fact of evil that is believed to be present in everyone from birth

**ori·gin·ate** B2 Ⓦ /əˈrɪdʒɪneɪt/ *verb* (*formal*) **1** B2 C1 [I] (+ *adv./prep.*) to happen or appear for the first time in a particular place or situation: *The disease is thought to have originated in the tropics.* **2** [T] ~ **sth** to create sth new: *Locke originated this theory in the 17th century.* **3** [I] to start in a particular place: ~ **in** ... *His flight originated in Japan.* ◊ **from/out of** ... *Flights originating out of Toronto should reach Edmonton without much problem.* ◊ ~ **at** ... *28 trains now originate and terminate at Tambaram.* ◊ ~ **from** ... *The call had originated from Jamaica/a cell phone.* ▶ **ori·gin·ator** *noun*

**ori·gin·ation** /əˌrɪdʒɪˈneɪʃn/ *noun* [U] (*formal*) the beginning or creation of sth: *Content providers can control the path their content takes from the point of origination to the end user.*

**ori·ole** /ˈɔːriəʊl/ *noun* **1** a North American bird: the male is black and orange and the female is yellow-green **2** a European bird, the male of which is bright yellow with black wings

**Oriya** /ɒˈriːjə; *NAmE* ɔːˈr-/ *noun* [U] a language spoken in Orissa in eastern India

**or·na·ment** *noun*, *verb*
- *noun* /ˈɔːnəmənt; *NAmE* ˈɔːrn-/ **1** [C] (*especially BrE*) an object that is used as decoration in a room, garden, etc. rather than for a particular purpose: *a china/glass/silver ornament* ◊ (*BrE*, *NAmE*) *Christmas tree ornaments* **2** [C] (*formal*) an object that is worn as jewellery **3** [U] (*formal*) the use of objects, designs, etc. as decoration: *The clock is simply for ornament; it doesn't work any more.* **4** ~ **to sth** (*formal*) a person or thing whose good qualities improve sth: *The building is an ornament to the city.* **5** **ornaments** [pl.] (*music*) features that are added when playing individual notes to make them more beautiful or interesting
- *verb* /ˈɔːnəment; *NAmE* ˈɔːrn-/ [usually passive] ~ **sth** (*formal*) to add decoration to sth **SYN** **decorate**: *a room richly ornamented with carving*

**or·na·men·tal** /ˌɔːnəˈmentl; *NAmE* ˌɔːrn-/ *adj.* used as decoration rather than for a practical purpose **SYN** **decorative**: *an ornamental fountain* ◊ *The chimney pots are purely ornamental.*

**or·na·men·ta·tion** /ˌɔːnəmenˈteɪʃn; *NAmE* ˌɔːrn-/ *noun* [U] the use of objects, designs, etc. to decorate sth

**or·nate** /ɔːˈneɪt; *NAmE* ɔːrˈn-/ *adj.* covered with a lot of decoration, especially when this involves very small or complicated designs: *a mirror in an ornate gold frame* ▶ **or·nate·ly** *adv.*: *ornately carved chairs*

**or·nery** /ˈɔːnəri; *NAmE* ˈɔːrn-/ *adj.* (*NAmE*, *informal*) easily annoyed and difficult to deal with

**or·ni·tholo·gist** /ˌɔːnɪˈθɒlədʒɪst; *NAmE* ˌɔːrnɪˈθɑːl-/ *noun* a person who studies birds ⊃ compare **BIRDWATCHER**

**or·ni·thol·ogy** /ˌɔːnɪˈθɒlədʒi; *NAmE* ˌɔːrnɪˈθɑːl-/ *noun* [U] the scientific study of birds ▶ **or·ni·tho·logic·al** /ˌɔːnɪθəˈlɒdʒɪkl; *NAmE* ˌɔːrnɪθəˈlɑːdʒ-/ *adj.*

**or·ogeny** /ɒˈrɒdʒəni; *NAmE* ɔːˈrɑːdʒ-/ *noun* [U] (*geology*) a process in which the outer layer of the earth is folded to form mountains

**orphan** /ˈɔːfn; *NAmE* ˈɔːrfn/ *noun*, *verb*
- *noun* a child whose parents are dead: *He was an orphan and lived with his uncle.* ◊ *orphan boys/girls*
- *verb* [usually passive] ~ **sb** to make a child an orphan: *She was orphaned in the war.*

**or·phan·age** /ˈɔːfənɪdʒ; *NAmE* ˈɔːrf-/ *noun* a home for children whose parents are dead

**ortho-** /ɔːθəʊ, ɔːθə, ɔːˈθɒ; *NAmE* ɔːrθəʊ, ɔːrθə, ɔːrˈθɑː/ *combining form* (in nouns, adjectives and adverbs) correct; standard: *orthodox* ◊ *orthography*

**ortho·don·tics** /ˌɔːθəˈdɒntɪks; *NAmE* ˌɔːrθəˈdɑːn-/ *noun* [U] the treatment of problems relating to the position of the teeth and JAWS ▶ **ortho·don·tic** *adj.*: *orthodontic treatment*

**ortho·don·tist** /ˌɔːθəˈdɒntɪst; *NAmE* ˌɔːrθəˈdɑːn-/ *noun* a dentist who treats problems relating to the position of the teeth and JAWS

**ortho·dox** /ˈɔːθədɒks; *NAmE* ˈɔːrθədɑːks/ *adj.* **1** (*especially of beliefs or behaviour*) generally accepted or approved of; following generally accepted beliefs **SYN** **traditional**: *orthodox medicine* **OPP** **unorthodox** ⊃ compare **HETERODOX** **2** following closely the traditional beliefs and practices of a religion: *an orthodox Jew* **3** **Orthodox** belonging to or connected with the Orthodox Church

**the ˌOrthodox ˈChurch** (*also* **the ˌEastern ˌOrthodox ˈChurch**) *noun* [sing.] a branch of the Christian Church in eastern Europe and Greece

**ortho·doxy** /ˈɔːθədɒksi; *NAmE* ˈɔːrθədɑːk-/ *noun* (*pl.* **-ies**) **1** [C, U] (*formal*) an idea or view that is generally accepted: *an economist arguing against the current financial orthodoxy* **2** [U, C, usually pl.] the traditional beliefs or practices of a religion, etc. **3** **Orthodoxy** [U] the Orthodox Church, its beliefs and practices

**or·thog·raphy** /ɔːˈθɒɡrəfi; *NAmE* ɔːrˈθɑːɡ-/ *noun* [U] (*formal*) the system of spelling in a language ▶ **ortho·graph·ic** /ˌɔːθəˈɡræfɪk; *NAmE* ˌɔːrθ-/ *adj.*

**ortho·paed·ics** (*US* **ortho·ped·ics**) /ˌɔːθəˈpiːdɪks; *NAmE* ˌɔːrθ-/ *noun* [U] the branch of medicine that deals with injuries and diseases of the bones or muscles ▶ **ortho·paed·ic** (*US* **ortho·ped·ic**) *adj.*: *an orthopaedic surgeon/hospital*

**Or·well·ian** /ɔːˈweliən; *NAmE* ɔːrˈw-/ *adj.* used to describe a political system in which a government tries to have complete control over people's behaviour and thoughts **ORIGIN** From the name of the English writer George Orwell, whose novel *Nineteen Eighty-Four* describes a government that has total control over the people.

**-ory** /əri; *BrE also* ri; *NAmE also* ɔːri/ *suffix* **1** (in adjectives) that does …; involving the action referred to: *explanatory* **2** (in nouns) a place for: *observatory*

**oryx** /ˈɒrɪks; *NAmE* ˈɔːr-/ *noun* a large ANTELOPE with long straight HORNS

**OS** /ˌəʊ ˈes/ *abbr.* **1** (*computing*) OPERATING SYSTEM **2** ORDINARY SEAMAN

**Oscar**™ /ˈɒskə(r); *NAmE* ˈɑːs-/ *noun* = **ACADEMY AWARD**™: *The movie was nominated for an Oscar.* ◊ *an Oscar nomination/winner*

**os·cil·late** /ˈɒsɪleɪt; *NAmE* ˈɑːs-/ *verb* **1** [I] ~ **(between A and B)** (*formal*) to keep changing from one extreme of feeling or behaviour to another, and back again **SYN** **swing**: *Her moods oscillated between depression and elation.* **2** [I] (*physics*) to keep moving from one position to another and back again: *Watch how the needle on the dial oscillates.* **3** [I] (*physics*) (of an electric current, radio waves, etc.) to change in strength or direction at regular INTERVALS

**os·cil·la·tion** /ˌɒsɪˈleɪʃn; *NAmE* ˌɑːs-/ *noun* (*formal*) **1** [U, sing.] a regular movement between one position and another or between one amount and another: *the oscillation of the compass needle* ◊ ~ **between A and B** *the economy's continual oscillation between growth and recession* **2** [C] ~ **(between A and B)** | ~ **(of sth) (against sth)** a single movement from one position to another of sth that is oscillating: *the oscillations of the pound against foreign currency* **3** [U, C] ~ **(between A and B)** a repeated change between different feelings, types of behaviour or ideas: *his oscillation, as a teenager, between science and art*

**os·cil·la·tor** /ˈɒsɪleɪtə(r); *NAmE* ˈɑːs-/ *noun* (*physics*) a piece of equipment for producing OSCILLATING electric currents

**os·cil·lo·scope** /əˈsɪləskəʊp; *NAmE* -skoʊp/ *noun* (*physics*) a piece of equipment that shows changes in electrical current as waves in a line on a screen

**os·mium** /ˈɒzmiəm; *NAmE* ˈɑːz-/ *noun* [U] (*symb.* **Os**) a chemical element. Osmium is a hard silver-white metal.

**os·mo·sis** /ɒzˈməʊsɪs; *NAmE* ɑːzˈmoʊ-/ *noun* [U] **1** (*biology or chemistry*) the slow steady passing of a liquid through a MEMBRANE (= a thin layer of material) as a result of there being different amounts of DISSOLVED substances on either side of the membrane: *Water passes into the roots of a plant by osmosis.* **2** the process of gradually learning or being influenced by sth, as a result of being in close contact with it ▶ **os·mot·ic** /ɒzˈmɒtɪk; *NAmE* ɑːzˈmɑːt-/ *adj.*: *osmotic pressure*

**os·prey** /ˈɒspreɪ; *NAmE* ˈɑːs-/ *noun* a large BIRD OF PREY (= a bird that kills other creatures for food) that eats fish

**os·se·ous** /ˈɒsiəs; *NAmE* ˈɑːs-/ *adj.* (*specialist*) made of or turned into bone

**os·sify** /ˈɒsɪfaɪ; *NAmE* ˈɑːs-/ *verb* [usually passive] (**os·si·fies**, **os·si·fy·ing**, **os·si·fied**, **os·si·fied**) **1** [I, T, usually passive] ~ **(sth)** (*formal*, *disapproving*) to become or make sth fixed and unable to change: *an ossified political system* **2** [I, T, usually passive] ~ **(sth)** (*specialist*) to become or make sth hard like bone ▶ **os·si·fi·ca·tion** /ˌɒsɪfɪˈkeɪʃn; *NAmE* ˌɑːs-/ *noun* [U]

**os·ten·sible** /ɒˈstensəbl; *NAmE* ɑːˈs-/ *adj.* [only before noun] (*formal*) seeming or stated to be real or true, when this is perhaps not the case **SYN** **apparent**: *The ostensible reason for his absence was illness.* ▶ **os·ten·sibly** /-bli/ *adv.*: *Troops were sent in, ostensibly to protect the civilian population.*

**os·ten·ta·tion** /ˌɒstenˈteɪʃn; *NAmE* ˌɑːs-/ *noun* [U] (*disapproving*) an EXAGGERATED display of wealth, knowledge or skill that is made in order to impress people

**os·ten·ta·tious** /ˌɒstenˈteɪʃəs; *NAmE* ˌɑːs-/ *adj.* **1** (*disapproving*) showing your wealth or status in a way that is intended to impress people **SYN** **showy**: *an ostentatious display of wealth* **2** (of an action) done in a very obvious way so that people will notice it: *He gave an ostentatious yawn.* ▶ **os·ten·ta·tious·ly** *adv.*: *ostentatiously dressed*

**osteo-** /ˈɒstiəʊ, ˌɒstiə, ˈɒstiɒ; *NAmE* ˈɑːstioʊ, ˌɑːstiə, ˈɑːstiɑː/ *combining form* (in nouns and adjectives) connected with bones: *osteopath*

**osteo·arth·ri·tis** /ˌɒstiəʊɑːˈθraɪtɪs; *NAmE* ˌɑːstioʊɑːrˈθ-/ *noun* [U] (*medical*) a disease that causes painful SWELLING (= the condition of being larger or rounder than normal) and permanent damage in the JOINTS of the body, especially the HIPS, knees and THUMBS

**osteo·path** /ˈɒstiəpæθ; *NAmE* ˈɑːs-/ *noun* a person whose job involves treating some diseases and physical problems by pressing and moving the bones and muscles ⊃ compare CHIROPRACTOR

**oste·op·athy** /ˌɒstiˈɒpəθi; *NAmE* ˌɑːstiˈɑːp-/ *noun* [U] the treatment of some diseases and physical problems by pressing and moving the bones and muscles ⊃ WORDFINDER NOTE at CURE ▶ **osteo·path·ic** /ˌɒstiəˈpæθɪk; *NAmE* ˌɑːs-/ *adj.*

**osteo·por·osis** /ˌɒstiəʊpəˈrəʊsɪs; *NAmE* ˌɑːs-/ (*also* **brittle 'bone disease**) *noun* [U] (*medical*) a condition in which the bones become weak and are easily broken, usually when people get older or because they do not eat enough of certain substances

**os·tra·cism** /ˈɒstrəsɪzəm; *NAmE* ˈɑːs-/ *noun* [U] (*formal*) the act of deliberately not including sb in a group or activity; the state of not being included

**os·tra·cize** (*BrE also* **-ise**) /ˈɒstrəsaɪz; *NAmE* ˈɑːs-/ *verb* (*usually passive*) ~ **sb** (*formal*) to refuse to let sb be a member of a social group; to refuse to meet or talk to sb **SYN** **shun**: *He was ostracized by his colleagues for refusing to support the strike.*

**os·trich** /ˈɒstrɪtʃ; *NAmE* ˈɑːs-/ *noun* **1** a very large African bird with a long neck and long legs, that cannot fly but can run very fast **2** (*informal*) a person who prefers to ignore problems rather than try and deal with them

**OTC** /ˌəʊ tiː ˈsiː/ *abbr.* = OVER-THE-COUNTER: *OTC medicines and food supplements* ⋄ *OTC trading of securities*

**other** ❶ **A1** **W** /ˈʌðə(r)/ *adj., pron.* **1** **A1** used to refer to people or things that are additional or different to people or things that have been mentioned or are known about: *Mr Harris and Mrs Bate and three other teachers were there.* ⋄ *Are there any other questions?* ⋄ *There seem to be no other survivors.* ⋄ *I can't see you now—some other time, maybe.* ⋄ *Two buildings were destroyed and many others damaged in the blast.* ⋄ *Some designs are better than others.* ⊃ compare ANOTHER **2** **A1** **the, my, your, etc. ~** used to refer to the second of two people or things: *My other sister is a doctor.* ⋄ *One son went to live in Australia and the other one was killed in a car crash.* ⋄ *He raised one arm and then the other.* ⋄ *You must ask one or other of your parents.* **3** **A1** **the, my, your, etc. ~** used to refer to the people or things that remain in a group: *I'll wear my other shoes—these are dirty.* ⋄ *'I like this one.' 'What about the other ones?'* ⋄ *I went swimming while the others played tennis.* **4** **A1** **the other …** used to refer to a place, direction, etc. that is the opposite to where you are, are going, etc: *I work on the other side of town.* ⋄ *He crashed into a car coming the other way.* ⋄ *He found me, not* **the other way round/around**. **IDM** **HELP** Most idioms containing **other** are at the entries for the nouns and verbs in the idioms, for example **in other words** is at **word**. **the other 'day/'morning/'evening/ 'week** recently: *I saw Jack the other day.* **other than** (usually used in negative sentences) **1** **B2** except: *I don't know any French people other than you.* ⋄ *We're going away in June but other than that I'll be here all summer.* **2** (*formal*)

---

1097

**ought to**

different or in a different way from; not: *I have never known him to behave other than selfishly.*

**other 'half** (*also* **better 'half**) *noun* (*informal, humorous*) the person that you are married to or your boyfriend or girlfriend

**other·ness** /ˈʌðənəs; *NAmE* ˈʌðərn-/ *noun* [U] (*formal*) the fact of being different or strange: *the otherness of an alien culture*

**other·wise** ❶ **B2** **W** /ˈʌðəwaɪz; *NAmE* ˈʌðərw-/ *adv.* **1** **B2** used to state what the result would be if sth did not happen or if the situation were different: *My parents lent me the money. Otherwise, I couldn't have afforded the trip.* ⋄ *Shut the window, otherwise it'll get too cold in here.* ⋄ *We're committed to the project. We wouldn't be here otherwise.* **2** apart from that: *There was some music playing upstairs. Otherwise the house was silent.* ⋄ *He was slightly bruised but otherwise unhurt.* **3** in a different way to the way mentioned; differently: *Bismarck, otherwise known as 'the Iron Chancellor'* ⋄ *It is not permitted to sell or otherwise distribute copies of past examination papers.* ⋄ *You know what this is about. Why* **pretend** *otherwise* (= that you do not)? ⋄ *I wanted to see him but he was otherwise engaged* (= doing sth else). **IDM** **or otherwise** used to refer to sth that is different from or the opposite of what has just been mentioned: *It was necessary to discover the truth or otherwise of these statements.* ⋄ *We insure against all damage, accidental or otherwise.* ⊃ more at KNOW *v.*

**other 'woman** *noun* [usually sing.] a woman with whom a man is having a sexual relationship, although he already has a wife or partner

**other-'worldly** *adj.* connected with spiritual thoughts and ideas rather than with ordinary life ▶ **other-'worldli·ness** *noun* [U]

**oti·ose** /ˈəʊtiəʊs; *NAmE* ˈoʊʃi-/ *adj.* (*formal*) having no useful purpose **SYN** **unnecessary**: *an otiose round of meetings*

**ot·itis** /əʊˈtaɪtɪs; *NAmE* oʊ-/ *noun* [U] (*medical*) painful SWELLING (= the condition of being larger or rounder than normal) of the ear, caused by an infection

**OTT** /ˌəʊ tiː ˈtiː/ *adj.* (*BrE, informal*) = OVER THE TOP: *Her make-up was a bit OTT.*

**otter** /ˈɒtə(r); *NAmE* ˈɑːt-/ *noun* a small animal that has four WEBBED feet (= with skin between the toes), a tail and thick brown fur. Otters live in rivers and eat fish.

**ot·to·man** /ˈɒtəmən; *NAmE* ˈɑːt-/ *noun* a piece of furniture like a large box with a soft top, used for storing things in and sitting on

**OU** /ˌəʊ ˈjuː/ *abbr.* (in the UK) Open University

**ou** /əʊ/ *noun* (*pl.* **os** *or* **ouens** /ˈəʊənz/; *SAfrE*) = OKE

**ouch** /aʊtʃ/ *exclamation* used to express sudden pain: *Ouch! That hurt!*

**oud** /uːd/ *noun* a musical instrument similar to a LUTE played mainly in Arab countries

**ought to** ❶ **B1** /ɔːt tə, *before vowels and finally* tu/ *modal verb* (*negative* **ought not to**, *short form especially BrE* **oughtn't to**) **1** **B1** used to say what is the right thing to do: *They ought to apologize.* ⋄ *They ought to have apologized* (= but they didn't). ⋄ *Such things ought not to be allowed.* ⋄ *He oughtn't to have been driving so fast.* ⋄ (*formal*) *'Ought I to write to say thank you?' 'Yes, I think you ought (to).'* **HELP** Questions beginning with **ought** are rare; it is more usual to begin with *Do you think*: *Do you think I ought to write and say thank you?* ⊃ note at SHOULD **2** **B1** used to say what you expect or would like to happen: *Children ought to be able to read by the age of 7.* ⋄ *Nurses ought to earn more.* **3** **B1** used to say what you advise or recommend: *We ought to be leaving now.* ⋄ *This is delicious. You ought to try some.* ⋄ *You ought to have come to the meeting. It was interesting.* **4** used to say what has probably happened or is probably true: *If he started out at nine, he ought to be here by now.* ⋄ *That ought to be enough food for the four of us.* ⋄ *Oughtn't the water to have boiled by now?* ⊃ note at MODAL

---

❶ Oxford Phrasal Academic Lexicon (OPAL) written and spoken word lists | **W** OPAL written word list | **S** OPAL spoken word list

# Ouija board

**Ouija board™** /ˈwiːdʒə bɔːd; *NAmE* bɔːrd/ *noun* a board marked with letters of the alphabet and other signs, used in SEANCES to receive messages said to come from people who are dead

**ounce** /aʊns/ *noun* **1** [C] (*abbr.* **oz**) (in Britain and North America) a unit for measuring weight, 1/16 of a pound, equal to 28.35 GRAMS ⊃ see also FLUID OUNCE **2** [sing.] **~ of sth** (*informal*) (used especially with negatives) a very small quantity of sth: *There's not an ounce of truth in her story.* **IDM** see PREVENTION

**our** ⓘ A1 /ɑː(r), ˈaʊə(r)/ *det.* (the possessive form of *we*) **1** A1 belonging to us; connected with us: *our daughter/dog/house* ◇ *We showed them some of our photos.* ◇ *Our main export is rice.* ◇ *And now, over to our Rome correspondent…* **2** Our used to refer to or address God or a holy person: *Our Father* (= God) ◇ *Our Lady* (= the Virgin Mary)

**ours** ⓘ B1 /ɑːz, ˈaʊəz; *NAmE* ɑːrz, ˈaʊərz/ *pron.* **1** B1 the one or ones that belong to us: *Their house is very similar to ours, but ours is bigger.* ◇ *No, those are Ellie's kids. Ours are upstairs.* ◇ *He's a friend of ours.* **2** (*BrE, informal*) our home: *Do you fancy coming to ours for Sunday dinner?*

**our·selves** ⓘ A2 /ɑːˈselvz, ˌaʊəˈselvz; *NAmE* ɑːrˈselvz, ˌaʊərˈselvz/ *pron.* **1** A2 the reflexive form of *we*; used when you and another person or other people together cause and are affected by an action: *We shouldn't blame ourselves for what happened.* ◇ *Let's just relax and enjoy ourselves.* ◇ *We'd like to see it for ourselves.* **2** B1 used to emphasize *we* or *us*; sometimes used instead of these words: *We've often thought of going there ourselves.* ◇ *The only people there were ourselves.*
**IDM** (all) by our'selves **1** alone; without anyone else **2** without help (all) to our'selves for us alone to have or use; not shared with others: *We had the pool all to ourselves.*

**-ous** /əs/ *suffix* (in adjectives) having the nature or quality of: *poisonous* ◇ *mountainous* ▶ **-ously** /əsli/ (in adverbs): *gloriously* **-ousness** /əsnəs/ (in nouns): *spaciousness*

**oust** /aʊst/ *verb* to force sb out of a job or position of power, especially in order to take their place: **~ sb (as sth)** *He was ousted as chairman.* ◇ **~ sb (from sth)** *The rebels finally managed to oust the government from power.*

**oust·er** /ˈaʊstə(r)/ *noun* (*NAmE*) the act of removing sb from a position of authority in order to put sb else in their place; the fact of being removed in this way: *the president's ouster by the military*

**out** ⓘ A1 /aʊt/ *adv., prep., noun, adj., verb*
■ *adv., prep.* **HELP** For the special uses of **out** in phrasal verbs, look at the entries for the verbs. For example **burst out** is in the phrasal verb section at **burst**. **1** A1 away from the inside of a place or thing: *She ran out into the corridor.* ◇ *She shook the bag and some coins fell out.* ◇ **~ of sth** *I got out of bed.* ◇ *He opened the box and out jumped a frog.* ◇ *Out you go!* (= used to order sb to leave a room) ◇ (*informal*) *He ran out the door.* **OPP** in **2** A1 (of people) away from or not at home or their place of work: *I called Liz but she was out.* ◇ *Let's go out this evening* (= for example to a restaurant or club). ◇ *We haven't had a night out for weeks.* ◇ **~ of sth** *Mr Green is out of town this week.* ◇ *I got an out of office reply to my email.* **OPP** in **3** outside; not in a building: *It's cold out.* ◇ *There were children playing out in the street.* **4** B1 used to show that sth/sb is removed from a place, job, etc: *This detergent is good for getting stains out.* ◇ *We want this government out.* ◇ **~ of sth** *He got thrown out of the restaurant.* **5** B1 away from the edge of a place: *The boy dashed out into the road.* ◇ **~ of sth** *Don't lean out of the window.* **6** B1 **~ of sth/sb** used to show where sth comes from: *He drank his beer out of the bottle.* ◇ *a romance straight out of a fairy tale* ◇ *I paid for the damage out of my savings.* ◇ *We'll get the truth out of her.* **7** B1 **~ of sth** used to show what sth is made from: *a statue made out of bronze* **8** B1 **~ of sth** used to show that sth does not have any of sth: *We're out of milk.* ◇ *He's been out of work for six months.* ◇ *You're out of luck—she left ten minutes ago.* **9** B1 **~ of sth** used to show that sb/sth is not or no longer in a particular state or condition: *Try and stay out of trouble.* ◇ *I watched the car until it was out of sight.* **10** B1 **~ (of sth)** used to show that sb is no longer involved in sth: *It was an awful job and I'm glad to be out of it.* ◇ *He gets out of the army in a few weeks.* ◇ *They'll be out* (= of prison) *on bail in no time.* ◇ *Brown goes on to the semi-finals but Lee is out.* **11** B1 **~ of sth** from a particular number or set: *You scored six out of ten.* ◇ *Two out of three people think the President should resign.* **12** B1 clearly and loudly so that people can hear: *to call/cry/shout out* ◇ *Read it out loud.* ◇ *Nobody spoke out in his defence.* **13** B2 **~ (of sth)** a long or a particular distance away from a place or from land: *She's working out in Australia.* ◇ *He lives right out in the country.* ◇ *The boats are all out at sea.* ◇ *The ship sank ten miles out of Stockholm.* **14** B2 available to everyone; known to everyone: *When does her new book come out?* ◇ *Word always gets out* (= people find out about things) *no matter how careful you are.* ◇ *Out with it!* (= say what you know) **15** **~ of sth** used to show the reason why sth is done: *I asked out of curiosity.* ◇ *She did it out of spite.* **16** (of a book, etc.) not in the library; borrowed by sb else: *The book you wanted is out on loan.* **17** (of the TIDE) at or towards its lowest point on land: *I like walking on the wet sand when the tide is out.* **OPP** in **18** if the sun, moon or stars are or come out, they can be seen from the earth and are not hidden by clouds **19** (of flowers) fully open: *There should be some snowdrops out by now.* **20** (in CRICKET, baseball, etc.) if a team or team member is out, it is no longer their turn with the BAT: *The West Indies were all out for 364* (= after scoring 364 RUNS in CRICKET). **OPP** in **21** (in games) if a player is **out**, they can no longer take part in the game: *If you have no more cards, you are out. The winner is the one with the most cards.* **22** (in tennis, etc.) if the ball is **out**, it landed outside the line: *The umpire said the ball was out.* **OPP** in **23** **~ (in sth)** not correct or exact; wrong: *I was slightly out in my calculations.* ◇ *Your guess was a long way out* (= completely wrong). ◇ *The estimate was out by more than $100.* **24** not possible or not allowed: *Swimming is out until the weather gets warmer.* **25** not fashionable: *Black is out this year.* **26** (of fire, lights or burning materials) not or no longer burning or lit: *Suddenly all the lights went out.* ◇ *The fire had burnt itself out.* **27** at an end: *It was summer and school was out.* ◇ *She was to regret her words before the day was out.* **28** unconscious: *He was out for more than an hour and came round in the hospital.* ◇ *She was knocked out cold.* **29** (*BrE, informal*) on strike **30** to the end; completely: *Hear me out before you say anything.* ◇ *We left them to fight it out* (= settle a disagreement by fighting or arguing). ⊃ see also ALL-OUT
**IDM** be out for sth / to do sth to be trying to get or do sth: *I'm not out for revenge.* ◇ *She's out for what she can get* (= trying to get something for herself). ◇ *The company is out to capture the Canadian market.* ˌout and aˈbout **1** able to go outside again after an illness **2** travelling around a place: *We've been out and about talking to people all over the country.* ˈout of here (*informal*) going or leaving: *As soon as I get my money I'm out of here!* ˈout of it (*informal*) **1** sad because you are not included in sth: *We've only just moved here so we feel a little out of it.* **2** not aware of what is happening, usually because of drinking too much alcohol, or taking drugs ⊃ more at IN *adv.*
■ *noun* [sing.] a way of avoiding having to do sth: *She was desperately looking for an out.* **IDM** see IN *n.*
■ *adj.* (*informal*) having told other people that you are GAY or LESBIAN: *an out gay man* ◇ *I had been out since I was 17.*
■ *verb* **1** **~ sb** to say publicly that sb is GAY or LESBIAN, especially when they would prefer to keep the fact a secret: *He is the latest politician to be outed by gay activists.* **2** **~ sb/sth (as sth)** to say sth publicly about sb/sth that they would prefer to keep secret: *The man who claimed to have found the diaries has been outed as a fraud.*

**out-** /aʊt/ *prefix* **1** (in verbs) greater, better, further, longer, etc: *outnumber* ◇ *outwit* ◇ *outgrow* ◇ *outlive* **2** (in nouns and adjectives) outside; OUTWARD; away from: *outbuildings* ◇ *outpatient* ◇ *outlying* ◇ *outgoing*

**out·age** /ˈaʊtɪdʒ/ *noun* (especially *NAmE*) a period of time when the supply of electricity, etc. is not working: *a power outage*

**ˌout-and-ˈout** *adj.* [only before noun] in every way **SYN** complete: *What she said was an out-and-out lie.*

**out·back** /ˈaʊtbæk/ noun **the outback** [sing.] the area of Australia that is a long way from the coast and the towns, where few people live

**out·bid** /ˌaʊtˈbɪd/ verb (**out·bid·ding**, **out·bid**, **out·bid**) ~ sb (**for sth**) to offer more money than sb else in order to buy sth, for example at an AUCTION

**out·board** /ˈaʊtbɔːd/ NAmE -bɔːrd/ adj. [usually before noun] (*specialist*) on, towards or near the outside of a ship or an aircraft

**outboard ˈmotor** (*also* ˌoutboard ˈengine, ˈout·board) noun an engine that you can fix to the back of a small boat

**out·bound** /ˈaʊtbaʊnd/ adj. travelling from a place rather than arriving in it: *outbound flights/passengers* OPP **inbound**

**out·box** /ˈaʊtbɒks; NAmE -bɑːks/ noun (*computing*) the place on a computer where new email messages that you write are stored before they are sent

**ˈout box** (*US*) (*BrE* **ˈout tray**) noun (in an office) a container on your desk for letters or documents that are waiting to be sent out or passed to sb else ⇒ compare IN TRAY

**out·break** ʔ+ C1 /ˈaʊtbreɪk/ noun the sudden start of sth unpleasant, especially violence or a disease: *the outbreak of war* ◇ *an outbreak of typhoid* ◇ *Outbreaks of rain are expected in the afternoon.* ⇒ WORDFINDER NOTE at HEALTH

**out·build·ing** /ˈaʊtbɪldɪŋ/ noun [usually pl.] a building such as a SHED or STABLE that is built near to, but separate from, a main building

**out·burst** /ˈaʊtbɜːst; NAmE -bɜːrst/ noun **1** a sudden strong expression of an emotion: *an outburst of anger* ◇ *She was alarmed by his violent outburst.* **2** a sudden increase in a particular activity or attitude: *an outburst of racism*

**out·cast** /ˈaʊtkɑːst; NAmE -kæst/ noun a person who is not accepted by society or by a particular group: *People with the disease were often treated as social outcasts.* ▶ **out·cast** adj.

**out·class** /ˌaʊtˈklɑːs; NAmE -ˈklæs/ verb [often passive] ~ sb/sth to be much better than sb you are competing against: *Kennedy was outclassed 0–6 0–6 in the final.*

**out·come** ʔ B2 O /ˈaʊtkʌm/ noun the result or effect of an action or event: *The likely outcome is a compromise.* ◇ *We are confident of a positive outcome.* ◇ *It is difficult to predict the final outcome.* ◇ *Four possible outcomes have been identified.* ◇ **regardless of the ~** *These costs are payable regardless of the outcome of the case.* ⇒ SYNONYMS at RESULT

**out·crop** /ˈaʊtkrɒp; NAmE -krɑːp/ noun a large mass of rock that stands above the surface of the ground

**out·cry** /ˈaʊtkraɪ/ noun [C, U] (*pl.* **-ies**) ~ (**at/over/against sth**) a reaction of anger or strong protest shown by people in public: *an outcry over the proposed change* ◇ *The new tax provoked a public outcry.* ◇ *There was outcry at the judge's statement.*

**out·dated** /ˌaʊtˈdeɪtɪd/ adj. no longer useful because of being old-fashioned: *outdated equipment* ◇ *These figures are now outdated.* ⇒ compare OUT OF DATE

**out·dis·tance** /ˌaʊtˈdɪstəns/ verb ~ sb/sth to leave sb/sth behind by going faster, further, etc.; to be better than sb/sth SYN **outstrip**

**out·do** /ˌaʊtˈduː/ verb (**out·does** /-ˈdʌz/, **out·did** /-ˈdɪd/, **out·done** /-ˈdʌn/) ~ sb/sth to do more or better than sb else SYN **beat**: *Sometimes small firms can outdo big business when it comes to customer care.* ◇ *Not to be outdone (= not wanting to let sb else do better), she tried again.*

**out·door** ʔ B1 /ˈaʊtdɔː(r)/ adj. [only before noun] used, happening or located outside rather than in a building: *outdoor pursuits/recreation/activities* ◇ *outdoor clothing* ◇ *an outdoor swimming pool* ◇ *I'm not really the outdoor type (= I prefer indoor activities).* OPP **indoor**

**out·doors** ʔ B1 /ˌaʊtˈdɔːz; NAmE -ˈdɔːrz/ adv., noun
- **adv.** ʔ B1 outside, rather than in a building: *The rain prevented them from eating outdoors.* OPP **indoors**
- **noun the outdoors** [sing.] the countryside, away from buildings and busy places: *They both have a love of the outdoors.* ◇ *Come to Canada and enjoy the great outdoors.*

1099 **outgoing**

**out·doors·man** /ˌaʊtˈdɔːzmən; NAmE -ˈdɔːrz-/, **out·doors·woman** /ˌaʊtˈdɔːzwʊmən; NAmE -ˈdɔːrz-/ noun (*pl.* **out·doors·men** /-mən/ *or* **out·doors·women** /-wɪmɪn/) (*especially NAmE*) a man or woman who spends a lot of time doing outdoor sports and activities, especially in the countryside

**out·doors·y** /ˌaʊtˈdɔːzi; NAmE -ˈdɔːrzi/ adj. (*NAmE, informal*) enjoying outdoor sports and activities, especially in the countryside

**outer** ʔ B2 /ˈaʊtə(r)/ adj. [only before noun] **1** on the outside of sth SYN **external**: *the outer layers of the skin* **2** ʔ B2 furthest from the inside or centre of sth: *I walked along the outer edge of the track.* ◇ *the outer suburbs of the city* ◇ *Outer London/Mongolia* ◇ (*figurative*) *to explore the outer (= most extreme) limits of human experience* OPP **inner**

**ˈouter belt** (*US*) (*BrE* **ˈring road**) noun a road that is built around a city or town to reduce traffic in the centre

**outer·most** /ˈaʊtəməʊst; NAmE -tərm-/ adj. [only before noun] furthest from the inside or centre: *the outermost planet* ◇ *He fired and hit the outermost ring of the target.* OPP **innermost**

**ˌouter ˈspace** noun [U] = SPACE (1): *radio waves from outer space*

**outer·wear** /ˈaʊtəweə(r); NAmE -tərwer/ noun [U] clothes such as coats that you wear over other clothing, especially outside

**out·fall** /ˈaʊtfɔːl/ noun the place where a river, pipe, etc. flows out into the sea: *a sewage outfall*

**out·field** /ˈaʊtfiːld/ noun, adv.
- **noun** [sing.] the outer part of the field in baseball, CRICKET and some other sports ⇒ compare INFIELD
- **adv.** in or to the outfield

**out·field·er** /ˈaʊtfiːldə(r)/ noun (in CRICKET and baseball) a player in the outfield

**out·fit** ʔ+ B2 /ˈaʊtfɪt/ noun, verb
- **noun 1** ʔ+ B2 [C] a set of clothes that you wear together, especially for a particular occasion or purpose: *She was wearing an expensive new outfit.* ◇ *a wedding outfit* ◇ *a cowboy/Superman outfit (= one that you wear for fun in order to look like the type of person mentioned)* **2** [C + *sing./pl. v.*] (*informal*) a group of people working together as an organization, business, team, etc: *a market research outfit* ◇ *This was the fourth album by the top rock outfit.* **3** [C] a set of equipment that you need for a particular purpose: *a bicycle repair outfit*
- **verb** [often passive] (**-tt-**) ~ sb/sth (**with sth**) (*especially NAmE*) to provide sb/sth with equipment or clothes for a special purpose SYN **equip**: *The ship was outfitted with a 12-bed hospital.*

**out·fit·ter** (*also* **out·fit·ters**) /ˈaʊtfɪtə(r)/ noun **1** (*old-fashioned, BrE*) a shop that sells men's clothes or school uniforms **2** (*NAmE*) a shop that sells equipment for camping and other outdoor activities

**out·flank** /ˌaʊtˈflæŋk/ verb **1** ~ sb/sth to move around the side of an enemy or opponent, especially in order to attack them from behind **2** ~ sb/sth to gain an advantage over sb, especially by doing sth unexpected SYN **out-manoeuvre**

**out·flow** /ˈaʊtfləʊ/ noun [usually sing.] ~ (**of sth/sb**) (**from sth**) the movement of a large amount of money, liquid, people, etc. out of a place: *There was a capital outflow of $22 billion in 2008.* ◇ *a steady outflow of oil from the tank* ◇ *the outflow of refugees* OPP **inflow**

**out·fox** /ˌaʊtˈfɒks; NAmE -ˈfɑːks/ verb ~ sb to gain an advantage over sb by being cleverer than they are SYN **outwit**

**out·going** adj. **1** /ˌaʊtˈɡəʊɪŋ/ liking to meet other people, enjoying their company and being friendly towards them SYN **sociable**: *an outgoing personality* **2** [only before noun] /ˈaʊtɡəʊɪŋ/ leaving the position of responsibility mentioned: *the outgoing president/government* OPP **incoming** **3** [only before noun] /ˈaʊtɡəʊɪŋ/ going away from a particular place rather than arriving in it: *This telephone should*

# outgoings

be used for outgoing calls. ◇ *outgoing flights/passengers* ◇ *the outgoing tide* **OPP** incoming

**out·goings** /ˈaʊtɡəʊɪŋz/ *noun* [pl.] (*BrE*) the amount of money that a person or a business has to spend regularly, for example every month **SYN** expenditure: *low/high outgoings* ◇ *Write down your incomings and outgoings.*

**ˈout-group** *noun* the people who do not belong to a particular IN-GROUP in a society

**out·grow** /ˌaʊtˈɡrəʊ/ *verb* (**out·grew** /-ˈɡruː/, **out·grown** /-ˈɡrəʊn/) **1** ~ **sth** to grow too big to be able to wear or fit into sth **SYN** grow out of sth: *She's already outgrown her school uniform.* ◇ *The company has outgrown its offices.* **2** ~ **sb** to grow taller, larger or more quickly than another person: *He's already outgrown his older brother.* **3** ~ **sth** to stop doing sth or lose interest in sth as you become older **SYN** grow out of sth: *He's outgrown his passion for rock music.*

**out·growth** /ˈaʊtɡrəʊθ/ *noun* **1** (*specialist*) a thing that grows out of sth else: *The eye first appears as a cup-shaped outgrowth from the brain.* **2** (*formal*) a natural development or result of sth: *The law was an outgrowth of the 2008 presidential election.*

**out·gun** /ˌaʊtˈɡʌn/ *verb* [often passive] (-**nn**-) ~ **sb/sth** to have greater military strength than sb: (*figurative*) *The England team was completely outgunned.*

**out·house** /ˈaʊthaʊs/ *noun* **1** (*BrE*) a small building, such as a SHED, outside a main building **2** (*especially NAmE*) a toilet in a small building of its own

**out·ing** /ˈaʊtɪŋ/ *noun* **1** [C] ~ (**to …**) a trip that you go on for pleasure or education, usually with a group of people and lasting no more than one day **SYN** excursion: *a family outing* ◇ *We went on an outing to London.* ⊃ SYNONYMS at TRIP **2** [C] (*sport, informal*) an occasion when sb takes part in a competition **3** [U, C] the practice of naming people as GAY or LESBIAN in public, when they do not want anyone to know

**out·land·ish** /aʊtˈlændɪʃ/ *adj.* (*usually disapproving*) strange or extremely unusual **SYN** bizarre: *outlandish costumes/ideas* ▸ **outˈland·ish·ly** *adv.*

**out·last** /ˌaʊtˈlɑːst; *NAmE* -ˈlæst/ *verb* ~ **sb/sth** to continue to exist or take part in an activity for a longer time than sb/sth: *He can outlast anyone on the dance floor.*

**out·law** /ˈaʊtlɔː/ *verb, noun*
■ *verb* **1** ~ **sth** to make sth illegal **SYN** ban: *plans to outlaw the carrying of knives* ◇ *the outlawed nationalist party* **2** ~ **sb** (in the past) to make sb an outlaw
■ *noun* (used especially about people in the past) a person who has done sth illegal and is hiding to avoid being caught; a person who is not protected by the law: *Robin Hood, the world's most famous outlaw*

**out·lay** /ˈaʊtleɪ/ *noun* [C, U] ~ (**on sth**) the money that you have to spend in order to start a new project: *The business quickly repaid the initial outlay on advertising.* ◇ *a massive financial/capital outlay* ⊃ SYNONYMS at COST

**out·let** /ˈaʊtlet/ *noun* **1** a shop or an organization that sells goods made by a particular company or of a particular type: *The business has 34 retail outlets in this state alone.* **2** a shop that sells goods of a particular make at reduced prices: *the Nike outlet in the outlet mall* **3** ~ (**for sth**) a way of expressing or making good use of strong feelings, ideas or energy: *She needed to find an outlet for her many talents and interests.* ◇ *Sport became the perfect outlet for his aggression.* **4** a pipe or hole through which liquid or gas can flow out: *a sewage outlet* ◇ *an outlet pipe* **OPP** inlet **5** (*also* **re·cep·tacle**) (*both NAmE*) (*also* **socket** *BrE and NAmE*) (*BrE* **ˈpower point**) a device in a wall that you put a PLUG into (= a small plastic object with two or three metal pins) in order to connect electrical equipment to the power supply of a building

**out·lier** /ˈaʊtlaɪə(r)/ *noun* **1** a person or thing that is different from or in a position away from others in the group: *They are corporate outliers, people who just don't fit into the culture of the company.* **2** (*statistics*) a data point on a GRAPH or in a set of results that is very much bigger or smaller than the next nearest data point: *If the outliers are removed from the data, the overall results do change significantly.*

**out·line** /ˈaʊtlaɪn/ *verb, noun*
■ *verb* **1** ~ **sth** to give a description of the main facts or points involved in sth **SYN** sketch: ~ **sth** *He outlined his plan to leave St. Petersburg.* ◇ ~ **sth to sb** *We outlined our proposals to the committee.* ◇ ~ **what, how, etc …** *Let me outline what I have in mind.* ◇ ~ **sth + adv./prep.** *For the reasons outlined above, unemployment is likely to remain high.* **2** [usually passive] to show or mark the outer edge of sth: *outlined against sth They saw the huge building outlined against the sky.*
■ *noun* [C, U] **1** a description of the main facts or points involved in sth: ~ **of sth** *This is a brief outline of the events.* ◇ *You should draw up a plan or outline for the essay.* ◇ **in ~** *The book describes in outline the main findings of the research.* ◇ *an outline agreement/proposal/plan* **2** the line that goes around the edge of sth, showing its main shape but not the details: ~ **of sth** *At last we could see the dim outline of an island.* ◇ *an outline map/sketch* ◇ **in ~** *She drew the figures in outline.*

**out·live** /ˌaʊtˈlɪv/ *verb* **1** ~ **sb** to live longer than sb: *He outlived his wife by three years.* **2** ~ **sth** to continue to exist after sth else has ended or disappeared: *The machine had outlived its usefulness* (= was no longer useful).

**out·look** /ˈaʊtlʊk/ *noun* [usually sing.] **1** the attitude to life and the world of a particular person, group or culture: *Travel broadens your outlook.* ◇ *a/an positive/optimistic outlook* ◇ ~ **on sth** *He had a practical outlook on life.* ◇ **in ~** *Most Western societies are liberal in outlook.* **2** the likely future for sb/sth; what is likely to happen **SYN** prospect: *the country's economic outlook* ◇ ~ **for sth** *The outlook for jobs is bleak.* ◇ *The outlook* (= the probable weather) *for the weekend is dry and sunny.* **3** (*formal*) a view from a particular place: *The house has a pleasant outlook over the valley.*

**out·ly·ing** /ˈaʊtlaɪɪŋ/ *adj.* [only before noun] far away from the cities of a country or from the main part of a place: *outlying areas*

**out·man·oeuvre** (*US* **out·ma·neu·ver**) /ˌaʊtməˈnuːvə(r)/ *verb* ~ **sb/sth** to do better than an opponent by acting in a way that is cleverer or shows more skill: *The president has so far managed to outmanoeuvre his critics.*

**out·moded** /ˌaʊtˈməʊdɪd/ *adj.* (*disapproving*) no longer fashionable or useful: *an outmoded attitude*

**out·num·ber** /ˌaʊtˈnʌmbə(r)/ *verb* ~ **sb/sth** to be greater in number than sb/sth: *The demonstrators were heavily outnumbered by the police.* ◇ *In this profession, women outnumber men by two to one* (= there are twice as many women as men).

**ˌout-of-ˈbody exˈperience** *noun* a feeling of being outside your own body, especially when you feel that you are watching yourself from a distance

**ˌout of ˈdate** *adj.* **1** old-fashioned or without the most recent information and therefore no longer useful: *These figures are very out of date.* ◇ *Suddenly she felt old and out of date.* ◇ *an out-of-date map* ◇ *out-of-date technology* ⊃ compare OUTDATED **2** no longer current or legally acceptable: *an out-of-date driving licence* ⊃ see also UP TO DATE

**ˌout-of-ˈpocket** *adj.* ~ **expenses/costs/expenditure/spending** small business expenses that you pay yourself, with your employer paying you back later: *On business trips she has some travel and other out-of-pocket expenses.* ⊃ see also IN/OUT OF POCKET at POCKET *noun*

**ˌout-of-ˈstate** *adj.* [only before noun] (*US*) coming from or happening in a different state: *out-of-state license plates*

**ˌout-of-the-ˈway** *adj.* far from a town or city: *a little out-of-the-way place on the coast*

**ˌout-of-ˈtown** *adj.* [only before noun] **1** located away from the centre of a town or city: *out-of-town superstores* **2** coming from or happening in a different place: *an out-of-town guest* ◇ *an out-of-town performance*

**ˌout-of-ˈwork** *adj.* [only before noun] unemployed: *an out-of-work actor*

**out·pace** /ˌaʊtˈpeɪs/ *verb* ~ **sb/sth** to go, rise, improve, etc. faster than sb/sth **SYN** outstrip: *He easily outpaced the other runners.* ◇ *Demand is outpacing production.*

**out·pa·tient** /ˈaʊtpeɪʃnt/ *noun* a person who goes to a hospital for treatment but does not stay there: *an outpatient clinic* ⇨ compare INPATIENT

**out·per·form** /ˌaʊtpəˈfɔːm; NAmE -pərˈfɔːrm/ *verb* ~ sb/ sth to achieve better results than sb/sth ▸ **out·per·form·ance** /ˌaʊtpəˈfɔːməns; NAmE -pərˈfɔːr-/ *noun* [U]

**out·place·ment** /ˈaʊtpleɪsmənt/ *noun* [U] (*business*) the process of helping people to find new jobs after they have been made unemployed

**out·play** /ˌaʊtˈpleɪ/ *verb* ~ sb to play much better than sb you are competing against: *We were totally outplayed and lost 106–74.*

**out·point** /ˌaʊtˈpɔɪnt/ *verb* ~ sb (especially in boxing) to defeat sb by scoring more points

**out·post** /ˈaʊtpəʊst/ *noun* 1 a small military camp away from the main army, used for watching an enemy's movements, etc. 2 a small town or group of buildings in a lonely part of a country: *a remote outpost* ◇ *the last outpost of civilization*

**out·pour·ing** /ˈaʊtpɔːrɪŋ/ *noun* 1 [usually pl.] a strong and sudden expression of feeling: *spontaneous outpourings of praise* 2 a large amount of sth produced in a short time: *a remarkable outpouring of new ideas*

**out·put** ?+ B2 ⦿ /ˈaʊtpʊt/ *noun, verb*
- *noun* [U, sing.] 1 ?+ B2 the amount of sth that a person, a machine or an organization produces: *Manufacturing output has increased by 8 per cent.* ⇨ WORDFINDER NOTE at INDUSTRY 2 (*computing*) the information, results, etc. produced by a computer: *data output* ◇ *an output device* ⇨ compare INPUT 3 the power, energy, etc. produced by a piece of equipment: *an output of 100 watts* 4 a place where energy, power, information, etc. leaves a system: *Connect a cable to the output.*
- *verb* (**out·put·ting, out·put, out·put** or **out·put·ting, out·put·ted, out·put·ted**) ~ sth (*computing*) to supply or produce information, results, etc: *Computers can now output data much more quickly.* ⇨ compare INPUT

**out·rage** ?+ C1 /ˈaʊtreɪdʒ/ *noun, verb*
- *noun* 1 ?+ [U] a strong feeling of shock and anger: *The judge's remarks caused public outrage.* ◇ *She was filled with a strong sense of moral outrage.* ◇ *Environmentalists have expressed outrage at the ruling.* 2 ?+ [C] an act or event that is violent, cruel or very wrong and that shocks people or makes them very angry SYN **atrocity**: *No one has yet claimed responsibility for this latest terrorist outrage.*
- *verb* ?+ C1 [often passive] ~ sb to make sb very shocked and angry: *He was outraged at the way he had been treated.*

**out·ra·geous** /aʊtˈreɪdʒəs/ *adj.* 1 offensive and unacceptable SYN **scandalous**: *outrageous behaviour* ◇ *'That's outrageous!' he protested.* 2 very unusual and intended to shock people slightly: *She says the most outrageous things sometimes.* ◇ *outrageous clothes* ▸ **out·ra·geous·ly** *adv.*: *an outrageously expensive meal* ◇ *They behaved outrageously.*

**out·ran** /ˌaʊtˈræn/ *past tense* of OUTRUN

**out·rank** /ˌaʊtˈræŋk/ *verb* ~ sb to be of higher rank, quality, etc. than sb

**outré** /ˈuːtreɪ; NAmE uːˈtreɪ/ *adj.* (*from French, formal*) very unusual in a way that sometimes shocks

**out·reach** /ˈaʊtriːtʃ/ *noun* [U] the activity of an organization that provides a service or advice to people in the community, especially those who cannot or are unlikely to come to an office, a hospital, etc. for help: *an outreach and education programme* ◇ *outreach workers* ◇ *efforts to expand the outreach to black voters*

**out·rider** /ˈaʊtraɪdə(r)/ *noun* a person who rides a motorcycle or a horse in front of or next to the vehicle of an important person in order to give protection

**out·rig·ger** /ˈaʊtrɪɡə(r)/ *noun* a wooden structure that is fixed to the side of a boat or ship in order to keep it steady in the water; a boat fitted with such a structure

**out·right** /ˈaʊtraɪt/ *adj., adv.*
- *adj.* [only before noun] 1 complete and total: *an outright ban/rejection/victory* ◇ *She was the outright winner.* ◇ *No one party is expected to gain an outright majority.* 2 open and direct: *There was outright opposition to the plan.*

1101 **outside lane**

- *adv.* 1 in a direct way and without trying to hide anything: *Why don't you ask him outright if it's true?* ◇ *She couldn't help herself and she laughed outright.* 2 clearly and completely: *Neither candidate won outright.* ◇ *The group rejects outright any negotiations with the government.* 3 not gradually; immediately: *Most of the crash victims were killed outright.* ◇ *We had saved enough money to buy the house outright.*

**out·run** /ˌaʊtˈrʌn/ *verb* (**out·run·ning, out·ran** /-ˈræn/, **out·run**) 1 ~ sb/sth to run faster or further than sb/sth: *He couldn't outrun his pursuers.* 2 ~ sb/sth to develop faster than sth SYN **outstrip**: *Demand for the new model is outrunning supply.*

**out·sell** /ˌaʊtˈsel/ *verb* (**out·sold, out·sold** /-ˈsəʊld/) ~ sb/ sth to sell more or to be sold in larger quantities than sb/ sth: *We are now outselling all our competitors.* ◇ *This year the newspaper has outsold its main rival.*

**out·set** /ˈaʊtset/ *noun*
IDM **at/from the ˈoutset (of sth)** at/from the beginning of sth: *I made it clear right from the outset that I disapproved.*

**out·shine** /ˌaʊtˈʃaɪn/ *verb* (**out·shone, out·shone** /ˌaʊtˈʃɒn; NAmE -ˈʃoʊn/) ~ sb/sth to be more impressive than sb/sth; to be better than sb/sth

**out·side** ⓣ A1 *adv., prep., noun, adj.*
- *adv.* /ˌaʊtˈsaɪd/ 1 ? A1 not in a room, building or container but on or to the outside of it: *I'm seeing a patient—please wait outside.* ◇ *The house is painted green outside.* 2 ? A1 not inside a building: *It's warm enough to eat outside.* ◇ *Go outside and see if it's raining.* OPP **inside**
- *prep.* /ˌaʊtˈsaɪd/ (*also* **outside of** *especially in NAmE*) 1 ? A2 on or to a place on the outside of sth: *You can park your car outside our house.* OPP **inside** 2 ? B1 away from or not in a particular place: *It's the biggest theme park outside the United States.* ◇ *We live in a small village just outside Leeds.* 3 ? B2 not part of sth: *The matter is outside my area of responsibility.* ◇ *You may do as you wish outside working hours.* OPP **within** 4 more than the amount of time mentioned: *The winning time was just nine seconds outside the world record.* ⇨ compare INSIDE (2) 5 **outside of** apart from: *There was nothing they could do, outside of hoping things would get better.*
- *noun* /ˌaʊtˈsaɪd/ (*usually* **the outside**) 1 ? A2 [C, usually sing.] the outer side or surface of sth SYN **exterior**: *The outside of the house needs painting.* ◇ **from the ~** *You can't open the door from the outside.* 2 ? A2 [sing.] the area that is near or around a building, etc: *I walked around the outside of the building.* ◇ **from the ~** *I didn't go into the temple—I only saw it from the outside.* 3 [sing.] the part of a road nearest to the middle: **on the ~** *Always overtake on the outside.* 4 [sing.] the part of a curving road or track furthest from the inner or shorter side of the curve OPP **inside**
IDM **at the ˈoutside** at the most; as a maximum: *There was room for 20 people at the outside.* **on the outˈside** 1 used to describe how sb appears or seems: *On the outside she seems calm, but I know she's worried.* 2 not in prison: *Life on the outside took some getting used to again.*
- *adj.* /ˈaʊtsaɪd/ [only before noun] 1 ? A2 of, on or facing the outer side SYN **external**: *The outside walls are damp.* 2 ? A2 not located in the main building; going out of the main building SYN **external**: *an outside toilet* ◇ *You have to pay to make outside calls.* ◇ *I can't get an outside line.* 3 ? B2 not included in or connected with your group, organization, country, etc: *We plan to use an outside firm of consultants.* ◇ *She has a lot of outside interests* (= not connected with her work). ◇ *They felt cut off from the outside world* (= from other people and from other things that were happening). 4 used to say that sth is very unlikely: *They have only an outside chance of winning.* ◇ *150 is an outside estimate* (= it is very likely to be less).

**outside ˈbroadcast** *noun* (*BrE*) a programme filmed or recorded away from the main studio

**outside ˈlane** (*BrE*) (*NAmE* **ˈpassing lane**) *noun* the part of a major road such as a MOTORWAY or INTERSTATE nearest the middle of the road, where vehicles drive fastest and can go past vehicles ahead

# outsider 1102

**out·sider** /ˌaʊtˈsaɪdə(r)/ noun **1** a person who is not accepted as a member of a society, group, etc: *Here she felt she would always be an outsider.* ⇨ WORDFINDER NOTE at SOCIETY **2** a person who is not part of a particular organization or profession: *They have decided to hire outsiders for some of the key positions.* ◊ *To an outsider it may appear to be a glamorous job.* **3** a person or an animal taking part in a race or competition that is not expected to win: *The race was won by a rank outsider* (= a complete outsider).

**out·size** /ˈaʊtsaɪz/ (also **out·sized** /ˈaʊtsaɪzd/) adj. [usually before noun] **1** larger than the usual size: *an outsize desk* **2** designed for large people: *outsize clothes*

**out·skirts** /ˈaʊtskɜːts; NAmE -skɜːrts/ noun [pl.] the parts of a town or city that are furthest from the centre: **on the ~ (of sth)** *They live on the outskirts of Milan.* ⇨ WORDFINDER NOTE at LOCATION

**out·smart** /ˌaʊtˈsmɑːt; NAmE -ˈsmɑːrt/ verb **~ sb** to gain an advantage over sb by being cleverer than they are **SYN** outwit: *She always managed to outsmart her political rivals.*

**out·source** /ˈaʊtsɔːs; NAmE -sɔːrs/ verb [T, I] **~ (sth)** (business) to arrange for sb outside a company to do work or provide goods for that company: *We outsource all our computing work.* ▶ **out·sourc·ing** noun [U]

**out·spend** /ˌaʊtˈspend/ verb (**out·spent**, **out·spent** /-ˈspent/) **~ sb/sth** to spend more money on sth than sb else: *The US far outspends its peer nations when it comes to healthcare costs per capita.*

**out·spoken** /ˌaʊtˈspəʊkən/ adj. saying exactly what you think, even if this shocks or offends people **SYN** blunt: *an outspoken opponent of the leader* ◊ *outspoken comments* ◊ **~ in sth** *She was outspoken in her criticism of the plan.* ⇨ SYNONYMS at HONEST ▶ **out·spoken·ly** adv. **out·spoken·ness** /-kənnəs/ noun [U]

**out·spread** /ˌaʊtˈspred/ adj. (formal) spread out completely: *The bird soared high, with outspread wings.*

**out·stand·ing** /aʊtˈstændɪŋ/ adj. **1** extremely good; excellent: *an outstanding player/achievement/success* ◊ *an area of outstanding natural beauty* ⇨ SYNONYMS at EXCELLENT **2** (of payment, work, problems, etc.) not yet paid, done, solved, etc: *She has outstanding debts of over £500.* ◊ *A lot of work is still outstanding.* **3** [usually before noun] very obvious or important **SYN** prominent: *the outstanding features of the landscape*

**out·stand·ing·ly** /aʊtˈstændɪŋli/ adv. **1** used to emphasize the good quality of sth **SYN** remarkably: *outstandingly successful* **2** extremely well: *He performed well but not outstandingly.*

**out·sta·tion** /ˈaʊtsteɪʃn/ noun, adj.
■ noun a branch of a company or an organization that is far from the HEADQUARTERS (= the place from which the company or organization is controlled)
■ adj. (IndE) working or studying in a place where you do not live: *The business school has accommodation for outstation students.*

**ˈoutstation cheque** noun (IndE) a CHEQUE from a bank account in one place that is exchanged for money in another city, state, etc.

**out·stay** /ˌaʊtˈsteɪ/ verb IDM see WELCOME n.

**out·stretched** /ˌaʊtˈstretʃt/ adj. (of parts of the body) stretched or spread out as far as possible: *He ran towards her with arms outstretched/with outstretched arms.*

**out·strip** /ˌaʊtˈstrɪp/ verb (**-pp-**) **1 ~ sth** to become larger, more important, etc. than sb/sth: *Demand is outstripping supply.* **2 ~ sth** to be faster, better or more successful than sb you are competing against **SYN** surpass: *Their latest computer outstrips all its rivals.* **3 ~ sb** to run faster than sb in a race so that you pass them

**outta** (also **outa**) /ˈaʊtə/ prep. used for writing the way 'out of' is sometimes pronounced in informal speech: *I'm outta here!* (= I'm leaving now.)

**ˈout-take** noun a piece of a film that is not included in the final film, for example because it contains a mistake

**ˈout-there** adj. (NAmE, informal) (of people) different, confident, having strong opinions and attracting attention to yourself; (of ideas) different from what most people consider normal, but exciting: *Wow, this is such an out-there character. This role is probably going to be cool.* ◊ *It may be totally out-there but I think it could work.*

**ˈout tray** (BrE) (US **ˈout box**) noun (in an office) a container on your desk for letters or documents that are waiting to be sent out or passed to sb else ⇨ compare IN TRAY

**out·vote** /ˌaʊtˈvəʊt/ verb [usually passive] **~ sb/sth** to defeat sb/sth by winning a larger number of votes **SYN** vote sb/sth↔down: *His proposal was outvoted by 10 votes to 8.*

**out·ward** /ˈaʊtwəd; NAmE -wərd/ adj., adv.
■ adj. [only before noun] **1** connected with the way people or things seem to be rather than with what is actually true: *Mark showed no outward signs of distress.* ◊ *She simply observes the outward forms of religion.* ◊ *To all outward appearances* (= as far as it was possible to judge from the outside) *they were perfectly happy.* **OPP** inward **2** going away from a particular place, especially one that you are going to return to: *the outward voyage/journey* **3** away from the centre or a particular point: *outward movement* ◊ *outward investment* (= in other countries) ◊ *Managers need to become more outward-looking* (= more open to new ideas). **OPP** inward
■ adv. = OUTWARDS

**ˌoutward ˈbound** adj. going away from home or a particular place

**the ˌOutward ˈBound ˈTrust** [sing.] (also **Outward Bound**™) [U] noun an international organization that provides training in outdoor activities, including sports, for young people

**out·ward·ly** /ˈaʊtwədli; NAmE -wərd-/ adv. on the surface; in appearance: *Though badly frightened, she remained outwardly composed.* ◊ *Outwardly, the couple seemed perfectly happy.* **OPP** inwardly

**out·wards** /ˈaʊtwədz; NAmE -wərdz/ (BrE) (also **out·ward** NAmE, BrE) adv. **~ (from sth)** towards the outside; away from the centre or from a particular point: *The door opens outwards.* ◊ *Factories were spreading outwards from the old heart of the town.* **OPP** inwards

**out·weigh** /ˌaʊtˈweɪ/ verb **~ sth** to be greater or more important than sth: *The advantages far outweigh the disadvantages.*

**out·wit** /ˌaʊtˈwɪt/ verb (**-tt-**) **~ sb/sth** to defeat sb/sth or gain an advantage over them by doing sth clever **SYN** outsmart: *Somehow he always manages to outwit his opponents.*

**out·with** /ˌaʊtˈwɪθ/ prep. (ScotE) outside of sth; not within sth

**ouzo** /ˈuːzəʊ/ noun [U, C] a strong alcoholic drink from Greece, made from ANISEED and usually drunk with water

**ova** /ˈəʊvə/ pl. of OVUM

**oval** /ˈəʊvl/ adj., noun
■ adj. like an egg in shape: *an oval face*
■ noun **1** an oval shape **2** (AustralE) a ground for Australian Rules football

**the ˌOval ˈOffice** noun [sing.] **1** the office of the US President in the White House **2** a way of referring to the US President and the part of the government that is controlled by the President: *Congress is waiting to see how the Oval Office will react.*

**ovary** /ˈəʊvəri/ noun (pl. **-ies**) **1** either of the two organs in a woman's body that produce eggs; a similar organ in female animals, birds and fish **2** the part of a plant that produces seeds ⇨ VISUAL VOCAB page V7 ▶ **ovar·ian** /əʊˈveəriən; NAmE -ˈver-/ adj. [only before noun]: *ovarian cancer*

**ova·tion** /əʊˈveɪʃn/ noun enthusiastic CLAPPING by an audience as a sign of their approval: *to give sb a huge/rapturous/rousing ovation* ◊ *The soloist got a ten-minute standing ovation* (= in which people stand up from their seats). ⇨ WORDFINDER NOTE at PERFORMANCE

**oven** /ˈʌvn/ *noun* the part of a cooker that is like a box with a door on the front, in which food is cooked or heated: *Take the cake out of the oven.* ◇ *Bake in a preheated oven for 15–20 minutes.* ◇ *a gas/an electric oven* ◇ *a cool/hot/moderate oven* ◇ *Open a window, it's like an oven in here!* ⊃ compare MICROWAVE IDM see BUN

**ˈoven glove** (*also* **ˈoven mitt**) *noun* a glove made of thick material, used for holding hot dishes from an oven

**ovenˈproof** /ˈʌvnpruːf/ *adj.* suitable for use in a hot oven: *an ovenproof dish*

**over** /ˈəʊvə(r)/ *prep., adv., noun*
- *prep.* HELP For the special uses of **over** in phrasal verbs, look at the entries for the verbs. For example **get over sth** is in the phrasal verb section at **get**. **1** resting on the surface of sb/sth and partly or completely covering them/it: *She put a blanket over the sleeping child.* ◇ *He wore an overcoat over his suit.* ◇ *She put her hand over her mouth to stop herself from screaming.* **2** in or to a position higher than but not touching sb/sth; above sb/sth: *They held a large umbrella over her.* ◇ *The balcony juts out over the street.* ◇ *There was a lamp hanging over the table.* **3** from one side of sth to the other; across sth: *a bridge over the river* ◇ *They ran over the grass.* ◇ *They had a wonderful view over the park.* **4** so as to cross sth and be on the other side: *She climbed over the wall.* **5** falling from or down from a place: *The car had toppled over the cliff.* ◇ *He didn't dare look over the edge.* **6** on the far or opposite side of sth: *He lives over the road.* **7 all ~** in or on all or most parts of sth: *Snow is falling all over the country.* ◇ *They've travelled all over the world.* ◇ *There were papers lying around all over the place.* **8** more than a particular time, amount, cost, etc: *over 3 million copies sold* ◇ *She stayed in Lagos for over a month.* ◇ *He's over sixty.* **9** used to show that sb has control or authority: *She has only the director over her.* ◇ *He ruled over a great empire.* ◇ *She has editorial control over what is included.* **10** during sth: *We'll discuss it over lunch.* ◇ *Over the next few days they got to know the town well.* ◇ *She has not changed much over the years.* ◇ *He built up the business over a period of ten years.* ◇ *We're away over (= until after) the New Year.* **11** past a particular difficult stage or situation: *She's over the worst of the recession.* ◇ *It took her ages to get over her illness.* **12** because of or relating to sth; about sth: *an argument over money* ◇ *a disagreement over the best way to proceed* **13** using sth; by means of sth: *We heard it over the radio.* ◇ *She wouldn't tell me over the phone.* **14** louder than sth: *I couldn't hear what he said over the noise of the traffic.* ⊃ note at ABOVE
  IDM **over and aˈbove** in addition to sth: *There are other factors over and above those we have discussed.*
- *adv.* HELP For the special uses of **over** in phrasal verbs, look at the entries for the verbs. For example **take sth over** is in the phrasal verb section at **take**. **1** across a street, an open space, etc: *I stopped and crossed over.* ◇ *He rowed us over to the other side of the lake.* ◇ *They have gone over to France.* ◇ *This is my aunt who's over from Canada.* ◇ *I went over (= across the room) and asked her name.* ◇ *Put it down over there.* **2** downwards and away from the correct position standing UPRIGHT: *Try not to knock that vase over.* ◇ *The wind must have blown it over.* **3** from one side to another side: *She turned over onto her front.* ◇ *The car skidded off the road and rolled over and over.* **4** so as to cover sb/sth completely: *The lake was frozen over.* ◇ *Cover her over with a blanket.* **5** above; more: *children of 14 and over* ◇ *You get an A grade for scores of 75 and over.* **6** not used or needed: *If there's any food left over, put it in the fridge.* **7** ended: *By the time we arrived the meeting was over.* ◇ *Thank goodness that's over!* ◇ *I was glad when it was over and done with.* **8** again: *He repeated it several times over until he could remember it.* ◇ (*NAmE*) *It's all wrong—you'll have to do it over.* **9** used to talk about sb/sth changing position: *He's gone over to the enemy (= joined them).* ◇ *Please change the wheels over (= for example, put the front wheels at the back).* ◇ *Let's ask some friends over (= to our home).* ◇ *Hand over the money!* **10** used when communicating by radio: *Message received. Over (= it is your turn to speak).* ◇ *Message understood. Over and out.*
  IDM **(all) over aˈgain** a second time from the beginning: *He did the work so badly that I had to do it all over again* 

myself. **over aˈgainst sth** in contrast with sth **ˌover and ˈover (aˌgain)** many times; repeatedly: *I've told you over and over again not to do that.* **ˌover to ˈyou** used to say that it is sb's turn to do sth
- *noun* (in CRICKET) a series of six balls BOWLED by the same person

**over-** /ˈəʊvə(r)/ *prefix* (in nouns, verbs, adjectives and adverbs) **1** more than usual; too much: *overproduction* ◇ *overload* ◇ *over-optimistic* ◇ *overconfident* ◇ *overanxious* **2** completely: *overjoyed* **3** upper; outer; extra: *overcoat* ◇ *overtime* **4** over; above: *overcast* ◇ *overhang*

**overˈachieve** /ˌəʊvərəˈtʃiːv/ *verb* **1** [I] to do better than expected in your studies or work **2** [I] to try too hard to be successful in your work ▸ **overˈachiever** *noun*

**overˈact** /ˌəʊvərˈækt/ *verb* [I, T] **~(sth)** (*disapproving*) to behave in a way that is EXAGGERATED and not natural, especially when you are acting a part in a play

**overˈactive** /ˌəʊvərˈæktɪv/ *adj.* [usually before noun] **1** (of an organ or part of the body) causing harm by doing sth too much: *an overactive thyroid* **2** of sb's imagination) too active, especially so that they imagine things that are not true: *She suffers from an overactive imagination.*

**ˈover·age** /ˈəʊvəreɪdʒ/ *adj.* too old to be allowed to do a particular thing

**overˈall** *adj., adv., noun*
- *adj.* [only before noun] including all the things or people that are involved in a particular situation; general: *There will be winners in each of three age groups, and one overall winner.* ◇ *The coach is happy with the overall performance of the team this season.* ◇ *The overall quality of the articles is good.* ◇ *The overall cost of my trip is £171.40.*
- *adv.* /ˌəʊvərˈɔːl/ **1** including everything or everyone; in total: *The company will invest $1.6m overall in new equipment.* **2** generally; when you consider everything: *Overall, this is a very useful book.* ⊃ LANGUAGE BANK at CONCLUSION
- *noun* /ˈəʊvərɔːl/ **1** (*BrE*) [C] a loose coat worn over other clothes to protect them from dirt, etc: *The lab assistant was wearing a white overall.* **2** **overalls** (*BrE*) (*NAmE* **coveralls**) [pl.] a loose piece of clothing like a shirt and trousers in one piece, made of heavy cloth and usually worn over other clothing by workers doing dirty work: *The mechanic was wearing a pair of blue overalls.* ⊃ compare BOILER SUIT **3** **overalls** (*also* **bib overalls**) (*both NAmE*) (*BrE* **dunˈgarees**) [pl.] a piece of clothing that consists of trousers with an extra piece of cloth covering the chest, held up by narrow pieces of cloth over the shoulders

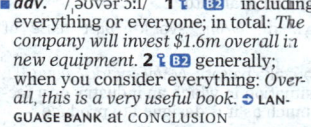
overalls/coveralls

dungarees/overalls

**overall maˈjority** *noun* [usually sing.] **1** more votes in an election or vote than all the other people or parties together **2** the difference between the number of members that the government has in a parliament and the number that all the other political parties have together: *a huge 101-seat overall majority*

**overamˈbitious** /ˌəʊvəræmˈbɪʃəs/ *adj.* **1** unsuccessful or likely to be unsuccessful because of needing too much effort, money or time: *Her plans were overambitious.* **2** (*disapproving*) too determined to be successful, rich, powerful, etc.

**overˈarching** /ˌəʊvərˈɑːtʃɪŋ; *NAmE* -ˈɑːrtʃ-/ *adj.* [usually before noun] (*formal*) very important, because it includes or influences many things

**ˈover·arm** /ˈəʊvərɑːm; *NAmE* -ɑːrm/ (*especially BrE*) (*also* **ˈoverˌhand** *especially in NAmE*) *adv.* if you throw a ball **overarm**, you throw it by moving your arm backwards then lifting it high above your shoulder ▸ **ˈover·arm** (*especially*

**overate**

*BrE*) (also **over·hand** especially in *NAmE*) *adj.*: *an overarm throw* ⊃ compare UNDERARM

**over·ate** /ˌəʊvəˈret, -ˈeɪt; *NAmE* -ˈeɪt/ *past tense* of OVEREAT

**over·awe** /ˌəʊvəˈrɔː/ *verb* [usually passive] **~ sb** to impress sb so much that they feel nervous or frightened ▶ **over·awed** *adj.*

**over·bal·ance** /ˌəʊvəˈbæləns; *NAmE* -vərˈb-/ *verb* [I, T] **~ (sb/sth)** (especially *BrE*) to lose your balance and fall; to make sb/sth lose their balance and fall: *He overbalanced and fell into the water.*

**over·bear·ing** /ˌəʊvəˈbeərɪŋ; *NAmE* -vərˈber-/ *adj.* (*disapproving*) trying to control other people in an unpleasant way SYN domineering: *an overbearing manner*

**over·bite** /ˈəʊvəbaɪt; *NAmE* -vərb-/ *noun* [usually sing.] (*specialist*) a condition in which a person or animal's upper JAW is too far forward in relation to their lower JAW

**over·blown** /ˌəʊvəˈbləʊn; *NAmE* -vərˈb-/ *adj.* **1** that is made to seem larger, more impressive or more important than it really is SYN **exaggerated 2** (of flowers) past the best, most beautiful stage

**over·board** /ˈəʊvəbɔːd; *NAmE* -vərbɔːrd/ *adv.* over the side of a boat or a ship into the water: *to fall/jump overboard* ◊ *Huge waves washed him overboard.* IDM **go ˈoverboard** (*informal*) to be too excited or enthusiastic about sth or about doing sth: *Don't go overboard on fitness.* **throw sb/sth ˈoverboard** to get rid of sb/sth that you think is not useful

**over·book** /ˌəʊvəˈbʊk; *NAmE* -vərˈb-/ *verb* [T, I] **~(sth)** to sell more tickets on a plane or reserve more rooms in a hotel than there are places available: *The flight was heavily overbooked.* ⊃ compare DOUBLE-BOOK

**over·bridge** /ˈəʊvəbrɪdʒ; *NAmE* -vərb-/ *noun* a bridge over a railway or road

**over·bur·den** /ˌəʊvəˈbɜːdn; *NAmE* -vərˈbɜːrdn/ *verb* [usually passive] **~ sb/sth (with sth)** to give sb/sth more work, worry, etc. than they can deal with

**over·came** /ˌəʊvəˈkeɪm; *NAmE* -vərˈk-/ *past tense* of OVERCOME

**over·cap·acity** /ˌəʊvəkəˈpæsəti; *NAmE* -vərk-/ *noun* [U, sing.] (*business*) the situation in which an industry or a factory cannot sell as much as it is designed to produce

**over·cast** /ˌəʊvəˈkɑːst; *NAmE* -vərˈkæst/ *adj.* covered with clouds; not bright: *an overcast sky/day* ◊ *Today it will be dull and overcast.*

**over·charge** /ˌəʊvəˈtʃɑːdʒ; *NAmE* -vərˈtʃɑːrdʒ/ *verb* [T, I] **~ (sb) (for sth)** to make sb pay too much for sth: *Make sure they don't overcharge you for the drinks.* ◊ *We were overcharged by £5.* OPP **undercharge**

**over·coat** /ˈəʊvəkəʊt; *NAmE* -vərk-/ *noun* a long warm coat worn in cold weather

**over·come** 0̃+ B2 /ˌəʊvəˈkʌm; *NAmE* -vərˈk-/ *verb* (**over·came** /-ˈkeɪm/, **over·come**) **1** 0̃+ B2 **~ sth** to succeed in dealing with or controlling a problem that has been preventing you from achieving sth: *She overcame injury to win the Olympic gold medal.* ◊ *The two parties managed to overcome their differences on the issue.* **2** 0̃+ C1 **~ sb/sth** to defeat sb: *In the final game Sweden easily overcame France.* **3** 0̃+ C1 [usually passive] **~ sb** to affect sb very strongly SYN **overwhelm**: *Her parents were overcome with grief at the funeral.* ◊ *The dead woman had been overcome by smoke.*

**over·com·pen·sate** /ˌəʊvəˈkɒmpənseɪt; *NAmE* -vərˈkɑːm-/ *verb* [I] **~ (for sth) (by doing sth)** to do too much when trying to correct a problem and so cause a different problem: *She overcompensated for her shyness by talking too much and laughing too loud.*

**over·con·fi·dent** /ˌəʊvəˈkɒnfɪdənt; *NAmE* -vərˈkɑːn-/ *adj.* too confident

**over·cook** /ˌəʊvəˈkʊk; *NAmE* -vərˈk-/ *verb* **~sth** to cook food for too long

**over·crowd·ed** /ˌəʊvəˈkraʊdɪd; *NAmE* -vərˈk-/ *adj.* (of a place) with too many people or things in it: *overcrowded cities/prisons* ◊ *Too many poor people are living in overcrowded conditions.*

**over·crowd·ing** /ˌəʊvəˈkraʊdɪŋ; *NAmE* -vərˈk-/ *noun* [U] the situation when there are too many people or things in one place

**over·de·vel·oped** /ˌəʊvədɪˈveləpt; *NAmE* -vərd-/ *adj.* that has grown too large: *overdeveloped muscles* ◊ *an overdeveloped sense of humour* ▶ **over·de·velop** *verb* **~ sth** **over·develop·ment** *noun* [U]

**over·do** /ˌəʊvəˈduː; *NAmE* -vərˈduː/ *verb* (**over·does** /-ˈdʌz/, **over·did** /-ˈdɪd/, **over·done** /-ˈdʌn/) **1** **~ sth** to do sth too much; to make sth seem larger, better, worse or more important than it really is: *She really overdid the sympathy* (= and so did not seem sincere). **2** **~ sth** to use too much of sth: *Don't overdo the salt in the food.* ◊ *Use illustrations where appropriate but don't overdo it.* **3** [usually passive] **~ sth** to cook sth for too long: *The fish was overdone and very dry.* IDM **overˈdo it/things** to work, study, etc. too hard or for too long: *He's been overdoing things recently.* ◊ *I overdid it in the gym and hurt my back.*

**over·dose** /ˈəʊvədəʊs; *NAmE* -vərd-/ *noun, verb*
■ *noun* too much of a drug taken at one time, so that it is dangerous: *a drug/drugs overdose* ◊ *She took a massive overdose of sleeping pills.* ⊃ WORDFINDER NOTE at DRUG
■ *verb* (also *informal* **OD**) [I] **~ (on sth)** to take too much of a drug at one time, so that it is dangerous: *He had overdosed on heroin.* ◊ (*figurative*) *I had overdosed on sun.*

**over·draft** /ˈəʊvədrɑːft; *NAmE* -vərdræft/ *noun* the amount of money that you owe to a bank when you have spent more money than is in your bank account; an arrangement that allows you to do this: *She had run up an overdraft of £3000.* ◊ *to pay off/clear an overdraft* ⊃ WORDFINDER NOTE at LOAN

**over·draw** /ˌəʊvəˈdrɔː; *NAmE* -vərˈd-/ *verb* [T, I] (**over·drew** /-ˈdruː/, **over·drawn** /-ˈdrɔːn/) **~(sth)** (especially *BrE*) to take out more money from a bank account than it contains: *Customers who overdraw their accounts will be charged a fee.*

**over·drawn** /ˌəʊvəˈdrɔːn; *NAmE* -vərˈd-/ *adj.* **1** [not usually before noun] (of a person) having taken more money out of your bank account than you have in it: *I'm overdrawn by £100.* **2** (of a bank account) with more money taken out than was paid in or left in: *an overdrawn account* ◊ *Your account is £200 overdrawn.*

**over·dressed** /ˌəʊvəˈdrest; *NAmE* -vərˈd-/ *adj.* (*usually disapproving*) wearing clothes that are too formal or too smart for a particular occasion OPP **underdressed**

**over·drive** /ˈəʊvədraɪv; *NAmE* -vərd-/ *noun* (*old-fashioned*) an extra high GEAR in a vehicle, used when you are driving at high speeds: *to be in overdrive* IDM **go into ˈoverdrive** to start being very active and working very hard: *As the wedding approached, the whole family went into overdrive.*

**over·dub** /ˌəʊvəˈdʌb; *NAmE* -vərˈd-/ *verb* (**-bb-**) **~ sb/sth** to record new sounds over the sounds on an original recording so that both can be heard

**over·due** /ˌəʊvəˈdjuː; *NAmE* -vərˈduː/ *adj.* **1** not paid, done, returned, etc. by the required or expected time: *an overdue payment/library book* ◊ *The rent is now overdue.* ◊ *Her baby is two weeks overdue.* ◊ *This car is overdue for a service.* **2** that should have happened or been done before now: *overdue reforms* ◊ *A book like this is long overdue.*

**over ˈeasy** *adj.* (*NAmE*) (of fried eggs) turned over when almost cooked and fried for a short time on the other side

**over·eat** /ˌəʊvəˈriːt/ *verb* (**over·ate** /ˌəʊvəˈret, -ˈeɪt; *NAmE* -ˈeɪt/, **over·eaten** /ˌəʊvəˈriːtn/) [I] to eat more than you need or more than is healthy ▶ **over·eat·ing** *noun* [U]: *She went through periods of compulsive overeating.*

**over-ˈegg** *verb* IDM **over-egg the ˈpudding** used to say that you think sb has done more than is necessary, or has added unnecessary details to make sth seem better or worse than it really is: *If you're telling lies, keep it simple—never over-egg the pudding.*

**over·em·pha·sis** /ˌəʊvəˈremfəsɪs/ *noun* [U, sing.] **~(on sth)** too much emphasis or importance: *an overemphasis* on curing illness rather than preventing it ▶ **over·empha·size, -ise** /-fəsaɪz/ verb: ~ **sth** The importance of preparation cannot be overemphasized.

**over·esti·mate**
- **verb** /ˌəʊvər'estɪmeɪt/ ~ **sth** to estimate sth to be larger, better, more important, etc. than it really is: *They overestimated his ability when they promoted him.* ◊ *The importance of these findings **cannot be overestimated** (= is very great).* **OPP** **underestimate** ▶ **over·esti·mation** noun [U, C]
- **noun** /ˌəʊvər'estɪmət/ [usually sing.] an estimate about the size, cost, etc. of sth that is too high **OPP** **underestimate**

**over·ex·cited** /ˌəʊvərɪk'saɪtɪd/ adj. too excited and not behaving in a calm or sensible way: *Don't get the children overexcited just before bedtime.*

**over·ex·pose** /ˌəʊvərɪk'spəʊz/ verb [usually passive] ~ **sth** to affect the quality of a photograph or film by allowing too much light to enter the camera **OPP** **underexpose** **2** ~ **sb/sth** to allow sb/sth to be seen too much on television, in the newspapers, etc: *The club is careful not to let the younger players be overexposed, and rarely allows them to be interviewed.* ▶ **over·ex·pos·ure** /-'spəʊʒə(r)/ noun [U]

**over·ex·tend·ed** /ˌəʊvərɪk'stendɪd/ adj. [not usually before noun] involved in more work or activities, or spending more money, than you can manage without problems ▶ **over·ex·tend** verb: ~ **yourself** *They should not overextend themselves on the mortgage.*

**over·feed** /ˌəʊvə'fiːd/ NAmE -vər'f-/ verb (**over·fed, over·fed** /-'fed/) ~ **sb/sth** to give sb/sth too much food ▶ **over·fed** adj. **OPP** **underfed**

**over·fish·ing** /ˌəʊvə'fɪʃɪŋ/ NAmE -vər'f-/ noun [U] the process of taking so many fish from the sea, a river, etc. that the number of fish in it becomes very low

**over·flow** verb, noun
- **verb** /ˌəʊvə'fləʊ; NAmE -vər'f-/ **1** [I, T] to be so full that the contents go over the sides: *The bath is overflowing!* ◊ ~ **with sth** *Plates overflowed with party food.* ◊ *(figurative) Her heart overflowed with love.* ◊ ~ **sth** *The river overflowed its banks.* **2** [I] ~ **(with sth)** (of a place) to have too many people in it: *The streets were overflowing with the crowds.* ◊ *The hospitals are **filled to overflowing** (= with patients).* **3** [I, T] ~ **(into sth)** | ~ **(sth)** to spread beyond the limits of a place or container that is too full: *The meeting overflowed into the street.*
- **noun** /ˌəʊvəfləʊ; NAmE -vərf-/ **1** [U, sing.] a number of people or things that do not fit into the space available: *A new office block was built to accommodate the overflow of staff.* ◊ *an overflow car park* **2** [U, sing.] the action of liquid flowing out of a container, etc. that is already full; the liquid that flows out: *an overflow of water from the lake* ◊ *(figurative) an overflow of powerful emotions* **3** [also **overflow pipe**] [C] a pipe that allows extra liquid to flow away safely when a container is full **4** [C, usually sing.] *(computing)* a fault that happens because a number or data item is too large for the computer to represent it exactly

**over·fly** /ˌəʊvə'flaɪ; NAmE -vər'f-/ verb [T, I] (**over·flies, over·fly·ing, over·flew** /-'fluː/, **over·flown** /-'fləʊn/) ~ **(sth)** to fly over a place: *We overflew the war zone, taking photographs.* ◊ *the noise from overflying planes* ▶ **over·flight** noun

**over·graze** /ˌəʊvə'greɪz; NAmE -vər'g-/ verb ~ **sth** if land is **overgrazed**, it is damaged by having too many animals feeding on it

**over·ground** /'əʊvəɡraʊnd; NAmE -vərg-/ adv. *(BrE)* on or above the surface of the ground, rather than under it: *The new railway line will run overground.* ▶ **over·ground** adj.: *overground trains* ⇒ compare **UNDERGROUND**

**over·grown** /ˌəʊvə'ɡrəʊn; NAmE -vər'g-/ adj. **1** (of gardens, etc.) covered with plants that have been allowed to grow wild and have not been controlled: *an overgrown path* ◊ ~ **with sth** *The garden's completely overgrown with weeds.* **2** *(often disapproving)* that has grown too large: *an overgrown village* ◊ *They act like a pair of overgrown children (= they are adults but they behave like children).*

**over·growth** /'əʊvəɡrəʊθ; NAmE -vərg-/ noun [U, sing.] *(specialist)* too much growth of sth, especially sth that grows on or over sth else ⇒ compare **UNDERGROWTH**

**over·hand** /'əʊvəhænd; NAmE -vərh-/ adj., adv. (especially NAmE) = **OVERARM**

**over·hang** verb, noun
- **verb** /ˌəʊvə'hæŋ; NAmE -vər'h-/ (**over·hung, over·hung** /-'hʌŋ/) [T, I] ~ **(sth)** to stick out over and above sth else: *His big fat belly overhung his belt.* ◊ *The path was cool and dark with overhanging trees.*
- **noun** /'əʊvəhæŋ; NAmE -vərh-/ **1** the part of sth that sticks out over and above sth else: *The roof has an overhang to protect the walls from the rain.* **2** the amount by which sth hangs over and above sth else **3** [usually sing.] *(business, especially NAmE)* the state of being extra to what is required; the things that are extra: *attempts to reduce the overhang of unsold goods*

**over·haul** noun, verb
- **noun** /'əʊvəhɔːl; NAmE -vərh-/ an examination of a machine or system, including doing repairs on it or making changes to it: *a complete/major overhaul* ◊ *A radical overhaul of the tax system is necessary.*
- **verb** /ˌəʊvə'hɔːl; NAmE -vər'h-/ **1** ~ **sth** to examine every part of a machine, system, etc. and make any necessary changes or repairs: *The engine has been completely overhauled.* **2** ~ **sb** to come from behind a person you are competing against in a race and go past them **SYN** **overtake**: *He managed to overhaul the leader on the final lap.*

**over·head** /ˌəʊvə'hed; NAmE -vərh-/ adv., adj., noun
- **adv.** above your head; in the sky: *Planes flew overhead constantly.* ◊ *Thunder boomed in the sky overhead.*
- **adj.** **1** above your head; raised above the ground: *overhead power lines* **2** [only before noun] connected with the general costs of running a business or an organization, for example paying for rent or electricity: *overhead costs*
- **noun** /'əʊvəhed; NAmE -vərh-/ [U] *(especially NAmE)* = **OVERHEADS**

**overhead pro·jector** noun *(abbr.* **OHP** /ˌəʊ eɪtʃ 'piː/) a piece of equipment that projects an image onto a wall or screen so that many people can see it ⇒ compare **DATA PROJECTOR, SLIDE PROJECTOR**

**over·heads** /'əʊvəhedz; NAmE -vərh-/ noun [pl.] *(especially BrE)* (also **over·head** [U] *especially in NAmE*) regular costs that you have when you are running a business or an organization, such as rent, electricity, wages, etc. ⇒ **SYNONYMS** at **COST**

**over·hear** /ˌəʊvə'hɪə(r); NAmE -vər'hɪr/ verb (**over·heard, over·heard** /-'hɜːd; NAmE -vər'hɜːrd/) to hear, especially by accident, a conversation in which you are not involved: ~ **sb/sth** *I overheard a conversation between two boys on the bus.* ◊ *We talked quietly so as not to be overheard.* ◊ ~ **sb doing sth** *We overheard them arguing.* ◊ ~ **sb do sth** *I overheard him say he was going to France.* ⇒ compare **EAVESDROP**

**over·heat** /ˌəʊvə'hiːt; NAmE -vər'h-/ verb **1** [I, T] to become or to make sth become too hot: *The engine is overheating.* ◊ ~ **sth** *It's vital not to overheat the liquid.* **2** [I] (of a country's economy) to be too active, with rising prices ▶ **over·heat·ing** noun [U]

**over·heated** /ˌəʊvə'hiːtɪd; NAmE -vər'h-/ adj. **1** too hot: *Don't sleep in an overheated room.* **2** too interested or excited: *the figment of an overheated imagination* **3** (of a country's economy) too active in a way that may cause problems

**over·hung** /ˌəʊvə'hʌŋ; NAmE -vər'h-/ past tense of **OVERHANG**

**over·in·dulge** /ˌəʊvərɪn'dʌldʒ/ verb **1** [I] ~ **(in sth)** to have too much of sth nice, especially food or drink **2** [T] ~ **sb** to give sb more than is good for them: *His mother overindulged him.*

**over·in·flated** /ˌəʊvərɪn'fleɪtɪd/ adj. **1** (of a price or value) too high: *overinflated house prices* **2** made to seem better, worse, more important, etc. than it really is **SYN** **exaggerated** **3** filled with too much air: *Overinflated tyres burst more easily.*

**over·joyed** /ˌəʊvə'dʒɔɪd; NAmE -vər'dʒ-/ adj. [not before noun] extremely happy or pleased **SYN** **delighted**: ~ **(at sth)** *He was overjoyed at my success.* ◊ ~ **(to do sth)** *We*

# overkill

were overjoyed to hear their good news. ◊ ~ **(that ...)** She was overjoyed that her article had been published.

**over·kill** /ˈəʊvəkɪl; NAmE -vərk-/ noun [U] (disapproving) too much of sth that reduces the effect it has: *There is a danger of overkill if you plan everything too carefully.*

**over·laid** /ˌəʊvəˈleɪd; NAmE -vərˈl-/ past tense, past part. of OVERLAY

**over·land** /ˈəʊvəlænd; NAmE -vərl-/ adj. across the land; by land, not by sea or by air: *an overland route* ▶ **over·land** *adv.*: *to travel overland*

**over·lap** W *verb, noun*
■ *verb* /ˌəʊvəˈlæp; NAmE -vərˈl-/ (**-pp-**) **1** [T, I] ~ **one thing overlaps another**, or the two things overlap, part of one thing covers part of the other: *A fish's scales overlap each other.* ◊ *The floor was protected with overlapping sheets of newspaper.* **2** [T] ~ **sth** to make two or more things overlap: *You will need to overlap the pieces of wood slightly.* **3** [I, T] ~ **(sth)** if two events overlap or overlap each other, the second one starts before the first one has finished **4** [I, T] to cover part of the same area of interest, knowledge, responsibility, etc.: *Our jobs overlap slightly, which sometimes causes difficulties.* ◊ ~ **(with) sth** *The language of science overlaps with that of everyday life.*
■ *noun* /ˈəʊvəlæp; NAmE -vərl-/ **1** [C, U] ~ **(between sth and sth)** a shared area of interest, knowledge, responsibility, etc.: *There is (a) considerable overlap between the two subjects.* **2** [C, U] the amount by which one thing covers another thing: *an overlap of 5cm on each roof tile* **3** [U, sing.] a period of time in which two events or activities happen together: *There will be an overlap of a week while John teaches Ann the job.*

**over·lay** *verb, noun*
■ *verb* /ˌəʊvəˈleɪ; NAmE -vərˈl-/ (**over·laid, over·laid** /-ˈleɪd/) [usually passive] **1** ~ **sth (with sth)** (specialist) to put sth on top of a surface so as to cover it completely; to lie on top of a surface: *wood overlaid with gold* **2** ~ **sth (with sth)** (literary) to add sth, especially a feeling or quality, to sth else so that it seems to cover it: *The place was overlaid with memories of his childhood.*
■ *noun* /ˈəʊvəleɪ; NAmE -vərl-/ **1** a clear sheet with drawings, figures, etc. on it that can be placed on top of another sheet in order to change it: *An overlay showing population can be placed on top of the map.* **2** a thing that is laid on top of or covers sth else: *an overlay of fibreglass insulation*

**over·leaf** /ˌəʊvəˈliːf; NAmE -vərˈl-/ adv. on the other side of the page of a book, etc: *Complete the form overleaf.* ◊ *The changes are explained in detail overleaf.*

**over·lie** /ˌəʊvəˈlaɪ; NAmE -vərˈl-/ verb [I, T] (**over·ly·ing**, **over·lay** /-ˈleɪ/, **over·lain** /-ˈleɪn/) ~ **(sth)** (specialist) to lie over sth: *overlying rock*

**over·load** *verb, noun*
■ *verb* /ˌəʊvəˈləʊd; NAmE -vərˈl-/ [often passive] **1** ~ **sth** to put too great a load on sth: *an overloaded truck* **2** ~ **sb (with sth)** to give sb too much of sth: *He's overloaded with responsibilities.* ◊ *Don't overload the students with information.* **3** ~ **sth** to put too great a demand on a computer, an electrical system, etc. causing it to fail
■ *noun* /ˈəʊvələʊd; NAmE -vərl-/ [U, sing.] too much of sth: *In these days of technological change we all suffer from information overload.*

**over·long** /ˌəʊvəˈlɒŋ; NAmE -vərˈlɔːŋ/ (NAmE also **overly long**) adj. too long: *an overlong agenda*

**over·look** /ˌəʊvəˈlʊk; NAmE -vərˈl-/ verb **1** ~ **sth** to fail to see or notice sth **SYN** miss: *He seems to have overlooked one important fact.* **2** ~ **sth** to see sth wrong or bad but decide to ignore it **SYN** turn a blind eye (to sth): *We could not afford to overlook such a serious offence.* **3** ~ **sth** if a building, etc. overlooks a place, you can see that place from the building: *a restaurant overlooking the lake* ◊ *Our back yard is overlooked by several houses.* **4** ~ **sb (for sth)** to not consider sb for a job or position, even though they might be suitable **SYN** pass over: *She's been overlooked for promotion several times.*

**over·lord** /ˈəʊvəlɔːd; NAmE -vərlɔːrd/ noun (especially in the past) a person who has power over many other people: *feudal overlords*

**over·ly** /ˈəʊvəli; NAmE -vərli/ adv. (before an adjective) too; very **SYN** excessively: *I'm not overly fond of pasta.* ◊ *We think you are being overly optimistic.*

**over·much** /ˌəʊvəˈmʌtʃ; NAmE -vərˈm-/ (NAmE also **overly much**) adv. (especially with a negative verb) too much; very much: *She didn't worry overmuch about it.* ▶ **over·much** *adj.*

**over·night** *adv., adj.*
■ *adv.* /ˌəʊvəˈnaɪt; NAmE -vərˈn-/ **1** during or for the night: *We stayed overnight in London after the theatre.* **2** suddenly or quickly: *Don't expect it to improve overnight.*
■ *adj.* /ˈəʊvənaɪt; NAmE -vərn-/ [only before noun] **1** happening during the night; for a night: *an overnight flight* ◊ *overnight accommodation* ◊ *She took only an overnight bag* (= containing the things needed for a night spent away from home). **2** happening suddenly or quickly: *The play was an overnight success.*

**over·op·ti·mis·tic** adj. **1** too confident that sth will be successful: *I'm not over-optimistic about my chances of getting the job.* **2** showing more confidence that sth will be successful than is shown to be right or reasonable by later events: *The sales forecasts turned out to be over-optimistic.*

**over·pass** /ˈəʊvəpɑːs; NAmE -vərpæs/ (NAmE) (BrE **fly-over**) noun a bridge that carries one road over another one ⊃ compare UNDERPASS

**over·pay** /ˌəʊvəˈpeɪ; NAmE -vərˈp-/ verb [usually passive] (**over·paid, over·paid** /-ˈpeɪd/) ~ **sb** to pay sb too much; to pay sb more than their work is worth **OPP** underpay ▶ **over·pay·ment** noun [C, U]

**over·play** /ˌəʊvəˈpleɪ; NAmE -vərˈp-/ verb ~ **sth** to give too much importance to sth **OPP** underplay
**IDM** **overplay your ˈhand** to fail to achieve success by judging your position to be stronger than it really is

**over·popu·lated** /ˌəʊvəˈpɒpjuleɪtɪd; NAmE -vərˈpɑːp-/ adj. (of a country or city) with too many people living in it ▶ **over·popu·la·tion** /ˌəʊvəˌpɒpjuˈleɪʃn; NAmE -vərˌpɑːp-/ noun [U]: *the problems of overpopulation*

**over·power** /ˌəʊvəˈpaʊə(r); NAmE -vərˈp-/ verb **1** ~ **sb** to defeat or gain control over sb completely by using greater strength: *Police finally managed to overpower the gunman.* **2** ~ **sb/sth** to be so strong or great that it affects sb/sth seriously **SYN** overwhelm: *Her beauty overpowered him.* ◊ *The flavour of the garlic overpowered the meat.*

**over·power·ing** /ˌəʊvəˈpaʊərɪŋ; NAmE -vərˈp-/ adj. very strong or powerful: *an overpowering smell of fish* ◊ *an overpowering personality* ◊ *The heat was overpowering.* ▶ **over·power·ing·ly** adv.

**over·priced** /ˌəʊvəˈpraɪst; NAmE -vərˈp-/ adj. too expensive; costing more than it is worth ⊃ SYNONYMS at EXPENSIVE

**over·print** /ˌəʊvəˈprɪnt; NAmE -vərˈp-/ verb ~ **A (on B)** ~ **B with A** to print sth on a document, etc. that already has printing on it

**over·pro·duce** /ˌəʊvəprəˈdjuːs; NAmE -vərprəˈduːs/ verb [T, I] ~ **(sth)** to produce more of sth than is wanted or needed ▶ **over·pro·duc·tion** /-ˈdʌkʃn/ noun [U]

**over·pro·tect·ive** /ˌəʊvəprəˈtektɪv; NAmE -vərp-/ adj. (disapproving) too anxious to protect sb from being hurt, in a way that limits their freedom: *overprotective parents*

**over·quali·fied** /ˌəʊvəˈkwɒlɪfaɪd; NAmE -vərˈkwɑːl-/ adj. having more experience or training than is necessary for a particular job, so that people do not want to employ you

**over·ran** /ˌəʊvəˈræn/ past tense of OVERRUN

**over·rate** /ˌəʊvəˈreɪt; NAmE -vərˈr-/ verb [usually passive] ~ **sb/sth** to have too high an opinion of sb/sth; to put too high a value on sb/sth: *In my opinion, Hirst's work has been vastly overrated.* **OPP** underrate

**over·reach** /ˌəʊvəˈriːtʃ; NAmE -vərˈr-/ verb [T, I] ~ **(yourself)** to fail by trying to achieve more than is possible: *In making these promises, the company had clearly overreached itself.*

**over·react** /ˌəʊvəriˈækt; NAmE -vərɪˈ-/ verb [I] ~ **(to sth)** to react too strongly, especially to sth unpleasant ▶ **over·re·ac·tion** /-ˈækʃn/ noun [sing., U]

**over·ride** /ˌəʊvəˈraɪd; NAmE -vərˈr-/ verb (**over·rode** /-ˈrəʊd/, **over·rid·den** /-ˈrɪdn/) **1** ~ **sth** to use your authority to reject sb's decision, order, etc. **SYN** **overrule**: *The chairman overrode the committee's objections and signed the agreement.* **2** ~ **sth** to be more important than sth: *Considerations of safety override all other concerns.* **3** ~ **sth** to interrupt the action of a device that usually works by itself in order to control it yourself: *A special code is needed to override the time lock.*

**over·rid·ing** /ˌəʊvəˈraɪdɪŋ; NAmE -vərˈr-/ adj. [only before noun] more important than anything else in a particular situation: *the overriding factor/consideration/concern* ◊ *Their overriding aim was to keep costs low.*

**over·ripe** /ˌəʊvərˈraɪp/ adj. too RIPE: *overripe fruit*

**over·rule** /ˌəʊvəˈruːl; NAmE -vərˈr-/ verb [often passive] ~ **sb/sth** to change a decision or reject an idea from a position of greater power **SYN** **override**: *to overrule a decision/an objection* ◊ *The verdict was overruled by the Supreme Court.*

**over·run** /ˌəʊvəˈrʌn/ verb (**over·ran** /-ˈræn/, **over·run**) **1** [T, often passive] ~ **sth** (especially of sth bad or not wanted) to fill or spread over an area quickly, especially in large numbers: *The house was completely overrun with mice.* ◊ *Enemy soldiers had overrun the island.* **2** [I, T] to take more time or money than was intended: *Her lectures never overrun.* ◊ *You've overrun your time by 10 minutes.* ▶ **over·run** /ˈəʊvərʌn/ noun: *a cost overrun*

**over·seas** 🔽+ B2 /ˌəʊvəˈsiːz; NAmE -vərˈs-/ adj., adv.
■ *adj.* 🔽+ B2 connected with foreign countries, especially those separated from your country by the sea or ocean: *The firm is expanding into overseas markets.* ◊ *overseas development/trade* ◊ *overseas visitors/students* ◊ *This was her first overseas trip as prime minister.* ⊃ compare HOME
■ *adv.* 🔽+ B2 to or in a foreign country, especially those separated from your country by the sea or ocean **SYN** **abroad**: *to live/work/go overseas* ◊ *The product is sold both at home and overseas.*

**over·see** 🔽+ C1 /ˌəʊvəˈsiː; NAmE -vərˈs-/ verb (**over·saw** /-ˈsɔː/, **over·seen** /-ˈsiːn/) ~ **sb/sth** to watch sb/sth and make sure that a job or an activity is done correctly **SYN** **supervise**

**over·seer** /ˈəʊvəsɪə(r); NAmE -vərsɪr/ noun **1** (*old-fashioned*) a person whose job is to make sure that other workers do their work **2** a person or an organization that is responsible for making sure that a system is working as it should

**over·sell** /ˌəʊvəˈsel; NAmE -vərˈs-/ verb (**over·sold**, **over·sold** /-ˈsəʊld/) [often passive] **1** ~ **sb/sth/yourself** to say that sb/sth is better than they really are: *He has a tendency to oversell himself.* **2** ~ **sth** (*business*) to sell too much or more of sth than is available: *The seats on the plane were oversold.*

**over·sen·si·tive** /ˌəʊvəˈsensɪtɪv; NAmE -vərˈs-/ adj. too easily upset or offended

**over·sexed** /ˌəʊvəˈsekst; NAmE -vərˈs-/ adj. (*usually disapproving*) having stronger sexual desire than is usual

**over·shadow** /ˌəʊvəˈʃædəʊ; NAmE -vərˈʃ-/ verb [often passive] **1** ~ **sb/sth** to make sb/sth seem less important, be successful: *He had always been overshadowed by his elder sister.* **2** ~ **sth** to make an event less pleasant than it should be **SYN** **cloud**: *News of the accident overshadowed the day's events.* **3** ~ **sth** to throw a shadow over sth: *The garden is overshadowed by tall trees.*

**over·share** /ˌəʊvəˈʃeə(r); NAmE -vərˈʃer/ verb [I] (*disapproving*) to give more information than people want to hear about your personal life: *Her tendency to overshare is sometimes embarrassing!* ▶ **over·sharer** noun **over·sharing** noun

**over·shoot** /ˌəʊvəˈʃuːt; NAmE -vərˈʃ-/ verb (**over·shot**, **over·shot** /-ˈʃɒt; NAmE -ˈʃɑːt/) **1** [T, I] to go further than the place you intended to stop or turn: ~ **sth** *The aircraft overshot the runway.* ◊ ~ **(sth) (by sth)** *She had overshot by 20 metres.* **2** ~ **sth (by sth)** to do more or to spend more money than you originally planned: *The department may overshoot its cash limit this year.*

**over·sight** /ˈəʊvəsaɪt; NAmE -vərs-/ noun **1** [C, U] the fact of making a mistake because you forget to do sth or you

### 1107 overtake

do not notice sth: *I didn't mean to leave her name off the list; it was an oversight.* **2** [U] (*formal*) the state of being in charge of sb/sth: *The committee has oversight of finance and general policy.*

**over·sim·plify** /ˌəʊvəˈsɪmplɪfaɪ; NAmE -vərˈs-/ verb (T, I) (**over·sim·pli·fies**, **over·sim·pli·fy·ing**, **over·sim·pli·fied**, **over·sim·pli·fied**) ~ **(sth)** to describe a situation, a problem, etc. in a way that is too simple and ignores some of the facts: *It's easy to oversimplify the issues involved.* ◊ *an oversimplified view of human nature* ▶ **over·sim·pli·fi·ca·tion** /ˌəʊvəˌsɪmplɪfɪˈkeɪʃn; NAmE -vərˌs-/ noun [C, usually sing., U]: *This is a gross oversimplification of the facts.* ⊃ compare SIMPLIFICATION

**over·sized** /ˈəʊvəsaɪzd; NAmE -vərs-/ (also less frequent **over·size** /ˈəʊvəsaɪz; NAmE -vərs-/) adj. bigger than the normal size; too big

**over·sleep** /ˌəʊvəˈsliːp; NAmE -vərˈs-/ verb (**over·slept**, **over·slept** /-ˈslept/) [I] to sleep longer than you intended: *I overslept and missed the bus.* ⊃ WORDFINDER NOTE at SLEEP

**over·spend** /ˌəʊvəˈspend; NAmE -vərˈs-/ verb (**over·spent**, **over·spent** /-ˈspent/) [I, T] to spend too much money or more than you planned: ~ **(on sth)** *The company has overspent on marketing.* ◊ ~ **sth** *Many departments have overspent their budgets this year.* ▶ **over·spend** /ˈəʊvəspend; NAmE -vərs-/ noun [sing.] (*BrE*): *a £1 million overspend* **over·spent** /ˌəʊvəˈspent; NAmE -vərˈs-/ adj.: *The organization is heavily overspent.*

**over·spill** /ˈəʊvəspɪl; NAmE -vərs-/ noun [U, sing.] (*BrE*) people who move out of a city because it is too crowded to an area where there is more space: *New towns were designed to house London's overspill.*

**over·staffed** /ˌəʊvəˈstɑːft; NAmE -vərˈstæft/ adj. (of a company, office, etc.) having more workers than are needed **OPP** **understaffed**

**over·state** /ˌəʊvəˈsteɪt; NAmE -vərˈs-/ verb ~ **sth** to say sth in a way that makes it seem more important than it really is **SYN** **exaggerate**: *He tends to overstate his case when talking politics.* ◊ *The seriousness of the crime cannot be overstated.* **OPP** **understate** ▶ **over·state·ment** /ˈəʊvəsteɪtmənt; NAmE -vərs-/ noun [C, U]: *It is not an overstatement to say a crisis is imminent.*

**over·stay** /ˌəʊvəˈsteɪ; NAmE -vərˈs-/ verb ~ **sth** to stay longer than the length of time you are expected or allowed to stay: *They overstayed their visa.* **IDM** see WELCOME *n.*

**over·step** /ˌəʊvəˈstep; NAmE -vərˈs-/ verb (-pp-) ~ **sth** to go beyond what is normal or allowed: *to overstep your authority* ◊ *He tends to overstep the boundaries of good taste.* **IDM** **overstep the ˈmark/ˈline** to behave in a way that people think is not acceptable

**over·stock** /ˌəʊvəˈstɒk; NAmE -vərˈstɑːk/ verb **1** [T, I] ~ **(sth)** to buy or make more of sth than you need or can sell **2** [T, I] ~ **(sth)** to put too many animals in a place where there is not enough room or food for them

**over·stretch** /ˌəʊvəˈstretʃ; NAmE -vərˈs-/ verb ~ **sb/sth/yourself** (*especially BrE*) to do more than you are capable of; to make sb/sth do more than they are capable of: *This will overstretch the prison service's resources.* ◊ *Credit cards can tempt you to overstretch yourself* (= spend more money than you can afford). ▶ **over·stretched** adj.: *overstretched muscles* ◊ *overstretched services*

**over·sub·scribed** /ˌəʊvəsəbˈskraɪbd; NAmE -vərs-/ adj. if an activity, service, etc. is **oversubscribed**, there are fewer places, tickets, etc. than the number of people who are asking for them

**overt** /əʊˈvɜːt, ˈəʊvɜːt; NAmE əʊˈvɜːrt, ˈəʊvɜːrt/ adj. [usually before noun] (*formal*) done in an open way and not secretly: *There was little overt support for the project.* ⊃ compare COVERT ▶ **overt·ly** adv.: *overtly political activities*

**over·take** /ˌəʊvəˈteɪk; NAmE -vərˈt-/ verb (**over·took** /-ˈtʊk/, **over·taken** /-ˈteɪkən/) **1** [T, I] ~ **(sb/sth)** (*especially BrE*) to go past a moving vehicle or person ahead of you because you are going faster than they are: *He pulled out to overtake a truck.* ◊ *It's dangerous to overtake on a bend.* **2** [T] ~ **sb/sth** to become greater in number, amount or importance than sth else **SYN** **outstrip**: *Nuclear energy*

# overtax

may overtake oil as the main fuel. ◊ We mustn't let ourselves be overtaken by our competitors. **3** [T, often passive] ~ **sb/sth** if sth unpleasant **overtakes** a person, it unexpectedly starts to happen and to affect them: *The climbers were overtaken by bad weather.* ◊ *Sudden panic overtook her.* ◊ *Our original plan was overtaken by events* (= the situation changed very rapidly) *and we had to make a new one.*

**over·tax** /ˌəʊvəˈtæks; NAmE -vərˈt-/ *verb* **1** ~ **sb/sth/yourself** to do more than you are able or want to do; to make sb/sth do more than they are able or want to do: *to overtax your strength* ◊ *Take it easy. Don't overtax yourself.* **2** ~ **sb/sth** to make a person or an organization pay too much tax

**over-the-counter** *adj.* (*abbr.* **OTC**) [only before noun] **1** (of drugs and medicines) that can be obtained without a PRESCRIPTION (= a written order from a doctor) **2** (*business, NAmE*) (of stocks and shares) not appearing in an official STOCK EXCHANGE list

**over·think** /ˌəʊvəˈθɪŋk; NAmE -vərˈθ-/ *verb* [T, I] (**overthought, overthought** /-ˈθɔːt/) to think about sth too much or for too long: *He has a tendency to overthink things.*

**over·throw** *verb, noun*
- *verb* /ˌəʊvəˈθrəʊ; NAmE -vərˈθ-/ (**overthrew** /-ˈθruː/, **overthrown** /-ˈθrəʊn/) ~ **sb/sth** to remove a leader or a government from a position of power by force: *The president was overthrown in a military coup.*
- *noun* /ˈəʊvəθrəʊ; NAmE -vərθ-/ [usually sing.] the act of taking power by force from a leader or government

**over·time** /ˈəʊvətaɪm; NAmE -vərt-/ *noun* [U] **1** time that you spend working at your job after you have worked the normal hours: *to do/work overtime* ◊ *overtime pay/earnings/hours* ◊ *The union announced a ban on overtime.* ⇨ WORDFINDER NOTE at PAY **2** the money sb earns for doing overtime: *They pay $150 a day plus overtime.* **3** (*NAmE*) (*BrE* ˌextra ˈtime) (*sport*) a set period of time that is added to the end of a sports game, etc., if there is no winner at the end of the normal period
IDM **be working ˈovertime** (*informal*) to be very active or too active: *There was nothing to worry about. It was just her imagination working overtime.*

**over·tired** /ˌəʊvəˈtaɪəd; NAmE -vərˈtaɪərd/ *adj.* extremely tired, so that you are easily annoyed

**over·tone** /ˈəʊvətəʊn; NAmE -vərt-/ *noun* [usually pl.] an attitude or an emotion that is suggested and is not expressed in a direct way: *There were political overtones to the point he was making.* ⇨ compare UNDERTONE

**over·took** /ˌəʊvəˈtʊk; NAmE -vərˈt-/ *past tense* of OVERTAKE

**over·train** /ˌəʊvəˈtreɪn; NAmE -vərˈt-/ *verb* [I] (of an athlete) to train too hard or for too long

**over·ture** /ˈəʊvətʃʊə(r); NAmE -vərtʃər, -tʃʊr/ *noun* **1** a piece of music written as an introduction to an OPERA or a BALLET: *Prokofiev's overture to 'Romeo and Juliet'* **2** [usually pl.] ~ **(to sb)** a suggestion or an action by which sb tries to make friends, start a business relationship, have discussions, etc. with sb else: *He began making overtures to a number of merchant banks.*

**over·turn** /ˌəʊvəˈtɜːn; NAmE -vərˈtɜːrn/ *verb* **1** [I, T] if sth **overturns**, or if sb **overturns** it, it turns into a position in which the top of it is where the bottom of it normally is or on its side: *The car skidded and overturned.* ◊ ~ **sth** *He stood up quickly, overturning his chair.* **2** [T] ~ **sth** to officially decide that a legal decision, etc. is not correct, and to make it no longer legally recognized: *to overturn a decision/conviction/verdict* ◊ *His sentence was overturned by the appeal court.* **3** to show that a belief or an idea is not correct: *She completely overturned my preconceptions about film stars.*

**over·use** /ˌəʊvəˈjuːz; NAmE -vərˈj-/ *verb* ~ **sth** to use sth too much or too often: *'Nice' is a very overused word.* ▶ **over·use** /-ˈjuːs/ *noun* [U, sing.]

**over·value** /ˌəʊvəˈvæljuː; NAmE -vərˈv-/ *verb* [often passive] ~ **sth** to put too high a value on sth: *Intelligence cannot be overvalued.* ◊ (*business*) *overvalued currencies/stocks*

**over·view** /ˈəʊvəvjuː; NAmE -vərvjuː/ *noun* a general description or an outline of sth SYN **survey** ⇨ LANGUAGE BANK at ABOUT

**over·ween·ing** /ˌəʊvəˈwiːnɪŋ; NAmE -vərˈw-/ *adj.* [only before noun] (*formal, disapproving*) showing that you are too confident or proud SYN **arrogant**

**over·weight** /ˌəʊvəˈweɪt; NAmE -vərˈw-/ *adj.* **1** (of people) too heavy, in a way that may be unhealthy: *She was only a few pounds overweight.* OPP **underweight** ⇨ compare OBESE ⇨ note at FAT **2** above an allowed weight: *overweight baggage*

**over·whelm** /ˌəʊvəˈwelm; NAmE -vərˈw-/ *verb* [often passive] **1** ~ **sb** to have such a strong emotional effect on sb that it is difficult for them to resist or know how to react SYN **overcome**: *She was overwhelmed by feelings of guilt.* ◊ *The beauty of the landscape overwhelmed me.* **2** ~ **sb** to defeat sb completely SYN **overpower**: *The army was overwhelmed by the rebels.* **3** ~ **sb** to be so bad or so great that a person cannot deal with it; to give too much of a thing to a person: *We were overwhelmed by requests for information.* **4** ~ **sb/sth** (*literary*) (of water) to cover sb/sth completely SYN **flood**

**over·whelm·ing** /ˌəʊvəˈwelmɪŋ; NAmE -vərˈw-/ *adj.* very great or very strong; so powerful that you cannot resist it or decide how to react: *The evidence against him was overwhelming.* ◊ *The overwhelming majority of those present were in favour of the plan.* ◊ *an overwhelming sense of loss* ◊ *She had the almost overwhelming desire to tell him the truth.* ◊ *You may find it somewhat overwhelming at first.* ▶ **over·whelm·ing·ly** *adv.*: *They voted overwhelmingly against the proposal.*

**over·win·ter** /ˌəʊvəˈwɪntə(r); NAmE -vərˈw-/ *verb* [I, T] ~ **(sth)** (of animals, birds and plants) to spend the winter months in a place; to stay alive or to keep sth alive during the winter ⇨ compare WINTER

**over·work** /ˌəʊvəˈwɜːk; NAmE -vərˈwɜːrk/ *verb, noun*
- *verb* [I, T] to work too hard; to make a person or an animal work too hard: *You look tired. Have you been overworking?* ◊ ~ **sb/sth** *She overworks her staff.*
- *noun* [U] the fact of working too hard: *His illness was brought on by money worries and overwork.*

**over·worked** /ˌəʊvəˈwɜːkt; NAmE -vərˈwɜːrkt/ *adj.* **1** made to work too hard or too much: *overworked nurses* **2** (of words or phrases) used too often so that the meaning or effect has become weaker

**over·write** /ˌəʊvəˈraɪt; NAmE -vərˈr-/ *verb* (**over·wrote** /-ˈrəʊt/, **over·writ·ten** /-ˈrɪtn/) ~ **sth** (*computing*) to replace information on the screen or in a file by putting new information over it

**over·wrought** /ˌəʊvəˈrɔːt; NAmE -vərˈr-/ *adj.* very worried and upset; excited in a nervous way SYN **distraught**

**over·zeal·ous** /ˌəʊvəˈzeləs; NAmE -vərˈz-/ *adj.* showing too much energy or enthusiasm: *An overzealous fan ran onto the stage during the concert.*

**ovi·duct** /ˈəʊvɪdʌkt/ *noun* (*anatomy*) either of the tubes that carry eggs from the OVARIES in women and female animals

**ovoid** /ˈəʊvɔɪd/ *adj.* (*formal*) like an egg in shape ▶ **ovoid** *noun*

**ovu·late** /ˈɒvjuleɪt; NAmE ˈɑːv-/ *verb* [I] (of a woman or a female animal) to produce an egg (called an OVUM), from the OVARY ▶ **ovu·la·tion** /ˌɒvjuˈleɪʃn; NAmE ˌɑːv-/ *noun* [U]: *methods of predicting ovulation*

**ovule** /ˈɒvjuːl, ˈəʊv-; NAmE ˈəʊv-/ *noun* (*biology*) the part of the OVARY of a plant containing the female cell, which becomes the seed when it is FERTILIZED ⇨ VISUAL VOCAB page V7

**ovum** /ˈəʊvəm/ *noun* (*pl.* **ova** /-və/) (*biology*) a female cell of an animal or a plant that can develop into a young animal or plant when FERTILIZED

**ow** /aʊ/ *exclamation* used to express sudden pain: *Ow! That hurt!*

**owe** /əʊ/ *verb* (not used in the progressive tenses) **1** ~ **sb sth** to have to pay sb for sth that you have already received or return money that you have borrowed: ~ **sb sth** *She still owes her father £3000.* ◊ (*figurative*)

I'm still owed three days' leave. ◊ **~sth** He owes me money than he can afford to pay. ◊ **~ sb sth (for sth)** She still owes £3000 to her father ◊ **~ sb sth for sth** How much do I owe you for the groceries? **2** [B2] to feel that you ought to do sth for sb or give them sth, especially because they have done sth for you: *~ sth to sb I owe a debt of gratitude to all my family.* ◊ *You owe it to your staff to be honest with them.* ◊ *~sb sth You owe me a favour!* ◊ *Thanks for sticking up for me—I owe you one* (= I owe you a favour). ◊ *I think you owe us an explanation.* ◊ *I think we're owed an apology.* **HELP** The passive is not used in this meaning except with a person as the subject: *An apology is owed to us.* **3** to exist or be successful because of the help or influence of sb/sth: *~ sth to sb/sth He owes his success to hard work.* ◊ *The play owes much to French tragedy.* ◊ *I owe everything to him.* ◊ *~ sb sth I owe him everything.* ◊ *I knew that I owed the surgeon my life.* **4** **~ allegiance / loyalty / obedience (to sb)** (*formal*) to have to obey and support sb who is in a position of authority or power

**ow·ing** /ˈəʊɪŋ/ *adj.* [not before noun] money that is **owing** has not been paid yet: *£100 is still owing on the loan.*

**ˈowing to** *prep.* because of: *The game was cancelled owing to torrential rain.*

**owl** /aʊl/ *noun* a BIRD OF PREY (= a bird that kills other creatures for food) with large round eyes, that hunts at night. Owls are traditionally thought to be wise: *An owl hooted nearby.* ⊃ see also BARN OWL, NIGHT OWL

**owl·et** /ˈaʊlət/ *noun* a young OWL

**owl·ish** /ˈaʊlɪʃ/ *adj.* looking like an OWL, especially because you are wearing round glasses, and therefore seeming serious and intelligent ▶ **owl·ish·ly** *adv.*: *She blinked at them owlishly.*

**own** [key] [A1] /əʊn/ *adj., pron., verb*
■ *adj., pron.* **1** [A1] used to emphasize that sth belongs to or is connected with sb: *It was her own idea.* ◊ *I saw it with my own eyes* (= I didn't hear about it from somebody else). ◊ *Is the car your own?* ◊ *Your day off is your own* (= you can spend it as you wish). ◊ *Our children are grown up and have children of their own.* ◊ **For reasons of his own** (= particular reasons that perhaps only he knew about), *he refused to join the club.* ◊ *The accident happened through no fault of her own.* ◊ *He wants to come into the business on his own terms.* ◊ *I need a room of my own.* ◊ *I have my very own room at last.* ◊ *Most people want to live in their own homes as they age.* **HELP** **Own** cannot be used after an article: *I need my own room.* ◊ *I need an own room.* ◊ *It's good to have your own room.* ◊ *It's good to have the own room.* **2** [A1] done or produced by and for yourself: *She makes all her own clothes.* ◊ *He has to cook his own meals.*
**IDM** **ˌcome into your/its ˈown** to have the opportunity to show how good or useful you are or sth is: *When the traffic's this bad, a bicycle really comes into its own.* **ˌget your ˈown ˌback (on sb)** (*informal*) to do sth to sb in return for harm they have done to you; to get REVENGE: *I'll get my own back on him one day, I swear!* **ˌhold your ˈown (against sb/sth) (in sth)** to remain in a strong position when sb is attacking you, competing with you, etc: *Business isn't good but we're managing to hold our own.* ◊ *She can hold her own against anybody in an argument.* ◊ *The patient is holding her own although she is still very sick.* **(all) on your ˈown 1** [B1] alone; without anyone else: *I'm all on my own today.* ◊ *She lives on her own.* ⊃ note at ALONE **2** [B1] without help: *He did it on his own.* ⊃ more at MIND *n.*, RIGHT *n.*, SOUND *n.*
■ *verb* (not used in the progressive tenses) **1** [A2] **~sth** to have sth that belongs to you, especially because you have bought it: *Do you own your house or do you rent it?* ◊ *I don't own anything of any value.* ◊ *Most of the apartments are privately owned.* ◊ *An American-owned company* **2** [T] **~sth** (*business*) to manage and take responsibility for sth: *The successful candidate will be responsible for owning and achieving sales targets.*
**IDM** **beˌhave / ˌact as if you ˈown the place** | **ˌthink you ˈown the place** (*disapproving*) to behave in a very confident way that annoys other people, for example by telling them what to do
**PHRV** **ˌown ˈup (to sth/to doing sth)** to admit that you are responsible for sth bad or wrong **SYN** *confess*: *I'm still waiting for someone to own up to the breakages.*

**ˌown-ˈbrand** (*also* **ˌown-ˈlabel**) (*both BrE*) (*US* **ˈstore-brand**) *adj.* used to describe goods that are marked with the name of the shop in which they are sold rather than with the name of the company that produced them

**owner** [key] [A2] /ˈəʊnə(r)/ *noun* a person who owns sth: *a dog/pet/gun owner* ◊ *a business/property/store owner* ◊ *The painting has been returned to its rightful owner.* ◊ *He's now the proud owner of a cottage in Wales.* ⊃ see also HOMEOWNER, LANDOWNER

**ˌowner-ˈoccupied** *adj.* (of a house, etc.) lived in by the owner rather than rented to sb else

**ˌowner-ˈoccupier** *noun* a person who owns the house, flat, etc. that they live in

**own·er·ship** [key] [B2] /ˈəʊnəʃɪp/; *NAmE* -nərʃ-/ *noun* [U] the fact of owning sth: *a growth in home ownership* ◊ *Ownership of the land is currently being disputed.* ◊ *to be in joint/ private/public ownership* ◊ *The restaurant is under new ownership.*

**ˌown ˈgoal** *noun* [usually sing.] **1** (in football (soccer)) a goal that is scored by mistake by a player against his or her own team **2** something that you do that achieves the opposite of what you wanted and that brings you a disadvantage

**ˌown-ˈlabel** *adj.* (*BrE*) = OWN-BRAND

**owt** /aʊt/ *pron.* (*BrE, dialect, informal*) anything: *I didn't say owt.*

**ox** /ɒks; *NAmE* ɑːks/ *noun* (*pl.* **oxen** /ˈɒksn; *NAmE* ˈɑːk-/) **1** a BULL (= a male cow) that has been CASTRATED (= had part of its sex organs removed), used, especially in the past, for pulling farm equipment, etc. ⊃ compare BULLOCK, STEER **2** (*old-fashioned*) any cow or BULL on a farm ⊃ see also CATTLE

**oxbow**

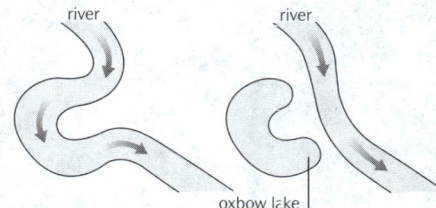

oxbow lake

**oxbow** /ˈɒksbəʊ; *NAmE* ˈɑːks-/ *noun* (*specialist*) a bend in a river that almost forms a full circle; a lake that forms when this bend is separated from the river

**Ox·bridge** /ˈɒksbrɪdʒ; *NAmE* ˈɑːks-/ *noun* [U] the universities of Oxford and Cambridge, when they are thought of together: *an Oxbridge education* ⊃ compare IVY LEAGUE, RED-BRICK

**ox·ford** /ˈɒksfəd; *NAmE* ˈɑːksfərd/ *noun* **1** **oxfords** [pl.] (*especially NAmE*) leather shoes that fasten with LACES ⊃ compare LACE-UP **2** [U] = OXFORD CLOTH: *an oxford shirt*

**ˌoxford ˈcloth** (*also* **ˈox·ford**) *noun* [U] (*NAmE*) a type of heavy cotton cloth used mainly for making shirts

**oxi·dant** /ˈɒksɪdənt; *NAmE* ˈɑːk-/ *noun* (*chemistry*) a substance that makes another substance combine with OXYGEN

**oxide** /ˈɒksaɪd; *NAmE* ˈɑːk-/ *noun* [U, C] (*chemistry*) a COMPOUND of OXYGEN and another chemical element: *iron oxide* ◊ *an oxide of tin*

**oxi·dize** (*BrE also* **-ise**) /ˈɒksɪdaɪz; *NAmE* ˈɑːk-/ *verb* [T, I] **~ (sth)** (*chemistry*) to remove one or more ELECTRONS from a substance, or to combine or to make sth combine with OXYGEN, especially when this causes metal to become covered with RUST ▶ **oxi·da·tion** /ˌɒksɪˈdeɪʃn; *NAmE* ˌɑːk-/ *noun* [U] ⊃ compare REDUCE, REDUCTION

**Oxon** /ˈɒksɒn; *NAmE* ˈɑːksɑːn/ *abbr.* (used after degree titles) of Oxford University: *Alice Tolley MA (Oxon)*

**ox·tail** /ˈɒksteɪl; *NAmE* ˈɑːks-/ *noun* [U, C] meat from the tail of a cow, used especially for making soup: *oxtail soup*

**oxy·gen** /ˈɒksɪdʒən/; *NAmE* /ˈɑːk-/ *noun* [U] (*symb.* O) a chemical element. Oxygen is a gas that is present in air and water and is necessary for people, animals and plants to live.

**oxy·gen·ate** /ˈɒksɪdʒəneɪt/; *NAmE* /ˈɑːk-/ *verb* ~ sth (*specialist*) to supply sth with oxygen ▶ **oxy·gen·ation** /ˌɒksɪdʒəˈneɪʃn/; *NAmE* /ˌɑːk-/ *noun* [U]

**ˈoxygen mask** *noun* a device placed over the nose and mouth through which a person can breathe oxygen, for example in an aircraft or a hospital

**oxy·moron** /ˌɒksɪˈmɔːrɒn/; *NAmE* /ˌɑːksɪˈmɔːrɑːn/ *noun* (*specialist*) a phrase that combines two words that seem to be the opposite of each other, for example *a deafening silence*

**oy** = OI

**oys·ter** /ˈɔɪstə(r)/ *noun* a large flat SHELLFISH. Some types of oyster can be eaten and others produce shiny white JEWELS called PEARLS: *Oyster beds, on the mudflats, are a form of fish farming.* ⊃ picture at SHELLFISH IDM see WORLD

**oys·ter·catch·er** /ˈɔɪstəkætʃə(r)/; *NAmE* -stərk-, -ketʃ-/ *noun* a black bird with long legs and a long red BEAK that lives near the coast and feeds on SHELLFISH

**ˈoyster mushroom** *noun* a type of wide, flat FUNGUS that grows on trees and that you can eat

**oy vey** /ˌɔɪ ˈveɪ/ *exclamation* used to show that you are disappointed or sad (mainly by Yiddish speakers or Jewish people)

**Oz** /ɒz/; *NAmE* /ɑːz/ *noun* [U] (*BrE, AustralE, NZE, informal*) Australia

**oz** *abbr.* (in writing) OUNCE(S): *4 oz sugar*

**ozone** /ˈəʊzəʊn/ *noun* [U] **1** (*chemistry*) a poisonous gas with a strong smell that is a form of OXYGEN **2** (*BrE, informal*) air near the sea that smells fresh and pure

**ˌozone-ˈfriend·ly** *adj.* not containing substances that will damage the OZONE LAYER

**ˈozone hole** *noun* an area in the ozone layer where the amount of OZONE has been very much reduced so that harmful RADIATION from the sun can pass through it

**ˈozone layer** *noun* [sing.] a layer of OZONE high above the earth's surface that helps to protect the earth from harmful RADIATION from the sun

**Oz·zie** /ˈɒzi/; *NAmE* /ˈɔːzi/ = AUSSIE

# Pp

**P** (*also* **p**) /piː/ *noun* [C, U] (*pl.* **Ps**, **P's**, **p's** /piːz/) the 16th letter of the English alphabet: *'Pizza' begins with (a) P/'P'.* **IDM** see MIND *v.*

**p** (*also* **p.**) *abbr.* **1** (*pl.* **pp.**) page: *See p. 34 and pp. 63–72.* **2** /piː/ PENNY/PENCE: *a 30p stamp* **3** (*music*) quietly (from Italian 'piano') ⊃ see also P. AND P., P. AND H.

**PA** /ˌpiː ˈeɪ/ *noun* **1** PUBLIC ADDRESS SYSTEM: *Announcements were made over the PA.* **2** (*especially BrE*) a person who works as a secretary or an assistant for one person (the abbreviation for 'personal assistant'): *~ to sb the PA to the Managing Director*

**Pa** *abbr.* (in writing) PASCAL

**pa** /pɑː/ *noun* (*old-fashioned, informal*) father: *I used to know your pa.*

**p.a.** *abbr.* per year (from Latin 'per annum'): *an increase of 3% p.a.*

**paan** (*also* **pan**) /pɑːn/ *noun* [U, C] (*IndE*) a BETEL leaf, usually folded into a shape with three sides and filled with SPICES for eating

**PAC** /pæk/ *abbr.* POLITICAL ACTION COMMITTEE

**pace¹** 🛈 **B2** /peɪs/ *noun, verb* ⊃ see also PACE²
- *noun* **1** 🛈 **B2** [sing., U] the speed at which sb/sth walks, runs or moves: *at a …~ to set off at a steady/gentle/leisurely pace* ◇ *Congestion frequently reduces traffic to walking pace.* ◇ *The ball gathered pace as it rolled down the hill.* ◇ *The runners have noticeably quickened their pace.* **2** 🛈 **B2** [sing., U] the speed at which sth happens: *~ of sth It is difficult to keep up with the rapid pace of change.* ◇ *I prefer the relaxed pace of life in the country.* ◇ *We encourage all students to work at their own pace* (= as fast or as slow as they can). ◇ *at a …~ The American economy has grown at a record pace.* ◇ *Rumours of corruption and scandal gathered pace* (= increased in number). **3** [C] an act of stepping once when walking or running; the distance travelled when doing this **SYN** **step**: *She took two paces forward.* **4** [U] the fact of sth happening, changing, etc. quickly: *He gave up his job in advertising because he couldn't stand the pace.* ◇ *The novel lacks pace* (= it develops too slowly).
⊃ see also FAST-PACED ⊃ see also PACY
**IDM** **go through your ˈpaces | show your ˈpaces** to perform a particular activity in order to show other people what you are capable of doing **keep ˈpace (with sb/sth)** to move, increase, change, etc. at the same speed as sb/sth: *She found it hard to keep pace with him as he strode off.* ◇ *Until now, wage increases have always kept pace with inflation.* **off the ˈpace** (in sport) behind the leader or the leading group in a race or a competition: *Last year's champion is still three shots off the pace* (= in golf). **put sb/sth through their/its ˈpaces** to give sb/sth a number of tasks to perform in order to see what they are capable of doing **set the ˈpace 1** to do sth at a particular speed or to a particular standard so that other people are then forced to copy it if they want to be successful: *The company is no longer setting the pace in the home computer market.* **2** (in a race) to run faster than the other people taking part, at a speed that they then try to copy ⊃ more at FORCE *v.*, SNAIL
- *verb* **1** 🛈 **B2** [I, T] to walk up and down in a small area many times, especially because you are feeling nervous or angry: *+ adv./prep. She paced up and down outside the room.* ◇ *~ sth Ted paced the floor restlessly.* **2** [T] *~ sth* to set the speed at which sth happens or develops: *He paced his game skilfully.* **3** [T] *~ yourself* to find the right speed or rhythm for your work or an activity so that you have enough energy to do what you have to do: *He'll have to learn to pace himself in this job.*
**PHR V** **ˌpace sth↔ˈoff/ˈout** to measure the size of sth by walking across it with regular steps

**pace²** /ˈpɑːkeɪ, ˈpɑːtʃeɪ, ˈpeɪsi/ *prep.* (from Latin, *formal*) used before a person's name to politely disagree with what they have said: *The evidence suggests, pace Professor Jones, that …* (= Professor Jones has a different opinion). ⊃ see also PACE¹

**ˈpace bowler** *noun* = FAST BOWLER

**ˈpace-maker** /ˈpeɪsmeɪkə(r)/ *noun* **1** an electronic device that is put inside a person's body to help their heart beat regularly **2** (*also* **pace-setter** *especially in NAmE*) a person or an animal that begins a race quickly so that the other people taking part will try to copy the speed and run a fast race: (*figurative*) *The big banks have been the pacesetters in developing the system.* **3** (*also* **pace-setter** *especially in NAmE*) a person or team that is winning in a sports competition: *The local club are now only one point off the pacemakers.*

**ˈpace-man** /ˈpeɪsmæn/ *noun* (*pl.* **-men** /-men/) = FAST BOWLER

**ˈpace-setter** /ˈpeɪssetə(r)/ *noun* (*especially NAmE*) = PACEMAKER

**pacey** = PACY

**pa-chinko** /pəˈtʃɪŋkəʊ/ *noun* [U] (*from Japanese*) a Japanese form of PINBALL, in which you can win prizes

**pachy-derm** /ˈpækɪdɜːm/ *noun* (*specialist*) a type of animal with a very thick skin, for example an elephant

**pa-cif-ic** /pəˈsɪfɪk/ *adj.* [usually before noun] (*literary*) peaceful or loving peace

**Paˌcific ˈDaylight Time** *noun* [U] (*abbr.* **PDT**) the time used in summer in the western parts of Canada and the US that is seven hours earlier than UTC

**the Paˌcific ˈRim** *noun* [sing.] the countries around the Pacific Ocean, especially the countries of eastern Asia, considered as an economic group

**Paˌcific ˈStandard Time** *noun* [U] (*abbr.* **PST**) the time used in winter in the western parts of Canada and the US that is eight hours earlier than UTC

**Paˌcific ˈtime** *noun* [U] the standard time on the west coast of the US and Canada

**paci-fier** /ˈpæsɪfaɪə(r)/ (*NAmE*) (*BrE* **dummy**) *noun* a rubber or plastic object with a special shape that a baby SUCKS on with its lips and tongue

**paci-fism** /ˈpæsɪfɪzəm/ *noun* [U] the belief that war and violence are always wrong

**paci-fist** /ˈpæsɪfɪst/ *noun* a person who believes that war and violence are always wrong and refuses to fight in a war ⊃ compare CONSCIENTIOUS OBJECTOR ▸ **paci-fist** *adj.* [usually before noun]: *pacifist beliefs*

**pa-cify** /ˈpæsɪfaɪ/ *verb* (**paci-fies**, **paci-fy-ing**, **paci-fied**, **paci-fied**) **1** *~ sb* to make sb who is angry or upset become calm and quiet **SYN** **placate**: *The baby could not be pacified.* ◇ *The speech was designed to pacify the irate crowd.* **2** *~ sth* to bring peace to an area where there is fighting or a war ▸ **paci-fi-ca-tion** /ˌpæsɪfɪˈkeɪʃn/ *noun* [U]

**pack** 🛈 **A2** /pæk/ *verb, noun*
- *verb*
- **PUT INTO CONTAINER 1** 🛈 **A2** [I, T] to put clothes, etc. into a bag in preparation for a trip away from home: *I haven't packed yet.* ◇ *~ sth I haven't packed my suitcase yet.* ◇ *I packed my bags and left.* ◇ *Did you pack the camera?* ◇ *~ A with B He packed a bag with a few things and was off.* ◇ *~ B into A He packed a few things into a bag.* ◇ *~ sb sth I've packed you some food for the journey.* **OPP** unpack **2** 🛈 **A2** [T] to put sth into a container so that it can be stored, transported or sold: *~ sth (up) (in/into sth) The pottery was packed in boxes and shipped to the US.* ◇ *I carefully packed up the gifts.* **OPP** unpack
- **PROTECT 3** [T] *~ sth (in/with sth)* to protect sth that breaks easily by surrounding it with soft material: *The paintings were carefully packed in newspaper.*
- **PRESERVE FOOD 4** [T] *~ sth (in sth)* to preserve food in a particular substance: *fish packed in ice*
- **FILL 5** [I, T] to fill sth with a lot of people or things: *+ adv./prep. We all packed together into one car.* ◇ *~ sth (with sth) Fans packed the hall to see the band.* ⊃ see also PACKED, PACKED OUT
- **SNOW/SOIL 6** [T] *~ sth (down)* to press sth such as snow or soil to form a thick hard mass: *Pack the earth down around the plant.* ◇ *a patch of packed snow*
- **CARRY GUN 7** [T] *~ (sth)* (*NAmE, informal*) to carry a gun: *to pack a gun* ◇ *Is he packing?*

# package

- STORM 8 [T] ~ sth to have sth: *A storm packing 75 mph winds swept across the area last night.*

**IDM** **pack a (powerful, real, etc.) 'punch** (*informal*) 1 (of a BOXER) to be capable of hitting sb very hard 2 to have a powerful effect on sb: *The advertising campaign packs quite a punch.* **pack your 'bags** (*informal*) to leave a person or place permanently, especially after an argument ⊃ more at SEND

**PHR V** **pack a'way** to be capable of being folded up small when it is not being used: *The tent packs away in a small bag.* **pack sth ↔ a'way** to put sth in a box, etc. when you have finished using it: *We packed away the summer clothes.* **pack sb ↔ in** [no passive] (of plays, performers, etc.) to attract a lot of people to see it/them: *The show is still packing them in.* **pack sth ↔ in** (*informal*) to stop doing sth **SYN** **give up**: *She decided to pack in her job.* ◇ (*especially BrE*) *Pack it in* (= stop behaving badly or annoying me), *you two!* **pack sb/sth 'in/'into sth** 1 to do a lot of things in a limited period of time: *You seem to have packed a lot into your life!* 2 to put a lot of things or people into a limited space **SYN** **cram**: *They've managed to pack a lot of information into a very small book.* **pack 'into sth** to go somewhere in large numbers so that all available space is filled **SYN** **cram**: *Over 80 000 fans packed into the stadium to watch the final.* ⊃ see also PACK *verb* **pack sb ↔ off (to …)** (*informal*) to send sb somewhere, especially because you do not want them with you: *My parents always packed me off to bed early.* **pack sth ↔ out** (of shows, performers, etc.) to attract enough people to completely fill a theatre, etc: *The band can still pack out concert halls.* ⊃ see also PACKED OUT **pack 'up** (*informal, especially BrE*) (of a machine) to stop working: *The TV's packed up again.* **pack 'up | pack sth ↔ 'up** 1 to put your possessions into a bag, etc. before leaving a place: *Are you packing up already? It's only 4 o'clock.* ◇ *We arrived just as the musicians were packing up their instruments.* 2 (*BrE, informal*) to stop doing sth, especially a job **SYN** **give up**: *What made you pack up a good job like that?* ⊃ see also PACK *verb*

■ *noun*

- CONTAINER 1 **B1** [C] (*especially NAmE*) a container, usually made of paper, that holds a number of the same thing or an amount of sth, ready to be sold: *~ of sth a pack of cigarettes/gum* ◇ *You can buy the envelopes in packs of ten.* ⊃ compare PACKAGE, PACKET ⊃ see also BLISTER PACK, FLAT PACK, POWER PACK, SIX-PACK
- SET 2 **B1** [C] a set of different things that are supplied together for a particular purpose: *Send for your free information pack today.*
- THINGS TIED FOR CARRYING 3 [C] a number of things that are wrapped or tied together, especially for carrying: *donkeys carrying packs of wool* ◇ (*figurative*) *Everything she told us is a pack of lies* (= a story that is completely false).
- LARGE BAG 4 [C] a large bag that you carry on your back: *We passed a group of walkers, carrying huge packs.* ⊃ see also BACKPACK *noun*, FANNY PACK
- OF ANIMALS 5 [C + sing./pl. v.] a group of animals that hunt together or are kept for hunting: *packs of savage dogs* ◇ *wolves hunting in packs* ◇ *a pack of hounds* ⊃ WORDFINDER NOTE at HUNT
- OF PEOPLE 6 [C + sing./pl. v.] a group of similar people or things, especially one that you do not like or approve of: *We avoided a pack of journalists waiting outside.* ◇ *He's the leader of the pack.* ⊃ see also RAT PACK 7 [C + sing./pl. v.] all the people who are behind the leaders in a race, competition, etc: *measures aimed at keeping the company ahead of the pack*
- OF CARDS 8 (*especially BrE*) (*also* **deck** *NAmE, BrE*) [C] a complete set of 52 PLAYING CARDS: *a pack of cards*
- OF CUBS/BROWNIES 9 [C + sing./pl. v.] an organized group of CUBS/CUB SCOUTS or BROWNIES: *to join a Brownie pack*
- FOR WOUND 10 [C] a hot or cold piece of soft material that holds liquid, used for treating a wound ⊃ see also FACE PACK, ICE PACK, MUD PACK **IDM** see JOKER

**pack·age** **B1** /ˈpækɪdʒ/ *noun, verb*

■ *noun* 1 **B1** (*especially NAmE*) = PARCEL: *A large package has arrived for you.* ⊃ compare PACK 2 **B1** (*NAmE*) a box, bag, etc. in which things are packed or wrapped; the contents of a box, etc: *Check the list of ingredients on the side of the package.* ◇ *~ of sth a package of hamburger buns* ⊃ compare PACKET 3 **B2** (*also* **'package deal**) a set of items or ideas that must be bought or accepted together: *an aid/a rescue package* ◇ *~ of sth a package of measures to help small businesses* 4 the pay and other benefits that sb gets from their employer: *Some CEOs received pay packages of over $10 million.* 5 (*also* **'software package**) (*computing*) a set of related programs for a particular type of task, sold and used as a single unit: *The system came with a database software package.*

■ *verb* [often passive] 1 **B2** to put sth into a box, bag, etc. to be sold or transported: *~ sth packaged food/goods* ◇ *~ sth up The orders were already packaged up, ready to be sent.* ◇ *~ sth in sth The fan is packaged in a bare white box.* ◇ *We package our products in recyclable materials.* 2 *~ sb/sth (as sth)* to present sb/sth in a particular way: *an attempt to package news as entertainment*

**'package store** *noun* (*US*) = LIQUOR STORE

**'package tour** (*BrE also* **'package holiday**) *noun* a holiday that is organized by a company at a fixed price and includes the cost of travel, hotels, etc. ⊃ WORDFINDER NOTE at HOLIDAY

**pack·ag·ing** /ˈpækɪdʒɪŋ/ *noun* [U] 1 materials used to wrap or protect goods that are sold in shops: *Attractive packaging can help to sell products.* 2 the process of wrapping goods: *His company offers a flexible packaging service for the food industry.*

**'pack animal** *noun* an animal used for carrying loads, for example a horse

**packed** /pækt/ *adj.* 1 extremely full of people **SYN** **crowded**: *The restaurant was packed.* ◇ *The show played to packed houses* (= large audiences). 2 containing a lot of a particular thing: *~ with sth The book is packed with information.* ◇ *~-packed an information-packed book* ⊃ see also ACTION-PACKED, JAM-PACKED 3 pressed closely together: *The birds' nests are lined with tightly packed leaves.* 4 [not before noun] (*informal*) having put everything you need into cases, boxes, etc. before you go somewhere: *I'm all packed and ready to go.* ⊃ see also PRE-PACKED

**packed 'lunch** *noun* (*BrE*) a meal of sandwiches, fruit, etc. that is prepared at home and eaten at school, work, etc. ⊃ compare BAG LUNCH, BOX LUNCH

**packed 'out** *adj.* [not before noun] (*informal, especially BrE*) completely full of people or things: *Opera houses are packed out wherever she sings.*

**pack·er** /ˈpækə(r)/ *noun* a person, machine or company that puts food, goods, etc. into containers to be sold or sent to sb

**packet** **B2** /ˈpækɪt/ *noun* 1 **B2** (*BrE*) a small container made of paper or card in which goods are packed for selling: *a packet of biscuits/cigarettes/crisps* ⊃ compare PACK, PACKAGE ⊃ see also PAY PACKET, WAGE PACKET 2 **B2** a small object wrapped in paper or put into a thick ENVELOPE so that it can be sent by mail, carried easily or given as a present: *A packet of photographs arrived with the mail.* 3 **B2** (*NAmE*) (*BrE* **sa·chet**) a closed plastic or paper package that contains a very small amount of liquid or a powder: *a packet of instant cocoa mix* 4 [sing.] (*BrE, informal*) a large amount of money: *That car must have cost a packet.* 5 (*computing*) a piece of information that forms part of a message sent through a computer network 6 (*NAmE*) a set of documents that are supplied together for a particular purpose: *a training packet*

**pack·horse** /ˈpækhɔːs; *NAmE* -hɔːrs/ *noun* a horse that is used to carry heavy loads

**'pack ice** *noun* [U] a large mass of ice floating in the sea, formed from smaller pieces that have frozen together

**pack·ing** /ˈpækɪŋ/ *noun* [U] 1 the act of putting your possessions, clothes, etc. into bags or boxes in order to take or send them somewhere: *Have you finished your packing?* 2 material used for wrapping around objects to protect them, especially before sending them somewhere: (*BrE*) *The price includes postage and packing.*

**'pack rat** *noun* 1 (*NAmE*) a person who collects and stores things that they do not really need 2 a small North

American animal like a mouse that collects small sticks, etc. in its hole

**pact** /pækt/ noun ~ (between A and B) | ~ (with sb) (to do sth) a formal agreement between two or more people, groups or countries, especially one in which they agree to help each other: *a non-aggression pact* ◇ *They have made a pact with each other not to speak about their differences in public.* ⇨ see also SUICIDE PACT

**pacy** (also **pacey**) /ˈpeɪsi/ adj. (BrE, informal) **1** (of a book, film, etc.) having a story that develops quickly **2** able to run quickly **SYN** fast: *a pacy winger who can also score goals*

**pad** ⟨+⟩ **C1** /pæd/ noun, verb
■ **noun**
- OF SOFT MATERIAL **1** ⟨+⟩ **C1** a thick piece of soft material that is used, for example, for cleaning or protecting sth or for holding liquid: *medicated cleansing pads for sensitive skin* ◇ *sanitary pads* (= that a woman uses during her PERIOD)
- OF PAPER **2** ⟨+⟩ **C1** a number of pieces of paper for writing or drawing on, that are fastened together at one edge: *a sketch/writing pad* ⇨ see also LEGAL PAD, NOTEPAD
- OF ANIMAL'S FOOT **3** the soft part under the foot of a cat, dog, etc.
- FOR CLEANING **4** a small piece of rough material used for cleaning pans, surfaces, etc: *a scouring pad*
- FOR SPACECRAFT/HELICOPTER **5** a flat surface where a SPACECRAFT or a helicopter takes off and lands ⇨ see also HELIPAD, LAUNCH PAD
- FOR PROTECTION **6** [usually pl.] a piece of thick material that you wear in some sports, for example football and CRICKET, to protect parts of your body: *knee pads* ⇨ see also SHIN PAD, SHOULDER PAD
- OF WATER PLANTS **7** the large flat leaf of some water plants, especially the WATER LILY: *floating lily pads* ⇨ see also LILY PAD
- FLAT/APARTMENT **8** [usually sing.] (informal) the place where sb lives, especially a flat ⇨ see also BACHELOR PAD, BRAKE PAD, INK PAD, KEYPAD
■ **verb** (-dd-)
- ADD SOFT MATERIAL **1** [T, often passive] to put a layer of soft material in or on sth in order to protect it, make it thicker or change its shape: *a padded jacket* ◇ *a padded envelope* (= for sending delicate objects) ◇ *be padded with sth* *All the sharp corners were padded with foam.*
- WALK QUIETLY **2** [I] + adv./prep. to walk with quiet steps: *She padded across the room to the window.*
- BILLS **3** [T] ~ sth (NAmE) to dishonestly add items to bills to obtain more money: *to pad bills/expense accounts*
**PHRV** **pad sth ↔ out** **1** to put soft material into a piece of clothing in order to change its shape **2** to make sth such as an article, seem longer or more impressive by adding things that are unnecessary: *The report was padded out with extracts from previous documents.*

**ˌpadded ˈcell** noun a room in a hospital for mentally ill people, with soft walls to prevent violent patients from injuring themselves

**pad·ding** /ˈpædɪŋ/ noun [U] **1** soft material that is placed inside sth to make it more comfortable or to change its shape **2** words that are used to make a speech, piece of writing, etc. longer, but that do not contain any interesting information

**pad·dle** /ˈpædl/ noun, verb
■ **noun 1** [C] a short POLE with a flat wide part on one or both ends, that you hold in both hands and use for moving a small boat, especially a CANOE, through water ⇨ compare OAR **2** [C] a tool or part of a machine that is like a paddle in shape, especially one used for mixing food **3 a paddle** [sing.] (BrE) an act or period of walking in shallow water with no shoes or socks: *Let's go for a paddle.* **4** [C] (NAmE) a BAT used for playing TABLE TENNIS **5** [C] (NAmE) a piece of wood with a handle, used in the past for hitting children as a punishment **IDM** see CREEK
■ **verb 1** [I, T] to move a small boat through water using a paddle: (+ adv./prep.) *We paddled downstream for about a mile.* ◇ ~ sth (+ adv./prep.) *We paddled the canoe along the coast.* **2** (BrE) (NAmE **wade**) [I] to walk or stand with no shoes or socks in shallow water in the sea, a lake, etc: *The children have gone paddling.* **3** [I] to swim with short movements of your hands or feet up and down ⇨ WORDFINDER NOTE at SWIMMING **4** [T] ~ sb/sth (NAmE) to hit a child with a flat piece of wood as a punishment

**paddle-board·ing** /ˈpædlbɔːdɪŋ; NAmE -bɔːrd-/ noun [U] the sport of moving on the water while lying, KNEELING or standing on a board, using your arms or a PADDLE to move yourself along ▸ **paddle-board** noun

**ˈpaddle steamer** (BrE) (NAmE **paddle wheeler** /ˈpædlwiːlə(r)/) (also **ˈpaddle boat** NAmE, BrE) noun an old-fashioned type of boat moved forward by a large wheel or wheels driven by STEAM

**ˈpaddle wheel** noun a large wheel on a boat that has boards around its outer edge and is driven by STEAM to move the boat through the water: *There were two paddle wheels, one on each side of the ship.*

**ˈpaddling pool** (BrE) (NAmE **ˈwading pool**) noun a shallow swimming pool for children to play in, especially a small plastic one that you fill with water

**pad·dock** /ˈpædək/ noun **1** a small field in which horses are kept ⇨ WORDFINDER NOTE at HORSE **2** (in horse racing or motor racing) an area where horses or cars are taken before a race and shown to the public **3** (AustralE, NZE) any field or area of land that has fences around it

**Paddy** /ˈpædi/ noun (pl. **-ies**) (informal) an offensive word for a person from Ireland

**paddy** /ˈpædi/ noun (pl. **-ies**) **1** (also **ˈpaddy field**) a field in which rice is grown: *a rice paddy* **2** [usually sing.] (BrE, informal) a state of being angry or in a bad mood **SYN** temper: *The news put him in a bit of a paddy.*

**pad·kos** /ˈpædkɒs; NAmE ˈpɑːdkɔːs/ SAfrE [ˈpɛtkɒs] noun [U] (SAfrE) food that you take with you to eat while on a journey

**pad·lock** /ˈpædlɒk; NAmE -lɑːk/ noun, verb
■ **noun** a type of lock that is used to fasten two things together or to fasten one thing to another. Padlocks are used with chains on gates, etc.
■ **verb** to lock sth with a padlock: ~ sth to sth *She always padlocked her bike to the railings.* ◇ ~ sth *The doors were padlocked.*

**padre** /ˈpɑːdreɪ/ noun (often used as a form of address) a priest, or other Christian minister, especially in the armed forces ⇨ compare CHAPLAIN

**ˌpad ˈthai** noun [U, C] a dish from Thailand made with a type of NOODLES made from rice, SPICES, egg, vegetables and sometimes meat or SEAFOOD

**paean** /ˈpiːən/ noun (literary) a song of praise or victory

**paed-** /piːd, ped/ (BrE) (NAmE **ped-**) combining form (in nouns and adjectives) connected with children: *paediatrician*

**paedia·tri·cian** (BrE) (NAmE **pediatrician**) /ˌpiːdiəˈtrɪʃn/ noun a doctor who studies and treats the diseases of children ⇨ WORDFINDER NOTE at SPECIALIST

**paedi·at·rics** (BrE) (NAmE **pediatrics**) /ˌpiːdiˈætrɪks/ noun [U] the branch of medicine that deals with children and their diseases ▸ **paedi·at·ric** (BrE) (NAmE **pedi-**) adj. [only before noun]: *paediatric surgery*

**paedo·phile** (BrE) (NAmE **pedo-**) /ˈpiːdəfaɪl; NAmE also ˈped-/ noun a person who is sexually attracted to children

**paedo·philia** (BrE) (NAmE **pedo-**) /ˌpiːdəˈfɪliə; NAmE also ˌped-/ noun [U] the condition of being sexually attracted to children

# paella

**pa·el·la** /paɪˈelə/ noun [U, C] a Spanish dish of rice, chicken, fish and vegetables, cooked and served in a large shallow pan

**pagan** /ˈpeɪɡən/ noun **1** a person who holds religious beliefs that are not part of any of the world's main religions **2** (often disapproving) used in the past by Christians to describe a person who did not believe in Christianity ▶ **pagan** adj.: a pagan festival **pa·gan·ism** noun [U]

**page** 🔑 A1 /peɪdʒ/ noun, verb
■ noun **1** 🔑 A1 (abbr. **p**) one side or both sides of a sheet of paper in a book, magazine, etc: *Turn to page 64.* ◇ *She slowly turned the pages of the album.* ◇ *a blank page* ◇ *the sports/news pages of the newspaper* ◇ **on a~** *The photograph was on the front page of every newspaper.* ◇ **over the~** *The address is over the page* (= on the next page). ⊃ see also FRONT PAGE, FULL-PAGE, TITLE PAGE, YELLOW PAGES™ **2** 🔑 A1 a section of data or information that can be shown on a computer screen at any one time: *to visit/view a page* ◇ *to load/refresh/update a page* ◇ *The page was really slow to load.* ◇ **on a~** *The message was posted on the company's official Facebook page.* ⊃ see also HOME PAGE, LANDING PAGE, WEB PAGE **3** (literary) an important event or period of history: *a glorious page of Arab history* **4** (especially NAmE) = PAGEBOY **5** (NAmE) a student who works as an assistant to a member of the US Congress **6** (in the Middle Ages) a boy or young man who worked for a KNIGHT while training to be a knight himself
**IDM** **on the same ˈpage** if two or more people or groups are **on the same page**, they agree about what they are trying to achieve **turn the ˈpage** to begin doing things in a different way and thinking in a more positive way after a period of difficulties ⊃ more at PRINT v.
■ verb **1** ~ **sb** to call sb's name over a PUBLIC ADDRESS SYSTEM in order to find them and give them a message: *Why don't you have him paged at the airport?* **2** ~ **sb** to contact sb by sending a message to their PAGER: *Page Dr Green immediately.*
**PHRV** ˌpage ˈthrough sth (NAmE) to quickly turn the pages of a book, magazine, etc. and look at them without reading them carefully or in detail **SYN** **flick through sth, leaf through sth**

**pa·geant** /ˈpædʒənt/ noun **1** a public entertainment in which people dress in historical costumes and give performances of scenes from history **2** (NAmE) a competition for young women in which their beauty, personal qualities and skills are judged: *a beauty pageant* ⊃ compare BEAUTY CONTEST **3** ~ **(of sth)** (literary) something that is considered as a series of interesting and different events: *life's rich pageant*

**pa·geant·ry** /ˈpædʒəntri/ noun [U] impressive and exciting events and ceremonies involving a lot of people wearing special clothes: *the pageantry of royal occasions*

**page·boy** /ˈpeɪdʒbɔɪ/ noun **1** (also **page** especially in NAmE) a small boy who helps or follows a bride during a marriage ceremony ⊃ compare BRIDESMAID **2** (also **page**) (old-fashioned) a boy or young man, usually in uniform, employed in a hotel to open doors, deliver messages for people, etc. **3** a HAIRSTYLE for women in which the hair is shoulder-length and turned under at the ends

**pager** /ˈpeɪdʒə(r)/ noun a small electronic device that you carry around with you and that shows a message or lets you know when sb is trying to contact you, for example by making a sound ⊃ see also BEEPER, BLEEPER

**ˈpage-turner** noun (informal) a book that is very exciting

**ˈpage view** noun one visit to a single page on a website: *a surge in page views*

**pa·gin·ate** /ˈpædʒɪneɪt/ verb ~ **sth** (specialist) to give a number to each page of a book, piece of writing, etc.

**pa·gin·ation** /ˌpædʒɪˈneɪʃn/ noun [U] (specialist) the process of giving a page number to each page of a book; the page numbers given

**pa·goda** /pəˈɡəʊdə/ noun a TEMPLE (= religious building) in South or East Asia in the form of a tall tower with several levels, each of which has its own roof that extends beyond the walls

**pah** /pɑː/ exclamation used to represent the sound that people make when they disagree with sth or think sth is very bad

**paid** /peɪd/ adj., verb
■ adj. **1** [usually before noun] (of work, etc.) for which people receive money: *Neither of them is currently in paid employment.* ◇ *a highly paid job* **OPP** **unpaid** ⊃ see also LOW-PAID, WELL PAID **2** [usually before noun] (of a person) receiving money for doing work: *Men still outnumber women in the paid workforce.* ◇ *a poorly paid teacher* **OPP** **unpaid** ⊃ see also POST-PAID
**IDM** **put ˈpaid to sth** (informal) to stop or destroy sth, especially what sb plans or wants to do
■ verb past tense, past part. of PAY

**ˌpaid-ˈup** adj. [only before noun] **1** having paid all the money necessary to be a member of a club or an organization: *a fully paid-up member* **2** (BrE, informal) strongly supporting sb/sth: *a fully paid-up environmental campaigner*

**pail** /peɪl/ noun (NAmE or old-fashioned) an open container with a handle, used for carrying or holding liquids, sand, etc. **SYN** **bucket**: *She filled the pail with fresh water.*

**pain** 🔑 A2 /peɪn/ noun, verb
■ noun ⊃ see also PAINS **1** 🔑 A2 [U, C] the feelings that you have in your body when you have been hurt or when you are ill: *a cry of pain* ◇ **in~** *She was clearly in a lot of pain.* ◇ **~in sth** *He felt a sharp pain in his knee.* ◇ *patients suffering from back pain* ◇ *stomach/chest/abdominal/back pains* ◇ *You get more aches and pains as you get older.* ◇ *The booklet contains information on pain relief during labour.* ◇ *This cream should help to relieve the pain.* ◇ *to feel/experience/suffer pain* ⊃ see also GROWING PAINS ⊃ HOMOPHONES at PANE ⊃ WORDFINDER NOTE at HEALTH **2** 🔑 A2 [U, C] mental or emotional difficulty: **the~ of (doing) sth** *the pain of separation* ◇ *I never meant to cause her pain.* ◇ *the pleasures and pains of growing old* **3** [C] (informal) a person or thing that is very annoying: *She can be a real pain when she's in a bad mood.* ◇ *It's a pain having to go all that way for just one meeting.*
**IDM** **no ˌpain, no ˈgain** (saying) used to say that you need to suffer if you want to achieve sth **on/under pain of sth** (formal) with the threat of having sth done to you as a punishment if you do not obey: *They were required to cut pollution levels, on pain of a £10 000 fine if they disobeyed.* **a pain in the ˈneck** (BrE also **a pain in the ˈarse/ˈbackside**) (NAmE also **a pain in the ˈass/ˈbutt**) (informal) a person or thing that is very annoying
■ verb (not used in the progressive tenses) (formal) to cause sb pain or make them unhappy **SYN** **hurt**: ~ **sb** *She was deeply pained by the accusation.* ◇ (old use) *The wound still pained him occasionally.* ◇ **it pains sb to do sth** *It pains me to see you like this.* ◇ **it pains sb that …** *It pained him that she would not acknowledge him.* ⊃ HOMOPHONES at PANE

**ˈpain barrier** noun [usually sing.] the moment at which sb doing hard physical activity feels the greatest pain, after which the pain becomes less: *He broke through the pain barrier at 25 kilometres and went on to win his first marathon.*

**pained** /peɪnd/ adj. showing that sb is feeling annoyed or upset: *a pained expression/voice*

**pain·ful** 🔑 B1 /ˈpeɪnfl/ adj. **1** 🔑 B1 causing you pain: *Is your back still painful?* ◇ *a painful death* ◇ *My ankle is still too painful to walk on.* **2** 🔑 B1 causing you to feel upset or embarrassed: *a painful experience/memory* ◇ **~ (for sb) (to do sth)** | **~ to do sth** *Their efforts were painful to watch.* ◇ **~ doing sth** *It was painful watching them get it all wrong.* **3** 🔑 B2 unpleasant or difficult to do **SYN** **trying**: *Applying for jobs can be a long and painful process.*

**pain·ful·ly** /ˈpeɪnfəli/ adv. **1** extremely, and in a way that makes you feel annoyed, upset, etc: *Their son was painfully shy.* ◇ *The dog was painfully thin.* ◇ *He was painfully aware of his lack of experience.* ◇ *Progress has been painfully slow.* **2** in a way that causes you physical or emotional pain: *He banged his knee painfully against the desk.* **3** with a lot of effort and difficulty: *painfully acquired experience*

**pain·kill·er** /ˈpeɪnkɪlə(r)/ noun a drug that reduces pain: *She's on* (= taking) *painkillers.* ▶ **pain·kill·ing** adj. [only before noun]: *painkilling drugs/injections*

▼ **SYNONYMS**

**painful**

sore • raw • inflamed • excruciating • burning • itchy

These words all describe sth that causes you physical pain.

**painful** causing you physical pain. NOTE **Painful** can describe a part of the body, illness, injury, treatment or death: *Is your knee still painful?* ◇ *a series of painful injections* ◇ *a slow and painful death*

**sore** (of a part of the body) painful and often red, especially because of infection or because a muscle has been used too much: *a sore throat* ◇ *Their feet were sore after hours of walking.*

**raw** (of a part of the body) red and painful, for example because of an infection or because the skin has been damaged: *The skin on her feet had been rubbed raw.*

**inflamed** (of a part of the body) painful, red and hot because of an infection or injury: *The wound had become inflamed.*

**excruciating** extremely painful. NOTE **Excruciating** can describe feelings, treatments or death but not parts of the body: *an excruciating throat/back/knee.*

**burning** painful and giving a feeling of being very hot: *She felt a burning sensation in her throat.*

**itchy** giving an uncomfortable feeling on your skin that makes you want to scratch; having this feeling: *an itchy rash* ◇ *I feel itchy all over.*

PATTERNS
- sore / inflamed / itchy **eyes**
- raw / inflamed / itchy **skin**
- a painful / an excruciating **death**
- a painful / burning **sensation**
- excruciating / burning **pain**

**pain·less** /ˈpeɪnləs/ *adj.* **1** causing you no pain: *a painless death* ◇ *The treatment is painless.* **2** not unpleasant or difficult to do: *The interview was relatively painless.* ▶ **pain·less·ly** *adv.*

**ˈpain point** *noun* a problem or difficulty, usually one identified by a business as one that it can provide the solution to: *It was a product that solved a very real pain point for consumers.*

**pains** /peɪnz/ *noun* [pl.] ⇨ see also GROWING PAINS
IDM ▶ **be at pains to do sth** to put a lot of effort into doing sth correctly: *She was at great pains to stress the advantages of the new system.* **for your ˈpains** (*especially BrE, often ironic*) as payment, reward or thanks for sth you have done: *I told her what I thought and got a mouthful of abuse for my pains!* **take (great) pains (to do sth) | go to great pains (to do sth)** to put a lot of effort into doing sth: *The couple went to great pains to keep their plans secret.* **take (great) pains with / over sth** to do sth very carefully: *He always takes great pains with his lectures.*

**pains·tak·ing** /ˈpeɪnzteɪkɪŋ/ *adj.* [usually before noun] done with a lot of care, effort and attention to detail SYN **thorough**: *painstaking research* ◇ *The event had been planned with painstaking attention to detail.* ▶ **pains·tak·ing·ly** *adv.*

**paint** ❶ A1 /peɪnt/ *noun, verb*
■ *noun* **1** [U] a liquid that is put on surfaces to give them a particular colour; a layer of this liquid when it has dried on a surface: *white paint* ◇ *gloss/matt/acrylic paint* ◇ *The woodwork has recently been given a fresh coat of paint.* ◇ *Wet paint!* (= used as a sign) ◇ *The paint is starting to peel off.* ◇ *The house is desperately in need of a lick of paint* (= a new coat of paint). ⇨ see also GREASEPAINT, OIL PAINT, SPRAY PAINT, WARPAINT **2** A2 **paints** [pl.] tubes or blocks of paint used for painting pictures: *oil paints*
■ *verb* **1** A1 [T, often passive] to cover a surface or object with paint: *~ sth (with sth) Paint the shed with weather-resistant paint.* ◇ *a brightly painted barge* ◇ **have sth painted** *We've had the house painted.* ◇ *~ sth + adj. The walls were painted yellow.* **2** A2 [T, I] to make a picture or design using paints: *~ sth/sb to paint portraits/pictures* ◇ *A friend painted the children for me* (= painted a picture of the children). ◇ *~ sth on sth Slogans had been painted on the walls.* ◇ *~ (sth) in sth She paints in oils.* ◇ *~ sth in sth a portrait painted in oils* ◇ *My mother paints well.* **3** [T] to give a particular impression of sb/sth SYN **portray**: *~ sb/sth as sth The article paints them as a bunch of petty criminals.* ◇ *~ sb/sth in ... The documentary painted her in a bad light.* **4** [T] *~ sth* to put colour ed MAKE-UP on your nails, lips, etc.
IDM **paint a (grim, gloomy, rosy, etc.) ˈpicture of sb/sth** to describe sb/sth in a particular way; to give a particular impression of sb/sth: *The report paints a vivid picture of life in the city.* ◇ *Journalists paint a grim picture of conditions in the camps.* **paint the town ˈred** (*informal*) to go to a lot of different bars, clubs, etc. and enjoy yourself **paint sth with a broad ˈbrush** to describe sth in a general way, ignoring the details ⇨ more at BLACK *adj.*
PHRV **ˌpaint sth↔ˈout** to cover part of a picture, sign, etc. with another layer of paint **ˌpaint ˈover sth** to cover sth with a layer of paint: *We painted over the dirty marks on the wall.*

**paint·ball** /ˈpeɪntbɔːl/ *noun* [U] a game in which people shoot balls of paint at each other

**paint·brush** /ˈpeɪntbrʌʃ/ *noun* a brush that is used for painting ⇨ picture at LADDER

**ˌpaint-by-ˈnumbers** *adj.* [only before noun] **1** (of pictures) having sections with different numbers showing which colours should be used to fill them in **2** (*disapproving*) used to describe sth that is produced without using the imagination: *He accused the government of relying on paint-by-numbers policies.*

**ˈpaint chip** *noun* a small piece of paint that has broken off sth or the small area where the paint has come off

**paint·er** ❶ A2 /ˈpeɪntə(r)/ *noun* **1** A2 a person whose job is painting buildings, walls, etc: *He works as a painter and decorator.* **2** A2 an artist who paints pictures: *a famous painter* ◇ *a portrait/landscape painter* **3** a rope fastened to the front of a boat, used for tying it to a post, ship, etc.

**paint·er·ly** /ˈpeɪntəli; *NAmE* -tərli/ *adj.* typical of artists or painting SYN **artistic**

**paint·ing** ❶ A1 /ˈpeɪntɪŋ/ *noun* **1** A1 [C] a picture that has been painted: *~ (of sb/sth) Canaletto's paintings of Venice* ◇ *~ by sb an exhibition of paintings by American artists* ⇨ see also CAVE PAINTING, OIL PAINTING, WALL PAINTING ⇨ SYNONYMS at PICTURE

WORDFINDER background, canvas, exhibition, foreground, frame, fresco, portrait, watercolour

**2** A1 [U] the act or art of using paint to produce pictures: *Her hobbies include music and painting.* ◇ *the great British tradition of landscape painting* ⇨ see also GENRE PAINTING **3** A1 [U] the act of putting paint onto the surface of objects, walls, etc: *painting and decorating* ◇ *We can do the painting ourselves.*

**ˈpaint job** *noun* the act or result of putting paint on an object, usually as the final layer or for decoration

**ˈpaint stripper** *noun* [U] a liquid used to remove old paint from surfaces

**paint·work** /ˈpeɪntwɜːk; *NAmE* -wɜːrk/ *noun* [U] (*especially BrE*) the layer of paint on the surface of a door, wall, car, etc: *The paintwork is beginning to peel.*

**pair** ❶ A1 /peə(r); *NAmE* per/ *noun, verb*
■ *noun*
• TWO THINGS THE SAME **1** A1 [C] *~ (of sth)* two things of the same type, especially when they are used or worn together: *a pair of shoes/boots* ◇ *a pair of gloves/earrings* ◇ *a huge pair of eyes* ◇ *The vase is one of a matching pair.*
• TWO PARTS JOINED **2** A1 [C] *~ (of sth)* an object consisting of two parts that are joined together: *a pair of trousers/pants/jeans* ◇ *a pair of glasses/binoculars/scissors* ◇ *Buy one pair of glasses and get a second pair free.* HELP A plural verb is sometimes used with **pair** in the singular in senses 1 and 2: *My last pair don't fit any more.* In informal *NAmE* some people use **pair** as a plural form: *three pair of shoes.*

# pairing

This is not considered correct in written English. ⇒ HOMOPHONES at PEAR
- **TWO PEOPLE** 3 [A1] [C + sing./pl. v.] two people who are doing sth together or who have a particular relationship: *Get pairs of students to act out the dialogue in front of the class.* ◊ *Get the students to do the exercise as pair work* (= two students work together). ◊ (*informal*) *I've had enough of the pair of you!* HELP In BrE a plural verb is usually used: *A pair of children were kicking a ball about.* ◊ *The pair are planning a trip to India together.*
- **TWO ANIMALS/BIRDS** 4 [C + sing./pl. v.] two animals or birds of the same type that are producing young together: *a breeding pair* ◊ *a pair of swans*
- **TWO HORSES** 5 [C] two horses working together to pull a CARRIAGE: *a carriage and pair* ⇒ see also AU PAIR

IDM **in ˈpairs** in groups of two objects or people: *Students worked in pairs on the project.* **I've only got one pair of ˈhands** (*informal*) used to say that you are too busy to do anything else **a pair of ˈhands** (*informal*) a person who can do, or is doing, a job: *We need an extra pair of hands if we're going to finish on time.* ⇒ more at SAFE *adj.*

■ *verb*
- **MAKE GROUPS OF TWO** 1 [T, usually passive] to put people or things into groups of two: *be paired with sb/sth Each blind student was paired with a sighted student.* ◊ *be paired (together) All the shoes on the floor were neatly paired.*
⇒ HOMOPHONES at PEAR
- **OF ANIMALS/BIRDS** 2 [I] (*specialist*) to come together in order to produce young: *Many of the species pair for life.*

PHRV **pair ˈoff (with sb)** | **pair sb ↔ ˈoff (with sb)** to come together, especially in order to have a romantic relationship; to bring two people together for this purpose: *It seemed that all her friends were pairing off.* ◊ *He's always trying to pair me off with his cousin.* **pair ˈup (with sb)** | **pair sb ↔ ˈup (with sb)** to come together or to bring two people together to work, play a game, etc.

**pair·ing** /ˈpeərɪŋ; NAmE ˈper-/ *noun* 1 [C] two people or things that work together or are placed together; the act of placing them together: *They take on a Chinese pairing in the next round of the World Table Tennis Championships.* 2 [U] (in the British Parliament) the practice of an MP agreeing with an MP of a different party that neither of them will vote in a debate so that they do not need to attend the debate

**paisa** /ˈpaɪsɑː, -sə/ *noun* (*pl.* **paise** /ˈpaɪseɪ, -sə/) a coin of India, Pakistan and Nepal. There are one hundred paise in a RUPEE.

**pais·ley** /ˈpeɪzli/ *noun* [U] a detailed pattern of curved shapes that look like feathers, used especially on cloth: *a paisley tie*

**Pai·ute** /ˈpaɪuːt/ *noun* (*pl.* **Pai·ute** or **Pai·utes**) a member of a Native American people many of whom live in the southwestern US

**pa·ja·mas** (*NAmE*) (*BrE, CanE* **py·ja·mas**) /pəˈdʒɑːməz; *NAmE* -ˈdʒæm-/ *noun* [pl.] a loose jacket and trousers worn in bed

**pak choi** /ˌpæk ˈtʃɔɪ/ (*BrE*) (*NAmE* **bok choy**) *noun* [U] a type of CHINESE CABBAGE with long dark green leaves and thick white STEMS

**Pak·eha** /ˈpɑːkɪhɑː/ *noun* (*NZE*) a white person from New Zealand (that is, not a Maori)

**Paki** /ˈpæki/ *noun* (*BrE, informal, taboo*) a very offensive word for a person from Pakistan, especially one living in the UK. The word is sometimes also used for people from India or Bangladesh.

**pa·kora** /pəˈkɔːrə/ *noun* a flat piece of spicy South Asian food consisting of meat or vegetables fried in BATTER

**PAL** /pæl/ *noun* [U] a television broadcasting system that is used in most of Europe ⇒ compare NTSC

**pal** /pæl/ *noun, verb*
■ *noun* 1 (*informal, becoming old-fashioned*) a friend: *We've been pals for years.* ⇒ see also PEN PAL 2 (*informal*) used to address a man in an unfriendly way: *If you try to take what's mine, pal, I'll make you sorry!* ▶ **pally** *adj.*: *I got very pally* (= friendly) *with him.*

■ *verb* (-ll-)
PHRV **pal aˈround (with sb)** (*informal, especially NAmE*) to do things with sb as a friend: *I palled around with him and his sister at school.* **pal ˈup (with sb)** (*BrE*) (*NAmE* **buddy ˈup (to/with sb)**) (*informal*) to become friendly with sb: *They palled up while they were at college.*

**pal·ace** 🔑 [A2] /ˈpæləs/ *noun* 1 [A2] [C] the official home of a king, queen, president, etc: *Buckingham Palace* ◊ *the royal/presidential palace* 2 (*often* **the Palace**) [sing.] a way of referring to the people who live or work in a palace, especially the British royal family and their advisers: *The Palace last night refused to comment on the reports.* ◊ *a Palace spokesman* 3 [C] any large impressive house: *The Old Town has a whole collection of churches, palaces and mosques.* 4 [C] (*old-fashioned*) (sometimes used in the names of buildings) a large public building, such as a hotel or cinema: *the Strand Palace Hotel*

**palace ˈcoup** (*also* **palace revoˈlution**) *noun* a situation in which a political leader has their power taken away from them by sb within the same party, etc.

**palaeo-** /ˈpæliəʊ, pelɪəʊ, pæliˈɒ; *NAmE* peɪliəʊ, peɪliˈɑː/ (*especially BrE*) (*NAmE usually* **paleo-**) *combining form* (in nouns, adjectives and adverbs) connected with ancient times

**palae·og·raphy** (*especially BrE*) (*NAmE usually* **pale·og·raphy**) /ˌpæliˈɒɡrəfi, peɪl-; *NAmE* ˌpeɪliˈɑːɡ-/ *noun* [U] the study of ancient writing systems ▶ **palae·og·rapher** (*also* **pale·og·rapher**) /ˌpæliˈɒɡrəfə(r), peɪl-; *NAmE* ˌpeɪliˈɑːɡrəfər/ *noun*

**Palaeo·lith·ic** (*especially BrE*) (*NAmE usually* **Paleo-**) /ˌpæliəˈlɪθɪk, peɪl-; *NAmE* peɪl-/ *adj.* from or connected with the early part of the Stone Age

**palae·on·tolo·gist** (*especially BrE*) (*NAmE usually* **paleo-**) /ˌpæliɒnˈtɒlədʒɪst, peɪl-; *NAmE* ˌpeɪliɑːnˈtɑːl-/ *noun* a person who studies FOSSILS

**palae·on·tology** (*especially BrE*) (*NAmE usually* **paleo-**) /ˌpæliɒnˈtɒlədʒi, peɪl-; *NAmE* ˌpeɪliɑːnˈtɑːl-/ *noun* [U] the study of FOSSILS (= the parts of dead animals or plants in rocks) as a guide to the history of life on earth

**pal·at·able** /ˈpælətəbl/ *adj.* 1 (of food or drink) having a pleasant or acceptable taste 2 **~ (to sb)** pleasant or acceptable to sb: *Some of the dialogue has been changed to make it more palatable to an American audience.* OPP **unpalatable**

**pal·atal** /ˈpælətl/ *noun* (*phonetics*) a speech sound made by placing the tongue against or near the hard PALATE of the mouth, for example /j/ at the beginning of *yes* ▶ **pal·atal** *adj.*

**pal·ate** /ˈpælət/ *noun* 1 the top part of the inside of the mouth: *the hard/soft palate* (= the hard/soft part at the front/back of the palate) ⇒ see also CLEFT PALATE 2 [usually sing.] the ability to recognize and/or enjoy good food and drink: *a menu to tempt even the most jaded palate* (= a person who has eaten so much rich food and become bored of it)

**pa·la·tial** /pəˈleɪʃl/ *adj.* [usually before noun] (of a room or building) very large and impressive, like a palace SYN **splendid**

**pal·at·in·ate** /pəˈlætɪnət/ *noun* 1 [C] the area ruled by a Count Palatine (= a political leader with the power of a king or queen) 2 **the Palatinate** [sing.] the land of the German Empire that was ruled over by the Count Palatine of the Rhine

**pal·at·ine** /ˈpælətaɪn/ *adj.* [only before noun] 1 (of an official, in the past) having the power in a particular area that a king or queen usually has 2 (of an area of land) ruled over by sb who has the power of a king or queen

**pa·la·ver** /pəˈlɑːvə(r); *NAmE also* -ˈlæv-/ *noun* (*informal*) 1 [U, sing.] (*BrE*) a lot of unnecessary activity, excitement or trouble, especially caused by sth that is not important SYN **fuss**: *What's all the palaver about?* ◊ *What a palave it is, trying to get a new visa!* 2 [U] (*NAmE*) talk that does not have any meaning SYN **nonsense**: *He's talking palaver.*

**pale** ⓣ B1 /peɪl/ adj., verb, noun
■ **adj.** (**paler**, **pal·est**) **1** B1 (of a person, their face, etc.) having skin that is very light in colour; having skin that has less colour than usual because of illness, a strong emotion, etc: *a pale complexion* ◇ *pale with fear/shock* ◇ *to go/turn/grow pale* ◇ *You look pale. Are you OK?* ◇ *The ordeal left her looking pale and drawn.* **2** ⓣ B1 light in colour; containing a lot of white: *pale blue eyes* ◇ *a paler shade of green* ◇ *a pale sky* **OPP** **dark, deep 3** ⓣ B1 (of light) not strong or bright: *the cold pale light of dawn* ⊃ see also PALLID, PALLOR ▸ **pale·ly** /ˈpeɪlli/ *adv.*: *Mark stared palely* (= with a pale face) *at his plate.* **pale·ness** *noun* [U]
■ **verb** [I] ~ **(at sth)** to become paler than usual: *She* (= her face) *paled visibly at the sight of the police car.* ◇ *The blue of the sky paled to a light grey.*
**IDM** ˈpale beside/next to sth | ˈpale in/by comparison (with/to sth) | ˈpale into insigˈnificance to seem less important when compared with sth else: *Last year's riots pale in comparison with this latest outburst of violence.*
■ **noun**
**IDM** be·yond the ˈpale considered by most people to be unacceptable or unreasonable: *His remarks were clearly beyond the pale.* ◇ *She has put herself beyond the pale* (= behaved in a way that is not acceptable).

**pale·face** /ˈpeɪlfeɪs/ *noun* (used in films, etc.) a name for a white person, said to have been used by Native Americans

**paleo-** (*NAmE*) = PALAEO-

**pal·ette** /ˈpælət/ *noun* **1** a thin board with a hole in it for the THUMB to go through, used by an artist for mixing colours on when painting **2** [usually sing.] (*specialist*) the colours used by a particular artist: *Greens and browns are typical of Ribera's palette.*

ˈpalette knife *noun* a knife with a BLADE (= metal cutting part) that bends easily and has a round end, used by artists and in cooking

**pal·imp·sest** /ˈpælɪmpsest/ *noun* **1** an ancient document from which some or all of the original text has been removed and replaced by a new text **2** (*formal*) something that has many different layers of meaning or detail

**pal·in·drome** /ˈpælɪndrəʊm/ *noun* a word or phrase that reads the same backwards as forwards, for example *madam* or *nurses run*

**pal·ing** /ˈpeɪlɪŋ/ *noun* [C, usually pl., U] a metal or wooden post that is pointed at the top; a fence made of these posts

**pal·is·ade** /ˌpælɪˈseɪd/ *noun* **1** a fence made of strong wooden or metal posts that are pointed at the top, especially used to protect a building in the past **2** **palisades** [pl.] (*US*) a line of high steep CLIFFS, especially along a river or by the sea or ocean

**pall** /pɔːl/ *noun*, *verb*
■ **noun 1** [usually sing.] ~ **of sth** a thick dark cloud of sth: *a pall of smoke/dust* ◇ (*figurative*) *News of her death cast a pall over the event.* **2** a cloth spread over a COFFIN (= a box used for burying a dead person in)
■ **verb** [I] (not used in the progressive tenses) ~ **(on sb)** to become less interesting to sb over a period of time because they have done or seen it too much: *Even the impressive scenery began to pall on me after a few hundred miles.*

**pal·la·dium** /pəˈleɪdiəm/ *noun* [U] (*symb.* **Pd**) a chemical element. Palladium is a rare silver-white metal that looks like PLATINUM.

ˈpall-bearer *noun* a person who helps to carry or walks next to the COFFIN at a FUNERAL

**pal·let** /ˈpælət/ *noun* **1** a heavy wooden or metal base that can be used for moving or storing goods **2** a cloth bag filled with STRAW, used for sleeping on

**pal·lia·tive** /ˈpæliətɪv/ *noun* **1** (*medical*) a medicine or medical treatment that reduces pain without curing its cause ⊃ WORDFINDER NOTE at CURE **2** (*formal*, *usually disapproving*) an action, a decision, etc. that is designed to make a difficult situation seem better without actually solving the cause of the problems ▸ **pal·lia·tive** *adj.* [usually before noun]: *palliative treatment* ◇ *short-term palliative measures*

1117 **pampas**

**pal·lid** /ˈpælɪd/ *adj.* **1** (of a person, their face, etc.) pale, especially because of illness: *a pallid complexion* **2** (of colours or light) not strong or bright, and therefore not attractive: *a pallid sky*

**pal·lor** /ˈpælə(r)/ *noun* [U] a pale colour of the face, especially because of illness or fear: *Her cheeks had an unhealthy pallor.*

**pally** /ˈpæli/ *adj.* ⊃ PAL

**palm** ⓣ+ B2 /pɑːm/ *noun*, *verb*
■ **noun 1** ⓣ+ B2 (also ˈpalm tree) a straight tree with a mass of long leaves at the top, growing in tropical countries. There are several types of palm tree, some of which produce fruit: *a date palm* ◇ *a coconut palm* ◇ *palm leaves/fronds/groves* ⊃ VISUAL VOCAB page V6 **2** the inner surface of the hand between the WRIST and the fingers: *He held the bird gently in the palm of his hand.* ◇ *sweaty palms* ◇ *to read sb's palm* (= to say what you think will happen to sb by looking at the lines on their palm)
**IDM** have sb in the ˈpalm of your ˈhand to have complete control or influence over sb ⊃ more at CROSS v., GREASE v.
■ **verb** ~ **sth** to hide a coin, card, etc. in your hand, especially when performing a trick
**PHRV** ˌpalm sb ˈoff (**with sth**) (*informal*) to persuade sb to believe an excuse or an explanation that is not true, in order to stop them asking questions or complaining ˌpalm sth↔ˈoff (**on/onto sb**) | ˌpalm sb↔ˈoff (**with sth**) (*informal*) to persuade sb to accept sth that has no value or that you do not want, especially by tricking them: *She's always palming the worst jobs off on her assistant.* ◇ *Make sure he doesn't try to palm you off with faulty goods.* ˌpalm sth ˈoff as sth (*informal*) to tell sb that sth is better than it is, especially in order to sell it: *They were trying to palm the table off as a genuine antique.*

**pal·metto** /pælˈmetəʊ/ *noun* (*pl.* -**os**) a small PALM tree that grows in the south-eastern US

**palm·is·try** /ˈpɑːmɪstri/ *noun* [U] the art of telling what a person is like and what will happen to them by looking at the lines on the PALM of their hand

ˈpalm oil *noun* [U] oil obtained from the fruit of some types of PALM tree, used in cooking and in making soap, CANDLES, etc.

**Palm ˈSunday** *noun* [U, C] (in the Christian Church) the Sunday before Easter

**palmy** /ˈpɑːmi/ *adj.* (**palm·ier**, **palmi·est**) used to describe a time in the past when life was good: *That's a picture of me in my palmier days.*

**palo·mino** /ˌpæləˈmiːnəʊ/ *noun* (*pl.* -**os**) a horse that is a cream or gold colour with a white MANE and tail

**palp·able** /ˈpælpəbl/ *adj.* that is easily noticed by the mind or the senses: *a palpable sense of relief* ◇ *The tension in the room was almost palpable.* ▸ **palp·ably** /-bli/ *adv.*: *It was palpably clear what she really meant.*

**pal·pate** /pælˈpeɪt/ *verb* ~ **sth** (*medical*) to examine part of the body by touching it ▸ **pal·pa·tion** /-ˈpeɪʃn/ *noun* [U]

**pal·pi·tate** /ˈpælpɪteɪt/ *verb* [I] (of the heart) to beat rapidly and/or in an IRREGULAR way especially because of fear or excitement

**pal·pi·ta·tions** /ˌpælpɪˈteɪʃnz/ *noun* [pl.] a physical condition in which your heart beats very quickly and in an IRREGULAR way: *Too much caffeine can cause heart palpitations.*

**palsy** /ˈpɔːlzi/ *noun* [U] (*old-fashioned*) PARALYSIS (= loss of control or feeling in part or most of the body), especially when the arms and legs shake without control ⊃ see also CEREBRAL PALSY ▸ **pal·sied** /-zid/ *adj.*

**pal·try** /ˈpɔːltri/ *adj.* [usually before noun] **1** (of an amount) too small to be considered as important or useful **SYN** **meagre**: *This account offers a paltry 1 per cent return on your investment.* ◇ *a paltry sum* **2** having no value or useful qualities: *a paltry gesture*

**pam·pas** /ˈpæmpəs; *NAmE also* -pəz/ *noun* (*usually* **the pampas**) [sing. + sing./pl. v.] the large area of land in South America that has few trees and is covered in grass

**pampas grass** noun [U] a type of tall grass from South America that is often grown in gardens for its long silver-white flowers that look like feathers

**pam·per** /ˈpæmpə(r)/ verb ~ sb (sometimes disapproving) to take care of sb very well and make them feel as comfortable as possible SYN cosset: *Pamper yourself with our new range of beauty treatments.* ◊ *a spoilt and pampered child*

**pamph·let** /ˈpæmflət/ noun a very thin book with a paper cover, containing information about a particular subject SYN leaflet

**pamph·let·eer** /ˌpæmfləˈtɪə(r); NAmE -ˈtɪr/ noun a person who writes pamphlets on particular subjects

**pan**[1] 🔑 B1 /pæn/ noun, verb
■ noun 1 🔑 B1 a container, usually made of metal, with a handle or handles, used for cooking food in: *pots and pans* ◊ *a large stainless steel pan* ⊃ see also FRYING PAN, SAUCEPAN 2 🔑 B1 the amount contained in a pan: *a pan of boiling water* 3 (NAmE) (BrE **tin**) a metal container used for cooking food in: *a cake pan* 4 either of the dishes on a pair of SCALES that you put things into in order to weigh them 5 (BrE) the bowl of a toilet ⊃ see also BEDPAN, DUSTPAN, OIL PAN, SALT PAN
IDM **go down the ˈpan** (BrE, informal) to fail completely: *My career was going down the pan.* ⊃ more at FLASH n.
■ verb (-nn-) 1 [T, usually passive] (informal) to severely criticize sth such as a play or a film SYN **slate**: **be panned (by sb)** *The television series was panned by critics and viewers alike.* 2 [I, T] if a television or video camera **pans** somewhere, or a person **pans** or **pans a camera**, the camera moves in a particular direction, to follow an object or to film a wide area: + adv./prep. *The camera panned back to the audience.* ◊ ~ sth + adv./prep. *He panned the camera along the row of faces.* 3 [I, T] ~(for) sth to wash soil or small stones in a pan to find gold or other valuable minerals: *panning for gold*
PHR V **ˌpan ˈout** (of events or a situation) to develop in a particular way: *I'm happy with the way things have panned out.*

**pan**[2] /pɑːn/ = PAAN

**pan-** /pæn/ combining form (in adjectives and nouns) including all of sth; connected with the whole of sth: *pan-African* ◊ *pandemic*

**pana·cea** /ˌpænəˈsiːə/ noun ~(for sth) something that will solve all the problems of a particular situation

**pan·ache** /pəˈnæʃ; NAmE also -ˈnɑːʃ/ noun [U] the quality of being able to do things in a lively and confident way that other people find attractive SYN **flair**, **style**

**pan·ama** /ˈpænəmə/ (also ˌpanama ˈhat) noun a man's hat made from fine STRAW

**pan·cake** /ˈpænkeɪk/ noun 1 [C] a thin flat round cake made from a mixture of flour, eggs and milk that is fried on both sides, usually eaten hot for breakfast in the US, and in the UK either as a DESSERT with sugar, jam, etc. or as a main course with meat, cheese, etc. 2 [U] thick MAKE-UP for the face, used especially in the theatre IDM see FLAT adj.

**ˈPancake Day** noun (informal) the day before the beginning of Lent, when people traditionally eat PANCAKES ⊃ compare SHROVE TUESDAY

**ˈpancake race** noun a traditional race in the UK on Pancake Day, in which each runner keeps throwing a PANCAKE into the air from a pan

**pan·cetta** /pænˈtʃetə/ noun [U] (from Italian) meat from the BELLY of a pig that has been CURED (= preserved using salt or smoke)

**pan·chay·at** /pʌnˈtʃaɪət/ noun (in some South Asian countries) 1 a village council 2 the official organization that governs local areas in the country, outside large towns

**pan·creas** /ˈpæŋkriəs/ noun an organ near the stomach that produces INSULIN and a liquid that helps the body to DIGEST food ⊃ VISUAL VOCAB page V1 ▶ **pan·cre·at·ic** /ˌpæŋkriˈætɪk/ adj. [only before noun]

**panda** /ˈpændə/ noun 1 (also ˌgiant ˈpanda) a large black and white animal like a bear that lives in China and is very rare 2 (also ˌred ˈpanda) an Asian animal like a RACCOON, with red-brown fur and a long thick tail

**pan·dal** /ˈpændl/ noun (IndE) a large tent used at social events

**pan·dem·ic** /pænˈdemɪk/ noun a disease that spreads over a whole country or the whole world ▶ **pan·dem·ic** adj.: *a pandemic disease* ⊃ compare ENDEMIC, EPIDEMIC

**pan·de·mo·nium** /ˌpændəˈməʊniəm/ noun [U] a situation in which there is a lot of noise and activity with a great lack of order, especially because people are feeling angry or frightened SYN **chaos**: *Pandemonium broke out when the news was announced.*

**pan·der** /ˈpændə(r)/ verb
PHR V **ˈpander to sth/sb** (disapproving) to do what sb wants, or try to please them, especially when this is not acceptable or reasonable: *to pander to sb's wishes* ◊ *The speech was pandering to racial prejudice.*

**p. and h.** (also **p. & h.**) /ˌpiː ən ˈeɪtʃ/ abbr. (NAmE) postage and handling ⊃ compare P. AND P.

**pan·dit** /ˈpændɪt/ (also **pun·dit**) noun 1 a Hindu priest or wise man 2 (IndE) a teacher 3 (IndE) a musician with a lot of skill

**Pandora's box** /pænˌdɔːrəz ˈbɒks; NAmE ˈbɑːks/ noun [sing., U] a process that, if started, will cause many problems: *This court case could open a Pandora's box of similar claims.* ORIGIN From the Greek myth in which **Pandora** was created by the god Zeus and sent to the earth with a box containing many evils. When she opened the box, the evils came out and infected the earth.

**p. and p.** (also **p. & p.**) /ˌpiː ən ˈpiː/ abbr. (BrE) postage and packing (= the cost of packing sth and sending it by post): *Add £2 for p. and p.* ⊃ compare P. AND H., S AND H

**pane** /peɪn/ noun a single sheet of glass in a window: *a pane of glass* ◊ *a windowpane*

▼ **HOMOPHONES**

**pain** • **pane** /peɪn/
• **pain** noun: *These pills should ease the pain.*
• **pain** verb: *It did pain him to see his ex happily married.*
• **pane** noun: *The burglars got in by breaking a pane of glass in a door.*

**pan·eer** (also **panir**) /pəˈnɪə(r); NAmE -ˈnɪr/ noun [U] a type of soft cheese used in Asian cooking

**pan·egyr·ic** /ˌpænəˈdʒɪrɪk/ noun (formal) a speech or piece of writing praising sb/sth

**panel** 🔑 B2 /ˈpænl/ noun, verb
■ noun 1 🔑 B2 [C] a square or RECTANGULAR piece of wood, glass or metal that forms part of a larger surface such as a door or wall: *One of the glass panels in the front door was cracked.* ◊ *wooden fence panels* ⊃ see also SOLAR PANEL 2 🔑 B2 [C] a flat board in a vehicle or on a machine where the controls and instruments are fixed: *an instrument/a display panel* ◊ *a control panel* 3 [C] a piece of metal that forms part of the outer frame of a vehicle 4 [C] a piece of cloth that forms part of a piece of clothing: *The trousers have double thickness knee panels for extra protection.* 5 🔑 B2 [C + sing./pl. v.] a group of specialists who give their advice or opinion about sth; a group of people who discuss topics of interest on television or radio: *an advisory panel* ◊ *a judging panel* ◊ *a panel of experts/judges* ◊ *on a ~ We have two politicians on tonight's panel.* ◊ *a panel discussion* 6 (also ˈjury panel) [C] (both especially NAmE) = JURY
■ verb [usually passive] (-ll-, US -l-) to cover or decorate a surface with flat pieces of wood, glass, etc: **be panelled (in sth)** *The walls were panelled in oak.* ◊ *a glass-/wood-panelled door*

**pan·el·ling** (US **pan·el·ing**) /ˈpænlɪŋ/ noun [U] square or RECTANGULAR pieces of wood used to cover and decorate walls, ceilings, etc.

**pan·el·list** (US **pan·el·ist**) /ˈpænəlɪst/ noun a person who is a member of a panel answering questions during a discussion, for example on radio or television

**panel van** (*AustralE, NZE, SAfrE*) (*NAmE* **panel truck**) *noun* a small van, especially one without windows at the sides or seats for passengers

**pan-fry** *verb* (**pan-fries, pan-frying, pan-fried, pan-fried**) ~ sth to fry food in a pan in shallow fat: *pan-fried chicken*

**pang** /pæŋ/ *noun* a sudden strong feeling of physical or emotional pain: *hunger pangs/pangs of hunger* ◊ *a sudden pang of jealousy*

**panga** /ˈpæŋɡə/ *EAfrE* [ˈpaŋga] *noun* (*EAfrE, SAfrE*) a large heavy knife that is used for cutting grass or small sticks or for removing WEEDS

**Pan·gaea** /pænˈdʒiːə/ *noun* [sing.] (*geology*) an extremely large area of land which existed millions of years ago, made up of all the present continents

**pan·go·lin** /ˈpæŋɡəlɪn/ *noun* a small animal from Africa or Asia that eats insects, and has a long nose, tongue and tail, and hard SCALES on its body

**pan·han·dler** /ˈpænhændlə(r)/ *noun* (*NAmE, informal*) a person who asks other people for money in the street ▶ **pan·han·dle** *verb* [I]

**panic** /ˈpænɪk/ *noun, verb*
■ *noun* [U, C, usually sing.] **1** a sudden feeling of great fear that cannot be controlled and prevents you from thinking clearly: *a moment of panic* ◊ *They were in a state of panic.* ◊ **in ~** *Office workers fled in panic as the fire took hold.* ◊ *There's no point getting into a panic about the exams.* ◊ *a panic attack* (= a condition in which you suddenly feel very anxious, causing your heart to beat faster, etc.) ◊ *a panic decision* (= one that is made when you are in a state of panic) ⊃ SYNONYMS at FEAR **2** a situation in which people are made to feel very anxious or frightened, causing them to act quickly and without thinking carefully: *News of the losses caused (a) panic among investors.* ◊ *Careful planning at this stage will help to avoid a last-minute panic.* ◊ *There's no panic* (= we do not need to rush), *we've got plenty of time.* ◊ *panic buying/selling* (= the act of buying/selling things quickly and without thinking carefully because you are afraid that a particular situation will become worse)
IDM **'panic stations** (*BrE, informal*) a situation in which people feel very anxious and there is a lot of confused activity, especially because there is a lot to do in a short period of time
■ *verb* [I, T] (**-ck-**) to suddenly feel frightened so that you cannot think clearly and you say or do sth stupid, dangerous, etc.; to make sb do this: *I panicked when I saw smoke coming out of the engine.* ◊ *~ sb/sth The gunfire panicked the horses.*
PHRV **'panic sb into doing sth** [usually passive] to make sb act too quickly because they are afraid of sth

**'panic button** *noun* a button that sb working in a bank, etc. can press to call for help if they are in danger
IDM **press/push the 'panic button** to react in a sudden or extreme way to sth unexpected that has frightened you

**pan·icky** /ˈpænɪki/ *adj.* (*informal*) very anxious about sth; feeling or showing panic SYN **hysterical**

**'panic room** (*also* **'safe room**) *noun* a room in a home or an office building where people can go to avoid a dangerous situation

**'panic-stricken** *adj.* extremely anxious about sth, in a way that prevents you from thinking clearly SYN **hysterical**

**pa·nini** /pəˈniːni/ (*also* **pa·nino** /pəˈniːnəʊ/) *noun* (*pl.* **pa·nini** or **pa·ninis**) a sandwich made with Italian bread, usually toasted

**panir** = PANEER

**pan·nier** /ˈpæniə(r)/ *noun* each of a pair of bags or boxes carried on either side of the back wheel of a bicycle or motorcycle; each of a pair of BASKETS carried on either side of its back by a horse or DONKEY

**pan·oply** /ˈpænəpli/ *noun* [sing., U] (*formal*) a large and impressive number or collection of sth SYN **array**

**pan·or·ama** /ˌpænəˈrɑːmə; *NAmE* -ˈræmə/ *noun* **1** a view of a wide area of land SYN **vista**: *There is a superb panorama of the mountains from the hotel.* ⊃ SYNONYMS at VIEW **2** a description, study or set of pictures that presents all the different aspects or stages of a particular subject, event, etc. ▶ **pan·or·am·ic** /ˌpænəˈræmɪk/ *adj.* [usually before noun]: *a panoramic view over the valley*

**'pan pipes** *noun* [pl.] (*BrE*) (*NAmE also* **'pan-pipe** [C]) a musical instrument made of a row of pipes of different lengths that you play by blowing across the open ends

**pansy** /ˈpænzi/ *noun* (*pl.* **-ies**) **1** a small garden plant with brightly coloured flowers **2** (*taboo, slang*) an offensive word for a GAY man

**pant** /pænt/ *verb* [I, T] to breathe quickly with short breaths, usually with your mouth open, because you have been doing some physical exercise, or because it is very hot: *She finished the race panting heavily.* ◊ *She could hear him panting up the stairs* (= running up and breathing quickly). ◊ *He found her panting for breath at the top of the hill.* ◊ **+ speech** *'Wait for me!' he panted.* ▶ **pant** *noun* [usually pl.]: *His breath came in short pants.* ⊃ see also PANTS IDM see PUFF *v.*
PHRV **'pant for/after sb/sth** to want sth/sb very much: *The end of the novel leaves you panting for more.*

**pan·ta·loons** /ˌpæntəˈluːnz/ *noun* [pl.] **1** women's loose trousers with wide legs that fit tightly at the ankles **2** (in the past) men's tight trousers fastened at the foot

**pan·the·ism** /ˈpænθiɪzəm/ *noun* [U] **1** the belief that God is present in all natural things **2** belief in many or all gods ▶ **pan·the·ist** /-ɪst/ *noun* **pan·the·ist·ic** /ˌpænθiˈɪstɪk/ *adj.*

**pan·theon** /ˈpænθiən; *NAmE* -θiɑːn/ *noun* **1** (*specialist*) all the gods of a nation or people: *the ancient Egyptian pantheon* **2** (*formal*) a group of people who are famous within a particular area of activity **3** a TEMPLE (= religious building) built in honour of all the gods of a nation; a building in which famous dead people of a nation are buried or honoured

**pan·ther** /ˈpænθə(r)/ *noun* **1** a LEOPARD (= a large wild animal of the cat family), especially a black one **2** (*NAmE*) = PUMA

**pantie girdle** = PANTY GIRDLE

**pan·ties** /ˈpæntiz/ (*especially NAmE*) (*BrE also* **knick·ers**) *noun* [pl.] a piece of women's underwear that covers the body from the middle part to the tops of the legs
IDM **get your 'panties in a bunch** (*NAmE*) (*BrE* **get your 'knickers in a twist**) (*informal*) to become angry, confused or upset

**panto** /ˈpæntəʊ/ *noun* (*pl.* **-os**) (*BrE, informal*) = PANTOMIME

**panto·mime** /ˈpæntəmaɪm/ *noun* **1** (*also BrE, informal* **panto**) [C, U] (in the UK) a type of play with music, dancing and jokes, that is based on a FAIRY TALE and is usually performed at Christmas **2** [U, C, usually sing.] the use of movement and the expression of your face to communicate sth or to tell a story SYN **mime** **3** [C, usually sing.] (*BrE*) a silly and confused situation SYN **farce**

**pantomime 'dame** (*also* **dame**) *noun* (*BrE*) a female character in a PANTOMIME, that is usually played by a man

**pantomime 'horse** *noun* (*BrE*) a character in a PANTOMIME that is supposed to be a horse, played by two people in a special costume

**pan·try** /ˈpæntri/ *noun* (*pl.* **-ies**) a cupboard or small room in a house, used for storing food SYN **larder** ⊃ see also FOOD PANTRY

**pants** ❶ /pænts/ *noun* [pl.] **1** (*BrE*) UNDERPANTS or KNICKERS: *a pair of pants* **2** (*especially NAmE*) trousers: *a new pair of pants* ◊ *ski/sweat/dress pants* ◊ *I started patting at my pants pocket.* ⊃ see also CAPRI PANTS, CARGO PANTS, HALF PANTS, HOT PANTS **3** (*BrE, slang*) (also used as an adjective) something you think is of poor quality SYN **rubbish**: *Their new album is absolute pants!* ◊ *Do we have to watch this pants programme?*
IDM **bore, scare, etc. the 'pants off sb** (*informal*) to make sb extremely bored, frightened, etc. ⊃ more at ANT, CATCH *v.*, SEAT *n.*, WEAR *v.*, WET *v.*

**pant·suit** /ˈpæntsuːt/ *noun* (*NAmE*) (*BrE* **'trouser suit**) *noun* a woman's suit of jacket and pants

# pantsula

**pant·sula** /ˌpæntˈsuːlə/ *noun* [U] a style of South African dancing in which each person takes a turn to perform dance movements in front of a group of other dancers who are in a circle

**panty girdle** (*also* **pantie girdle**) /ˈpænti ɡɜːdl; *NAmE* ɡɜːrdl/ *noun* a tight piece of women's underwear that combines KNICKERS and a GIRDLE

**panty·hose** /ˈpæntihəʊz/ (*NAmE*) (*BrE* **tights**) *noun* [pl.] a piece of clothing made of very thin cloth that fits closely over a woman's HIPS, legs and feet ⇨ compare STOCKING

**pap** /pæp/ (*BrE*) *noun, verb*
■ *noun* **1** [U] (*disapproving*) books, magazines, television programmes, etc. that have no real value **2** [U] soft or almost liquid food eaten by babies or people who are ill **3** *SAfrE* [pɒp] [U] (*SAfrE*) PORRIDGE made with flour from MAIZE **4** [C] = PAPARAZZO
■ *verb* (**-pp-**) ~ *sb* to follow a famous person around and take a photograph of them without their permission: *She can't even go to the gym without being papped.*

**papa** /pəˈpɑː; *NAmE* ˈpɑːpə/ *noun* (*BrE, old-fashioned or NAmE*) used to talk about or to address your father

**pap·acy** /ˈpeɪpəsi/ *noun* **1 the papacy** [sing.] the position or the authority of the POPE **2** [C, usually sing.] the period of time when a particular POPE is in power

**papad** /ˈpɑːpəd/ *noun* (*IndE*) a POPPADOM

**papal** /ˈpeɪpl/ *adj.* [only before noun] connected with the POPE: *papal authority* ◇ *a papal visit to Mexico*

**pap·ar·azzo** /ˌpæpəˈrætsəʊ; *NAmE* ˌpɑːpəˈrɑːt-/ (*also* **pap** /pæp/) *noun* (*pl.* **pap·ar·azzi** /ˌpæpəˈrætsi; *NAmE* ˌpɑːpəˈrɑːt-/) [usually pl.] a photographer who follows famous people around in order to get interesting photographs of them to sell to a newspaper

**pa·paya** /pəˈpaɪə/ (*BrE also* **paw·paw**) *noun* a tropical fruit with yellow and green skin, that is orange or red inside with round black seeds ⇨ VISUAL VOCAB page V4

**paper** 0̶ A1 /ˈpeɪpə(r)/ *noun, verb*
■ *noun*
- FOR WRITING/WRAPPING **1** A1 [U] (often in compounds) the thin material that you write and draw on and that is also used for wrapping and packing things: *a piece/sheet of paper* ◇ *a slip/scrap of paper* ◇ *a package wrapped in brown paper* ◇ *recycled paper* ◇ **on/onto** ~ *The image is copied onto paper.* ◇ *He brought his lunch in a brown paper bag.* ◇ *a paper cup/plate/napkin*
- NEWSPAPER **2** A1 [C] a newspaper: *the daily/morning paper* ◇ *the local paper* ◇ *Have you seen today's paper?* ◇ **in the** ~ *I read about it in the paper.* ◇ *The papers* (= newspapers in general) *soon got hold of the story.*
- DOCUMENTS **3** A2 **papers** [pl.] pieces of paper with writing on them, such as letters, pieces of work or private documents: *His desk was covered with books and papers.* ◇ *a stack/pile of papers* **4** A2 **papers** [pl.] official documents that prove your identity, give you permission to do sth, etc: *identity papers* ◇ *The couple filed divorce papers at Los Angeles court on Monday.* ⇨ see also WORKING PAPERS at WORKING PAPER
- EXAM **5** A2 [C] (*BrE*) a set of exam questions on a particular subject; the answers that people write to the questions: *The geography paper was hard.* ◇ *She spent the evening marking exam papers.* ⇨ WORDFINDER NOTE at EXAM
- ARTICLE **6** B1 [C] an academic article about a particular subject that is written by and for specialists: *a recent paper in the Journal of Medicine* ◇ ~ **on sth** *He has published a research paper on the topic.* ◇ *She was invited to give a paper* (= a talk) *at an international scientific congress.* **7** [C] (*NAmE*) a piece of written work done by a student: *Your grade will be based on four papers and a final exam.* ◇ **on sth** *I'm writing a paper on 'Macbeth'.* ⇨ see also TERM PAPER
- ON WALLS **8** [C, U] paper that you use to cover and decorate the walls of a room: *The room was damp and the paper was peeling off.* HELP There are many other compounds ending in **paper**. You will find them at their place in the alphabet.
IDM **on paper 1** when you put sth **on paper**, you write it down **2** judged from written information only, but not proved in practice: *The idea looks good on paper.* ⇨ more at PEN *n.*, WORTH *adj.*
■ *verb* ~ **sth** to decorate the walls of a room by covering them with WALLPAPER
PHRV **paper 'over sth 1** to cover a wall with WALLPAPER in order to hide sth SYN wallpaper: *The previous owners had obviously papered over any damp patches.* **2** to try to hide a problem in a way that is temporary and not likely to be successful: *The government is trying to paper over the cracks in the cabinet.* ◇ *We can't just paper over the problem.*

**paper·back** /ˈpeɪpəbæk; *NAmE* -pərb-/ *noun* [C, U] a book that has a thick paper cover: *a cheap paperback* ◇ **in** ~ *When is it coming out in paperback?* ◇ *a paperback book/edition* ⇨ compare HARDBACK

**paper boy**, **paper girl** *noun* a boy or girl who delivers newspapers to people's houses

**pa·per·chase** /ˈpeɪpətʃeɪs; *NAmE* -pərtʃ-/ *noun* **1** (*BrE*) a game in which one runner drops pieces of paper for the other runners to follow **2** (*NAmE, informal*) the fact of producing too much work on paper

**paper clip** *noun* a piece of bent wire or plastic that is designed to hold loose sheets of paper together

**paper cutter** *noun* (*US*) a device with a long sharp BLADE for cutting paper SYN guillotine

**paper·knife** /ˈpeɪpənaɪf; *NAmE* -pərn-/ *noun* (*pl.* **-knives** /-naɪvz/) (*especially BrE*) (*NAmE usually* **letter opener**) a knife used for opening ENVELOPES

**paper·less** /ˈpeɪpələs; *NAmE* -pərl-/ *adj.* using computers, phones, etc. rather than paper to exchange information: *the paperless office* ◇ *a system of paperless business transactions*

**paper 'money** *noun* [U] money that is made of paper, not coins SYN note

**paper 'plate** *noun* a plate made of thick card that can be thrown away after it is used

**'paper-pusher** *noun* (*NAmE*) = PEN-PUSHER

**paper 'round** (*BrE*) (*NAmE* **paper route**) *noun* the job of delivering newspapers to houses; the route taken when doing this

**paper shop** *noun* (*BrE*) = NEWSAGENT

**paper-'thin** *adj.* (of objects) very thin and DELICATE: *paper-thin slices of meat* ⇨ compare WAFER-THIN

**paper 'tiger** *noun* a person, a country or a situation that seems or claims to be powerful or dangerous but is not really

**paper 'towel** *noun* **1** [C] a thick sheet of paper that you use to dry your hands **2** [U] (*NAmE*) (*BrE* **'kitchen paper**, **'kitchen roll**, **'kitchen towel**) thick paper on a roll, used for cleaning up liquid, food, etc.

**'paper trail** *noun* (*informal*) a series of documents that provide evidence of what you have done or what has happened: *He was a shrewd lawyer with a talent for uncovering paper trails of fraud.*

**paper·weight** /ˈpeɪpəweɪt; *NAmE* -pərw-/ *noun* a small heavy object that you put on top of loose papers to keep them in place

**paper·work** /ˈpeɪpəwɜːk; *NAmE* -pərwɜːrk/ *noun* [U] **1** the written work that is part of a job, such as filling in forms or writing letters and reports: *We're trying to cut down on the amount of paperwork involved.* **2** all the documents that you need for sth, such as a court case or buying a house: *How quickly can you prepare the paperwork?*

**pa·pery** /ˈpeɪpəri/ *adj.* like paper; thin and dry

**pa·pier mâché** /ˌpæpieɪ ˈmæʃeɪ; *NAmE* ˌpeɪpər məˈʃeɪ, ˌpæpjeɪ/ *noun* (*from French*) paper mixed with GLUE (= a sticky substance) or flour and water, that is used to make attractive objects

**pap·il·loma** /ˌpæpɪˈləʊmə; *NAmE* -ˈloʊ-/ *noun* (*medical*) a small part like a WART that grows on the skin and is not usually harmful

**pap·ist** /ˈpeɪpɪst/ *noun* (*offensive*) an offensive word for a Roman Catholic, used by some Protestants ▶ **pap·ist** *adj.*

**pa·poose** /pəˈpuːs/ *noun* a type of bag that can be used for carrying a baby in, on your back or in front of you

**pap·ri·ka** /pəˈpriːkə; BrE also ˈpæprɪkə/ noun [U] a red powder made from a type of PEPPER, used in cooking as a SPICE ⊃ VISUAL VOCAB page V8

**ˈPap smear** (NAmE) (BrE **ˈsmear test**, **smear**, **ˈcervical ˈsmear**) noun a medical test in which a very small amount of TISSUE from a woman's CERVIX is removed and examined for cancer cells

**pa·py·rus** /pəˈpaɪrəs/ noun (pl. **pa·pyri** /-riː/) **1** [U] a tall plant with thick STEMS that grows in water, especially in Africa **2** [U] paper made from the STEMS of the papyrus plant, used in ancient Egypt for writing and drawing on **3** [C] a document or piece of paper made of papyrus

**par** /pɑː(r)/ noun [U] **1** (in golf) the number of shots a good player should need to complete a course or to hit the ball into a particular hole: *a par five hole* ◊ *Par for the course is 72.* **2** (also **ˈpar value**) (business) the value that a share in a company had originally: *at ~ to be redeemed at par* IDM **below/under ˈpar** less well, good, etc. than is usual or expected: *Teaching in some subjects has been well below par.* **be ˌpar for the ˈcourse** (disapproving) to be just what you would expect to happen or expect sb to do in a particular situation SYN **norm**: *Starting early and working long hours is par for the course in this job.* **on a ˌpar / ˈlevel with sb / sth** as good, bad, important, etc. as sb/sth else **up to ˈpar** as good as usual or as good as it should be SYN **up to scratch**

**par.** (also **para.**) abbr. (in writing) paragraph: See par. 3.

**para** /ˈpærə/ noun (informal) = PARATROOPER

**para-** /pærə/ prefix (in nouns and adjectives) **1** outside; beyond: *paranormal* **2** similar to but not official or not fully qualified: *paramilitary* ◊ *a paramedic*

**par·able** /ˈpærəbl/ noun a short story that teaches a moral or spiritual lesson, especially one of those told by Jesus as recorded in the Bible

**para·bola** /pəˈræbələ/ noun (geometry) a curve like the path of an object thrown into the air and falling back to earth ⊃ picture at CONIC SECTION ▸ **para·bol·ic** /ˌpærəˈbɒlɪk; NAmE -ˈbɑːl-/ adj.: *parabolic curves*

**para·ceta·mol** /ˌpærəˈsiːtəmɒl, -ˈset-; NAmE -mɑːl/ (BrE) (NAmE **acet·amino·phen**) noun [U, C] (pl. **para·ceta·mol** or **para·ceta·mols**) a drug used to reduce pain and a high temperature: *Do you have any paracetamol?* ◊ *Take two paracetamol(s) and try to sleep.*

**para·chute** /ˈpærəʃuːt/ noun, verb

▪ **noun** (also informal **chute**) a device that is attached to people or objects to make them fall slowly and safely when they are dropped from an aircraft. It consists of a large piece of thin cloth that opens out in the air: *Planes dropped supplies by parachute.* ◊ *a parachute drop/jump* ◊ *a parachute regiment* ⊃ see also GOLDEN PARACHUTE ⊃ WORDFINDER NOTE at AIRCRAFT

*parachute*

▪ **verb 1** [I] (+ adv. / prep.) to jump from an aircraft using a parachute: *The pilot was able to parachute to safety.* ◊ *She regularly goes parachuting.* **2** [T] ~ sb / sth + adv. / prep. to drop sb/sth from an aircraft by parachute

**para·chut·ist** /ˈpærəʃuːtɪst/ noun a person who jumps from a plane using a parachute

**para·clin·ical** /ˌpærəˈklɪnɪkl/ adj. (specialist) related to the parts of medicine, especially laboratory sciences, that are not directly involved in the care of patients

**par·ade** 🔊+ B2 /pəˈreɪd/ noun, verb

▪ **noun**
• PUBLIC CELEBRATION **1** 🔊+ B2 [C] a public celebration of a special day or event, usually with bands in the streets and decorated vehicles SYN **procession**: *the Lord Mayor's parade* ◊ *St Patrick's Day parade in New York* ⊃ WORDFINDER NOTE at CELEBRATE
• OF SOLDIERS **2** [C, U] a formal occasion when soldiers MARCH or stand in lines so that they can be INSPECTED (= looked at and approved) by their officers or other important people: *a military parade* ◊ *on ~ They stood as straight as soldiers on parade.* ◊ (figurative) *The latest software will be on parade at the exhibition.* ⊃ see also IDENTIFICATION PARADE
• SERIES **3** [C] a series of things or people: *Each generation passes through a similar parade of events.*
• ROW OF SHOPS **4** [C] (especially BrE) (often in names) a street with a row of small shops: *a shopping parade* IDM see RAIN v.

▪ **verb**
• WALK TO CELEBRATE / PROTEST **1** [I] (+ adv. / prep.) to walk somewhere in a formal group of people, in order to celebrate or protest about sth: *The victorious team will parade through the city tomorrow morning.*
• SHOW IN PUBLIC **2** [I] + adv. / prep. to walk around in a way that makes other people notice you: *People were parading up and down showing off their finest clothes.* **3** [T] ~ sb / sth + adv. / prep. to show sb/sth in public so that people can see them/it: *The trophy was paraded around the stadium.* ◊ *The prisoners were paraded in front of the crowd.* ◊ (figurative) *He is not one to parade his achievements.*
• OF SOLDIERS **4** [I, T] to come together, or to bring soldiers together, in order to MARCH (= walk formally) in front of other people: + adv. / prep. *The crowds applauded as the guards paraded past.* ◊ *~ sb + adv. / prep. The colonel paraded his men before the Queen.*
• PRETEND **5** [I, T] to pretend to be, or to make sb/sth seem to be, good or important when they are not: *~ as sth myth parading as fact* ◊ *~ sb / sth / yourself as sth He paraded himself as a loyal supporter of the party.*

**paˈrade ground** noun a place where soldiers gather to MARCH or to be INSPECTED (= looked at and approved) by an officer or an important visitor

**para·digm** /ˈpærədaɪm/ noun **1** (specialist or formal) a typical example or pattern of sth: *a paradigm for students to copy* ◊ *The war was a paradigm of the destructive side of human nature.* **2** (grammar) a set of all the different forms of a word: *verb paradigms* ▸ **para·dig·mat·ic** /ˌpærədɪɡˈmætɪk/ adj.

**ˈparadigm shift** noun a great and important change in the way sth is done or thought about

**para·dise** /ˈpærədaɪs/ noun **1** (often **Paradise**) [U] (in some religions) a perfect place where people are said to go when they die SYN **heaven**: *The ancient Egyptians saw paradise as an idealized version of their own lives.* **2** [C] a place that is extremely beautiful and that seems perfect, like heaven: *a tropical paradise* **3** [C] a perfect place for a particular activity or kind of person: *The area is a birdwatcher's paradise.* **4** [U] a state of perfect happiness SYN **bliss**: *Being alone is his idea of paradise.* ⊃ see also FOOL'S PARADISE **5** **Paradise** [U] (in the Bible) the garden of Eden, where Adam and Eve lived ⊃ see also BIRD OF PARADISE

**para·dox** /ˈpærədɒks; NAmE -dɑːks/ noun **1** [C] a person, thing or situation that has two opposite features and therefore seems strange: *He was a paradox—a loner who loved to chat to strangers.* ◊ *It is a curious paradox that professional comedians often have unhappy personal lives.* **2** [C, U] a statement containing two opposite ideas that make it seem impossible or unlikely, although it is probably true; the use of this in writing: *'More haste, less speed' is a well-known paradox.* ◊ *It's a work full of paradox and ambiguity.* ⊃ WORDFINDER NOTE at IMAGE ▸ **para·dox·ical** /ˌpærəˈdɒksɪkl; NAmE -ˈdɑːk-/ adj.: *It is paradoxical that some of the poorest people live in some of the richest areas of the country.* **para·dox·ical·ly** /-kli/ adv.: *Paradoxically, the less she ate, the fatter she got.*

**par·af·fin** /ˈpærəfɪn/ (also **ˈparaffin oil**) (both BrE) (NAmE **kero·sene**) noun [U] a type of oil obtained from PETROLEUM and used as a fuel for heat and light: *a paraffin heater / lamp / stove*

# paraffin wax

**paraffin wax** noun [U] a soft white substance that is made from PETROLEUM or coal, and is used especially for making CANDLES

**para·glider** /ˈpærəɡlaɪdə(r)/ noun **1** a structure consisting of a big thin piece of cloth like a PARACHUTE, with a HARNESS which is attached to a person when they jump from a high place in the sport of paragliding **2** a person who does paragliding

**para·glid·ing** /ˈpærəɡlaɪdɪŋ/ noun [U] a sport in which you wear a special structure like a PARACHUTE, jump from a high place and are carried along by the wind before coming down to earth: *to go paragliding*

**para·gon** /ˈpærəɡən; *NAmE* -ɡɑːn/ noun a person who is perfect or who is a perfect example of a particular good quality: *I make no claim to be a paragon.* ◇ *He wasn't the paragon of virtue she had expected.*

**para·graph** /ˈpærəɡrɑːf; *NAmE* -ɡræf/ noun (*abbr.* **par., para.**) a section of a piece of writing, usually consisting of several sentences dealing with a single subject. The first sentence of a paragraph starts on a new line: *an opening/introductory paragraph* ◇ *Write a paragraph on each of the topics given below.* ◇ *See paragraph 15 of the handbook.*

**para·graph·ing** /ˈpærəɡrɑːfɪŋ; *NAmE* -ɡræf-/ noun [U] the way that a piece of writing is divided into paragraphs

**para·keet** (*also* **parra·keet**) /ˈpærəkiːt/ noun a small bird of the PARROT family, usually with a long tail

**para·legal** /ˌpærəˈliːɡl/ noun (*especially NAmE*) a person who is trained to help a lawyer ▶ **para·legal** *adj.*

**par·all·ax** /ˈpærəlæks/ noun [U] (*specialist*) the effect by which the position or direction of an object appears to change when the object is seen from different positions

**par·al·lel** /ˈpærəlel/ *adj., noun, verb*

■ *adj.* **1** two or more lines that are **parallel** to each other are the same distance apart at every point: *parallel lines* ◇ *~ to/with sth The road and the canal are parallel to each other.* ⊃ picture at LINE **2** very similar or taking place at the same time: *a parallel case* ◇ *parallel trends* ◇ *Though still a committed painter, in 1978 she launched a parallel career as a photographer.* **3** (*computing*) involving several computer operations at the same time: *parallel processing* ▶ **par·al·lel** *adv.*: *The road and the canal run parallel to each other.* ◇ *The plane flew parallel to the coast.*

■ *noun* **1** [C, U] a person, a situation, an event, etc. that is very similar to another, especially one in a different place or time SYN **equivalent**: *These ideas have parallels in Freud's thought too.* ◇ *This tradition has no parallel in our culture.* ◇ *without ~ This is an achievement without parallel in modern times.* **2** [C, usually pl.] similar features: *There are interesting parallels between the 1960s and the late 1990s.* ◇ *It is possible to* **draw a parallel between** (= find similar features in) *their experience and ours.* **3** (*also* **parallel of ˈlatitude**) [C] an imaginary line around the earth that is always the same distance from the EQUATOR; this line on a map: *the 49th parallel* IDM **in ˈparallel (with sth/sb)** with and at the same time as sth/sb else: *The new degree and the existing certificate courses would run in parallel.*

■ *verb* **1** ~ sth to be similar to sth; to happen at the same time as sth: *Their legal system parallels our own.* ◇ *The rise in unemployment is paralleled by an increase in petty crime.* **2** ~ sth to be as good as sth SYN **equal**: *a level of achievement that has never been paralleled* ⊃ compare UNPARALLELED

**parallel ˈbars** noun [pl.] two bars on posts that are used for doing GYMNASTIC exercises

**parallel ˈimports** noun [pl.] (*economics*) goods that are imported into a country without the permission of the company that produced them, and sold at a lower price than the company sells them at

**par·al·lel·ism** /ˈpærəlelɪzəm/ noun [U, C] (*formal*) the state of being similar; a similar feature: *I think he exaggerates the parallelism between the two cases.*

**par·al·lelo·gram** /ˌpærəˈleləɡræm/ noun (*geometry*) a flat shape with four straight sides, the opposite sides being the same distance apart at every point and equal to each other

**parallelograms**

square    rectangle

rhombus    rhomboid

**parallel ˈprocessing** noun [U] (*computing*) the division of a process into different parts, which are performed at the same time by different PROCESSORS in a computer

**Para·lym·pian** (*also* **paralympian**) /ˌpærəˈlɪmpiən/ noun a person who competes in the Paralympics ▶ **Paralympian** (*also* **paralympian**) *adj.*

**the Para·lym·pics** /ðə ˌpærəˈlɪmpɪks/ noun [pl.] an international ATHLETICS competition for people who are DISABLED (= unable to use a part of the body completely or easily because of a physical condition, an illness, an injury, etc.)

**para·lyse** (*BrE*) (*NAmE* **para·lyze**) /ˈpærəlaɪz/ verb [often passive] **1** ~ sb to make sb unable to feel or move all or part of their body: *The accident left him paralysed from the waist down.* ◇ (*figurative*) *paralysing heat* ◇ (*figurative*) *She stood there, paralysed with fear.* **2** ~ sth to prevent sth from functioning normally: *The airport is still paralysed by the strike.*

**par·aly·sis** /pəˈræləsɪs/ noun (*pl.* **par·aly·ses** /-ləsiːz/) **1** [U, C] a loss of control of, and sometimes feeling in, part or most of the body, caused by disease or an injury to the nerves: *paralysis of both legs* **2** [U] the condition of being unable to move, act, function, etc: *The strike caused total paralysis in the city.*

**para·lyt·ic** /ˌpærəˈlɪtɪk/ *adj.* **1** [not before noun] (*BrE, informal*) very drunk **2** [usually before noun] (*formal*) suffering from paralysis; making sb unable to move: *a paralytic illness* ◇ *paralytic fear*

**para·med·ic** /ˌpærəˈmedɪk/ noun a person whose job is to help people who are sick or injured, but who is not a doctor or a nurse: *Paramedics treated the injured at the roadside.* ⊃ WORDFINDER NOTE at ACCIDENT ▶ **para·med·ic·al** /-dɪkl/ *adj.*: *paramedical staff*

**par·am·eter** /pəˈræmɪtə(r)/ noun [usually before noun] (*formal*) something that decides or limits the way in which sth can be done: *to set/define the parameters* ◇ *We had to work within the parameters that had already been established.*

**para·mili·tary** /ˌpærəˈmɪlətri; *NAmE* -teri/ *adj., noun*

■ *adj.* [usually before noun] **1** a **paramilitary** organization is an illegal group that is organized like an army: *a right-wing paramilitary group* **2** helping the official army of a country: *paramilitary police, such as the CRS in France*

■ *noun* [usually pl.] (*pl.* **-ies**) **1** a member of an illegal paramilitary group or organization **2** a member of an organization that helps the official army of a country

**para·mount** /ˈpærəmaʊnt/ *adj.* **1** more important than anything else: *This matter is of paramount importance.* ◇ *Safety is paramount.* ⊃ LANGUAGE BANK at VITAL **2** (*formal*) having the highest position or the greatest power: *China's paramount leader* ▶ **para·mount·cy** /-si/ noun [U]

**par·amour** /ˈpærəmʊə(r); *NAmE* -mʊr/ noun (*old-fashioned or literary*) a person that sb is having a romantic or sexual relationship with SYN **lover**

**para·noia** /ˌpærəˈnɔɪə/ noun [U] **1** (*medical*) a mental illness in which a person wrongly believes that other people are trying to harm them, that they are sb very important, etc. ⊃ WORDFINDER NOTE at CONDITION **2** (*informal*) fear of other people when there is no evidence or reason for this

**para·noid** /ˈpærənɔɪd/ *adj., noun*

■ *adj.* (*also less frequent* **para·noiac** /ˌpærəˈnɔɪæk; *NAmE* -ˈnɔɪk/) **1** afraid of other people for no reason or suspecting that they are trying to harm you, when really they are not: *She's getting really paranoid about what other people say about her.* ⊃ SYNONYMS at AFRAID **2** suffering from a mental illness in which you wrongly believe that other people are trying to harm you or that you are very

b **b**ad | d **d**id | f **f**all | g **g**et | h **h**at | j **y**es | k **c**at | l **l**eg | m **m**an | n **n**ow | p **p**en | r **r**ed

important: *paranoid delusions* ◊ *paranoid schizophrenia* ◊ *a paranoid killer*
- **noun** (*also* **para·noiac** /ˌpærəˈnɔɪæk; *NAmE* -ˈnɔʊɪk/) a person who suffers from paranoia

**para·nor·mal** /ˌpærəˈnɔːml; *NAmE* -ˈnɔːrml/ *adj.* **1** that cannot be explained by science or reason and that seems to involve mysterious forces SYN **supernatural 2 the paranormal** *noun* [sing.] events or subjects that are paranormal SYN **supernatural**

**para·pet** /ˈpærəpɪt, -pet/ *noun* **1** a low wall along the edge of a bridge, a roof, etc. to stop people from falling **2** a wall or barrier placed in order to protect soldiers from being shot: (*figurative*) *He was not prepared to* **put his head above the parapet** *and say what he really thought* (= he did not want to risk doing it).

**para·pher·na·lia** /ˌpærəfəˈneɪliə; *NAmE* -fər-/ *noun* [U] a large number of objects or personal possessions, especially the equipment that you need for a particular activity: *skiing paraphernalia* ◊ *an electric kettle and all the paraphernalia for making tea and coffee*

**para·phrase** /ˈpærəfreɪz/ *verb, noun*
- **verb** [T, I] ~ **(sth)** to express what sb has said or written using different words, especially in order to make it easier to understand: *Try to paraphrase the question before you answer it.*
- **noun** a statement that expresses sth that sb has written or said using different words, especially in order to make it easier to understand

**para·ple·gia** /ˌpærəˈpliːdʒə/ *noun* [U] PARALYSIS (= loss of control or feeling) in the legs and lower body

**para·ple·gic** /ˌpærəˈpliːdʒɪk/ *noun* a person who suffers from paraplegia ▶ **para·ple·gic** *adj.*

**para·psych·ology** /ˌpærəsaɪˈkɒlədʒi; *NAmE* -ˈkɑːl-/ *noun* [U] the study of mental powers that seem to exist but that cannot be explained by scientific knowledge

**para·quat** /ˈpærəkwɒt; *NAmE* -kwɑːt/ *noun* [U] an extremely poisonous liquid used to kill plants that are growing where they are not wanted

**para·sail·ing** /ˈpærəseɪlɪŋ/ *noun* [U] the sport of being pulled up into the air behind a boat while wearing a special PARACHUTE

**para·site** /ˈpærəsaɪt/ *noun* **1** a small animal or plant that lives on or inside another animal or plant and gets its food from it **2** (*disapproving*) a person who always relies on or benefits from other people and gives nothing back

**para·sit·ic** /ˌpærəˈsɪtɪk/ (*also less frequent* **para·sit·ical** /ˌpærəˈsɪtɪkl/) *adj.* **1** caused by a parasite: *a parasitic disease/infection* **2** living on another animal or plant and getting its food from it: *a parasitic mite* **3** (*disapproving*) (of a person) always relying on or benefiting from other people and giving nothing back ▶ **para·sit·ical·ly** /-kli/ *adv.*

**para·sol** /ˈpærəsɒl; *NAmE* -sɔːl/ *noun* **1** a type of light umbrella that women in the past carried to protect themselves from the sun **2** a large umbrella that is used for example on beaches or outside restaurants to protect people from hot sun ⇒ compare SUNSHADE

**para·statal** /ˌpærəˈsteɪtl/ *adj.* (*specialist*) (of an organization) having some political power and serving the state

**par·atha** /pəˈrɑːtə/ *noun* a type of South Asian bread made without YEAST, usually fried on a GRIDDLE

**para·troop·er** /ˈpærətruːpə(r)/ (*also informal* **para**) *noun* a member of the paratroops

**para·troops** /ˈpærətruːps/ *noun* [pl.] soldiers who are trained to jump from planes using a PARACHUTE ▶ **paratroop** *adj.* [only before noun]: *a paratroop regiment*

**par·boil** /ˈpɑːbɔɪl; *NAmE* ˈpɑːrb-/ *verb* ~ **sth** to boil food, especially vegetables, until it is partly cooked

**par·cel** /ˈpɑːsl; *NAmE* ˈpɑːrsl/ *noun, verb*
- **noun 1** (*especially BrE*) (*NAmE usually* **pack·age**) something that is wrapped in paper or put into a thick ENVELOPE so that it can be sent by mail, carried easily or given as a present: *There's a parcel and some letters for you.* ◊ *She was carrying a parcel of books under her arm.* ◊ *The prisoners were allowed food parcels.* **2** a piece of land: *50 five-acre parcels have been sold.* **3** (*especially BrE*) a

1123 **parent**

small amount of food that is wrapped in sth, usually PASTRY, before it is cooked: *filo pastry parcels* IDM see PART *n.*
- **verb** (*especially BrE*) (**-ll-**, *US* **-l-**) ~ **sth (up)** to wrap sth up and make it into a parcel: *She parcelled up the books to send.*
PHRV **parcel sth↔out** to divide sth into parts or between several people: *The land was parcelled out into small lots.*

ˈ**parcel bomb** *noun* (*BrE*) a bomb that is sent to sb in a package and that explodes when the package is opened

**parch** /pɑːtʃ; *NAmE* pɑːrtʃ/ *verb* ~ **sth** (especially of hot weather) to make an area of land very dry

**parched** /pɑːtʃt; *NAmE* pɑːrtʃt/ *adj.* **1** very dry, especially because the weather is hot: *dry parched land* ◊ *soil parched by drought* ◊ *She licked her parched lips.* **2** (*informal*) very thirsty: *Let's get a drink—I'm parched.*

ˌ**parched ˈrice** *noun* [U] rice that has been pressed flat and dried, used in Asian cooking

**parch·ment** /ˈpɑːtʃmənt; *NAmE* ˈpɑːrtʃ-/ *noun* **1** [U] material made from the skin of a sheep or GOAT, used in the past for writing on: *parchment scrolls* **2** [U] a type of thick paper, used for a particular purpose **3** [C] a document written on a piece of parchment

**pard·ner** /ˈpɑːdnə(r); *NAmE* ˈpɑːrd-/ *noun* (*NAmE, informal, non-standard*) a way of saying or writing 'partner' in informal speech

**par·don** /ˈpɑːdn; *NAmE* ˈpɑːrdn/ *exclamation, noun, verb*
- **exclamation 1** (*also* ˈ**pardon me** *especially in NAmE*) used to ask sb to repeat sth because you did not hear it or did not understand it: *'You're very quiet today.' 'Pardon?' 'I said you're very quiet today.'* **2** (*also* ˈ**pardon me**) used by some people to say 'sorry' when they have said or done sth wrong, usually by accident
- **noun 1** (*BrE also* ˌ**free ˈpardon**) [C] (*law*) an official decision not to punish sb for a crime, or to say that sb is not guilty of a crime: *to ask/grant/receive a pardon* ◊ *a royal/presidential pardon* **2** [U] (*formal*) ~ **(for sth)** the action of forgiving sb for sth SYN **forgiveness**: *He asked her pardon for having deceived her.* IDM see BEG
- **verb** (not usually used in the progressive tenses) **1** ~ **sb** to officially allow sb who has been found guilty of a crime to leave prison and/or avoid punishment: *She was pardoned after serving ten years of a life sentence.* **2** to forgive sb for sth they have said or done (used in many expressions when you want to be polite) SYN **excuse**: ~ **sth** *Pardon my ignorance, but what is a 'duplex'?* ◊ *The place was, if you'll pardon the expression, a dump.* ~ **sb (for sth/for doing sth)**: *You could be pardoned for thinking* (= it is easy to understand why people think) *that education is not the government's priority.* ◊ *Pardon me for interrupting you.* ◊ ~ **sb/sb's doing sth** *Pardon my asking, but is that your husband?*
IDM ˈ**pardon me** (*informal*) **1** (*especially NAmE*) used to ask sb to repeat sth because you did not hear it or do not understand it **2** used by some people to say 'sorry' when they have done sth wrong or made a rude noise by accident ⇒ see also I BEG YOUR PARDON at BEG **pardon me for ˈdoing sth** used to show that you are upset or offended by the way that sb has spoken to you: *'Oh, just shut up!' 'Well, pardon me for breathing!'* ⇒ more at FRENCH *n.*

**par·don·able** /ˈpɑːdnəbl; *NAmE* ˈpɑːrd-/ *adj.* that can be forgiven or excused SYN **excusable** OPP **unpardonable**

**pare** /peə(r); *NAmE* per/ *verb* **1** to remove the thin outer layer of sth, especially of fruit: ~ **sth** *She pared the apple.* ◊ ~ **sth from sth** *First, pare the rind from the lemon.* ◊ ~ **sth off/away** *He pared away the excess glue with a razor blade.* ⇒ see also PARING KNIFE **2** [often passive] to gradually reduce the size or amount: **be pared back/down (to sth)** *The training budget has been pared back to a minimum.* ◊ *The workforce has been* **pared to the bone** (= reduced to the lowest possible level). **3** ~ **sth** (*especially BrE*) to cut away the edges of sth, especially your nails, in order to make them smooth and neat ⇒ see also PARINGS ○ HOMOPHONES at PEAR

**par·ent** /ˈpeərənt; *NAmE* ˈper-/ *noun* **1** [usually pl.] a person's father or mother: *He's still living*

**parentage** 1124

with his parents. ◊ *Sue and Ben have recently become parents.* ◊ *her **adoptive** parents* (= who have legally adopted her as their child) ⇒ see also SINGLE PARENT, STEP-PARENT ⇒ WORDFINDER NOTE at FAMILY **2** (often used as an adjective) an animal or a plant which produces other animals or plants: *the parent bird/tree* **3** (often used as an adjective) an organization that produces and owns or controls smaller organizations of the same type: *a parent bank and its subsidiaries* ◊ *the parent company*

**par·ent·age** /ˈpeərəntɪdʒ; NAmE ˈper-/ *noun* [U] the origin of a person's parents and who they are: *a young American of German parentage* ◊ *Nothing is known about her parentage and background.*

**par·en·tal** ⓛ+ **C1** /pəˈrentl/ *adj.* [usually before noun] connected with a parent or parents: *parental responsibility/ rights* ◊ *parental choice in education* ◊ *the parental home*

**paˌrental conˈtrols** *noun* [pl.] (*also* **paˌrental ˈlock** [C]) a feature that is offered in some computer, mobile phone and digital television services, that enables parents or other adults to control children's access to material that is not suitable for them ▶ **parental control** *adj.* [only before noun]: *parental control software*

**paˌrental ˈleave** *noun* [U] time when a parent is allowed to be away from work to care for a child: *paid/unpaid parental leave* ◊ *fathers who take parental leave* ⇒ see also FAMILY LEAVE, MATERNITY LEAVE, PATERNITY LEAVE

**par·en·thesis** /pəˈrenθəsɪs/ *noun* (*pl.* **par·en·theses** /-θəsiːz/) **1** a word, sentence, etc. that is added to a speech or piece of writing, especially in order to give extra information. In writing, it is separated from the rest of the text using brackets, commas or DASHES. **2** (*formal* or *NAmE*) (*BrE* **bracket**, **ˌround ˈbracket**) [usually pl.] either of a pair of marks, ( ) placed around extra information in a piece of writing or part of a problem in mathematics: **in parentheses** *Irregular forms are given in parentheses.*

**par·en·thet·ical** /ˌpærənˈθetɪkl/ (*also* **par·en·thet·ic** /ˌpærənˈθetɪk/) *adj.* [usually before noun] (*formal*) given as extra information in a speech or piece of writing: *parenthetical remarks* ▶ **par·en·thet·ical·ly** /-kli/ *adv.*

**par·ent·hood** /ˈpeərənthʊd; NAmE ˈper-/ *noun* [U] the state of being a parent: *the joys of parenthood*

**par·ent·ing** /ˈpeərəntɪŋ; NAmE ˈper-/ *noun* [U] the process of caring for your child or children: *good/poor parenting* ◊ *parenting skills*

**par·en·tis** /pəˈrentɪs/ ⇒ IN LOCO PARENTIS

**parents-in-law** *noun* [pl.] the parents of your husband or wife ⇒ see also IN-LAWS

**ˌparent-ˈteacher association** *noun* = PTA

**par excellence** /ˌpɑːr ˈeksəlɑːns; NAmE ˌpɑːr ˌeksəˈlɑːns/ *adj.* (*from French*) (only used after the noun it describes) better than all the others of the same kind; a very good example of sth: *She turned out to be an organizer par excellence.* ▶ **par excellence** *adv.*: *Chemistry was par excellence the laboratory science of the early nineteenth century.*

**par·iah** /pəˈraɪə/ *noun* a person who is not acceptable to society and is avoided by everyone SYN **outcast** HELP This meaning of **pariah** is considered offensive in southern India.

**paring knife** /ˈpeərɪŋ naɪf; NAmE ˈper-/ *noun* a small sharp knife, used especially for cutting and PEELING fruit ⇒ see also PARE (1)

**par·ings** /ˈpeərɪŋz; NAmE ˈper-/ *noun* [pl.] thin pieces that have been cut off sth: *cheese parings* ⇒ see also PARE

**par·ish** ⓛ+ **C1** /ˈpærɪʃ/ *noun* **1** ⓛ+ **B1** [C] an area that has its own church and that a priest is responsible for: *a parish church/priest* ◊ *He is vicar of a large rural parish.* **2** (*also* **civil parish**) [C] (in England) a small country area that has its own elected local government: *the parish council* **3** [C + sing./pl. v.] the people living in a particular area, especially those who go to church **4** [C] (in the US state of Louisiana) a county

**par·ish·ad** /ˈpʌrɪʃʌd; NAmE ˈpɑːrɪʃɑːd/ *noun* (*IndE*) a council

**ˌparish ˈclerk** *noun* an official who organizes the affairs of a church in a particular area

**pa·rish·ion·er** /pəˈrɪʃənə(r)/ *noun* a person living in a PARISH, especially one who goes to church regularly

**ˌparish ˈregister** *noun* a book that has a list of all the BAPTISMS, marriages and FUNERALS that have taken place at a particular PARISH church

**par·ity** /ˈpærəti/ *noun* (*pl.* **-ies**) **1** [U] **~ (with sb/sth)** | **~ (between A and B)** (*formal*) the state of being equal, especially the state of having equal pay or status: *Prison officers are demanding pay parity with the police force.* **2** [U, C] **~ (with sth)** | **~ (between A and B)** (*finance*) the fact of the units of money of two different countries being equal: *to achieve parity with the dollar*

**park** ⓘ **A1** /pɑːk; NAmE pɑːrk/ *noun, verb*

■ *noun* **1** ⓛ **A1** [C] an area of public land in a town or a city where people go to walk, play and relax: *Hyde Park* ◊ **in the ~** *We went for a walk in the park.* ◊ *A public park will be built around the complex.* ◊ *a park bench* ⇒ see also NATIONAL PARK **2** ⓛ **A2** [C] (in compounds) an area of land used for a particular purpose: *a business/science park* ◊ *a wildlife park* ◊ *a park ranger* ⇒ see also AMUSEMENT PARK, BUSINESS PARK, CAR PARK, INDUSTRIAL PARK, NATIONAL PARK, RETAIL PARK, SAFARI PARK, SCIENCE PARK, THEME PARK, WATER PARK **3** [C] (in the UK) an area of land, usually with fields and trees, attached to a large country house **4** [C] (*NAmE*) a piece of land for playing sports, especially baseball ⇒ see also BALLPARK **5** **the park** [sing.] (*BrE*) a football (soccer) or rugby field: *the fastest man on the park* IDM see WALK *n.* ⇒ see also MOTOR PARK

■ *verb* **1** ⓛ **A1** [I, T] to leave a vehicle that you are driving in a particular place for a period of time: *He parked and went inside.* ◊ **~ + adv./prep.** *You can't park here.* ◊ *He's parked very badly.* ◊ **~ sth + adv./prep.** *You can't park the car here.* ◊ *a badly parked truck* ◊ *A red van was parked in front of the house.* ◊ **~ sth** *My mother parked the car.* ◊ *a parked car* ⇒ see also DOUBLE-PARK **2** [T] **~ sth + adv./ prep.** (*informal*) to leave sth in a convenient place until you need it: *Just park your bags in the hall until your room is ready.* **3** [T] **~ yourself + adv./prep.** (*informal*) to sit or stand in a particular place for a period of time: *She parked herself on the edge of the bed.* **4** [T] **~ sth** (*business, informal*) to decide to leave an idea or issue to be dealt with or considered at a later meeting: *Let's park that until our next meeting.* PHRV **ˌpark ˈup** | **ˌpark sth↔ˈup** (*especially BrE* or *AustralE*) to park your vehicle somewhere for a while: *People want to be able to park up and pop into the shop.* ◊ *I couldn't get parked up anywhere near the restaurant.*

**parka** /ˈpɑːkə; NAmE ˈpɑːrkə/ *noun* a very warm jacket or coat with a HOOD that often has fur inside

**park·ade** /pɑːˈkeɪd; NAmE pɑːrk-/ *noun* (*CanE*) a parking garage for many cars

**ˌpark and ˈride** *noun* a system designed to reduce traffic in towns in which people park their cars on the edge of a town and then take a special bus or train to the town centre; the area where people park their cars before taking the bus: *Use the park and ride.* ◊ *I've left my car in the park and ride.* ◊ *a park-and-ride service*

**park·ing** ⓘ **A2** /ˈpɑːkɪŋ; NAmE ˈpɑːrk-/ *noun* [U] **1** ⓛ **A2** the act of stopping a vehicle at a place and leaving it there for a period of time: *There is no parking here between 9 a.m. and 6 p.m.* ◊ *I managed to find a parking space.* ◊ *a parking fine* (= for parking illegally) **2** ⓛ **B2** a space or an area for leaving vehicles: *The hotel is centrally situated with ample free parking.*

**ˈparking brake** *noun* (*NAmE*) = HANDBRAKE

**ˈparking garage** *noun* (*NAmE*) (*BrE* **multi-storey ˈcar park**, **multi-ˈstorey**) *noun* a large building with several floors for parking cars in

**ˈparking lot** *noun* (*NAmE*) an area where people can leave their cars ⇒ compare CAR PARK

**ˈparking meter** (*also* **meter**) *noun* a machine next to the road that you put money into when you park your car next to it

**ˈparking ticket** (*also* **ticket**) *noun* an official notice that is put on your car when you have parked illegally, ordering you to pay money

**Par·kin·son's dis·ease** /ˈpɑːkɪnsnz dɪziːz; NAmE ˈpɑːrk-/ (also **par·kin·son·ism** /ˈpɑːkɪnsənɪzəm; NAmE ˈpɑːrk-/) noun [U] a disease of the nervous system that gets worse over a period of time and causes the muscles to become weak and the arms and legs to shake

**ˈParkinson's law** noun [U] (humorous) the idea that work will always take as long as the time available for it

**park·land** /ˈpɑːklænd; NAmE ˈpɑːrk-/ noun [U] open land with grass and trees, for example around a large house in the country

**par·kour** /pɑːˈkɔː(r); NAmE pɑːrˈk-/ noun [U] the sport of moving through a city by running, jumping and climbing under, around and through things ⇒ compare FREE RUNNING ORIGIN From French *parcours du combatant*, a type of military training.

**park·way** /ˈpɑːkweɪ; NAmE ˈpɑːrkweɪ/ noun (NAmE) a wide road with trees and grass along the sides or middle

**par·lance** /ˈpɑːləns; NAmE ˈpɑːrl-/ noun [U] (formal) a particular way of using words or expressing yourself, for example one used by a particular group: *in common/legal/modern parlance* ◊ *A Munro, in climbing parlance, is a Scottish mountain exceeding 3000 feet.*

**par·lay** /ˈpɑːleɪ; NAmE ˈpɑːrl-/ verb
PHRV **ˈparlay sth into sth** (NAmE) to use or develop sth such as money or a skill to make it more successful or worth more: *She hopes to parlay her success as a model into an acting career.*

**par·ley** /ˈpɑːli; NAmE ˈpɑːrli/ noun, verb
■ noun (old-fashioned) a discussion between enemies or people who disagree, in order to try and find a way of solving a problem
■ verb [I] ~ (with sb) (old-fashioned) to discuss sth with sb in order to solve a problem

**par·lia·ment** 🔑 B2 /ˈpɑːləmənt; NAmE ˈpɑːrl-/ noun 1 🔑 B2 [C] the group of people who are elected to make and change the laws of a country: *The German parliament is called the 'Bundestag'.* ⇒ see also EUROPEAN PARLIAMENT 2 🔑 B2 **Parliament** [U] the parliament of some countries, including the United Kingdom. In the UK, **Parliament** consists of the HOUSE OF COMMONS and the HOUSE OF LORDS: *a Member of Parliament* ◊ *an Act of Parliament* ◊ *in ~ The issue was debated in Parliament.* ◊ *to win a seat in Parliament* ◊ *to be elected to Parliament* 3 (also **Parliament**) [C, U] a particular period during which a parliament is working; Parliament as it exists between one GENERAL ELECTION and the next: *We are now into the second half of the parliament.* ◊ *to dissolve Parliament* (= formally end its activities) *and call an election* ⇒ see also HOUSES OF PARLIAMENT, HUNG ⇒ WORDFINDER NOTE at GOVERNMENT

WORDFINDER Act, bill, chamber, coalition, election, law, legislation, politician, vote

**par·lia·men·tar·ian** /ˌpɑːləmənˈteəriən; NAmE ˌpɑːrləmənˈter-/ noun a member of a parliament, especially one with a lot of skill and experience

**par·lia·men·tary** 🔑+ C1 /ˌpɑːləˈmentri; NAmE ˌpɑːrl-/ adj. [usually before noun] connected with a parliament; having a parliament: *parliamentary elections* ◊ *a parliamentary democracy* ⇒ compare UNPARLIAMENTARY

**parliamentary private ˈsecretary** noun = PPS

**parliamentary ˈprivilege** noun [U] the special right of Members of Parliament to speak freely in Parliament, especially about another person, without risking legal action: *He made the allegation under the protection of parliamentary privilege.*

**parliamentary ˈsecretary** noun a Member of Parliament who works in a government department below the minister

**parliamentary underˈsecretary** noun (in the UK) a Member of Parliament in a government department, below a minister in rank

**par·lour** (US **par·lor**) /ˈpɑːlə(r); NAmE ˈpɑːrl-/ noun 1 (old-fashioned) a room in a private house for sitting in, entertaining visitors, etc. 2 (in compounds) (especially NAmE) a shop that provides particular goods or services: *a beauty/*

---

1125 **Parsee**

*an ice-cream parlour* ⇒ see also FUNERAL PARLOUR, MASSAGE PARLOUR

**ˈparlour game** (US **ˈparlor game**) noun a game played in the home, especially a word game or guessing game

**par·lous** /ˈpɑːləs; NAmE ˈpɑːrl-/ adj. (formal) (of a situation) very bad and very uncertain; dangerous SYN perilous

**Par·mesan** /ˈpɑːmɪzæn; ˌpɑːməˈzæn; NAmE ˈpɑːrməzɑːn, -zæn/ (also **Parmesan ˈcheese**) noun [U] a type of very hard Italian cheese that is usually GRATED and eaten on Italian food

**pa·ro·chial** /pəˈrəʊkiəl/ adj. 1 [usually before noun] (formal) connected with a church PARISH: *parochial schools* ◊ *a member of the parochial church council* 2 (disapproving) only interested in small issues that happen in your local area and not interested in more important things ▶ **pa·ro·chial·ism** noun [U]: *the parochialism of a small community*

**paˈrochial school** noun (NAmE) a private school supported by a particular Christian church ⇒ compare FAITH SCHOOL

**par·od·ist** /ˈpærədɪst/ noun a person who writes parodies

**par·ody** /ˈpærədi/ noun, verb
■ noun (pl. **-ies**) 1 [C, U] a piece of writing, music, acting, etc. that deliberately copies the style of sb/sth in order to be humorous: *a parody of a horror film* ⇒ WORDFINDER NOTE at COMEDY 2 [C] (disapproving) something that is such a bad or an unfair example of sth that it seems silly SYN travesty: *The trial was a parody of justice.*
■ verb (par·odies, par·ody·ing, par·odied, par·odied) ~ sb/sth to copy the style of sb/sth in an EXAGGERATED way, especially in order to make people laugh SYN lampoon

**par·ole** /pəˈrəʊl/ noun, verb
■ noun [U] permission that is given to a prisoner to leave prison before the end of their sentence on condition that they behave well: *to be eligible for parole* ◊ *on ~ She was released on parole.* ⇒ WORDFINDER NOTE at PRISON
■ verb [usually passive] to give a prisoner permission to leave prison before the end of their sentence on condition that they behave well: **be paroled** *She was paroled after two years.*

**par·ox·ysm** /ˈpærəksɪzəm/ noun 1 ~ **of sth** a sudden strong feeling or expression of an emotion that cannot be controlled: *paroxysms of hate* ◊ *a paroxysm of laughter* 2 (medical) a sudden short attack of pain, causing physical shaking that cannot be controlled

**par·quet** /ˈpɑːkeɪ; NAmE pɑːrˈkeɪ/ noun [U] a type of floor that consists of flat pieces of wood fixed together in a pattern: *parquet flooring* ⇒ compare WOODBLOCK

**parra·keet** = PARAKEET

**parri·cide** /ˈpærɪsaɪd/ noun [U, C] (formal) the crime of killing your father, mother or a close relative; a person who is guilty of this crime ⇒ compare FRATRICIDE, MATRICIDE, PATRICIDE

**par·rot** /ˈpærət/ noun, verb
■ noun a tropical bird with a curved BEAK. There are several types of parrot, most of which have bright feathers. Some are kept as pets and can be trained to copy human speech. IDM see SICK adj.
■ verb ~ sb/sth (disapproving) to repeat what sb else has said without thinking about what it means

**parry** /ˈpæri/ verb (par·ries, parry·ing, par·ried, par·ried) 1 [T, I] ~ (sth) to defend yourself against sb who is attacking you by pushing their arm, weapon, etc. to one side SYN deflect: *He parried a blow to his head.* ◊ *The shot was parried by the goalie.* 2 [T] ~ sth | + speech to avoid having to answer a difficult question, criticism, etc., especially by replying in the same way SYN fend off: *She parried all questions about their relationship.* ▶ **parry** noun (pl. **-ies**)

**parse** /pɑːz; NAmE pɑːrs/ verb ~ sth (grammar) to divide a sentence into parts and describe the grammar of each word or part

**Par·see** (also **Parsi**) /ˌpɑːˈsiː; ˈpɑːsiː; NAmE ˌpɑːrˈsiː, ˈpɑːrsiː/ noun a member of a religious group whose ANCESTORS originally came from Persia and whose religion is Zoroastrianism

# parsimonious

**par·si·mo·ni·ous** /ˌpɑːsɪˈməʊniəs; NAmE ˌpɑːrs-/ adj. (formal) extremely unwilling to spend money **SYN** **mean** ▶ **par·si·mo·ni·ous·ly** adv.

**par·si·mony** /ˈpɑːsɪməni; NAmE ˈpɑːrsəmoʊni/ noun [U] (formal) the fact of being extremely unwilling to spend money **SYN** **meanness**

**pars·ley** /ˈpɑːsli; NAmE ˈpɑːrs-/ noun [U] a plant with curly green leaves that are used in cooking as a HERB and to decorate food: *fish with parsley sauce* ⇨ VISUAL VOCAB page V8

**pars·nip** /ˈpɑːsnɪp; NAmE ˈpɑːrs-/ noun [C, U] a long pale yellow root vegetable ⇨ VISUAL VOCAB page V5

**par·son** /ˈpɑːsn; NAmE ˈpɑːrsn/ noun **1** (old-fashioned) an Anglican VICAR or PARISH priest **2** (informal) a Protestant CLERGYMAN

**par·son·age** /ˈpɑːsənɪdʒ; NAmE ˈpɑːrs-/ noun a parson's house

**part** 🔑 **A1** ⊙ /pɑːt; NAmE pɑːrt/ noun, verb, adv.
■ noun
- SOME **1** 🔑 **A1** [U] ~ of sth some but not all of a thing: *We spent part of the time in the museum.* ◇ *Part of the building was destroyed in the fire.* ◇ *Voters are given only part of the story* (= only some of the information). ◇ *Part of me feels sorry for him* (= I feel a little sorry for him, but not very sorry).
- PIECE **2** 🔑 **A1** [C] a section, piece or feature of sth: ~ **of sth** *The mountains are covered with snow for a large part of the year.* ◇ *Making mistakes is an integral part of the learning process.* ◇ *an important/essential part of the project* ◇ **in parts** *The novel is good in parts.* ◇ *The procedure can be divided into two parts.* ◇ *The worst part was having to wait three hours in the rain.*
- MEMBER **3** 🔑 **A1** [U] ~ **of sth** an element or member of sth; a person or thing that helps to make up a whole or belongs in it: *Snacks can be part of a healthy eating plan.* ◇ *You need to be able to work as part of a team.*
- OF BODY/PLANT **4** 🔑 **A1** [C] a separate piece or area of a human or animal body or of a plant: *the parts of the body* ◇ *body parts* ⇨ see also PRIVATE PARTS
- OF MACHINE **5** 🔑 **A1** [C] a piece of a machine or structure: *aircraft/car/engine parts* ◇ *the working parts of the machinery* ◇ *spare parts*
- REGION/AREA **6** 🔑 **A1** [C] ~ **(of sth)** an area or a region of the world, a country, a town, etc: *the northern part of town* ◇ *different parts of the world/country* ◇ *Which part of Japan do you come from?* ◇ *Come and visit us if you're ever in our part of the world.* **7 parts** [pl.] (old-fashioned, informal) a region or an area: *She's not from these parts.* ◇ *He's just arrived back from foreign parts.*
- OF BOOK/SERIES **8** 🔑 **A1** [C] (abbr. **pt**) a section of a book, television series, etc., especially one that is published or broadcast separately: *The documentary was screened in four parts.* ◇ *Henry IV, Part II* ◇ *The final part will be shown next Sunday evening.*
- FOR ACTOR **9** 🔑 **B1** [C] a role played by an actor in a play, film, etc.; the words spoken by an actor in a particular role: *She played the part of Juliet.* ◇ (figurative) *He's always playing a part* (= pretending to be sth that he is not). ◇ **~ in sth** *He got a small part in a West End play.* ◇ **in a ~** *She was very good in the part.*
- INVOLVEMENT **10** [C, usually sing., U] the way in which sb/sth is involved in an action or situation: *Luck played a big part in their success.* ◇ *She plays an active part in local politics.* ◇ *We all have a part to play in the fight against crime.* ◇ *He had no part in the decision.* ◇ *I want no part of this sordid business.*
- IN MUSIC **11** [C] music for a particular voice or instrument in a group singing or playing together: *the clarinet part* ◇ *four-part harmony*
- EQUAL PORTION **12** [C] a unit of measurement that allows you to compare the different amounts of substances in sth: *Add three parts wine to one part water.*
- IN HAIR **13** (NAmE) (BrE **part·ing**) [C] a line on a person's head where the hair is divided with a COMB
- **IDM** **the best/better part of sth** most of sth, especially a period of time; more than half of sth: *The journey took her the better part of an hour.* **for the 'most part** mostly; usu-

ally: *The contributors are, for the most part, professional scientists.* ⇨ LANGUAGE BANK at GENERALLY **for 'my, 'his, 'their, etc. part** used to express your own, his, their, etc. opinion or feelings about sth **SYN** **personally** **in 'part** 🔑 **B2** partly; to some extent: *Her success was due in part to luck.* **look/dress the 'part** to have an appearance or wear clothes suitable for a particular job, role or position **a man/woman of (many) 'parts** a person with many skills **on the part of sb/on sb's part** made or done by sb: *It was an error on my part.* **part and parcel of sth** a normal part of sth: *Keeping the accounts is part and parcel of my job.* **part of the 'furniture** (informal) a person or thing that you are so used to seeing that you no longer notice them: *I worked there so long that I became part of the furniture.* **take sth in good 'part** (BrE) to accept sth slightly unpleasant without complaining or being offended **take 'part (in sth)** 🔑 **A2** to be involved in sth **SYN** **participate**: *to take part in a discussion/demonstration/fight/celebration* ◇ *How many countries took part in the last Olympic Games?* **take sb's 'part** (BrE) to support sb, for example in an argument **SYN** **side with**: *His mother always takes his part.* ⇨ more at DISCRETION, LARGE adj., SUM n.

■ verb
- LEAVE SB **1** [I] (formal) if a person **parts** from another person, or two people **part**, they leave each other: *We parted at the airport.* ◇ *I hate to part on such bad terms.* ◇ **~ from sb** *He has recently parted from his wife* (= they have started to live apart). ⇨ see also PARTING
- KEEP APART **2** [T, often passive] ~ **sb (from sb)** (formal) to prevent sb from being with sb else: *I hate being parted from the children.* ◇ *The puppies were parted from their mother at birth.*
- MOVE AWAY **3** [I, T] if two things or parts of things **part** or you **part** them, they move away from each other: *The crowd parted in front of them.* ◇ *The elevator doors parted and out stepped the President.* ◇ **~ sth** *Her lips were slightly parted.* ◇ *She parted the curtains a little and looked out.*
- HAIR **4** [T] ~ **sth** to divide your hair into two sections with a COMB, creating a line that goes from the back of your head to the front: *He parts his hair in the middle.* ⇨ see also PARTING

**IDM** **part 'company (with/from sb)** (also **part 'ways (with/from sb)**) **1** to leave sb; to end a relationship with sb: *This is where we part company* (= go in different directions). ◇ *The band have parted company with their manager.* ◇ *The band and their manager have parted company.* **2** to disagree with sb about sth: *Weber parted company with Marx on a number of important issues.*

**PHR V** **'part with sth** to give sth to sb else, especially sth that you would prefer to keep: *Make sure you read the contract before parting with any money.*

■ adv. (often in compounds) consisting of two things; to some extent but not completely: *She's part French, part English.* ◇ *His feelings were part anger, part relief.* ◇ *The course is part funded by the European Commission.* ◇ *He is part owner of a farm in France.*

**par·take** /pɑːˈteɪk; NAmE pɑːrt-/ verb (**par·took** /-ˈtʊk/, **par·taken** /-ˈteɪkən/) (formal) **1** [I] ~ **(of sth)** (old-fashioned or humorous) to eat or drink sth especially sth that is offered to you: *Would you care to partake of some refreshment?* **2** [I] ~ **(in sth)** (old-fashioned) to take part in an activity: *They preferred not to partake in the social life of the town.* **PHR V** **par'take of sth** (formal) to have some of a particular quality: *His work partakes of the aesthetic fashions of his time.*

**par·terre** /pɑːˈteə(r); NAmE pɑːrˈter/ noun (from French) **1** a flat area in a garden, with plants arranged in a formal design **2** (especially NAmE) the lower level in a theatre where the audience sits, especially the area below the BALCONY

**part ex'change** noun [U] (BrE) a way of buying sth, such as a car, in which you give your old one as part of the payment for a more expensive one: **in~** *We'll take your old car in part exchange.* ▶ **part-ex'change** verb ~ **sth**

**par·the·no·gen·esis** /ˌpɑːθənəʊˈdʒenɪsɪs; NAmE ˌpɑːrθ-/ noun [U] (biology) the process of producing new plants or animals from an OVUM that has not been FERTILIZED ▶ **par·theno·gen·et·ic** /ˌpɑːθənəʊdʒəˈnetɪk; NAmE ˌpɑːrθ-/ adj.

*parthenogenetic species* **par·the·no·gen·et·ic·al·ly** /-kli/ *adj.: These organisms reproduce parthenogenetically.*

**par·tial** ? **C1** Ⓦ /ˈpɑːʃl/ *NAmE* /ˈpɑːrʃl/ *adj.* **1** ? **C1** not complete or whole: *It was only a partial solution to the problem.* ◊ *a partial eclipse of the sun* **2** [not before noun] **~ to sb/sth** (*old-fashioned*) liking sb/sth very much: *I'm not partial to mushrooms.* **3** [not usually before noun] **~ (towards sb/sth)** (*disapproving*) showing or feeling too much support for one person, team, idea, etc., in a way that is unfair **SYN** **biased** **OPP** **impartial**

**par·ti·al·ity** /ˌpɑːʃiˈæləti/ *NAmE* /ˌpɑːrʃ-/ *noun* (*formal*) **1** [U] (*disapproving*) unfair support for one person, team, idea, etc. **SYN** **bias** **OPP** **impartiality 2** [sing.] **~ for sth/sb** a feeling of liking sth/sb very much **SYN** **fondness**: *She has a partiality for exotic flowers.*

**par·tial·ly** ? **C1** Ⓦ /ˈpɑːʃəli/ *NAmE* /ˈpɑːrʃ-/ *adv.* partly; not completely: *The road was partially blocked by a fallen tree.* ◊ *a society for the blind and partially sighted* (= people who can see very little). ➔ note at PARTLY

**par·ti·ci·pant** ? **B2** Ⓦ /pɑːˈtɪsɪpənt/ *NAmE* pɑːrˈt-/ *noun* a person who is taking part in an activity or event: *The average age of study participants was 48 years.* ◊ **~ in sth** *He has been an active participant in the discussion.*

**par·ti·ci·pate** ? **B1** Ⓦ /pɑːˈtɪsɪpeɪt/ *NAmE* pɑːrˈt-/ *verb* [I] (*rather formal*) **~ (in sth)** to take part in or become involved in an activity: *She didn't participate in the discussion.* ◊ *We encourage students to participate fully in the running of the college.* ◊ *The women actively participated in the creation of the artwork.*

**par·ti·ci·pa·tion** ? **B2** Ⓦ /pɑːˌtɪsɪˈpeɪʃn/ *NAmE* /pɑːˌr-t-/ *noun* [U] the act of taking part in an activity or event: *a show with lots of audience participation* ◊ **~ in sth** *A back injury prevented active participation in any sports for a while.*

**par·ti·ci·pa·tory** /pɑːˌtɪsɪˈpeɪtəri/ *NAmE* pɑːrˌtɪsəpətɔːri/ *adj.* [usually before noun] allowing everyone in a society, business, etc. to give their opinions and to help make decisions: *Participatory democracy is a fundamental principle of cooperative businesses.*

**par·ti·ciple** /ˈpɑːtɪsɪpl/ *NAmE* /ˈpɑːrtɪsɪpl/ *noun* (*grammar*) (in English) a word formed from a verb, ending in *-ing* (= the PRESENT PARTICIPLE) or *-ed, -en*, etc. (= the PAST PARTICIPLE) ▶ **par·ti·ci·pial** /ˌpɑːtɪˈsɪpiəl/ *NAmE* /ˌpɑːrt-/ *adj.* ➔ see also PAST PARTICIPLE, PRESENT PARTICIPLE

**par·ticle** /ˈpɑːtɪkl/ *NAmE* /ˈpɑːrt-/ *noun* **1** a very small piece of sth: *particles of dust/gold* ➔ see also ALPHA PARTICLE, BETA PARTICLE, ELEMENTARY PARTICLE, SUBATOMIC PARTICLE **2** (*grammar*) an adverb or a preposition that can combine with a verb to make a phrasal verb: *In 'She tore up the letter', the word 'up' is a particle.*

**particle physics** *noun* [U] the scientific study of very small pieces of matter that are parts of an ATOM

**par·ticu·lar** ? **A2** Ⓞ /pəˈtɪkjələ(r)/ *NAmE* pərˈt-/ *adj., noun*

■ *adj.* **1** ? **A2** [only before noun] used to emphasize that you are referring to one individual person, thing or type of thing and not others **SYN** **specific**: *Is there a particular type of book he enjoys?* ◊ *In this particular case, the owners were not local but Indian.* **2** ? **A2** [only before noun] greater than usual; special: *We must pay particular attention to this point.* ◊ *These documents are of particular interest.* **3** very definite about what you like and careful about what you choose **SYN** **fussy**: *She's very particular about her clothes.* **IDM** **in par·ticu·lar 1** ? **B1** especially or particularly: *He loves science fiction in particular.* ➔ LANGUAGE BANK at EMPHASIS **2** ? **B1** special or specific: *Peter was lying on the sofa doing nothing in particular.* ◊ *Is there anything in particular you'd like for dinner?* ◊ *She directed the question at no one in particular.*

■ *noun* (*formal*) **1** [usually pl.] a fact or detail, especially one that is officially written down: *The police officer took down all the particulars of the burglary.* ◊ *The nurse asked me for my particulars* (= personal details such as your name, address, etc.). ◊ *The new contract will be the same in every particular as the old one.* **2 particulars** [pl.] written information and details about a property, business, job, etc:

*Application forms and further particulars are available from the Personnel Office.*

**par·ticu·lar·ity** /pəˌtɪkjəˈlærəti/ *NAmE* pərˌt-/ *noun* (*pl. -ies*) (*formal*) **1** [U] the quality of being individual or unique: *the particularity of each human being* **2** [U] attention to detail; being exact **3 particularities** [pl.] the special features or details of sth

**par·ticu·lar·ize** (*BrE also* **-ise**) /pəˈtɪkjələraɪz/ *NAmE* pərˈt-/ *verb* [I, T] (*formal*) to give details of sth, especially one by one; to give particular examples of sth

**par·ticu·lar·ly** ? **B1** Ⓞ /pəˈtɪkjələli/ *NAmE* pərˈtɪkjələrli/ *adv.* especially; more than usual or more than others: *particularly useful/important/interesting* ◊ *Traffic is bad, particularly in the city centre.* ◊ *I enjoyed the play, particularly the second half.* ◊ *The task was not particularly* (= not very) *difficult.* ◊ *'Did you enjoy it?' 'No, not particularly* (= not very much).'

**par·ticu·late** /pɑːˈtɪkjələt, -leɪt/ *NAmE* pɑːrˈt-/ *adj., noun*

■ *adj.* relating to, or in the form of, PARTICLES: *particulate pollution*

■ *noun* **particulates** [pl.] matter in the form of PARTICLES: *the effects of diesel particulates on human health*

**part·ing** /ˈpɑːtɪŋ/ *NAmE* /ˈpɑːrt-/ *noun, adj.*

■ *noun* **1** [U, C] the act or occasion of leaving a person or place: *the moment of parting* ◊ *We had a tearful parting at the airport.* **2** (*BrE*) (*NAmE* **part**) [C] a line on a person's head where the hair is divided with a COMB: *a side/centre parting* **3** [U, C] the act or result of dividing sth into parts: *the parting of the clouds* **IDM** **a/the ˌparting of the ˈways** a point at which two people or groups of people decide to separate

■ *adj.* [only before noun] said or done by sb as they leave: *a parting kiss* ◊ *His parting words were 'I love you.'* **IDM** **ˌparting ˈshot** a final remark, especially an unkind one, that sb makes as they leave

**par·ti·san** /ˈpɑːtɪzæn, ˌpɑːtɪˈzæn/ *NAmE* /ˈpɑːrtəzn/ *adj., noun*

■ *adj.* (*often disapproving*) showing too much support for one person, group or idea, especially without considering it carefully **SYN** **one-sided**: *Most newspapers are politically partisan.* **OPP** **non-partisan**

■ *noun* **1** a person who strongly supports a particular leader, group or idea **SYN** **follower 2** a member of an armed group that is fighting secretly against enemy soldiers who have taken control of its country ▶ **par·ti·san·ship** /ˈpɑːtɪzænʃɪp/ *NAmE* /ˈpɑːrtəzn-/ *noun* [U]

**par·ti·tion** /pɑːˈtɪʃn/ *NAmE* pɑːrˈt-/ *noun, verb*

■ *noun* **1** [C] a wall or screen that separates one part of a room from another: *a glass partition* ◊ *partition walls* **2** [U] the division of one country into two or more countries: *the partition of Germany after the war*

■ *verb* [often passive] to divide sth into parts: **~ sth** *to partition a country* ◊ **~ sth into sth** *The room is partitioned into three sections.*

**PHRV** **par·ˌtition sth↔ˈoff** to separate one area, one part of a room, etc. from another with a wall or screen

**par·ti·tive** /ˈpɑːtətɪv/ *NAmE* /ˈpɑːrt-/ *noun* (*grammar*) a word or phrase that shows a part or quantity of sth: *In 'a spoonful of sugar', the word 'spoonful' is a partitive.* ▶ **par·ti·tive** *adj.*

**part·ly** ? **B2** Ⓞ /ˈpɑːtli/ *NAmE* /ˈpɑːrt-/ *adv.* to some extent; not completely: *Some people are unwilling to attend the classes partly because of the cost involved.* ◊ *He was only partly responsible for the accident.* ◊ *Two factors at least partly explain her success.*

▼ **WHICH WORD?**

**partly / partially**

● **Partly** and **partially** both mean 'not completely': *The road is partly/partially finished.* **Partly** is especially used to talk about the reason for something, often followed by **because** or **due to**: *I didn't enjoy the trip very much, partly because of the weather.* **Partially** should be used when you are talking about physical conditions: *His mother is partially blind.*

**part·ner** ❶ **A1** /ˈpɑːtnə(r); NAmE ˈpɑːrt-/ noun, verb
- **noun 1 A1** a person that you are doing an activity with, such as dancing or playing a game: *a dance/tennis partner* ⇒ see also BIRTH PARTNER, SPARRING PARTNER⇒ WORDFINDER NOTE at DANCE **2 A2** the person that you are married to or having a sexual relationship with: *Come to the New Year disco and bring your partner!* ◇ *a sexual/romantic partner* ⇒ see also CIVIL PARTNER, DOMESTIC PARTNER ⇒ WORDFINDER NOTE at LOVE **3 B1** one of the people who owns a business and shares the profits, etc.: *a business partner* ◇ ~ **in sth** *a partner in a law firm* ⇒ see also SILENT PARTNER, SLEEPING PARTNER **4 B1** a country or an organization that has an agreement with another country or organization: *a trading partner*
- **verb 1** [T] ~ **sb** to be sb's partner in a dance, game, etc: *Gerry offered to partner me at tennis.* **2** (of a company) to be involved in a business project with another company: ~ **with sb/sth** *Freshfoods usually partners with other companies to share risk.*

**part·ner·ship** **B2+** /ˈpɑːtnəʃɪp; NAmE ˈpɑːrtnərʃ-/ noun **1 B2+** [U] the state of being a partner in business: *to be in/to go into partnership* ◇ **in ~ with sb/sth** *He developed his own program in partnership with an American expert.* **2 B2** [C, U] a relationship between two people, organizations, etc.; the state of having this relationship: *Marriage should be an equal partnership.* ◇ ~ **with sb/sth** *the school's partnership with parents* ◇ **between A and B** *a partnership between the United States and Europe* ⇒ see also CIVIL PARTNERSHIP **3 B2+** [C] a business owned by two or more people who share the profits: *a junior member of the partnership*

**part of ˈspeech** noun (*grammar*) one of the classes into which words are divided according to their grammar, such as noun, verb, adjective, etc. **SYN word class** ⇒ WORDFINDER NOTE at DICTIONARY

**par·took** /pɑːˈtʊk; NAmE pɑːrt-/ *past tense* of PARTAKE

**par·tridge** /ˈpɑːtrɪdʒ; NAmE ˈpɑːrt-/ noun [C, U] (*pl.* **partridges** or **partridge**) a brown bird with a round body and a short tail, that people hunt for sport or food; the meat of this bird

**part-ˈtime** **B2+** adj., adv. (*abbr.* **PT**) for part of the day or week in which people work: *She's looking for a part-time job.* ◇ *to study on a part-time basis* ◇ *part-time workers* ◇ *I'm only part-time at the moment.* ◇ *Liz works part-time from 10 till 2.* ⇒ compare FULL-TIME ⇒ WORDFINDER NOTE at WORK

**part-ˈtimer** noun a person who works part-time

**par·tur·ition** /ˌpɑːtʃəˈrɪʃn; NAmE ˌpɑːrtʃ-/ noun [U] (*specialist*) the act of giving birth

**ˈpart-way** adv. some of the way: *They were part-way through the speeches when he arrived.*

**party** ❶ **A1** /ˈpɑːti; NAmE ˈpɑːrti/ noun, verb
- **noun** (*pl.* -**ies**) **1 A1** [C] (especially in compounds) a social occasion, often in a person's home, at which people eat, drink, talk, dance and enjoy themselves: *a dinner/tea/cocktail party* ◇ *at a ~ I was at a birthday party for my friend's five-year-old daughter.* ◇ *to have/throw/give a party* ◇ *Did you go to the party?* ◇ *party games* ⇒ WORDFINDER NOTE at CELEBRATE **2 B1** (*also* **Party**) [C + sing./pl. v.] a political organization that you can vote for in elections and whose members have the same aims and ideas: *Do you belong to a political party?* ◇ *the ruling/opposition party* ◇ *the Democratic/Republican/Conservative/Labour Party* ◇ *the party leader/conference* ◇ *a party member/activist/official* ⇒ see also ALL-PARTY **3 B2** [C + sing./pl. v.] a group of people who are doing sth together such as travelling or visiting somewhere: *The school is taking a party of 40 children to France.* ◇ *The theatre gives a 10 per cent discount to parties of more than ten.* ⇒ see also SEARCH PARTY, WORKING PARTY **4** [C] (*formal*) one of the people or groups of people involved in a legal agreement or argument: *the guilty/innocent party* ◇ *The contract can be terminated by either party with three months' notice.* ⇒ see also INJURED PARTY, THIRD PARTY **HELP** There are many other compounds ending in **party**. You will find them at their place in the alphabet.

**IDM** ▸ **be (a) party to sth** (*formal*) to be involved in an agreement or action: *to be party to a decision* ◇ *He refuses to be a party to any violence.* **bring sth to the ˈparty/ˈtable** to contribute sth useful to a discussion, project, etc: *What Hislop brought to the party was real commitment and energy.*
- **verb** (**parties, partying, partied, partied**) [I] (*informal*) to enjoy yourself, especially by eating, drinking alcohol and dancing: *They were out partying every night.*

**ˈparty animal** noun (*informal*) a person who enjoys parties, being with a lot of other people and staying up late: *I'm not really a party animal but I like quiet dinners with friends.*

**ˈparty favor** (*also* **favor**) noun [usually pl.] (NAmE) a small gift given to children at a party

**ˈparty-goer** noun a person who enjoys going to parties or who is a guest at a particular party

**ˈparty line** noun [usually sing.] the official opinions and policies of a political party, which members are expected to support **IDM** ⇒ see TOE v.

**ˈparty piece** noun (*BrE, informal*) a thing that sb often does to entertain people, especially at parties, for example singing a song

**party poˈlitical** adj. [only before noun] (*especially BrE*) made by or relating to a political party: *a party political broadcast*

**party ˈpolitics** noun [U + sing./pl. v.] political activity that involves getting support for a particular political party or attacking another party: *The President should stand above party politics.* ◇ *Many people think that party politics should not enter into local government.*

**ˈparty pooper** noun (*informal*) a person who does not want to take part in a pleasant activity and stops other people from having fun

**party ˈspirit** noun [U] the sort of mood in which you can enjoy a party and have fun

**party ˈwall** noun a wall that divides two buildings or rooms and belongs to both owners

**par·venu** /ˈpɑːvənjuː; NAmE ˈpɑːrvənuː/ noun (*pl.* -**us**) (*formal, disapproving*) a person from a low social or economic position who has suddenly become rich or powerful

**pas·cal** noun **1** /ˈpæskl/ [C] (*abbr.* **Pa**) the standard unit for measuring pressure **2 Pascal, PASCAL** /pæˈskæl/ [U] a language used for writing programs for computer systems

**pas·chal** /ˈpɑːskl; NAmE ˈpæs-/ adj. (*formal*) **1** relating to Easter **2** relating to the Jewish Passover

**pas de deux** /ˌpɑː də ˈdɜː/ noun (*pl.* **pas de deux** /ˌpɑː də ˈdɜː/) (*from French*) a dance, often part of a BALLET, that is performed by two people

**pash·mina** /pæʃˈmiːnə/ noun a long piece of cloth made of fine soft wool from a type of GOAT and worn by a woman around the shoulders

**Pashto** /ˈpæʃtəʊ/ noun [U] the official language of Afghanistan, also spoken in northern Pakistan

**pass** ❶ **A2** /pɑːs; NAmE pæs/ verb, noun
- **verb**
• **TEST/EXAM 1 A2** [I, T] to achieve the required standard in an exam, a test, etc: *I'm not really expecting to pass first time.* ◇ ~ **sth** *She hasn't passed her driving test yet.* **OPP fail** ⇒ HOMOPHONES at PAST **2** [T] ~ **sb** to test sb and decide that they are good enough, according to an agreed standard: *The examiners passed all the candidates.* **OPP fail**
• **MOVE 3 B1** [I, T] to move past or to the other side of sb/sth: *Several people were passing but nobody offered to help.* ◇ *I hailed a passing taxi.* ◇ ~ **sb/sth** *to pass a barrier/sentry/checkpoint* ◇ *You'll pass a bank on the way to the train station.* ◇ *She passed me in the street without even saying hello.* ◇ (*especially NAmE*) *There was a truck behind that was trying to pass me.* **HELP** The usual word in British English in the last example is **overtake**. **4 B1** [I] + **adv./prep.** to go or move in the direction mentioned: *The procession passed slowly along the street.* ◇ *A plane passed low overhead.* **5** [T] ~ **sth + adv./prep.** to make sth move in the direction or into the position mentioned: *He passed the rope around the post three times to secure it.*

- **GIVE 6** 🔑 **B1** [T] to give sth to sb by putting it into their hands or in a place where they can easily reach it: **~ sth** *Pass the salt, please.* ◇ **~ sth to sb** *He passed a note to his friend.* ◇ **~ sb sth** *Pass me the salt.* **7** [T] **~ sth (to sb)** to give sb information or a message: *His wife had been passing information to the police.*
- **BALL 8** 🔑 **B1** [T, I] (in ball games) to kick, hit or throw the ball to a player of your own side: **~ sth (to sb)** *He passed the ball to Sterling.* ◇ **~ (to sb)** *Why do they keep passing back to the goalie?*
- **TIME 9** 🔑 **B1** [I] when time **passes**, it goes by: *Almost fifty years have passed since that day.* ◇ *We grew more anxious with every passing day.* **10** 🔑 **B1** [T] **~ sth** to spend time, especially when you are bored or waiting for sth: *We sang songs to pass the time.* ◇ *How do you pass the long winter nights?*
- **END 11** 🔑 **B1** [I] to come to an end; to be over: *They waited for the storm to pass.*
- **CHANGE 12** [I] **~ from sth to/into sth** to change from one state or condition to another: *She had passed from childhood to early womanhood.*
- **AFTER DEATH 13** [I] **~ to sb** to be given to another person after first belonging to sb else, especially after the first person has died: *On his death, the title passed to his eldest son.*
- **BECOME GREATER 14** [T] **~ sth** (of an amount) to become greater than a particular total **SYN exceed**: *Unemployment has now passed the three million mark.*
- **LAW/PROPOSAL 15** 🔑 **B2** [T, I] to accept a proposal, law, etc. by voting; to be accepted in this way: **~ sth** *to pass a bill/law/resolution* ◇ **~ (by sth)** *The bill passed by 360 votes to 280.*
- **HAPPEN 16** [I] to be allowed: *I don't like it, but I'll let it pass* (= will not object). ◇ *Her remarks passed without comment* (= people ignored them). **17** [I] to happen; to be said or done: **~ (between A and B)** *They'll never be friends again after all that has passed between them.* ◇ **+ adj.** *His departure passed unnoticed.*
- **NOT KNOW 18** [I] **~ (on sth)** to say that you do not know the answer to a question, especially during a QUIZ: *'What's the capital of Peru?' 'I'll have to pass on that one.'* ◇ *'Who wrote "Catch-22"?' 'Pass* (= I don't know).*'*
- **NOT WANT 19** [I] **~ (on sth)** to say that you do not want sth that is offered to you: *Thanks. I'm going to pass on dessert, if you don't mind.*
- **SAY/STATE STH 20** [T] **~ sth** to say or state sth, especially officially: *The court waited in silence for the judge to pass sentence.* ◇ *It's not for me to pass judgement on your behaviour.* ◇ *The man smiled at the girl and passed a friendly remark.*
- **BELIEF/UNDERSTANDING 21** [T] **~ belief, understanding, etc.** (*formal*) to go beyond the limits of what you can believe, understand, etc.: *It passes belief* (= is impossible to believe) *that she could do such a thing.*
- **IN CARD GAMES 22** [I] to refuse to play a card or make a BID when it is your turn
- **FROM THE BODY 23** [T] **~ sth** to send sth out from the body as or with waste matter: *If you're passing blood you ought to see a doctor.*

**IDM** ⟩ **come to 'pass** (*old use*) to happen **not pass your 'lips 1** if words do not pass your lips, you say nothing **2** if food or drink does **not pass your lips**, you eat or drink nothing **pass the 'hat round/around** (*informal*) to collect money from a number of people, for example to buy a present for sb **pass 'muster** to be accepted as of a good enough standard **pass the time of 'day (with sb)** to say hello to sb and have a short conversation with them **pass 'water** (*formal*) to URINATE

**PHR V** ⟩ **,pass sth↔a'round** (*BrE also* **,pass sth↔'round**) to give sth to another person, who gives it to sb else, etc. until everyone has seen it: *Can you pass these pictures around for everyone to look at, please?* **'pass as sb/sth** = PASS FOR/AS SB/STH **,pass a'way 1** (*also* **,pass 'on**) to die. People say 'pass away' to avoid saying 'die': *His mother passed away last year.* **2** to stop existing: *civilizations that have passed away* **,pass 'by (sb/sth)** to go past: *The procession passed right by my front door.* **,pass sb/sth 'by** to happen without affecting sb/sth: *She feels that life is passing her by* (= that she is not enjoying the opportunities and pleasures of life). **,pass sth↔'down** [often passive] to give or teach sth to your children or to people younger than you, who will then give or teach it to those who live after them, and so on **SYN hand down** **'pass for/as sb/sth** to be accepted as sb/sth: *He speaks the language so well he could easily pass for a German.* ◇ *We had some wine—or what passes for wine in that area.* **,pass into sth** to become a part of sth: *Many foreign words have passed into the English language.* **,pass 'off** (*BrE*) (of an event) to take place and be completed in a particular way: *The demonstration passed off peacefully.* **,pass sb/yourself 'off as sb/sth** to pretend that sb/sth is sth they are not: *He escaped by passing himself off as a guard.* **,pass 'on** = PASS AWAY **,pass sth↔'on (to sb)** to give sth to sb else, especially after receiving it or using it yourself: *Pass the book on to me when you've finished with it.* ◇ *I passed your message on to my mother.* ◇ *Much of the discount is pocketed by retailers instead of being passed on to customers.* **,pass 'out** to become unconscious **SYN faint** **,pass 'out (of sth)** (*BrE*) to leave a military college after finishing a course of training: *a passing-out ceremony* **,pass sb↔'over** to decide not to promote sb in a job, especially when they deserve it or think that they deserve it: *He was passed over in favour of a younger man.* **,pass 'over sth** to ignore or avoid sth **SYN overlook**: *They chose to pass over her rude remarks.* **,pass sth↔'round** = PASS STH AROUND **,pass 'through ...** to go through a town, etc., stopping there for a short time but not staying: *We were passing through, so we thought we'd come and say hello.* **,pass sth↔'up** (*informal*) to choose not to make use of a chance, an opportunity, etc.: *Imagine passing up an offer like that!*

■ noun
- **OFFICIAL DOCUMENT 1** 🔑 **B1** an official document or ticket that shows that you have the right to enter or leave a place, to travel on a bus or train, etc.: *a boarding pass* (= for a plane) ◇ *There is no admittance without a security pass.* ⊃ see also BUS PASS
- **IN EXAM 2** 🔑 **B1** (*especially BrE*) a successful result in an exam or test: *She got a pass in French.* ◇ *12 passes and 3 fails* ◇ *Two A-level passes are needed for this course.* ◇ *The pass mark is 50 per cent.* ◇ *The school has a 90 per cent pass rate* (= 90 per cent of students pass their exams).
- **OF BALL 3** (in some sports) an act of hitting or throwing the ball to another player in your team: *a long pass to Turner* ◇ *a back pass to the goalkeeper*
- **THROUGH MOUNTAINS 4** a road or way over or through mountains: *a mountain pass*
- **MOVING PAST/OVER 5** an act of going or moving past or over sth: *The helicopter made several passes over the village before landing.*
- **STAGE IN PROCESS 6** a stage in a process, especially one that involves separating things from a larger group: *In the first pass all the addresses are loaded into the database.*

**IDM** ⟩ **come to such a 'pass** (*also* **come to a pretty 'pass**) (*old-fashioned or humorous*) to reach a sad or difficult state: *Things have come to a such a pass when we can't afford to pay the heating bills!* **make a pass at sb** (*informal*) to try to start a sexual relationship with sb

**pass·able** /ˈpɑːsəbl; *NAmE* ˈpæs-/ *adj.* **1** fairly good but not excellent **SYN satisfactory 2** [not usually before noun] if a road or a river is **passable**, it is not blocked and you can travel along or across it **OPP impassable**

**pass·ably** /ˈpɑːsəbli; *NAmE* ˈpæs-/ *adv.* in a way that is acceptable or good enough **SYN reasonably**: *He speaks passably good French.*

## pas·sage 🔑 B2 /ˈpæsɪdʒ/ noun
- **LONG NARROW WAY 1** 🔑 **B2** (*also* **pas·sage·way** /ˈpæsɪdʒweɪ/) [C] a long narrow area with walls on either side that connects one room or place with another **SYN corridor**: *A dark narrow passage led to the main hall.*
- **IN THE BODY 2** [C] a tube in the body through which air, liquid, etc. passes: *blocked nasal passages* ⊃ see also BACK PASSAGE
- **SECTION FROM BOOK 3** 🔑 **B2** [C] a short section from a book, piece of music, etc. **SYN excerpt, extract**: *Read the following passage and answer the questions below.* ◇ **~ from/in sth** *a passage from the Bible*
- **OF TIME 4** [*sing.*] **the ~ of time** (*literary*) the process of time passing: *Her confidence grew with the passage of time.*

# passbook 1130

- **OF BILL IN PARLIAMENT** 5 [sing.] the process of discussing a BILL in a parliament so that it can become law: *The bill is now guaranteed an easy passage through the House of Representatives.*
- **JOURNEY BY SHIP** 6 [sing.] a journey from one place to another by ship: *Her grandfather had **worked his passage** (= worked on a ship to pay for the journey) to America.*
- **GOING THROUGH** 7 [sing.] **a ~ (through sth)** a way through sth: *The officers forced a passage through the crowd.* 8 [U] (*formal*) the action of going across, through or past sth: *Large trees may obstruct the passage of light.* 9 [U, C, usually sing.] **~ (+ adv./prep.)** the permission to travel across a particular area of land: *We were promised a speedy passage through the border.* ⇒ see also SAFE PASSAGE
⇒ see also BIRD OF PASSAGE, RITE OF PASSAGE

**pass·book** /ˈpɑːsbʊk; *NAmE* ˈpæs-/ *noun* a small book containing a record of the money you put into and take out of an account at a BUILDING SOCIETY or a bank

**passé** /ˈpæseɪ, ˈpɑː-; *NAmE* pæˈseɪ/ *adj.* [not usually before noun] (*from French, disapproving*) no longer fashionable SYN **outmoded**

**pas·sen·ger** ⓘ **A2** /ˈpæsɪndʒə(r)/ *noun* **1** ⓘ **A2** a person who is travelling in a car, bus, train, plane or ship and who is not driving it or working on it: *airline/cruise/rail/bus passengers* **2** (*informal, disapproving, especially BrE*) a member of a group or team who does not do as much work as the others: *The firm cannot afford to carry passengers.*

**passenger seat** *noun* the seat in a car which is next to the driver's seat

**passer-by** *noun* (*pl.* **passers-by**) a person who is going past sb/sth by chance, especially when sth unexpected happens: *Police asked passers-by if they had seen the accident.* ⇒ SYNONYMS at WITNESS

**pass-fail** *adj.* (*US*) connected with a grading system for school classes, etc. in which a student passes or fails rather than receiving a grade as a letter (for example, A or B) ▶ **pass-fail** *adv.*: *to take a class pass-fail*

**pas·sim** /ˈpæsɪm/ *adv.* (*from Latin*) used in the notes to a book or an article to show that a particular name or subject appears in several places in it

**pass·ing** ⓘ **C1** /ˈpɑːsɪŋ; *NAmE* ˈpæs-/ *noun, adj.*
- *noun* [U] **1** ⓘ **C1** **the ~ of time/the years** the process of time going by **2** ⓘ **C1** (*formal*) the fact of sth ending or of sb dying: *When the government is finally brought down, no one will mourn its passing.* ◇ *the passing of the old year (= on New Year's Eve)* ◇ *Many will mourn her passing (= her death, when you do not want to say this directly).* **3** ⓘ **C1** **the ~ of sth** the act of making sth become a law: *the passing of a resolution/law*
- IDM **in passing** done or said when your main focus is sth different SYN **casually**: *He only mentioned it in passing and didn't give any details.*
- *adj.* [only before noun] **1** lasting only for a short period of time and then disappearing SYN **brief**: *a passing phase/thought/interest* ◇ *He makes only a passing reference to the theory in his book (= it is not the main subject of his book).* ◇ *She bears more than a passing resemblance to (= looks very like) your sister.* **2** going past: *the noise of passing cars* **3** going by in time: *I love him more with each passing day.* **4** **~ grade/mark** (*NAmE*) a mark that achieves the required standard in an exam, a test, etc.

**passing lane** (*NAmE*) (*BrE* **outside lane**) *noun* the part of a major road such as a MOTORWAY or INTERSTATE nearest the middle of the road, where vehicles drive fastest and can go past vehicles ahead

**passing shot** *noun* (in tennis) a shot which goes past your opponent, and which he or she cannot reach

**pas·sion** ⓘ **B1** /ˈpæʃn/ *noun* **1** ⓘ **B1** [U, C] a very strong feeling of love, hate, anger, enthusiasm, etc.: *I admire the passion and commitment shown by the players.* ◇ **with ~** *She argued her case with considerable passion.* ◇ *a crime of passion (= caused by strong feelings of sexual JEALOUSY)* ◇ *Passions were running high (= people were angry and emotional) at the meeting.* **2** ⓘ **B1** [C] a very strong feeling of liking sth; a hobby, an activity, etc. that you like very much: *Music is his true passion.* ◇ **~for sth** *She left her job to pursue her lifelong passion for painting.* **3** [U] **~ (for sb)** a very strong feeling of sexual love: *His passion for her made him blind to everything else.* **4** [sing.] (*formal*) a state of being very angry SYN **rage**: *She flies into a passion if anyone even mentions his name.* **5 the Passion** [sing.] (in Christianity) the SUFFERING and death of Jesus Christ

**pas·sion·ate** ⓘ **B2** /ˈpæʃənət/ *adj.* **1** ⓘ **B2** having or showing strong feelings of sexual love or of anger, etc: *to have a passionate nature* ▶ WORDFINDER NOTE at LOVE **2** ⓘ **B2** having or showing strong feelings of enthusiasm for sth or belief in sth: *a passionate interest in music* ◇ *a passionate defender of civil liberties* ▶ **pas·sion·ate·ly** *adv.*: *He took her in his arms and kissed her passionately.* ◇ *They are all passionately interested in environmental issues.*

**passion fruit** *noun* [C, U] (*pl.* **passion fruit**) a small tropical fruit with a thick purple skin and many seeds inside ⇒ VISUAL VOCAB page V4

**pas·sion·less** /ˈpæʃnləs/ *adj.* without emotion or enthusiasm

**Passion play** *noun* a play about the suffering and death of Jesus Christ

**pas·sive** ⓘ **C1** /ˈpæsɪv/ *adj., noun*
- *adj.* **1** ⓘ **C1** accepting what happens or what people do without trying to change anything or oppose them: *He played a passive role in the relationship.* ◇ *a passive observer of events* **2** (*grammar*) connected with the form of a verb used when the subject is affected by the action of the verb, for example *He was bitten by a dog.* ⇒ compare ACTIVE ▶ **pas·sive·ly** *adv.*
- *noun* (*also* **passive 'voice**) [sing.] (*grammar*) the form of a verb used when the subject is affected by the action of the verb ⇒ compare ACTIVE

**passive-ag'gressive** *adj.* being angry without expressing your anger openly, but resisting people in authority by refusing to do what they want or to accept responsibility for your actions: *He exhibited passive-aggressive tendencies.*

**passive re'sistance** *noun* [U] a way of opposing a government or an enemy by peaceful means, often by refusing to obey laws or orders

**passive 'smoking** *noun* [U] the act of breathing in smoke from other people's cigarettes

**pas·siv·ity** /pæˈsɪvəti/ *noun* [U] the state of accepting what happens without reacting or trying to fight against it

**pass key** *noun* = MASTER KEY

**Pass·over** /ˈpɑːsəʊvə(r); *NAmE* ˈpæs-/ *noun* [U, C] the Jewish religious festival and holiday in memory of the escape of the Jews from Egypt

**pass·port** ⓘ **A1** /ˈpɑːspɔːt; *NAmE* ˈpæspɔːrt/ *noun* **1** ⓘ **A1** an official document that identifies you as a citizen of a particular country, and that you may have to show when you enter or leave a country: *a **valid** passport* ◇ *a South African passport* ◇ *I was stopped as I went through **passport control** (= where passports are checked).* ◇ *EU passport holders* ⇒ WORDFINDER NOTE at AIRPORT **2 ~ to sth** a thing that makes sth possible or enables you to achieve sth SYN **key**: *The only passport to success is hard work.*

**pass·word** ⓘ **B2** /ˈpɑːswɜːd; *NAmE* ˈpæswɜːrd/ *noun* **1** ⓘ **B2** a series of letters, numbers, etc. that you must type into a computer or computer system in order to be able to use it: *Enter a username and password to get into the system.* ⇒ WORDFINDER NOTE at FILE **2** ⓘ **B2** a secret word or phrase that you need to know in order to be allowed into a place

**past** ⓘ **A1** /pɑːst; *NAmE* pæst/ *adj., noun, prep., adv.*
- *adj.* **1** ⓘ **A1** gone by in time: *in past years/centuries* ◇ *in times past* ◇ *The time for discussion is past.* **2** ⓘ **A1** [only before noun] gone by recently; just ended: *in the past year/month/week* ◇ *I've seen her several times over the past few days.* ◇ *The past month has been really busy at work.* **3** ⓘ **A1** [only before noun] belonging to an earlier time: *From past experience I'd say he'd probably forgotten the time.* ◇ *past and present students of the college* ◇ *Let's forget about who was more to blame — it's all past history.* ◇ *past events*

| æ cat | ɑː father | e bed | ɜː fur | ə about | ɪ sit | iː see | i happy | ɒ got (*BrE*) | ɔː saw | ʌ cup | ʊ put | uː too |

**4** [only before noun] (*grammar*) connected with the form of a verb used to express actions in the past: *the past tense*

■ **noun 1** **the past** [sing.] the time that has gone by; things that happened in an earlier time: *in~ I used to go there often in the past.* ◊ *the recent/distant past* ◊ *She looked back on the past without regret.* ◊ *of~ Writing letters seems to be a thing of the past.* **2** [C] a person's past life or career; the history of a place, country, group, etc: *We don't know anything about his past.* ◊ *Little remains from the city's glorious past.* **3** **the past** [sing.] (*grammar*) = PAST TENSE: *The past of 'shine' is 'shone'.* see BLAST *n.*, DISTANT, LIVE¹

■ **prep. 1** (*NAmE also* **after**) later than sth: *half past two* ◊ *ten (minutes) past six* ◊ *There's a bus at twenty minutes past the hour* (= at 1.20, 2.20, etc.)*.* ◊ *We arrived at two o'clock and left at ten past* (= ten minutes past two)*.* ◊ *It was past midnight when we got home.* **2** on or to the other side of sb/sth: *We live in the house just past the church.* ◊ *He hurried past them without stopping.* ◊ *He just walked* **straight past us! 3** above or further than a particular point or stage: *Unemployment is now past the 3 million mark.* ◊ *The flowers are past their best.* ◊ *He's past his prime.* ◊ *She's long past retirement age.* ◊ *Honestly, I'm* **past caring** *what happens* (= I can no longer be bothered to care)*.*

**IDM** **past it** (*BrE, informal*) too old to do what you used to be able to do; too old to be used for its normal function: *In some sports you're past it by the age of 25.* ◊ *That coat is looking decidedly past it.*

■ **adv. 1** from one side of sth to the other: *She smiled at me as she walked past.* **2** used to describe time passing by: *A week went past and nothing had changed.* ◆ see also FLY-PAST

▼ **HOMOPHONES**

**passed ♦ past** /pɑːst; *NAmE* pæst/
- **passed** *verb* (past tense, past participle of PASS): *You've passed all your exams—well done!*
- **past** *adj.*: *It's arguably the best novel of the past 20 years.*
- **past** *noun*: *Let's put the past behind us and move on.*
- **past** *prep.*: *You shouldn't be up, it's past your bedtime!*

**pasta** /'pæstə; *NAmE* 'pɑːs-/ *noun* [U] an Italian food from flour, water and sometimes eggs, formed into different shapes and usually served with a sauce. It is hard when dry and soft when cooked.

**paste** /peɪst/ *noun, verb*
■ **noun 1** [sing.] a soft wet mixture, usually made of a powder and a liquid: *She mixed the flour and water to a smooth paste.* **2** [C] (especially in compounds) a smooth, soft mixture of meat, fish, etc. that is spread on bread or used in cooking: *meat/fish/tomato paste* **3** [U] a type of GLUE that is used for sticking paper to things: *wallpaper paste* **4** [U] a substance like glass, that is used for making artificial JEWELS, for example diamonds
■ **verb 1** [T] ~ **sth + adv. / prep.** to stick sth to sth else using GLUE or paste: *He pasted the pictures into his scrapbook.* ◊ *Paste the two pieces together.* ◊ *Paste down the edges.* **2** [T] ~ **sth** to make sth by sticking pieces of paper together: *The children were busy cutting and pasting paper hats.* **3** [T, I] ~ **(sth)** (*computing*) to copy or move text into a document from another place or another document: *This function allows you to* **cut and paste** *text.* ◊ *It's quicker to copy and paste than to retype.*

**pas·tel** /'pæstl; *NAmE* pæ'stel/ *noun* **1** [U] soft coloured PIGMENT (= a powder that is mixed with liquid to make paint), used for drawing pictures: **in** ~ *drawings in pastel* **2** **pastels** [pl.] small sticks containing PIGMENT for drawing: *a box of pastels* **3** [C] a picture drawn with pastels **4** [C] a pale DELICATE colour: *The whole house was painted in soft pastels.*

**pas·teur·ize** (*BrE also* -**ise**) /'pɑːstʃəraɪz; *NAmE* 'pæs-/ *verb* ~ **sth** to heat a liquid, especially milk, to a particular temperature and then cool it, in order to kill harmful bacteria
▶ **pas·teur·iza·tion**, -**isa·tion** /ˌpɑːstʃəraɪˈzeɪʃn; *NAmE* ˌpæstʃərəˈz-/ *noun* [U]

**pas·tiche** /pæˈstiːʃ/ *noun* **1** [C, U] a work of art, piece of writing, etc. that is created by deliberately copying the style of sb/sth else: *a pastiche of the classic detective story* **2** [C] a work of art, etc. that consists of a variety of different styles

**pas·tille** /'pæstəl; *NAmE* pæ'stiːl/ *noun* (*especially BrE*) a small sweet that you eat by keeping it in your mouth, especially one that tastes of fruit or that contains medicine for a SORE throat (= a painful throat because of an infection): *fruit pastilles* ◊ *throat pastilles*

**pas·time** /'pɑːstaɪm; *NAmE* 'pæs-/ *noun* something that you enjoy doing when you are not working **hobby** ◆ SYNONYMS at INTEREST

**past·ing** /'peɪstɪŋ/ *noun* [sing.] (*especially BrE*) **1** a heavy defeat in a game or competition **2** an instance of being hit very hard as a punishment **thrashing**

**pas·tis** /pæˈstiːs/ *noun* [U, C] (*pl.* **pas·tis**) (*from French*) a strong alcoholic drink, usually drunk before a meal, that tastes of ANISEED

**past 'master** *noun* ~ **(at sth / at doing sth)** a person who is very good at sth because they have a lot of experience in it **expert**: *She's a past master at getting what she wants.*

**pas·tor** /'pɑːstə(r); *NAmE* 'pæs-/ *noun* a minister in charge of a Christian church or group, especially in some NONCONFORMIST churches

**pas·tor·al** /'pɑːstərəl; *NAmE* 'pæs-/ *adj.* **1** relating to the work of a priest or teacher in giving help and advice on personal matters, not just those connected with religion or education: *pastoral care* **2** showing country life or the countryside, especially in a romantic way: *a pastoral scene/poem/symphony* **3** relating to the farming of animals: *agricultural and pastoral practices*

**pas·tor·al·ism** /'pɑːstərəlɪzəm; *NAmE* 'pæs-/ *noun* [U] a way of keeping animals such as CATTLE, sheep, etc. that involves moving them from place to place to find water and food ▶ **pas·tor·al·ist** *noun, adj.*

**past par'ticiple** *noun* (*grammar*) the form of a verb that in English ends in -*ed*, -*en*, etc. and is used with the verb *have* to form PERFECT tenses such as *I have eaten*, with the verb *be* to form passive sentences such as *It was destroyed*, or sometimes as an adjective as in *an upset stomach* ◆ compare PRESENT PARTICIPLE

**the past 'perfect** (*also the* ˌpast ˌperfect 'tense, **the plu·per·fect**) *noun* [sing.] (*grammar*) the form of a verb that expresses an action completed before a particular point in the past, formed in English with *had* and the past participle

**pas·trami** /pəˈstrɑːmi/ *noun* [U] cold spicy smoked beef

**pas·try** /'peɪstri/ *noun* (*pl.* -**ies**) **1** [U] a mixture of flour, fat and water or milk that is rolled out flat to be a base or cover for a PIE, etc. ◆ see also CHOUX PASTRY, FILO PASTRY, PUFF PASTRY **2** [C] a small cake made using pastry ◆ see also DANISH PASTRY

**'pastry chef** (*also less frequent* 'pastry cook) *noun* a professional cook whose main job is to make PASTRY, cakes, etc.

**the past 'tense** (*also* **the past**) *noun* [sing.] (*grammar*) the form of a verb used to describe actions in the past: *The past tense of 'take' is 'took'.*

**pas·tur·age** /'pɑːstʃərɪdʒ; *NAmE* 'pæs-/ *noun* [U] (*specialist*) land where animals can feed on grass **pasture**, **pastureland**

**pas·ture** /'pɑːstʃə(r); *NAmE* 'pæs-/ *noun, verb*
■ **noun 1** [U, C] land covered with grass that is suitable for feeding animals on: *an area of permanent/rough/rich pasture* ◊ *high mountain pastures* ◊ *The cattle were* **put out to pasture***.* **2** **pastures** [pl.] the circumstances of your life, work, etc: *I felt we were off to* **greener pastures** (= a better way of life)*.* ◊ (*BrE*) *She decided it was time to move on to* **pastures new** (= a new job, place to live, etc.)*.*
■ **verb** ~ **sth** to put animals in a field to feed on grass

**pas·ture·land** /'pɑːstʃəlænd; *NAmE* 'pæstʃərl-/ *noun* [U, pl.] land where animals can feed on grass **pasturage**, **pasture**

**pasty¹** /'pæsti/ *noun* (*pl.* -**ies**) (*BrE*) a small PIE containing meat and/or vegetables ◆ see also CORNISH PASTY

# pasty

**pasty²** /ˈpeɪsti/ *adj.* pale and not looking healthy SYN **pallid**: *a pasty face/complexion*

**pat** /pæt/ *verb, noun, adj., adv.*
- *verb* (-tt-) to touch sb/sth gently several times with your hand flat, especially to show kind feelings: *~ sth She patted the dog on the head.* ◊ *He patted his sister's hand consolingly.* ◊ *~ sth + adj. Pat your face dry with a soft towel.*
- IDM **pat sb/yourself on the ˈback** (*informal*) to praise sb or yourself for doing sth well
- *noun* **1** [usually sing.] a gentle friendly touch with your open hand or with a flat object: *a pat on the head* ◊ *He gave her knee an affectionate pat.* **2** **~ of butter** a small, soft, flat piece of butter
- IDM **a ˌpat on the ˈback (for sth/for doing sth)** (*informal*) praise or approval for sth that you have done well: *He deserves a pat on the back for all his hard work.*
- *adj.* (*usually disapproving*) (of an answer, a comment, etc.) too quick, easy or simple; not seeming natural or realistic SYN **glib**: *The ending of the novel is a little too pat to be convincing.* ◊ *There are no pat answers to these questions.*
- *adv.*
- IDM **have/know sth off ˈpat** (*BrE*) (*NAmE* **have/know sth down ˈpat**) to know sth perfectly so that you can repeat it at any time without having to think about it: *He had all the answers off pat.* **stand ˈpat** (*especially NAmE*) to refuse to change your mind about a decision you have made or an opinion you have

**patch** /pætʃ/ *noun, verb*
- *noun*
  - • SMALL AREA **1** a small area of sth, especially one which is different from the area around it: *a black dog with a white patch on its back* ◊ *a bald patch on the top of his head* ◊ *damp patches on the wall* ◊ *patches of dense fog*
  - • PIECE OF MATERIAL **2** a small piece of material that is used to cover a hole in sth or to make a weak area stronger, or as decoration: *I sewed patches on the knees of my jeans.* **3** a piece of material that you wear over an eye, usually because the eye is damaged: *He had a black patch over one eye.* ⇒ see also EYEPATCH **4** (*NAmE*) (*BrE* **badge**) a piece of material that you SEW onto clothes as part of a uniform **5** a piece of material that people can wear on their skin to help them to stop smoking: *nicotine patches*
  - • PIECE/AREA OF LAND **6** a small piece of land, especially one used for growing vegetables or fruit: *a vegetable patch* **7** (*BrE, informal*) an area that sb works in, knows well or comes from: *He knows every house in his patch.* ◊ *She has had a lot of success in her home patch.*
  - • DIFFICULT TIME **8** (*informal, especially BrE*) a period of time of the type mentioned, usually a difficult or unhappy one: *to go through a bad/difficult/sticky patch* ⇒ see also PURPLE PATCH
  - • IN COMPUTING **9** a small piece of code (= instructions that a computer can understand) which can be added to a computer program to improve it or to correct a fault: *Follow the instructions below to download and install the patch.*
  - IDM **be not a ˈpatch on sb/sth** (*informal, especially BrE*) to be much less good, attractive, etc. than sb/sth else
- *verb* **~ sth (with sth)** to cover a hole on a worn place, especially in clothes, with a piece of cloth or other material SYN **mend**: *patched jeans* ◊ *to patch a hole in the roof*
- PHRV **ˌpatch sb/sth ˈthrough (to sb/sth)** to connect phone or electronic equipment temporarily: *She was patched through to London on the satellite link.* **ˌpatch sth↔toˈgether** to make sth from several different parts, especially in a quick careless way: *They hope to be able to patch together a temporary settlement.* **ˌpatch sth/sb↔ˈup** (*rather informal*) **1** to repair sth, especially in a temporary way by adding a new piece of material or a patch: *Just to patch the boat up will cost £10000.* **2** to treat sb's injuries, especially quickly or for the present time only: *The doctor will soon patch you up.* **3** to try to stop arguing with sb and be friends again: *They've managed to patch up their differences.* ◊ *Have you tried patching things up with her?* **4** to agree on sth, especially after long discussions and even though the agreement is not exactly what everyone wants: *They managed to patch up a deal.*

**patch·ouli** /pəˈtʃuːli; *BrE also* ˈpætʃuli/ *noun* [U] a PERFUME made with oil from the leaves of a south-east Asian bush

▼ SYNONYMS

**patch**
dot • mark • spot

These are all words for a small part on a surface that is a different colour from the rest.

**patch** an area of sth, especially one which is different from the area around it: *a white dog with a black patch on its head* ◊ *patches of dense fog*

**dot** a small round mark on sth, especially one that is printed: *The letters 'i' and 'j' have dots over them.* ◊ *The island is a small green dot on the map.*

**mark** an area of colour that is easy to notice on the body of a person or animal: *The horse had a white mark on its head.*

**spot** a small round area that is a different colour or feels different from the surface it is on: *Which has spots, a leopard or a tiger?*

PATTERNS
- a patch / dot / mark / spot **on** sth
- **with** patches / dots / marks / spots
- a **blue** / **black** / **red**, etc. patch / dot / mark / spot

**patch·work** /ˈpætʃwɜːk; *NAmE* -wɜːrk/ *noun* **1** [U] a type of NEEDLEWORK in which small pieces of cloth of different colours or designs are SEWN together: *a patchwork quilt* **2** [sing.] a thing that is made up of many different pieces or parts: *a patchwork of different styles and cultures* ◊ *From the plane, the landscape was just a patchwork of fields.*

**patchy** /ˈpætʃi/ *adj.* **1** existing or happening in some places and not others SYN **uneven**: *patchy fog* ◊ *The grass was dry and patchy.* **2** (*NAmE also* **spotty**) not complete; good in some parts, but not in others: *a patchy knowledge of Spanish* ◊ *It was a patchy performance.* ▶ **patch·ily** /-tʃəli/ *adv.* **patch·iness** *noun* [U]

**pate** /peɪt/ *noun* (*old use or humorous*) the top part of the head, especially where there is no hair on it: *The sun beat down on his bald pate.*

**pâté** /ˈpæteɪ; *NAmE* pɑːˈteɪ/ *noun* [U] a soft mixture of meat or fish that has been cut into very small pieces, served cold and used for spreading on bread, etc.

**pâté de foie gras** /ˌpæteɪ də ˌfwɑː ˈɡrɑː; *NAmE* pɑːˌteɪ/ (*also* **ˌfoie ˈgras**) *noun* [U] (*from French*) an expensive type of pâté made from the LIVER of a GOOSE or DUCK

**pa·tel·la** /pəˈtelə/ *noun* (*pl.* **pa·tel·lae** /-liː/) (*anatomy*) the KNEECAP

**pa·tent** /ˈpætnt/ *noun, adj., verb*
- *noun* /ˈpætnt; *BrE also* ˈpeɪt-/ [C, U] an official right to be the only person to make, use or sell a product or an invention; a document that proves this: **~ on** sth *to apply for/obtain/take out a patent on an invention* ◊ **by ~** *The device was protected by patent.* ◊ *patent applications/laws* ◊ *the US Patent Office*
- *adj.* /ˈpeɪtnt; *NAmE also* ˈpæt-/ [only before noun] **1** (of a product) made or sold by a particular company: *patent medicines* **2** (*formal*) used to emphasize that sth bad is very clear and obvious SYN **blatant**: *It was a patent lie.*
- *verb* /ˈpætnt; *BrE also* ˈpeɪt-/ **~ sth** to obtain a patent for an invention or a process

**pa·tent·ee** /ˌpætnˈtiː; *BrE also* ˌpeɪt-/ *noun* a person or an organization that holds the patent for sth

**patent leather** /ˌpeɪtnt ˈleðə(r); *NAmE* ˌpæt-/ *noun* [U] a type of leather with a hard shiny surface, used especially for making shoes and bags

**pa·tent·ly** /ˈpeɪtntli; ˈpæt-; *NAmE* ˈpæt-/ *adv.* (*formal*) without doubt SYN **clearly**: *Her explanation was patently ridiculous.* ◊ *It was patently obvious that she was lying.*

**pa·ter·nal** /pəˈtɜːnl; *NAmE* -ˈtɜːrnl/ *adj.* **1** connected with being a father; typical of a kind father: *paternal love* ◊ *He gave me a piece of paternal advice.* **2** related through the father's side of the family: *my paternal grandmother* (= my father's mother) ▶ **pa·ter·nal·ly** /-nəli/ *adv.*: *He smiled paternally at them.* ⇒ compare MATERNAL

**pa·ter·nal·ism** /pəˈtɜːnəlɪzəm; NAmE -ˈtɜːrn-/ noun [U] (sometimes disapproving) the system in which a government or an employer protects the people who are governed or employed by providing them with what they need, but does not give them any responsibility or freedom of choice ▶ **pa·ter·nal·is·tic** /pəˌtɜːnəˈlɪstɪk; NAmE -ˌtɜːrn-/ (also **pa·ter·nal·ist**) adj.: a paternalistic employer

**pa·ter·nity** /pəˈtɜːnəti; NAmE -ˈtɜːrn-/ noun [U] the fact of being the father of a child: He refused to admit paternity of the child. ⇒ compare MATERNITY

**paˈternity leave** noun [U] time that the father of a new baby is allowed to have away from work ⇒ see also FAMILY LEAVE, MATERNITY LEAVE, PARENTAL LEAVE

**paˈternity suit** (also **paˈternity case**) noun a court case that is intended to prove who a child's father is, especially so that he can be ordered to give the child financial support

**path** ⓘ B1 /pɑːθ; NAmE pæθ/ (pl. **paths** /pɑːðz; NAmE pæðz/) noun 1 ⓘ B1 a way or track that is built or is made by the action of people walking: a dirt/gravel/concrete path ◊ *Follow the path through the woods.* ◊ *along/down a~* They walked along the cliff path to the next town. ◊ *The path led up a steep hill.* ◊ *a coastal path* ⇒ see also BRIDLE PATH, CYCLE PATH, FOOTPATH 2 ⓘ B2 a plan of action or a way of achieving sth **SYN** pathway: *a career path* ◊ *~to sth* the path to success ◊ *on a~* Here are some pointers to set you on the right path. ⇒ see also CRITICAL PATH 3 ⓘ B2 [usually sing.] a line along which sb/sth moves; the space in front of sb/sth as they move **SYN** way: *Three men blocked her path.* ◊ *into/out of the~of sth* He threw himself into the path of an oncoming vehicle. ◊ *in sth's/sb's~* The avalanche forced its way down the mountain, crushing everything in its path. ⇒ see also FLIGHT PATH IDM see BEAT v., CROSS v., LEAD¹ v., PRIMROSE, RESISTANCE, SMOOTH v.

**path·et·ic** /pəˈθetɪk/ adj. **1** making you feel sad **SYN** pitiful: *a pathetic and lonely old man* ◊ *The starving children were a pathetic sight.* **2** (informal, disapproving) weak and not successful **SYN** feeble: *a pathetic excuse* ◊ *She made a pathetic attempt to smile.* ◊ *You're pathetic!* ▶ **path·et·ic·al·ly** /-kli/ adv.: *He cried pathetically.* ◊ *a pathetically shy woman*

**paˌthetic ˈfallacy** noun [U, sing.] (in art and literature) the act of describing animals and things as having human feelings

**path·find·er** /ˈpɑːθfaɪndə(r); NAmE ˈpæθ-/ noun **1** a person, group or thing that goes before others and shows the way over unknown land **2** a person, group or thing that finds a new way of doing sth **SYN** trailblazer: *The company is a pathfinder in computer technology.*

**patho-** /pæθəʊ, pæθə; BrE also pəˈθɒ; NAmE also pəˈθɑː/ combining form (in nouns, adjectives and adverbs) connected with disease: *pathogenesis ◊ pathophysiology*

**patho·gen** /ˈpæθədʒən/ noun (specialist) a thing that causes disease ▶ **patho·gen·ic** /ˌpæθəˈdʒenɪk/ adj.

**patho·gen·esis** /ˌpæθəˈdʒenɪsɪs/ noun (medical) the way in which a disease develops

**patho·logic·al** /ˌpæθəˈlɒdʒɪkl/ adj. **1** not reasonable or sensible; impossible to control: *pathological fear/hatred/violence* ◊ *a pathological liar* (= a person who cannot stop telling lies) **2** caused by, or connected with, disease or illness: *pathological depression* **3** (specialist) connected with pathology ▶ **patho·logic·al·ly** /-kli/ adv.: *pathologically jealous*

**path·olo·gist** /pəˈθɒlədʒɪst; NAmE -ˈθɑːl-/ noun a doctor who studies pathology and examines dead bodies to find out the cause of death ⇒ compare MEDICAL EXAMINER

**path·ology** /pəˈθɒlədʒi; NAmE -ˈθɑːl-/ noun **1** [U] (medical) the scientific study of diseases **2** [C] an aspect of sb's behaviour that is extreme and unreasonable and that they cannot control

**pathos** /ˈpeɪθɒs; NAmE -θɑːs/ noun [U] (in writing, speech and plays) the power of a performance, description, etc. to make you feel sympathy or be sad

**path·way** ⓘ C1 /ˈpɑːθweɪ; NAmE ˈpæθ-/ noun **1** ⓘ C1 a track that serves as a path: *They came out of the woods and onto a pathway.* **2** ⓘ C1 a plan of action or way of achieving sth **SYN** path: *We help students define and develop a clear career pathway.* **3** (biology) a route formed by a chain of nerve cells along which electrical signals travel from one part of the body to another: *neural pathways*

**pa·tience** ⓘ B2 /ˈpeɪʃns/ noun [U] **1** ⓘ B2 *~(with sb/sth)* the ability to stay calm and accept a delay or sth annoying without complaining: *She has little patience with* (= will not accept or consider) *such views.* ◊ *People have lost patience with* (= have become annoyed about) *the slow pace of reform.* ◊ *I have run out of patience with her.* ◊ *My patience is wearing thin* (= I do not have much patience left). ◊ *Teaching children with special needs requires patience and understanding.* **2** ⓘ B2 the ability to spend a lot of time doing sth difficult that needs a lot of attention and effort: *It takes time and patience to photograph wildlife.* ◊ *I don't have the patience to do jigsaw puzzles.* **3** (BrE) (NAmE **solitaire**) a card game for only one player IDM see TRY v.

**pa·tient** ⓘ A2 /ˈpeɪʃnt/ noun, adj.
■ noun **1** ⓘ A2 a person who is receiving medical treatment, especially in a hospital: *cancer/AIDS/heart patients* ◊ *critically ill/elderly patients* ◊ *Hospitals are treating more patients than ever before.* ◊ *~with sth* patients with heart disease ◊ *patient care/safety* ⇒ WORDFINDER NOTE at DOCTOR **2** ⓘ A2 a person who receives treatment from a particular doctor, dentist, etc: *He's one of Dr Shaw's patients.* ⇒ see also PRIVATE PATIENT **3** (grammar) the person or thing that is affected by the action of the verb. In the sentence 'I started the car', the patient is *car.* ⇒ compare AGENT
■ adj. ⓘ B2 able to wait for a long time or accept annoying behaviour or difficulties without becoming angry: *You'll just have to be patient and wait till I'm finished.* ◊ *~with sb/sth* She's very patient with young children. ▶ **pa·tient·ly** adv.: *Everyone waited patiently for me to get it right.*

**pat·ina** /ˈpætɪnə; NAmE pəˈtiːnə/ noun [usually sing.] **1** a green, black or brown layer that forms on the surface of some metals **2** a thin layer that forms on other materials; the shiny surface that develops on wood or leather when it is POLISHED: *(figurative) He looked relaxed and elegant and had the patina of success.*

**patio** /ˈpætiəʊ/ noun (pl. **-os**) a flat hard area outside, and usually behind, a house where people can sit: *on the~ Let's have lunch out on the patio.*

**ˈpatio ˌdoor** noun [usually pl.] (especially BrE) a large glass sliding door that leads to a garden or BALCONY

**pa·tis·serie** /pəˈtiːsəri/ noun (from French) **1** [C] a shop that sells cakes, etc. **2** [U] (also **pa·tis·series** [pl.]) (formal) cakes

**pat·ois** /ˈpætwɑː/ noun (pl. **pat·ois** /-wɑːz/) a form of a language, spoken by people in a particular area, that is different from the standard language of the country

**patri·arch** /ˈpeɪtriɑːk; NAmE -ɑːrk/ noun **1** the male head of a family or community ⇒ compare MATRIARCH **2** an old man that people have a lot of respect for **3 Patriarch** the title of a most senior BISHOP (= a senior priest) in the Orthodox or Roman Catholic Church

**patri·arch·al** /ˌpeɪtriˈɑːkl; NAmE -ˈɑːrkl/ adj. **1** ruled or controlled by men; giving power and importance only to men: *a patriarchal society* **2** connected with a patriarch ⇒ compare MATRIARCHAL

**patri·arch·ate** /ˈpeɪtriɑːkət; NAmE -ɑːrk-/ noun (formal) **1** the title, position or period of office of a Patriarch **2** the area governed by a Patriarch

**patri·archy** /ˈpeɪtriɑːki; NAmE -ɑːrki/ noun [C, U] (pl. **-ies**) a society, system or country that is ruled or controlled by men ⇒ compare MATRIARCHY

**pa·tri·cian** /pəˈtrɪʃn/ adj. (formal) connected with or typical of the highest social class **SYN** aristocratic ▶ **pa·tri·cian** noun ⇒ compare PLEBEIAN

**patri·cide** /ˈpætrɪsaɪd/ noun [U, C] (formal) the crime of killing your father; a person who is guilty of this crime ⇒ compare FRATRICIDE, MATRICIDE, PARRICIDE

**patri·lin·eal** /ˌpætrɪˈlɪniəl/ adj. (formal) used to describe the relationship between father and child that continues in a family with each generation, or sth that is based on

# patrimony

this relationship: *In that society, inheritance of land is patrilineal* (= the children get the land that their father owned). ⊃ compare MATRILINEAL

**pat·ri·mony** /ˈpætrɪməni; NAmE -moʊni/ *noun* [sing.] (*formal*) **1** property that is given to sb when their father dies SYN **inheritance 2** the works of art and TREASURES of a nation, church, etc. SYN **heritage**

**pat·riot** /ˈpætriət, ˈpeɪt-; NAmE ˈpeɪt-/ *noun* a person who loves their country and who is ready to defend it against an enemy

**pat·ri·ot·ic** /ˌpætriˈɒtɪk, ˌpeɪt-; NAmE ˌpeɪtriˈɑːt-/ *adj.* having or expressing a great love of your country: *a patriotic man who served his country well* ◇ *patriotic songs* ▶ **pat·ri·ot·ic·al·ly** *adv.* /-kli/

**pat·ri·ot·ism** /ˈpætriətɪzəm, ˈpeɪt-; NAmE ˈpeɪt-/ *noun* [U] love of your country and the desire to defend it

**pa·trol** /pəˈtroʊl/ *noun, verb*
■ *noun* **1** [C, U] the act of going to different parts of a building, an area, etc. to make sure that there is no trouble or crime: *Security guards make regular patrols at night.* ◇ **on** ~ *a police car on patrol* **2** [C] a group of soldiers, vehicles, etc. that patrol an area: *a naval/police patrol* ◇ *a patrol car/boat* **3** [C] a group of about six BOY SCOUTS or GIRL GUIDES/GIRL SCOUTS that forms part of a larger group
■ *verb* (-ll-) [T, I] ~(sth) to go around an area or a building at regular times to check that it is safe and that there is no trouble: *Troops patrolled the border day and night.* ◇ *to patrol the streets/area* ◇ *Guards can be seen patrolling everywhere.*

**pa·trol·man** /pəˈtroʊlmən/, **pa·trol·woman** /pəˈtroʊlwʊmən/ *noun* (*pl.* **-men** /-mən/, **-women** /-wɪmɪn/) **1** (in the US) a police officer who walks or drives around an area to make sure that there is no trouble or crime: *Patrolman Don Lilly* **2** (in the UK) an official of an association for car owners who goes to give help to drivers who have a problem with their cars

**pat·ron** /ˈpeɪtrən/ *noun* **1** a person who gives money and support to artists and writers: *Frederick the Great was the patron of many artists.* **2** a famous person who supports an organization such as a charity and whose name is used in the advertisements, etc. for the organization **3** (*formal*) a person who uses a particular shop, restaurant, etc: *Patrons are requested not to smoke.*

**pat·ron·age** /ˈpætrənɪdʒ, ˈpeɪt-/ *noun* [U] **1** the support, especially financial, that is given to a person or an organization by a patron: *Patronage of the arts comes from businesses and private individuals.* **2** the system by which an important person gives help or a job to sb in return for their support **3** (*especially NAmE*) the support that a person gives a shop, restaurant, etc. by spending money there

**pat·ron·ess** /ˌpeɪtrəˈnes/ *noun* a female PATRON ⊃ note at GENDER

**pat·ron·ize** (*BrE also* **-ise**) /ˈpætrənaɪz; NAmE ˈpeɪt-/ *verb* **1** [T, I] ~(sb) (*disapproving*) to treat sb in a way that seems friendly, but which shows that you think that they are not very intelligent, experienced, etc: *Some television programmes tend to patronize children.* **2** [T] ~sth (*formal*) to be a regular customer of a shop, restaurant, etc. *The club is patronized by students and locals alike.* **3** [T] ~sb/sth to help a particular person, organization or activity by giving them money: *She patronizes many contemporary British artists.*

**pat·ron·iz·ing** (*BrE also* **-is·ing**) /ˈpætrənaɪzɪŋ; NAmE ˈpeɪt-/ *adj.* (*disapproving*) showing that you think you are better or more intelligent than sb else SYN **superior**: *a patronizing smile* ◇ *I was only trying to explain; I didn't want to sound patronizing.* ▶ **pat·ron·iz·ing·ly, -is·ing·ly** *adv.*: *He patted her hand patronizingly.*

**patron ˈsaint** *noun* a Christian SAINT who is believed to protect a particular place or group of people: *St Patrick, Ireland's patron saint* ◇ *St Christopher, patron saint of travellers*

**patsy** /ˈpætsi/ *noun* (*pl.* **-ies**) (*informal, especially NAmE*) a weak person who is easily cheated or tricked, or who is forced to take the blame for sth that sb else has done wrong

**pat·ter** /ˈpætə(r)/ *noun, verb*
■ *noun* **1** [sing.] the sound that is made by sth repeatedly hitting a surface quickly and lightly: *the patter of rain on the roof* ◇ *the patter of feet/footsteps* **2** [U, sing.] fast continuous talk by sb who is trying to sell you sth or entertain you: *sales patter*
IDM ▶ **the patter of tiny feet** (*informal or humorous*) a way of referring to children when sb wants, or is going to have, a baby: *We can't wait to hear the patter of tiny feet.*
■ *verb* **1** [I] + *adv./prep.* to make quick, light sounds as a surface is being hit several times: *Rain pattered against the window.* **2** [I] + *adv./prep.* to walk with light steps in a particular direction: *I heard her feet pattering along the corridor.*

**pat·tern** /ˈpætn; NAmE -tərn/ *noun, verb*
■ *noun* **1** the regular way in which sth happens or is done: *changing patterns of urban life* ◇ *We have no way of predicting next year's weather patterns.* ◇ *stress/intonation/speech patterns* ◇ *Wages in both sectors have followed a similar pattern.* ⊃ see also HOLDING PATTERN **2** [usually sing.] ~**for sth** an excellent example to copy: *This system sets the pattern for others to follow.* **3** a regular arrangement of lines, shapes, colours, etc. for example as a design on material, carpets, etc: *a pattern of diamonds and squares* ◇ *a shirt with a floral pattern*

**WORDFINDER** band, check, dot, fleck, speckle, splash, spot, streak, stripe

**4** a design, set of instructions or shape to cut around that you use in order to make sth: *a knitting pattern* ◇ *She bought a dress pattern and some material.* **5** a small piece of material, paper, etc. that helps you choose the design of sth SYN **sample**: *wallpaper patterns*
■ *verb* **1** ~ sth to form a regular arrangement of lines or shapes on sth: *Frost patterned the window.* ◇ *a landscape patterned by vineyards* **2** ~ sth (*specialist*) to cause a particular type of behaviour to develop: *Adult behaviour is often patterned by childhood experiences.*
PHRV ˈpattern sth on sth (*BrE*) (*NAmE* ˈpattern sth after sth) [usually passive] to use sth as a model for sth; to copy sth: *a new approach patterned on Japanese ideas*

**pat·terned** /ˈpætənd; NAmE -tərnd/ *adj.* decorated with a pattern: *patterned wallpaper* ◇ ~**with sth** *cups patterned with yellow flowers*

**pat·tern·ing** /ˈpætnɪŋ; NAmE -tərn-/ *noun* [U] **1** (*specialist*) the forming of fixed ways of behaving by copying or repeating sth: *cultural patterning* ◇ *the patterning of husband-wife roles* **2** the arrangement of shapes or colours to make patterns: *a red fish with black patterning*

**patty** /ˈpæti/ *noun* (*pl.* **-ies**) (*especially NAmE*) meat, fish, etc. cut into very small pieces and formed into a small round flat shape: *a hamburger patty*

**pau·city** /ˈpɔːsəti/ *noun* [sing.] ~ **(of sth)** (*formal*) a small amount of sth; less than enough of sth: *a paucity of information*

**paunch** /pɔːntʃ/ *noun* a fat stomach on a man ▶ **paunchy** *adj.*

**pau·per** /ˈpɔːpə(r)/ *noun* (*old use*) a very poor person

**pause** /pɔːz/ *verb, noun*
■ *verb* **1** [I] to stop talking or doing sth for a short time before continuing: *Anita paused for a moment, then said: 'All right'.* ◇ *The woman spoke almost without pausing for breath* (= very quickly). ◇ *I paused at the door and looked back.* ◇ *Pausing only to pull on a sweater, he ran out of the house.* **2** [T] ~ sth to stop a video, etc. for a short time using the pause button: *She paused the movie to go and answer the door.*
■ *noun* **1** [C] a period of time during which sb stops talking or stops what they are doing: *There was a long pause before she answered.* ◇ *After a brief pause, they continued climbing.* ◇ ~ **in sth** *David waited for a pause in the conversation so he could ask his question.* ◇ **without** ~ *The rain fell without pause.* **2** [C] (*especially BrE*) (*also* **fer·mata** *especially in NAmE*) (*music*) a sign (⌒) over a note or a REST to show that it should be longer than usual **3** [U] (*also* ˈpause

**button**) a control that allows you to stop a video, etc. for a short time: *Press pause to stop the film.*
**IDM** **give (sb) ˈpause** (*also* **give (sb) pause for ˈthought**) (*formal*) to make sb think seriously about sth or hesitate before doing sth ⊃ more at PREGNANT

**pav·ane** /pəˈvæn, -ˈvɑːn/ (*also* **pavan** /ˈpævən/) *noun* a slow dance popular in the 16th and 17th centuries; a piece of music for this dance

**pave** /peɪv/ *verb* [often passive] **~ sth (with sth)** to cover a surface with large flat stones: *a paved area near the back door*
**IDM** **ˌpave the ˈway (for sb/sth)** to create a situation in which sb will be able to do sth or sth can happen: *This decision paved the way for changes in employment rights for women.* ⊃ more at ROAD, STREET *n.*

**pave·ment** /ˈpeɪvmənt/ *noun* **1** [C] (*BrE*) (*NAmE* **ˈside·walk**) a flat part at the side of a road for people to walk on: *a pavement cafe* **2** [C, U] any area of flat stones on the ground: *a mosaic pavement* **3** [U] (*NAmE*) the surface of a road: *Two cars skidded on the icy pavement.*

**ˈpavement artist** (*BrE*) (*NAmE* **ˈsidewalk artist**) *noun* an artist who draws pictures in CHALK on the PAVEMENT, hoping to get money from people who pass

**pa·vil·ion** /pəˈvɪliən/ *noun* **1** a temporary building used at public events and exhibitions: *the US pavilion at the Trade Fair* **2** (*BrE*) a building next to a sports ground, used by players and people watching the game: *a cricket pavilion* **3** (*NAmE*) a large building used for sports or entertainment: *the Pauley Pavilion, home of the university's basketball team* **4** a building that is meant to be more beautiful than useful, built as a shelter in a park or used for concerts and dances: *his first show at the Winter Gardens Pavilion, Blackpool*

**pav·ing** /ˈpeɪvɪŋ/ *noun* [U] **1** a surface of flat stones or material like stone on the ground: *Weeds grew through the cracks in the paving.* **2** the stones or material that are used to make a flat surface on the ground: *We'll use concrete paving.*

**ˈpaving stone** *noun* a flat, usually square, piece of stone that is used to make a hard surface for walking on **SYN** **flagstone**

**pav·lova** /pævˈləʊvə/ *noun* a cold DESSERT (= sweet dish) made of MERINGUE, cream and fruit

**Pav·lov·ian** /pævˈləʊviən/ *adj.* (of an animal's or human's reaction) happening in response to a particular STIMULUS: *Her yawn was a Pavlovian response to my yawn.* **ORIGIN** From the name of the Russian scientist, I P Pavlov, who carried out experiments on dogs, showing how they could be conditioned to react to certain stimuli.

**paw** /pɔː/ *noun, verb*
▪ *noun* **1** the foot of an animal that has claws or nails ⊃ VISUAL VOCAB page V2 **2** (*informal*) a person's hand: *Take your filthy paws off me!*
▪ *verb* **1** [I, T] (of an animal) to SCRATCH or touch sth repeatedly with a paw: **~ at sth** *The dog pawed at my sleeve.* ◊ **~ sth** *The stallion pawed the ground impatiently.* **2** [T] **~ sb** (*sometimes humorous*) to touch sb in a rough sexual way that they find offensive

**pawn** /pɔːn/ *noun, verb*
▪ *noun* **1** a CHESS piece of the smallest size and least value. Each player has eight pawns at the start of a game. **2** a person or group whose actions are controlled by more powerful people: *The hostages are being used as political pawns.*
**IDM** **in pawn** if sth is **in pawn**, it has been pawned: *All her jewellery was in pawn.*
▪ *verb* **~ sth** to leave an object with a pawnbroker in exchange for money. The object is returned to the owner if he or she pays back the money within an agreed period of time. If not, it can be sold.

**pawn·broker** /ˈpɔːnbrəʊkə(r)/ *noun* a person who lends money in exchange for articles left with them. If the money is not paid back by a particular time, the pawnbroker can sell the article.

**Paw·nee** /pɔːˈniː/ *noun* (*pl.* **Paw·nee** *or* **Paw·nees**) a member of a Native American people, many of whom live in the US state of Oklahoma

**pawn·shop** /ˈpɔːnʃɒp; *NAmE* -ʃɑːp/ *noun* a pawnbroker's shop

**paw·paw** /ˈpɔːpɔː/ *noun* (*BrE*) = PAPAYA

# pay ⓘ A1 /peɪ/ *verb, noun*

▪ *verb* (**paid, paid** /peɪd/) **1** A1 [I, T] to give sb money for work, goods, services, etc: *Who's paying?* ◊ **for sth** *I'll pay for the tickets.* ◊ **sb for sth** *Let me pay you for your time.* ◊ **~ for sb to do sth** *Her parents paid for her to go to Canada.* ◊ **~ sb to do sth** *Would you mind paying the taxi driver?* ◊ **~ sb sth** *She's paid $200 a day.* ◊ **~ sth** *Let me pay the bill.* ◊ **~ by sth** *Are you paying by card?* ◊ **(in) sth** to pay (in) cash ◊ **~ sth for sth** *She pays £200 a week for this apartment.* ◊ **~ sb/sth to do sth** *I don't pay you to sit around all day doing nothing!* ⊃ see also LOW-PAID, PRE-PAY, WELL PAID ⊃ WORDFINDER NOTE at EMPLOY **2** A1 [T] to give sb money that you owe them: **~ sth** *to pay a fee/bill/fine/debt* ◊ *to pay your rent* ◊ *Everyone has to pay their taxes.* ◊ **~ sth to sb** *Membership fees should be paid to the secretary.* ◊ **~ sb sth** *He still hasn't paid me the money he owes me.* **3** A2 [I, T] (of an employer or a job) to give or provide a particular amount of money for the work that sb does: *Software firms generally pay well* (= pay high salaries). ◊ *jobs that pay less than £10 an hour* **4** A2 [T] used with some nouns to show that you are giving or doing the thing mentioned: **~ sth** *Most of the students weren't paying attention.* ◊ **~ sth to sth/sb** *The director paid tribute to all she had done for the charity.* ◊ *He paid a visit to Japan last year.* ◊ **~ sb sth** *I'll pay you a visit when I'm next in town.* **5** B2 [I, T] to produce a profit; to result in some advantage for sb: *It's hard to make farming pay.* ◊ *Crime doesn't pay.* ◊ **it pays to do sth** *It pays to keep up to date with your work.* ◊ **it pays sb to do sth** *It would probably pay you to hire an accountant.* **6** [I] to suffer or be punished for your beliefs or actions: **~ for sth** *You'll pay for that remark!* ◊ **~ with sth** *Many people paid with their lives* (= they died).
**IDM** **the ˌdevil/ˌhell to ˈpay** (*informal*) a lot of trouble: *There'll be hell to pay when he finds out.* **he who ˌpays the ˈpiper calls the ˈtune** (*saying*) the person who provides the money for sth can also control how it is spent **not pay sb/sth any ˈmind** (*NAmE*) to give no attention to sb/sth: *People call him names sometimes, but he doesn't pay them any mind.* **pay ˈcourt to sb** (*old-fashioned*) to treat sb with great respect in order to gain favour with them **ˌpay for itˈself** (of a new system, sth you have bought, etc.) to save as much money as it cost: *The rail pass will pay for itself after about two trips.* **pay ˌgood ˈmoney for sth** used to emphasize that sth cost(s) a lot of money, especially if the money is wasted: *I paid good money for this jacket, and now look at it—it's ruined!* **pay its ˈway** (of a business, etc.) to make enough money to pay what it costs to keep it going: *The bridge is still not paying its way.* **pay the/a ˈpenalty/ˈprice (for sth/for doing sth)** to suffer because of bad luck, a mistake or sth you have done: *He looked terrible this morning. I think he's paying the penalty for all those late nights.* ◊ *They're now paying the price for past mistakes.* ◊ *She thinks that any inconvenience is **a price worth paying** for living in such a beautiful place.* **pay your ˈdues** **1** to work hard and gain experience, so that you deserve success or respect **2** to do what is required or expected of you: *Vick paid his dues* (= completed his punishment), *and since being released from prison has been a model citizen.* **pay your reˈspects (to sb)** (*formal*) to visit sb or to send a message of good wishes as a sign of respect for them: *Many came to pay their last respects* (= by attending sb's funeral). **pay through the ˈnose (for sth)** (*informal*) to pay too much money for sth **pay your ˈway** to pay for everything yourself without having to rely on anyone else's money **ˌyou pays your ˌmoney and you ˌtakes your ˈchoice** (*informal, especially BrE*) used for saying that there is very little difference between two or more things that you can choose ⊃ more at ARM *n.*, HEED *n.*, ROB
**PHRV** **ˌpay sb ˈback (sth) | ˌpay sth↔ˈback (to sb)** to return money that you borrowed from sb **SYN** **repay:** *I'll pay you back next week.* ◊ *You can pay back the loan over a period of three years.* ◊ *Did he ever pay you back that $100 he owes you?* **ˌpay sb ˈback (for sth)** to punish sb for making you or sb else suffer: *I'll pay him back for making*

# payable

me look like a fool in front of everyone. ⇒ related noun PAYBACK **pay sth↔'down** (especially NAmE) to reduce an amount of money that you owe by paying some of it: *She used the money to pay down her mortgage.* **pay sth↔'in** | **pay sth 'into sth** to put money into a bank account: *I paid in a cheque this morning.* ◇ *I'd like to pay some money into my account.* **pay 'off** (informal) (of a plan or an action, especially one that involves risk) to be successful and bring good results: *The gamble paid off.* **pay sb↔'off 1** to pay sb what they have earned and tell them to leave their job: *The crew were paid off as soon as the ship docked.* **2** (informal) to give sb money to prevent them from doing sth or talking about sth illegal or dishonest that you have done: *All the witnesses had been paid off.* ⇒ related noun PAY-OFF **pay sth↔'off** to finish paying money owed for sth: *We paid off our mortgage after fifteen years.* **pay sth↔'out 1** to pay a large sum of money for sth: *I had to pay out £500 to get my car repaired.* ⇒ related noun PAYOUT **2** to pass a length of rope through your hands **pay 'up** to pay all the money that you owe to sb, especially when you do not want to or when the payment is late: *I had a hard time getting him to pay up.*

■ **noun** [U] the money that sb gets for doing regular work: *Her job is hard work, but the pay is good.* ◇ *workers on low pay* ◇ *Her monthly take-home pay after taxes $2 600.* ◇ *the principle of equal pay for equal work* ◇ *a pay increase/cut* (BrE) *a pay rise* ◇ (NAmE) *a pay raise* ◇ *a 3 per cent pay offer* ◇ *the pay gap between men and women* ⇒ see also HAZARD PAY, SICK PAY ⇒ SYNONYMS at INCOME

**WORDFINDER** bonus, commission, deduction, earn, overtime, rise, salary, tax, wage

**IDM** **in the pay of sb/sth** (usually disapproving) working for sb or for an organization, often secretly

**pay·able** /ˈpeɪəbl/ adj. [not before noun] **1** that must be paid or can be paid: *A 10 per cent deposit is payable in advance.* ◇ *The price is payable in monthly instalments.* **2** when a CHEQUE, etc. is made **payable to** sb, their name is written on it and they can then pay it into their bank account

**pay and dis'play** noun [U] (BrE) a system of car parking in which you buy a ticket from a machine for a period of time and put it in the window of the car

**pay as you 'earn** noun [U] = PAYE ⇒ compare WITH-HOLDING TAX

**pay-as-you-'go** adj. connected with a system of paying for a service just before you use it rather than paying for it later: *pay-as-you-go phones*

**pay·back** /ˈpeɪbæk/ noun [C, U] **1** the money that you receive back on money that you have invested (especially when this is equal to the amount that you invested to start with); the time that it takes to get your money back: *a 10-year payback* **2** the advantage or reward that sb receives for sth they have done; the act of paying sth back: *His victory was seen as payback for all the hard work he'd put in during training.* ◇ (informal) *It's payback time!* (= a person will have to suffer for what they have done)

**'pay channel** noun a television channel that you must pay for separately in order to watch it

**'pay cheque** (BrE) (US **pay·check** /ˈpeɪtʃek/) noun **1** the CHEQUE that you are given when your salary or wages are paid to you **2** (especially NAmE) a way of referring to the amount of money that you earn: *a huge paycheck*

**pay·day** /ˈpeɪdeɪ/ noun [U, C] the day on which you get your wages or salary: *Friday is payday.*

**payday 'loan** noun a small amount of money that sb borrows for a short time at a high rate of interest, agreeing that they will pay it back when they receive their next wages ▶ **payday 'lender** noun **payday 'lending** noun

**'pay dirt** noun [U] (especially NAmE) earth that contains valuable minerals or metal such as gold

**IDM** **hit/strike 'pay dirt** (informal) to suddenly be in a successful situation, especially one that makes you rich

**PAYE** /ˌpiː eɪ waɪ ˈiː/ abbr. pay as you earn (a British system of paying income tax in which money is taken from

your wages by your employer and paid to the government)

**payee** /ˌpeɪˈiː/ noun (specialist) a person that money or a CHEQUE is paid to

**'pay envelope** (NAmE) (BrE **'pay packet**, **'wage packet**) noun an ENVELOPE containing your wages; the amount a person earns

**payer** /ˈpeɪə(r)/ noun a person who pays or who has to pay for sth: *mortgage payers* ◇ *The company are not very good payers* (= they are slow to pay their bills, or they do not pay their employees well).

**pay-for-per'formance** adj. [only before noun] (NAmE) paying more or less money depending on how well a person does their job: *There has been an increase in pay-for-performance plans all over the US.* ⇒ compare PERFORMANCE (3), PERFORMANCE-RELATED

**'pay gap** (also **'wage gap**) noun the difference between the amount that two different groups of people are paid: *efforts to close the gender pay gap*

**paying 'guest** noun a person who pays to live in sb's house with them, usually for a short time

**pay·load** /ˈpeɪləʊd/ noun **1** the passengers or goods on a vehicle, especially an aircraft, for which payment is received **2** the equipment carried by a SPACECRAFT or satellite **3** the EXPLOSIVE power of a bomb or a MISSILE

**pay·mas·ter** /ˈpeɪmɑːstə(r)/; NAmE -mæs-/ noun **1** (usually disapproving) a person or group of people that pays another person or organization and therefore can control their actions **2** an official who pays the wages in the army, a factory, etc.

**pay·ment** ❶ B1 /ˈpeɪmənt/ noun **1** ❶ B1 [U] the act of paying sb/sth or of being paid: *payment in cash/by cheque* ◇ *~ for sth payment for goods/services* ◇ *on ~ of sth The public has right of access on payment of a fee.* ⇒ see also NON-PAYMENT **2** ❶ B1 [C] a sum of money paid or expected to be paid: *a cash payment* ◇ *It's important to make the payments on time.* ◇ *mortgage/interest payments* ◇ *~ on sth They are finding it difficult to meet the payments on their car.* ⇒ see also BALANCE OF PAYMENTS, DOWN PAYMENT **3** [U, sing.] a reward or an act of thanks for sth you have done **SYN** recompense: *~ (for sth) Is this all the payment I get for my efforts?* ◇ *in ~ for sth We'd like you to accept this gift in payment for your kindness.*

**IDM** **on payment of sth** after sth has been paid: *Entry is only allowed on payment of the full registration fee.*

**'pay-off** noun (informal) **1** a payment of money to sb so that they will not cause you any trouble or to make them keep a secret **SYN** bribe **2** a payment of money to sb to persuade them to leave their job **3** an advantage or a reward from sth you have done

**pay·ola** /peɪˈəʊlə/ noun [U] (NAmE, informal) the practice of giving or taking payments for doing sth illegal, especially for illegally influencing the sales of a particular product **SYN** bribery

**pay·out** /ˈpeɪaʊt/ noun a large amount of money that is given to sb: *an insurance payout* ◇ *a lottery payout*

**'pay packet** (also **'wage packet**) (both BrE) (NAmE **'pay envelope**) noun an ENVELOPE containing your wages; the amount a person earns

**pay-per-view** noun [U] a system of television broadcasting in which you pay to watch a particular programme, such as a film or a sports event

**pay·phone** /ˈpeɪfəʊn/ noun a phone, usually in a public place, that is operated using coins or a card

**pay·roll** /ˈpeɪrəʊl/ noun **1** a list of people employed by a company showing the amount of money to be paid to each of them: *We have 500 people on the payroll.* **2** [usually sing.] the total amount paid in wages by a company

**'payroll tax** noun [C, U] a tax that is based on the wages paid to employees and is paid either by employers or partly by employers and partly by employees

**pay·slip** /ˈpeɪslɪp/ (BrE) (NAmE **'pay stub**) noun a piece of paper given to an employee that shows how much money they have been paid and how much has been taken away for tax, etc.

## peace dividend

### ▼ SYNONYMS

**payment**
premium • contribution • subscription • repayment • deposit • instalment

These are all words for an amount of money that you pay or are expected to pay, or for the act of paying.

**payment** an amount of money that you pay or are expected to pay; the act of paying: *ten monthly payments of $50* ◊ *payment in advance*

**premium** an amount of money that you pay once or regularly for an insurance policy; an extra payment added to the basic rate; a higher amount of money than usual: *an insurance premium* ◊ *a premium for express delivery*

**contribution** a sum of money that you pay regularly to your employer or the government in order to pay for benefits such as health insurance, a pension, etc: *You can increase your monthly contributions to the pension plan.*

**subscription** an amount of money you pay in advance to receive a service: *a subscription to Netflix*

**repayment** (*BrE*) an amount of money that you pay regularly to a bank, etc. until you have returned all the money that you owe; the act of paying this money: *the repayments on the loan*

**deposit** an amount of money that you pay as the first part of a larger payment: *We've put down a 5 per cent deposit on the house.*

**instalment** one of a number of payments that you make regularly over a period of time until you have paid for sth: *We paid for the car by/in instalments.*

PATTERNS
- (a/an) **annual/monthly/regular** payment/premium/contributions/subscription/repayment/deposit/instalment
- payment/repayment **in full**
- to **pay** a(n) premium/contribution/subscription/deposit/instalment
- to **make** a payment/repayment/deposit
- to **meet/keep up (with)** (the) payment(s)/the premiums/(the) repayment(s)/the instalments

ˌpay ˈTV (*also* ˈpay television) *noun* [U] a system of television broadcasting in which you pay to watch particular television programmes or channels

ˈpay·wall /ˈpeɪwɔːl/ *noun* a feature of a website that prevents users from accessing certain web pages unless they have paid to use the website: **behind a ~** *The most interesting pages on the site are behind a paywall.*

**PB** /ˌpiː ˈbiː/ *abbr.* PERSONAL BEST

**PBS** /ˌpiː biː ˈes/ *abbr.* the Public Broadcasting Service (an organization in the US that broadcasts television programmes to local stations that do not show advertisements)

**PC** /ˌpiː ˈsiː/ *noun, abbr.*
- *noun* a computer that is designed for one person to use at work or at home (the abbreviation for 'personal computer')
- *abbr.* **1** (*BrE*) POLICE CONSTABLE ⊃see also WPC **2** POLITICALLY CORRECT

**PCB** /ˌpiː siː ˈbiː/ *noun* printed circuit board

**PCP** /ˌpiː siː ˈpiː/ *noun* **1** PRIMARY CARE PHYSICIAN **2** PRIMARY CARE PROVIDER

**PCSO** /ˌpiː siː es ˈəʊ/ *noun* (in England and Wales) a person who is not a police officer but works in an area to help the work of the police (the abbreviation for 'police community support officer')

**pct.** *abbr.* (NAmE) (in writing) per cent: *Today our sales in Eastern Europe amount to 18 pct.*

**PDA** /ˌpiː diː ˈeɪ/ *noun* (*informal*) the act of two people showing their feelings for each other in a place where others can see them (the abbreviation for 'public display of affection'): *The couple showed plenty of PDA while hanging out poolside.*

**PDF** /ˌpiː diː ˈef/ *noun* (*computing*) a file format that allows a document to be sent electronically and look exactly the same when viewed on different computer systems (the abbreviation for 'Portable Document Format'): *I'll send it to you as a PDF* (= a PDF file).

**p.d.q.** /ˌpiː diː ˈkjuː/ *abbr.* (*informal*) pretty damn/damned quick (= very fast): *Make sure you get here p.d.q.*

**PDT** /ˌpiː diː ˈtiː/ *abbr.* PACIFIC DAYLIGHT TIME

**PE** (*BrE*) (*US* **P.E.**) /ˌpiː ˈiː/ *noun* [U] sport and exercise that is taught in schools (the abbreviation for 'physical education'): *a PE class*

**pea** /piː/ *noun* a small round green seed, eaten as a vegetable. Several peas grow together inside a long thin POD on a climbing plant also called a pea: *frozen peas* ◊ *pea soup* ⊃VISUAL VOCAB page V5 ⊃see also CHICKPEA, MUSHY PEAS, SNOW PEA, SPLIT PEA, SWEET PEA

**peace** ⓘ A2 /piːs/ *noun* **1** ⚹A2 [U, sing.] a situation or a period of time in which there is no war or violence in a country or an area: *world peace* ◊ *in~ The two communities live together in peace.* ◊ *at~ The countries have been at peace for more than a century.* ◊ *peace talks/negotiations* ◊ *the peace process* ◊ *a peace treaty/accord/agreement/deal* ◊ *~ between A and B The negotiators are trying to* **make peace** *between the warring factions.* ◊ *to* **bring/promote/achieve/ensure peace** ◊ *After years of war, the people long for a* **lasting peace.**

WORDFINDER agreement, armistice, ceasefire, disengage, negotiate, reparations, surrender, treaty, truce

**2** ⚹B2 [U] the state of being calm or quiet: *She lay back and enjoyed the peace of the summer evening.* ◊ *I would work better if I had some* **peace and quiet.** ◊ *I need to check that she is all right, just for my own* **peace of mind** (= so that I do not have to worry). ◊ **at~(with yourself)** *He never really felt at peace with himself.* ◊ (*law*) *They were charged with* **disturbing the peace** (= behaving in a noisy and violent way). ◊ **in~** *He just wants to be left in peace* (= not to be disturbed). **3** ⚹B2 [U] the state of living in friendship with sb without arguing: **in~(with sb)** *They simply can't seem to live in peace with each other.* ◊ **at~ with sb/sth** *She felt at peace with the world.* ⊃see also BREACH *noun*, JUSTICE OF THE PEACE

**IDM** ▸ **hold your ˈpeace/ˈtongue** (*old-fashioned*) to say nothing although you would like to give your opinion **make (your) peace with sb** to end an argument with sb, usually by saying you are sorry ⊃more at WICKED *n.*

### ▼ HOMOPHONES

**peace • piece** /piːs/
- **peace** *noun*: *Hopes for peace between the two nations are fading.*
- **piece** *noun*: *Here's an interesting piece of information.*

### ▼ WHICH WORD?

**peace / peacefulness**
- The noun **peace** can be used to talk about a peaceful state or situation: *world peace* ◊ *I just need some peace and quiet.* **Peacefulness** is not a common word. It means 'the quality of being peaceful'.

**peace·able** /ˈpiːsəbl/ *adj.* (*formal or literary*) **1** not involving or causing argument or violence SYN **peaceful**: *A peaceable settlement has been reached.* **2** not liking to argue; wishing to live in peace with others SYN **peaceful, calm**: *a peaceable character* ▸ **peace·ably** /-bli/ *adv.*

**the ˈPeace Corps** *noun* [sing.] a US organization that sends young Americans to work in other countries without pay in order to create international friendship

**ˈpeace dividend** *noun* [usually sing.] money previously spent on weapons and the defence of a country and now available to be used for other things because of a reduction in a country's military forces

# peaceful

**peace·ful** ❶ B1 /ˈpiːsfl/ adj. **1** ⚡ B1 not involving a war, violence or argument: *a peaceful protest/demonstration* ◊ *a peaceful resolution to the war* **2** B1 quiet and calm; not worried or upset in any way SYN **tranquil**: *a peaceful atmosphere* ◊ *peaceful sleep* ◊ *It's so peaceful out here in the country.* ◊ *She lives a peaceful existence in a mountain village.* **3** ⚡ B1 trying to create peace or to live in peace; not liking violence or argument SYN **peaceable**: *a peaceful religion/society* ◊ *The aims of the organization are wholly peaceful.* ▶ **peace·ful·ly** /-fəli/ adv.: *The siege has ended peacefully.* ◊ *The baby slept peacefully.* **peace·ful·ness** noun [U]

**peace·keep·er** /ˈpiːskiːpə(r)/ noun **1** a member of a military force who has been sent to help stop people fighting in a place where war or violence is likely **2** a person who tries to stop people arguing or fighting: *She's the peacekeeper in that family.*

**peace·keep·ing** /ˈpiːskiːpɪŋ/ adj. [only before noun] intended to help stop people fighting and prevent war or violence in a place where this is likely: *peacekeeping operations* ◊ *a United Nations peacekeeping force*

**peace-loving** adj. preferring to live in peace and to avoid arguments and fighting SYN **peaceable**

**peace·maker** /ˈpiːsmeɪkə(r)/ noun a person who tries to persuade people or countries to stop arguing or fighting and to make peace

**peace·nik** /ˈpiːsnɪk/ noun (informal, sometimes disapproving) a PACIFIST (= sb who believes war and violence are always wrong and refuses to fight)

**peace offering** noun a present given to sb to show that you are sorry for sth or want to make peace after an argument

**peace officer** noun (NAmE) a person whose job is to make people obey the law

**peace pipe** noun a TOBACCO pipe offered and smoked as a symbol of peace by Native Americans

**peace process** noun [usually sing.] a series of talks and agreements designed to end war or violence between two groups

**peace·time** /ˈpiːstaɪm/ noun [U] a period of time when a country is not at war ⊃ compare WARTIME

**peach** /piːtʃ/ noun, adj.
- noun **1** [C] a round fruit with soft red and yellow skin, that is yellow inside with a large rough seed: *a peach tree* ⊃ VISUAL VOCAB page V2 ⊃ compare NECTARINE **2** [sing.] ~ (of a …) (old-fashioned, informal) a particularly good or attractive person or thing **3** [U] a colour between pink and orange
- adj. between pink and orange in colour

**peachy** /ˈpiːtʃi/ adj. **1** like a peach in colour or appearance: *pale peachy skin* **2** (NAmE, informal) fine; very nice: *Everything is just peachy.*

**pea coat** (also **pea jacket**) noun a type of thick short coat

**pea·cock** /ˈpiːkɒk/ NAmE -kɑːk/ noun a large male bird with long blue and green tail feathers that it can spread out like a fan: *as proud as a peacock* ⊃ see also PEAHEN

**pea·fowl** /ˈpiːfaʊl/ noun (pl. **pea·fowl**) a large PHEASANT found mainly in Asia. The male is called a peacock and the female is called a peahen.

**pea-green** adj. bright green in colour, like PEAS ▶ **pea green** noun [U]

**pea·hen** /ˈpiːhen/ noun a large brown bird, the female of the peacock

**peak** ⚡+ C1 /piːk/ noun, verb, adj.
- noun **1** ⚡+ C1 [usually sing.] the point when sb/sth is best, most successful, strongest, etc. SYN **height**: *Traffic reaches its peak between 8 and 9 in the morning.* ◊ *the peaks and troughs of married life* ◊ *at the ~ of sth She's at the peak of her career.* ⊃ compare OFF-PEAK ⚡+ ❶ the pointed top of a mountain; a mountain with a pointed top: *a mountain peak* ◊ *snow-capped/jagged peaks* ◊ *The climbers made camp halfway up the peak.* ⊃ HOMOPHONES at PEEK ⊃ WORDFINDER NOTE at MOUNTAIN **3** any narrow and pointed shape, edge, etc.: *Whisk the egg whites into stiff peaks.* **4** (BrE) (NAmE **bill**, **visor**) the stiff front part of a cap that sticks out above your eyes
- verb [I] to reach the highest point or value: *Oil production peaked in the early 1980s.* ◊ *Unemployment peaked at 17 per cent.* ◊ *an athlete who peaks* (= produces his or her best performance) *at just the right time* ⊃ HOMOPHONES at PEEK ⊃ WORDFINDER NOTE at TREND
- adj. [only before noun] used to describe the highest level of sth, or a time when the greatest number of people are doing sth or using sth: *It was a time of peak demand for the product.* ◊ *March is one of the peak periods for our business.* ◊ *The athletes are all in peak condition.* ◊ *We need extra help during the peak season.* ⊃ compare OFF-PEAK

**peaked** /piːkt/ adj. **1** having a peak **2** (NAmE) (BrE **peaky**) ill or pale

**peak 'oil** noun [U] the point in time when world oil production reaches its highest rate, after which it goes into permanent decline

**peak 'rate** noun the busiest time, which is therefore charged at the highest rate: *peak-rate phone calls*

**peak time** (also **peak 'viewing time**) noun (BrE) = PRIME TIME

**peaky** /ˈpiːki/ (BrE, informal) (NAmE **peaked**) adj. ill or pale: *You're looking a little peaky. Are you OK?*

**peal** /piːl/ noun, verb
- noun **1** ~ (of sth) a loud sound or series of sounds: *She burst into peals of laughter.* ◊ *A peal of thunder broke overhead.* **2** the loud ringing sound of a bell: *a peal of bells rang out* **3** a set of bells that all have different notes; a musical pattern that can be rung on a set of bells
- verb **1** [I] ~ (out) (of bells) to ring loudly: *The bells of the city began to peal out.* **2** [I] ~ (with sth) to suddenly laugh loudly: *Ellen pealed with laughter.*

**pea·nut** /ˈpiːnʌt/ noun **1** (BrE also **ground·nut**) [C] a nut that grows underground in a thin shell: *a packet of salted peanuts* ◊ *peanut oil* ⊃ VISUAL VOCAB page V8 **2 peanuts** [pl.] (informal) a very small amount of money: *He gets paid peanuts for doing that job.*

**peanut 'butter** noun [U] a thick soft substance made from peanuts, usually eaten spread on bread: *a peanut butter sandwich*

**pear** /peə(r); NAmE per/ noun a yellow or green fruit that is narrow at the top and wide at the bottom: *a pear tree* ⊃ VISUAL VOCAB page V4 ⊃ see also PRICKLY PEAR

▼ HOMOPHONES

**pair • pare • pear** /peə(r); NAmE per/
- **pair** noun: *He was dressed in a pair of jeans and a white T-shirt.*
- **pair** verb: *The teacher decided to pair able students with those who were struggling.*
- **pare** verb: *They had to pare the novel down for a two-hour film.*
- **pear** noun: *Dessert was a delicious poached pear in red wine.*

**pearl** /pɜːl; NAmE pɜːrl/ noun **1** [C] a small hard shiny white ball that forms inside the shell of an OYSTER and is of great value as a JEWEL: *a string of pearls* ◊ *a pearl necklace* ◊ *She was wearing her pearls* (= a NECKLACE of PEARLS). **2** [C] a copy of a pearl that is made artificially **3** [U] = MOTHER-OF-PEARL: *pearl buttons* **4** [C, usually sing.] a thing that looks like a pearl in shape or colour: *pearls of dew on the grass* **5** [C] a thing that is very highly valued: *She is a pearl among women.*
- IDM **cast, throw, etc. pearls before 'swine** to give or offer valuable things to people who do not understand their value **a pearl of 'wisdom** (usually ironic) a wise remark: *Thank you for those pearls of wisdom.*

**pearly** /ˈpɜːli; NAmE ˈpɜːrli/ adj. like a pearl in colour: *pearly white teeth*

**the Pearly 'Gates** noun [pl.] (humorous) the gates of heaven

**pear-shaped** adj. **1** like a pear in shape **2** a pear-shaped person is much wider around the lower part of their body than around the top part

**IDM** go 'pear-shaped (BrE, informal) if things **go pear-shaped**, they go wrong

**peas·ant** ⓘ+ **C1** /'peznt/ noun **1** ⓘ+ **C1** (especially in the past, or in poorer countries) a farmer who owns or rents a small piece of land: *peasant farmers* **2** (informal, disapproving) a person who is rude, behaves badly or has little education **SYN** lout

**peas·ant·ry** /'pezntri/ noun [sing. + sing./pl. v.] all the peasants in a region or country: *the local peasantry*

**peat** /pi:t/ noun [U] a soft black or brown substance formed from old or dying plants just under the surface of the ground, especially in cool wet areas. It is burned as a fuel or used to improve garden soil: *peat bogs* ▶ **peaty** /'pi:ti/ adj.: *peaty soils*

**peb·ble** /'pebl/ noun a smooth, round stone that is found in or near water

**pebbly** /'pebli/ adj. covered with pebbles: *a pebbly beach*

**pecan** /'pi:kən, pɪ'kæn; NAmE pɪ'ka:n/ noun the nut of the American **pecan tree** with a smooth pink-brown shell ⊃ VISUAL VOCAB page V8

**pecca·dillo** /,pekə'dɪləʊ/ noun (pl. **-oes** or **-os**) a small unimportant thing that sb does wrong

**pec·cary** /'pekəri/ (pl. **-ies**) noun an animal like a pig, which lives in the southern US, Mexico and Central and South America

**peck** /pek/ verb, noun
■ verb **1** [I, T] (of birds) to move the BEAK forward quickly and hit or bite sth: **~(at sth)** *A robin was pecking at crumbs on the ground.* ◊ **~ sth** *A bird had pecked a hole in the sack.* ◊ **~ sth out** *Vultures had pecked out the dead goat's eyes.* **2** [T] (informal) to kiss sb lightly and quickly: **~ sb on sth** *He pecked her on the cheek as he went out.* ◊ **~ sth** *She pecked his cheek.*
**IDM a/the 'pecking order** (informal, often humorous) the order of importance in relation to one another among the members of a group **SYN** hierarchy: *New Zealand is at the top of the pecking order of rugby nations.*
**PHR V** '**peck at sth** to eat only a very small amount of a meal because you are not hungry **SYN** pick at
■ noun **1** (informal) a quick kiss: *He gave her a friendly peck on the cheek.* **2** an act of pecking sb/sth: *The budgerigar gave a quick peck at the seed.*

**peck·er** /'pekə(r)/ noun (slang, especially NAmE) a PENIS

**peck·ish** /'pekɪʃ/ adj. (BrE, informal) slightly hungry

**pecs** /peks/ noun [pl.] (informal) = PECTORALS

**pec·tin** /'pektɪn/ noun [U] (chemistry) a substance similar to sugar that forms in fruit that is ready to eat, and is used to make JAM thick and solid as it is cooked

**pec·toral** /'pektərəl/ adj., noun
■ adj. (anatomy) relating to or connected with the chest or breast: *pectoral muscles* ⊃ VISUAL VOCAB page V2
■ noun **pectorals** (also informal **pecs**) [pl.] the muscles of the chest

**pe·cu·liar** ⓘ+ **C1** /pɪ'kju:liə(r)/ adj. **1** ⓘ+ **C1** strange or unusual, especially in a way that is unpleasant or makes you worried: *a peculiar smell/taste* ◊ *The meat tasted rather peculiar.* ◊ *There was something peculiar in the way he smiled.* ◊ *I had a peculiar feeling we'd met before.* ◊ *For some peculiar reason, she refused to come inside.* ⊃ compare ODD **2 ~(to sb/sth)** belonging or relating to one particular place, situation, person, etc., and not to others: *a humour that is peculiar to American sitcoms* ◊ *a species of bird peculiar to Asia* ◊ *He has his own peculiar style which you'll soon get used to.* ◊ *the peculiar properties of mercury* **3** (BrE, informal) slightly ill **IDM** see FUNNY

**pe·cu·li·ar·ity** /pɪ,kju:li'ærəti/ noun (pl. **-ies**) **1** [C] a strange or unusual feature or habit: *a physical peculiarity* **2** [C] a feature that only belongs to one particular person, thing, place, etc. **SYN** characteristic: *the cultural peculiarities of the English* **3** [U] the fact of being strange or unusual

**pe·cu·li·ar·ly** /pɪ'kju:liəli; NAmE -ərli/ adv. **1** very; more than usually **SYN** particularly, especially: *These plants are peculiarly prone to disease.* **2** in a way that relates to or is especially typical of one particular person, thing, place, etc. **SYN** uniquely: *He seemed to believe that it*

1139 **pedestrianize**

*was a peculiarly British problem.* **3** in a strange or unusual way

**pe·cu·ni·ary** /pɪ'kju:niəri; NAmE -nieri/ adj. (formal) relating to or connected with money: *pecuniary advantage*

**ped-** /pi:d, ped/ (NAmE) (BrE **paed-**) combining form (in nouns and adjectives) connected with children

**peda·gogic** /,pedə'gɒdʒɪk; NAmE -'gɑ:dʒ-/ (also **peda·gogical** /,pedə'gɒdʒɪkl; NAmE -'gɑ:dʒ-/) adj. (formal) relating to teaching methods: *pedagogic principles* ▶ **peda·gogic·al·ly** /-kli/ adv.

**peda·gogue** /'pedəgɒg; NAmE -gɑ:g/ noun (old use or formal) a teacher; a person who likes to teach people things, especially because they think they know more than other people

**peda·gogy** /'pedəgɒdʒi; NAmE -gɑ:dʒi/ noun [U] (specialist) the study of teaching methods

**pedal** /'pedl/ noun, verb
■ noun **1** a flat bar on a machine such as a bicycle, car, etc. that you push down with your foot in order to make parts of the machine move or work: *I couldn't reach the pedals on her bike.* ◊ *She pressed her foot down sharply on the brake pedal.* ⊃ see also GAS PEDAL ⊃ WORDFINDER NOTE at CYCLING **2** a bar on a musical instrument such as a piano or an organ that you push with your foot in order to control the sound
**IDM put the pedal to the metal** (also **with the pedal to the metal**) (NAmE, informal) **1** (to go) at full speed; (to drive) with the ACCELERATOR of the car pressed to the floor: *We drove through the night flat-out, with the pedal to the metal.* **2** to use as much effort as possible; with as much effort as possible: *I'm still putting the pedal to the metal here at work.*
■ verb (**-ll-**, US **-l-**) **1** [I, T] to ride a bicycle somewhere: **+ adv./prep.** *I saw her pedalling along the towpath.* ◊ *He jumped on his bike and pedalled off.* ◊ **~ sth + adv./prep.** *She pedalled her bicycle up the track.* **2** [I, T] to turn or press the pedals on a bicycle or other machine: (**+ adv./prep.**) *You'll have to pedal hard up this hill.* ◊ **~ sth** *She had been pedalling her exercise bike all morning.* ⊃ see also BACK-PEDAL

**ped·ant** /'pednt/ noun (disapproving) a person who is too concerned with small details or rules especially when learning or teaching

**pe·dan·tic** /pɪ'dæntɪk/ adj. (disapproving) too worried about small details or rules ▶ **pe·dan·tic·al·ly** /-kli/ adv.

**ped·ant·ry** /'pedntri/ noun [U] (disapproving) too much attention to small details or rules

**ped·dle** /'pedl/ verb **1 ~ sth** to try to sell goods by going from house to house or from place to place: *He worked as a door-to-door salesman peddling cloths and brushes.* ◊ *to peddle illegal drugs* **2 ~ sth** (usually disapproving) to spread an idea or story in order to get people to accept it: *to peddle malicious gossip* ◊ *This line* (= publicly stated opinion) *is being peddled by all the government spokesmen.*

**ped·dler** /'pedlə(r)/ noun **1** (BrE) a person who sells illegal drugs or stolen goods: *a drug peddler* **2** (NAmE) (BrE **ped·lar**) a person who in the past travelled from place to place trying to sell small objects

**ped·es·tal** /'pedɪstl/ noun the base that a column, statue, etc. rests on: *a pedestal basin* (= a WASHBASIN supported by a column) ◊ *I replaced the vase carefully on its pedestal*
**IDM to put/place sb on a 'pedestal** to admire sb so much that you do not see their faults ⊃ more at KNOCK v.

**ped·es·trian** /pə'destriən/ noun, adj.
■ noun a person walking in the street and not travelling in a vehicle: *a pedestrian walkway/bridge* ⊃ compare MOTORIST ⊃ WORDFINDER NOTE at TRAFFIC
■ adj. without any imagination or excitement; boring **SYN** unimaginative

**pe,destrian 'crossing** (BrE) (NAmE **cross·walk**) noun a part of a road where vehicles must stop to allow people to cross ⊃ see also ZEBRA CROSSING

**ped·es·tri·an·ize** (BrE also **-ise**) /pə'destriənaɪz/ verb [usually passive] to make a street or part of a town into an area

Oxford Phrasal Academic Lexicon (OPAL) written and spoken word lists | **W** OPAL written word list | **S** OPAL spoken word list

# pedestrian precinct

that is only for people who are walking, not for vehicles
▶ **ped·es·tri·an·iza·tion**, **-isa·tion** /pəˌdestriənaɪˈzeɪʃn; *NAmE* -nəˈz-/ *noun* [U]

**pe·destrian ˈprecinct** (*BrE*) (*NAmE* **pe·destrian ˈmall**) *noun* a part of a town, especially a shopping area, that vehicles are not allowed to enter

**pedia·tri·cian** (*NAmE*) (*BrE* **paedia·tri·cian**) /ˌpiːdiəˈtrɪʃn/ *noun* a doctor who studies and treats the diseases of children

**pedi·at·rics** (*NAmE*) (*BrE* **paedi·at·rics**) /ˌpiːdiˈætrɪks/ *noun* [U] the branch of medicine that deals with children and their diseases▶ **pedi·at·ric** (*NAmE*) (*BrE* **paedi-**) *adj.*

**pedi·cab** /ˈpedikæb/ *noun* a small vehicle with three wheels, operated by PEDALS like a bicycle, used as a taxi in some countries⇨ see also RICKSHAW

**pedi·cure** /ˈpedikjʊə(r); *NAmE* -kjʊr/ *noun* [C, U] care and treatment of the feet and TOENAILS⇨ compare MANICURE

**pedi·gree** /ˈpedɪgriː/ *noun, adj.*
■ *noun* **1** [C] the parents, grandparents, etc. of an animal that are all of the same BREED (= type); an official record showing this: *dogs with good pedigrees* (= their ANCESTORS are known and of the same breed) **2** [C, U] a person's family history or the background of sth, especially when this is impressive: *She was proud of her long pedigree.* ◊ *The product has a pedigree going back to the last century.*
■ *adj.* (*BrE*) (*NAmE usually* **pedi·greed**) [only before noun] (of an animal) coming from a family of the same BREED that has been officially recorded for a long time and is thought to be of a good quality: *pedigree sheep*

**pedi·ment** /ˈpedɪmənt/ *noun* (*architecture*) the part in the shape of a TRIANGLE above the entrance of a building in the ancient Greek style

**ped·lar** (*BrE*) (*NAmE* **ped·dler**) /ˈpedlə(r)/ *noun* a person who in the past travelled from place to place trying to sell small objects

**ped·ometer** /pɪˈdɒmɪtə(r); *NAmE* -ˈdɑːm-/ *noun* an instrument for measuring how far you have walked

**pedo·phile** (*NAmE*) (*BrE* **paedo-**) /ˈpiːdəfaɪl; *NAmE also* ˈped-/ *noun* a person who is sexually attracted to children

**pedo·philia** (*NAmE*) (*BrE* **paedo-**) /ˌpiːdəˈfɪliə; *NAmE also* ˌped-/ *noun* [U] the condition of being sexually attracted to children; sexual activity with children

**pee** /piː/ *verb, noun*
■ *verb* [I] (*informal*) (**peed**, **peed**) to pass waste liquid from your body SYN *urinate*. SYN *to pee*.
■ *noun* (*informal*) **1** [sing.] an act of passing liquid waste from your body: (*BrE*) *to go for a pee* ◊ *to have a pee* ◊ (*NAmE*) *to take a pee* **2** [U] liquid waste passed from your body; URINE

**peek** /piːk/ *verb* **1** [I] to look at sth quickly and secretly because you should not be looking at it SYN *peep*: *No peeking!* ◊ *+ adv./prep. She peeked at the audience from behind the curtain.* ◊ *I couldn't resist peeking in the drawer.* **2** [I] **~ out/over/through, etc.** to be just able to be seen: *Her feet peeked out from the end of the blanket.* ▶ **peek** *noun* [sing.]: *I took a quick peek inside.* ⇨ see also SNEAK PEEK

▼ HOMOPHONES
**peak** • **peek** • **pique** /piːk/
- **peak** *noun*: *Mount McKinley is the highest peak in North America.*
- **peak** *verb*: *Birdsong tends to peak in the spring mating season.*
- **peek** *verb*: *I have to peek out from behind a cushion when watching horror films.*
- **peek** *noun*: *She sneaked a peek at her watch.*
- **pique** *noun*: *He smashed his racket in a fit of pique.*
- **pique** *verb*: *He knew the cutting remark would pique his friend's vanity.*

**peek·aboo** /ˈpiːkəbuː/ (*BrE also* **peep-bo**) *noun* [U] a simple game played to entertain young children, in which you keep hiding your face and then showing it again, saying 'Peekaboo!' or 'Peep-bo!'

**peel** /piːl/ *verb, noun*
■ *verb* **1** [T] **~sth** to take the outer layer off fruit, vegetables, etc: *to peel an orange/a banana* ◊ *Have you peeled the potatoes?* **2** [T, I] to remove a layer, etc. from the surface of sth; to come off the surface of sth: **~sth away/off/back** *Carefully peel away the lining paper.* ◊ **~away/off/back** *The label will peel off if you soak it in water.* ◊ **~sth from sth** *He peeled the wet clothes from his back.* **3** [I] **~(off)** (of a layer that covers sth) to come off in narrow or small pieces: *The wallpaper was beginning to peel.* **4** [I] (of a surface) to lose narrow or small pieces of sth that covers sth: *Put on some cream to stop your nose from peeling.* ◊ *The walls have begun to peel.* IDM see EYE *n.*
PHRV **ˌpeel ˈoff** to leave a group of vehicles, aircraft, etc. and turn to one side: *The leading car in the motorcade peeled off to the right.* ˌpeel **ˈoff** | ˌpeel (sth) ↔ **off** (*informal*) to remove some or all of your clothes: *You look hot—why don't you peel off?* ◊ *He peeled off his shirt.* ˌpeel **ˈout** (*NAmE*, *informal*) to leave quickly and in a noisy way, especially in a car, on a motorcycle, etc.
■ *noun* **1** [U, C] the thick outer layer of some fruits and vegetables: *orange/lemon peel* ◊ (*NAmE also*) *an orange/a lemon peel*⇨ VISUAL VOCAB page V4⇨ compare RIND, SKIN, ZEST **2** **peels** [pl.] (*NAmE*) = PEELINGS

**peel·er** /ˈpiːlə(r)/ *noun* (usually in compounds) a special type of knife for taking the skin off fruit and vegetables: *a potato peeler*

**peel·ings** /ˈpiːlɪŋz/ (*NAmE also* **peels**) *noun* [pl.] the skin of fruit or vegetables that has been removed

**peep** /piːp/ *verb, noun*
■ *verb* **1** [I] **(+ adv./prep.)** to look quickly and secretly at sth, especially through a small opening: *We caught her peeping through the keyhole.* ◊ *Could I just peep inside?* ◊ *He was peeping at her through his fingers.* **2** [I] **+ adv./prep.** to be just able to be seen: *The tower peeped above the trees.* ◊ *The sun peeped out from behind the clouds.* **3** [I, T] **~(sth)** to make a short high sound; to make sth make this sound
■ *noun* **1** [C, usually sing.] a quick or secret look at sth: *Dave took a quick peep at the last page.* **2** [sing.] (*informal*) something that sb says or a sound that sb makes: *We did not hear a peep out of the baby all night.* **3** [C] a short high sound like the one made by a young bird or by a WHISTLE (= a small metal or plastic tube that you blow to make a high sound) **4** (*also* ˌpeep ˈpeep) [C] (*BrE*) a word for the sound of a car's HORN, used especially by children

**peep-bo** /ˈpiːp bəʊ; ˈpiːpəʊ/ *noun* [U] (*BrE*) = PEEKABOO

**peep·hole** /ˈpiːphəʊl/ *noun* a small opening in a wall, door, etc. that you can look through

**Peeping ˈTom** *noun* (*disapproving*) a person who likes to watch people secretly when they are taking off their clothes SYN *voyeur*

**peeps** /piːps/ *noun* [pl.] (*informal*) people, especially friends, colleagues or people that you are addressing in a group email, blog, etc: *I spoke to the marketing peeps this morning.*

**ˈpeep show** *noun* **1** a series of moving pictures in a box that you look at through a small opening **2** a type of show in which sb pays to watch a woman take off her clothes in a small room

**peer** B2 /pɪə(r); *NAmE* pɪr/ *noun, verb*
■ *noun* **1** B2 [usually pl.] a person who is the same age or who has the same social status as you: *She enjoys the respect of her peers.* ◊ *Children are worried about failing in front of their peers.* ◊ *Peer pressure is strong among young people* (= they want to be like other people of the same age). **2** C1 (in the UK) a member of the NOBILITY or the HOUSE OF LORDS: *MPs and peers from all parties met to discuss the issue.*⇨ see also LIFE PEER, PEERESS
■ *verb* [I] **(+ adv./prep.)** to look closely or carefully at sth, especially when you cannot see it clearly: *We peered into the shadows.* ◊ *He went to the window and peered out.* ◊ *She kept peering over her shoulder.* ◊ *He peered closely at the photograph.*⇨ SYNONYMS at STARE

**peer·age** /ˈpɪərɪdʒ; *NAmE* ˈpɪr-/ *noun* **1** [sing.] all the peers as a group: *a member of the peerage* **2** [C] the rank of a peer or peeress

**peer·ess** /ˈpɪərəs; NAmE ˈpɪrəs/ noun a female PEER

**ˈpeer group** noun a group of people of the same age or social status: *She gets on well with her peer group.* ◊ *peer-group pressure*

**peer·less** /ˈpɪələs; NAmE ˈpɪrl-/ adj. better than all others of its kind SYN **unsurpassed**: *a peerless performance*

**ˈpeer pressure** noun [U] pressure from people of your age or social group to behave like them in order to be liked or accepted: *Teenagers are highly influenced by peer pressure.*

**peer reˈview** noun [U, C] a judgement on a piece of scientific or other professional work by others working in the same area: *All research proposals are subject to peer review before selection.* ▸ **peer-reˈviewed** adj.: *peer-reviewed journals*

**peer-to-ˈpeer** adj. [only before noun] (*computing*) (of a computer system) in which each computer can act as a SERVER for the others, allowing data to be shared without the need for a central server ⊃ compare CLIENT-SERVER

**peeve** /piːv/ noun
IDM ▸ **sb's pet ˈpeeve** (*especially NAmE*) (*BrE usually* **sb's pet ˈhate**) something that you particularly dislike

**peeved** /piːvd/ adj. ~ **(about/at/by sth)** (*informal*) annoyed: *He sounded peeved about not being told.*

**peev·ish** /ˈpiːvɪʃ/ adj. easily annoyed, often by things that are not important SYN **irritable** ▸ **peev·ish·ly** adv.

**peewee** /ˈpiːwiː/ noun, adj.
■ noun (NAmE, informal) a person or thing that is very small or smaller than usual: *I was a real peewee until I turned 13.*
■ adj. (NAmE, informal) very small; relating to small children: *Our 8-year-old is in a peewee baseball league.*

**pegs**

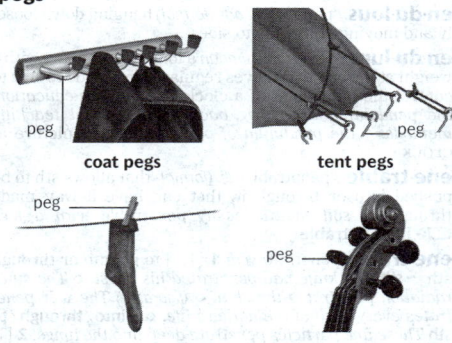

coat pegs    tent pegs
clothes peg / clothespin    tuning pegs

**peg** /peg/ noun, verb
■ noun 1 a short piece of wood, metal or plastic used for holding things together, hanging things on, marking a position, etc: *There's a peg near the door to hang your coat on.* 2 (*also* **tent peg**) a small pointed piece of wood or metal that you attach to the ropes of a tent and push into the ground in order to hold the tent in place 3 (*also* **clothes peg**) (*both BrE*) (*NAmE* **clothes·pin**) a piece of wood or plastic used for attaching wet clothes to a clothes line 4 (*also* **tuning peg**) a short piece of wood, metal or plastic that you turn to make the strings of a musical instrument tighter or looser 5 (*IndE*) a small amount of a drink, especially a strong alcoholic one: *a peg of whisky*
IDM ▸ **bring/take sb ˈdown a peg (or two)** to make sb realize that they are not as good, important, etc. as they think they are: *He needed to be taken down a peg or two.* **ˌoff the ˈpeg** (*BrE*) (*NAmE* **off the ˈrack**) (of clothes) made to a standard average size and not made especially to fit you: *He buys his clothes off the peg.* ◊ *off-the-peg fashions* **a peg to ˈhang sth on** something that gives you an excuse or opportunity to discuss or explain sth ⊃ more at SQUARE adj.
■ verb (-gg-) 1 to fasten sth with pegs: ~ *sth (out)* + adv./prep. *All their wet clothes were pegged out on the line.* ◊ ~ *sth to sth She was busy pegging her tent to the ground.* 2 [usually passive] to fix or keep prices, wages, etc. at a particular level: **be pegged (at sth)** *Pay increases will be pegged at 5 per cent.* ◊ **be pegged (to sth)** *Loan repayments are pegged to your income.* 3 ~ **sb as sth** (NAmE, informal) to think of sb in a particular way: *She pegged him as a big spender.* IDM see LEVEL adj.
PHRV ▸ **ˌpeg aˈway (at sth)** (*informal, especially BrE*) to continue working hard at sth or trying to achieve sth difficult **ˌpeg sb/sth⇿ˈback** (*especially BrE*) (*especially in sport*) to stop sb/sth from winning or increasing the amount by which they are ahead: *Each time we scored we were pegged back minutes later.* **ˌpeg ˈout** (BrE, informal) to die

**pe·jora·tive** /pɪˈdʒɒrətɪv; NAmE -ˈdʒɔːr-/ adj. (*formal*) a word or remark that is **pejorative** expresses DISAPPROVAL or criticism SYN **derogatory**: *I'm using the word 'academic' here in a pejorative sense.* ▸ **pe·jora·tive·ly** adv.

**Pe·kin·ese** (*also* **Pe·king·ese**) /ˌpiːkɪˈniːz/ noun (pl. **Pe·kin·ese** or **Pe·kin·eses**) a very small dog with long soft hair, short legs and a flat nose

**pe·la·gic** /pəˈlædʒɪk/ adj. (*specialist*) connected with, or living in, the parts of the sea that are far from land

**peli·can** /ˈpelɪkən/ noun a large bird that lives near water, with a bag of skin under its long BEAK for storing food

**pelican ˈcrossing** noun (in the UK) a place on a road where you can stop the traffic and cross by operating a set of TRAFFIC LIGHTS

**pel·lagra** /pəˈlægrə; NAmE -ˈlɑːg-/ noun [U] a disease caused by a lack of good food, that causes the skin to CRACK (= break) and may lead to mental illness

**pel·let** /ˈpelɪt/ noun 1 a small hard ball of any substance, often of soft material that has become hard: *food pellets for chickens* 2 a very small metal ball that is fired from a gun

**Pel·man·ism** /ˈpelmənɪzəm/ noun [U] a game in which players must remember cards or other objects that they have seen

**pel·met** /ˈpelmɪt/ (*also* **val·ance** *especially in NAmE*) noun a narrow piece of wood or cloth above a window that hides the curtain RAIL

**the pelo·ton** /ðə ˈpelətɒn; NAmE -tɑːn/ noun [sing.] (from French) the main group of riders in a bicycle race

**pelt** /pelt/ verb, noun
■ verb 1 [T] ~ **sb (with sth)** to attack sb by throwing things at them: *The children pelted him with snowballs.* 2 [I] ~ **(down)** (of rain) to fall very heavily 3 [I] + adv./prep. (*informal*) to run somewhere very fast SYN **dash**: *We pelted down the hill after the car.*
■ noun the skin of an animal, especially with the fur or hair still on it
IDM ▸ **(at) full ˈpelt/ˈtilt** as fast as possible

**ˌpelvic ˈfloor** noun (*anatomy*) the muscles at the base of the ABDOMEN, attached to the pelvis

**pel·vis** /ˈpelvɪs/ noun the wide curved set of bones at the bottom of the body that the legs and SPINE are connected to ⊃ VISUAL VOCAB page V1 ▸ **pel·vic** /-vɪk/ adj. [only before noun]: *the pelvic bones*

**pen** ⓘ A1 /pen/ noun, verb
■ noun 1 ⓘ A1 (often in compounds) an instrument made of plastic or metal used for writing with INK (= coloured liquid for writing, etc.): *to use pen and paper* ◊ **in** ~ *a message written in red pen* (= using a red pen) ◊ **from the** ~ **of sb** (*figurative*) *a new book from the pen of* (= written by) *Zadie Smith* ⊃ see also BALLPOINT PEN at BALLPOINT, FELT-TIP PEN, FOUNTAIN PEN, LIGHT PEN 2 a small piece of land surrounded by a fence in which farm animals are kept: *a sheep pen* 3 (NAmE, informal) = PENITENTIARY
IDM ▸ **the ˌpen is ˌmightier than the ˈsword** (*saying*) people who write books, poems, etc. have a greater effect on history and human affairs than soldiers and wars **ˌput pen to ˈpaper** to write or start to write sth ⊃ more at SLIP n.
■ verb (-nn-) 1 ~ **sth** (*formal*) to write sth: *He penned a letter to the local paper.* 2 ~ **sb/sth (in/up)** to shut an animal or a person in a small space: *At clipping time sheep need to be penned.* ◊ *The whole family were penned up in one room for a month.*

# penal 1142

**pen·al** /ˈpiːnl/ *adj.* [usually before noun] **1** connected with or used for punishment, especially by law: *penal reforms* ◊ *the penal system* ◊ *Criminals could at one time be sentenced to penal servitude* (= prison with hard physical work). ◊ *a penal colony* (= a place where criminals were sent as a punishment in the past) **2** that can be punished by law: *a penal offence* **3** very severe: *penal rates of interest*

**'penal code** *noun* a system of laws connected with crime and punishment

**pen·al·ize** (*BrE also* **-ise**) /ˈpiːnəlaɪz/ *verb* **1** ~ **sb** (**for sth**) to punish sb for breaking a rule or law by making them suffer a disadvantage: *You will be penalized for poor spelling.* **2** to punish sb for breaking a rule in a sport or game by giving an advantage to their opponent: ~ **sb** (**for sth**) *He was penalized for time-wasting.* ◊ ~ **sth** *Foul play will be severely penalized.* **3** ~ **sb** to put sb at a disadvantage by treating them unfairly: *The new law appears to penalize the poorest members of society.*

**pen·al·ty** /ˈpenəlti/ *noun* (*pl.* -**ies**) **1** a punishment for breaking a law, rule or contract: *to impose a penalty* ◊ *Assault carries a maximum penalty of seven years' imprisonment.* ◊ ~ **for (doing) sth** *The penalty for travelling without a ticket is £100.* ◊ *Contractors who fall behind schedule incur heavy financial penalties.* ◊ *a penalty clause in a contract* ◊ **without** ~ *You can withdraw money from the account at any time without penalty.* ◊ **on** ~ **of sth** *The Romans prohibited the teaching of the Torah on penalty of death.* ⇒ see also DEATH PENALTY **2** ~ (**of sth**) a disadvantage suffered as a result of sth: *One of the penalties of fame is loss of privacy.* **3** (in sports and games) a disadvantage given to a player or a team when they break a rule: *He incurred a ten-second penalty in the first round.* **4** (in football (soccer) and some other similar sports) a chance to score a goal or point without any defending players, except the GOALKEEPER, trying to stop it; the goal or point that is given if it is successful. This chance is given because the other team has broken the rules: *Two minutes later Ford equalized with a penalty.* ◊ *We were awarded a penalty after a late tackle.* ◊ *I volunteered to take the penalty* (= be the person who tries to score the goal/point) ◊ *He missed a penalty in the last minute of the game.* **IDM** see PAY *v.*

**'penalty area** (*BrE also* **'penalty box, area**) *noun* (in football (soccer)) the area in front of the goal. If the defending team breaks the rules within this area, the other team is given a penalty.

**'penalty box** *noun* **1** (*BrE*) = PENALTY AREA **2** (in ICE HOCKEY) an area next to the ice where a player who has broken the rules must wait for a short time

**'penalty kick** (*BrE also* **'spot kick**) *noun* a kick that is taken as a PENALTY in the game of football (soccer)

**'penalty point** *noun* (*BrE*) a note on sb's DRIVING LICENCE showing they have committed an offence while driving

**'penalty 'shoot-out** *noun* (in football (soccer)) a way of deciding the winner when both teams have the same score at the end of a game. Each team is given a number of chances to kick the ball into the goal and the team that scores the most goals wins.

**'penalty spot** *noun* (in football (soccer), hockey etc.) the point on the pitch from which a player takes a penalty

**pen·ance** /ˈpenəns/ *noun* **1** [C, usually sing., U] (especially in particular religions) an act that you give yourself to do, or that a priest gives you to do, in order to show that you are sorry for sth bad you have done wrong: *an act of penance* ◊ ~ **for sth** *to do penance for your sins* **2** [sing.] something that you have to do even though you do not like doing it: *She regards living in New York as a penance; she hates big cities.*

**pen-and-'ink** *adj.* [usually before noun] drawn with a pen: *pen-and-ink drawings*

**pence** /pens/ (*BrE*) (*abbr.* **p**) *pl.* of PENNY

**pen·chant** /ˈpɒ̃ʃɒ̃; *NAmE* ˈpentʃənt/ *noun* ~ **for sth** a special liking for sth **SYN** **fondness**: *She has a penchant for champagne.*

**pen·cil** /ˈpensl/ *noun, verb*
■ *noun* **1** [C, U] a narrow piece of wood, or a metal or plastic case, containing a black or coloured substance, used for drawing or writing: *I'll get a pencil and paper.* ◊ *coloured pencils* ◊ *I need to sharpen my pencil.* ◊ **in** ~ *She scribbled a note in pencil.* ◊ *a pencil drawing/sketch* ⇒ see also EYEBROW PENCIL
■ *verb* (**-ll-**, *US* **-l-**) ~ **sth** to write, draw or mark sth with a pencil: *a pencilled portrait* ◊ *A previous owner had pencilled 'First Edition' inside the book's cover.*
**PHRV** **'pencil sth/sb**⇔**'in** to write down sb's name or details of an arrangement with them that you know might have to be changed later: *We've pencilled in a meeting for Tuesday afternoon.* ◊ *Shall I pencil you in for Friday?* (= for a meeting)

**'pencil case** *noun* a small bag, etc. for holding pencils and pens

**'pencil pusher** *noun* (*NAmE*) = PEN-PUSHER

**'pencil sharpener** *noun* a small device with a BLADE (= cutting edge) inside, used for making pencils sharp

**'pencil skirt** *noun* a narrow straight skirt

**pen·dant** /ˈpendənt/ *noun* a piece of jewellery that you wear around your neck on a chain

**pend·ing** /ˈpendɪŋ/ *prep., adj.*
■ *prep.* (*formal*) while waiting for sth to happen; until sth happens: *He was released on bail pending further inquiries.*
■ *adj.* (*formal*) **1** waiting to be decided or settled: *Nine cases are still pending.* ◊ *a pending file/tray* (= where you put letters, etc. you are going to deal with soon) **2** going to happen soon **SYN** **imminent**: *An election is pending in Italy.* ◊ *his pending departure*

**'pen drive** *noun* = FLASH DRIVE

**pen·du·lous** /ˈpendʒələs/ *adj.* (*formal*) hanging down loosely and moving from side to side

**pen·du·lum** /ˈpendʒələm/ *noun* a long straight part with a weight at the end that moves regularly from side to side to control the movement of a clock: (*figurative*) *In education, the pendulum has swung back to traditional teaching methods.* ◊ *the pendulum of public opinion* ⇒ picture at CLOCK

**pene·trable** /ˈpenɪtrəbl/ *adj.* (*formal*) that allows sth to be pushed into or through it; that can have a way made through it: *soil that is easily penetrable with a fork* **OPP** **impenetrable**

**pene·trate** /ˈpenətreɪt/ *verb* **1** [T, I] to go into or through sth: ~ **sth** *The knife had penetrated his chest.* ◊ *The sun's radiation penetrates the skin.* ◊ (*figurative*) *The war penetrates every area of the nation's life.* ◊ ~ **into/through/to sth** *These fine particles penetrate deep into the lungs.* **2** [T, I] to succeed in entering or joining an organization, a group, etc. especially when this is difficult to do: ~ **sth** *They had penetrated airport security.* ◊ *The party has been penetrated by extremists.* ◊ *This year the company has been trying to penetrate new markets* (= to start selling their products there). ◊ ~ **into sth** *The troops had penetrated deep into enemy lines.* **3** [T] ~ **sth** to see or show a way into or through sth: *Our eyes could not penetrate the darkness.* ◊ *The flashlights barely penetrated the gloom.* **4** [T] ~ **sth** to understand or discover sth that is difficult to understand or is hidden: *Science can penetrate many of nature's mysteries.* **5** [I, T] to be understood or realized by sb: *I was at the door before his words penetrated.* ◊ ~ **sth** *None of my advice seems to have penetrated his thick skull* (= he has not listened to any of it). **6** [T] ~ **sb/sth** (of a man) to put the PENIS into the VAGINA or ANUS of a sexual partner

**pene·trat·ing** /ˈpenətreɪtɪŋ/ *adj.* **1** (of sb's eyes or the way they look at you) making you feel uncomfortable because the person seems to know what you are thinking: *penetrating blue eyes* ◊ *a penetrating gaze/look/stare* **2** (of a sound or voice) loud and hard **SYN** **piercing**: *Her voice was shrill and penetrating.* **3** showing that you have understood sth quickly and completely: *a penetrating comment/criticism/question* **4** spreading deeply or widely: *a penetrating smell* ◊ *the penetrating cold/damp*

**pene·tra·tion** /ˌpenəˈtreɪʃn/ *noun* [U] **1** the act or process of making a way into or through sth: *The floor is sealed to* *prevent water penetration.* ◊ *the company's successful penetration of overseas markets* **2** the act of a man putting his PENIS into his partner's VAGINA or ANUS

**pen·e·tra·tive** /ˈpenətrətɪv; *NAmE* -treɪt-/ *adj.* **1** (of sexual activity) involving putting the PENIS into sb's VAGINA or ANUS: *penetrative sex* **2** able to make a way into or through sth: *penetrative weapons* **3** detailed and complete: *a penetrative survey*

**pen·friend** /ˈpenfrend/ (*BrE*) (*also* **pen pal** *NAmE, BrE*) *noun* a person that you make friends with by writing letters or emails, often sb you have never met

**pen·guin** /ˈpeŋgwɪn/ *noun* a black and white bird that lives in the Antarctic. Penguins cannot fly but use their wings for swimming. There are several types of penguin, some of them very large but some of them quite small.

**peni·cil·lin** /ˌpenɪˈsɪlɪn/ *noun* [U] a substance obtained from MOULD, used as a drug to treat or prevent infections caused by bacteria; a type of ANTIBIOTIC

**pen·ile** /ˈpiːnaɪl/ *adj.* [only before noun] (*specialist*) relating to the PENIS

**pen·in·sula** /pəˈnɪnsjələ; *NAmE* -səl-/ *noun* an area of land that is almost surrounded by water but is joined to a larger piece of land: *the Iberian peninsula* (= Spain and Portugal)

**pen·in·su·lar** /pəˈnɪnsjələ(r); *NAmE* -səl-/ *adj.* on or connected with a peninsula: *peninsular Spanish* (= that is spoken in Spain, not in Latin America)

**penis** /ˈpiːnɪs/ *noun* the organ on the body of a man or male animal that is used for URINATING and sex

**peni·tence** /ˈpenɪtəns/ *noun* [U] a feeling of being sorry because you have done sth wrong

**peni·tent** /ˈpenɪtənt/ *adj., noun*
■ *adj.* feeling or showing that you are sorry for having done sth wrong SYN **remorseful**
■ *noun* a person who shows that they are sorry for doing sth wrong, especially a religious person who wants God to forgive them

**peni·ten·tial** /ˌpenɪˈtenʃl/ *adj.* (*formal*) showing that you are sorry for having done sth wrong

**peni·ten·tiary** /ˌpenɪˈtenʃəri/ *noun* (*pl. -ies*) (*also informal* **pen**) (*both NAmE*) a prison

**pen·knife** /ˈpennaɪf/ *noun* (*pl.* **-knives** /ˈpennaɪvz/) (*also* **pock·et·knife** *especially NAmE*) a small knife with one or more metal BLADES that fold down into the handle

penknife
blade

**pen·man·ship** /ˈpenmənʃɪp/ *noun* [U] (*formal*) the art of writing by hand; skill in doing this

**'pen name** *noun* a name used by a writer instead of their real name SYN **nom de plume** ⇒ compare PSEUDONYM

**pen·nant** /ˈpenənt/ *noun* **1** a long narrow pointed flag, for example one used on a ship to give signals **2** (in the US) a flag given to the team that wins in a sports league, especially in baseball

**pen·ni·less** /ˈpenɪləs/ *adj.* having no money; very poor SYN **destitute** ⇒ SYNONYMS at POOR

**penny** ❶ A2 /ˈpeni/ *noun* (*pl.* **pen·nies** or **pence** /pens/) HELP In senses 1 and 2, **pennies** is used to refer to the coins, and **pence** to refer to an amount of money. In sense 3, the plural is **pennies**. **1** ❷ A2 (*abbr.* **p**) a small British coin and unit of money. There are 100 pence in one pound (£1): *He had a few pennies in his pocket.* ◊ *That will be 45 pence, please.* ◊ *They cost 20p each.* **2** (*abbr.* **d**) a British coin in use until 1971. There were twelve pennies in one SHILLING and twenty shillings in a pound. **3** ❷ A2 (*NAmE*) a cent: *The fee ranges from a few pennies to $30 or more.* IDM **every 'penny** all of the money: *We collected £700 and every penny went to charity.* **in for a 'penny, in for a 'pound** (*saying*) used to say that since you have started to do sth, it is worth spending as much time or money as you need to in order to complete it **not a 'penny** no money at all: *It didn't cost a penny.* **the 'penny drops** (*informal, especially BrE*) used to say that sb has finally understood or realized sth that they had not understood

or realized before **a ˌpenny for your 'thoughts** | **a penny for them** (*saying*) used to ask sb what they are thinking about **turn up like a bad 'penny** (*informal*) (of a person) to appear when they are not welcome or not wanted, especially when this happens regularly **ˌtwo / ten a 'penny** (*BrE*) (*NAmE* **a ˌdime a 'dozen**) very common and therefore not valuable ⇒ more at PINCH *v.*, PRETTY *adj.*, SPEND *v.*

**'penny-pinching** *adj.* (*disapproving*) unwilling to spend money SYN **mean** ▶ **'penny-pinching** *noun* [U]

**'penny whistle** *noun* = TIN WHISTLE

**'pen pal** (*especially NAmE*) (*BrE also* **pen·friend**) *noun* a person that you make friends with by writing letters or emails, often sb you have never met

**'pen-pusher** (*especially BrE*) (*NAmE usually* **'paper-pusher**, **'pencil pusher**) *noun* (*informal, disapproving*) a person with a boring job, especially in an office, that involves a lot of writing

**pen·sion**¹ ❶ B2 /ˈpenʃn/ *noun, verb* ⇒ see also PENSION²
■ *noun* ❷ B2 an amount of money paid regularly by a government or company to sb who has retired from work: *a state pension* ◊ *to receive a retirement pension* ◊ *on a ~ She was struggling to live on a small pension.* ◊ *I've been paying into a private pension for years.* ◊ *a pension fund* ◊ *a pension scheme/plan* ⇒ see also OLD-AGE PENSION
■ *verb*
PHRV **ˌpension sb 'off** (*especially BrE*) [usually passive] to allow or force sb to retire and to pay them a pension: *He was pensioned off and his job given to a younger man.* ◊ (*informal, figurative*) *That car of yours should have been pensioned off years ago.*

**pen·sion**² /ˈpɒ̃sjɒ̃; *NAmE* ˌpɑːnsiˈəʊn/ *noun* (*from French*) a small, usually cheap, hotel in some European countries, especially France ⇒ see also PENSION¹

**pen·sion·able** /ˈpenʃənəbl/ *adj.* giving sb the right to receive a pension: *people of pensionable age* ◊ *pensionable pay*

**pen·sion·er** /ˈpenʃənə(r)/ *noun* (*especially BrE*) a person who is receiving a pension, especially from the government ⇒ see also OAP, OLD-AGE PENSIONER, SENIOR CITIZEN ⇒ WORDFINDER NOTE at OLD

**'pension plan** (*BrE usually* **'pension scheme**) (*NAmE also* **reˈtirement plan**) *noun* a system in which you, and usually your employer, pay money regularly into a fund while you are employed. You are then paid a PENSION when you retire.

**'pension pot** *noun* (*BrE, informal*) the total amount of money that a person has invested to provide an income for when they retire

**pen·sive** /ˈpensɪv/ *adj.* thinking deeply about sth, especially because you are sad or worried: *to be in a pensive mood* ◊ *to look pensive* ▶ **pen·sive·ly** *adv.*

**penta-** /ˈpentə, penˈtæ/ *combining form* (in nouns, adjectives and adverbs) five; having five: *pentagon* ◊ *pentathlon*

**penta·gon** /ˈpentəgən; *NAmE* -gɑːn/ *noun* **1** [C] (*geometry*) a flat shape with five straight sides and five angles ⇒ picture at POLYGON **2 the Pentagon** [sing.] the building near Washington DC that is the HEADQUARTERS of the US Department of Defense and the military leaders: *a spokesman for the Pentagon*

**pen·tag·on·al** /penˈtægənl/ *adj.* (*geometry*) having five sides

**penta·gram** /ˈpentəgræm/ *noun* a flat shape of a star with five points, formed by five straight lines. Pentagrams are often used as magic symbols.

**pen·tam·eter** /penˈtæmɪtə(r)/ *noun* [C, U] (*specialist*) a line of poetry with five stressed syllables; the rhythm of poetry with five stressed syllables to a line

**pent·ath·lon** /penˈtæθlən/ *noun* a sporting event in which people compete in five different sports (running, riding, swimming, shooting and FENCING) ⇒ compare BIATHLON, DECATHLON, HEPTATHLON, TRIATHLON

# pentatonic 1144

**pen·ta·ton·ic** /ˌpentəˈtɒnɪk; NAmE -ˈtɑːn-/ adj. (music) related to or based on a SCALE of five notes

**Pente·cost** /ˈpentɪkɒst; NAmE -kɔːst/ noun [U, C] (BrE also **Whit 'Sunday**) (in the Christian Church) the 7th Sunday after Easter when Christians celebrate the Holy Spirit coming to the APOSTLES

**Pente·cos·tal** /ˌpentɪˈkɒstl; NAmE -ˈkɔːs-/ adj. connected with a group of Christian Churches that emphasize the gifts of the Holy Spirit, such as the power to make sick people healthy again ▶ **Pente·costal·ism** /ˌpentɪˈkɒstəlɪzəm; NAmE -ˈkɔːs-/ noun [U] **Pente·costal·ist** noun

**pent·house** /ˈpenthaʊs/ noun an expensive and comfortable flat or set of rooms at the top of a tall building

**pent-up** /ˌpent ˈʌp/ adj. **1** (of feelings, energy, etc.) that cannot be expressed or released: *pent-up frustration/ energy* **2** having feelings that you cannot express: *She was too pent-up to speak.*

**pen·ul·ti·mate** /pəˈnʌltɪmət/ adj. [only before noun] immediately before the last one SYN **next/second to last**: *the penultimate chapter/day/stage*

**pen·um·bra** /pəˈnʌmbrə/ noun (specialist) **1** an area of shadow which is between fully dark and fully light **2** (astronomy) the shadow made by the earth or the moon during a PARTIAL ECLIPSE ⊃ compare UMBRA

**pen·ury** /ˈpenjəri/ noun [U] (formal) the state of being very poor SYN **poverty**

**peon** /ˈpiːən; NAmE ˈpiːɑːn/ noun **1** a worker on a farm in Latin America **2** (NAmE, humorous) a person with a hard or boring job that is not well paid and not considered important

**peony** /ˈpiːəni/ noun (pl. **-ies**) a garden plant with large round white, pink or red flowers

**people** 🔑 A1 /ˈpiːpl/ noun, verb
■ noun **1** 👥 A1 [pl.] human beings; men, women and children HELP The plural form **persons** is formal. Use **people** in most ordinary contexts.: *At least ten people were killed in the crash.* ◊ *There were a lot of people at the party.* ◊ *Many young people are out of work.* ◊ *older people* ◊ *They are just ordinary people.* **2** 👥 A1 [pl.] humans in general; everyone: *We want to change the way people think.* ◊ *People want fresh, local food.* ◊ *He wanted to help people fulfil their potential.* HELP Use **everyone** or **everybody** instead of 'all people'. **3** 👥 A1 [C] all the people who live in a particular place or belong to a particular country, race, etc: *the American/French people* ◊ *black/white people* ◊ *people of colour* (= people who are not white) ◊ *the indigenous peoples of Mexico* ⊃ see also TOWNSPEOPLE **4** A1 [pl.] men and women who work in a particular type of job or are involved in a particular area of activity: *a meeting with business people and bankers* ◊ *These garments are intended for professional sports people.* **5** 👥 A2 **the people** [pl.] the ordinary citizens of a country rather than those who govern or have a special position in society: *the life of the common people* ◊ *It was felt that the government was no longer in touch with the people.* ⊃ see also LITTLE PEOPLE **6** sb's ~ [pl.] (literary) the men, women and children that a person leads: *The king urged his people to prepare for war.* **7** sb's ~ [pl.] the men and women who work for you or support you: *I've had my people watching the house for a few days.* **8** (informal) guests or friends: *I'm having people to dinner this evening.* **9** [pl.] (old-fashioned) the men, women and children that you are closely related to, especially your parents, grandparents, etc: *She's spending the holidays with her people.* ⊃ see also BOAT PEOPLE, STREET PEOPLE, TRADESPEOPLE

IDM **of ˌall ˈpeople** when you say **of all people**, you are emphasizing that sb is the person you would most or least expect to do sth: *She of all people should know the answer to that.* **a ˌman/ˌwoman of the ˈpeople** (especially of a politician) a man/woman who understands and supports ordinary people **ˌpeople (who live) in ˌglass ˈhouses shouldn't throw ˈstones** (saying) you should not criticize other people, because they will easily find ways of criticizing you ⊃ more at THING

■ verb [usually passive] to live in a place or fill it with people: **be peopled by sb** *The town was peopled largely by workers from the car factory and their families.* ◊ **be peopled with sth** *The ballroom was peopled with guests.*

**ˈpeople carrier** (BrE) (also **ˌmini-ˈvan** especially in NAmE) noun a large car, like a van, designed to carry up to eight people

**ˈpeople person** noun [sing.] (informal) a person who enjoys, and is good at, being with and talking to other people

**ˈpeople power** noun [U] (informal) the pressure that is placed on politics, business, etc. when large numbers of the public express or act upon their opinions

**ˈpeople skills** noun [pl.] the set of abilities that enables sb to develop and maintain good relationships with people, especially in a work environment

**ˈpeople smuggling** (especially BrE) (also **ˌhuman ˈsmuggling** especially in NAmE) noun [U] the crime of illegally transporting people across international borders ▶ **ˈpeople smuggler** (especially BrE) (also **ˌhuman ˈsmuggler** especially in NAmE) noun

**ˈpeople trafficking** noun [U] (BrE) = HUMAN TRAFFICKING

**ˈpeople-watching** noun [U] the act of spending time looking at different kinds of people in a public place because you find this interesting

**Pe·oria** /piˈɔːriə/ noun a small city in the US state of Illinois. The opinions of the people who live there are considered to be typical of opinions in the whole of the US: *Ask yourself what the folks in Peoria will think of it.*

**pep** /pep/ verb, noun
■ verb (**-pp-**)
PHRV **ˌpep sb/sthˌup** (informal) to make sb/sth more interesting or full of energy SYN **liven up**: *Pep up meals by adding more unusual spices.* ◊ *A walk in the fresh air will pep you up.*
■ noun [U] energy and enthusiasm

**pep·per** 🔑 A1 /ˈpepə(r)/ noun, verb
■ noun **1** 👥 A1 [U] a powder made from dried BERRIES (called PEPPERCORNS), used to give a hot, spicy taste to food: *Season with salt and pepper* ◊ *freshly ground pepper* ⊃ see also BLACK PEPPER, CAYENNE, WHITE PEPPER **2** (BrE) (also **ˈsweet ˈpepper** BrE, NAmE) (NAmE **ˈbell pepper**) [C, U] a hollow fruit, usually red, green or yellow, eaten as a vegetable either raw or cooked ⊃ VISUAL VOCAB page V5
■ verb ~ **sth** to put pepper on food: *peppered steak* ◊ *Salt and pepper the potatoes.*
PHRV **ˈpepper sb/sth with sth** [usually passive] to hit sb/ sth with a series of small objects, especially bullets SYN **spray** **ˈpepper sth with sth** [often passive] to include large numbers of sth in sth: *He peppered his speech with jokes.*

**ˌpepper-and-ˈsalt** (also **ˌsalt-and-ˈpepper**) adj. (especially of hair) having two colours that are mixed together, especially a dark colour and a light one

**pep·per·corn** /ˈpepəkɔːn; NAmE -pərkɔːrn/ noun a dried BERRY from a tropical plant, that is GROUND (= broken and pressed) to make pepper ⊃ VISUAL VOCAB page V8

**ˌpeppercorn ˈrent** noun (BrE) a very low rent

**pep·per·mint** /ˈpepəmɪnt; NAmE -pərm-/ noun **1** [U] a type of MINT (= a plant used to add taste to food that produces an oil with a strong taste) ⊃ compare SPEARMINT **2** [C] a sweet made with peppermint oil to give it a strong taste

**pep·per·oni** /ˌpepəˈrəʊni/ noun [U] a type of spicy SAUSAGE: *a pepperoni pizza*

**ˈpepper pot** (especially BrE) (NAmE usually **ˈpepper shaker**) noun a small container with holes in the top, used for putting pepper on food

**ˈpepper spray** noun [C, U] a chemical substance made from hot peppers that causes sb's eyes, nose and throat to STING (= be painful) when it is SPRAYED on them

**pep·pery** /ˈpepəri/ adj. **1** tasting of pepper **2** easily annoyed: *a peppery old man*

**ˈpep pill** noun (informal) a pill (= tablet) containing a drug that gives you more energy or makes you happy for a short time

**peppy** /ˈpepi/ adj. (**pep·pier, pep·pi·est**) (informal, especially NAmE) lively and full of energy or enthusiasm: *a peppy advertising jingle*

**ˈpep rally** noun (NAmE, informal) a meeting of school students before a sports event to encourage support for the team: (figurative) *The Democrats held a pep rally on Capitol Hill yesterday.*

**pep·sin** /ˈpepsɪn/ noun [U] (biology) a substance in the stomach that breaks down PROTEINS in the process of DIGESTION

**ˈpep talk** noun (informal) a short speech intended to encourage sb to work harder, try to win, have more confidence, etc.

**pep·tic ulcer** /ˌpeptɪk ˈʌlsə(r)/ noun an ULCER in the DIGESTIVE SYSTEM, especially in the stomach

**pep·tide** /ˈpeptaɪd/ noun (chemistry) a chemical consisting of two or more AMINO ACIDS joined together

**per** ❶ A2 ◎ /pə(r), strong form pɜː(r)/ prep. used to express the cost or amount of sth for each person, number used, distance travelled, etc: *Rooms cost £50 per person, per night.* ◇ *60 miles per hour*
IDM **as per sth** following sth that has been decided: *The work was carried out as per instructions.* **as per ˈnormal/ˈusual** (informal) in the way that is normal or usual; as often happens: *Everyone blamed me as per usual.*

**per·am·bu·la·tion** /pəˌræmbjuˈleɪʃn/ noun [C] (formal or humorous) a slow walk or journey around a place, especially one made for pleasure ▶ **per·am·bu·late** verb /pəˈræmbjuleɪt/ [I, T] ~ (sth)

**per·am·bu·la·tor** /pəˈræmbjuleɪtə(r)/ noun **1** (specialist) a device consisting of a wheel on a long handle, which is pushed along the ground to measure distances **2** (old-fashioned, BrE) = PRAM

**per annum** /pər ˈænəm/ adv. (abbr. **p.a.**) (from Latin) for each year: *earning £30 000 per annum*

**per cap·ita** /pə ˈkæpɪtə; NAmE pər/ adj., adv. (from Latin) for each person: *Per capita income rose sharply last year.* ◇ *average earnings per capita*

**per·ceive** ❷+ B2 ◎ /pəˈsiːv; NAmE pər-/ verb (formal) **1** ❷+ B2 to understand or think of sb/sth in a particular way SYN see: ~ sb/sth/yourself (as sth) *This discovery was perceived as a major breakthrough.* ◇ *She did not perceive herself as disabled.* ◇ *~sb/sth to be/have sth They were widely perceived to have been unlucky.* HELP This pattern is usually used in the passive. **2** ❷+ C1 to notice or become aware of sth: *~ sth I perceived a change in his behaviour.* ◇ *that… She perceived that all was not well.* ◇ *~ sb/sth to be/have sth The patient was perceived to have difficulty in breathing.* HELP This pattern is usually used in the passive.

WORD FAMILY
**perceive** verb
**perception** noun
**perceptive** adj.
**perceptible** adj.
(≠ imperceptible)

**per cent** ❶ A2 ◎ (especially BrE) (NAmE usually **per·cent**) /pə ˈsent; NAmE pər/ (symb. **%**) noun, adj., adv.
■ noun ❷ A2 (pl. **per cent, per·cent**) ~ (**of sth/sb**) one part in every hundred: *Poor families spend about 80 to 90 per cent of their income on food.* ◇ *What per cent of the population is/are overweight?* ◇ *Sales increased by 5 percent last year.*
IDM see HUNDRED
■ adj., adv. ❷ A2 by, in or for every hundred: *a 15 per cent rise in price* ◇ *House prices dropped 8 per cent last year.*
IDM see HUNDRED

**per·cent·age** ❶ B1 ⓦ /pəˈsentɪdʒ; NAmE pər-/ noun **1** ❷ B1 [C + sing./pl. v.] the number, amount or rate of sth, expressed as if it is part of a total that is 100; a part or share of a whole: *~ of sth/sb What percentage of the population is/are overweight?* ◇ *A high percentage of the female staff are part-time workers.* ◇ *a large/small/low percentage* ◇ *as a ~ The figure is expressed as a percentage.* ◇ *The results were analysed in percentage terms.* ◇ *Interest rates are expected to rise by one percentage point* (= a unit of one per cent). **2** [C, usually sing.] a share of the profits of sth: *He gets a percentage for every car sold.*

---

# percipient

▼ **GRAMMAR POINT**
**expressing percentages**
• Percentages (= numbers of per cent) are written in words as *twenty-five per cent* and in figures as 25%.
• If a percentage is used with an uncountable or a singular noun the verb is generally singular: *90% of the land is cultivated.*
• If the noun is singular but represents a group of people, the verb is singular in NAmE but in BrE it may be singular or plural: *Eighty per cent of the work force is/are against the strike.*
• If the noun is plural, the verb is plural: *65% of children play computer games.*

**per·cent·ile** /pəˈsentaɪl; NAmE pər-/ noun (specialist) one of the 100 equal groups that a larger group of people can be divided into, according to their place on a scale measuring a particular value: *Overall these students rank in the 21st percentile on the tests—that is, they did worse than 79 per cent of all children taking the test.*

**per·cep·tible** /pəˈseptəbl; NAmE pər-/ adj. **1** (formal) great enough for you to notice it SYN **noticeable**: *a perceptible change/increase/decline/impact* ◇ *The price increase has had no perceptible effect on sales.* ◇ *Her foreign accent was barely perceptible.* **2** (specialist) that you can notice or feel with your senses: *the perceptible world* OPP **imperceptible** ▶ **per·cep·tibly** /-bli/ adv.: *Income per head rose perceptibly.* ◇ *It was perceptibly colder.*

**per·cep·tion** ❷+ B2 ⓦ /pəˈsepʃn; NAmE pər-/ noun **1** ❷+ B2 [U, C] (formal) an idea, a belief or an image you have as a result of how you see or understand sth: *a campaign to change public perception of the police* ◇ *~that… There is a general public perception that standards in schools are falling.* **2** ❷+ C1 [U] (specialist or formal) the way you notice things, especially with the senses: *our perception of reality* ◇ *visual perception* ⮕ see also EXTRASENSORY PERCEPTION **3** ❷+ C1 [U] (formal) the ability to understand the true nature of sth SYN **insight**: *She showed great perception in her assessment of the family situation.*

**per·cep·tive** /pəˈseptɪv; NAmE pər-/ adj. **1** (approving) having or showing the ability to see or understand things quickly, especially things that are not obvious: *a highly perceptive comment* ◇ *It was very perceptive of you to notice that.* **2** (specialist or formal) connected with seeing, hearing and understanding: *our innate perceptive abilities* ▶ **per·cep·tive·ly** adv. **per·cep·tive·ness** noun [U]

**per·cep·tual** /pəˈseptʃuəl; NAmE pər-/ adj. [only before noun] (specialist) relating to the ability to PERCEIVE things or the process of PERCEIVING: *perceptual skills*

**perch** /pɜːtʃ; NAmE pɜːrtʃ/ verb, noun
■ verb **1** [I] ~ (**on sth**) (of a bird) to land and stay on a branch, etc: *A robin was perching on the fence.* **2** [I, T] (informal) to sit or to make sb sit on sth, especially on the edge of it: *~ (on sth) We perched on a couple of high stools at the bar.* ◇ *~ sb/yourself (on sth) She perched herself on the edge of the bed.* ⮕ SYNONYMS at SIT **3** [I] (also **be perched** [T]) to be placed on the top or the edge of sth: *+ adv./prep. The hotel perched precariously on a steep hillside.*
■ noun **1** a place where a bird rests, especially a branch or bar for this purpose, for example in a bird's CAGE **2** a high seat or position: *He watched the game from his precarious perch on top of the wall.* **3** (pl. **perch**) a FRESHWATER fish that is sometimes used for food IDM see KNOCK v.

**per·chance** /pəˈtʃɑːns; NAmE pərˈtʃæns/ adv. (old use) perhaps

**perched** /pɜːtʃt; NAmE pɜːrtʃt/ adj. **1** ~ **on, etc. sth** (especially of a bird) sitting or resting on sth: *There was a bird perched on the roof.* **2** ~ **on, etc. sth** placed in a high and/or dangerous position: *a hotel perched high on the cliffs*

**per·cipi·ent** /pəˈsɪpiənt; NAmE pər-/ adj. (formal) having or showing the ability to understand things, especially things that are not obvious SYN **perceptive**

**per·co·late** /ˈpɜːkəleɪt/ *NAmE* /ˈpɜːrk-/ *verb* **1** [I] (+ *adv.* / *prep.*) (of a liquid, gas, etc.) to move gradually through a surface that has very small holes or spaces in it: *Water had percolated down through the rocks.* **2** [I] to gradually become known or spread through a group or society: *It had percolated through to us that something interesting was about to happen.* **3** [T, I] ~ **(sth)** to make coffee in a percolator; to be made in this way ▶ **per·co·la·tion** /ˌpɜːkəˈleɪʃn/ *NAmE* /ˌpɜːrk-/ *noun* [U]

**per·co·la·tor** /ˈpɜːkəleɪtə(r)/ *NAmE* /ˈpɜːrk-/ *noun* a pot for making coffee, in which boiling water is forced up a central tube and then comes down again through the coffee

**per·cus·sion** /pəˈkʌʃn/ *NAmE* /pərˈk-/ *noun* **1** [U] musical instruments that you play by hitting them with your hand or with a stick, for example drums: *percussion instruments* ◊ **on** ~ *The track features Joey Langton on percussion.* **2 the percussion** [sing.] (*also* **per'cussion section**) [C] the players of percussion instruments in an ORCHESTRA ⊃ compare BRASS, STRING, WOODWIND

**per·cus·sion·ist** /pəˈkʌʃənɪst/ *NAmE* /pərˈk-/ *noun* a person who plays percussion instruments

**per·cus·sive** /pəˈkʌsɪv/ *NAmE* /pərˈk-/ *adj.* (*specialist*) connected with sounds made by hitting things, especially PERCUSSION instruments

**per·cu·tan·eous** /ˌpɜːkjuːˈteɪniəs/ *NAmE* /ˌpɜːrk-/ *adj.* (*medical*) made or done through the skin: *a percutaneous injection*

**per diem** /ˌpɜː ˈdiːem/ *NAmE* /ˌpɜːr-/ *adj., noun* (*from Latin, especially NAmE*)
- *adj.* [only before noun] (of money) for each day: *a per diem allowance* ▶ **per diem** *adv.*: *He agreed to pay at specified rates per diem.*
- *noun* [U, C] money paid, for example to employees, for things they need to buy every day: *He will get $14000 a year in per diem to help with the higher costs of living in Washington.*

**per·di·tion** /pɜːˈdɪʃn/ *NAmE* /pɜːrˈd-/ *noun* [U] (*formal*) punishment that lasts forever after death

**pere·grin·ation** /ˌperəɡrɪˈneɪʃn/ *noun* [usually pl.] (*literary or humorous*) a journey, especially a long slow one

**pere·grine** /ˈperɪɡrɪn/ (*also* **peregrine 'falcon**) *noun* a grey and white BIRD OF PREY (= a bird that kills other creatures for food) that can be trained to hunt for sport

**per·emp·tory** /pəˈremptəri/ *adj.* (*formal, disapproving*) (especially of sb's manner or behaviour) expecting to be obeyed immediately and without questioning or refusing: *a peremptory summons* ◊ *The letter was peremptory in tone.*

**per·en·nial** /pəˈreniəl/ *adj., noun*
- *adj.* **1** continuing for a very long time; happening again and again: *the perennial problem of water shortage* ◊ *that perennial favourite, hamburgers* **2** (of plants) living for two years or more ▶ **per·en·ni·al·ly** /-əli/ *adv.*: *a perennially popular subject*
- *noun* any plant that lives for more than two years ⊃ compare ANNUAL, BIENNIAL

**per·fect** 🔊 **A1** *adj., verb, noun*
- *adj.* /ˈpɜːfɪkt/ *NAmE* /ˈpɜːrf-/ **1** **A1** having everything that is necessary; complete and without faults or weaknesses: *in perfect condition* ◊ *a perfect set of teeth* ◊ *Well I'm sorry—but nobody's perfect* (= used when sb has criticized you). ◊ *In a perfect world, everybody would have everything they needed.* **2** **A1** completely correct; exact and accurate: *She speaks perfect English.* ◊ *a perfect fit/match* ◊ *What perfect timing!* ⊃ see also PICTURE-PERFECT **3** **A1** the best of its kind: *a perfect example of the painter's early style* ◊ *the perfect crime* (= one in which the criminal is never discovered) **4** **A1** excellent; very good: *The weather was perfect.* ⊃ SYNONYMS at EXCELLENT **5** **A1** ~ **(for sb/sth)** exactly right for sb/sth **SYN** **ideal**: *Hawaii is the perfect place for a honeymoon.* ◊ *She's the perfect candidate for the job.* ◊ *'Will 2.30 be OK for you?' 'Perfect, thanks.'* **6** [only before noun] total; complete: *I don't know him—he's a perfect stranger.* **7** (*grammar*) connected with the form of a verb that consists of part of the verb *have* with the past participle of the main verb, used to express actions completed by the present or a particular point in the past or future: *'I have eaten' is the present perfect tense of the verb 'to eat', 'I had eaten' is the past perfect and 'I will have eaten' is the future perfect.* ⊃ see also FUTURE PERFECT, PAST PERFECT, PRESENT PERFECT **IDM** see PRACTICE *n.*, WORLD
- *verb* /pəˈfekt/ *NAmE* /pərˈf-/ ~ **sth** to make sth perfect or as good as you can: *As a musician, she has spent years perfecting her technique.*
- *noun* /ˈpɜːfɪkt/ *NAmE* /ˈpɜːrf-/ **the perfect** (*also* **the ˌperfect 'tense**) [sing.] (*grammar*) the form of a verb that expresses actions completed by the present or a particular point in the past or future, formed in English with part of the verb *have* and the past participle of the main verb ⊃ see also FUTURE PERFECT, PAST PERFECT, PRESENT PERFECT

**per·fec·tion** /pəˈfekʃn/ *NAmE* /pərˈf-/ *noun* [U, sing.] **1** the state of being perfect: *physical perfection* ◊ *The novel achieves a perfection of form that is quite new.* ◊ *His performance was perfection* (= sth perfect). ◊ **to** ~ *The fish was cooked to perfection.* **2** the act of making sth perfect by doing the final improvements: *They have been working on the perfection of the new model.*

**per·fec·tion·ist** /pəˈfekʃənɪst/ *NAmE* /pərˈf-/ *noun* (*sometimes disapproving*) a person who likes to do things perfectly and is not satisfied with anything less ▶ **per·fec·tion·ism** /-nɪzəm/ *noun* [U]

**per·fect·ly** 🔊 **B1** 🅂 /ˈpɜːfɪktli/ *NAmE* /ˈpɜːrf-/ *adv.* **1** **B1** completely: *It's perfectly normal to feel like this.* ◊ *It's perfectly good as it is* (= it doesn't need changing). ◊ *I thought he'd be upset, but he seems perfectly fine.* ◊ *You know perfectly well what I mean.* ◊ *To be perfectly honest, I didn't want to go anyway.* ◊ *He stood perfectly still until the danger had passed.* ◊ *'Do you understand?' 'Perfectly.'* **2** **B1** in a perfect way: *The TV works perfectly now.* ◊ *This dress fits perfectly.*

**ˌperfect 'pitch** *noun* [U] (*music*) the ability to identify or sing a musical note correctly without the help of an instrument

**ˌperfect 'storm** *noun* [sing.] (*especially NAmE*) an occasion when several bad things happen at the same time, creating a situation that could not be worse

**per·fidi·ous** /pəˈfɪdiəs/ *NAmE* /pərˈf-/ *adj.* (*literary*) that cannot be trusted **SYN** **treacherous**

**per·fidy** /ˈpɜːfədi/ *NAmE* /ˈpɜːrf-/ *noun* [U] (*literary*) unfair treatment of sb who trusts you **SYN** **treachery**

**per·for·ate** /ˈpɜːfəreɪt/ *NAmE* /ˈpɜːrf-/ *verb* ~ **sth** to make a hole or holes through sth: *The explosion perforated his eardrum.* ◊ *a perforated line* (= a row of small holes in paper, made so that a part can be torn off easily)

**per·for·ation** /ˌpɜːfəˈreɪʃn/ *NAmE* /ˌpɜːrf-/ *noun* **1** [C, usually pl.] a small hole in a surface, often one of a series of small holes: *Tear the sheet of stamps along the perforations.* **2** [U] (*medical*) the process of splitting or tearing in such a way that a hole is left: *Excessive pressure can lead to perforation of the stomach wall.*

**per·force** /pəˈfɔːs/ *NAmE* /pərˈfɔːrs/ *adv.* (*old use* or *formal*) because it is necessary or cannot be avoided **SYN** **necessarily**

**per·form** 🔊 **A2** 🅂 /pəˈfɔːm/ *NAmE* /pərˈfɔːrm/ *verb* **1** **A2** [T, I] ~ **(sth)** to entertain an audience by playing a piece of music, acting in a play, etc.: *to perform a song/dance/play* ◊ *The play was first performed in 2007.* ◊ *I'm looking forward to seeing you perform.* ◊ *I'd love to see them perform live* (= in a live show, not a recording). ◊ *What do you like about performing on stage?* ⊃ WORDFINDER NOTE at CONCERT **2** **B1** [T] ~ **sth** to do sth, such as a piece of work, task or duty **SYN** **carry out**: *She performs an important role in our organization.* ◊ *A computer can perform many tasks at once.* ◊ *to perform a function/duty* ◊ *to perform an analysis/a test/an experiment* ◊ *to perform a ceremony/ritual* **3** **B1** [I] to work or function well or badly: *to perform well/poorly/badly* ◊ *England's players perform better for their clubs than for their country.* ◊ *They gather information on how businesses are performing.* **IDM** see MIRACLE

**per·form·ance** /pəˈfɔːməns; NAmE pərˈfɔːrm-/ noun 1 [C] the act of performing a play, concert or some other form of entertainment: *The performance starts at seven.* ◇ *an evening performance* ◇ *one of the band's rare live performances* ◇ *~ of sth They gave a performance of Ravel's String Quartet* ◇ *by sb/sth a series of performances by the Kirov Ballet* ⊃ see also COMMAND PERFORMANCE

| WORDFINDER cue, dresser, matinee, opening night, ovation, prompter, rehearsal, stage manager |
|---|

2 [C] the way a person performs in a play, concert, etc: *She gave the greatest performance of her career.* ◇ *Both actors deliver outstanding performances.* ◇ *an excellent/a fine/an impressive performance* 3 [U, C] how well or badly you do sth; how well or badly sth works: *the country's economic performance* ◇ *It was an impressive performance by the French team.* ◇ *He criticized the recent poor performance of the company.* ◇ *The team has continued to improve performance.* ◇ *high-performance* (= very powerful) *cars* ◇ *performance indicators* (= things that show how well or badly sth is working) ⊃ compare PAY-FOR-PERFORMANCE, PERFORMANCE-RELATED 4 [U, sing.] (*formal*) the act or process of performing a task, an action, etc: *She has shown enthusiasm in the performance of her duties.* ◇ *He did not want a repeat performance of the humiliating defeat he had suffered.* 5 [sing.] (*informal, especially BrE*) an act that involves a lot of effort or trouble, sometimes when it is not necessary SYN **carry-on**: *It's such a performance getting the children off to school in the morning.*

**per'formance art** *noun* [U] an art form in which an artist gives a performance, rather than producing a physical work of art

**per'formance-enhancing** *adj.* [only before noun] (used especially about drugs that have been banned from use in sport) that people take so that they will be more successful in a sports competition: *steroids and other performance-enhancing drugs*

**per'formance-related** *adj.* [only before noun] depending on how well a person does their job: *Is there any evidence that performance-related pay actually improves performance?* ⊃ compare PAY-FOR-PERFORMANCE, PERFORMANCE (3)

**per'formance review** (*also* **appraisal** *especially in BrE*) *noun* a meeting in which an employee discusses with their manager how well they have been doing their job; the system of holding such meetings

**per·form·er** /pəˈfɔːmə(r); NAmE pərˈfɔːrm-/ *noun* 1 a person who performs for an audience in a show, concert, etc: *a brilliant/polished/seasoned performer* 2 a person or thing that behaves or works in the way mentioned: *He was a poor performer at school and left with no qualifications.* ◇ *VW is the star performer of the motor industry this year.*

**the per'forming 'arts** *noun* [pl.] arts such as music, dance and drama which are performed for an audience

**per·fume** /ˈpɜːfjuːm; NAmE pərˈfjuːm/ *noun, verb*
■ *noun* [C, U] 1 a liquid, often made from flowers, that you put on your skin to make yourself smell nice SYN **fragrance, scent**: *a bottle of expensive perfume* ◇ *We stock a wide range of perfumes.* ◇ *the perfume counter of the store* ◇ *She was wearing too much perfume.* 2 a pleasant, often sweet, smell SYN **scent**: *the heady perfume of the roses*
■ *verb* [often passive] 1 ~ sth (with sth) (*literary*) (especially of flowers) to make the air in a place smell pleasant SYN **scent**: *The garden was perfumed with the smell of roses.* 2 ~ sth (with sth) to put perfume in or on sth: *She perfumed her bath with fragrant oils.* ▶ **per·fumed** *adj.*: *perfumed soap*

**per·fum·ery** /pəˈfjuːməri; NAmE pərˈf-/ *noun* (*pl.* **-ies**) 1 [C] a place where perfumes are made and/or sold 2 [U] the process of making perfume

**per·func·tory** /pəˈfʌŋktəri; NAmE pərˈf-/ *adj.* (*formal*) (of an action) done as a duty or habit, without real interest, attention or feeling: *a perfunctory nod/smile* ◇ *They only made a perfunctory effort.* ▶ **per·func·tor·ily** /-trəli/ *adv.*: *to nod/smile perfunctorily*

---

# period

**per·gola** /ˈpɜːɡələ; NAmE ˈpɜːrɡ-/ *noun* a wooden structure in a garden for plants to grow over and people to sit or walk under

**per·haps** /pəˈhæps, præps; NAmE pərˈhæps/ *adv.* 1 possibly SYN **maybe**: *'Are you going to come?' 'Perhaps. I'll see how I feel.'* ◇ *Perhaps he's forgotten.* 2 used when you want to make a statement or opinion less definite: *This is perhaps his best novel to date.* 3 used when making a rough estimate: *a change which could affect perhaps 20 per cent of the population* 4 used when you agree or accept sth unwillingly, or do not want to say that you think sth is bad: *'You could do it yourself.' 'Yeah, perhaps.'* 5 used when making a polite request, offer or suggestion: *Perhaps it would be better if you came back tomorrow.* ◇ *I think perhaps you've had enough to drink tonight.*

▼ LANGUAGE BANK

**perhaps**

Making an opinion sound less definite

- Most cybercrime involves traditional crimes, such as theft and fraud, being committed in new ways. Phishing is **perhaps/possibly/probably** the best-known example of this.
- It **seems/appears** that the more personal data which organizations collect, the more opportunity there is for this data to be lost or stolen.
- It **seems clear that** introducing national ID cards would do little to prevent identity theft.
- It **could be argued that** the introduction of national ID cards might actually make identity theft easier.
- It **is possible that/It may be that** the only way to protect ourselves against DNA identity theft is to avoid the creation of national DNA databases.

⊃ LANGUAGE BANK at IMPERSONAL, OPINION

**per·igee** /ˈperɪdʒiː/ *noun* (*astronomy*) the point in the ORBIT of the moon, a planet or other object in space when it is nearest the planet, for example the earth, around which it turns ⊃ compare APOGEE ⊃ picture at ORBIT

**peril** /ˈperəl/ *noun* (*formal or literary*) 1 [U] serious danger: *in ~ The country's economy is now in grave peril.* ◇ *The heroine finds herself in mortal peril.* 2 [C, usually pl.] *~ (of sth)* the fact of sth being dangerous or harmful: *a warning about the perils of drug abuse*
IDM ► **do sth at your (own) 'peril** used to warn sb that if they do sth, it may be dangerous or cause them problems

**per·il·ous** /ˈperələs/ *adj.* (*formal or literary*) very dangerous SYN **hazardous** ▶ **per·il·ous·ly** *adv.*: *We came perilously close to disaster.*

**per·im·eter** /pəˈrɪmɪtə(r)/ *noun* 1 the outside edge of an area of land: *Guards patrol the perimeter of the estate.* ◇ *a perimeter fence/track/wall* 2 (*mathematics*) the total length of the outside edge of an area or a shape ⊃ compare CIRCUMFERENCE

**peri·natal** /ˌperɪˈneɪtl/ *adj.* (*specialist*) at or around the time of birth: *perinatal care* ◇ *perinatal mortality*

**peri·neum** /ˌperɪˈniːəm/ *noun* (*pl.* **peri·nea** /-ˈniːə/) (*anatomy*) the area between the ANUS and the SCROTUM or VULVA

**period** /ˈpɪəriəd; NAmE ˈpɪr-/ *noun, adv., adj.*
■ *noun*
• LENGTH OF TIME 1 a particular length of time: *a long/an extended period* ◇ *a short/brief period* ◇ *~ of sth a period of transition/uncertainty/expansion* ◇ *a period of two years/six months/four weeks* ◇ *a two-year/six-month/four-week period* ◇ *All these changes happened over a period of time.* ◇ *A year-to-year lease has no fixed time period.* ◇ *for a ~ The offer is available for a limited period only.* ◇ *over a ~ The hall will be closed over a 2-year period.* ◇ *during a ~ We know little of her life during that period.* ⊃ see also COOLING-OFF PERIOD 2 a length of time in the life of a particular person or in the history of a particular country: *Which period of history would you most like to have lived in?* ◇ *the post-war period* ◇ *Like Picasso, she too had a blue period.* ◇ *Most teenagers go through a period of rebelling.*

# periodic

**3** (*geology*) a length of time which is a division of an ERA. A period is divided into EPOCHS: *the Jurassic period*
- LESSON **4** any of the parts that a day is divided into at a school, college, etc. for study: '*What do you have next period?*' '*French.*' ◇ *a free/study period* (= for private study)
- WOMAN **5** the flow of blood each month from the body of a woman who is not pregnant: *period pains* ◇ *monthly periods* ◇ *When did you last have a period?* ᑐ compare MENSTRUATION
- PUNCTUATION **6** (*NAmE*) (*BrE* **full 'stop**) the mark (.) used at the end of a sentence and in some abbreviations, for example *e.g.*
- **adv.** (*especially NAmE*) (*BrE also* **full 'stop**) (*informal*) used at the end of a sentence to emphasize that there is nothing more to say about a subject: *The answer is no, period!*
- **adj.** [only before noun] having a style typical of a particular time in history: *period costumes/furniture*

**peri·od·ic** /ˌpɪəriˈɒdɪk/ *NAmE* /ˌpɪriˈɑːd-/ (also *less frequent* **peri·od·ical** /ˌpɪəriˈɒdɪkl/ *NAmE* /ˌpɪriˈɑːd-/) *adj.* [usually before noun] happening fairly often and regularly: *Periodic checks are carried out on the equipment.* ▶ **peri·od·ic·al·ly** /-kli/ *adv.*: *Mailing lists are updated periodically.*

**peri·od·ical** /ˌpɪəriˈɒdɪkl/ *NAmE* /ˌpɪriˈɑːd-/ *noun* a magazine that is published every week, month, etc., especially one that is about an academic subject

**the ˌperiodic ˈtable** *noun* [sing.] (*chemistry*) a list of all the chemical elements, arranged according to their ATOMIC NUMBER

**peri·odon·tal** /ˌperiəˈdɒntl/ *NAmE* -ˈdɑːn-/ *adj.* (*medical*) related to or affecting the parts of the mouth that surround and support the teeth

**peri·odon·titis** /ˌperiədɒnˈtaɪtɪs; *NAmE* -dɑːn-/ *noun* [U] (*medical*) a condition in which the area around the teeth becomes painful and SWOLLEN (= larger than normal), which may make the teeth fall out

**ˈperiod piece** *noun* **1** a play, film, etc. that is set in a particular period of history **2** an object, piece of furniture, etc. that was made during a particular period of history and is typical of that period

**peri·pat·et·ic** /ˌperɪpəˈtetɪk/ *adj.* (*formal*) going from place to place, for example in order to work: *a peripatetic music teacher*

**per·iph·eral** /pəˈrɪfərəl/ *adj., noun*
- **adj.** **1** (*formal*) not as important as the main aim, part, etc. of sth: *peripheral information* ◇ **~ to sth** *Fund-raising is peripheral to their main activities.* **2** (*specialist*) connected with the outer edge of a particular area: *the peripheral nervous system* ◇ *peripheral vision* **3** (*computing*) (of equipment) connected to a computer: *a peripheral device* ▶ **per·iph·er·al·ly** /-rəli/ *adv.*
- **noun** (*computing*) a piece of equipment that is connected to a computer: *monitors, printers and other peripherals*

**per·iph·ery** /pəˈrɪfəri/ *noun* [usually sing.] (*pl.* **-ies**) (*formal*) **1** the outer edge of a particular area: **on the ~ of sth** *industrial development on the periphery of the town* ◇ *The condition makes it difficult for patients to see objects at the periphery of their vision.* **2** the less important part of sth, for example of a particular activity or of a social or political group: **on the ~ of sth** *minor parties on the periphery of American politics*

**peri·scope** /ˈperɪskəʊp/ *noun* a device consisting of a long tube containing mirrors that enable the user to see over the top of sth, used especially in a SUBMARINE (= a ship that can operate UNDERWATER) to see above the surface of the sea

**per·ish** /ˈperɪʃ/ *verb* **1** [I] (*formal* or *literary*) (of people or animals) to die, especially in a sudden violent way: *A family of four perished in the fire.* **2** [I] (*formal*) to be lost or destroyed: *Early buildings were made of wood and have perished.* **3** [I, T] **~(sth)** (*BrE*) if a material such as rubber **perishes** or **is perished**, it becomes damaged, weaker or full of holes
- IDM **perish the ˈthought** (*informal* or *humorous*) used to say that you find a suggestion unacceptable or that you hope that sth will never happen: *Me get married? Perish the thought!*

**per·ish·able** /ˈperɪʃəbl/ *adj.* (especially of food) likely to DECAY or go bad quickly: *perishable goods/foods*

**per·ish·ables** /ˈperɪʃəblz/ *noun* [pl.] (*specialist*) types of food that DECAY or go bad quickly

**per·ished** /ˈperɪʃt/ *adj.* [not before noun] (*BrE*, *informal*) (of a person) very cold: *We were perished.*

**per·ish·ing** /ˈperɪʃɪŋ/ *adj.* (*BrE*, *informal*) **1** extremely cold SYN **freezing**: *It's perishing outside!* ◇ *I'm perishing!* **2** [only before noun] (*old-fashioned*) used to show that you are annoyed about sth: *I've had enough of this perishing job!*

**peri·stal·sis** /ˌperɪˈstælsɪs/ *noun* [U] (*biology*) the wave-like movements of the INTESTINE, etc. caused when the muscles pull tight and relax

**peri·ton·eum** /ˌperɪtəˈniːəm/ *noun* (*pl.* **peri·ton·eums** or **peri·ton·ea** /-ˈniːə/) (*anatomy*) the MEMBRANE (= very thin layer of TISSUE) on the inside of the ABDOMEN that covers the stomach and other organs

**peri·ton·itis** /ˌperɪtəˈnaɪtɪs/ *noun* [U] (*medical*) a serious condition in which the inside wall of the body becomes SWOLLEN (= larger than normal) and very painful

**peri·win·kle** /ˈperiwɪŋkl/ *noun* **1** [C, U] a small plant that grows along the ground **2** (*BrE also* **win·kle**) [C] a small SHELLFISH, like a SNAIL, that can be eaten

**per·jure** /ˈpɜːdʒə(r)/ *NAmE* /ˈpɜːrdʒ-/ *verb* **~ yourself** (*law*) to tell a lie in court after you have sworn to tell the truth ▶ **per·jurer** /ˈpɜːdʒərə(r)/ *NAmE* /ˈpɜːrdʒ-/ *noun*

**per·jury** /ˈpɜːdʒəri/ *NAmE* /ˈpɜːrdʒ-/ *noun* [U] (*law*) the crime of telling a lie in court after you have sworn to tell the truth: *to commit perjury*

**perk** /pɜːk/ *NAmE* pɜːrk/ *noun, verb*
- **noun** (*also formal* **per·quis·ite**) [usually pl.] something you receive as well as your wages for doing a particular job: *Perks offered by the firm include a car and free health insurance.* ◇ (*figurative*) *Not having to get up early is just one of the perks of being retired.*
- **verb**
- PHRV **ˌperk ˈup** | **ˌperk sb**↔**ˈup** (*informal*) to become or to make sb become more cheerful or lively, especially after they have been ill or sad SYN **brighten**: *He soon perked up when his friends arrived.* **ˌperk ˈup** | **ˌperk sth**↔**ˈup** (*informal*) to increase, or to make sth increase in value, etc: *Share prices had perked up slightly by close of trading.* **ˌperk sth**↔**ˈup** (*informal*) to make sth more interesting, more attractive, etc. SYN **liven up**: *ideas for perking up bland food*

**perky** /ˈpɜːki/ *NAmE* /ˈpɜːrki/ *adj.* (**perk·ier, perki·est**) (*informal*) cheerful and full of energy ▶ **perki·ness** *noun* [U]

**perm** /pɜːm/ *NAmE* pɜːrm/ *noun, verb*
- **noun** a way of changing the style of your hair by using chemicals to create CURLS that last for several months: *to have a perm*
- **verb** [often passive] **~ sth** to give sb's hair a perm: *to have your hair permed* ◇ *a shampoo for permed hair*

**perma·cul·ture** /ˈpɜːməkʌltʃə(r)/ *NAmE* /ˈpɜːrm-/ *noun* [U] an approach to life and growing food that copies the way things happen in nature in order to create ways for people to live without damaging the environment

**perma·frost** /ˈpɜːməfrɒst/ *NAmE* /ˈpɜːrməfrɔːst/ *noun* [U] (*specialist*) a layer of soil that is permanently frozen, in very cold regions of the world

**perma·link** /ˈpɜːməlɪŋk/ *NAmE* /ˈpɜːrm-/ *noun* a HYPERLINK that is always linked to the same electronic document, even if the document is replaced: *On my homepage you can click on the permalink to any of my blog posts.*

**per·man·ence** /ˈpɜːmənəns/ *NAmE* /ˈpɜːrm-/ (*also less frequent* **per·man·ency** /ˈpɜːmənənsi/ *NAmE* /ˈpɜːrm-/) *noun* [U] the state of lasting for a long time or for all time in the future: *The spoken word is immediate but lacks permanence.* ◇ *We no longer talk of the permanence of marriage.*

**per·man·ent** 🔑 B2 /ˈpɜːmənənt/ *NAmE* /ˈpɜːrm-/ *adj., noun*
- **adj.** 🔑 B2 lasting for a long time or for all time in the future; existing all the time: *a permanent job* ◇ *permanent staff* ◇ *They are now living together on a permanent basis.* ◇ *The accident has not done any permanent damage.* ◇ *a*

*permanent fixture* (= a person or an object that is always in a particular place) **OPP** *temporary*
- *noun* (*old-fashioned*, *NAmE*) = PERM

**per·man·ent·ly** ?+ **B2** /ˈpɜːmənəntli; *NAmE* ˈpɜːrm-/ *adv.* in a way that lasts for a long time or for all time in the future; in a way that exists all the time: *The stroke left his right side permanently damaged.* ◊ *She had decided to settle permanently in France.* **OPP** *temporarily*

**permanent ˈresident** *noun* a person who has been given the right to live and work in a country for as long as they want (but is not a citizen with the right to vote, etc.)

**Permanent ˈResident Card** *noun* an official card that shows that sb from another country is allowed to live and work in Canada

**Permanent Under'secretary** (*also* **Permanent ˈSecretary**) *noun* a senior officer in the British CIVIL SERVICE who advises a SECRETARY OF STATE ⊃ compare UNDERSECRETARY

**permanent ˈwave** *noun* (*old-fashioned*) = PERM

**per·me·able** /ˈpɜːmiəbl; *NAmE* ˈpɜːrm-/ *adj.* (*specialist*) allowing a liquid or gas to pass through: *permeable rocks* ◊ **to sth** *The skin of amphibians is permeable to water.* **OPP** *impermeable* ▶ **per·mea·bil·ity** /ˌpɜːmiəˈbɪləti; *NAmE* ˌpɜːrm-/ *noun* [U]

**per·me·ate** /ˈpɜːmieɪt; *NAmE* ˈpɜːrm-/ *verb* (*formal*) **1** [T, I] (of a liquid, gas, etc.) to spread to every part of an object or a place: **~ sth** *The smell of leather permeated the room.* ◊ **+ adv./prep.** *rainwater permeating through the ground* **2** [T, I] (of an idea, an influence, a feeling, etc.) to affect every part of sth: **~ sth** *a belief that permeates all levels of society* ◊ **+ adv./prep.** *Dissatisfaction among the managers soon permeated down to members of the workforce.* ▶ **per·me·ation** /ˌpɜːmiˈeɪʃn; *NAmE* ˌpɜːrm-/ *noun* [U] (*formal*)

**per·mis·sible** /pəˈmɪsəbl; *NAmE* pərˈm-/ *adj.* (*formal*) acceptable according to the law or a particular set of rules: *permissible levels of nitrates in water* ◊ **~ (for sb) (to do sth)** *It is not permissible for employers to discriminate on grounds of age.*

**per·mis·sion** ? **A2** /pəˈmɪʃn; *NAmE* pərˈm-/ *noun* **1** ? **A2** [U] the act of allowing sb to do sth, especially when this is done by sb in a position of authority: **~ for sth** *You must ask permission for all major expenditure.* ◊ **~ to do sth** *After much persuasion, permission was granted to speak to the refugees at the camp.* ◊ *All minors must seek parental permission to marry.* ◊ **for sb/sth to do sth** *No official permission has been given for the event to take place.* ◊ **~ from sb/sth (to do sth)** *He had to get permission from his parents to audition for the show.* ◊ **without ~** *She took the car without permission.* **2** [C, *usually pl.*] an official written statement allowing sb to do sth: *The publisher is responsible for obtaining the necessary permissions to reproduce illustrations.* ⊃ see also PLANNING PERMISSION

▼ **EXPRESS YOURSELF**

**Asking for permission/a favour**

You are more likely to get what you want if you can ask for it politely. Here are some ways of asking whether you may do something:
- **Would you mind if** *I opened the window?*
- **Could I possibly** *borrow your phone?*
- **I hate to ask, but could I please** *borrow your phone?* (*NAmE*)
- **Do you happen to have** *a pair of gloves I could borrow for the evening?*
- **Would it be all right if** *I left five minutes early?*
- **Is there any chance that we could** *stay at your house the night before our flight?*
- **Would it be OK to** *leave my bag here?*

Responses:
- **Yes, of course.**
- **Go ahead.**
- **That's fine.**
- **I'd rather you didn't,** *if you don't mind.*
- **I'd prefer it** *if you asked somebody else.*
- **If there's someone else you can ask, I'd be grateful.**

**per·mis·sive** /pəˈmɪsɪv; *NAmE* pərˈm-/ *adj.* allowing or showing a freedom of behaviour that many people do not approve of, especially in sexual matters: *permissive attitudes* ◊ *permissive parents* (= who allow their children a lot of freedom) ▶ **per·mis·sive·ness** *noun* [U]

**per·mit** ? **B2** **W** *verb*, *noun*
- *verb* /pəˈmɪt; *NAmE* pərˈm-/ (**-tt-**) (*formal*) **1** ? **B2** [T, often passive] to allow sb to do sth or to allow sth to happen: **be permitted** *Mobile phones are not permitted in the examination room.* ◊ **be permitted sth** *We were not permitted any contact with each other.* ◊ **be permitted to do sth** *Visitors are not permitted to take photographs.* ◊ **~ sth** *The owners have been unwilling to permit the use of their land.* ◊ **~ sb/yourself sth** *Jim permitted himself a wry smile.* ◊ **~ sb/yourself to do sth** *The bill was designed to permit new fathers to take time off work.* ◊ (*formal*) *Permit me to offer you some advice.* ⊃ **EXPRESS YOURSELF** at FORBID **2** ? **B2** [I, T] to make sth possible: *We hope to visit the cathedral, if time permits.* ◊ *I'll come tomorrow, weather permitting* (= if the weather is fine). ◊ **~ sth** *The password permits access to all files on the hard disk.* ◊ **~ sb/sth to do sth** *Cash machines permit you to withdraw money at any time.*
- *noun* ? **B2** /ˈpɜːmɪt; *NAmE* ˈpɜːrm-/ an official document that gives sb the right to do sth, especially for a limited period of time: *a parking/building permit* ◊ **to apply for a permit** ◊ **for sth** *The agency issued permits for exploratory drilling.* ⊃ see also LEARNER'S PERMIT, WORK PERMIT

**per·mu·ta·tion** /ˌpɜːmjuˈteɪʃn; *NAmE* ˌpɜːrm-/ *noun* [*usually pl.*] any of the different ways in which a set of things can be ordered: *The possible permutations of x, y and z are xyz, xzy, yxz, yzx, zxy and zyx.*

**per·ni·cious** /pəˈnɪʃəs; *NAmE* pərˈn-/ *adj.* (*formal*) having a very harmful effect on sb/sth, especially in a way that is not easily noticed

**per·nick·ety** /pəˈnɪkəti; *NAmE* pərˈn-/ (*especially BrE*) (*NAmE usually* **per·snick·ety**) *adj.* (*informal*, *disapproving*) worrying too much about details that are not important; showing this **SYN** *fussy*

**per·or·ation** /ˌpɜːrəˈreɪʃn; *NAmE* ˌpɜːrə-/ *noun* (*formal*) **1** the final part of a speech in which the speaker gives a summary of the main points **2** (*disapproving*) a long speech that is not very interesting

**per·ox·ide** /pəˈrɒksaɪd; *NAmE* -ˈrɑːk-/ (*also* **hydrogen peˈroxide**) *noun* [U] a clear liquid used to kill bacteria and to BLEACH hair (= make it lighter): *a woman with peroxide blonde hair*

**perp** /pɜːp; *NAmE* pɜːrp/ *noun* (*NAmE*, *informal*) = PERPETRATOR: *The perp stole a police car and got away.*

**per·pen·dicu·lar** /ˌpɜːpənˈdɪkjələ(r); *NAmE* ˌpɜːrp-/ *adj.*, *noun*
- *adj.* **1** **~ (to sth)** forming an angle of 90° with another line or surface; VERTICAL and going straight up: *Are the lines perpendicular to each other?* ◊ *The staircase was almost perpendicular* (= very steep). **2** **Perpendicular** (*architecture*) connected with a style of architecture common in England in the 14th and 15th centuries
- *noun* **the perpendicular** [*sing.*] a line, position or direction that is exactly perpendicular: *The wall is a little out of the perpendicular.*

**per·pet·rate** /ˈpɜːpətreɪt; *NAmE* ˈpɜːrp-/ *verb* (*formal*) to commit a crime or do sth wrong or evil: **~ sth** *to perpetrate a crime/fraud/massacre* ◊ **~ sth against/upon/on sb** *violence perpetrated against women and children* ▶ **per·pet·ra·tion** /ˌpɜːpəˈtreɪʃn; *NAmE* ˌpɜːrp-/ *noun* [U]

**per·pet·ra·tor** /ˈpɜːpətreɪtə(r); *NAmE* ˈpɜːrp-/ (*also NAmE*, *informal* **perp**) *noun* a person who commits a crime or does sth that is wrong or evil: *the perpetrators of the crime*

**per·pet·ual** /pəˈpetʃuəl; *NAmE* pərˈp-/ *adj.* **1** [*usually before noun*] continuing for a long period of time without stopping or being interrupted **SYN** *continuous*: *the perpetual noise of traffic* ◊ *We lived for years in a perpetual state of fear.* **2** [*usually before noun*] frequently repeated, in a way that is annoying **SYN** *continual*: *How can I work with these perpetual interruptions?* **3** [*only before noun*] (of a job or position) lasting for the whole of sb's life: *He was*

**perpetual motion**

elected perpetual president. ◇ (humorous) She's a perpetual student. ▶ **per·pet·u·al·ly** /-əli/ adv.

**per·petual 'motion** noun [U] a state in which sth moves continuously without stopping, or appears to do so: We're all in a state of perpetual motion in this office (= we're always moving around or changing things).

**per·petu·ate** /pəˈpetʃueɪt; NAmE pərˈp-/ verb (formal) to make sth such as a bad situation, a belief, etc. continue for a long time: ~ **sth** to perpetuate injustice ◇ Comics tend to perpetuate the myth that 'boys don't cry'. ◇ ~ **itself** This system perpetuated itself for several centuries. ▶ **per·petu·ation** /pəˌpetʃuˈeɪʃn; NAmE pərˌp-/ noun [U].

**per·petu·ity** /ˌpɜːpəˈtjuːəti; NAmE ˌpɜːrpəˈtuː-/ noun [U] **IDM** **in perpetuity** (formal) for all time in the future **SYN** **forever**: They do not own the land in perpetuity.

**per·plex** /pəˈpleks; NAmE pərˈp-/ verb [usually passive] ~ **sb**
**it perplexes sb that…** if sth **perplexes** you, it makes you confused or worried because you do not understand it **SYN** **puzzle**: They were perplexed by her response. ▶ **per·plex·ing** adj.: a perplexing problem

**per·plexed** /pəˈplekst; NAmE pərˈp-/ adj. confused and anxious because you are unable to understand sth; showing this: a perplexed expression ◇ She looked perplexed. ▶ **per·plex·ed·ly** /-ˈpleksɪdli/ adv.

**per·plex·ity** /pəˈpleksəti; NAmE pərˈp-/ noun (pl. -ies) (formal) **1** [U] the state of feeling confused and worried because you do not understand sth **SYN** **confusion**: in ~ Most of them just stared at her in perplexity. **2** [C, usually pl.] something that is difficult to understand: the perplexities of life

**per·quis·ite** /ˈpɜːkwɪzɪt; NAmE ˈpɜːrk-/ noun (formal) **1** [usually pl.] = **PERK** **2** ~ **(of sb)** something to which sb has a special right because of their social position: Politics used to be the perquisite of the property-owning classes.

**perry** /ˈperi/ noun [U, C] a slightly sweet alcoholic drink made from the juice of **PEARS** ⇒ compare **CIDER**

**per se** /ˌpɜː ˈseɪ; NAmE ˌpɜːr/ adv. (from Latin) used meaning 'by itself' to show that you are referring to sth on its own, rather than in connection with other things: The drug is not harmful per se, but is dangerous when taken with alcohol.

**per·se·cute** /ˈpɜːsɪkjuːt; NAmE ˈpɜːrs-/ verb [often passive] **1** ~ **sb (for sth)** to treat sb in a cruel and unfair way, especially because of their race, religion or political beliefs: Throughout history, people have been persecuted for their religious beliefs. ◇ persecuted minorities ⇒ **WORDFINDER NOTE** at **EQUAL** **2** ~ **sb** to deliberately annoy sb all the time and make their life unpleasant **SYN** **harass**: Why are the media persecuting him like this? ▶ **per·se·cu·tion** /ˌpɜːsɪˈkjuːʃn; NAmE ˌpɜːrs-/ noun [U, C]: the victims of religious persecution

**per·se·cu·tor** /ˈpɜːsɪkjuːtə(r); NAmE ˈpɜːrs-/ noun a person who treats another person or group of people in a cruel and unfair way

**per·se·ver·ance** /ˌpɜːsɪˈvɪərəns; NAmE ˌpɜːrsəˈvɪr-/ noun [U] (approving) the quality of continuing to try to achieve a particular aim despite difficulties: They showed great perseverance in the face of difficulty. ◇ The only way to improve is through hard work and dogged perseverance.

**per·se·vere** /ˌpɜːsɪˈvɪə(r); NAmE ˌpɜːrsəˈvɪr/ verb [I] (approving) to continue trying to do or achieve sth despite difficulties: ~ **(in sth/in doing sth)** Despite a number of setbacks, they persevered in their attempts to fly around the world in a balloon. ◇ ~ **(with sth/sb)** She persevered with her violin lessons. ◇ You have to persevere with difficult students.

**per·se·ver·ing** /ˌpɜːsɪˈvɪərɪŋ; NAmE ˌpɜːrsəˈvɪr-/ adj. [usually before noun] (approving) being determined to achieve a particular aim despite difficulties

**Per·sian** /ˈpɜːʃn; NAmE ˈpɜːrʒn/ noun **1** [C] a person from ancient Persia, or modern Persia, now called Iran **2** (also **Farsi**) [U] the official language of Iran **3** [C] = **PERSIAN CAT** ▶ **Per·sian** adj.

**Persian 'carpet** (also **Persian 'rug**) noun a carpet of traditional design from Iran, made by hand from silk or wool

**Persian 'cat** (also **Per·sian**) noun a type of cat with long hair, short legs and a round flat face

**per·sim·mon** /pəˈsɪmən; NAmE pərˈs-/ noun a sweet fruit that looks like a large orange tomato ⇒ **VISUAL VOCAB** page V4

**per·sist** /pəˈsɪst; NAmE pərˈs-/ verb **1** [I, T] to continue to do sth despite difficulties or opposition, in a way that can seem unreasonable: ~ **in doing sth** Why do you persist in blaming yourself for what happened? ◇ ~ **in sth** She persisted in her search for the truth. ◇ ~ **with sth** He persisted with his questioning. ◇ + **speech** 'So, did you agree or not?' he persisted. **2** [I] to continue to exist: If the symptoms persist, consult your doctor.

**per·sist·ence** /pəˈsɪstəns; NAmE pərˈs-/ noun [U] **1** the fact of continuing to try to do sth despite difficulties, especially when other people are against you and think that you are being annoying or unreasonable: His persistence was finally rewarded when the insurance company agreed to pay for the damage. ◇ It was her sheer persistence that wore them down in the end. **2** the state of continuing to exist for a long period of time: the persistence of unemployment in the 1970s and 1980s

**per·sist·ent** /pəˈsɪstənt; NAmE pərˈs-/ adj. **1** determined to do sth despite difficulties, especially when other people are against you and think that you are being annoying or unreasonable: How do you deal with persistent salesmen who won't take no for an answer? ◇ a persistent offender (= a person who continues to commit crimes after they have been caught and punished) **2** continuing for a long period of time, or repeated frequently, especially in a way that is annoying and cannot be stopped **SYN** **unrelenting**: persistent rain ◇ a persistent cough ▶ **per·sist·ent·ly** adv.: They have persistently denied claims of illegal dealing. ◇ persistently high interest rates

**per·sistent vegetative 'state** noun (medical) a condition in which a person's body is kept working by medical means but the person shows no sign of brain activity

**per·snick·ety** /pəˈsnɪkəti; NAmE pərˈs-/ adj. (NAmE) = **PERNICKETY**

**per·son** /ˈpɜːsn; NAmE ˈpɜːrsn/ noun (pl. **people** /ˈpiːpl/) **HELP** The plural form **persons** is used in some formal language. **1** a human as an individual: What sort of person would do a thing like that? ◇ He's a fascinating person. ◇ **as a ~** What is she like as a person? ◇ He's just the person we need for the job. ◇ I had a letter from the people who used to live next door. ◇ I'm not really a city person (= I don't really like cities). ⇒ see also **LITTLE PERSON**, **PEOPLE PERSON** **HELP** Use **everyone** or **everybody** instead of 'all people'. **2** (formal or disapproving) a human, especially one who is not identified: A certain person (= sb that I do not wish to name) told me about it. ◇ The price is $40 per person. ◇ This vehicle is licensed to carry 4 persons. (= in a notice) ◇ (law) The verdict was murder by a person or persons unknown. ⇒ see also **BUSINESS PERSON**, **DISPLACED PERSON**, **MISSING PERSON**, **NON-PERSON**, **VIP**, **YOUNG PERSON** **3** **-person** (in compounds) a person working in the area of business mentioned; a person connected with the thing mentioned: a salesperson ◇ a spokesperson **4** (grammar) any of the three classes of personal pronouns. The **first person** (I/we) refers to the person(s) speaking; the **second person** (you) refers to the person(s) spoken to; the **third person** (he/she/it/they) refers to the person(s) or thing(s) spoken about. **IDM** **about/on your 'person** (formal) if you have or carry sth **about/on your person**, you carry it about with you, for example in your pocket **in 'person** if you do sth **in person**, you go somewhere and do it yourself, instead of doing it by letter, asking sb else to do it, etc. **in the person of sb** (formal) in the form or shape of sb: Help arrived in the person of his mother. ⇒ more at **RESPECTER**

**per·sona** /pəˈsəʊnə; NAmE pərˈs-/ noun (pl. **per·son·ae** /pəˈsəʊnaɪ; NAmE pərˈs-/ or **per·so·nas**) (formal) the aspects of a person's character that they show to other people, especially when their real character is different: His public persona is quite different from the family man described in the book. ⇒ see also **DRAMATIS PERSONAE**

**per·son·able** /ˈpɜːsənəbl; *NAmE* ˈpɜːrs-/ *adj.* (of a person) attractive to other people because of having a pleasant appearance and character

**per·son·age** /ˈpɜːsənɪdʒ; *NAmE* ˈpɜːrs-/ *noun* (*formal*) an important or famous person: *a royal personage*

**per·son·al** ⓘ **A1** Ⓦ /ˈpɜːsənl; *NAmE* ˈpɜːrs-/ *adj.*
- **YOUR OWN 1** **A1** [usually before noun] your own; not belonging to or connected with anyone else: *The novel is written from* ***personal experience****.* ◇ *personal effects/belongings/possessions* ◇ *I take* ***personal responsibility*** *for the incident.* ◇ *Of course, this is just a personal opinion.* ◇ *a personal preference/view* ◇ *Her art is* ***deeply personal****.* ◇ ***intensely/highly personal*** ◇ *I need my* ***own personal*** *space.* ◇ *The software is for personal use only* (= no one else can use it).
- **BETWEEN INDIVIDUALS 2** **A1** [only before noun] between individual people who know each other: *Having good* ***personal relationships*** *is the most important thing for me.* ◇ *She is a personal friend of mine.*
- **PRIVATE 3** **A2** connected with a person's private life, rather than their job or official position: *I try not to let work interfere with my* ***personal life****.* ◇ ***personal information/data/details*** (= information about you that not everyone can know) ◇ *The letter was marked 'Personal'.* ◇ *I'd like to talk to you about a personal matter.*
- **DONE BY PERSON 4** **A2** [only before noun] done by a particular person rather than by sb who is acting for them: *The President made a personal appearance at the event.* ◇ *I shall give the matter my personal attention.*
- **DONE FOR PERSON 5** **A2** [only before noun] made or done for a particular person rather than for a large group of people or people in general: *We offer a personal service to all our customers.* ◇ *a personal pension plan* (= a pension organized by a private company for one particular person)
- **OFFENSIVE 6** **B1** referring to a particular person's character, appearance, opinions, etc. in a way that is offensive: *Try to avoid making personal remarks.* ◇ *I felt the criticism crossed the line and became a personal attack.* ◇ *It's nothing personal* (= I do not wish to offend you) *but I have to correct you on that point.*
- **CONNECTED WITH BODY 7** **B1** [only before noun] connected with a person's body: *personal cleanliness/hygiene* ◇ *This insurance policy covers you against* ***personal injury*** *or death.* **IDM** see CLOSE² *adj.*

**ˌpersonal ˈad** *noun* a private advertisement in a newspaper, etc., especially from sb looking for a romantic or sexual partner

**ˌpersonal alˈlowance** *noun* (in the UK) the amount of money you are allowed to earn each year before you have to pay INCOME TAX

**ˌpersonal asˈsistant** *noun* ⇒ PA (2)

**ˌpersonal ˈbest** *noun* (*abbr.* **PB**) the best result that you have ever had in an event such as a race or other competition: *She won the race with a personal best of 2 minutes 22.*

**ˌpersonal ˈcolumn** *noun* a part of a newspaper or magazine for private messages or personal advertisements

**ˌpersonal comˈputer** *noun* (*abbr.* **PC**) a computer that is designed for one person to use at work or at home ⇒ compare MAINFRAME

**ˌpersonal ˈday** *noun* (*NAmE*) a day that you take off work for personal reasons, but not because you are ill or on holiday

**ˌpersonal exˈemption** *noun* (in the US) the amount of money you are allowed to earn each year before you have to pay INCOME TAX. You are allowed one personal exemption for each person that you support financially, including yourself.

**ˌpersonal ˈinjury** *noun* [U] (*law*) physical injury, rather than damage to property or to sb's reputation

**per·son·al·ity** ⓘ **A2** /ˌpɜːsəˈnæləti; *NAmE* ˌpɜːrs-/ *noun* (*pl.* **-ies**) **1** **A2** [C, U] the various aspects of a person's character that combine to make them different from other people: *His wife has a strong personality.* ◇ *He maintained order by sheer force of personality.* ◇ *normal human* ***personality traits*** (= qualities), *such as shyness* ◇ *Partici-*

1151  **personification**

*pants identified their own personality type and explored the implications.* ◇ *There are likely to be tensions and* ***personality clashes*** *in any social group.* **2** **B1** [U] the qualities of a person's character that make them interesting and attractive: *We need someone with lots of personality to head the project.* **3** **B2** [C] a famous person, especially one who works in entertainment or sport **SYN** celebrity: *a well-known TV/radio/sports personality* ◇ *personalities from the world of music* **4** [C] a person whose strong character attracts attention: *Their son is a real personality.* **5** [U] the qualities of a place or thing that make it interesting and different **SYN** character: *The problem with many modern buildings is that they lack personality.*

**perˈsonality cult** (*also* **cult of perˈsonality**) *noun* (*disapproving*) a situation in which people are encouraged to show extreme enthusiasm and love for a famous person, especially a political leader

**perˈsonality disorder** *noun* (*specialist*) a serious mental condition in which sb's behaviour makes it difficult for them to have normal relationships with other people or a normal role in society

**per·son·al·ize** (*BrE also* **-ise**) /ˈpɜːsənəlaɪz; *NAmE* ˈpɜːrs-/ *verb* **1** [usually passive] **~ sth** to mark sth in some way to show that it belongs to a particular person: *All the towels were personalized with their initials.* **2 ~ sth** to design or change sth so that it is suitable for the needs of a particular person: *All our courses are personalized to the needs of the individual.* **3 ~ sth** to refer to particular people when discussing a general subject: *The mass media tends to personalize politics.* ▸ **per·son·al·ized**, **-ised** *adj.*: *a highly personalized service* ◇ (*BrE*) *a personalized number plate* (= on a car)

**per·son·al·ly** ⓘ **B1** /ˈpɜːsənəli; *NAmE* ˈpɜːrs-/ *adv.*
**1** **B1** used to show that you are giving your own opinion about sth: *Personally, I prefer the second option.* ◇ *'Is it worth the effort?' 'Speaking personally, yes.'* **2** **B1** by a particular person rather than by sb acting for them: *All emails will be answered personally.* ◇ *Do you know him personally* (= have you met him, rather than just knowing about him from other people)? **3** **B1** in a way that is connected with one particular person rather than a group of people **SYN** individually: *He was personally criticized by inspectors for his incompetence.* ◇ *You will be held* ***personally responsible*** *for any loss or breakage.* **4** **B1** in a way that is intended to be offensive: *I'm sure she didn't mean it personally.* **5** **B1** in a way that is connected with sb's personal life rather than with their job or official position: *Have you had any dealings with any of the suspects, either personally or professionally?*

**IDM ˌtake sth ˈpersonally** to be offended by sth: *I'm afraid he took your remarks personally.*

**ˌpersonal ˈpronoun** *noun* (*grammar*) any of the pronouns *I*, *you*, *he*, *she*, *it*, *we*, *they*, *me*, *him*, *her*, *us*, *them*

**ˌpersonal ˈshopper** *noun* a person whose job is to help sb else buy things, either by going with them around a shop or by doing their shopping for them

**ˌpersonal ˈspace** *noun* [U] the space directly around where you are standing or sitting: *He leaned towards her and she stiffened at this invasion of her personal space.*

**ˌpersonal ˈstatement** *noun* a written description of your achievements and interests, included as part of an application for a job or a place at university or college

**ˌpersonal ˈtrainer** *noun* a person who is paid by sb to help them exercise, especially by deciding what types of exercise are best for them ⇒ WORDFINDER NOTE at FIT

**perˌsona non ˈgrata** /pɜːˌsəʊnə nɒn ˈɡrɑːtə, ˈneɪn; *NAmE* pɜːrˌsoʊnə nɑːn/ *noun* [U] (*from Latin*) a person who is not welcome in a particular place because of sth they have said or done, especially one who is told to leave a country by the government

**per·soni·fi·ca·tion** /pəˌsɒnɪfɪˈkeɪʃn; *NAmE* pərˌsɑːn-/ *noun* **1** [C, usually *sing.*] **~ of sth** a person who has a lot of a particular quality or characteristic **SYN** epitome: *She was the personification of elegance.* **2** [U, C] the practice of representing objects, qualities, etc. as humans, in art and

# personify

literature; an object, quality, etc. that is represented in this way: *the personification of autumn in Keats's poem*

**per·son·ify** /pəˈsɒnɪfaɪ; NAmE pərˈsɑːn-/ verb (**per·soni·fies, per·soni·fy·ing, per·soni·fied, per·soni·fied**) **1** ~ **sth** to be an example of a quality or characteristic, or to have a lot of it SYN **typify**: *These children personify all that is wrong with the education system.* ◇ *He is kindness personified.* **2** [usually passive] **be personified (as sb)** to show or think of an object, quality, etc. as a person: *The river was personified as a goddess.*

**per·son·nel** ?+ C1 /ˌpɜːsəˈnel; NAmE ˌpɜːrs-/ noun **1** ?+ C1 [pl.] the people who work for an organization or one of the armed forces: *skilled personnel* ◇ *sales/technical/medical/security/military, etc. personnel* **2** ?+ C1 [U + sing./pl. v.] the department in a company that deals with employing and training people SYN **human resources**: *the personnel department/manager* ◇ *She works in personnel.* ◇ *Personnel is/are currently reviewing pay scales.*

**per·sonˈnel carrier** noun a military vehicle for carrying soldiers ⊃ see also ARMOURED PERSONNEL CARRIER

**ˌperson-to-ˈperson** adj. [usually before noun] **1** happening between two or more people who deal directly with each other rather than through another person: *Technical support is offered on a person-to-person basis.* **2** (*especially NAmE*) (of a phone call) made by calling the OPERATOR (= a person who works at a TELEPHONE EXCHANGE) and asking to speak to a particular person. If that person is not available, the call does not have to be paid for: *a person-to-person call*

**per·spec·tive** ⓘ B2 ⓞ /pəˈspektɪv; NAmE pərˈs-/ noun **1** ?+ B2 [C] a particular attitude towards sth; a way of thinking about sth SYN **viewpoint**: *a global/historical perspective* ◇ **from a ...** ~ *Try to see the issue from a different perspective.* ◇ **from the ~ of sb/sth** *a report that looks at the education system from the perspective of deaf people* ◇ **on sth** *The exhibition provides us with a unique perspective on her work.* **2** [U] the ability to think about problems and decisions in a reasonable way without making them seem worse or more important than they really are: *She was aware that she was losing all sense of perspective.* ◇ *Try to keep these issues in perspective.* ◇ *Talking to others can often help to put your own problems into perspective.* ◇ *It is important not to let things get out of perspective.* **3** [U] the art of creating an effect of depth and distance in a picture by representing people and things that are far away as being smaller than those that are nearer the front: **in** ~ *We learnt how to draw buildings in perspective.* ◇ **out of** ~ *The tree on the left is out of perspective.* **4** [C] (*formal*) a view, especially one in which you can see far into the distance: *a perspective of the whole valley*

**Per·spex**™ /ˈpɜːspeks; NAmE ˈpɜːrs-/ (*BrE*) (*NAmE* **Plexi·glas**™) noun [U] a strong clear plastic material that is often used instead of glass

**per·spi·ca·cious** /ˌpɜːspɪˈkeɪʃəs; NAmE ˌpɜːrs-/ adj. (*formal*) able to understand sb/sth quickly and accurately; showing this: *a perspicacious remark* ▸ **per·spi·ca·city** /-ˈkæsəti/ noun [U]

**per·spir·ation** /ˌpɜːspəˈreɪʃn; NAmE ˌpɜːrs-/ noun [U] **1** drops of liquid that form on your skin when you are hot SYN **sweat**: *Beads of perspiration stood out on his forehead.* ◇ *Her skin was damp with perspiration.* **2** the act of perspiring: *Perspiration cools the skin in hot weather.*

**per·spire** /pəˈspaɪə(r); NAmE pərˈs-/ verb [I] (*formal*) to produce SWEAT on your body SYN **sweat**

**per·suade** ⓘ B1 /pəˈsweɪd; NAmE pərˈs-/ verb **1** ?+ B1 to make sb do sth by giving them good reasons for doing it: ~ **sb to do sth** *Try to persuade him to come.* ◇ ~ **sb** *Please try and persuade her.* ◇ *She's always easily persuaded.* ◇ ~ **sb into (doing) sth** *I allowed myself to be persuaded into entering the competition.* ◇ ~ **sb out of (doing) sth** *There was no way to persuade him out of it* (= persuade him not to do it). **2** ?+ B1 to make sb believe that sth is true SYN **convince**: ~ **sb/yourself that** ... *It will be difficult to persuade them that there's no other choice.* ◇ *She had persuaded herself that life was not worth living.* ◇ ~ **sb No one**

▼ **WHICH WORD?**

**persuade / convince**

- The main meaning of **persuade** is to make someone agree to do something by giving them good reasons for doing it: *I tried to persuade her to see a doctor.* The main meaning of **convince** is to make someone believe that something is true: *He convinced me he was right.*
- It is quite common, however, for each of these words to be used with both meanings, especially for **convince** to be used as a synonym for **persuade**: *I persuaded/convinced her to see a doctor.* Some speakers of *BrE* think that this is not correct.

*was persuaded by his arguments.* ◇ ~ **sb of sth** (*formal*) *I am still not fully persuaded of the plan's merits.*

**per·sua·sion** /pəˈsweɪʒn; NAmE pərˈs-/ noun **1** [U] the act of persuading sb to do sth or to believe sth: *It didn't take much persuasion to get her to tell us where he was.* ◇ *After a little gentle persuasion, he agreed to come.* ◇ *She has great powers of persuasion.* **2** [C, U] a particular set of beliefs, especially about religion or politics: *politicians of all persuasions* ◇ *every shade of religious persuasion*

**per·sua·sive** /pəˈsweɪsɪv; NAmE pərˈs-/ adj. able to persuade sb to do or believe sth: *persuasive arguments* ◇ *He can be very persuasive.* ▸ **per·sua·sive·ly** adv.: *They argue persuasively in favour of a total ban on handguns.* **per·sua·sive·ness** noun [U]

**pert** /pɜːt; NAmE pɜːrt/ adj. **1** (especially of a girl or young woman) showing a lack of respect, often in a humorous way SYN **impudent**: *a pert reply* **2** (of a part of the body) small and with an attractive shape: *a pert nose* ◇ *pert features* ▸ **pert·ly** adv.

**per·tain** /pəˈteɪn; NAmE pərˈt-/ verb [I] (*formal*) to exist or to apply in a particular situation or at a particular time: *Living conditions are vastly different from those pertaining in their country of origin.* ◇ *Those laws no longer pertain.*
**PHRV** **perˈtain to sth/sb** (*formal*) to be connected with sth/sb: *the laws pertaining to adoption*

**per·tin·ent** /ˈpɜːtɪnənt; NAmE ˈpɜːrtn-/ adj. (*formal*) appropriate to a particular situation SYN **relevant**: *a pertinent question/fact* ◇ ~ **to sth** *Please keep your comments pertinent to the topic under discussion.* ▸ **per·tin·ent·ly** adv. **per·tin·ence** /ˈpɜːtɪnəns; NAmE ˈpɜːrtn-/ noun [U]

**per·turb** /pəˈtɜːb; NAmE pərˈtɜːrb/ verb ~ **sb** (*formal*) to make sb worried or anxious SYN **alarm**: *Her sudden appearance did not seem to perturb him in the least.* ▸ **per·turbed** /pəˈtɜːbd; NAmE pərˈtɜːrbd/ adj.: *a perturbed young man* ◇ ~ **at/about sth** *She didn't seem perturbed at the change of plan.* OPP **unperturbed**

**per·turb·ation** /ˌpɜːtəˈbeɪʃn; NAmE ˌpɜːrtərˈb-/ noun **1** [U] (*formal*) the state of feeling anxious about sth SYN **alarm 2** [C, U] (*specialist*) a small change in the quality, behaviour or movement of sth: *temperature perturbations*

**pertussis** /pəˈtʌsɪs; NAmE pərˈt-/ noun [U] (*medical*) = WHOOPING COUGH

**per·use** /pəˈruːz/ verb ~ **sth** (*formal* or *humorous*) to read sth, especially in a careful way: *A copy of the report is available for you to peruse at your leisure.* ▸ **per·usal** /-ˈruːzl/ noun [U, sing.]: *The agreement was signed after careful perusal.*

**perv** (*also* **perve**) /pɜːv; NAmE pɜːrv/ noun (*informal*) **1** = PERVERT **2** (*AustralE, NZE*) a look at sb/sth that shows sexual interest in them or it, in an unpleasant way

**per·vade** /pəˈveɪd; NAmE pərˈv-/ verb ~ **sth** (*formal*) to spread through and be easy to notice in every part of sth SYN **permeate**: *a pervading mood of fear* ◇ *the sadness that pervades most of her novels* ◇ *The entire house was pervaded by a sour smell.*

**per·va·sive** /pəˈveɪsɪv; NAmE pərˈv-/ adj. existing in all parts of a place or thing; spreading gradually to affect all parts of a place or thing: *a pervasive smell of damp* ◇ *A sense of social change is pervasive in her novels.* ▸ **per·va·sive·ly** adv. **per·va·sive·ness** noun [U]

**per·verse** /pəˈvɜːs; NAmE pərˈvɜːrs/ adj. showing a deliberate and determined desire to behave in a way that most people think is wrong, unacceptable or unreasonable: *a* *perverse decision* (= one that most people do not expect and think is wrong) ◊ *She finds a perverse pleasure in upsetting her parents.* ◊ *Do you really mean that or are you just being **deliberately perverse**?* ▶ **per·verse·ly** *adv.*: *She seemed perversely proud of her criminal record.* **per·vers·ity** /pəˈvɜːsəti; *NAmE* pərˈvɜːrs-/ *noun* [U]: *He refused to attend out of sheer perversity.*

**per·ver·sion** /pəˈvɜːʃn; *NAmE* pərˈvɜːrʒn/ *noun* [U, C] **1** behaviour that most people think is not normal or acceptable, especially when it is connected with sex; an example of this type of behaviour: *sexual perversion* ◊ *sadomasochistic perversions* **2** the act of changing sth that is good or right into sth that is bad or wrong; the result of this: *the perversion of justice* ◊ *Her account was a perversion of the truth.*

**per·vert** *verb, noun*
- *verb* /pəˈvɜːt; *NAmE* pərˈvɜːrt/ **1** ~ **sth** to change a system, process, etc. in a bad way so that it is not what it used to be or what it should be: *Some scientific discoveries have been perverted to create weapons of destruction.* **2** ~ **sb/sth** to affect sb in a way that makes them act or think in an unacceptable or IMMORAL way SYN **corrupt**: *Some people believe that television can pervert the minds of children.* IDM **pervert the course of ˈjustice** (*BrE*) (*NAmE* **ob'struct justice**) (*law*) to tell a lie or to do sth in order to prevent the police, etc. from finding out the truth about a crime
- *noun* /ˈpɜːvɜːt; *NAmE* ˈpɜːrvɜːrt/ (*also informal* **perv**) a person whose sexual behaviour is not thought to be normal or acceptable by most people SYN **deviant**: *a sexual pervert*

**per·verted** /pəˈvɜːtɪd; *NAmE* pərˈvɜːrt-/ *adj.* not thought to be normal or acceptable by most people: *sexual acts, normal and perverted* ◊ *She was having difficulty following his perverted logic.* ◊ *They clearly take a perverted pleasure in watching others suffer.*

**pesky** /ˈpeski/ *adj.* [only before noun] (*especially NAmE, informal*) annoying: *pesky insects*

**peso** /ˈpeɪsəʊ/ *noun* (*pl.* **-os**) the unit of money in many Latin American countries and the Philippines

**pes·sary** /ˈpesəri/ *noun* (*pl.* **-ies**) **1** a small piece of solid medicine that is placed inside a woman's VAGINA and left to DISSOLVE, used to cure an infection or to prevent her from becoming pregnant ➔ see also SUPPOSITORY **2** a device that is placed inside a woman's VAGINA to support the WOMB

**pes·sim·ism** /ˈpesɪmɪzəm/ *noun* [U] ~ (**about/over sth**) a feeling that bad things will happen and that sth will not be successful: *There is a mood of pessimism in the company about future job prospects.* OPP **optimism**

**pes·sim·ist** /ˈpesɪmɪst/ *noun* a person who always expects bad things to happen: *You don't have to be a pessimist to realize that we're in trouble.* OPP **optimist**

**pes·sim·is·tic** /ˌpesɪˈmɪstɪk/ *adj.* ~ (**about sth**) expecting bad things to happen or sth not to be successful; showing this: *They appeared surprisingly pessimistic about their chances of winning.* ◊ *a pessimistic view of life* ◊ *I think you're being far too pessimistic.* OPP **optimistic** ▶ **pes·sim·is·tic·al·ly** /-kli/ *adv.*

**pest** /pest/ *noun* **1** an insect or animal that destroys plants, food, etc: *insect/plant/garden pests* ◊ *a pest control officer* **2** (*informal*) an annoying person or thing: *That child is being a real pest.*

**pes·ter** /ˈpestə(r)/ *verb* [T, I] to annoy sb, especially by asking them sth many times SYN **badger**: ~ **sb for sth** *Journalists pestered neighbours for information.* ◊ ~ **sb with sth** *He has been pestering her with phone calls for over a week.* ◊ ~ **sb** *The horses were continually pestered by flies.* ◊ ~ (**sb to do sth**) *The kids kept pestering me to read to them.*

**pesti·cide** /ˈpestɪsaɪd/ *noun* [C, U] a chemical used for killing pests, especially insects: *vegetables grown without the use of pesticides* ◊ *crops sprayed with pesticide* ➔ see also HERBICIDE, INSECTICIDE

**pesti·lence** /ˈpestɪləns/ *noun* [U, sing.] (*old use* or *literary*) any disease that spreads quickly and kills a lot of people

**pes·tle** /ˈpesl/ *noun* a small heavy tool with a round end used for pressing things to a powder in a special bowl called a MORTAR

---

1153 **petition**

**pesto** /ˈpestəʊ/ *noun* [U] an Italian sauce made of BASIL leaves, PINE NUTS, cheese and oil

**PET** *noun* [U] **1** /ˌpiː iː ˈtiː/ an artificial substance used to make materials for packaging food, including plastic drinks bottles (the abbreviation for 'polyethylene terephthalate') **2** /pet/ (*medical*) a process that produces an image of your brain or of another part inside your body (the abbreviation for 'positron emission tomography'): *a PET scan* **3** /pet/ a British test, now called 'B1 Preliminary', that measures a person's ability to speak and write English as a foreign language at an INTERMEDIATE level (the abbreviation for 'Preliminary English Test')

**pet** ⓘ A2 /pet/ *noun, verb, adj.*
- *noun* **1** A2 an animal, a bird, etc. that you have at home for pleasure, rather than one that is kept for work or food: *Do you have any pets?* ◊ *a pet dog/hamster* ◊ *a family pet* ◊ *pet food* ◊ *a pet owner* ◊ *a pet shop* (= where animals are sold as pets) **2** (*usually disapproving*) a person who is given special attention by sb, especially in a way that seems unfair to other people SYN **favourite**: *She's the teacher's pet.* **3** (*BrE, informal*) used when speaking to sb to show kind feelings or to be friendly: *What's wrong, pet?* ◊ *Be a pet* (= be kind) *and post this letter for me.*
- *verb* (**-tt-**) **1** [T] ~ **sb/sth** to touch or move your hand gently over an animal or a child in a kind and loving way **2** [I] (*informal*) (of two people) to kiss and touch each other in a sexual way ➔ see also PETTING
- *adj.* [only before noun] that you are very interested in: *his pet subject/theory/project, etc.* ➔ see also PET NAME IDM **sb's pet ˈhate** (*BrE*) (*NAmE* **sb's pet ˈpeeve**) something that you particularly dislike

**petal** /ˈpetl/ *noun* a DELICATE coloured part of a flower. The head of a flower is usually made up of several petals around a central part. ➔ VISUAL VOCAB page V7

**pe·tard** /peˈtɑːd; *NAmE* -ˈtɑːrd/ *noun* IDM see HOIST *v.*

**Peter** /ˈpiːtə(r)/ *noun* IDM see ROB

**peter** /ˈpiːtə(r)/ *verb* PHRV **ˌpeter ˈout** to gradually become smaller, quieter, etc. and then end: *The campaign petered out for lack of support.* ◊ *The road petered out into a dirt track.*

**ˌPeter ˈPan** *noun* a person who looks unusually young for their age, or who behaves in a way that would be more appropriate for sb younger ORIGIN From a story by J M Barrie about a boy with magic powers who never grew up.

**peth·id·ine** /ˈpeθədiːn/ *noun* [U] a drug used to reduce severe pain, especially for women giving birth

**petit bourgeois** /ˌpeti ˈbʊəʒwɑː; *NAmE* ˈbʊrʒ-/ (*also* **petty ˈbourgeois**) *noun* (*pl.* **petits/petty bourgeois**) (*from French, disapproving*) a member of the lower middle class in society, especially one who thinks that money, work and social position are very important ▶ **petit ˈbourgeois** (*also* **petty ˈbourgeois**) *adj.* [usually before noun]

**pe·tite** /pəˈtiːt/ *adj.* (*from French, approving*) (of a girl, woman or her figure) small and thin: *a petite blonde*

**the pe·tite bourgeoi·sie** (*also* **petty bourgeoi·sie**) *noun* [sing.] (*from French*) the lower middle class in society

**pe·ti·tion** ⓘ C1 /pəˈtɪʃn/ *noun, verb*
- *noun* **1** ⓘ C1 ~ (**against/for sth**) a written document signed by a large number of people that asks sb in a position of authority to do or change sth: *Would you like to sign our petition against experiments on animals?* ◊ *to present/deliver a petition* ◊ *to start/launch a petition* **2** ~ (**for sth**) (*law*) an official document asking a court to take a particular course of action: *Her husband has already filed a petition for divorce.* **3** (*formal*) a formal prayer to God or request to sb in authority
- *verb* **1** [I, T] to make a formal request to sb in authority, especially by sending them a petition: ~ **for/against sth** *Local residents have successfully petitioned against the siting of a prison in their area.* ◊ ~ **sb/sth (for sth)** *The group intends to petition Parliament for reform of the law.* ◊ ~ **sb/sth to do sth** *Parents petitioned the school to review its admission policy.* **2** [I, T] ~ (**sb**) (**for sth**) | ~ **sb/sth to do sth** to formally ask for sth in court: *to petition for divorce*

**pe·ti·tion·er** /pəˈtɪʃənə(r)/ noun **1** a person who organizes or signs a petition **2** (*law*) a person who asks a court to take a particular course of action **3** (*formal*) a person who makes a formal request to sb in authority

**ˈpet name** noun a name you use for sb instead of their real name, as a sign of love of friendship

**ˈpet·rel** /ˈpetrəl/ noun a black and white bird that can fly over the sea a long way from land

**ˈPetri dish** /ˈpetri dɪʃ, ˈpiː-/ noun a shallow covered dish used for growing bacteria, etc. in

**petri·fied** /ˈpetrɪfaɪd/ adj. **1** extremely frightened SYN **terrified**: *a petrified expression* ◇ *~ (of sth) I'm petrified of snakes.* ◇ *They were petrified with fear* (= so frightened that they were unable to move or think). ◇ *~ (that ...) She was petrified that the police would burst in at any moment.* **2** [only before noun] **petrified** trees, insects, etc. have died and been changed into stone over a very long period of time: *a petrified forest*

**pet·rify** /ˈpetrɪfaɪ/ verb (**petri·fies**, **petri·fy·ing**, **petri·fied**, **petri·fied**) **1** [T] *~ sb* to make sb feel extremely frightened SYN **terrify 2** [I, T] *~ (sth)* to change or to make sth change into a substance like stone

**petro-** /ˈpetrəʊ, petrə; *BrE also* pəˈtrɒ; *NAmE also* pəˈtrɑː/ *combining form* (in nouns, adjectives and adverbs) **1** connected with rocks: *petrology* **2** connected with petrol: *petrochemical*

**petro·chem·ical** /ˌpetrəʊˈkemɪkl/ noun any chemical substance obtained from PETROLEUM oil or natural gas: *the petrochemical industry*

**petro·dol·lar** /ˈpetrəʊdɒlə(r); *NAmE* -dɑːl-/ noun a unit of money that is used for calculating the money earned by countries that produce and sell oil

**pet·rol** 🛈 A2 /ˈpetrəl/ (*BrE*) (*NAmE* **gas**, **gas·oline**) noun [U] a liquid obtained from PETROLEUM, used as fuel in car engines, etc: *to fill a car up with petrol* ◇ *to run out of petrol* ◇ *The car has a 2-litre petrol engine.* ◇ *an increase in petrol prices* ◇ *leaded/unleaded petrol* ⇒ compare DIESEL

**ˈpetrol bomb** noun (*BrE*) = MOLOTOV COCKTAIL

**ˈpetrol bunk** noun (*IndE*) a petrol station

**pet·rol·eum** /pəˈtrəʊliəm/ noun [U] mineral oil that is found under the ground or the sea and is used to produce petrol, PARAFFIN, DIESEL oil, etc.

**peˌtroleum ˈjelly** (*NAmE also* **pet·rol·atum** /ˌpetrəˈleɪtəm/) noun [U] a soft clear substance obtained from petroleum, used to HEAL (= make better) injuries on the skin or to make machine parts move together more smoothly SYN **Vaseline™**

**pet·rol·ogy** /pəˈtrɒlədʒi; *NAmE* -ˈtrɑːl-/ noun [U] the scientific study of how rocks are made and what they are made of ⇒ compare LITHOLOGY

**ˈpetrol station** (*BrE*) (*NAmE* **ˈgas station**) (*also* **ˈfilling station**, **ˈservice station** *NAmE, BrE*) noun a place at the side of a road where you take your car to buy petrol, oil, etc.

**petti·coat** /ˈpetikəʊt/ noun (*old-fashioned*) a piece of women's underwear like a thin dress or skirt, worn under a dress or skirt SYN **slip**

**pet·ting** /ˈpetɪŋ/ noun [U] the activity of kissing and touching sb, especially in a sexual way: *heavy petting* (= sexual activity which avoids PENETRATION)

**ˈpetting zoo** noun a ZOO with animals that children can touch

**pet·tish** /ˈpetɪʃ/ adj. behaving in an angry or SULKY way, especially because you cannot have or do what you want SYN **petulant** ▸ **pet·tish·ly** adv.

**petty** /ˈpeti/ adj. **1** [usually before noun] (*disapproving*) small and unimportant SYN **minor**: *petty squabbles* ◇ *a petty bureaucrat/official* (= who does not have much power or authority, although they might pretend to) **2** (*disapproving*) caring too much about small and unimportant matters, especially when this is unkind to other people SYN **small-minded**: *How could you be so petty?* **3** (*law*) (of a crime or criminal) not very serious: *petty crime/theft* ◇ *a petty criminal/thief* ⇒ compare GRAND THEFT ▸ **petti·ness** noun [U]

**petty ˈbourgeois** noun, adj. = PETIT BOURGEOIS

**the petty bourˈgeoi·sie** noun [sing.] = PETITE BOURGEOISIE

**petty ˈcash** noun [U] a small amount of money kept in an office for small payments

**petty ˈofficer** noun (*abbr.* **PO**) a sailor of middle rank in the NAVY

**petu·lant** /ˈpetʃələnt/ adj. behaving in an angry or SULKY way, especially because you cannot do or have what you want SYN **pettish** ▸ **petu·lant·ly** adv. **petu·lance** /-ləns/ noun [U]

**pe·tu·nia** /pəˈtjuːniə; *NAmE* -ˈtuː-/ noun a garden plant with white, pink, purple or red flowers

**pew** /pjuː/ noun a long wooden seat in a church
IDM **take a ˈpew!** (*BrE, informal, humorous*) used to tell sb to sit down

**pew·ter** /ˈpjuːtə(r)/ noun [U] a grey metal made by mixing tin with LEAD, used especially in the past for making cups, dishes, etc.; objects made from pewter

**pey·ote** /peɪˈəʊti/ noun **1** (*also* **mes·cal**) [C, U] a small, blue-green CACTUS that contains a powerful drug that affects people's minds **2** [U] the drug that comes from this plant

**PG** /ˌpiː ˈdʒiː/ abbr. (*BrE*) parental guidance (used to show that some scenes in a film may not be suitable for young children) ⇒ compare U

**PG-13** /ˌpiː dʒiː ˈθɜːtiːn; *NAmE* ˈθɜːrt-/ abbr. (in the US) parental guidance under 13 (used to show that some scenes in a movie may not be suitable for children under the age of 13): *The movie is rated PG-13.* ⇒ compare G (1), NC-17, R (5)

**PGCE** /ˌpiː dʒiː siː ˈiː/ noun a British teaching qualification taken by people who have a university degree (the abbreviation for 'Postgraduate Certificate in Education')

**pH** /ˌpiː ˈeɪtʃ/ noun [sing.] (*chemistry*) a measurement of the level of ACID or ALKALI in a SOLUTION or substance. In the pH range of 0 to 14 a reading of below 7 shows an ACID and of above 7 shows an alkali: *a pH of 7.5* ◇ *to test the pH level of the soil* ⬛ WORDFINDER NOTE at CHEMISTRY

**phago·cyte** /ˈfæɡəsaɪt/ noun (*biology*) a type of cell present in the body that is able to take in and destroy bacteria and other small cells

**phal·anx** /ˈfælæŋks; *NAmE* ˈfeɪl-/ noun (*formal*) **1** (*pl.* **phal·anxes**) a group of people or things standing very close together **2** (*pl.* **pha·lan·ges** /fəˈlændʒiːz/) (*anatomy*) a bone of the finger or toe

**phal·lic** /ˈfælɪk/ adj. of or like a phallus: *phallic symbols*

**phal·locen·tric** /ˌfæləʊˈsentrɪk/ adj. (*formal*) related to men, male power, or the phallus as a symbol of male power ▸ **phal·locen·trism** /-trɪzəm/ noun [U]

**phal·lus** /ˈfæləs/ noun **1** (*specialist*) the male sexual organ, especially when it is ERECT (= stiff) **2** a model or an image of the male sexual organ that represents power and FERTILITY

**phan·tasm** /ˈfæntæzəm/ noun (*formal*) a thing seen in the imagination SYN **illusion**

**phan·tas·ma·goria** /ˌfæntæzməˈɡɒriə; *NAmE* -ˈɡɔːr-/ noun [sing.] (*formal*) a changing scene of real or imagined figures, for example as seen in a dream or created as an effect in a film ▸ **phan·tas·ma·gor·ical** /-ˈrɪkl/ adj.

**phan·tasy** /ˈfæntəsi/ noun [C, U] (*old use*) = FANTASY

**phan·tom** /ˈfæntəm/ noun, adj.
■ noun **1** a ghost: *the phantom of his dead father* **2** a thing that exists only in your imagination
■ adj. [only before noun] **1** like a ghost: *a phantom horseman* **2** existing only in your imagination: *phantom profits* ◇ *phantom illnesses* ◇ *a phantom pregnancy* (= a condition in which a woman seems to be pregnant but in fact is not)

**phar·aoh** /ˈfeərəʊ; *NAmE* ˈfer-/ noun a political leader of ancient Egypt

**Phari·see** /ˈfærɪsiː/ noun **1** a member of an ancient Jewish group who followed religious laws and teaching very strictly **2** (*disapproving*) a person who is very proud of the fact that they have high religious and moral standards, but who does not care enough about other people SYN **hypocrite**

**pharma** /ˈfɑːmə; NAmE ˈfɑːrmə/ (also **Pharma**, **Big Pharma**) noun [U] (informal) pharmaceutical companies as an industry

**pharma·ceut·ical** /ˌfɑːməˈsuːtɪkl, -ˈsjuː-; NAmE ˌfɑːrməˈsuː-/ adj., noun
- adj. [only before noun] connected with making and selling medical drugs: *pharmaceutical products* ◊ *the pharmaceutical industry*
- noun [usually pl.] (*specialist*) a medical drug: *the development of new pharmaceuticals* ◊ *the pharmaceuticals industry*

**pharma·cist** /ˈfɑːməsɪst; NAmE ˈfɑːrm-/ noun **1** (NAmE also, old-fashioned **drug·gist**) a person whose job is to prepare medicines and sell or give them to the public in a shop or in a hospital: *We had to wait for the pharmacist to make up her prescription.* ⇨ compare CHEMIST **2 pharmacist's** (*pl.* **pharma·cists**) (*BrE*) a shop that sells medicines: *They sell vitamin supplements at the pharmacist's.* ⇨ compare CHEMIST ⇨ see also PHARMACY

**pharma·colo·gist** /ˌfɑːməˈkɒlədʒɪst; NAmE ˌfɑːrməˈkɑːl-/ noun a scientist who studies pharmacology

**pharma·col·ogy** /ˌfɑːməˈkɒlədʒi; NAmE ˌfɑːrməˈkɑːl-/ noun [U] the scientific study of drugs and their use in medicine ▸ **pharma·co·logic·al** /ˌfɑːməkəˈlɒdʒɪkl; NAmE ˌfɑːrməkəˈlɑːdʒ-/ adj.: *pharmacological research*

**pharma·co·poeia** (NAmE also **pharma·co·peia**) /ˌfɑːməkəˈpiːə; NAmE ˌfɑːrm-/ noun (*specialist*) an official book containing a list of medicines and drugs and instructions for their use

**phar·macy** /ˈfɑːməsi; NAmE ˈfɑːrm-/ noun (pl. -ies) **1** [C] a shop, or part of one, that sells medicines and drugs ⇨ compare CHEMIST, DRUGSTORE **2** [C] a place in a hospital where medicines are prepared ⇨ see also DISPENSARY **3** [U] the study of how to prepare medicines and drugs ⇨ **WORDFINDER NOTE** at MEDICINE

**pha·ryn·geal** /fəˈrɪndʒiəl, ˌfærɪnˈdʒiːəl/ adj., noun
- adj. (*medical*) relating to the pharynx
- noun (also **pharyngeal 'consonant**) (*phonetics*) a speech sound produced by the root of the tongue using the pharynx

**pha·ryn·gitis** /ˌfærɪnˈdʒaɪtɪs/ noun [U] (*medical*) a condition in which the throat is red and painful

**phar·ynx** /ˈfærɪŋks/ noun (pl. **pha·ryn·ges** /fəˈrɪndʒiːz/) (*anatomy*) the soft area at the top of the throat where the passages to the nose and mouth connect with the throat ⇨ **VISUAL VOCAB** page V1

**phase** ⓘ B2 ⓞ /feɪz/ noun, verb
- noun **1** ⓘ B2 a stage in a process of change or development: *during the **initial/final phase*** ◊ *the testing phase of the project* ◊ *This technology is still in an **early phase of development**.* ◊ *~ **in sth** an important phase in your career* ◊ *His anxiety about the work was just **a passing phase**.* ◊ *During his stay in Spain, his work entered a new phase.* ◊ *She's **going through a difficult phase**.* **2** each of the shapes of the moon as we see it from the earth at different times of the month
  - IDM **in phase / out of phase (with sth)** (*BrE*) working/not working together in the right way: *The traffic lights were out of phase.*
- verb [usually passive] to arrange to do sth gradually in stages over a period of time: **be phased** *Closure of the hospitals was phased over a three-year period.* ◊ *the phased withdrawal of troops from the area*
  - PHR V **phase sth↔in** [usually passive] to introduce or start using sth gradually in stages over a period of time: *The new tax will be phased in over two years.* **phase sth↔out** [usually passive] to stop using sth gradually in stages over a period of time: *Subsidies to farmers will be phased out by next year.*

**phat** /fæt/ adj. (*slang*) very good

**PhD** (also **Ph.D.** especially in NAmE) /ˌpiː eɪtʃ ˈdiː/ noun a university degree of a very high level that is given to sb who has done research in a particular subject (the abbreviation for 'Doctor of Philosophy'): *to be/have/do a PhD* ◊ *Anne Thomas, PhD*

**phea·sant** /ˈfeznt/ noun [C, U] (pl. **phea·sants** or **phea·sant**) a large bird with a long tail, the male of which is brightly coloured. People sometimes shoot pheasants for sport or food. Meat from this bird is also called pheasant: (*BrE*) *to shoot pheasant* ◊ (*NAmE*) *to hunt pheasant* ◊ *roast pheasant* ⇨ **VISUAL VOCAB** page V2

**phe·nol** /ˈfiːnɒl; NAmE -nɔːl/ noun [U] (*chemistry*) a poisonous white chemical. When DISSOLVED in water it is used as an ANTISEPTIC and DISINFECTANT, usually called CARBOLIC.

**phen·ology** /fəˈnɒlədʒi; NAmE -ˈnɑːl-/ noun [U] the study of patterns of events in nature, especially in the weather and in the behaviour of plants and animals

**phe·nom** /fəˈnɒm, ˈfiːnɒm; NAmE fəˈnɑːm, ˈfiːnɑːm/ noun (NAmE, informal) a person or thing that is very successful or impressive SYN **phenomenon**

**phe·nom·enal** /fəˈnɒmɪnl; NAmE -ˈnɑːm-/ adj. very great or impressive SYN **extraordinary**: *The product has been a phenomenal success.*

**phe·nom·en·al·ly** /fəˈnɒmɪnəli; NAmE -ˈnɑːm-/ adv. **1** in a very great or impressive way SYN **extraordinarily**: *This product has been phenomenally successful* **2** extremely; very: *phenomenally bad weather*

**phe·nom·en·ology** /fɪˌnɒmɪˈnɒlədʒi; NAmE -ˌnɑːmɪˈnɑːl-/ noun [U] the branch of philosophy that deals with what you see, hear, feel, etc. in contrast to what may actually be real or true about the world ▸ **phe·nom·eno·logic·al** /fɪˌnɒmɪnəˈlɒdʒɪkl; NAmE -ˌnɑːmɪnəˈlɑːdʒ-/ adj.

**phe·nom·enon** ⓘ B2 ⓞ /fəˈnɒmɪnən; NAmE -ˈnɑːm-/ noun (pl. **phe·nom·ena** /-mɪnə/) **1** ⓘ B2 a fact or an event in nature or society, especially one that is not fully understood: *cultural/natural phenomena* ◊ *~ **of sth** the **global phenomenon** of climate change* **2** (pl. NAmE **phe·nom·enons**) a person or thing that is very successful or impressive

**phe·no·type** /ˈfiːnətaɪp/ noun (*biology*) the set of characteristics of a living thing, resulting from its combination of GENES and the effect of its environment ⇨ compare GENOTYPE

**phero·mone** /ˈferəməʊn/ noun (*biology*) a substance produced by an animal as a chemical signal, often to attract another animal of the same species

**phew** /fjuː/ *exclamation* a sound that people make to show that they are hot, tired, or happy that sth bad has finished or did not happen: *Phew, it's hot in here!* ◊ *Phew, I'm glad that's all over.* ⇨ compare WHEW

**phi** /faɪ/ noun the 21st letter of the Greek alphabet (Φ, φ)

**phial** /ˈfaɪəl/ (also **vial** especially in NAmE) noun (*formal*) a small glass container, for medicine or PERFUME

**Phi Beta 'Kappa** noun (in the US) a society for college and university students who are very successful in their studies

**phil·an·der·er** /fɪˈlændərə(r)/ noun (*old-fashioned, disapproving*) a man who has sexual relationships with many different women

**phil·an·der·ing** /fɪˈlændərɪŋ/ noun [U] (*old-fashioned, disapproving*) behaviour in which a man has sexual relationships with many different women SYN **womanizing** ▸ **phil·an·der·ing** adj. [only before noun]

**phil·an·throp·ist** /fɪˈlænθrəpɪst/ noun a rich person who helps the poor and those in need, especially by giving money

**phil·an·thropy** /fɪˈlænθrəpi/ noun [U] the practice of helping the poor and those in need, especially by giving money ▸ **phil·an·throp·ic** /ˌfɪlənˈθrɒpɪk; NAmE -ˈθrɑːp-/ adj.: *philanthropic work* **phil·an·throp·ic·al·ly** /-kli/ adv.

**phila·tel·ist** /fɪˈlætəlɪst/ noun (*specialist*) a person who collects or studies stamps

**phil·ately** /fɪˈlætəli/ noun [U] (*specialist*) the collection and study of stamps ▸ **phila·tel·ic** /ˌfɪləˈtelɪk/ adj.

**-phile** /faɪl/ *combining form* (in nouns and adjectives) liking a particular thing; a person who likes a particular thing: *Anglophile* ◊ *bibliophile* ⇨ compare -PHOBE

**phil·har·mon·ic** /ˌfɪlɑːˈmɒnɪk; NAmE -ɑːrˈmɑːn-/ adj. used in the names of ORCHESTRAS, music societies, etc: *the Berlin Philharmonic (Orchestra)*

**-philia** /filiə/ combining form (in nouns) love of sth, especially connected with a sexual attraction that is not considered normal: *paedophilia* ⊃ compare **-PHOBIA**

**phil·is·tine** /ˈfɪlɪstaɪn; NAmE -stiːn/ noun (disapproving) a person who does not like or understand art, literature, music, etc. ▸ **phil·is·tine** adj.: *philistine attitudes* **phil·is·tin·ism** /ˈfɪlɪstɪnɪzəm/ noun [U] *the philistinism of the tabloid press*

**Phil·lips** /ˈfɪlɪps/ adj. (of a screw or SCREWDRIVER) with a part that has the shape of a cross for turning ⊃ compare **FLATHEAD, SLOTTED**

**philo-** /ˈfɪlə/; *BrE also* /fəˈlɒ/; *NAmE also* /fəˈlɑː/ (*also* **phil-** /fɪl, fəl/) combining form (in nouns, adjectives, verbs and adverbs) liking: *philanthropy*

**phil·olo·gist** /fəˈlɒlədʒɪst; NAmE -ˈlɑːl-/ noun a person who studies philology

**phil·ology** /fəˈlɒlədʒi; NAmE -ˈlɑːl-/ noun [U] the scientific study of the development of language or of a particular language ▸ **phil·olo·gic·al** /ˌfɪləˈlɒdʒɪkl; NAmE -ˈlɑːdʒ-/ adj.

**phil·oso·pher** /fəˈlɒsəfə(r); NAmE -ˈlɑːs-/ noun **1** a person who studies or writes about philosophy: *the Greek philosopher Aristotle* **2** a person who thinks deeply about things: *He seems to be a bit of a philosopher.*

**the phiˌlosopher's ˈstone** noun [sing.] an imaginary substance that, in the past, people believed could change any metal into gold or silver, or could make people live forever

**phil·oso·phic·al** /ˌfɪləˈsɒfɪkl; NAmE -ˈsɑːf-/ (also **phil·osoph·ic** /ˌfɪləˈsɒfɪk; NAmE -ˈsɑːf-/) adj. **1** connected with philosophy: *the philosophical writings of Kant* · *philosophic debate* **2** ~ (about sth) (approving) having a calm attitude towards a difficult or disappointing situation SYN **stoic**: *He was philosophical about losing and said that he'd be back next year to try again.* ▸ **phil·oso·phic·al·ly** /-kli/ adv.: *This kind of evidence is philosophically unconvincing.* · *She took the bad news philosophically.*

**phil·oso·phize** (*BrE also* **-ise**) /fəˈlɒsəfaɪz; NAmE -ˈlɑːs-/ verb [I] ~ (about / on sth) to talk about sth in a serious way, especially when other people think this is boring: *He spent the evening philosophizing on the meaning of life.* ▸ **phil·oso·phiz·ing, -is·ing** noun [U]

**phil·oso·phy** /fəˈlɒsəfi; NAmE -ˈlɑːs-/ noun **1** [U] ~ (of sth) the study of the nature and meaning of the universe and of human life: *the philosophy of science* · *a professor of philosophy* · *a degree in philosophy* ⊃ see also **NATURAL PHILOSOPHY** **2** [C, U] a particular set or system of beliefs resulting from the search for knowledge about life and the universe: *Buddhist/Eastern/Hindu philosophy* · *the philosophy of Aristotle* **3** [C] ~ (of sth) a set of beliefs or an attitude to life that guides sb's behaviour: *Her philosophy of life is to take every opportunity that presents itself.*

**phish·ing** /ˈfɪʃɪŋ/ noun [U] the activity of tricking people by getting them to give their identity, bank account numbers, etc. over the internet or by email, and then using these to steal money from them

**phle·bot·omy** /fləˈbɒtəmi; NAmE -ˈbɑːt-/ noun [C, U] (pl. -ies) (medical) the opening of a **VEIN** in order to remove blood or put another liquid in

**phlegm** /flem/ noun [U] **1** the thick substance that forms in the nose and throat, especially when you have a cold **2** the ability to remain calm in a situation that is difficult or frightening

**phleg·mat·ic** /flegˈmætɪk/ adj. not easily made angry or upset SYN **calm**: *a phlegmatic temperament* ▸ **phleg·mat·ic·al·ly** /-kli/ adv.

**phloem** /ˈfləʊem/ noun [U] (biology) the material in a plant containing very small tubes that carry sugars produced in the leaves around the plant ⊃ compare **XYLEM**

**phlox** /flɒks; NAmE flɑːks/ noun **1** a tall garden plant with groups of white, blue or red flowers with a sweet smell **2** a low, spreading plant with small white, blue or pink flowers

**-phobe** /fəʊb/ combining form (in nouns) a person who dislikes a particular thing or particular people: *Anglophobe* ⋄ *xenophobe* ⊃ compare **-PHILE**

**pho·bia** /ˈfəʊbiə/ noun **1** a strong unreasonable fear of sth: *He has a phobia about flying.* **2** **-phobia** (in nouns) a strong unreasonable fear of or feeling of hate for a particular thing: *claustrophobia* (= fear of being in a small closed space) ⋄ *xenophobia* (= strong dislike or fear of people from other countries) ⊃ compare **-PHILIA**

**pho·bic** /ˈfəʊbɪk/ noun **1** a person who has a strong unreasonable fear of or feeling of hate for sth: *cat phobics* **2** **-phobic** (in adjectives) having a strong unreasonable fear of or feeling of hate for a particular thing: *claustrophobic* ⋄ *xenophobic* ▸ **pho·bic** adj.: *phobic anxiety*

**phoe·nix** /ˈfiːnɪks/ noun (in stories) a magic bird that lives for several hundred years before burning itself and then being born again from its **ASHES**: *to rise like a phoenix from the ashes* (= to be powerful or successful again)

**phone** ❶ A1 /fəʊn/ (*also rather formal* **tele·phone**) noun, verb
▪ noun **1** A1 [C] a piece of equipment for talking to people who are not in the same place as you: *I have to make a phone call.* ⋄ *The phone rang and Pat answered it.* ⋄ *Can someone answer the phone?* ⋄ *I hadn't got my phone with me.* ⋄ *Please switch off your phones before the show begins.* ⋄ *a phone conversation/interview* ⋄ *Here is our list of top new phone apps.* **2** A1 [U, sing.] the system for talking to sb else using a phone: **by~** *They like to do business by phone.* ⋄ **on the ~** *I talk to my family on the phone.* ⋄ **over the ~** *I can't talk about this over the phone.* ⋄ *a phone bill* ⊃ see also **CELL PHONE, FEATURE PHONE, FLIP PHONE, MOBILE PHONE, PAYPHONE, TELEPHONE** noun ⊃ **EXPRESS YOURSELF** at **MESSAGE** **3** A1 [C] the part of a LANDLINE phone that you hold in your hand and speak into: *to pick up the phone* ⋄ *to put the phone down* ⋄ *to take the phone off the hook* (= so that no one can call) ⊃ see also **TELEPHONE** noun **4** **-phone** (in nouns) an instrument that uses or makes sound: *dictaphone* ⋄ *xylophone* **5** **-phone** (in adjectives and nouns) speaking a particular language; a person who does this: *anglophone* ⋄ *francophone* **6** (phonetics) a sound made in speech, especially when not considered as part of the sound system of a particular language ⊃ compare **PHONEME**
**IDM** be on the ˈphone **1** to be using the phone: *He's been on the phone to Kate for more than an hour.* **2** (BrE) to have a phone in your home or place of work: *They're not on the phone at the holiday cottage.*
▪ verb **1** A1 (especially BrE) (BrE also **phone ˈup**) [I, T] to make a phone call to sb SYN **call**: *I was just phoning up for a chat.* ⋄ ~ **back** *Could you phone back later?* ⋄ ~ **sb/sth** *Don't forget to phone New York.* ⋄ *For reservations, phone 020 281 3964.* ⋄ *Someone phoned the police.* ⊃ **WORDFINDER NOTE** at **CALL**
**PHRV** ˌphone ˈin (especially BrE) **1** to make a phone call to the place where you work: + adj. *Three people have phoned in sick already this morning.* **2** to make a phone call to a radio or television station: *Listeners are invited to phone in with their comments.* ⊃ related noun **PHONE-IN** ˌphone sth↔ˈin (especially BrE) to make a phone call to the place where you work in order to give sb some information: *I need you to phone the story in before five.*

▼ BRITISH/AMERICAN

**phone / call / ring**

Verbs
- In BrE, **to phone, to ring** and **to call** are the usual ways of saying **to telephone**. In NAmE the most common word is **call**, but **phone** is also used. Speakers of NAmE do not say **ring**. **Telephone** is very formal and is used mainly in BrE.

Nouns
- You can use **call** or **phone call** (more formal) in both BrE and NAmE: *Were there any phone calls for me?* ⋄ *How do I make a local call?* The idiom **give sb a call** is also common: *I'll give you a call tonight.* In informal BrE you could also say: *I'll give you a ring tonight.*

**ˈphone book** noun = **TELEPHONE DIRECTORY**

**phone booth** (also **telephone booth**) noun a place that is partly separated from the surrounding area, containing a public phone, in a hotel, restaurant, in the street, etc.

**phone box** (also **telephone box**, **call box**) (all BrE) noun a small unit with walls and a roof, containing a public phone, in the street, etc.

**phone call** noun = CALL (2)

**phone-card** /ˈfəʊnkɑːd; NAmE -kɑːrd/ noun (NAmE also **calling card**) 1 a plastic card that you can use in some public phones instead of money 2 (NAmE) a card with a number on it that you use in order to pay to make a call from any phone. The cost of the call is charged to your account and you pay it later.

**phone hacking** noun [U] the activity of finding a way to access the information stored on sb else's phone without their permission, especially to listen to their VOICEMAIL: *£1 million in damages has been paid out to victims of phone hacking.* ▶ **phone hacker** noun

**phone-in** (BrE) (NAmE **call-in**) noun a radio or television programme in which people can phone and make comments or ask questions about a particular subject ⊃ WORDFINDER NOTE at RADIO

**phon-eme** /ˈfəʊniːm/ noun (phonetics) any one of the set of smallest units of speech in a language that make the difference between one word and another. In English, the /s/ sound in *sip* and the /z/ sound in *zip* represent two different phonemes. ⊃ compare GRAPHEME ▶ **phon-em-ic** /fəˈniːmɪk/ adj.

**phone number** noun = TELEPHONE NUMBER

**phone tapping** (also rather formal **telephone tapping**) noun [U] the practice of connecting a piece of equipment to a phone in order to listen secretly to other people's phone conversations

**phon-et-ic** /fəˈnetɪk/ adj. 1 using special symbols to represent each different speech sound: *the International Phonetic Alphabet* ◊ *a phonetic symbol/transcription* 2 (of a spelling or spelling system) that closely matches the sounds represented: *Spanish spelling is phonetic, unlike English spelling.* 3 connected with the sounds of human speech ▶ **phon-et-ic-al-ly** /-kli/ adv.

**phon-et-ics** /fəˈnetɪks/ noun [U] the study of speech sounds and how they are produced ⊃ WORDFINDER NOTE at PRONUNCIATION ▶ **phon-et-ician** /ˌfəʊnəˈtɪʃn; BrE also ˌfɒn-; NAmE also ˌfɑːn-/ noun

**pho-ney** (also **phony** especially in NAmE) /ˈfəʊni/ adj., noun
- adj. (**pho-nier**, **pho-ni-est**) (informal, disapproving) not real or true; false, and trying to trick people SYN **fake**: *She spoke with a phoney Russian accent.*
- noun (pl. **-neys** or **-nies**) (informal) a person who is not honest or sincere; a thing that is not real or true

**phoney war** noun [sing.] (BrE) a period of time when two groups are officially at war but not actually fighting

**phon-ic** /ˈfɒnɪk; NAmE ˈfɑːn-/ adj. 1 (specialist) relating to sound; relating to sounds made in speech 2 **-phonic** (in adjectives) connected with an instrument that uses or makes sound: *telephonic*

**phon-ics** /ˈfɒnɪks; NAmE ˈfɑːn-/ noun [U] a method of teaching people to read based on the sounds that letters represent

**phono-** /ˈfəʊnəʊ, fəʊnə; BrE also fəˈnɒ; NAmE also fəˈnɑː/ (also **phon-** /fəʊn, fəʊn/) combining form (in nouns, adjectives and adverbs) connected with sound or sounds: *phonetic*

**phono-graph** /ˈfəʊnəɡrɑːf; NAmE -ɡræf/ noun (old-fashioned) = RECORD PLAYER

**phon-ology** /fəˈnɒlədʒi; NAmE -ˈnɑːl-/ noun [U] (linguistics) the speech sounds of a particular language; the study of these sounds ▶ **phono-logic-al** /ˌfəʊnəˈlɒdʒɪkl; ˌfɒn-; NAmE ˌfəʊnəˈlɑːdʒɪkl; ˌfɑːn-/ adj.: *phonological analysis* **phon-olo-gist** /fəˈnɒlədʒɪst; NAmE -ˈnɑːl-/ noun

**phony** (especially NAmE) = PHONEY

**phooey** /ˈfuːi/ exclamation used when you think sb/sth is wrong or silly ▶ **phooey** noun [U]: *It's all phooey!*

**phos-phate** /ˈfɒsfeɪt; NAmE ˈfɑːs-/ noun [C, U] (chemistry) any COMPOUND containing phosphorus, used in industry or for helping plants to grow: *phosphate-free washing powder*

**phos-phor-es-cent** /ˌfɒsfəˈresnt; NAmE ˌfɑːs-/ adj. (specialist) 1 producing a small amount of light in the dark ⊃ compare FLUORESCENT 2 producing light without heat or with so little heat that it cannot be felt ▶ **phos-phor-es-cence** /-sns/ noun [U]

**phos-phor-ic acid** /ˌfɒsˌfɒrɪk ˈæsɪd; NAmE ˌfɑːsˌfɔːr-/ noun [U] a substance used in FERTILIZERS and in the production of DETERGENTS and food

**phos-phorus** /ˈfɒsfərəs; NAmE ˈfɑːs-/ noun [U] (symb. P) a chemical element. Phosphorus is found in several different forms, including as a poisonous, pale yellow substance that shines in the dark and starts to burn as soon as it is placed in air.

**photo** 🅣 🅐🅵 /ˈfəʊtəʊ/ noun (pl. **-os**) = PHOTOGRAPH: *a colour/black-and-white photo* ◊ *wedding/family photos* ◊ *your passport/profile photo* ◊ *I'll take a photo of you.* 🅗🅔🅛🅟 The usual phrase in NAmE is **take a picture**. ◊ *Fans snapped photos of the event.* ◊ *She posted a photo of the two of them on her Facebook page.* ◊ *The actor shared a photo on Instagram.* ◊ *I've uploaded my holiday photos.* ◊ *to send/tweet a photo* ◊ *to release/publish a photo* ◊ *Visit the photo gallery on our website to see pictures from the event.* ⊃ SYNONYMS at PHOTOGRAPH ⊃ EXPRESS YOURSELF at DESCRIBE

**photo-** /ˈfəʊtəʊ; BrE also fəˈtɒ; NAmE also fəˈtɑː/ combining form (in nouns, adjectives, verbs and adverbs) 1 connected with light: *photosynthesis* 2 connected with photography: *photogenic*

**photo-bomb** /ˈfəʊtəʊbɒm; NAmE -bɑːm/ verb (informal) 1 [T, I] ~ (sth) to prevent a photograph from being taken in the way intended by suddenly appearing or doing sth unexpected as the picture is taken 2 [T] ~ sb to suddenly appear or do sth unexpected while a photograph is being taken of sb: *He photobombed the actress as she was posing for the press.* ▶ **photo-bomb** noun: *A fan decided to drop a photobomb on the reporter.* **photo-bomb-er** noun **photo-bomb-ing** noun [U]

**photo booth** noun a small structure with walls and a roof where you can put money in a machine and get photographs of yourself in a few minutes

**photo-call** /ˈfəʊtəʊkɔːl/ noun a time that is arranged in advance when newspaper photographers are invited to take photographs of sb: *The president joined the team for a photocall.*

**photo-cell** /ˈfəʊtəʊsel/ noun = PHOTOELECTRIC CELL

**photo-chem-ical** /ˌfəʊtəʊˈkemɪkl/ adj. (chemistry) caused by or relating to the chemical action of light: *photochemical smog*

**photo-copier** /ˈfəʊtəʊkɒpiə(r); NAmE -kɑːp-/ (also **copier** especially in NAmE) noun a machine that makes copies of documents, etc. by photographing them

**photo-copy** /ˈfəʊtəʊkɒpi; NAmE -kɑːpi/ noun, verb
- noun (also **copy**) (pl. **-ies**) a copy of a document, etc. made by a machine that photographs and then prints: *Make as many photocopies as you need.*
- verb (**photo-cop-ies**, **photo-copy-ing**, **photo-cop-ied**, **photo-cop-ied**) (also **copy** especially in BrE) 1 [T, I] ~ (sth) to make a photocopy of sth: *a photocopied letter* ◊ *Can you get these photocopied for me by 5 o'clock?* ◊ *I seem to have spent most of the day photocopying.* 2 [I] ~ well/badly (of printed material) to produce a good/bad photocopy: *The comments in pencil haven't photocopied very well.*

**photo-elec-tric** /ˌfəʊtəʊɪˈlektrɪk/ adj. using an electric current that is controlled by light

**photoelectric cell** (also **photo-cell**) noun an electric device that uses a stream of light. When the stream is broken it shows that sb/sth is present, and can be used to control alarms, machines, etc.

**photo finish** noun [usually sing.] the end of a race in which the leading runners or horses are so close together that only a photograph of them passing the finishing line can show which is the winner

**photo-gen-ic** /ˌfəʊtəʊˈdʒenɪk/ adj. looking attractive in photographs: *I'm not very photogenic.*

# photograph

**pho·to·graph** 🔊 `A1` /ˈfəʊtəɡrɑːf/ NAmE -ɡræf/ noun, verb
- **noun** 🔊 `A1` (also **photo**) a picture that is made by using a camera that stores images in digital form or that has a film sensitive to light inside it: *aerial photographs of the crash site* ◇ *colour/black-and-white photographs* ◇ *I spent the day **taking photographs** of the city.* ◇ *to post/upload a photograph* ◇ *to publish/release a photograph* HELP The usual phrase in NAmE is **take pictures**.
- **verb 1** 🔊 `A2` [T] to take a photograph of sb/sth: ~ *sb/sth* *a workshop on photographing wildlife* ◇ *a beautifully photographed book* (= with very good photographs in it) ◇ ~ *sb/ sth + adj.* *She refused to be photographed nude.* ◇ ~ *sb/sth doing sth* *They were photographed playing with their children.* **2** [I] ~ **well, badly,** etc. to look or not look attractive in photographs: *Some people just don't photograph well.*

▼ **SYNONYMS**

**photograph**
picture • photo • shot • snapshot/snap • print

These are all words for a picture that has been made using a camera.

**photograph** a picture that has been made using a camera: *a photograph of the house* ◇ *Can I take a photograph?*

**picture** a photograph: *We had our picture taken in front of the hotel.*

**photo** a photograph: *a passport photo*

PHOTOGRAPH, PICTURE OR PHOTO?
**Photograph** is slightly more formal and **photo** is slightly less formal. **Picture** is used especially in the context of photographs in newspapers, magazines and books.

**shot** a photograph: *I tried to get a shot of him in the water.* NOTE **Shot** often places more emphasis on the process of taking the photograph, rather than the finished picture.

**snapshot/snap** an informal photograph that is taken quickly, and not by a professional photographer: *holiday snaps*

**print** a copy of a photograph that is produced from film or from a digital camera: *a set of prints*

PATTERNS
- a **colour** photograph / picture / photo / snap / print
- to **take** a photograph / picture / photo / shot / snapshot

**pho·tog·raph·er** 🔊 `B1` /fəˈtɒɡrəfə(r)/; NAmE -ˈtɑːɡ-/ noun a person who takes photographs, especially as a job: *a wedding/wildlife/fashion photographer*

**photo·graph·ic** /ˌfəʊtəˈɡræfɪk/ adj. connected with photographs or photography: *photographic equipment/film/images* ◇ *They produced a photographic record of the event.* ◇ *His paintings are almost photographic in detail.*
▶ **pho·to·graph·ic·al·ly** /-kli/ adv.

**photo·graphic ˈmemory** noun [usually sing.] the ability to remember things accurately and in great detail after seeing them

**pho·tog·raphy** 🔊 `B1` /fəˈtɒɡrəfi; NAmE -ˈtɑːɡ-/ noun [U] the art, process or job of taking photographs or filming sth: *Her hobbies include hiking and photography.* ◇ *digital photography* ◇ *colour/black-and-white photography* ◇ *fashion photography by David Burn* ◇ *Did you see the film about Antarctica? The photography was superb!*

**photo·jour·nal·ism** /ˌfəʊtəʊˈdʒɜːnəlɪzəm; NAmE -ˈdʒɜːrn-/ noun [U] the work of gathering and preparing news stories using mainly photographs, especially in a magazine

**photo·jour·nal·ist** /ˌfəʊtəʊˈdʒɜːnəlɪst; NAmE -ˈdʒɜːrn-/ noun a person whose job is to take photographs that illustrate and report news stories

**photo·mon·tage** /ˌfəʊtəʊmɒnˈtɑːʒ; NAmE -mɑːn-/ noun [C, U] a picture which is made up of different photographs put together; the technique of producing these pictures

**pho·ton** /ˈfəʊtɒn; NAmE -tɑːn/ noun (physics) a unit of ELECTROMAGNETIC energy

**ˈphoto opportunity** noun an occasion when a famous person arranges to be photographed doing sth that will impress the public

**photo·recep·tor** /ˈfəʊtəʊrɪseptə(r)/ noun (biology) a cell or an organ in the body that is sensitive to light

**photo·sensi·tive** /ˌfəʊtəʊˈsensətɪv/ adj. (specialist) reacting to light, for example by changing colour or producing an electrical signal

**ˈphoto shoot** noun an occasion when a photographer takes pictures of sb, for example a famous person, fashion model, etc. for use in a magazine, etc: *I went on a photo shoot to Rio with him.*

**photo·shop** /ˈfəʊtəʊʃɒp; NAmE -ʃɑːp/ (also **Photoshop**) verb (-pp-) ~ sth to change a picture or photograph using computer software: *I'm sure this picture has been photoshopped.*

**photo·syn·thesis** /ˌfəʊtəʊˈsɪnθəsɪs/ noun [U] (biology) the process by which green plants turn CARBON DIOXIDE and water into food using energy obtained from light from the sun

**photo·syn·the·size** (BrE also **-ise**) /ˌfəʊtəʊˈsɪnθəsaɪz/ verb [I, T] ~ (sth) (biology) (of plants) to make food by means of photosynthesis

**photo·vol·ta·ic** /ˌfəʊtəʊvɒlˈteɪɪk; NAmE -vɑːl-/ adj. (physics) relating to the production of electricity at the meeting point of two substances that have been exposed to light: *a photovoltaic cell*

**phras·al** /ˈfreɪzl/ adj. of or connected with a phrase

**ˌphrasal ˈverb** noun (grammar) a verb combined with an adverb or a preposition, or sometimes both, to give a new meaning, for example *go in for, win over* and *see to*

**phrase** 🔊 `A1` /freɪz/ noun, verb
- **noun 1** 🔊 `A1` a group of words that have a particular meaning when used together: *a memorable/catchy phrase* ◇ *'Start slowly' is the key phrase for the first-time marathon runner.* ⇨ see also CATCHPHRASE **2** 🔊 `A1` (grammar) a small group of words (usually without a FINITE verb) that together have a particular meaning and that typically form part of a sentence. 'the green car' and 'on Friday morning' are phrases. ⇨ SYNONYMS at WORD ⇨ see also NOUN PHRASE **3** (music) a short series of notes that form a unit within a longer passage in a piece of music IDM see COIN v., TURN n.
- **verb 1** [T] to say or write sth in a particular way: ~ *sth (+ adv. / prep.)* *a carefully phrased remark* ◇ *I agree with what he says, but I'd have phrased it differently.* ◇ ~ *sth as sth* *Her order was phrased as a suggestion.* **2** [I, T] ~ (sth) to divide a piece of music into small groups of notes; to play or sing these in a particular way, especially in an effective way

**ˈphrase book** noun a book containing lists of common expressions translated into another language, especially for people visiting a foreign country

**phrase·ology** /ˌfreɪziˈɒlədʒi; NAmE -ˈɑːl-/ noun [U] (formal) the particular way in which words and phrases are arranged when saying or writing sth

**phras·ing** /ˈfreɪzɪŋ/ noun [U] **1** the words used to express sth: *The phrasing of the report is ambiguous.* **2** (music) the way in which a musician or singer divides a piece of music into phrases by stopping for a short time in suitable places

**phren·ology** /frəˈnɒlədʒi; NAmE -ˈnɑːl-/ noun [U] the study of the shape of the human head, which some people think is a guide to a person's character ▶ **phren·olo·gist** noun

**phwoah** (also **phwoor, phwoar**) /ˈfwɔːə/ exclamation (BrE, informal) used when you find sth or sb very impressive and attractive, especially in a sexual way

**ˈphyllo pastry** (NAmE) (BrE **ˈfilo pastry**) /ˌfiːləʊ ˈpeɪstri/ (NAmE also **phyllo**, BrE also **filo**) noun [U] a type of thin PASTRY, used in layers

**phylum** /ˈfaɪləm/ noun (pl. **phyla** /-lə/) (biology) a group into which animals, plants, etc. are divided, smaller than a

KINGDOM and larger than a CLASS ⇒ compare GENUS ⇒ WORDFINDER NOTE at BREED ⇒ VISUAL VOCAB page V3

**phys·ic·al** ❶ **A2** ⓞ /ˈfɪzɪkl/ adj., noun
■ adj.
- **THE BODY 1** **A2** [usually before noun] connected with a person's body rather than their mind: *physical activity/fitness* ◇ *physical appearance* ◇ *physical disabilities/injuries* ◇ *The ordeal has affected both her mental and physical health.* ◇ *He tends to avoid all physical contact.*
- **REAL THINGS 2** **B1** [only before noun] connected with things that actually exist or are present and can be seen, felt, etc. rather than things that only exist in a person's mind: *the physical world* ◇ *the physical properties* (= the colour, weight, shape, etc.) *of copper* ◇ *She was intimidated by his physical presence.*
- **NATURE/SCIENCE 3** **B2** [only before noun] according to the laws of nature: *It is a physical impossibility to be in two places at once.* **4** **B2** [only before noun] connected with the scientific study of forces such as heat, light, sound, etc. and how they affect objects: *physical laws*
- **SPORTS/ACTIVITIES 5** **B2** involving a lot of physical contact or activity: *Rugby is a very physical sport.*
- **SEX 6** **B2** involving sex: *physical love* ◇ *They are having a physical relationship.* ◇ *Their relationship was purely physical.*
- **PERSON 7** (*informal*) (of a person) liking to touch other people a lot: *She's not very physical.*
- **VIOLENT 8** (*informal*) violent (used to avoid saying this in a direct way): *Are you going to cooperate or do we have to get physical?*
■ noun (also ˌphysical examiˈnation) a medical examination of a person's body, for example to check that they are fit enough to do a particular job

**ˌphysical eduˈcation** noun = PE

**ˌphysical geˈography** noun [U] **1** the scientific study of the natural features on the surface of the earth, for example mountains and rivers **2** the way in which the natural features of a place are arranged: *the physical geography of Scotland*

**phys·ic·al·ity** /ˌfɪzɪˈkæləti/ noun [U] (*formal*) the quality of being physical rather than emotional or spiritual

**phys·ic·al·ly** /ˈfɪzɪkli/ adv. **1** in a way that is connected with a person's body rather than their mind: *physically fit/active* ◇ *physically disabled people* ◇ *He is in good health, both physically and mentally.* ◇ *I felt physically sick before the exam.* ◇ *I don't find him physically attractive.* ◇ *to be physically abused/assaulted/attacked* **2** according to the laws of nature or what is likely: *It's physically impossible to finish by the end of the week.*

**ˌphysical ˈscience** noun [U] (*also* **the ˌphysical ˈsciences** [pl.]) the areas of science involving the study of natural forces and things that are not alive, for example physics and chemistry ⇒ compare LIFE SCIENCE

**ˌphysical ˈtherapist** (US) (BrE **ˌphysio·therˈap·ist**, *informal* **physio**) noun a person whose job is to give patients physical therapy

**ˌphysical ˈtherapy** (US) (BrE **ˌphysio·therˈapy**, *informal* **physio**) noun [U] the treatment of disease, injury or weakness in the JOINTS or muscles by exercises, MASSAGE and the use of light and heat

**ˌphysical ˈtraining** noun = PT

**phyˈsician's asˈsistant** (also **phyˌsician asˈsistant**) noun (*abbr.* **PA**) (*NAmE*) a person who is qualified to assist a doctor and to do basic medical procedures

**phys·ician** **C1** /fɪˈzɪʃn/ noun (*especially NAmE*) a doctor, especially one who is a specialist in general medicine and not surgery ⇒ compare SURGEON **HELP** This word is now old-fashioned in BrE. **Doctor** or **GP** is used instead.

**physi·cist** /ˈfɪzɪsɪst/ noun a scientist who studies physics: *a nuclear physicist* ⇒ see also NUCLEAR PHYSICIST

**phys·ics** ❶ **A2** /ˈfɪzɪks/ noun [U] the scientific study of MATTER and energy and the relationships between them, including the study of forces, heat, light, sound, electricity and the structure of ATOMS: *a degree in physics* ◇ *quantum/theoretical physics* ◇ *the laws of physics* ◇ *the physics laboratory/department* ◇ *~ of sth to study the physics of*

the electron ⇒ see also ASTROPHYSICS, GEOPHYSICS, NUCLEAR PHYSICS, PARTICLE PHYSICS, QUANTUM PHYSICS

**WORDFINDER** amplitude, atom, energy, fission, force, frequency, gravity, molecule, nuclear

**physio** /ˈfɪziəʊ/ noun (*pl.* **-os**) (*BrE, informal*) **1** [U] = PHYSIOTHERAPY **2** [C] = PHYSIOTHERAPIST

**physio-** /ˈfɪziəʊ, ˌfɪziə; *BrE also* fɪziˈɒ; *NAmE also* fɪziˈɑː/ *combining form* (in nouns, adjectives and adverbs) **1** connected with nature **2** connected with PHYSIOLOGY

**physi·ognomy** /ˌfɪziˈɒnəmi; *NAmE* -ˈɑːn-/ noun (*pl.* **-ies**) (*formal*) the shape and features of a person's face

**physi·olo·gist** /ˌfɪziˈɒlədʒɪst; *NAmE* -ˈɑːl-/ noun a scientist who studies physiology

**physi·ology** /ˌfɪziˈɒlədʒi; *NAmE* -ˈɑl-/ noun **1** [U] the scientific study of the normal functions of living things: *the department of anatomy and physiology* **2** [U, sing.] the way in which a particular living thing functions: *plant physiology* ◇ *the physiology of the horse* ▸ **physio·logical** /ˌfɪziəˈlɒdʒɪkl/ *NAmE* -ˈlɑːdʒ-/ *adj.*: *the physiological effect of space travel* **physio·logic·ally** /-kli/ *adv.*

**physio·ther·ap·ist** /ˌfɪziəʊˈθerəpɪst/ (*also informal* **physio**) (*both BrE*) (*US* **ˌphysical ˈtherapist**) noun a person whose job is to give patients physiotherapy

**physio·ther·apy** /ˌfɪziəʊˈθerəpi/ (*also informal* **physio**) (*both BrE*) (*US* **ˌphysical ˈtherapy**) noun [U] the treatment of disease, injury or weakness in the JOINTS or muscles by exercises, MASSAGE and the use of light and heat ⇒ WORDFINDER NOTE at CURE

**phys·ique** /fɪˈziːk/ noun [C, U] the size and shape of a person's body **SYN** **build**: *He has the physique of a rugby player.* ◇ *a powerful physique*

**pi** /paɪ/ noun **1** (*geometry*) the symbol π used to show the RATIO of the CIRCUMFERENCE of (= distance around) a circle to its DIAMETER (= distance across), that is 3.14159 ... **2** the 16th letter of the Greek alphabet (Π, π)

**pi·an·is·simo** /piəˈnɪsɪməʊ/ *adv.* (*abbr.* **pp**) (*music, from Italian*) very quietly **OPP** **fortissimo** ▸ **pi·an·is·simo** *adj.*

**pi·an·ist** /ˈpɪənɪst; *NAmE* piːə-/ noun a person who plays the piano: *a concert pianist* ◇ *a jazz pianist*

**piano** ❶ **A1** noun, adv.
■ noun **A1** /piˈænəʊ/ (*pl.* **-os**) (*also old-fashioned, formal* **pi·ano·forte** /piˌænəʊˈfɔːteɪ; *NAmE* -ˈfɔːrt-/) a large musical instrument played by pressing the black and white keys on the keyboard. The sound is produced by small HAMMERS hitting the metal strings inside the piano: *to play the piano* ◇ *on ~ She was accompanied by her husband on piano.* ◇ *classical/jazz piano music* ◇ *a piano teacher/lesson* ◇ *Ravel's piano concerto in G* ⇒ see also GRAND PIANO, PLAYER PIANO, THUMB PIANO, UPRIGHT PIANO
■ *adv.* /ˈpjɑːnəʊ/ (*abbr.* **p**) (*music, from Italian*) played or sung quietly **OPP** **forte** ▸ **piano** *adj.*

**piˌano acˈcordion** noun a type of ACCORDION that you press buttons and keys on to produce the different notes

**Pi·an·ola™** /ˌpiːəˈnəʊlə/ noun a piano that plays itself by means of a piano roll **SYN** **player piano**

**piˈano roll** noun a roll of paper full of very small holes that controls the movement of the keys in a PLAYER PIANO

**pi·azza** /piˈætsə; *NAmE* -ˈɑːzə/ noun a public square, especially in an Italian town

**pic** /pɪk/ noun (*informal*) a picture

**pic·ar·esque** /ˌpɪkəˈresk/ *adj.* (*formal*) connected with literature that describes the adventures of a person who is sometimes dishonest but easy to like: *a picaresque novel*

**Pic·ca·dilly ˈCir·cus** /ˌpɪkədɪli ˈsɜːkəs; *NAmE* ˈsɜːrk-/ noun (*BrE*) used to describe a place that is very busy or crowded: *It's been like Piccadilly Circus in this house all morning.* **ORIGIN** From the name of a busy area in the centre of London where several large roads meet and where there is always a lot of traffic.

**pic·colo** /ˈpɪkələʊ/ noun (*pl.* **-os**) a musical instrument of the WOODWIND group, like a small FLUTE that plays high notes

# pick 1160

**pick** ❶ A2 /pɪk/ *verb, noun*

■ **verb 1** ⚹ A2 [T] (*rather informal*) to choose sb/sth from a group of people or things: *~sb/sth Pick a number from one to twenty.* ◊ *They are picking the final team this weekend.* ◊ *It's time to pick a side* (= decide who you support). ◊ *At the beach we picked a spot to sit down.* ◊ *~sb/sth to do sth He has been picked to play in this week's game.* ◊ *~sb/sth for sth Have you been picked for the team?* ◊ *~sb/sth as sth It was picked as the best film in the competition.* ⊃ SYNONYMS at CHOOSE ⊃ see also HAND-PICKED **2** ⚹ B1 [T] *~sth* to take flowers, fruit, etc. from the plant or the tree where they are growing: *to pick grapes/strawberries/cotton* ◊ *flowers freshly picked from the garden* ◊ *to go blackberry picking* **3** ⚹ B2 [T] to pull or remove sth or small pieces of sth from sth else, especially with your fingers: *~sth + adv./prep. She picked bits of fluff from his sweater.* ◊ *~sth to pick your nose* (= put your finger inside your nose to remove dried MUCUS) ◊ *~sth + adj. The dogs picked the bones clean* (= ate all the meat from the bones). **4** [I, T] *~(sth)* (*NAmE*) = PLUCK

IDM ▸ **pick and 'choose** to choose only those things that you like or want very much: *You have to take any job you can get—you can't pick and choose.* ▸ **pick sb's 'brains** (*informal*) to ask sb a lot of questions about sth because they know more about the subject than you do ▸ **pick a 'fight/'quarrel (with sb)** to deliberately start a fight or an argument with sb ▸ **pick 'holes in sth** to find the weak points in sth such as a plan, suggestion, etc: *It was easy to pick holes in his arguments.* ▸ **pick a 'lock** to open a lock without a key, using sth such as a piece of wire ▸ **pick sb's 'pocket** to steal sth from sb's pocket without them noticing ⊃ related noun PICKPOCKET ▸ **pick up the 'bill, 'tab, etc. (for sth)** (*informal*) to pay for sth: *The company picked up the tab for his hotel room.* ◊ *The government will continue to pick up college fees for some students.* ▸ **pick up the 'pieces** to return or to help sb return to a normal situation, particularly after a shock or a disaster: *You cannot live your children's lives for them; you can only be there to pick up the pieces when things go wrong.* ▸ **pick up 'speed** to go faster ▸ **pick up the 'threads** to return to an earlier situation or way of life after a period doing sth else ▸ **pick your 'way (across, along, among, over, through sth)** to walk carefully, choosing the safest, driest, etc. place to put your feet: *She picked her way delicately over the rough ground.* ▸ **pick a 'winner 1** to choose a horse, etc. that you think is most likely to win a race **2** (*informal*) to make a very good choice ⊃ more at BONE *n.*, PIECE *n.*, RIPE, SHRED *n.*

PHRV ▸ **'pick at sth 1** to eat food slowly, taking small amounts or bites because you are not hungry **2** to pull or touch sth several times: *He tried to undo the knot by picking at it with his fingers.* ▸ **'pick sb↔'off** (*informal*) to aim carefully at a person, an animal or an aircraft, especially one of a group, and then shoot them: *Snipers were picking off innocent civilians.* ▸ **'pick sth↔'off** to remove sth from such as a tree, a plant, etc: *Pick off all the dead leaves.* ▸ **'pick on sb/sth 1** to treat sb unfairly, by blaming, criticizing or punishing them: *She was picked on by the other girls because of her size.* **2** to choose sb/sth: *He picked on two of her statements which he said were untrue.* ▸ **'pick sb/sth↔'out 1** to choose sb/sth carefully from a group of people or things SYN **select**: *She was picked out from dozens of applicants for the job.* ◊ *He picked out the ripest peach for me.* **2** to recognize sb/sth from among other people or things: *See if you can pick me out in this photo.* ▸ **'pick sth↔'out 1** to play a tune on a musical instrument slowly without using written music: *He picked out the tune on the piano with one finger.* **2** to discover or recognize sth after careful study: *Read the play again and pick out the major themes.* **3** to make sth easy to see or hear: *a sign painted cream, with the lettering picked out in black* ▸ **'pick sth↔'over** | **'pick 'through sth** to examine a group of things carefully, especially to choose the ones you want: *Pick over the lentils and remove any little stones.* ◊ *I picked through the facts of the case.* ▸ **'pick 'up 1** to get better, stronger, etc.; to improve: *Trade usually picks up in the spring.* ◊ *The wind is picking up now.* ◊ *Sales have picked up 14 per cent this year.* ⊃ related noun PICKUP **2** (*informal*) to start again; to continue: *Let's pick up where we left off yesterday.* **3** (*especially NAmE, informal*) to put things away and make things neat, especially for sb else: *All I seem to do is cook, wash and pick up after the kids.* ▸ **'pick 'up** | **'pick sth 'up** to answer a phone: *The phone rang and rang and nobody picked up.* ▸ **'pick sb↔'up 1** to go somewhere in your car and collect sb who is waiting for you SYN **collect**: *I'll pick you up at five.* **2** to allow sb to get into your vehicle and take them somewhere: *The bus picks up passengers outside the airport.* **3** to rescue sb from the sea or from a dangerous place, especially one that is difficult to reach: *A lifeboat picked up survivors.* **4** (*informal, often disapproving*) to start talking to sb you do not know because you want to have a sexual relationship with them: *He goes to clubs to pick up girls.* ⊃ related noun PICKUP **5** (*informal*) (of the police) to arrest sb: *He was picked up by police and taken to the station for questioning.* **6** to make sb feel better: *Try this—it will pick you up.* ⊃ related noun PICK-ME-UP ▸ **'pick sb/sth↔'up** ⚹ A2 to take hold of sb/sth and lift them/it up: *She went over to the crying child and picked her up.* ▸ **'pick sth↔'up 1** to get information or a skill by chance rather than by making a deliberate effort: *to pick up bad habits* ◊ *Here's a tip I picked up from my mother.* ◊ *She picked up Spanish when she was living in Mexico.* **2** to identify or recognize sth: *Scientists can now pick up early signs of the disease.* **3** to collect sth from a place: *I picked up my coat from the cleaners.* ⊃ related noun PICKUP **4** to receive an electronic signal, sound or picture: *We were able to pick up the BBC World Service.* **5** (*informal*) to buy sth, especially cheaply or by chance: *We managed to pick up a few bargains at the auction.* **6** (*informal*) to get or obtain sth: *I seem to have picked up a terrible cold from somewhere.* ◊ *I picked up £30 in tips today.* **7** to find and follow a route: *to pick up the scent of an animal* ◊ *We can pick up the motorway in a few miles.* **8** to return to an earlier subject or situation in order to continue it SYN **take up**: *He picks up this theme again in later chapters of the book.* **9** to notice sth that is not very obvious; to see sth that you are looking for: *I picked up the faint sound of a car in the distance.* **10** (*especially NAmE*) to put things away neatly: *Will you pick up all your toys?* **11** (*NAmE*) to put things away and make a room neat: *to pick up a room* ▸ **'pick 'up on sth 1** to notice sth and perhaps react to it: *She failed to pick up on the humour in his remark.* **2** to return to a point that has already been mentioned or discussed: *If I could just pick up on a question you raised earlier.* ▸ **'pick sb 'up on sth** to mention sth that sb has said or done that you think is wrong: *I knew he would pick me up on that slip sooner or later.* ▸ **'pick yourself 'up** to stand up again after you have fallen: *He just picked himself up and went on running.* ◊ (*figurative*) *She didn't waste time feeling sorry for herself—she just picked herself up and carried on.*

■ **noun 1** ⚹ B2 [sing.] (*rather informal*) an act of choosing sth: *Take your pick* (= choose). ◊ *The winner gets first pick of the prizes.* **2** [C] (*informal*) a person or thing that is chosen: *She was his pick for best actress.* ⊃ SYNONYMS at CHOICE **3** [sing.] **the ~ of sth** (*rather informal*) the best thing or things in a group: *We're reviewing the pick of this month's new books.* ◊ *I think we got the pick of the bunch* (= the best in the group). **4** [C] = PICKAXE: *picks and shovels* **5** [C] (*informal*) = PLECTRUM ⊃ see also ICE PICK, TOOTHPICK

**'pick-and-mix** *adj.* (*BrE*) used to describe a way of putting sth together by choosing things from among a large variety of different items: *a pick-and-mix programme of study*

**'pick·axe** (*NAmE also* **pick·ax**) /ˈpɪkæks/ (*also* **pick**) *noun* a large heavy tool that has a curved metal bar with sharp ends fixed at the centre to a wooden handle. It is used for breaking rocks or hard ground. ⊃ picture at AXE

**'pick·er** /ˈpɪkə(r)/ *noun* a person or machine that picks flowers, vegetables, etc: *cotton pickers*

**picket** /ˈpɪkɪt/ *noun, verb*

■ **noun 1** a person or group of people who stand outside the entrance to a building in order to protest about sth, especially in order to stop people from entering a factory, etc. during a strike; an occasion at which this happens: *Five pickets were arrested by police.* ◊ *I was on picket duty at the time.* ◊ *a mass picket of the factory* ⊃ see also PICKETER ⊃ WORDFINDER NOTE at UNION **2** a soldier or group of soldiers guarding a military base **3** a pointed piece of wood

that is fixed in the ground, especially as part of a fence: *a picket fence*
- **verb** [T, I] **~ (sth)** to stand outside somewhere such as your place of work to protest about sth or to try and persuade people to join a strike: *200 workers were picketing the factory.* ◊ *Striking workers picketed outside the gates.*

**pick·et·er** /ˈpɪkɪtə(r)/ noun (*NAmE*) a person who takes part in a picket

**picket·ing** /ˈpɪkɪtɪŋ/ noun [U] the activity of standing outside the entrance to a building in order to protest about sth and stop people from entering the building: *mass picketing of the factory*

**ˈpicket line** noun a line or group of PICKETS: *Fire crews refused to cross the picket line.*

**pick·ings** /ˈpɪkɪŋz/ noun [pl.] something, especially money, that can be obtained from a particular situation in an easy or a dishonest way: *There were only slim pickings to be made at the fair.* ◊ *There are rich pickings to be had by investing in this sort of company.* ◊ *The strike affecting the country's largest airline is producing easy pickings for smaller companies.*

**pickle** /ˈpɪkl/ noun, verb
- **noun 1** [C, usually pl.] (*BrE*) a vegetable that has been preserved in VINEGAR or salt water and has a strong taste, served cold with meat, salads, etc. **2** [U] (*BrE*) a cold thick spicy sauce made from fruit and vegetables that have been boiled, often sold in JARS and served with meat, cheese, etc. **3** (*NAmE*) (*BrE* **gher·kin**) [U, C] a small CUCUMBER that has been preserved in VINEGAR before being eaten
- **IDM** **in a ˈpickle** (*informal*) in a difficult or unpleasant situation
- **verb ~ sth** to preserve food in VINEGAR or salt water

**pickled** /ˈpɪkld/ adj. **1** (of food) preserved in VINEGAR: *pickled cabbage/herring/onions* **2** (*old-fashioned, informal*) drunk

**ˈpick-me-up** noun (*informal*) something that makes you feel better, happier, healthier, etc., especially medicine or an alcoholic drink: (*figurative*) *This deal would offer the best possible pick-me-up to the town's ailing economy.*

**pick·off** /ˈpɪkɒf; *NAmE* -ɔːf/ noun (in baseball) a situation in which a player running to a BASE is out because a FIELDER or the PITCHER suddenly throws the ball to that base

**pick·pocket** /ˈpɪkpɒkɪt; *NAmE* -pɑːk-/ noun a person who steals money, etc. from other people's pockets, especially in crowded places

**pick-up** /ˈpɪkʌp/ noun, adj.
- **noun 1** (*also* **ˈpickup truck**) [C] a vehicle with low sides and no roof at the back used, for example, by farmers **2** [C] a person sb meets for the first time, for example in a bar, with whom they start a sexual relationship: *casual pickups* **3** [C] **~ (in sth)** an improvement: *a pickup in the housing market* **4** [U, C] an occasion when sb/sth is collected: *Goods are delivered not later than noon on the day after pickup.* **5** [C] the part of a record player or musical instrument that changes electrical signals into sound, or sound into electrical signals **6** [U] (*NAmE*) a vehicle's ability to ACCELERATE (= increase in speed)
- **adj.** [only before noun] (*NAmE*) (of a sports game) often not planned in advance and that anyone who wants to can join in: *A group of kids started a pickup game of basketball on the street outside.*

**picky** /ˈpɪki/ adj. (*informal*) (of a person) liking only particular things and difficult to please **SYN** **fussy**

**ˌpick-your-ˈown** adj. [only before noun] (of fruit or vegetables) picked by the customer on the farm where they are grown: *pick-your-own strawberries*

**pic·nic** /ˈpɪknɪk/ noun, verb
- **noun 1** an occasion when people pack a meal and take it to eat outdoors, especially in the countryside: *It's a nice day. Let's go for a picnic.* ◊ *We had a picnic beside the river.* **2** the meal, usually consisting of sandwiches, salad and fruit, etc. that you take with you when you go on a picnic: *Let's eat our picnic by the lake.* ◊ *a picnic lunch* ◊ *a picnic basket*
- **IDM** **be no ˈpicnic** (*informal*) to be difficult and cause a lot of problems: *Bringing up a family when you're unemployed is no picnic.*

# picture

- **verb** [I] (**-ck-**) to have a picnic: *No picnicking allowed* (= on a sign)

**pic·nick·er** /ˈpɪknɪkə(r)/ noun a person who is having a picnic

**pico-** /ˈpiːkəʊ, paɪkəʊ/ *combining form* (*specialist*) (in nouns; used in units of measurement) $10^{-12}$; one million millionth

**pictographs**

 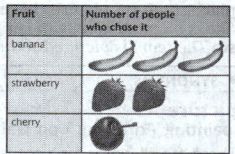

**picto·graph** /ˈpɪktəɡrɑːf; *NAmE* -ɡræf/ (*also* **picto·gram** /ˈpɪktəɡræm/) noun **1** a picture representing a word or phrase **2** a diagram that uses pictures to represent amounts or numbers of a particular thing

**pic·tor·ial** /pɪkˈtɔːriəl/ adj. [usually before noun] **1** using or containing pictures: *Pictorial representation of statistics or data in a chart is a kind of pictogram.* **2** connected with pictures: *pictorial traditions* ▶ **pic·tori·al·ly** /-əli/ adv.

**pic·ture** 0ʷ A1 S /ˈpɪktʃə(r)/ noun, verb
- **noun**
- **PAINTING/DRAWING 1** A1 [C] a painting or drawing, etc. that shows a scene, a person or thing: *a book with lots of pictures in it* ◊ **~ of sb/sth** *A picture of flowers hung on the wall.* ◊ *The children were drawing pictures of their pets.* ◊ *She wanted a famous artist to paint her picture* (= a picture of herself).
- **PHOTOGRAPH 2** A1 [C] a photograph: *to take a picture* ◊ *We had our picture taken in front of the hotel.* ◊ *The picture shows the couple together on their yacht.* ◊ **~ of sb/sth** *She posted a picture of the two of them on her Facebook page.* ◊ *The star shared the picture on Twitter.* ◊ *to upload/send/tweet a picture* ⊃ SYNONYMS at PHOTOGRAPH ⊃ EXPRESS YOURSELF at DESCRIBE
- **ON TV 3** A1 [C] **~ (of sb/sth)** an image on a television screen: *You are looking at live pictures of midtown Manhattan.* ◊ *poor picture quality*
- **DESCRIPTION 4** B1 [C, usually sing.] a description that gives you an idea in your mind of what sth is like: *We've only got scraps of information, not the full picture.* ◊ **~ of sth** *The writer paints a gloomy picture of the economy.* ◊ *From news reports a picture emerges of a country in crisis.*
- **MENTAL IMAGE 5** B2 [C, usually sing.] **~ (of sb/sth)** a mental image or memory of sth: *I have a vivid picture of my grandfather smiling down at me when I was very small.*
- **GENERAL SITUATION 6 the picture** [sing.] the general situation relating to sb/sth: *Just a few years ago the picture was very different.* ◊ *The overall picture for farming is encouraging.*
- **MOVIES 7** [C] a film: *The movie won nine Academy Awards, including Best Picture.* ◊ **in pictures** (*especially NAmE*) *I believe her husband's in pictures* (= he acts in movies or works in the movie industry). ⊃ see also MOTION PICTURE **8 the pictures** [pl.] (*old-fashioned, informal*) the cinema: *Shall we go to the pictures tonight?*
- **IDM** **be/look a ˈpicture** to look very beautiful or special **be the picture of ˈhealth, ˈguilt, ˈmisery, etc.** (*informal*) to look extremely healthy, guilty, unhappy, etc. **get the ˈpicture** (*informal*) to understand a situation, especially one that sb is describing to you: *'I pretended that I hadn't heard.' 'I get the picture.'* **in/out of the ˈpicture** (*informal*) involved/not involved in a situation: *Morris is likely to win, with Jones out of the picture now.* **put/keep sb in the ˈpicture** (*informal*) to give sb the information they need in order to understand a situation: *Just to put you in the picture—there have been a number of changes here recently.* ⊃ more at BIG adj., PAINT v., PRETTY adj.
- **verb**
- **IMAGINE 1** B2 to imagine sb/sth; to create an image of sb/sth in your mind: **~ sb/sth** *I could picture the scene clearly.* ◊ **~ sb/sth as sth** *We found it hard to picture him as the*

**picture book** 1162

father of teenage sons. ◊ **~ sb/sth doing sth** When he did not come home she pictured him lying dead on the roadside somewhere. ◊ **~ what, how, etc…** I tried to picture what it would be like to live alone.
- **DESCRIBE 2** (often passive) to describe or present sb/sth in a particular way **SYN** portray: **be pictured as sth** Before the trial Liz had been pictured as a frail woman dominated by her husband.
- **SHOW IN PHOTOGRAPH 3** [usually passive] to show sb/sth in a photograph or picture: **be pictured** (+ adv./prep./adj.) She is pictured here with her parents. ◊ **be pictured doing sth** The team is pictured setting off on their European tour.

▼ **SYNONYMS**

**picture**
painting • drawing • portrait • print • sketch
These are all words for a scene, person or thing that has been represented on paper by drawing, painting, etc.
**picture** a scene, person or thing that has been represented on paper using a pencil, a pen or paint: *The children were drawing pictures of their pets.*
**painting** a picture that has been made using paint: *a collection of paintings by American artists*
**drawing** a picture that has been made using a pencil or pen, not paint: *a pencil/charcoal drawing*
**portrait** a painting, drawing or photograph of a person, especially of the head and shoulders: *Vermeer's 'Portrait of the artist in his studio'* ◊ *a self-portrait* (= a painting that you do of yourself)
**print** a picture that has been copied from a painting using photography: *a Renoir print*
**sketch** a simple picture that is drawn quickly and does not have many details: *I usually do a few very rough sketches before I start on a painting.*

PATTERNS
- to **draw** a picture/portrait/sketch
- to **paint** a picture/portrait
- to **make** a painting/drawing/portrait/print/sketch
- to **do** a painting/drawing/portrait/sketch

**ˈpicture book** noun a book with a lot of pictures, especially one for children
**ˌpicture-ˈperfect** adj. (NAmE) exactly right in appearance or in the way things are done
**ˌpicture-ˈpostcard** adj. [only before noun] (especially BrE) (of places) very pretty: *a picture-postcard village*
**ˈpicture ˌpostcard** noun (old-fashioned) a POSTCARD with a picture on one side
**ˈpicture rail** noun a narrow piece of wood attached to the walls of a room below the ceiling and used for hanging pictures from
**pic·tur·esque** /ˌpɪktʃəˈresk/ adj. **1** (of a place, building, scene, etc.) pretty, especially in a way that looks old-fashioned **SYN** quaint: *a picturesque cottage/setting/village* **2** (of language) producing strong mental images by using unusual words: *a picturesque description of life at sea* ▸ **pic·tur·esque·ly** adv.: *The inn is picturesquely situated on the banks of the river.*
**ˈpicture window** noun a very large window made of a single piece of glass
**pic·tur·ize** (BrE also **-ise**) /ˈpɪktʃəraɪz/ verb **~ sth** (IndE) to adapt a story or play as a film; to create a film SEQUENCE to go with a song: *The novel has been picturized twice.* ▸ **pic·tur·iza·tion, -isa·tion** /ˌpɪktʃəraɪˈzeɪʃn; NAmE -rəˈz-/ noun [C, U]: *It was one of the few song picturizations that created magic with both music and visuals.*
**pid·dling** /ˈpɪdlɪŋ/ adj. [only before noun] (informal, disapproving) small and unimportant **SYN** trivial
**pidgin** /ˈpɪdʒɪn/ noun [U] **1** a simple form of a language, especially English, Portuguese or Dutch, with a limited number of words, that are used together with words from a local language. It is used when people who do not speak the same language need to talk to each other. **2 Pidgin** =

TOK PISIN **3** ~ **English, French, Japanese, etc.** a way of speaking a language that uses simple words and forms, used when a person does not speak the language well, or when he or she is talking to sb who does not speak the language well: *I tried to get my message across in my pidgin Italian.*

**pie** /paɪ/ noun [C, U] a baked dish of fruit or meat and/or vegetables with PASTRY on the bottom, sides and top: *a slice of apple pie* ◊ *a steak and kidney pie* ◊ **Help yourself to some more pie.** ◊ *a pie dish* ⊃ see also APPLE PIE, BANOFFI PIE, COTTAGE PIE, CUSTARD PIE, MINCE PIE, MUD PIE, PORK PIE, POT PIE, SHEPHERD'S PIE

**IDM** **a ˌpiece/ˌslice/ˌshare of the ˈpie** (BrE also **a ˌslice/ˌshare of the ˈcake**) a share of the available money or benefits that you believe you have a right to: *The company is demanding a larger slice of the corporate pie.* **ˌpie in the ˈsky** (informal) an event that sb talks about that seems very unlikely to happen: *This talk of moving to Australia is all just pie in the sky.* ⊃ more at AMERICAN adj., EASY adj., EAT, FINGER n., NICE

**pie·bald** /ˈpaɪbɔːld/ adj. (of a horse) with areas on it of two colours, usually black and white **SYN** pinto ⊃ compare SKEWBALD ▸ **pie·bald** noun

**piece** ❶ **A1** /piːs/ noun, verb

■ noun
- **SEPARATE AMOUNT 1** ❓ **A1** [C] (used especially with *of* and uncountable nouns) an amount of sth that has been cut or separated from the rest of it; a standard amount of sth: **~ of sth** *She wrote something on a small piece of paper.* ◊ *a piece of wood/metal* ◊ *a large piece of land* ◊ *a piece of cake* ◊ *a piece of cheese/meat/bread* ◊ *a small/little/tiny piece of sth* ◊ **into pieces** *He cut the pizza into bite-sized pieces.*
- **PART 2** ❓ **A1** [C, usually pl.] one of the bits or parts that sth breaks into: **~ of sth** *There were tiny pieces of glass all over the road.* ◊ **to pieces** *The boat had been smashed to pieces on the rocks.* ◊ **tear/rip sth to pieces** ◊ **in pieces** *The vase lay in pieces on the floor.* **3** ❓ **A1** [C] one of the parts that sth is made of: **to~** *He took the clock to pieces.* ◊ **~ of sth** *a missing piece of the puzzle* ◊ *The bridge was taken down piece by piece.* ◊ *a 500-piece jigsaw* ⊃ see also ONE-PIECE, TWO-PIECE, THREE-PIECE
- **SINGLE ITEM 4** ❓ **A1** [C] **~ (of sth)** (used especially with uncountable nouns) a single item of a particular type, especially one that forms part of a set: *a piece of equipment/furniture* ◊ *a piece of clothing/luggage* ◊ *a 28-piece dinner service* ⊃ see also MANTELPIECE **5** ❓ **A1** [C] **~ of sth** used with many uncountable nouns to describe a single example or an amount of sth: *a piece of information/evidence/advice/news/legislation* ◊ *a piece of software* ◊ *This is a superb piece of work.* ◊ *The building is a piece of history* (= of historical interest or importance). ◊ *You should eat at least two pieces of fruit a day.* **6** ❓ **A1** [C] a single item of writing, art, music, etc. that sb has produced or created; a short item of writing from a longer work: **~ of sth** *a piece of music/art* ◊ *a fine piece of writing* ◊ *They performed pieces by Bach and Handel.* ◊ **~ from sth** *She read a piece from 'Alice in Wonderland'.* ⊃ HOMOPHONES at PEACE
- **NEWS ARTICLE 7** [C] an article in a newspaper or magazine or a broadcast on television or radio: *The Washington Post ran a series of opinion pieces criticizing the policy.* ◊ **~ about/on sth** *Did you see her piece about the internet in the paper today?* ⊃ see also SET PIECE
- **COIN 8** [C] a coin of the value mentioned: *a 50p piece* ◊ *a five-cent piece*
- **IN CHESS, ETC. 9** [C] one of the small figures or objects that you move around in games such as CHESS
- **SHARE OF STH 10** [sing.] **~ of sth** (especially NAmE) a part or share of sth: *companies seeking a piece of the market*
- **GUN 11** [C] (NAmE, slang) a gun **HELP** You will find other compounds ending in **piece** at their place in the alphabet.

**IDM** **a/some ˌpiece of ˈwork** (NAmE, informal) used to express the fact that you admire sb or find them funny, often when they have done sth that surprises you: *You're some piece of work, Jack, do you know that?* **ˌfall to ˈpieces 1** (usually used in the progressive tenses) (of things) to become very old and in bad condition because of long use **SYN** fall apart: *Our car is falling to pieces, we've had it so long.* **2** (of a person, an organization, a plan, etc.) to stop working; to be destroyed: *He's worried the business will fall to pieces without him.* **ˌgive sb a ˌpiece of your ˈmind**

(*informal*) to tell sb that you think their behaviour is bad or are angry with them **go to ˈpieces** (*informal*) (of a person) to be so upset or afraid that you cannot manage to live or work normally **(all) in one ˈpiece** (*informal*) safe; not damaged or hurt, especially after a journey or dangerous experience: *They were lucky to get home in one piece.* **(all) of a ˈpiece** (*formal*) **1** all the same or similar: *The houses are all of a piece.* **2** all at the same time: *The house was built all of a piece in 1754.* **pick/pull/tear sb/sth to ˈpieces/ˈshreds** (*informal*) to criticize sb, or their work or ideas, very severely **a ˌpiece of ˈcake** (*informal*) a thing that is very easy to do **a ˌpiece of ˈpiss** (*BrE*, *taboo*, *slang*) a thing that is very easy to do ⟹ more at ACTION *n.*, BIT, BLOW *v.*, LONG *adj.*, NASTY, PICK *v.*, PIE, SAY *v.*, VILLAIN

■ *verb*

**PHRV** **ˌpiece sth↔toˈgether** **1** to understand a story, situation, etc. by taking all the facts and details about it and putting them together: *Police are trying to piece together the last hours of her life.* **2** to put all the separate parts of sth together to make a complete whole **SYN** **assemble**: *to piece together a jigsaw*

▼ **VOCABULARY BUILDING**

### Pieces

If you want to talk about a small amount or one example of something that is normally an uncountable noun, there is a range of words you can use. You must choose the right one to go with the substance you are talking about.

- **Piece** and (*BrE*, *informal*) **bit** are very general words and can be used with most uncountable nouns: *a piece of paper/wood/string/cake/fruit/meat/work/research/advice* ◊ *a bit of paper/work/chocolate/luck*
- A **slice** is a thin flat piece: *a slice of bread/cake/salami/cheese/pie/apple* ◊ (*figurative*) *a slice of life*
- A **chunk** is a thick, solid piece: *a chunk of cheese/bread/rock* ◊ *a chunk of land* (= a fairly large piece)
- A **lump** is a piece of something solid without any particular shape: *a lump of coal/rock/mud*
- A **fragment** is a very small piece of something that is broken or damaged: *fragments of glass* ◊ (*figurative*) *fragments of conversation* It can also be used with countable nouns to mean a small part of something: *a fragment of the story*
- A **speck** is a tiny piece of powder: *a speck of dust/dirt* You can also say: *a speck of light*
- **Drop** is used with liquids: *a drop of water/rain/blood/milk/whisky*
- A **pinch** is as much as you can hold between your finger and thumb: *a pinch of salt/cinnamon*
- A **portion** is enough for one person: *a portion of chicken*

**pièce de réˈsistˌance** /ˌpjes də reˈzɪstɑ̃s; *NAmE* ˌpjes də ˌreziːˈstɑːns/ *noun* [usually sing.] (*pl.* **pièces de réˌsistˌance** /ˌpjes də reˈzɪstɑ̃s; *NAmE* ˌpjes də ˌreziːˈstɑːns/) (*from French*) the most important or impressive part of a group or series of things

**piece·meal** /ˈpiːsmiːl/ *adj.* [usually before noun] (*often disapproving*) done or happening gradually at different times and often in different ways, rather than carefully planned at the beginning: *a piecemeal approach to dealing with the problem* ◊ *piecemeal changes* ▶ **piece·meal** *adv.*: *The reforms were implemented piecemeal.*

**ˈpiece rate** *noun* an amount of money paid for each thing or amount of sth that a worker produces

**piece·work** /ˈpiːswɜːk; *NAmE* -wɜːrk/ *noun* [U] work that is paid for by the amount done and not by the hours worked ▶ **ˈpiece·workˌer** *noun*

**ˈpie chart** *noun* a diagram consisting of a circle that is divided into sections to show the size of particular amounts in relation to the whole ⟹ **LANGUAGE BANK** at ILLUSTRATE, PROCESS¹ ⟹ picture at CHART

**pied** /paɪd/ *adj.* (especially of birds) of two or more different colours, especially black and white

**pied-à-terre** /ˌpjeɪd ɑːˈteə(r); *NAmE* ˈter/ *noun* (*pl.* **pieds-à-terre** /ˌpjeɪd ɑːˈteə(r); *NAmE* ˈter/) (*from French*) a small flat, usually in a town, that you do not live in as your main home but keep for use when necessary

**ˌPied ˈPiper** *noun* a person who persuades a lot of other people to follow them or do sth with them **ORIGIN** From the old German story of the Pied Piper of Hamelin, who made first rats and later children follow him by playing beautiful music on his pipe.

**pier** /pɪə(r); *NAmE* pɪr/ *noun* **1** a long structure built in the sea and joined to the land at one end, often with places of entertainment on it ⟹ **WORDFINDER NOTE** at SEA **2** a long low structure built in a lake, river or the sea and joined to the land at one end, used by boats to allow passengers to get on and off **SYN** **landing stage** **3** (*specialist*) a large strong piece of wood, metal or stone that is used to support a roof, wall, bridge, etc.

**pierce** /pɪəs; *NAmE* pɪrs/ *verb* **1** [T, I] to make a small hole in sth, or to go through sth, with a sharp object: ~ **sth** *The arrow pierced his shoulder.* ◊ *He pierced another hole in his belt with his knife.* ◊ *to have your ears/nose, etc. pierced* (= to have a small hole made in your ears/nose, etc. so that you can wear jewellery there) ~ **sb**: (*figurative*) *She was pierced to the heart with guilt.* ◊ ~ **through sth** *The knife pierced through his coat.* **2** [T, I] ~ **(through) sth** (*literary*) (of light, sound, etc.) to be suddenly seen or heard: *Sirens pierced the silence of the night.* ◊ *Shafts of sunlight pierced the heavy mist.* **3** [T, I] ~ **(through) sth** to force a way through a barrier **SYN** **penetrate**: *They failed to pierce the Liverpool defence.*

**pierc·ing** /ˈpɪəsɪŋ; *NAmE* ˈpɪrs-/ *adj.*, *noun*

■ *adj.* **1** [usually before noun] (of eyes or the way they look at sb) seeming to notice things about another person that would not normally be noticed, especially in a way that makes that person feel anxious or embarrassed: *She looked at me with piercing blue eyes.* ◊ *a piercing look* **2** [usually before noun] (of sounds) very high, loud and unpleasant **SYN** **shrill**: *a piercing shriek* ◊ *She has such a piercing voice.* **3** [only before noun] (of feelings) affecting you very strongly, especially in a way that causes you pain: *piercing sadness* **4** (of the wind or cold) very strong and feeling as if it can pass through your clothes and skin **5** [only before noun] sharp and able to make a hole in sth: *The animal is covered in long piercing spines.* ▶ **pierc·ing·ly** *adv.*: *His eyes were piercingly blue.* ◊ *The weather remained piercingly cold.*

■ *noun* **1** [U] = BODY PIERCING **2** [C] the hole that is made in your ear, nose or some other part of your body so that you can wear jewellery there: *She has a tongue piercing.*

**pietà** /pjeɪˈtɑː/ *noun* (*art*) a picture or sculpture of the Virgin Mary holding the dead body of Christ

**piety** /ˈpaɪəti/ *noun* [U] the state of having or showing a deep respect for sb/sth, especially for God and religion; the state of being PIOUS **OPP** **impiety**

**pif·fle** /ˈpɪfl/ *noun* [U] (*old-fashioned*, *informal*) ideas, statements or beliefs that you think are silly or not true **SYN** **nonsense**, **rubbish**

**pig** 🅞 **A1** /pɪɡ/ *noun*, *verb*

■ *noun* **1** 🅐 **A1** (*also* **hog** *especially in NAmE*) an animal with pink, black or brown skin, short legs, a broad nose and a short curly tail. Pigs are kept on farms for their meat (called PORK) or live in the wild: *a pig farmer* ◊ *Pigs were grunting and squealing in the yard.* ⟹ see also BOAR, PIGLET, SOW², SUCKLING PIG, SWINE, GUINEA PIG **2** (*informal*, *disapproving*) an unpleasant or offensive person; a person who is dirty or GREEDY: *Arrogant pig!* ◊ *Don't be such a pig!* ◊ *The greedy pig's eaten all the biscuits!* ◊ *She made a pig of herself with the ice cream* (= ate too much). ◊ *He's a real male chauvinist pig* (= a man who does not think women are equal to men). **3** (*slang*) an offensive word for a police officer

**IDM** **make a ˈpig's ear (out) of sth** (*BrE*, *informal*) to do sth badly; to make a mess of sth **(buy) a ˌpig in a ˈpoke** (*BrE*, *informal*) if you **buy a pig in a poke**, you buy sth without seeing it or knowing if it is good enough **a ˌpig of a ˈsth** (*BrE*, *informal*) a difficult or unpleasant thing or task: *I've had a pig of a day.* **ˌpigs might ˈfly** (*BrE*) (*NAmE* **when pigs ˈfly**) (*ironic*, *saying*) used to show that you do not believe sth will ever happen: *'With a bit of luck, we'll be finished by the end of the year.' 'Yes, and pigs might fly!'*

# pigeon

■ *verb* (*BrE*, *informal*) (**-gg-**) to eat too much of sth: **~ sth** *I had a whole box of chocolates and pigged the lot!* ◊ **~ yourself (on sth)** *Don't give me cakes—I'll just pig myself.*
**PHRV** ˌpig ˈout (on sth) (*informal*) to eat too much food: *They pigged out on pizza.*

**pi·geon** /ˈpɪdʒɪn/ *noun* a fat grey and white bird with short legs. Pigeons are common in cities and also live in woods and fields where people shoot them for sport or food: *the sound of pigeons cooing* ⇒ compare DOVE¹ ⇒ see also CARRIER PIGEON, CLAY PIGEON, HOMING PIGEON, WOOD PIGEON
**IDM** be sb's ˈpigeon (*BrE*, *old-fashioned*) to be sb's responsibility or business ⇒ more at CAT

**pi·geon·hole** /ˈpɪdʒɪnhəʊl/ *noun*, *verb*
■ *noun* one of a set of small boxes that are fixed on a wall and open at the front, used for putting letters, messages, etc. in; one of a similar set of boxes that are part of a desk, used for keeping papers, documents, etc. in: *If you can't come, leave a note in my pigeonhole.*
■ *verb* **1** **~ sb/sth (as sth)** to decide that sb/sth belongs to a particular group or type without thinking deeply enough about it and considering what other qualities they might have **SYN** **categorize**, **label**: *be pigeonholed as sth He has been pigeonholed as a children's writer.* **2** **~ sth** to decide to deal with sth later or to forget it **SYN** **shelve**: *Plans for a new school have been pigeonholed.*

**pig·gery** /ˈpɪɡəri/ *noun* (*pl.* **-ies**) a place where pigs are kept especially in order to produce young

**piggy** /ˈpɪɡi/ *noun*, *adj.*
■ *noun* (*pl.* **-ies**) a child's word for a pig
■ *adj.* [only before noun] (*informal*, *disapproving*) (of a person's eyes) like those of a pig

**pig·gy·back** /ˈpɪɡibæk/ *noun*, *verb*
■ *noun* a ride on sb's back, while he or she is walking: *Give me a piggyback, Daddy!* ◊ *a piggyback ride* ▶ **ˈpig·gy·back** *adv.*: *to ride piggyback*
■ *verb*
**PHRV** ˈpiggyback on sb/sth to use sth that already exists as a support for your own work; to use a larger organization, etc. for your own advantage

**ˈpiggy bank** *noun* a container in the shape of a pig, with a narrow opening in the top for putting coins in, used by children to save money ⇒ compare MONEY BOX

**ˌpiggy in the ˈmiddle** (also **ˌpig in the ˈmiddle**) (*both BrE*) (*NAmE* ˌmonkey in the ˈmiddle) *noun* **1** a children's game where two people throw a ball to each other over the head of another person who tries to catch it **2** a person who is caught between two people or groups who are fighting or arguing

**pig-ˈheaded** *adj.* unwilling to change your opinion about sth, in a way that other people think is annoying and unreasonable **SYN** **obstinate**, **stubborn** ▶ **pig-ˈheaded·ness** *noun* [U]

**ˈpig iron** *noun* [U] a form of iron that is not pure

**pig·let** /ˈpɪɡlət/ *noun* a young pig

**pig·ment** /ˈpɪɡmənt/ *noun* [U, C] **1** a substance that exists naturally in people, animals and plants and gives their skin, leaves, etc. a particular colour **2** a coloured powder that is mixed with a liquid to produce paint, etc.

**pig·men·ta·tion** /ˌpɪɡmənˈteɪʃn/ *noun* [U] the presence of pigments in skin, hair, leaves, etc. that causes them to be a particular colour

**pig·ment·ed** /ˈpɪɡmentɪd/ *adj.* (especially of skin) having a natural colour

**pigmy** *noun*, *adj.* = PYGMY

**pig·skin** /ˈpɪɡskɪn/ *noun* **1** [U] leather made from the skin of a pig **2** [sing.] (*NAmE*, *informal*) the ball used in AMERICAN FOOTBALL

**pig·sty** /ˈpɪɡstaɪ/ (also **sty**) *noun* (*pl.* **-ies**) (*NAmE also* **pig·pen** /ˈpɪɡpen/) **1** [C] a small building or area where pigs are kept **2** [sing.] (*informal*) a very dirty or untidy place

**pig·swill** /ˈpɪɡswɪl/ *noun* [U] = SWILL

**pig·tail** /ˈpɪɡteɪl/ (*BrE*) (also **braid** *NAmE*, *BrE*) *noun* hair that is tied together into one or two bunches and TWISTED into a

PLAIT or PLAITS, worn either at the back of the head or one on each side of the head: **in pigtails** *She wore her hair in pigtails.* ⇒ compare PONYTAIL

**pike** /paɪk/ *noun*, *verb*
■ *noun* **1** (*pl.* **pike**) a large FRESHWATER fish with very sharp teeth **2** a weapon with a sharp BLADE (= metal cutting edge) on a long wooden handle, used in the past by soldiers on foot **3** (*NAmE*) = TURNPIKE **4** (*dialect*) a pointed top of a hill in the north of England
**IDM** come down the ˈpike (*NAmE*, *informal*) to happen; to become easy to notice: *We're hearing a lot about new inventions coming down the pike.*
■ *verb*
**PHRV** ˌpike ˈout (*AustralE*, *NZE*, *informal*) to decide not to do sth that you had agreed to do ˌpike ˈon sb (*AustralE*, *NZE*, *informal*) to fail to provide the help or support that sb hoped for or expected

**pike·staff** /ˈpaɪksta:f; *NAmE* -stæf/ *noun* **IDM** see PLAIN *adj.*

**pikey** /ˈpaɪki/ *noun* (*BrE*, *informal*, *offensive*) **1** an offensive name for a GYPSY **2** an offensive word for a person who is poor and not educated: *He referred to them as dirty pikey scum.*

**pilaf** (also **pilaff**) /ˈpiːlæf; *NAmE* pɪˈlɑːf/ (also **pilau**, **pulao** /ˈpiːlaʊ; *NAmE* pɪˈlaʊ/) *noun* [U, C] a hot spicy Eastern dish of rice and vegetables and often pieces of meat or fish

**pi·las·ter** /pɪˈlæstə(r)/ *noun* (*specialist*) a flat column that sticks out from the wall of a building, used as decoration

**Pi·la·tes** /pɪˈlɑːtiːz/ *noun* [U] a system of stretching and pushing exercises using special equipment, which help make your muscles stronger and make you able to bend parts of your body more easily

**pil·chard** /ˈpɪltʃəd; *NAmE* -tʃərd/ *noun* a small sea fish that is used for food

**pile** /paɪl/ *noun*, *verb*
■ *noun* ⇒ see also PILES **1** [C] a number of things that have been placed on top of each other: **~ of sth** *a pile of clothes/paper* ◊ *I found it in a pile of documents on his desk.* ◊ **in/into a ~** *The hats were stacked in neat piles.* **2** [C] **~ (of sth)** a mass of sth that is high in the middle and wider at the bottom than at the top **SYN** **heap**: *piles of dirty washing* ◊ *a pile of rubble* **3** [C, usually pl.] **~ of sth** (*informal*) a lot of sth: *He made a pile of cash on the sale of his house.* ◊ *He walked out leaving a pile of debt behind him.* **4** [U, sing.] the short THREADS, pieces of wool, etc. that form the soft surface of carpets and some types of cloth such as VELVET: *a deep-pile carpet* **5** [C] a large wooden, metal or stone post that is fixed into the ground and used to support a building, bridge, etc. **6** [C] (*formal* or *humorous*) a large impressive building
**IDM** (at the) ˈbottom/ˈtop of the ˈpile in the least/most important position in a group of people or things **make a/ your ˈpile** (*informal*) to make a lot of money
■ *verb* **1** [T] to put things one on top of another; to form a pile: **~ sth** *She piled the boxes one on top of the other.* ◊ *The clothes were piled high on the chair.* ◊ **~ sth up** *Snow was piled up against the door.* ◊ **~ sth + adv./prep.** *We piled sandbags against the doors.* **2** [T] to put sth on/into sth; to load sth with sth: **~ A with B** *The sofa was piled high with cushions.* ◊ **~ B on(to) A** *He piled as much food as he could onto his plate.* ◊ **~ B in(to) A** *She piled everything into her suitcase.* ⇒ see also STOCKPILE *verb* **3** [I] + **adv./prep.** (*informal*) (of a number of people) to go somewhere quickly without order or control: *The coach finally arrived and we all piled on.*
**IDM** ˌpile on the ˈagony/ˈgloom (*especially BrE*, *informal*) to make an unpleasant situation worse: *Bosses piled on the agony with threats of more job losses.*
**PHRV** ˌpile ˈon (especially of a person's weight) to increase quickly: *The weight just piled on while I was abroad.* ˌpile sth↔ˈon **1** to make sth increase rapidly: *The team piled on the points in the first half of the game.* ◊ *I've been piling on the pounds* (= I have put on weight) *recently.* **2** to express a feeling in a much stronger way than is necessary: *Don't pile on the drama! ◊ Things aren't really that bad—she does tend to* **pile it on**. **3** to give sb more or too much of sth: *The German team* **piled on the pressure** *in the last 15 minutes.* ˌpile sth ˈon(to) sb to give sb a lot of sth to do, carry, etc: *He felt his boss was*

piling too much work on him. **pile 'up** to become larger in quantity or amount **SYN accumulate**: *Work always piles up at the end of the year.*

**'pile-driver** /ˈpaɪldraɪvə(r)/ *noun* **1** (*BrE*, *informal*) a very heavy kick or hard hit **2** a machine for forcing heavy posts into the ground

**piles** /paɪlz/ *noun* [pl.] VEINS at or near the ANUS that have become painful and SWOLLEN (= larger than normal) **SYN haemorrhoids**

**'pile-up** *noun* a road accident involving several vehicles crashing into each other: *Three people died in a multiple pile-up in freezing fog.*

**pil·fer** /ˈpɪlfə(r)/ *verb* [I, T] to steal things of little value or in small quantities, especially from the place where you work: **~(from sb/sth)** *He was caught pilfering.* ◊ **~sth (from sb/sth)** *She regularly pilfered stamps from work.* ▸ **pil·fer·age** /-fərɪdʒ/ *noun* [U] (*formal*): *pilferage of goods* **pil·fer·er** *noun*: *Certain types of goods are preferred by pilferers.* **pil·fer·ing** *noun* [U]: *We know that pilfering goes on.*

**pil·grim** /ˈpɪlgrɪm/ *noun* **1** a person who travels to a holy place for religious reasons: *Muslim pilgrims on their way to Mecca* ◊ *Christian pilgrims visiting Lourdes* **2 Pilgrim** a member of the group of English people (**the Pilgrim 'Fathers**) who sailed to America on the ship *The Mayflower* in 1620 and started a COLONY in Massachusetts

**pil·grim·age** /ˈpɪlgrɪmɪdʒ/ *noun* [C, U] **1** a journey to a holy place for religious reasons: *to go on/make a pilgrimage* **2** a journey to a place that is connected with sb/sth that you admire or respect: *His grave has become a place of pilgrimage.* ⇨ WORDFINDER NOTE at JOURNEY

**pill** ஃ+ B2 /pɪl/ *noun*, *verb*
■ *noun* **1** ஃ+ B2 [C] a small flat round piece of medicine that you SWALLOW whole, without biting it: *a vitamin pill* ⇨ see also PEP PILL, POISON PILL, SLEEPING PILL **2 the pill** or **the Pill** [sing.] a pill that some women take to prevent them becoming pregnant: *the contraceptive pill* ◊ *on the ~ to be/go on the pill* ⇨ see also MORNING-AFTER PILL **3** [C] (*NAmE*) an annoying person
**IDM** **sugar/sweeten the pill** to do sth that makes an unpleasant situation seem less unpleasant **SYN sugar-coat** ⇨ more at BITTER *adj.*
■ *verb* [I] (of a piece of clothing, especially one made of wool) to become covered in very small balls of FIBRE

**pil·lage** /ˈpɪlɪdʒ/ *verb* [I, T, often passive] to steal things from a place or person, especially in a war, using violence **SYN plunder**: *The rebels went looting and pillaging.* ◊ **be pillaged** *The town had been pillaged and burned.* ◊ **be pillaged from sth** *Works of art were pillaged from churches and museums.* ▸ **pil·lage** *noun* [U]: *They brought back horrific accounts of murder and pillage.* **pil·la·ger** *noun* ⇨ compare LOOT, PLUNDER

**pil·lar** /ˈpɪlə(r)/ *noun* **1** a large round stone, metal or wooden post that is used to support a bridge, the roof of a building, etc., especially when it is part of an attractive design **2** a large round stone, metal or wooden post that is built to remind people of a famous person or event **SYN column 3 ~ of sth** a mass of sth that is like a pillar in shape: *a pillar of smoke/rock* **4 ~ of sth** a strong supporter of sth; an important member of sth: *He was a pillar of the Church.* ◊ *a pillar of society* **5 ~ of sth** a person who has a lot of a particular quality: *She is a pillar of strength in a crisis.* **6** a basic part or feature of a system, organization, belief, etc: *the central pillar of this theory*
**IDM** **be driven, pushed, etc. from pillar to 'post** to be forced to go from one person or situation to another without achieving anything

**'pillar box** *noun* (*BrE*, *old-fashioned*) a tall red metal box in the street, used for putting letters in which are being sent by post ⇨ compare LETTER BOX, POSTBOX

**pil·lared** /ˈpɪləd; *NAmE* -lərd/ *adj.* [only before noun] (of a building or part of a building) having PILLARS

**pill·box** /ˈpɪlbɒks; *NAmE* -bɑːks/ *noun* a small shelter for soldiers, often partly underground, from which a gun can be fired

**pil·lion** /ˈpɪliən/ *noun* a seat for a passenger behind the driver of a motorcycle: *a pillion passenger/seat* ▸ **pil·lion** *adv.*: *to ride pillion*

**pil·lock** /ˈpɪlək/ *noun* (*BrE*, *slang*) a stupid person

**pil·lory** /ˈpɪləri/ *verb*, *noun*
■ *verb* [often passive] (**pil·lor·ies**, **pil·lory·ing**, **pil·lor·ied**, **pil·lor·ied**) **~ sb** to criticize sb strongly in public: *He was regularly pilloried by the press for his radical ideas.*
■ *noun* (*pl.* **-ies**) a wooden frame, with holes for the head and hands, which people were locked into in the past as a punishment ⇨ compare STOCK

**pil·low** /ˈpɪləʊ/ *noun*, *verb*
■ *noun* **1** a square or RECTANGULAR piece of cloth filled with soft material, used to rest your head on in bed: *She lay back against the pillows.* ◊ *pillow talk* (= conversations in bed between lovers) ◊ *He lay back on the grass using his backpack as a pillow.* ⇨ see also THROW PILLOW **2** (*NAmE*) = CUSHION
■ *verb* **~ sth (+ adv./prep.)** (*literary*) to rest sth, especially your head, on an object: *She lay on the grass, her head pillowed on her arms.*

**'pillow·case** /ˈpɪləʊkeɪs/ (*also* **'pil·low-slip** /ˈpɪləʊslɪp/) *noun* a cloth cover for a PILLOW, that can be removed

**pilot** ⓘ A2 /ˈpaɪlət/ *noun*, *verb*, *adj.*
■ *noun* **1** ஃ A2 a person who operates the controls of an aircraft, especially as a job: *an airline pilot* ◊ *a fighter/helicopter pilot* ◊ *The accident was caused by pilot error.* ⇨ see also AUTOMATIC PILOT, AUTOPILOT, CO-PILOT, TEST PILOT ⇨ WORDFINDER NOTE at AIRCRAFT **2** a person with special knowledge of a difficult area of water, for example, the entrance to a HARBOUR, whose job is to guide ships through it **3** a single television programme that is made in order to find out whether people will like it and want to watch further programmes **4** = PILOT LIGHT
■ *verb* **1 ~ sth** to fly an aircraft or guide a ship; to act as a pilot: *The plane was piloted by the instructor.* ◊ *The captain piloted the boat into a mooring.* **2 ~ sth (through sth)** to guide sb/sth somewhere, especially through a complicated place or system: *She piloted a bill on the rights of part-time workers through parliament.* **3 ~ sth** to test a new product, idea, etc. with a few people or in a small area before it is introduced everywhere
■ *adj.* [only before noun] done on a small scale in order to see if sth is successful enough to do on a large scale: *a pilot project/study/survey* ◊ *a pilot episode* (= of a radio or television series)

**'pilot light** (*also* **pilot**) *noun* a small flame that burns all the time, for example on a gas BOILER, and lights a larger flame when the gas is turned on

**'pilot officer** *noun* (*abbr.* **PO**) an officer of the lowest rank in the British AIR FORCE

**'pilot whale** *noun* a small WHALE that lives in warm seas

**Pils** /pɪlz, pɪls/ (*also* **Pilsner** /ˈpɪlznə(r), ˈpɪlsnə(r)/) *noun* [U] a type of strong light-coloured beer originally made in what is now the Czech Republic

**Pima** /ˈpiːmə/ *noun* (*pl.* **Pima** or **Pimas**) *noun* a member of a Native American people, many of whom live in the US state of Arizona

**pi·mento** /pɪˈmentəʊ/ *noun* (*pl.* **-os**) a small red PEPPER with a mild taste

**pimp** /pɪmp/ *noun*, *verb*
■ *noun* a man who controls PROSTITUTES and lives on the money that they earn
■ *verb* **1** [I] **~ (for sb)** to get customers for a PROSTITUTE **2 ~ sb (to sb)** to provide sb as a PROSTITUTE **3** [T] (*informal*) to add things to sth to make it look or sound better, especially by making it more individual: **~ sth** *Pimp your car with stylish custom wheels!* ◊ **~ sth up** *I would love to pimp the songs up.*

**pim·per·nel** /ˈpɪmpənel; *NAmE* -pərn-/ *noun* a small wild plant with red, white or blue flowers

**pim·ple** /ˈpɪmpl/ *noun* a small raised red spot on the skin ⇨ compare SPOT ⇨ see also GOOSE PIMPLES ▸ **pim·ply** /-pli/ *adj.*: *pimply skin* ◊ *a pimply youth*

**PIN** /pɪn/ (*also* **'PIN number**) *noun* a number given to you, for example by a bank, so that you can use a plastic card to

# pin

take out money from a cash machine (the abbreviation for 'personal identification number') ⊃ see also CHIP AND PIN

**pin** ❶ **B1** /pɪn/ noun, verb

■ noun
- FOR FASTENING/JOINING **1** **B1** a short thin piece of stiff wire with a sharp point at one end and a round head at the other, used especially for fastening together pieces of cloth when SEWING ⊃ see also BOBBY PIN, DRAWING PIN, HAIRPIN, PINS AND NEEDLES, SAFETY PIN
- JEWELLERY **2** a short thin piece of stiff wire with a sharp point at one end and an item of decoration at the other, worn as jewellery: *a diamond pin* **3** (*especially NAmE*) = BROOCH
- BADGE **4** (*especially NAmE*) a type of BADGE that is fastened with a pin at the back: *He supports the group and wears its pin on his lapel.*
- MEDICAL **5** a piece of steel used to support a bone in your body when it has been broken
- ELECTRICAL **6** one of the metal parts that stick out of an electric PLUG and fit into a SOCKET: *a 2-pin plug* ⊃ picture at PLUG
- IN GAMES **7** a wooden or plastic object that is like a bottle in shape and that players try to knock down in games such as BOWLING ⊃ see also TENPIN
- IN GOLF **8** a stick with a flag on top of it, placed in a hole so that players can see where they are aiming for
- LEGS **9** **pins** [pl.] (*informal*) a person's legs
- ON SMALL BOMB **10** a small piece of metal on a HAND GRENADE that stops it from exploding and is pulled out just before the HAND GRENADE is thrown ⊃ see also ROLLING PIN

**IDM** **for two 'pins** (*BrE, old-fashioned*) used to say that you would like to do sth, even though you know that it would not be sensible: *I'd kill him for two pins.* ⊃ more at HEAR

■ verb (-nn-)
- FASTEN/JOIN **1** **B1** ~ sth + adv./prep. to attach sth onto another thing or fasten things together with a pin, etc: *She pinned the badge onto her jacket.* ◇ *A message had been pinned to the noticeboard.* ◇ *Pin all the pieces of material together.* ◇ *She always wears her hair pinned back.*
- PREVENT MOVEMENT **2** ~ sb/sth + adv./prep. to make sb unable to move by holding them or pressing them against sth: *They pinned him against a wall and stole his wallet.* ◇ *He grabbed her arms and pinned them to her sides.* ◇ *They found him pinned under the wreckage of the car.*

**IDM** **pin (all) your 'hopes on sb/sth** (*also* **pin your 'faith on sb/sth**) to rely on sb/sth completely for success or help: *The company is pinning its hopes on the new project.*

**PHRV** **pin sb↔'down 1** to make sb unable to move by holding them with a lot of force: *Two men pinned him down until the police arrived.* **2** to find sb and make them answer a question or tell you sth you need to know: *I need the up-to-date sales figures but I can never pin him down at the office.* **pin sb↔'down (to sth/doing sth)** to make sb make a decision or say clearly what they think or what they intend to do: *It's difficult to pin her down to fixing a date for a meeting.* **pin sth↔'down** to explain or understand sth exactly: *The cause of the disease is difficult to pin down precisely.* **pin sth on sb** to make sb be blamed for sth, especially for sth they did not do: *No one would admit responsibility. They all tried to pin the blame on someone else.* ◇ *You can't pin this one on me—I wasn't even there!*

**pi·na co·lada** /ˌpiːnə kəˈlɑːdə/ noun [C, U] an alcoholic drink made by mixing RUM with PINEAPPLE juice and COCONUT

**pina·fore** /ˈpɪnəfɔː(r)/ noun **1** (*also* **pinafore dress**) (*both especially BrE*) (*NAmE usually* **jumper**) a loose dress without SLEEVES (= arms), usually worn over a BLOUSE or sweater **2** (*old-fashioned*) (*also informal* **pinny**) (*both BrE*) a long loose piece of clothing without SLEEVES (= arms), worn by women over the front of their clothes to keep them clean, for example when cooking ⊃ compare APRON **3** a loose piece of clothing like a dress without SLEEVES (= arms), worn by children over their clothes to keep them clean, or by young girls over a dress

**pi·ña·ta** (*also* **pi·na·ta**) /ˈpɪnˈjɑːtə/ noun (*especially NAmE*) (*from Spanish*) a brightly decorated figure, filled with toys and sweets, which children try to hit with a stick with

their eyes covered in order to break it open, as a party game

**pin·ball** /ˈpɪnbɔːl/ noun [U] a game played on a **'pinball machine**, in which the player sends a small metal ball up a sloping board and scores points as it BOUNCES off objects. The player tries to prevent the ball from reaching the bottom of the machine by pressing two buttons at the side.

**pin·board** /ˈpɪnbɔːd; *NAmE* -bɔːrd/ noun (*BrE*) a board made of CORK that is fixed to an indoor wall, on which you can display messages, notices, etc.

**pin·cer** /ˈpɪnsə(r)/ noun **1** **pincers** [pl.] a tool made of two crossed pieces of metal, used for holding things and pulling things, for example nails out of wood: *a pair of pincers* **2** [C] one of a pair of curved CLAWS of some types of animal, for example CRABS and LOBSTERS ⊃ VISUAL VOCAB page V3

**'pincer movement** noun [usually sing.] a military attack in which an army attacks the enemy from two sides at the same time

**pinch** /pɪntʃ/ verb, noun

■ verb
- PRESS **1** [T] ~ sb/sth/yourself to take a piece of sb's skin and press it together hard with your THUMB and the finger next to it: *My sister's always pinching me and it really hurts.* ◇ *He pinched the baby's cheek playfully.* ◇ (*figurative*) *She had to pinch herself to make sure she was not dreaming.* **2** [T] ~ sth (+ adv./prep.) to hold sth tightly between the THUMB and finger or between two things that are pressed together: *Pinch the nostrils together between your thumb and finger to stop the bleeding.* ◇ *a pinched nerve in the neck* **3** [I, T] to place the THUMB and a finger of one hand on the screen of an electronic device such as a mobile phone or small computer and move them together or apart, to make the image on the screen appear smaller or larger ⊃ see also FLICK, SPREAD, TAP
- OF A SHOE **4** [I, T] ~ (sb/sth) if sth such as a shoe **pinches** part of your body, it hurts you because it is too tight: *These new shoes pinch.*
- STEAL **5** [T] ~ sth (from sb/sth) (*BrE, informal*) to steal sth, especially sth small and not very valuable **SYN** nick: *Who's pinched my pen?*
- COST TOO MUCH **6** [T] ~ sb/sth to cost a person or an organization a lot of money or more than they can spend: *Higher interest rates are already pinching the housing industry.*
- ARREST **7** [T] ~ sb (*BrE, old-fashioned, informal*) to arrest sb: *I was pinched for dangerous driving.*

**IDM** **pinch 'pennies** (*informal*) to try to spend as little money as possible

**PHRV** **pinch 'in/'out** to place the THUMB and a finger of one hand on the screen of a device such as a mobile phone or small computer and move them together or apart, to make the image or text on the screen appear smaller or larger: *Pinch in on the home page.* ◇ *You can pinch out to zoom in on the map.* **pinch sth↔'off/'out** to remove sth by pressing your THUMB and fingers together and pulling

■ noun
- ACT OF PRESSING **1** an act of pressing a part of sb's skin together hard with your THUMB and finger, especially in order to hurt them: *She gave him a pinch on the arm to wake him up.*
- SMALL AMOUNT **2** the amount of sth that you can hold between your finger and THUMB: *a pinch of salt*

**IDM** **at a 'pinch** (*BrE*) (*NAmE* **in a 'pinch**) used to say that sth could be done or used in a particular situation if it is really necessary: *We can get six people round this table at a pinch.* ⊃ more at FEEL v., SALT n.

**pinched** /pɪntʃt/ adj. (of a person's face) pale and thin, especially because of illness, cold or worry

**'pinch-hit** verb **1** [I] (in baseball) to hit the ball for another player **2** [I] ~ (for sb) (*NAmE, informal*) to do sth for sb else who is suddenly unable to do it

**'pinch run** verb [I] (in baseball) to take the place of a player who is on a BASE: *Gordon pinch ran for Gomez.*

**pin·cush·ion** /ˈpɪnkʊʃn/ noun a small thick PAD made of cloth, used for sticking pins in when they are not being used

**pine** /paɪn/ noun, verb
- **noun 1** [C, U] (also **pine tree** [C]) an EVERGREEN forest tree with leaves like needles: *pine forests* ◇ *pine needles* ◇ *a Scots pine* **2** (also **pine-wood**) [U] the pale soft wood of the pine tree, used in making furniture, etc: *a pine table*
- **verb** [I] to become very sad because sb has died or gone away: *She pined for months after he'd gone.*
- **PHR V** **pine a'way** to become very sick and weak because you miss sb/sth very much: *After his wife died, he just pined away.* **'pine for sb/sth** to want or miss sb/sth very much: *She was pining for the mountains of her native country.*

**pin-eal** /ˈpaɪniəl/ (also **pi'neal gland**) noun (anatomy) a small organ in the brain that releases a HORMONE

**pine-apple** /ˈpaɪnæpl/ noun [C, U] a large tropical fruit with thick rough skin and stiff leaves on top, that is sweet and yellow inside with a lot of juice: *fresh pineapple* ◇ *a tin of pineapple chunks* ◇ *pineapple juice* ⇒ VISUAL VOCAB page V4 **IDM** see ROUGH adj.

**pine cone** noun the hard dry fruit of the PINE tree

**pine marten** noun a small wild animal with a long body, short legs and sharp teeth. Pine martens live in forests and eat smaller animals.

**pine nut** (BrE also **pine kernel**) noun the white seed of some PINE trees, used in cooking

**pine-wood** /ˈpaɪnwʊd/ noun [U] = PINE (2)

**ping** /pɪŋ/ noun, verb
- **noun** a short high sound made when a hard object hits sth that is made of metal or glass
- **verb 1** [I, T] ~ (sth) to make a short, high ringing sound; to make sth produce this sound: *The microwave pinged.* **2** (NAmE) (BrE **pink**) [I] (of a car engine) to make knocking sounds because the fuel is not burning correctly **3** [T] ~ sth to test whether an internet connection is working by sending a signal to a computer and waiting for a reply **4** [T] ~ sth (to sb) | ~ sb (informal) to send an email or a text message to sb: *I'll ping it to you later.*

**ping-er** /ˈpɪŋə(r)/ noun a device that makes a series of short high sounds, for example on a cooker to tell you that the cooking time has ended

**ping-pong** (BrE, informal) (NAmE **Ping-Pong™**) (also **table tennis**) noun [U] a game played like tennis with BATS and a small plastic ball on a table with a net across it

**pin-head** /ˈpɪnhed/ noun the very small flat surface at one end of a pin

**pin-hole** /ˈpɪnhəʊl/ noun a very small hole, especially one made by a pin

**pin-ion** /ˈpɪnjən/ verb ~ sb/sth + adv./prep. to hold or tie sb, especially by their arms, so that they cannot move: *His arms were pinioned to his sides.* ◇ *They were pinioned against the wall.*

**pink** 🔸 **A1** /pɪŋk/ adj., noun, verb
- **adj. 1** 🔸 **A1** pale red in colour: *pale pink roses* ◇ *She went bright pink with embarrassment.* ⇒ see also SALMON PINK, SHOCKING PINK **2** [only before noun] (BrE) connected with GAY people: *the pink pound* (= money spent by GAYS and LESBIANS as an influence in the economy) **3** (informal, disapproving, politics) having or showing slightly LEFT-WING political views ⇒ compare RED ▶ **pink·ness** noun [U] **IDM** see TICKLE v.
- **noun 1** 🔸 **A1** the colour that is produced when you mix red and white together: *She was dressed in pink.* ◇ *The bedroom was decorated in pale pinks.* **2** [C] a garden plant with pink, red or white flowers that have a sweet smell
- **verb** (BrE) (NAmE **ping**) [I] (of a car engine) to make knocking sounds because the fuel is not burning correctly

**pink 'gin** noun **1** [U, C] an alcoholic drink made from GIN mixed with ANGOSTURA that gives it a bitter taste **2** [C] a glass of pink gin

**pink-ish** /ˈpɪŋkɪʃ/ adj. fairly pink in colour

**pinko** /ˈpɪŋkəʊ/ noun (pl. **-os** or **-oes**) **1** (NAmE, informal, disapproving) a COMMUNIST or a SOCIALIST **2** (BrE, informal) a person who is slightly LEFT-WING in their ideas, but not very ⇒ compare RED ▶ **pinko** adj.

---

# pioneer

**'pink slip** noun (NAmE, informal) a letter given to sb to say that they must leave their job

**pinky** (also **pinkie**) /ˈpɪŋki/ noun (pl. **-ies**) (NAmE, ScotE) the smallest finger of the hand **SYN** **little finger**: *a pinky ring* (= worn on the smallest finger)

**pin-na-cle** /ˈpɪnəkl/ noun **1** [usually sing.] ~ **of sth** the most important or successful part of sth: *the pinnacle of her career* **2** a small pointed stone decoration built on the roof of a building **3** a high pointed piece of rock, especially at the top of a mountain

**pinny** /ˈpɪni/ noun (pl. **-ies**) (BrE, informal) = PINAFORE (2)

**Pinoc-chio** /pɪˈnəʊkiəʊ/ noun a character in a children's story who changes from a wooden figure into a boy. Whenever he tells a lie, his nose grows longer: *Cartoons showed the Minister as a long-nosed Pinocchio.*

**pin-point** /ˈpɪnpɔɪnt/ verb, adj., noun
- **verb 1** ~ sth to find and show the exact position of sb/sth or the exact time that sth happened: *He was able to pinpoint on the map the site of the medieval village.* **2** ~ sth to be able to give the exact reason for sth or to describe sth exactly: *The report pinpointed the areas most in need of help.*
- **adj.** if sth is done with **pinpoint accuracy**, it is done exactly and in exactly the right position: *The pilots bombed strategic targets with pinpoint accuracy.*
- **noun** a very small area of sth, especially light

**pin-prick** /ˈpɪnprɪk/ noun **1** a very small area of sth, especially light: *His eyes narrowed to two small pinpricks.* **2** a very small hole in sth, especially one that has been made by a pin **3** something that annoys you even though it is small and unimportant

**pins and 'needles** noun [U] an uncomfortable feeling in a part of your body, caused when a normal flow of blood returns after it has been partly blocked, especially because you have been sitting or lying in an uncomfortable position: *to have pins and needles* **IDM** **be on 'pins and 'needles** (NAmE) = (BE) ON TENTERHOOKS at TENTERHOOKS

**pin-stripe** /ˈpɪnstraɪp/ noun **1** [C] one of the thin white VERTICAL lines printed on dark cloth that is used especially for making business suits **2** [U, C] dark cloth with white vertical lines printed on it; a suit made from this cloth: *a pinstripe suit* ▶ **pin-striped** adj. [only before noun]: *a pinstriped suit* ◇ *a pinstriped official* (= who is wearing a pinstriped suit)

**pint** /paɪnt/ noun **1** (abbr. **pt**) a unit for measuring liquids and some dry goods, equal to 0.568 of a LITRE in the UK and some other countries, and 0.473 of a LITRE in the US. There are 8 pints in a GALLON: *a pint of beer/milk* ◇ *We'd better get a couple of extra pints* (= of milk) *tomorrow.* ◇ *Add half a pint of cream.* **2** (BrE) a pint of beer (especially in a pub): *Do you want to go for a pint later?* ◇ *a pint/half-pint glass*

**pinto** /ˈpɪntəʊ/ adj. (NAmE) (of a horse) with areas on it of two colours, usually black and white **SYN** **piebald** ▶ **pinto** noun (pl. **-os**)

**'pinto bean** noun a type of curved bean with coloured marks on the skin

**'pint-sized** adj. (informal) (of people) very small

**pin-up** noun **1** a picture of an attractive person, especially one who is not wearing many clothes, that is put on a wall for people to look at **2** a person who appears in a pin-up

**pin-wheel** /ˈpɪnwiːl/ noun (NAmE) **1** (BrE **wind-mill**) a toy with curved plastic parts that form the shape of a flower which turns round on the end of a stick when you blow on it **2** = CATHERINE WHEEL

**Pin-yin** /ˌpɪnˈjɪn/ noun [U] the standard system of ROMAN spelling in Chinese

**pi-on-eer** 🔸+ **C1** /ˌpaɪəˈnɪə(r)/; NAmE -ˈnɪr/ noun, verb
- **noun 1** 🔸+ **C1** ~ (in/of sth) a person who is the first to study and develop a particular area of knowledge, culture, etc. that other people then continue to develop **SYN** **trailblazer**: *a pioneer in the field of microsurgery* ◇ *a computer pioneer* ◇ *a pioneer aviator* ◇ *a pioneer design* (= one that introduces new ideas, methods, etc.) **2** 🔸+ **C1** one of the first people to go to a particular area in order to live and

# pioneering

work there: *Early pioneers settled on both sides of the Maple River.* ◊ *the pioneer spirit* ⊃ **WORDFINDER NOTE** at **EXPLORE**
- *verb* ~ sth when sb **pioneers** sth, they are one of the first people to do, discover or use sth new: *a new technique pioneered by surgeons in a London hospital*

**pi·on·eer·ing** /ˌpaɪəˈnɪərɪŋ; NAmE -ˈnɪr-/ *adj.* [usually before noun] introducing ideas and methods that have never been used before: *pioneering work on infant mortality* ◊ *the pioneering days of radio*

**pious** /ˈpaɪəs/ *adj.* **1** having or showing a deep respect for God and religion **SYN devout**: *pious acts* **OPP impious** ⊃ see also **PIETY 2** (*disapproving*) pretending to be religious, moral or good in order to impress other people **SYN sanctimonious**: *pious sentiments* **3** ~ hope something that you want to happen but is unlikely to be achieved: *Such reforms seem likely to remain little more than pious hopes.* ▶ **pi·ous·ly** *adv.*

**pip** /pɪp/ *noun, verb*
- *noun* **1** (especially *BrE*) (*NAmE* usually **seed**) the small hard seed that is found in some types of fruit: *an apple/orange pip* ⊃ **VISUAL VOCAB** page V4 **2 the pips** [pl.] (*BrE*) a series of short high sounds, especially those used when giving the exact time on the radio **3** (*NAmE*) one of the small round marks showing the value on DICE and DOMINOES; one of the marks showing the value and SUIT of a PLAYING CARD
- *verb* (-pp-) ~ sb (*BrE, informal*) to beat sb in a race, competition, etc. by only a small amount or at the last moment: *She pipped her rival for the gold medal.* ◊ *He was pipped at/to the post for the top award.*

## pipes

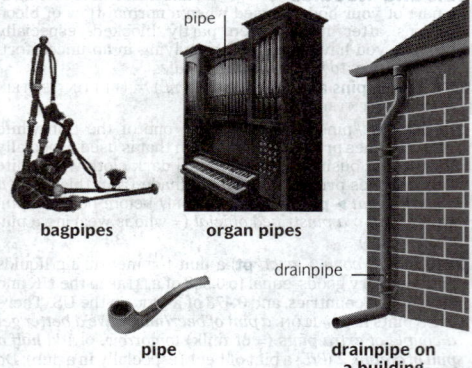

bagpipes · organ pipes · drainpipe · pipe · drainpipe on a building

**pipe** /paɪp/ *noun, verb*
- *noun* **1** [C, U] a tube through which liquids and gases can flow: *water pipes* ◊ *steel/copper pipes* ◊ *a burst pipe* ◊ *a leaking gas pipe* ◊ *PVC pipe is commonly used in building and construction.* ⊃ see also **DRAINPIPE**, **EXHAUST** *noun*, **WINDPIPE 2** [C] a narrow tube with a bowl at one end, used for smoking TOBACCO: *to smoke a pipe* ◊ *He puffed on his pipe.* ◊ *pipe tobacco* ⊃ see also **PEACE PIPE 3** [C] a musical instrument in the shape of a tube, played by blowing ⊃ see also **PAN PIPES 4** [C] any of the tubes from which sound is produced in an organ **5 pipes** [pl.] = **BAGPIPES** ⊃ see also **HALFPIPE**
- *verb* **1** [T] ~ sth (+ *adv./prep.*) to send water, gas, oil, etc. through a pipe from one place to another: *to pipe oil across the desert* ◊ *Water is piped from the reservoir to the city.* **2** [T] ~ sth (+ *adv./prep.*) [usually passive] to send sounds or signals through a wire or cable from one place to another: *The speech was piped over a public address system.* **3** [T, I] ~ (sb) to play music on a pipe or the BAGPIPES, especially to welcome sb who has arrived: *Passengers were piped aboard ship at the start of the cruise.* ◊ *a prize for piping and drumming* **4** [I, T] (+ *speech*) to speak or sing in a high voice or with a high sound: *Outside a robin piped.* **5** [T] ~ sth (on sth) to decorate food, especially a cake, with thin lines of ICING, etc. by forcing it out of a special bag or tube: *The cake had 'Happy Birthday' piped on it.*

**PHRV** ˌpipe ˈdown (*informal*) used especially in orders, to tell sb to stop talking or to be less noisy ˌpipe ˈup (with sth) (*informal*) to begin to speak: *The person next to me piped up with a silly comment.* ◊ + *speech* '*I know the answer,' piped up a voice at the back of the room.*

**ˈpipe band** *noun* a MARCHING BAND consisting of BAGPIPES and drums

**ˈpipe bomb** *noun* a bomb that sb makes themselves and that is contained in a pipe

**ˈpipe cleaner** *noun* a short piece of wire, covered with soft material, used for cleaning inside a TOBACCO pipe

**ˌpiped ˈmusic** *noun* [U] (*BrE*) recorded music that is played continuously in shops, restaurants, etc. **SYN Muzak**™

**ˈpipe dream** *noun* a hope or plan that is impossible to achieve or not practical

**pipe·line** /ˈpaɪplaɪn/ *noun* a series of pipes that are usually underground and are used for carrying oil, gas, etc. over long distances
**IDM** in the ˈpipeline something that is **in the pipeline** is being discussed, planned or prepared and will happen or exist soon

**ˈpipe organ** *noun* = **ORGAN**

**piper** /ˈpaɪpə(r)/ *noun* a person who plays music on a pipe or the BAGPIPES **IDM** see **PAY** *v.*

**pip·ette** /pɪˈpet; *NAmE* paɪ-/ *noun* (*specialist*) a narrow tube used in a laboratory for measuring or transferring small amounts of liquids

**pipe·work** /ˈpaɪpwɜːk; *NAmE* -wɜːrk/ *noun* [U] the pipes used for carrying oil, gas or water around a machine, building, etc.

**pip·ing** /ˈpaɪpɪŋ/ *noun, adj.*
- *noun* [U] **1** a pipe or pipes of the type or length mentioned: *ten metres of lead piping* **2** a long thin folded piece of cloth, often with a length of string inside, used to decorate a piece of clothing, a CUSHION, etc: *a uniform with gold piping* **3** lines of cream or ICING as decoration on a cake **4** the sound of a pipe or pipes being played
- *adj.* (of a person's voice) high

**ˌpiping ˈhot** *adj.* (of liquids or food) very hot

**pipit** /ˈpɪpɪt/ *noun* (often in compounds) a small brown bird with a pleasant song: *a meadow/rock/tree pipit*

**pip·squeak** /ˈpɪpskwiːk/ *noun* (*old-fashioned, informal*) a person that you think is unimportant or does not deserve respect because they are small or young

**pi·quancy** /ˈpiːkənsi/ *noun* [U] the quality of being piquant: *The tart flavour of the cranberries adds piquancy.* ◊ *The situation has an added piquancy since the two men are also rivals in love.*

**pi·quant** /ˈpiːkənt/ *adj.* **1** having a pleasantly strong or spicy taste **2** exciting and interesting

**pique** /piːk/ *noun, verb*
- *noun* [U] (*formal*) annoyed or bitter feelings that you have, usually because you believe that you have not been treated with enough respect: *When he realized nobody was listening to him, he left in a fit of pique.* ⊃ **HOMOPHONES** at **PEEK**
- *verb* ~ sb/sth (*formal*) to make sb annoyed or upset **SYN wound**¹ ⊃ **HOMOPHONES** at **PEEK** ▶ **piqued** *adj.* [not before noun]: *She couldn't help feeling a little piqued by his lack of interest.*
**IDM** ˌpique sb's ˈinterest, curiˈosity, etc. to make sb very interested in sth

**piqué** /ˈpiːkeɪ/ *noun* [U] a type of stiff cloth with a raised pattern

**pir·acy** /ˈpaɪrəsi/ *noun* [U] **1** the crime of attacking ships at sea in order to steal from them **2** the act of making illegal copies of DVDs, computer programs, books, etc. in order to sell them: *software piracy* ⊃ see also **PIRATE**

**pir·anha** /pɪˈrɑːnə/ *noun* a small South American FRESHWATER fish that attacks and eats live animals

**pir·ate** /ˈpaɪrət/ *noun, verb*
- *noun* **1** (especially in the past) a person on a ship who attacks other ships at sea in order to steal from them:

*a pirate ship* **2** **C1** (often used as an adjective) a person who makes illegal copies of books, computer programs, etc., in order to sell them: *a pirate edition* ◊ *software pirates* **3** (often used as an adjective) a person or an organization that broadcasts illegally: *a pirate radio station* ⊃ see also PIRACY ▶ **pir·at·ical** /paɪˈrætɪkl/ *adj*.
■ *verb* ~ **sth** to copy and use or sell sb's work or a product without permission and without having the right to do so: *pirated computer games*

**pir·ou·ette** /ˌpɪruˈet/ *noun* a fast turn in a circle that a person, especially a BALLET dancer, makes on one foot ▶ **pir·ou·ette** *verb* [I]: *She pirouetted across the stage.*

**Pis·ces** /ˈpaɪsiːz/ *noun* **1** [U] the 12th sign of the ZODIAC, the Fishes **2** [sing.] a person born when the sun is in this sign, that is between 20 February and 20 March ▶ **Pis·cean** /-siən/ *noun, adj.*

**piss** /pɪs/ *verb, noun* (*taboo, slang*)
■ *verb* [I] to URINATE **HELP** A more polite way of expressing this is **go to the toilet / loo** (*BrE*), **go to the bathroom** (*NAmE*) or simply **go** (*NAmE*), (*BrE*).
**IDM** ˌpiss yourˈself (ˈlaughing) to laugh very hard
**PHR V** ˌpiss aˈbout/aˈround (*BrE*) to waste time by behaving in a silly way **HELP** A more polite, informal way of saying this is **mess about** (*BrE*) or **mess around** (*BrE* and *NAmE*). ˌpiss sb aˈbout/aˈround (*BrE*) to treat sb in a way that is deliberately not helpful to them or wastes their time **HELP** A more polite, informal way of saying this is **mess sb about/around**. ˌpiss ˈdown (*BrE*) to rain heavily ˌpiss ˈoff (especially *BrE*) (usually used in orders) to go away: *Why don't you just piss off and leave me alone?* ˌpiss sb↔ˈoff to make sb annoyed or bored: *Her attitude really pisses me off.*
■ *noun* (*taboo, slang*) **1** [U] = URINE **2** [sing.] an act of URINATING: *to go for a piss*
**IDM** be on the ˈpiss (*BrE*) to be out at a pub, club, etc. and drinking a large amount of alcohol take the ˈpiss (out of sb/sth) (*BrE*) to make fun of sb, especially by copying them or laughing at them for reasons they do not understand ⊃ more at PIECE *n*.

**pissed** /pɪst/ *adj.* **1** (*BrE, taboo, slang*) drunk **2** (*NAmE, slang*) (also ˌpissed ˈoff *BrE, NAmE*) very angry or annoyed: *I'm pissed off with the way they've treated me.*

**piss-ˈpoor** *adj.* (*taboo, slang*) **1** of a very low standard: *That band really was piss-poor.* **2** not having enough money for basic needs

**ˈpiss-take** *noun* (*BrE, taboo, slang*) a joke that is intended to make sb/sth seem silly

**ˈpiss-up** *noun* (*BrE, taboo, slang*) an occasion when a large amount of alcohol is drunk **HELP** A more polite, informal word for this is **booze-up**.

**pis·ta·chio** /pɪˈstæʃiəʊ, -ˈstɑːʃ-/ *noun* (*pl. -os*) **1** (also piˈstachio nut) [C] the small green nut of an Asian tree ⊃ VISUAL VOCAB page V8 **2** [U] a pale green colour

**piste** /piːst/ *noun* a track of solid snow prepared for skiing on ⊃ see also OFF-PISTE

**pis·til** /ˈpɪstɪl/ *noun* (*biology*) the female organs of a flower, which receive the POLLEN and produce seeds

**pis·tol** /ˈpɪstl/ *noun* a small gun that you can hold and fire with one hand: *an automatic pistol* ◊ *a starting pistol* (= used to signal the start of a race) ⊃ see also AIR PISTOL, WATER PISTOL

**ˈpistol-whip** *verb* ~ **sb** to hit sb with the BUTT of a pistol many times

**pis·ton** /ˈpɪstən/ *noun* a part of an engine that consists of a short CYLINDER that fits inside a tube and moves up and down or backwards and forwards to make other parts of the engine move

**pit** **+** **C1** /pɪt/ *noun, verb*
■ *noun*
• DEEP HOLE **1** **+** **C1** [C] a large deep hole in the ground: *We dug a deep pit in the yard.* ◊ *The body had been dumped in a pit.* ⊃ see also SNAKE PIT **2** [C] (especially in compounds) a deep hole in the ground from which minerals are dug out: *a chalk/gravel pit*
• MINE **3** [C] = COAL MINE: *pit closures* ◊ (*BrE*) *He went down the pit* (= started work as a MINER) *when he left school.* ⊃ see also OPEN-PIT
• IN SKIN **4** [C] a small shallow hole in the surface of sth, especially a mark left on the surface of the skin by some disease, such as CHICKENPOX ⊃ see also PITTED
• IN FRUIT **5** [C] (especially *NAmE*) = STONE (5): *a peach pit* ⊃ VISUAL VOCAB page V4
• IN MOTOR RACING **6 the pits** [pl.] (*BrE*) (*NAmE* usually **the pit** [C]) a place near the track where cars can stop for fuel, new tyres, etc. during a race ⊃ see also PIT STOP
• IN THEATRE **7** [C] = ORCHESTRA PIT ⊃ see also MOSH PIT
• PART OF BODY **8** [C] (*NAmE, informal*) = ARMPIT
• IN BUSINESS **9** [C] (*NAmE*) the area of a STOCK EXCHANGE where a particular product is traded: *the corn pit* ⊃ compare FLOOR ⊃ see also SANDPIT
**IDM** be the ˈpits (*informal*) to be very bad or the worst example of sth the pit of your/the ˈstomach the bottom of the stomach where people say they feel strong feelings, especially fear: *He had a sudden sinking feeling in the pit of his stomach.* ⊃ more at BOTTOMLESS

■ *verb* (**-tt-**)
• MAKE HOLES **1** to make marks or holes on the surface of sth: ~ **sth** *Smallpox scars had pitted his face.* ◊ **be pitted with sth** *The surface of the moon is pitted with craters.*
• FRUIT **2** (*BrE also* **stone**) ~ **sth** to remove the stone from the inside of a fruit: *pitted olives*
**PHR V** ˈpit sb/sth against sth to test sb or their strength, intelligence, etc. in a struggle or contest against sb/sth else: *Lawyers and accountants felt that they were being pitted against each other.* ◊ *a chance to pit your wits against the world champions* (= in a test of your intelligence)

**pita**, **ˈpita bread** *noun* [U] (*NAmE*) = PITTA

**pit-a-pat** /ˌpɪt ə ˈpæt/ (*also* ˈpitter-patter) *adv.* with quick light steps or beats: *Her heart went pit-a-pat.* ▶ **pit-a-ˈpat** (*also* ˈpitter-patter) *noun* [sing.]: *I could hear the pit-a-pat of feet in the corridor.*

**ˈpit bull ˈterrier** (*also* ˈpit bull) *noun* a small, strong, aggressive dog, sometimes used in dog fights where people bet on which dog will win

**pitch** **ⓘ** **B2** /pɪtʃ/ *noun, verb*
■ *noun*
• FOR SPORT **1** **?** **B2** (*BrE*) (*also* **field** *NAmE, BrE*) [C] an area of ground specially prepared and marked for playing a sports game: *a football pitch* ◊ *a cricket/rugby/hockey pitch*
• OF SOUND **2** [sing., U] how high or low a sound is, especially a musical note: *A basic sense of rhythm and pitch is essential in a music teacher.* ⊃ see also PERFECT PITCH
• DEGREE/STRENGTH **3** [sing., U] the degree or strength of a feeling or activity; the highest point of sth: *a frenetic pitch of activity* ◊ *Speculation has reached such a pitch that a decision will have to be made immediately.* ⊃ see also FEVER PITCH
• TO SELL STH **4** [C, usually sing.] talk or arguments used by a person trying to sell things or persuade people to do sth: *an aggressive sales pitch* ◊ *the candidate's campaign pitch* ◊ *Each company was given ten minutes to make its pitch.*
• IN BASEBALL **5** [C] an act of throwing the ball; the way in which it is thrown ⊃ SYNONYMS at THROW
• BLACK SUBSTANCE **6** [U] a black sticky substance made from oil or coal, used on roofs or the wooden boards of a ship to stop water from coming through
• IN STREET/MARKET **7** [C] (*BrE*) a place in a street or market where sb sells things, or where sb performs in order to entertain people outdoors
• CAMPING **8** (*BrE*) (*NAmE* **camp·site**) a place in a CAMPSITE where you can put up one tent or park one CARAVAN, etc: *Pitches to rent from only £15 per night.*
• OF SHIP/AIRCRAFT **9** [U] (*specialist*) the movement of a ship up and down in the water or of an aircraft in the air ⊃ compare ROLL
• OF ROOF **10** [sing., U] (*specialist*) the degree to which a roof slopes

piston

Oxford Phrasal Academic Lexicon (OPAL) written and spoken word lists | OPAL written word list | OPAL spoken word list

# pitch and putt

**IDM** **make a ˈpitch for sb/sth** | **make a ˈpitch to sb** to make a determined effort to get sth or to persuade sb of sth ⊃ more at QUEER v.

■ verb

- **THROW** **1** [T] ~ **sb/sth + adv./prep.** to throw sb/sth with force: *The explosion pitched her violently into the air.* ◊ (figurative) *The new government has already been pitched into a crisis.*
- **IN SPORTS** **2** [I, T] ~**(sth)** (in baseball) to throw the ball to the person who is BATTING **3** [I, T] ~**(sth) + adv./prep.** (of the ball in the games of golf and CRICKET) to hit the ground; to make the ball hit the ground: *The ball pitched a yard short of the hole.* **4** [T, I] ~**(sth)** (in golf) to hit the ball in a high curve
- **FALL** **5** [I] + **adv./prep.** to fall heavily in a particular direction: *With a cry she pitched forward.*
- **OF SHIP/AIRCRAFT** **6** [I] to move up and down on the water or in the air: *The sea was rough and the ship pitched and rolled all night.* ⊃ compare ROLL (12)
- **SET LEVEL** **7** [T] to set sth at a particular level: ~**sth** (+ **adv./prep./adj.**) *They have pitched their prices too high.* ◊ ~**sth (at sth)** *The test was pitched at too low a level for the students.*
- **TRY TO SELL** **8** [T] to aim or direct a product or service at a particular group of people: ~**sth (at sb)** *The new software is being pitched at banks.* ◊ ~**sth (as sth)** *Orange juice is to be pitched as an athlete's drink.* **9** [T, I] to try to persuade sb to buy sth, to give you sth or to make a business deal with you: ~**sth** *Representatives went to Japan to pitch the company's newest products.* ◊ ~**(for sth)** *We were pitching against a much larger company for the contract.*
- **SOUND/MUSIC** **10** [T] ~**sth + adj.** to produce a sound or piece of music at a particular level: *You pitched that note a little flat.* ◊ *The song was pitched too low for my voice.* ⊃ see also HIGH-PITCHED, LOW-PITCHED
- **TENT** **11** [T] ~**sth** to set up a tent or a camp for a short time: *We could pitch our tent in that field.* ◊ *They pitched camp for the night near the river.* ⊃ see also PITCHED

**IDM** **pitch a ˈstory/ˈline/ˈyarn (to sb)** (*informal*) to tell sb a story or make an excuse that is not true

**PHRV** **ˌpitch ˈin (with sb/sth)** (*informal*) to join in and help with an activity, by doing some of the work or by giving money, advice, etc.: *Everyone pitched in with the work.* ◊ *Local companies pitched in with building materials and labour.* **ˌpitch sth↔ˈin** to give a particular amount of money in order to help with sth: *We all pitched in $10 to buy her a gift.* **ˌpitch ˈinto sb** (*informal*) to attack or criticize sb: *She started pitching into me as soon as I arrived.* **ˌpitch ˈinto sth** (*informal*) to start an activity with enthusiasm: ~**doing sth** *I rolled up my sleeves and pitched into cleaning the kitchen.* **ˌpitch ˈup** (*BrE, informal*) to arrive somewhere, especially late or without planning **SYN** turn up: *You can't just pitch up and expect to get in without a ticket.*

**ˌpitch and ˈputt** noun [U] golf played on a very small course

**ˌpitch-ˈblack** adj. completely black or dark

**ˌpitch-ˈdark** adj. completely dark

**pitched** /pɪtʃt/ adj. (of a roof) sloping; not flat

**ˌpitched ˈbattle** noun **1** a fight that involves a large number of people: *The demonstration escalated into a pitched battle with the police.* **2** a military battle fought with soldiers arranged in prepared positions

**pitch·er** /ˈpɪtʃə(r)/ noun **1** (*NAmE*) (*BrE* **jug**) a container with a handle and a LIP, for holding and pouring liquids: *a pitcher of water* ⊃ picture at JUG **2** (*BrE*) a large CLAY container with a small opening and one or two handles, used especially in the past, for holding liquids ⊃ picture at JUG **3** (in baseball) the player who throws the ball to the BATTER

**pitch·fork** /ˈpɪtʃfɔːk; *NAmE* -fɔːrk/ noun a farm tool in the shape of a large fork with a long handle and two or three sharp metal points, used especially for lifting and moving HAY (= dried grass), etc.

**ˈpitch invasion** noun (*BrE*) an occasion when a crowd of people who are watching a sports game run onto the field, for example to celebrate sth or protest about sth

**pitch-out** /ˈpɪtʃaʊt/ noun **1** (in baseball) a ball deliberately thrown so that it is too far out to hit so that the CATCHER can throw it to get a player out who is running between BASES **2** (in AMERICAN FOOTBALL) a ball thrown to the side

**pit·eous** /ˈpɪtiəs/ adj. [usually before noun] (*literary*) deserving PITY or causing you to feel PITY **SYN** pathetic: *a piteous cry/sight* ▶ **pit·eous·ly** adv.

**pit·fall** /ˈpɪtfɔːl/ noun a danger or difficulty, especially one that is hidden or not obvious at first: *the potential pitfalls of buying a house*

**pith** /pɪθ/ noun [U] **1** a soft dry white substance inside the skin of oranges and some other fruits ⊃ VISUAL VOCAB page V4 **2** the essential or most important part of sth: *the pith of her argument*

**ˈpith helmet** noun a light hard hat worn to give protection from the sun in very hot countries

**pithy** /ˈpɪθi/ adj. (*approving*) (**pith·i·er**, **pithi·est**) (of a comment, piece of writing, etc.) short but expressed well and full of meaning ▶ **pith·ily** /-θɪli/ adv.: *pithily expressed*

**piti·able** /ˈpɪtiəbl/ adj. (*formal*) **1** deserving PITY or causing you to feel PITY: *The refugees were in a pitiable state.* **2** not deserving respect: *a pitiable lack of talent* ▶ **piti·ably** /-bli/ adv.

**piti·ful** /ˈpɪtɪfl/ adj. **1** deserving PITY or causing you to feel PITY **SYN** pathetic: *The horse was a pitiful sight* (= because it was very thin or sick). **2** not deserving respect **SYN** poor: *a pitiful effort/excuse/performance* ▶ **piti·fully** /-fəli/ adv.: *The dog was whining pitifully.* ◊ *She was pitifully thin.* ◊ *The fee is pitifully low.*

**piti·less** /ˈpɪtiləs/ adj. **1** showing no PITY; cruel **SYN** callous: *a pitiless killer/tyrant* **2** very cruel or severe, and never ending **SYN** relentless: *a scorching, pitiless sun* ▶ **piti·less·ly** adv.

**piton** /ˈpiːtɒn; *NAmE* -tɑːn/ noun a short pointed piece of metal used in rock-climbing. The piton is fixed into the rock and has a rope attached to it through a ring at the other end.

**ˈpit stop** noun **1** (in motor racing) an occasion when a car stops during a race for more fuel, etc. **2** (*NAmE, informal*) a short stop during a long trip for a rest, a meal, etc.

**pitta** (*BrE*) (*NAmE* **pita**) /ˈpiːtə; *BrE also* ˈpɪtə/ (*also* **ˈpitta bread**, **ˈpita bread**) noun [U, C] a type of flat bread in the shape of an OVAL that can be split open and filled

**pit·tance** /ˈpɪtns/ noun [usually sing.] a very small amount of money that sb receives, for example as a wage, and that is hardly enough to live on: *to pay sb a pittance* ◊ *to work for a pittance*

**pit·ted** /ˈpɪtɪd/ adj. **1** having small marks or holes in the surface **2** (of fruit) having had the large hard seed (= the PIT) removed: *pitted olives*

**pitter-patter** /ˈpɪtə pætə(r); *NAmE* ˈpɪtər/ adv., noun = PIT-A-PAT

**pi·tu·it·ary** /pɪˈtjuːɪtəri; *NAmE* -ˈtuːəteri/ (*also* **piˈtuitary gland**) noun a small organ at the base of the brain that produces HORMONES that influence growth and sexual development

**pity** /ˈpɪti/ noun, verb

■ noun **1** [sing.] used to show that you are disappointed about sth **SYN** shame: *a ~ (that …) It's a pity that you can't stay longer.* ◊ *'I've lost it!' 'Oh, what a pity.'* ◊ *What a pity that she didn't tell me earlier.* ◊ *This dress is really nice. Pity it's so expensive.* ◊ *Oh, that's a pity.* ◊ *It would be a great pity if you gave up now.* ◊ *a ~ to do sth It seems a pity to waste this food.* **2** [U] a sad feeling caused by the pain and troubles of others: *I took pity on her and lent her the money.* ◊ (*formal*) *I beg you to have pity on him.* ◊ *I don't want your pity.* ◊ *a look/feeling/surge of pity* ◊ ~ **for sb/sth** *I could only feel pity for what they were enduring.*

**IDM** **more's the ˈpity** (*informal*) unfortunately: *'Was the bicycle insured?' 'No, more's the pity!'*

■ verb (**pit·ies**, **pit·ied**, **pit·ied**) (not used in the progressive tenses) to feel sorry for sb because of their situation; to feel pity for sb: ~**sb** *He pitied people who were stuck in*

**WORD FAMILY**
pity noun, verb
pitiful adj.
pitiless adj.
pitiable adj.
piteous adj.

*dead-end jobs.* ◊ *Compulsive gamblers are more* **to be pitied** *than condemned.* ◊ **~ sb doing sth** *I pity her having to work such long hours.*

**pi·ty·ing** /ˈpɪtiɪŋ/ *adj.* [usually before noun] showing PITY for sb, often in a way that shows that you think you are better than them: *a pitying look/smile* ▸ **pity·ing·ly** *adv.*

**pivot** /ˈpɪvət/ *noun, verb*
■ *noun* **1** the central point, pin or column on which sth turns or balances **2** the central or most important person or thing: *West Africa was the pivot of the cocoa trade.* ◊ *The pivot on which the old system turned had disappeared.*
■ *verb* [I, T] **~ (sth) (+ adv./prep.)** to turn or balance on a central point (= a pivot); to make sth do this: *Windows that pivot from a central point are easy to clean.* ◊ *She pivoted around and walked out.*
**PHRV** ˈpivot aˈround/ˈon sth (of an argument, a theory, etc.) to depend completely on sth **SYN** hinge on

**piv·otal** /ˈpɪvətl/ *adj.* of great importance because other things depend on it: *a pivotal role in European affairs*

**pix** /pɪks/ *noun* [pl.] *(informal)* photographs or pictures: *They showed us their wedding pix.*

**pixel** /ˈpɪksl/ *noun (computing)* any of the small individual areas on a computer screen, which together form the whole image

**pix·el·ate** *(also* **pix·el·late***)* /ˈpɪksəleɪt/ *verb* **1 ~ sth** to divide an image into PIXELS **2 ~ sth** to show an unclear image on television, consisting of a small number of large PIXELS, especially in order to hide sb's identity

**pixie** /ˈpɪksi/ *noun* (in stories) a creature like a small person with pointed ears, who has magic powers

**pizza** /ˈpiːtsə/ *noun* [C, U] an Italian dish consisting of a flat round bread base with cheese, tomatoes, vegetables, meat, etc. on top: *a ham and mushroom pizza* ◊ *Is there any pizza left?*

**pizz·azz** /pɪˈzæz/ *noun* [U] *(informal)* a lively and exciting quality or style **SYN** flair: *We need someone with youth, glamour and pizzazz.*

**piz·zeria** /ˌpiːtsəˈriːə/ *(NAmE also* **ˈpizza parlor***) noun* a restaurant that serves mainly pizzas

**pizzi·cato** /ˌpɪtsɪˈkɑːtəʊ/ *adj., adv. (from Italian, music)* played using the fingers instead of a BOW to pull at the strings of a musical instrument such as a VIOLIN

**Pl.** *abbr.* (used in written addresses) PLACE: *Grosvenor Pl.*

**pl.** *abbr.* (in writing) plural

**plac·ard** /ˈplækɑːd; *NAmE* -kɑːrd/ *noun* a large written or printed notice that is put in a public place or carried on a stick in a MARCH (= a formal walk to protest about sth): *They were carrying placards and banners demanding that he resign.* ⊃ WORDFINDER NOTE at PROTEST

**pla·cate** /pləˈkeɪt; *NAmE* ˈpleɪkeɪt/ *verb* **~ sb** to make sb feel less angry about sth **SYN** pacify: *a placating smile* ◊ *The concessions did little to placate the students.*

**pla·ca·tory** /pləˈkeɪtəri; *NAmE* ˈpleɪkətɔːri/ *adj. (formal)* designed to make sb feel less angry by showing that you are willing to satisfy or please them: *a placatory remark/smile/gesture*

## place 🔵 A1 /pleɪs/ *noun, verb*
■ *noun*
- **POSITION/POINT/AREA 1** 🔑 **A1** [C] a particular position, point or area: *in a ~ Keep your purse in a safe place.* ◊ *~ where… Is this the place where it happened?* ◊ *~ for sth This would be a good place for a picnic.* ◊ **to do sth** *If you're looking for a new service provider, this list is a good place to start.* ⊃ see also NO PLACE
- **CITY/TOWN/BUILDING 2** 🔑 **A1** [C] a particular city, town, building, etc: *I can't remember all the places we visited in Thailand.* ◊ *The police searched the place.* ◊ *Let's get out of this place!* ◊ **to do sth** *We were looking for a place to eat.* ◊ *a place to live/stay* **3** 🔑 **A1** [C] (especially in compounds or phrases) a building or an area of land used for a particular purpose: *The town has many excellent eating places.* ◊ **~ of sth** *(formal)* *churches and other places of worship* ◊ *(formal) He can usually be contacted at his place of work.* ⊃ see also DWELLING PLACE, HIDING PLACE, MEETING PLACE ⊃ see also RESTING PLACE

1171 **place**

- **AREA ON SURFACE 4** 🔑 **A1** [C] a particular area on a surface, especially on a person's body: **in … places** *He broke his arm in three places.* ◊ **in places** *The paint was peeling off the wall in places.*
- **IN BOOK/SPEECH, ETC. 5** 🔑 **B1** [C] a point in a book, speech, piece of music, etc., especially one that sb has reached at a particular time: *She had marked her place with a bookmark.* ◊ *Excuse me, I seem to have **lost my place**.* ◊ **in … places** *The audience laughed in all the right places.*
- **CORRECT POSITION 6** 🔑 **B1** [C] the natural or correct position for sth: **~ (in/on sth) (to do sth)** *Is there a place on the form to put your address?* ◊ **in sth's ~** *Put it back in its place when you've finished with it.*
- **SEAT 7** 🔑 **B1** [C] a position, seat, etc., especially one that is available for or being used by a person or vehicle: *Come and sit here—I've **saved you a place**.* ◊ *I don't want to **lose my place** in the line.* ◊ *Would you like to **change places** with me so you can see better?* ◊ *I've **set a place** for you at the table.*
- **AT UNIVERSITY/SCHOOL 8** 🔑 **B1** [C] an opportunity to take part in sth, especially to study at a school or university or on a course: *She's been offered a place at Bath to study Business.* ◊ *There are very few places left on the course.*
- **IN SPORTS TEAM 9** 🔑 **B1** [C] the position of being a member of a sports team: *She has **won a place** in the Olympic team.* ◊ *He **lost his place** in the first team.*
- **IN RACE/COMPETITION 10** 🔑 **B1** [C, usually sing.] a position among the winners of a race or competition; a position in the next stage of a competition: **in … ~** *He finished in third place.* ◊ **~ in sth** *Victory earned them a place in the final.*
- **ROLE/IMPORTANCE 11** 🔑 **B1** [sing.] the role or importance of sb/sth in a particular situation, usually in relation to others: **~ in sth** *He is assured of his **place in history**.* ◊ *It took her a while to **find her place** in the world.* ◊ *Anecdotes have no **place in** (= are not acceptable in) an academic essay.* ◊ *Accurate reporting **takes second place to** lurid detail.* ◊ *My father believed that people should **know their place** (= behave according to their social position).* ◊ *It's **not your place** (= your role) to give advice.*
- **HOME 12** 🔑 **B1** [sing.] *(informal)* a house or flat; a person's home: *What about dinner at **my place**?* ◊ *I'm fed up with living with my parents, so I'm looking for a **place of my own**.*
- **SAFE AREA 13** [C] (usually with a negative) a suitable or safe area for sb to be: *These streets are **no place for** a child to be out alone at night.*
- **MATHEMATICS 14** [C] the position of a figure after a DECIMAL POINT ⊃ see also DECIMAL PLACE
- **STREET/SQUARE 15 Place** [sing.] *(abbr.* **Pl.***)* used as part of a name for a short street or square: *66 Portland Place*

**IDM** all ˌover the ˈplace *(BrE also* all ˌover the ˈshop*) (US also* all ˌover the ˈlot*) (informal)* **1** everywhere: *New restaurants are appearing all over the place.* **2** not neat or tidy; not well organized: *Your calculations are all over the place* (= completely wrong). be ˈgoing places *(informal)* to be getting more and more successful in your life or career: *a young architect who's really going places* be in a ˌgood, ˌbad, ˌdark, etc. ˈplace *(also less frequent* be in a ˌgood, ˌbad, ˌdark, etc. ˈspace*)* to be feeling happy, sad, worried, etc. about sth; to be in a good, bad, unhappy, etc. state: *I'm happy now. I'm in a good place.* ˌchange/ˌswap ˈplaces (with sb) (usually used in negative sentences) to be in sb else's situation: *I'm perfectly happy—I wouldn't change places with anyone.* fall/slot into ˈplace if sth complicated or difficult to understand **falls** or **slots into place**, it becomes organized or clear in your mind ˌgive ˈplace to sb/sth *(formal)* to be replaced by sb/sth **SYN** give way to: *Houses and factories gave place to open fields as the train gathered speed.* have/hold a ˌplace in sb's ˈheart to be very dear to sb: *He'll always have a place in my heart.* if I ˌwas/were in ˈyour place used to introduce a piece of advice you are giving to sb: *If I were in your place, I'd resign immediately.* in the ˈfirst place 🔑 **B2** used at the end of a sentence to talk about why sth was done or whether it should have been done or not: *I still don't understand why you chose that name in the first place.* ◊ *I should never have taken that job in the first place.* in the ˈfirst, ˈsecond, etc. ˈplace used at the beginning of a sentence to introduce the different points you are making in an argument: *Well, in the first place he has all the right*

# placebo

qualifications. **in 'my, 'your, etc. place** in my, your, etc. situation: *I wouldn't like to be in your place.* **in 'place 1** [B2] (*also* **into 'place**) in the correct position; ready for sth: *Carefully lay each slab in place.* ◊ *The receiver had already clicked into place.* **2** [B2] working or ready to work: *All the arrangements are now in place for their visit.* **3** (*NAmE*) = ON THE SPOT at SPOT *n.* (3) **in (the) place of sb/sth | in sb's/sth's 'place** instead of sb/sth: *You can use milk in place of cream in this recipe.* ◊ *He was unable to come to the ceremony, but he sent his son to accept the award in his place.* **out of 'place 1** not in the correct place: *Some of these files seem to be out of place.* **2** not suitable for a particular situation: *Her remarks were out of place.* ◊ *I felt completely out of place among all these successful people.* **a place in the 'sun** a position in which you are comfortable or have an advantage over other people **put yourself in sb else's/sb's 'place** to imagine that you are in sb else's situation: *Of course I was upset—just put yourself in my place.* **put sb in their 'place** to make sb feel stupid or embarrassed for showing too much confidence: *At first she tried to take charge of the meeting but I soon put her in her place.* **take 'place** [A2] to happen, especially after previously being arranged or planned: *The film festival takes place in Octob* ◊ *We may never discover what took place that night.* **take sb's/sth's 'place | take the place of sb/sth** to replace sb/sth: *She couldn't attend the meeting so her assistant took her place.* ◊ *Computers have taken the place of typewriters in most offices.* **take your 'place 1** to go to the physical position that is necessary for an activity: *Take your places for dinner.* **2** to take or accept the status in society that is correct or that you deserve ⊃ more at HAIR, HEART *n.*, HIGH *adj.*, LIGHTNING *n.*, OWN *v.*, PRIDE *n.*, RIGHT *adj.*, ROCK *n.*

■ *verb*
- IN POSITION **1** [B1] [T] ~ sth + *adv./prep.* to put sth in a particular place, especially when you do it carefully or deliberately: *He placed his hand on her shoulder.* ◊ *A bomb had been placed under the seat.* ◊ *The parking areas in the town are few, but strategically placed.*
- ATTITUDE **2** [B2] [T] ~ sth on sth/sb/doing sth used to express the attitude sb has towards sth/sb: *They place a high value on punctuality.* ◊ *Great importance is placed on education.* ◊ *We have always placed emphasis on delivering customer satisfaction.*
- BET/ORDER/ADVERTISEMENT **3** [B2] [T] ~ sth to give instructions about sth or make a request for sth to happen: *to place an order/a bet* ◊ *We placed an advertisement for a cleaner in the local paper.*
- IN SITUATION **4** [T] ~ sb/yourself + *adv./prep.* (more formal than *put*) to put sb/yourself in a particular situation: *to place sb in command* ◊ *She was placed in the care of an uncle.* ◊ *His resignation placed us in a difficult position.* ◊ *The job places great demands on me.*
- FIND HOME/JOB **5** [T] to find a suitable job, home, etc. for sb: *~ sb (in sth) The agency placed about 2000 secretaries last year.* ◊ *~ sb with sb/sth The children were placed with foster parents.*
- GIVE RANK **6** [T] ~ sb/sth + *adv./prep.* to decide that sb/sth has a particular position or rank compared with other people or things: *I would place her among the top five tennis players in the world.* ◊ *Nursing attracts people who place relationships high on their list of priorities.*
- IN RACE **7** [T, I] used to describe a person, a team, a horse, etc. finishing in a particular position in a race: *~ sb/sth + adj. He was placed fifth in last Saturday's race.* **~ (sth)** (*BrE*): *My horse has been placed several times* (= it was among the first three or four to finish the race). ◊ (*NAmE*) *His horse placed in the last race* (= it was among the first three to finish the race, usually in second place).
- RECOGNIZE **8** [T] ~ sb/sth (usually used in negative sentences) to recognize sb/sth and be able to identify them/it: *I've seen her before but I just can't place her.* ◊ *His accent was impossible to place.*

[IDM] **be well, ideally, uniquely, better, etc. placed for sth/to do sth 1** to be in a good, very good, etc. position or have a good, etc. opportunity to do sth: *Engineering graduates are well placed for a wide range of jobs.* ◊ *The company is ideally placed to take advantage of the new legislation.* **2** to be located in a pleasant or convenient place: *The hotel is well placed for restaurants, bars and clubs.* ⊃ more at PEDESTAL, PREMIUM *n.*, RECORD *n.*

▼ SYNONYMS

**place**

site • area • position • point • location • scene • spot • venue

These are all words for a particular area or part of an area, especially one used for a particular purpose or where sb/sth is situated or happens.

**place** a particular point, area, city, town, building, etc., especially one used for a particular purpose or where a particular thing happens: *This would be a good place for a picnic.*

**site** the place where sth, especially a building, is or will be located; a place where sth happened or that is used for a particular purpose: *They've chosen a site for the new school.*

**area** a part of a room, building or particular space that is used for a special purpose; a particular place on an object: *the hotel reception area* ◊ *Move the cursor to a blank area on the screen.*

**position** the place where a person or thing is located; the place where sb/sth is meant to be: *From his position at the top of the hill, he could see the harbour.* [NOTE] The **position** of sb/sth is often temporary: the place where sb/sth is at a particular time.

**point** a particular place within an area, where sth happens or is supposed to happen: *the point at which the river divides*

**location** a place where sth happens or exists, especially a place that is not named or not known: *The company is moving to a new location.*

**scene** a place where sth happens, especially sth unpleasant: *the scene of the accident*

**spot** a particular point or area, especially one that has a particular character or where sth particular happens: *The lake is one of the local beauty spots.*

**venue** the place where people meet for an organized event such as a performance or sports event.

PATTERNS
- **at** a place/site/position/point/location/scene/spot/venue
- **in** a(n) place/area/position/location/venue
- the place/site/point/location/spot/venue **where** …
- the **right** place/site/position/location/spot/venue
- a **central** site/position/location/venue
- the/sb's/sth's **exact/precise** place/site/position/point/location/spot

**pla·cebo** /pləˈsiːbəʊ/ *noun* (*pl.* **-os**) a substance that has no physical effects, given to patients who do not need medicine but think that they do, or used when testing new drugs: *the placebo effect* (= the effect of taking a placebo and feeling better) ⊃ WORDFINDER NOTE at MEDICINE

**'place card** *noun* a small card with a person's name on it, placed on a table to show where they are to sit

**place·hold·er** /ˈpleɪshəʊldə(r)/ *noun* **1** (*specialist*) a symbol or piece of text that temporarily replaces sth that is missing **2** (*linguistics*) an item which is necessary in a sentence, but does not have real meaning, for example the word 'it' in 'It's a shame she left.'

**'place kick** *noun* (in rugby and AMERICAN FOOTBALL) a kick made by putting the ball on the ground first

**place·man** /ˈpleɪsmən/ *noun* (*pl.* **-men** /-mən/) (*BrE, disapproving*) a person who is given an official position as a reward for supporting a politician or government

**'place mat** *noun* a MAT on a table on which a person's plate is put

**place·ment** [+] [B2] /ˈpleɪsmənt/ *noun* **1** [+] [B2] [U] the act of finding sb a suitable job or place to live: *a job placement service* ◊ *a placement with a foster family* **2** [+] [B2] (*also* **'work placement**) [C, U] (*BrE*) a job, often as part of a course of study, where you get some experience of a particular kind of work: *The course includes a placement in Year 3.* ◊ **on ~** *The third year is spent on placement in selected*

| æ cat | ɑː father | e bed | ɜː fur | ə about | ɪ sit | iː see | i happy | ɒ got (*BrE*) | ɔː saw | ʌ cup | ʊ put | uː too |

*companies.* ⊃ compare INTERNSHIP, WORK EXPERIENCE **3** ⊞⊞ [U] the act of placing sth somewhere: *This procedure ensures correct placement of the catheter.* ⊃ see also ADVANCED PLACEMENT™, PRODUCT PLACEMENT

**'placement test** *noun* a test which is designed to find the appropriate level for students in a course or programme of study

**'place name** *noun* a name of a town or other place

**pla·cen·ta** /pləˈsentə/ (*usually* **the placenta**) *noun* (*anatomy*) an organ inside the UTERUS of a pregnant woman or animal to which the baby is attached and that is necessary to feed and protect the baby ⊃ compare AFTERBIRTH

**pla·cen·tal** /pləˈsentl/ *adj.* [usually before noun] **1** (*medical*) of or related to the PLACENTA **2** (*biology*) having a PLACENTA: *placental mammals*

**'place setting** *noun* a set or an arrangement of knives, forks and spoons, and/or plates and dishes for one person

**pla·cid** /ˈplæsɪd/ *adj.* **1** (of a person or an animal) not easily excited or annoyed: *a placid baby/horse* OPP **high-spirited 2** calm and peaceful, with very little movement SYN **tranquil**: *the placid waters of the lake* ▸ **pla·cid·ity** /pləˈsɪdəti/ *noun* [U] **pla·cid·ly** /ˈplæsɪdli/ *adv.*

**pla·cing** /ˈpleɪsɪŋ/ *noun* the position of sb/sth in a race or a competition or in a list arranged in order of success: *He needs a high placing in today's qualifier to reach the final.*

**pla·giar·ism** /ˈpleɪdʒərɪzəm/ *noun* [U, C] (*disapproving*) an act of plagiarizing sth; sth that has been plagiarized: *There were accusations of plagiarism.* ◊ *a text full of plagiarisms* ▸ **pla·giar·ist** /-rɪst/ *noun*

**pla·giar·ize** (*BrE also* **-ise**) /ˈpleɪdʒəraɪz/ *verb* [T, I] ~ (**sth**) (*disapproving*) to copy another person's ideas, words or work and pretend that they are your own: *He was accused of plagiarizing his colleague's results.*

**plague** /pleɪɡ/ *noun, verb*
■ *noun* **1** (*also* **the plague**) [U] = BUBONIC PLAGUE: *an outbreak of plague* **2** [C] any disease that spreads quickly and kills a lot of people SYN **epidemic**: *the plague of AIDS* **3** [C] ~ **of** sth large numbers of an animal or insect that come into an area and cause great damage: *a plague of locusts/rats, etc.* IDM see AVOID
■ *verb* **1** ~ sb/sth (**with** sth) to cause pain or trouble to sb/ sth over a period of time SYN **trouble**: *to be plagued by doubt* ◊ *Financial problems are plaguing the company.* ◊ *The team has been plagued by injury this season.* **2** ~ **sb** (**with** sth) to annoy sb or create problems, especially by asking for sth, demanding attention, etc. SYN **hound**: *Rock stars have to get used to being plagued by autograph hunters.*

**plaice** /pleɪs/ *noun* [C, U] (*pl.* **plaice**) a flat sea fish that is used for food

**plaid** /plæd/ *noun* **1** [U] a type of thick cloth with a pattern of lines and squares of different colours and WIDTHS, especially a TARTAN pattern **2** [C] a long piece of plaid made of wool, worn over the shoulders as part of the Scottish national dress

**Plaid Cymru** /ˌplaɪd ˈkʌmri/ *noun* [U + sing./pl. v.] (*WelshE*) a Welsh political party that wants Wales to be an independent state

**plain** ⓘ ⓑ₂ /pleɪn/ *adj., noun, adv.*
■ *adj.* (**plain·er**, **plain·est**) **1** ⓑ₂ not decorated or complicated; simple: *a plain but elegant dress* ◊ *plain food* ◊ *The interior of the church was plain and simple.* ◊ *plain yogurt* (= without sugar or fruit) ⊃ compare FANCY **2** ⓑ₂ without marks or a pattern on it: *covers in plain or printed cotton* ◊ *Write on plain paper* (= without lines). **3** ⓑ₂ easy to see or understand SYN **clear**: *He made it plain that we should leave.* ◊ *The facts were plain to see.* ◊ *It was a rip-off, plain and simple.* ◊ ~ **to sb** *It is all very plain to me.* ◊ **from sth (that ...)** *What is quite plain from the evidence before me is (that) the figures are false.* ⊃ SYNONYMS at CLEAR **4** not trying to trick anyone; honest and direct: *The plain fact is that nobody really knows.* ◊ *a politician with a reputation for* ***plain speaking*** **5** [only before noun] used to emphasize that sth is very ordinary, not special in any way SYN **everyday**: *You don't need any special skills for this job, just plain common sense.* **6** (especially of a woman) not beautiful or attractive **7** describing a simple STITCH used in KNITTING ▸ **plain·ness** /ˈpleɪnnəs/ *noun* [U]
IDM **be plain 'sailing** (*NAmE* **be clear/smooth 'sailing**) to be simple and free from trouble **in plain 'English** simply and clearly expressed, without using technical language **(as) plain as a 'pikestaff | (as) plain as 'day | (as) plain as the nose on your 'face** very obvious
■ *noun* (*also* **plains** [pl.]) a large area of flat land: *the flat coastal plain of Thassos* ◊ *the Great Plains* ⊃ see also FLOODPLAIN
■ *adv.* (*informal*) used to emphasize how bad, stupid, etc. sth is: *plain stupid/wrong*

▼ HOMOPHONES

**plain • plane** /pleɪn/

- **plain** *adj.*: *She likes plain food, without sauces or cheese.*
- **plain** *noun*: *Wheat is still grown on the Lombardy plain.*
- **plane** *noun*: *They recently flew into London on a private plane.*
- **plane** *verb*: *You may need to plane the surface for a smoother fit.*

▼ SYNONYMS

**plain**

simple • stark • bare • unequivocal

These words all describe statements, often about sth unpleasant, that are very clear, not trying to hide anything, and not using more words than necessary.

**plain** used for talking about a fact that other people may not like to hear; honest and direct in a way that other people may not like: *The plain fact is that nobody really knows.*

**simple** [only before noun] used for talking about a fact that other people may not like to hear; very obvious and not complicated by anything else: *The simple truth is that we just can't afford it.*

PLAIN OR SIMPLE?

When it is being used to emphasize facts that other people may not like to hear, **plain** is usually used in the expression *the plain fact/truth is that ...* **Simple** can be used in this way too, but it can also be used in a wider variety of structures and collocations (such as *recson and matter*): *The problem was due to the simple fact that ...* ◊ *The problem was due to the plain fact that ...* ◊ *for the plain reason that ...* ◊ *It's a plain matter of ...* Expressions with **simple** often suggest impatience with other people's behaviour.

**stark** (*rather formal*) used for describing an unpleasant fact or difference that is very obvious: *The stark truth is that there is not enough money left.* NOTE The *simple/plain truth* may be sth that some people do not want to hear, but it may be good for them to hear it anyway. The *stark truth* is sth particularly unpleasant and has no good side to it at all.

**bare** [only before noun] the most basic or simple, with nothing extra: *She gave me only the bare facts of the case.*

**unequivocal** (*formal*) expressing your opinion or intention very clearly and firmly: *The reply was an unequivocal 'no'.*

PATTERNS

- the plain/simple/stark/bare/unequivocal **truth**
- a(n) plain/simple/stark/bare/unequivocal **fact/ statement**
- a(n) plain/simple/unequivocal **answer**

**'plain·chant** /ˈpleɪntʃɑːnt/ *NAmE* -tʃænt/ *noun* [U] = PLAINSONG

**plain 'chocolate** *noun* [U] (*BrE*) = DARK CHOCOLATE

**plain 'clothes** *noun* [pl.] ordinary clothes, not uniform, when worn by police officers on duty: *officers in plain clothes* ⊃ WORDFINDER NOTE at POLICE ▸ **plain-'clothes** *adj.* [only before noun]: *plain-clothes police officers*

**plain 'flour** (*BrE*) (*NAmE* **all-purpose 'flour**) *noun* [U] flour that does not contain BAKING POWDER ⊃ compare SELF-RAISING FLOUR

# plainly

**plain·ly** /ˈpleɪnli/ adv. **1** in a way that is easy to see, hear, understand or believe SYN **clearly**: *The sea was plainly visible in the distance.* ◇ *The lease plainly states that all damage must be paid for.* ◇ *She had no right to interfere in what was plainly a family matter.* ◇ *Plainly* (= obviously) *something was wrong.* **2** using simple words to say sth in a direct and honest way: *To put it plainly, he's a crook.* **3** in a simple way, without decoration: *She was plainly dressed and wore no make-up.*

**plain·song** /ˈpleɪnsɒŋ; NAmE -sɔːŋ/ (also **plain·chant**) noun [U] a type of church music for voices alone, used since the Middle Ages

**plain-ˈspoken** (also **plain-ˈspeaking**) adj. saying what you think in very simple, direct language: *a plain-spoken man*

**plaint** /pleɪnt/ noun **1** (*BrE, law*) a complaint made against sb in court **2** (*literary*) a sad call or sound

**plain text** noun [U] (*specialist*) data that is stored in the form of ASCII (= a standard code used so that data can be moved between computers that use different programs). Plain text cannot be FORMATTED (= displayed in a particular way on the screen).

**plain·tiff** /ˈpleɪntɪf/ (also *less frequent* **com·plain·ant**) noun (*law*) a person who makes a formal complaint against sb in court ⇨ compare DEFENDANT

**plaint·ive** /ˈpleɪntɪv/ adj. sounding sad, especially in a weak, complaining way SYN **mournful**: *a plaintive cry/voice* ▶ **plaint·ive·ly** adv.

**plait** /plæt/ (*BrE*) (also **braid** *especially in NAmE*) noun, verb
■ noun a long piece of sth, especially hair, that is divided into three parts and TWISTED together: **in plaits** *She wore her hair in plaits*
■ verb ~ sth to TWIST three or more long pieces of hair, rope, etc. together to make one long piece

**plan** 🅞 A1 /plæn/ noun, verb
■ noun
• INTENTION **1** 🅞 A1 something that you intend to do or achieve: ~ **for sth** *Do you have any plans for the summer?* ◇ ~ **to do sth** *There are no plans to build new offices.* ◇ *Your best plan* (= the best thing to do) *would be to go by car.* ◇ *There's been a change of plan.* ◇ *We can't change our plans now.* ⇨ SYNONYMS at PURPOSE
• ARRANGEMENT **2** 🅞 A1 a set of things to do in order to achieve sth, especially one that has been considered in detail in advance: *a business/development/management plan* ◇ *an action plan* ◇ *a plan of action* ◇ *a five-point plan* ◇ *a three-year plan* ◇ ~ **for sth** *We need to make plans for the future.* ◇ ~ **for doing sth** *Both sides agreed to a detailed plan for keeping the peace.* ◇ ~ **to do sth** *The government has announced plans to create one million new training places.* ◇ **according to** ~ *Let's hope everything will go according to plan.* ◇ **under a** ~ *Under this plan, 98% of all Americans will get a tax cut.* ⇨ see also GAME PLAN, MASTER PLAN
• MAP **3** 🅞 A2 a detailed map of a building, town, etc: *a plan of the museum* ◇ *a street plan of the city*
• DRAWING **4** 🅞 B1 [*usually pl.*] (*specialist*) a detailed drawing of a machine, building, etc. that shows its size, shape and measurements: *The original plans of its building have not survived.* ◇ ~ **for sth** *The architect is drawing up plans for the new offices.* ⇨ compare ELEVATION (4), GROUND PLAN
**5** 🅞 B1 a diagram that shows how sth will be arranged: *a seating plan* (= showing where each person will sit, for example at a dinner) ◇ *a floor plan* (= showing how furniture is arranged) ⇨ see also FLOOR PLAN
• MONEY **6** (*especially in compounds*) a way of investing money for the future or buying insurance for sth: *a savings plan* ◇ *a health plan* ⇨ see also INSTALLMENT PLAN, PENSION PLAN, RETIREMENT PLAN ⇨ see also AMERICAN PLAN, OPEN-PLAN
IDM **ˌmake a ˈplan** (*SAfrE*) to think of sth you can do to solve a problem or make sth happen: *It's going to be difficult to find the time but I'll make a plan.* ⇨ more at SOUND v.

■ verb (-nn-)
• MAKE ARRANGEMENTS **1** 🅞 A1 [T, I] to make detailed arrangements for sth you want to do in the future: ~ **sth** *to plan a trip* ◇ *We planned the day down to the last detail.* ◇ *Everything went exactly as planned.* ◇ ~ **sth for sth** *A meeting has been planned for early next year.* ◇ ~ **for sth** *It's never too early to start planning for the future.* ◇ ~ **how, what, etc…** *I've been planning how I'm going to spend the day.* ◇ ~ **that…** *They planned that the two routes would connect.* ◇ ~ **ahead** *You can avoid a lot of stress by planning ahead.* ◇ *a well-planned campaign*
• INTEND/EXPECT **2** 🅞 A1 [I, T] to intend or expect to do sth: ~ **on doing sth** *We hadn't planned on going anywhere this evening.* ◇ ~ **to do sth** *She originally planned to be a doctor.* ◇ ~ **sth** *We're planning a trip to France in the spring—are you interested?*
• DESIGN **3** 🅞 A2 [T] ~ **sth** to make a design or an outline for sth: *to plan an essay/a garden* ◇ *The architects planned and designed the building with students in mind.*
PHRV **ˌplan sth↔ˈout** to plan carefully and in detail sth that you are going to do in the future: *Plan out your route before you go.* ◇ *She has her career all planned out.*

**Plan ˈA** noun [sing.] the thing or things sb intends to do if everything happens as they expect

**pla·nar** /ˈpleɪnə(r)/ adj. (*specialist*) of or related to a flat surface

**Plan ˈB** noun [sing.] the thing or things sb intends to do if their first plan is not successful: *If Plan A fails, go to Plan B.*

**plane** 🅞 A1 /pleɪn/ noun, adj., verb
■ noun **1** 🅞 A1 (*BrE also* **aero·plane**) (also **air·plane** *especially in NAmE*) a flying vehicle with wings and one or more engines: *a passenger/fighter/military/private plane* ◇ *to board a plane* ◇ *The plane took off an hour late.* ◇ *The plane landed in Geneva.* ◇ **by** ~ *She left by plane for Berlin.* ◇ *a plane ticket* ◇ *a plane crash* ⇨ HOMOPHONES at PLAIN

spirit level

bit | chuck

plane | drill

WORDFINDER cabin crew, charter, flight path, in-flight, land, long-haul, refuel, take-off, travel

**2** (*geometry*) any flat or level surface, or an imaginary flat surface through or joining material objects: *the horizontal/vertical plane* **3** a level of thought, existence or development: *to reach a higher plane of achievement* **4** a tool with a BLADE (= sharp metal part) set in a flat surface, used for making the surface of wood smooth by cutting very thin layers off it
■ adj. [*only before noun*] (*specialist*) completely flat; level: *a plane surface*
■ verb **1** [T] to make a piece of wood smoother or flatter with a PLANE: ~ **sth** *Plane the surface down first.* ◇ ~ **sth + adj.** *Then plane the wood smooth.* ⇨ HOMOPHONES at PLAIN
**2** [I] (of a bird) to fly without moving the wings, especially high up in the air **3** [I] (of a boat, etc.) to move quickly across water, only just touching the surface

**plane-load** /ˈpleɪnləʊd/ noun the number of people or the amount of goods that can be carried in a plane: *two plane-loads of refugees*

**planer** /ˈpleɪnə(r)/ noun an electric tool for making wooden surfaces smooth

**planet** 🅞 A2 /ˈplænɪt/ noun **1** 🅞 A2 [C] a large round object in space that moves around a star (such as the sun) and receives light from it: *the planets of our solar system* ◇ *the planet Earth/Venus/Mars* ⇨ WORDFINDER NOTE at EARTH
**2** 🅞 A2 **the planet** [sing.] used to mean 'the world', especially when talking about the environment: *the battle to save the planet*
IDM **to be on another ˈplanet** | **what ˈplanet is sb on?** (*informal, humorous*) used to suggest that sb's ideas are not realistic or practical: *He thinks being a father is easy. What planet is he on?*

**plan·et·ar·i·um** /ˌplænɪˈteəriəm; NAmE -ˈter-/ noun (pl. -iums) a building with a curved ceiling to represent the sky at night, with moving images of the planets and stars, used to educate and entertain people

**plan·et·ary** /ˈplænətri; NAmE -teri/ adj. [only before noun] (specialist) relating to a planet or planets: *a planetary system*

**ˈplane tree** noun a tree with spreading branches and broad leaves, that is often found in towns in northern countries

**plan·gent** /ˈplændʒənt/ adj. (literary) (of sounds) loud, deep and sad **SYN** plaintive: *the plangent sound of the harpsichord*

**plank** /plæŋk/ noun **1** a long narrow flat piece of wood that is used for making floors, etc: *a plank of wood* ◊ *a wooden plank* **2** a main point in the policy of an organization, especially a political party: *The central plank of the bill was rural development.* **IDM** see THICK adj., WALK v.

**plank·ing** /ˈplæŋkɪŋ/ noun [U] **1** planks used to make a floor, etc. **2** the activity of lying face down with your arms by your sides in an unusual or dangerous place in order to take a photograph to put on the internet or SOCIAL MEDIA: *Recent tragedies did little to decrease the popularity of planking.*

**plank·ton** /ˈplæŋktən/ noun [U + sing./pl. v.] the very small forms of plant and animal life that live in water

**ˌplanned eˈconomy** (also ˌcomˌmand eˈconomy) noun an economy in which production, prices and incomes are decided and fixed by the central government

**plan·ner** /ˈplænə(r)/ noun **1** (also ˌtown ˈplanner, NAmE also ˌcity ˈplanner) a person whose job is to plan the growth and development of a town ⊃ see also CITY PLANNER, TOWN PLANNER **2** a person who makes plans for a particular area of activity: *curriculum planners* **3** a book, chart, computer program, etc. that contains dates and is used for recording information, arranging meetings, etc: *a journey planner* ◊ *a wall planner*

**plan·ning** **❶** **B1** /ˈplænɪŋ/ noun [U] **1 ʔ B1** the act or process of making plans for sth: *financial planning* ◊ *After months of careful planning the event went without a hitch.* ◊ *We are currently in the planning stages.* ⊃ see also FAMILY PLANNING, SUCCESSION PLANNING **2** = TOWN PLANNING: *She now works in urban planning.* ◊ *to submit a planning application*

**ˈplanning permission** noun [U] (BrE) official permission to build a new building or change one that already exists

**plant** **❶** **A1** /plɑːnt; NAmE plænt/ noun, verb
■ noun
• LIVING THING **1 ʔ A1** [C] a living thing that grows in the earth and usually has a STEM, leaves and roots, especially one that is smaller than a tree or bush: *flowering plants* ◊ *a tomato/potato plant* ◊ *It's becoming more popular to grow plants organically.* ◊ *The area is home to many rare plant species.* ⊃ see also BEDDING PLANT, HOUSEPLANT, POT PLANT ⊃ VISUAL VOCAB page V7
• FACTORY **2 ʔ B1** [C] a factory or place where power is produced or an industrial process takes place: *a nuclear power plant* ◊ *a processing/manufacturing plant* ◊ *a chemical/steel/coal plant* ⊃ see also POWER PLANT, SEWAGE PLANT ⊃ SYNONYMS at FACTORY ⊃ WORDFINDER NOTE at FACTORY
• MACHINES **3** [U] the large machines that are used in industrial processes: *The company has been investing in new plant and equipment.*
• STH ILLEGAL **4** [C, usually sing.] (informal) something that sb has deliberately placed among another person's clothes or possessions in order to make them appear guilty of a crime
• PERSON **5** [C] a person who joins a group of criminals or enemies in order to live there and secretly report information about their activities
■ verb
• SEEDS/PLANTS **1 ʔ A2** ~ sth to put plants, seeds, etc. in the ground to grow: *to plant a tree/seed/crop* ◊ *Plant the bulbs in pots for a spring display.* **2 ʔ A2** [often passive] to cover or supply a garden, area of land, etc. with plants: *~sth The children are planting a garden next to the school.* ◊ *be planted with sth The field had been ploughed and planted with corn.*
• PUT IN POSITION **3** ~ sth/yourself + adv./prep. to place sth or yourself in a particular place or position: *They planted a flag on the summit.* ◊ *He planted himself squarely in front of us.*
• BOMB **4** ~ sth (+ adv./prep.) to hide sth such as a bomb in a place where it will not be found
• STH ILLEGAL **5** ~ sth (on sb) to hide sth, especially sth illegal, in sb's clothing, possessions, etc. so that when it is found it will look as though they committed a crime: *He claims that the drugs were planted on him.*
• PERSON **6** ~ sb (in sth) to send sb to join a group, etc., especially in order to make secret reports on its members
• THOUGHT/IDEA **7** ~ sth (in sth) to make sb think or believe sth, especially without them realizing that you gave them the idea: *He planted the first seeds of doubt in my mind.*
**PHRV** ˌplant sth↔ˈout to put plants in the ground so that they have enough room to grow

**plan·tain** /ˈplæntɪn, -tem/ noun **1** [C, U] a fruit like a large banana, but less sweet, that is cooked and eaten as a vegetable **2** [C] a wild plant with small green flowers and broad flat leaves that spread out close to the ground

**plan·tar** /ˈplæntə(r)/ adj. [only before noun] (anatomy) of or related to the bottom of the foot

**ˈplantar wart** (NAmE) (BrE verˈruca) noun a small hard spot like a WART on the bottom of the foot, which can be easily spread from person to person

**plan·ta·tion** /plɑːnˈteɪʃn; NAmE plæn-/ noun **1** a large area of land, especially in a hot country, where crops such as coffee, sugar, rubber, etc. are grown: *a banana/coffee plantation* **2** a large area of land that is planted with trees to produce wood: *conifer/forestry plantations*

**plant·er** /ˈplɑːntə(r); NAmE ˈplæn-/ noun **1** an attractive container to grow a plant in **2** a person who owns or manages a PLANTATION in a tropical country: *a tea planter* **3** a machine that plants seeds, etc.

**plant·ing** /ˈplɑːntɪŋ; NAmE ˈplæn-/ noun [U, C] an act of planting sth; sth that has just been planted: *The Tree Council promotes tree planting.* ◊ *These bushes are fairly recent plantings.*

**ˈplant pot** noun a container for growing plants in

**plaque** /plɑːk; BrE also plæk/ noun **1** [C] a flat piece of stone, metal, etc., usually with a name and dates on, attached to a wall in memory of a person or an event **2** [U] a soft substance that forms on teeth and encourages the growth of harmful bacteria ⊃ compare SCALE

**plasma** /ˈplæzmə/ (also **plasm** /ˈplæzəm/) noun [U] **1** (biology or medical) the clear liquid part of blood, in which the blood cells, etc. float **2** (physics) a gas that contains approximately equal numbers of positive and negative electric charges and is present in the sun and most stars

**ˈplasma screen** noun a type of television or computer screen that is larger and thinner than most screens and produces a very clear image

**ˈplasma TV** noun a television set with a plasma screen

**plas·ter** /ˈplɑːstə(r); NAmE ˈplæs-/ noun, verb
■ noun **1** [U] a substance made of LIME, water and sand, that is put on walls and ceilings to give them a smooth hard surface: *an old house with crumbling plaster and a leaking roof* ⊃ WORDFINDER NOTE at CONSTRUCTION **2** (also less frequent ˌplaster of ˈParis) [U] a white powder that is mixed with water and becomes very hard when it dries, used especially for making copies of statues or holding broken bones in place: *a plaster bust of Julius Caesar* ◊ **in~** (BrE) *She broke her leg a month ago and it's still in plaster.* **3** (also ˈsticking plaster) (both BrE) (also ˈBand-Aid™ NAmE, BrE) [C, U] a piece of material that be stuck to the skin to protect a small wound or cut; this material ⊃ WORDFINDER NOTE at HURT
■ verb **1** ~ sth to cover a wall, etc. with plaster **2** ~ sb/sth/ yourself in/with sth to cover sb/sth with a wet or sticky substance: *She plastered herself in suntan lotion.* ◊ *We were plastered from head to foot with mud.* **3** [usually

# plasterboard

passive) to make your hair flat and stick to your head: **be plastered + adv./prep.** *His wet hair was plastered to his head.* **4** [often passive] to completely cover a surface with pictures or posters: **A is plastered with B** *Her bedroom wall was plastered with photos of him.* ◊ **B is plastered over A** *She had photos of him plastered all over her bedroom wall.*
**PHRV** ˌplaster ˈover sth to cover sth such as a CRACK (= long narrow hole) or an old wall with plaster: *The old windows have been filled and plastered over.*

**plas·ter·board** /ˈplɑːstəbɔːd; NAmE ˈplæstərbɔːrd/ (NAmE also **drywall**) noun [U] a building material made of two sheets of thick paper with plaster set between them, used for inside walls and ceilings

**ˈplaster cast** noun **1** (also **cast**) a case made of PLASTER OF PARIS that covers a broken bone and protects it **2** a copy of sth, made from PLASTER OF PARIS: *They took a plaster cast of the teeth for identification purposes.*

**plas·tered** /ˈplɑːstəd; NAmE ˈplæstərd/ adj. [not before noun] (*informal*) drunk: *to be/get plastered*

**plas·terer** /ˈplɑːstərə(r); NAmE ˈplæs-/ noun a person whose job is to put plaster on walls and ceilings

**plaster of Paris** /ˌplɑːstər əv ˈpærɪs; NAmE ˌplæs-/ noun [U] = PLASTER (2)

**plas·ter·work** /ˈplɑːstəwɜːk; NAmE ˈplæstərwɜːrk/ noun [U] the dry PLASTER on ceilings when it has been formed into shapes and patterns for decoration

**plas·tic** ❶ A2 /ˈplæstɪk/ noun, adj.
■ noun **1** A2 [U, C, usually pl.] a light strong material that is produced by chemical processes and can be formed into shapes when heated. There are many different types of plastic, used to make different objects and FABRICS: *The pipes should be made of plastic.* ◊ *a sheet of clear plastic* ◊ *recycled plastic* **2** **plastics** [U] the science of making plastics **3** [U] (*informal*) a way of talking about CREDIT CARDS: *Do they take plastic?*
■ adj. **1** A2 made of plastic: *a plastic bag/bottle/cup* **2** (of a material or substance) easily formed into different shapes **SYN** **malleable**: *Clay is a plastic substance.* **3** (*disapproving*) that seems artificial; false; not real or sincere **SYN** **false**: *TV game show hosts with their banal remarks and plastic smiles*

**ˌplastic ˈbullet** noun a bullet made of plastic, that is intended to injure but not to kill people

**ˌplastic exˈplosive** noun [U, C] an EXPLOSIVE that is used to make bombs

**Plas·ti·cine**™ /ˈplæstəsiːn/ noun [U] (*BrE*) a soft substance like CLAY that is made in different colours, used especially by children for making models

**plas·ti·city** /plæˈstɪsəti/ noun [U] (*specialist*) the quality of being easily made into different shapes

**ˌplastic ˈsurgeon** noun a doctor who is qualified to perform plastic surgery

**ˌplastic ˈsurgery** noun [U] medical operations to repair injury to a person's skin, or to improve a person's appearance

**ˈplastic wrap** (also **Saran Wrap**™) (both NAmE) (BrE **ˈcling film**) noun [U] a thin clear plastic material that sticks to a surface and to itself, used especially for wrapping food

**plate** ❶ A2 /pleɪt/ noun, verb
■ noun
• FOOD **1** A2 [C] a flat, usually round, dish that you put food on: *sandwiches on a plate* ◊ *dinner/serving plates* ◊ *They filled their plates with spaghetti.* ⇒ see also PAPER PLATE, SIDE PLATE **2** A2 [C] **~ of sth** = PLATEFUL: *a plate of sandwiches* ◊ *two large plates of pasta* **3** [C] (*especially NAmE*) a whole main course of a meal, served on one plate: *Try the seafood plate.*
• FOR STRENGTH **4** B2 [C] a thin flat piece of metal, used especially to join or make sth stronger: *The tanks were mainly constructed of steel plates.* ◊ *She had a metal plate inserted in her arm.*
• FOR INFORMATION **5** [C] a flat piece of metal with some information on it, for example sb's name: *A brass plate beside the door said 'Dr Alan Tate'.* ⇒ see also NAMEPLATE
• ON VEHICLE **6** [usually pl.] the pieces of metal or plastic at the front and back of a vehicle with numbers and letters on it ⇒ see also L-PLATE, LICENSE PLATE, NUMBER PLATE
• SILVER/GOLD **7** [U] ordinary metal that is covered with a thin layer of silver or gold: *The cutlery is plate, not solid silver.* ⇒ see also GOLD PLATE, SILVER PLATE, TINPLATE **8** [U] dishes, bowls, etc. that are made of silver or gold
• ON ANIMAL **9** [C] (*biology*) one of the thin flat pieces of HORN or bone that cover and protect an animal: *the armadillo's protective shell of bony plates*
• GEOLOGY **10** [C] one of the very large pieces of rock that form the earth's surface and move slowly: *the Pacific plate* ◊ *Earthquakes are caused by two tectonic plates bumping into each other.* ⇒ see also PLATE TECTONICS
• PRINTING/PHOTOGRAPHY **11** [C] a photograph that is used as a picture in a book, especially one that is printed on a separate page on high quality paper: *The book includes 55 colour plates.* ◊ *See plate 4.* **12** [C] a sheet of metal, plastic, etc. that has been treated so that words or pictures can be printed from it: *a printing plate* **13** [C] a thin sheet of glass, metal, etc. that is covered with chemicals so that it reacts to light and can form an image, used in larger or older cameras
• IN MOUTH **14** [C] a thin piece of plastic with wire or artificial teeth attached to it which fits inside your mouth in order to make your teeth straight ⇒ compare BRACE, DENTURES
• IN BASEBALL **15** [sing.] (*NAmE*) = HOME PLATE
• IN CHURCH **16** (*usually* **the plate**) [sing.] a flat dish that is used to collect money from people in a church ⇒ see also BREASTPLATE, HOTPLATE
**IDM** have enough/a lot/too much on your ˈplate (*informal*) to have a lot of work or problems, etc. to deal with ⇒ more at HAND v., STEP v.
■ verb [usually passive] **1** to cover a metal with a thin layer of another metal, especially gold or silver: **be plated (with sth)** *a silver ring plated with gold* ◊ *platinum-plated jewellery* ⇒ see also GOLD-PLATED, SILVER-PLATED **2** to cover sth with sheets of metal or another hard substance: **be plated (with sth)** *The walls of the vault were plated with steel.* ◊ *nickel-plated wire*

**plat·eau** /ˈplætəʊ; NAmE plæˈtoʊ/ noun, verb
■ noun (pl. **plat·eaux** /-əʊz; NAmE plæˈtoʊz/ or **plat·eaus**) **1** an area of flat land that is higher than the land around it **2** a time of little or no change after a period of growth or progress: *Inflation has reached a plateau.* ⇒ WORDFINDER NOTE at TREND
■ verb [I] **~ (out)** to stay at a steady level after a period of growth or progress: *Unemployment has at last plateaued out.*

**plate·ful** /ˈpleɪtfʊl/ (also **plate**) noun the amount of food that you can put on a plate: *She ate three platefuls of spaghetti.*

**ˌplate ˈglass** noun [U] very clear glass of good quality, made in thick sheets, used for doors, windows of shops, etc.

**plate-ˈglass** adj. (*BrE*) used about universities in the UK) built in the 1960s, in contrast to older universities ⇒ compare OXBRIDGE, RED-BRICK (2)

**plate·let** /ˈpleɪtlət/ noun a very small part of a cell in the blood, shaped like a disc in shape. Platelets help to CLOT the blood from a cut or wound.

**ˌplate tecˈtonics** noun [U] (*geology*) the movements of the large sheets of rock (called PLATES) that form the earth's surface; the scientific study of these movements

**plat·form** ❶ A2 /ˈplætfɔːm; NAmE -fɔːrm/ noun
• AT TRAIN STATION **1** A2 the raised flat area next to the track at a train station where you get on or off the train: (*BrE*) *What platform does it go from?* ◊ (*BrE*) *The train now standing at platform 1 is for Leeds.* ⇒ compare TRACK ⇒ WORDFINDER NOTE at TRAIN
• FOR PERFORMERS **2** B1 a flat surface raised above the level of the ground or floor, used by public speakers or performers so that the audience can see them **SYN** **rostrum**: *Coming onto the platform now is tonight's conductor, Jane Glover.* ◊ *Representatives of both parties shared a platform* (= they spoke at the same meeting).
• RAISED SURFACE **3** B1 a raised level surface, for example one that equipment stands on or is operated from: *an oil/*

gas platform ◊ a viewing platform giving stunning views over the valley ◊ a launch platform (= for SPACECRAFT)
- COMPUTING **4** the type of computer system or the software that is used: a multimedia platform ◊ a mobile gaming platform ⟹ WORDFINDER NOTE at COMPUTER
- POLITICS/OPINIONS **5** [usually sing.] the aims of a political party and the things that they say they will do if they are elected to power: They are campaigning on an anti-immigration platform. **6** an opportunity or a place for sb to express their opinions publicly or make progress in a particular area: She used the newspaper column as a platform for her feminist views.
- SHOES **7** a type of shoe with a high, thick SOLE; the sole on such a shoe: platform shoes
- ON BUS **8** (BrE) the open part at the back of a DOUBLE-DECKER bus where you get on or off

▼ BRITISH/AMERICAN

**platform / track**
- In British stations the platforms, where passengers get on and off trains, have numbers: The Edinburgh train is waiting at platform 4.
- In stations in the US, it is the track that the train travels along that has a number: The train for Chicago is on track 9.

**'platform game** (also **plat·form·er** /ˈplætfɔːmə(r); NAmE -fɔːrm-/) noun a computer game in which the player controls a character who jumps and climbs between platforms at different positions on the screen

**plat·ing** /ˈpleɪtɪŋ/ noun [U] **1** a thin layer of a metal, especially silver or gold, on another metal **2** a layer of pieces of sth, especially of metal plates: armour plating

**plat·in·um** /ˈplætɪnəm/ noun [U] (symb. **Pt**) a chemical element. Platinum is a silver-grey PRECIOUS METAL, used in making expensive jewellery and in industry.

**platinum 'blonde** noun (informal) a woman whose hair is a very pale silver colour, especially because it has been coloured with chemicals; this colour of hair ▶ **platinum 'blonde** adj.

**plati·tude** /ˈplætɪtjuːd; NAmE -tuːd/ noun (disapproving) a comment or statement that has been made very often before and is therefore not interesting ▶ **plati·tud·in·ous** /ˌplætɪˈtjuːdɪnəs; NAmE -ˈtuːdən-/ adj. (formal)

**pla·ton·ic** /pləˈtɒnɪk; NAmE -ˈtɑːn-/ adj. (of a relationship) friendly but not involving sex: platonic love ◊ Their relationship is strictly platonic. ⟹ WORDFINDER NOTE at FRIEND

**Pla·ton·ism** /ˈpleɪtənɪzəm/ noun [U] (philosophy) the ideas of the ancient Greek PHILOSOPHER Plato and those who followed him ▶ **Pla·ton·ist** /-nɪst/ adj., noun

**pla·toon** /pləˈtuːn/ noun a small group of soldiers that is part of a COMPANY and commanded by a LIEUTENANT

**platte·land** /ˈplætəlænd/ SAfrE /ˈplətɛnt/ noun [U] (SAfrE) remote country districts; rural areas

**plat·ter** /ˈplætə(r)/ noun a large plate that is used for serving food: a silver platter ◊ I'll have the fish platter [= several types of fish and other food served on a large plate). IDM see SILVER n.

**platy·pus** /ˈplætɪpəs/; NAmE -pəs/ (also ˌduck-billed ˈplatypus) noun an Australian animal that is covered in fur and has a BEAK like a DUCK, WEBBED feet (= with skin between the toes) and a flat tail. Platypuses lay eggs but give milk to their young.

**plau·dits** /ˈplɔːdɪts/ noun [usually pl.] (formal) praise and approval: His work **won him plaudits** from the critics.

**plaus·ible** /ˈplɔːzəbl/ adj. **1** (of an excuse or explanation) reasonable and likely to be true: Her story sounded perfectly plausible. ◊ The only plausible explanation is that he forgot. **OPP** implausible **2** (disapproving) (of a person) good at sounding honest and sincere, especially when trying to trick people: She was a plausible liar. ▶ **plausi·bil·ity** /ˌplɔːzəˈbɪləti/ noun [U] **plaus·ibly** /ˈplɔːzəbli/ adv.: He argued very plausibly that the claims were true.

1177 **play**

**play** 🔊 **A1** /pleɪ/ verb, noun

■verb
- OF CHILDREN **1** **A1** [I, T] to do things for pleasure, as children do; to enjoy yourself, rather than work: You'll have to play inside today. ◊ There's a time to work and a time to play. ◊ ~**with sb/sth** A group of kids were playing with a ball in the street. ◊ I haven't got anybody to play with! ◊ ~ **sth** Let's play a different game. ⟹ SYNONYMS at ENTERTAINMENT **2** **A1** [T, no passive, I] to pretend to be or do sth for fun: ~ **sth** Let's play pirates. ◊ ~ **at (doing) sth** They were playing at being cowboys. ⟹ see also ROLE-PLAY
- SPORTS/GAMES **3** **A1** [T, I] to be involved in a game; to compete against sb in a game: ~ **sth** to play football/cards ◊ ~ **sth with/against sb** I usually play chess with my brother. ◊ ~ **sb** France are playing Wales tomorrow. ◊ ~ **sb at sth** Have you played her at squash yet? ◊ ~ **for sb** He plays for Cleveland. ◊ ~ **against sb** France are playing against Wales on Saturday. ◊ ~ **with sb** I like football, but I don't have anyone to play with. ◊ + **adv./prep.** Evans played very well. **4** [I] to take a particular position in a sports team: + **adv./prep.** Who's playing on the wing? ◊ + noun I've never played right back before. **5** [T] ~ **sb (+ adv./prep.)** to include sb in a sports team: I think we should play Matt on the wing. **6** [T] ~ **sth** to make contact with the ball and hit or kick it in the way mentioned: She played the ball and ran forward. ◊ He played a backhand volley. **7** [T] ~ **sth** (in CHESS) to move a piece in CHESS, etc: She played her bishop. **8** [T, I] ~ **(sth)** (in card games) to put a card face upwards on the table, showing its value: to play your ace/a trump ◊ He played out of turn!
- MUSIC **9** **A1** [T, I] to perform music on a musical instrument: ~ **(sth)** She played Mozart's Piano Concerto No. 20. ◊ In the distance a band was playing. ◊ He sat in the corner, playing softly on his guitar. ◊ ~ **sth on sth** He played a tune on his harmonica. ◊ ~ **sth to sb** Play that new piece to us. ◊ ~ **sb sth** Play us that new piece. **10** **A1** [T] ~ **sth** to have the skill of performing on a musical instrument: Do you **play a musical instrument?** ◊ to play the piano/violin/flute ◊ I'm learning to play my sax. **11** [T] ~ **sth** to use an MP3 player, a CD player, etc. to make it possible to hear a song, an album, a CD, etc: I played some music to drown out the noise. ◊ They're always playing that song on the radio. **12** [I] (of a song, an album, etc.) to be heard: My favourite song was playing on the radio.
- VIDEO/DVD **13** **A1** [I, T] (of a video or DVD) to start working; to make a video on DVD start working: These videos won't play on my computer. ◊ ~ **sth** Click below to play videos.
- ACT/PERFORM **14** **A2** [T, I] to act in a play, film, etc.; to act the role of sb: ~ **sth** to play a role/part ◊ The part of Elizabeth was played by Cate Blanchett. ◊ He had always wanted to play Othello. ◊ ~ **opposite sb** She played opposite Brad Pitt (= she and Brad Pitt played the two leading roles). **15** **B1** [I, T] to pretend to be sth that you are not: The children were dressed as soldiers, but they were just playing. ◊ + **adj.** I decided it was safer to play dead. ◊ + noun She enjoys playing the wronged wife. **16** [T] ~ **the sth** to behave as though you are a particular type of person: This is no time to play the hero. **17** [I] ~ **(to sb)** (of a play or show) to be performed: A production of 'Carmen' was playing to packed houses. **18** [T] ~ **sth** (of a band, theatre company, etc.) to give a performance in a particular place: The band are playing 11 cities around the country. ◊ I've played some fantastic venues.
- HAVE EFFECT **19** **B1** [T] ~ **a part/role (in sth/in doing sth)** to have an effect or influence on sth: Social media played an important part in the last election. ◊ High environmental temperatures may also play a role.
- TRICK **20** **B1** [T] ~ **a trick/tricks (on sb)** to trick sb for fun: Children ran around the village playing tricks. ◊ I played a trick on him just to see his reaction.
- SITUATION **21** [T] ~ **sth + adv./prep.** to deal with a situation in the way mentioned: He played the situation carefully for maximum advantage.
- NOT DO STH SERIOUSLY **22** [T, I] (often disapproving) to do sth without being serious about it or putting much effort into it: ~ **at (doing) sth** They were playing at being villains, like in the movies. ◊ ~ **sth (with sth)** Officials are playing politics with farm programs.

# playable

- **BE WILLING TO HELP** 23 [I] (usually in negative sentences) (*informal*) to be willing to work with other people in a helpful way, especially so that sb can get what they want: *He needs another loan, but the bank won't play.*
- **OF LIGHT/A SMILE** 24 [I] + adv./prep. to move or appear quickly and lightly, often changing direction or shape: *Sunlight played on the surface of the lake.*
- **OF FOUNTAIN** 25 [I] when a FOUNTAIN **plays**, it produces a steady stream of water

**IDM HELP** Most idioms containing **play** are at the entries for the nouns and adjectives in the idioms, for example **play the game** is at **game**. **have money, time, etc. to ˈplay with** (*informal*) to have plenty of money, time, etc. for doing sth **ˈplay with yourself** (*informal*) to MASTURBATE **what is sb ˈplaying at?** used to ask in an angry way about what sb is doing: *What do you think you are playing at?*

**PHRV** **ˌplay aˈround (with sb/sth)** (*also* **ˌplay aˈbout (with sb/sth)** *especially in BrE*) **1** to behave or treat sth in a careless way: *Don't play around with my tools!* **2** (*informal*) to have a sexual relationship with sb, usually with sb who is not your usual partner: *Her husband is always playing around.* **ˌplay aˈlong (with sb/sth)** to pretend to agree with sb/sth: *I decided to play along with her idea.* **ˌplay aˈway (from home)** **1** (of a sports team) to play a match at the opponent's ground or stadium **2** (*BrE*) (of a person who is married or who has a regular sexual partner) to have a secret sexual relationship with sb else **ˌplay sth↔ˈback (to sb)** to play music, film, etc. that has been recorded on a tape, video, etc: *Play that last section back to me again.* ⇨ related noun PLAYBACK **ˌplay sth↔ˈdown** to try to make sth seem less important than it really is **SYN** downplay **OPP** **play sth up** **ˌplay A ˈoff against B** (*BrE*) (*NAmE also* **ˈplay A off B**) to put two people or groups in competition with each other, especially in order to get an advantage for yourself: *She played her two rivals off against each other and got the job herself.* ⇨ related noun PLAY-OFF **ˌplay ˈon** (*sport*) to continue to play; to start playing again: *The home team claimed a penalty but the referee told them to play on.* **ˌplay onˈupon sth** to take advantage of sb's feelings, etc. **SYN** exploit: *Advertisements often play on people's fears.* **ˌplay sth↔ˈout** when an event **is played out**, it happens **SYN** enact: *Their love affair was played out against the backdrop of war.* **ˌplay yourself/itself ˈout** to become weak and no longer useful or important **ˌplay ˈup** / **ˌplay sb ˈup** (*especially BrE, informal*) **1** to behave badly: *The kids have been playing up all day.* **2** to cause sb problems or pain: *My shoulder is playing me up today.* **ˌplay sth↔ˈup** to try to make sth seem more important than it really is **SYN** overplay **OPP** **play sth down** **ˈplay with sb/sth** to treat sb who is emotionally attached to you in a way that is not serious and which can hurt their feelings: *She tends to play with men's emotions.* ◊ *She realized that Patrick was merely playing with her.* **ˈplay with sth** **1** to keep touching or moving sth: *She was playing with her hair.* ◊ *Stop playing with your food!* **2** to use things in different ways to produce an interesting or humorous effect, or to see what effect they have: *In this poem Fitch plays with words which sound alike.* ◊ *The composer plays with the exotic sounds of Japanese instruments.*

■ **noun**

- **IN THEATRE** 1 **A2** [C] a piece of writing performed by actors in a theatre or on television or radio: *a stage/radio play* ◊ *to put on/stage a play* ◊ *to produce/direct a play* ◊ *~ by sb a play by Shakespeare* ⇨ see also MORALITY PLAY, PASSION PLAY ⇨ WORDFINDER NOTE at ACTOR

**WORDFINDER** act, cast, drama, entrance, exit, line, role, scene, speech

- **CHILDREN** 2 **A2** [U] things that people, especially children, do for pleasure rather than as work: *the importance of learning through play* ◊ *at~ the happy sounds of children at play* ◊ *a children's play area*
- **IN SPORT** 3 **B1** [U] the playing of a game: *Rain stopped play.* ◊ *There was some excellent play in yesterday's match.* ◊ *This video game has fast and exciting game play.* ⇨ see also FAIR PLAY, FOUL PLAY 4 [C] (*NAmE*) an action or move in a game: *He made several nice defensive plays.*
- **ACTIVITY/INFLUENCE** 5 **B2** [U] the activity or operation of sth; the influence of sth on sth else: *the free play of market forces* ◊ *in~ More powerful forces are in play.* ◊ *The financial crisis has brought new factors into play.* ◊ *Personal feelings should not come into play when you are making business decisions.*
- **IN ROPE** 6 [U] the possibility of free and easy movement: *We need more play in the rope.*
- **OF LIGHT/A SMILE** 7 [U] (*literary*) a light, quick movement that keeps changing: *the play of sunlight on water*

**IDM** **have a ˈplay (with sth)** to spend time playing with a toy, game, etc: *I had a play with the new computer game.* **in/out of ˈplay** (*sport*) (of a ball) inside/outside the area allowed by the rules of the game: *She just managed to keep the ball in play.* **make a ˈplay for sb/sth** to try to obtain sth; to do things that are intended to produce a particular result: *She was making a play for the sales manager's job.* **make great/much ˈplay of sth** to emphasize the importance of a particular fact: *He made great play of the fact that his uncle was a duke.* **a play on ˈwords** the humorous use of a word or phrase that can have two different meanings **SYN** pun ⇨ more at CALL v., CHILD, STATE n., WORK n.

**playˈable** /ˈpleɪəbl/ *adj.* **1** (of a piece of music or a computer game) easy to play **2** (of a sports field) in a good condition and suitable for playing on **OPP** unplayable

**ˈplay-acting** *noun* [U] behaviour that seems to be honest and sincere when in fact the person is pretending ▶ **ˈplay-act** *verb* [I]: *He thought she was play-acting but in fact she had really hurt herself.*

**ˈplay-back** /ˈpleɪbæk/ *noun* [U, C, usually sing.] the act of playing music, showing a film or listening to a phone message that has been recorded before; a recording that you listen to or watch again

**ˈplayback singer** *noun* (*IndE*) a singer who records songs to be used in a film where actors pretend to sing

**ˈplay-bill** /ˈpleɪbɪl/ *noun* **1** a printed notice advertising a play **2** (*NAmE*) a theatre programme

**ˈplay-book** /ˈpleɪbʊk/ *noun* **1** (*sport*) (especially in AMERICAN FOOTBALL) a book or set of notes with descriptions and diagrams of the actions or moves that a team can use **2** a set of rules or way of doing sth: *The competition took their sales approach right out of our playbook.*

**ˈplay-boy** /ˈpleɪbɔɪ/ *noun* a rich man who spends his time enjoying himself

**ˌplay-by-ˈplay** *noun* [usually sing.] (*NAmE*) a report on what is happening in a sports game, given as the game is being played

**ˈplay date** *noun* an arrangement that parents make for their children to play together at a particular time and place

**ˌplayed ˈout** *adj.* [not before noun] (*informal*) no longer having any influence or effect

**playˈer** **A1** /ˈpleɪə(r)/ *noun* **1 A1** a person who takes part in a game or sport: *a football/tennis/chess player* ◊ *top/star players* ◊ *a game for four players* ⇨ see also FRANCHISE PLAYER **2** a company or person involved in a particular area of business or politics: *The company has emerged as a major player in the London property market.* ⇨ see also TEAM PLAYER **3 B1** (in compounds) a machine for producing the sound or pictures that have been recorded on CDs, etc: *a DVD/CD player* **4 A1** (usually in compounds) a person who plays a musical instrument: *a trumpet/bass player* **5** (*old-fashioned*) (especially in names) an actor: *Phoenix Players present 'Romeo and Juliet'.*

**ˌplayer piˈano** *noun* a piano that plays itself by means of a PIANO ROLL **SYN** Pianola™

**ˈplay-ful** /ˈpleɪfl/ *adj.* **1** full of fun; wanting to play: *a playful puppy* **2** (of a remark, an action, etc.) made or done in fun; not serious **SYN** light-hearted: *He gave her a playful punch on the arm.* ▶ **ˈplay-ful-ly** /-fəli/ *adv.* **ˈplay-ful-ness** *noun* [U]

**ˈplay-goer** /ˈpleɪɡəʊə(r)/ *noun* = THEATREGOER

**ˈplay-ground** /ˈpleɪɡraʊnd/ *noun* **1** an outdoor area where children can play, especially at a school or in a park ⇨ compare SCHOOLYARD ⇨ see also ADVENTURE PLAYGROUND **2** a place where a particular type of people go to enjoy themselves: *The resort is a playground of the rich and famous.*

**play·group** /ˈpleɪɡruːp/ (also **play·school**) (both *BrE*) *noun* [C, U] a place where children who are below school age go regularly to play together and to learn through playing ⊃ compare NURSERY SCHOOL

**play·house** /ˈpleɪhaʊs/ *noun* **1** used in names of theatres: *the Liverpool Playhouse* **2** (*BrE also* ˈ**Wendy house**) a model of a house large enough for children to play in

**play·ing** /ˈpleɪɪŋ/ *noun* **1** [U] the way in which sb plays sth, especially a musical instrument: *The orchestral playing is superb.* **2** [C] the act of playing a piece of music: *repeated playings of the National Anthem*

ˈ**playing card** (also **card**) *noun* any one of a set of 52 cards with numbers and pictures printed on one side, which are used to play various card games: (*BrE*) *a pack of (playing) cards* ◇ (*NAmE*) *a deck of (playing) cards*

ˈ**playing field** *noun* a large area of grass, usually with lines marked on it, where people play sports and games: *the school playing fields* IDM see LEVEL *adj.*, LEVEL *v.*

**play·let** /ˈpleɪlət/ *noun* a short play

**play·list** /ˈpleɪlɪst/ *noun* a list of songs and pieces of music that you create to play on a music app, computer, etc.

**play·maker** /ˈpleɪmeɪkə(r)/ *noun* a player in a team game who starts attacks or brings other players on the same side into a position in which they could score

**play·mate** /ˈpleɪmeɪt/ *noun* a friend with whom a child plays ⊃ WORDFINDER NOTE at FRIEND

ˈ**play-off** *noun* a match, or a series of them, between two players or teams with equal points or scores to decide who the winner is: *They lost to Chicago in the play-offs.*

**play·pen** /ˈpleɪpen/ *noun* a frame with wooden bars or NETTING that surrounds a small area in which a baby or small child can play safely

**play·room** /ˈpleɪruːm, -rʊm/ *noun* a room in a house for children to play in

**play·scheme** /ˈpleɪskiːm/ *noun* (*BrE*) a project that provides organized activities for children, especially during school holidays

**play·school** /ˈpleɪskuːl/ *noun* (*BrE*) = PLAYGROUP

**play·suit** /ˈpleɪsuːt/ *noun* **1** a piece of clothing for babies or small children that covers the body, arms and legs **2** (*BrE*) a set of clothes that children wear for fun so that they look like a particular person: *a Spiderman playsuit* **3** a piece of women's underwear that covers the upper body to the tops of the legs

**play·thing** /ˈpleɪθɪŋ/ *noun* **1** a person or thing that you treat like a toy, without really caring about them or it: *She was an intelligent woman who refused to be a rich man's plaything.* **2** (*old-fashioned*) a toy: *The teddy bear was his favourite plaything.*

**play·time** /ˈpleɪtaɪm/ *noun* [U, C] **1** (*especially BrE*) a time at school when teaching stops for a short time and children can play **2** a time for playing and having fun: *With so much homework to do, her playtime is now very limited.*

**play·wright** /ˈpleɪraɪt/ *noun* a person who writes plays for the theatre, television or radio SYN dramatist ⊃ compare SCREENWRITER, SCRIPTWRITER

**plaza** /ˈplɑːzə; *NAmE* ˈplæzə/ *noun* (*especially NAmE*) **1** a public outdoor square especially in a town where Spanish is spoken **2** a small shopping centre, sometimes also with offices: *a downtown shopping plaza* **3** (also **service plaza**) (*both NAmE*) (*BrE* **service station**) an area and building next to a HIGHWAY where you can buy food and gas, use the bathroom, etc.: *They stopped at a plaza on the interstate.* ⊃ see also TOLL PLAZA

**plc** /ˌpiː el ˈsiː/ (also **PLC**) *abbr.* (*BrE*) public limited company (used after the name of a company or business): *Lloyds Bank plc*

**plea** 🔑 C1 /pliː/ *noun* **1** 🔑 C1 (*formal*) a serious emotional request, especially for sth needing action now: ~ **for sth** *She made an impassioned plea for help.* ◇ ~ **(to sb) (to do sth)** *a plea to industries to stop pollution* ◇ *He refused to listen to her tearful pleas.* **2** 🔑 C1 (*law*) a statement made by sb or for sb who is accused of a crime: *a plea of guilty/not guilty* ◇ *to enter a guilty plea* ⊃ WORDFINDER NOTE at TRIAL **3** ~ **of sth** (*law*) a reason given to a court for doing or not doing sth: *He was charged with murder, but got off on a plea of insanity.*

ˈ**plea bargain·ing** *noun* [U] (*law*) the process of making an arrangement in court by which a person admits to being guilty of a smaller crime in the hope of receiving less severe punishment for a more serious crime ⊃ compare COP A PLEA ▶ ˈ**plea bargain** *noun*: *He reached a plea bargain with the authorities.*

**plead** 🔑+ C1 /pliːd/ *verb* (**pleaded**, **pleaded**, *NAmE also* **pled**, **pled** /pled/) **1** 🔑+ C1 [I, T] to ask sb for sth in a very strong and serious way SYN **beg**: ~**(with sb) (to do sth)** *She pleaded with him not to go.* ◇ ~**(with sb) (for sth)** *I was forced to plead for my child's life.* ◇ *pleading eyes* ◇ ~ **to do sth** *He pleaded to be allowed to see his mother one more time.* ◇ **+ speech** *'Do something!' she pleaded.* **2** 🔑+ C1 [I, T, no passive] to state in court that you are guilty or not guilty of a crime: (**+ adj.**) *to plead guilty/not guilty* ◇ *How do you plead?* (= said by the judge at the start of the trial) ◇ ~ **sth** *He advised his client to plead insanity* (= say that he/she was mentally ill and therefore not responsible for his/her actions). **3** [T] ~ **sth** to present a case to a court: *They hired a top lawyer to plead their case.* **4** 🔑+ C1 [T, I] to argue in support of sb/sth: ~ **sth** *She appeared on television to plead the cause of political prisoners everywhere.* ◇ ~ **for sb/sth** *The United Nations has pleaded for a halt to the bombing.* **5** [T, no passive] ~ **sth (for sth)** | ~ **that …** to give sth as an explanation or excuse for sth: *He pleaded family problems for his lack of concentration.*

**plead·ing** /ˈpliːdɪŋ/ *noun* **1** [C, U] an act of asking for sth that you want very much, in an emotional way: *He refused to give in to her pleadings.* **2** [C, usually pl.] (*law*) a formal statement of sb's case in court ⊃ see also SPECIAL PLEADING

**plead·ing·ly** /ˈpliːdɪŋli/ *adv.* in an emotional way that shows that you want sth very much but are not certain that sb will give it to you: *He looked pleadingly at her.*

**pleas·ant** 🔑 B1 /ˈpleznt/ *adj.* (**pleas·ant·er**, **pleas·ant·est**) HELP more pleasant and most pleasant are more common **1** 🔑 B1 fun, attractive, or giving pleasure: *a pleasant evening/atmosphere/walk* ◇ *What a pleasant surprise!* ◇ *to live in pleasant surroundings* ◇ *music that is pleasant to the ear* ◇ *a pleasant environment to work in* ◇ **it is ~ to do sth** *It was pleasant to be alone again.* **2** 🔑 B1 friendly and polite: *a pleasant young man* ◇ *a pleasant smile/voice/manner* ◇ ~ **to sb** *Please try to be pleasant to our guests.* OPP **unpleasant** ▶ **pleas·ant·ly** *adv.*: *a pleasantly cool room* ◇ *I was pleasantly surprised by my exam results.* ◇ *'Can I help you?' he asked pleasantly.* **pleas·ant·ness** *noun* [U]: *She remembered the pleasantness of the evening.*

**pleas·ant·ry** /ˈplezntri/ *noun* [C, usually pl., U] (*pl.* **-ies**) (*formal*) a friendly remark made in order to be polite: *After exchanging the usual pleasantries, they got down to serious discussion.*

**please** 🔑 A1 /pliːz/ *exclamation*, *verb*
■ *exclamation* **1** 🔑 A1 used as a polite way of asking for sth or telling sb to do sth: *Please sit down.* ◇ *Two coffees, please.* ◇ *Quiet please!* ◇ *Please could I leave early today?* **2** 🔑 A1 used to add force to a request or statement: *Please don't leave me here alone.* ◇ *Please, please don't forget.* ◇ *Please, I don't understand what I have to do.* **3** 🔑 A1 used as a polite way of accepting sth: *'Would you like some help?' 'Yes, please.'* ◇ *'Coffee?' 'Please.'* **4** **Please!** (*informal*, *often humorous*) used to ask sb to stop behaving badly: *Children, please! I'm trying to work.* ◇ *John! Please!* **5** **Please**/**P-lease** /pəˈliːz/ used when you are replying to sb who has said sth that you think is stupid: *Oh, please! You cannot be serious.*
■ *verb* **1** 🔑 A2 [T, I] ~ **(sb)** to make sb happy: *You can't please everybody.* ◇ *Children are usually easy to please.* ◇ *There's just no pleasing some people* (= some people are impossible to please). ◇ *I did it to please my parents.* ◇ *She's always very eager to please.* OPP **displease 2** [I] often used after *as* or *what*, *where*, etc. to mean 'to want', 'to choose' or 'to

# pleased

like' to do sth: *You may stay as long as you please.* ◇ *She always does exactly as she pleases.* ◇ *I'm free now to live wherever I please.*

**IDM** **if you ˈplease** 1 (*old-fashioned*, *formal*) used when politely asking sb to do sth: *Take a seat, if you please.* 2 (*especially BrE*, *old-fashioned*) used to say that you are annoyed or surprised at sb's actions: *And now, if you please, he wants me to rewrite the whole thing!* **ˈplease the ˈeye** to be very attractive to look at **ˌplease ˈGod** used to say that you very much hope or wish that sth will happen or not happen: *Please God, don't let him be dead.* **ˌplease yourˈself** (*informal*) used to tell sb that you are annoyed with them and do not care what they do: *'I don't think I'll bother finishing this.' 'Please yourself.'* **ˌplease yourˈself | ˌdo as you ˈplease** to be able to do whatever you like: *There were no children to cook for, so we could just please ourselves.*

▼ **EXPRESS YOURSELF**

**Asking for something**

Whether you are in shops or restaurants or in somebody's home, you can use polite questions to get what you want:
- *Could I have a glass of water, please?*
- *Do you have any decaffeinated coffee?*
- *I'd like tea with sugar, please.*
- *I'll have the pasta with salad, please.*

Responses:
- *Certainly.*
- *I'm sorry, we don't have any left.*
- *Yes, of course. Here you are / go.*

**pleased** ❶ A2 /pliːzd/ *adj.* 1 A2 feeling happy about sth: *You're coming? I'm so pleased.* ◇ **~ with sb/sth** *She was very pleased with her exam results.* ◇ **~ at sth** *She seemed pleased at our success.* ◇ **~ about sth** *You're looking very pleased about something.* ◇ **~ for sb** *I'm very pleased for you both.* ◇ **~ (that)...** *I'm really pleased (that) you're feeling better.* ⇨ SYNONYMS at GLAD 2 **~ to do sth** happy or willing to do sth: *We are always pleased to be able to help.* ◇ *I was pleased to hear you've been promoted.* ◇ *Aren't you pleased to see me?* ◇ (*especially BrE*) **Pleased to meet you** (= said when you are introduced to sb). ◇ *We are pleased to announce that the winner of our competition is...* ◇ *Thank you for your invitation, which I am very pleased to accept.*

**IDM** **ˌfar from ˈpleased | ˌnone / ˌnot too ˈpleased | ˌnot best ˈpleased** not pleased; angry: *She was none too pleased at having to do it all again.* **ˌonly too ˈpleased (to do sth)** very happy or willing to do sth: *We're only too pleased to help.* **ˈpleased with yourself** (*often disapproving*) too proud of sth you have done: *He was looking very pleased with himself.* ⇨ more at PUNCH

**pleas·ing** /ˈpliːzɪŋ/ *adj.* that gives you pleasure or makes you feel satisfied: *a pleasing design* ◇ **~ to sb/sth** *The new building was pleasing to the eye.* ⇨ SYNONYMS at SATISFYING
▶ **pleas·ing·ly** *adv.*: *She had a pleasingly direct manner.*

**pleas·ur·able** /ˈpleʒərəbl/ *adj.* (*formal*) giving pleasure **SYN** enjoyable: *a pleasurable experience* ◇ *We do everything we can to make your trip pleasurable.*

**pleas·ur·ably** /ˈpleʒərəbli/ *adv.* with pleasure: *He sipped his coffee pleasurably.*

**pleas·ure** ❶ B1 /ˈpleʒə(r)/ *noun* 1 ❶ B1 [U] a state of feeling or being happy or satisfied **SYN** enjoyment: *for ~ to read for pleasure* ◇ **in (doing) sth** *He takes no pleasure in his work.* ◇ **~ from / out of (doing) sth** *He gets a lot of pleasure out of watching his children perform.* ◇ **~ of (doing) sth** *She had the pleasure of seeing him look surprised.* ◇ **at (doing) sth** *I was touched by her genuine pleasure at her mother's present.* ◇ *It gives me great pleasure to introduce our guest speaker.* ⇨ SYNONYMS at FUN 2 ❶ B1 [U] the activity of enjoying yourself, especially in contrast to working: *Are you in Paris on business or pleasure?* ⇨ SYNONYMS at ENTERTAINMENT 3 ❶ B1 [C] a thing that makes you happy or satisfied: **~ of sth** *the simple pleasures of the countryside* ◇ *the pleasures and pains of everyday life*

◇ **it is a ~ to do sth** *It's a pleasure to meet you.* ◇ *'Thanks for doing that.' 'It's a pleasure.'* ⇨ compare DISPLEASURE
**IDM** **at your / sb's ˈpleasure** (*formal*) as you want; as sb else wants: *The land can be sold at the owner's pleasure.* **ˌmy ˈpleasure** used as a polite way of replying when sb thanks you for doing sth, to show that you were happy to do it **ˌwith ˈpleasure** used as a polite way of accepting or agreeing to sth: *'May I sit here?' 'Yes, with pleasure.'* ⇨ more at GUILTY

▼ **SYNONYMS**

**pleasure**
delight • joy • privilege • treat • honour

These are all words for things that make you happy or that you enjoy.

**pleasure** a thing that makes you happy or satisfied: *the pleasures and pains of everyday life* ◇ *It's been a pleasure meeting you.*

**delight** a thing or person that brings you great pleasure: *the delights of living in the country*

**joy** a thing or person that brings you great pleasure or happiness: *the joys and sorrows of childhood*

**PLEASURE, DELIGHT OR JOY?**

A **delight** or **joy** is greater than a **pleasure**; a person, especially a child, can be a **delight** or **joy**, but not a **pleasure**; **joys** are often contrasted with **sorrows**, but **delights** are not.

**privilege** (*rather formal*) something that you are proud and lucky to have the opportunity to do: *It was a great privilege to hear her sing.*

**treat** (*informal*) a thing that sb enjoyed or is likely to enjoy very much: *You've never been to this area before? Then you're in for a real treat.*

**honour** (*formal*) something that you are very pleased or proud to do because people are showing you great respect: *It was a great honour to be invited here today.*

**PATTERNS**
- the pleasures / delights / joys **of sth**
- It's a great pleasure / joy **to me that ...**
- It's a pleasure / delight / joy / privilege / treat / honour **to do sth**
- It's a pleasure / delight / joy **to see / find ...**
- a pleasure / delight / joy **to behold / watch**
- a **real** pleasure / delight / joy / privilege / treat
- a **great** pleasure / joy / privilege / honour
- a **rare** joy / privilege / treat / honour

**ˈpleasure boat** (*also* **ˈpleasure craft**) *noun* a boat used for short pleasure trips

**pleat** /pliːt/ *noun* a permanent fold in a piece of cloth, made by SEWING the top or side of the fold

**pleat·ed** /ˈpliːtɪd/ *adj.* having pleats: *a pleated skirt*

**plea·ther** /ˈpleðə(r)/ *noun* [U] a plastic material that looks like leather: *a pleather jacket* **ORIGIN** From **plastic** and **leather**

**pleb** /pleb/ *noun* (*informal*, *disapproving*) an offensive word for an ordinary person, especially one who is poor or not well educated

**plebe** /pliːb/ *noun* (*US*, *informal*) a first-year student at a military or NAVAL college in the US

**ple·beian** /pləˈbiːən/ *adj.*, *noun*
▪ *adj.* 1 connected with ordinary people or people of the lower social classes 2 (*disapproving*) having or showing no culture or education: *plebeian tastes*
▪ *noun* (*usually disapproving*) a person from a lower social class (used originally in ancient Rome) ⇨ compare PATRICIAN

**pleb·is·cite** /ˈplebɪsaɪt; *BrE also* -sɪt/ *noun* **~ (on sth)** (*politics*) a vote by the people of a country or a region on an issue that is very important **SYN** referendum: *to hold a plebiscite on the country's future system of government*

**plec·trum** /ˈplektrəm/ *noun* (*pl.* **ˈplec·trums** or **ˈplec·tra** /-trə/) (*also informal* **pick**) a small piece of metal, plastic, etc. used for PLUCKING the strings of a guitar or similar instrument

**pled** /pled/ (NAmE) past tense, past part. of PLEAD

**pledge** ?+ B1 /pledʒ/ verb, noun
- verb 1 ?+ B1 [T] to formally promise to give or do sth: ~ **sth** *Japan has pledged $100 million in humanitarian aid.* ◊ *The government pledged their support for the plan.* ◊ **~ sth to sb/sth** *We all had to pledge allegiance to the flag* (= state that we are loyal to our country). ◊ **~ to do sth** *The group has pledged to continue campaigning.* ◊ **~ (that) … ** *The group has pledged that they will continue campaigning.* 2 [T] to make sb or yourself formally promise to do sth SYN swear: **~ sb/yourself (to sth)** *They were all pledged to secrecy.* ◊ **~ sb/yourself to do sth** *The government has pledged itself to root out corruption.* 3 [T] **~ sth** to leave sth with sb as a pledge 4 [I, T] (NAmE) **~ sth** to promise to become a junior member of a FRATERNITY or SORORITY: *Do you think you'll pledge this semester?* ◊ **~ sth** *My brother pledged Sigma Nu* (= promised to join the Sigma Nu FRATERNITY)
- noun 1 ?+ B1 a serious promise SYN **commitment**: **~ (of sth)** *a pledge of support* ◊ **~ to do sth** *Will the government honour its* **election pledge** *not to raise taxes?* ◊ **~ that …** *Management has* **made a pledge** *that there will be no job losses this year.* 2 a sum of money or sth valuable that you leave with sb to prove that you will do sth or pay back money that you owe
- IDM **sign/take the 'pledge** (old-fashioned) to make a promise never to drink alcohol

**the Pledge of Al'legiance** noun [sing.] a formal promise to be LOYAL to the US, which Americans make standing in front of the flag with their right hand on their heart

**plen·ary** /ˈpliːnəri/ adj., noun
- adj. [only before noun] (formal) 1 (of meetings, etc.) to be attended by everyone who has the right to attend: *The new committee holds its first* **plenary session** *this week.* ⊃ WORDFINDER NOTE at CONFERENCE 2 without any limit; complete: *The Council has plenary powers to administer the agreement.*
- noun (pl. **-ies**) a plenary meeting

**pleni·po·ten·tiary** /ˌplenɪpəˈtenʃəri; NAmE -ʃieri/ noun (pl. **-ies**) (specialist) a person who has full powers to take action, make decisions, etc. to represent their government, especially in a foreign country ▶ **pleni·po·ten·tiary** adj.: *plenipotentiary powers*

**pleni·tude** /ˈplenɪtjuːd; NAmE -tuːd/ noun [sing., U] (formal) a large amount of sth SYN **abundance**

**plent·eous** /ˈplentiəs/ adj. (literary) = PLENTIFUL

**plen·ti·ful** /ˈplentɪfl/ (also literary **plent·eous**) adj. available or existing in large amounts or numbers SYN **abundant**: *a plentiful supply of food* ◊ *In those days jobs were plentiful.* ▶ **plen·ti·ful·ly** /-fəli/ adv.: *Evidence is plentifully available.* ◊ *She kept them plentifully supplied with gossip.*

**plenty** 🔵 B1 /ˈplenti/ pron., adv., noun, det.
- pron. ?+ B1 **~ (of sth)** a large amount; as much or as many as you need: *plenty of eggs/money/time* ◊ *'Do we need more milk?' 'No, there's plenty in the fridge.'* ◊ *They always gave us plenty to eat.* ◊ *We had plenty to talk about.* ⊃ note at MANY, MUCH
- adv. 1 **~ more (of) (sth)** a lot: *We have plenty more of them in the warehouse.* ◊ *There's plenty more paper if you need it.* 2 **~ big, long, etc. enough (to do sth)** (informal) more than big, long, etc. enough: *The rope was plenty long enough to reach the ground.* 3 (NAmE) a lot; very: *We talked plenty about our kids.* ◊ *You can be married and still be plenty lonely.* IDM see FISH n.
- noun [U] (formal) a situation in which there is a large supply of food, money, etc: *Everyone is happier* **in times of plenty.** ◊ **in ~** *We had food and drink in plenty.*
- det. (NAmE or informal) a lot of: *There's plenty room for all of you!*

**ple·num** /ˈpliːnəm/ noun a meeting attended by all the members of a committee, etc.; a PLENARY meeting

**pleth·ora** /ˈpleθərə/ noun [sing.] (formal) an amount that is greater than is needed or can be used SYN **excess**

**pleura** /ˈplʊərə; NAmE ˈplʊrə/ noun (pl. **pleurae** /-riː/) (anatomy) one of the two MEMBRANES that surround the lungs

1181 **plot**

**pleur·isy** /ˈplʊərəsi; NAmE ˈplʊr-/ noun [U] a serious illness that affects the inner surface of the chest and lungs, causing severe pain in the chest or sides

**Plexi·glas**™ /ˈpleksɪɡlɑːs; NAmE -ɡlæs/ (NAmE) (BrE **Perspex**™) noun [U] a strong clear plastic material that is often used instead of glass

**plexus** ⊃ SOLAR PLEXUS

**pli·able** /ˈplaɪəbl/ adj. 1 easy to bend without breaking SYN **flexible** 2 (of people) easy to influence or control SYN **impressionable**

**pli·ant** /ˈplaɪənt/ adj. 1 soft and bending easily: *The leather is soft and pliant.* 2 (sometimes disapproving) willing to accept change; easy to influence or control: *He was deposed and replaced by a more pliant successor.* ▶ **pli·ancy** /-ənsi/ noun [U]

**pli·ers** /ˈplaɪəz; NAmE -ərz/ noun [pl.] a metal tool with handles, used for holding things and TWISTING and cutting wire: *a pair of pliers* ⊃ picture at SPANNER

**plight** /plaɪt/ noun, verb
- noun [sing.] a difficult and sad situation: *the plight of the homeless* ◊ *The African elephant is in a desperate plight.*
- verb
- IDM **plight your 'troth** (old use or humorous) to make a promise to a person saying that you will marry them; to marry sb

**plim·soll** /ˈplɪmsəl, -səʊl/ (also **pump**) (also old-fashioned **'gym shoe**) (all BrE) noun a light simple sports shoe made of CANVAS (= strong cotton cloth) with a rubber SOLE: *a pair of plimsolls*

**plinth** /plɪnθ/ noun a block of stone on which a column or statue stands

**plod** /plɒd; NAmE plɑːd/ verb (**-dd-**) [I, T] to walk slowly with heavy steps, especially because you are tired SYN **trudge**: **+ adv./prep.** *We plodded on through the rain.* ◊ **~ your way + adv./prep.** *I watched her plodding her way across the field.* ▶ **plod** noun [sing.]
- PHRV **plod a'long/'on** to make very slow progress, especially with difficult or boring work SYN **slog**

**plod·der** /ˈplɒdə(r); NAmE ˈplɑːd-/ noun a person who works slowly and steadily but without imagination

**plod·ding** /ˈplɒdɪŋ; NAmE ˈplɑːd-/ adj. working or doing sth slowly and steadily, especially in a way that other people think is boring

**plonk** /plɒŋk; NAmE plɑːŋk/ verb, noun
- verb (especially BrE) (NAmE usually **plunk**) (informal) 1 **~ sth + adv./prep.** to put sth down on sth, especially noisily or carelessly: *He plonked the books down on the table.* 2 **~ yourself (down)** to sit down heavily or carelessly: *He just plonked himself down and turned on the TV.*
- noun (especially BrE, informal) 1 [U] cheap wine that is not of good quality 2 [C, usually sing.] a low sound like that of sth heavy falling and hitting a surface: *She sat down with a plonk.*

**plonk·er** /ˈplɒŋkə(r); NAmE ˈplɑːŋ-/ noun (BrE, slang) a stupid person

**plop** /plɒp; NAmE plɑːp/ noun, verb
- noun [usually sing.] a short sound like that of a small object dropping into water
- verb (**-pp-**) 1 [I] **+ adv./prep.** to fall, making a plop: *The frog plopped back into the water.* ◊ *A tear plopped down onto the page she was reading.* 2 [T] **~ sth + adv./prep.** to drop sth into sth, especially a liquid, so that it makes a plop: *Can you just plop some ice in my drink?* 3 [T, I] **~ (yourself) (down)** to sit or lie down heavily or in a relaxed way

**plot** 🔵 B1 /plɒt; NAmE plɑːt/ noun, verb
- noun 1 ?+ B1 [C, U] **~ (about sth)** the series of events that form the story of a novel, play, film, etc: *a conventional plot about love and marriage* ◊ *The book is well organized in terms of plot.* ⊃ WORDFINDER NOTE at BOOK

**WORDFINDER** dialogue, ending, flashback, narrate, scenario, scene, storyline, tension, twist

# plotter

**2** 🔑 B2 [C] a secret plan made by a group of people to do sth wrong or illegal **SYN** **conspiracy**: *~(to do sth) a murder plot* ◊ *~against sb Police uncovered a plot against the president.* **3** [C] a small piece of land that is used or intended for a special purpose: *She bought a small plot of land to build a house on.* ◊ *a vegetable plot* ⊃ SYNONYMS at LAND
**IDM** **lose the ˈplot** (*BrE, informal*) to lose your ability to understand or deal with what is happening **the plot ˈthickens** (*humorous*) used to say that a situation is becoming more complicated and difficult to understand
■ *verb* (-tt-) **1** 🔑 B2 [I, T] to make a secret plan to harm sb, especially a government or its leader **SYN** **conspire**: *~(with sb) (against sb) They were accused of plotting against the state.* ◊ *~(with sb) to do sth They were plotting to overthrow the government.* ◊ *~sth Military officers were suspected of plotting a coup.* **2** [T] *~sth (on sth)* to mark sth on a map, for example the position or course of sth: *The earthquake centres had been plotted on a world map.* **3** [T] *~sth (on sth)* to make a diagram or chart from some information: *We carefully plotted each patient's response to the drug on a chart.* **4** [T] *~sth (on sth)* to mark points on a GRAPH and draw a line or curve connecting them: *First, plot the temperature curve on the graph.* **5** [T] *~sth* to write the plot of a novel, play, etc: *a tightly-plotted thriller*

**plot·ter** /ˈplɒtə(r); *NAmE* ˈplɑːt-/ *noun* **1** a person who makes a secret plan to harm sb **SYN** **conspirator** **2** a device that turns data from a computer into a GRAPH

**plough** (*BrE*) (*NAmE* **plow**) /plaʊ/ *noun, verb*
■ *noun* **1** [C] a large piece of farming equipment with one or several curved BLADES (= metal cutting parts), pulled by a TRACTOR or by animals. It is used for digging and turning over soil, especially before seeds are planted. ⊃ see also SNOWPLOUGH *noun* **2** **the Plough** (*BrE*) (*NAmE* **the ˈBig ˈDipper**) [sing.] a group of seven bright stars that can only be seen from the northern half of the world
**IDM** **under the ˈplough** (*BrE, formal*) (of land) used for growing crops, not for keeping animals on **SYN** **arable**
■ *verb* [T, I] *~(sth)* to dig and turn over a field or other area of land with a plough: *ploughed fields*
**IDM** **plough a lonely, your own, etc., ˈfurrow** (*literary*) to do things that other people do not do, or be interested in things that other people are not interested in
**PHRV** **ˌplough sthˌ↔ˈback (in/into sth)** | **ˌplough sthˌ↔ˈback ˈin** **1** to turn over growing crops, grass, etc. with a plough and mix them into the soil to improve its quality **2** to put money made as profit back into a business in order to improve it: *The money was all ploughed back into the company.* **ˌplough ˈinto sb/sth** (especially of a vehicle or its driver) to crash violently into sth, especially because you are driving too fast or not paying enough attention: *A truck ploughed into the back of the bus.* **ˌplough sth ˈinto sth** to invest a large amount of money in a company or project: *The government has ploughed more than $20 billion into building new schools.* **ˌplough ˈon (with sth)** to continue doing sth that is difficult or boring: *No one was listening to her, but she ploughed on regardless.* **ˌplough (your way) ˈthrough sth** **1** to force a way through sth: *She ploughed her way through the waiting crowds.* **2** (of a vehicle or an aircraft) to go violently through sth, out of control: *The plane ploughed through the trees.* **3** to make slow progress through sth difficult or boring, especially a book, a report, etc: *I had to plough through dozens of legal documents.* **ˌplough sthˌ↔ˈup** **1** to turn over a field or other area of land with a plough to change it from grass, for example, to land for growing crops **2** to break up the surface of the ground by walking or driving across it again and again: *The paths get all ploughed up by motorbikes.*

**plough·man** (*BrE*) (*NAmE* **plow·man**) /ˈplaʊmən/ *noun* (*pl.* -men /-mən/) a man whose job is guiding a plough, especially one pulled by animals

**ploughman's ˈlunch** (*also* **ˈploughman's**) *noun* (*BrE*) a cold meal of bread, cheese, PICKLE and salad, often served in pubs

**plough·share** (*BrE*) (*NAmE* **plow·share**) /ˈplaʊʃeə(r); *NAmE* -ʃer/ (*NAmE also* **share**) *noun* the broad curved BLADE (= metal cutting part) of a plough **IDM** see SWORD

**plover** /ˈplʌvə(r); *NAmE also* ˈploʊv-/ *noun* a bird with long legs and a short tail that lives on wet ground

**plow, plow·man, plow·share** (*NAmE*) = PLOUGH, PLOUGHMAN, PLOUGHSHARE

**ploy** /plɔɪ/ *noun* words or actions that are carefully planned to get an advantage over sb else **SYN** **manoeuvre**: *a clever marketing ploy* ◊ *~to do sth It was all a ploy to distract attention from his real aims.* ◊ *~for doing sth a ploy for deflecting criticism*

**pluck** /plʌk/ *verb, noun*
■ *verb*
• HAIR **1** [T] *~sth (out)* to pull out hairs with your fingers or with TWEEZERS: *She plucked out a grey hair.* ◊ *expertly plucked eyebrows*
• CHICKEN, ETC. **2** [T] *~sth* to pull the feathers off a dead bird, for example a chicken, in order to prepare it for cooking
• MUSICAL INSTRUMENT **3** (*NAmE also* **pick**) [T, I] *~(at) sth* to play a musical instrument, especially a guitar, by pulling the strings with your fingers: *to pluck the strings of a violin* ◊ *He took the guitar and plucked at the strings.*
• REMOVE SB/STH **4** [T] *~sb (from sth) (to sth)* to remove sb from a place or situation, especially one that is unpleasant or dangerous: *Police plucked a drowning girl from the river yesterday.* ◊ *Survivors of the wreck were plucked to safety by a helicopter.* ◊ *She was plucked from obscurity to instant stardom.* **5** [T] *~sth (from sth)* to take hold of sth and remove it by pulling it: *He plucked the wallet from the man's grasp.*
• FRUIT/FLOWER **6** [T] *~sth (from sth)* (*old-fashioned or literary*) to pick a fruit, flower, etc. from where it is growing: *I plucked an orange from the tree.*
**IDM** **pluck sth out of the ˈair** to say a name, number, etc. without thinking about it, especially in answer to a question: *I just plucked a figure out of the air and said : 'Would £1000 seem reasonable to you?'* **pluck up (the) ˈcourage (to do sth)** to make yourself do sth even though you are afraid to do it: *I finally plucked up the courage to ask her for a date.*
**PHRV** **ˈpluck at sth** to hold sth with the fingers and pull it gently, especially more than once **SYN** **tug**: *The child kept plucking at his mother's sleeve.* ◊ (*figurative*) *The wind plucked at my jacket.*
■ *noun* [U] (*old-fashioned, informal*) the quality of being brave and determined: *It takes a lot of pluck to do what she did.*

**plucky** /ˈplʌki/ *adj.* (**pluck·ier**, **plucki·est**) (*informal*) having a lot of courage; being very determined **SYN** **brave**
▶ **pluck·ily** *adv.*

**plugs**

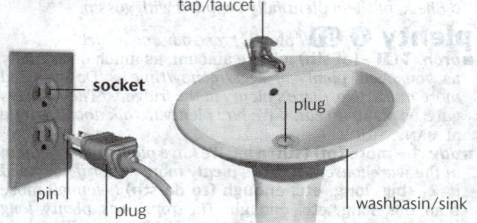

**plug** 🔑 C1 /plʌg/ *verb, noun*
■ *verb* (-gg-)
• FILL HOLE **1** 🔑 C1 *~sth (up)* to fill a hole with a substance or piece of material that fits tightly into it: *He plugged the hole in the pipe with an old rag.*
• PROVIDE STH MISSING **2** 🔑 C1 *~sth* to provide sth that has been missing from a particular situation and is needed in order to improve it: *A cheaper range of products was introduced to plug the gap at the lower end of the market.*
• BOOK/MOVIE **3** *~sth* (*informal*) to give praise or attention to a new book, film, etc. in order to encourage people to buy it or see it **SYN** **promote**: *She came on the show to plug her latest album.*

- **SHOOT** 4 ~ sb (NAmE, old-fashioned, informal) to shoot sb

**PHR V** ˌplug aˈway (at sth) to continue working hard at sth, especially sth that you find difficult ˌplug sth↔ˈin | ˌplug sth ˈinto sth to connect a piece of electrical equipment to the main supply of electricity or to another piece of electrical equipment: *Is the printer plugged in?* **OPP** unplug ˌplug sth ˈinto sth 1 = PLUG STH IN 2 to connect a computer to a computer system: *All our computers are plugged into the main network.* ˌplug ˈinto sth 1 (of a piece of electrical equipment) to be able to be connected to the main supply of electricity or to another piece of electrical equipment: *This Bluetooth speaker plugs into any standard outlet.* 2 to become involved with a particular activity or group of people: *The company has doubled its profits since plugging into lucrative overseas markets.*

■ noun
- **ELECTRICAL EQUIPMENT 1** a small plastic object with two or three metal pins that connects a piece of electrical equipment to the main supply of electricity: *a three-pin plug* ◊ *I'll have to change the plug on my hairdryer.* **2** (especially BrE, informal) a small opening in a wall, by which you connect a piece of electrical equipment to the main supply of electricity **SYN** socket: *Can I use this plug for my iron?* **3** a small object that connects a wire from one piece of electrical equipment to an opening in another: *the plug from the computer to the printer* ⊃ see also JACK PLUG
- **IN ENGINE 4** = SPARK PLUG
- **IN BATH/SINK 5** a thick round piece of plastic, rubber or metal that you put into the hole in a bath or a SINK to stop the water flowing out: *She pulled out the plug and let the water drain away.* ⊃ SYNONYMS at LID
- **IN HOLE 6** a round piece of material that fits into a hole and blocks it: *She took the plug of cotton wool from her ear.* ⊃ see also EARPLUG **7** (NAmE) = STOPPER ⊃ SYNONYMS at LID
- **FOR SCREW 8** a small plastic tube that you put into a hole in a wall so that it will hold a SCREW
- **FOR BOOK/MOVIE 9** (informal) praise or attention that sb gives to a new book, film, etc. in order to encourage people to buy or see it: *He managed to get in a plug for his new book.* **IDM** see PULL v.

ˌPlug and ˈPlay noun [U] (computing) a system that makes it possible for a piece of equipment, such as a printer, to be connected to a computer and to work immediately, without the user needing to do anything ▶ ˌplug-and-ˈplay adj.: *plug-and-play peripherals*

**plug-hole** /ˈplʌɡhəʊl/ (BrE) (US drain) noun a hole in a bath, SINK, etc. where the water flows away and into which a plug fits
**IDM** (go) down the ˈplughole (BrE) = (GO) DOWN THE DRAIN at DRAIN n.

ˈplug-in adj., noun
■ adj. [only before noun] **1** able to be connected to an electricity supply using a plug: *a plug-in kettle* **2** (computing) able to be added to a computer system so that it can do more things: *a plug-in graphics card*
■ noun **1** (computing) a piece of computer software that can be added to a system so that it can do more things **2** (CanE) a connection to an electricity supply in a garage, etc. so that you can use an electric HEATER to warm the engine of a car, so that it starts more easily

**plum** /plʌm/ noun, adj.
■ noun **1** [C] a soft round fruit with smooth red or purple skin, that is sweet inside with a large flat seed: *a plum tree* ⊃ VISUAL VOCAB page V4 **2** [U, C] a dark colour between red and purple
■ adj. [only before noun] (of a job, etc.) considered very good and worth having: *She's landed a plum job at the BBC.*

**plum·age** /ˈpluːmɪdʒ/ noun [U] the feathers covering a bird's body

**plumb** /plʌm/ verb, adv.
■ verb ~ sth (literary) to try to understand or succeed in understanding sth mysterious **SYN** fathom: *She spent her life plumbing the mysteries of the human psyche.*
**IDM** plumb the depths of sth to be or to experience an extreme example of sth unpleasant: *His latest novel plumbs the depths of horror and violence.* ◊ *The team's poor performances plumbed new depths last night when they lost 10–2.*

**PHR V** ˌplumb sth↔ˈin (especially BrE) to connect a WASHING MACHINE, toilet, etc. to the water supply in a building
■ adv. **1** (used before prepositions) exactly: *He was standing plumb in the middle of the road.* **2** (NAmE, old-fashioned, informal) completely: *He's plumb crazy.*

**plumb·er** /ˈplʌmə(r)/ noun a person whose job is to fit and repair things such as water pipes, toilets, etc.

**plumb·ing** /ˈplʌmɪŋ/ noun [U] **1** the system of pipes, etc. that supply water to a building **2** the work of a plumber

**plume** /pluːm/ noun **1** a cloud of sth that rises and curves upwards in the air: *a plume of smoke* **2** a large feather: *a black hat with an ostrich plume* **3** a group of feathers or long thin pieces of material tied together and often used as a decoration ⊃ see also NOM DE PLUME

**plumed** /pluːmd/ adj. having or decorated with a plume or plumes: *a plumed helmet*

**plum·met** /ˈplʌmɪt/ verb [I] to fall suddenly and quickly from a high level or position **SYN** plunge: *Share prices plummeted to an all-time low.* ◊ *Her spirits plummeted at the thought of meeting him again.* ◊ *The jet plummeted into a row of houses.* ⊃ WORDFINDER NOTE at TREND

**plummy** /ˈplʌmi/ adj. **1** (BrE, informal, usually disapproving) (of a voice) having a sound that is typical of upper-class English people: *a plummy accent* **2** like a PLUM in colour, taste, etc.

**plump** /plʌmp/ adj., verb
■ adj. (plump·er, plump·est) **1** having a soft, round body; slightly fat: *a short, plump woman* ◊ *a plump face* **2** looking soft, full and attractive to use or eat: *plump cushions* ◊ *plump tomatoes* ▶ **plump·ness** noun [U]
■ verb ~ sth (up) to make sth larger, softer and rounder: *He leaned forward while the nurse plumped up his pillows.*
**PHR V** ˈplump for sb/sth (informal) to choose sb/sth from a number of people or things, especially after thinking carefully

ˌplum ˈpudding noun [U, C] (BrE, old-fashioned) a hot PUDDING (= sweet dish) like a dark fruit cake, traditionally eaten in the UK at Christmas **SYN** Christmas pudding

ˌplum toˈmato noun a type of tomato that is long and thin, rather than round

**plun·der** /ˈplʌndə(r)/ verb, noun
■ verb [I, T] to steal things from a place, especially using force during a time of war **SYN** pillage: *The troops crossed the country, plundering and looting as they went.* ◊ ~ sth (of sth) *The abbey had been plundered of its valuables.* ◊ ~ sth (from sth) *Only a small amount of the money that he plundered from his companies has been recovered.* ⊃ compare LOOT(1) ▶ **plun·der·er** noun
■ noun [U] **1** the act of plundering **2** things that have been stolen, especially during a war, etc. **SYN** loot ⊃ compare PILLAGE

**plunge** /plʌndʒ/ verb, noun
■ verb **1** [I, T] to move or make sb/sth move suddenly forwards and/or downwards: + adv./prep. *She lost her balance and plunged 100 feet to her death.* ◊ *The train left the track and plunged down the embankment.* ◊ ~ sb/sth + adv./prep. *The earthquake plunged entire towns over the edge of the cliffs.* **2** [I] (of prices, temperatures, etc.) to decrease suddenly and quickly **SYN** plummet: *Stock markets plunged at the news of the coup.* ◊ *This year profits plunged by 40 per cent.* **3** [I] + adv./prep. (of a road, surface, etc.) to slope down steeply: *The track plunged down into the valley.* **4** [I] to move up and down suddenly and violently: *The horse plunged and reared.* ◊ (figurative) *His heart plunged* (= because of a strong emotion).
**PHR V** ˌplunge ˈin | ˌplunge ˈinto sth **1** to jump into sth, especially with force: *The pool was declared open and eager swimmers plunged in.* **2** to start doing sth in an enthusiastic way, especially without thinking carefully about what you are doing: *She was about to plunge into her story when the phone rang.* ◊ *He's always plunging in at the deep end* (= becoming involved in difficult situations without being well enough prepared). ˌplunge sth ˈin | ˌplunge sth ˈinto sth to push sth quickly and with force into sth else: *She plunged the knife deep into his chest.*

**plunge into sth 1** = PLUNGE IN **2** to experience sth unpleasant: *The country plunged deeper into recession.*
**plunge sb/sth into sth** to make sb/sth experience sth unpleasant: *The news plunged them into deep depression.* ◇ *There was a flash of lightning and the house was plunged into darkness.*
- **noun** [usually sing.] **1** a sudden movement downwards or away from sth SYN **drop**: *The calm water ends there and the river begins a headlong plunge.* **2 ~ (in sth)** a sudden decrease in an amount or the value of sth SYN **drop 3 ~ into sth** the act of becoming involved in a situation or activity: *The company is planning a deeper plunge into the commercial market.* **4** an act of jumping or DIVING into water; a quick swim: *She went for a plunge.*
IDM **take the ˈplunge** (*informal*) to decide to do sth important or difficult, especially after thinking about it for a long time

**ˈplunge pool** *noun* a small deep artificial pool filled with cold water, especially one that you jump into in order to get cooler after a SAUNA

**plun·ger** /ˈplʌndʒə(r)/ *noun* **1** a part of a piece of equipment that can be pushed down **2** a piece of equipment used for clearing kitchen and bathroom pipes, that consists of a rubber cup fixed to a handle

**plun·ging** /ˈplʌndʒɪŋ/ *adj.* [only before noun] (of a dress, BLOUSE, etc.) cut in a deep V shape at the front: *a plunging neckline*

**plunk** /plʌŋk/ *verb* (*informal*) **1 ~ sth + adv./prep.** (*NAmE*) = PLONK: *He plunked the package down on the desk.* **2 ~ sth** to play a guitar, a keyboard, etc. with your fingers and produce a rough unpleasant sound ▶ **plunk** *noun*: *the plunk, plunk of the banjo*
PHRV **ˈplunk down sth** to pay money for sth, especially a large amount

**plu·per·fect** /ˌpluːˈpɜːfɪkt; *NAmE* -ˈpɜːrf-/ *noun* (*grammar*) = PAST PERFECT

**plural** /ˈplʊərəl; *NAmE* ˈplʊr-/ *noun, adj.*
- **noun** (*abbr.* **pl.**) (*grammar*) a form of a noun or verb that refers to more than one person or thing: *The plural of 'child' is 'children'.* ◇ **in the ~** *The verb should be in the plural.* ⊃ compare SINGULAR
- **adj. 1** (*abbr.* **pl.**) (*grammar*) connected with or having the plural form: *Most plural nouns in English end in 's'.* **2** relating to more than one: *a plural society* (= one with more than one RACIAL, religious, etc. group)

**plur·al·ism** /ˈplʊərəlɪzəm; *NAmE* ˈplʊr-/ *noun* [U] (*formal*) **1** the existence of many different groups of people in one society, for example people of different races or of different political or religious beliefs: *cultural pluralism* **2** the belief that it is possible and good for different groups of people to live together in peace in one society **3** (*usually disapproving*) the fact of having more than one job or position at the same time, especially in the Church

**plur·al·ist** /ˈplʊərəlɪst; *NAmE* ˈplʊr-/ *adj., noun*
- **adj.** (*also* **plur·al·is·tic** /ˌplʊərəˈlɪstɪk; *NAmE* ˌplʊr-/) **1** (of a society) having many different groups of people and different political parties in it: *a pluralist democracy* **2** (*philosophy*) not based on a single set of principles or beliefs: *a pluralist approach to politics*
- **noun 1** a person who believes that it is possible and good for different groups of people to live together in peace in our society **2** a person who has more than one job or position at the same time, especially in the Church

**plur·al·ity** /plʊəˈræləti; *NAmE* plʊˈr-/ *noun* (*pl.* **-ies**) **1** [C, usually sing.] (*formal*) a large number: *a plurality of influences* **2** [C, usually sing.] (*US, politics*) the number of votes given to one person, political party, etc. when this number is less than 50% but more than any other single person, etc. receives: *In order to be elected, the candidate needs only a plurality of the votes cast.* ⊃ compare MAJORITY (3) **3** [U] (*grammar*) the state of being plural

**plus¹** /plʌs/ *prep., adj., noun, conj.*
- **prep. 1** used when the two numbers or amounts mentioned are being added together: *Two plus five is seven.* ◇ *The cost is £22, plus £1 for postage.* **2** as well as sth/sb; and also: *We have to fit five of us plus all our gear in the car.* OPP minus
IDM **ˌplus or ˈminus** used when the number mentioned may actually be more or less by a particular amount: *The margin of error was plus or minus three percentage points.* ⊃ compare GIVE OR TAKE
- **adj. 1** used after a number to show that the real number or amount is more than the one mentioned: *The work will cost £10000 plus.* **2** above zero: *The temperature is plus four degrees.* OPP minus **3** [only before noun] used to describe an aspect of sth that you consider to be a good thing: *One of the hotel's plus points is that it is very central.* ◇ *On the plus side, all the staff are enthusiastic.* OPP minus **4** [not before noun] (used in a system of grades) slightly higher than the grade A, B, etc: *I got B plus (B+) in the test.* OPP minus
- **noun 1** (*informal*) an advantage; a good thing: *Knowledge of French is a plus in her job.* ◇ *There were a lot of pluses in the performance.* ◇ **~ for sb/sth** *Ease of use is a big plus for any game.* **2** (*also* **ˈplus sign**) the symbol (+), used in mathematics: *He put a plus instead of a minus.* OPP minus
- **conj.** (*informal*) used to add more information SYN **furthermore**: *I've got too much on at work. Plus my father is not well.*

**plus²** /plʌs/
IDM **plus ça change** /ˌpluː sæ ˈʃɒʒ; *NAmE* ˌpluː sɑː ˈʃɑːnʒ/ (from French, *saying*) used as a way of saying that people and situations never really change over time, although they may appear to

**plush** /plʌʃ/ *noun, adj.*
- **noun** [U] a type of silk or cotton cloth with a thick soft surface made of a mass of THREADS: *red plush armchairs*
- **adj.** (*informal*) very comfortable; expensive and of good quality SYN **luxurious**: *a plush hotel*

**plus-ˈminus** *adv.* (*SAfrE*) (used when you are giving a figure that is not exact) approximately: *'How many people were there?' 'Plus-minus thirty.'*

**ˈplus-size** (*also* **ˈplus-sized**) *adj.* [usually before noun] **1** (of women's clothes) designed to fit larger women: *plus-size clothing/fashions* **2** (of a woman) large or fat HELP It is not polite to call sb *fat*. **Plus-size** is a polite and positive word to describe larger women.: *plus-size models*

**Pluto** /ˈpluːtəʊ/ *noun* one of a number of round objects in space that are not as large as planets but which go around the sun. In August 2006, the International Astronomical Union declared that Pluto should be called a DWARF PLANET because it is smaller and has different characteristics from the other planets in our SOLAR SYSTEM; in 2008 it declared that DWARF PLANETS further from the sun than Neptune could also be called plutoids.

**plu·toc·racy** /pluːˈtɒkrəsi; *NAmE* -ˈtɑːk-/ *noun* (*pl.* **-ies**) **1** [U] government by the richest people of a country **2** [C] a country governed by the richest people in it

**plu·to·crat** /ˈpluːtəkræt/ *noun* (*often disapproving*) a person who is powerful because of their wealth

**plu·to·nium** /pluːˈtəʊniəm; *NAmE* -ˈtoʊ-/ *noun* [U] (*symb.* **Pu**) a chemical element. Plutonium is RADIOACTIVE and is used in nuclear weapons and in producing nuclear energy.

**ply** /plaɪ/ *verb, noun*
- **verb** (**plies**, **ply·ing**, **plied**, **plied**) **1** [I, T] (*literary or IndE*) (of ships, buses, etc.) to travel regularly along a particular route or between two particular places: **+ adv./prep.** *Ferries ply across a narrow strait to the island.* ◇ *Buses ply regularly to and from these places.* ◇ **~ sth** *canals plied by gondolas and steam boats* **2** [T] **~ sth** (*formal*) to use a tool, especially with skill: *The tailor delicately plied his needle.*
IDM **ply for ˈhire/ˈtrade/ˈbusiness** (*BrE*) to look for customers, passengers, etc. in order to do business: *taxis plying for hire outside the theatre* **ply your ˈtrade** to do your work or business
PHRV **ˈply sb with sth 1** to keep giving sb large amounts of sth, especially food and/or drink **2** to keep asking sb questions: *He plied me with questions from the moment he arrived.*
- **noun** [U] (especially in compounds) a measurement of wool, rope, wood, etc. that tells you how thick it is: *four-ply knitting yarn*

**ply·wood** /ˈplaɪwʊd/ noun [U] board made by sticking thin layers of wood on top of each other: *plywood furniture*

**plz** /pliːz/ adv. (informal, non-standard) an informal way of writing 'please', for example in an email or text to a friend: *For details plz look at this website.* **HELP** You should not write this form in formal or standard writing.

**PM** /ˌpiː ˈem/ noun
▪ noun (informal) **1** (especially BrE) the main minister and leader of the government in some countries (the abbreviation for 'prime minister'): *an interview with the PM* **2** a private message (= one that only the person who wrote it and the person who they sent it to can read) on SOCIAL MEDIA or an online FORUM
▪ verb [T, I] (**PM'd**, **PM'd** or **PMed**, **PMed**) (informal) to send sb a private message (= one that only the person who wrote it and the person who they sent it to can read) on SOCIAL MEDIA or an online FORUM: *~ sb (sth) You should PM me your address.* ◊ *~ sth (to sb) I'll PM my address to you.* ◊ **+ adv./prep.** *She PM'd back right away.*

**p.m.** (NAmE also **P.M.**) /ˌpiː ˈem/ abbr. after 12 o'clock NOON (from Latin 'post meridiem'): *The appointment is at 3 p.m.* ⊃ compare A.M.

**PMS** /ˌpiː em ˈes/ (also **PMT** /ˌpiː em ˈtiː/ BrE) noun [U] physical and emotional problems such as pain and feeling depressed that many women experience before their PERIOD (= flow of blood) each month. PMS/PMT are abbreviations for 'premenstrual syndrome/tension'. ⊃ see also PREMENSTRUAL

**pneu·mat·ic** /njuːˈmætɪk; NAmE nuː-/ adj. [usually before noun] **1** filled with air: *a pneumatic tyre* **2** worked by air under pressure: *pneumatic tools*

**pneu.matic ˈdrill** (BrE) (NAmE **jack·ham·mer**) noun a large powerful tool, worked by air pressure, used especially for breaking up road surfaces

**pneu·mo·nia** /njuːˈməʊniə; NAmE nuː-/ noun [U] a serious illness affecting one or both lungs that makes breathing difficult

**PO** abbr. (in writing) **1** THE POST OFFICE ⊃ see also PO BOX **2** POSTAL ORDER

**poach** /pəʊtʃ/ verb **1** [T] *~ sth* to cook food, especially fish, gently in a small amount of liquid: *poached salmon* **2** [T] *~ sth* to cook an egg gently in nearly boiling water after removing its shell **3** [T, I] *~ (sth)* to illegally hunt birds, animals or fish on sb else's property or without permission: *The elephants are poached for their tusks.* ⊃ WORDFINDER NOTE at HUNT **4** [T, I] to take and use sb/sth that belongs to sb/sth else, especially in a secret, dishonest or unfair way: *~ sb/sth from sb/sth The company poached the contract from their main rivals.* ◊ *~ (sb/sth) Several of our employees have been poached by a rival firm.* ◊ *I hope I'm not poaching on your territory* (= doing sth that is actually your responsibility).

**poach·er** /ˈpəʊtʃə(r)/ noun **1** a person who illegally hunts birds, animals or fish on sb's else's property **2** a special pan for POACHING eggs **3** (also **ˈgoal poacher**) (especially in football (soccer)) a player who waits near the opposite team's goal in order to try to score if they get the ball
**IDM** **ˌpoacher turned ˈgamekeeper** (especially BrE) a person who has changed from one situation or attitude to the opposite one, especially sb who used to oppose people in authority but is now in a position of authority

**ˈPO box** /ˌpiː əʊ ˈbɒks; NAmE bɑːks/ (also **ˌpost office ˈbox**) noun used as a kind of address, so that mail can be sent to a post office where it is kept until it is collected: *Radio Netherlands, PO box 222, Hilversum*

**pocked** /pɒkt; NAmE pɑːkt/ adj. having holes or hollow marks on the surface **SYN** pitted

**pocket** /ˈpɒkɪt; NAmE ˈpɑːk-/ noun, verb
▪ noun
• IN CLOTHING **1** A2 a small piece of material like a small bag SEWN into or onto a piece of clothing so that you can carry things in it: *a jacket/coat/shirt/trouser pocket* ◊ *a back/a hip/an inside pocket* ◊ *in/into a ~ I put the note in my pocket.* ◊ *She reached into her pocket and pulled out her phone.* ◊ *out of/from a ~ Take your hands out of your pockets!* ⊃ see also BREAST POCKET, HIP POCKET

1185 **pod**

• SMALL CONTAINER **2** A2 a small bag or container fastened to sth so that you can put things in it, for example, in a car door or in a bag: *Information about safety procedures is in the pocket in front of you* (= on a plane).
• MONEY **3** [usually sing.] used to talk about the amount of money that you have to spend: *We have holidays to suit every pocket.* ◊ *He had no intention of paying for the meal out of his own pocket.* ◊ *The Foundation is reputed to have very deep pockets* (= to have a lot of money).
• SMALL GROUP/AREA **4** a small group or area that is different from everyone or everything around it: *There are still a few isolated pockets of resistance to the new regime.* ◊ *a pocket of air* ⊃ see also AIR POCKET
• IN BILLIARDS, ETC. **5** any of the holes or nets around the edges of the table used in the games of BILLIARDS, POOL or SNOOKER, which you have to hit the ball into
**IDM** **be in sb's ˈpocket** to be controlled or strongly influenced by sb **be/live in each other's ˈpockets** (BrE) if two people are or live in each other's pockets, they are too close to each other or spend too much time with each other **have sb in your ˈpocket** to have influence or power over sb, for example, a police officer or a politician, especially by threatening them or by offering them money **have sth in your ˈpocket** to be certain to win sth **in/out of ˈpocket** (especially BrE) having gained/lost money as a result of sth: *That one mistake left him thousands of pounds out of pocket.* ⊃ compare OUT-OF-POCKET ⊃ more at BURN v., DIP v., HAND n., LINE v., PICK v.
▪ verb
• PUT INTO POCKET **1** *~ sth* to put sth into your pocket: *She paid for the drink and pocketed the change without counting it.*
• MONEY **2** *~ sth* to take or keep sth, especially an amount of money, that does not belong to you: *He regularly charges passengers more than the normal fare and pockets the difference.* **3** *~ sth* to earn or win an amount of money: *Last year, she pocketed over $1 million in advertising contracts.*
• IN BILLIARDS, ETC. **4** *~ sth* (in the games of BILLIARDS, POOL and SNOOKER) to hit a ball into a POCKET **SYN** pot

**pock·et·book** /ˈpɒkɪtbʊk; NAmE ˈpɑːk-/ noun **1** (NAmE) used to refer to the financial situation of a person or country. (In the past it was a small flat case for carrying papers or money.): *Many foreign goods are too expensive for American pocketbooks.* ◊ *The increase is likely to hit the pocketbooks of consumers.* **2** (especially BrE) a small book for writing in **SYN** notebook **3** (NAmE, old-fashioned) = HANDBAG

**pock·et·ful** /ˈpɒkɪtfʊl; NAmE ˈpɑːk-/ noun the amount a pocket holds: *a pocketful of coins*

**pock·et·knife** /ˈpɒkɪtnaɪf; NAmE ˈpɑːk-/ noun (especially NAmE) = PENKNIFE

**ˈpocket money** noun [U] **1** (especially BrE) (also **allowance** especially in NAmE) a small amount of money that parents give their children, usually every week or every month **2** a small amount of money that you can spend on things you need or want ⊃ compare SPENDING MONEY

**ˈpocket-sized** (also **ˈpocket-size**) adj. small enough to fit into your pocket or to be carried easily; smaller than the standard size

**ˈpocket ˈveto** noun (in the US) a method by which the President can stop a new law from being introduced by not signing it and keeping it until a session of Congress has finished

**pock·mark** /ˈpɒkmɑːk; NAmE ˈpɑːkmɑːrk/ noun a hollow mark on the skin, often caused by disease or infection

**pock·marked** /ˈpɒkmɑːkt; NAmE ˈpɑːkmɑːrkt/ adj. covered with hollow marks or holes: *a pockmarked face* ◊ *The district is pockmarked with caves.*

**pod** /pɒd; NAmE pɑːd/ noun **1** a long thin case filled with seeds that develops from the flowers of some plants, especially PEAS and beans: *a pea pod* ◊ *a vanilla pod* ⊃ VISUAL VOCAB pages V5, V8 **2** a small plastic container with sth inside it: *single-use coffee pods* **3** a long narrow container that is hung under an aircraft and used to carry fuel, equipment, weapons, etc. **4** part of a SPACECRAFT or a boat

# podcast

that can be separated from the main part **5** [C] a small group of sea animals, such as DOLPHINS or WHALES, swimming together: *a pod of adult dolphins*

**pod·cast** /ˈpɒdkɑːst; NAmE ˈpɑːdkæst/ *noun* a digital AUDIO file that can be taken from the internet and played on a computer or a device that you can carry with you: *To listen to the podcast, click on the link below.* ▶ WORDFINDER NOTE at RADIO ▶ **pod·caster** *noun*: *The US has an estimated 60 million podcasters.* **pod·cast·ing** *noun* [U]: *Podcasting could turn into an audio form of blogging.*

**podgy** /ˈpɒdʒi/ ; NAmE ˈpɑːdʒi/ (*BrE*) (*also* **pudgy** NAmE, BrE) *adj.* (*informal, usually disapproving*) slightly fat: *podgy arms*

**po·dia·trist** /pəˈdaɪətrɪst/ *noun* (*especially* NAmE) = CHIROPODIST

**po·dia·try** /pəˈdaɪətri/ *noun* [U] (*especially* NAmE) = CHIROPODY

lectern      podium      podium/rostrum

**po·dium** /ˈpəʊdiəm/ *noun* **1** a small platform that a person stands on when giving a speech or CONDUCTING an ORCHESTRA, etc. SYN **rostrum 2** (in sports) three platforms of different levels on which winners stand, usually to receive prizes: *The pair just missed out on a podium finish when they took fourth place.* **3** (*NAmE*) = LECTERN

**Po·dunk** /ˈpəʊdʌŋk/ *adj.* (*US, informal*) (of a town) small and not important or interesting ORIGIN *From a place name of southern New England.*

**poem** ⓘ B1 /ˈpəʊɪm; NAmE ˈpəʊəm/ *noun* a piece of writing in which the words are chosen for their sound and the images they suggest, not just for their obvious meanings. The words are arranged in separate lines, usually with a repeated rhythm, and often the lines RHYME at the end: *His collected poems were published after the war.*

**poet** ⓘ B1 /ˈpəʊɪt; NAmE ˈpəʊət/ *noun* a person who writes poems: *an internationally renowned poet* ◊ *the Romantic poets*

**poet·ess** /ˌpəʊɪˈtes/ *noun* (*old-fashioned*) a woman who writes poems

**poet·ic** /pəʊˈetɪk/ (*also less frequent* **poet·ical** /pəʊˈetɪkl/) *adj.* **1** [only before noun] connected with poetry; being poetry: *poetic language* ◊ *Byron's Poetical Works* **2** (*approving*) like or suggesting poetry, especially because it shows imagination and deep feeling SYN **lyrical**: *There is a poetic quality to her playing.* IDM *see* LICENCE ▶ **poet·ic·al·ly** /-kli/ *adv.*

**po·etic ˈjustice** *noun* [U] a situation in which sth bad happens to sb, and you think that this is what they deserve

**poet·ics** /pəʊˈetɪks/ *noun* [U] **1** the art of writing poetry **2** the study of poetry, literature, etc.

**Poet ˈLaureate** *noun* **1** (especially in the UK) a person who has been officially chosen to write poetry for the country's important occasions **2** (*especially NAmE*) a person whose poetry is considered to be the best, or most typical of their country or region

**poet·ry** ⓘ B1 /ˈpəʊɪtri; NAmE ˈpəʊətri/ *noun* **1** ? [U] poems in general; poems as a genre of literature SYN **verse**: *lyric/epic poetry* ◊ *to write poetry* ◊ *a poetry reading* ⇨ compare PROSE ⇨ WORDFINDER NOTE at WRITE

WORDFINDER couplet, image, lyric, recite, refrain, rhyme, scansion, stanza, verse

**2** [U, sing.] (*approving*) a quality of beauty, style and feeling: *There was poetry in all her gestures.*

**po-faced** /ˌpəʊ ˈfeɪst/ *adj.* (*BrE, informal, disapproving*) looking very serious and as though you do not approve of sb/sth

**pogo stick** /ˈpəʊgəʊ stɪk/ *noun* a POLE with a bar to stand on and a spring at the bottom, that you jump around on for fun

**pog·rom** /ˈpɒgrəm; NAmE ˈpəʊg-/ *noun* the organized killing of large numbers of people, because of their race or religion (originally the killing of Jews in Russia)

**poign·ant** /ˈpɔɪnjənt/ *adj.* having a strong effect on your feelings, especially in a way that makes you feel sad SYN **moving**: *a poignant image/moment/memory, etc.* ◊ *Her face was a poignant reminder of the passing of time.* ▶ **poign·ancy** /ˈpɔɪnjənsi/ *noun* [U]: *the poignancy of parting and separation* ◊ *Of particular poignancy was the photograph of their son with his sisters, taken the day before he died.* **poign·ant·ly** *adv.*

**poin·set·tia** /ˌpɔɪnˈsetiə/ *noun* a tropical plant with large red or pink leaves that grow to look like flowers, often grown indoors in pots

**point** ⓘ A1 ⓞ /pɔɪnt/ *noun, verb*
■ *noun*
- OPINION/FACT **1** ? A1 [C] a thing that sb says or writes giving their opinion or stating a fact: *She made several interesting points in the article.* ◊ *I take your point* (= understand and accept what you are saying). ◊ *He's just saying that to prove a point* (= to show his idea is right). ◊ *OK, you've made your point!* ⇨ *see also* TALKING POINT
- MAIN IDEA **2** ? B1 [C] (*usually* **the point**) the main or most important idea in sth that is said or done: *The point is you shouldn't have to wait so long to see a doctor.* ◊ *I wish he would get to the point* (= say it quickly). ◊ *I'll come straight to the point: we need more money.* ◊ *Do you see my point* (= understand)? ◊ *I think I missed the point* (= did not understand). ◊ *You have a point* (= your idea is right)—*it would be better to wait till this evening.* ◊ *'There won't be anywhere to park.' 'Oh, that's a (good) point.'* (= I had not thought of that) ◊ *It just isn't true. That's the whole point* (= the only important fact). ◊ *'He's been married before.' 'That's beside the point'* (= not important). ◊ *I know it won't cost very much but that's not the point* (= not the important thing).
- PURPOSE **3** ? B1 [U, sing.] the purpose or aim of sth: *What's the point of all this violence?* ◊ *'Why don't you try again?' 'What's the point?'* ◊ *~ of doing sth I don't see the point of doing it all again.* ◊ *~ in doing sth There's no point in getting angry.* ⇨ SYNONYMS at PURPOSE
- DETAIL **4** ? B1 [C] a particular detail or fact: *Can you explain that point again?* ◊ *Summarize the main points of the argument.* ◊ *I should like to highlight the key points.* ◊ *An important point has been missed out.* ◊ *You raise an interesting point.* ⇨ *see also* ACTION POINT
- QUALITY **5** ? B1 [C] a particular quality or feature that sb/sth has: *Tact is not one of her strong points.* ◊ *Read the manual to learn the program's finer points* (= small details). ◊ *Living in Scotland has its good points but the weather is not one of them.* ◊ *One of the hotel's plus points* (= good features) *is that it is very central.* ⇨ *see also* SELLING POINT
- TIME **6** ? B1 [C] a particular time or stage of development: *We had reached the point when there was no money left.* ◊ **at/on the ~ of sth** *The climber was at the point of death when they found him.* ◊ **at one, some, this, etc.~** *At one point he looked like winning.* ◊ *Many people suffer from mental illness at some point in their lives.* ◊ **At this point in time** *we just have to wait.* ◊ **At this point I don't care what you decide to do.** ◊ **up to/until that ~** *Up to that point we were living in London.* ⇨ *see also* HIGH POINT, LOW POINT, MID-POINT, PAIN POINT, SATURATION POINT, STARTING POINT, STICKING POINT, TIPPING POINT, TURNING POINT
- PLACE **7** ? B1 [C] a particular place or area: *I'll wait for you at the meeting point in the arrivals hall.* ◊ *the point at which the river divides* ◊ *Draw a line from point A to point B.* ◊ *No parking beyond this point.* ⇨ SYNONYMS at PLACE ⇨ *see also* ENTRY POINT, FOCAL POINT, JUMPING-OFF POINT, PRESSURE POINT, RALLYING POINT, THREE-POINT TURN, TOUCH POINT, TRIG POINT, VANISHING POINT, VANTAGE POINT

- **DIRECTION 8** [C] one of the marks of direction around a COMPASS: *the points of the compass* (= N, S, E, W, etc.)
- **IN COMPETITION 9** [A2] [C] (*abbr.* **pt**) an individual unit that adds to a score in a game or sports competition: *to win/lose a point* ◇ *Australia finished 20 points ahead.* ◇ **~ for (doing) sth** *Players score points for finding words not found by any other player.* ◇ **on points** *They won on points* (= by scoring more points rather than by completely defeating their opponents.) ⊃ see also BREAK POINT, BROWNIE POINT, EXPERIENCE POINTS, GAME POINT, MATCH POINT, PENALTY POINT, SET POINT
- **MEASUREMENT 10** [C] a mark or unit on a scale of measurement: *The party's share of the vote fell by ten* **percentage points**. ⊃ see also BOILING POINT, FREEZING POINT, GRADE POINT AVERAGE, MELTING POINT, PRICE POINT
  **11** [C] a unit of credit towards an award or benefit: *Applicants are awarded points on criteria such as education, skills and knowledge of English.*
- **SHARP END 12** [B2] [C] the sharp, thin end of sth: *the point of a pencil/knife/pin* ⊃ see also BALLPOINT, GUNPOINT, KNIFEPOINT
- **LAND 13** [C] (*also* **Point**) a narrow piece of land that stretches into the sea: *The ship sailed around the point.* ◇ *Pagoda Point*
- **PUNCTUATION 14** [C] a small round mark used in writing, especially the one that separates a whole number from the part that comes after it: *two point six (2.6)* ◇ *a decimal point* ◇ *We broadcast on ninety-five point nine (95.9) FM.* ⊃ see also BULLET POINT, FULL STOP *noun*
- **OF LIGHT/COLOUR 15** [C] a very small DOT of light or colour: *The stars were points of light in the sky.*
- **FOR ELECTRICITY 16** [C] (*BrE*) a place in a wall, etc. where a piece of equipment can be connected to electricity: *a power/shaver/telephone point*
- **IN BALLET 17 points** [pl.] = POINTE
- **ON RAILWAY TRACK 18 points** [pl.] (*BrE*) (*NAmE* **switch** [C]) a piece of track at a place where a railway line divides that can be moved to allow a train to change tracks
- **SIZE OF LETTERS 19** [U] a unit of measurement for the size of letters in printing or on a computer screen, etc: *Change the text to 10 point.*

**IDM** **if/when it comes to the ˈpoint** used when you have to decide sth or say what you really think: *When it comes to the point, he always changes his mind.* **in point of ˈfact** used to say what is true in a situation: *In point of fact, she is their adopted daughter.* **make a ˈpoint of doing sth** to be or make sure you do sth because it is important or necessary: *I made a point of closing all the windows before leaving the house.* **ˌmore to the ˈpoint** used to say that sth is more important than sth else: *I couldn't do the job—I've never been to Spain and, more to the point, I don't speak Spanish.* **on point** (*NAmE*) **1** appropriate or relevant to the situation: *The quotation was directly on point.* ◇ *Let's stay on point.* **2** (*informal*) perfect; exactly right for the occasion: *The music here is totally on point.* **on the ˈpoint of doing sth** to be close to doing sth; to be going to do sth very soon **SYN** **be about to do sth**: *I was just on the point of calling you.* **ˌpoint of ˈcontact** a place where you go or a person that you speak to when you are dealing with an organization: *The receptionist is the first point of contact most people have with the clinic.* **a ˌpoint of deˈparture 1** a place where a journey starts **2** (*formal*) an idea, a theory or an event that is used to start a discussion, an activity, etc. **a ˌpoint of ˈhonour** a thing that sb considers to be very important for their honour or reputation **the ˌpoint of ˌno reˈturn** the time when you must continue with what you have decided to do, because it is not possible to get back to an earlier situation **ˌpoint ˈtaken** used to say that you accept that sb else is right when they have disagreed with you or criticized you: *Point taken. Let's drop the subject.* **to the ˈpoint** expressed in a simple, clear way without any extra information or feelings **SYN** **pertinent**: *The letter was short and to the point.* **to the ˈpoint of (doing) sth** to a degree that can be described as sth: *He was rude to the point of being aggressive.* **up to a (certain) ˈpoint** to some extent; to some degree but not completely: *I agree with you up to a point.* ⊃ more at BELABOUR, CASE *n.*, FINE *adj.*, LABOUR *v.*, MOOT *adj.*, SCORE *v.*, SORE *adj.*, STRETCH *v.*

■ *verb*

- **SHOW WITH FINGER 1** [B1] [I, T, no passive] to stretch out your finger or sth held in your hand towards sb/sth in order to show sb where a person or thing is: **~ at sb/sth** *'What's your name?' he asked, pointing at the child with his pen.* ◇ **~ to sb/sth** *He pointed to the spot where the house used to stand.* ◇ **~ towards sb/sth** *He said my name and pointed towards me.* ◇ **~ (+ adv./prep.)** *She pointed in my direction.* ◇ *It's rude to point!* ◇ **~ sth (+ adv./prep.)** *She pointed her finger in my direction.* ◇ **~ with sth (+ adv./prep.)** *She pointed with her finger at the map.*
- **AIM 2** [B1] [T] **~ sth (at sb/sth)** to aim sth at sb/sth: *He pointed the gun at her head.*
- **FACE DIRECTION 3** [B1] [I] **+ adv./prep.** to face in or be directed towards a particular direction: *The telescope was pointing in the wrong direction.* ◇ *The signpost pointed straight ahead.* ◇ *A compass needle points north.*
- **ON A COMPUTER 4** [I, T] to direct your CURSOR at a particular point on the screen; to link to a particular web page: *Shopping on the Web is pretty simple—you just point and click and wait.* ◇ **~ sth at/to sth** *Point your browser to www.oxfordlearnersdictionaries.com.*
- **LEAD TO 5** [I, T] to lead to or suggest a particular development or logical argument: **+ adv./prep.** *The evidence seems to point in that direction.* ◇ **~ the way + adv./prep.** *The fans are looking to the new players to point the way to victory.*
- **SHOW THE WAY 6** [T] to show sb which way to go: **~ sb + adv./prep.** *I wonder if you could point me in the right direction for the bus station.* ◇ **~ the way (+ adv./prep.)** *A series of yellow arrows pointed the way to reception.*
- **TOES 7** [T] **~ sth** to stretch your toes and foot so that they form a straight line with your leg *Reach up with your arms and point your toes.*
- **WALL 8** [T] **~ sth** to put MORTAR (= a mixture of sand, water, etc that becomes hard when dry) between the BRICKS, stones, etc. used to build a wall

**IDM** **point a/the ˈfinger (at sb)** to accuse sb of doing sth: *The article points an accusing finger at the authorities.* ⊃ related noun FINGER-POINTING

**PHRV** **ˌpoint sb/sth↔ˈout (to sb)** to stretch your finger out towards sb/sth in order to show sb which person or thing you are referring to: *I'll point him out to you next time he comes in.* **ˌpoint ˈout (to sb)** [B1] **| ˌpoint sth↔ˈout (to sb)** [B1] to mention sth in order to give sb information about it or make them notice it: *She tried in vain to point out to him the unfairness of his actions.* ◇ *He pointed out the dangers of driving alone.* ◇ **point out (to sb) that …** *I should point out that not one of these paintings is original.* ◇ **+ speech** *'It's not very far,' she pointed out.* ⊃ LANGUAGE BANK at ARGUE **ˌpoint to ˈsth 1** to mention sth that you think is important and/or the reason why a particular situation exists: *The board of directors pointed to falling productivity to justify their decision.* **2** to suggest that sth is true or likely: *All the signs point to a successful year ahead.* **ˌpoint sth↔ˈup** (*formal*) to emphasize sth so that it becomes easier to notice **SYN** **highlight**: *The conference merely pointed up divisions in the party.*

**ˌpoint-and-ˈclick** *adj.* [usually before noun] (*computing*) able to be used with a mouse

**ˌpoint-and-ˈshoot** *adj.* (of a camera) easy to use, without a person needing to move or change controls on it

**ˌpoint-ˈblank** *adj.* [only before noun] **1** (of a shot) fired with the gun touching or very close to the person or thing it is aimed at: *The officer was shot dead* **at point-blank range**. **2** (of sth that is said) very definite and direct and not very polite **SYN** **blunt**: *a point-blank refusal* ▶ **ˌpoint-ˈblank** *adv.*: *She fired point-blank at his chest.* ◇ *He refused point-blank to be photographed.*

**pointe** /pwæt/ *noun* [U] (*also* **pointes** /pwæt/, **points** [pl.]) the hard tops of the toes of a kind of shoe that a BALLET dancer balances on

**point·ed** [B2] /ˈpɔɪntɪd/ *adj.* **1** [B2] having a sharp end: *a pointed chin* ◇ *pointed teeth* ◇ *a pointed instrument* ⊃ see also POINTY **2** aimed in a clear and often critical way against a particular person or their behaviour: *a pointed comment/remark* ◇ *His words were a pointed reminder of her position.*

# pointedly

**point·ed·ly** /ˈpɔɪntɪdli/ *adv.* in a way that is clearly intended to show what you mean or to express criticism: *She yawned and looked pointedly at her watch.*

**point·er** /ˈpɔɪntə(r)/ *noun* **1** (*informal*) a piece of advice: *Here are some pointers on how to go about the writing task.* **2** ~ (to sth) a sign that sth exists; a sign that shows how sth may develop in the future: *The surge in car sales was regarded as an encouraging pointer to an improvement in the economy.* **3** a thin piece of metal that points to the numbers on a DIAL on a piece of equipment for measuring sth **4** a stick used to point to things on a map or picture on a wall **5** (*computing*) a small symbol, for example an ARROW, that marks a point on a computer screen **6** a large dog used in hunting, trained to stand still with its nose pointing towards the birds that are being hunted

**ˈpoint guard** *noun* (in basketball) the player who directs the team's attacking players ▸ compare SHOOTING GUARD

**poin·til·lism** /ˈpɔɪntɪlɪzəm, ˈpwæn-/ *noun* [U] a style of painting that was developed in France in the late nineteenth century in which very small marks of colour are used to build up the picture ▸ **poin·til·list** /-lɪst/ *adj.* **poin·til·list** *noun*: *Seurat, the French pointillist*

**point·ing** /ˈpɔɪntɪŋ/ *noun* [U] the MORTAR (= a mixture of sand, water, etc. that becomes hard when dry) that is put in the spaces between the BRICKS or stones in a wall to hold them together; the method of filling in the spaces with MORTAR

**ˈpointing device** *noun* (*computing*) a mouse or other device which allows you to move the CURSOR on a computer screen

**point·less** /ˈpɔɪntləs/ *adj.* having no purpose; not worth doing: *We searched until we knew it would be pointless to continue.* ▸ **point·less·ly** *adv.*: *He argued pointlessly with his parents.* **point·less·ness** *noun* [U]: *the pointlessness of war*

**ˈpoint man** *noun* a soldier who goes in front of the others to look for danger: (*NAmE, figurative*) *the president's point man on education* (= the person who is responsible for it)

**point of ˈorder** *noun* (*pl.* **points of order**) (*formal*) a question about whether the rules of behaviour in a formal discussion or meeting are being followed correctly

**point of ˈreference** *noun* (*pl.* **points of reference**) something that you already know that helps you understand a situation or explain sth to sb

**point of ˈsale** *noun* [usually sing.] the place where a product is sold: **at the ~** *More information on healthy foods should be provided at the point of sale.*

**point of ˈuse** *noun* [usually sing.] the place where a product or a service is actually used: **at the ~** *Medical care is still free at the point of use.*

**point of ˈview** *noun* (*pl.* **points of view**) **1** the particular attitude or opinion that sb has about sth: *Why can't you ever see my point of view?* ◊ *There are a number of different points of view on this issue.* ◊ *From my point of view* (= as far as I am concerned), *the party was a complete success.* **2** a particular way of considering or judging a situation SYN **angle**: *These statistics are important from an ecological point of view.* ◊ *The book is written from the father's point of view.*

**point-to-ˈpoint** *noun* (*BrE*) a race on horses that goes over a marked course across fields and has fences or walls for the horses to jump over

**pointy** /ˈpɔɪnti/ *adj.* (*informal*) with a point at one end SYN **pointed**: *pointy ears* ◊ (*humorous*) *Don't try to argue when you find yourself at the pointy end of a knife* (= when sb is threatening you with a knife).

**the ˈpointy end** *noun* [sing.] (*informal*) = BUSINESS END (1)

**poise** /pɔɪz/ *noun, verb*
■ *noun* [U] **1** a calm and confident manner with control of your feelings or behaviour **2** the ability to move or stand in an attractive way with good control of your body
■ *verb* [I, T] to be or hold sth steady in a particular position, especially above sth else: **+ adv./prep.** *The hawk poised in mid-air ready to swoop.* ◊ *~ sth/yourself to do sth He was poising himself to launch a final attack.* ◊ *~ sth/yourself + adv./prep. She poised the javelin in her hand before the throw.*

**poised** /pɔɪzd/ *adj.* **1** [not before noun] in a position that is completely still but is ready to move at any moment: **~ (on, above, over, etc. sth)** *Tina was tense, her hand poised over the telephone.* ◊ *He stopped writing and looked at me, pen poised.* ◊ *~ to do sth The cat crouched in the grass, poised to jump.* **2** [not before noun] **~ (in, on, above, etc. sth)** in a position that is balanced but likely to change in one direction or another: *The cup was poised on the edge of the chair.* ◊ (*figurative*) *The world stood poised between peace and war.* **3** [not before noun] completely ready for sth or to do sth SYN **set**: **~ for sth** *The economy is poised for recovery.* ◊ *~ to do sth Kate is poised to become the highest-paid supermodel in the fashion world.* **4** having a calm and confident manner and in control of your feelings and behaviour SYN **assured**: *He is a remarkably poised young man.*

**poi·son** ❶ B1 /ˈpɔɪzn/ *noun, verb*
■ *noun* [C, U] **1** ❶ B1 a substance that causes death or harm if it gets into the body: *Some mushrooms contain a deadly poison.* ◊ *How did he die? Was it poison?* ◊ *The dog was killed by rat poison* (= poison intended to kill RATS). ◊ *to hunt with poison arrows* ◊ *bombs containing poison gas* **2** an idea, a feeling, etc. that is extremely harmful: *the poison of racial hatred*
IDM ⊃ see MAN *n.*
■ *verb* **1** ❶ B1 **~ sb/yourself | ~ sb/yourself with sth** to harm or kill a person or an animal by giving them poison: *He was accused of poisoning his wife.* **2** ❶ B1 to put poison in or on sth: *~ sth a poisoned arrow Someone had been poisoning his food.* ◊ *~ sth with sth The chocolates had been poisoned with cyanide.* **3** ~ sth to have a bad effect on sth: *His comment served only to poison the atmosphere still further.* ◊ *She succeeded in poisoning their minds against me.*
IDM **a ˌpoisoned ˈchalice** (*especially BrE*) a thing that seems attractive when it is given to sb but which soon becomes unpleasant

**poi·son·er** /ˈpɔɪzənə(r)/ *noun* a person who murders sb by using poison

**poi·son·ing** /ˈpɔɪzənɪŋ/ *noun* [U, C] **1** the fact or state of poison having got into the body: *a series of deaths caused by carbon monoxide poisoning* ◊ *At least 10000 children are involved in accidental poisonings every year.* **2** the act of killing or harming sb/sth by giving them poison: *The police suspected poisoning.* ◊ *The rats were controlled by poisoning.* ⊃ see also BLOOD POISONING, FOOD POISONING

**poison ˈivy** *noun* [U] a North American climbing plant that causes painful spots on the skin when you touch it

**poi·son·ous** ❶ B1 /ˈpɔɪzənəs/ *adj.* **1** ❶ B1 causing death or illness if SWALLOWED or taken into the body SYN **toxic**: *poisonous chemicals/fumes/plants* ◊ *This gas is highly poisonous.* ◊ *~ to sb/sth The leaves of certain trees are poisonous to cattle.* **2** ❶ B1 (of animals and insects) producing a poison that can cause death or illness if the animal or insect bites you SYN **venomous**: *poisonous snakes* **3** extremely unpleasant or unfriendly: *the poisonous atmosphere in the office*

**ˌpoison ˈpen letter** *noun* an unpleasant letter that is not signed and is intended to upset the person who receives it

**poison ˈpill** *noun* (*informal, business*) a form of defence used by a company to prevent, or to reduce the effect of, a TAKEOVER that they do not want, for example by selling some of their important possessions

**poke** /pəʊk/ *verb, noun*
■ *verb* **1** [T] to quickly push your fingers or another object into sb/sth SYN **prod**: *~ sb/sth with sth She poked him in the ribs with her elbow.* ◊ *~ sth into sth She poked her elbow into his ribs.* ◊ *~ sb/sth I'm sick of being poked and prodded by doctors.* ◊ *She got up and poked the fire* (= to make it burn more strongly). **2** [T] *~ sth + adv./prep.* to push sth somewhere or move it in a particular direction with a small quick movement: *He poked his head around the corner to check that nobody was coming.* ◊ *Someone had poked a message under the door.* ◊ *Don't poke her eye out with that stick!* **3** [I] **+ adv./prep.** if an object is **poking out of, through**, etc. sth, you can see a part of it that is no longer covered by sth else: *The end of the cable was left*

poking out of the wall. ◊ *Clumps of grass poked up through the snow.* **4** [T] **~ a hole in sth (with sth)** to make a hole in sth by pushing your finger or another object into it: *The kids poked holes in the ice with sticks.* **5** [T] **~ sb** (*taboo, slang*) (of a man) to have sex with sb

**IDM** **poke ˈfun at sb/sth** to say unkind things about sb/sth in order to make other people laugh at them **SYN** **ridicule**: *Her novels poke fun at the upper class.* ⇒ more at NOSE *n*.

**PHRV** **ˌpoke aˈround** (*also* **ˌpoke aˈbout** *especially in BrE*) (*informal*) to look for sth, especially sth that is hidden among other things that you have to move: *The police spent the day poking around in his office but found nothing.* ◊ (*figurative*) *We've had journalists poking around and asking a lot of questions.* **ˈpoke at sth** to push a pointed object, your finger, etc. at sth repeatedly with small quick movements: *He poked at the spaghetti with a fork.*

■ *noun* **1** [C, usually sing.] the action of quickly pushing your fingers or another object into sb/sth: *to give the fire a poke* ◊ *He gave me a poke in the ribs to wake me up.* **2** [U] (*BrE*) power in a car: *I prefer something with a bit more poke.*

**IDM** **have a ˌpoke aˈround** (*informal*) to look carefully around a place to see what you can find; to try to find out information about sb/sth **ˌtake a ˈpoke at sb/sth** (*NAmE, old-fashioned, informal*) to make an unkind remark about sb/sth; to laugh at sb/sth ⇒ more at PIG *n*.

**poker** /ˈpəʊkə(r)/ *noun* **1** [U] a card game for two or more people, in which the players bet on the values of the cards they hold **2** [C] a metal stick for moving or breaking up coal in a fire

**ˈpoker-faced** *adj.* (*informal*) with an expression on your face that does not show what you are thinking or feeling ▶ **ˈpoker face** *noun*: *He maintained a poker face.*

**ˈpoker machine** *noun* (*AustralE*) = SLOT MACHINE (2)

**poky** /ˈpəʊki/ *adj.* (**poki·er**, **poki·est**) (*informal*) **1** (*especially BrE*) (of a room or a building) too small; without much space **SYN** **cramped**: *a poky little room* **2** (*also* **pokey**) (*both NAmE*) extremely slow and annoying

**pol** /pɒl; *NAmE* pɑːl/ *noun* (*NAmE, informal*) = POLITICIAN

**polar** /ˈpəʊlə(r)/ *adj.* [only before noun] **1** connected with, or near the North or South Pole: *the polar regions* ◊ *polar explorers* **2** (*specialist*) connected with the POLES (= the positive and negative ends) of a MAGNET: *polar attraction* **3** (*formal*) used to describe sth that is the complete opposite of sth else: *The parents' position is often the polar opposite of the child's.*

**ˈpolar bear** *noun* a white bear that lives near the North Pole

**po·lar·ity** /pəˈlærəti/ *noun* [U] **1 ~ (between A and B)** (*formal*) the situation when two TENDENCIES, opinions, etc. oppose each other: *the growing polarity between the left and right wings of the party* **2** [U, C] (*physics*) the condition of having two POLES with opposite qualities

**po·lar·ize** (*BrE also* **-ise**) /ˈpəʊləraɪz/ *verb* **1** [I, T] to separate or make people separate into two groups with completely opposite opinions: *Public opinion has polarized on this issue.* ◊ **~ sth** *The issue has polarized public opinion.* **2** [T] **~ sth** (*physics*) to make waves of light, etc. VIBRATE in a single direction **3** [T] **~ sth** (*physics*) to give polarity to sth: *to polarize a magnet* ▶ **po·lar·iza·tion**, **-isa·tion** /ˌpəʊlərəˈzeɪʃn; *NAmE* -rəˈz-/ *noun* [U, C]

**Po·lar·oid™** /ˈpəʊlərɔɪd/ *noun* **1** [C] (*also* **Polaroid ˈcamera**) a camera that can produce a printed photograph within a few seconds **2** [C] a printed photograph that has been produced by a Polaroid camera **3** [U] a clear substance that is put on SUNGLASSES and car windows to make the sun seem less bright: *Polaroid sunglasses* **4** **Polaroids** [pl.] (*also* **ˌPolaroid ˈsunglasses**) SUNGLASSES that have a layer of Polaroid on them

**pole** ¹⁺ ⓒ¹ /pəʊl/ *noun, verb*

■ *noun* **1** ¹⁺ ⓒ¹ a long thin straight piece of wood or metal, especially with the end placed in the ground, used as a support: *a tent pole* ◊ *a ski pole* ◊ *a curtain pole* ⇒ see also BARBER'S POLE, BARGEPOLE, FLAGPOLE, SKI POLE, TELEGRAPH POLE, TELEPHONE POLE, TOTEM POLE ⇒ picture at TENT **2** ¹⁺ ⓒ¹ either of the two points at the opposite ends of the line on which the earth or any other planet turns: *the North/South Pole* **3** (*physics*) either of the two ends of a MAGNET, or the positive or negative points of an electric

1189    **police department**

battery **4** either of two opposite or very different extremes: *Their opinions were at opposite poles of the debate.*

**IDM** **be ˌpoles aˈpart** to be widely separated; to have no interests that you share **up the ˈpole** (*BrE, old-fashioned, informal*) crazy ⇒ more at GREASY, TOUCH *v*.

■ *verb* [T, I] **~ (sth) + adv./prep.** to move a boat by pushing on the bottom of a river, etc. with a pole

**pole-axe** (*BrE*) (*US usually* **pole-ax**) /ˈpəʊlæks/ *verb* **~ sb 1** to hit sb very hard so that they fall down and cannot stand up again **2** [usually passive] **~ sb** to surprise or shock you so much that you do not know what to say or do **SYN** **dumbfound**

**pole·cat** /ˈpəʊlkæt/ *noun* **1** a small European wild animal with a long thin body, dark brown fur and a strong unpleasant smell **2** (*NAmE*) = SKUNK

**ˈpole dancing** *noun* [U] sexually exciting dancing that is performed in a bar or club, with the dancer moving his or her body around a long thin straight piece of wood or metal ▶ **ˈpole dancer** *noun*

**po·lem·ic** /pəˈlemɪk/ *noun* (*formal*) **1** [C] a speech or a piece of writing that argues very strongly for or against sth/sb **2** [U] (*also* **polemics** [pl.]) the practice or skill of arguing strongly for or against sth/sb: *Her speech was memorable for its polemic rather than its substance.*

**po·lem·ic·al** /pəˈlemɪkl/ (*also less frequent* **po·lem·ic**) *adj.* (*formal*) involving strong arguments for or against sth, often in opposition to the opinion of others

**po·lemi·cist** /pəˈlemɪsɪst/ *noun* (*formal*) a person who uses POLEMIC with skill

**po·lenta** /pəˈlentə; *NAmE* pəʊˈl-/ *noun* [U] **1** a yellow food made with MAIZE flour, used in Italian cooking **2** the flour used to make polenta

**ˈpole position** *noun* [U, C] **1** the leading position at the start of a race involving cars or bicycles **2** the leading position in a competition or contest: *in ~ She's in pole position to grab the Olympic 100m gold.*

**the ˈPole Star** *noun* [sing.] the star that is above the North Pole in the sky

**the ˈpole vault** *noun* [sing.] a sporting event in which people try to jump over a high bar, using a long thin straight piece of wood or FIBREGLASS to push themselves off the ground ▶ **ˈpole-vaulter** *noun* **ˈpole-vaulting** *noun* [U]

**po·lice** ❶ ⓐ¹ /pəˈliːs/ *noun, verb*

■ *noun* ¹⁺ ⓐ¹ (*often* **the police**) [pl.] an official organization whose job is to make people obey the law and to prevent and solve crime; the people who work for this organization: *Get out of the house or I'll call the police.* ◊ *The police arrested three men and took them for questioning.* ◊ *Police are investigating the break-in.* ◊ *Armed police soon arrived on the scene.* ◊ *a police car* ⇒ see also MILITARY POLICE, RIOT POLICE, SECRET POLICE, THOUGHT POLICE ⇒WORDFINDER NOTE at LAW

**WORDFINDER** arrest, charge, cordon, detain, detective, interrogate, plain clothes, raid, undercover

■ *verb* **1 ~ sth** (of the police, army, etc.) to go around a particular area to make sure that nobody is breaking the law there: *The border will be policed by UN officials.* **2 ~ sth** (of a committee, etc.) to make sure that a particular set of rules is obeyed **SYN** **monitor**: *The profession is policed by its own regulatory body.*

**poˈlice commissioner** *noun* (*especially NAmE*) = COMMISSIONER

**poˌlice ˈconstable** (*also* **constable**) *noun* (*abbr.* **PC**) (in the UK and some other countries) a police officer of the lowest rank: *Police Constable Jordan*

**poˈlice department** *noun* (in the US) the police organization of a particular city

**po·lice dog** noun a dog that is trained to help police in their work, for example by finding or attacking suspected criminals

**po·lice force** noun the police organization of a country, district or town

**po·lice·man** 🔊 **A1** /pəˈliːsmən/ noun (pl. **-men** /-mən/) a male police officer: *a plain-clothes/uniformed policeman* ⇒ note at GENDER

**po·lice officer** (also **officer**) noun a member of the police

**po·lice pro'cedural** noun a television series, film or novel that focuses on the procedures that the police use to solve a crime

**po·lice state** noun (*disapproving*) a country where people's freedom, especially to travel and to express political opinions, is controlled by the government, with the help of the police

**po·lice station** (*NAmE also* **'station house**) noun the office of a local police force: *The suspect was taken to the nearest police station for questioning.*

**po·lice·wo·man** /pəˈliːswʊmən/ noun (pl. **-women** /-wɪmɪn/) a female police officer ⇒ note at GENDER

**po·licing** /pəˈliːsɪŋ/ noun [U] **1** the activity of keeping order in a place with police: *community policing* **2** the activity of controlling an industry, an activity, etc. to make sure that people obey the rules

**pol·icy** 🔊 **B1** 🅦 /ˈpɒləsi; *NAmE* ˈpɑːl-/ noun (pl. **-ies**) **1** ⚡**B1** [C, U] a plan of action agreed or chosen by a political party, a business, etc.: **~ on sth** *the present government's policy on education* ◇ *The company has adopted a firm policy on shoplifting.* ◇ **to implement/pursue a policy** ◇ **~ of (doing) sth** *We have a policy of refusing to comment on such matters.* ◇ *US foreign/economic policy* ◇ *The document does not represent government policy.* ◇ *a change/shift in policy* ◇ *a policy adviser/decision* **2** [C, U] (*formal*) a principle that you believe in that influences how you behave; a way in which you usually behave: *She is following her usual policy of ignoring all offers of help.* ◇ (*saying*) *Honesty is the best policy.* **3** [C] a written statement of a contract of insurance: *Check the terms of the policy before you sign.* ⇒ WORDFINDER NOTE at INSURANCE

**pol·icy·hold·er** /ˈpɒləsihəʊldə(r); *NAmE* ˈpɑːl-/ noun (*formal*) a person or group that has paid for insurance protection

**pol·icy·maker** /ˈpɒləsimeɪkə(r); *NAmE* ˈpɑːl-/ noun a person who is responsible for or involved in developing plans of action for a political party, business, etc. ▶ **policymaking** noun [U]: *evidence-based policymaking*

**polio** /ˈpəʊliəʊ/ (also *formal* **polio·my·el·itis** /ˌpəʊliəʊˌmaɪəˈlaɪtɪs/) noun [U] a disease that affects the central nervous system and can cause temporary or permanent PARALYSIS (= loss of control or feeling in part or most of the body)

**pol·ish** /ˈpɒlɪʃ; *NAmE* ˈpɑːl-/ noun, verb
■ *noun* **1** [U, C] a substance used when rubbing a surface to make it smooth and shiny: *furniture/floor/shoe/silver polish* ◇ *wax polish* ⇒ *see also* NAIL POLISH **2** [sing.] an act of polishing sth: *I give it a polish now and again.* **3** [sing.] the shiny appearance of sth after it has been polished 🔸 **lustre**, **sheen 4** [U] a high quality of performance achieved with great skill 🔸 **brilliance**: *She played the cello with the polish of a much older musician.* **5** [U] high standards of behaviour; being polite 🔸 **refinement** 🅘🅓🅜 *see* SPIT *n.*
■ *verb* **1** [T, I] to make sth smooth and shiny by rubbing it: **~ (sth)** *Polish shoes regularly to protect the leather.* ◇ **~ sth with sth** *He polished his glasses with a handkerchief.* **2** [T] to make changes to sth in order to improve it: **~ sth** *The statement was carefully polished and checked before release.* ◇ **~ sth up** *The hotel has polished up its act* (= improved its service) *since last year.*
🅟🅗🅡🅥 **polish sb↔'off** (*especially NAmE, informal*) to kill sb **polish sth↔'off** (*informal*) to finish sth, especially food, quickly: *He polished off the remains of the apple pie.*

**pol·ished** /ˈpɒlɪʃt; *NAmE* ˈpɑːl-/ adj. **1** shiny as a result of POLISHING 🔸 **gleaming 2** confident, impressive and/or showing a lot of skill 🔸 **fine**

**pol·ish·er** /ˈpɒlɪʃə(r); *NAmE* ˈpɑːl-/ noun a machine for POLISHING sth: *a floor polisher*

**pol·it·buro** /ˈpɒlɪtbjʊərəʊ; *NAmE* ˈpɑːlɪtbjʊr-/ noun (pl. **-os**) the most important committee of a Communist party, with the power to decide on policy

**po·lite** 🔊 **A2** /pəˈlaɪt/ adj. (**po·liter**, **po·litest**) 🅗🅔🅛🅟 more polite *and* most polite *are also common* **1** ⚡**A2** **~ (to sb)** having or showing good manners and respect for the feelings of others 🔸 **courteous**: *Please be polite to our guests.* ◇ *Our waiter was very polite and helpful.* 🅞🅟🅟 **impolite 2** ⚡**B2** socially correct but not always sincere: *I don't know how to make polite conversation.* ◇ *The performance was greeted with polite applause.* **3** [only before noun] from a class of society that believes it is better than others: *'Bum' is not a word we use in polite company.* ▶ **po·lite·ly** *adv.* **po·lite·ness** noun [U]

**pol·it·ic** /ˈpɒlətɪk; *NAmE* ˈpɑːl-/ adj. (*formal*) (of actions) based on good judgement 🔸 **prudent, wise**: *It seemed politic to say nothing.* ⇒ *see also* BODY POLITIC

**pol·it·ical** 🔊 **B1** /pəˈlɪtɪkl/ adj. **1** ⚡**B1** connected with the state, government or public affairs: *a monarch without political power* ◇ *He was a political prisoner* (= one who was put in prison for holding opinions that the government thought dangerous). **2** ⚡**B1** connected with the different groups working in politics, especially their policies and the competition between them: *a political party/leader/opponent* ◇ *Peace organizations are being used as fronts for political agendas.* **3** (of people) interested in or active in politics: *She became very political at university.* ◇ *I'm not a political animal* (= person who is interested in politics). **4** connected with power, status, etc. within an organization, rather than with matters of principle: *I suspect that he was dismissed for political reasons.* ⇒ *see also* POLITICALLY

**po·litical 'action committee** noun (*abbr.* **PAC**) (in the US) a group of people who collect money to support the candidates and policies that will help them achieve their political and social aims

**po·litical a'sylum** noun [U] (*formal*) = ASYLUM

**po·litical 'capital** noun [U] the advantage over a political opponent that you can get from a particular situation: *He accused his opponents of trying to* **make political capital** *out of the tragedy.*

**po·litical cor'rectness** noun [U] (*sometimes disapproving*) the principle of avoiding language and behaviour that may offend particular groups of people

**po·litical e'conomy** noun [U] the study of how nations organize the production and use of wealth

**po·litical ge'ography** noun [U] the way in which the world is divided into different countries, especially as a subject of study

**pol·it·ic·al·ly** /pəˈlɪtɪkli/ adv. in a way that is connected with politics: *a politically sensitive issue* ◇ *politically motivated crimes* ◇ *It makes sense politically as well as economically.*

**po·litically cor'rect** adj. (*abbr.* **PC**) used to describe language or behaviour that deliberately tries to avoid offending particular groups of people

**po·litically incor'rect** adj. failing to avoid language or behaviour that may offend particular groups of people

**po·litical 'science** (also **pol·it·ics**) noun [U] the study of government and politics

**po·litical 'scientist** noun an expert in political science

**pol·it·ician** 🔊 **B1** /ˌpɒləˈtɪʃn; *NAmE* ˌpɑːl-/ noun **1** ⚡**B1** (also *NAmE, informal* **pol**) a person whose job involves politics, especially as an elected member of parliament, etc.: *democratically elected politicians* ◇ *Opposition politicians have called for fresh elections.* ◇ *a local politician* (= one who works in local government) ⇒ WORDFINDER NOTE at PARLIAMENT **2** (*disapproving*) a person who is good at using different situations in an organization to try to get power or advantage for himself or herself

**pol·it·i·cize** (*BrE* also **-ise**) /pəˈlɪtɪsaɪz/ *verb* [often passive] **1 ~ sth** to make sth a political issue: *The highly politicized issue of unemployment* **2 ~ sb/sth** to make sb/sth become more involved in politics: *The rural population has become increasingly politicized in recent years.* ▶ **pol·it·i·ciza·tion, -isa·tion** /pəˌlɪtɪsaɪˈzeɪʃn; *NAmE* -səˈz-/ *noun* [U]: *the politicization of education*

**pol·it·ick·ing** /ˈpɒlətɪkɪŋ; *NAmE* ˈpɑːl-/ *noun* [U] (*often disapproving*) political activity, especially to win support for yourself

**pol·it·ico** /pəˈlɪtɪkəʊ/ *noun* (*pl.* **-os**) (*informal, disapproving*) a politician; a person who is active in politics

**pol·it·ics** ❶ 〈B1〉 /ˈpɒlətɪks; *NAmE* ˈpɑːl-/ *noun* **1** 〈B1〉 [U + sing./pl. v.] the activities involved in getting and using power in public life, and being able to influence decisions that affect a country or a society: *world/international politics* ◊ *domestic/national/local politics* ◊ **in ~** *She is aiming for a career in politics.* ◊ *a major figure in British politics* ◊ *Have you considered going into politics* (= trying to become a Member of Parliament, Congress, etc.)? ⊃ see also PARTY POLITICS **2** 〈B2〉 [U + sing./pl. v.] (*disapproving*) matters connected with getting or using power within a particular group or organization: *I don't want to get involved in office politics.* ◊ *the internal politics of the legal profession* ◊ *racial/gender/sexual politics* (= connected with relationships of different groups in society) ◊ **the ~ of sth** *the politics of identity/race/gender* ⊃ see also IDENTITY POLITICS **3** [pl.] a person's political views or beliefs: *His politics are extreme.* **4** [U] = POLITICAL SCIENCE: *a degree in Politics* **5** [sing.] a system of political beliefs; a state of political affairs: *A politics of the future has to engage with new ideas.* ⊃ WORDFINDER NOTE at GOVERNMENT

**pol·ity** /ˈpɒləti; *NAmE* ˈpɑːl-/ *noun* (*pl.* **-ies**) (*specialist*) **1** [C] a society as a political unit **2** [U] the form or process of government

**polka** /ˈpɒlkə; *NAmE* ˈpəʊl-/ *noun* a fast dance for two people together that was popular in the 19th century; a piece of music for this dance

**ˈpolka dot** *noun* one of many small round marks that together form a pattern, especially on cloth: *a polka-dot tie* ⊃ compare SPOT

**poll** 〈B1+〉 〈C1〉 /pəʊl/ *noun, verb*
■ *noun* **1** 〈B1+〉 〈C1〉 (*also* **oˈpinion poll**) [C] the process of questioning people who are representative of a larger group in order to get information about the general opinion 〈SYN〉 **survey**: *to carry out/conduct a poll* ◊ *A recent poll suggests some surprising changes in public opinion.* **2** 〈B1+〉 〈C1〉 [C] (*also* **the polls** [pl.]) the process of voting at an election; the process of counting the votes: *The final result of the poll will be known tomorrow.* ◊ *Thursday is traditionally the day when Britain goes to the polls* (= when elections are held). ◊ *Polls close* (= voting ends) *at 9 p.m.* ⊃ SYNONYMS at ELECTION **3** [sing.] the number of votes given in an election 〈SYN〉 **ballot**: *Labour is ahead in the poll.* ◊ *They gained 20 per cent of the poll.* ⊃ see also DEED POLL, EXIT POLL, STRAW POLL ⊃ WORDFINDER NOTE at DEMOCRACY
■ *verb* **1** [T, I] to receive a particular number of votes in an election: *~ sth They polled 39 per cent of the vote in the last election.* ◊ *+ adv./prep. The Republicans have polled well* (= received many votes) *in recent elections.* **2** [T, usually passive] **~ sb** to ask a large number of members of the public what they think about sth 〈SYN〉 **survey**: *Over 50 per cent of those polled were against the proposed military action.*

**pol·len** /ˈpɒlən; *NAmE* ˈpɑːl-/ *noun* [U] fine powder, usually yellow, that is formed in flowers and carried to other flowers of the same kind by the wind or by insects, to make those flowers produce seeds

**ˈpollen count** *noun* [usually sing.] a number that shows the amount of pollen in the air, used to warn people whose health is affected by it

**ˈpollen tube** *noun* (*biology*) a tube that grows when pollen lands on the STIGMA (= a part of the female organ) of a flower to carry the male cell to the OVULE (= the part that contains the female cell)

**pol·lin·ate** /ˈpɒləneɪt/; *NAmE* ˈpɑːl-/ *verb* **~ sth** to put POLLEN into a flower or plant so that it produces seeds: *flowers* pollinated by bees/the wind ▶ **pol·lin·ation** /ˌpɒləˈneɪʃn; *NAmE* ˌpɑːl-/ *noun* [U]

**poll·ing** /ˈpəʊlɪŋ/ *noun* [U] **1** the activity of voting: *Polling has been heavy since 8 a.m.* **2** the act of asking questions as part of an opinion POLL

**ˈpolling booth** (*especially BrE*) (*NAmE* usually **ˈvoting booth**) *noun* a small place in a POLLING STATION, separated from the surrounding area, where people vote by marking a card, etc.

**ˈpolling day** *noun* [U, C] (*BrE*) a day on which people vote in an election: *a week before polling day*

**ˈpolling station** (*especially BrE*) (*NAmE* usually **ˈpolling place**) *noun* a building where people go to vote in an election

**polli·wog** (*also* **polly·wog**) /ˈpɒlɪwɒg; *NAmE* ˈpɑːliwɑːg/ *noun* (*NAmE*) = TADPOLE

**poll·ster** /ˈpəʊlstə(r)/ *noun* a person who makes or asks the questions in an OPINION POLL

**ˈpoll tax** *noun* a tax that must be paid at the same rate by every person or every adult in a particular area

**pol·lu·tant** /pəˈluːtənt/ *noun* (*formal*) a substance that pollutes sth, especially air and water

**pol·lute** /pəˈluːt/ *verb* to add dirty or harmful substances to land, air, water, etc. so that it is no longer pleasant or safe to use: **~ sth** *the exhaust fumes that are polluting our cities* ◊ **~ sth by/with sth** *The river has been polluted with toxic waste from local factories.* ◊ (*figurative*) *a society polluted by racism*

**pol·luter** /pəˈluːtə(r)/ *noun* a person, company, country, etc. that causes pollution

**pol·lu·tion** ❶ 〈A2〉 /pəˈluːʃn/ *noun* [U] **1** 〈A2〉 the process of making air, water, soil, etc. dirty; the state of being dirty: *air/water pollution* ◊ *to reduce pollution levels* **2** 〈A2〉 substances that make air, water, soil, etc. dirty: *beaches covered with pollution* **3** *noise/light ~* harmful or annoying levels of noise, or of artificial light at night

**Polly·anna** /ˌpɒliˈænə; *NAmE* ˌpɑːl-/ *noun* [usually sing.] a person who is always cheerful and expects only good things to happen 〈ORIGIN〉 From the name of a character created by the US writer of children's stories, Eleanor Hodgman Porter.

**polly·wog** = POLLIWOG

**polo** /ˈpəʊləʊ/ *noun* [U] a game in which two teams of players riding on horses try to hit a ball into a goal using MALLETS (= sticks with a block of wood at one end) ⊃ see also WATER POLO

**pol·on·aise** /ˌpɒləˈneɪz; *NAmE* ˌpɑːlə-/ *noun* a slow Polish dance that was popular in the 19th century; a piece of music for this dance

**ˈpolo neck** (*BrE*) (*NAmE* **ˈturtle·neck**) *noun* a high round COLLAR made when the neck of a piece of clothing is folded over; a piece of clothing with a polo neck: *a polo-neck sweater* ◊ *You can wear a polo neck with that jacket.*

**po·lo·nium** /pəˈləʊniəm/ *noun* [U] (*symb.* **Po**) a chemical element. Polonium is a RADIOACTIVE metal that is present in nature when URANIUM DECAYS.

**ˈpolo shirt** (*NAmE* also **ˈgolf shirt**) *noun* an informal shirt with short SLEEVES, a COLLAR and a few buttons at the neck

**pol·ter·geist** /ˈpəʊltəɡaɪst, ˈpɒl-; *NAmE* ˈpəʊltərɡ-/ *noun* a ghost that makes loud noises and throws objects

**poly** /ˈpɒli; *NAmE* ˈpɑːli/ *noun* (*pl.* **polys**) (*BrE, informal*) = POLYTECHNIC

**poly-** /ˈpɒli; *BrE* also ˈpɒli; *NAmE* also ˈpɑːli/ *combining form* (in nouns, adjectives and adverbs) many: *polygamy* ◊ *polyphonic*

**poly·an·dry** /ˈpɒliændri; *NAmE* ˈpɑːli-/ *noun* [U] (*specialist*) the custom of having more than one husband at the same time ⊃ compare POLYGAMY ▶ **poly·an·drous** /-drəs/ *adj.*

# polycarbonate

**pol·y·car·bon·ate** /ˌpɒliˈkɑːbənət; NAmE ˌpɑːliˈkɑːrb-/ noun [U, C] (specialist) a very strong, clear plastic used, for example, in windows and LENSES

**poly·clinic** /ˈpɒliklɪnɪk; NAmE ˈpɑːl-/ noun (BrE) a medical centre that is not part of a hospital, where both general doctors and specialists work

**poly·es·ter** /ˌpɒliˈestə(r); NAmE ˈpɑːliestər/ noun [U] a strong material made of FIBRES (called polyesters) which are produced by chemical processes, often mixed with other materials and used especially for making clothes: *a cotton and polyester shirt*

**poly·ethyl·ene** /ˌpɒliˈeθəliːn; NAmE ˌpɑːl-/ (NAmE **poly·thene**) noun [U] a strong, thin plastic material, used especially for making bags or for wrapping things in

**pol·yg·amy** /pəˈlɪɡəmi/ noun [U] (specialist) the custom of having more than one wife at the same time ⇨ compare POLYANDRY ▶ **pol·yg·am·ist** noun **pol·yg·am·ous** adj.: *a polygamous marriage/society*

**poly·glot** /ˈpɒliɡlɒt; NAmE ˈpɑːliɡlɑːt/ adj. (formal) knowing, using or written in more than one language SYN **multilingual**: *a polyglot nation* ▶ **poly·glot** noun

### polygons

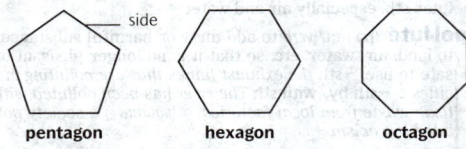

pentagon    hexagon    octagon

**poly·gon** /ˈpɒliɡən; NAmE ˈpɑːliɡɑːn/ noun (geometry) a flat shape with at least three straight sides and angles, and usually five or more ▶ **pol·yg·on·al** /pəˈlɪɡənl/ adj.

**poly·graph** /ˈpɒliɡrɑːf; NAmE ˈpɑːliɡræf/ noun (specialist) = LIE DETECTOR

**poly·he·dron** /ˌpɒliˈhiːdrən; NAmE ˌpɑːl-/ noun (pl. **poly·he·dra** /-drə/ or **poly·he·drons**) (geometry) a solid shape with many flat sides, usually more than six ▶ **poly·he·dral** /-drəl/ adj.

**poly·math** /ˈpɒlimæθ; NAmE ˈpɑːl-/ noun (formal, approving) a person who knows a lot about many different subjects

**poly·mer** /ˈpɒlimə(r); NAmE ˈpɑːl-/ noun (chemistry) a substance consisting of large MOLECULES (= groups of ATOMS) that are made from combinations of small simple MOLECULES

**poly·mer·ize** (BrE also **-ise**) /ˈpɒliməraɪz; NAmE ˈpɑːl-/ verb [I, T] ~ (sth) (chemistry) to combine, or to make units of a chemical combine, to make a POLYMER: *The substance polymerizes to form a hard plastic.* ▶ **poly·mer·iza·tion**, **-isa·tion** /ˌpɒlimeraɪˈzeɪʃn; NAmE ˌpɑːlɪməriˈz-/ noun [U]

**poly·morph·ous** /ˌpɒliˈmɔːfəs; NAmE ˌpɑːliˈmɔːrf-/ (also **poly·morph·ic** /ˌpɒliˈmɔːfɪk; NAmE ˌpɑːliˈmɔːrf-/) adj. (formal or specialist) having or passing through many stages of development

**poly·no·mial** /ˌpɒliˈnəʊmiəl; NAmE ˌpɑːl-/ noun (mathematics) an expression that has more than one group of numbers or letters, joined by the sign + or −: *Students learn how to factor polynomials.* ⇨ compare BINOMIAL (1) ▶ **poly·no·mial** adj.: *a polynomial equation*

**polyp** /ˈpɒlɪp; NAmE ˈpɑːl-/ noun **1** (medical) a small mass of cells that develops inside the body, especially in the nose, that is caused by disease but is not usually harmful **2** a small and very simple sea creature with a body like a tube in shape

**pol·yph·ony** /pəˈlɪfəni/ noun [U] (music) the combination of several different patterns of musical notes sung together to form a single piece of music SYN **counterpoint** ▶ **poly·phon·ic** /ˌpɒliˈfɒnɪk; NAmE ˌpɑːliˈfɑːn-/ adj.

**poly·pro·pyl·ene** /ˌpɒliˈprəʊpəliːn; NAmE ˌpɑːl-/ noun [U] a strong plastic often used for objects such as toys or chairs that are made in a MOULD

**poly·semy** /pəˈlɪsɪmi/ noun [U] (linguistics) the fact of having more than one meaning ▶ **poly·sem·ous** /pəˈlɪ-məs; NAmE ˌpɑːliˈsiːməs/ adj.: *polysemous words*

**poly·styr·ene** /ˌpɒliˈstaɪriːn; NAmE ˌpɑːl-/ (also **Styrofoam™** especially in NAmE) noun [U] a very light soft plastic that is usually white, used especially for making containers that prevent heat loss: *polystyrene cups*

**poly·syl·lable** /ˈpɒlisɪləbl; NAmE ˈpɑːl-/ noun (specialist) a word of several (usually more than three) syllables ▶ **poly·syl·lab·ic** /ˌpɒlisɪˈlæbɪk; NAmE ˌpɑːl-/ adj.

**poly·tech·nic** /ˌpɒliˈteknɪk; NAmE ˌpɑːl-/ (also BrE, informal **poly**) noun (in England, Wales and Northern Ireland in the past) a college for higher education, especially in scientific and technical subjects. Most polytechnics are now called, and have the same status as, universities.

**poly·the·ism** /ˈpɒliθiːɪzəm; NAmE ˈpɑːl-/ noun [U] the belief that there is more than one god ⇨ compare MONOTHEISM ▶ **poly·the·is·tic** /ˌpɒliθiːˈɪstɪk; NAmE ˌpɑːl-/ adj.

**poly·thene** /ˈpɒliθiːn; NAmE ˈpɑːl-/ (BrE) (NAmE **poly·ethyl·ene**) noun [U] a strong thin plastic material, used especially for making bags or for wrapping things in: *a polythene bag*

**poly·tun·nel** /ˈpɒlitʌnl; NAmE ˈpɑːl-/ noun a long low structure covered with plastic, used for growing seeds or young plants outdoors

**poly·un·sat·ur·ated fat** /ˌpɒliʌnˌsætʃəreɪtɪd ˈfæt; NAmE ˌpɑːl-/ noun [C, U] a type of fat found, for example, in seeds and vegetable oils, which does not encourage the harmful development of CHOLESTEROL: *foods that are high in polyunsaturated fats* ⇨ see also MONOUNSATURATED FAT, SATURATED FAT, TRANS-FATTY ACID, UNSATURATED FAT ▶ **poly·un·sat·ur·ates** /ˌpɒliʌnˈsætʃərəts; NAmE ˌpɑːl-/ noun [pl.]: *foods that are high in polyunsaturates (= polyunsaturated fats)*

**poly·ur·eth·ane** /ˌpɒliˈjʊərəθeɪn; NAmE ˌpɑːliˈjʊr-/ noun [U] (specialist) a type of plastic material used in making paint, GLUE (= a sticky substance), etc.

**poly·va·lent** /ˌpɒliˈveɪlənt; NAmE ˌpɑːl-/ adj. **1** (chemistry) having a VALENCY of 3 or more **2** (formal) having many different functions or forms: *polyvalent managerial skills* ▶ **poly·va·lence** /-ləns/ noun [U]

**poly·vi·nyl chlor·ide** /ˌpɒlivaɪnl ˈklɔːraɪd; NAmE ˌpɑːl-/ noun [U] = PVC

**pom** /pɒm; NAmE pɑːm/ noun = POMMY

**pom·ade** /pəˈmeɪd, -ˈmɑːd/ noun (old-fashioned) [U, C] a liquid that is put on the hair to make it look shiny and smell nice

**pom·egran·ate** /ˈpɒmɪɡrænɪt; NAmE ˈpɑːm-/ noun a round fruit with thick smooth skin, that is red inside and full of large seeds ⇨ VISUAL VOCAB page V4

**pom·mel** /ˈpɒml; NAmE ˈpɑːl-/ noun **1** the higher front part of a SADDLE on a horse **2** the round part on the end of the handle of a SWORD

**'pommel horse** noun a large object on four legs with two handles on top, which GYMNASTS put their hands on and move their body and legs around

**pommy** /ˈpɒmi; NAmE ˈpɑːmi/ noun (pl. **-ies**) (also **pom**) (AustralE, NZE, informal) an offensive word for a British person

**pomp** /pɒmp; NAmE pɑːmp/ noun [U] the impressive clothes, decorations, music, etc. and traditional customs that are part of an official occasion or ceremony: *all the pomp and ceremony of a royal wedding* IDM **pomp and ˈcircumstance** formal and impressive ceremony

**pom-pom** /ˈpɒm pɒm; NAmE ˈpɑːm pɑːm/ (also **pom·pon** /ˈpɒmpɒn; NAmE ˈpɑːmpɑːn/) noun **1** a small ball made of wool, used for decoration, especially on a hat SYN **bobble 2** (especially in the US) a large round bunch of thin pieces of plastic, tied to a handle, used by CHEERLEADERS

**pom·pous** /ˈpɒmpəs; NAmE ˈpɑːm-/ adj. (disapproving) showing that you think you are more important than other people, especially by using long and formal words SYN **pretentious**: *a pompous official* ▶ **pom·pos·ity** /pɒmˈpɒsəti; NAmE pɑːmˈpɑːs-/ noun [U]: *The prince's manner* was informal, without a trace of pomposity. **pom·pous·ly** /ˈpɒmpəsli/ *NAmE* /pɑːm-/ *adv.*

**poncey** (*also* **poncy**) /ˈpɒnsi/ *NAmE* /ˈpɑːn-/ *adj.* (*BrE, disapproving, informal*) trying to be impressive in a way that is silly and not natural: *I don't want to go to some poncey restaurant—I just want something to eat!*

**pon·cho** /ˈpɒntʃəʊ/ *NAmE* /ˈpɑːn-/ *noun* (*pl.* **-os**) a type of coat without arms, made from one piece of cloth with a hole in the middle for the head to go through

**pond** /pɒnd/ *NAmE* /pɑːnd/ *noun* **1** a small area of still water, especially one that is artificial: *a fish pond* **2** (*informal, humorous*) the Atlantic Ocean: *across the ~ Critics across the pond have been queueing up to heap praise on the movie.* **IDM** see BIG *adj.*

**pon·der** /ˈpɒndə(r)/ *NAmE* /ˈpɑːn-/ *verb* [I, T] (*formal*) to think about sth carefully for a period of time **SYN** **consider**: *~ on/over sth She pondered over his words.* ◊ *~sth The senator pondered the question for a moment.* ◊ *~whether, what, etc… They are pondering whether the money could be better used elsewhere.* ◊ *+ speech 'I wonder why,' she pondered aloud.*

**pon·der·ous** /ˈpɒndərəs/ *NAmE* /ˈpɑːn-/ *adj.* (*formal*) **1** (*disapproving*) (of speech and writing) too slow and careful; serious and boring **SYN** **tedious 2** moving slowly and heavily, able to move only slowly **SYN** **laboured**: *She watched the cow's ponderous progress.* ▸ **pon·der·ous·ly** *adv.* **pon·der·ous·ness** *noun* [U]

**pong** /pɒŋ/ *NAmE* /pɑːŋ/ *noun* (*BrE, informal*) a strong unpleasant smell ▸ **pong** *verb* [I]: *That cheese pongs!*

**pon·tiff** /ˈpɒntɪf/ *NAmE* /ˈpɑːn-/ *noun* (*formal*) the POPE (= the leader of the Roman Catholic Church)

**pon·tif·ic·al** /pɒnˈtɪfɪkl/ *NAmE* /pɑːn-/ *adj.* (*formal*) connected with a POPE

**pon·tifi·cate** *verb, noun*
▪ *verb* /pɒnˈtɪfɪkeɪt/ *NAmE* /pɑːn-/ [I] *~(about/on sth)* (*disapproving*) to give your opinions about sth in a way that shows that you think you are right
▪ *noun* /pɒnˈtɪfɪkət/ *NAmE* /pɑːn-/ the official position or period in office of a POPE

**pon·toon** /pɒnˈtuːn/ *NAmE* /pɑːn-/ *noun* **1** [C] a temporary floating platform built across several boats or hollow structures, especially one used for tying boats to **2** [C] a boat or hollow structure that is one of several used to support a floating platform or bridge: *a pontoon bridge* **3** [U] (*BrE*) = BLACKJACK (1)

**pony** /ˈpəʊni/ *noun, verb*
▪ *noun* (*pl.* **-ies**) **1** a type of small horse ⊃ see also SHETLAND PONY **2** (*BrE, slang*) £25 ⊃ see also ONE-TRICK PONY **IDM** see DOG *n.*, SHANK
▪ *verb* (**po·nies, pony·ing, po·nied, po·nied**)
**PHRV** **pony ˈup sth** (*NAmE, informal*) to pay money for sth: *Each guest had to pony up $40 for the meal.*

**pony·tail** /ˈpəʊniteɪl/ *noun* a bunch of hair tied at the back of the head so that it hangs like a horse's tail ⊃ compare PIGTAIL

**pony-trekking** *noun* [U] (*BrE*) the activity of riding PONIES in the countryside for pleasure: *to go pony-trekking*

**Ponzi scheme** /ˈpɒnzi skiːm/ *NAmE* /ˈpɑːn-/ *noun* a plan for making money that involves encouraging people to invest by offering them a high rate of interest and using their money to pay earlier INVESTORS. When there are not enough new INVESTORS, people who have recently invested lose their money. **ORIGIN** From Charles Ponzi, who organized the first scheme of this kind in the US in 1919.

**poo** (*also* **pooh**) /puː/ (*both BrE*) (*also* **poop** *especially in NAmE*) *noun* [U, C] a child's word for the solid waste that is passed through the BOWELS **SYN** **faeces**: *dog poo* ◊ *I want to do a poo!* ▸ **poo** (*also* **pooh**) *verb* [I]

**pooch** /puːtʃ/ *noun* (*informal*) a dog

**poo·dle** /ˈpuːdl/ *noun* **1** a dog with thick curly hair that is sometimes cut into special shapes **2** (*BrE, informal*) a person who is too willing to do what sb else tells them to do

**poof** /pʊf/ *noun, exclamation*
▪ *noun* (*also* **poof·ter** /ˈpʊftə(r)/) (*BrE, taboo, slang*) an offensive word for a GAY man

▪ *exclamation* used when talking about sth disappearing suddenly: *He walked through—and vanished. Poof! Like that.*

**pooh** /puː/ *exclamation, noun, verb*
▪ *exclamation* (*especially BrE*) **1** used to express great dislike at a bad smell: *Pooh! It stinks!* **2** used to say that you think sb's idea, suggestion, etc. is not very good or that you do not believe what sb has said: *'I might lose my job for this.' 'Oh, pooh, nobody will care.'*
▪ *noun, verb* = POO

**pooh-ˈpooh** *verb ~sth* (*informal*) to say that a suggestion, an idea, etc. is not true or not worth thinking about

**pool** /puːl/ *noun, verb*
▪ *noun*
• FOR SWIMMING **1** [C] = SWIMMING POOL: *an indoor/outdoor pool* ◊ *Does the hotel have a pool?* ◊ *relaxing by the pool* ⊃ see also INFINITY POOL, PADDLING POOL, PLUNGE POOL, WADING POOL
• OF WATER **2** [C] a small area of still water, especially one that has formed naturally: *freshwater/thermal pools* ⊃ see also ROCK POOL, TIDE POOL
• OF LIQUID/LIGHT **3** [C] *~(of sth)* a small amount of liquid or light lying on a surface: *The body was lying in a pool of blood.* ◊ *a pool of light*
• GROUP OF THINGS/PEOPLE **4** [C] *~(of sth)* a supply of things or money that is shared by a group of people and can be used when needed: *a pool of cars used by the firm's sales force* ◊ *a pool car* ⊃ see also GENE POOL **5** [C] *~(of sth)* a group of people available for work when needed: *a pool of cheap labour*
• GAME **6** [U] a game for two people played with 16 balls on a table, often in pubs and bars. Players use CUES (= long sticks) to try to hit the balls into pockets at the edge of the table: *a pool table* ◊ *to shoot* (= play) *pool* ⊃ compare BILLIARDS, SNOOKER
▪ *verb ~sth* to collect money, information, etc. from different people so that it can be used by all of them: *The students work individually, then pool their ideas in groups of six.* ◊ *Police forces across the country are pooling resources in order to solve this crime.*

**pool·room** /ˈpuːlruːm, -rʊm/ *noun* (*NAmE*) **1** a place for playing a game of POOL **2** a BETTING SHOP

**pool·side** /ˈpuːlsaɪd/ *noun* [sing.] the area around a swimming pool: *lazing at the poolside* ◊ *a poolside bar*

**poop** /puːp/ *noun, verb*
▪ *noun* **1** (*also* **ˈpoop deck**) [C] the raised part at the back end of a ship ⊃ compare STERN **2** [U] (*especially NAmE*) (*BrE usually* **poo**) (*informal*) a child's word for the solid waste that is passed through the BOWELS: *dog poop on the sidewalk* **3** [U] (*especially NAmE, old-fashioned, informal*) information about sth, especially the most recent news
▪ *verb* (*NAmE, informal*) **1** (*BrE usually* **poo**) [I] to pass solid waste from the BOWELS: *The dog just pooped in the kitchen!* **2** [T] *~sb (out)* to make sb very tired
**PHRV** **poop ˈout** to stop working or functioning

**pooped** /puːpt/ (*also* **ˌpooped ˈout**) *adj.* [not before noun] (*especially NAmE, informal*) very tired

**pooper scoop·er** /ˈpuːpə skuːpə(r)/ *NAmE* /ˈpuːpər/ (*also* **ˈpoop scoop**) *noun* (*informal*) a tool used by dog owners for removing their dogs' solid waste from the streets, parks, etc.

## poor /pɔː(r), pʊə(r)/ *NAmE* /pʊr, pɔːr/ *adj.* (**poor·er, poor·est**)

• HAVING LITTLE MONEY **1** having very little money; not having enough money for basic needs: *They were too poor to buy shoes for the kids.* ◊ *We aim to help the poorest families.* ◊ *It's among the poorer countries of the world.* **OPP** **rich** ⊃ see also DIRT POOR **2** **the poor** *noun* [pl.] people who have very little money: *They provided food and shelter for the poor.* **OPP** **the rich** ⊃ see also WORKING POOR

**WORDFINDER** beg, benefit, charity, homeless, hostel, poverty, shanty town, sweatshop, unemployment

• UNFORTUNATE **3** [only before noun] deserving sympathy: *Have you heard about poor old Harry? His wife's left*

# poorhouse 1194

him. ◊ *It's hungry—the poor little thing.* ◊ *'I have stacks of homework to do.' 'Oh, you poor thing.'*
- **NOT GOOD 4** **B1** not good; of a quality that is low or lower than expected: *the party's **poor** performance in the election* ◊ *The food was of very **poor** quality.* ◊ *to be in **poor** health* ◊ *It was raining heavily and visibility was poor.* ◊ *to have a poor opinion of sb* (= to not think well of sb) ◊ see also PISS-POOR **5** **B1** [usually before noun] (of a person) not good at sth: *a poor swimmer* ◊ *a poor judge of character* ◊ *She's a good teacher but a poor manager.* ◊ *~ **at (doing) sth** Many companies are poor at dealing with telephone complaints.*
- **HAVING LITTLE OF STH 6** **B2** **~ in sth** having very small amounts of sth: *a country poor in natural resources* ◊ *soil poor in nutrients* **OPP** rich ◊ see also TIME-POOR

**IDM** **be/come a poor second, third, etc.** (*especially BrE*) to finish a long way behind the winner in a race, competition, etc. **the ˌpoor man's ˈsb/ˈsth** a person or thing that is similar to but of a lower quality than a particular famous person or thing: *Sparkling white wine is the poor man's champagne.*

▼ SYNONYMS

**poor**

disadvantaged • needy • impoverished • deprived • penniless • hard up

These words all describe sb who has very little or no money and therefore cannot satisfy their basic needs.

**poor** having very little money; not having enough money for basic needs: *They were too poor to buy shoes for the kids.*

**disadvantaged** having less money and fewer opportunities than most people in society: *socially disadvantaged sections of the community*

**needy** poor: *It's a charity that provides help for needy children.*

**impoverished** (*journalism*) poor: *Thousands of impoverished peasants are desperate to move to the cities.*

**deprived** [usually before noun] without enough food, education, and all the things that are necessary for people to live a happy and comfortable life

POOR, NEEDY, IMPOVERISHED OR DEPRIVED?

**Poor** is the most general of these words and can be used to describe yourself, another individual person, people as a group, or a country or an area. **Needy** is mostly used to describe people considered as a group: it is not used to talk about yourself or individual people: *poor/needy children/families* ◊ *They were too needy to buy shoes for the kids.* **Impoverished** is used, especially in journalism, to talk about poor countries and the people who live there. To talk about poor areas in rich countries, use **deprived**.

**penniless** (*literary*) having no money; very poor: *He died penniless in Paris.*

**hard up** (*informal*) having very little money, especially for a short period of time: *I was always hard up as a student.*

PATTERNS
- poor/disadvantaged/needy/impoverished/deprived/penniless/hard-up **people/families**
- poor/disadvantaged/needy/impoverished/deprived **areas**
- poor/disadvantaged/impoverished **countries**
- a(n) poor/disadvantaged/impoverished/deprived **background**

**poor·house** /ˈpɔːhaʊs, ˈpʊəh-; *NAmE* ˈpʊrh-, ˈpɔːr-/ (*BrE also* **work·house**) noun (in the UK in the past) a building where very poor people were sent to live and given work to do

**the ˌPoor ˈLaw** noun a group of laws used in Britain in the past to control the help that was given to poor people

**poor·ly** /ˈpɔːli, ˈpʊəli; *NAmE* ˈpʊrli, ˈpɔːr-/ *adv., adj.*
- *adv.* in a way that is not good enough **SYN** badly: *a poorly attended meeting* (= at which there are not many people) ◊ *poorly designed* ◊ *The job is relatively poorly paid.* ◊ *Our candidate fared poorly in the election* (= did not get many votes). ◊ *Healthcare in the capital compares poorly with that in the rest of the country.*
- *adj.* [not usually before noun] (*BrE, informal*) ill: *She felt poorly.*

**poor·ness** /ˈpɔːnəs, ˈpʊən-; *NAmE* ˈpʊrn-, ˈpɔːr-/ noun [U] the state of not having a good quality or feature: *The poorness of the land makes farming impossible.*

**ˌpoor reˈlation** noun something that is not treated with as much respect as other similar things because it is not thought to be as good, important or successful: *The short story is often considered to be a poor relation to the novel.*

**poo·tle** /ˈpuːtl/ verb [I] **+ adv./prep.** (*BrE, informal*) to move or travel without any hurry: *She pootled along in her old car.*

**pop** **A2** /pɒp; *NAmE* pɑːp/ *noun, adj., verb, adv.*
- *noun*
- MUSIC **1** **A2** (*also* **ˈpop music**) [U] popular music of the sort that has been popular since the 1950s, usually with a strong rhythm and simple tunes, often contrasted with rock, SOUL and other forms of popular music: *rock, pop and soul* ◊ *The album covers a range of genres—from mainstream pop to jazz.* ◊ see also SYNTH-POP
- SOUND **2** [C] a short, sharp, EXPLOSIVE sound: *The cork came out of the bottle with a loud pop.*
- DRINK **3** [U] (*old-fashioned, informal*) a sweet FIZZY drink (= with bubbles) that is not alcoholic
- FATHER **4** [sing.] (*especially NAmE, old-fashioned, informal*) used as a word for 'father', especially as a form of address: *Hi, Pop!*

**IDM** **have/take a ˈpop (at sb)** (*BrE, informal*) to attack sb physically or in words **…a pop** (*especially NAmE, informal*) costing a particular amount for each one: *We can charge $50 a pop.*

- *adj.* [only before noun]
- MUSIC/STYLE **1** **A2** connected with modern popular music: *a pop song* ◊ *a pop star/singer* ◊ *a pop band/group* ◊ *a pop concert* **2** made in a modern popular style: *pop culture*
- *verb* (-pp-)
- MAKE SOUND **1** [I+] **C1** [I, T] ~(sth) to make a short EXPLOSIVE sound; to cause sth to make this sound: *the sound of corks popping* **2** [I+] **C1** [T, I] ~(sth) to BURST, or make sth BURST (= break apart or open), with a short EXPLOSIVE sound: *She jumped as someone popped a balloon behind her.*
- GO QUICKLY **3** [I+] **C1** [I] + **adv./prep.** (*informal*) to go somewhere quickly, suddenly or for a short time: *I'll pop over and see you this evening.* ◊ *Why don't you pop in* (= visit us) *for a drink next time you're in the area?*
- PUT QUICKLY **4** [I+] **C1** [T] ~ **sth/sb + adv./prep.** (*especially BrE, informal*) to put sth/sb somewhere quickly, suddenly or for a short time: *He popped his head around the door and said hello.* ◊ *I'll pop the books in* (= deliver them) *on my way home.* ◊ *Pop your bag on here.*
- APPEAR SUDDENLY **5** [I+] **C1** [I] + **adv./prep.** to suddenly appear, especially when not expected: *The window opened and a dog's head popped out.* ◊ *An idea suddenly popped into his head.* ◊ (*computing*) *The dialog box pops up every time I try to close the browser.*
- OF EARS **6** [I] if your ears **pop** when you are going up or down in a plane, etc., the pressure in them suddenly changes
- OF EYES **7** [I] if your eyes **pop** or **pop out**, they suddenly open fully because you are surprised or excited: *Her eyes nearly popped out of her head when she saw them.*
- TAKE DRUGS **8** [T] ~ **sth** (*informal*) to take a lot of a drug, regularly: *She's been popping pills for months.* **9** [T] ~ **the hood** (*NAmE*) to open the BONNET of a car

**IDM** **pop your ˈclogs** (*BrE, humorous*) to die **pop the ˈquestion** (*informal*) to ask sb to marry you **PHRV** **ˌpop ˈoff** (*informal*) to die **ˌpop sth↔ˈon** (*BrE, informal*) **1** to put on a piece of clothing: *I'll just pop on a sweater and meet you outside.* **2** to turn on a piece of electrical equipment

- *adv.*

**IDM** **go ˈpop** to BURST (= to break open) or explode with a sudden short sound: *The balloon went pop.*

**pop.** *abbr.* population: *pop. 200000*

**ˈpop art** (*also* **Pop Art**) noun [U] a style of art, developed in the 1950s and 1960s, that was based on popular culture and used material such as advertisements, film images, etc.

**pop·corn** /ˈpɒpkɔːn; NAmE ˈpɑːpkɔːrn/ noun [U] a type of food made from grains of MAIZE that are heated until they explode, forming light white balls that are then covered with salt or sugar

**ˈpop culture** (also ˌpopular ˈculture) noun [U] (sometimes disapproving) TV shows, books, toys, etc. that are popular among ordinary people in a particular society: *Mickey Mouse has become a part of American pop culture.*

**pope** /pəʊp/ (often **the Pope**) noun the leader of the Roman Catholic Church, who is also the Bishop of Rome: *the election of a new pope* ◇ *Pope Francis* ◇ *a visit from the Pope* ⇒ see also PAPACY, PAPAL
**IDM** **Is the Pope (a) ˈCatholic?** (*humorous*) used to say that there is no doubt that sth is true: *'Will they arrive late?' 'Is the Pope a Catholic?'*

**popery** /ˈpəʊpəri/ noun [U] (*taboo*) an offensive way of referring to Roman Catholicism

**ˈpop-eyed** adj. (*informal*) having eyes that are wide open, especially because you are very surprised, excited or frightened

**ˈpop·gun** /ˈpɒpɡʌn; NAmE ˈpɑːp-/ noun a toy gun that fires small objects such as CORKS and makes a short sharp noise

**pop·ish** /ˈpəʊpɪʃ/ adj. [usually before noun] (*taboo, offensive*) used by some people to describe sb/sth that is connected with Roman Catholicism

**pop·lar** /ˈpɒplə(r); NAmE ˈpɑːp-/ noun a tall straight tree with soft wood

**ˈpop music** noun = POP

**pop·over** /ˈpɒpəʊvə(r); NAmE ˈpɑːp-/ noun (NAmE) a type of food made from a mixture of eggs, milk and flour which rises to form a hollow shell when it is baked

**poppa** /ˈpɒpə; NAmE ˈpɑːpə/ noun (NAmE, *informal*) used by children to talk about or to address their father ⇒ see also PAPA, POP noun

**pop·pa·dom** /ˈpɒpədəm; NAmE ˈpɑːp-/ noun a type of thin round South Asian bread that is fried in oil and often served with CURRY

**pop·per** /ˈpɒpə(r); NAmE ˈpɑːp-/ noun (BrE) = PRESS STUD

**pop·pet** /ˈpɒpɪt; NAmE ˈpɑːp-/ noun (BrE, *informal*) used to talk to or about sb you like or love, especially a child

**ˌpop psyˈchology** noun [U] the use by ordinary people of simple or fashionable ideas from psychology in order to understand or explain people's feelings and emotional problems

**poppy** /ˈpɒpi; NAmE ˈpɑːpi/ noun (pl. **-ies**) a wild or garden plant, with a large DELICATE flower that is usually red, and small black seeds. OPIUM is obtained from one type of poppy: *poppy fields/seeds* ⇒ VISUAL VOCAB page V7

**ˈpoppy·cock** /ˈpɒpikɒk; NAmE ˈpɑːpikɑːk/ noun [U] (*old-fashioned, informal*) ideas, statements or beliefs that you think are silly or not true **SYN** nonsense

**ˈpop quiz** noun (NAmE) a short test that is given to students without any warning

**Pop·sicle**™ /ˈpɒpsɪkl; NAmE ˈpɑːp-/ (NAmE) (BrE **ice lolly**, *informal* **lolly**) noun a piece of ice that tastes of fruit, served on a stick

**popu·lace** /ˈpɒpjələs; NAmE ˈpɑːp-/ noun [sing. + sing. / pl. v.] (*formal*) (usually **the populace**) all the ordinary people of a particular country or area: *He had the support of large sections of the local populace.* ◇ *The populace at large is/ are opposed to sudden change.*

**popu·lar** ⓘ A1 Ⓢ /ˈpɒpjələ(r); NAmE ˈpɑːp-/ adj.
**1** A1 liked or enjoyed by a large number of people: *an extremely/immensely popular TV show* ◇ *This is one of our most popular designs.* ◇ **~ with sb** *These policies are unlikely to prove popular with middle-class voters.* ◇ *I'm not very popular with my parents* (= they are annoyed with me) *at the moment.* ◇ **~ among sb** *Pizza is more popular among younger adults.* ◇ (*ironic*) *'Our dog got into the neighbour's garden again!' 'You'll be popular.'* **OPP** unpopular **2** Ⓑ B2 [only before noun] (*sometimes disapproving*) right or appropriate for the taste and knowledge of ordinary people: *popular music/songs/culture/fiction* ◇ *the popular press* **3** Ⓑ B2 [only before noun] (of ideas, beliefs and opinions) shared by a large number of people: *a popular misconception* ◇ *Contrary to popular belief, women cause fewer road accidents than men.* ◇ *Popular opinion was divided on the issue.* ◇ *By popular demand, the tour has been extended by two weeks.* **4** [only before noun] connected with the ordinary people of a country: *The party still has widespread popular support.* ◇ *a share of the popular vote* **IDM** see WISDOM

**ˌpopular ˈculture** noun [U] (*sometimes disapproving*) = POP CULTURE

**ˌpopular etyˈmology** noun [U] = FOLK ETYMOLOGY

**ˌpopular ˈfront** noun a political group or party that has SOCIALIST aims

**popu·lar·ity** ⓘ B2 /ˌpɒpjuˈlærəti; NAmE ˌpɑːp-/ noun [U] the state of being liked, enjoyed or supported by a large number of people: *the increasing popularity of cycling* ◇ *Her novels have gained in popularity over recent years.* ◇ **~ with/among sb** *to win/lose popularity with the students*

**popu·lar·ize** (BrE also **-ise**) /ˈpɒpjələraɪz; NAmE ˈpɑːp-/ verb **1 ~ sb/sth** to make a lot of people know about sth and enjoy it: *The programme did much to popularize little-known writers.* **2 ~ sth** to make a difficult subject easier to understand for ordinary people: *He spent his life popularizing natural history.* ▶ **popu·lar·iza·tion, -isa·tion** /ˌpɒpjələraɪˈzeɪʃn; NAmE ˌpɑːpjələrəˈz-/ noun [U]

**popu·lar·ly** /ˈpɒpjələli; NAmE ˈpɑːpjələrli/ adv. **1** by a large number of people **SYN** commonly: *a popularly held belief* ◇ *the UN Conference on Environment and Development, popularly known as the 'Earth Summit'* **2** by the ordinary people of a country **SYN** democratically: *a popularly elected government*

**ˈpopular vote** noun **1** [U, C] the act of voting by the people in a country or an area who have the right to vote: *The head of government is the prime minister, elected by popular vote for a four-year term.* **2** (often **the popular vote**) [C, usually sing.] the choice expressed in an election by the majority of people who vote (but which may not necessarily determine who wins the election, depending on the system used): *It is possible to win the popular vote but still lose the electoral vote.* ⇒ compare ELECTORAL VOTE (2)

**popu·late** /ˈpɒpjuleɪt; NAmE ˈpɑːp-/ verb **1** [often passive] **~ sth** to live in an area and form its population **SYN** inhabit: *a heavily/densely/sparsely/thinly populated country* ◇ *The island is populated largely by sheep.* ◇ (*figurative*) *the amazing characters that populate her novels* **2 ~ sth** to move people or animals to an area to live there: *The French began to populate the island in the 15th century.* **3 ~ sth** (*computing*) to add data to a document

**popu·la·tion** ⓘ A2 Ⓞ /ˌpɒpjuˈleɪʃn; NAmE ˌpɑːp-/ noun **1** Ⓐ A2 [C + sing. / pl. v., U] all the people who live in a particular area, city or country; the total number of people who live there: *One third of the world's population consumes/consume two thirds of the world's resources.* ◇ *The country has a total population of 65 million.* ◇ *The entire population of the town was at the meeting.* ◇ *countries with ageing populations* ◇ *Muslims make up 55 per cent of the population.* ◇ *areas of dense/sparse population* (= where many/not many people live) **2** Ⓐ A2 [C + sing. / pl. v.] a particular group of people or animals living in a particular area: *the adult/student/working population* ◇ *the rural/urban population* ◇ *The disease is relatively uncommon in the general population.* ◇ *The prison population* (= the number of people in prison) *is continuing to rise.* ◇ *Oil spillages are disastrous for fish populations.* ⇒ WORDFINDER NOTE at CITY

**popuˈlation exˌplosion** noun a sudden large increase in the number of people or animals living in an area

**popu·lism** /ˈpɒpjəlɪzəm; NAmE ˈpɑːp-/ noun [U] a type of politics that claims to represent the opinions and wishes of ordinary people ▶ **popu·list** /-lɪst/ noun: *a party of populists* **popu·list** adj. [usually before noun]: *a populist leader*

**popu·lous** /ˈpɒpjələs; NAmE ˈpɑːp-/ adj. (*formal*) where a large number of people live: *one of America's most populous states*

**pop-up**

**pop-up** *adj., noun* [only before noun]
- *adj.* **1** (of a book, etc.) containing a picture that stands up when the pages are opened: *a pop-up birthday card* **2** (of an electric TOASTER) that pushes the bread quickly upwards when it is ready **3** (of a computer menu, etc.) that can be brought to the screen quickly while you are working on another document: *a pop-up menu/window* **4** a pop-up shop, restaurant, etc. is a business that opens quickly somewhere and is designed to only use that location for a short period of time: *The airline opened a pop-up shop to promote its winter sale.*
- *noun* **1** a computer menu, window, etc. that can be brought to the screen quickly while you are working on another document; a computer window, especially one containing an advertisement, that appears on the screen although it has not been requested: *an advertising pop-up* **2** a shop, restaurant, etc. that opens quickly somewhere and is designed to only use that location for a short period of time: *The designers opened a pop-up in the main shopping area as part of the fashion event.*

**por·cel·ain** /ˈpɔːsəlɪn; NAmE ˈpɔːrs-/ *noun* [U, C] a hard, white, shiny substance made by baking CLAY and used for making DELICATE cups, plates and other objects; objects that are made of this: *a porcelain figure*

**porch** /pɔːtʃ; NAmE pɔːrtʃ/ *noun* **1** a small area at the entrance to a building, such as a house or a church, that is covered by a roof and often has walls **2** (NAmE) = VERANDA

**por·cine** /ˈpɔːsaɪn; NAmE ˈpɔːrs-/ *adj.* (*formal*) like a pig; connected with pigs

**por·cu·pine** /ˈpɔːkjupaɪn; NAmE ˈpɔːrk-/ *noun* an animal covered with long, stiff parts like needles (called QUILLS), which it can raise to protect itself when it is attacked

**pore** /pɔː(r)/ *noun, verb*
- *noun* one of the very small holes in your skin that SWEAT can pass through; one of the similar small holes in the surface of a plant or a rock ⇒ see also POROUS
- *verb*
**PHRV** **'pore over sth** to look at or read sth very carefully **SYN** *examine*: *His lawyers are poring over the small print in the contract.*

**pork** /pɔːk; NAmE pɔːrk/ *noun* [U] **1** meat from a pig that has not been CURED (= preserved using salt or smoke): *roast pork* ◊ *pork chops* ◊ *a leg of pork* ⇒ compare BACON, GAMMON, HAM ⇒ see also PULLED PORK **2** (NAmE, *informal*) = PORK BARREL

**'pork barrel** *noun* [U] (NAmE, *informal*) local projects that are given a lot of government money in order to win votes; the money that is used

**pork·er** /ˈpɔːkə(r); NAmE ˈpɔːrk-/ *noun* a pig that is made fat and used as food

**pork 'pie** *noun* [C, U] (in the UK) a small PIE filled with PORK and usually eaten cold

**pork 'scratchings** (BrE) (US **pork rinds**) *noun* [pl.] hard pieces of pig skin that are fried and eaten cold, often sold in bags as a SNACK

**porky** /ˈpɔːki; NAmE ˈpɔːrki/ *noun, adj.*
- *noun* (*pl.* **-ies**) (*also* **porky 'pie**) (BrE, *slang*) a statement that is not true; a lie: *to tell porkies*
- *adj.* (*informal, disapproving*) (of people) fat

**porn** /pɔːn; NAmE pɔːrn/ *noun* [U] (*informal*) = PORNOGRAPHY ⇒ see also HARD PORN, SOFT PORN

**porno** /ˈpɔːnəʊ; NAmE ˈpɔːrn-/ *adj.* [usually before noun] (*informal*) = PORNOGRAPHIC: *a porno movie*

**porn·og·raph·er** /pɔːˈnɒɡrəfə(r); NAmE pɔːrˈnɑːɡ-/ *noun* (*disapproving*) a person who produces or sells pornography

**porno·graph·ic** /ˌpɔːnəˈɡræfɪk; NAmE ˌpɔːrn-/ (*also informal* **porno**) *adj.* [usually before noun] (*disapproving*) intended to make people feel sexually excited by showing NAKED people or sexual acts, usually in a way that many other people find offensive: *pornographic movies/magazines*

**porn·og·raphy** /pɔːˈnɒɡrəfi; NAmE pɔːrˈnɑːɡ-/ *noun* [U] (*also informal* **porn**) (*disapproving*) magazines, DVDs, websites, etc. that describe or show NAKED people and sexual acts in order to make people feel sexually excited, especially in a way that many other people find offensive: *child pornography*

**por·os·ity** /pɔːˈrɒsəti; NAmE -ˈrɑːs-/ *noun* [U] (*specialist*) the quality or state of being porous

**por·ous** /ˈpɔːrəs/ *adj.* having many small holes that allow water or air to pass through slowly: *porous material/rocks/surfaces*

**por·phy·ria** /pɔːˈfɪriə; NAmE pɔːrˈf-/ *noun* [U] (*medical*) a disease of the blood that causes mental problems and makes the skin sensitive to light

**por·poise** /ˈpɔːpəs; NAmE ˈpɔːrp-/ *noun* a sea animal that looks like a large fish with a pointed mouth. Porpoises are similar to DOLPHINS but smaller.

**por·ridge** /ˈpɒrɪdʒ; NAmE ˈpɔːr-/ *noun* [U] **1** (*especially BrE*) (NAmE *usually* **oat·meal**) a type of soft, thick, white food made by boiling OATS in milk or water, eaten hot, especially for breakfast **2** (EAfrE) a type of thick drink made by boiling flour with water

**port** 🔊 **B1** /pɔːt; NAmE pɔːrt/ *noun, verb*
- *noun* **1** 🔊 **B1** [C] a town or city with a HARBOUR, especially one where ships load and unload goods: *a container/fishing port* ◊ *Rotterdam is a major port.* ◊ *the port city of Gdansk* **2** 🔊 **B1** [C, U] (*abbr.* **Pt.**) a place where ships load and unload goods or shelter from storms: *a naval port* ◊ **in/into ~** *The ship spent four days in port.* ◊ *They reached port at last.* ◊ *port of entry* (= a place where people or goods can enter a country) ⇒ see also AIRPORT, FREE PORT, HELIPORT, SEAPORT **3** (*also* **port 'wine**) [U] a strong sweet wine, usually dark red, that is made in Portugal. It is usually drunk at the end of a meal. **4** [C] a glass of port **5** [U] the side of a ship or aircraft that is on the left when you are facing forward: *the port side* ⇒ compare STARBOARD **6** [C] (*computing*) a place on a computer where you can attach another piece of equipment, often using a cable: *the modem port* ⇒ see also SERIAL PORT
**IDM** **any port in a 'storm** (*saying*) if you are in great trouble, you take any help that is offered
- *verb* **1** **~ sth (from sth) (to sth)** (*computing*) to copy software from one system or machine to another: *Is there a problem with apps ported from another platform?* **2** **~ sth (to sth)** to continue to use the same number when you change from one phone company to another: *how to port your number to a new mobile phone*

**port·able** /ˈpɔːtəbl; NAmE ˈpɔːrt-/ *adj., noun*
- *adj.* **1** that is easy to carry or to move: *a portable TV* ◊ (*figurative*) *a portable loan/pension* (= that can be moved if you change banks, jobs, etc.) **2** (*computing*) (of software) written in such a way that it can be run on computers of different types ▶ **port·abil·ity** /ˌpɔːtəˈbɪləti; NAmE ˌpɔːrt-/ *noun* [U]: *The new light cover increases this model's portability.*
- *noun* a small version of a machine, such as a television or computer, that is easy to carry: *new video games for consoles and portables*

**port·age** /ˈpɔːtɪdʒ; NAmE ˈpɔːrt-/ *noun* [U] the act of carrying boats or goods between two rivers

**Porta-john**™ /ˈpɔːtə dʒɒn; NAmE ˈpɔːrtə dʒɑːn/ *noun* (NAmE) = PORTAPOTTY

**Porta·kabin**™ /ˈpɔːtəkæbɪn; NAmE ˈpɔːrt-/ *noun* (BrE) a small building that can be moved from place to place by a vehicle, designed to be used as a temporary office, etc.

**por·tal** /ˈpɔːtl; NAmE ˈpɔːrtl/ *noun* **1** [usually pl.] (*formal or literary*) a large, impressive gate or entrance to a building **2** (*computing*) a website that is used as a point of entry to the internet, where information has been collected that will be useful to a person interested in particular kinds of things: *a business/news/shopping portal*

**Porta-loo**™ /ˈpɔːtəluː; NAmE ˈpɔːrt-/ (BrE) (NAmE **portapotty**, **Porta-john**™) *noun* (*pl.* **-oos**) a toilet inside a small light building that can be moved from place to place

**'portal vein** (*also* **he patic 'portal vein**) *noun* (*anatomy*) a VEIN that takes blood from the stomach and other organs near the stomach to the LIVER

**porta·potty** (*also* **Porta Potti**™) /ˈpɔːtəpɒti; NAmE ˈpɔːrtəpɑːti/ *noun* (*pl.* **-ies**) **1** (NAmE) (BrE **Portaloo**™) (NAmE *also* **Porta-john**™) a toilet inside a small light building that can be moved from place to place **2** (*BrE*) a toilet that you can take with you when you are travelling

**port·cul·lis** /pɔːtˈkʌlɪs; *NAmE* pɔːrt-/ *noun* a strong, heavy iron gate that can be raised or let down at the entrance to a castle

**por·tend** /pɔːˈtend; *NAmE* pɔːrˈt-/ *verb* ~ **sth** (*formal*) to be a sign or warning of sth that is going to happen in the future, especially sth bad or unpleasant SYN **foreshadow**

**por·tent** /ˈpɔːtent; *NAmE* ˈpɔːrt-/ *noun* (*literary*) a sign or warning of sth that is going to happen in the future, especially when it is sth unpleasant SYN **omen**

**por·tent·ous** /pɔːˈtentəs; *NAmE* pɔːrˈt-/ *adj.* **1** (*literary*) important as a sign or a warning of sth that is going to happen in the future, especially when it is sth unpleasant: *a portentous sign* **2** (*formal, disapproving*) very serious and intended to impress people SYN **pompous**: *a portentous remark* ▸ **por·tent·ous·ly** *adv.* **por·tent·ous·ness** *noun* [U]

**por·ter** /ˈpɔːtə(r); *NAmE* ˈpɔːrt-/ *noun* **1** a person whose job is carrying people's bags and other loads, especially at a train station, an airport or in a hotel **2** (*BrE*) a person whose job is to move patients from one place to another in a hospital **3** (*BrE*) a person whose job is to be in charge of the entrance to a hotel, large building, college, etc.: *the night porter* ◊ *The hotel porter will get you a taxi.* ⟹ compare DOORMAN **4** (*NAmE*) a person whose job is helping passengers on a train, especially in a SLEEPING CAR

**port·folio** /pɔːtˈfəʊliəʊ; *NAmE* pɔːrtˈfoʊlioʊ/ *noun* (*pl.* **-os**) **1** a thin flat case used for carrying documents, drawings, etc.: *I left my portfolio on the train.* **2** a collection of photographs, drawings, etc. that you use as an example of your work, especially when applying for a job: *She spent most of last year getting her portfolio together.* **3** (*finance*) a set of shares owned by a particular person or organization: *an investment/share portfolio* ⟹ WORDFINDER NOTE at INVEST **4** (*especially BrE, formal*) the particular area of responsibility of a government minister: *the defence portfolio* ◊ *He resigned her portfolio.* ◊ *He was asked to join as a minister without portfolio* (= one without responsibility for a particular government department). **5** the range of products or services offered by a particular company or organization: *a portfolio of wines*

**port·hole** /ˈpɔːthəʊl; *NAmE* ˈpɔːrt-/ *noun* a round window in the side of a ship or an aircraft

**por·tico** /ˈpɔːtɪkəʊ; *NAmE* ˈpɔːrt-/ *noun* (*pl.* **-oes** or **-os**) (*formal*) a roof that is supported by columns, especially one that forms the entrance to a large building

**por·tion** /ˈpɔːʃn; *NAmE* ˈpɔːrʃn/ *noun, verb*
- *noun* **1** one part of sth larger: *a substantial/significant portion of the population* ◊ *Only a small portion of the budget is spent on books.* ◊ *The central portion of the bridge collapsed.* **2** an amount of food that is large enough for one person: *a generous portion of meat* ◊ *She cut the cake into six small portions.* **3** [usually sing.] a part of sth that is shared with other people SYN **share**: *You must accept a portion of the blame for this crisis.*
- *verb* to divide sth into parts or portions: ~ **sth** *The factory portions and packs over 12 000 meals a day.* ◊ ~ **sth out** *Land was portioned out among the clans.*

**port·ly** /ˈpɔːtli; *NAmE* ˈpɔːrt-/ *adj.* [usually before noun] (especially of an older man) rather fat SYN **stout**

**port·man·teau** /pɔːtˈmæntəʊ; *NAmE* pɔːrtˈmæntoʊ/ *noun, adj.*
- *noun* (*pl.* **portmanteaus** or **portmanteaux** /-təʊz/) (*old-fashioned*) a large, heavy bag that opens into two parts
- *adj.* [only before noun] consisting of a number of different items that are combined into a single thing: *a portmanteau course* ◊ *'Depression' is a portmanteau condition.*

**port·manteau word** *noun* a word that is invented by combining the beginning of one word and the end of another and keeping the meaning of each. For example *motel* is a portmanteau word that is a combination of *motor* and *hotel*.

**ˌport of ˈcall** *noun* (*pl.* **ports of call**) **1** a port where a ship stops during a journey **2** (*informal*) a place where you go or stop for a short time, especially when you are going to several places: *My first port of call in town was the bank.*

1197 **posit**

**por·trait** /ˈpɔːtreɪt, -trət; *NAmE* ˈpɔːrtrət/ *noun* **1** ~ (**of sb**) a painting, drawing or photograph of a person, especially of the head and shoulders: *a portrait of his wife* ◊ *He had his portrait painted in uniform.* ◊ *a portrait painter* ⟹ SYNONYMS at PICTURE ⟹ WORDFINDER NOTE at PAINTING ⟹ see also SELF-PORTRAIT **2** ~ (**of sb/sth**) a detailed description of sb/sth SYN **depiction**: *a portrait of life at the French court* **3** (used especially before another noun) the way of printing a document in which the top of the page is one of the shorter sides ⟹ compare LANDSCAPE (4)

**por·trait·ist** /ˈpɔːtreɪtɪst, -trət-; *NAmE* ˈpɔːrtrət-/ *noun* a person who makes portraits

**por·trait·ure** /ˈpɔːtrətʃə(r); *NAmE* ˈpɔːrtrət-/ *noun* [U] the art of making portraits; the portraits that are made

**por·tray** /pɔːˈtreɪ; *NAmE* pɔːrˈt-/ *verb* **1** ~ **sb/sth** to show sb/sth in a picture; to describe sb/sth in a piece of writing SYN **depict**: *The painting portrays the duke's third wife.* ◊ *His war poetry vividly portrays life in the trenches.* **2** ~ **sb/sth** (**as sb/sth**) to describe or show sb/sth in a particular way, especially when this does not give a complete or accurate impression of what they are like SYN **represent**: *Throughout the trial, he portrayed himself as the victim.* **3** ~ **sb/sth** to act a particular role in a film or play SYN **play**: *Her father will be portrayed by Jim Broadbent.*

**por·tray·al** /pɔːˈtreɪəl; *NAmE* pɔːrˈt-/ *noun* [C, U] the act of showing or describing sb/sth in a picture, play, book, etc.; a particular way in which this is done: *The article examines the portrayal of gay men in the media.* ◊ *He is best known for his chilling portrayal of Hannibal Lecter.*

**Por·tu·guese** /ˌpɔːtʃuˈɡiːz; *NAmE* ˌpɔːrtʃ-/ *adj., noun*
- *adj.* from or connected with Portugal
- *noun* **1** [C] (*pl.* **Por·tu·guese**) a person from Portugal **2** [U] the language used in Portugal and Brazil and some other countries

**pose** /pəʊz; *NAmE* poʊz/ *verb, noun*
- *verb* **1** [T] ~ **sth** to create a threat, problem, etc. that has to be dealt with: *to pose a threat/risk/challenge/danger* ◊ *The task poses no special problems.* **2** [T] ~ **a question** (*formal*) to ask a question, especially one that needs serious thought **3** [I] ~ (**for sb/sth**) to sit or stand in a particular position in order to be painted, drawn or photographed: *The delegates posed for a group photograph.* **4** [I] ~ **as sb** to pretend to be sb in order to trick other people: *The gang entered the building posing as workmen.* **5** [I] (usually used in the progressive tenses) (*disapproving*) to dress or behave in a way that is intended to impress other people: *I saw him out posing in his new sports car.*
- *noun* **1** a particular position in which sb stands, sits, etc., especially in order to be painted, drawn or photographed: *He adopted a relaxed pose for the camera.* **2** (*disapproving*) a way of behaving that is not sincere and is intended to impress or trick people SYN **affectation** IDM see STRIKE v.

**poser** /ˈpəʊzə(r); *NAmE* ˈpoʊz-/ *noun* **1** (*informal*) a difficult question or problem SYN **puzzler** **2** (*also* **pos·eur** (*disapproving*)) a person who behaves or dresses in a way that is intended to impress other people and is not sincere

**pos·eur** /pəʊˈzɜː(r); *NAmE* poʊˈzɜːr/ *noun* = POSER (2)

**posh** /pɒʃ; *NAmE* pɑːʃ/ *adj.* (**posh·er, posh·est**) (*informal*) **1** attractive and expensive SYN **stylish**: *a posh hotel* ◊ *You look very posh in your new suit.* **2** (*BrE, sometimes disapproving*) typical of or used by people who belong to a high social class: *a posh accent/voice* ◊ *They live in the posh part of town.* ◊ *They pay for their children to go to a posh school.* ▸ **posh** *adv.*: (*BrE*) *to talk posh*

**posho** *noun* **1** /ˈpɒʃəʊ; *NAmE* ˈpɑːʃ-/ [C] (*pl.* **-os**) (*BrE, informal, disapproving*) a person from a high social class **2** /ˈpəʊʃəʊ; *EAfrE* [ˈpoʃo] [U] (*EAfrE*) a type of flour made from MAIZE: *a posho mill*

**posit** /ˈpɒzɪt; *NAmE* ˈpɑːz-/ *verb* ~ **sth** | ~ **that …** (*formal*) to suggest or accept that sth is true so that it can be used as the basis for an argument or discussion SYN **postulate**: *Most religions posit the existence of life after death.*

# position 1198

**po·si·tion** 🔑 A2 ⊙ /pəˈzɪʃn/ noun, verb

■ **noun**
- **PLACE 1** 🔑 A2 [C] the place where sb/sth is located: *Where would be the best position for the lights?* ◇ **from a/your ~** *From his position on the cliff top, he had a good view of the harbour.* ◇ **in a ~** *These plants will grow well in a sheltered position.* ⊃ SYNONYMS at PLACE **2** 🔑 A2 [C, U] the place where sb/sth is meant to be; the correct place: *He took up his position by the door.* ◇ **in ~** *Is everybody in position?* ◇ *The dancers all got into position.*
- **WAY SB/STH IS PLACED 3** 🔑 A2 [C, U] the way in which sb is sitting or standing, or the way in which sth is arranged: *a sitting/standing/kneeling position* ◇ *The soldiers had to stand for hours without changing position.* ◇ **in a ... ~** *Keep the box in an upright position.* ◇ *Make sure that you are working in a comfortable position.* ⊃ see also LOTUS POSITION, MISSIONARY POSITION, RECOVERY POSITION
- **SITUATION 4** 🔑 B1 [C, usually sing.] the situation that sb is in, especially when it affects what they can and cannot do: *The company's financial position is not certain.* ◇ **in your ~** *What would you do in my position?* ◇ **in a ... ~** *This put him and his colleagues in a difficult position.* ◇ **to be in a position of power/strength/authority** ◇ **in a ~ to do sth** *I'm afraid I am not in a position to help you.* ⊃ note at SITUATION
- **OPINION 5** 🔑 B2 [C] an opinion on or an attitude towards a particular subject: *She has made her position very clear.* ◇ **to change/reconsider/shift your position** ◇ **~ on sth** *the party's position on education reforms* ◇ **~ that ...** *My parents always took the position that early nights meant healthy children.*
- **LEVEL OF IMPORTANCE 6** 🔑 B2 [C, U] a person or organization's level of importance when compared with others: *the position of women in society* ◇ *the company's dominant position in the world market* ◇ *Wealth and position (= high social status) were not important to her.*
- **JOB 7** 🔑 B2 [C] (formal) a job SYN post: *He held a senior position in a large company.* ◇ *I should like to apply for the position of Sales Director.* ◇ *We need more women in leadership positions.* ⊃ SYNONYMS at JOB
- **IN RACE/COMPETITION 8** [C] a place in a race, competition, or test, when compared to others: *United's 3-0 win moved them up to third position.* ⊃ see also POLE POSITION
- **IN SPORT 9** [C] the place where sb plays and the responsibilities they have in some team games: *What position does he play?*
- **IN WAR 10** [C, usually pl.] a place where a group of people involved in fighting have put men and guns: *They attacked the enemy positions at dawn.*

■ **verb** 🔑 B2 to put sb/sth in a particular position SYN **place**: **~ sb/sth/yourself + adv./prep.** *She quickly positioned herself behind the desk.* ◇ *Large television screens were positioned at either end of the stadium.* ◇ **be positioned to do sth** *The company is now well positioned to compete in foreign markets.* ▶ **po·si·tion·ing** noun [U]

**po·si·tion·al** /pəˈzɪʃənəl/ adj. [only before noun] (specialist or sport) connected with the position of sb/sth: *The team has made some positional changes because two players are injured.*

**po'sition paper** noun a written report from an organization or a government department that explains or recommends a particular course of action

**posi·tive** 🔑 A1 ⊙ /ˈpɒzətɪv; NAmE ˈpɑːz-/ adj., noun

■ **adj.**
- **EFFECTIVE/USEFUL 1** 🔑 A1 good or useful: *have a positive impact/effect* ◇ *The contributions have a positive impact on the lives of hundreds of children.* ◇ *The only positive outcome of that day was that our country came together.* OPP **negative 2** 🔑 A2 expressing agreement or support: *It's always nice to get positive feedback.* ◇ *We've had a very positive response to the idea.* OPP **negative 3** 🔑 B1 directed at dealing with sth or producing a successful result: *We must take positive steps to deal with the problem.* ◇ *In the last few years, positive changes have been made.* OPP **negative**
- **CONFIDENT 4** 🔑 B1 thinking about what is good in a situation; feeling confident and sure that sth good will happen: *a positive attitude/outlook* ◇ **~ about sth** *She tried to be more positive about her new job.* ◇ *On the positive side,* *profits have increased.* ◇ *The report ended on a positive note.* ◇ *There were times when it was difficult to remain positive.* OPP **negative**
- **SCIENTIFIC TEST 5** 🔑 B1 showing clear evidence that a particular substance or medical condition is present: *a positive pregnancy test* ◇ *The athlete tested positive for steroids.* ◇ *to be HIV positive* OPP **negative**
- **SURE/DEFINITE 6** 🔑 B2 [not before noun] (of a person) completely sure that sth is correct or true: **~ about sth** *I can't be positive about what time it happened.* ◇ **~ (that) ...** *She was positive that he had been there.* ◇ *'Are you sure?' 'Positive.'* ⊃ SYNONYMS at SURE **7** 🔑 B2 giving clear and definite proof or information SYN **conclusive**: *The results show a positive correlation between exercise and self-esteem.* ◇ (formal) *This is proof positive that he stole the money.* **8** [only before noun] (informal) complete and definite SYN **absolute**: *He has a positive genius for upsetting people.* ◇ *It was a positive miracle that we survived.*
- **GRAMMAR 9** (also **affirmative**) (of a statement) expressing sth that is true, did happen, etc.; not containing words such as 'no', 'not', 'never', etc. OPP **negative**
- **NUMBER/QUANTITY 10** greater than zero OPP **negative**
- **ELECTRICITY 11** (specialist) containing or producing the type of electricity that is carried by a PROTON: *a positive charge* ◇ *the positive terminal of a battery* OPP **negative**

■ **noun**
- **GOOD QUALITY 1** 🔑 B2 [C] a good or useful quality or aspect: *What are the positives and negatives of going this route?*
- **RESULT OF TEST 2** 🔑 B2 [C] the result of a test or an experiment that shows that a substance or condition is present: *The result can be a false positive—indicating a problem where none actually exists.* OPP **negative**
- **IN PHOTOGRAPHY 3** [C] (specialist) a developed film showing light and dark areas and colours as they actually were, especially one printed from a NEGATIVE

**positive discrimin·ation** (BrE) (also **affirmative 'action** NAmE, BrE) noun [U] the practice or policy of making sure that a particular number of jobs, etc. are given to people from groups that are often treated unfairly because of their race, sex, etc. ⊃ compare REVERSE DISCRIMINATION

**posi·tive·ly** ⓦ /ˈpɒzətɪvli; NAmE ˈpɑːz-/ adv. **1** used to emphasize the truth of a statement, especially when this is surprising or when it contrasts with a previous statement: *The instructions were not just confusing, they were positively misleading.* **2** in a way that shows you are thinking of the good things about a situation, not the bad: *Very few of those interviewed spoke positively about their childhood.* ◇ *Thinking positively is one way of dealing with stress.* OPP **negatively 3** in a way that shows you approve of or agree with sth/sb: *The industry has responded positively to these developments.* OPP **negatively 4** in a way that leaves no possibility of doubt SYN **conclusively**: *Her attacker has now been positively identified by police.* **5** (specialist) in a way that contains or produces the type of electricity that is opposite to that carried by an ELECTRON: *positively charged protons* OPP **negatively**

**posi·tiv·ism** /ˈpɒzətɪvɪzəm; NAmE ˈpɑːz-/ noun [U] a system of philosophy based on things that can be seen or proved, rather than on ideas ⊃ see also LOGICAL POSITIVISM ▶ **posi·tiv·ist** /-vɪst/ noun **posi·tiv·ist** adj.: *a positivist approach*

**posi·tron** /ˈpɒzɪtrɒn; NAmE ˈpɑːzɪtrɑːn/ noun (physics) a PARTICLE in an ATOM which has the same mass as an ELECTRON and an equal but positive charge ⊃ WORDFINDER NOTE at ATOM

**poss** /pɒs; NAmE pɑːs/ adj. [not before noun] (BrE, informal) possible: *I'll be there if poss.* ◇ *as soon as poss*

**posse** /ˈpɒsi; NAmE ˈpɑːsi/ noun **1** (informal) a group of people who are similar in some way, or who spend time together: *a little posse of helpers* **2** (in the US in the past) a group of people who were brought together by a SHERIFF (= an officer of the law) in order to help him catch a criminal **3** (informal) a group of young men involved in crime connected with drugs

**pos·sess** 🔑 B2 /pəˈzes/ verb (not used in the progressive tenses) **1** 🔑 B2 **~ sth** (formal) to have or own sth: *He was charged with possessing a shotgun without a licence.* ◇

*The gallery possesses a number of the artist's early works.* **2** [B2] **~ sth** (*formal*) to have a particular quality or feature: *I'm afraid he doesn't possess a sense of humour.* **3 ~ sb** (*literary*) (of a feeling, an emotion, etc.) to have a powerful effect on sb and control the way that they think, behave, etc. **4 ~ sb to do sth** (used in negative sentences and questions) to make sb do sth that seems strange or unreasonable: *What possessed him to say such a thing?*

**pos·sessed** /pəˈzest/ *adj.* [not before noun] **~ (by sth)** (of a person or their mind) controlled by an evil spirit: *She has convinced herself that she is possessed by the devil.*
**IDM** **be possessed of sth** (*formal*) to have a particular quality or feature: *She was possessed of exceptional powers of concentration.* **like a man / woman posˈsessed** | **like one posˈsessed** with a lot of force or energy: *He flew out of the room like a man possessed.*

**pos·ses·sion** ❶ [A2] /pəˈzeʃn/ *noun*
• HAVING/OWNING **1** [A2] [C, usually pl.] something that you own or have with you at a particular time **SYN** belongings: *personal possessions* ◇ *One of Jane's most prized possessions was her photo album.* ⊃ SYNONYMS at THING **2** [B1] [U] (*formal*) the state of having or owning sth: **~ of sth** *The possession of a passport is essential for foreign travel.* ◇ *On her father's death, she came into possession of* (= received) *a vast fortune.* ◇ *You cannot legally take possession of the property* (= start using it after buying it) *until three weeks after the contract is signed.* ◇ **in sb's ~** *The manuscript is just one of the treasures in their possession.* ◇ **in~ of sth** *The gang was caught in possession of stolen goods.* ◇ *drug possession*
• IN SPORT **3** [U] the state of having control of the ball: *to win/get/lose possession of the ball*
• LAW **4** [U] the state of having illegal drugs or weapons with you at a particular time: *She was charged with possession.*
• COUNTRY **5** [C] (*formal*) a country that is controlled or governed by another country
• BY EVIL SPIRIT **6** [U] the situation when sb's mind is believed to be controlled by the Devil or by an evil spirit
**IDM** **possession is nine tenths of the ˈlaw** (*saying*) if you already have or control sth, it is difficult for sb else to take it away from you, even if they have the legal right to it

**pos·ses·sive** /pəˈzesɪv/ *adj., noun*
■ *adj.* **1 ~ (of / about sb / sth)** demanding total attention or love; not wanting sb to be independent: *Some parents are too possessive of their children.* **2 ~ (of / about sth)** not liking to lend things or share things with others: *Jimmy's very possessive about his toys.* **3** [usually before noun] (*grammar*) showing that sth belongs to sb/sth: *possessive pronouns* (= yours, theirs, etc.). ▶ **posˈses·sive·ly** *adv.*: *'That's mine!' she said possessively.* **posˈses·sive·ness** *noun* [U]: *I couldn't stand his jealousy and possessiveness.*
■ *noun* (*grammar*) **1** [C] a pronoun or a form of a word that expresses the fact that sth belongs to sb/sth: *'Ours' and 'their' are possessives.* **2 the possessive** *noun* [sing.] the special form of a word that expresses belonging ⊃ compare GENITIVE

**pos·ses·sor** /pəˈzesə(r)/ *noun* (*formal or humorous*) a person who owns or has sth **SYN** owner: *He is now the proud possessor of a driving licence.*

**pos·si·bil·ity** ❶ [A2] ⊙ /ˌpɒsəˈbɪləti; *NAmE* ˌpɑːs-/ *noun* (*pl.* **-ies**) **1** [A2] [C, U] a thing that may happen or be true; the fact that sth might happen or be true, but is not certain: *Bankruptcy is a real possibility if sales don't improve.* ◇ *What had seemed impossible now seemed a distinct possibility.* ◇ **~ that …** *There's a strong possibility that it will rain.* ◇ **~ of sth** *He refused to rule out the possibility of a tax increase.* ◇ **~ of doing sth** *I am excited about the possibility of going to the Olympics.* **OPP** impossibility **2** [B1] [C] one of the different things that you can do in a particular situation: *The possibilities are endless.* ◇ *Selling the house is just one possibility that is open to us.* ◇ *to consider / investigate a wide range of possibilities* ◇ **~ of doing sth** *She explored the possibility of studying in the US.* ⊃ SYNONYMS at OPTION **3** [B1] [U, usually pl.] something that gives you a chance to achieve sth **SYN** opportunity: *possibilities for sth There are countless possibilities for future research.* ◇ **possibilities for doing sth** *The course offers a range of exciting possibilities for developing your skills.* **4 possibil-**ities [pl.] if sth **has possibilities**, it can be improved or made successful **SYN** potential: *The house is in a bad state of repair but it has possibilities.*
**IDM** **within / beyond the bounds / realms of possibility** possible/not possible: *A successful outcome is not beyond the realms of possibility.*

**pos·si·ble** ❶ [A1] ⊙ /ˈpɒsəbl; *NAmE* ˈpɑːs-/ *adj., noun*
■ *adj.* **1** [A1] [not usually before noun] that can be done or achieved: **~ to do sth** *New technology has made it possible to communicate more easily.* ◇ **it is ~ to do sth** *It is possible to get there by bus.* ◇ **it is ~ for sb to do sth** *Would it be possible for me to leave a message for her?* ◇ *This wouldn't have been possible without you.* ◇ *I'd like the money back by next week if possible.* ◇ *Use public transport whenever possible* (= when you can). ◇ *We spent every possible moment on the beach.* **OPP** impossible ⊃ EXPRESS YOURSELF at FORBID, PERMISSION **2** [A1] that might exist or happen but is not certain to: *the possible side effects of the drug* ◇ *Frost is possible, although unlikely, at this time of year.* ◇ **it is ~ (that) …** *It is quite possible that the river will flood again.* ◇ *With the possible exception of the Beatles, no other band has become so successful so quickly.* ◇ *'Do you think he'll resign?' 'Anything's possible where he's concerned.'* ⊃ LANGUAGE BANK at PERHAPS **3** [A1] reasonable or acceptable in a particular situation: *There are several possible explanations.* **4** used after adjectives to emphasize that sth is the best, worst, etc. of its type: *It was the best possible surprise anyone could have given me.* ◇ *Don't leave your packing until the last possible moment.*
**IDM** **as quickly, much, soon, etc. as ˈpossible** [B1] as quickly, much, soon, etc. as you can: *We will get your order to you as soon as possible.* ⊃ more at WORLD, WORST *n.*
■ *noun* a person or thing that is suitable for a particular job, purpose, etc. and might be chosen: *Out of all the people interviewed, there are only five possibles.*

**pos·si·bly** ❶ [B1] /ˈpɒsəbli; *NAmE* ˈpɑːs-/ *adv.* **1** [B1] used to say that sth might exist, happen or be true, but you are not certain **SYN** perhaps: *It was possibly their worst performance ever.* ◇ *She found it difficult to get on with her, possibly because of the difference in their ages.* ◇ *'Will you be around next week?' 'Possibly.'* ⊃ LANGUAGE BANK at PERHAPS ⊃ EXPRESS YOURSELF at LIKELY **2** [B1] used with *can / could* to emphasize that you are surprised, annoyed, etc. about sth: *You can't possibly mean that!* **3** [B1] used with *could* to ask sb politely to do sth: *Could you possibly open that window?* **4** [B1] used with *can / could* to say that sb will do or has done as much as they can in order to make sth happen: *I will come as soon as I possibly can.* ◇ *They tried everything they possibly could to improve the situation.* **5** used with negatives, especially *can't / couldn't*, to say strongly that you cannot do sth or that sth cannot or could not happen or be done: *I can't possibly tell you that!* ◇ *You can't possibly carry all those bags.* ◇ *'Let me buy it for you.' 'That's very kind of you, but I couldn't possibly* (= accept).*'*

**pos·sum** /ˈpɒsəm; *NAmE* ˈpɑːs-/ *noun* (*AustralE*, *NZE* or *NAmE*, *informal*) = OPOSSUM
**IDM** **play ˈpossum** (*informal*) to pretend to be asleep or not aware of sth, in order to trick sb

**post** ❶ [A1] /pəʊst/ *noun, verb*
■ *noun*
• LETTERS **1** [A1] (*BrE*) (*also* mail *NAmE*, *BrE*) [U] the official system used for sending and delivering letters, packages, etc: **by ~** *I'll send the original to you by post.* ◇ **in the ~** *I'll put the documents in the post to you tomorrow.* ◇ *My application got lost in the post.* **2** [A1] (*BrE*) (*also* mail *NAmE*, *BrE*) [U] letters, packages, etc. that are sent and delivered: *There was a lot of post this morning.* ◇ *Have you opened your post yet?* **3** [A1] (*BrE*) [U, sing.] an occasion during the day when letters, etc. are collected or delivered: *to catch / miss the post* ◇ **in the ~** *The parcel came in this morning's post.* ◇ *Payment should be sent by return of post* (= immediately).
• INTERNET **4** [A2] (*also* ˈpost·ing) [C] a message sent to a discussion group on the internet; a piece of writing that forms part of a blog: *I love reading her posts because I learn so much.* ◇ **~ about sb / sth** *She wrote a post about*

# post-

the experience on her blog. ◊ **~by sb** *This post by Mark Brady is very interesting.* ⊃ see also BLOG POST
- **JOB 5** [C] a job, especially an important one in a large organization **SYN** **position**: *an academic/a government post* ◊ *She took up a teaching post at Basle University.* ◊ *to resign (from)/quit/leave a post* ◊ *The company has been unable to fill the post.* ◊ *He has held the post for three years.* ⊃ SYNONYMS at JOB **6** (*especially NAmE*) (*BrE usually* **posting**) an act of sending sb to a particular place to do their job, especially for a limited period of time: *an overseas post*
- **FOR SOLDIER/GUARD 7** [C] the place where sb, especially a soldier, does their job: *a police/military/customs/border post* ◊ *an observation post* ◊ *The guards were ordered not to leave their posts.* ⊃ see also COMMAND POST, LAST POST, STAGING POST, TRADING POST
- **WOOD/METAL 8** [C] (often in compounds) a piece of wood or metal that is set in the ground in a position pointing upwards, especially to support sth or to mark a point: *She tied the dog to a post.* ◊ *corner posts* (= that mark the corners of a sports field) ⊃ see also BEDPOST, GATEPOST, LAMP POST, SIGNPOST *noun*
- **END OF RACE 9 the post** [*sing.*] the place where a race finishes, especially in horse racing ⊃ see also FIRST-PAST-THE-POST, WINNING POST
- **FOOTBALL 10** [C, usually sing.] = GOALPOST: *The ball hit the post and bounced in.* **IDM** see DEAF, PILLAR

■ **verb**
- **LETTERS 1** (*BrE*) (*NAmE* **mail**) [T] to send a letter, etc. to sb by post: **~sth** *The cost of posting a letter has gone up again.* ◊ **~sth off** *Have you posted off your order yet?* ◊ **~sth to sb** *Is it OK if I post the documents to you next week?* ◊ **~sb sth** *Is it OK if I post you the documents next week?* ⊃ compare MAIL 2 (*BrE*) (*NAmE* **mail**) [T] **~sth** to put a letter, etc. into a POSTBOX: *Could you post this letter for me?*
- **STH THROUGH HOLE 3** [T] **~sth + adv./prep.** to put sth through a hole into a container: *Let yourself out and post the keys through the letter box.*
- **GIVE INFORMATION 4** [T, I] to put information or pictures on a website: **~sth on sth** *More details will be posted on the website tomorrow.* ◊ **~sth** *Many thanks to all who have posted comments.* ◊ *to post a video/picture/photo/message/link* ◊ **on sth** *The photos have been provided by fans who post on the message board.* ⊃ see also CROSS POST **5** [T] (*especially NAmE*) to announce sth publicly or officially, especially financial information or a warning: **~sth** *The company posted a $1.1 billion loss.* ◊ *A snow warning was posted for Ohio.* ◊ **be posted + adj.** *The aircraft and its crew were posted missing.*
- **SB FOR JOB 6** [T, usually passive] to send sb to a place for a period of time as part of their job: **be posted + adv./prep.** *She's been posted to Washington for two years.* ◊ *Most of our employees get posted abroad at some stage.*
- **SOLDIER/GUARD 7** [T, usually passive] to put sb, especially a soldier, in a particular place so that they can guard a building or area: **be posted + adv./prep.** *Guards have been posted along the border.*
- **PUBLIC NOTICE 8** [T, often passive] to put a notice, etc. in a public place so that people can see it **SYN** **display**: **be posted + adv./prep.** *A copy of the letter was posted on the noticeboard.*
- **PAY MONEY TO COURT 9** [T] **~bail/(a) bond** (*especially NAmE*) to pay money to a court so that a person accused of a crime can go free until their trial: *She was released after posting $100 cash bond and her driver's license.*
**IDM** **keep sb ˈposted (about/on sth)** to regularly give sb the most recent information about sth and how it is developing

**post-** /pəʊst/ *prefix* (in nouns, verbs and adjectives) after: *a postgraduate* ◊ *a post-Impressionist* ◊ *the post-1945 period* ⊃ compare ANTE-, PRE-

**postˈage** /ˈpəʊstɪdʒ/ *noun* [U] the cost of sending a letter, etc. by post: *an increase in postage rates* ◊ *How much was the postage on that letter?* ◊ (*BrE*) *All prices include postage and packing.* ◊ (*NAmE*) *All prices include postage and handling.*

**ˈpostage stamp** *noun* (*formal*) = STAMP

**ˈpostal** /ˈpəʊstl/ *adj.* [only before noun] **1** connected with the official system for sending and delivering letters, etc:

---

▼ **BRITISH/AMERICAN**

### post / mail

**Nouns**
- In *BrE* the official system used for sending and delivering letters, parcels/packages, etc. is usually called the **post**. In *NAmE* it is usually called the **mail**: *I'll put an application form in the post/mail for you today.* ◊ *Send your fee by post/mail to this address.* **Mail** is sometimes used in *BrE* in such expressions as: *the Royal Mail.* **Post** occurs in *NAmE* in such expressions as: *the US Postal Service.*
- In *BrE* **post** is also used to mean the letters, parcels/packages, etc. that are delivered to you. **Mail** is the usual word in *NAmE* and is sometimes also used in *BrE*: *Was there any post/mail this morning?* ◊ *I sat down to open my post/mail.*

**Verbs**
- Compare: *I'll post the letter when I go out.* (*BrE*) and *I'll mail the letter when I go out.* (*NAmE*)

**Compounds**
- Note these words: **postman** (*BrE*), **mailman / mail carrier** (both *NAmE*); **postbox** (*BrE*), **mailbox** (*NAmE*) Some compounds are used in both *BrE* and *NAmE*: **post office**, **postcard**, **mail order**.

---

*your full postal address* ◊ *the postal service/system* ◊ *postal charges* **2** (*especially BrE*) involving things that are sent by post: *postal bookings*
**IDM** **go ˈpostal** (*especially NAmE, informal*) to become very angry: *He went postal when he found out.*

**ˈpostal ballot** *noun* (*BrE*) a system of voting on a particular issue in which everyone sends their vote by post

**ˈpostal code** *noun* (*BrE, CanE*) = POSTCODE

**ˈpostal order** (*BrE*) (*also* **ˈmoney order** *NAmE, BrE*) *noun* (*abbr.* **PO**) an official document that you can buy at a bank or a post office and send to sb so that they can exchange it for money

**ˈpostal service** *noun* **1** a system of collecting and delivering letters, etc: *a good postal service* **2 the Postal Service** (*US*) (*BrE* **the ˈPost Office**) the national organization in many countries that is responsible for collecting and delivering letters, etc.

**ˈpostal vote** (*BrE*) (*NAmE* **ˈabsentee ˈballot**) *noun* a vote in an election that you can send when you cannot be present

**ˈpost·bag** /ˈpəʊstbæɡ/ *noun* (*BrE*) **1** (*also* **ˈmail·bag** *NAmE, BrE*) [usually sing.] all the letters, emails, etc. received by a newspaper, a TV station, a website, or an important person at a particular time or about a particular subject: *We had a huge postbag on the subject from our readers.* **2** = MAILBAG (1)

**ˈpost·box** /ˈpəʊstbɒks/ *noun* a public box, for example in the street, that you put letters into when you send them ⊃ compare PILLAR BOX

**ˈpost·card** /ˈpəʊstkɑːd; *NAmE* -kɑːrd/ (*also* **card**) *noun* a card used for sending messages by post without an ENVELOPE, especially one that has a picture on one side: *colourful postcards of California* ◊ *Send us a postcard from Venice!* ◊ *Send your answers on a postcard to the above address.* ⊃ see also PICTURE POSTCARD

**ˈpost·code** /ˈpəʊstkəʊd/ (*BrE*) (*also* **ˈpostal code** *BrE, CanE*) *noun* a group of letters and numbers that are used as part of an address

letter box / mail slot

front door

postbox

mailboxes

so that post can be separated into groups and delivered more quickly ⇒ see also ZIP CODE

**postcode 'lottery** noun [sing.] (*BrE*) a situation in which the amount or type of medical treatment that is provided to people depends on the particular area of the country they live in

**post-coital** /ˌpəʊst ˈkɔɪtl, ˈkəʊɪ-; *NAmE* ˈkəʊɪtl/ *adj.* [usually before noun] happening or done after SEXUAL INTERCOURSE

**ˌpost-ˈdate** *verb* **1** ~ sth to write a date on a CHEQUE that is later than the actual date so that the CHEQUE cannot be CASHED (= exchanged for money) until that date ⇒ compare BACKDATE **2** ~ sth to happen, exist or be made at a later date than sth else in the past ◉◉◉ predate

**post-doc** /ˈpəʊstdɒk; *NAmE* -dɑːk/ *noun* (*informal*) **1** a person who is doing advanced research after completing a PHD: *She continued at Stanford as a postdoc.* **2** a position where sb does advanced research after completing a PHD: *I've applied for a postdoc.*

**post-doc-tor-al** /ˌpəʊstˈdɒktərəl; *NAmE* -ˈdɑːk-/ *adj.* (usually before noun) connected with advanced research or study that is done after a PHD has been completed

**pos-ter** ⓞ A2 /ˈpəʊstə(r)/ *noun* **1** A2 a large notice, often with a picture on it, that is put in a public place to advertise sth: *campaign/election posters ◊ a poster campaign* (= an attempt to educate people about sth by using posters) ⇒ compare PLACARD ⇒ WORDFINDER NOTE at ADVERTISE **2** A2 a large picture that is printed on paper and put on a wall as decoration: *posters of her favourite pop stars* **3** a person who posts a message on a MESSAGE BOARD (= a place on a website where people can read or write messages)

**ˈposter child** (*also* **ˈposter boy**, **ˈposter girl**) *noun* (*especially NAmE*) **1** a child with a particular illness or other problem whose picture appears on a poster advertising an organization that helps children with that illness or problem **2** (*often humorous*) a person who is seen as representing a particular quality or activity: *He is the poster child for incompetent government.*

**pos-ter-ior** /pɒˈstɪəriə(r); *NAmE* pɑːˈstɪr-/ *adj., noun*
- *adj.* [only before noun] (*specialist*) located behind sth or at the back of sth ◉◉◉ anterior
- *noun* (*humorous*) the part of your body that you sit on; your bottom

**pos-teri-ori** ⇒ A POSTERIORI

**pos-ter-ity** /pɒˈsterəti/ *noun* [U] (*formal*) all the people who will live in the future: *Their music has been preserved for posterity. ◊ Posterity will remember him as a great man.*

**post-grad** /ˈpəʊstɡræd/ *noun* (*informal*) a POSTGRADUATE

**post-gradu-ate** /ˌpəʊstˈɡrædʒuət/ (*also informal* **post-grad**) *noun* (*especially BrE*) a person who already holds a first degree and who is doing advanced study or research; a graduate student: *postgraduate students ◊ a postgraduate course* ⇒ note at STUDENT

**ˌpost-ˈhaste** *adv.* (*literary*) as quickly as you can: *to depart post-haste*

**post hoc** /ˌpəʊst ˈhɒk; *NAmE* ˈhɑːk/ *adj.* (*from Latin, formal*) (of an argument, etc.) happening after the event, especially when one event is the cause of another: *a post hoc explanation* ▸ **post hoc** *adv.*

**post-hu-mous** /ˈpɒstjəməs; *NAmE* ˈpɑːs-/ *adj.* [usually before noun] happening, done, published, etc. after a person has died: *a posthumous award for bravery* ▸ **post-hu-mous-ly** *adv.*

**post-ie** /ˈpəʊsti/ *noun* (*BrE, informal*) = POSTMAN

**post-in-ˈdus-trial** *adj.* [only before noun] (of a place or society) no longer relying on heavy industry (= the production of steel, large machines, etc.)

**post-ing** /ˈpəʊstɪŋ/ *noun* **1** (*especially BrE*) (*NAmE usually* **post**) an act of sending sb to a particular place to do their job, especially for a limited period of time: *an overseas posting* **2** = POST (6)

**Post-it™** (*also* **ˈPost-it™ note**) *noun* a small piece of coloured, sticky paper that you use for writing a note on, and that can be easily removed

**post-man** /ˈpəʊstmən/, **post-woman** /ˈpəʊstwʊmən/ *noun* (*pl.* **-men** /-mən/, **-women** /-wɪmɪn/) (*also informal* **post-ie**) (*all BrE*) (*NAmE* **ˈmail-man**, **ˈmail carrier**) a person whose job is to collect and deliver letters, etc. ⇒ note at GENDER

**post-mark** /ˈpəʊstmɑːk; *NAmE* -mɑːrk/ *noun* an official mark placed over the stamp on a letter, etc. that shows when and where it was posted and makes it impossible to use the stamp again ▸ **post-mark** *verb* [usually passive]: *~ sth The card was postmarked Tokyo 9th March.*

**post-mas-ter** /ˈpəʊstmɑːstə(r); *NAmE* -mæs-/, **post-mis-tress** /ˈpəʊstmɪstrəs/ *noun* a person who is in charge of a post office

**post-mod-ern** /ˌpəʊstˈmɒdn; *NAmE* -ˈmɑːdərn/ *adj.* connected with or influenced by postmodernism

**post-mod-ern-ism** /ˌpəʊstˈmɒdənɪzəm; *NAmE* -ˈmɑːdərn-/ *noun* [U] a style and movement in art, architecture, literature, etc. in the late 20th century that reacted against modern styles, for example by mixing features from traditional and modern styles ⇒ compare MODERNISM ▸ **post-mod-ern-ist** /-nɪst/ *noun, adj.* [usually before noun]

**post-mortem** /ˌpəʊst ˈmɔːtəm; *NAmE* ˈmɔːrt-/ *noun* **1** (*also* **ˌpost-ˌmortem examiˈnation**) a medical examination of the body of a dead person in order to find out how they died ⓢⓨⓝ autopsy: *to do/conduct/carry out a post-mortem ◊ ~ on sb The post-mortem on the child revealed that she had been poisoned.* **2** ~ (on sth) a discussion or an examination of an event after it has happened, especially in order to find out why it failed: *to hold a post-mortem on the party's election defeat*

**post-natal** /ˌpəʊstˈneɪtl/ (*NAmE or formal* **post-partum**) *adj.* [only before noun] connected with the period after the birth of a child: *postnatal care* ⇒ compare ANTENATAL, PRENATAL

**ˌpostnatal deˈpression** (*BrE*) (*NAmE* **ˌpost-partum deˈpression**) *noun* [U] a medical condition in which a woman feels very sad and anxious in the period after her baby is born

**ˈpost office** *noun* **1** [C] a place where you can buy stamps, send letters, etc.: *Where's the main post office? ◊ You can buy your stamps at the post office. ◊ a post office counter* **2** the **ˈPost Office** [sing.] (*abbr.* **PO**) the national organization in many countries that is responsible for collecting and delivering letters, etc.: *He works for the Post Office.*

**ˈpost office box** *noun* = PO BOX

**ˌpost-ˈop-era-tive** (*also informal* **ˌpost-ˈop**) *adj.* [only before noun] (*medical*) connected with the period after a medical operation: *post-operative complications/pain/care* ⇒ compare INTRAOPERATIVE, PREOPERATIVE

**ˌpost-ˈpaid** *adj.* [only before noun] that you can send free because the charge has already been paid: *a post-paid envelope* ▸ **ˌpost-ˈpaid** *adv.*

**post-partum** /ˌpəʊst ˈpɑːtəm; *NAmE* ˈpɑːrt-/ (*NAmE also* **postpartum**) *adj.* [only before noun] (*NAmE or formal*) = POSTNATAL

**ˌpost-ˌpartum deˈpression** (*also* **ˌpost ˌpartum deˈpression**) (*both NAmE*) (*BrE* **ˌpostnatal deˈpression**) *noun* [U] a medical condition in which a woman feels very sad and anxious in the period after her baby is born

**post-pone** ⓞ+ B1 /pəˈspəʊn; *NAmE* pəʊs-/ *verb* to arrange for an event, etc. to take place at a later time or date than originally planned ⓢⓨⓝ put off: *~ sth The game has already been postponed three times. ◊ ~ sth to/until sth We'll have to postpone the meeting until next week. ◊ ~ doing sth It was an unpopular decision to postpone building the new hospital.* ⇒ compare CANCEL ▸ **post-pone-ment** *noun* [U, C]: *Riots led to the postponement of local elections.*

**post-pran-dial** /ˌpəʊstˈprændiəl/ *adj.* [usually before noun] (*formal or humorous*) happening immediately after a meal

**post-proˈduc-tion** *adj.* [usually before noun] **post-production** work on music or on films is done after recording or filming: *post-production editing* ▸ **ˌpost-proˈduc-tion**

noun [U]: *The movie is now in post-production and will be released next month.*

**post room** (*BrE*) (*also* **mailroom** *especially in NAmE*) *noun* the department of a company that deals with sending and receiving mail

**post·script** /ˈpəʊstskrɪpt/ *noun* **1** (*abbr.* **PS**) ~ **(to sth)** an extra message that you add at the end of a letter after you sign your name **2** ~ **(to sth)** extra facts or information about a story, an event, etc. that are added after it has finished

**post·season** /ˈpəʊstsiːzn/ *adj., noun*
■ *adj.* [only before noun] (*especially NAmE*) taking place after the end of the regular sports season, when teams play additional games to decide which team is best in a particular sport: *The postseason games, leading up to the finals, should be very exciting.* ⊃ compare PRESEASON
■ *noun* [usually sing.] (*especially NAmE*) the period of time after the regular sports season: *The team is expected to do well in the postseason.* ⊃ compare PRESEASON

**post-trau·matic ˈstress disorder** *noun* [U] (*medical*) (*abbr.* **PTSD**) a medical condition in which a person suffers mental and emotional problems resulting from an experience that shocked them very much

**post-ˈtruth** *adj.* [usually before noun] relating to circumstances in which people respond more to feelings and beliefs than to facts: *post-truth politics* ⊃ compare FAKE NEWS

**pos·tu·late** *verb, noun*
■ *verb* /ˈpɒstjʊleɪt/; *NAmE* /ˈpɑːs-/ ~ **sth** | ~ **that ...** (*formal*) to suggest or accept that sth is true so that it can be used as the basis for a theory, etc. **SYN** **posit**: *They postulated a 500-year lifespan for a plastic container.*
■ *noun* (*formal*) /ˈpɒstjʊlət/; *NAmE* /ˈpɑːs-/ a statement that is accepted as true, that forms the basis of a theory, etc.

**pos·tural** /ˈpɒstʃərəl/; *NAmE* /ˈpɑːs-/ *adj.* (*formal*) connected with the way you hold your body when sitting or standing

**pos·ture** /ˈpɒstʃə(r)/; *NAmE* /ˈpɑːs-/ *noun, verb*
■ *noun* **1** [U, C] the position in which you hold your body when standing or sitting: *a comfortable/relaxed posture* ⋄ *Try to maintain an upright posture.* ⋄ *Good posture is essential when working at the computer.* ⋄ *Back pains can be the result of poor posture.* **2** [C, usually sing.] ~ **(towards sb/sth)** your attitude to a particular situation or the way in which you deal with it: *The company has adopted an aggressive posture towards its rivals.*
■ *verb* [I] ~ **(as sth)** (*disapproving*) to pretend to be sth that you are not by saying and doing things in order to impress or trick people

**pos·tur·ing** /ˈpɒstʃərɪŋ/; *NAmE* /ˈpɑːs-/ *noun* [U, C] (*disapproving*) behaviour that is not natural or sincere but is intended to attract attention or to have a particular effect

**post·viral ˈsyn·drome** /ˌpəʊst'vaɪrəl ˈsɪndrəʊm/ (*also* **postviral faˈtigue syndrome**) *noun* [U] a condition that follows a VIRAL infection, in which sb feels extremely weak and tired, and which can last for a long time

**post-ˈwar** *adj.* [usually before noun] existing, happening or made in the period after a war, especially the Second World War: *the post-war years*

**post·woman** ⊃ POSTMAN

**posy** /ˈpəʊzi/ *noun* (*pl.* **-ies**) a small bunch of flowers

**pot** /pɒt; *NAmE* pɑːt/ *noun, verb*
■ *noun*
• FOR COOKING **1** [C] a deep round container used for cooking things in: *pots and pans*
• CONTAINER **2** [C] (*especially BrE*) a container made of glass, CLAY or plastic, used for storing food in: *a pot of jam* ⋄ *a yoghurt pot* **3** [C] (*especially in compounds*) a container of various kinds, made for a particular purpose: *a coffee pot* ⋄ *a pencil pot* ⋄ *Is there any more tea in the pot?* ⊃ see also CHAMBER POT, CHIMNEY POT, FLOWERPOT, LOBSTER POT, MELTING POT, PEPPER POT, PLANT POT, POTTED **4** [C] the amount contained in a pot: *They drank a pot of coffee.* **5** [C] a bowl, etc. that is made by a POTTER
• MONEY **6** **the pot** [sing.] (*especially NAmE*) the total amount of money that is bet in a card game **7** **the pot** [sing.] (*especially*

*cially NAmE*) all the money given by a group of people in order to do sth together, for example to buy food, or available for a particular purpose ⊃ see also KITTY, PENSION POT
• DRUG **8** [U] (*informal*) = CANNABIS: *pot smoking*
• SHOT **9** [C] = POTSHOT: *He took a pot at the neighbour's cat with his air rifle.*
• IN BILLIARDS, ETC. **10** [C] (in the game of BILLIARDS, POOL or SNOOKER) the act of hitting a ball into one of the pockets around the edge of the table
• STOMACH **11** [C] (*informal*) = POT BELLY
**IDM** **go to ˈpot** (*informal*) to become much less good because people are not working hard or taking care of things: *Her handwriting's gone to pot since she started using a computer all the time.* **the pot calling the kettle ˈblack** (*saying, informal*) used to say that you should not criticize sb for a fault that you have yourself, **pot ˈluck** when you take **pot luck**, you choose sth or go somewhere without knowing very much about it, but hope that it will be good, pleasant, etc: *It's pot luck whether you get good advice or not.* ⋄ *You're welcome to stay to supper, but you'll have to take pot luck* (= eat whatever is available). ⊃ see also POTLUCK, **ˈpots of money** (*BrE, informal*) a very large amount of money ⊃ more at GOLD *n.*, MELTING POT, WATCH *v.*
■ *verb* (**-tt-**)
• PLANT **1** ~ **sth** to put a plant into a FLOWERPOT filled with soil
• IN BILLIARDS, ETC. **2** ~ **sth** (in the games of BILLIARDS, POOL and SNOOKER) to hit a ball into one of the pockets (= holes at the corners and edges of the table) **SYN** **pocket**: *He potted the black to take a 7–3 lead.*
• SHOOT **3** ~ **sth** to kill an animal or a bird by shooting it ⊃ see also POTTED

**pot·able** /ˈpəʊtəbl/ *adj.* (*formal*) (of water) safe to drink

**pot·ash** /ˈpɒtæʃ/; *NAmE* /ˈpɑːt-/ *noun* [U] a chemical containing potassium, used to improve soil for farming and in making soap

**po·tas·sium** /pəˈtæsiəm/ *noun* [U] (*symb.* **K**) a chemical element. Potassium is a soft silver-white metal that exists mainly in COMPOUNDS which are used in industry and farming.

**po·tato** /pəˈteɪtəʊ/ *noun* [C, U] (*pl.* **-oes**) a round white vegetable with a brown or red skin that grows underground as part of a plant also called a potato: *Will you peel the potatoes for me?* ⋄ *baked/roast/fried potatoes* ⊃ VISUAL VOCAB page V5 ⊃ see also BAKED POTATO, COUCH POTATO, HOT POTATO, JACKET POTATO, MASHED POTATO, MEAT AND POTATOES, MEAT-AND-POTATOES, SMALL POTATOES, SWEET POTATO

**poˈtato ˈcrisp** (*BrE*), **poˈtato chip** (*NAmE*) *noun* = CRISP, CHIP

**poˈtato masher** *noun* a kitchen UTENSIL (= tool) for MASHING potatoes

**pot-ˈbellied** *adj.* (of people and animals) having a large stomach that sticks out ▶ **pot ˈbelly** (*also informal* **pot**) *noun*

**pot·boil·er** /ˈpɒtbɔɪlə(r)/; *NAmE* /ˈpɑːt-/ *noun* (*disapproving*) a book, a play, etc. that is produced only to earn money quickly

**po·tency** /ˈpəʊtnsi/ *noun* (*pl.* **-ies**) **1** [U, C] the power that sb/sth has to affect your body or mind: *the potency of desire* ⋄ *If you keep a medicine too long, it may lose its potency.* **2** [U] the ability of a man to have sex

**po·tent** /ˈpəʊtnt/ *adj.* **1** having a strong effect on your body or mind: *a potent drug* ⋄ *a very potent alcoholic brew* ⋄ *a potent argument* **2** powerful: *a potent force* ⊃ see also IMPOTENT ▶ **po·tent·ly** *adv.*

**po·ten·tate** /ˈpəʊtnteɪt/ *noun* (*literary, often disapproving*) a political leader who has a lot of power, especially when this is not limited by a parliament, etc.

**po·ten·tial** /pəˈtenʃl/ *adj., noun*
■ *adj.* [only before noun] that can develop into sth or be developed in the future **SYN** **possible**: *potential customers/buyers/investors/clients* ⋄ *We have compiled a list*

æ cat | ɑː father | e bed | ɜː fur | ə about | ɪ sit | iː see | i happy | ɒ got (*BrE*) | ɔː saw | ʌ cup | ʊ put | uː too

of 10 **potential** *candidates.* ◊ **potential** *risks* ◊ *a* **potential** *threat* ◊ *the* **potential** *impact of the latest surge in oil prices* ◊ *First we need to identify actual and* **potential** *problems.*
- **noun 1** [U] the possibility of sth happening or being developed or used: **~ for sth** *the potential for change* ◊ **~ for doing sth** *The European marketplace offers excellent potential for increasing sales.* ◊ **~ of sth** *the huge potential of the American market* ◊ **~ to do sth** *The disease has the potential to cause a global health emergency.* **2** [U] qualities that exist and can be developed **SYN** **promise**: *All children should be encouraged to realize their full potential.* ◊ *to reach/fulfil/achieve your potential* ◊ *John shows great potential in the swimming pool.* ◊ **as sb/sth** *She has great potential as an artist.* ◊ **to do sth** *He has the potential to become a world-class musician.* ◊ **with~** *We're looking for a trainee with potential.* **3** [U, C] (*physics*) the difference in VOLTAGE between two points in an electric field or CIRCUIT

**po·tential 'energy** *noun* [U] (*physics*) the form of energy that an object gains as it is lifted

**po·ten·ti·al·ity** /pəˌtenʃiˈæləti/ *noun* (*pl.* **-ies**) (*formal*) a power or a quality that exists and is capable of being developed: *We often underestimate our potentialities.*

**po·ten·tial·ly** /pəˈtenʃəli/ *adv.* used to say that sth may develop into sth **SYN** **possibly**: *a potentially dangerous situation*

**po·ten·ti·om·eter** /pəˌtenʃiˈɒmɪtə(r); NAmE -ˈɑːm-/ *noun* **1** a device for measuring differences in electrical POTENTIAL **2** a device for varying electrical RESISTANCE, used, for example, in volume controls

**pot·head** /ˈpɒthed; NAmE ˈpɑːt-/ *noun* (*informal, disapproving*) a person who smokes CANNABIS

**pot·hole** /ˈpɒthəʊl; NAmE ˈpɑːt-/ *noun* **1** a large rough hole in the surface of a road that is formed by traffic and bad weather **2** a deep hole that is formed in rock, especially by the action of water

**pot·hol·ing** /ˈpɒthəʊlɪŋ; NAmE ˈpɑːt-/ *noun* [U] = CAVING: *to go potholing* ▶ **pot·holer** *noun* = CAVER

**po·tion** /ˈpəʊʃn/ *noun* (*literary*) a drink of medicine or poison; a liquid with magic powers: *a magic/love potion* ◊ (*humorous*) *I've tried all sorts of drugs, creams, pills and potions.*

**potjie** /ˈpɔɪki/ *SAfrE* [ˈpɔɪki] *noun* (*SAfrE*) **1** a round pot, usually with three legs, that is made from CAST IRON and used for cooking food slowly over a fire **2** a meal that is prepared in a pot like this: *a chicken potjie*

**pot·luck** /ˌpɒtˈlʌk; NAmE ˌpɑːt-/ *noun* (NAmE) a meal to which each guest brings some food, which is then shared out among the guests

**'pot pie** *noun* [C, U] (NAmE) meat, vegetables, etc. baked in a deep dish with PASTRY on top: *a chicken pot pie*

**'pot plant** *noun* (BrE) = HOUSEPLANT

**pot·pourri** /ˌpəʊpʊˈriː/ *noun* (from French) **1** [U, C] a mixture of dried flowers and leaves used for making a room smell pleasant **2** [sing.] a mixture of various things that were not originally intended to form a group: *a potpourri of tunes*

**'pot roast** *noun* a piece of meat cooked slowly in a pot ▶ **'pot-roast** *verb* **~ sth**

**pot·shot** /ˈpɒtʃɒt; NAmE ˈpɑːtʃɑːt/ (*also* **pot**) *noun* (*informal*) a shot that sb fires without aiming carefully: *Somebody took a potshot at him as he drove past.* ◊ (*figurative*) *The newspapers took constant potshots at (= criticized) the president.*

**pot·tage** /ˈpɒtɪdʒ; NAmE ˈpɑːt-/ *noun* [U] (*old use*) soup or STEW

**pot·ted** /ˈpɒtɪd; NAmE ˈpɑːt-/ *adj.* [only before noun] **1** planted in a pot: *potted plants* **2** (BrE) (of a book, or a story) in a short simple form: *a potted history of England* **3** (BrE) **potted** meat or fish has been cooked and preserved in a small container

**pot·ter** /ˈpɒtə(r); NAmE ˈpɑːt-/ *verb, noun*
- **verb** (BrE) (NAmE **putter**) [I] **+ adv./prep.** to do things or move without hurrying, especially when you are doing sth that you enjoy and that is not important: *I spent the day pottering around the house.*
- **noun** a person who makes CLAY pots by hand

**'potter's wheel** *noun* a piece of equipment with a flat disc that goes round, on which potters put wet CLAY in order to shape it into pots

**pot·tery** /ˈpɒtəri; NAmE ˈpɑːt-/ *noun* (*pl.* **-ies**) **1** [U] pots, dishes, etc. made with CLAY that are baked in an oven, especially when they are made by hand: *Roman pottery* ◊ *a piece of pottery* **2** [U] the CLAY that some dishes and pots are made of: *a jug made of blue-glazed pottery* **3** [U] the skill of making pots and dishes from CLAY, especially by hand: *a pottery class* **4** [C] a place where CLAY pots and dishes are made

**'potting shed** *noun* a small building where seeds and young plants are grown in pots before they are planted outside

**potty** /ˈpɒti; NAmE ˈpɑːti/ *adj., noun*
- **adj.** (BrE, *informal, becoming old-fashioned*) (**pot·tier**, **pot·ti·est**) **1** crazy: *The kids are driving me potty!* **2** **~ about sb/sth** liking sb/sth a lot
- **noun** (*pl.* **-ies**) (*informal*) a bowl that very young children use when they are too small to use a toilet ⇒ compare CHAMBER POT

**potty-'mouthed** *adj.* (*especially NAmE, informal*) using rude, offensive language **SYN** **foul-mouthed**: *a potty-mouthed comedian*

**'potty-train** *verb* **~ sb** to teach a small child to use a potty or toilet ▶ **'potty-trained** *adj.*; **'potty-training** *noun* [U]

**POTUS** /ˈpəʊtəs/ *abbr.* (*especially US*) President of the United States: *In primaries, the moderate candidate for POTUS generally wins.* ⇒ see also FLOTUS, SCOTUS

**pouch** /paʊtʃ/ *noun* **1** a small bag, usually made of leather, and often carried in a pocket or attached to a belt: *a tobacco pouch* ◊ *She kept her money in a pouch around her neck.* **2** a large bag for carrying letters, especially official ones ⇒ see also DIPLOMATIC POUCH at DIPLOMATIC BAG **3** a pocket of skin on the stomach of some female MARSUPIAL animals, such as KANGAROOS, in which they carry their young ⇒ VISUAL VOCAB page V2 **4** a pocket of skin in the CHEEKS (= sides of the face below the eyes) of some animals, such as HAMSTERS, in which they store food

**poult·ice** /ˈpəʊltɪs/ *noun* a soft substance spread on a cloth, sometimes heated, and put on the skin to reduce pain or SWELLING

**poult·ry** /ˈpəʊltri/ *noun* **1** [pl.] chickens, DUCKS and GEESE, kept for their meat or eggs: *to keep poultry* ◊ *poultry farming* ⇒ VISUAL VOCAB page V2 **2** [U] meat from chickens, DUCKS and GEESE: *Eat plenty of fish and poultry.*

**pounce** /paʊns/ *verb* [I] to move suddenly forwards in order to attack or catch sb/sth: *The lion crouched ready to pounce.* ◊ **~ on/upon sb/sth** *The muggers pounced on her as she got out of the car.* ◊ *Hegerberg pounced on the loose ball and scored.*
**PHRV** **'pounce on/upon sth** to quickly notice sth that sb has said or done, especially in order to criticize it **SYN** **seize on/upon**: *His comments were pounced upon by the press.*

**pound** /paʊnd/ *noun, verb*
- **noun**
  - **MONEY 1** [C] (*also specialist* **pound 'sterling**) (*symb.* £) the unit of money in the UK, worth 100 pence: *a ten-pound note* ◊ *a pound coin* ◊ *I've spent £25 on food today.* ◊ *What would you do if you won a million pounds?* ⇒ see also STERLING *noun* **2** [C] the unit of money of several other countries: *His salary will be about 5 000 Egyptian pounds per month.* **3** **the pound** [sing.] (*finance*) the value of the British pound compared with the value of the money of other countries: *the strength/weakness of the pound against other currencies* ◊ *The pound fell sharply to a record low against the yen.*
  - **WEIGHT 4** [C] (*abbr.* **lb**) (in Britain and North America) a unit for measuring weight, equal to 0.454 of a KILOGRAM: *half a pound of butter* ◊ *They cost two dollars a pound.* ◊ *I've lost six and a half pounds since I started my diet.*
  - **FOR CARS 5** [C] a place where vehicles that have been parked illegally are kept until their owners pay to get them back

# pound cake

- **FOR DOGS** 6 [C] a place where dogs that have been found in the street without their owners are kept until their owners claim them
- **IDM** (have, get, want, etc.) your pound of 'flesh the full amount that sb owes you, even if this will cause them trouble or difficulty **ORIGIN** From Shakespeare's *Merchant of Venice*, in which the moneylender Shylock demanded a pound of flesh from Antonio's body if he could not pay back the money he borrowed. ⊃ more at PENNY, PREVENTION

■ *verb*
- **HIT** 1 [I, T] to hit sth/sb hard many times, especially in a way that makes a lot of noise **SYN** hammer: *~ at/against/ on sth Heavy rain pounded on the roof.* ◇ *Someone was pounding at the door.* ◇ *~ away (at/against/on sth) The factory's machinery pounded away day and night.* ◇ *~ sb/ sth (with sth) She pounded him with her fists.* ⊃ SYNONYMS at BEAT
- **WALK NOISILY** 2 [I] + adv./prep. to move with noisy steps: *She pounded along the corridor after him.*
- **OF HEART/BLOOD** 3 [I] to beat quickly and loudly: *Her heart was pounding with excitement.* ◇ *The blood was pounding (= making a beating noise) in his ears.* ◇ *Her head began to pound.* ◇ *a pounding headache*
- **BREAK INTO PIECES** 4 [T] *~ sth (to/into sth)* to hit sth many times in order to break it into smaller pieces: *The seeds were pounded to a fine powder.*
- **ATTACK WITH BOMBS** 5 [T] *~ sth* to attack an area with a large number of bombs over a period of time: *The area is still being pounded by rebel guns.*
- **OF MUSIC** 6 [I] *~ (out)* to be played loudly: *Rock music was pounding out from the jukebox.*

**PHRV** pound sth↔'out to play music loudly on a musical instrument: *to pound out a tune on the piano*

**'pound cake** noun [C, U] (NAmE) a plain yellow cake made with eggs, fat, flour and sugar

**pound·er** /ˈpaʊndə(r)/ noun (in compounds) 1 something that weighs the number of pounds mentioned: *a three-pounder (= a fish, for example, that weighs 3lb)* 2 a gun that fires a SHELL that weighs the number of pounds mentioned: *an eighteen-pounder*

**pound·ing** /ˈpaʊndɪŋ/ noun [usually sing.] 1 a very loud repeated noise, such as the sound of sth hitting sth else hard; the sound or the feeling of your heart beating strongly: *We were awoken by a pounding at the door.* ◇ *There was a pounding in his head.* 2 an occasion when sth is hit hard or attacked and severely damaged **SYN** batter·ing: *The boat took a pounding in the gale.* ◇ *(figurative) The team took a pounding (= were badly defeated).*

**'pound sign** noun 1 the symbol (£) that represents a pound in British money 2 (NAmE) = hash, 'hash sign: *the symbol (#), especially one on a phone*

**pour** /pɔː(r)/ verb 1 [T] to make a liquid or other substance flow from a container in a continuous stream, especially by holding the container at an angle: *~ sth + adv./prep. Pour the sauce over the pasta.* ◇ *~ sth Although I poured it carefully, I still managed to spill some.* 2 [T, I] to serve a drink by letting it flow from a container into a cup or glass: *~ sth Will you pour the coffee?* ◇ *~ sb sth I've poured you a cup of tea.* ◇ *~ sth for sb I've poured a cup of tea for you.* ◇ *~ sth out I'm in the kitchen, pouring out drinks.* ◇ *Shall I pour?* 3 [I, T] when rain pours down or when it's pouring (with) rain, rain is falling heavily: *It's pouring outside.* ◇ *~ down The rain continued to pour down.* ◇ *(BrE) ~ with rain It's pouring with rain.* ◇ *(NAmE) ~ (down) rain It's pouring rain outside.* 4 [I] + adv./prep. (of liquid, smoke, light, etc.) to flow quickly in a continuous stream: *Tears poured down his cheeks.* ◇ *Thick black smoke was pouring out of the roof.* 5 [I] + adv./prep. to come or go somewhere continuously in large numbers **SYN** flood: *The crowd poured into the streets.* ◇ *Commuters came pouring out of the station.*

**IDM** pour oil on troubled 'water(s) to try to settle an argument ⊃ more at COLD *adj.*, HEART *n.*, RAIN *v.*, SCORN *n.*

**PHRV** pour sth 'into sth to provide a large amount of money for sth: *The government has poured millions into the education system.* · **pour 'out** when feelings or sb's words pour out they are expressed, usually after they

have been kept hidden for some time: *The whole story then came pouring out.* · **pour sth↔'out** to express your feelings or give an account of sth, especially after keeping them or it secret or hidden: *She poured out her troubles to me over a cup of coffee.* ⊃ related noun OUTPOURING

**pout** /paʊt/ verb [I, T] *~ (sth)* | *+ speech* if you pout, pout your lips or if your lips pout, you push out your lips, to show you are annoyed or to look sexually attractive: *He pouted angrily.* ◇ *Her lips pouted invitingly.* ◇ *models pouting their lips for the camera* ► **pout** noun: *Her lips were set in a pout of annoyance.* **pouty** *adj.*: *pouty lips*

**pout·ine** /puːˈtiːn/ noun [U] (CanE) a dish of FRENCH FRIES with cheese CURDS on top, served with a sauce (usually GRAVY)

**pov·erty** /ˈpɒvəti; NAmE ˈpɑːvərti/ noun 1 [U] the state of being poor: *conditions of extreme/abject poverty* ◇ *to alleviate poverty* ◇ *in ~ Many elderly people live in poverty.* ◇ *The government is aiming to reduce child poverty (= the number of children living below the poverty line).* ⊃ WORDFINDER NOTE at POOR ⊃ see also FUEL POVERTY 2 [U, sing.] a lack of sth; poor quality: *There is a poverty of colour in her work.*

**the 'poverty line** (also **the 'poverty level** especially in US) noun [sing.] the official level of income that is necessary to be able to buy the basic things you need such as food and clothes and to pay for somewhere to live: **below** *~ A third of the population is living below the poverty line.*

**'poverty-stricken** *adj.* extremely poor; with very little money

**'poverty trap** noun [usually sing.] a situation in which a person stays poor even when they get a job because the money they receive from the government is reduced

**POW** /ˌpiː əʊ ˈdʌbljuː/ noun a person, usually a member of the armed forces, who is captured by the enemy during a war and kept in a prison camp until the war has finished (the abbreviation for 'prisoner of war'): *a POW camp*

**pow** /paʊ/ exclamation used to express the sound of an explosion, a gun firing or sb hitting sb else

**pow·der** /ˈpaʊdə(r)/ noun, verb
■ noun 1 [U, C] a dry mass of very small fine pieces or grains: *milk/chilli/cocoa powder* ◇ *lumps of chalk crushed to a fine white powder* ◇ *The snow was like powder.* ◇ *a wide range of cleaning fluids and powders* ◇ *The mustard is sold in powder form.* ⊃ see also BAKING POWDER, CURRY POWDER, MILK POWDER, SOAP POWDER, TALCUM POWDER, WASHING POWDER 2 [U] a very fine, soft, dry substance that you can put on your face to make it look smooth and dry ⊃ see also FACE POWDER 3 [U] = GUNPOWDER
**IDM** keep your 'powder dry (old-fashioned) to remain ready for a possible emergency · take a 'powder (NAmE, informal) to leave suddenly; to run away
■ verb *~ sth* to put powder on sth: *She powdered her face and put on her lipstick.*
**IDM** powder your 'nose (old-fashioned) a polite way of referring to the fact that a woman is going to the toilet: *I'm just going to powder my nose.*

**powder 'blue** *adj.* very pale blue in colour ► **powder 'blue** noun [U]

**pow·dered** /ˈpaʊdəd; NAmE -dərd/ *adj.* 1 (of a substance that is naturally liquid) dried and made into powder: *powdered milk* 2 CRUSHED (= pressed and broken) and made into a powder: *powdered chalk* 3 covered with powder: *her powdered cheeks*

**powdered 'milk** noun [U] = MILK POWDER

**powdered 'sugar** noun [U] (US) = CONFECTIONER'S SUGAR

**'powder keg** noun a dangerous situation that may suddenly become very violent

**'powder puff** noun a round thick piece of soft material that you use for putting powder on your face

**'powder room** noun 1 a polite word for a women's toilet in a public building 2 (NAmE) a small room in a house containing a WASHBASIN and a toilet, usually for guests to use **SYN** half bath

**pow·dery** /ˈpaʊdəri/ *adj.* like powder; covered with powder: *a light fall of powdery snow* ◇ *powdery cheeks*

**power** /ˈpaʊə(r)/ noun, verb

■ noun
- **CONTROL 1** [U] the ability to control people or things: **~ to do sth** He has the power to make things very unpleasant for us. ◊ **over sb/sth** The aim is to give people more power over their own lives. ◊ **in your ~** She had him completely in her power (= was able to do what she liked with him). ◊ In those days the king exercised real political power. **2** [U] political control of a country or an area: **to take/seize/lose power** ◊ **in ~** The present regime has been in power for two years. ◊ The party came to power at the last election. ◊ They are hoping to return to power. ◊ a **power struggle** between rival factions within the party ⊃ see also BALANCE OF POWER
- **ENERGY 3** [U] energy that can be collected and used to operate a machine, to make electricity, etc: **nuclear/wind/solar power** ◊ **engine power** ◊ They used these streams to generate power for the mill. ⊃ **WORDFINDER NOTE** at ELECTRICITY ⊃ see also HORSEPOWER **4** [U] the public supply of electricity: They've switched off the power. ◊ the **power supply/grid** ◊ a **power failure** (also especially in NAmE) a **power outage 5** [U] the quality of having great power or force, or of being very effective: The ship was helpless against the power of the storm. ◊ It was a performance of great power. ⊃ see also FIREPOWER, STAYING POWER **6** [U] physical strength used in action; physical strength that sb possesses and might use: **with ~** He hit the ball with as much power as he could. ◊ the sheer physical power of the man
- **ABILITY 7** [U] (in people) the ability or opportunity to do sth: **in your ~** I will do everything in my power to help you. ◊ **within your ~** It is not within my power (= I am unable) to help you. **8** [U] (also **powers** [pl.]) a particular ability of the body or mind: Spiderman uses his powers to fight crime. ◊ **~ of sth** He had lost the power of speech. ◊ He had to use all his powers of persuasion. **9 powers** [pl.] all the abilities of a person's body or mind: At 26, he is **at the height of his powers** and ranked fourth in the world.
- **AUTHORITY 10** [C, usually pl., U] the right or authority of a person or group to do sth: The powers of the police must be clearly defined. ◊ This sort of **abuse of power** is unacceptable. ◊ **~ to do sth** The Secretary of State has the power to approve the proposals. ◊ **of sth** The president has the power of veto over all new legislation. ⊃ see also POWER OF ATTORNEY
- **COUNTRY 11** [C] a country with a lot of influence in world affairs, or with great military strength: **world powers** ◊ **major European powers** such as France and Germany ⊃ see also SUPERPOWER
- **INFLUENCE 12** [U] (in compounds) strength or influence in a particular area of activity: These companies have enormous **economic power**. ◊ the exercise of **military power** ◊ **air/sea power** (= military strength in the air/at sea) ◊ The **purchasing power** of today's youth is higher than ever. ⊃ see also BARGAINING POWER, SOFT POWER **13** [U] the influence of a particular thing or group within society: Hollywood star power ◊ **~ of sth** the power of the media ⊃ see also BLACK POWER, GIRL POWER, PEOPLE POWER
- **MATHEMATICS 14** [C, usually sing.] the number of times that an amount is to be multiplied by itself: **to the ~ of sth** 4 to the power of 3 is $4^3$ (= 4×4×4=64).
- **OF LENS 15** [U] the amount by which a LENS can make objects appear larger: the power of a microscope/telescope
- **GOOD/EVIL SPIRIT 16** [C] a good or evil spirit that controls the lives of others: the powers of darkness (= the forces of evil) ⊃ see also FLOWER POWER
- IDM **do sb a 'power of good** (old-fashioned, informal) to be very good for sb's physical or mental health **more power to sb's 'elbow** (BrE, old-fashioned, informal) used to encourage sb or express support for their actions **the (real) power behind the 'throne** the person who really controls an organization, a country, etc. in contrast to the person who is legally in charge **the powers that 'be** (often ironic) the people who control an organization, a country, etc. ⊃ more at CORRIDOR, SWEEP v.

■ verb
- **SUPPLY ENERGY 1** [T, usually passive] to supply a machine or vehicle with the energy that makes it work: **be powered (by sth)** The aircraft is powered by a jet engine. ◊ **~ sth** The plant generates enough energy to power a town of 6 000 people.
- **MOVE QUICKLY 2** [I, T] to move or move sth very quickly and with great power in a particular direction: **+ adv./prep.** He powered through the water. ◊ **~ sth + adv./prep.** She powered her way into the lead. ◊ He powered his header past the goalie.

PHRV **power 'down | power sth↔'down** (also **power 'off, power sth↔'off**) to stop a machine, especially a computer, by turning off the electricity supply: We were told to power down at 9.45. ◊ Power off your PC. OPP **power sth↔up, power up power sth↔up | power 'up** (also **power sth↔'on, power 'on**) to prepare a machine to start working by supplying it with electricity, etc.; (of a machine) to start working: Back at the hotel, I powered up my laptop. ◊ The system wouldn't power on. OPP **power down, power↔sth down**

**power-assisted 'steering** noun [U] (BrE) = POWER STEERING

**'power base** noun the area or the people that provide the main support for a politician or a political party

**'power-boat** /ˈpaʊəbəʊt; NAmE -boʊt/ noun a fast boat with a powerful engine that is used especially for racing

**'power broker** noun a person who has a strong influence on who has political power in an area

**'power couple** noun a couple in which both partners are famous and successful at what they do

**'power cut** (BrE) (NAmE **'power outage**) noun a situation in which the supply of electricity is interrupted; a period of time when this happens

**'power dressing** noun [U] a style of dressing in which people in business wear formal and expensive clothes to emphasize how important they and their jobs are

**powered** /ˈpaʊəd; NAmE -ərd/ adj. (usually in compounds) operated by a form of energy such as electricity or by the type of energy mentioned: a powered wheelchair ◊ a solar-powered calculator ⊃ see also HIGH-POWERED

**power·ful** /ˈpaʊəfl; NAmE -ərfl/ adj. **1** (of people) being able to control and influence people and events SYN **influential**: an incredibly powerful organization ◊ The US remains the most powerful nation in the world. ◊ She is still a powerful figure in the party. ◊ a rich and powerful man **2** having great power or force; very effective: a powerful engine ◊ a powerful voice ◊ Capitalism is an immensely powerful force in modern society. ◊ Gene technology is a very powerful tool. **3** having a strong effect on your thoughts, feelings or body: a powerful image/symbol/speech ◊ Nicotine is a powerful drug. ◊ Her background has had a powerful influence on her film-making. ◊ A successful prosecution would send a powerful message. **4** (of a person or an animal) physically strong SYN **muscular**: a powerful body ◊ a powerful athlete ▸ **power·ful·ly** /-fəli/ adv.: a powerfully emotive song ◊ He is powerfully built (= he has a large strong body). ◊ She argued powerfully for reform.

**'power grab** noun (informal) an attempt by a person or group to take more authority for themselves, usually by taking it from another person or group

**power·house** /ˈpaʊəhaʊs; NAmE -ərh-/ noun **1** a group or an organization that is strong and effective in its activities: China has been described as an 'emerging economic powerhouse'. **2** a person who is very strong and full of energy

**power·less** /ˈpaʊələs; NAmE -ərl-/ adj. **1** without power to control or to influence sb/sth SYN **helpless**: powerless minorities ◊ When the enemy attacked, we were completely powerless against them. **2 ~ to do sth** completely unable to do sth: I saw what was happening, but I was powerless to help. ▸ **power·less·ness** noun [U]: a feeling/sense of powerlessness

**power·lift·ing** /ˈpaʊəlɪftɪŋ; NAmE -ərl-/ noun [U] the sport of lifting weights in three different ways, in a set order ▸ **power·lift·er** noun

**'power line** noun a thick wire that carries electricity: overhead power lines

**power nap** noun a short sleep that sb has during the day in order to get back their energy ▶ **power-nap** verb [I] (-pp-)

**power of at'torney** noun [U, C] (pl. **powers of attorney**) (law) the right to act as the representative of sb in business or financial matters; a document that gives sb this right

**power outage** (NAmE) (BrE **power cut**) noun a situation in which the supply of electricity is interrupted; a period of time when this happens

**power pack** noun a device that stores and supplies electrical power. Power packs are usually designed to be easy to carry with you.

**power plant** (BrE also **power station**) noun a building or group of buildings where electricity is produced

**power play** noun [U] **1** (in ICE HOCKEY) a situation in which one team has more players than another because a player is off the ice as a punishment **2** a way of behaving that shows or increases a person's power, especially in a relationship: *political power play*

**power point** noun (BrE) = SOCKET (1)

**power politics** noun [U + sing./pl. v.] a situation in which a person, group or country tries to control a situation by using their power, threats of force, etc.

**power-sharing** noun [U] a policy or system in which different groups or political parties share responsibility for making decisions, taking political action, etc.

**power shower** noun (BrE) a shower that has an electric PUMP to make the water come out fast

**power station** (BrE) (also **power plant** NAmE, BrE) noun a building or group of buildings where electricity is produced: *a coal-fired power station ◊ a nuclear power station* ⊃ WORDFINDER NOTE at ENERGY

**power steering** (BrE also **power-assisted steering**) noun [U] (in a vehicle) a system that uses power from the engine to help the driver change direction

**power-up** noun **1** [U] the moment when a machine is switched on and starts working: *Does the computer beep on power-up?* **2** [C] in computer games, an advantage that a character can get if a player wins a certain number of points, for example more strength

**power user** noun (computing) a person who can use the more advanced features of computer software

**pow·wow** /ˈpaʊwaʊ/ noun **1** a meeting of Native Americans **2** (informal or humorous) a meeting for discussion

**pox** /pɒks; NAmE pɑːks/ noun **the pox** [sing.] (old use) **1** a disease spread by sexual contact SYN syphilis **2** = SMALLPOX

**poxy** /ˈpɒksi; NAmE ˈpɑːk-/ adj. [only before noun] (BrE, informal) if sb describes sth as poxy, they think it has little value or importance

**pp** abbr. **1 pp.** pages: *See pp. 100–117.* **2** (also **p.p.**) /ˌpiː ˈpiː/ (especially BrE) used in front of a person's name when sb signs a business letter for that person: *pp Chris Baker* (= from Chris Baker, but signed by sb else because Chris Baker is away) **3** (music) very quietly (from Italian 'pianissimo')

**ppi** /ˌpiː piː ˈaɪ/ abbr. (computing) pixels per inch (a measure of the quality of images)

**PPS** /ˌpiː piː ˈes/ noun a Member of Parliament in the UK who is given the job of helping a minister (the abbreviation for 'Parliamentary Private Secretary')

**PPV** /ˌpiː piː ˈviː/ abbr. PAY-PER-VIEW

**PR** /ˌpiː ˈɑː(r)/ noun [U] **1** the business of giving the public information about a particular organization or person in order to create a good impression (the abbreviation for 'public relations'): *a PR department/agency/campaign ◊ The article is very good PR for the theatre.* **2** a system that gives each party in an election a number of seats in relation to the number of votes its candidates receive (the abbreviation for 'proportional representation')

**prac·tic·able** /ˈpræktɪkəbl/ adj. (formal) able to be done; likely to be successful SYN feasible, workable: *at the earliest practicable opportunity ◊ as soon as (is) practicable ◊ The only practicable alternative is to postpone the meeting. ◊ Employers should provide a safe working environment, as far as is reasonably practicable.* ⊃ compare IMPRACTICABLE ▶ **prac·tic·abil·ity** /ˌpræktɪkəˈbɪləti/ noun [U]: *We were doubtful about the practicability of the plan.* **prac·tic·ably** /ˈpræktɪkəbli/ adv.: *Please reply as soon as is practicably possible.*

**prac·tical** ❶ B1 ⦿ /ˈpræktɪkl/ adj., noun

■ adj.
• CONNECTED WITH REAL THINGS **1** B1 connected with real situations rather than with ideas or theories: *to have gained practical experience of the work ◊ practical advice ◊ the practical implications of the proposal ◊ There are some obvious practical applications of the research. ◊ In practical terms, it means spending less. ◊ Of how much practical use was the conference?* ⊃ compare THEORETICAL
• LIKELY TO WORK **2** B1 ~ (for sb) (to do sth) (of an idea, a method or a course of action) right or sensible; likely to be successful SYN workable: *It wouldn't be practical for us to go all that way just for the weekend.* OPP impractical
• USEFUL **3** B2 (of things) useful or suitable: *a practical little car, ideal for the city* OPP impractical
• SENSIBLE **4** B2 (of a person) sensible and realistic: *Let's be practical and work out the cost first.* OPP impractical
• GOOD AT MAKING THINGS **5** (of a person) good at making or repairing things SYN handy: *Bob's very practical. He does all the odd jobs around the house.*
• ALMOST TOTAL **6** [only before noun] almost complete or total SYN virtual: *She married a practical stranger.*
IDM **for (all) ˈpractical purposes** used when you are stating what the reality of a situation is: *There's still another ten minutes of the game to go, but for practical purposes it's already over.*

■ noun (BrE) a lesson or an exam in science or technology in which students have to do or make things, not just read or write about them ⊃ WORDFINDER NOTE at EXAM

**prac·ti·cal·ity** /ˌpræktɪˈkæləti/ noun **1** [U] the quality of being suitable, or likely to be successful SYN feasibility: *I have doubts about the practicality of their proposal.* **2** [U] the quality of being sensible and realistic: *I was impressed by her practicality.* **3** **practicalities** [pl.] the real facts and circumstances rather than ideas or theories: *It sounds like a good idea; let's look at the practicalities and work out the costs.*

**practical ˈjoke** noun a trick that is played on sb to make them look stupid and to make other people laugh ▶ **practical ˈjoker** noun

**prac·tic·al·ly** /ˈpræktɪkli/ adv. **1** almost; very nearly SYN virtually: *The theatre was practically empty. ◊ I meet famous people practically every day. ◊ My essay is practically finished now. ◊ There's practically no difference between the two options.* ⊃ note at ALMOST **2** in a realistic or sensible way; in real situations: *Practically speaking, we can't afford it. ◊ It sounds like a good idea, but I don't think it will work practically.* ⊃ compare THEORETICALLY

**practical ˈnurse** noun (NAmE) a nurse with practical experience but less training than a REGISTERED NURSE

**prac·tice** ❶ A1 ⦿ /ˈpræktɪs/ noun, verb

■ noun
• FOR IMPROVING SKILL **1** A1 [U, C] doing an activity or training regularly so that you can improve your skill; the time you spend doing this: *conversation practice ◊ There's a basketball practice every Friday evening. ◊* with ~ *With practice you will become more skilled. ◊* ~ in doing sth *I've had a lot of practice in saying 'no' recently!* ⊃ see also FIRE PRACTICE, TEACHING PRACTICE
• ACTION NOT IDEAS **2** B2 [U] action rather than ideas: *the theory and practice of teaching ◊ She's determined to put her new ideas into practice.*
• WAY OF DOING STH **3** B2 [U, C] a way of doing sth that is the usual or expected way in a particular organization or situation: *common/current/standard practice ◊ Everyone knows it is good business practice to listen to your customers. ◊ religious practices ◊ I am constantly adopting new practices on my farm. ◊* ~ of doing sth *We will follow*

*the practice* of going in alphabetical order. ⇒ see also BEST PRACTICE, CODE OF PRACTICE
- **HABIT/CUSTOM 4** [C] a thing that is done regularly; a habit or a custom: *~ of doing sth the German practice of giving workers a say in how their company is run* ◊ **it is sb's ~ to do sth** *It is his practice to read several books a week.*
- **OF DOCTOR/LAWYER 5** [U, C] the work or the business of some professional people such as doctors, dentists and lawyers; the place where they work: *the practice of medicine* ◊ *clinical/medical practice* ◊ *in ~ My solicitor is no longer in practice.* ◊ *a successful medical/dental/law practice* ⇒ see also FAMILY PRACTICE, GENERAL PRACTICE, GROUP PRACTICE, PRIVATE PRACTICE ⇒ **WORDFINDER NOTE** at DOCTOR

**IDM** ▶ **be/get out of 'practice** to be/become less good at doing sth than you were because you have not spent time doing it recently: *Don't ask me to speak French! I'm out of practice.* **in 'practice** in reality: *Prisoners have legal rights, but in practice these rights are not always respected.* **,practice makes 'perfect** (*saying*) a way of encouraging people by telling them that if you do an activity regularly and try to improve your skill, you will become very good at it

■ **verb** A1 (*US*) = PRACTISE: *to practice the piano every day* ◊ *The team is practicing for their big game on Friday.* ◊ *They practiced the dance until it was perfect.* ◊ *She's practicing medicine in Philadelphia.*

**prac·tise** 🔊 A1 (*US* **prac·tice**) /ˈpræktɪs/ *verb* 1 B1 [I, T] to do an activity or train regularly so that you can improve your skill: *You need to practise every day.* ◊ *~ for sth She's practising for her piano exam.* ◊ *~ sth I've been practising my serve for weeks.* ◊ *~ (sth) on sb/sth He usually wants to practise his English on me.* ◊ *~ doing sth Practise reversing the car into the garage.* 2 B2 [I, T] to work as a doctor, lawyer, etc: *There are over 50000 solicitors practising in England and Wales.* ◊ *~ as sth She practised as a barrister for many years.* ◊ *~ sth to practise law/medicine* 3 [T] *~ sth* (*formal*) to do sth regularly as part of your normal behaviour: *to practise self-restraint/safe sex* ◊ *Do you still practise your religion?*
**IDM** ▶ **practise what you 'preach** to do the things yourself that you tell other people to do

**prac·tised** (*US* **-ticed**) /ˈpræktɪst/ *adj.* good at doing sth because you have been doing it regularly: *She's only 18 but she's already a practised composer.* ◊ *It took a practised eye to spot the difference.* ◊ *~ in sth He has good ideas but he isn't practised in the art of marketing.*

**prac·tis·ing** (*US* **-ticing**) /ˈpræktɪsɪŋ/ *adj.* [only before noun] taking an active part in a particular religion, profession, etc: *a practising Christian/teacher*

**prac·ti·tion·er** 🔊 C1 🅦 /prækˈtɪʃənə(r)/ *noun* (*formal*) 1 🔊 C1 a person who works in a profession, especially medicine or law: *dental practitioners* ◊ *a qualified practitioner* ⇒ see also FAMILY PRACTITIONER, GENERAL PRACTITIONER, NURSE PRACTITIONER 2 a person who regularly does a particular activity, especially one that requires skill: *one of the greatest practitioners of science fiction*

**prae·sid·ium** (*especially BrE*) = PRESIDIUM

**prag·mat·ic** /præɡˈmætɪk/ *adj.* solving problems in a practical and sensible way rather than by having fixed ideas or theories **SYN** **realistic**: *a pragmatic approach to management problems* ▶ **prag·mat·ic·ally** /-kli/ *adv.*

**prag·mat·ics** /præɡˈmætɪks/ *noun* [U] (*linguistics*) the study of the way in which language is used to express what sb really means in particular situations, especially when the actual words used may appear to mean sth different

**prag·ma·tism** /ˈpræɡmətɪzəm/ *noun* [U] (*formal*) thinking about solving problems in a practical and sensible way rather than by having fixed ideas and theories ▶ **prag·ma·tist** /-tɪst/ *noun*

**prairie** /ˈpreəri; *NAmE* ˈpreri/ *noun* [C, U] a flat, wide area of land in North America and Canada, without many trees and originally covered with grass

**'prairie dog** *noun* a small brown North American animal of the SQUIRREL family that lives in holes on the prairies

**'prairie wolf** *noun* = COYOTE

**praise** 🔊 B2 /preɪz/ *noun, verb*
■ *noun* [U] 1 B2 (*also less frequent* **praises** [pl.]) words that show that you approve of and admire sb/sth: *The team coach singled out two players for special praise.* ◊ *~ for sth His teachers are full of praise for the progress he's making.* ◊ *~ (for sth) from sb His latest movie has won high praise from the critics.* ◊ *Critics heaped/lavished/showered praise on her latest movie.* ◊ *to deserve/earn/garner praise* ◊ *in ~ of sb She wrote poems in praise of freedom.* ◊ *They always* **sing his praises** (= praise him very highly). 2 B2 the expression of thanks to or respect for God: *hymns/songs of praise* ◊ *~ to sb joyous singing and praise to God* **IDM** see DAMN *v.*
■ *verb* 1 B2 to say that you approve of and admire sb/sth **SYN** **compliment**: *~ sb/sth She praised his cooking.* ◊ *a highly praised film* ◊ *~ sb/sth for sth He praised his team for their performance.* ◊ *~ sb/sth as sth Critics praised the work as highly original.* 2 B2 *~ sb* to express your thanks to or your respect for God: *Praise the Lord.* ◊ *Allah be praised.*
**IDM** ▶ **praise sb/sth to the 'skies** to praise sb/sth a lot

▼ **HOMOPHONES**
**praise • prays • preys** /preɪz/
- **praise** *noun*: *This organization has never received the praise and recognition it deserves.*
- **praise** *verb*: *Always praise your child for making an effort.*
- **prays** *verb* (*third person of* PRAY): *Aeneas prays to Jupiter, who sends rain.*
- **preys** *verb* (*third person of* PREY): *The snake preys on small mammals and birds.*

**'praise singer** (*also* **'praise poet**) *noun* (*SAfrE*) (in traditional African society) a person who writes and performs music and poetry in order to praise a leader or other important person

**praise·worthy** /ˈpreɪzwɜːði; *NAmE* -wɜːrði/ *adj.* (*formal*) deserving praise **SYN** **commendable**: *a praiseworthy achievement*

**pra·line** /ˈprɑːliːn, ˈpreɪl-; *NAmE* ˈpreɪl-/ *noun* [U] a sweet substance made of nuts and boiled sugar, often used to fill chocolates

**pram** /præm/ (*BrE*) (*NAmE* **'baby carriage**) *noun* a small vehicle on four wheels for a baby to go out in, pushed by a person on foot ⇒ **WORDFINDER NOTE** at BABY ⇒ picture at PUSHCHAIR

**prana** /ˈprɑːnə/ *noun* [U] (in Hindu philosophy) the force that keeps all life in existence

**prance** /prɑːns; *NAmE* præns/ *verb* 1 [I] + *adv./prep.* to move quickly with EXAGGERATED steps so that people will look at you: *The lead singer was prancing around with the microphone.* 2 [I] (of a horse) to move with high steps

**prang** /præŋ/ *verb* *~ sth* (*BrE, informal*) to damage a vehicle in an accident ▶ **prang** *noun*

**prank** /præŋk/ *noun* a trick that is played on sb as a joke: *a childish prank* ▶ **prank** *verb*: *~ sb* (*informal*) *I felt really stupid when I realized I'd been pranked.* **prank·ster** /ˈpræŋkstə(r)/ *noun*: *Student pranksters have done considerable damage to the school buildings.*

**prat** /præt/ *noun* (*BrE, informal*) a stupid person

**prat·fall** /ˈprætfɔːl/ *noun* (*especially NAmE*) 1 an embarrassing mistake 2 a fall on your bottom

**prat·tle** /ˈprætl/ *verb* [I] *~ (on/away) (about sb/sth)* (*old-fashioned, often disapproving*) to talk a lot about things that are not important: *~ on/away about sb/sth She prattled on about her children all evening.* ▶ **prat·tle** *noun* [U]

**prawn** /prɔːn/ *noun* [C, U] (*especially BrE*) (*NAmE usually* **shrimp**) a SHELLFISH that can be eaten, with ten legs and a long tail. Prawns turn pink when cooked. ⇒ **VISUAL VOCAB** page V3

**praxis** /ˈpræksɪs/ *noun* [U] (*philosophy*) a way of doing sth; the use of a theory or a belief in a practical way

# pray

**pray** /preɪ/ verb, adv.
- **verb 1** [I, T] to speak to God, especially to give thanks or ask for help: *They knelt down and prayed.* ◊ *~ for sb/sth I'll pray for you.* ◊ *to pray for peace* ◊ *to sb (for sb/sth) She prayed to God for an end to her sufferings.* ◊ *~ (that)... We prayed (that) she would recover from her illness.* ◊ *to do sth He prayed to be forgiven.* ◊ *+ speech 'Please God don't let it happen,' she prayed.* ◆ HOMOPHONES at PRAISE **2** [I, T] to hope very much that sth will happen: *~ for sth We're praying for good weather on Saturday.* ◊ *~ (that)... I prayed that nobody would notice my mistake.*
- **adv.** (*old use* or *ironic*) used to mean 'please' when you are asking a question or telling sb to do sth: *What, pray, is the meaning of this?* ◊ *Pray continue.*

**prayer** /preə(r); NAmE prer/ noun **1** [C] words that you say to God giving thanks or asking for help: *to say your prayers* ◊ *~ for sb/sth prayers for the sick* ◊ *He arrived at that very moment, as if in answer to her prayer.* ◊ *Their prayers were answered and the child was found safe and well.* ◊ *to sb/sth She stopped saying nightly prayers to God.* **2** [C] a fixed form of words that you can say when you speak to God: *It was a prayer she had learnt as a child.* ⇒ see also LORD'S PRAYER **3** [U] (**in**) *~ the act or habit of praying: They knelt in prayer.* ◊ *We believe in the power of prayer.* **4** **prayers** [pl.] a religious meeting that takes place regularly in which people say prayers **5** [C, usually sing.] a thing that you hope for very much: *My prayer is that one day he will walk again.* IDM see WING n.
- IDM **not have a ˈprayer (of doing sth)** to have no chance of succeeding (in doing sth)

**ˈprayer book** noun a book that contains prayers, for use in religious services

**prayerful** /ˈpreəfl; NAmE ˈprerfl/ adj. **1** involving the act of praying: *The group stands silently prayerful for a moment as the candle is lit.* **2** (of a person) tending to pray a lot; believing very strongly in a religion: *He was a very humble and prayerful person.*

**ˈprayer meeting** noun a religious meeting when people say prayers to God

**ˈprayer rug** (*also* **ˈprayer mat**) noun a small carpet on which Muslims rest their knees when they are saying prayers

**ˌpraying ˈmantis** (*also* **mantis**) noun a large green insect that eats other insects. The female praying mantis often eats the male.

**pre-** /priː/ prefix (in verbs, nouns and adjectives) before: *preheat* ◊ *precaution* ◊ *pre-war* ◊ *preseason training* (= before a sports season starts) ⇒ compare ANTE-, POST-

**preach** /priːtʃ/ verb **1** [I, T] to give a religious talk in a public place, especially in a church during a service: *She preached to the congregation about forgiveness.* ◊ *~ sth The minister preached a sermon on the parable of the lost sheep.* **2** [T, I] to tell people about a particular religion, way of life, system, etc. in order to persuade them to accept it: *~ sth to preach the word of God* ◊ *He preached the virtues of capitalism to us.* ◊ *~ (about sth) She preached about the benefits of a healthy lifestyle.* **3** [I] (*disapproving*) to give sb advice on moral standards, behaviour, etc., especially in a way that they find annoying or boring: *I'm sorry, I didn't mean to preach.* ◊ *~ at sb You're preaching at me again!*
- IDM **preach to the conˈverted** (*also* **preach to the ˈchoir** *especially in NAmE*) to speak to people in support of views that they already hold ⇒ more at PRACTISE

**preacher** /ˈpriːtʃə(r)/ noun a person, often a member of the CLERGY, who gives religious talks and often performs religious ceremonies, for example in a church: *a preacher famous for her inspiring sermons* ◊ *a lay preacher* (= who is not a priest, etc. but who has been trained to give religious talks)

**preachy** /ˈpriːtʃi/ adj. (*informal, disapproving*) trying to give advice or to persuade people to accept an opinion on what is right and wrong

**preamble** /priˈæmbl/ noun [C, U] (*formal*) an introduction to a book or a written document; an introduction to sth you say: *in a ~ The aims of the treaty are stated in its preamble.* ◊ *without ~ She gave him the bad news without preamble.*

**prearranged** /ˌpriːəˈreɪndʒd/ adj. planned or arranged in advance SYN predetermined

**pre-ˈbook** verb [I, T] (*BrE*) to arrange to have sth such as a room, table, seat, or ticket in advance: *You are advised to pre-book.* ◊ *~ sth Accommodation is cheaper if you pre-book it.*

**precancerous** /ˌpriːˈkænsərəs/ adj. (*medical*) that will develop into cancer if not treated: *precancerous cells*

**precarious** /prɪˈkeəriəs; NAmE -ˈker-/ adj. **1** (of a situation) not safe or certain; dangerous: *He earned a precarious living as an artist.* ◊ *The museum is in a financially precarious position.* **2** likely to fall or cause sb to fall: *That ladder looks very precarious.* ◊ *The path down to the beach is very precarious in wet weather.* ▶ **precariously** adv.: *The economy is precariously close to recession.* ◊ *He balanced the glass precariously on the arm of his chair.* **precariousness** noun [U]

**precast** /ˌpriːˈkɑːst; NAmE -ˈkæst/ adj. (of some building materials) made into blocks ready to use: *precast concrete slabs*

**precaution** /prɪˈkɔːʃn/ noun [usually pl.] **1** ~ (**against sth**) something that is done in advance in order to prevent problems or to avoid danger: *safety precautions* ◊ *precautions against fire* ◊ *You must take all reasonable precautions to protect yourself and your family.* ◊ *I'll keep the letter as a precaution.* **2** **precautions** [pl.] a way of referring to CONTRACEPTION: *We didn't take any precautions and I got pregnant.* ▶ **precautionary** /prɪˈkɔːʃənəri; NAmE -neri/ adj.: *He was kept in the hospital overnight as a precautionary measure.*

**precede** /prɪˈsiːd/ verb (*formal*) **1** ~ sb/sth to happen before sth or come before sth/sb in order: *the years preceding the war* ◊ *His resignation was preceded by weeks of speculation.* ◊ *She preceded me in the job.* **2** ~ sb + adv./prep. to go in front of sb: *She preceded him out of the room.* **3** ~ sth with sth to do or say sth to introduce sth else: *She preceded her speech with a vote of thanks to the committee.*

**precedence** /ˈpresɪdəns/ noun [U] ~ (**over sb/sth**) the condition of being more important than sb else and therefore coming or being dealt with first SYN **priority**: *She had to learn that her wishes did not take precedence over other people's needs.* ◊ *The speakers came on to the platform in order of precedence* (= the most important one first).

**precedent** /ˈpresɪdənt/ noun **1** [C, U] an official action or decision that has happened in the past and that is seen as an example or a rule to be followed in a similar situation later: *The ruling set a precedent for future libel cases.* **2** [C, U] a similar action or event that happened earlier: *historical precedents* ◊ *There is no precedent for a disaster on this scale.* ◊ *without ~ Such protests are without precedent in recent history.* **3** [U] the way that things have always been done SYN **tradition**: *to break with precedent* (= to do sth in a different way) ⇒ see also UNPRECEDENTED

**preceding** /prɪˈsiːdɪŋ/ adj. [only before noun] happening before sth; coming before sth/sb in order: *See the preceding chapter.* ◊ *It had happened during the preceding year.*

**precept** /ˈpriːsept/ noun [C, U] (*formal*) a rule about how to behave or what to think SYN **principle**

**precinct** /ˈpriːsɪŋkt/ noun **1** (*BrE*) a commercial area in a town where cars cannot go: *a pedestrian/shopping precinct* **2** (*NAmE*) one of the parts into which a town or city is divided in order to organize elections **3** (*NAmE*) a part of a city that has its own police station; the police station in this area: *Detective Hennessy of the 44th precinct* ◊ *The murder occurred just a block from the precinct.* **4** [usually pl.] (*formal*) the area around a place or a building, sometimes surrounded by a wall: *the cathedral/college precincts* ◊ *within the precincts of the castle*

**precious** /ˈpreʃəs/ adj., adv.
- **adj. 1** rare and worth a lot of money: *a precious vase* ◊ *The crown was set with precious jewels—diamonds, rubies and emeralds.* ⇒ see also PRECIOUS METAL, PRECIOUS

STONE, SEMI-PRECIOUS ⇒ SYNONYMS at VALUABLE. valuable or important and not to be wasted: *Clean water is a precious commodity in that part of the world.* ◇ *You're wasting precious time!* **3** loved or valued very much **SYN** treasured: *precious memories/possessions* ◇ *~ to sb You are infinitely precious to me.* **4** [only before noun] (*informal*) used to show you are angry that another person thinks sth is very important: *I didn't touch your precious car!* **5** (*disapproving*) (especially of people and their behaviour) very formal, EXAGGERATED and not natural in what you say and do **SYN** affected ▶ **pre·cious·ness** noun [U]: *the preciousness of an old friendship* ◇ *His writings reveal an unattractive preciousness of style.*

■ *adv.* **~ little/few** (*informal*) used to emphasize the fact that there is very little of sth or that there are very few of sth: *There's precious little to do in this town.*

**precious metal** noun [C, U] a very valuable metal such as gold or silver

**precious stone** (*also* **stone**) noun a rare valuable stone, such as a diamond, that is used in jewellery ⇒ see also SEMI-PRECIOUS

**preci·pice** /ˈpresəpɪs/ noun a very steep side of a high CLIFF, mountain or rock: (*figurative*) *The country was now on the edge of a precipice* (= very close to disaster). ⇒ see also PRECIPITOUS ⇒ WORDFINDER NOTE at MOUNTAIN

**pre·cipi·tate** verb, adj., noun

■ verb /prɪˈsɪpɪteɪt/ (*formal*) **1** ~ sth to make sth, especially sth bad, happen suddenly or sooner than it should **SYN** bring on, spark: *His resignation precipitated a leadership crisis.* **2** ~ sb/sth into sth to suddenly force sb/sth into a particular state or condition: *The assassination of the president precipitated the country into war.*

■ *adj.* /prɪˈsɪpɪtət/ (*formal*) (of an action or a decision) happening very quickly or suddenly and usually without enough care and thought ▶ **pre·cipi·tate·ly** adv.: *to act precipitately*

■ *noun* /prɪˈsɪpɪteɪt/ (*chemistry*) a solid substance that has been separated from a liquid in a chemical process

**pre·cipi·ta·tion** /prɪˌsɪpɪˈteɪʃn/ noun **1** [U] (*specialist*) rain, snow, etc. that falls; the amount of this that falls: *an increase in annual precipitation* ⇒ WORDFINDER NOTE at RAIN **2** [U, C] (*chemistry*) a chemical process in which solid material is separated from a liquid

**pre·cipit·ous** /prɪˈsɪpɪtəs/ adj. (*formal*) **1** very steep, high and often dangerous **SYN** sheer: *precipitous cliffs* ◇ *a precipitous drop at the side of the road* **2** sudden and great **SYN** abrupt: *a precipitous decline in exports* **3** done very quickly, without enough thought or care **SYN** hasty: *a precipitous action* ▶ **pre·cipit·ous·ly** adv.: *The land dropped precipitously down to the rocky shore.* ◇ *The dollar plunged precipitously.* ◇ *We don't want to act precipitously.* ⇒ see also PRECIPICE

**pré·cis** /ˈpreɪsiː; NAmE preɪˈsiː/ noun [C, U] (pl. **pré·cis** /ˈpreɪsiːz; NAmE preɪˈsiːz/) a short version of a speech or a piece of writing that gives the main points or ideas **SYN** summary: *to write/give/make a précis of a report* ▶ **pré·cis** verb (**pré·cises** /-siːz/, **pré·cis·ing** /ˈpreɪsiːɪŋ/, NAmE preɪˈsiːɪŋ/, **pré·cised**, **pré·cised** /-siːd/): *~ sth* to précis a scientific report

**pre·cise** /prɪˈsaɪs/ adj. **1** clear and accurate **SYN** exact: *precise details/instructions/measurements* ◇ *Can you give a more precise definition of the word?* ◇ *I can be reasonably precise about the time of the incident.* **2** [only before noun] used to emphasize that sth happens at a particular time or in a particular way: *We were just talking about her when, at that precise moment, she walked in.* ◇ *Doctors found it hard to establish the precise nature of her illness.* **3** taking care to be exact and accurate, especially about small details **SYN** meticulous: *a skilled and precise worker* ◇ *small, precise movements* ◇ (*disapproving*) *She's rather prim and precise.* **IDM** **to be (more) precise** used to show that you are giving more detailed and accurate information about sth you have just mentioned: *The shelf is about a metre long—well, 98cm, to be precise.*

**pre·cise·ly** /prɪˈsaɪsli/ adv. **1** exactly: *They look precisely the same to me.* ◇ *That's precisely what I meant.* ◇ *It's not clear precisely how the accident happened.* ◇ *The meeting starts at 2 o'clock precisely.* **2** 

# predatory

accurately; carefully: *to describe sth precisely* ◇ *She pronounced the word very slowly and precisely.* **3** used to emphasize that sth is very true or obvious: *It's precisely because I care about you that I don't like you staying out late.* **4** used to emphasize that you agree with a statement, especially because you think it is obvious or is similar to what you have just said: *'It's not that easy, is it?' 'No, precisely.'*

**IDM** **more precisely** used to show that you are giving more detailed and accurate information about sth you have just mentioned: *The problem is due to discipline, or, more precisely, the lack of discipline, in schools.* ⇒ LANGUAGE BANK at I.E.

**pre·ci·sion** /prɪˈsɪʒn/ noun [U] the quality of being exact, accurate and careful **SYN** accuracy: **with ~** *He chose his words with precision.* ◇ *done with mathematical precision* ◇ *Historians can't estimate the date with any (degree of) precision.* ◇ *precision instruments/tools*

**pre·clude** /prɪˈkluːd/ verb (*formal*) to prevent sth from happening or sb from doing sth; to make sth impossible: *~ sth Lack of time precludes any further discussion.* ◇ *~ sb from doing sth My lack of interest in the subject precluded me from gaining much enjoyment out of it.* ◇ *~ (sb) doing sth His religious beliefs precluded him/his serving in the army.*

**pre·co·cious** /prɪˈkəʊʃəs/ adj. (*sometimes disapproving*) (of a child) having developed particular abilities and ways of behaving at a much younger age than usual: *a precocious child who started her acting career at the age of 5* ◇ *sexually precocious* ◇ *From an early age she displayed a precocious talent for music.* ▶ **pre·co·cious·ly** adv.: *a precociously talented child* **pre·co·city** /prɪˈkɒsəti; NAmE -ˈkɑːs-/ (*also* **pre·co·cious·ness**) noun [U] (*formal*): *his unusual precocity*

**pre·cog·ni·tion** /ˌpriːkɒɡˈnɪʃn; NAmE -kɑːɡ-/ noun [U] (*formal*) the knowledge that sth will happen in the future, which sb has because of a dream or a sudden feeling

**pre-Columbian** /ˌpriː kəˈlʌmbiən/ adj. (*specialist*) connected with North and South America and their cultures before the arrival of Columbus in 1492

**pre·con·ceived** /ˌpriːkənˈsiːvd/ adj. [only before noun] (of ideas, opinions, etc.) formed before you have enough information or experience of sth: *Before I started the job, I had no preconceived notions of what it would be like.*

**pre·con·cep·tion** /ˌpriːkənˈsepʃn/ noun [C, usually pl., U] an idea or opinion that is formed before you have enough information or experience **SYN** assumption: *a book that will challenge your preconceptions about rural life* ⇒ compare MISCONCEPTION

**pre·con·di·tion** /ˌpriːkənˈdɪʃn/ noun **~ (for/of sth)** something that must happen or exist before sth else can exist or be done **SYN** prerequisite: *A ceasefire is an essential precondition for negotiation.*

**pre-cooked** /ˌpriːˈkʊkt/ adj. (of food) prepared and partly cooked in advance so that it can be quickly heated and eaten later

**pre·cur·sor** /prɪˈkɜːsə(r); NAmE -ˈkɜːrs-/ noun **~ (of/to sth)** (*formal*) a person or thing that comes before sb/sth similar and that leads to or influences its development **SYN** forerunner

**pre-cut** adj. cut in advance and ready to use

**pre·date** /ˌpriːˈdeɪt/ (*also* **ante-date**) verb **~ sth** to be built or formed, or to happen, at an earlier date than sth else in the past: *Few of the town's fine buildings predate the earthquake of 1755.* **OPP** post-date

**pre·da·tion** /prɪˈdeɪʃn/ noun [U] (*specialist*) the act of an animal killing and eating other animals

**preda·tor** /ˈpredətə(r)/ noun [C, U] **1** an animal that kills and eats other animals: *Some animals have no natural predators.* **2** (*disapproving*) a person or an organization that uses weaker people for their own advantage: *to protect domestic industry from foreign predators*

**preda·tory** /ˈpredətri; NAmE -tɔːri/ adj. **1** (*specialist*) (of animals) living by killing and eating other animals **2** (of people) using weaker people for their own financial or

**predatory lending**

sexual advantage: *a predatory insurance salesman* ◇ *a predatory look*

**pre·da·tory 'lending** *noun* [U] the practice of lending money to people who cannot afford to pay it back, often by hiding the true cost of the loan

**pre·da·tory 'pricing** *noun* [U] (*business*) the fact of a company selling its goods at such a low price that other companies can no longer compete and have to stop selling similar goods

**pre·dawn** /ˌpriːˈdɔːn/ *adj.* [only before noun] in or relating to the part of the day just before the first light appears: *The aircraft took off in the predawn darkness.*

**pre·de·cease** /ˌpriːdɪˈsiːs/ *verb* ~ **sb** (*law*) to die before sb: *His wife predeceased him.*

**pre·de·ces·sor** /ˈpriːdəsesə(r); *NAmE* ˈpred-/ *noun* **1** a person who did a job before sb else: *The new president reversed many of the policies of his predecessor.* **2** a thing, such as a machine, that has been followed or replaced by sth else ⊃ compare SUCCESSOR

**pre·des·tin·ation** /ˌpriːdestɪˈneɪʃn/ *noun* [U] the theory or the belief that everything that happens has been decided or planned in advance by God or by FATE and that humans cannot change it

**pre·des·tined** /ˌpriːˈdestɪnd/ *adj.* ~ **(to do sth)** (*formal*) already decided or planned by God or by FATE: *It seems she was predestined to be famous.*

**pre·de·ter·mine** /ˌpriːdɪˈtɜːmɪn; *NAmE* -ˈtɜːrm-/ *verb* ~ **sth** (*formal*) to decide sth in advance so that it does not happen by chance: *The sex of the embryo is predetermined at fertilization.* ▶ **pre·de·ter·mined** *adj.*: *An alarm sounds when the temperature reaches a predetermined level.*

**pre·de·ter·miner** /ˌpriːdɪˈtɜːmɪnə(r); *NAmE* -ˈtɜːrm-/ *noun* (*grammar*) a word that can be used before a determiner, such as *all* in *all the students* or *twice* in *twice the price*

**pre·dica·ment** /prɪˈdɪkəmənt/ *noun* a difficult or an unpleasant situation, especially one where it is difficult to know what to do SYN **quandary**: *the club's financial predicament* ◇ *I'm in a terrible predicament.*

**predi·cate** *noun*, *verb*
■ *noun* /ˈpredɪkət/ (*grammar*) a part of a sentence containing a verb that makes a statement about the subject of the verb, such as *went home* in *John went home*. ⊃ compare OBJECT
■ *verb* /ˈpredɪkeɪt/ (*formal*) **1** [usually passive] ~ **sth on/upon sth** to base sth on a particular belief, idea or principle: *Democracy is predicated upon the rule of law.* **2** ~ **that** … | ~ **sth** to state that sth is true: *The article predicates that the market collapse was caused by weakness of the dollar.*

**pre·dica·tive** /prɪˈdɪkətɪv; *NAmE* ˈpredɪkeɪtɪv/ *adj.* (*grammar*) (of an adjective) coming after a verb such as *be*, *become*, *get*, *seem*, *look*. Many adjectives, for example *old* can be either predicative as in *The man is very old*, or ATTRIBUTIVE as in *an old man*. Some, like *asleep*, can only be predicative. ▶ **pre·dica·tive·ly** *adv.*

**pre·dict** /prɪˈdɪkt/ *verb* to say that sth will happen in the future SYN **forecast**: ~ **sth** *a reliable method of predicting earthquakes* ◇ *Nobody could predict the outcome.* ◇ *to predict the future* ◇ ~ **what, whether, etc.** … *It is impossible to predict what will happen.* ◇ ~ **(that)** … *She predicted (that) the election result would be close.* ◇ *it was predicted that* … *It was predicted that inflation would continue to fall.* ◇ **sb/sth is predicted to do sth** *The trial is predicted to last for months.* ⊃ LANGUAGE BANK at EXPECT

**pre·dict·able** /prɪˈdɪktəbl/ *adj.* **1** if sth is predictable, you know in advance that it will happen or what it will be like: *a predictable result* ◇ *The ending of the book was entirely predictable.* ◇ *In March and April, the weather is much less predictable.* **2** (*often disapproving*) behaving or happening in a way that you would expect and therefore boring: *He's very nice, but I find him rather dull and predictable.* ▶ **pre·dict·abil·ity** /prɪˌdɪktəˈbɪləti/ *noun* [U] **pre·dict·ably** /prɪˈdɪktəbli/ *adv.*

**pre·dic·tion** /prɪˈdɪkʃn/ *noun* [C, U] a statement that says what you think will happen; the act of making such a statement: *The results of the experiment confirmed our predictions.* ◇ ~ **about/on sth** *I've learned not to make predictions about the weather.* ◇ ~ **that** … *Not many people agree with the government's prediction that the economy will improve.* ◇ ~ **for sb/sth** *What are your predictions for the economy?* ⊃ LANGUAGE BANK at EXPECT

**pre·dict·ive** /prɪˈdɪktɪv/ *adj.* [usually before noun] **1** (*formal*) connected with the ability to show what will happen in the future: *the predictive power of science* **2** (of a computer program) allowing you to enter text on a computer or a mobile phone more quickly by using the first few letters of each word to predict what you want to say: *predictive text input* ◇ *predictive messaging*

**pre·dict·or** /prɪˈdɪktə(r)/ *noun* (*formal*) something that can show what will happen in the future: *Cholesterol level is not a strong predictor of heart disease in women.*

**pre·di·lec·tion** /ˌpriːdɪˈlekʃn; *NAmE* ˌpredlˈek-/ *noun* (usually *sing.*) ~ **(for sth)** (*formal*) if you have a predilection for sth, you like it very much SYN **liking**, **preference**

**pre·dis·pose** /ˌpriːdɪˈspəʊz; *NAmE* -ˈspoʊz/ *verb* (*formal*) **1** to influence sb so that they are likely to think or behave in a particular way: ~ **sb to sth** *He believes that some people are predisposed to criminal behaviour.* ◇ ~ **sb to do sth** *Her good mood predisposed her to enjoy the play.* **2** ~ **sb to sth** to make it likely that you will suffer from a particular illness: *Stress can predispose people to heart attacks.*

**pre·dis·pos·ition** /ˌpriːdɪspəˈzɪʃn/ *noun* [C, U] ~ **(to/towards sth)** | ~ **(to do sth)** (*formal*) a condition that makes sb/sth likely to behave in a particular way or to suffer from a particular disease: *a genetic predisposition to liver disease*

**pre·dom·in·ance** /prɪˈdɒmɪnəns; *NAmE* -ˈdɑːm-/ *noun* **1** [sing.] the situation of being greater in number or amount than other things or people SYN **preponderance**: *a predominance of female teachers in elementary schools* **2** [U] the state of having more power or influence than others SYN **dominance**

**pre·dom·in·ant** /prɪˈdɒmɪnənt; *NAmE* -ˈdɑːm-/ *adj.* **1** most obvious or easy to notice: *a predominant feature* ◇ *Yellow is the predominant colour this spring in the fashion world.* **2** having more power or influence than others SYN **dominant**: *a predominant culture*

**pre·dom·in·ant·ly** /prɪˈdɒmɪnəntli; *NAmE* -ˈdɑːm-/ (*also less frequent* **pre·dom·in·ate·ly** /prɪˈdɒmɪnətli; *NAmE* -ˈdɑːm-/) *adv.* mostly; mainly: *She works in a predominantly male environment.* ⊃ LANGUAGE BANK at GENERALLY

**pre·dom·in·ate** /prɪˈdɒmɪneɪt; *NAmE* -ˈdɑːm-/ *verb* **1** [I] to be greater in amount or number than sth/sb else in a place, group, etc: *a colour scheme in which red predominates* ◇ *Women predominated in the audience.* **2** [I] ~ **(over sb/sth)** to have the most influence or importance: *Private interest was not allowed to predominate over the public good.*

**pre·e'clamp·sia** *noun* [U] (*medical*) a condition in which a pregnant woman has high BLOOD PRESSURE, which can become serious if it is not treated

**pree·mie** /ˈpriːmi/ *noun* (*NAmE*, *informal*) a PREMATURE baby

**pre-'eminent** *adj.* (*formal*) more important, more successful or of a higher standard than others: *Dickens was pre-eminent among English writers of his day.* ▶ **pre-'eminence** *noun* [U]: *to achieve pre-eminence in public life*

**pre-'empt** /ˌpriːˈempt/ *verb* **1** ~ **sth** to prevent sth from happening by taking action to stop it: *A good training course will pre-empt many problems.* **2** ~ **sb/sth** to do or say sth before sb else does: *She was just about to apologize when he pre-empted her.* **3** ~ **sth** (*NAmE*) to replace a planned programme on the television: *The scheduled programme will be pre-empted by a special news bulletin.*

**pre-'emption** /ˌpriːˈempʃn/ *noun* [U] (*business*) the opportunity given to one person or group to buy goods, shares, etc: *Existing shareholders will have pre-emption rights.*

**pre-'emptive** /ˌpriːˈemptɪv/ *adj.* [usually before noun] done to stop sb taking action, especially action that will be harmful to yourself: *a pre-emptive attack/strike on the military base*

**preen** /priːn/ verb **1** [T, I] ~ **(yourself)** (usually disapproving) to spend a lot of time making yourself look attractive and then admiring your appearance: *Will you stop preening yourself in front of the mirror?* **2** [T] ~ **yourself (on sth)** (usually disapproving) to feel very pleased with yourself about sth and show other people how pleased you are **3** [I, T] ~ **(itself)** (of a bird) to clean itself or make its feathers smooth with its BEAK

**pre-e'xist** verb [I] to exist from an earlier time: *a pre-existing medical condition* ▶ **pre-e'xistent** adj.

**pre·fab** /ˈpriːfæb/ noun (informal) a prefabricated building: *prefabs built after the war*

**pre·fab·ri·cated** /ˌpriːˈfæbrɪkeɪtɪd/ adj. (especially of a building) made in sections that can be put together later ▶ **pre·fab·ri·ca·tion** /ˌpriːfæbrɪˈkeɪʃn/ noun [U]

**pref·ace** /ˈprefəs/ noun, verb
- **noun** an introduction to a book, especially one that explains the author's aims ⊃ compare FOREWORD
- **verb 1** ~ **sth (with sth)** to provide a book or other piece of writing with a preface: *He prefaced the diaries with a short account of how they were discovered.* **2** ~ **sth by/with sth** | ~ **sth by doing sth** (formal) to say sth before you start making a speech, answering a question, etc: *I must preface my remarks with an apology.*

**prefa·tory** /ˈprefətri/; NAmE -tɔːri/ adj. [only before noun] (formal) acting as a PREFACE or an introduction to sth: *a prefatory note*

**pre·fect** /ˈpriːfekt/ noun **1** (in some British schools) an older student with some authority over younger students and some other responsibilities and advantages **2** (also **Prefect**) an officer responsible for an area of local government in some countries, for example France, Italy and Japan

**pre·fec·ture** /ˈpriːfektʃə(r)/ noun an area of local government in some countries, for example France, Italy and Japan

**pre·fer** 🛈 **A1** 🅢 /prɪˈfɜː(r)/ verb (**-rr-**) (not usually used in the progressive tenses) to like one thing or person better than another; to choose one thing rather than sth else because you like it better: ~ **sth** *'Coffee or tea?' 'I'd prefer tea, thanks.'* ◇ *I would prefer it if you didn't tell anyone.* ◇ *A local firm is to be preferred.* ◇ ~ **sth to sth** *I much prefer jazz to rock music.* ◇ ~ **sth over sth** *A few people still prefer landlines over mobiles.* ◇ ~ **sth + adj.** *I prefer my coffee black.* ◇ ~ **to do sth** *I much prefer to travel by train.* ◇ *I prefer not to think about it.* ◇ ~ **sb/sth to do sth** *Would you prefer me to stay?* ◇ ~ **doing sth** *I prefer playing in defence.* ◇ ~ **that …** (formal) *I would prefer that you did not mention my name.* **IDM** see CHARGE n. ⊃ note at WANT

▼ EXPRESS YOURSELF

**Expressing a preference**

These are ways of stating what your preferred choice is. Note that we sometimes discount our own expertise or authority before expressing our preference:
- *I like the red one **better than/more than** the green one.*
- *I **prefer** beef to lamb.*
- *I'd **prefer** to wait here.*
- *I'd **rather** go to the concert than the play.*
- *I think I'd **rather** stay in than go out tonight.*
- *I like swimming **better than** jogging.*
- *I think that colour's **much more attractive**.*
- *It doesn't really matter to me **whether** we eat here or go out.* (especially NAmE)
- *I don't really mind **whether** we talk now or later.* (BrE)
- *I'm **happy either way**.* (NAmE)
- *I don't really care **either way**.*
- *If it were up to me, I'd choose the green one.*
- *If you ask me, the old one looks better than the new one.*
- *I'm not an expert but Design B seems more eye-catching.*

**pref·er·able** /ˈprefrəbl/ adj. more attractive or more suitable; to be preferred to sth: ~ **(to sth)** *Anything was preferable to the tense atmosphere at home.* ◇ ~ **(to doing sth)** *He finds country life infinitely preferable to living in the city.* ◇ ~ **(to do sth)** *It would be preferable to employ two people, not one.* ▶ **pref·er·ably** /-bli/ adv.: *We're looking for a new house, preferably one near the school.*

**pref·er·ence** 🛈 **B2** 🅦 /ˈprefrəns/ noun **1** 🛈 **B2** [U, sing.] a greater interest in or desire for sb/sth than sb/sth else: *It's a matter of **personal preference**.* ◇ *I can't say that I have any particular preference.* ◇ ~ **for sb/sth** *Many people expressed a strong preference for the original plan.* ◇ *Let's make a list of possible speakers, **in order of preference**.* **2** 🛈 **B2** [C] a thing that is liked better or best: *a study of consumer preferences* ⊃ SYNONYMS at CHOICE

**IDM** **give (a) preference to sb/sth** to treat sb/sth in a way that gives them an advantage over other people or things: *Preference will be given to graduates of this university.* **in preference to sb/sth** rather than sb/sth: *She was chosen in preference to her sister.*

**pref·er·en·tial** /ˌprefəˈrenʃl/ adj. [only before noun] giving an advantage to a particular person or group: *Don't expect to get preferential treatment.* ▶ **pref·er·en·tial·ly** /-ʃəli/ adv.

**pre·fer·ment** /prɪˈfɜːmənt; NAmE -ˈfɜːrm-/ noun [U] (formal) the fact of being given a more important job or a higher rank **SYN** promotion

**pre·fig·ure** /ˌpriːˈfɪɡə(r); NAmE -ˈfɪɡjər/ verb ~ **sth** to suggest or show sth that will happen in the future

**pre·fix** /ˈpriːfɪks/ noun, verb
- **noun 1** (grammar) a letter or group of letters added to the beginning of a word to change its meaning, such as *un-* in *unhappy* and *pre-* in *preheat* ⊃ compare AFFIX, SUFFIX **2** a word, letter or number that is put before another: *Car insurance policies have the prefix MC (for motor car).* **3** (old-fashioned) a title such as *Dr* or *Mrs* used before a person's name
- **verb** to add letters or numbers to the beginning of a word or number: ~ **A to B** *American members have the letters US prefixed to their code numbers.* ◇ ~ **B with A** *Their code numbers are prefixed with US.*

**preg·gers** /ˈpreɡəz; NAmE -ɡərz/ adj. [not before noun] (BrE, informal) pregnant

**preg·nancy** 🛈 **C1** /ˈpreɡnənsi/ noun [U, C] (pl. **-ies**) the state of being pregnant: *a pregnancy test* ◇ *during ~* *Many women experience sickness during pregnancy.* ◇ *unplanned/unwanted pregnancies* ◇ *the increase in teenage pregnancies* ⊃ see also ECTOPIC PREGNANCY

**preg·nant** 🛈 **B2** /ˈpreɡnənt/ adj. **1** 🛈 **B2** (of a woman or female animal) having a baby or young animal developing inside her/its body: *My wife is pregnant.* ◇ ~ **with …** *I was pregnant with our third child at the time.* ◇ *a **heavily pregnant** woman* (= one whose baby is nearly ready to be born) ◇ *to **get/become/fall pregnant*** ◇ *He got his girlfriend pregnant and they're getting married.* ◇ *She's six months pregnant.*

**WORDFINDER** antenatal, child, conception, fetus, maternity leave, miscarriage, morning sickness, scan, womb

**2** ~ **with sth** (formal) full of a quality or feeling: *Her silences were pregnant with criticism.*

**IDM** **a pregnant 'pause/'silence** an occasion when nobody speaks, although people are aware that there are feelings or thoughts to express

**pre·heat** /ˌpriːˈhiːt/ verb ~ **sth** to heat an oven to a particular temperature before you put food in it to cook

**pre·hen·sile** /prɪˈhensaɪl; NAmE -sl/ adj. (specialist) (of a part of an animal's body) able to hold things: *the monkey's prehensile tail* ⊃ VISUAL VOCAB page V2

**pre·his·toric** /ˌpriːhɪˈstɒrɪk; NAmE -ˈstɔːr-/ adj. connected with the time in history before information was written down: *in prehistoric times* ◇ *prehistoric man/remains/animals/burial sites*

**pre·his·tory** /ˌpriːˈhɪstri/ noun **1** [U] the period of time in history before information was written down **2** [sing.] the earliest stages of the development of sth: *the prehistory of capitalism*

**pre-in'stall** verb = PRELOAD

**pre·judge** /ˌpriːˈdʒʌdʒ/ verb ~ **sth** (formal) to make a judgement about a situation before you have all the necessary information: *They took care not to prejudge the issue.*

# prejudice 1212

**pre·ju·dice** /ˈpredʒədɪs/ *noun, verb*
- *noun* [U, C] an unreasonable dislike of or PREFERENCE for a person, group, custom, etc., especially when it is based on their race, religion, sex, etc: *a victim of racial prejudice* ◇ *Their decision was based on ignorance and prejudice.* ◇ *~against sb/sth There is little prejudice against workers from other EU states.* ◇ *in favour of sb/sth I must admit to a prejudice in favour of British universities.*
- IDM **without 'prejudice (to sth)** (*law*) without affecting any other legal matter: *They agreed to pay compensation without prejudice* (= without admitting GUILT).
- *verb* **1** ~ **sb (against sth)** to influence sb so that they have an unfair or unreasonable opinion about sb/sth SYN **bias**: *The prosecution lawyers have been trying to prejudice the jury against her.* **2** ~ **sth** (*formal*) to have a harmful effect on sth: *Any delay will prejudice the child's welfare.*

**pre·ju·diced** /ˈpredʒədɪst/ *adj.* having an unreasonable dislike of or PREFERENCE for sb/sth, especially based on their race, religion, sex, etc: *Few people will admit to being racially prejudiced.* ◇ ~(**against/in favour of sb/sth**) *They are prejudiced against older applicants.* ◇ (*humorous*) *I think it's an excellent article, but then I'm prejudiced—I wrote it.*

**pre·ju·di·cial** /ˌpredʒəˈdɪʃl/ *adj.* ~(**to sth**) (*formal*) harming or likely to harm sb/sth SYN **damaging**: *developments prejudicial to the company's future*

**prel·ate** /ˈprelət/ *noun* (*formal*) a priest of high rank in the Christian Church, such as a BISHOP or CARDINAL

**prelim** /ˈpriːlɪm/ *noun* [usually pl.] (*informal*) a game, race, etc. in the early stages of a sports competition that determines who will continue to compete: *He finished second in the prelims and will advance to the finals.*

**pre·lim·in·ary** /prɪˈlɪmɪnəri; *NAmE* -neri/ *adj., noun*
- *adj.* happening before a more important action or event SYN **initial**: *After a few preliminary remarks he announced the winners.* ◇ *preliminary results/findings/enquiries* ◇ *the preliminary rounds of the contest* ◇ ~**to sth** *pilot studies preliminary to a full-scale study*
- *noun* (*pl.* **-ies**) a **preliminary** is an action or event that is done in preparation for sth: *I'll skip the usual preliminaries and come straight to the point.* ◇ *England was lucky to get through the preliminaries* (= the preliminary stages in a sports competition). ◇ ~**to (doing) sth** *Research will be needed as a preliminary to taking a decision.*

**pre·load** /ˌpriːˈləʊd/ (*also* **pre-in'stall**) *verb* ~ **sth** to load sth in advance: *The PC comes with office software preloaded.*
▶ **pre·load** /ˈpriːləʊd/ *noun*

**prel·ude** /ˈpreljuːd/ *noun* **1** a short piece of music, especially an introduction to a longer piece **2** ~ (**to sth**) an action or event that happens before another more important one and forms an introduction to it

**pre·mar·ital** /ˌpriːˈmærɪtl/ *adj.* [only before noun] happening before marriage: *premarital sex*

**pre·ma·ture** /ˈpremətʃə(r); *NAmE* ˌpriːməˈtʃʊr, -ˈtʊr/ *adj.* **1** happening before the normal or expected time: *his premature death at the age of 37* **2** (of a birth or a baby) happening or being born before the normal length of PREGNANCY has been completed: *The baby was four weeks premature.* ◇ *a premature birth after only thirty weeks* ➔ WORDFINDER NOTE at BABY **3** happening or made too soon: *a premature conclusion/decision/judgement* ◇ *It is premature to talk about success at this stage.* ▶ **pre·ma·ture·ly** *adv.*: *The child was born prematurely.* ◇ *Her hair became prematurely white.*

**'pre-med** *noun* (*informal*) **1** [U] (*especially NAmE*) a course or set of classes that students take in preparation for medical school **2** [C] (*especially NAmE*) a student who is taking classes in preparation for medical school **3** [U] = PREMEDICATION

**pre·medi·ca·tion** /ˌpriːˌmedɪˈkeɪʃn/ (*also informal* **pre-med**) *noun* [U] drugs given to sb in preparation for an operation or other medical treatment

**pre·medi·tated** /ˌpriːˈmedɪteɪtɪd/ *adj.* (of a crime or bad action) planned in advance: *a premeditated attack* ◇ *The killing had not been premeditated.* OPP **unpremeditated**
▶ **pre·medi·ta·tion** /ˌpriːˌmedɪˈteɪʃn/ *noun* [U]

**pre·men·strual** /ˌpriːˈmenstruəl/ *adj.* happening or experienced before MENSTRUATION: *Many women suffer from premenstrual tension/syndrome, causing headaches and depression.* ➔ see also PMS

**prem·ier** /ˈpremiə(r); *NAmE* prɪˈmɪr/ *adj., noun*
- *adj.* [only before noun] most important, famous or successful: *one of the country's premier chefs* ◇ (*BrE, sport*) *the Premier League/Division*
- *noun* **1** used especially in newspapers, etc. to mean 'prime minister' **2** (in Canada) the first minister of a PROVINCE or TERRITORY

**premi·ere** /ˈpremieə(r); *NAmE* prɪˈmɪr/ *noun, verb*
- *noun* the first public performance of a film or play: *the world premiere of his new play* ◇ *The movie will have its premiere in July.* ➔ see also SEASON PREMIERE
- *verb* [T, I] ~ (**sth**) to perform a play or piece of music or show a film to an audience for the first time; to be performed or shown to an audience for the first time: *The play was premiered at the Birmingham Rep in 2014.* ◇ *His new movie premieres in New York this week.*

**the ˌPremier ˈLeague** *noun* [sing.] the football (= soccer) league in England and Wales that has the best teams in it

**prem·ier·ship** /ˈpremiəʃɪp; *NAmE* prɪˈmɪrʃɪp/ *noun* [sing.] **1** the period or position of being prime minister: *during Theresa May's premiership* **2** (*often* **the Premiership**) the former name for the football league in England and Wales that has the best teams in it, now called the PREMIER LEAGUE **3** a professional league for the best RUGBY UNION teams in England

**prem·ise** /ˈpremɪs/ (*BrE also, less frequent* **prem·iss**) /ˈpremɪs/ *noun* (*formal*) a statement or an idea that forms the basis for a reasonable line of argument: *the basic premise of her argument* ◇ *a false premise* ◇ *His reasoning is based on the premise that all people are equally capable of good and evil.*

**prem·ised** /ˈpremɪst/ *adj.* ~ **on/upon sth** (*formal*) based on a particular idea or belief that is considered to be true: *Traditional economic analysis is premised on the assumption that more is better.*

**prem·ises** /ˈpremɪsɪz/ *noun* [pl.] the building and land near to it that a business owns or uses: *business/commercial/industrial premises* ◇ **on the ~** *No alcohol may be consumed on the premises.* ◇ **off the ~** *Police were called to escort her off the premises.* ➔ SYNONYMS at BUILDING

**pre·mium** /ˈpriːmiəm/ *noun, adj.*
- *noun* **1** an amount of money that you pay once or regularly for an insurance policy: *a monthly premium of £6.25* ➔ SYNONYMS at PAYMENT ➔ WORDFINDER NOTE at INSURANCE **2** an extra payment added to the basic rate: *You have to pay a high premium for express delivery.* ◇ *A premium of 10 per cent is paid out after 20 years.* ◇ *a premium-rate phone number*
- IDM **at a 'premium 1** if sth is **at a premium**, there is little of it available and it is difficult to get: *Space is at a premium in a one-bedroomed apartment.* **2** at a higher than normal price: *Shares are selling at a premium.* **put/place/set a premium on sb/sth** to think that sb/sth is particularly important or valuable
- *adj.* [only before noun] very high (and higher than usual); of high quality: *premium prices/products*

**pre·molar** /ˌpriːˈməʊlə(r)/ *noun* a tooth that is between the CANINE and MOLAR teeth. An adult human normally has eight of these teeth: two at the top and two at the bottom on both sides of the mouth. ➔ compare INCISOR, WISDOM TOOTH

**pre·moni·tion** /ˌpreməˈnɪʃn; ˌpriːm-/ *noun* a feeling that sth is going to happen, especially sth unpleasant: ~ (**of sth**) *a premonition of disaster* ◇ ~ (**that...**) *He had a premonition that he would never see her again.* ▶ **pre·moni·tory** /prɪˈmɒnɪtəri; *NAmE* -ˈmɑːnɪtɔːri/ *adj.* (*formal*): *a premonitory dream*

**pre·natal** /ˌpriːˈneɪtl/ (*especially NAmE*) (*BrE also* **ante·natal**) *adj.* relating to the medical care given to pregnant women ➔ compare POSTNATAL

**pre·nup·tial agreement** /ˌpriː ˌnʌpʃl əˈgriːmənt/ (*also informal* **pre-nup** /ˈpriːnʌp/) *noun* an agreement made by a couple before they get married in which they say how their money and property is to be divided if they get divorced

**pre·occu·pa·tion** /priˌɒkjuˈpeɪʃn; NAmE -ˌɑːk-/ noun 1 [U, C] ~ (with sth) a state of thinking about sth continuously; sth that you think about frequently or for a long time SYN **obsession**: *She found his preoccupation with money irritating.* ◊ *His current preoccupation is the appointment of the new manager.* 2 [U] a mood created by thinking or worrying about sth and ignoring everything else: *She spoke slowly, in a state of preoccupation.*

**pre·occu·pied** /priˈɒkjupaɪd; NAmE -ˈɑːk-/ adj. ~ (with sth) thinking and/or worrying continuously about sth so that you do not pay attention to other things: *He was too preoccupied with his own thoughts to notice anything wrong.*

**pre·occupy** /priˈɒkjupaɪ; NAmE -ˈɑːk-/ verb (**pre·occu·pies**, **pre·occu·py·ing**, **pre·occu·pied**, **pre·occu·pied**) ~ **sb** if sth is **preoccupying** you, you think or worry about it very often or all the time

**pre·op·era·tive** /priˈɒpərətɪv; NAmE -ˈɑːp-/ adj. [only before noun] (*medical*) (also *informal* **pre-op**) connected with the period before a medical operation: *a preoperative appointment* ⊃ compare INTRAOPERATIVE, POST-OPERATIVE

**pre·or·dained** /ˌpriːɔːˈdeɪnd; NAmE -ɔːrˈd-/ adj. (*formal*) already decided or planned by God or by FATE SYN **pre-destined**: *Is everything we do preordained?* ◊ ~ **to do sth** *They seemed preordained to meet.*

**pre-order** *verb, noun*
- *verb* ~ **sth** to place an order for a product before it is available
- *noun* [C, U] an order for a product that is not yet available: *You can place a pre-order now at the link below.* ◊ *The game is now available for pre-order.*

**pre-ˈowned** adj. (*NAmE*) not new; owned by sb else before SYN **second-hand**

**prep** /prep/ noun, verb
- *noun* [U] (*BrE*) (in some private schools) school work that is done at the end of the day after lessons
- *verb* (**-pp-**) 1 [T, I] (especially *NAmE*, *informal*) to prepare (sth): ~ **sth** *Prep the vegetables in advance.* ◊ ~ **(for sth)** *They're prepping for college.* 2 [T] ~ **sb** (*specialist*) to prepare sb for a medical operation

**pre-ˈpacked** (also **pre-ˈpackaged**) adj. (of goods, especially food) put into packages before being sent to shops to be sold: *pre-packed sandwiches*

**pre·paid** /ˌpriːˈpeɪd/ (*BrE also* **pre-pay**) adj. paid for in advance: *a prepaid mobile phone* ◊ *A prepaid envelope is enclosed* (= so you do not have to pay the cost of sending a letter).

**prep·ar·ation** ⓘ B2 /ˌprepəˈreɪʃn/ noun 1 B2 [U] the act or process of getting ready for sth or making sth ready: *food preparation* ◊ ~ **for sth** *Preparation for the party started early.* ◊ *Careful preparation for the exam is essential.* ◊ **in** ~ *The third book in the series is currently in preparation.* ◊ **in** ~ **for sth** *The team has been training hard in preparation for the big game.* ◊ ~ **of sth** *She helped in the preparation of several of his manuscripts.* 2 B2 [C, usually pl.] things that you do to get ready for sth or make sth ready: ~ **for sth** *The country is making preparations for war.* ◊ *Was going to college a good preparation for your career?* ◊ ~ **to do sth** *We made preparations to move to new offices.* ◊ *wedding preparations* 3 [C] a substance that has been specially prepared for use as a medicine, COSMETIC, etc: *a pharmaceutical preparation* ◊ *preparations for the hair and skin*

**pre·para·tory** /prɪˈpærətri; NAmE -tɔːri/ adj. (*formal*) done in order to prepare for sth: *preparatory meetings* ◊ ~ **to sth** *Security checks had been carried out preparatory to* (= to prepare for) *the President's visit.*

**preˈparatory school** (also **ˈprep school**) noun 1 (in the UK) a private school for children between the ages of 7 and 13 ⊃ compare PUBLIC SCHOOL 2 (in the US) a school, usually a private one, that prepares students for college

**pre·pare** ⓘ A1 /prɪˈpeə(r); NAmE -ˈper/ verb 1 A1 [T, I] to make sb or sth ready to be used or to do sth: ~ **sth/sb (for sb/sth)** *to prepare a report* ◊ ~ **sb/sth to do sth** *The* 

---

1213　　　**pre-qualifying**

*training has prepared me to deal with any medical issue.* ◊ ~ **for sth** *We all set about preparing for the party.* 2 A1 [I, T] to make yourself ready to do sth or for sth that you expect to happen: *I had no time to prepare.* ◊ ~ **for sth** *The whole class is working hard preparing for the exams.* ◊ ~ **yourself (for sth)** *The police are preparing themselves for trouble at the demonstration.* ◊ ~ **to do sth** *I was preparing to leave.* ◊ ~ **yourself to do sth** *The troops prepared themselves to go into battle.* 3 A1 [T] ~ **sth** to make food ready to be eaten: *He was in the kitchen preparing lunch.* 4 [T] ~ **sth (from sth)** to make a medicine or chemical substance, for example by mixing other substances together: *remedies prepared from herbal extracts*
IDM **prepare the ˈground (for sth)** to make it possible or easier for sth to be achieved: *The committee will prepare the ground for next month's meeting.*

**pre·pared** ⓘ B1 /prɪˈpeəd; NAmE -ˈperd/ adj. 1 B1 [not before noun] ready and able to deal with sth: *We'll be better prepared next time.* ◊ *When they set out they were **well prepared**.* ◊ ~ **for sth** *I was not prepared for all the problems it caused.* OPP **unprepared** ⊃ see also ILL-PREPARED 2 B1 ~ **to do sth** willing to do sth: *We are not prepared to accept these conditions.* ◊ *How much are you prepared to pay?* OPP **unwilling** 3 B1 done, made, written, etc. in advance: *The police officer read out a prepared statement.*

**pre·pared·ness** /prɪˈpeərɪdnəs; NAmE -ˈperd-/ noun [U] ~ **(to do sth)** (*formal*) the state of being ready or willing to do sth: *I was surprised by his preparedness to break the law.* ◊ *The troops are in a state of preparedness.*

**pre-ˈpay** adj. (*BrE*) = PREPAID: *pre-pay phones*

**pre·pay·ment** /ˌpriːˈpeɪmənt/ noun [U] payment in advance: *a prepayment plan*

**pre·pon·der·ance** /prɪˈpɒndərəns; NAmE -ˈpɑːn-/ noun (*formal*) [sing.] if there is a **preponderance** of one type of people or things in a group, there are more of them than others SYN **predominance**

**pre·pon·der·ant** /prɪˈpɒndərənt; NAmE -ˈpɑːn-/ adj. [usually before noun] (*formal*) larger in number or more important than other people or things in a group
▶ **pre·pon·der·ant·ly** adv.

**pre·pone** /prɪˈpəʊn/ verb ~ **sth** (*IndE*, *informal*) to move sth to an earlier time than was originally planned

**prep·os·ition** /ˌprepəˈzɪʃn/ noun (*grammar*) a word or group of words, such as *in*, *from*, *to*, *out of* and *on behalf of*, used before a noun or pronoun to show place, position, time or method ▶ **prep·os·ition·al** /-ʃənl/ adj.: *a prepositional phrase* (= a preposition and the noun following it, for example *at night* or *after breakfast*)

**pre·pos·sess·ing** /ˌpriːpəˈzesɪŋ/ adj. (especially after a negative) (*formal*) attractive in appearance SYN **appealing**: *He was not a prepossessing sight.* ⊃ compare UNPREPOSSESSING

**pre·pos·ter·ous** /prɪˈpɒstərəs; NAmE -ˈpɑːs-/ adj. (*formal*) 1 completely unreasonable, especially in a way that shocks or annoys you SYN **outrageous**: *These claims are absolutely preposterous!* 2 unusual in a way that is silly or that shocks you SYN **outrageous**: *The band were famous for their preposterous clothes and haircuts.* ▶ **pre·pos·ter·ous·ly** adv.: *a preposterously expensive bottle of wine*

**prep·py** (*also* **prep·pie**) /ˈprepi/ noun (*pl.* **-ies**) (*NAmE*, *informal*) a young person who goes or went to an expensive private school and who dresses and acts in a way that is thought to be typical of such a school ▶ **prep·py** (*also* **prep·pie**) adj.: *a preppy image* ◊ *preppy clothes*

**pre-proˈduction** adj. [usually before noun] done before the process of producing sth, especially a film, begins: *the pre-production script* ▶ **pre-proˈduction** noun [U]

**prep school** noun = PREPARATORY SCHOOL

**pre-ˈqualifying** adj. [only before noun] relating to a competition or game in which teams or players take part to decide if they are good enough to be in another competition: *players who fail at the pre-qualifying stage* ▶ **pre-ˈqualifier** noun

# prequel

**pre·quel** /ˈpriːkwəl/ noun a book or a film about events that happened before those in a popular book or film that has already appeared: *Fans waited for years for the first Star Wars prequel.* ⇨ compare SEQUEL

**Pre-Raphael·ite** /ˌpriːˈræfiəlaɪt/ noun, adj.
- noun a member of a group of British nineteenth-century artists who painted in a style similar to Italian artists of the fourteenth and fifteenth centuries, before the time of Raphael
- adj. **1** connected with or in the style of the Pre-Raphaelites: *Pre-Raphaelite paintings* **2** (especially of a woman) looking like a person in a painting by one of the Pre-Raphaelites, for example with pale skin and long, thick, dark red hair

**pre-re·cord** verb ~ sth to record music, a television programme, etc. in advance, so that it can be broadcast or used later

**pre·reg·is·ter** /ˌpriːˈredʒɪstə(r)/ verb [I] ~ (for sth) (*especially NAmE*) to register for sth before the usual time or before sth starts ▶ **pre·reg·is·tra·tion** /ˌpriːredʒɪˈstreɪʃn/ noun [U]

**pre·requi·site** /ˌpriːˈrekwəzɪt/ noun [usually sing.] ~ (for / of / to sth) (*formal*) something that must exist or happen before sth else can happen or be done SYN **precondition**: *A degree is an essential prerequisite for employment at this level.* ⇨ compare REQUISITE ▶ **pre·requi·site** adj. [only before noun]: *prerequisite knowledge*

**pre·roga·tive** /prɪˈrɒɡətɪv; NAmE -ˈrɑːɡ-/ noun (*formal*) a right or advantage belonging to a particular person or group because of their importance or social position: *In many countries education is still the prerogative of the rich.* ◇ *the royal prerogative* (= the special rights of a king or queen)

**pres·age** /ˈpresɪdʒ, prɪˈseɪdʒ/ verb ~ sth (*literary*) to be a warning or sign that sth will happen, usually sth unpleasant ▶ **pre·sage** /ˈpresɪdʒ/ noun: *the first presages of winter*

**Pres·by·ter·ian** /ˌprezbɪˈtɪəriən; NAmE -ˈtɪr-/ noun a member of a branch of the Christian Protestant Church that is the national Church of Scotland and one of the largest Churches in the US. It is governed by ELDERS who are all equal in rank. ▶ **Pres·by·ter·ian** adj. **Pres·by·ter·ian·ism** noun [U]

**pres·by·tery** /ˈprezbɪtri; NAmE -teri/ noun (pl. -ies) **1** a local council of the Presbyterian Church **2** a house where a Roman Catholic priest lives **3** part of a church, near the east end, beyond the CHOIR

**pre·school** /ˈpriːskuːl/ noun a school for children between the ages of about two and five SYN **nursery school**

**pres·ci·ent** /ˈpresiənt; NAmE ˈpreʃnt/ adj. (*formal*) knowing or appearing to know about things before they happen ▶ **pres·ci·ence** /ˈpresiəns; NAmE ˈpreʃns/ noun [U]

**pre·scribe** /prɪˈskraɪb/ verb **1** (of a doctor) to tell sb to take a particular medicine or have a particular treatment; to write a PRESCRIPTION for a particular medicine, etc.: ~ sth *Valium is usually prescribed to treat anxiety.* ◇ ~ (sb) sth (for sth) *He may be able to prescribe you something for that cough.* ⇨ WORDFINDER NOTE at DOCTOR **2** (of a person or an organization with authority) to say what should be done or how sth should be done SYN **stipulate**: ~ sth *The prescribed form must be completed and returned to this office.* ◇ ~ that … *Police regulations prescribe that an officer's number must be clearly visible.* ◇ ~ which, what, etc … *The syllabus prescribes precisely which books should be studied.*

**pre·scrip·tion** /prɪˈskrɪpʃn/ noun **1** [C] an official piece of paper on which a doctor writes the type of medicine you should have, and which enables you to get it from a CHEMIST'S: ~ **for sth** *The doctor gave me a prescription for antibiotics.* ◇ **on** ~ (*BrE*) *Antibiotics are only available on prescription.* ◇ **by** ~ (*NAmE*) *Antibiotics are only available by prescription.* ◇ *They are not available without a prescription.* ◇ *prescription drugs/medication(s)* **2** [C] medicine that your doctor has ordered for you: *The pharmacist will make up your prescription.* ◇ *a prescription charge* (= in Britain, the money you must pay for a medicine your doctor has ordered for you) **3** [U] the act of prescribing medicine: *The prescription of drugs is a doctor's responsibility.* **4** [C] ~ (for sth) (*formal*) a plan or a suggestion for making sth happen or for improving it: *a prescription for happiness*

**pre·scrip·tive** /prɪˈskrɪptɪv/ adj. **1** (*formal*) telling people what should be done: *prescriptive methods of teaching* **2** (*linguistics*) telling people how a language should be used, rather than describing how it is used OPP **descriptive** **3** (*specialist*) (of rights and institutions) made legal or acceptable because they have existed for a long time: *prescriptive powers*

**pre·season** /ˌpriːˈsiːzn/ adj., noun
- adj. [only before noun] (*especially NAmE*) taking place before the regular sports season begins: *She suffered an ankle sprain during preseason practice.* ⇨ compare POSTSEASON
- noun [usually sing.] (*especially NAmE*) the period of time before the regular sports season begins: *Herndon missed portions of the preseason.* ⇨ compare POSTSEASON

**pre·select** /ˌpriːsɪˈlekt/ verb ~ sb/sth to choose sb/sth in advance

**pre-'sell** verb (**pre-sold**, **pre-sold**) **1** ~ sth to help sell a product, service, etc., especially one that is not yet available, by using advertising and other techniques to attract consumers' attention: *Putting a trial version on your website is a great way of pre-selling your product.* **2** ~ sth to sell sth in advance of when it is available: *These farmers pre-sell their crops.*

**pres·ence** /ˈprezns/ noun **1** [U] (of a person) the fact of being in a particular place: *He hardly seemed to notice my presence.* ◇ (*formal*) *Your presence is requested at the meeting.* ◇ ~ **of sb** *the increased presence of Asian actors in Hollywood* OPP **absence** **2** [U] ~ (of sth) (of a thing or a substance) the fact of being in a particular place or thing: *The test can identify the presence of abnormalities in the unborn child.* OPP **absence** **3** [sing.] a group of people, especially soldiers, who have been sent to a place to deal with a particular situation: *The government is maintaining a heavy police presence in the area.* ◇ *a military presence* **4** [C, usually sing.] (*literary*) a person or spirit that you cannot see but that you feel is near: *She felt a presence behind her.* **5** [U, sing.] (*approving*) the quality of making a strong impression on other people by the way you talk or behave; a person who has this quality: *a man of great presence* ◇ *She has a strong voice but absolutely no stage presence.* ◇ *She has a great screen presence.*
IDM **in the 'presence of sb** | **in sb's 'presence** with sb in the same place: *The document was signed in the presence of two witnesses.* ◇ *She asked them not to discuss the matter in her presence.* **in the 'presence of sth** when sth exists in a particular place: *Litmus paper turns red in the presence of an acid.* **make your 'presence 'felt** to do sth to make people very aware of the fact that you are there; to have a strong influence on a group of people or a situation

**presence of 'mind** noun [U] the ability to react quickly and stay calm in a difficult or dangerous situation: *The boy had the presence of mind to turn off the gas.*

**pres·ent** adj., noun, verb
- adj. /ˈpreznt/ **1** [only before noun] existing or happening now: *I am not satisfied with the present situation.* ◇ *the present owner of the house* ◇ *a list of all club members, past and present* ◇ *We do not have any more information at the present time.* ◇ *A few brief comments are sufficient for present purposes.* ⇨ note at ACTUAL ⇨ see also PRESENT DAY **2** [not before noun] (of a person) being in a particular place: *I wasn't present when the doctor examined him.* ◇ **~ at sth** *There were 200 people present at the meeting.* OPP **absent** **3** [not before noun] ~ (in sth) (of a thing or a substance) existing in a particular place or thing: *The threat of force was always present.* ◇ *Levels of pollution present in the atmosphere are increasing.* OPP **absent**
IDM **all present and cor'rect** (*BrE*) (*NAmE* **all present and ac'counted for**) used to say that all the things or people who should be there are now there **present company ex'cepted** (*informal*) used after being rude or critical about sb to say that the people you are talking to are not included in the criticism
- noun /ˈpreznt/ **1** a thing that you give to sb as a gift: *What can I get him for a birthday present?* ◇ *Christmas/*

*wedding presents* ◊ **as a~** *He gave her the painting as a present.* ◊ **~ for sb** *We have a present for you.* ◊ **from sb** *That dress was a present from my sister.* **2** [A1] (*usually* **the present**) [sing.] the time now: **in the~** *You've got to forget the past and start living in the present.* ◊ **at~** *I'm sorry he's out at present* (= now). ◊ **to the~** *The book covers the period from the early 1990s to the present.* **3 the present** [sing.] (*grammar*) = PRESENT TENSE IDM see MOMENT, TIME *n.*

■ *verb* /prɪˈzent/

• STH TO BE CONSIDERED **1** [A2] to show or offer sth for other people to look at or consider: **~ sth** *Are you presenting a paper at the conference?* ◊ *to present evidence/data* ◊ *to present your results/findings* ◊ **~ sth to sb** *The committee will present its final report to Parliament in June.* ◊ **~ sth for sth** *Eight options were presented for consideration.*
• GIVE **2** [B2] to give sth to sb, especially formally at a ceremony: **~ sth** *The local MP will start the race and present the prizes.* ◊ **~ sb with sth** *Last year she was presented with an award for lifetime achievement.* ◊ **~ sth to sb** *The sword was presented by the family to the museum.*
• STH IN PARTICULAR WAY **3** [B2] to show or describe sth/sb in a particular way: **~ sth** *The company has decided it must present a more modern image.* ◊ **~ yourself + adv./prep.** *You need to present yourself better.* ◊ **~ sth/sb/yourself as sth** *He likes to present himself as a radical politician.* ◊ *The article presents these proposals as misguided.*
• PROBLEM/OPPORTUNITY **4** to cause sth to happen or be experienced: **~ sth** *The course presents an excellent learning opportunity.* ◊ *to present problems/challenges* ◊ *to present a threat/risk/danger* ◊ **~ sb with sth** *Your request shouldn't present us with any problems.*
• ITSELF **5** (of an opportunity, a solution, etc.) to suddenly happen or become available SYN **arise:** **~ itself** *One major problem did present itself, though.* ◊ *As soon as the opportunity presented itself, she would get another job.* ◊ **~itself to sb** *Thankfully, a solution presented itself to him surprisingly soon.*
• RADIO/TV PROGRAMME **6** **~ sth** (*BrE*) to appear in a radio or television programme and introduce the different items in it: *She used to present a gardening programme on TV.*
• PLAY/BROADCAST **7** **~ sth** to produce a show, play, broadcast, etc. for the public: *Compass Theatre Company presents a new production of 'King Lear'.*
• INTRODUCE SB **8** **~ sb (to sb)** (*formal*) to introduce sb formally, especially to sb of higher rank or status: *May I present my fiancé to you?*
• YOURSELF **9** **~ yourself at, for, in, etc.** (*formal*) to officially appear somewhere: *You will be asked to present yourself for interview.* ◊ *She was ordered to present herself in court on 20 May.*
• EXPRESS STH **10** **~ sth (to sb)** (*formal*) to offer or express sth in speech or writing: *Please allow me to present my apologies.*
• CHEQUE/BILL **11** **~ sth** to give sb a CHEQUE or bill that they should pay: *A cheque presented by Mr Jackson was returned by the bank.* ◊ *The builders presented a bill for several hundred pounds.*
IDM **preˌsent ˈarms** (of soldiers) to hold a RIFLE straight upwards in front of the body as a mark of respect

**preˈsent·able** /prɪˈzentəbl/ *adj.* **1** looking clean and attractive and suitable to be seen in public: *I must go and make myself presentable before the guests arrive.* **2** acceptable: *You're going to have to do a lot more work on this essay before it's presentable.*

**preˌsen·ˈta·tion** ⓘ B1 Ⓦ /ˌprezn'teɪʃn; *NAmE* ˌpriːzn-/ *noun* **1** B1 [C] **~ (on/about sb/sth)** a meeting at which sth, especially a new product or idea, or piece of work, is shown to a group of people: *The sales manager will give a presentation on the new products.* **2** B2 [U] the act of showing sth or of giving sth to sb: *The trial was adjourned following the presentation of new evidence to the court.* ◊ *The presentation of prizes began after the speeches.* ◊ *The Mayor will make the presentation* (= hand over the gift) *herself.* ◊ **on~ of sth** *Members will be admitted on presentation of a membership card.* **3** B2 [U] the way in which sth is offered, shown, explained, etc. to others: *Improving the product's presentation* (= the way it is wrapped, advertised, etc.) *should increase sales.* ◊ *The main emphasis of the training will be on presentation skills.*

**4** [C] the series of computer slides (= images) that are shown with the talk when sb gives a presentation at a meeting: *I've put my presentation on a memory stick.* **5** [C] a ceremony or formal occasion during which a gift or prize is given **6** [C] a performance of a play, etc. in a theatre **7** [C, U] (*medical*) the position in which a baby is lying in the mother's body just before birth

**preˌsen·ˈta·tion·al** /ˌprezn'teɪʃənl; *NAmE* ˌpriːzn-/ *adj.* [only before noun] connected with the act of showing, explaining or offering sth to other people, especially a new product, a policy or a performance: *a course on developing presentational skills*

**the ˌpresent ˈday** *noun* [sing.] the situation that exists in the world now, rather than in the past or the future: *a study of European drama, from Ibsen to the present day* ▸ **ˌpresent-ˈday** *adj.* [only before noun]: *present-day fashions* ◊ *present-day America*

**preˈsent·er** /prɪˈzentə(r)/ *noun* **1** (*BrE*) a person who introduces the different sections of a radio or television programme: *a TV presenter* ➔ see also ANNOUNCER, HOST *noun* **2** a person who makes a speech or talks to an audience about a particular subject: *conference presenters* **3** (*NAmE*) a person who gives sb a prize at a ceremony

**preˈsen·ti·ment** /prɪˈzentɪmənt/ *noun* (*formal*) a feeling that sth is going to happen, especially sth unpleasant SYN **foreboding:** *a presentiment of disaster*

**ˈpres·ent·ly** [C1] /ˈprezntli/ *adv.* **1** [C1] (*especially NAmE*) at the time you are speaking or writing; now SYN **currently:** *The crime is presently being investigated by the police.* ◊ *These are the courses presently available.* HELP In this meaning **presently** usually comes before the verb, adjective or noun that it refers to. **2** [C1] used to show that sth happened after a short time: *Presently, the door opened again and three men stepped out.* HELP In this meaning **presently** usually comes at the beginning of a sentence. **3** [C1] used to show that sth will happen soon SYN **shortly:** *She'll be here presently.* HELP In this meaning **presently** usually comes at the end of a sentence.

▼ BRITISH/AMERICAN
**presently**
■ In both *BrE* and *NAmE*, **presently** can mean 'soon' or 'after a short time': *I'll be with you presently.* In *NAmE* the usual meaning of **presently** is 'at the present time' or 'now': *She is presently living in Milan.* ◊ *There is presently no cure for the disease.* This use is becoming more accepted in *BrE*, but **at present** or **currently** are usually used.

**ˌpresent ˈparticiple** *noun* (*grammar*) the form of the verb that in English ends in *-ing* and is used with the verb *to be* to form progressive tenses such as *I was running* or sometimes as an adjective as in *running water* ➔ compare PAST PARTICIPLE

**the ˌpresent ˈperfect** *noun* [sing.] (*grammar*) the form of a verb that expresses an action done in a time period up to the present, formed in English with the present tense of *have* and the past participle of the verb, as in *I have eaten*

**the ˌpresent ˈtense** (*also* **the present**) *noun* [usually sing.] (*grammar*) the form of a verb that expresses an action that is happening now or at the time of speaking

**ˌpres·er·ˈva·tion** [C1] /ˌprezə'veɪʃn; *NAmE* -zər'v-/ *noun* [U] **1** [C1] the act of keeping sth in its original state or in good condition: *building/environmental/food preservation* ◊ *a preservation group/society* **2** the act of making sure that sth is kept: *The central issue in the strike was the preservation of jobs.* **3** the degree to which sth has not been changed or damaged by age, weather, etc: *The paintings were in an excellent state of preservation.* ➔ see also SELF-PRESERVATION

**ˌpres·er·ˈva·tion·ist** /ˌprezə'veɪʃənɪst; *NAmE* -zər'v-/ *noun* a person who works to keep old buildings or areas of the countryside in their original condition and to prevent them from being destroyed

**preˌser·ˈvation order** *noun* (in the UK) a document that makes it illegal to change or destroy a building, a tree or

# preservative

part of the countryside, because of its beauty or historical interest

**pre·ser·va·tive** /prɪˈzɜːvətɪv; NAmE -ˈzɜːrv-/ noun [C, U] a substance used to prevent food or wood from DECAYING (= being destroyed by natural processes): *The juice contains no artificial preservatives.* ◊ *(a) wood preservative* ▸ **pre·ser·va·tive** *adj.* [only before noun]

**pre·serve** ❶ B2 /prɪˈzɜːv; NAmE -ˈzɜːrv/ *verb, noun*
■ *verb* **1** B2 ~ sth to keep a particular quality, feature, etc.; to make sure that sth is kept: *He was anxious to preserve his reputation.* ◊ *Efforts to preserve the peace have failed.* **2** B2 [often passive] to keep sth in its original state in good condition: ~ sth/sb *a perfectly preserved 14th century house* ◊ (*humorous*) *Is he really 60? He's remarkably well preserved.* ◊ ~ sth + adj. *This vase has been preserved intact.* **3** B2 to prevent sth, especially food, from DECAYING (= being destroyed by natural processes) by treating it in a particular way: ~ sth *Wax polish preserves wood and leather.* ◊ ~ sth in sth *olives preserved in brine* **4** ~ sb/sth (from sth) to keep sb/sth alive, or safe from harm or danger SYN save: *The society was set up to preserve endangered species from extinction.* ⇨ compare CONSERVE
■ *noun* **1** [sing.] ~ (of sb) an activity, a job, an interest, etc. that is thought to be suitable for one particular person or group of people: *Football is no longer the preserve of men.* ◊ *in the days when nursing was a female preserve* **2** [C, usually pl., U] a type of jam made by boiling fruit with a large amount of sugar **3** [C, usually pl., U] (*especially BrE*) a type of PICKLE made by cooking vegetables with salt or VINEGAR **4** [C] (*NAmE*) = RESERVE **5** [C] an area of private land or water where animals and fish are kept for people to hunt

**pre·server** /prɪˈzɜːvə(r); NAmE -ˈzɜːrv-/ *noun* **1** [C] a person who makes sure that a particular situation does not change: *The police are the preservers of law and order.* **2** [C, U] a substance used to prevent wood from DECAYING (= being destroyed by natural processes) ⇨ see also LIFE PRESERVER

**pre·set** /ˌpriːˈset/ *verb* (**pre·set·ting, pre·set, pre·set**) **1** to set the controls of a piece of electrical equipment so that it will start to work at a particular time: ~ sth to do sth *You can preset the radiators to come on when you need them to.* ◊ ~ sth *to preset TV channels/radio stations* (= to set the controls so that particular channels are selected when you press particular buttons) **2** [usually passive] ~ sth to decide sth in advance: *They kept to the preset route.*

**pre·side** ⓘ+ C1 /prɪˈzaɪd/ *verb* [I] (*formal*) to lead or be in charge of a meeting, ceremony, etc: *the presiding judge* ◊ ~ at/over sth *They asked if I would preside at the committee meeting.* ◊ (*figurative*) *The party presided over one of the worst economic declines in the country's history* (= it was in power when the decline happened).

**presi·dency** ⓘ+ C1 /ˈprezɪdənsi/ *noun* [usually sing.] (*pl. -ies*) the job of being president of a country or an organization; the period of time sb holds this job: *the current holder of the EU presidency* ◊ *He was a White House official during the Bush presidency.*

**presi·dent** ❶ A2 /ˈprezɪdənt/ *noun* **1** A2 (*also* **President**) the leader of a REPUBLIC, for example the US: *Several presidents attended the funeral.* ◊ *the President of the United States* ◊ *President Trump is due to visit the country next month.* ◊ *Do you have any comment, Mr President?* ⇨ see also VICE-PRESIDENT (1) ⇨ WORDFINDER NOTE at CONGRESS **2** B1 (*also* **President**) the person in charge of some organizations, clubs, colleges, etc: *to be made president of the students' union* **3** B2 (*especially NAmE*) the person in charge of a bank or a commercial organization: *the bank president* ◊ *the president of Columbia Pictures* ⇨ see also VICE-PRESIDENT (2)

**president-elect** *noun* (*pl.* **presidents-elect**) a person who has been elected to be president but who has not yet begun the job

**presi·den·tial** ⓘ+ C1 /ˌprezɪˈdenʃl/ *adj.* connected with the position or activities of a president: *a presidential campaign/candidate/election* ◊ *a presidential system of government*

**Presidents' Day** *noun* (in the US) a legal holiday on the third Monday in February, in memory of the birthdays of George Washington and Abraham Lincoln

**pre·sid·ium** (*also* **prae·sid·ium** *especially in BrE*) /prɪˈsɪdiəm/ *noun* a permanent committee that makes important decisions as part of a government or large political organization, especially in COMMUNIST countries

**press** ❶ B1 /pres/ *noun, verb*
■ *noun*
• NEWSPAPERS **1** B1 (*often* **the Press**) [sing. + sing./pl. v.] newspapers and magazines: *the local/national/foreign press* ◊ *the popular/tabloid press* (= newspapers with a lot of pictures and stories about famous people) ◊ *the music/sporting press* (= newspapers and magazines about music/sport) ◊ *Unlike the American, the British press operates on a national scale.* ◊ *in the* ~ *The case has been widely reported in the press.* ◊ *the freedom of the Press/press freedom* (= the freedom to report any events and express opinions) ◊ *The event is bound to attract wide press coverage* (= it will be written about in many newspapers). ⇨ see also GUTTER PRESS **2** B2 **the press, the Press** [sing. + sing./pl. v.] the journalists and photographers who work for newspapers and magazines: *The Press was/were not allowed to attend the trial.* **3** [sing., U] the type or amount of reports that newspapers write about sb/sth: *The airline has had a bad press recently* (= journalists have written unpleasant things about it).
• PUBLISHING/PRINTING **4** [C, U] a machine for printing books, newspapers, etc.; the process of printing them: *We were able to watch the books rolling off the presses.* ◊ *These prices are correct at the time of going to press.* ◊ *a story that is hot off the press* (= has just appeared in the newspapers) ⇨ see also PRINTING PRESS **5** [C] a business that prints and publishes books: *Oxford University Press*
• EQUIPMENT FOR PRESSING **6** [C] (especially in compounds) a piece of equipment that is used for creating pressure on things, to make them flat or to get liquid from them: *a trouser press* ◊ *a garlic press* ⇨ see also FRENCH PRESS™, GARLIC PRESS
• ACT OF PUSHING **7** [C, usually sing.] an act of pushing sth with your hand or with a tool that you are holding: *He gave the bell another press.* ◊ *Those shirts need a press* (= with an iron).
• CROWD **8** [sing.] a large number of people or things competing for space or movement SYN throng: *the press of bodies all moving the same way*
• CUPBOARD **9** [C] (*IrishE, ScotE*) a large cupboard, usually with shelves, for holding clothes, books, etc. ⇨ see also BENCH PRESS
■ *verb*
• PUSH **1** B1 [T, I] to push part of a device, etc. in order to make it work: ~ sth *to press a button/key* ◊ ~ sth + adj. *He pressed the lid firmly shut.* ◊ (+ *adv./prep.*) *Press here to open.* ◊ *She pressed down hard on the gas pedal.* ⇨ picture at SQUEEZE **2** B1 [T, I] to push sth closely against sth; to be pushed in this way: ~ sth/sb/yourself against sth *She pressed her face against the window.* ◊ ~ sth to sth *He pressed a handkerchief to his nose.* ◊ ~ sth together *She pressed her lips together.* ◊ ~ against sth *His body was pressing against hers.* **3** [T] ~ sth into/onto sth to put sth in a place by pushing it: *He pressed a coin into her hand and moved on.* **4** [T] ~ sth to put gentle pressure on sb's hand or arm, especially to show care or kind feelings **5** [I] + *adv./prep.* (of people in a crowd) to move in the direction mentioned by pushing: *The photographers pressed around the royal visitors.* ◊ (*figurative*) *A host of unwelcome thoughts were pressing in on him.*
• TRY TO PERSUADE **6** [T] to make strong efforts to persuade or force sb to do sth SYN push, urge: ~ sb *If pressed, he will admit that he knew about the affair.* ◊ ~ sb for sth *The bank is pressing us for repayment of the loan.* ◊ ~ sb to do sth *They are pressing us to make a quick decision.* ◊ ~ sb into (doing) sth *Don't let yourself be pressed into doing something you don't like.*
• POINT/CLAIM/CASE **7** [T] ~ sth to express or repeat sth with force: *I don't want to press the point, but you do owe me $200.* ◊ *She is still pressing her claim for compensation.* ◊ *They were determined to press their case at the highest level.*

ⓘ Oxford 3000 | ⓘ+ Oxford 5000 | A1 A2 B1 B2 C1 CEFR level | PHRV phrasal verb(s) | IDM idiom(s)

- **MAKE FLAT/SMOOTH 8** [T] to make sth flat or smooth by using force or putting sth heavy on top: *~sth pressed flowers* (= pressed between the pages of a book) ◊ *~sth + adj. Press the soil flat with the back of a spade.* **9** [T] *~sth* to make clothes smooth using a hot iron ⓢⓨⓝ **iron**: *My suit needs pressing.*
- **FRUIT/VEGETABLES 10** [T] *~sth* to get the juice out of fruit or vegetables by using force or weight
- **METAL 11** [T] to make sth from a material, using pressure: *~sth to press a CD* ◊ *~sth from/out of sth The car bodies are pressed out of sheets of metal.*

**ⒾⒹⓂ** ˌpress (the) ˈflesh (*informal*) (of a famous person or politician) to say hello to people by shaking hands ˌpress sth ˈhome to get as much advantage as possible from a situation by attacking or arguing in a determined way: *to press home an attack/an argument/a point* ◊ *Simon saw she was hesitating and pressed home his advantage.* ˌpress sb/sth into ˈservice to use sb/sth for a purpose that they were not trained or intended for because there is nobody or nothing else available: *Every type of boat was pressed into service to rescue passengers from the sinking ferry.* ⊃ more at BUTTON *n*., CHARGE *n*., PANIC BUTTON

**ⓅⒽⓇⓋ** ˌpress aˈhead/ˈon (with sth) to continue doing sth in a determined way; to hurry forward: *The company is pressing ahead with its plans for a new warehouse.* ◊ *'Shall we stay here for the night?' 'No, let's press on.'* ˌpress for sth to keep asking for sth ⓢⓨⓝ **demand**, **push for**: *They continued to press for a change in the law.* ˌpress sth on sb to try to make sb accept sth, especially food or drink, although they may not want it: *She kept pressing cake on us.*

ˈpress agency *noun* = NEWS AGENCY

ˈpress agent (*also NAmE*, *informal* **flack**) *noun* a person whose job is to supply information and advertising material about a particular actor, musician, theatre, etc. to newspapers, radio or television

ˈpress box *noun* a special area or a room at a sports ground where sports journalists sit

ˈpress conference (*especially BrE*) (*NAmE usually* ˈnews conference) *noun* a meeting at which sb talks to a group of journalists in order to answer their questions or to make an official statement: *to hold/give a press conference*

ˈpress corps *noun* (*pl.* **press corps**) a group of journalists who work in or go to a particular place to report on an event

ˈpress cutting (*BrE*) (*also* ˈpress clipping *NAmE, BrE*) *noun* = CUTTING

**pressed** /prest/ *adj*. **1** [not before noun] *~(for sth)* not having enough of sth, especially time or money: *I'm really pressed for cash at the moment.* ⊃ see also HARD-PRESSED **2** made flat using force, a heavy object or a hot iron: *pictures made with pressed flowers* ◊ *neatly pressed trousers*

ˈpress gallery *noun* an area in a parliament building or a court for journalists to sit in

ˈpress gang *noun* a group of people who were employed in the past to force men to join the army or NAVY

ˈpress-gang *verb ~sb (into sth/into doing sth)* (*informal*) to force sb to do sth that they do not want to do

ˈpres·sie = PREZZIE

**press·ing** /ˈpresɪŋ/ *adj*., *noun*
- *adj*. [usually before noun] **1** needing to be dealt with immediately ⓢⓨⓝ **urgent**: *I'm afraid I have some pressing business to attend to.* ◊ *There is a pressing need for more specialist nurses.* **2** difficult to refuse or to ignore: *a pressing invitation*
- *noun* an object, especially a record, made by using pressure or weight to shape a piece of metal, plastic, etc.; a number of such objects that are made at one time: *The initial pressing of the group's album has already sold out.*

ˈpress·man /ˈpresmæn/ *noun* (*pl.* **-men** /-men/) (*BrE, informal*) a journalist

ˈpress office *noun* the office of a large organization, political party or government department that answers questions from journalists and provides them with information

ˈpress officer *noun* a person who is in charge of or works for a press office

# pressure

ˈpress release *noun* an official statement made to journalists by a large organization, a political party or a government department

ˈpress secretary *noun* a person who works for a politician or a political organization and gives information about them to journalists, the newspapers, etc.

ˈpress stud (*also* ˈpop·per) (*both BrE*) (*NAmE* **snap**) *noun* a type of button used for fastening clothes, consisting of two metal or plastic sections that can be pressed together

press-up/push-up      sit-up

ˈpress-up (*BrE*) (*also* ˈpush-up *NAmE, BrE*) *noun* [usually pl.] an exercise in which you lie on your stomach and raise your body off the ground by pressing down on your hands until your arms are straight

**pres·sure** 🔑 Ⓑ⓵ 🔊 /ˈpreʃə(r)/ *noun*, *verb*
- *noun*
- **PERSUASION/FORCE 1** ❗ Ⓑ⓵ [U] the act of trying to persuade or to force sb to do sth: *~for sth The pressure for change continued to mount.* ◊ *~(on sb) (to do sth) There is intense pressure on her to resign.* ◊ *We must bring pressure to bear on our government to reverse this decision.* ⊃ see also PEER PRESSURE
- **STRESS 2** ❗ Ⓑ⓵ [U] (*also* **pressures** [pl.]) difficulties and worries that are caused by the need to achieve or to behave in a particular way: *You need to be able to handle pressure in this job.* ◊ *~of sth She was unable to attend because of the pressure of work.* ◊ *~on sb The economic pressures on small businesses are intense.*
- **WHEN STH PRESSES 3** ❗ Ⓑ⓶ [U] the force or weight with which sth presses against sth else: *The nurse applied pressure to his arm to stop the bleeding.* ◊ *The barriers gave way under the pressure of the crowd.* ◊ *Last year he had brain surgery to relieve pressure from a blood clot.*
- **OF GAS/LIQUID 4** ❗ Ⓑ⓶ [U, C] the force produced by a particular amount of gas or liquid in a container or a limited

---

▼ **SYNONYMS**

**pressure**

stress • tension • strain

These are all words for the feelings of worry caused by the problems in sb's life.

**pressure** difficulties and feelings of worry that are caused by the need to achieve sth or to behave in a particular way: *She was unable to attend because of the pressures of work.*

**stress** pressure or worry caused by the problems in sb's life: *stress-related illnesses*

**PRESSURE OR STRESS?**

It is common to say that sb *is suffering from stress*, while **pressure** may be the thing that causes **stress**.

**tension** a feeling of worry and stress that makes it impossible to relax: *nervous tension*

**strain** pressure on sb/sth because they have too much to do or manage; the problems or worry that this produces: *I found it a strain looking after four children.*

**PATTERNS**
- to be **under** pressure/stress/strain
- **considerable** pressure/stress/tension/strain
- to **cause** stress/tension/strain
- to **cope with** the pressure/stress/tension/strain
- to **relieve/release** the pressure/stress/tension/strain
- to be **suffering from** stress/tension

# pressure cooker

space; the amount of this: *air/water pressure* ◊ *Check the tyre pressure* (= the amount of air in a tyre) *regularly.* ⇨ see also BLOOD PRESSURE, HIGH PRESSURE, LOW PRESSURE
- **EFFECT ON STH** **5** [U] **~ (on sb)** the effect that sth has on the way a situation develops, especially when this causes problems: *This puts upward pressure on prices.* ◊ *The high unemployment rate was exerting downward pressure on wage growth.* ◊ *~ to relieve/ease the pressure on sth*
- **OF ATMOSPHERE** **6** [U] the force of the atmosphere on the earth's surface: *A band of high/low pressure is moving across the country.* ⇨ see also ATMOSPHERIC

**IDM** **put ˈpressure on sb (to do sth)** to force or to try to persuade sb to do sth **under ˈpressure 1** if a liquid or a gas is kept **under pressure**, it is forced into a container so that when the container is opened, the liquid or gas escapes quickly **2** being forced to do sth: *The director is under increasing pressure to resign.* ◊ *Hospital staff are coming under pressure to work longer hours.* **3** made to feel anxious about sth you have to do: *The team performs well under pressure.*

■ *verb* [often passive] (*especially NAmE*; *BrE also* **presˈsurˌize**) **~ sb (into sth / into doing sth)** | **~ sb to do sth** to persuade sb to do sth, especially by making them feel that they have to or should do it: *Don't let yourself be pressured into making a hasty decision.*

**ˈpressure cooker** *noun* **1** a strong metal pot with a tight LID (= cover), that cooks food quickly by STEAM under high pressure **2** a situation that is difficult or dangerous because people are likely to become anxious or violent

**ˈpressure group** *noun* a group of people who try to influence the government and ordinary people's opinions in order to achieve the action they want, for example a change in a law: *the environmental pressure group 'Greenpeace'* ⇨ compare LOBBY (3) ⇨ see also INTEREST GROUP

**ˈpressure hose** *noun* a long tube that is strong enough for liquid to pass through it at high pressure

**ˈpressure point** *noun* **1** a place on the surface of the body that is sensitive to pressure, for example where an artery can be pressed against a bone to stop the loss of blood **2** a place or situation where there is likely to be trouble

**ˈpressure suit** *noun* a suit which can be filled with air, used to protect the person wearing it from low air pressure, for example while flying a plane very high in the atmosphere

**ˈpressure washer** *noun* a machine that cleans things by SPRAYING them with water under high pressure

**presˈsurˌize** (*BrE also* -**ise**) /ˈpreʃəraɪz/ *verb* **1** (*BrE*) (*also* **presˈsure** *NAmE, BrE*) [often passive] to persuade sb to do sth, especially by making them feel that they have to or should do it: **~ sb (into sth / into doing sth)** *She was pressurized into accepting the job.* ◊ **~ sb to do sth** *He felt that he was being pressurized to resign.* **2** [usually passive] **~ sth** to keep the air pressure in a SUBMARINE, an aircraft, etc. the same as it is on earth ▶ **presˌsurˌizaˈtion, -isaˈtion** /ˌpreʃəraɪˈzeɪʃn; *NAmE* -rəˈz-/ *noun* [U]

**presˈtige** /preˈstiːʒ/ *noun, adj.*
■ *noun* [U] the respect and value that sb/sth has because of their social position, or what they have done **SYN** **status**: *personal prestige* ◊ *There is a lot of prestige attached to owning a car like this.* ◊ *jobs with low prestige*
■ *adj.* [only before noun] **1** that brings respect and importance: *a prestige job* **2** admired and respected because it looks important and expensive **SYN** **luxury**: *a prestige car*

**presˈtiˌgious** /preˈstɪdʒəs; *NAmE* -ˈstiːdʒ-/ *adj.* [usually before noun] respected and admired as very important or of very high quality: *a prestigious award* ◊ *a highly prestigious university*

**presto** /ˈprestəʊ/ *exclamation, adv., adj., noun*
■ *exclamation* (*NAmE*) (*BrE* **hey ˈpresto**) **1** something that people say when they have just done sth so quickly and easily that it seems to have been done by magic **2** something that people say just before they finish a magic trick

■ *adv., adj.* (used as an instruction in a piece of music) very quickly
■ *noun* (*pl.* **-os**) a piece of music that should be performed very quickly

**preˈsumˌably** /prɪˈzjuːməbli; *NAmE* -ˈzuː-/ *adv.* used to say that you think that sth is probably true: *Presumably this is where the accident happened.* ◊ *You'll be taking the car, presumably?* ◊ *I couldn't concentrate, presumably because I was so tired.*

**preˈsume** /prɪˈzjuːm; *NAmE* -ˈzuːm/ *verb* **1** [I, T] to suppose that sth is true, although you do not have actual proof **SYN** **assume**: *They are very expensive, I presume?* ◊ *'Is he still abroad?' 'I presume so.'* ◊ **~ (that) ...** *I presumed (that) he understood the rules.* ◊ **it is presumed that ...** *Little is known of the youngest son; it is presumed that he died young.* ◊ **~ sb/sth to be/have sth** *I presumed him to be her husband.* **2** [T] to accept that sth is true until it is shown not to be true, especially in court: **~ sb/sth + adj.** *Twelve passengers are missing, presumed dead.* ◊ *In English law, a person is presumed innocent until proved guilty.* ◊ **~ sth** *We must presume innocence until we have proof of guilt.* ◊ **~ sb/sth to be/have sth** *We must presume them to be innocent until we have proof of guilt.* **3** [T] **~ sth** (*formal*) to accept sth as true or existing and to act on that basis: *The course seems to presume some previous knowledge of the subject.* **4** [I] **~ to do sth** (*formal*) to behave in a way that shows a lack of respect by doing sth that you have no right to do: *I wouldn't presume to tell you how to run your own business.*

**PHRV** **preˈsume on/upon sb/sth** (*formal*) to make use of sb's friendship by asking them for more than you should: **presume on/upon sb/sth to do sth** *I felt it would be presuming on our personal relationship to keep asking her for help.*

**preˈsumpˌtion** /prɪˈzʌmpʃn/ *noun* **1** [C] something that is thought to be true or likely: *There is a general presumption that the doctor knows best.* **2** [U] (*formal*) behaviour that is too confident and shows a lack of respect for other people **3** [U, C] (*law*) the act of supposing that sth is true, although it has not yet been proved or is not certain: *Everyone is entitled to the presumption of innocence until they are proved to be guilty.*

**preˈsumpˌtive** /prɪˈzʌmptɪv/ *adj.* [usually before noun] (*formal or specialist*) likely to be true, based on the facts that are available ⇨ see also HEIR PRESUMPTIVE

**preˈsumpˌtuˌous** /prɪˈzʌmptʃuəs/ *adj.* [not usually before noun] too confident, in a way that shows a lack of respect for other people

**preˈsupˌpose** /ˌpriːsəˈpəʊz/ *verb* (*formal*) **1** **~ sth** to accept sth as true or existing and act on that basis, before it has been proved to be true **SYN** **presume**: *Teachers sometimes presuppose a fairly high level of knowledge by the students.* **2** **~ that ...** | **~ sth** to depend on sth in order to exist or be true **SYN** **assume**: *His argument presupposes that it does not matter who is in power.*

**preˌsupˌpoˈsiˌtion** /ˌpriːsʌpəˈzɪʃn/ *noun* [C, U] (*formal*) something that you believe to be true and use as the beginning of an argument even though it has not been proved; the act of believing it is true **SYN** **assumption**: *theories based on presupposition and coincidence*

**pre-ˈtax** *adj.* [only before noun] before the tax has been taken away: *pre-tax profits/losses/income*

**pre-ˈteach** *verb* **~ sth** to teach sth, especially new words, to students before a test or exercise

**pre-ˈteen** *noun* a young person of about 11 or 12 years of age ▶ **pre-ˈteen** *adj.* [usually before noun]: *the pre-teen years*

**preˈtence** (*BrE*) (*NAmE* **preˈtense**) /prɪˈtens; *NAmE* ˈpriː-tens/ *noun* **1** [U, sing.] the act of behaving in a particular way, in order to make other people believe sth that is not true: *Their friendliness was only pretence.* ◊ **~ of doing sth** *By the end of the evening she had abandoned all pretence of being interested.* ◊ **~ of sth** *He made no pretence of great musical knowledge.* ◊ **~ that ...** *She was unable to keep up the pretence that he loved him.* **2** [U, C, usually sing.] (*formal or literary*) a claim that you have a particular quality or skill: **~ (to sth)** *a woman with some pretence to beauty* ◊ **~ (to doing sth)** *I make no pretence to being an expert on the subject.* **IDM** see FALSE

**pre·tend** /prɪˈtend/ verb, adj.
- verb 1 [I, T] to behave in a particular way, in order to make other people believe sth that is not true: *I'm tired of having to pretend all the time.* ◊ *Of course I was wrong; it would be hypocritical to pretend otherwise.* ◊ ~**to sb that** ... *He pretended to his family that everything was fine.* ◊ ~**(that)** ... *We pretended (that) nothing had happened.* ◊ ~**to do sth** *I pretended to be asleep.* ◊ *She didn't love him, though she pretended to.* ~ sth (formal): *She pretended an interest she did not feel.* **2** [I, T] (especially of children) to imagine that sth is true as part of a game: *They didn't have any real money so they had to pretend.* ◊ ~**(that)** ... *Let's pretend (that) we're astronauts.* **3** [I, T] (usually used in negative sentences and questions) to claim to be, do or have sth, especially when this is not true: ~**to sth** *I can't pretend to any great musical talent.* ◊ ~**(that)** ... *I don't pretend (that) I know much about the subject, but* ... ◊ ~**to be/do/have sth** *The book doesn't pretend to be a great work of literature.*
- adj. [usually before noun] (informal) (often used by children) not real, imaginary: *pretend cakes*

**pre·tend·er** /prɪˈtendə(r)/ noun ~ **(to sth)** a person who claims they have a right to a particular title even though other people disagree with them

**pre·tense** (NAmE) = PRETENCE

**pre·ten·sion** /prɪˈtenʃn/ noun [C, usually pl., U] **1** the act of trying to appear more important, intelligent, etc. than you are in order to impress other people: *intellectual pretensions* ◊ *The play mocks the pretensions of the new middle class.* ◊ *He spoke without pretension.* **2** a claim to be or to do sth: ~ **to (doing) sth** *a building with no pretensions to architectural merit* ◊ ~ **(to do sth)** *The movie makes no pretension to reproduce life.*

**pre·ten·tious** /prɪˈtenʃəs/ adj. (disapproving) trying to appear important, intelligent, etc. in order to impress other people; trying to be sth that you are not, in order to impress: *That's a pretentious name for a dog!* ◊ *It was just an ordinary house—nothing pretentious.* ◊ *He's so pretentious!* ⟶ compare UNPRETENTIOUS ▸ **pre·ten·tious·ly** adv. **pre·ten·tious·ness** noun [U]

**the pret·er·ite** /ðə ˈpretərət/ (NAmE also **pret·erit**) noun [sing.] (grammar) a form of a verb that expresses the past

**pre·term** /ˌpriːˈtɜːm; NAmE -ˈtɜːrm/ adj. born or happening after a short PREGNANCY, especially one that is less than 37 weeks: *caring for low birthweight and preterm babies* ◊ *a preterm birth/delivery* ▸ **preterm** adv.: *Babies born preterm are at greater risk of needing hospitalization.*

**pre·ter·nat·ural** /ˌpriːtəˈnætʃrəl; NAmE ˌpretərˈn-, -ˈpriːt-/ adj. [only before noun] (formal) that does not seem natural; that cannot be explained by natural laws ▸ **pre·ter·nat·ur·al·ly** /-rəli/ adv.: *The city was preternaturally quiet.*

**pre·test** /ˈpriːtest/ noun a test that you take to find out how much you already know or can do before learning or doing sth ▸ **pre·test** verb ~ sb

**pre·text** /ˈpriːtekst/ noun a false reason that you give for doing sth, usually sth bad, in order to hide the real reason; an excuse: **(as a)** ~ **for (doing) sth** *The incident was used as a pretext for intervention in the area.* ◊ **on/under the** ~ **of doing sth** *He left the party early on the pretext of having work to do.* ◊ ~ **to do sth** *Be careful not to give him a pretext to report you.* ⟶ SYNONYMS at REASON

**pre·trial** /ˌpriːˈtraɪəl/ adj. [only before noun] in or connected with the time before a court case begins: *He testified at a pretrial hearing.*

**pret·tify** /ˈprɪtɪfaɪ/ verb (**pret·ti·fies**, **pret·ti·fy·ing**, **pret·ti·fied**, **pret·ti·fied**) ~ **sth** (usually disapproving) to try to make sth pretty, often with the result that it looks worse or false

**pretty** /ˈprɪti/ adv., adj.
- adv. (with adjectives and adverbs) (rather informal) **1** to some extent; fairly: *The game was pretty good.* ◊ *I'm pretty sure I'll be going.* ◊ *It's pretty hard to explain.* ◊ *I'm going to have to find a new apartment pretty soon.* ⟶ note at QUITE **2** very: *That performance was pretty impressive.* ◊ *Things are looking pretty good!*

**IDM** **pretty ˈmuch/ˈwell** (BrE also **pretty ˈnearly**) (NAmE also **pretty ˈnear**) (informal) almost; almost completely: *One dog looks pretty much like another to me.* ⟶ more at SIT
- adj. (**pret·tier**, **pret·ti·est**) **1** (especially of a woman, or a girl) attractive without being very beautiful: *a pretty face* ◊ *a very pretty girl* ◊ *You look so pretty in that dress!* ⟶ SYNONYMS at BEAUTIFUL **2** (of places or things) attractive and pleasant to look at or to listen to without being large, beautiful or impressive: *pretty clothes* ◊ *a pretty garden* ◊ *a pretty name* ▸ **pret·tily** /-tɪli/ adv. (especially BrE): *She laughed prettily.* ◊ *The rooms are simply but prettily furnished.* **pret·ti·ness** noun [U]: *the prettiness of youth*

**IDM** **as ˌpretty as a ˈpicture** (old-fashioned) very pretty **not just a pretty ˈface** (humorous) used to emphasize that you have particular skills or qualities: *'I didn't know you could play the piano.' 'I'm not just a pretty face, you know!'* **not a pretty ˈsight** (humorous) not pleasant to look at: *You should have seen him in his swimming trunks—not a pretty sight!* **a pretty ˈpenny** (old-fashioned) a lot of money ⟶ more at PASS n.

**pret·zel** /ˈpretsl/ noun a small dry biscuit in the shape of a KNOT or stick, tasting of salt and often served with drinks at a party

pretzel
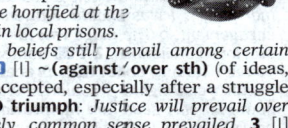

**pre·vail** /prɪˈveɪl/ verb (formal) **1** [I] to exist or be very common at a particular time or in a particular place: ~ **in sth** *We were horrified at the conditions prevailing in local prisons.* ◊ ~ **among sb** *Those beliefs still prevail among certain social groups.* **2** [I] ~ **(against/over sth)** (of ideas, opinions, etc.) to be accepted, especially after a struggle or an argument SYN **triumph**: *Justice will prevail over tyranny.* ◊ *Fortunately, common sense prevailed.* **3** [I] ~ **(against/over sb)** to defeat an opponent, especially after a long struggle
**PHRV** **preˈvail on/upon sb to do sth** to persuade sb to do sth: *I'm sure he could be prevailed upon to give a talk.*

**pre·vail·ing** /prɪˈveɪlɪŋ/ adj. [only before noun] **1** existing or most common at a particular time SYN **current**, **predominant**: *the prevailing economic conditions* ◊ *the attitude towards science prevailing at the time* ◊ *The prevailing view seems to be that they will find her guilty.* **2** the **prevailing wind** in an area is the one that blows over it most frequently ⟶ WORDFINDER NOTE at WIND[1]

**preva·lence** /ˈprevələns/ noun [U] (formal) the fact of existing or being very common at a particular time or in a particular place

**preva·lent** /ˈprevələnt/ adj. ~ **(among sb)** | ~ **(in sb/sth)** (formal) that exists or is very common at a particular time or in a particular place SYN **common**, **widespread**: *a prevalent view* ◊ *These prejudices are particularly prevalent among people living in the North.*

**pre·vari·cate** /prɪˈværɪkeɪt/ verb [I, T] (+ speech) (formal) to avoid giving a direct answer to a question in order to hide the truth SYN **beat about the bush**: *Stop prevaricating and come to the point.* ▸ **pre·vari·ca·tion** /prɪˌværɪˈkeɪʃn/ noun [U, C]

**pre·vent** /prɪˈvent/ verb to stop sb from doing sth; to stop sth from happening: ~ **sth/sb** *The accident could have been prevented.* ◊ *Maddie would have joined the army if an injury had not prevented her.* ◊ ~ **sb/sth from doing sth** *He is prevented by law from holding a licence.* ◊ ~ **sb/sth doing sth** (BrE) *Nothing would prevent him speaking out against injustice.* ▸ **pre·vent·able** adj.: *preventable diseases/accidents*

**pre·ven·tion** /prɪˈvenʃn/ noun [U] the act of stopping sth bad from happening: *accident/crime prevention* ◊ *the prevention of disease* ◊ *a fire prevention officer*
**IDM** **preˌvention is better than ˈcure** (BrE) (US **an ounce of preˌvention is better than a pound of ˈcure**) (saying) it is better to stop sth bad from happening rather than try to deal with the problems after it has happened

## preventive

**pre·vent·ive** /prɪˈventɪv/ (also **pre·venta·tive** /prɪˈventətɪv/) adj. [only before noun] intended to try to stop sth that causes problems or difficulties from happening: *preventive medicine* ◊ *The police were able to take preventive action and avoid a possible riot.* ⊃ compare CURATIVE

**pre·view** /ˈpriːvjuː/ noun, verb
- noun **1** an occasion at which you can see a film, a show, etc. before it is shown to the general public: *a press preview* (= for journalists only) ◊ *a special preview of our winter fashion collection* ⊃ see also SNEAK PREVIEW **2** a description in a newspaper or a magazine that tells you about a film, a television programme, etc. before it is shown to the public: *Turn to page 12 for a preview of next week's programmes.* **3** (NAmE) = TRAILER (4) **4** a chance to see what sth will be like before it happens or is shown: *Click on the print preview button.*
- verb **1** ~ sth to see a film, a television programme, etc. before it is shown to the general public and write an account of it for a newspaper or magazine: *The exhibition was previewed in last week's issue.* **2** ~ sth (especially NAmE) to give sb a short account of sth that is going to happen, be studied, etc: *The professor previewed the course for us.*

**pre·vi·ous** 🅱🅱1 ⓞ /ˈpriːviəs/ adj. [only before noun] **1** 🅱1 happening or existing before the event or object that you are talking about ⓢⓨⓝ **prior**: *No previous experience is necessary for this job.* ◊ *The car has had only one previous owner.* ◊ *She is his daughter from a previous marriage.* ◊ *I was unable to attend because of a previous engagement.* ◊ *The judge will take into consideration any previous convictions.* **2** 🅱1 immediately before the time you are talking about ⓢⓨⓝ **preceding**: *the previous year/month/week/night* ◊ *I couldn't believe it when I heard the news. I'd only seen him the previous day.* ▶ **pre·vi·ous to** prep.: *Previous to this, she'd always been well.*

**pre·vi·ous·ly** ⓞ 🅱1 🅦 /ˈpriːviəsli/ adv. at a time before the time that you are talking about: *The building had previously been used as a hotel.* ◊ *I had visited them three days previously.*

**pre-ˈwar** adj. [usually before noun] happening or existing before a war, especially before the Second World War: *the pre-war years* ◊ *pre-war Britain*

**pre-wash** verb, noun
- verb /ˌpriːˈwɒʃ/; NAmE ˈwɑːʃ/ **1** ~ sth to wash cloth before it is used, or clothing before it is sold **2** ~ sth to give clothing an extra wash before the main wash, especially in a machine
- noun /ˈpriːwɒʃ/; NAmE wɑːʃ/ [C] an extra wash before the main wash **2** [U] a substance which is applied to clothing before washing, in order to make it cleaner

**prey** 🅸+ 🅲1 /preɪ/ noun, verb
- noun [U, sing.] **1** 🅸+ 🅲1 an animal, a bird, etc. that is hunted, killed and eaten by another: *The lion will often stalk its prey for hours.* ◊ *birds of prey* (= birds that kill for food) ⊃ WORDFINDER NOTE at HUNT **2** 🅸+ 🅲1 a person who is harmed or tricked by sb, especially for dishonest purposes: *Elderly people are easy prey for dishonest salesmen.* ⓘⓓⓜ **be/fall ˈprey to sth** (formal) **1** (of an animal) to be killed and eaten by another animal or bird **2** (of a person) to be harmed or affected by sth bad
- verb
ⓘⓓⓜ **prey on sb's ˈmind** (of a thought, problem, etc.) to make sb think and worry about it all the time
ⓟⓗⓡⓥ **ˈprey on/upon sb/sth 1** (of an animal or a bird) to hunt and kill another animal for food ⊃ HOMOPHONES at PRAISE **2** to harm sb who is weaker than you, or make use of them in a dishonest way to get what you want: *Bogus social workers have been preying on old people living alone.*

**prez** /prez/ noun (informal) president

**prez·zie** (also **pres·sie**) /ˈprezi/ noun (BrE, informal) a present that you give sb, for example for their birthday

**price** ⓞ 🅰1 /praɪs/ noun, verb
- noun **1** 🅰1 [C, U] the amount of money that you have to pay for sth: *Boat for sale, price £8000* ◊ *house/oil/share prices* ◊ *rising/falling prices* ◊ *to raise/increase prices* ◊ *to lower/cut/reduce prices* ◊ *~ for sth to charge a high/reasonable/low price for sth* ◊ *to pay/charge a price for sth* ◊ *Can you give me a price for the work* (= tell me how much you will charge)? ◊ *Children over five must pay (the) full price for the ticket.* ◊ **in ~** *Most new technology comes down in price with time.* ◊ **at a ~** *They sell quality art supplies at discount prices.* ◊ **price rises/increases/hikes/cuts** ⊃ see also ASKING PRICE, COST PRICE, CUT-PRICE, HALF-PRICE, HAMMER PRICE, MARKET PRICE, LIST PRICE, PURCHASE PRICE, SELLING PRICE, STICKER PRICE **2** 🅸+ 🅱2 [sing.] the unpleasant things that you must do or experience in order to achieve sth or as a result of achieving sth: *Criticism is part of the price of leadership.* ◊ **~ for (doing) sth** *Loneliness is a high price to pay for independence in your old age.* ◊ *Giving up his job was a small price to pay for his children's happiness.* ◊ **at a …~** *His success came at a high price.* **3** [C] (in horse racing) the numbers that tell you how much money you will receive if the horse that you bet on wins the race ⓢⓨⓝ **odds**: *Six to one is a good price for that horse.* ⊃ see also STARTING PRICE
ⓘⓓⓜ **at ˈany price** whatever the cost or the difficulties may be: *We want peace at any price.* **at a ˈprice 1** costing a lot of money: *You can buy strawberries all year round, but at a price.* **2** involving sth unpleasant: *He'll help you—at a price!* **beyond ˈprice** (formal or literary) extremely valuable or important **everyone has their ˈprice** (saying) you can persuade anyone to do sth by giving them more money or sth that they want **not at ˈany price** used to say that no amount of money would persuade you to do or to sell sth: *I wouldn't work for her again—not at any price!* **a ˈprice on sb's head** an amount of money that is offered for capturing or killing sb **put a ˈprice on sth** to say how much sth valuable is worth: *They haven't yet put a price on the business.* ◊ *You can't put a price on that sort of loyalty.* **ˈwhat price …?** (BrE, informal) **1** used to say that you think that sth you have achieved may not be worth all the problems and difficulties it causes: *What price fame and fortune?* **2** used to say that sth seems unlikely: *What*

---

### ▼ SYNONYMS

**price**

cost • value • expense • worth

These words all refer to the amount of money that you have to pay for sth.

**price** the amount of money that you have to pay for an item or service: *house prices* ◊ *How much are these? They don't have a price on them.* ◊ *I can't afford it at that price.*

**cost** the amount of money that you need in order to buy, make or do sth: *A new computer system has been installed at a cost of £80 000.*

**value** how much sth is worth in money or other goods for which it can be exchanged: *The winner will receive a prize to the value of £1000.* ⓝⓞⓣⓔ Especially in British English, **value** can also mean how much sth is worth compared with its price: *This restaurant is excellent value* (= is worth the money it costs).

**PRICE, COST OR VALUE?**
The **price** is what sb asks you to pay for an item or service: *to ask/charge a high price* ◊ *to ask/charge a high cost/value*. Obtaining or achieving sth may have a **cost**; the **value** of sth is how much other people would be willing to pay for it: *house prices* ◊ *the cost of moving house* ◊ *The house now has a market value of one million pounds.*

**expense** the money that you spend on sth; sth that makes you spend money: *The garden was transformed at great expense.* ◊ *Running a car is a big expense.*

**worth** the financial value of sb/sth: *He has a personal net worth of $10 million.* ⓝⓞⓣⓔ **Worth** is more often used to mean the practical or moral value of sth.

**PATTERNS**
- the **high** price/cost/value
- the **real/true** price/cost/value/worth
- to **put/set** a price/value **on** sth
- to **increase/reduce** the price/cost/value/expense
- to **raise/double/lower** the price/cost/value
- to **cut** the price/cost

price England winning the World Cup? ⇨ more at CHEAP
adj., PAY v.
- **verb 1** [T, usually passive, I] to fix the price of sth at a particular level: **be priced + adv./prep.** *The main courses are all reasonably priced.* ◊ *These goods are priced too high.* ◊ **be priced at sth** *The tickets are priced at $100 each.* **2 ~ sth (up)** to write or stick tickets on goods to show how much they cost **3 ~ sth** to compare the prices of different types of the same thing: *We priced various models before buying this one.*
- IDM **price yourself/sth out of the 'market** to charge such a high price for your goods, services, etc. that nobody wants to buy them

**'price controls** noun [pl.] (*economics*) limits that a government puts on the price of goods at particular times, such as when there is not enough of sth, when there is a war, etc.

**'price-fixing** noun [U] the practice of companies agreeing not to sell goods below a particular price

**'price index** noun = RETAIL PRICE INDEX

**price·less** /ˈpraɪsləs/ adj. **1** extremely valuable or important: *a priceless collection of antiques* ◊ *priceless information* ⇨ SYNONYMS at VALUABLE **2** (*informal*) extremely funny: *You should have seen his face—it was priceless!*

**'price point** noun (*business*) one of the possible prices that a company can charge for a product or service in order to create a high demand for it

**'price tag** noun a label on sth that shows how much you must pay: (*figurative*) *There is a £50 million price tag on the team's star player.* ⇨ picture at LABEL

**'price war** noun a situation in which companies or shops keep reducing the prices of their products and services in order to attract customers away from their competitors

**pricey** /ˈpraɪsi/ adj. (**prici·er, prici·est**) (*informal*) expensive ⇨ SYNONYMS at EXPENSIVE

**pri·cing** /ˈpraɪsɪŋ/ noun [U] the act of deciding how much to charge for sth: *competitive pricing* ◊ *pricing policy* ⇨ see also PREDATORY PRICING, ROAD PRICING

**prick** /prɪk/ verb, noun
- **verb 1** [T] to make a very small hole in sth with a sharp point: **~ sth** *He pricked the balloon and burst it.* ◊ **~ sth with sth** *Prick holes in the paper with a pin.* **2** [T] **~ sth (on sth)** to make a small hole in the skin so that it hurts or blood comes out: *She pricked her finger on a needle.* **3** [I, T] to make sb feel a slight pain as if they were being pricked: *He felt a pricking sensation in his throat.* ◊ **~ sth** *Tears pricked her eyes.*
- IDM **prick your 'conscience | your 'conscience pricks you** to make you feel guilty about sth; to feel guilty about sth: *Her conscience pricked her as she lied to her sister.* **prick (up) your 'ears 1** (of an animal, especially a horse or dog) to raise the ears **2** (*also* **your 'ears prick up**) (of a person) to listen carefully because you have just heard sth interesting; to listen out for sth you might hear: *Her ears pricked up at the sound of his name.*
- **noun 1** (*taboo, slang*) a PENIS **2** (*taboo, slang*) an offensive word for a stupid or unpleasant man: *Don't be such a prick!* **3** an act of making a very small hole in sth with a sharp point: *I'm going to give your finger a little prick with this needle.* **4** a slight pain caused by a sharp point or sth that feels like a sharp point: *You will feel a tiny prick in your arm.* ◊ *He could feel the hot prick of tears in his eyes.*

**prickle** /ˈprɪkl/ verb, noun
- **verb 1** [T, I] **~ (sth)** to give sb an unpleasant feeling on their skin, as if a lot of small sharp points are pushing into it: *The rough cloth prickled my skin.* ◊ *His moustache prickled when he kissed me.* **2** [I] **~ (with sth)** (of skin, eyes, etc.) to feel strange and unpleasant because you are frightened, angry, excited, etc: *Her eyes prickled with tears.* ◊ *The hairs on the back of my neck prickled when I heard the door open.* ◊ (*figurative*) *He prickled* (= became angry) *at the suggestion that it had been his fault.*
- **noun 1** a small sharp part on the STEM or leaf of a plant or on the skin of some animals: *a cactus covered in prickles* **2** a slight STINGING feeling on the skin: *a prickle of fear/excitement*

**prick·ly** /ˈprɪkli/ adj. (**prick·lier, prick·li·est**) **1** covered with prickles: *a prickly bush* **2** causing you to feel as if your skin is touching sth that is covered with prickles: *a prickly feeling* **3** (*informal*) (of a person) easily annoyed or offended SYN **touchy 4** (of a decision, an issue, etc.) difficult to deal with because people have very different ideas about it SYN **thorny**: *Let's move on to the prickly subject of taxation reform.*

**prickly 'heat** noun [U] a skin condition, common in hot countries, that causes small red spots that ITCH

**prickly 'pear** noun **1** a type of CACTUS with PRICKLES (= sharp parts like needles), with yellow flowers **2** the pink and yellow fruit of the prickly pear that is like a PEAR in shape and can be eaten

**'prick-teaser** (*also* **'prick-tease**) noun (*taboo, slang*) = COCK-TEASER

**pride** /praɪd/ noun, verb
- **noun**
- • PLEASURE **1** [U, sing.] a feeling of being pleased or satisfied that you get when you or people who are connected with you have done sth well or own sth that other people admire: *The sight of her son graduating filled her with pride.* ◊ *Success in sport is a source of national pride.* ◊ **~ in sth** *I take (a) pride in my work.* ◊ **~ in doing sth** *We take great pride in offering the best service in town.* ◊ **with ~** *I looked with pride at what I had achieved.* ⇨ SYNONYMS at SATISFACTION **2** [sing.] **the ~ of sth** a person or thing that makes people feel pleased or satisfied: *The new sports stadium is the pride of the town.*
- • RESPECT FOR YOURSELF **3** [U] the feeling of respect that you have for yourself: *Pride would not allow him to accept the money.* ◊ *Her pride was hurt.* ◊ *Losing his job was a real blow to his pride.* ◊ *It's time to swallow your pride* (= hide your feelings of pride) *and ask for your job back.* ⇨ see also GAY PRIDE **4** [U] (*disapproving*) the feeling that you are better or more important than other people: *She was full of pride and arrogance and despised ordinary people.* ⇨ see also PROUD
- • LIONS **5** [C + sing./pl. v.] a group of lions
- IDM **sb's pride and 'joy** a person or thing that causes sb to feel very pleased or satisfied **pride comes/goes before a 'fall** (*saying*) if you have too high an opinion of yourself or your abilities, sth will happen to make you look stupid **pride of 'place** the position in which sth is most easily seen, that is given to the most important thing in a particular group
- **verb**
- PHRV **'pride yourself on (doing) sth** [no passive] to be proud of sth: *She had always prided herself on her appearance.*

**priest** /priːst/ noun **1** a person who is qualified to perform religious duties and ceremonies in the Roman Catholic, Anglican and Orthodox Churches: *a parish priest* ◊ *the ordination of women priests* ⇨ compare CHAPLAIN, CLERGYMAN, MINISTER, VICAR **2** (*feminine* **priest·ess** /priːˈstes; *NAmE* ˈpriːstəs/) a person who performs religious ceremonies in some religions that are not Christian: *a Hindu/Buddhist priest* ⇨ see also HIGH PRIEST

**priest·hood** /ˈpriːsthʊd/ noun **1 the priesthood** [sing.] the job or position of being a priest: *to enter the priesthood* (= to become a priest) **2** all the priests of a particular religion or country

**priest·ly** /ˈpriːstli/ adj. [usually before noun] connected with a priest; like a priest

**'priest's hole** noun a secret space in a house where Catholic priests hid in the past at times when Catholicism was against the law in England

**prig** /prɪɡ/ noun (*disapproving*) a person who behaves in a morally correct way and who shows that they think what other people do is bad ▸ **prig·gish** adj. **prig·gish·ness** noun [U]

**prim** /prɪm/ adj. (**prim·mer, prim·mest**) **1** (*disapproving*) (of a person) always behaving in a careful and formal way, and easily shocked by anything that is rude: *You can't tell her*

# prima ballerina 1222

that joke—she's much too **prim and proper**. **2** formal and neat SYN **demure**: *a prim suit with a high-necked collar* ▶ **prim·ly** *adv.*: *'You're not supposed to say that,' she said primly.*

**prima ballerina** /ˌpriːmə ˌbæləˈriːnə/ *noun* the main woman dancer in a BALLET company

**pri·macy** /ˈpraɪməsi/ *noun* (*pl.* **-ies**) (*formal*) **1** [U] the fact of being the most important person or thing: *a belief in the primacy of the family* **2** [C] the position of an ARCHBISHOP

**prima donna** /ˌpriːmə ˈdɒnə; *NAmE* ˈdɑːnə/ *noun* **1** the main woman singer in an OPERA performance or an OPERA company **2** (*disapproving*) a person who thinks they are very important because they are good at sth, and who behaves badly when they do not get what they want

**prim·aeval** (*BrE*) = PRIMEVAL

**prima facie** /ˌpraɪmə ˈfeɪʃi/ *adj.* [only before noun] (*from Latin, law*) based on what at first seems to be true, although it may be proved false later: *prima facie evidence* ▶ **prima facie** *adv.*: *Prima facie, there is a strong case against him.*

**primal** /ˈpraɪml/ *adj.* [only before noun] (*formal*) connected with the earliest origins of life; very basic SYN **primeval**: *the primal hunter-gatherer* ◊ *a primal urge/fear*

**pri·mar·ily** /praɪˈmerəli; *BrE also* ˈpraɪmərəli/ *adv.* mainly SYN **chiefly**: *a course designed primarily for specialists* ◊ *The problem is not primarily a financial one.*

**pri·mary** /ˈpraɪməri; *NAmE* -meri/ *adj.*, *noun*
■ *adj.* **1** [only before noun] (*especially BrE*) connected with the education of children between the ages of about five and eleven: *primary teachers* ⇒ compare ELEMENTARY, SECONDARY, TERTIARY **2** [usually before noun] main; most important; basic SYN **prime**: *our primary objective/goal/purpose* ◊ *Our primary concern must be the children.* ◊ *Good healthcare is of primary importance.* ◊ *The film's primary focus is on two families.* **3** [usually before noun] (*formal or specialist*) developing or happening first; earliest: *primary causes* ◊ *The disease is still in its primary stage.*
■ *noun* (*pl.* **-ies**) (*also* **primary e'lection**) (in the US) an election in which people in a particular area vote to choose a candidate for a future important election: *the Illinois primary* ◊ *the presidential primaries* ⇒ WORDFINDER NOTE at CONGRESS

**primary 'care** (*also* **primary 'health care**) *noun* [U] the medical treatment that you receive first when you are ill, for example from your family doctor

**primary 'care physician** *noun* (*abbr.* **PCP**) (*especially NAmE*) (*BrE usually* **GP**, **general practitioner**) a doctor who is trained in general medicine and who treats patients in a local community rather than at a hospital

**primary 'care provider** *noun* (*abbr.* **PCP**) a company or organization that provides primary care

**primary 'colour** (*US* **primary 'color**) *noun* one of the three colours, red, yellow and blue, that can be mixed together to make all other colours

**primary 'health care** *noun* = PRIMARY CARE

**primary 'industry** *noun* [U, C] (*economics*) the section of industry that provides RAW MATERIALS to be made into goods, for example farming and MINING

**primary 'school** *noun* **1** (*BrE*) a school for children between the ages of 4 or 5 and 11 **2** (*NAmE, old-fashioned*) = ELEMENTARY SCHOOL ⇒ compare SECONDARY SCHOOL

**primary 'source** *noun* a document, etc. that contains information obtained by research or by observing sb/sth carefully, not taken from other books, etc. ⇒ compare SECONDARY SOURCE

**primary 'stress** *noun* [C, U] (*phonetics*) the strongest stress that is put on a syllable in a word or a phrase when it is spoken ⇒ compare SECONDARY STRESS

**pri·mate** *noun* **1** /ˈpraɪmeɪt/ any animal that belongs to the group of MAMMALS that includes humans, APES and monkeys ⇒ VISUAL VOCAB page V2 **2** /ˈpraɪmət, -meɪt/ an ARCHBISHOP (= a priest of very high rank in the Christian Church): *the Primate of all England* (= the Archbishop of Canterbury)

**prime** /praɪm/ *adj.*, *noun*, *verb*
■ *adj.* [only before noun] **1** main; most important; basic: *My prime concern is to protect my property.* ◊ *The care of the environment is of prime importance.* ◊ *He's the police's prime suspect in this case.* ⇒ SYNONYMS at MAIN **2** of the best quality; excellent: *prime (cuts of) beef* ◊ *The store has a prime position in the mall.* **3** a **prime example** of sth is one that is typical of it: *The building is a prime example of 1960s architecture.* **4** most likely to be chosen for sth; most suitable: *The house is isolated and a prime target for burglars.* ◊ *He's a prime candidate for promotion.*
■ *noun* **1** [sing.] the time in your life when you are strongest or most successful: *a young woman in her prime* ◊ *He was barely 30 and in the prime of (his) life.* ◊ *These flowers are long past their prime.* **2** [C] = PRIME NUMBER
■ *verb* **1** to prepare sb for a situation so that they know what to do, especially by giving them special information SYN **brief**: *~ sb (with sth) They had been primed with good advice.* ◊ *~ sb (for sth) She was ready and primed for action.* ◊ *~ sb to do sth He had primed his friends to give the journalists as little information as possible.* **2** *~ sth* to make sth ready for use or action: *The bomb was primed, ready to explode.* **3** *~ sth* to prepare wood, metal, etc. for painting by covering it with a special paint that helps the next layer of paint to stay on
IDM **prime the 'pump** to encourage the growth of a new or weak business or industry by putting money into it

**prime 'cost** (*also* **first cost**) *noun* [C, U] (*business*) the cost of sth calculated by adding the cost of materials used to make it and the cost of paying sb to make it, but not including costs that are connected with running a business, such as rent and electricity

**prime 'minister** (*also* **Prime 'Minister**) *noun* (*abbr.* **PM**) the main minister and leader of the government in some countries

**prime 'mover** *noun* a person or thing that starts sth and has an important influence on its development

**prime 'number** (*also* **prime**) *noun* (*mathematics*) a number that can be divided exactly only by itself and 1, for example 7, 17 and 41

**primer** *noun* **1** /ˈpraɪmə(r)/ [U, C] a type of paint that is put on wood, metal, etc. before it is painted to help the paint to stay on the surface **2** /ˈpraɪmə(r); *NAmE* ˈpriː-/ [C] (*NAmE*) a book that contains basic instructions: *The President doesn't need a primer on national security.* **3** /ˈpraɪmə(r); *NAmE* ˈpriː-/ [C] (*old-fashioned*) a book for teaching children how to read, or containing basic facts about a school subject

**prime 'rate** *noun* (in the US) the lowest rate of interest at which business customers can borrow money from banks ⇒ compare BASE RATE

**prime 'rib** *noun* [U, C] (*NAmE*) a piece of beef that is cut from the RIB section of the animal

**prime 'time** (*BrE also* **peak time**, **peak 'viewing time**) *noun* [U] the time when the greatest number of people are watching television or listening to the radio: *prime-time television*

**pri·meval** (*BrE also* **prim·aeval**) /praɪˈmiːvl/ *adj.* [usually before noun] **1** from the earliest period of the history of the world, very ancient: *primeval forests* **2** (*formal*) (of a feeling, or a desire) very strong and not based on reason, as if from the earliest period of human life: *primeval urges*

**primi·tive** /ˈprɪmətɪv/ *adj.*, *noun*
■ *adj.* **1** [usually before noun] belonging to a very simple society with no industry, etc: *primitive tribes* ◊ *primitive beliefs* **2** [usually before noun] belonging to an early stage in the development of humans or animals: *primitive man* **3** very simple and old-fashioned, especially when sth is also not convenient and comfortable SYN **crude**: *The methods of communication used during the war were primitive by today's standards.* ◊ *The facilities on the campsite were very primitive.* **4** [usually before noun] (of a feeling or a desire) very strong and not based on reason, as if from the earliest period of human life: *a primitive instinct* ▶ **primi·tive·ly** *adv.* **primi·tive·ness** *noun* [U]
■ *noun* **1** an artist of the period before the Renaissance; an example of work from this period **2** an artist who paints in a very simple style like a child; an example of the work of such an artist

**prim·i·tiv·ism** /ˈprɪmɪtɪvɪzəm/ noun [U] a belief that simple forms and ideas are the most valuable, expressed as a philosophy or in art or literature

**primo·geni·ture** /ˌpraɪməʊˈdʒenɪtʃə(r)/ noun [U] (law) the system in which the oldest son in a family receives all the property when his father dies

**prim·or·dial** /praɪˈmɔːdiəl; NAmE -ˈmɔːrd-/ adj. [usually before noun] (formal) **1** existing at or from the beginning of the world SYN primeval **2** (of a feeling or a desire) very basic SYN primeval: *primordial impulses*

**primp** /prɪmp/ verb [I, T] **~ (sth/yourself)** (often disapproving) to make yourself look attractive by arranging your hair, putting on MAKE-UP, etc.

**prim·rose** /ˈprɪmrəʊz/ noun **1** [C] a small wild plant that produces pale yellow flowers in spring ⊃ VISUAL VOCAB page V7 **2** (also ˌprimrose ˈyellow) [U] a pale yellow colour ▶ **prim·rose** (also ˌprimrose ˈyellow) adj. IDM **the primrose ˈpath** (literary) an easy life that is full of pleasure but that causes you harm in the end

**prim·ula** /ˈprɪmjələ/ noun a type of primrose that is often grown in gardens

**Pri·mus™** /ˈpraɪməs/ (also ˈPrimus stove) noun a small cooker that you can move around that burns oil. It is used especially by people who are camping.

**prince** 🅘 B1 /prɪns/ noun **1** a male member of a royal family who is not king, especially the son or GRANDSON of the king or queen: *the royal princes* ◊ *Prince Charles* ◊ *~ of … the Prince of Wales* ⊃ see also CROWN PRINCE **2** the male ruler of a small country or state that has a royal family; a male member of this family, especially the son or GRANDSON of the ruler: *~ of … the prince of Orange* ◊ *Prince Albert of Monaco* **3** (in some European countries) a NOBLEMAN **4** *~ of/among sth* (literary) a man who is thought to be one of the best in a particular field: *the prince of comedy*

ˌPrince ˈCharming noun [sing.] (usually humorous) a man who seems to be a perfect boyfriend or husband because he is very attractive, kind, etc. ORIGIN From the hero of some European fairy tales, for example *Cinderella* and *Sleeping Beauty*.

ˌPrince ˈConsort noun a title sometimes given to the husband of a queen who is himself a prince: *Prince Albert, the Prince Consort*

**prince·ling** /ˈprɪnslɪŋ/ noun (usually disapproving) a prince who rules a small or unimportant country

**prince·ly** /ˈprɪnsli/ adj. [usually before noun] **1** (usually ironic) (of a sum of money) large or generous: *I bought a bike for the princely sum of £20!* **2** (old-fashioned, formal) very grand; generous: *princely buildings* ◊ *a princely gift* **3** connected with a prince; like a prince

**prin·cess** 🅘 B1 /ˌprɪnˈses, ˈprɪnses; NAmE ˈprɪnses/ noun **1** a female member of a royal family who is not a queen, especially the daughter or GRANDDAUGHTER of the king or queen: *the royal princesses* ◊ *Princess Anne* ⊃ see also CROWN PRINCESS **2** the wife of a prince: *~ of … the Princess of Wales* **3** (disapproving) a young woman who has always been given everything that she wants, and who thinks that she is better than other people **4** (BrE, informal) used as a form of address by a man to a girl or young woman: *Is something the matter, princess?*

ˌPrincess ˈRoyal noun a title often given to the oldest daughter of a British king or queen

**prin·ci·pal** B2 /ˈprɪnsəpl/ adj., noun
■ *adj.* B2 [only before noun] most important; main: *The principal reason for this omission is lack of time.* ◊ *New roads will link the principal cities of the area.* ⊃ SYNONYMS at MAIN
■ *noun* **1** C1 (BrE, CanE) the person who is in charge of a college or (in Scotland and Canada) a university: *Peter Brown, principal of St John's College* ⊃ see also DEAN **2** C1 (NAmE) (BrE ˌhead ˈteacher) a teacher who is in charge of a school: *Principal Ray Smith* **3** [usually sing.] (finance) an amount of money that you lend to sb or invest to earn interest **4** the person who has the most important part in a play, an OPERA, etc. **5** (specialist) a person that you are representing, especially in business or law

---

# print

▼ HOMOPHONES

**principal • principle** /ˈprɪnsəpl/
• **principal** adj.: *They were joined on stage by their principal conductor.*
• **principal** noun: *The college is excited to announce the appointment of a new principal.*
• **principle** noun: *Many green activists oppose GM crops on principle.*

ˌprincipal ˈboy noun (BrE) the main male role in a PANTOMIME, usually played by a woman

**prin·ci·pal·ity** /ˌprɪnsɪˈpæləti/ noun (pl. -ies) **1** [C] a country that is ruled by a prince: *the principality of Monaco* **2 the Principality** [sing.] (BrE) Wales

**prin·ci·pal·ly** /ˈprɪnsəpli/ adv. mainly SYN chiefly: *The book is aimed principally at beginners.* ◊ *No new power stations have been built, principally because of the cost.*

ˌprincipal ˈparts noun [pl.] (grammar) the forms of a verb from which all the other forms can be made. In English these are the infinitive (for example *swim*), the past tense (*swam*) and the past participle (*swum*).

**prin·ci·ple** 🅘 B2 /ˈprɪnsəpl/ noun **1** B2 [C, usually pl., U] a moral rule or a strong belief that influences your actions: *He has high moral principles.* ◊ *Stick to your principles and tell him you won't do it.* ◊ *against your principles I refuse to lie about it; it's against my principles.* ◊ *on ~ He doesn't invest in the arms industry on principle.* ◊ *She refuses to allow her family to help her as a matter of principle.* ⊃ HOMOPHONES at PRINCIPAL **2** B2 [C] a law, a rule or a theory that sth is based on: *The same principles apply to both humans and animals.* ◊ *~of (doing) sth There are three fundamental principles of teamwork.* ◊ *to learn the basic/general principles of sth* ◊ *~for (doing) sth draft principles for the management of shared natural resources* ◊ *~behind sth The principle behind it is very simple.* **3** B2 [C] a belief that is accepted as a reason for acting or thinking in a particular way: *The welfare of the child is the guiding principle of the family courts.* ◊ *They were accused of violating the principles of democracy.* ◊ *~that … the application of the principle that men and women should receive equal pay for equal work* **4** B2 [C, U] a general or scientific rule that explains how sth works or why sth happens: *~(that …) the principle that heat rises* ◊ *in~ A tidal current turbine is similar in principle to a windmill.*
IDM **in ˈprinciple 1** if something can be done in principle, there is no good reason why it should not be done although it has not yet been done and there may be some difficulties: *In principle there is nothing that a human can do that a machine might not be able to do one day.* **2** in general but not in detail: *They have agreed to the proposal in principle but we still have to negotiate the terms.*

**prin·cipled** /ˈprɪnsəpld/ adj. **1** having strong beliefs about what is right and wrong; based on strong beliefs: *a principled woman* ◊ *to take a principled stand against abortion* OPP unprincipled **2** based on rules or truths: *a principled approach to language teaching*

**print** 🅘 A2 /prɪnt/ verb, noun
■ *verb*
• LETTERS/PICTURES **1** A2 [T, I] to produce letters, pictures, etc. on paper using a machine that puts INK (= coloured liquid) on the surface: *~(sth) I'm printing a copy of the document for you.* ◊ *(computing) Click on the icon when you want to print.* ◊ *be printed with sth Each card is printed with a different message.* ⊃ WORDFINDER NOTE at FILE
• BOOKS/NEWSPAPERS **2** A2 [T] *~sth* to produce books, newspapers, etc. by printing them in large quantities: *They printed 30000 copies of the book.*
• PUBLISH **3** A2 *~sth* [T] to publish sth in printed form: *The photo was printed in all the national newspapers.*
• PHOTOGRAPH **4** [T] *~sth (from sth)* to produce a photograph on paper from a digital file or from film
• WRITE **5** [T, I] *~(sth)* to write without joining the letters together: *Print your name and address clearly in the space provided.*

Ⓞ Oxford Phrasal Academic Lexicon (OPAL) written and spoken word lists | Ⓦ OPAL written word list | Ⓢ OPAL spoken word list

# printable

- **MAKE MARK** **6** [T] ~ **sth (in/on sth)** to make a mark on a soft surface by pressing: *The tracks of the large animal were clearly printed in the sand.* ◊ *(figurative) The memory of that day was indelibly printed on his brain.*
- **MAKE DESIGN** **7** [T] to make a design on a surface or cloth by pressing a surface against it which has been coloured with INK or DYE: ~ **A on B** *They had printed their own design on the T-shirt.* ◊ ~ **B with A** *A T-shirt printed with their own design*

**IDM** the ˌprinted ˈword/ˈpage what is published in books, newspapers, etc: *the power of the printed word* ⇒ more at LICENCE, WORTH *adj.*
**PHRV** ˌprint sth↔ˈoff/ˈout to produce a document or information from a computer in printed form ⇒ related noun PRINTOUT

■ **noun**
- **LETTERS/NUMBERS** **1** [U] letters, words, numbers, etc. that have been printed onto paper: *The tiny print was hard to read without my glasses.* ◊ **in ...~** *in large/small/bold print* ◊ *the print edition/version of the dictionary* ⇒ see also FINE PRINT, SMALL PRINT
- **NEWSPAPERS/BOOKS** **2** [U] used to refer to the business of producing newspapers, magazines and books: *the print media* ◊ *print unions*
- **MARK** **3** [C, usually pl.] a mark left by your finger, foot, etc. on the surface of sth: *His prints were found on the gun.* ◊ *There were paw prints everywhere.* ⇒ see also FINGERPRINT, FOOTPRINT
- **PICTURE** **4** [C] a picture that is cut into wood or metal then covered with INK (= coloured liquid for printing, drawing, etc.) and printed onto paper; a picture that is copied from a painting using photography: *a framed set of prints* ⇒ see also SCREEN PRINT ⊃ SYNONYMS at PICTURE
- **PHOTOGRAPH** **5** [C] a photograph produced from film: *How many sets of prints would you like?* ◊ *a colour print* ⊃ SYNONYMS at PHOTOGRAPH
- **CLOTH** **6** [U, C] cotton cloth that has a pattern printed on it; *this pattern: a cotton print dress* ◊ *a floral print* ⇒ see also BLUEPRINT

**IDM** get into ˈprint to be published: *By the time this gets into print, they'll already have left the country.* **in ˈprint 1** (of a book) still available from the company that publishes it **2** (of a person's work) printed in a book, newspaper, etc: *It was the first time he had seen his name in print.* **out of ˈprint** (of a book) no longer available from the company that publishes it

**print·able** /ˈprɪntəbl/ *adj.* (usually used with a negative) suitable to be repeated in writing and read by people: *His comment when he heard the news was not printable* (= was very rude). **OPP** unprintable

**printed ˈcircuit** *noun* a CIRCUIT for electricity in a piece of electronic equipment that uses thin pieces of metal instead of wires to carry the current

**print·er** /ˈprɪntə(r)/ *noun* **1** a machine for printing text on paper, especially one connected to a computer: *a colour printer* ◊ *a printer cartridge* ⇒ see also INKJET PRINTER, LASER PRINTER **2** a person or a company whose job is printing books, etc. **3** **printer's** (*pl.* **printers**) a place where books, etc. are printed

**print·ing** /ˈprɪntɪŋ/ *noun* **1** [U] the act of producing letters, pictures, patterns, etc. on sth by pressing a surface covered with INK (= coloured liquid for printing, drawing, etc.) against it: *the invention of printing* ◊ *colour printing* **2** [C] the act of printing a number of copies of a book at one time: *The book is in its sixth printing.* **3** [U] a type of writing when you write all the letters separately and do not join them together

**ˈprinting press** *noun* a machine that produces books, newspapers, etc. by pressing a surface covered in INK (= coloured liquid for writing, drawing, etc.) onto paper

**print·mak·ing** /ˈprɪntmeɪkɪŋ/ *noun* [U] the process of creating pictures or designs by printing them from specially prepared plates or blocks ▶ **print·maker** *noun*

**print on deˈmand** *noun* (*abbr.* POD /ˌpiː əʊ ˈdiː/) a system of printing books only when a customer wants one: *The titles are available through print on demand.* ◊ *This is a print-on-demand title.*

**print·out** /ˈprɪntaʊt/ *noun* [U, C] a page or set of pages containing information in printed form from a computer: *a printout of text downloaded from the internet* ⇒ compare READ-OUT

**ˈprint run** *noun* (*specialist*) the number of copies of a book, magazine, etc. printed at one time

**print·works** /ˈprɪntwɜːks; NAmE -wɜːrks/ *noun* (*pl.* **printworks**) (*BrE*) a factory where patterns are printed on cloth

**prion** /ˈpriːɒn; NAmE ˈpriːɑːn/ *noun* (*biology*) a very small unit of PROTEIN that is believed to be the cause of brain diseases such as BSE, CJD and SCRAPIE

**prior** /ˈpraɪə(r)/ *adj., noun*
■ *adj.* [only before noun] (*formal*) **1** happening or existing before sth else or before a particular time: *Although not essential, some prior knowledge of statistics is desirable.* ◊ *This information must not be disclosed without prior written consent.* ◊ *Visits are by prior arrangement.* ◊ *Please give us prior notice if you need an evening meal.* ◊ *She will be unable to attend because of a prior engagement.* **2** already existing and therefore more important: *They have a prior claim to the property.* **3** **prior to** before sth: *during the week prior to the meeting*
■ *noun* (*feminine* **pri·or·ess** /ˈpraɪərəs; *BrE also* ˌpraɪəˈres/) **1** a person who is in charge of a group of MONKS or NUNS living in a PRIORY **2** (in an ABBEY) a person next in rank below an ABBOT or ABBESS

**pri·ori** ⊃ A PRIORI

**pri·or·it·ize** (*BrE also* -ise) /praɪˈɒrətaɪz; NAmE -ˈɔːr- -ˈɑːr-/ *verb* **1** [T, I] ~ **(sth)** to put tasks, problems, etc. in order of importance, so that you can deal with the most important first: *You should make a list of all the jobs you have to do and prioritize them.* **2** [T] ~ **sth** (*formal*) to treat sth as being more important than other things: *The organization was formed to prioritize the needs of older people.* ▶ **pri·ori·tiz·ation, -isa·tion** /praɪˌɒrətaɪˈzeɪʃn; NAmE -ˌɔːrətəˈz-; -ˌɑːr-/ *noun* [U]

**pri·or·ity** /praɪˈɒrəti; NAmE -ˈɔːr-; -ˈɑːr-/ *noun* (*pl.* -**ies**) **1** [C] something that you think is more important than other things and should be dealt with first: *a high/low priority* ◊ *Education is a top priority.* ◊ *Our first priority is to improve standards.* ◊ *Financial security was high on his list of priorities.* ◊ *You need to get your priorities right* (= decide what is important to you). ◊ (*NAmE*) *You need to get your priorities straight.* **2** [U] the most important place among various things that have to be done or among a group of people **SYN** precedence: *Club members will be given priority.* ◊ *The search for a new vaccine will take priority over all other medical research.* ◊ *Priority cases, such as homeless families, get dealt with first.* **3** [U] (*BrE*) the right of a vehicle to go before other traffic at a particular place on a road **SYN** right of way: *Buses have priority at this junction.*

**pri·ory** /ˈpraɪəri/ *noun* (*pl.* -**ies**) a building where a community of MONKS or NUNS lives, which is smaller and less important than an ABBEY

**prise** (*especially BrE*) (*NAmE* **prize**) /praɪz/ (*also* **pry** *especially in NAmE*) *verb* to use force to separate sth from sth else: ~ **sth + adv./prep.** *He prised her fingers from the bag and took it from her.* ◊ ~ **sth + adj.** *She used a knife to prise open the lid.*
**PHRV** ˌprise sth↔ˈout (of sb) | ˌprise sth from sb to force sb to give you information about sth/sth

**prism** /ˈprɪzəm/ *noun* **1** (*geometry*) a solid figure with ends that are PARALLEL (= the same distance apart at every point) and of the same size and shape, and with sides whose opposite edges are equal and PARALLEL ⇒ picture at SOLID **2** a clear glass or plastic object, often with ends in the shape of a TRIANGLE, which separates light that passes through it into the colours of the RAINBOW

**pris·mat·ic** /prɪzˈmætɪk/ *adj.* **1** (*specialist*) using or containing a prism; in the shape of a prism **2** (*literary*) (of colours) formed by a prism; very bright and clear

**prison** /ˈprɪzn/ *noun* **1** [C, U] a building where people are kept as a punishment for a crime they have committed, or while they are waiting for trial **SYN** jail: *He was sent to prison for five years.* ◊ **in ~ (for**

sth / for doing sth) *Her son is in prison for murder.* ◇ **out of ~ When did she get out of prison?** ◇ *a **maximum-security prison** ◇ a **prison sentence/term** ◇ a **prison cell** ◇ the **prison population** (= the total number of prisoners in a country) ◇ (BrE) a **prison officer** ◇ (NAmE) a **prison guard*** ⊃ see also OPEN PRISON ⊃ note at SCHOOL

**WORDFINDER** cell, death row, discharge, justice, parole, probation, remission, sentence, warder

**2** [U] the system of keeping people in prisons: *the prison service/system* ◇ *The government insists that 'prison works'.* **3** [C] a place or situation from which sb cannot escape: *His hospital room had become a prison.*

**'prison camp** *noun* a guarded camp where prisoners, especially prisoners of war or political prisoners, are kept

**pris·on·er** /ˈprɪznə(r)/ *noun* **1** a person who is kept in prison as a punishment, or while they are waiting for trial: *The number of prisoners serving life sentences has fallen.* ◇ *They called for the **prisoners to be released**.* ◇ *They are demanding the release of all political prisoners.* **2** a person who has been captured, for example by an enemy, and is being kept somewhere: *He was **taken prisoner** by rebel soldiers.* ◇ *They are **holding her prisoner** and demanding a large ransom.* ◇ (figurative) *She is afraid to go out and has become a virtual prisoner in her own home.*

**prisoner of 'conscience** *noun* (*pl.* **prisoners of conscience**) a person who is kept in prison because of his or her political or religious beliefs

**prisoner of 'war** *noun* (*pl.* **prisoners of war**) (*abbr.* **POW**) a person, usually a member of the armed forces, who is captured by the enemy during a war and kept in a prison camp until the war has finished

**'prison visitor** *noun* (in the UK) a person who visits people in prison in order to help them, and who does not get paid for doing so

**prissy** /ˈprɪsi/ *adj.* (*informal, disapproving*) too careful to always behave correctly and appearing easily shocked by rude behaviour, etc. **SYN** **prudish**

**pris·tine** /ˈprɪstiːn/ *adj.* **1** fresh and clean, as if new **SYN** **immaculate**: *The car is **in pristine condition**.* **2** not developed or changed in any way; left in its original condition **SYN** **unspoiled**: *pristine, pollution-free beaches*

**priv·acy** /ˈprɪvəsi; NAmE ˈpraɪ-/ *noun* [U] **1** the state of being alone and not watched or interrupted by other people: *She was longing for some peace and privacy.* ◇ *I value my privacy.* ◇ **in the ~ of sth** *He read the letter later in the privacy of his own room.* **2** the state of being free from the attention of the public: *freedom of speech and the right to privacy* ◇ *privacy rights/issues* ◇ *She complained that the photographs were an invasion of her privacy.*

**pri·vate** /ˈpraɪvət/ *adj., noun*
■ *adj.*
• **NOT PUBLIC 1** [usually before noun] belonging to or for the use of a particular person or group; not for public use: *The sign said, '**Private** property. Keep out.'* ◇ *a **private** jet* ◇ *Those are my father's **private** papers.* ◇ *The hotel has 110 bedrooms, all with **private** bathrooms.* ⊃ see also SEMIPRIVATE
• **CONVERSATION/MEETING 2** intended for or involving a particular person or group of people, not for people in general or for others to know about: *a **private** conversation* ◇ *We agreed to **keep** our arrangement **private**.* ◇ *They were sharing a **private** joke.* ◇ *Senior defence officials held **private** talks.*
• **FEELINGS/INFORMATION 3** that you do not want other people to know about **SYN** **secret**: *her **private** thoughts and feelings*
• **NOT OWNED/RUN BY STATE 4** [usually before noun] owned or managed by an individual person or an independent company rather than by the state: *a **private** firm/business/hospital* ◇ *The painting is now in a **private** collection.* ◇ *The area has attracted substantial **private** investment.* **OPP** **public 5** (of education or medical care) provided for a fee by an individual person or an independent organization rather than by the state: *She gives private*

1225 **private secretary**

*English lessons at weekends.* ◇ (BrE) *If I can afford it, I think I'll **go private** (= pay for medical care rather than use the government service).* **6** [only before noun] working or acting for yourself rather than for the state or for a group or company: *a **private** contractor/investigator* ◇ *a **private** citizen/individual* ◇ *We got the money from a **private** investor.*
• **NOT WORK 7** [usually before noun] not connected with your work or official position: *a politician's **private** life* ◇ *She claimed she was acting in a **private** capacity.*
• **QUIET 8** where you are not likely to be interrupted; quiet: *Let's go somewhere a bit more private.* **OPP** **public**
• **PERSON 9** [usually before noun] not wanting to share thoughts and feelings with other people: *He's a very private person.*
• **MONEY 10** that you receive from property or other sources but do not have to earn: *He has a **private** income.*
▶ **pri·vate·ly** *adv.*: *Can we speak privately?* ◇ *In public he supported the official policy, but privately he was sure it would fail.* ◇ *a privately owned company* ◇ *Their children were educated privately.* ◇ *She smiled, but privately she was furious.*
■ *noun* **1** [C] (*abbr.* **Pte**) a soldier of the lowest rank in the army: *Private (John) Smith* **2 privates** [pl.] (*informal*) = PRIVATE PARTS

**IDM** **in 'private** with nobody else present: *Is there somewhere we can discuss this in private?* ⊃ compare IN PUBLIC

**private 'company** (*also* **private limited 'company**) *noun* (*business*) a business that may not offer its shares for sale to the public ⊃ compare PUBLIC COMPANY, PLC

**private de'tective** (*also* **private in'vestigator**) (*also informal* **private 'eye**) *noun* a detective who is not in the police, but who can be employed to find out information, find a missing person, follow sb, etc.

**private 'enterprise** *noun* [U] the economic system in which industry or business is owned by independent companies or private people and is not controlled by the government ⊃ compare FREE ENTERPRISE

**private 'equity** *noun* [U] (*finance*) investment made in a company, usually a small one, whose shares are not bought and sold by the public

**priv·at·eer** /ˌpraɪvəˈtɪə(r); NAmE -ˈtɪr/ *noun* a ship used in the past for attacking and stealing from other ships

**private 'law** *noun* [U] (*law*) the branch of the law that relates to individual people and their property

**private 'member** *noun* (in the British political system) a member of parliament who is not a minister in the government

**private 'member's bill** *noun* (in the British political system) a law that is suggested by a member of parliament who is not a minister in the government and that is not part of the government's plans

**private 'parts** (*also informal* **pri·vates**) *noun* [pl.] a polite way of referring to the sexual organs without saying their names

**private 'patient** *noun* (in the UK) a person who is treated by a doctor outside the National Health Service and who pays for their treatment

**private 'practice** *noun* **1** [U] (of a profession) the fact of working on your own or in a small independent company rather than as an employee of the government or a large company: **in ~** *Most solicitors in England and Wales are in private practice.* **2** [U, C] (in the UK) the fact of providing medical care outside the National Health Service, which people must pay for; a place providing this care

**private 'school** (*also* **independent 'school**) *noun* a school that receives no money from the government and where the education of the students is paid for by their parents ⊃ compare FREE SCHOOL, PUBLIC SCHOOL, STATE SCHOOL

**private 'secretary** *noun* **1** a secretary whose job is to deal with the more important and personal affairs of a business person **2** a CIVIL SERVANT who acts as an assistant to a senior government official ⊃ see also PARLIAMENTARY PRIVATE SECRETARY

s see | t tea | v van | w wet | z zoo | ʃ shoe | ʒ vision | tʃ chain | dʒ jam | θ thin | ð this | ŋ sing

**the ˌprivate ˈsector** noun [sing.] the part of the economy of a country that is not under the direct control of the government ⇒ compare PUBLIC SECTOR, THIRD SECTOR

**ˌprivate ˈsoldier** noun a soldier of the lowest rank

**ˌprivate ˈview** (also ˌprivate ˈviewing) noun an occasion when a few people are invited to look at an exhibition of paintings before it is open to the public

**pri·va·tion** /praɪˈveɪʃn/ noun [C, usually pl., U] (formal) a lack of the basic things that people need for living **SYN** hardship: *the privations of poverty* ◊ *They endured years of suffering and privation.*

**pri·vat·iza·tion** /ˌpraɪvətaɪˈzeɪʃn; NAmE -təˈz-/ noun [U] the act of selling a business or an industry so that it is no longer owned by the government: *There were fears that privatization would lead to job losses.*

**pri·vat·ize** (BrE also **-ise**) /ˈpraɪvətaɪz/ verb ~ sth to sell a business or an industry so that it is no longer owned by the government **SYN** denationalize **OPP** nationalize

**priv·et** /ˈprɪvɪt/ noun [U] a bush with small dark green leaves that remain on the bush and stay green all year, often used for garden HEDGES: *a privet hedge*

**priv·il·ege** /ˈprɪvəlɪdʒ/ noun, verb
- **noun 1** [C] a special right or advantage that a particular person or group of people has: *Education should be a universal right and not a privilege.* ◊ *You can enjoy all the benefits and privileges of club membership.* **2** [U] (disapproving) the rights and advantages that rich and powerful people in a society have: *As a member of the nobility, his life had been one of wealth and privilege.* **3** [sing.] something that you are proud and lucky to have the opportunity to do **SYN** honour: *I hope to have the privilege of working with them again.* ◊ *It was a great privilege to hear her sing.* ⇒ SYNONYMS at PLEASURE **4** [C, U] (specialist) a special right to do or say things without being punished: *parliamentary privilege* (= the special right of members of parliament to say particular things without risking legal action) ⇒ see also EXECUTIVE PRIVILEGE, PARLIAMENTARY PRIVILEGE
- **verb** ~ sb/sth (formal) to give sb/sth special rights or advantages that others do not have **SYN** favour: *education policies that privilege the children of wealthy parents*

**priv·il·eged** /ˈprɪvəlɪdʒd/ adj. **1** (sometimes disapproving) having special rights or advantages that most people do not have: *Those in authority were in a privileged position.* ◊ *She comes from a privileged background.* ◊ *In those days, only a privileged few had the vote.* **2** [not before noun] having an opportunity to do sth that makes you feel proud **SYN** honoured: *We are privileged to welcome you as our speaker this evening.* **3** (law) (of information) known only to a few people and legally protected so that it does not have to be made public **SYN** confidential

**privy** /ˈprɪvi/ adj., noun
- **adj.** ~ to sth (formal) allowed to know about sth secret: *She was not privy to any information contained in the letters.*
- **noun** (pl. **-ies**) (old-fashioned) a toilet, especially an outdoor one

**the ˌPrivy ˈCouncil** noun [sing. + sing./pl. v.] (in the UK) a group of people who advise the king or queen on political affairs ▸ **ˌPrivy ˈCouncillor** noun

**the ˌprivy ˈpurse** noun [sing.] (in the UK) an amount of money that the government gives to the king or queen to pay his or her private expenses plus some official expenses

**prize** /praɪz/ noun, adj., verb
- **noun 1** an award that is given to a person who wins a competition, race, etc. or who does very good work: *She was awarded the Nobel Peace Prize.* ◊ *He won first prize in the woodwind section.* ◊ *The prize went to the grey long-haired cat.* ◊ ~ for (doing) sth *There are no prizes for guessing* (= it is very easy to guess) *who she was with.* ◊ *a cash prize of $5000* ◊ *His film took the top prize at Cannes last year.* ◊ *I won £500 in prize money.* ⇒ see also BOOBY PRIZE, CONSOLATION PRIZE, NOBEL PRIZE ⇒ WORDFINDER NOTE at COMPETITION **2** something very important or valuable that is difficult to achieve or obtain: *World peace is the greatest prize of all.*
- **adj.** [only before noun] **1** (especially of an animal, a flower or a vegetable) good enough to win a prize in a competition: *prize cattle* **2** being a very good example of its kind: *a prize student* ◊ *He's a prize specimen of the human race!* ◊ (informal) *She's a prize idiot* (= very silly).
- **verb 1** [usually passive] to value sth highly **SYN** treasure: ~ sth *an era when honesty was prized above all other virtues* ◊ ~ sth for sth *Oil of cedarwood is highly prized for its use in perfumery.* **2** (NAmE) = PRISE

**prized** /praɪzd/ adj. [only before noun] very valuable to sb: *I lost some of my most prized possessions in the fire.*

**prize·fight** /ˈpraɪzfaɪt/ noun a BOXING match that is fought for money, especially when the match has not been officially LICENSED ▸ **prize·fight·er** noun **prize·fight·ing** noun [U]

**ˈprize-giving** noun (BrE) a ceremony at which prizes are given to people who have done very good work

**prize·win·ner** (also **prize winner**) /ˈpraɪzwɪnə(r)/ noun a person who has won a prize ▸ **ˈprize-winning** adj. [only before noun]: *a prizewinning story*

**pro** /prəʊ/ noun, adj., prep.
- **noun** (pl. **pros**) (informal) a person who works as a professional, especially in a sport: *a golf pro* ◊ *He handled the situation like an old pro* (= sb who has a lot of experience). **IDM** **the pros and ˈcons** the advantages and disadvantages of sth: *We weighed up the pros and cons.*
- **adj.** (especially NAmE) (in sport) professional: *a pro wrestler* ◊ *pro football* ◊ *a young boxer who's just turned pro*
- **prep.** (informal) if sb is pro sb/sth, they are in favour of or support that person or thing: *He has always been pro the environment.* ⇒ compare ANTI

**pro-** /prəʊ/ prefix (in adjectives) in favour of; supporting: *pro-democracy* ⇒ compare ANTI-

**pro·act·ive** /ˌprəʊˈæktɪv/ adj. (of a person or policy) controlling a situation by making things happen rather than waiting for things to happen and then reacting to them ⇒ compare REACTIVE ▸ **pro·act·ive·ly** adv.

**pro-am** /ˌprəʊ ˈæm/ adj. [only before noun] (in sport) involving both professional and AMATEUR players: *a pro-am golf tournament* ▸ **pro-ˈam** noun: *to play in a pro-am*

**prob·abil·ist·ic** /ˌprɒbəbəˈlɪstɪk; NAmE ˌprɑːb-/ adj. [usually before noun] (specialist) (of methods, arguments, etc.) based on the idea that, as we cannot be certain about things, we can base our beliefs or actions on what is likely

**prob·abil·ity** /ˌprɒbəˈbɪləti; NAmE ˌprɑːb-/ noun (pl. **-ies**) **1** [U, C] how likely sth is to happen **SYN** likelihood: *The probability is that prices will rise rapidly.* ◊ *There seemed to be a high probability of success.* **2** [C] a thing that is likely to happen: *A fall in interest rates is a strong probability in the present economic climate.* ◊ *It now seems a probability rather than just a possibility.* **3** [C, U] (mathematics) a RATIO showing the chances that a particular thing will happen: *There is a 60 per cent probability that the population will be infected with the disease.* **IDM** **in ˌall probaˈbility ...** it is very likely that: *In all probability he failed to understand the consequences of his actions.* ⇒ more at BALANCE n.

**prob·able** /ˈprɒbəbl; NAmE ˈprɑːb-/ adj., noun
- **adj.** likely to happen, to exist or to be true: *the probable cause/explanation/outcome* ◊ *highly/quite/most probable* ◊ *It is probable that the disease has a genetic element.* ⇒ compare IMPROBABLE
- **noun** ~ (for sth) (especially BrE) a person or an animal that is likely to win a race or to be chosen for a team

**ˌprobable ˈcause** noun [U] (especially NAmE, law) good reason to think that a crime has been committed: *If there is probable cause, a judge can rule to give a search warrant.*

**prob·ably** /ˈprɒbəbli; NAmE ˈprɑːb-/ adv. used to say that sth is likely to happen or to be true: *You're probably right.* ◊ *I think that's probably true.* ◊ *It'll probably be OK.* ◊ *It was the best known and probably the most popular of her songs.* ◊ *'Is he going to be there?' 'Probably.'* ◊ *'Do we need the car?' 'Probably not.'* ◊ *As you probably* know, I'm going to be changing jobs soon. ◊ *The two cases are most probably connected.* ⇒ LANGUAGE BANK at PERHAPS

**pro·bate** /ˈprəʊbeɪt/ *noun, verb*
- *noun* [U] (*law*) the fact of officially proving that a WILL (= a legal document that says what is to happen to a person's property when they die) is correct according to the law
- *verb* ~ **sth** (*NAmE, law*) to prove that a WILL is correct according to the law

**pro·ba·tion** /prəˈbeɪʃn; *NAmE* proʊˈb-/ *noun* [U] **1** (*law*) a system that allows a person who has committed a crime not to go to prison if they behave well and if they see an official (called a PROBATION OFFICER) regularly for a fixed period of time: *He was given two years' probation.* ◊ **on** ~ *The prisoner was put on probation.* ⇒ WORDFINDER NOTE at PRISON **2** a time of training and testing when you start a new job to see if you are suitable for the work: *a period of probation* ⇒ WORDFINDER NOTE at TRAINING **3** (*NAmE*) a fixed period of time during which a student who has behaved badly or not worked hard must improve their work or their behaviour ▶ **pro·ba·tion·ary** /prəˈbeɪʃnəri; *NAmE* proʊˈbeɪʃəneri/ *adj.*: *a probationary period* ◊ *young probationary teachers*

**pro·ba·tion·er** /prəˈbeɪʃnə(r); *NAmE* proʊˈb-/ *noun* **1** a person who is new in a job and is being watched to see if they are suitable **2** a person who is seeing a PROBATION OFFICER because of having committed a crime

**proˈbation officer** *noun* a person whose job is to check on people who are on probation and help them

**probe** /prəʊb/ *noun, verb*
- *noun* **1** ~ (**into sth**) (used especially in newspapers) a complete and careful investigation of sth: *a police probe into the financial affairs of the company* **2** (*also* **ˈspace probe**) a SPACECRAFT without people on board which obtains information and sends it back to earth **3** (*specialist*) a long, thin metal tool used by doctors for examining inside the body **4** (*specialist*) a small device put inside sth and used by scientists to test sth or record information
- *verb* **1** [I, T] to ask questions in order to find out secret or hidden information about sb/sth SYN **investigate**: ~ (**into sth**) *He didn't like the media probing into his past.* ◊ ~ **sth** *a TV programme that probed government scandals in the 1990s* ◊ + **speech** *'Then what happened?' he probed.* **2** [T] ~ **sth** to touch, examine or look for sth, especially with a long, thin instrument: *The doctor probed the wound for signs of infection.* ◊ *Searchlights probed the night sky.*

**prob·ing** /ˈprəʊbɪŋ/ *adj.* **1** intended to discover the truth: *They asked a lot of probing questions.* **2** examining sb/sth closely: *She looked away from his dark probing eyes.* ▶ **prob·ing** *noun* [U, C]: *the journalist's unwanted probings*

**pro·biot·ic** /ˌprəʊbaɪˈɒtɪk; *NAmE* -ˈɑːt-/ *adj.* [only before noun] encouraging the growth of bacteria that have a good effect on the body: *probiotic products/yogurt/cheese*

**prob·ity** /ˈprəʊbəti/ *noun* [U] (*formal*) the quality of being completely honest: *financial probity*

**prob·lem** 🅞 A1 🅞 /ˈprɒbləm; *NAmE* ˈprɑːb-/ *noun, adj.*
- *noun* **1** A1 a thing that is difficult to deal with or to understand: *big/serious/major problems* ◊ *She has a lot of health problems.* ◊ *financial/social/technical problems* ◊ *Let me know if you have any problems.* ◊ *to address/tackle/solve a problem* ◊ (*especially NAmE*) *to fix a problem* ◊ *If he chooses Mary it's bound to cause problems.* ◊ *The problem first arose in 2018.* ◊ ~ **with sth** *There is a problem with this argument.* ◊ ~ **of sth** *the problem of drug abuse* ◊ ~ **of doing sth** *Most students face the problem of funding themselves while they are studying.* ◊ ~ **for sb** *Unemployment is a very real problem for graduates now.* ◊ *It's a nice table! The only problem is (that) it's too big for our room.* ◊ *Stop worrying about their marriage—it isn't your problem.* ◊ *There's no history of heart problems* (= disease connected with the heart) *in our family.* ⇒ see also ATTITUDE PROBLEM, TEETHING PROBLEMS **2** a question that can be answered by using logical thought or mathematics: *mathematical problems* ◊ *to find the answer to the problem* ⇒ WORDFINDER NOTE at MATHS
- IDM **have a ˈproblem with sth/sb** to disagree with or object to sth/sb: *I have no problem with you working at* home tomorrow. ◊ (*informal*) *We are going to do this my way. Do you have a problem with that?* (= showing that you are impatient with the person that you are speaking to) **ˈit's / that's not ˈmy problem** (*informal*) used to show that you do not care about sb else's difficulties **no ˈproblem** (*informal*) **1** 🅞 A1 (*also* **not a ˈproblem**) used to show that you are happy to help sb or that sth will be easy to do: *'Can I pay by credit card?' 'Yes, no problem.'* **2** 🅞 A1 used after sb has thanked you or said they are sorry for sth: *'Thanks for the ride.' 'No problem.'* **that's ˈher/ˈhis/ˈtheir/ˈyour problem** (*informal*) used to show that you think a person should deal with their own difficulties **what's your ˈproblem?** (*informal*) used to show that you think sb is being unreasonable: *What's your problem?—I only asked if you could help me for ten minutes.*
- *adj.* [only before noun] causing problems for other people or yourself: *She was a problem child, always in trouble with the police.* ◊ *a new approach to problem drinking*

**prob·lem·at·ic** /ˌprɒbləˈmætɪk; *NAmE* ˌprɑːb-/ (*also less frequent* **prob·lem·at·ic·al** /ˌprɒbləˈmætɪkl; *NAmE* ˌprɑːb-/) *adj.* difficult to deal with or to understand; full of problems; not certain to be successful: *The situation is more problematic than we first thought.* OPP **unproblematic**

**ˈproblem-solving** *noun* [U] the act of finding ways of dealing with problems

**pro ˈbono** /ˌprəʊ ˈbəʊnəʊ/ *adj.* [only before noun] (*from Latin*) (especially of legal work) done without asking for payment ▶ **pro ˈbono** *adv.*

**pro·bos·cis** /prəˈbɒsɪs; *NAmE* proʊˈbɑːs-, -skɪs/ *noun* (*pl.* **pro·bos·ces** /prəˈbɒsiːz; *NAmE* proʊˈbɑːs-, -skiːz/, **pro·bos·cises**) (*specialist*) **1** the long flexible nose of some animals, such as an elephant **2** the long thin mouth, like a tube, of some insects **3** (*humorous*) a large human nose

**probs** /prɒbz; *NAmE* prɑːbz/ *noun* [pl.]
- IDM **no ˈprobs** (*informal*) used to mean 'there is no problem': *I can let you have it by next week. No probs.*

**pro·ced·ure** 🅞 B2 🅞 /prəˈsiːdʒə(r)/ *noun* **1** 🅞 B2 [C, U] a way of doing sth, especially the usual or correct way: *emergency/safety/disciplinary procedures* ◊ *Making a complaint is quite a simple procedure.* ◊ *The school in this case did not follow the correct procedure.* ◊ **to follow normal/standard/the proper procedure** ◊ ~ **for (doing) sth** *The procedure for logging on to the network involves a password.* **2** [U] the official or formal way of doing sth, especially in business, law or politics: *court/legal/parliamentary procedure* **3** [C] (*medical*) a medical operation: *a routine surgical procedure* ◊ *to perform/undergo a procedure* ⇒ WORDFINDER NOTE at OPERATION ▶ **pro·ced·ural** /-dʒərəl/ *adj.* (*formal*): *procedural rules* ⇒ see also POLICE PROCEDURAL

**pro·ceed** 🅞 B2 /prəˈsiːd; *NAmE* proʊs-/ *verb* 🅞 B2 **1** [I] ~ **(with sth)** to continue doing sth that has already been started; to continue being done: *We're not sure whether we still want to proceed with the deal.* ◊ *Work is proceeding slowly.* **2** 🅞 B2 [I] ~ **to do sth** to do sth next, after having done sth else first SYN **go on**: *He outlined his plans and then proceeded to explain them in more detail.* ◊ (*humorous*) *Having said she wasn't hungry, she then proceeded to order a three-course meal.* **3** 🅞 B2 [I] + **adv./prep.** (*formal*) to move or travel in a particular direction: *The marchers proceeded slowly along the street.* ◊ *Passengers for Rome should proceed to Gate 32 for boarding*
- PHRV **proˈceed against sb** (*law*) to start a court case against sb **proˈceed from sth** (*formal*) to be caused by or be the result of sth

**pro·ceed·ing** 🅞 C1 /prəˈsiːdɪŋ/ *noun* (*formal*) **1** 🅞 C1 [C, usually pl.] the process of using a court to settle an argument or to deal with a complaint: *court/legal/judicial proceedings* ◊ *bankruptcy/divorce/extradition proceedings* ◊ ~ **(against sb) (for sth)** *There was enough evidence to bring criminal proceedings against her.* **2** 🅞 C1 **proceedings** [pl.] an event or a series of actions: *The Mayor will open the proceedings at the City Hall tomorrow.* ◊ *We watched the proceedings from the balcony.* **3** **proceedings** [pl.] the official written report of a meeting, etc.

# proceeds

**pro·ceeds** /ˈprəʊsiːdz/ noun [pl.] the money that you receive when you sell sth or organize a performance, etc.; profits: *She sold her car and bought a piano with the proceeds.* ◇ *~ of/from sth The proceeds of the concert will go to charity.*

**pro·cess¹** /ˈprəʊses; NAmE ˈprɑːs-/ noun, verb ◇ see also PROCESS²

■ noun 1 a series of things that are done in order to achieve a particular result: *the consultation/planning process* ◇ *Each time we have to go through the whole decision-making process again.* ◇ *I'm afraid getting things changed will be a slow process.* ◇ *mental/cognitive/thought processes* ◇ *~ of doing sth They began the difficult process of reforming the education system.* ◇ *Find which food you are allergic to by a process of elimination.* ◇ **in the ~ of doing sth** *We're in the process of selling our house.* ◇ **in the ~** *I was moving some furniture and I twisted my ankle in the process* (= while I was doing it). ◇ see also PEACE PROCESS  2 a series of things that happen, especially ones that result in natural changes: *the ageing/healing process* ◇ *It's a normal part of the learning process.* 3 a method of doing or making sth, especially one that is used in industry: *manufacturing processes* ◇ *She is involved in the production process from start to finish.* ◇ see also FOUR-COLOUR PROCESS ◇ **WORDFINDER NOTE** at FACTORY ◇ see also DUE PROCESS OF LAW

■ verb 1 [often passive] to treat raw material, food, etc. in order to change it, preserve it, etc: **(be) processed** *Most of the food we buy is processed in some way.* ◇ *processed cheese/meats*  2 [often passive] ~ sth to deal officially with a document, request, etc: *It will take a week for your application to be processed.*  3 [often passive] ~ sth (*computing*) to perform a series of operations on data in a computer  4 ~ sth / ~ what, how, etc ... to understand the meaning of sth that has happened or been said: *My brain slowly processed the fact that I was free to leave.*

## LANGUAGE BANK

**process**
Describing a process
- This diagram **illustrates the process** of paper-making. / This diagram **shows how** paper is made.
- **First / First of all**, logs are delivered to a paper mill, where the bark is removed and the wood is cut into small chips.
- **Next / Second**, the wood chips are pulped, either using chemicals or in a pulping machine.
- Pulping breaks down the internal structure of the wood and **enables / allows** the natural oils **to** be removed.
- **Once / After** the wood has been pulped, the pulp is bleached **in order to** remove impurities. / ...is bleached **so that** impurities **can** be removed.
- **The next stage is to** feed the pulp into the paper machine, where it is mixed with water **and then** poured onto a wire conveyor belt.
- **As** the pulp travels along the conveyor belt, the water drains away. **This causes** the solid material **to** sink to the bottom, forming a layer of paper.
- **At this point** the new paper is still wet, **so** it is passed between large heated rollers, which press out the remaining water and **simultaneously** dry the paper / ...dry the paper **at the same time**.
- **The final stage is to** wind the paper onto large rolls. / **Finally**, the paper is wound onto large rolls.
◇ note at FIRSTLY, LASTLY
◇ LANGUAGE BANK at CONCLUSION, FIRST

**pro·cess²** /prəˈses/ verb [I] + adv./prep. (*formal*) to walk or move along slowly in, or as if in, a procession ◇ see also PROCESS¹

**pro·cess·ing** /ˈprəʊsesɪŋ; NAmE ˈprɑːs-/ noun [U]  1 the treatment of raw material, food, etc. in order to change it, preserve it, etc: *the food processing industry* ◇ *a sewage processing plant*  2 the process of dealing officially with a document, request, etc: *errors in the processing of financial transactions* ◇ see also BATCH PROCESSING, CENTRAL PROCESSING UNIT, DATA PROCESSING,

NATURAL LANGUAGE PROCESSING, PARALLEL PROCESSING, WORD PROCESSING

**pro·ces·sion** /prəˈseʃn/ noun  1 [C, U] a line of people or vehicles that move along slowly, especially as part of a ceremony; the act of moving in this way: *a funeral procession* ◇ *a torchlight procession* ◇ *The procession made its way down the hill.* ◇ **in ~** *Groups of unemployed people from all over the country marched in procession to the capital.*  2 [C] a number of people who come one after the other: *A procession of waiters appeared bearing trays of food.*

**pro·ces·sion·al** /prəˈseʃənl/ adj. [only before noun] used in a procession, especially a religious one; connected with a procession

**pro·ces·sor** /ˈprəʊsesə(r); NAmE ˈprɑːs-/ noun  1 a machine, person or company that processes things: *The company is Ireland's largest dairy processor.* ◇ see also FOOD PROCESSOR  2 (*computing*) a part of a computer that controls all the other parts of the system **SYN** central processing unit ◇ see also MICROPROCESSOR, WORD PROCESSOR

**pro-ˈchoice** adj. believing that a pregnant woman should be able to choose to have an ABORTION if she wants ◇ compare ANTI-CHOICE, PRO-LIFE

**pro·claim** /prəˈkleɪm/ verb (*formal*)  1 to publicly and officially tell people about sth important **SYN** declare: ~ sth *The president proclaimed a state of emergency.* ◇ *~ that... The charter proclaimed that all states would have their own government.* ◇ *~ sb/sth/yourself + noun He proclaimed himself emperor.* ◇ *~ sb/sth/yourself to be / have sth Steve checked the battery and proclaimed it to be dead.* ◇ *~ how, what, etc... The senator proclaimed how shocked he was at the news.* ◇ *+ speech 'We will succeed,' she proclaimed.*  2 to show sth clearly; to be a sign of sth: *~ sth This building, more than any other, proclaims the character of the town.* ◇ *~ sb/sth + noun His accent proclaimed him a Scot.* ◇ *~ sb/sth to be / have sth His accent proclaimed him to be a Scot.*

**proc·lam·ation** /ˌprɒkləˈmeɪʃn; NAmE ˌprɑːk-/ noun [C, U] an official statement about sth important that is made to the public; the act of making an official statement

**pro·cliv·ity** /prəˈklɪvəti/ noun (pl. -ies) ~ (for sth / for doing sth) (*formal*) a natural desire or need that makes you tend to do sth, often sth bad **SYN** propensity: *his sexual/criminal proclivities* ◇ *the government's proclivity for spending money*

**pro·cras·tin·ate** /prəˈkræstɪneɪt/ verb [I] (*formal, disapproving*) to delay doing sth that you should do, usually because you do not want to do it ▶ **pro·cras·tin·ation** /prəˌkræstɪˈneɪʃn/ noun [U]

**pro·cre·ate** /ˈprəʊkrieɪt/ verb [I, T] ~ (sth) (*formal*) to produce children or baby animals **SYN** reproduce ▶ **pro·cre·ation** /ˌprəʊkriˈeɪʃn/ noun [U]: *They believe that sex is primarily for procreation.*

**proc·tor** /ˈprɒktə(r); NAmE ˈprɑːk-/ (NAmE) (BrE in·vigi·la·tor) noun a person who watches people while they are taking an exam to make sure that they have everything they need, that they keep to the rules, etc. ▶ **proc·tor** (NAmE) (BrE in·vigi·late) verb [T, I] ~ (sth)

**proc·ur·ator fis·cal** /ˌprɒkjʊreɪtə ˈfɪskl; NAmE ˌprɑːkjʊreɪtər/ noun (pl. proc·ur·ators fis·cal) (in Scotland) a public official whose job is to decide whether people who are suspected of a crime should be brought to trial

**pro·cure** /prəˈkjʊə(r); NAmE -ˈkjʊr/ verb  1 [T] (*formal*) to obtain sth, especially with difficulty: *~ sth (for sb/sth) She managed to procure a ticket for the concert.* ◇ *They procured a copy of the report for us.* ◇ *~ sb sth They procured us a copy of the report.*  2 [T, I] ~ (sb) to provide a PROSTITUTE for sb: *He was accused of procuring under-age girls.*

**pro·cure·ment** /prəˈkjʊəmənt; NAmE -ˈkjʊrm-/ noun [U] (*formal*) the process of obtaining supplies of sth, especially for a government or an organization

**prod** /prɒd; NAmE prɑːd/ verb, noun

■ verb (-dd-)  1 [T, I] to push sb/sth with your finger or with a pointed object **SYN** poke: *~ sb/sth (+ adv./prep.) She prodded him in the ribs to wake him up.* ◇ *~ at sb/sth He prodded at his breakfast with a fork.*  2 [T] ~ sb (into sth /

**into doing sth)** to try to make sb do sth, especially when they are unwilling: *She finally prodded him into action.*
■ **noun 1** the act of pushing sb with your finger or with a pointed object SYN **dig**: *She gave him a sharp prod with her umbrella.* **2** (*informal*) an act of encouraging sb or of reminding sb to do sth: *If they haven't replied by next week, you'll have to call them and give them a prod.* **3** an instrument like a stick that is used for prodding animals

**prod·ding** /ˈprɒdɪŋ; NAmE ˈprɑːd-/ *noun* [U] the act of encouraging sb to do sth: *He needed no prodding.*

**prod·igal** /ˈprɒdɪɡl; NAmE ˈprɑːd-/ *adj.* (*formal, disapproving*) too willing to spend money or waste time, energy or materials ▸ SYN **extravagant** ▶ **prod·ig·al·ity** /ˌprɒdɪˈɡæləti; NAmE ˌprɑːd-/ *noun* [U]
IDM **the/a prodigal ('son)** a person who leaves home and wastes their money and time on a life of pleasure, but who later is sorry about this and returns home

**pro·di·gious** /prəˈdɪdʒəs/ *adj.* [usually before noun] (*formal*) very large or powerful and causing surprise; impressive SYN **colossal, enormous**: *a prodigious achievement/memory/talent* ◊ *USB sticks can store prodigious amounts of information.* ▶ **pro·di·gious·ly** *adv.*: *a prodigiously talented musician*

**prod·igy** /ˈprɒdədʒi; NAmE ˈprɑːd-/ *noun* (*pl.* **-ies**) a young person whose intelligence or skill is unusually good for their age: *a child/an infant prodigy* ◊ *a musical prodigy*

**pro·duce** 🔊 **A2** 🔊
*verb, noun*

| | WORD FAMILY |
|---|---|
| ■ *verb* /prəˈdjuːs; NAmE -ˈduːs/ | **produce** *verb* |
| • GOODS **1** **A2** ~ sth to make things to be sold, especially in large quantities SYN **manufacture**: *Our company mainly produces goods for export.* ◊ *The local factory produces electronic components.* ⇨ SYNONYMS at MAKE, PRODUCT ⇨ see also MASS-PRODUCE | **producer** *noun* |
| | **production** *noun* |
| | **productive** *adj.* (≠ unproductive) |
| | **productively** *adv.* |
| | **product** *noun* |
| | **produce** *noun* |

• MAKE NATURALLY **2** **A2** ~ sth to grow or make sth as part of a natural process; to have a baby or young animal: *The region produces over 50 per cent of the country's wheat.* ◊ *Our cat produced kittens last week.* ◊ *Her duty was to produce an heir to the throne.* ◊ ~ **sth from sth** *The wine is produced from Chardonnay grapes.*
• CREATE WITH SKILL **3** **B1** ~ sth to create sth, especially when skill is needed: *She produced a delicious meal out of a few leftovers.* ◊ *By 1912 he was producing purely abstract works.*
• RESULT/EFFECT **4** **B1** ~ sth to cause a particular result or effect SYN **bring about**: *A phone call to the manager produced the result she wanted.* ◊ *His words failed to produce the desired effect.* ◊ *The drug produces a feeling of excitement.*
• SHOW/BRING OUT **5** to show sth or make sth appear from somewhere: ~ **sth from/out of sth** *He produced a letter from his pocket.* ◊ ~ **sth** *She failed to produce any evidence to support these claims.*
• PERSON **6** ~ sb if a town, country, etc. **produces** sb with a particular skill or quality, the person comes from that town, country, etc: *He is the greatest athlete this country has ever produced.*
• MOVIE/PLAY **7** ~ sth to be in charge of preparing a film, play, etc. for the public to see: *She produced a TV series about adopted children.*
■ *noun* **B2** /ˈprɒdjuːs; NAmE ˈproʊduːs, ˈprɑː-/ [U] things that have been made or grown, especially things connected with farming: *The shop sells only fresh local produce.* ◊ *It says on the label 'Produce of France'.*

**pro·du·cer** 🔊 **B1** 🔊 /prəˈdjuːsə(r); NAmE -ˈduː-/ *noun*
**1** **B1** a person, a company or a country that grows or makes food, goods or materials: *French wine producers* ◊ *Libya is a major oil producer.* ◊ *the world's largest producer of uranium* ⇨ compare CONSUMER **2** **B1** a person who is in charge of the practical and financial aspects of making a film or play: *a film producer* ◊ *He is an executive producer of the film.* ⇨ compare DIRECTOR (3) **3** a person or company that arranges for sb to make a programme for radio or television, or a record, CD, etc: *an independent television producer*

---

**prod·uct** 🔊 **A1** 🔊 /ˈprɒdʌkt; NAmE ˈprɑːd-/ *noun*
**1** **A1** [C, U] a thing that is grown, produced or created, usually for sale: *food/agricultural/software products* ◊ *He has eliminated dairy products from his diet.* ◊ *to develop/produce/market/sell a product* ◊ *to buy/purchase a product* ◊ *investment in product development* ◊ *We have just launched a new product on to the market.* ◊ *The bank offers a whole range of financial products and services.* ◊ (*business*) *We need new product to sell (= a new range of products).* ⇨ see also END PRODUCT, GROSS DOMESTIC PRODUCT, GROSS NATIONAL PRODUCT **2** **B2** [C] a thing produced during a natural, chemical or industrial process: *One product of any combustion reaction is carbon monoxide.* ⇨ see also BY-PRODUCT, WASTE PRODUCT **3** [C] ~ **of sth** a person or thing that is the result of sth: *The child is the product of a broken home.* **4** [C, U] a cream or liquid that you put on your hair or skin to make it look better: *This product can be used on wet or dry hair.* **5** (*mathematics*) [C] a quantity obtained by multiplying one number by another: *The product of 21 and 16 is 336.*

▼ SYNONYMS

**product**
goods • commodity • merchandise • produce
These are all words for things that are produced to be sold.
**product** a thing that is produced or grown, usually to be sold: *to create/develop/launch a new product*
**goods** things that are produced to be sold: *cotton/leather goods* ◊ *electrical goods*
**commodity** (*economics*) a product or raw material that can be bought and sold, especially between countries: *rice, flour and other basic commodities*
**merchandise** [U] goods that are bought or sold; things that you can buy that are connected with or advertise a particular event or organization: *official Olympic merchandise*
GOODS OR MERCHANDISE?
Choose **goods** if the emphasis is on what the product is made of or what it is for: *leather/household goods*. Choose **merchandise** if the emphasis is less on the product itself and more on its brand or the fact of buying/selling it.
**produce** [U] things that have been grown or made, especially things connected with farming: *We sell only fresh local produce.*
PATTERNS
• **consumer/industrial** products/goods/commodities
• **household** products/goods
• **farm** products/produce
• **luxury** products/goods/commodities
• to **sell/market** a product/goods/a commodity/merchandise/produce
• to **export** a product/goods/a commodity/merchandise
• to **buy/purchase** a product/goods/a commodity/merchandise/produce

**pro·duc·tion** 🔊 **B1** 🔊 /prəˈdʌkʃn/ *noun* **1** **B1** [U] the process of growing or making food, goods or materials, especially large quantities: *food/oil production* ◊ *Production of the new aircraft will start next year.* ◊ *in ~ The new model will be in production by the end of the year.* ◊ *The car goes into production later this year.* ◊ *This model went out of production last year.* ◊ *production costs/processes* ⇨ see also MASS PRODUCTION ⇨ WORDFINDER NOTE at FACTORY **2** **B1** [U] the quantity of goods that is produced: *a decline/an increase in production* ◊ *The goal is to increase production by 40%.* **3** **B1** [U] the act or process of making sth naturally: *Eating cheese stimulates the production of saliva.* **4** **B2** [C, U] a film, play or broadcast that is prepared for the public; the act of preparing a film, play, etc: *a new production of 'King Lear'* ◊ *He wants a career in film production.* ◊ *in ~ Series four is currently in production.*
IDM **on production of sth** (*formal*) when you show sth: *Discounts only on production of your student ID card.*

**pro'duction line** (*also* **as'sembly line**) *noun* a line of workers and machines in a factory, along which a product

**pro·duction number** *noun* a scene in a musical play or a film where a lot of people sing and dance

**pro'duction values** *noun* [pl.] the quality of a film, play, music concert, etc. in terms of the money spent on making it look good: *The film benefits from a strong cast and high production values.*

**pro·duct·ive** /prəˈdʌktɪv/ *adj.* **1** making goods or growing crops, especially in large quantities: *highly productive farming land* ◊ *productive workers* **OPP** **unproductive** **2** doing or achieving a lot ■ **fruitful**: *a productive meeting* ◊ *My time spent in the library was very productive.* ⊃ compare COUNTERPRODUCTIVE **3** ~ **of sth** (*formal*) resulting in sth or causing sth: *a play productive of the strongest emotions* ▶ **pro·duct·ive·ly** *adv.*: *to use land more productively* ◊ *It's important to spend your time productively.*

**pro·duct·iv·ity** /ˌprɒdʌkˈtɪvəti; *NAmE* ˌproʊd-, ˌprɑːd-/ *noun* [U] the rate at which a worker, a company or a country produces goods, and the amount produced, compared with how much time, work and money is needed to produce them: *high/improved/increased productivity* ◊ *Wage rates depend on levels of productivity.*

**product ˈplacement** *noun* [U, C] the use of particular products in films or television programmes in a way that makes people notice them, as a form of advertising ⊃ WORDFINDER NOTE at ADVERTISE

**prof** /prɒf; *NAmE* prɑːf/ *noun* (*informal*) = PROFESSOR: *a college prof*

**Prof.** /prɒf; *NAmE* prɑːf/ *abbr.* (in writing) PROFESSOR: *Prof. Mike Harrison*

**pro·fane** /prəˈfeɪn/ *adj.*, *verb*
■ *adj.* **1** (*formal*) having or showing a lack of respect for God or religion: *profane language* **2** (*specialist*) not connected with religion or holy things ■ **secular**: *songs of sacred and profane love*
■ *verb* ~ **sth** (*formal*) to treat sth holy with a lack of respect

**pro·fan·ity** /prəˈfænəti; *NAmE also* proʊˈf-/ *noun* (*pl.* **-ies**) (*formal*) **1** [U] behaviour that shows a lack of respect for God or holy things **2** [C, usually pl.] swear words, or religious words used in a way that shows a lack of respect for God or holy things: *He uttered a stream of profanities.*

**pro·fess** /prəˈfes/ *verb* (*formal*) **1** to claim that sth is true or correct, especially when it is not: ~ **sth** *She still professes her innocence.* ◊ ~ **to be / have sth** *I don't profess to be an expert in this subject.* **2** to state openly that you have a particular belief, feeling, etc. ■ **declare**: ~ **sth** *In this scene the couple finally profess their love for each other.* ◊ ~ **yourself + adj.** *She professed herself satisfied with the progress so far.* **3** ~ **sth** to belong to a particular religion: *to profess Christianity/Islam/Judaism*

**pro·fessed** /prəˈfest/ *adj.* [only before noun] **1** used to describe a belief or a position that sb has publicly made known: *a professed Christian/anarchist* **2** used to describe a feeling or an attitude that sb says they have but which may not be sincere: *These, at least, were their professed reasons for pulling out of the deal.*

**pro·fes·sion** /prəˈfeʃn/ *noun* **1** [C] a type of job that needs special training or skill, especially one that needs a high level of education: *the medical/legal/teaching profession* ◊ *to enter/go into/join a profession* ◊ (*BrE*) *the caring professions* (= that involve looking after people) ◊ *She was at the very top of her profession.* ◊ *by ~ He was a lawyer by profession.* ⊃ SYNONYMS at WORK **2** ~ **the profession** [sing. + sing./pl. v.] all the people who work in a particular type of profession: *The legal profession has/have always resisted change.* **3** ~ **the professions** [pl.] the traditional jobs that need a high level of education and training, such as being a doctor or a lawyer: *employment in industry and the professions* **4** [C] ~ **of sth** a statement about what you believe, feel or think about sth, that is sometimes made publicly ■ **declaration**: *a profession of faith*

**pro·fes·sion·al** /prəˈfeʃnəl/ *adj.*, *noun*
■ *adj.* **1** doing sth as a paid job rather than as a hobby: *professional athletes/players* ◊ *After he won the amateur championship he turned professional.* **OPP** **amateur** **2** (of sport) done as a paid job rather than as a hobby: *In professional sport winning is everything.* **OPP** **amateur** **3** [only before noun] connected with a job that needs special training or skill, especially one that needs a high level of education: *professional qualifications/skills* ◊ *professional standards/practice* ◊ *an opportunity for professional development* ◊ *He may need professional help.* **4** (of people) having a job which needs special training and a high level of education: *Most of the people on the course were professional women.* **5** showing that sb is well trained and has a lot of skill ■ **competent**: *He dealt with the problem in a highly professional way.* **OPP** **amateur** **6** connected with the standards that are expected in a particular profession: *professional conduct/misconduct* **OPP** **unprofessional** ⊃ compare NON-PROFESSIONAL
■ *noun* **1** a person who does a job that needs special training and a high level of education: *the terms that doctors and other health professionals use* **2** (*also informal* **pro**) a person who does a sport or other activity as a paid job rather than as a hobby: *a top golf professional* **OPP** **amateur** **3** (*also informal* **pro**) a person who has a lot of skill and experience: *This was clearly a job for a real professional.* **OPP** **amateur**

**pro·fessional ˈfoul** *noun* (*BrE*) (in sport, especially football (soccer)) the act of deliberately breaking a rule in order to prevent the other team from gaining an advantage, especially to prevent them from scoring a goal

**pro·fes·sion·al·ism** /prəˈfeʃnəlɪzəm/ *noun* [U] **1** the high standard that you expect from a person who is well trained in a particular job: *We were impressed by the professionalism of the staff.* **2** great skill and ability: *the power and professionalism of her performance* **3** the practice of using professional players in sport: *Increased professionalism has changed the game radically.*

**pro·fes·sion·al·ize** (*BrE also* **-ise**) /prəˈfeʃnəlaɪz/ *verb* [usually passive] ~ **sth** to make an activity more professional, for example by paying people who take part in it ▶ **pro·fes·sion·al·iza·tion, -isa·tion** /prəˌfeʃnəlaɪˈzeɪʃn; *NAmE* -lə'z-/ *noun* [U]: *the increasing professionalization of sports*

**pro·fes·sion·al·ly** /prəˈfeʃnəli/ *adv.* **1** in a way that is connected with a person's job or training: *You need a complete change, both professionally and personally.* **2** in a way that shows skill and experience: *The product has been marketed very professionally.* **3** by a person who has the right skills and qualifications: *The burglar alarm should be professionally installed.* **4** as a paid job, not as a hobby: *After the injury, he never played professionally again.*

**pro·fes·sor** /prəˈfesə(r)/ (*also informal* **prof**) *noun* (*abbr.* **Prof.**) **1** (*especially BrE*) (*NAmE* **full professor**) a university teacher of the highest rank: *Professor (Ann) Williams* ◊ ~ **of sth** *to be appointed professor of economics at Cambridge* ◊ *He was made (a) professor at the age of 40.* **HELP** **Full professor** is used to describe the rank of university teacher, and not as a title. **2** (*NAmE*) a teacher at a university or college: *a university/college professor* ◊ *a chemistry/law professor* ◊ ~ **of sth** *a professor of psychology/political science* ⊃ compare ASSISTANT PROFESSOR, ASSOCIATE PROFESSOR

**pro·fes·sor·ial** /ˌprɒfəˈsɔːriəl; *NAmE* ˌproʊf-, ˌprɑːf-/ *adj.* connected with a professor; like a professor: *professorial duties* ◊ *His tone was almost professorial.*

**pro·fes·sor·ship** /prəˈfesəʃɪp; *NAmE* -sərʃ-/ *noun* the rank or position of a university professor: *a visiting professorship* ◊ *She was appointed to a professorship in Economics at Princeton.*

**prof·fer** /ˈprɒfə(r); *NAmE* ˈprɑːf-/ *verb* (*formal*) **1** ~ **sth (to sb)** | ~ **sb sth** to offer sth to sb, by holding it out to them: *'Try this,' she said, proffering a plate.* **2** to offer sth such as advice or an explanation: ~ **sth (to sb)** *What advice would you proffer to someone starting up in business?* ◊ ~ **sb sth** *What advice would you proffer her?* ◊ ~ **itself** *A solution proffered itself.*

**pro·fi·cient** /prəˈfɪʃnt/ *adj.* able to do sth well because of training and practice: *I'm a reasonably proficient driver.* ◊

~ **in (doing) sth** *She's proficient in several languages.* ◊ *~ at (doing) sth He's proficient at his job.* ▶ **pro·fi·ciency** /-ʃnsi/ *noun* [U]: *to develop proficiency* ◊ *a certificate of language proficiency* ◊ *~ in/at (doing) sth a high level of oral proficiency in English*

## pro·file ❶ A2 Ⓦ /ˈprəʊfaɪl/ *noun, verb*

■ *noun* **1** ʳ A2 a description of sb/sth that gives useful information: *We first build up a detailed profile of our customers and their requirements.* ◊ *You can update your Facebook profile* (= your description of yourself on a SOCIAL MEDIA website). **2** ʳ B2 the general impression that sb/sth gives to the public and the amount of attention they receive: *Her popularity has done great things for the profile of the sport.* ◊ *The deal will certainly raise the company's international profile.* **3** the outline of a person's face when you look from the side, not the front: *his strong profile* ◊ *in~ a picture of the president in profile* **4** the edge or outline of sth that you see against a background: *the profile of the tower against the sky*
ⒾⒹⓂ **a high/low ˈprofile** the amount of attention sb/sth has from the public: *This issue has had a high profile in recent months.* ◊ *I advised her to keep a low profile for the next few days* (= not to attract attention).
■ *verb* **~ sb/sth** to give or write a description of sb/sth that gives the most important information: *His career is profiled in this month's journal.*

**pro·fil·ing** /ˈprəʊfaɪlɪŋ/ *noun* [U] the act of collecting useful information about sb/sth so that you can give a description of them or it: *customer profiling* ◊ *offender profiling* ⊃ see also RACIAL PROFILING ▶ **pro·fil·er** /-lə(r)/ *noun*

## profit ❶ B1 /ˈprɒfɪt; NAmE ˈprɑːf-/ *noun, verb*

■ *noun* **1** ʳ B1 [C, U] the money that you make in business or by selling things, especially after paying the costs involved: *annual/pre-tax/corporate profits* ◊ *Profits before tax grew from £615m to £1168m.* ◊ *a rise/an increase/a jump/a drop/a fall in profits* ◊ *to maximize/increase profits* ◊ *to report/post profits of £50 million* ◊ *The club may turn a profit* (= make a profit) *by the end of the year.* ◊ *The sale generated record profits.* ◊ *Net profit* (= after you have paid costs and tax) *was up 16.1 per cent.* ◊ *The business recorded a gross profit of* (= before you pay costs and tax) *£1.45 million last year* ◊ *The division's profit margins are being squeezed.* ◊ *The directors are driven only by the profit motive.* ◊ *~ on sth The company made a healthy profit on the deal.* ◊ *~ from sth Profit from exports rose 7.7 per cent.* ◊ *The radio station earns a profit from its advertising.* ◊ *at a~ We should be able to sell the house at a huge profit.* ◊ *for~ The agency is voluntary and not run for profit.* Ⓞⓟⓟ **loss** ⊃ see also NON-PROFIT, NOT-FOR-PROFIT ⊃ HOMOPHONES at PROPHET ⊃ WORDFINDER NOTE at MONEY **2** [U] (*formal*) the advantage that you get from doing sth: *Future lawyers could study this text with profit.*
■ *verb* [I, T] (*formal*) to get sth useful from a situation; to be useful to sb or give them an advantage: *~ (from sth) Farmers are profiting from the new legislation.* ◊ *~ (by sth) We tried to profit by our mistakes* (= learn from them). ◊ *~ sth Many local people believe the development will profit them.*
⊃ HOMOPHONES at PROPHET

**prof·it·able** ʳ+ C1 /ˈprɒfɪtəbl; NAmE ˈprɑːf-/ *adj.* **1** ʳ+ C1 that makes or is likely to make money: *a highly profitable business* ◊ *It is usually more profitable to sell direct to the public.* ⊃ SYNONYMS at SUCCESSFUL **2** that gives sb an advantage or a useful result ⓢⓨⓝ **rewarding**: *She spent a profitable afternoon in the library.* ▶ **prof·it·abil·ity** /ˌprɒfɪtəˈbɪləti; NAmE ˌprɑːf-/ *noun* [U]: *to increase profitability* **prof·it·ably** /ˈprɒfɪtəbli; NAmE ˈprɑːf-/ *adv.*

**ˌprofit and ˈloss account** *noun* (*business*) a list that shows the amount of money that a company has earned, how much it has spent, and the total profit or loss that it has made in a particular period of time

**prof·it·eer·ing** /ˌprɒfɪˈtɪərɪŋ; NAmE ˌprɑːfɪˈtɪr-/ *noun* [U] (*disapproving*) the act of making a lot of money in an unfair way, for example by asking very high prices for things that are hard to get ▶ **prof·it·eer** *noun*

**pro·fit·er·ole** /prəˈfɪtərəʊl/ (*especially BrE*) *noun* a small cake in the shape of a ball, made of light PASTRY, filled with cream and usually with chocolate on top ⊃ compare CREAM PUFF (1), ECLAIR

**prof·it·less** /ˈprɒfɪtləs; NAmE ˈprɑːf-/ *adj.* (*formal*) producing no PROFIT or useful result

**ˈprofit-making** *adj.* [usually before noun] (of a company or a business) that makes or will make a profit

**ˈprofit margin** (also **margin**) *noun* (*business*) the difference between the cost of buying or producing sth and the price that it is sold for

**ˈprofit-sharing** *noun* [U] the system of dividing all or some of a company's profits among its employees

**ˈprofit-taking** *noun* [U] (*business*) the sale of shares in companies whose value has increased

**ˈprofit warning** (*BrE also* **ˈprofits warning**) *noun* (*business*) a statement from a company informing the people who invest in it that profits will be lower than expected: *The company issued a profit warning following disappointing sales in October and November.*

**prof·li·gate** /ˈprɒflɪɡət; NAmE ˈprɑːf-/ *adj.* (*formal, disapproving*) using money, time, materials, etc. in a careless way ⓢⓨⓝ **wasteful**: *profligate spending* ▶ **prof·li·gacy** /-ɡəsi/ *noun* [U]

**pro-form** *noun* (*grammar*) a word that depends on another part of the sentence or text for its meaning, for example 'her' in 'I like Ruth but I don't love her.'

**pro forma** /ˌprəʊ ˈfɔːmə; NAmE ˈfɔːrmə/ *adj.* (*from Latin*) [usually before noun] **1** (especially of a document) prepared in order to show the usual way of doing sth or to provide a standard method: *a pro forma letter* ◊ *pro forma instructions* **2** (of a document) sent in advance: *a pro forma invoice* (= a document that gives details of the goods being sent to a customer) **3** done because it is part of the usual way of doing sth, although it has no real meaning: *a pro forma debate* ▶ **pro forma** *noun*: *I enclose a pro forma for you to complete, sign and return.*

**pro·found** ʳ+ C1 /prəˈfaʊnd/ *adj.* **1** ʳ+ C1 very great; felt or experienced very strongly: *profound changes in the earth's climate* ◊ *My father's death had a profound effect on us all.* **2** ʳ+ C1 showing great knowledge or understanding: *profound insights* ◊ *a profound book* **3** ʳ+ C1 needing a lot of study or thought: *profound questions about life and death* **4** (*medical*) very serious; complete: *profound disability*

**pro·found·ly** /prəˈfaʊndli/ *adv.* **1** in a way that has a very great effect on sb/sth: *We are profoundly affected by what happens to us in childhood.* **2** (*medical*) very seriously; completely: *profoundly deaf*

**pro·fund·ity** /prəˈfʌndəti/ *noun* (*pl.* **-ies**) (*formal*) **1** [U] the quality of understanding or dealing with a subject at a very serious level ⓢⓨⓝ **depth**: *He lacked profundity and analytical precision.* **2** [U] the fact of being very great, serious or powerful: *the profundity of her misery* **3** [C, usually pl.] something that sb says that shows great understanding: *His profundities were lost on the young audience.*

**pro·fuse** /prəˈfjuːs/ *adj.* produced in large amounts: *profuse apologies/thanks* ◊ *profuse bleeding* ▶ **pro·fuse·ly** *adv.*: *to bleed profusely* ◊ *to apologize profusely*

**pro·fu·sion** /prəˈfjuːʒn/ *noun* [sing. + sing./pl. v., U] (*formal or literary*) a very large quantity of sth ⓢⓨⓝ **abundance**: *a profusion of colours* ◊ *in ~ Roses grew in profusion against the old wall.*

**pro·geni·tor** /prəʊˈdʒenɪtə(r)/ *noun* (*formal*) **1** a person or thing from the past that a person, animal or plant that is alive now is related to ⓢⓨⓝ **ancestor**: *He was the progenitor of a family of distinguished actors.* **2** a person who starts an idea or a development: *the progenitors of modern art*

**pro·geny** /ˈprɒdʒəni; NAmE ˈprɑːdʒ-/ *noun* [pl.] (*formal or humorous*) a person's children; the young of animals and plants: *He was surrounded by his numerous progeny.*

**pro·ges·ter·one** /prəˈdʒestərəʊn/ *noun* [U] a HORMONE produced in the bodies of women and female animals which prepares the body to become pregnant and is also used in CONTRACEPTION ⊃ compare OESTROGEN, TESTOSTERONE

# prognosis

**prog·no·sis** /prɒgˈnəʊsɪs; NAmE prɑːg-/ noun (pl. **prog·no·ses** /-ˈnəʊsiːz/) **1** (medical) an opinion, based on medical experience, of the likely development of a disease or an illness **2** (formal) a judgement about how sth is likely to develop in the future SYN **forecast**: *The prognosis is for more people to work part-time in the future.* ▶ **prog·nos·tic** /prɒgˈnɒstɪk; NAmE prɑːgˈnɑːs-/ adj.

**prog·nos·ti·ca·tion** /prɒgˌnɒstɪˈkeɪʃn; NAmE prɑːgˌnɑːs-/ noun (formal) a thing that sb says will happen in the future: *gloomy prognostications*

**pro·gram** ⓘ A2 /ˈprəʊɡræm/ noun, verb
■ noun
- **1** A2 a set of instructions in code that control the operations or functions of a computer: *You'll need to download and install the program on your computer.* ◇ *To **run the program**, simply click the icon.* ⊃ WORDFINDER NOTE at COMPUTER

WORDFINDER code, data, functionality, input, interface, keyword, operating system, retrieve, software

**2** A2 (NAmE) = PROGRAMME: *a TV program* ◇ *an intense training program* ◇ *the university's graduate programs* ◇ *a week-long program of lectures*
■ verb (**-mm-**, NAmE also **-m-**)
- **1** B1 [I, T] to give a computer, etc. a set of instructions to make it perform a particular task: *In this class, students will learn how to program.* ◇ *~ sth (to do sth) The computer is programmed to warn users before information is deleted.* ⊃ compare PROGRAMME **2** (NAmE) = PROGRAMME

**pro·gram·mable** /prəʊˈɡræməbl, ˈprəʊɡræməbl/ NAmE ˈprəʊɡræməbl/ adj. (of a computer or electrical device) able to accept instructions that control how it operates or functions

**pro·gram·mat·ic** /ˌprəʊɡrəˈmætɪk/ adj. [usually before noun] (formal) connected with, suggesting or following a plan: *programmatic reforms*

**pro·gram·mat·ical·ly** /ˌprəʊɡrəˈmætɪkli/ adv. (formal) **1** in a way that is connected with, suggests or follows a plan: *Programmatically, not a great deal separated the two parties in the electoral contest last year.* **2** by using a computer program: *Is it better to make the change manually or programmatically?*

**pro·gramme** ⓘ A1 Ⓦ (BrE) (NAmE **pro·gram**) /ˈprəʊɡræm/ noun, verb
■ noun
- ON TV/RADIO **1** A1 something that people watch on television or listen to on the radio: *a news programme* ◇ *a TV/ television/radio programme* ◇ *~on/about sth Did you see that programme on India last night?* ⊃ WORDFINDER NOTE at RADIO

WORDFINDER chat show, documentary, drama, game show, news, quiz, reality TV, sitcom

- PLAN **2** B1 a plan of things that will be done or included in the development of sth: *the country's nuclear weapons/ space programme* ◇ *We have recently launched a research programme.* ◇ *~for sb a training programme for new staff* ◇ *~ of sth The government is implementing a programme of reform.*
- COURSE OF STUDY **3** B1 (NAmE) a course of study: *a school/ an educational programme* ⊃ note at COURSE
- ORDER OF EVENTS **4** B1 an organized order of performances or events SYN **line-up**: *The concert is the highlight of the festival's musical programme.* ◇ *~of sth a week-long programme of lectures* ◇ *What's the programme for* (= what are we going to do) *tomorrow?*
- FOR PLAY/CONCERT **5** a thin book or a piece of paper that gives you information about a play, a concert, etc.: *a theatre programme* ⊃ WORDFINDER NOTE at CONCERT
- OF MACHINE **6** a series of actions done by a machine, such as a WASHING MACHINE: *Select a cool programme for woollen clothes.*

IDM **get with the ˈprogramme** (BrE) (NAmE **get with the ˈprogram**) (informal) (usually in orders) used to tell sb that they should change their attitude and do what they are supposed to be doing
■ verb
- PLAN **1** [usually passive] to plan for sth to happen, especially as part of a series of planned events: **be programmed (for sth)** *The final section of road is programmed for completion next month.*
- PERSON/ANIMAL **2** [usually passive] to make a person, an animal, etc. behave in a particular way, so that they do it without thinking about it: **be programmed to do sth** *Human beings are genetically programmed to learn certain kinds of language.*
- MACHINE **3** *~ sth (to do sth)* to give a machine instructions to do a particular task: *She programmed the central heating to come on at eight.*

ˌprogrammed ˈlearning noun [U] a method of study in which a subject is divided into very small parts and the student must be successful in one part before he or she can go on to the next

**pro·gram·mer** /ˈprəʊɡræmə(r)/ noun a person whose job is writing computer programs

**pro·gram·ming** B1+ B2 /ˈprəʊɡræmɪŋ/ noun [U] **1** B1+ B2 the process of writing and testing computer programs: *programming languages* **2** the planning of which television or radio programmes to broadcast: *politically balanced programming*

**pro·gress** ⓘ A2 Ⓞ noun, verb
■ noun /ˈprəʊɡres; NAmE ˈprɑːɡ-, -ɡrəs/ [U] **1** A2 the process of improving or developing, or of getting nearer to achieving or completing sth: *I think we're **making progress**.* ◇ *economic/scientific/technological progress* ◇ *slow/ steady/rapid/good progress* ◇ *~ in (doing) sth Police are **making significant progress** in fighting computer crime.* ◇ *~ on sth There's been no sign of progress on this issue.* ◇ *They asked for a **progress report** on the building work.* **2** movement forwards or towards a place: *We watched his slow progress down the steep slope.* ◇ *There wasn't much traffic so we made good progress.*
IDM **in ˈprogress** (formal) happening at this time: *Work on the new offices is now in progress.* ◇ *Please be quiet— examination in progress.* ⊃ see also WORK IN PROGRESS
■ verb /prəˈɡres/ **1** B2 [I] to improve or develop over a period of time; to make progress SYN **advance**: *The course allows students to progress at their own speed.* ◇ *Work on the new road is progressing slowly.* ◇ *~ (from sth) (to sth) He soon progressed from the basics to more difficult work.* **2** [I] + adv./prep. (formal) to move forward: *The line of traffic progressed slowly through the town.* ◇ (figurative) *Cases can take months to progress through the courts.* **3** [I] to go forward in time SYN **go on**: *The weather became colder as the day progressed.*

**pro·gres·sion** Ⓦ /prəˈɡreʃn/ noun **1** [U, C] the process of developing gradually from one stage or state to another: *opportunities for career progression* ◇ *the rapid progression of the disease* ◇ *~ (from sth) (to sth) a natural progression from childhood to adolescence* **2** [C] a number of things that come in a series ⊃ see also ARITHMETIC PROGRESSION, GEOMETRIC PROGRESSION

**pro·gres·sive** B1+ B2 Ⓦ /prəˈɡresɪv/ adj., noun
■ adj. **1** B1+ B2 in favour of new ideas, modern methods and change: *progressive schools* OPP **retrogressive 2** B1+ C1 happening or developing steadily: *a progressive reduction in the size of the workforce* ◇ *a progressive muscular disease* **3** (also **con·tinu·ous**) (grammar) connected with the form of a verb (for example *I am waiting* or *It is raining*) that is made from a part of *be* and the present participle. Progressive forms are used to express an action that continues for a period of time. ▶ **pro·gres·siv·ism** noun [U]: *political progressivism*
■ noun (usually pl.) a person who is in favour of new ideas, modern methods and change: *political battles between progressives and conservatives*

**pro·gres·sive·ly** /prəˈɡresɪvli/ adv. (often with a comparative) steadily and continuously: *The situation was becoming progressively more difficult.* ◇ *The pain got progressively worse.*

**prog rock** /ˈprɒɡ rɒk; NAmE ˈprɑːɡ rɑːk/ (also **pro·gres·sive ˈrock**) noun [U] a style of rock music that includes elements of other kinds of music, including jazz

**pro·hibit** /prəˈhɪbɪt; NAmE also prəʊˈh-/ verb (formal) **1** [often passive] to stop sb from being done or used especially by law SYN **forbid**: ~ sth *a law prohibiting the sale of alcohol* ◊ **~ sb from doing sth** *Soviet citizens were prohibited from travelling abroad.* ◊ **~(sb) doing sth** *The policy prohibits smoking on school grounds.* **2** ~ **sth/sb from doing sth** to make sth impossible to do SYN **prevent**: *The high cost of equipment prohibits many people from taking up this sport.*

**pro·hib·it·ed** /prəˈhɪbɪtɪd; NAmE also prəʊˈh-/ adj. (formal) not allowed; banned: *prohibited substances* ◊ *Smoking on site is strictly prohibited.*

**pro·hib·ition** /ˌprəʊɪˈbɪʃn/ noun **1** [U] (formal) the act of stopping sth being done or used, especially by law: *the prohibition of smoking in public areas* **2** [C] **~ (against/ on sth)** (formal) a law or a rule that stops sth being done or used: *a prohibition against selling alcohol to people under the age of 18* **3 Prohibition** [U] (in the US) the period of time from 1920 to 1933 when it was illegal to make and sell alcoholic drinks

**pro·hib·ition·ist** /ˌprəʊɪˈbɪʃənɪst/ noun a person who supports the act of making sth illegal, especially the sale of alcoholic drinks

**pro·hibi·tive** /prəˈhɪbətɪv; NAmE also prəʊˈh-/ adj. **1** (of a price or a cost) so high that it prevents people from buying sth or doing sth SYN **exorbitant**: *prohibitive costs* ◊ *The price of property in the city is prohibitive.* **2** preventing people from doing sth by law: *prohibitive legislation* **3** (NAmE) (of a person taking part in an election or a competition) extremely likely to win: *Miami began the day a prohibitive Super Bowl favorite.* ▶ **pro·hibi·tive·ly** adv.: *Car insurance can be prohibitively expensive for young drivers.*

**pro·ject** ⓘ A1 W noun, verb
■ noun /ˈprɒdʒekt; NAmE ˈprɑːdʒ-/
• SCHOOL/COLLEGE WORK **1** A1 a piece of work involving careful study of a subject over a period of time, done by school or college students: *a history project* ◊ **~ on sth** *My class is doing a project on medieval towns.* ◊ *The final term will be devoted to project work.*
• PLANNED WORK **2** B1 a planned piece of work that is designed to find information about sth, to produce sth new, or to improve sth: *We worked on various projects together.* ◊ *to fund/finance a project* ◊ *to undertake/complete a project* ◊ *a building/construction project* ◊ **~ to do sth** *They've set up a research project to investigate the harmful effects of air pollution.* ◊ *a project manager/team*
• SET OF AIMS/ACTIVITIES **3** a set of aims, ideas or activities that sb is interested in or wants to bring to people's attention: *The party attempted to assemble its aims into a focused political project.*
• HOUSING **4** (NAmE) = HOUSING PROJECT: *Going into the projects alone can be dangerous.*
■ verb /prəˈdʒekt/
• ESTIMATE **1** B2 [T, usually passive] to estimate what the size, cost or amount of sth will be in the future based on what is happening now SYN **forecast**: **be projected** *A growth rate of 4 per cent is projected for next year.* ◊ **be projected at sth** *The overall cost is projected at $11 billion.* ◊ **be projected to do sth** *Unemployment is projected to rise to over 5 per cent next year.* ◊ **it is projected that ...** *It is projected that the unemployment rate will fall.*
• PLAN **2** B2 [T, usually passive] to plan an activity, a project etc. for a time in the future: **be projected** *The next edition of the book is projected for publication in March.* ◊ *The projected housing development will go ahead next year.*
• LIGHT/IMAGE **3** B2 [T] **~ sth (on/onto sth)** to make light, an image, etc. fall onto a flat surface or screen: *They projected the digital image onto the model's surface.*
• STICK OUT **4** [I] **+ adv./prep.** to stick out beyond an edge or a surface SYN **protrude**: *a building with balconies projecting out over the street*
• PRESENT YOURSELF **5** [T] to present sb/sth/yourself to other people in a particular way, especially one that gives a good impression: **~ sth** *They sought advice on how to project a more positive image of their company.* ◊ **~ sb/sth/yourself (as sb/sth)** *He projected himself as a man worth listening to.*
• SEND/THROW UP OR AWAY **6** [T] **~ sth/sb (+ adv./prep.)** to send or throw sth up or away from yourself: *Actors must*

1233 **prolific**

*learn to project their voices.* ◊ (figurative) *the powerful men who would project him into the White House*
PHRV **proˈject sth onto sb** (psychology) to imagine that other people have the same feelings, problems, etc. as you, especially when this is not true

**pro·ject·ile** /prəˈdʒektaɪl; NAmE -tl/ noun, adj.
■ noun (formal or specialist) **1** an object, such as a bullet, that is fired from a gun or other weapon **2** any object that is thrown as a weapon
■ adj. (formal or specialist) very fast and with a lot of force: *projectile motion* ◊ *The virus causes projectile (= sudden and violent) vomiting.*

**pro·jec·tion** ⓘ C1 W /prəˈdʒekʃn/ noun
• ESTIMATE **1** C1 [C] an estimate or a statement of what figures, amounts, or events will be in the future, or what they were in the past, based on what is happening now: *to make forward/backward projections of population figures* ◊ *Sales have exceeded our projections.*
• OF IMAGE **2** [U, C] the act of putting an image of sth onto a surface; an image that is shown in this way: *the projection of three-dimensional images on a computer screen* ◊ *laser projections*
• OF SOLID SHAPE **3** [C] (specialist) a solid shape or object as represented on a flat surface: *map projections*
• STH THAT STICKS OUT **4** [C] something that sticks out from a surface: *tiny projections on the cell*
• OF VOICE/SOUND **5** [U] the act of making your voice, a sound, etc. AUDIBLE (= able to be heard) at a distance: *voice projection*
• PSYCHOLOGY **6** [U] the act of imagining that sb else is thinking the same as you and is reacting in the same way
• OF THOUGHTS/FEELINGS **7** [C, U] the act of giving a form and structure to inner thoughts and feelings: *The idea of God is a projection of humans' need to have something greater than themselves.*

**pro·jec·tion·ist** /prəˈdʒekʃənɪst/ noun a person whose job is to show films by operating a projector

**pro·ject·or** /prəˈdʒektə(r)/ noun a piece of equipment for projecting photographs, films or computer slides onto a screen ⊃ see also DATA PROJECTOR, OVERHEAD PROJECTOR, SLIDE PROJECTOR

**pro·lapse** /ˈprəʊlæps/ noun (medical) a condition in which an organ of the body has slipped forward or down from its normal position

**prole** /prəʊl/ noun (BrE, old-fashioned, informal) an offensive word for a WORKING CLASS person

**pro·le·tar·ian** /ˌprəʊləˈteəriən; NAmE -ˈter-/ adj. connected with ordinary people who earn money by working, especially those who do not own any property ⊃ compare BOURGEOIS ▶ **pro·le·tar·ian** noun

**the pro·le·tar·iat** /ðə ˌprəʊləˈteəriət; NAmE -ˈter-/ noun [sing. + sing./pl. v.] (specialist) (used especially when talking about the past) the class of ordinary people who earn money by working, especially those who do not own any property ⊃ compare BOURGEOISIE

**pro-ˈlife** adj. [usually before noun] opposed to ABORTION: *the pro-life movement* ◊ *a pro-life campaigner* ⊃ compare PRO-CHOICE

**pro·lif·er·ate** /prəˈlɪfəreɪt/ verb [I] to increase rapidly in number or amount SYN **multiply**: *Books and articles on the subject have proliferated over the last year.*

**pro·lif·er·ation** /prəˌlɪfəˈreɪʃn/ noun [U, sing.] the sudden increase in the number or amount of sth; a large number of a particular thing: *attempts to prevent cancer cell proliferation* ◊ *a proliferation of personal computers*

**pro·lif·ic** /prəˈlɪfɪk/ adj. **1** (of an artist, a writer, etc.) producing many works, etc: *a prolific author* ◊ *a prolific goalscorer* ◊ *one of the most prolific periods in her career* **2** (of plants, animals, etc.) producing a lot of fruit, flowers, young, etc. **3** able to produce enough food, etc. to keep many animals and plants alive: *prolific rivers* **4** existing in large numbers: *a pop star with a prolific following of teenage fans* ▶ **pro·lif·ic·al·ly** /-kli/ adv.: *to write prolifically* ◊ *animals that breed prolifically*

# prolix

**pro·lix** /ˈprəʊlɪks/ *adj.* (*formal*) (of writing, a speech, etc.) using too many words and therefore boring ▶ **pro·lix·ity** /prəʊˈlɪksəti/ *noun* [U]

**pro·logue** /ˈprəʊlɒg; *NAmE* -lɔːg/ *noun* a speech, etc. at the beginning of a play, book or film that introduces it ⊃ compare EPILOGUE

**pro·long** /prəˈlɒŋ; *NAmE* -ˈlɔːŋ/ *verb* ~ **sth** to make sth last longer SYN **extend**: *The operation could prolong his life by two or three years.* ◇ *Don't prolong the agony* (= of not knowing sth)—*just tell us who won!*

**pro·lon·ga·tion** /ˌprəʊlɒŋˈgeɪʃn; *NAmE* -lɔːŋ-/ *noun* [U, sing.] (*formal*) the act of making sth last longer: *the artificial prolongation of human life*

**pro·longed** /prəˈlɒŋd; *NAmE* -ˈlɔːŋd/ *adj.* continuing for a long time: *a prolonged illness* ◇ *a prolonged period of dry weather*

**prom** /prɒm; *NAmE* prɑːm/ *noun* **1** (especially in the US) a formal dance, especially one that is held at a HIGH SCHOOL: *the senior prom* **2** (*BrE*, *informal*, *becoming old-fashioned*) = PROMENADE: *to walk along the prom* **3** (*BrE*) = PROMENADE CONCERT: *the last night of the proms*

**prom·en·ade** /ˌprɒməˈnɑːd; *NAmE* ˌprɑːməˈneɪd/ *noun*, *verb*
- *noun* **1** (*also informal* **prom**) (*both BrE*, *becoming old-fashioned*) a public place for walking, usually a wide path next to the sea **2** (*old-fashioned*) a walk that you take for pleasure or exercise, especially by the sea, in a public park, etc.
- *verb* [I] (*old-fashioned*) to walk up and down in a relaxed way, by the sea, in a public park, etc.

**promenade concert** (*also informal* **prom**) (*both BrE*) *noun* a concert at which many of the audience stand up or sit on the floor

**Pro·me·thean** /prəˈmiːθiən/ *adj.* doing things in an individual and original way and showing no respect for authority and rules ORIGIN From the Greek myth in which **Prometheus**, a Titan, stole fire from the gods and gave it to humans.

**prom·in·ence** /ˈprɒmɪnəns; *NAmE* ˈprɑːm-/ *noun* [U, sing.] the state of being important, well known or easy to notice: *a young actor who has recently risen to prominence* ◇ *She has achieved a prominence she hardly deserves.* ◇ ~ **as sth** *The study of local history has gained prominence as an academic discipline.*

**prom·in·ent** /ˈprɒmɪnənt; *NAmE* ˈprɑːm-/ *adj.* **1** important or well known: *a prominent politician* ◇ *He played a prominent part in the campaign.* ◇ *She was prominent in the fashion industry.* **2** easily seen SYN **noticeable**: *The church tower was a prominent feature in the landscape.* ◇ *The story was given a prominent position on the front page.* **3** sticking out from sth: *a prominent nose* ◇ *prominent cheekbones* ▶ **prom·in·ent·ly** *adv.*: *The photographs were prominently displayed on her desk.* ◇ *Problems of family relationships feature prominently in her novels.*

**pro·mis·cu·ous** /prəˈmɪskjuəs/ *adj.* **1** (*disapproving*) having many sexual partners: *promiscuous behaviour* ◇ *a promiscuous lifestyle* ◇ *to be sexually promiscuous* **2** (*formal*, *often disapproving*) taken from a wide range of sources, especially without careful thought: *promiscuous reading* ◇ *a stylistically promiscuous piece of music* ▶ **prom·is·cu·ity** /ˌprɒmɪsˈkjuːəti; *NAmE* ˌprɑːm-/ *noun* [U]: *sexual promiscuity* **prom·is·cu·ous·ly** *adv.*

**prom·ise** /ˈprɒmɪs; *NAmE* ˈprɑːm-/ *verb*, *noun*
- *verb* **1** [I, T] to tell sb that you will definitely do or not do sth, or that sth will definitely happen: *'We haven't got time to go to the park.' 'But you promised!'* ◇ ~ **to do sth** *The college principal promised to look into the matter.* ◇ *'Promise not to tell anyone!' 'I promise.'* ◇ *They arrived at 7.30 as they had promised.* ◇ ~ **sth** *The government has promised a full investigation into the disaster.* ◇ *I'll see what I can do but I can't promise anything.* ◇ ~ **(that) ...** *The brochure promised (that) the local food would be superb.* ◇ ~ **sb (that) ...** *You promised me (that) you'd be home early tonight.* ◇ ~ **sth to sb** *He promised the money to his grandchildren.* ◇ ~ **sb sth** *He promised his grandchildren the money,* ◇ **yourself sth** *I've promised myself some fun when the exams are over.* ◇ ~ **(sb) + speech** *'I'll be back soon,' she promised.* **2** [T] to make sth seem likely to happen; to show signs of sth: *it promises to be sth It promises to be an exciting few days.* ◇ ~ **sth** *There were dark clouds overhead promising rain.* IDM **I (can) promise you** (*informal*) used as a way of encouraging or warning sb about sth: *I can promise you, you'll have a wonderful time.* ◇ *If you don't take my advice, you'll regret it, I promise you.* **promise (sb) the 'earth/ 'moon/'world** (*informal*) to make promises that will be impossible to keep
- *noun* **1** [C] a statement that tells sb that you will definitely do or not do sth: *to make/keep/fulfil/break a promise* ◇ *You haven't gone back on your promise, have you?* ◇ *The minister was under attack for a series of broken promises.* ◇ ~ **to do sth** *She kept her promise to visit her aunt regularly.* ◇ ~ **to sb** *He had now to deliver on his promises to the Canadian electorate.* ◇ ~ **from/by sb** *These are empty promises from a party not in a position to honour them.* ◇ *It is unlikely that these laws will be changed, despite promises by the Prime Minister.* ◇ ~ **of sth** *The government failed to keep its promise of lower taxes.* ◇ ~ **(that ...)** *Do I have your promise that you won't tell anyone about this?* IDM see LICK *n.* **2** [U] a sign that sb/sth will be successful SYN **potential**: *Her work shows great promise.* ◇ *Their research holds considerable promise.* ◇ *He failed to fulfil his early promise.* ◇ *Their future was full of promise.* ◇ ~ **for sth** *Stem cell research offers real promise for the treatment of currently incurable diseases.* **3** [U, sing.] ~ **of sth** a sign, or a reason for hope that sth may happen, especially sth good: *The day dawned bright and clear, with the promise of warm, sunny weather.*

**the Promised Land** *noun* [sing.] a place or situation where you expect to be happy, safe, etc.

**prom·is·ing** /ˈprɒmɪsɪŋ; *NAmE* ˈprɑːm-/ *adj.* showing signs of being good or successful: *He was voted the most promising new actor for his part in the movie.* ◇ *The weather doesn't look very promising.* ▶ **prom·is·ing·ly** *adv.*: *The day began promisingly with bright sunshine.*

**prom·is·sory note** /ˈprɒmɪsəri nəʊt; *NAmE* ˈprɑːmɪsɔːri-/ *noun* (*specialist*) a signed document containing a promise to pay a stated amount of money before a particular date

**promo** /ˈprəʊməʊ/ *adj.* [only before noun] (*informal*) connected with advertising (= PROMOTING) sb/sth, especially a new pop record: *a promo video* ▶ **promo** *noun* (*pl.* **-os**): *to make pop promos*

**prom·on·tory** /ˈprɒməntri; *NAmE* ˈprɑːməntɔːri/ *noun* (*pl.* **-ies**) a long narrow area of high land that goes out into the sea SYN **headland** ⊃ WORDFINDER NOTE AT COAST

**pro·mote** /prəˈməʊt/ *verb* **1** to help sell a product, service, etc. or make it more popular by advertising it or offering it at a special price: ~ **sth** *The band has gone on tour to promote their new album.* ◇ *This trade fair will help businesses from Malawi to promote their products.* ◇ ~ **sth as sth** *The area is being promoted as a tourist destination.* **2** ~ **sth** to help sth to happen or develop SYN **encourage**: *to promote democracy/peace/ understanding/health* ◇ *to promote the development/use of sth* ◇ *policies to promote economic growth* ◇ *a campaign to promote awareness of environmental issues* **3** [often passive] to move sb to a higher rank or more senior job: ~ **sb** *She worked hard and was soon promoted.* ◇ ~ **sb (from sth) (to sth)** *He has been promoted to sergeant.* OPP **demote** **4** ~ **sth (from sth) (to sth)** to move a sports team from playing with one group of teams to playing in a better group: *They were promoted to the First Division last season.* OPP **relegate**

**pro·moter** /prəˈməʊtə(r)/ *noun* **1** a person or company that organizes or provides money for an artistic performance or a sporting event **2** ~ **of sth** a person who tries to persuade others about the value or importance of sth SYN **champion**: *She became a leading promoter of European integration.*

**pro·mo·tion** /prəˈməʊʃn/ *noun* **1** [U, C] a move to a more important job or rank in a company or an organization: *The new job is a promotion for him.* ◇ ~ **to sth** *Her promotion to Sales Manager took everyone by surprise.*

◊ *a job with excellent* **promotion** *prospects* **2** [U] **~ (to sth)** a move by a sports team from playing in one group of teams to playing in a better group: *the team's promotion to the First Division* **OPP** **relegation** **3** [U, C] activities done in order to increase the sales of a product or service; a set of advertisements for a particular product or service: *Her job is mainly concerned with sales and promotion.* ◊ *We are doing a special promotion of Chilean wines.* ⊃ see also CROSS-PROMOTION ⊃ SYNONYMS at ADVERTISEMENT ⊃ WORDFINDER NOTE at SHOP **4** [U] **~ of sth** (*formal*) activity that encourages people to believe in the value or importance of sth, or that helps sth to succeed: *a society for the promotion of religious tolerance*

**pro·mo·tion·al** /prə'məʊʃənl/ *adj.* connected with advertising: *promotional material*

**prompt** /prɒmpt; *NAmE* prɑːmpt/ *verb, adj., noun, adv.*

■ *verb* **1** [T] to make sb decide to do sth; to cause sth to happen **SYN** **provoke**: **~ sth** *The discovery of the bomb prompted an increase in security.* ◊ *His speech prompted an angry outburst from a man in the crowd.* ◊ **~ sb to do sth** *The thought of her daughter's wedding day prompted her to lose some weight.* **2** [T] to encourage sb to speak by asking them questions or suggesting words that they could say: **~ sb** *She was too nervous to speak and had to be prompted.* **~ sb to do sth** (*computing*): *The program will prompt you to enter data where required.* ◊ **~ (sb) + speech** *'And then what happened?' he prompted.* **3** [T, I] **~ (sb)** to follow the text of a play and remind the actors what the words are if they forget their lines

■ *adj.* **1** done without delay **SYN** **immediate**: *Prompt action was required as the fire spread.* ◊ *Prompt payment of the invoice would be appreciated.* **2** [not before noun] (of a person) acting without delay; arriving at the right time **SYN** **punctual**: *Please be prompt when attending these meetings.* ▶ **prompt·ness** *noun* [U]

■ *noun* **1** a word or words said to an actor, to remind them what to say next when they have forgotten **2** (*computing*) a sign on a computer screen that shows that the computer has finished doing sth and is ready for more instructions

■ *adv.* exactly at the time mentioned: *The meeting will begin at ten o'clock prompt.*

**prompt·er** /'prɒmptə(r); *NAmE* 'prɑːmp-/ *noun* a person who prompts actors in a play ⊃ WORDFINDER NOTE at PERFORMANCE

**prompt·ing** /'prɒmptɪŋ; *NAmE* 'prɑːmp-/ *noun* [U] (*also* **promptings** [pl.]) an act of persuading sb to do sth: *He wrote the letter without further prompting.* ◊ *Never again would she listen to the promptings of her heart.*

**prompt·ly** /'prɒmptli; *NAmE* 'prɑːmpt-/ *adv.* **1** without delay: *She deals with all the correspondence promptly and efficiently.* **2** exactly at the correct time or at the time mentioned **SYN** **punctually**: *They arrived promptly at two o'clock.* **3** (always used before the verb) immediately: *She read the letter and promptly burst into tears.*

**pro·mul·gate** /'prɒmlgeɪt; *NAmE* 'prɑːm-/ *verb* (*formal*) **1** [usually passive] **~ sth** to spread an idea, a belief, etc. among many people **2** **~ sth** to announce a new law or system officially or publicly ▶ **pro·mul·ga·tion** /ˌprɒml-'geɪʃn; *NAmE* ˌprɑːml-/ *noun* [U]

**prone** /prəʊn/ *adj.* **1** likely to suffer from sth or to do sth bad **SYN** **liable**: **~ to sth** *prone to injury* ◊ *Working without a break makes you more prone to error.* ◊ **~ to do sth** *Tired drivers were found to be particularly prone to ignore warning signs.* **2 -prone** (in adjectives) likely to suffer or do the thing mentioned: *error-prone* ◊ *injury-prone* ⊃ see also ACCIDENT-PRONE **3** (*formal*) lying flat with the front of your body touching the ground **SYN** **prostrate**: *The victim lay prone without moving.* ◊ *He was found lying in a prone position.* ⊃ compare SUPINE ▶ **prone·ness** /'prəʊnnəs/ *noun* [U] **~ (to sth)**: *proneness to depression*

**prong** /prɒŋ; *NAmE* prɔːŋ/ *noun* **1** each of the two or more long pointed parts of a fork **2** each of the separate parts of an attack, argument, etc. that move towards a place, subject, etc. from different positions **3** **-pronged** (in adjectives) having the number or type of prongs mentioned: *a two-pronged fork* ◊ *a three-pronged attack*

1235

**pro·noun** /'prəʊnaʊn/ *noun* (*grammar*) a word that is used instead of a noun or noun phrase, for example *he, it, hers, me, them,* etc.: *demonstrative/interrogative/possessive/relative pronouns* ⊃ see also IMPERSONAL PRONOUN, INDEFINITE PRONOUN, PERSONAL PRONOUN

**pro·nounce** 🔊 **A2**

/prə'naʊns/ *verb* **1** **A2** [T] **~ sth** to make the sound of a word or letter in a particular way: *Very few people can pronounce my name correctly.* ◊ *The 'b' in* lamb *is not pronounced.* ⊃ see also PRONUNCIATION, UNPRONOUNCEABLE **2** [T, I] (*formal*) to give a judgement, opinion or statement formally, officially or publicly: **~ sth** *to pronounce an opinion* ◊ *The judge will pronounce sentence today.* ◊ **~ sb/sth + noun** *She pronounced him the winner of the competition.* ◊ *I now pronounce you husband and wife* (= in a marriage ceremony). ◊ **~ sb/sth + adj.** *She was pronounced dead on arrival at the hospital.* ◊ **~ sb/sth to be/have sth** *He pronounced the country to be in a state of war.* ◊ **~ that …** *She pronounced that an error had been made.* ◊ **+ speech** *'It's pneumonia,' he pronounced gravely.* ◊ **~ for sb/sth** *The judge pronounced for* (= in favour of) *the defendant.*

**PHRV** **pro'nounce on/upon sth** (*formal*) to state your opinion on sth, or give a decision about sth: *The minister will pronounce on further security measures later today.*

WORD FAMILY
**pronounce** *verb*
**pronunciation** *noun*
**unpronounceable** *adj.*
**mispronounce** *verb*

**pro·nounce·able** /prə'naʊnsəbl/ *adj.* (of sounds or words) that can be pronounced **OPP** **unpronounceable**

**pro·nounced** /prə'naʊnst/ *adj.* very obvious, easy to notice or strongly expressed **SYN** **definite**: *He walked with a pronounced limp.* ◊ *She has very pronounced views on art.*

**pro·nounce·ment** /prə'naʊnsmənt/ *noun* **~ (on sth)** (*formal*) a formal public statement

**pronto** /'prɒntəʊ; *NAmE* 'prɑːn-/ *adv.* (*informal*) quickly; immediately: *I expect to see you back here, pronto!*

**pro·nun·ci·ation** /prəˌnʌnsi'eɪʃn/ *noun* **1** [U, C] the way in which a language or a particular word or sound is pronounced: *a guide to English pronunciation* ◊ *There is more than one pronunciation of 'garage'.*

**WORDFINDER** cluster, consonant, diphthong, elide, intonation, phonetics, stress, tone, voiced

**2** [sing.] the way in which a particular person pronounces the words of a language: *Your pronunciation is excellent.* ⊃ WORDFINDER NOTE at DICTIONARY

**proof** 🔊 **B2** /pruːf/ *noun, adj., verb*

■ *noun* **1** **B2** [U, C] information, documents, etc. that show that sth is true **SYN** **evidence**: *conclusive/definitive/scientific proof* ◊ *The police suspected him of dealing drugs, but they didn't* **have** *any* **proof.** ◊ *to* **require/need proof** ◊ **~ of sth** *Can you* **provide** *any* **proof** *of identity?* ◊ *Keep the receipt as proof of purchase.* ◊ *These results are a* **further proof** *of his outstanding ability.* ◊ **~ (that) …** *There is no proof that the knife belonged to her.* ◊ *Today's unemployment figures are* **proof positive** *the government's economic plan isn't working.* ◊ *In criminal cases the* **burden of proof** (= requirement to provide proof) *is on the prosecution.* ◊ *plans to lower the* **standard of proof** *required to convict people of crimes under the Terrorism Act* **2** [U] the process of testing whether sth is true or a fact: *Is the claim capable of proof?* ⊃ see also BURDEN OF PROOF **3** [C] (*mathematics*) a way of proving that a statement is true or that what you have calculated is correct **4** [C, usually pl.] a copy of printed material which is produced so that mistakes can be corrected: *She was checking the proofs of her latest novel.* **5** [U] a standard used to measure the strength of alcoholic drinks

**IDM** **the proof of the 'pudding (is in the 'eating)** (*saying*) you can only judge if sth is good or bad when you have tried it ⊃ more at LIVING *adj.*

■ *adj.* **1** **~ against sth** (*formal*) that can resist the damaging or harmful effects of sth: *The sea wall was not proof against the strength of the waves.* **2** (in compounds) that can resist

# proof of concept

or protect against the thing mentioned: *rainproof/windproof clothing* ◊ *The car has childproof locks on the rear doors.* ◊ *an inflation-proof pension plan*
- **verb 1** ~ **sth** to put a special substance on sth, especially cloth, to protect it against water, fire, etc: *proofed canvas* **2** ~ **sth** to produce a test copy of a piece of printed work so that mistakes can be corrected: *colour proofing*

**ˌproof of ˈconcept** *noun* [U, C, usually sing.] evidence that shows that a business proposal, design idea, etc. will work, usually based on an experiment or a PILOT project: *It is important to demonstrate proof of concept.*

**proof·read** /ˈpruːfriːd/ *verb* [T, I] (**proof·read**, **proof·read** /-red/) ~ **(sth)** to read and correct a piece of written or printed work: *Has this document been proofread?* ▸ **ˈproof·read·er** *noun*: *to work as a proofreader for a publishing company*

**prop** /prɒp/ *NAmE* prɑːp/ *noun, verb*
- *noun* **1** a piece of wood, metal, etc. used to support sth or keep it in position: *Rescuers used props to stop the roof of the tunnel collapsing.* ◊ *a pit prop* (= one used in a coal mine) **2** a person or thing that gives help or support to sb/sth that is weak **3** [usually pl.] a small object used by actors during the performance of a play or in a film: *He is responsible for all the stage props and lighting.* ⊃ WORDFINDER NOTE at STAGE **4** (*also* **ˌprop ˈforward**) (in rugby) a player on either side of the front row of a SCRUM
- *verb* (**-pp-**) to support an object by leaning it against sth, or putting sth under it, etc.; to support a person in the same way: ~ **sth/sb/yourself (up) (against sth)** *He propped his bike against the wall.* ◊ *She propped herself up on one elbow.* ◊ *He lay propped against the pillows.* ◊ ~ **sth + adj.** *The door was propped open.*
- **PHRV** **ˌprop sth↔ˈup 1** to prevent sth from falling by putting sth under it to support it **SYN** SHORE UP **2** (*often disapproving*) to help sth that is having difficulties: *The government was accused of propping up declining industries.*

**propa·ganda** /ˌprɒpəˈɡændə/ *NAmE* ˌprɑːp-/ *noun* [U] (*usually disapproving*) ideas or statements that may be false or present only one side of an argument that are used in order to gain support for a political leader, party, etc: *enemy propaganda* ◊ *a propaganda campaign*

**propa·gand·ist** /ˌprɒpəˈɡændɪst/ *NAmE* ˌprɑːp-/ *noun* (*formal, usually disapproving*) a person who creates or spreads propaganda ▸ **propa·gand·ist** *adj.* [only before noun]: *a propagandist organization*

**propa·gand·ize** (*BrE also* **-ise**) /ˌprɒpəˈɡændaɪz/ *NAmE* ˌprɑːp-/ *verb* [I, T] ~ **(sb/sth)** (*formal, disapproving*) to spread PROPAGANDA; to influence people using PROPAGANDA

**propa·gate** /ˈprɒpəɡeɪt/ *NAmE* ˈprɑːp-/ *verb* **1** [T] ~ **sth** (*formal*) to spread an idea, a belief or a piece of information among many people: *Television advertising propagates a false image of the ideal family.* **2** [T, I] ~ **(sth)** (*specialist*) to produce new plants from a parent plant: *The plant can be propagated from seed.* ◊ *Plants won't propagate in these conditions.* ▸ **propa·ga·tion** /ˌprɒpəˈɡeɪʃn/ *NAmE* ˌprɑːp-/ *noun* [U]

**propa·ga·tor** /ˈprɒpəɡeɪtə(r)/ *NAmE* ˈprɑːp-/ *noun* a box for propagating plants in

**pro·pane** /ˈprəʊpeɪn/ *noun* [U] a gas used as a fuel for cooking and heating: *a propane gas cylinder*

**pro·pel** /prəˈpel/ *verb* (**-ll-**) [often passive] **1** ~ **sth (+ adv./prep.)** to move, drive or push sth forward or in a particular direction: *mechanically propelled vehicles* ◊ *He succeeded in propelling the ball across the line.* **2** ~ **sb + adv./prep.** to force sb to move in a particular direction or to get into a particular situation: *He was grabbed from behind and propelled through the door.* ◊ *Fury propelled her into action.* ◊ *This picture propelled her to international stardom.* ⊃ see also PROPULSION

**pro·pel·lant** /prəˈpelənt/ *noun* [C, U] **1** a gas that forces out the contents of an AEROSOL **2** a thing or substance that propels sth, for example the fuel that fires a ROCKET

**pro·pel·ler** /prəˈpelə(r)/ *noun* a device with two or more long, flat BLADES that turn quickly and cause a ship or an aircraft to move forward

**pro·pen·sity** /prəˈpensəti/ *noun* (*pl.* **-ies**) (*formal*) a natural desire or need that makes you tend to behave in a particular way **SYN** INCLINATION: ~ **for (doing) sth** *He showed a propensity for violence.* ◊ ~ **to do sth** *She has a propensity to exaggerate.*

**proper** 🔊 B1 /ˈprɒpə(r)/; *NAmE* ˈprɑːp-/ *adj.* **1** B1 [only before noun] (*especially BrE*) right, appropriate or correct; according to the rules: *We should have had a proper discussion before voting.* ◊ *Please follow the proper procedures for dealing with complaints.* ◊ *Manufacturers provide these directions to indicate the proper use of their products* ◊ *It is vital that they're given the proper training.* ◊ *Nothing is in its proper place.* **2** B1 [only before noun] (*BrE, informal*) that you consider to be real and of a good enough standard: *I haven't had a proper meal in days.* ◊ *Eat some proper food, not just toast and jam!* ◊ *When are you going to get a proper job?* **3** socially and morally acceptable: *It is right and proper that parents take responsibility for their children's attendance at school.* ◊ *The development was planned without proper regard to the interests of local people.* ◊ *He is always perfectly proper in his behaviour.* **OPP** IMPROPER ⊃ see also PROPRIETY **4** [after noun] according to the most exact meaning of the word: *The celebrations proper always begin on the last stroke of midnight.* **5** [only before noun] (*BrE, informal*) complete: *We're in a proper mess now.* **6** ~ **to sth** (*formal*) belonging to a particular type of thing; natural in a particular situation or place: *They should be treated with the dignity proper to all individuals created by God.*
- **IDM** **ˌgood and ˈproper** (*BrE, informal*) completely; to the greatest extent possible: *That's messed things up good and proper.*

**prop·er·ly** 🔊 B1 /ˈprɒpəli/; *NAmE* ˈprɑːpərli/ *adv.* **1** B1 (*especially BrE*) in a way that is correct and/or appropriate: *How much money do we need to do the job properly?* ◊ *The television isn't working properly.* ◊ *Make sure the letter is properly addressed.* ◊ *Businesses should ensure that staff are properly trained in how to use new systems.* **2** in a way that is socially or morally acceptable: *You acted perfectly properly in approaching me first.* ◊ *When will these kids learn to behave properly?* **OPP** IMPROPERLY **3** really; in fact: *He had usurped powers that properly belonged to parliament.* ◊ *The subject is not, properly speaking* (= really), *a science.*

**ˌproper ˈnoun** (*also* **ˌproper ˈname**) *noun* (*grammar*) a word that is the name of a person, a place, an institution, etc. and is written with a capital letter, for example *Tom, Mrs Jones, Rome, Texas, the Rhine, the White House* ⊃ compare ABSTRACT NOUN, COMMON NOUN

**prop·er·tied** /ˈprɒpətid/ *NAmE* ˈprɑːpərt-/ *adj.* [only before noun] (*formal*) owning property, especially land

**prop·erty** 🔊 B1 /ˈprɒpəti/; *NAmE* ˈprɑːpərti/ *noun* (*pl.* **-ies**) **1** B1 [U] a thing or things that are owned by sb; a possession or possessions: *personal/stolen property* ◊ *This building is government property.* ◊ *Be careful not to damage other people's property.* ⊃ see also INTELLECTUAL PROPERTY, LOST PROPERTY, PUBLIC PROPERTY ⊃ SYNONYMS at THING **2** B2 [U] land and buildings: *The price of property has risen enormously.* ◊ *A sign indicates that it is now private property.* ◊ *commercial/residential property* ◊ *property prices/values/taxes* ◊ *a property developer/owner* ◊ *property development/investment* ◊ *a slump in the property market* ⊃ see also COMMUNITY PROPERTY ⊃ SYNONYMS at BUILDING **3** B2 [C] (*formal*) a building or buildings and the surrounding land: *to own/buy/purchase/acquire/sell a property* ◊ *rental/investment properties* ◊ *There are a lot of empty properties in the area.* ⊃ SYNONYMS at BUILDING **4** [C, usually pl.] (*formal*) a quality or characteristic that sth has: *Compare the physical properties of the two substances.* ◊ *a plant with medicinal properties*

**proph·ecy** /ˈprɒfəsi/ *NAmE* ˈprɑːf-/ *noun* (*pl.* **-ies**) **1** [C] a statement that sth will happen in the future, especially one made by sb with religious or magic powers: *to fulfil a prophecy* (= make it come true) **2** [U] (*formal*) the power of being able to say what will happen in the future: *She was believed to have the gift of prophecy.*

**proph·esy** /ˈprɒfəsaɪ/ *NAmE* ˈprɑːf-/ *verb* (**proph·es·ies**, **proph·esy·ing**, **proph·es·ied**, **proph·es·ied**) to say what will happen in the future (done in the past using religious or magic powers): **~sth** *to prophesy war* ◊ **~ that …** *She prophesied that she would win a gold medal.* ◊ **+ speech** *'It will end in disaster,' he prophesied.*

**proph·et** /ˈprɒfɪt; NAmE ˈprɑːf-/ *noun* **1** [C] (in the Christian, Jewish and Muslim religions) a person sent by God to teach the people and give them messages from God **2 the Prophet** [sing.] Muhammad, who founded the religion of Islam **3** [C] a person who claims to know what will happen in the future **4** [C] **~ (of sth)** a person who teaches or supports a new idea, theory, etc: *William Morris was one of the early prophets of socialism.* **5 the Prophets** [pl.] the name used for some books of the Old Testament and the Hebrew Bible [IDM] see DOOM *n.*

▼ **HOMOPHONES**

**profit • prophet** /ˈprɒfɪt; NAmE ˈprɑːf-/

- **profit** *noun: She's only interested in making a quick profit.*
- **profit** *verb: Patents allowed inventors to profit from ownership of their inventions.*
- **prophet** *noun: With his long white beard, he looks like an Old Testament prophet.*

**proph·et·ess** /ˌprɒfɪˈtes, ˈprɒfɪtes; NAmE ˈprɑːfɪtəs/ *noun* a woman who is a prophet

**proph·et·ic** /prəˈfetɪk/ *adj.* (*formal*) **1** correctly stating or showing what will happen in the future: *Many of his warnings proved prophetic.* **2** like or connected with a prophet or prophets: *the prophetic books of the Old Testament* ▸ **proph·et·ic·al·ly** /-kli/ *adv.*

**prophy·lac·tic** /ˌprɒfəˈlæktɪk; NAmE ˌproʊf-/ *adj., noun*
■ *adj.* (*medical*) done or used in order to prevent a disease: *prophylactic treatment* ▸ **prophy·lac·tic·al·ly** /-kli/ *adv.*
■ *noun* **1** (*medical*) a medicine, device or course of action that prevents disease **2** (*NAmE, formal*) = CONDOM

**prophy·laxis** /ˌprɒfəˈlæksɪs; NAmE ˌproʊf-/ *noun* [U] (*medical*) action that is taken in order to prevent disease

**pro·piti·ate** /prəˈpɪʃieɪt/ *verb* **~ sb** (*formal*) to stop sb from being angry by trying to please them SYN **placate**: *Sacrifices were made to propitiate the gods.* ▸ **pro·piti·ation** /prəˌpɪʃiˈeɪʃn/ *noun* [U]

**pro·pi·tious** /prəˈpɪʃəs/ *adj.* **~ (for sth/sb)** (*formal*) likely to produce a successful result: *It was not a propitious time to start a new business.*

**pro·pon·ent** /prəˈpəʊnənt/ *noun* **~ (of sth)** (*formal*) a person who supports an idea or course of action SYN **advocate**

**pro·por·tion** 🔊+ 🔊 ○ /prəˈpɔːʃn; NAmE -ˈpɔːrʃn/ *noun*
- **PART OF WHOLE 1** 🔊+ 🔊 [C + sing. / pl. v.] a part or share of a whole: *Water covers a large proportion of the earth's surface.* ◊ *Loam is a soil with roughly equal proportions of clay, sand and silt.* ◊ *A significant proportion of the books have been translated from other languages.* ◊ *A higher proportion of Americans go on to higher education than is the case in Britain.*
- **RELATIONSHIP 2** 🔊+ 🔊 [U] the relationship of one thing to another in size, amount, etc. SYN **ratio**: **~ of sth to sth** *The proportion of men to women in the college has changed dramatically over the years.* ◊ **in the ~** … *The basic ingredients are limestone and clay in the proportion 2:1.* ◊ **in ~ to sth** *The room is very long in proportion to* (= relative to) *its width.* **3** 🔊+ 🔊 [U, C, usually pl.] the correct relationship in size, degree, importance, etc. between one thing and another or between the parts of a whole: **in ~ (to sth)** *You haven't drawn the figures in the foreground in proportion.* ◊ **out of ~ (with sth)** *The head is out of proportion with the body.* ◊ *an impressive building with fine proportions* ◊ (*figurative*) *Always try to keep a* **sense of proportion** (= the relative importance of different things).
- **SIZE/SHAPE 4** 🔊+ 🔊 **proportions** [pl.] the measurements of sth; its size and shape: *This method divides the task into more manageable proportions.* ◊ *a food shortage that could soon* **reach crisis proportions** ◊ *a room of fairly generous proportions*
- **MATHEMATICS 5** [U] the equal relationship between two pairs of numbers, as in the statement '4 is to 8 as 6 is to 12'
[IDM] ˌkeep sth in proˈportion to react to sth in a sensible way and not think it is worse or more serious than it really

is ˌout of (all) proˈportion (to sth) larger, more serious, etc. in relation to sth than is necessary or appropriate: *They earn salaries out of all proportion to their ability.* ◊ *The media have blown the incident up out of all proportion.*

▼ **GRAMMAR POINT**

**proportion**

- If **proportion** is used with an uncountable or a singular noun, the verb is generally singular: *A proportion of the land is used for agriculture.*
- If **the proportion of** is used with a plural countable noun, or a singular noun that represents a group of people, the verb is usually singular, but with **a (large, small, etc.) proportion** of a plural verb is often used, especially in BrE: *The proportion of small cars on America's roads is increasing.* ◊ *A high proportion of five-year-olds have teeth in poor condition.*

▼ **LANGUAGE BANK**

**proportion**

Describing fractions and proportions

- According to this pie chart, **a third of** students' leisure time is spent watching TV.
- **One in five** hours is / are spent socializing.
- Socializing **accounts for / makes up / comprises** about 20 per cent of leisure time.
- Students spend **twice as much** time playing computer games as doing sport.
- **Three times as many** hours are spent playing computer games as reading.
- The figure for playing computer games **is three times higher than** the figure for reading.
- **The largest proportion of** time is spent playing computer games.

⊃ note at HALF
⊃ SYNONYMS at CONSIST
⊃ LANGUAGE BANK at EXPECT, FALL, ILLUSTRATE, INCREASE

**pro·por·tion·al** 🔊 /prəˈpɔːʃənl; NAmE -ˈpɔːrʃ-/ *adj.* **~ (to sth)** increasing or decreasing in size, amount or degree according to changes in sth else: *Salary is proportional to years of experience.* ◊ *to be* **directly/inversely proportional** *to sth* ▸ **pro·por·tion·al·ly** *adv.*: *Families with children spend proportionally less per person than families without children.*

**pro·por·tion·al·ity** /prəˌpɔːʃəˈnæləti; NAmE -ˌpɔːrʃ-/ *noun* [U] (*formal*) the principle that an action, a punishment, etc. should not be more severe than is necessary

**proˌportional ˌrepreˈsenˈtation** *noun* [U] (*abbr.* **PR**) a system that gives each party in an election a number of seats in relation to the number of votes its candidates receive ⊃ compare FIRST-PAST-THE-POST

**pro·por·tion·ate** /prəˈpɔːʃənət; NAmE -ˈpɔːrʃ-/ *adj.* **~ (to sth)** (*formal*) increasing or decreasing in size, amount or degree according to changes in sth else SYN **proportional**: *The number of accidents is proportionate to the increased volume of traffic.* ⊃ compare DISPROPORTIONATE ▸ **pro·por·tion·ate·ly** *adv.*: *Prices have risen but wages have not risen proportionately.*

**pro·por·tioned** /prəˈpɔːʃnd; NAmE -ˈpɔːrʃ-/ *adj.* (used especially after an adverb) having parts that relate in size to other parts in the way that is described: *a well-proportioned living room* ◊ *She was tall and perfectly proportioned.*

**pro·posal** 🔊 🔊 🔊 /prəˈpəʊzl/ *noun* **1** 🔊 🔊 [C, U] a formal suggestion or plan; the act of making a suggestion: *to submit/present/put forward a proposal* ◊ *to consider/discuss a proposal* ◊ *to accept/approve/support/reject a proposal* ◊ **~ to do sth** *a proposal to build more office accommodation* ◊ **~ that** … *His proposal that the system should be changed was rejected.* ◊ **~ for sth** *The proposal for a new high-speed railway met with strong opposition.* ◊ **~ on sth** *When will the minister publish his proposals on reform of the health service?* ◊ **~ by / from sb** *two recent*

| s see | t tea | v van | w wet | z zoo | ʃ shoe | ʒ vision | tʃ chain | dʒ jam | θ thin | ð this | ŋ sing |

# propose

proposals by Vancouver City Council ◊ **under a~** *Under these proposals, the Commission will be significantly strengthened.* ◊ *The Republicans in Congress will vote for the president's* **budget proposal.** ◊ **WORDFINDER NOTE** at DEAL **2** [C] an act of formally asking sb to marry you

**pro·pose** /prəˈpəʊz/ *verb*
- **SUGGEST PLAN 1** [T] (*formal*) to suggest a plan, an idea, etc. for people to think about and decide on: *~ sth The government proposed changes to the voting system.* ◊ *The three countries had proposed a plan for him to hand over power to a chosen successor.* ◊ *What would you propose?* ◊ *~ that … She proposed that the book be banned.* (*BrE also*) *She proposed that the book should be banned.* ◊ **it is proposed that …** *It was proposed that the president be elected for a period of two years.* ◊ *~ doing sth He proposed changing the name of the company.* ◊ **it is proposed to do sth** *It was proposed to pay the money from public funds.*
- **INTEND 2** [T] (*formal*) to intend to do sth: *~ to do sth What do you propose to do now?* ◊ *~ doing sth How do you propose getting home?*
- **MARRIAGE 3** [I, T] to ask sb to marry you: *He was afraid that if he proposed she might refuse.* ◊ *~ to sb She proposed to me!* ◊ *~ sth (to sb) to propose marriage* ⇒ **WORDFINDER NOTE** at WEDDING
- **AT FORMAL MEETING 4** [T] to suggest sth at a formal meeting and ask people to vote on it: *~ sb (for/as sth) I propose Tom Ellis for chairman.* ◊ *~ sth to propose a motion* (= to be the main speaker in support of an idea at a formal debate) ⇒ compare OPPOSE, SECOND¹ ⇒ **WORDFINDER NOTE** at DEBATE
- **SUGGEST EXPLANATION 5** [T] *~ sth* (*formal*) to suggest an explanation of sth for people to consider **propound**: *She proposed a possible solution to the mystery.*

**IDM propose a ˈtoast (to sb) | propose sb's ˈhealth** to ask people to wish sb health, happiness and success by raising their glasses and drinking: *I'd like to propose a toast to the bride and groom.*

**pro·poser** /prəˈpəʊzə(r)/ *noun* a person who formally suggests sth at a meeting ⇒ compare SECONDER

**prop·os·ition** /ˌprɒpəˈzɪʃn/ /NAmE ˌprɑːp-/ *noun*, *verb*
- *noun* **1** an idea or a plan of action that is suggested, especially in business: *I'd like to put a business proposition to you.* ◊ *He was trying to make it look like an attractive proposition.* **2** a thing that you intend to do; a problem, task or person to be dealt with **matter**: *Getting a work permit in the UK is not always a simple proposition.* **3** (*also* **Proposition**) (*in the US*) a suggested change to the law that people can vote on: *How did you vote on Proposition 8?* **4** (*formal*) a statement that expresses an opinion: *Her assessment is based on the proposition that power corrupts.* **5** (*mathematics*) a statement of a THEOREM, and an explanation of how it can be proved ▶ **prop·os·ition·al** /-ʃənl/ *adj.*
- *verb* *~ sb* to say in a direct way to sb that you would like to have sex with them: *She was propositioned by a strange man in the bar.*

**pro·pound** /prəˈpaʊnd/ *verb* *~ sth* (*formal*) to suggest an idea or explanation of sth for people to consider **propose, put forward**: *the theory of natural selection, first propounded by Charles Darwin*

**pro·pri·etary** /prəˈpraɪətri/ /NAmE -teri/ *adj.* [usually before noun] **1** (of goods) made and sold by a particular company and protected by a REGISTERED TRADEMARK: *a proprietary medicine* ◊ *proprietary brands* ◊ *a proprietary name* **OPP non-proprietary 2** relating to an owner or to the fact of owning sth: *The company has a proprietary right to the property.*

**pro·pri·etor** /prəˈpraɪətə(r)/ *noun* (*formal*) the owner of a business, a hotel, etc: *newspaper proprietors* ▶ **pro·pri·etor·ship** /prəˈpraɪətəʃɪp/ /NAmE -tərʃ-/ *noun* [U]

**pro·pri·etor·ial** /prəˌpraɪəˈtɔːriəl/ *adj.* (*formal*) relating to an owner or to the fact of owning sth: *proprietorial rights* ◊ *He laid a proprietorial hand on her arm* (= as if he owned her). ▶ **pro·pri·etor·ial·ly** *adv.*

**pro·pri·ety** /prəˈpraɪəti/ *noun* (*formal*) **1** [U] moral and social behaviour that is considered to be correct and acceptable: *Nobody questioned the propriety of her being there alone.* **OPP impropriety 2 the proprieties** [pl.] the rules of correct behaviour **etiquette**: *They were careful to observe the proprieties.*

**props** /prɒps/ /NAmE prɑːps/ *noun* [pl.] *~ (to sb)* (*informal*) used to show that you appreciate what sb has done because it is good: *Props to all of you who helped out over there.* ◊ *I gotta give props to the bass player.* **ORIGIN** Props here means 'proper respect or recognition'.

**pro·pul·sion** /prəˈpʌlʃn/ *noun* [U] (*specialist*) the force that drives sth forward: *wind/steam/jet propulsion* ⇒ see also PROPEL ▶ **pro·pul·sive** /-ˈpʌlsɪv/ *adj.*

**pro rata** /ˌprəʊ ˈrɑːtə/ *adj.* (*from Latin, formal*) (of a payment or share of sth) calculated according to how much of sth has been used, the amount of work done, etc. **proportionate**: *If costs go up, there will be a pro rata increase in prices.* ▶ **pro rata** *adv.*: *Prices will increase pro rata.*

**pro·sa·ic** /prəˈzeɪɪk/ /NAmE prəʊˈz-/ *adj.* (*usually disapproving*) **1** ordinary and not showing any imagination **unimaginative**: *a prosaic style* **2** not interesting or romantic **mundane**: *the prosaic side of life* ▶ **pro·saic·al·ly** /-kli/ *adv.*

**pro·scen·ium** /prəˈsiːniəm/ *noun* the part of the stage in a theatre that is in front of the curtain: *a traditional theatre with a proscenium arch* (= one that forms a frame for the stage where the curtain is opened) ⇒ **WORDFINDER NOTE** at STAGE

**prosciutto** /prəˈʃuːtəʊ/ /NAmE also prəʊˈʃ-/ *noun* [U] (*from Italian*) a type of Italian HAM that is served in very thin slices

**pro·scribe** /prəˈskraɪb/ /NAmE prəʊˈs-/ *verb* *~ sth* (*formal*) to say officially that sth is banned: *proscribed organizations* ▶ **pro·scrip·tion** /-ˈskrɪpʃn/ *noun* [U, C]

**prose** /prəʊz/ *noun* [U] writing that is not poetry: *the author's clear elegant prose* (= style of writing)

**Pro·secco™** /prəˈsekəʊ/ *noun* [U, C] (*pl.* **-os**) an Italian SPARKLING white wine (= one with bubbles) ⇒ compare CHAMPAGNE

**pros·ecute** /ˈprɒsɪkjuːt/ /NAmE ˈprɑːs-/ *verb* **1** [T, I] to officially charge sb with a crime in court: *The police decided not to prosecute.* ◊ *~ sb/sth Trespassers will be prosecuted* (= a notice telling people to keep out of a particular area). ◊ *~ sb/sth for (doing) sth The company was prosecuted for breaching the Health and Safety Act.* ⇒ **WORDFINDER NOTE** at LAW **2** [I, T] *~ (sb)* to be a lawyer in a court case for a person or an organization that is charging sb with a crime: *the prosecuting counsel/lawyer/attorney* ◊ *James Spencer, prosecuting, claimed that the witness was lying.* **3** [T] *~ sth* (*formal*) to continue taking part in or doing sth: *They had overwhelming public support to prosecute the war.*

**pros·ecu·tion** /ˌprɒsɪˈkjuːʃn/ /NAmE ˌprɑːs-/ *noun* **1** [U, C] the process of trying to prove in court that sb is guilty of a crime (= of prosecuting them); the process of being officially charged with a crime in court: *Prosecution for a first minor offence rarely leads to imprisonment.* ◊ *He threatened to bring a private prosecution against the doctor.* ⇒ **WORDFINDER NOTE** at TRIAL **2 the prosecution** [sing. + sing./pl. v.] a person or an organization that prosecutes sb in court, together with the lawyers, etc: *He was a witness for the prosecution.* ◊ *The prosecution has/have failed to prove its/their case.* ◊ *defence and prosecution* ◊ *a prosecution lawyer* **3** [U] (*formal*) the act of making sth happen or continue

**pros·ecu·tor** /ˈprɒsɪkjuːtə(r)/ /NAmE ˈprɑːs-/ *noun* **1** a public official who charges sb officially with a crime and prosecutes them in court: *the public/state prosecutor* **2** a lawyer who leads the case against a DEFENDANT in court: *The prosecutor rose to give the opening address.* ⇒ see also CROWN PROSECUTOR

**pros·elyt·ize** (*BrE also* **-ise**) /ˈprɒsələtaɪz/ /NAmE ˈprɑːs-/ *verb* [I] (*formal, often disapproving*) to try to persuade other people to accept your beliefs, especially about religion or politics

**ˈprose poem** *noun* a piece of writing that uses the language and ideas associated with poetry, but is not in VERSE form

**pro shop** *noun* a shop at a golf club that sells or repairs golf equipment, usually run by a professional player who works at that club

**pros·ody** /ˈprɒsədi; *NAmE* ˈprɑːs-/ *noun* [U] **1** (*specialist*) the patterns of sounds and rhythms in poetry; the study of this **2** (*phonetics*) the part of PHONETICS that deals with stress and INTONATION as opposed to individual speech sounds ▶ **pro·sodic** /prəˈsɒdɪk; *NAmE* prəˈsɑːd-/ *adj.*

**pros·pect** 🔊 **B2** *noun, verb*

■ *noun* /ˈprɒspekt; *NAmE* ˈprɑːs-/ **1** 🔊 [U, sing.] the possibility that sth will happen: *~ of (doing) sth There is no immediate prospect of peace.* ◊ *~ (that) … There's a reasonable prospect that his debts will be paid.* ◊ **in ~** *A place in the semi-finals is in prospect* (= likely to happen). **2** 🔊 **B2** [sing.] an idea of what might or will happen in the future: *an exciting prospect* ◊ *Travelling alone around the world is a daunting prospect.* ◊ *~ of doing sth The prospect of becoming a father filled him with alarm.* **3** 🔊 **B2** **prospects** [pl.] the chances of being successful: *good job/employment/career prospects* ◊ *industries with excellent growth prospects* ◊ *At 25 he was an unemployed musician with no prospects.* ◊ **prospects for sth** *Long-term prospects for the economy have improved.* ◊ **prospects of sth** *Their prospects of success are slight.* **4** [C] *~ (for sth)* a person who is likely to be successful in a competition or in a particular career: *She is one of Canada's best prospects for a gold medal.* **5** [C] (*formal*) a wide view of an area of land, etc: *a delightful prospect of the lake*

■ *verb* /prəˈspekt; *NAmE* ˈprɑːspekt/ [I] *~ (for sth)* to search an area for gold, minerals, oil, etc: *Thousands moved to the area to prospect for gold.* ◊ (*figurative*) *to prospect for new clients*

**pro·spect·ive** 🔊+ **C1** /prəˈspektɪv/ *adj.* [usually before noun] **1** 🔊+ **C1** expected to do sth or to become sth **SYN** **potential**: *a prospective buyer* **2** 🔊+ **C1** expected to happen soon **SYN** **forthcoming**: *They are worried about prospective changes in the law.*

**pro·spect·or** /prəˈspektə(r); *NAmE* ˈprɑːspektər/ *noun* a person who searches an area for gold, minerals, oil, etc.

**pro·spec·tus** /prəˈspektəs/ *noun* **1** a book, document or web page that gives information about a school, college, etc. in order to advertise it ⊃ **WORDFINDER NOTE** at ADVERTISE **2** (*business*) a document that gives information about a company's shares before they are offered for sale

**pros·per** /ˈprɒspə(r); *NAmE* ˈprɑːs-/ *verb* [I] to develop in a successful way; to be successful, especially in making money **SYN** **thrive**

**pros·per·ity** 🔊+ **C1** /prɒˈsperəti/ *noun* [U] the state of being successful, especially in making money **SYN** **affluence**: *Our future prosperity depends on economic growth.* ◊ *The country is enjoying a period of* **peace and prosperity**.

**pros·per·ous** /ˈprɒspərəs; *NAmE* ˈprɑːs-/ *adj.* (*formal*) rich and successful **SYN** **affluent**: *prosperous countries* ⊃ **SYNONYMS** at **RICH**

**pros·tate** /ˈprɒsteɪt; *NAmE* ˈprɑːs-/ (*also* **prostate gland**) *noun* a small organ in men, near the BLADDER, that produces a liquid in which SPERM is carried

**pros·thesis** /ˈprɒsθɪsɪs; *NAmE* prɑːs-/ *noun* (*pl.* **prostheses** /-ˈθiːsiːz/) (*medical*) an artificial part of the body, for example a leg, an eye or a tooth ▶ **pros·thet·ic** /-ˈθetɪk/ *adj.*: *a prosthetic arm*

**pros·thet·ics** /prɒsˈθetɪks; *NAmE* prɑːs-/ *noun* **1** [pl.] artificial parts of the body **2** [U] the activity of making or attaching artificial body parts

**pros·ti·tute** /ˈprɒstɪtjuːt; *NAmE* ˈprɑːstɪtuːt/ *noun, verb*

■ *noun* a person who has sex for money

■ *verb* **1** *~ sth/yourself* (*disapproving*) to use your skills, abilities, etc. to do sth that earns you money but that other people do not respect because you are capable of doing sth better: *Many felt he was prostituting his talents by writing Hollywood scripts.* **2** *~ yourself* to work as a prostitute

**pros·ti·tu·tion** /ˌprɒstɪˈtjuːʃn; *NAmE* ˌprɑːstɪˈtuː-/ *noun* [U] **1** the work of a prostitute: *Many women were forced into prostitution.* ◊ **child prostitution** **2** *~ of sth* (*formal*) the use of your abilities on sth of little value

---

1239 **protection**

**pros·trate** *adj., verb*

■ *adj.* /ˈprɒstreɪt; *NAmE* ˈprɑːs-/ (*formal*) **1** lying on the ground and facing downwards **SYN** **prone**: *They fell prostrate in worship.* ◊ *He stumbled over Luke's prostrate body.* ⊃ compare SUPINE (1) **2** *~ (with sth)* so shocked, upset, etc. that you cannot do anything: *She was prostrate with grief after her son's death.*

■ *verb* /prɒˈstreɪt; *NAmE* ˈprɑːstreɪt/ **1** *~ yourself* to lie on your front with your face looking downwards, especially as a way of showing respect for God or a god **2** [usually passive] *~ sb* to make sb feel weak, shocked, and unable to do anything **SYN** **overcome**: *He was expecting to find her prostrated by the tragedy.* ◊ *For months he was* **prostrated with grief**.

**pros·tra·tion** /prɒˈstreɪʃn; *NAmE* prɑːs-/ *noun* [U] (*formal*) **1** extreme physical weakness: *a state of prostration brought on by the heat* **2** the action of lying with your face downwards, especially as a way of showing respect for God or a god

**prot·ag·on·ist** /prəˈtæɡənɪst/ *noun* (*formal*) **1** the main character in a play, film or book ⊃ compare HERO ⊃ **WORDFINDER NOTE** at CHARACTER **2** one of the main people in a real event, especially a competition, battle or struggle **3** an active supporter of a policy or movement, especially one that is trying to change sth **SYN** **champion**: *a leading protagonist of the conservation movement*

**pro·tea** /ˈprəʊtiə/ *noun* **1** a type of bush found in South Africa with large flowers with thick orange or pink outer leaves **2** the flower itself, which is one of South Africa's national symbols

**pro·tean** /ˈprəʊtiən, prəʊˈtiːən/ *adj.* (*literary*) able to change quickly and easily: *a protean character*

**pro·te·ase** /ˈprəʊtieɪz/ *noun* (*biology*) a substance in the body that breaks down PROTEINS and PEPTIDES

**pro·tect** 🔊 **A2** 🔊 /prəˈtekt/ *verb* **1** **A2** [T, I] to make sure that sb/sth is not harmed, injured, damaged, etc: *~ sb/sth/yourself to protect children/citizens/civilians/ consumers/workers* ◊ *the section of the treaty that protects the rights of employees* ◊ *Each company is fighting to protect its own commercial interests.* ◊ *~ sb/sth/yourself against/from sth Troops have been sent to protect aid workers against attack.* ◊ *They huddled together to protect themselves from the wind.* ◊ *~ against/from sth a paint that helps protect against rust* **2** **A2** [T, usually passive] *~ sth* to introduce laws that make it illegal to kill, harm or damage a particular animal, area of land, building, etc: *the need to protect the environment* ◊ **to be protected by sth** *Polar bears have been protected by law in Norway since 1973.* **3** [T, usually passive] *~ sth* to help an industry in your own country by taxing goods from other countries so that there is less competition: *protected markets* **4** [T, I] *~ (sb/ sth) (against sth)* to provide sb/sth with insurance against fire, injury, damage, etc: *Many policies do not protect you against personal injury.* **5** [T] *~ sb/sth (against/from sth)* (*computing*) to limit access to data, a web page, etc., for example by using PASSWORDS or ENCRYPTION (= special codes): *All these pages are password-protected.*

**pro·tec·tion** 🔊 **B2** 🔊 /prəˈtekʃn/ *noun* **1** 🔊 **B2** [U] the act of protecting sb/sth; the state of being protected: *~ against/from sth Wear clothes that provide adequate protection against the wind and rain.* ◊ *~ of/for sb/sth (against/from sth) We seek to ensure the protection of human rights.* ◊ **under ~** *He asked to be put under police protection.* ◊ **data protection laws** **2** 🔊 **B2** [C, U] a thing that protects sb/sth against sth: *~ (against/from sth) The plastic sheeting is not a complete protection against the rain.* ◊ **as (a) ~ (against/from sth)** *He wears a helmet as protection.* **3** [U] insurance against fire, injury, damage, etc: *Our policy offers complete protection against fire and theft.* **4** [U] the system of helping an industry in your own country by taxing foreign goods: *The government is ready to introduce protection for the car industry.* **5** [U] the system of paying criminals so that they will not attack your business or property: *to pay* **protection money** ◊ *to run a* **protection racket**

---

u *actual* | aɪ *my* | aʊ *now* | eɪ *say* | əʊ *go* | ɔɪ *boy* | ɪə *near* | eə *hair* | ʊə *pure*

# protectionism

**pro·tec·tion·ism** /prəˈtekʃənɪzəm/ noun [U] the principle or practice of protecting a country's own industry by taxing foreign goods ▶ **pro·tec·tion·ist** /-nɪst/ adj.: protectionist policies

**proˈtection order** noun ~ (against sb) a set of legal measures that are intended to stop sb from harming sb else: He breached the protection order by phoning his ex-wife on two occasions.

**pro·tect·ive** /prəˈtektɪv/ adj. **1** [only before noun] providing or intended to provide protection: Workers should wear full protective clothing. ◇ a protective layer of varnish ◇ a protective barrier against the sun's rays **2** having or showing a wish to protect sb/sth: He put a protective arm around her shoulders. ◇ ~ towards sb/sth She had been fiercely protective towards him as a teenager. ◇ ~ of sb/sth He was extremely protective of his role as advisor. ◇ Parents can easily become over-protective of their children (= want to protect them too much). **3** intended to give an advantage to your own country's industry: protective tariffs ▶ **pro·tect·ive·ly** adv.: She clutched her bag protectively. **pro·tect·ive·ness** noun [U]

**proˌtective ˈcustody** noun [U] the state of being kept in prison for your own safety

**pro·tect·or** /prəˈtektə(r)/ noun a person, an organization or a thing that protects sb/sth: I regarded him as my friend and protector. ◇ the company's image as a protector of the environment ◇ Hard hats and ear protectors are provided.

**pro·tect·or·ate** /prəˈtektərət/ noun **1** [C] a country that is controlled and protected by a more powerful country ⊃ compare COLONY **2** [U] the state or period of being controlled and protected by another country

**pro·tégé** (feminine **pro·té·gée**) /ˈprɒtəʒeɪ; NAmE ˈproʊt-/ noun (from French) a young person who is helped in their career and personal development by a more experienced person: a protégé of the great violinist Yehudi Menuhin

**pro·tein** /ˈprəʊtiːn/ noun [C, U] a substance, found within all living things, that forms the structure of muscles, organs, etc. There are many different proteins and they are an essential part of what humans and animals eat to help them grow and stay healthy: essential proteins and vitamins ◇ protein deficiency ◇ Peas, beans and lentils are a good source of vegetable protein. ⊃ see also ENZYME ⊃ WORDFINDER NOTE at BIOLOGY

**ˈprotein shake** noun a drink that looks like a MILKSHAKE and contains a lot of protein. People drink protein shakes for health reasons such as to gain muscle, lose weight or have more energy.

**pro tem** /ˌprəʊ ˈtem/ adv. (from Latin) for now, but not for a long time SYN temporarily: A new manager will be appointed pro tem. ▶ **pro tem** adj.: A pro tem committee was formed from existing members.

**pro·test** noun, verb

■ **noun** /ˈprəʊtest/ [U, C] the expression of strong dislike of or opposition to sth; a statement or an action that shows this: to hold/organize/join a protest ◇ violent/anti-war protests ◇ The riot began as a peaceful protest. ◇ mass/street protests ◇ a protest march/movement ◇ Unions have called for a day of protest on 24 February. ◇ The announcement raised a storm of protest. ◇ ~ at sth There have been mounting protests at the treatment of asylum seekers by the government. ◇ in ~ (at sth) The director resigned in protest at the decision. ◇ ~ over sth protests over plans to close the museum ◇ without ~ She accepted the charge without protest. ◇ ~ against sth The workers staged a protest against the proposed changes in their contracts. ◇ as a ~ (against sth) They have decided not to attend the Bonn conference as a protest. ◇ ~ from/by sb The building work will go ahead, despite protests from local residents. ⊃ WORDFINDER NOTE at UNION

**WORDFINDER** civil disobedience, demonstrate, hunger strike, march, occupy, placard, riot, sabotage, uprising

IDM **under ˈprotest** unwillingly and after expressing DISAGREEMENT: She wrote a letter of apology but only under protest.

■ **verb** /prəˈtest/; NAmE also /ˈproʊtest/ **1** [I, T] to say or do sth to show that you disagree with sth or think it is bad, especially publicly: There's no use protesting, I won't change my mind. ◇ ~ **about/against/at sth** Students took to the streets to protest against the decision. ◇ The victim's widow protested at the leniency of the sentence. ◇ ~ **sth**: (NAmE) They fully intend to protest the decision. ⊃ SYNONYMS at COMPLAIN **2** [T] to state clearly that sth is true, especially when you have been accused of sth or when other people do not believe you: ~ **sth** She has always protested her innocence. ◇ ~ **that** … He protested that the journey was too far by car. ◇ + **speech** 'That's not what you said earlier!' Jane protested.

**Prot·est·ant** /ˈprɒtɪstənt; NAmE ˈproːt-/ noun a member of a part of the Western Christian Church that separated from the Roman Catholic Church in the 16th century: He's a Protestant. ▶ **Prot·est·ant** adj.: The majority of the population is Protestant. ◇ a Protestant church/country **Prot·est·ant·ism** noun [U]

**prot·est·ation** /ˌprɒtəˈsteɪʃn; NAmE ˌproːt-, ˌproʊt-/ noun [C, U] (formal) a strong statement that sth is true, especially when other people do not believe you: She repeated her protestation of innocence. ◇ Despite his protestation to the contrary, he was extremely tired.

**pro·test·er** /prəˈtestə(r), ˈprəʊtestə(r)/ noun a person who makes a public protest SYN demonstrator: Thousands of protesters marched through the city.

**ˈprotest vote** noun **1** [C] a vote for a person or party not because you support them but because you want to prevent another person or party from succeeding: People were really casting a protest vote against the leadership of the Democratic Party rather than endorsing the far left. **2** [sing.] the total number of protest votes in an election: The Communist Party appeared to benefit from the protest vote.

**proto-** /ˈprəʊtəʊ, ˈprəʊtə/ combining form (in nouns and adjectives) original; from which others develop: prototype ◇ proto-modernist painters

**proto·col** /ˈprəʊtəkɒl; NAmE -kɔːl/ noun **1** [U] a system of fixed rules and formal behaviour used at official meetings, usually between governments: a breach of protocol ◇ the protocol of diplomatic visits **2** [C] (specialist) the first or original version of an agreement, especially a TREATY between countries, etc.; an extra part added to an agreement or TREATY: the first Geneva Protocol ◇ It is set out in a legally binding protocol which forms part of the treaty. **3** [C] (computing) a set of rules that control the way data is sent between computers **4** [C] (specialist) a plan for performing a scientific experiment or medical treatment

**pro·ton** /ˈprəʊtɒn; NAmE -taːn/ noun (physics) a very small piece of matter (= a substance) with a positive electric charge that forms part of the NUCLEUS (= central part) of an ATOM ⊃ see also ELECTRON, NEUTRON ⊃ WORDFINDER NOTE at ATOM

**proto·plasm** /ˈprəʊtəplæzəm/ noun [U] (biology) a soft, clear substance like JELLY that forms the living part of an animal or plant cell ⊃ compare CYTOPLASM

**proto·type** /ˈprəʊtətaɪp/ noun ~ (for/of sth) the first design of sth from which other forms are copied or developed: the prototype of the modern bicycle ▶ **proto·typ·ical** /ˌprəʊtəˈtɪpɪkl/ adj.

**proto·zoan** /ˌprəʊtəˈzəʊən/ noun (pl. **proto·zoans** or **proto·zoa** /-ˈzəʊə/) (biology) a very small living thing, usually with only one cell, that can only be seen under a MICROSCOPE ▶ **proto·zoan** adj.

**pro·tract·ed** /prəˈtræktɪd; NAmE also proʊˈt-/ adj. (formal) lasting longer than expected or longer than usual SYN prolonged: protracted delays/disputes/negotiations

**pro·tract·or** /prəˈtræktə(r); NAmE also proʊˈt-/ noun an instrument for measuring and drawing angles, usually made from a half circle of clear plastic with degrees (0° to 180°) marked on it

**pro·trude** /prəˈtruːd; NAmE proʊˈt-/ verb [I] (formal) to stick out from a place or a surface: protruding teeth ◇ ~ **from sth** He hung his coat on a nail protruding from the wall.

**pro·tru·sion** /prəˈtruːʒn; NAmE proʊ't-/ noun [C, U] (formal) a thing that sticks out from a place or surface; the fact of doing this: *a protrusion on the rock face*

**pro·tu·ber·ance** /prəˈtjuːbərəns; NAmE proʊˈtuː-/ noun (formal) a round part that sticks out from a surface SYN **bulge**

**proud** ⓣ B1 /praʊd/ adj., adv.
■ *adj.* (**proud·er**, **proud·est**)
• PLEASED 1 B1 feeling pleased and satisfied about sth that you own or have done, or are connected with: *proud parents* ◊ *the proud owner of a new car* ◊ **~ of sb / sth / yourself (for doing sth)** *Your achievements are something to be proud of.* ◊ *Barry was proud of the fact that he had never missed a day's work in his life.* ◊ *He was proud of himself for not giving up.* ◊ **~ to be / do sth** *I feel very proud to be a part of the team.* ◊ *I'm proud to say it's now been 17 days since I last smoked.* ◊ **~ (that) …** *She was proud that her daughter had so much talent.* ⊃ see also HOUSE-PROUD ⊃ SYNONYMS at GLAD 2 ⓣ B2 [only before noun] causing sb to feel proud: *This is the proudest moment of my life.* ◊ *The car had been his proudest possession.*
• FEELING TOO IMPORTANT 3 ⓣ B2 (*disapproving*) feeling that you are better and more important than other people SYN **arrogant**: *She comes across as proud and arrogant.* ◊ *He was too proud now to be seen with his former friends.*
• HAVING SELF-RESPECT 4 ⓣ B2 having respect for yourself and not wanting to lose the respect of others: *They were a proud and independent people.* ◊ *Don't be too proud to ask for help.*
• BEAUTIFUL / TALL 5 (*literary*) beautiful, tall and impressive: *The sunflowers stretched tall and proud to the sun.* ⊃ see also PRIDE IDM see PUNCH
■ *adv.*
IDM **do sb ˈproud** (*BrE*, *old-fashioned*) to treat sb very well by giving them a lot of good food, entertainment, etc. **do yourself / sb ˈproud** to do sth that makes you proud of yourself or that makes other people proud of you

**proud·ly** /ˈpraʊdli/ adv. 1 in a way that shows that sb is proud of sth: *She proudly displayed her prize.* 2 (*literary*) in a way that is large and impressive: *The Matterhorn rose proudly in the background.*

**prov·able** /ˈpruːvəbl/ adj. that can be shown to be true SYN **verifiable**

**prove** ⓣ B1 /pruːv/ verb (**proved**, **proved** or **proved**, **proven** /ˈpruːvn/; *BrE also* /ˈprəʊvn/ *especially in NAmE*) HELP In *BrE* **proved** is the more common form. Look also at **proven**.
• SHOW STH IS TRUE 1 ⓣ B1 [T] to use facts, evidence, etc. to show that sth is true: **~ sth** *They hope this new evidence will prove her innocence.* ◊ *'I know you're lying.' 'Prove it!'* ◊ *He felt he needed to prove his point* (= show other people that he was right). ◊ *Are you just doing this to prove a point?* ◊ *What are you trying to prove?* ◊ *I certainly don't have anything to prove—my record speaks for itself.* ◊ **~ sth to sb** *Just give me a chance and I'll prove it to you.* ◊ **~ (that)** *This proves (that) I was right.* ◊ **~ sb / sth / yourself + adj. / noun** *She was determined to prove everyone wrong.* ◊ *In this country, you are innocent until proved guilty.* ◊ **~ sb / sth / yourself to be sth** *You've just proved yourself to be a liar.* ◊ **~ what, how, etc …** *This just proves what I have been saying for some time.* ◊ **it is proved that …** *Can it be proved that he did commit these offences?* OPP **disprove** ⊃ LANGUAGE BANK at EVIDENCE ⊃ see also PROOF *verb*
• BE 2 ⓣ B2 linking *verb* if sth **proves** dangerous, expensive, etc. or if it **proves to be** dangerous, etc., you discover that it is dangerous, etc. over a period of time SYN **turn out**: **+ adj.** *The strategy has proved successful.* ◊ *It was proving extremely difficult to establish the truth.* ◊ **+ noun** *The play proved a great success.* ◊ **~ to be sth** *The promotion proved to be a turning point in his career.*
• YOURSELF 3 ⓣ B2 [T] **~ yourself (to sb)** to show other people how good you are at doing sth or that you are capable of doing sth: *He constantly feels he has to prove himself to others.* 4 [T] **~ yourself + adj. / noun | ~ yourself to be sth** to show other people that you are a particular type of

| **WORD FAMILY** |
|---|
| **prove** *verb* (≠ disprove) |
| **proof** *noun* |
| **proven** *adj.* (≠ unproven) |

person or that you have a particular quality: *He proved himself determined to succeed.*
• OF BREAD 5 [I] to SWELL (= become larger or rounder) before being baked because of the action of YEAST SYN **rise** IDM see EXCEPTION

**proven** /ˈpruːvn; *BrE also* ˈprəʊvn/ adj., verb
■ *adj.* [only before noun] tested and shown to be true: *a student of proven ability* ◊ *It is a proven fact that fluoride strengthens growing teeth.* OPP **unproven**
IDM **not ˈproven** (in Scottish law) a VERDICT (= decision) at a trial that there is not enough evidence to show that sb is guilty or innocent, and that they must be set free
■ *verb past part.* of PROVE

**prov·en·ance** /ˈprɒvənəns; NAmE ˈprɑːv-/ noun [U, C] (*specialist*) the place that sth originally came from SYN **origin**: *All the furniture is of English provenance.* ◊ *There's no proof about the provenance of the painting* (= whether it is genuine or not).

**pro-verb** /ˈprəʊ vɜːb; NAmE vɜːrb/ noun (*grammar*) a verb that depends on another verb for its meaning for example 'do' in 'she likes chocolate and so do I'.

**prov·erb** /ˈprɒvɜːb; NAmE ˈprɑːvɜːrb/ noun a well-known phrase or sentence that gives advice or says sth that is generally true, for example 'Waste not, want not.'

**pro·verb·ial** /prəˈvɜːbiəl; NAmE -ˈvɜːrb-/ adj. 1 [only before noun] used to show that you are referring to a particular proverb or well-known phrase: *Let's not count our proverbial chickens.* 2 [not usually before noun] well known and talked about by a lot of people SYN **famous**: *Their hospitality is proverbial.* ▸ **pro·verb·ial·ly** /-əli/ adv.

**pro·vide** ⓣ A2 Ⓦ /prəˈvaɪd/ verb 1 ⓣ A2 to give sth to sb or make it available for them to use SYN **supply**: **~ sth** *Please provide the following information.* ◊ *The exhibition provides an opportunity for local artists to show their work.* ◊ *Please answer questions in the space provided.* ◊ **~ sth for sb** *We are here to provide a service for the public.* ◊ **~ sb with sth** *We are here to provide the public with a service.* ◊ **~ sth to sb** *We provide financial support to low-income families.* 2 **~ that …** (*formal*) (of a law or rule) to state that sth will or must happen SYN **stipulate**: *The final section provides that any work produced for the company is thereafter owned by the company.* ⊃ see also PROVISION *noun*
PHRV **proˈvide against sth** (*formal*) to make preparations to deal with sth bad or unpleasant that might happen in the future **proˈvide for sb** to give sb the things that they need to live, such as food, money and clothing **proˈvide for sth** (*formal*) 1 to make preparations to deal with sth that might happen in the future 2 (of a law, rule, etc.) to make it possible for sth to be done: *The legislation provides for the detention of suspected terrorists for up to seven days.*

**pro·vided** /prəˈvaɪdɪd/ (*also* **pro·vid·ing**) *conj.* **~ (that) …** used to say what must happen or be done to make it possible for sth else to happen SYN **if**: *We'll buy everything you produce, provided of course the price is right.* ◊ *Provided that you have the money in your account, you can withdraw up to £300 a day.*

**provi·dence** /ˈprɒvɪdəns; NAmE ˈprɑːv-/ (*also* **Providence**) *noun* [U] (*formal*) God, or a force that some people believe controls our lives and the things that happen to us, usually in a way that protects us SYN **fate**: *to trust in divine providence.* IDM see TEMPT

**provi·dent** /ˈprɒvɪdənt; NAmE ˈprɑːv-/ adj. (*formal*) careful in planning for the future, especially by saving money SYN **prudent** OPP **improvident**

**provi·den·tial** /ˌprɒvɪˈdenʃl; NAmE ˌprɑːv-/ adj. (*formal*) lucky because it happens at the right time, but without being planned SYN **timely** ▸ **provi·den·tial·ly** /-ʃəli/ adv.

**pro·vider** /prəˈvaɪdə(r)/ noun a person or an organization that supplies sb with sth they need or want: *training / childcare providers* ◊ *We are one of the largest providers of employment in the area.* ◊ *The eldest son is the family's sole provider* (= the only person who earns money). ⊃ see also ACCESS PROVIDER, CONTENT PROVIDER, PRIMARY CARE PROVIDER, SERVICE PROVIDER

---

Ⓞ Oxford Phrasal Academic Lexicon (OPAL) written and spoken word lists | Ⓦ OPAL written word list | Ⓢ OPAL spoken word list

# providing

**pro·vid·ing** /prəˈvaɪdɪŋ/ *conj.* = PROVIDED

**prov·ince** /ˈprɒvɪns; *NAmE* ˈprɑːv-/ *noun* **1** [C] one of the areas that some countries are divided into with its own local government: *the provinces of Canada* **2** **the provinces** [pl.] all the parts of a country except the capital city: *The show will tour the provinces after it closes in London.* ◇ *a shy young man from the provinces* **3** [sing.] (*formal*) a person's particular area of knowledge, interest or responsibility: *Such decisions are normally the province of higher management.* ◇ *I'm afraid the matter is outside my province* (= I cannot or need not deal with it).

**pro·vin·cial** /prəˈvɪnʃl/ *adj., noun*
■ *adj.* **1** [only before noun] connected with one of the large areas that some countries are divided into, with its own local government: *provincial assemblies/elections* **2** [only before noun] (*sometimes disapproving*) connected with the parts of a country that do not include the capital city, especially when these are regarded as lacking culture or modern ideas: *a provincial town* ⮕ WORDFINDER NOTE at LOCATION **3** (*disapproving*) unwilling to consider new or different ideas or things **SYN** narrow-minded ▸ **pro·vin·cial·ly** /-ʃəli/ *adv.*
■ *noun* (*often disapproving*) a person who lives in or comes from a part of the country that is not near the capital city, especially when regarded as lacking culture or modern ideas

**pro·vin·cial·ism** /prəˈvɪnʃəlɪzəm/ *noun* [U] (*disapproving*) the attitude of people who are unwilling to consider new or different ideas or things

**ˈproving ground** *noun* a place where sth such as a new machine, vehicle or weapon can be tested: *It's an ideal proving ground for the new car.* ◇ (*figurative*) *The club is the proving ground for young boxers.*

**pro·vi·sion** /prəˈvɪʒn/ *noun, verb*
■ *noun* **1** [U, C, usually sing.] the act of supplying sb with sth that they need or want; sth that is supplied: *housing provision* ◇ *The government is responsible for the provision of healthcare.* ◇ *There is no provision for anyone to sit down here.* ◇ *The provision of specialist teachers is being increased.* **2** [U, C] ~ **for sb/sth** preparations that you make for sth that might or will happen in the future: *He had already made provisions for* (= planned for the financial future of) *his wife and children before the accident.* ◇ *You should make provision for things going wrong.* **3** **provisions** [pl.] supplies of food and drink, especially for a long journey **4** [C] a condition or an arrangement in a legal document: *under the provisions of sth Under the provisions of the lease, the tenant is responsible for repairs.* ⮕ see also PROVIDE
■ *verb* [often passive] ~ **sb/sth (with sth)** (*formal*) to supply sb/sth with enough of sth, especially food, to last for a particular period of time

**pro·vi·sion·al** /prəˈvɪʒənl/ *adj.* **1** arranged for the present time only and likely to be changed in the future **SYN** temporary: *a provisional government* ◇ *provisional arrangements* **2** arranged, but not yet definite: *The booking is only provisional.* ▸ **pro·vi·sion·al·ly** /-nəli/ *adv.*: *The meeting has been provisionally arranged for Friday.*

**proˌvisional ˈlicence** (*BrE*) (*NAmE* ˈlearner's permit) *noun* an official document that you must have when you start to learn to drive

**pro·viso** /prəˈvaɪzəʊ/ *noun* (*pl.* **-os**) (*formal*) a condition that must be accepted before an agreement can be made **SYN** provision: *Their participation is subject to a number of important provisos.* ◇ *He agreed to their visit with the proviso that they should stay no longer than one week.*

**pro·vo·ca·teur** /prəˌvɒkəˈtɜː(r); *NAmE* -vɑːk-/ *noun* = AGENT PROVOCATEUR

**provo·ca·tion** /ˌprɒvəˈkeɪʃn; *NAmE* ˌprɑːv-/ *noun* [U, C] the act of doing or saying sth deliberately in order to make sb angry or upset; something that is done or said to cause this: **under** ~ *He reacted violently only under provocation.* ◇ **without** ~ *The terrorists can strike at any time without provocation.* ◇ *She bursts into tears at the slightest provocation.* ◇ *So far the police have refused to respond to their provocations.*

**pro·voca·tive** /prəˈvɒkətɪv; *NAmE* -ˈvɑːk-/ *adj.* **1** intended to make people angry or upset; intended to make people argue about sth: *a provocative remark* ◇ *He doesn't really mean that—he's just being deliberately provocative.* **2** intended to make sb sexually excited: *a provocative smile* ▸ **pro·voca·tive·ly** *adv.*

**pro·voke** /prəˈvəʊk/ *verb* **1** ~ **sth** to cause a particular reaction or have a particular effect: *The announcement provoked a storm of protest.* ◇ *The article was intended to provoke discussion.* ◇ *Dairy products may provoke allergic reactions in some people.* **2** to say or do sth that you know will annoy sb so that they react in an angry way **SYN** goad: ~ **sb** *Be careful what you say—he's easily provoked.* ◇ ~ **sb into (doing) sth** *The lawyer claimed his client was provoked into acts of violence by the defendant.* ◇ ~ **sb to do sth** *An attack on their city will only provoke them to retaliate.*

**prov·ost** /ˈprɒvəst; *NAmE* ˈproʊvoʊst/ (*also* **Provost**) *noun* **1** (in the UK) the person in charge of a college at some universities **2** (in the US) a senior official who manages the affairs of some colleges and universities **3** (in Scotland) the head of a council in some towns, cities and districts ⮕ compare MAYOR **4** the head of a group of priests belonging to a particular CATHEDRAL

**prow** /praʊ/ *noun* (*formal* or *literary*) the pointed front part of a ship or boat

**prow·ess** /ˈpraʊəs/ *noun* [U] (*formal*) great skill at doing sth: *academic/sporting prowess*

**prowl** /praʊl/ *verb, noun*
■ *verb* **1** [I, T] (+ *adv./prep.*) | ~ **sth** (of an animal) to move quietly and carefully around an area, especially when hunting: *The tiger prowled through the undergrowth.* **2** [I, T] (+ *adv./prep.*) | ~ **sth** to move quietly and carefully around an area, especially with the intention of committing a crime: *A man was seen prowling around outside the factory just before the fire started.* **3** [T, I] ~ **sth** | (+ *adv./prep.*) to walk around a room, an area, etc., especially because you are bored, anxious, etc. and cannot relax: *He prowled the empty rooms of the house at night.*
■ *noun*
IDM **(be/go) on the ˈprowl** (of an animal or a person) moving quietly and carefully, hunting or looking for sth: *There was a fox on the prowl near the chickens.* ◇ *an intruder on the prowl*

**prowl·er** /ˈpraʊlə(r)/ *noun* a person who follows sb or who moves around quietly outside their house, especially at night, in order to frighten them, harm them or steal sth from them

**prox·imal** /ˈprɒksɪml; *NAmE* ˈprɑːk-/ *adj.* (*anatomy*) located towards the centre of the body

**prox·im·ate** /ˈprɒksɪmət; *NAmE* ˈprɑːk-/ *adj.* [usually before noun] (*specialist*) nearest in time, order, etc. to sth

**prox·im·ity** /prɒkˈsɪməti; *NAmE* prɑːk-/ *noun* [U] (*formal*) the state of being near sb/sth in distance or time: ~ **(of sb/sth) (to sb/sth)** *The proximity of the college to London makes it very popular.* ◇ **in the** ~ **of sth** *a house in the proximity of* (= near) *the motorway* ◇ **in … (to sb/sth)** *The area has a number of schools in close proximity to each other.* ◇ *the death of two members of her family in close proximity*

**proxy** /ˈprɒksi; *NAmE* ˈprɑːk-/ *noun* (*pl.* **-ies**) **1** [U] the authority that you give to sb to do sth for you, when you cannot do it yourself: **by** ~ *You can vote either in person or by proxy.* ◇ *a proxy vote* **2** [C, U] a person who has been given the authority to represent sb else: *Your proxy will need to sign the form on your behalf.* ◇ *They were like proxy parents to me.* ◇ **for sb** *She is acting as proxy for her husband.* **3** [C] ~ **for sth** (*formal* or *specialist*) something that you use to represent sth else that you are trying to measure or calculate: *The number of patients on a doctor's list was seen as a good proxy for assessing how hard they work.*

**ˈproxy war** *noun* a war started by a major power that does not itself become involved

**Pro·zac™** /ˈprəʊzæk/ *noun* [C, U] a drug used to treat the illness of DEPRESSION: **on** ~ *She's been on Prozac for two years.*

**prude** /pruːd/ *noun* (*disapproving*) a person that you think is too easily shocked by things connected with sex

**pru·dent** /ˈpruːdnt/ adj. (formal) sensible and careful when you make judgements and decisions; avoiding unnecessary risks: *a prudent businessman* ◇ *a prudent decision/investment* ◇ *It might be more prudent to get a second opinion before going ahead.* **OPP** **imprudent** ▶ **pru·dence** /-dns/ noun [U] (formal) ⊃ SYNONYMS at CARE **pru·dent·ly** adv.

**prud·ery** /ˈpruːdəri/ noun [U] (formal, disapproving) the attitude or behaviour of people who seem very easily shocked by things connected with sex

**prud·ish** /ˈpruːdɪʃ/ adj. (disapproving) very easily shocked by things connected with sex **SYN** strait-laced ▶ **prud·ish·ness** noun [U]

**prune** /pruːn/ noun, verb
■ noun a dried PLUM that is often eaten cooked: *stewed prunes*
■ verb **1** to cut off some of the branches from a tree, bush, etc. so that it will grow better and stronger: ~ sth *When should you prune apple trees?* ◇ *He pruned the longer branches off the tree.* ◇ ~ sth back *The hedge needs pruning back.* **2** ~ sth (back) to make sth smaller by removing parts; to cut out parts of sth: *Staff numbers have been pruned back to 175.* ◇ *Prune out any unnecessary details.* ▶ **prun·ing** noun [U]: *All roses require annual pruning.* ◇ *The company would benefit from a little pruning here and there.*

**pruri·ent** /ˈprʊəriənt/; NAmE ˈprʊr-/ adj. (formal, disapproving) having or showing too much interest in things connected with sex ▶ **pruri·ence** /ˈprʊəriəns; NAmE ˈprʊr-/ noun [U]

**pry** /praɪ/ verb (**pries**, **pry·ing**, **pried**, **pried** /praɪd/) **1** [I] ~ (into sth) to try to find out information about other people's private lives in a way that is annoying or rude: *I'm sick of you prying into my personal life!* ◇ *I'm sorry. I didn't mean to pry.* ◇ *She tried to keep the children away from the prying eyes of the world's media.* **2** (especially NAmE) = PRISE

**PS** /ˌpiː ˈes/ noun something written at the end of a letter to introduce some more information or sth that you have forgotten (the abbreviation for 'postscript'): *PS Don't mention this to Ben.* ◇ *She added a PS asking me to water the plants.*

**psalm** /sɑːm/ noun a song, poem or prayer that praises God, especially one in the Bible: *the Book of Psalms*

**psal·ter** /ˈsɔːltə(r)/ noun a book containing a collection of songs and poems, (called PSALMS), with their music, that is used in a church

**pseud** /sjuːd/; BrE also sjuːd/ noun (BrE, informal, disapproving) a person who pretends to know a lot about a particular subject in order to impress other people ▶ **pseud** adj.

**pseudo-** /ˈsuːdəʊ/; BrE also ˈsjuːdəʊ/ combining form (in nouns, adjectives and adverbs) not what sb claims it is; false or pretended: *pseudo-intellectual* ◇ *pseudoscience*

**pseudo·nym** /ˈsuːdənɪm/; BrE also ˈsjuː-/ noun a name used by sb, especially a writer, instead of their real name: **under a ~** *She writes under a pseudonym.* ⊃ compare PEN NAME ▶ **pseud·onym·ous** /suːˈdɒnɪməs, sjuː-; NAmE suːˈdɑːn-/ adj.

**psi** /psaɪ, saɪ/ noun the 23rd letter of the Greek alphabet (Ψ, ψ)

**p.s.i.** /ˌpiː es ˈaɪ/ abbr. pounds per square inch (used for giving the pressure of tyres, etc.)

**psor·ia·sis** /səˈraɪəsɪs/ noun [U] (medical) a skin disease that causes rough red areas where the skin comes off in small pieces

**psst** /pst/ exclamation the way of writing the sound people make when they want to attract sb's attention quietly: *Psst! Let's get out now before they see us!*

**PST** /ˌpiː es ˈtiː/ abbr. **1** PACIFIC STANDARD TIME **2** provincial sales tax (a tax that is added to the price of goods in some parts of Canada)

**psych** /saɪk/ verb
**PHRV** **psych sb↔'out (of sth)** (informal) to make an opponent feel less confident by saying or doing things that make you seem better, stronger, etc. than them **psych sb/yourself 'up (for sth)** (informal) to prepare sb/yourself mentally for sth difficult or unpleasant: *I'd got myself all psyched up for the interview and then it was called off at the last minute.* ⊃ see also PSYCHED

**psy·che** /ˈsaɪki/ noun (formal) the mind; your deepest feelings and attitudes: *the human psyche* ◇ *She knew, at some deep level of her psyche, that what she was doing was wrong.*

**psyched** /saɪkt/ adj. [not before noun] (especially NAmE, informal) excited, especially about sth that is going to happen

**psy·che·delia** /ˌsaɪkəˈdiːliə/ noun [U] music, art, fashion, etc. that is created as a result of the effects of psychedelic drugs

**psy·che·del·ic** /ˌsaɪkəˈdelɪk/ adj. [usually before noun] **1** (of drugs) causing the user to see and hear things that are not there or that do not exist (= to HALLUCINATE) **2** (of art, music, clothes, etc.) having bright colours, strange sounds, etc. like those that are experienced when taking psychedelic drugs

**psy·chi·at·ric** /ˌsaɪkiˈætrɪk/ adj. relating to PSYCHIATRY or to mental illness: *psychiatric disorders* ◇ *a psychiatric hospital/nurse/patient* ◇ *psychiatric treatment* ⊃ compare MENTAL

**psych·iat·rist** /saɪˈkaɪətrɪst/ noun a doctor who studies and treats mental illnesses ⊃ WORDFINDER NOTE at SPECIALIST

**psych·iatry** /saɪˈkaɪətri/ noun [U] the study and treatment of mental illness

**psy·chic** /ˈsaɪkɪk/ adj., noun
■ adj. **1** (also less frequent **psych·ical** /ˈsaɪkɪkl/) connected with strange powers of the mind and not able to be explained by natural laws **SYN** **paranormal**: *psychic energy/forces/phenomena/powers* ◇ *psychic healing* **2** (of a person) seeming to have strange mental powers and to be able to do things that are not possible according to natural laws: *She claims to be psychic and helps people to contact the dead.* ◇ *How am I supposed to know—I'm not psychic!* **3** (also less frequent **psych·ical**) (formal) connected with the mind rather than the body ▶ **psych·ic·al·ly** /ˈsaɪkɪkli/ adv.
■ noun a person who claims to have strange mental powers so that they can do things that are not possible according to natural laws, such as predicting the future and speaking to dead people

**psycho-** /ˈsaɪkəʊ, saɪkə; BrE also saɪˈkɒ; NAmE also saɪˈkɑː/ (also **psych-** /saɪk/) combining form (in nouns, adjectives and adverbs) connected with the mind: *psychology* ◇ *psychiatric*

**psy·cho** /ˈsaɪkəʊ/ noun (pl. -os) (informal) a person who is mentally ill and who behaves in a very strange violent way ▶ **psy·cho** adj.

**psy·cho·active** /ˌsaɪkəʊˈæktɪv/ adj. (specialist) (of a drug) affecting the mind

**psy·cho·ana·lyse** (BrE) (NAmE -yze) /ˌsaɪkəʊˈænəlaɪz/ (also **ana·lyse**, **ana·lyze**) verb ~ sb to treat or study sb using psychoanalysis

**psy·cho·ana·ly·sis** /ˌsaɪkəʊəˈnæləsɪs/ (also **an·aly·sis**) noun [U] a method of treating sb with mental problems by asking them to talk about past experiences and feelings in order to try to find explanations for their present problems ▶ **psy·cho·ana·lyt·ic** /ˌsaɪkəʊˌænəˈlɪtɪk/ adj. [only before noun]: *a psychoanalytic approach* **psy·cho·ana·lyt·ic·al·ly** /-kli/ adv.

**psy·cho·ana·lyst** /ˌsaɪkəʊˈænəlɪst/ (also **ana·lyst**) noun a person who treats patients using psychoanalysis

**psy·cho·bab·ble** /ˈsaɪkəʊbæbl/ noun [U] (informal, disapproving) the language that people use when they talk about feelings and emotional problems, that sounds very scientific, but really has little meaning

**psy·cho·drama** /ˈsaɪkəʊdrɑːmə/ noun **1** a way of treating people who are mentally ill by encouraging them to act events from their past to help them understand their feelings **2** a play or film that makes the minds and feelings of the characters more important than the events

**psy·cho·kin·esis** /ˌsaɪkəʊkɪˈniːsɪs, -kaɪ-/ noun [U] the act of moving an object by using the power of the mind

**psy·cho·lin·guis·tics** /ˌsaɪkəʊlɪŋˈɡwɪstɪks/ *noun* [U] the study of how the mind processes and produces language ▶ **psy·cho·lin·guis·tic** /-ˈɡwɪstɪk/ *adj.*

**psy·cho·logic·al** /ˌsaɪkəˈlɒdʒɪkl/; *NAmE* -ˈlɑːdʒ-/ *adj.* **1** [usually before noun] connected with a person's mind and the way in which it works: *the psychological development of children* ◊ *Abuse can lead to both psychological and emotional problems.* ◊ *Her symptoms are more psychological than physical* (= imaginary rather than real). ◊ *Victory in the last game gave them a psychological advantage over their opponents.* ◊ *a psychological novel* (= one that examines the minds of the characters) **2** [only before noun] connected with the study of psychology: *psychological research* ▶ **psy·cho·logic·al·ly** /-kli/ *adv.*: *psychologically harmful* ◊ *Psychologically, the defeat was devastating.*
**IDM** the ˌpsychological ˈmoment the best time to do sth in order for it to be successful

**psycho·logical ˈwarfare** *noun* [U] things that are said and done in order to make an opponent believe that they cannot win a war, a competition, etc.

**psych·olo·gist** /saɪˈkɒlədʒɪst; *NAmE* -ˈkɑːl-/ *noun* a scientist who studies and is trained in psychology: *to see a psychologist* ◊ *to go to a psychologist* ◊ *an educational psychologist* ◊ *a clinical psychologist* (= one who treats people with mental DISORDERS or problems) ⊃ see also SOCIAL PSYCHOLOGIST

**psych·ology** /saɪˈkɒlədʒi; *NAmE* -ˈkɑːl-/ *noun* **1** [U] the scientific study of the mind and how it influences behaviour: *clinical/educational/child/sport psychology* ⊃ compare POP PSYCHOLOGY ⊃ see also SOCIAL PSYCHOLOGY **2** [sing.] the kind of mind that sb has that makes them think or behave in a particular way: *~ of sb the psychology of small boys* ◊ *Watching the shoppers at the sales gave her a first-hand insight into crowd psychology.* **3** [sing.] how the mind influences behaviour in a particular area of life: *~ of sth the psychology of interpersonal relationships*

**psy·cho·met·ric** /ˌsaɪkəˈmetrɪk/ *adj.* [only before noun] (*specialist*) used for measuring mental abilities and processes: *psychometric testing*

**psy·cho·path** /ˈsaɪkəpæθ/ *noun* a person suffering from a serious mental illness that causes them to behave in a violent way towards other people ▶ **psy·cho·path·ic** /ˌsaɪkəˈpæθɪk/ *adj.*: *a psychopathic disorder/killer*

**psy·cho·path·ology** /ˌsaɪkəʊpəˈθɒlədʒi; *NAmE* -ˈθɑːl-/ *noun* **1** [U] the scientific study of mental DISORDERS **2** [C] a DISORDER that affects sb's mind or their behaviour

**psych·osis** /saɪˈkəʊsɪs/ *noun* [C, U] (*pl.* **psych·oses** /-ˈkəʊsiːz/) a serious mental illness that makes a person lose contact with reality ⊃ see also PSYCHOTIC ⊃ WORDFINDER NOTE at CONDITION

**psy·cho·somat·ic** /ˌsaɪkəʊsəˈmætɪk/ *adj.* **1** (of an illness) caused by mental problems, such as stress and worry, rather than physical problems **2** (*specialist*) connected with the relationship between the mind and the body

**psy·cho·ther·apy** /ˌsaɪkəʊˈθerəpi/ (*also* **ther·apy**) *noun* [U] the treatment of mental illness by discussing sb's problems with them rather than by giving them drugs ▶ **psy·cho·ther·ap·ist** (*also* **ther·ap·ist**) *noun*

**psych·ot·ic** /saɪˈkɒtɪk; *NAmE* -ˈkɑːt-/ *noun* (*medical*) a person suffering from severe mental illness ▶ **psych·ot·ic** *adj.*: *a psychotic disorder/illness* ◊ *a psychotic patient* ⊃ see also PSYCHOSIS

**psy·cho·trop·ic** /ˌsaɪkəˈtrəʊpɪk/ *adj.* [usually before noun] (*medical*) relating to drugs or substances that affect a person's mental state: *psychotropic medication/drugs*

**PT** *abbr.* **1** /ˌpiː ˈtiː/ (*BrE*) physical training (sport and physical exercise that is taught in schools, in the army, etc.) **2** (*also* **P/T**) (in writing) PART-TIME: *The course is 1 year FT, 2 years PT.*

**pt** (*also* **pt.** especially in *NAmE*) *abbr.* (in writing) **1** part: *Shakespeare's Henry IV Pt 2* **2** PINT **3** point: *The winner scored 10 pts.* **4 Pt.** (especially on a map) port: *Pt. Moresby*

**PTA** /ˌpiː tiː ˈeɪ/ *abbr.* parent-teacher association (a group run by parents and teachers in a school that organizes social events and helps the school in different ways)

**ptar·mi·gan** /ˈtɑːmɪɡən; *NAmE* ˈtɑːrm-/ *noun* a type of GROUSE (= a bird with a fat body and feathers on its legs), found in mountain areas and in Arctic regions

**Pte** *abbr.* (*BrE*) (in writing) PRIVATE (= a soldier of the lowest rank in the army): *Pte Jim Hill*

**ptero·dac·tyl** /ˌterəˈdæktɪl/ *noun* a flying REPTILE that lived millions of years ago

**PTO** /ˌpiː tiː ˈəʊ/ *abbr.* (*BrE*) please turn over (written at the bottom of a page to show that there is more on the other side)

**PTSD** /ˌpiː tiː es ˈdiː/ *abbr.* = POST-TRAUMATIC STRESS DISORDER

**Pty** *abbr.* proprietary (used in the names of some companies in Australia and South Africa): *Computer Software Packages Pty Ltd*

**pub** /pʌb/ (*also formal* **ˌpublic ˈhouse**) (*both BrE*) *noun* a building where people go to drink and meet their friends. Pubs serve alcoholic and other drinks, and often also food: *We're all going to the pub after work.* ◊ (*informal*) *They've gone down the pub for a drink.* ◊ **in a ~** *They spent the whole evening in the pub.* ◊ **at a ~** *He is one of the regulars at the pub.* ◊ *I got home from the pub just after 11.* ◊ *a pub lunch* ◊ *the landlord of the local pub*

**ˈpub crawl** *noun* (*BrE, informal*) a visit to several pubs, going straight from one to the next, drinking at each of them

**pube** /pjuːb/ *noun* [usually pl.] (*informal*) a pubic hair

**pu·berty** /ˈpjuːbəti; *NAmE* -bərti/ *noun* [U] the period of a person's life during which their sexual organs develop and they become capable of having children: *to reach puberty* ⊃ WORDFINDER NOTE at YOUNG ⊃ see also ADOLESCENCE

**pubes** /ˈpjuːbiːz/ *noun* **1** (*pl.* **pubes**) the lower front part of the body, above the legs, covered by hair in adults **2** *pl.* of PUBIS

**pu·bes·cent** /pjuːˈbesnt/ *adj.* [usually before noun] (*formal*) in the period of a person's life when they are changing physically from a child to an adult

**pubic** /ˈpjuːbɪk/ *adj.* [only before noun] connected with the part of a person's body near their sexual organs: *pubic hair* ◊ *the pubic bone*

**pubis** /ˈpjuːbɪs/ *noun* (*pl.* **pubes** /-biːz/) one of the two bones that form the sides of the PELVIS

**pub·lic** /ˈpʌblɪk/ *adj., noun*
■ *adj.*
- OF ORDINARY PEOPLE **1** [only before noun] connected with ordinary people in society in general: *The campaign is designed to increase public awareness of the issues.* ◊ *Levels of waste from the factory may be a danger to public health.* ◊ *Why would the closure of hospitals be in the public interest* (= useful to ordinary people)? ◊ *The government had to bow to public pressure.*
- FOR EVERYONE **2** [only before noun] provided, especially by the government, for the use of people in general: *a public education system* ◊ *a public library* OPP private
- OF GOVERNMENT **3** [only before noun] connected with the government and the services it provides: *public money/spending/funding* ◊ *He spent much of his career in public office* (= working in the government). ◊ (*BrE*) *the public purse* (= the money that the government can spend) ◊ *The rail industry is no longer in public ownership* (= controlled by the government). OPP private
- SEEN/HEARD BY PEOPLE **4** known to people in general: *Details of the government report have not yet been made public.* ◊ *a public figure* (= a person who is well known because they are often on the television, radio, etc.) ◊ *She entered public life* (= started a job in which she became known to the public) *at the age of 25.* **5** open to people in general; intended to be seen or heard by people in general: *There is a ban on smoking in public places.* ◊ *A public meeting to discuss the issue will be held tomorrow night.* ◊ *This may be the band's last public appearance together.*

---

æ cat | ɑː father | e bed | ɜː fur | ə about | ɪ sit | iː see | i happy | ɒ got (*BrE*) | ɔː saw | ʌ cup | ʊ put | uː too

- **PLACE 6** ⟨*B1*⟩ where there are a lot of people who can see and hear you: *Let's go somewhere a little less public.* ◇ **OPP** **private** ▶ **pub·lic·ly** /-kli/ *adv.*: *a publicly owned company* ◇ *He later publicly apologized for his comments.* ◇ *This information is not publicly available.* **IDM** **go ˈpublic 1** to tell people about sth that is a secret **2** (of a company) to start selling shares on the STOCK EXCHANGE **in the public ˈeye** well known to many people through television, newspapers, the internet, etc: *She doesn't want her children growing up in the public eye.* ⊃ more at KNOWLEDGE

■ *noun* [sing. + sing. / pl. v.]
- **ORDINARY PEOPLE 1** ⟨*A2*⟩ **the public** ordinary people in society in general: *The palace is now open to the public.* ◇ *There have been many complaints from members of the public.* ◇ *The public has/have a right to know what is contained in the report.* ⊃ see also GENERAL PUBLIC
- **GROUP OF PEOPLE 2** a group of people who share a particular interest or who are involved in the same activity: *the theatre-going public* ◇ *She is an author who knows how to keep her public* (= the people who buy her books) *satisfied.* **IDM** **in ˈpublic** ⟨*B1*⟩ when other people, especially people you do not know, are present: *She doesn't like to be seen in public without her make-up on.* ⊃ compare IN PRIVATE ⊃ more at DIRTY *adj.*

**public ˈaccess** *noun* [U] **1** the right of people in general to go into particular buildings or areas of land or to obtain particular information: *public access to the countryside* **2** (in the US and some other countries) the right of people in general to use television or radio channels to present their own programmes: *a public access channel*

**public adˈdress system** *noun* (*abbr.* **PA system** /ˌpiː ˈeɪ sɪstəm/, **PA**) an electronic system that uses MICROPHONES and LOUDSPEAKERS to make music, voices, etc. louder so that they can be heard by everyone in a particular place or building

**public afˈfairs** *noun* [pl.] issues and questions about social, economic, political or business activities, etc. that affect ordinary people in general

**pub·li·can** /ˈpʌblɪkən/ *noun* **1** (*BrE, formal*) a person who owns or manages a pub **2** (*AustralE, NZE*) a person who owns or manages a hotel

**pub·li·ca·tion** ⟨*T*⟩ ⟨*B2*⟩ /ˌpʌblɪˈkeɪʃn/ *noun* **1** ⟨*B2*⟩ [U, C] the act of printing a book, a magazine, etc. and making it available to the public; a book, a magazine, etc. that has been published: *the publication date* ◇ *~of sth the publication of his first novel* ◇ *~on sth a list of recent publications on this subject* ◇ *~in sth Her article has been accepted for publication in the June issue of the journal.* ◇ *in a ~ Her work has appeared in a wide variety of mainstream publications.* ◇ *the publication by the European Commission of an agriculture information pack* **2** ⟨*B2*⟩ [U] the act of printing sth in a newspaper, report, etc. so that the public knows about it: *~of sth a delay in the publication of the exam results* ◇ *The newspaper continues to defend its publication of the photographs.*

**public ˈbar** *noun* (in the UK) a bar in a pub with simple or less comfortable furniture than the other bars ⊃ compare LOUNGE BAR

**public ˈcompany** (*also* **public limited ˈcompany**) (*both BrE*) (*NAmE* **public corpoˈration**) *noun* (*abbr.* **plc, PLC**) a company that sells shares in itself to the public

**public conˈvenience** *noun* (*BrE, formal*) a public building containing toilets that are provided for anyone to use

**public corpoˈration** *noun* **1** (*NAmE*) (*BrE* **public ˈcompany**, **public limited ˈcompany**) a company that sells shares in itself to the public **2** (*BrE*) an organization that is owned by the government and that provides a national service

**public deˈfender** *noun* (in the US) a lawyer who is paid by the government to defend people in court if they cannot pay for a lawyer themselves

**public doˈmain** *noun* [sing.] something that is in the **public domain** is available for everyone to use or to discuss and is not secret: *The information has been placed in the public domain.* ◇ *public domain software*

**public eduˈcation** *noun* [U] **1** (*especially NAmE*) (*BrE usually* **state eduˈcation**) education in schools, colleges and universities provided by the government **2** the process of giving the public information or training about a particular subject

**public ˈenemy** *noun* a person who has done, or is believed to have done, a very bad thing, especially sth that is harmful to society: *public enemy number one* (= the person or thing that is most frightening or that is most hated)

**public ˈholiday** *noun* = HOLIDAY (3)

**public ˈhouse** *noun* (*BrE, formal*) = PUB

**public ˈhousing** *noun* [U] (in the US) houses and flats that are built by the government for people who do not have enough money to pay for private accommodation ⊃ compare SOCIAL HOUSING

**pub·li·cist** /ˈpʌblɪsɪst/ *noun* a person whose job is to make sth known to the public, for example a new product, actor, etc.

**pub·li·city** ⟨*T+*⟩ ⟨*B2*⟩ /pʌbˈlɪsəti/ *noun* [U] **1** ⟨*T+*⟩ ⟨*B2*⟩ the attention that is given to sb/sth by newspapers, television, etc: *good/bad/adverse publicity* ◇ *There has been a great deal of publicity surrounding his disappearance.* ◇ *The trial took place amid a blaze of* (= a lot of) *publicity.* **2** ⟨*T+*⟩ ⟨*B2*⟩ the business of attracting the attention of the public to sth/sb; the things that are done to attract attention: *She works in publicity.* ◇ *There has been a lot of advance publicity for her new film.* ◇ *publicity material* ◇ *a publicity campaign* ◇ *The band dressed up as the Beatles as a publicity stunt.* ⊃ SYNONYMS at ADVERTISEMENT

**pub·li·cize** (*BrE also* **-ise**) /ˈpʌblɪsaɪz/ *verb* **~sth** to make sth known to the public; to advertise sth: *They flew to Europe to publicize the plight of the refugees.* ◇ *a much/highly/widely publicized speech* (= that has received a lot of attention on television, in newspapers, etc.) ◇ *He was in London publicizing his new biography of Kennedy.* ⊃ WORDFINDER NOTE at ADVERTISE

**public limited ˈcompany** *noun* (*BrE*) (*abbr.* **plc**) = PUBLIC COMPANY

**public ˈnuisance** *noun* **1** [sing., U] (*law*) an illegal act that causes harm to people in general: *He was charged with committing (a) public nuisance.* **2** [C, usually sing.] (*informal*) a person or thing that annoys a lot of people

**public oˈpinion** *noun* [U] the opinions that people in society have about an issue: *The media has a powerful influence on public opinion.*

**public ˈproperty** *noun* [U] **1** (*law*) land, buildings, etc. that are owned by the government and can be used by everyone **2** a person or thing that everyone has a right to know about: *Sophie became public property when she married into the royal family.*

**public ˈprosecutor** *noun* (in the UK) a lawyer who works for the government and tries to prove people guilty in court ⊃ see also DISTRICT ATTORNEY

**public reˈlations** *noun* **1** [U] (*abbr.* **PR**) the business of giving the public information about a particular organization or person in order to create a good impression: *She works in public relations.* ◇ *a public relations exercise* **2** [pl.] the state of the relationship between an organization and the public: *Sponsoring the local team is good for public relations.*

**public ˈschool** *noun* [C, U] **1** (in Britain, especially in England) a private school for young people between the ages of 13 and 18, whose parents pay for their education. The students often live at the school while they are studying: *He was educated at (a) public school.* ⊃ compare PREPARATORY SCHOOL, PRIVATE SCHOOL **2** (in the US, Australia, New Zealand and other countries) a free local school paid for by the government ⊃ compare STATE SCHOOL

**the public ˈsector** *noun* [sing.] (*economics*) the part of the economy of a country that is owned or controlled by the government ⊃ compare PRIVATE SECTOR, THIRD SECTOR

**public ˈservant** *noun* a person who is employed by the state or in local government or who is an elected

# public service 1246

representative: *pay increases for public servants* ◊ *a long and outstanding career as a public servant*

**public 'service** *noun* **1** [C] a service such as education or transport that a government or an official organization provides for people in general in a particular society: *to improve public services in the area* ◊ *a public service broadcast* **2** [C, U] something that is done to help people rather than to make a profit: *to perform a public service* **3** [U] the government and government departments: *to work in public service* ◊ *public service workers*

**public 'service broadcasting** *noun* [U] radio and television programmes broadcast by organizations such as the BBC in the UK that are independent of government but are financed by public money ⊃ **WORDFINDER NOTE** at RADIO

**public 'spending** *noun* [U] the amount of money that is spent by the government: *The government is keen to cut public spending.*

**public-'spir·it·ed** *adj.* willing to do things that will help other people in society: *a public-spirited act* ◊ *That was very public-spirited of you.* ▶ **public 'spirit** *noun* [U]

**public 'television** *noun* [U] (*NAmE*) a television service that shows mainly educational programmes and is paid for by the government, the public and some companies

**public 'transit** *noun* [U] (*NAmE*) = MASS TRANSIT

**public 'transport** (*BrE*) (*NAmE* **public transpor'tation**) *noun* [U] the system of buses, trains, etc. provided by the government or by companies, which people use to travel from one place to another: *to travel on/by public transport* ◊ *Most of us use public transport to get to work.*

**public u'tility** *noun* (*formal*) a company that supplies essential services such as gas, water and electricity to the public

**public 'works** *noun* [pl.] building work, such as that of hospitals, schools and roads, that is paid for by the government

**pub·lish** 🅐 **A2** 🅢 /ˈpʌblɪʃ/ *verb* **1** 🅐 **A2** [T] ~ sth to produce a book, magazine, CD-ROM, etc. and sell it to the public: *to publish a book/novel/magazine/paper* ◊ *The first edition was published in 2007.* ◊ *He works for a company that publishes reference books.* ◊ *Most of our titles are also published on CD-ROM.* ◊ *Many plays were published anonymously.* ⊃ **WORDFINDER NOTE** at BOOK **2** 🅑 **B1** [T] ~ sth to print a letter, an article, etc. in a newspaper or magazine: ~ sth *to publish a story/letter/comment/review* ◊ *to publish an article/interview* ◊ ~ sth in sth *Pictures of the suspect were published in all the daily papers.* **3** 🅑 **B2** [T] ~ sth to make information available to the public **SYN** **release**: *to publish work/research/results* ◊ *The findings of the committee will be published on Friday.* ◊ ~ sth on sth *according to the information published on their website* ◊ *The report will be published on the internet.* **4** 🅑 **B1** [T, I] (of an author) to have your work printed and sold to the public: *University teachers are under pressure to publish.* ◊ ~ sth *She hasn't published anything for years.*

**pub·lish·er** /ˈpʌblɪʃə(r)/ *noun* a person or company that prepares and prints books, magazines, newspapers or electronic products and makes them available to the public

**pub·lish·ing** 🅐+ **B2** /ˈpʌblɪʃɪŋ/ *noun* [U] the profession or business of preparing and printing books, magazines, CD-ROMs, etc. and selling or making them available to the public: *a publishing house/company* ⊃ see also DESKTOP PUBLISHING, DIGITAL PUBLISHING, ELECTRONIC PUBLISHING

**puce** /pjuːs/ *adj.* between red and purple in colour: *His face was puce with rage.* ▶ **puce** *noun* [U]

**puck** /pʌk/ *noun* **1** a hard flat rubber disc that is used as a ball in ICE HOCKEY **2** (*computing*) a pointing device that looks like a computer mouse and is used to control the movement of the CURSOR on a computer screen

**puck·er** /ˈpʌkə(r)/ *verb* [I, T] ~(sth) (up) to form or to make sth form small folds or lines: *His face puckered, and he was ready to cry.* ◊ *She puckered her lips.* ◊ *puckered fabric*

**puck·ish** /ˈpʌkɪʃ/ *adj.* [usually before noun] (*literary*) enjoying playing tricks on other people **SYN** **mischievous**

**pud** /pʊd/ *noun* (*BrE*, *informal*) = PUDDING

**pud·ding** /ˈpʊdɪŋ/ (*BrE*, *informal* **pud**) *noun* [U, C] **1** (*BrE*) a sweet dish eaten at the end of a meal: *What's for pudding?* ◊ *I haven't made a pudding today.* **SYN** **afters**, **dessert**, **sweet 2** (*BrE*) a hot sweet dish, often like a cake, made from flour, fat and eggs with fruit, jam, etc. in or on it: *treacle pudding* ⊃ see also BREAD-AND-BUTTER PUDDING, CHRISTMAS PUDDING, PLUM PUDDING, RICE PUDDING, SPONGE PUDDING **3** (*BrE*) a hot dish like a PIE with soft PASTRY made from flour, fat and eggs and usually filled with meat: *a steak and kidney pudding* **4** (*especially NAmE*) a cold DESSERT (= a sweet dish) like cream that tastes of fruit, chocolate, etc: *chocolate pudding* ⊃ see also BLACK PUDDING, YORKSHIRE PUDDING **IDM** see OVER-EGG, PROOF *n.*

**pud·dle** /ˈpʌdl/ *noun* a small amount of water or other liquid, especially rain, that has collected in one place on the ground ⊃ **WORDFINDER NOTE** at RAIN

**pudgy** /ˈpʌdʒi/ (*BrE also* **podgy**) *adj.* (*informal*, *usually disapproving*) slightly fat

**Pue·blo** /ˈpweblaʊ/ *noun* (*pl.* **Pue·blo** *or* **Pue·blos**) *noun* a member of a group of Native American people who live in the US states of Arizona and New Mexico

**pue·blo** /ˈpweblaʊ/ *noun* (*pl.* **-os**) (from *Spanish*) a town or village in Latin America or the south-western US, especially one with traditional buildings

**pu·er·ile** /ˈpjʊəraɪl; *NAmE* ˈpjʊərəl/ *adj.* (*disapproving*) silly; suitable for a child rather than an adult **SYN** **childish**

**puff** /pʌf/ *verb*, *noun*

■ *verb* **1** [I, T] to be smoking a cigarette, pipe, etc.: ~(at/on sth) *He puffed (away) on his pipe.* ◊ ~ sth *I sat puffing my cigar.* **2** [I, T] to make smoke or STEAM blow out in clouds; to blow out in clouds: ~ sth (out) *Chimneys were puffing out clouds of smoke.* ◊ ~(out) *Steam puffed out.* **3** [I, T] (+ speech) (*informal*) to breathe loudly and quickly, especially after you have been running **SYN** **gasp**: *I was starting to puff a little from the climb.* ⊃ see also PUFFED, PUFFED OUT at PUFFED **4** [I] + adv./prep. to move in a particular direction, sending out small clouds of smoke or STEAM: *The train puffed into the station.*
**IDM** **be puffed up with 'pride, etc.** to be too full of PRIDE, etc. **puff and 'pant** (*also* **puff and 'blow** *informal*) to breathe quickly and loudly through your mouth after physical effort ⊃ more at HUFF *v.*
**PHRV** **puff sth↔'out** to make sth bigger and rounder, especially by filling it with air: *She puffed out her cheeks.* **puff 'up**; **puff sth↔'up** to become bigger and rounder or to make sth bigger and rounder, especially by filling it with air: *Her cheeks puffed up.* ◊ *The frog puffed itself up.*

■ *noun* **1** [C] an act of breathing in sth such as smoke from a cigarette, or drugs: *He had a few puffs at the cigar.* ◊ *Take two puffs from the inhaler every four hours.* **2** [C] a small amount of air, smoke, etc. that is blown from somewhere: *a puff of wind* ◊ *Puffs of white smoke came from the chimney.* ◊ (*figurative*) *Any chance of success seemed to vanish in a puff of smoke* (= to disappear quickly). **3** [C] a hollow piece of light PASTRY that is filled with cream, jam, etc. ⊃ see also CREAM PUFF **4** (*NAmE also* **'puff piece**) [C] (*informal*, *usually disapproving*) a piece of writing or speech that praises sb/sth too much **5** [U] (*especially BrE*, *informal*) breath: *The hill was very steep and I soon ran out of puff.* ⊃ see also POWDER PUFF

**puff·ball** /ˈpʌfbɔːl/ *noun* a FUNGUS with a round brown head, that BURSTS (= breaks open) when it is ready to release its seeds

**puffed** /pʌft/ (*also* **puffed 'out**) *adj.* [not before noun] (*BrE*, *informal*) breathing quickly and with difficulty because you have been taking a lot of physical exercise

**puff·er** /ˈpʌfə(r)/ *noun* **1** (*informal*) a type of INHALER (= a small device containing medicine that you breathe in through your mouth, for people who have problems with breathing) **2** = PUFFERFISH

**puff·er·fish** /ˈpʌfəfɪʃ; NAmE -fərf-/ noun (pl. **puffer-fish** or **puffer-fishes**) (also **puff·er**) a poisonous fish that lives in warm seas and fills with air when it is in danger

**puf·fin** /ˈpʌfɪn/ noun a black and white bird with a large, brightly coloured BEAK that lives near the sea, common in the N Atlantic ⊃ VISUAL VOCAB page V2

**ˈpuff ˈpastry** noun [U] a type of light PASTRY that forms many thin layers when baked, used for making PIES, cakes, etc.

**ˈpuff piece** noun (NAmE) = PUFF (4)

**puffy** /ˈpʌfi/ adj. (**puff·ier**, **puffi·est**) **1** (of eyes, faces, etc.) looking SWOLLEN (= larger or rounder than normal): *Her eyes were puffy from crying.* **2** (of clouds, etc.) looking soft, round and white ▶ **puffi·ness** noun [U]

**pug** /pʌɡ/ noun a small dog with short hair and a wide flat face with deep folds of skin

**pu·gil·ist** /ˈpjuːdʒɪlɪst/ noun (old-fashioned) a BOXER ▶ **pu·gil·ism** /-lɪzəm/ noun [U] **pu·gil·is·tic** /ˌpjuːdʒɪˈlɪstɪk/ adj.

**pug·na·cious** /pʌɡˈneɪʃəs/ adj. (formal) having a strong desire to argue or fight with other people SYN **bellicose** ▶ **pug·na·cious·ly** adv. **pug·na·city** /-ˈnæsəti/ noun [U]

**puja** /ˈpuːdʒɑː/ noun **1** a Hindu ceremony of WORSHIP **2** an OFFERING (= a gift that is given to a god) at the ceremony

**pu·jari** /puːˈdʒɑːri/ noun a Hindu priest

**puke** /pjuːk/ verb [I, T] ~ (sth) (up) (informal) to VOMIT: *The baby puked all over me this morning.* ◊ *That guy makes me puke!* (= makes me angry) ◊ *I puked up my dinner.* ▶ **puke** noun [U]: *to be covered in puke*

**pukka** /ˈpʌkə/ adj. (BrE) **1** (old-fashioned) what sb claims it is; not a copy; appropriate in a particular social situation **2** (informal) of very good quality

**pulao** (also **pilau**) /ˈpiːlaʊ; NAmE pɪˈlaʊ/ noun [U, C] = PILAF

**Pul·it·zer Prize** /ˈpʊlɪtsə praɪz, ˈpjuːl-; NAmE -zər praɪz/ noun [C, usually sing.] in the US, one of the prizes that are given each year for excellent work in literature, music, or JOURNALISM

# pull ⓞ A2

/pʊl/ verb, noun

■ verb

- MOVE/REMOVE STH **1** A2 [I, T] to take hold of sth and use force in order to move it or try to move it towards yourself: *You push and I'll pull.* ◊ *Don't pull so hard or the handle will come off.* ◊ ~ **at/on sth** *I pulled on the rope to see if it was secure.* ◊ *He pulled at her coat sleeve.* ◊ ~**sth** *Stop pulling her hair!* ◊ ~**sb/sth + adv./prep.** *She pulled him gently towards her.* ◊ *He smiled and pulled her closer.* ◊ ~**sth + adj.** *Pull the door shut.* **2** A2 [T] to remove sth from a place by pulling: ~**sth** *If these weeds are not pulled, they will spread rapidly.* ◊ *He pulled a knife and stabbed the man.* ◊ ~**sth + adj./prep.** *Pull the plug out.* ◊ *She pulled off her boots.* ◊ *He pulled a gun on me* (= took out a gun and aimed it at me). **3** A2 [T] ~ **sb/sth + adv./prep.** to move sb/sth in a particular direction by pulling: *Pull your chair nearer the table.* ◊ *He pulled on his sweater.* ◊ *She took his arm and pulled him along.* **4** A2 [T] ~**sth** to hold or be attached to sth and move it along behind you: *In this area oxen are used to pull carts.* ◊ *a car pulling a trailer*
- BODY **5** B1 [I, T] to move your body or a part of your body in a particular direction, especially using force: ~ **adv./prep.** *He tried to kiss her but she pulled away.* ◊ ~**sth/yourself + adv./prep.** *The dog snapped at her and she quickly pulled back her hand.* ◊ ~**sth/yourself + adj.** *John pulled himself free and ran off.*
- CURTAINS **6** B1 [T] ~**sth** to open or close curtains, etc. SYN **draw**: *Pull the curtains—it's dark outside.*
- MUSCLE **7** B1 [T] ~**sth** to damage a muscle, etc. by using too much force: *to pull a muscle/ligament/tendon* ◊ *He pulled a hamstring in training.* ⊃ SYNONYMS at INJURE
- SWITCH **8** B1 [T] ~**sth** to move a switch, etc. towards yourself or down in order to operate a machine or piece of equipment: *Pull the lever to start the motor.* ◊ *Don't pull the trigger!*
- VEHICLE/ENGINE **9** [I, T] ~**(sth) to the right/the left/one side** to move or make a vehicle move to the side: *The wheel is pulling to the left.* ◊ *She pulled the car to the right to avoid the dog.* **10** [I] (of an engine) to work hard and use a lot of power: *The old car pulled hard as we drove slowly up the hill.*
- BOAT **11** [I, T] ~**(sth) (+ adv./prep.)** to use OARS to move a boat along: *They pulled towards the shore.*
- CROWD/SUPPORT **12** [T] ~**sb/sth (in)** to attract the interest or support of sb/sth: *They pulled in huge crowds on their latest tour.*
- ATTRACT SEXUALLY **13** [T, I] ~**(sb)** (BrE, informal) to attract sb sexually and get them to spend the evening with you: *He can still pull the girls.* ◊ *She's hoping to pull tonight.*
- TRICK/CRIME **14** [T] ~**sth** (informal) to succeed in playing a trick on sb, committing a crime, etc: *He's pulling some sort of trick on you.*
- CANCEL **15** [T] ~**sth** (informal) to cancel an event; to stop showing an advertisement, etc: *The gig was pulled at the last moment.*

IDM **like pulling ˈteeth** (informal) used to say that it is very difficult to make sb do sth: *It's like pulling teeth trying to get him to talk.* **pull a ˈfast one (on sb)** (slang) to trick sb **pull in different/opposite diˈrections** to have different aims that cannot be achieved together without causing problems **pull sb's ˈleg** (informal) to play a joke on sb, usually by making them believe sth that is not true **pull the ˈother one (—it's got ˈbells on)** (BrE, informal) used to show that you do not believe what sb has just said **pull out all the ˈstops** (informal) to make the greatest effort possible to achieve sth **pull the ˈplug on sb/sth** (informal) to put an end to sb's project, a plan, etc. **pull your ˈpunches** (informal) (usually used in negative sentences) to express sth less strongly than you are able to, for example to avoid upsetting or shocking sb: *Her articles certainly don't pull any punches.* **pull sth/a ˈrabbit out of the ˈhat** (informal) to suddenly produce sth as a solution to a problem **pull ˈrank (on sb)** (informal) to make use of your place or status in society or at work to make sb do what you want **pull the ˈrug (out) from under sb's ˈfeet** (informal) to take help or support away from sb suddenly **pull your ˈsocks up** (BrE, informal) to try to improve your performance, work, behaviour, etc: *You're going to have to pull your socks up.* **pull ˈstrings (for sb)** (NAmE also **pull ˈwires**) (informal) to use your influence in order to get an advantage for sb **pull the ˈstrings** to control events or the actions of other people **pull up ˈstakes** (NAmE) (BrE **pull up ˈsticks**) to suddenly move from your house and go to live somewhere else **pull your ˈweight** to work as hard as everyone else in a job, an activity, etc. **pull the ˈwool over sb's eyes** (informal) to hide your real actions or intentions from sb by making them believe sth that is not true ⊃ more at BOOTSTRAP *n.*, FACE *n.*, HORN *n.*, PIECE *n.*

PHRV **ˌpull aˈhead (of sb/sth)** to move in front of sb/sth: *The cyclists were together until the bend, when Tyler pulled ahead.* **ˌpull sb/sth aˈpart** to separate people or animals that are fighting **ˌpull sth aˈpart** to separate sth into pieces by pulling different parts of it in different directions **ˈpull at sth** = PULL ON/AT STH **ˌpull aˈway (from sth)** (of a vehicle) to start moving: *They waved as the bus pulled away.* **ˌpull ˈback 1** (of an army) to move back from a place SYN **withdraw 2** to decide not to do sth that you were intending to do, because of possible problems SYN **withdraw**: *Their sponsors pulled back at the last minute.* **ˌpull sb↔ˈback** to make an army move back from a place **ˌpull ˈback | ˌpull sth↔ˈback** (sport) to improve a team's position in a game: *Rangers pulled back to 4–3.* **ˌThey pulled back a goal just before half-time.** **ˌpull sb ˈdown** (especially US) to make sb less happy, healthy or successful **ˌpull sth↔ˈdown 1** to destroy a building completely SYN **demolish 2** = PULL STH IN/DOWN **ˌpull sb↔ˈin** (informal) to bring sb to a police station in order to ask them questions about a crime **ˌpull sth↔ˈin/ˈdown** to earn the large amount of money mentioned SYN **make**: *I reckon she's pulling in over $100000.* **ˌpull ˈin (to sth) 1** (of a train) to enter a station and stop **2** (BrE) (of a vehicle or its driver) to move to the side of the road or to the place mentioned and stop: *The police car signalled to us to pull in.* **ˌpull ˈoff | ˌpull ˈoff sth** (of a vehicle or its driver) to leave the road in order to stop for a short time **ˌpull sth↔ˈoff** (informal) to succeed in doing sth difficult: *We pulled off the deal.* ◊ *I never thought you'd pull it off.* **ˈpull on/at sth** to take long deep breaths from a cigarette, etc. **ˌpull ˈout** (of a vehicle or its driver) to move away from the side of the road, etc: *A car suddenly*

---

ⓞ Oxford Phrasal Academic Lexicon (OPAL) written and spoken word lists | Ⓦ OPAL written word list | Ⓢ OPAL spoken word list

# pullback

*pulled out in front of me.* **pull ˈout (of sth)** 1 (of a train) to leave a station 2 to move away from sth or stop being involved in it SYN **withdraw**: *The project became so expensive that we had to pull out.* **pull sb/sth ˈout (of sth)** to make sb/sth move away from sth or stop being involved in it SYN **withdraw**: *They are pulling their troops out of the war zone.* ⇨ related noun PULL-OUT **pull ˈover** (of a vehicle or its driver) to move to the side of the road in order to stop or let sth pass **pull sb/sth↔ˈover** (of the police) to make a driver or vehicle move to the side of the road **pull ˈthrough | pull ˈthrough sth** 1 to get better after a serious illness, operation, etc: *The doctors think she will pull through.* 2 to succeed in doing sth very difficult: *It's going to be tough but we'll pull through it together.* **pull sb ˈthrough | pull sb ˈthrough sth** 1 to help sb get better after a serious illness, operation, etc. 2 to help sb succeed in doing sth very difficult: *I relied on my instincts to pull me through.* **pull toˈgether** to act, work, etc. together with other people in an organized way and without fighting **pull yourˈself toˈgether** to take control of your feelings and behave in a calm way: *Stop crying and pull yourself together!* **pull ˈup** (of a vehicle or its driver) to stop: *He pulled up at the traffic lights.* **pull sb ˈup** (*BrE*, *informal*) to criticize sb for sth that they have done wrong

■ **noun**
- **TRYING TO MOVE STH** 1 ⓘ B1 [C] an act of trying to make sth move by taking hold of it and using force to bring it towards you: *I gave the door a sharp pull and it opened.*
- **PHYSICAL FORCE** 2 [sing.] **the~(of sth)** a strong physical force that makes sth move in a particular direction: *the earth's gravitational pull*
- **ATTRACTION** 3 [C, usually sing.] **the~(of sth)** the fact of sth attracting you or having a strong effect on you: *The magnetic pull of the city was hard to resist.*
- **INFLUENCE** 4 [U] (*informal*) power and influence over other people: *people who have a lot of pull with the media*
- **ON CIGARETTE/DRINK** 5 [C] **~(at/on sth)** an act of taking a deep breath of smoke from a cigarette, etc. or a deep drink of sth: *She took a long pull on her cigarette.*
- **WALK UP HILL** 6 [C, usually sing.] (*BrE*) a difficult walk up a steep hill: *It's a long pull up to the summit.*
- **MUSCLE INJURY** 7 [C] an injury to a muscle caused by using too much force
- **HANDLE/ROPE** 8 [C] (especially in compounds) something such as a handle or rope that you use to pull sth: *a bell/door pull* ⇨ see also RING PULL

IDM **on the ˈpull** (*BrE*, *slang*) (of a person) trying to find a sexual partner

**pullˈback** /ˈpʊlbæk/ *noun* 1 an act of taking soldiers away from an area 2 a time when prices are reduced, or when fewer people want to buy sth

**ˈpull date** (*US*) (*BrE* **ˈsell-by date**) *noun* the date printed on food packages, etc. after which the food must not be sold

**ˈpull-down** *adj.* 1 designed to be used by being pulled down: *a pull-down bed* 2 **~ menu** (*computing*) a list of possible choices that appears on a computer screen below a menu title

**pulled ˈpork** *noun* [U] meat from a pig that is cooked very slowly, often with smoke, until it is so soft you can pull it into small pieces with your hands

**pulˈlet** /ˈpʊlɪt/ *noun* a young chicken, especially one that is less than one year old

**pulˈley** /ˈpʊli/ *noun* a wheel or set of wheels over which a rope or chain is pulled in order to lift or lower heavy objects: *a system of ropes and pulleys* ⇨ picture at BLOCK AND TACKLE

**ˈpulling power** (*BrE*) (*NAmE* **ˈdrawing power**) *noun* [U] the ability of sb/sth to attract customers, supporters, an audience, etc.

**Pullˈman** /ˈpʊlmən/ *noun* (*pl.* **Pullˈmans**) a type of very comfortable coach on a train

**ˈpull-out** *noun*, *adj.*
- *noun* 1 a part of a magazine, newspaper, etc. that can be taken out easily and kept separately: *an eight-page pull-out on health* ◊ *a pull-out guide* 2 an act of taking an army away from a particular place; an act of taking an organization out of a system
- *adj.* [only before noun] (*especially NAmE*) a **pull-out** bed, COUCH, etc. can be kept hidden when not in use and pulled out when it is needed

**pullˈover** /ˈpʊləʊvə(r)/ *noun* (*especially BrE*) a KNITTED piece of clothing made of wool or cotton for the upper part of the body, with long SLEEVES and no buttons SYN **jumper**, **sweater**

**ˈpull tab** (*also* **tab**) (*both NAmE*) (*BrE* **ˈring pull**) *noun* a small piece of metal with a ring attached which is pulled to open cans of food, drink, etc.

**ˈpull-up** (*also* **ˈchin-up** *especially in NAmE*) *noun* [usually pl.] an exercise in which you hold onto a high bar above your head and pull yourself up towards it

**pulˈmonˈary** /ˈpʌlmənəri/; *NAmE* -neri/ *adj.* [only before noun] (*medical*) connected with the lungs

**pulp** /pʌlp/ *noun*, *verb*
- *noun* 1 [sing., U] a soft wet substance that is made especially by pressing hard on sth: *Cook the fruit gently until it forms a pulp.* ◊ *His face had been beaten to a pulp* (= very badly beaten). 2 [U] a soft substance that is made by pressing hard on wood, cloth or other material that is mixed with water and chemicals, and that is then used to make paper: *paper/wood pulp* 3 [U] the soft part inside some fruit and vegetables SYN **flesh** 4 (especially in noun compounds) writing that is of poor quality but popular and often SENSATIONAL: *a writer of pulp fiction* ▶ **pulpy** *adj.*: *Cook the fruit slowly until soft and pulpy.*
- *verb* **~ sth** to press hard on or beat sth so that it becomes soft and wet: *Unsold copies of the novel had to be pulped.* ◊ *pulped fruit*

**ˈpulp ˈfiction** *noun* [U] fiction that is badly written and often intended to shock people

---

▼ **SYNONYMS**

## pull
**drag • draw • haul • tow • tug**

These words all mean to move sth in a particular direction, especially towards or behind you.

**pull** to hold sth and move it in a particular direction; to hold or be attached to a vehicle and move it along behind you: *Pull the chair nearer the table.* ◊ *They use oxen to pull their carts.*

**drag** to pull sb/sth in a particular direction or behind you, usually along the ground, and especially with effort: *The sack is too heavy to lift—you'll have to drag it.*

**draw** (*formal*) to move sb/sth by pulling them/it gently; to pull a vehicle such as a carriage: *I drew my chair closer to the fire.* ◊ *a horse-drawn carriage*

**haul** to pull sb/sth to a particular place with a lot of effort: *Fishermen were hauling in their nets.*

**DRAG OR HAUL?**
You usually **drag** sth behind you along the ground; you usually **haul** sth towards you, often upwards towards you. **Dragging** sth often needs effort, but **hauling** sth always does.

**tow** to pull a car, boat or light plane behind another vehicle, using a rope or chain: *Our car was towed away by the police.*

**tug** to pull sb/sth hard in a particular direction: *She tried to escape but he tugged her back.*

**PATTERNS**
- to pull/drag/draw/haul/tow/tug sb/sth **along/down/towards** sth
- to pull/drag/draw/haul/tow sb/sth **behind** you
- to pull/drag/draw/haul a **cart/sledge**
- to pull/draw a **coach/carriage**
- to pull/haul/tow a **truck**
- **horses** pull/draw/haul sth
- **dogs** pull/drag/haul sth

**pul·pit** /ˈpʊlpɪt/ *noun* a small platform in a church that is like a box and is high above the ground, where a priest, etc. stands to speak to the people

**pul·sar** /ˈpʌlsɑː(r)/ *noun* (*astronomy*) a star that cannot be seen but that sends out regular rapid radio signals ⊃ compare QUASAR

**pul·sate** /pʌlˈseɪt; *NAmE* ˈpʌlseɪt/ *verb* **1** [I] to make strong regular movements or sounds: *pulsating rhythms* ◊ *a pulsating headache* ◊ *Lights were pulsating in the sky.* **2** [I] to be full of excitement or energy **SYN** *buzz*: *a pulsating game* ◊ *~ with sth The streets were pulsating with life.*
▶ **pul·sa·tion** /pʌlˈseɪʃn/ *noun* [C, U]

**pulse** ʔ+ C1 /pʌls/ *noun*, *verb*
■ *noun* **1** ʔ+ C1 [usually sing.] the regular beat of the heart as it sends blood around the body, that can be felt in different places, especially on the inside part of the WRIST; the number of times the heart beats in a minute: *a strong/weak pulse* ◊ *an abnormally high pulse rate* ◊ *The doctor took/felt my pulse.* ◊ *Fear sent her pulse racing* (= made it beat very quickly). **2** a strong regular beat in music **SYN** *rhythm*: *the throbbing pulse of the drums* **3** a single short increase in the amount of light, sound or electricity produced by a machine, etc: *pulse waves* ◊ *sound pulses* **4** **pulses** [pl.] the seeds of some plants that are eaten as food, such as PEAS and LENTILS **IDM** SEE FINGER *n*.
■ *verb* **1** [I] to move, beat or flow with strong regular movements or sounds **SYN** *throb*: *A vein pulsed in his temple.* ◊ *the pulsing rhythm of the music* **2** [I] *~ (with sth)* to be full of a feeling such as excitement or energy **SYN** *buzz*: *The auditorium pulsed with excitement.*

**pul·ver·ize** (*BrE also* **-ise**) /ˈpʌlvəraɪz/ *verb* **1** *~ sth* (*formal*) to make sth into a fine powder by pressing or CRUSHING it **2** *~ sb/sth* (*informal*, *especially BrE*) to defeat or destroy sb/sth completely **SYN** *crush*: *We pulverized the opposition.*

**puma** /ˈpjuːmə; *NAmE* ˈpuː-/ (*especially BrE*) (*NAmE usually* **cou·gar**) (*NAmE also* **mountain lion**, **pan·ther**) *noun* a large American wild animal of the cat family, with yellow-brown or grey fur

**pum·ice** /ˈpʌmɪs/ (*also* **pumice stone**) *noun* [U] a type of grey stone that comes from VOLCANOES and is very light in weight. It is used in powder form for cleaning and POLISHING, and in pieces for rubbing on the skin to make it softer.

**pum·mel** /ˈpʌml/ *verb* (**-ll-**, *US* **-l-**) [T, I] to keep hitting sb/sth hard, especially with your FISTS (= tightly closed hands): *~ sb/sth* (*with sth*) *He pummelled the pillow with his fists.* ◊ (*figurative*) *She pummelled* (= strongly criticized) *her opponents.* ◊ *~ (at sth) Her fists pummelled at his chest.*

**pump** ʔ+ C1 /pʌmp/ *verb*, *noun*
■ *verb* **1** ʔ+ C1 [T] to make water, air, gas, etc. flow in a particular direction by using a pump or sth that works like a pump: *~ sth (+ adv./prep.) The engine is used for pumping water out of the mine.* ◊ *The heart pumps blood around the body.* ◊ *~ sth + adj. The lake had been pumped dry.* **2** [I] *+ adv./prep.* (of a liquid) to flow in a particular direction as if it is being forced by a pump: *Blood was pumping out of his wound.* **3** [T] *~ sth (+ adv./prep.)* to move sth quickly up and down or in and out: *He kept pumping my hand up and down.* ◊ *I pumped the handle like crazy.* **4** [I] to move quickly up and down or in and out: *She sprinted for the line, legs pumping.* ◊ *My heart was pumping with excitement.* **5** [T] *~ sb (for sth)* (*informal*) to try to get information from sb by asking them a lot of questions: *See if you can pump him for more details.*
**IDM** *pump* ˈ*bullets,* ˈ*shots, etc. into sb* to fire a lot of bullets into sb *pump sb* ˈ*full of sth* to fill sb with sth, especially drugs: *They pumped her full of painkillers.* *pump* ˈ*iron* (*informal*) to do exercises in which you lift heavy weights in order to make your muscles stronger *pump sb's ˈstomach* to remove the contents of sb's stomach using a pump, because they have SWALLOWED sth harmful
**PHRV** *pump sth* ˈ*into sth* | *pump sth* ˈ*in* to put a lot of money into sth: *He pumped all his savings into the business.* *pump sth* ˈ*into sb* to force a lot of sth into sb: *It's difficult to pump facts and figures into tired students.* *pump sth*↔ˈ*out* (*informal*) to produce sth in large amounts: *loudspeakers pumping out rock music* ◊ *Our cars pump out thousands of tonnes of poisonous fumes every year.* *pump sb*↔ˈ*up* [usually passive] to make sb feel more excited or determined *pump sth*↔ˈ*up* **1** to fill a tyre, etc. with air using a pump **2** (*informal*) to increase the amount, value or volume of sth: *Interest rates were pumped up last week.*
■ *noun* **1** ʔ+ C1 a machine that is used to force liquid, gas or air into or out of sth: (*BrE*) *a petrol pump* ◊ (*NAmE*) *a gas pump* ◊ *a foot/hand pump* (= that you work by using your foot or hand) ◊ *a bicycle pump* ⊃ see also AIR PUMP, BREAST PUMP **2** (*BrE*) = PLIMSOLL **3** (*especially NAmE*) (*BrE* **court shoe**) a woman's formal shoe that is plain and does not cover the top part of the foot **4** (*BrE*) a woman's light, soft, flat shoe worn for dancing or exercise; a similar style of shoe worn as a fashion item: *ballet pumps* ⊃ see also FIST PUMP **IDM** SEE HAND *n*., PRIME *v*.

ˈ**pump-action** *adj.* [only before noun] (of a gun or other device) worked by quickly pulling or pressing part of it in and out or up and down: *a pump-action shotgun* ◊ *a pump-action spray*

**pump·kin** /ˈpʌmpkɪn/ *noun* [U, C] a large, round vegetable with thick orange skin. The seeds can be dried and eaten and the soft part inside can be cooked as a vegetable or in sweet PIES: *Pumpkin pie is a traditional American dish served on Thanksgiving.* ⊃ VISUAL VOCAB page V5

ˈ**pump room** *noun* (especially in the past) the room at a SPA where people go to drink the special water

**pun** /pʌn/ *noun*, *verb*
■ *noun* the clever or humorous use of a word that has more than one meaning, or of words that have different meanings but sound the same: *We're banking on them lending us the money—no pun intended!* ◊ *~ on sth The song's title is a pun on 'sweet' and 'suite'.* ⊃ compare WORDPLAY ⊃ WORDFINDER NOTE *at* COMEDY
■ *verb* [I] (**-nn-**) to make a pun

**Punch** /pʌntʃ/ *noun*
**IDM** (**as**) ˌ**pleased /** ˌ**proud as** ˈ**Punch** very pleased/proud

**punch** ʔ+ C1 /pʌntʃ/ *verb*, *noun*
■ *verb* **1** ʔ+ C1 to hit sb/sth hard with your FIST (= closed hand): *~ sb/sth He was kicked and punched as he lay on the ground.* ◊ *He was punching the air in triumph.* ◊ *~ sb/sth in/on sth She punched him on the nose.* **2** ʔ+ C1 to make a hole in sth with a PUNCH or some other sharp object: *~ sth to punch a time card* ◊ *~ sth in/through sth The machine punches a row of holes in the metal sheet.* **3** *~ sth* to press buttons or keys on a computer, phone, etc. in order to operate it: *I punched the button to summon the elevator.*
▶ **punch·er** *noun*: *He's one of boxing's strongest punchers.*
**IDM** ˌ**punch above your** ˈ**weight** to be or try to be more successful than others in doing sth that normally requires more skill, experience, money, etc. than you have: *This player seems to be able to constantly punch above his weight.*
**PHRV** ˌ**punch** ˈ**in/** ˈ**out** (*NAmE*) to record the time you arrive at/leave work by putting a card into a special machine ⊃ see also CLOCK IN/ON *at* CLOCK, CLOCK OUT/OFF *at* CLOCK ˌ**punch sth**↔ˈ**in** | ˌ**punch sth** ˈ**into sth** to put information into a computer by pressing the keys: *He punched in the security code.* ˌ**punch sb** ˈ**out** (*NAmE*, *informal*) to hit sb so hard that they fall down ˌ**punch sth**↔ˈ**out 1** to press a combination of buttons or keys on a computer, phone, etc: *He picked up the telephone and punched out his friend's number.* **2** to make a hole in sth or knock sth out by hitting it very hard: *I felt as if all my teeth had been punched out.* **3** to cut sth from paper, wood, metal, etc. with a special tool ˌ**punch sth**↔ˈ**up** (*NAmE*) **1** to press keys on a computer in order to get sth up on screen: *Ruby punched up the video and they all watched.* **2** (*informal*) to make sth more interesting, more powerful or more fun: *They really need to punch up the action scenes.*
■ *noun* **1** ʔ+ C1 [C] a hard hit made with the FIST (= closed hand): *a punch in the face* ◊ *Hill threw a punch at the police officer.* ◊ *a knockout punch* ◊ *He shot out his right arm and landed a punch on Lorrimer's nose.* ⊃ see also SUCKER PUNCH **2** [U] the power to interest people: *It's a well-constructed crime story, told with speed and punch.* **3** [C] a tool or machine for cutting holes in paper, leather or

metal: *a hole punch* **4** [U] a hot or cold drink made by mixing water, fruit juice, SPICES and usually wine or another alcoholic drink IDM see BEAT v., PACK v., PULL v., ROLL v.

**Punch and Judy show** /ˌpʌntʃ ən ˈdʒuːdi ʃəʊ/ *noun* (in the UK) a traditional type of entertainment for children in which PUPPETS are used to tell stories about Punch, who is always fighting with his wife Judy

**punch-bag** /ˈpʌntʃbæɡ/ (*BrE*) (*NAmE* **ˈpunching bag**) *noun* a heavy leather bag, hung on a rope, which is hit with the FISTS (= closed hands), especially by BOXERS as part of training, or as a form of exercise

**punch-ball** /ˈpʌntʃbɔːl/ *noun* a heavy leather ball, fixed on a spring, which is hit with the FISTS (= closed hands), especially by BOXERS as a part of training, or as a form of exercise

**punch-bowl** /ˈpʌntʃbəʊl/ *noun* a bowl used for serving PUNCH (4)

**punch-drunk** *adj.* **1** (of a BOXER) confused as a result of being hit on the head many times **2** unable to think clearly; in a confused state

**ˈpunching bag** (*NAmE*) (*BrE* **punch-bag**) *noun* a heavy leather bag, hung on a rope, which is hit with the FISTS (= closed hands), especially by BOXERS as part of training, or as a form of exercise

**punch-line** /ˈpʌntʃlaɪn/ (*also NAmE, informal* **ˈtag line**) *noun* the last few words of a joke that make it funny

**ˈpunch-up** *noun* (*BrE, informal*) a physical fight SYN **brawl**

**punchy** /ˈpʌntʃi/ *adj.* (**punch-ier, punchi-est**) (of a speech, song, etc.) having a strong effect because it expresses sth clearly in only a few words

**punc-tili-ous** /pʌŋkˈtɪliəs/ *adj.* (*formal*) very careful to behave correctly or to perform your duties exactly as you should: *a punctilious host* ▸ **punc-tili-ous-ly** *adv.* **punc-tili-ous-ness** *noun* [U]

**punc-tual** /ˈpʌŋktʃuəl/ *adj.* happening or doing sth at the arranged or correct time; not late: *She has been reliable and punctual.* ◊ *a punctual start at 9 o'clock* ▸ **punc-tu-al-ity** /ˌpʌŋktʃuˈæləti/ *noun* [U] **punc-tu-al-ly** /ˈpʌŋktʃuəli/ *adv.*: *They always pay punctually.*

**punc-tu-ate** /ˈpʌŋktʃueɪt/ *verb* **1** [T, often passive] ~ **sth (with sth)** to interrupt sth fairly often and regularly: *Her speech was punctuated by bursts of applause.* **2** [I, T] ~ **(sth)** to divide writing into sentences and phrases by using special marks, for example commas, question marks, etc.

**punc-tu-ation** /ˌpʌŋktʃuˈeɪʃn/ *noun* [U] the marks used in writing that divide sentences and phrases; the system of using these marks

**punctuˈation mark** *noun* a sign or mark used in writing to divide sentences and phrases

**punc-ture** /ˈpʌŋktʃə(r)/ *noun, verb*
■ *noun* **1** (*BrE*) a small hole in a tyre made by a sharp point that allows air to escape: *I had a puncture on the way and arrived late.* ⊃ compare FLAT (6) **2** a small hole, especially in the skin, made by a sharp point ⊃ see also LUMBAR PUNCTURE
■ *verb* **1** [T, I] ~ **(sth)** to make a small hole in sth; to get a small hole: *to puncture a tyre* ◊ *She was taken to the hospital with broken ribs and a punctured lung.* ◊ *One of the front tyres had punctured.* **2** [T] ~ **sth** to suddenly make sb feel less confident, proud, etc: *to puncture sb's confidence*

**pun-dit** /ˈpʌndɪt/ *noun* **1** a person who knows a lot about a particular subject and who often talks about it in public SYN **expert 2** = PANDIT

**pun-dit-ry** /ˈpʌndɪtri/ *noun* [U] the activity of giving expert opinions on a subject in the media: *football/political punditry*

**pun-gent** /ˈpʌndʒənt/ *adj.* **1** having a strong taste or smell: *the pungent smell of burning rubber* ⊃ SYNONYMS at BITTER ⊃ WORDFINDER NOTE at TASTE **2** direct and having a strong effect: *pungent criticism* ▸ **pun-gency** /-dʒənsi/ *noun* [U] **pun-gent-ly** *adv.*

**pun·ish** /ˈpʌnɪʃ/ *verb* **1** [I, T] to make sb suffer because they have broken the law or done sth wrong: ~ **sb** *Those responsible for this crime will be severely punished.* ◊ ~ **sb by doing sth** *My parents used to punish me by not letting me watch TV.* ◊ ~ **sb for (doing) sth** *He was punished for refusing to answer their questions.* ◊ *Damages are not designed to punish, but to compensate for the loss sustained.* ⊃ WORDFINDER NOTE at LAW **2** [T] ~ **sth (by/with sth)** to set the punishment for a particular crime: *In those days murder was always punished with the death penalty.* **3** [T] ~ **yourself (for sth)** to blame yourself for sth that has happened

**pun·ish·able** /ˈpʌnɪʃəbl/ *adj.* (of a crime) that can be punished, especially by law: *Giving false information to the police is a punishable offence.* ◊ ~ **by/with sth** *a crime punishable by/with imprisonment*

**pun·ish·ing** /ˈpʌnɪʃɪŋ/ *adj.* [usually before noun] long and difficult and making you work hard so you become very tired: *The President has a punishing schedule for the next six months.*

**pun·ish·ment** /ˈpʌnɪʃmənt/ *noun* **1** [U, C] an act or a way of punishing sb: *to inflict/impose/mete out punishment* ◊ ~ **for (doing) sth** *What is the punishment for murder?* ◊ *There is little evidence that harsher punishments deter any better than more lenient ones.* ◊ *The punishment should fit the crime.* ◊ **as (a)** ~ *He was sent to his room as a punishment.* ◊ ~ **of sb** *new approaches to the punishment of offenders* ⊃ see also CAPITAL PUNISHMENT, CORPORAL PUNISHMENT **2** [U] rough treatment: *The carpet by the door takes the most punishment.*

**pu·ni·tive** /ˈpjuːnətɪv/ *adj.* [usually before noun] (*formal*) **1** intended as punishment: *There are calls for more punitive measures against people who drink and drive.* ◊ (*law*) *He was awarded punitive damages.* **2** very severe and that people find very difficult to pay: *punitive taxes* ▸ **pu·ni·tive·ly** *adv.*

**Pun-jabi** /pʊnˈdʒɑːbi/ *noun* **1** [C] a person from the Punjab area in north-west India and Pakistan **2** [U] the language of people from the Punjab ▸ **Pun-jabi** *adj.*

**punk** /pʌŋk/ *noun* **1** (also **ˌpunk ˈrock**) [U] a type of loud and aggressive rock music popular in the late 1970s and early 1980s: *a punk band* **2** (also **ˌpunk ˈrocker**) [C] a person who likes punk music and dresses like a punk musician, for example by wearing metal chains, leather clothes and having brightly coloured hair: *a punk haircut* **3** [C] (*especially NAmE, informal*) a young man or boy who behaves in a rude or violent way SYN **lout**

**pun-kah** /ˈpʌŋkə, -kɑː/ *noun* **1** (*IndE*) an electric fan **2** (in India in the past) a large cloth fan that hung from the ceiling and that was moved by pulling a string

**ˈpun-net** /ˈpʌnɪt/ *noun* (*BrE*) a small box or BASKET that soft fruit is often sold in

**punt** /pʌnt/ *noun, verb*
■ *noun* **1** a long shallow boat with a flat bottom and square ends which is moved by pushing the end of a long POLE against the bottom of a river **2** (*BrE, informal*) a bet: *The investment is little more than a punt.* **3** (in rugby or AMERICAN FOOTBALL) a long kick made after dropping the ball from your hands
IDM **take/have a ˈpunt** (*BrE, informal*) **1** ~ **(on sth/sb)** to choose sth that involves some risk: *Adventurous new investors might want to have a punt.* **2** ~ **(at sth/doing sth)** to try to do sth: *He took a punt at explaining why he'd done it.*
■ *verb* **1** [I, T] ~ **(sth) (+ adv./prep.)** to travel in a punt, especially for pleasure: *We spent the day punting on the river.* ◊ *to go punting* **2** [T] ~ **sth (+ adv./prep.)** (in rugby or AMERICAN FOOTBALL) to drop a ball from your hands and kick it before it reaches the ground

**punt-er** /ˈpʌntə(r)/ *noun* (*BrE, informal*) **1** a person who buys or uses a particular product or service SYN **customer**: *It's important to keep the punters happy.* **2** a person who bets money on the result of a horse race

**puny** /ˈpjuːni/ *adj.* (**puni-er, puni-est**) (*disapproving*) **1** small and weak SYN **feeble**: *The lamb was a puny little thing.* **2** not very impressive: *They laughed at my puny efforts.*

**pup** /pʌp/ *noun* **1** = PUPPY **2** a young animal of various species (= types): *a seal pup*

**IDM** **sell sb/buy a pup** (*BrE*, *old-fashioned*, *informal*) to sell sb sth/to buy sth that has no value or is worth much less than the price paid

**pupa** /ˈpjuːpə/ *noun* (*pl.* **pupae** /-piː/) an insect in the stage of development between a LARVA and an adult insect ⊃ compare CHRYSALIS ▶ **pupal** /-pəl/ *adj.* [usually before noun]

**pu·pate** /pjuːˈpeɪt; *NAmE* ˈpjuːpeɪt/ *verb* [I] (*biology*) to develop into a pupa

**pupil** ⓘ B2 /ˈpjuːpl/ *noun* 1 B2 (*especially BrE*, *becoming old-fashioned*) a person who is being taught, especially a child in a school: *school pupils* ◊ *a former/past pupil* ◊ *How many pupils does the school have?* ◊ *She now teaches only private pupils.* ⊃ SYNONYMS at STUDENT 2 B2 a person who is taught artistic, musical, etc. skills by an expert: *~ of sb The painting is by a pupil of Rembrandt.* 3 the small round black area at the centre of the eye: *Her pupils were dilated.* ⊃ compare IRIS

**pup·pet** /ˈpʌpɪt/ *noun* 1 a model of a person or an animal that can be made to move, for example by pulling strings attached to parts of its body or by putting your hand inside it. A puppet with strings is also called a MARIONETTE: *a hand puppet* ◊ *a puppet show* ⊃ see also GLOVE PUPPET, HAND PUPPET, SOCK PUPPET 2 (*usually disapproving*) a person or group whose actions are controlled by another: *The occupying forces set up a puppet government.*

**pup·pet·eer** /ˌpʌpɪˈtɪə(r); *NAmE* -ˈtɪr/ *noun* a person who performs with puppets

**pup·pet·ry** /ˈpʌpɪtri/ *noun* [U] the art and skill of making and using puppets

**puppy** /ˈpʌpi/ *noun* (*pl.* **-ies**) (*also* **pup**) 1 a young dog: *a litter of puppies* ◊ *a Labrador puppy* 2 (*old-fashioned*, *informal*) a proud or rude young man

**puppy love** *noun* [U] feelings of love that a young person has for sb else and that adults do not think is very serious

**pur·chase** ⓘ B2 /ˈpɜːtʃəs; *NAmE* ˈpɜːrtʃ-/ *verb*, *noun*
■ *verb* B2 (*formal*) to buy sth: *~ sth Please ensure that you purchase your ticket in advance.* ◊ *to purchase an item/a product* ◊ *to purchase a property/home* ◊ *~ sth from sb The equipment can be purchased from your local supplier.* ◊ *~ sth for sth They purchased the land for $1 million.* ◊ (*figurative*) *Victory was purchased* (= achieved) *at too great a price.*
■ *noun* (*formal*) 1 B2 [U, C] the act or process of buying sth: *to make a purchase* (= buy sth) ◊ *Keep your receipt as proof of purchase.* ◊ *Many developers were delaying the purchase of land until later in the year.* ◊ *The company has just announced its 27 million purchase of Park Hotel.* ◊ *An illustrated catalogue is available for purchase.* ◊ *~ from sb/sth Our intention is to increase purchases from local suppliers.* ◊ *~ by sb Such massive purchases by single investors were extremely rare.* ⊃ WORDFINDER NOTE at BUY ⊃ see also COMPULSORY PURCHASE, HIRE PURCHASE 2 B2 [C] something that you have bought: *major purchases, such as a new car* ◊ *If you are not satisfied with your purchase we will give you a full refund.* 3 [U, *sing.*] (*specialist*) a strong hold on sth with the hands or feet, for example when you are climbing SYN **grip**: *She tried to get a purchase on the slippery rock.*

**'purchase price** *noun* [usually *sing.*] (*formal*) the price that is paid for sth you buy ⊃ compare ASKING PRICE, COST PRICE, SELLING PRICE

**pur·chaser** /ˈpɜːtʃəsə(r); *NAmE* ˈpɜːrtʃ-/ *noun* (*formal*) a person who buys sth ⊃ compare BUYER

**pur·chas·ing** /ˈpɜːtʃəsɪŋ; *NAmE* ˈpɜːrtʃ-/ *noun* [U] (*business*) the activity of buying things, especially for a company

**'purchasing power** *noun* [U] 1 money that people have available to buy goods with: *The cost of houses has risen faster than purchasing power.* 2 the amount that a unit of money can buy: *the peso's purchasing power*

**pur·dah** /ˈpɜːdə; *NAmE* ˈpɜːrdə/ *noun* [U] the system in some Muslim societies by which women live in a separate part of a house or cover their faces so that men do not see them: *in ~ to be in purdah* ◊ *He kept his daughters in virtual purdah.*

1251 **Purim**

**pure** ⓘ B2 Ⓢ /pjʊə(r); *NAmE* pjʊr/ *adj.* (**purer** /ˈpjʊərə(r); *NAmE* ˈpjʊr-/, **purest** /ˈpjʊərɪst; *NAmE* ˈpjʊr-/)
• NOT MIXED 1 B2 [usually before noun] not mixed with anything else; with nothing added: *pure gold* ◊ *These shirts are 100% pure cotton.* ◊ *The patient was given pure oxygen to breathe.* ◊ *Classical dance in its purest form requires symmetry and balance.*
• CLEAN 2 B2 clean and not containing any harmful substances: *a bottle of pure water* ◊ *The air was sweet and pure.* OPP **impure**
• COMPLETE 3 B2 [only before noun] complete and total: *They met by pure chance.* ◊ *She laughed with pure joy.* ◊ *That woman is pure evil.*
• COLOUR/SOUND/LIGHT 4 B2 very clear; perfect: *beaches of pure white sand* ◊ *a pure voice*
• MORALLY GOOD 5 without evil thoughts or actions, especially sexual ones; morally good: *to lead a pure life* ◊ *His motives were pure.* OPP **impure**
• SUBJECT YOU STUDY 6 [only before noun] about increasing knowledge of the subject rather than using knowledge in practical ways: *pure mathematics* ◊ *technology as opposed to pure science subjects* ⊃ compare APPLIED
• BREED/RACE 7 not mixed with any other BREED or race, etc: *These cattle are one of the purest breeds in Britain.* ⊃ see also PURIFY, PURITY
**IDM** **pure and simple** used after the noun that it refers to in order to emphasize that there is nothing but the thing you have just mentioned involved in sth: *It's laziness, pure and simple.*

**purée** /ˈpjʊəreɪ; *NAmE* pjʊˈreɪ/ *noun*, *verb*
■ *noun* [U, C] food in the form of a thick liquid made by pressing and mixing fruit or cooked vegetables in a small amount of water: *apple purée*
■ *verb* (**pur·éed**, **pur·éed**) *~ sth* to make food into a purée

**pure·ly** ⓘ+ /ˈpjʊəli; *NAmE* ˈpjʊrli/ *adv.* only; completely: *I saw the letter purely by chance.* ◊ *The charity is run on a purely voluntary basis.* ◊ *She took the job purely and simply for the money.*

**pur·ga·tive** /ˈpɜːɡətɪv; *NAmE* ˈpɜːrɡ-/ *noun* (*formal*) a substance, especially a medicine, that causes your BOWELS to empty SYN **laxative** ▶ **pur·ga·tive** *adj.*

**pur·ga·tory** /ˈpɜːɡətri; *NAmE* ˈpɜːrɡətɔːri/ *noun* [U] 1 (*usually* **Purgatory**) (in Roman Catholic teaching) a place or state in which the souls of dead people suffer for the bad things they did when they were living, so that they can become pure enough to go to heaven 2 (*informal*, *humorous*) any place or state in which sb suffers: *Getting up at four every morning is sheer purgatory.* ⊃ compare HELL (2)

**purge** /pɜːdʒ; *NAmE* pɜːrdʒ/ *verb*, *noun*
■ *verb* 1 to remove people from an organization, often violently, because their opinions or activities are unacceptable to the people in power: *~ sth (of sb) His first act as leader was to purge the party of extremists.* ◊ *~ sb (from sth) He purged extremists from the party.* 2 (*formal*) to make yourself/sb/sth pure, healthy or clean by getting rid of bad thoughts or feelings: *~ yourself/sb/sth (of sth) We need to purge our sport of racism.* ◊ *~ sth (from sth) Nothing could purge the guilt from her mind.*
■ *noun* the act of removing people, often violently, from an organization because their views are unacceptable to the people who have power

**puri·fier** /ˈpjʊərɪfaɪə(r); *NAmE* ˈpjʊr-/ *noun* a device that removes substances that are dirty, harmful or not wanted: *an air/water purifier*

**purify** /ˈpjʊərɪfaɪ; *NAmE* ˈpjʊr-/ *verb* (**puri·fies**, **puri·fy·ing**, **puri·fied**, **puri·fied**) 1 *~ sth* to make sth pure by removing substances that are dirty, harmful or not wanted: *One tablet will purify a litre of water.* 2 *~ sb/sth/yourself* to make sb pure by removing evil from their souls: *Hindus purify themselves by bathing in the River Ganges.* 3 *~ sth (from sth)* (*specialist*) to take a pure form of a substance out of another substance that contains it ▶ **puri·fi·ca·tion** /ˌpjʊərɪfɪˈkeɪʃn; *NAmE* ˌpjʊr-/ *noun* [U]: *a water purification plant*

**Pu·rim** /ˈpʊərɪm, pʊˈriːm; *NAmE* ˈpʊrɪm/ *noun* [U] a Jewish festival that is celebrated in the spring

# purist

**pur·ist** /ˈpjʊərɪst; NAmE ˈpjʊr-/ noun a person who thinks things should be done in the traditional way and who has strong opinions on what is correct in language, art, etc. ▶ **pur·ism** /-rɪzəm/ noun [U]

**pur·itan** /ˈpjʊərɪtən; NAmE ˈpjʊr-/ noun, adj.
- noun **1** (usually disapproving) a person who has very strict moral attitudes and who thinks that pleasure is bad **2 Puritan** a member of a Protestant group of Christians in England in the 16th and 17th centuries who wanted to WORSHIP God in a simple way
- adj. **1 Puritan** connected with the Puritans and their beliefs **2** = PURITANICAL

**pur·it·an·ical** /ˌpjʊərɪˈtænɪkl; NAmE ˌpjʊr-/ (also **pur·itan**) adj. (usually disapproving) having very strict moral attitudes: *Their parents had a puritanical streak and didn't approve of dancing.*

**pur·itan·ism** /ˈpjʊərɪtənɪzəm; NAmE ˈpjʊr-/ noun [U] **1 Puritanism** the beliefs and practices of the Puritans **2** very strict moral attitudes

**pur·ity** /ˈpjʊərəti; NAmE ˈpjʊr-/ noun [U] the state or quality of being pure: *The purity of the water is tested regularly.* ◊ *spiritual purity* **OPP** impurity

**pur·loin** /pɜːˈlɔɪn, ˈpɜːlɔɪn; NAmE pɜːrl-/ verb ~ **sth (from sb/sth)** (formal or humorous) to steal sth or use it without permission

**pur·ple** 🔑 **A2** /ˈpɜːpl; NAmE ˈpɜːrpl/ adj., noun
- adj. **1** 🔑 **A1** having the colour of blue and red mixed together: *a purple flower/dress* ◊ *His face was purple with rage.* **2** ~ **prose/passage** writing or a piece of writing that is too grand in style
- noun 🔑 **A1** [U, C] the colour of blue and red mixed together: *She was dressed in purple.* ◊ *the startling pinks and purples of the dresses*

ˌPurple ˈHeart noun a MEDAL given to a member of the armed forces of the US who has been wounded in battle

ˈpurple patch noun (BrE) a period of success or good luck

**purp·lish** /ˈpɜːpəlɪʃ; NAmE ˈpɜːrp-/ adj. similar to purple in colour: *purplish lips*

**pur·port** verb, noun
- verb /pəˈpɔːt; NAmE pərˈpɔːrt/ ~ **to be/have sth** (formal) to claim to be sth or to have done sth, when this may not be true **SYN** profess: *The book does not purport to be a complete history of the period.*
- noun /ˈpɜːpɔːt; NAmE ˈpɜːrpɔːrt/ [sing.] **the** ~ **of sth** (formal) the general meaning of sth

**pur·ported** /pəˈpɔːtɪd; NAmE pərˈpɔːrt-/ adj. [only before noun] (formal) that has been stated to have happened or to be true, when this might not be the case: *the scene of the purported crime* ▶ **pur·port·ed·ly** adv.: *a letter purportedly written by Mozart*

**pur·pose** 🔑 **A2** 🔊 /ˈpɜːpəs; NAmE ˈpɜːrp-/ noun
**1** 🔑 **A2** [C] the intention, aim or function of sth; the thing that sth is supposed to achieve: *Our campaign's main purpose is to raise money.* ◊ *The purpose of the book is to provide a complete guide to the university.* ◊ *Giving too much advance notice would defeat the purpose of the inspection.* ◊ **for the** ~ **of sth/of doing sth** *A meeting was called for the purpose of appointing a new treasurer.* ◊ *The experiments serve no useful purpose* (= are not useful). **2** 🔑 **B2** **purposes** [pl.] what is needed in a particular situation: *for … purposes These gifts count as income for tax purposes.* ◊ **for the purposes of sth** *For the purposes of this study, the three groups have been combined.* **3** 🔑 **B2** [C, U] meaning that is important and valuable to you: *Volunteer work gives her life a sense of purpose.* **4** [U] the ability to plan sth and work successfully to achieve it **SYN** determination: *He has enormous confidence and strength of purpose.* ⊃ see also CROSS PURPOSES
**IDM** **on ˈpurpose** not by accident; deliberately: *He did it on purpose, knowing it would annoy her.* **to ˌlittle/no ˈpurpose** (formal) with little/no useful effect or result ⊃ more at FIT adj., INTENT n., PRACTICAL adj.

## SYNONYMS

### purpose
aim • intention • plan • point • idea

These are all words for talking about what sb/sth intends to do or achieve.

**purpose** what sth is supposed to achieve; what sb is trying to achieve: *Our campaign's main purpose is to raise money.*

**aim** what sb is trying to achieve; what sth is supposed to achieve: *She went to London with the aim of finding a job.* ◊ *Our main aim is to increase sales in Europe.*

**PURPOSE OR AIM?**
Your **purpose** for doing something is your reason for doing it; your **aim** is what you want to achieve. **Aim** can suggest that you are only trying to achieve sth; **purpose** gives a stronger sense of achievement being certain. **Aim** can be sb's aim or the aim of sth. **Purpose** is more usually the purpose of sth: you can talk about sb's purpose but that is more formal.

**intention** what you intend to do: *I have no intention of going to the wedding.* ◊ *She's full of good intentions but they rarely work out.*

**plan** what you intend to do or achieve: *There are no plans to build new offices.*

**INTENTION OR PLAN?**
Your **intentions** are what you want to do, especially in the near future; your **plans** are what you have decided or arranged to do, often, but not always, in the longer term.

**point** (rather informal) the purpose or aim of sth: *What's the point of all this violence?* ◊ *The point of the lesson is to compare the two countries.*

**idea** (rather informal) the purpose of sth; sb's aim: *The whole idea of going was so that we could meet her new boyfriend.* ◊ *What's the idea behind this?*

**POINT OR IDEA?**
**Point** is a more negative word than **idea**. If you say *What's the point …?* you are suggesting that there is no point; if you say *What's the idea …?* you are genuinely asking a question. **Point**, but not **idea**, is used to talk about things you feel annoyed or unhappy about: *There's no idea in …* ◊ *I don't see the idea of ….*

**PATTERNS**
- with the purpose/aim/intention/idea of doing sth
- sb's intention/plan to do sth
- to have a(n) purpose/aim/intention/plan/point
- to achieve/fulfil a(n) purpose/aim

ˌpurpose-ˈbuilt adj. (BrE) designed and built for a particular purpose

**pur·pose·ful** /ˈpɜːpəsfl; NAmE ˈpɜːrp-/ adj. having a useful purpose; acting with a clear aim and with DETERMINATION: *Purposeful work is an important part of the regime for young offenders.* ◊ *She looked purposeful and determined.* ▶ **pur·pose·ful·ly** /-fəli/ adv. **pur·pose·ful·ness** noun [U]

**pur·pose·less** /ˈpɜːpəsləs; NAmE ˈpɜːrp-/ adj. having no meaning, use or clear aim **SYN** meaningless, pointless: *purposeless destruction*

**pur·pose·ly** /ˈpɜːpəsli; NAmE ˈpɜːrp-/ adv. on purpose; deliberately: *He sat down, purposely avoiding her gaze.*

**pur·pos·ive** /ˈpɜːpəsɪv; NAmE ˈpɜːrp-/ adj. (formal) having a clear and definite purpose **SYN** purposeful

**purr** /pɜː(r)/ verb **1** [I] when a cat **purrs**, it makes a low continuous sound in the throat, especially when it is happy or comfortable **2** [I] (of a machine or vehicle) to make a low continuous sound; to move making such a sound: *a purring engine* ◊ *The car purred away.* **3** [I, T] (+ **speech**) to speak in a low and gentle voice, for example to show you are happy or satisfied, or because you want to attract sb or get them to do sth: *He was purring with satisfaction.* ▶ **purr** (also **pur·ring**) noun [sing.]: *the purr of a cat/a car engine*

**purse** /pɜːs; NAmE pɜːrs/ noun, verb
- noun **1** [C] (especially BrE) a small bag made of leather, plastic, etc. for carrying coins and often also paper

money, cards, etc., used especially by women: *I took a coin out of my purse and gave it to the child.* ⊃compare CHANGE PURSE, WALLET **2** [C] (*NAmE*) = HANDBAG **3** [sing.] the amount of money that is available to a person, an organization or a government to spend: *We have holidays to suit every purse.* ◊ *Should spending on the arts be met out of the public purse* (= from government money)? ⊃see also PRIVY PURSE **4** [C] (*sport*) a sum of money given as a prize in a boxing match IDM see SILK
■ *verb* ~ **your lips** to form your lips into a small tight round shape, for example to show that you do not approve of sth

**pur·ser** /'pɜːsə(r)/ *NAmE* 'pɜːrs-/ *noun* an officer on a ship who is responsible for taking care of the passengers, and for the accounts

**the 'purse strings** *noun* [pl.] a way of referring to money and how it is controlled or spent: *Who holds the purse strings in your house?* ◊ *The government will have to tighten the purse strings* (= spend less).

**pur·su·ance** /pə'sjuːəns/ *NAmE* pər'suː-/ *noun*
IDM **in pursuance of sth** (*formal* or *law*) in order to do sth; in the process of doing sth: *They may need to borrow money in pursuance of their legal action.*

**pur·su·ant** /pə'sjuːənt/ *NAmE* pər'suː-/ *adj.* ~ **to sth** (*formal* or *law*) according to or following sth, especially a rule or law SYN **in accordance with sth**

**pur·sue** ⊕ B2 /pə'sjuː; *NAmE* pər'suː/ *verb* (*formal*)
**1** ⊕ ~ **sth** to do sth or try to achieve sth over a period of time: *to pursue a goal* ◊ *to pursue an aim/objective* ◊ *We intend to pursue this policy with determination.* ◊ *She wishes to pursue a medical career.* ◊ *I was determined to pursue my dream of becoming an actor.* **2** ⊕ B2 to continue to discuss, find out about or be involved in sth: *to pursue an agenda/a strategy/a claim* ◊ *The Crown Prosecution Service is unwilling to pursue the case.* ◊ *We have decided not to pursue the matter.* ◊ *She wanted the freedom to pursue her own interests.* ◊ *He was still pursuing his studies.* ◊ *Other companies are pursuing the same course.* ◊ *The government has actively pursued a campaign against the militants.* **3** ⊕ ~ **sb/sth** to follow or go after sb/sth, especially in order to catch them: *She left the theatre, hotly pursued by the press.* ◊ *Police pursued the car at high speed.*

**pur·suer** /pə'sjuːə(r)/ *NAmE* pər'suː-/ *noun* a person who is following or going after sb

**pur·suit** ⊕ B2 /pə'sjuːt/ *NAmE* pər'suːt/ *noun* **1** ⊕ B2 [U] the act of looking for or trying to get sth: ~ **of sth** *the pursuit of happiness/knowledge/profit* ◊ **in** ~ **of sth** *She travelled the world in pursuit of her dreams.* **2** ⊕ C1 [U] the act of following or going after sb, especially in order to catch them: **in** ~ *We drove away with two police cars in pursuit* (= following). ◊ *I galloped off on my horse with Rosie in **hot pursuit** (= following quickly behind).* **3** ⊕ C1 [C, usually *pl.*] something that you give your time and energy to, that you do as a hobby SYN **hobby, pastime**: *outdoor/leisure/artistic pursuits*

**puru·lent** /'pjʊərələnt/ *NAmE* 'pjʊr-/ *adj.* (*medical*) containing or producing PUS: *a purulent discharge from the wound*

**pur·vey** /pə'veɪ/ *NAmE* pər'v-/ *verb* ~ **sth** (*formal*) to supply food, services or information to people

**pur·vey·or** /pə'veɪə(r)/ *NAmE* pər'v-/ *noun* (*formal*) a person or company that supplies sth

**pur·view** /'pɜːvjuː; *NAmE* 'pɜːrvjuː/ *noun* [U]
IDM **within/outside the purview of sth** (*formal*) within/outside the limits of what a person, an organization, etc. is responsible for; dealt/ not dealt with by a document, law, etc.

**pus** /pʌs/ *noun* [U] a thick yellow or green liquid that is produced in a wound as a result of an infection

**push** ⊕ A2 /pʊʃ/ *verb, noun*
■ *verb*
• USING HANDS/ARMS/BODY **1** ⊕ A2 [I, T] to use your hands, arms or body in order to make sb/sth move forward or away from you; to move part of your body into a particular position: *We pushed and pushed but the piano wouldn't move.* ◊ *Push hard when I tell you to.* ◊ *You push and I'll pull.* ◊ ~ **at sth** *She pushed at the door but it wouldn't budge.* ◊ ~ **sb/sth** *He walked slowly up the hill pushing his bike.* ◊

1253 **push**

*Somebody pushed me and I fell over.* ◊ *When you push the gate, it doesn't open.* ◊ ~ **sb/sth + adv./prep.** *She pushed the cup towards me.* ◊ *He pushed his chair back and stood up.* ◊ *He tried to kiss her but she pushed him away.* ◊ *She pushed her face towards him.* ◊ ~ **sth + adj.** *I pushed the door open.* **2** ⊕ A2 [I, T] to use force to move past sb/sth using your hands, arms, etc: *People were pushing and shoving to get to the front.* ◊ ~ + **adv./prep.** *The fans pushed against the barrier.* ◊ ~ **your way + adv./prep.** *Try and push your way through the crowd.*
• SWITCH/BUTTON **3** ⊕ A2 [T] ~ **sth** to press a switch, button, etc., for example in order to make a machine start working: *I pushed the button for the top floor.*
• AFFECT STH **4** ⊕ B2 [T] ~ **sth + adv./prep.** to affect sth so that it reaches a particular level or state: *This development could push the country into recession.* ◊ *The rise in interest rates will push prices up.*
• PERSUADE **5** ⊕ B2 [T] to persuade or encourage sb to do sth that they may not want to do: ~ **sb into (doing) sth** *My teacher pushed me into entering the competition.* ◊ ~ **sb to do sth** *No one pushed you to take the job, did they?*
• WORK HARD **6** ⊕ B2 [T] ~ **sb/yourself** to make sb work hard: *The music teacher really pushes her pupils.* ◊ *Lucy should push herself a little harder.*
• PUT PRESSURE ON SB **7** [T] ~ **sb (+ adv./prep.)** (*informal*) to put pressure on sb and make them angry or upset: *Her parents are very tolerant, but sometimes she pushes them too far.*
• NEW IDEA/PRODUCT **8** [T] ~ **sth** (*informal*) to try hard to persuade people to accept or agree with a new idea, buy a new product, etc: *The interview gave him a chance to push his latest movie.* ◊ *She didn't want to push the point any further at that moment.* ◊ *He continues to push his own political agenda.*
• SELL DRUGS **9** [T] ~ **sth** (*informal*) to sell illegal drugs
• OF ARMY **10** [I] + **adv./prep.** to move forward quickly through an area: *The army pushed (on) towards the capital.*
IDM **be ,pushing '40, '50, etc.** (*informal*) to be nearly 40, 50, etc. years old **be pushing up (the) 'daisies** (*old-fashioned, humorous*) to be dead and buried in the ground **push the 'boat out** (*BrE, informal*) to spend a lot of money on enjoying yourself or celebrating sth SYN **splash out** **push the 'boundaries/'limits** to attempt to go beyond what is allowed or thought to be possible: *We aim to push the boundaries of what we can achieve.* **push the en'velope** (*informal*) to go beyond the limits of what is allowed or thought to be possible: *He is a performer who consistently pushes the envelope of TV comedy.* **push your 'luck** | **push it/things** (*informal*) to take a risk because you have successfully avoided problems in the past: *You didn't get caught last time, but don't push your luck!* **push sb over/ to the 'edge** to force sb to lose control of their behaviour, usually after a particular event or series of events: *Losing his job finally pushed him over the edge.* **push sth to the back of your 'mind** to try to forget about sth unpleasant: *I tried to push the thought to the back of my mind.* ⊃more at BUTTON *n.*, PANIC BUTTON
PHRV **push sb a'round** (*BrE also* **push sb a'bout**) to give orders to sb in a rude or unpleasant way **push a'head/ 'forward (with sth)** to continue with a plan in a determined way: *The government is pushing ahead with its electoral reforms.* **push sth↔'aside** to avoid thinking about sth: *He pushed aside the feelings of fear.* **push 'back (on sth)** (*especially NAmE*) to oppose or resist a plan, an idea or a change **push sth 'back** to make the time or date of a meeting, etc. later than originally planned: *The start of the game was pushed back from 2p.m. to 4p.m.* **'push for sth | 'push sb for sth** to repeatedly ask for sth or try to make sth happen because you think it is very important: *The pressure group is pushing for a ban on GM foods.* ◊ *I'm going to have to push you for an answer.* **push 'forward** to continue moving or travelling somewhere, especially when it is a long distance or difficult **push yourself 'forward** to make other people think about and notice you or sb else: *She had to push herself forward to get a promotion.* **push 'in** (*BrE*) (*NAmE* **cut 'in**) to go in front of other people who are waiting, in a way that is rude and unfair **push 'off 1** (*BrE, informal*) used to tell sb

# pushback

rudely to go away: *Hey, what are you doing? Push off!* **2** to move away from land in a boat, or from the side of a swimming pool, etc. ,**push 'on** to continue with a journey or an activity: *We rested for a while then pushed on to the next camp.* ,**push sb↔'out** to make sb leave a place or an organization ,**push sth↔'out** to produce sth in large quantities: *factories pushing out cheap cotton shirts* ,**push sb/sth 'over** to make sb/sth fall to the ground by pushing them: *Sam pushed me over in the playground.* ⇨ see also PUSHOVER ,**push sth↔'through** to get a new law or plan officially accepted: *The government is pushing the changes through before the election.*

■ noun
- USING HANDS/ARMS/BODY **1** 🔑 B1 an act of pushing sth/sb: *She gave him a gentle push.* ◊ *The car won't start. Can you give it a push?* ◊ (*figurative*) **At the push of a button** (= very easily) *he could get a whole list of names.*
- OF ARMY **2** a large and determined military attack: *a final push against the enemy* ◊ (*figurative*) *The firm has begun a major push into the European market.*
- EFFORT **3** ~ **for sth** a determined effort to achieve sth: *The push for reform started in 2007.* **4** an act of encouraging sb to do sth: *He wants to open his own business, but needs a push in the right direction to get him started.*

IDM **at a 'push** (*BrE, informal*) used to say that sth is possible, but only with difficulty: *We can provide accommodation for six people at a push.* **give sb/get the 'push 1** (*BrE, informal*) to dismiss sb/to be dismissed from your job SYN **fire**: *They gave him the push after only six weeks.* **2** (*BrE, informal*) to end a romantic relationship with sb; to be told that a romantic relationship with sb is over: *He was devastated when his girlfriend gave him the push.* **when ,push comes to 'shove** (*informal*) when there is no other choice; when everything else has failed

**push·back** /ˈpʊʃbæk/ noun [U] (*especially NAmE*) the act of opposing or resisting a plan, an idea or a change: *The plan was abandoned because the pushback from the military was so strong.*

**push·bike** /ˈpʊʃbaɪk/ noun (*BrE, old-fashioned*) a bicycle

**'push-button** adj. [only before noun] operated by pressing buttons with your fingers: *a push-button phone* ▶ **'push-button** noun

pushchair/ stroller     pram / baby carriage     carrycot

**push·chair** /ˈpʊʃtʃeə(r); NAmE -tʃer/ (BrE) (NAmE **stroll·er**) (also **buggy** BrE and NAmE) noun a small folding seat on wheels in which a small child sits and is pushed along

**pushed** /pʊʃt/ adj. [not before noun] (*informal*) **1** ~ (**to do sth**) having difficulty doing sth: *You'll be hard pushed to finish this today.* **2** ~ **for sth** not having enough of sth: *to be pushed for money/time* **3** busy: *I know you're pushed, but can you make tomorrow's meeting?*

**push·er** /ˈpʊʃə(r)/ noun (*informal*) a person who sells illegal drugs: *drug pushers* ⇨ see also PAPER-PUSHER, PEN-PUSHER, PENCIL PUSHER

**push·over** /ˈpʊʃəʊvə(r); NAmE -oʊ-/ noun (*informal*) **1** a thing that is easy to do or win: *The game will be a pushover.* **2** a person who is easy to persuade or influence: *I don't think she'll agree—she's no pushover.*

**push-pin** /ˈpʊʃpɪn/ noun (*NAmE*) a type of DRAWING PIN with a coloured plastic head that is not flat

**push-start** verb ~ **sth** (*especially BrE*) to push a vehicle in order to make the engine start ▶ **'push-start** noun ⇨ see also KICK-START verb

**'push-up** (*especially NAmE*) (*BrE also* **'press-up**) noun [usually pl.] an exercise in which you lie on your stomach and raise your body off the ground by pressing down on your hands until your arms are straight ⇨ picture at PRESS-UP

**pushy** /ˈpʊʃi/ adj. (**push·ier**, **pushi·est**) (*informal, disapproving*) trying hard to get what you want, especially in a way that seems rude: *a pushy salesman* ▶ **pushi·ness** noun [U]

**pu·sil·lan·im·ous** /ˌpjuːsɪˈlænɪməs/ adj. (*formal*) frightened to take risks SYN **cowardly**

**puss** /pʊs/ noun **1** (*especially BrE*) used when you are calling or talking to a cat **2** (*especially NAmE, informal*) a person's face or mouth

**pussy** /ˈpʊsi/ noun (pl. **-ies**) **1** a child's word for a cat **2** (*taboo, slang*) the female sexual organs, especially the VULVA

**pussy·cat** /ˈpʊsikæt/ noun (*informal*) **1** a child's word for a cat **2** a person who is kind and friendly, especially when you would not expect them to be like this: *He's just a pussycat really, once you get to know him.*

**pussy·foot** /ˈpʊsifʊt/ verb [I] ~ (**about/around**) (*informal, usually disapproving*) to be careful or anxious about expressing your opinion in case you upset sb

**pus·tule** /ˈpʌstjuːl; NAmE ˈpʌstʃuːl/ noun (*formal or medical*) a spot on the skin containing PUS

**put** 🛈 A1 /pʊt/ verb (**put·ting**, **put**, **put**)
- IN PLACE/POSITION **1** 🔑 A1 ~ **sth + adv./prep.** to move sth into a particular place or position: *Put the cases down there, please.* ◊ *Did you put sugar in my coffee?* ◊ *Put your hand up if you need more paper.* **2** ~ **sth + adv./prep.** to move sth into a particular place or position using force: *He put his fist through a glass door.* **3** 🔑 B1 ~ **sb/sth + adv./prep.** to cause sb/sth to go to a particular place: *Her family put her into a nursing home.* ◊ *It was the year the Americans put a man on the moon.*
- ATTACH **4** 🔑 A2 ~ **sth + adv./prep.** to attach or fix sth to sth else: *We had to put new locks on all the doors.*
- WRITE **5** 🔑 A1 ~ **sth (+ adv./prep.)** to write sth or make a mark on sth: *Put your name here.* ◊ *Friday at 11? I'll put it in my diary.* ◊ *I couldn't read what she had put.*
- INTO STATE/CONDITION **6** 🔑 B1 ~ **sb/sth + adv./prep.** to bring sb/sth into the state or condition mentioned: *I was put in charge of the office.* ◊ *The incident put her in a bad mood.* ◊ **Put yourself in my position.** *What would you have done?* ◊ *I tried to* **put the matter into perspective.** ◊ *Don't go* **putting yourself at risk.** ◊ *It was time to* **put his suggestion into practice.** ◊ *This new injury will* **put him out of action** *for several weeks.*
- AFFECT SB/STH **7** 🔑 B1 ~ **sth on/onto/to sth** to make sb/sth feel sth or be affected by sth: *Her new job has put a great strain on her.* ◊ *They* **put pressure on** *her to resign.* ◊ *It's time you* **put a stop to** *this childish behaviour.*
- EXPRESS **8** 🔑 B2 ~ **sth + adv./prep.** to express or state sth in a particular way: *She put it very tactfully.* ◊ **Put simply,** *we accept their offer or go bankrupt.* ◊ *I was,* **to put it mildly,** *annoyed* (= I was extremely angry). ◊ *He was too trusting —or,* **to put it another way,** *he had no head for business.* ◊ *The meat was—* **how shall I put it?** *—a little overdone.* ◊ *As T.S. Eliot puts it …* ◊ *She had never tried to* **put** *this feeling* **into words.** ◊ *Can you help me put this letter into good English, please?*
- GIVE VALUE/RANK **9** ~ **sth on sth** to give or attach a particular level of importance, trust, value, etc. to sth: *Our company puts the emphasis on quality.* ◊ *He put a limit on the amount we could spend.* **10** ~ **sb/sth + adv./prep.** to consider sb/sth to belong to the class or level mentioned: *I'd put her in the top rank of modern novelists.*
- IN SPORT **11** ~ **sth** to throw the SHOT

IDM HELP Most idioms containing **put** are at the entries for the nouns and adjectives in the idioms, for example **put your foot in it** is at **foot**. **I wouldn't put it 'past sb (to do sth)** (*informal*) used to say that you think sb is capable of doing sth wrong, illegal, etc. **put it a'bout** (*BrE, informal*) to have many sexual partners **put it to sb that …** to suggest sth to sb to see if they can argue against it: *I put it to you that you are the only person who had a motive for the crime.* **put one 'over on sb** (*informal*) to persuade sb to believe sth that is not true: *Don't try to put one over on me!* **put sb 'through it** (*especially BrE, informal*) to force sb to experience sth difficult or unpleasant: *They really put me* through it (= asked me difficult questions) *at the interview.* **put to'gether** used when comparing or contrasting sb/sth with a group of other people or things to mean 'combined' or 'in total': *Your department spent more last year than all the others put together.* **put up or 'shut up** (*especially BrE*) used to tell sb to stop just talking about sth and actually do it, show it, etc.

**PHRV** **put sth↔a'bout** (*BrE, informal*) to tell a lot of people news, information, etc. that may be false: **put it about that …** *Someone's been putting it about that you plan to resign.*
**'put sth above sth** = PUT STH BEFORE/ABOVE STH
**put yourself/sth↔a'cross/'over (to sb)** to communicate your ideas, feelings, etc. successfully to sb: *She's not very good at putting her views across.*
**put sth↔a'side** 1 to ignore or forget sth, usually a feeling or difference of opinion **SYN** **disregard**: *They decided to put aside their differences.* 2 to stop working on one task in order to start another one: *He put aside his studies in order to pursue a political career.* 3 to save sth or keep it available to use: *We put some money aside every month for our retirement.* ◇ *I put aside half an hour every day to write my diary.*
**'put sb/sth at sth** to calculate sb/sth to be a particular age, weight, amount, etc: *The damage to the building is put at over $1 million.*
**put sb↔a'way** [often passive] (*informal*) to send sb to prison, to a mental hospital, etc. **put sth↔a'way** 1 to put sth in the place where it is kept because you have finished using it: *I'm just going to put the car away* (= in the garage). 2 to save money to spend later: *She has a few thousand dollars put away for her retirement.* 3 (*informal*) to eat or drink large quantities of sth: *He must have put away a bottle of whisky last night.*
**put sth↔'back** 1 to return sth to its usual place or to the place where it was before it was moved: *If you use something, put it back!* 2 to move sth to a later time or date **SYN** **postpone**: *The meeting has been put back to next week.* 3 to cause sth to be delayed: *Poor trading figures put back our plans for expansion.* 4 to move the hands of a clock so that they show the correct earlier time: *Remember to put your clocks back tonight* (= because the time has officially changed).
**put sth before/above sth** to treat sth as more important than sth else
**put sth be'hind you** to try to forget about an unpleasant experience and think about the future
**put sth↔'by** (*especially BrE*) (*also* **put sth↔a'side**) to save money for a particular purpose: *I'm putting by part of my wages every week to buy a bike.*
**put 'down** (of an aircraft or its pilot) to land: *He put down in a field.* **put sb↔'down** (*informal*) to make sb look or feel stupid, especially in front of other people ⊃ related noun PUT-DOWN **put sth↔'down** 1 to stop holding sth and place it on a table, shelf, etc: *Put that knife down before you hurt somebody!* ◇ (*figurative*) *It's a great book. I couldn't put it down* (= stop reading it). ◇ (*BrE*) *She put the phone down on me* (= ended the call before I had finished speaking). 2 to write sth; to make a note of sth: *The meeting's on the 22nd. Put it down in your diary.* 3 to pay part of the cost of sth: *We put a five per cent deposit down on the house.* 4 to stop sth by force **SYN** **crush**: *to put down a rebellion* ◇ *The military government is determined to put down all opposition.* 5 [often passive] to kill an animal, usually by giving it a drug, because it is old or sick: *We had to have our cat put down.* 6 to put a baby to bed: *Can you be quiet—I've just put the baby down.* 7 to present sb formally for discussion by a parliament or committee **SYN** **table**: *to put down a motion/an amendment* **put sb 'down as sth** to consider or judge sb to be a particular type of person: *I'd put them both down as retired teachers.* **put sb 'down for sth** to put sb's name on a list, for sth: *Put me down for three tickets for Saturday.* ◇ *They've put their son down for the local school.*
**put sth down to sth** to consider that sth is caused by sth **SYN** **attribute**: *What do you put her success down to?*
**put sth↔'forth** (*formal*) = PUT STH↔OUT
**put yourself/sb↔'forward** to suggest yourself/sb as a candidate for a job or position: *Can I put you/your name forward for club secretary?* **put sth↔'forward** 1 B2 to suggest sth for discussion: *to put forward a suggestion* 2 to

move sth to an earlier time or date: *We've put the wedding forward by one week.* 3 to move the hands of a clock to the correct later time: *Remember to put your clocks forward tonight* (= because the time has officially changed).
**put sb↔'in** to elect a political party to govern a country: *Who will the voters put in this time?* **put sth↔'in** 1 to fix equipment or furniture into position so that it can be used **SYN** **install**: *We're having a new shower put in.* 2 to include sth in a letter, story, etc. 3 to interrupt another speaker in order to say sth: *Could I put in a word?* ◇ **+ speech** *'But what about us?' he put in.* 4 to officially make a claim, request, etc: *The company has put in a claim for damages.* 5 **put in a (…) performance** to give a performance of sth, especially one of a particular kind: *All the actors put in great performances.* 6 (*also* **put sth into sth**) to spend a lot of time or make a lot of effort doing sth: *She often puts in twelve hours' work a day.* **put sth into doing sth** *He's putting a lot of work into improving his French.* ⊃ related noun INPUT 7 (*also* **put sth into sth**) to use or give money: **put sth into doing sth** *He's put all his savings into buying that house.* **put 'in (at …)** | **put 'into …** (of a boat or its sailors) to enter a port: *They put in at Lagos for repairs.* **OPP** **put 'out (to …/from …)** **put 'in for sth** (*especially BrE*) to officially ask for sth: *Are you going to put in for that job?* **put yourself/sb/sth 'in for sth** to enter yourself/sb/sth for a competition
**put sth 'into sth** 1 to add a quality to sth: *He put as much feeling into his voice as he could.* 2 = PUT STH↔IN (6, 7)
**put sb↔'off** 1 to cancel a meeting or an arrangement that you have made with sb: *It's too late to put them off now.* 2 to make sb dislike sb/sth or not trust them/it: *She's very clever but her manner does tend to put people off.* ◇ *Don't be put off by how it looks—it tastes delicious.* ⊃ see also OFF-PUTTING 3 (*also* **put sb 'off sth**) to interrupt sb who is trying to give all their attention to sth that they are doing: *Don't put me off when I'm trying to concentrate.* ◇ *The sudden noise put her off her game.* 4 (*BrE*) (of a vehicle or its driver) to stop in order to allow sb to leave: *I asked the bus driver to put me off at the station.* **put sb 'off sth/sb** to make sb lose interest in or enthusiasm for sth/sb: *He was put off science by bad teaching.* ◇ **put sb off doing sth** *The accident put her off driving for life.* **put sth↔'off** to change sth to a later time or date **SYN** **postpone, delay**: *We've had to put off our wedding until September.* ◇ **put off doing sth** *He keeps putting off going to the dentist.*
**put sb 'on** 1 to give sb the phone so that they can talk to the person at the other end: *Hi, Dad—can you put Nicky on?* 2 (usually used in the progressive tenses) (*NAmE, informal*) to try to make sb believe sth that is not true, usually as a joke **SYN** **have sb on**: *Oh, come on, you know I was only putting you on.* **put sth↔'on** 1 B2 A2 to dress yourself in sth: *Hurry up! Put your coat on!* **OPP** **take sth↔off** 2 to apply sth to your skin, face, etc: *She's just putting on her make-up.* 3 to switch on a piece of equipment: *I'll put the kettle on for tea.* ◇ *She put on the brakes suddenly.* 4 to start to play recorded music or a video: *Do you mind if I put some music on?* 5 to start cooking food, especially on top of a cooker: *I just need to put the potatoes on.* 6 to become heavier, especially by the amount mentioned **SYN** **gain**: *She looks like she's put on weight.* ◇ *He must have put on several kilos.* 7 (*BrE*) to provide sth specially: *The city is putting on extra buses during the summer.* 8 to produce or present a play, a show, etc: *The local drama club is putting on 'Macbeth'.* 9 to pretend to have a particular feeling, quality, way of speaking, etc: *He put on an American accent.* ◇ *I don't think she was hurt. She was just putting it on.* **put sth 'on sth** 1 to add an amount of money or a tax to the cost of sth: *The government has put ten pence on the price of twenty cigarettes.* 2 to bet money on sth: *I've never put money on a horse.* ◇ *I put £5 on him to win.*
**put sb 'onto sb/sth** 1 to tell the police, etc. about where a criminal is or about a crime: *What first put the police onto the scam?* 2 to tell sb about sb/sth that they may like or find useful: *Who put you onto this restaurant—it's great!*
**put 'out (for sb)** (*NAmE, slang*) to agree to have sex with sb **put yourself 'out (for sb)** (*informal*) to make a special effort to do sth for sb: *Please don't put yourself out on*

# putative

*my account.* **put sb ↔ out 1** to cause sb trouble, extra work, etc. SYN **inconvenience**: *I hope our arriving late didn't put them out.* **2 be put out** to be upset or offended: *He looked really put out.* **3** to make sb unconscious: *These pills should put him out for a few hours.* **put sth ↔ out 1** to take sth out of your house and leave it, for example for sb to collect: (*BrE*) *to put the rubbish out* ◇ (*NAmE*) *to put the garbage/trash out* **2** to place sth where it will be noticed and used: *Have you put out clean towels for the guests?* **3** to stop sth from burning or shining: *to put out a candle/cigarette/light* ◇ *Firefighters soon put the fire out.* **4** to produce sth, especially for sale: *The factory puts out 500 new cars a week.* ⊃ related noun OUTPUT **5** to publish or broadcast sth: *Police have put out a description of the man they wish to question.* **6** to give a job or task to a worker who is not your employee or to a company that is not part of your own group or organization: *A lot of the work is put out to freelancers.* **7** to make a figure, result, etc. wrong: *The rise in interest rates put our estimates out by several thousands.* **8** to push a bone out of its normal position SYN **dislocate**: *She fell off her horse and put her shoulder out.* **9** (*also formal* **put sth ↔ forth**) to develop or produce new leaves, SHOOTS, etc. **put out (to .../ from ...)** (of a boat or its sailors) to leave a port: *to put out to sea* ◇ *We put out from Liverpool.* OPP **put in (at ...)** **put yourself/sth 'over (to sb)** = PUT YOURSELF/STH ↔ ACROSS/OVER (TO SB) **put sth ↔ through** to continue with and complete a plan, programme, etc: *We managed to put the deal through.* **put sb 'through sth 1** to make sb experience sth very difficult or unpleasant: *You have put your family through a lot recently.* **2** to arrange or pay for sb to attend a school, college, etc: *He put all his children through college.* **put sb 'through (to sb/...)** to connect sb by phone: *Could you put me through to the manager, please?* **put sb to sth** to cause sb trouble, difficulty, etc: *I hope we're not putting you to too much trouble.* **put sth to sb 1** to offer a suggestion to sb so that they can accept or reject it: *Your proposal will be put to the board of directors.* **2** to ask sb a question: *The audience is now invited to put questions to the speaker.* **put sth ↔ to'gether** B2 to make or prepare sth by fitting or collecting parts together: *to put together a model plane/an essay/a meal* ◇ *I think we can put together a very strong case for the defence.* **put sth towards sth** to give money to pay part of the cost of sth: *Here's $100 to put towards your ski trip.* **put 'up sth 1** to show a particular level of skill, DETERMINATION, etc. in a fight or contest: *They surrendered without putting up much of a fight.* ◇ *The team put up a great performance* (= played very well). **2** to suggest an idea, etc. for other people to discuss: *to put up an argument/case/a proposal* **put sb ↔ up 1** to let sb stay at your home: *We can put you up for the night.* **2** to suggest or present sb as a candidate for a job or position: *The Green Party hopes to put up more candidates in the next election.* **put sth ↔ up** B1 to build sth or place sth somewhere: *to put up a building/fence/memorial/tent* ⊃ SYNONYMS at BUILD **2** B1 to fix sth in a place where it will be seen SYN **display**: *to put up a notice* **3** to raise sth or put it in a higher position: *to put up a flag* ◇ *She's put her hair up.* **4** to raise or increase sth: *They've put up the rent by £20 a month.* **5** to provide or lend money: *A local businessman has put up the £500 000 needed to save the club.* **put 'up (at ...)** (*especially BrE*) to stay somewhere for the night: *We put up at a motel.* **put 'up for sth** | **put yourself 'up for sth** to offer yourself as a candidate for a job or position: *She is putting up for election to the committee.* **put sb 'up to sth** (*informal*) to encourage or persuade sb to do sth wrong or stupid: *Some of the older boys must have put him up to it.* **put 'up with sb/sth** to accept sb/sth that is annoying, unpleasant, etc. without complaining SYN **tolerate**: *I don't know how she puts up with him.* ◇ *I'm not going to put up with their smoking any longer.*

**pu·ta·tive** /ˈpjuːtətɪv/ *adj.* [only before noun] (*formal or law*) believed to be the person or thing mentioned SYN **presumed**: *the putative father of this child*

**'put-down** *noun* (*informal*) a remark or criticism that is intended to make sb look or feel stupid

**'put-on** *noun* [usually sing.] (*NAmE*) something that is done to trick or cheat people

**pu·tong·hua** /ˌpuːtʊŋˈhwɑː; *NAmE* -tʊŋ-/ *noun* [U] the standard spoken form of modern Chinese, based on the form spoken in Beijing⊃ compare MANDARIN

**pu·tre·fac·tion** /ˌpjuːtrɪˈfækʃn/ *noun* [U] (*formal*) the process of DECAYING, especially that of a dead body

**pu·trefy** /ˈpjuːtrɪfaɪ/ *verb* (**pu·tre·fies, pu·tre·fy·ing, pu·tre·fied, pu·tre·fied**) [I] (*formal*) to DECAY and smell very bad SYN **rot**

**pu·trid** /ˈpjuːtrɪd/ *adj.* **1** (of dead animals or plants) DECAYING and therefore smelling very bad SYN **foul**: *the putrid smell of rotten meat* **2** (*informal*) very unpleasant: *a putrid pink colour*

**putsch** /pʊtʃ/ *noun* (from German) a sudden attempt to remove a government by force

**putt** /pʌt/ *verb* [I, T] ~ (**sth**) (in golf) to hit the ball gently when it is on the short grass near the hole, so that it rolls across the ground a short distance into or towards the hole ▸ **putt** *noun*

**putt·er** /ˈpʌtə(r)/ *verb, noun*
■ *verb* **1** (of a boat or vehicle) to make a repeated low sound as it moves slowly: *the puttering of the engine as it reduced speed* **2** (*NAmE*) (*BrE* **pot·ter**) [I] (+ *adv./prep.*) to do things or move without hurrying, especially when you are doing sth that you enjoy and that is not important: *I spent the morning puttering around the house.*
■ *noun* (in the game of golf) the type of CLUB that is used for putting (= hitting the ball short distances)

**'putting green** *noun* a small GOLF COURSE on an area of smooth short grass where people can practise PUTTING

**putty** /ˈpʌti/ *noun* [U] a soft sticky substance that becomes hard when it is dry and that is used for fixing glass into window frames IDM **(like) putty in sb's 'hands** easily controlled or influenced by another person: *She'll persuade him. He's like putty in her hands.*

**'put-upon** *adj.* treated in an unfair way by sb because they take advantage of the fact that you are kind or willing to do things: *his much put-upon wife*

**putz** /pʌts/ *verb, noun*
■ *verb* [I] ~ **around** (*NAmE, informal*) to waste time not doing anything useful or important
■ *noun* (*NAmE, informal*) a stupid person

**puz·zle** /ˈpʌzl/ *noun, verb*
■ *noun* **1** B2 a game, etc. that you have to think about carefully in order to answer it or do it: *a crossword puzzle* ◇ *a book of puzzles for children* **2** C1 [usually sing.] something that is difficult to understand or explain SYN **mystery** **3** (*especially NAmE*) = JIGSAW
■ *verb* ~ **sb** to make sb feel confused because they do not understand sth SYN **baffle**: *What puzzles me is why he left the country without telling anyone.* ▸ **puz·zling** /ˈpʌzlɪŋ/ *adj.*: *one of the most puzzling aspects of the crime* PHRV **'puzzle over sth** to think hard about sth in order to understand or explain it **puzzle sth ↔ 'out** to find the answer to a difficult or confusing problem by thinking carefully SYN **work out**: *puzzle out why, what, etc ... He was trying to puzzle out why he had been brought to the house.*

**puz·zled** /ˈpʌzld/ *adj.* unable to understand sth or the reason for sth SYN **baffled**: *She had a puzzled look on her face.* ◇ ~ **about sth** *You look very puzzled about something.* ◇ ~ **as to sth** *Scientists are puzzled as to why the whale had swum to the shore.*

**puzzle·ment** /ˈpʌzlmənt/ *noun* [U] (*formal*) a feeling of being confused because you do not understand sth: *She frowned in puzzlement.*

**puz·zler** /ˈpʌzlə(r)/ *noun* (*informal*) something that makes you feel confused SYN **poser**

**PVC** /ˌpiː viː ˈsiː/ *noun* [U] a strong plastic material used for a wide variety of products, such as clothing, pipes, covers, etc. (the abbreviation for 'polyvinyl chloride')

**PVR** /ˌpiː viː ˈɑː(r)/ noun a device that records video onto a hard disk or other memory device, using digital technology (the abbreviation for 'personal video recorder') **SYN** DVR

**p.w.** abbr. (BrE) per week: *Rent is £100 p.w.*

**pwn** /poʊn/ verb ~ sb (informal) to completely defeat sb, especially in a video game; to be completely successful against sb/sth: *I'm going to pwn some noobs* (= players who do not have much experience) *in this game.*

**pygmy** (also **pigmy**) /ˈpɪɡmi/ noun, adj.
■ noun (pl. **-ies**) **1 Pygmy** a member of a race of very short people living in parts of Africa and south-east Asia **2** (disapproving) a very small person or thing or one that is weak in some way: *He regarded them as intellectual pygmies.*
■ adj. [only before noun] used to describe a plant or species (= type) of animal that is much smaller than other similar kinds: *a pygmy shrew*

**py·ja·ma** /pəˈdʒɑːmə/; NAmE -ˈdʒæmə/ noun loose trousers tied at the WAIST and worn by men or women in some Asian countries: *He was dressed in a pyjama and kurta, ideal for a summer evening.*

**py·ja·mas** (US **pa·ja·mas**) /pəˈdʒɑːməz/; NAmE -ˈdʒæm-/ noun [pl.] a loose jacket and trousers worn in bed: *a pair of pyjamas* ▶ **py·jama** (US **pa·jama**) adj. [only before noun]: *pyjama bottoms* **IDM** see CAT

**py·lon** /ˈpaɪlən; NAmE also -lɑːn/ noun a tall metal structure that is used for carrying electricity wires high above the ground

**pyra·mid** /ˈpɪrəmɪd/ noun **1** a large building with a square or TRIANGULAR base and sloping sides that meet in a point at the top. The ancient Egyptians built stone pyramids as places to bury their kings and queens. **2** (geometry) a solid shape with a square or TRIANGULAR base and sloping sides that meet in a point at the top ⇒ picture at SOLID **3** an object or a pile of things that has the shape of a pyramid: *a pyramid of cans in a shop window* **4** an organization or a system in which there are fewer people at each level as you get near the top: *a management pyramid* ▶ **pyr·am·idal** /-mɪdl/ adj.

**'pyramid scheme** noun an illegal way of making money, in which people are persuaded to invest money or sell a product and to persuade others to do the same, with the later INVESTORS paying money to the earlier INVESTORS, until the payment structure collapses and most people lose their money

**pyre** /ˈpaɪə(r)/ noun a large pile of wood on which a dead body is placed and burned in a FUNERAL ceremony

**pyr·eth·rum** /paɪˈriːθrəm/ noun **1** [C] a type of flower grown especially in Kenya **2** [U] a substance made from this flower and used for killing insects

**Pyrex**™ /ˈpaɪreks/ noun [U] a type of hard glass that does not break at high temperatures, and is often used to make dishes for cooking food in

**pyr·ites** /paɪˈraɪtiːz; NAmE pəˈr-/ (BrE) (NAmE **pyrite** /ˈpaɪraɪt/) noun [U] a shiny yellow mineral that is made up of SULPHUR and a metal such as iron: *iron/copper pyrites*

**pyro·mania** /ˌpaɪrəʊˈmeɪniə/ noun [U] (specialist) a mental illness that causes a strong desire to set fire to things

**pyro·maniac** /ˌpaɪrəʊˈmeɪniæk/ noun **1** (specialist) a person who suffers from pyromania **2** (informal, humorous) a person who enjoys making or watching fires

**pyro·tech·nics** /ˌpaɪrəˈtekniks/ noun **1** [pl. + sing./pl. v.] (specialist) FIREWORKS or a display of FIREWORKS **2** [pl.] (formal) a clever and complicated display of skill, for example by a musician, writer or speaker: *guitar pyrotechnics* ▶ **pyro·tech·nic** adj. [usually before noun]

**Pyr·rhic vic·tory** /ˌpɪrɪk ˈvɪktəri/ noun a victory that is not worth winning because the winner has suffered or lost so much in winning it **ORIGIN** From **Pyrrhus**, the king of Epirus who defeated the Romans in 279 BC but lost many of his own men.

**Py·thag·oras' the·orem** /paɪˌθæɡərəsɪz ˈθɪərəm; pəˌθæɡərəsɪz ˈθiː-, ˈθɪr-/ (NAmE **Py·thag·orean the·orem** /paɪˌθæɡəˌriːən ˈθɪərəm; NAmE pəˌθæɡəˌriːən ˈθiː-ə, ˈθɪr-/) noun (geometry) the rule that, in a RIGHT-ANGLED TRIANGLE, the SQUARE of the HYPOTENUSE (= the side opposite the RIGHT ANGLE) is equal to the squares of the other two sides added together

**py·thon** /ˈpaɪθən; NAmE -θɑːn/ noun a large tropical snake that kills animals for food by winding its long body tightly around them

# Qq

**Q** /kjuː/ *noun, abbr.*
- *noun* (also **q**) [C, U] (*pl.* **Qs, Q's, q's** /kjuːz/) the 17th letter of the English alphabet: *'Queen' begins with (a) Q/'Q'.* ⊃ see also Q-TIP™
- *abbr.* question IDM see MIND *v.*

**QA** /ˌkjuː ˈeɪ/ *abbr.* = QUALITY ASSURANCE

**Qa·ba·lah** /kəˈbɑːlə, ˈkæbələ/ = KABBALAH

**QC** /ˌkjuː ˈsiː/ *noun, abbr.* (in the UK) the highest level of BARRISTER, who can speak for the government in court. QC is the abbreviation for 'Queen's Counsel' and is used when there is a queen in the UK. ⊃ compare KC

**QE** /ˌkjuː ˈiː/ *abbr.* = QUANTITATIVE EASING

**QED** (also **Q.E.D.** especially in US) /ˌkjuː iː ˈdiː/ *abbr.* that is what I wanted to prove and I have proved it (from Latin 'quod erat demonstrandum')

**qib·lah** (also **qibla, kiblah, kibla**) /ˈkɪblə/ *noun* [sing.] the direction of the Kaaba (the holy building at Mecca), towards which Muslims turn when they are PRAYING

**QR code**™ /ˌkjuː ˈɑː kəʊd; NAmE ˈɑːr/ *noun* a pattern of black and white squares that contains information, often a web address, that can be read by the camera on a smartphone (the abbreviation for 'quick response code')

**qt** *abbr.* (in writing) QUART

**Q-tip**™ *noun* (NAmE) = COTTON BUD

**qua** /kweɪ, kwɑː/ *prep.* (*from Latin, formal*) as sth; in the role of sth: *The soldier acted qua soldier, not as a human being.* ⊃ see also SINE QUA NON

**quack** /kwæk/ *noun, verb*
- *noun* **1** the sound that a DUCK makes **2** (*informal, disapproving*) a person who dishonestly claims to have medical knowledge or skills: *quack doctors* ◊ *I've got a check-up with the quack* (= the doctor) *next week.*
- *verb* [I] when a DUCK **quacks**, it makes the noise that is typical of ducks

**quack·ery** /ˈkwækəri/ *noun* [U] the methods or behaviour of sb who pretends to have medical knowledge

**quad** /kwɒd; NAmE kwɑːd/ *noun* **1** = QUADRANGLE **2** = QUADRUPLET ⊃ see also QUADS

**quad bike** (*BrE*) (NAmE **four-'wheeler**) *noun* a motorcycle with four large wheels, used for riding over rough ground, often for fun ⊃ see also ATV

**quad·ran·gle** /ˈkwɒdræŋɡl; NAmE ˈkwɑːd-/ *noun* (*formal*) (also rather informal **quad**) an open square area that has buildings all around it, especially in a school or college

**quad·ran·gu·lar** /kwɒdˈræŋɡjələ(r); NAmE kwɑːd-/ *adj.* **1** (*geometry*) (of a shape) having four sides and flat rather than solid **2** (of a sporting competition) involving four teams or individuals who each compete against all the others

**quad·rant** /ˈkwɒdrənt; NAmE ˈkwɑːd-/ *noun* **1** (*geometry*) a quarter of a circle or of its CIRCUMFERENCE (= the distance around it) ⊃ picture at CIRCLE **2** an instrument for measuring angles, especially to check your position at sea or to look at stars

**quad·rat·ic** /kwɒˈdrætɪk; NAmE kwɑːd-/ *adj.* (*mathematics*) involving an unknown quantity that is multiplied by itself once only: *a quadratic equation*

**quadri-** /ˈkwɒdri, kwɒˈdrɪ; NAmE kwɑːdri, kwɑːˈdrɪ/ (also **quadr-**) *combining form* (in nouns, adjectives and adverbs) four; having four: *quadrilateral* ◊ *quadruplet*

**quad·ri·ceps** /ˈkwɒdrɪseps; NAmE ˈkwɑːd-/ *noun* (*pl.* **quadri·ceps**) (also informal **quads**) (*anatomy*) the large muscle at the front of the THIGH

**quad·ri·lat·eral** /ˌkwɒdrɪˈlætərəl; NAmE ˌkwɑːd-/ *noun* (*geometry*) a flat shape with four straight sides ▸ **quad·ri·lat·eral** *adj.*

**quad·rille** /kwəˈdrɪl/ *noun* a dance for four or more couples in a square, popular in the past

**quad·ril·lion** /kwɒˈdrɪljən; NAmE kwɑːˈd-/ *number* the number $10^{15}$, or 1 followed by 15 zeros

**quad·ri·ple·gic** /ˌkwɒdrɪˈpliːdʒɪk; NAmE ˌkwɑːd-/ *noun* a person who is permanently unable to use their arms and legs ▸ **quadri·ple·gic** *adj.* **quadri·ple·gia** /-dʒə/ *noun* [U]

**quad·ru·ped** /ˈkwɒdruped; NAmE ˈkwɑːd-/ *noun* (*specialist*) any creature with four feet ⊃ compare BIPED

**quad·ru·ple** /ˈkwɒdrupl; NAmE kwɑːˈdruːpl/ *verb, adj., det.*
- *verb* [I, T] **~ (sth)** to become four times bigger; to make sth four times bigger: *Sales have quadrupled in the last five years.*
- *adj.* [only before noun], *det.* **1** consisting of four parts, people or groups: *a quadruple alliance* **2** being four times as much or as many: *a quadruple whisky* ◊ *This year we produced quadruple the amount produced in 2013.*

**quad·ru·plet** /ˈkwɒdruplət; NAmE kwɑːˈdruːplət/ (also **quad**) *noun* one of four children born at the same time to the same mother

**quads** /kwɒdz; NAmE kwɑːdz/ *noun* [pl.] (*informal*) = QUADRICEPS

**quaff** /kwɒf; NAmE kwæf, kwɑːf/ *verb* **~ sth** (*old-fashioned* or *literary*) to drink a large amount of sth quickly

**quag·mire** /ˈkwæɡmaɪə(r); BrE also ˈkwɒɡ-/ *noun* **1** an area of soft wet ground SYN bog **2** a difficult or dangerous situation SYN morass

**quail** /kweɪl/ *noun, verb*
- *noun* [C, U] (*pl.* **quails** or **quail**) a small brown bird, whose meat and eggs are used for food; the meat of this bird
- *verb* [I] **~ (at / before sb / sth)** (*literary*) to feel frightened or to show that you are frightened

**quaint** /kweɪnt/ *adj.* attractive in an unusual or old-fashioned way: *quaint old customs* ◊ *a quaint seaside village* ▸ **quaint·ly** *adv.* **quaint·ness** *noun* [U]

**quake** /kweɪk/ *verb, noun*
- *verb* **1** [I] **~ (with sth)** (of a person) to shake because you are very frightened or nervous SYN tremble: *Quaking with fear, Polly slowly opened the door.* **2** [I] (of the earth or a building) to move or shake violently: *The ground quaked as the bomb exploded.*
- *noun* (*informal*) = EARTHQUAKE

**Quaker** /ˈkweɪkə(r)/ *noun* a member of the Society of Friends, a Christian religious group that meets without any formal ceremony and is strongly opposed to violence and war ▸ **Quaker** *adj.*: *a Quaker school*

**quali·fi·ca·tion** ⓘ B1 /ˌkwɒlɪfɪˈkeɪʃn; NAmE ˌkwɑːl-/ *noun* **1** B1 [C, usually pl.] (*BrE*) an exam that you have passed or a course of study that you have successfully completed: *academic/educational/professional/vocational qualifications* ◊ *a coaching/teaching/nursing qualification* ◊ *He left school with no formal qualifications.* ◊ *to have qualifications* ◊ *to gain/get/obtain/possess/achieve qualifications* ◊ *In this job, experience counts for more than paper qualifications.* **~ in sth** *Too many school-leavers lack basic qualifications in English and Maths.* ⊃ WORDFINDER NOTE at STUDY **2** [C] a skill or type of experience that you need for a particular job or activity: *What qualifications do radio presenters require?* **~ for sth** *Previous teaching experience is a necessary qualification for the job.* ⊃ WORDFINDER NOTE at APPLY **3** [C, U] information that you add to a statement to limit the effect that it has or the way it is applied SYN proviso: *I accept his theories, but not without certain qualifications.* ◊ *The plan was approved without qualification.* **4** [U] the fact of passing an exam, completing a course of training or reaching the standard necessary to do a job or take part in a competition: *Nurses in training should be given a guarantee of employment following qualification.* ◊ *A victory in this game will earn them qualification for the World Cup.*

**quali·fied** ⓘ B1 /ˈkwɒlɪfaɪd; NAmE ˈkwɑːl-/ *adj.* **1** B1 having passed the exams or completed the training that are necessary in order to do a particular job; having the experience to do a particular job: *a qualified teacher* ◊ *a qualified instructor/accountant/nurse/doctor* ◊ *qualified staff/personnel* ◊ *to be highly qualified* ◊ *to be suitably/fully qualified* ◊ **~ for sth** *She's extremely well qualified for the job.* ◊ **~ to do sth** *I'm not qualified to teach in state schools.* **2** B1 [not before noun] **~ to do sth** having the practical knowledge or skills to do sth: *I don't know much about it, so I don't feel qualified to comment.* **3** [usually before noun] (of approval, support, etc.) limited in some way: *The plan was given only qualified support.* ◊ *The project was only a qualified success.*

**quali·fier** /ˈkwɒlɪfaɪə(r); NAmE ˈkwɑːl-/ noun **1** a person or team that has defeated others in order to enter a particular competition **2** a game or match that a person or team has to win in order to enter a particular competition: *a World Cup qualifier* **3** (*grammar*) a word, especially an adjective or adverb, that describes another word in a particular way: *In 'the open door', 'open' is a qualifier, describing the door.*

**quali·fy** ⓘ B1 /ˈkwɒlɪfaɪ; NAmE ˈkwɑːl-/ verb (qualifies, qualifying, qualified, qualified)
- FOR JOB **1** ⓣ B1 [I] to reach the standard of ability or knowledge needed to do a particular job, for example by completing a course of study or passing exams: *How long does it take to qualify?* ◊ **~ as sth** *He qualified as a doctor last year.* ◊ **in sth** *She spent seven years qualifying in law.*
  ➲ WORDFINDER NOTE at TRAINING
- GIVE SKILLS/KNOWLEDGE **2** ⓣ B1 [T] to give sb the skills and knowledge they need to do sth: **~ sb for sth** *This training course will qualify you for a better job.* ◊ **~ sb to do sth** *The test qualifies you to drive heavy vehicles.*
- FOR COMPETITION **3** ⓣ B1 [I] to be of a high enough standard to enter a competition; to defeat another person or team in order to enter or continue in a competition: *He failed to qualify.* ◊ **~ for sth** *South Korea qualified for the finals when they beat Italy 6–1.*
- HAVE/GIVE RIGHT **4** ⓣ B2 [I, T] to have or give sb the right to do sth: *To qualify, you must have lived in this country for at least three years.* ◊ **~ for sth** *If you live in the area, you qualify for a parking permit.* ◊ **~ sb (for sth)** *Paying a fee doesn't automatically qualify you for membership.*
- FIT DESCRIPTION **5** [I, T] to have the right qualities to be described as a particular thing: **~ (as sth)** *Do you think this dress qualifies as evening wear?* ◊ **~ sth (as sth)** *It's an old building, but that doesn't qualify it as an ancient monument!*
- STATEMENT **6** [T] **~ sth** | **~ what…** to add sth to a previous statement to make the meaning less strong or less general: *I want to qualify what I said earlier—I didn't mean he couldn't do the job, only that he would need supervision.*
- GRAMMAR **7** [T] **~ sth** (of a word) to describe another word in a particular way: *In 'the open door', 'open' is an adjective qualifying 'door'.*

**quali·ta·tive** Ⓦ /ˈkwɒlɪtətɪv; NAmE ˈkwɑːlɪteɪt/ adj. [usually before noun] connected with what sth is like or how good it is, rather than with how much of it there is: *qualitative analysis/research* ◊ *There are qualitative differences between the two products.* ➲ compare QUANTITATIVE ▶ **quali·ta·tive·ly** adv.: *qualitatively different*

**qual·ity** ⓘ A2 Ⓞ /ˈkwɒləti; NAmE ˈkwɑːl-/ noun, adj.
■ **noun** (*pl.* **-ies**) **1** ⓣ A2 [U, C] the standard of sth when it is compared to other things like it; how good or bad sth is: *Improving the quality of care for nursing home residents is a priority.* ◊ *When costs are cut product quality suffers.* ◊ **of…~** *to be of good/poor/top quality* ◊ *goods of a high quality* ◊ *high-quality goods* ◊ **in~** *a decline in water quality* ➲ see also AIR QUALITY **2** ⓣ B1 [U] a high standard 🅢🅨🅝 **excellence**: *We aim to provide quality at reasonable prices.* ◊ **of~** *contemporary writers of quality* **3** ⓣ B1 [C] a thing that is part of a person's character, especially sth good: *personal qualities such as honesty and generosity* ◊ *to have leadership qualities* **4** [C, U] a feature of sb/sth, especially one that makes them different from sb/sth else: *the special quality of light and shade in her paintings* **5** [C] (*BrE*) = QUALITY NEWSPAPER
■ **adj. 1** [only before noun] used especially by people trying to sell goods or services to say that sth is of a high quality: *We specialize in quality furniture.* ◊ *quality service at a competitive price* **2** (*BrE, slang*) very good: *'What was the film like?' 'Quality!'*

**ˈquality asˈsurance** (*abbr.* **QA**) *noun* [U] the practice of managing the way goods are produced or services are provided to make sure they are kept at a high standard

**ˈquality conˈtrol** *noun* [U] the practice of checking goods as they are being produced, to make sure that they are of a high standard

**ˈquality ˈnewspaper** (*also less frequent* **qualˈity**) *noun* (*BrE*) a newspaper that deals seriously with issues and has a high standard of editing and comment ➲ compare TABLOID (2)

**ˈquality of ˈlife** *noun* [U] the level of health, comfort and happiness that a particular person or group has: *Their quality of life improved dramatically when they moved to France.* ➲ compare STANDARD OF LIVING

**ˈquality time** *noun* [U] time spent giving your full attention to sb, especially to your children or partner after work

**qualm** /kwɑːm, kwɔːm/ *noun* [usually pl.] **~ (about sth)** a feeling of doubt or worry about whether what you are doing is right 🅢🅨🅝 **misgiving**: *He had been working very hard so he had no qualms about taking a few days off.*

**quan·dary** /ˈkwɒndəri; NAmE ˈkwɑːn-/ *noun* [usually sing.] (*pl.* **-ies**) the state of not being able to decide what to do in a difficult situation 🅢🅨🅝 **dilemma**: **in a~** *George was in a quandary—should he go or shouldn't he?*

**quango** /ˈkwæŋɡəʊ/ *noun* (*pl.* **-os**) (*often disapproving*) (in the UK) an organization dealing with public matters, started by the government, but working independently and with its own legal powers

**quanta** /ˈkwɒntə; NAmE ˈkwɑːn-/ *pl.* of QUANTUM

**quan·ti·fier** /ˈkwɒntɪfaɪə(r); NAmE ˈkwɑːn-/ *noun* (*grammar*) a determiner or pronoun that expresses quantity, for example 'all' or 'both'

**quan·tify** Ⓦ /ˈkwɒntɪfaɪ; NAmE ˈkwɑːn-/ *verb* (**quan·ti·fies**, **quan·ti·fy·ing**, **quan·ti·fied**, **quan·ti·fied**) **~ sth** to describe or express sth as an amount or a number: *The risks to health are impossible to quantify.* ▶ **quan·ti·fi·able** /ˈkwɒntɪfaɪəbl, ˌkwɒntɪˈfaɪəbl/ NAmE /ˈkwɑːntɪfaɪəbl, ˌkwɑːntɪˈfaɪəbl/ *adj.*: *quantifiable data* **quan·ti·fi·ca·tion** /ˌkwɒntɪfɪˈkeɪʃn; NAmE ˌkwɑːn-/ *noun* [U]

**quan·ti·ta·tive** Ⓦ /ˈkwɒntɪtətɪv; NAmE ˈkwɑːntəteɪtɪv/ *adj.* connected with the amount or number of sth rather than with how good it is: *quantitative analysis/research* ◊ *There is no difference between the two in quantitative terms.* ➲ compare QUALITATIVE ▶ **quan·ti·ta·tive·ly** adv.

**ˈquantitative ˈeasing** (*abbr.* **QE**) *noun* [U] the introduction of new money into a country's money supply by a central bank

**quan·tity** ⓘ A2 Ⓞ /ˈkwɒntəti; NAmE ˈkwɑːn-/ *noun* (*pl.* **-ies**) **1** ⓣ A2 [C, U] an amount or a number of sth: **~ of sth** *a large/small quantity of sth* ◊ *vast/huge quantities of food* ◊ **in … quantities** *a product that is cheap to produce in large quantities* ◊ **in … ~** *Is it available in sufficient quantity?* **2** ⓣ A2 [U] the measurement of sth by saying how much of it there is: *The data is limited in terms of both quality and quantity.* **3** ⓣ B1 [C, U] a large amount or number of sth: **~ of sth** *The police found a quantity of drugs at his home.* ◊ *I was overwhelmed by the sheer quantity of information available.* ◊ *Their latest album isn't selling in anything like the quantities that their first one did.* ◊ **in ~** *It's cheaper to buy goods in quantity.* 🅘🅓🅜 see UNKNOWN *adj.*

**ˈquantity surˈveyor** *noun* (*BrE*) a person whose job is to calculate the quantity of materials needed for building sth, how much it will cost and how long it will take

**quan·tum** /ˈkwɒntəm; NAmE ˈkwɑːn-/ *noun* (*pl.* **quanta** /-tə/) (*physics*) a very small quantity of ELECTROMAGNETIC energy

**ˈquantum ˈleap** (*also less frequent* **ˌquantum ˈjump**) *noun* a sudden, great and important change, improvement or development

**ˌquantum meˈchanics** *noun* [U] (*physics*) the branch of MECHANICS that deals with movement and force in pieces of matter smaller than ATOMS

**ˈquantum ˈphysics** *noun* [U] the branch of science that investigates the principles of QUANTUM THEORY to understand the behaviour of PARTICLES at the ATOMIC and SUB-ATOMIC level

# quantum theory

**quantum theory** *noun* [U] (*physics*) a theory based on the idea that energy can only be changed in units that cannot be divided

**quar·an·tine** /ˈkwɒrəntiːn; NAmE ˈkwɔːr-/ *noun, verb*
- *noun* [U] a period of time when an animal or a person that has or may have a disease is kept away from others in order to prevent the disease from spreading: **in ~** *The dog was kept in quarantine for six months.* ◇ *quarantine regulations*
- *verb* [T, I] **~ (sth/sb)** to put an animal or a person into quarantine; to go into quarantine

**quark** /kwɑːk; NAmE kwɑːrk, kwɔːrk/ *noun* **1** [C] (*physics*) a very small part of matter (= a substance). There are several types of quark and it is thought that PROTONS, NEUTRONS, etc. are formed from them. **2** [U] a type of soft cheese from central Europe, similar to CURD CHEESE

**quar·rel** /ˈkwɒrəl; NAmE ˈkwɑːr-/ *noun, verb*
- *noun* **1** [C] an angry argument or DISAGREEMENT between people, often about a personal matter: *a family quarrel* ◇ **~ with sb** *He did not mention the quarrel with his wife.* ◇ **~ about/over sth** *They had a quarrel about money.* ◇ **~ between A and B** *Were you at any time aware of a quarrel between the two of them?* **2** [U] **~ (with sb/sth)** (especially in negative sentences) a reason for complaining about sb/sth or for disagreeing with sb/sth: *We have no quarrel with his methods.* IDM see PICK *v.*
- *verb* [I] (-**ll**-, *US* -**l**-) to have an angry argument or DISAGREEMENT: *My sister and I used to quarrel all the time.* ◇ **~ (with sb) (about/over sth)** *She quarrelled with her brother over their father's will.*
- PHRV **ˈquarrel with sb/sth** to disagree with sb/sth: *Nobody could quarrel with your conclusions.*

**quar·rel·some** /ˈkwɒrəlsəm; NAmE ˈkwɑːr-/ *adj.* (of a person) often arguing with other people SYN argumentative

**quarry** /ˈkwɒri; NAmE ˈkwɑːri/ *noun, verb*
- *noun* (*pl.* -**ies**) **1** [C] a place where large amounts of stone, etc. are dug out of the ground: *a slate quarry* ◇ *the site of a disused quarry* ⊃ compare MINE **2** [sing.] an animal or a person that is being hunted or followed SYN **prey**: *The hunters lost sight of their quarry in the forest.* ◇ *The photographers pursued their quarry through the streets.*
- *verb* [usually passive] (**quar·ries, quarry·ing, quar·ried, quar·ried**) to take stone, etc. out of a quarry: **A is quarried (from/out of B)** *The local rock is quarried from the hillside.* ◇ **B is quarried (for A)** *The area is being quarried for limestone.* ▸ **quarrying** *noun* [U]: *There has been quarrying in the area for centuries.*

**quart** /kwɔːt; NAmE kwɔːrt/ *noun* (*abbr.* **qt**) a unit for measuring liquids, equal to 2 PINTS or about 1.14 LITRES in the UK and Canada, and 0.95 of a LITRE in the US

**quar·ter** ❶ A1 /ˈkwɔːtə(r); NAmE ˈkwɔːrt-/ *noun, verb*
- *noun*
- **1 OF 4 PARTS 1** ❶ A1 (*also* **fourth** *especially in NAmE*) [C] one of four equal parts of sth: **~ of sth** *a quarter of an hour/a century* ◇ *a quarter of a mile/million* ◇ *Almost a quarter of respondents reported employment discrimination.* ◇ *The programme lasted an hour and a quarter.* ◇ *Cut the apple into quarters.* ◇ *The theatre was about three quarters full.* ⊃ note at HALF
- **15 MINUTES 2** ❶ A1 [C] a period of 15 minutes either before or after every hour: *It's (a) quarter to four now—I'll meet you at (a) quarter past.* ◇ (*NAmE also*) *It's quarter of four now—I'll meet you at quarter after.*
- **3 MONTHS 3** [C] a period of three months, used especially as a period for which bills are paid or a company's income is calculated
- **PART OF TOWN 4** [C, usually sing.] a district or part of a town: *the historic quarter of the city* ◇ *As a student in Paris, she loved the Latin quarter.*
- **PERSON/GROUP 5** [C] a person or group of people, especially as a source of help, information or a reaction: *Support for the plan came from an unexpected quarter.* ◇ *The news was greeted with dismay in some quarters.*
- **25 CENTS 6** [C] a coin of the US and Canada worth 25 cents
- **ROOMS TO LIVE IN 7 quarters** [pl.] rooms that are provided for soldiers, servants, etc. to live in: *We were moved to more comfortable living quarters.* ◇ *the servants'/officers' quarters*
- **OF MOON 8** [C] the period of time twice a month when we can see a quarter of the moon: *The moon is in its first quarter.*
- **IN SPORT 9** [C] one of the four periods of time into which a game of AMERICAN FOOTBALL is divided
- **WEIGHT 10** [C] (*BrE*) a unit for measuring weight, a quarter of a pound; 4 OUNCES **11** [C] a unit for measuring weight, 28 pounds in the UK or 25 pounds in the US; a quarter of a HUNDREDWEIGHT
- **PITY 12** [U] (*literary*) kind treatment of an enemy or opponent who is in your power SYN **mercy**: *His rivals knew that they could expect no quarter from such a ruthless adversary.* IDM see CLOSE² *adj.*
- *verb*
- **DIVIDE INTO 4 1 ~ sth** to cut or divide sth into four parts: *She peeled and quartered an apple.*
- **PROVIDE ROOMS 2 ~ sb (+ adv./prep.)** (*formal*) to provide sb with a place to eat and sleep: *The soldiers were quartered in the town.*

**quar·ter·back** /ˈkwɔːtəbæk; NAmE ˈkwɔːrtərb-/ *noun, verb*
- *noun* (in AMERICAN FOOTBALL) the player who directs the team's attacking play and passes the ball to other players at the start of each attack
- *verb* **1** [I] (in AMERICAN FOOTBALL) to play as a quarterback **2** [T] **~ sth** (*NAmE*) to direct or organize sth

**ˈquarter day** *noun* (*BrE, specialist*) the first day of a QUARTER (= a period of three months) on which payments must be made, for example at the STOCK EXCHANGE

**quar·ter·deck** /ˈkwɔːtədek; NAmE ˈkwɔːrtərd-/ *noun* a part of the upper level of a ship, at the back, that is used mainly by officers

**quarter-ˈfinal** *noun* (in sports or competitions) one of the four games, matches or contests to decide the players or teams for the SEMI-FINALS of a competition ▸ **quarter-ˈfinalist** *noun*

**ˈQuarter Horse** *noun* (*NAmE*) a small type of horse that can run very fast over short distances

**quar·ter·ly** /ˈkwɔːtəli; NAmE ˈkwɔːrtərli/ *adj., adv., noun*
- *adj.* produced or happening every three months: *a quarterly meeting of the board* ▸ **quar·ter·ly** *adv.*: *to pay the rent quarterly*
- *noun* (*pl.* -**ies**) a magazine, etc. published four times a year

**quar·ter·mas·ter** /ˈkwɔːtəmɑːstə(r); NAmE ˈkwɔːrtərmæs-/ *noun* an officer in the army who is in charge of providing food, uniforms and accommodation

**ˈquarter note** (*NAmE*) (*BrE* **crot·chet**) *noun* (*music*) a note that lasts half as long as a MINIM ⊃ picture at MUSIC

**ˈquarter-tone** *noun* (*music*) a quarter of a TONE on a musical SCALE, for example half of the INTERVAL (= the difference) between the notes E and F

**quar·tet** /kwɔːˈtet; NAmE kwɔːrˈt-/ *noun* **1** [C + sing./ pl. v.] a group of four musicians or singers who play or sing together: *the Amadeus Quartet* **2** [C] a piece of music for four musicians or singers: *a Beethoven string quartet* **3** [C + sing./ pl. v.] a set of four people or things: *the last in a quartet of novels*

**quar·tile** /ˈkwɔːtaɪl; NAmE ˈkwɔːrtaɪl, -tl/ *noun* (*statistics*) one of four equal groups into which a set of things can be divided according to the DISTRIBUTION of a particular VARIABLE: *women in the fourth quartile of height* (= the shortest 25% of women) ⊃ compare QUINTILE

**quarto** /ˈkwɔːtəʊ; NAmE ˈkwɔːrt-/ *noun* (*pl.* -**os**) (*specialist*) **1** [U] a size of page made by folding a standard sheet of paper twice to make eight pages **2** [C] a book with pages in quarto size

**quartz** /kwɔːts; NAmE kwɔːrts/ *noun* [U] a hard mineral, often in CRYSTAL form, that is used to make very accurate clocks and watches

**qua·sar** /ˈkweɪzɑː(r)/ *noun* (*astronomy*) a large object like a star, that is far away and that shines very brightly and occasionally sends out strong radio signals ⊃ compare PULSAR

**quash** /kwɒʃ; NAmE kwɑːʃ/ *verb* **1 ~ sth** (*law*) to officially say that a decision made by a court is no longer legally acceptable or correct SYN **overturn**: *His conviction was* later quashed by the Court of Appeal. **2** ~ **sth** to take action to stop sth from continuing SYN **suppress**: *The rumours were quickly quashed.*

**quasi-** /ˈkweɪzaɪ, kweɪsaɪ, kwɑːzi/ *combining form* (in adjectives and nouns) **1** that appears to be sth but is not really so: *a quasi-scientific explanation* **2** partly; almost: *a quasi-official body*

**quat·rain** /ˈkwɒtreɪn/; *NAmE* /ˈkwɑːt-/ *noun* (*specialist*) a poem or VERSE of a poem that has four lines

**qua·ver** /ˈkweɪvə(r)/ *verb, noun*
■ *verb* [I, T] (+ **speech**) if sb's voice **quavers**, it is unsteady, usually because the person is nervous or afraid: *'I'm not safe here, am I?' she asked in a quavering voice.* ▶ **qua·very** *adj.*: *a quavery voice*
■ *noun* **1** (*BrE*) (*NAmE* **eighth note**) (*music*) a note that lasts half as long as a CROTCHET ⊃ picture at MUSIC **2** [usually sing.] a shaking sound in sb's voice

**quay** /kiː/ *noun* a platform in a HARBOUR where boats come in to load, etc: *A crowd was waiting on the quay.*

▼ HOMOPHONES
**key • quay** /kiː/
• **key** *noun*: *She quietly turned the key in the lock.*
• **key** *adj.*: *Fresh eggs are a key ingredient for a tasty cake.*
• **key** *verb*: *Customers have to key their PIN for amounts over £30.*
• **quay** *noun*: *The constant coming and going of ferries makes the quay a bustling place.*

**quay·side** /ˈkiːsaɪd/ *noun* [usually sing.] a quay and the area near it: *crowds waiting on/at the quayside to welcome them*

**queasy** /ˈkwiːzi/ *adj.* **1** feeling sick; wanting to VOMIT SYN **nauseous 2** slightly nervous or worried about sth ▶ **queas·ily** /-zəli/ *adv.* **queasi·ness** *noun* [U]

**Que·chua** /ˈketʃwə/ *noun* [U] a language originally spoken by the Quechua people of South America, now spoken in Peru, Bolivia, Chile, Colombia and Ecuador

**queen** 🔑 A2 /kwiːn/ *noun*
• FEMALE RULER **1** 🔑 A2 the female ruler of an independent state that has a royal family: *to be crowned queen* ◊ *kings and queens* ◊ ~ *of ... the Queen of Norway* ◊ *Queen Victoria* **2** 🔑 A2 (*also* **queen consort**) the wife of a king: *Henry VII and his queen, Elizabeth of York* ◊ ~ *of ... The King and Queen of Denmark attended the wedding.*
• BEST IN GROUP **3** ~ (**of sth**) a woman, place or thing that is thought to be one of the best in a particular group or area: *the queen of fashion* ◊ *a movie queen* ◊ *Venice, queen of the Adriatic* ⊃ see also DRAMA QUEEN
• AT FESTIVAL **4** a woman or girl chosen to perform official duties at a festival or celebration: *a carnival queen* ◊ *a May queen* (= at a festival to celebrate the coming of spring) ◊ *a homecoming queen* ⊃ see also BEAUTY QUEEN
• IN CHESS **5** the most powerful piece used in the game of CHESS that can move any number of squares in any direction
• IN CARDS **6** a PLAYING CARD with the picture of a queen on it
• INSECT **7** a large female insect that lays eggs for the whole group: *a queen bee*
• GAY **8** (*taboo, informal*) an offensive word for a GAY man who behaves like a woman IDM ⊃ see UNCROWNED

**queen ˈbee** *noun* **1** a female bee that produces eggs for the whole group of bees in a HIVE ⊃ compare DRONE, WORKER **2** a woman who behaves as if she is the most important person in a particular place or group

**queen·ly** /ˈkwiːnli/ *adj.* of, like or suitable for a queen

**queen ˈmother** *noun* a title given to the wife of a king who has died and who is the mother of the new king or queen: *Queen Elizabeth, the Queen Mother*

**Queen's ˈCounsel** *noun* = QC

**the Queen's ˈEnglish** *noun* [U] (*old-fashioned*) the English language as written and spoken correctly by educated people in the UK HELP 'The Queen's English' is used when the United Kingdom has a queen, and 'the King's English' when it has a king.

---

1261 **question**

**Queen's ˈevidence** *noun* [U] (*law*) (in the UK) if a criminal **turns Queen's evidence**, he or she gives evidence against the people who committed a crime with him or her

**the Queen's ˈSpeech** *noun* [sing.] in the UK, a statement read by the Queen at the start of a new Parliament, which contains details of the government's plans

**queer** /kwɪə(r)/; *NAmE* /kwɪr/ *adj., noun, verb*
■ *adj.* (**queer·er, queer·est**) **1** (*old-fashioned*) strange or unusual SYN **odd**: *His face was a queer pink colour.* **2** (*taboo, slang*) an offensive way of describing a GAY person, especially a man, which is, however, also used by some gay people about themselves IDM see FISH *n.*
■ *noun* (*taboo, slang*) an offensive word for a GAY person, especially a man, which is, however, also used by some gay people about themselves
■ *verb*
IDM **queer sb's ˈpitch | queer the ˈpitch (for sb)** (*BrE, informal*) to cause sb's plans to fail or to destroy their chances of getting sth

**quell** /kwel/ *verb* (*formal*) **1** ~ **sth/sb** to stop sth such as violent behaviour or protests: *Extra police were called in to quell the disturbances.* ◊ (*figurative*) *She started to giggle, but Bob quelled her with a look.* **2** ~ **sth** to stop or reduce strong or unpleasant feelings SYN **calm**: *to quell your fears*

**quench** /kwentʃ/ *verb* **1** ~ **your thirst** to drink so that you no longer feel thirsty SYN **slake 2** ~ **sth** (*formal*) to stop a fire from burning SYN **extinguish**: *Firemen tried to quench the flames raging through the building.*

**queru·lous** /ˈkwerələs/ *adj.* (*formal disapproving*) complaining; showing that you are annoyed SYN **peevish** ▶ **queru·lous·ly** *adv.*

**query** 🔑+ C1 /ˈkwɪəri/; *NAmE* /ˈkwɪri/ *noun, verb*
■ *noun* (*pl.* **-ies**) **1** 🔑+ C1 a question, especially one asking for information or expressing a doubt about sth: *Our assistants will be happy to answer your queries.* ◊ *If you have a query about your insurance policy, contact our helpline.* **2** 🔑+ C1 a question mark to show that sth has not been finished or decided: *Put a query against Jack's name—I'm not sure if he's coming.*
■ *verb* (**quer·ies, query·ing, quer·ied, quer·ied**) **1** to express doubt about whether sth is correct or not or what sth means: ~ **sth** *We queried the bill as it seemed far too high.* ◊ *I'm not in a position to query their decision.* ◊ ~ **what, whether, etc ...** *Both novels query what it means to be American.* **2** to ask a question; to put a question to sb: + **speech** *'Who will be leading the team?' queried Simon.* ◊ ~ **sb** (*especially NAmE*) *I queried a few people on the subject.*

**ˈquery language** *noun* [C, U] (*computing*) a system of words and symbols that you type in order to ask a computer to give you information from a DATABASE or an information system

**quesa·dilla** /ˌkeɪsəˈdiːə/ *noun* a Mexican dish consisting of a TORTILLA (= flat, round bread) filled with cheese and sometimes meat or other ingredients, folded in half and fried

**quest** 🔑+ C1 /kwest/ *noun, verb*
■ *noun* 🔑+ C1 (*formal or literary*) a long search for sth, especially for some quality such as happiness: ~ **for sth** *the quest for happiness/knowledge/truth* ◊ **in** ~ **of sth** *He set off in quest of adventure.*
■ *verb* [I] ~ (**for sth**) (*formal or literary*) to search for sth that is difficult to find

**ques·tion** 🔑 A1 🔊 /ˈkwestʃən/ *noun, verb*
■ *noun* **1** 🔑 A1 [C] a sentence, phrase or word that asks for information: *to ask/answer a question* ◊ *Does anyone have any questions?* ◊ *The question is, how much are they going to pay you?* ◊ *The big question is, why did they do it?* ◊ (*formal*) *The question arose as to whether or not he knew of the situation.* ◊ ~ **about sth** (*formal*) *He put a question to the minister about the recent reforms.* ◊ *I hope the police don't ask any awkward questions.* ◊ **open questions** *that don't just need 'Yes' or 'No' as an answer.* ⊃ see also INDIRECT QUESTION, LEADING QUESTION, QUESTION TAG, REPORTED QUESTION **2** 🔑 A1 [C] a task or request for information that is intended to test your

## questionable

knowledge or understanding, for example in an exam or a competition: *Question 3 was very difficult.* ◊ **on sth** *In the exam there's sure to be a question on energy.* **3** ? B1 [C] a matter or topic that needs to be discussed or dealt with: *This is an issue that raises many important questions.* ◊ **~ of sth** *Let's look at the question of security.* ◊ *The question that needs to be addressed is one of funding.* ◊ **about sth** *Questions remain about how she was appointed.* ◊ *Which route is better remains an open question* (= it is not decided). **4** ? A2 [U, C] doubt or not being certain about sth: *His suitability for the job is open to question.* ◊ **beyond ~** *Her honesty is beyond question.* ◊ **without ~** *Her version of events was accepted without question.* ◊ *This case brings into question the whole purpose of the law.* ◊ *The safety of the system has recently come into question.* ◊ *His ability has never been called into question.* ◊ **as to/about sth** *I did have some questions as to his motive in coming.*

IDM ▶ **good ˈquestion!** (*informal*) used to show that you do not know the answer to a question: '*How much is all this going to cost?*' '*Good question!*' **in ˈquestion** **1** that is being discussed: *On the day in question we were in Cardiff.* **2** in doubt; uncertain: *The future of public transport is not in question.* **just/merely/only a question of (doing) sth** used to say that sth is not difficult to predict, explain, do, etc: *It's merely a question of time before the business collapses.* ◊ *It's just a question of deciding what you really want.* **out of the ˈquestion** impossible or not allowed and therefore not worth discussing: *Another trip abroad this year is out of the question.* **there is/was no question of sth happening/of sb doing sth** there is/was no possibility of sth: *There was no question of his/him cancelling the trip so near the departure date.* ⊃ more at BEG, MOOT *adj.*, POP *v.*

■ *verb* **1** ? A2 **~ sb (about/on sth)** | **+ speech** [often passive] to ask sb questions about sth, especially officially: *Two men are being questioned by police.* ◊ *She was arrested and questioned about the fire.* ◊ *The students were questioned on the books they had been studying.* ⊃ see also CROSS-QUESTION **2** ? B1 to have or express doubts about sth: **~ sth** *I just accepted what he told me. I never thought to question it.* ◊ *At times I question the wisdom of that decision.* ◊ *I seriously question his ability to do his job.* **~ whether, what, etc…** *He questioned whether the accident was solely the truck driver's fault.*

▼ EXPRESS YOURSELF

### Dealing with questions

If you give a talk, for example at a conference, you need to explain to the audience when they can ask questions, and deal with the questions they ask:

- *There will be time for questions at the end, if you'd like to save them up till then.*
- *If you don't mind, we'll take all of your questions at the end of the presentation.*
- *We've set aside/We're saving the last 15 minutes for questions.*
- *If you have questions, please feel free to ask them as we go along.*
- *That's an interesting point. Perhaps I can answer it like this…*
- *I'm not sure I understand your question.*
- *If I understand your question correctly, what you're asking is…*
- *That's something we probably need to look into further.*
- *Does that answer your question?*
- *I hope that answers your question.*
- *Can I come back to that point later?*

**ques·tion·able** /ˈkwestʃənəbl/ *adj.* **1** that you have doubts about because you think it is not accurate or correct SYN **debatable**: *The conclusions that they come to are highly questionable.* ◊ *it is ~ whether…* *It is questionable whether this is a good way of solving the problem.* **2** likely to be dishonest or morally wrong SYN **suspect**: *Her motives for helping are questionable.* ▶ **ques·tion·ably** /-bli/ *adv.*

**ques·tion·er** /ˈkwestʃənə(r)/ *noun* a person who asks questions, especially in a broadcast programme or a public debate

**ques·tion·ing** /ˈkwestʃənɪŋ/ *noun, adj.*
■ *noun* [U] the activity of asking sb questions: *He was taken to the police station for questioning.* ◊ *They faced some hostile questioning over the cost of the project.*
■ *adj.* showing that you need information, or that you have doubts: *a questioning look* ◊ *She raised a questioning eyebrow.* ▶ **ques·tion·ing·ly** *adv.*

**ˈquestion mark** *noun* the mark (?) used in writing after a question
IDM **a ˈquestion mark over/against sth** used to say that sth is not certain: *There's still a big question mark hanging over his future with the team.*

**ques·tion·naire** ?+ B2 /ˌkwestʃəˈneə(r)/, *NAmE* -ˈner/ *noun* **~ (on/about sth)** a written list of questions that are answered by a number of people so that information can be collected from the answers: *to complete a questionnaire* ◊ (*BrE*) *to fill in a questionnaire* ◊ (*especially NAmE*) *to fill out a questionnaire*

**ˈquestion tag** (*also* **ˈtag question**) *noun* (*grammar*) a phrase such as *isn't it?* or *don't you?* that you add to the end of a statement in order to turn it into a question or check that the statement is correct, as in *You like mushrooms, don't you?*

## queue ⓘ B1 /kjuː/ *noun, verb*

■ *noun* **1** ? B1 (*BrE*) (*NAmE* **line**) a line of people, cars, etc. waiting for sth or to do sth: *There were long queues at polling stations.* ◊ *the bus queue* ◊ *the front/head/back/end of the queue* ◊ **~ for sth** *I had to join a queue for the toilets.* ◊ **~ of sb/sth** *There was a queue of traffic waiting to turn right.* ◊ **in a ~** *How long were you in the queue?* ◊ *I took my place in the queue.* ⊃ HOMOPHONES at CUE **2** (*computing*) a list of items of data stored in a particular order IDM see JUMP *v.*

■ *verb* (*pres. part.* **queu·ing** *or* **queue·ing**) **1** ? B1 [I] (*BrE*) to wait in a line of people, vehicles, etc. in order to do sth, get sth or go somewhere: **~ (up) for sth** *Queue here for taxis.* ◊ *We had to queue up for an hour for the tickets.* ◊ *You have to queue to get in at weekends.* ⊃ HOMOPHONES at CUE **2** [T, I] **~ (sth)** (*computing*) to add tasks to other tasks so that they are ready to be done in order; to come together to be done in order: *The system queues the jobs before they are processed.*
PHRV **be ˈqueuing up (for sth/to do sth)** if people are said to be queuing up for sth or to do sth, a lot of them want to have it or do it: *Italian football clubs are queuing up to sign the young star.*

**ˈqueue-jumping** *noun* [U] (*BrE*) a situation in which a person moves to the front of a queue to get served before other people who have been waiting longer

**quib·ble** /ˈkwɪbl/ *verb, noun*
■ *verb* [I] **~ (about/over sth)** to argue or complain about a small matter or an unimportant detail: *It isn't worth quibbling over such a small amount.*
■ *noun* a small complaint or criticism, especially one that is not important: *minor quibbles*

**quiche** /kiːʃ/ *noun* [C, U] an open PIE filled with a mixture of eggs and milk with meat, vegetables, cheese, etc. ⊃ compare FLAN, TART

## quick ⓘ A1 /kwɪk/ *adj., adv., noun*

■ *adj.* (**quick·er, quick·est**) **1** ? A1 done with speed; taking or lasting a short time: *a quick look/check/search* ◊ *She gave him a quick glance.* ◊ *Let's take a quick break.* ◊ *There's no quick fix for this problem.* ◊ *Let me just ask one quick question.* ◊ *Thanks for the quick response.* ◊ *These cakes are very quick and easy to make.* ◊ *Would you like a quick drink?* ◊ *It's quicker by train.* ◊ *Are you sure this is the quickest way?* ◊ *Have you finished already? That was quick!* ◊ *His quick thinking saved her life.* ◊ *He fired three shots in quick succession.* ⊃ see also DOUBLE QUICK **2** ? A1 moving or doing sth fast: *a quick learner* ◊ **~ to do sth** *The kids were quick to learn.* ◊ *She was quick* (= too quick) *to point out the mistakes I'd made.* ◊ *Her quick hands suddenly stopped moving.* ◊ *Try to be quick! We're late already.* ◊ *Once again, his quick wits* (= ability to think quickly) *got him out of an awkward situation.* ◊ (*NAmE, informal*) *He's a quick study* (= he learns quickly). **3** ? A1 [only before noun] happening very soon or without delay: *We need to make a* quick decision. ◊ The company wants quick results. ◊ The doctor said she'd make a quick recovery. ⊃ note at FAST

**IDM** ▶ **quick and 'dirty** (informal) used to describe sth that is usually complicated, but is being done quickly and simply in this case: Read our quick-and-dirty guide to creating a website. ⊃ more at BUCK n., DRAW n., MARK n., TEMPER n., UPTAKE

■ adv. (quick·er, quick·est) **1** quickly; fast: Come as quick as you can! ◊ Let's see who can get there quickest. ◊ It's another of his schemes to **get rich quick**. **2** **quick-** (in adjectives) doing the thing mentioned quickly: quick-thinking ◊ quick-growing

**IDM** **(as) quick as a 'flash** very quickly: Quick as a flash she was at his side.

■ noun **the quick** [sing.] the soft, sensitive area under your nails: She has bitten her nails down to the quick.

**IDM** **cut sb to the 'quick** to upset sb very much by doing or saying sth unkind

---

▼ WHICH WORD?

**quick / quickly / fast**

- **Quickly** is the usual adverb from **quick**: I quickly realized that I was on the wrong train. ◊ My heart started to beat more quickly.
- **Quick** is sometimes used as an adverb in very informal language, especially as an exclamation: Come on! Quick! They'll see us! **Quicker** is used more often: My heart started to beat much quicker. ◊ The quicker I get you away from here, the better.
- **Fast** is more often used when you are talking about the speed that somebody or something moves at: How fast can a cheetah run? ◊ Can't you drive any faster? ◊ You're driving too quickly. There is no word **fastly**.

---

**quick·en** /ˈkwɪkən/ verb (formal) **1** [I, T] to become quicker or make sth quicker: She felt her heartbeat quicken as he approached. ◊ ~ sth He quickened his pace to catch up with them. **2** [I, T] ~(sth) to become more active; to make sth more active: His interest quickened as he heard more about the plan.

**quick-'fire** adj. [only before noun] (of a series of things) done or said very fast, one after the other: a series of quick-fire questions

**quickie** /ˈkwɪki/ noun (informal) **1** a thing that only takes a short time: I've got a question—it's just a quickie. ◊ a quickie divorce **2** a sexual act that takes a very short time

**quick·lime** /ˈkwɪklaɪm/ noun [U] = LIME

**quick·ly** 🔵 **A1** 🅢 /ˈkwɪkli/ adv. **1** **A1** fast: She walked quickly away. ◊ The disease spreads quickly. ◊ The last few weeks have gone quickly (= the time seems to have passed quickly). ◊ The tool makes it possible to create websites quickly and easily. **2** **A1** soon; after a short time: to act/respond quickly ◊ The authorities moved quickly to quell the violence. ◊ He replied to my letter very quickly. ◊ It quickly became clear that she was dying. ◊ I quickly realized that this was a big mistake. ◊ He scored a stunning goal, quickly followed by another. ⊃ note at QUICK

**quick·ness** /ˈkwɪknəs/ noun [U] the quality of being fast, especially at thinking, etc: She was known for the quickness of her wit. ◊ He amazes me with his quickness and eagerness to learn.

**'quick one** noun (BrE, informal) a drink, usually an alcoholic one, taken quickly

**quick·sand** /ˈkwɪksænd/ noun [U] (also **quicksands** [pl.]) **1** deep wet sand that you sink into if you walk on it **2** a situation that is dangerous or difficult to escape from

**quick·sil·ver** /ˈkwɪksɪlvə(r)/ noun, adj.
■ noun [U] (old use) = MERCURY
■ adj. [only before noun] (literary) changing or moving very quickly: his quicksilver temperament

**quick·step** /ˈkwɪkstep/ noun a dance for two people together, with a lot of fast steps; a piece of music for this dance

**'quick-'witted** adj. able to think quickly; intelligent: a quick-witted student/response **OPP** **slow-witted**

**quid** /kwɪd/ noun (pl. **quid**) (BrE, informal) one pound in money: Can you lend me five quid?

---

**IDM** **not the full 'quid** (AustralE, NZE, informal) not very intelligent **quids 'in** in a position of having made a profit, especially a good profit

**quid pro quo** /ˌkwɪd prəʊ ˈkwəʊ/ noun [sing.] (from Latin) a thing given in return for sth else

**qui·es·cent** /kwiˈesnt/ adj. **1** (formal) quiet; not active **2** (medical) (of a disease, etc.) not developing, especially when this is probably only a temporary state **SYN** **dormant** ▶ **qui·es·cence** /-sns/ noun [U]

**quiet** 🔵 **A1** /ˈkwaɪət/ adj., noun, verb

■ adj. (qui·et·er, qui·et·est) **1** **A1** making very little noise: her quiet voice ◊ a quieter, more efficient engine ◊ Could you **keep the kids quiet** while I'm on the phone? ◊ He **went very quiet** (= did not say much) so I knew he was upset. ◊ 'Be quiet,' said the teacher. ◊ She crept downstairs (as) quiet as a mouse. **2** **A1** without many people or much noise or activity: a quiet street/town ◊ It is a quiet place with just a handful of shops, bars and restaurants. ◊ They lead a quiet life. ◊ After a month of political tensions, things are relatively quiet. ◊ Business is usually quieter at this time of year. ◊ They had a quiet wedding. **3** **A1** peaceful; without being interrupted: to have a quiet drink ◊ They were enjoying a quiet moment by the lake. ◊ I was looking forward to a quiet evening at home. **4** **A1** (of a person) tending not to talk very much: She was quiet and shy. **5** (of a feeling or an attitude) definite but not expressed in an obvious way: He had an air of quiet authority. ▶ **quiet·ness** noun [U]: the quietness of the countryside ◊ His quietness worried her.

**IDM** **keep quiet about sth | keep sth quiet** to say nothing about sth; to keep sth secret: I've decided to resign but I'd rather you kept quiet about it.

■ noun [U] the state of being calm and without much noise: the quiet of his own room ◊ the quiet of the early morning ◊ I go to the library for a little peace and quiet.

**IDM** **on the 'quiet** without telling anyone **SYN** **secretly**

■ verb [I, T] (especially NAmE) to become calmer or less noisy; to make sb/sth calmer or less noisy **SYN** **calm down**. ~(down) The demonstrators quieted down when the police arrived. ◊ ~ sb/sth (down) He's very good at quieting the kids.

**quiet·en** /ˈkwaɪətn/ verb [I, T] ~(sb/sth) (down) (BrE) to become calmer or less noisy; to make sb/sth calmer or less noisy: The chatter of voices gradually quietened. ◊ Things seem to have quietened down a bit this afternoon (= we are not so busy, etc.).

**quiet·ly** 🔵 **A2** /ˈkwaɪətli/ adv. **1** **A2** in a way that makes very little noise: to ask/speak/talk quietly ◊ to move/stand quietly ◊ a quietly spoken woman ◊ 'I'm sorry,' she said quietly. **2** **A2** in a peaceful way; without being interrupted: I spent a few hours quietly relaxing. ◊ He noticed the woman sitting quietly at the bar. **3** without many people or much noise or activity: Sometimes a business begins quietly, as a hobby maybe, in a spare bedroom. **4** in a definite, but not obvious, way: He is quietly confident that they can succeed (= he is confident, but he is not talking about it too much).

**quiet·ude** /ˈkwaɪətjuːd/; NAmE -tuːd/ noun [U] (literary) the state of being still and quiet **SYN** **calm**

**quiff** /kwɪf/ noun (especially BrE) a piece of hair at the front of the head that is brushed upwards and backwards

**quill** /kwɪl/ noun **1** (also **quill feather**) a large feather from the wing or tail of a bird **2** (also **quill 'pen**) a pen made from a quill feather **3** one of the long sharp stiff SPINES on a PORCUPINE

**quilt** /kwɪlt/ noun a warm cover for a bed, made of two layers with soft material between them, often held in place and decorated with lines of STITCHING: a patchwork quilt ⊃ compare COMFORTER (2), DUVET

**quilt·ed** /ˈkwɪltɪd/ adj. (of clothes, etc.) made of two layers of cloth with soft material between them, held in place by lines of STITCHES: a quilted jacket

**quilt·ing** /ˈkwɪltɪŋ/ noun [U] the work of making a QUILT; cloth that is used for this

# quin

**quin** /kwɪn/ noun (BrE, informal) = QUINTUPLET

**quince** /kwɪns/ noun a hard bitter yellow fruit used for making jam, etc. It grows on a tree, also called a quince: *quince jelly* ◊ *a flowering quince*

**quin·ine** /ˈkwɪniːn; NAmE ˈkwaɪnaɪn/ noun [U] a drug made from the BARK of a South American tree, used in the past to treat MALARIA

**qui·noa** /ˈkiːnwɑː, kiˈnəʊə/ noun [U] a South American plant, grown for its seeds, used as food and to make alcoholic drinks; the seeds of the quinoa plant

**quint** /kwɪnt/ noun (NAmE, informal) = QUINTUPLET

**quint·es·sence** /kwɪnˈtesns/ noun [sing.] **1 the ~ of sth** (formal) the perfect example of sth: *It was the quintessence of an English manor house.* **2 the ~ of sth** (formal) the most important features of sth SYN **essence**: *a painting that captures the quintessence of Viennese elegance* ▶ **quint·es·sen·tial** /ˌkwɪntɪˈsenʃl/ adj.: *He was the quintessential tough guy.* **quint·es·sen·tial·ly** /-ʃəli/ adv.

**quin·tet** /kwɪnˈtet/ noun **1** [C + sing./pl. v.] a group of five musicians or singers who play or sing together: *the Miles Davis Quintet* **2** [C] a piece of music for five musicians or singers: *a string quintet*

**quin·tile** /ˈkwɪntaɪl/ noun (statistics) one of five equal groups into which a set of things can be divided according to the DISTRIBUTION of a particular VARIABLE: *men in the first quintile of weight* (= the heaviest 20% of men) ⊃ compare QUARTILE

**quin·tu·ple** /ˈkwɪntjupl; NAmE kwɪnˈtuːpl/ adj., det., verb
■ adj. [only before noun], det. **1** consisting of five parts, people, or groups **2** being five times as much or as many
■ verb [I, T] ~ (sth) to become five times bigger; to make sth five times bigger: *Sales have quintupled over the past few years.*

**quin·tu·plet** /ˈkwɪntʊplət; NAmE kwɪnˈtʌplət/ (also BrE, informal **quin**) (also NAmE, informal **quint**) noun one of five children born at the same time to the same mother

**quip** /kwɪp/ noun, verb
■ noun a quick and clever remark: *to make a quip*
■ verb (-pp-) + speech to make a quick and clever remark

**quirk** /kwɜːk; NAmE kwɜːrk/ noun, verb
■ noun **1** an aspect of sb's personality or behaviour that is a little strange SYN **peculiarity 2** a strange thing that happens, especially by accident: *By a strange quirk of fate they had booked into the same hotel.* ▶ **quirky** adj.: *a quirky sense of humour*
■ verb [T, I] ~ (sth) (especially NAmE) to TWIST your mouth or EYEBROWS suddenly; (of your mouth or eyebrows) to move in this way: *David quirked an eyebrow and smirked slightly.* ◊ *Her lips quirked suddenly.*

**quis·ling** /ˈkwɪzlɪŋ/ noun (disapproving) a person who helps an enemy that has taken control of his or her country SYN **collaborator**

**quit** 🔑 B1 /kwɪt/ verb (**quit·ting**, **quit**, **quit**) (BrE also **quit·ting**, **quit·ted**, **quit·ted**) **1** 🔑 B1 [I, T] (informal) to leave your job, school, etc: *If I don't get more money I'll quit.* ◊ **~ as sth** *He has decided to quit as manager of the team.* ◊ **~ sth** *to quit your job* ◊ *He quit the show last year because of bad health.* ◊ (NAmE) *She quit school at 16.* **2** 🔑 B1 [T, I] (especially NAmE, informal) to stop doing sth: **doing sth** *I've quit smoking.* ◊ **~ sth** *Just quit it!* ◊ *We only just started. We're not going to quit now.* **3** [T, I] ~ (sth) to leave the place where you live: *We decided it was time to quit the city.* ◊ *The landlord gave them all notice to quit.* **4** [I, T] ~ (sth) to close a computer program or application: *I quit the app and restarted it.*

**quite** 🔑 A1 /kwaɪt/ adv. **1** 🔑 A1 (BrE) (not used with a negative) to some degree SYN **fairly**, **pretty**: *quite good/interesting/common/difficult* ◊ *I quite like opera.* ◊ *He plays quite well.* ◊ **~ a** ... *He's quite a good player.* HELP When **quite** is used with an adjective before a noun, it comes before *a* or *an*. You can say: *It's quite a small house* or: *Their house is quite small* but not: *It's a quite small house.* **2** 🔑 B1 to the greatest possible degree SYN **completely**, **absolutely** SYN **entirely**: *quite amazing/delicious/empty/*

1264

*perfect* ◊ *The two species are in fact* **quite** *different from one another.* ◊ *He made it* **quite** *clear that he never wanted to see her again.* ◊ *I've had* **quite enough** *of your tantrums.* ◊ *Are you* **quite sure**? ◊ *I* **quite agree**. ◊ **Quite apart from** *all the work, he had financial problems.* ◊ **not~** *Unfortunately it is* **not quite** *as simple as that.* ◊ *I* **don't quite know** *what to do next.* ◊ (BrE) *The theatre was* **not quite** (= was almost) *full.* ◊ *It's like being in the Alps, but not quite.* ◊ *I've* **never quite** *understood why she's so successful.* ◊ *'I almost think she prefers animals to people.' 'Quite right too,'* said Bill.
**3** 🔑 B1 to a great degree; very; really: *I'm quite happy to wait for you.* ◊ *You'll be quite comfortable here.* ◊ *I can see it quite clearly.* ◊ (NAmE) *'You've no intention of coming back?' 'I'm quite sorry, but no, I have not.'* **4** (also formal **quite so**) (BrE) used to agree with sb or show that you understand them: *'He's bound to feel shaken after his accident.' 'Quite.'*
IDM **'quite a/the sth** (also informal **'quite some sth**) used to show that a person or thing is particularly impressive or unusual in some way: *This is quite a different problem.* ◊ *She's quite a beauty.* ◊ *We found it quite a change when we moved to London.* ◊ *He's quite the little gentleman, isn't he?* ◊ *It must be quite some car.* **quite a 'lot (of sth)** 🔑 B2 (also BrE, informal **quite a 'bit**) a large number or amount of sth: *They drank quite a lot of wine.* **'quite some sth 1** a large amount of sth: *She hasn't been seen for quite some time.* **2** (informal) = QUITE A/THE STH ⊃ more at CONTRARY[1] n., FEW pron.

▼ **WHICH WORD?**

**quite / fairly / rather / pretty**
Look at these examples:
● *The exam was fairly difficult.*
● *The exam was quite difficult.*
● *The exam was rather difficult.*
● **Quite** is a little stronger than **fairly**, and **rather** is a little stronger than **quite**. **Rather** is not very common in NAmE; **pretty** has the same meaning and this is used in informal BrE too: *The exam was pretty difficult.*
● In BrE **quite** has two meanings: *I feel quite tired today* (= fairly tired). With adjectives that describe an extreme state ('non-gradable' adjectives) it means 'completely' or 'absolutely': *I feel quite exhausted.* With some adjectives, both meanings are possible. The speaker's stress and intonation will show you which is meant: *Your essay is 'quite good* (= fairly good—it could be better); *Your essay is quite 'good* (= very good, especially when this is unexpected).
● In NAmE **quite** usually means something like 'very', not 'fairly' or 'rather'. **Pretty** is used instead for this sense.

**quits** /kwɪts/ adj.
IDM **be quits (with sb)** (informal) when two people are quits, they do not owe each other anything, especially money: *I'll give you £5 and then we're quits.* ⊃ more at CALL v., DOUBLE n.

**quit·ter** /ˈkwɪtə(r)/ noun (often disapproving) a person who gives up easily and does not finish a task they have started

**quiver** /ˈkwɪvə(r)/ verb, noun
■ verb [I] to shake slightly; to make a slight movement SYN **tremble**: *Her lip quivered and then she started to cry.*
■ noun **1** an emotion that has an effect on your body; a slight movement in part of your body: *He felt a quiver of excitement run through him.* ◊ *Jane couldn't help the quiver in her voice.* **2** a case for carrying ARROWS

**quix·ot·ic** /kwɪkˈsɒtɪk; NAmE -ˈsɑːt-/ adj. (formal) having or involving ideas or plans that show imagination but are usually not practical ORIGIN From the character Don Quixote in the novel by Miguel de Cervantes, whose adventures are a result of him trying to achieve or obtain things that are impossible.

**quiz** /kwɪz/ noun, verb
■ noun (pl. **quiz·zes**) **1** a competition or game in which people try to answer questions to test their knowledge: *a general knowledge quiz* ◊ *a television quiz show* ⊃ WORD-FINDER NOTE at PROGRAMME **2** (especially NAmE) an informal test given to students: *a reading comprehension quiz* ⊃ see also POP QUIZ ⊃ note at EXAM

■ *verb* [often passive] (-zz-) **1** to ask sb a lot of questions about sth in order to get information from them SYN **question**: ~ **sb (about sb/sth)** *Four men are being quizzed by police about the murder.* ◊ *Police have been granted an extra 24 hours to quiz the men.* ◊ ~ **sb on/over sth** *We were quizzed on our views about education.* **2** ~ **sb (on sth)** (*NAmE*) to give students an informal test: *You will be quizzed on chapter 6 tomorrow.*

**quiz·master** /ˈkwɪzmɑːstə(r); *NAmE* -mæs-/ *noun* (*BrE*) a person who asks the questions in a QUIZ, especially on television or the radio

**quiz·zical** /ˈkwɪzɪkl/ *adj.* (of an expression) showing that you are slightly surprised: *a quizzical expression* ▶ **quiz·zi·cal·ly** /-kli/ *adv.*: *She looked at him quizzically.*

**quoit** /kɔɪt, kwɔɪt/ *noun* **1** [C] a ring that is thrown onto a small post in the game of quoits **2 quoits** [U] a game in which rings are thrown onto a small post

**quoll** /kwɒl; *NAmE* kwɑːl/ *noun* a small animal with short legs, a long tail and brown fur with white spots, that lives in the forests of Australia and parts of Papua New Guinea

**Quorn™** /kwɔːn; *NAmE* kwɔːrn/ *noun* [U] a substance made from a type of FUNGUS, used in cooking instead of meat

**quorum** /ˈkwɔːrəm/ *noun* [sing.] the smallest number of people who must be at a meeting before it can begin or decisions can be made

**quota** ?+ C1 /ˈkwəʊtə; *NAmE* ˈkwoʊtə/ *noun* **1** ?+ C1 [C] ~ **(on sth)** a limited number or amount of people or things that is officially allowed: *to introduce a strict import quota on grain* ◊ *a quota system for accepting refugees* **2** [C] an amount of sth that sb expects or needs to have or achieve: *I'm going home now—I've done my quota of work for the day.* **3** [sing.] (*politics*) (in a system of PROPORTIONAL REPRESENTATION) a fixed number of votes that a candidate needs in order to be elected: *He was 76 votes short of the quota.*

**quot·able** /ˈkwəʊtəbl/ *adj.* (of a statement) interesting or funny and worth repeating

**quota·tion** ⓞ B1 /kwəʊˈteɪʃn; *NAmE* kwoʊ-/ *noun* **1** ?+ B1 (*rather formal*) (*also rather informal* **quote**) [C] a group of words or a short piece of writing taken from a book, play, speech, etc. and repeated because it is interesting or useful: *a dictionary of quotations* ◊ ~ **from sth** *The book began with a quotation from Goethe.* ⊃ see also MISQUOTATION **2** [U] the act of repeating sth interesting or useful that another person has written or said: *The writer illustrates his point by quotation from a number of sources.* **3** [C] (*rather formal*) (*also rather informal* **quote**) a statement of how much money a particular piece of work will cost SYN **estimate**: *You need to get a written quotation before they start work.* **4** [C] (*finance*) a statement of the current value of goods or shares: *the latest quotations from the Stock Exchange.*

**quo'tation marks** (*also informal* **quotes**) (*BrE also* **in·verted commas**) *noun* [pl.] a pair of marks (' ') or (" ") placed around a word, sentence, etc. to show that it is what sb said or wrote, that it is a title or that you are using it in an unusual way

**quote** ⓞ B1 Ⓢ /kwəʊt/ *verb, noun*
■ *verb*
• REPEAT EXACT WORDS **1** ?+ B1 [T, I] to repeat the exact words that another person has said or written: ~ **sth** *to quote Shakespeare* ◊ ~ **sth from sth** *He quoted a passage from the minister's speech.* ◊ ~ **from sth** *They quoted from the Bible.* ◊ ~ **sb/sth in sth** *Quote this reference number in all correspondence.* ◊ *He was widely quoted in the American media.* ◊ ~ **sb** *to quote an expert/an official/a source* ◊ *The minister claimed he had been selectively quoted.* ◊ ~ **sb as doing sth** *The President was quoted in the press as saying that he disagreed with the decision.* ◊ *She said, and I quote, 'Life is meaningless without love.'* ◊ ~ **sb on sth** *'It will all be gone tomorrow.' 'Can I quote you on that?'* ◊ *Don't quote me on this* (= this is not an official statement), *but I think he is going to resign.* ◊ ~ + **speech** *'The man who is tired of London is tired of life,' he quoted.* ⊃ see also MISQUOTE
• GIVE EXAMPLE **2** [T] to mention an example of sth to support what you are saying: ~ **(sb) sth** *Can you quote me an instance of when this happened?* ◊ ~ **sth as sth** *an example that is often quoted as evidence of mismanagement* ⊃ SYNONYMS at MENTION
• GIVE PRICE **3** [T, I] ~ **(sb) (sth) (for sth/for doing sth)** to tell a customer how much money you will charge them for a job, service or product: *They quoted us £300 for installing a shower unit.* **4** [T] ~ **sth (at sth)** (*finance*) to give a market price for shares, gold or foreign money: *Yesterday the pound was quoted at $1.8285, unchanged from Monday.* **5** [T] ~ **sth** (*finance*) to give the prices for a business company's shares on a STOCK EXCHANGE: *Several football clubs are now quoted on the Stock Exchange.*
IDM **'quote ( ... 'unquote)** (*informal*) used to show the beginning (and end) of a word, phrase, etc. that has been said or written by sb else: *It was quote, 'the hardest decision of my life', unquote, and one that he lived to regret.*
■ *noun* (*rather informal*)
• EXACT WORDS **1** ?+ B1 (*also rather formal* **quotation**) a group of words or a short piece of writing taken from a book, play, speech, etc. and repeated because it is interesting or useful: *The essay was full of quotes.* ◊ ~ **from sth** *a quote from a New York Times article*
• PRICE **2** = QUOTATION (3): *Their quote for the job was way too high.*
• PUNCTUATION **3 quotes** [pl.] = QUOTATION MARKS: **in** ~ *If you take text from other sources, place it in quotes.*

**quoth** /kwəʊθ/ *verb* + **speech** (*old use or humorous*) used meaning 'said' before 'I', 'he' or 'she'

**quo·tid·ian** /kwəʊˈtɪdiən/ *adj.* (*formal*) ordinary; typical of what happens every day SYN **day-to-day**

**quo·tient** /ˈkwəʊʃnt/ *noun* (*mathematics*) a number which is the result when one number is divided by another ⊃ see also INTELLIGENCE QUOTIENT

**Qur'an** = KORAN

**q.v.** /ˌkjuː ˈviː/ *abbr.* used in books to tell a reader that there is more information in another part of the book (from Latin 'quod vide')

**QWERTY** /ˈkwɜːti; *NAmE* ˈkwɜːrti/ *adj.* [usually before noun] (of a keyboard on a computer or TYPEWRITER) with the keys arranged with Q, W, E, R, T and Y on the left of the top row of letters (which is the usual way for an English-language keyboard)

# Rr

**R** /ɑː(r)/ noun, abbr.

■ **noun** (also **r**) [C, U] (pl. **Rs**, **R's**, **r's** /ɑːz/; NAmE ɑːrz/) the 18th letter of the English alphabet: *'Rose' begins with (an) R/ 'R'*. ⇨ see also A & R, R & R **IDM** see THREE

■ **abbr. 1** (BrE) Queen; King (from Latin 'Regina'; 'Rex'): *Elizabeth R*. **2 R.** (especially on maps) River: *R. Trent* **3** (also **R.** especially in NAmE) (in politics in the US) REPUBLICAN **4** (BrE) Royal: *the RAC* (= Royal Automobile Club) **5** (in the US) RESTRICTED (= a label for a movie that is not suitable for people under the age of 17 to see without an adult present) ⇨ compare G (1), NC-17, PG-13 ⇨ see also R & B, R & D

**r** abbr. (in writing) right: *l to r: Jane, Elizabeth and Mary*

**rabbi** /ˈræbaɪ/ noun a Jewish religious leader or a teacher of Jewish law: *the Chief Rabbi* (= the leader of Jewish communities in a particular country) ◊ *Rabbi Sacks*

**rab·bin·ical** /rəˈbɪnɪkl/ (also **rab·bin·ic**) adj. connected with rabbis or Jewish law or teaching

**rab·bit** /ˈræbɪt/ noun, verb
■ **noun 1** [C] a small animal with soft fur, long ears and a short tail. Rabbits live in holes in the ground or are kept as pets or for food: *a rabbit hutch* ⇨ compare HARE **2** [U] meat from a rabbit **IDM** see BREED v., PULL v.
■ **verb** [I] **go rabbiting** to hunt or shoot rabbits
**PHR V** **ˈrabbit on (about sb/sth)** (BrE, informal, disapproving) to talk continuously about things that are not important or interesting **SYN** chatter

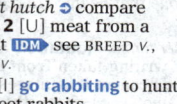
rabbit

**ˈrabbit warren** (also **war·ren**) noun **1** a system of holes and underground tunnels where wild rabbits live **2** (disapproving) a building or part of a city with many narrow passages or streets: *The council offices were a real rabbit warren*.

hare

**rab·ble** /ˈræbl/ noun (sing. + sing./pl. v.) (disapproving) **1** a large group of noisy people who are or may become violent **SYN** mob: *a drunken rabble* **2** the **rabble** ordinary people or people who are considered to have a low social position **SYN** the masses: *a speech that appealed to the rabble*

**ˈrabble-rouser** noun (usually disapproving) a person who makes speeches to crowds of people intending to make them angry or excited, especially for political aims
▸ **ˈrabble-rousing** adj. **ˈrabble-rousing** noun [U]

**rabid** /ˈræbɪd/; BrE also /ˈreɪb-/ adj. **1** [usually before noun] (disapproving) (of a type of person) having very strong feelings about sth and acting in an unacceptable way: *rabid right-wing fanatics* ◊ *the rabid tabloid press* **2** [usually before noun] (of feelings or opinions) violent or extreme: *rabid speculation* **3** suffering from rabies: *a rabid dog* ▸ **rabid·ly** adv.

**ra·bies** /ˈreɪbiːz/ noun [U] a disease of dogs and other animals that causes MADNESS and death. Animals with the disease can pass it to humans by biting them. ⇨ compare HYDROPHOBIA

**rac·coon** (also **ra·coon**) /rəˈkuːn/; NAmE ræˈk-/ noun **1** [C] a small North American animal with grey-brown fur, black marks on its face and a thick tail **2** [U] the fur of the raccoon

**race** 🔊 **A2** **W** /reɪs/ noun, verb
■ **noun**
• COMPETITION **1** 🔊 **A2** [C] a competition between people, animals, vehicles, etc. to see which one is the faster or fastest: *a boat/horse race* ◊ *a five-kilometre road race* ◊ *Who won the race?* ◊ *Shall we have a race to the end of the beach?* ◊ **between A and B** *a race between the two best runners of the club* ◊ **against sb** *He's already in training for the big race against Bailey.* ◊ **in a~** *Their horse came third in the race last year.* ⇨ see also DRAG RACE, EGG-AND-SPOON RACE, HORSE RACE, OBSTACLE RACE, PANCAKE RACE, SACK RACE **2** 🔊 **B2** [sing.] a situation in which a number of people, groups, organizations, etc. are competing, especially for political power or to achieve sth first: *~ for sth Who will win the race for the White House?* ◊ *~ **to do sth** The race is on (= has begun) to find a cure for the disease.* ◊ *in a ~ He has taken a lead in the presidential race.* ⇨ see also ARMS RACE, RAT RACE, SPACE RACE
• FOR HORSES **3** the **races** [pl.] a series of horse races that happen at one place on a particular day: *to go to the races*
• PEOPLE **4** 🔊 **B1** [C, U] one of the main groups that humans can be divided into according to their physical differences, for example the colour of their skin; the fact of belonging to one of these groups: *This custom is found in people of all races throughout the world.* ◊ *people of mixed race* ◊ *legislation against discrimination on the grounds of race or gender* ⇨ WORDFINDER NOTE at EQUAL **5** [C] a group of people who share the same language, history, culture, etc: *the Nordic races* ◊ *He admired Canadians as a hardy and determined race.* ⇨ see also HUMAN RACE
• ANIMALS/PLANTS **6** [C] a BREED or type of animal or plant: *a race of cattle*
**IDM** **a ˌrace against ˈtime/the ˈclock** a situation in which you have to do sth or finish sth very fast before it is too late **ˌrace to the ˈbottom** (economics) a situation in which companies and countries compete with each other to produce goods as cheaply as possible by paying low wages and giving workers poor conditions and few rights ⇨ more at HORSE n.

■ **verb**
• COMPETE **1** 🔊 **A2** [I, T] to compete against sb/sth to see who can go faster or the fastest, do sth first, etc.; to take part in a race or races: *They raced to a thrilling victory in the relay.* ◊ *She'll be racing for the senior team next year.* ◊ *~ against sb/sth Who will he be racing against in the next round?* ◊ *~ sb/sth We raced each other back to the car.* ◊ *~ to do sth Television companies are racing to be the first to screen his life story.* **2** [T] *~ sth* to make an animal or a vehicle compete in a race: *to race dogs/horses/pigeons* ◊ *to race motorbikes*
• MOVE FAST **3** 🔊 **B1** [I, T] to move very fast; to move sb/sth very fast: *+ adv./prep. He raced up the stairs.* ◊ *The days seemed to race past.* ◊ *~ sb/sth + adv./prep. The injured man was raced to the hospital.* ◊ *She raced her car through the narrow streets of the town.*
• OF HEART/MIND/THOUGHTS **4** [I] to function very quickly because you are afraid, excited, etc: *My mind raced as I tried to work out what was happening.* ◊ *My heart was racing with fear.*
• OF ENGINE **5** [I] to run too fast: *The truck came to rest against a tree, its engine racing.*

**ˈrace car** (NAmE) (also **ˈracing car** BrE, NAmE) noun a car that has been specially designed for motor racing

**ˈrace card** noun
**IDM** **play the ˈrace card** (disapproving) if you accuse sb of **playing the race card**, you mean that you think they are using complaints about RACISM to gain sympathy or an advantage

**race·course** /ˈreɪskɔːs/; NAmE -kɔːrs/ (BrE) (NAmE **race·track**) noun a track where horses race and the buildings, etc. that are connected with it

**race-goer** /ˈreɪsɡəʊə(r)/; NAmE -ɡoʊər/ noun (BrE) a person at a horse race; person who often goes to horse races

**race·horse** /ˈreɪshɔːs/; NAmE -hɔːrs/ noun a horse that is BRED and trained to run in races

**ˈrace meeting** noun (BrE) a series of races, especially for horses, held at one course over one day or several days

**racer** /ˈreɪsə(r)/ noun **1** a person or an animal that competes in races: *Italy's champion downhill racer* ⇨ see also

**BOY RACER** **2** a car, boat, etc. designed for racing: *an ocean racer*

**race re'lations** *noun* [pl.] the relationships between people of different races who live in the same community

**'race riot** *noun* violent behaviour between people of different races living in the same community

**race-track** /'reɪstræk/ *noun* **1** a track for races between runners, cars, bicycles, etc: *You can't cross the road—it's like a racetrack.* **2** (*NAmE*) (*BrE* **race-course**) a track where horses race and the buildings, etc. that are connected with it

**race-way** /'reɪsweɪ/ *noun* (*NAmE*) a track for racing cars or horses

**ra-cial** /'reɪʃl/ *adj.* **1** [only before noun] happening or existing between people of different races: *racial hatred/prejudice/tension/violence* ◊ *racial equality* ◊ *They have pledged to end racial discrimination in areas such as employment.* **2** [usually before noun] connected with a person's race: *racial minorities* ◊ *a person's racial origin* ▶ **ra-cial-ly** /-ʃəli/ *adv.*: *The attacks were not racially motivated.* ◊ *racially mixed schools*

**ra-cial-ism** /'reɪʃəlɪzəm/ *noun* [U] (*BrE, old-fashioned, disapproving*) = RACISM

**ra-cial-ist** /'reɪʃəlɪst/ *noun, adj.* (*BrE, old-fashioned, disapproving*) = RACIST

**racial 'profiling** *noun* [U] the fact of police officers, etc. suspecting that sb has committed a crime based on the colour of their skin or their race rather than on any evidence

**ra-cing** /'reɪsɪŋ/ *noun* [U] **1** (*also* **'horse racing**) the sport of racing horses: *He used to watch the racing on TV in the afternoons.* ◊ (*especially NAmE, AustralE, NZE*) *the racing industry* ⇒ *see also* FLAT RACING **2** (usually in compounds) any sport that involves competing in races: *yacht/motorcycle racing* ◊ *road/street racing* ◊ *a racing driver* ⇒ *see also* AUTO RACING, DRAG RACING, MOTOR RACING, STOCK-CAR RACING

**'racing car** (*NAmE also* **'race car**) *noun* a car that has been specially designed for motor racing

**ra-cism** /'reɪsɪzəm/ *noun* **1** the unfair treatment of people who belong to a different race; violent behaviour towards them: *a victim of racism* ◊ *ugly outbreaks of racism* **2** the belief that some races of people are better than others: *irrational racism*

**ra-cist** /'reɪsɪst/ *adj., noun*
■ *adj.* having the belief that some races of people are better than others; showing this through violent and unfair treatment of people of other races: *racist attitudes/remarks* ◊ *racist thugs/attacks*
■ *noun* a person who believes that some races of people are better than others and may show this in violent or unfair treatment of people of other races: *He's a racist.*

**rack** /ræk/ *noun, verb*
■ *noun* **1** (often in compounds) a piece of equipment, usually made of metal or wooden bars, that is used for holding things or for hanging things on: *a vegetable/wine/plate/toast rack* ◊ *I looked through a rack of clothes at the back of the shop.* ⇒ *see also* LUGGAGE RACK, ROOF RACK **2** (usually **the rack**) an instrument of TORTURE, used in the past for punishing and hurting people. Their arms and legs were tied to the wooden frame and then pulled in opposite directions, stretching the body. **3** ~ **of lamb/pork** a particular piece of meat that includes the front RIBS and is cooked in the oven **4** a part of a machine that consists of a bar with parts that a wheel or GEAR can fit into
**IDM** **go to 'rack and 'ruin** to get into a bad condition: *They let the house go to rack and ruin.* **off the 'rack** (*NAmE*) (*BrE* **off the 'peg**) (of clothes) made to a standard average size and not made specially to fit you **on the 'rack** feeling extreme pressure, worry or pain
■ *verb* (*also less frequent* **wrack**) [often passive] to make sb suffer great physical or mental pain: **be racked by/with sth** *to be racked with/by guilt* ◊ *Her face was racked with pain.* ◊ ~ **sb/sth** *Violent sobs racked her whole body.* ◊ (*BrE*) *a racking cough*

racks

plate rack

wine rack

vegetable rack

toast rack

magazine rack

luggage rack

roof rack

**IDM** **rack your 'brain(s)** to think very hard or for a long time about sth: *She racked her brains, trying to remember exactly what she had said.*
**PHRV** **rack 'up sth** to collect sth, such as profits or losses in a business, or points in a competition: *The company racked up $200 million in losses in two years.* ◊ *In ten years of boxing he racked up a record 176 wins.*

**racket** /'rækɪt/ *noun* **1** [sing.] (*informal*) a loud unpleasant noise **SYN** **din**: *Stop making that terrible racket!* **2** [C] (*informal*) a dishonest or illegal way of getting money: *a protection/extortion/drugs, etc. racket* **3** (*also* **rac-quet**) [C] a piece of sports equipment used for hitting the ball, etc. in the games of tennis, SQUASH or BADMINTON. It has an OVAL frame, with strings stretched across and down it. ⇒ *compare* BAT **4 rackets, racquets** [U] a game for two or four people, similar to SQUASH, played with rackets and a small hard ball in a court with four walls

**rack-et-eer** /ˌrækə'tɪə(r); *NAmE* -'tɪr/ *noun* (*disapproving*) a person who makes money through dishonest or illegal activities ▶ **rack-et-eer-ing** *noun* [U]

**ra-con-teur** /ˌrækɒn'tɜː(r); *NAmE* -kɑːn-/ *noun* (*from French*) a person who is good at telling stories in an interesting and humorous way

**ra-coon** = RACCOON

**rac-quet** = RACKET

**rac-quet-ball** /'rækɪtbɔːl/ *noun* [U] a game played especially in the US by two or four players on a COURT with four walls, using RACKETS and a small hollow rubber ball

**racy** /'reɪsi/ *adj.* (**raci-er, raci-est**) having a style that is exciting and fun, sometimes in a way that is connected with sex: *a racy novel*

**rad** /ræd/ *adj., noun*
■ *adj.* (*especially NAmE, old-fashioned, slang*) very good
■ *noun* (*physics*) a unit for measuring the effect of RADIATION

**radar** /'reɪdɑː(r)/ *noun* [U] a system that uses radio waves to find the position and movement of objects, for example planes and ships, when they cannot be seen: *They located the ship by radar.* ◊ *a radar screen* ⇒ *compare* SONAR
**IDM** **below/under the 'radar** used to say that people are not aware of sth: *Experts say a lot of corporate crime stays under the radar.* **on/off the 'radar (screen)** used to say that people's attention is on or not on sth: *The issue of terrorism is back on the radar screen.*

**'radar trap** *noun* = SPEED TRAP

**ra-dial** /'reɪdiəl/ *adj., noun*
■ *adj.* having a pattern of lines, etc. that go out from a central point towards the edge of a circle: *the radial pattern of public transport facilities* ▶ **ra-dial-ly** /-əli/ *adv.*

# radian

**radian** *noun* (BrE also **radial ˈtyre**) (NAmE also **radial ˈtire**) a car tyre with strong CORDS inside the material of the tyre that are set at an angle towards the centre of the wheel and make the tyre stronger and safer

**ra·dian** /ˈreɪdiən/ *noun* (*geometry*) a unit used to measure an angle, equal to the angle at the centre of a circle whose ARC is the same length as the circle's RADIUS

**ra·di·ance** /ˈreɪdiəns/ *noun* [U] **1** a special bright quality that shows in sb's face, for example because they are very happy or healthy **2** warm light shining from sth

**ra·di·ant** /ˈreɪdiənt/ *adj.* **1** showing great happiness, love or health: *a radiant smile* ◊ *The bride looked radiant.* ◊ *~with sth She was radiant with health.* **2** giving a warm bright light: *The sun was radiant in a clear blue sky.* **3** [only before noun] (*specialist*) sent out in RAYS from a central point: *the radiant heat/energy of the sun* ▸ **ra·di·ant·ly** *adv.*: *radiantly happy* ◊ *He smiled radiantly.*

**ra·di·ate** /ˈreɪdieɪt/ *verb* **1** [T, I] if a person **radiates** a particular quality or emotion, or if it **radiates** from them, people can see it very clearly: *~sth He radiated self-confidence and optimism.* ◊ *~from sb the energy that seemed to radiate from her* **2** [T, I] if sth **radiates** heat, light or energy or heat, etc. **radiates** from it, the heat is sent out in all directions **SYN** **give off sth**: *The hot stars radiate energy.* ◊ *~(from sth) Heat radiates from the stove.* **3** [I] *+ adv./prep.* (of lines, etc.) to spread out in all directions from a central point: *Five roads radiate from the square.* ◊ *The pain started in my stomach and radiated all over my body.*

**ra·di·ation** /ˌreɪdiˈeɪʃn/ *noun* **1** [U, C] powerful and very dangerous RAYS that are sent out from RADIOACTIVE substances: *high levels/doses of radiation that damage cells* ◊ *the link between exposure to radiation and childhood cancer* ◊ *a radiation leak from a nuclear power station* ◊ *radiation sickness* ◊ *the radiations emitted by radium* ⇒ see also GAMMA RADIATION **2** [U] heat, energy, etc. that is sent out in the form of RAYS: *ultraviolet radiation* ◊ *electromagnetic radiation from power lines* **3** (*also* **radiˈation therapy**) [U] the treatment of cancer and other diseases using radiation ⇒ compare CHEMOTHERAPY, RADIOTHERAPY

**ra·di·ator** /ˈreɪdieɪtə(r)/ *noun* **1** a hollow metal device for heating rooms. Radiators are usually connected by pipes through which hot water is sent: *a central heating system with a radiator in each room* **2** a device for cooling the engine of a vehicle or an aircraft

**rad·ical** /ˈrædɪkl/ *adj., noun*

- *adj.* [usually before noun] **1** relating to the most basic and important parts of sth; complete and detailed **SYN** **far-reaching**: *the need for radical changes in education* ◊ *demands for radical reform of the law* ◊ *radical differences between the sexes* **2** new, different and likely to have a great effect: *radical ideas* ◊ *a radical solution to the problem* ◊ *radical proposals* **3** in favour of extreme and complete political or social change: *the radical wing of the party* ◊ *radical politicians/students/writers* ⇒ WORDFINDER NOTE at CAPITALISM **4** (*NAmE, old-fashioned, slang*) very good▸ **rad·ical·ly** /-kli/ *adv.*: *The new methods are radically different from the old.* ◊ *Attitudes have changed radically.*
- *noun* **1** a person with radical opinions: *political radicals* **2** (*chemistry*) a group of ATOMS that behave as a single unit in a number of COMPOUNDS ⇒ see also FREE RADICAL

**rad·ical·ism** /ˈrædɪkəlɪzəm/ *noun* [U] belief in RADICAL ideas and principles, especially on political and social issues

**rad·ical·ize** (*BrE also* **-ise**) /ˈrædɪkəlaɪz/ *verb* **~sb/sth** to make sb more extreme or RADICAL in their opinions on political or social issues: *Recent events have radicalized opinion on educational matters.* ◊ *The war has angered and radicalized a new generation of fighters.* ▸ **rad·ical·iza·tion** (*BrE also* **-isa·tion**) /ˌrædɪkəlaɪˈzeɪʃn; NAmE -ləˈz-/ *noun* [U]: *growing political radicalization in the country* ◊ *preventing the radicalization of young people*

**rad·icchio** /ræˈdiːkiəʊ/ *noun* [U] a type of CHICORY (= a leaf vegetable) with dark red leaves

**radii** /ˈreɪdiaɪ/ *pl.* of RADIUS

**radio** /ˈreɪdiəʊ/ *noun, verb*

- *noun* **1** [U, sing.] the activity of broadcasting programmes for people to listen to; the programmes that are broadcast: *The play was written specially for radio.* ◊ *I listen to the radio on the way to work.* ◊ **on ~** *The interview was broadcast on radio and television.* ◊ **on the ~** *Did you hear the interview with him on the radio?* ◊ *national radio* ◊ *a radio programme/show/broadcast/interview* ◊ *a radio station/network* ◊ *a radio host* ◊ *FM/commercial radio* ◊ *digital/satellite radio* ⇒ see also TALK RADIO

> **WORDFINDER** air, announce, bulletin, jingle, phone-in, podcast, programme, public service broadcasting, station

**2** [C] a piece of equipment used for listening to programmes that are broadcast to the public: *to turn the radio on/off* ◊ *to have the radio on* ◊ *a car radio* ⇒ see also CLOCK RADIO **3** [U] the process of sending and receiving messages through the air using ELECTROMAGNETIC waves: **by ~** *He was unable to contact Blake by radio.* ◊ *to keep in radio contact* ◊ *radio frequencies/signals/communications/waves* **4** [C] a piece of equipment, for example on ships or planes, for sending and receiving radio signals: **on/over a ~** *They heard the gale warning over the ship's radio.*

- *verb* [I, T] (**ra·dio·ing, ra·dioed, ra·dioed**) to send a message to sb by radio: **~for sth** *The police officer radioed for help.* ◊ **~sth to sb/sth** *The warning was radioed to headquarters.*

**radio-** /ˈreɪdiəʊ; BrE also ˈreɪdiˈɒ; NAmE also ˈreɪdiˈɑː/ *combining form* (in nouns, adjectives and adverbs) **1** connected with radio waves or broadcasting: *radio-controlled* **2** connected with RADIOACTIVITY: *radiotherapy*

**radio·active** /ˌreɪdiəʊˈæktɪv/ *adj.* sending out powerful and very dangerous RAYS when the NUCLEI (= central parts) of ATOMS are broken up▸ **radio·activ·ity** /ˌreɪdiəʊækˈtɪvəti/ *noun* [U]: *the study of radioactivity* ◊ *a rise in the level of radioactivity*

**radio aˈstronomy** *noun* [U] the part of ASTRONOMY that studies radio waves sent out by objects in space

**ˈradio button** *noun* (*computing*) (on a computer screen) a small circle that you click on in order to make a particular choice. The radio button is then marked with a DOT (= a small round mark) to show that it has been selected.

**radio·car·bon** /ˌreɪdiəʊˈkɑːbən; NAmE -ˈkɑːrb-/ *noun* [U] (*specialist*) a RADIOACTIVE form of CARBON that is present in the materials of which living things are formed, used in CARBON DATING: *radiocarbon analysis*

**ˌradiocarbon ˈdating** *noun* [U] (*formal*) = CARBON DATING

**ˌradio-conˈtrolled** *adj.* controlled from a distance by radio signals

**radi·og·raph·er** /ˌreɪdiˈɒɡrəfə(r); NAmE -ˈɑːɡ-/ *noun* a person working in a hospital whose job is to take X-RAY photographs to help with medical examinations

**radi·og·raphy** /ˌreɪdiˈɒɡrəfi; NAmE -ˈɑːɡ-/ *noun* [U] the process or job of taking X-RAY photographs

**radio·iso·tope** /ˌreɪdiəʊˈaɪsətəʊp/ *noun* (*chemistry*) a form of a chemical element which sends out RADIATION

**ˈradio jockey** *noun* (*IndE*) a person whose job is to introduce different sections of a programme or play recorded popular music on the radio

**radi·olo·gist** /ˌreɪdiˈɒlədʒɪst; NAmE -ˈɑːl-/ *noun* a doctor who is trained in radiology ⇒ WORDFINDER NOTE at SPECIALIST

**radi·ology** /ˌreɪdiˈɒlədʒi; NAmE -ˈɑːl-/ *noun* [U] the study and use of different types of RADIATION in medicine, for example to treat diseases

**radio·met·ric** /ˌreɪdiəʊˈmetrɪk/ *adj.* relating to a measurement of RADIOACTIVITY▸ **radio·met·ric·ally** /-kli/ *adv.*: *These rocks have been dated radiometrically at two billion years old.*

**ˈradio telescope** *noun* a piece of equipment that receives radio waves from space and is used for finding stars and the position of SPACECRAFT, etc.

---

æ cat | ɑː father | e bed | ɜː fur | ə about | ɪ sit | iː see | i happy | ɒ got (*BrE*) | ɔː saw | ʌ cup | ʊ put | uː too

**radio·ther·apy** /ˌreɪdiəʊˈθerəpi/ noun [U] the treatment of disease by RADIATION: *a course of radiotherapy* ⇒ compare CHEMOTHERAPY ⇒ WORDFINDER NOTE at CURE ▶ **radio-thera·pist** noun

**ˈradio wave** noun a low-energy ELECTROMAGNETIC wave, especially when used for long-distance communication

**rad·ish** /ˈrædɪʃ/ noun [C, U] a small red and white root vegetable with a strong taste, eaten raw in salads: *a bunch of radishes* ⇒ VISUAL VOCAB page V5

**ra·dium** /ˈreɪdiəm/ noun [U] (*symb.* **Ra**) a chemical element. Radium is a white RADIOACTIVE metal used in the treatment of diseases such as cancer.

**ra·dius** /ˈreɪdiəs/ noun (pl. **radii** /-diaɪ/) **1** a straight line between the centre of a circle and any point on its outer edge; the length of this line ⇒ picture at CIRCLE ⇒ compare DIAMETER **2** a round area that covers the distance mentioned from a central point: **within a …** *They deliver to within a 5-mile radius of the store.* **3** (*anatomy*) the shorter bone of the two bones in the lower part of the arm between the ELBOW and the WRIST, on the same side as the THUMB ⇒ VISUAL VOCAB page V1 ⇒ see also ULNA

**radon** /ˈreɪdɒn; *NAmE* -dɑːn/ noun [U] (*symb.* **Rn**) a chemical element. Radon is a RADIOACTIVE gas used in the treatment of diseases such as cancer.

**RAF** /ˌɑːr eɪ ˈef, ræf/ abbr. Royal Air Force (the British AIR FORCE): *He was an RAF pilot.*

**raf·fia** /ˈræfiə/ noun [U] soft material that looks like string and is made from the leaves of a type of PALM tree, used for making BASKETS, MATS, etc. or for tying things

**raff·ish** /ˈræfɪʃ/ adj. (of sb's behaviour, clothes, etc.) not very acceptable according to some social standards, but interesting and attractive

**raf·fle** /ˈræfl/ noun, verb
- *noun* a way of making money for a particular project or organization. People buy tickets with numbers on them and some of these numbers are later chosen to win prizes. ⇒ compare LOTTERY
- *verb* ~ sth to give sth as a prize in a raffle

**raft** /rɑːft; *NAmE* ræft/ noun **1** a flat structure made of pieces of wood tied together and used as a boat or floating platform **2** a small boat made of rubber or plastic that is filled with air: *an inflatable raft* **3** [usually sing.] **~ of sth** (*informal*) a large number or amount of sth: *a whole raft of new proposals*

**raft·er** /ˈrɑːftə(r); *NAmE* ˈræf-/ noun [C, usually pl.] one of the sloping pieces of wood that support a roof

**raft·ing** /ˈrɑːftɪŋ; *NAmE* ˈræf-/ noun [U] the sport or activity of travelling down a river on a RAFT: *We went white-water rafting on the Colorado River.*

**rag** /ræɡ/ noun, verb
- *noun* **1** [C, U] a piece of old, often torn, cloth used especially for cleaning things **2** [C] (*informal*, *usually disapproving*) a newspaper that you believe to be of low quality: *the local rag* **3** [C] a piece of RAGTIME music **4** [U, C] (*BrE*) an event or a series of events organized by students each year to raise money for charity: *rag week*
- **IDM** **in ˈrags** wearing very old torn clothes: *The children were dressed in rags.* **ˌlose your ˈrag** (*BrE*, *informal*) to get angry **(from) ˌrags to ˈriches** from being extremely poor to being very rich: *a rags-to-riches story* ⇔ *Hers was a classic tale of rags to riches.* ⇒ more at WAVE v.
- *verb* (**-gg-**) ~ **sb** (**about sth**) (*old-fashioned*) to laugh at and/ or play tricks on sb **SYN** tease
- **PHRV** **ˈrag on sb** (*NAmE*, *informal*) to complain to sb about their behaviour, work, etc.

**raga** /ˈrɑːɡə/ noun a traditional pattern of notes used in Indian music; a piece of music based on one of these patterns

**raga-muf·fin** (*also* **ragga-muf·fin**) /ˈræɡəmʌfɪn/ noun **1** [C] a person, usually a child, who is wearing old clothes that are torn and dirty **2** [C] (*especially BrE*) a person who likes or performs RAGGA music **3** [U] = RAGGA

**rag-bag** /ˈræɡbæɡ/ noun [sing.] a collection of things that appear to have little connection with each other: *a ragbag of ideas*

**ˈrag ˌdoll** noun a soft DOLL made from pieces of cloth

---

# raid

**rage** /reɪdʒ/ noun, verb
- *noun* **1** [U, C] a feeling of violent anger that is difficult to control: *His face was dark with rage.* ◇ *to be shaking/trembling/speechless with rage* ◇ **in a ~** *Sue stormed out of the room in a rage.* ◇ *He flies into a rage if you even mention the subject.* **2** [U] (in compounds) anger and violent behaviour caused by a particular situation: *a case of trolley rage in the supermarket* ⇒ see also AIR RAGE, ROAD RAGE
- **IDM** **be all the ˈrage** (*informal*) to be very popular and fashionable: *It was 1711 and Italian opera was all the rage.*
- *verb* **1** [I, T] to show that you are very angry about sth or with sb, especially by shouting **SYN** rail: **~ (at/against/about sb/sth)** *He raged against the injustice of it all.* ◇ **+ speech** *'That's unfair!' she raged.* **2** [I] **~ (on)** (of a storm, a battle, an argument, etc.) to continue in a violent way: *The riots raged for three days.* ◇ *The blizzard was still raging outside.* **3** [I] **(+ adv./prep.)** (of an illness, a fire, etc.) to spread very quickly: *Forest fires were raging out of control.* ◇ *A flu epidemic raged through Europe.* **4** [I] (*AustralE, NZE, slang*) to go out and enjoy yourself

**ragga** /ˈræɡə/ (*also* **ragga-muf·fin, rag-muf·fin**) noun [U] a type of dance music from the West Indies that contains features of REGGAE and HIP-HOP

**ragga·muf·fin** = RAGAMUFFIN

**rag·ged** /ˈræɡɪd/ adj. **1** (of clothes) old and torn **SYN** shabby **2** (of people) wearing old or torn clothes: *ragged children* **3** having an outline, an edge or a surface that is not straight or even: *ragged clouds* ◇ *a ragged coastline* **4** not smooth or regular; not showing control or careful preparation: *I could hear the sound of his ragged breathing.* ◇ *Their performance was still very ragged.* **5** (*informal*) very tired, especially after physical effort ▶ **rag·ged·ly** adv.: *raggedly dressed* ◇ *She was breathing raggedly.* **rag·ged·ness** noun [U]
- **IDM** **ˌrun sb ˈragged** (*informal*) to make sb do a lot of work or make a big effort so that they become tired

**ra·ging** /ˈreɪdʒɪŋ/ adj. [only before noun] **1** (of feelings or emotions) very strong: *a raging appetite/thirst* ◇ *raging jealousy* **2** (of natural forces) very powerful: *a raging storm* ◇ *The stream had become a raging torrent.* ◇ *The building was now a raging inferno.* **3** (of a pain or an illness) very strong or painful: *a raging headache* **4** very serious, causing strong feelings and continuing over a period of time: *His speech has provoked a raging debate.*

**ra·gout** /ˈræɡuː, ˈræɡuː/ noun [C, U] (*from French*) a hot dish of meat and vegetables boiled together with various SPICES

**rag·tag** /ˈræɡtæɡ/ adj. [usually before noun] (*informal*) (of a group of people or an organization) not well organized; giving a bad impression: *a ragtag band of rebels*

**rag·time** /ˈræɡtaɪm/ noun [U] an early form of jazz, especially for the piano, first played by African American musicians in the early 1900s

**rag·weed** /ˈræɡwiːd/ noun [U] a North American plant with small green flowers that contain a lot of POLLEN, which causes HAY FEVER in some people

**rag·wort** /ˈræɡwɜːt; *NAmE* -wɜːrt/ noun [U] a wild plant with yellow flowers, poisonous to cows and horses

**raid** /reɪd/ noun, verb
- *noun* **1** [+] [C] a short surprise attack on an enemy by soldiers, ships or aircraft: *to conduct/launch a raid* ◇ **~on sth** *The air force carried out a bombing raid on enemy bases.* ◇ **~ against sth** *The raids against military targets continued.* ⇒ see also AIR RAID **2** [+] [C] a surprise visit by the police looking for criminals or for illegal goods or drugs: *They were arrested during a dawn raid.* ◇ **~ on sth** *He was injured during a police raid on his nightclub.* ⇒ WORDFINDER NOTE at POLICE **3** [+] [C] an attack on a building, etc. in order to commit a crime: *an armed bank raid* ◇ **~ on sth** *Two customers foiled a raid on a local post office.*
- *verb* **1** [+] [C] **~ sth** (of police) to visit a person or place without warning to look for criminals, illegal goods, drugs, etc. **2** [+] [C] **~ sth** (of soldiers, fighting planes, etc.) to attack a place without warning: *Villages along the border are regularly raided.* ◇ *a raiding party* (= a group of soldiers, etc. that attack a place) **3** [+] [C] **~ sth** to enter a

# raider

place, usually using force, and steal from it SYN **plunder, ransack**: *Many treasures were lost when the tombs were raided in the last century.* ◊ *(humorous) I caught him raiding the fridge again* (= taking food from it).

**raid·er** /'reɪdə(r)/ *noun* a person who makes a criminal raid on a place: *armed/masked raiders*

**rail** ⓘ B2 /reɪl/ *noun, verb*
- *noun* **1** ⓘ+ B2 [C] a wooden or metal bar placed around sth as a barrier or to provide support: *She leaned on the ship's rail and gazed out to sea.* ⊃ see also GUARD RAIL, HANDRAIL **2** ⓘ+ B2 [C] a bar fixed to the wall for hanging things on: *a picture/curtain/towel rail* ⊃ see also PICTURE RAIL, TOWEL RAIL **3** ⓘ+ B2 [C, usually pl.] each of the two metal bars that form the track that trains run on **4** ⓘ+ B2 [U] (often before another noun) railways as a means of transport: *by~ to travel by rail* ◊ *rail travel/services/fares* ◊ *a rail link/network* IDM **get back on the 'rails** (*informal*) to become successful again after a period of failure, or to begin functioning normally again **go off the 'rails** (*informal*) **1** to start behaving in a way that is strange or unacceptable, for example drinking a lot or taking drugs **2** to lose control and stop functioning correctly: *The company has gone badly off the rails in recent years.* ⊃ more at JUMP *v.*
- *verb* [I, T] ~ (at/against sth/sb) | + speech (*formal*) to complain about sth/sb in a very angry way SYN **rage**: *She railed against the injustice of it all.* PHRV **rail sth 'in/'off** to separate an area or object from others by placing rails around it

**rail·car** /'reɪlkɑː(r)/ *noun* = CAR (2)

**rail·card** /'reɪlkɑːd; NAmE -kɑːrd/ *noun* (*BrE*) a card that allows sb to travel by train at a reduced price

**rail·head** /'reɪlhed/ *noun* (*specialist*) the point at which a railway ends

**rail·ing** /'reɪlɪŋ/ *noun* [C, usually pl.] a fence made of metal bars that go straight upwards; one of these bars: *iron/metal railings* ◊ *I chained my bike to the park railings.* ◊ *She leaned out over the railing.*

**rail·man** /'reɪlmən/ *noun* (*pl.* **-men** /-mən/) (*BrE*) = RAILWAYMAN

**rail·road** /'reɪlrəʊd/ *noun, verb*
- *noun* (*NAmE*) (*BrE* **rail·way**) **1** (*BrE also* **railway line**) a track with RAILS on which trains run: *railroad tracks* **2** a system of tracks, together with the trains that run on them, and the organization and people needed to operate them: *This town got a lot bigger when the railroad came in the 1860s.*
- *verb* [usually passive] **1** ~ **sb** (**into sth/into doing sth**) to force sb to do sth before they have had enough time to decide whether or not they want to do it SYN **bulldoze 2** ~ **sth** (**through/through sth**) to make a group of people accept a decision, law, etc. quickly by putting pressure on them: *The bill was railroaded through the House.* **3** ~ **sb** (*NAmE*) to decide that sb is guilty of a crime, without giving them a fair trial

**'railroad crossing** (*also* **'grade crossing**) (*NAmE*) (*BrE* **,level 'crossing**) *noun* a place where a road crosses a railroad at the same level (not on a bridge)

**rail·road·er** /'reɪlrəʊdə(r)/ *noun* (*NAmE*) (*BrE* **rail·way·man, rail·man**) (*both BrE*) (*NAmE* **rail·road·er**) a person who works for a railway company

**rail·way** ⓘ A2 /'reɪlweɪ/ (*NAmE* **rail·road**) *noun* **1** ⓘ+ A2 (*BrE also* **railway line**) a track with RAILS on which trains run: *The railway is still under construction.* ◊ *a disused railway* **2** ⓘ+ A2 a system of tracks, together with the trains that run on them, and the organization and people needed to operate them: **on the railways** *Her father worked on the railways.* ◊ *a railway station* ◊ *the Midland Railway* ◊ *a model railway*

**rail·way·man** /'reɪlweɪmən/ *noun* (*pl.* **-men** /-mən/) (*also* **rail·man**) (*both BrE*) (*NAmE* **rail·road·er**) a person who works for a railway company

**rai·ment** /'reɪmənt/ *noun* [U] (*old use*) clothing

---

**rain** ⓘ A1 /reɪn/ *noun, verb*
- *noun* **1** ⓘ+ A1 [U, sing.] water that falls from the sky in separate drops: *There will be rain in all parts tomorrow.* ◊ *The rain was falling more heavily now.* ◊ *Rain is forecast for the weekend.* ◊ **in the**~ *Don't go out in the rain.* ◊ *It's* **pouring with rain** (= raining very hard). ◊ *heavy/torrential/pouring/driving rain* ◊ *The rain poured down.* ◊ *It looks like rain* (= as if it is going to rain). ◊ *A light rain began to fall.* ◊ *I think I felt a drop of rain.* ◊ *Typically, we get nearly 5 inches of rain in June.* ◊ *rain clouds/showers* ⊃ HOMOPHONES at REIGN ⊃ see also ACID RAIN, RAINY

**WORDFINDER** downpour, drought, flash flood, monsoon, precipitation, puddle, shelter, shower, squall

**2 the rains** [pl.] the season of heavy continuous rain in tropical countries: *The rains come in September.* **3** [sing.] ~ **of sth** a large number of things falling from the sky at the same time: *a rain of arrows/bullets* IDM **come 'rain, come 'shine/(come) rain or 'shine** whether there is rain or sun; whatever happens: *He goes jogging every morning, rain or shine.* ⊃ more at RIGHT *adj.*
- *verb* **1** ⓘ+ A1 [I] when **it rains**, water falls from the sky in drops: *Is it raining?* ◊ *It had been raining hard all night.* ◊ *It was still raining heavily.* ◊ *It rained and rained and didn't stop for days.* ◊ *It started to rain.* ⊃ HOMOPHONES at REIGN **2** [I, T] to fall or to make sth fall on sb/sth in large quantities: ~(**down**) (**on sb/sth**) *Bombs rained (down) on the city's streets.* ◊ *Falling debris rained on us from above.* ◊ *He covered his face as the blows rained down on him* (= he was hit repeatedly). ◊ ~ **sth** (**down**) (**on sb/sth**) *The volcano erupted, raining hot ash over a wide area.* IDM **be raining cats and 'dogs** (*informal*) to be raining heavily **it never rains but it 'pours** (*BrE*) (*NAmE* **when it rains, it 'pours**) (*saying*) used to say that when one bad thing happens to you, other bad things happen soon after **rain on sb's 'parade** (*informal*) to prevent sb from enjoying an event; to cause sb's plans to fail PHRV **be rained 'off** (*BrE*) (*NAmE* **be rained 'out**) (of an event) to be cancelled or to have to stop because it is raining: *The game has been rained off again.*

▼ **VOCABULARY BUILDING**

**Rain and storms**

Rain
- **Drizzle** is fine light rain.
- A **shower** is a short period of rain.
- A **downpour** or a **cloudburst** is a heavy fall of rain that often starts suddenly.
- When it is raining very hard you can say that it is **pouring**. In informal *BrE* you can also say that it is **bucketing down** or **chucking it down**. You can also say: *The heavens opened.*

Storms
- A **cyclone** and a **typhoon** are types of violent tropical storms with very strong winds.
- A **hurricane** has very strong winds and is usually at sea.
- A **monsoon** is a period of very heavy rain in particular countries, or the wind that brings this rain.
- A **squall** is a sudden strong, violent wind, usually in a rainstorm or snowstorm.
- A **tornado** (or *informal* **twister**) has very strong winds which move in a circle, often with a long narrow cloud.
- A **whirlwind** moves very fast in circles and causes a lot of damage.
- A **blizzard** is a snowstorm with very strong winds.
- **Tempest** is used mainly in literary language to describe a violent storm.

**'rain barrel** (*NAmE*) (*BrE* **'water butt**) *noun* a large BARREL for collecting rain as it flows off a roof

**rain·bow** /'reɪnbəʊ/ *noun* a curved band of different colours that appears in the sky when the sun shines through rain: *all the colours of the rainbow*

**,rainbow coa'lition** *noun* a political group formed by different parties who agree to work together, especially one that includes one or more very small parties

**rainbow 'nation** noun [usually sing.] (approving) a name used to describe the people of South Africa because of their many races and cultures

**rainbow 'trout** noun [C, U] type of TROUT (= a fish that is often eaten as food, and often caught in the sport of fishing)

**'rain check** noun (especially NAmE) a ticket that can be used later if a game, show, etc. is cancelled because of rain
**IDM take a rain check (on sth)** (especially NAmE, informal) to refuse an offer or invitation but say that you might accept it later: *'Are you coming for a drink?' 'Can I take a rain check?—I must get this finished tonight.'*

**'rain-coat** /ˈreɪnkəʊt/ noun a long light coat that keeps you dry in the rain

**'rain date** noun (NAmE) an alternative date when an event will take place if it has to be cancelled on the original date because of rain: *July 15 is our annual fun day (rain date July 22).*

**'rain-drop** /ˈreɪndrɒp; NAmE -drɑːp/ noun a single drop of rain

**'rain-fall** /ˈreɪnfɔːl/ noun [U, C] the total amount of rain that falls in a particular area in a particular amount of time; an occasion when rain falls: *There has been below average rainfall this month.* ◊ *an average annual rainfall of 10 cm*
➾ **WORDFINDER NOTE** at CLIMATE

**'rain-for-est** /ˈreɪnfɒrɪst; NAmE -fɔːr-/ noun [C, U] a thick forest in tropical parts of the world that have a lot of rain: *the Amazon rainforest* ➾ compare CLOUD FOREST

**'rain-maker** /ˈreɪnmeɪkə(r)/ noun **1** (especially NAmE, business) a person who makes a business grow and become successful **2** a person who is believed to have the power to make rain fall, especially among Native Americans

**'rain-out** /ˈreɪnaʊt/ noun (NAmE) an occasion when bad weather prevents an event from starting or finishing

**'rain-storm** /ˈreɪnstɔːm; NAmE -stɔːrm/ noun a heavy fall of rain

**'rain-water** /ˈreɪnwɔːtə(r)/ noun [U] water that has fallen as rain: *a barrel for collecting rainwater*

**rainy** /ˈreɪni/ adj. (rain-ier, rain-iest) having or bringing a lot of rain: *a rainy day* ◊ *the rainy season* ◊ *the rainiest place in Britain*
**IDM save, keep, etc. sth for a ˌrainy ˈday** to save sth, especially money, for a time when you will really need it

**raise** ⓞ A2 /reɪz/ verb, noun
■ **verb**
- **MOVE UPWARDS 1** ⓘ A2 ~ sth to lift or move sth to a higher level: *She raised the gun and fired.* ◊ *He raised a hand in greeting.* ◊ *She raised her eyes from her work.* **OPP lower**¹
➾ HOMOPHONES at RAZE ➾ note at RISE ➾ see also CURTAIN-RAISER **2** ⓘ B1 ~ sb/sth/yourself (+ adv./prep.) to move sb/sth/yourself to a standing, sitting or VERTICAL position: *Somehow we managed to raise her to her feet.* ◊ *He raised himself up on one elbow.* **OPP lower**¹
- **INCREASE 3** ⓘ B1 to increase the amount or level of sth: ~ sth *to raise prices/taxes* ◊ *We need to raise public awareness of the issue.* ◊ ~ sth to sth *They raised their offer to $500.* ◊ *Don't tell her about the job until you know for sure—we don't want to raise her hopes* (= make her hope too much). ◊ *I've never heard him even raise his voice* (= speak louder because he was angry).
- **COLLECT MONEY/PEOPLE 4** ⓘ B1 ~ sth to bring or collect money or people together; to manage to get or form sth: *We are raising money for charity.* ◊ *They are holding a quiz to help raise funds for the club.* ◊ *He set about raising an army.* ➾ see also FUNDRAISER
- **MENTION SUBJECT 5** ⓘ B2 ~ sth to mention sth for people to discuss or sb to deal with **SYN broach**: *The book raises many important questions.* ◊ *I have raised this issue with the environmental health office.* ◊ *Local residents have raised concerns about late-night noise.*
- **CAUSE/PRODUCE 6** ~ sth to cause or produce a feeling or reaction: *to raise doubts in people's minds* ◊ *The plans for the new development have raised angry protests from local residents.* ◊ *It wasn't an easy audience but he raised a laugh with his joke.* ◊ *It had been a difficult day but she managed to raise a smile.* **7** ~ sth to make sth happen or

1271 **rake**

appear: *She raised the alarm when he failed to return home.* ◊ *The horses' hooves raised a cloud of dust.* ➾ see also FIRE-RAISER
- **CHILD/ANIMAL 8** ⓘ B2 (especially NAmE) to care for a child or young animal until it is able to take care of itself: ~ sb/sth *She raised five children on her own.* ◊ *kids raised on a diet of hamburgers* ◊ ~ sb/sth (as) sth *They raised her (as) a Catholic.* ◊ *I was born and raised a city boy.* ➾ compare BRING SB↔UP
- **FARM ANIMALS/CROPS 9** ~ sth to BREED (= keep and produce young from) particular farm animals; to grow particular crops: *to raise cattle/corn*
- **END STH 10** ~ sth to end the limits on sb/sth: *to raise a blockade/ban/siege*
- **ON RADIO/PHONE 11** ~ sb to contact sb and speak to them by radio or phone: *We managed to raise him on his mobile phone.*
- **DEAD PERSON 12** ~ sb (from sth) to make sb who has died come to life again **SYN resurrect**: *Christians believe that God raised Jesus from the dead.*
- **IN CARD GAMES 13** ~ sb sth to make a higher bet than another player in a card game: *I'll raise you another hundred dollars.*
- **MATHEMATICS 14** ~ sth **to the power of sth** to multiply an amount by itself a particular number of times: *3 raised to the power of 3 is 27* (= 3×3×3).
- **BUILD 15** ~ sth (especially NAmE) to build sth: *Our priority will be to raise a boundary wall and prevent trespassing.*
**IDM raise a/your hand against/to sb** to hit or threaten to hit sb **raise the ˈbar** to set a new, higher standard of quality or performance: *The factory has raised the bar on productivity, food safety and quality.* **OPP lower**¹ ➾ compare SET THE BAR **raise your ˈeyebrows (at sth)** [often passive] to show that you think sth is bad or are surprised by sth: *Eyebrows were raised when he arrived without his wife.* **raise your ˈglass (to sb)** to hold up your glass and wish sb happiness, good luck, etc. before you drink **raise ˈhell** (informal) to protest angrily, especially in a way that causes trouble for sb **raise the ˈroof** to produce or make sb produce a lot of noise in a building, for example by shouting or CHEERING **raise sb's ˈspirits** to make sb feel more cheerful or brave **SYN cheer up** ➾ more at ANTE, HACKLES, LIFT v., SIGHT n., TEMPERATURE
**PHRV raise sth to sb/sth** to build or place a statue, etc. somewhere in honour or memory of sb/sth: *The town raised a memorial to those killed in the war.*
■ **noun** (NAmE) (BrE **rise**) an increase in the money you are paid for the work you do ➾ HOMOPHONES at RAZE

**raised** /reɪzd/ adj. **1** higher than the area around: *a raised platform* **2** at a higher level than normal: *the sound of raised voices* ◊ *Smokers often have raised blood pressure.*

**rai-sin** /ˈreɪzn/ noun a dried GRAPE, used in cakes, etc.

**rais-ing** /ˈreɪzɪŋ/ noun [U, sing.] the act of raising sth: *consciousness raising* ◊ *a raising of standards in schools* ➾ see also FUNDRAISING

**rai-son d'être** /ˌreɪzɒ̃ ˈdetrə; NAmE ˌreɪzoʊn ˈdetrə/ noun [sing.] (from French) the most important reason for sb's/sth's existence: *Work seems to be her sole raison d'être.*

**raita** /ˈraɪtə/ noun [U] a South Asian dish of raw vegetables cut into small pieces and mixed with YOGURT

**the Raj** /ðə ˈrɑːdʒ; BrE also ˈrɑːʒ/ noun [sing.] British rule in India before 1947

**raja** (also less frequent **rajah**) /ˈrɑːdʒə/ noun an Indian king or prince who ruled over a state in the past

**rake** /reɪk/ noun, verb
■ **noun 1** [C] a garden tool with a long handle and a row of metal points at the end, used for gathering fallen leaves and making soil smooth **2** [C] (in the past) a man, especially a rich and fashionable one, who was thought to have low moral standards, for example because he drank or GAMBLED a lot or had sex with a lot of women **3** [sing.] the amount by which sth, especially the stage in a theatre, slopes
■ **verb 1** [T, I] to pull a rake over a surface in order to make it level or to remove sth: ~ (sth) (+ adv./prep.) *The leaves had been raked into a pile.* ◊ (figurative) *She raked a comb through her hair.* ◊ ~ sth + adj. *First rake the soil smooth.*

# raked

**2** [T] ~ **sth (with sth)** to point a camera, light, gun, etc. at sb/sth and move it slowly from one side to the other: *They raked the streets with machine-gun fire.* ◊ *Searchlights raked the grounds.* **3** [I] **+ adv./prep.** to search a place carefully for sth: *She raked around in her bag for her keys.* **4** [T, I] ~ **(sth)** to SCRATCH the surface of sth with a sharp object, especially your nails
**IDM** **rake sb over the ˈcoals** (*NAmE*) (*BrE* **haul sb over the ˈcoals**) to criticize sb severely because they have done sth wrong
**PHR V** ˌrake ˈin sth (*informal*) to earn a lot of money, especially when it is done easily: *The movie raked in more than $300 million.* ◊ *She's been raking it in since she started her new job.* ˌrake ˈover sth (*informal*, *disapproving*) to examine sth that happened in the past in great detail and keep talking about it, when it should be forgotten: *She had no desire to rake over the past.* ˌrake sth↔ˈup (*informal*, *disapproving*) to mention sth unpleasant that happened in the past and that other people would like to forget

**raked** /reɪkt/ *adj.* placed on a slope: *raked seating*
**rak·ish** /ˈreɪkɪʃ/ *adj.* **1** (of a man) acting like a RAKE (2) (= in a way that is not moral, etc.) **SYN** **dissolute** **2** if you wear a hat at a **rakish angle**, it is not straight on your head and it makes you look relaxed and confident **SYN** **jaunty** ▸ **rak·ish·ly** *adv.*
**ra·kyat** /ˈrɑːkjɑːt/ *SEAsianE* [ˈrakjat] *noun* [pl.] (*SEAsianE*) ordinary people: *The government should help the rakyat to get affordable homes.*

**rally** 🔊 **C1** /ˈræli/ *noun*, *verb*
■ *noun* **1** 🔊 **C1** [C] a large public meeting, especially one held to support a particular idea or political party: *to attend/hold a rally* ◊ *a peace/protest rally* ◊ *a mass rally in support of the strike* ⊃ see also PEP RALLY **2** 🔊 **C1** [C] a race for cars, motorcycles, etc. over public roads: *the Monte Carlo rally* ◊ *rally driving* **3** [C] (in tennis and similar sports) a series of hits of the ball before a point is scored **4** [sing.] (in sport or on the Stock Exchange) an act of returning to a strong position after a period of difficulty or weakness **SYN** **recovery**: *After a furious late rally, they finally scored.* ◊ *a rally in shares on the stock market*
■ *verb* (**ral·lies**, **rally·ing**, **ral·lied**, **ral·lied**) **1** 🔊 **C1** [I, T] to come together or bring people together in order to help or support sb/sth: ~ **around/behind sb/sth** *The cabinet rallied behind the Prime Minister.* ◊ ~ **to sb/sth** *Many national newspapers rallied to his support.* ◊ ~ **sb/sth (around/behind/to sb/sth)** *They have rallied a great deal of support for their campaign.* **2** [I] to become healthier, stronger, etc. after a period of illness, weakness, etc. **SYN** **recover**: *He never really rallied after the operation.* ◊ *The champion rallied to win the second set 6–3.* **3** [I] (*finance*) (especially of share prices or a country's money) to increase in value after falling in value **SYN** **recover**: *The company's shares had rallied slightly by the close of trading.* ◊ *The pound rallied against the dollar.*
**PHR V** ˌrally aˈround | ˌrally aˈround sb (*also especially BrE* ˌrally ˈround, ˌrally ˈround sb) (of a group of people) to work together in order to help sb who is in a difficult or unpleasant situation

**rally·cross** /ˈrælikrɒs; *NAmE* -krɔːs/ *noun* [U] a form of motor racing in which cars are driven both over rough ground and on roads
**ˈrallying cry** *noun* a phrase or an idea that is used to encourage people to support sb/sth
**ˈrallying point** *noun* a person, a group, an event, etc. that makes people come together in support of sth
**RAM** /ræm/ *noun* [U] computer memory in which data can be changed or removed and can be looked at in any order (the abbreviation for 'random-access memory'): *16 gigabytes of RAM*
**ram** /ræm/ *verb*, *noun*
■ *verb* (**-mm-**) **1** ~ **sth** (of a vehicle, a ship, etc.) to drive into or hit another vehicle, ship, etc. with force, sometimes deliberately: *Two passengers were injured when their taxi was rammed from behind by a bus.* **2** ~ **sth + adv./prep.** to push sth somewhere with force: *She rammed the key into the lock.* ◊ (*figurative*) *The spending cuts had been rammed through Congress.*
**IDM** ˌram sth↔ˈhome (*especially BrE*) to emphasize an idea, argument, etc. very strongly to make sure people listen to it ⊃ more at THROAT
**PHR V** ˌram ˈinto sth | ˌram sth ˈinto sth to hit against sth or to make sth hit against sth with force: *He rammed his truck into the back of the one in front.*
■ *noun* **1** a male sheep ⊃ compare EWE **2** a part in a machine that is used for hitting sth very hard or for lifting or moving things: *hydraulic rams* ⊃ see also BATTERING RAM

**Ram·adan** /ˈræmədæn; *NAmE* ˌrɑːməˈdɑːn/ *noun* [U, C] the 9th month of the Muslim year, when Muslims do not eat or drink between DAWN and SUNSET

**ram·ble** /ˈræmbl/ *verb*, *noun*
■ *verb* **1** [I] **+ adv./prep.** (*especially BrE*) to walk for pleasure, especially in the countryside: *We spent the summer rambling in Ireland.* **2** [I] to talk about sb/sth in a confused way, especially for a long time: *He had lost track of what he was saying and began to ramble.* ◊ ~ **(on) (about sb/sth)** *What is she rambling on about now?* **3** [I] **(+ adv./prep.)** (of plants) to grow in many different directions, especially over other plants or objects: *Climbing plants rambled over the front of the house.* ⊃ see also RAMBLING
■ *noun* **1** (*especially BrE*) a long walk for pleasure: *to go for a ramble in the country* **2** a long confused speech or piece of writing: *She went into a long ramble about the evils of television.*

**ram·bler** /ˈræmblə(r)/ *noun* **1** (*especially BrE*) a person who walks in the countryside for pleasure, especially as part of an organized group **2** a plant, especially a ROSE, that grows up walls, fences, etc.

**ram·bling** /ˈræmblɪŋ/ *adj.*, *noun*
■ *adj.* **1** (of a building) spreading in various directions with no particular pattern **SYN** **sprawling** **2** (of a speech or piece of writing) very long and confused **SYN** **incoherent**: *a rambling letter* ⊃ WORDFINDER NOTE at STORY **3** (of a plant) growing or climbing in all directions, for example up a wall: *a rambling rose*
■ *noun* **1** [U] the activity of walking for pleasure in the countryside **2** **ramblings** [pl.] speech or writing that continues for a long time without saying much and seems very confused: *the ramblings of a madman*

**Rambo** /ˈræmbəʊ/ *noun* (*informal*) a very strong and aggressive man **ORIGIN** From the name of the main character in David Morrell's novel *First Blood*, which was made popular in three films/movies in the 1980s.

**ram·bunc·tious** /ræmˈbʌŋkʃəs/ *adj.* (*especially NAmE*, *informal*) = RUMBUSTIOUS
**ram·bu·tan** /ræmˈbuːtn/ *noun* a red tropical fruit with soft pointed parts on its skin and a slightly bitter sharp taste
**ram·ekin** /ˈræmɪkɪn/ *noun* a small dish for baking and serving food for one person
**ramen** /ˈrɑːmən/ *noun* [U] thin Asian NOODLES, usually served in a light soup
**ram·ifi·ca·tion** /ˌræmɪfɪˈkeɪʃn/ *noun* [usually pl.] one of a number of complicated and unexpected results that follow an action or a decision **SYN** **complication**: *These changes are bound to have widespread social ramifications.*

**ramp** /ræmp/ *noun*, *verb*
■ *noun* **1** a slope that joins two parts of a road, path, building, etc. when one is higher than the other: *Ramps should be provided for wheelchair users.* **2** (*NAmE*) (*BrE* **slip road**) a road used for driving onto or off a major road such as a MOTORWAY or INTERSTATE: *a freeway exit ramp* ⊃ see also OFF-RAMP, ON-RAMP **3** a slope or set of steps that can be moved, used for loading a vehicle or getting on or off a plane: *a loading ramp* **4** (*IndE*) the long stage that models walk on during a fashion show **SYN** **catwalk**, **runway**
■ *verb*
**PHR V** ˌramp sth↔ˈup to make sth increase in amount

**ram·page** *noun*, *verb*
■ *noun* /ˈræmpeɪdʒ/ [usually sing.] a sudden period of wild and violent behaviour, often causing damage and

DESTRUCTION: *Gangs of youths* **went on the rampage** *in the city yesterday.*
- **verb** /ˈræmpeɪdʒ, ræmˈpeɪdʒ/ [I] **+ adv. / prep.** (of people or animals) to move through a place in a group, usually breaking things and causing damage SYN **run amok**: *a herd of rampaging elephants*

**ram·pant** /ˈræmpənt/ *adj.* **1** (of sth bad) existing or spreading everywhere in a way that cannot be controlled SYN **unchecked**: *rampant inflation/corruption* ◇ *Unemployment is now rampant in most of Europe.* **2** (of plants) growing thickly and very fast in a way that cannot be controlled ▸ **ram·pant·ly** *adv.*

**ram·part** /ˈræmpɑːt; NAmE -pɑːrt/ *noun* [usually pl.] a high wide wall of stone or earth with a path on top, built around a castle, town, etc. to defend it

**ram·rod** /ˈræmrɒd; NAmE -rɑːd/ *noun* a long straight piece of iron used in the past to push EXPLOSIVE into a gun
IDM **ramrod ˈstraight | (as) straight as a ˈramrod** (of a person) with a very straight back and looking serious and formal

**ram·shackle** /ˈræmʃækl/ *adj.* **1** (of buildings, vehicles, furniture, etc.) in a very bad condition and needing repair SYN **tumbledown 2** (of an organization or a system) badly organized or designed and not likely to last very long SYN **rickety**

**ran** /ræn/ *past tense of* RUN

**ranch** /rɑːntʃ; NAmE ræntʃ/ *noun* a large farm, especially in North America or Australia, where cows, horses, sheep, etc. are BRED (= kept in order to produce young): *a cattle/sheep ranch* ◇ **ranch hands** (= the people who work on a ranch) ⊃ *see also* DUDE RANCH IDM *see* BET *v.*

**ranch·er** /ˈrɑːntʃə(r); NAmE ˈræn-/ *noun* a person who owns, manages or works on a ranch: *a cattle rancher*

**ˈranch house** *noun* **1** a house on a ranch **2** (*NAmE*) a house built all on one level, that is very wide but not very deep from front to back and has a roof that is not very steep ⊃ *compare* BUNGALOW

**ranch·ing** /ˈrɑːntʃɪŋ; NAmE ˈræn-/ *noun* [U] the activity of running a RANCH: *cattle/sheep ranching*

**ran·cid** /ˈrænsɪd/ *adj.* if food containing fat is **rancid**, it tastes or smells unpleasant because it is no longer fresh: *Butter soon goes/turns* (= becomes) *rancid in this heat.*

**ran·cour** (*NAmE* **ran·cor**) /ˈræŋkə(r)/ *noun* (*formal*) feelings of hate and a desire to hurt other people, especially because you think that sb has done sth unfair to you SYN **bitterness**: *without ~ She learned to accept criticism without rancour.* ▸ **ran·cor·ous** /-kərəs/ *adj.*: *a rancorous legal battle*

**rand** /rænd, rɑːnt/ *noun* (*pl.* **rand**) **1** [C] the unit of money in the Republic of South Africa **2 the Rand** /-/ [sing.] (in South Africa) a large area around Johannesburg where gold is mined and where there are many cities and towns

**R & B** /ˌɑːr ən ˈbiː/ *abbr.* RHYTHM AND BLUES

**R & D** /ˌɑːr ən ˈdiː/ *abbr.* RESEARCH AND DEVELOPMENT

**ran·dom** ?+ B2 ◯ /ˈrændəm/ *adj.*, *noun*
- *adj.* **1** ?+ B2 [usually before noun] done, chosen, etc. without sb deciding in advance what is going to happen, or without any regular pattern: *the random killing of innocent people* ◇ *a random sample/selection* (= in which each thing has an equal chance of being chosen) ◇ (*informal*) *I find and play a lot of random stuff—Bach, blues, bebop.* ◇ *She dodged the random items that were on the concrete floor.* **2** [only before noun] (*informal*) (especially of a person) not known or not identified: *Some random guy gave me a hundred bucks.* **3** (*informal*) a thing or person that is **random** is strange and does not make sense, often in a way that interests you or makes you laugh: *Mom, you are so random!* ◇ *The humour is great because it's just so random and unhinged from reality.* ▸ **ran·dom·ly** *adv.*: *The winning numbers are randomly selected by computer.* ◇ *My phone seems to switch itself off randomly.* **ran·dom·ness** *noun* [U]: *It introduced an element of randomness into the situation.*
- *noun*
IDM **at ˈrandom** without deciding in advance what is going to happen, or without any regular pattern: *She opened the book at random* (= not at any particular page) *and started reading.* ◇ *The terrorists fired into the crowd at random.* ◇ *Names were chosen at random from a list.*

**ˌrandom ˈaccess** *noun* [U] (*computing*) the ability in a computer to go straight to data items without having to read through items stored previously

**ˌrandom-ˌaccess ˈmemory** *noun* [U] (*computing*) = RAM

**ran·dom·ize** W (*BrE also* **-ise**) /ˈrændəmaɪz/ *verb* **~ sth** (*specialist*) to use a method in an experiment, a piece of research, etc. that gives every item an equal chance of being considered; to put things in a RANDOM order

**R & R** /ˌɑːr ən ˈɑː(r)/ *abbr.* **1** rest and recreation (doing things for pleasure rather than working) **2** (*medical*) rescue and resuscitation

**randy** /ˈrændi/ *adj.* (**ran·dier**, **ran·di·est**) (*BrE*, *informal*) sexually excited: *to feel/get randy*

**ranee** = RANI

**rang** /ræŋ/ *past tense of* RING²

**range** 0 B1 ◯ /reɪndʒ/ *noun*, *verb*
- *noun*
- VARIETY **1** ?ᴱ B1 [C, usually sing.] a variety of things of a particular type: **~ of sth** *The hotel offers a* **wide range** *of facilities.* ◇ *There is a* **full range** *of activities for children.* ◇ *a narrow/limited range of options* **across a ~** *Employees across a range of occupations were surveyed.* ◇ **over a ~** *We have reached agreement over a* **range of issues***.*
- OF PRODUCTS **2** ?ᴱ B2 [C] **~ (of sth)** a set of products of a particular type: *our new* **range of hair products** ◇ *We are looking to expand our* **product range***.* ⊃ *see also* MID-RANGE, TOP OF THE RANGE
- LIMITS/EXTENT **3** ?ᴱ B2 [C, usually sing.] the limits between which sth varies: **in a ~** *Most of the students are in the 17–20* **age range***.* ◇ *It's difficult to find a house in our* **price range** (= that we can afford). ◇ **in the ~ of sth** *There will be an increase in the range of 0 to 3 per cent.* ◇ **within a ~** *Prices vary only within a narrow range.* **4** [C, usually sing.] the extent of sb's knowledge or abilities: *I think she has quite a* **limited range** *as an actor.* ◇ **~ of sth** *The range of his knowledge is impressive.* **5** [C, usual y sing.] **~ (of sth)** the area covered by or included in sth: *Her sculptures explore the range of human experience.*
- DISTANCE **6** [C, U] **~ (of sth)** the distance over which sth can be seen or heard: *The child was now out of her* **range of vision** (= not near enough for her to see). **7** [C, U] **~ (of sth)** the distance over which a gun or other weapon can hit things: *These missiles have a range of 300 miles.* ⊃ *see also* CLOSE-RANGE, LONG-RANGE, SHORT-RANGE **8** [C] **~ (of sth)** the distance that a vehicle will travel before it needs more fuel
- OF MOUNTAINS **9** [C] a line or group of mountains or hills: *the great* **mountain range** *of the Alps*
- FOR SHOOTING **10** [C] an area of land where people can practise shooting or where bombs, etc. can be tested: *a shooting range* ⊃ *see also* DRIVING RANGE, RIFLE RANGE
- OVEN **11** [C] a large piece of equipment that can burn various fuels and is kept hot all the time, used for cooking, especially in the past **12** [C] (*NAmE*) = STOVE: *Cook the meat on a low heat on top of the range.*
- FOR COWS **13 the range** [sing.] (*NAmE*) a large open area for keeping cows, etc. ⊃ *see also* FREE-RANGE
IDM **in / within ˈrange (of sth)** near enough to be reached, seen or heard: *He shouted angrily at anyone within range.* **out of ˈrange (of sth)** too far away to be reached, seen or heard: *The cat stayed well out of range of the children.* ⊃ *more at* CLOSE² *adj.*
- *verb*
- VARY **1** ?ᴱ B2 [I] to vary between two particular amounts, sizes, etc., including others between them: **~ from A to B** *Accommodation ranges from tourist class to luxury hotels.* ◇ **~ in sth** *His four daughters range in age from 9 to 15.* **~ between A and B** *Estimates of the damage range between $1 million and $5 million.* **2** ?ᴱ B2 [I] to include a variety of different things in addition to those mentioned: **~ from A to B** *She has had a number of different jobs, ranging from chef to swimming instructor.* ◇ **+ adv. / prep.** *The*

# rangefinder

*conversation ranged widely* (= covered a lot of different topics). ⊃ see also WIDE-RANGING
- **ARRANGE 3** [T, often passive] ~ **sb/sth/yourself + adv./prep.** (*formal*) to arrange people or things in a particular position or order: *The delegates ranged themselves around the table.* ◇ *Spectators were ranged along the whole route of the procession.*
- **MOVE AROUND 4** [I, T] to move around an area: **+ adv./prep.** *He ranges far and wide in search of inspiration for his paintings.* ◇ ~ **sth** *Her eyes ranged the room.*

**PHR V** **range yourself/sb a'gainst/'with sb/sth** [usually passive] to join with other people to oppose or support sb/sth: *The whole family seemed ranged against him.* **'range over sth** to include a variety of different subjects: *His lecture ranged over a number of topics.*

**range·find·er** /ˈreɪndʒfaɪndə(r)/ *noun* an instrument for estimating how far away an object is, used with a camera or gun

**ran·ger** /ˈreɪndʒə(r)/ *noun* **1** a person whose job is to take care of a park, a forest or an area of countryside **2 Ranger (Guide)** a girl who belongs to the part of the Guide Association in the UK for girls between the ages of 14 and 19 **3 Ranger** (*US*) a soldier who is trained to make quick attacks in enemy areas ⊃ compare COMMANDO

**rangy** /ˈreɪndʒi/ *adj.* (of a person or an animal) having long thin arms and/or legs

**rani** (*also* **ranee**) /ˈrɑːniː, rɑːˈniː/ *noun* an Indian queen; the wife of a RAJA

**rank** **B2** /ræŋk/ *noun, verb, adj.*
- *noun*
- **POSITION IN ORGANIZATION/ARMY, ETC. 1 B2** [U, C] the position, especially a high position, that sb has in a particular organization, society, etc: *She was not used to mixing with people of high social rank.* ◇ *He rose through the ranks to become managing director.* ◇ *Within months she was elevated to ministerial rank.* ◇ ~ **of sth** *Barons are the lowest rank of the nobility.* ⊃ see also RANKING *noun* **2 B2** [C, U] the position that sb has in the army, NAVY, police, etc: ~ **of sth** *He was soon promoted to the rank of captain.* ◇ *He rose steadily through the ranks and retired as a lieutenant-colonel* ◇ *officers of junior/senior rank* ◇ *officers and other ranks* (= people who are not officers) ◇ *The colonel was stripped of his rank* (= was given a lower position, especially as a punishment). ◇ **in ~** *a military commander similar in rank to a modern general* **3 the ranks** [pl.] the position of ordinary soldiers rather than officers; the army: *He served in the ranks for most of the war.* ◇ *He rose from the ranks* (= from being an ordinary soldier) *to become a warrant officer.* ◇ *a campaign to attract more women into the military ranks*
- **QUALITY 4** [sing.] the degree to which sb/sth is of high quality: *a painter of the first rank* ◇ *Britain is no longer in the front rank of world powers.* ◇ *The findings are arranged in rank order according to performance.*
- **MEMBERS OF GROUP 5 the ranks** [pl.] the members of a particular group or organization: *We have a number of international players in our ranks.* ◇ *At 50, he was forced to join the ranks of the unemployed.* ◇ *There were serious divisions within the party's own ranks.*
- **LINE/ROW 6** [C] a line or row of soldiers, police, etc. standing next to each other: *They watched as ranks of marching infantry passed the window.* **7** [C] a line or row of people or things: *massed ranks of spectators* ◇ *The trees grew in serried ranks* (= very closely together). ⊃ see also TAXI RANK

**IDM** **break 'ranks 1** (of soldiers, police, etc.) to fail to remain in line **2** (of the members of a group) to refuse to support the group or the organization of which they are members ⊃ more at CLOSE¹ *v.*, PULL *v.*
- *verb* (not used in the progressive tenses)
- **GIVE POSITION 1 B2** [T, I] to give sb/sth a particular position on a scale according to quality, importance, success, etc.; to have a position of this kind: ~ **sb/sth** *In most Australian elections, electors are required to rank all candidates.* ◇ ~ **sb/sth + adv./prep.** *The tasks have been ranked in order of difficulty.* ◇ *She is currently the highest ranked player in the world.* ◇ **top-ranked** *players* ◇ ~ **sb/sth as sth** *Forty-five per cent of respondents ranked health as* their number one priority. ◇ ~ **sb/sth as doing sth** *Voters regularly rank education as being more important than defence.* ◇ ~ **(sb/sth) + adj** *At the height of her career she ranked second in the world.* ◇ ~ **sb/sth + noun** *The university is ranked number one in the country for engineering.* ◇ ~ **as sth** *It certainly doesn't rank as his greatest win.* ◇ **+ adv./prep.** *The restaurant ranks among the finest in town.* ◇ *It would certainly rank high on any list of favourite children's books.* ◇ *This must rank with* (= be as good as) *the greatest movies ever made.* ◇ (*NAmE*) *You just don't rank* (= you're not good enough).
- **PUT IN LINE/ROW 2** [T, usually passive] ~ **sth** to arrange objects in a line or row
- *adj.* **1** having a strong unpleasant smell: *The house was full of the rank smell of urine.* **2** (*informal*) very unpleasant: *I think the whole situation's pretty rank.* **3** [only before noun] used to emphasize a particular quality, state, etc: *an example of rank stupidity/hypocrisy* ◇ *The winning horse was a rank outsider.* **4** (of plants, etc.) growing too thickly

**the ˌrank and 'file** *noun* [sing. + sing./pl. v.] **1** the ordinary soldiers who are not officers **2** the ordinary members of an organization: *the rank and file of the workforce* ◇ *rank-and-file members*

**'rank correlation** *noun* [U] (*statistics*) a method for finding to what extent two sets of numbers, each arranged in order, are connected or have an effect on each other

**rank·ing** **C1** /ˈræŋkɪŋ/ *noun, adj.*
- *noun* **1 C1** the position of sb/sth on a scale that shows how good or important they are in relation to other similar people or things, especially in sport: *He has improved his ranking this season from 67th to 30th.* ◇ *She has retained her No.1 world ranking.* **2 the rankings** [pl.] an official list showing the best players of a particular sport in order of how successful they are
- *adj.* (*especially NAmE*) having a high or the highest rank in an organization, etc: *a ranking diplomat* ◇ *He was the ranking officer* (= the most senior officer present at a particular time). ⊃ see also HIGH-RANKING, LOW-RANKING, MIDDLE-RANKING, TOP-RANKING

**ran·kle** /ˈræŋkl/ *verb* [I, T] if sth such as an event or a remark **rankles**, it makes you feel angry or upset for a long time: ~ **(sb)** *Her comments still rankled.* ◇ ~ **with sb** *His decision to sell the land still rankled with her.*

**ran·sack** /ˈrænsæk/ *verb* ~ **sth** to make a place untidy, causing damage, because you are looking for sth **SYN** **turn upside down**: *Burglars ransacked her home.*

**ran·som** /ˈrænsəm/ *noun, verb*
- *noun* [C, U] money that is paid to sb so that they will set free a person who is being kept as a prisoner by them: *The kidnappers demanded a ransom of £50000 from his family.* ◇ *a ransom demand/note* ◇ *ransom money* ◇ *They are refusing to pay ransom for her release.*

**IDM** **hold sb to 'ransom 1** to keep sb as a prisoner and demand that other people pay you an amount of money before you set them free **2** (*disapproving*) to take action that puts sb in a very difficult situation in order to force them to do what you want ⊃ more at KING
- *verb* ~ **sb** to pay money to sb so that they will set free the person that they are keeping as a prisoner: *The kidnapped children were all ransomed and returned home unharmed.*

**ran·som·ware** /ˈrænsəmweə(r); *NAmE* -wer/ *noun* [U] a type of software that is designed to block access to a computer system until a sum of money is paid

**rant** /rænt/ *verb* [I, T] ~ **(on) (about sth)** | ~ **at sb** | **+ speech** (*disapproving*) to speak or complain about sth in a loud and/or angry way ▶ **rant** *noun*

**IDM** **ˌrant and 'rave** (*disapproving*) to show that you are angry by shouting or complaining loudly for a long time

**rant·ings** /ˈræntɪŋz/ *noun* [pl.] loud or angry comments or speeches that continue for a long time

**rap** /ræp/ *noun, verb*
- *noun* **1** [C] a quick, sharp hit or knock: *There was a sharp rap on the door.* **2** [U] a type of popular music with a fast strong rhythm and words which are spoken fast, not sung: *a rap song/artist* **3** [C] *a rap song* **4** [C] (*NAmE, informal*) a criminal CONVICTION (= the fact of being found guilty of a crime): *a police rap sheet* (= a record of the crimes sb has committed) **5** [sing.] (*NAmE, informal*) an unfair judgement on sth or sb: *He denounced the criticisms as 'just one bum*

---

æ cat | ɑː father | e bed | ɜː fur | ə about | ɪ sit | iː see | i happy | ɒ got (*BrE*) | ɔː saw | ʌ cup | ʊ put | uː too

*rap after another.'* ◊ *Wolves get a bad rap, says a woman who owns three.* **IDM** **(give sb/get) a rap on/over/across the 'knuckles** (*informal*) (to give sb/receive) strong criticism for sth: *We got a rap over the knuckles for being late.* **take the 'rap (for sb/sth)** (*informal*) to be blamed or punished, especially for sth you have not done **SYN** **blame**: *She was prepared to take the rap for the shoplifting, though it had been her sister's idea.* ◊ more at BEAT *v.*
- **verb** (-pp-) **1** [I, T] to hit a hard object or surface several times quickly, making a noise: **(+ adv./prep.)** *She rapped angrily on the door.* ◊ **~sth (+ adv./prep.)** *He rapped the table with his pen.* **2** [T] **~sth (out)** | **+ speech** to say sth suddenly and quickly in a loud, angry way: *He walked through the store, rapping out orders to his staff.* **3** [T] **~sb/sth (for sth/for doing sth)** (used mainly in newspapers) to criticize sb severely, usually publicly: *Some of the teachers were rapped for poor performance.* **4** [I, T] **~(sth)** (*music*) to say the words of a rap ➾ see also RAPPER **IDM** **rap sb on/over the 'knuckles** | **rap sb's 'knuckles** (*informal*) to criticize sb for sth

> ▼ HOMOPHONES
>
> **rap ◆ wrap**
> - **rap** *noun*: *Hip-hop and rap have come to dominate the record charts.*
> - **rap** *verb*: *Teachers used to rap misbehaving pupils on the hand with a ruler.*
> - **wrap** *verb*: *We always wrap presents and leave them under the tree on Christmas Eve.*
> - **wrap** *noun*: *Cover the dough with plastic wrap and leave in the refrigerator.*

**ra·pa·cious** /rəˈpeɪʃəs/ *adj.* (*formal, disapproving*) wanting more money or goods than you need or have a right to **SYN** **grasping** ▸ **ra·pa·cious·ly** *adv.* **rap·ac·ity** /-ˈpæsəti/ *noun* [U]: *the rapacity of landowners seeking greater profit*

**rape** ⓘ+ **C1** /reɪp/ *noun, verb*
- *noun* **1** ⓘ+ **C1** [U, C] the crime, typically committed by a man, of forcing sb to have sex with him, especially using violence: *He was charged with rape.* ◊ *a rape victim* ◊ *an increase in the number of reported rapes* ➾ see also DATE RAPE, GANG RAPE, RAPIST, STATUTORY RAPE **2** [sing.] **~(of sth)** (*literary*) the act of destroying an area or damaging its beauty in a way that seems unnecessary **3** (*also* **oilseed 'rape**) [U] a plant with bright yellow flowers, grown as food for farm animals and for its seeds that are used to make oil
- *verb* ⓘ+ **C1** **~sb** (especially of a man) to force sb to have sex with him when they do not want to by threatening them or using violence ➾ see also GANG-RAPE, RAPIST

**rape·seed** /ˈreɪpsiːd/ [U] seeds of the rape plant, used mainly for cooking oil ➾ see also CANOLA

**rapid** ⓘ **B2** ⓦ /ˈræpɪd/ *adj.* happening quickly or in a short period of time: *rapid change/expansion/growth/development* ◊ *a rapid rise/increase/decline in sales* ◊ *The patient made a rapid recovery.* ◊ *a rapid pulse/heartbeat* ◊ *The guard fired four shots in rapid succession.* ◊ *Work proceeded at a rapid pace.* ◊ *The disease is spreading at a rapid rate.* ➾ note at FAST ▸ **rap·id·ity** /rəˈpɪdəti/ *noun* [U]: *the rapidity of economic growth* ◊ *The disease is spreading with alarming rapidity.*

**rapid-'fire** *adj.* [only before noun] **1** (of questions, comments, etc.) spoken very quickly, one after the other **2** (of a gun) able to shoot bullets very quickly, one after the other

**rap·id·ly** ⓘ **B2** ⓞ /ˈræpɪdli/ *adv.* very quickly; at a great rate: *to increase/spread/expand rapidly* ◊ *to change/develop/evolve rapidly* ◊ *a rapidly growing economy* ◊ *Crime figures are rising rapidly.* ◊ *The technology is rapidly changing.*

**rapid-re'sponse** *adj.* [only before noun] having the necessary training and equipment to be able to act quickly when there is an emergency such as an accident, an attack or a natural disaster: *a UN rapid-response unit* ◊ *rapid-response systems for early detection of the virus*

1275 **rare earth**

**rapids** /ˈræpɪdz/ *noun* [pl.] part of a river where the water flows very fast, usually over rocks: *to shoot the rapids* (= to travel quickly over them in a boat)

**rapid 'transit** *noun* [U] (*especially NAmE*) the system of fast public transport in cities, especially the SUBWAY ➾ see also TRANSIT *noun* (3)

**ra·pier** /ˈreɪpiə(r)/ *noun* a long, thin, light SWORD with a sharp point: (*figurative*) *rapier wit* (= very quick and sharp)

**rap·ist** /ˈreɪpɪst/ *noun* a person who forces sb to have sex when they do not want to (= RAPES them)

**rap·pel** /ræˈpel/ (*NAmE*) (*BrE* **ab·seil**) *verb* [I] (**-ll-**) **~(down, off, etc. sth)** to go down a steep CLIFF or rock while attached to a rope, pushing against the slope or rock with your feet ▸ **rap·pel** (*NAmE*) (*BrE* **ab·seil**) *noun* **rap·pel·ling** /-ˈpelɪŋ/ (*NAmE*) (*BrE* **abseiling**) *noun* [U]

**rap·per** /ˈræpə(r)/ *noun* a person who speaks the words of a RAP song

**rap·port** /ræˈpɔː(r)/ *noun* [sing., U] **~(with sb)** | **~(between A and B)** a friendly relationship in which people understand each other very well: *She understood the importance of establishing a close rapport with clients.*

**rap·por·teur** /ˌræpɔːˈtɜː(r); *NAmE* -pɔːrˈt-/ *noun* (from French, *specialist*) a person officially chosen by an organization to investigate a problem and report on it: *the UN special rapporteur on human rights*

**rap·proche·ment** /ræˈprɒʃmɒ̃, -ˈprəʊʃ-; *NAmE* ˌræprəʊʃˈmɑːn, -prɑːʃ-/ *noun* [sing., U] (from French, *formal*) a situation in which the relationship between two countries or groups of people becomes more friendly after a period during which they were enemies: **~(with sb)** *policies aimed at bringing about a rapprochement with China* ◊ **~(between A and B)** *There now seems little chance of rapprochement between the warring factions.* ➾ WORDFINDER NOTE at ALLY

**rapt** /ræpt/ *adj.* so interested in one particular thing that you are not aware of anything else: *a rapt audience* ◊ *She listened to the speaker with rapt attention.* ▸ **rapt·ly** *adv.*

**rap·tor** /ˈræptə(r)/ *noun* (*specialist*) any BIRD OF PREY (= a bird that kills other creatures for food)

**rap·ture** /ˈræptʃə(r)/ *noun* [U] (*formal*) a feeling of extreme pleasure and happiness **SYN** **delight**: *Charles listened with rapture to her singing.* ◊ *The children gazed at her in rapture.*
**IDM** **be in, go into, etc. 'raptures (about/over sb/sth)** to feel or express extreme pleasure or enthusiasm for sb/sth: *The critics went into raptures about her performance.* ◊ *The last minute goal sent the fans into raptures.*

**rap·tur·ous** /ˈræptʃərəs/ *adj.* [usually before noun] expressing extreme pleasure or enthusiasm for sb/sth **SYN** **ecstatic**: *rapturous applause* ➾ SYNONYMS at EXCITED ▸ **rap·tur·ous·ly** *adv.*

**rare** ⓘ **B1** /reə(r); *NAmE* rer/ *adj.* (**rarer, rar·est**) **1** ⓘ+ not done, happening, etc. very often: *a rare disease/occurrence/event* ◊ **it is~for sb/sth to do sth** *It's extremely rare for it to be this hot in April.* ◊ **it is~to do sth** *It is rare to find such loyalty these days.* ◊ *On the rare occasions when they met he hardly even dared speak to her.* ◊ *The bacteria can cause infection and, in rare cases, blindness.* ◊ *The current exhibition offers a rare opportunity to see his original drawings.* ◊ *In a rare moment of candour, she admitted that mistakes had been made.* ◊ *It was a rare* (= very great) *honour to be made a fellow of the college.* **2** ⓘ+ **B1** existing only in small numbers and therefore valuable or interesting: *a rare book* ◊ *a rare coin/stamp* ◊ *a rare breed* ◊ *a rare plant/bird/animal* ◊ *This species is extremely rare.* **3** (of meat) cooked for only a short time so that the inside is still red ➾ compare WELL DONE ➾ see also RARITY

**rare 'earth** (*also* **rare earth 'element**) *noun* any one of a group of chemical elements that have similar properties and tend to occur together in nature: *We import all of our rare earths from China.* ◊ *The bones were analysed for their rare earth element contents.* ◊ *Rare earth metals are used in virtually every electronic device.*

# rarefied

**rar·efied** /ˈreərɪfaɪd; NAmE ˈrer-/ adj. [usually before noun] **1** (often disapproving) understood or experienced by only a very small group of people who share a particular area of knowledge or activity: *the rarefied atmosphere of academic life* **2** (of air) containing less OXYGEN than usual

**rare 'gas** noun (chemistry) = NOBLE GAS

**rare·ly** ⓘ B1 /ˈreəli; NAmE ˈrerli/ adv. not very often: *She is rarely seen in public nowadays.* ◇ *The term is rarely used today.* ◇ *Irish coins minted before 1100 are rarely found.* ◇ *I only rarely get a chance to go to the theatre.* ◇ *We rarely agree on what to do.* ◇ *a rarely performed play* ◇ (formal) *Rarely has a debate attracted so much media attention.*

**rar·ing** /ˈreərɪŋ; NAmE ˈrer-/ adj. **~ to do sth** (informal) very enthusiastic about starting to do sth: *The new recruits arrived early, all dressed up and raring to go* (= to start). ◇ *She is raring to get back to work after her operation.*

**rar·ity** /ˈreərəti; NAmE ˈrer-/ noun (pl. -ies) **1** [C] a person or thing that is unusual and is therefore often valuable or interesting: *Women are still something of a rarity in senior positions in business.* ◇ *His collection of plants contains many rarities.* **2** (also less frequent **rare·ness** /ˈreənəs; NAmE ˈrern-/) [U] the quality of being rare: *The value of antiques will depend on their condition and rarity.*

**ras·cal** /ˈrɑːskl; NAmE ˈræs-/ noun **1** (humorous) a person, especially a child or man, who shows a lack of respect for other people and enjoys playing tricks on them: *Come here, you little rascal!* **2** (old-fashioned) a dishonest man ▸ **ras·cal·ly** /ˈrɑːskəli; NAmE ˈræs-/ adj.

**rash** /ræʃ/ noun, adj.
- noun **1** [C, usually sing.] an area of red spots on a person's skin, caused by an illness or a reaction to sth: *I woke up covered in a rash.* ◇ *I come out in a rash* (= a rash appears on my skin) *if I eat chocolate.* ◇ *The sun brought her out in* (= caused) *an itchy rash.* ◇ *a heat rash* (= caused by heat) ⇨ compare SPOT **2** [sing.] **~ (of sth)** a lot of sth; a series of unpleasant things that happen over a short period of time SYN **spate**: *a rash of movies about life in prison* ◇ *There has been a rash of burglaries in the area over the last month.*
- adj. (of people or their actions) doing sth that may not be sensible without first thinking about the possible results; done in this way SYN **reckless**: *a rash young man* ◇ **~ (to do sth)** *It would be rash to assume that everyone will agree with you on this.* ◇ *Think twice before doing anything rash.* ◇ *This is what happens when you make rash decisions.* ▸ **rash·ly** adv.: *She had rashly promised to lend him the money.* **rash·ness** noun [U]: *He bitterly regretted his rashness.*

**rash·er** /ˈræʃə(r)/ noun (especially BrE) a thin slice of BACON (= meat from the back or sides of a pig)

**rasp** /rɑːsp; NAmE ræsp/ noun, verb
- noun **1** [sing.] a rough, unpleasant sound **2** [C] a metal tool with a long BLADE covered with rows of sharp points, used for making rough surfaces smooth
- verb **1** [T, I] to say sth in a rough, unpleasant voice SYN **croak**: + **speech** '*Where have you been?*' *she rasped.* ◇ **~(sth) (out)** *He rasped out some instructions.* **2** [I] to make a rough unpleasant sound SYN **grate**: *a rasping cough/voice* **3** [T] **~ sth** to rub a surface with a rasp or with sth rough that works or feels like a rasp: *The wind rasped his face.*

**rasp·berry** /ˈrɑːzbəri; NAmE ˈræzberi/ noun (pl. -ies) **1** a small, dark red soft fruit that grows on bushes: *raspberry jam* ⇨ VISUAL VOCAB page V4 **2** (NAmE also **Bronx 'cheer**) (informal) a rude sound made by sticking out the tongue and blowing: *to blow a raspberry at sb*

**raspy** /ˈrɑːspi; NAmE ˈræs-/ adj. (of sb's voice) having a rough sound, as if the person has a SORE throat (= a painful throat because of an infection) SYN **croaky**

**Ras·ta·far·ian** /ˌræstəˈfeəriən; NAmE ˌrɑːstəˈfer-/ (also informal **Rasta** /ˈræstə; NAmE ˈrɑːs-/) noun a member of a Jamaican religious group that WORSHIPS the former Emperor of Ethiopia, Haile Selassie, and that believes that black people will one day return to Africa. Rastafarians often wear DREADLOCKS and have other particular patterns of behaviour and dress. ▸ **Ras·ta·far·ian** (also informal **Rasta**) adj. **Ras·ta·far·ian·ism** noun [U]

**rat** B2 /ræt/ noun, verb
- noun **1** B2 a small animal with a long tail, that looks like a large mouse, usually considered a PEST (= an animal which is disliked because it destroys food or spreads disease): *rat poison* ⇨ see also BROWN RAT, CANE RAT, COMMON RAT, PACK RAT, WATER RAT **2** (informal, disapproving) an unpleasant person, especially sb who treats their partner or friends badly, for example by leaving them or cheating them IDM see SINK v., SMELL v.
- verb (-tt-)
PHRV **'rat on sb** (NAmE also **rat sb out (to sb)**) (informal, disapproving) to tell sb in authority about sth wrong that sb else has done: *Where I come from, you don't rat on your friends.* **'rat on sth** (BrE, informal) to not do sth that you have agreed or promised to do SYN **renege**: *The government is accused of ratting on its promises to the unemployed.* **rat sb↔out (to sb)** (especially NAmE, informal, disapproving) = RAT ON SB: *Someone ratted us out to the police.*

**rata** ⇨ PRO RATA

**rata·touille** /ˌrætəˈtuːi, -ˈtwiː/ noun [U, C] a dish of onions, PEPPERS, AUBERGINES, COURGETTES and tomatoes cooked together

**rat·bag** /ˈrætbæg/ noun (BrE, slang) an unpleasant or horrible person

**ratchet** /ˈrætʃɪt/ noun, verb
- noun a wheel or bar with teeth along the edge and a metal piece that fits between the teeth, allowing movement in one direction only
- verb
PHRV **ratchet (sth)↔up** to increase, or make sth increase, repeatedly and by small amounts: *Overuse of credit cards has ratcheted up consumer debt to unacceptable levels.*

**rate** ⓘ A2 ⓞ /reɪt/ noun, verb
- noun **1** A2 [C] a measurement of the speed at which sth happens: **~ (of sth)** *Figures published today show another fall in the rate of inflation.* ◇ **at a/the ~ of sth** *Most people walk at an average rate of five kilometres an hour.* ◇ **at a ... ~ (that)** ... *At the rate you work, you'll never finish!* ⇨ see also BURN RATE, HEART RATE **2** A2 [C] a measurement of the number of times sth happens or sth does sth during a particular period: *We have seen a reduction in the crime rate over the last 12 months.* ◇ *a high success/failure rate* ◇ *the youth unemployment rate* ◇ **~ of sth** *a high/low/rising rate of unemployment* ◇ **at a/the ~ of sth** *Local businesses are closing at the rate of three a year.* ⇨ see also BIRTH RATE, BOUNCE RATE, CHURN RATE, DEATH RATE **3** B1 [C] a fixed amount of money that is charged or paid for sth: *exchange/interest/tax rates* ◇ *We offer special reduced rates for students.* ◇ *to cut/reduce/increase/raise interest rates* ◇ **~ of sth** *a low/high hourly rate of pay* ◇ *the basic rate of tax* (= the lowest amount that is paid by everyone) ◇ **at a ~ (of sth)** *We had to borrow money at a high rate of interest.* ◇ *a fixed-rate mortgage* (= one in which the amount of money paid back each month is fixed for a particular period) ⇨ see also BANK RATE, BASE RATE, FLAT RATE, LENDING RATE, PEAK RATE, PIECE RATE, PRIME RATE, SAVINGS RATE **4 rates** (also **business rates**) [pl.] (in the UK) a tax paid by businesses to a local authority for land and buildings that they use HELP In Northern Ireland **rates** are also a tax paid by anyone who owns a house. In the rest of the UK, **rates** on private homes have been replaced by the COUNCIL TAX. ⇨ SYNONYMS at TAX ⇨ see also FIRST-RATE, SECOND-RATE, THIRD-RATE
IDM **at ˌany 'rate** (informal) **1** used to say that a particular fact is true despite what has happened in the past or what may happen in the future: *Well, that's one good piece of news at any rate.* ◇ *I may be away on business next week but at any rate I'll be back by Friday.* **2** used to show that you are being more accurate about sth that you have just said: *He said he'll be coming tomorrow. At any rate, I think that's what he said.* **3** used to show that what you have just said is not as important as what you are going to say:

There were maybe 60 or 70 people there. **At any rate**, the room was packed. **at a rate of ˈknots** (*BrE*, *informal*) very quickly **at ˈthis / ˈthat rate** (*informal*) used to say what will happen if a particular situation continues to develop in the same way: *At this rate, we'll soon be bankrupt.* ⊃ more at GOING *adj.*

■ **verb** (not used in the progressive tenses) **1** [T, I] to have or think that sb/sth has a particular level of quality, value, etc: **~ sb / sth + adv. / prep.** *The university is highly rated for its research.* ◇ *They rated him highly as a colleague.* ◇ **~ sb / sth + adj.** *Voters continue to rate education high on their list of priorities.* ◇ **~ sb / sth (as) sth** *The show was rated (as) a success by critics and audiences.* ◇ **~ as sth** *The match rated as one of their worst defeats.* ◇ **+ adj.** *I'm afraid our needs do not rate very high with this administration.* **2** [T] **~ sth** (*informal*) to think that sb/sth is good: *What did you think of the movie? I didn't rate it myself.* ◇ *How did you rate her speech?* **3** [T, usually passive] to place sb/sth in a particular position on a scale in relation to similar people or things SYN **rank**: **be rated (+ adv. / prep.)** *The schools were rated according to their exam results.* ◇ *The difficulty of each exercise is rated on a scale of 1 to 5.* ◇ *It's a chance to watch six top-rated players.* ◇ **be rated + noun** *She is currently rated number two in the world.* **4** [T] **~ sth** to be good, important, etc. enough to be treated in a particular way SYN **merit**: *The incident didn't even rate a mention in the press.* **5** [T, usually passive] to state that a film or video is suitable for a particular audience: **be rated + noun** *The cartoon was rated PG.* ⊃ see also X-RATED, ZERO-RATED

▼ SYNONYMS

**rate**
charge • fee • rent • fine • fare • toll • rental
These are all words for an amount of money that is charged or paid for sth.

**rate** a fixed amount of money that is asked or paid for sth: *a low hourly rate of pay* ◇ *interest rates*

**charge** an amount of money that is asked for goods or services: *an admission charge*

**fee** (*rather formal*) an amount of money that you have to pay for professional advice or services, to go to a school or college, or to join an organization: *legal fees* ◇ *an annual membership fee*

**rent** an amount of money that you regularly have to pay for use of a building or room. NOTE In American English, **rent** can be used to mean **rental**: *The weekly rent on the car was over $300.*

**fine** a sum of money that must be paid as punishment for breaking a law or rule: *a parking fine*

**fare** the money that you pay to travel by bus, plane, taxi, etc.

**toll** an amount of money that you have to pay to use a particular road or bridge.

**rental** an amount of money that you have to pay to use sth for a particular period of time.

RENT OR RENTAL?
In British English **rent** is only money paid to use a building or room; for other items use **rental**. In American English **rent** can be used for both, but **rental** is still more common for other items.

PATTERNS
- (a) rate / charge / fee / rent / fine / fare / toll / rental **for** sth
- (a) rate / charge / fee / rent / toll / rental **on** sth
- **at** a rate / charge / fee / rent / fare / rental of …
- **for** a charge / fee
- to **pay** (a) rate / charge / fee / rent / fine / fare / toll / rental
- to **charge** (a) rate / fee / rent / fare / toll / rental

ˈrate cap *noun* (in the US) a limit placed on the amount of interest banks, etc. may charge

ˈrate·pay·er /ˈreɪtpeɪə(r)/ *noun* **1** (in the UK in the past) a person who paid taxes to the local authority on the buildings and land they owned **2** (in the US) a person who pays for services like electricity, gas, water, etc. to be provided for their home

**ra·ther** ❶ A2 ❷ /ˈrɑːðə(r); *NAmE* ˈræð-/ *adv.*, *exclamation*

■ *adv.* **1** A2 used to mean 'fairly' or 'to some degree', often when you are disappointed, surprised or expressing slight criticism: *rather odd / strange / unusual* ◇ *a rather large sum of money* ◇ *A rather small number of people turned up.* ◇ *They took a rather different approach.* ◇ *I thought it was a rather good idea.* ◇ *The instructions were rather complicated.* ◇ *She fell and hurt her leg rather badly.* ◇ *I didn't fail the exam; in fact I did rather well!* ◇ *It was a rather difficult question.* ◇ *It was rather a difficult question.* ◇ *He looks rather like his father.* ◇ *The patient has responded to the treatment rather better than expected.* ◇ *He was conscious that he was talking rather too much.* ⊃ note at QUITE **2** used with a verb to make a statement sound less strong: *I've always rather liked Charlie.* ◇ *I rather suspect we're making a mistake.* ◇ *We were rather hoping you'd be able to do it by Friday.* **3** B2 used to correct sth you have said, or to give more accurate information: *She worked as a secretary, or rather, a personal assistant.* ◇ *In the end he had to walk—or rather run—to the office.* ⊃ LANGUAGE BANK at I.E. **4** B2 used to introduce an idea that is different or opposite to the idea that you have stated previously: *The walls were not white, but rather a sort of dirty grey.* IDM **rather than** B1 instead of sb / sth: *I think I'll have a cold drink rather than coffee.* ◇ *Why didn't you ask for help, rather than trying to do it on your own?* **ˈrather you, him, etc. than ˈme** (*informal*) used for saying that you would not like to do sth that another person is going to do: *'I'm going climbing tomorrow.' 'Rather you than me!'* **would rather … (than)** B2 (usually reduced to *'d rather*) would prefer to: *She'd rather die than give a speech.* ◇ *'Do you want to come with us?' 'No, I'd rather not.'* ◇ *Would you rather walk or take the bus?* ◇ *'Do you mind if I smoke?' 'Well, I'd rather you didn't.'* ⊃ EXPRESS YOURSELF at PREFER

■ *exclamation* /ˌrɑːˈðɜː(r)/ (*BrE*, *old-fashioned*) used to agree with sb's suggestion: *'How about a trip to the beach?' 'Rather!'*

**rat·ify** /ˈrætɪfaɪ/ *verb* (**rati·fies**, **rati·fy·ing**, **rati·fied**, **rati·fied**) **~ sth** to make an agreement officially or legally VALID by voting for or signing it: *The treaty was ratified by all the member states.* ▸ **rati·fi·ca·tion** /ˌrætɪfɪˈkeɪʃn/ *noun* [U]

**rat·ing** ❷+ B2 W /ˈreɪtɪŋ/ *noun* **1** ❷+ B2 [C] a measurement of how good, popular, important, etc. sb / sth is, especially in relation to other people or things: *The poll gave an approval rating of 39 per cent for the president.* ◇ *Education has been given a high-priority rating by the new administration.* ⊃ see also CREDIT RATING **2 the ratings** [pl.] a set of figures that show how many people watch or listen to a particular television or radio programme, used to show how popular a programme is: *The show has gone up in the ratings.* **3** [C] a number or letter that shows which groups of people a particular film is suitable for: *The film was given a 15 rating by British censors.* ◇ *The movie carries an R rating.* **4** [C] (*BrE*) a sailor in the NAVY who is not an officer

**ratio** ❷+ C1 ❷ /ˈreɪʃiəʊ/ *noun* (*pl.* **-os**) the relationship between two groups of people or things that is represented by two numbers showing how much larger one group is than the other: *The school has a very high teacher-student ratio.* ◇ **~ of A to B** *What is the ratio of men to women in the department?* ◇ *The ratio of applications to available places currently stands at 100:1.*

**ra·tion** /ˈræʃn/ *noun*, *verb*

■ *noun* **1** [C] a fixed amount of food, fuel, etc. that you are officially allowed to have when there is not enough for everyone to have as much as they want, for example during a war: *the weekly butter ration* **2 rations** [pl.] a fixed amount of food given regularly to a soldier or to sb who is in a place where there is not much food available: *We're on short rations* (= allowed less than usual) *until fresh supplies arrive.* ◇ *Once these latest rations run out, the country will again face hunger and starvation.* **3** [sing.] **~ (of sth)** an amount of sth that is thought to be normal or fair: *As part of the diet, allow yourself a small daily ration of sugar.* ◇ *I've had my ration of problems for one day—you deal with it!*

■ *verb* [often passive] to limit the amount of sth that sb is allowed to have, especially because there is not enough of

# rational

it available: *be rationed Eggs were rationed during the war.* ◇ **be rationed to sth** *The villagers are rationed to two litres of water a day.* ⊃ see also RATIONING

**ra·tion·al** /ˈræʃnəl/ *adj.* **1** (of behaviour, ideas, etc.) based on reason rather than emotions: *a rational argument/choice/decision* ◇ *rational analysis/thought* ◇ *There is no rational explanation for his actions.* **2** (of a person) able to think clearly and make decisions based on reason rather than emotions **SYN** **reasonable**: *No rational person would ever behave like that.* **OPP** **irrational** ▶ **ra·tion·al·ity** /ˌræʃəˈnæləti/ *noun* [U]: *the rationality of his argument* **ra·tion·al·ly** /ˈræʃnəli/ *adv.*: *to act/behave/think rationally* ◇ *She argued her case calmly and rationally.*

**ra·tion·ale** /ˌræʃəˈnɑːl; *NAmE* -ˈnæl/ *noun* (**behind/for/of sth**) (*formal*) the principles or reasons which explain a particular decision, course of action, belief, etc. **SYN** **reason**: *What is the rationale behind these new exams?*

**ra·tion·al·ism** /ˈræʃnəlɪzəm/ *noun* [U] (*philosophy*) the belief that all behaviour, opinions, etc. should be based on reason rather than on emotions or religious beliefs

**ra·tion·al·ist** /ˈræʃnəlɪst/ *noun* a person who believes in rationalism ▶ **ra·tion·al·ist** (*also* **ra·tion·al·is·tic** /ˌræʃnəˈlɪstɪk/) *adj.* [usually before noun]: *a rationalistic position*

**ra·tion·al·ize** (*BrE also* **-ise**) /ˈræʃnəlaɪz/ *verb* **1** [T, I] **~(sth)** to find or try to find a logical reason to explain why sb thinks, behaves, etc. in a way that is difficult to understand: *an attempt to rationalize his violent behaviour* **2** [T, I] **~(sth)** (*BrE*) to make changes to a business, system, etc. in order to make it more efficient, especially by spending less money: *Twenty workers lost their jobs when the department was rationalized.* ⊃ SYNONYMS at CUT ▶ **ra·tion·al·iza·tion, -isa·tion** /ˌræʃnəlaɪˈzeɪʃn; *NAmE* -ləˈz-/ *noun* [U, C]: *No amount of rationalization could justify his actions.* ◇ *a need for rationalization of the industry*

**ra·tion·ing** /ˈræʃənɪŋ/ *noun* [U] the policy of limiting the amount of food, fuel, etc. that people are allowed to have when there is not enough for everyone to have as much as they want

**ˈrat pack** *noun* [sing. + sing./pl. v.] (*BrE, disapproving*) journalists and photographers who follow famous people around in a way which makes their lives unpleasant

**the ˈrat race** *noun* [sing.] (*disapproving*) the way of life of people living and working in a large city where people compete in an aggressive way with each other in order to be more successful, earn more money, etc.

**ˈrat run** *noun* (*BrE, informal*) a small road, especially one with houses on it, used by drivers during busy times when the main roads are full of traffic

**rats** /ræts/ *exclamation* (*informal*) used to show that you are annoyed about sth: *Rats! I forgot my glasses.*

**rat·tan** /ræˈtæn; ˈrætæn/ *noun* [U] a south-east Asian climbing plant with long thin strong STEMS used especially for making furniture: *a rattan chair*

**rat·tle** /ˈrætl/ *verb, noun*
- *verb* (*informal*) **1** [I, T] **~(sth)** to make a series of short loud sounds when shaking or hitting against sth hard; to make sth do this: *Every time a bus went past, the windows rattled.* **2** [I] **+ adv./prep.** (of a vehicle) to make a series of short loud sounds as it moves somewhere: *A convoy of trucks rattled by.* **3** [T] **~sb** to make sb nervous or frightened **SYN** **unnerve**: *He was clearly rattled by the question.* ⊃ see also SABRE-RATTLING
**IDM** **ˌrattle sb's ˈcage** (*informal*) to annoy sb: *Who's rattled his cage?*
**PHRV** **ˌrattle aˈround | ˌrattle aˈround sth** (*informal*) to be living, working, etc. in a room or building that is too big: *She spent the last few years alone, rattling around the old family home.* **ˌrattle sth↔ˈoff** to say sth from memory without having to think too hard: *She can rattle off the names of all the presidents of the US.* **ˌrattle ˈon (about sth)** (*informal*) to talk continuously about sth that is not important or interesting, especially in an annoying way
- *noun* **1** (*also* **ˈrat·tling**) [usually sing.] a series of short loud sounds made when hard objects hit against each other: *the rattle of gunfire* ◇ *From the kitchen came a rattling of cups and saucers.* ⊃ see also DEATH RATTLE **2** a baby's toy that makes a series of short loud sounds when it is shaken **3** a wooden object that is held in one hand and makes a series of short loud sounds when you turn it round, used, for example, by people watching a sports game

**ˈrattle·snake** /ˈrætlsneɪk/ (*also informal* **ˈrat·tler** /ˈrætlə(r)/) *noun* a poisonous American snake that makes a noise like a rattle with its tail when it is angry or afraid

**ratty** /ˈræti/ *adj.* (**rat·tier, rat·ti·est**) **1** (*BrE, informal*) becoming angry very easily **SYN** **grumpy, irritable**: *He gets ratty if he doesn't get enough sleep.* **2** (*NAmE, informal*) in bad condition **SYN** **shabby**: *long ratty hair* ◇ *a ratty old pair of jeans* **3** looking like a RAT

**rau·cous** /ˈrɔːkəs/ *adj.* sounding loud and rough: *raucous laughter* ◇ *a raucous voice* ◇ *a group of raucous young men* ▶ **rau·cous·ly** *adv.* **rau·cous·ness** *noun* [U]

**raunchy** /ˈrɔːntʃi/ *adj.* (*informal*) **1** intended to be sexually exciting **SYN** **sexy**: *a raunchy magazine* ◇ *Their stage act is a little too raunchy for television.* **2** (*NAmE*) looking dirty and untidy: *a raunchy old man*

**rav·age** /ˈrævɪdʒ/ *verb* [usually passive] **~sth** to damage sth badly **SYN** **devastate**: *a country ravaged by civil war*

**rav·ages** /ˈrævɪdʒɪz/ *noun* [pl.] **the ~of sth** (*formal*) the DESTRUCTION caused by sth: *the ravages of war* ◇ *Her looks had not survived the ravages of time.*

**rave** /reɪv/ *verb, noun*
- *verb* **1** [I, T] **~(about sb/sth) | + speech** to talk or write about sth in a very enthusiastic way: *The critics raved about his performance in 'Hamlet'.* **2** [I, T] **~(on) (at sb) (about sth) | + speech** to shout in a loud and emotional way at sb because you are angry with them; to talk or shout in a way that is not logical or sensible: *She was shouting and raving at them.* ◇ *He wandered the streets raving at passers-by.* **IDM** see RANT
- *noun* **1** (in the UK) a large party, held outside or in an empty building, at which people dance to fast electronic music and often take illegal drugs: *an all-night rave* **2** (*NAmE*) = RAVE REVIEW

**raven** /ˈreɪvn/ *noun, adj.*
- *noun* a large bird of the CROW family, with shiny black feathers and a rough, unpleasant call
- *adj.* [only before noun] (*literary*) (of hair) shiny and black: *raven-haired*

**raven·ing** /ˈrævnɪŋ/ *adj.* (*literary*) (especially of animals) aggressive and hungry: *He says the media are ravening wolves.*

**rav·en·ous** /ˈrævənəs/ *adj.* **1** (of a person or an animal) extremely hungry **SYN** **starving**: *What's for lunch? I'm absolutely ravenous.* **2** [only before noun] (of HUNGER) very great: *a ravenous appetite* ▶ **rav·en·ous·ly** *adv.*

**raver** /ˈreɪvə(r)/ *noun* (*BrE, informal*) **1** (*often humorous*) a person who likes going out and who has an exciting social life **2** a person who goes to RAVES

**ˈrave reˌview** (*NAmE also* **rave**) *noun* an article in a newspaper or magazine that is very enthusiastic about a particular film, book, etc.

**ra·vine** /rəˈviːn/ *noun* a deep, very narrow valley with steep sides

**rav·ing** /ˈreɪvɪŋ/ *adj., adv.*
- *adj.* [only before noun] **1** (of a person) talking or behaving in a way that shows they are crazy: *The man's a raving lunatic.* **2** used to emphasize a particular state or quality: *She's no raving beauty.*
- *adv.* **IDM** **(stark) raving ˈmad/ˈbonkers** (*informal*) completely crazy

**rav·ings** /ˈreɪvɪŋz/ *noun* [pl.] words that have no meaning, spoken by sb who is crazy: *He dismissed her words as the ravings of a hysterical woman.*

**ravi·oli** /ˌræviˈəʊli/ *noun* [U] PASTA in the shape of small squares filled with meat, cheese, etc., usually served with a sauce

**rav·ish** /ˈrævɪʃ/ *verb* (*literary*) **1** **~sb** (of a man) to force a woman to have sex **SYN** **rape** **2** [usually passive] **~sb** to give sb great pleasure

**rav·ish·ing** /ˈrævɪʃɪŋ/ adj. extremely beautiful SYN **gorgeous**: *a ravishing blonde* ▸ **rav·ish·ing·ly** adv.: *ravishingly beautiful*

**raw** 0 B2 /rɔː/ adj., noun
■ adj.
- FOOD **1** B2 not cooked: *raw meat* ◊ *raw eggs/vegetables* ◊ *These fish are often eaten raw.*
- MATERIALS **2** B2 [usually before noun] in its natural state; not yet changed, used or made into sth else: *raw sewage* ◊ *raw sugar/milk/cotton*
- INFORMATION **3** [usually before noun] not yet organized into a form in which it can be easily used or understood: *This information is only raw data and will need further analysis.*
- EMOTIONS/QUALITIES **4** [usually before noun] powerful and natural; not trained or showing control: *songs full of raw emotion* ◊ *He started with nothing but raw talent and determination.*
- PART OF BODY **5** red and painful because the skin has been damaged: *There were raw patches on her feet where the shoes had rubbed.* ⇨ SYNONYMS at PAINFUL
- PERSON **6** [usually before noun] new to a job or an activity and therefore without experience or skill: *a raw beginner* ◊ *raw recruits* (= for example, in the army)
- WEATHER **7** very cold: *a raw north wind* ◊ *It had been a wet, raw winter.*
- DESCRIPTION **8** honest, direct and sometimes SHOCKING: *a raw portrayal of working-class life* ◊ (*NAmE*) *raw language* (= containing many sexual details) ▸ **raw·ness** noun [U]
IDM **a raw ˈdeal** the fact of sb being treated unfairly: *Older workers often get a raw deal.*

■ noun
IDM **catch/touch sb on the ˈraw** (*BrE*) to upset sb by reminding them of sth they are particularly sensitive about **in the ˈraw 1** in a way that does not hide the unpleasant aspects of sth: *He spent a couple of months on the streets to experience life in the raw.* **2** (*especially NAmE*) with no clothes on SYN **naked** ⇨ more at NERVE *n.*

**raw·hide** /ˈrɔːhaɪd/ noun [U] natural leather that has not had any special treatment

**raw maˈterial** noun [C, U] a basic material that is used to make a product: *We have had problems with the supply of raw materials to the factory.* ◊ *These trees provide the raw material for high-quality paper.* ◊ (*figurative*) *The writer uses her childhood as raw material for this novel.* ⇨ WORDFINDER NOTE at INDUSTRY

**ray** ⇨ C1 /reɪ/ noun **1** ⇨ C1 a narrow line of light, heat or other energy: *the sun's rays* ◊ *ultraviolet rays* ◊ *The windows were shining in the reflected rays of the setting sun.* ⇨ HOMOPHONES at RAZE ⇨ WORDFINDER NOTE at SUN ⇨ see also BLU-RAY, CATHODE RAY TUBE, COSMIC RAYS, GAMMA RAYS at GAMMA RADIATION, X-RAY noun **2** ⇨ C1 ~ **of** sth a small amount of sth good or of sth that you are hoping for SYN **glimmer**: *There was just one small ray of hope.* **3** a sea fish with a large broad flat body and a long tail, that is used for food **4** (*also* **re**) (*music*) the second note of a MAJOR SCALE
IDM **catch/get/grab some ˈrays** (*informal*) to sit or lie in the sun, especially in order to get a SUNTAN **a ray of ˈsunshine** (*informal*) a person or thing that makes life brighter or more cheerful

**ˈray gun** noun (in SCIENCE FICTION stories) a gun that kills or injures people by sending out harmful rays

**rayon** /ˈreɪɒn; *NAmE* ˈreɪɑːn/ noun [U] a FIBRE made from CELLULOSE; a smooth material made from this, used for making clothes

**raze** /reɪz/ verb [usually passive] ~ **sth** to completely destroy a building, town, etc. so that nothing is left: *The village was razed to the ground.*

▼ **HOMOPHONES**
**raise · rays · raze** /reɪz/
- **raise** verb: *Raise your hand if you know the answer.*
- **raise** noun: *You work so hard, you deserve a raise!*
- **rays** noun (plural of RAY): *Rays of sunlight streamed through the window.*
- **raze** verb: *They wanted to raze the old town centre to make room for new architecture.*

---

1279 **reach**

**razor** /ˈreɪzə(r)/ noun an instrument that is used for removing hair by SHAVING: *an electric razor* ◊ *a disposable razor* ⇨ compare SHAVER ⇨ see also ELECTRIC RAZOR
IDM **be on the ˈrazor's edge | be on a ˈrazor edge** to be in a difficult situation where any mistake may be very dangerous

**ˈrazor blade** noun a thin sharp piece of metal that is used in a razor, especially one that can be thrown away when it is no longer sharp ⇨ picture at BLADE

**razor-ˈsharp** adj. **1** extremely sharp: *razor-sharp teeth* **2** showing that sb is extremely intelligent: *a razor-sharp mind*

**razor-ˈthin** adj. (*NAmE*) (of a victory in an election, etc.) won by a very small number of votes

**ˈrazor wire** noun [U] strong wire with small sharp points or BLADES sticking out, placed on top of walls and around areas of land to keep people out

**razz·ma·tazz** /ˌræzməˈtæz/ (*also* **raz·za·ma·tazz** /ˌræzəməˈtæz/) (*also* **razzle-ˈdazzle**) noun [U] *informal* a lot of noisy, exciting activity that is intended to attract people's attention: *The documentary focuses on the razzmatazz of an American political campaign.*

**RBI** /ˌɑː biː ˈaɪ; *NAmE* ˌɑːr/ noun (in baseball) a run scored by a player in the field as a result of another player who has hit the ball and who gets credit for the run (the abbreviation for 'run batted in')

**RC** /ˌɑː ˈsiː; *NAmE* ˌɑːr/ *abbr.* ROMAN CATHOLIC (= belonging to or connected with the part of the Christian Church that has the POPE as its leader)

**RCMP** /ˌɑː siː em ˈpiː; *NAmE* ˌɑːr/ *abbr.* Royal Canadian Mounted Police (the national police force of Canada)

**Rd** (*also* **Rd.** *especially in NAmE*) *abbr.* (used in written addresses) Road: *12 Ashton Rd*

**RDA** /ˌɑː diː ˈeɪ; *NAmE* ˌɑːr/ *abbr.* recommended daily allowance or recommended dietary allowance (the amount of a chemical, for example a vitamin or a mineral, which you should have every day)

**RE** /ˌɑː ˈiː; *NAmE* ˌɑːr/ noun [U] a school subject in which students learn about different religions (the abbreviation for 'religious education'): *an RE teacher*

**re**[1] /reɪ/ = RAY (4)

**re**[2] /riː/ *prep.* used at the beginning of a business letter, etc. to introduce the subject that it is about; used on an email that you are sending as a reply: *Re your letter of 1 September ...* ◊ *Re: travel expenses* ⇨ WORDFINDER NOTE at MESSAGE

**re-** /riː/ *prefix* (in verbs and related nouns, adjectives and adverbs) again: *reapply* ◊ *reincarnation* ◊ *reassuring*

**reach** 0 A2 S /riːtʃ/ verb, noun
■ verb
- ARRIVE **1** A2 [T] ~ **sth/sb** to arrive at the place that you have been travelling to: *They didn't reach the border until after dark.* ◊ *I hope this letter reaches you.* **2** B1 [T] ~ **sb** to come to sb's attention: *The rumours eventually reached the President.*
- LEVEL/SPEED/STAGE **3** B1 [T] ~ **sth** to increase to a particular level, speed, etc. over a period of time: *The conflict has now reached a new level of intensity.* ◊ *Daytime temperatures can reach 40°C.* ◊ *Her popularity reached its peak in the late 1990s.* **4** B1 [T] ~ **sth** to arrive at a particular point or stage of sth after a period of time: *We have a good chance of reaching the final.* ◊ *The problem has now reached crisis point.* ◊ *I have reached the stage in my career where I need a change.*
- ACHIEVE AIM **5** B1 [T] ~ **sth** to achieve a particular aim SYN **arrive at**: *Politicians again failed to reach an agreement.* ◊ *to reach a conclusion/decision/verdict/compromise* ⇨ see also FAR-REACHING
- WITH HAND/ARM **6** B1 [I, T] to stretch your hand towards sth in order to touch it, pick it up, etc.: **+ adv./prep.** *She reached inside her bag for a pen.* ◊ *I reached out to pat the dog.* ◊ **~ sth + adv./prep.** *He reached out his hand to touch her.* **7** B1 [I, T] to be able to stretch your hand far enough

# reachable

in order to touch sth, pick sth up, etc: **(+ adv. / prep.)** 'Grab the end of the rope.' 'I can't reach that far!' ◇ **~ sth** Can you reach the light switch from where you're sitting? **8** [T] to stretch your hand out or up in order to get sth for sb: **~ sth (down) for sb** Can you reach that box down for me? ◇ **~ sb (down) sth** Can you reach me down that box?
- **BE LONG ENOUGH 9** [I, T] to be big enough, long enough, etc. to arrive at a particular point: **+ adv. / prep.** The carpet only reached halfway across the room. ◇ **~ sth** Is the cable long enough to reach the socket?
- **CONTACT SB 10** [T] **~ sb** to communicate with sb, especially by phone: Do you know where I can reach him?
- **BE SEEN / HEARD BY SB 11** [T] **~ sb** to be seen or heard by sb: Through the internet we are able to reach a wider audience.
**IDM** **reach for the ˈstars** to try to be successful at sth that is difficult ◆ more at EAR
**PHRV** **ˌreach ˈout (to sb) 1** to show sb that you are interested in them and/or want to help them: The church needs to find new ways of reaching out to young people. **2** (especially NAmE) to contact sb in order to get help: If you have any questions or concerns, please reach out to us at this email address: …

■ **noun**
- **OF ARMS 1** [U, sing.] the distance over which you can stretch your arms to touch sth; the distance over which a particular object can be used to touch sth else: **beyond sb's ~** The shot was well beyond the reach of the goalkeeper. ◇ **out of sb's ~** Keep all medicines out of reach of children. ◇ **within sb's ~** He lashed out angrily, hitting anyone within his reach. ◇ Use shears with a long reach for cutting high hedges.
- **OF POWER / INFLUENCE 2** [U, sing.] the limit to which sb / sth has the power or influence to do sth: The brand now has **global reach**. ◇ **beyond sb / sth's ~** Such matters are beyond the reach of the law. ◇ **out of sb / sth's ~** Victory is now out of her reach. ◇ **within sb / sth's ~** The basic model is priced well within the reach of most people.
- **OF RIVER 3** [C, usually pl.] a straight section of water between two bends on a river: the **upper / lower reaches** of the Nile (= the part that is furthest from / nearest to the sea)
- **PLACE FAR FROM CENTRE 4 reaches** [pl.] **the outer, further, etc. ~ of sth** the parts of an area or a place that are a long way from the centre: the outer reaches of space ◇ (figurative) an exploration of the deepest reaches of the human mind
- **SECTIONS OF ORGANIZATION 5 reaches** [pl.] **the higher, lower, etc. ~ of sth** the higher, etc. sections of an organization, a system, etc: There are still few women in the upper reaches of the civil service. ◇ Many clubs in the lower reaches of the league are in financial difficulty.
**IDM** **within (easy) ˈreach (of sth)** close to sth: The house is within easy reach of schools and sports facilities.

**reach·able** /ˈriːtʃəbl/ adj. [not before noun] that is possible to reach: The farm is only reachable by car.

**re·acquaint** /ˌriːəˈkweɪnt/ verb **~ sb / yourself with sth** to let sb / yourself find out about sth again or get used to sth again: I'll need to reacquaint myself with this program—it's a long time since I've used it.

**react** /riˈækt/ verb **1** [I] to change or behave in a particular way as a result of or in response to sth: I nudged her but she didn't react. ◇ You never know how he is going to react. ◇ **~ to sth** Local residents have reacted angrily to the news. ◇ **~ (to sth) by doing sth** The market reacted by falling a further two points. ◇ **~ with sth** Her family reacted with horror when she told them. **2** [I] to become ill after eating, breathing, etc. a particular substance: **~ + adv.** Some patients may react adversely. ◇ **~ (+ adv.) to sth** People can react badly to certain food additives. **3** [I] **~ (with sth) | ~ (together)** (chemistry) (of substances) to experience a chemical change when coming into contact with another substance: Iron reacts with water and air to produce rust. ◆ WORDFINDER NOTE at CHEMISTRY
**PHRV** **reˌact aˈgainst sb / sth** to show dislike or opposition in response to sth, especially by deliberately doing the opposite of what sb wants you to do: He reacted strongly against the artistic conventions of his time.

**react·ant** /riˈæktənt/ noun (chemistry) a substance that takes part in and is changed by a chemical reaction

**re·ac·tion** /riˈækʃn/ noun
- **TO EVENT / SITUATION 1** [C, U] what you do, say or think as a result of sth that has happened: to **provoke / cause / get a reaction** ◇ **a positive / negative / adverse reaction** ◇ **~ to sth** What was his reaction to the news? ◇ Often our actions are based upon an **emotional reaction** to what someone has done or said to us. ◇ **in~to sth** A spokesman said the changes were not in reaction to the company's recent losses. ◇ **~ of sb** The **initial reaction** of the White House was favourable. ◇ **~ from sb** It's just another **knee-jerk reaction** from sections of the media. ◇ My **immediate reaction** was one of shock. ◇ There has been a **mixed reaction** to her appointment as director. ◇ I tried shaking him but there was no reaction.
- **CHANGE IN ATTITUDES 2** [C, usually sing., U] **~ against sth** a change in people's attitudes or behaviour caused by DISAPPROVAL of the attitudes, etc. of the past: The return to traditional family values is a reaction against the permissiveness of recent decades.
- **TO DRUGS 3** [C, U] a response by the body, usually a bad one, to a drug, chemical substance, etc: If you have a bad **reaction**, discontinue use immediately. ◇ **~ to sth** to have an **allergic reaction** to a drug ◇ Adverse reactions to certain foods can take a few days to manifest.
- **TO DANGER 4 reactions** [pl.] the ability to move quickly in response to sth, especially in danger: a skilled driver with quick reactions
- **SCIENCE 5** [C, U] (chemistry) a chemical change produced by two or more substances acting on each other: a **chemical reaction** ◇ **a nuclear reaction** ◇ To perform the test, add five drops of the solution to the compound and then observe the reaction. ◇ **~ of sth with sth** the reaction of oxygen with other atoms ◆ see also CHAIN REACTION **6** [U, C] (physics) a force shown by sth in response to another force, which is of equal strength and acts in the opposite direction
- **AGAINST PROGRESS 7** [U] opposition to social or political progress or change: The forces of reaction made change difficult.

**re·ac·tion·ary** /riˈækʃənri; NAmE -ʃəneri/ noun (pl. **-ies**) (disapproving) a person who is opposed to political or social change ▸ **re·ac·tion·ary** adj.: a reactionary government

**reˈaction time** noun [C, U] the amount of time it takes for a person or system to respond to sth

**re·acti·vate** /riˈæktɪveɪt/ verb **~ sth** to make sth start working or happening again after a period of time ▸ **re·acti·va·tion** /riˌæktɪˈveɪʃn/ noun [U]

**re·act·ive** /riˈæktɪv/ adj. **1** (formal) showing a reaction or response: The police presented a reactive rather than preventive strategy against crime. ◆ compare PROACTIVE **2** (chemistry) tending to show chemical change when mixed with another substance: highly reactive substances

**re·activ·ity** /ˌriːækˈtɪvəti/ noun (chemistry) the degree to which sth reacts, or is likely to react: Oxygen has high reactivity.

**re·act·or** /riˈæktə(r)/ (also **nuclear reˈactor**) noun a large structure used to produce nuclear energy

**read** /riːd/ verb, noun, adj.

■ **verb** /riːd/ (**read, read** /red/)
- **WORDS / SYMBOLS 1** [I, T] (not used in the progressive tenses) to look at and understand the meaning of written or printed words or symbols: She's still learning to read. ◇ Some children can **read and write** before they go to school. ◇ **~ sth** I can't read your writing. ◇ Can you read music? ◇ I'm trying to read the map. ◆ see also SIGHT-READ, SPEED-READ ◆ HOMOPHONES at REED **2** [I, T] to go through written or printed words, etc. in silence or speaking them to other people: I'm going to go to bed and read. ◇ **~ to sb / yourself** He liked reading to his grandchildren. ◇ **~ sth** to read a book / magazine / newspaper ◇ to read an article / a report / a letter / a blog / a review ◇ Have you read any Steinbeck (= novels by him)? ◇ one of the most **widely read** books in the world ◇ He read the poem **aloud**. ◇ **~ sth to sb / yourself** Go on—read it to us. ◇ **~ sb sth** She read us a story. ◆ see also PROOFREAD ◆ HOMOPHONES at RED

- **DISCOVER BY READING** 3 [I, T] (not used in the progressive tenses) to discover or find out about sb/sth by reading: *~ about-/of sth (in sth) I read about the accident in the local paper.* ◇ *~ that ... I read that he had resigned.* ◇ *~ sth I can't remember where I read it.* ◇ *~ sth in sth Don't believe everything you read in the papers.*
- **SB'S MIND/THOUGHTS** 4 [T] *~ sb's mind/thoughts* to guess what sb else is thinking
- **SB'S LIPS** 5 [T] *~ sb's lips* to look at the movements of sb's lips to learn what they are saying ⇒ see also LIP-READ
- **UNDERSTAND** 6 [T] to understand sth in a particular way **SYN** interpret: *~ sth How do you read the present situation?* ◇ *~ sth as sth Silence must not always be read as consent.*
- **OF A PIECE OF WRITING** 7 [T] **+ speech** to have sth written on it; to be written in a particular way: *The sign read 'No admittance'.* ◇ *I've changed the last paragraph. It now reads as follows ...* 8 [I] **+ adv./prep.** to give a particular impression when read: *Generally, the article reads very well.* ◇ *The poem reads like (= sounds as if it is) a translation.*
- **MEASURING INSTRUMENT** 9 [T] *~ sth* (of measuring instruments) to show a particular weight, pressure, etc: *What does the thermometer read?* 10 [T] *~ sth* to get information from a measuring instrument: *A man came to read the gas meter.*
- **HEAR** 11 [T] *~ sb* to hear and understand sb speaking on a radio set: *'Do you read me?' 'I'm reading you loud and clear.'*
- **REPLACE WORD** 12 [T] *~ A for B | ~ B as A* to replace one word, etc. with another when correcting a text: *For 'madam' in line 3 read 'madman'.*
- **SUBJECT AT UNIVERSITY** 13 [T, I] (*BrE, rather old-fashioned*) to study a subject, especially at a university: *~ sth I read English at Oxford.* ◇ *~ for sth She's reading for a law degree.*
- **COMPUTING** 14 [T] (of a computer or the person using it) to take information from a disk: *~ sth My computer can't read the CD-ROM you sent.* ◇ *~ sth into sth to read a file into a computer*

**IDM** **read between the 'lines** to look for or discover a meaning in sth that is not openly stated: *Reading between the lines, I think Clare needs money.* **read sb like a 'book** to understand easily what sb is thinking or feeling **read my 'lips** (*informal*) used to tell sb to listen carefully to what you are saying: *Read my lips: no new taxes (= I promise there will be no new taxes).* **read (sb) the 'Riot Act** (*BrE*) to tell sb with force that they must not do sth **ORIGIN** From an Act of Parliament passed in 1715 to prevent riots. It made it illegal for a group of twelve or more people to refuse to split up if they were ordered to do so and part of the Act was read to them. **take it/sth as 'read** (*BrE*) to accept sth without discussing it: *Can we take it as read that you want the job?*

**PHRV** **read sth↔'back (to sb)** to read a message, etc. to others in order to check that it is correct **read sth 'into sth** to think that sth means more than it really does: *Don't read too much into what she says.* **read 'on** to continue reading: *That's the story so far. Now read on...* **read sth↔'out (to sb)** to read sth using your voice, especially to other people **read sth↔'over/'through** to read sth carefully from beginning to end to look for mistakes or check details: *I read through the first paragraph again.* **read sth↔'up | read 'up on sb/sth** to read a lot about a subject: *I'll need to read up on the case before the meeting.*

- **noun** /riːd/ [sing.] (*informal*) 1 (*especially BrE*) an act or a period of reading sth: *I was having a quiet read when the phone rang.* 2 **a good, interesting, etc. ~** a book, an article, etc. that is good, etc: *His thrillers are always a gripping read.*
- **adj.** /red/ (used after an adverb) (of a person) having knowledge that has been gained from reading books, etc: *She's very widely read in law.* ⇒ see also WELL READ

**read·able** /ˈriːdəbl/ *adj.* 1 (of a book, article, etc.) that is easy, interesting and ENJOYABLE to read ⇒ WORDFINDER NOTE at STORY 2 (of written or printed words) clear and easy to read **SYN** legible ⇒ see also MACHINE-READABLE ▸ **read·abil·ity** /ˌriːdəˈbɪləti/ *noun* [U]

**read·er** **⓪** **A1** /ˈriːdə(r)/ *noun* 1 **A1** a person who reads, especially one who reads a lot or in a particular way: *an avid reader of science fiction* ◇ *a fast/slow reader* ◇ *And so, dear reader, our tale comes to its end.* ◇ *The reader is left to draw his or her own conclusions.* ⇒ see also SIGHT-READER 2 **A1** a person who reads a particular newspaper, magazine, etc: *readers' letters* ◇ *Are you a 'Times' reader?* ◇ *regular readers of this magazine* 3 an easy book that is intended to help people learn to read their own or a foreign language: *a series of graded English readers* 4 (*usually* **Reader**) a senior teacher at a British university just below the rank of a professor: *She is Reader in Music at Edinburgh.* 5 (*computing*) an electronic device that reads data stored in one form and changes it into another form so that a computer can perform operations on it ⇒ see also CARD READER, E-READER, FEED READER 6 (*specialist*) a machine that produces on a screen a large image of a text stored on a MICROFICHE or MICROFILM ⇒ see also MIND READER, NEWSREADER

**read·er·ship** /ˈriːdəʃɪp; *NAmE* -dərʃ-/ *noun* 1 [usually sing.] the number or type of people who read a particular newspaper, magazine, etc: *a readership of around 10000* ◇ *In its new format, the magazine hopes to attract a much wider readership.* 2 (*usually* **Readership**) **~ (in sth)** (*BrE*) the position of a READER at a university

**read·ily** **?+** **C1** **W** /ˈredɪli/ *adv.* 1 **?+** **C1** quickly and without difficulty **SYN** freely: *All ingredients are readily available from your local store.* 2 **?+** **C1** in a way that shows you do not object to sth **SYN** willingly: *Most people readily accept the need for laws.*

**readi·ness** /ˈredɪnəs/ *noun* 1 [U] **~ (for sth)** the state of being ready or prepared for sth: *Everyone has doubts about their readiness for parenthood.* 2 [U, sing.] **~ (of sb) (to do sth)** the state of being willing to do sth: *Over half the people interviewed expressed their readiness to die for their country.*

**read·ing** **⓪** **A1** **S** /ˈriːdɪŋ/ *noun*
- **ACTIVITY** 1 **?+** **A1** [U] the activity of sb who reads: *My hobbies include reading and painting.* ◇ *He needs more help with his reading.* ◇ *Are you any good at map reading?* ◇ *reading glasses* (= worn when reading) ◇ *a reading lamp/light* (= one that can be moved to shine light onto sth that you are reading) ◇ *~ on sth After extensive reading on the subject she set to work on an article.* ◇ *~ about sth He's done a lot of reading about the history of race relations.* 2 [sing.] an act of reading sth: *A closer* (= more detailed) *reading of the text reveals just how desperate he was feeling.*
- **BOOKS/ARTICLES** 3 **?** **A2** [U] books, articles, etc. that are intended to be read: *reading material* ◇ *reading matter* ◇ *a series of reading books for children* ◇ *a reading list* (= a list of books, etc. that students are expected to read for a particular subject) ◇ *further reading* (= at the end of a book, a list of other books that give more information about the same subject) ◇ *The report makes for interesting reading* (= it is interesting to read) ◇ *The article is not exactly light reading* (= it is serious and requires effort and concentration to understand). ◇ *~ for sb/sth His article should be compulsory reading for law students.* ◇ *Her assigned reading for English class was 'Great Expectations'.* ◇ *~ on sth a list of suggested reading on this topic*
- **WAY OF UNDERSTANDING** 4 [C] **~ (of sth)** the particular way in which you understand a book, situation, etc. **SYN** interpretation: *a literal reading of the text* ◇ *My own reading of events is less optimistic.*
- **MEASUREMENT** 5 [C] the amount or number shown on an instrument used for measuring sth: *Meter readings are taken every three months.*
- **EVENT** 6 [C] an event at which sth is read to an audience for entertainment; a piece of literature that is read at such an event: *a poetry reading* ◇ *The evening ended with a reading from her latest novel.*
- **FROM BIBLE** 7 [C] a short section from a holy text that is read to people as part of a religious service: *The reading today is from the Book of Daniel.*
- **IN PARLIAMENT** 8 [C] one of the stages during which a BILL (= a proposal for a new law) must be discussed and accepted by a parliament before it can become law

# reading age

**reading age** *noun* a person's ability to read, measured by comparing it with the average ability of children of a particular age: *a 30-year-old man with a reading age of eight*

**reading group** *noun* = BOOK GROUP

**reading list** *noun* a list of books, articles, etc. that students are expected to read for a particular subject

**reading room** *noun* a room in a library, club, etc. where people can read or study

**re·adjust** /ˌriːəˈdʒʌst/ *verb* **1** [I] to get used to a changed or new situation: *Children are highly adaptable—they just need time to readjust.* ◇ **~to (doing) sth** *Once again he had to readjust to living alone.* **2** [T] **~sth** to change or move sth slightly: *She got out of the car and readjusted her dress.* ▶ **re·adjust·ment** *noun* [C, U]: *He has made a number of readjustments to his technique.* ◇ *a painful period of readjustment*

**re·admit** /ˌriːədˈmɪt/ *verb* (**-tt-**) [often passive] **1 ~sb (to sth)** to allow sb to join a group, an organization or an institution again **2 ~sb (to sth)** to take sb into a hospital again after they had been allowed to leave: *He was readmitted only a week after being discharged.* ▶ **re·admis·sion** /-ˈmɪʃn/ *noun* [U, C] **~ (to sth)**

**read-only** /ˌriːd ˈəʊnli/ *adj.* (*computing*) (of memory, data or a file) able to be seen and read, but not changed: *Non-paying users will see these files in read-only mode.*

**read-only ˈmemory** *noun* [U] (*computing*) = ROM

**read-out** /ˈriːd aʊt/ *noun* (*computing*) a display of information on a computer screen ⊃ compare PRINTOUT

**read-through** /ˈriːd θruː/ *noun* an occasion when the words of a play are spoken by members of a theatre group, before they begin practising acting it

**ready** 🔑 **A1** /ˈredi/ *adj., verb, adv., noun*
- *adj.* (**read·ier**, **readi·est**)
- PREPARED/AVAILABLE **1** **A1** [not before noun] fully prepared for what you are going to do and able to start it immediately: *Just a minute—I'm almost ready.* ◇ **~ for sth** *I'm just getting the kids ready for school.* ◇ **~ to do sth** *Right, we're ready to go.* ◇ *We were getting ready to go out.* **2** **A1** [not before noun] having the experience, attitude, etc. that you need in order to be able to deal with sth: *Her husband wants to start a family, but she isn't ready.* ◇ **~ for sth** *I'm not sure if Karen is ready for marriage yet.* ◇ **~ to do sth** *He is clearly not ready to take on such an important role.* **3** **B1** [not before noun] completed and available to be used: *Come on, dinner's ready!* ◇ *The new building should be ready by 2020.* ◇ **~ for sth** *Can you help me get everything ready for the party?* ◇ **~ to do sth** *The contract will be ready to sign in two weeks.* **4** available to be used easily and immediately: *All the relevant records are ready to hand.* ◇ *a ready supply of wood* ◇ *a ready source of income* ⊃ see also READILY, READINESS, ROUGH AND READY
- WILLING **5** [not before noun] willing and quick to do or give sth: **~ for sth** *I was very angry and ready for a fight.* ◇ **~ with sth** *She's always ready with advice.* ◇ **~ to do sth** *He's always ready and willing to help.* ◇ *Don't be so ready to believe the worst about people.*
- LIKELY TO DO STH **6 ~ to do sth** likely to do sth very soon **SYN** on the point of: *She looked ready to collapse at any minute.*
- NEEDING STH **7 ~ for sth** needing sth as soon as possible: *Right, I'm ready for bed.* ◇ *After the long walk, we were all ready for a drink.*
- QUICK/CLEVER **8** [only before noun] quick and clever: *She has great charm and a ready wit.*
- **IDM** **make ˈready (for sth)** (*formal*) to prepare for sth; to prepare sth for sth: *to make ready for the President's visit* **ready, steady, ˈgo!** (*BrE*) (*also* **(get) ready, (get) set, go** *NAmE, BrE*) what you say to tell people to start a race **ˌready to ˈroll** (*informal*) ready to start
- *verb* (**read·ies, ready·ing, read·ied, read·ied**) **~ sb/yourself/sth (for sth)** | **~ sb/yourself/sth (to do sth)** (*formal*) to prepare sb/yourself/sth for sth: *British companies were readying themselves for big changes.*
- *adv.* (used before a past participle, especially in compounds) already done: *ready-cooked meals* ◇ *The concrete was ready mixed.*
- *noun* **read·ies** [pl.] (*also* **the ˈready** [sing.]) (*BrE, informal*) money that you can use immediately
- **IDM** **at the ˈready** available to be used immediately: *We all had our cameras at the ready.*

**ready-ˈmade** *adj.* **1** prepared in advance so that you can eat or use it immediately: *ready-made pastry* **2** (*old-fashioned*) (especially of clothes) made in standard sizes, not to the measurements of a particular customer: *a ready-made suit* **3** already provided for you so you do not need to produce or think about it yourself: *When he married her he also took on a ready-made family.*

**ˈready meal** *noun* (*BrE*) a meal that you buy already prepared and which only needs to be heated before you eat it

**ˈready ˈmoney** (*also* **ˌready ˈcash**) *noun* [U] (*informal*) money in the form of coins and notes that you can spend immediately

**ready-to-ˈwear** *adj.* (of clothes) made in standard sizes, not to the measurements of a particular customer

**re·affirm** /ˌriːəˈfɜːm; *NAmE* -ˈfɜːrm/ *verb* **~ sth** to state sth again in order to emphasize that it is still true ▶ **re·affirm·ation** /ˌriːæfəˈmeɪʃn; *NAmE* -fərˈm-/ *noun* [C, U]

**re·agent** /riˈeɪdʒənt/ *noun* (*chemistry*) a substance used to cause a chemical reaction, especially in order to find out if another substance is present

**real** 🔑 **A1** 🔊 /ˈriːəl; *BrE also* rɪəl/ *adj., adv.*
- *adj.*
- EXISTING/NOT IMAGINED **1 A1** actually existing or happening and not imagined or pretended: *a real danger/risk/threat/concern* ◇ *All the characters are based on real people.* ◇ *pictures of animals, both real and mythological* ◇ *In the movies guns kill people instantly, but it's not like that in real life.* ◇ *Politicians seem to be out of touch with the real world.* ◇ *The growth of violent crime is a very real problem.* ◇ *There's no real possibility of them changing their minds.* ◇ *We have a real chance of success.* ◇ *By the end of it I had a real sense of achievement.*
- TRUE/NOT FALSE **2 A1** not false or artificial: *Are those real flowers?* ◇ *real leather* **3 B1** [only before noun] actual or true, rather than what appears to be true: *Tell me the real reason.* ◇ *The real story is even more amazing.* ◇ *Judy Garland's real name was Frances Ethel Gumm.* ◇ *The real problem is a lack of investment in infrastructure.* ◇ *The real issue was whether the accused knew the goods were stolen.* ◇ *See the real Africa on one of our walking safaris.* ◇ *I couldn't resist the opportunity to meet a real live celebrity.* **4 A1** [only before noun] having all the important qualities that it should have to deserve to be called what it is called: *She never had any real friends at school.* ◇ *his first real kiss* ◇ *I had no real interest in politics.* ◇ *He was making a real effort to be nice to her.* ◇ *These measures have made a real difference to people's lives.* ◇ *She has not shown any real regret for what she did.*
- FOR EMPHASIS **5 B1** [only before noun] used to emphasize a state or quality: *He looks a real idiot.* ◇ *This accident could have produced a real tragedy.* ◇ *Her next play was a real contrast.* ◇ *It's been a real challenge, but we're determined to succeed.*
- MONEY/INCOME **6** [only before noun] when the effect of such things as price rises on the power of money to buy things is included in the sums: *Real wage costs have risen by 10 per cent in the past year.* ◇ *This represents a reduction of 5 per cent in real terms.*
- **IDM** **for ˈreal** what sb claims it is or serious: *This is not a fire drill—it's for real.* ◇ (*NAmE*) *He managed to convince voters that he was for real.* **ˌget ˈreal!** (*informal*) used to tell sb that they are behaving in a stupid or unreasonable way **ˌkeep it ˈreal** (*informal*) to act in an honest and natural way **the ˌreal ˈthing** (*informal*) actually what sb claims that sth is: *Are you sure it's the real thing (= love), not just infatuation?* ⊃ more at MCCOY, POWER *n.*
- *adv.* (*NAmE, ScotE, informal*) very: *That tastes real good.* ◇ *He's a real nice guy.* ◇ *I'm real sorry.*

**ˌreal ˈale** *noun* [U, C] (*BrE*) a type of beer that is made, stored and served in the traditional way (from a BARREL, without additional gas pressure)

**ˈreal estate** *noun* [U] (*especially NAmE*) **1** (*also* **realty**) property in the form of land or buildings: *My father sold real estate.* **2** the business of selling houses or land for building: *to work in real estate* **3** (*especially on a web page*) space that is useful or valuable: *A company's home page is its most valuable real estate.* ◊ *You can increase screen real estate by moving the taskbar to the right of the screen.*

**ˈreal esˈtate agent** (*also* **ˈRealtor™**) (*both NAmE*) (*BrE* **eˈstate agent**) *noun* a person whose job is to sell houses and land for people

**re·align** /ˌriːəˈlaɪn/ *verb* **1** ~ sth to change the position or direction of sth slightly: *The road was realigned to improve visibility.* **2** ~ sth to make changes to sth in order to adapt it to a new situation: *The company has been forced to realign its operations in the area.* **3** ~ yourself (with sb/sth) to change your opinions, policies, etc. so that they are the same as those of another person, group, etc: *The rebel MPs have realigned themselves with the opposition party.*
▶ **re·align·ment** *noun* [U, C]: ~ (of sth) the realignment of personal goals ◊ political realignments

**real·ism** /ˈriːəlɪzəm; *BrE also* ˈrɪə-/ *noun* [U] **1** a way of seeing, accepting and dealing with situations as they really are without being influenced by your emotions or false hopes: *There was a new mood of realism among the leaders at the peace talks.* **2** (of novels, paintings, films/movies, etc.) the quality of being very like real life **3** (*also* **Realism**) a style in art or literature that shows things and people as they are in real life ⊃ see also MAGIC REALISM, SOCIALIST REALISM ⊃ compare IDEALISM, ROMANTICISM

**real·ist** /ˈriːəlɪst; *BrE also* ˈrɪə-/ *noun* **1** a person who accepts and deals with a situation as it really is and does not try to pretend that it is different: *I'm a realist—I know you can't change people overnight.* **2** a writer, painter, etc. whose work represents things as they are in real life

**real·is·tic** 🔑 **B2** /ˌriːəˈlɪstɪk; *BrE also* ˌrɪə-/ *adj.* **1** 🔑 **B2** accepting in a sensible way what it is actually possible to do or achieve in a particular situation: *a realistic assessment/approach/view* ◊ **about sth** *We have to be realistic about our chances of winning.* ◊ **it is ~ (for sb) to do sth** *It is not realistic to expect people to spend so much money.* **2** 🔑 **B2** sensible and appropriate; possible to achieve **SYN** **feasible, viable**: *a realistic prospect/chance/possibility* ◊ *a realistic alternative/option* ◊ *We must set realistic goals.* ◊ *a realistic target* ◊ *to pay a realistic salary* **3** 🔑 **B2** representing things as they are in real life: *a realistic portrayal/depiction/picture* ◊ *a realistic drawing* ◊ *We try to make these training courses as realistic as possible.* ◊ *realistic graphics* **OPP** **unrealistic**

**real·is·tic·al·ly** /ˌriːəˈlɪstɪkli; *BrE also* ˌrɪə-/ *adv.* **1** used to say what you think can actually be achieved in a particular situation: *Realistically, there is little prospect of a ceasefire.* **2** in a way that shows sb accepts in a sensible way what it is actually possible to do or achieve: *How many can you realistically hope to sell?* ◊ *Kate spoke realistically about the task ahead.* **3** in a way that represents things as they are in real life: *a fireplace with realistically glowing coals*

**real·ity** 🔑 **B1** 🔊 /riˈæləti/ *noun* (*pl.* **-ies**) **1** 🔑 **B1** [U] the true situation and the problems that actually exist in life, in contrast to how you would like life to be: *She refuses to face reality.* ◊ *You're out of touch with reality.* ◊ *The reality is that there is not enough money to pay for this project.* **2** 🔑 **B2** [C] a thing that is actually experienced or seen, in contrast to what people might imagine: *Will time travel ever become a reality?* ◊ *As children they experienced the harsh realities of life.* ◊ *This decision reflects the realities of the political situation.* ⊃ see also VIRTUAL REALITY **3** [U] ~ television/TV/shows/series/contestants television/shows, etc. that use real people (not actors) in real situations, presented as entertainment: *a reality TV star* ◊ *the reality show 'Survivor'*
**IDM** ▶ **in reˈality** used to say that a situation is different from what has just been said or from what people believe: *Outwardly she seemed confident but in reality she felt extremely nervous.*

**reˈality check** *noun* [*usually sing.*] (*informal*) an occasion when you are reminded of how things are in the real world, rather than how you would like things to be

**reˈality TˈV** (*also* reˌality ˈtelevision) *noun* [U] television shows that are based on real people (not actors) in real situations, presented as entertainment ⊃ **WORDFINDER NOTE** at PROGRAMME

**real·iz·able** (*BrE also* **-is·able**) /ˈriːəlaɪzəbl; *BrE also* ˈrɪə-/ *adj.* **1** possible to achieve or make happen **SYN** **achievable**: *realizable objectives* **2** that can be sold and turned into money: *realizable assets*

**real·iza·tion** 🔑 **C1** (*BrE also* **-isa·tion**) /ˌriːəlaɪˈzeɪʃn; ˌrɪə-; *NAmE* ˌriːələˈz-/ *noun* **1** 🔑 **C1** [U, *sing.*] the process of becoming aware of sth **SYN** **awareness**: ~ of sth *the sudden realization of what she had done.* ◊ ~ that ... *There is a growing realization that changes must be made.* **2** 🔑 **C1** [U] ~ (of sth) the process of achieving a particular aim, etc. **SYN** **achievement**: *It was the realization of his greatest ambition.* **3** [U] ~ of your assets (*formal*) the act of selling sth that you own, such as property, in order to get the money that you need for sth **4** [U, C] ~ (of sth) (*formal*) the act of producing a sound, play, design, etc.; or the thing that is produced

**real·ize** 🔑 **A2** (*BrE also* **-ise**) /ˈriːəlaɪz; *BrE also* ˈrɪə-/ *verb*
• BE/BECOME AWARE **1** 🔑 **A2** [T, I] (not used in the progressive tenses) to understand or become aware of a particular fact or situation: ~ (that) ... *I didn't realize (that) you were so unhappy.* ◊ *The moment I saw her, I realized something was wrong.* ◊ *I finally came to realize that he would never change.* ◊ ~ how, what, etc ... *I don't think you realize how important this is to her.* ◊ ~ sth *Many families fail to realize the importance of a well-balanced diet* ◊ *Only later did she realize her mistake.* ◊ *I hope you realize the seriousness of this crime.* ◊ *The situation was more complicated than they had at first realized.* ◊ *They managed to leave without any of us realizing.* ◊ **it is realized that ...** *There was a cheer when it was realized that everyone was safely back.*
• ACHIEVE STH **2** 🔑 **B2** [T] ~ sth to achieve sth important that you very much want to do: *to realize your dream* ◊ *We try to help all students realize their full potential* (= be as successful as they are able to be). ◊ *She never realized her ambition of becoming a professional singer.*
• HAPPEN **3** [T, *usually passive*] ~ sth if sb's fears **are realized**, the things that they are afraid will happen, do happen: *His worst fears were realized when he saw that the door had been forced open.*
• SELL **4** [T] ~ your assets (*formal*) to sell things that you own, for example property, in order to get the money that you need for sth **SYN** **convert 5** [T] ~ sth (*formal*) (of goods, etc.) to be sold for a particular amount of money **SYN** **make**: *The paintings realized $2 million at auction.*
• MAKE STH REAL **6** [T] ~ sth (*formal*) to produce sth that can be seen or heard, based on written information or instructions: *The stage designs have been beautifully realized.*

**ˈreal-life** *adj.* [only before noun] actually happening or existing in life, not in books, stories or films: *a novel based on real-life events* ◊ *a real-life Romeo and Juliet* **OPP** **fictional**

**re·allo·cate** /ˌriːˈæləkeɪt/ *verb* ~ sth (to sb/sth) to change the way money or materials are shared between different people, groups, projects, etc. **SYN** **redistribute** ▶ **re·allo·ca·tion** /ˌriːˌæləˈkeɪʃn/ *noun* [U, C]

**real·ly** 🔑 **A1** /ˈriːəli; *BrE also* ˈrɪə-/ *adv.* **1** 🔑 **A1** used to emphasize an adjective or adverb: *That's a really good idea.* ◊ *It's really hard to find a decent job these days.* ◊ *It all went really well.* ◊ *This is a really nice place.* ◊ *Things are looking really bad for him.* ◊ *It's really important that I speak with her right away.* **2** 🔑 **A1** used to emphasize sth you are saying or an opinion you are giving: *I really want to go home now.* ◊ *I want to help—I really do.* ◊ *You really need to forget all about her.* ◊ *I really don't mind.* ◊ *He really likes you.* ◊ *I really enjoyed the film.* ◊ *I really, really hope you're right.* ◊ *I really and truly am in love this time.* **3** 🔑 **A1** used to express interest in or surprise at what sb is saying: *'We're going to Japan next month.' 'Oh, really?'* ◊ *'She's resigned.' 'Really? Are you sure?'* **4** 🔑 **A1** used to say what is actually the fact or the truth about sth: *What do you really think about it?* ◊ *Tell me what really happened.* ◊ *They are*

---

🅞 Oxford Phrasal Academic Lexicon (OPAL) written and spoken word lists | 🅦 OPAL written word list | 🅢 OPAL spoken word list

# realm

not really my aunt and uncle. ◊ *I can't believe I am really going to meet the princess.* **5** used, often in negative sentences, to reduce the force of sth you are saying: *I don't really agree with that.* ◊ *It doesn't really matter.* ◊ *'Did you enjoy the book?' 'Not really'* (= 'no' or 'not very much'). **HELP** The position of **really** can change the meaning of the sentence. **I don't really know** means that you are not sure about something; **I really don't know** emphasizes that you do not know. (Look at sense 2.) **6** used in questions and negative sentences when you want sb to say 'no': *Do you really expect me to believe that?* ◊ *I don't really need to go, do I?* **7** used to show that you think sth that sb has done is bad: *Really, you could have told us before.*

**realm** /relm/ *noun* **1** an area of activity, interest or knowledge: **in the ~ of sth** *in the realm of literature* ◊ *At the end of the speech he seemed to be moving into the realms of fantasy.* **2** (*formal*) a country ruled by a king or queen **SYN kingdom**: *the defence of the realm* **IDM** see POSSIBILITY

**real·politik** /reɪˈɑːlpəlɪtiːk; *NAmE* -pɑːl-/ *noun* [U] (*from German*) a system of politics that is based on the actual situation and needs of a country or political party rather than on moral principles

**real 'time** *noun* [U] (*computing*) the fact that there is only a very short time between a computer system receiving information and dealing with it: *To make the training realistic the simulation operates* **in real time.** ◊ *real-time missile guidance systems*

**Real·tor™** (also **real·tor**) /ˈriːəltə(r)/ *noun* (*NAmE*) = REAL ESTATE AGENT

**realty** /ˈriːəlti/ *noun* [U] (*especially NAmE*) = REAL ESTATE

**real-world** *adj.* [only before noun] existing in the real world and not specially invented for a particular purpose: *Teachers need to prepare their students to deal with real-world situations outside the classroom.*

**ream** /riːm/ *noun, verb*
- *noun* **1 reams** [pl.] (*informal*) a large quantity of writing: *She wrote reams in the exam.* **2** [C] (*specialist*) 500 sheets of paper
- *verb* **~ sb** (*NAmE, informal*) to treat sb unfairly or cheat them: *We got reamed on that deal.*
**PHRV ream sb⇔'out** (*NAmE, informal*) to criticize sb strongly because they have done sth wrong

**re·ani·mate** /riːˈænɪmeɪt/ *verb* ~ **sb/sth** (*formal*) to give sb/sth new life or energy

**reap** /riːp/ *verb* **1** [T] ~ **sth** to obtain sth, especially sth good, as a direct result of sth that you have done: *They are now reaping the rewards of all their hard work.* **2** [I, T] ~ **(sth)** to cut and collect a crop, especially WHEAT, from a field **SYN harvest**
**IDM reap a/the 'harvest** (*BrE*) to benefit or suffer as a direct result of sth that you have done **you reap what you 'sow** (*saying*) you have to deal with the bad effects or results of sth that you originally started

**reap·er** /ˈriːpə(r)/ *noun* a person or a machine that cuts and collects crops on a farm ⇒ see also GRIM REAPER

**re·appear** /ˌriːəˈpɪə(r); *NAmE* -ˈpɪr/ *verb* [I] to appear again after not being heard of or seen for a period of time: *She went upstairs and did not reappear until morning.* ▶ **re·appear·ance** /ˌriːəˈpɪərəns; *NAmE* -ˈpɪr-/ *noun* [U, sing.]

**re·apply** /ˌriːəˈplaɪ/ *verb* (**re·applies, re·apply·ing, re·applied, re·applied**) **1** [T] ~ **sth** to put another layer of a substance on a surface: *Sunblock should be reapplied every hour.* **2** [I] ~ **(for sth)** to make another formal request for sth: *Previous applicants for the post need not reapply.* **3** [T] ~ **sth** to use sth again, especially in a different situation: *Students are taught a number of skills that can be reapplied throughout their studies.*

**re·appoint** /ˌriːəˈpɔɪnt/ *verb* ~ **sb (as) sth | ~ sb (to sth)** to give sb the job that they used to have in the past: ~ **sb (as) sth** *After the trial he was reappointed (as) treasurer.*
▶ **re·appoint·ment** *noun* [U]

**re·appraisal** /ˌriːəˈpreɪzl/ *noun* [C, usually sing., U] the act of examining sth again to see if it needs to be changed **SYN reassessment**

**re·appraise** /ˌriːəˈpreɪz/ *verb* ~ **sth/sb** (*formal*) to think again about the value or nature of sth/sb to see if your opinion about it/them should be changed **SYN reassess**

**rear** /rɪə(r); *NAmE* rɪr/ *adj., noun, verb*
- *adj.* [only before noun] at or near the back of sth: *front and rear windows* ◊ *the rear entrance of the building*
- *noun* **1** (*usually* **the rear**) [sing.] the back part of sth: *A trailer was attached to the rear of the truck.* ◊ *There are toilets at both* **front and rear** *of the plane.* ◊ *A high gate blocks the only entrance* **to the rear.** ⇒ note at BACK **2** (*also* **rear 'end**) [C, usually sing.] (*informal*) the part of the body that you sit on **SYN backside, bottom**: *a kick in the rear*
**IDM bring up the 'rear** to be at the back of a line of people, or last in a race
- *verb* **1** [T] ~ **sb/sth** (often passive) to care for young children or animals until they are fully grown **SYN bring up, raise**: *She reared a family of five on her own.* **2** [T] ~ **sth** to keep and BREED (= produce young from) animals or birds, for example on a farm: *to rear cattle* **3** [I] ~ **(up)** (of an animal, especially a horse) to raise itself on its back legs, with the front legs in the air: *The horse reared, throwing its rider.* **4** [I] ~ **(up)** (of sth large) to seem to lean over you, especially in a way that makes you feel frightened: *The great bulk of the building reared up against the night sky.*
**IDM** see HEAD *n.*
**PHRV 'rear sb/sth on sth** [usually passive] to give a person or an animal a particular type of food, entertainment, etc. while they are young: *I was the son of sailors and reared on stories of the sea.*

**rear ad·miral** *noun* an officer of very high rank in the NAVY: *Rear Admiral Baines*

**rear 'end** *noun* **1** the back part of a vehicle **OPP front end 2** (*informal*) = REAR (2)

**rear-'end** *verb* ~ **sth/sb** (*informal*) (of a vehicle or driver) to drive into the back of another vehicle

**rear·guard** /ˈrɪəɡɑːd; *NAmE* ˈrɪrɡɑːrd/ *noun* (*usually* **the rearguard**) [sing. + sing./pl. v.] a group of soldiers that protect the back part of an army especially when the army is RETREATING after it has been defeated **OPP vanguard**

**rearguard 'action** *noun* [usually sing.] a struggle to change or stop sth even when it is not likely that you will succeed: *They have been* **fighting a rearguard action** *for two years to stop their house being demolished.*

**rear·ing** /ˈrɪərɪŋ; *NAmE* ˈrɪr-/ *noun* [U] **1** the process of caring for children as they grow up, teaching them how to behave as members of society **2** the process of BREEDING (= producing young from) animals or birds and caring for them as they grow: *livestock rearing*

**re·arm** /ˌriːˈɑːm; *NAmE* -ˈɑːrm/ *verb* [I, T] to obtain or supply sb with new or better weapons, armies, etc: *The country was forbidden to rearm under the terms of the treaty.* ◊ ~ **sb** *Rebel troops were being rearmed.* ▶ **re·arma·ment** /ˌriːˈɑːməmənt; *NAmE* -ˈɑːrm-/ *noun* [U]

**re·arrange** /ˌriːəˈreɪndʒ/ *verb* **1** ~ **sth/sb/yourself** to change the position or order of things; to change your position: *We've rearranged the furniture in the bedroom.* ◊ *She rearranged herself in another pose.* **2** ~ **sth** to change the time, date or place of an event **SYN reschedule**: *Can we rearrange the meeting for next Tuesday at two?* ▶ **re·arrange·ment** *noun* [C, U]

**rear-view 'mirror** *noun* a mirror in a car or other vehicle that allows the driver to see the traffic behind

**rear·ward** /ˈrɪəwəd; *NAmE* ˈrɪrwərd/ *adj.* (*formal*) at or near the back of sth: *rearward seats*

**rear-wheel 'drive** *noun* [U] a system in which power from the engine is sent to the back wheels of a vehicle
⇒ compare FRONT-WHEEL DRIVE

**rea·son** /ˈriːzn/ *noun, verb*
- *noun* **1** [C] a cause or an explanation for sth that has happened or that sb has done: *He said no but he didn't give a reason.* ◊ **~ for (doing) sth** *I have no particular reason for doubting him.* ◊ **~ behind sth** *There were a number of reasons behind her departure.* ◊ **~ (that) …** *We aren't going for the simple reason that we can't afford it.* ◊ **~ why …** *Give me one good reason why I should help you.* ◊ **for a~** *For some reason* (= one that I don't know or don't understand)

we all have to come in early tomorrow. ◊ *For this reason*, it's important to have friends who will support you. ◊ *The man attacked me for no apparent reason.* ◊ *people who, for whatever reason, are unable to support themselves* ◊ *for reasons of sth For reasons of security the door is always kept locked.* ◊ *'Why do you want to know?' 'No reason'* (= I do not want to say why). ◊ *'Why did she do that?' 'She must have her reasons'* (= secret reasons which she does not want to tell). ⊃ LANGUAGE BANK at THEREFORE ⊃ EXPRESS YOURSELF at WHY **2** ʔ **B2** [U] a fact that makes it right or fair to do sth: **~ to do sth** *They have reason to believe she is lying.* ◊ *We have every reason* (= have very good reasons) *to feel optimistic.* ◊ *~why … There is no reason why we should agree to this.* ◊ **~ for (doing) sth** *This result gives us all the more reason for optimism.* ◊ **with~** *She complained, with reason* (= rightly), *that she had been underpaid.* **3** ʔ **B2** [U] the power of the mind to think in a logical way, to understand and have opinions, etc: *Only human beings are capable of reason* (= of thinking in a logical way, etc.). ◊ *to lose your reason* (= become mentally ill) **4** ʔ **B2** [U] what is possible, practical or right: *I can't get her to listen to reason.* ◊ *Why can't they see reason?* ◊ *Look, you're supposed to be the voice of reason here.* ◊ **within~** *He's looking for a job and he's willing to do anything within reason.*

IDM **it ˌstands to ˈreason** (*informal*) it must be clear to any sensible person who thinks about it: *It stands to reason that they'll leave if you don't pay them enough.* ⊃ more at RHYME *n*.

■ *verb* **1** [T, I] **~ (that …)** **| + speech** to form a judgement about a situation by considering the facts and using your power to think in a logical way: *She reasoned that she must have left her bag on the train.* ◊ *They couldn't fire him, he reasoned. He was the only one who knew how the system worked.* **2** [I] to use your power to think and understand: *the human ability to reason*

PHRV **ˌreason sth ˈout** to try and find the answer to a problem by using your power to think in a logical way **SYN** figure out **ˈreason with sb** to talk to sb in order to persuade them to be more sensible: *I tried to reason with him, but he wouldn't listen.*

**rea·son·able** **⓵** **B2** **W** /ˈriːznəbl/ *adj*. **1** **B2** fair, practical, and sensible: **it is ~ (for sb) to do sth** *It is reasonable to assume that he knew beforehand that this would happen.* ◊ *Be reasonable! We can't work late every night.* ◊ *The prosecution has to prove beyond (a) reasonable doubt that he is guilty of murder.* ◊ *We have reasonable grounds for believing that you are responsible.* **OPP** unreasonable **2** ʔ **B2** acceptable and appropriate in a particular situation: *The police apparently thought this explanation perfectly reasonable.* ◊ *The judge said they had a reasonable expectation of privacy relating to the information concerned.* **3** ʔ **B2** (of prices) not too expensive **SYN** fair: *We sell good-quality food at reasonable prices.* ⊃ SYNONYMS at CHEAP **4** ʔ **B2** [usually before noun] fairly good, but not very good **SYN** average: *a reasonable standard of living* ◊ *The hotel was reasonable, I suppose* (= but not excellent).
▶ **rea·son·able·ness** *noun* [U]

**rea·son·ably** ʔ+ **B2** **W** /ˈriːznəbli/ *adv*. **1** ʔ+ **B2** to a degree that is fairly good but not very good: *The instructions are reasonably straightforward.* ◊ *She seems reasonably happy in her new job.* **2** ʔ+ **B2** in a logical and sensible way: *We tried to discuss the matter calmly and reasonably.* **3** ʔ+ **B2** in a fair way: *He couldn't reasonably be expected to pay back the loan all at once.* ◊ *The apartments are reasonably priced* (= not too expensive).

**rea·soned** /ˈriːznd/ *adj*. [only before noun] (of an argument, opinion, etc.) presented in a logical way that shows careful thought

**rea·son·ing** ʔ+ **C1** **W** /ˈriːznɪŋ/ *noun* [U] the process of thinking about things in a logical way; opinions and ideas that are based on logical thinking: *What is the reasoning behind this decision?* ◊ *This line of reasoning is faulty.*

**re·as·sem·ble** /ˌriːəˈsembl/ *verb* **1** [T] **~ sth** to fit the parts of sth together again after it has been taken apart: *We had to take the table apart and reassemble it upstairs.* **2** [I] to meet together again as a group after a break: *The class reassembled after lunch.*

▼ SYNONYMS

**reason**
explanation • grounds • basis • excuse • motive • justification • pretext

These are all words for a cause or an explanation for sth that has happened or that sb has done.

**reason** a cause or an explanation for sth that has happened or that sb has done; a fact that makes it right or fair to do sth: *He said no but he didn't give a reason.*

**explanation** a statement, fact or situation that tells you why sth has happened; a reason given for sth: *The most likely explanation is that his plane was delayed.* ◊ *She left the room abruptly without explanation.*

**grounds** (*rather formal*) a good or true reason for saying, doing or believing sth: *You have no grounds for complaint.*

**basis** (*rather formal*) the reason why people take a particular action: *On what basis will this decision be made?*

**excuse** a reason, either true or invented, that you give to explain or defend your behaviour; a good reason that you give for doing sth that you want to do for other reasons: *Late again! What's your excuse this time?* ◊ *It gave me an excuse to take the car.*

**motive** a reason that explains sb's behaviour: *There seemed to be no motive for the murder.*

**justification** (*rather formal*) a good reason why sth exists or is done: *I can see no possible justification for any further tax increases.*

**GROUNDS OR JUSTIFICATION?**

**Justification** is used to talk about finding or understanding reasons for actions, or trying to explain why it is a good idea to do sth. It is often used with words like *little*, *no*, *some*, *every*, *without*, and *not any*. **Grounds** is used more for talking about reasons that already exist, or that have already been decided, for example by law: *moral/economic grounds*.

**pretext** (*rather formal*) a false reason that you give for doing sth, usually sth bad, in order to hide the real reason: *He left the party early on the pretext of having to work.*

**PATTERNS**
- (a/an) reason/explanation/grounds/basis/excuse/motive/justification/pretext **for** sth
- the reason/motive **behind** sth
- **on the** grounds/basis/pretext **of/that** …
- (a) **good/valid** reason/explanation/grounds/excuse/motive/justification

**re·assert** /ˌriːəˈsɜːt; *NAmE* -ˈsɜːrt/ *verb* **1 ~ sth** to make other people recognize again your right or authority to do sth, after a period when this has been in doubt: *She found it necessary to reassert her position.* **2 ~ itself** to start to have an effect again, after a period of not having any effect: *He thought about giving up his job, but then common sense reasserted itself.* **3** to state again, clearly and definitely, that sth is true: **~ that …** *He reasserted that all parties should be involved in the talks.* **◊ ~ sth** *Traditional values have been reasserted.* ▶ **re·as·ser·tion** /ˌriːəˈsɜːʃn; *NAmE* -ˈsɜːrʃn/ *noun* [sing., U]

**re·assess** /ˌriːəˈses/ *verb* **~ sth** to think again about sth to decide if you need to change your opinion of it **SYN** reappraise ▶ **re·assess·ment** *noun* [U, C]

**re·assign** /ˌriːəˈsaɪn/ *verb* [often passive] **1 ~ sb (to sth)** to give sb a different duty, position or responsibility: *After his election defeat he was reassigned to the diplomatic service.* **2 ~ sth (to sb/sth)** to give sth to a different person or organization; to change the status of sth: *The case was reassigned to a different court.* ▶ **re·assign·ment** *noun* [U, C]

**re·as·sur·ance** /ˌriːəˈʃʊərəns, -ˈʃɔːr-; *NAmE* -ˈʃʊr-/ *noun* **1** [U] **~ (that …)** the fact of giving advice or help that takes away a person's fears or doubts: *to give/provide/offer reassurance* **2** [C] **~ (that …)** something that is said or

# reassure

done to take away a person's fears or doubts: *We have been given reassurances that the water is safe to drink.*

**re·assure** /ˌriːəˈʃʊə(r), -ˈʃɔː(r)/; *NAmE* -ˈʃʊr/ *verb* to say or do sth that makes sb less frightened or worried **SYN** put/set sb's mind at ease/rest: *~sb (about sth) They tried to reassure her, but she still felt anxious.* ◊ *~sb that… The doctor reassured him that there was nothing seriously wrong.*

**re·assur·ing** /ˌriːəˈʃʊərɪŋ, -ˈʃɔːr-; *NAmE* -ˈʃʊr-/ *adj.* making you feel less worried or uncertain about sth: *a reassuring smile* ◊ *It's reassuring (to know) that we've got the money if necessary.* ▶ **re·assur·ing·ly** *adv.*

**re·awaken** /ˌriːəˈweɪkən/ *verb* ~sth to make you feel a particular emotion again or to make you remember sth again **SYN** rekindle: *The place reawakened childhood memories.*

**re·bate** /ˈriːbeɪt/ *noun* **1** an amount of money that is paid back to you because you have paid too much: *a tax rebate* **2** an amount of money that is taken away from the cost of sth, before you pay for it **SYN** discount: *Buyers are offered a cash rebate.*

**rebel** C1 *noun, verb*
- *noun* /ˈrebl/ **1** C1 a person who fights against the government of their country: *rebel forces* ◊ *Armed rebels advanced towards the capital.* **2** C1 a person who opposes sb in authority over them within an organization, a political party, etc: *A number of Tory rebels are planning to vote against the government.* **3** C1 a person who does not like to obey rules or who does not accept normal standards of behaviour, dress, etc: *I've always been the rebel of the family.*
- *verb* /rɪˈbel/ [I] (-ll-) ~(against sb/sth) to fight against or refuse to obey an authority, for example a government, a system, your parents, etc: *He later rebelled against his strict religious upbringing.* ◊ *Most teenagers find something to rebel against.*

**re·bel·lion** C1 /rɪˈbeljən/ *noun* **1** C1 [U, C] an attempt by some of the people in a country to change their government, using violence **SYN** uprising: in ~(against sb/sth) *The north of the country rose in rebellion against the government.* ◊ *The army put down the rebellion.* **2** C1 [U, C] opposition to authority within an organization, a political party, etc: in ~(against sth) *Some members are in rebellion against proposed cuts in spending.* ◊ *The prime minister faces a rebellion from junior members of her party.* **3** C1 [U] opposition to authority; being unwilling to obey rules or accept normal standards of behaviour, dress, etc: *teenage rebellion*

**re·bel·li·ous** /rɪˈbeljəs/ *adj.* **1** unwilling to obey rules or accept normal standards of behaviour, dress, etc: *rebellious teenagers* ◊ *He has always had a rebellious streak.* ➔ WORDFINDER NOTE at YOUNG **2** opposed to the government of a country; opposed to those in authority within an organization: *rebellious cities/factions* ▶ **re·bel·li·ous·ly** *adv.*: *'I don't care!' she said rebelliously.* **re·bel·li·ous·ness** *noun* [U]

**re·birth** /ˌriːˈbɜːθ; *NAmE* -ˈbɜːrθ/ *noun* [U, sing.] **1** a period of new life, growth or activity: *the seasonal cycle of death and rebirth* **2** a spiritual change when a person's faith becomes stronger or they move to another religion

**re·boot** /ˌriːˈbuːt/ *verb* **1** [T, I] ~(sth) (*computing*) if you reboot a computer or it reboots, you switch it off and then start it again immediately ➔ WORDFINDER NOTE at COMPUTER **2** [T] ~sth to make sth, especially a series of films or TV programmes, start again or become successful again: *This film is the producer's second attempt to reboot the franchise.* ▶ **re·boot** /ˌriːˈbuːt/ *noun*: *After a reboot, the program started working again.* ◊ *a trailer for the upcoming 'Spider Man' reboot*

**re·born** /ˌriːˈbɔːn; *NAmE* -ˈbɔːrn/ *verb, adj.*
- *verb* **be reborn** (used only in the passive without *by*) **1** to become active or popular again **2** to be born again: *If you were reborn as an animal, which animal would you be?*
- *adj.* [usually before noun] **1** having become active again: *a reborn version of social democracy* **2** having experienced a complete spiritual change: *reborn evangelical Christians* ➔ see also BORN-AGAIN

**re·bound** *verb, noun*
- *verb* /rɪˈbaʊnd/ **1** [I] ~(from/off sth) to BOUNCE back after hitting sth: *The ball rebounded from the goalpost and Podolski headed it in.* **2** [I] ~(on sb) (*formal*) if sth that you do rebounds on you, it has an unpleasant effect on you, especially when the effect was intended for sb else **SYN** backfire **3** [I] (*business*) (of prices, etc.) to rise again after they have fallen **SYN** bounce back
- *noun* /ˈriːbaʊnd/ **1** (*sport*) a ball that hits sth and BOUNCES back **2** (in basketball) the act of catching the ball after a player has thrown it at the BASKET and has not scored a point **3** (*business*) a positive reaction that happens after sth negative

**IDM** on the ˈrebound while you are sad and confused, especially after a relationship has ended

**re·brand** /ˌriːˈbrænd/ *verb* ~sth/yourself to change the image of a company or an organization or one of its products or services, for example by changing its name or by advertising it in a different way: *In the 1990s the Labour Party rebranded itself as New Labour.* ▶ **re·brand·ing** *noun* [sing., U]: *a rebranding exercise* ◊ *a £5 million rebranding*

**re·buff** /rɪˈbʌf/ *noun* (*formal*) an act of unkindly refusing a friendly offer, request or suggestion **SYN** rejection: *Her offer of help was met with a sharp rebuff.* ▶ **re·buff** *verb*: *~sth They rebuffed her request for help.*

**re·build** C1 /ˌriːˈbɪld/ *verb* (re·built, re·built /-ˈbɪlt/) **1** [T, I] ~(sth) to build or put sth together again: *After the earthquake, the people set about rebuilding their homes.* ◊ *He rebuilt the engine using parts from cars that had been scrapped.* **2** [T] ~sth to make sth/sb complete and strong again: *When she lost her job, she had to rebuild her life completely.* ◊ *attempts to rebuild the shattered post-war economy*

**re·buke** /rɪˈbjuːk/ *verb* [often passive] ~sb (for sth/for doing sth) (*formal*) to speak severely to sb because they have done sth wrong **SYN** reprimand: *The company was publicly rebuked for having neglected safety procedures.* ▶ **re·buke** *noun* [C, U]: *He was silenced by her stinging rebuke.*

**rebus**

to be or not to be

**rebus** /ˈriːbəs/ *noun* a combination of pictures and letters which represent a word or phrase whose meaning has to be guessed

**rebut** /rɪˈbʌt/ *verb* (-tt-) ~sth (*formal*) to say or prove that a statement or criticism is false **SYN** refute ▶ **re·but·tal** /-ˈbʌtl/ *noun* [C, U]: *The accusations met with a firm rebuttal.*

**re·cal·ci·trant** /rɪˈkælsɪtrənt/ *adj.* (*formal*) unwilling to obey rules or follow instructions; difficult to control ▶ **re·cal·ci·trance** /-strəns/ *noun* [U]

**re·call** B2 *verb, noun*
- *verb* /rɪˈkɔːl/ **1** B2 [T, I] (*formal*) (not used in the progressive tenses) to remember sth **SYN** recollect: *~sth She could not recall his name.* ◊ *Many years later Muir recalled his days at Glasgow University.* ◊ *I cannot recall a time when the country faced such serious problems.* ◊ *'I may have; I don't recall,' she said.* ◊ *If I recall correctly, he lives in Luton.* ◊ *~(sb/sth) doing sth I can't recall meeting her before.* ◊ *~that… He recalled that she always came home late on Wednesdays.* ◊ *~what, when, etc. Can you recall exactly what happened?* ◊ *~+ speech 'It was on a Thursday in March,' he recalled.* **2** [T] *~sth* (not used in the progressive tenses) to make sb think of sth **SYN** evoke: *The poem recalls Eliot's 'The Waste Land'.* **3** [T] to order sb to return: *~sb Both countries recalled their ambassadors.* ◊ *~sb to sth He was recalled to military duty.* ◊ *They have both been recalled to the Welsh squad (= selected as members of the*

team after a time when they were not selected). **4** [T] ~ **sth** to ask for sth to be returned, often because there is sth wrong with it: *The company has recalled all the faulty hairdryers.*

■ **noun** /ˈriːkɔːl; rɪˈkɔːl/ **1** [U] the ability to remember sth that you have learned or sth that has happened in the past: *She has amazing powers of recall.* ◊ *to have **instant recall** (=* to be able to remember sth immediately) ◊ *to have **total recall** (=* to be able to remember all the details of sth) **2** [sing.] an official order or request for sb/sth to return, or for sth to be given back: *Thomas's recall to the Welsh team* ◊ *The manufacturer has issued a **product recall** over safety fears.*

**IDM** **beyond reˈcall** impossible to bring back to the original state; impossible to remember

**reˈcant** /rɪˈkænt/ *verb* [T, I] ~ **(sth)** *(formal)* to say, often publicly, that you no longer have the same belief or opinion that you had before ▶ **reˈcanˈtaˈtion** /ˌriːkænˈteɪʃn/ *noun* [C, U]

**recap** /ˈriːkæp/ *verb, noun*
■ *verb* [I, T] (**-pp-**) ~ **(on sth)** | ~ **sth** | ~ **what, where, etc …** = RECAPITULATE: *Let me just recap on what we've decided so far.*
■ *noun* = RECAPITULATION

**reˈcapˈituˈlate** /ˌriːkəˈpɪtʃuleɪt/ *verb* (*formal*) (*also* **recap**) [I, T] ~ **(on sth)** | ~ **sth** | ~ **what, where, etc …** to repeat or give a summary of what has already been said, decided, etc: *To recapitulate briefly, the three main points are these …* ▶ **reˈcapˈituˈlaˈtion** /ˌriːkəpɪtʃuˈleɪʃn/ *noun* [C, U] (*formal*) (*also* **recap**)

**reˈcapˈture** /ˌriːˈkæptʃə(r)/ *verb* **1** ~ **sth** to win back a place, position, etc. that was previously taken from you by an enemy or opponent: *Government troops soon recaptured the island.* **2** ~ **sb/sth** to catch a person or an animal that has escaped **3** ~ **sth** to bring back a feeling or repeat an experience that you had in the past: *He was trying to recapture the happiness of his youth.* ▶ **reˈcapˈture** *noun* [U]: *the recapture of towns occupied by the rebels*

**reˈcast** /ˌriːˈkɑːst; *NAmE* -ˈkæst/ *verb* (**reˈcast**, **reˈcast**) **1** ~ **sth (as sth)** to change sth by organizing or presenting it in a different way: *She recast her lecture as a radio talk.* **2** ~ **sb (as sth)** to change the actors or the role of a particular actor in a play, etc.

**recce** /ˈreki/ *noun* (*BrE, informal*) = RECONNAISSANCE: *to do a quick recce of an area*

**reˈcede** /rɪˈsiːd/ *verb* **1** [I] to move gradually away from sb or away from a previous position: *The sound of the truck receded into the distance.* ◊ *She watched his receding figure.* **2** [I] (especially of a problem, feeling or quality) to become gradually weaker or smaller: *The prospect of bankruptcy has now receded* (= it is less likely). ◊ *The pain was receding slightly.* **3** [I] (of hair) to stop growing at the front of the head: *a middle-aged man with receding hair/a receding hairline* **4** [I] **a receding chin** a CHIN (= part of the face below the mouth) that slopes backwards towards the neck

# reˈceipt ❶ **B1** /rɪˈsiːt/ *noun* **1** ❢ **B1** [C] a piece of paper or an electronic document that shows that goods or services have been paid for: *Can I have a receipt, please?* ◊ ~ **for sth** *Do you need a receipt for that?* ⇒ **WORD-FINDER NOTE** at BUY **2** ❢ **B2** [U] (*formal*) the act of receiving sth: ~ **of sth** *to acknowledge receipt of a letter* ◊ **on** ~ **of sth** *The goods will be dispatched on receipt of an order form.* ◊ **in** ~ **of sth** *Are you in receipt of any state benefits?* **3 receipts** [pl.] (*business*) money that a business, bank or government receives: *net/gross receipts*

**reˈceivˈable** /rɪˈsiːvəbl/ *adj.* (usually following a noun) (*business*) (of bills, accounts, etc.) for which money has not yet been received: *accounts receivable*

**reˈceivˈables** /rɪˈsiːvəblz/ *noun* [pl.] (*business*) money that is owed to a business

# reˈceive ❶ **A2** /rɪˈsiːv/ *verb*
• GET/ACCEPT **1** ❢ **A2** [T] (*rather formal*) to get or accept sth that is sent or given to you: ~ **sth** *to receive a letter/message/phone call* ◊ *to receive information/payment/thanks* ◊ ~ **sth from sb/sth** *He received an award for bravery from the police.*

1287 **reception**

• TREATMENT **2** ❢ **B1** [T] to experience or be given a particular type of treatment or attention: ~ **sth** *Her work has not received the attention it deserves.* ◊ *She received urgent hospital treatment.* ◊ ~ **sth from sb** *We have received overwhelming support from the local community.*
• IMPRESSION **3** ❢ **B1** ~ **sth** to form an idea or impression of sb/sth as a result of what you see, experience, etc: *I did not receive the impression that he was afraid.*
• INJURY **4** ❢ **B1** [T] ~ **sth** to be injured in a particular way: *to receive severe injuries* ◊ *She received only minor cuts and bruises.*
• REACT TO STH **5** ❢ **B2** [T, usually passive] to react to sth new, in a particular way: **be received + adv. / prep.** *The play was well received by the critics.* ◊ **be received with sth** *The proposals have been received with great enthusiasm.*
• GUESTS **6** [T, often passive] ~ **sb (with sth)** | ~ **sb (as sth)** (*formal*) to welcome or entertain a guest, especially formally: *He was received as an honoured guest at the White House.*
• AS MEMBER OF STH **7** [T] ~ **sb (into sth)** (*formal*) to officially recognize and accept sb as a member of a group: *Three young people were received into the Church at Easter.*
• TV/RADIO **8** [T] ~ **sth** to change broadcast signals into sounds or pictures on a television, radio, etc: *to receive programmes via satellite* **9** [T] ~ **sth/sb** to be able to hear a radio message that is being sent by sb: *I'm receiving you loud and clear.*
• STOLEN GOODS **10** [T, I] ~ **(sth)** (*especially BrE*) to buy or accept goods that you know have been stolen
• IN SPORT **11** [I, T] ~ **(sth)** (in tennis, etc.) to be the player that the SERVER hits the ball to: *She won the toss and chose to receive.*

**IDM** **be at / on the reˈceiving end (of sth)** (*informal*) to be the person that an action, etc. is directed at, especially an unpleasant one: *She found herself on the receiving end of a great deal of criticism.*

**reˈceived** /rɪˈsiːvd/ *adj.* [only before noun] (*formal*) accepted by most people as being correct: *The **received wisdom** is that they cannot win.*

**reˌceived proˌnunciˈation** *noun* [U] = RP

**reˈceiver** ❢+ **B2** /rɪˈsiːvə(r)/ *noun* **1** ❢+ **B2** the part of a phone that you hold close to your mouth and ear: *to pick up/lift/put down/replace the receiver* ⇒ *compare* HANDSET **2** ❢+ **B2** a piece of radio or television equipment that changes broadcast signals into sound or pictures: *a satellite/GPS receiver* ⇒ *compare* TRANSMITTER **3** (*BrE also* **ofˈficial reˈceiver**) (*law*) a person who is chosen by a court to be in charge of a company that is BANKRUPT: *to call in the receivers* **4** a person who receives sth: *Molly's more of a giver than a receiver.* **5** a person who buys or accepts stolen goods, knowing that they have been stolen **6** (in AMERICAN FOOTBALL ) a player who plays in a position in which the ball can be caught when it is being passed forward ⇒ *see also* WIDE RECEIVER

**reˈceiverˈship** /rɪˈsiːvəʃɪp; *NAmE* -vərʃ-/ *noun* [U] (*law*) the state of a business being controlled by an official receiver because it has no money

# reˈcent ❶ **A2** ❢ /ˈriːsnt/ *adj.* [usually before noun] that happened or began only a short time ago: *a recent study/report/survey* ◊ *his most recent visit to Poland* ◊ *There have been many changes in recent years.* ◊ *in recent months/weeks/days*

# reˈcentˈly ❶ **A2** ❢ /ˈriːsntli/ *adv.* not long ago: *a recently published book* ◊ *The company recently announced plans to lay off one-fifth of its workforce.* ◊ *We received a letter from him recently.* ◊ *Until recently they were living in York.* ◊ *I haven't seen them recently* (= it is some time since I saw them). ◊ *Have you used it recently* (= in the recent past)? ◊ *It's only recently that it's become a problem.*

**reˈcepˈtacle** /rɪˈseptəkl/ *noun* **1** ~ **(for sth)** (*formal*) a container for putting sth in **2** (*NAmE*) = OUTLET (5)

# reˈcepˈtion ❶ **A2** ❢ /rɪˈsepʃn/ *noun* **1** ❢ **A2** [U] (*especially BrE*) the area inside the entrance of a hotel, an office building, etc. where guests or visitors go first when they arrive: **in** ~ *We arranged to meet in reception at 6.30.* ◊ **at** ~ *I've left the keys at reception.* ◊ **on** ~ *I've been on reception*

# reception centre

(= working there) *the whole morning.* ◊ (*NAmE, BrE*) *the reception desk* ⊃ compare FRONT DESK ⊃ WORDFINDER NOTE at HOTEL **2** [C] a formal social occasion to welcome sb or celebrate sth: *a wedding reception* ⊃ WORDFINDER NOTE at WEDDING **3** [sing.] the type of welcome that is given to sb/sth: *The band got a rapturous reception from the crowd.* ◊ *Delegates gave him a warm reception as he called for more spending on education.* **4** [U] the quality of radio and television signals that are broadcast: *good/bad reception* ◊ *There was very poor reception on my phone.* **5** [U] the act of receiving or welcoming sb: *the reception of refugees from the war zone* **6** [U] (*also* **reception class** [C]) (in England and Wales) the first class at school for children aged 4 or 5: *My son is in reception.*

**re·cep·tion centre** (*especially US* **re·cep·tion center**) *noun* **1** a place where people can get information or advice: *The museum is building a new reception centre for visitors.* **2** a place where people, for example those without a home, can get help and temporary accommodation: *a reception centre for refugees*

**re·cep·tion class** *noun* = RECEPTION (6)

**re·cep·tion·ist** /rɪˈsepʃənɪst/ *noun* a person whose job is to deal with people arriving at or phoning a hotel, an office building, a doctor's surgery, etc. ⊃ WORDFINDER NOTE at DOCTOR

**re·cep·tion room** *noun* (*BrE*) (used especially when advertising houses for sale) a room in a house where people can sit, for example a living room or DINING ROOM

**re·cep·tive** /rɪˈseptɪv/ *adj.* ~ (**to sth**) willing to listen to or to accept new ideas or suggestions SYN **responsive**: *She was always receptive to new ideas.* ◊ *He gave an impressive speech to a receptive audience.* ▶ **re·cep·tive·ness** *noun* [U] **re·cep·tiv·ity** /ˌriːsepˈtɪvəti/ *noun* [U]: *receptivity to change*

**re·cep·tor** /rɪˈseptə(r)/ *noun* (*biology*) a sense organ or nerve ending in the body that reacts to changes such as heat or cold and makes the body react in a particular way

**re·cess** *noun, verb*
- *noun* /ˈriːses, rɪˈses/ **1** [C, U] a period of time during the year when the members of a parliament, committee, etc. do not meet **2** [C] a short break in a trial in court: *The judge called a short recess.* **3** (*NAmE*) (*BrE* **break**, **break time**) [U] a period of time between lessons at school **4** [C] a part of a wall that is set further back than the rest of the wall, forming a space SYN **alcove**: *a recess for books* **5** [C, usually pl.] the part of a place that is furthest from the light and hard to see or get to: *He stared into the dark recesses of the room.* ◊ (*figurative*) *The doubt was still there, in the deep recesses of her mind.*
- *verb* /rɪˈses/ [often passive] **1** [T, I] ~ (**sth**) (*NAmE*) to take or to order a recess: *The hearing was recessed for the weekend.* **2** [T] ~ **sth** (**in/into sth**) to put sth in a position that is set back into a wall, etc: *recessed shelves*

**re·ces·sion** /rɪˈseʃn/ *noun* **1** [C, U] a difficult time for the economy of a country, when there is less trade and industrial activity than usual and more people are unemployed: *the impact of the current recession on manufacturing* ◊ **in ~** *The economy is in deep recession.* ◊ *policies to pull the country out of recession* **2** [U] (*formal*) the movement backwards of sth from a previous position: *the gradual recession of the floodwater*

**re·ces·sion·ary** /rɪˈseʃənri/ *NAmE* -ʃəneri/ *adj.* [only before noun] connected with a recession or likely to cause one

**re·ces·sive** /rɪˈsesɪv/ *adj.* (*biology*) a **recessive** physical characteristic only appears in a child if it has two GENES for this characteristic, one from each parent ⊃ compare DOMINANT (2)

**re·charge** /ˌriːˈtʃɑːdʒ; *NAmE* -ˈtʃɑːrdʒ/ *verb* **1** [T, I] ~ (**sth**) to fill a battery with electrical power; to be filled with electrical power: *He plugged his razor in to recharge it.* ◊ *The drill takes about three hours to recharge.* **2** [I] (*informal*) to get back your strength and energy by resting for a time: *We needed the break in order to recharge.* ▶ **re·charge·able** *adj.*: *rechargeable batteries*
IDM **recharge your batteries** to get back your strength and energy by resting for a while

**re·cid·iv·ist** /rɪˈsɪdɪvɪst/ *noun* (*formal*) a person who continues to commit crimes, and seems unable to stop, even after being punished ▶ **re·cid·iv·ism** /-vɪzəm/ *noun* [U]

**re·cipe** /ˈresəpi/ *noun* **1** a set of instructions that tells you how to cook sth and the INGREDIENTS (= items of food) you need for it: **~ for sth** *a recipe for chicken soup* ◊ *vegetarian recipes* ◊ *a recipe book* **2** **~ for sth** a method or an idea that seems likely to have a particular result SYN **formula**: *His plans are a recipe for disaster.* ◊ *What's her recipe for success?*

**re·cipi·ent** /rɪˈsɪpiənt/ *noun* (*formal*) a person who receives sth: *recipients of awards*

**re·cip·ro·cal** /rɪˈsɪprəkl/ *adj.* involving two people or groups who agree to help each other or behave in the same way to each other: *The two colleges have a reciprocal arrangement whereby students from one college can attend classes at the other.* ▶ **re·cip·ro·cal·ly** /-kli/ *adv.*

**re·cip·ro·cate** /rɪˈsɪprəkeɪt/ *verb* **1** [T, I] to behave or feel towards sb in the same way as they behave or feel towards you: **~ sth** (**with sth**) *Her passion for him was not reciprocated.* ◊ **~ (with sth)** *I wasn't sure whether to laugh or to reciprocate with a remark of my own.* **2** [I] (*specialist*) to move backwards and forwards in a straight line: *a reciprocating action* ▶ **re·cip·ro·ca·tion** /rɪˌsɪprəˈkeɪʃn/ *noun* [U]

**reci·proci·ty** /ˌresɪˈprɒsəti; *NAmE* -ˈprɑːs-/ *noun* [U] (*formal*) a situation in which two people, countries, etc. provide the same help or advantages to each other

**re·cital** /rɪˈsaɪtl/ *noun* **1** a public performance of music or poetry, usually given by one person or a small group: *to give a piano recital* **2** a spoken description of a series of events, etc. that is often long and boring

**reci·ta·tion** /ˌresɪˈteɪʃn/ *noun* **1** [C, U] an act of saying a piece of poetry or literature that you have learned to an audience **2** [C] an act of talking or writing about a series of things: *She continued her recitation of the week's events.*

**reci·ta·tive** /ˌresɪtəˈtiːv/ *noun* [C, U] (*music*) a passage in an OPERA or ORATORIO that is sung in the rhythm of ordinary speech with many words on the same note ⊃ WORDFINDER NOTE at OPERA

**re·cite** /rɪˈsaɪt/ *verb* **1** [T, I] ~ (**sth**) (**to sb**) | ~ **what**… | **+ speech** to say a poem, piece of literature, etc. that you have learned, especially to an audience: *Each child had to recite a poem to the class.* ⊃ WORDFINDER NOTE at POETRY **2** [T] ~ **sth** (**to sb**) | ~ **what**… | **+ speech** to say a list or series of things: *They recited all their grievances to me.* ◊ *She could recite a list of all the kings and queens.*

**reck·less** /ˈrekləs/ *adj.* showing a lack of care about danger and the possible results of your actions SYN **rash**: *He showed a reckless disregard for his own safety.* ◊ *She was a good rider, but reckless.* ◊ *to cause death by reckless driving* ◊ **~ with sth** *He had always been reckless with money.* ▶ **reck·less·ly** *adv.*: *He admitted driving recklessly.* **reck·less·ness** *noun* [U]

**reckon** /ˈrekən/ *verb* **1** [T, I] ~ (**that**)… (especially *BrE, informal*) to think sth or have an opinion about sth: *I reckon (that) I'm going to get that job.* ◊ *He'll be famous one day. What do you reckon* (= do you agree)? ◊ *It's worth a lot of money, I reckon.* ◊ *'They'll never find out.' 'You reckon?'* (= I think you may be wrong about that) ⊃ SYNONYMS at THINK **2** **be reckoned** [T] (not used in the progressive tenses) to be generally considered to be sth: **be reckoned to be/have sth** *Children are reckoned to be more sophisticated nowadays.* ◊ **+ noun/adj.** *It was generally reckoned a success.* **3** [T] **~ to do sth** (*BrE, informal*) to expect to do sth: *We reckon to finish by ten.* **4** [T] to calculate an amount, a number, etc.: **~ sth** **be reckoned at sth** *The age of the earth is reckoned at about 4.6 billion years.* ◊ **~ (that)**… *They reckon (that) their profits are down by at least 20%.* ◊ **be reckoned to do sth** *The journey was reckoned to take about two hours.* IDM see NAME *n.*
PHRV **ˈreckon on sth** to expect sth to happen or to rely on sth happening: *They hadn't reckoned on a rebellion.* ◊ **reckon on doing sth** *We'd reckoned on having good weather.* **ˌreckon sth↔ˈup** (especially *BrE*) to calculate the total amount or number of sth: *He reckoned up the cost of everything in his mind.* **ˈreckon with sb/sth 1** [usually passive] to consider or treat sb/sth as a serious opponent, problem, etc: *They were already a political force* **to be reckoned with.**

**2** (usually used in negative sentences) to consider sth as a possible problem that you should be prepared for SYN **take sth into account**: **reckon with doing sth** *I didn't reckon with getting caught up in so much traffic.* '**reckon without sb/sth** (*especially BrE*) to not consider sb/sth as a possible problem that you should be prepared for SYN **not take sth into account**: *They had reckoned without the determination of the opposition.*

**reck·on·ing** /ˈrekənɪŋ/ *noun* **1** [U, C] the act of calculating sth, especially in a way that is not very exact: *By my reckoning you still owe me £5.* **2** [C, usually sing., U] a time when sb's actions will be judged to be right or wrong and they may be punished: *In the final reckoning truth is rewarded.* ◇ *Officials concerned with environmental policy predict that a day of reckoning will come.*
IDM **in/into/out of the ˈreckoning** (*especially BrE*) (especially in sport) among/not among those who are likely to win or be successful: *Wilshere is fit again and could come into the reckoning.*

**re·claim** /rɪˈkleɪm/ *verb* **1** to get sth back or to ask to have it back after it has been lost, taken away, etc.: ~ **sth** *You'll have to go to the police station to reclaim your wallet.* ◇ ~ **sth from sb/sth** *The team reclaimed the title from their rivals.* ⊃ see also BAGGAGE RECLAIM **2** ~ **sth (from sth)** to make land that is naturally too wet or too dry suitable to be built on, farmed, etc: *The site for the airport will be reclaimed from the swamp.* ◇ *reclaimed land* **3** [usually passive] ~ **sth** if a piece of land **is reclaimed by** desert, forest, etc., it turns back into desert, etc. after being used for farming or building **4** ~ **sth (from sth)** to obtain materials from waste products so that they can be used again ⊃ see also RECYCLE **5** ~ **sb (from sth)** to rescue sb from a bad or criminal way of life ▶ **rec·lam·ation** /ˌrekləˈmeɪʃn/ *noun* [U]: *land reclamation*

**re·clas·sify** /ˌriːˈklæsɪfaɪ/ *verb* (**re·clas·si·fies**, **re·clas·si·fy·ing**, **re·clas·si·fied**, **re·clas·si·fied**) ~ **sth** to put sth in a different class or category: *The drug is to be reclassified after trials showed it to be more harmful than previously thought.*

**re·cline** /rɪˈklaɪn/ *verb* **1** [I] ~ **(against/in/on sth)** (*formal*) to sit or lie in a relaxed way, with your body leaning backwards: *She was reclining on a sofa.* ◇ *a reclining figure* (= for example in a painting) **2** [I, T] ~ **(sth)** when a seat **reclines** or when you **recline** a seat, the back of it moves into a comfortable, sloping position: *a reclining chair*

**re·cliner** /rɪˈklaɪnə(r)/ (*also* **reˈcliner chair**) *noun* a soft comfortable chair with a back that can be pushed back at an angle so that you can lean back in it

**re·cluse** /rɪˈkluːs; *NAmE* ˈreklu:s/ *noun* a person who lives alone and likes to avoid other people: *a recluse* ▶ **re·clu·sive** /rɪˈkluːsɪv/ *adj.*: *a reclusive millionaire*

**rec·og·ni·tion** 🗣️ B2 OPAL /ˌrekəɡˈnɪʃn/ *noun* **1** 🗣️ B2 [U] the act of remembering who sb is when you see them, or of identifying what sth is: *He glanced briefly towards her but there was no sign of recognition.* ◇ *the automatic recognition of handwriting and printed text by computer* **2** 🗣️ C1 [sing., U] the act of accepting that sth exists, is true or is official: ~ **that** … *a growing recognition that older people have potential too* ◇ ~ **of sth** *There is a general recognition of the urgent need for reform.* ◇ ~ **as sth** *to seek international/official/formal recognition as a sovereign state* **3** 🗣️ C1 [U] public praise and reward for sb's work or actions: ~ **for sth** *She gained only minimal recognition for her work.* ◇ **in ~ of sth** *He received the award in recognition of his success over the past year.*
IDM **to change, alter, etc. beyond/out of (all) recogˈnition** to change so much that you can hardly recognize it: *The town has changed beyond recognition since I was last here.*

**rec·og·niz·able** (*BrE also* **-is·able**) /ˈrekəɡnaɪzəbl; *BrE also* ˌrekəɡˈnaɪzəbl/ *adj.* ~ **(as sth/sb)** easy to know or identify: *The building was easily recognizable as a prison.* ◇ *After so many years she was still instantly recognizable.* OPP **unrecognizable** ▶ **rec·og·niz·ably**, **-is·ably** /-bli/ *adv.*

**rec·og·ni·zance** (*BrE also* **-is·ance**) /rɪˈkɒɡnɪzəns; *NAmE* -ˈkɑːɡ-/ *noun* [U] (*law*) a promise by sb who is accused of a crime to appear in court on a particular date; a sum of money paid as a guarantee of this promise

**rec·og·nize** 🗣️ A2 OPAL (*BrE also* **-ise**) /ˈrekəɡnaɪz/ *verb* (not used in the progressive tenses) **1** 🗣️ A2 to know who sb is or what sth is when you see or hear them or it, because you have seen or heard them or it before: ~ **sb/sth** *I recognized him as soon as he came in the room.* ◇ *Do you recognize this tune?* ◇ ~ **sb/sth by/from sth** *I recognized her by her red hair.* ⊃ SYNONYMS at IDENTIFY **2** 🗣️ B2 to admit or to be aware that sth exists or is true SYN **acknowledge**: ~ **sth** *They recognized the need to take the problem seriously.* ◇ ~ **sth as sth** *Drugs were not recognized as a problem then.* ◇ ~ **sb/sth to be/have sth** *Drugs were not recognized to be a problem then.* ◇ ~ **how, what, etc** … *Nobody recognized how urgent the situation was.* ◇ ~ **that** … *We recognized that the task was not straightforward.* ◇ **it is recognized that** … *It is widely recognized that driver fatigue is a problem on motorways.* ⊃ SYNONYMS at ADMIT **3** 🗣️ B2 to accept and approve of sb/sth officially: ~ **sb/sth** *The UK has refused to recognize the new regime.* ◇ *These qualifications are recognized throughout the EU.* ◇ *internationally recognized human rights* ◇ **be recognized as sb/sth** *The organization has not been officially recognized as a trade union.* ◇ **be recognized to be/have sth** *He is recognized to be their natural leader.* **4** 🗣️ B2 **be recognized (as sth)** to be thought of as very good or important by people in general: *The book is now recognized as a classic.* ◇ *She's a recognized authority on the subject.* **5** ~ **sb/sth** to give sb official thanks for sth that they have done or achieved: *His services to the state were recognized with the award of a knighthood.*

**re·coil** *verb, noun*
▪ *verb* /rɪˈkɔɪl/ **1** [I] to move your body quickly away from sb/sth because you find them or it frightening or unpleasant SYN **flinch**: ~ **(from sb/sth)** *She recoiled from his touch.* ◇ ~ **at sth** *He recoiled in horror at the sight of the corpse.* **2** [I] ~ **(from sth/from doing sth)** | ~ **(at sth)** to react to an idea or a situation with strong dislike or fear SYN **shrink**: *She recoiled from the idea of betraying her own brother.* **3** [I] (of a gun) to move suddenly backwards when it is fired
▪ *noun* /ˈriːkɔɪl/ [U, sing.] a sudden movement backwards, especially of a gun when it is fired

**rec·ol·lect** /ˌrekəˈlekt/ *verb* [T, I] (not used in the progressive tenses) (*rather formal*) to remember sth, especially by making an effort to remember it SYN **recall**: ~ **(sth)** *She could no longer recollect the details of the letter.* ◇ *As far as I can recollect, she wasn't there on that occasion.* ◇ ~ **what, how, etc** … *I don't recollect what he said.* ◇ ~ **that** … *I recollect that we were all gathered in the kitchen.* ◇ ~ **(sb/sth) doing sth** *I recollect him/his saying that it was dangerous.* ◇ **+ speech** *'It was just before the war,' she recollected.*

**rec·ol·lec·tion** /ˌrekəˈlekʃn/ *noun* **1** [U] the ability to remember sth; the act of remembering sth SYN **memory**: ~ **(of doing sth)** *I have no recollection of meeting her before.* ◇ ~ **(of sth)** *My recollection of events differs from his.* ◇ **To the best of my recollection** (= if I remember correctly) *I was not present at that meeting.* **2** [C] a thing that you remember from the past SYN **memory**: *to have a clear/vivid/dim/vague recollection of sth*

**re·com·mence** /ˌriːkəˈmens/ *verb* [I, T] (*formal*) to begin again; to start doing sth again: *Work on the bridge will recommence next month.* ◇ ~ **(doing) sth** *The two countries agreed to recommence talks the following week.*

**rec·om·mend** 🗣️ A2 OPAL /ˌrekəˈmend/ *verb* **1** 🗣️ A2 to tell sb that sth is good or useful, or that sb would be suitable for a particular job, etc.: ~ **sb/sth** *The hotel's new restaurant comes highly recommended* (= a lot of people have praised it). ◇ ~ **sb/sth to sb** *I recommend the book to all my students.* ◇ ~ **sb/sth for sth/sb** *She was recommended for the post by a colleague.* ◇ ~ **sb/sth as sth** *The guidelines recommend low-fat dairy products as excellent sources of calcium* **2** 🗣️ A2 to advise a particular course of action; to advise sb to do sth: ~ **sth** *The report recommended a 10% pay increase.* ◇ *It is dangerous to exceed the recommended dose.* ◇ ~ **doing sth** *He recommended reading the book before seeing the movie.* ◇ ~ **against sth/against doing sth** *My doctor recommended against surgery.* ◇ ~ **(that)** … *I recommend that he see a lawyer.* ◇ **it is**

# recommendation

## SYNONYMS

### recommend
advise • advocate • urge

These words all mean to tell sb what you think they should do in a particular situation.

**recommend** to tell sb what you think they should do in a particular situation; to say what you think the price or level of sth should be: *We'd recommend you to book your flight early.* ◇ *a recommended price of $50*

**advise** to tell sb what you think they should do in a particular situation: *I'd advise you not to tell him.*

### RECOMMEND OR ADVISE?
**Advise** is a stronger word than **recommend** and is often used when the person giving the advice is in a position of authority: *Police are advising fans without tickets to stay away.* ◇ *Police are recommending fans without tickets to stay away.* *I advise you…* can suggest that you know better than the person you are advising: this may cause offence if they are your equal or senior to you. *I recommend…* mainly suggests that you are trying to be helpful and is less likely to cause offence. **Recommend** is often used with more positive advice to tell sb about possible benefits and **advise** with more negative advice to warn sb about possible dangers: *He advised reading the book before seeing the movie.* ◇ *I would recommend against going out on your own.*

**advocate** (*formal*) to support or recommend sth publicly: *The group does not advocate the use of violence.*

**urge** (*formal*) to recommend sth strongly: *The situation is dangerous and the UN is urging caution.*

### PATTERNS
- to recommend / advise / advocate / urge that …
- It is recommended / advised / advocated / urged that …
- to recommend / advise / urge sb to do sth
- to recommend / advise / advocate doing sth
- to **strongly** recommend / advise / advocate sb / sth

## EXPRESS YOURSELF

### Asking for and making a recommendation

When you need help making a choice, you can ask somebody to give you their view:
- *What would / do you recommend?*
- *What do you think would be best?*
- *Which of the options do you favour / prefer?*

Responses:
- *I can recommend the steak today.*
- *My favourite is the Corner Cafe.*
- *I'd recommend waiting a few months.*
- *I suggest you have another look at the house before you make a decision.*
- *If it were up to me / If you ask me / If it were my decision, I'd go for the cheaper one.*

**recommended that …** *It is strongly recommended that the machines should be checked every year.* ◇ **~ sb to do sth** *We'd recommend you to book your flight early.* ◇ **how, what, etc …** *Can you recommend how much we should charge?* **3 ~ sb / sth (to sb)** to make sb/sth seem attractive or good **SYN** **commend**: *This system has much to recommend it.*

**rec·om·men·da·tion** ⊙ B1 /ˌrekəmenˈdeɪʃn/ noun **1** ? B1 [C] an official suggestion about the best thing to do: *to accept/reject a recommendation* ◇ **~ for / on sth** *Her report lists numerous recommendations for the improvement of safety.* ◇ **~ to sb** *The committee made recommendations to the board on teachers' pay and conditions.* ◇ **~ from sb/sth** *We will be implementing all the recommendations from the report.* ◇ **on the ~ of sb / sth** *I had the operation on the recommendation of my doctor.* **2** ? B1 [U, C] the act of telling sb that sth is good or useful or that sb would be suitable for a particular job, etc: *It's best to find a builder through personal recommendation.* ◇ **on sb's ~** *We chose the hotel on their recommendation (= because they recommended it).* ◇ *Here's the list of my top restaurant recommendations.* **3** [C] (*especially NAmE*) a formal letter or statement that sb would be suitable for a particular job, etc. **SYN** **testimonial**

**rec·om·pense** /ˈrekəmpens/ noun, verb
- **noun** [U] (*formal*) something, usually money, that you are given because you have suffered in some way, or as a payment for sth: **~ (for sb / sth)** *There must be adequate recompense for workers who lose their jobs.* ◇ **in ~ (for sth)** *I received $1000 in recompense for loss of earnings.*
- **verb** **~ sb (for sth)** (*formal*) to do sth for sb or give them a payment for sth that they have suffered **SYN** **compensate**: *There was no attempt to recompense the miners for the loss of their jobs.*

**recon** /ˈriːkɒn; *NAmE* -kɑːn/ noun [C, U] (*NAmE, informal*) = **RECONNAISSANCE**

**rec·on·cile** /ˈrekənsaɪl/ verb (*formal*) **1 ~ sth (with sth)** to find an acceptable way of dealing with two or more ideas, needs, etc. that seem to be opposed to each other: *an attempt to reconcile the need for industrial development with concern for the environment* ◇ *It was hard to reconcile his career ambitions with the needs of his children.* **2** [usually passive] to make people become friends again after an argument or a DISAGREEMENT: **~ sb** *The pair were reconciled after Jackson made a public apology.* ◇ **~ sb with sb** *He has recently been reconciled with his wife.* **3 ~ sb / yourself (to sth)** to make sb/yourself accept an unpleasant situation because it is not possible to change it **SYN** **resign yourself to**: *He could not reconcile himself to the prospect of losing her.* ▶ **rec·on·cil·able** /ˌrekənˈsaɪləbl/ adj.

**rec·on·cili·ation** /ˌrekənsɪliˈeɪʃn/ noun **1** [sing., U] **~ (between A and B) | ~ (with sb)** an end to a DISAGREEMENT or conflict with sb and the start of a good relationship again: *Their change of policy brought about a reconciliation with Britain.* **2** [U] **~ (between A and B) | ~ (of A) (and / with B)** the process of making it possible for two different ideas, facts, etc. to exist together without being opposed to each other: *the reconciliation between environment and development*

**rec·on·dite** /ˈrekəndaɪt/ adj. (*formal*) not known about or understood by many people **SYN** **obscure**

**re·con·di·tion** /ˌriːkənˈdɪʃn/ verb [often passive] **~ sth** to repair a machine so that it is in good condition and works well **SYN** **overhaul**

**re·con·fig·ure** /ˌriːkənˈfɪɡə(r); *NAmE* -ˈfɪɡjər/ verb **~ sth** to make changes to the way that sth is arranged to work, especially computer equipment or a program: *You may need to reconfigure the firewall if you add a new machine to your network.*

**re·con·firm** /ˌriːkənˈfɜːm; *NAmE* -ˈfɜːrm/ verb **~ sth** to check again that sth is definitely correct or as previously arranged: *You have to reconfirm your flight 24 hours before travelling.*

**re·con·nais·sance** /rɪˈkɒnɪsns; *NAmE* -ˈkɑː.n-/ (*also BrE, informal* **recce**) (*also NAmE, informal* **recon**) noun [C, U] the activity of getting information about an area for military purposes, using soldiers, planes, etc: *to make an aerial reconnaissance of the island* ◇ *Time spent on reconnaissance is seldom wasted.* ◇ *a reconnaissance aircraft/mission/satellite* ⊃ **WORDFINDER NOTE** at **EXPLORE**

**re·con·nect** /ˌriːkəˈnekt/ verb [T, I] to connect sth again; to connect to sth again: **~ sth (to sth)** *I replaced the taps and reconnected the water supply.* ◇ **~ (to sth)** *Once you have removed the virus it is safe to reconnect to the internet.*

**re·con·noitre** (*US* -ter) /ˌrekəˈnɔɪtə(r); *NAmE also* ˌriːk-/ verb [I, T] **~ (sth)** to get information about an area, especially for military purposes, by using soldiers, planes, etc.

**re·con·quer** /ˌriːˈkɒŋkə(r); *NAmE* -ˈkɑːŋ-/ verb **~ sth** to take control again of a country or city by force, after having lost it

**re·con·sider** /ˌriːkənˈsɪdə(r)/ verb [T, I] **~ (sth) | ~ what, how, etc …** to think about sth again, especially because you might want to change a previous decision or opinion: *to reconsider your decision/position* ◇ *Recent information may persuade the board to reconsider.* ▶ **re·con·sider·ation** /ˌriːkənˌsɪdəˈreɪʃn/ noun [U, sing.]

**re·con·sti·tute** /ˌriːˈkɒnstɪtjuːt; NAmE -ˈkɑːnstɪtuːt/ verb **1** ~ **sth/itself (as sth)** (formal) to form an organization or a group again in a different way: *The group reconstituted itself as a political party.* **2** [usually passive] ~ **sth** to bring dried food, etc. back to its original form by adding water ▶ **re·con·sti·tu·tion** /ˌriːˌkɒnstɪˈtjuːʃn; NAmE -ˌkɑːnstɪˈtuː-/ noun [U]

**re·con·struct** ⓦ /ˌriːkənˈstrʌkt/ verb **1** ~ **sth (from sth)** to build or make sth again that has been damaged or that no longer exists: *They have tried to reconstruct the settlement as it would have been in Iron Age times.* **2** ~ **sth** to be able to describe or show exactly how a past event happened, using the information you have gathered: *Investigators are trying to reconstruct the circumstances of the crash.*

**re·con·struc·tion** ₹+ C1 ⓦ /ˌriːkənˈstrʌkʃn/ noun **1** ₹+ C1 [U] the process of changing or improving the condition of sth or the way it works; the process of putting sth back into the state it was in before: *the post-war reconstruction of Germany* ◊ *a reconstruction period* **2** ₹+ C1 [U] the activity of building again sth that has been damaged or destroyed: *the reconstruction of the sea walls* **3** ₹+ C1 [C] a copy of sth that no longer exists: *The doorway is a nineteenth-century reconstruction of Norman work.* **4** ₹+ C1 [C] an act of acting out events that are known to have happened, in order to try and get more information or better understanding about what happened, especially a crime: *Last night police staged a reconstruction of the incident.* **5 Reconstruction** [U] (in the US) the period after the Civil War when the southern states returned to the US and laws were passed that gave rights to African Americans

**re·con·struct·ive** /ˌriːkənˈstrʌktɪv/ adj. [only before noun] (of medical treatment) that involves RECONSTRUCTING part of a person's body because it has been badly damaged or because the person wants to change its shape: *reconstructive surgery*

**re·con·vene** /ˌriːkənˈviːn/ verb [I, T] ~ **(sth)** if a meeting, parliament, etc. **reconvenes** or if sb **reconvenes** it, it meets again after a break

**re·cord** ⓘ A2 ⓦ noun, verb
■ noun /ˈrekɔːd; NAmE -kərd/
• **WRITTEN ACCOUNT 1** ₹ A2 [C] a written account of sth that is kept so that it can be looked at and used in the future: *You should keep a record of your expenses.* ◊ *medical/dental records* ◊ *It was the worst flood since records began.* ◊ **according to… records** *According to official records, there were 21 murders in the city that year.* ◊ **on** ~ *Last summer was the wettest on record.* ◊ *people who leave no trace in the historical record* (= written documents that provide evidence about the past)
• **HIGHEST/BEST 2** ₹ A2 [C] the best result or the highest or lowest level that has ever been reached, especially in sport: *She holds the world record for the 100 metres.* ◊ **to break the record** (= to achieve a better result than there has ever been before) ◊ **to set a new record** ◊ *There was a record number of candidates for the post.* ◊ *I got to work in record time.* ◊ *Unemployment has reached a record high* (= the highest level ever). ⊃ **WORDFINDER NOTE** at SPORT
• **OF SB/STH'S PAST 3** ₹ B1 [sing.] the facts that are known about sb/sth's past behaviour, character, achievements, etc: *The airline has a good safety record.* ◊ ~ **on sth** *The report criticizes the government's record on housing.* ◊ ~**of sth** *He has an impressive record of achievement.* ⊃ see also TRACK RECORD **4** [C] rocks, FOSSILS, the parts of buildings and objects found in the ground, etc. that provide evidence about the past: *Fossil records suggest that the region was covered in water until relatively recently.* ◊ *evidence in the geological/archaeological record*
• **OF CRIMES 5** (*also* **criminal ˈrecord**) [C] the fact of having committed crimes in the past: *Does he have a record?*
• **MUSIC 6** [C] a thin, round piece of plastic on which music, etc. is recorded: *to play a record* ◊ *a record collection* ⊃ see *also* VINYL (2) **7** [C] a piece or collection of music released as a record, or on CD, the internet, etc: *a record company* (= one which produces and sells records) ◊ *The band had a hit record in 1973.* ◊ *His new record is available on CD or as a download.* ⊃ see *also* ALBUM (2)
**IDM** **(just) for the ˈrecord 1** used to show that you want what you are saying to be officially written down and

1291 **recount**

remembered **2** used to emphasize a point that you are making, so that the person you are speaking to takes notice: *And, for the record, he would be the last person I'd ask.* **off the ˈrecord** if you told sb sth **off the record**, it is not yet official and you do not want them to repeat it publicly **put/place sth on (the) ˈrecord** | **be/go on (the) ˈrecord (as saying…)** to say sth publicly or officially so that it may be written down and repeated: *He didn't want to go on the record as either praising or criticizing the proposal.* **put/set the ˈrecord straight** to give people the correct information about sth in order to make it clear that what they previously believed was in fact wrong ⊃ more *at* BROKEN *adj.*, MATTER *n.*
■ verb /rɪˈkɔːd; NAmE -ˈkɔːrd/
• **KEEP ACCOUNT 1** ₹ A2 [T] to keep a permanent account of facts or events by writing them down, filming them, storing them in a computer, etc: ~ **sth** *Her childhood is recorded in the diaries of those years.* ◊ *You should record all your expenses during your trip.* ◊ ~**how, what, etc…** *His job is to record how politicians vote on major issues.* ◊ ~**that…** *She recorded in her diary that they crossed the Equator on 15 June.* ◊ **it is recorded that…** *It is recorded that, by the year 630, four hundred monks were attached to the monastery.*
• **SOUND/MUSIC/FILM 2** ₹ A2 [T, I] to make a copy of music, a film, etc. or to convert sound or a performance into a permanent form, so that you can listen to or watch it again: ~**(sth)** *Did you remember to record that programme for me?* ◊ *a recorded concert* ◊ *Tell me when the machine starts recording.* ◊ ~ **sb/sth doing sth** *He recorded the class rehearsing before the performance.* ⊃ see *also* PRE-RECORD, TAPE-RECORD
• **MUSIC 3** ₹ A2 [T, I] ~**(sth)** to perform music so that it can be copied, stored and played back: *The band is back in the US recording their new album.* ◊ *to record a song* ◊ *They spent the summer touring and recording.*
• **MAKE OFFICIAL STATEMENT 4** [T] ~ **sth** to make an official or legal statement about sth: *The coroner recorded a verdict of accidental death.*
• **OF MEASURING INSTRUMENT 5** [T] ~ **sth** | ~**what, how, etc…** to show a particular measurement or amount: *The thermometer recorded a temperature of 40°C.*
• **SCORE/RESULT 6** [T] ~ **sth** to achieve a particular score or result: *The team recorded their first win of the season.*

**ˈrecord-breaker** *noun* a person or thing that achieves a better result or higher level than has ever been achieved before ▶ **ˈrecord-breaking** *adj.* [only before noun]: *a record-breaking jump*

**reˌcorded deˈlivery** (*BrE*) (*NAmE* **ˌcertified ˈmail**) *noun* [U] a method of sending a letter or package in which the person sending it gets an official note to say it has been posted and the person receiving it must sign a form when it is delivered: *I'd like to send this (by) recorded delivery.* ⊃ compare REGISTERED MAIL

**re·cord·er** /rɪˈkɔːdə(r); NAmE -ˈkɔːrd-/ *noun* **1** (in compounds) a machine for recording sound or pictures or both: *a tape/cassette/video/DVD recorder* ⊃ see *also* FLIGHT RECORDER **2** a musical instrument in the shape of a pipe that you blow into, with holes that you cover with your fingers **3** a judge in a court in some parts of the UK and the US **4** a person who keeps a record of events or facts

**ˈrecord holder** *noun* a person who has achieved the best result which has been achieved in a sport

**re·cord·ing** ⓘ A2 ⓦ /rɪˈkɔːdɪŋ; NAmE -ˈkɔːrd-/ *noun* **1** ₹ A2 [C] sound or pictures that have been recorded on computer files or on CD, DVD, video, etc: ~ **of sb/sth** *a video recording of the wedding* ⊃ see *also* DIGITAL RECORDING, TAPE RECORDING **2** ₹ A2 [U] the process of making a record, film, radio or television show, etc: ~ **of sth** *during the recording of the show* ◊ *a recording studio/session/artist* ◊ *the recording industry* (= the industry that records and sells music) **3** [U, sing.] the process or act of writing down and storing information for official purposes: *the recording of financial transactions*

**ˈrecord player** *noun* a piece of equipment for playing records in order to listen to the music, etc. on them

**re·count¹** ₹+ C1 /rɪˈkaʊnt/ *verb* (*formal*) to tell sb about sth, especially sth that you have experienced: ~ **sth (to sb)** *a*

# recount

She was asked to *recount the details of the conversation to the court.* ◊ **~ what, how, etc…** *They recounted what had happened during those years.* ◊ **+ speech** *'It was before the war,' he recounted.*

**re·count²** /ˌriːˈkaʊnt/ *verb* **~ sth** to count sth again, especially votes ▶ **re·count** /ˈriːkaʊnt/ *noun: The defeated candidate demanded a recount.*

**re·coup** /rɪˈkuːp/ *verb* **~ sth** (*formal*) to get back an amount of money that you have spent or lost **SYN recover**: *We hope to recoup our initial investment in the first year.*

**re·course** /rɪˈkɔːs; *NAmE* ˈriːkɔːrs/ *noun* [U] (*formal*) the fact of having to, or being able to, use sth that can provide help in a difficult situation: *Your only recourse is legal action.* ◊ **~ to sth** *The government, when necessary, has recourse to the armed forces.* ◊ **without ~ to sth** *She made a complete recovery without recourse to surgery.*

**re·cover** ⓘ B2 /rɪˈkʌvə(r)/ *verb*
- **FROM ILLNESS 1** B2 [I] **~ (from sth)** to get well again after being ill, hurt, etc: *He's still recovering from his operation.* ◊ *She remains in serious condition, but is expected to recover.* ◊ **WORDFINDER NOTE** at HEALTH
- **FROM STH UNPLEASANT 2** B2 [I] **~ (from sth)** to return to a normal state after an unpleasant or unusual experience or a period of difficulty: *It can take many years to recover from the death of a loved one.* ◊ *The economy is at last beginning to recover.*
- **MONEY 3** [T] **~ sth (from sb/sth)** to get back the same amount of money that you have spent or that is owed to you **SYN recoup**: *He is unlikely to ever recover his legal costs.*
- **STH LOST/STOLEN 4** [T] to get back or find sth that was lost, stolen or missing: **~ sth** *The police eventually recovered the stolen paintings.* ◊ **~ sth from sb/sth** *Six bodies were recovered from the wreckage.*
- **POSITION/STATUS 5** [T] **~ sth** to win back a position, level, status, etc. that has been lost **SYN regain**: *The team recovered its lead in the second half.*
- **SENSES/EMOTIONS 6** [T] to get back the use of your senses, control of your emotions, etc. **SYN regain**: **~ sth** *It took her a few minutes to recover consciousness.* ◊ *to recover your sight* ◊ **~ yourself** *She seemed upset but quickly recovered herself.* ▶ **re·covered** *adj.* [not before noun]: *She is now fully recovered from her injuries.*

**re·cov·er·able** /rɪˈkʌvərəbl/ *adj.* **1** that you can get back after it has been spent or lost: *Travel expenses will be recoverable from the company.* **2** that can be obtained from the ground: *recoverable oil reserves*

**re·cov·ery** B2+ B2 Ⓦ /rɪˈkʌvəri/ *noun* (*pl.* **-ies**) **1** B2+ B2 [U, C, usually sing.] **~ (from sth)** the process of becoming well again after an illness or injury: *My father has made a full recovery from the operation.* ◊ *to make a remarkable/ quick/speedy/slow recovery* ◊ *She is on the road to* (= making progress towards) *recovery.* **2** B2+ C1 [U, C, usually sing.] the process of improving or becoming stronger again: *The government is forecasting an economic recovery.* ◊ *The economy is showing signs of recovery.* ◊ **~ in sth** *a recovery in consumer spending* **3** [U] **~ (of sth)** the action or process of getting sth back that has been lost or stolen: *There is a reward for information leading to the recovery of the missing diamonds.* **4** [U] (*also* **re'covery room** [C]) the room in a hospital where patients are kept immediately after an operation

**re'covery position** *noun* [sing.] a position lying on the side, with the arms and legs carefully placed, that helps a person who is not conscious to breathe

**re·create** /ˌriːkriˈeɪt/ *verb* **~ sth** to make sth that existed in the past exist or seem to exist again: *The movie recreates the glamour of 1940s Hollywood.* ▶ **re·cre·ation** /-ˈeɪʃn/ *noun* [C, U]: *The writer attempts a recreation of the sights and sounds of his childhood.*

**rec·re·ation** /ˌrekriˈeɪʃn/ *noun* **1** [U] the fact of people doing things for pleasure, when they are not working: *the need to improve facilities for leisure and recreation* ◊ *the increasing use of land for recreation* **2** [C] a particular activity that sb does when they are not working **SYN hobby, pastime**: *His recreations include golf, football and shooting.* ⊃ **SYNONYMS** at ENTERTAINMENT

**rec·re·ation·al** /ˌrekriˈeɪʃənl/ *adj.* connected with activities that people do for pleasure when they are not working: *recreational activities/facilities* ◊ *These areas are set aside for public recreational use.*

**recre·ational 'drug** *noun* a substance that some people take because they enjoy the mental and physical effects that it has: *He said that he hadn't taken legal or illegal recreational drugs.*

**recre·ational 'vehicle** *noun* (*NAmE*) (*BrE* **ˈcamp·er**, **ˈcamper van**) (*also* **motor·home** *NAmE, BrE*) *noun* (*abbr.* **RV**) a large vehicle designed for people to live and sleep in when they are travelling

**recre'ation ground** *noun* (*BrE*) an area of land used by the public for sports and games

**recre'ation room** (*also NAmE, informal* **'rec room**) *noun* **1** a room in a school, a hospital, an office building, etc. in which people can relax, play games, etc. **2** (*NAmE*) a room in a private house used for games, entertainment, etc.

**re·crim·in·ation** /rɪˌkrɪmɪˈneɪʃn/ *noun* [C, usually pl., U] an angry statement that sb makes accusing sb else of sth, especially in response to a similar statement from them: *bitter recriminations* ◊ *We spent the rest of the evening in mutual recrimination.* ▶ **re·crim·in·atory** /rɪˈkrɪmɪnətri; *NAmE* -tɔːri/ *adj.*

**'rec room** /ˈrek ruːm, rʊm/ *noun* (*NAmE, informal*) = RECREATION ROOM

**re·cruit** B2+ B2 /rɪˈkruːt/ *verb, noun*
- *verb* **1** B2+ B2 [T, I] to find new people to join a company, an organization, the armed forces, etc.: **~ (sb)** *The police are trying to recruit more officers from ethnic minorities.* ◊ *He's responsible for recruiting at all levels.* ◊ **~ sb to sth** *They recruited several new members to the club.* ◊ **~ sb to do sth** *They recruited more staff to deal with the complaints.* **2** [T] **~ sb to do sth** to persuade sb to do sth, especially to help you: *We were recruited to help peel the vegetables.* **3** [T] **~ sth** to form a new army, team, etc. by persuading new people to join it: *to recruit a task force* ▶ **re·cruit·er** *noun*
- *noun* **1** B2+ B2 a person who has recently joined the armed forces or the police: *the training of new recruits* ◊ *He spoke of us scornfully as raw recruits* (= people without training or experience). **2** B2+ B2 a person who joins an organization, a company, etc: *attempts to attract new recruits to the nursing profession*

**re·cruit·ment** B2+ B2 /rɪˈkruːtmənt/ *noun* [U] the act or process of finding new people to join a company, an organization, the armed forces, etc: *the recruitment of new members* ◊ *a recruitment drive* ◊ *a recruitment consultant/ agency*

**rec·tal** /ˈrektəl/ *adj.* (*anatomy*) relating to the RECTUM

**rect·angle** /ˈrektæŋɡl/ *noun* a flat shape with four straight sides, two of which are longer than the other two, and four angles of 90° ⊃ **picture** at PARALLELOGRAM ▶ **rect·angu·lar** /rekˈtæŋɡjələ(r)/ *adj.*

**rect·ify** /ˈrektɪfaɪ/ *verb* (**rec·ti·fies**, **rec·ti·fy·ing**, **rec·ti·fied**, **rec·ti·fied**) **~ sth** (*formal*) to put right sth that is wrong **SYN correct**: *to rectify a fault* ◊ *We must take steps to rectify the situation.* ▶ **rec·ti·fi·able** /ˌrektɪˈfaɪəbl/ *adj.*: *The damage will be easily rectifiable.* **rec·ti·fi·ca·tion** /ˌrektɪfɪˈkeɪʃn/ *noun* [U]

**rec·ti·lin·ear** /ˌrektɪˈlɪniə(r)/ *adj.* (*specialist*) **1** in a straight line: *rectilinear motion* **2** having straight lines: *rectilinear forms*

**rec·ti·tude** /ˈrektɪtjuːd; *NAmE* -tuːd/ *noun* [U] (*formal*) the quality of thinking or behaving in a correct and honest way **SYN uprightness**

**recto** /ˈrektəʊ/ *noun* (*pl.* **-os**) (*specialist*) the page on the right side of an open book ⊃ **compare** VERSO

**rec·tor** /ˈrektə(r)/ *noun* **1** an Anglican priest who is in charge of a particular area (called a PARISH). In the past a rector received an income directly from this area. ⊃ **compare** VICAR **2** (in the UK) the head of certain universities, colleges or schools

**rec·tory** /ˈrektəri/ *noun* (*pl.* **-ies**) *noun* a house where the rector of a church lives, or lived in the past

**rec·tum** /ˈrektəm/ noun (pl. **rec·tums** or **recta** /-tə/-) (*anatomy*) the end section of the tube where food waste collects before leaving the body through the ANUS ⇒ VISUAL VOCAB page V1

**re·cum·bent** /rɪˈkʌmbənt/ adj. [usually before noun] (*formal*) (of a person's body or position) lying down

**re·cu·per·ate** /rɪˈkuːpəreɪt/ verb (*formal*) **1** [I] ~ **(from sth)** to get back your health, strength or energy after being ill, tired, injured, etc. SYN **recover**: *He's still recuperating from his operation.* **2** [T] ~ **sth** to get back money that you have spent or lost SYN **recoup, recover**: *He hoped to recuperate at least some of his losses.* ▸ **re·cu·per·ation** /rɪˌkuːpəˈreɪʃn/ noun [U]: *It was a period of rest and recuperation.*

**re·cu·pera·tive** /rɪˈkuːpərətɪv/ adj. (*formal*) helping you to get better after you have been ill, very tired, etc.

**recur** /rɪˈkɜː(r)/ verb (**-rr-**) [I] to happen again or a number of times: *This theme recurs several times throughout the book.* ◇ *a recurring illness/problem/nightmare, etc.*

**re·cur·rence** /rɪˈkʌrəns; *NAmE* -ˈkɜːr-/ noun [C, usually sing., U] if there is **a recurrence of** sth, it happens again: *attempts to prevent a recurrence of the problem*

**re·cur·rent** /rɪˈkʌrənt; *NAmE* -ˈkɜːr-/ adj. that happens again and again: *recurrent infections* ◇ *Poverty is a recurrent theme in her novels.*

**re·cur·sion** /rɪˈkɜːʃn; *NAmE* -ˈkɜːrʒn/ noun [U] (*mathematics*) the process of repeating a FUNCTION, each time applying it to the result of the previous stage

**re·cur·sive** /rɪˈkɜːsɪv; *NAmE* -ˈkɜːrs-/ adj. (*specialist*) involving a process that is applied repeatedly

**re·cus·ant** /ˈrekjʊzənt; *NAmE* rəˈkjuːzənt/ noun (*formal*) a person who refuses to do what a rule or person in authority says they should do ▸ **re·cus·ancy** /ˈrekjʊzənsi/ noun [U]

**recuse** /rɪˈkjuːz/ verb ~ **sb / yourself (from sth)** (*especially NAmE*) to excuse a judge, lawyer or member of the JURY from a case in court because they may not be able to act fairly: *The judge recused himself from the case because he knew a member of the family.*

**re·cyc·lable** /ˌriːˈsaɪkləbl/ adj. able to be recycled

**re·cycle** 🔑 A2 /ˌriːˈsaɪkl/ verb **1** 🔑 A2 ~ **sth** to treat things that have already been used so that they can be used again: *to recycle waste/rubbish* ◇ *recycled materials* **2** ~ **sth** to use the same ideas, methods, jokes, etc. again: *He recycled all his old jokes.* ▸ **re·cyc·ling** noun [U]: *the recycling of glass* ◇ *a recycling plant*

**red** 🔑 A1 /red/ adj., noun
- adj. (**red·der, red·dest**) **1** 🔑 A1 having the colour of blood or fire: *bright/light/dark red lipstick* ◇ *The lights (= traffic lights) changed to red before I could get across.* **2** 🔑 A1 (of hair or an animal's fur) red-brown in colour: *her flaming red hair* ◇ *a red squirrel* ⇒ see also RED DEER, REDHEAD **3** 🔑 A2 (of the face) bright red or pink, especially because you are angry, embarrassed or ashamed: *I felt my face go red.* ◇ (*BrE*) *She went red as a beetroot.* ◇ (*NAmE*) *She went red as a beet.* **4** (of the eyes) BLOODSHOT (= with thin lines of blood in them) or surrounded by red or very pink skin: *Her eyes were red from crying.* **5** (*informal, politics, sometimes disapproving*) having very LEFT-WING political opinions ⇒ compare PINK **6** (*politics*) (of an area in the US) having more people who vote for the REPUBLICAN candidate than the DEMOCRATIC one: *red states/counties* OPP **blue** ▸ **red·ness** noun [U, sing.]: *You may notice redness and swelling after the injection.*
  **IDM** ▸ **red in ˈtooth and ˈclaw** involving opposition or competition that is violent and without sympathy: *nature, red in tooth and claw* **a red rag to a ˈbull** (*BrE*) (*NAmE* **like waving a red flag in front of a ˈbull**) used to talk about sth that is likely to make sb very angry ⇒ more at PAINT *v.*
- noun **1** 🔑 A1 [C, U] the colour of blood or fire: *She often wears red.* ◇ *the reds and browns of the woods in the fall (= of the leaves)* ◇ *I've marked the corrections in red (= in red ink).* ◇ *The traffic lights were on red.* **2** [U, C] red wine: *Would you prefer red or white?* ◇ *an Italian red* **3** [C] (*informal, disapproving, politics*) a person with very LEFT-WING political opinions ⇒ compare PINKO

**IDM** ▸ **be in the ˈred** (*informal*) to owe money to your bank because you have spent more than you have in your account: *The company has plunged $37 million into the red.* ⇒ compare BE IN THE BLACK see ˈred (*informal*) to become very angry

▼ HOMOPHONES

**read • red** /red/
- **read** verb (past tense, past participle of READ): *Have you read his new novel yet?*
- **red** adj.: *She's that girl over there in the red dress.*
- **red** noun: *The red of the setting sun glowed on the horizon.*

**re·dact** /rɪˈdækt/ verb [usually passive] (*formal*) to remove information from a document because you do not want the public to see it: **be redacted (from sth)** *All sensitive personal information has been redacted from the public documents.* ▸ **re·dac·tion** /-ˈdækʃn/ noun [C, U]

**red aˈlert** noun [U, sing.] a situation in which you are prepared for sth dangerous to happen; a warning of this: *Following the bomb blast, local hospitals have been put on red alert.*

**red ˈblood cell** (also **ˈred cell**) (*biology* **eryth·ro·cyte**) noun any of the red-coloured cells in the blood that carry OXYGEN

**red-ˈblooded** adj. [usually before noun] (*informal*) full of strength and energy, often sexual energy SYN **virile**: *red-blooded young males*

**red ˈbox** noun (*BrE*) a box used by a government minister to hold official documents

**ˈred-brick** adj. [usually before noun] **1** (of buildings, walls, etc.) built with BRICKS (= hard blocks of baked earth that are used for building) of a red-brown colour: *red-brick cottages* **2** (*becoming old-fashioned*) (of universities in the UK) built in the late nineteenth or early twentieth century, in contrast to older universities, such as Oxford and Cambridge ⇒ compare OXBRIDGE

**red·bush** /ˈredbʊʃ/ noun [U] = ROOIBOS

**red ˈcard** noun (in football (soccer) and some other games) a card shown by the REFEREE to a player who has broken the rules of the game and is not allowed to play for the rest of the game ⇒ compare YELLOW CARD

**red ˈcarpet** (usually **the red carpet**) noun [sing.] a piece of red carpet laid on the ground for an important visitor to walk on when he or she arrives: *I didn't expect to be given the red carpet treatment!*

**ˈred cell** noun = RED BLOOD CELL

**red·coat** /ˈredkəʊt/ noun **1** a British soldier in the past **2** (in the UK) a worker at a HOLIDAY CAMP who entertains and helps guests

**the Red ˈCrescent** noun [sing.] the name used by national branches in Muslim countries of the International Movement of the Red Cross and the Red Crescent, an organization that takes care of people suffering because of war or natural disasters

**the Red ˈCross** noun [sing.] an international organization that takes care of people suffering because of war or natural disasters. Its full name is the International Movement of the Red Cross and the Red Crescent.

**red ˈdeer** noun (pl. **red deer**) a DEER with large ANTLERS (= parts on its head that are like branches in shape), which has a red-brown coat in summer

**red·den** /ˈredn/ verb [I, T] ~ **(sth)** to become red; to make sth red: *The sky was reddening.* ◇ *He stared at her and she reddened.* ◇ ~ **with sth** *He could feel his face reddening with embarrassment.*

**red·dish** /ˈredɪʃ/ adj. fairly red in colour

**red ˈdwarf** noun (*astronomy*) a small, old star that is not very hot

**re·dec·or·ate** /ˌriːˈdekəreɪt/ verb [I, T] to put new paint and/or paper on the walls of a room or house: *We've just redecorated.* ◇ ~ **sth** *The house has been fully redecorated.* ▸ **re·dec·or·ation** /ˌriːˌdekəˈreɪʃn/ noun [U]

# redeem

**re·deem** /rɪˈdiːm/ *verb* **1** ~ sb/sth to make sb/sth seem less bad **SYN** **compensate**: *The excellent acting wasn't enough to redeem a weak plot.* ◊ *The only **redeeming feature** of the job* (= good thing about it) *is the salary.* ⊃ **SYNONYMS** at SAVE **2** ~ **yourself** to do sth to improve the opinion that people have of you, especially after you have done sth bad: *He has a chance to redeem himself after last week's mistakes.* **3** → **sb** (in Christianity) to save sb from the power of evil: *Jesus Christ came to redeem us from sin.* **4** ~ **sth** to pay the full sum of money that you owe sb; to pay a debt: *to redeem a loan/mortgage* **5** ~ **sth** to exchange sth such as shares or VOUCHERS for money or goods: *This voucher can be redeemed at any of our branches.* **6** ~ **sth** to get back a valuable object from sb by paying them back the money you borrowed from them in exchange for the object: *He was able to redeem his watch from the pawnshop.* **7** ~ **a pledge / promise** (*formal*) to do what you have promised that you will do

**re·deem·able** /rɪˈdiːməbl/ *adj.* ~ **(against sth)** that can be exchanged for money or goods: *These vouchers are redeemable against any future purchase.*

**the Re·deem·er** /ðə rɪˈdiːmə(r)/ *noun* [sing.] (*literary*) Jesus Christ

**re·define** /ˌriːdɪˈfaɪn/ *verb* to change the nature or limits of sth; to make people consider sth in a new way: ~ **sth** *The new constitution redefined the powers of the president.* ◊ ~ **what, how,** *etc…* *We need to redefine what we mean by democracy.* ▸ **re·def·in·ition** /ˌriːdefɪˈnɪʃn/ *noun* [U, C]

**re·demp·tion** /rɪˈdempʃn/ *noun* [U] **1** (*formal*) the act of saving or state of being saved from the power of evil; the act of REDEEMING: *the redemption of the world from sin* **2** (*finance*) the act of exchanging shares for money (= of REDEEMING them)
**IDM** **beyond / past reˈdemption** too bad to be saved or improved

**re·demp·tive** /rɪˈdemptɪv/ *adj.* (*formal*) that saves you from the power of evil: *the redemptive power of love*

**re·deploy** /ˌriːdɪˈplɔɪ/ *verb* [often passive] to move sb/sth to a new position or job: ~ **sth** *Our troops are to be redeployed elsewhere.* ◊ ~ **sb/sth to sth** *Most of the employees will be redeployed to other parts of the company.* ▸ **re·deploy·ment** *noun* [U, C]: *the redeployment of staff/resources*

**re·design** /ˌriːdɪˈzaɪm/ *verb* ~ **sth** to design sth again, in a different way ▸ **re·design** /ˌriːdɪˈzaɪn/ *noun* [U, C]

**re·develop** /ˌriːdɪˈveləp/ *verb* [T, I] ~ **(sth)** to change an area by building new roads, houses, factories, etc: *The city has plans to redevelop the site.* ▸ **re·devel·op·ment** *noun* [U, C]: *inner-city redevelopment*

**ˈred-eye** *noun* **1** (*also* **ˈred-eye ˈflight**) [C] (*especially* NAmE, *informal*) a flight in a plane at night, on which you cannot expect to get enough sleep: *We took the red-eye to Boston.* **2** [U] the appearance of having red eyes that people sometimes have in photographs taken using flash

**ˌred-ˈfaced** *adj.* with a red face, especially because you are embarrassed or angry

**ˌred ˈflag** *noun* **1** a flag used to warn people of danger **2** a red flag as a symbol of revolution or COMMUNISM

**ˌred ˈgiant** *noun* (*astronomy*) a large star towards the end of its life that is relatively cool and gives out a red light

**ˌred-ˈhanded** *adj.* **IDM** see CATCH *v.*

**ˈred·head** /ˈredhed/ *noun* (*sometimes offensive*) a person who has red hair ⊃ compare BLONDE, BRUNETTE ⊃ **WORDFINDER NOTE** at BLONDE ▸ **ˌred-ˈheaded** *adj.*: *a red-headed girl*

**ˌred ˈherring** *noun* an unimportant fact, idea, event, etc. that takes people's attention away from the important ones **ORIGIN** From the custom of using the smell of a smoked, dried herring (which was red) to train dogs to hunt.

**ˌred-ˈhot** *adj.* **1** (of metal or sth burning) so hot that it looks red: *Red-hot coals glowed in the fire.* **2** showing strong feeling: *her red-hot anger* **3** (*informal*) new, exciting and of great interest to people: *a red-hot issue* **4** used to describe the person, animal or team that is considered almost certain to win a race, etc: *The race was won by the red-hot favourite.*

---

**redid** /ˌriːˈdɪd/ *past tense* of REDO

**ˌRed ˈIndian** (*also* **ˈred-skin**) *noun* (*old-fashioned*, *taboo*) a very offensive word for a Native American

**re·dir·ect** /ˌriːdəˈrekt, -daɪˈr-/ *noun*
- *verb* **1** [T] ~ **sth (to sth)** to use sth, for example money, in a different way or for a different purpose: *Resources are being redirected to this important new project.* **2** [T, I] to send sth to a different address or in a different direction: ~ **sth (to sth)** *Enquiries on this matter are being redirected to the press office.* ◊ ~ **to sth** *That URL currently redirects to a Facebook page.* ▸ **re·dir·ec·tion** /-ˈrekʃn/ *noun* [sing., U]: *a sudden redirection of economic policy* ◊ *the redirection of mail*
- *noun* (*computing*) /ˈriːdərekt/ an instance of redirecting sth from one address to another; a facility that redirects sth: *Spammers are starting to use automatic redirects.*

**re·dis·cover** /ˌriːdɪˈskʌvə(r)/ *verb* ~ **sth** to find again sth that had been forgotten or lost ▸ **re·dis·cov·ery** *noun* [U, C] (*pl.* **-ies**)

**re·dis·trib·ute** /ˌriːdɪˈstrɪbjuːt; BrE *also* ˌriːdɪstrɪ-/ *verb* ~ **sth (from sb/sth) (to sb/sth)** to share sth out among people in a different way: *Wealth needs to be redistributed from the rich to the poor.* ▸ **re·dis·tri·bu·tion** /ˌriːdɪstrɪˈbjuːʃn/ *noun* [U, sing.]: *the redistribution of wealth* **re·dis·tribu·tive** /ˌriːdɪˈstrɪbjətɪv/ *adj.*

**re·dis·trict** /ˌriːˈdɪstrɪkt/ *verb* [T, I] ~ **(sth)** (US) to change the official borders between districts

**ˈred-letter day** *noun* an important day, or a day that you will remember, because of sth good that happened then **ORIGIN** From the custom of using red ink to mark holidays and festivals on a calendar.

**ˌred ˈlight** *noun* a signal telling the driver of a vehicle to stop: *to go through a red light* (= not stop at one)

**ˈred-light district** *noun* a part of a town where there are many PROSTITUTES

**ˌred ˈline** *noun* an issue or a demand that one person or group refuses to change their opinion about during a DISAGREEMENT or NEGOTIATIONS: *The issue of sovereignty is a red line that cannot be crossed.*

**ˌred ˈmeat** *noun* [U] meat that is dark brown in colour when it has been cooked, such as beef and LAMB ⊃ compare WHITE MEAT

**ˈred·neck** /ˈrednek/ *noun* (*informal*) an offensive word for a person who lives in a country area of the US, has little education and has strong conservative political opinions

**redo** /ˌriːˈduː/ *verb* (**re·does** /-ˈdʌz/, **redid** /-ˈdɪd/, **re·done** /-ˈdʌn/) ~ **sth** to do sth again or in a different way: *A whole day's work had to be redone.* ◊ *We've just redone the bathroom* (= decorated it again).

**redo·lent** /ˈredələnt/ *adj.* [not before noun] (*literary*) **1** ~ **of / with sth** making you think of the thing mentioned: *an atmosphere redolent of the sea and ships* **2** ~ **of / with sth** smelling strongly of the thing mentioned: *a kitchen redolent with the smell of baking* ▸ **redo·lence** /-ləns/ *noun* [U]

**re·double** /ˌriːˈdʌbl/ *verb* ~ **sth** to increase sth or make it stronger: *The leading banks are expected to **redouble their efforts** to keep the value of the dollar down.* ◊ *redoubled enthusiasm*

**re·doubt** /rɪˈdaʊt/ *noun* **1** (*literary*) a place or situation in which sb/sth is protected when they are being attacked or threatened **2** a small building from which soldiers can fight and defend themselves

**re·doubt·able** /rɪˈdaʊtəbl/ *adj.* (*formal*) if a person is redoubtable, they have very strong qualities that make you respect them and perhaps feel afraid of them **SYN** **formidable**

**re·dound** /rɪˈdaʊnd/ *verb*
**PHRV** **reˈdound to sth** (*formal*) to improve the impression that people have of you: *Their defeat redounds to the glory of those whom they attacked.*

**ˌred ˈpanda** *noun* = PANDA (2)

**ˌred ˈpepper** *noun* **1** [C, U] a hollow red fruit that is eaten, raw or cooked, as a vegetable **2** [U] (*especially* NAmE) = CAYENNE

**re·draft** /ˌriːˈdrɑːft/ *NAmE* -ˈdræft/ *verb* ~ **sth** to write an article, a letter, etc. again in order to improve it or make changes ▶ **re·draft** /ˈriːdrɑːft; *NAmE* -dræft/ *noun*

**re·draw** /ˌriːˈdrɔː/ *verb* (**re·drew** /-ˈdruː/, **re·drawn** /-ˈdrɔːn/) ~ **sth** to make changes to sth such as the borders of a country or region, a plan, an arrangement, etc: *After the war the map of Europe was redrawn.* ◊ *to* **redraw the boundaries** *between male and female roles in the home*

**re·dress** /rɪˈdres/ *verb*, *noun*
■ *verb* ~ **sth** (*formal*) to correct sth that is unfair or wrong **SYN** **right**: *to redress an injustice*
**IDM** **redress the ˈbalance** to make a situation equal or fair again
■ *noun* [U] (*formal*) payment, etc. that you should get for sth wrong that has happened to you or harm that you have suffered **SYN** **compensation**: *to have little prospect of redress* ◊ ~ **for/against sth** *to seek legal redress for unfair dismissal*

**re·dress·al** /rɪˈdresl/ *noun* [U] (*especially IndE*) = REDRESS

**red·shirt** /ˈredʃɜːt; *NAmE* -ʃɜːrt/ *noun* (*NAmE*) a college sports player who does not play for one year in order to be allowed to play for an extra year later ▶ **redshirt** *verb* [T, I] ~ **(sb)**: *He was redshirted in his freshman season at Florida State.* ◊ *He redshirted this past year.*

**red·skin** /ˈredskɪn/ *noun* (*old-fashioned, taboo, offensive*) = RED INDIAN

**red ˈtape** *noun* [U] (*disapproving*) official rules that seem more complicated than necessary and prevent things from being done quickly: *bureaucratic red tape* **ORIGIN** From the custom of tying up official documents with red or pink tape.

**re·duce** 🅞 **A2** 🅞 /rɪˈdjuːs; *NAmE* -ˈduːs/ *verb* **1** 🅐 [T, I] to make sth less or smaller in size, quantity, price, etc.; to become less or smaller in size, quantity, etc: ~ **sth** *Reduce speed now* (= on a sign). ◊ *Giving up smoking reduces the risk of heart disease.* ◊ *to reduce costs/numbers* ◊ *a reduced rate/price* ◊ ~ **sth by sth** *Costs have been reduced by 20% over the past year.* ◊ ~ **sth from sth to sth** *The number of employees was reduced from 40 to 25.* ◊ ~ **sth to sth** *The skirt was reduced to £10 in the sale.* ◊ ~ **in sth** *Towards the coast, the hills gradually reduce in size.* **2** [T, I] ~ **(sth)** if you **reduce** a liquid or a liquid **reduces**, you boil it so that it becomes less in quantity **3** [I] (*NAmE, informal*) to lose weight by limiting the amount and type of food that you eat: *a reducing plan* **4** [T] ~ **sth** (*chemistry*) to add one or more ELECTRONS to a substance or to remove OXYGEN from a substance ⇒ compare OXIDIZE
**IDM** **reˌduced ˈcircumstances** the state of being poorer than you were before. People say 'living in reduced circumstances' to avoid saying 'poor'.
**PHRV** **reˈduce sb/sth (from sth) to (doing) sth** [usually passive] to force sb/sth into a particular state or condition, usually a worse one: *a beautiful building reduced to rubble* ◊ *She was reduced to tears by their criticisms.* ◊ *They were reduced to begging in the streets.* **reˈduce sth to sth** to change sth to a more general or simpler form: *We can reduce the problem to two main issues.*

**re·du·cible** /rɪˈdjuːsəbl; *NAmE* -ˈduː-/ *adj.* (used especially in negative sentences) ~ **to sth** (*formal*) that can be described or considered in terms of one simple factor: *The problem is not reducible to one of money.*

**re·duc·tio ad ab·sur·dum** /rɪˌdʌktiəʊ æd æbˈsɜːdəm; *NAmE* -ˈsɜːrd-/ *noun* [U, C] (*from Latin, philosophy*) a method of proving that sth is not true by showing that its result is not logical or sensible

**re·duc·tion** 🅞 **B2** 🅦 /rɪˈdʌkʃn/ *noun* **1** 🅘 **B2** [C, U] an act of making sth less or smaller; the state of being made less or smaller: ~ **in sth** *a 33% reduction in the number of hospital beds available* ◊ *a drastic reduction in costs* ◊ *a significant/substantial reduction in spending* **2** 🅘 **B2** [C] an amount of money by which sth is made cheaper: *price reductions* ⇒ WORDFINDER NOTE at BUY **3** [C] a copy of a photograph, map, picture, etc. that is made smaller than the original one **OPP** **enlargement 4** [U, C] (*chemistry*) the fact of adding one or more ELECTRONS to a substance or of removing OXYGEN from a substance ⇒ compare OXIDATION **5** a sauce made by boiling a liquid until it becomes thick

**re·duc·tion·ism** /rɪˈdʌkʃənɪzəm/ *noun* [U] (*formal, often disapproving*) the belief that complicated things can be explained by considering them as a combination of simple parts ▶ **re·duc·tion·ist** /-nɪst/ *adj., noun*

**re·duc·tive** /rɪˈdʌktɪv/ *adj.* (*formal, often disapproving*) that tries to explain sth complicated by considering it as a combination of simple parts

**re·dun·dancy** /rɪˈdʌndənsi/ *noun* (*pl.* **-ies**) **1** [U, C, usually pl.] (*BrE*) the situation when sb has to leave their job because there is no more work available for them: *Thousands of factory workers are facing redundancy.* ◊ *to accept/take* **voluntary redundancy** (= to offer to leave your job) ◊ *the threat of* **compulsory redundancies** ◊ *redundancy payments* ⇒ see also LAY-OFF **2** [U] (*formal or specialist*) the state of not being necessary or useful: *Natural language is characterized by redundancy* (= words are used that are not really necessary for sb to understand the meaning).

**re·dun·dant** /rɪˈdʌndənt/ *adj.* **1** (*BrE*) (of a person) without a job because there is no more work available for you in a company: *to be* **made redundant** *from your job* ◊ *redundant employees* **2** not needed or useful: *The picture has too much redundant detail.* ▶ **re·dun·dant·ly** *adv.*

**re·du·pli·cate** /ˌriːˈdjuːplɪkeɪt; *NAmE* -ˈduː-/ *verb* [I, T] ~ **(sth/itself)** to make a copy of sth in order to form another of the same kind: *These cells are able to reduplicate themselves.*

**re·du·pli·ca·tive** /rɪˈdjuːplɪkətɪv; *NAmE* -ˈduːplɪkeɪt-/ *adj.* (used about words) repeating a syllable or other part of the word, often with a slight change: *Reduplicative expressions like 'mishmash' and 'nitty-gritty' illustrate the playful nature of English.*

**re·dux** /ˈriːdʌks/ *adj.* [after noun] brought back into use or made popular again: *The 1980s were far more than just the 1950s redux.*

**red ˈwine** *noun* **1** [U, C] wine that gets its red colour from the skins of the GRAPES **2** [C] a glass of red wine ⇒ compare ROSÉ, WHITE WINE

**red·wood** /ˈredwʊd/ *noun* **1** [C] a very tall type of tree that grows especially in California and Oregon: *giant redwoods* **2** [U] the red wood of the redwood tree

**ˈred zone** *noun* [sing.] (IN AMERICAN FOOTBALL) the area within 20 YARDS of a team's GOAL LINE

**reed** /riːd/ *noun* **1** a tall plant like grass with a hollow STEM that grows in or near water: *reed beds* (= where they grow) ⇒ VISUAL VOCAB page V7 **2** a small thin piece of CANE, metal or plastic in some musical instruments such as the OBOE or the CLARINET that moves very quickly when air is blown over it, producing a sound

▼ HOMOPHONES
**read** • **reed** /riːd/
• **read** *verb*: *She can read Arabic, but she can't speak it.*
• **reed** *noun*: *A saxophone is another instrument that uses a reed.*

**re-ˈeducate** *verb* ~ **sb** to teach sb to think or behave in a new or different way ▶ **re-eduˈcation** *noun* [U]

**reedy** /ˈriːdi/ *adj.* [usually before noun] **1** (of a voice or sound) high and not very pleasant **2** full of reeds: *reedy river banks*

**reef** /riːf/ *noun*, *verb*
■ *noun* **1** a long line of rocks or sand near the surface of the sea: *a coral reef* ⇒ see also BARRIER REEF **2** a part of a sail that can be tied or rolled up to make the sail smaller in a strong wind
■ *verb* ~ **sth** (*specialist*) to make a sail smaller by tying or rolling up part of it

**reef·er** /ˈriːfə(r)/ *noun* **1** (*also* **ˈreefer jacket**) a short thick jacket made of wool, usually dark blue, with two rows of buttons **2** (*old-fashioned, slang*) a cigarette containing MARIJUANA

# reek

**reek** /riːk/ *verb, noun*
- *verb* **1** [I] ~ **(of sth)** to smell very strongly of sth unpleasant: *His breath reeked of tobacco.* **2** [I] ~ **(of sth)** (*disapproving*) to make you think that sth unpleasant, wrong or dishonest is involved in a situation: *Her denials reeked of hypocrisy.*
- *noun* [sing.] a strong unpleasant smell SYN **stench**

**reel** /riːl/ *noun, verb*
- *noun* **1** (*especially BrE*) (*also especially NAmE* **spool**) a round object around which you wind such things as THREAD, wire or film; a reel together with the film, wire, THREAD, etc. that is wound around it: *a cotton reel ◊ a reel on a fishing rod ◊ reels of magnetic tape ◊ a new reel of film ◊ The hero was killed in the final reel* (= in the final part of the film). **2** a fast Scottish, Irish or American dance, usually for two or four couples; a piece of music for this dance
- *verb* **1** [I] (+ *adv.*/*prep.*) to move in a very unsteady way, for example because you are drunk or have been hit SYN **stagger**: *I punched him on the chin, sending him reeling backwards.* **2** [I] ~ **(at/from/with sth)** to feel very shocked or upset about sth: *I was still reeling from the shock.* **3** [I] to seem to be turning round and round: *When he opened his eyes, the room was reeling.*
- **PHR V** **reel sth ↔ 'in/'out** to wind sth on/off a reel: *I slowly reeled the fish in.* **reel sth ↔ 'off** to say or repeat sth quickly without having to stop or think about it: *She immediately reeled off several names.*

**re-e'lect** *verb* to elect sb again: **~ sb (to sth)** *She was re-elected to parliament.* ◊ **~ sb (as) sth** *The committee voted to re-elect him (as) chairman.* ▶ **re-e'lection** *noun* [U]: (*BrE*) *to stand for re-election* ◊ (*NAmE*) *to run for re-election*

**re-e'merge** *verb* [I] to appear somewhere again: *The cancer may re-emerge years later.*

**re-e'nact** *verb* **~ sth** to repeat the actions of a past event, especially as an entertainment: *Members of the English Civil War Society will re-enact the battle.* ▶ **re-e'nactment** *noun*

**re-'enter** *verb* [T, I] ~ **(sth)** to return to a place or to an area of activity that you used to be in: *Adams decided to re-enter politics after the war.*

**re-'entry** *noun* [U] **1** ~ **(into sth)** the act of returning to a place or an area of activity that you used to be in: *She feared she would not be granted re-entry into Britain.* ◊ *a re-entry programme for nurses* (= for nurses returning to work after a long time doing sth else) **2** the return of a SPACECRAFT into the earth's atmosphere

**re-e'valuate** *verb* **~ sth** to think about sth again, especially in order to form a new opinion about it ▶ **re-e'valu'ation** *noun* [C, U]

**reeve** /riːv/ *noun* a law officer in England in the past

**re-e'xamine** *verb* **~ sth** to examine or think about sth again, especially because you may need to change your opinion SYN **reassess**: *All the evidence needs to be re-examined.* ▶ **re-e'xami'nation** *noun* [U, sing.]

**ref** /ref/ *noun, verb* (*informal*)
- *noun* = REFEREE: *The game's not over till the ref blows the whistle.*
- *verb* (-ff-) ~ **sth** = REFEREE: *The game was badly reffed.*

**ref.** /ref/ *abbr.* reference (used especially in business as a way of identifying sth such as a document): *our ref.: 3498*

**re·fec·tory** /rɪˈfektəri/ *noun* (*pl.* **-ies**) a large room in which meals are served, especially in a religious institution and in some schools and colleges in the UK

**refer** /rɪˈfɜː(r)/ *verb* (-rr-) to send sb/sth to sb/sth for help, advice or a decision: **~ sb/sth to sb/sth** *My doctor referred me to a specialist.* ◊ *The case was referred to the Court of Appeal.* ◊ (*formal*) *May I refer you to my letter of 14 May?* ◊ **~ sb (for sth)** *She was referred for evaluation and treatment.*
- **PHR V** **re'fer to sb/sth (as sth)** to mention or speak about sb/sth: *The victims were not referred to by name.* ◊ *Her mother never referred to him again.* ◊ *You know who I'm referring to.* ◊ *He referred to the fact that the vessel had not undergone a refit since 1987.* ◊ *She always referred to Ben as 'that nice man'.* ⊃ SYNONYMS at MENTION **re'fer to sb/sth 1** to describe or be connected to sb/sth: *The star refers to items which are intended for the advanced learner.* ◊ *The term 'Arts' usually refers to humanities and social sciences.* ◊ *This paragraph refers to the events of last year.* ⊃ LANGUAGE BANK at DEFINE **2** to look at sth or ask a person for information SYN **consult**: *You may refer to your notes if you want.* ◊ *to refer to a dictionary*

**re·fer·able** /rɪˈfɜːrəbl, ˈrefrəbl/ *adj.* **~ to sth** (*formal*) that can be related to sth else: *These symptoms may be referable to virus infection rather than parasites.*

**ref·er·ee** /ˌrefəˈriː/ *noun, verb*
- *noun* **1** (*also informal* **ref**) the official who controls the game in some sports: *He was sent off for arguing with the referee.* ⊃ see also ASSISTANT REFEREE ⊃ compare UMPIRE **2** (*BrE*) a person who gives information about your character and ability, usually in a letter, for example when you are applying for a job **3** a person who is asked to settle an argument: *to act as a referee between the parties involved* **4** a person who reads and checks the quality of an academic article before it is published
- *verb* **1** (*also informal* **ref**) [I, T] to act as the referee in a game: *a refereeing decision* ◊ **~ sth** *Who refereed the final?* **2** [T] **~ sth** to read and check the quality of an academic article before it is published

**referee's as'sistant** *noun* = ASSISTANT REFEREE

**ref·er·ence** /ˈrefrəns/ *noun, verb*
- *noun*
- • MENTIONING SB/STH **1** [C, U] a thing you say or write that mentions sb/sth else; the act of mentioning sb/sth: **~ to sb/sth** *She made no reference to her illness but only to her future plans.* ◊ *the President's passing reference to* (= brief mention of) *the end of the war* ◊ **~ to doing sth** *The book is full of references to growing up in India.*
- • LOOKING FOR INFORMATION **2** [U] the act of looking at sth for information: **for ~** *A copy of the booklet is given to the employee for reference.* ◊ *I wrote down the name of the hotel for future reference* (= because it might be useful in the future). ◊ *The library contains many popular works of reference* (= books that contain facts and information). ⊃ see also POINT OF REFERENCE
- • NUMBER/WORD/SYMBOL **3** [C] (*abbr.* **ref.**) a number, word or symbol that shows where sth is on a map, or where you can find a piece of information: *The map reference is Y4.* ◊ *Please quote your reference number when making an enquiry.* ⊃ WORDFINDER NOTE at MAP
- • ASKING FOR ADVICE **4** [U] ~ **(to sb/sth)** (*formal*) the act of asking sb for help or advice: *The emergency nurse can treat minor injuries without reference to a doctor.*
- • FOR NEW JOB **5** [C] a letter written by sb who knows you, giving information about your character and abilities, especially to a new employer: *I'm sure she'll give you a good reference.* **6** [C] a person who agrees to write a reference, for you, for example when you are applying for a job SYN **referee**: *My previous boss will act as a reference for me.* ⊃ WORDFINDER NOTE at APPLY
- • IN BOOK **7** [C] a note in a book that tells you where a particular piece of information comes from: *There is a list of references at the end of each chapter.* ◊ **~ to sth** *References to previous research are listed in an appendix.* ⊃ see also CROSS REFERENCE, FRAME OF REFERENCE, TERMS OF REFERENCE
- **IDM** **in/with reference to** (*formal*) used to say what you are talking or writing about: *With reference to your letter of July 22...*
- *verb* ~ **sth** (*formal*) to refer to sth; to provide a book, etc. with references: *Each chapter is referenced, citing literature up to 2018.* ⊃ see also CROSS-REFERENCE

**'reference book** *noun* a book that contains facts and information, that you look at when you need to find out sth particular

**'reference library** *noun* a library containing books that can be read in the library but cannot be borrowed ⊃ compare LENDING LIBRARY

**'reference point** *noun* a standard by which sth can be judged or compared

**ref·er·en·dum** /ˌrefəˈrendəm/ *noun* [C, U] (*pl.* **ref·er·en·dums** or **ref·er·enda** /-də/) an occasion when all the people of a country can vote on an important issue: **~ on sth** *Switzerland decided to hold a referendum on joining the*

EU. ◇ by ~ *The changes were approved by referendum.* ⊃ **WORDFINDER NOTE** at DEMOCRACY ⊃ note at ELECTION

**re·fer·ral** /rɪˈfɜːrəl/ *noun* [U, C] ~ **(to sb/sth)** the act of sending sb who needs professional help to a person or place that can provide it: *illnesses requiring referral to hospitals* ◇ *to make a referral*

**re·fill** *verb, noun*
■ *verb* /ˌriːˈfɪl/ ~ **sth (with sth)** to fill sth again: *He refilled her glass.* ▶ **re·fill·able** /-ˈfɪləbl/ *adj.*: *a refillable gas cylinder*
■ *noun* /ˈriːfɪl/ **1** another drink of the same type: *Would you like a refill?* **2** an amount of sth, sold in a cheap container, that you use to fill up a more expensive container that is now empty

**re·fi·nance** /ˌriːˈfaɪnæns/ *verb* [T, I] ~ **(sth)** (*finance*) to borrow money in order to pay a debt

**re·fine** /rɪˈfaɪn/ *verb* **1** ~ **sth** to make a substance pure by taking other substances out of it: *the process of refining oil/sugar* **2** ~ **sth** to improve sth by making small changes to it

**re·fined** /rɪˈfaɪnd/ *adj.* **1** [usually before noun] (of a substance) made pure by having other substances taken out of it: *refined sugar* **2** (of a person) polite, well educated and able to judge the quality of things; having the sort of manners that are considered typical of a high social class **SYN** **cultured, genteel** **OPP** **unrefined**

**re·fine·ment** /rɪˈfaɪnmənt/ *noun* **1** [C] a small change to sth that improves it **SYN** **enhancement**: *This particular model has a further refinement.* **2** [C, U] ~ **of sth** a thing that is an improvement on an earlier, similar thing; the quality of being improved in this way: ~ **of sth** *The new plan is a refinement of the one before.* **3** [U] the process of improving sth or of making sth pure: *the refinement of industrial techniques* ◇ *the refinement of uranium* **4** [U] the quality of being polite and well educated and able to judge the quality of things; the state of having the sort of manners that are considered typical of a high social class **SYN** **gentility**: *a person of considerable refinement* ◇ *an atmosphere of refinement*

**re·finer** /rɪˈfaɪnə(r)/ *noun* a person or company that refines substances such as sugar or oil: *oil refiners*

**re·fin·ery** /rɪˈfaɪnəri/ *noun* (*pl.* **-ies**) a factory where a substance such as oil is REFINED (= made pure)

**refit** /ˌriːˈfɪt/ *verb* (**-tt-**) ~ **sth** to repair or fit new parts, equipment, etc. to sth: *He spent £70000 refitting his yacht.* ▶ **refit** /ˈriːfɪt/ *noun*: *The ship has undergone a complete refit.*

**re·flate** /ˌriːˈfleɪt/ *verb* [T, I] ~ **(sth)** (*economics*) to increase the amount of money that is used in a country, usually in order to increase the demand for goods ⊃ compare DEFLATE, INFLATE ▶ **re·fla·tion** /-ˈfleɪʃn/ *NAmE* -ʃənəri/ *adj.*: *reflationary policies*

**re·flect** ⓘ **B1** ⓞ /rɪˈflekt/ *verb* **1** **B1** [T, usually passive] to show the image of sb/sth on the surface of sth such as a mirror, water or glass: **be reflected (in sth)** *His face was reflected in the mirror.* ◇ *She could see herself reflected in his eyes.* **2** **B1** [T, I] to throw back light, heat, sound, etc. from a surface: ~ **sth** *The windows reflected the bright afternoon sunlight.* ◇ ~ **sth + adv./prep.** *When the sun's rays hit the earth, a lot of the heat is reflected back into space.* ◇ ~ + **adv./prep.** *The sun reflected dully off the stone walls.* **3** **B1** [T] ~ **sth** to show or be a sign of the nature of sth or of sb's attitude or feeling: *Our newspaper aims to reflect the views of the local community.* ◇ *This year's figures simply reflect the fact that we have fewer people out of work.* **4** **B2** [I, T] to think carefully and deeply about sth: *Before I decide, I need time to reflect.* ◇ ~ **on/upon sth** *She was left to reflect on the implications of her decision.* ◇ ~ **that** ... *On the way home he reflected that the interview had gone well.* ◇ ~ **how, what, etc** ... *She reflected how different it could have been.* ◇ + **speech** *'It could all have been so different,' she reflected.* **IDM** **reflect well, badly, etc. on sb/sth** to make sb/sth appear to be good, bad, etc. to other people: *This incident reflects badly on everyone involved.*

**re·flect·ance** /rɪˈflektəns/ *noun* [U, C] (*physics*) a measure of how much light is reflected off a surface, considered as a part of the total light that shines onto it

1297 **reforestation**

**re·flected ˈglory** *noun* [U] (*disapproving*) praise or approval that is given to sb, not because of sth that they have done, but because of sth that sb connected with them has done: *She basked in the reflected glory of her daughter's success.*

**re·flec·tion** ⓡ **C1** ⓞ (*BrE, also old-fashioned* **re·flex·ion**) /rɪˈflekʃn/ *noun* **1** ⓡ **C1** [C] an image in a mirror, on a shiny surface, on water, etc: *He admired his reflection in the mirror.* **2** [U] the action or process of sending back light, heat, sound, etc. from a surface **3** ⓡ **C1** [C] a sign that shows the state or nature of sth: *Your clothes are often a reflection of your personality.* ◇ **on sth** *The increase in crime is a* **sad reflection on** (= shows sth bad about) *our society today.* **4** ⓡ **C1** [U] careful thought about sth, sometimes over a long period of time: *A week off would give him time for reflection.* ◇ **on** ~ *She decided on reflection to accept his offer after all.* ⊃ see also SELF-REFLECTION **5** [C, usually pl.] your written or spoken thoughts about a particular subject or topic: *a book of her reflections on childhood* **6** [C] an account or a description of sth: *The article is an accurate reflection of events that day.*

**re·flect·ive** /rɪˈflektɪv/ *adj.* **1** (*formal*) thinking deeply about things **SYN** **thoughtful**: *a quiet and reflective man* **2** reflective surfaces send back light or heat: *reflective car number plates* ◇ *On dark nights children should wear reflective clothing.* **3** ~ **of sth** typical of a particular situation or thing; showing the state or nature of sth: *His abilities are not reflective of the team as a whole.* ◇ *Everything you do or say is reflective of your personality.* ▶ **re·flect·ive·ly** *adv.*: *She sipped her wine reflectively.*

**re·flect·iv·ity** /ˌriːflekˈtɪvəti, rɪˌflek-/ *noun* [U] (*physics*) the degree to which a material reflects light or RADIATION

**re·flect·or** /rɪˈflektə(r)/ *noun* **1** a surface that reflects light **2** a small piece of special glass or plastic that is put on a bicycle, or on clothing, so that it can be seen at night when light shines on it

**re·flex** /ˈriːfleks/ *noun* an action or a movement of your body that happens naturally in response to sth and that you cannot control; sth that you do without thinking: *The doctor tested her reflexes.* ◇ *to have* **quick/slow reflexes** ◇ *a* **reflex response/reaction** ◇ *Only the goalkeeper's reflexes* (= his ability to react quickly) *stopped the ball from going in.* ◇ *Almost as a* **reflex action**, *I grab my pen as the phone rings.*

**ˈreflex ˈangle** *noun* an angle of more than 180° ⊃ picture at ANGLE ⊃ compare ACUTE ANGLE, OBTUSE ANGLE, RIGHT ANGLE

**re·flex·ion** (*BrE, old-fashioned*) = REFLECTION

**re·flex·ive** /rɪˈfleksɪv/ *adj.* a **reflexive** word or form of a word shows that the action of the verb affects the person who performs the action: *In 'He cut himself', 'cut' is a reflexive verb and 'himself' is a reflexive pronoun.*

**re·flex·ology** /ˌriːfleksˈɒlədʒi; *NAmE* -ˈɑːl-/ *noun* [U] a type of alternative treatment in which sb's feet are rubbed in a particular way in order to cure a health problem in other parts of their body or to make them feel mentally relaxed ⊃ WORDFINDER NOTE at TREATMENT ▶ **re·flex·olo·gist** *noun*

**re·float** /ˌriːˈfləʊt/ *verb* ~ **sth** to make a boat or ship float again, for example after it has become stuck on the bottom in shallow water

**re·flux** /ˈriːflʌks/ *noun* [U] (*medical*) the fact of the liquid contents of the stomach flowing back into the OESOPHAGUS: *He has* **acid reflux**.

**re·focus** /ˌriːˈfəʊkəs/ *verb* (**-s-** or **-ss-**) **1** [I, T] to give attention, effort, etc. to sth new or different: ~ **(on/upon sb/sth)** *Policy must refocus on people instead of places.* ◇ ~ **sth (on/upon sb/sth)** *We need to refocus attention on the real issues facing this country.* **2** [I, T] (of your eyes, a camera, etc.) to adapt to or be changed again so that things can be seen clearly; to change sth again so that you can see things clearly

**re·for·est·ation** /ˌriːfɒrɪˈsteɪʃn; *NAmE* -fɔːr-/ (*BrE also* **re·affor·est·ation**) *noun* [U] (*specialist*) the act of planting new trees in an area where there used to be a forest ⊃ compare DEFORESTATION

**re·form** /rɪˈfɔːm; NAmE -ˈfɔːrm/ noun, verb
- noun [U, C] change that is made to a social system, an organization, etc. in order to improve or correct it: *a government committed to reform* ◇ *economic/electoral/constitutional, etc. reform* ◇ *the reform of the educational system* ◇ *reforms in education* ◇ *far-reaching/major/sweeping reforms*
- verb 1 [T] ~ sth to improve a system, an organization, a law, etc. by making changes to it: *proposals to reform the social security system* ◇ *The law needs to be reformed.* 2 [I, T] to improve your behaviour; to make sb do this: *He has promised to reform.* ◇ ~ sb *She thought she could reform him.* ▸ re·formed *adj.*: *a reformed character*

**re-form** /ˌriːˈfɔːm; NAmE ˈfɔːrm/ verb [I, T] to form again or form sth again, especially into a different group or pattern: *The band is re-forming after 23 years.* ◇ ~ sth *The party has recently been re-formed.*

**re·format** /ˌriːˈfɔːmæt; NAmE -ˈfɔːrm-/ verb (-tt-) ~ sth (computing) to give a new FORMAT to a computer disk

**ref·or·ma·tion** /ˌrefəˈmeɪʃn; NAmE -fər-/ noun 1 [U] (formal) the act of improving or changing sb/sth 2 **the Reformation** [sing.] new ideas in religion in 16th century Europe that led to attempts to reform (= change and improve) the Roman Catholic Church and to the forming of the Protestant Churches; the period of time when these changes were taking place

**re·forma·tory** /rɪˈfɔːmətri; NAmE -ˈfɔːrmətɔːri/ noun (pl. -ies) (also **reˈform school**) (NAmE) (BrE, old-fashioned) a type of school that young criminals are sent to instead of prison

**Reˈformed Church** noun [sing.] a church that has accepted the principles of the REFORMATION, especially a Calvinist one

**re·form·er** /rɪˈfɔːmə(r); NAmE -ˈfɔːrm-/ noun a person who works to achieve political or social change

**re·form·ist** /rɪˈfɔːmɪst; NAmE -ˈfɔːrm-/ adj. wanting or trying to change political or social situations ▸ re·form·ist noun

**re·for·mu·late** /ˌriːˈfɔːmjuleɪt; NAmE -ˈfɔːrm-/ verb 1 ~ sth to create or prepare sth again: *It is never too late to reformulate your goals.* 2 ~ sth to say or express sth in a different way: *Let me try to reformulate the problem.* ▸ re·for·mu·la·tion /ˌriːˌfɔːmjuˈleɪʃn; NAmE -ˌfɔːrm-/ noun [U, C]

**re·fract** /rɪˈfrækt/ verb ~ sth (physics) (of water, air, glass, etc.) to make waves, such as those of light, sound or energy, change direction when they go through at an angle: *Light is refracted when passed through a prism.* ▸ re·frac·tion /-ˈfrækʃn/ noun [U]

**re·fract·ive** /rɪˈfræktɪv/ adj. (physics) causing, caused by or relating to refraction

**reˌfractive ˈindex** noun (physics) a measurement of how much an object or a substance refracts light

**re·fract·or** /rɪˈfræktə(r)/ noun (physics) something such as a LENS which REFRACTS light (= causes it to change direction)

**re·frac·tory** /rɪˈfræktəri/ adj. 1 (formal) (of a person) difficult to control; behaving badly 2 (medical) (of a disease or medical condition) difficult to treat or cure

**re·frain** /rɪˈfreɪn/ verb, noun
- verb [I] (formal) to stop yourself from doing sth, especially sth that you want to do SYN desist: ~ (from sth) *They appealed to the protesters to refrain from violence.* ◇ ~ from doing sth *Please refrain from smoking.*
- noun 1 a comment or complaint that is often repeated: *Complaints about poor food in schools have become a familiar refrain.* 2 the part of a song or a poem that is repeated after each VERSE SYN chorus ⊃ WORDFINDER NOTE at POETRY

**re·fresh** /rɪˈfreʃ/ verb 1 [T] ~ sb/yourself to make sb feel less tired or less hot: *The long sleep had refreshed her.* ◇ *He refreshed himself with a cool shower.* 2 [T] ~ sth (especially NAmE, informal) to fill sb's glass or cup again: *Let me refresh your glass.* 3 [T] ~ **your/sb's memory** to remind yourself/sb of sth, especially with the help of sth that can be seen or heard SYN jog: *He had to refresh his memory by looking at his notes.* 4 [T, I] ~ **(sth)** (computing) to make the most recent information show, for example on an internet page: *Click here to refresh this document.* ◇ *The page refreshes automatically.* ⊃ WORDFINDER NOTE at COMMAND

**reˈfresher course** (also **re·fresh·er** especially in NAmE) noun a short period of training to improve your skills or to teach you about new ideas and developments in your job

**re·fresh·ing** /rɪˈfreʃɪŋ/ adj. 1 pleasantly new or different: *It made a refreshing change to be taken seriously for once.* 2 making you feel less tired or hot: *a refreshing drink/shower* ▸ re·fresh·ing·ly adv.: *refreshingly different* ◇ *The house was refreshingly cool inside.*

**re·fresh·ment** /rɪˈfreʃmənt/ noun 1 **refreshments** [pl.] drinks and small amounts of food that are provided or sold to people in a public place or at a public event: *Light refreshments will be served during the break.* 2 [U] (formal) food and drink: *In York we had a short stop for refreshment.* ◇ *Can we offer you some refreshment?* ◇ *a refreshment room/kiosk/tent* ◇ (humorous) *liquid refreshment (= alcoholic drink)* 3 [U] (formal) the fact of making sb feel stronger or less tired or hot: *a place to rest and find refreshment for mind and body*

**refried beans** /ˌriːfraɪd ˈbiːnz/ noun [pl.] beans that have been boiled and fried in advance and are heated again when needed, used especially in Mexican cooking

**re·friger·ate** /rɪˈfrɪdʒəreɪt/ verb ~ sth (formal) to make food, etc. cold in order to keep it fresh or preserve it: *Once opened, this product should be kept refrigerated.* ◇ *a refrigerated lorry/truck* ▸ re·friger·ation /rɪˌfrɪdʒəˈreɪʃn/ noun [U]: *Keep all meat products under refrigeration.*

**re·friger·ator** /rɪˈfrɪdʒəreɪtə(r)/ noun (formal or NAmE) = FRIDGE: *This dessert can be served straight from the refrigerator.*

**re·fuel** /ˌriːˈfjuːəl/ verb [T, I] (-ll-, US -l-) ~ **(sth)** to fill sth, especially a plane, with fuel in order to continue a journey; to be filled with fuel: *to refuel a plane* ◇ *The planes needed to refuel before the next mission.* ◇ *a refuelling stop* ⊃ WORDFINDER NOTE at PLANE

**ref·uge** /ˈrefjuːdʒ/ noun 1 [U] shelter or protection from danger, trouble, etc: *A further 300 people have taken refuge in the US embassy.* ◇ *a place of refuge* ◇ ~ from sb/sth *They were forced to seek refuge from the fighting.* ◇ *As the situation at home got worse she increasingly took refuge in her work.* 2 [C] a place, person or thing that provides shelter or protection for sb/sth: *a wetland refuge for birds* ◇ ~ from sb/sth *He regarded the room as a refuge from the outside world.* 3 [C] a building that provides a temporary home for people in need of shelter or protection from sb/sth: *a women's refuge* ◇ *a refuge for the homeless* 4 (BrE) = TRAFFIC ISLAND

**refu·gee** /ˌrefjuˈdʒiː/ noun a person who has been forced to leave their country or home, because there is a war or for political, religious or social reasons: *a steady flow of refugees from the war zone* ◇ *political/economic refugees* ◇ *a refugee camp* ⊃ SYNONYMS at IMMIGRANT

**re·fund** noun, verb
- noun /ˈriːfʌnd/ a sum of money that is paid back to you, especially because you paid too much or because you returned goods to a shop: *a tax refund* ◇ *to claim/demand/receive a refund* ◇ *If there is a delay of 12 hours or more, you will receive a full refund of the price of your trip.* ⊃ WORDFINDER NOTE at BUY
- verb /rɪˈfʌnd/ to give sb their money back, especially because they have paid too much or because they are not satisfied with sth they bought SYN reimburse: ~ sth *Tickets cannot be exchanged or money refunded.* ◇ ~ sth to sb *We will refund your money to you in full if you are not entirely satisfied.* ◇ ~ sb sth *We will refund you your money in full.* ▸ re·fund·able adj.: *a refundable deposit* ◇ *Tickets are not refundable.*

**re·fur·bish** /ˌriːˈfɜːbɪʃ; NAmE -ˈfɜːrb-/ verb ~ sth to clean and decorate a room, building, etc. in order to make it more attractive, more useful, etc. ▸ re·fur·bish·ment (also *informal* **re·furb** /ˈriːfɜːb; *NAmE* -fɜːrb/ *noun* [U, C]: *The hotel is closed for refurbishment.*

**re·fusal** ⚑+ C1 /rɪˈfjuːzl/ *noun* [U, C] an act of saying or showing that you will not do, give or accept sth: *the refusal of a request/an invitation/an offer* ◇ *a blunt/flat/curt refusal* ◇ **~ to do sth** *His refusal to discuss the matter is very annoying.* ⊃ see also FIRST REFUSAL

**re·fuse¹** ❶ A2 /rɪˈfjuːz/ *verb* 1 ⚑ A2 [I, T] to say or show that you will not do sth that sb has asked you to do: *Go on, ask her; she can hardly refuse.* ◇ **~ to do sth** *He flatly refused to discuss the matter.* ◇ *She refused to accept that there was a problem.* ◇ **sth** *The demand for an apology was pointedly refused.* 2 ⚑ A2 [T, I] **~ (sth)** to say that you do not want sth that has been offered to you SYN **turn sb/sth↔down**: *I politely refused their invitation.* ◇ *The job offer was simply too good to refuse.* 3 ⚑ A2 [T] to say that you will not allow sth; to say that you will not give or allow sb sth that they want or need SYN **deny**: **~ sth** *He refused our request for an interview.* ◇ *The authorities refused permission for the new housing development.* ◇ **~ sb sth** *They refused him a visa.* ◇ *She would never refuse her kids anything.* 4 [T] (of a thing) to fail to do what you want or expect it to do: *The car refused to start.* ◇ *The problem simply refuses to go away.*

**re·fuse²** /ˈrefjuːs/ *noun* [U] (*formal*) waste material that has been thrown away SYN **rubbish**: *domestic/household refuse* ◇ *the city refuse dump* ◇ *refuse collection/disposal* ⊃ note at RUBBISH

**refuse collector** (*BrE*) (*NAmE* **ˈgarbage collector**) *noun* (*formal*) = DUSTMAN

**re·fuse·nik** /rɪˈfjuːznɪk/ *noun* a person who refuses to obey an order or law as a protest

**re·fute** /rɪˈfjuːt/ *verb* (*formal*) 1 **~ sth** to prove that sth is wrong SYN **rebut**: *to refute an argument/a theory, etc.* 2 **~ sth** to say that sth is not true or fair SYN **deny**: *She refutes any suggestion that she behaved unprofessionally.*
▶ **re·fut·able** /-ˈfjuːtəbl/ *adj.* **refu·ta·tion** /ˌrefjuˈteɪʃn/ *noun* [C, U]: *a refutation of previously held views*

**reg** /redʒ/ *abbr.* (*BrE*, *informal*) REGISTRATION: *an 18 reg car* = *a car with '18' in its* REGISTRATION NUMBER, *showing the year that it was registered*)

**re·gain** ⚑+ C1 /rɪˈɡeɪn/ *verb* 1 ⚑+ C1 **~ sth** to get back sth you no longer have, especially an ability or a quality: *I struggled to regain some dignity.* ◇ *The party has regained control of the region.* ◇ *She paused on the edge, trying to regain her balance.* ◇ *He did not regain consciousness* (= wake up after being unconscious) *for several days.* 2 **~ sth** (*literary*) to get back to a place that you have left: *They finally managed to regain the beach.*

**regal** /ˈriːɡl/ *adj.* typical of a king or queen, and therefore impressive: *regal power* ◇ *the regal splendour of the palace* ◇ *She dismissed him with a regal gesture.* ⊃ compare ROYAL
▶ **re·gal·ly** /-ɡəli/ *adv.*

**re·gale** /rɪˈɡeɪl/ *verb*
PHRV **reˈgale sb with sth** to entertain sb with stories, jokes, etc: *He regaled us with tales of his days as a jazz pianist.*

**re·galia** /rɪˈɡeɪliə/ *noun* [U] the special clothes that are worn or objects that are carried at official ceremonies

**re·gard** ❶ B2 ⓦ /rɪˈɡɑːd; *NAmE* -ˈɡɑːrd/ *verb*, *noun*
■ *verb* 1 ⚑ B2 [often passive] to think about sb/sth in a particular way: **~ sb/sth + adv./prep.** *Her work is very highly regarded.* ◇ **~ sb/sth/yourself as sth** *He regards himself as a patriot.* ◇ *She is widely regarded as the current leader's natural successor.* 2 **~ sb/sth (+ adv./prep.)** (*formal*) to look at sb/sth, especially in a particular way SYN **contemplate**: *He regarded us suspiciously.*
IDM **as reˈgards sb/sth** (*formal*) relating to or in connection with sb/sth: *I have little information as regards her fitness for the post.* ◇ *As regards the first point in your letter …*
■ *noun* 1 ⚑ B2 [U] (*formal*) attention to or thought and care for sb/sth: **~ for sb/sth** *to have scant/little/no regard for sb/sth* ◇ *Social services should pay proper regard to the needs of inner-city areas.* ◇ **without ~ to sb/sth** *He was driving without regard to speed limits.* 2 ⚑ [U] (*formal*) respect for sb/sth: *He held her in high regard* (= had a good opinion of her). ◇ **~ for sb/sth** *I had great regard for his abilities.*

1299

# **regardless of**

⊃ see also SELF-REGARD 3 **regards** [pl.] used to send good wishes to sb at the end of an email or letter, or when asking sb to give your good wishes to another person who is not present: *With best/kind regards, Yours …* ◇ *Give your brother my regards when you see him.*
IDM **have reˈgard to sth** (*formal* or *law*) to remember and think carefully about sth: *It is always necessary to have regard to the terms of the contract.* **in ˈthis/ˈthat reˈgard** (*formal*) relating to what has just been mentioned: *I have nothing further to say in this regard.* **in/with reˈgard to sb/sth** (*formal*) relating to sb/sth: *a country's laws in regard to human rights* ◇ *The company's position with regard to overtime is made clear in their contracts.*

▼ **SYNONYMS**

**regard**

call • find • consider • see • view

These words all mean to think about sb/sth in a particular way.

**regard** to think of sb/sth in a particular way: *He seemed to regard the whole thing as a joke.*

**call** to say that sb/sth has particular qualities or characteristics: *I wouldn't call German an easy language.*

**find** to have a particular feeling or opinion about sth: *You may find your illness hard to accept.*

**consider** to think of sb/sth in a particular way: *Who do you consider (to be) responsible for the accident?*

**REGARD OR CONSIDER?**
These two words have the same meaning, but they are used in different patterns and structures. In this meaning **consider** must be used with a complement or clause: you can *consider sb/sth to be sth* or *consider sb/sth as sth*, although very often the *to be* or *as* is left out: *He considers himself an expert.* ◇ *They are considered a high-risk group.* You can also *consider that sb/sth is sth* and again, the *that* can be left out. **Regard** is used in a narrower range of structures. The most frequent structure is *regard sb/sth as sth*; the *as* cannot be left out: *I regard him a close friend.* You cannot: *regard sb/sth to be sth* or *regard that sb/sth is sth.* However, **regard** (but not **consider** in this meaning) can also be used without a noun or adjective complement but with just an object and adverb (*sb/sth is highly regarded*) or adverbial phrase (*regard sb/sth with suspicion/jealousy/admiration*).

**see** to have an opinion of sth: *Try to see things from her point of view.*

**view** to think of sb/sth in a particular way: *How do you view your position within the company?* NOTE **View** has the same meaning as **regard** and **consider** but is slightly less frequent and slightly less formal. The main structures are *view sb/sth as sb/sth* (you cannot leave out the *as*) and *view sb/sth with sth.*

**PATTERNS**
• to regard/consider/see/view sb/sth **as** sth
• to regard/consider/see/view sb/sth **from** a particular point of view
• to find/consider sb/sth **to be** sth
• generally/usually regarded/considered/seen/viewed as sth
• to regard/consider/view sb/sth **favourably/unfavourably**

**re·gard·ing** /rɪˈɡɑːdɪŋ; *NAmE* -ˈɡɑːrd-/ *prep.* relating to sb/sth; about sb/sth: *She has said nothing regarding your request.* ◇ *Call me if you have any problems regarding your work.*

**re·gard·less** ⚑+ C1 /rɪˈɡɑːdləs; *NAmE* -ˈɡɑːrd-/ *adv.* paying no attention, even if the situation is bad or there are difficulties: *The weather was terrible but we carried on regardless.*

**reˈgardless of** ⓦ *prep.* paying no attention to sth/sb; treating sth/sb as not being important: *The club welcomes all new members regardless of age.* ◇ *He went ahead and did it, regardless of the consequences.* ◇ *The amount will be*

# regatta

paid to everyone regardless of whether they have children or not.

**re·gatta** /rɪˈɡætə; NAmE also -ˈɡɑːtə/ noun a sporting event in which races between ROWING BOATS or SAILING BOATS are held

**Re·gency** /ˈriːdʒənsi/ adj. [usually before noun] of or in the style of the period 1811–20 in the UK, when George, Prince of Wales, was REGENT (= ruled the country in place of the king, his father): *Regency architecture*

**re·gency** /ˈriːdʒənsi/ noun (pl. -ies) a period of government by a REGENT (= a person who rules a country in place of the king or queen)

**re·gen·er·ate** /rɪˈdʒenəreɪt/ verb 1 [T] ~ sth to make an area, institution, etc. develop and grow strong again: *The money will be used to regenerate the commercial heart of the town.* 2 [I, T] (*biology*) to grow again; to make sth grow again: *Once destroyed, brain cells do not regenerate.* ◇ ~ sth/itself *If the woodland is left alone, it will regenerate itself in a few years.* ▸ **re·gen·er·ation** /rɪˌdʒenəˈreɪʃn/ noun [U]: *economic regeneration* ◇ *the regeneration of cells in the body* **re·gen·er·ative** /rɪˈdʒenərətɪv/ adj.: *the regenerative powers of nature*

**re·gent** /ˈriːdʒənt/ (*also* **Regent**) noun a person who rules a country because the king or queen is too young, old, ill, etc: *to act as regent* ▸ **re·gent** (*also* **Regent**) adj. [after noun]: *the Prince Regent*

**reg·gae** /ˈreɡeɪ/ noun [U] a type of popular music with strong rhythms, developed in Jamaica in the 1960s

**reg·gae·ton** /ˈreɡeɪtɒn; NAmE -tɑːn/ noun [U] a type of dance music, developed in Puerto Rico in the 1980s, which is a mixture of REGGAE, SALSA and HIP-HOP or RAP, and which often includes words that are sung or spoken in Spanish

**reggo** = REGO

**regi·cide** /ˈredʒɪsaɪd/ noun [U, C] (*formal*) the crime of killing a king or queen; a person who is guilty of this crime

**re·gime** /reɪˈʒiːm/ noun 1 a method or system of government, especially one that has not been elected in a fair way: *a fascist/totalitarian/military, etc. regime* ◇ *an oppressive/brutal regime* 2 a method or system of organizing or managing sth: *Our tax regime is one of the most favourable in Europe.* 3 = REGIMEN: *a dietary regime*

**reˈgime change** noun [U, C, usually sing.] the situation when one government is replaced by another, especially using military force

**regi·men** /ˈredʒɪmən/ (*also* **re·gime**) noun (*medical or formal*) a set of rules about food and exercise or medical treatment that you follow in order to stay healthy or to improve your health

**regi·ment** /ˈredʒɪmənt/ noun [C + sing./pl. v.] 1 a large group of soldiers that is commanded by a COLONEL ⇒ WORDFINDER NOTE at ARMY 2 (*formal*) a large number of people or things

**regi·men·tal** /ˌredʒɪˈmentl/ adj. [only before noun] connected with a particular regiment of soldiers: *a regimental flag* ◇ *regimental headquarters*

**regi·ment·ed** /ˈredʒɪmentɪd/ adj. (*disapproving*) 1 involving strict discipline and/or organization: *The school imposes a very regimented lifestyle on its students.* 2 arranged in strict groups, patterns, etc: *regimented lines of trees* ▸ **regi·men·ta·tion** /ˌredʒɪmenˈteɪʃn/ noun [U]: *She rebelled against the regimentation of school life.*

**Re·gina** /rɪˈdʒaɪnə; NAmE -ˈdʒiːnə/ noun [U] (*BrE, from Latin, formal*) a word meaning 'queen', used, for example, in the titles of legal cases which are brought by the state when there is a queen in the UK: *Regina v Jones* ⇒ compare REX

**re·gion** /ˈriːdʒən/ noun 1 [C] a large area of land, usually without exact limits or borders: *mountainous/coastal regions* ◇ *one of the most densely populated regions of North America* ◇ *in the ~ There are more than two million people living in the region.* 2 [C] one of the areas that a country is divided into, that has its own customs and/or its own government: *the Basque region of Spain* 3 **the regions** [pl.] (*BrE*) all of a country except the capital city 4 [C] a part of the body, usually

one that has a particular character or problem: *pains in the abdominal region*

**IDM** ▸ **in the ˈregion of** used when you are giving a number, price, etc. to show that it is not exact **SYN** approximately: *He earns somewhere in the region of €50000.*

**re·gion·al** /ˈriːdʒənl/ adj. [usually before noun] of or relating to a region: *services available at a local and regional level* ◇ *the conflict between regional and national interests* ◇ *a regional assembly/council/government* ▸ **re·gion·al·ly** /-nəli/ adv.: *regionally based television companies*

**re·gion·al·ism** /ˈriːdʒənəlɪzəm/ noun 1 [C] a feature of a language that exists in a particular part of a country, and is not part of the standard language 2 [U] the desire of the people who live in a particular region of a country to have more independent control in political and economic decisions

**reg·is·ter** /ˈredʒɪstə(r)/ verb, noun

■ verb
- **PUT NAME ON LIST** 1 [T, I] to record your/sb's/sth's name on an official list: *You can also register online.* ◇ ~ sb/sth *The site has 114 million registered users.* ◇ *We expect about 50 per cent of registered voters to vote in the election.* ◇ ~ sb + adj. *She is officially registered disabled.* ◇ ~ (sb/sth) with sb/sth *to register with a doctor/dentist* ◇ ~ (sb/sth) for sth *About 700 people registered for the conference.* ◇ ~ (sb) to do sth *More than 5 000 people registered to take part in the contest.* ⇒ WORDFINDER NOTE at CONFERENCE
- **GIVE OPINION PUBLICLY** 2 [T] ~ sth (*formal*) to make your opinion known officially or publicly: *China has registered a protest over foreign intervention.*
- **ON MEASURING INSTRUMENT** 3 [I, T] if a measuring instrument **registers** an amount or sth **registers** an amount on a measuring instrument, the instrument shows or records that amount: + noun *The thermometer registered 32°C.* ◇ *The earthquake registered 3 on the Richter scale.* ◇ ~ sth *The stock exchange has registered huge losses this week.*
- **SHOW FEELING** 4 [T, no passive, I] ~ (sth) (*formal*) to show or express a feeling: *Her face registered disapproval.* ◇ *Shock registered on everyone's face.*
- **NOTICE STH** 5 [T, no passive, I] (often used in negative sentences) ~ (sth) to notice sth and remember it; to be noticed: *He barely registered our presence.* ◇ *I told her my name, but it obviously didn't register.*
- **LETTER/PACKAGE** 6 [T, usually passive] ~ sth to send sth by mail, paying extra money to protect it against loss or damage: *Can I register this, please?* ◇ *a registered letter*

■ noun
- **LIST OF NAMES** 1 [C] an official list or record of names, items, etc.; a book that contains such a list: *The bride and groom signed the register.* ◇ ~ of sb/sth *They keep a register of all those who have contributed to the fund.* ◇ (*BrE*) *Teacher took the register* (= checked who was present at school). ◇ (*BrE*) *Dr Shaw was struck off the medical register for misconduct.* ⇒ see also ELECTORAL REGISTER, PARISH REGISTER
- **OF VOICE/INSTRUMENT** 2 [C] the range, or part of a range, of a human voice or a musical instrument: *in the upper/middle/lower register*
- **OF WRITING/SPEECH** 3 [C, U] (*linguistics*) the level and style of a piece of writing or speech, that is usually appropriate to the situation that it is used in: *The essay suddenly switches from a formal to an informal register.* ⇒ WORDFINDER NOTE at DICTIONARY
- **FOR HOT/COLD AIR** 4 [C] (*NAmE*) an opening, with a cover that you can have open or shut, that allows hot or cold air from a heating or cooling system into a room ⇒ compare VENT
- **MACHINE** 5 [C] (*NAmE*) = CASH REGISTER

**ˌregistered ˈmail** (*BrE also* **ˌregistered ˈpost**) noun [U] a method of sending a letter or package in which the person sending it can claim money if it arrives late or is lost or damaged ⇒ compare RECORDED DELIVERY

**ˌregistered ˈnurse** noun (*abbr.* **RN**) 1 (*NAmE*) a nurse who has a degree in NURSING and who has passed an exam to be allowed to work in a particular state 2 (*BrE*) a nurse who has an official qualification

**registered 'trademark** noun (symb. ®) the sign or name of a product, etc. that is officially recorded and protected so that nobody else can use it

**'register office** noun the official way of referring to a REGISTRY OFFICE

**regis·trar** /ˌredʒɪˈstrɑː(r); NAmE ˈredʒɪstrɑːr/ noun **1** a person whose job is to keep official records, especially of births, marriages and deaths **2** the senior officer who organizes the affairs of a college or university **3** a doctor working in a British hospital who is training to become a specialist in a particular area of medicine: *a paediatric registrar* ⊃ compare CONSULTANT, RESIDENT

**regis·tra·tion** ? + B2 /ˌredʒɪˈstreɪʃn/ noun **1** ? + B2 [U, C] the act of making an official record of sth/sb: *the registration of letters and parcels* ◊ *the registration of students for a course* ◊ *registration fees* ◊ *the registration of a child's birth* **2** [U, C] a document showing that an official record has been made of sth ⊃ compare LOGBOOK **3** [C] (*BrE*) = REGISTRATION NUMBER **4** [U] (*BrE*) the time when a teacher looks at the list of students on the class register and checks that the students are present

**regi'stration number** (*also* **regis·tra·tion**) (*both BrE*) (*NAmE* **license (plate) number**) noun the series of letters and numbers that are shown on a NUMBER PLATE at the front and back of a vehicle to identify it

**regi'stration plate** noun (*BrE*) = NUMBER PLATE

**regis·try** /ˈredʒɪstri/ noun (*pl.* **-ies**) a place where registers are kept; an official list or register

**'registry office** (*also* **'register office**) noun (in the UK) a place where CIVIL marriages (= that do not involve a religious ceremony) are performed and where records of births, marriages and deaths are made: *to get married in/at a registry office*

**rego** (*also* **reggo**) /ˈredʒəʊ/ noun (*pl.* **-os**) (*AustralE, NZE, informal*) a REGISTRATION for a car, etc.

**re·gress** /rɪˈɡres/ verb [I] **~ (to sth)** (*formal, usually disapproving*) to return to an earlier or less advanced form or way of behaving

**re·gres·sion** /rɪˈɡreʃn/ noun [U, C] **~ (to sth)** (*formal, usually disapproving*) the process of going back to an earlier or less advanced form or state

**re·gres·sive** /rɪˈɡresɪv/ adj. **1** becoming or making sth less advanced: *The policy has been condemned as a regressive step.* **2** (*specialist*) (of taxes) having less effect on the rich than on the poor

**re·gret** ⓘ B2 /rɪˈɡret/ verb, noun

■ *verb* (**-tt-**) **1** ? B2 to feel sorry about sth you have done or about sth that you have not been able to do: **~ sth** *If you don't do it now, you'll only regret it.* ◊ *The decision could be one he lives to regret.* ◊ *'I've had a wonderful life,' she said, 'I don't regret a thing.'* ◊ **~ doing sth** *He bitterly regretted ever having mentioned it.* ◊ **~ what, how, etc …** *I deeply regret what I said.* ◊ **~ that** *I regret that I never got to meet him in person.* **2** ? B2 (*formal*) used to say in a polite or formal way that you are sorry or sad about a situation: **~ sth** *The airline regrets any inconvenience.* ◊ **~ that** *I regret that I am unable to accept your kind invitation.* ◊ **~ to do sth** *We regret to inform you that your application has not been successful.* ◊ *it is regretted that … It is to be regretted that so many young people leave school without qualifications.* ⊃ WORDFINDER NOTE at SORRY

■ *noun* ? B2 [U, C] a sad feeling because of sth that has happened or sth that you have done or not done: *a feeling/pang/twinge of regret* ◊ *What is your greatest regret (= the thing that you are most sorry about doing or not doing)?* ◊ **with ~** *It is with great regret that I accept your resignation.* ◊ **~ at (doing) sth** *She expressed her regret at the decision.* ◊ **~ for (doing) sth** *There has still been no official expression of regret for their deaths.* ◊ *He said he felt **deep regret** for having been part of a government that had brutally violated human rights.*

**re·gret·ful** /rɪˈɡretfl/ adj. feeling or showing that you are sad or disappointed because of sth that has happened or sth that you have done or not done SYN **rueful**: *a regretful look*

**re·gret·ful·ly** /rɪˈɡretfəli/ adv. **1** in a way that shows you are sad or disappointed about sth: *'I'm afraid not,' he said*

1301 **regular**

▼ **WHICH WORD?**

**regretfully / regrettably**

● **Regretfully** and **regrettably** can both be used as sentence adverbs to show that you are sorry about something and wish the situation were different: *Regretfully, some jobs will be lost.* ◊ *Regrettably, some jobs will be lost.*

● **Regretfully** can also be used to mean 'in a way that shows you are sad or disappointed about something': *He sighed regretfully.*

*regretfully.* ◊ *Emma shook her head regretfully.* **2** used to show that you are sorry that sth is the case and you wish the situation were different SYN **regrettably**: *Regretfully, mounting costs have forced the museum to close.*

**re·gret·table** /rɪˈɡretəbl/ adj. **~ (that …)** (*formal*) that you are sorry about and wish had not happened: *It is regrettable that the police were not informed sooner.* ◊ *The loss of jobs is highly regrettable.* ▶ **re·gret·tably** /-bli/ adv.: *Regrettably, crime has been increasing in this area.*

**re·group** /ˌriːˈɡruːp/ verb **1** [T, I] **~ (sth) (for sth)** to arrange the way people or soldiers work together in a new way, especially in order to continue fighting or attacking sb: **~ (sth)** *They regrouped their forces and renewed the attack.* ◊ *After its election defeat, the party needs to regroup.* **2** [I] (of a person) to return to a normal state after an unpleasant experience or a period of difficulty, and become ready to make an effort again with new enthusiasm or strength: *Summer is a time to relax, regroup and catch up on all those things you've been putting off all year.*

**regu·lar** ⓘ A2 /ˈreɡjələ(r)/ adj., noun

■ *adj.*

● **FOLLOWING PATTERN 1** ? A2 following a pattern, especially with the same time or space in between each thing and the next: *A light flashed at regular intervals.* ◊ *There is a regular bus service to the airport.* ◊ *regular meetings/visits* ◊ *The equipment is checked on a regular basis.* ◊ *She writes a regular column for a national newspaper.* OPP **irregular**

● **FREQUENT 2** ? A2 done or happening often: *Do you take regular exercise?* ◊ *I'm still in regular contact with friends I met at university.* ◊ *a painter whose work is a regular feature of the Summer Exhibition* OPP **irregular 3** ? A2 [only before noun] (of people) doing the same thing or going to the same place often: *regular readers/customers/users* ◊ *She is a regular contributor to many journals and magazines* ◊ *He was a regular visitor to her house.*

● **GRAMMAR 4** ? A2 (especially of verbs or nouns) changing their form in the same way as most other verbs and nouns: *The past participle of regular verbs ends in '-ed'.* OPP **irregular**

● **USUAL 5** ? B1 [only before noun] usual: *I couldn't see my regular doctor today.* ◊ *On Monday he would have to return to his regular duties.* ◊ *the last match of the regular season*

● **STANDARD SIZE 6** ? B1 (*especially NAmE*) of a standard size: *Regular or large fries?*

● **ORDINARY 7** ? B1 [only before noun] (*especially NAmE*) ordinary; without any special or extra features: *Do you want regular or diet cola?* ◊ (*approving*) *He's just a regular guy who loves his dog.*

● **EVEN 8** ? B2 having an even shape: *a face with regular features* OPP **irregular**

● **PERMANENT 9** ? B2 lasting or happening over a long period: *a regular income* ◊ *She couldn't find any regular employment.*

● **SOLDIER 10** [only before noun] belonging to or connected with the permanent armed forces or police force of a country: *the regular army* ◊ *regular soldiers* OPP **irregular**

● **FOR EMPHASIS 11** (*informal*) used for emphasis to show that sb/sth is an exact or clear example of the thing mentioned: *The whole thing was a regular disaster.*

IDM **(as) regular as 'clockwork** very regularly; happening at the same time in the same way: *He is home by six every day, regular as clockwork.*

# regularity

■ noun
- **CUSTOMER 1** a customer who often goes to a particular shop, pub, restaurant, etc: *He's one of our regulars.*
- **MEMBER OF TEAM 2** a person who often plays in a particular team, takes part in a particular television show, etc: *We are missing six first-team regulars because of injury.*
- **SOLDIER 3** a professional soldier who belongs to a country's permanent army

**regu·lar·ity** /ˌreɡjuˈlærəti/ *noun* **1** [U] the fact that the same thing happens again and again, and usually with the same length of time between each time it happens: *Aircraft passed overhead* **with monotonous regularity**. **2** [U] the fact that sth is arranged in an even way or in an organized pattern: *the striking regularity of her features* **3** [C] a thing that has a pattern to it: *They had observed regularities in the behaviour of the animals.* ⇨ compare IRREGULARITY

**regu·lar·ize** (*BrE also* **-ise**) /ˈreɡjələraɪz/ *verb* ~ **sth** to make a situation that already exists legal or official: *Illegal immigrants were given the opportunity to regularize their position.*

**regu·lar·ly** 🅘 🅱🅱 /ˈreɡjələli; *NAmE* -lərli/ *adv.* **1** 🅱🅱 at regular INTERVALS or times: *We meet regularly to discuss the progress of the project.* **2** 🅱🅱 often: *He admitted that he regularly used drugs.* **3** 🅱🅱 in an even or balanced way: *The plants were spaced regularly, about 50 cm apart.*

**regu·late** 🅱🅱 /ˈreɡjuleɪt/ *verb* **1** 🅱🅱 [T, I] ~ **(sth)** to control sth by means of rules: *The department is responsible for regulating the insurance industry.* ◊ *The activities of credit companies are regulated by law.* **2** 🅱🅱 [T] ~ **sth** to control the speed, pressure, temperature, etc. in a machine or system: *This valve regulates the flow of water.*

**regu·la·tion** 🅘 🅱🅱 🅦 /ˌreɡjuˈleɪʃn/ *noun, adj.*
■ *noun* **1** 🅱🅱 [C, usually pl.] an official rule made by a government or some other authority: *too many rules and regulations* ◊ **the strict regulations** *governing the sale of weapons* ◊ *to comply with the regulations* ◊ **against regulations** *It's against safety regulations to fix these doors open.* ◊ **under the regulations** *Under the new regulations spending on office equipment will be strictly controlled.* **2** [U] controlling sth by means of rules: *the voluntary regulation of the press* ⇨ see also SELF-REGULATION
■ *adj.* [only before noun] that must be worn or used according to the official rules: *in regulation uniform*

**regu·la·tor** 🅱🅱 🅒🅒 /ˈreɡjuleɪtə(r)/ *noun* **1** 🅒🅒 a person or an organization that officially controls an area of business or industry and makes sure that it is operating fairly: *Ofgas, the gas industry regulator* **2** 🅒🅒 a device that controls sth such as speed, temperature or pressure: *a pressure regulator*

**regu·la·tory** 🅱🅱 🅒🅒 /ˈreɡjələtəri; *NAmE* -tɔːri/ *adj.* [usually before noun] having the power to control an area of business or industry and make sure that it is operating fairly: *regulatory bodies/authorities/agencies*

**re·gur·gi·tate** /rɪˈɡɜːdʒɪteɪt; *NAmE* -ˈɡɜːrdʒ-/ *verb* **1** ~ **sth** (*formal*) to bring food that has been SWALLOWED back up into the mouth again **2** ~ **sth** (*disapproving*) to repeat sth you have heard or read without really thinking about it or understanding it ▶ **re·gur·gi·ta·tion** /rɪˌɡɜːdʒɪˈteɪʃn; *NAmE* -ˌɡɜːrdʒ-/ *noun* [U]

**rehab** /ˈriːhæb/ *noun* [U] the process of helping to cure sb who has a problem with drugs or alcohol: *to go into rehab* ◊ *a rehab clinic* ⇨ WORDFINDER NOTE at DRUG

**re·habili·tate** /ˌriːəˈbɪlɪteɪt/ *verb* **1** ~ **sb** to help sb to have a normal, useful life again after they have been very ill or in prison for a long time: *a unit for rehabilitating drug addicts* **2** ~ **sb (as sth)** to begin to consider that sb is good or acceptable after a long period during which they were considered bad or unacceptable: *He played a major role in rehabilitating Magritte as an artist.* **3** ~ **sth** to return a building or an area to its previous good condition

**re·habili·ta·tion** 🅒🅒 /ˌriːəˌbɪlɪˈteɪʃn/ *noun* [U] **1** 🅒🅒 the process of helping sb to have a normal, useful life again after they have been very ill or in prison for a long time: *a drug rehabilitation centre* ◊ *the rehabilitation of* *offenders* **2** the act of starting to consider that sb is good or acceptable after a long period during which they were considered bad or unacceptable: *the rehabilitation of Magritte as an artist* **3** the process of returning a building, place or area of activity to its previous good condition: *the rehabilitation of the steel industry*

**re·hash** /ˌriːˈhæʃ/ *verb* ~ **sth** (*disapproving*) to arrange ideas, pieces of writing or pieces of film into a new form but without any great change or improvement: *He just rehashes songs from the 60s.* ▶ **re·hash** /ˈriːhæʃ/ *noun* [sing.] (*disapproving*): *The movie is just a rehash of the best TV episodes.*

**re·hear** /ˌriːˈhɪə(r); *NAmE* -ˈhɪr/ *verb* (**re·heard**, **re·heard** /ˌriːˈhɜːd; *NAmE* -ˈhɜːrd/) ~ **sth** (*law*) to hear or consider a case again in court

**re·hear·ing** /ˌriːˈhɪərɪŋ; *NAmE* -ˈhɪr-/ *noun* (*law*) an opportunity for a case to be heard or considered again in court

**re·hearsal** /rɪˈhɜːsl; *NAmE* -ˈhɜːrsl/ *noun* **1** [C, U] time that is spent practising a play or piece of music in preparation for a public performance: *to have a rehearsal* ◊ *We only had six days of rehearsal.* ◊ **in ~** *Our new production of 'Hamlet' is currently in rehearsal.* ◊ *a rehearsal room* ⇨ see also DRESS REHEARSAL ⇨ WORDFINDER NOTE at PERFORMANCE **2** [C, usually sing.] ~ **(for sth)** an experience or event that helps to prepare you for sth that is going to happen in the future: *These training exercises are designed to be a rehearsal for the invasion.* **3** [C, usually sing.] ~ **of sth** (*formal*) the act of repeating sth that has been said before: *We listened to his lengthy rehearsal of the arguments.*

**re·hearse** /rɪˈhɜːs; *NAmE* -ˈhɜːrs/ *verb* **1** [I, T] to practise or make people practise a play, piece of music, etc. in preparation for a public performance: ~ **(for sth)** *We were given only two weeks to rehearse.* ◊ ~ **sth/sb** *Today, we'll just be rehearsing the final scene.* ◊ *The actors were poorly rehearsed.* **2** [T] to prepare in your mind or practise privately what you are going to do or say to sb: ~ **sth** *She walked along rehearsing her excuse for being late.* ◊ ~ **what, how, etc ...** *She mentally rehearsed what she would say to Jeff.* **3** [T] ~ **sth** (*formal, usually disapproving*) to repeat ideas or opinions that have often been expressed before

**re·heat** /ˌriːˈhiːt/ *verb* ~ **sth** to heat cooked food again after it has been left to go cold

**re·home** /ˌriːˈhəʊm/ *verb* ~ **sth** to find a new owner for a pet, especially a dog or cat, usually after caring for it for a time: *The organization rescues stray dogs and rehomes them.*

**re·house** /ˌriːˈhaʊz/ *verb* ~ **sb** to provide sb with a different home to live in: *Thousands of earthquake victims are still waiting to be rehoused.*

**reign** 🅱🅱 /reɪn/ *noun, verb*
■ *noun* **1** 🅒🅒 the period during which a king, queen, EMPEROR, etc. rules: **in/during a ~** *The house was built during the reign of Henry VIII.* **2** the period during which sb is in charge of an organization, a team, etc. ⇨ WORDFINDER NOTE at KING
■ *verb* **1** 🅒🅒 [I] to rule as king, queen, EMPEROR, etc: *the reigning monarch* ◊ *Queen Victoria reigned from 1837 to 1901.* ◊ ~ **over sb/sth** *Herod reigned over Palestine at that time.* **2** [I] ~ **(over sb/sth)** to be the best or most important in a particular situation or area of skill: *the reigning champion* ◊ *In the field of classical music, he still reigns supreme.* **3** [I] (*literary*) (of an idea, a feeling or an atmosphere) to be the most obvious feature of a place or moment: *At last silence reigned* (= there was complete silence).

▼ **HOMOPHONES**

**rain • reign • rein** /reɪn/
- **rain** *noun*: *Look at that rain! We'll be drenched if it doesn't stop.*
- **rain** *verb*: *Take an umbrella—it's going to rain.*
- **reign** *noun*: *The country changed dramatically during her long reign.*
- **reign** *verb*: *Henry Bolingbroke was soon to reign in England as Henry IV.*
- **rein** *noun*: *She's been given free rein to spend the money however she wants.*
- **rein** *verb*: *They should learn to rein in their opinions, otherwise they'll offend somebody.*

**re·ig·nite** /ˌriːɪɡˈnaɪt/ *verb* [I, T] to start burning again; to make sth start burning again: *The oven burners reignite automatically if blown out.* ◊ **~ sth** *You may need to reignite the pilot light.* ◊ (*figurative*) *Their passion was reignited by a romantic trip to Venice.*

**reign of ˈterror** *noun* (*pl.* **reigns of terror**) a period during which there is a lot of violence and many people are killed by the political leader or people in power

**reiki** /ˈreɪki/ *noun* [U] (*from Japanese*) a method of making sick people well again based on the idea that energy can be directed into a person's body by touch

**re·im·burse** /ˌriːɪmˈbɜːs; *NAmE* -ˈbɜːrs/ *verb* (*formal*) to pay back money to sb which they have spent or lost: **~ sth** *We will reimburse any expenses incurred.* ◊ **~ sb (for sth)** *You will be reimbursed for any loss or damage caused by our company.* ▸ **re·im·burse·ment** *noun* [U]

**rein** /reɪn/ *noun, verb*
- *noun* **1** [C, usually pl.] a long narrow leather band that is attached to a metal bar in a horse's mouth (= a BIT) and is held by the rider in order to control the horse: *She pulled gently on the reins.* ➔ WORDFINDER NOTE at HORSE **2 reins** [pl.] (*BrE*) a pair of long narrow pieces of cloth or other material worn by a small child and held by an adult in order to stop the child from walking off and getting lost **3 the reins** [pl.] the state of being in control or the leader of sth: *It was time to* **hand over the reins** *of power* (= to give control to sb else). ◊ *The vice-president was forced to* **take up the reins** *of office.*
- IDM **give/allow sb/sth free/full ˈrein** | **give/allow free/full ˈrein to sth** to give sb complete freedom of action; to allow a feeling to be expressed freely: *The designer was given free rein.* ◊ *The script allows full rein to her larger-than-life acting style.* ➔ HOMOPHONES at REIGN ➔ more at TIGHT *adj.*
- *verb*
- PHRV **ˌrein sb/sth↔ˈback** | **ˌrein sth↔ˈin 1** to start to control sb/sth more strictly SYN **check**: *We need to rein back public spending.* ◊ *She kept her emotions tightly reined in.* ➔ HOMOPHONES at REIGN **2** to stop a horse or make it go more slowly by pulling back the reins

**re·in·car·nate** /ˌriːɪnkɑːˈneɪt; *NAmE* ˌriːɪnˈkɑːrneɪt/ *verb* [T, often passive, I] **~ (sb/sth) (as sb/sth)** to be born again in another body after you have died; to make sb be born again in this way: *They believe humans are reincarnated in animal form.*

**re·in·car·na·tion** /ˌriːɪnkɑːˈneɪʃn; *NAmE* -kɑːrˈn-/ *noun* **1** [U] the belief that after sb's death their soul lives again in a new body **2** [C, usually sing.] a person or an animal whose body contains the soul of a dead person

**rein·deer** /ˈreɪndɪə(r); *NAmE* -dɪr/ *noun* (*pl.* **rein·deer** or **rein·deers**) a large DEER with long ANTLERS (= hard parts on the head that are like branches), that lives in cold northern regions: *herds of reindeer*

**re·inforce** /ˌriːɪnˈfɔːs; *NAmE* -ˈfɔːrs/ *verb* **1** ʔ+ B2 **~ sth** to make a feeling, an idea, etc. stronger: *Such jokes tend to reinforce racial stereotypes.* ◊ *The climate of political confusion has only reinforced the country's economic decline.* ◊ *Success in the talks will reinforce his reputation as an international statesman.* **2** ʔ+ C1 **~ sth** to make a structure or material stronger, especially by adding another material to it: *All buildings are now reinforced to withstand earthquakes.* ◊ *reinforced steel* **3 ~ sth** to send more people or equipment in order to make an army, etc. stronger: *The UN has undertaken to reinforce its military presence along the borders.*

**reinforced ˈconcrete** *noun* [U] CONCRETE (= a hard building material) with metal bars or wires inside to make it stronger

**re·inforce·ment** /ˌriːɪnˈfɔːsmənt; *NAmE* -ˈfɔːrs-/ *noun* **1 reinforcements** [pl.] extra soldiers or police officers who are sent to a place because more are needed: *to send in reinforcements* **2** [U, sing.] the act of making sth stronger, especially a feeling or an idea

**re·instate** /ˌriːɪnˈsteɪt/ *verb* **1 ~ sb/sth (in/as sth)** to give back a job or position that had been taken away from sb: *He was reinstated in his post.* **2 ~ sth (in/as sth)** to return sth to its previous position or status SYN **restore**: *There have been repeated calls to reinstate the death penalty.* ▸ **re·instate·ment** *noun* [U]

**re·insur·ance** /ˌriːɪnˈʃʊərəns, -ˈʃɔːr-; *NAmE* -ˈʃʊr-/ *noun* [U] (*finance*) the practice of one insurance company buying insurance from another company against any losses that result from claims that are made against it

**re·inter·pret** /ˌriːɪnˈtɜːprət; *NAmE* -ˈtɜːrp-/ *verb* **~ sth** to interpret sth in a new or different way ▸ **re·inter·pret·ation** /ˌriːɪnˌtɜːprəˈteɪʃn; *NAmE* -ˌtɜːrp-/ *noun* [C, U]

**re·intro·duce** /ˌriːɪntrəˈdjuːs; *NAmE* -ˈduːs/ *verb* **1** to start to use sth again SYN **bring back**: **~ sth** *to reintroduce the death penalty* ◊ **~ sth to sth** *plans to reintroduce trams to the city* **2 ~ sth (to sth)** to put a type of animal, bird or plant back into a region where it once lived: *The centre has a fifty per cent success rate of reintroducing animals to the wild.* ▸ **re·intro·duc·tion** /ˌriːɪntrəˈdʌkʃn/ *noun* [U, C]

**re·invent** /ˌriːɪnˈvent/ *verb* **~ sth/yourself (as sth)** to present yourself/sth in a new form or with a new image: *The former wild man of rock has reinvented himself as a respectable family man.*
IDM **reinvent the ˈwheel** to waste time creating sth that already exists and works well

**re·invest** /ˌriːɪnˈvest/ *verb* [T, I] **~ (sth)** to put profits that have been made on an investment back into the same investment or into a new one ▸ **re·invest·ment** *noun* [U, C]

**re·in·vig·or·ate** /ˌriːɪnˈvɪɡəreɪt/ *verb* **~ sth/sb** to give new energy or strength to sth/sb: *We need to reinvigorate the economy of the area.* ◊ *I felt reinvigorated after a rest and a shower.*

**re·issue** *verb, noun*
- *verb* /ˌriːˈɪʃuː/ to publish or produce again a book, record, etc. that has not been available for some time: **~ sth** *The novel was reissued in paperback.* ◊ **~ sth as sth** *old jazz recordings reissued as digital downloads*
- *noun* /ˈriːɪʃuː/ an old book or record that has been published or produced again after not being available for some time

**re·iter·ate** /riˈɪtəreɪt/ *verb* (*formal*) to repeat sth that you have already said, especially to emphasize it: **~ sth** *to reiterate an argument/a demand/an offer* ◊ **~ that…** *Let me reiterate that we are fully committed to this policy.* ◊ **+ speech** *'I said "money",' he reiterated.* ▸ **re·iter·ation** /riˌɪtəˈreɪʃn/ *noun* [sing.]: *a reiteration of her previous statement*

**re·ject** ❶ B1 ❷ *verb, noun*
- *verb* /rɪˈdʒekt/
- • ARGUMENT/IDEA/PLAN **1** ʔ B1 **~ sth** to refuse to accept or consider sth: *to reject an argument/a hypothesis/a notion/a plan* ◊ *to reject a claim/an offer/a request/an application* ◊ *The prime minister rejected any idea of reforming the system.* ◊ *The proposal was firmly rejected.*
- • SB FOR JOB **2** ʔ B1 **~ sb** to refuse to accept sb for a job, position, etc: *Please reject the following candidates…* ◊ *I've been rejected by all the universities I applied to.*
- • NOT USE/PUBLISH **3** ʔ B1 **~ sth** to decide not to use, sell, publish, etc. sth because its quality is not good enough: *Imperfect articles are rejected by our quality control.*
- • NEW ORGAN **4** ʔ B1 **~ sth** (of the body) to not accept a new organ after a TRANSPLANT operation, by producing substances that attack the organ: *Her body has already rejected two kidneys.*
- • NOT LOVE **5** ʔ B1 **~ sb/sth** to fail to give a person or an animal enough love or care: *The lioness rejected the smallest cub, which died.* ◊ *When her husband left home she felt rejected and useless.*
- *noun* /ˈriːdʒekt/
- • STH THAT CANNOT BE USED **1** something that cannot be used or sold because there is sth wrong with it
- • PERSON **2** a person who has not been accepted as a member of a team, society, etc: *one of society's rejects*

**re·jec·tion** ʔ+ C1 ❶ /rɪˈdʒekʃn/ *noun* **1** ʔ+ C1 the act of refusing to accept or consider sth: *Her proposal met with unanimous rejection.* **2** ʔ+ C1 the act of refusing to accept sb for a job, position, etc: *a rejection letter* (= a letter in which you are told, for example, that you have

# rejig

not been accepted for a job) **3** [+] [C1] the decision not to use, sell, publish, etc. sth because its quality is not good enough: *I've had letters of rejection from several publishers.* ◇ *Everyone from George Orwell to JK Rowling has had* **rejection slips** (= formal notice from a publisher that a book, etc. is rejected). **4** the failure of sb's body to accept a new organ after a TRANSPLANT operation: *He had a second lung transplant after rejection of the first.* **5** failure to give a person or an animal enough love or care: *painful feelings of rejection*

**re·jig** /ˌriːˈdʒɪɡ/ *verb* (-**gg**-) (*BrE*) (*US* **re·jig·ger** /ˌriːˈdʒɪɡə(r)/) ~ **sth** (*informal*) to make changes to sth; to arrange sth in a different way

**re·joice** /rɪˈdʒɔɪs/ *verb* [I, T] (*formal*) to express great happiness about sth: *When the war ended, people finally had cause to rejoice.* ◇ ~ **at/in/over sth** *The motor industry is rejoicing at the cut in car tax.* ◇ ~ **to do sth** *They rejoiced to see their son well again.* ◇ ~ **that ...** *I rejoice that justice has prevailed.*

[IDM] **rejoice in the name of ...** (*BrE, humorous*) to have a name that sounds funny: *He rejoiced in the name of Owen Owen.*

**re·joic·ing** /rɪˈdʒɔɪsɪŋ/ *noun* [U] (*also* **rejoicings** [pl.]) the happy celebration of sth: *a time of great rejoicing*

**re·join¹** /ˌriːˈdʒɔɪn/ *verb* [T, I] ~ **(sb/sth)** to join sb/sth again after leaving them: *to rejoin a club* ◇ *She turned off her phone and rejoined them at the table.* ◇ *The path goes through a wood before rejoining the main road.*

**re·join²** /rɪˈdʒɔɪn/ *verb* + **speech** | ~ **that ...** (*formal*) to say sth as an answer, especially sth quick, critical or funny [SYN] **retort**: *'You're wrong!' she rejoined.*

**re·join·der** /rɪˈdʒɔɪndə(r)/ *noun* [usually sing.] (*formal*) a reply, especially a quick, critical or funny one [SYN] **retort**

**re·ju·ven·ate** /rɪˈdʒuːvəneɪt/ *verb* ~ **sb/sth** to make sb/sth look or feel younger, more lively or more modern ▸ **re·ju·ven·ation** /rɪˌdʒuːvəˈneɪʃn/ *noun* [U]

**re·kin·dle** /ˌriːˈkɪndl/ *verb* ~ **sth** (*formal*) to make a feeling or relationship become active again [SYN] **reawaken**: *to rekindle feelings/hopes*

**re·lapse** *noun, verb*

- *noun* /ˈriːlæps/ [C, U] the fact of becoming ill again after making an improvement: *to have/suffer a relapse* ◇ *a risk of relapse* ⊃ WORDFINDER NOTE *at* HEALTH
- *verb* /rɪˈlæps/; *NAmE also* ˈriːlæps/ [I] ~ **(into sth)** to go back into a previous condition or into a worse state after making an improvement: *They relapsed into silence.* ◇ *He relapsed into his old bad habits.* ◇ *Two days after leaving the hospital she relapsed into a coma.*

**re·late** [T] [B1] [W] /rɪˈleɪt/ *verb* **1** [B1] show or make a connection between two or more things [SYN] **connect**: ~ **sth** *I found it difficult to relate the two ideas in my mind.* ◇ ~ **A to B** *In the future, pay increases will be related to productivity.* **2** [B2] (*formal*) to give a spoken or written report of sth; to tell a story: ~ **sth** *Then he related a story about his days working in a research laboratory.* ◇ ~ **sth to sb** *He related the facts of the case to journalists.* ◇ ~ **how, what, etc. ...** *She related how he had run away from home as a boy.* ◇ ~ **that ...** *The story relates that an angel appeared and told him to sing.*

[PHRV] **re·late to sth/sb** **1** [B1] to be connected with sth/sb; to refer to sth/sb: *We shall discuss the problem as it relates to our specific case.* ◇ *The second paragraph relates to the situation in Scotland.* ◇ *theories relating to education and learning* **2** to be able to understand and have sympathy with sb/sth [SYN] **empathize**: *Many adults can't relate to children.* ◇ *Our product needs an image that people can relate to.*

**re·lated** [T] [B1] [O] /rɪˈleɪtɪd/ *adj.* **1** [B1] connected with sth/sb in some way: ~ **to sth/sb** *The amount of protein you need is directly related to your lifestyle.* ◇ *These problems are closely related.* ◇ *a related issue* ◇ *a stress-related illness* [OPP] **unrelated** **2** [B1] in the same family: *We're distantly related.* ◇ ~ **to sb** *Are you related to Margaret?* ◇ ~ **by sth** *The Logans and the Fishers were related by marriage.* ◇ *We were closely related by blood.* **3** [B1] belonging to the same group: *related species* ◇ ~ **to sth** *The llama is related to the camel.* ▸ **re·lat·ed·ness** *noun* [U]

**re·la·tion** [T] [B1] [O] /rɪˈleɪʃn/ *noun* **1** [B1] **relations** [pl.] the way in which two people, groups or countries behave towards each other or deal with each other: *diplomatic/international/foreign relations* ◇ *US-Chinese relations* ◇ *teacher-student relations* ◇ ~ **with sb/sth** *Relations with neighbouring countries are under strain at present.* ◇ ~ **between A and B** *We seek to improve relations between our two countries.* ◇ (*formal*) *to have* **sexual relations** (= to have sex) ⊃ see also INDUSTRIAL RELATIONS, PUBLIC RELATIONS, RACE RELATIONS **2** [B1] [U, C] the way in which two or more things are connected: ~ **between A and B** *the relation between rainfall and crop yields* ◇ ~ **to sth** *the relation of the farmer to the land* ◇ *The fee they are offering bears no relation to the amount of work involved.* ◇ **in** ~ **to sth** (*formal*) *I have some comments to make in relation to* (= about) *this matter.* ◇ *Its brain is small in relation to* (= compared with) *its body.* **3** [C] a person who is in the same family as sb else [SYN] **relative**: *a close/near/distant relation of mine* ◇ *a relation by marriage* ◇ *a party for friends and relations* ◇ *He's called Brady too, but we're no relation* (= not related). ◇ ~ **to sb** *Is he any relation to you?* ⊃ WORDFINDER NOTE *at* FAMILY ⊃ see also BLOOD RELATION, POOR RELATION

> WORDFINDER ancestor, branch, descent, dynasty, family tree, genealogy, generation, inherit, trace

**re·la·tion·al** /rɪˈleɪʃənl/ *adj.* (*formal or specialist*) existing or considered in relation to sth else

**re·la·tion·al ˈdata·base** *noun* (*computing*) a DATABASE that recognizes relationships between different pieces of information

**re·la·tion·ship** [T] [A2] [O] /rɪˈleɪʃnʃɪp/ *noun* **1** [A2] [C] the way in which two people, groups or countries behave towards each other or deal with each other: *a personal/working relationship* ◇ ~ **between A and B** *The relationship between the police and the local community has improved.* ◇ ~ **with sb** *She has a very close relationship with her sister.* ◇ *I have established a good working relationship with my boss.* ⊃ see also LOVE-HATE RELATIONSHIP ⊃ WORDFINDER NOTE *at* ALLY **2** [A2] [C] a loving and/or sexual friendship between two people: *Their affair did not develop into a long-term relationship.* ◇ *It was his first sexual relationship.* ◇ ~ **with sb** *She was having a relationship with a younger man.* ◇ ~ **between A and B** *The relationship between Joe and Carmen is at the heart of the film.* ◇ **in a** ~ *Are you in a relationship?* ⊃ WORDFINDER NOTE *at* LOVE **3** [B1] [C, U] the way in which two or more things are connected: ~ **between A and B** *They examine the relationship between poverty and crime.* ◇ ~ **to sth** *This comment bore no relationship to the subject of our conversation.* ◇ **in** ~ **to sth** *They measured height in relationship to weight.* **4** [B1] [C, U] the way in which a person is related to sb else in a family: *a father-son relationship* ◇ ~ **between A and B** *I'm not sure of the exact relationship between them— I think they're cousins.*

**rela·tive** [T] [B1] [W] /ˈrelətɪv/ *adj., noun*

- *adj.* **1** [B1] considered and judged by being compared with sth else: *the relative merits of the two plans* ◇ *We need to assess the relative importance of each of these factors.* **2** [B1] (*grammar*) referring to an earlier noun, sentence or part of a sentence: *In 'the man who came', 'who' is a relative pronoun and 'who came' is a relative clause.* **3** [B2] [only before noun] that exists or that has a particular quality only when compared with sth else [SYN] **comparative**: *They now live in relative comfort* (= compared with how they lived before). ◇ *We won the game with relative ease.* ◇ *It's all relative though, isn't it? We never had any money when I was a kid and $500 was a fortune to us.* ⊃ compare ABSOLUTE
[IDM] **relative to sb/sth** **1** in comparison with sb/sth else; in relation to sb/sth: *the position of the sun relative to the earth* ◇ *The company employs too many people relative to the size of its business.* **2** having a connection with sb/sth; concerning sb/sth: *the facts relative to the case*
- *noun* **1** [B1] a person who is in the same family as sb else [SYN] **relation**: *a close/distant relative* ◇ *her friends and*

*relatives* **2** B1 a thing that belongs to the same group as sth else: *The ibex is a distant relative of the mountain goat.*

**relative a,tomic ˈmass** (*also* **a,tomic ˈmass**, **a,tomic ˈweight**) *noun* (*chemistry*) the average MASS of all the naturally occurring ATOMS of a chemical element

**relative ˈdensity** (*also* **speˌcific ˈgravity**) *noun* [U] (*chemistry*) the mass of a substance divided by the mass of the same volume of water or air

**rela·tive·ly** ⓘ B2 ⓞ /ˈrelətɪvli/ *adv.* to a fairly large degree, especially in comparison to sth else: *relatively large/small/high/low* ◊ *I found the test **relatively** easy.* ◊ *We had **relatively** few applications for the job.*
IDM **ˈrelatively speaking** used when you are comparing sth with all similar things: *Relatively speaking, these jobs provide good salaries.*

**rela·tiv·ism** /ˈrelətɪvɪzəm/ *noun* [U] (*formal*) the belief that truth and right and wrong cannot be judged generally but can be judged only in relation to other things, such as your personal situation ▸ **rela·tiv·ist** /-vɪst/ *adj.*: *a relativist view* ▸ **rela·tiv·ist** *noun*

**rela·tiv·ity** /ˌreləˈtɪvəti/ *noun* [U] **1** (*physics*) Einstein's theory of the universe based on the principle that all movement is relative and that time is a fourth DIMENSION related to space **2** (*formal*) the state of being relative and only able to be judged when compared with sth else

**re·launch** *verb* /ˌriːˈlɔːntʃ/ ~ sth to start or present sth again in a new or different way, especially a product for sale ▸ **re·launch** /ˈriːlɔːntʃ/ *noun*

**relax** ⓘ A1 /rɪˈlæks/ *verb* **1** A1 [I] to rest while you are doing sth that you enjoy, especially after work or effort SYN unwind: *Just relax and enjoy the movie.* ◊ *I'm going to spend the weekend just relaxing.* ◊ **~ with sth** *When I get home from work I like to relax with the newspaper.* **2** B1 [I, T] to become or make sb become calmer and less worried: *I'll only relax when I know you're safe.* ◊ *Relax! Everything will be OK.* **3** B1 [I, T] to become or make sth become less tight or stiff: *Allow your muscles to relax completely.* ◊ **~ sth** *The massage relaxed my tense back muscles.* ◊ *He relaxed his grip on her arm.* ◊ (*figurative*) *The dictator refuses to relax his grip on power.* **4** B2 [T] ~ sth to allow rules, laws, etc. to become less strict: *to relax rules/restrictions/regulations/requirements* **5** [T] ~ sth to allow your attention or effort to become weaker: *You cannot afford to relax your concentration for a moment.*

**re·lax·ant** /rɪˈlæksənt/ *noun* (*medical*) a drug that is used to make the body relax: *a muscle relaxant*

**re·lax·ation** /ˌriːlækˈseɪʃn/ *noun* **1** [U, C] a way of resting and enjoying yourself; time spent resting and enjoying yourself: *I go hill-walking for relaxation.* ◊ *Fishing is his favourite relaxation.* ◊ *a few days of relaxation* ⊃ SYNONYMS at ENTERTAINMENT **2** [U] the state of feeling calm and not anxious or worried: *Some people take up yoga to aid relaxation.* ◊ *relaxation techniques* **3** [U] the fact of a part of the body, especially a muscle, becoming less tight: *an ointment that helps muscle relaxation* **4** [U, C, *usually sing.*] the act of making a rule or some form of control less strict or severe: *the relaxation of foreign currency controls* ◊ *a relaxation of travel restrictions*

**re·laxed** ⓘ B1 /rɪˈlækst/ *adj.* **1** B1 (of a person) calm and not anxious or worried: *She had a very relaxed manner.* ◊ **~ about sth** *I'm feeling more **relaxed** about the future now.* **2** B1 (of a place) calm and informal: *a family-run hotel with a **relaxed** atmosphere* **3** B1 not caring too much about discipline or making people follow rules SYN laid-back: **~ about sth** *She's pretty relaxed about her children's viewing habits.*

**re·lax·ing** ⓘ B1 /rɪˈlæksɪŋ/ *adj.* helping you to rest and become less anxious: *a relaxing evening with friends*

**re·lay** *verb, noun*
▪ *verb* /ˈriːleɪ, rɪˈleɪ/ **1** ~ sth (to sb) to receive and send on information, news, etc. to sb: *He relayed the message to his boss.* ◊ *Instructions were relayed to him by phone.* **2** ~ sth (to sb) to broadcast television or radio signals: *The game was relayed by satellite to audiences all over the world.*

▪ *noun* /ˈriːleɪ/ **1** (*also* **ˈrelay race**) a race between teams in which each member of the team runs or swims one section of the race: *the 4×100m relay* ◊ *a relay team* ◊ *the sprint relay* **2** a fresh set of people or animals that take the place of others that are tired or have finished a period of work: **in relays** *Rescuers worked in relays to save the trapped miners.* **3** an electronic device that receives radio or television signals and sends them on again with greater strength: *a relay station*

**re·lease** ⓘ B1 ⓦ /rɪˈliːs/ *verb, noun*
▪ *verb*
• SET SB FREE **1** B1 to let sb come out of a place where they have been kept or stuck and unable to leave or move: ~ sb *to release a prisoner* ◊ **~ sb from sth** *to release sb from prison/jail/hospital*
• STOP HOLDING STH **2** B2 to stop holding sth or stop it from being held so that it can move, fly, fall, etc. freely SYN **let go, let loose**: **~ sth** *He refused to release her arm.* ◊ *Intense heat is released in the reaction.* ◊ **~ sth into sth** *the need to limit the amount of greenhouse gases being released into the atmosphere*
• FEELINGS **3** B2 ~ sth to express feelings such as anger or worry in order to get rid of them: *She burst into tears, releasing all her pent-up emotions.*
• PART OF MACHINE **4** B2 ~ sth to remove sth from a fixed position, allowing sth else to move or function: *to release the clutch/handbrake/switch*
• MAKE AVAILABLE **5** B2 to make information available to the public: **~ sth** *to release a statement/report/document/poll/study* ◊ *to release figures/results/information/data* ◊ *Police have released no further details about the accident.* ◊ **~ sth to sb** *The suspect's name has not been released to the public.* **6** B2 ~ sth to make a film, recording or other product available to the public: *He's planning to release a solo album.* ◊ *to release a film/video* **7** ~ sth to make sth available that had previously been limited: *The new building programme will go ahead as soon as the government releases the funds.*
• FREE SB FROM DUTY **8** to free sb from a duty, responsibility, contract, etc. ~ sb *The club is releasing some of its older players.* ◊ **~ sb from sth** *The new law released employers from their obligation to recognize unions.*
• MAKE LESS TIGHT **9** ~ sth to make sth less tight: *You need to release the tension in these shoulder muscles.*

▪ *noun*
• SETTING SB/STH FREE **1** B1 [U, sing.] the act of setting a person or an animal free; the state of being set free: **~ of sb/sth** *The government has been working to secure the release of the hostages.* ◊ **~ (of sb/sth) from sth** *Following his release from prison, he moved to London.* ⊃ *see also* DAY RELEASE, WORK RELEASE
• MAKING STH AVAILABLE **2** B2 [U, sing.] the act of making a film, recording or other product available to the public: *The new software is planned for release in April.* ◊ *The movie goes on general release* (= will be widely shown in cinemas) *next week.* **3** B2 [C] a thing that is made available to the public, especially a new film or music recording: *recent/new releases* ◊ *the latest releases* **4** B2 [U, sing.] the act of making information available to the public: *the release of the report* ◊ *The company issued a news release after the board meeting.*
• OF GAS/CHEMICAL **5** B2 [U, C] the act of letting a gas, chemical, etc. move or flow freely: *Release of these hormones gives the body a temporary increase in strength and energy.* ◊ **~ of sth into sth** *the release of carbon dioxide into the atmosphere* ◊ *to monitor radiation releases* ⊃ *see also* TIME-RELEASE
• FROM UNPLEASANT FEELING **6** [U, sing.] the feeling that you are free from pain, worry or some other unpleasant feeling: *a sense of release after the exam* ◊ *I think her death was a merciful release.* ⊃ *see also* PRESS RELEASE

**rele·gate** /ˈrelɪɡeɪt/ *verb* **1** ~ sb/sth (to sth) to give sb a lower or less important position, rank, etc. than before: *She was then relegated to the role of assistant.* ◊ *He relegated the incident to the back of his mind.* **2** [*usually passive*] ~ sth (*BrE*) to move a sports team from playing with one group of teams to playing in a lower group OPP **promote**

# relent

▶ **rele·ga·tion** /ˌrelɪˈɡeɪʃn/ *noun* [U]: *teams threatened with relegation*

**re·lent** /rɪˈlent/ *verb* (*formal*) **1** [I] to finally agree to sth after refusing **SYN** **give in (to sb/sth)**: '*Well, wait a little while then,*' *she said, finally relenting.* **2** [I] to become less determined, strong, etc: *After two days the rain relented.* ◇ *The police will not relent in their fight against crime.*

**re·lent·less** /rɪˈlentləs/ *adj.* **1** not stopping; not getting less strong **SYN** **unrelenting**: *her relentless pursuit of perfection* ◇ *The sun was relentless.* **2** refusing to give up or be less strict or severe: *a relentless enemy* ▶ **re·lent·less·ly** *adv.*

**rele·vance** ?+ **C1 W** /ˈreləvəns/ (*also* **rele·vancy** /ˈreləvənsi/) *noun* [U] **1** ?+ **C1** a close connection with the subject you are discussing or the situation you are in: *I don't see the relevance of your question.* ◇ **~to sth** *What he said has no direct relevance to the matter in hand.* **OPP** **irrelevance** **2** ?+ **C1** the fact of being valuable and useful to people in their lives and work: *a classic play of contemporary relevance*

**rele·vant** ? **B2** O /ˈreləvənt/ *adj.* **1** ? **B2** closely connected with the subject you are discussing or the situation you are in: *relevant information/facts/documents/factors* ◇ *The incident is still under investigation by the relevant authorities.* ◇ **~to sb/sth** *These comments are not directly relevant to this inquiry.* **OPP** **irrelevant** **2** ?+ **B2** the fact of being valuable and useful to people in their lives and work: *Her novel is still relevant today.* ◇ **~to sb/sth** *Past imperial glories are hardly relevant to the present day.* ▶ **rele·vant·ly** *adv.*: *The applicant has experience in teaching and, more relevantly, in industry.*

**re·li·abil·ity** ?+ **C1 W** /rɪˌlaɪəˈbɪləti/ *noun* [U] **1** ?+ **C1** the quality of being able to be trusted to do what sb wants or needs **SYN** **dependability**: *The incident cast doubt on her motives and reliability.* **2** ?+ **C1** the quality of being likely to be correct or true: *The reliability of these results has been questioned.* ◇ *Lawyers sought to cast doubt on the reliability of her statements.* **3** ?+ **C1** the quality of being able to work or operate for long periods without breaking down or needing attention: *The aircraft has an exceptional record of reliability.* **OPP** **unreliability**

**re·li·able** ? **B1 W** /rɪˈlaɪəbl/ *adj.* **1** ?+ **B1** that can be trusted to do sth well; that you can rely on **SYN** **dependable**: *We are looking for someone who is reliable and hard-working.* ◇ *a reliable friend* **2** ?+ **B1** that is likely to be correct or true: *reliable information/data* ◇ *Our information comes from a reliable source.* ◇ *a reliable witness* **3** able to work or operate for long periods without breaking down or needing attention: *My car's not as reliable as it used to be.* **OPP** **unreliable** ▶ **re·li·ably** /-bli/ *adv.*: *I am reliably informed* (= told by sb who knows the facts) *that the company is being sold.*

**re·li·ance** **W** /rɪˈlaɪəns/ *noun* [U, sing.] **~(on/upon sb/sth)** the state of needing sb/sth in order to survive, be successful, etc.; the fact of being able to rely on sb/sth **SYN** **dependence**: *Heavy reliance on one client is risky when you are building up a business.* ◇ *Such learning methods encourage too great a reliance upon the teacher.* ◇ *The study programme concentrates more on group work and places less reliance on* (= depends less on) *lectures.* ◇ *I wouldn't place too much reliance on* (= trust) *these figures.*

**re·li·ant** /rɪˈlaɪənt/ *adj.* **~on/upon sb/sth** needing sb/sth in order to survive, be successful, etc. **SYN** **dependent**: *The hostel is heavily reliant upon charity.* ⊃ *see also* SELF-RELIANT

**relic** /ˈrelɪk/ *noun* **1 ~(of/from sth)** an object, a tradition, a system, etc. that has survived from the past: *The building stands as the last remaining relic of the town's cotton industry.* ◇ *Videotapes may already seem like relics of a bygone era.* **2** a part of the body or clothing of a holy person, or sth that they owned, that is kept after their death and respected as a religious object: *holy relics*

**re·lief** ? **B2** /rɪˈliːf/ *noun*
• REMOVAL OF ANXIETY/PAIN **1** ? **B2** [U, sing.] the feeling of happiness that you have when sth unpleasant stops or does not happen: *I felt a huge **sense of relief** when I heard they were all OK.* ◇ *We all **breathed a sigh of relief** when he left.* ◇ **Much to my relief** *the car was not damaged.* ◇ *News of their safety **came as a great relief.*** ◇ **~to sb** *This was a great relief to him.* ◇ **~that ...** *His mother spoke of her relief that he was now safely home.* ◇ **~at (doing) sth** *She expressed relief at the outcome of the investigation.* **2** ? **B2** [U] the act of removing or reducing pain, worry, etc: *modern methods of **pain relief*** ◇ **~of sth** *the relief of symptoms/suffering/poverty/pain* ◇ **~from sth** *The drugs only provided temporary relief from the pain.*
• HELP **3** ? **B2** [U] food, money, medicine, etc. that is given to help people in places where there has been a war or natural disaster **SYN** **aid**: *disaster relief* ◇ *relief efforts/operations* ⊃ *see also* DEBT RELIEF **4** [U] (*especially NAmE*) financial help given by the government to people who need it
• ON TAX **5** [U] = TAX RELIEF: *relief on mortgage interest payments*
• STH DIFFERENT **6** ? **B2** [U, sing.] something that is interesting or fun that replaces sth boring, difficult or unpleasant for a short period of time: *a few moments of light relief in an otherwise dull performance* ◇ *There was little **comic relief** in his speech.* ◇ **~from sth** *The calm of the countryside came as a welcome relief from the hustle and bustle of city life.*
• WORKERS **7** [C + sing./pl. v.] (often used as an adjective) a person or group of people that replaces another when they have finished working for the day or when they are sick: *The next crew relief comes on duty at 9 o'clock.* ◇ *relief drivers*
• FROM ENEMY **8** [sing.] **~of ...** the act of freeing a town, etc. from an enemy army that has surrounded it
• IN ART **9** [U, C] a way of decorating wood, stone, etc. by cutting designs into the surface of it so that some parts stick out more than others; a design that is made in this way: *The column was decorated **in high relief*** (= with designs that stick out a lot) *with scenes from Greek mythology.* ◇ *The bronze doors are covered with sculpted reliefs.*
• MAKING STH EASY TO NOTICE **10** [U] the effect of colours, light, etc. that makes an object easier to notice than others around it: *The snow-capped mountain stood **out in sharp relief** against the blue sky.* **11** [U] the quality of a particular situation, problem, etc. that makes it easier to notice than before: *Their differences have been **thrown into sharp relief** by the present crisis.*

**re·lief road** *noun* (*BrE*) a road that vehicles can use to avoid an area of heavy traffic, especially a road built for this purpose

**re·lieve** ?+ **B2** /rɪˈliːv/ *verb* **1** ?+ **B2** **~sth** to remove or reduce an unpleasant feeling or pain: *to relieve the symptoms of a cold* ◇ *to relieve anxiety/guilt/stress* ◇ *Being able to tell the truth at last seemed to relieve her.* **2** ?+ **C1** **~sth** to make a problem less serious **SYN** **alleviate**: *efforts to relieve poverty* ◇ *to relieve traffic congestion* **3** **~sth** to make sth less boring, especially by introducing sth different: *We played cards to relieve the boredom of the long wait.* ◇ *The black and white pattern is relieved by tiny coloured flowers.* **4** **~sb** to replace sb at the end of their period of duty: *to relieve a sentry* ◇ *You'll be relieved at six o'clock.* **5** **~sth** to free a town, etc. from an enemy army that has surrounded it. **6 ~yourself** a polite way of referring to going to the toilet: *I had to relieve myself behind a bush.*
**PHRV** **reˈlieve sb of sth 1** to help sb by taking sth heavy or difficult from them: *Let me relieve you of some of your bags.* ◇ *The new secretary will relieve us of some of the paperwork.* **2** (*informal*, *ironic*) to steal sth from sb: *A boy with a knife relieved him of his wallet.* **3** to dismiss sb from a job, position, etc: *General Beale was relieved of his command.*

**re·lieved** ?+ **B2** /rɪˈliːvd/ *adj.* feeling happy because sth unpleasant has stopped or has not happened; showing this: *She sounded relieved.* ◇ **~to see, hear, find, etc. sth** *You'll be relieved to know your jobs are safe.* ◇ **~(that) ...** *I'm just relieved that nobody was hurt.* ◇ *They exchanged relieved glances.* ⊃ SYNONYMS *at* GLAD

**re·liever** /rɪˈliːvə(r)/ *noun* **1** (especially in compounds) a thing or person that removes or reduces pain, feelings of worry or unhappiness, or a problem: *a pain reliever* (= a drug used to reduce or remove pain) ◊ *Exercise can be a great stress reliever.* **2** (*also* **re·lief pitcher**) (in baseball) a PITCHER (= the player who throws the ball) who enters the game in place of the previous pitcher

**re·li·gion** ❶ **B1** /rɪˈlɪdʒən/ *noun* **1** **B1** [U] the belief in the existence of a god or gods, and the activities that are connected with the WORSHIP of them, or in the teachings of a spiritual leader: *Is there always a conflict between science and religion?* ◊ *He believed in God but had no interest in organized religion.* ◊ *by ~ They are Jewish by religion.* **2** **B1** [C] one of the systems of faith that are based on the belief in the existence of a particular god or gods, or in the teachings of a spiritual leader: *the Jewish religion* ◊ *Christianity, Islam and other world religions* ◊ *The law states that everyone has the right to practise their own religion.* **3** [sing.] a particular interest or influence that is very important in your life: *For him, football is an absolute religion.*
**IDM** **get re'ligion** (*informal*, *disapproving*) to suddenly start believing in a religion

**re·ligi·os·ity** /rɪˌlɪdʒiˈɒsəti; NAmE -ˈɑːs-/ *noun* [U] (*formal*, *sometimes disapproving*) the state of being religious or too religious

**re·li·gious** ❶ **B1** /rɪˈlɪdʒəs/ *adj.* **1** **B1** [only before noun] connected with religion or with a particular religion: *religious beliefs/convictions/faith* ◊ *religious freedom/liberty* ◊ *religious traditions/practices/ceremonies* ◊ *religious education* (= education about religion) ◊ *religious instruction* (= instruction in a particular religion) ◊ *religious groups/leaders* **2** **B1** (of a person) believing strongly in a particular religion and obeying its laws and practices **SYN** **devout**: *a deeply religious man* ▸ **re·li·gious·ness** *noun* [U]

**re·li·gious·ly** /rɪˈlɪdʒəsli/ *adv.* **1** very carefully or regularly: *She followed the instructions religiously.* **2** in a way that is connected with religion: *Were you brought up religiously?*

**re'ligious school** *noun* (*NAmE*) **1** [U, C] a school supported by a SYNAGOGUE, church, etc. and attended in addition to an ordinary school ⊃ *compare* SUNDAY SCHOOL **2** (*BrE* **faith school**) [C] a school especially for children of a particular religion

**re·lin·quish** /rɪˈlɪŋkwɪʃ/ *verb* (*formal*) to stop having sth, especially when this happens unwillingly **SYN** **give sth↔up**: *~ sth He was forced to relinquish control of the company.* ◊ *They had relinquished all hope that she was alive.* ◊ *~ sth to sb She relinquished possession of the house to her sister.*

**reli·quary** /ˈrelɪkwəri; NAmE -kweri/ *noun* (*pl.* **-ies**) a container in which a RELIC of a holy person is kept

**rel·ish** /ˈrelɪʃ/ *verb*, *noun*
- *verb* to get great pleasure from sth; to want very much to do or have sth **SYN** **enjoy**: *~ sth to relish a challenge* ◊ *to relish the chance/opportunity to do sth* ◊ *I don't relish the prospect of getting up early tomorrow.* ◊ *~ (sb/sth) doing sth Nobody relishes cleaning the oven.*
- *noun* **1** [U] great pleasure: *with~ She savoured the moment with obvious relish.* **2** [U, C] a cold, thick, spicy sauce made from fruit and vegetables that have been boiled, that is served with meat, cheese, etc.

**re·live** /ˌriːˈlɪv/ *verb* *~ sth* to experience sth again, especially in your imagination: *He relives the horror of the crash every night in his dreams.*

**rel·lie** /ˈreli/ *noun* (*AustralE*, *NZE*, *informal*) a relative: *All the rellies will be at the party.*

**re·load** /ˌriːˈləʊd/ *verb* **1** [I, T] *~(sth)* to put more bullets into a gun, more film into a camera, etc. **2** [T] *~ sth* to put data or a program into the memory of a computer again **3** [T] *~ sth* to fill a container, vehicle, machine, etc. again

**re·locate** /ˌriːləʊˈkeɪt; NAmE ˌriːˈləʊkeɪt/ *verb* [I, T] (especially of a company or workers) to move or to move sb/sth to a new place to work or operate: *The firm may be forced to relocate from New York to Stanford.* ◊ *~ sth The company relocated its head office to Stanford.* ▸ **re·loca·tion** /ˌriːləʊˈkeɪʃn/ *noun* [U]: *relocation costs*

**re·luc·tant** **B2+** **C1** /rɪˈlʌktənt/ *adj.* hesitating before doing sth because you do not want to do it or because you are not sure that it is the right thing to do: *reluctant agreement* ◊ *He finally gave a reluctant smile.* ◊ *a reluctant hero* (= a person who does not want to be called a hero) **OPP** **eager**
▸ **re·luc·tance** /-ˈlʌktəns/ *noun* [U, sing.]: *~(to do sth) There is still some reluctance on the part of employers to become involved in this project.* ◊ *They finally agreed to our terms with a certain reluctance.* **re·luc·tant·ly** *adv.*: *We reluctantly agreed to go with her.*

**rely** ❶ **B2** ❸ /rɪˈlaɪ/
*verb* (**re·lies**, **rely·ing**, **re·lied**, **re·lied**)
**PHRV** **re·ly on/upon sb/sth 1** **B2** to need or depend on sb/sth: *The charity relies solely on donations from the public.* ◊ *rely on/upon sb/sth for sth As babies, we rely entirely on others for food.* ◊ *rely on/upon sb/sth to do sth These days we rely heavily on computers to organize our work.* ◊ *rely on/upon sb/sth doing sth The industry relies on the price of raw materials remaining low.* **2** **B2** to trust or have faith in sb/sth: *You should rely on your own judgement.* ◊ *rely on/upon sb/sth to do sth You can rely on me to keep your secret.* ◊ *He can't be relied on to tell the truth.* ◊ *rely on/upon sb/sth for sth I couldn't rely on John for information.* ⊃ SYNONYMS *at* TRUST

**WORD FAMILY**
**rely** *verb*
**reliable** *adj.* (≠ unreliable)
**reliably** *adv.*
**reliability** *noun* (≠ unreliability)
**reliance** *noun*

**REM** /rem, ˌɑːr iː ˈem/ *abbr.* rapid eye movement (describes a period of sleep during which you dream and your eyes make many small movements) ⊃ WORDFINDER NOTE *at* SLEEP

**re·made** /ˌriːˈmeɪd/ *past tense*, *past part.* of REMAKE

**re·main** ❶ **B1** /rɪˈmeɪn/ *verb* (*rather formal*) (not usually used in the progressive tenses) **1** **B1** linking verb to continue to be sth; to be still in the same state or condition: *~ + adj. to remain silent* ◊ *Train fares are likely to remain unchanged.* ◊ *It remains unclear whether Russia will in fact agree to the meeting.* ◊ *The museum will remain open to the public throughout the building work.* ◊ *~ + noun Her identity remains a mystery.* ◊ *As a result, sanctions remained in place.* **2** **B1** [I] to still be present after the other parts have been removed, used, etc.; to continue to exist: *Very little of the house remained after the fire.* ◊ *There were only ten minutes remaining.* **3** **B1** [I] *~ + adv./prep.* to stay in the same place; to not leave: *They remained in Mexico until June.* ◊ *The plane remained on the ground.* ◊ *She left, but I remained behind.* **4** **B2** [I] to still need to be done, said or dealt with: *~ to do sth It remains to be seen* (= it will only be known later) *whether you are right.* ◊ *There remained one significant problem.* ◊ *Of course, problems remain.* ◊ *Questions remain about the president's honesty.* ◊ *I feel sorry for her, but the fact remains (that) she lied to us.* ⊃ LANGUAGE BANK *at* NEVERTHELESS **IDM** *see* ALOOF

**re·main·der** **B2+** **C1** /rɪˈmeɪndə(r)/ *noun*, *verb*
- *noun* **1** **B2+** **C1** (*usually* **the remainder**) [sing. + sing./pl. v.] the people, things or time that remain **SYN** **rest**: *I kept some of his books and gave away the remainder.* **HELP** When **the remainder** refers to a plural noun, the verb is plural: *Most of our employees work in New York; the remainder are in London.* **2** [C, *usually sing.*] (*mathematics*) the numbers left after one number has been SUBTRACTED from another, or one number has been divided into another: *Divide 2 into 7, and the answer is 3, remainder 1.* ⊃ *compare* DIVISOR **3** [C] a book that has been remaindered
- *verb* [I, T, *usually passive*] *~(sth)* to reduce the price of a book that did not get sold at its original price

**Re·main·er** /rɪˈmeɪnə(r)/ *noun* (*ErE*) a person believing that the UK should remain in the European Union and not supporting BREXIT **OPP** **Leaver**

**re·main·ing** /rɪˈmeɪnɪŋ/ *adj.* [only before noun] still needing to be done or dealt with: *The remaining twenty patients were transferred to another hospital.* ◊ *Any remaining tickets for the concert will be sold on the door.* ⊃ *see also* REMAIN

# remains

**re·mains** /rɪˈmeɪnz/ noun [pl.] **1** ~ (of sth) the parts of sth that are left after the other parts have been used, eaten, removed, etc: *She fed the remains of her lunch to the dog.* **2** the parts of ancient objects and buildings that have survived and are discovered in the present day: *prehistoric remains* ◇ *the remains of a Roman fort* **3** (*formal*) the body of a dead person or animal: *They had discovered human remains.*

**re·make** noun, verb
- **noun** /ˈriːmeɪk/ a new or different version of an old film or song
- **verb** /ˌriːˈmeɪk/ (re·made, re·made /-ˈmeɪd/) ~ sth to make a new or different version of sth such as an old film or song; to make sth again: *'The Seven Samurai' was remade in Hollywood as 'The Magnificent Seven'.*

**re·mand** /rɪˈmɑːnd/ NAmE -ˈmænd/ verb, noun
- **verb** [usually passive] to send sb away from a court to wait for their trial which will take place at a later date: **be remanded** (+ adv./prep.) *The two men were charged with burglary and remanded in custody* (= sent to prison until their trial). ◇ *She was remanded on bail* (= allowed to go free until the trial after leaving a sum of money with the court).
- **noun** [U] the process of keeping sb in prison while they are waiting for their trial: **on** ~ *He is currently being held on remand.* ◇ *a remand prisoner*

**re·mark** /rɪˈmɑːk/ NAmE -ˈmɑːrk/ noun, verb
- **noun 1** [C] something that you say or write which expresses an opinion, a thought, etc. about sb/sth **SYN** comment: *to make a remark* ◇ ~ **by sb** *The controversy intensified following remarks by the President of the European Commission.* ◇ *What exactly did you mean by that last remark?* ➔ note at STATEMENT **2** [U] (*old-fashioned or formal*) the quality of being important or interesting enough to be noticed **SYN** note: *The exhibition contains nothing that is worthy of remark.*
- **verb** [I, T] to say or write a comment about sth/sb **SYN** comment: ~ **on/upon sb/sth** *The judges remarked on the high standard of entries for the competition.* ◇ ~ **how** *She remarked how tired I was looking.* ◇ ~ **(to sb) + speech** *'It's much colder than yesterday,' he remarked casually.* ◇ ~ **(to sb) that...** *Critics remarked that the play was not original.* ◇ **be remarked on** *The similarities between the two have often been remarked on.* ➔ SYNONYMS at COMMENT

**re·mark·able** /rɪˈmɑːkəbl/ NAmE -ˈmɑːrk-/ adj. unusual or surprising in a way that causes people to take notice **SYN** astonishing: *a remarkable achievement/career/talent* ◇ *She was a truly remarkable woman.* ◇ ~ **for sth** *The area is remarkable for its scenery.* ◇ ~ **that...** *It is remarkable that nobody noticed sooner.* **OPP** unremarkable

**re·mark·ably** /rɪˈmɑːkəbli/ NAmE -ˈmɑːrk-/ adv. in a way that is unusual or surprising and causes people to take notice **SYN** astonishingly: *The car is in remarkably good condition for its age.* ◇ *Remarkably, nobody was killed.*

**re·marry** /ˌriːˈmæri/ verb (re·mar·ries, re·marry·ing, re·mar·ried, re·mar·ried) [I] to marry again after being divorced or after your husband or wife has died ▶ **re·mar·riage** /-rɪdʒ/ noun [U, C]

**re·mas·ter** /ˌriːˈmɑːstə(r)/ NAmE -ˈmæs-/ verb ~ sth to make a new MASTER copy of a recording in order to improve the sound quality: *All the tracks have been digitally remastered from the original tapes.*

**re·match** /ˈriːmætʃ/ noun [usually sing.] a match or game played again between the same people or teams, especially because neither side won the first match or game

**re·medi·al** /rɪˈmiːdiəl/ adj. [only before noun] **1** aimed at solving a problem, especially when this involves correcting or improving sth that has been done wrong: *remedial treatment* (= for a medical problem) ◇ *Remedial action must be taken now.* **2** connected with school students who are slower at learning than others: *remedial education* ◇ *a remedial class*

**re·me·di·ation** /rɪˌmiːdiˈeɪʃn/ noun [U] (NAmE) the process of improving sth or correcting sth that is wrong, especially changing or stopping damage to the environment: *remediation of contaminated soil* ▶ **re·medi·ate** /rɪˈmiːdieɪt/ verb ~ sth (NAmE): *The problems need to be detected and remediated quickly.*

**rem·edy** /ˈremədi/ noun, verb
- **noun** (*pl.* -ies) **1** a way of dealing with or improving an unpleasant or difficult situation **SYN** solution: ~ **for sth** *There is no simple remedy for unemployment.* ◇ ~ **to sth** *There are a number of possible remedies to this problem.* **2** a treatment or medicine to cure a disease or reduce pain that is not very serious: *a herbal remedy* ◇ ~ **for sth** *an excellent home remedy for sore throats* **3** ~ **(against sth)** (*law*) a way of dealing with a problem, using the processes of the law **SYN** redress: *Holding copyright provides the only legal remedy against unauthorized copying.*
- **verb** (rem·ed·ies, rem·edy·ing, rem·ed·ied, rem·ed·ied) ~ **sth** to correct or improve sth **SYN** right: *to remedy a problem* ◇ *This situation is easily remedied.*

**re·mem·ber** /rɪˈmembə(r)/ verb (not usually used in the progressive tenses)
- **SB/STH FROM THE PAST 1** [T, I] to have or keep an image in your memory of an event, a person, a place, etc. from the past: ~ **sb/sth** *This is Carla. Do you remember her?* ◇ *I don't remember my first day at school.* ◇ *I'll always remember this holiday.* ◇ ~ **sb/sth as sth** *He still remembered her as the lively teenager he'd known years before.* ◇ ~ **sb/sth from sth** *I remember her from university.* ◇ ~ **sb/sth with sth** *He will be remembered with affection by all who knew him.* ◇ *As far as I can remember, this is the third time we've met.* ◇ ~ **doing sth** *I remember seeing pictures of him when I was a child.* ◇ ~ **sb/sth doing sth** *I can still vividly remember my grandfather teaching me to play cards.* ◇ ~ **(that)**... *I remember (that) we used to go and see them most weekends.* ➔ note at WANT
- **FACT/INFORMATION 2** [T, I] to bring back to your mind a fact, piece of information, etc. that you knew: *If I remember correctly, you were supposed to collect the keys on your way here.* ◇ ~ **sth** *I'm sorry—I can't remember your name.* ◇ ~ **how, what, etc.** *Can you remember how much money we spent?* ◇ ~ **(that)**... *Remember that we're going out tonight.* **3** [T] to keep an important fact in your mind: ~ **(that)**... *Remember (that) you may feel sleepy after taking the pills.* ◇ *It is important to remember that exercise and a balanced diet are the foundation of any successful fitness plan.* ◇ *it is remembered that*... *It should be remembered that the majority of accidents happen in the home.*
- **STH YOU HAVE TO DO 4** [T] to not forget to do sth; to actually do what you have to do: ~ **to do sth** *Remember to call me when you arrive!* ◇ ~ **sth** *Did you remember your homework* (= to bring it)? **HELP** Notice the difference between **remember doing sth** and **remember to do sth**: *I remember posting the letter* means 'I have an image in my memory of doing it'; *I remembered to post the letter* means 'I didn't forget to do it.'
- **IN PRAYERS 5** [T] ~ **sb** to think about sb with respect, especially when saying a prayer **SYN** commemorate: *a church service to remember the war dead*
- **GIVE PRESENT 6** [T] ~ **sb/sth** to give money, a present, etc. to sb/sth: *My aunt always remembers my birthday* (= by sending a card or present). ◇ *His grandfather remembered him* (= left him money) *in his will.*

**IDM** **be (best) reˈmembered for sth** | **be (best) reˈmembered as sth** to be famous or known for a particular thing that you have done in the past: *He is best remembered as the man who brought jazz to England.*

**PHRV** **reˈmember me to sb** (*especially BrE*) used to ask sb to give your good wishes to sb else: *Remember me to your parents.*

**re·mem·brance** /rɪˈmembrəns/ noun **1** [U] the act or process of remembering an event in the past or a person who is dead: **in** ~ **of sb/sth** *A service was held in remembrance of local soldiers killed in the war.* ◇ *a remembrance service* ◇ (*formal*) *He smiled at the remembrance of their first kiss.* **2** [C] (*formal*) an object that causes you to remember sb/sth; a memory of sb/sth: *The cenotaph stands as a remembrance of those killed during the war.*

**Reˈmembrance Sunday** (also **Reˈmembrance Day**) noun the Sunday nearest to the 11 November on which those killed in war, especially the wars of 1914–18 and

1939–45, are remembered in ceremonies and church services in the UK and some other countries ⇒ see also MEMORIAL DAY, VETERANS DAY

**re·mind** ❶ B1 /rɪˈmaɪnd/ *verb* to help sb remember sth, especially sth important that they must do: ~ **sb/yourself** *I'm sorry, I've forgotten your name. Can you remind me?* ◊ *That* (= what you have just said, done, etc.) *reminds me, I must get some cash.* ◊ *'You need to finish that essay.' 'Don't remind me'* (= I don't want to think about it).' ◊ ~ **sb/yourself about/of sth** *'Don't forget the camera.' 'Remind me about it nearer the time.'* ◊ ~ **sb/yourself to do sth** *Remind me to phone Alan before I go out.* ◊ ~ **sb/yourself (that) …** *Passengers are reminded that smoking is not allowed on this train.* ◊ *The bathroom mirror constantly reminds me that I am getting old.* ◊ ~ **sb/yourself what, how, etc** … *Can someone remind me what I should do next?* ◊ ~ **sb/yourself + speech** *'You had an accident,' he reminded her.*
PHRV **reˈmind sb of sb/sth** if sb/sth **reminds** you of sb/sth else, they make you remember or think about the other person, place, thing, etc. because they are similar in some way: *You remind me of your father when you say that.* ◊ *That smell reminds me of France.*

**re·mind·er** C1 /rɪˈmaɪndə(r)/ *noun* 1 + C1 ~ **(of sb/sth)** | ~ **(that …)** something that makes you think about or remember sth/sb, that you have forgotten or would like to forget: *The sheer size of the cathedral is a constant reminder of the power of religion.* ◊ *The incident served as a timely reminder of just how dangerous mountaineering can be.* 2 + C1 a letter or note informing sb that they have not done sth: *If an invoice is not paid within seven days, we automatically send out a reminder.*

**rem·in·isce** /ˌremɪˈnɪs/ *verb* [I] ~ **(about sth/sb)** to think, talk or write about a happy time in your past: *We spent a happy evening reminiscing about the past.*

**rem·in·is·cence** /ˌremɪˈnɪsns/ *noun* 1 [C, usually pl.] a spoken or written description of sth that sb remembers about their past life SYN **memory**: *The book is a collection of his reminiscences about the actress.* ◊ *reminiscences of a wartime childhood* 2 [U] the act of remembering things that happened in the past SYN **recollection** 3 [C, usually pl.] something that reminds you of sth similar: *Her music is full of reminiscences of African rhythms.*

**rem·in·is·cent** /ˌremɪˈnɪsnt/ *adj.* 1 ~ **of sb/sth** reminding you of sb/sth: *The way he laughed was strongly reminiscent of his father.* 2 [only before noun] (*formal*) showing that you are thinking about the past, especially in a way that causes you pleasure: *a reminiscent smile*

**re·miss** /rɪˈmɪs/ *adj.* [not before noun] (*formal*) not giving sth enough care and attention SYN **negligent**: ~ **(of sb) (to do sth)** *It was remiss of them not to inform us of these changes sooner.* ◊ ~ **in (doing) sth** *She had clearly been remiss in her duty.*

**re·mis·sion** /rɪˈmɪʃn/ *noun* [U, C] 1 a period during which a serious illness improves for a time and the patient seems to get better: **in** ~ *The patient has been in remission for the past six months.* ◊ *The symptoms reappeared after only a short remission.* 2 (*BrE*) a reduction in the amount of time sb spends in prison, especially because they have behaved well ⇒ WORDFINDER NOTE at PRISON 3 (*formal*) an act of reducing or cancelling the amount of money that sb has to pay: *New businesses may qualify for tax remission.* ◊ *There is a partial remission of fees for overseas students.*

**remit** *noun, verb*
■ *noun* /ˈriːmɪt, rɪˈmɪt/ [usually sing.] (*BrE*) the area of activity over which a particular person or group has authority, control or influence: **outside the ~ of sb/sth** *Such decisions are outside the remit of this committee.* ◊ **within the ~ of sb/sth** *In future, staff recruitment will fall within the remit of the division manager.* ◊ ~ **to do sth** *a remit to report on medical services*
■ *verb* /rɪˈmɪt/ (-tt-) (*formal*) 1 to send money, etc. to a person or place SYN **forward**: ~ **sth to sb** *Payment will be remitted to you in full.* 2 ~ **sth** to cancel or free sb from a debt, duty, punishment, etc. SYN **cancel**: *to remit a fine* ◊ *to remit a prison sentence* ⇒ see also UNREMITTING

PHRV **reˈmit sth to sb** [usually passive] (*law*) to send a matter to an authority so that a decision can be made: *The case was remitted to the Court of Appeal.*

**re·mit·tance** /rɪˈmɪtns/ *noun* 1 [C] (*formal*) a sum of money that is sent to sb in order to pay for sth: *Please return the completed form with your remittance.* 2 [U] the act of sending money to sb in order to pay for sth SYN **payment**: *Remittance can be made by cheque or credit card.*

**re·mix** /ˌriːˈmɪks/ *verb* ~ **sth** to make a new version of a recorded piece of music by using a machine to arrange the separate parts of the recording in a different way, add new parts, etc. ▶ **reˈmix** /ˈriːmɪks/ (*also* **mix**) *noun* **reˈmixer** /ˈriːmɪksə(r)/ *noun*: *the skills of remixer Tom Moulton*

**rem·nant** /ˈremnənt/ *noun* 1 [usually pl.] a part of sth that is left after the other parts have been used, removed, destroyed, etc. SYN **remains**: *The woods are remnants of a huge forest which once covered the whole area.* 2 a small piece of cloth that is left when the rest has been sold

**re·model** /ˌriːˈmɒdl/; *NAmE* -ˈmɑːdl/ *verb* (-ll-, *US* -l-) ~ **sth** to change the structure or shape of sth

**re·mold** (*US*) = REMOULD

**rem·on·strance** /rɪˈmɒnstrəns; *NAmE* -ˈmɑːn-/ *noun* [C, U] (*formal*) a protest or complaint

**rem·on·strate** /ˈremənstreɪt; *NAmE* rɪˈmɑːnstreɪt/ *verb* [I, T] ~ **(with sb) (about sth)** | **+ speech** (*formal*) to protest or complain about sth/sb: *They remonstrated with the official about the decision.*

**re·morse** /rɪˈmɔːs/; *NAmE* -ˈmɔːrs/ *noun* [U] the feeling of being extremely sorry for sth wrong or bad that you have done: *I felt guilty and full of remorse.* ◊ ~ **for (doing) sth** *He was filled with remorse for not believing her.* ⇒ WORDFINDER NOTE at SORRY ▶ **reˈmorse·ful** /-fl/ *adj.* **reˈmorse·ful·ly** /-fəli/ *adv.*

**re·morse·less** /rɪˈmɔːsləs; *NAmE* -ˈmɔːrs-/ *adj.* 1 (especially of an unpleasant situation) seeming to continue or become worse in a way that cannot be stopped SYN **relentless**: *the remorseless increase in crime* 2 cruel and having or showing no regret for sth wrong or bad you have done SYN **merciless**: *a remorseless killer* ▶ **reˈmorse·less·ly** *adv.*

**re·mort·gage** /ˌriːˈmɔːɡɪdʒ; *NAmE* -ˈmɔːrɡ-/ *verb* [I, T] ~ **(sth)** to arrange a second MORTGAGE on your house or apartment, or to increase or change your first one ▶ **reˈmort·gage** /ˈriːmɔːɡɪdʒ; *NAmE* -mɔːrɡ-/ *noun*

**re·mote** ❶ B1 /rɪˈməʊt/ *adj., noun*
■ *adj.* (**reˈmoter, reˈmotest**)
• PLACE 1 B1 far away from places where other people live SYN **isolated**: *a remote village/island/location/region* ◊ *a remote community* ◊ *a remote part of the country* ◊ *one of the remotest areas of the world* ◊ ~ **from sth** *The site is remote from major population centres.*
• TIME 2 B2 [only before noun] far away in time SYN **distant**: *in the remote past/future* ◊ *a remote ancestor* (= who lived a long time ago)
• RELATIVES 3 [only before noun] (of people) not closely related SYN **distant**: *a remote cousin*
• COMPUTER/SYSTEM 4 that you can connect to from far away, using an electronic link: *a remote terminal/database/server*
• DIFFERENT 5 ~ **(from sth)** very different from sth: *His theories are somewhat remote from reality.*
• NOT FRIENDLY 6 (of people or their behaviour) not very friendly or interested in other people SYN **aloof, distant**
• VERY SMALL 7 not very great SYN **slight**: *There is still a remote chance that they will find her alive.* ◊ *I don't have the remotest idea what you're talking about.* ▶ **reˈmote·ness** *noun* [U]: *the geographical remoteness of the island* ◊ *His remoteness made her feel unloved.*
■ *noun* (*informal*) = REMOTE CONTROL

**reˌmote ˈaccess** *noun* [U] the use of a computer system, etc. that is in another place, that you can connect to when you are far away, using an electronic link

**reˌmote conˈtrol** *noun* 1 [U] the ability to operate a machine from a distance using radio or electrical signals: **by ~** *It works by remote control.* ◊ *a remote-control camera*

# remotely

**2** (also informal **re·mote**) [C] a device that allows you to operate a television, etc. from a distance SYN **zapper**: *I can't find the remote control.* ▶ **re·mote-con'trolled** *adj.: remote-controlled equipment*

**re·mote·ly** /rɪˈməʊtli/ *adv.* **1** (usually in negative sentences) to a very slight degree SYN **slightly**: *It wasn't even remotely funny* (= it wasn't at all funny). ◊ *The two incidents were only remotely connected.* **2** from a distance: *remotely operated* **3** far away from places where other people live: *The church is remotely situated on the north coast of the island.*

**re·mote 'sensing** *noun* [U] the use of satellites to search for and collect information about the earth

**re·mould** (US **re·mold**) /ˌriːˈməʊld/ *verb* ~ **sth** (*formal*) to change sth such as an idea, a system, etc: *attempts to remould policy to make it more acceptable*

**re·mount** /ˌriːˈmaʊnt/ *verb* **1** [I, T] ~ **(sth)** to get on a horse, bicycle, etc. again after getting off it or falling off it **2** [T] ~ **sth** to organize and begin sth a second time

**re·mov·able** /rɪˈmuːvəbl/ *adj.* [usually before noun] that can be taken off or out of sth SYN **detachable**

**re·moval** /rɪˈmuːvl/ *noun* **1** [U] the act of taking sth away from a particular place: *Clearance of the site required the removal of a number of trees.* ◊ *the removal of a tumour* **2** [U] the act of getting rid of sth: *stain removal* ◊ *the removal of trade barriers* **3** [U] the act of dismissing sb from their job SYN **dismissal**: *events leading to the removal of the president from office* **4** [C] (*BrE*) an act of taking furniture, etc. from one house to another: *house removals* ◊ *a removal company/firm* ◊ *When are the removal men coming?*

**re·mov·al·ist** /rɪˈmuːvəlɪst/ *noun* (*AustralE*) a person or company that takes furniture, etc. from one house or building to another

**re'moval van** (also **'furniture van**) (both BrE) (NAmE **'moving van**) *noun* a large van used for moving furniture and other goods from one home or business to another

**re·move** /rɪˈmuːv/ *verb, noun*
■ *verb* **1** to take sb/sth away from a place: ~ **sb/sth** *Illegally parked vehicles will be removed.* ◊ ~ **sb/sth from sb/sth** *He removed his hand from her shoulder.* ◊ *Remove the pan from the heat and continue to stir the sauce.* **2** ~ **sth** to take off clothing, etc. from the body: *She removed her glasses and rubbed her eyes.* **3** ~ **sth** to get rid of sth unpleasant, dirty, etc.; to make sth disappear: ~ **sth** *She has had the tumour removed.* ◊ *Considerable progress has been made in removing barriers to trade within the EU.* ◊ ~ **sth from sb/sth** *The police instructed the author to remove the offending material from the website.* **4** ~ **sb from sth** to dismiss sb from their position or job: *The elections removed the government from power.*
IDM **be far/further/furthest removed from sth** to be very different from sth; to not be connected with sth: *Many of these books are far removed from the reality of the children's lives.* **once, twice, etc. re'moved** (of a cousin) belonging to a different generation: *He's my cousin's son so he's my first cousin once removed.*
■ *noun* [C, U] (*formal*) an amount by which two things are separated: *Charlotte seemed to be living at one remove from reality.*

**re·mover** /rɪˈmuːvə(r)/ *noun* **1** [U, C] (usually in compounds) a substance used for getting rid of marks, paint, etc: *nail varnish remover* ◊ *stain remover* ⊃ see also STAPLE REMOVER **2** [usually pl.] (*BrE*) a person or company whose job is to take furniture, etc. from one house to another: *a firm of removers*

**re·mu·ner·ate** /rɪˈmjuːnəreɪt/ *verb* [usually passive] ~ **sb (for sth)** (*formal*) to pay sb for work that they have done

**re·mu·ner·ation** /rɪˌmjuːnəˈreɪʃn/ *noun* [U, C] (*formal*) an amount of money that is paid to sb for the work they have done

**re·mu·nera·tive** /rɪˈmjuːnərətɪv/ *adj.* [usually before noun] (*formal*) paying a lot of money: *remunerative work*

**re·nais·sance** /rɪˈneɪsns/ *NAmE* /ˈrenəsɑːns/ *noun* [sing.] **1 the Renaissance** the period in Europe during the four-teenth, fifteenth and sixteenth centuries when people became interested in the ideas and culture of ancient Greece and Rome and used these influences in their own art, literature, etc: *Renaissance art* **2** a situation when there is new interest in a particular subject, form of art, etc. after a period when it was not very popular SYN **revival**: *to experience a renaissance*

**Re'naissance man** *noun* a person who is good at a lot of things and has a lot of interests, especially writing and painting

**renal** /ˈriːnl/ *adj.* [usually before noun] (*medical*) relating to or involving the KIDNEYS: *renal failure*

**re·name** /ˌriːˈneɪm/ *verb* to give sb/sth a new name: ~ **sth** *to rename a street* ◊ ~ **sth + noun** *Leningrad was renamed St Petersburg.*

**rend** /rend/ *verb* (**rent, rent** /rent/) ~ **sth** (*old use* or *literary*) to tear sth apart with force or violence: *The women rend their clothes in grief.* ◊ (*figurative*) *a country rent in two by civil war* ◊ (*figurative*) *Loud screams rent the air.* ⊃ see also HEART-RENDING

**ren·der** /ˈrendə(r)/ *verb*
• CAUSE SB/STH TO BE STH **1** ~ **sb/sth + adj.** (*formal*) to cause sb/sth to be in a particular state or condition SYN **make**: *to render sth harmless/useless/ineffective* ◊ *Hundreds of people were rendered homeless by the earthquake.*
• GIVE HELP **2** ~ **sth** (*formal*) to give sb sth, especially in return for sth or because it is expected: ~ **sth to sb/sth** *They rendered assistance to the disaster victims.* ◊ *to render a service to sb* ◊ ~ **sb sth to render sb a service** ◊ ~ **sth** *It was payment for services rendered.*
• PRESENT STH **3** ~ **sth** (*formal*) to present sth, especially when it is done officially SYN **furnish**: *The committee was asked to render a report on the housing situation.*
• EXPRESS/PERFORM **4** ~ **sth** (*formal*) to express or perform sth: *He stood up and rendered a beautiful version of 'Summertime'.* ◊ *The artist has rendered the stormy sea in dark greens and browns.*
• TRANSLATE **5** to express sth in a different language SYN **translate**: ~ **sth (as sth)** *The Italian phrase can be rendered as 'I did my best'.* ◊ ~ **sth (into sth)** *It's a concept that is difficult to render into English.*
• WALL **6** ~ **sth** (*specialist*) to cover a wall with a layer of PLASTER or CEMENT
• MELT **7** ~ **sth (down)** to make fat liquid by heating it; to melt sth

**ren·der·ing** /ˈrendərɪŋ/ *noun* **1** [C] the performance of a piece of music, a role in a play, etc.; the particular way in which sth is performed SYN **interpretation, rendition**: *her dramatic rendering of Lady Macbeth* **2** [C] a piece of writing that has been translated into a different language; the particular way in which it has been translated: *a faithful rendering of the original text* **3** [U, C] (*specialist*) a layer of PLASTER or CEMENT that is put on a BRICK or stone wall in order to make it smooth

**ren·dez·vous** /ˈrɒndɪvuː, -deɪ-/ *NAmE* /ˈrɑːn-/ *noun, verb*
■ *noun* (*pl.* **ren·dez·vous** /-vuːz/) (*from French*) **1** ~ **(with sb)** an arrangement to meet sb at a particular time and place **2** a place where people have arranged to meet **3** a bar, etc. that is a popular place for people to meet: *a lively Paris rendezvous*
■ *verb* [I] (**ren·dez·voused, ren·dez·voused** /-vuːd/) ~ **(with sb)** (*from French*) to meet at a time and place that have been arranged in advance

**ren·di·tion** /renˈdɪʃn/ *noun* **1** [C] the performance of sth, especially a song or piece of music; the particular way in which it is performed SYN **interpretation 2** (also **ex,traordinary ren'dition**) [U] (especially in the US) the practice of sending foreign suspects to be questioned in another country where the laws about the treatment of prisoners are less strict

**rene·gade** /ˈrenɪɡeɪd/ *noun* (*formal, disapproving*) **1** (often used as an adjective) a person who leaves one political, religious, etc. group to join another that has very different views **2** a person who opposes and lives outside a group or society that they used to belong to SYN **outlaw**

**re·nege** /rɪˈniːɡ, -neɪɡ; *NAmE* -neɡ/ *verb* [I] ~ **(on sth)** (*formal*) to break a promise, an agreement, etc. SYN **go back on**: *to renege on a deal/debt/contract*

**renew** /rɪˈnjuː; NAmE -ˈnuː/ verb **1** ~ sth to begin sth again after it stopped or was interrupted **SYN** **resume**: *The army renewed its assault on the capital.* ◇ *We have to renew our efforts to attract young players.* ◇ *The annual dinner is a chance to renew acquaintance with old friends.* **2** ~ sth to make sth legally acceptable for a further period of time: *to renew a licence/lease/subscription/contract* ◇ *How do I go about renewing my passport?* ◇ *I'd like to renew these library books* (= arrange to borrow them for a further period of time). **3** ~ sth to emphasize sth by saying or stating it again **SYN** **reiterate, repeat**: *to renew an appeal/a request/a complaint* ◇ *Community leaders have renewed calls for a peaceful settlement.* ◇ *The project is to go ahead following renewed promises of aid from the UN.* **4** ~ sth to change sth that is old or damaged and replace it with sth new of the same kind: *The wiring in your house should be renewed every ten to fifteen years.*

**re·new·able** /rɪˈnjuːəbl; NAmE -ˈnuː-/ adj. **1** [usually before noun] (of energy and natural resources) that is replaced naturally or controlled carefully and can therefore be used without the risk of using it all up: *renewable sources of energy such as wind and solar power* **2** (of a contract, ticket, etc.) that can be made legally acceptable for a further period of time after it has finished: *a renewable lease* ◇ *The work permit is not renewable.* **OPP** **non-renewable**

**re·new·ables** /rɪˈnjuːəblz; NAmE -ˈnuː-/ noun [pl.] types of energy that can be replaced naturally such as energy produced from wind or water: *renewables such as hydro-electricity and solar energy* ◇ *investment in renewables* **HELP** **Renewables** are more commonly referred to as **renewable energy (sources)**.

**re·newal** /rɪˈnjuːəl; NAmE -ˈnuː-/ noun [C, U] **1** ~ (of sth) a situation in which sth begins again after it stopped or was interrupted: *a renewal of interest in traditional teaching methods* **2** the act of making a contract, etc. legally acceptable for a further period of time after it has finished: *The lease comes up for renewal at the end of the month.* ◇ *the renewal date* **3** a situation in which sth is replaced, improved or made more successful: *economic renewal* ◇ **urban renewal** (= the act of improving the buildings, etc. in a particular area)

**re·newed** /rɪˈnjuːd; NAmE -ˈnuːd/ adj. [usually before noun] happening again with increased interest or strength: *Renewed fighting has been reported on the border.* ◇ *with renewed enthusiasm*

**ren·min·bi** /ˈrenmɪnbi/ noun (pl. **ren·min·bi**) **1** the renminbi [sing.] the money system of China **2** = YUAN

**ren·net** /ˈrenɪt/ noun [U] a substance that makes milk thick and SOUR and is used in making cheese

**re·nounce** /rɪˈnaʊns/ verb (formal) **1** ~ sth to state officially that you are no longer going to keep a title, position, etc. **SYN** **give sth↔up**: *to renounce a claim/title/privilege/right* **2** ~ sth to state publicly that you no longer have a particular belief or that you will no longer behave in a particular way: *to renounce ideals/principles/beliefs, etc.* ◇ *a joint declaration renouncing the use of violence* **3** ~ sb/sth to state publicly that you no longer wish to have a connection with sb/sth because you DISAPPROVE of them **SYN** **disown**: *He had renounced his former associates.* ⊃ see also RENUNCIATION

**reno·vate** /ˈrenəveɪt/ verb ~ sth to repair and paint an old building, a piece of furniture, etc. so that it is in good condition again ▶ **reno·va·tion** /ˌrenəˈveɪʃn/ noun [U, C, usually pl.]: *buildings in need of renovation* ◇ *There will be extensive renovations to the hospital.*

**re·nown** /rɪˈnaʊn/ noun [U] (formal) the state of being famous and receiving respect because of sth you have done that people admire: *He won renown as a fair judge.* ◇ *a pianist of some/international/great renown*

**re·nowned** /rɪˈnaʊnd/ adj. famous and respected **SYN** **celebrated, noted**: *a renowned author* ◇ ~ **as sth** *It is renowned as one of the region's best restaurants.* ◇ ~ **for sth** *She is renowned for her patience.*

**rent** /rent/ noun, verb
■ noun **1** [U, C] an amount of money that you regularly pay so that you can use a house, room, etc: *I earn just about enough to **pay the rent**.* ◇ *a month's rent in advance* ◇ *a high/low/fair rent* ◇ **on sth** *The rent on the two-bedroom flat was £250 a week.* ◇ **at a…~** *The supply of housing at affordable rents became inadequate.* ◇ (BrE) *a rent book* (= used to record payments of rent) ⊃ see also GROUND RENT, PEPPERCORN RENT ⊃ compare HIRE **2** [U, C] (especially NAmE) = RENTAL (1) **3** [C] (old use or literary) a torn place in a piece of material or clothing
**IDM** **for rent** (especially NAmE) (especially on printed signs) available to rent
■ verb **1** [T, I] to regularly pay money to sb so that you can use sth that they own, such as a house, a room, some land, etc: *Are you looking to buy or rent?* ◇ ~ **sth** *to rent a house/an apartment* ◇ *to live in rented accommodation/housing/property* ◇ *We're looking for a house to rent in the area.* ◇ ~ **sth from sb** *Who do you rent the land from?* **2** [T] to allow sb to use sth that you own such as a house or some land in exchange for regular payments: ~ **sth (out)** *We rented our house out for a year when we went abroad.* ◇ ~ **sth (out) to sb** *He rents rooms in his house to students.* ◇ *The land is rented out to other farmers.* ◇ ~ **sb sth** *She agreed to rent me the room.* **3** [T] ~ **sth** (especially NAmE) to pay money to sb so that you can use sth for a short period of time: *to rent a film/movie/DVD* ◇ *We rented a car for the week and explored the area.* ⊃ compare HIRE **4** [I] (NAmE) to be available for sb to use if they pay a particular amount of money: *The apartment rents for $500 a month.* **5** past tense, past part of REND

▼ BRITISH/AMERICAN

**rent / hire / let**

Verbs
- You can **hire** something for a short period of time (BrE only), but **rent** something for a longer period: *We can hire bikes for a day to explore the town.* ◇ *We don't own our TV, we rent it.*
- In NAmE, **rent** is always used. It is sometimes now used in BrE instead of **hire**, too.
- The owners of a thing can **hire** it **out** for a short period: (BrE) *Do you hire out bikes?* Or they can **rent (out)/let (out)** a building, etc: *We rent out rooms in our house to students.*
- Outside a building you could see: (BrE) **To let** (especially NAmE) **For rent**.
- To **hire** can also mean to employ somebody, especially in NAmE: *We hired a new secretary.*

⊃ see also LEASE verb

Nouns
- The amount of money that you pay to rent something is **rent** or **rental** (more formal). When you hire something you pay a **hire charge** (BrE). On a sign outside a shop you might see: (BrE) *Bikes for hire.*

⊃ see also LET, LEASE, HIRE noun

**rent-a-** /ˈrent ə/ combining form (informal, often humorous) (in nouns and adjectives) showing that the thing mentioned can be rented: *rent-a-car* ◇ *rent-a-crowd*

**ren·tal** /ˈrentl/ noun **1** [also **rent** especially in NAmE] [U, C, usually sing.] the amount of money that you pay to use sth for a particular period of time: *Telephone charges include line rental.* ⊃ **SYNONYMS** at RATE **2** [U] the act of renting sth or an arrangement to rent sth: *the world's largest car rental company* ◇ (especially NAmE) *a rental car* ◇ *a minimum rental period of three months* ⊃ compare HIRE **3** [C] (especially NAmE) a house, car or piece of equipment that you can rent: *'Is this your own car?' 'No, it's a rental.'*

**ˈrent boy** noun (BrE) a young male PROSTITUTE

**rent·ed** /ˈrentɪd/ adj. that you pay rent for: *a rented studio*

**rent·er** /ˈrentə(r)/ noun **1** a person who rents sth: *house buyers and renters* **2** (NAmE) a person or an organization that provides sth for people to rent: *the nation's biggest automobile renter*

**ˌrent-ˈfree** adj. for which no rent is paid: *rent-free housing* ▶ **ˌrent-ˈfree** adv.

# rentier

**ren·tier** /'rɒntieɪ; NAmE ˌrɑːn'tjeɪ/ noun (specialist) a person who lives from money earned from property and investments

**'rent-seeking** adj. (disapproving, economics) trying to change or control public policy or economic conditions in order to increase your own profits: *rent-seeking behaviour* ▶ **'rent-seeking** noun [U]

**re·nun·ci·ation** /rɪˌnʌnsi'eɪʃn/ noun (formal) **1** [U, C] an act of stating publicly that you no longer believe sth or that you are giving sth up: *the renunciation of violence* **2** [U] the act of rejecting physical pleasures, especially for religious reasons **SYN** self-denial⊃ see also RENOUNCE

**re·occur** /ˌriːə'kɜː(r)/ verb (-rr-) to happen again or a number of times **SYN** recur

**re·of·fend** /ˌriːə'fend/ verb [I] to commit a crime again: *Without help, many released prisoners will reoffend.* ▶ **re·of·fend·er** noun

**re·open** /ˌriː'əʊpən/ verb **1** [T, I] **~(sth)** to open a shop, theatre, etc. again, or to be opened again, after being closed for a period of time: *The school was reopened just two weeks after the fire.* ◇ *The store will reopen at 9 a.m. on 2 January.* **2** [T, I] **~(sth)** to deal with or begin sth again after a period of time; to start again after a period of time: *to reopen a discussion* ◇ *The police have decided to reopen the case.* ◇ *Management have agreed to reopen talks with the union.* ◇ *The trial reopened on 6 March.* ▶ **re·open·ing** noun [U, sing.]
**IDM** **re,open old 'wounds** to remind sb of sth unpleasant that happened or existed in the past

**re·order** /ˌriː'ɔːdə(r); NAmE -'ɔːrd-/ verb **1** [T, I] **~(sth)** to ask sb to supply you with more of a product: *Please quote this reference number when reordering stock.* **2** [T] **~sth** to change the order in which sth is arranged

**re·organ·ize** (BrE also -ise) /ˌriː'ɔːɡənaɪz; NAmE -'ɔːrɡ-/ verb [T, I] **~(sth)** to change the way in which sth is organized or done ▶ **re·organ·iza·tion, -isa·tion** /ˌriːˌɔːɡənaɪ'zeɪʃn; NAmE -ˌɔːrɡənə'z-/ noun [U, C]: *the reorganization of the school system*

**re·ori·ent** /ˌriː'ɔːrient/ verb **1** **~sb/sth (to/towards/away from sb/sth)** to change the focus or direction of sb/sth: *Other governments may reorient their foreign policies away from the United States.* **2** **~yourself** to find your position again in relation to everything that is around or near you ▶ **re·orien·ta·tion** /ˌriːˌɔːriən'teɪʃn/ noun [U]

**Rep.** abbr. (in American politics) **1** REPRESENTATIVE **2** REPUBLICAN

**rep** /rep/ noun (informal) **1** [C] = SALES REP, REPRESENTATIVE **2** [C] a person who speaks officially for a group of people, especially at work: *a union rep* **3** [U] (informal) the type of work of a theatre company in which different plays are performed for short periods of time (the abbreviation for 'repertory')

**re·pack·age** /ˌriː'pækɪdʒ/ verb **1** **~sth** to change the boxes, bags, etc. in which a product is sold **2** **~sth/sb** to present sth/sb in a new way: *She earns more since she repackaged herself as a business consultant.*

**re·paid** /rɪ'peɪd/ past tense, past part. of REPAY

**re·pair** ❶ **A2** /rɪ'peə(r); NAmE -'per/ verb, noun
■ verb **1** **A2** **~sth** to fix sth that is broken, damaged or torn: *to repair a car/television* ◇ *He has had surgery to repair the damage.* ◇ *It's almost 15 years old. It isn't worth having it repaired.* **2** **B1** **~sth** to say or do sth in order to improve a bad or unpleasant situation **SYN** right: *to repair relations/a relationship* ◇ *It was too late to repair the damage done to their relationship.* ▶ **re·pair·er** noun: *TV repairers*
**PHRV** **re'pair to...** (formal or humorous) to go to a particular place
■ noun **B1** [C, U] an act of repairing sth: *They agreed to pay the costs of any repairs.* ◇ *The building was in need of repair.* ◇ **beyond~** *The car was damaged beyond repair (= it was too badly damaged to be repaired).* ◇ **under~** *The hotel is currently under repair (= being repaired).* ◇ *The bridge will remain closed until essential repair work has been carried out.* ◇ **~of sth** *They agreed to pay for the repair of any damage done.* ◇ **~to sth** *The money was to be used for repairs to the school.*
**IDM** **in good, bad, etc. re'pair | in a good, bad, etc. state of re'pair** (formal) in good, etc. condition

**re·pair·able** /rɪ'peərəbl; NAmE -'per-/ adj. [not usually before noun] that can be repaired **OPP** irreparable

**re·pair·man** /rɪ'peəmæn; NAmE -'perm-/ noun (pl. -men /-men/) (also **re·pair·er** especially in BrE) a person whose job is to repair things: *a TV repairman*

**rep·ar·ation** /ˌrepə'reɪʃn/ noun **1 reparations** [pl.] money that is paid by a country that has lost a war, for the damage, injuries, etc. that it has caused⊃ **WORDFINDER NOTE** at PEACE **2** [U] the act of giving sth to sb or doing sth for them in order to show that you are sorry that you have caused them to suffer: *Offenders should be forced to make reparation to the community.*

**rep·ar·tee** /ˌrepɑː'tiː; NAmE -pɑːr'tiː/ noun [U] clever and funny comments and replies that are made quickly

**re·past** /rɪ'pɑːst; NAmE -'pæst/ noun (old-fashioned or formal) a meal

**re·pat·ri·ate** /ˌriː'pætrieɪt; NAmE -'peɪt-/ verb **1** **~sb** (formal) to send or bring sb back to their own country: *The refugees were forcibly repatriated.* **2** **~sth** (business) to send money or profits back to your own country ▶ **re·pat·ri·ation** /ˌriːˌpætri'eɪʃn; NAmE -ˌpeɪt-/ noun [U, C]: *the repatriation of immigrants/profits* ◇ *a voluntary repatriation programme*

**re·pay** /rɪ'peɪ/ verb (**re·paid, re·paid** /-'peɪd/) **1** to pay back the money that you have borrowed from sb: **~sth** *to repay a debt/loan/mortgage* ◇ *I'll repay the money I owe them next week.* ◇ **~sth to sb** *The advance must be repaid to the publisher if the work is not completed on time.* ◇ **~sb** *When are you going to repay them?* ◇ **~sb sth** *I fully intend to repay them the money that they lent me.* **2** to give sth to sb or do sth for them in return for sth that they have done for you **SYN** recompense: **~sb (for sth)** *How can I ever repay you for your generosity?* ◇ **~sth (with sth)** *Their trust was repaid with fierce loyalty.* **3** **~sth** (formal) if sth repays your attention, interest, study, etc., it is worth spending time to look at it, etc: *The report repays careful reading.*

**re·pay·able** /rɪ'peɪəbl/ adj. that can or must be paid back: *The loan is repayable in monthly instalments.*

**re·pay·ment** /rɪ'peɪmənt/ noun **1** [U] the act of paying back money that you have borrowed from a bank, etc: *The loan is due for repayment by the end of the year.* **2** [C, usually pl.] a sum of money that you pay regularly to a bank, etc. until you have returned all the money that you owe: *We were unable to meet (= pay) the repayments on the loan.* ◇ *mortgage repayments*⊃ **SYNONYMS** at PAYMENT

**re'payment mortgage** noun (BrE) a type of MORTGAGE in which you pay regular sums of money to the bank, etc. until you have returned all the money and interest that you owe⊃ compare ENDOWMENT MORTGAGE

**re·peal** /rɪ'piːl/ verb **~sth** if a government or other group or person with authority **repeals** a law, that law no longer has any legal force ▶ **re·peal** noun [U]

**re·peat** ❶ **A1** /rɪ'piːt/ verb, noun
■ verb
• SAY/WRITE AGAIN **1** **A1** [T] to say or write sth again or more than once: **~sth** *to repeat a question/a claim/an assertion/a warning* ◇ *She repeated the word several times.* ◇ *I'm sorry—could you repeat that?* ◇ *She kept repeating his name softly over and over again.* ◇ **~yourself** *Do say if I'm repeating myself (= if I have already said this).* ◇ **~that...** *He's fond of repeating that the company's success is all down to him.* ◇ **+ speech** *'Are you really sure?' she repeated.* **2** **A1** [I, T] used to emphasize sth that you have already said: *The claims are, I repeat, totally unfounded.* ◇ **~sth** *I am not, repeat not, travelling in the same car as him!*
• WHAT SB ELSE SAID **3** **A1** [T] to say sth that sb else has said, especially in order to learn it: **~sth (after sb)** *Listen and repeat each sentence after me.* ◇ **~what...** *Can you repeat*

**WORD FAMILY**
**repeat** verb, noun
**repeatable** adj.
 (≠ unrepeatable)
**repeated** adj.
**repeatedly** adv.
**repetition** noun
**repetitive** adj.
**repetitious** adj.

what I've just said word for word? **4** [T] to tell sb sth that you have heard or been told by sb else: **~ sth to sb** *I don't want you to repeat a word of this to anyone.* ◇ **~ sth** *The rumour has been widely repeated in the press.*
- **DO AGAIN 5** [T, I] to do or produce sth again or more than once: **~ sth** *to repeat a mistake/process* ◇ *to repeat an experiment/exercise* ◇ *Organizers are hoping to repeat the success of last year's event.* ◇ *These offers are unlikely to be repeated.* ◇ *The programmes will be repeated next year.* ◇ *Lift and lower the right leg 20 times. Repeat with the left leg.*
- **HAPPEN AGAIN 6** [T, I] to happen more than once in the same way: **~ sth/itself** *History has a strange way of repeating itself.* ◇ *a repeating pattern/design*
- **OF FOOD 7** [I] **~ (on sb)** (*BrE, informal*) if food repeats, you can taste it for some time after you have eaten it: *Do you find that onions repeat on you?*

■ *noun* **1** an event that is very similar to sth that happened before: **~ of sth** *She didn't want a repeat performance of what had happened the night before.* ◇ (*business*) *a repeat order* (= for a further supply of the same goods) ◇ *a repeat offender* (= sb who commits a crime again) **2** a television or radio programme that has been broadcast before: *'Is it a new series?' 'No, a repeat.'* **3** (*music*) a passage that is repeated

**re·peat·able** /rɪˈpiːtəbl/ *adj.* [not usually before noun] **1** (of a comment, etc.) (usually in negative sentences) polite and not offensive: *His reply was not repeatable.* **2** that can be repeated **OPP unrepeatable**

**re·peat·ed** /rɪˈpiːtɪd/ *adj.* [only before noun] happening, said or done many times: *She did not respond to repeated requests for interviews.* ◇ *The marriage failed despite repeated attempts to save it.* ▶ **re·peat·ed·ly** *adv.*: *The victim had been stabbed repeatedly in the chest.*

**re·peat·er** /rɪˈpiːtə(r)/ *noun* (*specialist*) a gun that you can fire several times without having to load it again

**repel** /rɪˈpel/ *verb* (**-ll-**) **1** [T] **~ sb/sth** (*formal*) to successfully fight sb who is attacking you, your country, etc. and drive them away: *to repel an attack/invasion/invader* ◇ *Troops repelled an attempt to infiltrate the south of the island.* ◇ (*figurative*) *The reptile's prickly skin repels nearly all of its predators.* **2** [T] **~ sth** to drive, push or keep sth away: *a cream that repels insects* ◇ *The fabric has been treated to repel water.* **3** [T] **~ sb** (not used in the progressive tenses) to make sb feel horror or DISGUST **SYN disgust, repulse**: *I was repelled by the smell.* **4** [T, I] **~ (sth)** (*specialist*) if one thing **repels** another, or if two things **repel** each other, an electrical or MAGNETIC force pushes them apart: *Like poles repel each other.* **OPP attract** ⊃ see also REPULSION, REPULSIVE

**re·pel·lent** /rɪˈpelənt/ *adj., noun*
■ *adj.* **1** **~ (to sb)** (*formal*) very unpleasant; causing strong dislike **SYN repulsive**: *Their political ideas are repellent to most people.* **2** (in compounds) not letting a particular substance, especially water, pass through it: *water-repellent cloth*
■ *noun* [U, C] **1** a substance that is used for keeping insects away from you: (*an*) *insect repellent* ◇ *mosquito repellent* **2** a substance that is used on cloth, stone, etc. to prevent water from passing through it: (*a*) *water repellent*

**re·pent** /rɪˈpent/ *verb* [I, T] (*formal*) to feel and show that you are sorry for sth bad or wrong that you have done: *God welcomes the sinner who repents.* ◇ **of sth** *She had repented of what she had done.* ◇ **~ sth** *He came to repent his hasty decision* (= wished he had not taken it). ⊃ WORD-FINDER NOTE at SORRY

**re·pent·ance** /rɪˈpentəns/ *noun* [U] **~ (for sth)** (*formal*) the fact of showing that you are sorry for sth wrong that you have done **SYN contrite, remorse**: *He shows no sign of repentance.*

**re·pent·ant** /rɪˈpentənt/ *adj.* (*formal*) feeling or showing that you are sorry for sth wrong that you have done **SYN contrite, remorseful** **OPP unrepentant**

**re·per·cus·sion** /ˌriːpəˈkʌʃn; *NAmE* -pərˈk-/ *noun* [usually pl.] an indirect and usually bad result of an action or event that may happen some time afterwards **SYN consequence**: *The collapse of the company will have repercussions for the whole industry.* ⊃ SYNONYMS at RESULT

**rep·er·toire** /ˈrepətwɑː(r); *NAmE* -pərt-/ *noun* **1** (*also formal* **rep·er·tory**) all the plays, songs, pieces of music, etc. that a performer knows and can perform: *a pianist with a wide repertoire* **2** all the things that a person is able to do: *a young child's growing verbal repertoire*

**rep·er·tory** /ˈrepətri; *NAmE* -pərtɔːri/ *noun* **1** (*also informal* **rep**) [U] the type of work of a theatre company in which different plays are performed for short periods of time: *an actor in repertory* ◇ *a repertory company* **2** [C] (*formal*) = REPERTOIRE (1)

**repe·ti·tion** /ˌrepəˈtɪʃn/ *noun* **1** [U, C] the fact of doing or saying the same thing many times: *learning by repetition* **2** [C] a thing that has been done or said before: *We do not want to see a repetition of last year's tragic events.*

**repe·ti·tious** /ˌrepəˈtɪʃəs/ *adj.* (*often disapproving*) involving sth that is often repeated, in a way that becomes boring: *a long and repetitious speech* ▶ **repe·ti·tious·ly** *adv.* **repe·ti·tious·ness** *noun*

**re·peti·tive** /rɪˈpetətɪv/ *adj.* **1** saying or doing the same thing many times, so that it becomes boring **SYN monotonous**: *a repetitive task* **2** repeated many times: *a repetitive pattern of behaviour* ▶ **re·peti·tive·ly** *adv.* **re·peti·tive·ness** *noun* [U]

**re·phrase** /ˌriːˈfreɪz/ *verb* **~ sth** to say or write sth using different words in order to make the meaning clearer

**re·place** /rɪˈpleɪs/ *verb* **1** **~ sb/sth** to be used instead of sb/sth else; to do sth instead of sb/sth else **SYN take over (from sth)**: *The new design will eventually replace all existing models.* ◇ *She replaced her husband as the local doctor.* **2** to remove sb/sth and put another person or thing in their place: **~ sb/sth** *He will be difficult to replace when he leaves.* ◇ **~ sb/sth with/by sb/sth** *It is not a good idea to miss meals and replace them with snacks.* **3** **~ sth** to change sth that is old, damaged, etc. for a similar thing that is newer or better: *We're thinking of replacing our phone system.* ◇ *to replace a window/roof* **4** **~ sth (+ adv./prep.)** to put sth back in the place where it was before: *I replaced the cup carefully in the saucer.* ◇ *to replace the handset* (= after using the phone).

**re·place·able** /rɪˈpleɪsəbl/ *adj.* that can be replaced **OPP irreplaceable**

**re·place·ment** /rɪˈpleɪsmənt/ *noun* **1** [U] the act of replacing one thing with another, especially sth that is newer or better: *the replacement of worn car parts* **2** [C] a thing that replaces sth, especially because the first thing is old, broken, etc.: *a hip replacement* ◇ *replacement windows* **3** [C] **~ (for sb)** a person who replaces another person in an organization, especially in their job: *We need to find a replacement for Sue.* ⊃ see also HORMONE REPLACEMENT THERAPY

**re·play** *noun, verb*
■ *noun* /ˈriːpleɪ/ **1** (*sport*) a game that is played again because neither side won in the previous game **2** the playing again of a short section of a film, tape, etc. especially to look at or listen to sth more carefully: *The replay showed that the ball was over the line.* ⊃ see also ACTION REPLAY, INSTANT REPLAY **3** (*informal*) something that is repeated or happens in exactly the same way as it did before: *This election will not be a replay of the last one.*
■ *verb* /ˌriːˈpleɪ/ **1** [usually passive] **~ sth** to play a sports game again because neither team won the first game **2** **~ sth** to play again a video, music recording or video game: *The police replayed footage of the accident over and over again.* ◇ (*figurative*) *He replayed the scene in his mind.*

**re·plen·ish** /rɪˈplenɪʃ/ *verb* **~ sth (with sth)** (*formal*) to make sth full again by replacing what has been used **SYN top up**: *to replenish food and water supplies* ◇ *Allow me to replenish your glass.* ▶ **re·plen·ish·ment** *noun* [U]

**re·plete** /rɪˈpliːt/ *adj.* **1** [not before noun] **~ (with sth)** (*formal*) filled with sth; with a full supply of sth: *literature replete with drama and excitement* **2** (*old-fashioned or formal*) very full of food

# replica 1314

**rep·li·ca** /ˈreplɪkə/ noun a very good or exact copy of sth: *a replica of the Eiffel Tower* ◊ *The weapon used in the raid was a replica.* ◊ *replica guns*

**rep·li·cate** /ˈreplɪkeɪt/ verb **1** [T] ~ sth (formal) to copy sth exactly **SYN** duplicate: *Subsequent experiments failed to replicate these findings.* **2** [T, I] ~ (itself) (specialist) (of a virus or a MOLECULE) to produce exact copies of itself: *The drug prevents the virus from replicating itself.* ▶ **rep·lic·able** /-kəbl/ adj.: *The design is easily replicable.* **rep·li·ca·tion** /ˌreplɪˈkeɪʃn/ noun [U, C]

**reply** 🔊 A2 /rɪˈplaɪ/ verb, noun
■ verb (re·plies, re·ply·ing, re·plied, re·plied) **1** 🔊 A2 [I, T] to say or write sth as an answer to sth/sb: *She didn't even bother to reply.* ◊ *~ to sb/sth to reply to a question/an email/a query* ◊ *~ (to sb/sth) with sth She simply replied with a smile.* ◊ *+ speech 'I won't let you down,' he replied confidently.* ◊ *~ that … The senator replied that he was not in a position to comment.* ⊃ note at ANSWER **2** [I] *~ (with sth)* to do sth as a reaction to sth that sb has said or done: *The terrorists replied to the government's statement with more violence.*
■ noun 🔊 A2 [C, U] an act of replying to sth/sb in speech, writing or by some action: *I asked her what her name was but she made no reply.* ◊ *~ to sth I got some interesting replies to my post about online banking.* ◊ *in ~ to sth (formal) I am writing in reply to your letter of 16 March.* ◊ *(BrE) a reply-paid envelope* (= on which you do not have to put a stamp because it has already been paid for) ◊ *without ~ (BrE) Morocco scored four goals without reply to win the game.* ⊃ note at ANSWER

**re·port** 🔊 A1 **W** /rɪˈpɔːt; NAmE -ˈpɔːrt/ noun, verb
■ noun
- **OF NEWS 1** 🔊 A1 a written or spoken account of an event, especially one that is published or broadcast: *Are these news reports true?* ◊ *media/press/newspaper reports* ◊ *~ on sth And now over to Jim Muir, for a report on the South African election.* ◊ *according to a~ According to this evening's weather report, there will be snow tomorrow.* ⊃ WORD-FINDER NOTE at JOURNALIST
- **INFORMATION 2** 🔊 A1 a spoken or written description of sth containing information that sb needs to have: *a police report* ◊ *The company has just released its annual report.* ◊ *~ on sth You need to compile a report on your findings.* ⊃ see also SELF-REPORT noun
- **OFFICIAL STUDY 3** 🔊 A1 an official document written by a group of people who have examined a particular situation or problem: *to release/issue a report* ◊ *~ on sth The committee will publish its report on the health service next week.* ◊ *according to a~ According to the report, we are facing an obesity crisis.*
- **STORY 4** 🔊 B1 [pl.] a story or piece of information that may or may not be true: **reports of sth** *There are unconfirmed reports of a shooting in the capital.* ◊ **reports that** *… We are hearing reports that she has quit.*
- **ON STUDENT'S WORK 5** (BrE) (NAmE re·port card) a written statement about a student's work at school, college, etc: *a school report* ◊ *to get a good/bad report*
- **EMPLOYEE 6** (BrE, business) an employee whose work is the responsibility of a particular manager: *a weekly meeting with my direct reports*
- **OF GUN 7** the sound of an explosion or of a gun being fired **SYN** bang, blast: *a loud report*

**IDM** of bad / good re'port (formal) talked about by people in a bad/good way

■ verb
- **GIVE INFORMATION 1** 🔊 A2 [T, I] to give people information about sth that you have heard, seen, done, etc.: *~ sth The crash happened seconds after the pilot reported engine trouble.* ◊ *Call me urgently if you have anything to report.* ◊ *~ on sth (to sb) The committee will report on its research next month.* ◊ *~ (sb/sth) doing sth The neighbours reported seeing him leave the building around noon.* ◊ *~ sb/sth + adj. The doctor reported the patient fully recovered.* ◊ *~ sb/sth as (doing) sth The house was reported as being in excellent condition.* ◊ **be reported to be / have sth** *The house was reported to be in excellent condition.* ◊ *~ (that) … Employers reported that graduates were deficient in writing and problem-solving skills.* ◊ *~ what, how, etc … She failed to report what had occurred.* ◊ *+ speech 'The cabin's empty,' he reported.* ⊃ see also SELF-REPORT verb
- **NEWS/STORY 2** 🔊 A2 [T, I] to present a written or spoken account of an event in a newspaper, on television, etc: *~ sth The stabbing was widely reported in the press.* ◊ *~ (that) … The TV news reported that several people had been arrested.* ◊ **it is reported (that)** *… It was reported that several people had been arrested.* ◊ *~ on sth She reports on royal stories for the BBC.* ◊ *~ from sth She has reported from many war zones.* **3** 🔊 B1 **be reported** [T] used to show that sth has been stated, and you do not know if it is true or not: **be reported to do sth** *She is reported to earn over $1 million a year.* ◊ **be reported as (doing) sth** *The president is reported as saying that he needs a break.* ◊ **it is reported (that)** *… It was reported that changes were being considered.*
- **CRIME/ACCIDENT, ETC. 4** 🔊 A2 [T] to tell a person in authority about a crime, an accident, an illness, etc. or about sth bad that sb has done: *~ sth (to sb) Have you reported the incident to the police?* ◊ *a decrease in the number of reported cases of AIDS* ◊ *~ sb (to sb) for (doing) sth He's already been reported twice for arriving late.* ◊ *~ sb/sth + adj. She has reported her daughter missing.*
- **ARRIVE 5** 🔊 B2 [I] to tell sb that you have arrived, for example for work or for a meeting with sb: *~ for sth You should report for duty at 9.30 a.m.* ◊ *~ to sb/sth All visitors must report to the reception desk on arrival.*

**PHR V** re·port ˈback to return to a place, especially in order to work again: *Take an hour for lunch and report back at two.* re·port ˈback (on sth) (to sb) to give sb information about sth that they have asked you to find out about: *Find out as much as you can about him and report back to me.* ◊ *One person in the group should be prepared to report back to the class on your discussion.* ◊ **report back that** *… They reported back that no laws had actually been broken.* re·ˈport to sb (not used in the progressive tenses) (business) if you **report to** a particular manager in an organization that you work for, they are officially responsible for your work and tell you what to do

> ▼ SYNONYMS
>
> **report**
> story • account • version
>
> These are all words for a written or spoken account of events.
>
> **report** a written or spoken account of an event, especially one that is published or broadcast: *Are these newspaper reports true?*
>
> **story** an account, often spoken, of what happened to sb or of how sth happened; a report of events in a newspaper, magazine or news broadcast: *It was many years before the full story was made public.* ◊ *the front-page story*
>
> **account** a written or spoken description of sth that has happened: *She gave the police a full account of the incident.*
>
> REPORT OR ACCOUNT?
> A **report** is always of recent events, especially news. An **account** may be of recent or past events.
>
> **version** a description of an event from the point of view of a particular person or group of people: *She gave us her version of what had happened that day.*
>
> PATTERNS
> - a report / story **about** sth
> - a **brief / short** report / story / account
> - a **full** report / story / account / version
> - a **news** report / story
> - to **give** a(n) report / account / version

**re·por·tage** /ˌrepɔːˈtɑːʒ, rɪˈpɔːtɪdʒ; NAmE rɪˈpɔːrtɪdʒ, ˌrepɔːrˈtɑːʒ/ noun [U] (formal) the reporting of news or the typical style in which this is done in newspapers, or on TV and radio

**re·port·ed·ly** 🔊+ C1 /rɪˈpɔːtɪdli; NAmE -ˈpɔːrt-/ adv. according to what some people say: *The band have reportedly decided to split up.*

**re·ˌported ˈquestion** noun (grammar) = INDIRECT QUESTION

**re·ported 'speech** (also **indirect 'speech**) noun [U] (grammar) a report of what sb has said that does not use their exact words: *In reported speech, '"I'll come later," he said.' becomes 'He said he'd come later.'*

**re·port·er** ⓘ A2 /rɪˈpɔːtə(r)/; NAmE -ˈpɔːrt-/ noun a person who collects and reports news for newspapers, radio or television: *a news/a newspaper/an investigative reporter* ◇ *a reporter from the 'New York Times'* ⊃ compare JOURNALIST ⊃ see also COURT REPORTER, CUB REPORTER

**re·port·ing** ℹ️ B2 Ⓦ /rɪˈpɔːtɪŋ/; NAmE -ˈpɔːrt-/ noun [U] the presenting of and writing about news on television and radio, and in newspapers: *accurate/balanced/objective reporting* ◇ (BrE) *Reporting restrictions on the trial have been lifted* (= it can now legally be reported).

**re·pose** /rɪˈpəʊz/ noun, verb
■ **noun** [U] (literary) a state of rest, sleep or feeling calm
■ **verb** (literary) **1** [I] + *adv./prep.* (of an object) to be or be kept in a particular place **2** [I] + *adv./prep.* (of a person) to lie or rest in a particular place

**re·posi·tory** /rɪˈpɒzɪtri/; NAmE -ˈpɑːzətɔːri/ noun (pl. **-ies**) (formal) **1** a place where sth is stored in large quantities **2** a person or book that is full of information: *My father is a repository of family history.*

**re·pos·sess** /ˌriːpəˈzes/ verb [usually passive] to take back property or goods from sb who has arranged to buy them but who still owes money for them and cannot pay: **be repossessed** *First I lost my job, then my house was repossessed.* ⊃ compare FORECLOSE

**re·pos·ses·sion** /ˌriːpəˈzeʃn/ noun **1** [U, C] the act of repossessing property, goods, etc: *families threatened with repossession* ◇ *a repossession order* **2** [C] a house, car, etc. that has been repossessed: *Auctions are the best place for buying repossessions.*

**rep·re·hen·sible** /ˌreprɪˈhensəbl/ adj. (formal) morally wrong and deserving criticism SYN **deplorable**

**rep·re·sent** ⓘ B1 Ⓞ /ˌreprɪˈzent/ verb
• ACT/SPEAK FOR SB **1** ℹ️ B1 [often passive] *~sb/sth* to be a member of a group of people and act or speak for them at an event, a meeting, etc: *The competition attracted over 500 contestants representing eight different countries.* ◇ *Local businesses are well represented on the committee* (= there are a lot of people from them on the committee). ◇ *The President was represented at the ceremony by the Vice-President.* **2** ℹ️ B1 *~sb/sth* to act or speak officially for sb and defend their interests: *The union represents over 200 000 teachers.* ◇ *The association was formed to represent the interests of women artists.* ◇ *Ms Dale is representing the defendant* (= is his/her lawyer) *in the case.*
• IN SPORT **3** ℹ️ B1 *~sth* to take part in a sports event for a particular country, city, etc: *He's been chosen to represent Scotland in next year's World Cup Finals.*
• BE SYMBOL **4** ℹ️ B1 *~sth* (not used in the progressive tenses) to be a symbol of sth SYN **symbolize**: *Each colour on the chart represents a different department.* ◇ *Wind direction is represented by arrows.*
• BE EQUAL TO **5** ℹ️ B2 *linking verb + noun* (not used in the progressive tenses) to be sth SYN **constitute**: *This contract represents 20% of the company's annual revenue.* ◇ *to represent value for money* ◇ *He got rid of anyone who represented a threat to his authority.*
• BE PRESENT **6** ℹ️ B2 *be represented* to be present in sth to a particular degree: *Women and men were represented equally on the teams.*
• BE EXAMPLE OF **7** ℹ️ B2 [no passive] *~sth* to be an example or expression of sth SYN **be typical of**: *a project representing all that is good in the community* ◇ *Those comments do not represent the views of us all.*
• IN PICTURE **8** *~sb/sth* (as *sb/sth*) (formal) to show sb/sth, especially in a picture SYN **depict**: *The carvings represent a hunting scene.* ◇ *The results are represented in fig. 3 below.*
• DESCRIBE **9** *~sb/sth* (as *sth*) (formal) to present or describe sb/sth in a particular way, especially when this may not be fair: *The king is represented as a villain in the play.* ◇ *The risks were represented as negligible.*
• MAKE FORMAL STATEMENT **10** *~sth* (*to sb*) | *~that …* (formal) to make a formal statement to sb in authority to make

your opinions known or to protest *They represented their concerns to the authorities.*

**rep·re·sen·ta·tion** ℹ️+ C1 Ⓞ /ˌreprɪzenˈteɪʃn/ noun **1** ℹ️+ C1 [U, C] the act of presenting sb/sth in a particular way; something that shows or describes sth SYN **portray·al**: *the negative representation of single mothers in the media* ◇ *The snake swallowing its tail is a representation of infinity.* **2** ℹ️+ C1 [U] the fact of having representatives who will speak or vote for you or act in your place: *The green movement lacks effective representation in Parliament.* ◇ *The accused was not allowed legal representation.* ⊃ see also PROPORTIONAL REPRESENTATION **3 representations** [pl.] (*especially BrE, formal*) formal statements made to sb in authority, especially in order to make your opinions known or to protest: *We have made representations to the prime minister, but without success.*

**rep·re·sen·ta·tion·al** /ˌreprɪzenˈteɪʃənl/ adj. **1** (specialist) (especially of a style of art or painting) trying to show things as they really are ⊃ compare ABSTRACT **2** involving the act of representing sb/sth: *local representational democracy*

**rep·re·sen·ta·tive** ⓘ B2 Ⓦ /ˌreprɪˈzentətɪv/ noun, adj.
■ **noun 1** ℹ️ B2 a person who has been chosen to speak or vote for sb else or for a group of people, or to take the place of sb else: *our elected representatives in government* ◇ *a union/legal representative* ◇ *He was the Queen's representative at the ceremony.* ◇ *~ of sb/sth a representative of the UN* ◇ *~ from sth The committee includes representatives from industry.* ⊃ WORDFINDER NOTE at UNION **2** ℹ️ B2 (also informal **rep**) a person who works for a company and travels around selling its products: *a sales representative* ◇ *She's our representative in France.* **3** a person who is typical of a particular group: *The singer is regarded as a representative of the youth of her generation.* **4 Representative** (abbr. **Rep.**) (in the US) a member of the House of Representatives, the Lower House of Congress; a member of the House of Representatives in the lower house of a state parliament
■ **adj. 1** ℹ️ *~ (of sb/sth)* typical of a particular group of people; that is a typical example of sth: *Is a questionnaire answered by 500 people truly representative of the population as a whole?* ◇ *The painting is not representative of his work of the period.* **2** ℹ️ B2 [usually before noun] containing or including examples of all the different types of people or things in a large group: *a representative sample of teachers* **3** (of a system of government, etc.) consisting of people who have been chosen to speak or vote for the rest of a group: *a representative democracy* OPP **unrepresentative**

**re·press** /rɪˈpres/ verb **1** *~sth* to try not to have or show an emotion, a feeling, etc. SYN **control**: *to repress a smile* ◇ *He burst in, making no effort to repress his fury.* **2** [often passive] *~sb/sth* to use political and/or military force to control a group of people and limit their freedom SYN **put down, suppress**

**re·pressed** /rɪˈprest/ adj. **1** (of a person) having emotions or desires that are not allowed to be expressed **2** (of emotions) not expressed openly: *repressed anger*

**re·pres·sion** /rɪˈpreʃn/ noun [U] **1** the act of using force to control a group of people and limit their freedom: *government repression* **2** the act of controlling strong emotions and desires and not allowing them to be expressed so that they no longer seem to exist: *sexual repression*

**re·pres·sive** /rɪˈpresɪv/ adj. **1** (of a system of government) controlling people by force and limiting their freedom SYN **dictatorial, tyrannical**: *a repressive regime/measure/law* **2** controlling emotions and desires and not allowing them to be expressed ▸ **re·pres·sive·ly** adv. **re·pres·sive·ness** noun [U]

**re·prieve** /rɪˈpriːv/ verb, noun
■ **verb** [usually passive] (not usually used in the progressive tenses) **1** *~sb* to officially cancel or delay a punishment for a prisoner who is CONDEMNED to death: *a reprieved murderer* **2** *~sth* to officially cancel or delay plans to close sth or end sth: *70 jobs have been reprieved until next April.*

# reprimand

**rep·ri·mand** /ˈreprɪmɑːnd/ *NAmE* -mænd/ *verb* ~ **sb (for sth/for doing sth)** | + **speech** (*formal*) to tell sb officially that you do not approve of them or their actions **SYN** **rebuke**: ~ **sb for sth** *The officers were severely reprimanded for their unprofessional behaviour.* ► **rep·ri·mand** *noun* [C, U]: *He received a severe reprimand for his behaviour.*

**re·print** *verb, noun*
- *verb* /ˌriːˈprɪnt/ [usually passive] ~ **sth** to print more copies of a book, an article, etc. with few or no changes
- *noun* /ˈriːprɪnt/ **1** an act of printing more copies of a book because all the others have been sold **2** a book that has been reprinted

**re·pris·al** /rɪˈpraɪzl/ *noun* [C, U] a violent or aggressive act towards sb because of sth bad that they have done towards you **SYN** **retaliation**: *They did not want to give evidence for fear of reprisals.* ◇ **in ~ for sth** *They shot ten hostages in reprisal for the assassination of their leader.*

**re·prise** /rɪˈpriːz/ *noun* [usually sing.] a repeated part of sth, especially a piece of music

**re·proach** /rɪˈprəʊtʃ/ *noun, verb*
- *noun* (*formal*) **1** [U] blame or criticism for sth you have done: *His voice was full of reproach.* ◇ **above/beyond ~** *The captain's behaviour is beyond reproach* (= so good that you cannot criticize it). **2** [C] a word or remark expressing blame or criticism: *He listened to his wife's bitter reproaches.* **3** [U] a state of shame or loss of honour: *Her actions brought reproach upon herself.* **4** [sing.] ~ **(to sb/sth)** a person or thing that brings shame on sb/sth **SYN** **discredit**: *Such living conditions are a reproach to our society.*
- *verb* (*formal*) **1** ~ **sb (for sth/for doing sth)** | ~ **sb (with sth/with doing sth)** | ~ **(sb)** + **speech** to blame or criticize sb for sth that they have done or not done, because you are disappointed in them: *She was reproached by colleagues for leaking the story to the press.* **2** ~ **yourself (for sth/for doing sth)** | ~ **yourself (with sth)** to feel guilty about sth that you think you should have done in a different way: *He reproached himself for not telling her the truth.*

**re·proach·ful** /rɪˈprəʊtʃfl/ *adj.* expressing blame or criticism: *a reproachful look* ► **re·proach·ful·ly** /-fəli/ *adv.*

**rep·ro·bate** /ˈreprəbeɪt/ *noun* (*formal or humorous*) a person who behaves in a way that society thinks is not moral ► **rep·ro·bate** *adj.* [only before noun]

**re·pro·cess** /ˌriːˈprəʊses/ *verb* ~ **sth** to treat waste material so that it can be used again: *All these countries reprocess nuclear fuel.*

**re·pro·duce** /ˌriːprəˈdjuːs; *NAmE* -ˈduːs/ *verb* **1** [T] ~ **sth** to make a copy of a picture, piece of text, etc: *It is illegal to reproduce these worksheets without permission from the publisher.* ◇ *The photocopier reproduces colours very well.* **2** [T] ~ **sth** to produce sth very similar to sth else in a different medium or context; to make sth happen again in the same way: *The atmosphere of the novel is successfully reproduced in the movie.* ◇ *I was able to reproduce the same results with subsequent tests.* **3** [I, T] if people, plants, animals, etc. **reproduce** or **reproduce themselves**, they produce young: *Most reptiles reproduce by laying eggs on land.* ◇ ~ **itself** *cells reproducing themselves* (= making new ones) ► **re·pro·du·cible** /ˌriːprəˈdjuːsəbl; *NAmE* -ˈduː-/ *adj.*

**re·pro·duc·tion** /ˌriːprəˈdʌkʃn/ *noun* **1** [U] the act or process of producing babies, young animals or plants: *sexual reproduction* **2** [U] the act or process of producing copies of a document, book, picture, etc: *Use a black pen on white paper to ensure good reproduction.* **3** [U] the quality of recorded sound: *Digital recording gives excellent sound reproduction.* **4** [C] a thing that has been reproduced, especially a copy of a work of art: *a catalogue with colour reproductions of the paintings for sale* ◇ *reproduction furniture* (= furniture made as a copy of an earlier style)

**re·pro·duct·ive** /ˌriːprəˈdʌktɪv/ *adj.* [only before noun] connected with REPRODUCING babies, young animals or plants: *reproductive organs*

**re·proof** /rɪˈpruːf/ *noun* (*formal*) **1** [U] blame or DISAPPROVAL: *His words were a mixture of pity and reproof.* **2** [C] a remark that expresses blame or disapproval **SYN** **rebuke**: *She received a mild reproof from the teacher.*

**re·prove** /rɪˈpruːv/ *verb* ~ **sb (for sth/for doing sth)** | ~ **(sb)** + **speech** (*formal*) to tell sb that you do not approve of sth that they have done **SYN** **rebuke**: *He reproved her for rushing away.* ► **re·prov·ing** *adj.* [usually before noun]: *a reproving glance* **re·prov·ing·ly** *adv.*

**rep·tile** /ˈreptaɪl; *NAmE* also -tl/ *noun* any animal that has cold blood and skin covered in SCALES, and that lays eggs. Snakes, CROCODILES and TORTOISES are all reptiles. ⊃ **VISUAL VOCAB** page V3 ⊃ compare AMPHIBIAN ► **rep·til·ian** /repˈtɪliən/ *adj.*: *our reptilian ancestors* ◇ (*figurative*) *He licked his lips in an unpleasantly reptilian way.*

**re·pub·lic** /rɪˈpʌblɪk/ *noun* a country that is governed by a president and politicians elected by the people and where there is no king or queen: *newly independent republics* ◇ *the Republic of Ireland* ⊃ see also BANANA REPUBLIC ⊃ compare MONARCHY

**re·pub·lic·an** /rɪˈpʌblɪkən/ *noun, adj.*
- *noun* **1** a person who supports a form of government with a president and politicians elected by the people and with no king or queen ⊃ compare ROYALIST **2 Republican** (*abbr.* R, Rep.) a member or supporter of the Republican Party of the US ⊃ compare DEMOCRAT **3 Republican** a person from Northern Ireland who believes that Northern Ireland should be part of the Republic of Ireland and not part of the United Kingdom ⊃ compare LOYALIST
- *adj.* **1** connected with or like a republic; supporting the principles of a republic: *a republican government/movement* **2** (*also* **Republican**) (*abbr.* R, Rep.) connected with the Republican Party in the US **3** (*also* **Republican**) connected with or supporting the Republicans in Northern Ireland ► **re·pub·lic·an·ism** (*also* **Re·pub·lic·an·ism**) *noun* [U]: *a strong commitment to Republicanism*

**the Re·publican Party** *noun* [sing.] one of the two main political parties in the US, usually considered to support conservative views, and to want to limit the power of central government ⊃ compare DEMOCRATIC PARTY

**re·pu·di·ate** /rɪˈpjuːdieɪt/ *verb* (*formal*) **1** ~ **sth** to refuse to accept sth **SYN** **reject**: *to repudiate a suggestion* **2** ~ **sth** to say officially and/or publicly that sth is not true **SYN** **deny**: *to repudiate a report* **3** ~ **sb** (*old-fashioned*) to refuse to be connected with sb any longer **SYN** **disown**: *He repudiated his first wife and married her sister.* ► **re·pu·di·ation** /rɪˌpjuːdiˈeɪʃn/ *noun* [U]

**re·pug·nance** /rɪˈpʌɡnəns/ *noun* [U] (*formal*) a very strong feeling of dislike for sth **SYN** **repulsion**: *She was trying to overcome her physical repugnance for him.*

**re·pug·nant** /rɪˈpʌɡnənt/ *adj.* [not usually before noun] (*formal*) making you feel strong dislike **SYN** **repulsive**: *We found his suggestion absolutely repugnant.* ◇ ~ **to sb** *The idea of eating meat was repugnant to her.*

**re·pulse** /rɪˈpʌls/ *verb* (*formal*) **1** [usually passive] ~ **sb** to make sb feel strong dislike **SYN** **repel, disgust**: *I was repulsed by the horrible smell.* **2** ~ **sb/sth** to fight sb who is attacking you and drive them away **SYN** **repel**: *to repulse an attack/invasion/offensive* **3** ~ **sb/sth** to refuse to accept sb's help, attempts to be friendly, etc. **SYN** **reject**: *Each time I tried to help I was repulsed.* ◇ *She repulsed his advances.*

**re·pul·sion** /rɪˈpʌlʃn/ *noun* [U] **1** a feeling of very strong dislike of sth that you find extremely unpleasant **2** (*physics*) the force by which objects tend to push each other away: *the forces of attraction and repulsion* ⊃ see also REPEL ⊃ compare ATTRACTION

**re·pul·sive** /rɪˈpʌlsɪv/ *adj.* **1** causing a feeling of strong dislike; very unpleasant **SYN** **disgusting**: *a repulsive sight/smell/habit* ◇ *What a repulsive man!* ⊃ SYNONYMS at DISGUSTING **2** (*physics*) causing repulsion (= a force that pushes away): *repulsive forces* ► **re·pul·sive·ly** *adv.*: *repulsively ugly*

**re·pur·pose** /ˌriːˈpɜːpəs; *NAmE* -ˈpɜːrp-/ *verb* ~ **sth** to change sth slightly in order to make it suitable for a new purpose: *Content repurposed from old media is legitimate internet content.*

**rep·ut·able** /ˈrepjətəbl/ *adj.* that people consider to be honest; having a good reputation SYN **respected**: *a reputable dealer/company/supplier* ⊃ compare DISREPUTABLE

**repu·ta·tion** ⓘ B2 /ˌrepjuˈteɪʃn/ *noun* [C, U] the opinion that people have about what sb/sth is like, based on what has happened in the past: *to have a good/bad reputation* ◊ *to build/earn a reputation* ◊ *~ as sth She soon established a reputation as a first-class cook.* ◊ *~ for (doing) sth The company enjoys an international reputation for quality of design.* ◊ *to damage/tarnish/ruin sb's reputation* ◊ *The weather in England is living up to its reputation* (= is exactly as expected).

**re·pute** /rɪˈpjuːt/ *noun* [U] (*formal*) the opinion that people have of sb/sth SYN **reputation**: *of (...) ~ She is a writer of international repute.* ◊ *My parents were artists of (some) repute* (= having a very good reputation).

**re·puted** /rɪˈpjuːtɪd/ *adj.* [not usually before noun] generally thought to be sth or to have done sth, although this is not certain SYN **rumoured**: *~ (to be sth) He is reputed to be the best heart surgeon in the country.* ◊ *~ (to have done sth) The house is wrongly reputed to have been the poet's birthplace.* ◊ *She sold her share of the company for a reputed £7 million.* ▶ **re·puted·ly** *adv.*

**re·quest** ⓘ B2 /rɪˈkwest/ *noun, verb*
- *noun* **1** B2 the action of asking for sth formally and politely; a thing that you formally ask for: *~ for sth a request for information* ◊ *They made a request for further aid.* ◊ *~ to do sth He submitted a request to adopt a flexible working routine.* ◊ *to grant a request* ◊ *to refuse/decline/reject/deny a request* ◊ *at sb's ~* | *at the ~ of sth He was there at the request of his manager* (= because his manager had asked him to go). ◊ *on ~ Application forms are available on request.* ◊ *~ that... She left her address with a request that any mail should be sent on to her.* **2** an instruction to a computer to perform a task **3** a song or tune that sb asks to have played on a radio programme: *The next request is from a listener in Aberdeen.*
- *verb* B1 (*formal*) to ask for sth or ask sb to do sth in a polite or formal way: *~ sth She requested permission to film at the White House.* ◊ *~ sth from sb/sth The government has requested information from the companies involved in the scandal.* ◊ *be requested to do sth Visitors are requested not to touch the exhibits.* ◊ *~ that... She requested that no one be told of her decision until the next meeting.* ◊ *+ speech 'Please come with me,' he requested.*

**re·quiem** /ˈrekwiəm, -kwiem/ (*also* **requiem 'mass**) *noun* **1** a Christian ceremony for a person who has recently died, at which people say prayers for his or her soul **2** a piece of music for this ceremony

**re·quire** ⓘ B1 ⓦ /rɪˈkwaɪə(r)/ *verb* (not usually used in the progressive tenses) (*formal*) **1** B1 to need sth; to depend on sb/sth: *~ sth These pets require a lot of care and attention.* ◊ *This condition requires urgent treatment.* ◊ *Do you require anything else?* (= in a shop/store, for example) ◊ *~ sb/sth to do sth True marriage requires us to show trust and loyalty.* ◊ *~ that... The situation required that he be present.* ◊ (*BrE also*) *The situation required that he should be present.* ◊ *~ doing sth Lentils do not require soaking before cooking.* **2** B2 [often passive] to make sb do or have sth, especially because it is necessary according to a particular law or set of rules: *be required (by sth) The wearing of seat belts is required by law.* ◊ *'Hamlet' is required reading* (= must be read) *for this course.* ◊ *Several students failed to reach the required standard.* ◊ *be required of sb What exactly is required of a receptionist* (= what are they expected to do)? ◊ *be required to do sth All candidates will be required to take a short test.* ◊ *~ that... We require that you comply with the following rules:...* ⊃ SYNONYMS at DEMAND

**re·quire·ment** ⓘ B2 ⓦ /rɪˈkwaɪəmənt/; *NAmE* -ərm-/ *noun* (*formal*) **1** B2 (*usually* **requirements**) [pl.] something that you need or want: *the basic requirements of life* ◊ *a software solution to meet your requirements* ◊ *All products can be customized to suit your specific requirements.* ◊ *These goods are surplus to requirements* (= more

1317 **research**

than we need). **2** B2 something that you must have in order to do sth else: *to meet/fulfil/satisfy the requirements* ◊ *What is the minimum entry requirement for this course?*

**requis·ite** /ˈrekwɪzɪt/ *adj., noun*
- *adj.* [only before noun] (*formal*) necessary for a particular purpose: *She lacks the requisite experience for the job.*
- *noun* (*formal*) something that you need for a particular purpose: *toilet requisites* (= soap, TOOTHPASTE, etc.) ◊ *~ for/of sth A university degree has become a requisite for entry into most professions.* ⊃ compare PREREQUISITE

**requi·si·tion** /ˌrekwɪˈzɪʃn/ *noun, verb*
- *noun* [C, U] a formal, official written request or demand for sth: *the requisition of ships by the government* ◊ *a requisition form/order*
- *verb ~ sth* to officially demand the use of a building, vehicle, etc., especially during a war or an emergency: *The school was requisitioned as a military hospital.*

**re·quite** /rɪˈkwaɪt/ *verb ~ sth* (*formal*) to give sth such as love, a favour, kind treatment, etc. in return for what sb has given you: *requited love* ⊃ compare UNREQUITED

**reroute** /ˌriːˈruːt/; *NAmE also* -ˈraʊt/ *verb ~ sth* to change the route that a road, vehicle, phone call, etc. normally follows

**rerun** *noun, verb*
- *noun* /ˈriːrʌn/ **1** a television programme that is shown again: *reruns of old TV shows* **2** an event, such as a race or competition, that is held again **3** something that is done in the same way as sth in the past: *We wanted to avoid a rerun of last year's disastrous trip.*
- *verb* /ˌriːˈrʌn/ (**re·run·ning**, **reran** /-ˈræn/, **rerun**) **1** *~ sth* to show a film, television programme, etc. again **2** *~ sth* to do sth again in a similar way: *to rerun an experiment* **3** *~ sth* to run a race again

**re·sale** /ˈriːseɪl/ *noun* [U] the sale to another person of sth that you have bought: *the resale value of a car*

**re·sched·ule** /ˌriːˈʃedjuːl/; *NAmE* -ˈskedʒuː-/ *verb* [often passive] *~ sth (for/to sth)* to change the time at which sth has been arranged to happen, especially so that it takes place later: *The meeting has been rescheduled for next week.* **2** *~ sth* (*finance*) to arrange for sb to pay back money that they have borrowed at a later date than was originally agreed ▶ **re·sched·ul·ing** *noun* [U, sing.]

**re·scind** /rɪˈsɪnd/ *verb ~ sth* (*formal*) to officially state that a law, contract, decision, etc. no longer has any legal force SYN **revoke**

**re·scis·sion** /rɪˈsɪʒn/ *noun* (*formal*) the act of cancelling or ending a law, an order, or an agreement

**res·cue** ⓘ B2 /ˈreskjuː/ *verb, noun*
- *verb* B2 to save sb/sth from a dangerous or harmful situation: *~ sb/sth from sth/sb The coastguard rescued six people from the sinking boat.* ◊ *You rescued me from an embarrassing situation.* ◊ *~ sb/sth from doing sth He rescued a child from drowning.* ◊ *~ sb/sth The hostages were rescued and brought to safety.* ◊ *~ sb/sth + adj. She had despaired of ever being rescued alive.* ⊃ SYNONYMS at SAVE ▶ **res·cuer** *noun*
- *noun* **1** B2 [U] the act of saving sb/sth from a dangerous or difficult situation; the fact of being saved: *We had given up hope of rescue.* ◊ *A wealthy benefactor came to their rescue with a generous donation.* ◊ *a rescue operation/mission* ◊ *a mountain rescue team* ◊ *rescue helicopters/boats/workers* **2** B2 [C] an occasion when sb/sth is saved from a dangerous or difficult situation: *Ten fishermen were saved in a daring sea rescue.*

**ˈrescue worker** *noun* a person whose job is to try to save people from dangerous or difficult situations, especially after an accident or a disaster: *Rescue workers are working under very difficult conditions to find survivors from the blast.*

**re·search** ⓘ A2 ⓦ *noun, verb*
- *noun* ⓘ A2 /rɪˈsɜːtʃ, ˈriːsɜːtʃ/; *NAmE* ˈriːsɜːrtʃ, rɪˈsɜːrtʃ/ [U] a careful study of a subject, especially in order to discover new facts or information about it: *scientific/medical/academic research* ◊ *to do/conduct/undertake research* ◊ *I've done some research to find out the cheapest way of travelling there.* ◊ *~ into sth He has carried out extensive*

# researcher 1318

research into renewable energy sources. ◊ **~on sth/sb** *Recent research on deaf children has produced some interesting findings about their speech.* ◊ **according to~** *According to recent research, more people are going to the movies than ever before.* ◊ *a research project/grant* HELP The plural form **researches** is also sometimes used in *BrE*, but is much less frequent: *What have their researches shown?* ⇨ WORDFINDER NOTE at SCIENCE ⇨ see also ACTION RESEARCH, MARKET RESEARCH, OPERATIONAL RESEARCH

■ **verb** ⓘ A2 /rɪˈsɜːtʃ/ NAmE rɪˈsɜːrtʃ/ [I, T] to study sth carefully and try to discover new facts about it: **~(sth)** *to research a topic/subject* ◊ *She's in New York researching her new book* (= finding facts and information to put in it). ◊ *They spent days researching in the school library.* ◊ **~how, what, etc…** *We have to research how the product will actually be used.*

**reˈsearch and deˈvelopment** *noun* [U] (*abbr.* **R & D**) (in industry, etc.) work that tries to find new products and processes or to improve existing ones

**re·search·er** ⓘ A2 Ⓦ /rɪˈsɜːtʃə(r), ˈriːsɜːtʃə(r)/ NAmE /rɪˈsɜːrtʃər, ˈriːsɜːrtʃər/ *noun* a person who studies sth carefully and tries to discover new facts about it: *European researchers say olive oil could help prevent cancer.* ◊ **~in sth** *a leading researcher in the field of artificial intelligence*

**re·sect** /rɪˈsekt/ *verb* **~sth** (*medical*) to cut out part of an organ or a piece of TISSUE from the body ▶ **re·sec·tion** /-ˈsekʃn/ *noun* [U, C]

**re·sell** /ˌriːˈsel/ *verb* (**re·sold, re·sold** /-ˈsəʊld/) **~sth** to sell sth that you have bought: *He resells the goods at a profit.*

**re·sem·blance** /rɪˈzembləns/ *noun* [C, U] the fact of being or looking similar to sb/sth SYN **likeness**: *a striking/close/strong resemblance* ◊ *family resemblances* ◊ **~to sb/sth** *She bears an uncanny resemblance to Dido.* ◊ *The movie bears little resemblance to the original novel.* ◊ **~between A and B** *The resemblance between the two signatures was remarkable.*

**re·sem·ble** ⓘ+ C1 /rɪˈzembl/ *verb* [no passive] (not used in the progressive tenses) **~sb/sth** to look like or be similar to another person or thing: *She closely resembles her sister.* ◊ *So many hotels resemble each other.* ◊ *The plant resembles grass in appearance.*

**re·sent** /rɪˈzent/ *verb* to feel bitter or angry about sth, especially because you feel it is unfair: **~sth/sb** *I deeply resented her criticism.* ◊ **~doing sth** *He bitterly resents being treated like a child.* ◊ **~sb doing sth** *She resented him making all the decisions.* ◊ (*formal*) *She resented his making all the decisions.*

**re·sent·ful** /rɪˈzentfl/ *adj.* feeling bitter or angry about sth that you think is unfair: *a resentful look* ◊ **~of/at/about sth** *They seemed to be resentful of our presence there.* ◊ *She was resentful at having been left out of the team.* ▶ **re·sent·ful·ly** /-fəli/ *adv.*

**re·sent·ment** /rɪˈzentmənt/ *noun* [U, sing.] **~(towards/against sb)** a feeling of anger or unhappiness about sth that you think is unfair: *to feel/harbour/bear resentment towards/against sb* ◊ *She could not conceal the deep resentment she felt at the way she had been treated.*

**re·ser·va·tion** ⓘ B1 /ˌrezəˈveɪʃn; NAmE -zərˈv-/ *noun* **1** [C] an arrangement for a seat on a plane or train, a room in a hotel, etc. to be kept for you: *I'll call the restaurant and make a reservation.* ◊ *We have a reservation in the name of Grant.* ⇨ WORDFINDER NOTE at HOTEL ⇨ compare BOOKING **2** [C, U] a feeling of doubt about a plan or an idea SYN **misgiving**: *reservations about sb/sth I have serious reservations about his ability to do the job.* ◊ **without~** *They support the measures without reservation* (= completely). **3** (*also* **reˈserve**) [C] an area of land in the US that is kept separate for Native Americans to live in **4** [C] = RESERVATION POLICY ⇨ see also CENTRAL RESERVATION

**ˌreserˈvation policy** (*also* **re·ser·va·tion**) *noun* [U] (in India) the policy of keeping a fixed number of jobs or places in schools, colleges, etc. for people who are members of SCHEDULED CASTES, SCHEDULED TRIBES or other BACKWARD CLASSES

**re·serve** ⓘ B2 /rɪˈzɜːv; NAmE -ˈzɜːrv/ *noun, verb*

■ *noun*
• SUPPLY **1** ⓘ B2 [C, usually pl.] a supply of sth that is available to be used in the future or when it is needed: *cash/foreign currency reserves* ◊ *large oil and gas reserves* ◊ **~of sth** *He discovered unexpected reserves of strength.* ⇨ see also GOLD RESERVE
• PROTECTED LAND **2** ⓘ B2 (*NAmE also* **pre·serve**) [C] a piece of land that is a protected area for animals, plants, etc: *a wildlife/forest reserve* ⇨ see also GAME RESERVE, NATURE RESERVE **3** [C] = RESERVATION (3)
• QUALITY/FEELING **4** [U] the quality that sb has when they do not talk easily to other people about their ideas, feelings, etc. SYN **reticence**: *She found it difficult to make friends because of her natural reserve.* **5** [U] (*formal*) a feeling that you do not want to accept or agree to sth, etc. until you are quite sure that it is all right to do so: **with~** *Any contract should be treated with reserve until it has been checked.* ◊ **without~** *She trusted him without reserve* (= completely).
• IN SPORT **6** [C] an extra player who plays in a team when one of the other players is injured or not available to play **7 the reserves** [pl.] a team that is below the level of the main team
• MILITARY FORCE **8 the reserve** [sing.] (*also* **the reserves** [pl.]) an extra military force, etc. that is not part of a country's regular forces, but is available to be used when needed: *the Army Reserve* ◊ *the reserve police*
• PRICE **9** (*also* **reˈserve price**) [C] the lowest price that sb will accept for sth, especially sth that is sold at an AUCTION

IDM **in reˈserve** available to be used in the future or when needed: *The money was being kept in reserve for their retirement.* ◊ *200 police officers were held in reserve.*

■ *verb* **1** ⓘ B2 to ask for a seat, table, room, etc. to be available for you or sb else at a future time SYN **book**: **~sth for sb/sth** *I'd like to reserve a table for three for eight o'clock.* ◊ **~sth** *I've reserved a room in the name of Jones.* ⇨ compare BOOK **2** ⓘ B2 **~sth for sb/sth** to keep sth for sb/sth, so that it cannot be used by any other person or for any other reason: *These seats are reserved for special guests.* **3 ~sth** to have or keep a particular power: *The management reserves the right to refuse admission.* ◊ (*law*) *All rights reserved* (= nobody else can publish or copy this).

IDM **reˌserve (your) deˈcision/ˈjudgement** to not decide or make a judgement about sth until a later time: *I'd prefer to reserve judgement until I know all the facts.*

**reˈserve bank** *noun* **1** (in the US) a regional bank that operates according to the policies of the FEDERAL RESERVE SYSTEM **2** (*AustralE, NZE, SAfrE*) a central bank

**re·served** /rɪˈzɜːvd; NAmE -ˈzɜːrvd/ *adj.* (of a person or their character) slow or unwilling to show feelings or express opinions SYN **shy** ⇨ compare UNRESERVED

**re·serv·ist** /rɪˈzɜːvɪst; NAmE -ˈzɜːrv-/ *noun* a soldier, etc. who is a member of the RESERVES (= a military force that can be used in an emergency)

**res·er·voir** /ˈrezəvwɑː(r); NAmE -zərv-/ *noun* **1** a natural or artificial lake where water is stored before it is taken by pipes to houses, etc. **2** (*formal*) a large amount of sth that is available to be used **3** (*specialist*) a place in an engine or a machine where a liquid is kept before it is used

**reset** /ˌriːˈset/ *verb* (**re·set·ting, reset, reset**) **1 ~sth (to sth)** | **~sth to do sth** to change a machine, an instrument or a control so that it gives a different time or number or is ready to use again: *You need to reset your watch to local time.* **2** [*often passive*] **~sth** to place sth in the correct position again: *to reset a broken bone*

**re·set·tle** /ˌriːˈsetl/ *verb* **1** [T, usually passive, I] to help people go and live in a new country or area; to go and live in a new country or area: (**be resettled**) **+ adv./prep.** *Many of the refugees were resettled in Britain and Canada.* **2** [T, usually passive] to start to use an area again as a place to live: **be resettled** *The region was only resettled 200 years later.* **3** [I, T] **~(yourself)** to make yourself comfortable in a new position: *The birds flew around and then resettled on the pond.* ▶ **re·set·tle·ment** *noun* [U]: *the resettlement of refugees* ◊ *a resettlement agency*

**re·shape** /ˌriːˈʃeɪp/ *verb* **~sth** to change the shape or structure of sth

**re·shuf·fle** /ˌriːˈʃʌfl/ (*also less frequent* **shuf·fle**) *verb* [T, I] **~(sth)** to change around the jobs that a group of people do, for example in a government: *The prime minister eventually decided against reshuffling the Cabinet.* ▶ **re·shuf·fle** /ˈriːʃʌfl/ *noun*: *a Cabinet reshuffle*

**res·ide** /rɪˈzaɪd/ *verb* [I] + *adv.* / *prep.* (*formal*) to live in a particular place: *He returned to Britain in 1939, having resided abroad for many years.*
**PHRV re·side in sb/sth** to be in sb/sth; to be caused by sth: *The source of the problem resides in the fact that the currency is too strong.* **re·side in/with sb/sth** (of a power, a right, etc.) to belong to sb/sth **SYN be vested in**: *The ultimate authority resides with the board of directors.*

**resi·dence** /ˈrezɪdəns/ *noun* (*formal*) **1** [C] a house, especially a large or impressive one: *a desirable family residence for sale* (= for example, in an advertisement) ◊ *10 Downing Street is the British Prime Minister's official residence.* **2** [U] the state of living in a particular place: *They were not able to take up residence in their new home until the spring.* ◊ *Please state your occupation and place of residence.* ◊ *in ~ The flag flies when the Queen is in residence.* ⊃ see also HALL OF RESIDENCE **3** (*also* **resi·dency**) [U] permission to live in a country that is not your own: *They have been denied residence in this country.* ◊ *a residence permit*
**IDM in ˈresidence** (of a writer, an artist, a musician, etc.) having an official position in a particular place such as a college or university: *creative writing classes given by the writer in residence*

**ˈresidence hall** *noun* (*NAmE*) = HALL OF RESIDENCE

**resi·dency** /ˈrezɪdənsi/ *noun* (*pl.* **-ies**) (*formal*) **1** [U] = RESIDENCE (3): *She has been granted permanent residency in Britain.* **2** [U, C] the period of time that an artist, a writer or a musician spends working for a particular institution **3** [U] the state of living in a particular place: *a residency requirement for students* **4** [U, C] (*especially NAmE*) the period of time when a doctor working in a hospital receives special advanced training **5** (*also* **resi·dence**) [C] the official house of sb such as an AMBASSADOR

**resi·dent** /ˈrezɪdənt/ *noun, adj.*
■ *noun* **1** a person who lives in a particular place or who has their home there: *a resident of the United States* ◊ *The proposals sparked concern among local residents.* ⊃ see also PERMANENT RESIDENT **2** (*formal*) a person who is staying in a hotel: *The hotel restaurant is open to non-residents.* **3** a doctor working in a hospital in the US who is receiving special advanced training ⊃ compare REGISTRAR
■ *adj.* living in a particular place: *the town's resident population* (= not tourists or visitors) ◊ *to be resident abroad/in the UK* ◊ *Tom's our resident expert* (= our own expert) *on foreign movies.*

**ˈresident ˈalien** *noun* (*NAmE, law*) a person from another country who has permission to stay in the US

**resi·den·tial** /ˌrezɪˈdenʃl/ *adj.* [usually before noun] **1** (of an area of a town) suitable for living in; consisting of houses rather than factories or offices: *a quiet residential area* ⊃ WORDFINDER NOTE *at* LOCATION **2** (of a job, a course, etc.) requiring a person to live at a particular place; offering living accommodation: *a residential language course* ◊ *a residential home for the elderly* ◊ *residential care for children*

**ˈresidents' association** *noun* a group of people who live in a particular area and join together to discuss the problems of that area

**re·sid·ual** /rɪˈzɪdjuəl; *NAmE* -dʒu-/ *adj.* [only before noun] (*formal*) left at the end of a process **SYN outstanding**: *There are still a few residual problems with the computer program.*

**re·sidu·ary** /rɪˈzɪdjuəri; *NAmE* -dʒueri/ *adj.* **1** (*law*) left from the money and property of a person who has died after all debts, gifts, etc. have been paid **2** (*specialist*) left at the end of a process

**resi·due** /ˈrezɪdjuː; *NAmE* -duː/ *noun* **1** [C] a small amount of sth that remains at the end of a process: *pesticide residues in fruit and vegetables* **2** (*law*) the part of the money, property, etc. of a person who has died that remains after all the debts, gifts, etc. have been paid: *The residue of the estate was divided equally among his children.*

**re·sign** /rɪˈzaɪn/ *verb* [I, T] to officially tell sb that you are leaving your job, an organization, etc: *She was forced to resign due to ill health.* ◊ *~ as sth He resigned as manager after eight years.* ◊ *~ from sth Two members resigned from the board in protest.* ◊ *~ sth My father resigned his directorship last year.*
**PHRV re·ˈsign yourself to sth** to accept sth unpleasant that cannot be changed or avoided: *She resigned herself to her fate.* ◊ **resign yourself to doing sth** *We had to resign ourselves to making a loss on the sale.*

**res·ig·na·tion** /ˌrezɪɡˈneɪʃn/ *noun* **1** [U, C] the act of giving up your job or position; the occasion when you do this: *a letter of resignation* ◊ *There were calls for her resignation from the board of directors.* ◊ *Further resignations are expected.* **2** [C] a letter, for example to your employers, to say that you are giving up your job or position: *to offer/hand in/tender your resignation* ◊ *We haven't received his resignation yet.* **3** [U] the quality of being willing to accept a difficult or unpleasant situation that you cannot change: *They accepted their defeat with resignation.*

**re·signed** /rɪˈzaɪnd/ *adj.* being willing to calmly accept sth unpleasant or difficult that you cannot change: *a resigned sigh* ◊ *~ to (doing) sth He was resigned to never seeing his birthplace again.* ▶ **re·sign·ed·ly** /-ˈzaɪnɪdli/ *adv.*: *'I suppose you're right,' she said resignedly.*

**re·sili·ence** /rɪˈzɪliəns/ (*also less frequent* **re·sili·ency** /rɪˈzɪliənsi/) *noun* **1** the ability of people or things to recover quickly after sth unpleasant, such as shock, injury, etc. **2** the ability of a substance to return to its original shape after it has been bent, stretched or pressed

**re·sili·ent** /rɪˈzɪliənt/ *adj.* **1** able to recover quickly after sth unpleasant such as shock, injury, etc: *He'll get over it—young people are amazingly resilient.* **2** (of a substance) returning to its original shape after being bent, stretched, or pressed ▶ **re·sili·ent·ly** *adv.*

**resin** /ˈrezɪn; *NAmE* -zn/ *noun* [C, U] **1** a sticky substance that is produced by some trees and is used in making VARNISH, medicine, etc. **2** an artificial substance similar to resin, used in making plastics ▶ **res·in·ous** /ˈrezɪnəs/ *adj.*: *the resinous scent of pine trees*

**re·sist** /rɪˈzɪst/ *verb* **1** [T, I] to refuse to accept sth and try to stop it from happening **SYN oppose**: *~ sth They are determined to resist pressure to change the law.* ◊ *~ doing sth The bank strongly resisted cutting interest rates.* ◊ *Residents who oppose the plans are threatening to resist.* **2** [I, T] to fight back when attacked; to use force to stop sth from happening: *He tried to pin me down, but I resisted.* ◊ *~ sth She was charged with resisting arrest.* **3** [T] (usually in negative sentences) to stop yourself from having sth you like or doing sth you very much want to do: *~ sth I finished the cake. I couldn't resist it.* ◊ *The Chancellor resisted the temptation to raise business taxes.* ◊ *I found the temptation to miss the class too hard to resist.* ◊ *~ doing sth He couldn't resist showing off his new car.* **4** [T] *~ sth* to not be harmed or damaged by sth: *A healthy diet should help your body resist infection.* ◊ *The castle was built to resist attack.*

**re·sist·ance** /rɪˈzɪstəns/ *noun* **1** [U, sing.] dislike of or opposition to a plan, an idea, etc.; the act of refusing to obey: *As with all new ideas it met with resistance.* ◊ *~ to sb/sth There has been a lot of resistance to this new law.* ◊ *Resistance to change has nearly destroyed the industry.* **2** [U, sing.] the act of using force to oppose sb/sth: *armed resistance* ◊ *The defenders put up a strong resistance.* ◊ *~ to sb/sth The demonstrators offered little or no resistance to the police.* ⊃ see also PASSIVE RESISTANCE **3** [U, sing.] *~ (to sth)* the power not to be affected by sth: *AIDS lowers the body's resistance to infection.* **4** [U, sing.] *~ (to sth)* a force that stops sth moving or makes it move more slowly: *wind/air resistance* (= in the design of planes or cars) **5** [U, C] (*physics*) (*symb* R) the opposition of a substance or device to the flow of an electrical current **6** (*often* **the Resistance**) [sing. + sing./pl. v.] a secret organization that resists the authorities, especially in a country that an enemy has control of: *resistance fighters* ⊃ see also PIÈCE DE RÉSISTANCE

# resistant

**IDM** **(choose, follow, take, etc.) the line/path of least re·sist·ance** (to choose, etc.) the easiest way of doing sth
**re·sist·ant** W /rɪˈzɪstənt/ adj. **1** ~ **(to sth)** not affected by sth; able to resist sth: *plants that are resistant to disease* **2** ~ **(to sth)** opposing sth and trying to stop it happening: *Elderly people are not always resistant to change.* **3** **-resistant** (in adjectives) not damaged by the thing mentioned: *disease-resistant plants* ◇ *fire-resistant materials* ⊃ see also HEAT-RESISTANT, WATER-RESISTANT
**re·sist·er** /rɪˈzɪstə(r)/ noun a person who resists sb/sth
**re·sist·ive** /rɪˈzɪstɪv/ adj. **1** able to survive or deal with the action or effect of sth **2** (*physics*) relating to electrical RESISTANCE ▸ **re·sist·iv·ity** /ˌriːzɪˈstɪvəti/ noun [U, C]
**re·sist·or** /rɪˈzɪstə(r)/ noun (*physics*) a device that has RESISTANCE to an electric current in a CIRCUIT
**re·sit** /ˌriːˈsɪt/ verb (*BrE*) [T, I] (**re·sit·ting, resat, resat** /-ˈsæt/) (also **re·take** *BrE, NAmE*) ~ **(sth)** to take an exam or a test again, usually after failing it the first time ⊃ WORDFINDER NOTE at EXAM ▸ **re·sit** /ˈriːsɪt/ (also **re·take**) noun: *Students are only allowed one resit.*
**re·size** /ˌriːˈsaɪz/ verb ~ **sth** to make sth bigger or smaller, especially an image on a computer screen
**re·skill** /ˌriːˈskɪl/ verb [I, T] ~ **(sb)** to learn new skills so that you can do a new job; to teach sb new skills
**reso·lute** /ˈrezəluːt/ adj. strong and determined: *resolute leadership* ◇ *He became even more resolute in his opposition to the plan.* **OPP** irresolute ▸ **reso·lute·ly** adv.: *They remain resolutely opposed to the idea.* **reso·lute·ness** noun [U]
**reso·lu·tion** 𝒞+ B2 W /ˌrezəˈluːʃn/ noun **1** 𝒞+ B2 [C] a definite decision to do or not to do sth: *Have you made any New Year's resolutions* (= for example, to give up smoking from 1 January)? ◇ ~ **to do sth** *She made a resolution to visit her relatives more often.* **2** 𝒞+ C1 [C] a formal statement of an opinion agreed on by a committee or a council, especially by means of a vote: *to pass/adopt/approve a resolution* ⊃ see also JOINT RESOLUTION **3** 𝒞+ C1 [U, sing.] the act of solving or settling a problem, argument, etc. **SYN** settlement: *dispute/conflict resolution* ◇ ~ **to sth** *Hopes of a peaceful resolution to the conflict were fading.* **4** [U] the quality of being resolute or determined **SYN** resolve: *The reforms owe a great deal to the resolution of one man.* **5** [U, sing.] the power of a computer screen, printer, etc. to give a clear image, depending on the size of the DOTS (= marks) that make up the image: *The graphics look fine, even at low resolution.* ⊃ see also HIGH-RESOLUTION, LOW-RESOLUTION
**re·solve** 𝒞 B2 W /rɪˈzɒlv/; *NAmE* -ˈzɑːlv/ verb, noun
■ verb (*formal*) **1** 𝒞 B2 [T] ~ **sth/itself** to find an acceptable solution to a problem or difficulty **SYN** settle: *to resolve an issue/a dispute/a conflict/a crisis* ◇ *Attempts are being made to resolve the problem of security in schools.* **2** [T, I] to make a definite decision to do sth: ~ **to do sth** *He resolved not to tell her the truth.* ◇ ~ **(that) …** *She resolved that she would never see him again.* ◇ ~ **on doing sth** *We had resolved on making an early start.* **3** [T] (of a committee, meeting, etc.) to reach a decision by means of a formal vote: *it is resolved that …* *It was resolved that the matter be referred to a higher authority.* ◇ ~ **that …** *They resolved that the matter be referred to a higher authority.* ◇ ~ **to do sth** *The Supreme Council resolved to resume control over the national press.*
**PHRV** **re·solve sth into sth** | **re·solve sth into sth 1** to separate or to be separated into its parts: *to resolve a complex argument into its basic elements* **2** (of sth seen or heard at a distance) to gradually turn into a different form when it is seen or heard more clearly: *The orange light resolved itself into four lanterns.* **3** to gradually become or be understood as sth: *The discussion eventually resolved itself into two main issues.*
■ noun [U] (*formal*) a determined desire to achieve sth **SYN** resolution: *The difficulties in her way merely strengthened her resolve.* ◇ ~ **to do sth** *The government reiterated its resolve to uncover the truth.*
**re·solved** /rɪˈzɒlvd/; *NAmE* -ˈzɑːlvd/ adj. [not before noun] ~ **(to do sth)** (*formal*) determined: *I was resolved not to see him.*

**res·on·ance** /ˈrezənəns/ noun **1** [U] (*formal*) (of sound) the quality of being resonant: *Her voice had a strang and thrilling resonance.* **2** [C, U] (*specialist*) the sound or other VIBRATION produced in an object by sound or VIBRATIONS of a similar frequency from another object **3** [U, C] (*formal*) (in a piece of writing, music, etc.) the power to bring images, feelings, etc. into the mind of the person reading or listening; the images, etc. produced in this way
**res·on·ant** /ˈrezənənt/ adj. **1** (*formal*) (of sound) deep, clear and continuing for a long time: *a deep resonant voice* **2** (*specialist*) causing sounds to continue for a long time **SYN** resounding: *resonant frequencies* **3** (*literary*) having the power to bring images, feelings, memories, etc. into your mind: *a poem filled with resonant imagery* ▸ **res·on·ant·ly** adv.
**res·on·ate** /ˈrezəneɪt/ verb (*formal*) **1** [I] (of a voice, an instrument, etc.) to make a deep, clear sound that continues for a long time **2** [I] (of a place) to be filled with sound; to make a sound continue longer **SYN** resound: *a resonating chamber* ◇ ~ **with sth** *The room resonated with the chatter of 100 people.* **3** [I] ~ **(with sb/sth)** to remind sb of sth; to be similar to what sb thinks or believes: *These issues resonated with the voters.* **4** [I] ~ **(with sth)** (*literary*) to be full of a particular quality or feeling: *She makes a simple story resonate with complex themes and emotions.*
**res·on·ator** /ˈrezəneɪtə(r)/ noun (*specialist*) a device for making sound louder and stronger, especially in a musical instrument

**re·sort** 𝒞 B2 /rɪˈzɔːt/; *NAmE* -ˈzɔːrt/ noun, verb
■ noun **1** 𝒞 B2 [C] a place where a lot of people go on holiday: *seaside/ski/mountain resorts* ◇ *a popular tourist resort* (*BrE also*) *a popular holiday resort* ◇ *the resort town of Byron Bay* ⊃ WORDFINDER NOTE at TOURIST **2** [U] ~ **to sth** the act of using sth, especially sth bad or unpleasant, because nothing else is possible **SYN** recourse: *There are hopes that the conflict can be resolved without resort to violence.* **3** **the first/last/final** ~ the first or last course of action that you should or can take in a particular situation: *Strike action should be regarded as a last resort, when all attempts to negotiate have failed.* ◇ *In the last resort* (= in the end) *everyone must decide for themselves.*
■ verb
**PHRV** **re·sort to sth** to make use of sth, especially sth bad, as a means of achieving sth, often because there is no other possible solution **SYN** recourse: *They felt obliged to resort to violence.* ◇ **re·sort to doing sth** *We may have to resort to using untrained staff.*
**re·sound** /rɪˈzaʊnd/ verb (*formal*) **1** [I] ~ **(through sth)** (of a sound, voice, etc.) to fill a place with sound: *Laughter resounded through the house.* ◇ (*figurative*) *The tragedy resounded around the world.* **2** [I] ~ **(with/to sth)** (of a place) to be filled with sound: *The street resounded to the thud of marching feet.*
**re·sound·ing** /rɪˈzaʊndɪŋ/ adj. [only before noun] **1** very great **SYN** emphatic: *a resounding victory/win/defeat* ◇ *The evening was a resounding success.* **2** (of a sound) very loud and continuing for a long time **SYN** resonant ▸ **re·sound·ing·ly** adv.
**re·source** 𝒞 B1 O /rɪˈsɔːs, -ˈzɔːs/; *NAmE* ˈriːsɔːrs, rɪˈsɔːrs/ noun, verb
■ noun **1** 𝒞 B1 [C, usually pl.] a supply of sth that a country, an organization or a person has and can use, especially to increase their wealth: *the exploitation of minerals and other natural resources* ◇ *They promote the use of renewable resources like soybean oil.* ◇ *The school does the best it can with limited resources* (= money). ◇ *Think carefully about how you allocate resources.* ◇ *We agreed to pool our resources* (= so that everyone gives sth). ⊃ see also HUMAN RESOURCES **2** 𝒞 B1 [C] something that can be used to help achieve an aim, especially a book, equipment, etc. that provides information for teachers and students: *The website is an invaluable educational resource.* ◇ *This is an online resource for anyone interested in digital design.* ◇ *Time is your most valuable resource, especially in examinations.* ◇ *a library resource centre* **3** **resources** [pl.] personal qualities such as courage and imagination that help you deal with difficult situations: *He has no inner resources and hates being alone.*

■ *verb* ~ sth to provide sth with the money or equipment that is needed: *Schools in the area are still inadequately resourced.*

**re·source·ful** /rɪˈsɔːsfl, -ˈzɔːs-; NAmE -ˈsɔːrs-/ *adj.* (*approving*) good at finding ways of doing things and solving problems, etc. **SYN** enterprising ▸ **re·source·ful·ly** /-fəli/ *adv.* **re·source·ful·ness** *noun* [U]

**re·spawn** /ˌriːˈspɔːn/ *verb* [I, T] ~ **(sb/sth)** if a character that has been killed in a video game respawns or is respawned, that character appears again in the game

**re·spect** ❶ **B1** Ⓦ /rɪˈspekt/ *noun, verb*
■ *noun* **1** ⓘ **B1** [U, *sing.*] ~ **(for sb/sth)** a strong feeling of approval of sb/sth because of their good qualities or achievements: *I have the **utmost respect** for her and her work.* ◇ *They feel a deep and **mutual respect** for each other.* ◇ *It was a noble effort that **deserves respect**.* ◇ *You did a great job. **Respect**!* (= used to praise sb) ⊃ see also SELF-RESPECT **OPP** disrespect **2** ⓘ **B1** [U, *sing.*] polite behaviour towards or care for sb/sth that you think is important: ~ **for sb/sth** *to show a lack of respect for authority* ◇ *They have a deep respect for the natural world.* ◇ *Everyone has a right to be **treated with respect**.* ◇ *A two-minute silence was held as a **mark of respect**.* **OPP** disrespect **3** ⓘ **B2** [C] **in ... ~** a particular aspect or detail of sth: *In this respect we are very fortunate.* ◇ *There was one respect, however, in which they differed.*
**IDM** **in respect of sth** (*formal or business*) **1** about; relating to: *A writ was served on the firm in respect of their unpaid bill.* **2** in payment for sth: *money received in respect of overtime worked* **with reˈspect | with all due reˈspect** (*formal*) used when you are going to disagree, usually quite strongly, with sb: *With all due respect, the figures simply do not support you on this.* **with respect to sth** (*formal or business*) in connection with: *The two groups were similar with respect to income and status.* ⊃ more at PAY *v.*
■ *verb* **1** ⓘ **B1** (not usually used in the progressive tenses) ~ **sb/sth** to have a very good opinion of sb/sth; to admire sb/sth: *I respect Jack's opinion on most subjects.* ◇ *a much loved and **highly respected** teacher* ◇ ~ **sb/sth for sth** *She had always been honest with me, and I respect her for that.* **2** ⓘ **B1** ~ **sth** to be careful about sth; to make sure you do not do sth that might be considered wrong: *Employers must respect employees' privacy.* ◇ *I respect your right to disagree.* ◇ *She promised to respect our wishes.* **3** ⓘ **B1** ~ **sth** to agree not to break a law, principle, etc.: *The new leader has promised to respect the constitution.*

**re·spect·abil·ity** /rɪˌspektəˈbɪləti/ *noun* [U] the fact of being considered socially acceptable

**re·spect·able** /rɪˈspektəbl/ *adj.* **1** considered by society to be acceptable, good or correct: *a highly respectable neighbourhood* ◇ *a respectable married man* ◇ *Go and make yourself look respectable.* **OPP** disreputable **2** fairly good; that there is no reason to be ashamed of **SYN** acceptable: *a perfectly respectable result* ▸ **re·spect·ably** /-bli/ *adv.*: *respectably dressed*

**re·spect·er** /rɪˈspektə(r)/ *noun*
**IDM** **be no respecter of ˈpersons, age, class, etc.** to treat everyone in the same way, without being influenced by their importance, wealth, etc.

**re·spect·ful** /rɪˈspektfl/ *adj.* showing or feeling respect: *The onlookers stood at a respectful distance.* ◇ *We were brought up to be respectful of authority.* **OPP** disrespectful ▸ **re·spect·ful·ly** /-fəli/ *adv.*: *He listened respectfully.*

**re·spect·ing** /rɪˈspektɪŋ/ *prep.* (*formal*) in connection with **SYN** **with respect to sth**: *information respecting the child's whereabouts*

**re·spect·ive** ⓘ+ **C1** /rɪˈspektɪv/ *adj.* [only before noun] belonging or relating separately to each of the people or things already mentioned: *They are each recognized specialists in their respective fields.* ◇ *the respective roles of men and women in society*

**re·spect·ive·ly** ⓘ+ **C1** Ⓦ /rɪˈspektɪvli/ *adv.* in the same order as the people or things already mentioned: *Julie and Mark, aged 17 and 19 respectively.*

**res·pir·ation** /ˌrespəˈreɪʃn/ *noun* [U] (*formal*) the act of breathing: *Blood pressure and respiration are also recorded.*

1321   **responsibility**

**res·pir·ator** /ˈrespəreɪtə(r)/ *noun* **1** a piece of equipment that makes it possible for sb to breathe over a long period when they are unable to do so naturally: *She was **put on a respirator**.* **2** a device worn over the nose and mouth to allow sb to breathe in a place where there is a lot of smoke, gas, etc.

**re·spira·tory** /rəˈspɪrətri, ˈrespərətri; NAmE ˈrespərətɔːri/ *adj.* connected with breathing: *the respiratory system* ◇ *respiratory diseases*

**res·pite** /ˈrespaɪt; NAmE -pɪt/ *noun* [*sing.*, U] **1** ~ **(from sth)** a short break or escape from sth difficult or unpleasant: *The drug brought a brief respite from the pain.* ◇ *There was no respite from the suffocating heat.* ◇ *She continued to work without respite.* ◇ **respite care** (= temporary care arranged for old, mentally ill, etc. people so that the people who usually care for them can have a rest) ⊃ **SYNONYMS** at REST **2** a short delay allowed before sth difficult or unpleasant must be done **SYN** **reprieve**: *His creditors agreed to give him a temporary respite.*

**re·splen·dent** /rɪˈsplendənt/ *adj.* ~ **(in sth)** (*formal or literary*) brightly coloured in an impressive way: *He glimpsed Sonia, resplendent in a red dress.* ▸ **re·splen·dent·ly** *adv.*

**re·spond** ❶ ⓘ **A2** Ⓞ /rɪˈspɒnd; NAmE -ˈspɑːnd/ *verb* **1** ⓘ **A2** [I, T] (*rather formal*) to give a spoken or written answer to sb/sth **SYN** **reply**: *I asked him his name, but he didn't respond.* ◇ ~ **to sth/sb** *The government did not respond to our questions.* ◇ + **speech** '*I'm not sure,*' *she responded.* ◇ ~ **that ...** *When asked about the company's future, the director responded that he remained optimistic.* ⊃ note at ANSWER **2** ⓘ **A2** [I] to do sth as a reaction to sth that sb has said or done **SYN** **react**: ~ **(to sth)** *How did they respond to the news?* ◇ ~ **by doing sth** *The government responded by banning all future demonstrations.* **3** ⓘ **A2** [I] ~ **(to sth)** to react quickly or in the correct way to sth/sb: *The car responds very well to the controls.* ◇ *You can rely on him to **respond to a challenge**.* **4** [I] ~ **(to sth)** to improve as a result of a particular kind of treatment: *The infection did not respond to the drugs.*

**re·spond·ent** /rɪˈspɒndənt; NAmE -ˈspɑːn-/ *noun* **1** a person who answers questions, especially in a survey: *60 per cent of the respondents agreed with the suggestion.* **2** (*law*) a person who is accused of sth

**re·spond·er** ⊃ FIRST RESPONDER

**re·sponse** ❶ ⓘ **A2** Ⓞ /rɪˈspɒns; NAmE -ˈspɑːns/ *noun* **1** ⓘ **A2** [C, U] a spoken or written answer: *She made no response.* ◇ ~ **to sb/sth** *I received an **immediate response** to my request.* ◇ **in ~ to sth** *I am writing in response to your enquiry.* ◇ **in ~** *Jack just nodded in response.* **2** ⓘ **A2** [C, U] a reaction to sth that has happened or been said: *The news provoked an **angry response**.* ◇ *a **positive response**.* ◇ *I knocked on the door but there was no response.* ◇ ~ **to sb/sth** *There has been little response to our appeal for funds.* ◇ **in ~ to sth** *The product was developed in response to demand.* ⊃ see also IMMUNE RESPONSE, RAPID-RESPONSE **3** [C, usually *pl.*] a part of a church service that the people sing or speak as an answer to the part that the priest sings or speaks

**reˈsponse time** *noun* the length of time that a person or system takes to react to sth: *The average response time to emergency calls was 9 minutes.*

**re·spon·si·bil·ity** ❶ **B1** Ⓦ /rɪˌspɒnsəˈbɪləti; NAmE -ˌspɑːn-/ *noun* (*pl.* **-ies**) **1** ⓘ **B1** [U, C] a duty to deal with or take care of sb/sth, so that you may be blamed if sth goes wrong: *to be in a position of responsibility* ◇ *It's time for someone to **take responsibility** and get the job done.* ◇ ~ **for sth** *She **assumed responsibility** for recruitment.* ◇ ~ **for doing sth** *They have responsibility for ensuring the rules are enforced.* ◇ ~ **to do sth** *It is their responsibility to ensure the rules are enforced.* ◇ *parental rights and responsibilities* ◇ *She is no longer able to fulfil her responsibilities.* **2** ⓘ **B1** [U] ~ **(for sth)** blame for sth bad that has happened: *The bank refuses to **accept responsibility** for the mistake.* ◇ *Nobody has **claimed responsibility** for the bombing.* ◇ *It is for the court to decide who **bears responsibility**.* ◇ *We **take full responsibility** for any errors in the text.* ⊃ see also DIMINISHED RESPONSIBILITY **3** ⓘ **B1** [U, C] a moral duty to

# responsible

do sth or to help or take care of sb because of your job, position, etc: **~to/towards sb** *She feels a strong sense of responsibility towards her employees.* ◊ **~ to do sth** *I think we have a moral responsibility to help these countries.* ⇒ see also CORPORATE RESPONSIBILITY

**re·spon·sible** ⓘ B1 Ⓦ /rɪˈspɒnsəbl; *NAmE* -ˈspɑːn-/ *adj.*

- HAVING JOB/DUTY **1** B1 having the job or duty of doing sth or taking care of sb/sth, so that you may be blamed if sth goes wrong: **~ for doing sth** *Mike is responsible for designing the entire project.* ◊ **~ for sb/sth** *Even where parents no longer live together, they each continue to be responsible for their children.* ◊ *I'd like to talk to whoever is responsible here.*
- CAUSING STH **2** B1 **~ (for sth)** being able to be blamed for sth: *Who's responsible for this mess?* ◊ *He is mentally ill and cannot be held responsible for his actions.* ◊ *Everything will be done to bring those responsible to justice.* **3** B2 **~(for sth)** being the cause of sth: *Cigarette smoking is responsible for about 90 per cent of deaths from lung cancer.*
- RELIABLE **4** B2 (of people, organizations or their actions or behaviour) **~(with sth)** that you can trust and rely on SYN **conscientious**: *The child should be accompanied by a parent or other responsible adult.* ◊ *The firm specializes in socially responsible investments.* OPP **irresponsible**
- JOB **5** B2 [usually before noun] needing sb who can be trusted and relied on; involving important duties: *a responsible position*
- TO SB IN AUTHORITY **6** **~ to sb/sth** having to report to sb/sth with authority or in a higher position and explain to them what you have done: *The Council of Ministers is responsible to the Assembly.*

**re·spon·sibly** /rɪˈspɒnsəbli; *NAmE* -ˈspɑːn-/ *adv.* in a sensible way that shows you can be trusted: *to act responsibly* OPP **irresponsibly**

**re·spon·sive** /rɪˈspɒnsɪv; *NAmE* -ˈspɑːn-/ *adj.* **1** [not usually before noun] **~ (to sb/sth)** reacting quickly and in a positive way: *Firms have to be responsive to consumer demand.* ◊ *A flu virus that is not responsive to treatment* **2** **~ (to sb/sth)** reacting with interest or enthusiasm SYN **receptive**: *The club is responsive to new ideas.* ◊ *a responsive and enthusiastic audience* **3** (*computing*) used to describe a website, etc. that changes to suit the kind of device you are using, for example by changing the size of the text or the way that items are arranged on the screen OPP **unresponsive** ▶ **re·spon·sive·ly** *adv.* **re·spon·sive·ness** *noun* [U]

**re·spray** /ˌriːˈspreɪ/ *verb* **~ sth** to change the colour of sth, especially a car, by SPRAYING it with paint ▶ **re·spray** /ˈriːspreɪ/ *noun* [usually sing.]

**rest** ⓘ A2 /rest/ *noun, verb*

■ *noun*
- REMAINING PART/PEOPLE/THINGS **1** A2 **the rest** [sing.] the part of sth that remains: *Take what you want and throw the rest away.* ◊ **the ~ of sth** *The country enjoys friendly relations with the rest of the world.* ◊ *How would you like to spend the rest of the day?* ◊ *I'm not doing this job for the rest of my life.* **2** A2 **the rest** [pl.] the people or things that remain; the others: *The first question was difficult, but the rest were pretty easy.* ◊ **the ~ of sth** *Don't blame Alex. He's human, like the rest of us.*
- PERIOD OF RELAXING **3** A2 [C, U] a period of relaxing, sleeping or doing nothing after a period of activity: *I had a good night's rest.* ◊ *We stopped for a well-earned rest.* ◊ **~ from sth** *to have/take a rest from all your hard work* ◊ *Try to get some rest—you have a busy day tomorrow.* ⇒ see also CHAPEL OF REST
- SUPPORT **4** [C] (often in compounds) an object that is used to support or hold sth: *an armrest* (= for example on a seat or chair)
- IN MUSIC **5** [C, U] a period of silence between notes; a sign that shows a rest between notes ⇒ picture at MUSIC

IDM **and (all) the ˈrest (of it)** (*informal*) used at the end of a list to mean everything else that you might expect to be on the list: *He wants a big house and an expensive car and all the rest of it.* **and the ˈrest** (*informal*) used to say that the actual amount or number of sth is much higher than sb has stated: *'It cost 250 pounds…' 'And the rest, and the rest!'* **at ˈrest 1** (*specialist*) not moving: *At rest the insect looks like a dead leaf.* **2** dead and therefore free from trouble or worry. People say 'at rest' to avoid saying 'dead': *She now lies at rest in the churchyard.* **come to ˈrest** to stop moving: *The car crashed through the barrier and came to rest in a field.* ◊ *His eyes came to rest on Clara's face.* **for the ˈrest** (*BrE, formal*) apart from that; considering other matters: *The book has some interesting passages about the author's childhood. For the rest, it is extremely dull.* **give it a ˈrest** (*informal*) used to tell sb to stop talking about sth because they are annoying you **give sth a ˈrest** (*informal*) to stop doing sth for a while **lay sb to ˈrest** to bury sb. People say 'to lay sb to rest' to avoid saying 'to bury' sb: *George was laid to rest beside his parents.* **lay/put sth to ˈrest** to stop sth by showing it is not true: *The announcement finally laid all the speculation about their future to rest.* **the rest is ˈhistory** used when you are telling a story to say that you do not need to tell the end of it, because everyone knows it already ⇒ more at MIND *n.*, WICKED *n.*

■ *verb*
- RELAX **1** A2 [I, T] to relax, sleep or do nothing after a period of activity or illness; to not use a part of your body for some time: *The doctor told me to rest.* ◊ (*figurative*) *He won't rest* (= will never be satisfied) *until he finds her.* ◊ **~ sth** *He had to rest his injured knee for six weeks.* ⇒ see also RESTED
- SUPPORT **2** B1 [T, I] to support sth by putting it on or against sth; to be supported in this way: **~ sth + adv./prep.** *Rest your head on my shoulder.* ◊ *He rested his chin in his hands.* ◊ **+ adv./prep.** *Their bikes were resting against the wall.*
- BE LEFT **3** [I] if you let a matter rest, you stop discussing it or dealing with it: *The matter cannot rest there—I intend to sue.*
- BE BURIED **4** [I] **+ adv./prep.** to be buried. People say 'rest' to avoid saying 'be buried': *She rests beside her husband in the local cemetery.* ◊ *May he rest in peace.* ⇒ see also RIP

IDM **rest asˈsured (that …)** (*formal*) used to emphasize that what you say is true or will definitely happen: *You may rest assured that we will do all we can to find him.* **ˌrest your ˈcase 1 I rest my case** (*sometimes humorous*) used to say that you do not need to say any more about sth because you think that you have proved your point **2** (*law*) used by lawyers in court to say that they have finished presenting their case: *The prosecution rests its case.* ⇒ more at EASY *adv.*, GOD, LAUREL

PHRV **ˈrest on/upon sb/sth 1** to depend or rely on sb/sth: *All our hopes now rest on you.* **2** to look at sb/sth: *Her eyes rested on the piece of paper in my hand.* **ˈrest on sth** to be based on sth: *The whole argument rests on a false*

---

# SYNONYMS

## rest

**break • respite • time out • breathing space**

These are all words for a short period of time spent relaxing.

**rest** a period of relaxing, sleeping or doing nothing after a period of activity: *We stopped for a well-earned rest.*

**break** a short period of time when you stop what you are doing and rest or eat: *Let's take a break.* NOTE In British English **break** is a period of time between lessons at school. The North American English word is **recess**.

**respite** a short break from sth difficult or unpleasant: *The drug brought a brief respite from the pain.*

**time out** (*especially NAmE, informal*) time for resting or relaxing away from your usual work or studies: *Take time out to relax by the pool.*

**breathing space** a short rest in the middle of a period of mental or physical effort: *This delay gives the party a breathing space in which to sort out its policies.*

**PATTERNS**
- (a) rest/break/respite/time out **from** sth
- to **have/take** (a) rest/break/time out
- to **give sb** (a) rest/break/respite/breathing space

assumption. **rest with sb (to do sth)** (*formal*) if it rests with sb to do sth, it is their responsibility to do it: *It rests with management to justify their actions.* ◊ *The final decision rests with the doctors.*

**rest area**, **rest stop** *noun* (*NAmE*) an area next to an important road where people can stop their cars to rest, eat food, etc. ⊃ compare LAY-BY

**re·start** /ˌriːˈstɑːt; *NAmE* -ˈstɑːrt/ *verb* [I, T] ~ **(sth)** to start again, or to make sth start again, after it has stopped: *to restart a game* ◊ *The doctors struggled to restart his heart.*
▶ **re·start** /ˈriːstɑːt; *NAmE* -stɑːrt/ *noun*

**re·state** /ˌriːˈsteɪt/ *verb* ~ **sth** (*formal*) to say sth again or in a different way, especially so that it is more clearly or strongly expressed ▶ **re·state·ment** *noun* [U]

**res·taur·ant** ⓘ 🅰️🅱️ /ˈrestrɒnt; *NAmE* -strɑːnt, -stərɑːnt/ *noun* a place where you can buy and eat a meal: *an Italian/a fast-food restaurant* ◊ *We had a meal in a restaurant.* ◊ *We went to my favourite restaurant to celebrate.* ◊ *a restaurant chain/owner* ⊃ compare CAFE ⊃ WORDFINDER NOTE at EAT

**WORDFINDER** à la carte, course, cuisine, menu, order, reservation, service charge, speciality, waiter

**restaurant car** *noun* (*BrE*) = DINING CAR

**res·taura·teur** /ˌrestərəˈtɜː(r)/ *noun* (*formal*) a person who owns and manages a restaurant

**rest·ed** /ˈrestɪd/ *adj.* feeling healthy and full of energy because you have had a rest: *I awoke feeling rested and refreshed.* ⊃ see also REST *noun*

**rest·ful** /ˈrestfl/ *adj.* that makes you feel relaxed and peaceful **SYN** calm: *a hotel with a restful atmosphere*

**rest home** *noun* a place where old or sick people are cared for

**rest house** *noun* (in parts of Asia and Africa) a house or HUT that you can pay to stay in like a hotel room, especially in wild country

**resting place** *noun* 1 a GRAVE (= where a dead person is buried). People say 'resting place' to avoid saying 'grave': *her final/last resting place* 2 a place where you can rest

**res·ti·tu·tion** /ˌrestɪˈtjuːʃn; *NAmE* -ˈtuː-/ *noun* [U] 1 ~ **(of sth) (to sb/sth)** (*formal*) the act of giving back sth that was lost or stolen to its owner **SYN** restoration 2 ~ **(of sth) (to sb/sth)** (*law*) payment, usually money, for some harm or wrong that sb has suffered

**rest·ive** /ˈrestɪv/ *adj.* (*formal*) unable to stay still, or unwilling to be controlled, especially because you feel bored or not satisfied ▶ **rest·ive·ness** *noun* [U]

**rest·less** /ˈrestləs/ *adj.* 1 unable to stay still or be happy where you are, because you are bored or need a change: *The audience was becoming restless.* ◊ *After five years in the job, he was beginning to feel restless.* 2 without real rest or sleep **SYN** disturbed: *a restless night* ▶ **rest·less·ly** *adv.*: *He moved restlessly from one foot to the other.* **rest·less·ness** *noun* [U]

**re·stock** /ˌriːˈstɒk; *NAmE* -ˈstɑːk/ *verb* [T, I] ~ **(sth) (with sth)** to fill sth with new or different things to replace those that have been used, sold, etc.; to get a new supply of sth

**res·tor·ation** 🅱️🅲️ /ˌrestəˈreɪʃn/ *noun* 1 🅱️🅲️ [U, C] the work of repairing and cleaning an old building, a painting, etc. so that its condition is as good as it originally was: *restoration work* ▶ **for** ~ *The Palace is closed for restoration.* 2 🅲️ [U, C] ~ **of sth** the act of bringing back a system, a law, etc. that existed previously: *the restoration of democracy/the monarchy* 3 [U] ~ **(of sth) (to sb/sth)** the act of returning sth to its correct place, condition or owner: *the restoration of the Elgin marbles to Greece* 4 **the Restoration** [sing.] the time in Britain after 1660 when, following a period with no king or queen, Charles II became king: *Restoration comedy/poetry* (= written during and after this time)

**re·stora·tive** /rɪˈstɒrətɪv; *NAmE* -ˈstɔːr-/ *adj., noun*
■ *adj.* 1 (*formal*) making you feel strong and healthy again: *the restorative power of fresh air* 2 (*medical*) connected with treatment that repairs the body or a part of it: *restorative dentistry/surgery*

■ *noun* (*old-fashioned*) a thing that makes you feel better, stronger, etc.

**re·store** 🅱️🅲️ /rɪˈstɔː(r)/ *verb* 1 🅱️🅲️ to bring back a situation or feeling that existed before: ~ **sth** *The measures are intended to restore public confidence in the economy.* ◊ *Order was quickly restored after the riots.* ◊ *The operation restored his sight* (= made him able to see again). ◊ ~ **sth to sb** *Peace has now been restored to the area.* 2 🅲️🅱️ ~ **sb/sth to sth** to bring sb/sth back to a former condition, place or position: *He is now fully restored to health.* ◊ *We hope to restore the garden to its former glory* (= make it as beautiful as it used to be). 3 🅲️🅱️ ~ **sth** to repair a building, work of art, piece of furniture, etc. so that it looks as good as it did originally: *Her job is restoring old paintings.* 4 ~ **sth** to bring a law, tradition, way of working, etc. back into use **SYN** reintroduce: *to restore ancient traditions* ◊ *Some people argue that the death penalty should be restored.* 5 ~ **sth (to sb/sth)** (*formal*) to give sth that was lost or stolen back to sb: *The police have now restored the painting to its rightful owner.*

**re·storer** /rɪˈstɔːrə(r)/ *noun* a person whose job is to repair old buildings, works of art, etc. so that they look as they did when new

**re·strain** /rɪˈstreɪn/ *verb* 1 to stop sb/sth from doing sth, especially by using physical force: ~ **sb/sth** *The prisoner had to be restrained by the police.* ◊ *He placed a restraining hand on her arm.* ◊ ~ **sb/sth from (doing) sth** *They have obtained an injunction restraining the company from selling the product.* 2 to stop yourself from feeling an emotion or doing sth that you would like to do: ~ **sth** *John managed to restrain his anger.* ◊ ~ **yourself (from sth/from doing sth)** *She had to restrain herself from crying out in pain.* 3 ~ **sth** to stop sth that is growing or increasing from becoming too large **SYN** bring/get/keep sth under control: *The government is taking steps to restrain inflation.*

**re·strained** /rɪˈstreɪnd/ *adj.* 1 showing calm control rather than emotion: *her restrained smile* 2 not too brightly coloured or decorated **SYN** discreet: *The costumes and lighting in the play were restrained.*

**re·straining order** *noun* ~ **(against sb)** (*especially NAmE*) an official order given by a judge which demands that sth must or must not be done. A restraining order does not require a trial in court but only lasts for a limited period of time. ⊃ compare INJUNCTION

**re·straint** 🅲️🅲️ /rɪˈstreɪnt/ *noun* 1 🅲️🅲️ [C, usually pl.] ~ **(on sb/sth)** a rule, a fact, an idea, etc. that limits or controls what people can do: *The government has imposed export restraints on some products* ⊃ SYNONYMS at LIMIT 2 🅲️🅲️ [U] the act of controlling or limiting sth because it is necessary or sensible to do so: *wage restraint* ◊ **without** ~ *They said that they would fight without restraint* (= completely freely) *for what they wanted.* 3 🅲️ [U] the quality of behaving calmly and with control **SYN** self-control: *The police appealed to the crowd for restraint.* ◊ *He exercised considerable restraint in ignoring the insults.* 4 [U] (*formal*) the use of physical force to control sb who is behaving in a violent way: *the physical restraint of prisoners* 5 [C] (*formal*) a type of SEAT BELT or safety device: *Children must use an approved child restraint or adult seat belt.*

**re·strict** 🅱️🅲️ /rɪˈstrɪkt/ *verb* 1 🅱️🅲️ to limit the size, amount or range of sth: ~ **sth to sth** *Speed is restricted to 30 mph in towns.* ◊ *We restrict the number of students per class to ten.* ◊ ~ **sth** *Fog severely restricted visibility.* ◊ *Having small children tends to restrict your freedom.* 2 🅲️🅱️ ~ **sth** to stop sb/sth from moving or acting freely **SYN** impede: *The long skirt restricted her movements.* 3 🅲️🅱️ ~ **sth (to sb)** to control sth with rules or laws: *Access to the club is restricted to members only.* 4 ~ **yourself/sb (to sth/to doing sth)** to allow yourself or sb to have only a limited amount of sth or to do only a particular kind of activity: *I restrict myself to one cup of coffee a day.*

**re·stricted** /rɪˈstrɪktɪd/ *adj.* 1 limited or small in size or amount: *a restricted space* ◊ *a restricted range of foods* 2 limited in what you are able to do: *In those days women led fairly restricted lives.* ◊ *Her vision is restricted in one eye.* 3 controlled by rules or laws: *to allow children only*

# restriction

restricted access to the internet ◇ (*BrE*) *a restricted area* (= limited by laws about speed or parking) ◇ **~ to sb/sth** *The tournament is restricted to players under the age of 23.* **4** [usually before noun] (of a place) only open to people with special permission, especially because it is secret or dangerous: *to enter a restricted zone* **5** (*BrE*) officially secret and only available to people with special permission **SYN** **classified**: *a restricted document* **OPP** **unrestricted**

**re·stric·tion** /rɪˈstrɪkʃn/ *noun* **1** [C] *a rule or law that limits what you can do or what can happen*: *import/speed/travel restrictions* ◇ **~ on sth** *to impose/place a restriction on sth* ◇ *The government has agreed to lift restrictions on press freedom.* ⇒ **SYNONYMS** at **LIMIT** **2** [U] *the act of limiting or controlling sb/sth*: *sports clothes that prevent any restriction of movement* **3** [C] *a thing that limits the amount of freedom you have*: *the restrictions of a prison* ⇒ **WORDFINDER NOTE** at **FREEDOM**

**re·strict·ive** /rɪˈstrɪktɪv/ *adj.* **1** *preventing people from doing what they want*: *restrictive laws* **2** (*also* **defining**) (*grammar*) (of **RELATIVE CLAUSES**) *explaining which particular person or thing you are talking about rather than giving extra information about them. In 'The books which are on the table are mine', 'which are on the table' is a restrictive relative clause.* ▶ **re·strict·ive·ly** *adv.*

**rest·room** /ˈrestruːm, -rʊm/ *noun* (*NAmE*) *a room with a toilet in a public place, such as a theatre or restaurant*

**re·struc·ture** /ˌriːˈstrʌktʃə(r)/ *verb* [T, I] **~ (sth)** *to organize sth such as a system or a company in a new and different way* ▶ **re·struc·tur·ing** *noun* [U, C, usually sing.]

**re·sult** /rɪˈzʌlt/ *noun, verb*

■ *noun*
- **CAUSED BY STH** **1** [C] *a thing that is caused or produced because of sth else*: *to yield/achieve/produce a result* ◇ **~ of sth** *The company's failure was a direct result of bad management.* ◇ *This book is the result of 25 years of research.* ◇ *The end result* (= the final one) *of her hard work was a place at medical school.* ◇ **as a~** *He made one big mistake, and, as a result, lost his job.* ◇ **as a~ of sth** *She died as a result of her injuries.* ◇ **with the~ that...** *The farm was flooded, with the result that the crop was lost.* ◇ **with... results** *He decided to get involved, with disastrous results.* ⇒ **LANGUAGE BANK** at **BECAUSE OF, CONSEQUENTLY**
- **OF GAME/ELECTION** **2** [C] *the final score or the name of the winner in a sports event, competition, election, etc*: *the election results* ◇ *the football results* ◇ **~ of sth** *They will announce the result of the vote tonight.* **3** [C, usually sing.] (*BrE, informal*) *a victory or a success*: *We badly need to get a result from this match.*
- **OF EXAM** **4** [C, usually pl.] (*BrE*) *the mark or grade you get in an exam or in a number of exams*: *Have you had your results yet?*
- **OF TEST/RESEARCH** **5** [C, usually pl.] *the information that you get from a scientific test or piece of research*: *Other research has yielded similar results.* ◇ *The doctor will explain your blood test results.* ◇ **~ of sth** *the results of a study* ◇ *The results of our experiment indicate that environmental factors play a part.* ⇒ **WORDFINDER NOTE** at **SCIENCE**
- **OF COMPUTER SEARCH** **6** [C, usually pl.] *the information that you get from a computer search*: *The user can control how the search results are displayed.*
- **SUCCESS** **7** **results** [pl.] *things that are achieved successfully*: *The project is beginning to show results.* ◇ *a coach who knows how to get results from his players* ◇ *For best results, defrost fully before use.*
- **OF BUSINESS** **8** [C, usually pl.] *the amount of profit or loss made by a business over a particular period of time*: *Companies are required by law to report their financial results on a quarterly basis.* ◇ *to announce/publish results*

■ *verb* **1** **~ in sth** *to make sth happen*: *A heavy frost could result in loss of the crop.* ◇ **result in sb/sth doing sth** *These policies resulted in many elderly people suffering hardship.* ⇒ **LANGUAGE BANK** at **CAUSE** **2** [I] *to happen because of sth else that happened first*: *When water levels rise, flooding results.* ◇ **~ from sth** *job losses resulting from changes in production* ◇ *It was a large explosion and the resulting damage was extensive.*

---

▼ **SYNONYMS**

## result
consequence • outcome • repercussion

These are all words for a thing that is caused because of sth else.

**result** *a thing that is caused or produced by sth else*: *She died as a result of her injuries.* ◇ *This book is the result of 25 years of research.*

**consequence** (*rather formal*) *a result of sth that has happened, especially a bad result*: *This decision could have serious consequences for the industry.* **NOTE** **Consequences** is used most frequently to talk about possible negative results of an action. It is commonly used with such words as *adverse, dire, disastrous, fatal, harmful, negative, serious, tragic* and *unfortunate*. Even when there is no adjective, **consequences** often suggests negative results.

**outcome** *the result of an action or process*: *We are waiting to hear the final outcome of the negotiations.*

### RESULT OR OUTCOME?
**Result** is often used to talk about things that are caused directly by sth else: *Aggression is often the result of fear.* **Outcome** is more often used to talk about what happens at the end of a process when the exact relation of cause and effect is less clear: *Aggression is often the outcome of fear.* **Result** is often used after an event to talk about what happened. **Outcome** is often used before an action or process to talk about what is likely to happen.

**repercussion** (*rather formal*) *an indirect and usually bad result of an action or event that may happen some time afterwards.*

### PATTERNS
- to have consequences/repercussions **for** sb/sth
- **with** the result/consequence/outcome **that...**
- a(n)/the **possible** result/consequences/outcome/repercussions
- a(n)/the **likely/inevitable** result/consequences/outcome
- (a/an) **negative** results/consequences/outcome/repercussions
- **far-reaching/serious** results/consequences/repercussions
- to **have** a result/consequences/an outcome/repercussions

---

**re·sult·ant** /rɪˈzʌltənt/ *adj.* [only before noun] (*formal*) *caused by the thing that has just been mentioned*: *the growing economic crisis and resultant unemployment*

**re·sume** /rɪˈzjuːm; *NAmE* -ˈzuːm/ *verb* (*formal*) **1** [T, I] *if you resume an activity, or if it resumes, it begins again or continues after being interrupted*: **~(sth)** *to resume talks/negotiations* ◇ *She resumed her career after an interval of six years.* ◇ *The noise resumed, louder than before.* ◇ **~ doing sth** *He got back in the car and resumed driving.* **2** [T] **~ your seat/place/position** *to go back to the seat or place that you had before*

**ré·sumé** /ˈrezjuːmeɪ; *NAmE* -zəm-/ *noun* **1 ~ (of sth)** *a short summary or account of sth*: *a brief résumé of events so far* **2** (*NAmE*) (*BrE* **cur·ricu·lum vitae**) *a written record of your education and the jobs you have done, that you send when you are applying for a job*

**re·sump·tion** /rɪˈzʌmpʃn/ *noun* [sing., U] (*formal*) *the act of beginning sth again after it has stopped*: *We are hoping for an early resumption of peace talks.*

**re·sup·ply** /ˌriːsəˈplaɪ/ *verb* **~ sb (with sth)** *to give sb new supplies of sth they need; to give sth to sb again in a different form* ▶ **re·supply** /ˌriːsəˈplaɪ/ *noun*

**re·sur·face** /ˌriːˈsɜːfɪs; *NAmE* -ˈsɜːrf-/ *verb* **1** [I] *to come to the surface again after being* **UNDERWATER** *or under the ground*: *The submarine resurfaced.* ◇ (*figurative*) *All the old hostilities resurfaced when they met again.* **2** [T] **~ sth** *to put a new surface on a road, path, etc.*

**re·sur·gence** /rɪˈsɜːdʒəns; *NAmE* -ˈsɜːrdʒ-/ *noun* [sing., U] *the return and growth of an activity that had stopped*

**re·sur·gent** /rɪˈsɜːdʒənt; NAmE -ˈsɜːrdʒ-/ adj. [usually before noun] (formal) becoming stronger or more popular again

**res·ur·rect** /ˌrezəˈrekt/ verb **1** ~ **sth** to bring back into use sth such as a belief, a practice, etc. that had disappeared or been forgotten **SYN** revive **2** ~ **sb** to bring a dead person back to life **SYN** raise

**res·ur·rec·tion** /ˌrezəˈrekʃn/ noun **1** **the Resurrection** [sing.] (in the Christian religion) the time when Jesus Christ returned to life again after his death; the time when all dead people will become alive again, when the world ends **2** [U, sing.] a new beginning for sth which is old or which had disappeared or become weak

**re·sus·ci·tate** /rɪˈsʌsɪteɪt/ verb ~ **sb**/**sth** to make sb start breathing again or become conscious again after they have almost died **SYN** revive: *He had a heart attack and all attempts to resuscitate him failed.* ◊ (figurative) *efforts to resuscitate the economy* ▸ **re·sus·ci·ta·tion** /rɪˌsʌsɪˈteɪʃn/ noun [U]: *frantic attempts at resuscitation* ⊃ see also MOUTH-TO-MOUTH RESUSCITATION

**re·tail¹** 🔑+ B2 /ˈriːteɪl/ noun, adv., verb ⊃ see also RETAIL²
▪ noun 🔑+ B2 [U] the selling of goods to the public, usually through shops: *The recommended retail price is £9.99.* ◊ *department stores and other retail outlets* ⊃ *the retail trade* ⊃ compare WHOLESALE ▸ **re·tail** adv.: *to buy/sell retail* (= in a shop)
▪ verb **1** [T] ~ **sth** to sell goods to the public, usually through shops: *The firm manufactures and retails its own range of sportswear.* **2** [I] ~ **at**/**for sth** (business) to be sold at a particular price: *The book retails at £14.95.*

**re·tail²** /ˈriːteɪl/ verb ~ **sth (to sb)** (formal) to tell people about sth, especially about a person's behaviour or private life **SYN** recount¹: *She retailed the neighbours' activities with relish.* ⊃ see also RETAIL¹

**re·tail·er** /ˈriːteɪlə(r)/ noun a person or business that sells goods to the public

**re·tail·ing** /ˈriːteɪlɪŋ/ noun [U] the business of selling goods to the public, usually through shops: *career opportunities in retailing* ⊃ compare WHOLESALING

**ˈretail park** noun (BrE) an area containing a group of large shops, located outside a town

**ˌretail ˈprice index** (also **ˈprice index**) noun [sing.] (abbr. **RPI**) (in the UK) a list of the prices of some ordinary goods and services which shows how much these prices change each month ⊃ see also CONSUMER PRICE INDEX

**ˌretail ˈtherapy** noun [U] (usually humorous) the act of going shopping and buying things in order to make yourself feel more cheerful: *I was ready for a little retail therapy.*

**re·tain** 🔑 B2 /rɪˈteɪn/ verb (rather formal) **1** 🔑 B2 ~ **sth** to keep sth; to continue to have sth **SYN** preserve: *to retain your independence* ◊ *He struggled to retain control of the situation.* ◊ *The house retains much of its original charm.* ◊ *She retained her tennis title for the third year.* **2** 🔑 B2 ~ **sth** to continue to hold or contain sth: *a soil that retains moisture* ◊ *This information is no longer retained within the computer's main memory.* ◊ (figurative) *She has a good memory and finds it easy to retain facts.* **3** ~ **sb**/**sth** (law) if a member of the public **retains** sb such as a lawyer, he or she pays money regularly or in advance so the lawyer, etc. will do work for him or her: *a retaining fee* ◊ *to retain the services of a lawyer* ⊃ see also RETENTION, RETENTIVE

**re·tain·er** /rɪˈteɪnə(r)/ noun **1** a sum of money that is paid to sb to make sure they will be available to do work when they are needed: *The agency will pay you a monthly retainer.* **2** (BrE) a small amount of rent that you pay for a room, etc. when you are not there in order to keep it available for your use **3** (NAmE) a device that keeps a person's teeth straight after they have had ORTHODONTIC treatment with BRACES **4** (old-fashioned) a servant, especially one who has been with a family for a long time

**re·tain·ing** /rɪˈteɪnɪŋ/ adj. [only before noun] (specialist) intended to keep sth in the correct position: *a retaining wall* (= one that keeps the earth or water behind it in position)

**re·take** verb, noun
▪ verb /ˌriːˈteɪk/ (**re·took** /-ˈtʊk/, **re·taken** /-ˈteɪkən/) **1** ~ **sth** (especially of an army) to take control of sth such as a town again: *Government forces moved in to retake the city.* ◊ (figurative) *Moore fought back to retake the lead later in the race.* **2** = RESIT
▪ noun /ˈriːteɪk/ **1** the act of filming a scene in a film again, because it was not right before **2** = RESIT

**re·tali·ate** /rɪˈtælieɪt/ verb [I] to do sth harmful to sb because they have harmed you first **SYN** revenge: ~ **(against sb/sth)** *to retaliate against an attack* ◊ **(by doing sth/with sth)** *The boy hit his sister, who retaliated by kicking him.* ▸ **re·tali·atory** /rɪˈtæliətri/; NAmE -tɔːri/ adj.: *retaliatory action*

**re·tali·ation** /rɪˌtæliˈeɪʃn/ noun [U] action that a person takes against sb who has harmed them in some way **SYN** reprisal: ~ **(against sb/sth) (for sth)** *retaliation against UN workers* ◊ **in** ~ **(for sth)** *The shooting may have been in retaliation for the arrest of the terrorist suspects.*

**re·tard** verb, noun
▪ verb /rɪˈtɑːd; NAmE -ˈtɑːrd/ ~ **sth** (formal) to make the development or progress of sth slower **SYN** delay, slow: *The progression of the disease can be retarded by early surgery.* ▸ **re·tard·ation** /ˌriːtɑːˈdeɪʃn; NAmE -tɑːrˈd-/ noun [U]: *Many factors can lead to growth retardation in unborn babies.*
▪ noun /ˈriːtɑːd; NAmE -tɑːrd/ (taboo, slang) an offensive way of describing sb who is not intelligent, has not developed normally or who you think is stupid

**re·tard·ed** /rɪˈtɑːdɪd; NAmE -ˈtɑːrd-/ adj. (old-fashioned, offensive) less developed mentally than is normal for a particular age **SYN** backward

**retch** /retʃ/ verb [I] to make sounds and movements as if you are VOMITING but do not actually do so **SYN** heave: *The smell made her retch.*

**re·tell** /ˌriːˈtel/ verb (**re·told**, **re·told** /-ˈtəʊld/) ~ **sth** to tell a story again, often in a different way

**re·ten·tion** /rɪˈtenʃn/ noun [U] (formal) **1** the action of keeping sth rather than losing it or stopping it: *The company needs to improve its training and retention of staff.* **2** the action of keeping liquid, heat, etc. inside sth rather than letting it escape: *Eating too much salt can cause fluid retention.* **3** the ability to remember things: *Visual material aids the retention of information.* ⊃ see also RETAIN

**re·ten·tive** /rɪˈtentɪv/ adj. (of the memory) able to store facts and remember things easily ⊃ see also RETAIN

**re·test** /ˌriːˈtest/ verb ~ **sb**/**sth** to test sb/sth again: *Subjects were retested one month later.*

**re·think** /ˌriːˈθɪŋk/ verb (**re·thought**, **re·thought** /-ˈθɔːt/) [T, I] ~ **(sth)** to think again about an idea, a course of action, etc., especially in order to change it: *to rethink a plan* ▸ **re·think** /ˈriːθɪŋk/ (also **re·think·ing** /ˌriːˈθɪŋkɪŋ/) noun [sing.]: *to have a radical rethink of company policy*

**reti·cent** /ˈretɪsnt/ adj. (formal) unwilling to tell people about things **SYN** reserved, uncommunicative: *She was shy and reticent.* ◊ ~ **about sth** *He was extremely reticent about his personal life.* ▸ **reti·cence** /-sns/ noun [U]

**re·ticu·la·ted** /rɪˈtɪkjuleɪtɪd/ adj. (specialist) built, arranged or marked like a net or network, with many small squares or sections

**ret·ina** /ˈretɪnə/ noun (pl. **ret·inas** or **ret·inae** /-niː/) a layer of TISSUE at the back of the eye that is sensitive to light and sends signals to the brain about what is seen ▸ **ret·inal** /-nl/ [usually before noun], adj.

**ret·inue** /ˈretɪnjuː; NAmE -tənuː/ noun [C + sing./pl. v.] a group of people who travel with an important person to provide help and support **SYN** entourage

**re·tire** 🔑 B1 /rɪˈtaɪə(r)/ verb
• **FROM JOB 1** 🔑 B1 [I, T] to leave your job and stop working, especially because you have reached a particular age or because you are ill; to tell sb they must stop doing their job: *The company's official retiring age is 65.* ◊ ~ **from sth** *She was forced to retire early from teaching because of ill health.* ◊ ~ **to sth** *My dream is to retire to a villa in France.* ◊ ~ **as sth** *He has no plans to retire as editor of the magazine.* ◊ ~ **sb** *She was retired on medical grounds.* ⊃ WORDFINDER NOTE at EMPLOY

# retired

- **IN SPORT** **2** [I] to stop competing during a game, race, etc., usually because you are injured: ~ **(from sth)** *She fell badly, spraining her ankle, and had to retire.* ◊ **+ adj.** *He retired hurt in the first five minutes of the game.*
- **FROM/TO A PLACE 3** [I] (*formal*) to leave a place, especially to go somewhere quieter or more private: *The jury retired to consider the evidence.* ◊ **~to sth** *After dinner he likes to retire to his study.*
- **OF ARMY 4** [I] (*formal*) to move back from a battle in order to organize your soldiers in a different way
- **GO TO BED 5** [I] (*literary*) to go to bed: *I retired late that evening.*
- **IN BASEBALL 6** [T] **~sb** to make a player or team have to stop their turn at BATTING: *He retired twelve batters in a row.*

**re·tired** ⓘ **B1** /rɪˈtaɪəd; *NAmE* -ərd/ *adj.* having retired from work: *a retired doctor/teacher/officer/general* ◊ *Dad is retired now.*

**re·tir·ee** /rɪˌtaɪəˈriː/ *noun* (*NAmE*) a person who has stopped working because of their age

**re·tire·ment** ⚡+ **B2** /rɪˈtaɪəmənt; *NAmE* -ərm-/ *noun* **1** ⚡+ **B2** [U, C] the fact of stopping work because you have reached a particular age; the time when you do this: *At 60, he was now approaching retirement.* ◊ *Susan is going to take early retirement* (= retire before the usual age). ◊ *retirement age* ◊ *a retirement pension* **2** ⚡+ **B2** [U, sing.] the period of your life after you have stopped work at a particular age: *to provide for retirement* ◊ *We all wish you a long and happy retirement.* ◊ **in ~** *Up to a third of one's life is now being spent in retirement.* **3** ⚡ **C1** [U] ~ **(from sth)** the act of stopping a particular type of work, especially in sport, politics, etc.; the period of your life after a career in sport, politics, etc: *He announced his retirement from football.* ◊ *She came out of retirement to win two gold medals at the championships.*

**re·tirement community** *noun* a group of homes for older or retired people, with facilities offering activities and services: *My parents' retirement community has its own golf course.*

**re·tirement home** (*BrE also* **old 'people's home**) *noun* a place where old people live and are cared for

**re·tirement plan** *noun* (*NAmE*) = PENSION PLAN

**re·tir·ing** /rɪˈtaɪərɪŋ/ *adj.* preferring not to spend time with other people **SYN** *shy*: *a quiet, retiring man*

**re·told** /ˌriːˈtəʊld/ past tense, past part. of RETELL

**re·tool** /ˌriːˈtuːl/ *verb* **1** [T, I] ~**(sth)** to replace or change the machines or equipment in a factory so that it can produce new or better goods **2** [T] ~**sth** (*NAmE, informal*) to organize sth in a new or different way

**re·tort** /rɪˈtɔːt; *NAmE* -ˈtɔːrt/ *verb, noun*
- *verb* to reply quickly to a comment, in an angry, offended or humorous way: **+ speech** '*Don't be ridiculous!*' *Pat retorted angrily.* ◊ ~**that** … *Sam retorted that it was my fault as much as his.*
- *noun* **1** a quick, angry or humorous reply **SYN** **rejoinder, riposte**: *She bit back* (= stopped herself from making) *a sharp retort.* **2** a closed bottle with a long narrow bent SPOUT that is used in a laboratory for heating chemicals

**re·touch** /ˌriːˈtʌtʃ/ *verb* ~**sth** to make small changes to a picture or photograph so that it looks better

**re·trace** /rɪˈtreɪs/ *verb* **1** ~**sth** to go back along exactly the same path or route that you have come along: *She turned around and began to retrace her steps towards the house.* **2** ~**sth** to make the same trip that sb else has made in the past: *They are hoping to retrace the epic voyage of Christopher Columbus.* **3** ~**sth** to find out what sb has done or where they have been: *Detectives are trying to retrace her movements on the night she disappeared.*

**re·tract** /rɪˈtrækt/ *verb* **1** ~**sth** (*formal*) to say that sth you have said earlier is not true or correct or that you did not mean it: *He made a false confession which he later retracted.* ◊ *They tried to persuade me to retract my words.* **2** [T] ~**sth** (*formal*) to refuse to keep an agreement, a promise, etc: *to retract an offer* **3** [I, T] (*specialist*) to move back into the main part of sth; to pull sth back into the main part of sth: *The animal retracted into its shell.* ◊ ~**sth** *The undercarriage was fully retracted.*

**re·tract·able** /rɪˈtræktəbl/ *adj.* that can be moved or pulled back into the main part of sth: *a knife with a retractable blade*

**re·trac·tion** /rɪˈtrækʃn/ *noun* (*formal*) **1** [C] a statement saying that sth you previously said or wrote is not true: *He demanded a full retraction of the allegations against him.* **2** [U] (*specialist*) the act of pulling sth back (= of retracting it): *the retraction of a cat's claws*

**re·train** /ˌriːˈtreɪn/ *verb* [I, T] to learn, or to teach sb, a new type of work, a new skill, etc: ~**(sb) (as sth)** *She retrained as a teacher.* ◊ ~**sb to do sth** *Staff have been retrained to use the new technology.* ▶ **re·train·ing** *noun* [U]

**re·tread** *noun, verb*
- *noun* /ˈriːtred/ **1** (*disapproving*) a book, film, song, etc. that contains ideas that have been used before **2** a tyre made by putting a new rubber surface on an old tyre
- *verb* /ˌriːˈtred/ (**retrod** /ˌriːˈtrɒd; *NAmE* -ˈtrɑːd/, **retrodden** /ˌriːˈtrɒdn; *NAmE* -ˈtrɑːdn/) **HELP** In sense 3, **retreaded** /ˌriːˈtredɪd/ is used for the past tense and past participle. **1** ~**sth** to go back along a route that you have already travelled along: *You'll often have to retread the same ground to find the exit.* ◊ *You'll have to retread certain areas in the normal course of gameplay.* ◊ (*figurative*) *It feels like this discussion is just retreading old ground.* **2** ~**sth** (*disapproving*) to make a new version of a book, film, song, etc., usually one that is not as interesting as the original: *The author retreads an old and familiar story.* **3** ~**sth** to put a new rubber surface on an old tyre

**re·treat** ⚡+ **C1** /rɪˈtriːt/ *noun, verb*
- *noun*
- **FROM DANGER/DEFEAT 1** ⚡+ **C1** [C, usually sing., U] a movement away from a place or an enemy because of danger or defeat: *Napoleon's retreat from Moscow* ◊ *The army was in full retreat* (= retreating very quickly). ◊ *to sound the retreat* (= to give a loud signal for an army to move away)
- **ESCAPE 2** ⚡+ **C1** [C, usually sing., U] ~ **(from/into sth)** an act of trying to escape from a particular situation to one that you think is safer or more pleasant **SYN** **escape**: *Is watching television a retreat from reality?*
- **CHANGE OF DECISION 3** [C, usually sing.] an act of changing a decision because of criticism or because a situation has become too difficult: *The Senator made an embarrassing retreat from his earlier position.*
- **QUIET PLACE 4** [C] a quiet, private place that you go to in order to get away from your usual life: *a country retreat* **5** [U, C] a period of time when sb stops their usual activities and goes to a quiet place for prayer and thought; an organized event when people can do this: *He went into retreat and tried to resolve the conflicts within himself.* ◊ *to go on a Buddhist retreat* **IDM** see BEAT *v.*
- *verb*
- **FROM DANGER/DEFEAT 1** ⚡+ **C1** [I] to move away from a place or an enemy because you are in danger or because you have been defeated: *The army was forced to retreat after suffering heavy losses.* ◊ *We retreated back down the mountain.* **OPP** **advance**
- **MOVE AWAY/BACK 2** ⚡+ **C1** [I] to move away or back **SYN** **recede**: *He watched her retreating figure.* ◊ *The flood waters slowly retreated.*
- **TO QUIET PLACE 3** ⚡+ **C1** [I] (+ *adv./prep.*) to escape to a place that is quieter or safer **SYN** **retire**: *Bored with the conversation, she retreated to her bedroom.* ◊ (*figurative*) *He retreated into a world of fantasy.*
- **CHANGE DECISION 4** [I] + *adv./prep.* to change your mind about sth because of criticism or because a situation has become too difficult **SYN** **back off (from sth)**: *The government had retreated from its pledge to reduce class sizes.*
- **FINANCE 5** [I] + *noun* to lose value: *Share prices retreated 45p to 538p.*

**re·trench** /rɪˈtrentʃ/ *verb* **1** [I] (*formal*) (of a business, government, etc.) to spend less money; to reduce costs **2** [T] ~**sb** (*AustralE, NZE, SAfrE*) to tell sb that they cannot continue working for you ▶ **re·trench·ment** *noun* [U, C]: *a period of retrenchment*

**re·trial** /ˌriːˈtraɪəl/ noun [usually sing.] a new trial of a person whose criminal offence has already been judged once in court

**ret·ri·bu·tion** /ˌretrɪˈbjuːʃn/ noun [U] ~ (for sth) (formal) severe punishment for sth seriously wrong that sb has done: *People are seeking retribution for the latest terrorist outrages.* ◊ *fear of divine retribution* (= punishment from God) ▶ **re·tribu·tive** /rɪˈtrɪbjətɪv/ adj. [usually before noun]: *retributive justice*

**re·trieval** /rɪˈtriːvl/ noun [U] **1** (formal) the process of getting sth back, especially from a place where it should not be SYN **recovery**: *The ship was buried, beyond retrieval, at the bottom of the sea.* ◊ **beyond** ~ (figurative) *By then the situation was beyond retrieval* (= impossible to put right). **2** (computing) the process of getting back information that is stored on a computer: *methods of information retrieval*

**re·trieve** /rɪˈtriːv/ verb **1** (formal) to bring or get sth back, especially from a place where it should not be SYN **recover**: *~ sth from sb/sth She bent to retrieve her comb from the floor.* ◊ *~ sth The police have managed to retrieve some of the stolen money.* **2** (computing) to find and get back data or information that has been stored in the memory of a computer: *~ sth from sb/sth to retrieve information from the database* ◊ *~ sth The program allows you to retrieve items quickly by searching under a keyword.* ⊃ WORDFINDER NOTE at PROGRAM **3** ~ sth to make a bad situation better; to get back sth that was lost: *You can only retrieve the situation by apologizing.* ▶ **re·triev·able** /-ˈtriːvəbl/ adj. OPP **irretrievable**

**re·triever** /rɪˈtriːvə(r)/ noun a large dog used in hunting to bring back birds that have been shot ⊃ see also GOLDEN RETRIEVER

**retro** /ˈretrəʊ/ adj. using styles or fashions from the recent past: *the current Seventies retro trend*

**retro-** /retrəʊ, retrə/ prefix (in nouns, adjectives and adverbs) back or backwards: *retrograde* ◊ *retrospective*

**retro·active** /ˌretrəʊˈæktɪv/ adj. (formal) = RETROSPECTIVE ▶ **retro·active·ly** adv.: *The ruling should be applied retroactively.*

**retro·fit** /ˈretrəʊfɪt/ verb (-tt-) ~ sth to put a new piece of equipment into a machine that did not have it when it was built; to provide a machine with a new part, etc: *Voice recorders were retrofitted into planes already in service.* ◊ *They retrofitted the plane with improved seating.* ▶ **retro·fit** noun

**retro·grade** /ˈretrəɡreɪd/ adj. (formal, disapproving) (of an action) making a situation worse or returning to how sth was in the past: *The closure of the factory is a retrograde step.*

**retro·gres·sive** /ˌretrəˈɡresɪv/ adj. (formal, disapproving) returning to old-fashioned ideas or methods instead of making progress OPP **progressive**

**retro·spect** /ˈretrəspekt/ noun
IDM **in ˈretrospect** thinking about a past event or situation, often with a different opinion of it from the one you had at the time: *In retrospect, I think that I was wrong.* ◊ *The decision seems extremely odd, in retrospect.*

**retro·spec·tion** /ˌretrəˈspekʃn/ noun [U] (formal) thinking about past events or situations

**retro·spect·ive** /ˌretrəˈspektɪv/ adj., noun
■ adj. **1** thinking about or connected with sth that happened in the past **2** (also less frequent, formal **retro·active**) (of a new law or decision) intended to take effect from a particular date in the past rather than from the present date: *retrospective legislation* ◊ *retrospective pay awards* ▶ **retro·spect·ive·ly** adv.: *She wrote retrospectively about her childhood.* ◊ *The new rule will be applied retrospectively.*
■ noun a public exhibition of the work that an artist has done in the past, showing how his or her work has developed

**retro·virus** /ˈretrəʊvaɪrəs/ noun any of a group of viruses that includes HIV. Retroviruses multiply by making changes to DNA. ⊃ see also ANTIRETROVIRAL

**retry** /ˌriːˈtraɪ/ verb (re·tries, re·try·ing, re·tried, re·tried) **1** [T] ~ sb/sth to examine a person or case again in court **2** [I] to make another attempt to do sth, especially on a computer

---

1327 **return**

**re·turn** /rɪˈtɜːn; NAmE -ˈtɜːrn/ verb, noun
■ verb
• COME/GO BACK **1** [I] to come or go back from one place to another: *~ to… She's returning to Australia tomorrow after six months in Europe.* ◊ *He had recently returned to this country after living in Spain.* ◊ *~ from… I returned from work to find the house empty.* ◊ *People were returning home for the weekend.*
• BRING/GIVE BACK **2** [T] to bring, give, put or send sth back to sb/sth: *~ sb/sth to sb/sth We had to return the hairdryer to the store because it was faulty.* ◊ *I must return some books to the library.* ◊ *~ sth He refused to return our money.* ◊ *~ sb/sth + adj. I returned the letter unopened.*
• OF FEELING/SITUATION **3** [I] to come back again SYN **reappear, resurface**: *The following day the pain returned.* ◊ *There's a chance the cancer will return.*
• TO PREVIOUS SUBJECT/ACTIVITY **4** [I] ~ to sth to start discussing a subject you were discussing earlier, or doing an activity you were doing earlier: *He returns to this topic later in the report.* ◊ *She looked up briefly then returned to her sewing.* ◊ *The doctor may allow her to return to work next week.*
• TO PREVIOUS STATE **5** [I] ~ to sth to go back to a previous state: *Train services have returned to normal after the strike.*
• DO/GIVE THE SAME **6** [T] ~ sth to do or give sth to sb because they have done or given the same to you first; to have the same feeling about sb that they have about you: *to return a smile/gaze/greeting* ◊ *If you assist people when they ask for help, it is more likely they will return the favour.* ◊ *She phoned him several times but he was too busy to return her call.* ◊ *'You were both wonderful!' 'So were you!' we said, returning the compliment.* ◊ *He did not return her love.* ◊ *to return fire* (= to shoot at sb who is shooting at you)
• IN TENNIS **7** [T] ~ sth to hit the ball back to your opponent during a game: *to return a service/shot*
• A VERDICT **8** [T] ~ a verdict to give a decision about sth in court: *The jury returned a verdict of not guilty.*
• ELECT POLITICIAN **9** [T, usually passive] ~ sb (to sth) | ~ sb (as sth) (BrE) to elect sb to a political position
• PROFIT/LOSS **10** [T] ~ sth (business) to give or produce a particular amount of money as a profit or loss: *to return a high rate of interest* ◊ *Last year the company returned a loss of £157 million.*

■ noun
• COMING BACK **1** [sing.] the action of arriving in or coming back to a place that you were in before: *~ of sb/sth (to …) (from …) A week had passed since their return to Geneva.* ◊ *on/upon sb/sth's ~ He was met by his brother on his return from Italy.* ◊ *on the return flight/journey/trip/visit*
• GIVING/SENDING BACK **2** [U, sing.] the action of giving, putting or sending sth/sb back: *~ of sth/sb We would appreciate the prompt return of books to the library.* ◊ *The judge ordered the return of the child to his mother.* ◊ *Write your return address* (= the address that a reply should be sent to) *on the back of the envelope.*
• OF FEELING/STATE **3** [sing.] the situation when a feeling or state that has not been experienced for some time starts again SYN **reappearance**: *~ of sth the return of spring* ◊ *a return of my doubts*
• TO PREVIOUS SITUATION/ACTIVITY **4** [sing.] the action of going back to an activity or a situation that you used to do or be in: *~ to sth his return to power* ◊ *This film is a welcome return to form for the groundbreaking director.*
• PROFIT **5** [U, C] the amount of profit that you get from sth SYN **earnings, yield**: *a high rate of return on capital* ◊ *the return on investment* ◊ *annual/investment returns* ◊ *farmers seeking to improve returns from their crops*
• OFFICIAL REPORT **6** [C] an official report or statement that gives particular information to the government or another body: *census returns* ◊ *election returns* (= the number of votes for each candidate in an election) ◊ *US citizens living in Canada must file tax returns under both systems.* ⊃ see also TAX RETURN
• TICKET **7** [C] (BrE) = RETURN TICKET: *'Brighton, please.' 'Single or return?'* ◊ *A return is cheaper than two singles.* ◊ *the return fare to London* ⊃ see also DAY RETURN **8** [C] a ticket

R

# returnable 1328

for the theatre or a sports game that was bought by sb but is given back to be sold again
- **ON COMPUTER** **9** [U] (also **re'turn key** [C]) the button that you press on a computer when you reach the end of an instruction, or to begin a new line: *To exit this option, press return.* ⊃ **WORDFINDER NOTE** at **KEYBOARD**
- **IN TENNIS** **10** [C] (in tennis and some other sports) the action of hitting the ball, etc. back to your opponent: *a powerful return of serve*

**IDM** ▶ **by re'turn (of 'post)** (*BrE*) using the next available post; as soon as possible: *Please reply by return of post.* **in re'turn (for sth)** **1** as a way of thanking sb or paying them for sth they have done: *Can I buy you lunch in return for your help?* **2** as a response or reaction to sth: *I asked her opinion, but she just asked me a question in return.* ⊃ more at DIMINISH, HAPPY, POINT *n.*, SALE

▼ **SYNONYMS**

**return**
come back • go back • get back • turn back

These words all mean to come or go back from one place to another.

**return** to come or go back from one place to another: *I waited a long time for him to return.* **NOTE** **Return** is slightly more formal than the other words in this group, and is used more often in writing or formal speech.

**come back** to return. **NOTE** **Come back** is usually used from the point of view of the person or place that sb returns to: *Come back and visit again soon!*

**go back** to return to the place you recently or originally came from or that you have been to before. **NOTE** **Go back** is usually used from the point of view of the person who is returning: *Do you ever want to go back to China?*

**get back** to arrive back somewhere, especially at your home or the place where you are staying: *What time did you get back last night?*

**turn back** to return the way that you came, especially because sth stops you from continuing: *The weather got so bad that we had to turn back.*

**PATTERNS**
- to return / come back / go back / get back **to / from / with** sth
- to return / come back / go back / get back / turn back **again**
- to return / come back / go back / get back **home / to work**
- to return / come back / get back **safely**

**re·turn·able** /rɪˈtɜːnəbl; *NAmE* -ˈtɜːrn-/ *adj.* **1** (*formal*) that can or must be given back after a period of time: *A returnable deposit is payable on arrival.* ◊ *The application form is returnable not later than 7th June.* **2** (of bottles and containers) that can be taken back to a shop in order to be used again **OPP** **non-returnable**

**re'turn address** *noun* the address that a letter should be returned to if it cannot be delivered

**re·turn·ee** /rɪˌtɜːˈniː; *NAmE* -ˌtɜːrˈniː/ *noun* [usually pl.] (*especially NAmE*) a person who returns to their own country, after living in another country

**re·turn·er** /rɪˈtɜːnə(r); *NAmE* -ˈtɜːrn-/ *noun* (*BrE*) a person who goes back to work after not working for a long time

**re'turning officer** *noun* (*BrE*) an official in a particular area who is responsible for arranging an election and announcing the result

**re'turn 'match** (also **re'turn 'game**) *noun* (*especially BrE*) a second match or game between the same two players or teams

**re'turn 'ticket** (also **re-turn**) (*both BrE*) (*NAmE* **round-trip 'ticket**) *noun* a ticket for a journey to a place and back again

**re'turn 'visit** *noun* a trip to a place that you have been to once before, or a trip to see sb who has already come to see you: *This hotel is worth a return visit.* ◊ *The US president is making a return visit to Moscow.*

**re·tweet** /ˌriːˈtwiːt/ *verb* if you retweet a message written by another user on the Twitter SOCIAL MEDIA service, the message can be seen by all of the people who regularly receive messages from you ▶ **retweet** /ˈriːtwiːt/ *noun*

**re·unify** /ˌriːˈjuːnɪfaɪ/ *verb* [often passive] (**re·uni·fies, re·uni·fy·ing, re·uni·fied, re·uni·fied**) ~ **sth** to join together two or more regions or parts of a country so that they form a single political unit again ▶ **re·uni·fi·ca·tion** /ˌriːˌjuːnɪfɪˈkeɪʃn/ *noun* [U]: *the reunification of Germany*

**re·union** /ˌriːˈjuːniən/ *noun* **1** [C] a social occasion or party attended by a group of people who have not seen each other for a long time: *a family reunion* ◊ *the school's annual reunion* ◊ *a reunion of the class of '85* **2** [C, U] ~ **(with sb)** | ~ **(between A and B)** the act of people coming together again after they have been apart for some time: *an emotional reunion between mother and son* ◊ *Christmas is a time of reunion.* **3** [U] the action of becoming a single group or organization again: *the reunion of the Church of England with the Church of Rome*

**re·unite** /ˌriːjuˈnaɪt/ *verb* [T, I] **1** [usually passive] to bring two or more people together again after they have been separated for a long time; to come together again: ~ **A with / and B** *Last night she was reunited with her children.* ◊ ~ **(sb)** *The family was reunited after the war.* ◊ *There have been rumours that the band will reunite for a world tour.* **2** ~ **(sth)** to join together again separate areas or separate groups within an organization, a political party, etc.; to come together again: *As leader, his main aim is to reunite the party.*

**re·us·able** /ˌriːˈjuːzəbl/ *adj.* that can be used again: *reusable plastic bottles*

**reuse** /ˌriːˈjuːz/ *verb* ~ **sth** to use sth again: *Please reuse your envelopes.* ▶ **reuse** /-ˈjuːs/ *noun* [U]

**Rev.** /rev/ (*BrE also* **Revd**) *abbr.* (used before a name) REVEREND: *Rev. Jesse Jackson*

**rev** /rev/ *verb, noun*
- *verb* [T, I] (-vv-) ~ **(sth) (up)** when you **rev** an engine or it **revs**, it runs quickly: *The taxi driver revved up his engine.* ◊ *I could hear the car revving outside.*
- *noun* (*informal*) a complete turn of an engine, used when talking about an engine's speed **SYN** revolution: *4 000 revs per minute* ◊ *The needle on the rev counter soared.*

**re·value** /ˌriːˈvæljuː/ *verb* **1** [T] ~ **sth** to estimate the value of sth again, especially giving it a higher value **2** [T, I] ~ **(sth)** to increase the value of the money of a country when it is exchanged for the money of another country: *The yen is to be revalued.* **OPP** devalue ▶ **re·valu·ation** /ˌriːˌvæljuˈeɪʃn/ *noun* [U, C, usually sing.]: *the revaluation of the pound*

**re·vamp** /ˌriːˈvæmp/ *verb* ~ **sth** (*informal*) to make changes to the form of sth, usually to improve its appearance ▶ **re·vamp** /ˈriːvæmp/ *noun* [sing.]

**re·veal** 🔊 **B2** 🟦 /rɪˈviːl/ *verb, noun*
- *verb* **1** 🔊 **B2** to make sth known to sb **SYN** disclose: ~ **sth** *to reveal a secret* ◊ *A series of flashbacks reveal the details of the tragedy.* ◊ ~ **sth to sb** *The doctors did not reveal the truth to him.* ◊ ~ **(that)** … *The report reveals that the company made a loss of £20 million last year.* ◊ *it is revealed that* … *It was revealed that important evidence had been suppressed.* ◊ ~ **how, what, etc** … *Officers could not reveal how he died.* ◊ ~ **sb / sth to be / have sth** *Salted peanuts were recently revealed to be the nation's favourite snack.* ◊ ~ **sb / sth as sth** *He has been revealed as a traitor.* ⊃ LANGUAGE BANK at EVIDENCE **2** 🔊 **B2** to show sth that previously could not be seen **SYN** display: ~ **sth** *He laughed, revealing a line of white teeth.* ◊ *The door opened to reveal a cosy little room.* ◊ ~ **yourself** *She crouched in the dark, too frightened to reveal herself.* ⊃ see also REVELATION, REVELATORY, FAIL *noun* (2)
- *noun* (*informal*) the moment when a previously secret piece of information is made known, such as the winner of a prize, or the solution to a mystery in a film or TV drama: *The big reveal at the end of the movie answers all questions.*

**re·veal·ing** /rɪˈviːlɪŋ/ *adj.* **1** giving you interesting information that you did not know before: *The document provided a revealing insight into the government's priorities.* ◊

*The answers the children gave were extremely revealing.* **2** (of clothes) allowing more of sb's body to be seen than usual: *a revealing blouse* ▶ **re·veal·ing·ly** *adv.*: *He spoke revealingly about his problems.*

**re·veille** /rɪˈvæli; NAmE ˈrevəli/ *noun* [U] a tune that is played to wake soldiers in the morning; the time when it is played

**revel** /ˈrevl/ *verb, noun*
■ *verb* [I] (-ll-, US -l-) to spend time enjoying yourself in a noisy, enthusiastic way SYN **make merry**
PHRV **ˈrevel in sth** to enjoy sth very much: *She was clearly revelling in all the attention.* ◊ **revel in doing sth** *Some people seem to revel in annoying others.*
■ *noun* [usually pl.] (*literary*) noisy celebrations

**reve·la·tion** C1 /ˌrevəˈleɪʃn/ *noun* **1** [C] ~ (about/concerning sth) | ~ (that ...) a fact that people are made aware of, especially one that has been secret and is surprising SYN **disclosure**: *startling/sensational revelations about her private life* **2** [C] the act of making people aware of sth that has been secret SYN **disclosure**: *The company's financial problems followed the revelation of a major fraud scandal.* **3** [C, U] something that is considered to be a sign or message from God ⊃ see also REVEAL
IDM **come as/be a revelation (to sb)** to be a completely new or surprising experience; to be different from what was expected

**rev·ela·tory** /ˌrevəˈleɪtəri; NAmE ˈrevələtɔːri/ *adj.* (*formal*) making people aware of sth that they did not know before: *a revelatory insight* ⊃ see also REVEAL

**rev·el·ler** (US **rev·el·er**) /ˈrevələ(r)/ *noun* a person who is having fun in a noisy way, usually with a group of other people and often after drinking alcohol

**rev·el·ry** /ˈrevlri/ *noun* [U] (also **rev·el·ries** [pl.]) noisy fun, usually involving a lot of eating and drinking SYN **festivity, merrymaking**: *We could hear sounds of revelry from next door.* ◊ *New Year revelries*

**re·venge** /rɪˈvendʒ/ *noun, verb*
■ *noun* [U] **1** something that you do in order to make sb suffer because they have made you suffer: *an act of revenge* ◊ *~ for sth She is seeking revenge for the murder of her husband.* ◊ *in ~ for sth The bombing was in revenge for the assassination.* ◊ *~ on sb/sth He swore to take (his) revenge on his political enemies.* ◊ *revenge attacks/killings* **2** ~ (for sth) (*sport*) the defeat of a person or team that defeated you in a previous game: *The team wanted to get revenge for their defeat earlier in the season.*
■ *verb*
PHRV **reˈvenge yourself on sb | be reˈvenged on sb** (*literary*) to punish or hurt sb because they have made you suffer: *She vowed to be revenged on them all.* ⊃ note at AVENGE

**rev·enue** B2 /ˈrevənjuː; NAmE -nuː/ *noun* [U] (also **revenues** [pl.]) the money that a government receives from taxes or that an organization, etc. receives from its business SYN **receipts**: *a shortfall in tax revenue* ◊ *a slump in oil revenues* ◊ *The company's annual revenues rose by 30%.*

**ˌRevenue and ˈCustoms** *noun* = HM REVENUE AND CUSTOMS

**ˈrevenue stream** *noun* the money that a company or person earns from a particular activity; a means by which a company or person earns money: *Hiring the venue out for weddings will create an additional revenue stream.*

**re·verb** /ˈriːvɜːb; NAmE -vɜːrb/ *noun* [U] a sound effect that can be changed by electronic means to give music more or less of an ECHO

**re·ver·ber·ate** /rɪˈvɜːbəreɪt; NAmE -ˈvɜːrb-/ *verb* **1** [I] (of a sound) to be repeated several times as it is reflected off different surfaces SYN **echo**: *Her voice reverberated around the hall.* **2** [I] ~ (with/to sth) (of a place) to seem to shake because of a loud noise: *The hall reverberated with the sound of music and dancing.* **3** [I] (*formal*) to have a strong effect on people for a long time or over a large area: *Repercussions of the case continue to reverberate through the financial world.*

**re·ver·ber·ation** /rɪˌvɜːbəˈreɪʃn; NAmE -ˌvɜːrb-/ *noun* **1** [C, usually pl., U] a loud noise that continues for some time

after it has been produced because of the surfaces around it SYN **echo 2 reverberations** [pl.] the effects of sth that happens, especially unpleasant ones that spread among a large number of people SYN **repercussion**

**re·vere** /rɪˈvɪə(r); NAmE -ˈvɪr/ *verb* [usually passive] ~ **sb (as sth)** (*formal*) to admire and respect sb/sth very much SYN **idolize**

**rev·er·ence** /ˈrevərəns/ *noun* [U] ~ (for sb/sth) (*formal*) a feeling of admiring and respecting sb/sth very much: *The poem conveys his deep reverence for nature.*

**Rev·er·end** /ˈrevərənd/ *adj.* [only before noun] **Reverend** (*abbr.* **Rev.**) the title of a member of the clergy that is also sometimes used to talk to or about one: *the Reverend Charles Dodgson* ◊ *Good morning, Reverend.* ⊃ see also RIGHT REVEREND

**rev·er·ent** /ˈrevərənt/ *adj.* (*formal*) showing deep respect SYN **respectful** ▶ **rev·er·ent·ly** *adv*

**rev·er·en·tial** /ˌrevəˈrenʃl/ *adj.* (*formal*) showing deep respect: *His name was always mentioned in almost reverential tones.* ▶ **rev·er·en·tial·ly** /-ʃəli/ *adv.*: *She lowered her voice reverentially.*

**rev·erie** /ˈrevəri/ *noun* [C, U] (*formal*) a state of thinking about pleasant things, almost as though you are dreaming SYN **daydream**: *She was jolted out of her reverie as the door opened.*

**re·ver·sal** /rɪˈvɜːsl; NAmE -ˈvɜːrsl/ *noun* **1** [C, U] ~ (of sth) a change of sth so that it is the opposite of what it was: *a complete/dramatic/sudden reversal of policy* ◊ *the reversal of a decision* ◊ *The government suffered a total reversal of fortune(s) last week.* **2** [C] a change from being successful to having problems or being defeated: *the team's recent reversal* ◊ *The company's financial problems were only a temporary reversal.* **3** [C, U] an exchange of positions or functions between two or more people: *It's a complete role reversal/reversal of roles* (= for example when a child cares for a parent).

**re·verse** C1 /rɪˈvɜːs; NAmE -ˈvɜːrs/ *verb, noun, adj.*
■ *verb*
• CHANGE TO OPPOSITE **1** C1 [T] ~ **sth** to change sth completely so that it is the opposite of what it was before: *Falling birth rates may reverse the trend towards early retirement.* ◊ *The government has failed to reverse the economic decline.* ◊ *It is sometimes possible to arrest or reverse the disease.* **2** C1 [T] ~ **sth** to change a previous decision, law, etc. to the opposite one SYN **revoke**: *The Court of Appeal reversed the decision.* **3** C1 [T] ~ **sth** to turn sth the opposite way around or change the order of sth around: *Writing is reversed in a mirror.* ◊ *You should reverse the order of these pages.*
• EXCHANGE TWO THINGS **4** C1 [T] ~ **sth** to exchange the positions or functions of two things: *It felt as if we had reversed our roles of parent and child.* ◊ *She used to work for me, but our situations are now reversed.*
• YOURSELF **5** C1 [T] ~ **yourself (on sth)** (NAmE) to admit you were wrong or to stop having a particular position in an argument: *He has reversed himself on a dozen issues.*
• VEHICLE **6** C1 [I, T] (*especially BrE*) when a vehicle or its driver **reverses** or the driver **reverses** a vehicle, the vehicle goes backwards: *He reversed around the corner.* ◊ *She reversed into a parking space.* ◊ *Caution! This truck is reversing.* ◊ *~ sth Now reverse the car.* ⊃ compare BACK
• PHONE CALL **7** [T] ~ **(the) charges** (*BrE*) to make a phone call that will be paid for by the person you are calling, not by you: *I want to reverse the charges, please.* ⊃ see also COLLECT *adj.*
■ *noun*
• OPPOSITE **1** C1 **the reverse** [sing.] the opposite of what has just been mentioned: *This problem is the reverse of the previous one.* ◊ *Although I expected to enjoy living in the country, in fact the reverse is true.* ◊ *In the south, the reverse applies.* ◊ *It wasn't easy to persuade her to come —quite the reverse.*
• BACK **2 the reverse** [sing.] the back of a coin, piece of material, piece of paper, etc. ⊃ compare OBVERSE (2)
• IN VEHICLE **3** (*also* **reˈverse ˈgear**) [U] the machine in a vehicle used to make it move backwards: *Put the car in/ into reverse.*

# reverse-charge

- LOSS/DEFEAT **4** [C] (*formal*) a loss or defeat; a change from success to failure SYN **setback**: *Property values have suffered another reverse.* ◇ *a damaging political reverse*

IDM **go/put sth into re'verse** to start to happen or to make sth happen in the opposite way: *In 2008 economic growth went into reverse.* **in re'verse** in the opposite order or way SYN **backwards**: *The secret number is my phone number in reverse.* ◇ *We did a similar trip to you, but in reverse.*

- **adj.** [only before noun]
- OPPOSITE **1** ?+ C1 opposite to what has been mentioned: *to travel in the reverse direction* ◇ *The winners were announced in reverse order* (= the person in the lowest place was announced first). ◇ *The experiment had the reverse effect to what was intended.*
- BACK **2** opposite to the front: *Iron the garment on the reverse side.*

**re'verse-'charge** *adj.* a **reverse-charge** phone call is paid for by the person who receives the call, not by the person who makes it ▶ **re,verse-'charge** *adv.*: *I didn't have any money so I had to call reverse-charge.*

**re,verse dis,crimi'nation** *noun* [U] (*disapproving*) the practice or policy of making sure that a particular number of jobs, etc. are given to people from groups that are often treated unfairly because of their race, sex, etc. HELP The term **reverse discrimination** is nearly always used in a disapproving way; to describe this policy in a way that is not necessarily disapproving use **positive discrimination** or **affirmative action**.

**re,verse engi'neering** *noun* [U] the copying of another company's product after examining it carefully to find out how it is made

**re,vers·ible** /rɪˈvɜːsəbl; NAmE -ˈvɜːrs-/ *adj.* **1** (of clothes, materials, etc.) that can be turned inside out and worn or used with either side showing: *a reversible jacket* **2** (of a process, an action or a disease) that can be changed so that sth returns to its original state or situation: *Is the trend towards privatization reversible?* ◇ *reversible kidney failure* OPP **irreversible** ▶ **re,vers·ibil·ity** /rɪˌvɜːsəˈbɪləti; NAmE -ˈvɜːrs-/ *noun* [U]

**re'versing light** (*BrE*) (*NAmE* **'backup light**) *noun* a white light at the back of a vehicle that comes on when the vehicle moves backwards

**re·ver·sion** /rɪˈvɜːʃn; NAmE -ˈvɜːrʒn/ *noun* **1** [U, sing.] ~ (**to sth**) (*formal*) the act or process of returning to a former state or condition: *a reversion to traditional farming methods* **2** [U, C] (*law*) the return of land or property to sb: *the reversion of Hong Kong to China*

**re·vert** /rɪˈvɜːt; NAmE -ˈvɜːrt/ *verb* [I] (+ **adv./prep.**) (*IndE, rather formal*) to reply: *Excellent openings—kindly revert with your updated CV.*
PHRV **re'vert to sb/sth** (*law*) (of property, rights, etc.) to return to the original owner again ⊃ see also REVERSION **re'vert to sth** (*formal*) **1** to return to a former state; to start doing sth again that you used to do in the past: *After her divorce she reverted to her maiden name.* ◇ *Try not to revert to your old eating habits.* **2** to return to an earlier topic or subject: *So, to revert to your earlier question…* ◇ *The conversation kept reverting to the events of March 6th.*

**re·view** ⓘ A2 Ⓦ /rɪˈvjuː/ *noun, verb*
- *noun* **1** ?+ A2 [C, U] a report in a newspaper or magazine or on the internet, television or radio, in which sb gives their opinion of a book, play, film, product, etc.; the act of writing this kind of report: *a book review* ◇ *She gave the film a glowing review.* ◇ *He submitted his latest novel for review.* ⊃ see also RAVE REVIEW ⊃ WORDFINDER NOTE at NEWSPAPER **2** ?+ A2 [C, U] (*especially NAmE*) an act of looking again at sth you have studied or written, especially in order to prepare for an exam: *We need to do the review for the test tomorrow.* ◇ *We'll have time at the end of class for review.* **3** ?+ B2 [C, U] an examination of sth, with the intention of changing it if necessary: *The government has embarked on a systematic review of transport policy.* ◇ *The proposals are available for review online.* ◇ **under** ~ *The terms of the contract are under review.* ◇ **up for** ~ *His parole application is up for review next week.* ◇ *a review board/panel* ⊃ see also JUDICIAL REVIEW, PERFORMANCE REVIEW **4** ?+ B2 [C] an examination of all the relevant information on a subject or on a series of events: *to conduct/undertake a review of customer complaints* ◇ *a comprehensive review of current scientific knowledge on the subject* ◇ *The* **literature review** *suggests a number of areas for further study.* ⊃ see also PEER REVIEW **5** [C] (*formal*) a ceremony that involves an official INSPECTION of soldiers, etc. by an important visitor
- *verb* **1** ?+ A2 [T] ~ **sth** to write a report of a book, play, film, product, etc. in which you give your opinion of it: *Please rate and review your purchase on our website.* ◇ *The book was favourably reviewed by most critics.* **2** ?+ B2 [T, I] (*especially NAmE*) to look again at sth you have studied, especially in order to prepare for an exam: ~ **sth** *We will be reviewing all the topics covered this semester.* ◇ ~ **for sth** *Jonas helped me review for the test.* **3** [T] ~ **sth** (*especially NAmE*) to check a piece of work to see if there are any mistakes **4** ?+ B2 [T] ~ **sth** to carefully examine or consider sth again, especially so that you can decide if it is necessary to make changes SYN **reassess**: *The government will review the situation later in the year.* ◇ *The company is reviewing its business travel policy.* ◇ *to review a case/the evidence* ⊃ SYNONYMS at EXAMINE **5** ?+ B2 [T] ~ **sth** to read or study information about sth, especially in order to reach an opinion about it: *to review records/documents/data* ◇ *Let's start by reviewing the evidence.* ◇ *This paper reviews the literature on the subject.* **6** [T] ~ **sth** to think about past events, for example to try to understand why they happened SYN **take stock (of sth)**: *to review your failures and triumphs* **7** [T] ~ **sb/sth** to make an official INSPECTION of a group of soldiers, etc. in a military ceremony

**re·view·er** /rɪˈvjuːə(r)/ *noun* **1** a person who writes reviews of books, films or plays **2** a person who examines or considers sth carefully, for example to see if any changes need to be made

**re·vile** /rɪˈvaɪl/ *verb* [usually passive] ~ **sb** (**for sth/for doing sth**) (*formal*) to criticize sb/sth in a way that shows how much you dislike them

**re·vise** ⓘ B1 /rɪˈvaɪz/ *verb* **1** ?+ B1 [T] ~ **sth** to change your opinions or plans, for example because of sth you have learned: *I can see I will have to revise my opinions of his abilities now.* ◇ *The government may need to revise its policy in the light of this report.* **2** ?+ B1 [T] ~ **sth** to change sth, such as a book or an estimate, in order to correct or improve it: *a revised edition of a textbook* ◇ *I'll prepare a revised estimate for you.* ◇ ~ **sth up/down** *We may have to revise this figure upwards.* **3** ?+ B2 [I, T] (*BrE*) to prepare for an exam by looking again at work that you have done: *I can't come out tonight. I have to revise.* ◇ ~ **for sth** *I spent the weekend revising for my exam.* ◇ ~ **sth** *I'm revising Geography today.* ⊃ WORDFINDER NOTE at EXAM

**re·vi·sion** ?+ B2 /rɪˈvɪʒn/ *noun* **1** ?+ B2 [C] a change or set of changes to sth: *He made some minor revisions to the report before printing it out.* **2** ?+ B2 [U, C] the act of changing sth, or of examining sth with the intention of changing it: *a system in need of revision* ◇ *a revision of trading standards* **3** ?+ B2 [U] (*BrE*) the process of learning work for an exam: *Have you started your revision yet?*

**re·vi·sion·ism** /rɪˈvɪʒənɪzəm/ *noun* [U] (*often disapproving, politics*) ideas that are different from, and want to change, the main ideas or practices of a political system, especially MARXISM ▶ **re·vi·sion·ist** /-nɪst/ *noun*: *bourgeois revisionists* **re·vi·sion·ist** *adj.*: *revisionist historians*

**re·visit** /ˌriːˈvɪzɪt/ *verb* **1** ~ **sth** to visit a place again, especially after a long period of time **2** ~ **sth** to return to an idea or a subject and discuss it again: *It's an idea that may be worth revisiting at a later date.*

**re·vit·al·ize** (*BrE also* **-ise**) /ˌriːˈvaɪtəlaɪz/ *verb* ~ **sth** to make sth stronger, more active or more healthy: *measures to revitalize the inner cities* ▶ **re·vit·al·iza·tion, -isa·tion** /ˌriːˌvaɪtəlaɪˈzeɪʃn; NAmE -ləˈz-/ *noun* [U]: *the revitalization of the steel industry*

**re·vival** ?+ C1 /rɪˈvaɪvl/ *noun* **1** ?+ C1 [U, C] an improvement in the condition or strength of sth: *the revival of trade* ◇ *an economic revival* **2** ?+ C1 [C, U] the process of sth becoming or being made popular or fashionable again: *a religious revival* ◇ *Jazz is enjoying a revival.* ◇ *a revival of interest in folk music* **3** [C] a new production of a play that has not been performed for some time: *a revival of Peter Shaffer's 'Equus'*

**re·vival·ism** /rɪˈvaɪvəlɪzəm/ *noun* [U] **1** the process of creating interest in sth again, especially religion **2** the practice of using ideas, designs, etc. from the past: *revivalism in architecture*

**re·vival·ist** /rɪˈvaɪvəlɪst/ *noun* a person who tries to make sth popular again ▶ **re·vival·ist** *adj.*: *revivalist movements* ◊ *a revivalist preacher*

**re·vive** ʇ+ B1 /rɪˈvaɪv/ *verb* **1** ʇ+ B1 [I, T] to become, or to make sb/sth become, conscious or healthy and strong again: *The flowers soon revived in water.* ◊ *The economy is beginning to revive.* ◊ *~ sb/sth The paramedics couldn't revive her.* ◊ *This movie is intended to revive her flagging career.* **2** ʇ+ B1 *~ sth* to make sth start being used or done again: *This quaint custom should be revived.* ◊ *She has been trying to revive the debate over equal pay.* **3** [T] *~ sth* to produce again a play, etc. that has not been performed for some time: *This 1930s musical is being revived at the National Theatre.* ⊃ see also REVIVAL

**re·viv·ify** /ˌriːˈvɪvɪfaɪ/ *verb* (**re·vivi·fies**, **re·vivi·fy·ing**, **re·vivi·fied**, **re·vivi·fied**) *~ sth* (*formal*) to give new life or health to sth SYN revitalize

**revo·ca·tion** /ˌrevəˈkeɪʃn/ *noun* [U, C] (*formal*) the act of cancelling a law, etc.: *the revocation of planning permission*

**re·voke** /rɪˈvəʊk/ *verb* *~ sth* (*formal*) to officially cancel sth so that it is no longer legally acceptable

**re·volt** /rɪˈvəʊlt/ *noun, verb*

■ *noun* [C, U] a protest against authority, especially that of a government, often involving violence; the action of protesting against authority SYN **uprising**: *the Peasants' Revolt of 1381* ◊ *to lead a revolt* ◊ *The army quickly crushed the revolt.* ◊ *the biggest back-bench revolt this government has ever seen* ◊ *Attempts to negotiate peace ended in armed revolt.* ◊ **in** *~* (*formal*) *The people rose in revolt.*

■ *verb* **1** [I] to take violent action against the people in power SYN **rebel**, **rise**: *The peasants threatened to revolt.* ◊ *~ against sb/sth Finally the people revolted against the military dictatorship.* ⊃ see also REVOLUTION **2** [I] *~(against sth)* to behave in a way that is the opposite of what sb expects of you, especially in protest SYN **rebel**: *Teenagers often revolt against parental discipline.* **3** [T] *~ sb* to make you feel horror SYN **disgust**, **nauseate**, **sicken**: *All the violence in the movie revolted me.* ◊ *The way he ate his food revolted me.* ⊃ see also REVULSION

**re·volt·ing** /rɪˈvəʊltɪŋ/ *adj.* extremely unpleasant SYN **disgusting**, **nauseating**: *a revolting smell* ◊ *a revolting little man* ⊃ SYNONYMS at DISGUSTING ▶ **re·volt·ing·ly** *adv.*: *revoltingly ugly*

**revo·lu·tion** ⓘ B2 /ˌrevəˈluːʃn/ *noun* **1** ʇ B2 [C, U] an attempt, by a large number of people, to change the government of a country, especially by violent action: *a socialist revolution* ◊ *the outbreak of the French Revolution in 1789* ◊ *to start a revolution* ◊ *a country on the brink of revolution* ⊃ see also COUNTER-REVOLUTION, REVOLT *noun* **2** ʇ B2 [C] a great change in conditions, ways of working, beliefs, etc. that affects large numbers of people: *a cultural/social/scientific, etc. revolution* ◊ *~ in sth A revolution in information technology is taking place.* ⊃ see also INDUSTRIAL REVOLUTION **3** [C, U] a complete CIRCULAR movement around a point: *The disk rotates at up to 500 revolutions per minute.* ◊ **around sth** *the revolution of the earth around the sun* ⊃ see also REVOLVE

**revo·lu·tion·ary** ʇ+ C1 /ˌrevəˈluːʃənəri/; *NAmE* -neri/ *adj., noun*

■ *adj.* **1** ʇ+ C1 [usually before noun] connected with political revolution: *a revolutionary leader* ◊ *revolutionary uprisings* **2** ʇ+ C1 involving a great or complete change: *a revolutionary idea* ◊ *a time of rapid and revolutionary change*

■ *noun* (*pl.* **-ies**) a person who starts or supports a revolution, especially a political one: *socialist revolutionaries*

**revo·lu·tion·ize** (*BrE also* **-ise**) /ˌrevəˈluːʃənaɪz/ *verb* *~ sth* to completely change the way that sth is done: *Aerial photography has revolutionized the study of archaeology.*

**re·volve** /rɪˈvɒlv; *NAmE* -ˈvɑːlv/ *verb* [I] to go in a circle around a central point: *The fan revolved slowly.* ◊ *The earth revolves on its axis.*

PHRV **re·volve around sth** (*also* **re·volve round sth** *especially in BrE*) to move around sth in a circle: *The earth revolves around the sun.* **re·volve around sb/sth** (*also* **re·volve round sb/sth** *especially in BrE*) to have sb/sth as the main interest or subject: *His whole life revolves around surfing.* ◊ *She thinks that the world revolves around her.*

**re·volver** /rɪˈvɒlvə(r); *NAmE* -ˈvɑːl-/ *noun* a small gun that has a container for bullets that turns around so that shots can be fired quickly without having to stop to put more bullets in

**re·volv·ing** /rɪˈvɒlvɪŋ; *NAmE* -ˈvɑːl-/ *adj.* [usually before noun] able to turn in a circle: *a revolving chair* ◊ *The theatre has a revolving stage.*

**re·volving ˈdoor** *noun* **1** a type of door in an entrance to a large building that turns around in a circle as people go through it **2** used to talk about a place or an organization that people enter and then leave again very quickly: *The company became a revolving-door workplace.*

**revue** /rɪˈvjuː/ *noun* [C, U] a show in a theatre, with songs, dances, jokes, short plays, etc., often about recent events

revolving door

**re·vul·sion** /rɪˈvʌlʃn/ *noun* [U, sing.] (*formal*) a strong feeling of horror SYN **disgust**, **repugnance**: *Most people viewed the bombings with revulsion.* ◊ **at sth** *She felt a deep sense of revulsion at the violence.* ◊ **against sth** *I started to feel a revulsion against their decadent lifestyle.* ⊃ see also REVOLT *noun*

**re·ward** ⓘ B2 /rɪˈwɔːd; *NAmE* -ˈwɔːrd/ *noun, verb*

■ *noun* **1** ʇ B2 [C, U] a thing that you are given because you have done sth good, worked hard, etc.: *a financial reward* ◊ *~ for (doing) sth a reward for good behaviour* ◊ *You deserve a reward for being so helpful.* ◊ *Winning the match was just reward for the effort the team had made.* ◊ *The company is now reaping the rewards of their investments.* **2** B2 [C] an amount of money that is offered to sb for helping the police to find a criminal or for finding sth that is lost: *~ for sth A £100 reward has been offered for the return of the necklace.* IDM see VIRTUE

■ *verb* ʇ B2 [often passive] to give sth to sb because they have done sth good, worked hard, etc.: *~ sb for sth She was rewarded for her efforts with a cash bonus.* ◊ *~ sb for doing sth He rewarded us handsomely* (= with a lot of money) *for helping him.* ◊ *~ sb with sth She started singing to the baby and was rewarded with a smile.* ◊ *~ sb/sth Our patience was finally rewarded.*

**re·ward·ing** /rɪˈwɔːdɪŋ; *NAmE* -ˈwɔːrd-/ *adj.* **1** (of an activity, etc.) worth doing; that makes you happy because you think it is useful or important: *a rewarding experience/job* ⊃ SYNONYMS at SATISFYING **2** producing a lot of money SYN **profitable**: *Teaching is not very financially rewarding* (= is not very well paid). OPP **unrewarding**

**re·wind** /ˌriːˈwaɪnd/ *verb* (**re·wound**, **re·wound** /-ˈwaʊnd/) [T, I] *~ (sth)* to make sth such as a film or a recording go back to the beginning or to an earlier point

**re·wire** /ˌriːˈwaɪə(r)/ *verb* *~ sth* to put new electrical wires into a building or piece of equipment

**re·word** /ˌriːˈwɜːd; *NAmE* -ˈwɜːrd/ *verb* *~ sth* to write or say sth again using different words in order to make it clearer or more acceptable ▶ **re·word·ing** *noun* [C, U]

**re·work** /ˌriːˈwɜːk; *NAmE* -ˈwɜːrk/ *verb* *~ sth* to make changes to sth in order to improve it or make it more suitable ▶ **re·work·ing** *noun* [C, U]: *The movie is a reworking of the Frankenstein story.*

---

ⓘ Oxford Phrasal Academic Lexicon (OPAL) written and spoken word lists | Ⓦ OPAL written word list | Ⓢ OPAL spoken word list

**re·writ·able** /ˌriːˈraɪtəbl/ *adj.* (*computing*) able to be used again for different data: *a rewritable CD*

**re·write** /ˌriːˈraɪt/ *verb* (**re·wrote** /-ˈrəʊt/, **re·writ·ten** /-ˈrɪtn/) ~ **sth** to write sth again in a different way, usually in order to improve it or because there is some new information: *I intend to rewrite the story for younger children.* ◊ *This essay will have to be completely rewritten.* ◊ *an attempt to rewrite history* (= to present historical events in a way that shows or proves what you want them to) ▶ **re·write** /ˈriːraɪt/ *noun*

**Rex** /reks/ *noun* [U] (*BrE, from Latin, formal*) a word meaning 'king', used, for example, in the titles of legal cases brought by the state when there is a king in the UK: *Rex v Jones* ⇨ compare REGINA

**RGN** /ˌɑː dʒiː ˈen; *NAmE* ˌɑːr/ *noun* (*BrE*) registered general nurse

**r.h.** *abbr.* (in writing) RIGHT HAND

**rhap·sod·ize** (*BrE also* **-ise**) /ˈræpsədaɪz/ *verb* [I, T] ~ **(about / over sth)** + **speech** (*formal*) to talk or write with great enthusiasm about sth SYN **be in, go into,** etc. **raptures (about / over sb / sth)**

**rhap·sody** /ˈræpsədi/ *noun* (*pl.* **-ies**) **1** (often in titles) a piece of music that is full of feeling and is not regular in form: *Liszt's Hungarian Rhapsodies* **2** (*formal*) the expression of great enthusiasm or happiness in speech or writing ▶ **rhap·sod·ic** /ræpˈsɒdɪk; *NAmE* -ˈsɑːd-/ *adj.*

**rhe·sus monkey** /ˈriːsəs mʌŋki/ *noun* a small South Asian monkey, often used in scientific experiments

**rhet·oric** /ˈretərɪk/ *noun* [U] **1** (*formal, often disapproving*) speech or writing that is intended to influence people, but that is not completely honest or sincere: *the rhetoric of political slogans* ◊ *empty rhetoric* **2** (*formal*) the art of using language in speech or writing in a special way that influences or entertains people SYN **eloquence, oratory**

**rhet·or·ical** /rɪˈtɒrɪkl; *NAmE* -ˈtɔːr-/ *adj.* **1** (of a question) asked only to make a statement or to produce an effect rather than to get an answer: *'Don't you care what I do?' he asked, but it was a rhetorical question.* **2** (*formal, often disapproving*) (of a speech or piece of writing) intended to influence people, but not completely honest or sincere **3** (*formal*) connected with the art of RHETORIC: *the use of rhetorical devices such as metaphor and irony* ▶ **rhet·oric·al·ly** /-kli/ *adv.*: *'Do you think I'm stupid?' she asked rhetorically.* ◊ *a rhetorically structured essay*

**rhet·or·ician** /ˌretəˈrɪʃn/ *noun* (*specialist*) a person who shows skill in the art of formal rhetoric

**rheuˌmatic ˈfever** *noun* [U] a serious disease that causes a high temperature with SWELLING and pain in the JOINTS

**rheu·ma·tism** /ˈruːmətɪzəm/ *noun* [U] a disease that makes the muscles and JOINTS painful, stiff and SWOLLEN (= larger than normal) ▶ **rheum·at·ic** /ruˈmætɪk/ *adj.*: *rheumatic pains*

**rheuma·toid arth·ritis** /ˌruːmətɔɪd ɑːˈθraɪtɪs; *NAmE* ɑːr-/ *noun* [U] (*medical*) a disease that gets worse over a period of time and causes painful SWELLING (= the condition of being larger than normal) and permanent damage in the JOINTS of the body, especially the fingers, WRISTS, feet and ankles

**rheuma·tol·ogy** /ˌruːməˈtɒlədʒi; *NAmE* -ˈtɑːl-/ *noun* [U] the study of the diseases of JOINTS and muscles, such as RHEUMATISM and ARTHRITIS

**rhine·stone** /ˈraɪnstəʊn/ *noun* a clear stone that is intended to look like a diamond, used in cheap jewellery

**rhin·itis** /raɪˈnaɪtɪs/ *noun* [U] (*medical*) a condition in which the inside of the nose becomes SWOLLEN (= larger than normal) and painful, caused by an infection or an ALLERGY

**rhino** /ˈraɪnəʊ/ *noun* (*pl.* **-os**) (*informal*) = RHINOCEROS: *a black/white rhino* ◊ *rhino horn*

**rhi·noceros** /raɪˈnɒsərəs; *NAmE* -ˈnɑːs-/ *noun* (*pl.* **rhi·noceros** or **rhi·nocer·oses**) (*also informal* **rhino**) a large heavy animal with very thick skin and either one or two HORNS on its nose, that lives in Africa and Asia

**rhi·zome** /ˈraɪzəʊm/ *noun* (*specialist*) the thick STEM of some plants, such as IRIS and MINT, that grows along or under the ground and has roots and STEMS growing from it

**rho** /rəʊ/ *noun* the 17th letter of the Greek alphabet (Ρ, ρ)

**rho·dium** /ˈrəʊdiəm/ *noun* [U] (*symb.* **Rh**) a chemical element. Rhodium is a hard silver-white metal that is usually found with PLATINUM.

**rhodo·den·dron** /ˌrəʊdəˈdendrən/ *noun* a bush with large red, purple, pink or white flowers

**rhom·boid** /ˈrɒmbɔɪd/ *NAmE* ˈrɑːm-/ *noun* (*geometry*) a flat shape with four straight sides, with only the opposite sides and angles equal to each other ⇨ picture at PARALLELOGRAM

**rhom·bus** /ˈrɒmbəs/ *NAmE* ˈrɑːm-/ *noun* (*geometry*) a flat shape with four equal sides and four angles which are not 90°. ⇨ picture at PARALLELOGRAM

**rhu·barb** /ˈruːbɑːb; *NAmE* -bɑːrb/ *noun* [U] **1** the thick red STEMS of a garden plant, also called rhubarb, that are cooked and eaten as a fruit: *rhubarb pie* ⇨ VISUAL VOCAB page V4 **2** a word that a group of actors repeat on stage to give the impression of a lot of people talking at the same time

**rhumba** = RUMBA

**rhyme** /raɪm/ *noun, verb*
■ *noun* **1** [C] a word that has the same sound or ends with the same sound as another word: *Can you think of a rhyme for 'beauty'?* **2** [C] a short poem in which the last word in the line has the same sound as the last word in another line, especially the next one: *children's rhymes and stories* ⇨ see also NURSERY RHYME **3** [U] the use of words in a poem or song that have the same sound, especially at the ends of lines: *the poet's use of rhyme* ◊ **in ~** *a story in rhyme* ⇨ WORDFINDER NOTE at POETRY
IDM **there's no ˌrhyme or ˈreason to / for sth** | **without ˌrhyme or ˈreason** if there is **no rhyme or reason to sth** or it happens **without rhyme or reason**, it happens in a way that cannot be easily explained or understood
■ *verb* **1** [I] ~ **(with sth)** if two words, syllables, etc. **rhyme**, or if one **rhymes** with the other, they have or end with the same sound: *'Though' rhymes with 'low'.* ◊ *'Tough' and 'through' don't rhyme.* ◊ *rhyming couplets* **2** [T] ~ **sth (with sth)** to put words that sound the same together, for example when you are writing poetry: *You can rhyme 'girl' with 'curl'.* **3** [I] (of a poem) to have lines that end with the same sound: *I prefer poems that rhyme.*

**ˈrhyming ˌslang** *noun* [U] a way of talking in which you use words or phrases that rhyme with the word you mean, instead of using that word. For example in COCKNEY rhyming slang 'apples and pears' means 'stairs'.

**rhythm** /ˈrɪðəm/ *noun* [C, U] **1** a strong regular repeated pattern of sounds or movements: *to dance to the rhythm of the music* ◊ *the rhythm of her breathing* ◊ *music with a fast/slow/steady rhythm* ◊ *jazz rhythms* ◊ **in ~** *He can't seem to play in rhythm.* ◊ **in ~ with sth** *The boat rocked up and down in rhythm with the sea.* ◊ *a dancer with a natural sense of rhythm* (= the ability to move in time to a fixed beat) ⇨ WORDFINDER NOTE at SING **2** a regular pattern of changes or events: *the rhythm of the seasons* ◊ *biological/body rhythms* ◊ *You'll soon get into a rhythm.* ⇨ see also BIORHYTHM

**ˌrhythm and ˈblues** *noun* [U] (*abbr.* **R & B**) a type of music that is a mixture of BLUES and jazz and has a strong rhythm

**ˈrhythm guiˌtar** *noun* [U] a guitar style that consists mainly of CHORDS played with a strong rhythm ⇨ compare LEAD GUITAR

**rhyth·mic** /ˈrɪðmɪk/ (*also less frequent* **rhyth·mic·al** /ˈrɪðmɪkl/) *adj.* having a regular pattern of sounds, movements or events: *music with a fast, rhythmic beat* ◊ *the rhythmic ticking of the clock* ▶ **rhyth·mic·al·ly** /-kli/ *adv.*

**ˈrhythm section** *noun* the part of a band that supplies the rhythm, usually consisting of drums, BASS, and sometimes piano

**rial** (*also* **riyal**) /riːˈɑːl, ˈriːɑːl; *NAmE* riːˈɔːl/ *noun* **1** the unit of money in Iran and Oman **2** *usually* **riyal** the unit of money in Saudi Arabia, Qatar and Yemen

**rib** /rɪb/ *noun, verb*
- *noun* **1** [C] any of the curved bones that are connected to the SPINE and surround the chest: *a broken/bruised/cracked rib* ◇ *Stop poking me in the ribs!* ⊃ see also FALSE RIB, FLOATING RIB, RIBCAGE ⊃ VISUAL VOCAB page V1 **2** [U, C] a piece of meat with one or more bones from the ribs of an animal ⊃ see also PRIME RIB, SHORT RIBS, SPARE RIB **3** [C] a curved piece of wood, metal or plastic that forms the frame of a boat, roof, etc. and makes it stronger **4** [U, C] a way of KNITTING (= making clothing using wool and two long needles) that produces a pattern of straight lines up and down in which some are raised higher than others: *a rib cotton sweater* IDM see DIG *v.*
- *verb* (**-bb-**) ~ **sb (about/over sth)** (*old-fashioned, informal*) to laugh at sb and make jokes about them, but in a friendly way SYN **tease**

**rib·ald** /ˈrɪbld, ˈraɪbɔːld/ *adj.* (of language or behaviour) referring to sex in a rude but humorous way

**ribbed** /rɪbd/ *adj.* (especially of material for clothes) having raised lines: *a ribbed sweater*

**rib·bing** /ˈrɪbɪŋ/ *noun* [U] **1** a pattern of raised lines in KNITTING (= the activity of making clothing out of wool) or on a surface **2** (*old-fashioned, informal*) the act of making fun of sb in a friendly way SYN **tease**

**rib·bon** /ˈrɪbən/ *noun* **1** [U, C] a narrow piece of material, used to tie things or for decoration: *a present tied with yellow ribbon* ◇ *lengths of velvet ribbon* ◇ *She was wearing two blue silk ribbons in her hair.* **2** [C] something that is long and narrow in shape: *The road was a ribbon of moonlight.* **3** [C] a ribbon in special colours, or tied in a special way, that is given to sb as a prize or as a military honour, or that is worn by sb to show that they belong to a particular political party ⊃ compare ROSETTE **4** [C] a long narrow piece of material containing INK (= coloured liquid for writing, drawing, etc.) that you put into TYPEWRITERS and some computer printers
IDM **cut a/the 'ribbon (on sth)** **1** to officially open a building, road, etc. with a special ceremony that typically involves cutting a ribbon across the entrance: *The prince cut the ribbon to officially open the building.* **2** to officially start sth, such as a business project or activity: *Today we're happy to cut the ribbon on a project that will improve safety for cyclists.* **cut/tear, etc. sth to 'ribbons** to cut/tear, etc. sth very badly

**rib·cage** /ˈrɪbkeɪdʒ/ *noun* the structure of curved bones (called RIBS), that surrounds and protects the chest ⊃ VISUAL VOCAB page V1

**'rib-eye** (*also* **rib-eye 'steak**) *noun* a piece of beef which is cut from outside the RIBS

**ribo·fla·vin** /ˌraɪbəˈfleɪvɪn/ *noun* [U] a vitamin which is important for producing energy, found in milk, LIVER, eggs and green vegetables

**rice** ⊕ A1 /raɪs/ *noun* [U] short, narrow white or brown grain grown on wet land in hot countries as food; the plant that produces this grain: *a grain of rice* ◇ *boiled/steamed/fried rice* ◇ *long-/short-grain rice* ◇ *brown rice* (= without its outer layer removed) ◇ *rice paddies* (= rice fields) ⊃ see also JOLLOF RICE, PARCHED RICE, WILD RICE ⊃ VISUAL VOCAB page V8

**'rice paper** *noun* [U] a type of very thin paper made from tropical plants, used as a base for some types of cake

**rice 'pudding** *noun* [U, C] a DESSERT (= a sweet dish) made from rice cooked with milk and sugar

**rich** ⊕ A1 /rɪtʃ/ *adj.* (**rich·er, rich·est**)
- WITH A LOT OF MONEY **1** A1 having a lot of money or property: *one of the richest women in the world* ◇ *to get/grow/become rich* ◇ *She longed to be rich and famous.* ⊃ see also CASH-RICH OPP **poor 2 the rich** *noun* [pl.] people who have a lot of money or property: *It's a favourite resort for the rich and famous.* OPP **the poor 3** A1 (of a country) producing a lot of wealth so that many of its people can live at

a high standard: *the richest countries/economies/nations* OPP **poor**
- CONTAINING/PROVIDING STH **4** B1 (often in compounds) containing or providing a large supply of sth: **~in sth** *Oranges are rich in vitamin C.* ◇ *The area is rich in wildlife.* ◇ *His novels are a rich source of material for the movie industry.* ◇ *iron-rich rocks* OPP **poor**
- FULL OF VARIETY **5** B2 very interesting and full of variety: *the region's rich history and culture* ◇ *She leads a rich and varied life.*
- FOOD **6** B2 containing a lot of fat, butter, eggs, etc. and making you feel full quickly: *a rich, creamy sauce* ◇ *The chocolate orange fondant was too rich for me.*
- SOIL **7** containing the substances that make it good for growing plants in SYN **fertile**: *a rich, well-drained soil* OPP **poor**
- COLOURS/SOUNDS **8** (of colours, sounds, smells and tastes) strong or deep; very beautiful or attractive: *rich dark reds* ◇ *the rich sound of the organ*
- EXPENSIVE **9** (*literary*) expensive and beautiful SYN **sumptuous**: *The rooms were decorated with rich fabrics.*
- CRITICISM **10** (*especially BrE, informal*) used to say that a criticism sb makes is surprising and not reasonable, because they have the same fault: *Me? Lazy? That's rich, coming from you!* ⊃ compare RICHNESS IDM see STRIKE *v.*

▼ SYNONYMS

**rich**
**wealthy** • **prosperous** • **affluent** • **well off** • **comfortable**

These words all describe sb/sth that has a lot of money, property or valuable possessions.

**rich** (of a person) having a lot of money, property or valuable possessions; (of a country or city) producing a lot of wealth so that many of its people can live at a high standard

**wealthy** rich

RICH OR WEALTHY?
There is no real difference in meaning between these two words. Both are very frequent, but **rich** is more frequent and can be used in some fixed phrases where **wealthy** cannot: *He's stinking/filthy wealthy.* ◇ *It's a favourite resort for the wealthy and famous.*

**prosperous** (*rather formal*) rich and successful

**affluent** (*rather formal*) rich and with a good standard of living: *affluent Western countries*

PROSPEROUS OR AFFLUENT?
Both **prosperous** and **affluent** are used to talk about people and places. **Prosperous** is used much more than **affluent** to talk about times and periods. **Affluent** is often used to contrast rich people or societies with poor ones. Being **prosperous** is nearly always seen as a good thing: *It's good to see you looking so prosperous.* ◇ *It's good to see you looking so affluent.*

**well off** (often used in negative sentences) rich: *His family is not very well off.* NOTE The opposite of **well off** is **badly off**, but this is not very frequent; it is more common to say that sb is *not well off*.

**comfortable** having enough money to buy what you want without worrying about the cost: *They're not millionaires, but they're certainly very comfortable.*

PATTERNS
- a(n) rich/wealthy/prosperous/affluent/well-off **family**
- a rich/wealthy/prosperous/well-off **man/woman**
- a(n) rich/wealthy/prosperous/affluent **country/city**

**riches** /ˈrɪtʃɪz/ *noun* [pl.] large amounts of money and valuable or beautiful possessions: *a career that brought him fame and riches* ◇ *material riches* IDM see EMBARRASSMENT, RAG *n.*

**rich·ly** /ˈrɪtʃli/ *adv.* **1** in a beautiful and expensive manner: *a richly decorated room* **2** used to express the fact that sth

# richness

has a pleasant strong colour, taste or smell: *a richly flavoured sauce* ◊ *The polished floor glowed richly.* **3** in a generous way: *She was richly rewarded for all her hard work.* **4** in a way that people think is right and are correct SYN **thoroughly**: *richly deserved success* ◊ *richly earned respect* **5** used to express the fact that the quality or thing mentioned is present in large amounts: *richly varied countryside* ◊ *a richly atmospheric novel*

**rich·ness** /ˈrɪtʃnəs/ *noun* [U] the state of being rich in sth, such as colour, minerals or interesting qualities: *the richness and variety of marine life* ⊃ compare WEALTH

**the Rich·ter scale** /ðə ˈrɪktə skeɪl; *NAmE* -tər-/ *noun* [sing.] a system for measuring how strong an earthquake is: *an earthquake measuring 7.1 on the Richter scale*

**ricin** /ˈraɪsɪn/ *noun* [U] a very poisonous substance obtained from the seeds of the CASTOR OIL plant

**rick** /rɪk/ *noun, verb*
- *noun* a large pile of HAY or STRAW that is built in a regular shape and covered to protect it from rain
- *verb* ~ **sth** (*BrE*) (*US* SYN **sprain**) to injure a part of your body by TWISTING it suddenly

**rick·ets** /ˈrɪkɪts/ *noun* [U] a disease of children caused by a lack of good food that makes the bones become soft and badly formed, especially in the legs

**rick·ety** /ˈrɪkəti/ *adj.* not strong or well made; likely to break: *a rickety chair*

**rick·shaw** /ˈrɪkʃɔː/ *noun* a small, light vehicle with two wheels used in some Asian countries to carry passengers. The rickshaw is pulled by sb walking or riding a bicycle. ⊃ see also AUTORICKSHAW, CYCLE RICKSHAW

**rico·chet** /ˈrɪkəʃeɪ; *BrE also* -ʃet/ *verb, noun*
- *verb* [I] (**rico·chet·ing** /ˈrɪkəʃeɪɪŋ/, **rico·cheted**, **rico·cheted** /-ʃeɪd/, *BrE also* **rico·chet·ting** /ˈrɪkəʃetɪŋ/, **rico·chet·ted**, **rico·chet·ted** /-tɪd/) + *adv./prep.* (of a moving object) to hit a surface and come off it fast at a different angle: *The bullet ricocheted off a nearby wall.*
- *noun* **1** [C] a ball, bullet or stone that ricochets: *A woman protester was killed by a ricochet.* **2** [U] the action of ricocheting: *the ricochet of bricks and bottles off police riot shields*

**ri·cotta** /rɪˈkɒtə; *NAmE* -ˈkɑːtə/ *noun* [U] a type of soft white Italian cheese

**ric·tus** /ˈrɪktəs/ *noun* (*formal*) a wide TWISTED or smiling mouth that does not look natural or relaxed

**rid** ⓘ B2 /rɪd/ *verb* (**rid·ding, rid, rid**)
- IDM **be ˈrid of sb/sth** (*formal*) to be free of sb/sth that has been annoying you or that you do not want: *She wanted to be rid of her parents and their authority.* ◊ *I was glad to be rid of the car when I finally sold it.* ◊ (*BrE*) *He was a nuisance and we're all well rid of him* (= we'll be much better without him). **get ˈrid of sb/sth** ⓘ B2 to make yourself free of sb/sth that is annoying you or that you do not want; to throw sth away: *Try and get rid of your visitors before I get there.* ◊ *The problem is getting rid of nuclear waste.* ◊ *I can't get rid of this headache.* ◊ *We got rid of all the old furniture.* ⊃ more at WANT *v.*
- PHR V **ˈrid sb/sth of sb/sth** (*formal*) to remove sth that is causing a problem from a place, group, etc: *Further measures will be taken to rid our streets of crime.* **ˈrid yourself of sb/sth** (*formal*) to make yourself free from sb/sth that is annoying you or causing you a problem: *to rid yourself of guilt* ◊ *He wanted to rid himself of the burden of the secret.*

**rid·dance** /ˈrɪdns/ *noun* [U]
- IDM **good ˈriddance (to sb/sth)** an unkind way of saying that you are pleased that sb/sth has gone: *'Goodbye and good riddance!' she said to him angrily as he left.*

**rid·den** /ˈrɪdn/ *adj., verb*
- *adj.* (usually in compounds) full of a particular unpleasant thing: *a disease-ridden slum* ◊ *a class-ridden society* ◊ *She was guilt-ridden at the way she had treated him.* ◊ *She was ridden with guilt.* ⊃ see also ANGST-RIDDEN
- *verb past part.* of RIDE

**rid·dle** /ˈrɪdl/ *noun, verb*
- *noun* **1** a question that is difficult to understand, and that has a surprising answer, that you ask sb as a game: *Stop talking in riddles* (= saying things that are confusing)—*say what you mean.* ◊ *Bilbo solves the riddle that unlocks the door to the mountain.* **2** a mysterious event or situation that you cannot explain SYN **mystery**: *the riddle of how the baby died*
- *verb* [usually passive] ~ **sb/sth (with sth)** to make a lot of holes in sb/sth: *The car was riddled with bullets.*
- IDM **be ˈriddled with sth** to be full of sth, especially sth bad or unpleasant: *His body was riddled with cancer.* ◊ *Her typing was slow and riddled with mistakes.*

**ride** ⓘ A1 /raɪd/ *verb, noun*
- *verb* (**rode** /rəʊd/, **rid·den** /ˈrɪdn/)
  - • HORSE **1** A1 [I, T] to sit on an animal, especially a horse, and control it as it moves: *I learnt to ride as a child.* ◊ + *adv./prep.* *They rode along narrow country lanes.* ◊ *He was riding on a large black horse.* ◊ ~ **sth** *to ride a horse* ◊ *He's ridden six winners so far this year* (= in horse racing). ⊃ HOMOPHONES at ROAD **2 go ˈriding** (*BrE*) (*NAmE* **go ˈhorseback riding**) [I] to spend time riding a horse for pleasure: *How often do you go riding?*
  - • BICYCLE/MOTORCYCLE **3** A1 [T, I] to sit on and control a bicycle, motorcycle, etc: ~ **sth** (+ *adv./prep.*) *The boys were riding their bikes around the streets.* ◊ *He rode a Harley Davidson.* ◊ + *adv./prep.* *The ground there is too rough to ride over.* ⊃ WORDFINDER NOTE at CYCLING
  - • IN VEHICLE **4** A1 [I, T] to travel in a vehicle, especially as a passenger: + *adv./prep.* *I walked back while the others rode in the car.* ◊ ~ **sth** (+ *adv./prep.*) (*NAmE*) *to ride a train/the subway/an elevator* ◊ (*NAmE*) *She rode the bus to school every day.* ⊃ see also PARK AND RIDE
  - • ON WATER/AIR **5** [I, T] to float or be supported on water or air: (+ *adv./prep.*) *We watched the balloon riding high above the fields.* ◊ ~ **sth** *surfers riding the waves*
  - • GO THROUGH AREA **6** [T] ~ **sth** to go through or over an area on a horse, bicycle, etc: *We rode the mountain trails.*
  - • CRITICIZE **7** [T] ~ **sb** (*NAmE*) to criticize or TEASE sb in an annoying way: *Why is everybody riding me today?*
- IDM **be riding for a ˈfall** to be doing sth that involves risks and that may end in disaster **be riding ˈhigh** to be successful or very confident **let sth ˈride** to decide to do nothing about a problem that you know you may have to deal with later **ride the ˈcrest of sth** to enjoy great success or support because of a particular situation or event: *The band is riding the crest of its last tour.* **ride ˈherd on sb/sth** (*NAmE, informal*) to keep watch or control over sb/sth: *police riding herd on crowds of youths on the streets* **ride ˈshotgun** (*especially NAmE, informal*) to travel in the front passenger seat of a car or truck **ride a/the ˈwave of sth** to enjoy or be supported by the particular situation or quality mentioned: *Schools are riding a wave of renewed public interest.* ⊃ more at ROUGHSHOD, WISH *n.*
- PHR V **ˈride on sth** (usually used in the progressive tenses) to depend on sth: *My whole future is riding on this interview.* **ride sth↔ˈout** to manage to survive a difficult situation or time without having to make great changes: *The company did well to ride out the storm.* **ride ˈup** (of clothing) to move gradually upwards, out of position: *Short skirts tend to ride up when you sit down.*
- *noun*
  - • IN VEHICLE **1** A2 a short journey in a vehicle, on a bicycle, etc: *a train ride through beautiful countryside* ◊ *It's a ten-minute bus ride from here to town.* ◊ *Steve gave me a ride on his motorbike.* ◊ *We went for a ride on our bikes.* ◊ *a bike/boat/car/taxi ride* **2** A2 (*NAmE*) (*BrE* **lift**) a free ride in a car, etc. to a place you want to get to: *She hitched a ride to the station.* ◊ *We managed to get a ride into town when we missed the bus.* **3** B1 the kind of journey you make in a car, etc: *a smooth/comfortable/bumpy ride* ◊ (*figurative*) *The new legislation faces a bumpy ride* (= will meet with opposition and difficulties).
  - • ON HORSE **4** A2 a short journey on a horse, etc: *a pony ride* ◊ *The kids had a ride on an elephant at the zoo.* ◊ *He goes for a ride most mornings.*
  - • AT FUNFAIR **5** a large machine at a FUNFAIR or AMUSEMENT PARK that you ride on for fun or excitement; an occasion

when you go on one of these: *The rides are free.* ◊ *a roller coaster ride* ⊃ see also THRILL RIDE

**IDM** **come / go along for the ˈride** (*informal*) to join in an activity for pleasure but without being seriously interested in it **have a rough / an easy ˈride** | **give sb a rough / an easy ˈride** (*informal*) to experience/not experience difficulties when you are doing sth; to make things difficult/easy for sb: *He will be given a rough ride at the party conference.* **take sb for a ˈride** (*informal*) to cheat or trick sb: *It's not a pleasant feeling to discover you've been taken for a ride by someone you trusted.* ⊃ more at FREE *adj.*

**ˈride-off** *noun* (*NAmE*) = JUMP-OFF

**rider** /ˈraɪdə(r)/ *noun* **1** a person who rides a horse, bicycle or motorcycle: *Three riders* (= people riding horses) *were approaching.* ◊ *horses and their riders* ◊ *She's an experienced rider.* ◊ *a motorcycle dispatch rider* ⊃ see also DISPATCH RIDER **2** ~ **(to sth)** an extra piece of information that is added to an official document

**ridge** /rɪdʒ/ *noun, verb*
- *noun* **1** a narrow area of high land along the top of a line of hills; a high pointed area near the top of a mountain: *walking along the ridge* ◊ *the north-east ridge of the Matterhorn* ⊃ WORDFINDER NOTE at MOUNTAIN **2** a raised line on the surface of sth; the point where two sloping surfaces join: *The ridges on the soles of my boots stopped me from slipping.* ◊ *the ridge of the roof* **3** [usually sing.] ~ **(of high pressure)** (*specialist*) a long narrow area of high pressure in the atmosphere ⊃ compare TROUGH
- *verb* [usually passive] ~ **sth** to make narrow raised lines or areas on the surface of sth

**ridged** /rɪdʒd/ *adj.* (of an object or area) with raised lines on the surface

**ridi·cule** /ˈrɪdɪkjuːl/ *noun, verb*
- *noun* [U] unkind comments that make fun of sb/sth or make them look silly **SYN** **mockery**: *She is an object of ridicule in the tabloid newspapers.* ◊ *to hold sb up to ridicule* (= make fun of sb publicly)
- *verb* ~ **sb/sth** to make sb/sth look silly by laughing at them or it in an unkind way **SYN** **make fun of sb/sth**

**ri·dic·u·lous** ʔ+ **B2** /rɪˈdɪkjələs/ (*also also informal* **ridic** /rɪˈdɪk/) *adj.* very silly or unreasonable **SYN** **absurd, ludicrous**: *I look ridiculous in this hat.* ◊ *Don't be ridiculous! You can't pay £50 for a T-shirt!* ▸ **ri·dic·u·lous·ly** *adv.*: *The meal was ridiculously expensive.* **ri·dic·u·lous·ness** *noun* [U] **IDM** see SUBLIME *n.*

**rid·ing** /ˈraɪdɪŋ/ *noun* **1** (*BrE also* **ˈhorse riding**) (*NAmE also* **ˈhorseback riding**) [U] the sport or activity of riding horses: *I'm taking riding lessons.* ◊ *riding boots* ◊ (*BrE*) *to go riding* ◊ (*NAmE*) *to go horseback riding* **2** **Riding** [C] one of the three former parts of the English county of Yorkshire called the **East Riding**, the **North Riding** and the **West Riding** **ORIGIN** From an Anglo-Saxon word meaning 'one third'.

**rife** /raɪf/ *adj.* [not before noun] **1** if sth bad or unpleasant is **rife** in a place, it is very common there **SYN** **widespread**: *It is a country where corruption is rife.* ◊ *Rumours are rife that he is going to resign.* **2** ~ **(with sth)** full of sth bad or unpleasant: *Los Angeles is rife with gossip about the stars' private lives.*

**riff** /rɪf/ *noun* **1** a short repeated pattern of notes in popular music or jazz: *a guitar riff* **2** ~ **(on sth)** a MONOLOGUE (= long speech by one person) on a particular subject, especially a funny one that you make up as you are speaking: *an extended riff on the pitfalls of contemporary romance* ▸ **riff** *verb* [I]: *riffing guitars* ◊ **on sth** *Most comedians can riff on politics.*

**rif·fle** /ˈrɪfl/ *verb* [I, T] to turn over papers or the pages of a book quickly and without reading them all **SYN** **leaf**: ~ **through sth** *He was riffling through the papers on his desk.* ◊ ~ **sth** *to riffle the pages of a book*

**riff-raff** /ˈrɪf ræf/ *noun* [U + sing./pl. v.] (*disapproving*) an offensive way of referring to people of low social class or people who are not considered socially acceptable

# right

**rifle** ʔ+ **C1** /ˈraɪfl/ *noun, verb*
- *noun* ʔ+ **C1** a gun with a long BARREL which you hold to your shoulder to fire ⊃ see also AIR RIFLE
- *verb* **1** [I, T] ~ **(through) sth** to search quickly through sth in order to find or steal sth: *She rifled through her clothes for something suitable to wear.* **2** [T] ~ **sth** to steal sth from somewhere: *His wallet had been rifled.* **3** [T] ~ **sth + adv./prep.** to kick a ball very hard and straight in a game of football (soccer)

**rifle·man** /ˈraɪflmən/ *noun* (*pl.* **-men** /-mən/) a soldier who carries a rifle

**ˈrifle range** *noun* **1** [C] a place where people practise shooting with rifles **2** [U] the distance that a bullet from a rifle will travel

**rift** /rɪft/ *noun* **1** a serious break in the relationship between people or organizations **SYN** **breach, division**: *The rift within the party deepened.* ◊ *Efforts to heal the rift between the two countries have failed.* **2** a large break or opening in the ground, rocks or clouds

**ˈrift valley** *noun* a valley with steep sides formed when two TECTONIC PLATES move apart from each other

**rig** /rɪɡ/ *verb, noun*
- *verb* (**-gg-**) [usually passive] **1** ~ **sth** to arrange or influence sth in a dishonest way in order to get the result that you want **SYN** **fix**: *He said the election had been rigged.* ◊ *to rig a vote* ◊ *to rig the market* (= to cause an artificial rise or fall in prices, in order to make a profit) **2** ~ **sth (with sth)** to provide a ship or boat with ropes, sails, etc.; to fit the sails, etc. in position **3** ~ **sth (up) (with sth)** to fit equipment somewhere, sometimes secretly: *The lights had been rigged (up) but not yet tested.* ◊ *The car had been rigged with about 300 pounds of explosive.*
**PHRV** **ˌrig sb / sth / yourself↔ˈout (in / with sth)** [often passive] (*old-fashioned*) to provide sb/sth with a particular kind of clothes or equipment: *I was accepted for the job and rigged out in a uniform.* **ˌrig sth↔ˈup** to make or to build sth quickly, using whatever materials are available: *We managed to rig up a shelter for the night.*
- *noun* **1** (especially in compounds) a large piece of equipment that is used for taking oil or gas from the ground or the bottom of the sea: *an oil rig* **2** the way that the MASTS and sails on a boat, etc. are arranged **3** (*NAmE, informal*) a large lorry **4** equipment that is used for a special purpose: *a CB radio rig*

**rig·ging** /ˈrɪɡɪŋ/ *noun* [U] **1** the ropes that support the MASTS and sails of a boat or ship **2** the act of influencing sth in a dishonest way in order to get the result that you want: *vote rigging*

**right** ❶ **A1** ⓦ /raɪt/ *adj., adv., noun, verb, exclamation*
- *adj.*
- **TRUE/CORRECT 1** ʔ **A1** true or correct as a fact: *Did you get the answer right?* ◊ *'What's the right time?' '10.37.'* ◊ *That's exactly right.* ◊ *'David, isn't it?' 'Yes, that's right.'* (*informal*) *It was Monday you went to see Angie, right?* ◊ *Let me get this right* (= understand correctly)—*you want us to do an extra ten hours' work for no extra pay?* **OPP** **wrong** ⊃ SYNONYMS at TRUE **2** ʔ **A1** [not before noun] correct in your opinion or judgement: ~ **about sth** *You were quite right about the weather.* ◊ ~ **to do sth** *They're absolutely right to be cautious.* ◊ *'It's not easy.' 'Yeah, you're right.'* ◊ ~ **in doing sth** *Am I right in thinking we've met before?* **OPP** **wrong 3** ʔ **A2** correct for a particular situation or thing, or for a particular person: *Have you got the right money* (= the exact amount) *for the bus fare?* ◊ *What's the right way to do this?* ◊ *You're not holding it the right way up.* ◊ *Are you sure you've got that on the right way round?* ◊ *This is a step in the right direction.* ◊ *Next time we'll get it right.* ◊ *She's definitely the right person for the job* ◊ ~ **for sb** *I'm glad you split up. She wasn't right for you.* ◊ *I was waiting for the right moment to ask him.* ◊ *I think we made the right decision.* **OPP** **wrong** ⊃ see also MR RIGHT
- **MORALLY GOOD 4** ʔ **A1** [not usually before noun] morally good or acceptable; correct according to law or a person's duty: *I hope we're doing the right thing.* ◊ *to feel/seem right*

# right 1336

◇ **~to do sth** *You were quite right to criticize him.* ◇ *it's ~to do sth It's only right to warn you of the risk.* ◇ *it's ~ that... It's right that he should be punished.* **OPP** wrong
- **NORMAL** 5 [A2] [not before noun] in a normal or good enough condition: *I don't feel quite right today* (= I feel ill). ◇ *Things aren't right between her parents.* ◇ *If only I could have helped put matters right.* ◇ *That sausage doesn't smell right.* **OPP** wrong
- **FASHIONABLE/IMPORTANT** 6 [B1] socially fashionable or important: *She knows all the right people* (= for example, people who can help her in her career).
- **NOT LEFT** 7 [A1] [only before noun] of, on or towards the side of the body that is towards the east when a person faces north: *your right hand/arm/foot/leg* ◇ *Keep on the right side of the road.* ◇ *Take a right turn at the intersection.* **OPP** left ⊃ see also RIGHT-WING
- **COMPLETE** 8 [only before noun] (*BrE, informal, especially disapproving*) used to emphasize sth bad: *You made a right mess of that!* ◇ *I felt a right idiot.* ⊃ see also ALL RIGHT *adj.*
▶ **right·ness** *noun* [U]: *the rightness* (= justice) *of their cause* ◇ *the rightness of his decision*
**IDM** **be in the right place at the right time** to be able to take advantage of opportunities when they come: *His success was down to being in the right place at the right time.* **give your right 'arm for sth/to do sth** (*informal*) used to say that sb is willing to give up a lot in order to have or do sth that they really want: *I'd have given my right arm to have been there with them.* **(not) in your right 'mind** (not) mentally normal ⊃ SYNONYMS at MAD **(as) right as 'rain** (*informal*) in excellent health or condition **right e'nough** (*informal*) certainly; in a way that cannot be denied: *You heard me right enough* (= so don't pretend that you did not). **right 'on** (*informal*) used to express strong approval or support ⊃ see also RIGHT-ON **right side 'up** (*NAmE*) with the top part turned to the top; in the correct, normal position: *I dropped my toast, but luckily it fell right side up.* **OPP** upside down **she'll be right** (*AustralE, informal*) used to say that everything will be all right, even if there is a problem now **too 'right** (*BrE, informal*) used to say that there is no doubt about sth: *'We need to stick together.' 'Too right!'* ◇ *'I'll have to do it again.' 'Too right you will.'* ⊃ more at BUTTON *n.*, FOOT *n.*, HEAD *n.*, HEART *n.*, IDEA, MIGHT *n.*, NOTE *n.*, SIDE *n.*, TRACK *n.*

■ *adv.*
- **NOT LEFT** 1 [A1] on or to the right side: *Turn right at the end of the street.* **OPP** left
- **EXACTLY** 2 [A2] + *adv./prep.* exactly; directly: *Lee was standing right behind her.* ◇ *I'm right behind you on this one* (= I am supporting you). ◇ *The wind was right in our faces.* ◇ *The bus came right on time.* ◇ *The tour starts right here.*
- **COMPLETELY** 3 [B1] + *adv./prep.* all the way; completely: *They drove right up to the door.* ◇ *Everything is planned right down to the last detail.* ◇ *I'm right out of ideas.* ◇ *She kept right on swimming until she reached the other side.*
- **IMMEDIATELY** 4 [B1] + *adv./prep.* immediately; without delay: *I'll be right back.* ◇ *They left right after lunch.* ◇ *She'll be right with you* (= she is coming very soon). ◇ *I knew right from the start what was going to happen.*
- **CORRECTLY** 5 [B1] correctly: *You guessed right.* **OPP** wrong
- **IN A GOOD WAY** 6 [B1] in the way that things should happen or are supposed to happen; in a way that is morally good: *Nothing's going right for me today.* ◇ *You did right to tell me about it.* **OPP** wrong
**IDM** **right and 'left** (*also* **right, left and 'centre**, **left, right and 'centre**) (*informal*) in all directions; everywhere: *She owes money right and left.* **right a'way/'off** immediately; without delay: *I want it sent right away.* ◇ *I told him right off what I thought of him.* **right 'now** 1 [A1] at this moment: *He's not in the office right now.* 2 [A1] immediately: *Do it right now!* **right off the 'bat** (*especially NAmE, informal*) immediately; without delay: *We both liked each other right off the bat.* **see sb right** (*informal*) to make sure that sb has all they need or want: *You needn't worry about money—I'll see you right.* ⊃ more at GATE, HIT *v.*, SERVE *v.*, STREET *n.*, WORD *n.*

■ *noun*
- **NOT LEFT SIDE** 1 [A1] the/sb's right [sing.] the right side or direction: *on the ~ (of sb/sth) Take the first street on the right.* ◇ *to the ~ (of sb/sth) Keep over to the right.* ◇ *on/to sb's ~ She seated me on her right.* ◇ *from the ~ Look out for traffic coming from the right.* ◇ *Arabic script is read from right to left.* ◇ *the top/bottom/far right* **OPP** left 2 [A1] [sing.] the first, second, etc. ~ the first, second, etc. road on the right side: *Take the first right, then the second left.* **OPP** left 3 a right [sing.] a turn to the right: *Take a right at the traffic lights.* ◇ (*NAmE also*) *to make a right* ◇ (*informal*) *to hang a right* **OPP** left
- **MORAL/LEGAL CLAIM** 4 [B1] [C, U] a moral or legal claim to have or get sth or to behave in a particular way: *They had fought hard for equal rights.* ◇ *to defend your basic/fundamental rights* ◇ *~ to sth Everyone has a right to a fair trial.* ◇ *~ to do sth You have no right to stop me from going in there.* ◇ *What gives you the right to do that?* ◇ *She had every right to be angry.* ◇ *within your rights to do sth You're quite within your rights to ask for your money back.* ◇ **by rights** *By rights* (= if things were fair) *half the money should be mine.* ◇ **by ~** *The property belongs to her by right.* ◇ **~ of sth** *There is no right of appeal against the decision.* ◇ *the gay rights movement* ⊃ see also ANIMAL RIGHTS, CIVIL RIGHTS, DIVINE RIGHT, HUMAN RIGHT, WOMEN'S RIGHTS
- **STH MORALLY GOOD** 5 [B1] [U, C] what is morally good or correct: *She doesn't understand the difference between right and wrong.* ◇ *They both had some right on their side.* ◇ **in the ~** *He wouldn't apologize. He knew he was in the right* (= had justice on his side). ◇ *It was difficult to establish the rights and wrongs* (= the true facts) *of the matter.* **OPP** wrong
- **FOR BOOK/MOVIE, ETC.** 6 [B2] rights [pl.] the authority to perform, publish, film, etc. a particular work, event, etc: *He sold the rights for $2 million.* ◇ *~ to sth She got $1.5 million for the film rights to her book.*

---

▼ **SYNONYMS**

**right**
**correct**

Both these words describe a belief, opinion, decision or method that is suitable or the best one for a particular situation.

**right** if sb is right to do or think sth, that is a good thing to do or think in that situation: *You're right to be cautious.* ◇ *You made the right decision.* ◇ *'It's not easy.' 'Yes, you're right.'*

**correct** (of a method, belief, opinion or decision) right and suitable in a particular situation: *What's the correct way to shut the machine down?* ◇ *I don't think she's correct to say he's incompetent.*

**RIGHT OR CORRECT?**
- **Correct** is more formal than **right**. It is more often used for methods and **right** is more often used for beliefs, opinions and decisions.

**PATTERNS**
- right/correct **about** sb/sth
- right/correct **to do** sth
- right/correct **in thinking/believing/saying** sth
- the right/correct **decision/judgement/conclusion**
- the right/correct **way/method/approach**
- **absolutely/quite** right/correct

---

▼ **WHICH WORD?**

**right / rightly**
- **Right** and **rightly** can both be used as adverbs. In the sense 'correctly' or 'in the right way', **right** is the usual adverb. It is only used after verbs: *He did it right.* ◇ *Did I spell your name right?* **Rightly** cannot be used like this. In formal language **correctly** is used: *Is your name spelled correctly?*
- The usual meaning of **rightly** is 'for a good reason' and it comes before an adjective: *They are rightly proud of their children.* It can be used to mean 'correctly' before a verb or in particular phrases: *As you rightly say, we have a serious problem.* In *NAmE* **rightly** is not at all common.

- POLITICS 7 **B1** **the right**, **the Right** [sing. + sing./pl. v.] political groups that most strongly support the CAPITALIST system; part of a political party whose members are most conservative ⊃ compare RIGHT WING: *The Right made great gains in the recent elections.* ◊ *the far/extreme right* ◊ **on the ~ (of sth)** *He's on the extreme right of the party.* **OPP** left ⊃ see also ALT-RIGHT, CENTRE-RIGHT, HARD RIGHT
- IN BOXING 8 [C] a hard hit that is made with your right hand **OPP** left

**IDM** **bang to 'rights** (*BrE*) (*NAmE* **dead to 'rights**) (*informal*) with definite proof that you have committed a crime, so that you cannot claim to be innocent: *We've got you bang to rights handling stolen property.* **do 'right by sb** (*old-fashioned*) to treat sb fairly **in your own 'right** because of your personal qualifications or efforts, not because of your connection with sb else: *She sings with a rock band, but she's also a jazz musician in her own right.* **put/set sb/sth to 'rights** to correct sb/sth; to put things in their right places or right order: *It took me ages to put things to rights after the workmen had left.* ⊃ more at WORLD, WRONG *n.*

■ *verb*
- RETURN TO POSITION 1 ~ **sb/sth/yourself** to return sb/sth/ yourself to the normal position, standing or sitting UPRIGHT: *They learnt to right a capsized canoe.* ◊ *At last the plane righted itself and flew on.*
- CORRECT 2 ~ **sth** to correct sth that is wrong or not in its normal state **SYN** right: *Righting the economy will demand major cuts in expenditure.*

**IDM** **right a 'wrong** to do sth to correct an unfair situation or sth bad that you have done

■ *exclamation* (*BrE, informal*) **1** used to show that you accept a statement or an order: '*You may find it hurts a little at first.*' '*Right.*' ◊ '*Barry's here.*' '*Oh, right.*' **2** used to get sb's attention to say that you are ready to do sth, or to tell them to do sth: *Right! Let's get going.* **3** used to check that sb agrees with you or has understood you: *So that's twenty of each sort, right?* ◊ *And I didn't think any more of it, right, but Mum says I should see a doctor.* **4** (*ironic*) used to say that you do not believe sb or that you disagree with them: '*I won't be late tonight.*' '*Yeah, right.*'

**'right angle** *noun* an angle of 90°: *Place the table* **at right angles/at a right angle** *to the wall* ⊃ picture at ANGLE, TRIANGLE ⊃ compare ACUTE ANGLE, OBTUSE ANGLE, REFLEX ANGLE

**'right-angled** *adj.* having or consisting of a right angle

**'right-angled 'triangle** (*especially BrE*) (*NAmE usually* **right 'triangle**) *noun* a flat shape with three straight sides and one right angle ⊃ picture at TRIANGLE

**right 'brain** *noun* [U, sing.] the right side of the human brain, that is thought to be used for creating new ideas and to be where emotions come from ⊃ compare LEFT BRAIN

**right-'click** *verb* [T, I] ~ **sth** | ~ **(on sth)** to choose a particular function or item on a computer screen, etc., by pressing the button on a mouse that is on the right side

**right·eous** /ˈraɪtʃəs/ *adj.* (*formal*) **1** morally right and good: *a righteous God* **2** that you think is morally acceptable or fair: *righteous anger/indignation, etc.* ▸ see also SELF-RIGHTEOUS ▸ **right·eous·ly** *adv.* **right·eous·ness** *noun* [U]

**right 'field** *noun* [sing.] (in baseball) the part of the field to the right of the BATTER

**right·ful** /ˈraɪtfl/ *adj.* [only before noun] (*formal*) that is correct, right or legal **SYN** proper: *The stolen car was returned to its* **rightful** *owner.* ▸ **right·ful·ly** /-fəli/ *adv.*: *She was only claiming what was rightfully hers.*

**'right-hand** *adj.* [only before noun] **1** on the right side of sth: *on the right-hand side of the road* ◊ *the top right-hand corner of the screen* **2** intended for use by your right hand: *a right-hand glove* **OPP** **left-hand**

**right-hand 'drive** *adj.* (of a vehicle) with the driver's seat and STEERING WHEEL on the right side **OPP** **left-hand drive**

**right-'handed** *adj.* **1** a person who is **right-handed** uses their right hand for writing, using tools, etc. **2** a right-handed tool is designed to be used with the right hand **OPP** **left-handed** ▸ **right-'handed** *adv.*

**right-'hander** *noun* **1** a person who uses their right hand for writing, using tools, etc. **2** a hit with the right hand **OPP** **left-hander**

**right-hand 'man** *noun* [sing.] a person who helps sb a lot and who they rely on, especially in an important job: *the President's right-hand man*

**Right 'Honourable** *adj.* [only before noun] (*abbr.* **Rt Hon**) **1 the Right Honourable ...** a title of respect used when talking to or about a person of high social rank, especially a lord **2 the/my Right Honourable ...** the title of respect used by Members of Parliament in the UK when talking to or about a senior Member of Parliament during a debate ⊃ compare HONOURABLE

**right·ist** /ˈraɪtɪst/ *noun* a person who supports RIGHT-WING political parties and their ideas **SYN** **right-winger** **OPP** **leftist** ▸ **right·ist** *adj.*

**right·ly** /ˈraɪtli/ *adv.* **1** for a good reason **SYN** justifiably: *The school was rightly proud of the excellent exam results.* ◊ *He was proud of his beautiful house, and rightly so.* ◊ *Quite rightly, the environment is of great concern.* ◊ *Rightly or wrongly, many older people are afraid of violence in the streets.* **2** in a correct or accurate way: *As she rightly pointed out, the illness can affect adults as well as children.* ◊ *I can't rightly say what happened.* ◊ *I don't rightly know where he's gone.* ◊ *If I remember rightly, there's a train at six o'clock.* ⊃ note at RIGHT

**right-'minded** (*also* **right-'thinking**) *adj.* (*approving*) (of a person) having beliefs and opinions that most people approve of

**right·most** /ˈraɪtməʊst/ *adj.* [only before noun] furthest to the right

**right-of-'centre** *adj.* = CENTRE-RIGHT

**right of 'way** *noun* (*pl.* **rights of way**) **1** [U] (*especially BrE*) legal permission to go onto or through another person's land: *Private property—no right of way.* **2** [C] (*especially BrE*) a public path that goes through private land **3** [U] the right to drive across or into a road before another vehicle: *I had right of way at the junction.* ◊ *Whose right of way is it?*

**right-'on** *adj.* (*BrE, informal, sometimes disapproving*) having political opinions or being aware of social issues that are fashionable and LEFT-WING: *right-on middle-class intellectuals*

**(the) Right 'Reverend** *adj.* [only before noun] (*abbr.* **Rt Rev**, **Rt Revd**) a title of respect used when talking about a BISHOP (= a senior priest)

**'rights issue** *noun* (*business*) an opportunity to buy shares in a company at a cheaper price, offered to people who already own some shares in it

**right·size** /ˈraɪtsaɪz/ *verb* [I, T] ~ **(sth)** (*business*) to change the size of a company in order to reduce costs, especially by reducing the number of employees

**right-'thinking** *adj.* = RIGHT-MINDED

**right 'triangle** *noun* (*NAmE*) = RIGHT-ANGLED TRIANGLE

**right·ward** /ˈraɪtwəd; *NAmE* -wərd/ (*also* **right·wards** *especially in BrE*) *adj.* **1** on or to the right: *a rightward movement* **2** towards more RIGHT-WING political ideas: *a rightward shift in voting patterns* ▸ **right·ward** (*also* **right·wards**) *adv.*

**the 'right wing** *noun* **1** [sing. + sing./pl. v.] the part of a political party whose members are least in favour of social change: *He is on the right wing of the party.* **2** [C, U] an attacking player or a position on the right side of the field in a sports game **OPP** **left wing**

**right-'wing** *adj.* strongly supporting the CAPITALIST system: *right-wing policies* **OPP** **left-wing**

**right-'winger** *noun* **1** a person on the right wing of a political party: *She is a prominent Tory right-winger.* **2** a person who plays on the right side of the field in a sports game **OPP** **left-winger**

# rigid

**rigid** /ˈrɪdʒɪd/ adj. **1** (often disapproving) (of rules, methods, etc.) very strict and difficult to change SYN **inflexible**: *The curriculum was too narrow and too rigid.* ◇ *His rigid adherence to the rules made him unpopular.* **2** (often disapproving) (of a person) not willing to change their ideas or behaviour SYN **inflexible**: *rigid attitudes* **3** (of an object or substance) stiff and difficult to move or bend: *a rigid support for the tent* ◇ *She sat upright, her body rigid with fear.* ◇ *(figurative) I was bored rigid* (= extremely bored). ▶ **ri·gid·ity** /rɪˈdʒɪdəti/ noun [U, C]: *the rigidity of the law on this issue* ◇ *the rigidity of the metal bar* **ri·gid·ly** /ˈrɪdʒɪdli/ adv.: *The speed limit must be rigidly enforced.* ◇ *She stared rigidly ahead.*

**rig·ma·role** /ˈrɪɡməroʊl/ noun [U, sing.] **1** a long and complicated process that is annoying and seems unnecessary: *I couldn't face the whole rigmarole of getting a work permit again.* **2** a long and complicated story

**rigor mor·tis** /ˌrɪɡə ˈmɔːtɪs; NAmE -ɡər ˈmɔːrt-/ noun [U] the process by which the body becomes stiff after death

**rig·or·ous** /ˈrɪɡərəs/ adj. **1** done carefully and with a lot of attention to detail SYN **thorough**: *a rigorous analysis* **2** demanding that particular rules, processes, etc. are strictly followed SYN **strict**: *The work failed to meet their rigorous standards.* ▶ **rig·or·ous·ly** adv.: *The country's press is rigorously controlled.*

**rig·our** (US **rigor**) /ˈrɪɡə(r)/ noun **1** [U] the fact of being careful and paying great attention to detail: *academic/intellectual/scientific, etc. rigour* **2** [U] (formal) the fact of being strict or severe SYN **severity**: *This crime must be treated with the full rigour of the law.* **3** **the rigours of sth** [pl.] the difficulties and unpleasant conditions of sth: *The plants were unable to withstand the rigours of a harsh winter.*

**the Rig Veda** /ðə ˌrɪɡ ˈveɪdə/ noun [sing.] the oldest and most important of the Vedas (= Hindu holy texts)

**rile** /raɪl/ verb ~ **sb** | **it riles sb that ...** to annoy sb or make them angry SYN **anger**: *Nothing ever seemed to rile him.* IDM **be/get (all) riled up** (especially NAmE, informal) to be or get very annoyed

**Riley** /ˈraɪli/ noun IDM see LIFE

**rim** /rɪm/ noun, verb
■ noun **1** the edge of sth in the shape of a circle: *He looked at them over the rim of his glass.* ◇ *The rims of her eyes were red with crying.* ◇ *spectacles with gold rims* ⊃ picture at EDGE **2** the metal edge of a wheel onto which the tyre is fixed **3** **-rimmed** adj. having a particular type of rim: *gold-rimmed spectacles* ◇ *red-rimmed eyes* (= for example, from crying) ⊃ see also HORN-RIMMED
■ verb [often passive] (**-mm-**) ~ **sth** (formal) to form an edge around sth

**rime** /raɪm/ noun [U] (literary) FROST

**rim·less** /ˈrɪmləs/ adj. [only before noun] (of glasses) having LENSES (= the clear parts that you look through) that are not surrounded by frames

**rind** /raɪnd/ noun **1** [U] the thick outer layer of some types of fruit: *lemon rind* ⊃ compare PEEL, SKIN, ZEST **2** [U, C] the thick outer skin of some foods such as BACON and some types of cheese

**ring¹** 🔊 A2 /rɪŋ/ noun, verb ⊃ see also RING²
■ noun
• JEWELLERY **1** 🔊 A2 [C] a piece of jewellery that you wear on your finger, consisting of a round band of gold, silver, etc., sometimes decorated with PRECIOUS STONES: *a gold ring* ◇ *a diamond ring* (= a ring with a diamond on it) ⊃ see also ENGAGEMENT RING, NOSE RING, SIGNET RING, WEDDING RING
• CIRCLE **2** 🔊 B1 [C] an object in the shape of a circle with a large hole in the middle: *a key ring* ◇ *curtain rings* ◇ *onion rings* ⊃ see also KEY RING **3** 🔊 B1 [C] a round mark or shape: *She had dark rings around her eyes from lack of sleep.* ◇ *The children sat on the floor in a ring.*

## rings

children in a ring

key ring

diamond ring

gas ring

boxing ring

gas ring on a cooker/range

• FOR PERFORMANCE/COMPETITION **4** [C] an area in which animals or people perform or compete, with seats around the outside for the audience: *a boxing ring* ◇ *a circus ring* ⊃ see also BULLRING
• FOR COOKING **5** [C] (especially BrE) a small flat place on a cooker that is heated by gas or electricity and is used for cooking on SYN **burner**: *to turn off the gas ring* ⊃ see also GAS RING
• GROUP OF PEOPLE **6** [C] a group of people who are working together, especially in secret or illegally: *a spy ring* ◇ *a drugs ring*
IDM **run rings around/round sb** (informal) to be much better at doing sth than sb else ⊃ more at BRASS, HAT
■ verb (**ringed**, **ringed**)
• SURROUND **1** [often passive] ~ **sb/sth (with sth)** to surround sb/sth: *Thousands of demonstrators ringed the building.*
• BIRD'S LEG **2** ~ **sth** to put a metal ring around a bird's leg so that it can be easily identified in the future
• DRAW CIRCLE **3** ~ **sth** (especially BrE) to draw a circle around sth SYN **circle**: *Ring the correct answer in pencil.*

**ring²** 🔊 A2 /rɪŋ/ verb, noun ⊃ see also RING¹
■ verb (**rang** /ræŋ/, **rung** /rʌŋ/)
• TELEPHONE **1** 🔊 A2 (BrE) (also **call** NAmE, BrE) [T, I] to phone sb/sth: ~ **sb/sth up** *I'll ring you up later.* ◇ *He rang up the police station.* ◇ ~ **sb/sth** *When is the best time to ring New York?* ◇ ~ **(up)** *David rang up while you were out.* ◇ *He said he was ringing from London.* ◇ *I'm ringing about your advertisement in the paper.* ◇ *She rang to say she'd be late.* ◇ ~ **for sth** *Could you ring for a cab?* ⊃ note at PHONE **2** 🔊 A2 [I] (of a phone) to make a sound because sb is trying to phone you: *Will you answer the telephone if it rings?*
• BELL **3** 🔊 A2 [T, I] if you **ring a bell** or if a bell **rings**, it produces a sound: ~ **(sth)** *Someone was ringing the doorbell.* ◇ *The church bells rang.* ◇ ~ **for sb/sth** *Just ring for the nurse* (= attract the nurse's attention by ringing a bell) *if you need her.*
• WITH SOUND **4** [I] ~ **(with sth)** (literary) to be full of a sound; to fill a place with sound SYN **resound**: *The house rang with children's laughter.* ◇ *Applause rang through the hall.*
• WITH QUALITY **5** [I] ~ **(with sth)** to be full of a particular quality: *His words rang with pride.*
• OF EARS **6** [I] to be uncomfortable and be unable to hear clearly, usually because you have heard a loud noise, etc: *The music was so loud it made my ears ring.*
IDM **ring a bell** (informal) to sound familiar to you, as though you have heard it before: *His name rings a bell but I can't think where we met.* **ring the 'changes (with sth)** (BrE) to make changes to sth in order to have greater variety: *Ring the changes with a new colour.* **ring in your 'ears/'head** to make you feel that you can still hear sth: *His warning was still ringing in my ears.* **ring off the 'hook** (usually used in the progressive tenses) (of a phone) to ring many times, with one phone call after another: *The*

phone has been ringing off the hook with offers of help. **ring 'true / 'hollow / 'false** to give the impression of being sincere/true or not sincere/true: *It may seem a strange story but it rings true to me.* ⇒ more at ALARM *n.*

**PHRV** **ring a'round** = RING ROUND (SB/STH) **ring 'back | ring sb⇿'back** (*BrE*) to phone sb again, for example because they were not there when you called earlier, or to return a call they made to you: *He isn't here now—could you ring back later?* ⋄ *I'll ask Simon to ring you back when he gets in.* **ring 'in** (*BrE*) to phone a television or radio show, or the place where you work **ring 'in sth** to ring bells to celebrate sth, especially the new year **ring 'off** (*BrE*) to put down the phone because you have finished speaking: *He rang off before I could explain.* ⇒ WORDFINDER NOTE at CALL **ring 'out** to be heard loudly and clearly: *A number of shots rang out.* **ring 'round / a'round (sb / sth)** (*BrE*) to phone a number of people in order to organize sth or to get some information, etc: *I rang round all the travel agents in the area.* **ring 'through (to sb)** (*BrE*) to make a phone call to sb, especially within the same building: *Reception just rang through to say my visitor has arrived.* **ring sth⇿ 'up** to enter the cost of goods being bought in a shop on a CASH REGISTER by pressing the buttons; to make sales of a particular value: *She rang up all the items on the till.* ⋄ *The company rang up sales of $166 million last year.*

■ **noun**
- **OF BELL 1** [C] the sound that a bell makes; the act of ringing a bell: *There was a ring at the door.* ⋄ *He gave a couple of loud rings on the doorbell.*
- **SOUND 2** [sing.] a loud, clear sound: *the ring of horse's hooves on the cobblestones*
- **QUALITY 3** [sing.] ~ **(of sth)** a particular quality that words, sounds, etc. have: *His explanation has a ring of truth about it.* ⋄ *Her protestation of innocence had a hollow ring to it* (= did not sound sincere). ⋄ *The story had a familiar ring to it* (= as if I had heard it before).

**IDM** **give sb a 'ring** (*BrE, informal*) to make a phone call to sb: *I'll give you a ring tomorrow.* ⇒ note at PHONE

**ring-back** /'rɪŋbæk/ *(also* **Callback™***) noun* [U, C] a phone service that you can use if you call sb and their phone is being used, so that your phone will ring when the line is free; a call made using this service

**'ring binder** *noun* a file for holding papers, in which metal rings go through the edges of the pages, holding them in place

**ringed** /rɪŋd/ *adj.* [only before noun] **1** having a ring or rings on: *a ringed finger* **2** (especially of an animal or bird) having a mark or marks like a ring on it: *a ringed plover*

**ringer** /'rɪŋə(r)/ *noun* **1** = BELL-RINGER **2** a device that makes a ringing sound, for example on a phone **3** a horse or person that takes part in a race illegally, for example by using a false name **IDM** see DEAD *adj.*

**ring-ette** /rɪŋ'et/ *noun* [U] a Canadian game similar to ICE HOCKEY, played with a straight stick and rubber ring, especially by women

**'ring-fence** *verb* (*BrE*) **1** ~ **sth** (*finance*) to protect a particular sum of money by putting limits on it so that it can only be used for a particular purpose **2** ~ **sth** to protect sth by putting limits on it so that it can only be used by particular people or for a particular purpose: *All employees can access the parts of the Intranet that are not ring-fenced.* ▶ **'ring fence** *noun*: *The government has promised to put a ring fence around funding for education.*

**'ring finger** *noun* the finger next to the smallest one, especially on the left hand, on which a wedding ring is traditionally worn

**ring-ing** /'rɪŋɪŋ/ *adj., noun*
■ *adj.* [only before noun] **1** (of a sound) loud and clear **2** (of a statement, etc.) powerful and made with a lot of force: *a ringing endorsement of her leadership*
■ *noun* [sing., U] an act or a sound of ringing: *There was an unpleasant ringing in my ears.* ⇒ see also BELL-RINGING

**ring-lead-er** /'rɪŋliːdə(r)/ *noun* (*disapproving*) a person who leads others in crime or in causing trouble

# riot shield

**ring-let** /'rɪŋlət/ *noun* [usually pl.] a long CURL of hair hanging down from sb's head

**ring-mas-ter** /'rɪŋmɑːstə(r); *NAmE* -mæs-/ *noun* a person in charge of a CIRCUS performance

**'ring pull** (*BrE*) (*NAmE* **'pull tab, tab**) *noun* a small piece of metal with a ring attached which is pulled to open cans of food, drink, etc.

**'ring road** (*BrE*) (*US* **'outer belt**) *noun* a road that is built around a city or town to reduce traffic in the centre

**ring-side** /'rɪŋsaɪd/ *noun* [U] the area closest to the space in which a BOXING match or CIRCUS takes place: *According to law, a doctor must be present at the ringside.* ⋄ *a ringside seat*

**ring-tone** /'rɪŋtəʊn/ *noun* the sound a phone makes when sb is calling you. Ringtones are often short tunes, and the word is especially used to refer to the different sounds mobile phones make when they ring.

**'ring toss** /'rɪŋtɒs; *NAmE* -tɔːs/ (*NAmE*) (*BrE* **hoopla**) *noun* [U] a game in which players try to throw rings over objects in order to win them as prizes

**ring-worm** /'rɪŋwɜːm; *NAmE* -wɜːrm/ *noun* [U] a skin disease that produces small, round, red areas on the skin

**rink** /rɪŋk/ *noun* **1** = ICE RINK **2** = SKATING RINK

**rinse** /rɪns/ *verb, noun*
■ *verb* **1** ~ **sth (with sth)** to wash sth with clean water only, not using soap: *Rinse the cooked pasta with boiling water.* **2** to remove the soap from sth with clean water after washing it: ~ **sth** *Always rinse your hair thoroughly.* ⋄ ~ **sth out** *Make sure you rinse all the soap out.* ⇒ SYNONYMS at CLEAN **3** ~ **sth + adv. / prep.** to remove dirt, etc. from sth by washing it with clean water: *She rinsed the mud from her hands.* ⋄ *I wanted to rinse the taste out of my mouth.* ⇒ WORDFINDER NOTE at LIQUID
**PHRV** **rinse sth⇿ 'out** to make sth clean, especially a container, by washing it with water: *Rinse the cup out before use.*
■ *noun* **1** [C] an act of rinsing sth: *I gave the glass a rinse.* ⋄ *Fabric conditioner is added during the final rinse.* **2** [C, U] a liquid that you put on your hair when it is wet in order to change its colour: *a blue rinse* **3** [C, U] a liquid used for cleaning the mouth and teeth

**riot** /'raɪət/ *noun, verb*
■ *noun* **1** [C] a situation in which a group of people behave in a violent way in a public place, often as a protest: *One prison guard was killed when a riot broke out in the jail.* ⋄ *Shortages eventually led to food riots.* ⇒ RACE RIOT ⇒ WORDFINDER NOTE at PROTEST **2** [sing.] ~ **of sth** (*formal*) a collection of a lot of different types of the same thing: *The garden was a riot of colour.* **3** *a* **riot** [sing.] (*old-fashioned, informal*) a person or an event that is very funny
**IDM** **run 'riot 1** (of people) to behave in a way that is violent and/or not under control **SYN** **rampage**: *They let their kids run riot.* **2** if your imagination, a feeling, etc. **runs riot**, you allow it to develop and continue without trying to control it **3** (of plants) to grow and spread quickly ⇒ more at READ *v.*
■ *verb* [I] (of a crowd of people) to behave in a violent way in a public place, often as a protest ▶ **'riot-er** *noun*: *Rioters set fire to parked cars.* **'riot-ing** *noun* [U]: *Rioting broke out in the capital.*

**'riot gear** *noun* [U] the clothes and equipment used by the police when they are dealing with riots

**riot-ous** /'raɪətəs/ *adj.* [usually before noun] **1** (*formal or law*) noisy and/or violent, especially in a public place: *riotous behaviour* ⋄ *The organizers of the march were charged with assault and riotous assembly.* **2** noisy, exciting and fun **SYN** **uproarious**: *a riotous party* ⋄ *riotous laughter*

**riot-ous-ly** /'raɪətəsli/ *adv.* extremely *riotously funny*

**'riot police** *noun* [pl.] police who are trained to deal with people RIOTING

**'riot shield** (*also* **shield**) *noun* a piece of equipment made from strong plastic, used by the police to protect themselves from angry crowds

# RIP

**RIP** (also **R.I.P.** especially in US) /ˌɑːr aɪ ˈpiː/ abbr. rest in peace (often written on GRAVES)

**rip** /rɪp/ verb, noun

- **verb** (-pp-) **1** [T, I] to tear sth or to become torn, often suddenly or violently: **~ (sth)** *I ripped my jeans on the fence.* ◊ *The flags had been ripped in two.* ◊ *I heard the tent rip.* ◊ **~ sth + adj.** *She ripped the letter open.* **2** [T] **~ sth + adv./prep.** to remove sth quickly or violently, often by pulling it: *He ripped off his tie.* ◊ *The carpet had been ripped from the stairs.* **3** [T] **~ sth** (*computing*) to copy sound or video files from a website or CD on to a computer **4** **~ sth** (*computing*) to change text or images into a form in which they can be displayed on a screen or printed
  - **IDM** **let ˈrip** | **let sth ˈrip** (*informal*) **1** to go or allow sth such as a car to go as fast as possible: *Once on the open road, he let rip.* ◊ *Come on Steve—let her rip.* **2** to do sth or to allow sth to happen as fast as possible: *This would cause inflation to let rip again.* **let ˈrip (at sb)** (*informal*) to speak or do sth with great force, enthusiasm, etc. and without control: *When she gets angry with her boyfriend, she really lets rip at him.* ◊ *The group let rip with a single from their new album.* **rip sb/sth aˈpart/to ˈshreds/to ˈbits, etc.** to destroy sth; to criticize sb very strongly ⊃ more at HEART *n.*, LIMB
  - **PHRV** **ˈrip at sth** to attack sth violently, usually by tearing or cutting it **rip ˈinto sb (for/with sth)** to criticize sb and tell them that you are very angry with them **rip ˈinto/ˈthrough sb/sth** to go very quickly and violently into or through sb/sth: *A bullet ripped into his shoulder.* **rip sb↔ˈoff** [usually passive] (*informal*) to cheat sb, by making them pay too much, by selling them sth of poor quality, etc: *Tourists complain of being ripped off by local cab drivers.* ⊃ related noun RIP-OFF **rip sth↔ˈoff** (*informal*) to steal or illegally copy sth: *Thieves broke in and ripped off five computers.* **rip sth↔ˈup** to tear sth into small pieces: *He ripped up the letter and threw it in the fire.*
- **noun** [usually sing.] **1** a long tear in cloth, paper, etc. **2** = RIP CURRENT

**ri·par·ian** /raɪˈpeəriən; NAmE -ˈper-/ adj. [usually before noun] **1** (*specialist*) growing in, living in, or relating to areas of wet land near to a river or stream **2** (*law*) on, near or relating to the bank of a river

**ˈrip current** (also **rip**) noun a strong current of water that flows away from the coast

**ripe** /raɪp/ adj. (**riper**, **rip·est**) **1** (of fruit or crops) fully grown and ready to be eaten **OPP** unripe **2** (of cheese) having a taste that has fully developed **SYN** mature **3** (of a smell) strong and unpleasant **4** **~ (for sth)** ready or suitable for sth to happen: *This land is ripe for development.* ◊ *The conditions were ripe for social change.* ◊ *Reforms were promised when the time was ripe.* ▸ **ripe·ness** noun [U]
- **IDM** **ripe for the ˈpicking** offering sb an ideal opportunity to gain an advantage **a/the ripe old age (of …)** an age that is considered to be very old: *He lived to the ripe old age of 91.*

**ripen** /ˈraɪpən/ verb [I, T] **~ (sth)** to become ripe; to make sth ripe

**ˈrip-off** noun (*informal*) **1** [usually sing.] something that is not worth what you pay for it: *$70 for a T-shirt! What a rip-off!* **2 ~ (of sth)** a copy of sth, especially one that is less expensive or not as good as the original thing: *The single is a rip-off of a 70s hit.*

**ri·poste** /rɪˈpɒst; NAmE -ˈpoʊst/ noun (*formal*) **1** a quick and clever reply, especially to criticism **SYN** retort: *a witty riposte* **2** a course of action that takes place in response to sth that has happened: *The US delivered an early riposte to the air attack.* ▸ **ri·poste** verb [T, I] (+ **speech**)

**ripped** /rɪpt/ adj. **1** (of clothes or fabric) badly torn: *ripped blue jeans* **2** (*informal*) having strong muscles that you can see clearly: *I'm not trying to get ripped—I just want to stay fit.*

**rip·per** /ˈrɪpə(r)/ noun, adj.
- **noun** (*informal*) **1** [C] a person who is very good at SNOWBOARDING **2** [U] (*especially AustralE*) a thing that is particularly good: **a ~ of a sth** *He's a ripper of a bloke to have a beer with.*
- **adj.** (*especially AustralE*, *informal*) particularly good; excellent

**rip·ple** /ˈrɪpl/ noun, verb
- **noun 1** a small wave on the surface of a liquid, especially water in a lake, etc: *The air was so still that there was hardly a ripple on the pond's surface.* **2** a thing that looks or moves like a small wave: *ripples of sand* **3** [usually sing.] **~ of sth** a sound that gradually becomes louder and then quieter again: *a ripple of applause/laughter* **4** [usually sing.] **~ of sth** a feeling that gradually spreads through a person or group of people: *A ripple of fear passed through him.* ◊ *The announcement sent a ripple of excitement through the crowd.*
  - **IDM** **create/make ˈripples/a ˈripple** to be noticed and have an impact: *It's a film that promises to create ripples.*
- **verb 1** [I, T] to move or to make sth move in very small waves: *The sea rippled and sparkled.* ◊ *rippling muscles* ◊ **~ sth** *The wind rippled the wheat in the fields.* **2** [I] **+ adv./prep.** (of a feeling, etc.) to spread through a person or a group of people like a wave: *A gasp rippled through the crowd.*

**ˈripple effect** noun a situation in which an event or action has an effect on sth, which then has an effect on sth else: *His resignation will have a ripple effect on the whole department.* ⊃ compare DOMINO EFFECT

**ˈrip-roaring** adj. [only before noun] (*informal*) **1** noisy, exciting and/or full of activity: *a rip-roaring celebration* **2 ~ success** a great success

**Rip Van Winkle** /ˌrɪp væn ˈwɪŋkl/ noun a person who is surprised to find how much the world has changed over a period of time **ORIGIN** From the name of a character in a short story by the US writer Washington Irving. He sleeps for 20 years and wakes up to find that the world has completely changed.

**rise** /raɪz/ verb, noun

- **verb** (**rose** /rəʊz/, **risen** /ˈrɪzn/)
  - • **MOVE UPWARDS 1** [I] to come or go upwards; to reach a higher level or position: *The curtain rose to reveal an empty stage.* ◊ **+ adv./prep.** *Smoke was rising from the chimney.* ◊ *The river has risen by several metres.*
  - • **INCREASE 2** [I] to increase in amount or number: *Prices are still rising.* ◊ **~ in sth** *to rise in value/price* ◊ *Global temperatures could rise three degrees or more.* ◊ **~ by sth** *Unemployment rose by 3%.* ◊ **~ to sth** *Interest rates rose to a six-year high.* ◊ *to rise sharply/dramatically/rapidly/ steeply* ◊ *to rise steadily/slightly* ⊃ LANGUAGE BANK at INCREASE
  - • **OF SUN/MOON 3** [I] when the sun, moon, etc. **rises**, it appears above the HORIZON: *The sun rises in the east.* **OPP** set ⊃ WORDFINDER NOTE at SUN
  - • **BECOME POWERFUL/IMPORTANT 4** [I] to become more successful, important, powerful, etc: *a rising young politician* ◊ **+ adv./prep.** *He rose to prominence in the 90s.* ◊ *You could rise to the top if you work hard.* ◊ *She rose through the ranks to become managing director.*
  - • **GET UP 5** [I] **(+ adv./prep.)** (*formal*) to get up from a lying, sitting or KNEELING position **SYN** get up: *We are accustomed to rising (= getting out of bed) early.* ◊ *They rose from the table.* ◊ *She rose to her feet.* ⊃ SYNONYMS at STAND
  - • **END MEETING 6** [I] (*formal*) (of a group of people) to end a meeting **SYN** adjourn: *The House (= members of the House of Commons) rose at 10p.m.*
  - • **OF SOUND 7** [I] if a sound **rises**, it becomes louder and higher: *Her voice rose angrily.*
  - • **OF WIND 8** [I] if the wind **rises**, it begins to blow more strongly **SYN** get up
  - • **OF FEELING 9** [I] (*formal*) if a feeling **rises** inside you, it begins and gets stronger: *He felt anger rising inside him.* ◊ *Her spirits rose (= she felt happier) at the news.*
  - • **OF YOUR COLOUR 10** [I] (*formal*) if your colour **rises**, your face becomes pink or red because you are embarrassed

- **OF HAIR 11** [I] if hair **rises**, it stands up instead of lying flat: *The hair on the back of my neck rose when I heard the scream.*
- **FIGHT 12** [I] ~ **(up) (against sb/sth)** (*formal*) to begin to fight against your government or leader or against a foreign army SYN **rebel**: *The peasants rose in revolt.* ◇ *He called on the people to rise up against the invaders.*
  ⊃ related noun UPRISING
- **START TO BE SEEN 13** [I] (*formal*) to be able to be seen above everything that is around: *Mountains rose in the distance.*
- **OF LAND 14** [I] if land **rises**, it slopes upwards: *The ground rose steeply all around.*
- **OF BEGINNING OF RIVER 15** [I] + adv./prep. a river **rises** where it begins to flow: *The Thames rises in the Cotswold hills.*
- **OF BREAD/CAKES 16** [I] when bread, cakes, etc. **rise**, they become larger and rounder because of the action of YEAST or BAKING POWDER
- **OF DEAD PERSON 17** [I] ~ **(from sth)** to come to life again: *to rise from the dead* ◇ (*figurative*) *Can a new party rise from the ashes of the old one?*

**IDM** ,rise and 'shine (*old-fashioned*) usually used in orders to tell sb to get out of bed and be active ⊃ more at HACKLES, HEIGHT
**PHRV** ,rise a'bove sth **1** to not be affected or limited by problems, offensive remarks, etc: *She had the courage and determination to rise above her physical disability.* **2** to be wise enough or morally good enough not to do sth wrong or not to think the same as other people: *I try to rise above prejudice.* **3** to be of a higher standard than other things of a similar kind: *His work rarely rises above the mediocre.* 'rise to sth **1** to show that you are able to deal with an unexpected situation, problem, etc: *Luckily, my mother rose to the occasion.* ◇ *He was determined to rise to the challenge.* **2** to react when sb is deliberately trying to make you angry or get you interested in sth: *I refuse to rise to that sort of comment.* ◇ *As soon as I mentioned money, he rose to the bait.*

■ noun
- **INCREASE 1** B1 [C] an increase in an amount, a number or a level: *The industry is feeling the effects of recent price rises.* ◇ *a rapid temperature rise* ◇ ~ **in sth** *There has been a sharp rise in the number of people out of work.* ◇ *a five per cent rise in train fares* ◇ ~ **of sth** *a rise of 10%* ⊃ LANGUAGE BANK at INCREASE **2** B1 [C] (*BrE*) (*NAmE* **raise**) an increase in the money you are paid for the work you do: *I'm going to ask for a rise.* ◇ *He criticized the huge pay rises awarded to industry bosses.* ⊃ WORDFINDER NOTE at PAY
- **IN POWER/IMPORTANCE 3** B2 [sing.] the act of becoming more important, successful, powerful, etc: ~ **of sb/sth** *the rise of fascism in Europe* ◇ *the rise and fall of the British Empire* ◇ ~ **to sth** *the party's rise to power* ◇ *her meteoric rise to stardom*
- **A MOVEMENT UPWARDS 4** B2 [sing.] a movement upwards: *She watched the gentle rise and fall of his chest as he slept.*
- **SLOPING LAND 5** [C] an area of land that slopes upwards SYN **slope**: *The church was built at the top of a small rise.*
  ⊃ see also HIGH-RISE, LOW-RISE

**IDM** get a 'rise out of sb to make sb react in an angry way by saying sth that you know will annoy them, especially as a joke give 'rise to sth (*formal*) to cause sth to happen or exist: *The novel's success gave rise to a number of sequels.*

**ris·er** /ˈraɪzə(r)/ noun **1** early/late ~ a person who usually gets out of bed early/late in the morning **2** (*specialist*) the part that goes up between two steps in a set of stairs ⊃ compare TREAD ⊃ picture at STAIRCASE

**ris·ible** /ˈrɪzəbl/ adj. (*formal, disapproving*) deserving to be laughed at rather than taken seriously SYN **ludicrous**, **ridiculous**

**ris·ing** /ˈraɪzɪŋ/ noun a situation in which a group of people protest against, and try to get rid of, a government, a leader, etc. SYN **revolt**, **uprising**

**risk** O B1 O /rɪsk/ noun, verb
■ noun **1** B1 [C, U] the possibility of sth bad happening at some time in the future; a situation that could be dangerous or have a bad result: *The health risks are very low.* ◇ ~ **of sth** *a high risk of failure* ◇ *The study found a slightly increased risk of cancer in this group.* ◇ *to reduce/minimize*

1341

# risk

▼ WHICH WORD?

**rise / raise**

**Verbs**
- **Raise** is a verb that must have an object and **rise** is used without an object. When you **raise** something, you lift it to a higher position or increase it: *He raised his head from the pillow.* ◇ *We were forced to raise the price.* When people or things **rise**, they move from a lower to a higher position: *She rose from the chair.* ◇ *The helicopter rose into the air.* **Rise** can also mean 'to increase in number or quantity': *Costs are always rising.*

**Nouns**
- The noun **rise** means a movement upwards or an increase in an amount or quantity: *a rise in interest rates.* In *BrE* it can also be used to mean an increase in pay: *Should I ask my boss for a rise?* In *NAmE* this is a **raise**: *a three per cent pay raise.* **Rise** can also mean the process of becoming more powerful or important: *his dramatic rise to power.*

*the risk of sth* ◇ ~ **of doing sth** *Smoking can increase the risk of developing heart disease.* ◇ ~ **(that) ...** *There is still a risk that the whole deal will fall through.* ◇ ~ **to sb/sth** *The chemicals pose little risk* (= are not dangerous) *to human health.* ◇ *Make sure you understand the risks and benefits.* ◇ *Cigarette smoking is a risk factor for this disease.* ⊃ see also HIGH-RISK, LOW-RISK **2** B1 [C] a person or thing that is likely to cause problems or danger at some time in the future: *Those old boxes in the corridor are a fire risk.* ◇ *a safety/health risk* ◇ ~ **to sth/sb** *The group was considered to be a risk to national security.* ⊃ see also SECURITY RISK **3** [C] **a good/bad/poor ~** a person or business that a bank or an insurance company is willing/unwilling to lend money or sell insurance to because they are likely/unlikely to pay back the money, etc: *With five previous claims, he's now a bad insurance risk.* ⊃ WORDFINDER NOTE at INSURANCE ⊃ see also HIGH-RISK, LOW-RISK

**IDM** at 'risk B1 in danger of sth unpleasant or harmful happening: *As with all diseases, certain groups will be more at risk than others.* ◇ *If we go to war, innocent lives will be put at risk.* ◇ ~ **of/from (doing) sth** *Journalists in the zone are at serious risk of being kidnapped.* at the 'risk of doing sth used to introduce sth that may sound stupid or may offend sb: *At the risk of showing my ignorance, how exactly does the internet work?* at risk to yourself/sb/sth with the possibility of harming yourself/sb/sth: *He dived in to save the dog at considerable risk to his own life.* do sth at your own 'risk to do sth even though you have been warned about the possible dangers and will have to take responsibility for anything bad that happens: *Persons swimming beyond this point do so at their own risk* (= on a notice). ◇ *Valuables are left at their owner's risk* (= on a notice). run a/the 'risk (of sth/of doing sth) | run 'risks to be or put yourself in a situation in which sth bad could happen to you: *People who are overweight run a risk of a heart attack or stroke.* ◇ *We don't want to run the risk of losing their business.* ◇ *Investment is all about running risks.* take a 'risk | take 'risks to do sth even though you know that sth bad could happen as a result: *That's a risk I'm not prepared to take.* ◇ *You have no right to take risks with other people's lives.*

■ verb **1** B1 ~ **sth** to put sth valuable or important in a dangerous situation, in which it could be lost or damaged: *He risked his life to save her.* ◇ ~ **sth on sth** *He risked all his money on a game of cards.* ◇ ~ **sth for sth** *They were willing to risk everything for their liberty.* **2** B1 to do sth that may mean that you get into a situation which is unpleasant or harmful for you: ~ **sth** *There was no choice. If they stayed there, they risked death.* ◇ ~ **(sb/sth) doing sth** *These families risked losing everything.* **3** B1 to do sth that you know is not really a good idea or may not succeed: ~ **sth** *He risked a glance at her furious face.* ◇ *They risked the wrath of the government* (= risked making them angry) *by leaking the story.* ◇ *It was a difficult decision but we decided to*

# risk assessment

risk it. ◊ **~ doing sth** *We've been advised not to risk travelling in these conditions.* **IDM** **risk life and ˈlimb** | **risk your ˈneck** to risk being killed or injured in order to do sth

**ˈrisk assessment** *noun* [C, U] (*business*) the act of identifying possible risks, calculating how likely they are to happen and estimating what effects they might have, especially in the context of a company taking responsibility for the safety of its employees or members of the public: *The employer has an obligation to carry out a risk assessment.*

**ˈrisk-averse** *adj.* not willing to do sth if it is possible that sth bad could happen as a result: *We live in a risk-averse culture.* ◊ *In business you cannot be innovative and risk-averse at the same time.*

**ˈrisk-taking** *noun* [U] the practice of doing things that involve risks in order to achieve sth

**risky** /ˈrɪski/ *adj.* (**riskˑier**, **riskiˑest**) **HELP** You can also use **more risky** and **most risky**. involving the possibility of sth bad happening **SYN** **dangerous**: *Life as an aid worker can be a risky business* (= dangerous). ◊ *a risky investment* ◊ *It's far too risky to generalize from one set of results.*
▶ **riskˑily** /-skɪli/ *adv.* **riskiˑness** *noun* [U]

**risˑotto** /rɪˈzɒtəʊ; *NAmE* -ˈsɔːt-, -ˈzɔː-/ *noun* [C, U] (*pl.* **-os**) an Italian dish of rice cooked with vegetables, meat, etc.

**risˑqué** /ˈrɪskeɪ; *NAmE* rɪˈskeɪ/ *adj.* a **risqué** performance, comment, joke, etc. shocks people slightly, usually because it is about sex

**Ritˑalin**™ /ˈrɪtəlɪn/ *noun* a drug given to children who suffer from ATTENTION DEFICIT DISORDER, to help them become calmer and concentrate better

**rite** /raɪt/ *noun* a ceremony performed by a particular group of people, often for religious purposes: *funeral rites* ◊ *initiation rites* (= performed when a new member joins a secret society) ⊃ see also LAST RITES

**rite of ˈpassage** *noun* a ceremony or an event that marks an important stage in sb's life

**ritˑual** /ˈrɪtʃuəl/ *noun, adj.*
- *noun* [C, U] **1** a series of actions that are always performed in the same way, especially as part of a religious ceremony: *religious rituals* ◊ *She objects to the ritual of organized religion.* **2** something that is done regularly and always in the same way: *Sunday lunch with the in-laws has become something of a ritual.*
- *adj.* [only before noun] **1** done as part of a ritual or ceremony: *ritual chanting* **2** always done or said in the same way, especially when this is not sincere: *ritual expressions of sympathy* ▶ **rituˑalˑly** /-əli/ *adv.*: *The goat was ritually slaughtered.*

**ritˑualˑisˑtic** /ˌrɪtʃuəˈlɪstɪk/ *adj.* [usually before noun] **1** connected with the rituals performed as part of a ceremony: *a ritualistic act of worship* **2** always done or said in the same way, especially when this is not sincere

**rituˑalˑize** (*BrE also* **-ise**) /ˈrɪtʃuəlaɪz/ *verb* [usually passive] ~ **sth** (*formal*) to do sth in the same way or pattern every time: *ritualized expressions of grief*

**ritzy** /ˈrɪtsi/ *adj.* (*informal*) expensive and fashionable **ORIGIN** From the *Ritz*, the name of several very comfortable and expensive hotels in London and other cities.

**rival** /ˈraɪvl/ *noun, adj., verb*
- *noun* a person, company or thing that competes with another in sport, business, etc: *The two teams have always been rivals.* ◊ *Marlowe was Shakespeare's **main rival** at the beginning of his career.* ◊ *the company's **nearest/closest rival** in the business* ◊ *This latest design **has no rivals** (= it is easily the best design available).* ◊ *~ **for sth** She has no rivals for the job.* ◊ *~ **to sb/sth** Grand it may be, but this cathedral is no rival to the great cathedral of Amiens.* ⊃ see also ARCH-RIVAL
- *adj.* (of a person, company, thing, etc.) competing with another person, company, thing, etc: *a rival bid/claim/offer* ◊ *fighting between rival groups/factions* ◊ *He was shot by a member of a rival gang.*
- *verb* (-ll-, *NAmE also* -l-) ~ **sb/sth** (**for/in sth**) to be as good, impressive, etc. as sb else **SYN** **compare with/to**: *You will find scenery to rival anything you can see in the Alps.* ⊃ see also UNRIVALLED

**riˑvalˑry** /ˈraɪvlri/ *noun* [C, U] (*pl.* **-ries**) a state in which two people, companies, etc. are competing for the same thing: *~ (**with sb/sth**) (**for sth**) a fierce rivalry for world supremacy* ◊ *~ (**between A and B**) (**for sth**) There is a certain amount of friendly rivalry between the teams.* ◊ *political rivalries* ◊ *sibling rivalry* (= between brothers and sisters)

**riven** /ˈrɪvn/ *adj.* [not before noun] **1** ~ (**by/with sth**) (*formal*) (of a group of people) divided because of DISAGREEMENTS, especially in a violent way: *a party riven by internal disputes* **2** ~ (**by/with sth**) (*formal*) (of an object) divided into two or more pieces

**river** /ˈrɪvə(r)/ *noun* **1** (*abbr.* **R.**) a natural flow of water that continues in a long line across land to the sea: *the River Thames* ◊ *the Hudson River* ◊ *on the banks of the river* (= the ground at the side of a river) ◊ *up/down ~ to travel up/down river* (= in the opposite direction to/in the same direction as the way in which the river is flowing) ◊ *the mouth of the river* (= where it enters the sea) ◊ *in the ~ Can we swim in the river?* ◊ *on the ~ a boat on the river* ◊ *They have a house on the river* (= beside it).

**WORDFINDER** bend, course, current, dam, downstream, estuary, source, tributary, waterfall

**2** ~ (**of sth**) a large amount of liquid that is flowing in a particular direction: *Rivers of molten lava flowed down the mountain.* **IDM** SEE SELL *v.*

**ˈriverˑbank** /ˈrɪvəbæŋk; *NAmE* -vərb-/ *noun* the ground at the side of a river: *on the riverbank*

**ˈriver bed** *noun* the area of ground over which a river usually flows: *a dried-up river bed*

**ˈriver blindness** *noun* [U] (*medical*) a tropical skin disease caused by a PARASITE of certain flies that are found in rivers, which can also cause a person to become blind

**ˈriverˑfront** /ˈrɪvəfrʌnt; *NAmE* -vərf-/ *noun* (*especially NAmE*) an area of land next to a river with buildings, shops, restaurants, etc. on it

**riverˑine** /ˈrɪvəraɪn/ *adj.* [usually before noun] (*specialist*) on, near, or relating to a river or the banks of a river

**ˈriverˑside** /ˈrɪvəsaɪd; *NAmE* -vərs-/ *noun* [sing.] the ground along either side of a river: *a riverside path* ◊ *a walk by the riverside*

**rivet** /ˈrɪvɪt/ *noun, verb*
- *noun* a metal pin that is used to fasten two pieces of leather, metal, etc. together
- *verb* [usually passive] **1** to hold sb's interest or attention so completely that they cannot look away or think of anything else: **be riveted (by sth)** *I was absolutely riveted by her story.* ◊ **be riveted on sb/sth** *My eyes were riveted on the figure lying in the road.* ◊ **be riveted to sth** *The film keeps you riveted to the screen.* **2** ~ **sth** to fasten sth with rivets: *The steel plates were riveted together.* **IDM** see SPOT *n.*

**rivˑetˑing** /ˈrɪvɪtɪŋ/ *adj.* so interesting or exciting that it holds your attention completely **SYN** **engrossing**

**riviˑera** /ˌrɪviˈeərə; *NAmE* -ˈerə/ *noun* (*often* **Riviera**) an area by the sea that is warm and popular for holidays, especially the Mediterranean coast of France: *the French Riviera*

**rivuˑlet** /ˈrɪvjələt/ *noun* (*formal*) a very small river; a small stream of water or other liquid

**riyal** = RIAL

**RM** *abbr.* (in writing) (in the UK) Royal Marine ⊃ see also MARINE *noun*

**RN** *abbr.* (in writing) **1** REGISTERED NURSE **2** (in the UK) Royal Navy

**RNA** /ˌɑːr en ˈeɪ/ *noun* [U] (*chemistry*) a chemical present in all living cells; like DNA it is a type of NUCLEIC ACID

**roach** /rəʊtʃ/ *noun* **1** (*NAmE, informal*) = COCKROACH: *The apartments were infested with rats and roaches.* **2** (*pl.*

**roach**) a small European FRESHWATER fish **3** (slang) the end part of a cigarette containing MARIJUANA

**road** 🔑 **A1** /rəʊd/ noun **1** ❓ **A1** a hard surface built for vehicles to travel on: *a main/major/minor road* ◊ *a country/mountain road* ◊ *The house is on a very busy road.* ◊ **along/up/down the ~** *They live just down the road* (= further on the same road). ◊ **by~** *It takes about five hours by road* (= driving). ◊ *It's difficult to* **cross the road** *safely around here.* ◊ *road accidents/safety/users* ➲ see also ACCESS ROAD, A-ROAD, B-ROAD, DIRT ROAD, OFF-ROAD, RELIEF ROAD, RING ROAD, SIDE ROAD, SLIP ROAD, TOLL ROAD ➲ WORDFINDER NOTE at CAR

**WORDFINDER** bypass, carriageway, diversion, hard shoulder, lane, lay-by, motorway, roundabout, signpost

**2** ❓ **A1** **Road** (*abbr.* **Rd**) used in names of roads, especially in towns: *35 York Road* ◊ *We live in/on Kingston Road.* **3** the way to achieving sth: *on the* **~ to sth** *to be on the road to recovery* ◊ *We have discussed privatization, but we would prefer not to go down that particular road.* ➲ see also HIGH ROAD

**IDM** **(further) along/down the ˈroad** | **years down the ˈroad** at some time in the future: *There are certain to be more job losses further down the road.* **ˈany road** (NEngE) = ANYWAY **off the ˈroad** (of a car) not in good enough condition to be legally driven on public roads **one for the ˈroad** (*informal*) a last alcoholic drink before you leave a party, etc. **on the ˈroad 1** travelling, especially for long distances or periods of time: *The band has been on the road for six months.* **2** (of a car) in good condition so that it can be legally driven: *It will cost about £500 to get the car back on the road.* **3** moving from place to place, and having no permanent home: *Life on the road can be very hard.* **the road to ˌhell is paved with good inˈtentions** (*saying*) it is not enough to intend to do good things; you must actually do them ➲ more at END *n.*, HIT *v.*, RUBBER *n.*, SHOW *n.*

▼ **HOMOPHONES**

**road • rode • rowed** /rəʊd/

- **road** noun: *Follow the road around to the left.*
- **rode** verb (*past tense of* RIDE): *I rode a camel when I was on holiday.*
- **rowed** verb (*past tense of* ROW¹): *She took the oars and rowed quickly down the river.*

**ˈroad bike** *noun* a bicycle with narrow tyres designed for use on roads, as opposed to rough ground or racing tracks, especially used in long-distance road races ➲ compare HYBRID (4), MOUNTAIN BIKE

**ˈroad·block** /ˈrəʊdblɒk; NAmE -blɑːk/ *noun* **1** a barrier put across the road by the police or army so that they can stop and search vehicles **2** (NAmE) something that stops a plan from going ahead

**ˈroad·house** /ˈrəʊdhaʊs/ *noun* (NAmE, *old-fashioned*) a restaurant or bar on a main road in the country

**roadie** /ˈrəʊdi/ *noun* (*informal*) a person who works with a band of musicians on tour, and helps move and set up their equipment

**ˈroad·kill** /ˈrəʊdkɪl/ *noun* **1** [U] an animal, or animals, that have been killed by a car on the road **2** [C, U] the killing of an animal by a car hitting it on the road

**ˈroad map** *noun* **1** a map that shows the roads of an area, especially one that is designed for a person who is driving a car **2** a set of instructions or suggestions about how to do sth or find out about sth

**ˈroad movie** *noun* a film which is based on a journey made by the main character or characters

**ˈroad pricing** *noun* [U] the system of making drivers pay to use busy roads at certain times

**ˈroad rage** *noun* [U] a situation in which a driver becomes extremely angry or violent with the driver of another car because of the way they are driving

**ˈroad·run·ner** /ˈrəʊdrʌnə(r)/ *noun* a North American bird of the CUCKOO family, that lives in desert areas and can run very fast

▼ **MORE ABOUT…**

**roads**

Roads and streets

- In a town or city, **street** is the most general word for a road with houses and buildings on one or both sides: *a street map of London*. **Street** is not used for roads between towns, but streets in towns are often called **Road**: *Oxford Street* ◊ *Mile End Road*. A **road map** of a country shows you the major routes between, around and through towns and cities.
- Other words used in the names of streets include: **Circle, Court, Crescent, Drive, Hill** and **Way**. **Avenue** suggests a wide street lined with trees. A **lane** is a narrow street between buildings or, in *BrE*, a narrow country road.

The high street

- **High street** is used in *BrE*, especially as a name, for the main street of a town, where most shops, banks, etc. are: *the shoe shop in the High Street* ◊ *high street shops*. In *NAmE* **Main Street** is often used as a name for this street.

Larger roads

- British and American English use different words for the roads that connect towns and cities. **Motorways**, (for example, the M57) in *BrE*, **freeways**, **highways** or **interstates**, (for example State Route 347, Interstate 94, the Long Island Expressway) in *NAmE*, are large divided roads built for long-distance traffic to avoid towns.
- A **ring road** (*BrE*)/ an **outer belt** (*NAmE*) is built around a city or town to reduce traffic in the centre. This can also be called a **beltway** in *NAmE*, especially when it refers to the road around Washington D.C. A **bypass** passes around a town or city rather than through the centre.

**ˈroad·show** /ˈrəʊdʃəʊ/ *noun* a travelling show arranged by a radio or television programme, or by a magazine, company or political party

**ˈroad·side** /ˈrəʊdsaɪd/ *noun* [sing.] the edge of the road: *a roadside cafe* ◊ **by the ~** *She sat down by the roadside.*

**ˈroad sign** *noun* a sign near a road giving information or instructions to drivers

**ˈroad·ster** /ˈrəʊdstə(r)/ *noun* (*old-fashioned*) a car with no roof and two seats

**ˈroad tax** *noun* [U] (in the UK) a tax that sb who owns a motor vehicle must pay to drive on the roads ➲ WORDFINDER NOTE at CAR

**ˈroad test** *noun* **1** a test to see how a vehicle functions or what condition it is in **2** (NAmE) = DRIVING TEST

**ˈroad-test** *verb* **~ sth** to test a vehicle to see how it functions or what condition it is in

**ˈroad train** *noun* (*especially AustralE*) a large lorry pulling one or more TRAILERS

**ˈroad trip** *noun* (*especially NAmE, informal*) a trip made in a car over a long distance

**ˈroad warrior** *noun* (*NAmE, informal*) **1** [C] a person who travels a lot for their job and does a lot of work while travelling **2** **road warriors** [pl.] a sports team that plays well away from their home sports ground: *The Chicago Blackhawks have been road warriors all season long.*

**ˈroad·way** /ˈrəʊdweɪ/ *noun* [C, U] a road or the part of a road used by vehicles

**ˈroad·works** /ˈrəʊdwɜːks; NAmE -wɜːrks/ *noun* [pl.] (*BrE*) (*NAmE* **ˈroad·work** [U]) repairs that are being done to the road; an area where these repairs are being done ➲ WORDFINDER NOTE at TRAFFIC

**ˈroad·worthy** /ˈrəʊdwɜːði; NAmE -wɜːrði/ *adj.* (of a vehicle) in a safe condition to drive ▶ **ˈroad·worthi·ness** *noun* [U]

# roam

**roam** /rəʊm/ *verb* **1** [I, T] to walk or travel around an area without any definite aim or direction **SYN** **wander**: **+ adv./prep.** *The sheep are allowed to roam freely on this land.* ◇ **~ sth** *to roam the countryside/the streets* **2** [I, T] (of the eyes or hands) to move slowly over every part of sb/sth: **~ over sth/sb** *His gaze roamed over her.* ◇ **~ sth/sb** *Her eyes roamed the room.*

**roam·ing** /ˈrəʊmɪŋ/ *noun* [U] using a mobile phone by connecting to a different company's network, for example when you are in a different country: *international roaming charges*

**roan** /rəʊn/ *noun* an animal, especially a horse, that has hair of two colours mixed together: *a strawberry roan* (= with a mixture of brown and grey hair that looks pink) ▶ **roan** *adj.* [only before noun]

**roar** /rɔː(r)/ *verb, noun*
- *verb* **1** [I] to make a very loud, deep sound: *We heard a lion roar.* ◇ *The gun roared deafeningly.* ◇ *The engine roared to life* (= started noisily). **2** [I, T] to shout sth very loudly: *The crowd roared.* ◇ **~ sth (out)** *The fans roared (out) their approval.* ◇ **+ speech** *'Stand back,' he roared.* **3** [I] to laugh very loudly: *He looked so funny, we all roared.* ◇ **~ with laughter** *It made them roar with laughter.* **4** [I] **+ adv./prep.** (of a vehicle or its rider/driver) to move very fast, making a lot of noise: *She put her foot down and the car roared away.* **5** [I] (of a fire) to burn brightly with a lot of flames, heat and noise **IDM** see **VICTORY**
- *noun* **1** a loud deep sound made by an animal, especially a lion, or by sb's voice: *His speech was greeted by a roar of applause.* ◇ *roars of laughter* **2** a loud continuous noise made by the wind or sea, or by a machine: *I could barely hear above the roar of traffic.*

**roar·ing** /ˈrɔːrɪŋ/ *adj.* [only before noun] **1** making a continuous loud deep noise: *All we could hear was the sound of roaring water.* **2** (of a fire) burning with a lot of flames and heat ⊃ see also **RIP-ROARING**
**IDM** **do a ˈroaring trade (in sth)** (*informal*) to sell a lot of sth very quickly ˌroaring ˈdrunk extremely drunk and noisy ˌa ˌroaring sucˈcess (*informal*) a very great success **the ˌroaring ˈtwenties** *noun* [pl.] the years from 1920 to 1929, considered as a time when people were confident and cheerful

**roast** /rəʊst/ *verb, noun, adj.*
- *verb* **1** [T, I] **~ (sth)** to cook food, especially meat, without liquid in an oven or over a fire; to be cooked in this way: *to roast a chicken* ◇ *the smell of roasting meat* ⊃ see also **POT-ROAST, SPIT-ROAST** **2** [T, I] **~ (sth)** to cook nuts, beans, etc. in order to dry them and turn them brown; to be cooked in this way: *roasted chestnuts* **3** [T] **~ sb** (*informal or humorous*) to be very angry with sb; to criticize sb strongly **4** [I, I] **~ (sth)** (*informal*) to become or to make sth become very hot in the sun or by a fire: *She could feel her skin beginning to roast.*
- *noun* **1** (*BrE also* **joint**) a large piece of meat that is cooked whole in the oven: *the Sunday roast* ⊃ see also **POT ROAST** **2** (*NAmE*) (often in compounds) a party that takes place in sb's garden at which food is cooked over an open fire: *a hot dog roast* **3** (*NAmE*) an event, especially a meal, at which people celebrate sb's life by telling funny stories about them
- *adj.* [only before noun] cooked in an oven or over a fire: *roast chicken/potatoes*

**roast·ing** /ˈrəʊstɪŋ/ *adj., noun*
- *adj.* **1** [only before noun] used for roasting meat, vegetables, etc: *a roasting dish* **2** (*also* ˌroasting ˈhot) so hot that you feel uncomfortable: *a roasting hot day*
- *noun* [sing.] an occasion when sb is criticized severely: *They got a roasting at the next meeting.*

**rob** /rɒb/ *NAmE* /rɑːb/ *verb* (**-bb-**) **~ sb/sth (of sth)** to steal money or property from a person or place: *to rob a bank* ◇ *The tomb had been robbed of its treasures.*
**IDM** ˌrob sb ˈblind (*informal*) to cheat or trick sb so that they lose a lot of money ˌrob the ˈcradle (*NAmE, informal*) to have a sexual relationship with a much younger person ˌrob ˌPeter to pay ˈPaul (*saying*) to borrow money from one person to pay back what you owe to another person; to take money from one thing to use for sth else
**PHRV** ˈrob sb/sth of sth [often passive] to prevent sb having sth that they need or deserve **SYN** **deprive**: *A last-minute goal robbed the team of victory.* ◇ *He had been robbed of his dignity.*

**rob·ber** /ˈrɒbə(r)/ *NAmE* /ˈrɑːb-/ *noun* a person who steals from a person or place, especially using violence or threats: *a bank robber*

**rob·bery** /ˈrɒbəri/ *NAmE* /ˈrɑːb-/ *noun* [U, C] (*pl.* **-ies**) the crime of stealing money or goods from a bank, shop, person, etc., especially using violence or threats: *armed robbery* (= using a gun, knife, etc.) ◇ *There has been a spate of robberies in the area recently.* ⊃ compare **BURGLARY, THEFT** **IDM** see **DAYLIGHT, HIGHWAY**

**robe** /rəʊb/ *noun, verb*
- *noun* **1** a long loose outer piece of clothing, especially one worn as a sign of rank or office at a special ceremony: *coronation robes* ◇ *cardinals in scarlet robes* **2** = **BATHROBE**
- *verb* [usually passive] **~ sb/yourself (in sth)** (*formal*) to dress sb/yourself in long loose clothes or in the way mentioned: *a robed choir* ◇ *The priests were robed in black.*

**robin** /ˈrɒbɪn/ *NAmE* /ˈrɑːb-/ *noun* **1** a small brown European bird with a red breast **2** a grey American bird with a red breast, larger than a European robin ⊃ see also **ROUND ROBIN**

**Robin ˈHood** *noun* a person who takes or steals money from rich people and gives it to poor people **ORIGIN** From the name of a character in traditional English stories who lived in a forest, robbing rich people and giving money to poor people.

**robo·call** /ˈrəʊbəʊkɔːl/ *noun* (*NAmE, informal, disapproving*) a phone call from a company that is trying to sell you sth, using a computer-operated DIALLING system to call your number, and a recorded message

**robot** /ˈrəʊbɒt/ *NAmE* /-bɑːt/ *noun* **1** a machine that can perform a complicated series of tasks by itself: *These cars are built by robots.* ◇ *a robot arm* **2** (especially in stories) a machine that is made to look like a human and that can do some things that a human can do: *a toy robot* ◇ *The action starts when an army of giant robots invades Manhattan.* **3** (*SAfrE*) a TRAFFIC LIGHT: *Turn left at the first robot.*

**ro·bot·ic** /rəʊˈbɒtɪk/ *NAmE* /-ˈbɑːt-/ *adj.* **1** connected with robots: *a robotic arm* **2** like a robot, making stiff movements, speaking without feeling or expression, etc.

**ro·bot·ics** /rəʊˈbɒtɪks/ *NAmE* /-ˈbɑːt-/ *noun* [U] the science of designing and operating robots

**ro·bust** /rəʊˈbʌst/ *adj.* **1** strong and healthy: *She was almost 90, but still very robust.* **2** strong; able to survive being used a lot and not likely to break **SYN** **sturdy**: *a robust piece of equipment* **3** (of a system or an organization) strong and not likely to fail or become weak: *robust economic growth* **4** strong and determined; showing that you are sure about what you are doing are saying **SYN** **vigorous**: *The company is taking a more robust approach to management.* ▶ **ro·bust·ly** *adv.*: *The furniture was robustly constructed.* ◇ *They defended their policies robustly.* **ro·bust·ness** *noun* [U]

**rock** /rɒk/ *NAmE* /rɑːk/ *noun, verb*
- *noun*
  - **HARD MATERIAL 1** [U, C] the hard solid material that forms part of the surface of the earth and some other planets: *They drilled through several layers of rock to reach the oil.* ◇ *a cave with striking rock formations* (= shapes made naturally from rock) ◇ *The tunnel was blasted out of solid rock.* ◇ *volcanic/igneous/sedimentary rocks* **2** [C] a mass of rock standing above the earth's surface or in the sea: *the Rock of Gibraltar* ◇ *The ship crashed into the infamous Sker Point rocks and broke into three pieces.* **3** [C] a large single piece of rock: *They clambered over the rocks at the foot of the cliff.* ◇ *The sign said 'Danger: falling rocks'.*
  - **STONE 4** [C] (*NAmE*) a small stone: *Protesters pelted the soldiers with rocks.*

- **MUSIC** 5 A2 (also ˈrock music) [U] a type of loud popular music, developed in the 1960s, with a strong beat played on electric guitars and drums: *punk/indie/classic rock* ◊ *a rock band/star/concert* ⇒ see also FOLK ROCK, GARAGE ROCK, GLAM ROCK, HARD ROCK, PROG ROCK
- **SWEET/CANDY** 6 (*BrE*) [U] a type of hard sweet made in long sticks, often sold in places where people go on holiday by the sea: *a stick of Brighton rock*
- **JEWEL** 7 [C, usually pl.] (*NAmE, informal*) a PRECIOUS STONE, especially a diamond
- **PERSON** 8 [C, usually sing.] a person who is emotionally strong and who you can rely on: *He is my rock.*

IDM (ˌcaught/ˌstuck) between a ˈrock and a ˈhard place in a situation where you have to choose between two things, both of which are unpleasant ˌget your ˈrocks off (*slang*) 1 to have an ORGASM 2 to do sth that you really enjoy ˌon the ˈrocks 1 a relationship or business that is on the rocks is having difficulties and is likely to fail soon: *Sue's marriage is on the rocks.* 2 (of drinks) served with pieces of ice but no water: *Scotch on the rocks* ⇒ more at LIVE¹, STEADY *adj.*

■ verb
- **MOVE GENTLY** 1 B1+ C1 [I, T] to move gently backwards and forwards or from side to side; to make sb/sth move in this way: (+ *adv./prep.*) *The boat rocked from side to side in the waves.* ◊ *She was rocking backwards and forwards in her seat.* ◊ ~ *sb/sth* (+ *adv./prep.*) *He rocked the baby gently in his arms.*
- **SHOCK** 2 B1+ C1 [T, often passive] ~ sb/sth (*rather informal*) to shock sb/sth very much or make them afraid: *The country was rocked by a series of political scandals.* ◊ *The news rocked the world.*
- **SHAKE** 3 [I, T] to shake or to make sth shake violently: *The house rocked when the bomb exploded.* ◊ ~ **sth** *The town was rocked by an earthquake.* ◊ (*figurative*) *The scandal rocked the government* (= made the situation difficult for it).
- **DANCE** 4 [I] (*old-fashioned*) to dance to rock music
- **BE GOOD** 5 sth rocks [I] (*slang*) used to say that sth is very good: *Her new movie rocks!*
- **FASHION** 6 [T] ~ sth (*informal*) to wear sth or have a style of clothing, hair, etc. that makes you look attractive or confident: *How to rock the retro look.* ◊ *She rocked a red leather skirt at the award ceremony.*

IDM rock the ˈboat (*informal*) to do sth that upsets a situation and causes problems: *She was told to keep her mouth shut and not rock the boat.* ⇒ more at FOUNDATION

PHR V rock ˈout to perform or dance to rock music loudly and with a lot of energy

**rocka·billy** /ˈrɒkəbɪli; *NAmE* ˈrɑːk-/ *noun* [U] a type of American music that combines ROCK AND ROLL and country music

ˌrock and ˈroll (also ˌrock 'n' ˈroll) *noun* [U] a type of music popular in the 1950s with a strong beat and simple tunes

ˌrock ˈbottom *noun* [U] (*informal*) the lowest point or level that is possible: *Prices hit rock bottom.* ◊ *The marriage had reached rock bottom.* ▶ ˌrock-ˈbottom *adj.*: *rock-bottom prices*

ˈrock climbing *noun* [U] the sport or activity of climbing steep rock surfaces: *to go rock climbing*

**rock·er** /ˈrɒkə(r); *NAmE* ˈrɑːk-/ *noun* 1 one of the two curved pieces of wood on the bottom of a rocking chair 2 (*especially NAmE*) = ROCKING CHAIR 3 **Rocker** (*BrE*) a member of a group of young people in the UK, especially in the 1960s, who liked to wear leather jackets, ride motorcycles and listen to ROCK AND ROLL music ⇒ compare MOD 4 a person who performs, dances to or enjoys rock music

IDM be ˌoff your ˈrocker (*informal*) to be crazy

**rock·ery** /ˈrɒkəri; *NAmE* ˈrɑːk-/ *noun* (*pl.* -ies) (also ˈrock garden) a garden or part of a garden consisting of an arrangement of large stones with plants growing among them

**rocket** B1+ B2 /ˈrɒkɪt; *NAmE* ˈrɑːk-/ *noun, verb*
■ noun 1 B1+ B2 [C] a SPACECRAFT in the shape of a tube that is driven by a stream of gases let out behind it when fuel is burned inside: *a space rocket* ◊ *The rocket was launched in 2007.* ◊ *The idea took off like a rocket* (= it immediately became popular). ⇒ WORDFINDER NOTE at SPACE 2 B1+ C1 [C] a MISSILE (= a weapon that travels through the air) that carries a bomb and is driven by a stream of burning gases: *a rocket attack* 3 [C] a FIREWORK that goes high into the air and then explodes with coloured lights 4 [U] (*BrE*) (*NAmE* aruˈgula) a plant with long green leaves that have a strong taste and are eaten raw in salads ⇒ VISUAL VOCAB page V5

IDM to give sb a ˈrocket | to get a ˈrocket (*BrE, informal*) to speak angrily to sb because they have done sth wrong; to be spoken to angrily for this reason

■ verb 1 [I] (+ *adv./prep.*) to increase very quickly and suddenly SYN shoot up: *rocketing prices* ◊ *Unemployment has rocketed up again.* ◊ *The total has rocketed from 376 to 532.* 2 [I] + *adv./prep.* to move very fast: *The car rocketed out of a side street.* 3 [I, T] to achieve or to make sb/sth achieve a successful position very quickly: ~ (**sb/sth**) **to sth** *The band rocketed to stardom with their first single.* 4 [T] ~ **sth** to attack a place with rockets

**rock·et·ry** /ˈrɒkɪtri; *NAmE* ˈrɑːk-/ *noun* [U] the area of science which deals with ROCKETS and with sending rockets into space; the use of rockets

ˈrocket science *noun* [U]

IDM it's not ˈrocket science (*informal*) used to emphasize that sth is easy to do or understand SYN brain surgery: *Go on, you can do it. It's not exactly rocket science, is it?*

ˈrocket scientist *noun* (used especially in negative sentences) (*informal*) an extremely intelligent person: *You don't need to be a rocket scientist to figure out that this plan will not work.*

ˈrock face *noun* a surface of rock that goes straight upwards, especially on a mountain

**rock·fall** /ˈrɒkfɔːl; *NAmE* ˈrɑːk-/ *noun* the fact of rocks falling down; a pile of rocks that have fallen

ˈrock garden *noun* = ROCKERY

ˌrock-ˈhard *adj.* extremely hard or strong

ˈrocking chair (also ˈrock·er *especially in NAmE*) *noun* a chair with two curved pieces of wood under it that allow it to move backwards and forwards

ˈrocking horse *noun* a wooden horse for children that can be made to ROCK backwards and forwards

ˈrock music *noun* [U] = ROCK

ˌrock 'n' ˈroll /ˌrɒk ən ˈrəʊl; *NAmE* ˈrɑːk-/ *noun* [U] = ROCK AND ROLL

ˈrock pool (*BrE*) (*NAmE* ˈtide pool) *noun* a small amount of water that collects between the rocks by the sea

ˈrock salt *noun* [U] a kind of salt that comes from the ground ⇒ compare SEA SALT

ˌrock ˈsolid *adj.* 1 that you can trust not to change or to disappear: *The support for the party was rock solid.* 2 extremely hard and not likely to break

**rocky** /ˈrɒki; *NAmE* ˈrɑːki/ *adj.* (**rockˈier, rockˈiest**) 1 made of rock; full of rocks: *a rocky coastline* ◊ *rocky soil* 2 difficult and not certain to continue or to be successful: *a rocky marriage*

**ro·coco** (also **Ro·coco**) /rəˈkəʊkəʊ/ *adj.* used to describe a style of architecture, furniture, etc. that has a lot of decoration, especially in the shape of CURLS; used to describe a style of literature or music that has a lot of detail and decoration. The rococo style was popular in the 18th century.

**rod** B1+ C1 /rɒd; *NAmE* rɑːd/ *noun* 1 B1+ C1 (often used in compounds) a long straight piece of wood, metal or glass 2 = FISHING ROD: *fishing with rod and line* ⇒ WORDFINDER NOTE at FISHING 3 (also **the rod**) (*old-fashioned*) a stick that is used for hitting people as a punishment: *There used to be a*

# rode

saying: *'Spare the rod and spoil the child.'* **4** (*NAmE*, *slang*) a small gun ⇨ see also FUEL ROD, HOT ROD
**IDM** **make a rod for your own back** to do sth that will cause problems for you in the future ⇨ more at BEAT v., RULE v.

**rode** /rəʊd/ *past tense* of RIDE ⇨ HOMOPHONES at ROAD

**ro·dent** /ˈrəʊdnt/ *noun* any small animal that belongs to a group of animals with strong sharp front teeth. Mice, RATS and SQUIRRELS are all rodents. ⇨ VISUAL VOCAB page V2

**rodeo** /ˈrəʊdiəʊ, rəʊˈdeɪəʊ/ *noun* (*pl.* **-os**) a public competition, especially in the US, in which people show their skill at riding wild horses and catching CATTLE with ropes

**roe** /rəʊ/ *noun* **1** [U, C] the mass of eggs inside a female fish ('**hard** roe) or the SPERM of a male fish ('**soft** roe), used as food: *cod's roe* **2** [C] = ROE DEER

**'roe deer** *noun* (*pl.* **roe deer**) (*also* **roe**) a small European and Asian DEER

**ROFL** /ˈrɒfl; *NAmE* ˈrɑːfl/ (*also* **ROTFL**) *abbr.* (*informal*) (especially in text message, on SOCIAL MEDIA, etc.) roll(ing) on the floor laughing (used to show that you find sth extremely funny): *He did the funniest dance I've ever seen. ROFL.* ⇨ compare LOL

**roger** /ˈrɒdʒə(r)/ *NAmE* ˈrɑːdʒ-/ *exclamation, verb*
■ *exclamation* people say **Roger!** in communication by radio to show that they have understood a message
■ *verb* ~ **sb** (*BrE*, *taboo*, *slang*) (of a man) to have sex with sb

**rogue** /rəʊɡ/ *noun, adj.*
■ *noun* **1** (*humorous*) a person who behaves badly, but despite this is quite attractive: *He's a bit of a rogue, but very charming.* **2** (*old-fashioned*) a man who is not honest or moral **SYN** rascal: *a rogues' gallery* (= a collection of pictures of criminals)
■ *adj.* [only before noun] **1** (of an animal) living apart from the main group, and possibly dangerous **2** behaving in a different way from other similar people or things, often causing damage: *a rogue gene* ◇ *a rogue police officer*
**IDM** **go 'rogue** (*informal*) to suddenly start doing sth unexpected, especially sth dangerous, wrong or against the rules: *Denzel Washington plays a CIA agent gone rogue.*

**roguish** /ˈrəʊɡɪʃ/ *adj.* (*usually approving*) (of a person) pleasant and funny but looking as if they might do sth wrong: *a roguish smile* ▶ **roguish·ly** *adv.*

**roil** /rɔɪl/ *verb* **1** [T] (*NAmE*) ~ **sb** = RILE **2** [T] (*literary*) (of a liquid, cloud, surface, etc.) to move quickly and violently in different directions; to make a liquid, cloud, surface, etc. move quickly and violently in different directions: (*figurative*) *The collapse of the mortgage sector has roiled markets.* ▶ **roil·ing** *adj.*: *the roiling sea*

**roko** /ˈrəʊkəʊ/ *noun* (*IndE*) a public meeting or MARCH (= organized walk by many people) at which people show that they are protesting against or supporting sb/sth, especially one that involves blocking a railway or road: *Activists staged a rail roko to protest against the minister's decision.*

**role** ⓘ **A2** ⓞ /rəʊl/ *noun* **1** **A2** an actor's part in a play, film, etc: *a lead/leading/starring role* ◇ *the* ~ *of sb He played the role of Sonny in 'The Godfather'.* ⇨ WORDFINDER NOTE at ACTOR **2** **A2** the function or position that sb has or is expected to have in an organization, in society or in a relationship: *the changing role of women* ◇ *~ in sth the artist's role in society* ◇ *~ as sb He is stepping down from his role as chair.* ◇ *In many marriages there has been a complete role reversal* (= change of roles) *with the man staying at home and the woman going out to work.* **3** **B1** the degree to which sb/sth is involved in a situation or an activity and the effect that they have on it: *A cup of tea often serves* **an important** *social role.* ◇ *a key/leading/central/crucial/vital role* ◇ *~ in doing sth The media play a major role in influencing people's opinions.* ◇ *~ in sth UK scientists have taken a lead role in the project.* ◇ *~ of sb/sth in sth the role of diet in the prevention of disease* ◇ *~ as sth The company has cemented its role as a leader in the industry.*

## HOMOPHONES

**role • roll** /rəʊl/
- **role** *noun*: *She's playing the role of Elizabeth Bennet.*
- **roll** *noun*: *The soup is served with a freshly baked roll.*
- **roll** *verb*: *Everyone must roll the dice, and the player with the highest number starts.*

**'role model** *noun* a person that people admire and try to copy

**'role-play** *noun* [U, C] a learning activity in which you behave in the way sb else would behave in a particular situation: *Role-play allows students to practise language in a safe situation.* ▶ **'role-play** *verb* [I, T] ~ **(sth)**

**'role-playing game** *noun* (*abbr.* **RPG**) a game, often an online or computer game, in which players pretend to be imaginary characters who take part in adventures, especially in situations from FANTASY literature

**rolls**

roll of cloth  roll of tape
bread rolls  roll of toilet paper

**roll** ⓘ **B1** /rəʊl/ *verb, noun*
■ *verb*
- **TURN OVER 1 B1** [I, T] to turn over and over and move in a particular direction; to make a round object do this: + *adv./prep. The ball rolled down the hill.* ◇ *We watched the waves rolling onto the beach.* ◇ *~ sth + adv./prep. Delivery men were rolling barrels across the yard.* **2 B1** [I, T] to turn over and over or round and round while remaining in the same place; to make sth do this: *Her eyes rolled.* ◇ + *adv./prep. a dog rolling in the mud* ◇ *~ sth She rolled her eyes* (= to show surprise or disapproval). ◇ *~ sth + adv./prep. He was rolling a pencil between his fingers.* **3 B1** [I, T] to turn over to face a different direction; to make sb/sth do this: *~ over (onto sth) She rolled over to let the sun brown her back.* ◇ *~ onto sth He rolled onto his back.* ◇ *~ sb/sth over (onto sth) I rolled the baby over onto its stomach.* ◇ *~ sb/sth onto sth She rolled the patient onto his side.* ⇨ HOMOPHONES at ROLE **4 B2** [T] *~ sth* to throw DICE in a game: *Each player rolls their dice.* ◇ *Roll a six to start.*
- **MOVE (AS IF) ON WHEELS 5 B1** [I, T] to move smoothly on wheels or as if on wheels; to make sth do this: + *adv./prep. The car began to roll back down the hill.* ◇ *The traffic rolled slowly forwards.* ◇ *~ sth + adv./prep. He rolled the trolley across the room.*
- **OF CLOUDS/WAVES 6** [I] + *adv./prep.* to move or flow forward in a steady way: *Mist was rolling in from the sea.* ◇ *the sound of waves rolling in to the shore*
- **MAKE BALL/TUBE 7 B2** [T, I] to make sth/yourself into the shape of a ball or tube: *~ sth into sth I rolled the string into a ball.* ◇ *~ sth up We rolled up the carpet.* ◇ *a rolled-up newspaper* ◇ *The hedgehog rolled (up) into a ball.* ⇨ compare UNROLL **8** [T] *~ sth* to make a cigarette yourself by putting TOBACCO on special paper and forming it into a tube: *He leaned on the table and rolled a cigarette.* ◇ *I always roll my own* (= make my own cigarettes).
- **FOLD CLOTHING 9 B2** [T] to fold the edge of a piece of clothing, etc. over and over on itself to make it shorter: *~ sth up Roll up your sleeves.* ◇ *~ sth + adv./prep. She rolled her jeans to her knees.*
- **MAKE STH FLAT 10** [T] *~ sth (out)* to make sth flat by pushing sth heavy over it: *Roll the pastry on a floured surface.*
- **WRAP UP 11** [T] to wrap or cover sb/sth/yourself in sth: *~ sb/sth/yourself in sth Roll the meat in the breadcrumbs.* ◇ *~ sb/sth/yourself up in sth He rolled himself up in the blanket.*
- **OF SHIP/PLANE/WALK 12** [I, T] *~ (sth) (+ adv./prep.)* to move or make sth move from side to side: *He walked with*

*a rolling gait.* ◊ *The ship was rolling heavily to and fro.* ⊃ compare PITCH
- **MAKE SOUND** **13** [I, T] to make a long continuous sound: *rolling drums* ◊ *Thunder rolled.* ◊ *~sth to roll your r's* (= by letting your tongue VIBRATE with each 'r' sound)
- **MACHINE** **14** [I, T] when a machine **rolls** or sb **rolls** it, it operates: *They had to repeat the scene because the cameras weren't rolling.* ◊ *~sth Roll the cameras!*

**IDM** **be ˌrolling in ˈmoney/it** (*informal*) to have a lot of money **let's ˈroll** (*informal, especially NAmE*) used to suggest to a group of people that you should all start doing sth or going somewhere **ˌrolled into ˈone** combined in one person or thing: *Banks are several businesses rolled into one.* **ˌrolling in the ˈaisles** (*informal*) laughing a lot: *She soon had us rolling in the aisles.* **a ˌrolling ˌstone gathers no ˈmoss** (*saying*) a person who moves from place to place, job to job, etc. does not have a lot of money, possessions or friends but is free from responsibilities **ˌroll on …!** (*BrE, informal*) used to say that you want sth to happen or arrive soon: *Roll on Friday!* **ˌroll up your ˈsleeves** to prepare to work or fight **ˌroll with the ˈpunches** to adapt yourself to a difficult situation ⊃ more at BALL *n.*, GRAVE¹ *n.*, HEAD *n.*, READY *adj.*, TONGUE *n.*

**PHRV** **ˌroll aˈround** (*BrE also* **ˌroll aˈbout**) to be laughing so much that you can hardly control yourself **ˌroll sth↔ˈback** **1** to reduce the power or importance of sth; to REVERSE the progress made with sth: *Many of the gains made in the last 20 years have been rolled back.* **2** to push sth further away: (*figurative*) *to roll back the frontiers of space* **3** (*NAmE*) to reduce prices, etc: *to roll back inflation* **ˌroll sth↔ˈdown** **1** to open or close sth by turning a handle: *He rolled down his car window and started shouting at them.* **2** to make a rolled piece of clothing, etc. hang or lie flat: *to roll down your sleeves* **ˌroll ˈin** (*informal*) **1** to arrive in great numbers or amounts: *Offers of help are still rolling in.* **2** to arrive late at a place, without seeming worried or sorry: *Steve rolled in around lunchtime.* **ˌroll sth↔ˈout** **1** to make sth flat by pushing sth over it: *Roll out the pastry.* **2** to officially make a new product available or start a new political CAMPAIGN **SYN** **launch**: *The new model is to be rolled out in July.* ⊃ related noun ROLL-OUT **ˌroll ˈover** (*informal*) to be easily defeated without even trying: *We can't expect them to just roll over for us.* **ˌroll sb ˈover** (*BrE, informal*) to defeat sb easily: *They rolled us over in the replay.* **ˌroll sth↔ˈover** (*specialist*) to allow money that sb owes to be paid back at a later date: *The bank refused to roll over the debt.* ⊃ related noun ROLLOVER **ˌroll ˈup** (*informal*) to arrive: *Bill finally rolled up two hours late.* ◊ *Roll up! Roll up!* (= used to invite people who are passing to form an audience) **ˌroll sth↔ˈup** to open or close sth by turning a handle: *She rolled up all the blinds.*

■ *noun*
- **BREAD** **1** B1 (*also* **bread ˈroll**) [C] a small LOAF of bread for one person: *Soup and a roll* ◊ *a chicken/cheese, etc. roll* (= filled with chicken/cheese, etc.) ⊃ compare BUN ⊃ **HOMOPHONES** *at* ROLE ⊃ *see also* EGG ROLL, JELLY ROLL, SAUSAGE ROLL, SPRING ROLL, SWISS ROLL
- **OF PAPER/CLOTH, ETC.** **2** B2 [C] a long piece of paper, cloth, etc. that has been wrapped around itself or a tube several times so that it forms the shape of a tube: *~ of sth a roll of fabric/wrapping paper* ◊ *in a~ Wallpaper is sold in rolls.* ⊃ *see also* TOILET ROLL
- **OF SWEETS/CANDY** **3** [C] *~(of sth)* (*NAmE*) a paper tube wrapped around sweets, etc: *a roll of mints*
- **OF BODY** **4** [sing.] an act of rolling the body over and over: *The kittens were enjoying a roll in the sunshine.* **5** [C] a physical exercise in which you roll your body on the ground, moving your back and legs over your head: *a forward/backward roll*
- **OF SHIP/PLANE** **6** [U] the act of moving from side to side so that one side is higher than the other ⊃ compare PITCH
- **OF FAT** **7** [C] an area of too much fat on your body, especially around the middle part: *Rolls of fat hung over his belt.*
- **LIST OF NAMES** **8** [C] an official list of names: *the electoral roll* (= a list of all the people who can vote in an election) ◊ *The chairman called/took the roll* (= called out the names

on a list to check that everyone was present). ⊃ *see also* PAYROLL
- **SOUND** **9** [C] *~(of sth)* a deep continuous sound: *the distant roll of thunder* ◊ *a drum roll*
- **OF DICE** **10** [C] an act of rolling a DICE: *The order of play is decided by the roll of a dice.*
- **PHONETICS** **11** [C] = TRILL (3)

**IDM** **be on a ˈroll** (*informal*) to be experiencing a period of success at what you are doing: *Don't stop me now—I'm on a roll!* **a ˌroll in the ˈhay** (*informal*) an act of having sex with sb

**ˈroll-back** /ˈrəʊlbæk/ *noun* [sing., U] (*especially NAmE*) **1** a reduction in a price or in pay, to a past level **2** the act of changing a situation, law, etc. back to what it was before

**ˈroll bar** *noun* a metal bar over the top of a car without a roof, used to make the car stronger and to protect passengers if the car turns over

**ˈroll call** *noun* [U, sing.] the reading of a list of names to a group of people to check who is there: *Roll call will be at 7 a.m.* ◊ *The guest list reads like a roll call of the nation's heroes.*

**ˌrolled ˈoats** *noun* [pl.] OATS that have had their shells removed before being CRUSHED (= broken and pressed), used especially for making PORRIDGE

**roll-er** /ˈrəʊlə(r)/ *noun* **1** a piece of wood, metal or plastic, like a tube in shape, that rolls over and over, used as a tool or as part of a machine, for example to make sth flat or to move sth: *Flatten the surface of the grass with a roller.* ◊ *a paint roller* ◊ *the heavy steel rollers under the conveyor belt* ◊ *We'll need to move the piano on rollers.* ⊃ picture at LADDER ⊃ *see also* STEAMROLLER *noun* **2** a long, powerful wave in the sea: *Huge Atlantic rollers crashed onto the rocks.* **3** a small plastic tube that hair is rolled around to make it curly **SYN** **curler**: *heated rollers* ◊ *in rollers Her hair was in rollers.* ⊃ *see also* HIGH ROLLER

**roll-er-ball** /ˈrəʊləbɔːl; *NAmE* -lərb-/ *noun* **1** a type of BALLPOINT pen **2** = TRACKBALL

**Roll-er-blade**™ /ˈrəʊləbleɪd; *NAmE* -lərb-/ *noun* a type of IN-LINE SKATE ▶ **ˈroll-er-blade** *verb* [I]

**ˈroller blind** *noun* a roll of cloth that is fixed at the top of a window and can be pulled up and down to cover the window

**ˈroller coaster** *noun* **1** a track at a FAIRGROUND that goes up and down very steep slopes and that people ride on in a small train for fun and excitement: *a roller-coaster ride* **2** a situation that keeps changing very quickly: *The last few weeks have been a real roller coaster.*

**ˈroller skate** (*also* **skate**) *noun, verb*
- *noun* a type of boot with two pairs of small wheels attached to the bottom: *a pair of roller skates*
- *verb* [I] to move over a hard surface wearing roller skates
▶ **ˈroller skating** (*also* **skat-ing**) *noun* [U]

**rol-lick-ing** /ˈrɒlɪkɪŋ; *NAmE* ˈrɑːl-/ *adj., noun*
- *adj.* [only before noun] cheerful and often noisy **SYN** **exuberant**: *a rollicking comedy*
- *noun* (*BrE, informal*) angry criticism for sth bad sb has done: *He gave us both a rollicking.*

**roll-ing** /ˈrəʊlɪŋ/ *adj.* [only before noun] **1** (of hills or countryside) having gentle slopes ⊃ **WORDFINDER NOTE** *at* LANDSCAPE **2** done in regular stages or at regular INTERVALS over a period of time: *a rolling programme of reform*

**ˈrolling mill** *noun* a machine or factory that produces flat sheets of metal

**ˈrolling pin** *noun* a wooden or glass kitchen UTENSIL (= a tool) in the shape of a tube, used for rolling PASTRY flat

**ˈrolling stock** *noun* [U] the engines, trains, etc. that are used on a railway

**ˌroll of ˈhonour** (*US* **ˈhonor roll**) *noun* [usually sing.] a list of people who are being praised officially for sth they have done

# roll-on

**'roll-on** adj. [only before noun] spread or put on the body using a ball that moves around in the top of a bottle or container: *a roll-on deodorant* ▶ **'roll-on** noun

**roll-on roll-'off** adj. [usually before noun] (abbr. **ro-ro**) (BrE) (of a ship) designed so that cars can be driven straight on and off: *a roll-on roll-off car ferry*

**'roll-out** noun an occasion when a company, the government, etc. introduces or starts to use a new product or service

**roll-over** /'rəʊləʊvə(r)/ noun 1 [U] (specialist) the act of allowing money that is owed to be paid at a later date 2 [U, C] (BrE) a prize of money in a competition or LOTTERY in a particular week, that is added to the prize given in the following week if nobody wins it: *a rollover jackpot* 3 [U] (especially NAmE) the turning over of a vehicle during an accident

**Rolls-Royce™** /ˌrəʊlz 'rɔɪs/ noun 1 (also informal **Rolls™**) a large, comfortable and expensive make of car made by a company in the UK 2 **the ~ of sth** (BrE) something that is thought of as an example of the highest quality of a type of thing: *This is the Rolls-Royce of canoes.*

**'roll-up** noun (BrE, informal) a cigarette that you make yourself with TOBACCO and special paper

**roly-poly** /ˌrəʊli 'pəʊli/ adj., noun
- adj. [only before noun] (informal) (of people) short, round and fat SYN **plump**
- noun (pl. **-ies**) (also **roly-poly 'pudding**) [U, C] (BrE) a hot DESSERT (= a sweet dish) made from SUET PASTRY spread with jam and rolled up

**ROM** /rɒm; NAmE rɑːm/ noun [U] computer memory that contains instructions or data that cannot be changed or removed (the abbreviation for 'read-only memory') ⊃ compare **CD-ROM**

**the Roma** /ðə 'rəʊmə/ noun [pl.] the ROMANI people: *the Roma population of eastern Europe*

**ro-maine** /rəʊ'meɪn/ (NAmE) (BrE also **cos lettuce**) noun [C, U] a type of LETTUCE with long, narrow leaves that form a tall HEAD

**Roman** /'rəʊmən/ adj., noun
- adj. 1 connected with ancient Rome or the Roman Empire: *a Roman road/temple/villa* ◊ *Roman Britain* 2 connected with the modern city of Rome 3 connected with the Roman Catholic Church 4 **roman** used to describe ordinary printing type that does not lean forward: *Definitions in this dictionary are printed in roman type.* ⊃ compare **ITALIC**
- noun 1 [C] a member of the ancient Roman REPUBLIC or EMPIRE 2 [C] a person from the modern city of Rome 3 **roman** [U] the ordinary style of printing that uses small letters that do not lean forward ⊃ compare **ITALICS**
- IDM see **ROME**

**the ˌRoman 'alphabet** noun [sing.] the alphabet that is used in English and in most western European languages

**ˌRoman 'Catholic** (also **Cath-olic**) noun (abbr. **RC**) a member of the part of the Christian Church that has the POPE as its leader ▶ **ˌRoman 'Catholic** (also **Cath-olic**) adj. **ˌRoman Ca'tholicism** (also **Cath-oli-cism**) noun [U]

**Ro-mance** /rəʊ'mæns; NAmE 'rəʊmæns/ adj. [only before noun] **Romance** languages, such as French, Italian and Spanish, are languages that developed from Latin

**ro-mance** /rəʊ'mæns, 'rəʊmæns; NAmE 'rəʊmæns/ noun, verb
- noun 1 [C] an exciting, usually short, relationship between two people who are in love with each other: *a holiday romance* ◊ *They had a whirlwind romance.* 2 [U] love or the feeling of being in love; *Spring is here and romance is in the air.* ◊ *How can you put the romance back into your marriage?* 3 [C] a story about a love affair: *She's a compulsive reader of romances.* 4 [U] a feeling of excitement and adventure, especially connected with a particular place or activity: *the romance of travel* 5 [C] a story of excitement and adventure, often set in the past: *medieval romances*
- verb 1 [I] to tell stories that are not true or to describe sth in a way that makes it seem more exciting or interesting than it really is 2 [T] **~sb** to have or to try to have a romantic relationship with sb

**Ro·man·esque** /ˌrəʊmə'nesk/ adj. used to describe a style of architecture that was popular in western Europe from the 10th to the 12th centuries and that had round ARCHES, thick walls and tall PILLARS ⊃ see also **NORMAN**

**Rom·ani** (also **Rom·any**) /'rɒməni; BrE also 'rɒm-; NAmE also rɑːm-/ noun (pl. **-ies**) 1 [C] a member of a race of people, originally from Asia, who traditionally travel around and live in CARAVANS ⊃ see also **ROMA**, **GYPSY** 2 [U] the language of Romani people ▶ **Rom·ani** (also **Rom·any**) adj. [usually before noun]

**ˌRoman 'law** noun the legal system of the ancient Romans, and the basis for CIVIL LAW in many countries

**ˌRoman 'numeral** noun one of the letters used by the ancient Romans to represent numbers and still used today, in some situations. In this system I=1, V=5, X=10, L=50, C=100, D=500, M=1000 and these letters are used in combinations to form other numbers: *Henry VIII* © BBC MMXIX (2019) ⊃ compare **ARABIC NUMERAL** ⊃ picture at **IDEOGRAM**

**Romano-** /rəʊmə'nəʊ; BrE also rəmə'nəʊ/ combining form (in nouns and adjectives) Roman: *Romano-British pottery*

**ro·man·tic** ⓘ B1 /rəʊ'mæntɪk/ adj., noun
- adj. 1 B1 connected with or about love or a sexual relationship: *a romantic candlelit dinner* ◊ *a romantic comedy* ◊ *I'm not interested in a romantic relationship.* ⊃ WORDFINDER NOTE at **LOVE** 2 B1 (of people) showing feelings of love: *Why don't you ever give me flowers? I wish you'd be more romantic.* 3 B1 beautiful in a way that makes you think of love or feel strong emotions: *romantic music* ◊ *romantic mountain scenery* 4 B2 having an attitude to life where imagination and the emotions are especially important; not looking at situations in a realistic way: *a romantic view of life* ◊ *When I was younger, I had romantic ideas of becoming a writer.* 5 **Romantic** [usually before noun] used to describe literature, music or art, especially of the nineteenth century, that is about strong feelings, imagination and a return to nature, rather than reason, order and INTELLECTUAL ideas: *the Romantic movement* ◊ *Keats is one of the greatest Romantic poets.* ▶ **ro·man·tic·al·ly** /-kli/ adv.: *to be romantically involved with sb* ◊ *Their names have been linked romantically.* ◊ *He talked romantically of the past and his youth.*
- noun 1 a person who is emotional and has a lot of imagination, and who has ideas and hopes that may not be realistic: *a hopeless romantic* ◊ *He was a romantic at heart and longed for adventure.* 2 **Romantic** a writer, a musician or an artist who writes, etc. in the style of Romanticism

**ro·man·ti·cism** /rəʊ'mæntɪsɪzəm/ noun [U] 1 (also **Romanticism**) a style and movement in art, music and literature in the late 18th and early 19th century, in which strong feelings, imagination and a return to nature were more important than reason, order and INTELLECTUAL ideas ⊃ compare **REALISM** 2 the fact of seeing people, events and situations as more exciting and interesting than they really are 3 strong feelings of love; the fact of showing emotion, love, etc.

**ro·man·ti·cize** (BrE also **-ise**) /rəʊ'mæntɪsaɪz/ verb [T, I] **~(sth)** to make sth seem more attractive or interesting than it really is: *romanticizing the past* ◊ *a romanticized picture of parenthood*

**rom·com** /'rɒmkɒm; NAmE 'rɑːmkɑːm/ noun (informal) a humorous film or TV show that is about love; a romantic comedy

**Rome** /rəʊm/ noun
- IDM **Rome wasn't built in a 'day** (saying) used to say that a complicated task will take a long time and should not be rushed **when in 'Rome (do as the 'Romans do)** (saying) used to say that when you are in a foreign country, or a situation you are not familiar with, you should behave in the way that the people around you behave

**romeo** (also **Romeo**) /'rəʊmiəʊ/ noun (pl. **-os**) (often humorous) a man who has sex with a lot of women ORIGIN From the name of the young hero of Shakespeare's play *Romeo and Juliet*.

**romp** /rɒmp; NAmE rɑːmp/ *verb, noun*
- *verb* [I] (+ *adv./prep.*) to play in a happy and noisy way: *kids romping around in the snow*
- **IDM** **romp home/to victory** to easily win a race or competition: *Their horse romped home in the 2 o'clock race.* ◊ *The Dutch team romped to a 5–1 victory over Celtic.*
- **PHR V** **romp a'way/a'head** (*BrE*, *informal*) to increase, make progress or win quickly and easily **romp 'through (sth)** (*BrE*, *informal*) to do sth easily and quickly: *She romped through the exam questions.*
- *noun* (often used in newspapers) (*informal*) **1** [C] a sexual experience that is not serious: *politicians involved in sex romps with call girls* **2** [C] a funny book, play or film that is full of action or adventure **3** [sing.] an easy victory in a sports competition: *They won in a 5–1 romp.*

**ron·da·vel** /ˈrɒndɑːvl; NAmE ˈrɑːndəvel/ SAfrE [rɔnˈdɑːvl/ *noun* (SAfrE) a round HUT with a pointed roof that is usually made from THATCH (= dried grass)

**rondo** /ˈrɒndəʊ; NAmE ˈrɑːn-/ *noun* (*pl.* **-os**) a piece of music in which the main tune is repeated several times, sometimes forming part of a longer piece

**roo** /ruː/ *noun* (*informal*) = KANGAROO

**roof** 🔊 **A2** /ruːf/ *noun, verb*
- *noun* (*pl.* **roofs**) **1** 🔊 **A2** the structure that covers or forms the top of a building or vehicle: *a flat/sloping/pitched roof* ◊ *Offices on the upper floors have access to a roof terrace.* ◊ *a tin/slate/tiled/thatched roof* ◊ *Tim climbed on to the garage roof.* ◊ *The roof of the car was not damaged in the accident.* ⇒ see also GREEN ROOF, SUNROOF **2 -roofed** (in adjectives) having the type of roof mentioned: *flat-roofed buildings* **3** the top of an underground space such as a tunnel or CAVE **4 ~ of your mouth** the top of the inside of your mouth
- **IDM** **go through the 'roof 1** (of prices, etc.) to rise or increase very quickly **2** (*also* **hit the 'roof**) (*informal*) to become very angry **have a 'roof over your head** to have somewhere to live **under one 'roof** | **under the same 'roof** in the same building or house: *There are various stores and restaurants all under one roof.* ◊ *I don't think I can live under the same roof as you any longer.* **under your 'roof** in your home: *I don't want her under my roof again.* ⇒ more at CAT, RAISE *v.*
- *verb* [often passive] to cover sth with a roof; to put a roof on a building: *~ sth (in/over) The shopping centre is not roofed over.* ◊ *~ sth with/in sth Their cottage was roofed with green slate.*

**roof·er** /ˈruːfə(r)/ *noun* a person whose job is to repair or build roofs

**'roof garden** *noun* a garden on the flat roof of a building

**roof·ing** /ˈruːfɪŋ/ *noun* [U] **1** material used for making or covering roofs **2** the process of building roofs

**'roof rack** (*also* **'luggage rack** especially in *NAmE*) *noun* a metal frame fixed to the roof of a car and used for carrying bags, cases and other large objects ⇒ picture at RACK

**roof·top** /ˈruːftɒp; NAmE -tɑːp/ *noun* the outside part of the roof of a building: *From the hill we looked out over the rooftops of Athens.* ◊ *The prisoners staged a rooftop protest.*
- **IDM** **shout, etc. sth from the 'rooftops** to talk about sth in a very public way: *He was in love and wanted to shout it from the rooftops.*

**rooi·bos** /ˈrɔɪbɒs; NAmE -bɔːs/ SAfrE [ˈrɔɪbɔs] (*also* **red bush**) *noun* [U] (SAfrE) a type of bush grown in South Africa whose leaves are dried and used to make tea: *rooibos tea*

**rook** /rʊk/ *noun* **1** a large black bird of the CROW family. Rooks build their NESTS in groups at the tops of trees. **2** = CASTLE (2)

**rook·ery** /ˈrʊkəri/ *noun* (*pl.* **-ies**) a group of trees in which ROOKS have built their NESTS

**rookie** /ˈrʊki/ *noun* (*informal*) **1** (especially in *NAmE*) a person who has just started a job or an activity and has very little experience **2** (*NAmE*) a member of a sports team in his or her first full year of playing that sport

# 1349 root

**room** 🔊 **A1** /ruːm, rʊm/ *noun, verb*
- *noun*
- **IN BUILDING 1** 🔊 **A1** [C] a part of a building that has its own walls, floor and ceiling and is usually used for a particular purpose: *I heard him enter the room.* ◊ **in the/sb's ~** *They were in the next room and we could hear every word they said.* ◊ *I don't want to watch television. I'll be in the other room* (= a different room). ◊ *I think Simon is in his room* (= bedroom). ◊ *a dining/living/sitting room* **HELP** There are many compounds ending in **room**. You will find them at their place in the alphabet.
- **-ROOMED/-ROOM 2** (in adjectives) having the number of rooms mentioned: *a three-roomed/three-room apartment*
- **IN HOTEL 3** 🔊 **A1** [C] a bedroom in a hotel, etc: *a double/single room* ◊ *I just stayed in my hotel room.* ◊ *She lets out rooms to students.*
- **PLACE TO LIVE 4 rooms** [pl.] (*BrE*, *old-fashioned*) a set of two or more rooms that you rent to live in **SYN lodgings**: *They lived in rooms in Kensington.*
- **SPACE 5** 🔊 **B1** [U] empty space that can be used for a particular purpose: *I'll move the table—it takes up too much room.* ◊ **~ for sb/sth** *Is there enough room for me in the car?* ◊ *How can we make room for all the furniture?* ◊ **~ to do sth** *The bar was so packed there was hardly room to move.* ◊ **~ for sb to do sth** *I left room for Zac to sit beside me.* ◊ *There's plenty of room in the attic.*
- **POSSIBILITY 6** [U] the possibility of sth existing or happening; the opportunity to do sth: **~ for sth** *He had to be certain. There could be no room for doubt.* ◊ *There's some room for improvement in your work* (= it is not as good as it could be). ◊ **~ to do sth** *It is important to give children room to think for themselves.*
- **PEOPLE 7** [sing.] all the people in a room: *The whole room burst into applause.*
- **IDM** **no room to swing a 'cat** (*informal*) when sb says **there's no room to swing a cat**, they mean that a room is very small and that there is not enough space ⇒ more at ELEPHANT, MANOEUVRE *n.*, SMOKE *n.*
- *verb* [I] **~ (with sb)** | **~ (together)** (*NAmE*) to rent a room somewhere; to share a rented room or flat with sb: *She and Nancy roomed together at college.*

**room·ful** /ˈruːmfʊl, ˈrʊm-/ *noun* [sing.] a large number of people or things that are in a room: *He announced his resignation to a roomful of reporters.*

**roomie** /ˈruːmi, ˈrʊmi/ *noun* (*NAmE*, *informal*) = ROOM-MATE

**'rooming house** *noun* (*NAmE*) a building where rooms with furniture can be rented for living in

**'room-mate** (*BrE*) (*NAmE* **room·mate**) *noun* (*also NAmE*, *informal* **roomie**) **1** a person that you share a room with, especially at a college or university **2** (*NAmE*) (*BrE* **flatmate**) a person who shares an apartment with one or more others

**'room service** *noun* [U] a service provided in a hotel, by which guests can order food and drink to be brought to their rooms: *He ordered coffee from room service.* ⇒ WORD-FINDER NOTE at HOTEL

**'room temperature** *noun* [U] the normal temperature inside a building: *at ~ Serve the wine at room temperature.*

**roomy** /ˈruːmi, ˈrʊmi/ *adj.* (**room·ier**, **roomi·est**) (*approving*) having a lot of space inside **SYN spacious**: *a surprisingly roomy car* ▸ **roomi·ness** *noun* [U].

**roost** /ruːst/ *noun, verb*
- *noun* a place where birds sleep **IDM** see RULE *v.*
- *verb* [I] (of birds) to rest or go to sleep somewhere **IDM** see HOME *adv.*

**roost·er** /ˈruːstə(r)/ *noun* (*especially NAmE*) (*BrE also* **cock**) *noun* an adult male chicken ⇒ compare HEN

**root** 🔊 **B2** 🌐 /ruːt/ *noun, verb*
- *noun*
- **OF PLANT 1** 🔊 **B2** [C] the part of a plant that grows under the ground and takes in water and minerals that it sends to the rest of the plant: *deep spreading roots* ◊ *Tree roots can cause damage to buildings.* ◊ **by the roots** *I pulled the plant*

🔵 Oxford Phrasal Academic Lexicon (OPAL) written and spoken word lists | 🟢 OPAL written word list | 🔵 OPAL spoken word list

# root beer

up by the roots (= including the roots). ◊ **root vegetables/ crops** (= plants whose roots you can eat, such as carrots) ⇒ VISUAL VOCAB pages V5, V6, V7 ⇒ see also GRASSROOTS, TAPROOT
- **OF HAIR/TOOTH/NAIL 2** [C] the part of a hair, tooth, nail or tongue that attaches it to the rest of the body: *hair that is blonde at the ends and dark at the roots*
- **MAIN CAUSE OF PROBLEM 3** [C, usually sing.] the main cause of sth, such as a problem or difficult situation: **~ of sth** *Money, or love of money, is said to be the root of all evil.* ◊ *We have to get to the root of the problem.* ◊ **at the ~ of sth** *What lies at the root of his troubles is a sense of insecurity.* ◊ *What would you say was the root cause of the problem?*
- **ORIGIN 4** [C, usually pl.] the origin or basis of sth: *Flamenco may have its roots in Arabic music.*
- **CONNECTION WITH PLACE 5** **roots** [pl.] the feelings or connections that you have with a place because you have lived there or your family came from there: *I'm proud of my Italian roots.* ◊ *After 20 years in America, I still feel my roots are in England.*
- **OF WORD 6** [C] (*linguistics*) the part of a word that has the main meaning and that its other forms are based on; a word that other words are formed from: *'Comfort' is the root of 'comfortable', 'comfortably', 'discomfort' and 'uncomfortable'.*
- **MATHEMATICS 7** [C] a quantity which, when multiplied by itself a particular number of times, produces another quantity ⇒ see also CUBE ROOT, SQUARE ROOT

IDM **put down ˈroots 1** (of a plant) to develop roots **2** to settle and live in one place: *After ten years travelling the world, she felt it was time to put down roots somewhere.* **ˌroot and ˈbranch** completely and in a way that affects every part of sth: *The government set out to destroy the organization root and branch.* ◊ *root-and-branch reforms* **take ˈroot 1** (of a plant) to develop roots **2** (of an idea) to become accepted widely: *Fortunately, militarism failed to take root in Europe as a whole.*

■ *verb*
- **OF PLANTS 1** [I, T] ~ (sth) to grow roots; to cause or encourage a plant to grow roots
- **SEARCH 2** [I] to search for sth by moving things or turning things over SYN rummage: ~ (**about/around**) **for sth** *pigs rooting for food* ◊ *Who's been rooting around in my desk?* ◊ ~ (**through sth**) (**for sth**) *'It must be here somewhere,' she said, rooting through the suitcase.*
- **SEX 3** [I, T] ~ (sb) (*AustralE, NZE, taboo, slang*) to have sex with sb

PHRV **ˈroot for sb** [no passive] (usually used in the progressive tenses) (*informal*) to support or encourage sb in a sports competition or when they are in a difficult situation: *We're rooting for the Bulls.* ◊ *Good luck—I'm rooting for you!* **ˌroot sth/sb↔ˈout 1** to find the person or thing that is causing a problem and remove or get rid of them **2** to find sb/sth after searching for a long time **ˌroot sth↔ˈup** to dig or pull up a plant with its roots

**ˈroot beer** *noun* **1** [U, C] a sweet FIZZY drink (= with bubbles), that does not contain alcohol, made from GINGER and the roots of other plants. It is drunk especially in the US. **2** [C] a bottle, can or glass of root beer

**ˈroot canal** *noun* the space inside the root of a tooth

**ˈroot directory** *noun* (*computing*) a file that contains all the other files in a program, system, etc.

**root·ed** /ˈruːtɪd/ *adj.* **1** ~ **in sth** developing from or being strongly influenced by sth: *His problems are deeply rooted in his childhood experiences.* **2** fixed in one place; not moving or changing: *She was rooted to her chair.* ◊ *Their life is rooted in Chicago now.* ◊ *Racism is still deeply rooted in our society.* ⇒ see DEEP-ROOTED **3** (*AustralE, slang*) extremely tired **4** (*AustralE, slang*) too old or broken to use IDM see SPOT *n.*

**root·less** /ˈruːtləs/ *adj.* having nowhere that you really think of as home, or as the place where you belong: *She had had a rootless childhood moving from town to town.* ▸ **ˈroot·less·ness** *noun* [U]

**rootsy** /ˈruːtsi/ *adj.* (*informal*) (of music) belonging to a particular tradition, and not changed from the original style

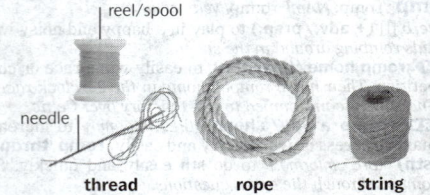
reel/spool
needle
thread  rope  string

**rope** /rəʊp/ *noun, verb*
■ *noun* **1** [C, U] very strong thick string made by TWISTING thinner strings, wires, etc. together: *The rope broke and she fell 50 metres onto the rocks.* ◊ *We tied his hands together with rope.* ◊ *The anchor was attached to a length of rope.* ◊ *Coils of rope lay on the quayside.* ⇒ see also JUMP ROPE, SKIPPING ROPE, TOW ROPE **2 the ropes** [pl.] the fence made of rope that is around the edge of the area where a BOXING or WRESTLING match takes place **3** [C] a number of similar things attached together by a string or THREAD: *a rope of pearls*

IDM **give sb enough ˈrope** to allow sb freedom to do what they want, especially in the hope that they will make a mistake or look silly: *The question was vague, giving the interviewee enough rope to hang herself.* **on the ˈropes** (*informal*) very close to being defeated **show sb/know/ learn the ˈropes** (*informal*) to show sb/know/learn how a particular job should be done ⇒ more at END *n.*, MONEY

■ *verb* **1** to tie one person or thing to another with a rope: ~ **A and B together** *The thieves had roped the guard's feet together.* ◊ ~ **A to B** *I roped the goat to a post.* **2** ~ **sth** to tie sth with a rope so that it is held tightly and safely: *I closed and roped the trunk.* **3** ~ **sth** (*especially NAmE*) to catch an animal by throwing a circle of rope around it SYN lasso

PHRV **ˌrope sb↔ˈin** | **ˌrope sb ˈinto sth** [usually passive] (*informal*) to persuade sb to join in an activity or to help to do sth, even when they do not want to: **be roped in to do sth** *Everyone was roped in to help with the show.* ◊ **be roped into doing sth** *Ben was roped into making coffee for the whole team.* **ˌrope sth↔ˈoff** to separate an area from another one, using ropes, to stop people from entering it: *Police roped off the street to investigate the accident.*

**ˈrope ladder** *noun* a LADDER made of two long ropes connected by short pieces of wood or metal with equal spaces between

**ropy** (also **ropey**) /ˈrəʊpi/ *adj.* (*BrE, informal*) **1** not in good condition; of bad quality: *We spent the night in a ropy old tent.* **2** feeling slightly ill

**ro-ro** /ˈrəʊ rəʊ/ *abbr.* (*BrE*) ROLL-ON ROLL-OFF

**Ror·schach test** /ˈrɔːʃɑːk test; *NAmE* ˈrɔːrʃɑːrk-/ *noun* (*psychology*) a test in which people have to say what different shapes made by INK (= coloured liquid for printing, drawing, etc.) make them think of

**rort** /rɔːt; *NAmE* rɔːrt/ *noun* (*AustralE, NZE, informal*) a dishonest thing that sb does: *a tax rort* ▸ **rort** *verb* [T, I]: ~ (**sth**) *He was an expert at rorting the system* (= getting the best out of it for himself without actually doing anything illegal).

**ros·ary** /ˈrəʊzəri/ *noun* (*pl.* **-ies**) **1** [C] a string of BEADS that are used by some Roman Catholics for counting prayers as they say them **2 the Rosary** [sing.] the set of prayers said by Roman Catholics while counting rosary BEADS

**rose** /rəʊz/ *noun, adj., verb*
■ *noun* **1** [C] a flower with a sweet smell that grows on a bush with THORNS (= sharp points) on its STEMS: *a bunch of red roses* ◊ *a rose bush/garden* ◊ *a climbing/rambling rose* ⇒ VISUAL VOCAB page V7 **2** (also **ˌrose ˈpink**) [U] a pink colour **3** [C] a piece of metal or plastic with small holes in it that is attached to the end of a pipe or WATERING CAN so that the water comes out in a fine SPRAY when you are watering plants ⇒ see also ENGLISH ROSE

IDM **be coming up ˈroses** (*informal*) (of a situation) to be developing in a successful way **a ˌrose by any other**

**name would smell as ˈsweet** (*saying*) what is important is what people or things are, not what they are called ⇨ more at BED *n.*, SMELL *v.*
- **adj.** (*also* ˌrose ˈpink) pink in colour
- **verb** past tense of RISE

▼ **HOMOPHONES**

**rose • rows** /rəʊz/

- **rose** *noun*: He gave me a single red rose.
- **rose** *verb* (*past tense of* RISE): Prices rose 2 per cent in December.
- **rows** *noun* (*plural of* ROW¹): Five rows of chairs were set out facing the whiteboard.
- **rows** *verb* (*third person of* ROW¹): She rows across the river, helping passengers reach the other side.

**rosé** /ˈrəʊzeɪ; NAmE rəʊˈzeɪ/ *noun* [U, C] (*from French*) a light pink wine: *a bottle of rosé* ◊ *an excellent rosé* ⇨ compare RED WINE, WHITE WINE

**rose·bud** /ˈrəʊzbʌd/ *noun* the flower of a ROSE before it is open

**ˈrose-coloured** (*US* ˈrose-colored) *adj.* **1** pink in colour **2** (*also* ˈrose-tinted) used to describe an idea or a way of looking at a situation as being better or more positive than it really is: *He tends to view the world through rose-coloured spectacles.* ◊ *a rose-tinted vision of the world*

**ˈrose hip** *noun* = HIP

**rose·mary** /ˈrəʊzməri; NAmE -meri/ *noun* [U] a bush with small narrow leaves that smell sweet and are used in cooking as a HERB ⇨ VISUAL VOCAB page V8

**Ros·etta Stone** /rəʊˌzetə ˈstəʊn/ *noun* [sing.] something, especially a discovery, that helps people to understand or find an explanation for a mystery or an area of knowledge that not much was known about ORIGIN From the name of an ancient stone with writing in three different languages on it that was found near Rosetta in Egypt in 1799. It has helped archaeologists to understand and translate many of the ancient Egyptian texts.

**ros·ette** /rəʊˈzet/ *noun* **1** a round decoration made of RIBBON that is worn by supporters of a political party or sports team, or to show that sb has won a prize ⇨ picture at MEDAL **2** a thing that has the shape of a ROSE: *The leaves formed a dark green rosette.*

**ˈrose water** *noun* [U] a liquid with a sweet smell made from ROSES, used as a PERFUME or in cooking

**ˈrose·wood** /ˈrəʊzwʊd/ *noun* [U] the hard red-brown wood of a tropical tree, that has a pleasant smell and is used for making expensive furniture

**Rosh Hash·ana** (*also* Rosh Hashˌanah) /ˌrɒʃ həˈʃɑːnə; NAmE ˌrɑːʃ / *noun* [U] the Jewish New Year festival, held in September

**rosin** /ˈrɒzɪn; NAmE ˈrɑːzn/ *noun* [U] a substance that a player uses on the BOW of a musical instrument such as a VIOLIN so that it makes a better sound when it moves across the strings ▸ **rosin** *verb* ~ *sth*

**ros·ter** /ˈrɒstə(r); NAmE ˈrɑːs-/ *noun, verb*
- *noun* **1** a list showing the tasks that different people have to do at different times within an organization SYN **rota**: *a duty roster* **2** a list of the names of people who are available to do a job, play in a team, etc.: *They have a number of outstanding players on their roster.*
- *verb* [usually passive] (*BrE*) to put sb's name on a roster: **be rostered (for sth/to do sth)** *The driver was rostered for Sunday.*

**ros·trum** /ˈrɒstrəm; NAmE ˈrɑːs-/ *noun* (*pl.* **rosˈtrums** *or* **ros·tra** /-trə/) a small raised platform that a person stands on to make a speech, CONDUCT music, receive a prize, etc. SYN **podium** ⇨ picture at PODIUM

**rosy** /ˈrəʊzi/ *adj.* (**rosi·er**, **rosi·est**) **1** pink and pleasant in appearance: *She had rosy cheeks.* **2** likely to be good or successful SYN **hopeful**: *The future is looking very rosy for our company.* ◊ *She painted a rosy picture of their life together in Italy* (= made it appear to be very good and perhaps better than it really was). IDM see GARDEN *n.*

**rot** /rɒt; NAmE rɑːt/ *verb, noun*
- *verb* [I, T] (**-tt-**) to DECAY, or make sth DECAY, naturally and gradually SYN **decompose**: *rotting leaves* ◊ *~ (away) The window frame had rotted away completely.* ◊ (*figurative*) *prisoners thrown in jail and left to rot* ◊ *~ sth Too much sugar will rot your teeth.* ⇨ see also ROTTEN
- *noun* [U] **1** the process or state of DECAYING and falling apart: *The wood must not get damp as rot can quickly result.* ⇨ see also DRY ROT **2 the rot** used to describe the fact that a situation is getting worse: *The rot set in last year when they reorganized the department.* ◊ *The team should manage to stop the rot if they play well this week.* **3** (*BrE, old-fashioned*) silly things that sb says SYN **nonsense**, **rubbish**: *Don't talk such rot!*

**rota** /ˈrəʊtə/ *noun* (*BrE*) a list of tasks that need to be done and the people who will do them in turn SYN **roster**: *Dave organized a cleaning rota.*

**ro·tary** /ˈrəʊtəri/ *adj., noun*
- *adj.* [only before noun] **1** (of a movement) moving in a circle around a central fixed point: *rotary motion* **2** (of a machine or piece of equipment) having parts that move in this way: *a rotary engine*
- *noun* (*pl.* **-ies**) (*NAmE*) = TRAFFIC CIRCLE

**ro·tate** /rəʊˈteɪt; NAmE ˈrəʊteɪt/ *verb* **1** [I, T] to move or turn around a central fixed point; to make sth do this: *Stay well away from the helicopter when its blades start to rotate.* ◊ *~ about/around sth winds rotating around the eye of a hurricane* ◊ *~ sth Rotate the wheel through 180 degrees.* **2** [I, T] if a job **rotates**, or if people **rotate** a job, they regularly change the job or regularly change who does the job: *+ adv./prep. The EU presidency rotates among the members.* ◊ *When I joined the company, I rotated around the different sections.* ◊ *~ sth We rotate the night shift so no one has to do it all the time.* ▸ **ro·tat·ing** *adj.* [only before noun]: *rotating parts*

**ro·ta·tion** /rəʊˈteɪʃn/ *noun* **1** [U] the action of an object moving in a circle around a central fixed point: *the daily rotation of the earth on its axis* **2** [C] one complete movement in a circle around a fixed point: *This switch controls the number of rotations per minute.* **3** [U, C] the act of regularly changing the thing that is being used in a particular situation, or of changing the person who does a particular job: *crop rotation/the rotation of crops* (= changing the crop that is grown on an area of land in order to protect the soil) ◊ **in ~** *The committee is chaired by all the members in rotation.* ▸ **ro·ta·tion·al** /-ʃənl/ *adj.* [only before noun]

**ROTC** /ˈrɒtsi; NAmE ˈrɑːt-/ *abbr.* (*US*) Reserve Officers' Training Corps (an organization for students in the US who are training to be military officers while they are studying)

**rote** /rəʊt/ *noun* [U] (often used as an adjective) the process of learning sth by repeating it until you remember it rather than by understanding the meaning of it: **by ~** *to learn by rote* ◊ *rote learning/memorization*

**ROTFL** *abbr.* (*informal*) = ROFL

**roti** /ˈrəʊti/ *noun* [U, C] **1** a type of South Asian bread that is cooked on a GRIDDLE **2** (*IndE*) bread of any kind

**ro·tis·serie** /rəʊˈtɪsəri/ *noun* (*from French*) a piece of equipment for cooking meat that turns it around on a long straight piece of metal (called a SPIT)

**rotor** /ˈrəʊtə(r)/ *noun* a part of a machine that turns around a central point: *rotor blades on a helicopter*

**rot·ten** /ˈrɒtn; NAmE ˈrɑːtn/ *adj., adv.*
- *adj.* **1** (of food, wood, etc.) that has DECAYED and cannot be eaten or used: *the smell of rotten vegetables* ◊ *The fruit is starting to go rotten.* ◊ *rotten floorboards* **2** [usually before noun] (*informal*) very bad SYN **terrible**: *I've had a rotten day!* ◊ *What rotten luck!* ◊ *She's a rotten singer.* ◊ **~ at (doing) sth** *I'm rotten at maths.* **3** [not usually before noun] (*informal*) dishonest: *The organization is rotten to the core.* **4** [not before noun] (*informal*) looking or feeling ill: *She felt rotten.* **5** [not before noun] (*informal*) feeling guilty about sth you have done: *I feel rotten about leaving them behind.*

# Rottweiler

**6** [only before noun] (*informal*) used to emphasize that you are angry or upset about sth: *You can keep your rotten money!* ▶ **rot·ten·ness** /-tnnəs/ *noun* [U] **IDM** see APPLE
■ *adv.* (*informal*) to a large degree; very much: *The children were spoilt rotten.*

**Rott·weiler** /ˈrɒtwaɪlə(r), ˈrɒtvaɪ-; *NAmE* ˈrɑːtwaɪl-/ *noun* a large dog that can be very aggressive

**ro·tund** /rəʊˈtʌnd/ *adj.* (*formal or humorous*) having a fat round body **SYN** **plump**: *the rotund figure of Mr Stevens* ▶ **ro·tund·ity** *noun* [U]

**ro·tunda** /rəʊˈtʌndə/ *noun* a round building or hall, especially one with a curved roof (= a DOME)

**rou·ble** (*especially BrE*) (*NAmE usually* **ruble**) /ˈruːbl/ *noun* the unit of money in Russia

**rouge** /ruːʒ/ *noun* [U] (*from French, old-fashioned*) a red powder used by women for giving colour to their CHEEKS (= the sides of the face) ▶ **rouge** *verb* ~ **sth**

**rough** ⓘ B1 /rʌf/ *adj., noun, verb, adv.*
■ *adj.* (**rough·er, rough·est**)
• NOT SMOOTH **1** ⓘ B1 having a surface that is not even or regular: *rough ground* ◊ *The skin on her hands was hard and rough.* ◊ *Trim rough edges with a sharp knife.* **OPP** **smooth**
• NOT EXACT **2** ⓘ B2 not exact; not including all details **SYN** **approximate**: *a rough calculation/estimate of the cost* ◊ *I've got a rough idea of where I want to go.* ◊ *There were about 20 people there, at a rough guess.* ◊ *a rough draft of a speech* ◊ *a rough sketch*
• VIOLENT **3** ⓘ B2 not gentle or careful; violent: *This watch is not designed for rough treatment.* ◊ *They complained of rough handling by the guards.* ◊ *rough kids* ◊ *Don't try any rough stuff with me!* **4** ⓘ B2 where there is a lot of violence or crime: *the roughest neighbourhood in the city* ⮕ WORD-FINDER NOTE at LOCATION
• SEA/WEATHER **5** ⓘ B2 having large and dangerous waves; wild and with storms: *It was too rough to sail that night.*
• DIFFICULT **6** difficult and unpleasant **SYN** **tough**: *He's had a really rough time recently* (= he's had a lot of problems). ◊ *We'll get someone in to do the rough work* (= the hard physical work). ◊ *You two are obviously going through a rough patch right now.*
• NOT WELL **7** (*BrE*) not feeling well: *You look rough—are you OK?* ◊ *I had a rough night* (= I didn't sleep well).
• PLAIN/BASIC **8** simply made and not finished in every detail; plain or basic: *rough wooden tables* ◊ *a rough track* ◊ (*BrE*) *rough paper for making notes on*
• NOT SMOOTH **9** not smooth or pleasant to taste, listen to, etc: *a rough wine/voice* ▶ **rough·ness** *noun* [U] ⮕ see also ROUGHLY
**IDM** **a ˌrough ˈdeal** the fact of being treated unfairly **(have some) ˌrough ˈedges** | **be rough around the ˈedges** (to have some) small parts, for example in a performance or in your character, that are not yet as good as they should be: *The ballet still had some rough edges.* ◊ *He had a few rough edges knocked off at school.* ◊ *The films are very rough around the edges.* **the ˌrough end of the ˈpineapple** (*AustralE, informal*) a situation in which sb is treated badly or unfairly ⮕ more at RIDE *n*.
■ *noun*
• IN GOLF **1** **the rough** [sing.] the part of a golf course where the grass is long, making it more difficult to hit the ball ⮕ compare FAIRWAY
• DRAWING/DESIGN **2** [C] (*specialist*) the first version of a drawing or design that has been done quickly and without much detail
• VIOLENT PERSON **3** [C] (*old-fashioned, informal*) a violent person: *a gang of roughs*
**IDM** **in ˈrough** (*especially BrE*) if you write or draw sth **in rough**, you make a first version of it, not worrying too much about mistakes or details **take the ˌrough with the ˈsmooth** to accept the unpleasant or difficult things that happen in life as well as the good things ⮕ more at BIT

■ *verb*
**IDM** **ˈrough it** (*informal*) to live in a way that is not very comfortable for a short time: *We can sleep on the beach. I don't mind roughing it for a night or two.*
**PHRV** **ˌrough sth↔ˈout** to draw or write sth without including all the details: *I've roughed out a few ideas.* **ˌrough sb↔ˈup** to hurt sb by hitting or kicking them: *He claimed that guards had roughed him up in prison.*
■ *adv.* using force or violence: *Do they always play this rough?*
**IDM** **ˌlive/ˌsleep ˈrough** (*BrE*) to live or sleep outdoors, usually because you have no home and no money: *young people sleeping rough on the streets* ⮕ related noun ROUGH SLEEPER

**ˈrough·age** /ˈrʌfɪdʒ/ *noun* [U] the part of food that helps to keep a person healthy by keeping the BOWELS working and moving other food quickly through the body **SYN** **fibre**

**ˌrough and ˈready** *adj.* [usually before noun] **1** simple and prepared quickly but good enough for a particular situation: *a rough-and-ready guide to the education system* **2** (of a person) not very polite, educated or fashionable

**ˌrough and ˈtumble** *noun* [U, sing.] **1** ~ (**of sth**) a situation in which people compete with each other and are aggressive in order to get what they want: *the rough and tumble of politics* **2** noisy and slightly violent behaviour when children or animals are playing together

**ˈrough cut** *noun* the first version of a film, after the different scenes have been put together

**ˈrough-cut** *verb* ~ **sth** to cut sth quickly, without paying attention to the exact size

**ˌrough ˈdiamond** (*BrE*) (*NAmE* **ˌdiamond in the ˈrough**) *noun* a person who has many good qualities even though they do not seem to be very polite, educated, etc.

**rough·en** /ˈrʌfn/ *verb* [I, T] to become rough; to make sth rough: *His voice roughened with every word.* ◊ ~ **sth** *Cold weather roughens your skin.*

**ˌrough-ˈhewn** *adj.* [only before noun] **1** (of stone, wood, etc.) cut in a way that leaves it with a rough surface: *rough-hewn walls* ◊ (*figurative*) *the rough-hewn features of his face* **2** (*formal*) (of a person or their behaviour) not very polite or educated

**ˈrough·house** /ˈrʌfhaʊz/ *verb* [I, T] ~ (**sb**) (*NAmE, informal*) to fight sb or play with sb roughly: *Quit roughhousing, you two!*

**ˈrough·ing** /ˈrʌfɪŋ/ *noun* [U] (in ICE HOCKEY and AMERICAN FOOTBALL) an illegal use of force, for which a PENALTY may be given

**ˌrough ˈjustice** *noun* [U] **1** punishment that does not seem fair: *It was rough justice that they lost in the closing seconds of the game.* **2** treatment that is fair but not official or expected: *There was a certain amount of rough justice in his downfall.*

**rough·ly** ⓘ+ B2 S /ˈrʌfli/ *adv.* **1** ⓘ+ B2 approximately but not exactly: *Sales are up by roughly 10 per cent.* ◊ *We live roughly halfway between here and the coast.* ◊ *They all left at roughly the same time.* ◊ **Roughly speaking**, *we receive about fifty letters a week on the subject.* **2** ⓘ+ B2 using force or not being careful and gentle: *He pushed her roughly out of the way.* ◊ '*What do you want?*' *she demanded roughly.* **3** in a way that does not leave a smooth surface: *roughly plastered walls*

**ˈrough·neck** /ˈrʌfnek/ *noun* (*informal*) **1** (*especially NAmE*) a man who is noisy, rude and aggressive **2** a man who works on an OIL RIG

**rough·shod** /ˈrʌfʃɒd; *NAmE* -ʃɑːd/ *adv.*
**IDM** **ˌride, etc. ˈroughshod over sb** (*especially BrE*) (*NAmE usually* **run ˈroughshod over sb**) to treat sb badly and not worry about their feelings

**ˈrough ˈsleeper** *noun* (*BrE*) a person who has no home and sleeps outside, especially on the streets of a town or city: *The charity provides shelter for rough sleepers.* ⮕ see also LIVE/SLEEP ROUGH at ROUGH *adv.*

**rou·lette** /ruːˈlet/ *noun* [U] a GAMBLING game in which a ball is dropped onto a moving wheel that has holes with numbers on it. Players bet on which hole the ball will be in when the wheel stops. ⊃ **WORDFINDER NOTE** at GAMBLING ⊃ see also RUSSIAN ROULETTE

**round** ⓘ A2 /raʊnd/ *adj., adv., prep., noun, verb*

■ *adj.* (**round·er**, **round·est**) **1** A2 having a shape like a circle or a ball: *a round plate* ◊ *These glasses suit people with round faces.* ◊ *The fruit are small and round.* ◊ *Rugby isn't played with a round ball.* ◊ *the discovery that the world is round* ◊ *The child was watching it all with big round eyes* (= showing interest). ◊ *a T-shirt with a round neck* ⊃ see also ROUND-TABLE **2** 🔑 A2 having a curved shape: *the round green hills of Donegal* ◊ *round brackets* (= in writing) ◊ *She had a small mouth and round pink cheeks.* **3** 🔑 B2 [only before noun] a **round** figure or amount is one that is given as a whole number, usually one ending in 0: *Make it a round figure—say forty dollars.* ◊ *Two thousand is a nice round number—put that down.* ◊ *Well, in round figures* (= not giving the exact figures) *we've spent twenty thousand so far.* ⊃ see also YEAR-ROUND ▶ **round·ness** *noun* [U]: *His face had lost its boyish roundness.*

■ *adv.* (especially *BrE*) (*NAmE* usually **around**) **HELP** For the special uses of **round** in phrasal verbs, look at the verb entries. For example, the meaning of **come round to sth** is given in the phrasal verb section of the entry for **come**. **1** 🔑 A2 moving in a circle: *Everybody joins hands and dances round.* ◊ *How do you make the wheels go round?* ◊ *The children were spinning round and round.* ◊ (*figurative*) *The thought kept going round and round in her head.* ⊃ see also MERRY-GO-ROUND **2** 🔑 A2 measuring or marking the edge or outside of sth: *a young tree measuring only 18 inches round* ◊ *They've built a high fence all round to keep intruders out.* **3** 🔑 A2 on all sides of sb/sth: *A large crowd had gathered round to watch.* **4** 🔑 A2 at various places in an area: *People stood round waiting for something to happen.* **5** 🔑 A2 in a circle or curve to face another way or the opposite way: *He turned the car round and drove back again.* ◊ *She looked round at the sound of his voice.* **6** 🔑 A2 to the other side of sth: *We walked round to the back of the house.* ◊ *The road's blocked—you'll have to drive the long way round.* **7** 🔑 A2 from one place, person, etc. to another: *They've moved all the furniture round.* ◊ *He went round interviewing people about local traditions.* ◊ *Pass the biscuits round.* ◊ *Have we enough cups to go round?* **8** 🔑 A2 (*informal*) to or at a particular place, especially where sb lives: *I'll be round in an hour.* ◊ *We've invited the Frasers round this evening.* ⊃ note at AROUND
**IDM** **round a'bout 1** approximately: *We're leaving round about ten.* ◊ *A new roof will cost round about £3000.* **2** in the area near a place: *in Oxford and the villages round about* ⊃ more at TIME *n.*

■ *prep.* (especially *BrE*) (*NAmE* usually **around**) **1** 🔑 A2 in a circle: *the first woman to sail round the world* ◊ *The earth moves round the sun.* **2** 🔑 A2 on, to or from the other side of sth: *Our house is round the next bend.* ◊ *There she is, coming round the corner.* ◊ (*figurative*) *There must be a way round* (= a way of solving) *the problem.* **3** 🔑 A2 on all sides of sb/sth; surrounding sb/sth: *She put her arms round him.* ◊ *He had a scarf round his neck.* ◊ *They were all sitting round the table.* **4** 🔑 A2 in or to many parts of sth: *She looked all round the room.* **5** to fit in with particular people, ideas, etc: *He has to organize his life round the kids.* ⊃ note at AROUND
**IDM** **round 'here** near where you are now or where you live: *There are no decent schools round here.* ⊃ more at MILLSTONE

■ *noun*
- **IN COMPETITIONS 1** 🔑 B2 a stage in a competition or sports event: *the qualifying rounds of the National Championships* ◊ *She made it through to the final round.* **2** a stage in a BOXING or WRESTLING match: *The fight only lasted five rounds.* **3** a complete game of golf; a complete way around the course in some other sports, such as SHOWJUMPING: *We played a round of golf.* ◊ *the first horse to jump a clear round* ⊃ **WORDFINDER NOTE** at COMPETITION
- **STAGE IN PROCESS 4** 🔑 B2 a set of events which form part of a longer process: *the next round of peace talks* ◊ *the final round of voting in the election*

**1353** **rounded**

- **REGULAR ACTIVITIES/ROUTE 5** a regular series of activities: *the daily round of school life* ◊ *Her life is one long round of parties and fun.* **6** a regular route that sb takes when delivering or collecting sth; a regular series of visits that sb makes: **on your~** *Dr Green was on her daily ward rounds.* ◊ (*BrE*) *a postman on his delivery round* ⊃ see also PAPER ROUND
- **DRINKS 7** a number of drinks bought by one person for all the others in a group: *a round of drinks* ◊ *It's my round* (= it is my turn to pay for the next set of drinks).
- **BREAD 8** (*BrE*) a whole slice of bread; sandwiches made from two whole slices of bread: *Who's for another round of toast?* ◊ *two rounds of beef sandwiches*
- **CIRCLE 9** a round object or piece of sth: *Cut the pastry into rounds.*
- **OF APPLAUSE/CHEERS 10 ~ of applause/cheers** a short period during which people show their approval of sb/sth by CLAPPING: *There was a great round of applause when the dance ended.*
- **SHOT 11** a single shot from a gun; a bullet for one shot: *They fired several rounds at the crowd.* ◊ *We only have three rounds of ammunition left.*
- **SONG 12** (*music*) a song for two or more voices in which each sings the same tune but starts at a different time
**IDM** **do/go the 'rounds (of sth) 1** (*BrE*) (*NAmE* **make the 'rounds**) if news or a joke **does the rounds**, it is passed on quickly from one person to another **2** (*BrE*) (*also* **make the 'rounds** *NAmE, BrE*) to go around from place to place, especially when looking for work or support for a political campaign, etc. ⊃ see also WHIP-ROUND **in the 'round 1** (of a work of art) made so that it can be seen from all sides: *an opportunity to see Canova's work in the round* **2** (of a theatre or play) with the people watching all around a central stage

■ *verb* **1** [T] **~ sth** to go around a corner of a building, a bend in the road, etc: *The boat rounded the tip of the island.* ◊ *We rounded the bend at high speed.* **2** [T, I] **~ (sth)** to make sth into a round shape; to form into a round shape: *She rounded her lips and whistled.* ◊ *His eyes rounded with horror.* **3** [T] **~ sth (up/down) (to sth)** to increase or decrease a number to the next highest or lowest whole number
**PHRV** **round sth↔'off (with sth) 1** (*NAmE also* **round sth↔'out**) to finish an activity or complete sth in a good or suitable way: *She rounded off the tour with a concert at Carnegie Hall.* **2** to take the sharp or rough edges off sth: *You can round off the corners with sandpaper.* **'round on sb** to suddenly speak angrily to sb and criticize or attack them **SYN** **turn on**: *He rounded on journalists, calling them 'a pack of vultures'.* **round sb/sth↔'up 1** to find and gather together people, animals or things: *I rounded up a few friends for a party.* ◊ *The cattle are rounded up in the evenings.* **2** if police or soldiers **round up** a group of people, they find them and arrest or capture them ⊃ related noun ROUND-UP

**round·about** /ˈraʊndəbaʊt/ *noun, adj.*

■ *noun* (*BrE*) **1** (*NAmE* **'traffic circle**, **ro·tary**) a place where two or more roads meet, forming a circle that all traffic must go around in the same direction: *At the roundabout, take the second exit.* ⊃ **WORDFINDER NOTE** at ROAD ⊃ see also MINI-ROUNDABOUT **2** (*NAmE* **'merry-go-round**) a round platform for children to play on in a park, etc. that is pushed round while the children are sitting on it ⊃ picture at MERRY-GO-ROUND **3** (*BrE*) = MERRY-GO-ROUND (1)
**IDM** see SWING *n.*

■ *adj.* [usually before noun] not done or said using the shortest, simplest or most direct way possible: *It was a difficult and roundabout trip.* ◊ *He told us, in a very roundabout way, that he was thinking of leaving.*

**round bracket** *noun* (*BrE*) = BRACKET

**round·ed** /ˈraʊndɪd/ *adj.* [usually before noun] **1** having a round shape: *a surface with rounded edges* ◊ *rounded shoulders* **2** having a wide variety of qualities that combine to produce sth pleasant, complete and balanced: *a smooth rounded taste* ◊ *a fully rounded education* ⊃ see also WELL ROUNDED

# roundel

**roun·del** /ˈraʊndl/ noun (specialist) a round design that is used as a decoration or to identify an aircraft

**round·ers** /ˈraʊndəz/; NAmE -dərz/ noun [U] a British game played especially in schools by two teams using a BAT and ball. Each player tries to hit the ball and then run around the four sides of a square before the other team can return the ball. ⇒ compare BASEBALL

**Round·head** /ˈraʊndhed/ noun a person who supported Parliament against the King in the English Civil War (1642–49) ⇒ compare CAVALIER

**round·house** /ˈraʊndhaʊs/ noun a hard hit made with the FIST (= closed hand) where the arm moves around in a wide curve

**ˈroundhouse kick** noun a move in KARATE and other MARTIAL ARTS, in which you turn on one foot as you make a high kick with the other

**round·ly** /ˈraʊndli/ adv. (used to describe a negative action) strongly or by a large number of people: *The report has been roundly criticized.* ◊ *They were roundly defeated* (= they lost by a large number of points).

**ˌround ˈrobin** noun 1 (sport) a competition in which every player or team plays every other player or team 2 a letter intended to be read by many people that is copied and sent to each one: *I always send a round robin letter with all our news to friends at Christmas.*

**ˌround-ˈtable** adj. [only before noun] (of discussions, meetings, etc.) at which everyone is equal and has the same rights: *round-table talks*

**ˌround-the-ˈclock** (also ˌa round-the-ˈclock) adj. [only before noun] lasting or happening all day and night: *round-the-clock nursing care* ⇒ see also CLOCK

**ˈround trip** noun [C, U] a journey to a place and back again: *a 30-mile round trip to work* ◊ (NAmE) *It's 30 miles round trip to work.* ▶ **ˈround-ˈtrip** adj. [only before noun] (NAmE): *a round-trip ticket* ⇒ see also RETURN TICKET

**ˈround-up** noun [usually sing.] 1 a summary of the most important points of a particular subject, especially the news: *We'll be back after the break with a round-up of today's other stories.* 2 an act of bringing people or animals together in one place for a particular purpose

**round·worm** /ˈraʊndwɜːm; NAmE -wɜːrm/ noun a small WORM that lives in the INTESTINES of pigs, humans and some other animals

**rouse** /raʊz/ verb 1 (formal) to wake sb up, especially when they are sleeping deeply: **~sb from sleep/bed** *The telephone roused me from my sleep at 6 a.m.* ◊ **~sb** *Nicky roused her with a gentle nudge.* 2 to make sb want to start doing sth when they were not active or interested in doing it: **~sb/yourself (to sth)** *A lot of people were roused to action by the appeal.* ◊ **~sb/yourself to do sth** *Richard couldn't rouse himself to say anything in reply.* ◊ **~sb from sth** *We finally managed to rouse her from her lethargy.* 3 **~sth** (formal) to make sb feel a particular emotion: *to rouse sb's anger* ◊ *What roused your suspicions* (= what made you suspicious)? 4 [usually passive] to make sb angry, excited or full of emotion: **be roused** *Chris is not easily roused.* ⇒ see also AROUSE

> **HOMOPHONES**
> **rouse • rows** /raʊz/
> • **rouse** verb: *We were unable to rouse him from his sleep.*
> • **rows** noun (plural of ROW²): *They keep having rows over who does more work around the house.*

**rous·ing** /ˈraʊzɪŋ/ adj. [usually before noun] 1 full of energy and enthusiasm: *a rousing cheer* ◊ *The team was given a rousing reception by the fans.* 2 intended to make other people feel enthusiastic about sth: *a rousing speech* ⇒ see also RABBLE-ROUSING

**roust** /raʊst/ verb **~sb (from sth)** (NAmE) to worry or upset sb or make them move from a place

**rout** /raʊt/ noun, verb
■ noun [sing.] a situation in which sb is defeated easily and completely in a battle or competition
IDM **put sb to ˈrout** (literary) to defeat sb easily and completely
■ verb **~sb** to defeat sb completely in a competition, a battle, etc: *The Buffalo Bills routed the Atlanta Falcons 41–14.*

**route** ⓘ A2 /ruːt; NAmE also raʊt/ noun, verb
■ noun 1 A2 a way that you follow to get from one place to another: *Motorists are advised to find an alternative route.* ◊ **~(from A) to B** *the quickest route from Florence to Rome* ◊ **~+ adv./prep.** *a key route through the city centre* ◊ *an escape route* ⇒ see also EN ROUTE 2 A2 a fixed way along which a bus, train, etc. regularly travels or goods are regularly sent: *The house is not on a bus route.* ◊ *shipping/supply routes* ◊ *a cycle route* (= a path that is only for CYCLISTS) ⇒ see also TRADE ROUTE 3 B2 a particular way of achieving sth: *to go down/take/follow a particular route* ◊ **~to (doing) sth** *the route to success* 4 used before the number of a main road in the US: *Route 66*
■ verb (**rout·ing**, **rout·ed**, **rout·ed**) **~sb/sth (+ adv./prep.)** to send sb/sth by a particular route: *Satellites route data all over the globe.*

**ˈroute one** noun [U] (BrE) (in football (soccer)) kicking the ball a long way towards your opponent's end, used as a direct way of attacking, rather than passing the ball between players

**rout·er¹** /ˈruːtə(r); NAmE also ˈraʊt-/ noun (computing) a device that sends data to the appropriate parts of a computer network: *a wireless router* ⇒ WORDFINDER NOTE at COMPUTER

**rout·er²** /ˈraʊtə(r)/ noun an electric tool which cuts shallow lines in surfaces

**rou·tine** ⓘ A1 /ruːˈtiːn/ noun, adj.
■ noun 1 A1 [C, U] the normal order and way in which you regularly do things: *to settle/get/fall into a routine* ◊ *Make exercise a part of your daily routine.* ◊ *We clean and repair the machines as a matter of routine.* 2 B1 [U] (disapproving) a situation in which life is boring because things are always done in the same way: *She needed a break from routine.* 3 [C] a series of movements, jokes, etc. that are part of a performance: *to do/perform a dance routine* 4 [C] (computing) a list of instructions that enable a computer to perform a particular task
■ adj. [usually before noun] 1 B2 done or happening as a normal part of a particular job, situation or process: *routine enquiries/questions/tests/screening* ◊ *The fault was discovered during a routine check.* 2 B2 not unusual or different in any way: *He died of a heart attack during a routine operation.* 3 B2 (disapproving) ordinary and boring SYN **dull, humdrum**: *a routine job* ◊ *This type of work rapidly becomes routine.* ▶ **rou·tine·ly** adv.: *Visitors are routinely checked as they enter the building.*

**ˈrouting number** (US) (BrE ˈsort code) noun a number that is used to identify a particular bank

**roux** /ruː/ noun [C, U] (pl. **roux**) (from French) a mixture of fat and flour heated together until it forms a mass, used for making sauces

**rove** /rəʊv/ verb 1 [I, T] (formal) to travel from one place to another, often with no particular purpose SYN **roam**: **+ adv./prep.** *A quarter of a million refugees roved around the country.* ◊ **~sth** *bands of thieves who roved the countryside* 2 [I] **(+ adv./prep.)** if sb's eyes **rove**, they keep looking in different directions

**rover** /ˈrəʊvə(r)/ noun (literary) a person who likes to travel a lot rather than live in one place

**rov·ing** /ˈrəʊvɪŋ/ adj. [usually before noun] travelling from one place to another and not staying anywhere permanently: *a roving reporter for ABC news*
IDM **have a roving ˈeye** (old-fashioned) to always be looking for the chance to have a new sexual relationship

**row¹** ⓘ B1 /rəʊ/ noun, verb ⇒ see also ROW²
■ noun 1 B1 a number of people standing or sitting next to each other in a line; a number of objects arranged in a line: **~of sb/sth** *a row of trees* ◊ **in a~** *We sat in a row at the*

back of the room. ◊ *The vegetables were planted in neat rows.* ⇨ **HOMOPHONES** at ROSE **2** [?] **B1** a line of seats in a cinema, theatre, etc: **in the ...** ~ *Let's sit in the back row.* ◊ *Our seats are five rows from the front.* **3** [?] **B1** a line of numbers or words arranged one after the other across the page in a table: *The top row of Table 2 shows the current values.* ⇨ compare COLUMN (2) **4** a complete line of STITCHES in KNITTING or CROCHET (= ways of making clothing, etc. out of wool) **5** Row used in the name of some roads: *Manor Row* **6** [usually sing.] an act of ROWING a boat; the period of time spent doing this: *We went for a row on the lake.* ⇨ see also DEATH ROW, SKID ROW
**IDM** **in a 'row 1** if sth happens several times **in a row**, it happens in exactly the same way each time, and nothing different happens in the time between: *This is her third win in a row.* **2** if sth happens for several days, etc. **in a row**, it happens on each of those days: *Inflation has fallen for the third month in a row.* ⇨ more at DUCK *n.*
▪ *verb* **1** [I, T] to move a boat through water using OARS (= long thin straight pieces of wood with flat ends): *We rowed around the island.* ◊ ~ *sth Grace rowed the boat out to sea again.* ⇨ **HOMOPHONES** at ROAD, ROSE **2** [T] ~ **sb** (+ **adv./ prep.**) to take sb somewhere in a boat with OARS: *The fisherman rowed us back to the shore.*
**PHR V** **row 'back** [I] to change an earlier statement, opinion or promise: *The government is now trying to row back on its commitments.*

**row²** /raʊ/ *noun, verb* ⇨ see also ROW¹
▪ *noun* (*especially BrE, informal*) **1** [C] ~ **(about / over sth)** a serious argument between people, organizations, etc. about sth: *A row has broken out over education.* **2** [C] a noisy argument between two or more people **SYN** quarrel: *She left him after a blazing row.* ◊ *family rows* ◊ *He had a row with his son.* ⇨ **HOMOPHONES** at ROUSE **3** [sing.] a loud unpleasant noise **SYN** din, racket: *Who's making that row?*
▪ *verb* [I] (*BrE, informal*) to have a noisy argument: *Mike and Sue are always rowing.* ◊ ~ **(with sb) (about sb/sth)** *She had rowed with her parents about her boyfriend.*

**rowan** /ˈrəʊən/; *BrE also* /ˈraʊ-/ (*also* **rowan tree**, **mountain 'ash**) *noun* a small tree that has red BERRIES in the autumn

**row·boat** /ˈrəʊbəʊt/ (*NAmE*) (*BrE* **rowing boat**) *noun* a small open boat that you move using OARS

**rowdy** /ˈraʊdi/ *adj.* (**row·dier**, **row·di·est**) (of people) making a lot of noise or likely to cause trouble **SYN** disorderly: *a rowdy crowd at the pub* ▶ **row·di·ly** /-dəli/ *adv.* **row·di·ness** *noun* [U] **rowdy** *noun* (*pl.* **-ies**): *rowdies and troublemakers*

**'rowdy sheet** *noun* (*IndE*) a record kept in a police station of the names of people that the police have charged with a crime **SYN** charge sheet

**rowdy 'sheeter** *noun* (*IndE*) a person who has been found guilty of multiple crimes in the past

**rower** /ˈrəʊə(r)/ *noun* a person who ROWS a boat

**row house** /ˈrəʊ haʊs/ (*also* **'town house**) (*both NAmE*) (*BrE* **terraced 'house**) *noun* a house that is one of a row of houses that are joined together on each side

**row·ing** /ˈrəʊɪŋ/ *noun* [U] the sport or activity of travelling in a boat using OARS: *to go rowing*

**'rowing boat** (*BrE*) (*NAmE* **row·boat**) *noun* a small open boat that you move using OARS

**'rowing machine** *noun* a piece of sports equipment on which you make the same movements as sb who is ROWING a boat ⇨ picture at EXERCISE BIKE

**royal** **①** **B1** /ˈrɔɪəl/ *adj., noun*
▪ *adj.* [only before noun] **1** [?] **B1** connected with or belonging to the king or queen of a country: *the royal family* ◊ *a royal wedding* ⇨ compare REGAL ⇨ WORDFINDER NOTE at KING **2** (*abbr.* **R**) used in the names of organizations that serve or are supported by a king or queen: *the Royal Navy* ◊ *the Royal Society for the Protection of Birds* **3** impressive; suitable for a king or queen **SYN** splendid: *We were given a royal welcome.*
▪ *noun* [usually pl.] (*informal*) a member of a royal family

1355 **RT**

**the Royal A'cademy** (*also* **the Royal A'cademy of 'Arts**) *noun* [sing.] a British organization whose members are famous artists. Its building in London contains an art school and space for exhibitions.

**royal as'sent** *noun often* **the royal assent** [U] (in the UK) the act of signing an Act of Parliament by the king or queen so that it becomes law

**royal 'blue** *adj.* deep bright blue ▶ **royal 'blue** *noun* [U]

**Royal Com'mission** *noun* ~ **(on / into sth)** | ~ **(to do sth)** (in the UK) a group of people who are officially chosen to examine a particular law or subject and suggest any changes or new laws that should be introduced

**Royal 'Highness** *noun* Her / His / Your Royal Highness a title of respect used when talking to or about a member of the royal family (apart from the queen or king, who is 'Her/His/Your Majesty'): *Their Royal Highnesses, the Duke and Duchess of Kent*

**roy·al·ist** /ˈrɔɪəlɪst/ *noun* a person who believes that a country should have a king or queen **SYN** monarchist ⇨ compare REPUBLICAN ▶ **roy·al·ist** *adj.*

**roy·al·ly** /ˈrɔɪəli/ *adv.* (*old-fashioned*) very well; in a very impressive way or to a great degree

**the Royal 'Mail** *noun* (in the UK) the service that collects and delivers letters

**roy·alty** /ˈrɔɪəlti/ *noun* (*pl.* **-ies**) **1** [U] one or more members of a royal family: *The gala evening was attended by royalty and politicians.* ◊ *We were treated like royalty.* **2** [C, usually pl.] a sum of money that is paid to sb who has written a book, piece of music, etc. each time that it is sold or performed: *All royalties from the album will go to charity.* ◊ **in royalties** *She received £2000 in royalties.* **3** [C, usually pl.] a sum of money that is paid by an oil or mining company to the owner of the land that they are working on

**royal 'warrant** *noun* [usually sing.] a king's or queen's permission for a company to supply goods to them and to advertise this fact on the company's products, etc.

**the royal "we'** *noun* [sing.] the use of 'we' instead of 'I' by a single person, as used traditionally by kings and queens in the past

**RP** /ˌɑː ˈpiː; *NAmE* ˌɑːr/ *noun* [U] a widely recognized accent of British English, associated with education, broadcasting and the South of England. (the abbreviation for 'received pronunciation')

**RPG** /ˌɑː piː ˈdʒiː; *NAmE* ˌɑːr/ *noun* = ROLE-PLAYING GAME

**RPI** /ˌɑː piː ˈaɪ; *NAmE* ˌɑːr/ *abbr.* RETAIL PRICE INDEX

**rpm** /ˌɑː piː ˈem; *NAmE* ˌɑːr/ *abbr.* revolutions per minute (a measurement of the speed of an engine, a computer HARD DRIVE, etc.)

**R-rated** *adj.* (*NAmE*) (of a movie) rated 'restricted', meaning that no one younger than 17 will be allowed to see it unless an adult goes with them: *R-rated films*

**RRP** /ˌɑːr ɑː ˈpiː; *NAmE* ˌɑːr/ *abbr.* recommended retail price

**RRSP** /ˌɑːr ɑːr es ˈpiː; *NAmE* ˌɑːr/ *abbr.* (*CanE*) registered retirement savings plan (a special type of savings plan in which you can save money without paying taxes on it until you stop working when you are older)

**RSI** /ˌɑːr es ˈaɪ/ *noun* [U] pain and SWELLING, especially in the arms and hands, caused by performing the same movement many times in a job or an activity (the abbreviation for 'repetitive strain injury' or 'repetitive stress injury')

**RSS** /ˌɑːr es ˈes/ *abbr.* (*computing*) Really Simple Syndication (a standard system for the distribution of information, especially news, from an internet publisher to internet users)

**RSVP** (*BrE*) (*also* **R.S.V.P.** *US, BrE*) /ˌɑːr es viː ˈpiː; *NAmE* ˌɑːr/ *abbr.* (written on invitations) please reply (from French 'répondez s'il vous plaît')

**RT** *abbr.* (in writing) RETWEET (used when you want to show that a message that you put on the Twitter SOCIAL MEDIA service was originally written by another person): *RT*

# RTA 1356

@EddieSmith Great new menu at the Burger Shack www.theburgershack.com

**RTA** /ˌɑː tiː ˈeɪ; *NAmE* ˌɑːr/ *abbr.* (*BrE*) road traffic accident

**RTF** /ˌɑː tiː ˈef; *NAmE* ˌɑːr/ *abbr.* (*computing*) rich text format (a type of file containing data that can be used with different programs or systems): *an RTF file*

**Rt Hon** *abbr.* (*BrE*) (in writing) RIGHT HONOURABLE

**Rt Revd** (*also* **Rt. Rev.**) *abbr.* (*BrE*) (in writing) RIGHT REVEREND

**rub** ⓘ B2 /rʌb/ *verb, noun*
- *verb* (**-bb-**) **1** B2 [T, I] to move your hand, a cloth, etc. backwards and forwards over a surface while pressing it: *~ sth He sat up on the hard bunk and rubbed his eyes.* ◊ *~ sth + adv./prep. He rubbed a hand wearily over his eyes.* ◊ *~ sth/yourself with sth Rub the surface with sandpaper before painting.* ◊ *~ sth/yourself against sth The cat rubbed itself against my legs.* ◊ *~ against sth Animals had been rubbing against the trees.* ◊ *~ sth/yourself + adj. Rub the surface smooth.* ◊ *~ + noun I rubbed a clear patch on the window with my fingers.* **2** B2 [T, I] to press two surfaces against each other and move them backwards and forwards; to be pressed together and move in this way: *~ (together) She rubbed her hands in delight.* ◊ *~ together It sounded like two pieces of wood rubbing together.* **3** B2 [I, T] (of a surface) to move backwards and forwards many times against sth while pressing it, especially causing pain or damage: *The back of my shoe is rubbing.* ◊ *~ on/against sth The wheel is rubbing on the mudguard.* ◊ *~ sth (+ adj.) The horse's neck was rubbed raw* (= until the skin came off) *where the rope had been.* **4** B2 [T] to spread a liquid or other substance over a surface while pressing it: *~ sth into/onto sth She rubbed the lotion into her skin.*
- IDM **rub sb's 'nose in it** (*informal*) to keep reminding sb in an unkind way of their past mistakes **rub ˈsalt into the wound | rub ˈsalt into sb's wounds** to make a difficult experience even more difficult for sb **rub ˈshoulders with sb** (*NAmE also* **rub ˈelbows with sb**) to meet and spend time with a famous person, socially or as part of your job **rub sb up the wrong ˈway** (*BrE*) (*NAmE* **rub sb the wrong ˈway**) (*informal*) to make sb annoyed or angry, often without intending to, by doing or saying sth that offends them ⊃ more at TWO
- PHRV **rub aˈlong (with sb/together)** (*BrE, informal*) (of two people) to live or work together in a friendly enough way **rub sb/yourself/sth↔ˈdown** to rub the skin of a person, horse, etc. hard with sth to make it clean and dry **rub sth↔ˈdown** to make sth smooth by rubbing it with a special material **rub it ˈin** | **rub sth ˈin** (no passive) to keep reminding sb of sth they feel embarrassed about and want to forget: *I know I was stupid; you don't have to rub it in.* **rub ˈoff (on/onto sb)** (of personal qualities, behaviour, opinions, etc.) to become part of a person's character as a result of that person spending time with sb who has those qualities, etc: *Her sense of fun has rubbed off on her children.* **rub sth↔ˈoff (sth) | rub ˈoff** to remove sth or to be removed by rubbing: *She rubbed off the dead skin.* ◊ *The gold colouring had begun to rub off.* ◊ (*BrE*) *If you write on the whiteboard, rub it off at the end of the lesson.* **rub sb↔ˈout** (*NAmE, slang*) to murder sb **rub sth↔ˈout** (*BrE*) (*also* **erase** *NAmE, BrE*) to remove the marks made by a pencil, etc., using a RUBBER: *to rub out a mistake*
- *noun* **1** [C, usually sing.] an act of rubbing a surface: *She gave her knee a quick rub.* **2** **the rub** [sing.] (*formal or humorous*) a problem or difficulty: *The hotel is in the middle of nowhere and there lies the rub. We don't have a car.*

**rub·ber** ⓘ B2 /ˈrʌbə(r)/ *noun, adj.*
- *noun* **1** B2 [U] a strong substance that can be stretched and does not allow liquids to pass through it, used for making tyres, boots, etc. It is made from the liquid (= SAP) inside a tropical plant or is produced using chemicals: *a ball made of rubber* ◊ *a rubber tree* ⊃ see also FOAM RUBBER *at* FOAM **2** [C] (*BrE*) (*also* **eraser** *NAmE, BrE*) a small piece of rubber or a similar substance, used for

removing pencil marks from paper; a piece of soft material used for removing CHALK marks from a BLACKBOARD or pen from a WHITEBOARD **3** [C] (*informal, especially NAmE*) = CONDOM **4** [C] (in some card games or sports) a competition consisting of a series of games or matches between the same teams or players
- IDM **where the ˌrubber meets the ˈroad** (*NAmE*) the point at which sth is tested and you really find out whether it is successful or true: *Here's where the rubber meets the road: will consumers actually buy the product?* ⊃ more at BURN *v.*
- *adj.* ⓘ B2 [usually before noun] made of rubber: *a rubber ball* ◊ *rubber gloves*

**ˌrubber ˈband** (*BrE also* **eˌlastic ˈband**) *noun* a thin round piece of rubber used for holding things together

**ˌrubber ˈboot** (*NAmE*) (*BrE* **ˈwelˑlingˑton**, **ˌwellington ˈboot**, *informal* **welly**) *noun* one of a pair of long rubber boots, usually reaching almost up to the knee, that you wear to stop your feet getting wet

**ˌrubber ˈbullet** *noun* a bullet made of rubber intended to injure but not to kill people, used by the army or police to control violent crowds

**ˌrubber ˈdinghy** *noun* a small boat made of rubber that is filled with air

**ˌrubber ˈduck** *noun* **1** a plastic toy in the shape of a duck, usually yellow, for playing with in the bath **2** (*SAfrE, informal*) a small boat made of rubber that is filled with air, especially one with a motor

**rub·ber·ized** (*BrE also* **-ised**) /ˈrʌbəraɪzd/ *adj.* [only before noun] covered with rubber: *rubberized cloth*

**ˌrubber ˈstamp** *noun* **1** a small tool that you hold in your hand and use for printing the date, the name of an organization, etc. on a document **2** (*disapproving*) a person or group that gives approval to the actions or decisions of others without considering them: *Parliament is seen as a rubber stamp for decisions made elsewhere.*

**ˌrubber-ˈstamp** *verb* *~ sth* (*often disapproving*) to give official approval to a law, plan, decision, etc., especially without considering it carefully

**rub·bery** /ˈrʌbəri/ *adj.* **1** looking or feeling like rubber: *The eggs were overcooked and rubbery.* ⊃ WORDFINDER NOTE *at* CRISP **2** (of legs or knees) feeling weak and unable to support your weight

**rub·bing** /ˈrʌbɪŋ/ *noun* a copy of writing or a design on a piece of stone or metal that is made by placing a piece of paper over it and rubbing with CHALK, a pencil, etc.

**ˈrubbing alcohol** (*NAmE*) (*BrE* **ˌsurgical ˈspirit**) *noun* [U] a clear liquid, consisting mainly of alcohol, used for cleaning wounds, etc.

**rub·bish** ⓘ A2 /ˈrʌbɪʃ/ *noun, verb*
- *noun* [U] **1** A2 (*especially BrE*) things that you throw away because you no longer want or need them: *a rubbish bag/bin* ◊ *a rubbish dump/heap/tip* ◊ *The streets were littered with rubbish.* ◊ *garden/household rubbish* ⊃ WORDFINDER NOTE *at* WASTE ⊃ see also GARBAGE, TRASH *noun* **2** B1 (*BrE, informal*) (also used as an adjective) something that you think is of poor quality: *I thought the play was rubbish!* ◊ *Do we have to listen to this rubbish music?* **3** B1 (*BrE, informal*) comments, ideas, etc. that you think are stupid or wrong SYN **nonsense**: *Rubbish! You're not fat.* ◊ *You're talking a load of rubbish—it's true!*
- *verb* (*BrE*) (*NAmE* **trash**) *~ sb/sth* to criticize sb/sth severely or treat them as though they are of no value

**rub·bishy** /ˈrʌbɪʃi/ *adj.* (*BrE, informal*) of very poor quality SYN **trashy**: *rubbishy old films*

**rub·ble** /ˈrʌbl/ *noun* [U] broken stones, etc. from a building or wall that has been destroyed or damaged: *The bomb reduced the houses to rubble.* ⊃ WORDFINDER NOTE *at* CONSTRUCTION

**ˈrub-down** *noun* **1** the act of rubbing sb/sth with a cloth or special material, for example to make a person dry or to make sth dry, clean or smooth: *You may need to give the*

### BRITISH/AMERICAN
**rubbish / garbage / trash / refuse**
- **Rubbish** is the usual word in *BrE* for the things that you throw away because you no longer want or need them. **Garbage** and **trash** are both used in *NAmE*. Inside the home, **garbage** tends to mean waste food and other wet material, while **trash** is paper, card and dry material.
- In *BrE*, you put your **rubbish** in a **dustbin** in the street to be collected by the **dustmen**. In *NAmE*, your **garbage** and **trash** goes in a **garbage can / trashcan** in the street and is collected by **garbage men / collectors**.
- **Refuse** is a formal word and is used in both *BrE* and *NAmE*. **Refuse collector** is the formal word for a dustman or garbage collector.

floor a rub-down with glasspaper. **2** (*NAmE*) the act of rubbing and pressing a person's body with the hands to reduce pain in the muscles and JOINTS SYN **massage**

**Rube Gold·berg** /ˌruːb ˈɡəʊldbɜːɡ; *NAmE* -bɜːrɡ/ (*NAmE*) (*BrE* **Heath Rob·in·son**) *adj.* [only before noun] (*humorous*) (of machines and devices) having a very complicated design, especially when used to perform a very simple task; not practical

**ru·bella** /ruːˈbelə/ *noun* [U] (*medical*) = GERMAN MEASLES

**the Ru·bi·con** /ðə ˈruːbɪkən; *NAmE* -kɑːn/ *noun* [sing.] the point at which a decision has been taken which can no longer be changed: *Today we cross the Rubicon. There is no going back.* ORIGIN From the *Rubicon*, a stream which formed the border between Italy and Gaul. When Julius Caesar broke the law by crossing it with his army in 49BC, it led inevitably to war.

**ru·bid·ium** /ruːˈbɪdiəm/ *noun* [U] (*symb.* **Rb**) a chemical element. Rubidium is a rare soft silver-coloured metal that reacts strongly with water and burns when it is brought into contact with air.

**Rubik's Cube™** /ˈruːbɪks kjuːb/ *noun* a PUZZLE consisting of a plastic CUBE covered with coloured squares that you turn to make each side of the cube a different colour

**ruble** (especially *NAmE*) = ROUBLE

**ru·bric** /ˈruːbrɪk/ *noun* (*formal*) a title or set of instructions written in a book, an exam paper, etc.

**ruby** /ˈruːbi/ *noun* (*pl.* **-ies**) **1** [C, U] a dark red PRECIOUS STONE: *a ruby ring* **2** [U] a dark red colour ▶ **ruby** *adj.*: *ruby lips*

**ruby 'wedding** (*BrE*) (*US* ˌruby anni'versary) (*also* ˌruby 'wedding anniversary *US*, *BrE*) *noun* the 40th anniversary of a wedding ⇨ compare DIAMOND WEDDING, GOLDEN WEDDING, SILVER WEDDING

**ruched** /ruːʃt/ *adj.* (of cloth, clothes, etc.) SEWN so that they hang in folds: *ruched curtains*

**ruck** /rʌk/ *noun, verb*
■ *noun* **1** [C] (in rugby) a group of players who gather round the ball when it is lying on the ground and push each other in order to get the ball **2** [sing.] a group of people standing closely together or fighting **3 the ruck** [sing.] (*disapproving*) ordinary people or events: *She saw marriage to him as a way out of the ruck.*
■ *verb* [I] (in rugby) to take part in a ruck
PHRV ˌruck 'up | ˌruck sth↔'up (of cloth) to form untidy folds; to make sth do this: *Your dress is rucked up at the back.*

**ruck·sack** /ˈrʌksæk/ (*BrE*) (*also* **back·pack** *NAmE*, *BrE*) *noun* a bag that you carry on your back, made of strong material and often used by people who go climbing or walking

**ruckus** /ˈrʌkəs/ *noun* [sing.] (especially *NAmE*, *informal*) a situation in which there is a lot of noise, activity and argument SYN **commotion**

**ruc·tions** /ˈrʌkʃnz/ *noun* [pl.] (especially *BrE*) angry protests or arguments: *There'll be ructions if her father ever finds out.*

**rud·der** /ˈrʌdə(r)/ *noun* a piece of wood or metal at the back of a boat or an aircraft that is used for controlling its direction

---

**rud·der·less** /ˈrʌdələs; *NAmE* -dərl-/ *adj.* (*formal*) with nobody in control; not knowing what to do

**ruddy** /ˈrʌdi/ *adj., adv.*
■ *adj.* **1** (of a person's face) looking red and healthy: *ruddy cheeks* ◊ *a ruddy complexion* **2** (*literary*) red in colour: *a ruddy sky* **3** [only before noun] (*BrE*, *informal*) a mild swear word that some people use to show that they are annoyed: *I can't get the ruddy car to start!*
■ *adv.* (*BrE*, *informal*) a mild swear word used by some people to emphasize what they are saying, especially when they are annoyed: *There was a ruddy great hole in the ceiling.*

**rude** ⓘ A2 /ruːd/ *adj.* (**ruder**, **rud·est**) **1** A2 having or showing a lack of respect for other people and their feelings SYN **impolite**: *a rude comment/remark* ◊ *She is bossy, rude and arrogant.* ◊ *~to sb The man was downright rude to us.* ◊ *~(to sb) about sth She was very rude about my driving.* ◊ *~to do sth It's rude to speak when you're eating.* **2** (*especially BrE*) (*NAmE* usually **crude**) connected with sex or the body in a way that people find offensive or embarrassing: *a rude gesture* ◊ *Someone made a rude noise.* ◊ *The joke is too rude to repeat.* **3** [only before noun] (*formal*) sudden, unpleasant and unexpected: *Those expecting good news will get a rude shock.* ◊ *If the players think they can win this match easily, they are in for a rude awakening.* **4** (*literary*) made in a simple, basic way SYN **primitive**: *rude shacks* ▶ **rude·ness** *noun* [U]: *She was critical to the point of rudeness.*
IDM in rude 'health (*BrE*, *old-fashioned*) looking or feeling very healthy

### ▼ SYNONYMS
**rude**
cheeky • insolent • disrespectful • impolite • impertinent • discourteous

These are all words for people showing a lack of respect for other people.

**rude** having or showing a lack of respect for other people and their feelings: *Why are you so rude to your mother?* ◊ *It's rude to speak when you're eating.*

**cheeky** (*BrE*, *informal*) (especially of children) rude in a funny or an annoying way: *You cheeky monkey!* ◊ *a cheeky grin*

**insolent** (*rather formal*) very rude, especially to sb who is older or more important NOTE **Insolent** is used especially to talk about the behaviour of children towards adults.

**disrespectful** (*rather formal*) showing a lack of respect for sb / sth: *Some people said he had been disrespectful to the president in his last speech.*

**impolite** (*rather formal*) not behaving in a pleasant way that follows the rules of society: *Some people think it is impolite to ask someone's age.* NOTE **Impolite** is often used in the phrases *It seemed impolite* and *It would be impolite*.

**impertinent** (*rather formal*) not showing respect for sb who is older or more important NOTE **Impertinent** is often used by people such as parents and teachers when they are telling children that they are angry with them for being rude: *Don't be impertinent!*

**discourteous** (*formal*) having bad manners and not showing respect: *He didn't wish to appear discourteous.*

**PATTERNS**
- rude / cheeky / disrespectful / impolite / discourteous **to** sb
- rude / impolite / impertinent **to do sth**

**rude·ly** /ˈruːdli/ *adv.* **1** in a way that shows a lack of respect for other people and their feelings: *They brushed rudely past us.* ◊ *'What do you want?' she asked rudely.* **2** in a way that is sudden, unpleasant and unexpected: *I was rudely awakened by the phone ringing.*

**ru·di·men·tary** /ˌruːdɪˈmentri/ *adj.* **1** (*formal*) dealing with only the most basic matters or ideas SYN **basic**: *They were given only rudimentary training in the job.* **2** (*formal or*

# rudiments

*specialist*) not highly or fully developed **SYN** **basic**: *Some dinosaurs had only rudimentary teeth.*

**ru·di·ments** /ˈruːdɪmənts/ *noun* [pl.] **the ~ (of sth)** (*formal*) the most basic or essential facts of a particular subject, skill, etc. **SYN** **basics**

**rue** /ruː/ *verb* (**rue·ing**, **ruing**, **rued**, **rued**) ~ sth (*old-fashioned or formal*) to feel bad about sth that happened or sth that you did because it had bad results **SYN** **regret**: *He rued the day they had bought such a large house.*

**rue·ful** /ˈruːfl/ *adj.* feeling or showing that you are sad or sorry: *a rueful smile* ▶ **rue·ful·ly** /-fəli/ *adv.*: *'So this is goodbye,' she said ruefully.*

**ruff** /rʌf/ *noun* **1** a ring of coloured or marked feathers or fur around the neck of a bird or an animal **2** a wide stiff white COLLAR with many folds in it, worn especially in the 16th and 17th centuries

**ruf·fian** /ˈrʌfiən/ *noun* (*old-fashioned*) a violent man, especially one who commits crimes **SYN** **thug**

**ruf·fle** /ˈrʌfl/ *verb, noun*
■ *verb* **1** to alter the smooth surface of sth, so that it is not even: ~ *sth She ruffled his hair affectionately.* ◊ ~ *sth up The bird ruffled up its feathers.* **2** (often *passive*) ~ sb to make sb annoyed, worried or upset **SYN** **fluster**: *She was obviously ruffled by his question.* ◊ *He never gets ruffled, even under pressure.*
**IDM** **ruffle sb's/a few ˈfeathers** (*informal*) to annoy or upset sb or a group of people: *The senator's speech ruffled a few feathers in the business world.* ⮕ more at SMOOTH *v.*
■ *noun* [usually pl.] a narrow piece of cloth that is SEWN in folds and is used to decorate a piece of clothing at the neck or WRISTS **SYN** **frill**

**ruf·fled** /ˈrʌfld/ *adj.* decorated with ruffles **SYN** **frilled**: *a ruffled blouse*

**rug** /rʌɡ/ *noun* **1** a piece of thick material like a small carpet that is used for covering or decorating part of a floor: *a hearth rug* (= in front of a FIREPLACE) **2** (*BrE*) a piece of thick warm material, like a BLANKET, that is used for wrapping around your legs to keep warm **3** (*informal, humorous*) = TOUPEE **IDM** SEE PULL *v.*, SWEEP *v.*

**rugby** ⓘ B1 (*sometimes* **Rugby**) /ˈrʌɡbi/ (*also* **rugby ˈfootball**) *noun* [U] a game played by two teams of 13 or 15 players, using an OVAL ball which may be kicked or carried. Teams try to put the ball over the other team's line: *to play a game of rugby* ◊ *a rugby club/match/player/team* **ORIGIN** Named after Rugby school, where the game was first played.

**ˌRugby ˈLeague** *noun* [U] a form of rugby, with 13 players in a team

**ˌRugby ˈUnion** (*also informal* **ˈrug·ger** *especially in BrE*) *noun* [U] a form of rugby, with 15 players in a team

**rug·ged** /ˈrʌɡɪd/ *adj.* **1** (of the landscape) not level or smooth and having rocks rather than plants or trees: *rugged cliffs* ◊ *They admired the rugged beauty of the coastline.* ⮕ WORDFINDER NOTE at LANDSCAPE **2** [usually before *noun*] (*approving*) (of a man's face) having strong, attractive features **3** [usually before *noun*] (of a person) determined to succeed in a difficult situation, even if this means using force or upsetting other people: *a rugged individualist* **4** (of equipment, clothing, etc.) strong and designed to be used in difficult conditions: *A less rugged vehicle would never have made the trip.* ◊ *rugged outdoor clothing* ▶ **rug·ged·ly** *adv.*: *ruggedly handsome* **rug·ged·ness** *noun* [U]

**rug·ger** /ˈrʌɡə(r)/ *noun* (*informal, especially in BrE*) = RUGBY UNION

**ruin** /ˈruːɪn/ *verb, noun*
■ *verb* **1** ~ sth to damage sth so badly that it loses all its value, pleasure, etc. **SYN** **spoil, wreck**: *The bad weather ruined our trip.* ◊ *That one mistake ruined his chances of getting the job.* ◊ *My new shoes got ruined in the mud.* **2** ~ sb/sth to make sb/sth lose all their money, their position, etc: *If she loses the court case it will ruin her.* ◊ *The country was ruined by the war.*
■ *noun* **1** [U] the state or process of being destroyed or severely damaged: *A large number of churches fell into ruin after the revolution.* **2** [C] (*also* **ruins** [pl.]) the parts of a building that remain after it has been destroyed or severely damaged: *The old mill is now little more than a ruin.* ◊ *We visited the ruins of a Norman castle.* ◊ (*figurative*) *He was determined to build a new life out of the ruins of his career.* **3** [U] the fact of having no money, of having lost your job, position, etc: *The divorce ultimately led to his ruin.* ◊ *The bank stepped in to save the company from financial ruin.* **4** [sing.] something that causes a person, company, etc. to lose all their money, job, position, etc. **SYN** **downfall**: *Gambling was his ruin.*
**IDM** **in ˈruins** destroyed or severely damaged: *Years of fighting have left the area in ruins.* ◊ *The scandal left his reputation in ruins.* ⮕ more at RACK *n.*

**ruin·ation** /ˌruːɪˈneɪʃn/ *noun* [U] (*formal*) the process of destroying sth/sb or being destroyed **SYN** **destruction**: *Urban development has led to the ruination of vast areas of countryside.*

**ru·ined** /ˈruːɪnd/ *adj.* [only before *noun*] (of a building, town, etc.) destroyed or severely damaged so that only parts remain: *a ruined castle*

**ruin·ous** /ˈruːɪnəs/ *adj.* (*formal*) **1** costing a lot of money and more than you can afford: *ruinous legal fees* **2** causing serious problems or damage **SYN** **devastating**: *The decision was to prove ruinous.* **3** (of a town, building, etc.) destroyed or severely damaged: *The buildings were in a ruinous state.* ▶ **ruin·ous·ly** *adv.*: *ruinously expensive*

**rule** ⓘ A1 ⓞ /ruːl/ *noun, verb*
■ *noun*
• **OF ACTIVITY/GAME 1** A1 [C] a statement of what may, must or must not be done in a particular situation or when playing a game: *She laid down strict rules for her tenants, including prompt payment of rent.* ◊ *the rules of golf/tennis/football* ◊ *to follow/obey a rule* ◊ *to break/violate a rule* ◊ *to enforce/apply a rule* ◊ *You can't just change the rules to suit yourself.* ◊ **against the rules** *It's against all the rules and regulations.* ◊ **under ... rules** *These products are banned under international rules.* ⮕ see also GROUND RULE
• **OF SYSTEM 2** A1 [C] a statement of what is possible according to a particular system, for example the grammar of a language: *the basic rules of grammar*
• **ADVICE 3** B1 [C] a statement of what you are advised to do in a particular situation: *The first rule is to make eye contact with your interviewer.* ◊ ~ **for doing sth** *There are no hard and fast rules for planning healthy meals.* ⮕ see also GOLDEN RULE
• **HABIT/NORMALLY TRUE 4** [C, usually *sing.*] a habit; the normal state of things; what is true in most cases: *He makes it a rule never to borrow money.* ◊ *Cold winters here are the exception rather than the rule* (= are rare).
• **GOVERNMENT/CONTROL 5** B2 [U] the government of a country or control of a group of people by a particular person, group or system: *military/civilian/democratic rule* ◊ **under ... ~** *The country was still under colonial rule.* ◊ **majority rule** (= government by the political party that most people have voted for) ⮕ WORDFINDER NOTE at FREEDOM ⮕ see also HOME RULE, SELF-RULE
• **MEASURING TOOL 6** [C] a measuring instrument with a straight edge ⮕ see also SLIDE RULE
**IDM** **as a (general) ˈrule** usually but not always: *I go to bed early as a rule.* ◊ *As a general rule, vegetable oils are better for you than animal fats.* **bend/stretch the ˈrules** to change the rules to suit a particular person or situation **play by sb's (own) ˈrules** if sb *plays by their own rules* or makes other people *play by their rules*, they set the conditions for doing business or having a relationship **play by the ˈrules** to deal fairly and honestly with people **the rule of ˈlaw** the condition in which all members of society, including its political leaders, accept the authority of the law **a rule of ˈthumb** a practical method of doing or measuring sth, usually based on past experience rather than on exact measurement **the rules of the ˈgame** the standards of behaviour that most people accept or that actually operate in a particular area of life or business **work to ˈrule** to follow the rules of your job in a very strict way in order to cause delay, as a form of protest

æ cat | ɑː father | e bed | ɜː fur | ə about | ɪ sit | iː see | i happy | ɒ got (*BrE*) | ɔː saw | ʌ cup | ʊ put | uː too

against your employer or your working conditions ⊃ see also WORK-TO-RULE ⊃ more at EXCEPTION
- verb
- GOVERN/CONTROL **1** [T, I] to control and have authority over a country, a group of people, etc: **~(sth)** *At that time, King John ruled England.* ◇ *The film is set in an imagined future in which machines rule the world.* ◇ *(figurative) Eighty million years ago, dinosaurs ruled the earth.* ◇ *(figurative) After the revolution, anarchy ruled.* ◇ **~over sb/sth** *She once ruled over a vast empire.* **2** [T, often passive] **~sth** (*often disapproving*) to be the main thing that influences and controls sb/sth: *The pursuit of money ruled his life.* ◇ *We live in a society where we are ruled by the clock.*
- GIVE OFFICIAL DECISION **3** [I, T] to give an official decision about sth pronounce: **~on sth** *The court will rule on the legality of the action.* ◇ **~against/in favour of sb/sth** *The judge ruled against/in favour of the plaintiff.* ◇ **~sb/sth + adj.** *The deal may be ruled illegal.* ◇ **~sb/sth to be/have sth** *The deal was ruled to be illegal.* ◇ **~that...** *The court ruled that the women were unfairly dismissed.* ◇ **it is ruled that...** *It was ruled that the women had been unfairly dismissed.*
- DRAW STRAIGHT LINE **4** [T] **~sth** to draw a straight line using sth that has a hard straight edge: *Rule a line at the end of every piece of work.*

IDM **rule the ˈroost** (*informal*) to be the most powerful member of a group **rule (sb/sth) with a rod of ˈiron** to control a person or a group of people very severely ⊃ more at COURT *n.*, DIVIDE *v.*, HEART *n.*
PHRV **ˌrule ˈoff** | **ˌrule sth↔ˈoff** to separate sth from the next section of writing by drawing a line below it **ˌrule sb/sth↔ˈout 1** rule sb/sth out (as sth) to state that sth is not possible or that sb/sth is not suitable exclude: *Police have not ruled out the possibility that the man was murdered.* ◇ *The proposed solution was ruled out as too expensive.* **2** to prevent sb from doing sth; to prevent sth from happening: *His age effectively ruled him out as a possible candidate.* **ˌrule sb ˈout of sth** [*usually passive*] (*in sport*) to state that a player, runner, etc. will not be able to take part in a sporting event; to prevent a player from taking part: *He has been ruled out of the match with a knee injury.*

ˈrule book *noun* (*usually* **the rule book**) the set of rules that must be followed in a particular job, organization or game

ruled /ruːld/ *adj.* ruled paper has lines printed across it

ruler /ˈruːlə(r)/ *noun* **1** a person who rules or governs **2** a straight narrow piece of wood, plastic or metal, marked in CENTIMETRES or inches, used for measuring or for drawing straight lines

ˈrul·ing C1 /ˈruːlɪŋ/ *noun, adj.*
- *noun* **1** **~(on sth)** an official decision made by sb in a position of authority, especially a judge: *The court will make its ruling on the case next week.*
- *adj.* [*only before noun*] having control over a particular group, country, etc: *the ruling party* ◇ *the ruling class/elite*

rum /rʌm/ *noun, adj.*
- *noun* **1** [U, C] a strong alcoholic drink made from the juice of SUGAR CANE **2** [C] a glass of rum
- *adj.* [*usually before noun*] (*BrE, old-fashioned, informal*) strange odd, peculiar

rumba (*also* rhumba) /ˈrʌmbə/ *noun* a fast dance originally from Cuba; a piece of music for this dance

rum·ble /ˈrʌmbl/ *verb, noun*
- *verb* **1** [I] to make a long deep sound or series of sounds: *The machine rumbled as it started up.* ◇ *thunder rumbling in the distance* ◇ *I'm so hungry my stomach's rumbling.* **2** [I] + adv./prep. to move slowly and heavily, making a rumbling sound: *tanks rumbling through the streets* **3** [T] **~sb** (*BrE, informal*) to discover the truth about sb or what they are trying to hide: *They knew they had been rumbled.* **4** [I] (*NAmE, informal*) (of a gang of young people) to fight against another gang
PHRV **ˈrumble on** (*especially BrE*) (of an argument, a disagreement, etc.) to continue slowly and steadily for a long time: *Discussions rumble on over the siting of the new airport.*

- *noun* **1** [U, C] **~(of sth)** a long deep sound or series of sounds: *the rumble of thunder* ◇ *Inside, the noise of the traffic was reduced to a distant rumble.* ◇ (*figurative*) *Although an agreement has been reached, rumbles of resentment can still be heard.* **2** [C] (*NAmE, informal*) a fight in the street between two or more gangs

ˈrumble strip *noun* (*informal*) a series of raised narrow areas across a road or along its edge that make a loud noise when a vehicle drives over them in order to warn the driver to go slower or that he or she is too close to the edge of the road

rum·bling /ˈrʌmblɪŋ/ *noun* **1** (also used as an adjective) a long deep sound or series of sounds: *the rumblings of thunder* ◇ *a rumbling noise* ◇ (*figurative*) *the rumblings of discontent* **2** [*usually pl.*] things that people are saying that may not be true rumour: *There are rumblings that the election may have to be postponed.*

rum·bus·tious /rʌmˈbʌstʃəs/ (*especially BrE*) (*NAmE usually* ram·bunc·tious) *adj.* [*usually before noun*] (*informal*) full of energy in a cheerful and noisy way boisterous

ru·min·ant /ˈruːmɪnənt/ *noun* (*specialist*) any animal that brings back food from its stomach to its mouth and CHEWS it again. Cows and sheep are both ruminants. ▶ ru·min·ant *adj.*: ruminant animals

ru·min·ate /ˈruːmɪneɪt/ *verb* [I, T] **~(on/over/about sth)** | **+ speech** (*formal*) to think deeply about sth ponder ▶ ru·min·ation /ˌruːmɪˈneɪʃn/ *noun* [C, U]

ru·mina·tive /ˈruːmɪnətɪv; *NAmE* -neɪt-/ *adj.* (*formal*) tending to think deeply and carefully about things pensive, thoughtful: *in a ruminative mood* ▶ ru·mina·tive·ly *adv.*

rum·mage /ˈrʌmɪdʒ/ *verb, noun*
- *verb* [I] + adv./prep. to move things around carelessly while searching for sth: *She was rummaging around in her bag for her keys.* ◇ *I rummaged through the contents of the box until I found the book I wanted.*
- *noun* [*sing.*] the act of looking for sth among a group of other objects in a way that makes them untidy: *Have a rummage around in the drawer and see if you can find a pen.*

ˈrummage sale *noun* (*especially NAmE*) (*BrE usually* **ˈjumble sale**) *noun* a sale of old or used clothes, etc. to make money for a church, school or other organization ⊃ compare GARAGE SALE, YARD SALE

rummy /ˈrʌmi/ *noun* [U] a simple card game in which players try to collect particular combinations of cards

ru·mour C1 (*US* rumor) /ˈruːmə(r)/ *noun, verb*
- *noun* C1 [C, U] a piece of information, or a story, that people talk about, but that may not be true: *to start/spread a rumour* ◇ **~of sth** *There are widespread rumours of job losses.* ◇ **~about sth** *Some malicious rumours are circulating about his past.* ◇ **~that...** *I heard a rumour that they are getting married.* ◇ *Many of the stories are based on rumour.* ◇ **Rumour has it** (= people say) *that he was murdered.*
- *verb* **be rumoured** to be reported as a rumour and possibly not true: *it is rumoured that...* *It's widely rumoured that she's getting promoted.* ◇ **~to be/have sth** *He was rumoured to be involved in the crime.* ▶ ru·moured *adj.* [*only before noun*]: *He denied his father's rumoured love affair.*

ˈrumour mill (*US* ˈrumor mill) *noun* used to refer to the process by which rumours and GOSSIP are started and spread among a group of people: *The rumour mill has been churning out* (= producing) *reports that they're getting a divorce.*

rump /rʌmp/ *noun* **1** [C] the round area at the top of the back legs of an animal that has four legs **2** [U] (*also* **ˈrump ˈsteak** [C, U]) a piece of good quality meat cut from the rump of a cow **3** [C, *usually sing.*] (*humorous*) the part of the body that you sit on backside **4** [*sing.*] (*BrE*) the small or unimportant part of a group or an organization that remains when most of its members have left

**rum·ple** /ˈrʌmpl/ verb ~ sth to make sth untidy or not smooth and neat: *She rumpled his hair playfully.* ◊ *The bed was rumpled where he had slept.*

**rum·pus** /ˈrʌmpəs/ noun [usually sing.] (*informal*) a lot of noise that is made especially by people who are complaining about sth ⟨SYN⟩ **commotion**: *to cause a rumpus*

**run** ⓘ A1 /rʌn/ verb, noun

■ verb (**running, ran** /ræn/, **run**)

- **MOVE FAST ON FOOT 1** A1 [I] to move using your legs, going faster than when you walk: *Can you run as fast as Mike?* ◊ *They turned and ran when they saw us coming.* ◊ *She came running to meet us.* ◊ + adv./prep. *The dogs ran off as soon as we appeared.* **HELP** In spoken English *run* can be used with **and** plus another verb, instead of with **to** and the infinitive, especially to tell somebody to hurry and do something: *Run and get your swimsuits, kids.* ◊ *I ran and knocked on the nearest door.* **2** A1 ~ sth to travel a particular distance by running: *Who was the first person to run a mile in under four minutes?* ⊃ see also MILE **3** A1 [I] (*sometimes* **go running**) to run as a sport: *She used to run when she was at college.* ◊ *I often go running before work.*
- **RACE 4** A1 [I, T] to take part in a race: ~ in sth *He will be running in the 100 metres tonight.* ◊ *There are only five horses running in the first race.* ◊ ~ sth *to run a marathon* ◊ *Farah ran a fine race to take the gold medal.* ⊃ see also RUNNER (1) **5** [T, often passive] ~ sth to make a race take place: *The Derby will be run in spite of the bad weather.*
- **HURRY 6** [I] + adv./prep. to hurry from one place to another: *I've spent the whole day running around after the kids.* ⊃ see also RAT RUN
- **MANAGE 7** B1 [T] ~ sth to be in charge of a business, campaign, etc: *to run a hotel/store/language school* ◊ *He has no idea how to run a business.* ◊ *Stop trying to run my life* (= organize it) *for me.* ◊ *The shareholders want more say in how the company is run.* ◊ *Both candidates have run a good campaign.* ◊ *state-run industries* ⊃ see also RUNNING noun (2)
- **PROVIDE 8** B2 [T] ~ sth to make a service, course of study, etc. available to people ⟨SYN⟩ **organize**: *The college runs summer courses for foreign students.*
- **BUSES/TRAINS 9** B1 [I] to travel on a particular route: *Buses to Oxford run every half hour.* ◊ + adv./prep. *All the trains are running late* (= are leaving later than planned). **10** [T] ~ sth (+ adv./prep.) to make buses, trains, etc. travel on a particular route: *They run extra trains during the rush hour.*
- **VEHICLE/MACHINE 11** B2 [I, T] to operate or function; to make sth do this: *Stan had the chainsaw running.* ◊ ~ on sth *Our van runs on* (= uses) *diesel.* ◊ ~ sth *Could you run the engine for a moment?* **12** [I, T] when a computer program or system **runs** or sb **runs** it, it operates: *You may find that some apps are running slowly.* ◊ *There are too many programs running on your computer.* ◊ ~ sth *You can run the program overnight.* ◊ *My PC runs Windows 10.* **13** [I, T] if a recording on a tape **runs** or sb **runs** it, it plays: *He didn't know the tape was still running.* ◊ ~ sth (+ adv./prep.) *Can you run the tape back a few minutes?* **14** [T] ~ sth (*BrE*) to own and use a vehicle or machine: *I can't afford to run a car on my salary.*
- **DRIVE SB 15** [T] ~ sb + adv./prep. (*informal*) to drive sb to a place in a car: *Shall I run you home?*
- **MOVE SOMEWHERE 16** B2 [I] + adv./prep. to move, especially in a particular direction: *The car ran off the road into a ditch.* ◊ *A shiver ran down my spine.* ◊ *The sledge ran smoothly over the frozen snow.* ◊ *The old tramlines are still there but now no trams run on them.* **17** B2 [T] ~ sth + adv./prep. to move sth in a particular direction: *She ran her fingers nervously through her hair.* ◊ *I ran my eyes over the page.*
- **LEAD/STRETCH 18** B2 [I, T] to lead or stretch from one place to another; to make sth do this: + adv./prep. *He had a scar running down his left cheek.* ◊ *The road runs parallel to the river.* ◊ ~ sth (+ adv./prep.) *We ran a cable from the lights to the stage.*
- **LIQUID 19** B2 [I] + adv./prep. to flow: *The tears ran down her cheeks.* ◊ *Water was running all over the bathroom floor.* **20** [T] to make liquid flow: ~ sth (into sth) *She ran hot water into the bucket.* ◊ *to run the hot tap* (= to turn it so that water flows from it) ◊ ~ sth for sb *I'll run a bath for you.* ◊ ~ sb sth *I'll run you a bath.* **21** B2 [I] to send out a liquid: *Who left the tap running?* ◊ *Your nose is running* (= MUCUS *is flowing from it*). ◊ *The smoke makes my eyes run.* **22** [I] (usually used in the progressive tenses) ~ with sth to be covered with a liquid: *His face was running with sweat.* ◊ *The bathroom floor was running with water.*
- **OF COLOUR 23** [I] if the colour **runs** in a piece of clothing, etc. when it gets wet, the colour comes out of the material and spreads into other pieces of clothing, etc. in the same water: *The colour ran and made all my underwear pink.*
- **MELT 24** [I] (of a solid substance) to melt: *The wax began to run.* ⊃ see also RUNNY
- **BE/BECOME 25** B2 [I] + adj. to become different in a particular way, especially a bad way: *The river ran dry* (= stopped flowing) *during the drought.* ◊ *Supplies are running low.* ◊ *We've run short of milk.* ◊ *You've got your rivals running scared.* **26** [I] ~ at sth to be at or near a particular level: *Inflation was running at 26 per cent.*
- **CONTINUE FOR TIME 27** [I] ~ (for sth) to continue for a particular period of time without stopping: *Her last musical ran for six months on Broadway.* ◊ *This debate will run and run!* **28** [I] ~ (for sth) to operate or be legally acceptable for a particular period of time: *The permit runs for three months.* ◊ *The lease on my house only has a year left to run.*
- **HAPPEN 29** [I] (usually used in the progressive tenses) to happen or progress at the time or in the way mentioned: + adv./prep. *Programmes are running a few minutes behind schedule this evening.* ◊ *Her life had always run smoothly before.* ◊ *The murderer was given three life sentences, to run concurrently.*
- **IN ELECTION 30** B2 [I] to be a candidate in an election for a political position, especially in the US: *Obama ran a second time in 2012.* ◊ ~ for sb/sth *to run for president* ◊ ~ in sth *to run in the election* ⊃ compare STAND
- **GUNS, DRUGS, ETC. 31** [T] ~ sth (+ adv./prep.) to bring or take sth into a country illegally and secretly ⟨SYN⟩ **smuggle**: *He used to run guns across the border.* ⊃ see also RUNNER
- **OF STORY/ARGUMENT 32** [I, T] to have particular words, contents, etc: *Their argument ran something like this ...* ◊ + speech *'Ten shot dead by gunmen,' ran the newspaper headline.*
- **OF NEWSPAPER/MAGAZINE 33** [T] ~ sth to print and publish an item or a story: *On advice from their lawyers they decided not to run the story.*
- **A TEST/CHECK 34** [T] ~ a test, a check, an experiment, etc. to do a test, an experiment, etc: ~ sth (on sth) *The doctors decided to run some more tests on the blood samples.*
- **OF TIGHTS/STOCKINGS 35** [I] (*NAmE*) if TIGHTS or STOCKINGS **run**, a long thin hole appears in them ⟨SYN⟩ **ladder**

⟨IDM⟩ **HELP** Most idioms containing **run** are at the entries for the nouns and adjectives in the idioms, for example **run riot** is at *riot*. **come ˈrunning** to be pleased to do what sb wants: *She knew she had only to call and he would come running.* **ˈrun for it** (often used in orders) to run in order to escape from sb/sth **up and ˈrunning** working fully and correctly: *It will be a lot easier when we have the database up and running.*

⟨PHRV⟩ **ˌrun aˈcross sb/sth** to meet sb or find sth by chance **ˌrun ˈafter sb** (*informal*) to try to have a romantic or sexual relationship with sb ⟨SYN⟩ **pursue**: *He's always running after younger women.* **ˌrun ˈafter sb/sth** to run to try to catch sb/sth ⟨SYN⟩ **pursue**
**ˌrun aˈlong** (*old-fashioned, informal*) used in orders to tell sb, especially a child, to go away
**ˌrun aˈround with sb** (*NAmE also* **ˌrun ˈwith sb**) (*usually disapproving*) to spend a lot of time with sb: *She's always running around with older men.*
**ˌrun ˈat sb** [no passive] to run towards sb to attack or as if to attack them: *He ran at me with a knife.*
**ˌrun aˈway (from sb/ ...)** to leave sb/a place suddenly; to escape from sb/a place: *He ran away from home at the age of thirteen.* ◊ *Looking at all the accusing faces, she felt a sudden urge to run away.* ⊃ related noun RUNAWAY **ˌrun aˈway from sth** to try to avoid sth because you are shy, lack confidence, etc: *You can't just run away from the situation.* **ˌrun aˈway with you** if a feeling **runs away**

**with you**, it gets out of your control: *Her imagination tends to run away with her.* ˌrun aˈway/ˈoff with sb | ˌrun aˈway/ˈoff (together) to leave home, your husband, wife, etc. in order to have a relationship with another person: *She ran away with the next-door neighbour.* ◊ *She and the next-door neighbour ran away together.* ˌrun aˈway with sth **1** to win sth clearly or easily **2** to believe sth that is not true: *I don't want you to run away with the impression that all I do is have meetings all day.* ˌrun back ˈover sth to discuss or consider sth again ⓢⓨⓝ review: *I'll run back over the procedure once again.* ˌrun sth ˈby/ˈpast sb (*informal*) to show sb sth or tell sb about an idea in order to see their reaction to it ˌrun ˈdown **1** to lose power or stop working: *The battery has run down.* **2** to gradually stop functioning or become smaller in size or number: *British manufacturing industry has been running down for years.* ⊃ related noun RUNDOWN ˌrun sth↔ˈdown **1** to make sth lose power or stop working: *If you leave your headlights on you'll soon run down the battery.* **2** to make sth gradually stop functioning or become smaller in size or number: *The company is running down its sales force.* ⊃ related noun RUNDOWN ˌrun sb/sth↔ˈdown **1** (of a vehicle or its driver) to hit sb/sth and knock them/it to the ground **2** to criticize sb/sth in an unkind way: *He's always running her down in front of other people.* **3** to find sb/sth after a search ˌrun sb↔ˈin (*old-fashioned, informal*) to arrest sb and take them to a police station ˌrun sth↔ˈin (*BrE*) (in the past) to prepare the engine of a new car for normal use by driving slowly and carefully: (*figurative*) *Whatever system you choose, it must be run in properly.* ˌrun ˈinto sb (*informal*) to meet sb by chance: *Guess who I ran into today!* ˌrun ˈinto sth **1** to enter an area of bad weather while travelling: *We ran into thick fog on the way home.* **2** to experience difficulties, etc: *Be careful not to run into debt.* ◊ *to run into danger/trouble/difficulties* **3** to reach a particular level or amount: *Her income runs into six figures* (= is more than £100000, $100000, etc.). ˌrun ˈinto sb/sth to crash into sb/sth: *The bus went out of control and ran into a line of people.* ˌrun sth ˈinto sb/sth to make a vehicle crash into sb/sth: *He ran his car into a tree.* ˌrun ˈoff (*BrE*) (of a liquid) to flow out of a container ˌrun sth↔ˈoff **1** to copy sth on a machine: *Could you run off twenty copies of the agenda?* **2** to cause a race to be run: *The heats of the 200 metres will be run off tomorrow.* **3** to make a liquid flow out of a container ˌrun ˈoff with sth | ˌrun ˈoff (together) = RUN AWAY/OFF WITH SB ˌrun ˈoff with sth to steal sth and take it away: *The treasurer had run off with the club's funds.* ˌrun ˈon to continue without stopping; to continue longer than is necessary or expected: *The meeting will finish promptly—I don't want it to run on.* ˌrun ˈon sth [no passive] if your thoughts, a discussion, etc. **run on** a subject, you think or talk a lot about that subject ˌrun ˈout **1** ⓐ② if a supply of sth **runs out**, it is used up or finished: *Time is running out for the trapped miners.* **2** if an agreement or a document **runs out**, it no longer has any legal force ⓢⓨⓝ expire ˌrun ˈout (of sth) ⓑ① to use up or finish a supply of sth: *We ran out of fuel.* ◊ *Could I have a cigarette? I seem to have run out.* ˌrun ˈout on sb (*informal*) to leave sb that you live with, especially when they need your help ˌrun sb↔ˈout [often passive] (in CRICKET) to make a player stop BATTING by hitting the WICKET with the ball before the player has completed his or her run ˌrun ˈover if a container or its contents **run over**, the contents come over the edge of the container ⓢⓨⓝ overflow ˌrun sb/sth↔ˈover (of a vehicle or its driver) to knock a person or an animal down and drive over their body or a part of it: *Two children were run over and killed.* ◊ *My dog almost got run over.* ˌrun ˈover (sth) to take more time or spend more money than was planned: *My work meetings always run over.* ◊ *The project ran over time and budget.* ˌrun ˈover sth to read through or practise sth quickly: *She ran over her notes before giving the lecture.* ˌrun sth ˈpast sb = RUN STH BY/PAST SB: *Run that past me again.* ˌrun sb↔ˈthrough (*literary*) to kill sb by sticking a knife, SWORD, etc. through them ˌrun ˈthrough sth **1** to discuss,

repeat or read sth quickly: *He ran through the names on the list.* ◊ *Could we run through your proposals once again?* **2** [no passive] to pass quickly through sth: *An angry murmur ran through the crowd.* ◊ *Thoughts of revenge kept running through his mind.* **3** [no passive] to be present in every part of sth: *A deep melancholy runs through her poetry.* **4** to perform, act or practise sth: *Can we run through Scene 3 again, please?* ⊃ related noun RUN-THROUGH **5** to use up or spend money carelessly: *She ran through the entire amount within two years.* ˌrun ˈto sth **1** to be of a particular size or amount: *The book runs to nearly 800 pages.* **2** (*especially BrE*) if you or your money will **not run to sth**, you do not have enough money for sth: *Our funds won't run to a trip abroad this year.* ˌrun sth↔ˈup **1** to allow a bill, debt, etc. to reach a large total ⓢⓨⓝ accumulate: *How had he managed to run up so many debts?* **2** to make a piece of clothing quickly, especially by SEWING: *to run up a blouse* **3** to raise sth, especially a flag ˌrun ˈup against sth to experience a difficulty: *The government is running up against considerable opposition to its tax reforms.* ˌrun ˈwith sb = RUN AROUND WITH SB ˌrun ˈwith sth to accept or start to use a particular idea or method: *OK, let's run with Jan's suggestion.*

■ **noun**

- ON FOOT **1** ⓕ ⓐ② [C] an act of running; a period of time spent running or the distance that sb runs: *I go for a run every morning.* ◊ *a five-mile run* ◊ *Catching sight of her he broke into a run* (= started running). ◊ *I decided to **make a run for it*** (= to escape by running). ◊ **at a~** *She took the stairs at a run.* ⊃ see also FUN RUN
- TRIP **2** [C] a trip by car, plane, boat, etc., especially a short one or one that is made regularly: *They took the car out for a run.* ⊃ see also RAT RUN, SCHOOL RUN
- OF SUCCESS/FAILURE **3** [C] a period of sth good or bad happening; a series of successes or failures ⓢⓨⓝ spell: *a run of good/bad luck* ◊ *Liverpool lost to Leeds, ending an unbeaten run of 18 games.*
- OF PLAY/MOVIE **4** [C] a series of performances of a play or film: *The show had a record-breaking run in the London theatre.*
- OF PRODUCT **5** [C] the amount of a product that a company decides to make at one time: *The first print run of 6000 copies sold out.*
- MONEY **6** [C, usually sing.] **~on the dollar, pound**, etc. a situation when many people sell dollars, etc. and the value of the money falls **7** [C, usually sing.] **~on a bank** a situation when many people suddenly want to take their money out of a bank
- SUDDEN DEMAND **8** [C, usually sing.] **~on sth** a situation when many people suddenly want to buy sth ⓢⓨⓝ rush: *There's been a run on barbecues with the hot weather.*
- WAY THINGS HAPPEN **9** [sing.] **the~of sth** the way things usually happen; the way things seem to be happening on a particular occasion: *In the normal run of things the only exercise he gets is climbing in and out of taxis.* ◊ (*BrE*) *Wise scored in the 15th minute against the run of play* (= although the other team had seemed more likely to score).
- IN SPORTS **10** [C] a sloping track used in skiing and some other sports: *a ski/toboggan run* **11** [C] a point scored in the game of CRICKET or baseball: *Our team won by four runs.* ⊃ see also HOME RUN
- IN ELECTION **12** [sing.] (*NAmE*) an act of trying to get elected to public office: *He made an unsuccessful run for governor in 2008.*
- FOR ANIMALS/BIRDS **13** [C] (often in compounds) an area with a fence, walls, etc. in which animals or birds are kept as pets or on a farm: *a chicken run*
- IN MUSIC **14** [C] a series of notes sung or played quickly up or down the SCALE
- IN CARD GAMES **15** [C] a series of cards held by one player
- IN TIGHTS/STOCKINGS **16** [C] (*NAmE*) = LADDER
- ILLNESS **17 the runs** [pl.] (*informal*) = DIARRHOEA ⊃ see also DRY RUN, DUMMY RUN, TEST RUN, TRIAL RUN

ⓘⓓⓜ **the ˌcommon, ˌgeneral, ˌordinary, ˌusual ˈrun (of sth)** the average type of sth: *He was very different from the*

# runabout

*general run of movie stars.* **give sb a (good) run for their 'money** to make sb try very hard, using all their skill and effort, in order to beat you in a game or competition **give sb/get/have the 'run of sth** to give sb/get/have permission to make full use of sth: *Her dogs have the run of the house.* **on the 'run 1** trying to avoid being captured: *He's on the run from the police.* **2** (*informal*) continuously active and moving around: *I've been on the run all day and I'm exhausted.* ◇ *Here are some quick recipes for when you're eating on the run* (= in a hurry). ⊃ more at LONG *adj.*, SHORT *adj.*

**run·about** /ˈrʌnəbaʊt/ *noun* (*BrE, informal*) a small car, especially one used for short journeys

**run·around** /ˈrʌnəraʊnd/ *noun*
[IDM] **give sb the 'runaround** (*informal*) to treat sb badly by not telling them the truth, or by not giving them the help or the information they need, and sending them somewhere else

**run·away** /ˈrʌnəweɪ/ *adj., noun*
■ *adj.* [only before noun] **1** (of a person) having left without telling anyone: *runaway children* **2** (of an animal or a vehicle) not under the control of its owner, rider or driver: *a runaway horse/car* **3** happening very easily or quickly, and not able to be controlled: *a runaway winner/victory* ◇ *the runaway success of her first play* ◇ *runaway inflation*
■ *noun* a person who has suddenly left or escaped from sb/sth, especially a child who has left home without telling anyone: *teenage runaways living on the streets*

**run-'down** *adj.* **1** (of a building or place) in very bad condition; that has not been taken care of [SYN] **neglected:** *run-down inner-city areas* **2** (of a business, etc.) not as busy or as active as it used to be: *run-down transport services* **3** [not before noun] (of a person) tired or slightly ill, especially from working hard: *to be run-down*

**run·down** /ˈrʌndaʊn/ *noun* [usually sing.] **1 ~ (in/of sth)** (*BrE*) a reduction in the amount, size or activity of sth, especially a business: *a rundown of transport services* **2 ~ (on/of sth)** an explanation or a description of sth: *I can give you a brief rundown on each of the applicants.*

**rune** /ruːn/ *noun* **1** one of the letters in an alphabet that people in northern Europe used in ancient times and cut into wood or stone **2** a symbol that has a mysterious or magic meaning ▶ **runic** /ˈruːnɪk/ *adj.*: *runic inscriptions*

**rung** /rʌŋ/ *noun, verb*
■ *noun* one of the bars that forms a step in a LADDER: *He put his foot on the bottom rung to keep the ladder steady.* ◇ (*figurative*) *to get a foot on the bottom rung of the career ladder*
■ *verb past part.* of RING²

**'run-in** *noun* **1 ~ (with sb)** (*informal*) an argument or a fight: *The fiery player has had numerous run-ins with referees.* **2 ~ (to sth)** (*BrE*) = RUN-UP

**run·ner** /ˈrʌnə(r)/ *noun* **1** a person or an animal that runs, especially one taking part in a race: *a long-distance/cross-country/marathon runner* ◇ *a list of runners* (= horses in a race) *and riders* ⊃ see also FORERUNNER, FRONT RUNNER, ROADRUNNER **2** (especially in compounds) a person who takes goods illegally into or out of a place: *a drug runner* ⊃ see also GUNRUNNER **3** a narrow piece of metal, plastic or wood that sth slides on or can move along on: *the runners of a sledge* **4** a plant STEM that grows along the ground and puts down roots to form a new plant **5** a long narrow piece of cloth or carpet on a piece of furniture or on the floor **6** a person in a company or an organization whose job is to take messages, documents, etc. from one place to another **7** (*CanE*) a shoe that is used for running or doing other sport in
[IDM] **do a 'runner** (*BrE, informal*) to leave or run away from somewhere in a hurry, especially to avoid paying a bill or receiving a punishment

**'runner bean** *noun* (also **'string bean**) (both *BrE*) a type of bean which is a long flat green POD growing on a climbing plant also called a runner bean. The pods are cut up, cooked and eaten as a vegetable.

**runner-'up** *noun* (*pl.* **runners-up**) a person or team that finishes second in a race or competition; a person or team that has not finished first but that wins a prize: *Winner: Kay Hall. Runner-up: Chris Platts.* ◇ *They finished runners-up behind Sweden.* ◇ *The runners-up will all receive a £50 prize.* ⊃ WORDFINDER NOTE at COMPETITION

**run·ning** /ˈrʌnɪŋ/ *noun, adj.*
■ *noun* [U] **1** the action or sport of running: *to go running* ◇ *long-distance/cross-country running* **2** the activity of managing or operating sth: *the day-to-day running of a business* ◇ *the running costs of a car* (= for example of fuel, repairs, insurance) **3** **-running** (in compounds) the activity of bringing sth such as drugs, guns, etc. into a country secretly and illegally: *drug-running*
[IDM] **in/out of the 'running (for sth)** (*informal*) having some/no chance of succeeding or achieving sth **make the 'running** (*BrE, informal*) to set the speed at which sth is done; to take the lead in doing sth
■ *adj.* **1** used after a number and a noun such as 'year' 'day' or 'time', to say that sth has happened in the same way several times, without a change: *She's won the championship three years running.* ◇ *It was the third day running that the train had been late.* ◇ *No party has won an election four times running.* **2** **running water** is water that is flowing somewhere or water that is supplied to a building and available to be used through TAPS: *I can hear the sound of running water.* ◇ *a remote cottage without electricity or running water* **3** [only before noun] lasting a long time; continuous [SYN] **ongoing:** *For years he had fought a running battle with the authorities over the land.* ◇ *a running argument* ◇ *His old raincoat became a running joke* (= people kept laughing at it). ⊃ see also LONG-RUNNING **4** **-running** (in compounds) running or flowing in the way mentioned: *a fast-running river*
[IDM] **(go and) take a running 'jump** (*old-fashioned, informal*) used to tell sb in a rude way to go away ⊃ more at ORDER *n.*

**'running back** *noun* (in AMERICAN FOOTBALL) an attacking player whose main job is to run forward carrying the ball

**running 'commentary** *noun* a continuous description of an event, especially a sporting event, that sb gives as it happens: *to give a running commentary on the game*

**'running mate** *noun* [usually sing.] (*politics*) (in the US) a person who is chosen by the candidate in an election, especially that for president, to support them and to have the next highest political position if they win: *The presidential nominee was advised to choose a woman as a running mate.* ⊃ WORDFINDER NOTE at CONGRESS

**'running order** *noun* [sing.] the order of the items in a television programme or a show; the order that members of a team will play in

**'running time** *noun* the amount of time that a film, a journey, etc. lasts

**'running 'total** *noun* the total number or amount of things, money, etc. that changes as you add each new item

**runny** /ˈrʌni/ *adj.* (**run·nier, run·ni·est**) **1** (of your nose or eyes) producing a lot of liquid, for example when you have a cold **2** having more liquid than is usual; not solid: *runny honey* ◇ *Omelettes should be runny in the middle.*

**'run-off** *noun* **1** [C] a second vote or competition that is held to find a winner because two people taking part in the first competition got the same result **2** [U, C] rain, water or other liquid that runs off land into streams and rivers

**run-of-the-'mill** *adj.* (*often disapproving*) ordinary, with no special or interesting features

**'run-out** *noun* (in CRICKET) a situation in which a player fails to complete a RUN before a player from the other team hits the WICKET with the ball, and so is OUT

**runt** /rʌnt/ *noun* **1** the smallest, weakest animal of the young that are born from the same mother at the same time: *the runt of the litter* **2** (*informal, disapproving*) a rude way of referring to sb who is small, weak or unimportant

**'run-through** *noun* a practice for a performance of a play, show, etc. [SYN] **rehearsal**

**run·time** /ˈrʌntaɪm/ noun **1** [C] the time that a film or DVD lasts **2** [U, C] (*computing*) the amount of time that a program takes to perform a task; the time when a program is performing a task **3** [C] (*computing*) a computer program that enables other computer programs to run inside it

**ˈrun-up** noun (*BrE*) **1** (*also less frequent* ˈ**run-in**) ~ (**to sth**) a period of time leading up to an important event; the preparation for this: *an increase in spending in the run-up to Christmas* ◇ *during the run-up to the election* **2** the act of running or the distance you run, to gain speed before you jump a long distance, throw a ball, etc.

**run·way** /ˈrʌnweɪ/ noun **1** a long narrow piece of ground with a hard surface that an aircraft takes off from and lands on **2** (*especially NAmE*) = CATWALK

**ru·pee** /ruːˈpiː/ noun the unit of money in India, Pakistan and some other countries

**rup·ture** /ˈrʌptʃə(r)/ noun, verb
- noun [C, U] **1** (*medical*) an injury in which sth inside the body breaks apart or BURSTS (= explodes): *the rupture of a blood vessel* **2** a situation when sth breaks or BURSTS: *ruptures of oil and water pipelines* **3** (*informal*) a HERNIA of the ABDOMEN: *I nearly gave myself a rupture lifting that pile of books.* **4** (*formal*) the ending of agreement or of good relations between people, countries, etc: *a rupture in relations between the two countries* ◇ *Nothing could heal the rupture with his father.*
- verb **1** [T, I] ~ (**sth/yourself**) (*medical*) to BURST or break apart sth inside the body; to be broken or BURST apart: *a ruptured appendix* ◇ *He ruptured himself* (= got a HERNIA) *trying to lift the piano.* **2** [T, I] ~ (**sth**) (*formal*) to make sth such as a container or a pipe break or BURST; to be broken or BURST: *The impact ruptured both fuel tanks.* ◇ *A pipe ruptured, leaking water all over the house.* **3** [T] ~ **sth** (*formal*) to make an agreement or good relations between people or countries end: *the risk of rupturing North-South relations*

**rural** 🔵 **B2** 🌐 /ˈrʊərəl; NAmE ˈrʊr-/ adj. [usually before noun] connected with or like the countryside: *rural areas* ◇ *the rural community/population* ◇ *a rural economy* ◇ *a rural way of life* ⊃ compare URBAN ⊃ WORDFINDER NOTE at LOCATION

**ˌrural ˈdean** noun = DEAN

**ruse** /ruːz/ noun a way of doing sth or of getting sth by cheating sb **SYN** trick

**rush** 🔵 **B2** /rʌʃ/ verb, noun
- verb
• MOVE FAST **1** ᛫ **B2** [I, T] to move or to do sth with great speed, often too fast: *We've got plenty of time; there's no need to rush.* ◇ + *adv./prep.* *Don't rush off, I haven't finished.* ◇ *I've been rushing around all day trying to get everything done.* ◇ *to* **rush to the aid/defence/rescue** *of sb* ◇ ~ **to do sth** *People rushed to buy shares in the company.* ◇ ~ **sth** *We had to rush our meal.*
• TAKE/SEND QUICKLY **2** ᛫ **B2** [T] ~ **sb/sth** + *adv./prep.* to transport or send sb/sth somewhere with great speed: *Ambulances rushed the injured to the hospital.* ◇ *Relief supplies were rushed in.*
• DO STH TOO QUICKLY **3** ᛫ **B2** [I, T] to do or to make sb do sth without thinking about it carefully: ~ **into sth/into doing sth** *We don't want to rush into having a baby.* ◇ ~ **sb** *Don't rush me. I need time to think about it.* ◇ ~ **sb into sth/into doing sth** *I'm not going to be rushed into anything.*
• LIQUID/AIR **4** [I] (+ *adv./prep.*) (of a liquid or air) to flow strongly: *The water rushed in through the hole in the ship's hull.*
• ATTACK **5** [T] ~ **sb/sth** to try to attack or capture sb/sth suddenly: *A group of prisoners rushed an officer and managed to break out.* ◇ *Fans rushed the stage after the concert.*
• IN AMERICAN FOOTBALL **6** [T] ~ **sb** (*NAmE*) to run into sb who has the ball **7** [I] (*NAmE*) to move forward and gain ground by carrying the ball and not passing it
• IN AMERICAN COLLEGES **8** [T] ~ **sb** (*NAmE*) to give a lot of attention to sb, especially to a student because you want

them to join your FRATERNITY or SORORITY: *He is being rushed by Sigma Nu.* **IDM** see FOOL *n.*, FOOT *n.*
**PHRV** ˌrush sth↔ˈout to produce sth very quickly: *The editors rushed out an item on the crash for the late news.* ˌrush sth↔ˈthrough | ˌrush sth ˈthrough sth to deal with official business very quickly by making the usual process shorter than usual: *to rush a bill through Parliament*
- noun
• FAST MOVEMENT **1** ᛫ **B2** [sing.] a sudden strong movement or action: ~ **for sth** *Shoppers made a rush for the exits.* ◇ **in a ~** *The words came out in a rush.* ◇ **in the ~ to do sth** *She was trampled in the rush to get out.* ◇ *They listened to the rush of the sea below.* ◇ *He had a* **rush of blood to the head** (= suddenly lost control of himself) *and punched the man.*
• HURRY **2** ᛫ **B2** [sing., U] a situation in which you are in a hurry and need to do things quickly: *What's the rush?* ◇ *'I'll let you have the book back tomorrow.' 'There's no rush.'* ◇ **in a ~** *I can't stop—I'm in a rush.* ◇ *a* **rush job** (= one that has been done quickly)
• BUSY SITUATION **3** ᛫ **B2** [sing.] a situation in which people are very busy and there is a lot of activity: *The evening rush was just starting.* ◇ *the Christmas rush*
• OF FEELING **4** [sing.] ~ (**of sth**) a sudden strong emotion or sign of strong emotion: *a sudden rush of excitement/fear/anger* **5** [sing.] a sudden feeling of extreme pleasure or excitement: *Parachuting will give you the rush of a lifetime.* ◇ *Users of the drug report experiencing a rush that lasts several minutes.*
• SUDDEN DEMAND **6** [sing.] ~ (**on/for sth**) a sudden large demand for goods, etc. **SYN** run: *There's been a rush on umbrellas this week.* ⊃ see also GOLD RUSH
• PLANT **7** [C, usually pl.] a tall plant like grass that grows near water. Its long thin STEMS can be dried and used for making BASKETS, the seats of chairs, etc: *rush matting*
• OF FILM/MOVIE **8 rushes** [pl.] (*specialist*) the first prints of a film before they have been EDITED
• IN AMERICAN FOOTBALL **9** [C] an occasion when a player or players run towards a player on the other team who has the ball: *There was a rush on the quarterback.* **10** [C] an occasion when a player runs forward with the ball: *Johnson carried the ball an average of 6 yards per rush.*
• IN AMERICAN COLLEGES **11** [sing] (*NAmE*) the time when parties are held for students who want to join a FRATERNITY or SORORITY: *rush week* ◇ *a rush party* **IDM** see BUM *n.*

**rushed** /rʌʃt/ adj. done too quickly or made to do sth too quickly **SYN** hurried: *It was a rushed decision made at the end of the meeting.* ◇ *Let's start work on it now so we're not too rushed at the end.* **IDM** see FOOT *n.*

**ˈrush hour** noun [C, usually sing., U] the time, usually twice a day, when the roads are full of traffic and trains are crowded because people are travelling to or from work: *the morning/evening rush hour* ◇ **at ~** | **in the ~** *Don't travel at rush hour/in the rush hour.* ◇ *rush-hour traffic*

**rus·set** /ˈrʌsɪt/ adj. red-brown in colour ▶ **rus·set** noun [U]: *leaves of russet and gold*

**Rus·sian** /ˈrʌʃn/ adj., noun
- adj. from or connected with Russia
- noun **1** [C] a person from Russia **2** [U] the language of Russia

**ˌRussian ˈdoll** noun one of a set of hollow painted figures which fit inside each other

**ˌRussian rouˈlette** noun [U] a dangerous game in which a person shoots at their own head with a gun that contains only one bullet (in a gun that can take six), so that the person does not know if the gun will fire or not: (*figurative*) *The airline was accused of playing Russian roulette with passenger safety.*

**Russo-** /ˈrʌsəʊ/ *combining form* (in nouns and adjectives) Russian: *Russo-Japanese relations*

**rust** /rʌst/ noun, verb
- noun [U] **1** a red-brown substance that is formed on some metals by the action of water and air: *pipes covered with rust* ◇ *rust spots* ◇ *a rust-coloured dress* ⊃ see also

# rust belt

RUSTY **2** a plant disease that causes red-brown spots; the FUNGUS that causes this disease
- **verb** [I, T] if metal **rusts** or sth **rusts** it, it becomes covered with rust **SYN** corrode: *old rusting farming implements* ◊ *Brass doesn't rust.* ◊ ~ *sth Water had got in and rusted the engine.* ▸ **rust·ed** *adj.*: *rusted iron* ⇒ see also RUSTY
- **PHRV** **rust a·way** to be gradually destroyed by rust

**'rust belt** *noun* (*especially US*) a region that used to have a lot of industry, but that has now decreased in importance and wealth, especially parts of the northern US where there were many factories that have now closed

**rus·tic** /ˈrʌstɪk/ *adj.*, *noun*
- *adj.* **1** (*approving*) typical of the country or of country people; simple: *an old cottage full of rustic charm* **2** made very simply of rough wood: *a rustic garden seat* ◊ *a rustic fence* ▸ **rus·ti·city** /rʌˈstɪsəti/ *noun* [U]
- *noun* (*disapproving* or *humorous*) a person who lives in or comes from the country

**rus·tle** /ˈrʌsl/ *verb*, *noun*
- *verb* **1** [I, T] ~ (sth) if sth dry and light **rustles** or you **rustle** it, it makes a sound like paper, leaves, etc. moving or rubbing together: *the sound of the trees rustling in the breeze* **2** [T] ~ sth to steal farm animals
- **PHRV** **rustle sth↔up (for sb)** (*informal*) to make or find sth quickly for sb and without planning: *I'm sure I can rustle you up a sandwich.* ◊ *She's trying to rustle up some funding for the project.*
- *noun* [sing.] a light dry sound like leaves or pieces of paper moving or rubbing against each other: *There was a rustle of paper as people turned the pages.* ◊ *I heard a faint rustle in the bushes.*

**rust·ler** /ˈrʌslə(r)/ *noun* a person who steals farm animals

**rust·ling** /ˈrʌslɪŋ/ *noun* **1** [U, C] the sound of light, dry things moving together: *the soft rustling of leaves* **2** [U] the act of stealing farm animals

**rusty** /ˈrʌsti/ *adj.* (**rust·ier**, **rusti·est**) **1** covered with RUST: *rusty metal* ◊ *a rusty old car* **2** [not usually before noun] (*informal*) (of a sport, skill, etc.) not as good as it used to be, because you have not been practising: *My tennis is very rusty these days.* ◊ *I haven't played the piano for ages—I may be a little rusty.* ▸ **rusti·ness** *noun* [U]

**rut** /rʌt/ *noun* **1** [C] a deep track that a wheel makes in soft ground **2** [C] a boring way of life that does not change: *I gave up my job because I felt I was stuck in a rut.* ◊ *If you don't go out and meet new people, it's easy to get into a rut.* **3** (*also* **the rut**) [U] the time of year when male animals, especially DEER, become sexually active ⇒ see also RUTTED, RUTTING

**ru·ta·baga** /ˈruːtəbeɪɡə/ (*NAmE*) (*BrE* **swede**) (*ScotE* **tur·nip**) *noun* [C, U] a large round yellow root vegetable ⇒ VISUAL VOCAB page V5

**ru·the·nium** /ruːˈθiːniəm/ *noun* [U] (*symb.* **Ru**) a chemical element. Ruthenium is a hard silver-white metal that breaks easily and is found in PLATINUM ORES.

**ruth·less** /ˈruːθləs/ *adj.* (*often disapproving*) (of people or their behaviour) hard and cruel; determined to get what you want and not caring if you hurt other people: *a ruthless dictator* ◊ *The way she behaved towards him was utterly ruthless.* ◊ *He has a ruthless determination to succeed.* ▸ **ruth·less·ly** *adv.* **ruth·less·ness** *noun* [U]

**rut·ted** /ˈrʌtɪd/ *adj.* (of a road or path) with deep tracks that have been made by wheels ⇒ see also RUT (1)

**rut·ting** /ˈrʌtɪŋ/ *adj.* (of male animals, especially DEER) in a time of sexual activity: *rutting deer* ◊ *the rutting season* ⇒ see also RUT (3)

**RV** /ˌɑːr ˈviː/ *NAmE* /ˌɑːr/ (*NAmE*) (*BrE* **camp·er**, **'camper van**) (*also* **motor·home** *NAmE*, *BrE*) *noun* a large vehicle designed for people to live and sleep in when they are travelling (the abbreviation for 'recreational vehicle')

**Rx** /ˌɑːr ˈeks/ *noun* (*NAmE*) **1** an official piece of paper on which a doctor writes the type of medicine you should have, and which enables you to get it from a CHEMIST'S (the written abbreviation for a doctor's 'prescription') **2** a solution to a problem: *There's no Rx for unemployment.*

**-ry** ⇒ -ERY

**rye** /raɪ/ *noun* [U] a plant that looks like BARLEY but that produces larger grain, grown as food for animals and for making flour and WHISKY; the grain of this plant: *rye bread* ◊ *rye whisky* ⇒ VISUAL VOCAB page V8

**'rye-grass** /ˈraɪɡrɑːs/ *NAmE* -græs/ *noun* [U] a type of grass which is grown as food for animals

# Ss

**S** /es/ *noun, abbr., symbol*
- *noun* (also **s**) [C, U] (*pl.* **Ss, S's, s's** /'esɪz/) the 19th letter of the English alphabet: *'Snow' begins with (an) S/'S'.*
- *abbr.* (in writing) **1** (*pl.* **SS**) Saint **2** (especially for sizes of clothes) small **3** (*NAmE also* **So.**) south; southern: *S Yorkshire* **4** SIEMENS ⊃ see also S AND H
- *symbol* (in writing) (*physics*) the symbol for ENTROPY

**-s, -es** HELP The pronunciation is formed by adding /z/ after vowels and voiced non-sibilants, /s/ after voiceless non-sibilants, and /ɪz/ after the sibilants /s z ʃ ʒ tʃ dʒ/. *suffix* **1** (makes the plural of regular nouns): *cats* ◊ *potatoes* **2** (makes the third person singular of regular verbs): *sees* ◊ *watches*

**-'s** *suffix, short form*
- *suffix* (added to nouns) **1** belonging to: *the woman's hat* ◊ *Peter's desk* ◊ *children's clothes* **2** used to refer to sb's home or, in British English, a particular shop: *Shall we go to David's (= David's house) tonight?* ◊ (*BrE*) *I'll call in at the chemist's on my way home*
- *short form* (*informal*) **1** used after *he, she* or *it* and *where, what, who* or *how* to mean 'is' or 'has': *She's still in the bath.* ◊ *What's he doing now?* ◊ *It's time to go now.* ◊ *Who's taken my pen?* ◊ *Where's he gone?* ◊ *It's gone wrong again.* **2** (used after *let* when making a suggestion that includes yourself and others) us: *Let's go out for lunch.*

**-s'** *suffix* (forming the end of plural nouns) belonging to: *the cats' tails* ◊ *their wives' jobs*

**SA** *abbr.* South Africa

**saag** (also **sag**) /sæg/ *BrE also* sɑːg/ *noun* [U] (*IndE*) = SPINACH

**sab·bath** /'sæbəθ/ *noun often* **the Sabbath** [sing.] (in Judaism and Christianity) the holy day of the week that is used for resting and WORSHIPPING God. For Jews this day is Saturday and for Christians it is Sunday: *to keep/break the Sabbath (= to obey/not obey the religious rules for this day)*

**sab·bat·ic·al** /sə'bætɪkl/ *noun* [C, U] a period of time when sb, especially a teacher at a university, is allowed to stop their normal work in order to study or travel: *to take a year's sabbatical* ◊ **on~** *He's on sabbatical this term.* ◊ *sabbatical term/year*

**saber** (*US*) = SABRE

**sabji** /'sʌbdʒi/ ; *NAmE* 'sɑːb-/ = SABZI

**sable** /'seɪbl/ *noun* **1** [C] a small animal from northern Asia with dark yellow-brown fur **2** [U] the skin and fur of the sable, used for making expensive coats and artists' brushes

**sabo·tage** /'sæbətɑːʒ/ *noun, verb*
- *noun* [U] **1** the act of doing deliberate damage to equipment, transport, machines, etc. to prevent an enemy from using them, or to protest about sth: *an act of economic/military/industrial sabotage* ◊ *Police investigating the train derailment have not ruled out sabotage.* ⊃ WORDFINDER NOTE at PROTEST **2** the act of preventing sth from being successful or being achieved, especially deliberately
- *verb* **1 ~sth** to damage or destroy sth deliberately to prevent an enemy from using it or to protest about sth: *The main electricity supply had been sabotaged by the rebels.* **2 ~sth** to prevent sth from being successful or being achieved, especially deliberately: *Protesters failed to sabotage the peace talks.* ◊ *The rise in interest rates sabotaged any chance of the firm's recovery.*

**sabo·teur** /,sæbə'tɜː(r)/ *noun* a person who does deliberate damage to sth to prevent an enemy from using it, or to protest about sth: *Saboteurs blew up a small section of the track.*

**sabre** (*US* **saber**) /'seɪbə(r)/ *noun* **1** a heavy SWORD with a curved BLADE (= metal cutting edge) **2** a light SWORD with a thin BLADE used in the sport of FENCING

**'sabre-rattling** (*US* 'saber-rattling) *noun* [U] the act, by a government, of trying to frighten the government of another country by threatening to use military force

**sabre-tooth** (*US* **saber-tooth**) /'seɪbətuːθ/; *NAmE* -bɑːrt-/ (*also* **sabre-toothed 'tiger**) (*US* **saber-toothed 'tiger**) *noun* a large animal of the cat family with two very long curved upper teeth, that lived thousands of years ago and is now EXTINCT

**sabzi** /'sʌbzi; *NAmE* 'sɑːb-/ (*also* **sabji**) *noun* [U, C] (*IndE*) vegetables, especially when cooked

**sac** /sæk/ *noun* a part inside the body of a person, an animal or a plant, that is like a bag in shape, has thin skin around it, and contains liquid or air

**sac·charin** /'sækərɪn/ *noun* [U] a sweet chemical substance used instead of sugar, especially by people who are trying to lose weight

**sac·char·ine** /'sækərɪn; *BrE also* -riːn/ (*also less frequent* **saccharin**) *adj.* (*disapproving*) (of people or things) too emotional in a way that seems EXAGGERATED SYN sentimental: *a saccharine smile* ◊ *saccharine songs*

**sa·chet** /'sæʃeɪ; *NAmE* sæ'ʃeɪ/ *noun* **1** (*BrE*) (*NAmE* **packet**) a closed plastic or paper package that contains a very small amount of liquid or a powder: *a sachet of sauce/sugar/shampoo* **2** a small bag containing dried HERBS or flowers that you put with your clothes to make them smell pleasant

**sack** /sæk/ *verb, noun*
- *verb* **1 ~sb** (especially *BrE, informal*) to dismiss sb from a job SYN fire: *She was sacked for refusing to work on Sundays.* **2 ~sth** (of an army, etc., especially in the past) to destroy things and steal property in a town or building: *Rome was sacked by the Goths in 410.* **3 ~sb** (in AMERICAN FOOTBALL) to knock down the QUARTERBACK
- PHRV **,sack 'out** (*NAmE, informal*) to go to sleep or to bed: *We watched a movie and sacked out on the couch.*
- *noun* **1** [C] a large bag with no handles, made of strong rough material or strong paper or plastic, used for storing and carrying, for example flour, coal, etc. **2** [C] (*NAmE*) a strong paper bag for carrying shopping **3** [C] the contents of a sack: *They got through a sack of potatoes.* ◊ (*NAmE*) *two sacks of groceries* **4 the sack** [sing.] (*BrE, informal*) being told by your employer that you can no longer continue working for a company, etc., usually because of sth that you have done wrong: *He got the sack for swearing.* ◊ *Her work was so poor that she was given the sack.* ◊ *Four hundred workers face the sack.* **5 the sack** [sing.] (especially *NAmE, informal*) a bed: *He caught them in the sack together.* **6** (*usually* **the sack**) [sing.] (*formal*) the act of stealing or destroying property in a captured town: *the sack of Rome* IDM see HIT *v.*

**sack·cloth** /'sækklɒθ; *NAmE* -klɔːθ/ (*also* **sack·ing**) *noun* [U] a type of rough cloth made from JUTE, etc., used for making sacks IDM **wear, put on, etc. ,sackcloth and 'ashes** to behave in a way that shows that you are sorry for sth that you have done

**sack·ful** /'sækfʊl/ *noun* the amount contained in a sack: *two sackfuls of flour*

**sack·ing** /'sækɪŋ/ *noun* **1** [C] an act of sacking sb (= dismissing them from their job) **2** [U] = SACKCLOTH

**'sack race** *noun* a race in which the competitors jump forward inside a sack

**sac·ra·ment** /'sækrəmənt/ *noun* (in Christianity) **1** [C] an important religious ceremony such as marriage, BAPTISM or COMMUNION **2 the sacrament** [sing.] the bread and wine that are eaten and drunk during the service of COMMUNION ▶ **sac·ra·men·tal** /,sækrə'mentl/ *adj.* [usually before noun]: *sacramental wine*

**sa·cred** /'seɪkrɪd/ *adj.* **1** connected with God or a god; considered to be holy: *a sacred image/shrine/temple* ◊ *sacred music* ◊ *Cows are sacred to Hindus.* **2** very important and treated with great respect; that must not be changed or challenged SYN sacrosanct: *Human life must always be sacred.* ◊ *For journalists nothing is sacred (= they write about anything).* ▶ **sa·cred·ness** *noun* ⊃ see also SANCTITY

# sacred cow

**sacred 'cow** noun (disapproving) a custom, system, etc. that has existed for a long time and that many people think should not be questioned or criticized

**sac·ri·fice** /ˈsækrɪfaɪs/ noun, verb
- noun [C, U] **1** the fact of giving up sth important or valuable to you in order to get or do sth that seems more important; sth that you give up in this way: *The makers of the product assured us that there had been no sacrifice of quality.* ◇ *Her parents made sacrifices so that she could have a good education.* ◇ *to make the ultimate/supreme sacrifice* (= to die for your country, to save a friend, etc.) **2** ~ **(to sb)** the act of offering sth to a god, especially an animal that has been killed in a special way; an animal, etc. that is offered in this way: *They offered sacrifices to the gods.* ◇ *a human sacrifice* (= a person killed as a sacrifice)
- verb **1** [T] to give up sth that is important or valuable to you in order to get or do sth that seems more important for yourself or for another person: ~ **sth for sb/sth** *She sacrificed everything for her children.* ◇ *The designers have sacrificed speed for fuel economy.* ◇ ~ **sth** *Would you sacrifice a football game to go out with a girl?* **2** [T, I] ~ **(sb/sth)** to kill an animal or a person and offer it or them to a god, in order to please the god

**sac·ri·fi·cial** /ˌsækrɪˈfɪʃl/ adj. [usually before noun] offered as a sacrifice: *a sacrificial lamb*

**sac·ri·lege** /ˈsækrəlɪdʒ/ noun [U, sing.] an act of treating a holy thing or place without respect: *(figurative) It would be sacrilege to alter the composer's original markings.* ▶ **sac·ri·le·gious** /ˌsækrəˈlɪdʒəs/ adj.

**sac·ris·tan** /ˈsækrɪstən/ noun a person whose job is to take care of the holy objects in a Christian church and to prepare the ALTAR for services

**sac·risty** /ˈsækrɪsti/ noun (pl. -ies) a room in a church where a priest prepares for a service by putting on special clothes and where various objects used in WORSHIP are kept SYN **vestry**

**sacro·sanct** /ˈsækrəʊsæŋkt/ adj. [not usually before noun] that is considered to be too important to change or question SYN **sacred**: *I'll work till late in the evening, but my weekends are sacrosanct.*

**sac·rum** /ˈseɪkrəm, ˈsæk-/ noun (pl. sacra /-krə/ or sac·rums) (anatomy) a bone in the lower back, between the two HIP bones of the PELVIS

**SAD** /sæd/ abbr. SEASONAL AFFECTIVE DISORDER

**sad** /sæd/ adj. (sad·der, sad·dest)
- UNHAPPY **1** unhappy or showing unhappiness: ~ **to do sth** *We are very sad to hear that you are leaving.* ◇ ~ **that…** *I was sad that she had to go.* ◇ ~ **about sth** *I felt terribly sad about it.* ◇ ~ **for sb/sth** *I felt so sad for her.* ◇ *She looked sad and tired.* ◇ *He gave a slight, sad smile.* **2** that makes you feel unhappy: *a sad story* ◇ ~ **to do sth** *It was sad to see them go.* ◇ ~ **(that)…** *It is sad that so many of his paintings have been lost.* ◇ *We had some sad news yesterday.* ◇ *He's a sad case—his wife died last year and he can't seem to manage without her.* ◇ *Sad to say* (= unfortunately) *the house has now been demolished.*
- UNACCEPTABLE **3** unacceptable; deserving blame or criticism SYN **deplorable**: *a sad state of affairs* ◇ *It's a sad fact that many of those killed were children.*
- BORING **4** (informal) boring or not fashionable: *You sad old man.* ◇ *You'd have to be sad to wear a shirt like that.*
- IN POOR CONDITION **5** in poor condition: *The salad consisted of a few leaves of sad-looking lettuce.* ⊃ see also SADLY, SADNESS

**sad·den** /ˈsædn/ verb [often passive] (formal) to make sb sad: ~ **sb** *We were deeply saddened by the news of her death.* ◇ ~ **sb to do sth** *Fans were saddened to see the former champion play so badly.* ◇ **it saddens sb that…** *It saddened her that people could be so cruel.*

**sad·dle** /ˈsædl/ noun, verb
- noun **1** a leather seat for a rider on a horse: *She swung herself into the saddle.* ⊃ see also SIDE-SADDLE **2** a seat on a bicycle or motorcycle ⊃ WORDFINDER NOTE at CYCLING **3** a piece of meat from the back of an animal
- IDM **in the 'saddle 1** in a position of responsibility, control or authority: *It's actually good to be back in the saddle after the holidays.* **2** riding a horse: *Three weeks after the accident he was back in the saddle.*
- verb ~ **sth** to put a saddle on a horse
- PHR V **saddle 'up** | **saddle sth↔ 'up** to put a saddle on a horse | **'saddle sb/yourself with sth** [often passive] to give sb/yourself an unpleasant responsibility, task, debt, etc: *I've been saddled with organizing the conference.* ◇ *The company was saddled with debts of £12 million.*

**saddle·bag** /ˈsædlbæɡ/ noun **1** one of a pair of bags put over the back of a horse **2** a bag attached to the back of a bicycle or motorcycle saddle

**sadhu** /ˈsɑːduː/ noun (pl. -us) a Hindu holy man, especially one who lives away from people and society

**sad·ism** /ˈseɪdɪzəm/ noun [U] **1** pleasure from watching or making sb suffer: *There's a streak of sadism in his nature.* **2** a need to hurt sb in order to get sexual pleasure ⊃ compare MASOCHISM

**sad·ist** /ˈseɪdɪst/ noun a person who gets pleasure, especially sexual pleasure, from hurting other people ▶ **sad·is·tic** /səˈdɪstɪk/ adj.: *He took sadistic pleasure in taunting the boy.* **sad·is·tic·al·ly** /-kli/ adv.

**sadly** /ˈsædli/ adv. **1** in a sad way: *'I'm so sorry,' she said sadly.* **2** unfortunately: *Sadly, after eight years of marriage they had grown apart.* **3** very much and in a way that makes you sad: *She will be sadly missed.* ◇ *If you think I'm going to help you again, you're sadly* (= completely) *mistaken.*

**sad·ness** /ˈsædnəs/ noun **1** [U, sing.] the feeling of being sad: *memories tinged with sadness* ◇ *I felt a deep sadness.* **2** [C, usually pl.] something which makes you sad: *our joys and sadnesses*

**sado·maso·chism** /ˌseɪdəʊˈmæsəkɪzəm/ noun [U] pleasure from hurting sb and being hurt, especially during sexual activity ▶ **sado·maso·chist** /-kɪst/ noun **sado·maso·chis·tic** /ˌseɪdəʊˌmæsəˈkɪstɪk/ adj.

**sae** /ˌes eɪ ˈiː/ noun (BrE) an ENVELOPE on which you have written your name and address and usually put a stamp so that sb else can use it to send sth to you (the abbreviation for 'stamped addressed envelope' or 'self-addressed envelope'): *Please enclose an sae for your test results.* ⊃ compare SASE

**sa·fari** /səˈfɑːri/ noun [U, C] **1** a trip to see or hunt wild animals, especially in east or southern Africa: **on ~** *to be/go on safari* ⊃ WORDFINDER NOTE at HUNT **2** (EAfrE) a journey; a period of time spent travelling or when you are not at home or at work: *I just got back from a month-long safari.* ◇ **on ~** *It arrived while I was on safari.* ⊃ WORDFINDER NOTE at JOURNEY

**sa'fari park** noun a park in which wild animals move around freely and are watched by visitors from their cars

**safe** /seɪf/ adj., noun
- adj. (safer, saf·est)
- PROTECTED **1** [not before noun] protected from any danger, harm or loss: *The children are quite safe here.* ◇ *She didn't feel safe on her own.* ◇ *Will the car be safe parked in the road?* ◇ ~ **from sb/sth** *They aimed to make the country safe from terrorist attacks.* ◇ *Your secret is safe with me* (= I will not tell anyone else). ◇ *Here's your passport. Now keep it safe.* OPP **unsafe**
- WITHOUT PHYSICAL DANGER **2** not likely to lead to any physical harm or danger: ~ **(for sb) (to do sth)** *Is the water here safe to drink?* ◇ *The street is not safe for children to play in.* ◇ *It is one of the safest cars in the world.* ◇ *Builders were called in to make the building safe.* OPP **unsafe**
- NOT HARMED/LOST **3** not harmed, damaged, lost, etc: *We were glad she let us know she was safe.* ◇ *The missing child was found safe and well.* ◇ *They turned up safe and sound.* ◇ *A reward was offered for the animal's safe return.*
- PLACE **4** where sb/sth is not likely to be in danger or to be lost: *We all want to live in safer cities.* ◇ *Keep your passport in a safe place.* ◇ *We watched the explosion from a safe distance.* OPP **unsafe**

- **WITHOUT RISK 5** A2 not involving much or any risk; not likely to be wrong or to upset sb: *a safe investment* ◊ *As I peruse the menu the only safe bet is the grilled chicken.* ◊ *a safe subject for discussion* ◊ **~ to do sth** *It's safe to assume (that) there will always be a demand for new software.* ◊ (*disapproving*) *The show was well performed, but so safe and predictable.*
- **PERSON 6** [usually before noun] doing an activity in a careful way SYN **careful**: *a safe driver*
- **LAW 7** based on good evidence: *a safe verdict* OPP **unsafe**
- **APPROVING 8** (*BrE, informal*) used by young people to show that they approve of sb/sth: *I like him, he's safe.* ◊ *That kid's safe.* **9** (*BrE, informal*) used by young people as a way of accepting sth that is offered: '*You want some?*' '*Yeah, safe.*' ⊃ see also **FAIL-SAFE**

IDM **better ˌsafe than ˈsorry** (*saying*) used to say that it is wiser to be too careful than to act too quickly and do sth you may later wish you had not | **in ˈsafe ˈhands** | **in the ˈsafe hands of sb** being taken care of well by sb: *I've left the kids in safe hands—with my parents.* ◊ *Their problem was in the safe hands of the experts.* **on the ˈsafe side** being especially careful; taking no risks: *I took some extra cash just to be on the safe side.* **play (it) ˈsafe** to be careful; to avoid risks **(as) ˌsafe as ˈhouses** (*BrE*) very safe **safe in the knowledge that** confident because you know that sth is true or will happen: *She went out safe in the knowledge that she looked fabulous.* **a safe pair of ˈhands** (*especially BrE*) a person that you can trust to do a job well ⊃ more at **BET** *n*.

- *noun* a strong metal box or cupboard with a complicated lock, used for storing valuable things in, for example, money or jewellery

ˌsafe ˈconduct (*also* ˌsafe ˈpassage) *noun* [U, C] official protection from being attacked, arrested, etc. when passing through an area; a document that promises this: *The guerrillas were promised safe conduct out of the country.*

ˈsafe deˌposit box (*also* ˌsafety deˈposit box) *noun* a metal box for storing valuable things, usually kept in a special room at a bank

ˈsafe·guard /ˈseɪfɡɑːd; *NAmE* -ɡɑːrd/ *verb, noun*
- *verb* [T, I] (*formal*) to protect sth/sb from loss, harm or damage; to keep sth/sb safe: **~ sth** *to safeguard a person's interests* ◊ *to safeguard jobs* ◊ **~ sth/sb against/from sth** *The new card will safeguard the company against fraud.* ◊ **~ against sth** *The leaflet explains how to safeguard against dangers in the home.*
- *noun* **~ (against sth)** something that is designed to protect people from harm, risk or danger: *Stronger legal safeguards are needed to protect the consumer.*

ˈsafe ˈhaven *noun* a place where sb can go to be safe from danger or attack

ˈsafe house *noun* a house used by people who are hiding, for example by criminals hiding from the police, or by people who are being protected by the police from other people who may wish to harm them

ˈsafe ˈkeeping *noun* [U] **1** the fact of sth being in a safe place where it will not be lost or damaged: *She had put her watch in her pocket for safe keeping.* **2** the fact of sb/sth being taken care of by sb who can be trusted: *The documents are in the safe keeping of our lawyers.*

safe·ly /ˈseɪfli/ *adv.* **1** without being harmed, damaged or lost: *The plane landed safely.* **2** in a way that does not cause harm or that protects sb/sth from harm: *The bomb has been safely disposed of.* ◊ *The money is safely locked in a drawer.* **3** without much possibility of being wrong: *We can safely say that he will accept the job.* **4** without any possibility of the situation changing: *I thought the kids were safely tucked up in bed.* **5** without any problems being caused; with no risk: *These recommendations can safely be ignored.*

ˈsafe mode *noun* [U] (*computing*) a way of starting a computer that makes it easier to find a problem without the risk of losing data

ˌsafe ˈpassage *noun* [U, C] = **SAFE CONDUCT**

ˈsafe room *noun* = **PANIC ROOM**

# 1367    saga

ˌsafe ˈseat *noun* (*BrE*) a **CONSTITUENCY** where a particular political party has a lot of support and their candidate is unlikely to be defeated in an election

ˌsafe ˈsex *noun* [U] sexual activity in which people try to protect themselves from AIDS and other sexual diseases, for example by using a **CONDOM**

ˈsafe space *noun* a place in which a person or a particular group of people can know that they will be free from harm or criticism: *The refuge provides a safe space for victims of domestic violence.*

safe·ty ⓘ B1 Ⓦ /ˈseɪfti/ *noun* (*pl.* **-ies**) **1** B1 [U] the state of being safe and protected from danger or harm: **in ~** *a place where children can play in safety* ◊ *He was kept in custody for his own safety.* ◊ *The police are concerned for the safety of the 12-year-old boy who has been missing for three days.* **2** B1 [U] the state of not being dangerous: *I'm worried about the safety of the treatment.* ◊ *a local campaign to improve road safety* ◊ *breaches of fire safety regulations* ◊ *safety concerns/issues* ◊ *The airline has an excellent safety record.* **3** B1 [U] a place where you are safe: **to ~** *I managed to swim to safety.* ◊ **from the ~ of sth** *We watched the lions from the safety of the car.* **4** [C] (*NAmE*) = **SAFETY CATCH** **5** [C] (*NAmE*) (*in* AMERICAN FOOTBALL) a defending player who plays in a position far away from the other team

IDM **ˈsafety ˈfirst** (*saying*) safety is the most important thing **there's ˌsafety in ˈnumbers** (*saying*) being in a group makes you safer and makes you feel more confident

ˈsafety belt *noun* = **SEAT BELT**

ˈsafety catch (*especially BrE*) (*NAmE usually* **safety**) *noun* a device that stops a gun from being fired or a machine from working by accident

ˌsafety deˈposit box *noun* = **SAFE DEPOSIT BOX**

ˈsafety glass *noun* [U] strong glass that does not break into sharp pieces

ˈsafety island *noun* (US) = **TRAFFIC ISLAND**

ˈsafety measure *noun* something that you do in order to prevent sth bad or dangerous from happening

ˈsafety net *noun* **1** an arrangement that helps to prevent disaster if sth goes wrong: *a financial safety net* ◊ *people who have fallen through the safety net and ended up homeless on the streets* **2** a net placed below **ACROBATS**, etc. to catch them if they fall

ˈsafety pin *noun* a pin with a point bent back towards the head, that is covered when closed so that it cannot hurt you

ˈsafety valve *noun* **1** a device that lets out **STEAM** or pressure in a machine when it becomes too great **2** a way of letting out feelings of anger, excitement, etc. without causing harm: *Exercise is a good safety valve for the tension that builds up at work.*

saf·flower /ˈsæflaʊə(r)/ *noun* [C, U] a plant with orange flowers, whose seeds produce an oil which is used in cooking

saf·fron /ˈsæfrən/ *noun* [U] **1** a bright yellow powder made from **CROCUS** flowers, used in cooking as a **SPICE** and to give colour to food ⊃ **VISUAL VOCAB** page V8 **2** a bright orange-yellow colour ▶ **saf·fron** *adj.*: *Buddhist monks in saffron robes*

sag[1] /sæɡ/ *verb* (**-gg-**) **1** [I] to hang or bend down in the middle, especially because of weight or pressure: *a sagging roof* ◊ *The tent began to sag under the weight of the rain.* ◊ *Your skin starts to sag as you get older.* **2** [I] to become weaker or fewer: *Their share of the vote sagged badly at the last election.* ▶ **sag** *noun* [U, C, usually sing.]: *Weight has caused the sag.* IDM see **JAW** *n*.

sag[2] *noun* = **SAAG**

saga /ˈsɑːɡə/ *noun* **1** a long traditional story about adventures and brave acts, especially one from Norway or Iceland **2** a long story about events over a period of many years: *a family saga* **3** a long series of events or

# sagacious

adventures and/or a report about them: *The front page is devoted to the continuing saga of the hijack.* ◊ (*humorous*) *the saga of how I missed the plane*

**sa·ga·cious** /səˈgeɪʃəs/ *adj.* (*formal*) showing good judgement and understanding **SYN** **wise** ▶ **sa·ga·ci·ty** /-ˈgæsəti/ *noun* [U]

**sage** /seɪdʒ/ *noun, adj.*
- *noun* **1** [U] a plant with flat, light green leaves that have a strong smell and are used in cooking as a HERB ⊃ VISUAL VOCAB page V8 **2** [C] (*formal*) a very wise person
- *adj.* (*literary*) wise, especially because you have a lot of experience ▶ **sage·ly** *adv.*: *She nodded sagely.*

**sage·brush** /ˈseɪdʒbrʌʃ/ *noun* [U] a plant with leaves that smell sweet that grows in dry regions in the western US; an area of ground covered with sagebrush

**saggy** /ˈsægi/ *adj.* (**sag·gier**, **sag·gi·est**) (*informal*) no longer stretched tight; hanging or sinking down in a way that is not attractive

**Sag·it·tar·ius** /ˌsædʒɪˈteəriəs; NAmE -ˈter-/ *noun* **1** [U] the 9th sign of the ZODIAC, the ARCHER **2** [sing.] a person born when the sun is in this sign, that is between 22 November and 20 December, approximately ▶ **Sag·it·tar·ian** /-riən/ *noun, adj.*

**sago** /ˈseɪɡəʊ/ *noun* [U] hard white grains made from the soft inside of a type of PALM tree, often cooked with milk to make a DESSERT: *sago pudding*

**sa·guaro** /səˈɡwɑːrəʊ/ *noun* (*pl.* **-os**) a very large CACTUS that grows in the southern US and Mexico

**sahib** /sɑːb, ˈsɑːhɪb; NAmE ˈsɑːhɪb, -hɪb/ *noun* used in India, especially in the past, to address a European man, especially one with some social or official status

**said** /sed/ **1** past tense, past part. of SAY **2** *adj.* [only before noun] (*formal or law*) = AFOREMENTIONED: *the said company*

**sail** 🔊 **A2** /seɪl/ *verb, noun*
- *verb* **1** **A2** [I, T] (of a boat or ship or the people on it) to travel on water using sails or an engine: **+ adv./prep.** *to sail into harbour* ◊ *The dinghy sailed smoothly across the lake.* ◊ *The ferry sails from Newhaven to Dieppe.* ◊ *one of the first people to sail around the world* ◊ *~sth to sail the Atlantic* **2** (*also* **go sailing**) [I, T] to control or travel on a boat with a sail, especially as a sport: *We spent the weekend sailing off the south coast.* ◊ *Do you go sailing often?* ◊ *~sth She sails her own yacht.* **3** [I] (of a boat or ship or the people in it) to begin a journey on water: *We sail at 2 p.m. tomorrow.* ◊ *~for sth He sailed for the West Indies from Portsmouth.* **4** [I] **+ adv./prep.** to move quickly and smoothly in a particular direction; (of people) to move in a confident manner: *clouds sailing across the sky* ◊ *The ball sailed over the goalie's head.* ◊ *She sailed past, ignoring me completely.*
  **IDM** **sail close to the ˈwind** to take a risk by doing sth that is dangerous or that may be illegal
  **PHRV** **sail ˈthrough (sth)** to pass an exam, a test, etc. without any difficulty
- *noun* **1** **B1** [C, U] a sheet of strong cloth which the wind blows against to make a boat or ship travel through the water: *As the boat moved down the river the wind began to fill the sails.* ◊ **under ~** *a ship under sail* (= using sails) ◊ *in the days of sail* (= when ships all used sails) ◊ *She moved away like a ship in full sail* (= with all its sails spread out). **2** **B1** [sing.] a trip in a boat or ship: *We went for a sail.* ◊ *a two-hour sail across the bay* **3** [C] a set of boards attached to the arm of a WINDMILL

▼ **HOMOPHONES**
**sail • sale** /seɪl/
- **sail** *verb*: *Thor managed to sail his raft across the Pacific Ocean.*
- **sail** *noun*: *Far out I could see a yacht with a white sail.*
- **sale** *noun*: *She will receive the profits from the sale of her property.*

**IDM** **set ˈsail (from/for …)** (*formal*) to begin a trip by sea: *a liner setting sail from New York* ◊ *We set sail (for I ance) at high tide.* ⊃ more at TRIM *v.*, WIND¹ *n.*

**sail·board** /ˈseɪlbɔːd; NAmE -bɔːrd/ (*also* **board**) *noun* = WINDSURFER (1) ▶ **sail·board·er** *noun* **sail·board·ing** *noun* [U]

**sail·boat** /ˈseɪlbəʊt/ (NAmE) (BrE **sailing boat**) *noun* a boat with sails

**sail·ing** 🔊 **A2** /ˈseɪlɪŋ/ *noun* **1** **A2** [U] the sport or activity of travelling in a boat with sails: *to go sailing* ◊ *a sailing club* **2** [C] one of the regular times that a ship leaves a port: *There are six sailings a day.* **IDM** see CLEAR *adj.*, PLAIN *adj.*

**ˈsailing boat** (BrE) (NAmE **sail·boat**) *noun* a boat with sails
**ˈsailing ship** *noun* a ship with sails

**sail·or** 🔊 **B1** /ˈseɪlə(r)/ *noun* **1** **B1** a person who works on a ship as a member of the crew: *a crew of two officers and 13 sailors* **2** **B1** a person who sails a boat: *My parents were keen sailors.*
**IDM** **a good/bad ˈsailor** a person who rarely/often becomes sick at sea

**saint** **C1** /seɪnt; *before names BrE also* snt/ *noun* **1** **C1** (*abbr.* **S**, **St**) a person that the Christian Church recognizes as being very holy, because of the way they have lived or died: *St John* ◊ *St Valentine's Day* ◊ *The children were all named after saints.* ⊃ see also PATRON SAINT **2** **C1** a very good, kind or patient person: *She's a saint to go on living with that man.* ◊ *His behaviour would try the patience of a saint.* ▶ **saint·hood** *noun* [U]

**saint·ed** /ˈseɪntɪd/ *adj.* [usually before noun] (*old-fashioned or humorous*) considered or officially stated to be a saint: *And how is my sainted sister?*

**saint·ly** /ˈseɪntli/ *adj.* like a SAINT; very holy and good: *to lead a saintly life* ▶ **saint·li·ness** *noun* [U]

**ˈsaint's day** *noun* (in the Christian Church) a day of the year when a particular SAINT is remembered and on which, in some countries, people who are named after that SAINT have celebrations

**saith** /seθ/ (*old use*) says

**sake¹** **C1** /seɪk/ *noun* ⊃ see also SAKE²
**IDM** **for Christ's, God's, goodness', heaven's, pity's, etc. ˈsake** used to emphasize that it is important to do sth or when you are annoyed about sth: *Do be careful, for goodness' sake.* ◊ *Oh, for heaven's sake!* ◊ *For pity's sake, help me!* **HELP** Some people find the use of **Christ**, **God** or **heaven** here offensive. **for sth's ˈsake** **C1** because of the interest or value sth has, not because of the advantages it may bring: *I believe in education for its own sake.* ◊ *art for art's sake* **for the sake of sb/sth** | **for sb's/sth's ˈsake** **C1** in order to help sb/sth or because you like sb/sth: *They stayed together for the sake of the children.* ◊ *You can do it. Please, for my sake.* ◊ *I hope you're right, for all our sakes* (= because this is important for all of us). **for the sake of sth** **C1** in order to get or keep sth: *The translation sacrifices naturalness for the sake of accuracy.* ◊ *She gave up smoking for the sake of her health.* ◊ *Let's suppose, for the sake of argument* (= in order to have a discussion), *that interest rates went up by 2 per cent.* **(just) for the ˈsake of it** for no particular reason: *Don't get married just for the sake of it.* ⊃ more at OLD

**sake²** (*also* **saki**) /ˈsɑːki/ *noun* [U, C] a Japanese alcoholic drink made from rice ⊃ see also SAKE¹

**sa·laam** /səˈlɑːm/ *verb* [I, T] **~(sb)** (in some Eastern countries) to say hello to sb in a formal way by bending forward at the middle part of your body and putting your right hand on your FOREHEAD ▶ **sa·laam** *noun*

**sal·able** (US) = SALEABLE

**sal·acious** /səˈleɪʃəs/ *adj.* (*formal*) (of stories, pictures, etc.) encouraging sexual desire or containing too much sexual detail ▶ **sal·acious·ness** *noun* [U]

**salad** 🔊 **A1** /ˈsæləd/ *noun* **1** **A1** [U, C] a mixture of raw vegetables such as LETTUCE, tomato and CUCUMBER, usually served with other food as part of a meal: *All main* courses come with salad or vegetables. ◊ Is cold meat and salad OK for lunch? ◊ a **side salad** (= a small bowl of salad served with the main course of a meal) ◊ a **salad bowl** (= a large bowl for serving salad in) ⊃ VISUAL VOCAB page V5 ⊃ see also CAESAR SALAD, GARDEN SALAD, GREEK SALAD, GREEN SALAD, SIDE SALAD **2** ⓘ A1 [C, U] (in compounds) meat, fish, cheese, etc. served with salad: *a chicken/tuna/seafood/egg salad* **3** ⓘ A1 [U, C] (in compounds) raw or cooked vegetables, etc. that are cut into small pieces, often mixed with MAYONNAISE and served cold with other food: *potato salad* ◊ *a pasta salad* ⊃ see also FRUIT SALAD **4** [C] any green vegetable, especially LETTUCE, that is eaten raw in a salad: *salad plants/leaves* ◊ *baby octopus served with salad greens*

IDM **your ˈsalad days** (*old-fashioned*) the time when you are young and do not have much experience of life

**ˈsalad bar** *noun* a place in a restaurant or supermarket where you can get a salad or ingredients to make a salad

**ˈsalad dressing** *noun* [U, C] = DRESSING

**sal·a·man·der** /ˈsæləmændə(r)/ *noun* an animal like a LIZ-ARD, with short legs and a long tail, that is an AMPHIBIAN (= lives on both land and in water) ⊃ VISUAL VOCAB page V3

**sa·lami** /səˈlɑːmi/ *noun* [U, C] (*pl.* **sa·lamis**) a type of large spicy SAUSAGE served cold in thin slices

**sal·ar·ied** /ˈsælərid/ *adj.* **1** (of a person) receiving a salary: *a salaried employee* **2** (of a job) for which a salary is paid: *a salaried position*

**sal·ary** ⓘ A2 /ˈsæləri/ *noun* (*pl.* **-ies**) money that employees receive for doing their job, especially professional employees or people working in an office, usually paid every month: *an annual salary of $40 000* ◊ *She earned a six-figure salary.* ◊ *a 9 per cent salary increase* ◊ (*BrE*) *He gets a basic salary plus commission.* ◊ (*NAmE*) *base salary* ⊃ compare WAGE ⊃ SYNONYMS at INCOME ⊃ WORDFINDER NOTE at PAY

**ˈsalary·man** /ˈsælərimæn/ *noun* (*pl.* **-men** /-men/) (especially in Japan) a WHITE-COLLAR worker (= one who works in an office)

**sal·bu·ta·mol** /sælˈbjuːtəmɒl; *NAmE* -mɔːl/ *noun* [U] a drug that is used in the treatment of medical conditions such as ASTHMA

**sale** ⓘ A2 /seɪl/ *noun* **1** ⓘ A2 [U, C] an act or the process of selling sth: *regulations governing the sale of alcoholic beverages* ◊ *She gets 10 per cent commission on each sale.* ◊ *We gave them our sales pitch* (= our explanation of why they should buy sth). ⊃ HOMOPHONES at SAIL ⊃ see also BILL OF SALE, POINT OF SALE **2** ⓘ A2 **sales** [pl.] the number of items sold: *They have to boost sales to make a profit.* ◊ *Retail sales fell in November by 10 per cent.* ◊ *ticket/car sales* ◊ *The company has seen record sales over the past year.* ◊ *sales are up/down Online sales were up by 12 per cent.* ◊ *the sales figures for May* **3** ⓘ A2 **sales** [U] (also **ˈsales department** [C]) the part of a company that deals with selling its products: *a sales and marketing director* ◊ *in~ She works in sales.* ◊ *He's a sales manager for a hotel group.* **4** ⓘ A2 [C] an occasion when a shop or business sells its products at a lower price than usual: *The sale starts next week.* ◊ *the January sales* ◊ **in the sales** *I bought a coat in the sales.* ⊃ WORDFINDER NOTE at SHOP ⊃ see also FIRE SALE **5** [C] an occasion when goods are sold, especially an AUC-TION: *a contemporary art sale* ⊃ see also BAKE SALE, BRING-AND-BUY SALE, CAR BOOT SALE, ESTATE SALE, GARAGE SALE, JUMBLE SALE, RUMMAGE SALE, YARD SALE

IDM ▸ **(up) for ˈsale** available to be bought, especially from the owner: *I'm sorry, it's not for sale.* ◊ *They've put their house up for sale.* ◊ *an increase in the number of stolen vehicles being offered for sale* ◊ *a 'for sale' sign* ▸ **on ˈsale 1** available to be bought, especially in a shop: *Tickets are on sale from the booking office.* ◊ *The new model goes on sale next month.* **2** (*especially NAmE, SAfrE*) being offered at a reduced price: *All video equipment is on sale today and tomorrow.* ▸ **(on) ˌsale or reˈturn** (*BrE*) (of goods) supplied with the agreement that any item that is not sold can be sent back without having to be paid for

**sale·able** (*US also* **sal·able**) /ˈseɪləbl/ *adj.* good enough to be sold; that sb will want to buy: *a saleable product* ◊ *not in saleable condition* OPP **unsaleable**

**ˈsale of ˈwork** *noun* (*pl.* **ˌsales of ˈwork**) (*BrE*) a sale of things made by members of an organization, such as a church, often to make money for charity

**ˈsale·room** /ˈseɪlruːm, -rʊm/ (*BrE*) (*NAmE* **ˈsales·room**) *noun* a room where goods are sold at an AUCTION

**ˈsales clerk** (*also* **clerk**) (*both NAmE*) (*BrE* **ˈshop assistant, asˈsistant**) *noun* a person whose job is to serve customers in a shop

**sales·man** /ˈseɪlzmən/, **sales·woman** /ˈseɪlzwʊmən/ *noun* (*pl.* **-men** /-mən/, **-women** /-wɪmɪn/) a man or woman whose job is to sell goods, for example, in a shop: *a car salesman* ⊃ note at GENDER

**sales·man·ship** /ˈseɪlzmənʃɪp/ *noun* [U] skill in persuading people to buy things

**sales·per·son** /ˈseɪlzpɜːsn; *NAmE* -pɜːrsn/ *noun* (*pl.* **-people**) a person whose job is to sell goods, for example, in a shop

**ˈsales rep** (*also formal* **ˈsales repreˈsentative, rep**) *noun* an employee of a company who travels around a particular area selling the company's goods to shops and other businesses

**ˈsales·room** /ˈseɪlzruːm, -rʊm/ (*NAmE*) (*BrE* **ˈsale·room**) *noun* a room where goods are sold at an AUCTION

**ˈsales slip** *noun* (*NAmE*) a piece of paper that shows that goods or services have been paid for SYN **receipt**

**ˈsales tax** *noun* [U, C] (in some countries) the part of the price you pay when you buy sth that goes to the government as tax

**sali·cyl·ic acid** /ˌsælɪsɪlɪk ˈæsɪd/ *noun* [U] a bitter chemical found in some plants, used in ASPIRIN (= a drug used for reducing pain and making your blood thinner)

**sa·li·ent** /ˈseɪliənt/ *adj.* [only before noun] most important or easy to notice: *She pointed out the salient features of the new design.* ◊ *He summarized the salient points.* ▸ **sa·li·ence** /-əns/ *noun* [U, sing.]: *This issue has been growing in salience.* ◊ ~ **for sb/sth** *The themes in the book have a special salience for adolescents.*

**sa·line** /ˈseɪlaɪn; *NAmE* -liːn/ *adj., noun*
■ *adj.* [usually before noun] (*specialist*) containing salt: *Wash the lenses in saline solution.* ▸ **sa·lin·ity** /səˈlɪnəti/ *noun* [U]: *to measure the salinity of the water*
■ *noun* [U] (*specialist*) a mixture of salt in water

**sa·liva** /səˈlaɪvə/ *noun* [U] the liquid that is produced in your mouth that helps you to SWALLOW food

**sa·liv·ary** /səˈlaɪvəri; ˈsælɪvəri; *NAmE* ˈsæləveri/ *adj.* (*specialist*) of or producing saliva

**sali·vate** /ˈsælɪveɪt/ *verb* [I] (*formal or humorous*) to produce more SALIVA in your mouth than usual, especially when you see or smell food: (*figurative*) *He was salivating over the thought of the million dollars.* ▸ **sali·va·tion** /ˌsælɪˈveɪʃn/ *noun* [U]

**sal·low** /ˈsæləʊ/ *adj., noun*
■ *adj.* (of a person's skin or face) having a slightly yellow colour that does not look healthy SYN **pasty**²
■ *noun* a type of WILLOW tree that does not grow very tall

**sally** /ˈsæli/ *noun, verb*
■ *noun* (*pl.* **sal·lies**) **1** a remark that is intended to entertain sb or make them laugh SYN **witticism 2** a sudden attack by an enemy
■ *verb* (**sal·lies, sally·ing, sal·lied, sal·lied**)
PHRV ▸ **ˌsally ˈforth/ˈout** (*old-fashioned or literary*) to leave a place in a determined or enthusiastic way

**sal·mon** /ˈsæmən/ *noun* [C, U] (*pl.* **sal·mon**) a large fish that has silver skin and is pink inside and is used for food. Salmon live in the sea but swim up rivers to lay their eggs: *a whole salmon* ◊ *smoked salmon* ◊ *wild and farmed salmon* ◊ *good weather conditions for salmon fishing*

**sal·mon·ella** /ˌsælməˈnelə/ *noun* [U] a type of bacteria that makes people sick if they eat food that contains it;

an illness caused by this bacteria: *cases of salmonella poisoning* ◊ *an outbreak of salmonella*

**salmon 'pink** *adj.* orange-pink in colour, like the inside of a salmon ▶ **salmon 'pink** *noun* [U]

**salon** /ˈsælɒn; *NAmE* səˈlɑːn/ *noun* **1** a shop that gives customers hair or beauty treatment or that sells expensive clothes: *a beauty salon* ◊ *a hairdressing salon* ⇒ see also BEAUTY SALON **2** (*old-fashioned*) a room in a large house used for entertaining guests **3** (in the past) a regular meeting of writers, artists and other guests at the house of a famous or important person: *a literary salon*

**sa·loon** /səˈluːn/ *noun* **1** (also **saˈloon car**) (both *BrE*) (*NAmE* **sedan**) a car with a BOOT (= space at the back for carrying things) that is separated from the part where the driver and passengers sit: *a five-seater family saloon* **2** (also **saˈloon bar**) (both *BrE*) = LOUNGE BAR **3** a bar where alcoholic drinks were sold in the western US and Canada in the past **4** a large comfortable room on a ship, used by the passengers to sit and relax in

**salsa** /ˈsælsə; *NAmE* ˈsɑːl-/ *noun* **1** [U] a type of Latin American dance music **2** [C, U] a dance performed to this music **3** [U] a spicy tomato sauce eaten with Mexican food

**salt** ⓘ A1 /sɔːlt; *BrE also* sɒlt/ *noun, verb, adj.*
■ *noun* **1** ⓘ [U] a white substance that is added to food to make it taste better or to preserve it. Salt is obtained from mines and is also found in SEAWATER. It is sometimes called ˌcommon ˈsalt to show that it is different from other chemical salts. Its chemical name is SODIUM CHLORIDE: *Pass the salt, please.* ◊ *a pinch of salt* (= a small amount of it) ◊ *Season with salt and pepper.* ◊ *table salt* ⇒ see also ROCK SALT, SEA SALT **2** [C] (*chemistry*) a chemical formed from a metal and an ACID: *mineral salts* ⇒ see also EPSOM SALTS **3 salts** [pl.] a substance that looks or tastes like salt: *bath salts* (= used to give a pleasant smell to bath water) ⇒ see also SMELLING SALTS
IDM **the salt of the ˈearth** a very good and honest person that you can always depend on **take sth with a ˈpinch of ˈsalt** (*NAmE also* **take sth with a ˈgrain of ˈsalt**) to be careful about believing that sth is completely true ⇒ more at DOSE *n.*, RUB *v.*, WORTH *adj.*
■ *verb* **1** [usually passive] **~ sth** to put salt on or in food: *salted peanuts* ◊ *a pan of boiling salted water* **2 ~ sth (down)** to preserve food with salt: *salted fish* **3 ~ sth** to put salt on roads to melt ice or snow
PHRV **ˌsalt sth↔aˈway** to save sth for the future, secretly and usually dishonestly: *She salted away the profits in foreign bank accounts.*
■ *adj.* [only before noun] containing, tasting of or preserved with salt: *salt water* ◊ *salt beef*

**salt-and-ˈpepper** *adj.* = PEPPER-AND-SALT

**ˈsalt cellar** *noun* **1** (*BrE*) (*NAmE also* **ˈsalt shaker**) a small container for salt, usually with one hole in the top, that is used at the table **2** (*NAmE*) a small open dish containing salt

**ˈsalt flats** *noun* [pl.] a flat area of land, covered with a layer of salt

**sal·tire** /ˈsɔːltaɪə(r), ˈsæl-/ *noun* **1** [C] a cross in the shape of an X, especially on a COAT OF ARMS or a flag **2 the Saltire** [sing.] the flag of Scotland, which is a white saltire on a blue background

**ˈsalt marsh** (*also* **ˈsalt meadow**) *noun* an area of open land near a coast that is regularly flooded with water from the sea

**ˈsalt pan** *noun* an area of low land where SEAWATER has EVAPORATED to leave salt

**salt·petre** (*US* **salt·peter**) /ˌsɔːltˈpiːtə(r); *BrE also* ˌsɒlt-/ *noun* [U] a white powder used for preserving food and making matches and GUNPOWDER

**ˈsalt shaker** *noun* (*NAmE*) = SALT CELLAR (1)

**ˈsalt truck** (*US*) (*BrE* **ˈgrit·ter**) *noun* a large vehicle used for putting salt, sand or GRIT on the roads in winter when there is ice on them

**ˈsalt water** *noun* [U] water containing salt; SEAWATER
▶ **ˈsalt-water** *adj.* [only before noun]: *saltwater fish* ⇒ compare FRESHWATER

**salty** /ˈsɔːlti; *BrE also* ˈsɒl-/ *adj.* (**saltˈier**, **saltiˈest**) **1** containing or tasting of salt: *salty food* ◊ *salty sea air* ⇒ compare SWEET **2** (*old-fashioned*) (of language or humour) funny and sometimes slightly rude ▶ **saltiˈness** *noun* [U]: *She could taste the saltiness of her tears.*

**sa·lu·bri·ous** /səˈluːbriəs/ *adj.* (*formal*) (of a place) pleasant to live in; clean and healthy

**salu·tary** /ˈsæljətri; *NAmE* -teri/ *adj.* having a good effect on sb/sth, though often seeming unpleasant: *a salutary lesson/experience/warning* ◊ *The accident was a salutary reminder of the dangers of climbing.*

**sa·lu·ta·tion** /ˌsæljuˈteɪʃn/ *noun* **1** [C, U] (*formal*) something that you say to welcome or say hello to sb; the action of welcoming or saying hello to sb **2** [C] (*specialist*) the words that are used in a letter to address the person you are writing to, for example 'Dear Sir'

**sa·lute** /səˈluːt/ *verb, noun*
■ *verb* **1** [I, T] to touch the side of your head with the fingers of your right hand to show respect, especially in the armed forces: *The sergeant stood to attention and saluted.* ◊ **~ sb/sth** *to salute the flag/an officer* **2** [T] **~ sb/sth** (*formal*) to show that you respect and admire sb/sth SYN acknowledge: *The players saluted the fans before leaving the field.* ◊ *The president saluted the courage of those who had fought for their country.*
■ *noun* **1** [C] the action of raising your right hand to the side of your head as a sign of respect, especially between soldiers and officers **2** [C, U] a thing that you say or do to show that you respect and admire sb/sth or to welcome sb: *He raised his hat as a friendly salute.* ◊ **to sb/sth** *His first words were a salute to the people of South Africa.* ◊ **in ~** *They all raised their glasses in salute.* **3** [C] an official occasion when guns are fired into the air to show respect for an important person: *a 21-gun salute*

**sal·vage** /ˈsælvɪdʒ/ *noun, verb*
■ *noun* [U] **1** the act of saving things that have been, or are likely to be, damaged or lost, especially in a disaster or an accident: *the salvage of the wrecked tanker* ◊ *a salvage company/operation/team* **2** the things that are saved from a disaster or an accident: *an exhibition of the salvage from the wreck*
■ *verb* **1** to save a badly damaged ship, etc. from being lost completely; to save parts or property from a damaged ship or from a fire, etc: **~ sth** *The wreck was salvaged by a team from the RAF.* ◊ *The house was built using salvaged materials.* ◊ **~ sth from sth** *We only managed to salvage two paintings from the fire.* **2 ~ sth** to manage to rescue sth from a difficult situation; to stop a bad situation from being a complete failure: *What can I do to salvage my reputation?* (= get a good reputation again) ◊ *He wondered what he could do to salvage the situation.* ◊ *United lost 5–2, salvaging a little pride with two late goals.*

**ˈsalvage yard** *noun* (*NAmE*) a place where old machines, cars, etc. are broken up so that the metal can be sold or used again

**sal·va·tion** /sælˈveɪʃn/ *noun* [U] **1** (in Christianity) the state of being saved from the power of evil: *to pray for the salvation of the world* **2** a way of protecting sb from danger, disaster, loss, etc: *Group therapy classes have been his salvation.*

**the Salˈvation ˈArmy** *noun* [sing.] a Christian organization whose members wear military uniforms and work to help poor people

**salve** /sælv, sɑːv; *NAmE* sæv/ *noun, verb*
■ *noun* [U, C] a substance that you put on a wound or painful skin to help it to get better or to protect it
■ *verb* **~ your conscience** (*formal*) to do sth that makes you feel less guilty

**sal·ver** /ˈsælvə(r)/ *noun* a large plate, usually made of metal, on which drinks or food are served at a formal event

**salvo** /ˈsælvəʊ/ *noun* (*pl.* **-os** *or* **-oes**) the act of firing several guns or dropping several bombs, etc. at the same time; a sudden attack: *The first salvo exploded a short distance away.* ◊ *(figurative)* *The newspaper article was* **the opening salvo** *in what proved to be a long battle.*

**sal·war** /sʌlˈwɑː(r)/ (*also* **shal·war**) *noun* light loose trousers that are tight around the ankles, sometimes worn by South Asian women: *a salwar kameez* (= a salwar worn with a KAMEEZ)

**Sa·mar·itan** /səˈmærɪtən/ *noun*
IDM **a good Sa'maritan** a person who gives help and sympathy to people who need it ORIGIN From the Bible story of a person from Samaria who helps an injured man that nobody else will help.

**the Sa·mar·itans** /ðə səˈmærɪtənz/ *noun* [pl.] a British charity that offers help to people who are worried, depressed, or in danger of killing themselves, by providing a phone number that they can ring in order to talk to sb

**samba** /ˈsæmbə/ *noun* a fast dance originally from Brazil; a piece of music for this dance

**same** 🔑 **A1** **S** /seɪm/ *adj., pron., adv.*
- *adj.* **1** **A1** exactly the one or ones referred to or mentioned; not different: *We have lived in the same house for twenty years.* ◊ *Our children go to the same school as theirs.* ◊ *She's still the same fun-loving person that I knew at college.* ◊ *This one works in exactly the same way as the other.* ◊ *They both said much the same thing.* ◊ *He used the very same* (= exactly the same) *words.* ◊ *I was relieved and sad at the same time.* **2** **A1** exactly like the one or ones referred to or mentioned: *I bought the same car as yours* (= another car of that type). ◊ *She was wearing the same dress that I had on.* ◊ *The same thing happened to me last week.*
IDM HELP Most idioms containing **same** are at the entries for the nouns and verbs in the idioms, for example **be in the same boat** is at **boat**. ˌsame ˈold, ˌsame ˈold (*informal*) used to say that a situation has not changed at all: *'How's it going?' 'Oh, same old, same old.'* **the same old story**, **stuff**, **nonsense**, **etc.** (*informal*) used to say that a situation or the excuses, products or entertainment being offered have not improved at all: *It's the same old story—budget cuts and government neglect.*
- *pron.* **1** **the ~ (as …)** the same thing or things: *I would do the same again.* ◊ *I think the same as you do about this.* ◊ *Just do the same as me* (= as I do). ◊ *His latest movie is just more of the same—exotic locations, car chases and a final shoot-out.* ◊ (*informal*) *'I'll have coffee.' 'Same for me, please* (= I will have one too)*.'* **2** **A1** **the ~ (as …)** having the same number, colour, size, quality, etc: *There are several brands and they're not all the same.* ◊ *I'd like one the same as yours.* **3** **the same** (*BrE*) the same person: *'Was that George on the phone?' 'The same* (= yes, it was George)*.'*
IDM **all / just the ˈsame** despite this SYN **nevertheless**: *He's not very reliable, but I like him just the same.* ◊ *'Will you stay for lunch?' 'No, but thanks all the same.'* **All the same, there's some truth in what she says.** **be all the ˈsame to sb** to not be important to sb: *I'd rather stay here, if it's all the same to you.* **one and the ˈsame** the same person or thing: *It turns out that her aunt and my cousin are one and the same.* **(the) ˌsame aˈgain** (*informal*) used to ask sb to serve you the same drink as before: *Same again, please!* ˌsame ˈhere (*informal*) (*also slang* **same**) used to say that sth is also true of you: *'I can't wait to see it.' 'Same here.'* **(the) ˌsame to ˈyou** (*also slang* **same**) used to answer a GREETING, an offensive remark, etc: *'Happy Christmas!' 'And the same to you!'* ◊ *'Get lost!' 'Same to you!'*
- *adv.* **A1** (*usually* **the same**) in the same way: *We treat boys exactly the same as girls.* ◊ (*informal*) *He gave me five dollars, same as usual.*

**same·ness** /ˈseɪmnəs/ *noun* [U] (*often disapproving*) the fact of being the same; a lack of variety: *She grew tired of the sameness of the food.*

ˈ**same-sex** *adj.* [only before noun] of the same sex; involving people of the same sex: *The child's same-sex parent acts as a role model.* ◊ *a same-sex relationship*

**samey** /ˈseɪmi/ *adj.* (*BrE, informal, disapproving*) not changing or different and therefore boring

1371

**sa·miti** /ˈsæmiti/ *noun* (*IndE*) a committee, a society or an association

**sa·mosa** /səˈməʊsə/ *noun* a type of hot spicy South Asian food consisting of a TRIANGLE of thin PASTRY filled with meat or vegetables and fried until it is hard and dry

**samp** /sæmp/ *noun* [U] (*SAfrE*) the inner parts of MAIZE seeds that are pressed and broken roughly; a type of PORRIDGE that is made from this

**sam·pan** /ˈsæmpæn/ *noun* a small boat with a flat bottom used along the coast and rivers of China

**sam·ple** 🔑 **B1** 🔊 /ˈsɑːmpl; NAmE ˈsæm-/ *noun, verb*
- *noun* **1** **B1** a number of people or things taken from a larger group and used in tests to provide information about the group: *The interviews were given to a random sample of students.* ◊ *The survey covers a representative sample of schools.* ◊ *The current study has a larger sample size than earlier studies.* **2** **B2** a small amount of a substance taken from a larger amount and tested in order to obtain information about the substance: *a blood/urine/tissue/DNA sample* ◊ *to collect/obtain/take a sample* ⮕ WORDFINDER NOTE at EXAMINE **3** **B2** a small amount or example of sth that can be looked at or tried to see what it is like: *'I'd like to see a sample of your work,' said the manager.* ◊ *a free sample of shampoo* **4** (*specialist*) a piece of recorded music or sound that is used in a new piece of music
- *verb* **1** **B2** **~ sth** to try a small amount of a particular food to see what it is like; to experience sth for a short time to see what it is like: *I sampled the delights of Greek cooking for the first time.* **2 ~ sb/sth** (*specialist*) to test, question, etc., part of sth or of a group of people in order to find out what the rest is like: *12 per cent of the children sampled said they prefer cats to dogs.* **3 ~ sth** (*specialist*) to record part of a piece of music, or a sound, in order to use it in a new piece of music

**sam·pler** /ˈsɑːmplə(r); NAmE ˈsæm-/ *noun* **1** a piece of cloth decorated with different STITCHES that people made in the past to show a person's skill at SEWING **2** a collection that shows typical examples of sth, especially pieces of music

**sam·pling** W /ˈsɑːmplɪŋ; NAmE ˈsæm-/ *noun* [U] **1** the process of taking a sample: *statistical sampling* **2** (*specialist*) the process of copying and recording parts of a piece of music in an electronic form so that they can be used in a different piece of music

ˈ**sampling error** *noun* (*statistics*) a situation in which a set of results or figures does not show a true situation, because the group of people or things it was based on was not typical of a wider group

**sam·urai** /ˈsæmuraɪ/ *noun* (*pl.* **sam·urai**) (*from Japanese*) (in the past) a member of a powerful military class in Japan

**sana·tor·ium** /ˌsænəˈtɔːriəm/ *noun* (*pl.* **-tor·iums**, **-tor·ia** /-riə/) (*NAmE also* **sani·tar·ium**) a place like a hospital where patients who have a long-term illness or who are getting better after an illness are treated

**sanc·tify** /ˈsæŋktɪfaɪ/ *verb* (**sanc·ti·fies**, **sanc·ti·fied**, **sanc·ti·fy·ing**, **sanc·ti·fied**) [usually passive] (*formal*) **1 ~ sth** to make sth holy **2 ~ sth** to make sth seem right or legal; to give official approval to sth: *This was a practice sanctified by tradition.* ▶ **sanc·ti·fi·ca·tion** /ˌsæŋktɪfɪˈkeɪʃn/ *noun* [U]

**sanc·ti·mo·ni·ous** /ˌsæŋktɪˈməʊniəs/ *adj.* (*disapproving*) giving the impression that you feel you are better and more moral than other people SYN **self-righteous** ▶ **sanc·ti·mo·ni·ous·ly** *adv.* **sanc·ti·mo·ni·ous·ness** *noun* [U]

**sanc·tion** **B2+** **C1** /ˈsæŋkʃn/ *noun, verb*
- *noun* **1** **B2+** **C1** [C, usually pl.] **~ (against sb)** an official order that limits trade, contact, etc. with a particular country, in order to make it do sth, such as obeying international law: *Trade sanctions were imposed against any country that refused to sign the agreement.* ◊ *The economic sanctions have been lifted.* ⮕ WORDFINDER NOTE at TRADE **2** [U] (*formal*) official permission or approval for an action or a change SYN **authorization**: *These changes will require the sanction of the court.* **3** [C] **~ (against sth)** a course of action

# sanctity

that can be used, if necessary, to make people obey a law or behave in a particular way **SYN** **penalty**: *The ultimate sanction will be the closure of the restaurant.*
- *verb* **1** ~ sth (*formal*) to give permission for sth to take place: *The government refused to sanction a further cut in interest rates.* **2** ~ sb/sth (*specialist*) to punish sb/sth; to impose a sanction on sth

**sanc·tity** /ˈsæŋktəti/ *noun* [U] **1** ~ (of sth) the state of being very important and worth protecting: *the sanctity of marriage* **2** the state of being holy: *a life of sanctity, like that of St Francis*

**sanc·tu·ary** /ˈsæŋktʃuəri; *NAmE* -tʃueri/ *noun* (*pl.* **-ies**) **1** [C] an area where wild birds or animals are protected and encouraged to produce young **SYN** **reserve**: *a bird/wildlife sanctuary* **2** [U] safety and protection, especially for people who are in danger of being attacked or captured: *to seek/find/take sanctuary in a place* ◊ *The government offered sanctuary to 4000 refugees.* ◊ *She longed for the sanctuary of her own home.* **3** [C, usually sing.] a safe place, especially one where people who are in danger of being attacked or captured can stay and be protected: *The church became a sanctuary for the refugees.* **4** [C] a holy building or the part of it that is considered the most holy

**sanc·tum** /ˈsæŋktəm/ *noun* [usually sing.] (*formal*) **1** a private room where sb can go and not be interrupted: *She once allowed me into her inner sanctum.* **2** a holy place

**sand** ❶ **B1** /sænd/ *noun, verb*
- *noun* **1** ❷ **B1** [U] a substance that consists of very small fine grains of rock. Sand is found on beaches, in deserts, etc: *a grain of sand* ◊ *coarse/fine sand* ◊ *Concrete is a mixture of sand and cement.* ◊ *The children were playing in the sand* (= for example, in a SANDPIT). **2** **B1** [U, C, usually pl.] a large area of sand on a beach or in the desert: *We went for a walk along the sand.* ◊ *miles of golden sands* ◊ *the burning desert sands* ⇒ SYNONYMS at COAST ⇒ see also SANDY **IDM** see HEAD *n.*, SHIFT *v.*
- *verb* ~ sth (down) to make sth smooth by rubbing it with SANDPAPER or using a SANDER

**san·dal** /ˈsændl/ *noun* a type of light open shoe that is worn in warm weather. The top part consists of leather bands that fasten the SOLE to your foot.

**san·dal·wood** /ˈsændlwʊd/ *noun* [U] a type of oil with a sweet smell that is obtained from a hard tropical wood (also called sandalwood) and is used to make PERFUME

**sand·bag** /ˈsændbæg/ *noun, verb*
- *noun* a bag filled with sand used to build a wall as a protection against floods or explosions
- *verb* (-gg-) **1** ~ sth to put sandbags in or around sth as protection against floods or explosions **2** ~ sb (*informal, especially NAmE*) to attack sb by criticizing them strongly; to treat sb badly

**sand·bank** /ˈsændbæŋk/ *noun* a raised area of sand in a river or the sea ⇒ WORDFINDER NOTE at SEA

**sand·bar** /ˈsændbɑː(r)/ *noun* a long mass of sand at the point where a river meets the sea that is formed by the movement of the water

**sand·blast** /ˈsændblɑːst; *NAmE* -blæst/ *verb* [often passive] ~ sth to clean, POLISH, decorate, etc. a surface by firing sand at it from a special machine

**sand·box** /ˈsændbɒks; *NAmE* -bɑːks/ *noun* **1** (*NAmE*) (*BrE* **sand·pit**) an area in the ground or a shallow container, filled with sand for children to play in **2** a test area on a computer system, where you can run software without affecting the HARDWARE or other software **3** a video game style that allows players to explore the game freely, make changes to the way it looks, or establish their own rules

**sand·cas·tle** /ˈsændkɑːsl; *NAmE* -kæsl/ *noun* a pile of sand made to look like a castle, usually made by a child on a beach

**ˈsand dune** *noun* = DUNE

**sand·er** /ˈsændə(r)/ *noun* an electric tool with a rough surface used for making wood smooth

**s and h** (*also* **s & h**) /ˌes ən ˈeɪtʃ/ *abbr.* (*NAmE*) shipping and handling ⇒ compare P. AND P.

**S & L** /ˌes ən ˈel/ *abbr.* SAVINGS AND LOAN ASSOCIATION

**sand·lot** /ˈsændlɒt; *NAmE* -lɑːt/ *adj.* [only before noun] (*NAmE*) (of a sport) played for fun rather than as a job for money: *sandlot baseball*

**the ˈsand·man** /ðə ˈsændmæn/ *noun* [sing.] an imaginary man who is said to help children get to sleep

**sand·paper** /ˈsændpeɪpə(r)/ *noun, verb*
- *noun* [U] strong paper with a rough surface covered with sand or a similar substance, used for rubbing surfaces in order to make them smooth
- *verb* (*also* **sand**) ~ sth (down) to make sth smooth by rubbing it with sandpaper

**sand·piper** /ˈsændpaɪpə(r)/ *noun* a small bird with long legs and a long BEAK that lives near rivers and lakes

**sand·pit** /ˈsændpɪt/ (*BrE*) (*NAmE* **sand·box**) *noun* an area in the ground or a shallow container, filled with sand for children to play in

**sand·stone** /ˈsændstəʊn/ *noun* [U] a type of stone that is formed of grains of sand tightly pressed together, used in building

**sand·storm** /ˈsændstɔːm; *NAmE* -stɔːrm/ *noun* a storm in a desert in which sand is blown into the air by strong winds

**ˈsand trap** (*also* **trap**) *noun* (both especially *NAmE*) = BUNKER

**sand·wich** ❶ **A1** /ˈsænwɪtʃ, -wɪdʒ/ *noun, verb*
- *noun* **A1** (*also BrE, informal* **sar·nie**) two slices of bread, often spread with butter, with a layer of meat, cheese, etc. between them: *a ham/tuna/egg sandwich* ◊ *a toasted sandwich* ⇒ see also CLUB SANDWICH, OPEN SANDWICH, OPEN-FACED SANDWICH
- *verb*
**PHRV** **ˈsandwich sb/sth beˈtween sb/sth** [usually passive] to fit sb/sth into a very small space between two other things or people, or between two times: *I was sandwiched between two fat men on the bus.* **ˌsandwich A and B toˈgether (with sth)** [usually passive] to put sth between two things to join them: *two small biscuits sandwiched together with chocolate*

**ˈsandwich board** *noun* a pair of boards with advertisements on them that sb wears at the front and back of their body as they walk around in public

**sandy** /ˈsændi/ *adj.* (**sand·ier**, **sandi·est**) **1** covered with or containing sand: *a sandy beach* ◊ *sandy soil* **2** (of hair) having a light colour, between yellow and red ⇒ WORDFINDER NOTE at BLONDE

**sane** /seɪn/ *adj.* (**saner**, **san·est**) **1** having a normal healthy mind; not mentally ill: *No sane person would do that.* ◊ *Being able to get out of the city at the weekend keeps me sane.* **2** sensible and reasonable: *the sane way to solve the problem* **OPP** **insane** ⇒ see also SANITY ▶ **sane·ly** *adv.*

**sang** /sæŋ/ *past tense of* SING

**san·geet** /sʌnˈɡiːt; *NAmE* sɑːŋˈɡ-/ *noun* (*IndE*) a celebration held before a Hindu wedding ceremony for the woman who is getting married and her friends and relatives

**sangh** /sæŋ/ *BrE also* sʌŋ/ *noun* (*IndE*) a group of people who meet regularly because they have the same interest or aim; an association: *The leader of the sangh appealed for peace.*

**san·goma** /sænˈɡəʊmə; *SAfrE* [sɛŋˈɡɔmə]/ *noun* (*SAfrE*) a person who is believed to have magic powers that can be used, for example, to find out why sb is ill or protect sb from being harmed

**san·gria** /sænˈɡriːə/ *noun* [U, C] (*from Spanish*) an alcoholic drink made of red wine mixed with fruit, and sometimes with LEMONADE or BRANDY added

**san·guin·ary** /ˈsæŋɡwɪnəri; *NAmE* -neri/ *adj.* (*formal*) involving or liking killing and blood

**san·guine** /ˈsæŋɡwɪn/ *adj.* ~ (about sth) (*formal*) cheerful and confident about the future **SYN** **optimistic**: *They are less sanguine about the company's long-term prospects.* ◊ *He tends to take a sanguine view of the problems involved.* ▶ **san·guine·ly** *adv.*

**sani·tar·ium** /ˌsænəˈteəriəm; NAmE -ˈter-/ noun (pl. -**tar·iums** or -**taria** /-riə/) (NAmE) = SANATORIUM

**sani·tary** /ˈsænətri; NAmE -teri/ adj. **1** [only before noun] connected with keeping places clean and healthy to live in, especially by removing human waste: *Overcrowding and poor sanitary conditions led to disease in the refugee camps.* ◊ *The hut had no cooking or sanitary facilities.* **2** clean; not likely to cause health problems **SYN hygienic**: *The new houses were more sanitary than the old ones had been.* **OPP insanitary**

**sanitary towel** (BrE) (NAmE **ˈsanitary napkin**) (also **ˈsanitary pad** BrE and NAmE) noun a thick piece of soft material that a woman wears between her legs to hold blood during her PERIOD ⊃ compare TAMPON

**sani·ta·tion** /ˌsænɪˈteɪʃn/ noun [U] the equipment and systems that keep places clean, especially by removing human waste: *disease resulting from poor sanitation*

**saniˈtation worker** noun (NAmE, formal) a person whose job is to remove waste from outside houses, etc. **SYN refuse collector**

**sani·tize** (BrE also -**ise**) /ˈsænɪtaɪz/ verb (formal) **1** ~ sth (disapproving) to remove the parts of sth that could be considered unpleasant: *This sanitized version of his life does not mention his time in prison.* **2** ~ sth to clean sth completely using chemicals to remove bacteria **SYN disinfect**

**san·ity** /ˈsænəti/ noun [U] **1** the state of having a normal healthy mind: *His behaviour was so strange that I began to question his sanity.* ◊ *to keep/preserve your sanity* **2** the state of being sensible and reasonable: *After a series of road accidents the police pleaded for sanity among drivers.* **OPP insanity** ⊃ see also SANE

**sank** /sæŋk/ past tense of SINK

**sans** /sænz/ prep. (from French, literary or humorous) without: *There were no potatoes so we had fish and chips sans the chips.*

**sansa** /ˈsænsə/ noun = THUMB PIANO

**San·skrit** /ˈsænskrɪt/ noun [U] an ancient language of India belonging to the Indo-European family, in which the Hindu holy texts are written and on which many modern languages are based

**Santa Claus** /ˌsæntə ˈklɔːz/ (also **Santa**) (BrE also **ˌFather ˈChristmas**) noun an imaginary old man with red clothes and a long white BEARD. Parents tell small children that he brings them presents at Christmas. ⊃ see also SECRET SANTA

**sap** /sæp/ noun, verb
■ noun **1** [U] the liquid in a plant or tree that carries food to all its parts: *Maple syrup is made from sap collected from the sugar maple tree.* **2** [C] (especially NAmE, informal) a stupid person that you can easily trick, or treat unfairly
■ verb (-**pp**-) ~ sth to make sth/sb weaker; to destroy sth gradually: *The hot sun sapped our energy.* ◊ ~ sb (of sth) *Years of failure have sapped him of his confidence.*

**sap·ling** /ˈsæplɪŋ/ noun a young tree

**sap·per** /ˈsæpə(r)/ noun (BrE) a soldier whose job is to build or repair roads, bridges, etc.

**sap·phic** /ˈsæfɪk/ adj. (formal) relating to LESBIANS ▶ **sap·phism** /-fɪzəm/ noun [U]

**sap·phire** /ˈsæfaɪə(r)/ noun **1** [C, U] a clear, bright blue PRECIOUS STONE **2** [U] a bright blue colour ▶ **sap·phire** adj.: *sapphire eyes*

**sappy** /ˈsæpi/ adj. (**sap·pier**, **sap·pi·est**) **1** (NAmE, informal) = SOPPY **2** (of plants) full of SAP

**sap·wood** /ˈsæpwʊd/ noun [U] the soft younger outer layers of the wood of a tree, inside the BARK ⊃ compare HEARTWOOD

**Saran Wrap**™ /səˌræn ˈræp/ noun (U) (NAmE) = PLASTIC WRAP

**sar·casm** /ˈsɑːkæzəm; NAmE ˈsɑːrk-/ noun [U] a way of using words that are the opposite of what you mean in order to be unpleasant to sb or to make fun of them: *'That will be useful,' she snapped with heavy sarcasm* (= she really thought it would not be useful at all). ◊ *a hint/touch/ trace of sarcasm in his voice*

**sar·cas·tic** /sɑːˈkæstɪk; NAmE sɑːrˈk-/ (also BrE, informal **sarky**) adj. showing or expressing sarcasm: *sarcastic comments* ◊ *a sarcastic manner* ◊ *'There's no need to be sarcastic,' she said.* ▶ **sar·cas·tic·ally** /-kli/ adv.

**sar·coma** /sɑːˈkəʊmə; NAmE sɑːrˈk-/ noun (medical) a harmful (= MALIGNANT) mass of cells (= a TUMOUR) that grows in certain parts of the body such as muscle or bone

**sar·copha·gus** /sɑːˈkɒfəɡəs; NAmE sɑːrˈkɑːf-/ noun (pl. **sar·cophagi** /-ɡaɪ/) a stone COFFIN (= box that a dead person is buried in), especially one that is decorated, used in ancient times

**sar·dine** /ˌsɑːˈdiːn; NAmE ˌsɑːrˈd-/ noun a small young sea fish (for example, a young PILCHARD) that is either eaten fresh or preserved in tins
**IDM** **(packed, crammed, etc.) like sarˈdines** (informal) pressed tightly together in a way that is uncomfortable or unpleasant

**sar·don·ic** /sɑːˈdɒnɪk; NAmE sɑːrˈdɑːn-/ adj. (disapproving) showing that you think that you are better than other people and do not take them seriously **SYN mocking**: *a sardonic smile* ▶ **sar·don·ic·ally** /-kli/ adv.

**sarge** /sɑːdʒ; NAmE sɑːrdʒ/ noun (informal) used to talk to or about a SERGEANT

**sari** /ˈsɑːri/ noun a long piece of cloth that is wrapped around the body and worn as the main piece of clothing by women in South Asia

**sarin** /ˈsɑːrɪn/ noun [U] a type of poisonous gas used in chemical weapons

**sarky** /ˈsɑːki/ adj. (**sark·ier**, **sarki·est**) (BrE, informal) = SARCASTIC

**sar·nie** /ˈsɑːni/ NAmE ˈsɑːrni/ noun (BrE, informal) = SANDWICH

**sar·ong** /səˈrɒŋ; NAmE -ˈrɔːŋ/ noun a long piece of cloth wrapped around the body from the middle part or the chest, worn by Malaysian and Indonesian men and women

**sar·panch** /ˈsɑːpʌntʃ; NAmE ˈsɑːrp-/ noun (in some South Asian countries) the head of a village

**SARS** /sɑːz; NAmE sɑːrz/ noun [U] an illness that is easily spread from person to person, which affects the lungs and can sometimes cause death (the abbreviation for 'severe acute respiratory syndrome'): *No new SARS cases have been reported in the region.*

**sar·tor·ial** /sɑːˈtɔːriəl; NAmE sɑːrˈt-/ adj. [only before noun] (formal) relating to clothes, especially men's clothes, and the way they are made or worn: *He is known for his sartorial elegance.* ▶ **sar·tor·ially** /-əli/ adv.

**SAS** /ˌes eɪ ˈes/ abbr. Special Air Service (a group of highly trained soldiers in the UK who are used on very secret or difficult military operations)

**SASE** /ˌes eɪ es ˈiː/ noun (NAmE) an ENVELOPE on which you have written your name and address and put a stamp so that sb else can use it to send sth to you (the abbreviation used in writing for 'self-addressed stamped envelope') ⊃ compare SAE

**sash** /sæʃ/ noun **1** a long piece of cloth worn around the middle part of the body or over one shoulder, especially as part of a uniform **2** either of a pair of windows, one above the other, that are opened and closed by sliding them up and down inside the frame

**sashay** /ˈsæʃeɪ; NAmE sæˈʃeɪ/ verb [I] + **adv./prep.** to walk in a very confident but relaxed way, especially in order to be noticed: *I watched her as she sashayed across the room.*

**sash·imi** /sæˈʃiːmi; NAmE sɑːˈʃ-/ noun [U] (from Japanese) a Japanese dish consisting of slices of raw fish, served with sauce

**ˈsash window** noun a window that consists of two separate parts, one above the other that you open by sliding one of the parts up or down

**Sas·quatch** /ˈsæskwætʃ, -kwɒtʃ; NAmE -kwɑːtʃ/ noun = BIGFOOT

# sass

**sass** /sæs/ noun, verb
- noun [U] (especially NAmE, informal) behaviour or talk that is rude and does not show respect
- verb ~ sb (NAmE, informal) to speak to sb in a rude way, without respect: *Don't sass your mother!*

**sas·sa·fras** /ˈsæsəfræs/ noun a North American tree with pleasant-smelling leaves and BARK. Its leaves are sometimes used to make a type of tea.

**Sas·sen·ach** /ˈsæsənæk, -næx/ noun (ScotE, disapproving or humorous) an English person ▶ **Sas·sen·ach** adj.

**sassy** /ˈsæsi/ adj. (**sas·sier**, **sas·si·est**) (informal, especially NAmE) **1** (disapproving) rude; showing a lack of respect **2** (approving) fashionable and confident: *his sassy, streetwise daughter*

**SAT** noun **1** SAT™ /ˌes eɪ ˈtiː/ (in the US) a test taken by HIGH SCHOOL students who want to go to a college or university (the abbreviation for 'Scholastic Assessment Test'): *to take the SAT* ◊ *I scored 1050 on the SAT.* ◊ *an SAT score* **2** /sæt/ (in England) a test taken by children at the ages of 7 and 11, now officially called NCT (the abbreviation for 'Standard Assessment Task')

**Sat.** abbr. (in writing) Saturday

**sat** /sæt/ past tense, past part. of SIT

**Satan** /ˈseɪtn/ noun the DEVIL

**sa·tan·ic** /səˈtænɪk; NAmE also seɪ-/ adj. **1** (often Sa·tan·ic) connected with the WORSHIP of Satan: *satanic cults* **2** (formal) morally bad and evil SYN demonic ▶ **sa·tan·ic·al·ly** /-kli/ adv.

**sa·tan·ism** /ˈseɪtənɪzəm/ noun [U] the WORSHIP of Satan ▶ **sa·tan·ist** /-nɪst/ noun

**satay** /ˈsæteɪ; NAmE ˈsɑːt-/ noun [U, C] a south-east Asian dish consisting of meat or fish cooked on sticks and served with a sauce made with PEANUTS

**satchel** /ˈsætʃəl/ noun a bag with a long STRAP, that you hang over your shoulder or wear on your back, used especially for carrying school books

**sat·com** (also **SAT·COM**) /ˈsætkɒm; NAmE -kɑːm/ noun [U] satellite communications

**sate** /seɪt/ verb ~ sth (formal) to satisfy a desire

**sated** /ˈseɪtɪd/ adj. [not usually before noun] ~ (with sth) (formal) having had so much of sth that you do not need any more: *sated with pleasure*

**sat·el·lite** /ˈsætəlaɪt/ noun **1** an electronic device that is sent into space and moves around the earth or another planet. It is used for communicating by radio, television, etc. and for gathering information: *a weather/communications/spy satellite* ◊ **by/via** ~ *The interview came live by satellite from Hollywood.* ◊ *satellite television/TV/radio* (= broadcast using a satellite) ◊ *a satellite broadcast/channel/picture* ⇒ WORDFINDER NOTE at SPACE **2** a natural object that moves around a larger natural object in space: *The moon is a satellite of earth.* **3** a town, a country or an organization that is controlled by and depends on another larger or more powerful one: *satellite states*

**'satellite dish** noun a piece of equipment that receives signals from a satellite, used to enable people to watch satellite television

**'satellite station** noun **1** a company that broadcasts television programmes using a satellite **2** a place where special equipment is used to follow the movements of satellites and receive information from them

**sati** (also **sut·tee**) /ˈsʌti:, sʌˈtiː/ noun **1** [U] the former practice in Hinduism of a wife burning herself with the body of her dead husband **2** [C] a wife who did this

**sa·ti·ate** /ˈseɪʃieɪt/ verb [usually passive] ~ sb/sth (formal) to give sb so much of sth that they do not feel they want any more ▶ **sa·ti·ation** /ˌseɪʃiˈeɪʃn/ noun [U]

**sa·ti·ety** /səˈtaɪəti/ noun [U] (formal or specialist) the state or feeling of being completely full of food, or of having had enough of sth

**satin** /ˈsætɪn; NAmE -tn/ noun, adj.
- noun [U] a type of cloth with a smooth shiny surface: *a white satin ribbon*
- adj. [only before noun] having the smooth shiny appearance of satin: *The paint has a satin finish.*

**sat·iny** /ˈsætɪni; NAmE ˈsætni/ adj. looking or feeling like satin: *her satiny skin*

**sat·ire** /ˈsætaɪə(r)/ noun [U, C] a way of criticizing a person, an idea or an institution in which you use humour to show their faults or weaknesses; a piece of writing that uses this type of criticism: *political/social satire* ◊ *a work full of savage/biting satire* ◊ *The novel is a stinging satire on American politics.*

**sa·tir·ic·al** /səˈtɪrɪkl/ (also less frequent **sa·tir·ic** /səˈtɪrɪk/) adj. using satire to criticize sb/sth: *a satirical magazine* ▶ **sa·tir·ic·al·ly** /-kli/ adv.

**sat·ir·ist** /ˈsætərɪst/ noun a person who writes or uses SATIRE

**sat·ir·ize** (BrE also **-ise**) /ˈsætəraɪz/ verb ~ sb/sth to use SATIRE to show the faults in a person, an organization, a system, etc.

**sat·is·fac·tion** /ˌsætɪsˈfækʃn/ noun **1** [U, C] the good feeling that you have when you have achieved sth or when sth that you wanted to happen does happen; sth that gives you this feeling: *to gain/get/derive satisfaction from sth* ◊ *a look/smile of satisfaction* ◊ **with**~ *She looked back on her career with great satisfaction.* ◊ *He had the satisfaction of seeing his book become a bestseller.* ◊ *She didn't want to give him the satisfaction of seeing her cry.* ◊ *The company is trying to improve customer satisfaction.* ◊ *He was enjoying all the satisfactions of being a parent.* ⇒ see also DISSATISFACTION **2** [U] the act of FULFILLING a need or desire: *the satisfaction of sexual desires* ◊ *the satisfaction of your ambitions* **3** [U] (formal) an acceptable way of dealing with a complaint, a debt, an injury, etc: *I complained to the manager but I didn't get any satisfaction.* IDM **to sb's satis'faction 1** if you do sth **to sb's satisfaction**, they are pleased with it: *The affair was settled to the complete satisfaction of the client.* **2** if you prove sth **to sb's satisfaction**, they believe or accept it: *Can you demonstrate to our satisfaction that your story is true?*

### WORD FAMILY
**satisfaction** noun (≠ dissatisfaction)
**satisfactory** adj. (≠ unsatisfactory)
**satisfy** verb
**satisfying** adj. (≠ unsatisfying)
**satisfied** adj. (≠ dissatisfied) (≠ unsatisfied)

**sat·is·fac·tory** /ˌsætɪsˈfæktəri/ adj. good enough for a particular purpose SYN acceptable: *a satisfactory explanation/answer/solution/conclusion* ◊ *The work is satisfactory but not outstanding.* ◊ *The existing law is not entirely/wholly satisfactory.* OPP unsatisfactory ▶ **sat·is·fac·tor·ily** /-rəli/ adv.: *Her disappearance has never been satisfactorily explained.* ◊ *Our complaint was dealt with satisfactorily.*

**sat·is·fied** /ˈsætɪsfaɪd/ adj. **1** pleased because you have achieved sth or because sth that you wanted to happen has happened: *a satisfied customer* ◊ ~ **with sb/sth** *She's pleased with what she's got.* OPP dissatisfied ⇒ SYNONYMS at HAPPY **2** believing or accepting that sth is true SYN convinced: ~ **(that)** … *I'm satisfied that they are telling the truth.* ◊ ~ **with sth** *She seemed satisfied with my explanation.* ⇒ compare UNSATISFIED

**sat·isfy** /ˈsætɪsfaɪ/ verb (sat·is·fies, sat·is·fy·ing, sat·is·fied, sat·is·fied) **1** ~ sb (not used in the progressive tenses) to make sb pleased by doing or giving them what they want: *Nothing satisfies him—he's always complaining.* ◊ *The proposed plan will not satisfy everyone.* **2** ~ sth to provide what is wanted, needed or asked for: *The food wasn't enough to satisfy his hunger.* ◊ *to satisfy sb's curiosity* ◊ *The education system must satisfy the needs of all children.* ◊ *We cannot satisfy demand for the product.* ◊ *to satisfy a requirement/condition/criterion* **3** (not used in the progressive tenses) (formal) to make sb certain

▼ SYNONYMS

**satisfaction**
happiness • pride • contentment • fulfilment
These are all words for the good feeling that you have when you are happy or when you have achieved sth.

**satisfaction** the good feeling that you have when you have achieved sth or when sth that you wanted to happen does happen: *He derived great satisfaction from knowing that his son was happy.*

**happiness** the good feeling that you have when you are happy: *Money can't buy you happiness.*

**pride** a feeling of being pleased or satisfied that you get when you or people who are connected with you have done sth well or own sth that other people admire: *The sight of her son graduating filled her with pride.*

**contentment** (*rather formal*) a feeling of being happy or satisfied with what you have: *They found contentment in living a simple life.*

**fulfilment** a feeling of being happy or satisfied with what you do or have done: *her search for personal fulfilment*

SATISFACTION, HAPPINESS, CONTENTMENT OR FULFILMENT?
- You can feel **satisfaction** at achieving almost anything, small or large; you feel **fulfilment** when you do sth useful and enjoyable with your life. **Happiness** is the feeling you have when things give you pleasure and can be quite a lively feeling; **contentment** is a quieter feeling that you get when you have learned to find pleasure in things.

PATTERNS
- satisfaction / happiness / pride / contentment / fulfilment **in** sth
- **real** satisfaction / happiness / pride / contentment / fulfilment
- **true** satisfaction / happiness / contentment / fulfilment
- **great** satisfaction / happiness / pride
- **quiet** satisfaction / pride / contentment
- **to feel** satisfaction / happiness / pride / contentment
- **to bring sb** satisfaction / happiness / pride / contentment / fulfilment
- **to find** satisfaction / happiness / contentment / fulfilment

sth is true or has been done: ~ *sb Her explanation did not satisfy the teacher.* ◊ ~ *sb of sth People need to be satisfied of the need for a new system.* ◊ ~ *sb/yourself (that) … Once I had satisfied myself (that) it was the right decision, we went ahead.*

**sat·is·fy·ing** /ˈsætɪsfaɪɪŋ/ *adj.* giving pleasure because it provides sth you need or want: *a satisfying meal* ◊ *a satisfying experience* ◊ **it is~to do sth** *It's satisfying to play a game really well.* ▸ **sat·is·fy·ing·ly** *adv.*

**sat·nav** (*also* **sat nav**) /ˈsætnæv/ *noun* [U, C] (*BrE*) a computer system that uses information obtained from satellites to guide the driver of a vehicle (the abbreviation for 'satellite navigation'): *The drivers all have satnav in the van.* ⊃ compare GPS

**sat·sang** /ˈsætsæŋ/; *BrE also* /ˈsʌtsʌŋ/ *noun* (*IndE*) a religious meeting where people read holy texts, think deeply about or talk about religious matters, etc.

**sat·suma** /sætˈsuːmə/ *noun* a type of small orange without seeds and with loose skin that comes off easily

**sat·ur·ate** /ˈsætʃəreɪt/ *verb* **1** ~ **sth** to make sth completely wet SYN **soak**: *The continuous rain had saturated the soil.* **2** [often passive] to fill sth/sb completely with sth so that it is impossible or USELESS to add any more: **be saturated (with/in sth)** *Newspapers were saturated with reports about the royal wedding.*

**sat·ur·ated** /ˈsætʃəreɪtɪd/ *adj.* **1** [not usually before noun] completely wet SYN **soaked** ⊃ SYNONYMS at WET **2** [usually before noun] (*chemistry*) if a chemical SOLUTION (= a liquid with sth DISSOLVED in it) is **saturated**, it contains the greatest possible amount of the substance that has been DISSOLVED in it: *a saturated solution of sodium chloride*

1375

▼ SYNONYMS

**satisfying**
rewarding • pleasing • gratifying • fulfilling
These words all describe an experience, activity or fact that gives you pleasure because it provides sth you need or want.

**satisfying** that gives you pleasure because it provides sth you need or want: *It's satisfying to play a game really well.*

**rewarding** (of an experience or activity) that makes you happy because you think it is useful or important; worth doing: *Nursing can be a very rewarding career.*

**pleasing** (*rather formal*) that gives you pleasure, especially to look at, hear or think about: *It was a simple but pleasing design.*

**gratifying** (*formal*) that gives you pleasure, especially because it makes you feel that you have done well: *It is gratifying to see such good results.*

**fulfilling** (of an experience or activity) that makes you happy, because it makes you feel your skills and talents are being used: *I'm finding the work much more fulfilling now.*

SATISFYING, REWARDING OR FULFILLING?
- Almost any experience, important or very brief, can be **satisfying**. **Rewarding** and **fulfilling** are used more for longer, more serious activities, such as jobs or careers. **Satisfying** and **fulfilling** are more about your personal satisfaction or happiness; **rewarding** is more about your sense of doing sth important and being useful to others.

PATTERNS
- a satisfying / rewarding / gratifying / fulfilling **experience / feeling**
- (a) satisfying / rewarding / fulfilling **job / career / work**
- **to find sth** satisfying / rewarding / pleasing / gratifying

⊃ WORDFINDER NOTE at LIQUID **3** [usually before noun] (of colours) very strong: *saturated reds*

**ˌsaturated ˈfat** *noun* [C, U] a type of fat found, for example, in butter, fried food and many types of meat, that is considered to be less healthy in the diet than other types of fat ⊃ see also MONOUNSATURATED FAT, POLYUNSATURATED FAT, TRANS-FATTY ACID, UNSATURATED FAT

**sat·ur·ation** /ˌsætʃəˈreɪʃn/ *noun* [U] **1** (*often figurative*) the state or process that happens when no more of sth can be accepted or added because there is already too much of it or too many of them: *a business beset by price wars and market saturation* (= the fact that no new customers can be found) ◊ **saturation bombing** *of the city* (= covering the whole city) ◊ *television's* **saturation coverage** (= so much coverage that it is impossible to avoid or add to it) *of the Olympics* **2** (*chemistry*) the degree to which sth is ABSORBED into sth else, expressed as a percentage of the greatest possible

**ˌsatuˈration point** *noun* [U, sing.] **1** the stage at which no more of sth can be accepted or added because there is already too much of it or too many of them: *The market for computer games has reached saturation point.* **2** (*chemistry*) the stage at which no more of a substance can be ABSORBED into a liquid or VAPOUR

**Sat·ur·day** ❶ A1 /ˈsætədeɪ, -di; *NAmE* -tərd-/ *noun* [C, U] (*abbr.* **Sat.**) the day of the week after Friday and before Sunday HELP To see how **Saturday** is used, look at the examples at **Monday**. ORIGIN From the Old English for 'day of Saturn', translated from Latin *Saturni dies*.

**Sat·urn** /ˈsætɜːn, -tən; *NAmE* -tɜːrn/ *noun* a large planet in the SOLAR SYSTEM that has rings around it and is 6th in order of distance from the sun

**Sat·ur·na·lia** /ˌsætəˈneɪliə; *NAmE* -tərˈn-/ *noun* [U] an ancient Roman festival that took place in December, around the time that Christmas now takes place

# saturnine

**sat·ur·nine** /ˈsætənaɪn; NAmE -tərn-/ adj. (literary) (of a person or their face) looking serious and THREATENING

**satyr** /ˈsætə(r); NAmE ˈseɪt-, ˈsæt-/ noun (in ancient Greek stories) a god of the woods, with a man's face and body and a GOAT's legs and HORNS

**sauce** 🔊 A2 /sɔːs/ noun 1 🔊 A2 [C, U] a thick liquid that is eaten with food to add taste to it: *tomato/cranberry/chilli sauce* ◊ *chicken in a white sauce* ◊ *ice cream with a hot fudge sauce* ◊ *pasta sauce* (= sauce that is served with pasta)⊃ see also BARBECUE SAUCE, BROWN SAUCE, HOLLANDAISE SAUCE, SOY SAUCE, TARTARE SAUCE, WHITE SAUCE, WORCESTERSHIRE SAUCE 2 [U] (BrE, old-fashioned, informal) talk or behaviour that is annoying or shows no respect SYN **cheek**
IDM **what's sauce for the ˈgoose is ˌsauce for the ˈgander** (old-fashioned, saying) what one person is allowed to do, another person must be allowed to do in a similar situation

**sauce·pan** /ˈsɔːspən; NAmE -pæn/ (especially BrE) (NAmE usually **pot**) noun a deep round metal pot with a LID (= cover) and one long handle or two short handles, used for cooking things over heat

**sau·cer** /ˈsɔːsə(r)/ noun a small shallow round dish that a cup stands on; an object that is like this in shape: *cups and saucers* ⊃ see also FLYING SAUCER

**saucy** /ˈsɔːsi/ adj. (sau·ci·er, sau·ci·est) rude or referring to sex in a way that is humorous but not offensive SYN **cheeky**: *saucy jokes* ◊ *a saucy smile* ▶ **sau·cily** /-sɪli/ adv.

**sauer·kraut** /ˈsaʊəkraʊt; NAmE -ərk-/ noun [U] (from German) CABBAGE (= a type of green vegetable) that is preserved in salt water and then cooked

**sauna** /ˈsɔːnə, ˈsaʊnə/ noun a period of time in which you sit or lie in a room (also called a **sauna**) which has been heated to a very high temperature. Some saunas involve the use of STEAM: *a hotel with a swimming pool and sauna* ◊ *to have/take a sauna*

**saun·ter** /ˈsɔːntə(r)/ verb [I] + adv. / prep. to walk in a slow relaxed way SYN **stroll**: *He sauntered by, looking as if he had all the time in the world.* ▶ **saun·ter** noun [sing.]

**saus·age** /ˈsɒsɪdʒ; NAmE ˈsɔːs-/ noun [C, U] a mixture of meat, fat, bread, etc. cut into small pieces, put into a long tube of skin, cooked and eaten whole or served cold in thin slices: *beef/pork sausages* ◊ *200g of garlic sausage* ⊃ see also BLOOD SAUSAGE, LIVER SAUSAGE
IDM **not a ˈsausage** (BrE, old-fashioned, informal) nothing at all

**ˈsausage dog** noun (BrE, informal) = DACHSHUND

**ˈsausage meat** noun [U] the mixture of meat, fat, bread, etc. cut into small pieces and used for making sausages

**ˌsausage ˈroll** noun (BrE) a small tube of PASTRY filled with sausage meat and cooked

**sauté** /ˈsəʊteɪ; NAmE soʊˈteɪ/ verb (sauté·ing, sautéed, sautéed or sauté·ing, sautéd, sautéd) ~ sth to fry food quickly in a little hot fat ▶ **sauté** adj. [only before noun]: *sauté potatoes*

**sav·age** /ˈsævɪdʒ/ adj., noun, verb
■ adj. 1 aggressive and violent; causing great harm SYN **brutal**: *savage dogs* ◊ *She had been badly hurt in what police described as 'a savage attack'.* ◊ *savage public spending cuts* 2 involving very strong criticism: *The article was a savage attack on the government's record.* 3 [only before noun] (old-fashioned, taboo) an offensive way of referring to groups of people or customs that are considered to be simple and not highly developed SYN **primitive**: *a savage tribe* ▶ **sav·age·ly** adv.: *savagely attacked/criticized* ◊ *'No!' he snarled savagely.*
■ noun 1 (old-fashioned, taboo) an offensive word for sb who belongs to a people that is simple and not developed: *the development of the human race from primitive savages* 2 (literary) a cruel and violent person: *He described the attack as the work of savages.*
■ verb [usually passive] 1 (of an animal) to attack sb violently, causing serious injury: *be savaged (by sth)* *She was savaged to death by a bear.* 2 (formal) to criticize sb/sth severely: *be savaged (by sb)* *Her latest novel has been savaged by the critics.*

**sav·agery** /ˈsævɪdʒri/ noun [U] behaviour that is very cruel and violent SYN **violence**: *The police were shocked by the savagery of the attacks.*

**sa·van·nah** (also **sa·vanna**) /səˈvænə/ noun [C, U] a wide flat open area of land, especially in Africa, that is covered with grass but has few trees ⊃ compare VELD

**sav·ant** /ˈsævənt, səˈvɑːnt; NAmE səˈvɑːnt/ noun (formal) 1 a person with great knowledge and ability 2 a person who is less intelligent than others but who has particular unusual abilities that other people do not have ⊃ see also IDIOT SAVANT

**save** 🔊 A2 /seɪv/ verb, noun, prep., conj.
■ verb
• **KEEP SAFE** 1 🔊 A2 [T] to keep sb/sth safe from death, harm, loss, etc: ~ sb/sth *to save sb's life* ◊ *Doctors were unable to save her.* ◊ *He's trying to save their marriage.* ◊ *If you really want to save the planet, sell your car.* ◊ (figurative) *Thanks for doing that. You saved my life* (= helped me a lot). ◊ ~ sb/sth from sth *to save a rare species from extinction* ◊ ~ sb/sth from doing sth *She saved a little girl from falling into the water.*
• **MONEY** 2 🔊 A2 [I, T] to keep money instead of spending it, especially in order to buy a particular thing: *I'm not very good at saving.* ◊ ~ for sth *I'm saving for a new bike.* ◊ ~ up (for sth) *We've been saving up to go to Australia.* ◊ ~ sth *You should save a little each week.* ◊ *I've saved almost £100 so far.* ◊ ~ sth (up) (for sth) *He's been saving his allowance up for a new bike.*
• **NOT WASTE** 3 🔊 A2 [T, I] to avoid wasting sth or using more than necessary: ~ sth *to save time/energy/money* ◊ *Book early and save £50!* ◊ *We should try to save water.* ◊ ~ sth on sth *The government is trying to save £1 million on defence.* ◊ ~ sb sth (on sth) *If we go this way it will save us two hours on the trip.* ◊ ~ on sth *I save on fares by walking to work.*
• **KEEP FOR FUTURE / SOMEBODY ELSE** 4 🔊 A2 [T] to keep sth to use or enjoy in the future or for sb else to use: ~ sth (for sth/sb) *He's saving his strength for the last part of the race.* ◊ *We'll eat some now and save some for tomorrow.* ◊ *Save some food for me.* ◊ ~ sb sth *Save me some food.*
• **COMPUTING** 5 🔊 A2 [T, I] to make a computer keep data by putting a copy in a location where it will be stored: ~ sth (to sth) *Save data frequently.*
• **COLLECT STH** 6 [T] ~ sth to collect sth because you like it or for a special purpose: *I've been saving theatre programmes for years.* ◊ *If you save ten tokens you can get a T-shirt.*
• **AVOID STH BAD** 7 🔊 B2 [T] to avoid doing sth difficult or unpleasant; to make sb able to avoid doing sth difficult or unpleasant: ~ sb from doing sth *The prize money saved her from having to find a job.* ◊ ~ sth *She did it herself to save argument.* ◊ ~ sb sth *Thanks for sending that letter for me—it saved me a trip.* ◊ ~ doing sth *He's grown a beard to save shaving.* ◊ ~ sb doing sth *If you phone for an appointment, it'll save you waiting.*
• **IN SPORT** 8 [T, I] ~ (sth) (in football (soccer), etc.) to prevent an opponent's shot from going in the goal: *to save a penalty* ◊ *The goalie saved Johnson's long-range shot.* ◊ (BrE) *The goalie saved brilliantly from Johnson's long-range shot.*
• **IN CHRISTIAN BELIEF** 9 [T, I] ~ (sth) to prevent a person's soul from going to hell
IDM **not be able to do sth to ˌsave your ˈlife** (informal) to be completely unable to do sth: *He can't interview people to save his life.* **ˌsave sb's ˈbacon / ˈneck** (informal) to rescue sb from a very difficult situation **ˌsave the ˈday / situˈation** to prevent failure or defeat, when this seems certain to happen: *Salah's late goal saved the day for Liverpool.* **ˌsave (sb's) ˈface** to avoid or help sb avoid being embarrassed: *She was fired, but she saved face by telling everyone she'd resigned.* **ˌsave your ˈbreath** (informal) used to tell sb that it is not worth wasting time and effort saying sth because it will not change anything: *Save your breath—you'll never persuade her.* **ˌsave your (own) ˈskin / ˈhide / ˈneck** to try to avoid death, punishment, etc., especially by leaving others in an extremely difficult situation:

*To save his own skin,* he lied and blamed the accident on his friend.
- **noun** (in football (soccer), etc.) an action by the GOALKEEPER that stops a goal being scored: *He made a spectacular save.*
- **prep.** (also **save for**) (*old use* or *formal*) except *sth*: *They knew nothing about her save her name.*
- **conj.** (*old use* or *formal*) except: *They found out nothing more save that she had borne a child.*

▼ **SYNONYMS**

**save**
budget • economize • tighten your belt
These words all mean to spend less money.
**save** to keep money instead of spending it, often in order to buy a particular thing: *I'm saving for a new car.*
**budget** to be careful about the amount of money you spend; to plan to spend an amount of money for a particular purpose: *If we budget carefully we'll be able to afford the trip.*
**economize** to use less money, time, etc. than you normally use
**tighten your belt** (*rather informal*) to spend less money because there is less available: *With the price increases, we are all having to tighten our belts.*
PATTERNS
- to save up/budget **for** sth
- to **have to** save/budget/economize/tighten our belts
- to **try to/manage to** save/budget/economize

▼ **SYNONYMS**

**save**
rescue • bail out • redeem
These words all mean to prevent sb/sth from dying, losing sth, being harmed or embarrassed.
**save** to prevent sb/sth from dying, being harmed or destroyed or losing sth: *Doctors were unable to save him.* ◊ *a campaign to save the panda from extinction*
**rescue** to save sb/sth from a dangerous or harmful situation: *They were rescued by a passing cruise ship.*
**bail sb out** to rescue sb/sth from a difficult situation, especially by providing money: *Don't expect me to bail you out if it all goes wrong.*
**redeem** (*formal, religion*) to save sb from the power of evil: *He was a sinner, redeemed by the grace of God.*
NOTE Redeem is also used in non-religious language in the phrase **redeem a situation**, which means to prevent a situation from being as bad as it might be.
PATTERNS
- to save/rescue/redeem sb/sth **from** sth
- to save/rescue/redeem a **situation**
- to save/redeem **sinners/mankind**
- to rescue sb/bail sb out **financially**

**saver** /ˈseɪvə(r)/ *noun* **1** a person who saves money and puts it in a bank, etc. for future use **2** (often in compounds) something that helps you spend less money or use less of the thing mentioned: *a money/time saver* ⊃ see also LIFE-SAVER, SCREEN SAVER

**Savile Row** /ˌsævl ˈrəʊ/ *noun* a street in London with many shops that sell expensive clothes for men that are often specially made for each person: *He was wearing a Savile Row suit.*

**sav·ing** ❶ B2 /ˈseɪvɪŋ/ *noun* **1** ⚡ [C] an amount of sth such as time or money that you do not need to use or spend: **~ of sth** *Buy three and make a saving of 55p.* ◊ **~on sth** *With the new boiler you can make big savings on fuel bills.* ◊ *cost/energy savings* **2** ⚡ B2 **savings** [pl.] money that you have saved, especially in a bank, etc: *She spent her entire life savings* (= all the money she had saved throughout her life) *to furnish and equip the house.* **3 -saving** (in adjectives) that prevents the waste of the thing mentioned or stops it from being necessary: *energy-saving modifica-* tions ◊ *labour-saving devices* ◊ *space-saving fitted furniture* ⊃ see also DAYLIGHT SAVING TIME, FACE-SAVING, LIFE-SAVING, MONEY-SAVING, TIME-SAVING

**ˌsaving ˈgrace** *noun* [usually sing.] the one good quality that a person or thing has that prevents them or it from being completely bad

**ˈsavings account** (*BrE also* **deposit account**) *noun* a type of bank account that pays interest on the money that is left in it, but from which you cannot take the money out without giving notice or losing interest ⊃ compare CURRENT ACCOUNT

**ˌsavings and ˈloan association** (*US*) (*BrE* **ˈbuilding society**) *noun* (*abbr.* **S&L**) an organization like a bank that lends money to people who want to buy a house. People also save money with a savings and loan association.

**ˈsavings bank** *noun* a bank that offers accounts that you can put money into to earn interest

**ˈsavings rate** *noun* **1** the interest rate paid on a savings account **2** a measure of the amount of income saved rather than spent or paid in taxes by a group of people, a country, etc.

**sa·viour** (*US* **sa·vior**) /ˈseɪvjə(r)/ *noun* **1** [usually sing.] a person who rescues sb/sth from a dangerous or difficult situation: *The new manager has been hailed as the saviour of the club.* **2 the Saviour** [sing.] used in the Christian religion as another name for Jesus Christ

**sa·vory** (*US*) = SAVOURY

**sa·vour** (*US* **savor**) /ˈseɪvə(r)/ *verb, noun*
- **verb 1 ~ sth** to enjoy the full taste of sth, especially by eating or drinking it slowly SYN **relish**: *He ate his meal slowly, savouring every mouthful.* **2 ~ sth** to enjoy a feeling or an experience completely SYN **relish**: *I wanted to savour every moment.*
PHR V **ˈsavour of sth** [no passive] (*formal*) to seem to have an amount of sth, especially sth bad: *His recent comments savour of hypocrisy.*
- **noun** [usually sing.] (*formal* or *literary*) a taste or smell, especially a pleasant one: (*figurative*) *For Emma, life had lost its savour.*

**sa·voury** (*US* **sa·vory**) /ˈseɪvəri/ *adj., noun*
- **adj. 1** tasting of salt; not sweet: *savoury snacks* ⊃ WORD-FINDER NOTE at TASTE **2** having a pleasant taste or smell: *a savoury smell from the kitchen* ⊃ see also UNSAVOURY
- **noun** [usually pl.] (*pl.* **-ies**) a small amount of a food with a SALTY taste, not a sweet one, often served at a party, etc.

**savvy** /ˈsævi/ *noun, adj.*
- **noun** [U] (*informal*) practical knowledge or understanding of sth: *political savvy*
- **adj.** (**sav·vier, sav·vi·est**) (*informal*) having practical knowledge and understanding of sth; having COMMON SENSE: *savvy shoppers* ⊃ see also MEDIA-SAVVY, TECH-SAVVY

**saw** /sɔː/ *noun, verb*
- **noun** (often in compounds) a tool that has a long BLADE (= metal cutting part) with sharp points (called TEETH) along one of its edges. A saw is moved backwards and forwards by hand or driven by electricity and is used for cutting wood or metal. ⊃ see also CHAINSAW, CIRCULAR SAW, COPING SAW, HACKSAW, HANDSAW, JIGSAW

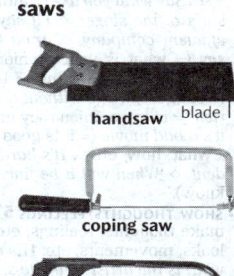

saws

handsaw  blade

coping saw

hacksaw

- **verb** (**sawed**, **sawn** /sɔːn/, *NAmE also* **sawed**, **sawed**)
**1** [I, T] to use a saw to cut sth: *The workmen sawed and hammered all day.* ◊ + **adv./prep.** *He accidentally sawed through a cable.* ◊ **~ sth (+ adv./prep.)** *She sawed the plank in half.*
**2** [I, T] **~ (away) (at sth)** |

**sawdust**

~ **sth** to move sth backwards and forwards on sth as if using a saw: *She sawed away at her violin.* ◊ *He was sawing energetically at a loaf of bread.* **3** past tense of SEE

**PHRV** **saw sth↔ˈdown** to cut sth and bring it to the ground using a saw: *The tree had to be sawn down.* **ˌsaw sth↔ˈoff | saw sth ˈoff sth** to remove sth by cutting it with a saw: *We sawed the dead branches off the tree.* **ˌsaw sth↔ˈup (into sth)** to cut sth into pieces with a saw: *We sawed the wood up into logs.*

**saw·dust** /ˈsɔːdʌst/ *noun* [U] very small pieces of wood that fall as powder when wood is cut with a saw

**saw·mill** /ˈsɔːmɪl/ *noun* a factory in which wood is cut into boards using machines

**sawn-off ˈshotgun** (*BrE*) (*NAmE* **sawed-off ˈshotgun**) *noun* a SHOTGUN with part of its BARREL cut off, to make it easier to hide

**sax** /sæks/ *noun* (*informal*) = SAXOPHONE

**Saxon** /ˈsæksn/ *noun* a member of a race of people once living in north-west Germany, some of whom settled in Britain in the 5th and 6th centuries ⇒ see also ANGLO-SAXON ▶ **Saxon** *adj*: *Saxon churches/kings*

**saxo·phone** /ˈsæksəfəʊn/ (*also informal* **sax**) *noun* a metal musical instrument that you blow into, used especially in jazz and dance music. A saxophone has a REED and belongs to the WOODWIND family.

**sax·oph·on·ist** /sækˈsɒfənɪst; *NAmE* ˈsæksəfəʊnɪst/ *noun* a person who plays the saxophone

**say** **A1** /seɪ/ *verb, noun, exclamation*
■ *verb* (**says** /sez/, **said, said** /sed/)
- **SPEAK 1** **A1** [I, T] to speak or tell sb sth, using words: + **speech** *'Hello!' she said.* ◊ *'That was marvellous,' said Daniel.* **HELP** In stories the subject often comes after **said**, **says** or **say** when it follows the actual words spoken, unless it is a pronoun.: ~ **sth** *Be quiet, I have something to say.* ◊ *Please say yes!* ◊ *I didn't believe a word she said.* ◊ *That's a terrible thing to say.* ◊ ~ **sth to sb** *She said nothing to me about it.* ◊ ~ **to sb/yourself + speech** *I said to myself* (= thought), *'That can't be right!'* ◊ ~ **(that)** … *He said (that) his name was Sam.* ◊ *Can I just say I'm not happy about this.* ◊ **it is said that** … *It is said that she lived to be over 100.* ◊ ~ **what, how, etc** … *She finds it hard to say what she feels.* ◊ *'Why can't I go out now?' 'Because I say so.'* ◊ ~ **to do sth** *He said to meet him here.* ◊ **be said to be/have sth** *He is said to have been a brilliant scholar.* ⇒ EXPRESS YOURSELF at INTERRUPT
- **REPEAT WORDS 2** **A1** [T] ~ **sth** to repeat words, phrases, etc: *to say a prayer* ◊ *Try to say that line with more conviction.*
- **GIVE WRITTEN INFORMATION 3** **A2** [T, no passive] (of sth that is written or can be seen) to give particular information or instructions: + **speech** *The notice said 'Keep Out'.* ◊ ~ **sth** *The clock said three o'clock.* ◊ ~ **(that)** … *The instructions say (that) we should leave it to set for four hours.* ◊ ~ **where, why, etc** … *The book doesn't say where he was born.* ◊ ~ **to do sth** *The guidebook says to turn left.*
- **EXPRESS OPINION 4** **B1** [T, I] to express an opinion on sth: ~ **sth** *Say what you like* (= although you disagree) *about her, she's a fine singer.* ◊ *I'll say this for them, they're a very efficient company.* ◊ *Anna thinks I'm lazy—what do you say* (= what is your opinion)? ◊ ~ **(that)** … *I can't say I blame her for resigning* (= I think she was right). ◊ *I say* (= suggest) *we go without them.* ◊ *I wouldn't say they were rich* (= in my opinion they are not rich). ◊ *That's not to say it's a bad movie* (= it is good but it is not without faults). ◊ ~ **what, how, etc** … *It's hard to say what caused the accident.* ◊ *'When will it be finished?' 'I couldn't say* (= I don't know).'
- **SHOW THOUGHTS/FEELINGS 5** **B1** [T] ~ **sth (about sth)** to make thoughts, feelings, etc. clear to sb by using words, looks, movements, etc: *His angry glance said it all.* ◊ *Just what is the artist trying to say in her work?*
- **SHOW WHAT SB/STH IS LIKE 6** **B1** [T] to show, sometimes indirectly, what sb/sth is like: ~ **sth** *That says it all really, doesn't it?* (= it shows clearly what is true) ◊ ~ **sth (to sb)** *(about sb/sth) The incident says an awful lot about his character.*
- **GIVE EXAMPLE 7** **B2** [T, no passive] to suggest or give sth as an example or a possibility: ~ **sth/sb** *You could learn the basics in, let's say, three months.* ◊ *Let's take any writer, say,* (= for example) *Dickens …* ◊ ~ **(that)** … *Say you lose your job: what would you do then?*

**IDM** **before you can say Jack ˈRobinson** (*old-fashioned*) very quickly; in a very short time **ˌgo without ˈsaying** to be very obvious or easy to predict: *Of course I'll help you. That goes without saying.* **have something, nothing, etc. to ˈsay for yourself** to be ready, unwilling, etc. to talk or give your views on sth: *She doesn't have much to say for herself* (= doesn't take part in conversation). ◊ *He had plenty to say for himself* (= he had a lot of opinions and was willing to talk). ◊ *Late again—what have you got to say for yourself* (= what is your excuse)? **have something to ˈsay (to sb) about sth** to be angry: *He knew that if he wasn't back by midnight, his parents would have something to say about it.* **ˌhaving ˈsaid that | that ˈsaid** (*informal*) used to introduce an opinion that makes what you have just said seem less strong: *I sometimes get worried in this job. Having said that, I enjoy doing it, it's a challenge.* **ˈI'll say!** (*old-fashioned*, *informal*) used for emphasis to say 'yes': *'Does she see him often?' 'I'll say! Nearly every day.'* **I ˈmust say** (*informal*) used to emphasize an opinion: *Well, I must say, that's the funniest thing I've heard all week.* **I ˈsay** (*BrE, old-fashioned, informal*) **1** used to express surprise, shock, etc: *I say! What a huge cake!* **2** used to attract sb's attention or introduce a new subject of conversation: *I say, can you lend me five pounds?* **it says a ˈlot, very ˈlittle, etc. for sb/sth** (*informal*) it shows a good/bad quality that sb/sth has: *It says a lot for her that she never lost her temper.* ◊ *It didn't say much for their efficiency that the order arrived a week late.* **I ˌwouldn't say ˈno (to sth)** (*informal*) used to say that you would like sth or to accept sth that is offered: *I wouldn't say no to a pizza.* ◊ *'Tea, Brian?' 'I wouldn't say no.'* **least said ˌsoonest ˈmended** (*BrE, saying*) a bad situation will pass or be forgotten most quickly if nothing more is said about it **the ˌless/ˌleast said the ˈbetter** the best thing to do is say as little as possible about sth **ˌnever say ˈdie** (*saying*) do not stop hoping **not say boo to a ˈgoose** (*BrE*) (*NAmE* **not say boo to ˈanyone**) to be very shy or gentle: *He's so nervous he wouldn't say boo to a goose.* **ˈnot to say** used to introduce a stronger way of describing sth: *a difficult, not to say impossible, task* **say ˈcheese** used to ask sb to smile before you take their photograph **say ˈno (to sth)** to refuse an offer, a suggestion, etc: *If you don't invest in this, you're saying no to a potential fortune.* **ˌsay no ˈmore** (*informal*) used to say that you understand exactly what sb means or is trying to say, so it is unnecessary to say anything more: *'They went to Paris together.' 'Say no more!'* **ˌsay your ˈpiece** to say exactly what you feel or think **say ˈwhat?** (*NAmE, informal*) used to express surprise at what sb has just said: *'He's getting married.' 'Say what?'* **say ˈwhen** used to ask sb to tell you when you should stop pouring a drink or serving food for them because they have enough **ˈthat is to say** in other words: *three days from now, that is to say on Friday* ⇒ see also I.E. **that ˈsaid** = HAVING SAID THAT v. **ˌthat's not ˈsaying much** used to say that sth is not very unusual or special: *She's a better player than me, but that's not saying much* (= because I am a very bad player). **ˌthere's no ˈsaying** used to say that it is impossible to predict what might happen: *There's no saying how he'll react.* **ˌthere's something, not much, etc. to be said for sth/ˌdoing sth** there are/are not good reasons for doing sth, believing sth or agreeing with sth **to ˌsay the ˈleast** without making sth seem better, worse, more serious, etc. than it really is: *I was surprised, to say the least.* **to say ˈnothing of sth** used to introduce a further fact or thing in addition to those already mentioned **SYN** **not to mention**: *It was too expensive, to say nothing of the time it wasted.* **ˌwell ˈsaid!** (*informal*) I agree completely: *'We must stand up for ourselves.' 'Well said, John.'* **what do/would you ˈsay (to sth/doing sth)** (*informal*) would you like sth/to do sth?: *What would you say to eating out tonight?* ◊ *Let's go away for a weekend. What do you say?* **what/whatever sb ˈsays, ˈgoes** (*informal, often humorous*) a particular person must

be obeyed: *Sarah wanted the kitchen painted green, and what she says, goes.* **whatever you 'say** (*informal*) used to agree to sb's suggestion because you do not want to argue **when ,all is ,said and 'done** when everything is considered: *I know you're upset, but when all's said and done it isn't exactly a disaster.* **who can 'say ( …)?** used to say that nobody knows the answer to a question: *Who can say what will happen next year?* **who 'says ( …)?** (*informal*) used to disagree with a statement or an opinion: *Who says I can't do it?* **who's to say ( …)?** used to say that sth might happen or might have happened in a particular way, because nobody really knows: *Who's to say we would not have succeeded if we'd had more time?* **you can say 'that again** (*informal*) I agree with you completely: *'He's in a bad mood today.' 'You can say that again!'* **you can't say 'fairer (than 'that)** (*BrE, informal*) used to say that you think the offer you are making is reasonable or generous: *Look, I'll give you £100 for it. You can't say fairer than that.* **you don't 'say!** (*informal, often ironic*) used to express surprise: *'They left without us.' 'You don't say!'* (= I'm not surprised) **you 'said it!** (*informal*) 1 (*BrE*) used to agree with sb when they say sth about themselves that you would not have been rude enough to say yourself: *'I know I'm not the world's greatest cook.' 'You said it!'* 2 (*NAmE*) used to agree with sb's suggestion ⇨ more at DARE *v.*, EASY *adv.*, ENOUGH *pron.*, GLAD, HEAR, LET *v.*, MEAN *v.*, MIND *v.*, NEEDLESS, SOON, SORRY *adj.*, SUFFICE, WORD *n.*
- **noun** [+ C1] [*sing.*, U] the right to influence sth by giving your opinion before a decision is made: *~ (in sth) We had no say in the decision to sell the company.* ◇ *People want a greater say in local government.* ◇ *~ on sth The judge has the final say on the sentence.*
  IDM **have your 'say** (*informal*) to have the opportunity to express yourself fully about sth: *She won't be happy until she's had her say.* ⇨ see also SAY YOUR PIECE at SAY *verb*
- **exclamation** (*NAmE, informal*) 1 used for showing surprise or pleasure: *Say, that's a nice haircut!* 2 used for attracting sb's attention or for making a suggestion or comment: *Say, how about going to a movie tonight?*

▼ WHICH WORD?

**say / tell**
- **Say** never has a person as the object. You **say something** or **say something to somebody**. **Say** is often used when you are giving somebody's exact words: *'Sit down,' she said.* ◇ *Anne said, 'I'm tired.'* ◇ *Anne said (that) she was tired.* ◇ *What did he say to you?* You cannot use 'say about', but **say something about** is correct: *I want to say something/a few words/a little about my family.* **Say** can also be used with a clause when the person you are talking to is not mentioned: *She didn't say what she intended to do.*
- **Tell** usually has a person as the object and often has two objects: *Have you told him the news yet?* It is often used with 'that' clauses: *Anne told me (that) she was tired.* **Tell** is usually used when somebody is giving facts or information, often with *what, where,* etc.: *Can you tell me when the movie starts?* (BUT: *Can you give me some information about the school?*) **Tell** is also used when you are giving somebody instructions: *The doctor told me to stay in bed.* ◇ *The doctor told me (that) I had to stay in bed.* OR: *The doctor said (that) I had to stay in bed.* NOT: *The doctor said me to stay in bed.*

**say·ing** /ˈseɪɪŋ/ *noun* a well-known phrase or statement that expresses sth about life that most people believe is wise and true: *'Accidents will happen',* **as the saying goes**.

**'say-so** *noun* [*sing.*] (*informal*) permission that sb gives to do sth: *Nothing could be done without her say-so.*
IDM **on sb's 'say-so** based on a statement that sb makes without giving any proof: *He hired and fired people on his partner's say-so.*

**scab** /skæb/ *noun* 1 [C] a hard dry layer that forms over and covers a wound on the skin as it gets better 2 [C] (*informal, disapproving*) a worker who refuses to join a strike or takes the place of sb on strike SYN **blackleg**

**scab·bard** /ˈskæbəd/; *NAmE* -bərd/ *noun* a cover for a SWORD that is made of leather or metal SYN **sheath**

1379 **scale**

**scab·by** /ˈskæbi/ *adj.* covered in scabs: *scabby knees*

**sca·bies** /ˈskeɪbiːz/ *noun* [U] a skin disease that causes ITCHING and small red raised spots

**scab·rous** /ˈskeɪbrəs, ˈskæb-/; *NAmE* ˈskæb-/ *adj.* 1 (*formal*) offensive in a sexual way SYN **indecent** 2 (*specialist*) having a rough surface SYN **scaly**: *scabrous skin*

**scads** /skædz/ *noun* [pl.] **~ (of sth)** (*especially NAmE, informal*) large numbers or amounts of sth: *scads of $20 bills*

**scaf·fold** /ˈskæfəʊld/ *noun* 1 a platform used when EXECUTING criminals by cutting off their heads or hanging them from a rope 2 a structure made of scaffolding, for workers to stand on when they are working on a building

**scaf·fold·ing** /ˈskæfəldɪŋ/ *noun* [U] POLES and boards that are joined together to make a structure for workers to stand on when they are working high up on the outside wall of a building ⇨ WORDFINDER NOTE at CONSTRUCTION

**scal·able** (*BrE also* **scale-able**) /ˈskeɪləbl/ *adj.* 1 used to describe a computer, a network, software, etc. that can be adapted to meet greater needs in the future: *A business database needs to be scalable.* ◇ *Many internet companies use highly scalable technology to reduce the requirement for many new employees.* 2 designed to work on a large or small scale, according to needs: *scalable graphics* ▸ **scal·abil·ity** (*BrE also* **scale-abil·ity**) /ˌskeɪləˈbɪləti/ *noun* [U]: *New database technology offers scalability for future growth.*

**sca·lar** /ˈskeɪlə(r)/ *adj.* (*mathematics*) (of a quantity) having size but no direction ⇨ compare VECTOR ▸ **sca·lar** *noun*

**scala·wag** /ˈskæləwæg/ (*NAmE*) (*especially BrE* **scally·wag**) *noun* (*informal*) a person, especially a child, who behaves badly, but not in a serious way SYN **scamp**

**scald** /skɔːld/ *verb, noun*
- **verb ~ sth/yourself** to burn yourself or part of your body with very hot liquid or STEAM: *Be careful not to scald yourself with the steam.* ◇ (*figurative*) *Tears scalded her eyes.* ⇨ SYNONYMS at BURN
- **noun** an injury to the skin from very hot liquid or STEAM

**scald·ing** /ˈskɔːldɪŋ/ (*also* **scalding 'hot**) *adj.* hot enough to scald: *scalding water* ◇ *scalding hot coffee* ◇ (*figurative*) *Scalding tears poured down her face.*

**scale** ⓘ B2 ⓞ /skeɪl/ *noun, verb*
- **noun**
- • SIZE 1 ⓘ B2 [*sing.*, U] the size or extent of sth, especially when compared with sth else: **on a … ~** *They entertain on a large scale* (= they hold expensive parties with a lot of guests). ◇ *Here was corruption on a grand scale.* ◇ *On a global scale, 77 per cent of energy is created from fossil fuels.* ◇ *to achieve* **economies of scale** *in production* (= to produce many items so the cost of producing each one is reduced) ◇ **~ of sth** *It was impossible to comprehend the* **full scale** *of the disaster.* ◇ *It was not until morning that the* **sheer scale** *of the damage could be seen* (= how great it was). ⇨ see also FULL-SCALE, LARGE-SCALE, SMALL-SCALE
- • RANGE OF LEVELS 2 ⓘ B2 [C] a range of levels or numbers used for measuring sth: *a five-point pay scale* ◇ *to evaluate performance on a scale from 1 to 10* ⇨ see also RICHTER SCALE, SLIDING SCALE, TIMESCALE 3 ⓘ B2 [C, *usually sing.*] the set of all the different levels of sth, from the lowest to the highest: *At the other end of the scale, life is a constant struggle to get enough to eat.* ◇ *the social scale*
- • MARKS FOR MEASURING 4 ⓘ B2 [C] a series of marks at regular points on an instrument that is used for measuring: *How much does it read on the scale?*
- • WEIGHING INSTRUMENT 5 ⓘ B2 **scales** [pl.] (*NAmE also* **scale**) an instrument for weighing people or things: *bathroom/ kitchen/weighing scales* ◇ (*figurative*) the **scales of justice** (= represented as the two pans on a BALANCE)
- • OF MAP/DIAGRAM/MODEL 6 ⓘ B2 [C] the relation between the actual size of sth and its size or a map, diagram or model that represents it: *a scale of 1:25000* ◇ *a scale model/drawing* ◇ *Both plans are drawn to the same scale.* ◇ **to ~** *Is this diagram to scale?* (= are its parts the same size and shape in relation to each other as they are in the thing represented?) ⇨ WORDFINDER NOTE at MAP

# scaleable

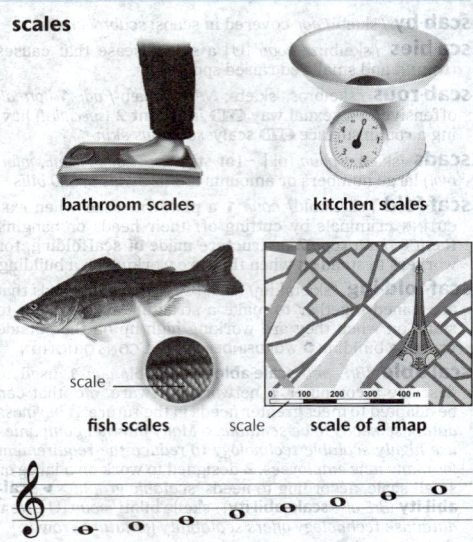

scales

bathroom scales · kitchen scales

fish scales · scale · scale of a map

the scale of C

- **IN MUSIC 7** [C] a series of musical notes moving upwards or downwards, with fixed INTERVALS between each note, especially a series of eight starting on a particular note: *the scale of C major* ◊ *to practise scales on the piano* ⇨ compare KEY, OCTAVE
- **OF FISH/REPTILE 8** [C] any of the thin plates of hard material that cover the skin of many fish and REPTILES ⇨ VISUAL VOCAB page V2
- **IN WATER PIPES, ETC. 9** (*BrE also* **fur**) [U] a hard white substance that is sometimes left inside water pipes and containers for heating water ⇨ see also LIMESCALE
- **ON TEETH 10** [U] a hard substance that forms on teeth, especially when they are not cleaned regularly ⇨ compare PLAQUE **IDM** see TIP *v.*

■ **verb**
- **CLIMB 1** ~ **sth** (*formal*) to climb to the top of sth very high and steep: *the first woman to scale the world's five highest peaks* ◊ (*figurative*) *He has scaled the heights of his profession.*
- **FISH 2** ~ **sth** to remove the small flat hard pieces of skin from a fish
- **TEETH 3** ~ **sth** to remove TARTAR from the teeth by SCRAPING: *The dentist scaled and polished my teeth.*
- **CHANGE SIZE 4** ~ **sth (from sth) (to sth)** (*specialist*) to change the size of sth: *Text can be scaled from 4 points to 108 points without any loss of quality.*

**PHRV** ˌscale sth↔ˈdown (*also* ˌscale sth↔ˈback) to reduce the number, size or extent of sth: *We are thinking of scaling down our training programmes next year.* ◊ *The IMF has scaled back its growth forecasts for the next decade.* ⇨ SYNONYMS at CUT ˌscale sth↔ˈup to increase the size or number of sth

**scale·able** (*BrE*) = SCALABLE
**sca·lene tri·angle** /ˌskeɪliːn ˈtraɪæŋɡl/ *noun* (*geometry*) a flat shape whose three sides are all of different lengths ⇨ picture at TRIANGLE
**scal·lion** /ˈskæliən/ *noun* (*NAmE*) = GREEN ONION, SPRING ONION
**scal·lop** /ˈskɒləp; *NAmE* ˈskæl-/ *noun, verb*
■ *noun* **1** a SHELLFISH that can be eaten, with two flat round shells that fit together: *a scallop shell* **2** any one of a series of small curves cut on the edge of a piece of cloth, PASTRY, etc. for decoration
■ *verb* (*usually passive*) ~ **sth** to decorate the edge of sth with small curves: *a scalloped edge*

**scally** /ˈskæli/ *noun* (*pl.* **-ies**) (*BrE, informal*) (used especially in Liverpool in NW England) a boy or young man who behaves badly or causes trouble
**scally·wag** /ˈskæliwæɡ/ (*BrE*) (*NAmE usually* **scala·wag**) *noun* (*informal*) a person, especially a child, who behaves badly, but not in a serious way **SYN** scamp
**scalp** /skælp/ *noun, verb*
■ *noun* **1** the skin that covers the part of the head where the hair grows **2** (in the past) the skin and hair that was removed from the head of a dead enemy as a sign of victory **3** (*informal*) a symbol of the fact that sb has been defeated or punished: *They have claimed some impressive scalps in their bid for the championship.*
■ *verb* **1** ~ **sb** to remove the skin and hair from the top of an enemy's head as a sign of victory **2** (*NAmE*) (*BrE* **tout**) ~ **sth** to sell tickets for a popular event illegally, at a price that is higher than the official price, especially outside a theatre, stadium, etc.
**scal·pel** /ˈskælpəl/ *noun* a small sharp knife used by doctors in medical operations ⇨ WORDFINDER NOTE at OPERATION
**scalp·er** /ˈskælpə(r)/ (*NAmE*) (*BrE* **tout**, **ˈticket tout**) *noun* a person who buys tickets for concerts, sports events, etc. and then sells them to other people at a higher price
**scaly** /ˈskeɪli/ *adj.* (**scal·ier**, **scali·est**) (of skin) covered with SCALES(8), or hard and dry, with small pieces that come off
**scam** /skæm/ *noun, verb*
■ *noun* (*informal*) a clever and dishonest plan for making money
■ *verb* (*informal*) (**-mm-**) to cheat sb in order to get sth, especially money, from them: ~ **sb (out of sth)** *He was arrested for scamming pensioners out of their savings.* ◊ ~ **sb into (doing) sth** *The company scams customers into buying software they don't need.*
**scamp** /skæmp/ *noun* (*old-fashioned*) a child who enjoys playing tricks and causing trouble **SYN** scallywag
**scam·per** /ˈskæmpə(r)/ *verb* [I] + *adv./prep.* (especially of children or small animals) to move quickly with short light steps
**scampi** /ˈskæmpi/ *noun* [U + *sing./pl. v.*] **1** (*BrE*) SHELLFISH (large PRAWNS or a type of small LOBSTER) covered with BREADCRUMBS or BATTER and fried: *scampi and chips* **2** (*also* **shrimp ˈscampi**) (*both NAmE*) a dish of large PRAWNS fried in butter and GARLIC

**scan** 🔊 **B1** /skæn/ *verb, noun*
■ *verb* (**-nn-**) **1** 🔊 **B1** [T, I] to look quickly but not very carefully at a document, etc.: ~ **sth (for sth)** *I scanned the list quickly for my name.* ◊ ~ **through sth (for sth)** *She scanned through the newspaper over breakfast.* ◊ ~ **for sth** *You should teach students to scan for essential information.* **2** [T] to look at every part of sth carefully, especially because you are looking for a particular thing or person **SYN** scrutinize: ~ **sth for sth** *He scanned the horizon for any sign of land.* ◊ ~ **sth** *She scanned his face anxiously.* **3** 🔊 **B2** [T] (*computing*) to pass light over a picture or document using a SCANNER in order to copy it and put it in the memory of a computer: ~ **sth** *How do I scan a photo and attach it to an email?* ◊ ~ **sth into sth** *The pencil image is scanned into a computer.* **4** 🔊 **B2** [T] ~ **sth** to get an image of an object, a part of sb's body, etc. on a computer by passing X-RAYS, ULTRASOUND waves or ELECTROMAGNETIC waves over it in a special machine: *Their brains are scanned so that researchers can monitor the progress of the disease.* **5** [T] ~ **sth** (of a light, RADAR, etc.) to pass across an area: *Concealed video cameras scan every part of the compound.* **6** [I, T] ~ **(sth)** (*computing*) (of a program) to examine a computer program or document in order to look for a virus: *This software is designed to scan all new files for viruses.* **7** [I] (of poetry) to have a regular rhythm according to fixed rules: *This line doesn't scan.*
**PHRV** ˌscan sth ˈinto sth | ˌscan sth ˈin (*computing*) to pass light over a picture or document using a SCANNER in order to copy it and put it in the memory of a computer: *Text and pictures can be scanned into the computer.*
■ *noun* **1** [C] a medical test in which a machine produces a picture of the inside of a person's body, or a baby inside its mother's body, on a computer screen: *to have a brain scan*

➲ WORDFINDER NOTE at EXAMINE, PREGNANT ➲ see also CAT SCAN, CT SCAN **2** [sing.] the act of looking quickly through sth written or printed, usually in order to find sth

**scan·dal** /ˈskændl/ noun **1** [C, U] behaviour or an event that people think is morally or legally wrong and causes public feelings of shock or anger: *a series of sex scandals* ◊ *to cause/create a scandal* ◊ *The scandal broke* (= became known to the public) *in May.* ◊ *There has been no hint of scandal during his time in office.* **2** [U] talk or reports about the very bad or wrong things that people have done or are thought to have done: *to spread scandal* ◊ *newspapers full of scandal* **3** [sing.] an action, attitude, etc. that you think is very wrong and not at all acceptable **SYN** disgrace: *it is a ~that … It is a scandal that such a large city has no orchestra.*

**scan·dal·ize** (*BrE also* -**ise**) /ˈskændəlaɪz/ *verb* ~ **sb** to do sth that shocks people very much **SYN** outrage: *She scandalized her family with her extravagant lifestyle.*

**scan·dal·ous** /ˈskændələs/ *adj.* **1** SHOCKING and unacceptable **SYN** disgraceful: *a scandalous waste of money* ◊ *it is scandalous that … It is scandalous that he has not been punished.* **2** [only before noun] containing talk about the very bad or wrong things that people have done or are thought to have done: *scandalous stories* ▶ **scan·dal·ous·ly** *adv.*: *scandalously low pay*

**Scan·di·navia** /ˌskændɪˈneɪviə/ *noun* [U] a cultural region in north-west Europe consisting of Norway, Sweden and Denmark and sometimes also Iceland, Finland and the Faroe Islands ▶ **Scan·di·navian** /-ən/ *adj., noun*

**scan·dium** /ˈskændiəm/ *noun* [U] (*symb.* **Sc**) a chemical element. Scandium is a silver-white metal found in various minerals.

**scan·ner** /ˈskænə(r)/ *noun* **1** a device for examining sth or recording sth using light, sound or X-RAYS: *The identity cards are examined by an electronic scanner.* ➲ see also BODY SCANNER **2** (*computing*) a device which copies pictures and documents so that they can be stored on a computer: *a document scanner* ➲ see also FLATBED SCANNER **3** a machine used by doctors to produce a picture of the inside of a person's body on a computer screen **4** a piece of equipment for receiving and sending RADAR signals

**scan·sion** /ˈskænʃn/ *noun* [U] (*specialist*) the rhythm of a line of poetry ➲ WORDFINDER NOTE at POETRY

**scant** /skænt/ *adj.* [only before noun] hardly any; not very much and not as much as there should be: *I paid scant attention to what she was saying.* ◊ *The firefighters went back into the house with scant regard for their own safety.*

**scanty** /ˈskænti/ *adj.* (**scant·ier**, **scanti·est**) **1** too little in amount for what is needed: *Details of his life are scanty.* **2** (of clothes) very small and not covering much of your body: *a scanty bikini* ▶ **scant·ily** /-təli/ *adv.*: *scantily dressed models*

**-scape** /skeɪp/ *combining form* (in nouns) a view or scene of: *landscape* ◊ *seascape* ◊ *moonscape*

**scape·goat** /ˈskeɪpɡəʊt/ *noun* a person who is blamed for sth bad that sb else has done or for some failure **SYN** fall guy: *She felt she had been made a scapegoat for her boss's incompetence.* ▶ **scape·goat** *verb* ~ **sb/sth**

**scap·ula** /ˈskæpjələ/ *noun* (*pl.* **scapu·lae** /-liː/ *or* **scapu·las**) (*anatomy*) the SHOULDER BLADE ➲ VISUAL VOCAB page V1

**scar** /skɑː(r)/ *noun, verb*
■ *noun* **1** a mark that is left on the skin after a wound has got better: *a scar on his cheek* ◊ *Will the operation* **leave a scar?** ◊ *scar tissue* **2** a permanent sad or painful feeling that a person is left with after an unpleasant experience: *His years in prison have left deep scars.* **3** something unpleasant or ugly that damages the appearance or public image of sth: *The town still bears the scars of war.* ◊ *Racism has been a scar on the game.* **4** an area of a hill or CLIFF where there is exposed rock and no grass
■ *verb* (-**rr**-) [usually passive] **1** (of a wound, etc.) to leave a mark on the skin after it has got better: **be/leave sb scarred** *His face was badly scarred.* **2** (of an unpleasant experience) to leave sb with a feeling of being very sad or with mental pain: **be/leave sb scarred** *The experience left her scarred for life.* **3** to damage the appearance of sth:

**be scarred (by sth)** *The hills are scarred by quarries.* ◊ *battle-scarred buildings*

**scar·ab** /ˈskærəb/ (*also* **ˈscarab beetle**) *noun* a large black BEETLE (= an insect with a hard shell); a design showing a scarab beetle

**scarce** /skeəs; NAmE skers/ *adj., adv.*
■ *adj.* (**scar·cer**, **scar·cest**) if sth is **scarce**, there is not enough of it and it is only available in small quantities: *scarce resources* ◊ *Details of the accident are scarce.* ◊ *Food was becoming scarce.*
**IDM** **make yourself ˈscarce** (*informal*) to leave somewhere and stay away for a time in order to avoid an unpleasant situation
■ *adv.* (*literary*) only just; almost not **SYN** scarcely: *I can scarce remember him.*

**scarce·ly** /ˈskeəsli; NAmE ˈskers-/ *adv.* **1** only just; almost not: *I can scarcely believe it.* ◊ *We scarcely ever meet.* ◊ *Scarcely a week goes by without some new scandal in the papers.* **2** used to say that sth happens immediately after sth else happens: *He had scarcely put the phone down when the doorbell rang.* ◊ *Scarcely had the game started when it began to rain.* **3** used to suggest that sth is not at all reasonable or likely: *It was scarcely an occasion for laughter.* ◊ *She could scarcely complain, could she?* ➲ note at HARDLY

**scar·city** /ˈskeəsəti; NAmE ˈskers-/ *noun* (*pl.* -**ies**) if there is a **scarcity** of sth, there is not enough of it and it is difficult to obtain it **SYN** shortage: *a time of scarcity* ◊ *a scarcity of resources*

**scare** /skeə(r); NAmE sker/ *verb, noun*
■ *verb* [T] to frighten sb: ~**sb** *You scared me.* ◊ **it scares sb to do sth** *It scared me to think I was alone in the building.* ➲ SYNONYMS at FRIGHTEN **2** [I] to become frightened: *He doesn't scare easily.* ➲ see also SCARY
**IDM** **scare the ˈshit out of sb | scare sb ˈshitless** (*taboo, slang*) to frighten sb very much ➲ more at DAYLIGHTS, DEATH, LIFE
**PHR V** **ˌscare sb↔aˈway/ˈoff** to make sb go away by frightening them: *They managed to scare the bears away.* **ˈscare sb into doing sth** to frighten sb in order to make them do sth: *Local businesses were scared into paying protection money.* **ˌscare sb↔ˈoff** to make sb afraid or nervous about doing sth, especially without intending to: *Rising prices are scaring customers off.* **ˌscare ˈup sth** (NAmE, *informal*) to find or make sth by using whatever is available: *I'll see if I can scare up enough chairs for us all.*
■ *noun* **1** [C] (used especially in newspapers) a situation in which a lot of people are frightened or worried about sth: *a health scare* ◊ *recent scares about pesticides in food* ◊ *a scare story* (= a news report that spreads more anxiety or fear about sth than is necessary) ◊ *to cause a major scare* ◊ *scare tactics* (= ways of persuading people to do sth by frightening them) ➲ see also BOMB SCARE **2** [sing.] a sudden feeling of fear: *You gave me a scare!* ◊ *We've had quite a scare.* ➲ see also SCARY

**scare·crow** /ˈskeəkrəʊ; NAmE ˈskerk-/ *noun* a figure made to look like a person, that is dressed in old clothes and put in a field to frighten birds away

**scared** /skeəd; NAmE skerd/ *adj.* frightened of sth or afraid that sth bad might happen: *The thieves got scared and ran away.* ◊ **~ of doing sth** *She is scared of going out alone.* ◊ **~ of sb/sth** *He's scared of heights.* ◊ **~ to do sth** *People are scared to use the buses late at night.* ◊ **~(that)…** *I'm scared (that) I'm going to fall.* ◊ **~ for sth** *We were scared for our lives* (= thought we would die). ◊ *I was scared to death* (= very frightened). ◊ *We were scared stiff* (= very frightened). ➲ SYNONYMS at AFRAID ➲ see also SHIT-SCARED **IDM** see SHADOW *n.*, WIT, WITLESS

**scaredy-cat** /ˈskeədi kæt; NAmE ˈskerd-/ (NAmE *also* **fraidy cat**) *noun* (*informal, disapproving*) a children's word for a person who is easily frightened

**scare·mon·ger** /ˈskeəmʌŋɡə(r); NAmE ˈskermɑːŋ-/ *noun* (*disapproving*) a person who spreads stories deliberately to

**scare quotes** 1382

make people frightened or nervous ▸ **scare‧monger‧ing** noun [U]

**'scare quotes** noun [pl.] QUOTATION MARKS that a writer puts around a word or phrase to show that it is used in an unusual way, usually one that the writer does not agree with: *This pronouncement came from the organization's 'scientific' committee (the scare quotes are mine).*

**scarf** /skɑːf; NAmE skɑːrf/ noun, verb
■ noun (pl. **scarves** /skɑːvz; NAmE skɑːrvz/ or *less frequent* **scarfs**) a piece of cloth that is worn around the neck, for example to keep warm or for decoration. Women also wear scarves over their shoulders or hair: *a woollen/silk scarf*
■ verb (NAmE) (BrE **scoff**) [I, T] ~ **(sth)** (informal) to eat a lot of sth quickly

**scari‧ly** /'skeərəli; NAmE 'skerəli/ adv. (informal) **1** in a frightening way: *He's become scarily thin in recent months.* **2** in a very interesting, unusual or surprising way: *His new girlfriend looks scarily like his ex.*

**scar‧let** /'skɑːlət; NAmE 'skɑːrl-/ adj. bright red in colour: *scarlet berries* ◊ *She went scarlet with embarrassment.* ▸ **scar‧let** noun [U]

**scarlet 'fever** noun [U] a serious disease that causes a high temperature and red marks on the skin

**scarp** /skɑːp; NAmE skɑːrp/ noun (specialist) a very steep slope

**scar‧per** /'skɑːpə(r); NAmE 'skɑːrp-/ verb [I] (BrE, informal) to run away; to leave: *The police arrived, so we scarpered.*

**Scart** (also **SCART**) /skɑːt; NAmE skɑːrt/ noun a device with 21 pins, used to connect video equipment to, for example, a television: *a Scart socket*

**scarves** /skɑːvz; NAmE skɑːrvz/ pl. of SCARF

**scary** 🛈 A2 /'skeəri; NAmE 'skeri/ adj. (**scari‧er**, **scari‧est**) (informal) frightening: *It was a really scary moment.* ◊ *a scary movie* ⇒ see also SCARE, SCARILY

**scat** /skæt/ noun [U] a style of jazz singing in which the voice is made to sound like a musical instrument

**scath‧ing** /'skeɪðɪŋ/ adj. criticizing sb or sth very severely in a way that shows no respect SYN withering: *a scathing attack on the new management* ◊ ~ **about sb/sth** *He was scathing about the government's performance.* ▸ **scath‧ing‧ly** adv.: *'Oh, she's just a kid,' he said scathingly.*

**scato‧logic‧al** /ˌskætə'lɒdʒɪkl; NAmE -'lɑːdʒ-/ adj. (formal) connected with human waste from the body in an unpleasant way: *scatological humour*

**scat‧ter** /'skætə(r)/ verb, noun
■ verb **1** [T] to throw or drop things in different directions so that they cover an area of ground: ~ **sth** *They scattered his ashes at sea.* ◊ ~ **sth on/over/around sth** *Scatter the grass seed over the lawn.* ◊ ~ **sth with sth** *Scatter the lawn with grass seed.* **2** [I, T] to move or to make people or animals move very quickly in different directions SYN disperse: *At the first gunshot, the crowd scattered.* ◊ ~ **sb/sth** *The explosion scattered a flock of birds roosting in the trees.*
■ noun [usually sing.] = SCATTERING

**scat‧ter‧brain** /'skætəbreɪn; NAmE -tərb-/ noun (informal) a person who is always losing or forgetting things and cannot think in an organized way ▸ **scat‧ter‧brained** adj.

**'scatter cushion** (BrE) (NAmE **'throw pillow**) noun a small CUSHION that can be placed on furniture, on the floor, etc. for decoration

**scat‧tered** /'skætəd; NAmE -tərd/ adj. spread far apart over a wide area or over a long period of time: *a few scattered settlements* ◊ *sunshine with scattered showers* ◊ *Her family are scattered around the world.*

**scat‧ter‧gun** /'skætəɡʌn; NAmE -tərɡ-/ (BrE) (NAmE usually **scat‧ter‧shot** /'skætəʃɒt; NAmE -tərʃɑːt/) adj. [only before noun] referring to a way of doing or dealing with sth by considering many different possibilities, people, etc. in a way that is not well organized: *The scattergun approach to*

marketing means that the campaign is not targeted at particular individuals.

**scat‧ter‧ing** /'skætərɪŋ/ (also *less frequent* **scat‧ter**) noun [usually sing.] a small amount or number of things spread over an area: *a scattering of houses*

**scatty** /'skæti/ adj. (**scat‧tier**, **scat‧ti‧est**) (BrE, informal) tending to forget things and behave in a slightly silly way

**scav‧enge** /'skævɪndʒ/ verb **1** [T, I] (of a person, an animal or a bird) to search through waste for things that can be used or eaten: ~ **sth (from sth)** *Much of their furniture was scavenged from other people's garbage.* ◊ ~ **(through sth) (for sth)** *Dogs and foxes scavenged through the trash cans for something to eat.* **2** [T, I] (of animals or birds) to eat dead animals that have been killed by another animal, by a car, etc.: ~ **sth** *Crows scavenge carrion left on the roads.* ◊ ~ **(on sth)** *Some fish scavenge on dead fish in the wild.*

**scav‧en‧ger** /'skævɪndʒə(r)/ noun an animal, a bird or a person that scavenges

**'scavenger hunt** noun a game in which players have to find various objects

**scen‧ario** 🛈+ B2 🅦 /sə'nɑːriəʊ; NAmE -'nær-/ noun (pl. -os) **1** 🛈+ B2 a description of how things might happen in the future: *Let me suggest a possible scenario.* ◊ *The worst-case scenario* (= the worst possible thing that could happen) *would be for the factory to be closed down.* ◊ *a nightmare scenario* **2** a written outline of what happens in a film or play SYN synopsis ⇒ WORDFINDER NOTE at FILM

**scene** 🛈 A2 /siːn/ noun
• PLACE **1** A2 [C, usually sing.] the place where sth happens, especially sth unpleasant: *the scene of the accident/crime/crash* ◊ *Police carried out a full search of the crime scene.* ◊ **on/at the ~** *Firefighters arrived on the scene within minutes.* ⇒ SYNONYMS at PLACE
• EVENT **2** 🛈+ A2 [C, usually pl.] an event or a situation that you see, especially one of a particular type: *The team's victory produced scenes of jubilation all over the country.* ◊ *She witnessed some very distressing scenes.*
• IN MOVIE/PLAY, ETC. **3** 🛈+ A2 [C] a part of a film, play or book in which the action happens in one place or is of one particular type: *sex/fight/action/battle scenes* ◊ *to film/shoot a scene* ⇒ WORDFINDER NOTE at PLOT **4** 🛈+ A2 [C] one of the small sections that a play or an OPERA is divided into: *Act I, Scene 2 of 'Macbeth'* ⇒ WORDFINDER NOTE at DRAMA
• AREA OF ACTIVITY **5** 🛈+ B1 **the scene, the ... scene** [sing.] (informal) a particular area of activity or way of life and the people who are part of it: *the art/club/punk scene* ◊ **on the ... ~** *a newcomer on the music scene* ◊ *Tarantino burst onto the cinema scene in the '90s.*
• VIEW **6** [C] a view that you see: *a delightful rural scene* ◊ *They went abroad for a change of scene* (= to see and experience new surroundings). ⇒ SYNONYMS at VIEW
• PAINTING/PHOTOGRAPH **7** [C] a painting, drawing, or photograph of a place and the things that are happening there: *an exhibition of Parisian street scenes*
• ARGUMENT **8** [C, usually sing.] a loud, angry argument, especially one that happens in public and is embarrassing: *She had made a scene in the middle of the party.* ◊ *'Please leave,' he said. 'I don't want a scene.'*
IDM **behind the 'scenes 1** in the part of a theatre, etc. that the public does not usually see: *The students were able to go behind the scenes to see how programmes are made.* **2** in a way that people in general are not aware of: *A lot of negotiating has been going on behind the scenes.* ◊ *behind-the-scenes work* **not sb's 'scene** (informal) not the type of thing that sb likes or enjoys doing **set the 'scene (for sth) 1** to create a situation in which sth can easily happen or develop: *His arrival set the scene for another argument.* **2** to give sb the information and details they need in order to understand what comes next: *The first part of the programme was just setting the scene.*

▼ HOMOPHONES

**scene** ◆ **seen** /siːn/

• **scene** noun: *A police officer attended the scene.*
• **seen** verb (past participle of SEE): *Have you seen the latest Star Wars movie?*

---

æ cat | ɑː father | e bed | ɜː fur | ə about | ɪ sit | iː see | i happy | ɒ got (BrE) | ɔː saw | ʌ cup | ʊ put | uː too

**scene-of-crime** adj. [only before noun] (BrE) relating to the part of the police service that examines the physical evidence of a crime that is present in the place where the crime was committed: *a scene-of-crime officer*

**scen·ery** /ˈsiːnəri/ noun [U] **1** the natural features of an area, such as mountains, valleys, rivers and forests, when you are thinking about them being attractive to look at: *The scenery is magnificent.* ◇ *to enjoy the scenery* ⊃ SYNONYMS at COUNTRY **2** the painted background that is used to represent natural features or buildings on a theatre stage ⊃ WORDFINDER NOTE at STAGE

**scenic** /ˈsiːnɪk/ adj. **1** [usually before noun] having beautiful natural scenery: *an area of scenic beauty* ◇ *They took the scenic route back to the hotel.* ◇ *a scenic drive* **2** [only before noun] connected with scenery in a theatre: *scenic designs* ▶ **scen·ic·al·ly** /-kli/ adv.: *scenically attractive areas*

**scent** /sent/ noun, verb
■ noun **1** [U, C] the pleasant smell that sth has: *The air was filled with the scent of wild flowers.* ◇ *These flowers have no scent.* **2** [U, C, usually sing.] the smell that a person or an animal leaves behind and that other animals such as dogs can follow SYN **trail**: *The dogs must have lost her scent.* **3** [U] (especially BrE) a liquid with a pleasant smell that you wear on your skin to make it smell nice SYN **perfume, fragrance**: *a bottle of scent* **4** [sing.] **~ of sth** the feeling that sth is present or is going to happen very soon: *The scent of victory was in the air.* IDM **on the 'scent (of sth)** close to discovering sth **put/throw sb off the 'scent** to do sth to stop sb from finding you or discovering sth
■ verb **1 ~ sth** to find sth by using the sense of smell: *The dog scented a rabbit.* **2 ~ sth** to begin to feel that sth exists or is about to happen SYN **sense**: *The press could scent a scandal.* ◇ *By then, the team was scenting victory.* **3** [often passive] **~ sth (with sth)** to give sth a particular, pleasant smell: *Roses scented the night air.*

▼ **HOMOPHONES**
cent • scent • sent /sent/
• **cent** *noun: Not one cent of their profits goes to charity.*
• **scent** *noun: The delicious scent of freshly baked bread floated to his window.*
• **sent** *noun (past tense, past participle of* SEND*): I sent her a thank you letter.*

**scent·ed** /ˈsentɪd/ adj. having a strong pleasant smell

**scep·ter** (US) = SCEPTRE

**scep·tic** (BrE) (NAmE **skep·tic**) /ˈskeptɪk/ noun a person who usually doubts that claims or statements are true, especially those that other people believe in ⊃ see also EUROSCEPTIC

**scep·tical** (BrE) (NAmE **skep·tical**) /ˈskeptɪkl/ adj. having doubts that a claim or statement is true or that sth will happen: *She looked highly sceptical.* ◇ **~ about sth** *I am sceptical about his chances of winning.* ◇ **~ of sth** *The public remain sceptical of these claims.* ▶ **scep·tical·ly** (BrE) (NAmE **skep·tical·ly**) /-kli/ adv.

**scep·ti·cism** (BrE) (NAmE **skep·ti·cism**) /ˈskeptɪsɪzəm/ noun [U, sing.] an attitude of doubting that claims or statements are true or that sth will happen: *Such claims should be regarded with a certain amount of scepticism.*

**scep·tre** (US **scep·ter**) /ˈseptə(r)/ noun a decorated ROD carried by a king or queen at ceremonies as a symbol of their power ⊃ compare MACE, ORB

**schaden·freude** /ˈʃɑːdnfrɔɪdə/ noun [U] (from German) a feeling of pleasure at the bad things that happen to other people

**sched·ule** /ˈʃedjuːl/ NAmE /ˈskedʒuːl/ noun, verb
■ noun **1** [C, U] a plan that lists all the work that you have to do and when you must do each thing: *I have a hectic schedule for the next few days.* ◇ *We're working to a tight schedule* (= we have a lot of things to do in a short time). ◇ **on ~** *Filming began on schedule* (= at the planned time). ◇ **ahead of ~** *The new bridge has been finished two years ahead of schedule.* ◇ **behind ~** *The tunnel project has already fallen behind schedule.* **2** [C] (NAmE) = TIMETABLE: *a train/flight schedule* ◇ *Besides a full school schedule, Kayla's week is jam-packed with other activities.* **3** [C] a list of the television and radio programmes that are on a particular channel and the times that they start: *The channel's schedules are filled with old films and repeats.* **4** [C] a written list of things, for example prices, rates or conditions: *tax schedules*
■ verb **1** [usually passive] to arrange for sth to happen at a particular time: **~ sth (for sth)** *The meeting is scheduled for Friday afternoon.* ◇ *One of the scheduled events is a talk on alternative medicine.* ◇ *We'll be stopping here for longer than scheduled.* ◇ **~ sb/sth to do sth** *I'm scheduled to arrive in LA at 5 o'clock.* **2 ~ sth (as sth)** (formal) to include sth in an official list of things: *The substance has been scheduled as a poison.* ▶ **sched·uler** noun: *The president's schedulers allowed 90 minutes for TV interviews.*

**scheduled 'caste** noun (in India) a CASTE (= division of society) that is listed in the Indian Constitution and recommended for special help in education and employment

**scheduled 'flight** noun a plane service that leaves at a regular time each day or week ⊃ compare CHARTER FLIGHT

**scheduled 'tribe** noun (in India) a TRIBE that is listed in the Indian Constitution and recommended for special help in education and employment

**schema** /ˈskiːmə/ noun (pl. **sche·mas** or **sche·mata** /ˈskiːmətə, skiːˈmɑːtə/) (specialist) an outline of a plan or theory

**sche·mat·ic** /skiːˈmætɪk/ adj. **1** (of a diagram) showing the main features or relationships but not the details: *a schematic diagram* **2** having a fixed plan or pattern: *The play has a very schematic plot.* ▶ **sche·mat·ic·al·ly** /-kli/ adv.: *The process is shown schematically in figure 3.*

**scheme** /skiːm/ noun, verb
■ noun **1** (BrE) a plan or system for doing or organizing sth: *a training scheme* ◇ **~ for doing sth** *a local scheme for recycling newspapers* ◇ **~ to do sth** *to introduce/operate a scheme to improve links between schools and industry* ◇ **under a ~** *Under the new scheme only successful schools will be given extra funding.* ◇ *to introduce/launch/run a scheme* ⊃ see also PENSION SCHEME at PENSION PLAN **2** a plan for getting money or some other advantage for yourself, especially one that involves cheating other people: **~ to do sth** *an elaborate scheme to avoid taxes* ⊃ see also PYRAMID SCHEME **3** an ordered system or arrangement: *It is a poem with a rhyme scheme and a defined structure.* ⊃ see also COLOUR SCHEME **4** (ScotE, informal) = HOUSING SCHEME (2) IDM **the/sb's 'scheme of things** the way things seem to be organized; the way sb wants everything to be organized: *This small annoyance isn't much in the grand scheme of things.* ◇ *I don't think marriage figures in his scheme of things.*
■ verb **1** [I, T] (disapproving) to make secret plans to do sth that will help yourself and possibly harm others SYN **plot**: **~ (against sb)** *She seemed to feel that we were all scheming against her.* ◇ **~ to do sth** *His colleagues, meanwhile, were busily scheming to get rid of him.* ◇ **~ sth** *Her enemies were scheming her downfall.* **2** [T] **~ sth** (SAfrE, informal) to think or form an opinion about sth: *What do you scheme?* ◇ *'Do you think he'll come?' 'I scheme so.'*

**schemer** /ˈskiːmə(r)/ noun (disapproving) a person who plans secretly to do sth for their own advantage

**schem·ing** /ˈskiːmɪŋ/ adj. (disapproving) often planning secretly to do sth for your own advantage, especially by cheating other people

**scherzo** /ˈskeətsəʊ/ NAmE /ˈskert-/ noun (pl. **-os**) (from Italian) a short, lively piece of music, that is often part of a longer piece

**schism** /ˈskɪzəm, ˈsɪ-/ noun [C, U] (formal) **~ (within/between sth)** strong DISAGREEMENT within an organization, especially a religious one, that makes its members

# schist

divide into separate groups ▶ **schis·mat·ic** /skɪzˈmætɪk, sɪz-/ *adj.*

**schist** /ʃɪst/ *noun* [U] a type of rock formed of layers of different minerals, that breaks naturally into thin flat pieces

**schiz·oid** /ˈskɪtsɔɪd/ *adj.* (*specialist*) similar to or suffering from schizophrenia: *schizoid tendencies*

**schizo·phre·nia** /ˌskɪtsəˈfriːniə; *NAmE also* -ˈfren-/ *noun* [U] a mental illness in which a person becomes unable to link thought, emotion and behaviour, leading to WITHDRAWAL from reality and personal relationships ⊃ WORDFINDER NOTE at CONDITION

**schizo·phren·ic** /ˌskɪtsəˈfrenɪk/ *noun, adj.*
- *noun* a person who suffers from schizophrenia
- *adj.* **1** suffering from schizophrenia **2** (*informal*) frequently changing your mind about sth or holding opinions about sth that seem to oppose each other

**schlep** (*also* **schlepp**) /ʃlep/ *verb* (**-pp-**) (*informal*) **1** [I] **+ adv./prep.** to go somewhere, especially if it is a slow, difficult journey, or you do not want to go **2** [T] **~ sth (+ adv./prep.)** to carry or pull sth heavy: *I'm not schlepping these suitcases all over town.* ORIGIN From Yiddish *shlepn*, 'to drag'. ▶ **schlep** (*also* **schlepp**) *noun* [sing.]

**schlock** /ʃlɒk; *NAmE* ʃlɑːk/ *noun* [U] (*NAmE, informal*) things that are cheap and of poor quality ▶ **schlocky** *adj.*: *a low-budget schlocky film*

**schmaltz** /ʃmɔːlts/ *noun* [U] (*informal, disapproving*) the fact of being too SENTIMENTAL: *At the end of the movie we drown in a sea of schmaltz.* ▶ **schmaltzy** *adj.* (**schmaltz·ier**, **schmaltzi·est**)

**schmo** (*also* **shmo**) /ʃməʊ/ *noun* (*pl.* **-oes**) (*NAmE, informal, disapproving*) a person who is stupid in an annoying way

**schmooze** /ʃmuːz/ *verb* [I, T] **~ (with) sb** (*informal*) to talk in an informal and friendly way with sb, especially in order to gain an advantage by persuading people to like you and do what you want SYN chat ▶ **schmooz·er** *noun*

**schmuck** /ʃmʌk/ *noun* (*informal, disapproving, especially NAmE*) a stupid person: *He's such a schmuck!*

**schnapps** /ʃnæps/ *noun* [U, C] (*from German*) a strong alcoholic drink made from grain

**schnau·zer** /ˈʃnaʊzə(r)/ *noun* a dog with short, rough and curly hair

**scholar** ⁺ B2 /ˈskɒlə(r); *NAmE* ˈskɑːl-/ *noun* **1** ⁺ B2 a person who knows a lot about a particular subject because they have studied it in detail: *a classical scholar* ◊ *He was the most distinguished scholar in his field.* **2** C1 a student who has been given a scholarship to study at a school, college or university: *a Rhodes scholar* **3** (*BrE, informal*) a clever person who works hard at school: *I was never much of a scholar.*

**schol·ar·ly** /ˈskɒləli; *NAmE* ˈskɑːlərli/ *adj.* **1** (of a person) spending a lot of time studying and having a lot of knowledge about an academic subject SYN **academic 2** connected with academic study SYN **academic**: *a scholarly journal*

**schol·ar·ship** ⁺ B2 /ˈskɒləʃɪp; *NAmE* ˈskɑːlərʃ-/ *noun* **1** ⁺ B2 [C] an amount of money given to sb by an organization to help pay for their education: *She won a scholarship to study at Stanford.* ◊ **on a ~** *He went to drama school on a scholarship.* **2** ⁺ C1 [U] the serious study of an academic subject and the knowledge and methods involved SYN **learning**: *a magnificent work of scholarship*

**scho·las·tic** /skəˈlæstɪk/ *adj.* (*only before noun*) (*formal*) **1** connected with schools and education: *scholastic achievements* **2** connected with scholasticism

**scho·las·ti·cism** /skəˈlæstɪsɪzəm/ *noun* [U] a system of philosophy, based on religious principles and writing, that was taught in universities in the Middle Ages

**school** 🔑 A1 /skuːl/ *noun, verb*
- *noun*
  - • WHERE CHILDREN LEARN **1** ⁺ A1 [C] a place where children go to be educated: *My brother and I went to the same school.* ◊ (*formal*) *Which school do they attend?* ◊ *I'm going to the school today to talk to Kim's teacher.* ◊ *school buildings* HELP There are many compounds ending in **school**. You will find them at their place in the alphabet. **2** ⁺ A1 [U] (used without *the* or *a*) the process of learning in a school; the time during your life when you go to a school: (*BrE*) *to start/leave school* ◊ (*NAmE*) *to start/quit school* ◊ *Where did you go to school?* ◊ (*BrE*) **at~** *All my kids are still at school.* ◊ (*NAmE*) **in~** *All my kids are still in school.* ◊ (*NAmE*) *to* **teach school** (= teach in a school) ◊ *The transition from school to work can be difficult.* **3** ⁺ A1 [U] (used without *the* or *a*) the time during the day when children are working in a school: *School begins at 9.* ◊ **after~** *Shall I meet you after school today?* ◊ **at/in~** *The kids are at/in school until 3.30.* ◊ **off~** *I'm off school this week.* ◊ *after-school activities* ◊ *The next day was Monday, a school day.*
  - • STUDENTS AND TEACHERS **4** ⁺ A2 **the school** [sing.] all the children or students and the teachers in a school: *I had to stand up in front of the whole school.*
  - • FOR PARTICULAR SKILL **5** ⁺ A1 [C, U] (often in compounds) a place where people go to learn a particular subject or skill: *a drama/language/riding school* ◊ *She wants to go to art school.* ⊃ see also CHARM SCHOOL, TRADE SCHOOL
  - • COLLEGE/UNIVERSITY **6** ⁺ A2 [C, U] (*NAmE, informal*) a college or university; the time that you spend there: *famous schools like Yale and Harvard* ◊ *Where did you go to school?* ⊃ see also GRAD SCHOOL, GRADUATE SCHOOL **7** ⁺ A2 [C, U] a department of a college or university that teaches a particular subject: *the business/law/medical school* ◊ **~ of sth** *the School of Dentistry* ◊ *He was determined to get into medical school.*
  - • OF WRITERS/ARTISTS **8** [C] a group of writers, artists, etc. whose style of work or opinions have been influenced by the same person or ideas: *the Dutch school of painting*
  - • OF FISH **9** [C] a large number of fish or other sea animals, swimming together: *a school of dolphins* ⊃ compare SHOAL ⊃ see also OLD SCHOOL
  - IDM **school(s) of ˈthought** a way of thinking that a number of people share: *There are two schools of thought about how this illness should be treated.* ⊃ more at COOL *adj.*, OLD
- *verb* (*formal*)
  - • YOURSELF/ANIMAL **1** to train sb/yourself/an animal to do sth: **~ sb/sth/yourself (in sth)** *to school a horse* ◊ *She had schooled herself in patience.* ◊ **~ sb/sth/yourself to do sth** *I have schooled myself to remain calm under pressure.*
  - • CHILD **2** **~ sb** to educate a child: *She should be schooled with her peers.*

> **GRAMMAR POINT**
> **school**
> • When a **school** is being referred to as an institution, you do not need to use *the*: *When do the children finish school?* When you are talking about a particular building, *the* is used: *I'll meet you outside the school.* **Prison, jail, court,** and **church** work in the same way: *Her husband spent three years in prison.*
> ⊃ note at COLLEGE, HOSPITAL

> **BRITISH/AMERICAN**
> **at / in school**
> • In *BrE* somebody who is attending school is **at school**: *I was at school with her sister.* In *NAmE* **in school** is used: *I have a ten-year-old in school.* **In school** in *NAmE* can also mean 'attending a university'.

**ˈschool age** *noun* [U] the age or period when a child normally attends school: *children of school age* ◊ *school-age children*

**ˈschool board** *noun* (*NAmE*) (in the US) a committee that is elected to be in charge of all the public schools in a particular area

**school·boy** /ˈskuːlbɔɪ/ *noun* a boy who attends school ⊃ SYNONYMS at STUDENT

**school·child** /ˈskuːltʃaɪld/ *noun* (*pl.* **school·chil·dren** /-tʃɪldrən/) (*also informal* **school·kid**) a child who attends school ⊃ SYNONYMS at STUDENT

**school council** noun **1** (BrE) (NAmE **student council**) a group of school students who have been elected by the other students to represent their views about decisions that affect the school **2** (NAmE) a group of people, including parents and teachers, elected or chosen to advise on the management of a school ⇒ compare GOVERNOR (3)

**school day** (also **school-day**) noun **1** a day of the week when students go to school: *I get up very early on school days.* **2** the part of the day that students spend at school: *The school day ends at 3 p.m.* ⇒ **schooldays** [pl.] the period in your life when you go to school: *She hadn't seen Laura since her schooldays.*

**school district** noun (in the US) an area that contains several schools that are governed together

**school friend** noun (especially BrE) a friend who attends or attended the same school as you: *She met up with some of her old (= former) school friends.*

**school-girl** /ˈskuːlɡɜːl; NAmE -ɡɜːrl/ noun a girl who attends school ⇒ SYNONYMS at STUDENT

**school-house** /ˈskuːlhaʊs/ noun **1** a school building, especially a small one in a village in the past **2** a house for a teacher next to a small school

**schoolie** /ˈskuːli/ noun (AustralE) a school student at the end of his or her time at school

**Schoolies Week** (also **Schoolies**) noun [U] (in Australia) a time in November or December each year when Year 12 (final-year) school students celebrate leaving school by having a holiday in a town with a beach

**school-ing** /ˈskuːlɪŋ/ noun [U] (formal) the education you receive at school: *secondary schooling* ◇ *He had very little schooling.*

**school-kid** /ˈskuːlkɪd/ noun (informal) = SCHOOLCHILD

**school-leaver** noun (BrE) a person who has just left school, especially when they are looking for a job: *the problem of rising unemployment among school-leavers*

**school-master** /ˈskuːlmɑːstə(r); NAmE -mæs-/, **school-mistress** /ˈskuːlmɪstrəs/ noun (especially BrE, old-fashioned) a teacher in a school, especially a private school ⇒ compare MASTER

**school-mate** /ˈskuːlmeɪt/ noun (especially BrE) a person who attends or attended the same school as you

**school-room** /ˈskuːlruːm, -rʊm/ noun (old-fashioned) a classroom

**the school run** noun [sing.] (BrE) the journey that parents make to take their children to school or to bring them home again

**school-teach-er** /ˈskuːltiːtʃə(r)/ noun a person whose job is teaching in a school

**school-work** /ˈskuːlwɜːk; NAmE -wɜːrk/ noun [U] work that students do at school or for school: *She is struggling to keep up with her schoolwork.*

**school-yard** /ˈskuːljɑːd; NAmE -jɑːrd/ noun (NAmE) an outdoor area of a school for children to play in ⇒ compare PLAYGROUND

**schoo-ner** /ˈskuːnə(r)/ noun **1** a sailing ship with two or more MASTS (= posts that support the sails) **2** (NAmE, AustralE, NZE) a tall glass for beer

**schtick** = SHTICK

**schtum** = SHTUM

**schwa** (also **shwa**) /ʃwɑː/ noun (phonetics) a vowel sound in parts of words that are not stressed, for example the 'a' in *about* or the 'e' in *moment*; the PHONETIC symbol for this, /ə/

**sci-at-ic** /saɪˈætɪk/ adj. [only before noun] (anatomy) of the HIP or of the nerve which goes from the PELVIS to the THIGH (= the **sciatic nerve**)

**sci-at-ica** /saɪˈætɪkə/ noun [U] pain in the back, HIP and outer side of the leg, caused by pressure on the sciatic nerve

**sci-ence** 🔵 **A1** 🔊 /ˈsaɪəns/ noun **1** **A1** [U] knowledge about the structure and behaviour of the natural and physical world, based on facts that you can prove, for example by experiments: *new developments in science and technology* ◇ *the advance of modern science* ◇ *the laws of science* ⇒ see also HARD SCIENCE, JUNK SCIENCE **2** **A1** [U] the study of science: *science students/teachers/classes* **3** **A1** [U, C] a particular branch of science: *medical/environmental science* ◇ *the biological sciences* ◇ *to study one of the sciences* ⇒ compare ART, HUMANITY ⇒ see also COMPUTER SCIENCE, DOMESTIC SCIENCE, EARTH SCIENCE, FOOD SCIENCE, INFORMATION SCIENCE, LIFE SCIENCE, NATURAL SCIENCE, PHYSICAL SCIENCE, POLITICAL SCIENCE, ROCKET SCIENCE, SOCIAL SCIENCE, SOIL SCIENCE **4** [sing.] a system for organizing the knowledge about a particular subject, especially one that deals with aspects of human behaviour or society: *a science of international politics* ⇒ see also CHRISTIAN SCIENCE, CREATION SCIENCE IDM see BLIND v.

> **WORDFINDER** analysis, evaluate, evidence, experiment, hypothesis, laboratory, research, result, study

**science fair** noun (NAmE) a competition in which students at a school compete to present the best science project

**science fiction** (also informal **sci-fi**) noun [U] (abbr. **SF**) a type of book, film, etc. that is based on imagined scientific discoveries of the future, and often deals with space travel and life on other planets

**science park** noun an area where there are a lot of companies or organizations involved in scientific research and development

**sci-en-tif-ic** 🔵 **B1** 🔊 /ˌsaɪənˈtɪfɪk/ adj. [usually before noun] **1** **B1** involving science; connected with science: *a scientific discovery/theory/fact* ◇ *scientific research/evidence/knowledge/methods* ◇ *the scientific community (= people who work in science)* **2** (of a way of doing sth or thinking) careful and logical: *He took a very scientific approach to management.* ◇ *We need to be more scientific about this problem.* OPP unscientific ⇒ compare NON-SCIENTIFIC ▶ **sci-en-tif-ic-al-ly** /-kli/ adv.

**sci-en-tism** /ˈsaɪəntɪzəm/ noun [U] **1** a way of thinking or expressing ideas that is considered to be typical of scientists **2** complete belief in scientific methods, or in the truth of scientific knowledge

**sci-en-tist** 🔵 **A1** /ˈsaɪəntɪst/ noun a person who studies or is an expert in one or more of the NATURAL SCIENCES (= for example, physics, chemistry or biology): *a research scientist* ◇ *nuclear/climate scientists* ◇ *scientists and engineers* ◇ *Scientists believe there is ice a few inches below the surface of Mars.* ⇒ see also CHRISTIAN SCIENTIST, COMPUTER SCIENTIST, POLITICAL SCIENTIST, ROCKET SCIENTIST, SOCIAL SCIENTIST

**Sci-en-tol-ogy**™ /ˌsaɪənˈtɒlədʒi; NAmE -ˈtɑːl-/ noun [U] a religious system based on getting knowledge of yourself and spiritual FULFILMENT through courses of study and training ▶ **sci-en-tolo-gist** noun

**sci-fi** /ˈsaɪ faɪ/ noun [U] (informal) = SCIENCE FICTION

**scimi-tar** /ˈsɪmɪtə(r); NAmE also -tɑːr/ noun a short curved SWORD with one sharp edge, used especially in Eastern countries

**scin-tilla** /sɪnˈtɪlə/ noun [sing.] (usually in negative sentences) **~ (of sth)** (formal) a very small amount of sth: *There is not a scintilla of truth in what she says.*

**scin-til-lat-ing** /ˈsɪntɪleɪtɪŋ/ adj. very clever, exciting and interesting: *a scintillating performance* ◇ *Statistics on unemployment levels hardly make for scintillating reading.*

**scion** /ˈsaɪən/ noun **1** (formal or literary) a young member of a family, especially a famous or important one **2** (specialist) a piece of a plant, especially one cut to make a new plant

**sci-rocco** = SIROCCO

**scis-sors** /ˈsɪzəz; NAmE -zərz/ noun [pl.] a tool for cutting paper or cloth that has two sharp BLADES (= cutting edges) with handles, joined together in the middle: *a pair of*

# sclera

**scissors** ⇒ see also NAIL SCISSORS ▶ **scis·sor** adj. [only before noun]: *The legs move in a scissor action.*

**sclera** /ˈsklɪərə; NAmE ˈsklɪrə/ noun (pl. **-rae** /-riː/ or **-ras**) (anatomy) the white part of the eye

**scler·osis** /skləˈrəʊsɪs; NAmE -ˈroʊ-/ noun [U] (medical) a condition in which soft TISSUE in the body becomes hard, in a way that is not normal ⇒ see also MULTIPLE SCLEROSIS ▶ **scler·otic** /skləˈrɒtɪk; NAmE -ˈrɑːt-/ adj.

**scoff** /skɒf; NAmE skɑːf/ verb 1 [I, T] ~ (at sb/sth) | + speech to talk about sb/sth in a way that makes it clear that you think they are stupid or silly **SYN** mock: *Don't scoff—she's absolutely right.* ◊ *He scoffed at our amateurish attempts.* 2 (BrE) (NAmE **scarf**) [T] ~ sth (informal) to eat a lot of sth quickly: *Who scoffed all the grapes?*

**scoff-law** /ˈskɒflɔː; NAmE ˈskɑːf-/ noun (NAmE, informal) a person who often breaks the law but in a way that is not very serious

**scold** /skəʊld; NAmE skoʊld/ verb [T, I] ~ sb (for sth/for doing sth) | (+ speech) (formal) to speak angrily to sb, especially a child, because they have done sth wrong **SYN** rebuke: *He scolded them for arriving late.* ▶ **scold·ing** noun [usually sing.]: *I got a scolding from my mother.*

**scoli·osis** /ˌskəʊliˈəʊsɪs; BrE also ˌskɒl-/ noun [U] (medical) a condition in which the SPINE is curved in a way that is not normal

**sconce** /skɒns; NAmE skɑːns/ noun an object that is attached to a wall, used for holding a CANDLE or an electric light: *The room is softly lit by wall sconces.*

**scone** /skəʊn; BrE also skɒn; NAmE also skɑːn/ noun a small round cake, sometimes with dried fruit in it and often eaten with butter, jam and cream spread on it

**scoop** /skuːp/ noun, verb
- noun 1 [C] a tool like a large spoon with a deep bowl, used for picking up substances in powder form like flour, or for serving food like ice cream: *Use an ice-cream scoop.* 2 [C] the amount picked up by a scoop: *two scoops of mashed potato* 3 [C] a piece of important or exciting news that is published in one newspaper before other newspapers know about it 4 **the scoop** [U] **the ~ on sb/sth** (NAmE, informal) the latest information about sb/sth, especially details that are not generally known: *I got the inside scoop on his new girlfriend.*
- verb 1 ~ sth (+ adv./prep.) to move or lift sth with a scoop or sth like a scoop: *She scooped ice cream into their bowls.* ◊ *First, scoop a hole in the soil.* ◊ *Scoop out the melon flesh.* 2 ~ sb/sth (up) (+ adv./prep.) to move or lift sb/sth with a quick continuous movement: *She scooped the child up in her arms.* ◊ *He quickly scooped his clothes from the chair.* 3 ~ sb/sth to publish a story before all the other newspapers, television companies, etc: *The paper had inside information and scooped all its rivals.* 4 ~ sth (informal) to win sth, especially a large sum of money or a prize: *He scooped £10000 on the lottery.*

**scooped** /skuːpt/ (also **scoop**) adj. [only before noun] (of the neck of a woman's dress, etc.) cut low and round: *a scooped neck/neckline*

**scoot** /skuːt/ verb [I] (+ adv./prep.) (informal) to go or leave somewhere in a hurry: *I'd better scoot or I'll be late.*

**scoot·er** /ˈskuːtə(r)/ noun 1 (BrE) (also **motor scooter** NAmE, BrE) a light motorcycle, usually with small wheels and a curved metal cover at the front to protect the rider's legs ⇒ see also MOBILITY SCOOTER 2 a vehicle, used especially by children, with two or three small wheels attached to a narrow board with a handle that rises straight up at the front. The rider holds the handle, puts one foot on the board and pushes against the ground with the other.

**scope** /skəʊp; NAmE skoʊp/ noun, verb
- noun [U] 1 the opportunity or ability to do or achieve sth **SYN** potential: ~ for sth *There's still plenty of scope for improvement.* ◊ *Her job offers very little scope for promotion.* ◊ ~ (for sb) (to do sth) *The extra money will give us the scope to improve our facilities.* ◊ **within sb's ~** *First try to do something that is within your scope.* 2 the range of things that a subject, an organization, an activity, etc. deals with: **in~** *Our powers are limited in scope.* ◊ **beyond/outside the ~ of sth** *This subject lies beyond the scope of our investigation.* 3 **-scope** (in nouns) an instrument for looking through or watching sth with: *microscope* ◊ *telescope*
- verb 1 ~ sth (informal) to look at or examine sth carefully and completely: *His eyes scoped the room, trying to spot her in the crowd.* 2 ~ sth (out) (informal) to examine sth carefully before you start work on it so that you know the size of the task: *The information helped us scope the project.*

**scorch** /skɔːtʃ; NAmE skɔːrtʃ/ verb 1 [T, I] ~ (sth) to burn and slightly damage a surface by making it too hot; to be slightly burned by heat: *I scorched my dress when I was ironing it.* ◊ *Don't stand so near the fire—your coat is scorching!* ⇒ SYNONYMS at BURN 2 [T, I] ~ (sth) to become or to make sth become dry and brown, especially from the heat of the sun or from chemicals: *scorched grass* ◊ *The leaves will scorch if you water them in the sun.* 3 [I] + adv./prep. (BrE, informal) to move very fast: *The car scorched off down the road.*

**scorched earth policy** noun (in a war) a policy of destroying anything in a particular area that may be useful to the enemy

**scorch·er** /ˈskɔːtʃə(r); NAmE ˈskɔːrtʃ-/ noun (informal) 1 a very hot day 2 (BrE) (used mainly in newspapers) a very good hit, shot, etc. in a sport: *a scorcher of a free kick*

**scorch·ing** /ˈskɔːtʃɪŋ; NAmE ˈskɔːrtʃ-/ adj. (informal) 1 very hot **SYN** baking 2 (especially BrE) used to emphasize how strong, powerful, etc. sth is: *a scorching critique of the government's economic policy*

**score** /skɔː(r)/ verb, noun
- verb
  - • GIVE/GET POINTS/GOALS 1 [I, T] to win points, goals, etc. in a game or competition: *Fraser scored again in the second half.* ◊ ~ sth *to score a goal/try/touchdown/victory/point/run* 2 [I] to keep a record of the points, goals, etc. won in a game or competition: *Who's going to score?* 3 [T, I] to gain marks in a test or an exam: ~ sth *She scored 98 per cent in the French test.* ◊ + adv./prep. *Girls usually score highly in language exams.* 4 [T] ~ sb/sth to give sth/sb a particular number of points: *The tests are scored by psychologists.* ◊ *Score each criterion on a scale of 1 to 5.* ◊ *a scoring system* 5 [T] ~ sth to be worth a particular number of points: *Each correct answer will score two points.*
  - • SUCCEED 6 [T, I] to succeed; to have an advantage: ~ (sth) *The army continued to score successes in the south.* ◊ *She's scored again with her latest blockbuster.* ◊ ~ **over sth** *Bicycles score over other forms of transport in towns.*
  - • ARRANGE/WRITE MUSIC 7 [T, usually passive] to arrange a piece of music for one or more musical instruments or for voices: **be scored for sth** *The piece is scored for violin, viola and cello.*
  - • CUT 8 [T] ~ sth to make a cut or mark on a surface: *Score the card first with a knife.*
  - • HAVE SEX 9 [I] ~ (with sb) (slang) (especially of a man) to have sex with a new partner: *Did you score last night?*
  - • BUY DRUGS 10 [T, I] ~ (sth) (slang) to buy or get illegal drugs
  - **IDM** **score a ˈpoint/ˈpoints (off/against/over sb)** = SCORE OFF SB
  - **PHRV** ˈscore off sb [no passive] (especially BrE) to show that you are better than sb, especially by making clever remarks, for example in an argument: *He was always trying to score off his teachers.* **score sth↔out/through** to draw a line or lines through sth: *Her name had been scored out on the list.*
- noun
  - • POINTS/GOALS, ETC. 1 [C] the number of points, goals, etc. scored by each player or team in a game or competition: *a high/low score* ◊ *What's the score now?* ◊ *The final*

score was 4–3. ◊ I'll **keep (the)** score. **2** 🔑 **A2** [C] (especially NAmE) the number of points sb gets for correct answers in a test: *test scores* ◊ *an IQ score of 120* ◊ *to get a* **high/low** score ⊃ see also CREDIT SCORE
- MUSIC **3** [C] a written or printed version of a piece of music showing what each instrument is to play or what each voice is to sing: *an orchestral score* ◊ *the score of Verdi's 'Requiem'* **4** [C] the music written for a film or play: *an award for best original score* ◊ *The* **musical score** *is magnificent and the performances are outstanding.*
⊃ WORDFINDER NOTE at OPERA
- TWENTY **5** [C] (*pl.* **score**) a set or group of 20 or approximately 20: *Several cabs and a score of cars were parked outside.* ◊ **by the ~** *Doyle's success brought imitators by the score* (= very many imitators). ◊ *the biblical age of three score years and ten* (= 70)
- MANY **6 scores** [pl.] very many: *There were scores of boxes and crates, all waiting to be checked and loaded.*
- CUT **7** [C] a cut in a surface, made with a sharp tool
- FACTS ABOUT SITUATION **8 the score** [sing.] (*informal*) the real facts about the present situation: *What's the score?* ◊ *You don't have to lie to me. I know the score.*
**IDM** **on 'that / 'this score** about that/this matter: *You don't have to worry on that score.* ⊃ more at EVEN v., SETTLE v.

**score-board** /'skɔːbɔːd; NAmE 'skɔːrbɔːrd/ noun a large board on which the score in a game or competition is shown

**score-card** /'skɔːkɑːd; NAmE 'skɔːrkɑːrd/ noun a card or piece of paper that people watching or playing a game can use to write the score on, or on which the score can be officially recorded

'**score draw** noun (*BrE*) the result of a football (soccer) match in which both teams score the same number of goals

**score-less** /'skɔːləs; NAmE 'skɔːrl-/ adj. (of a game) without either team getting any points, goals, etc: *a scoreless draw*

**score-line** /'skɔːlaɪn; NAmE 'skɔːrl-/ noun (*BrE*) (used mainly in newspapers) the final score or result in a game, competition, etc: *a 2–1 scoreline* ◊ *The team did not play as badly as the scoreline suggests.*

**scorer** /'skɔːrə(r)/ noun **1** (in sports) a player who scores points, goals, etc: *United's* **top scorer 2** a person who keeps a record of the points, goals, etc. scored in a game or competition **3 a high/low ~** a person who gets a high/low number of points in a test or an exam

'**score sheet** noun (*BrE*) a piece of paper on which the score of a game can be officially recorded
**IDM** **get your name on the 'score sheet** (*informal*) (used in newspapers) to score a goal, etc.

**scorn** /skɔːn; NAmE skɔːrn/ noun, verb
- ■ noun [U] a strong feeling that sb/sth is stupid or not good enough, usually shown by the way you speak **SYN** **contempt**: *Her fellow teachers greeted her proposal* **with scorn**. ◊ **~ for sb/sth** *They had nothing but scorn for his political views.*
**IDM** **pour / heap 'scorn on sb/sth** to speak about sb/sth in a way that shows that you do not respect them or have a good opinion of them
- ■ verb **1** **~ sb/sth** to feel or show that you think sb/sth is stupid and you do not respect them or it **SYN** **dismiss**: *She scorned their views as old-fashioned.* **2** (*formal*) to refuse to have or do sth because you are too proud: *~ sth to scorn an invitation* ◊ **~ to do sth** *She would have scorned to stoop to such tactics.* **IDM** see HELL

**scorn-ful** /'skɔːnfl; NAmE 'skɔːrn-/ adj. showing or feeling scorn **SYN** **contemptuous**: *a scornful laugh* ◊ **~ of sth** *He was scornful of such 'female' activities as cooking.* ▸ **scornfully** /-fəli/ adv.: *She laughed scornfully.*

**Scor·pio** /'skɔːpiəʊ; NAmE 'skɔːrp-/ noun **1** [U] the 8th sign of the ZODIAC, the SCORPION **2** [C] (*pl.* **-os**) a person born when the sun is in this sign, that is between 23 October and 21 November, approximately

**scor·pion** /'skɔːpiən; NAmE 'skɔːrp-/ noun a small creature like an insect with eight legs, two front CLAWS (= curved and pointed arms) and a long tail that curves over its back and can give a poisonous STING. Scorpions live in hot countries. ⊃ VISUAL VOCAB page V3

**Scot** /skɒt; NAmE skɑːt/ noun **1** a person from Scotland **2 the Scots** [pl.] the people of Scotland ⊃ note at SCOTTISH

**Scotch** /skɒtʃ; NAmE skɑːtʃ/ noun, adj.
- ■ noun **1** [U] the type of WHISKY made in Scotland: *a bottle of Scotch* **2** [C] a glass of Scotch: *Do you want a Scotch?*
- ■ adj. of or connected with Scotland ⊃ note at SCOTTISH

**scotch** /skɒtʃ; NAmE skɑːtʃ/ verb **~ sth** to stop sth from happening; to take action to end sth: *Plans for a merger have been scotched.* ◊ *Rumours that he had fled the country were promptly scotched by his wife.*

**Scotch 'bonnet** noun a type of very hot CHILLI

**Scotch 'egg** noun (*BrE*) a boiled egg covered with SAUSAGE MEAT and BREADCRUMBS, fried and eaten cold

'**Scotch tape**™ (*NAmE*) (*BrE* **Sello tape**™, '**sticky tape**) noun [U] clear plastic tape that is sticky on one side, used for sticking things together

**scot-'free** adv. (*informal*) without receiving the punishment you deserve: *They got off scot-free because of lack of evidence.* **ORIGIN** This idiom comes from the old English word 'scot' meaning 'tax'. People were scot-free if they didn't have to pay the tax.

**Scot·land Yard** /ˌskɒtlənd 'jɑːd; NAmE ˌskɑːtlənd 'jɑːrd/ noun [U + sing. / pl. v.] the main office of the London police, especially the department that deals with serious crimes in London: *Scotland Yard has/have been called in.* ◊ *Scotland Yard's Counter Terrorism Command*

**Scots** /skɒts; NAmE skɑːts/ adj., noun
- ■ adj. of or connected with Scotland, and especially with the English language as spoken in Scotland or the Scots language: *He spoke with a Scots accent.* ◊ *She comes from an old Scots family.*
- ■ noun [U] a language spoken in Scotland, closely related to English but with many differences

**Scot·tie** /'skɒti; NAmE 'skɑːti/ noun (*informal*) = SCOTTISH TERRIER

**Scot·tish** /'skɒtɪʃ; NAmE 'skɑːt-/ adj. of or connected with Scotland or its people: *the Scottish Highlands* ◊ *Scottish dancing*

▼ MORE ABOUT …
**describing things from Scotland**
- The adjective **Scottish** is the most general word used to describe the people and things of Scotland, while **Scots** is only used to describe its people, its law and especially its language: *Scottish dancing* ◊ *the Scottish parliament* ◊ *a well-known Scots poet* ◊ *a slight Scots accent.*
- The adjective **Scotch** is now mainly used in fixed expressions such as *Scotch whisky* and *Scotch broth* and sounds old-fashioned or insulting if it is used in any other way.
- The noun **Scotch** means whisky, and the noun **Scots** refers to a language spoken in Scotland, closely related to English. A person who comes from Scotland is a **Scot**: *The Scots won their match against England.*
⊃ note at BRITISH

**the** ˌ**Scottish** ˈ**National Party** noun [sing. + sing. / pl. v.] (*abbr.* **SNP**) a Scottish political party which wants Scotland to be an independent nation

**the** ˌ**Scottish** ˈ**Parliament** noun [sing. + sing. / pl. v.] the parliament elected by the people of Scotland which has powers to make its own laws in areas such as education and health

**Scottish 'terrier** (*also* **Scot·tie** *informal*) noun a small TERRIER (= type of dog) with rough hair and short legs

**SCOTUS** /'skəʊtəs; NAmE 'skoʊtəs/ abbr. (*especially US*) Supreme Court of the United States (the highest court in the US) ⊃ see also FLOTUS, POTUS

**scoun·drel** /'skaʊndrəl/ noun (*old-fashioned*) a man who treats other people badly, especially by not being honest or moral **SYN** **rogue**

# scour

**scour** /ˈskaʊə(r)/ *verb* **1** ~ sth (for sb/sth) to search a place or thing carefully and completely in order to find sb/sth **SYN** comb: *We scoured the area for somewhere to pitch our tent.* ◊ *He had been scouring the papers for weeks, looking for a job.* **2** ~ sth (out) to clean sth by rubbing its surface hard with rough material: *I had to scour out the pans.* **3** ~ sth (away/out) to make a passage, hole, or mark in the ground, rocks, etc. as the result of movement, especially over a long period: *The water had raced down the slope and scoured out the bed of a stream.* ◊ *We could see where the cartwheels had scoured the ground.*

**scourge** /skɜːdʒ/ *NAmE* skɜːrdʒ/ *noun, verb*
- *noun* **1** [usually sing.] ~ (of sb/sth) (*formal*) a person or thing that causes trouble, difficulty or mental pain: *the scourge of war/disease/poverty* ◊ *Inflation was the scourge of the 1970s.* **2** a WHIP used to punish people in the past
- *verb* **1** [usually passive] ~ sb (*literary*) to cause trouble, difficulty or mental pain to sb: *He lay awake, scourged by his conscience.* **2** ~ sb (*old use*) to hit sb with a scourge **SYN** whip

**Scouse** /skaʊs/ *noun* (*BrE, informal*) **1** (*also* **Scouser** /ˈskaʊsə(r)/) [C] a person from Liverpool in north-west England **2** [U] a way of speaking, used by people from Liverpool ▶ **Scouse** *adj.: a Scouse accent*

**scout** /skaʊt/ *noun, verb*
- *noun* **1 the Scouts** [U + sing./pl. v.] an organization (in the UK, officially called the '**Scout Association**') originally for boys, which trains young people in practical skills and does a lot of activities with them, for example camping: *to join the Scouts* **2** [C] (*BrE*) a boy or girl who is a member of the Scouts: *Both my brothers were scouts.* ◊ *a scout troop* ⇒ compare BROWNIE, CUB ⇒ see also BOY SCOUT, EXPLORER SCOUT, GIRL SCOUT, GUIDE **3** [C] a person, an aircraft, etc. sent ahead to get information about the enemy's position, strength, etc. ⇒ WORDFINDER NOTE at EXPLORE **4** [C] = TALENT SCOUT
- *verb* **1** [T, I] to search an area or various areas in order to find or discover sth: ~ sth (for sb/sth) *They scouted the area for somewhere to stay the night.* ◊ ~ (around) (for sb/sth) *The kids were scouting around for wood for the fire.* ◊ *a military scouting party* **2** [I, T] ~ (sb) to look for sports players, actors, musicians, etc. who have special ability, so you can offer them work: *He scouts for Manchester United.*
- **PHRV** **ˌscout sth↔ˈout** to find out what an area is like or where sth is, by searching: *We went ahead to scout out the lie of the land.*

**scout·ing** /ˈskaʊtɪŋ/ *noun* [U] the activities that boy and girl SCOUTS take part in; the Scout organization

**scout·master** /ˈskaʊtmɑːstə(r); *NAmE* -mæs-/ (*also* **scout leader**) *noun* an adult in charge of a group of SCOUTS (2)

**scowl** /skaʊl/ *verb, noun*
- *verb* [I] ~ (at sb/sth) to look at sb/sth in an angry or annoyed way **SYN** glower ⇒ WORDFINDER NOTE at EXPRESSION
- *noun* an angry look or expression: *He looked up at me with a scowl.*

**Scrab·ble™** /ˈskræbl/ *noun* [U] a board game in which players try to make words from letters printed on small plastic blocks and connect them to words that have already been placed on the board

**scrab·ble** /ˈskræbl/ *verb* [I] ~ (around/about) (for sth) | ~ + adv./prep. (*especially BrE*) to try to find or to do sth in a hurry or with difficulty, often by moving your hands or feet about quickly, without much control: *She scrabbled around in her bag for her glasses.* ◊ *He was scrabbling for a foothold on the steep slope.* ◊ *a sound like rats scrabbling on the other side of the wall*

**scrag·gly** /ˈskrægli/ *adj.* (*NAmE, informal*) thin and growing in a way that is not even: *a scraggly beard*

**scram** /skræm/ *verb* (-mm-) [I] (*old-fashioned, informal*) (usually used in orders) to go away quickly: *Scram! I don't want you here.*

**scram·ble** /ˈskræmbl/ *verb, noun*
- *verb*
  - **WALK/CLIMB 1** [I] + *adv./prep.* to move quickly, especially with difficulty, using your hands to help you **SYN** clamber: *She managed to scramble over the wall.* ◊ *He scrambled to his feet as we came in.*
  - **PUSH/FIGHT 2** [I] to push, fight or compete with others in order to get or to reach sth: ~ for sth *The audience scrambled for the exits.* ◊ ~ to do sth *Shoppers were scrambling to get the best bargains.*
  - **ACHIEVE STH WITH DIFFICULTY 3** [T] to manage to achieve sth with difficulty, in a hurry, without much control: ~ sth *Cork scrambled a 1–0 win over Sligo.* ◊ ~ sth + adv./prep. *Salah managed to scramble the ball into the net.*
  - **EGGS 4** [T, usually passive] ~ sth to cook an egg by mixing the white and yellow parts together and heating them, sometimes with milk and butter: *scrambled eggs*
  - **TELEPHONE/RADIO 5** [T, often passive] ~ sth to change the way that a phone or radio message sounds so that only people with special equipment can understand it: *scrambled satellite signals*
  - **CONFUSE THOUGHTS 6** [T] ~ sth to confuse sb's thoughts, ideas, etc. so that they have no order: *Alcohol seemed to have scrambled his brain.*
  - **AIRCRAFT 7** [T, usually passive, I] ~ (sth) to order that planes, etc. should take off immediately in an emergency; to take off immediately in an emergency: *A helicopter was scrambled to help rescue three young climbers.* ◊ *They scrambled as soon as the call came through.*
- *noun*
  - **DIFFICULT WALK/CLIMB 1** [sing.] a difficult walk or climb over rough ground, especially one in which you have to use your hands
  - **PUSH/FIGHT 2** [sing.] ~ (for sth) a situation in which people push, fight or compete with each other in order to get or do sth **SYN** free-for-all: *There was a mad scramble for the best seats.*
  - **MOTORCYCLE RACE 3** [C] a race for motorcycles over rough ground

**scram·bler** /ˈskræmblə(r)/ *noun* a device that changes radio or phone signals or messages so that they cannot be understood by other people

**scram·bling** /ˈskræmblɪŋ/ *noun* [U] (*BrE*) = MOTOCROSS

**scrap** /skræp/ *noun, verb*
- *noun* **1** [C] a small piece of sth, especially paper, cloth, etc.: *She scribbled his phone number on a scrap of paper.* ◊ (*figurative*) *scraps of information* ◊ (*figurative*) *She was just a scrap of a thing* (= small and thin). **2** [sing.] (usually with a negative) a small amount of sth **SYN** bit: *It won't make a scrap of difference.* ◊ *There's not a scrap of evidence to support his claim.* ◊ *a barren landscape without a scrap of vegetation* **3 scraps** [pl.] food left after a meal: *Give the scraps to the dog.* **4** [U] things that are not wanted or cannot be used for their original purpose, but which have some value for the material they are made of: **for~** *We sold the car for scrap* (= so that any good parts can be used again). ◊ *scrap metal* ◊ *a scrap dealer* (= a person who buys and sells scrap) **5** [C] (*informal*) a short fight or argument **SYN** squabble, scuffle: *He was always getting into scraps at school.* ⇒ see also SCRAPPY
- *verb* (-pp-) **1** [T, often passive] ~ sth to cancel or get rid of sth that is no longer practical or useful: *They had been forced to scrap plans for a new school building.* ◊ *The oldest of the aircraft were scrapped.* **2** [I] (*informal*) to fight with sb: *The bigger boys started scrapping.*

**scrap·book** /ˈskræpbʊk/ *noun* a book with empty pages where you can stick pictures, newspaper articles, etc.

**scrape** /skreɪp/ *verb, noun*
- *verb*
  - **REMOVE 1** [T] to remove sth from a surface by moving sth sharp and hard like a knife across it: ~ sth (+ *adv./prep.*) *She scraped the mud off her boots.* ◊ ~ sth + *adj.* *The kids had scraped their plates clean.*
  - **DAMAGE 2** [T] to rub sth by accident so that it gets damaged or hurt: ~ sth *She fell and scraped her knee.* ◊ ~ sth + *adv./prep.* *I scraped the side of my car on the wall.* ◊ *Sorry, I've scraped some paint off the car.* ◊ *The wire had scraped the skin from her fingers.*

---

æ cat | ɑː father | e bed | ɜː fur | ə about | ɪ sit | iː see | i happy | ɒ got (*BrE*) | ɔː saw | ʌ cup | ʊ put | uː too

- **MAKE SOUND 3** [I, T] to make an unpleasant noise by rubbing against a hard surface; to make sth do this: **(+ adv./ prep.)** *I could hear his pen scraping across the paper.* ◇ *We could hear her scraping away at the violin.* ◇ **~ sth (+ adv./ prep.)** *Don't scrape your chairs on the floor.*
- **WIN WITH DIFFICULTY 4** [T, I] **~ (sth)** to manage to win or to get sth with difficulty: *The team scraped a narrow victory last year.* ◇ *(BrE) I just scraped a pass in the exam.* ◇ *They scraped a living by playing music on the streets.* ◇ *The government scraped home* (= just won) *by three votes.*
- **MAKE HOLE IN GROUND 5** [T] **~ sth (out)** to make a hole or hollow place in the ground: *He found a suitable place, scraped a hole and buried the bag in it.*
- **PULL HAIR BACK 6** [T] **~ your hair back** to pull your hair tightly back, away from your face: *Her hair was scraped back from her face in a ponytail.*

**IDM** **scrape (the bottom of) the ˈbarrel** (*disapproving*) to have to use things or people that are not the best or most suitable because the ones that were the best or most suitable are no longer available ⊃ more at BOW¹ v.

**PHRV** **ˌscrape ˈby (on sth)** to manage to live on the money you have, but with difficulty: *I can just scrape by on what my parents give me.* **ˌscrape ˈin** | **ˌscrape ˈinto sth** to manage to get a job, a position, a place at college, etc., but with difficulty: *He scraped in with 180 votes.* ◇ *Our team just scraped into the semi-finals.* **ˌscrape sth↔ˈout** to remove sth from inside sth else, using sth sharp or hard like a knife: *Scrape out the flesh of the melon with a spoon.* **ˌscrape ˈthrough** | **ˌscrape ˈthrough sth** to succeed in doing sth with difficulty, especially in passing an exam: *I might scrape through the exam if I'm lucky.* **ˌscrape sth↔toˈgether/ˈup** to obtain or collect together sth, but with difficulty: *We managed to scrape together eight volunteers.*

■ *noun*
- **ACTION/SOUND 1** [sing.] the action or unpleasant sound of one thing rubbing roughly against another: *the scrape of iron on stone*
- **DAMAGE 2** [C] an injury or a mark caused by rubbing against sth rough: *She emerged from the overturned car with only a few scrapes and bruises.*
- **DIFFICULT SITUATION 3** [C] (*old-fashioned*) a difficult situation that you have caused yourself: *He was always getting into scrapes as a boy.*

**scraper** /ˈskreɪpə(r)/ *noun* a tool used for scraping, for example for scraping mud from shoes or ice from a car

**scrap·heap** /ˈskræphiːp/ *noun* a pile of things, especially of metal, that are no longer wanted or useful
**IDM** **on the ˈscrapheap** (*informal*) no longer wanted or considered useful

**scra·pie** /ˈskreɪpi/ *noun* [U] a serious disease that affects the NERVOUS SYSTEM of sheep

**scrap·ing** /ˈskreɪpɪŋ/ *noun* [usually pl.] a small amount of sth produced by SCRATCHING a surface (= rubbing it with sth hard or sharp)

**ˈscrap paper** *noun* [U] loose pieces of paper used for writing notes on

**scrappy** /ˈskræpi/ *adj.* (**scrap·pier**, **scrap·pi·est**) **1** consisting of individual sections, events, etc. that are not organized into a whole **SYN** **bitty**: *a scrappy essay* **2** (*especially BrE*) not tidy and often of poor quality: *The note was written on a scrappy bit of paper.* ⊃ see also SCRAP

**scrap·yard** /ˈskræpjɑːd; *NAmE* -jɑːrd/ (*BrE*) (*also* **junk·yard** *NAmE, BrE*) *noun* a place where old cars, machines, etc. are collected, so that parts of them, or the metal they are made of, can be sold to be used again

**scratch** /skrætʃ/ *verb, noun, adj.*

■ *verb*
- **RUB WITH YOUR NAILS 1** [T, I] to rub your skin with your nails, usually because it is ITCHING: **~ sth** *John yawned and scratched his chin.* ◇ **~ (yourself)** *The dog scratched itself behind the ear.* ◇ *Try not to scratch.* ◇ **~ at sth** *She scratched at the insect bites on her arm.*
- **CUT SKIN 2** [T, I] to cut or damage your skin slightly with sth sharp: **~ (sb/sth/yourself)** *I'd scratched my leg and it was bleeding.* ◇ *Does the cat scratch?* ◇ **~ sb/sth/ yourself on sth** *She scratched herself on a nail.*
- **DAMAGE SURFACE 3** [T] **~ sth** to damage the surface of sth, especially by accident, by making thin shallow marks on it: *Be careful not to scratch the furniture.* ◇ *The car's paintwork is badly scratched.*
- **MAKE/REMOVE MARK 4** [T] **~ sth + adv./prep.** to make or remove a mark, etc. on sth deliberately, by rubbing it with sth hard or sharp: *They scratched lines in the dirt to mark out a pitch.* ◇ *We scratched some of the dirt away.* ◇ (*figurative*) *You can scratch my name off the list.*
- **MAKE SOUND 5** [I] **(+ adv./prep.)** to make an annoying noise by rubbing sth with sth sharp: *His pen scratched away on the paper.*
- **A LIVING 6** [T] **~ a living** to make enough money to live on, but with difficulty
- **CANCEL 7** [T, I] to decide that sth cannot happen or sb/sth cannot take part in sth, before it starts: **~ sb/sth** *to scratch a rocket launch* ◇ **~ sb/sth from sth** *The horse was scratched from the race because of injury.* ◇ **~ (from sth)** *She had scratched because of a knee injury.*

**IDM** **scratch your ˈhead (over sth)** to think hard in order to find an answer to sth **scratch the ˈsurface (of sth)** to deal with, understand, or find out about only a small part of a subject or problem **you scratch ˈmy back and I'll scratch ˈyours** (*saying*) used to say that if sb helps you, you will help them, even if this is unfair to others

**PHRV** **ˌscratch aˈround (for sth)** (*BrE also* **ˌscratch aˈbout (for sth)**) to search for sth, especially with difficulty **ˌscratch sth↔ˈout** to remove a word, especially a name, from sth written, usually by putting a line through it

■ *noun*
- **MARK/CUT 1** [C] a mark, a cut or an injury made by scratching sb's skin or the surface of sth: *Her hands were covered in scratches from the brambles.* ◇ *a scratch on the paintwork* ◇ *It's only a scratch* (= a very slight injury). ◇ **without a~** *He escaped without a scratch* (= was not hurt at all).
- **SOUND 2** [sing.] the unpleasant sound of sth sharp or rough being rubbed against a surface
- **WITH YOUR NAILS 3** [sing.] the act of scratching a part of your body when it ITCHES: *Go on, have a good scratch!*

**IDM** **from ˈscratch 1** without any previous preparation or knowledge: *I learned German from scratch in six months.* **2** from the very beginning, not using any of the work done earlier: *They decided to dismantle the machine and start again from scratch.* **up to ˈscratch** as good as sth/sb should be **SYN** **satisfactory**: *His work simply isn't up to scratch.* ◇ *It'll take months to bring the band up to scratch.*

■ *adj.* (*BrE*) **1** put together in a hurry using whatever people or materials are available: *a scratch team* **2** (especially in golf) with no HANDICAP: *a scratch player*

**ˈscratch card** *noun* a card with an area that you remove by rubbing hard to find out if you have won a prize

**scratch·ings** ⊃ PORK SCRATCHINGS

**scratchy** /ˈskrætʃi/ *adj.* (**scratch·ier**, **scratchi·est**) **1** (of clothes or cloth) rough and unpleasant to the touch **SYN** **itchy** **2** (of a record, voice, etc.) making a rough, unpleasant sound like sth sharp being moved across a surface: *a scratchy recording of Mario Lanza* ◇ *a scratchy pen* **3** (of writing or drawings) done without care

**scrawl** /skrɔːl/ *verb, noun*

■ *verb* [T, I] to write sth in a careless untidy way, making it difficult to read **SYN** **scribble**: **~ sth (across/in/on/over sth)** *I tried to read his directions, scrawled on a piece of paper.* ◇ **~ across/in/on/over sth** *Someone had scrawled all over my notes.*

■ *noun* a careless untidy way of writing; sth written in this way **SYN** **scribble**: *Her signature was an illegible scrawl.* ◇ *I can't be expected to read this scrawl!* ◇ *The paper was covered in scrawls.*

**scrawny** /ˈskrɔːni/ *adj.* (**scrawn·ier**, **scrawni·est**) (*disapproving*) (of people or animals) very thin in a way that is not attractive

# scream

**scream** 🔑 B2 /skri:m/ *verb, noun*
■ *verb* 1 ᛭ B2 [I, T] to give a loud, high shout, because you are hurt, frightened, excited, etc. **SYN** shriek: *He covered her mouth to stop her from screaming.* ◊ *~ in/with sth The kids were screaming with excitement.* ◊ *~ out (in/with sth) People ran for the exits, screaming out in terror.* ◊ *~ yourself + adj. The baby was screaming itself hoarse.* ◊ *screaming fans* 2 ᛭ B2 [T, I] to shout sth in a loud, high voice because of fear, anger, etc. **SYN** yell: *+ speech 'Help!' she screamed.* ◊ *~(out) for sth/sb Someone was screaming for help.* ◊ *~at sb (to do sth) He screamed at me to stop.* ◊ *~sth (out) (at sb) She screamed abuse at him.* ◊ *~(out) that … His sister screamed out that he was crazy.* ⊃ SYNONYMS at SHOUT 3 [I] to make a loud, high noise; to move fast, making this noise **SYN** screech: *Lights flashed and sirens screamed.* ◊ *+ adv./prep. The powerboat screamed out to sea.*
**IDM** **scream blue ˈmurder** (*BrE*) (*NAmE* **scream bloody ˈmurder**) to scream loudly and for a long time, especially in order to protest about sth ⊃ more at KICK *v.*
**PHR V** **ˌscream ˈout (for sth)** to be in need of attention in a very obvious way **SYN** cry out: *These books scream out to be included in a list of favourites.*
■ *noun* 1 ᛭ B2 [C] a loud high shout made by sb who is hurt, frightened, excited, etc.; a loud high noise: *~ of sth She let out a scream of pain.* ◊ *They ignored the baby's screams.* ◊ *a blood-curdling/piercing/loud scream* 2 [*sing.*] (*old-fashioned, informal*) a person or thing that causes you to laugh: *He's a scream.*

**ˈscream·ing·ly** /ˈskri:mɪŋli/ *adv.* extremely: *It was screamingly obvious what we should do next.*

**scree** /skri:/ *noun* [U, C] an area of small loose stones, especially on a mountain, which may slide when you walk on them

**screech** /skri:tʃ/ *verb, noun*
■ *verb* 1 [I, T] to make a loud high unpleasant sound; to say sth using this sound: *Monkeys were screeching in the trees.* ◊ *The wind screeched in his ears.* ◊ *screeching brakes* ◊ *He screeched with pain.* ◊ *+ speech 'No, don't!' she screeched.* ◊ *~(sth) (at sb) He screeched something at me.* 2 [I] (*+ adv./prep.*) (of a vehicle) to make a loud high unpleasant noise as it moves: *The car screeched to a halt outside the hospital.* ◊ *A police car screeched out of a side street.*
■ *noun* a loud high unpleasant call or noise: *a screech of brakes/tyres* ◊ *She suddenly let out a screech.*

**screed** /skri:d/ *noun* a long piece of writing, especially one that is not very interesting

**screen** 🔑 A2 /skri:n/ *noun, verb*
■ *noun*
• **OF TV/COMPUTER** 1 ᛭ A2 [C] the flat surface at the front of a television, computer, or other electronic device, on which you see pictures or information: *a computer/television/TV screen* ◊ *a monitor with a 21-inch screen* ◊ *on the ~ The image came up on the screen for a few seconds.* ◊ *on ~ Information can be viewed on screen or printed out.* ◊ *the screen display* ⊃ **WORDFINDER NOTE** at COMPUTER ⊃ see also FLAT-SCREEN, ON-SCREEN, SECOND SCREEN
• **FILMS/MOVIES/TV** 2 ᛭ A2 [C] the large flat surface that films or pictures are shown on: *a cinema/movie screen* ◊ *an eight-screen cinema* ◊ *The movie will be coming to your screens shortly.* 3 ᛭ B1 (*often* **the screen**) [*sing.*, U] films or television in general: *He has adapted the play for the screen.* ◊ *on ~ Some actors never watch themselves on screen.* ◊ *She was a star of stage and screen* (= plays and films). ◊ *a screen actor* ⊃ see also BIG SCREEN, OFF-SCREEN, SILVER SCREEN, SMALL SCREEN 4 [C] the data or images shown on a computer screen: *Press the F1 key to display a help screen.* ◊ *Can you do a printout of this screen for me?* ◊ *I posted the screen grab on Twitter.* ⊃ see also HOME SCREEN
• **PIECE OF FURNITURE** 5 ᛭ B2 [C] a tall, flat piece of furniture or equipment that is fixed to a wall, etc. or that can be moved to divide a room or to keep one area hidden or separate: *The nurse put a screen around the bed.* ⊃ see also FIRE SCREEN
• **FOR HIDING/PROTECTING STH/SB** 6 [C] something that prevents sb from seeing or being aware of sth, or that protects sb/sth: *~(of sth) We planted a screen of tall trees.* ◊ *behind a ~ of sth* (*figurative*) *All the research was conducted behind a screen of secrecy.* ⊃ see also SMOKESCREEN, SUN-SCREEN, WINDSCREEN
• **ON WINDOW/DOOR** 7 [C] (*especially NAmE*) a wire or plastic net that is held in a frame and fastened on a window, or a door, to let in air but keep out insects: *screen doors*
• **IN CHURCH** 8 [C] a wood or stone structure in a church, that partly separates the main area from the ALTAR or CHOIR
• **CHECK** 9 [C] a system of checking a person or thing to find out whether or not sth, typically a disease, is present: *You should get a health screen every couple of years.* ◊ *Candidates for this position must be able to pass a drug screen.*
**IDM** see RADAR

■ *verb*
• **SHOW FILM/MOVIE/PROGRAMME** 1 ᛭ B2 [*usually passive*] *~ sth* to show a film, etc. in a cinema or on television: *a list of films to be screened as part of the festival*
• **FOR DISEASE** 2 [*often passive*] *~ sb (for sth)* to examine people in order to find out if they have a particular disease or illness: *Men over 55 should be regularly screened for prostate cancer.*
• **CHECK** 3 *~ sb* (of a company, an organization, etc.) to find out information about people who work or who want to work for you in order to make sure that they can be trusted: *Government employees may be screened by the security services.* 4 *~ sth* to check sth to see if it is suitable or if you want it: *I use my voicemail to screen my phone calls.*
• **HIDE STH/SB** 5 *~ sth/sb (from sth/sb)* to hide or protect sth/sb by placing sth in front of or around them **SYN** shield: *Dark glasses screened his eyes from the sun.*
**PHR V** **ˌscreen sth ↔ ˈoff** [*often passive*] to separate part of a room, etc. from the rest of it by putting a screen around it: *Beds can be screened off to give patients more privacy.*
**ˌscreen sb ↔ ˈout** to decide not to allow sb to join an organization, enter a country, etc. because you think they may cause trouble **ˌscreen sth ↔ ˈout** to prevent sth harmful from entering or going through sth: *The ozone layer screens out dangerous rays from the sun.*

**screen·er** /ˈskri:nə(r)/ *noun* a person who checks people and their bags at an airport

**screen·ing** ᛭ B2 /ˈskri:nɪŋ/ *noun* 1 ᛭ B2 [C] the act of showing a film or television programme: *This will be the movie's first screening in this country.* 2 ᛭ C1 [U, C] the testing or examining of a large number of people or things for disease, faults, etc: *breast cancer screening*

**ˈscreen name** *noun* a name or series of letters, numbers, etc. that a person uses on an INSTANT MESSAGING service, online FORUM, etc.

**ˈscreen·play** /ˈskri:npleɪ/ *noun* the words that are written for a film (= the script), together with instructions for how it is to be acted and filmed

**ˈscreen-print** *verb* [T, I] *~(sth)* to force INK (= coloured liquid for printing, drawing, etc.) or metal onto a surface through a screen of silk or artificial material to produce a picture ▶ **ˈscreen print** *noun*

**ˈscreen saver** (*also* **screen-saver**) *noun* a computer program that replaces a screen display on a computer with another, moving, display after a particular length of time

**ˈscreen·shot** /ˈskri:nʃɒt; *NAmE* -ʃɑ:t/ *noun* (*computing*) an image of the display on a screen, used when showing how a program works

**ˈscreen test** *noun* a test to see if sb is suitable to appear in a film

**ˈscreen time** *noun* [U] 1 the amount of time that is given to a particular subject, actor, etc. on film or television: *A lot of screen time in the film is devoted to flashbacks.* 2 time spent using a device such as a computer, television or tablet: *We try not to let our children have too much screen time.*

**screen·writer** /ˈskri:nraɪtə(r)/ *noun* a person who writes SCREENPLAYS ⊃ compare PLAYWRIGHT, SCRIPTWRITER

**screw** /skruː/ *verb, noun*

- *verb* **1** [T] ~ **sth + adv./prep.** to fasten one thing to another or make sth tight with a screw or screws: *The bookcase is screwed to the wall.* ◊ *You need to screw all the parts together.* ◊ *Now screw down the lid.* ⊃ compare UNSCREW **2** [T] to turn sth round and round in order to fasten it in place: ~ **sth + adv./prep.** *She screwed the cap back on the jar.* ◊ ~ **sth + adj.** *Screw the bolt tight.* ⊃ compare UNSCREW **3** [I] + **adv./prep.** to be attached by screwing: *The bulb should just screw into the socket.* ◊ *The lid simply screws on.* **4** [T] to use your hand to make sth, especially a piece of paper, form a tight ball: ~ **sth up (into sth)** *I screwed up the letter and threw it into the fire.* ◊ ~ **sth (up) into sth** *Screw the foil into a little ball.* ⊃ see also SCREWED-UP **5** [T] (*slang*) to cheat sb, especially by making them pay too much money for sth: ~ **sb** *We've been screwed.* ◊ ~ **sb for sth** *How much did they screw you for* (= how much did you have to pay)? **6** [T] ~ **sth from/out of sb** (*informal*) to force sb to give you sth: *They screwed the money out of her by threats.* **7** [I, T] ~ **(sb)** (*taboo, slang*) to have sex with sb
  **IDM** **screw 'him, 'you, 'that, etc.** (*taboo, slang*) an offensive way of showing that you are annoyed or do not care about sb/sth **screw up your 'courage** to force yourself to be brave enough to do sth: *I finally screwed up my courage and went to the dentist.* ⊃ more at HEAD *n*.
  **PHRV** **,screw a'round** (*taboo, slang*) to have sex with a lot of different people **,screw 'up** (*slang*) to deal with a situation very badly **SYN** **mess up**: *You really screwed up there!* ⊃ related noun SCREW-UP **,screw sb↔'up** (*slang*) to upset or confuse sb so much that they are not able to deal with problems in their life: *Her father's death really screwed her up.* ⊃ see also SCREWED-UP **,screw sth↔'up 1** to fasten sth with screws: *to screw up a crate* **2** (*BrE*) to fasten sth by turning it: *I screwed up the jar and put it back on the shelf.* **3** (*slang*) to do sth badly or cause sth to fail: *Don't screw it up this time.* ⊃ related noun SCREW-UP **,screw your 'eyes/'face↔up** to pull the muscles of your eyes or face tight because the light is too strong, you are in pain, etc: *He took a sip of the medicine and screwed up his face.*

- *noun* **1** [C] a thin pointed piece of metal like a nail with a raised SPIRAL line (called a THREAD) along it and a line or cross cut into its head. Screws are turned and pressed into wood, metal, etc. with a SCREWDRIVER in order to fasten two things together: *One of the screws is loose.* ◊ *Now tighten all the screws.* ⊃ picture at NAIL ⊃ see also ALLEN SCREW™, CORKSCREW *noun* **2** [C] an act of turning a screw **3** [*sing.*] (*taboo, slang*) an act of having sex **4** [*sing.*] (*taboo, slang*) a partner in sex: *a good screw* **5** [C] a PROPELLER on a ship, a boat or an aircraft **6** [C] (*BrE, slang*) a prison officer
  **IDM** **have a 'screw loose** (*informal*) to be slightly strange in your behaviour **put the 'screws on (sb)** to force sb to do sth by frightening and threatening them ⊃ more at TURN *n*.

**screw-ball** /ˈskruːbɔːl/ *noun* (*informal, especially NAmE*) a strange or crazy person

**'screw cap** *noun* = SCREW TOP: *screw-cap bottles/wine*

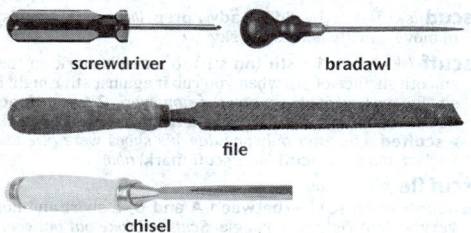
screwdriver    bradawl
file
chisel

**screw-driver** /ˈskruːdraɪvə(r)/ *noun* **1** a tool with a narrow BLADE (= metal part) that has a special shape at the end, used for turning SCREWS **2** a COCKTAIL (= an alcoholic drink) made from VODKA and orange juice

**screwed-'up** *adj*. **1** (*informal*) upset and anxious, especially because of sth bad that has happened to you in the past:
an extremely screwed-up kid **2** (*especially BrE*) TWISTED into a ball: *a screwed-up tissue* **3** if your face or eyes are **screwed-up**, the muscles are tight, because you are worried, in pain, etc., or because the light is too bright

**'screw top** (*also* **'screw cap**) *noun* a round top that you fasten on a bottle or JAR by turning it: *a screw-top bottle/jar*

**'screw-up** *noun* (*pl.* **screw-ups**) (*slang*) an occasion when you do sth badly or fail at sth

**screwy** /ˈskruːi/ *adj*. (**screwier**, **screwiest**) (*informal*) strange or crazy

**scrib·ble** /ˈskrɪbl/ *verb, noun*
- *verb* **1** [T, I] to write sth quickly and carelessly, especially because you do not have much time **SYN** **scrawl**: ~ **sth** *He scribbled a note to his sister before leaving.* ◊ ~ **sth down** *She scribbled down her phone number and pushed it into his hand.* ◊ ~ **(away)** *Throughout the interview the journalists scribbled away furiously.* **2** [I] **(+ adv./prep.)** to draw marks that do not mean anything: *Someone had scribbled all over the table in crayon.*
- *noun* **1** [U, *sing.*] careless and untidy writing **SYN** **scrawl**: *How do you expect me to read this scribble?* **2** [C, *usually pl.*] marks or pictures that seem to have no meaning **SYN** **scrawl**: *The page was covered with a mass of scribbles.*

**scrib·bler** /ˈskrɪblə(r)/ *noun* **1** (*disapproving* or *humorous*) a journalist, author or other writer **2** (*CanE*) a book with plain paper for writing in, especially for children at school

**scribe** /skraɪb/ *noun* a person who made copies of written documents before printing was invented

**scrim·mage** /ˈskrɪmɪdʒ/ *noun* **1** a confused struggle or fight **SYN** **scrum** **2** (in AMERICAN FOOTBALL) a period of play that begins with the ball being placed on the ground **3** (*NAmE*) a practice game of AMERICAN FOOTBALL, basketball, etc.

**scrimp** /skrɪmp/ *verb* [I] to spend very little money on the things that you need to live, especially so that you can save it to spend on sth else: *They scrimped and saved to give the children a good education.*

**scrip** /skrɪp/ *noun* (*business*) an extra share in a business, given out instead of a DIVIDEND

**script** /skrɪpt/ *noun, verb*
- *noun* **1** [C] a written text of a play, film, broadcast, talk, etc: *That line isn't in the original script.* **2** [U] writing done by hand: *She admired his neat script.* ⊃ see also MANUSCRIPT **3** [U, C] a set of letters in which a language is written **SYN** **alphabet**: *a document in Cyrillic script* (= used to write Russian and some other languages) **4** [C] (*BrE*) a candidate's written answer or answers in an exam **5** [U, C] (*computing*) a series of instructions for a computer, carried out in a particular order, for example when a link in a website is clicked: *The bug was caused by an error in the script.*
- *verb* [often passive] ~ **sth** to write the script for a film, play, etc.

**script·ed** /ˈskrɪptɪd/ *adj*. read from a script: *a scripted talk* **OPP** **unscripted**

**scrip·ture** /ˈskrɪptʃə(r)/ *noun* **1** **Scripture** [U] (*also* **the Scriptures** [*pl.*]) **2 scriptures** [*pl.*] the holy books of a particular religion: *Hindu scriptures* ▸ **scrip·tural** /-tʃərəl/ *adj*.: *scriptural references*

**script·writer** /ˈskrɪptraɪtə(r)/ *noun* a person who writes the words for films, television and radio plays ⊃ compare PLAYWRIGHT, SCREENWRITER

**scroll** /skrəʊl/ *noun, verb*
- *noun* **1** a long roll of paper for writing on **2** a decoration cut in stone or wood with a curved shape like a roll of paper
- *verb* [I, T] to move text on a computer screen up or down so that you can read different parts of it: **+ adv./prep.** *Use the arrow keys to scroll through the list of files.* ◊ *Scroll down to the bottom of the document.* ◊ ~ **sth** *Use the arrow keys to scroll the list of files.* ⊃ **WORDFINDER NOTE** at COMMAND

# scroll bar

**'scroll bar** noun (computing) a narrow area at the edge of a computer screen that you use to scroll through a file with, using a mouse

**Scrooge** /skruːdʒ/ noun [usually sing.] (informal, disapproving) a person who is very unwilling to spend money ORIGIN From **Ebenezer Scrooge**, a character in Charles Dickens' *A Christmas Carol* who is extremely mean.

**scro·tum** /ˈskrəʊtəm/ noun (pl. **scro·tums** or **scrota** /-tə/) the bag of skin that contains the TESTICLES in men and most male animals

**scrounge** /skraʊndʒ/ verb, noun
■ verb [T, I] (informal, disapproving) to get sth from sb by asking them for it rather than by paying or working for it SYN cadge (off/from sb) *He's always scrounging free meals off us.* ◇ *~ (for sth) What is she scrounging for this time?* ▶ **scroun·ger** noun: *a campaign against welfare scroungers*
■ noun
IDM **on the 'scrounge** (BrE, informal, disapproving) trying to get sth by persuading sb to give it to you

**scrub** /skrʌb/ verb, noun
■ verb (-bb-) 1 [T, I] to clean sth by rubbing it hard, especially with a brush and usually with soap and water: *~ sth/yourself I found him in the kitchen, scrubbing the floor.* ◇ *He stepped into the shower and scrubbed himself all over.* ◇ *~ sth/yourself down She scrubbed the counters down with bleach.* ◇ *~ at sth The woman scrubbed at her face with a tissue.* ◇ *~ sth/yourself + adj. Scrub the vegetables clean.* 2 [T] *~ sth* (informal) to cancel sth that you have arranged to do
PHRV **scrub sth↔off | scrub sth off sth** to remove sth from the surface of an object by rubbing it hard with a brush, etc: *This treatment involves scrubbing off the top layer of dead skin.* **scrub sth↔out** to clean the inside of sth by rubbing it hard with a brush and usually with soap and water **scrub 'up** 1 (of a doctor, nurse, etc.) to wash your hands and arms before performing a medical operation 2 **scrub up well** (BrE, informal) to look good when you make an effort: *Barry scrubs up well on a good day, as can be seen in this pic.*
■ noun 1 [sing.] an act of scrubbing sth: *I've given the floor a good scrub.* 2 [U] small bushes and trees: *The vegetation consisted of low scrub.* 3 (also **scrub·land**) [U] an area of dry land covered with small bushes and trees 4 **scrubs** [pl.] (specialist) the special clothes worn by SURGEONS when they are doing medical operations ➪ WORDFINDER NOTE at OPERATION

**scrub·ber** /ˈskrʌbə(r)/ noun 1 (BrE, informal) an offensive word for a PROSTITUTE or for a woman who has sex with a lot of men 2 a brush or other object that you use for cleaning things, for example pans

**'scrubbing brush** (BrE) (NAmE **'scrub brush**) noun a stiff brush for cleaning floors and other surfaces

**scrub·by** /ˈskrʌbi/ adj. 1 covered with small bushes and trees: *a scrubby hillside* 2 (of trees) small and not fully developed: *scrubby vegetation*

**scrub·land** /ˈskrʌblənd/ noun [U] = SCRUB

**scruff** /skrʌf/ noun (BrE, informal) a dirty or untidy person
IDM **by the scruff of the/sb's 'neck** roughly holding the back of an animal's or person's neck: *She grabbed him by the scruff of the neck and threw him out.*

**scruffy** /ˈskrʌfi/ adj. (**scruff·ier**, **scruffi·est**) (informal) dirty or untidy in appearance SYN shabby: *He looked a little scruffy.* ◇ *scruffy pair of jeans* ▶ **scruff·ily** /-fəli/ adv. **scruffi·ness** noun [U]

**scrum** /skrʌm/ noun 1 (also formal **scrum·mage**) a part of a rugby game when players from both sides link themselves together in a group, with their heads down, and push against the other side. The ball is then thrown between them and each side tries to get it. 2 the group of players who link themselves together in a scrum 3 (especially BrE) a crowd of people who are pushing each other: *There was a real scrum when the bus arrived.*

**scrum 'half** noun (in rugby) a player who puts the ball into the scrum

**scrum·mage** /ˈskrʌmɪdʒ/ noun, verb
■ noun (formal) = SCRUM
■ verb (also **scrum 'down**) [I] (sport) to form a SCRUM during a game of rugby

**scrump·tious** /ˈskrʌmpʃəs/ adj. (informal) tasting very good SYN delicious

**scrunch** /skrʌntʃ/ verb 1 [I] to make a loud sound like the one that is made when you walk on GRAVEL (= small stones) SYN crunch: *The snow scrunched underfoot.* 2 [T] *~ sth (up)* to cause sth to form a small round shape with your hand: *He scrunched up the note and threw it on the fire.* 3 [T] *~ sth (up)* to make sth become smaller or SQUEEZED together: *The hedgehog scrunched itself up into a ball.* ◇ *She scrunched up her face, as if about to cry.* 4 [T] *~ sth* to create a loose curly HAIRSTYLE by SQUEEZING the hair with the hands ▶ **scrunch** noun [sing.]: *the scrunch of tyres on the gravel*

**scrun·chy** (also **scrun·chie**) /ˈskrʌntʃi/ noun (pl. **-ies**) a RUBBER BAND covered in cloth used to fasten hair away from the face

**scru·ple** /ˈskruːpl/ noun, verb
■ noun [C, usually pl., U] a feeling that prevents you from doing sth that you think may be morally wrong: *I overcame my moral scruples.* ◇ *He had no scruples about spying on her.* ◇ *She is totally without scruples.*
■ verb [I] **not ~ to do sth** (formal) to be willing to do sth even if it might be wrong

**scru·pu·lous** /ˈskruːpjələs/ adj. 1 careful about paying attention to every detail SYN meticulous: *You must be scrupulous about hygiene when you're preparing a baby's feed.* ◇ *scrupulous attention to detail* 2 *~ (in sth/in doing sth)* careful to be honest and do what is right: *He was scrupulous in all his business dealings.* OPP unscrupulous ▶ **scru·pu·lous·ly** adv.: *Her house is scrupulously clean.* ◇ *to be scrupulously honest* **scru·pu·lous·ness** noun [U]

**scru·tin·eer** /ˌskruːtɪˈnɪə(r)/; NAmE -ˈnɪr/ noun (BrE) a person who checks that an election or other vote is organized correctly and fairly

**scru·tin·ize** (BrE also **-ise**) /ˈskruːtənaɪz/ verb *~ sb/sth* to look at or examine sb/sth carefully: *She leaned forward to scrutinize their faces.* ◇ *The statement was carefully scrutinized before publication.*

**scru·tiny** /ˈskruːtəni/ noun [U] (formal) careful and complete examination SYN inspection: *Her argument doesn't really stand up to scrutiny.* ◇ *Foreign policy has come under close scrutiny recently.* ◇ *The documents should be available for public scrutiny.*

**scuba diving** /ˈskuːbə daɪvɪŋ/ (also **scuba**) noun [U] the sport or activity of swimming UNDERWATER using special breathing equipment consisting of a container of air which you carry on your back and a tube through which you breathe the air: *to go scuba diving* ◇ *scuba gear/equipment* ▶ **'scuba diver** noun

**scud** /skʌd/ verb [I] (**-dd-**) + adv./prep. (literary) (of clouds) to move quickly across the sky

**scuff** /skʌf/ verb 1 *~ sth (on sth)* to make a mark on the smooth surface of sth when you rub it against sth rough: *I scuffed the heel of my shoe on the stonework.* 2 *~ your feet, heels, etc.* to drag your feet along the ground as you walk ▶ **scuffed** adj.: *After only one day, his shoes were already scuffed and dirty.* **scuff** (also **'scuff mark**) noun

**scuf·fle** /ˈskʌfl/ noun, verb
■ noun *~ (with sb)* | *~ (between A and B)* a short and not very violent fight or struggle: *Scuffles broke out between police and demonstrators.* ➪ SYNONYMS at FIGHT
■ verb 1 [I] *~ (with sb)* (of two or more people) to fight or struggle with each other for a short time, in a way that is not very serious: *She scuffled with photographers as she left her hotel.* 2 [I] + adv./prep. to move quickly making a quiet rubbing noise: *Some animal was scuffling in the bushes.*

**scuf·fling** /ˈskʌflɪŋ/ noun [U] a low noise made by sth moving around: *He could hear whispering and scuffling on the other side of the door.*

**scull** /skʌl/ noun, verb
- noun **1** [C, usually pl.] one of a pair of small OARS used by a single person ROWING a boat, one in each hand **2 sculls** [pl.] a race between small light boats with pairs of sculls: *single/double sculls* (= with one/two people in each boat) **3** [C] a small light boat used in sculls races
- verb [I] to ROW a boat using sculls

**scull·er** /ˈskʌlə(r)/ noun a person who ROWs with sculls

**scul·lery** /ˈskʌləri/ noun (pl. -ies) a small room next to the kitchen in an old house, originally used for washing dishes, etc.

**scull·ing** /ˈskʌlɪŋ/ noun [U] the sport of racing with SCULLS

**sculpt** /skʌlpt/ verb [usually passive] **1** to make figures or objects by CARVING or shaping wood, stone, CLAY, metal, etc.: ~ *sth (in sth)* *a display of animals sculpted in ice* ◊ ~ *sth (from/out of sth)* *The figures were sculpted from single blocks of marble.* **2** ~ *sth* to give sth a particular shape: *a coastline sculpted by the wind and sea*

**sculp·tor** /ˈskʌlptə(r)/ noun a person who makes sculptures

**sculp·ture** ❶ 🅱🅱 /ˈskʌlptʃə(r)/ noun **1** 🅱🅱 [C, U] a work of art that is a solid figure or object made by CARVING or shaping wood, stone, CLAY, metal, etc.: *a marble sculpture of Venus* ◊ *He collects modern sculpture.* **2** 🅱🅱 [U] the art of making sculptures: *the techniques of sculpture in stone* ▶ **sculp·tural** /-tʃərəl/ adj.: *sculptural decoration*

**sculp·tured** /ˈskʌlptʃəd/ NAmE -tʃərd/ adj. [usually before noun] **1** (of figures or objects) CARVED or SHAPED from wood, stone, CLAY, metal, etc. **2** (approving) (of part of the body) having a clear and attractive shape: *sculptured cheekbones*

**scum** /skʌm/ noun **1** [U, sing.] a layer of bubbles or an unpleasant substance that forms on the surface of a liquid: *Skim off any scum.* ◊ *stinking water covered by a thick green scum* **2** [U, pl.] (informal) an offensive word for people who you think are very bad: *Don't waste your sympathy on scum like that.* ◊ *Drug dealers are the scum of the earth* (= the worst people there are). ▶ **scummy** adj. (**scummier, scum·mi·est**): *scummy water* ◊ *scummy people dropping litter*

**scum·bag** /ˈskʌmbæg/ noun (slang, offensive) an unpleasant person

**scup·per** /ˈskʌpə(r)/ verb ~ *sth* (BrE, informal) to cause sb/sth to fail ⓢⓨⓝ foil: *The residents' protests scuppered his plans for developing the land.*

**scur·ril·ous** /ˈskʌrələs; NAmE ˈskɜːr-/ adj. (formal) very rude and offensive, and intended to damage sb's reputation: *scurrilous rumours* ▶ **scur·ril·ous·ly** adv.

**scurry** /ˈskʌri; NAmE ˈskɜːri/ verb [I] (**scur·ries, scurry·ing, scur·ried, scur·ried**) + adv./prep. to run with quick short steps ⓢⓨⓝ scuttle: *She said goodbye and scurried back to work.* ◊ *Ants scurried around the pile of rotting food.* ▶ **scurry** noun [sing.]

**scurvy** /ˈskɜːvi; NAmE ˈskɜːrvi/ noun [U] a disease caused by a lack of vitamin C from not eating enough fruit and vegetables

**scut·tle** /ˈskʌtl/ verb **1** [I] + adv./prep. to run with quick short steps ⓢⓨⓝ scurry: *She scuttled off when she heard the sound of his voice.* ◊ *He held his breath as a rat scuttled past.* **2** ~ *sth* to deliberately cause sth to fail ⓢⓨⓝ foil: *Shareholders successfully scuttled the deal.* **3** ~ *sth* to sink a ship deliberately by making holes in the side or bottom of it

**scuttle·butt** /ˈskʌtlbʌt/ noun [U] (NAmE, slang) stories about other people's private lives, that may be unkind or not true ⓢⓨⓝ gossip

**scuzzy** /ˈskʌzi/ adj. (**scuzz·ier, scuz·zi·est**) (informal, especially NAmE) dirty and unpleasant

**Scylla and Cha·ryb·dis** /ˌsɪlə ən kəˈrɪbdɪs/ noun used to refer to a situation in which an attempt to avoid one danger increases the risk from another danger ⓞⓡⓘⓖⓘⓝ From ancient Greek stories in which a female sea creature (called Scylla) tried to catch and eat sailors who passed between her cave and a whirlpool (called Charybdis).

**scythe** /saɪð/ noun, verb
- noun a tool with a long handle and a slightly curved BLADE (= sharp metal cutting edge), held in two hands and used for cutting long grass, etc.
- verb [T, I] ~ *(sth)* to cut grass, etc. with a scythe: *the scent of newly scythed grass*

**SD card** /ˌes ˈdiː kɑːd; NAmE kɑːrd/ noun a type of MEMORY CARD, used with digital cameras, mobile phones, music players, etc. (the abbreviation for 'secure digital card')

**the SDLP** /ˌðiː es diː el ˈpiː/ abbr. (in Northern Ireland) the Social Democratic and Labour Party (a political party of the left that is supported mainly by Catholics)

**SE** abbr. south-east; south-eastern: *SE Asia*

**sea** ❶ 🄰🄰 /siː/ noun **1** 🄰🄰 (often **the sea**) [U] (also literary **seas** [pl.]) (especially BrE) the salt water that covers most of the earth's surface and surrounds its continents and islands: *The waste was dumped in the sea.* ◊ *The wreck is lying at the bottom of the sea.* ◊ **by~** *to travel by sea* ◊ **by the~** *a cottage by the sea* ◊ *the sea off* (= near) *Japan* ◊ *We left port and headed for* **the open sea** (= far away from land). ◊ *the cold seas of the Arctic* ◊ *a hotel room with sea view* ⟹ HOMOPHONES at SEIZE ⟹ WORDFINDER NOTE at COAST ⟹ see also DEEP-SEA, HIGH SEAS, OCEAN

> **WORDFINDER** beach, coast, harbour, pier, sandbank, shoreline, surf, tide, wave

**2** 🄰🄰 [C] (often **Sea**, especially as part of a name) a large area of salt water that is part of an ocean or surrounded by land: *the North Sea* ◊ *the Caspian Sea* **3** 🄰🄰 [C] (also **seas** [pl.]) the movement of the waves of the sea: *The sea was very rough.* ◊ *The ship sank in heavy seas.* **4** [sing.] **~ of sth** a large amount of sth that stretches over a wide area: *He looked down at the sea of smiling faces before him.*

ⒾⒹⓂ **at ˈsea 1** on the sea, especially in a ship, or in the sea: *It happened on the second night at sea.* ◊ *They were lost at sea.* **2** confused and not knowing what to do: *I'm all at sea with these new regulations.* **go/run away to ˈsea** to become a sailor, to leave your home and family without permission to become a sailor **out to ˈsea** far away from land where the sea is deepest: *She fell overboard and was swept out to sea.* **put (out) to ˈsea** to leave a port or HARBOUR by ship or boat ⟹ more at DEVIL, FISH n.

> ▼ **BRITISH/AMERICAN**
> 
> **sea / ocean**
> 
> - In BrE, the usual word for the mass of salt water that covers most of the earth's surface is the **sea**. In NAmE, the usual word is the **ocean**: *A swimmer drowned in the sea/ocean this morning.*
> - The names of particular areas of seas, however, are fixed: *the Mediterranean Sea* ◊ *the Atlantic Ocean.*
> - **Sea/ocean** are also used if you go to the coast on holiday: *We're spending a week by the sea/at the ocean in June.* In NAmE it is also common to say: *We're going to the beach for vacation.*
> ⟹ note at COAST

**ˈsea air** noun [U] air near the sea, thought to be good for the health: *a breath of sea air*

**ˈsea anemone** noun a simple, brightly coloured sea creature that sticks onto rocks and looks like a flower

**the ˈsea·bed** /ðə ˈsiːbed/ noun [sing.] the floor of the sea

**sea·bird** /ˈsiːbɜːd; NAmE -bɜːrd/ noun a bird that lives close to the sea, for example on CLIFFS or islands, and gets its food from it ⟹ VISUAL VOCAB page V2

**sea·board** /ˈsiːbɔːd; NAmE -bɔːrd/ noun the part of a country that is along its coast: *Australia's eastern seaboard*

# seaborne

**sea·borne** /ˈsiːbɔːn; *NAmE* -bɔːrn/ *adj.* [only before noun] carried in ships: *a seaborne invasion*

**ˈsea breeze** *noun* a wind blowing from the sea towards the land

**ˈsea change** *noun* [usually sing.] a strong, clear and definite change in a situation

**ˈsea cucumber** *noun* an INVERTEBRATE animal that lives on the sea floor, with a long thick body like a WORM

**ˈsea dog** *noun* (*informal*) a sailor who is old or who has a lot of experience

**sea·farer** /ˈsiːfeərə(r); *NAmE* -fer-/ *noun* (*old-fashioned or formal*) a sailor

**sea·far·ing** /ˈsiːfeərɪŋ; *NAmE* -fer-/ *adj.* [only before noun] connected with work or travel on the sea: *a seafaring nation* ▶ **sea·far·ing** *noun* [U]

**ˈsea fish** *noun* (*pl.* **sea fish**) a fish that lives in the sea, rather than in rivers or lakes

**sea·food** /ˈsiːfuːd/ *noun* [U] fish and sea creatures that can be eaten, especially SHELLFISH: *a seafood restaurant* ◇ *a seafood cocktail*

**ˈsea fret** *noun* = FRET

**sea·front** /ˈsiːfrʌnt/ *often* **the seafront** (*BrE*) (*NAmE* **ocean-front**) *noun* [sing.] the part of a town facing the sea: *the grand houses along the seafront* ◇ *a seafront hotel* ⇒ compare BEACHFRONT

**sea·going** /ˈsiːɡəʊɪŋ/ *adj.* [only before noun] (of ships) built for crossing the sea

**sea·grass** /ˈsiːɡrɑːs; *NAmE* -ɡræs/ *noun* [U] a plant like grass that grows in or close to the sea

**sea-ˈgreen** *adj.* blue-green in colour, like the sea ▶ **ˈsea green** *noun* [U]

**sea·gull** /ˈsiːɡʌl/ *noun* = GULL: *a flock of seagulls*

**sea·horse** /ˈsiːhɔːs; *NAmE* -hɔːrs/ *noun* a small sea fish that swims in a VERTICAL position and has a head that looks like the head of a horse

**seal** /siːl/ *verb, noun*

■ *verb*
- CLOSE ENVELOPE **1** ~ **sth (up/down)** to close an ENVELOPE, etc. by sticking the edges of the opening together: *Make sure you've signed the cheque before sealing the envelope.* ◇ *a sealed bid* (= one that is kept in a sealed envelope and therefore remains secret until all other bids have been received)
- CLOSE CONTAINER **2** [often passive] ~ **sth (up) (with sth)** to close a container tightly or fill a small opening, etc., especially so that air, liquid, etc. cannot get in or out: *He sealed the bag tightly with sticky tape.* ◇ *The organs are kept in sealed plastic bags.*
- MAKE STH DEFINITE **3** ~ **sth** to make sth definite, so that it cannot be changed or argued about: *to seal a contract* ◇ *They drank a glass of wine to seal their new friendship.* ◇ *The discovery of new evidence sealed his fate* (= nothing could prevent what was going to happen to him).
- COVER SURFACE **4** [often passive] ~ **sth (with sth)** to cover the surface of sth with a substance in order to protect it: *The floors had been stripped and sealed with varnish.*
- CLOSE BORDERS/EXITS **5** ~ **sth** (of the police, army, etc.) to prevent people from passing through a place: *Troops have sealed the borders between the countries.* **IDM** see LIP, SIGN *v.*

**PHRV** **seal sth↔ˈin** to prevent sth that is contained in sth else from escaping **ˈseal sth in sth** to put sth in an ENVELOPE, container, etc. and seal it: *The body was sealed in a lead coffin.* **seal sth↔ˈoff** (of the police, army) to prevent people from entering a particular area

■ *noun*
- OFFICIAL MARK **1** [C] an official design or mark, STAMPED on a document to show that it is real and carries the authority of a particular person or organization: *The letter bore the president's seal.*
- MAKING STH DEFINITE **2** [sing.] a thing that makes sth definite: *The project has been given the government's seal of approval* (= official approval). ◇ *I looked upon the gift as a seal on our friendship.*
- ON CONTAINERS **3** [C] a substance, piece of material, etc. used to fill a small opening so that air, liquid, etc. cannot get in or out: *a jar with a rubber seal in the lid* ◇ *Only drink bottled water and check the seal isn't broken.*
- ON LETTERS/BOXES **4** [C] a piece of WAX (= a soft substance produced by bees), soft metal or paper that is placed across the opening of sth such as a letter or box and which has to be broken before the letter or box can be opened: *He broke the wax seal and unrolled the paper.* **5** [C] a piece of metal, a ring, etc. with a design on it, used for STAMPING a WAX or metal seal
- SEA ANIMAL **6** [C] a sea animal that eats fish and lives around coasts. There are many types of seal, some of which are hunted for their fur: *a colony of seals* ◇ *grey seals basking on the rocks*

**IDM** **set the ˈseal on sth** (*formal*) to make sth definite or complete: *Her election to the premiership set the seal on a remarkable political career.* **under ˈseal** (*formal*) (of a document) in a sealed ENVELOPE that cannot be opened before a particular time

**ˈsea lane** *noun* an official route at sea that is regularly used by ships

**seal·ant** /ˈsiːlənt/ (*also* **seal·er**) *noun* [U, C] a substance that is put onto a surface to stop air, water, etc. from entering or escaping from it

**ˈsea legs** *noun* [pl.] the ability to walk easily on a moving ship and not to feel sick at sea: *It won't take you long to find your sea legs.*

**seal·er** /ˈsiːlə(r)/ *noun* **1** [U, C] = SEALANT **2** [C] a person who hunts SEALS **3** [C] a ship used for hunting seals

**ˈsea level** *noun* [U, C] the average height of the sea, used as the basis for measuring the height of all places on land: *50 metres above sea level*

**sea·lift** /ˈsiːlɪft/ *noun* an operation to take people, soldiers, food, etc. to or from an area by ship, especially in an emergency

**seal·ing** /ˈsiːlɪŋ/ *noun* [U] the activity of hunting SEALS

**ˈsea lion** *noun* a large SEAL (= a sea animal with thick fur, that eats fish and lives around the coast) that lives by the Pacific Ocean

**seam** /siːm/ *noun* **1** a line along which two edges of cloth, etc. are joined by SEWN together: *a shoulder seam* ⇒ WORD-FINDER NOTE *at* SEW **2** a thin layer of coal or other material, between layers of rock under the ground: *They struck a rich seam of iron ore.* ◇ (*figurative*) *The book is a rich seam of information.* **3** a line where two edges meet, for example the edges of wooden boards

**IDM** **be bursting/bulging at the ˈseams** (*informal*) to be very full, especially of people **be falling/coming apart at the ˈseams** (*informal*) to be going very badly wrong and likely to stop functioning completely: *She was falling apart at the seams, spending most of her time in tears.* ⇒ more *at* FRAY *v.*

**sea·man** /ˈsiːmən/ *noun* (*pl.* **-men** /-mən/) a member of the NAVY or a sailor on a ship below the rank of an officer: *Seaman Bates* ◇ *a merchant seaman* ⇒ see also ABLE SEAMAN, ORDINARY SEAMAN

**sea·man·ship** /ˈsiːmənʃɪp/ *noun* [U] skill in sailing a boat or ship

**seamed** /siːmd/ *adj.* **1** having a seam or seams: *seamed stockings* **2** (*literary*) covered with deep lines: *an old man with a brown seamed face*

**ˈsea mile** *noun* = NAUTICAL MILE

**seam·less** /ˈsiːmləs/ *adj.* **1** without a SEAM: *seamless underwear* **2** with no spaces or breaks between one part and the next: *a seamless flow of talk* ▶ **seam·less·ly** *adv.*

**seam·stress** /ˈsiːmstrəs; *BrE also* ˈsem-/ *noun* (*old-fashioned*) a woman who can SEW and make clothes or whose job is SEWING and making clothes

**seamy** /ˈsiːmi/ *adj.* (**seam·ier**, **seami·est**) unpleasant or morally wrong **SYN** sordid: *a seamy sex scandal* ◇ *the seamier side of life*

**se·ance** /ˈseɪɒs; NAmE ˈseɪɑːns/ noun a meeting at which people try to make contact with and talk to the spirits of dead people

**sea·plane** /ˈsiːpleɪn/ noun a plane that can take off from and land on water

**sea·port** /ˈsiːpɔːt; NAmE -pɔːrt/ noun a town with a HARBOUR used by large ships: *the Baltic seaports*

**sea power** noun **1** [U] the ability to control the seas with a strong NAVY **2** [C] a country with a strong NAVY

**sear** /sɪə(r); NAmE sɪr/ verb **1** [T] ~ sth to burn the surface of sth in a way that is sudden and powerful: *The heat of the sun seared their faces.* ◊ *Sear the meat first (= cook the outside of it quickly at a high temperature) to retain its juices.* **2** [I, T] (*formal*) to cause sb to feel sudden and great pain: + *adv./prep. The pain seared along her arm.* ◊ *~ sb Feelings of guilt seared him.* ⊃ see also SEARING

**search** 🔑 A2 /sɜːtʃ; NAmE sɜːrtʃ/ noun, verb
■ **noun 1** 🔑 A2 an attempt to find sb/sth, especially by looking carefully for them/it: *~ for sb/sth In a long search for the murder weapon* ◊ *The search for a cure goes on.* ◊ *The search is on (= has begun) for someone to fill the post.* ◊ *~ of sth Detectives carried out a thorough search of the building.* ◊ *in~ of sb/sth She went into the kitchen in search of (= looking for) a drink.* ◊ *Eventually the search was called off.* ◊ *a search and rescue team* ⊃ see also WORD SEARCH **2** 🔑 A2 an act or the activity of looking for information on a computer or on the internet: *I've just done a search on the internet and came up with this website.* ◊ *~ for sth I did an image search for 'vinyl record'.* ◊ *~ on sth A Google search on her name yielded nothing.* ◊ *Our site is found on the first page of search results.* ⊃ see also BODY SEARCH, STRIP SEARCH
■ **verb 1** 🔑 A2 [I, T] to look carefully for sth/sb; to examine a particular place when looking for sth/sb: *~ for sth/sb She searched in vain for her passport.* ◊ *Police searched for clues in the area.* ◊ + *adv./prep. The customs officers searched through our bags.* ◊ *I've searched high and low for those files.* ◊ *~ sth His house had clearly been searched and the book was missing.* ◊ *~ sth for sth/sb Police searched the area for clues.* ◊ *Firefighters searched the buildings for survivors.* **2** 🔑 A2 [I, T] to look for information on a computer or on the internet: *~ for sth You can search for any word or phrase in the text.* ◊ *I searched online today for more information on sonic booms.* ◊ *~ sth The database can be searched by keyword, topic or source.* ◊ *~ sth for sth I searched the internet for recipes.* **3** 🔑 B1 [T] (especially of the police) to examine sb's clothes, their pockets, etc. in order to find sth that they may be hiding: *~ sb Visitors are regularly searched as they enter the building.* ◊ *~ sb for sth The youths were arrested and searched for anything that would incriminate them.* ⊃ see also STRIP-SEARCH **4** 🔑 B1 [I] *~* (**for sth**) to think carefully about sth, especially in order to find the answer to a problem: *He searched desperately for something to say.* ◊ *We are continually searching for ways to cut costs.* ⊃ see also SOUL-SEARCHING ▶ **search·er** noun
**IDM** ˈsearch me (*informal*) used to emphasize that you do not know the answer to sb's question: *'Why didn't she say anything?' 'Search me!'*
**PHRV** ˌsearch sb/sbˈout to look for sth/sb until you find them **SYN** track sth/sb down: *Fighter pilots searched out and attacked enemy aircraft.*

**search·able** /ˈsɜːtʃəbl; NAmE ˈsɜːrtʃ-/ adj. (of a computer DATABASE or network) having information organized in such a way that it can be searched for using a computer: *a searchable database*

**search engine** noun a computer program that searches the internet for information, especially by looking for documents containing a particular word or group of words ⊃ WORDFINDER NOTE at WEB

**search ˌengine optimiˈzation** (*BrE also* **-iˈsation**) noun [U] (*abbr.* SEO) the process of making a website appear high on a list of results given by a search engine

**search·ing** /ˈsɜːtʃɪŋ; NAmE ˈsɜːrtʃ-/ adj. [usually before noun] (of a look, a question, etc.) trying to find out the truth about sth; complete and serious: *a searching investigation/analysis/examination* ◊ *He gave her a long searching look.*

---

1395 **season**

◊ *The police asked him some searching questions.*
▶ **ˈsearch·ing·ly** adv.

**search·light** /ˈsɜːtʃlaɪt; NAmE ˈsɜːrtʃ-/ noun a powerful lamp that can be turned in any direction, used, for example, for finding people or vehicles at night

**ˈsearch party** noun [C + sing./pl v.] an organized group of people who are looking for a person or thing that is missing or lost

**ˈsearch term** noun a word or phrase that you key into a SEARCH ENGINE on the internet or the search function of a computer program in order to find the document, information, etc., that you are looking for

**ˈsearch warrant** noun an official document that allows the police to search a building, for example to look for stolen property

**sear·ing** /ˈsɪərɪŋ; NAmE ˈsɪr-/ adj. [usually before noun] **1** so strong that it seems to burn you *the searing heat of a tropical summer* ◊ *searing pain* **2** (of words or speech) powerful and critical: *a searing attack on the government*
▶ **ˈsear·ing·ly** adv. ⊃ see also SEAR

**sea salt** noun [U] a type of salt that is obtained from SEA-WATER ⊃ compare ROCK SALT

**sea·scape** /ˈsiːskeɪp/ noun a picture or view of the sea ⊃ compare TOWNSCAPE

**ˈsea shanty** noun (*BrE*) = SHANTY

**sea·shell** /ˈsiːʃel/ noun the shell of a small creature that lives in the sea, often found empty when the creature has died

**sea·shore** /ˈsiːʃɔː(r)/ (*usually* **the seashore**) noun [usually sing.] the land along the edge of the sea or ocean, usually where there is sand and rocks ⊃ SYNONYMS at COAST

**sea·sick** /ˈsiːsɪk/ adj. [not usually before noun] feeling sick or wanting to VOMIT when you are travelling on a boat or ship: *to be/feel/get seasick* ▶ **ˈsea·sick·ness** noun [U]

**sea·side** /ˈsiːsaɪd/ (*often* **the seaside**) noun [sing.] (*especially BrE*) an area that is by the sea, especially one where people go for a day or a holiday: *a trip to the seaside* ◊ *at/by the ~ a day at the seaside* ⊃ SYNONYMS at COAST ▶ **ˈsea·side** adj. [only before noun]: *a seaside resort* ◊ *a seaside vacation home*

**sea·son** 🔑 A2 /ˈsiːzn/ noun, verb
■ **noun 1** 🔑 A2 any of the four main periods of the year: spring, summer, autumn and winter: *the changing seasons* ⊃ see also GROWING SEASON **2** 🔑 A2 **the dry/rainy/wet ~** a period of the year in tropical countries when it is either very dry or it rains a lot **3** 🔑 B1 a period of time during a year when a particular activity happens or is done: *He scored his first goal of the season on Saturday.* ◊ *The female changes colour during the breeding season.* ◊ *The growing season for these trees varies depending on species.* ◊ *The hotels are always full during the peak season (= when most people are on holiday).* ◊ *the* **ˈholiday season** (*especially NAmE*) *the* **ˈtourist season** ◊ (*NAmE*) *the* **ˈholiday season** (= the time of Thanksgiving, Hanukkah, Christmas and New Year) ◊ (*BrE*) *the* **ˈfestive season** (= Christmas and New Year) ⊃ see also CLOSE SEASON, HIGH SEASON, LOW SEASON, MARCHING SEASON, OFF SEASON, OPEN SEASON, SILLY SEASON **4** a period of time in which a play is shown in one place; a series of plays, films or television programmes: *The play opens for a second season in London next week.* ◊ *a season of films by Alfred Hitchcock* **5** a period of time during one year when a particular style of clothes, hair, etc. is popular and fashionable: *This season's look is soft and romantic.* **6** (*especially NAmE*) a set of television or radio programmes that have the same characters or deal with the same subject **SYN** series: *The show begins its second season next week.*
**IDM** ˌbe in ˈseason | ˌcome into ˈseason **1** (of fruit or vegetables) be/become easily available and ready to eat because it is the right time of year for them **2** (of a female animal) be/become ready to have sex and produce young **SYN** **on heat** ˌout of ˈseason **1** (of fruit or vegetables) not

# seasonable

easily available because it is not the right time of year for them **2** at the times of year when few people go on holiday: *Hotels are cheaper out of season.* **season's greetings** used during the Christmas period to wish sb a pleasant holiday
- *verb* [T, I] **~ (sth) (with sth)** to add salt, pepper, etc. to food in order to make it taste better: *Season the lamb with garlic.* ◊ *Add the mushrooms, and season to taste* (= add as much salt, pepper, etc. as you think is necessary).

**sea·son·able** /ˈsiːznəbl/ *adj.* usual or suitable for the time of year: *seasonable temperatures* **OPP** **unseasonable**

**sea·son·al** /ˈsiːznəl/ *adj.* **1** happening or needed during a particular season; varying with the seasons: *seasonal workers brought in to cope with the Christmas period* ◊ *seasonal variations in unemployment figures* ⇒ **WORDFINDER NOTE** at **WORK** **2** typical of or suitable for the time of year, especially Christmas: *seasonal decorations* **OPP** **unseasonal** ▸ **sea·son·al·ly** /-nəli/ *adv.*: *seasonally adjusted unemployment figures* (= not including the changes that always happen in different seasons)

**seasonal af·fec·tive dis·order** *noun* [U] (*abbr.* **SAD**) a medical condition in which a person feels sad and tired during late autumn and winter when there is not much light from the sun

**sea·son·al·ity** /ˌsiːzəˈnæləti/ *noun* [U, sing.] (*specialist*) the fact of varying with the seasons: *a high degree of climatic seasonality*

**sea·soned** /ˈsiːznd/ *adj.* **1** [usually before noun] (of a person) having a lot of experience of a particular activity: *a seasoned campaigner/performer/traveller, etc.* **2** (of food) with salt, pepper, etc. added to it: *The sausage was very highly seasoned.* **3** (of wood) made suitable for use by being left outside

**season fiˈnale** *noun* (especially NAmE) the last show of a SEASON (= set of episodes) of a TV series

**sea·son·ing** /ˈsiːznɪŋ/ *noun* [U, C] a substance used to add taste to food, especially salt and pepper

**season ˈpremiere** (also **ˌseason ˈopener**) *noun* (especially NAmE) the first show of a new SEASON (= set of episodes) of a TV series: *The season premiere is scheduled for September 21.*

**ˈseason ticket** *noun* a ticket that you can use many times within a particular period, for example on a regular train or bus journey, or for a series of sports games at a particular stadium, and that costs less than paying separately each time: *an annual/a monthly/a weekly season ticket* ◊ *a season ticket holder*

**seat** 📖 **A2** /siːt/ *noun, verb*
- *noun*
- **PLACE TO SIT 1** 📖 **A2** a place where you can sit, for example a chair: *She sat back in her seat.* ◊ *He put his shopping on the seat behind him.* ◊ *Please take a seat* (= sit down). ◊ *Ladies and gentlemen, please take your seats* (= sit down). ◊ *the front/passenger seat* (= in a car) ◊ *the back/rear seats* ◊ *a child seat* (= for a child in a car) ◊ *a window/an aisle seat* (= on a plane or train) ◊ *a car/toilet seat* ◊ *We used the branch of an old tree as a seat.* ⇒ **SYNONYMS** at **SIT** ⇒ see also BACK SEAT, BOOSTER SEAT, BOX SEAT, BUCKET SEAT, CAR SEAT, EJECTOR SEAT, HOT SEAT, LOVE SEAT, PASSENGER SEAT, WINDOW SEAT
- **-SEATER 2** (in nouns and adjectives) with the number of seats mentioned: (*BrE*) *a ten-seater minibus* ◊ *an all-seater stadium* (= in which nobody is allowed to stand)
- **PART OF CHAIR 3** the part of a chair, etc. on which you actually sit: *a steel chair with a plastic seat*
- **IN PLANE/TRAIN/THEATRE 4** 📖 **A2** a place where you pay to sit in a plane, train, theatre, etc: *to book/reserve a seat* (= for a concert, etc.). ◊ *There are no seats left on that flight.*
- **OFFICIAL POSITION 5** 📖 **B2** an official position as a member of a parliament, council, committee, etc: *a seat on the city council/in Parliament/in Congress* ◊ *Republicans currently hold 51 seats in the Senate.* ◊ *to win/lose a seat* (= in an election) ◊ (*BrE*) *to take your seat* (= to begin your duties, especially in Parliament) ⇒ see also SAFE SEAT

- **TOWN/CITY 6** **~ of sth** (*formal*) a place where people are involved in a particular activity, especially a city that has a university or the offices of a government: *Washington is the seat of government of the US.* ◊ *a university town renowned as a seat of learning*
- **COUNTRY HOUSE 7** (*BrE*) = COUNTRY SEAT: *the family seat in Norfolk*
- **PART OF BODY 8** (*especially formal*) the part of the body on which a person sits **SYN** **bottom**
- **PART OF TROUSERS/PANTS 9** the part of a pair of trousers that covers a person's seat
**IDM** **be in the ˈdriving seat** (*BrE*) (*NAmE* **be in the ˈdriver's seat**) to be the person in control of a situation **(fly) by the seat of your ˈpants** (*informal*) to act without careful thought and without a plan that you have made in advance, hoping that you will be lucky and be successful **SYN** **wing it** ⇒ more at BACK SEAT, BUM *n.*, EDGE *n.*

- *verb*
- **SIT DOWN 1** 📖 **B2** **~ sb/yourself** (*formal*) to give sb a place to sit; to sit down in a place: *Please wait to be seated* (= in a restaurant, etc.). ◊ *Please be seated* (= sit down). ◊ *He seated himself behind the desk.* ⇒ **SYNONYMS** at **SIT**
- **OF BUILDING/VEHICLE 2** **~ sb** to have enough seats for a particular number of people: *The aircraft seats 200 passengers.*

**ˈseat belt** (*also* **ˈsafety belt**) *noun* a belt that is attached to the seat in a car or plane and that you fasten around yourself so that you are not thrown out of the seat if there is an accident: *Fasten your seat belts.*

**seat·ing** /ˈsiːtɪŋ/ *noun* [U] places to sit; seats: *The theatre has seating for about 500 people.* ◊ *The room had a seating capacity of over 200.* ◊ *the seating arrangements for the conference*

**seat·mate** /ˈsiːtmeɪt/ *noun* a person that you sit next to when you are travelling, especially on a plane

**ˈsea turtle** *noun* (*NAmE*) = TURTLE

**ˈsea urchin** (*also* **ˈur·chin**) *noun* a small sea creature with a round shell which is covered with SPIKES

**ˈsea wall** *noun* a large strong wall built to stop the sea from flowing onto the land

**sea·ward** /ˈsiːwəd; *NAmE* -wərd/ *adj.* towards the sea; in the direction of the sea: *the seaward side of the coastal road* ▸ **sea·ward** (*also* **sea·wards**) *adv.*: *Her gaze was fixed seawards.*

**sea·water** /ˈsiːwɔːtə(r)/ *noun* [U] water from the sea, which contains salt

**sea·way** /ˈsiːweɪ/ *noun* a passage from the sea through the land along which large ships can travel

**sea·weed** /ˈsiːwiːd/ *noun* [U, C] a plant that grows in the sea, or on rocks at the edge of the sea. There are many different types of seaweed, some of which are eaten as food.

**sea·worthy** /ˈsiːwɜːði; *NAmE* -wɜːrði/ *adj.* (of a ship) in a suitable condition to sail ▸ **sea·worthi·ness** *noun* [U]

**se·ba·ceous** /sɪˈbeɪʃəs/ *adj.* [usually before noun] (*biology*) producing a substance like oil in the body: *the sebaceous glands in the skin*

**sebum** /ˈsiːbəm/ *noun* [U] an oil-like substance produced by the SEBACEOUS GLANDS

**Sec.** (*US also* **Secy.**) *abbr.* (in writing) SECRETARY

**sec** /sek/ *noun* **a sec** [sing.] (*informal*) a very short time; a second: *Stay there. I'll be back in a sec.* ◊ *Hang on* (= wait) *a sec.*

**sec.** *abbr.* (in writing) second(s)

**seca·teurs** /ˌsekəˈtɜːz; *NAmE* -ˈtɜːrz/ *noun* [pl.] (*BrE*) a garden tool like a pair of strong SCISSORS, used for cutting plant STEMS and small branches: *a pair of secateurs*

**se·cede** /sɪˈsiːd/ *verb* [I] **~ (from sth)** (*formal*) (of a state, country, etc.) to officially leave a larger state or organization of states and become independent: *The Republic of Panama seceded from Colombia in 1903.*

**se·ces·sion** /sɪˈseʃn/ noun [U, C] ~ **(from sth)** the fact of an area or group becoming independent from the country or larger group that it belongs to

**se·ces·sion·ist** /sɪˈseʃənɪst/ adj. [only before noun] supporting or connected with secession ▶ **se·ces·sion·ist** noun: *a military campaign against the secessionists*

**se·clude** /sɪˈkluːd/ verb ~ **yourself/sb (from sb/sth)** (formal) to keep yourself/sb away from contact with other people

**se·cluded** /sɪˈkluːdɪd/ adj. (especially of a place) quiet and private: *a secluded spot/corner/beach*

**se·clu·sion** /sɪˈkluːʒn/ noun [U] the state of being private or of having little contact with other people: *the seclusion and peace of the island*

**sec·ond¹** 🅐🅰🅦 /ˈsekənd/ det., ordinal number, adv., noun, verb ⊃ see also SECOND²
■ det., ordinal number **1** 🅐 happening or coming next after the first in a series of similar things or people; 2nd: *This is the second time it's happened.* ◊ *Italy scored a second goal just after half-time.* ◊ *the second of June/June 2nd* ◊ *He was the second to arrive.* ◊ *We have one child and are expecting our second in July.* **2** 🅐 next in order of importance, size, quality, etc. to one other person or thing: *Osaka is Japan's second-largest city.* ◊ *Birmingham, the UK's second city* ◊ *Basketball is second only to soccer in global popularity.* ◊ *As a dancer, he is second to none* (= nobody is a better dancer than he is). **3** 🅑 [only before noun] another; in addition to one that you already own or use: *They have a second home in Tuscany.*
■ adv. **1** 🅐 after one other person or thing in order or importance: *She came second in the marathon.* ◊ *One of the smaller parties came a close second* (= nearly won). ◊ *I agreed to speak second.* ◊ *He is a writer first and a scientist second.* ◊ *I came second (to) last* (= the one before the last one) *in the race.* **2** 🅐 used to introduce the second of a list of points you want to make in a speech or piece of writing 🆂🆈🅽 *secondly*: *She did it first because she wanted to, and second because I asked her to.* ⊃ LANGUAGE BANK at FIRST, PROCESS¹
■ noun **1** 🅐 [C] (symb. ″) (abbr. **sec.**) a unit for measuring time. There are 60 seconds in one minute: *in … seconds She can run 100 metres in just over 11 seconds.* ◊ *for … seconds For several seconds he did not reply.* ◊ *every … seconds The light flashes every five seconds.* ◊ *per~ The water flows at about 1.5 metres per second.* **2** 🅐 [C] (also informal **sec**) a very short time 🆂🆈🅽 *moment*: *in a~ I'll be with you in a second.* ◊ *in/within seconds They had finished within seconds.* ⊃ see also SPLIT SECOND **3** [C] (symb. ″) a unit for measuring angles. There are 60 seconds in one minute: *1° 6′ 10″* (= one degree, six minutes and ten seconds) **4 seconds** [pl.] (informal) a second amount of the same food that you have just eaten: *Seconds, anybody?* **5** [C, usually pl.] an item that is sold at a lower price than usual because it is not perfect **6** (also **second gear**) [U] one of six or seven positions of the GEARS in a vehicle: *in~ When it's icy, move off in second.* **7** [C] a level of university degree at British universities. An *upper second* is a good degree and a *lower second* is average. ⊃ compare FIRST, THIRD **8** [C] a person whose role is to help and support sb else, for example in a BOXING match or in a formal DUEL in the past 🅸🅳🅼 see JUST adv., WAIT v.
■ verb ~ sth to state officially at a meeting that you support another person's idea, suggestion, etc. so that it can be discussed and/or voted on: *Any proposal must be seconded by two other members of the committee.* ◊ (informal) *'Thank God that's finished.' 'I'll second that!'* (= I agree) ⊃ compare PROPOSE ⊃ WORDFINDER NOTE at DEBATE

**sec·ond²** /sɪˈkɒnd; NAmE -ˈkɑːnd/ verb [usually passive] (especially BrE) to send an employee to another department, office, etc. in order to do a different job for a short period of time: **be seconded (from sth) (to sth)** *Each year two teachers are seconded to industry for six months.* ⊃ see also SECOND¹ ▶ **se·cond·ment** noun [U, C] (BrE): **on ~** *They met while she was on secondment from the Foreign Office.*

**sec·ond·ary** 🅑 🅑🅦 /ˈsekəndri; NAmE -deri/ adj.
**1** 🅑 [only before noun] connected with teaching children of 11–18 years: *secondary teachers* ◊ *the secondary cur-*

1397 **second-degree**

*riculum* ⊃ compare ELEMENTARY, PRIMARY, TERTIARY **2** 🅑 less important than sth else: *That is just a secondary consideration.* ◊ *Experience is what matters—age is of secondary importance.* ◊ ~ **to sth** *Raising animals was only secondary to other forms of farming.* **3** 🅑 [usually before noun] happening as a result of sth else: *a secondary infection* ◊ *a secondary effect* ◊ *a secondary colour* (= made from mixing two primary colours) ▶ **sec·ond·ar·ily** /ˈsekəndrəli; NAmE ˌsekənˈderəli/ adv.: *Their clothing is primarily functional and only secondarily decorative.*

**ˌsecondary eduˈcation** noun [U] (especially BrE) education for children between the ages of 11 and 18: *primary and secondary education*

**ˌsecondary ˈmodern** noun (in England, Wales and Northern Ireland until the 1970s) a school for young people between the ages of 11 and 16 who did not go to a GRAMMAR SCHOOL

**ˈsecondary school** noun (especially BrE) a school for young people between the ages of 11 and 16 or 18 ⊃ compare HIGH SCHOOL, PRIMARY SCHOOL

**ˈsecondary source** noun a book or other source of information where the writer has taken the information from some other source and not collected it himself or herself ⊃ compare PRIMARY SOURCE

**ˌsecondary ˈstress** noun [U, C] (phonetics) the second strongest stress that is put on a syllable in a word or a phrase when it is spoken ⊃ compare PRIMARY STRESS

**ˌsecond ˈbase** noun [sing.] (in baseball) the second of the four positions that players must reach in order to score points; the position of the player on the defending team near second base

**ˌsecond ˈbest** adj. **1** not as good as the best: *The two teams seemed evenly matched but Arsenal came off second best* (= lost). ◊ *my second-best suit* **2** not exactly what you want; not perfect: *a second-best solution* ▶ **ˌsecond ˈbest** noun [U]: *Sometimes you have to settle for* (= be content with) *second best.*

**ˌsecond ˈchamber** noun (especially BrE) = UPPER HOUSE

**ˌsecond ˈclass** noun **1** [U] a way of travelling on a train or ship that costs less and is less comfortable than FIRST CLASS. In the UK this is now usually called **ˈstandard class**. **2** [U] (in the UK) the class of mail that costs less and takes longer to arrive than FIRST CLASS **3** [U] (in the US) the system of sending newspapers and magazines by mail **4** [U, sing.] the second highest standard of degree given by a British university, often divided into upper second class and lower second class

**ˌsecond-ˈclass** adj. **1** (disapproving) (of a person) less important than other people: *Older people should not be treated as second-class citizens.* **2** of a lower standard or quality than the best: *a second-class education* **3** [only before noun] connected with the less expensive way of travelling on a train, ship, etc: *second-class carriages/compartments/passengers* **4** [only before noun] (in the UK) connected with letters, packages, etc. that you pay less to send and that are delivered less quickly: *second-class letters/stamps* **5** (in the US) connected with the system of sending newspapers and magazines by mail **6** [only before noun] used to describe a British university degree which is good but not of the highest class: *Applicants should have at least a second-class honours degree.* ▶ **ˌsecond ˈclass** adv.: *to send a letter second class* ◊ *to travel second class*

**the ˌSecond ˈComing** noun [sing.] a day in the future when Christians believe Jesus Christ will come back to earth

**ˌsecond ˈcousin** noun a child of a cousin of your mother or father

**ˌsecond-deˈgree** adj. [only before noun] **1** ~ **murder, assault, burglary, etc.** (especially NAmE) murder, etc. that is less serious than FIRST-DEGREE crimes **2** ~ **burns** burns of the second most serious of three kinds, causing BLISTERS but no permanent marks ⊃ compare FIRST-DEGREE, THIRD-DEGREE

---

Ⓞ Oxford Phrasal Academic Lexicon (OPAL) written and spoken word lists | Ⓦ OPAL written word list | Ⓢ OPAL spoken word list

**sec·ond·er** /ˈsekəndə(r)/ noun a person who SECONDS a proposal, etc. (= supports it so that it can be discussed) ⊃ compare PROPOSER

**ˌsecond-geneˈration** adj. **1** used to describe people who were born in the country they now live in but whose parents came to live there from another country: *She was a second-generation Japanese-American.* **2** (of a product, technology, etc.) at a more advanced stage of development than an earlier form: *second-generation handheld computers*

**ˌsecond-ˈguess** verb **1** [T] ~ sb/sth/yourself to guess what sb will do before they do it; to guess how you will feel in the future: *It was impossible to second-guess the decision of the jury.* **2** [T, I] ~ (sb/sth) (*especially NAmE*) to criticize sb after a decision has been made; to criticize sth after it has happened

**ˈsecond hand** noun the hand on some watches and clocks that shows seconds ⊃ picture at CLOCK

**ˌsecond-ˈhand** adj. **1** not new; owned by sb else before: *a second-hand bookshop* (= for selling second-hand books) ◊ (*especially BrE*) *second-hand cars* **2** (*often disapproving*) (of news, information, etc.) learned from other people, not from your own experience: *second-hand opinions* ▶ **second-ˈhand** adv.: *I bought the camera second-hand.* ◊ *I only heard about it second-hand.* ⊃ compare FIRST-HAND

**ˌsecond-hand ˈsmoke** noun smoke that is breathed in from other people smoking around you

**ˌsecond ˈhome** noun **1** [C] a house or flat that sb owns as well as their main home and uses, for example, for holidays **2** [sing.] a place where sb now lives and which they know as well as, and like as much as, the place where they grew up

**ˌsecond in comˈmand** noun ~ (to sb) a person who has the second highest rank in a group and takes charge when the leader is not there

**ˌsecond ˈlanguage** noun a language that sb learns to speak well and that they use for work or at school, but that is not the language they learned first: *ESL or English as a Second Language*

**ˌsecond ˈlanguage acquiˈsition** noun [U] (*abbr.* SLA) (*linguistics*) the learning of a second language

**ˌsecond lieuˈtenant** noun an officer of lower rank in the army or the US AIR FORCE just below the rank of a LIEUTENANT

**sec·ond·ly** ⓘ A2 🔊 /ˈsekəndli/ adv. used to introduce the second of a list of points you want to make in a speech or piece of writing: *Firstly, it's expensive, and secondly, it's too slow.*

**ˈsecond name** noun (*especially BrE*) **1** a family name or SURNAME **2** a second personal name or MIDDLE NAME: *His second name is Willem, after his grandfather.*

**ˌsecond ˈnature** noun [U] ~ (to sb) (to do sth) something that you do very easily and naturally, because it is part of your character or you have done it so many times

**the ˌsecond ˈperson** noun [sing.] (*grammar*) the form of a pronoun or verb used when addressing sb: *In the phrase 'you are', the verb 'are' is in the second person and the word 'you' is a second-person pronoun.* ⊃ compare FIRST PERSON, THIRD PERSON

**ˌsecond-ˈrate** adj. not very good or impressive ⓢⓨⓝ mediocre: *a second-rate player*

**ˈsecond screen** noun a mobile device used while watching television, especially to access additional content or apps: *a second-screen app* ▶ **ˌsecond-ˈscreen** verb [I]: *Many people are now second-screening on their mobile devices while watching TV.*

**ˌsecond ˈsight** noun [U] the ability that some people seem to have to know or see what will happen in the future or what is happening in a different place

**ˌsecond-ˈstring** adj. [only before noun] (*especially NAmE*) (usually of a player in a sports team) only used occasionally where sb/sth else is not available: *a second-string quarterback* ▶ **ˌsecond ˈstring** noun: *Wilson was a second string for New Zealand in last week's match.*

**ˌsecond ˈwind** noun [sing.] (*informal*) new energy that makes you able to continue with sth that had made you tired

**the ˌSecond World ˈWar** (*also* ˌWorld War ˈII) noun [sing.] the second large international war, which was fought between 1939 and 1945

**se·crecy** /ˈsiːkrəsi/ noun [U] the fact of making sure that nothing is known about sth; the state of being secret: *the need for absolute secrecy in this matter* ◊ *Everyone involved was sworn to secrecy.* ◊ *The whole affair is still shrouded in secrecy.*

**se·cret** ⓘ A2 /ˈsiːkrət/ adj., noun
■ adj. **1** A2 known about by only a few people; kept hidden from others: *secret information/meetings/talks* ◊ ~ from sb *He tried to keep it secret from his family.* ◊ *Details of the proposals remain secret.* ◊ *a secret passage leading to the beach* ⊃ see also TOP SECRET **2** ⓑ⒈ [only before noun] used to describe actions and behaviour that you do not tell other people about: *He's a secret drinker.* ◊ *her secret fears* **3** ~ (about sth) (of a person or their behaviour) liking to have secrets that other people do not know about; showing this ⓢⓨⓝ secretive: *They were so secret about everything.* ◊ *Jessica caught a secret smile flitting between the two of them.* ▶ **se·cret·ly** adv.: *The police had secretly filmed the conversations.* ◊ *She was secretly pleased to see him.*
■ noun **1** ⓑ⒈ [C] something that is known about by only a few people and not told to others: *Can you keep a secret?* ◊ *She will not reveal his secret.* ◊ *The location of the ship is a closely guarded secret.* ◊ *This bar is one of central London's best/worst kept secrets.* ◊ *Shall we let him in on* (= tell him) *the secret?* ◊ *He made no secret of his ambition* (= he didn't try to hide it). ◊ *It's no secret that the past few years have been challenging for the industry.* ⊃ see also OFFICIAL SECRET, TRADE SECRET **2** ⓑ⒈ (*usually* the secret) [sing.] the best or only way to achieve sth; the way a particular person achieves sth: ~ of sth *Careful planning is the secret of success.* ◊ ~ to (doing) sth *These animals may hold the secret to combating the virus.* **3** [C, usually pl.] a thing that is not yet fully understood or that is difficult to understand: *the secrets of the universe*
ⓘⓓⓜ **in ˈsecret** without other people knowing about it: *The meeting was held in secret.* ⊃ more at GUILTY, OPEN adj.

**ˈsecret agent** (*also* agent) noun a person who works secretly to obtain information for a government or other organization ⓢⓨⓝ spy

**sec·re·tar·ial** /ˌsekrəˈteəriəl; NAmE -ˈter-/ adj. involving or connected with the work of a secretary: *secretarial work*

**sec·re·tar·iat** /ˌsekrəˈteəriət, -riæt; NAmE -ˈteriət/ noun the department of a large international or political organization which is responsible for running it, especially the office of a SECRETARY GENERAL

**sec·re·tary** ⓘ A2 /ˈsekrətri; NAmE -teri/ noun (*pl.* -ies) (*abbr.* Sec.) **1** A2 a person who works in an office, working for another person, dealing with mail and phone calls, keeping records, arranging meetings with people, etc: *a legal/medical secretary* ◊ *Please contact my secretary to make an appointment.* ⊃ see also EXECUTIVE SECRETARY, PRIVATE SECRETARY **2** A2 an official of a club, society, etc. who deals with mail, keeping records and making business arrangements: *the membership secretary* ⊃ WORDFINDER NOTE at CLUB ⊃ see also GENERAL SECRETARY, SOCIAL SECRETARY **3** ⓑ⒉ **Secretary** = SECRETARY OF STATE ⊃ see also FOREIGN SECRETARY, HOME SECRETARY **4** ⓑ⒉ (in the US) the head of a government department, chosen by the president: *Secretary of the Treasury* **5** (in the UK) an assistant of a government minister, an AMBASSADOR, etc. ⊃ see also PARLIAMENTARY SECRETARY, PARLIAMENTARY PRIVATE SECRETARY, PRESS SECRETARY, UNDERSECRETARY

**ˌsecretary ˈgeneral** noun (*pl.* secretaries general *or* secretary generals) the person who is in charge of the department that deals with the running of a large international or political organization: *a former secretary general of NATO*

**Secretary of 'State** noun **1** (also **Sec·re·tary**) (in the UK) the head of an important government department: *the Secretary of State for Education* ◊ *the Education Secretary* **2** (in the US) the head of the government department that deals with foreign affairs

**se·crete** /sɪˈkriːt/ verb **1** ~ sth (of part of the body or a plant) to produce a liquid substance: *Insulin is secreted by the pancreas.* **2** ~ sth (in sth) (formal) to hide sth, especially sth small: *The drugs were secreted in the lining of his case.*

**se·cre·tion** /sɪˈkriːʃn/ noun (specialist) **1** [U] the process by which liquid substances are produced by parts of the body or plants: *the secretion of bile by the liver* **2** [C, usually pl.] a liquid substance produced by parts of the body or plants: *bodily secretions*

**se·cret·ive** /ˈsiːkrətɪv/ adj. ~ (about sth) tending or liking to hide your thoughts, feelings, actions, etc. from other people: *He's very secretive about his work.* ▶ **se·cret·ive·ly** adv. **se·cret·ive·ness** noun [U]

**ˌsecret poˈlice** noun [pl.] a police force that works secretly to make sure that citizens behave as their government wants

**ˌSecret ˈSanta** noun an arrangement in which each one of a group of friends or colleagues buys a small Christmas gift for one other. The person receiving the gift does not know who chose it.

**ˌsecret ˈservice** noun [usually sing.] a government department that is responsible for protecting its government's military and political secrets and for finding out the secrets of other governments

**sect** /sekt/ noun (sometimes disapproving) a small group of people who belong to a particular religion but who have some beliefs or practices which separate them from the rest of the group

**sect·ar·ian** /sekˈteəriən; NAmE -ˈter-/ adj. [usually before noun] (often disapproving) connected with the differences that exist between groups of people who have different religious views: *sectarian attacks/violence* ◊ *attempts to break down the sectarian divide in Northern Ireland*

**sect·ar·ian·ism** /sekˈteəriənɪzəm; NAmE -ˈter-/ noun [U] (often disapproving) strong support for one particular religious or political group, especially when this leads to violence between different groups

**sec·tion** ❶ **A1** ⊙ /ˈsekʃn/ noun, verb
■ **noun**
• **PART / PIECE 1 A1** [C] any of the parts into which sth is divided: ~ **of sth** *That section of the road is still closed.* ◊ *the tail section of the plane* ◊ *The library has a large biology section.* ⊃ see also CONIC SECTION, GOLDEN SECTION **2 A2** [C] a separate part of a structure from which the whole can be put together: *The shed comes in sections that you assemble yourself.*
• **OF DOCUMENT / BOOK 3 A1** [C] a separate part of a document, book, etc: *These issues will be discussed more fully in the next section.* ◊ *the sports section of the newspaper*
• **GROUP OF PEOPLE 4 B1** [C] a separate group within a larger group of people: ~ **of sth** *an issue that will affect large sections of the population* ◊ *the brass section of an orchestra* ⊃ see also RHYTHM SECTION
• **OF ORGANIZATION 5** [C] a department in an organization, institution, etc. **SYN** division: *He's the director of the finance section.*
• **DISTRICT 6** [C] (NAmE) a district of a town, city or county: *the Dorchester section of Boston*
• **MEASUREMENT 7** [C] (NAmE) a measure of land, equal to one square mile
• **DIAGRAM 8** [C] a drawing or diagram of sth as it would look if it were cut from top to bottom or from one side to the other: ~ **through sth** *The illustration shows a section through a leaf.* ◊ **in ~** *The architect drew the house in section.* ⊃ see also CROSS SECTION
• **MEDICAL 9** [C, U] (medical) the act of cutting or separating sth in an operation: *The surgeon performed a section (= made a cut) on the vein.* ⊃ see also CAESAREAN **10** [C] (medical, biology) a very thin flat piece cut from body TISSUE to

be looked at under a MICROSCOPE: *to examine a section from the kidney*
■ **verb**
• **MEDICAL / BIOLOGY 1** ~ **sth** (medical) to divide body TISSUE by cutting **2** ~ **sth** (biology) to cut animal or plant TISSUE into thin slices in order to look at it under a MICROSCOPE
• **MENTAL PATIENT 3** [often passive] ~ **sb** (BrE) to officially order a mentally ill person to go and receive treatment in a PSYCHIATRIC hospital, using a law that can force them to stay there until they are successfully treated
**PHRV** **ˌsection sth↔ˈoff** to separate an area from a larger one: *Parts of the town had been sectioned off.*

**sec·tion·al** /ˈsekʃənl/ adj. [usually before noun] **1** connected with one particular group within a community or an organization: *the sectional interests of managers and workers* **2** made of separate sections: *a sectional building* **3** connected with a CROSS SECTION of sth (= a surface or an image formed by cutting through sth from top to bottom): *a sectional drawing*

**sec·tor** ❶ **B2** Ⓦ /ˈsektə(r)/ noun **1 B2** a part of an area of activity, especially of a country's economy: *the service / banking / manufacturing / financial sector* ◊ **in a ~** *She works in the voluntary sector* (= organizations that do not make a profit). ◊ *the privileged sectors of society* ⊃ see also PRIVATE SECTOR, PUBLIC SECTOR, THIRD SECTOR **2 B2** a part of a particular area, especially an area under military control: *each sector of the war zone* **3** (geometry) a part of a circle lying between two straight lines drawn from the centre to the edge ⊃ picture at CIRCLE

**sec·tor·al** /ˈsektərəl/; NAmE also sekˈtɔːrəl/ adj. relating to a particular part of an area of activity, especially of a country's economy: *The party pursued sectoral interests rather than the interests of society as a whole.*

**secu·lar** **I+** **C1** /ˈsekjələ(r)/ adj. **1 I+ C1** not connected with spiritual or religious matters: *secular music* ◊ *We live in a largely secular society.* **2** (of priests) living among ordinary people rather than in a religious community

**secu·lar·ism** /ˈsekjələrɪzəm/ noun [U] (specialist) the belief that religion should not be involved in the organization of society, education, etc. ▶ **secu·lar·ist** adj. [usually before noun]

**secu·lar·iza·tion** (BrE also **-isa·tion**) /ˌsekjələraɪˈzeɪʃn; NAmE -rəˈz-/ noun [U] the process of removing the influence or power that religion has over sth

**secu·lar·ize** (BrE also **-ise**) /ˈsekjələraɪz/ verb [often passive] ~ **sth** to make sth SECULAR; to remove sth from the control or influence of religion: *a secularized society*

**se·cure** ❶ **B2** /sɪˈkjʊə(r); NAmE -ˈkjʊr/ verb, adj.
■ **verb** (formal)
• **GET STH 1 B2** to obtain or achieve sth, especially when this means using a lot of effort: ~ **sth** *to secure a contract / deal / funding* ◊ *The team managed to secure a place in the finals.* ◊ *The team were unable to secure a victory.* ◊ ~ **sth for sb / sth / yourself** *He secured a place for himself at law school.* ◊ ~ **sb / sth / yourself sth** *He secured himself a place at law school.*
• **FASTEN STH 2 B2** ~ **sth (to sth)** to attach or fasten sth so that it does not move: *She secured the rope firmly to the back of the car.*
• **PROTECT FROM HARM 3 B2** to protect sth so that it is safe and difficult to attack or damage: ~ **sth against sth** *to secure a property against intruders* ◊ ~ **sth from sth** *Have you properly secured your computer from viral attack?* ◊ (figurative) *a savings plan that will secure your child's future*
• **A LOAN 4** ~ **sth** to legally agree to give sb property or goods that are worth the same amount as the money that you have borrowed from them, if you are unable to pay the money back: *a loan secured on the house*
■ **adj.**
• **CERTAIN / SAFE 1 B2** likely to continue or be successful for a long time **SYN** safe: *a secure job / income* ◊ *It's not a very secure way to make a living.* ◊ *The future of the company looks secure.* **OPP** insecure **2 B2** where sb / sth cannot be harmed; that cannot be affected or harmed by sth

# security

**SYN** **safe**: *Parents are primarily concerned with leaving their children in a safe, **secure** environment.* ◊ *~ **against/from sth** Information must be stored so that it is secure from accidental deletion.*
- **HAPPY/CONFIDENT** **3** B2 feeling happy and confident about yourself or a particular situation: *At last they were able to feel **secure** about the future.* ◊ *She finished the match, **secure** in the knowledge that she was through to the next round.* **OPP** **insecure**
- **BUILDING/DOOR/ROOM** **4** B2 guarded and/or made stronger so that it is difficult for people to enter or leave: *Check that all windows and doors have been made as **secure** as possible.* ◊ *a **secure** unit for child offenders* **OPP** **insecure**
- **NOT LIKELY TO MOVE OR FALL** **5** B2 not likely to move, fall down, etc. **SYN** **stable**: *The aerial doesn't look very **secure** to me.* ◊ *It was difficult to maintain a **secure** foothold on the ice.* ◊ *(figurative) Our relationship was now on a more **secure** footing.* **OPP** **insecure** ▶ **se·cure·ly** *adv.*: *She locked the door securely behind her.* ◊ *Make sure the ropes are securely fastened.*

## se·cur·ity ❶ B1 W /sɪˈkjʊərəti; NAmE -ˈkjʊr-/ noun
(pl. -ies)
- **PROTECTION** **1** B1 [U] the activities involved in protecting a country, building or person against attack, danger, etc: *national/homeland security* (= the defence of a country) ◊ *~ **against sth** The bars are to provide security against break-ins.* ◊ *They carried out **security checks** at the airport.* ◊ *The visit took place amidst **tight security** (= the use of many police officers).* ◊ *the **security forces/services** (= the police, army, etc.)* ◊ *a **high/maximum security prison** (= for dangerous criminals)* ⊃ see also HIGH-SECURITY, MINIMUM SECURITY PRISON **2** B1 [U] a place at an airport where you go after your passport has been checked so that officials can find out if you are carrying illegal drugs or weapons: *My bag was emptied and searched when I went through security.* ◊ *It took ages to clear security and reach the departure lounge.* ⊃ **WORDFINDER NOTE** at AIRPORT **3** [U + sing./pl. v.] the department of a large company or organization that deals with the protection of its buildings, equipment and staff: *Security was/were called to the incident.* **4** B1 [U] protection against sth bad that might happen in the future: *financial security* ◊ *Job security* (= the guarantee that you will keep your job) *is a thing of the past.* ⊃ see also FOOD SECURITY, INFORMATION SECURITY
- **FEELING HAPPY/SAFE** **5** B2 [U] the state of feeling happy and safe from danger or worry: *the security of a loving family life* ◊ *She'd allowed herself to be lulled into a **false sense of security** (= a feeling that she was safe when in fact she was in danger).*
- **FOR A LOAN** **6** [U, C] a valuable item, such as a house, that you agree to give to sb if you are unable to pay back the money that you have borrowed from them: **as ~ for sth** *His home and business are being held as security for the loan.*
- **SHARES IN COMPANY** **7** **securities** [pl.] *(finance)* documents proving that sb is the owner of shares, etc. in a particular company ⊃ see also OLD AGE SECURITY, SOCIAL SECURITY

**seˈcurity blanket** *noun* **1** *(BrE also* **ˈcomfort blanket***)* a BLANKET or other object that a child holds in order to feel safe **2** something that provides protection against attack, danger, etc: *A firewall provides an essential security blanket for your computer network.* **3** *(BrE)* official orders or measures that prevent people from knowing about, seeing, etc. sth: *The government has thrown a security blanket around the talks.*

**the Seˈcurity Council** *(also the* **UN Seˈcurity Council***,* **the ˌUnited ˌNations Seˈcurity Council***) noun* [sing.] the part of the United Nations that tries to keep peace and order in the world, consisting of representatives of fifteen countries

**seˈcurity forces** *noun* [pl.] soldiers and police who are responsible for maintaining security in a city, region, etc: *a member of the security forces*

**seˈcurity guard** *noun* a person whose job is to guard a building, money, etc.

**seˈcurity risk** *noun* a person who cannot be given secret information because they are a danger to a particular country, organization, etc., especially because of their political beliefs

**Seˈcurity Service** *noun* a government organization that protects a country and its secrets from enemies

**Secy.** *abbr. (US)* = SEC.

**sedan** /sɪˈdæn/ *(NAmE) (BrE* **sal·oon**, **saˈloon car***) noun* a car with four doors and a BOOT (= space at the back for carrying things) which is separated from the part where the driver and passengers sit

**sed·ate** /sɪˈdeɪt/ *adj., verb*
■ *adj.* [usually before noun] **1** slow, calm and relaxed **SYN** **unhurried**: *We followed the youngsters at a more sedate pace.* **2** quiet, especially in a way that lacks excitement: *a sedate country town* ◊ *a sedate, sober man* ▶ **sed·ate·ly** *adv.*
■ *verb* [often passive] *~ **sb/sth** to give sb drugs in order to make them calm and/or to make them sleep **SYN** **tranquillize**: *Most of the patients are heavily sedated.*

**sed·ation** /sɪˈdeɪʃn/ *noun* [U] the act of giving sb drugs in order to make them calm or to make them sleep; the state that results from this: **under ~** *The victim's wife was last night being kept under sedation in the local hospital.*

**seda·tive** /ˈsedətɪv/ *noun* a drug that makes sb go to sleep or makes them feel calm and relaxed **SYN** **tranquillizer** ⊃ **WORDFINDER NOTE** at SLEEP ▶ **seda·tive** *adj.* [usually before noun]: *the sedative effect of the drug*

**sed·en·tary** /ˈsedntri; NAmE -teri/ *adj.* **1** (of work, activities, etc.) in which you spend a lot of time sitting down: *a **sedentary job/occupation/lifestyle*** **2** (of people) spending a lot of time sitting down and not moving: *He became increasingly sedentary in later life.* **3** *(specialist)* (of people or animals) that stay and live in the same place or area: *Rhinos are largely sedentary animals.* ◊ *a sedentary population*

**Seder** /ˈseɪdə(r)/ *noun* a Jewish CEREMONIAL service and dinner on the first night or first two nights of Passover

**sedge** /sedʒ/ *noun* [U] a plant like grass that grows in wet ground or near water

**sedi·ment** /ˈsedɪmənt/ *noun* [U] **1** the solid material that settles at the bottom of a liquid **2** *(geology)* sand, stones, mud, etc. carried by water or wind and left, for example, on the bottom of a lake, river, etc.

**sedi·ment·ary** /ˌsedɪˈmentri/ *adj. (geology)* connected with or formed from the sand, stones, mud, etc. that settle at the bottom of lakes, etc: *sedimentary rocks*

**sedi·men·ta·tion** /ˌsedɪmenˈteɪʃn/ *noun* [U] *(geology)* the process of a layer of sediment being created

**se·di·tion** /sɪˈdɪʃn/ *noun* [U] *(formal)* the use of words or actions that are intended to encourage people to oppose a government **SYN** **insurrection** ▶ **se·di·tious** /-ʃəs/ *adj.*: *seditious activity*

**se·duce** /sɪˈdjuːs; NAmE -ˈduːs/ *verb* **1** *~ **sb** to persuade sb to have sex with you, especially sb who is younger or who has less experience than you **2** *~ **sb** (into sth/into doing sth) to persuade sb to do sth that they would not usually agree to do by making it seem very attractive **SYN** **entice**: *The promise of huge profits seduced him into parting with his money.*

**se·du·cer** /sɪˈdjuːsə(r); NAmE -ˈduː-/ *noun* a person who persuades sb to have sex with them

**se·duc·tion** /sɪˈdʌkʃn/ *noun* **1** [U, C] the act of persuading sb to have sex with you: *Cleopatra's seduction of Caesar* **2** [C, usually pl., U] *~ (of sth)* the qualities or features of sth that make it seem attractive **SYN** **enticement**: *Who could resist the seductions of the tropical island?*

**se·duc·tive** /sɪˈdʌktɪv/ *adj.* **1** sexually attractive: *a seductive woman* ◊ *She used her most seductive voice.* **2** attractive in a way that makes you want to have or do sth **SYN** **tempting**: *The idea of retiring to the south of France is highly seductive.* ▶ **se·duc·tive·ly** *adv.* **se·duc·tive·ness** *noun* [U]

**se·duc·tress** /sɪˈdʌktrəs/ *noun* a woman who persuades sb to have sex with her

# see

**see** ⓘ A1 /siː/ *verb, noun*

■ **verb** (saw /sɔː/, seen /siːn/)

- **USE EYES 1** A1 [T, I] (not used in the progressive tenses) to become aware of sb/sth by using your eyes: ~ sb/sth *She looked for him but couldn't see him in the crowd.* ◇ *The opera was the place to see and be seen* (= by other important or fashionable people). ◇ ~ (that)... *He could see (that) she had been crying.* ◇ ~ what, how, etc... *Did you see what happened?* ◇ ~ sb/sth + adj. *I hate to see you unhappy.* ◇ ~ sb/sth doing sth *She was seen running away from the scene of the crime.* ◇ ~ sb/sth do sth *I saw you put the key in your pocket.* ◇ *sb/sth is seen to do sth He was seen to enter the building about the time the crime was committed.* ◇ (*figurative*) *The government not only has to do something, it must be seen to be doing something* (= people must be aware that it is doing sth). ◇ ~ + adv./prep. *The walls were too high to see over.* ⊃ HOMOPHONES at SEIZE **2** A1 [I] (not usually used in the progressive tenses) to have or use the power of sight: *She will never see again* (= she has become blind). ◇ *On a clear day you can see for miles from here.* ◇ **to ~ to do sth** *It was getting dark and I couldn't see to read.*
- **WATCH 3** A1 [T] (not usually used in the progressive tenses) to watch a game, television programme, performance, etc: ~ sth *Did you see that programme on Brazil last night?* ◇ *In the evening we went to see a movie.* ◇ ~ **sth on sth** *It's not the sort of thing you see on TV that often.* ⊃ SYNONYMS at LOOK
- **LOOK UP/ASK FOR INFORMATION 4** A1 [T, I] (used in orders) to look at sth in order to find information; to go to sb in order to ask for help or information: ~ sth/sb *See page 158.* ◇ *If you missed the session, see a member of staff for advice.* ◇ ~ + adv./prep. *See above/below for a breakdown of the costs.*
- **MEET BY CHANCE 5** A1 [T] ~ sb (not usually used in the progressive tenses) to be near and recognize sb; to meet sb by chance: *Guess who I saw at the party last night!*
- **VISIT 6** A1 [T] ~ sb/sth to visit sb/sth: *Come and see us again soon.*
- **HAVE MEETING 7** A1 [T] ~ sb (about sth) to have a meeting with sb: *You ought to see a doctor about that cough.* ◇ *What is it you want to see me about?*
- **SPEND TIME 8** B2 [T] (often used in the progressive tenses) ~ sb to spend time with sb: *Are you seeing anyone* (= having a romantic relationship with anyone)? ◇ *They've been seeing a lot of each other* (= spending a lot of time together) *recently*.
- **UNDERSTAND 9** B1 [I, T] (not usually used in the progressive tenses) to understand sth: *'It opens like this.' 'Oh, I see.'* ◇ ~ sth *He didn't see the joke.* ◇ *I don't think she saw the point of the story.* ◇ ~ *to see/the need for sth / I can see both sides of the argument.* ◇ *Make Lydia see reason* (= be sensible), *will you?* ◇ ~ (that)... *Can't you see (that) he's taking advantage of you?* ◇ ~ **that** *I don't see that it matters what Josh thinks.* ◇ ~ what, why, etc... *'It's broken.' 'Oh yes, I see what you mean.'* ◇ *'Can we go swimming?' 'I don't see why not* (= yes, you can).' ⊃ SYNONYMS at UNDERSTAND
- **HAVE OPINION 10** B1 [T] ~ sth + adv./prep. (not usually used in the progressive tenses) to have an opinion of sth: *I see things differently now.* ◇ *Try to see things from her point of view.* ◇ *The way I see it, you have three main problems.* ◇ *As far as I can see* (= in my opinion), *you've done nothing wrong.* ⊃ SYNONYMS at REGARD
- **IMAGINE 11** B1 [T] (not used in the progressive tenses) to consider sth as a future possibility; to imagine sb/sth as sth: ~ sb/sth/yourself doing sth *I can't see her changing her mind.* ◇ ~ sb/sth/yourself as sth *His colleagues see him as a future director.* ⊃ SYNONYMS at IMAGINE
- **FIND OUT 12** B1 [I, T] (not usually used in the progressive tenses) to find out sth by looking, asking or waiting: *'Has the mail come yet?' 'I'll just go and see.'* ◇ *'Is he going to get better?' 'I don't know, we'll just have to wait and see.'* ◇ *We'll have a great time, you'll see.* ◇ ~ what, how, etc... *Go and see what the kids are doing, will you?* ◇ *We'll have to see how it goes.* ◇ ~ (that)... *I see (that) interest rates are going up again.* ◇ **it is seen that**... *It can be seen that certain groups are more at risk than others.* **13** [I, T] (not usually used in the progressive tenses) to find out or decide sth by thinking or considering: *'Will you be able to help*

1401

*us?' 'I don't know, I'll have to see.'* ◇ *'Can I go to the party?' 'We'll see* (= I'll decide later).' ◇ ~ **what, whether, etc**... *I'll see what I can do to help.*
- **MAKE SURE 14** [T] (not usually used in the progressive tenses) ~ **that**... to make sure that you do sth or that sth is done: *See that all the doors are locked before you leave.*
- **EXPERIENCE 15** [T] (not used in the progressive tenses) ~ sth to experience or suffer sth: *He has seen a great deal in his long life.* ◇ *I hope I never live to see the day when computers finally replace books.* ◇ *It didn't surprise her—she had seen it all before.*
- **WITNESS EVENT 16** [T] (not used in the progressive tenses) ~ sth to be the time when an event happens: *The twentieth century saw dramatic changes in most areas of life.* **17** [T] (not used in the progressive tenses) ~ sth to be the place where an event happens SYN *witness*: *This stadium has seen many thrilling football games.*
- **HELP 18** [T] ~ sb + adv./prep. to go with sb to help or protect them: *I saw the old lady across* (= helped her cross) *the road.* ◇ *May I see you home* (= go with you as far as your house)? ◇ *My secretary will see you out* (= show you the way out of the building).

IDM HELP Most idioms containing **see** are at the entries for the nouns and adjectives in the idioms, for example **not see the wood for the trees** is at **wood**. **for all (the world) to 'see** that can be seen clearly; in a way that can be seen clearly **let me 'see / let's 'see** (*informal*) used when you are thinking or trying to remember sth: *Now let me see— how old is she now?* **see sth 'coming** to realize that there is going to be a problem before it happens: *We should have seen it coming. There was no way he could keep going under all that pressure.* **see for your'self** to find out or look at sth yourself in order to be sure that what sb is saying is true: *If you don't believe me, go and see for yourself!* **see sb/sth for what they 'are/it 'is** to realize that sb/sth is not as good, pleasant, etc. as they/it seem **seeing that...** (*also informal* **seeing as (how)**...) because of the fact that...: *Seeing that he's been off sick all week he's unlikely to come.* **'see you (a'round/'later/'soon)** A1 | **(I'll) be 'seeing you** (*informal*) goodbye: *I'd better be going now. See you!* **you 'see** B1 (*informal*) used when you are explaining sth: *You see, the thing is, we won't be finished before Friday.*

PHRV **'see about sth** to deal with sth: *I must see about* (= prepare) *lunch.* ◇ *He says he won't help, does he? Well, we'll soon see about that* (= I will demand that he does help). ◇ **see about doing sth** *I'll have to see about getting that roof repaired.* **'see sth in sb/sth** to find sb/sth attractive or interesting: *I don't know what she sees in him.* **see sb↔'off 1** to go to a station, an airport, etc. to say goodbye to sb who is starting a journey **2** (*BrE*) to force sb to leave a place, for example by threatening them or running

▼ SYNONYMS

**see**

spot • catch • glimpse

These words all mean to become aware of sb/sth by using your eyes, especially suddenly or when it is not easy to see them/it.

**see** to become aware of sb/sth by using your eyes: *She looked for him but couldn't see him in the crowd.* ◇ *He could see (that) she had been crying.*

**spot** to see or notice sb/sth, especially suddenly or when they are not easy to see or notice: *I've just spotted a mistake on the front cover.*

**catch** to see or notice sth for a moment, but not clearly or completely: *She caught sight of a car in the distance.* ◇ *He caught a glimpse of himself in the mirror.*

**glimpse** (*literary*) to see sb/sth for a moment, but not clearly or completely: *He'd glimpsed her through the window as she passed.*

PATTERNS
- to see/spot **that/how/what/where/who**...
- to **suddenly** see/spot/glimpse sb/sth

# seed

after them: *The dogs saw them off in no time.* **3** (*BrE*) to defeat sb in a game, fight, etc: *The home team saw off the challengers by 68 points to 47.* **see sb↔out** (not used in the progressive tenses) (*BrE*) to last longer than the rest of sb's life: *I've had this coat for years, and I'm sure it will see me out.* **see sth↔out** (not used in the progressive tenses) (*BrE*) to reach the end or last until the end of sth: *They had enough fuel to see the winter out.* ◊ *He saw out his career in Italy.* **see 'over sth** (*BrE*) to visit and look at a place carefully: *We need to see over the house before we can make you an offer.* **see 'through sb/sth** (not used in the progressive tenses) to realize the truth about sb/sth: *We saw through him from the start.* ◊ *I can see through your little game* (= I am aware of the trick you are trying to play on me). **see sth 'through** (not usually used in the progressive tenses) to not give up doing a task, project, etc. until it is finished: *She's determined to see the job through.* **see sb 'through | see sb 'through sth** (not used in the progressive tenses) to give help or support to sb for a particular period of time: *Her courage and good humour saw her through.* ◊ *I only have $20 to see me through the week.* **'see to sth** to deal with sth: *Will you see to the arrangements for the next meeting?* ◊ *Don't worry—I'll see to it.* ◊ *We'll have to get that door seen to* (= repaired). **'see to it that …** to make sure that …: *Can you see to it that the email goes out this afternoon?*

■ *noun* (*formal*) the district or office of a BISHOP or an ARCH-BISHOP: *the Holy See* (= the office of the POPE)

**seed** /siːd/ *noun, verb*

■ *noun*
- **OF PLANTS/FRUIT 1** [C, U] the small hard part produced by a plant, from which a new plant can grow: *a packet of wild flower seeds* ◊ *sesame seeds* ◊ *to sow/plant seeds* ◊ *These vegetables can be grown from seed.* ◊ *seed potatoes* (= used for planting) ⊃ VISUAL VOCAB pages V5, V8 ⊃ see also BIRDSEED **2** [C] (*NAmE*) = PIP ⊃ VISUAL VOCAB page V4
- **BEGINNING 3** [C, usually pl.] **~ (of sth)** the beginning of a feeling or development that continues to grow: *the seeds of rebellion* ◊ *This planted the seeds of doubt in my mind.*
- **IN TENNIS 4** [C] (especially in tennis) one of the best players in a competition. The seeds are given a position in a list to try and make sure that they do not play each other in the early parts of the competition: *The top seed won comfortably.* ◊ *the number one seed*
- **OF A MAN 5** [U] (*old-fashioned* or *humorous*) SEMEN **6** [U] (*literary*) all the people who are the children, GRANDCHILDREN, etc. of one man
- **IDM go/run to 'seed 1** (especially of a vegetable plant) to produce flowers and seeds as well as leaves **2** to become much less attractive or good because of lack of attention: *After his divorce, he let himself go to seed.* ⊃ more at SOW¹

■ *verb*
- **OF A PLANT 1** [I] to produce seeds **2** [T] **~ itself** to produce other plants using its own seeds
- **AREA OF GROUND 3** [T, usually passive] to plant seeds in an area of ground: **be seeded (with sth)** *The site has been seeded with prairie grasses and wildflowers.* ◊ *a newly seeded lawn*
- **IN TENNIS 4** [T, usually passive] to make sb a seed in a competition: **be seeded** *He has been seeded 14th at Wimbledon next week.*

**seed·bed** /ˈsiːdbed/ *noun* **1** an area of soil which has been specially prepared for planting seeds in **2** [usually sing.] **~ (of/for sth)** a place or situation in which sth can develop

**'seed corn** *noun* [U] **1** the grain that is kept for planting the next year's crops **2** people or things that will be successful or useful in the future

**seed·ed** /ˈsiːdɪd/ *adj.* **1** (especially of a tennis player) given a number showing that they are one of the best players in a particular competition: *a seeded player* **2** (of fruit) with the seeds removed: *seeded tomatoes*

**seed·less** /ˈsiːdləs/ *adj.* [usually before noun] (of fruit) having no seeds: *seedless grapes*

**seed·ling** /ˈsiːdlɪŋ/ *noun* a young plant that has grown from a seed

**'seed money** (also **'seed capital**) *noun* [U] money to start a new business, project, etc.

**seedy** /ˈsiːdi/ *adj.* (**seed·ier**, **seedi·est**) (*disapproving*) dirty and unpleasant, possibly connected with bad or illegal activities: *a seedy bar* ◊ *the seedy world of prostitution* ◊ *a seedy-looking man* ▶ **seedi·ness** *noun* [U]

**Seeing 'Eye dog™** *noun* (*NAmE*) = GUIDE DOG

**seek** /siːk/ *verb* (**sought**, **sought** /sɔːt/) (*formal*) **1** [T, I] to look for sb/sth: *Drivers are advised to seek alternative routes.* ◊ **~ for sth/sb** (*BrE*) *They sought in vain for somewhere to shelter.* **2** [T] to ask sb for sth; to try to obtain or achieve sth: **~ sth** *I think it's time we sought legal advice.* ◊ *They sought refuge in the mountain villages.* ◊ *The pilot sought permission to land.* ◊ **~ sth from sb** *She managed to calm him down and seek help from a neighbour.* ◊ **~ for sth/sb** (*BrE*) *They came seeking for the truth.* **3** [I] **~ to do sth** to try to do sth SYN attempt: *He sought to establish himself as a writer.* **4 -seeking** (in adjectives and nouns) looking for or trying to get the thing mentioned; the activity of doing this: *attention-seeking behaviour* ◊ *Voluntary work can provide a framework for job-seeking.* ⊃ see also HEAT-SEEKING, HIDE-AND-SEEK, RENT-SEEKING, SELF-SEEKING
- **IDM seek your 'fortune** (*literary*) to try to find a way to become rich, especially by going to another place
- **PHRV ,seek sb/sth 'out** to look for and find sb/sth, especially when this involves using a lot of effort

**seek·er** /ˈsiːkə(r)/ *noun* (often in compounds) a person who is trying to find or get the thing mentioned: *an attention/a publicity seeker* ◊ *seekers after the truth* ⊃ see also ASYLUM SEEKER, JOB SEEKER

**seem** /siːm/ *linking verb* **1** (not used in the progressive tenses) to give the impression of being or doing sth SYN appear: **+ adj.** *You seem happy.* ◊ *Do whatever seems best to you.* ◊ **+ noun** *He seems a nice man.* ◊ **~ to be sth** *She seems to be a smart woman.* ◊ **~ like sth** *It seemed like a good idea at the time.* ◊ **~ as though …** *It always seemed as though they would get married.* ◊ **it seems (to sb) (that) …** *It seems to me that teachers have to work pretty hard.* ◊ **~ to do/have sth** *They seem to know what they're doing.* **2** **~ to do/be/have sth** used to make what you say about your thoughts, feelings or actions less strong: *I seem to have left my book at home.* ◊ *I can't seem to* (= I've tried, but I can't) *get started today.* **3 it seems | it would seem** used to suggest that sth is true when you are not certain or when you want to be polite: **~ (that) …** *It would seem that we all agree.* ◊ **+ adj.** *It seems only reasonable to ask students to buy a dictionary.* ⊃ LANGUAGE BANK at IMPERSONAL, OPINION, PERHAPS

**seem·ing** /ˈsiːmɪŋ/ *adj.* [only before noun] (*formal*) appearing to be sth that may not be true SYN apparent: *a seeming impossibility* ◊ *She handled the matter with seeming indifference.*

**seem·ing·ly** /ˈsiːmɪŋli/ *adv.* **1** in a way that appears to be true but may in fact not be: *a seemingly stupid question* ◊ *a seemingly endless journey* **2** (*formal*) according to what you have read or heard SYN apparently: *Seemingly, he borrowed the money from the bank.*

**seem·ly** /ˈsiːmli/ *adj.* (*old-fashioned* or *formal*) appropriate for a particular social situation OPP unseemly

**seen** /siːn/ *past part.* OF SEE ⊃ HOMOPHONES at SCENE

**seep** /siːp/ *verb* [I] **+ adv./prep.** (especially of liquids) to flow slowly and in small quantities through sth or into sth SYN trickle: *Blood was beginning to seep through the bandages.* ◊ *Water seeped from a crack in the pipe.* ◊ (*figurative*) *Gradually the pain seeped away.*

**seep·age** /ˈsiːpɪdʒ/ *noun* [U, C, usually pl.] the process by which a liquid flows slowly and in small quantities through sth; the result of this process: *Water gradually escapes by seepage through the ground.* ◊ *oil seepages*

**seer** /sɪə(r)/; *NAmE* sɪr/ *noun* (*literary*) (especially in the past) a person who claims that they can see what is going to happen in the future SYN **prophet**

**'see-saw** (*especially BrE*) (*also* **see-saw** *especially in NAmE*) *noun, verb*
- *noun* **1** (*NAmE also* **'teeter-totter**) [C] a piece of equipment for children to play on consisting of a long flat piece of wood that is supported in the middle. A child sits at each end and makes the see-saw move up and down: *Can we go on the see-saw?* **2** [sing.] a situation in which things keep changing from one state to another and back again: *The match was a see-saw battle between the two teams.*
- *verb* [I] ~ **(from A to B)** to keep changing from one situation, opinion, emotion, etc. to another and back again: *Her emotions see-sawed from anger to fear.* ◊ *Share prices see-sawed all day.*

**seethe** /siːð/ *verb* [I] **1** to be extremely angry about sth but to try not to show other people how angry you are SYN **fume**: *She seethed silently in the corner.* ◊ ~ **with sth** *He marched off, seething with frustration.* ◊ ~ **at sth** *Inwardly he was seething at this challenge to his authority.* **2** ~ **(with sth)** (of a place) to be full of a lot of people or animals, especially when they are all moving around: *The resort is seething with tourists all year round.* ◊ *He became caught up in a seething mass of arms and legs.* **3** (*literary*) (of liquids) to move around quickly and violently: *The grey ocean seethed beneath them.*

**'see-through** *adj.* (of cloth) very thin so that you can see through it: *a see-through blouse*

**seg·ment** ⓘ+ C1 W *noun, verb*
- *noun* /ˈseɡmənt/ **1** ⓘ+ C1 a part of sth that is separate from the other parts or can be considered separately: *She cleaned a small segment of the painting.* ◊ *Lines divided the area into segments.* **2** one of the sections of an orange, a lemon, etc. ⊃ VISUAL VOCAB page V4 **3** (*geometry*) a part of a circle separated from the rest by a single line ⊃ picture at CIRCLE **4** (*phonetics*) the smallest speech sound that a word can be divided into
- *verb* /seɡˈment/ [often passive] ~ **sth** (*specialist*) to divide sth into different parts: *Market researchers often segment the population on the basis of age and social class.* ◊ *The worm has a segmented body* (= with different sections joined together).

**seg·men·ta·tion** /ˌseɡmenˈteɪʃn/ *noun* [U, C, usually pl.] (*specialist*) the act of dividing sth into different parts; one of these parts

**seg·re·gate** /ˈseɡrɪɡeɪt/ *verb* (*formal*) **1** ~ **sb (from sb)** to separate people of different races, religions or sexes and treat them in a different way: *a culture in which women are segregated from men* ◊ *a racially segregated community* ◊ *a segregated school* (= one for students of one race or religion only) OPP **integrate 2** ~ **sth (from sth)** to keep one thing separate from another: *Pedestrians are segregated from the traffic by a metal barrier.*

**seg·re·ga·tion** /ˌseɡrɪˈɡeɪʃn/ *noun* [U] (*formal*) **1** the act or policy of separating people of different races, religions or sexes and treating them in a different way: **racial/religious segregation** ◊ *segregation by age and sex* **2** ~ **(of A) (and/from B)** (*formal*) the act of separating people or things from a larger group: *The report recommends segregation of cyclists from both cars and pedestrians.*

**seg·re·ga·tion·ist** /ˌseɡrɪˈɡeɪʃənɪst/ *adj.* believing that people should be separated according to their sex, race or religion: *segregationist policies* ▶ **seg·re·ga·tion·ist** *noun*

**segue** /ˈseɡweɪ/ *verb* [I] + **adv./prep.** to move smoothly from one song, subject, place, etc. to another: *a spiritual that segued into a singalong chorus* ◊ *He then segued into a discussion of atheism.* ▶ **segue** *noun*

**Seg·way**™ /ˈseɡweɪ/ *noun* a vehicle with a motor and two wheels attached to a platform with a tall handle. The rider holds the handle and puts both feet on the platform.

**seine** /seɪn/ (*also* **'seine net**) *noun* a type of fishing net which hangs down in the water and is pulled together at the ends to catch fish

1403 **select**

**seis·mic** /ˈsaɪzmɪk/ *adj.* [only before noun] **1** connected with or caused by earthquakes: *seismic waves* **2** having a very great effect; of very great size: *a seismic shift in the political process*

**seis·mo·graph** /ˈsaɪzməɡrɑːf; *NAmE* -ɡræf/ *noun* an instrument that measures and records information about earthquakes

**seis·mol·ogy** /saɪzˈmɒlədʒi; *NAmE* -ˈmɑːl-/ *noun* [U] the scientific study of earthquakes ▶ **seis·mo·log·ic·al** /ˌsaɪzməˈlɒdʒɪkl; *NAmE* -ˈlɑːdʒ-/ *adj*.: *the National Seismological Institute* **seis·molo·gist** /ˌsaɪzˈmɒlədʒɪst; *NAmE* -ˈmɑːl-/ *noun*

**seize** ⓘ+ C1 /siːz/ *verb* **1** ⓘ+ C1 [T] to take sb/sth in your hand suddenly and using force SYN **grab**: ~ **sth from sb** *She tried to seize the gun from him.* ◊ ~ **sb/sth** *He seized her by the arm.* ◊ *She seized hold of my hand.* **2** ⓘ+ C1 [T] ~ **sth (from sb)** to take control of a place or situation, often suddenly and violently: *They seized the airport in a surprise attack.* ◊ *The army has seized control of the country.* ◊ *He seized power in a military coup.* **3** ⓘ+ C1 [T] ~ **sb** to arrest or capture sb: *The men were seized as they left the building.* **4** ⓘ+ C1 [T] ~ **sth** to take illegal or stolen goods away from sb: *A large quantity of drugs was seized during the raid.* **5** ⓘ+ C1 [T] ~ **a chance, an opportunity, the initiative, etc.** to be quick to make use of a chance, an opportunity, etc. SYN **grab**: *The party seized the initiative with both hands* (= quickly and with enthusiasm). **6** [T] ~ **sb** (of an emotion) to affect sb suddenly and deeply: *Panic seized her.* ◊ *He was seized by curiosity.* **7** [I] (*NAmE*) = SEIZE UP
PHRV **'seize on/upon sth** to suddenly show a lot of interest in sth, especially because you can use it to your advantage SYN **pounce on/upon**: *The rumours were eagerly seized upon by the local press.* **,seize 'up** (*NAmE also* **seize**) **1** if a machine **seizes up**, it no longer works because the parts are STUCK and cannot move **2** if a part of your body **seizes up**, you are unable to move it easily and it is often painful

▼ HOMOPHONES

seas • sees • seize /siːz/
- **seas** *noun* (*plural of* SEA): *The pirate was a renowned terror of the eastern seas.*
- **sees** *verb* (*third person of* SEE): *It's a secret—make sure nobody sees!*
- **seize** *verb*: *She was eager to seize any opportunity that was offered.*

**seiz·ure** /ˈsiːʒə(r)/ *noun* **1** [U, C] ~ **(of sth)** the use of legal authority to take sth from sb; an amount of sth that is taken in this way: *The court ordered the seizure of his assets.* ◊ *the largest ever seizure of cocaine at a British port* **2** [U] ~ **of sth** the act of using force to take control of a country, town, etc: *the army's seizure of power* ◊ *the seizure of Burma by Japan in 1942* **3** [C] (*o'd-fashioned*) a sudden attack of an illness, especially one that affects the brain

**sel·dom** ⓘ+ C1 /ˈseldəm/ *adv.* not often SYN **rarely**: *He had seldom seen a child with so much talent.* ◊ *She seldom, if ever, goes to the theatre.* ◊ *They seldom watch television these days.* ◊ (*literary*) *Seldom had he seen such beauty.*

**se·lect** ⓘ B2 W /sɪˈlekt/ *verb, adj.*
- *verb* **1** ⓘ B2 [T, I] to choose sb/sth from a group of people or things, usually according to a system: ~ **sb/sth for sth** *He hasn't been selected for the team.* ◊ *All our hotels have been carefully selected for the excellent value they provide.* ◊ ~ **sb/sth as sth** *She was selected as the parliamentary candidate for Bath.* ◊ ~ **sb/sth** *a randomly selected sample of 23 schools* ◊ *This model is available at selected stores only.* ◊ ~ **sb/sth to do sth** *Six theatre companies have been selected to take part in this year's festival.* ◊ ~ **what, which, etc.** *Select what you want from the options available.* ◊ ~ **from sth** *They could select from a range of choices depending on their interests and skills.* ⊃ SYNONYMS at CHOOSE **2** ~ **sth** (*computing*) to mark sth on a computer screen; to choose sth, especially from a menu: *Select the*

## select committee 1404

text you want to format by holding down the left button on your mouse. ◊ *Select 'New Mail' from the 'Send' menu.* ⊃ **WORDFINDER NOTE** at **COMMAND**
■ *adj.* **1** [only before noun] carefully chosen as the best out of a larger group of people or things: *a select wine list* ◊ *Only a select few* (= a small number of people) *have been invited to the wedding.* **2** (of a society, club, place, etc.) used by people who have a lot of money or a high social position **SYN exclusive**: *They live in a very select area.* ◊ *a select club*

**se**,**lect com**'**mittee** *noun* (in the UK) a small group of politicians or experts that have been chosen to examine a particular subject or problem

**se·lec·tion** **B2** /sɪˈlekʃn/ *noun* **1** **B2** [U] the process of choosing sb/sth from a group of people or things, usually according to a system: *She took a long time to make her selection.* ◊ *the random selection of numbers* ◊ *selection criteria* ◊ *the selection process* ⊃ see also **SELF-SELECTION** **2** **B2** [C] a number of people or things that have been chosen from a larger group: ~ *of sth A selection of readers' comments is published below.* ⊃ **SYNONYMS** at **CHOICE** **3** [C] a collection of things from which sth can be chosen **SYN choice, range**: ~ **of sth** *The showroom has a wide selection of kitchens.* ⊃ see also **NATURAL SELECTION**

**se**'**lection committee** *noun* a group of people who choose, for example, the members of a sports team

**se·lect·ive** **C1** /sɪˈlektɪv/ *adj.* **1** **C1** [usually before noun] affecting or involving only a small number of people or things from a larger group: *the selective breeding of cattle* ◊ *selective strike action* **2** **C1** ~ (**about/in sth**) tending to be careful about what or who you choose: *You will have to be selective about which information to include in the report.* ◊ *Their admissions policy is very selective.* ◊ *a selective school* (= one that chooses which children to admit, especially according to ability) ▸ **se·lect·ive·ly** *adv.*: *The product will be selectively marketed in the US* (= only in some areas). **se·lect·iv·ity** /sə,lek'tɪvəti/ *noun* [U]: *Schools are tending towards greater selectivity.*

**se**,**lective** '**service** *noun* [U] (*NAmE*) a system in which people have to spend a period of time in the armed forces by law

**se·lect·or** /sɪˈlektə(r)/ *noun* **1** (*BrE*) a person who chooses the members of a particular sports team **2** a device in an engine, a machine, etc. that allows you to choose a particular function

**sel·en·ium** /səˈliːniəm/ *noun* [U] (*symb.* **Se**) a chemical element. Selenium is a grey substance that is used in making electrical equipment and coloured glass. A lack of selenium in the human body can lead to illnesses such as DEPRESSION.

**self** **B2** /self/ *noun* (*pl.* **selves** /selvz/) **1** **B2** [C, usually sing.] the type of person you are, especially the way you normally behave, look or feel: *You'll soon be feeling your old self again* (= feeling well or happy again). ◊ *He's not his usual happy self this morning.* ◊ *Only with a few people could she be her real self* (= show what she was really like rather than what she pretended to be). **2** [U] (*also* **the self** [sing.]) (*formal*) a person's personality or character that makes them different from other people: *Many people living in institutions have lost their sense of self* (= the feeling that they are individual people). ◊ *the inner self* (= a person's emotional and spiritual character) ◊ *a lack of confidence in the self* **3** [U] (*formal*) your own advantage or pleasure rather than that of other people: *She didn't do it for any reason of self.* **4** [C] used to refer to a person: *You didn't hurt your little self, did you?* ◊ *We look forward to seeing Mrs Brown and your good self this evening.* **IDM** see FORMER *adj.*

**self-** /self/ *combining form* (in nouns and adjectives) of, to or by yourself or itself: *self-control* ◊ *self-addressed* ◊ *self-taught*

**self-ab**'**sorbed** *adj.* only thinking about or interested in yourself ▸ **self-ab**'**sorp·tion** *noun* [U]

**self-a**'**buse** /self əˈbjuːs/ *noun* [U] **1** behaviour by which a person does harm to himself or herself **2** (*old-fashioned*) = MASTURBATION

**self-**'**access** *noun* [U] a method of learning in which students choose their materials and use them to study on their own: *a self-access centre/library*

**self-actual·i**'**za·tion** *noun* [U] the fact of using your skills and abilities and achieving as much as you can possibly achieve **SYN self-realization**

**self-ad**'**dressed** *adj.* if an ENVELOPE is **self-addressed**, sb has written their own address on it

**self-ad**'**hesive** *adj.* [usually before noun] covered on one side with a sticky substance so that it can be stuck to sth without the use of GLUE, etc: *self-adhesive tape*

**self-a**'**nalysis** *noun* [U] the study of your own character and behaviour, especially your reasons for doing things

**self-ap**'**point·ed** *adj.* [usually before noun] (*usually disapproving*) giving yourself a particular title, job, etc., especially without the agreement of other people: *self-appointed experts*

**self-ap**'**prais·al** *noun* [U, C] an act or the process of judging your own work or achievements

**self-as**'**sembly** *adj.* (*BrE*) (of furniture) bought in several parts that you have to put together yourself: *cheap self-assembly kitchen units* ▸ **self-as**'**sembly** *noun* [U]: *kitchen units for self-assembly*

**self-as**'**sess·ment** *noun* [U] **1** the process of judging your own progress, achievements, etc. **2** (in the UK) a system of paying tax in which you calculate yourself how much you should pay

**self-as**'**sured** *adj.* having a lot of confidence in yourself and your abilities **SYN confident** ▸ **self-as**'**sur·ance** *noun* [U]

**self-a**'**wareness** *noun* [U] knowledge and understanding of your own character ▸ **self-a**'**ware** *adj.*

**self-**'**build** *noun* [U, C] (*BrE*) the building of homes by their owners; a home that is built in this way: *self-build houses*

**self-**'**catering** *adj.* [usually before noun] (*BrE*) a **self-catering** holiday is one which provides you with accommodation and the equipment that is necessary to cook your own meals: *self-catering accommodation* ⊃ **WORDFINDER NOTE** at **HOLIDAY** ▸ **self-**'**catering** *noun* [U] (*BrE*): *All prices are based on a week's self-catering in shared accommodation.*

**self-**'**centred** (*US* **self-**'**centered**) *adj.* (*disapproving*) tending to think only about yourself and not thinking about the needs or feelings of other people ▸ **self-**'**centred·ness** (*US* **self-**'**centered·ness**) *noun* [U]

**self-**'**checkout** *noun* a system that enables customers in a shop, especially a supermarket, to scan and pay for goods without help from a shop assistant

**self-con**'**fessed** *adj.* [only before noun] admitting that you are a particular type of person or have a particular problem, especially a bad one: *a self-confessed thief*

**self-**'**confident** *adj.* having confidence in yourself and your abilities **SYN self-assured, confident**: *a self-confident child* ◊ *a self-confident manner* ▸ **self-**'**confidence** *noun* [U]: *He has no self-confidence.*

**self-con·gratu·la·tion** *noun* [U] (*usually disapproving*) a way of behaving that shows that you think you have done sth very well and are pleased with yourself ▸ **self-con·gratu·la·tory** *adj.*: *The winners gave themselves a self-congratulatory round of applause.*

**self-**'**conscious** *adj.* **1** ~ (**about sth**) nervous or embarrassed about your appearance or what other people think of you: *He's always been self-conscious about being so short.* **2** (*often disapproving*) done in a way that shows you are aware of the effect that is being produced: *The humour of the play is self-conscious and contrived.* **OPP unselfconscious** ▸ **self-**'**conscious·ly** *adv.*: *She was self-consciously aware of his stare.* **self-**'**conscious·ness** *noun* [U]

**self-con**'**tained** *adj.* **1** not needing or depending on other people: *Her father was a quiet, self-contained man.* **2** able

b **b**ad | d **d**id | f **f**all | g **g**et | h **h**at | j **y**es | k **c**at | l **l**eg | m **m**an | n **n**ow | p **p**en | r **r**ed

to operate or exist without outside help or influence **SYN** independent: *a self-contained community* ◊ *Each chapter is self-contained and can be studied in isolation.* **3** [usually before noun] (*BrE*) (of a flat/an apartment) having its own kitchen, bathroom and entrance: *self-contained accommodation*

**self-contra·dict·ory** *adj.* containing two ideas or statements that cannot both be true ▶ **self-contra·dic·tion** *noun* [U]

**self-con·trol** *noun* [U] the ability to remain calm and not show your emotions even though you are feeling angry, excited, etc: *to lose/regain your self-control* ◊ *It took all his self-control not to shout at them.* ▶ **self-con·trolled** *adj.*

**self-cor·rect·ing** *adj.* [usually before noun] that corrects or changes itself without outside help: *The economic market is a self-correcting mechanism, that does not need regulation by government.*

**self-criti·cism** *noun* [U] the process of looking at and judging your own faults or weaknesses ▶ **self-critical** *adj.*: *Don't be too self-critical.*

**self-de·cep·tion** *noun* [U] the act of making yourself believe sth that you know is not true

**self-de·feat·ing** *adj.* causing more problems and difficulties instead of solving them; not achieving what you wanted to achieve but having an opposite effect: *Paying children too much attention when they misbehave can be self-defeating.*

**self-de·fence** (*US* **self-de·fense**) *noun* [U] **1** something you say or do in order to protect yourself when you are being attacked, criticized, etc: **in~** *The man later told police that he was acting in self-defence.* **2** the skill of being able to protect yourself from physical attack without using weapons: *I'm taking classes in self-defence.*

**self-de·lu·sion** *noun* [U] the act of making yourself believe sth that you know is not true

**self-de·nial** *noun* [U] the act of not having or doing the things you like, either because you do not have enough money, or for moral or religious reasons **SYN** abstinence

**self-depre·cat·ing** /ˌself ˈdeprəkeɪtɪŋ/ *adj.* done in a way that makes your own achievements or abilities seem unimportant: *He gave a self-deprecating shrug.* ▶ **self-depre·ca·tion** /ˌself deprəˈkeɪʃn/ *noun* [U]

**self-de·scribed** *adj.* [only before noun] using particular words to describe yourself, although your description may not be true or accurate: *He's a self-described 'nice guy'.* ⊃ compare SELF-STYLED

**self-de·struct** *verb* [I] (especially of a machine, etc.) to destroy itself, usually by exploding: *This tape will self-destruct in 30 seconds.* ◊ (*figurative*) *In the last half hour of the movie the plot rapidly self-destructs.*

**self-de·struc·tion** *noun* [U] the act of doing things to deliberately harm yourself ▶ **self-de·struc·tive** *adj.*

**self-de·ter·min·ation** *noun* [U] (*formal*) **1** the right of a country or a region and its people to be independent and to choose their own government and political system **SYN** independence **2** the right or ability of a person to control their own FATE

**self-de·vel·op·ment** *noun* [U] the process by which a person's character and abilities are developed: *Staff are encouraged to use the library for professional self-development.*

**self-dis·cip·line** *noun* [U] the ability to make yourself do sth, especially sth difficult or unpleasant: *It takes a lot of self-discipline to go jogging in winter.*

**self-dis·cov·ery** *noun* [U] the process of understanding more about yourself in order to make yourself happier: *David left his boring job to go on a journey of self-discovery.*

**self-doubt** *noun* [U, C] the feeling that you are not good enough

**self-drive** *adj.* [only before noun] (*BrE*) **1** a **self-drive** car is one that you hire and drive yourself **2** a **self-drive** holiday is one on which you use your own car or a car you hire to travel to the holiday area

**self-driving** (*also* **au·tono·mous**, **driver·less**) *adj.* (of a vehicle) that has the technology to drive itself without a person in control: *self-driving cars*

**self-educated** *adj.* having learned things by reading books, etc. rather than at school or college

**self-ef·facing** *adj.* not wanting to attract attention to yourself or your abilities **SYN** modest: *He was a shy, self-effacing man.* ▶ **self-ef·face·ment** *noun* [U]

**self-em·ployed** *adj.* working for yourself and not employed by a company, etc: *a self-employed musician* ◊ *retirement plans for the self-employed* (= people who are self-employed) ▶ **self-em·ploy·ment** *noun* [U]

**self-esteem** *noun* [U] a feeling of being happy with your own character and abilities **SYN** self-worth: *to have high/low self-esteem* ◊ *You need to build your self-esteem.*

**self-evident** *adj.* obvious and needing no further proof or explanation: *The dangers of such action are self-evident.* ◊ *a self-evident truth* ▶ **self-evident·ly** *adv.*

**self-exam·in·ation** *noun* [U] **1** the study of your own behaviour and beliefs to find out if they are right or wrong **2** the act of checking your body for any signs of illness

**self-ex·plana·tory** *adj.* easy to understand and not needing any more explanation

**self-ex·pres·sion** *noun* [U] the expression of your thoughts or feelings, especially through activities such as writing, painting, dancing, etc: *You should encourage your child's attempts at self-expression.*

**self-ful·fil·ling** *adj.* [usually before noun] a **self-fulfilling** PROPHECY is one that becomes true because people expect it to be true and behave in a way that will make it happen: *If you expect to fail, you will fail. It's a self-fulfilling prophecy.*

**self-ful·fil·ment** (*BrE*) (*NAmE* **self-ful·fill·ment**) *noun* [U] the feeling of being happy and satisfied that you have everything you want or need

**self-govern·ment** *noun* [U] the government or control of a country or an organization by its own people or members, not by others ▶ **self-govern·ing** *adj.*

**self-harm** *noun* [U] the practice of deliberately injuring yourself, for example by cutting yourself, as a result of having serious emotional or mental problems ▶ **self-harm** *verb* [I]: *As a teenager I was self-harming regularly.*

**self-help** *noun* [U] the act of relying on your own efforts and abilities in order to solve your problems, rather than depending on other people for help ▶ **self-help** *adj.* [only before noun]: *a self-help discussion group for people suffering from depression* (= whose members help each other)

**self-iden·tify** *verb* [I, T] to recognize that you have a particular characteristic or belong to a particular category: **~(as sth)** *to self-identify as Christian/Muslim/atheist* ◊ **~sth** *Students at the college have the right to self-identify their gender.* ▶ **self-iden·ti·fi·ca·tion** *noun* [U] **~(as sth)**: *her self-identification as a feminist*

**self-iden·tity** *noun* [U, sing.] the way sb considers their characteristics as a particular individual, especially in relation to the social environment they live or work in: *She has a strong sense of self-identity.* ◊ *Play can help children develop a positive self-identity.*

**selfie** /ˈselfi/ *noun* (*informal*) a photo of yourself that you take, typically with a smartphone or WEBCAM, and usually put on SOCIAL MEDIA

**selfie stick** *noun* a long stick on which you can put your camera or smartphone in order to take a photo of yourself from further away than if you hold the camera or phone in your hand

**self-image** *noun* the opinion or idea you have of yourself, especially of your appearance or abilities: *to have a positive/negative self-image*

**self-im·port·ant** *adj.* (*disapproving*) thinking that you are more important than other people **SYN** arrogant ▶ **self-im·port·ance** *noun* [U], **self-im·port·ant·ly** *adv.*

**self-im'posed** adj. [usually before noun] a **self-imposed** task, duty, etc. is one that you force yourself to do rather than one that sb else forces you to do

**self-im'prove·ment** noun [U] the process by which a person improves their knowledge, status, character, etc. by their own efforts

**self-in'duced** adj. (of illness, problems, etc.) caused by yourself: *self-induced vomiting*

**self-in'dulgent** adj. (disapproving) allowing yourself to have or do things that you like, especially when you do this too much or too often ▶ **self-in'dulgence** noun [U]

**self-in'flict·ed** adj. a **self-inflicted** injury, problem, etc. is one that you cause for yourself: *a self-inflicted wound*

**self-'interest** noun [U] (disapproving) the fact of sb only considering their own interests and of not caring about things that would help other people: *Not all of them were acting out of self-interest.* ▶ **self-'interest·ed** adj.

**self-in'volved** adj. thinking so much about yourself and your own interests that you do not pay enough attention to other people or things

**self·ish** /ˈselfɪʃ/ adj. (disapproving) caring only about yourself rather than about other people: *selfish behaviour* ◊ *Do you think I'm being selfish by not letting her go?* ◊ *What a selfish thing to do!* ◊ *It was selfish of him to leave all the work to you.* **OPP** unselfish, selfless ▶ **self·ish·ly** adv.: *She looked forward, a little selfishly, to a weekend away from her family.* **self·ish·ness** noun [U]

**self-'knowledge** noun [U] an understanding of yourself

**self·less** /ˈselfləs/ adj. (approving) thinking more about the needs, happiness, etc. of other people than about your own: *a life of selfless service to the community* **OPP** selfish ▶ **self·less·ly** adv. **self·less·ness** noun [U]

**self-'loathing** noun [U] a strong feeling of hating yourself

**self-'love** noun [U] the feeling that your own happiness and wishes are important

**self-'made** adj. [usually before noun] having become rich and successful through your own hard work rather than having had money given to you: *He was proud of the fact that he was a self-made man.*

**self-'manage·ment** noun [U] **1** the act of taking responsibility for your behaviour, health and happiness, or for the organization of your work activities: *This role requires strong self-management skills.* **2** the act of dealing with a medical condition, etc. by yourself: *self-management of chronic conditions*

**self-'medicate** verb [I, T] **1** to take medicine or drugs without getting permission from a doctor or without following a doctor's instructions: ~ *for sth A lot of people self-medicate for minor ailments like colds.* ◊ ~ *(sth) (with sth) She self-medicated her symptoms with herbal remedies.* **2** to drink or take drugs to reduce feelings of stress or try to improve other health problems: ~ *for sth He spent years abusing drugs to self-medicate for depression.* ◊ ~ *(sth) (with sth) People sometimes self-medicate their mental health issues with drugs or alcohol.*

**self-'motivated** adj. if a person is **self-motivated**, they are capable of hard work and effort without the need for pressure from others ▶ **self-moti'vation** noun [U]

**self-muti'lation** noun [U] the act of wounding yourself, especially when this is a sign of mental illness

**self-ob'sessed** adj. thinking or worrying continuously about your own life and circumstances so that you do not think of anything else; thinking only about yourself

**self-o'pinion·ated** adj. (disapproving) believing that your own opinions are always right and refusing to listen to those of other people **SYN** opinionated

**self-per'petu·at·ing** adj. continuing without any outside influence: *Revenge leads to a self-perpetuating cycle of violence.*

**self-'pity** noun [U] (often disapproving) a feeling of SADNESS for yourself, especially because of sth unpleasant or unfair that has happened to you: *She's not someone who likes to wallow in self-pity.* ▶ **self-'pitying** adj.

**self-'portrait** noun a painting, etc. that you do of yourself

**self-pos'sessed** adj. able to remain calm and confident in a difficult situation ▶ **self-pos'session** noun [U]: *He soon recovered his usual self-possession.*

**self-preser'vation** noun [U] the fact of protecting yourself in a dangerous or difficult situation: *She was held back by some sense of self-preservation.*

**self-pro'claimed** adj. (often disapproving) giving yourself a particular title, job, etc. without the agreement or permission of other people

**self-pro'motion** noun [U] (disapproving) the activity of making people notice you and your abilities, especially in a way that annoys other people: *The article was a piece of blatant self-promotion.*

**self-raising 'flour** (US **baking flour**, **self-rising 'flour**) noun [U] flour that contains BAKING POWDER ⊃ compare PLAIN FLOUR

**self-reali'zation** (BrE also **-isation**) noun [U] the fact of using your skills and abilities and achieving as much as you can possibly achieve **SYN** self-actualization

**self-referen·tial** /ˌself refəˈrenʃl/ adj. (specialist) (of a work of literature) referring to the fact of actually being a work of literature, or to the author, or to other works that the author has written

**self-re'flection** noun [U] serious thought about your own character and actions

**self-re'gard** noun [U] a good opinion of yourself, which is considered bad if you have too little or too much: *He suffers from a lack of self-regard.* ▶ **self-re'gard·ing** adj.: *His autobiography is nothing but self-regarding nonsense.*

**self-'regulat·ing** adj. something that is **self-regulating** controls itself: *a self-regulating economy* ▶ **self-regu'lation** noun [U]

**self-re'liant** adj. able to do or decide things by yourself, rather than depending on other people for help **SYN** independent ▶ **self-re'liance** noun [U]

**self-re'port** verb, noun
■ verb ~ sth | ~ whether, what, etc ... | ~ that ... to give details about an aspect of your life, typically relating to your physical or mental condition: *Participants in the survey had to self-report their health status.*
■ noun (often used before another noun) details that you provide about an aspect of your life, typically relating to your physical or mental condition: *a self-report questionnaire*

**self-re'spect** noun [U] a feeling of being proud of yourself and that what you do, say, etc. is right and good

**self-re'spect·ing** adj. [only before noun] (especially in negative sentences) being proud of yourself because you believe that what you do is right and good: *No self-respecting journalist would ever work for that newspaper.*

**self-re'straint** noun [U] the ability to stop yourself doing or saying sth that you want to because you know it is better not to: *She exercised all her self-restraint and kept quiet.*

**self-'righteous** adj. (disapproving) feeling or behaving as if what you say or do is always morally right, and other people are wrong **SYN** sanctimonious ▶ **self-'righteous·ly** adv. **self-'righteous·ness** noun [U]

**self-rising 'flour** (also **baking flour**) (both US **self-raising 'flour**) noun [U] flour that contains BAKING POWDER ⊃ compare ALL-PURPOSE FLOUR

**self-'rule** noun [U] the governing of a country or an area by its own people

**self-'sacrifice** noun [U] (approving) the act of not allowing yourself to have or do sth in order to help other people: *the courage and self-sacrifice of those who fought in the war* ▶ **self-'sacrifi·cing** adj.

**self·same** /ˈselfseɪm/ adj. [only before noun] **the, this, etc. selfsame ...** used to emphasize that two people or things are the same **SYN** identical: *Jane had been wondering that selfsame thing.*

---

æ cat | ɑː father | e bed | ɜː fur | ə about | ɪ sit | iː see | i happy | ɒ got (BrE) | ɔː saw | ʌ cup | ʊ put | uː too

**self-ˈsatisfied** *adj.* (*disapproving*) too pleased with yourself or your own achievements **SYN** smug: *He had a self-satisfied smirk on his face.* ▶ **self-satisˈfaction** *noun* [U]: *a look of self-satisfaction*

**self-ˈseeking** *adj.* (*disapproving*) interested only in your own needs and interests rather than thinking about the needs of other people ▶ **self-ˈseeking** *noun* [U]

**self-seˈlection** *noun* [U] a situation in which people decide for themselves to do sth rather than being chosen to do it ▶ **self-seˈlecting** *adj.*: *a self-selecting group* **self-seˈlected** *adj.*

**self-ˈservice** *adj.* [usually before noun] a **self-service** shop, restaurant, etc. is one in which customers serve themselves and then pay for the goods ▶ **self-ˈservice** *noun* [U]: *The cafe provides quick self-service at low prices.*

**self-ˈserving** *adj.* (*disapproving*) interested only in gaining an advantage for yourself

**self-ˈstarter** *noun* (*approving*) a person who is able to work on their own and make their own decisions without needing anyone to tell them what to do

**self-ˈstorage** *noun* [U] a service that provides a place where you can store things and a key so that you can get them when you need them: *self-storage facilities/units*

**self-ˈstudy** *noun* [U] the activity of learning about sth without a teacher to help you ▶ **self-ˈstudy** *adj.*: *self-study materials*

**self-ˈstyled** *adj.* [only before noun] (*disapproving*) using a name or title that you have given yourself, especially when you do not have the right to do it

**self-sufˈficient** *adj.* ~ **(in sth)** able to do or produce everything that you need without the help of other people: *The country is totally self-sufficient in food production.* ▶ **self-sufˈficiency** *noun* [U]

**self-supˈporting** *adj.* having enough money to be able to operate without financial help from other people

**self-suˈstaining** *adj.* able to continue in a healthy or successful state without help from anyone or anything else: *The solar panel project will help local communities become self-sustaining.* ⋄ *a self-sustaining population of wild fish*

**self-ˈtaught** *adj.* having learned sth by reading books, etc., rather than by sb teaching you: *a self-taught artist*

**self-ˈtitled** *adj.* [only before noun] (of an album, a TV show, etc.) having a title that is the same as the performer's or writer's name: *She was given her own comedy show, the self-titled 'Laura'.*

**self-ˈwilled** *adj.* (*disapproving*) determined to do what you want without caring about other people **SYN** headstrong

**self-ˈworth** *noun* [U] a feeling of confidence in yourself that you are a good and useful person **SYN** self-esteem

**sell** ⓘ **A1** /sel/ *verb, noun*
■ *verb* (**sold, sold** /səʊld/)
• **EXCHANGE FOR MONEY 1** ⓘ **A1** [T, I] to give sth to sb in exchange for money: ~**(sth)** *I recently sold my bike.* ⋄ *We offered them a good price but they wouldn't sell.* ⋄ ~**sth (to sb) (for sth)** *I sold my car to James for £800.* ⋄ ~**sb sth (for sth)** *I sold James my car for £800.* ⋄ ~**(sth) at sth** *They sold the business at a profit/loss* (= they gained/lost money when they sold it). ⇨ HOMOPHONES at CELL
• **OFFER FOR SALE 2** ⓘ **A1** [T] to offer sth for people to buy: ~**sth** *Most supermarkets sell a range of organic products.* ⋄ *They began selling spectacles in 1783.* ⋄ ~**sth for/at sth** *We sell these little notebooks at €1 each.* ⇨ compare CROSS-SELLING
• **BE BOUGHT 3** ⓘ **A2** [T, I] to be bought by people in the way or in the numbers mentioned; to be offered at the price mentioned: *The book sold well and was reprinted many times.* ⋄ *The new design just didn't sell* (= nobody bought it). ⋄ ~**sth** *The magazine sells 300 000 copies a week.* ⋄ ~**for/at sth** *The pens sell for just 50p each.*
• **PERSUADE 4** [I, T] to make people want to buy sth: *You may not like it but advertising sells.* ⋄ ~**sth** *It is quality not price that sells our products.* **5** [T] ~**sth/yourself (to sb)** to persuade sb that sth is a good idea, service, product, etc.; to persuade sb that you are the right person for a job, position, etc: *Now we have to try and sell the idea to management.* ⋄ *You really have to sell yourself at a job interview.*
• **TAKE MONEY/REWARD 6** [T] ~**yourself (to sb)** (*disapproving*) to accept money or a reward from sb for doing sth that is against your principles **SYN** prostitute ⇨ see also SALE
**IDM** ▶ **be ˈsold on sth** (*informal*) to be very enthusiastic about sth **sell your ˈbody** to have sex with sb in exchange for money **sell sb down the ˈriver** (*informal*) to give poor or unfair treatment to sb you have promised to help **ORIGIN** From the custom of buying and selling slaves on the plantations of the Mississippi River in America. Slaves who caused trouble for their masters could be sold to plantation owners lower down the river, where conditions would be worse. **sell sb/yourself ˈshort** to not value sb/yourself highly enough and show this by the way you treat or present them/yourself **sell your ˈsoul (to the devil)** to do anything, even sth really bad or dishonest, in return for money, success or power ⇨ more at HOT *adj.*, PUP
**PHR V** ▶ **sell sth↔ˈoff 1** to sell things cheaply because you want to get rid of them or because you need the money **2** to sell all or part of an industry, a company or land: *The Church sold off the land for housing.* ⇨ related noun SELL-OFF **sell sth↔ˈon** to sell to sb else sth that you have bought not long before: *She managed the business for a year and then sold it on.* **sell ˈout | be ˌsold ˈout** (of tickets for a concert, sports game, etc.) to be all sold: *The tickets sold out within hours.* ⋄ *This week's performances are completely sold out.* **sell ˈout (of sth) | be ˌsold ˈout (of sth)** to have sold all the available items, tickets, etc: *I'm sorry, we've sold out of bread.* ⋄ *We are already sold out for what should be a fantastic game.* **sell ˈout (to sb/sth) 1** (*disapproving*) to change or give up your beliefs or principles: *He's a talented screenwriter who has sold out to TV soap operas.* **2** to sell your business or a part of your business: *The company eventually sold out to a multinational media group.* ⇨ related noun SELL-OUT **sell ˈup | sell sth↔ˈup** (*especially BrE*) to sell your home, possessions, business, etc., usually because you are leaving the country or retiring

■ *noun* [sing.] (*informal*) **a hard, tough, easy, etc. ~** something that is difficult/easy to persuade people to buy or accept: *This policy is going to be a tough sell to the public.* ⇨ see also HARD SELL

**ˈsell-by date** (*BrE*) (*US* **ˈpull date**) *noun* the date printed on food packages, etc. after which the food must not be sold: *This milk is past its sell-by date.* ⋄ (*figurative*) *These policies are way past their sell-by dates.*

**sell·er** /ˈselə(r)/ *noun* **1** a person who sells sth: *a flower seller* ⋄ *The law is intended to protect both the buyer and the seller.* ⇨ compare VENDOR ⇨ see also BOOKSELLER **2** a **good, poor, etc. ~** a product that has been sold in the amounts or way mentioned: *This particular model is one of our biggest sellers.* ⇨ see also BESTSELLER
**IDM** ▶ **a ˌseller's ˈmarket** a situation in which people selling sth have an advantage, because there is not a lot of a particular item for sale, and prices can be kept high

**ˈselling point** *noun* a feature of sth that makes people want to buy or use it: *The price is obviously one of the main selling points.* ⋄ *Sales departments try to identify a product's USP or 'unique selling point'.*

**ˈselling price** *noun* the price at which sth is sold ⇨ compare ASKING PRICE, COST PRICE, PURCHASE PRICE

**ˈsell-off** *noun* **1** (*BrE*) the sale by the government of an industry or a service to individual people or private companies **2** (*NAmE, business*) the sale of a large number of STOCKS and SHARES, after which their value usually falls

**Sel·lo·tape™** /ˈseləteɪp/ (*also* **ˈsticky tape**) (*both BrE*) (*NAmE* **ˈScotch tape™**) *noun* [U] clear plastic tape that is sticky on one side, used for sticking things together: *a roll of Sellotape* ⋄ *The envelope was stuck down with Sellotape.*

**sel·lo·tape** /ˈseləteɪp/ *verb* ~**sth (to sth)** (*BrE*) to join or stick things together with Sellotape: *We found a note sellotaped to the front door.*

# sell-out

**'sell-out** noun [usually sing.] **1** a play, concert, etc. for which all the tickets have been sold: *Next week's final looks like being a sell-out.* ◇ *a sell-out tour* **2** a situation in which sb behaves badly towards a person or group who trusted them, by not doing sth that they promised to do, or by doing sth that they promised not to do: *The workers see the deal as a union sell-out to management.*

**selt·zer** /'seltsə(r)/ noun [U, C] FIZZY water (= with bubbles), usually containing minerals, used as a drink

**selves** /selvz/ pl. of SELF

**se·man·tic** /sɪ'mæntɪk/ adj. [usually before noun] (*linguistics*) connected with the meaning of words and sentences ▶ **se·man·tic·al·ly** /-kli/ adv.: *semantically related words*

**se·man·tics** /sɪ'mæntɪks/ noun [U] (*linguistics*) **1** the study of the meanings of words and phrases **2** the meaning of words, phrases or systems

**sema·phore** /'seməfɔː(r)/ noun, verb
▪ *noun* [U] a system for sending signals in which you hold your arms or two flags in particular positions to represent different letters of the alphabet
▪ *verb* [I, T] ~(sth) | ~that... to send a message to sb by semaphore or a similar system of signals

**semb·lance** /'sembləns/ noun [sing., U] ~ **of sth** (*formal*) a situation in which sth seems to exist although this may not, in fact, be the case: *The ceasefire brought about a semblance of order.* ◇ *Life at last returned to some semblance of normality.*

**semen** /'siːmən/ noun [U] the white liquid containing SPERM that is produced by the sex organs of men and male animals

**se·mes·ter** /sɪ'mestə(r)/ noun (especially in North America) one of the two periods that the school or college year is divided into: *the spring/fall semester* ⊃ compare TERM (2)

**semi** /'semi/ noun (pl. **semis**) **1** (*BrE*, *informal*) a SEMI-DETACHED house (= one that is joined to another house by one shared wall): *suburban semis* **2** (*NAmE*) = SEMI-TRAILER **3** = SEMI-FINAL

**semi-** /semi; NAmE also semaɪ/ prefix (in adjectives and nouns) half; partly: *semicircular* ◇ *semi-final*

**semi-'annual** (NAmE also **semi-an·nual**) adj. (*especially NAmE*) produced or happening twice each year SYN **biannual**: *The journal is published on a semi-annual basis.*

**semi-'arid** adj. (*specialist*) (of land or climate) dry; with little rain

**semi-auto'matic** adj. (of a gun) able to load bullets itself, and therefore very quickly, but not able to fire itself ▶ **semi-auto'matic** noun

**semi·breve** /'semibriːv/ noun (*BrE*) (NAmE **'whole note**) noun (*music*) a note that lasts as long as four CROTCHETS ⊃ picture at MUSIC

**semi·circle** /'semisɜːkl; NAmE 'semisɜːrkl, -maɪs-/ noun **1** (*geometry*) one half of a circle ⊃ picture at CIRCLE **2** a thing, or a group of people or things, like a semicircle in shape: *a semicircle of chairs* ◇ *We sat in a semicircle round the fire.* ▶ **semi·cir·cu·lar** /ˌsemi'sɜːkjələ(r)/ NAmE ˌsemi-'sɜːrk-, -maɪs-/ adj.: *a semicircular driveway*

**semi·colon** /ˌsemi'kəʊlən, -lɒn/ NAmE 'semikəʊlən, -maɪk-/ noun the mark (;) used to separate the parts of a complicated sentence or items in a detailed list, showing a break that is longer than a comma but shorter than a full stop ⊃ compare COLON

**semi·con·duct·or** /ˌsemikən'dʌktə(r)/ NAmE 'semikəndʌktər, -maɪk-/ noun (*specialist*) **1** a solid substance that CONDUCTS electricity in particular conditions, better than INSULATORS but not as well as CONDUCTORS **2** a device containing a semiconductor used in ELECTRONICS

**semi-de'tached** adj. (of a house) joined to another house by a wall on one side that is shared ⊃ compare DETACHED ⊃ see also TERRACED ▶ **semi-de'tached** (also informal **semi**) noun (*BrE*) ⊃ compare DUPLEX

**semi-'final** (also **semi**) noun one of the two games or parts of a sports competition that are held to decide who will compete in the last part (the FINAL): *He's through to the semi-final of the men's singles.* ▶ **semi-'finalist** noun: *They are semi-finalists for the fourth year in succession.*

**sem·inal** /'semɪnl/ adj. **1** (*formal*) very important and having a strong influence on later developments: *a seminal work/article/study* **2** [usually before noun] (*specialist*) of or containing SEMEN: *seminal fluid*

**sem·inar** /'semɪnɑː(r)/ noun **1** a class at a university or college when a small group of students and a teacher discuss or study a particular topic: *Teaching is by lectures and seminars.* ◇ *a graduate seminar* ◇ *a seminar room* ⊃ WORDFINDER NOTE at UNIVERSITY **2** a meeting for discussion or training: *a one-day management seminar*

**sem·in·ar·ian** /ˌsemɪ'neəriən; NAmE -'ner-/ noun a student in a seminary

**sem·in·ary** /'semɪnəri; NAmE -neri/ noun (pl. **-ies**) a college where priests, ministers or RABBIS are trained

**Sem·inole** /'semɪnəʊl/ noun (pl. **Sem·inole** or **Sem·in·oles**) a member of a Native American people, many of whom live in the US states of Oklahoma and Florida

**semi·otics** /ˌsemi'ɒtɪks; NAmE -'ɑːt-/ noun [U] the study of signs and symbols and of their meaning and use ▶ **semi·otic** adj.: *semiotic analysis*

**semi-'precious** adj. [usually before noun] (of a JEWEL) less valuable than the most valuable types of JEWELS

**semi-'private** /ˌsemi'praɪvət; NAmE also -'maɪ'p-/ adj. (NAmE) **1** shared by a small number of people, usually two: *a semiprivate hospital room* **2** partly private, but not completely: *The news spread via semiprivate social media networks.*

**semi-pro'fes·sion·al** adj. **semi-professional** musicians or sports players are paid for what they do, but do not do it as their main job ▶ **semi-pro'fes·sion·al** noun

**semi·quaver** /'semikweɪvə(r)/ (*BrE*) (NAmE **'sixteenth note**) noun (*music*) a note that lasts half as long as a QUAVER ⊃ picture at MUSIC

**semi-'skilled** adj. [usually before noun] (of workers) having some special training or qualifications, but less than SKILLED people: *a semi-skilled machine operator* ◇ *semi-skilled jobs* (= for people who have some special training)

**semi-'skimmed** adj. (*BrE*) (of milk) that has had some of the fat removed ⊃ compare SKIMMED MILK, WHOLE MILK

**Sem·ite** /'siːmaɪt, 'sem-; NAmE 'sem-/ noun a member of the peoples who speak Semitic languages, including Arabs and Jews

**Sem·it·ic** /sə'mɪtɪk/ adj. **1** of or connected with the language group that includes Hebrew and Arabic **2** of or connected with the people who speak Semitic languages, especially Hebrew and Arabic

**semi·tone** /'semitəʊn/ (*BrE*) (NAmE **'half step, 'half·tone**) noun (*music*) half a TONE on a musical SCALE, for example the INTERVAL between C and C♯ or between E and F ⊃ compare STEP

**'semi-trailer** (also **semi**) noun (*NAmE*) a TRAILER that has wheels at the back and is supported at the front by the vehicle that is pulling it

**semi-'tropical** adj. = SUBTROPICAL

**semo·lina** /ˌsemə'liːnə/ noun [U] **1** large hard grains of WHEAT pressed and used for making PASTA and sweet dishes **2** a sweet dish made from semolina and milk, eaten for DESSERT in the UK and for breakfast in the US

**sem·tex** /'semteks/ noun [U] a powerful EXPLOSIVE that is used for making bombs, often illegally

**SEN** /ˌes iː 'en/ (also **SEND** /send/) abbr. (*BrE*) special educational needs (the educational needs of children who have physical problems or difficulty learning). The official term **SEND** stands for 'special educational needs and disability'.

**Sen.** abbr. SENATOR: *Sen. John K Nordqvist*

**sen·ate** /'senət/ noun (usually **the Senate**) **1** [sing.] one of the two groups of elected politicians who make laws in some countries, for example in the US, Australia, Canada and France. The Senate is smaller than the other group but higher in rank. Many state parliaments in the US also have a Senate: *a member of the Senate* ◊ *a Senate committee* ⇨ compare CONGRESS, HOUSE OF REPRESENTATIVES ⇨ WORDFINDER NOTE at CONGRESS **2** [C, usually sing., U] (in some countries) the group of people who control a university: *the senate of Loughborough University* **3** [sing.] (in ancient Rome) the most important council of the government; the building where the council met

**sen·ator** ⁺ **C1** /'senətə(r)/ *noun* (*often* **Senator**) (*abbr.* **Sen.**) a member of a senate: *Senator McCarthy* ◊ *She has served as a Democratic senator for North Carolina since 2009.* ▶ **sen·at·or·ial** /ˌsenə'tɔːriəl/ *adj.* [only before noun]: *a senatorial candidate*

**send** ⓘ **A1** /send/ *verb* (**sent**, **sent** /sent/)
- BY MAIL/RADIO **1** **A1** to make sth go or be taken to a place, especially by post, email, radio, etc.: *~sth to send a letter/a package/an email* ◊ (*BrE*) *to send sth by post* ◊ (*NAmE*) *to send sth by mail* ◊ *~sth to sb/sth A radio signal was sent to the spacecraft.* ◊ *~sb sth I'll send you a text message.* ◊ *~sth back The laptop was faulty so I sent it back to the manufacturers.* ⓗ HOMOPHONES at SCENT
- MESSAGE **2** **A1** to tell sb sth by sending them a message: *~sth My parents send their love.* ◊ *~sth to sb Henry sent his regards to you.* ◊ (*figurative*) *What sort of message is that sending to young people?* ◊ *~sb sth He sent me word to come.* ◊ *~sth (that)… She sent word (that) she could not come.* ◊ *~to do sth* (*formal*) *She sent to say that she was coming home.*
- SB SOMEWHERE **3** **A1** to tell sb to go somewhere or to do sth; to arrange for sb to go somewhere: *~sb Ed couldn't make it so they sent me instead.* ◊ *~sb + adv./prep. She sent the kids to bed early.* ◊ *to send sb to prison/boarding school* ◊ *~sb to do sth I've sent Tom to buy some milk.*
- MAKE STH MOVE QUICKLY **4** to make sth/sb move quickly or suddenly: *~sth/sb doing sth Every step he took sent the pain shooting up his leg.* ◊ *The punch sent him flying.* ◊ *~sth/sb + adv./prep. The report sent share prices down a further 8p.*
- MAKE SB REACT **5** to make sb behave or react in a particular way: *~sb to do sth Her music always sends me to sleep.* ◊ *~sb into sth Her account of the visit sent us into fits of laughter.* ◊ *~sb + adj. All the publicity nearly sent him crazy.*
**IDM** **send sb ˈpacking** (*informal*) to tell sb clearly or rudely to go away ⇨ more at THING
**PHRV** **ˌsend aˈway (to sb) (for sth)** = SEND OFF (FOR STH)
**ˌsend sb↔ˈdown** (*BrE*) **1** (*informal*) to send sb to prison **2** (*old-fashioned*) to order a student to leave a university because of bad behaviour **ˌsend for sb** to ask or tell sb to come to you, especially in order to help you: *Send for a doctor, quickly!* **ˌsend for sth** to ask sb to bring or deliver sth to you: *His son found him and sent for help.* ◊ *She sent for the latest sales figures.* **ˌsend sb ˈforth** (*old-fashioned or literary*) to send sb away from you to another place **ˌsend ˈforth sth** (*formal*) to produce a sound, signal, etc. so that other people can hear it, receive it, etc: *He opened his mouth and sent forth a stream of noise.* **ˌsend sb↔ˈin** to order sb to go to a place to deal with a difficult situation: *Troops were sent in to restore order.* **ˌsend sth↔ˈin** to send sth by post to a place where it will be dealt with: *Have you sent in your application yet?* **ˌsend ˈoff (for sth)** | **ˌsend aˈway (to sb) (for sth)** to write to sb and ask them to send you sth by post: *I've sent off for some books for my course.* **ˌsend sb↔ˈoff** (*BrE*) (in a sports game) to order sb to leave the field because they have broken the rules of the game: *Bale was sent off for a foul in the second half.* ⇨ related noun SENDING-OFF **ˌsend sth↔ˈoff** to send sth to a place by post: *I'm sending the files off to my boss tomorrow.* **ˌsend sth↔ˈon 1** to send sth to a place so that it arrives before you get there: *We sent our furniture on by ship.* **2** to send a letter that has been sent to sb's old address to their new address **SYN** **forward 3** to send sth from one place/person to another: *They arranged for the information to be sent on to us.* **ˌsend ˈout for sth** to ask a restaurant or shop to deliver food to you at home or at work: *Let's send out for a pizza.* **ˌsend sth↔ˈout 1** to send sth to a lot of different

**1409** **senior citizen**

people or places: *Have the invitations been sent out yet?* **2** to produce sth, such as light, a signal, sound, etc. **SYN** **emit** **ˌsend sb/sth↔ˈup** (*informal*) to make people laugh at sb/sth by copying them/it in a funny way: *a TV programme that sends up politicians* ⇨ related noun SEND-UP **ˌsend sb↔ˈup** (*US, informal*) to send sb to prison

**sender** /'sendə(r)/ *noun* a person who sends sth: *If undelivered, please return to sender.*

**sending-ˈoff** *noun* (*pl.* **sendings-off**) (*BrE*) (in football (soccer)) a situation when a REFEREE tells a player to leave the field because they have broken the rules in a serious way

**ˈsend-off** *noun* (*informal*) an occasion when people come together to say goodbye to sb who is leaving: *Her colleagues gave her a good send-off.*

**ˈsend-up** *noun* (*informal*) an act of making sb/sth look silly by copying them in a funny way

**Seneca** /'senəkə/ *noun* (*pl.* **Seneca** or **Senecas**) a member of a Native American people, many of whom now live in the US states of New York and Ohio

**senescence** /sɪ'nesns/ *noun* [U] (*formal or specialist*) the process of becoming old and showing the effects of being old ▶ **senescent** /-'nesnt/ *adj.*

**senile** /'siːnaɪl/ *adj.* **1** behaving in a confused or strange way, and unable to remember things, because you are old: *I think she's going senile.* **2** (*medical*) (of a medical condition) caused by old age: *senile cataracts* ▶ **senility** /sə'nɪləti/ *noun* [U]: *an old man on the verge of senility*

**ˌsenile deˈmentia** *noun* [U] a term used in the past for a serious mental DISORDER in old people that causes loss of memory, loss of control of the body, etc.

**senior** ⓘ **B2** /'siːniə(r)/ *adj., noun*
■ *adj.*
- OF HIGH RANK **1** **B2** high in rank or status; higher in rank or status than others: *a senior official/officer/manager/executive* ◊ *a senior adviser/analyst/lecturer* ◊ *She is senior vice president of marketing.* ◊ *senior figures in the Labour party* ◊ *senior members of staff* ◊ *I have ten years' experience at senior management level.* ◊ (*BrE*) *Junior nurses usually work alongside more senior nurses.* **OPP** **junior**
- IN SPORT **2** **B2** [only before noun] for adults or people at a more advanced level: *to take part in senior competitions* ◊ *He won the senior men's 400 metres.*
- FOR OLDER PEOPLE **3** [only before noun] for SENIOR CITIZENS (= older people, especially those who have retired from work): *Get one third off rail fares with a senior railcard.* ◊ *senior discounts/concessions*
- FATHER **4 Senior** (*abbr.* **Snr**, **Sr**) used after the name of a man who has the same name as his son, to make it clear who is being referred to ⇨ compare JUNIOR
- SCHOOL/COLLEGE **5** [only before noun] (*BrE*) (of a school or part of a school) for children over the age of 11 or 13 **6** [only before noun] (*NAmE*) connected with the last year in HIGH SCHOOL or college: *the senior prom*
■ *noun*
- OLDER PERSON **1** a person who is older than sb else: *She was ten years his senior.* ◊ *My brother is my senior by two years.* ⇨ compare JUNIOR **2** (*especially NAmE*) = SENIOR CITIZEN
- HIGHER RANK **3** a person who is higher in rank or status: *She felt unappreciated both by her colleagues and her seniors.*
- IN SPORT **4** adults or people who have reached an advanced level: *tennis coaching for juniors and seniors*
- IN SCHOOL/COLLEGE **5** (*BrE*) a child at a senior school; an older child in a school **6** (in the US and some other countries) a student in the last year at a HIGH SCHOOL or college: *high school seniors* ⇨ compare SOPHOMORE

**ˌsenior ˈcitizen** (*also* **senior** *especially in NAmE*) *noun* an older person, especially sb who has retired from work. People often call sb a 'senior citizen' to avoid saying that they are old or using the expression 'old-age pensioner'.

**senior high school** (also **senior high**) noun (in the US and Canada) a school for young people between the ages of 14 and 18 ⊃ compare JUNIOR HIGH SCHOOL

**sen·ior·i·ty** /ˌsiːniˈɒrəti/ NAmE /ˌsiːniˈɔːr-/ noun [U] **1** the fact of being older or of a higher rank than others: *a position of seniority* **2** the rank that you have in a company because of the length of time you have worked there: *a lawyer with five years' seniority* ◇ *Should promotion be based on merit or seniority?*

**sen·sa·tion** ⁺ C1 /senˈseɪʃn/ noun **1** ⁺ C1 [C] a feeling that you get when sth affects your body: *a tingling/burning sensation* ◇ *I had a sensation of falling, as if in a dream.* **2** ⁺ C1 [U] the ability to feel through your sense of touch SYN **feeling**: *She seemed to have lost all sensation in her arms.* **3** ⁺ C1 [C, usually sing.] a general feeling or impression that is difficult to explain; an experience or a memory: *He had the eerie sensation of being watched.* ◇ *When I arrived, I had the sensation that she had been expecting me.* **4** ⁺ C1 [C, usually sing.] very great surprise, excitement, or interest among a lot of people; the person or the thing that causes this surprise: *News of his arrest caused a sensation.* ◇ *The band became a sensation overnight.*

**sen·sa·tion·al** /senˈseɪʃənl/ adj. **1** causing great surprise, excitement, or interest SYN **thrilling**: *The result was a sensational 4–1 victory.* **2** (*disapproving*) (of a newspaper, etc.) trying to get your interest by presenting facts or events as worse or more SHOCKING than they really are **3** (*informal*) extremely good; wonderful SYN **fantastic**: *You look sensational in that dress!* ▶ **sen·sa·tion·al·ly** /-nəli/ adv.: *They won sensationally against the top team.* ◇ *The incident was sensationally reported in the press.* ◇ *He's sensationally good-looking.*

**sen·sa·tion·al·ism** /senˈseɪʃənəlɪzəm/ noun [U] (*disapproving*) a way of getting people's interest by using words that are intended to shock you or by presenting facts and events as worse or more SHOCKING than they really are ▶ **sen·sa·tion·al·ist** /-lɪst/ adj.: *sensationalist headlines*

**sen·sa·tion·al·ize** (BrE also **-ise**) /senˈseɪʃənəlaɪz/ verb ~ sth (*disapproving*) to make a story seem more exciting or SHOCKING than it really is

**sense** ⓘ A2 O /sens/ noun, verb
■ noun
- UNDERSTANDING/JUDGEMENT **1** ⁺ A2 [sing.] ~ (of sth) an understanding about sth; an ability to judge sth: *One of the most important things in a partner is a sense of humour* (= the ability to find things funny or make people laugh). ◇ *He has a very good sense of direction* (= finds the way to a place easily). ◇ (*figurative*) *She has lost all sense of direction in her life* (= the idea of what she should do in her life). ◇ *Alex doesn't have any dress sense* (= does not know which clothes look attractive). **2** ⁺ B1 [U] good understanding and judgement; knowledge of what is sensible or practical behaviour: *You should have the sense to take advice when it is offered.* ◇ *There's no sense in* (= it is not sensible) *worrying about it now.* ◇ *Can't you talk sense* (= say sth sensible)? ◇ *There's a lot of sense in what Mary says.* ⊃ note at SENSIBLE ⊃ see also COMMON SENSE, GOOD SENSE
- MEANING **3** ⁺ B1 [C] the meaning that a word or phrase has; a way of understanding sth: *in … –* *The word 'love' is used in different senses by different people.* ◇ *education in its broadest sense* ◇ *He was a true friend, in every sense of the word* (= in every possible way). ◇ *In a sense* (= in one way) *it doesn't matter any more.* ◇ *In some senses* (= in one or more ways) *the criticisms were justified.* ◇ (*formal*) *In no sense can the issue be said to be resolved.* ◇ *in the – of sth I am using 'cold' in the sense of 'unfriendly'.* ◇ *There is a sense in which we are all to blame for the tragedy.*
- SIGHT/HEARING, ETC. **4** ⁺ B2 [C] one of the five powers (sight, hearing, smell, taste and touch) that your body uses to get information about the world around you: *the five senses* ◇ ~ *of sth Dogs have a keen sense* (= strong sense) *of smell.* ◇ *the sense organs* (= eyes, ears, nose, etc.) *I could hardly believe the evidence of my own senses* (= what I could see, hear, etc.). ⊃ see also SIXTH SENSE
- FEELING **5** ⁺ B2 [C] a feeling about sth important: ~ *of sth His career was guided by a strong sense of duty.* ◇ *a sense of*

*purpose/identity/urgency* ◇ *Helmets can give cyclists a false sense of security.* ◇ *He felt an overwhelming sense of loss.* ◇ ~ *(that) … I had the sense that he was worried about something.*
- NORMAL STATE OF MIND **6 senses** [pl.] a normal state of mind; the ability to think clearly: *If she threatens to leave, it should bring him to his senses.* ◇ *He waited for Dora to come to her senses and return.* ◇ (*old-fashioned*) *Are you out of your senses? You'll be killed!*

IDM **knock/talk some ˈsense into sb** to try and persuade sb to stop behaving in a stupid way, sometimes using rough or violent methods **make ˈsense 1** ⁺ A2 to have a meaning that you can easily understand: *This sentence doesn't make sense.* **2** ⁺ B1 to be a sensible thing to do: *It makes sense to buy the most up-to-date version.* **3** ⁺ B2 to be easy to understand or explain: *Who would send me all these flowers? It makes no sense.* ◇ *It all made perfect sense to me.* **make ˈsense of sth** to understand sth that is difficult or has no clear meaning **see ˈsense** to start to be sensible or reasonable **a sense of ocˈcasion** a feeling or understanding that an event is important or special: *Candles on the table gave the evening a sense of occasion.* ⊃ more at LEAVE *n.*
■ verb (not used in the progressive tenses)
- BECOME AWARE **1** ⁺ B2 to become aware of sth even though you cannot see it, hear it, etc.: ~ *sth Sensing danger, they started to run.* ◇ ~ *(that) … Lisa sensed that he did not believe her.* ◇ ~ *sb/sth doing sth He sensed someone moving around behind him.* ◇ ~ *sb/sth do sth He sensed something move in the bushes.* ◇ ~ *how, what, etc. … She could sense how nervous he was.*
- OF MACHINE **2** ~ *sth* to discover and record sth: *equipment that senses the presence of toxic gases*

**sense·less** /ˈsensləs/ adj. **1** (*disapproving*) having no meaning or purpose SYN **pointless**: *senseless violence* ◇ *His death was a senseless waste of life.* ◇ *It's senseless to continue any further.* **2** [not before noun] unconscious: *He was beaten senseless.* ◇ *She drank herself senseless.* **3** not using good judgement: *The police blamed senseless drivers who went too fast.* ▶ **sense·less·ly** adv.

**sens·ibil·ity** /ˌsensəˈbɪləti/ noun (pl. **-ies**) **1** [U, C] the ability to experience and understand deep feelings, especially in art and literature: *a man of impeccable manners, charm and sensibility* ◇ *artistic sensibility* **2 sensibilities** [pl.] a person's feelings, especially when the person is easily offended or influenced by sth: *The article offended her religious sensibilities.*

**sens·ible** ⓘ B1 /ˈsensəbl/ adj. **1** ⁺ B1 (of people and their behaviour) able to make good judgements based on reason and experience rather than emotion; practical: *She's a sensible sort of person.* ◇ *I think that's a very sensible idea.* ◇ ~ *about sth We have to be sensible about this.* ◇ *it is ~ (for sb) to do sth It is sensible to have contingency plans in place.* **2** (of clothes, etc.) useful rather than fashionable: *sensible shoes* **3** (*formal* or *literary*) aware of sth: *I am sensible of the fact that mathematics is not a popular subject.* OPP **insensible** HELP Use **silly** (sense 1) or **impractical** (senses 1 and 2) as the opposite for the other senses. ▶ **sens·ibly** /-bli/ adv.: *to behave sensibly* ◇ *He decided, very sensibly, not to drive when he was so tired.* ◇ *She's always very sensibly dressed.*

▼ WHICH WORD?
**sensible / sensitive**
**Sensible** and **sensitive** are connected with two different meanings of **sense**.
- **Sensible** refers to your ability to make good judgements: *She gave me some very sensible advice.* ◇ *It wasn't very sensible to go out on your own so late at night.*
- **Sensitive** refers to how easily you react to things and how much you are aware of things or other people: *a soap for sensitive skin* ◇ *This movie may upset a sensitive child.*

**sen·si·tive** ⓘ B2 W /ˈsensətɪv/ adj.
- TO PEOPLE'S FEELINGS **1** ⁺ B2 aware of and able to understand other people and their feelings: *a sensitive and*

*caring man* ◇ **~ to sth** *She is very sensitive to other people's feelings.* **OPP** **insensitive**
- **TO COLD/LIGHT/FOOD, ETC. 2** [B2] reacting quickly or more than usual to sth: **~ to sth** *My teeth are very sensitive to cold food.* ◇ *Young children are **particularly** sensitive to the harmful effects of pesticides.* **OPP** **insensitive** ⊃ see also TOUCH-SENSITIVE
- **TO ART/MUSIC/LITERATURE 3** [B2] able to understand art, music and literature and to express yourself through them: *an actor's sensitive reading of the poem*
- **EASILY UPSET 4** [B2] easily offended or upset: *You're far too sensitive.* ◇ **~ about sth** *He's very sensitive about his weight.* ◇ **~ to sth** *She's very sensitive to criticism.* **OPP** **insensitive**
- **INFORMATION/SUBJECT 5** [B2] that you have to treat with great care because it may offend people or make them angry or embarrassed: *sensitive information/data* ◇ *highly sensitive documents* ◇ *Healthcare is a politically sensitive issue.*
- **TO SMALL CHANGES 6** **~ (to sth)** able to measure very small changes: *a sensitive instrument* ◇ *(figurative) The Stock Exchange is very sensitive to political change.* **OPP** **insensitive** ⊃ see also CASE-SENSITIVE ▶ **sen·si·tive·ly** *adv.*: *He handled the matter sensitively.* ◇ *He writes sensitively.* **IDM** see NERVE *n.*

**sen·si·tiv·ity** [B2+] [C1] /ˌsensəˈtɪvəti/ *noun (pl. -ies)*
- **TO PEOPLE'S FEELINGS 1** [B2+] [C1] [U] **~ (to sth)** the ability to understand other people's feelings: *sensitivity to the needs of children* ◇ *She pointed out with tact and sensitivity exactly where he had gone wrong.*
- **TO ART/MUSIC/LITERATURE 2** [B2+] [C1] [U] the ability to understand art, music and literature and to express yourself through them: *She played with great sensitivity.*
- **BEING EASILY UPSET 3** [B2+] [C1] [U, C, usually pl.] the fact of being easily offended or upset by sth: *He's a mixture of anger and sensitivity.* ◇ *She was blind to the feelings and sensitivities of other people.* **OPP** **insensitivity**
- **OF INFORMATION/SUBJECT 4** [B2+] [C1] [U] the fact of needing to be treated very carefully because it may offend or upset people: *Confidentiality is important because of the sensitivity of the information.*
- **TO FOOD/COLD/LIGHT, ETC. 5** [B2+] [C1] [U, C, usually pl.] *(specialist)* the fact of reacting quickly or more than usual to sth: *food sensitivity* ◇ *allergies and sensitivities* ◇ *Some children develop a sensitivity to cow's milk.* ◇ *The eyes of some fish have a greater sensitivity to light than ours do.*
- **TO SMALL CHANGES 6** [U] the ability to measure very small changes: *the sensitivity of the test*

**sen·si·tize** (*BrE also* **-ise**) /ˈsensətaɪz/ *verb* [usually passive] **1** **~ sb/sth (to sth)** to make sb/sth more aware of sth, especially a problem or sth bad: *People are becoming more sensitized to the dangers threatening the environment.* **2** **~ sb/sth (to sth)** *(specialist)* to make sb/sth sensitive to physical or chemical changes, or to a particular substance ▶ **sen·si·tiza·tion, -isa·tion** /ˌsensətaɪˈzeɪʃn; *NAmE* -təˈz-/ *noun* [U]

**sen·sor** /ˈsensə(r)/ *noun* a device that can react to light, heat, pressure, etc. in order to make a machine, etc. do sth or show sth: *security lights with an infrared sensor* (= that come on when a person is near them)

**sen·sory** [W] /ˈsensəri/ *adj.* [usually before noun] *(specialist)* connected with your physical senses: *sensory organs* ◇ *sensory overload/deprivation*

**sen·sual** /ˈsenʃuəl/ *adj.* **1** connected with your physical feelings; giving pleasure to your physical senses, especially sexual pleasure: *sensual pleasure* **2** suggesting an interest in physical pleasure, especially sexual pleasure: *sensual lips* ◇ *He was darkly sensual and mysterious.* ▶ **sen·su·al·ity** /ˌsenʃuˈæləti/ *noun* [U]: *the sensuality of his poetry* **sen·su·al·ly** /ˈsenʃuəli/ *adv.*

**sen·su·ous** /ˈsenʃuəs/ *adj.* **1** giving pleasure to your senses: *sensuous music* ◇ *I'm drawn to the poetic, sensuous qualities of her paintings.* **2** suggesting an interest in sexual pleasure: *his full sensuous lips* ▶ **sen·su·ous·ly** *adv.* **sen·su·ous·ness** *noun* [U]

**sent** /sent/ *past tense, past part.* OF SEND ⊃ HOMOPHONES at SCENT

---

**sen·tence** [❶] [A1] /ˈsentəns/ *noun, verb*
■ *noun* **1** [A1] [C] *(grammar)* a set of words expressing a statement, a question or an order, usually containing a subject and a verb. In written English sentences begin with a capital letter and end with a full stop/period (.), a question mark (?) or an exclamation mark (!): *Does the sentence contain an adverb?* ◇ *I was too stunned to finish my sentence.* **2** [B2] [C, U] the punishment given by a court: *a jail/prison sentence* ◇ *The judge passed sentence* (= said what the punishment would be). ◇ *The prisoner has served* (= completed) *his sentence and will be released tomorrow.* ◇ **~ of sth** *a maximum/minimum sentence of five years* ◇ *The charges carry a sentence of up to ten years.* ◇ **~ for sth** *He received an 18-year sentence for attempted murder.* ◇ **under ~ (of sth)** *to be under sentence of death* ⊃ **WORDFINDER NOTE** at PRISON ⊃ see also COMMUNITY SENTENCE, DEATH SENTENCE, LIFE SENTENCE, SUSPENDED SENTENCE
■ *verb* [B2] [often passive] to say officially in court that sb is to receive a particular punishment: **~ sb (to sth)** *to be sentenced to death/life imprisonment* ◇ **~ sb to do sth** *The judge sentenced him to hang.*

**ˈsentence adverb** *noun (grammar)* an adverb that expresses the speaker's attitude towards, or gives the subject of, the whole of the rest of the sentence: *In 'Luckily, I didn't tell anyone' and 'Financially, we have a serious problem', 'luckily' and 'financially' are sentence adverbs.*

**sen·ten·tious** /senˈtenʃəs/ *adj. (formal, disapproving)* trying to sound important or intelligent, especially by expressing moral judgements ▶ **sen·ten·tious·ly** *adv.*

**sen·tient** /ˈsentiənt, ˈsenʃnt/ *adj.* [usually before noun] *(formal)* able to see or feel things through the senses: *Man is a sentient being.*

**sen·ti·ment** [B2+] [C1] /ˈsentɪmənt/ *noun* **1** [B2+] [C1] [C, U] *(formal)* a feeling or an opinion, especially one based on emotions: *the spread of nationalist sentiments* ◇ *This is a sentiment I wholeheartedly agree with.* ◇ *Public sentiment is against any change to the law.* **2** [B2+] [C1] [U] *(sometimes disapproving)* feelings of sympathy, romantic love, being sad, etc. which may be too strong or not appropriate: *There was no fatherly affection, no display of sentiment.* ◇ *There is no room for sentiment in business.*

**sen·ti·men·tal** /ˌsentɪˈmentl/ *adj.* **1** connected with your emotions, rather than reason: *She kept the letters for sentimental reasons.* ◇ *The ring wasn't worth very much but it had great sentimental value.* **2** *(often disapproving)* producing emotions such as sympathy, romantic love, or being sad, which may be too strong or not appropriate; feeling these emotions too much: *a slushy, sentimental love story* ◇ *He's not the sort of man who gets sentimental about old friendships.* **OPP** **unsentimental** ▶ **sen·ti·men·tal·ly** /-təli/ *adv.*

**sen·ti·men·tal·ist** /ˌsentɪˈmentəlɪst/ *noun (sometimes disapproving)* a person who is sentimental about things

**sen·ti·men·tal·ity** /ˌsentɪmenˈtæləti/ *noun* [U] *(disapproving)* the fact of being too sentimental

**sen·ti·men·tal·ize** (*BrE also* **-ise**) /ˌsentɪˈmentəlaɪz/ *verb* [T, I] **~ (sth)** *(disapproving)* to present sth in an emotional way, emphasizing its good aspects and not mentioning its bad aspects: *Jackie was careful not to sentimentalize country life.*

**sen·ti·nel** /ˈsentɪnl/ *noun (literary)* a soldier whose job is to guard sth **SYN** **sentry**: *(figurative) a tall round tower standing sentinel over the river*

**sen·try** /ˈsentri/ *noun (pl. -ies)* a soldier whose job is to guard sth: *to be on sentry duty*

**SEO** /ˌes iː ˈəʊ/ *abbr.* SEARCH ENGINE OPTIMIZATION

**sepal** /ˈsepl/ *NAmE* /ˈsiːpl/ *noun (specialist)* a part of a flower, like a leaf, that lies under and supports the PETALS (= the thin coloured parts that make up the head of the flower). Each flower has a ring of sepals called a CALYX. ⊃ **VISUAL VOCAB** page V7

**sep·ar·able** /ˈsepərəbl/ *adj.* **1** **~ (from sth)** that can be separated from sth, or considered separately: *The moral*

# separate

question is not entirely separable from the financial one. **2** (*grammar*) (of a phrasal verb) that can be used with the object going either between the verb and the PARTICLE or after the particle: *The phrasal verb 'tear up' is separable because you can say 'She tore the letter up' or 'She tore up the letter'.* **OPP inseparable** ▶ **sep·ar·abil·ity** /ˌsepərəˈbɪləti/ *noun* [U]

**sep·ar·ate** ❶ A2 ⓦ
*adj., verb*

| WORD FAMILY |
|---|
| separate *adj.* |
| separately *adv.* |
| separable *adj.* |
| (≠ inseparable) |
| separate *verb* |
| separated *adj.* |
| separation *noun* |

■ *adj.* /ˈseprət/ **1** ᵠ A2 forming a unit by itself; not joined to sth else: *They have begun to sleep in separate rooms.* ◊ *~ from sb/sth Raw meat must be kept separate from cooked meat.* **2** ᵠ A2 [usually before noun] different; not connected: *The companies now exist as two separate entities.* ◊ *~ from sth I try to keep my private life separate from my work.* ◊ *This is a completely separate matter.* ▶ **sep·ar·ate·ness** *noun* [U]: *Japan's long-standing sense of separateness and uniqueness*
**IDM go your separate 'ways 1** to end a relationship with sb **2** to go in a different direction from sb you have been travelling with ⊃ more at COVER *n.*

■ *verb* /ˈsepəreɪt/ **1** ᵠ B1 [I, T] to divide into different parts or groups; to divide things into different parts or groups: *Stir the sauce constantly so that it does not separate.* ◊ *~ sth Separate the eggs* (= separate the YOLK from the white)*.* ◊ *~ A from/and B It is impossible to separate belief from emotion.* ◊ *~ sth into sth Make a list of points and separate them into 'desirable' and 'essential'.* **2** ᵠ B1 [I, T] to move apart; to make people or things move apart: *South America and Africa separated 200 million years ago.* ◊ *~ from sth South America separated from Africa 200 million years ago.* ◊ *~ into sth We separated into several different search parties.* ◊ *~ sb/sth Police tried to separate the two men who were fighting.* ◊ *~ A from/and B Those suffering from infectious diseases were separated from the other patients.* ◊ *~ sb/sth into sth The children were separated into two groups.* **3** ᵠ B1 [T] to be between two people, areas, countries, etc. so that they are not touching or connected: *~ sb/sth A thousand kilometres separates the two cities.* ◊ *~ A from/and B A high wall separated our back yard from the playing field.* **4** ᵠ B1 [I] to stop living together as a couple with your husband, wife or partner: *They separated last year.* ◊ *~ from sb He separated from his wife after 20 years of marriage.* **5** [T] *~ sb/sth (from sb/sth)* to make sb/sth different in some way from sb/sth else ᴇʏɴ **divide**: *Politics is the only thing that separates us* (= that we disagree about)*.* ◊ *The judges found it impossible to separate the two contestants* (= they gave them equal scores)*.* ◊ *Only four points separate the top three teams.* **IDM** see MAN *n.*, SHEEP, WHEAT
**PHRV separate 'out (from sth) | separate sth↔'out (from sth)** to divide into different parts; to divide sth into different parts: *to separate out different meanings*

**sep·ar·at·ed** /ˈsepəreɪtɪd/ *adj.* no longer living with your husband, wife or partner: *Her parents are separated but not divorced.* ◊ *~ from sb He's been separated from his wife for a year.*

**sep·ar·ate·ly** ⓦ /ˈseprətli/ *adv.* as a separate person or thing; not together: *They were photographed separately and then as a group.* ◊ *Last year's figures are shown separately.* ◊ *~ from sb/sth That matter will be considered separately from the main agenda.*

**sep·ar·ates** /ˈseprəts/ *noun* [pl.] individual pieces of clothing, for example skirts, jackets, and trousers, that are designed to be worn together in different combinations

**sep·ar·ation** ᵠ C1 ⓦ /ˌsepəˈreɪʃn/ *noun* **1** ᵠ C1 [U, sing.] the act of separating people or things; the state of being separate: *~ from sb/sth the state's eventual separation from the federation* ◊ *~ between A and B the need for a clear separation between Church and State* ⊃ see also COLOUR SEPARATION **2** ᵠ C1 [C] a period of time that people spend apart from each other: *They were reunited after a separation of more than 20 years.* **3** ᵠ C1 [C] a decision that a husband and wife make to live apart while they are still legally married: *a legal separation* ⊃ compare DIVORCE

**sepa'ration anxiety** *noun* [U] feelings of worry that a young child experiences when a parent goes away

**the sepa'ration of 'powers** *noun* [sing.] the principle of the US Constitution that the political power of the government is divided between the President, Congress and the Supreme Court ⊃ compare CHECKS AND BALANCES

**sep·ar·at·ist** /ˈseprətɪst/ *noun* a member of a group of people within a country who want to separate from the rest of the country and form their own government: *Basque separatists* ▶ **sep·ar·at·ism** /-prətɪzəm/ *noun* [U] **sep·ar·at·ist** *adj.*: *a separatist movement*

**sep·ar·ator** /ˈsepəreɪtə(r)/ *noun* a machine for separating things

**Seph·ardi** /sɪˈfɑːdi; NAmE -ˈfɑːrdi/ *noun* (*pl.* **Seph·ar·dim** /-dɪm/) a Jew whose ANCESTORS came from Spain or North Africa ⊃ compare ASHKENAZI ▶ **Seph·ar·dic** /-dɪk/ *adj.*

**sepia** /ˈsiːpiə/ *noun* [U] **1** a brown substance used in INKS and paints and used in the past for printing photographs **2** a red-brown colour ▶ **sepia** *adj.* [usually before noun]: *sepia ink/prints/photographs*

**sepoy** /ˈsiːpɔɪ/ *noun* **1** in the past, an Indian soldier serving under a British or European officer **2** (*IndE*) a soldier or police officer of the lowest rank

**sep·sis** /ˈsepsɪs/ *noun* [U] (*medical*) an infection of part of the body in which PUS is produced

**Sep·tem·ber** ❶ A1 /sepˈtembə(r)/ *noun* [U, C] (*abbr.* **Sept.**) the 9th month of the year, between August and October **HELP** To see how **September** is used, look at the examples at **April**.

**sep·tet** /sepˈtet/ *noun* **1** [C + sing./pl. v.] a group of seven musicians or singers **2** [C] a piece of music for seven musicians or singers

**sep·tic** /ˈseptɪk/ *adj.* (of a wound or part of the body) containing harmful bacteria that cause infection: *a septic finger* ◊ *A dirty cut may go septic.*

**septi·cae·mia** (*BrE*) (*NAmE* **septi·ce·mia**) /ˌseptɪˈsiːmiə/ *noun* [U] (*medical*) infection of the blood by harmful bacteria ᴇʏɴ **blood poisoning**

**'septic tank** *noun* a large container, usually underground, that holds human waste from toilets until the action of bacteria makes it liquid enough to go into the ground

**sep·tua·gen·ar·ian** /ˌseptjuədʒəˈneəriən; NAmE -tʃuədʒəˈner-/ *noun* (*formal*) a person between 70 and 79 years old

**sep·tum** /ˈseptəm/ *noun* (*pl.* **septa** /-tə/) (*anatomy*) a thin part that separates two hollow areas, for example the part of the nose between the NOSTRILS

**se·pul·chral** /səˈpʌlkrəl/ *adj.* (*literary*) looking or sounding sad and serious; making you think of death ᴇʏɴ **funeral**: *He spoke in sepulchral tones.*

**se·pul·chre** (*US* **se·pul·cher**) /ˈseplkə(r)/ *noun* (*old use*) a place for a dead body, either cut in rock or built of stone

**se·quel** /ˈsiːkwəl/ *noun* **1** *~ (to sth)* a book, film, play, etc. that continues the story of an earlier one: *a sequel to the hit movie 'Madagascar'* ⊃ compare PREQUEL **2** [usually sing.] *~ (to sth)* something that happens after an earlier event or as a result of an earlier event: *There was an interesting sequel to these events later in the year.*

**se·quence** ❶ B2 ⓞ /ˈsiːkwəns/ *noun, verb*
■ *noun* **1** ᵠ B2 [C] *~ (of sth)* a set of events, actions, numbers, etc. which have a particular order and which lead to a particular result: *He described the sequence of events leading up to the robbery.* **2** ᵠ B2 [C, U] the order that events, actions, etc. happen in or should happen in: *in a … ~ The tasks had to be performed in a particular sequence.* ◊ *in ~ Number the pages in sequence.* ◊ **out of ~** *These pages are out of sequence.* **3** [C] a part of a film

that deals with one subject or topic or consists of one scene
■ *verb* **1** ~ **sth** (*specialist*) to arrange things into a sequence **2** ~ **sth** (*biology*) to identify the order in which a set of GENES or parts of MOLECULES are arranged: *The human genome has now been sequenced.* ▶ **se·quen·cing** *noun* [U]: *a gene sequencing project*

**the ˌsequence of ˈtenses** *noun* [sing.] (*grammar*) the rules according to which the tense of a SUBORDINATE CLAUSE depends on the tense of a main clause, so that, for example, '*I think that you are wrong*' becomes '*I thought that you were wrong*' in the past tense

**se·quen·cer** /ˈsiːkwənsə(r)/ *noun* an electronic instrument for recording and storing sounds so that they can be played later as part of a piece of music

**se·quen·tial** /sɪˈkwenʃl/ *adj.* (*formal*) following in order of time or place: *sequential data processing* ▶ **se·quen·tial·ly** /-ʃəli/ *adv.*: *data stored sequentially on a computer*

**se·ques·ter** /sɪˈkwestə(r)/ *verb* (*law*) **1** = SEQUESTRATE **2** ~ **sb** to keep a JURY together in a place, in order to prevent them from talking to other people about a court case, or learning about it in the newspapers, on television, etc.

**se·ques·tered** /sɪˈkwestəd; *NAmE* -stərd/ *adj.* [usually before noun] (*literary*) (of a place) quiet and far away from people

**se·ques·trate** /sɪˈkwestreɪt, ˈsɪkwestreɪt/ (*also* **se·ques·ter**) *verb* ~ **sth** (*law*) to take control of sb's property or ASSETS until a debt has been paid ▶ **se·ques·tra·tion** /ˌsiːkwəˈstreɪʃn; *NAmE also* ˌsek-/ *noun* [U, C]

**se·quin** /ˈsiːkwɪn/ *noun* a small round shiny disc SEWN onto clothing as decoration ▶ **se·quinned** (*BrE*) (*NAmE* **se·quined**) /-kwɪnd/ *adj.* [usually before noun]

**se·quoia** /sɪˈkwɔɪə/ *noun* a very tall North American tree, a type of redwood

**sera** /ˈsɪərə; *NAmE* ˈsɪrə/ *pl.* of SERUM

**ser·aph** /ˈserəf/ *noun* (*pl.* **ser·aph·im** /-rəfɪm/ *or* **ser·aphs**) an ANGEL of the highest rank ⊃ compare CHERUB

**ser·en·ade** /ˌserəˈneɪd/ *noun, verb*
■ *noun* **1** (in the past) a song or tune played or sung at night by a man outside the window of the woman he loves **2** a gentle piece of music in several parts, usually for a small group of instruments
■ *verb* ~ **sb** to sing or play music to sb (as done in the past by a man singing under her window to the woman he loved): *We were serenaded by a string quartet.*

**ser·en·dip·ity** /ˌserənˈdɪpəti/ *noun* [U] the fact of sth interesting or pleasant happening by chance ▶ **ser·en·dip·it·ous** /-təs/ *adj.*: *serendipitous discoveries*

**se·rene** /səˈriːn/ *adj.* calm and peaceful: *a lake, still and serene in the sunlight* ▶ **se·rene·ly** *adv.*: *serenely beautiful* ◇ *She smiled serenely.* **se·ren·ity** /-ˈrenəti/ *noun* [U, sing.]: *The hotel offers a haven of peace and serenity away from the bustle of the city.*

**serf** /sɜːf; *NAmE* sɜːrf/ *noun* (in the past) a person who was forced to live and work on land that belonged to a LANDOWNER whom they had to obey

**serf·dom** /ˈsɜːfdəm; *NAmE* ˈsɜːrf-/ *noun* [U] the system under which crops were grown by serfs; the state of being a serf: *the abolition of serfdom in Russia in 1861*

**serge** /sɜːdʒ; *NAmE* sɜːrdʒ/ *noun* [U] a type of strong cloth made of wool, used for making clothes: *a blue serge suit*

**ser·geant** /ˈsɑːdʒənt; *NAmE* ˈsɑːrdʒ-/ *noun* (*abbr.* **Sergt, Sgt**) **1** a member of one of the middle ranks in the army and the AIR FORCE, below an officer: *Sergeant Salter* ⊃ see also FLIGHT SERGEANT, STAFF SERGEANT **2** (in the UK) a police officer just below the rank of an INSPECTOR **3** (in the US) a police officer just below the rank of a LIEUTENANT or CAPTAIN ⊃ see also SARGE

**ˌsergeant ˈmajor** *noun* (often used as a title) **1** a soldier of middle rank in the British army who is responsible for helping the officer who organizes the affairs of a particular REGIMENT (= a large group of soldiers) **2** a soldier in the US army of the highest rank of NON-COMMISSIONED OFFICERS

---

1413 **serious**

**ser·ial** /ˈsɪəriəl; *NAmE* ˈsɪr-/ *adj., noun*
■ *adj.* **1** [only before noun] doing the same thing in the same way several times; done in the same way several times: *a serial rapist* ◇ *He is wanted for serial murder.* **2** [only before noun] (of a story, etc.) broadcast or published in several separate parts: *a novel in serial form* **3** [usually before noun] (*specialist*) arranged in a series: *tasks carried out in the same serial order* ▶ **seri·al·ly** /-riəli/ *adv.*
■ *noun* a story that is broadcast or published in several separate parts on television, on the radio, on the internet, in a magazine, etc.

▼ **HOMOPHONES**

**cereal** • **serial** /ˈsɪəriəl; *NAmE* ˈsɪr-/

• **cereal** *noun*: *A nutritious breakfast cereal can contribute to a healthy lifestyle.*
• **serial** *noun*: *All the female characters in this serial are very strong.*
• **serial** *adj.*: *The novel was first published in serial form.*

**seri·al·ize** (*BrE also* **-ise**) /ˈsɪəriəlaɪz; *NAmE* ˈsɪr-/ *verb* ~ **sth** to publish or broadcast sth in parts as a serial: *The novel was serialized on TV in six parts.* ▶ **seri·al·iza·tion, -isa·tion** /ˌsɪəriəlaɪˈzeɪʃn; *NAmE* ˌsɪriələˈz-/ *noun* [C, U]: *a newspaper serialization of the book*

**ˈserial killer** *noun* a person who murders several people one after the other in a similar way

**ˈserial number** *noun* a number put on a product, such as a camera, television, etc., in order to identify the particular product

**ˈserial port** *noun* (*computing*) a point on a computer where you connect a device such as a mouse that sends or receives data one BIT at a time

**ser·ies** /ˈsɪəriːz; *NAmE* ˈsɪr-/ *noun* (*pl.* **ser·ies**)
**1** [C] a set of television or radio programmes or PODCASTS that deal with the same subject or that have the same characters: *The first episode of the new series is on Saturday.* ◇ *Her stories have been made into a TV series.* ◇ *a drama/comedy series* **2** [C, usually sing.] several events or things of a similar kind that happen one after the other: ~ **of sth** *The incident sparked off a whole series of events that nobody had foreseen.* ◇ **in a** ~ **of sth** *This is the latest in a series of articles on the nature of modern society.* **3** [C] (*sport*) a set of sports games played between the same two teams: *the World Series* (= in baseball) ◇ *England have lost the Test series* (= of CRICKET matches) *against India.* **4** [U, C] (*specialist*) an electrical CIRCUIT in which the current passes through all the parts in the correct order

**serif** /ˈserɪf/ *noun* a short line at the top or bottom of some styles of printed letters: *a serif typeface*

**ser·ious** /ˈsɪəriəs; *NAmE* ˈsɪr-/ *adj.*
• **BAD 1** bad or dangerous: *a serious illness/offence/crime* ◇ *a serious problem/issue* ◇ *to cause serious injury/damage/harm* ◇ *They pose a serious threat to security.*
• **NOT SILLY 2** thinking about things in a careful and sensible way; not silly: *Be serious for a moment; this is important.* ◇ *I'm afraid I'm not a very serious person.* ⊃ SYNONYMS on page 1414
• **NOT JOKING 3** sincere about sth; not joking or meant as a joke: *Believe me, I'm deadly* (= extremely) *serious.* ◇ *Don't laugh, it's a serious suggestion.* ◇ ~ **about doing sth** *He knew it was time to get serious about losing weight.* ◇ ~ **about sb/sth** *He's really serious about Penny and wants to get engaged.* ◇ (*informal*) *You can't be serious!* (= you must be joking)
• **NEEDING THOUGHT 4** needing to be thought about carefully; not only for pleasure: *a serious article* ◇ *a serious newspaper* ◇ *an appreciation of serious music*
• **IMPORTANT 5** that must be treated as important: *serious questions/concerns/doubts* ◇ *It's time to give serious consideration to this matter.*
• **LARGE AMOUNT 6** (*informal*) used to emphasize that there is a large amount of sth: *You can earn serious money doing that.*

# seriously

**SYNONYMS**

**serious**
grave · earnest · solemn

These words all describe sb who thinks and behaves carefully and sensibly, but often without much joy or laughter.

**serious** thinking about things in a careful and sensible way; not laughing about sth: *He's not really a very serious person.* ◇ *Be serious for a moment; this is important.*

**grave** (*rather formal*) (of a person) serious in manner, as if sth sad, important, or worrying has just happened: *He looked very grave as he entered the room.*

**earnest** serious and sincere: *The earnest young doctor answered all our questions.*

**solemn** looking or sounding very serious, without smiling; done or said in a very serious and sincere way: *Her expression grew solemn.* ◇ *I made a solemn promise that I would return.*

**PATTERNS**
- a(n) serious/grave/earnest/solemn **expression/face**
- a serious/solemn **mood/atmosphere**

**ser·ious·ly** ❶ B1 /ˈsɪəriəsli; *NAmE* ˈsɪr-/ *adv.* **1** B1 in a serious way: *to be seriously ill/injured/wounded/hurt* ◇ *Smoking can seriously damage your health.* ◇ *You need to think seriously about your next career move.* ◇ *He is seriously considering opening a second restaurant.* **2** used at the beginning of a sentence to show a change from joking to being more serious: *Seriously though, it could be really dangerous.* **3** (*informal*) very; extremely: *They're seriously rich.*
**IDM** **take sb/sth ˈseriously** to think that sb/sth is important and deserves your attention and respect: *We take threats of this kind very seriously.* ◇ *Why can't you ever take anything seriously?*

**ser·ious·ness** /ˈsɪəriəsnəs; *NAmE* ˈsɪr-/ *noun* [U, sing.] the state of being serious: *He spoke with a seriousness that was unusual in him.*
**IDM** **in all ˈseriousness** very seriously; not as a joke

**ser·mon** /ˈsɜːmən; *NAmE* ˈsɜːrm-/ *noun* **1** a talk on a moral or religious subject, usually given by a religious leader during a service ⮕ SYNONYMS at SPEECH **2** (*informal, usually disapproving*) moral advice that a person tries to give you in a long talk

**sero·tonin** /ˌserəˈtəʊnɪn/ *noun* [U] a chemical in the brain that affects how messages are sent from the brain to the body, and also affects how a person feels

**ser·pent** /ˈsɜːpənt; *NAmE* ˈsɜːrp-/ *noun* (*literary*) a snake, especially a large one

**ser·pen·tine** /ˈsɜːpəntaɪn; *NAmE* ˈsɜːrpəntiːn/ *adj.* (*literary*) bending and TWISTING like a snake **SYN** **winding**: *the serpentine course of the river*

**ser·rated** /səˈreɪtɪd/ *adj.* having a series of sharp points on the edge like a SAW: *a knife with a serrated edge* ◇ *a serrated blade*

**ser·ra·tion** /seˈreɪʃn/ *noun* [usually pl.] a part on the edge of a knife or other tool that is sharp and pointed like a SAW

**serum** /ˈsɪərəm; *NAmE* ˈsɪr-/ *noun* (*pl.* **sera** /-rə/ or **ser·ums**) **1** [U] (*biology*) the thin liquid that remains from blood when the rest has CLOTTED **2** [U, C] (*medical*) serum taken from the blood of an animal and given to people to protect them from disease, poison, etc: *snakebite serum* **3** [U] any liquid like water in body TISSUE

**ser·vant** ❶ B1 /ˈsɜːvənt; *NAmE* ˈsɜːrv-/ *noun* **1** B1 a person who works in another person's house, and cooks, cleans, etc. for them: *a domestic servant* ◇ *They treat their mother like a servant.* ◇ *~ to sb She was working as a servant to the Smith family.* **2** *~ (to/of sth)* a person who works for a company or an organization ⮕ see also CIVIL SERVANT, PUBLIC SERVANT **3** *~ to/of sth* a person or thing that is controlled by sth: *He was willing to make himself a servant of his art.* **IDM** see OBEDIENT

**serve** ❶ A2 /sɜːv; *NAmE* sɜːrv/ *verb, noun*
■ *verb*
- **FOOD/DRINK 1** A2 [T, I] to give sb food or drink, for example at a restaurant or during a meal: *~(sth) Breakfast is served between 7 and 10 a.m.* ◇ *Pour the sauce over the pasta and serve immediately.* ◇ *Shall I serve?* ◇ *~sth with sth Serve the lamb with new potatoes and green beans.* ◇ *~sth to sb They served a wonderful meal to more than fifty delegates.* ◇ *~sb with sth The delegates were served with a wonderful meal.* ◇ *~sb sth She served us a delicious lunch.* ◇ *~sth + adj. The quiche can be served hot or cold.* **2** [T] *~sb/sth* (of an amount of food) to be enough for sb/sth: *This dish will serve four hungry people.*
- **CUSTOMERS 3** A2 [T, I] *~(sb)* (*especially BrE*) to help a customer or sell them sth in a shop: *Are you being served?* ◇ *She was serving behind the counter.*
- **BE USEFUL 4** B2 [T] *~sth/sb* to be useful to sb in achieving or satisfying sth: *These experiments serve no useful purpose.* ◇ *Most of their economic policies serve the interests of big business.* ◇ *How can we best serve the needs of future generations?* ◇ *His linguistic ability served him well in his chosen profession.*
- **PROVIDE STH 5** B2 [T] to provide an area or a group of people with a product or service: *~sb/sth The centre will serve the whole community.* ◇ *~sb/sth with sth The town is well served with buses and major road links.*
- **WORK 6** B2 [I, T] to work or perform duties for a person, an organization, a country, etc.; to spend a period of time in a particular job: *~as sth He served as a captain in the army.* ◇ *~under/with sb He served under Tony Blair in the 1990s.* ◇ *~+ adv./prep. She served in the medical corps.* ◇ *~sth/sb He proudly served his country during the war.* ◇ *She has already served two terms as mayor.* ◇ *He served the family faithfully for many years* (= as a servant).
- **BE SUITABLE 7** [I] *~(as sth)* to be suitable for a particular use, especially when nothing else is available: *The sofa will serve as a bed for a night or two.*
- **HAVE PARTICULAR RESULT 8** [I, T] to have a particular effect or result: *~as sth The judge said the punishment would serve as a warning to others.* ◇ *~to do sth The attack was unsuccessful and served only to alert the enemy.*
- **TIME IN PRISON 9** [T] *~sth* to spend a period of time in prison: *prisoners serving life sentences* ◇ *She is serving two years for theft.* ◇ *He has served time* (= been to prison) *before.*
- **OFFICIAL DOCUMENT 10** [T] (*law*) to give or send sb an official document, especially one that orders them to appear in court: *~sth (on sb) to serve sb with a writ/summons on sb* ◇ *~sb with sth to serve sb with a writ/summons*
- **IN SPORT 11** [I, T] (in tennis, etc.) to start playing by throwing the ball into the air and hitting it: *Who's serving?* ◇ *~sth She served an ace.*

**IDM** **it serves sb ˈright (for doing sth)** used to say that sth that has happened to sb is their own fault and they deserve it: *Left you, did she? It serves you right for being so selfish.* **serve your/its ˈturn** (*BrE*) to be useful for a particular purpose or period of time **serve two ˈmasters** (usually used in negative sentences) to support two different parties, principles, etc. at the same time ⮕ more at FIRST *adv.*, MEMORY

**PHR V** **ˌserve sth↔ˈout 1** to continue doing sth, especially working or staying in prison, for a fixed period of time that has been set: *He has three more years in prison before he's served out his sentence.* ◇ *BrE) They didn't want me to serve out my notice.* **2** (*BrE*) to share food or drink between a number of people: *I went around the guests serving out drinks.* **ˌserve sth↔ˈup 1** to put food onto plates and give it to people: *He served up a delicious meal.* **2** to give, offer or provide sth: *She served up the usual excuse.* ◇ *The teams served up some fantastic entertainment.*

■ *noun* (in tennis, etc.) the action of serving the ball to your opponent

**ser·ver** /ˈsɜːvə(r); *NAmE* ˈsɜːrv-/ *noun* **1** (*computing*) a computer program that controls or supplies information to several computers connected in a network; the main computer on which this program is run ⊃ see also CLIENT-SERVER **2** (*sport*) a player who is serving, for example in tennis **3** [usually pl.] a kitchen UTENSIL (= tool) used for putting food onto sb's plate: *salad servers* **4** (*NAmE*) a person who serves food in a restaurant; a waiter or WAITRESS **5** a person who helps a priest during a church service ⊃ see also TIME-SERVER

**'server farm** *noun* = DATA CENTRE

**ser·vice** ⓘ A2 ⓦ /'sɜːvɪs; *NAmE* 'sɜːrv-/ *noun*, *verb*

■ *noun*
- PROVIDING STH **1** ⓘ A2 [C] a system that provides sth that the public needs, organized by the government or a private company: *the ambulance/bus/postal service* ◊ *The government aims to improve public services, especially education.* ◊ *Essential services* (= the supply of water, gas, electricity) *will be maintained.* ⊃ see also EMERGENCY SERVICES, POSTAL SERVICE, PUBLIC SERVICE **2** ⓘ A2 (*also* Service) [C] an organization or a company that provides sth for the public or does sth for the government: *the prison service* ◊ *the BBC World Service* ⊃ see also CIVIL SERVICE, DIPLOMATIC SERVICE, FIRE SERVICE, HEALTH SERVICE, INTERNAL REVENUE SERVICE, NATIONAL HEALTH SERVICE, SECRET SERVICE, SECURITY SERVICE, SOCIAL SERVICES **3** ⓘ A2 [C, U] a business whose work involves doing sth for customers but not producing goods; the work that such a business does: *financial services* ◊ *the development of new goods and services* ◊ *We guarantee (an) excellent service.* ◊ *to provide/offer a service* ◊ *The number of people using the service has fallen.* ◊ *the service sector* (= the part of the economy involved in this type of business) ◊ *a service industry* ⊃ see also WIRE SERVICE
- IN HOTEL/SHOP/RESTAURANT **4** ⓘ B1 [U] the serving of customers in hotels, restaurants, and shops: *The food was good but the service was very slow.* ⊃ see also CUSTOMER SERVICE, ROOM SERVICE, SELF-SERVICE
- WORK FOR ORGANIZATION **5** ⓘ B2 [U] the work that sb does for an organization, etc., especially when it continues for a long time or is admired very much: *~ with sth She has just celebrated 25 years' service with the company.* ◊ *~ to sth He has retired after 30 years of dedicated service to the local community.* ◊ *The employees have good conditions of service.* ⊃ see also COMMUNITY SERVICE, JURY SERVICE at JURY DUTY
- ARMY, ETC. **6** ⓘ B2 [C, usually pl., U] the army, the NAVY and the AIR FORCE; the work done by people in them: *Most of the boys went straight into the services.* ◊ *He saw service in North Africa.* ◊ *a service family* ⊃ see also ACTIVE SERVICE, MILITARY SERVICE, NATIONAL SERVICE
- OF VEHICLE/MACHINE **7** [U] the use that you can get from a vehicle or machine; the state of being used: *That computer gave us very good service.* ◊ *in ~ This bus is not in service.* ◊ *out of~ The ship will be taken out of service within two years.* **8** [C, U] an examination of a vehicle or machine followed by any work that is necessary to keep it operating well: *a service engineer* ◊ (*BrE*) *I had taken the car in for a service.* ◊ (*NAmE*) *I had taken the car in for service.* ⊃ see also AFTER-SALES SERVICE
- SKILLS/HELP **9** [usually pl.] (*formal*) the particular skills or help that a person is able to offer: *You need the services of a good lawyer.* ◊ *~ as sb/sth He offered his services as a driver.*
- RELIGIOUS CEREMONY **10** ⓘ B2 [C] a religious ceremony: *a funeral/memorial service* ◊ *to hold/attend a service*
- BUS/TRAIN **11** [C, usually sing.] a bus, train, etc. that goes regularly to a particular place at a particular time: *the cancellation of the 10.15 service to Glasgow*
- ON MOTORWAY **12** services [sing. + sing./pl. v.] (*BrE*) a place next to a MOTORWAY where you can stop for petrol, a meal, the toilets, etc: *motorway services* ◊ *It's five miles to the next services.* ⊃ see also SERVICE AREA, SERVICE STATION
- IN TENNIS **13** [sing.] an act of hitting the ball in order to start playing; the way that you hit it SYN serve: *It's your service* (= your turn to start playing). ◊ *Her service has improved.*
- SET OF PLATES, ETC. **14** [C] a complete set of plates, dishes, etc. that match each other: *a tea service* (= cups, SAUCERS, a TEAPOT and plates, for serving tea) ⊃ see also DINNER SERVICE

- BEING SERVANT **15** [U] (*old-fashioned*) the state or position of being a servant: *to be in/go into service* (= to be/become a servant)
- OF OFFICIAL DOCUMENT **16** [U] (*law*) the formal giving of an official document, etc. to sb: *the service of a demand for payment* ⊃ see also LIP SERVICE

IDM **at the 'service of sb/sth | at sb's 'service** completely available for sb to use or to help sb: *Healthcare must be at the service of all who need it.* ◊ ('*formal* or *humorous*) *If you need anything, I am at your service.* **be of 'service (to sb)** (*formal*) to be useful or helpful: *Can I be of service to anyone?* **do sb a/no 'service** (*formal*) to do sth that is helpful/not helpful to sb: *She was doing herself no service by remaining silent.* ⊃ more at PRESS *v.*

■ *verb*
- VEHICLE/MACHINE **1** [usually passive] to examine a vehicle or machine and repair it if necessary so that it continues to work correctly: **have sth/be serviced** *We need to have the car serviced.*
- PROVIDE STH **2** [often passive] to provide people with sth they need, such as shops, or a transport system SYN serve: **be serviced by sth/sb** *Botley is well serviced by a regular bus route into Oxford.*
- PAY INTEREST **3** *~* sth (*finance*) to pay interest on money that has been borrowed: *The company can no longer service its debts.*

**ser·vice·able** /'sɜːvɪsəbl; *NAmE* 'sɜːrv-/ *adj.* of good enough quality to be used: *The carpet is worn but still serviceable.*

**'service area** *noun* (*BrE*) a place on a MOTORWAY where you can stop and buy food, petrol, have a meal, go to the toilet, etc.

**'service charge** *noun* **1** an amount of money that is added to a bill, as an extra charge for a service: *That will be $50, plus a service charge of $2.50.* **2** (*BrE*) an amount of money that is added to a bill in a restaurant, for example 10 per cent of the total, that goes to pay for the work of the staff ⊃ WORDFINDER NOTE at RESTAURANT **3** an amount of money that is paid to the owner of an apartment building for services such as putting out rubbish, cleaning the stairs, etc.

**'service club** *noun* (*NAmE*) an organization whose members do things to help their local community

**'service industry** *noun* [U, C] a business that provides services for customers

**ser·vice·man** /'sɜːvɪsmən; *NAmE* 'sɜːrv-/, **ser·vice·woman** /'sɜːvɪswʊmən; *NAmE* 'sɜːrv-/ *noun* (*pl.* -men /-mən/, -women /-wɪmɪn/) a man or woman who is a member of the armed forces ⊃ note at GENDER

**'service member** *noun* (*US*) a person who serves in a country's army, NAVY, etc.

**'service plaza** *noun* (*NAmE*) = PLAZA (3)

**'service provider** (*also less frequent* **'access provider**) *noun* a business company that provides a service to customers, especially one that connects customers to the internet: *an internet service provider*

**'service road** (*NAmE also* **'frontage road**) *noun* a side road that runs next to a main road, that you use to reach houses, shops, etc.

**'service station** *noun* **1** = GAS STATION, PETROL STATION **2** (*BrE*) (*NAmE* **'plaza**, **'service plaza**) an area and building next to a MOTORWAY where you can buy food and petrol, go to the toilet, etc: *a motorway service station*

**ser·vi·cing** /'sɜːvɪsɪŋ; *NAmE* 'sɜːrv-/ *noun* [U] **1** the act of checking and repairing a vehicle, machine, etc. to keep it in good condition: *Like any other type of equipment it requires regular servicing.* **2** (*finance*) the act of paying interest on money that has been borrowed: *debt servicing*

**ser·vi·ette** /ˌsɜːviˈet; *NAmE* ˌsɜːrv-/ *noun* (*BrE*) a piece of cloth or paper used at meals for protecting your clothes and cleaning your lips and fingers SYN napkin

# servile

**ser·vile** /ˈsɜːvaɪl; NAmE ˈsɜːrvl, -vaɪl/ adj. (disapproving) wanting too much to please sb and obey them ▶ **ser·vil·ity** /sɜːˈvɪləti; NAmE sɜːrˈv-/ noun [U]

**serv·ing** /ˈsɜːvɪŋ; NAmE ˈsɜːrv-/ noun an amount of food for one person: *This recipe will be enough for four servings.*

**ser·vi·tor** /ˈsɜːvɪtə(r); NAmE ˈsɜːrv-/ noun (old use) a male servant

**ser·vi·tude** /ˈsɜːvɪtjuːd; NAmE ˈsɜːrvɪtuːd/ noun [U] (formal) the condition of being a slave or being forced to obey another person SYN **slavery**

**servo** /ˈsɜːvəʊ; NAmE ˈsɜːrv-/ noun (pl. -os) (specialist) a part of a machine that controls a larger machine

**ses·ame** /ˈsesəmi/ noun [U] a tropical plant grown for its seeds and their oil, which are used in cooking: *sesame seeds*

**ses·sion** ⓘ B2 ⓢ /ˈseʃn/ noun **1** B2 [C] a period of time that is spent doing a particular activity: *a training/ practice session* ◊ *a therapy/counselling/group session* ⊃ see also JAM SESSION **2** B2 [C, U] a formal meeting or series of meetings of a court, a parliament, etc.; a period of time when such meetings are held: *a session of the UN General Assembly* ◊ *a special session of the US Supreme Court* ◊ **in** ~ *The court is now in session.* ⊃ see also COURT OF SESSION **3** [C] a school or university year **4** [C] an occasion when people meet to play music, especially Irish music, in a pub

**ˈsession musician** noun a musician who is hired to play on recordings but is not a permanent member of a band

**set** ⓘ B1 ⓞ /set/ verb, noun, adj.
■ verb (set·ting, set, set)
• CLOCK/MACHINE **1** B1 [T] ~ sth (+ adv./prep.) to prepare or arrange sth so that it is ready for use or in position: *She set the camera on automatic.* ◊ *I set my watch by (= make it show the same time as) the TV.* ◊ *Set the alarm for 7 o'clock.*
• TABLE **2** B1 [T] ~ a/the table (for sb/sth) to arrange knives, forks, etc. on a table for a meal: *Could you set the table for dinner?* ◊ *The table was set for six guests.*
• EXAMPLE/STANDARD, ETC. **3** B1 [T] ~ sth to fix sth so that others copy it or try to achieve it: *This could set a new fashion.* ◊ *They set high standards of customer service.* ◊ *I am unwilling to set a precedent.* ◊ *She set a new world record for the high jump.* ◊ *I rely on you to set a good example.*
• WORK/TASK **4** B1 [T] ~ sth to give sb a piece of work to do or a task or target to achieve: ~ sth *Who will be setting (= writing the questions for) the French exam?* ◊ ~ sth for sb *What books have been set (= are to be studied) for the English course?* ◊ ~ sth for sb/yourself *She's set a difficult task for herself.* ◊ ~ sb/yourself sth *She's set herself a difficult task.* ◊ ~ sb/yourself to do sth *I've set myself to finish the job by the end of the month.*
• ARRANGE **5** B1 [T] ~ sth to arrange or fix sth; to decide on sth: *They haven't set a date for their wedding yet.* ◊ *The government has set strict limits on public spending this year.* ◊ *We can't just let the global corporations set the agenda (= decide what is important) every time.*
• PLAY/BOOK/FILM **6** B1 [T, usually passive] to place the action of a play, novel or film in a particular place, time, etc: *be set + adv./prep. The novel is set in London in the 1960s.*
• BE LOCATED **7** B2 [T, usually passive] to be located in a particular place: *be ~ + adv./prep. The house is set in fifty acres of parkland.*
• PUT/START **8** B2 [T] ~ sth/sb + adv./prep. to put sth/sb in a particular place or position: *She set a tray down on the table.* ◊ *They ate everything that was set in front of them.* **9** B2 [T] to cause sb/sth to be in a particular state; to start sth happening: ~ sb/sth + adv./prep. *Her manner immediately set everyone at their ease.* ◊ *He pulled the lever and set the machine in motion.* ◊ *Demonstrators set two cars on fire.* ◊ *Demonstrators set fire to two cars.* ◊ ~ sb/sth + adj. *The hijackers set the hostages free.* ◊ ~ sb/ sth doing sth *Her remarks set me thinking.*
• OF SUN/MOON **10** B2 [I] to go down below the HORIZON: *We sat and watched the sun setting.* ⊃ see also SUNSET verb **OPP rise**
• JEWELLERY **11** [T, usually passive] to put a PRECIOUS STONE into a piece of jewellery: ~ A in B *She had the sapphire set in a gold ring.* ◊ ~ B with A *Her bracelet was set with emeralds.*
• BECOME HARD **12** [I] to become solid or hard: *Leave the concrete to set for a few hours.* ◊ + adj. *The glue had set hard.*
• FACE **13** [T, usually passive] ~ sth to fix your face into a determined expression: *Her jaw was set in a determined manner.*
• HAIR **14** [T] ~ sth to arrange sb's hair while it is wet so that it dries in a particular style: *She had her hair washed and set.*
• BONE **15** [T, I] ~ (sth) to put a broken bone into a fixed position and hold it there, so that it will join together again and get better; to get better in this way: *The surgeon set her broken arm.*
• FOR PRINTING **16** [T] ~ sth (specialist) to use a machine or computer to arrange writing and images on pages in order to prepare a book, newspaper, etc. for printing ⊃ see also TYPESETTER
• WORDS TO MUSIC **17** [T] ~ sth (to sth) to write music to go with words: *Schubert set many poems to music.* **HELP** Idioms containing **set** are at the entries for the nouns and adjectives in the idioms, for example **set the pace** is at **pace** n.

**PHRV ˈset about sb** (*BrE, old-fashioned, informal*) to attack sb | **ˈset about sth** | **ˌset about ˈdoing sth** [no passive] to start doing sth: *She set about the business of cleaning the house.* ◊ *We need to set about finding a solution.*
**ˌset sb aˈgainst sb** to make sb oppose a friend, relative, etc.: *She accused her husband of setting the children against her.* **ˌset sth (ˈoff) against sth 1** to judge sth by comparing good or positive qualities with bad or negative ones: *Set against the benefits of the new technology, there is also a strong possibility that jobs will be lost.* **2** (*finance*) to record sth as a business cost as a way of reducing the amount of tax you must pay: *to set capital costs off against tax*
**ˌset sb/sth aˈpart (from sb/sth)** to make sb/sth different from or better than others: *Her elegant style sets her apart from other journalists.* **ˌset sth↔aˈpart (for sth)** [usually passive] to keep sth for a special use or purpose: *Two rooms were set apart for use as libraries.*
**ˌset sth↔aˈside 1** to save or keep money, time, land, etc. for a particular purpose: *She tries to set aside some money every month.* ◊ *The government has set aside thousands of acres of land as protected wilderness.* ⊃ see also SET-ASIDE **2** to not consider sth, because other things are more important SYN **disregard**: *Let's set aside my personal feelings for now.* **3** (*law*) to officially state that a decision made by a court is not legally acceptable: *The verdict was set aside by the Appeal Court.*
**ˌset sth/sb↔ˈback** to delay the progress of sth/sb by a particular time: *The bad weather set back the building programme by several weeks.* ⊃ related noun SETBACK
**ˌset sb ˈback sth** [no passive] (*informal*) to cost sb a particular amount of money: *The repairs could set you back over £200.* **ˌset sth ˈback (from sth)** [usually passive] to place sth, especially a building, at a distance from sth: *The house is set well back from the road.*
**ˌset sb↔ˈdown** (*BrE*) (of a bus or train, or its driver) to stop and allow sb to get off: *Passengers may be set down and picked up only at the official stops.* **ˌset sth↔ˈdown 1** to write sth down on paper in order to record it **2** to give sth as a rule, principle, etc: *The standards were set down by the governing body.*
**ˌset ˈforth** (*literary*) to start a journey | **ˌset sth↔ˈforth** (*formal*) to present sth or make it known SYN **expound**: *The president set forth his views in a television broadcast.*
**ˌset ˈin** (of rain, bad weather, infection, etc.) to begin and seem likely to continue: *The rain seemed to have set in for the day.* **ˌset sth ˈin/ˈinto sth** [usually passive] to fasten sth into a flat surface so that it does not stick out from it: *a plaque set into the wall*
**ˌset ˈoff** to begin a journey: *We set off for London just after ten.* **ˌset sth↔ˈoff 1** to make a bomb, etc. explode: *A gang*

*of boys were setting off fireworks in the street.* **2** to make an alarm start ringing: *Opening this door will set off the alarm.* **3** to start a process or series of events: *Panic on the stock market set off a wave of selling.* **4** to make sth more attractive or easy to notice by being placed near it: *That blouse sets off the blue of her eyes.* ˌset sb ˈoff (doing sth) to make sb start doing sth such as laughing, crying or talking

ˌset ˈon/uˈpon sb [usually passive] to attack sb suddenly: *I opened the gate, and was immediately set on by a large dog.* ˌset sb/sth ˈon sb to make a person or an animal attack sb suddenly: *The farmer threatened to set his dogs on us.*

ˌset ˈout **1** 🔑 B2 to leave a place and begin a journey: *They set out on the last stage of their journey.* **2** to begin a job, task, etc. with a particular aim or goal: *She set out to break the world record.* ◇ *They succeeded in what they set out to do.* ˌset sth↔ˈout **1** to arrange or display things: *Her work is always very well set out.* **2** to present ideas, facts, etc. in an organized way, in speech or writing: *He set out his objections to the plan.* ◇ *She set out the reasons for her resignation in a long letter.*

ˌset ˈto (*old-fashioned, informal*) to begin doing sth in a busy or determined way

ˌset sb↔ˈup **1** to provide sb with the money that they need in order to do sth: *A bank loan helped to set him up in business.* **2** (*informal*) to make sb healthier, stronger, more lively, etc: *The break from work really set me up for the new year.* **3** (*informal*) to trick sb, especially by making them appear guilty of sth: *He denied the charges, saying the police had set him up.* ⊃ related noun SET-UP ˌset sth↔ˈup **1** 🔑 B1 to create sth or start it: *to set up a business* ◇ *A fund will be set up for the dead men's families.* **2** 🔑 B1 to build sth or put sth somewhere: *The police set up roadblocks on routes out of the city.* **3** 🔑 B1 to make a piece of equipment or a machine ready for use: *She set up her guitar and amp in her bedroom.* **4** 🔑 B1 to arrange for sth to happen: *I've set up a meeting for Friday.* **5** to start a process or a series of events: *The slump on Wall Street set up a chain reaction in stock markets around the world.* ⊃ related noun SET-UP ˌset (yourself) ˈup (as sth) to start running a business: *She took out a bank loan and set up on her own.* ◇ *After leaving college, he set himself up as a freelance photographer.*

■ **noun**

• GROUP **1** 🔑 B1 [C] ~ (of sth) a group of similar things that belong together in some way: *a set of six chairs* ◇ *a complete set of her novels* ◇ *a set of false teeth* ◇ *a new set of rules to learn* ◇ *You can borrow my keys—I have a spare set.* ⊃ see also BOX SET, TRAIN SET **2** 🔑 B1 [C] a group of objects used together, for example for playing a game: *a chess set* ⊃ see also TRAIN SET **3** [C + sing./pl. v.] (*sometimes disapproving*) a group of people who have similar interests and spend a lot of time together socially: *the smart set* (= rich, fashionable people) ◇ *Dublin's literary set* ⊃ see also JET SET

• TV/RADIO **4** [C] a piece of equipment for receiving television or radio signals: *a television/TV set*

• FOR PLAY/MOVIE **5** [C] the SCENERY used for a play, film, etc: *We need volunteers to help build and paint the set.* **6** [C, U] a place where a play is performed or part of a film is filmed: *The cast must all be on (the) set by 7 in the morning.*
⊃ WORDFINDER NOTE at DRAMA

• IN SPORT **7** [C] one section of a match in games such as tennis or VOLLEYBALL: *She won in straight sets* (= without losing a set).

• MATHEMATICS **8** [C] a group of things regarded as a unit because they all have particular qualities in common: *the set of all square numbers less than 50*

• POP MUSIC **9** [C] a series of songs or pieces of music that a musician or group performs at a concert

• CLASS **10** [C] (*BrE*) a group of school students with a similar ability in a particular subject: *She's in the top set for French.*

• OF FACE/BODY **11** [sing.] ~ of sth the way in which sb's face or body is fixed in a particular expression, especially one showing a feeling of being determined: *She admired the firm set of his jaw.*

• HAIR **12** [sing.] an act of arranging hair in a particular style while it is wet: *A shampoo and set costs £15.*

• BECOMING SOLID **13** [sing.] the state of becoming solid or hard

• ANIMAL'S HOME **14** [C] = SETT

• PLANT **15** [C] a young plant, SHOOT etc. for planting: *onion sets*

■ **adj.**

• IN POSITION **1** in a particular position: *a house set in 40 acres of parkland* ◇ *He had close-set eyes.*

• PLANNED **2** [usually before noun] planned or fixed: *Each person was given set jobs to do.* ◇ *The school funds a set number of free places.* ◇ *Mornings in our house always follow a set pattern.*

• OPINIONS/IDEAS **3** not likely to change: *set ideas/opinions/views on how to teach* ◇ *As people get older, they get set in their ways.*

• MEAL **4** [only before noun] (of a meal in a restaurant) having a fixed price and a limited choice of dishes: *a set dinner/lunch/meal* ◇ *Shall we have the set menu?*

• LIKELY/READY **5** likely to do sth; ready for sth or to do sth: ~ for sth *The team looks set for victory.* ◇ ~ to do sth *Interest rates look set to rise again.* ◇ *Be set to leave by 10 o'clock.* ⊃ LANGUAGE BANK at EXPECT

• FACE **6** [usually before noun] (of a person's expression) fixed; not natural: *a set smile* ◇ *His face took on a set expression.*

IDM be (dead) ˈset against sth/against doing sth to be strongly opposed to sth: *Why are you so dead set against the idea?* be ˈset on sth/on doing sth to want to do or have sth very much; to be determined to do sth ⊃ more at MARK n.

ˈset-aside noun [U] a system in which the government pays farmers not to use some of their land for growing crops; the land that the farmers are paid not to use

ˈset-back /ˈsetbæk/ noun a difficulty or problem that delays or prevents sth, or makes a situation worse: *The team suffered a major setback when their best player was injured.* ◇ *The breakdown in talks represents a temporary setback in the peace process.*

seth /seθ/ noun (IndE) **1** a MERCHANT (= a person who sells goods in large quantities) or BANKER (= a person with an important job in a bank) **2** a rich man **3** a title added to a name to indicate high social status

ˌset ˈpiece noun **1** a part of a play, film, piece of music, etc. that has a well-known pattern or style, and is used to create a particular effect **2** a move in a sports game that is well planned and practised

ˌset ˈpoint noun (especially in tennis) a point that, if won by a player, will win them the SET (7)

ˌset ˈsquare (*BrE*) (*NAmE* ˈtri·an·gle) noun an instrument for drawing straight lines and angles, made from a flat piece of plastic or metal in the shape of a TRIANGLE with one angle of 90°

sett (*also* set) /set/ noun a hole in the ground where a BADGER lives

set·tee /seˈtiː/ noun (*BrE*) a long comfortable seat with a back and arms, for two or more people to sit on SYN sofa, couch

set·ter /ˈsetə(r)/ noun **1** a large dog with long hair, sometimes used in hunting. There are several types of setter. **2** (often in compounds) a person who sets sth: *a quiz setter* ⊃ see also JET-SETTER, PACESETTER, TRENDSETTER

**set·ting** 🔑 B1 /ˈsetɪŋ/ noun **1** 🔑 B1 an environment where sth is located; the place at which sth happens: *a rural/an ideal/a beautiful/an idyllic setting* ◇ ~ for sth *It was the perfect setting for a wonderful Christmas.* ◇ in a ~ *The exhibition shows how bees can live happily in an urban setting.* ⊃ SYNONYMS at ENVIRONMENT **2** 🔑 B1 the place and time at which the action of a play, novel, etc. takes place: ~ for sth *London has been used as the setting for many films.* **3** 🔑 B1 a position at which the controls on a machine can be set, to set the speed, height, temperature, etc: *at/on a ~ The performance of the engine was tested at different settings.* **4** *usually* settings [pl.] the place on a computer or other electronic device where you can choose the way

# settle

that it works or looks; the particular choices that you make: *To change the size of the font, go to Settings.* ◇ *It's easy to* **change the settings** *on your device.* **5** (*music*) music written to go with a poem, etc: *Schubert's setting of a poem by Goethe* **6** a piece of metal in which a PRECIOUS STONE is fixed to form a piece of jewellery **7** a complete set of equipment for eating with (knife, fork, spoon, glass, etc.) for one person, arranged on a table: *a place setting*

**set·tle** ❶ **B2** /ˈsetl/ *verb, noun*

■ *verb*
- **END ARGUMENT 1** **B2** [T, I] to put an end to an argument or a DISAGREEMENT: *~ sth to settle a dispute/a matter/an issue* ◇ *to settle a case/lawsuit/claim* ◇ *It's time you settled your differences with your father.* ◇ *The company has agreed to settle out of court* (= come to an agreement without going to court). ◇ *~ with sb (for sth) The corporation later settled with the singer for $1.5 million.*
- **DECIDE/ARRANGE 2** **B2** [T, often passive] to decide or arrange sth finally: *~ sth It's all settled—we're leaving on the nine o'clock plane.* ◇ *Bob will be there?* ***That settles it.*** *I'm not coming.* ◇ *He had to settle his affairs* (= arrange all his personal business) *in Paris before he could return home.* ◇ ***it is settled that…*** *It's been settled that we leave on the nine o'clock plane.*
- **CHOOSE PERMANENT HOME 3** **B2** [I] *+ adv./prep.* to make a place your permanent home: *She settled in Vienna after her father's death.* **4** **B2** [T, usually passive, I] (of a group of people) to make your permanent home in a country or an area as COLONISTS: *~ sth This region was settled by the Dutch in the nineteenth century.* ◇ *~+ adv./prep. They settled on undeveloped land along the Mississippi.* ⇒ WORD-FINDER NOTE at EXPLORE
- **INTO COMFORTABLE POSITION/STATE 5** [I, T] to make yourself or sb else comfortable in a new position: *~ (back) (+ adv./prep.) Ellie settled back in her seat.* ◇ *~ sb/yourself (+ adv./prep.) He settled himself comfortably in his usual chair.* ◇ *I settled her on the sofa and put a blanket over her.* **6** [T] *~ sth + adv./prep.* to put sth carefully in a position so that it does not move: *She settled the blanket around her knees.* **7** [I, T] to become or make sb/sth become calm or relaxed: *The baby wouldn't settle.* ◇ *~ sb/sth I took a pill to help settle my nerves.* ◇ *This should settle your stomach.*
- **COME TO REST 8** [I] *~ (on/over sth)* to fall from above and come to rest on sth; to stay for some time on sth: *Dust had settled on everything.* ◇ *Two birds settled on the fence.* ◇ *I don't think the snow will settle* (= remain on the ground without melting). ◇ *His gaze settled on her face.*
- **SINK DOWN 9** [I, T] *~ (sth)* to sink slowly down; to make sth do this: *The contents of the package may have settled in transit.*
- **PAY MONEY 10** [T, I] to pay the money that you owe: *~ sth Please settle your bill before leaving the hotel.* ◇ *The insurance company is refusing to settle her claim.* ◇ *~ (up) (with sb) Let me settle with you for the meal.* ◇ *I'll pay now—we can settle up later.*

**IDM** ▸ **settle a ˈscore/accounts (with sb)** | **settle an old ˈscore** to hurt or punish sb who has harmed or cheated you in the past: *'Who would do such a thing?' 'Maybe someone with an old score to settle.'* ⇒ more at DUST *n.*

**PHRV** ▸ **settle ˈdown 1** to get into a comfortable position, either sitting or lying: *I settled down with a book.* **2** to start to have a quieter way of life, living in one place: *When are you going to get married and settle down?* **settle ˈdown** | **settle sb↔ˈdown** to become or make sb become calm, less excited, etc: *It always takes the class a while to settle down at the start of the lesson.* **settle (down) to sth** to begin to give your attention to sth: *They finally settled down to a discussion of the main issues.* ◇ *He found it hard to settle to his work.* ▸ **ˈsettle for sth** to accept sth that is not exactly what you want but is the best that is available: *In the end they had to settle for a draw.* ◇ *I couldn't afford the house I really wanted, so I had to settle for second best.* ▸ **settle ˈin** | **settle ˈinto sth** to start to feel comfortable in a new home, job, etc: *How are the kids settling into their new school?* ▸ **ˈsettle on sth** to choose or

make a decision about sth after thinking about it: *Have you settled on a name for the baby yet?* ▸ **ˈsettle sth on sb** (*law*) to formally arrange to give money or property to sb, especially in a WILL

■ *noun* an old-fashioned piece of furniture with a long wooden seat and a high back and arms, often also with a box for storing things under the seat

**set·tled** /ˈsetld/ *adj.* **1** not likely to change or move: *settled weather* ◇ *a settled way of life* **2** comfortable and happy with your home, job, way of life. **OPP** **unsettled**

**set·tle·ment** **B2+** **C1** /ˈsetlmənt/ *noun* **1** **B2+** **C1** [C] an official agreement that ends an argument between two people or groups: *to negotiate a peace settlement* ◇ *The management and unions have reached a settlement over new working conditions.* ◇ *an out-of-court settlement* (= money that is paid to sb or an agreement that is made to stop sb going to court) **2** **B2+** **C1** [U] the action of reaching an agreement: *the settlement of a dispute* **3** [C] (*law*) the conditions, or a document stating the conditions, on which money or property is given to sb: *a divorce/marriage/property settlement* **4** [U] the action of paying back money that you owe: *the settlement of a debt* ◇ **in ~ of sth** *She had to pay over $5 000 in settlement of her debts.* **5** **B2+** **C1** [C] a place where people have come to live and make their homes, especially where few or no people lived before: *signs of an Iron Age settlement* ⇒ see also INFORMAL SETTLEMENT **6** [U] the process of people making their homes in a place: *the settlement of the American West*

**ˈsettlement house** *noun* (*especially NAmE*) a public building in an area of a large city that has social problems, that provides social services such as advice and training to the people who live there

**set·tler** **B2+** **B2** /ˈsetlə(r)/ *noun* a person who goes to live in a new country or region: *Most of the settlers came from England.*

**ˈset-top ˈbox** *noun* a device that allows digital television from cable, satellite, the internet, etc. to be seen on a television set that does not have this feature built in (= as part of the television)

**ˈset-up** **B2+** **C1** *noun* [usually sing.] (*informal*) **1** **B2+** **C1** a way of organizing sth; a system: *I've only been here a couple of weeks and I don't really know the set-up.* **2** a situation in which sb tricks you or makes it seem as if you have done sth wrong: *He didn't steal the goods. It was a set-up.*

**sevak** /ˈseɪvək/ *NAmE* -vɑːk/ *noun* (*IndE*) **1** a male servant **2** a male SOCIAL WORKER

**seven** ❶ **A1** /ˈsevn/ *number* 7 **HELP** There are examples of how to use numbers at the entry for **five**.
**IDM** **the seven-year ˈitch** (*informal, humorous*), the desire for new sexual experience that is thought to be felt after seven years of marriage ⇒ more at SIX

**the ˌseven ˈseas** *noun* [pl.] all of the earth's oceans

**seven·teen** ❶ **A1** /ˌsevnˈtiːn/ *number* 17 ▸ **seven·teenth** /-ˈtiːnθ/ *ordinal number, noun*

**sev·enth** /ˈsevnθ/ *ordinal number, noun*
■ *ordinal number* 7th **HELP** There are examples of how to use ordinal numbers at the entry for **fifth**.
**IDM** **in seventh ˈheaven** extremely happy: *Now that he's been promoted he's in seventh heaven.*
■ *noun* each of seven equal parts of sth

**Seventh-Day Adventist** /ˌsevnθ deɪ ˈædvəntɪst/ *noun* a member of a Christian religious group that believes that Christ will soon return to Earth

**sev·enty** ❶ **A1** /ˈsevnti/ **1** **A1** *number* 70 **2** *noun* **the seventies** [pl.] numbers, years or temperatures from 70 to 79 ▸ **seven·ti·eth** /-əθ/ *ordinal number, noun* **HELP** There are examples of how to use ordinal numbers at the entry for **fifth**.
**IDM** **in your ˈseventies** between the ages of 70 and 79

**sever** /ˈsevə(r)/ *verb* (*formal*) **1** to cut sth into two pieces; to cut sth off sth: **~ sth** *to sever a rope* ◇ *a severed artery* ◇ **~ sth from sth** *His hand was severed from his arm.* **2** **~ sth** to completely end a relationship or all communication with sb **SYN** **break off**: *The two countries have severed all diplomatic links.*

**sev·eral** /ˈsevrəl/ det., pron., adj.
- **det., pron.** more than two but not very many: *Several letters arrived this morning.* ◊ *He's written several books about India.* ◊ *Several more people than usual came to the meeting.* ◊ *If you're looking for a photo of Alice you'll find several in here.* ◊ *Several of the paintings were destroyed in the fire.*
- **adj.** (*formal*) separate: *They said goodbye and went their several ways.*

**sev·er·ally** /ˈsevrəli/ adv. (*formal or law*) separately: *Tenants are jointly and severally liable for payment of the rent.*

**sev·er·ance** /ˈsevərəns/ noun [sing., U] (*formal*) **1** the act of ending a connection or relationship: *the severance of diplomatic relations* **2** the act of ending sb's work contract: *employees given notice of severance* ◊ **severance pay/terms**

**se·vere** /sɪˈvɪə(r); NAmE -ˈvɪr/ adj. (**se·verer**, **se·ver·est**) HELP more severe and most severe are more common.
- **VERY BAD 1** extremely bad or serious: *His injuries are severe.* ◊ *severe pain/depression/asthma* ◊ *a severe illness/disease* ◊ *severe weather/storms* ◊ *The fire has caused severe damage to the building.* ◊ *The victim suffered severe brain damage.* ◊ *a severe shortage of qualified staff* ◊ *If the pain becomes severe, you may wish to contact a doctor.*
- **PUNISHMENT 2** punishing sb in an extreme way when they break a particular set of rules SYN **harsh**: *a severe punishment/sentence/penalty* ◊ *~ on/with sb The courts are becoming more severe on young offenders.* ◊ *Her parents were never so severe with her older brother.*
- **NOT KIND 3** not kind or showing sympathy; not smiling or showing approval SYN **stern**: *a severe expression* ◊ *She was a severe woman who seldom smiled.*
- **VERY DIFFICULT 4** extremely difficult and requiring a lot of skill or ability SYN **stiff**: *The marathon is a severe test of stamina.*
- **STYLE/APPEARANCE/CLOTHING 5** (*disapproving*) extremely plain and without any decoration: *Modern furniture is a little too severe for my taste.* ◊ *Her hair was short and severe.* ▶ **se·ver·ity** /sɪˈverəti/ noun [U]: *A prison sentence should match the severity of the crime.* ◊ *The chances of a full recovery will depend on the severity of her injuries.* ◊ *the severity of the problem* ◊ *He frowned with mock severity.* ◊ *The elaborate facade contrasts strongly with the severity of the interior.*

**se·vere·ly** /sɪˈvɪəli; NAmE -ˈvɪrli/ adv. **1** very badly or seriously: *severely disabled* ◊ *areas severely affected by unemployment* ◊ *The crops were severely damaged.* **2** in an extreme or strict way SYN **harshly**: *Anyone breaking the law will be severely punished.* ◊ *a severely critical report* ◊ *Access to this information is severely restricted.* **3** in a way that is not kind and does not show sympathy or approval SYN **sternly**: *He looked severely at me.* **4** in a way that is extremely difficult and requires a lot of skill or ability: *Her patience was being severely tested.* **5** (*disapproving*) in an extremely plain style that lacks any decoration: *Her hair was tied severely in a bun.*

**sev·ika** /ˈseɪvɪkə/ noun (*IndE*) **1** a female servant **2** a female SOCIAL WORKER

**sew** /səʊ/ verb (**sewed**, **sewn** /səʊn/, **sewed**) **1** [I, T] to use a needle and THREAD to make STITCHES in cloth: *My mother taught me how to sew.* ◊ *to sew by hand/machine* ◊ *~ sth to sew a seam* ◊ HOMOPHONES at SOW¹ **2** [T] to make, repair or attach sth using a needle and THREAD: *~ sth She sews all her own clothes.* ◊ *~ sth on Can you sew a button on for me?* ◊ *Surgeons were able to sew the finger back on.* ◊ *~ sth + adv./prep. The jewel was sewn into the lining of his coat.*

WORDFINDER baste, bind, embroidery, hem, lining, seam, stitch, tack, thread

PHRV **sew sth↔up 1** to join or repair sth by sewing: *to sew up a seam* **2** [often passive] (*informal*) to arrange sth in an acceptable way: *It didn't take me long to sew up the deal.* ◊ *They think they have the election sewn up* (= they think they are definitely going to win).

**sew·age** /ˈsuːɪdʒ/ noun [U] used water and waste substances that are produced by human bodies, that are carried away from houses and factories through special pipes (= SEWERS): *a ban on the dumping of raw sewage* (= that has not been treated with chemicals) *at sea* ◊ *sewage disposal* ⊃ compare WASTEWATER ⊃ **WORDFINDER NOTE** at WASTE

**ˈsewage farm** noun (*BrE*) = SEWAGE WORKS

**ˈsewage plant** (also ˌsewage ˈtreatment plant) noun (*especially NAmE*) = SEWAGE WORKS

**ˈsewage works** (also ˌsewage ˈtreatment works, ˈsewage disˈposal works) noun [C + sing./pl. v.] (*all BrE*) a place where chemicals are used to clean sewage so that it can then be allowed to go into rivers, etc. or used to make MANURE

**sewer** /ˈsuːə(r)/ noun an underground pipe that is used to carry sewage away from houses, factories, etc.

**sew·er·age** /ˈsuːərɪdʒ/ noun [U] the system by which SEWAGE is carried away from houses, factories, etc. and is cleaned and made safe by adding chemicals to it

**ˈsewer grate** noun (*US*) = GRATE

**sew·ing** /ˈsəʊɪŋ/ noun [U] **1** the activity of making, repairing or decorating things made of cloth using a needle and THREAD: *knitting and sewing* **2** something that is being SEWN: *a pile of sewing*

**ˈsewing machine** noun a machine that is used for SEWING things that are made of cloth

**sewn** /səʊn/ past part. of SEW

**sex** /seks/ noun, verb
- **noun 1** [U, C] the state of being male or female: *How can you tell what sex a fish is?* ◊ *~ of sb/sth a process that allows couples to choose the sex of their baby* ◊ *Please indicate your sex and date of birth below.* ◊ **sex discrimination** (= the act of treating men and women differently in an unfair way) ⊃ compare GENDER **2** [C] either of the two groups that people, animals, and plants are divided into according to their function of producing young: *a member of the opposite sex* ◊ *people of the same sex* ⊃ see also FAIR SEX, SAME-SEX **3** [U] physical activity between two people in which they touch each other's sexual organs, and which may include SEXUAL INTERCOURSE: *~ with sb It is illegal to have sex with a person under the age of 16.* ◊ *gay sex* ◊ *a footballer involved in a sex scandal* ◊ *victims of sex abuse* ◊ *sex education in schools* ◊ *These drugs may affect your sex drive* (= your interest in sex and the ability to have it). ⊃ see also SAFE SEX, SEXUAL INTERCOURSE **4** **-sexed** (in adjectives) having the amount of sexual activity or desire mentioned: *a highly-sexed woman*
- **verb** *~ sth* (*specialist*) to examine an animal in order to find out whether it is male or female

PHRV **sex sb↔up** (*informal*) to make sb feel sexually excited ˌ**sex sth↔ˈup** (*informal*) to make sth seem more exciting and interesting: *The profession is trying to sex up its image.*

**sexa·gen·ar·ian** /ˌseksədʒəˈneəriən; NAmE -ˈner-/ noun a person between 60 and 69 years old

**ˈsex appeal** noun [U] the quality of being attractive in a sexual way: *He exudes sex appeal.*

**ˈsex change** noun [usually sing.] a medical operation in which parts of a person's body are changed so that they become a person of the opposite sex

**ˈsex chromosome** noun (*biology*) a CHROMOSOME that decides the sex of an animal or a plant ⊃ see also X CHROMOSOME, Y CHROMOSOME

**sex·ism** /ˈseksɪzəm/ noun [U] the unfair treatment of people, especially women, because of their sex; the attitude that causes this: *legislation designed to combat sexism in the workplace* ◊ *a study of sexism in language*

**sex·ist** /ˈseksɪst/ noun (*disapproving*) a person who treats other people, especially women, unfairly because of their sex or who makes offensive remarks about them ▶ **sex·ist** adj.: *a sexist attitude* ◊ *sexist language*

# sexless

**sex·less** /ˈsekslɪs/ adj. **1** that is neither male nor female, or does not seem to be either male or female: *a sexless figure* **2** in which there is no sexual desire or activity

ˈ**sex life** noun a person's sexual activities: *ways to improve your sex life*

ˈ**sex maniac** noun a person who wants to have sex more often than is normal and who thinks about it all the time

ˈ**sex object** noun a person considered only for their sexual attraction and not for their character or their intelligence

ˈ**sex offender** noun a person who has been found guilty of illegal sexual acts

**sex·ology** /sekˈsɒlədʒi; NAmE -ˈsɑːl-/ noun [U] the scientific study of human sexual behaviour ▶ **sex·olo·gist** noun

**sex·pot** /ˈsekspɒt; NAmE -pɑːt/ noun (informal, sometimes offensive) (used especially in newspapers and magazines) a person, especially a woman, who is thought to be sexually attractive

ˈ**sex symbol** noun a famous person who is thought by many people to be sexually attractive

**sext** /sekst/ verb [I, T] ~ (sb) to send sb sexual messages or photos showing NAKED people and sexual acts on a mobile phone ▶ **sext** noun **sext·ing** noun [U]

**sex·tant** /ˈsekstənt/ noun an instrument for measuring angles and distances, used to calculate the exact position of a ship or an aircraft

**sex·tet** /seksˈtet/ noun **1** [C + sing./pl. v.] a group of six musicians or singers who play or sing together **2** [C] a piece of music for six musicians or singers

**sex·ton** /ˈsekstən/ noun a person whose job is to take care of a church and the area around it, ring the church bell, etc.

**sex·ual** ⓘ B1 ○ /ˈsekʃuəl/ adj. **1** ⓘ B1 [usually before noun] connected with the physical activity of sex: *sexual behaviour/activity/desire* ◇ *sexual abuse/assault/violence* ◇ *They were not having a sexual relationship at the time.* ◇ *sexual orientation/identity* (= whether you are HETEROSEXUAL, GAY or BISEXUAL) **2** [only before noun] connected with the process of producing young: *the sexual organs* (= the PENIS, VAGINA, etc.) ◇ *sexual reproduction* **3** [usually before noun] connected with the state of being male or female: *sexual characteristics* ▶ **sex·ual·ly** /-ʃəli/ adv.: *sexually abused children* ◇ *She finds him sexually attractive.* ◇ *sexually explicit material* ◇ *The disease is a threat to anyone who is sexually active.*

ˌ**sexual haˈrassment** noun [U] unacceptable physical contact, comments about sex, etc., usually happening at work, that a person finds annoying and offensive

ˌ**sexual ˈintercourse** (also **inter·course**) noun [U] (formal) the physical activity of sex, usually describing the act of a man putting his PENIS inside a woman's VAGINA SYN **coitus**

**sexu·al·ity** ⓘ+ C1 Ⓦ /ˌsekʃuˈæləti/ noun [U] the feelings and activities connected with a person's sexual desires: *male/female sexuality* ◇ *He was confused about his sexuality.*

**sexu·al·ize** (BrE also **-ise**) /ˈsekʃuəlaɪz/ verb ~ sb/sth to make sb/sth seem sexually attractive ▶ **sexu·al·iza·tion**, **-isa·tion** /ˌsekʃuəlaɪˈzeɪʃn; NAmE -ləˈz-/ noun [U]

ˌ**sexually transˈmitted diˈsease** noun [C, U] (abbr. **STD**) any disease that is spread through sexual intercourse, such as SYPHILIS

ˈ**sex worker** noun a polite way of referring to a PROSTITUTE

**sexy** ⓘ+ B2 /ˈseksi/ adj. (**sex·ier**, **sexi·est**) **1** ⓘ+ B2 (of a person) sexually attractive: *the sexy lead singer* ◇ *She looked incredibly sexy in a black evening gown.* **2** ⓘ+ B2 sexually exciting: *sexy underwear* ◇ *a sexy look* **3** ⓘ+ C1 (of a person) sexually excited: *The music and wine began to make him feel sexy.* **4** ⓘ+ C1 (informal) exciting and interesting: *a sexy new range of software* ◇ *Accountancy just isn't sexy.* ▶ **sex·ily** /-səli/ adv. **sexi·ness** noun [U]

**SF** /ˌes ˈef/ abbr. SCIENCE FICTION

**SFX** /ˌes ef ˈeks/ abbr. SPECIAL EFFECTS

**SGML** /ˌes dʒi: em ˈel/ abbr. (computing) Standard Generalized Mark-up Language (a system used for marking text on a computer so that the text can be read on a different computer system or displayed in different forms)

**Sgt** (especially BrE) (also **Sgt.** NAmE, BrE) abbr. (in writing) SERGEANT: *Sgt Williams*

**sh** (also **shh**) /ʃ/ exclamation the way of writing the sound people make when they are telling sb to be quiet: *Sh! Keep your voice down!*

**shaadi** /ˈʃɑːdi/ noun (pl. **shaadis**) (IndE) a wedding or marriage

**sha·bash** /ʃɑːˈbɑːʃ/ exclamation (IndE) used to tell sb that they have done well at sth

**shabby** /ˈʃæbi/ adj. (**shab·bier**, **shab·bi·est**) **1** (of buildings, clothes, objects, etc.) in poor condition because they have been used a lot SYN **scruffy**: *She wore shabby old jeans and a T-shirt.* **2** (of a person) badly dressed in clothes that have been worn a lot SYN **scruffy**: *The old man was shabby and unkempt.* **3** (of behaviour) unfair or unreasonable SYN **shoddy**: *She tried to make up for her shabby treatment of him.* **4** (informal) not very good: *Roberts has scored eight goals so far this season. Not too shabby* (= very good) *for a player who only joined the team this year.* ▶ **shab·bily** /-bɪli/ adv.: *shabbily dressed* ◇ *I think you were very shabbily treated.* **shab·bi·ness** noun [U]

**shack** /ʃæk/ noun, verb
■ noun a small building, usually made of wood or metal, that has not been built well
■ verb
PHR V ˌshack ˈup with sb | be ˌshacked ˈup with sb (slang) to start/be living with sb that you have a sexual relationship with, but that you are not married to: *I hear he's shacked up with some woman.*

**shackle** /ˈʃækl/ noun, verb
■ noun **1** [C, usually pl.] a metal ring placed around a prisoner's WRIST or ankle and joined by a chain to sth, or to a shackle on the other wrist or ankle, to prevent the prisoner from escaping or moving easily **2** **shackles** [pl.] ~ (of sth) (formal) a particular state, set of conditions or circumstances, etc. that prevent you from saying or doing what you want: *a country struggling to free itself from the shackles of colonialism*
■ verb [often passive] **1** to put shackles on sb: **be shackled (to sth)** *The hostage had been shackled to a radiator.* ◇ *The prisoners were kept shackled during the trial.* **2** ~ sb/sth to prevent sb from behaving or speaking as they want

**shade** ⓘ B2 /ʃeɪd/ noun, verb
■ noun
• OUT OF SUN **1** ⓘ B2 [U] an area that is dark and cool under or behind sth, for example a tree or building, because the sun's light does not get to it: *~ of sth The shade of the pine tree provided some protection from the sun.* ◇ *in the ~ (of sth) The temperature can reach 40°C in the shade.* ◇ *We sat down in the shade of the wall.* **in ~** *These plants grow well in sun or shade.* ◇ *The trees provide shade for the animals in the summer.* ⇒ see also SHADY
• ON LAMP, ETC. **2** [C] a thing that you use to prevent light from coming through or to make sth bright: *I bought a new shade for the lamp.* ◇ *an eyeshade* ⇒ see also LAMPSHADE, SUNSHADE
• ON WINDOW **3** [C] (also ˈwindow shade) (both NAmE) = BLIND
• OF COLOUR **4** ⓘ B2 [C] a particular form of a colour, that is, how dark or light it is: *~ of sth a dark/light/pale/bright shade of blue* ⇒ SYNONYMS at COLOUR
• IN PICTURE **5** [U] the dark areas in a picture, especially the use of these to produce variety: *The painting needs more light and shade.*

- **OF OPINION/FEELING** 6 [C, usually pl.] **~of sth** a different kind or level of opinion, feeling, etc: *politicians of all shades of opinion* ◊ *The word has many shades of meaning.*
- **SLIGHTLY** 7 **a shade** [sing.] a little; slightly **SYN** touch: *He was feeling a shade disappointed.*
- **FOR EYES** 8 **shades** [pl.] (*informal*) = SUNGLASSES
- **GHOST** 9 [C] (*literary*) the spirit of a dead person; a ghost

**IDM** **put sb/sth in the 'shade** to be much better or more impressive than sb/sth: *I tried hard but her work put mine in the shade.* **shades of sb/sth** (*informal*) used when you are referring to things that remind you of a particular person, thing or time: *short skirts and long boots—shades of the 1960s*

■ *verb*
- **FROM DIRECT LIGHT** 1 to prevent direct light from reaching sth: **~sb/sth** *The courtyard was shaded by high trees.* ◊ **~sb/sth from/against sth** *She shaded her eyes against the sun.*
- **LAMP** 2 [usually passive] **~sth** to provide a screen for a lamp, light, etc. to make it less bright: *a shaded lamp*
- **PART OF PICTURE** 3 **~sth** to make a part of a drawing, etc. darker, for example with an area of colour or with pencil lines: **~sth** *What do the shaded areas on the map represent?* ◊ **~sth in** *I'm going to shade this part in.*
- **JUST WIN** 4 **~sth** (*BrE, informal*) to win a contest by scoring only a very small number of points, goals, etc. more than your opponent

**PHR V** **shade 'into sth** to change gradually into sth else, so that you cannot tell where one thing ends and the other thing begins: *The scarlet of the wings shades into pink at the tips.* ◊ *Distrust of foreigners can shade into racism.*

▼ **WHICH WORD?**

**shade / shadow**
- **Shade** [U] is an area or a part of a place that is protected from the heat of the sun and so is darker and cooler: *Let's sit in the shade for a while.*
- A **shadow** [C] is the dark shape made when a light shines on a person or an object: *As the sun went down we cast long shadows on the lawn.*
- **Shadow** [U] is an area of darkness in which it is difficult to distinguish things easily: *Her face was in deep shadow.*

**shad·ing** /ˈʃeɪdɪŋ/ *noun* 1 [U] the use of colour, pencil lines, etc. to give an impression of light and shade in a picture or to emphasize areas of a map, diagram, etc. 2 **shadings** [pl.] slight differences that exist between different aspects of the same thing

**shadow** 🅞 **B2** /ˈʃædəʊ/ *noun, verb, adj.*

■ *noun*
- **DARK SHAPE** 1 🅡 **B2** [C] the dark shape that sb/sth's form makes on a surface, for example on the ground, when they are between the light and the surface: *The children were having fun, chasing each other's shadows.* ◊ *The ship's sail cast a shadow on the water.* ◊ *The shadows lengthened as the sun went down.* ◊ (*figurative*) *He didn't want to cast a shadow on* (= spoil) *their happiness.* ◊ *note at* SHADE ◊ *picture at* SHADE
- **DARKNESS** 2 🅡 **B2** [U] (also **shadows** [pl.]) DARKNESS in a place or on sth, especially so that you cannot easily see who or what is there: **in the shadows** *I thought I saw a figure standing in the shadows.* ◊ **in~** *His face was deep in shadow, turned away from her.* ◊ *note at* SHADE
- **SMALL AMOUNT** 3 [sing.] **~of sth** a very small amount of sth **SYN** hint: *A shadow of a smile touched his mouth.* ◊ *She knew* **beyond a shadow of a doubt** (= with no doubt at all) *that he was lying.*
- **INFLUENCE** 4 [sing.] the strong (often bad) influence of sb/sth: *The new leader wants to escape from the shadow of his predecessor.* ◊ **under the~of sb/sth** *These people have been living for years under the shadow of fear.*
- **UNDER EYES** 5 **shadows** [pl.] dark areas under sb's eyes, because they are tired, etc.
- **SB THAT FOLLOWS SB** 6 [C] a person or an animal that follows sb else all the time
- **STH NOT REAL** 7 [C] a thing that is not real or possible to obtain: *You can't spend all your life chasing shadows.* ◊ *see also* EYESHADOW, FIVE O'CLOCK SHADOW

1421 **shake**

**IDM** **be frightened/nervous/scared of your own 'shadow** to be very easily frightened; to be very nervous **in/under the 'shadow of** 1 very close to: *The new market is in the shadow of the City Hall.* 2 when you say that sb is **in/under the shadow of** another person, you mean that they do not receive as much attention as that person ◊ *more at* FORMER *adj.*

■ *verb*
- **FOLLOW AND WATCH** 1 **~sb** to follow and watch sb closely and often secretly: *He was shadowed for a week by the secret police.* 2 **~sb** to be with sb who is doing a particular job, so that you can learn about it: *It is often helpful for teachers to shadow managers in industry.*
- **COVER WITH SHADOW** 3 **~sth** to cover sth with a shadow: *A wide-brimmed hat shadowed her face.* ◊ *The bay was shadowed by magnificent cliffs.* ◊ *see also* OVERSHADOW

■ *adj.* [only before noun] (*BrE, politics*) used to refer to senior politicians of the main opposition party who would become government ministers if their party won the next election: *the shadow Chancellor* ◊ *the shadow Cabinet*

**shad·owy** /ˈʃædəʊi/ *adj.* 1 dark and full of shadows: *Someone was waiting in the shadowy doorway.* 2 [usually before noun] difficult to see because there is not much light: *Shadowy figures approached them out of the fog.* 3 [usually before noun] that not much is known about: *the shadowy world of terrorism*

**shady** /ˈʃeɪdi/ *adj.* (**shadi·er**, **shadi·est**) 1 protected from direct light from the sun by trees, buildings, etc: *a shady garden* ◊ *We went to find somewhere cool and shady to have a drink.* 2 (of a tree, etc.) providing shade from the sun 3 [usually before noun] (*informal*) seeming to be dishonest or illegal: *a shady businessman/deal*

**shaft** /ʃɑːft; *NAmE* ʃæft/ *noun, verb*

■ *noun* 1 (often in compounds) a long, narrow passage that usually goes straight down in a building or underground, used especially for a lift or as a way of allowing air in or out: *a lift/elevator shaft* ◊ *a mineshaft* ◊ *a ventilation shaft* 2 the long narrow part of an ARROW, HAMMER, GOLF CLUB, etc. 3 (often in compounds) a metal bar that joins parts of a machine or an engine together, enabling power and movement to be passed from one part to another ◊ *see also* CAMSHAFT, CRANKSHAFT 4 [usually pl.] either of the two long POLES at the front of a CARRIAGE or CART between which a horse is fastened in order to pull it 5 **~of light, sunlight, etc.** (*literary*) a long, narrow area of light: *A shaft of moonlight fell on the lake.* ◊ (*figurative*) *a shaft of inspiration* 6 **~of pain, fear, etc.** (*literary*) a sudden strong feeling of pain, etc. that travels through your body: *Shafts of fear ran through her as she heard footsteps behind her.* 7 **~of sth** (*formal*) a clever remark that is intended to upset or annoy sb: *a shaft of wit*

**IDM** **give sb the 'shaft** (*NAmE, informal*) to treat sb unfairly

■ *verb* **~sb** (*informal*) to treat sb unfairly or cheat them

**shag** /ʃæɡ/ *noun, verb, adj.*

■ *noun* 1 [C, usually sing.] (*BrE, taboo, slang*) an act of sex with sb 2 [C] a large black bird with a long neck that lives near the sea

■ *verb* (**-gg-**) [I, T] **~(sb)** (*BrE, taboo, slang*) to have sex with sb

■ *adj.* [only before noun] used to describe a carpet, etc., usually made of wool, that has long THREADS

**shaggy** /ˈʃæɡi/ *adj.* (**shag·gier**, **shag·gi·est**) 1 (of hair, fur, etc.) long and untidy: *a shaggy mane of hair* 2 having long untidy hair, fur, etc: *a huge shaggy white dog*

**shah** /ʃɑː/ *noun* the title of the kings of Iran in the past

**shaikh** /ʃeɪk/ = SHEIKH

**shake** 🅞 **A2** /ʃeɪk/ *verb, noun*

■ *verb* (**shook** /ʃʊk/, **shaken** /ˈʃeɪkən/)
- **OBJECT/BUILDING/PERSON** 1 🅡 **A2** [I, T] to move or make sb/sth move with short quick movements from side to side or up and down: *The whole house shakes when a train goes past.* ◊ **~sb/sth (by sth)** *Shake the bottle well before use.* ◊ *He shook her violently by the shoulders.* ◊ **~sb/sth + adj.** *He knelt and gently shook her awake.* 2 🅡 **B1** [T] **~sth**

# shakedown

+ *adv./prep.* to move sth in a particular direction by shaking: *She bent down to shake a pebble out of her shoe.*
- **HANDS** **3** [T, I] to take sb's hand and move it up and down as a way of saying hello or to show that you agree about sth: ~ **hands (with sb)** *Do people in Italy shake hands when they meet?* ◊ *She refused to shake hands with him.* ◊ ~ **sb's hand** *He stepped forward and shook my hand.* ◊ ~ **(hands) on sth** *They shook hands on the deal* (= to show that they had reached an agreement).
- **YOUR HEAD** **4** [T] ~ **your head** to turn your head from side to side as a way of saying 'no' or to show that you are sad, feel doubt, etc: '*Drink?*' *he offered. She shook her head.*
- **YOUR FIST** **5** [T] ~ **your fist (at sb)** to show that you are angry with sb; to threaten sb by shaking your FIST (= closed hand)
- **OF BODY** **6** [I] to make short quick movements that you cannot control, for example because you are cold or afraid **SYN** **tremble**: *Her hands had started to shake.* ◊ ~ **with sth** *He was shaking with fear.* ◊ *I was shaking like a leaf.*
- **OF VOICE** **7** [I] ~ **(with sth)** (of sb's voice) to sound unsteady, usually because you are nervous, upset or angry
- **SHOCK SB** **8** [T] (not used in the progressive tenses) to shock or upset sb very much: ~ **sb** *He was badly shaken by the news of her death.* ◊ ~ **sb up** *The accident really shook her up.*
- **BELIEF/IDEA** **9** [T] ~ **sth** to make a belief or an idea less certain: *The incident had shaken her faith in him.* ◊ *This announcement is bound to shake the confidence of the industry.*
- **GET RID OF** **10** [T] to get rid of sth: ~ **sth off** *I can't seem to shake off this cold.* ◊ ~ **sth** *He couldn't shake the feeling that there was something wrong.*

**IDM** **shake in your 'boots / 'shoes** (*informal*) to be very frightened or nervous **shake a 'leg** (*old-fashioned, informal*) used to tell sb to start to do sth or to hurry ⇒ more at FOUNDATION

**PHRV** **shake 'down** (*informal*) (of a new situation or arrangement) to become established: *Let's wait and see how everything shakes down.* **shake sb/sth↔'down** (*NAmE, informal*) **1** to search a person or place completely and very carefully ⇒ related noun SHAKEDOWN **2** to threaten sb in order to get money from them **shake sb↔'off** to get away from sb who is following or running after you **shake sth↔'out** to open or spread sth by shaking, especially so that bits of dirt, dust, etc. come off it: *to shake out a duster* **shake sth↔'up** to make important changes in an organization, a profession, etc. in order to make it more efficient ⇒ related noun SHAKE-UP

■ *noun*
- **MOVEMENT** **1** [C, usually sing.] an act of shaking sb/sth: *She gave him a shake to wake him.* ◊ *Give the bottle a good shake before opening.* ◊ ~ **of sth** *He dismissed the idea with a firm shake of his head* (= turning it from side to side to mean 'no'). ⇒ see also HANDSHAKE
- **OF BODY** **2 the shakes** [pl.] (*informal*) a physical condition in which you cannot stop your body from shaking because of fear, illness, or because you have drunk too much alcohol: *I always get the shakes before exams.*
- **DRINK** **3** [C] = MILKSHAKE: *a strawberry shake* ⇒ see also PROTEIN SHAKE

**IDM** **in two 'shakes | in a couple of 'shakes** (*informal*) very soon ⇒ more at FAIR *adj.*, GREAT *adj.*

**shake·down** /ˈʃeɪkdaʊn/ *noun* (*NAmE, informal*) **1** a situation in which sb tries to force sb else to give them money using violence, threats, etc. **2** a complete and careful search of sb/sth: *a police shakedown of the area* **3** a test of a vehicle to see if there are any problems before it is used

**shaken** /ˈʃeɪkən/ (*also* ˌshaken 'up) *adj.* [not usually before noun] shocked, upset or frightened by sth

**shaker** /ˈʃeɪkə(r)/ *noun* **1** (often in compounds) a container that is used for shaking things: *a salt shaker* ◊ *a cocktail shaker* **2 Shaker** a member of a religious group in the US who live in a community in a very simple way and do not marry or have partners **IDM** see MOVER

**ˈshake-up** *noun* ~ **(in / of sth)** a situation in which a lot of changes are made to a company, an organization, etc. in order to improve the way in which it works: *a management shake-up*

**shak·ing** /ˈʃeɪkɪŋ/ *noun* [sing., U] the act of shaking sth/sb or the fact of being shaken

**shaky** /ˈʃeɪki/ *adj.* (**shaki·er, shaki·est**) **1** shaking and feeling weak because you are ill, emotional or old **SYN** **unsteady**: *Her voice sounded shaky on the phone.* ◊ *The old man was very shaky on his feet.* **2** not stable, steady or safe; not certain: *That ladder looks a little shaky.* ◊ (*figurative*) *Her memories of the accident are a little shaky.* ◊ (*figurative*) *The protesters are on shaky ground* (= it is not certain that their claims are valid). **3** not seeming very successful; likely to fail **SYN** **uncertain**: *Business is looking shaky at the moment.* ◊ *After a shaky start, they fought back to win 3–2.* ▶ **shaki·ly** /-kɪli/ *adv.*: '*Get the doctor,*' *he whispered shakily.*

**shale** /ʃeɪl/ *noun* [U] a type of soft stone that splits easily into thin flat layers ▶ **shaly** *adj.*

**ˈshale ˈgas** *noun* [U] gas that is found in shale: *the extraction of shale gas by fracking*

▼ **GRAMMAR POINT**

**shall / will**

- In modern English the traditional difference between **shall** and **will** has almost disappeared, and **shall** is not used very much at all, especially in NAmE. **Shall** is now only used with *I* and *we*, and often sounds formal and old-fashioned. People are more likely to say: *I'll* (= I will) *be late* and: '*You'll* (= you will) *apologize immediately.*' ◊ '*No I won't!*'.
- In BrE **shall** is still used with *I* and *we* in questions or when you want to make a suggestion or an offer: *What shall I wear to the party?* ◊ *Shall we order some coffee?* ◊ *I'll drive, shall I?*
⇒ note at SHOULD

▼ **EXPRESS YOURSELF**

**Offering to do something**

There are various ways of offering and accepting help:
- *Would you like me to help you with that?*
- *Can I give you a hand?*
- *Can I help you with that?*
- *Shall I carry that for you?* (BrE *or formal,* NAmE)
- *Would it help if I spoke to Julie before you call her?*
- *Let me take your bag.*
- *If there's anything I can do (to help), let me know.*

Responses:
- *That's very kind / nice / generous / thoughtful of you. Thank you.*
- *It's all right, thank you. I can manage / do it.*
- *Thanks. That would be very helpful.*

**shall** /ʃəl/, *strong form* /ʃæl/ *modal verb* (*negative* **shall not**, *short form* **shan't** /ʃɑːnt/; NAmE /ʃænt/, *pt* **should** /ʃʊd/, *negative* **should not**, *short form* **shouldn't** /ˈʃʊdnt/) (*especially BrE*) **1** (*becoming old-fashioned*) used with *I* and *we* for talking about or predicting the future: *This time next week I shall be in Scotland.* ◊ *We shan't be gone long.* ◊ *I said that I should be pleased to help.* **2** used in questions with *I* and *we* for making offers or suggestions or asking advice: *Shall I send you the book?* ◊ *What shall we do this weekend?* ◊ *Let's look at it again, shall we?* **3** (*old-fashioned or formal*) used to show that you are determined, or to give an order or instruction: *He is determined that you shall succeed.* ◊ *Candidates shall remain in their seats until all the papers have been collected.* ⇒ note at MODAL

**shal·lot** /ʃəˈlɒt; NAmE -ˈlɑːt/ *noun* a vegetable like a small onion with a very strong taste ⇒ VISUAL VOCAB page V5

**shal·low** /ˈʃæləʊ/ *adj.* (**shal·low·er, shal·low·est**) **1** not having much distance between the top or surface and the bottom: *a shallow dish/pan/bowl* ◊ *They* were playing in **the shallow end** (= of the swimming pool). ◊ *These fish are found in **shallow waters** around the coast.* **OPP** **deep 2** *(disapproving)* (of a person, an idea, a comment, etc.) not showing serious thought, feelings, etc. about sth **SYN** **superficial 3 shallow breathing** involves taking in only a small amount of air each time ▶ **shal·low·ly** *adv.*: *He was breathing shallowly.* **shal·low·ness** *noun* [U]

**the shal·lows** /ðə ˈʃæləʊz/ *noun* [pl.] a shallow place in a river or the sea

**sha·lom** /ʃəˈlɒm; *NAmE* -ˈloʊm/ *exclamation* a Hebrew word for 'hello' or 'goodbye' that means 'peace'

**shalt** /ʃælt/ *verb* ▶ **thou shalt** *(old use)* used to mean 'you shall', when talking to one person

**shal·war** /ʃʌlˈwɑː(r)/ = SALWAR

**sham** /ʃæm/ *noun, adj., verb*
■ *noun (disapproving)* **1** [sing.] a situation, feeling, system, etc. that is not as good or true as it seems to be: *She felt trapped in a sham of a marriage.* **2** [C, usually sing.] a person who pretends to be sth that they are not **3** [U] behaviour, feelings, words, etc. that are intended to make sb/sth seem to be better than they really are: *Their promises turned out to be full of sham and hypocrisy.*
■ *adj.* [only before noun] *(usually disapproving)* not what sb claims it is but intended to seem real **SYN** **false**: *a sham marriage*
■ *verb* (-mm-) [I, T] ~ **(sth)** | ~ + *adj.* to pretend sth: *Is he really sick or is he just shamming?*

**sha·man** /ˈʃeɪmən, ˈʃɑː-, ˈʃæm-/ *noun* a person in some religions and societies who is believed to be able to contact good and evil spirits and cure people of illnesses ▶ **sha·man·ic** /ʃəˈmænɪk/ *adj.*

**shamba** /ˈʃæmbə/ *EAfrE* /ˈʃamba/ *noun (EAfrE)* a small farm or a field that is used for growing crops

**sham·ble** /ˈʃæmbl/ *verb* [I] (+ *adv. / prep.*) to walk in a slow and lazy way or with difficulty, dragging your feet along the ground

**sham·bles** /ˈʃæmblz/ *noun* [sing.] *(informal)* **1** a situation in which there is a great lack of order or understanding **SYN** **mess**: *The press conference was a complete shambles.* ◊ *What a shambles!* ◊ **in a ~** *The government is in a shambles over Europe.* **2** a place which is dirty or untidy **SYN** **mess**: *The house was a shambles.*

**sham·bol·ic** /ʃæmˈbɒlɪk; *NAmE* -ˈbɑːl-/ *adj. (BrE, informal)* without order or organization **SYN** **chaotic, disorganized**

**shame** ⓘ B2 /ʃeɪm/ *noun, verb, exclamation*
■ *noun* **1** ⓘ B2 **a shame** [sing.] used to say that sth is a cause for feeling sad or disappointed **SYN** **pity**: **~ (that)** … *It's a shame that she wasn't here to see it.* ◊ **~ about sb/sth (doing sth)** *It's a shame about Tim, isn't it?* ◊ **~ (for sb/sth) to do sth** *It's a shame to see her wasting her talent like this.* **2** ⓘ B2 [U] the feelings of being sad, embarrassed and guilty that you have when you know that sth you have done is wrong or stupid: **with~** *His face burned with shame.* ◊ **in~** *She hung her head in shame.* ◊ **~of (doing) sth** *The king preferred death to the shame of defeat.* ◊ **~of sb/sth doing sth** *He could not live with the shame of other people knowing the truth.* **3** [U] *(formal)* (only used in questions and negative sentences) the ability to feel shame at sth you have done: *Have you no shame?* **4** [U] the loss of respect that is caused when you do sth wrong or stupid: *There is no shame in wanting to be successful.* ◊ *(formal) She felt that her failure would bring shame on her family.*
**IDM** **put sb/sth to ˈshame** to be much better than sb/sth: *Their presentation put ours to shame.* ˈ**shame on you, him, etc.** *(informal)* used to say that sb should feel ashamed for sth they have said or done ⊃ more at NAME *v.*
■ *verb* **1** ~ **sb** to make sb feel ashamed: *His generosity shamed them all.* **2** ~ **sb** *(formal)* to make sb feel that they have lost honour or respect: *You have shamed your family.*
**PHRV** ˈ**shame sb into doing sth** to persuade sb to do sth by making them feel ashamed not to do it: *She shamed her father into promising more help.*
■ *exclamation (SAfrE)* used to express sympathy, or to show that you like sb/sth: *Shame, she's so cute!*

**shame-faced** /ˌʃeɪmˈfeɪst/ *adj.* feeling or looking ashamed because you have done sth bad or stupid **SYN** **sheepish**: *a shamefaced smile* ▶ **shame-faced·ly** /ˌʃeɪmˈfeɪstli, -ˈfeɪsɪdli/ *adv.*

**shame·ful** /ˈʃeɪmfl/ *adj.* that should make you feel ashamed **SYN** **disgraceful**: *shameful behaviour* ◊ *It was shameful the way she was treated.* ▶ **shame·ful·ly** /-fəli/ *adv.*

**shame·less** /ˈʃeɪmləs/ *adj. (disapproving)* not feeling ashamed of sth you have done, although other people think you should **SYN** **unashamed** ▶ **shame·less·ly** *adv.* *(usually disapproving, sometimes approving)*: *The whole film is shamelessly romantic and glamorous.* **shame·less·ness** *noun* [U]

**sha·mi·ana** /ʃɑːmiˈɑːnə/ *noun (IndE)* a large tent used at social events

**sham·ing** /ˈʃeɪmɪŋ/ *adj.* causing sb to feel ashamed: *a shaming defeat by a less experienced team*

**sham·my** /ˈʃæmi/ *noun (pl. -ies) (also* **ˈshammy leather**) [U, C] *(informal)* = CHAMOIS (2)

**sham·poo** /ʃæmˈpuː/ *noun, verb*
■ *noun (pl. -os)* **1** [C, U] a liquid soap that is used for washing your hair; a similar liquid used for cleaning carpets, furniture covers or a car: *a shampoo for greasy hair* ◊ *carpet shampoo* **2** [C, usually sing.] an act of washing your hair using shampoo: *Rinse the hair thoroughly after each shampoo.* ◊ *a shampoo and set* (= an act of washing and styling sb's hair)
■ *verb* (**sham·poo·ing, sham·pooed, sham·pooed**) ~ **sth** to wash or clean hair, carpets, etc. with shampoo

**sham·rock** /ˈʃæmrɒk; *NAmE* -rɑːk/ *noun* a small plant with three leaves on each STEM. The shamrock is the national symbol of Ireland.

**shandy** /ˈʃændi/ *noun (pl. -ies) (especially BrE)* **1** [U, C] a drink made by mixing beer with LEMONADE **2** [C] a glass or can of shandy: *Two shandies, please.*

**shang·hai** /ˌʃæŋˈhaɪ/ *verb* (**shang·hai·ing** /-haɪɪŋ/, **shang·haied, shang·haied** /-ˈhaɪd/) ~ **sb (into doing sth)** *(old-fashioned, informal)* to trick or force sb into doing sth that they do not really want to do

**Shangri-La** /ˌʃæŋɡri ˈlɑː/ *noun* [sing.] a place that is extremely beautiful and where everything seems perfect, especially a place far away from modern life **ORIGIN** From the name of an imaginary valley in Tibet in James Hilton's novel *Lost Horizon*, where people do not grow old.

**shank** /ʃæŋk/ *noun* **1** the straight narrow part between the two ends of a tool or an object **2** the part of an animal's or a person's leg between the knee and ankle **3** the top part of the leg of an animal, cooked and eaten: *braised lamb shanks*

**shan't** /ʃɑːnt; *NAmE* ʃænt/ *short form* shall not

**shanti** /ˈʃɑːnti/ *noun* [U] *(IndE)* (often used in religious songs or prayers) peace

**shanty** /ˈʃænti/ *noun (pl. -ies)* **1** a small house, built of pieces of wood, metal and CARDBOARD, where very poor people live, especially on the edge of a big city **2** *(also* **sea shanty**) *(US* **chanty, chan·tey**) a song that sailors traditionally used to sing while pulling ropes, etc.

ˈ**shanty town** *noun* an area in or near a town where poor people live in shanties ⊃ WORDFINDER NOTE at POOR

**shape** ⓘ A2 /ʃeɪp/ *noun, verb*
■ *noun* **1** ⓘ A2 [C, U] the form of the outer edges or surfaces of sth; an example of sth that has a particular form: *a rectangular/spherical/cylindrical shape* ◊ *fantastic creatures that can change shape and be either visible or invisible* ◊ *You can recognize the fish by the shape of their fins.* ◊ *They have completely different body shapes.* ◊ **in~** *The island was originally circular in shape.* ◊ *Candles come in all shapes and sizes.* ◊ **in the~of sth** *The pool was in the shape of a heart.* ◊ *(figurative) The government provides*

# shaped

money in the shape of (= consisting of) grants and student loans. **2** [C] a person or thing that is difficult to see clearly SYN **figure**: *Ghostly shapes moved around in the dark.* **3** [U] the physical condition of sb/sth: *in …~ What sort of shape was the car in after the accident? ◇ He's in good shape for a man of his age.* **4** [U] the particular qualities or characteristics of sth: *Will new technology change the shape of broadcasting?*

**IDM** **get (yourself) into ˈshape** to take exercise, eat healthy food, etc. in order to become physically fit **get/ knock/lick sb into ˈshape** to train sb so that they do a particular job, task, etc. well **get/knock/lick sth into ˈshape** to make sth more acceptable, organized or successful: *I've got all the information together but it still needs knocking into shape.* **give ˈshape to sth** (*formal*) to express or explain a particular idea, plan, etc. **in ˈany (way,) shape or form** (*informal*) of any type: *I don't approve of violence in any shape or form.* **(get/keep/ stay) in ˈshape** (of a person) (to get/stay) in good physical condition: *You don't have to spend a fortune on gym membership to get in shape. ◇ I like to stay in shape.* **out of ˈshape 1** not having the normal shape: *The wheel had been twisted out of shape.* **2** (of a person) not in good physical condition **the shape of things to ˈcome** the way things are likely to develop in the future **take ˈshape** to develop and become more complete or organized **throw ˈshapes 1** (*BrE*) to dance: *She spent the whole evening throwing shapes on the dance floor.* **2** (*IrishE*) to behave in a way that makes you seem to threaten sb, especially by standing as though you are ready to fight, without actually becoming violent: *I was worried he might get violent but he was just throwing shapes.* ⊃ more at BENT *adj*.

■ **verb 1** [T] to make sth into a particular shape: *~A into B Shape the dough into a ball. ◇ ~sth This tool is used for shaping wood.* **2** [T] *~sb/sth* to have an important influence on the way that sb/sth develops: *You are helping to shape the future of this country. ◇ She had a leading role in shaping party policy.* **3** [I] *~to do sth* to prepare to do sth, especially hit or kick sth: *She was shaping to hit her second shot.*

**PHRV** **ˌshape ˈup 1** to develop in a particular way, especially in a good way: *Our plans are shaping up nicely (= showing signs that they will be successful).* **2** (*informal*) to improve your behaviour, work harder, etc: *If he doesn't shape up, he'll soon be out of a job.*

**shaped** /ʃeɪpt/ *adj.* having the type of shape mentioned: *a huge balloon shaped like a giant cow ◇ almond-shaped eyes ◇ an L-shaped room* ⊃ see also PEAR-SHAPED

**shape·less** /ˈʃeɪpləs/ *adj.* [usually before noun] (*often disapproving*) **1** not having any definite shape: *a shapeless sweater* **2** without clear organization SYN **unstructured**: *a shapeless and incoherent story* ▸ **shape·less·ly** *adv.* **shape·less·ness** *noun* [U]

**shape·ly** /ˈʃeɪpli/ *adj.* (especially of a woman's body) having an attractive curved shape

**ˈshape-shifter** *noun* (in stories) a person or an animal that is able to change into other people, animals or things: *In the film he plays a shape-shifter, who takes the form of people's worst fears.* ▸ **ˈshape-shifting** *adj.*

**shard** /ʃɑːd/ *NAmE* /ʃɑːrd/ (*also* **sherd**) *noun* a piece of broken glass, metal, etc: *shards of glass*

**share** /ʃeə(r)/ *NAmE* /ʃer/ *verb, noun*
■ *verb*
- **USE AT THE SAME TIME 1** [T, I] to have, use or experience sth at the same time as sb else: *There isn't an empty table. Would you mind sharing? ◇ ~sth to share a room/bed ◇ ~sth with sb Sue shares a house with three other students.*
- **DIVIDE BETWEEN PEOPLE 2** [T, I] to have part of sth while another person or other people also have part: *~sth with sb He shared the pie with her. ◇ The Hungarian king shared power with the Austrian emperor to form the Austro-Hungarian Empire.* **3** [T] *~sth (out) (among/ between sb)* to divide sth between two or more people:

*We shared the pizza between the four of us.* ⊃ see also JOB-SHARING, POWER-SHARING
- **GIVE SOME OF YOURS 4** [T, I] to give some of what you have to sb else; to let sb use sth that is yours: *John had no brothers or sisters and wasn't used to sharing. ◇ ~sth The conference is a good place to share information and exchange ideas. ◇ ~sth with sb This online resource will give farmers a new way to share knowledge with each other.*
- **FEELINGS/IDEAS/PROBLEMS 5** [T, I] to have the same feelings, ideas, experiences, etc. as sb else: *~sth to share a concern/an opinion ◇ shared values ◇ They shared a common interest in botany. ◇ a view that is widely shared ◇ ~sth with sb Sikhs share this belief with followers of other Indian religions. ◇ ~in sth I didn't really share in her love of animals.* **6** [T] to tell other people about your ideas, experiences, and feelings: *~sth to share thoughts/ideas/ feelings/memories ◇ Men often don't like to share their problems. ◇ The two friends shared everything—they had no secrets. ◇ Please share this on Facebook and Twitter so we can get the word out. ◇ The group listens while one person shares (= tells other people about their experiences, feelings, etc.). ◇ ~sth with sb Would you like to share your experience with the rest of the group?*
- **BLAME/RESPONSIBILITY 7** [T, I] to be equally involved in sth or responsible for sth: *~sth (with sb) Both drivers shared the blame for the accident. ◇ be shared between A and B Responsibility is shared between parents and teachers. ◇ ~in sth I try to get the kids to share in the housework.*

**IDM** **ˌshare and share aˈlike** (*saying*) used to say that everyone should share things equally and in a fair way ⊃ more at TROUBLE *n.*

■ *noun*
- **PART/AMOUNT OF STH 1** [C, usually sing.] one part of sth that is divided between two or more people: *~of sth Next year we hope to have a greater share of the market. ◇ The party won its biggest share of the vote since 1992. ◇ The new TV channel has continued to increase its share of advertising revenue.* ⊃ see also JOB-SHARE, MARKET SHARE, TIME-SHARE **2** [sing.] the part that sb has in a particular activity that involves several people: *We all did our share. ◇ ~of sth Everyone must accept their share of the blame.* **3** [sing.] an amount of sth that is thought to be normal or acceptable for one person or thing: *He always eats more than his share. ◇ ~of sth I've had my share of luck in the past.* **4** [C] the action of sending on a message on SOCIAL MEDIA for other people to see: *The campaign has already received 180000 shares on Twitter.*
- **IN BUSINESS 5** [C] any of the units of equal value into which a company is divided that are sold to raise money. People who own shares receive part of the company's profits: *to have/hold/own shares ◇ to buy/sell/trade shares ◇ The company's shares fell 4.37 per cent. ◇ ~in sth They acquired shares in the company earlier this year.* compare STOCK ⊃ WORDFINDER NOTE at INVEST ⊃ see also ORDINARY SHARE
- **FARM EQUIPMENT 6** [C] (*NAmE*) = PLOUGHSHARE **IDM** see CAKE *n.*, FAIR *adj.*, LION, PIE

**-share** /ʃeə(r)/ *NAmE* /ʃer/ *combining form* **1** (in nouns) an arrangement to divide sth between two or more people, groups, etc: *a job-share (= a job that is done by two people who each work for part of the week) ◇ (BrE) a nanny share (= an arrangement for sb to work for two families)* ⊃ see also TIMESHARE **2** (in verbs) using an arrangement in which two or more people or groups use or have the same thing: *(especially BrE) We encourage people to carshare to reduce congestion on the roads. ◇ (NAmE) to rideshare*

**share-crop·per** /ˈʃeəkrɒpə(r)/ *NAmE* /ˈʃerkrɑːp-/ *noun* (*especially NAmE*) a farmer who gives part of his or her crop as rent to the owner of the land

**share·hold·er** /ˈʃeəhəʊldə(r)/ *NAmE* /ˈʃerh-/ *noun* an owner of shares in a company or business ⊃ WORDFINDER NOTE at COMPANY

**share·hold·ing** /ˈʃeəhəʊldɪŋ/ *NAmE* /ˈʃerh-/ *noun* the amount of a company or business that sb owns in the form of shares

**ˈshare index** (*NAmE also* **ˈstock index**) *noun* [usually sing.] a list that shows the current value of shares on the STOCK MARKET, based on the prices of shares of particular companies

**ˈshare option** (*BrE*) (*NAmE* **ˈstock option**) *noun* a right given to employees to buy shares in their company at a fixed price

**ˈshare-ware** /ˈʃeəweə(r); *NAmE* ˈʃerwer/ *noun* [U] (*computing*) computer software (= programs, etc.) that is available free for a user to test, after which they must pay if they wish to continue using it ⊃ compare FREEWARE

**sha·ria** (*also* **sha·riah**) /ʃəˈriːə/ *noun* [U] the system of religious laws that Muslims follow

**ˈsharing economy** *noun* [usually sing.] an economic system in which people can share possessions, services, etc., usually by means of the internet: *The sharing economy lets people turn a quick profit by renting out rooms, cars or even washing machines.*

**shark** /ʃɑːk; *NAmE* ʃɑːrk/ *noun* **1** a large sea fish with very sharp teeth and a pointed FIN on its back. There are several types of shark, some of which can attack people swimming. ⊃ see also GREAT WHITE SHARK **2** (*informal, disapproving*) a person who is dishonest in business, especially sb who gives bad advice and gets people to pay too much for sth ⊃ see also LOAN SHARK IDM see JUMP *v*.

**sharp** 🔾 B1 /ʃɑːp; *NAmE* ʃɑːrp/ *adj.*, *adv.*, *noun*
■ *adj.* (**sharp·er**, **sharp·est**)
• EDGE/POINT **1** 🔾 B1 having a fine edge or point, especially of sth that can cut or make a hole in sth: *a sharp knife* ◇ *Toys with sharp edges are not suitable for young children.* OPP blunt
• RISE/DROP/CHANGE **2** 🔾 B2 [usually before noun] (especially of a change in sth) sudden, rapid and large: *a sharp drop in prices* ◇ *a sharp rise in crime* ◇ *a sharp increase in unemployment* ◇ *He heard a sharp intake of breath.*
• CLEAR/DEFINITE **3** 🔾 B2 [usually before noun] clear and definite: *a sharp outline* ◇ *The photograph is not very sharp* (= there are no clear contrasts between areas of light and shade). ◇ *She drew a sharp distinction between domestic and international politics.* ◇ *In sharp contrast to her mood, the clouds were breaking up to reveal a blue sky.* ◇ *The issue must be brought into sharper focus.*
• MIND/EYES **4** (of people or their minds, eyes, etc.) quick to notice or understand things or to react: *to have sharp eyes* ◇ *a girl of sharp intelligence* ◇ *a sharp sense of humour* ◇ *He kept a sharp lookout for any strangers.* ◇ *It was very sharp of you to see that!*
• CRITICAL **5** (of a person or what they say) critical or severe: *sharp criticism* ◇ *Emma has a sharp tongue* (= she often speaks in an unpleasant or unkind way). ◇ **~ with sb** *He was very sharp with me when I was late.*
• SOUNDS **6** [usually before noun] loud, sudden and often high in tone: *She read out the list in sharp, clipped tones.* ◇ *There was a sharp knock on the door.*
• FEELING **7** (of a physical feeling or an emotion) very strong and sudden, often like being cut or badly hurt SYN **intense**: *He winced as a sharp pain shot through his leg.* ◇ *Polly felt a sharp pang of jealousy.*
• CURVES **8** changing direction suddenly: *a sharp bend in the road* ◇ *a sharp turn to the left*
• TASTE/SMELL **9** strong and slightly bitter: *The cheese has a distinctively sharp taste.* ⊃ SYNONYMS at BITTER
• FROST/WIND **10** used to describe a very cold or very severe FROST or wind ⊃ see also RAZOR-SHARP
• CLEVER AND DISHONEST **11** (*disapproving*) (of a person or their way of doing business) clever but possibly dishonest: *His lawyer's a sharp operator.* ◇ *The firm had to face some sharp practice from competing companies.*
• CLOTHES **12** [usually before noun] (of clothes or the way sb dresses) fashionable and new: *The consultants were a group of men in sharp suits.* ◇ *Todd is a sharp dresser.*
• FACE/FEATURES **13** not full or round in shape: *a man with a thin face and sharp features* (= a pointed nose and chin)
• IN MUSIC **14** used after the name of a note to mean a note a SEMITONE higher: *the Piano Sonata in C sharp minor* OPP flat ⊃ compare NATURAL ⊃ picture at MUSIC **15** above

the correct PITCH (= how high or low a note sounds): *That note sounded sharp.* OPP flat ▶ **sharp·ness** *noun* [U, sing.]: *There was a sudden sharpness in her voice.*
IDM **not the sharpest knife in the ˈdrawer** | **not the sharpest tool in the ˈbox** (*informal, humorous*) not intelligent: *He's not exactly the sharpest knife in the drawer, is he?* **the ˈsharp end (of sth)** (*BrE, informal*) the place or position of greatest difficulty or responsibility: *He started work at the sharp end of the business, as a salesman.*
■ *adv.*
• EXACTLY **1** used after an expression for a time of day to mean 'exactly': *Please be here at seven o'clock sharp.*
• LEFT/RIGHT **2** (*BrE*) **~ left/right** turning suddenly to the left or right
• MUSIC **3** (*comparative* **sharp·er**, no *superlative*) above the correct PITCH (= how high or low a note sounds) OPP flat
IDM **look ˈsharp** (*BrE, informal*) used in orders to tell sb to be quick or to hurry: *You'd better look sharp or you'll be late.*
■ *noun* **1** (*music*) a note played a SEMITONE higher than the note that is named. The written symbol is (♯): *It's a difficult piece to play, full of sharps and flats.* OPP flat ⊃ compare NATURAL **2 sharps** [pl.] (*medical*) things with a sharp edge or point, such as needles and SYRINGES: *the safe disposal of sharps*

**sharp·en** /ˈʃɑːpən; *NAmE* ˈʃɑːrp-/ *verb* **1** [T, I] **~ (sth)** to make sth sharper; to become sharper: *This knife needs sharpening.* ◇ *The outline of the trees sharpened as it grew lighter.* **2** [I, T] **~ (sth)** if a sense or feeling **sharpens** or sth **sharpens** it, it becomes stronger and/or clearer: *The sea air sharpened our appetites.* **3** [T] **~ sth** to make an issue or topic of discussion clearer and more likely to produce a result: *There is a need to sharpen the focus of the discussion.* **4** [I, T] to become or make sth better, more effective, etc. than before SYN **improve**: **~ (up)** *He needs to sharpen up before the Olympic trials.* ◇ **~ sth (up)** *She's doing a course to sharpen her business skills.* **5** [I, T] **~ (sth)** if your voice **sharpens** or sth **sharpens** it, it becomes high and loud in an unpleasant way

**sharp·en·er** /ˈʃɑːpnə(r); *NAmE* ˈʃɑːrp-/ *noun* (usually in compounds) a tool or machine that makes things sharp: *a pencil sharpener* ◇ *a knife sharpener*

**ˌsharp-ˈeyed** *adj.* able to see very well and quick to notice things SYN **observant**: *A sharp-eyed reader spotted the mistake in yesterday's paper.*

**sharp·ish** /ˈʃɑːpɪʃ; *NAmE* ˈʃɑːrp-/ *adv.* (*BrE, informal*) quickly; in a short time

**sharp·ly** /ˈʃɑːpli; *NAmE* ˈʃɑːrp-/ *adv.* **1** in a critical, rough or severe way: *The report was sharply critical of the police.* ◇ *'Is there a problem?' he asked sharply.* **2** suddenly and by a large amount: *Profits fell sharply following the takeover.* ◇ *The road fell sharply to the sea.* **3** in a way that clearly shows the differences between two things: *Their experiences contrast sharply with those of other children.* **4** quickly and suddenly or loudly: *She moved sharply across the room to block his exit.* ◇ *He rapped sharply on the window.* **5** used to emphasize that sth has a sharp point or edge: *sharply pointed*

**ˈsharp sharp** (*also* **sharp**) *exclamation* (*SAfrE, informal*) **1** used to express approval or agreement **2** used as a greeting when people meet or part

**sharp·shoot·er** /ˈʃɑːpʃuːtə(r); *NAmE* ˈʃɑːrp-/ *noun* a person who shows skill at shooting a gun

**shat** /ʃæt/ *past tense*, *past part.* of SHIT

**shat·ter** 🔾 C1 /ˈʃætə(r)/ *verb* **1** 🔾 C1 [I, T] to suddenly break into small pieces; to make sth suddenly break into small pieces: **~ (into sth)** *He dropped the vase and it shattered into pieces on the floor.* ◇ *the sound of shattering glass* ◇ **~ sth (into sth)** *The explosion shattered all the windows in the building.* **2** 🔾 C1 [T, I] to destroy sth completely, especially sb's feelings, hopes or beliefs; to be destroyed in this way: **~ sth (into sth)** *Anna's self-confidence had been completely shattered.* ◇ *Her experience of divorce shattered her illusions about love.* ◇ **~ (into sth)** *My whole world shattered*

# shattered

into a million pieces. **3** [T] **~ sb** to make sb feel extremely shocked and upset: *The unexpected death of their son shattered them.*

**shat·tered** /ˈʃætəd/ *NAmE* -tərd/ *adj.* **1** very shocked and upset: *The experience left her feeling absolutely shattered.* **2** (*BrE, informal*) very tired SYN **exhausted**

**shat·ter·ing** /ˈʃætərɪŋ/ *adj.* **1** that shocks and upsets you very much: *a shattering experience* ◊ *The news of his death came as a shattering blow.* **2** very loud SYN **deafening**
▶ **shat·ter·ing·ly** *adv.*

**shauri** /ˈʃaʊri/ *EAfrE* [ˈʃaʊri] *noun* (*EAfrE*) something that needs to be discussed or decided; something that causes a problem

**shave** /ʃeɪv/ *verb, noun*
■ *verb* **1** [I, T] to cut hair from the skin, especially the face, using a RAZOR: *Mike cut himself shaving.* ◊ **~ sb/sth/yourself** *The nurse washed and shaved him.* ◊ *a shaved head* ⊃ see also SHAVEN **2** [T] **~ sth** to cut a small amount off a price, etc: *The firm had shaved profit margins.*
PHRV **shave sth↔ˈoff**, **shave sth ˈoff sth 1** to remove a BEARD or MOUSTACHE by shaving: *Charles decided to shave off his beard.* **2** to cut very thin pieces from the surface of wood, etc: *I had to shave a few millimetres off the door to make it shut.* **3** to reduce a number by a very small amount: *He shaved a tenth of a second off the world record.*
■ *noun* an act of shaving: *I need a shave.* ◊ *to have a shave*
IDM see CLOSE² *adj.*

**shaven** /ˈʃeɪvn/ *adj.* with all the hair removed by shaving: *a shaven head* ⊃ compare UNSHAVEN ⊃ see also CLEAN-SHAVEN

**shaver** /ˈʃeɪvə(r)/ (*also* eˌlectric ˈrazor, eˌlectric ˈshaver) *noun* an electric tool for removing hair by shaving ⊃ compare RAZOR

**ˈshaving cream**, **ˈshaving foam** *noun* [U] special cream or FOAM for spreading over the face with a **ˈshaving brush** before removing hair with a RAZOR

**shav·ings** /ˈʃeɪvɪŋz/ *noun* [pl.] thin pieces cut from a piece of wood, etc. using a sharp tool, especially a PLANE

**shawl** /ʃɔːl/ *noun* a large piece of cloth worn by a woman around the shoulders or head, or wrapped around a baby

**Shaw·nee** /ʃɔːˈniː/ *noun* (*pl.* **Shaw·nee** *or* **Shaw·nees**) a member of a Native American people, many of whom now live in the US state of Oklahoma

**she** 📖 A1 /ʃi, strong form ʃiː/ *pron., noun*
■ *pron.* **1** 📖 A1 (used as the subject of a verb) a female person or animal that has already been mentioned or is easily identified: *'What does your sister do?' 'She's a dentist.'* ◊ *Doesn't she* (= the woman we are looking at) *look like Sue?* ⊃ compare HER ⊃ note at GENDER **2** (*AustralE, NZE*) it (used to refer to sth not usually thought of as female)
■ *noun* **1** [sing.] (*informal*) a female: *What a sweet little dog. Is it a he or a she?* **2** **she-** (in compound nouns) a female animal: *a she-wolf*

**s/he** *pron.* used in writing by some people when the subject of the verb could be either female (she) or male (he): *If a student does not attend all the classes, s/he will not be allowed to take the exam.*

**shea butter** /ˈʃeɪ bʌtə(r), ˈʃiː/ *noun* a type of fat obtained from the nuts of the **ˈshea tree**, used in foods and COSMETICS

**sheaf** /ʃiːf/ *noun* (*pl.* **sheaves** /ʃiːvz/) **1** a number of pieces of paper tied or held together **2** a bunch of WHEAT tied together after being cut

**shear** /ʃɪə(r); *NAmE* ʃɪr/ *verb* (**sheared**, **sheared**, /ʃɔːn; *NAmE* ʃɔːrn/, **sheared**) **1** [T] **~ sth** to cut the wool off a sheep: *It was time for the sheep to be shorn.* ◊ *sheep shearing* **2** [T] **~ sth** (*formal*) to cut off sb's hair: *shorn hair* **3** [I, T] **~ (sth) (off)** (*specialist*) (especially of metal) to break under pressure; to cut through sth and make it break: *The bolts holding the wheel in place sheared off.*
PHRV **be ˈshorn of sth** (*literary*) to have sth important taken away from you: *Shorn of his power, the deposed king went into exile.*

**shears** /ʃɪəz; *NAmE* ʃɪrz/ *noun* [pl.] a garden tool like a very large pair of SCISSORS, used for cutting bushes and HEDGES: *a pair of garden shears*

**shear·water** /ˈʃɪəwɔːtə(r); *NAmE* ˈʃɪrwɔː-/ *noun* a bird with long wings that often flies low over the sea

**sheath** /ʃiːθ/ *noun* (*pl.* **sheaths** /ʃiːðz/) **1** a cover that fits closely over the BLADE (= sharp part) of a knife or other sharp weapon or tool ⊃ picture at SWORD **2** any layer that covers and fits closely over sth for protection: *the sheath around an electric cable* **3** (*BrE*) = CONDOM **4** a woman's dress that fits the body closely

**sheathe** /ʃiːð/ *verb* **1** **~ sth** (*literary*) to put a knife or SWORD into a sheath **2** [usually passive] **~ sth (in/with sth)** to cover sth in a material, especially in order to protect it

**sheaves** /ʃiːvz/ *pl.* of SHEAF

**she·bang** /ʃɪˈbæŋ/ *noun*
IDM **the whole sheˈbang** (*informal*) the whole thing; everything

**she·been** /ʃɪˈbiːn/ *noun* (*informal*) (especially in Ireland, Scotland and South Africa) a place where alcoholic drinks are sold, usually illegally

**shed** 📖+ C1 /ʃed/ *verb, noun*
■ *verb* (**shed·ding**, **shed**, **shed**)
• GET RID OF **1** 📖+ C1 **~ sth** (often used in newspapers) to get rid of sth that is no longer wanted: *The factory is shedding a large number of jobs.* ◊ *a quick way to shed unwanted pounds* (= extra weight or fat on your body) ◊ *Museums have been trying hard to shed their stuffy image.*
• DROP **2** **~ sth (+ adv./prep.)** (*formal*) to take off a piece of clothing: *Luke shed his clothes onto the floor.* **3** **~ sth** (*BrE*) (of a vehicle) to lose or drop what it is carrying: *The traffic jam was caused by a lorry shedding its load.*
• SKIN/LEAVES **4** **~ sth** if an animal **sheds** its skin, or a plant **sheds** leaves, it loses them naturally
• LIGHT **5** **~ sth (on/over sb/sth)** to send light over sth; to let light fall somewhere: *The candles shed a soft glow on her face.*
• TEARS **6** **~ tears** (*formal* or *literary*) to cry: *She shed no tears when she heard he was dead.*
• BLOOD **7** **~ blood** (*formal*) to kill or injure people, especially in a war ⊃ see also BLOODSHED IDM see LIGHT *n.*
■ *noun* (often in compounds) **1** a small simple building, usually made of wood or metal, used for keeping things in: *a bicycle shed* ◊ (*BrE*) *a garden shed* **2** (*BrE*) a large industrial building, used for working in or keeping equipment: *an engine shed* **3** (*AustralE, NZE*) a building with open sides where the wool is cut off sheep (= they are SHEARED) or where cows are MILKED ⊃ see also COWSHED, POTTING SHED, WOODSHED

**she'd** /ʃiːd/ *short form* **1** she had HELP **She'd** is only used when *had* is an auxiliary verb: *She'd just left school.* When *had* is the main verb, use the full form: *I'm glad she had a good time.* ◊ *I'm glad she'd a good time.* **2** she would

**shed·load** /ˈʃedləʊd/ *noun* **~ (of sth)** (*BrE, informal*) a large amount of sth, especially money: *The project cost a shedload of money.* ◊ *This should save you shedloads.*

**sheen** /ʃiːn/ *noun* [sing., U] a soft smooth shiny quality SYN **shine**: *hair with a healthy sheen*

**sheep** 📖 A1 /ʃiːp/ *noun* (*pl.* **sheep**) an animal with a thick coat, kept on farms for its meat (called MUTTON or LAMB) or its wool: *a flock of sheep* ◊ *Sheep were grazing in the fields.* ⊃ compare EWE, LAMB, RAM ⊃ see also BLACK SHEEP
IDM **like ˈsheep** (*disapproving*) if people behave **like sheep**, they all do what the others are doing, without thinking for themselves **sort out/separate the ˈsheep from the ˈgoats** to recognize the difference between people who are good at sth, intelligent, etc. and those who are not ⊃ more at COUNT *v.*, WELL *adv.*, WOLF *n.*

**ˈsheep dip** *noun* [U, C] a liquid which is used to kill insects, etc. in a sheep's coat; the container in which sheep are put to treat them with this

**sheep·dog** /ˈʃiːpdɒg; NAmE -dɔːg/ noun **1** a dog that is trained to help control sheep on a farm **2** (BrE) a dog of a type that is often used for controlling sheep, especially a COLLIE

**sheep·fold** /ˈʃiːpfəʊld/ noun an area in a field surrounded by a fence or wall where sheep are kept for safety

**sheep·herd·er** /ˈʃiːphɜːdə(r); NAmE -hɜːrd-/ noun (NAmE) = SHEPHERD

**sheep·ish** /ˈʃiːpɪʃ/ adj. looking or feeling embarrassed because you have done sth silly or wrong **SYN** shame-faced: *Mary gave her a sheepish grin.* ▸ **sheep·ish·ly** adv.

**sheep·skin** /ˈʃiːpskɪn/ noun [U, C] the skin of a sheep with the wool still on it: *a sheepskin coat/rug*

**sheer** **₵+** **C1** /ʃɪə(r); NAmE ʃɪr/ adj., adv., verb
■ adj. **1** **₵+** **C1** [only before noun] used to emphasize the size, degree or amount of sth: *The area is under threat from the sheer number of tourists using it.* ◇ *We were impressed by the sheer size of the cathedral.* **2** **₵+** **C1** [only before noun] complete and not mixed with anything else **SYN** utter: *The concert was sheer delight.* ◇ *I only agreed out of sheer desperation.* **3** very steep: *sheer cliffs/slopes* ◇ *Outside there was a sheer drop down to the sea below.* **4** (of cloth, etc.) thin, light and almost TRANSPARENT: *sheer nylon*
■ adv. straight up or down: *The cliffs rise sheer from the beach.* ◇ *The ground dropped sheer away at our feet.*
■ verb
**PHRV** **sheer aˈway/ˈoff (from sth)** to change direction suddenly, especially in order to avoid hitting sth: *(figurative) Her mind sheered away from images she did not wish to dwell on.*

**sheesh** /ʃiːʃ/ exclamation (informal) used to express the feeling of being extremely annoyed or finding it hard to believe sth: *I mean, sheesh, get back to work, Frankie!*

**sheet** **₵** **A2** **S** /ʃiːt/ noun
• ON BED **1** **₵ A2** a large piece of thin cloth used on a bed to lie on or lie under: *Have you changed the sheets* (= put clean sheets on the bed)? ◇ *He slid between the sheets and closed his eyes.* ◇ *white bed sheets* ⊃ see also DUST SHEET
• OF PAPER **2** **₵ A2** a piece of paper for writing or printing on, etc. usually in a standard size: *a ~ of sth a clean/blank sheet of paper* (= with no writing on it) ◇ *Pick up one of our free information sheets at reception.* ⊃ see also BALANCE SHEET, CHEAT SHEET, FACT SHEET, SCORE SHEET, STYLE SHEET
• FLAT THIN PIECE **3** **₵ B1** a flat thin piece of any material, normally square or RECTANGULAR: *~ of sth a sheet of glass/plastic/plywood/steel* ◇ *sheet metal* (= metal that has been made into thin sheets) ⊃ see also BAKING SHEET
• WIDE FLAT AREA **4** **₵ B1** a wide flat area of sth, covering the surface of sth else: *~ of sth The road was covered with a sheet of ice.* ⊃ see also ICE SHEET
• OF FIRE/WATER **5** a large moving mass of fire or water: *a sheet of flame* ◇ *The rain was coming down in sheets* (= very heavily).
• ON SAIL **6** (specialist) a rope or chain fastened to the lower corner of a sail to hold it and to control the angle of the sail **HELP** There are other compounds ending sheet. You will find them at their place in the alphabet. **IDM** see CLEAN adj.

**sheet·ing** /ˈʃiːtɪŋ/ noun [U] **1** metal, plastic, etc. made into flat thin pieces: *metal/plastic/polythene sheeting* **2** cloth used for making sheets for beds

**sheet ˈlightning** noun [U] LIGHTNING that appears as a broad area of light in the sky ⊃ compare FORKED LIGHTNING

**sheet ˈmusic** noun [U] printed music as opposed to recorded music; printed music published on separate sheets of paper that are not fastened together to form a book

**sheikh** /ʃeɪk, ʃiːk/ (also **shaikh** /ʃeɪk/) noun **1** an Arab prince or leader; the head of an Arab family, village, etc. **2** a leader in a Muslim community or organization

**sheila** /ˈʃiːlə/ noun (AustralE, NZE, slang) a girl or young woman

**shekel** /ˈʃekl/ noun the unit of money in Israel

---

1427 **shell shock**

**shelf** **₵** **B1** /ʃelf/ noun (pl. **shelves** /ʃelvz/) **1** **₵ B1** a flat board, made of wood, metal, glass, etc., fixed to the wall or forming part of a cupboard, BOOKCASE, etc., for things to be placed on: **on a ~** *The book I wanted was on the top shelf.* ◇ *supermarket shelves* ◇ (NAmE) *store shelves* ◇ *the powerful retailers who control what products get shelf space* ⊃ see also TOP-SHELF **2** (geology) a thing like a shelf in shape, especially a piece of rock sticking out from a CLIFF or from the edge of a mass of land under the sea ⊃ see also CONTINENTAL SHELF, ICE SHELF, SHELVE
**IDM** **off the ˈshelf** that can be bought immediately and does not have to be specially designed or ordered: *I bought this package off the shelf.* ⊃ compare OFF THE PEG ⊃ see also OFF-THE-SHELF **on the ˈshelf** (informal) **1** not wanted by anyone; not used **2** (old-fashioned) (especially of women) considered to be too old to get married ⊃ more at MARKET n.

**ˈshelf life** noun [usually sing.] the length of time that food, etc. can be kept before it is too old to be sold

**ˈshelf-stacker** noun a person whose job is to fill shelves with goods to be sold, especially in a supermarket

**shell** **₵** **B1** /ʃel/ noun, verb
■ noun **1** **₵ B1** [C, U] the hard outer part of eggs, nuts, some seeds, and some animals: *We collected shells on the beach.* ◇ *snail/oyster/clam shells* ◇ *walnut shells* ◇ *earrings made out of coconut shell* ⊃ see also EGGSHELL, NUTSHELL, SEASHELL, TORTOISESHELL ⊃ **VISUAL VOCAB** pages V3, V4, V8 ⊃ picture at SHELLFISH **2** [C] any object that looks like the shell of a SNAIL or sea creature: *pasta shells* **3** [C] a metal case filled with EXPLOSIVE, to be fired from a large gun: *mortar/artillery shells* **4** [C] (NAmE) = CARTRIDGE **5** [C] the walls or outer structure of sth, for example, an empty building or ship after a fire or a bomb attack: *The house was now a shell gutted by flames.* ◇ *(figurative) My life has been an empty shell since he died.* **6** [C] any structure that forms a hard outer frame: *the body shell of a car* **7** [sing.] the outer layer of sb's personality; how they seem to be or feel: *She had developed a shell of indifference.*
**IDM** **come out of your ˈshell** to become less shy and more confident when talking to other people **to go, retreat, etc. into your ˈshell** to become shyer and avoid talking to other people
■ verb **1** [T, I] **~ (sth)** to fire shells at sth: *They shelled the city all night.* ◇ *Just as they were leaving, the rebels started shelling.* **2** [T] **~ sth** to remove the shell or outer layer from nuts, PEAS, etc.
**PHRV** **ˌshell ˈout (for sth)** | **ˌshell sth↔ˈout (for sth)** (informal) to pay a lot of money for sth **SYN** fork out (for sth): *The band shelled out $100 000 for a mobile recording studio.*

**she'll** /ʃiːl/ short form she will

**shel·lac** /ʃəˈlæk, ˈʃelæk/ noun, verb
■ noun [U] a natural substance used in making varnish to protect surfaces and make them hard
■ verb (-ck-) **1** **~ sth** to cover sth with shellac **2** [usually passive] **~ sb** (NAmE, informal) to defeat sb very easily: *The Republicans got shellacked in the elections.*

**shell·fire** /ˈʃelfaɪə(r)/ noun [U] attacks or explosions caused by SHELLS being fired from large guns

**shell·fish** /ˈʃelfɪʃ/ noun (pl. shell·fish) a creature with a shell, that lives in water, especially one of the types that can be eaten. OYSTERS and CRABS are both shellfish. ⊃ compare CRUSTACEAN, MOLLUSC ⊃ picture on page 1428

**ˈshell game** noun (NAmE) **1** **the shell game** [sing.] a game in which three cups are moved around, and players must guess which is the one with a small object under it **2** [C] an act by an organization or a politician that tricks people in a clever way

**shell·ing** /ˈʃelɪŋ/ noun [U] the firing of SHELLS (3) from large guns: *We suffered weeks of heavy shelling.*

**ˈshell shock** noun [U] a mental illness that can affect soldiers who have been in battle for a long time

# shell-shocked 1428

**shellfish**

claw — lobster — mussel — clam — oyster — shell

**'shell-shocked** adj. **1** shocked, confused or anxious because of a difficult situation, and unable to think or act normally **2** suffering from shell shock

**shel·ter** 🔊 B2 /ˈʃeltə(r)/ noun, verb
- noun **1** 👤 B2 [U] the fact of having a place to live or stay, considered as a basic human need: Human beings need food, clothing and shelter. **2** 👤 B2 [U] protection from rain, danger, or attack: ~ from sth to take shelter from the storm ◊ The sand dunes provided shelter from the wind. ◊ ~ of sth The fox was running for the shelter of the trees. **3** 👤 B2 [C] (often in compounds) a structure built to give protection, especially from the weather or from attack: He helped construct temporary shelters in 10 villages before the rains came. ◊ an air-raid shelter ⇒ see also BUS SHELTER **4** [C] a building, usually owned by a charity, that provides a place to stay for people without a home, or protection for people or animals who have been badly treated: a night shelter for the homeless ◊ an animal shelter ⇒ see also HOSTEL, TAX SHELTER
- verb **1** 👤 B2 [T] to give sb/sth a place where they are protected from the weather or from danger; to protect sb/sth: ~ sb/sth from sth Trees shelter the house from the wind. ◊ ~ sb/sth helping the poor and sheltering the homeless ◊ Perhaps I sheltered my daughter too much (= protected her too much from unpleasant or difficult experiences). **2** 👤 B2 [I] to stay in a place that protects you from the weather or from danger: A bomb fell on the building, killing those who were sheltering inside. ◊ ~ from sth We sheltered from the rain in a doorway. ⇒ WORDFINDER NOTE at RAIN

**shel·tered** /ˈʃeltəd/; NAmE -tərd/ adj. **1** (of a place) protected from bad weather: a sheltered bay/beach **2** (sometimes disapproving) protected from the more unpleasant aspects or difficulties of life: She had a very sheltered childhood. ◊ They both lead very sheltered lives. **3** [only before noun] (BrE) (of houses, flats, etc.) designed for people, especially old people, who can still live fairly independent lives, but with staff available to help them if necessary: sheltered accommodation/housing ◊ a sheltered workshop for the blind

**shelve** /ʃelv/ verb **1** [T] ~ sth to decide not to continue with a plan, either for a short time or permanently **SYN** put on ice: The government has shelved the idea until at least next year. **2** [T] ~ sth to put books, etc. on a shelf **3** [I] (+ adv./ prep.) (of land) to slope downwards: The beach shelved gently down to the water.

**shelves** /ʃelvz/ pl. of SHELF

**shelv·ing** /ˈʃelvɪŋ/ noun [U] shelves; material for making shelves: wooden shelving

**'she-male** noun (informal) a TRANSSEXUAL, especially one who works as a PROSTITUTE

**she·nan·igans** /ʃɪˈnænɪɡənz/ noun [pl.] (informal) secret or dishonest activities that people find interesting and sometimes funny

**Sheng** /ʃeŋ/ EAfrE /ˈʃeŋ/ noun [U] (EAfrE) (in Kenya) a simple form of language that includes words from English, Kiswahili and other African languages, used especially between young people in cities

**shep·herd** /ˈʃepəd/; NAmE -pərd/ noun, verb
- noun (NAmE also **sheep·herd·er**) a person whose job is to take care of sheep
- verb ~ sb + adv./prep. to guide sb or a group of people somewhere, making sure they go where you want them to go

**shep·herd·ess** /ˌʃepəˈdes/; NAmE ˈʃepərdəs/ noun a woman who takes care of sheep

**shepherd's 'pie** noun [C, U] (especially BrE) a dish of LAMB (= meat from a young sheep) cut into very small pieces and covered with a layer of MASHED potato ⇒ compare COTTAGE PIE

**sher·bet** /ˈʃɜːbət/; NAmE ˈʃɜːrb-/ noun **1** [U] (BrE) a powder that tastes of fruit and FIZZES when you put it in your mouth, eaten as a sweet **2** [C, U] (NAmE, becoming old-fashioned) = SORBET

**sherd** /ʃɜːd/; NAmE ʃɜːrd/ noun = SHARD

**sher·iff** /ˈʃerɪf/ noun **1** (in the US) an elected officer responsible for keeping law and order in a county or town **2** (also **High 'Sheriff**) (in England and Wales) an officer representing the king or queen in counties, and some cities, who performs some legal duties and attends ceremonies **3** (in Scotland) a judge **4** (in Canada) an official who works in a court preparing court cases

**'sheriff court** noun a lower court in Scotland

**Sher·lock** /ˈʃɜːlɒk/; NAmE ˈʃɜːrlɑːk/ (also **Sherlock Holmes** /ˌʃɜːlɒk ˈhəʊmz/; NAmE ˌʃɜːrlɑːk/) noun (informal, sometimes ironic) a person who tries to find an explanation for a crime or sth mysterious or who shows that they understand sth quickly, especially sth that is not obvious: Oh, well done, Sherlock. Did you figure that out all by yourself? **ORIGIN** From Sherlock Holmes, a very clever detective in stories by Arthur Conan Doyle, published in the late 19th and early 20th centuries.

**Sherpa** /ˈʃɜːpə/; NAmE ˈʃɜːrpə/ noun a member of a Himalayan people, who often guide people in the mountains, sometimes carrying their bags, etc.

**sherry** /ˈʃeri/ noun (pl. **-ies**) **1** [U, C] a strong yellow or brown wine, originally from southern Spain. It is often drunk before meals: sweet/dry sherry ◊ cream sherry (= a type of very sweet sherry) ◊ fine quality sherries ◊ a sherry glass (= a type of small narrow wine glass) **2** [C] a glass of sherry: I'll have a sherry.

**sher·wani** /ʃɜːˈwɑːni/; NAmE ʃɜːrˈw-/ noun a knee-length coat with buttons up to the neck, sometimes worn by men from South Asia

**she's** short form **1** /ʃiː, ʃɪz/ she is **2** /ʃiːz/ she has **HELP** She's is only used to mean 'she has' when has is an auxiliary verb: She's just got here. When has is the main verb, use the full form: She has two children. ◊ She's two children.

**'Shetland pony** /ˈʃetlənd ˈpəʊni/ noun a very small, strong horse with a rough coat

**shh** = SH

**Shia** (also **Shi'a**) /ˈʃiːə/ noun (pl. **Shia** or **Shias**) **1** [U] one of the two main branches of the Islamic religion ⇒ compare SUNNI **2** [C] (also **Shi·ite, Shi'ite**) a member of the Shia branch of Islam

**shi·atsu** /ʃiˈætsuː/ noun [U] (from Japanese) = ACUPRESSURE

**shib·bo·leth** /ˈʃɪbəleθ/ noun (formal) **1** an old idea, principle or phrase that is no longer accepted by many people as important or appropriate to modern life **2** a custom, word, etc. that distinguishes one group of people from another **ORIGIN** From a Hebrew word meaning 'ear of corn'. In the Bible story, Jephthah, one of the leaders of the Gileadites, was able to use it as a test to tell which were his own men, because others found the 'sh' sound difficult to pronounce.

**shied** /ʃaɪd/ past tense, past part. of SHY

**shield** /ʃiːld/ noun, verb
- noun **1** a large piece of metal or leather carried by soldiers in the past to protect the body when fighting **2** = RIOT SHIELD **3** ~ (against sth) a person or thing used to protect sb/sth, especially by forming a barrier: Water is not an effective shield against the sun's more harmful rays. ◊ She hid her true feelings behind a shield of cold indifference. ⇒ see also HUMAN SHIELD **4** a plate or screen that protects a machine or the person using it from damage or

injury **5** an object in the shape of a shield, given as a prize in a sports competition, etc. ⇒ picture at MEDAL **6** a drawing or model of a shield showing a COAT OF ARMS **7** (*NAmE*) a police officer's BADGE

▪ **verb 1** to protect sb/sth from danger, harm or sth unpleasant: ~ **sth against sth** *I shielded my eyes against the glare.* ◇ ~ **sb/sth from sb/sth** *The ozone layer shields the earth from the sun's ultraviolet rays.* ◇ *You can't shield her from the truth forever.* ◇ ~ **sb/sth** *Police believe that somebody is shielding the killer.* **2** ~ **sth** to put a shield around a machine, etc. in order to protect the person using it

**shift** ⓘ **B1** ⊙ /ʃɪft/ *noun, verb*

▪ *noun*
- **PERIOD OF WORK 1** 🔊 **B1** [C] a period of time worked by a group of workers who start work as another group finishes: *to work a shift* ◇ *I've just finished an eight-hour shift.* ◇ **in shifts** *working in shifts* ◇ **on a~** *to be on the day/night shift at the factory* ◇ **shift workers/work** ⇒ see also GRAVEYARD SHIFT, SPLIT SHIFT **2** 🔊 **B1** [C + sing./pl. v.] the workers who work a particular shift: *The night shift has/have just come off duty.* ⇒ WORDFINDER NOTE at FACTORY
- **CHANGE 3** 🔊 **B2** [C] a change in opinion, mood, policy, etc: ~ **in sth** *Does the government's condemnation of the regime signal a shift in policy?* ◇ ~ **of sth** *a shift of emphasis* ⇒ see also PARADIGM SHIFT
- **ON COMPUTER 4** [U] (*also* **shift key** [*sing.*]) the system on a computer keyboard or TYPEWRITER that allows capital letters or a different set of characters to be typed; the key that operates this system ⇒ WORDFINDER NOTE at KEYBOARD
- **CLOTHING 5** [C] a woman's simple straight dress **6** [C] a simple straight piece of clothing worn by women in the past as underwear ⇒ see also DOPPLER SHIFT, STICK SHIFT

▪ *verb*
- **MOVE 1** 🔊 **B2** [I, T] to move, or move sth, from one position or place to another: *Lydia shifted uncomfortably in her chair.* ◇ ~ **(from sb/sth) to sb/sth** *The action of the novel shifts from Paris to London.* ◇ ~ **sth** *Could you help me shift some furniture?* ◇ ~ **sth (from sb/sth)** *He shifted his gaze from the child to her.* ◇ *More Japanese manufacturers are shifting production to China.* **2** [I, T] ~ **(yourself)** (*BrE, informal*) to move quickly SYN **hurry**
- **SITUATION/OPINION/POLICY 3** 🔊 **B2** [I] (of a situation, an opinion, a policy etc.) to change from one state, position, etc. to another: *Public attitudes towards marriage have shifted over the past 50 years.* ◇ ~ **(away from sb/sth) (to/towards sb/sth)** *The balance of power shifted away from workers towards employers.* **4** [T] to change your opinion of or attitude towards sth, or change the way that you do sth: ~ **sth** *We need to shift the focus of this debate.* ◇ ~ **sth (from …) (to/towards/toward …)** *The new policy shifted the emphasis away from fighting inflation.*
- **RESPONSIBILITY 5** [T] ~ **responsibility/blame (for sth) (onto sb)** to make sb else responsible for sth you should do or sth bad that you have done: *He tried to shift the blame for his mistakes onto his colleagues.*
- **REMOVE MARK 6** [T] ~ **sth** to remove sth such as a dirty mark SYN **get rid of sth**: *a detergent that shifts even the most stubborn stains*
- **SELL GOODS 7** [T] ~ **sth** to sell goods, especially goods that are difficult to sell: *They cut prices drastically to try and shift stock.*
- **IN VEHICLE 8** [I] (*NAmE*) to change the GEARS when you are driving a vehicle: *to shift into second gear*

IDM **ˌshift your ˈground** (*usually disapproving*) to change your opinion about a subject, especially during a discussion **(the) ˌshifting ˈsands (of sth)** used to describe a situation that changes so often that it is difficult to understand or deal with it
PHRV **ˌshift for yourˈself** (*BrE*) to do things without help from other people: *You're going to have to shift for yourself from now on.*

**shift·er** /ˈʃɪftə(r)/ *noun* (*especially NAmE*) the GEARBOX of a vehicle or the set of LEVERS on a bicycle for changing GEAR ⇒ see also SHAPE-SHIFTER

**shift·less** /ˈʃɪftləs/ *adj.* (*disapproving*) lazy and having no ambition to succeed in life

**shifty** /ˈʃɪfti/ *adj.* (**shift·ier, shift·iest**) (*informal*) seeming to be dishonest; looking guilty about sth SYN **furtive**: *shifty eyes* ◇ *to look shifty* ▸ **shift·ily** /-ɪli/ *adv.*

**shii·take** (*also* **shi·take**) /ʃɪˈtɑːki/ (*also* **shiitake ˈmushroom**) *noun* (*from Japanese*) a type of Japanese or Chinese MUSHROOM

**Shi·ite** (*also* **Shi'ite**) /ˈʃiːaɪt/ *noun* a member of the Shia branch of Islam ⇒ compare SUNNI ▸ **Shi·ite** (*also* **Shi'ite**) *adj.* [*usually before noun*]

**shil·ling** /ˈʃɪlɪŋ/ *noun* **1** a British coin and unit of money in use until 1971, worth 12 old pence. There were 20 shillings in one pound. **2** the unit of money in Kenya, Uganda, Tanzania and Somalia

**shim** /ʃɪm/ *noun* (*NAmE*) a thin piece of wood, rubber, metal, etc. which is thicker at one end than the other, that you use to fill a space between two things that do not fit well together

**shim·mer** /ˈʃɪmə(r)/ *verb, noun*
▪ *verb* [I] to shine with a soft light that seems to move slightly: *The sea was shimmering in the sunlight.* ⇒ SYNONYMS at SHINE
▪ *noun* [U, *sing.*] a shining light that seems to move slightly: *a shimmer of moonlight in the dark sky*

**shimmy** /ˈʃɪmi/ *verb* [I] (**shim·mies, shimmy·ing, shimmied, shim·mied**) + *adv./prep.* to dance or move in a way that involves shaking your shoulders and HIPS

**shin** /ʃɪn/ *noun, verb*
▪ *noun* the front part of the leg below the knee ⇒ VISUAL VOCAB page V1
▪ *verb* (**-nn-**)
PHRV **ˌshin ˈup/ˈdown sth** (*BrE*) (*NAmE* **ˈshinny ˈup/ˈdown sth**) (*informal*) to climb up or down sth quickly, using your hands and legs: *He shinned down the drainpipe and ran off.*

**ˈshin bone** *noun* the front and larger bone of the two bones in the lower part of the leg between the knee and the ankle SYN **tibia** ⇒ VISUAL VOCAB page V1

**shin·dig** /ˈʃɪndɪɡ/ *noun* (*informal*) a big noisy party

**shine** ⓘ **B1** /ʃaɪn/ *verb, noun*
▪ *verb* (**shone, shone** /ʃɒn; *NAmE* ʃoʊn/) HELP In sense 2 in *NAmE* **shined** can also be used for the past tense and past participle. In sense 3 **shined** is used for the past tense and past participle. **1** 🔊 **B1** [I] to produce or reflect light; to be bright: *The sun shone brightly in a cloudless sky.* ◇ ~ **on sb/sth** *the beauty of the moon shining on the waves* ◇ ~ **with sth** (*figurative*) *Her eyes were shining with excitement.* ◇ (*figurative*) *Excitement was shining in her eyes.* ⇒ SYNONYMS on page 1430 **2** 🔊 **B1** [T] (*NAmE also* **shined, shined**) ~ **sth** + *adv./prep.* to aim or point the light of a lamp, etc. in a particular direction: *He shone the flashlight around the cellar.* ◇ (*figurative*) *Campaigners are shining a spotlight on the world's diminishing natural resources.* **3** [T] (**shined, shined**) ~ **sth** to POLISH sth; to make sth smooth and bright: *He shined shoes and sold newspapers to make money.* **4** [I] to show that you are very good at sth: *He failed to shine academically but he was very good at sports.* ◇ *She has set a shining example of loyal service over four decades.* ⇒ see also SHINY, KNIGHT *n.*, RISE *v.*
PHRV **ˌshine ˈthrough (sth)** (of a quality) to be easy to see or notice: *Her old professional skills shone through.*
▪ *noun* [*sing.*] the bright quality that sth has when light is reflected on it: *a shampoo that gives your hair body and shine*
IDM **take a ˈshine to sb/sth** (*informal*) to begin to like sb very much as soon as you see or meet them **take the ˈshine off sth** (*informal*) to make sth seem much less good than it did at first ⇒ more at RAIN *n.*

**shiner** /ˈʃaɪnə(r)/ *noun* (*informal*) an area of dark skin that can form around sb's eye when they have been hit hard there SYN **black eye**

**shin·gle** /ˈʃɪŋɡl/ *noun* **1** [U] a mass of small smooth stones on a beach or at the side of a river: *a shingle beach* **2** [C, U] a small flat piece of wood that is used to cover a wall or roof of a building **3** [C] (*NAmE*) a board with a sign on it, in

# shingled  1430

## SYNONYMS

**shine**
gleam · glow · sparkle · glisten · shimmer · glitter · twinkle · glint

These words all mean to produce or reflect light.

**shine** to produce or reflect light, especially brightly: *The sun was shining and the sky was blue.*

**gleam** to shine with a clear bright or pale light, especially a reflected light: *Moonlight gleamed on the water.*

**glow** (often of sth hot or warm) to produce a steady light that is not very bright: *The end of his cigarette glowed red.*

**sparkle** to shine brightly with small flashes of light: *The diamonds sparkled in the light.*

**glisten** (of sth wet) to shine: *The road glistened wet after the rain.*

**shimmer** to shine with a soft light that seems to shake slightly: *Everything seemed to shimmer in the heat.*

**glitter** to shine brightly with small flashes of reflected light: *The ceiling of the cathedral glittered with gold.*

### SPARKLE OR GLITTER?

There is very little difference in meaning between these two words. **Glitter** can sometimes suggest a lack of depth, but this is more frequent in the figurative use of **glitter** as a noun: *the superficial glitter of show business*. **Sparkle** is also often used to talk about light reflected off a surface, but things that produce light can also sparkle: *Stars sparkled in the sky.*

**twinkle** to shine with a light that changes rapidly from bright to faint to bright again: *Stars twinkled in the sky.*

**glint** to give small bright flashes of reflected light: *The blade of the knife glinted in the darkness.*

### PATTERNS

- to shine / gleam / sparkle / glisten / shimmer / glitter / glint **on** sth
- to shine / gleam / glow / sparkle / glisten / shimmer / glitter / twinkle / glint **with** sth
- to shine / gleam / sparkle / glisten / shimmer / glitter / glint **in the sunlight**
- to shine / gleam / glisten / shimmer / glitter / glint **in the moonlight**
- the **stars** shine / sparkle / glitter / twinkle
- sb's **eyes** shine / gleam / glow / sparkle / glisten / glitter / twinkle / glint
- to shine / gleam / glow / glitter **brightly**
- to shine / gleam / glow / shimmer **softly**

front of a doctor's or lawyer's office: *He hung out his own shingle* (= started a business as a doctor or lawyer).

**shin·gled** /ˈʃɪŋɡld/ adj. (of a roof, building, etc.) covered with shingles

**shin·gles** /ˈʃɪŋɡlz/ noun [U] a disease that affects the nerves and produces a band of painful spots on the skin

**'shin guard** (BrE also **'shin pad**) noun a piece of thick material that is used to protect the lower front part of the leg when playing sports

**shinny** /ˈʃɪni/ verb, noun
- verb (**shin·nies**, **shinny·ing**, **shin·nied**, **shin·nied**)
  PHRV **'shinny up/down sth** (NAmE) (BrE **'shin up/down sth**) (informal) to climb up or down sth quickly, using your hands and legs
- noun (also **'shinny hockey**) [U] an informal form of ICE HOCKEY, played especially by children

**'shin splints** noun [pl.] sharp pain in the front parts of the lower legs caused by too much exercise, especially on a hard surface

**Shinto** /ˈʃɪntəʊ/ (also **Shin·to·ism** /ˈʃɪntəʊɪzəm/) noun a Japanese religion whose practices include the WORSHIP of ANCESTORS and a belief in nature spirits

**shinty** /ˈʃɪnti/ noun [U] a Scottish game similar to hockey, played with curved sticks by teams of twelve players

**shiny** ⓘ B1 /ˈʃaɪni/ adj. (**shini·er**, **shini·est**) smooth and bright; reflecting the light: *a shiny object/surface*
IDM **shiny new** (approving) very new and attractive: *shiny new stuff/software*

**ship** ⓘ A2 /ʃɪp/ noun, verb
- noun ⓘ A2 a large boat that carries people or goods by sea: **on a ~** *The others sailed on a later ship.* ◊ *a cargo/cruise/merchant ship* ◊ **by ~** *Raw materials and labour come by ship, rail or road.* ◊ *The captain gave the order to* **abandon ship** (= to leave the ship because it was sinking). ⊃ see also AIRSHIP, FACTORY SHIP, FLAGSHIP, LIGHTSHIP, SAILING SHIP
IDM see JUMP v., SINK v., TIGHT adj.
- verb (-pp-) **1** ⓘ B2 [T] **~ sb/sth + adv./prep.** to send or transport sb/sth by ship or by another means of transport: *The company ships its goods all over the world.* ◊ *He was arrested and shipped back to the UK for trial.* **2** [I, T] to be available to be bought; to make sth available to be bought: *The software is due to ship next month.* ◊ **~ sth** *The company continues to ship more computer systems than its rivals.* **3** [T] **~ water** (of a boat, etc.) to have water coming in over the sides **4** [T] **~ A and/with B** (informal) to think that two people should already be in a romantic relationship: *Some people are already shipping Alex and Meredith.*
PHRV **ship sb↔off** (disapproving) to send sb to a place where they will stay: *The children were shipped off to a boarding school at an early age.*

**-ship** /ʃɪp/ suffix (in nouns) **1** the state or quality of: *ownership* ◊ *friendship* **2** the status or office of: *citizenship* ◊ *professorship* **3** skill or ability as: *musicianship* **4** the group of: *membership*

**ship·board** /ˈʃɪpbɔːd/; NAmE -bɔːrd/ adj. [only before noun] happening on a ship: *shipboard romances*

**ship·build·er** /ˈʃɪpbɪldə(r)/ noun a person or company that builds ships ▸ **ship·build·ing** noun [U]: *the shipbuilding industry*

**ship·load** /ˈʃɪpləʊd/ noun as many goods or passengers as a ship can carry

**ship·mate** /ˈʃɪpmeɪt/ noun sailors who are **shipmates** are sailing on the same ship as each other

**ship·ment** /ˈʃɪpmənt/ noun **1** [U] the process of sending goods from one place to another: *The goods are ready for shipment.* ◊ *the illegal shipment of arms* ◊ *shipment costs* **2** [C] a load of goods that are sent from one place to another: *arms shipments* ◊ *a shipment of arms*

**ship·owner** /ˈʃɪpəʊnə(r)/ noun a person or company that owns a ship or ships

**ship·per** /ˈʃɪpə(r)/ noun a person or company that arranges for goods to be sent from one place to another, especially by ship

**ship·ping** ⓘ C1 /ˈʃɪpɪŋ/ noun [U] **1** ⓘ C1 ships in general or considered as a group: *The canal is open to shipping.* ◊ *international shipping lanes* (= routes for ships) **2** ⓘ C1 the activity of carrying people or goods from one place to another by ship or by some other means: *a shipping company* ◊ *We offer free shipping on orders over $50.* ⊃ WORDFINDER NOTE at INDUSTRY

**'ship's chandler** noun = CHANDLER

**ship·shape** /ˈʃɪpʃeɪp/ adj. [not usually before noun] clean and neat; in good condition and ready to use

**ship·wreck** /ˈʃɪprek/ noun, verb
- noun **1** [U, C] the loss or DESTRUCTION of a ship at sea because of a storm or because it hits rocks, etc: *They narrowly escaped shipwreck in a storm in the North Sea.* **2** [C] a ship that has been lost or destroyed at sea: *The contents of shipwrecks belong to the state.*
- verb **be shipwrecked** to be sailing in a ship that is then lost or destroyed at sea ▸ **ship·wrecked** adj.: *a shipwrecked sailor*

**ship·yard** /ˈʃɪpjɑːd/; NAmE -jɑːrd/ noun a place where ships are built or repaired: *shipyard workers*

**shire** /ˈʃaɪə(r)/ noun (BrE) **1** [C] (old use) a county **2** -shire /ʃə(r)/ combining form used in the names of some counties in Britain: *Hampshire* ◊ *Yorkshire* **3** **the Shires** (also **the Shire Counties**) [pl.] counties in central England that are in country areas

---

æ cat | ɑː father | e bed | ɜː fur | ə about | ɪ sit | iː see | i happy | ɒ got (BrE) | ɔː saw | ʌ cup | ʊ put | uː too

**'shire horse** noun a large powerful horse, used for pulling loads

**shirk** /ʃɜːk; NAmE ʃɜːrk/ verb [I, T] (disapproving) to avoid doing sth you should do, especially because you are too lazy: *Discipline in the company was strict and no one shirked.* ◊ **~ from sth/doing sth** *A determined burglar will not shirk from breaking a window to gain entry.* ◊ **~sth/doing sth** *She never shirked her responsibilities.* ▶ **shirk·er** noun

**shirt** ⓘ **A1** /ʃɜːt; NAmE ʃɜːrt/ noun a piece of clothing (usually for men), worn on the upper part of the body, made of light cloth, with SLEEVES and usually with a COLLAR and buttons down the front: *to wear a shirt* ◊ *He had a shirt and tie on.* ◊ *a long-sleeved/short-sleeved shirt* ⊃ see also DRESS SHIRT, HAIR SHIRT, HAWAIIAN SHIRT, NIGHTSHIRT, POLO SHIRT, SWEATSHIRT, T-SHIRT
**IDM** **keep your 'shirt on** (*informal*) used to tell sb not to get angry: *Keep your shirt on! It was only a joke.* **put your 'shirt on sb/sth** (BrE, *informal*) to bet all your money on sb/sth **the shirt off sb's 'back** anything that sb has, including the things they really need themselves, that sb else takes from them or they are willing to give

**'shirt-sleeve** /'ʃɜːtsliːv; NAmE 'ʃɜːrt-/ noun [usually pl.] an arm of a shirt
**IDM** **in (your) 'shirtsleeves** wearing a shirt without a jacket, etc. on top of it

**shi·sha** /'ʃiːʃə/ noun **1** [C] a HOOKAH (= a long pipe for smoking that passes smoke through a container of water to cool it) **2** [U] TOBACCO for smoking in a HOOKAH, especially when mixed with other things that make it taste good, such as MINT

**shish kebab** /'ʃɪʃ kɪbæb; NAmE -bɑːb/ noun (especially NAmE) = KEBAB

**shit** /ʃɪt/ exclamation, noun, verb, adj.
■ exclamation (*taboo, slang*) a swear word that many people find offensive, used to show that you are angry or annoyed: *Shit! I've lost my keys!* **HELP** Less offensive exclamations to use are **damn** or **darn it** (*especially NAmE*), and **blast** or **bother** (*BrE*).
■ noun (*taboo, slang*) **1** [U] solid waste matter from the BOWELS **SYN** excrement: *a pile of dog shit on the path* **HELP** A more polite way to express this example would be 'a pile of dog poo/poop'. **2** [sing.] an act of emptying solid waste matter from the BOWELS: *to have/take a shit* **3** [U] stupid remarks or writing **SYN** nonsense: *You're talking shit!* ◊ *She's so full of shit.* ⊃ see also BULLSHIT noun **4** [C] (*disapproving*) an unpleasant person who treats other people badly: *He's an arrogant little shit.* **5** [U] criticism or unfair treatment: *I'm not going to take any shit from them.*
**IDM** **beat, kick, etc. the 'shit out of sb** (*taboo, slang*) to attack sb violently so that you injure them **in the 'shit** | **in deep 'shit** (*taboo, slang*) in trouble: *I'll be in the shit if I don't get this work finished today.* **like 'shit** (*taboo, slang*) really bad, ill etc.; really badly: *I woke up feeling like shit.* ◊ *We get treated like shit in this job.* **no 'shit!** (*taboo, slang, often ironic*) used to show that you are surprised, impressed, etc. or that you are pretending to be **not give a 'shit (about sb/sth)** (*taboo, slang*) to not care at all about sb/sth: *He doesn't give a shit about anybody else.* **shit 'happens** (*taboo, slang*) used to express the idea that we must accept that bad things often happen without reason **when the shit hits the 'fan** (*taboo, slang*) when sb in authority finds out about sth bad or wrong that sb has done: *When the shit hits the fan, I don't want to be here.* ⊃ more at BUG v., CROCK, SCARE v.
■ verb (**shit·ting**, **shit, shit**) (*taboo, slang*) **HELP** **shat** /ʃæt/ and, in BrE, **shit·ted** are also used for the past tense and past participle. **1** [I, T] **~ (sth)** to empty solid waste matter from the BOWELS **HELP** A more polite way of expressing this is 'to go to the toilet/lavatory' (*BrE*), 'to go to the bathroom' (*NAmE*) or 'to go'. A more formal expression is 'to empty the bowels'. **2** [T] **~ yourself** to empty solid waste matter from the BOWELS by accident **3** [T] **~ yourself** to be very frightened
■ adj. (*taboo, slang, especially BrE*) very bad: *You're shit and you know you are!* ◊ *They're a shit team.*

1431

**shi·take** = SHIITAKE

**shite** /ʃaɪt/ exclamation, noun [U] (BrE, *taboo, slang*) another word for SHIT

**'shit-faced** adj. (*taboo, slang*) very drunk

**'shit-hole** /'ʃɪthəʊl/ noun (*taboo, slang*) a very dirty or unpleasant place

**'shit-house** /'ʃɪthaʊs/ noun (*taboo, slang*) a toilet

**'shit-less** /'ʃɪtləs/ adj. (*taboo, slang*) **IDM** see SCARE v.

**shit-'scared** adj. [not before noun] (*taboo, slang*) very frightened

**shitty** /'ʃɪti/ adj. (**shit·ti·er**, **shit·ti·est**) (*taboo, slang*) **1** unpleasant; very bad **2** unfair or unkind: *What a shitty way to treat a friend!*

**shiver** /'ʃɪvə(r)/ verb, noun
■ verb [I] (of a person) to shake slightly because you are cold, frightened, excited, etc: *Don't stand outside shivering—come inside and get warm!* ◊ *He shivered at the thought of the cold, dark sea.* ◊ **~ with sth** *to shiver with cold/fear/excitement/pleasure*
■ noun **1** [C] a sudden shaking movement of your body because you are cold, frightened, excited, etc: *The sound of his voice sent shivers down her spine.* ◊ *He felt a cold shiver of fear run through him.* **2 the shivers** [pl.] shaking movements of your body because of fear or a high temperature: *I don't like him. He gives me the shivers.* ◊ *Symptoms include headaches, vomiting and the shivers.*

**shiv·ery** /'ʃɪvəri/ adj. shaking with cold, fear, illness, etc.

**shmo** = SCHMO

**shoal** /ʃəʊl/ noun **1** a large number of fish swimming together as a group ⊃ compare SCHOOL (9) **2** a small hill of sand just below the surface of the sea

**shock** ⓘ **B2** /ʃɒk; NAmE ʃɑːk/ noun, verb
■ noun
• SURPRISE **1** ⓘ **B2** [C, usually sing., U] a strong feeling of surprise as a result of sth happening, especially sth unpleasant; the event that causes this feeling: *I got a terrible shock the other day.* ◊ *The news of my promotion came as a shock.* ◊ **in~** *She stared at him in shock for a moment.* ◊ *He's still in a state of shock* ◊ **~ of (doing) sth** *She still hadn't got over the shock of seeing him again.* ◊ **~ for sb/sth** *This must be quite a shock for you all.* ◊ **~ to sb/sth** *Her sudden death was a huge shock to the many people who knew her.* ⊃ see also CULTURE SHOCK, STICKER SHOCK
• MEDICAL **2** ⓘ **B2** [U] a serious medical condition, usually the result of injury in which a person has lost a lot of blood and they are extremely weak: *She was taken to hospital suffering from shock.* ◊ *He had gone into shock and was shaking violently.* ⊃ see also SHELL SHOCK, TOXIC SHOCK SYNDROME
• VIOLENT SHAKING **3** ⓘ **B2** [C, U] a violent shaking movement that is caused by an explosion, earthquake, etc: *The shock of the explosion could be felt six miles away.* ◊ *The bumper absorbs shock on impact.* ⊃ compare AFTERSHOCK
• FROM ELECTRICITY **4** ⓘ **B2** [C] = ELECTRIC SHOCK: *Don't touch that wire or you'll get a shock.*
• OF HAIR **5** [C, usually sing.] **~ of hair** a thick mass of hair on a person's head
**IDM** **shock 'horror** (BrE, *informal, often humorous*) used when you pretend to be shocked by sth that is not really very serious or surprising ⊃ see also SHOCK-HORROR
■ verb
• SURPRISE AND UPSET **1** ⓘ **B2** [T] to surprise and upset sb: **~sb** *President Kennedy's assassination in Dallas on November 22, 1963, shocked the world.* ◊ *The news had shocked her deeply.* ◊ **~sb that …** *It shocked her that he would do such a thing.* ◊ **~sb to do sth** *It shocked me to think that some people would be prepared to commit acts like these.* ⊃ SYNONYMS on page 1432
• OFFEND/DISGUST **2** ⓘ **B2** [I, T] (of bad language, immoral behaviour, etc.) to make sb feel offended or full of horror: *These movies deliberately set out to shock.* ◊ **~sb** *She enjoys shocking people by saying outrageous things.*

# shock absorber

## ▼ SYNONYMS

**shock**

appal • horrify • disgust • sicken • repel

These words all mean to surprise and upset sb very much.

**shock** [often passive] to surprise sb, usually in a way that upsets them: *We were all shocked at the news of his death.*

**appal** to shock and upset sb very much: *The brutality of the crime has appalled the public.*

**horrify** to make sb feel extremely shocked, upset or frightened: *The whole country was horrified by the killings.*

**disgust** to make sb feel shocked and almost ill because sth is so unpleasant: *The level of violence in the movie really disgusted me.*

**sicken** (BrE) to make sb feel very shocked, angry and almost ill because sth is so unpleasant: *The public is becoming sickened by these images of violence and death.*

**repel** [often passive] (*rather formal*) to make sb feel horror or disgust: *I was repelled by the smell of drink on his breath.*

### PATTERNS
- shocked/appalled/horrified/disgusted **at** sb/sth
- **to** shock/appal/horrify/disgust sb **that** …
- **to** shock/appal/horrify/disgust/sicken sb **to think/see/hear** …
- sb's **behaviour** shocks/appals sb
- **violence/an idea** shocks/appals/horrifies/disgusts sb

**'shock absorber** *noun* a device that is fitted to each wheel of a vehicle in order to reduce the effects of travelling over rough ground, so that passengers can be more comfortable

**shocked** 🔑 B2 /ʃɒkt; NAmE ʃɑːkt/ *adj.* **1** 🔑 B2 surprised and upset; showing that sb feels surprised and upset: *I was quite shocked when I found out what he'd done.* ◇ *~at/by sb/sth We were all shocked at the news of his death.* ◇ *~that … Neighbours were shocked that such an attack could happen in their area.* ◇ *~to do sth I was shocked to hear that he had resigned.* ◇ *He was **shocked to find out** that the school had no official policy for dealing with such cases.* ◇ *They seemed **shocked to see** her there.* ◇ *For a few minutes we stood in shocked silence.* **2** 🔑 B2 feeling offended or DISGUSTED: *She was trying very hard not to look shocked.* ◇ *~at/by sb/sth Many people were shocked by the sex scenes in the film.*

**shock·er** /'ʃɒkə(r); NAmE 'ʃɑːk-/ *noun* (*informal*) **1** a film, piece of news or person that shocks you **2** something that is of very low quality

**'shock-horror** *adj.* intending to make people very shocked or very angry: *a shock-horror advertising campaign* ⇒ see also SHOCK HORROR at SHOCK *noun*

**shock·ing** 🔑+ B2 /'ʃɒkɪŋ; NAmE 'ʃɑːk-/ *adj.* **1** 🔑+ B2 that offends or upsets people; that is morally wrong: *shocking behaviour* ◇ *shocking news* ◇ *It is shocking that they involved children in the crime.* ◇ *a shocking waste of money* **2** (*informal, especially BrE*) very bad: *The house was left in a shocking state.* ▶ **shock·ing·ly** *adv.*: *a shockingly high mortality rate*

**shocking 'pink** *adj.* very bright pink in colour ▶ **shocking 'pink** *noun* [U]

**'shock jock** *noun* (*informal, especially NAmE*) a DISC JOCKEY on a radio show who deliberately expresses opinions or uses language that many people find offensive

**shock·proof** /'ʃɒkpruːf; NAmE 'ʃɑːk-/ *adj.* made so that it cannot be damaged if it is dropped or hit: *My watch is shockproof and waterproof.*

**'shock tactics** *noun* [pl.] actions that are done to deliberately shock people in order to persuade them to do sth or to react in a particular way

**'shock therapy** (*also* **'shock treatment**) *noun* [U] a way of treating mental illness by giving ELECTRIC SHOCKS or a drug that has a similar effect

**'shock troops** *noun* [pl.] soldiers who are specially trained to make sudden attacks on the enemy

**'shock wave** *noun* **1** a movement of very high air pressure that is caused by an explosion, earthquake, etc. **2 shock waves** [pl.] feelings of shock that people experience when sth bad happens suddenly: *The murder sent shock waves through the whole community.*

**shod** /ʃɒd; NAmE ʃɑːd/ *adj., verb*
- *adj.* (*literary*) wearing shoes of the type mentioned: *She turned on her elegantly shod heel.*
- *verb* past tense, past part. of SHOE

**shoddy** /'ʃɒdi; NAmE 'ʃɑːdi/ *adj.* (**shod·dier**, **shod·di·est**) **1** (of goods, work, etc.) made or done badly and with not enough care SYN **second-rate**: *shoddy goods* ◇ *shoddy workmanship* **2** dishonest or unfair: *shoddy treatment* ▶ **shod·dily** /-dəli/ *adv.* **shod·di·ness** *noun* [U]

**shoe** 🔑 A1 /ʃuː/ *noun, verb*
- *noun* **1** 🔑 A1 one of a pair of objects usually made of leather or plastic that you wear on your feet: *a pair of shoes* ◇ *running shoes* ◇ *She soon regretted **wearing** her new **shoes**.* ◇ *He took his shoes and socks off.* ◇ *What's your shoe size?* ◇ *shoe polish* ⇒ see also ATHLETIC SHOE, COURT SHOE, DECK SHOE, GYM SHOE, SNOWSHOE, TENNIS SHOE, TRAINING SHOE **2** = HORSESHOE

  IDM **be in sb's shoes | put yourself in sb's shoes** to be in, or imagine that you are in, another person's situation, especially when it is an unpleasant or difficult one: *I wouldn't like to be in your shoes when they find out about it.* **if I were in 'your shoes** used to introduce a piece of advice you are giving to sb: *If I were in your shoes, I'd resign immediately.* **if the shoe fits (, wear it)** (NAmE) (BrE **if the cap fits (, wear it)**) if you feel that a remark applies to you, you should accept it and take it as a warning or criticism **the shoe is on the other 'foot** (NAmE) (BrE **the boot is on the other 'foot**) used to say that a situation has changed so that sb now has power or authority over the person who used to have power or authority over them ⇒ more at FILL v., SHAKE v., STEP v.
- *verb* (**shoe·ing**, **shod**, **shod**) /ʃɒd; NAmE ʃɑːd/ *~sth* to put one or more HORSESHOES on a horse: *The horses were sent to the blacksmith to be shod.*

**shoe·box** /'ʃuːbɒks; NAmE -bɑːks/ *noun* **1** a box in which a pair of new shoes is kept in a shop or delivered to a customer **2** (*disapproving*) a very small house with a square shape and no interesting features, especially one that is very similar to all the ones around it

**shoe·horn** /'ʃuːhɔːn; NAmE -hɔːrn/ *noun, verb*
- *noun* a curved piece of plastic or metal, used to help your heel slide into a shoe
- *verb* *~sth + adv./prep.* to succeed in putting sth into a small space or a place where it does not fit very easily: *They managed to shoehorn the material onto just one CD.*

**shoe·lace** /'ʃuːleɪs/ (*also* **lace**) (NAmE *also* **shoe·string**) *noun* a long thin piece of material like string that goes through the holes on a shoe and is used to fasten it: *a pair of shoelaces* ◇ *to **tie/untie** your **shoelaces*** ◇ *Your shoelace is undone.*

**shoe·maker** /'ʃuːmeɪkə(r)/ *noun* a person whose job is making shoes and boots ⇒ compare COBBLER ▶ **shoe·mak·ing** *noun* [U]

**shoe·shine** /'ʃuːʃaɪn/ *noun* [U] (*especially NAmE*) the activity of cleaning people's shoes for money: *a shoeshine stand on West 32nd Street*

**shoe·string** /'ʃuːstrɪŋ/ *noun, adj.*
- *noun* (NAmE) = SHOELACE

  IDM **on a 'shoestring** (*informal*) using very little money: *In the early years, the business was run on a shoestring.*
- *adj.* [only before noun] (*informal*) that uses very little money: *The club exists on a shoestring budget.*

**sho·gun** /'ʃəʊɡən/ *noun* (in the past) a Japanese military leader

**shojo** /'ʃəʊdʒəʊ/ *noun* [C, U] (*pl.* **shojo**) a Japanese form of COMIC STRIP for girls that is usually about personal and romantic relationships

**Shona** /ˈʃəʊnə/ noun [U] a language spoken by the Shona peoples of southern Africa, used in Zimbabwe and other parts of southern Africa

**shone** /ʃɒn; NAmE ʃəʊn/ past tense, past part. of SHINE

**sho·nen** /ˈʃəʊnən/ noun [C, U] (pl. **sho·nen**) a Japanese form of COMIC STRIP for boys that usually has a lot of exciting action and adventure: *The comic is one of Japan's top-selling shonen.*

**shonky** /ˈʃɒŋki; NAmE ˈʃɑːŋ-/ adj. (**shonk·ier**, **shonki·est**) (AustralE, NZE, informal) not honest or legal

**shoo** /ʃuː/ verb, exclamation
■ *verb* (**shoo·ing**, **shooed**, **shooed**) ~ sb/sth (+ adv./prep.) to make sb/sth go away or to another place, especially by saying 'shoo' and waving your arms and hands: *He shooed the dog out of the kitchen.*
■ *exclamation* used to tell a child or an animal to go away

**ˈshoo-in** noun ~ (for sth) | ~ (to do sth) (informal) a person or team that will win easily

**shook** /ʃʊk/ past tense, past part. of SHAKE

**shoot** ❶ B1 /ʃuːt/ verb, noun, exclamation
■ *verb* (**shot**, **shot** /ʃɒt; NAmE ʃɑːt/)
• WEAPON **1** B1 [I, T] to fire a gun or other weapon; to fire sth from a weapon: *Don't shoot—I surrender.* ◇ *The police rarely shoot to kill* (= try to kill the people they shoot at). ◇ ~ **at sb/sth** *troops shooting at the enemy* ◇ ~ **sth** *Have you ever shot a gun before?* ◇ ~ **sth at sb/sth** *She shot a bullet right at me but missed.* ⇨ HOMOPHONES at CHUTE **2** B1 [T] to kill or wound a person or an animal with a bullet, etc: ~ **sb/sth/yourself** *He shot himself during a fit of depression.* ◇ ~ **sb/sth/yourself in sth** *He was left brain-damaged after being shot in the head.* ◇ ~ **sb/sth/yourself with sth** *In the struggle the burglar was shot with his own gun.* ◇ *Three people were shot dead during the robbery.* **3** [T, I] (of a gun or other weapon) to fire bullets, etc: ~ **sth** *This is just a toy gun—it doesn't shoot real bullets.*
• FOR SPORT **4** B1 [T, I] ~ (**sth**) to hunt and kill birds and animals with a gun as a sport: *to shoot pheasants* ◇ *They go shooting in Scotland.*
• FILM/PHOTOGRAPH **5** [I, T] to make a film or photograph of sth: *Cameras ready? OK, shoot!* ◇ ~ **sth** (+ adv./prep.) *to shoot a film/video/scene* ◇ *Where was the movie shot?*
• MOVE QUICKLY **6** [I, T] to move suddenly or quickly in one direction; to make sb/sth move in this way: + **adv./prep.** *A plane shot across the sky.* ◇ *Her hand shot out to grab my wrist.* ◇ *Flames were shooting up through the roof.* ◇ (figurative) *The band's last single shot straight to number one in the charts.* ◇ ~ **sth** + **adv./prep.** *She shot out her hand to grab my wrist.*
• OF PAIN **7** [I] to move suddenly and quickly and be very sharp: *a shooting pain in the back* ◇ + **adv./prep.** *The pain shot up her arm.*
• DIRECT AT SB **8** [T, no passive] to direct sth at sb suddenly or quickly: ~ **sth at sb** *Journalists were shooting questions at the candidates.* ◇ *She shot an angry glance at him.* ◇ ~ **sb sth** *She shot him an angry glance.*
• IN SPORTS **9** [I, T] (in football (soccer), hockey, etc.) to try to kick, hit or throw the ball into a goal or to score a point: *He should have shot instead of passing.* ◇ (especially NAmE) ~ **sth** *After school we'd be on the driveway shooting hoops* (= playing basketball). **10** [T] ~ **sth** (informal) (in golf) to make a particular score in a complete round or competition: *She shot a 75 in the first round.*
• PLAY GAME **11** [T] ~ **sth** (especially NAmE) to play particular games: *to shoot pool*
IDM **be like shooting ˈfish in a ˈbarrel** (informal) used to emphasize how easy it is to do sth: *What do you mean you can't do it? It'll be like shooting fish in a barrel!* **have shot your ˈbolt** (informal) to have used all your power, money or supplies **shoot the ˈbreeze/ˈbull** (NAmE, informal) to have a conversation in an informal way SYN **chat**: *We sat around the bar, shooting the breeze.* **shoot from the ˈhip** to react quickly without thinking carefully first **shoot yourself in the ˈfoot** (informal) to do or say sth that will cause you a lot of trouble or harm, especially when you are trying to get an advantage for yourself **shoot it ˈout (with sb)** (informal) to fight against sb with guns, especially until one side is killed or defeated: *The gang decided to shoot it out with the police.* ⇨ related noun SHOOT-OUT **shoot the ˈmessenger** to blame the person who gives the news that sth bad has happened, instead of the person who is really responsible: *Don't shoot the messenger!* **ˌshoot your ˈmouth off (about sth)** (informal) **1** to talk about sth in a way that shows that you are too proud of it **2** to talk about sth that is private or secret **shoot the ˈrapids** to go in a boat over part of a river where the water flows very fast **shoot to ˈfame/ˈstardom** to suddenly become famous, especially as a singer or actor: *She shot to stardom in a Broadway musical.* ⇨ more at DIRTY adj.
PHRV **ˌshoot sb/sth↔ˈdown 1** to make sb/sth fall to the ground by shooting them/it: *Several planes were shot down by enemy fire.* **2** to be very critical of sb's ideas, opinions, etc: *His latest theory has been shot down in flames.* **ˈshoot for sth** (NAmE, informal) to try to achieve or get sth, especially sth difficult: *We've been shooting for a pay raise for months.* **ˌshoot ˈoff** (informal) to leave very quickly SYN **dash**: *I had to shoot off at the end of the meeting.* **ˌshoot sth ˈoff** (NAmE) to light FIREWORKS and make them go off SYN **let sth off**, **set sth off** **ˌshoot ˈthrough** (AustralE, NZE, informal) to leave, especially in order to avoid sb/sth: *I was only five when my Dad shot through.* **ˌshoot ˈup 1** to grow very quickly: *Their kids have shot up since I last saw them.* **2** to rise suddenly by a large amount: *Ticket prices shot up last year.* ⇨ LANGUAGE BANK at INCREASE **3** (slang) to INJECT an illegal drug directly into your blood **ˌshoot sth↔ˈup 1** to cause great damage to sth by shooting **2** [no passive] (slang) to INJECT an illegal drug directly into your blood
■ *noun*
• PLANT **1** [+] C1 the part that grows up from the ground when a plant starts to grow; a new part that grows on plants or trees: *new green shoots* ◇ *bamboo shoots* ⇨ VISUAL VOCAB page V7
• FILM/PHOTOGRAPHS **2** [+] C1 an occasion when sb takes professional photographs for a particular purpose or makes a film: *a fashion shoot* ⇨ HOMOPHONES at CHUTE ⇨ see also PHOTO SHOOT
• FOR SPORT **3** (especially BrE) an occasion when a group of people hunt and shoot animals or birds for sport; the land where this happens
■ *exclamation* **1** (NAmE) used to show that you are annoyed when you do sth stupid or when sth goes wrong (to avoid saying 'shit'): *Shoot! I've forgotten my book!* **2** (especially NAmE) used to tell sb to say what they want to say: *You want to tell me something? OK, shoot!*

**shoot·around** /ˈʃuːtəraʊnd/ noun (in basketball) an informal practice session, often on the morning of a game

**ˈshoot-'em-up** adj. (informal) a **shoot-'em-up** computer game, etc. is one involving a lot of violence with guns

**shoot·er** /ˈʃuːtə(r)/ noun **1** a person or weapon that shoots ⇨ see also SHARPSHOOTER, SIX-SHOOTER, STRAIGHT SHOOTER, TROUBLESHOOTER **2** (informal) a gun **3** (NAmE) (used especially in news reports) a person who uses a gun to kill people

**shoot·ing** ❶ B2 /ˈʃuːtɪŋ/ noun **1** B2 [C] a situation in which a person is shot with a gun: *Terrorist groups claimed responsibility for the shootings and bomb attacks.* ◇ *There was no direct link between the two fatal shootings.* **2** [U] the sport of shooting animals and birds with guns: *grouse shooting* ⇨ see also CLAY PIGEON SHOOTING **3** B2 [U] the process of filming a film: *Shooting began early this year.*

**ˈshooting gallery** noun **1** a place where people shoot guns at objects for practice or to win prizes **2** (especially NAmE) a place where people go to take drugs

**ˈshooting guard** noun (in basketball) a player whose job is to score points by making shots from a long distance away and also to stay close to opposing players to stop them from scoring; the position of this player ⇨ compare POINT GUARD

**ˈshooting match** noun an occasion when people or groups fight or attack each other

# shooting star

**IDM** **the whole ˈshooting match** (*BrE*, *informal*) everything, or a situation which includes everything

**ˌshooting ˈstar** (*also* **ˌfalling ˈstar**) *noun* a small METEOR (= a piece of rock in outer space) that travels very fast and burns with a bright light as it enters the earth's atmosphere

**ˈshoot-out** *noun* a fight that is fought with guns until one side is killed or defeated ⊃ see also PENALTY SHOOT-OUT

**shop** 🔊 **A1** /ʃɒp; *NAmE* ʃɑːp/ *noun*, *verb*

■ *noun*

- WHERE YOU BUY STH **1** 🔊 **A1** [C] (*especially BrE*) a building or part of a building where you can buy goods or services: *to open/close/run a shop* ◇ *There's a good selection of local shops.* ◇ (*BrE*) *a butcher's shop* ◇ (*NAmE*) *a butcher shop* ◇ (*BrE*) *I'm just going to the shops. Can I get you anything?* ⊃ see also BAKESHOP, BETTING SHOP, CHARITY SHOP, CHIP SHOP, COFFEE SHOP, CORNER SHOP, FACTORY SHOP, GIFT SHOP, JUNK SHOP, OP SHOP, PAPER SHOP, PRO SHOP, SMOKE SHOP, TEA SHOP

**WORDFINDER** assistant, buy, counter, display, fitting room, promotion, sale, store, till

- FOR MAKING/REPAIRING THINGS **2** (*also* **ˈworkˌshop**) [C] (*especially in compounds*) a place where things are made or repaired, especially part of a factory where a particular type of work is done: *a repair shop* ◇ *a paint shop* (= where cars or other items are painted) ⊃ see also BODY SHOP, MACHINE SHOP
- SHOPPING **3** [sing.] (*BrE*, *informal*) an act of going shopping, especially for food and other items needed in the house: *I do a weekly shop at the supermarket.*
- SCHOOL SUBJECT **4** (*also* **ˈshop class**) [U] (*both NAmE*) = INDUSTRIAL ARTS
- ROOM FOR TOOLS **5** (*also* **ˈworkˌshop**) [C] (*both NAmE*) a room in a house where tools are kept for making repairs to the house, building things out of wood, etc. ⊃ see also CLOSED SHOP, COP SHOP

**IDM** **all ˌover the ˈshop** (*BrE*, *informal*) = ALL OVER THE PLACE at PLACE *n*. **set up ˈshop** to start a business ⊃ more at BULL, CLOSE¹ *v*., MIND *v*., SHUT *v*., TALK *v*.

■ *verb* (-pp-)

- BUY **1** 🔊 **A1** [I] to buy things in shops: *I bumped into him when I was out shopping with my mother.* ◇ *to shop online* ◇ *They shop in the same supermarket.* ◇ ~ **for sth** *to shop for food* **2** 🔊 **A1** **go ˈshopping** [I] to spend time going to shops and looking for things to buy: *There should be plenty of time to go shopping before we leave New York.* ◇ *'Where's Mum?' 'She went shopping.'*
- TELL POLICE ABOUT SB **3** [T] ~ **sb (to sb)** (*BrE*, *informal*) to give information to sb, especially to the police, about sb who has committed a crime: *He didn't expect his own mother to shop him to the police.*

**PHRV** **ˌshop aˈround (for sth)** to compare the quality or prices of goods or services that are offered by different shops, companies, etc. so that you can choose the best: *Shop around for the best deal.*

**shopˈahoˌlic** /ˌʃɒpəˈhɒlɪk; *NAmE* ˌʃɑːpəˈhɔːl-/ *noun* (*informal*) a person who enjoys shopping very much and spends too much time or money doing it ▸ **shopˈahoˌlic** *adj.*

**ˈshop asˌsistant** (*also* **asˈsistant**) (*both BrE*) (*NAmE* **ˈsales clerk**, **clerk**) *noun* a person whose job is to serve customers in a shop

**ˈshop-bought** (*BrE*) (*NAmE* **ˈstore-bought**) *adj.* [only before noun] bought from a shop and not made at home: *shop-bought cakes*

**ˌshop ˈfloor** *noun* [sing.] **1** the area in a factory where the goods are made by the workers: *on the* ~ ◇ *to work on the shop floor* **2** the workers in a factory, not the managers ⊃ WORDFINDER NOTE at FACTORY

**ˈshop-front** /ˈʃɒpfrʌnt; *NAmE* ˈʃɑːp-/ (*BrE*) (*NAmE* **ˈstorefront**) *noun* the outside of a shop that faces the street

**ˈshop·house** /ˈʃɒphaʊs; *NAmE* ˈʃɑːp-/ *noun* (in south-east Asia) a shop that opens onto the street and is used as the owner's home

---

**shopˈkeepˌer** /ˈʃɒpkiːpə(r); *NAmE* ˈʃɑːp-/ (*also* **ˈstoreˌkeepˌer** *especially in NAmE*) *noun* a person who owns or manages a shop, usually a small one

**ˈshopˌliftˌing** /ˈʃɒplɪftɪŋ; *NAmE* ˈʃɑːp-/ *noun* [U] the crime of stealing goods from a shop by deliberately leaving without paying for them ▸ **ˈshop-lift** *verb* [I, T] ◇ ~ **(sth)** **ˈshopˌliftˌer** *noun*: *Shoplifters will be prosecuted.*

**ˈshopˌlot** /ˈʃɒplɒt; *NAmE* ˈʃɑːplɑːt/ *noun* (*SEAsianE*) the amount of space that a shop fills

**ˈshopˌper** /ˈʃɒpə(r); *NAmE* ˈʃɑːp-/ *noun* a person who buys goods from shops: *The streets were full of Christmas shoppers.* ⊃ see also MYSTERY SHOPPER, PERSONAL SHOPPER

**shopˈping** 🔊 **A1** /ˈʃɒpɪŋ; *NAmE* ˈʃɑːp-/ *noun* [U] **1** 🔊 **A1** the activity of going to shops and buying things or ordering them online: *to go shopping* ◇ (*BrE*) *When shall I do the shopping?* ◇ (*BrE*) *We do our shopping on Saturdays.* ◇ *I do all my clothes shopping online.* ◇ *a shopping basket* ⊃ see also COMPARISON SHOPPING, WINDOW SHOPPING **2** 🔊 **A2** (*especially BrE*) the things that you have bought from shops: *to put the shopping in the car*

**ˈshopping arˌcade** *noun* = ARCADE (3)

**ˈshopping bag** *noun* **1** a large, strong bag made of cloth, plastic, etc. used for carrying your shopping **2** (*NAmE*) (*BrE* **ˈcarrier bag**, **ˈcarrier**) a paper or plastic bag for carrying shopping

**ˈshopping cart** *noun* **1** (*NAmE*) (*BrE* **ˈshopping trolley**) a large BASKET on wheels into which you put the things that you want to buy as you push it round a store **2** (*especially NAmE* **cart**) (*BrE usually* **basket**) a feature on a website that records the items that you select to buy

**ˈshopping ˌcentre** (*BrE*) (*NAmE* **ˈshopping ˌcenter**) *noun* a group of shops built together, sometimes under one roof

**ˈshopping list** *noun* a list that you make of all the things that you need to buy when you go shopping: (*figurative*) *The union presented a shopping list of demands to the management.*

**ˈshopping mall** *noun* (*especially NAmE*) = MALL

**ˈshopping ˌtrolley** (*BrE*) (*NAmE* **ˈshopping cart**) *noun* a large BASKET on wheels into which you put things that you want to buy as you push it round a shop

**ˈshop-soiled** (*BrE*) (*NAmE* **shop-worn**) *adj.* (of goods) dirty or not in perfect condition because they have been in a shop for a long time: *a sale of shop-soiled goods at half price*

**ˈshop ˈsteward** *noun* (*especially BrE*) a person who is elected by members of a trade union in a factory or company to represent them in meetings with managers

**ˈshop talk** *noun* [U] talk about your work or your business

**ˈshop ˈwindow** (*BrE*) (*NAmE* **ˈstore window**) (*also* **ˈwindow**) *noun* the glass at the front of a shop and the area behind it where goods are shown to the public

**shopˈworn** /ˈʃɒpwɔːn; *NAmE* ˈʃɑːpwɔːrn/ (*NAmE*) (*BrE* **ˈshop-soiled**) *adj.* (of goods) dirty or not in perfect condition because they have been in a shop for a long time: (*figurative*) *a shopworn argument* (= that is no longer new or useful)

**shore** 🔊 **B2** /ʃɔː(r)/ *noun*, *verb*

■ *noun* **1** 🔊 **B2** [C, U] the land along the edge of the sea, the ocean or a lake: *a rocky/sandy shore* ◇ *to swim from the boat to the shore* ◇ *on the shores of sth* ◇ *a house on the shores of the lake* ◇ *off~* *The ship was anchored off shore.* ⊃ WORDFINDER NOTE at COAST **2** **the shore** [sing.] (*NAmE*) an area that is by the sea or ocean, especially one where people go for a day or a holiday: *Let's go to the shore.* **3** **shores** [pl.] (*especially literary*) a country, especially one with a coast: *foreign shores* ◇ *What brings you to these shores?*

■ *verb*

**PHRV** **ˌshore sth↔ˈup** **1** to support part of a building or other large structure by placing large pieces of wood or metal against or under it so that it does not fall down **2** to help to support sth that is weak or going to fail

**ˈshore·line** /ˈʃɔːlaɪn; *NAmE* ˈʃɔːrl-/ *noun* [usually sing.] the edge of the sea, the ocean or a lake: *a rocky shoreline* ◇

*The road follows the shoreline for a few miles.* ⇒ WORDFINDER NOTE at SEA

**shorn** /ʃɔːn/ NAmE /ʃɔːrn/ *past part.* OF SHEAR

**short** ❶ A1 /ʃɔːt/; NAmE /ʃɔːrt/ *adj., adv., noun, verb*

■ *adj.* (short·er, short·est)
- LENGTH/DISTANCE **1** A1 measuring or covering a small length or distance, or a smaller length or distance than usual: *He had **short** curly hair.* ◇ *a **short** walk/distance* ◇ *a **short** skirt* ◇ *She decided to cut her hair short.* OPP **long**
- HEIGHT **2** A1 (of a person) small in height: *He was a **short**, fat little man.* OPP **tall**
- TIME **3** A1 lasting or taking a small amount of time or less time than usual: *a **short** time/period/while* ◇ *The government is suggesting a relatively **short** consultation period.* ◇ *a programme of **short** films* ◇ *The **short** answer to your query is that he has acted completely illegally.* ◇ *a **short** book* (= that does not have many pages and so does not take long to read) ◇ *She has a very **short** memory* (= remembers only things that have happened recently). ◇ *I'm sorry it's such **short** notice—we didn't know ourselves until today.* OPP **long 4** [only before noun] (of a period of time) seeming to have passed very quickly: *Just two **short** years ago he was the best player in the country.* OPP **long**
- NOT ENOUGH **5** B2 [not before noun] not having enough of sth; being without sth: *I'm afraid I'm a little **short** (= of money) this month.* ◇ ~**of sth** *She is not **short** of excuses when things go wrong.* **6** ~**on sth** (*informal*) not having enough of a particular quality: *He was a big, strong guy but **short** on brains.* **7** [not before noun] not easily available; not supplying as much as you need: *Money was **short** at that time.* **8** [not before noun] ~**(of sth)** less than the number, amount or distance mentioned or needed: *Her last throw was only three centimetres **short** of the world record.* ◇ *The team was five players **short**.* ◇ *She was just **short** of her 90th birthday when she died.*
- OF BREATH **9** ~**of breath** having difficulty breathing, for example because of illness
- NAME/WORD **10** being a shorter form of a name or word: ~**for sth** *Call me Jo—it's **short** for Joanna.* ◇ **for ~** *file transfer protocol or FTP for **short***
- RUDE **11** [not before noun] ~**(with sb)** (of a person) speaking to sb using few words in a way that seems rude: *I'm sorry I was **short** with you earlier—I had other things on my mind.*
- VOWEL **12** (*phonetics*) a **short** vowel is pronounced for a shorter time than other vowels: *Compare the **short** vowel in 'full' and the long vowel in 'fool'.* OPP **long** ⇒ see also SHORTLY ▸ **short·ness** *noun* [U] *She suffered from **short**ness of breath.*

IDM **a brick short of a load, two sandwiches short of a 'picnic, etc.** (*informal*) (of a person) stupid; not very intelligent **get the short end of the 'stick** (NAmE) (BrE **draw the short 'straw**) to be the person in a group who is chosen or forced to perform an unpleasant duty or task **give sb/sth short 'shrift** | **get short 'shrift** to give sb little attention or sympathy; to get little attention or sympathy **have/be on a short 'fuse** to tend to get angry quickly and easily **in short 'order** quickly and without trouble **in the 'short run** relating to the immediate future: *In the **short** run, unemployment may fall.* **in short sup'ply** not existing in large enough quantities to satisfy demand: *Basic foodstuffs were in **short** supply.* ◇ *Sunshine will be in **short** supply for the west coast.* **little/nothing short of sth** used when you are saying that sth is almost true, or is equal to sth: *Last year's figures were little **short** of disastrous.* ◇ *The transformation has been nothing **short** of a miracle.* **make short 'work of sth/sb** to defeat, deal with sth/sb quickly: *Liverpool made **short** work of the opposition* (= in a football match). ◇ *He made **short** work of his lunch* (= ate it quickly). **short and 'sweet** (*informal*) not lasting a long time but pleasant while it lasts: *We haven't much time so I'll keep it **short** and sweet.* ⇒ more at LIFE, LONG *adj.*, MEASURE *n.*, NOTICE *n.*, TEMPER *n.*, TERM *n.*, THICK *adj.*

■ *adv.* (short·er, short·est) **1** if you **go short of** or **run short of sth**, you do not have enough of it: *I'd never let you go **short** of anything.* ◇ *Mothers regularly go **short** of food to ensure their children have enough.* ◇ *They had run **short** of fuel.* **2** not as far as you

need or expect: *All too often you pitch the ball **short**.* **3** before the time expected or arranged; before the natural time: *a career tragically cut **short** by illness* ◇ *I'm afraid I'm going to have to stop you **short** there, as time is running out.*

IDM **be caught 'short** (BrE *also* **be taken 'short**) **1** (BrE, *informal*) to suddenly feel a strong need to go to the toilet **2** to be put at a disadvantage **come 'short** (SAfrE, *informal*) to have an accident; to get into trouble **fall short of sth** | **fall short of the 'mark** to fail to reach the standard that you expected or need: *The hotel fell far **short** of their expectations.* **pull, bring, etc. sb up 'short** to make sb suddenly stop what they are doing: *I was brought up **short** by a terrible thought.* **short of (doing) sth** without sth; without doing sth; unless sth happens: *Short of a miracle, we're certain to lose.* ◇ *Short of asking her to leave* (= and we don't want to do that) *there's not a lot we can do about the situation.* ⇒ more at SELL *v.*, STOP *v.*

■ *noun* (*informal*) ⇒ see also SHORTS **1** (BrE) a small strong alcoholic drink, for example of WHISKY **2** a short film, especially one that is shown before the main film **3** (*informal*) = SHORT CIRCUIT

IDM **in 'short** in a few words: *His novels belong to a great but vanished age. They are, in **short**, old-fashioned.* ⇒ more at LONG *adj.*

■ *verb* [I, T] ~ **(sth) (out)** (*informal*) = SHORT-CIRCUIT

**short·age** B1+ B2 /ˈʃɔːtɪdʒ; NAmE /ˈʃɔːrt-/ *noun* [C, U] a situation when there is not enough of the people or things that are needed: *food/housing/water **shortages*** ◇ *a **shortage** of funds* ◇ *There is no **shortage** of* (= there are plenty of) *things to do in the town.*

**short·bread** /ˈʃɔːtbred/ NAmE /ˈʃɔːrt-/ (BrE *also* **short·cake**) *noun* [U] a rich biscuit made with flour, sugar and a lot of butter

**short·cake** /ˈʃɔːtkeɪk/ NAmE /ˈʃɔːrt-/ *noun* [U] **1** (BrE) = SHORTBREAD **2** a cake with a PASTRY base and cream and fruit on top: *strawberry **shortcake***

**short-'change** *verb* [often passive] **1** ~**sb** to give back less than the correct amount of money to sb who has paid for sth with more than the exact price: *I think I've been **short-changed** at the bar.* ⇒ WORDFINDER NOTE at BUY **2** ~**sb** to treat sb unfairly by not giving them what they have earned or deserve

**short 'circuit** (*also informal* **short**) *noun* a failure in an electrical CIRCUIT, when electricity travels along the wrong route because of damaged wires or a fault in the connections between the wires

**short-'circuit** (*also informal* **short**) *verb* **1** [I, T] ~**(sth)** to have a short circuit; to make sth have a short circuit: *The wires had short-circuited and burnt out.* **2** [T] ~**sth** to succeed in doing sth more quickly than usual, without going through all the usual processes

**short·com·ing** /ˈʃɔːtkʌmɪŋ; NAmE /ˈʃɔːrt-/ *noun* [usually pl.] a fault in sb's character, a plan, a system, etc. SYN **defect**

**short·cut** /ˈʃɔːtkʌt; NAmE /ˈʃɔːrt-/ *noun* **1** a quicker or shorter way of getting to a place: *You can take a **shortcut** across the field.* ◇ *a way of doing sth that is quicker than the usual way: There are no **shortcuts** to economic recovery.* **3** (*computing*) a record of the address of a file, website, or other data that is made so you can access the file, etc. quickly: *keyboard **shortcuts***

**short·en** /ˈʃɔːtn; NAmE /ˈʃɔːrtn/ *verb* [T, I] to make sth shorter; to become shorter: ~**(sth)** *Injury problems could **shorten** his career.* ◇ *a **shortened** version of the game* ◇ *In November the temperatures drop and the days **shorten**.* ◇ ~**sth to sth** *Her name's Katherine, generally **shortened** to Kate.* OPP **lengthen**

**short·en·ing** /ˈʃɔːtnɪŋ; NAmE /ˈʃɔːrt-/ *noun* [U] fat that is used for making PASTRY

**short·fall** /ˈʃɔːtfɔːl; NAmE /ˈʃɔːrt-/ *noun* ~**(of sth) (in sth)** if there is a **shortfall** in sth, there is less of it than you need or expect SYN **deficit**

**short·hair** /ˈʃɔːtheə(r); NAmE /ˈʃɔːrther/ *noun* a type of cat with short hair ⇒ compare LONGHAIR

# shorthand 1436

**short·hand** /ˈʃɔːthænd/ *NAmE* /ˈʃɔːrt-/ *noun* **1** (*NAmE also* **sten·og·raphy**) [U] a quick way of writing using special signs or abbreviations, used especially to record what sb is saying: *typing and shorthand* ◇ **in ~** *to take sth down in shorthand* ◇ *a shorthand typist* **2** [U, C, usually sing.] **~ (for sth)** a shorter way of saying or referring to sth, which may not be as accurate as the more complicated way of saying it

**ˌshort-ˈhanded** *adj.* [not usually before noun] not having as many workers or people who can help as you need ▶ **SYN** **short-staffed**

**ˈshort-haul** *adj.* [only before noun] that involves transporting people or goods over short distances, especially by plane ▶ **OPP** **long-haul**

**ˈshort-horn** /ˈʃɔːthɔːn/ *NAmE* /ˈʃɔːrthɔːrn/ *noun* a type of cow with short **HORNS**

**short·ie** = SHORTY

**ˈshort-list** /ˈʃɔːtlɪst/ *NAmE* /ˈʃɔːrt-/ *noun, verb*
- *noun* [usually sing.] a small number of candidates for a job, etc., who have been chosen from all the people who applied: *to draw up a shortlist* ◇ **~ for sth** *a shortlist for a literary prize* ◇ **on the ~ (for sth)** *The film is on the shortlist for Best Picture.* ⇨ **WORDFINDER NOTE** at APPLY
- *verb* [usually passive] (*BrE*) to put sb/sth on a shortlist for a job, prize, etc: **to be shortlisted (for sth)** *Candidates who are shortlisted for interview will be contacted by the end of the week.*

**short-lived** /ˌʃɔːt ˈlɪvd/ *NAmE* /ˌʃɔːrt ˈlɪvd, ˈlaɪvd/ *adj.* lasting only for a short time

**short·ly** /ˈʃɔːtli/ *NAmE* /ˈʃɔːrt-/ *adv.* **1** a short time; not long: *She arrived shortly after us.* ◇ *I saw him shortly before he died.* **2** soon: *I'll be ready shortly.* **3** in an angry and impatient way ▶ **SYN** **sharply**

**ˌshort-ˈrange** *adj.* [usually before noun] **1** (of weapons) designed to travel only over short distances: *short-range missiles* **2** (of plans, etc.) connected with a short period of time in the future: *a short-range weather forecast* ⇨ compare LONG-RANGE

**ˈshort ribs** *noun* [pl.] a piece of beef with some of the bones from the RIBS of the cow

**shorts** /ʃɔːts/ *NAmE* /ʃɔːrts/ *noun* [pl.] **1** short trousers that end above or at the knee: *a pair of tennis shorts* ◇ *He was wearing a T-shirt and shorts.* **2** (*NAmE*) = BOXER SHORTS

**ˌshort-ˈsighted** *adj.* **1** (*especially BrE*) (*NAmE usually* **near-sighted**) able to see things clearly only if they are very close to you ▶ **OPP** **long-sighted** **2** not thinking carefully about the possible effects of sth or what might happen in the future: *a short-sighted policy* ▶ **short ˈsight** (*also* **ˌshort-ˈsighted·ness**) *noun* [U]: *She suffered from short sight.* ◇ *Many people accused the government of short-sightedness.* ▶ **ˌshort-ˈsighted·ly** *adv.*

**ˌshort-ˈstaffed** *adj.* [not usually before noun] having fewer members of staff than you need or usually have ▶ **SYN** **short-handed** ⇨ see also UNDERSTAFFED

**ˈshort-stay** *adj.* [only before noun] (*BrE*) (of a place) where you only stay for a short time: *a short-stay car park*

**ˈshort·stop** /ˈʃɔːtstɒp/ *NAmE* /ˈʃɔːrtstɑːp/ *noun* (in baseball) a player who tries to stop balls that are hit between second and third base; the position of this player

**ˈshort ˈstory** *noun* a story, usually about imaginary characters and events, that is short enough to be read from beginning to end without stopping

**ˌshort-ˈtempered** *adj.* tending to become angry very quickly and easily

**ˌshort-ˈterm** *adj.* [usually before noun] lasting a short time; designed only for a short period of time in the future: *a short-term loan* ◇ *to find work on a short-term contract* ◇ *short-term plans* ◇ *a short-term solution to the problem* ◇ *His short-term memory* (= the ability to remember things that happened a short time ago) *is failing.* ⇨ compare LONG-TERM

**ˌshort-ˈtermism** *noun* [U] a way of thinking or planning that only considers the advantages or profits you could have now, rather than the effects in the future

**ˌshort ˈtime** *noun* [U] (*BrE*) if workers are put on **short time**, they work for fewer hours than usual, because there is not enough work to do or not enough money to pay them

**ˈshort wave** (*also* **short-wave**) *noun* [C, U] (*abbr.* **SW**) a radio wave with a length of between 10 and 100 metres; the band of radio waves of this length used for broadcasting: *a short-wave radio/transmitter* ◇ **on ~** *The BBC also broadcasts on short wave.* ⇨ compare LONG WAVE, MEDIUM WAVE

**shorty** (*also* **shortie**) /ˈʃɔːti/ *NAmE* /ˈʃɔːrti/ *noun* (*pl.* **-ies**) (*informal, often offensive*) a person who is shorter than average

**Sho·shone** /ʃəʊˈʃəʊni/ *noun* (*pl.* **Sho·shone** *or* **Sho·shones**) a member of a Native American people many of whom now live in the US state of Wyoming

**shot** /ʃɒt/ *NAmE* /ʃɑːt/ *noun, verb, adj.*
- *noun*
- **WITH GUN 1** [C] the act of firing a gun; the sound this makes: *We heard some shots in the distance.* ◇ **~ at sb/sth** *Someone took a shot at the car.* ◇ **~ to sth** *She was killed by a single shot to the head.* ⇨ see also GUNSHOT, POTSHOT **2** [C] **a good, bad, etc. ~** a person who shoots a gun in a particular way (well, badly, etc.)
- **IN SPORT 3** [C] an attempt to score a goal or point in a game: *He took a shot from the edge of the box.* ◇ **~ at/on sth** *Unfortunately her shot at goal missed.* ⇨ see also HOOK SHOT, JUMP SHOT **4** [C] an act of hitting the ball: *Good shot!* ◇ *Go on—take another shot.* ⇨ see also DROP SHOT, PASSING SHOT **5** (*often* **the shot**) [sing.] the heavy ball that is used in the sports competition called SHOT-PUT
- **PHOTOGRAPH 6** [C] a photograph: *I got some good shots of people at the party.* ⇨ **SYNONYMS** at PHOTOGRAPH ⇨ see also MUGSHOT, SCREENSHOT, SNAPSHOT
- **SCENE IN FILM 7** [C] a scene in a film that is filmed continuously by one camera: *the opening shot of a character walking across a desert*
- **BULLETS 8** (*also* **lead ˈshot**) [U] a large number of small metal balls that you fire together from a SHOTGUN ⇨ see also BUCKSHOT **9** [C] (*pl.* **shot**) a large stone or metal ball that was shot from a CANNON or large gun in the past
- **REMARK/ACTION 10** [C] a remark or an action that is usually one of a series, and is aimed against sb/sth that you are arguing or competing with: *This statement was the opening shot in the argument.* ◇ *The supermarket fired the first shot in a price war today.* ⇨ see also PARTING SHOT at PARTING *adj.*
- **ATTEMPT 11** [C, usually sing.] **~ (at sth/at doing sth)** (*informal*) the act of trying to do or achieve sth: *The team are looking good for a shot at the title.* ◇ *I've never produced a play before but I'll have a shot at it.* ◇ *I'm willing to give it a shot.* ◇ *Just give it your best shot* (= try as hard as you can) *and you'll be fine.* ⇨ see also A LONG SHOT at LONG *adj.*, ONE-SHOT
- **DRUG 12** [C] (*informal, especially NAmE*) a small amount of a drug that is put into your body using a SYRINGE ▶ **SYN** **injection**: *a flu shot* (= to protect you against flu) ◇ *a shot of morphine*
- **DRINK 13** [C] (*informal*) a small amount of a drink, especially a strong alcoholic one: *a shot of whisky*
- **OF SPACECRAFT 14** [C] (*especially in compounds*) the process of sending a SPACECRAFT into and through space: *The space shot was shown live on television.*
- **HORSE/DOG IN RACE 15** [sing.] (used with numbers) a horse, dog, etc. that has the particular chance of winning a race that is mentioned: *The horse is a 10–1 shot.*
- **IDM** **like a ˈshot** (*informal*) very quickly and without hesitating: *If I had the chance to go there, I'd go like a shot.* **a ˌshot across the/sb's ˈbows** something that you say or do as a warning to sb about what might happen if they do not change, etc. **a ˌshot in the ˈarm** something that encourages sb/sth or gives them the help they need ⇨ more at BIG *adj.*, CALL *v.*, DARK *n.*, LONG *adj.*, PARTING *adj.*
- *verb* past tense, past part. of SHOOT
- *adj.* **1 ~ (with sth)** (of cloth, hair, etc.) having another colour showing through or mixed with the main colour: *shot*

| æ cat | ɑː father | e bed | ɜː fur | ə about | ɪ sit | iː see | i happy | ɒ got (*BrE*) | ɔː saw | ʌ cup | ʊ put | uː too |

**silk** **2** [not before noun] (*informal*) in a very bad condition; destroyed: *The brakes on this car are shot.* ◇ *I'm shot—I'm too old for this job.* ◇ *After the accident his nerves were shot to pieces.*
**IDM** **be/get ˈshot of sb/sth** (*BrE*, *informal*) to get rid of sb/ sth so you no longer have the problems they cause: *I'll be glad to get shot of this car.* **shot through with sth** containing a lot of a particular colour, quality or feature: *a voice shot through with emotion*

**shot·gun** /ˈʃɒtɡʌn; *NAmE* ˈʃɑːt-/ *noun* a long gun that fires a lot of small metal bullets (called SHOT) and is used especially for shooting birds or animals ⇒ see also SAWN-OFF SHOTGUN **IDM** see RIDE v.

**ˌshotgun ˈwedding** (*also* ˌshotgun ˈmarriage) *noun* (*old-fashioned*, *informal*) a wedding that has to take place quickly because the woman is pregnant

**shot·mak·ing** /ˈʃɒtmeɪkɪŋ; *NAmE* ˈʃɑːt-/ *noun* [U] (in golf, tennis, etc.) a way of playing in which a player takes risks in order to win more points

**Sho·to·kan** /ˈʃəʊtəkɑːn/ *noun* [U] (*from Japanese*) a popular form of KARATE

**ˈshot-put** *noun often the* **shot-put** [sing.] (*also* **ˈshot-putting**, **ˌputting the ˈshot** [U]) the event or sport of throwing a heavy metal ball (called a SHOT) as far as possible

**should** ⓘ **A1** Ⓦ /ʃəd/, *strong form* /ʃʊd/ *modal verb* (*negative* **should not**, *short form* **shouldn't** /ˈʃʊdnt/) **1** ⁇ **A1** used to show what is right, appropriate, etc., especially when criticizing sb's actions: *You shouldn't drink and drive.* ◇ *He should have been more careful.* ◇ *A present for me? You shouldn't have!* (= used to thank sb politely) **2** ⁇ **A2** used for giving or asking for advice: *You should stop worrying about it.* ◇ *Should I call him and apologize?* ◇ *I should wait a little longer, if I were you.* ◇ (*ironic*) *'She doesn't think she'll get a job.' 'She should worry, with all her qualifications* (= she does not need to worry).' **3** ⁇ **B1** used to say that you expect sth is true or will happen: *We should arrive before dark.* ◇ *I should have finished the book by Friday.* ◇ *The roads should be less crowded today.* **4** ⁇ **B2** used to say that sth that was expected has not happened: *It should be snowing now, according to the weather forecast.* ◇ *The bus should have arrived ten minutes ago.* **5** ⁇ **B2** used as the past form of *shall* when reporting what sb has said: *He asked me what time he should come.* (= His words were: 'What time shall I come?') ◇ (*BrE*, *formal*) *I said (that) I should be glad to help.* **6** ⁇ **B2** (*BrE*) used after *that* when sth is suggested or arranged: *She recommended that I should take some time off.* ◇ *In order that training should be effective it must be planned systematically.* **HELP** In both *NAmE* and *BrE* this idea can be expressed without 'should': *She recommended that I take some time off.* ◇ *In order that training be effective…* **7** ⁇ **B2** used with *I* and *we* to give opinions that you are not certain about: *I should imagine it will take about three hours.* ◇ *'Is this enough food for everyone?' 'I should think so.'* ◇ *'Will it matter?' 'I shouldn't think so.'* **8** used for expressing strong agreement: *'I know it's expensive but it will last for years.' 'I should hope so too!'* ◇ *'Nobody will oppose it.' 'I should think not!'* **9 why, how, who, what ~ sb/sth do** used to refuse sth or to show that you are annoyed at a request; used to express surprise about an event or a situation: *Why should I help him? He's never done anything for me.* ◇ *How should I know where you've left your bag?* ◇ *I got on the bus and who should be sitting in front of me but Tony!* **10** used to tell sb that sth would surprise them or make them laugh if they saw or experienced it: *You should have seen her face when she found out!* ⇒ note at MODAL **11** used after *that* after many adjectives that describe feelings: *I'm anxious that we should allow plenty of time.* ◇ *I find it astonishing that he should be so rude to you.* **12** (*BrE*, *formal*) used with *I* and we in polite requests: *I should like to call my lawyer.* ◇ *We should be grateful for your help.* **13** (*BrE*, *formal*) used after *I* or *we* instead of *would* for describing what you would do if sth else happened first: *If I were asked to work on Sundays, I should resign.* **14** (*formal*) used to refer to a possible event or situation: *If you should change your mind, do let me know.* ◇ *In case you should need any help, here's my num-*

1437

*ber.* ◇ *Should anyone call* (= if anyone calls), *please tell them I'm busy.*

▼ **GRAMMAR POINT**

**should / ought / had better**

- **Should** and **ought to** are both used to say that something is the best thing or the right thing to do, but **should** is much more common: *You should take the baby to the doctor's.* ◇ *I ought to give up smoking.* In questions, **should** is usually used instead of **ought to**: *Should we call the doctor?*
- **Had better** can also be used to say what is the best thing to do in a situation that is happening now: *We'd better hurry or we'll miss the train.*
- You form the past by using **should have** or **ought to have**: *She should have asked for some help.* ◇ *You ought to have been more careful.*
- The forms **should not** or **shouldn't** (and **ought not to** or **oughtn't to**), which are rare in *NAmE* and formal in *BrE*) are used to say that something is a bad idea or the wrong thing to do: *You shouldn't drive so fast.*
- The forms **should not have** or **shouldn't have** and, much less frequently, **ought not to have** or **oughtn't to have** are used to talk about the past: *I'm sorry, I shouldn't have lost my temper.*

▼ **GRAMMAR POINT**

**should / would**

- In modern English, the traditional difference between **should** and **would** in reported sentences, conditions, requests, etc. has disappeared and **should** is not used very much at all. In spoken English the short form '**d** is usually used: *I said I'd (I would) be late.* ◇ *He'd (he would) have liked to have been an actor.* ◇ *I'd (I would) really prefer tea.*
- The main use of **should** now is to tell somebody what they ought to do, to give advice, or to add emphasis: *We should really go and visit them soon.* ◇ *You should have seen it!*

**shoul·der** ⓘ **A2** /ˈʃəʊldə(r)/ *noun*, *verb*

■ *noun*
- **PART OF BODY 1** ⁇ **A2** [C] either of the two parts of the body between the top of each arm and the neck: *over sb's ~ He slung the bag over his shoulder.* ◇ *on sb's ~ He carried the child on his shoulders.* ◇ *around sb's ~ He put an arm around her shoulders and pulled her close.* ◇ *She shrugged her shoulders* (= showing that she didn't know or care). ◇ *an off-the-shoulder dress* (= that does not cover the shoulders) ◇ *a shoulder injury* ⇒ VISUAL VOCAB page V1
- **-SHOULDERED 2** (in adjectives) having the type of shoulders mentioned: *broad-shouldered*
- **CLOTHING 3** ⁇ **A2** [C] the part of a piece of clothing that covers the shoulder: *a jacket with padded shoulders*
- **MEAT 4** [U, C] **~ (of sth)** meat from the top part of one of the front legs of an animal that has four legs
- **OF MOUNTAIN/BOTTLE, ETC. 5** [C] **~ (of sth)** a part of sth, such as a bottle or mountain, that is like a shoulder in shape: *The village lay just around the shoulder of the hill.*
- **SIDE OF ROAD 6** [C] (*NAmE*) an area of ground at the side of a road where vehicles can stop in an emergency: *No shoulder for next 5 miles* (= on a notice). ⇒ see also HARD SHOULDER

**IDM** **be looking over your ˈshoulder** to be anxious and have the feeling that sb is going to do sth unpleasant or harmful to you **on sb's ˈshoulders** if blame, GUILT, etc. is **on sb's shoulders**, they must take responsibility for it **put your shoulder to the ˈwheel** to start working very hard at a particular task **a shoulder to ˈcry on** used to describe a person who listens to your problems and gives you sympathy **ˌshoulder to ˈshoulder (with sb) 1** physically close to sb **2** as one group that has the same aims, opinions, etc. ⇒ more at CHIP *n.*, COLD *adj.*, HEAD *n.*, OLD, RUB *v.*, STRAIGHT *adv.*

**shoulder**

# shoulder bag

- **verb**
- ACCEPT RESPONSIBILITY **1** [T] ~ sth to accept the responsibility for sth: *to shoulder the responsibility/blame for sth* ◇ *women who shoulder the double burden of childcare and full-time work*
- PUSH WITH SHOULDER **2** [T, I] to push forward with your shoulder in order to get somewhere: ~ **your way** + *adv./prep. He shouldered his way through the crowd and went after her.* ◇ + *adv./prep. She shouldered past a woman with a screaming baby.* **3** [T] ~ **sb/sth** + *adv./prep.* to push sb/sth out of your way with your shoulder: *He shouldered the man aside.*
- CARRY ON SHOULDER **4** [T] ~ sth to carry sth on your shoulder: *She shouldered her bag and set off home.*

**ˈshoulder bag** *noun* a bag, especially a HANDBAG, that is carried over the shoulder with a long, narrow piece of leather, etc.

**ˈshoulder blade** *noun* either of the two large flat bones at the top of the back **SYN** scapula ⊃ VISUAL VOCAB page V1

**ˌshoulder-ˈhigh** *adj., adv.* as high as a person's shoulders: *a shoulder-high wall* ◇ *They carried him shoulder-high through the crowd.*

**ˈshoulder-length** *adj.* (especially of hair) long enough to reach your shoulders

**ˈshoulder pad** *noun* [usually pl.] **1** a small piece of thick cloth that is SEWN into the shoulder of a dress, jacket, etc. to make a person's shoulders look bigger **2** a piece of hard plastic that people wear under their shirts to protect their shoulders when playing AMERICAN FOOTBALL, ICE HOCKEY, etc.

**ˈshoulder strap** *noun* **1** a narrow piece of cloth on a dress or other piece of clothing that goes over your shoulder from the front to the back **2** a long narrow piece of cloth, leather, etc. that is attached to a bag so that you can carry it over your shoulder

## shout ⓘ A2 /ʃaʊt/ *verb, noun*

- **verb 1** A2 [I, T] to say sth in a loud voice; to speak loudly/angrily to sb: *Stop shouting and listen!* ◇ ~ **for sth** *I shouted for help but nobody came.* ◇ ~ **at sb/sth** *Then he started shouting and swearing at her.* ◇ ~ **at sb to do sth** *She shouted at him to shut the gate.* ◇ ~ **sth (at/to sb/sth)** *Protesters shouted slogans denouncing the war.* ◇ ~ **that …** *He shouted that he couldn't swim.* ◇ ~ **yourself** + *adj. She shouted herself hoarse, cheering on the team.* ◇ + **speech** *'Run!' he shouted.* **2** [I] to make a loud noise: *She could hear him shouting and screaming in the next room.* ◇ ~ **(out) (in/with sth)** *She shouted out in pain when she tried to move her leg.* **3** [I, T] (*AustralE, NZE*) to buy drinks or food for sb in a bar, restaurant, etc: *I'll shout—what are you drinking?* ◇ ~ **(sb) sth** *Who's going to shout me a drink?* **IDM** see ROOFTOP
- **PHRV** ˌshout sb ↔ ˈdown to shout so that sb who is speaking cannot be heard: *The speaker was shouted down by a group of protesters.* ˌshout sth ↔ ˈout to say sth in a loud voice so that it can be clearly heard: *Don't shout out all the answers.* ◇ + **speech** *'I'm over here!' I shouted out.*
- **noun 1** A2 a loud cry of anger, fear, excitement, etc: *angry shouts* ◇ ~ **of sth** *a shout of anger/encouragement* ◇ ~ **from sb/sth** *He ignored the loud shouts from the crowd outside.* **2** [usually sing.] (*BrE, informal*) a person's turn to buy drinks: *What are you drinking? It's my shout.* **IDM** ˌbe ˌin with a ˈshout (of sth/of doing sth) (*informal*) to have a good chance of winning sth or of achieving sth ˌgive sb a ˈshout (*informal*) to tell sb sth: *Give me a shout when you're ready.*

**ˈshout·ing** /ˈʃaʊtɪŋ/ *noun* [U] shouts from a number of people: *Didn't you hear all the shouting?* **IDM** ˌbe all ˌover bar the ˈshouting (*BrE*) (of an activity or a competition) to be almost finished or decided, so that there is no doubt about the final result ⊃ more at DISTANCE *n.*

**ˈshouting match** *noun* an argument when people shout loudly at each other ⊃ compare SLANGING MATCH

## ▼ SYNONYMS

### shout
yell • cry • scream • cheer • bellow • raise your voice

These words all mean to say sth in a very loud voice.

**shout** to say sth in a loud voice; to speak loudly and often angrily to sb: *Stop shouting and listen!* ◇ *'Run!' he shouted.*

**yell** to shout loudly, for example because you are angry, excited, frightened or in pain: *She yelled at the boy to get down from the wall.*

**cry** (*rather formal or literary*) to shout loudly: *She ran over to the window and cried for help.*

**scream** to shout sth in a loud high voice because you are afraid, angry or excited: *He screamed at me to stop.*

**cheer** (especially of a crowd of people) to shout loudly to show support or praise for sb, or to encourage them: *We all cheered as the team came onto the field.*

**bellow** to shout in a loud deep voice, especially because you are angry: *'Quiet!' the teacher bellowed.*

**raise your voice** to speak loudly to sb, especially because you are angry: *She never once raised her voice to us.*

### PATTERNS
- to shout / yell / cry / raise your voice **to** sb
- to shout / yell / scream / bellow **at** sb
- to shout / yell / cry out / scream / bellow **in** pain / anguish / rage, etc.
- to shout / yell / cry out / scream **for** joy / excitement / delight, etc.
- to shout / yell / cry out / scream **with** excitement / triumph, etc.
- to shout / yell / scream / bellow at sb **to do sth**
- to shout / yell / scream **abuse**
- to shout / yell / cry / scream **for help**

**ˈshout-out** *noun* (*informal*) a public expression of thanks or welcome, especially on radio or television or during a live performance: *This is a shout-out to all our sponsors and advertisers.*

**shouty** /ˈʃaʊti/ *adj.* (*informal*) doing or involving a lot of shouting: *a shouty conversation on the stairs*

## shove /ʃʌv/ *verb, noun*

- **verb 1** [I, T] to push sb/sth in a rough way: *The crowd was pushing and shoving to get a better view.* ◇ + *adv./prep. The door wouldn't open no matter how hard she shoved.* ◇ ~ **sb/sth (+ adv./prep.)** *He shoved her down the stairs.* **2** [T] ~ **sth** + *adv./prep.* (*informal*) to put sth somewhere roughly or carelessly: *She shoved the book into her bag and hurried off.* ◇ *He came over and shoved a piece of paper into my hand.* ◇ *Shove your suitcase under the bed.* **IDM** ˈshove it (*especially NAmE, informal*) used to say rudely that you will not accept or do sth: *'The boss wants that report now.' 'Yeah? Tell him he can shove it.'*
- **PHRV** ˌshove ˈoff (*BrE, informal*) used to tell sb rudely to go away ˌshove ˈup (*BrE, informal*) to move in order to make a space for sb to sit down next to you: *Shove up! Jan wants to sit down.*
- **noun** [usually sing.] a strong push: *You have to give the door a shove or it won't close.* **IDM** see PUSH *n.*

## shovel /ˈʃʌvl/ *noun, verb*

- **noun 1** a tool like a SPADE with a long handle and a broad metal part with curved edges, used for moving earth, snow, sand, etc: *workmen with picks and shovels* ◇ (*NAmE*) *The children took their pails and shovels to the beach.* ⊃ compare SPADE **2** the part of a large machine or vehicle that digs or moves earth
- **verb** (-ll-, *US* -l-) ~ **sth** (+ *adv./prep.*) to lift and move earth, stones, coal, etc. with a shovel: *A gang of workmen were shovelling rubble onto a truck.* ◇ *They went out in freezing conditions to shovel snow.* ◇ (*NAmE*) *to shovel the sidewalk/driveway* (= to remove snow) ◇ (*figurative*) *He sat at the table, shovelling food into his mouth.*

**ˈshovel-ready** *adj.* (of a construction project) at the stage where workers can be employed and building begun

# show

**show** /ʃəʊ/ verb, noun

■ **verb** (showed, shown /ʃəʊn/, showed) **HELP** The form showed is rare as a past participle.

- **MAKE CLEAR** **1** [T] (not usually used in the progressive tenses) to make sth clear; to prove sth: **~(that)** ... *The figures clearly **show** that her claims are false.* ◊ *The government's popularity is declining, as the polls **show**.* ◊ **~sb that** ... *Our research **showed** us that women were more interested in their health than men.* ◊ **~sth** *The report **showed** an increase in sales.* ◊ **~sb/sth to be/have sth** *His new book **shows** him to be a first-rate storyteller.* ◊ **~sb/sth doing sth** *Tax records **show** Shakespeare living near the Globe Theatre in 1599.* ◊ **~(sb) how, what, etc...** *This **shows** how people are influenced by TV advertisements.* ⊃ LANGUAGE BANK at ILLUSTRATE
- **LET SB SEE STH** **2** [T] to let sb see sth: **~sth** *You have to **show** your ticket as you go in.* ◊ **~sth to sb** *Have you **shown** your work to anyone?* ◊ **~sb** *Have you **shown** anyone your work?*
- **TEACH** **3** [T] to teach or demonstrate the way to do sth, for example by letting sb watch you do it or by explaining it: **~sth (to sb)** *She **showed** the technique to her students.* ◊ **~sb sth** *She **showed** her students the technique.* ◊ **~(sb) how, what, etc** ... *Can you **show** me how to do it?*
- **POINT** **4** [T] to point to sth so that sb can see where or what it is: **~sb sth** *He **showed** me our location on the map.* ◊ **~sb which, what, etc** ... *Show me which picture you drew.*
- **GUIDE** **5** [T] to lead or guide sb to a place: **~sb + adv./prep.** *The attendant **showed** us to our seats.* ◊ **~sb sth** *I'll go first and **show** you the way.* ⊃ SYNONYMS at TAKE
- **QUALITY/BEHAVIOUR/FEELING** **6** [T] to make it clear that you have a particular quality: **~sth** *to **show** great courage* ◊ **~sb sth** *She wants to **show** the world her ability.* ◊ **~yourself + adj./noun** *She had **shown** herself unable to deal with money.* ◊ **~yourself to be/have sth** *He has **shown** himself to be ready to make compromises.* ◊ **~that** ... *He has **shown** that he is ready to make compromises.* **7** [T] to behave in a particular way towards sb: **~sth** *I wanted to be there to **show** support.* ◊ **~sth for/to sb** *They **showed** no respect for their parents.* ◊ **~sb sth** *They **showed** their parents no respect.* **8** [I, T] if a feeling or quality **shows**, or if sb/sth **shows** it, it can be seen or noticed: *Fear **showed** in his eyes.* ◊ *They loved working together, and it **shows** (= it can be seen in their work).* ◊ *She **showed** no interest in my work.* ◊ *The market **shows** no sign of slowing down.* ◊ *Her second attempt **showed** a marked improvement.* ◊ **~how, what, etc** ... *She tried not to **show** how disappointed she was.*
- **BE ABLE TO BE SEEN** **9** [I, T] if sth **shows**, people can see it. If sth **shows** a mark, dirt, etc., the mark can be seen: *She had a warm woollen hat and scarf on that left only her eyes and nose **showing**.* ◊ **~sth** *Their new white carpet **showed** every mark.*
- **INFORMATION** **10** [T] (not usually used in the progressive tenses) to give particular information, or a time or measurement: **~sth** *The map **shows** the principal towns and rivers.* ◊ *The end-of-year accounts **show** a loss.* ◊ **~how, what, etc** ... *The flow chart **shows** how resources are allocated.*
- **OF PICTURE/PHOTOGRAPH** **11** [T] (not usually used in the progressive tenses) to be of sb/sth; to represent sb/sth: **~sb/sth (+ adv./prep.)** *She had objected to a photo **showing** her in a bikini.* ◊ **~sb/sth doing sth** *The painting **shows** St George slaying the dragon.*
- **FOR PUBLIC TO SEE** **12** [I, T] to be or make sth available for the public to see: *The movie is now **showing** at all major movie theaters.* ◊ **~sth** *The documentary will be **shown** on Sunday.* ◊ *She plans to **show** her paintings early next year.*
- **PROVE** **13** [T, no passive] (*informal*) to prove that you can do sth or are sth: **~sb (sth)** *They think I can't do it, but I'll **show** them!* ◊ **~yourself to be/have sth** *He has **shown** himself to be a caring father.* ◊ **~what, how, etc** ... *I'm giving him a chance to **show** what he can do.*
- **ARRIVE** **14** [I] (*especially NAmE, informal*) to arrive where you have arranged to meet sb or do sth: *I waited an hour but he didn't **show**.* ⊃ see also SHOW UP
- **ANIMAL** **15** [T] **~sth** to enter an animal in a competition

**IDM** **it goes to 'show** used to say that sth proves sth: *It just goes to **show** what you can do when you really try.* **show sb the 'door** to ask sb to leave, because they are no longer welcome **show your 'face** to appear among your friends or in public: *She stayed at home, afraid to **show** her face.* **show your 'hand/'cards** (*NAmE also* **tip your 'hand**) to make your plans or intentions known **show sb who's 'boss** to make it clear to sb that you have more power and authority than they have **show the 'way** to do sth first so that other people can follow **show 'willing** (*BrE*) to show that you are ready to help, work hard, etc. if necessary **(have) something, nothing, etc. to 'show for sth** (to have) something, nothing, etc. as a result of sth: *All those years of hard work, and nothing to **show** for it!* ⊃ more at FLAG *n.*, PACE¹ *n.*, ROPE *n.*

**PHRV** **,show sb a'round (sth)** (*BrE also* **,show sb 'round (sth)**) to be a guide for sb when they visit a place for the first time to show them what is interesting: *We were **shown** around the school by one of the students.* ◊ *Has anyone **shown** you around yet?* **,show 'off** (*informal, disapproving*) to try to impress others by talking about your abilities, possessions, etc: *He's just **showing** off because that girl he likes is here.* ⊃ related noun SHOW-OFF **,show sb/sth↔'off** to **show** people sb/sth that you are proud of: *She wanted to **show** off her new husband at the party.* ◊ **show off how, what, etc...** *He likes to **show** off how well he speaks French.* **,show sth↔'off** (*of clothing*) to make sb look attractive, by showing their best features: *a dress that **shows** off her figure* **,show sb 'round (sth)** (*BrE*) = SHOW SB AROUND (STH) **,show 'through** | **,show 'through sth** to be able to be seen behind or under sth else: *The writing on the other side of the page **shows** through.* ◊ (*figurative*) *When he spoke, his bitterness **showed** through.* ◊ *Veins **showed** through her pale skin.* **,show 'up** (*informal*) to arrive where you have arranged to meet sb or do sth: *It was getting late when she finally **showed** up.* **,show 'up** | **,show sth↔'up** to start to be able to be seen; to make sth start to be able to be seen: *a broken bone **showed** up on the X-ray* ◊ *The harsh light **showed** up the lines on her face.* **,show sb↔'up** **1** (*BrE, informal*) to make sb feel embarrassed by behaving badly: *He **showed** me up by snoring during the concert.* **2** to make sb feel embarrassed by doing sth better than them

■ **noun**

- **ENTERTAINMENT** **1** [C] a programme on television or the radio: *Millions of people watch the **show**.* ◊ *a TV/television/radio **show*** ◊ *a quiz **show*** ⊃ see also CHAT SHOW, GAME SHOW, ROADSHOW, TALK SHOW **2** [C] a theatre performance, especially one that includes singing and dancing: *to go to/see a **show*** ◊ *to put on/stage a **show*** ◊ *The book has been turned into a stage **show**.* ◊ *She's the star of the **show**!* ⊃ see also FLOOR SHOW, LIGHT SHOW, TALENT SHOW **3** [C] (*NAmE, informal*) a concert, especially of rock music
- **OF COLLECTION OF THINGS** **4** [C, U] an occasion when a collection of things are brought together for people to look at: *a dog/car/gun **show*** ◊ **on ~** *The paintings are on **show** until April.* ⊃ see also AIR SHOW, FASHION SHOW, FREAK SHOW, PEEP SHOW, SLIDE SHOW, TRADE SHOW
- **OF FEELING** **5** [C] an action or a way of behaving that shows how you feel **SYN** display: *a **show** of emotion/support* ◊ *a **show** of force/strength by the army*
- **INSINCERE ACT** **6** [U, sing.] something that is done only to give a good impression, but is not sincere: *He may seem charming, but it's all **show**!* ◊ **for ~** *She pretends to be interested in opera, but it's only for **show**.* ◊ *He made a great **show** of affection, but I knew he didn't mean it.*
- **COLOURFUL SIGHT** **7** [C, U] a brightly coloured or pleasant sight **SYN** display: *a lovely **show** of spring flowers*
- **EVENT/SITUATION** **8** [sing.] (*informal*) an event, a business or a situation where sth is being done or organized: *She runs the whole **show**. I won't interfere—it's your **show**.*
- **GOOD/POOR SHOW** **9** [C, usually sing.] (*especially BrE, informal*) something that is done in a particular way: *The team put on a good **show** in the competition.* ◊ *It's a poor **show** if he forgets your birthday.* ⊃ see also NO-SHOW

**O** Oxford Phrasal Academic Lexicon (OPAL) written and spoken word lists | **W** OPAL written word list | **S** OPAL spoken word list

# show-and-tell

**IDM** **for ˈshow** intended to be seen but not used: *These items are just for show—they're not for sale.* **ˌget the ˈshow on the ˈroad** (*informal*) to start an activity or a journey: *Let's get this show on the road!* **(ˌjolly) ˌgood ˈshow!** (*BrE, old-fashioned, informal*) used to show you like sth or to say that sb has done sth well **a show of ˈhands** a way of voting for or against something in which people raise their hands to vote ⊃ more at DOG *n.*, STEAL *v.*

**ˌshow-and-ˈtell** *noun* [U] an activity in which children have to bring sth to show their class and talk about it to them

**ˈshow-boat** /ˈʃəʊbəʊt/ *verb, noun*
■ *verb* [I] (*informal, often disapproving*) to behave in a way that tries to show people how clever, SKILFUL, etc. you are ▶ **ˈshow-boat·ing** *noun* [U]
■ *noun* (*NAmE*) a boat on which musical shows are performed

**ˈshow business** (*also informal* **ˈshow-biz** /ˈʃəʊbɪz/) *noun* [U] the business of providing public entertainment, for example in the theatre, in films or on television: *in ~ to be in show business* ◇ *show-business people/stars* ◇ *That's showbiz!*

**ˈshow·case** /ˈʃəʊkeɪs/ *noun* **1** [usually sing.] **~ (for sb/sth)** an event that presents sb's abilities or the good qualities of sth in an attractive way: *The festival was a showcase for young musicians.* **2** a box with a glass top or sides that is used for showing objects in a shop, museum, etc. ▶ **ˈshow·case** *verb*: **~ sth** *Jack found a film role that showcased all his talents.*

**ˈshow·down** /ˈʃəʊdaʊn/ *noun* [usually sing.] an argument, a fight or a test that will settle a DISAGREEMENT that has lasted for a long time: *Management are facing a showdown with union members today.* ◇ *Fans gathered outside the stadium for the final showdown (= the game that will decide the winner of the competition).*

**show·er** ❶ **A1** /ˈʃaʊə(r)/ *noun, verb*
■ *noun* **1** ❓ **A1** a piece of equipment producing a flow of water that you stand under to wash yourself; the small room or part of a room that contains a shower: **in the ~** *He's in the shower.* ◇ *an en-suite shower room* ◇ *a shower cubicle/curtain* ⊃ see also POWER SHOWER **2** ❓ **A1** the act of washing yourself with a shower: *a hot/cold shower* ◇ (*especially BrE*) **to have a shower** ◇ (*especially NAmE*) **to take a shower** ◇ *shower gel* **3** ❓ **B1** a short period of rain or snow: *scattered/heavy showers* ◇ *April showers* ◇ *We were caught in a heavy shower.* ◇ *rain/snow showers* ◇ *wintry showers (= of snow)* ◇ **~of sth** *a shower of rain/hail/hailstones* ⊃ WORDFINDER NOTE AT RAIN **4** a large number of things that arrive or fall together: *a meteor shower* ◇ *a shower of sparks from the fire* ◇ *a shower of kisses* **5** (*NAmE*) a party at which you give presents to a woman who is getting married or having a baby: *a bridal/baby shower*
■ *verb* **1** [I] to wash yourself under a shower: *She showered and dressed and went downstairs.* **2** [I] **~(down) on sb/ sth** | **~down** to fall onto sb/sth, especially in a lot of small pieces: *Volcanic ash showered down on the town after the eruption.* **3** [T] **~ sb with sth** to drop a lot of small things onto sb: *The bride and groom were showered with rice as they left the church.* ◇ *The roof collapsed, showering us with dust and debris.* **4** [T] to give sb a lot of sth: **~ sb with sth** *He showered her with gifts.* ◇ **~ sth on sb** *He showered gifts on her.*

**show·ery** /ˈʃaʊəri/ *adj.* (of the weather) with showers of rain often occurring: *a showery day*

**ˈshow-girl** /ˈʃəʊɡɜːl; *NAmE* -ɡɜːrl/ *noun* a female performer who sings and dances in a musical show

**ˈshow·ground** /ˈʃəʊɡraʊnd/ *noun* a large outdoor area where FAIRS, farm shows, etc. take place

**ˈshow house** (*also* **ˈshow home**) (*both BrE*) (*NAmE* **ˈmodel home**) *noun* a house in a group of new houses that has been painted and filled with furniture, so that people who might want to buy one of the houses can see what they will be like

**show·ing** /ˈʃəʊɪŋ/ *noun* **1** an act of showing a film: *There are three showings a day.* **2** [usually sing.] evidence of how well or how badly sb/sth is performing: *the strong/poor showing of the Green Party in the election* ◇ *On (= judging by) last week's showing, the team is unlikely to win today.*

**ˈshow-jump·ing** /ˈʃəʊdʒʌmpɪŋ/ *noun* [U] the sport of riding a horse and jumping over a set of fences as quickly as possible

**show·man** /ˈʃəʊmən/ *noun* (*pl.* **-men** /-mən/) **1** a person who is good at getting people's attention and does things in a way that entertains them **2** a person who organizes public entertainments, especially at FAIRGROUNDS

**show·man·ship** /ˈʃəʊmənʃɪp/ *noun* [U] skill in getting a lot of attention and doing things in a way that entertains people

**shown** /ʃəʊn/ *past part.* of SHOW

**ˈshow-off** *noun* (*informal, disapproving*) a person who tries to impress other people by showing how good he or she is at doing sth

**ˈshow·piece** /ˈʃəʊpiːs/ *noun* an excellent example of sth that people are meant to see and admire

**ˈshow·place** /ˈʃəʊpleɪs/ *noun* a place of great beauty, historical interest, etc. that is open to the public

**ˈshow·room** /ˈʃəʊruːm, -rʊm/ *noun* a large shop in which goods for sale, especially cars and electrical goods, are displayed: *a car showroom*

**ˈshow-stopper** *noun* (*informal*) a performance that is very impressive and receives a lot of APPLAUSE from the audience ▶ **ˈshow-stopping** *adj.* [only before noun]: *a show-stopping performance*

**ˈshow·time** /ˈʃəʊtaɪm/ *noun* [U] the time that a theatre performance will begin: *It's five minutes to showtime and the theatre is packed.* ◇ (*figurative, NAmE*) *Everybody ready? It's showtime!*

**ˈshow trial** *noun* an unfair trial of sb in court, organized by a government for political reasons, not in order to find out the truth

**showy** /ˈʃəʊi/ *adj.* (*often disapproving*) so brightly coloured, large or EXAGGERATED that it attracts a lot of attention **SYN** **ostentatious**: *showy flowers* ▶ **ˈshow·ily** /ˈʃəʊɪli/ *adv.* **ˈshowi·ness** /ˈʃəʊinəs/ *noun* [U]

**shrank** /ʃræŋk/ *past tense* of SHRINK

**ˈshrap·nel** /ˈʃræpnəl/ *noun* [U] small pieces of metal that are thrown out with a lot of force when a bomb explodes

**shred** /ʃred/ *verb, noun*
■ *verb* (**-dd-**) **~ sth** to cut or tear sth into small pieces: *Serve the fish on a bed of shredded lettuce.* ◇ *He was accused of shredding documents relating to the case (= putting them in a SHREDDER).*
■ *noun* **1** [usually pl.] a small thin piece that has been torn or cut from sth **SYN** **scrap**: *shreds of paper* ◇ *His jacket had been torn to shreds by the barbed wire.* **2** [usually sing.] **~ of sth** (used especially in negative sentences) a very small amount of sth: *There is not a shred of evidence to support his claim.*
**IDM** **in ˈshreds** **1** very badly damaged **SYN** **in tatters**: *The country's economy is in shreds.* ◇ (*figurative*) *Her nerves were in shreds.* **2** torn in many places: *The document was in shreds on the floor.* **pick/pull/tear sb/sth to ˈpieces/ ˈshreds** (*informal*) to criticize sb, or their work or ideas, very severely

**shred·der** /ˈʃredə(r)/ *noun* a machine that tears sth into small pieces, especially paper, so that nobody can read what was printed on it

**shrew** /ʃruː/ *noun* **1** a small animal like a mouse with a long nose **2** (*old-fashioned*) an angry unpleasant woman

**shrewd** /ʃruːd/ *adj.* (**shrewd·er, shrewd·est**) **1** clever at understanding and making judgements about a situation **SYN** **astute**: *a shrewd businessman* ◇ *She is a shrewd judge of character.* **2** showing good judgement and likely to be right: *a shrewd move* ◇ *I have a shrewd idea who the mystery caller was.* ▶ **ˈshrewd·ly** *adv.* **ˈshrewd·ness** *noun* [U]

**shrew·ish** /ˈʃruːɪʃ/ *adj.* (*old-fashioned*) (of women) always arguing and in a bad mood

**Shri** (also **Sri**) /ʃriː, sriː/ noun (IndE) **1** a title used before the names of gods or holy books, showing respect **2** a title of respect for a man

**shriek** /ʃriːk/ verb, noun
- verb **1** [I] to give a loud high shout, for example when you are excited, frightened or in pain SYN scream: ~ (in sth) *She shrieked in fright.* ◊ ~ with sth *The audience was shrieking with laughter.* ~ at sb (figurative): *The answer shrieked at her* (= was very obvious). **2** [T] to say sth in a loud, high voice SYN scream: ~ (sth) (at sb) *She was shrieking abuse at them as they carried her off.* ◊ + speech *'Look out!' he shrieked.*
- noun a loud high shout, for example one that you make when you are excited, frightened or in pain: *She let out a piercing shriek.* ◊ *a shriek of delight*

**shrift** /ʃrɪft/ noun IDM see SHORT adj.

**shrike** /ʃraɪk/ noun a bird with a strong BEAK, that catches small birds and insects and sticks them on THORNS

**shrill** /ʃrɪl/ adj., verb
- adj. (**shrill·er, shrill·est**) **1** (of sounds or voices) very high and loud, in an unpleasant way SYN piercing: *a shrill voice* **2** loud and determined but often unreasonable: *shrill demands/protests* ▶ **shrilly** /ˈʃrɪli/ adv. **shrill·ness** /ˈʃrɪlnəs/ noun [U]
- verb **1** [I] to make an unpleasant high loud sound: *Behind him, the telephone shrilled.* **2** [T] + speech to say sth in a loud, high voice SYN shriek: *'Wait for me!' she shrilled.*

**Shri·mati** (also **Sri·mati**) /ˈʃriːmʌti, ˈsriː-/ noun (IndE) a title of respect for a woman, especially a married woman: *Shrimati Sonia Gandhi*

**shrimp** /ʃrɪmp/ noun (pl. **shrimps** or **shrimp**) **1** a small SHELLFISH that can be eaten, like a PRAWN but smaller. Shrimps turn pink when cooked. **2** (NAmE) = PRAWN: *grilled shrimp* ⇒ VISUAL VOCAB page V3

**shrimp·ing** /ˈʃrɪmpɪŋ/ noun [U] the activity of catching shrimps: *a shrimping net* ▶ **shrimp·er** noun (especially NAmE): *shrimpers and fishermen in the Gulf of Mexico*

**shrimp ˈscampi** noun [U] (NAmE) = SCAMPI (2)

**shrine** /ʃraɪn/ noun **1** a place where people come to WORSHIP because it is connected with a holy person or event: *to visit the shrine of Mecca* ◊ *a shrine to the Virgin Mary* **2** ~ (for sb) | ~ (to sb/sth) a place that people visit because it is connected with sb/sth that is important to them: *Wimbledon is a shrine for all lovers of tennis.*

**shrink** /ʃrɪŋk/ verb, noun
- verb (**shrank** /ʃræŋk/, **shrunk**, **shrunk**, **shrunk** /ʃrʌŋk/) **1** [I, T] ~ (sth) to become smaller, especially when washed in water that is too hot; to make clothes, cloth, etc. smaller in this way: *My sweater shrank in the wash.* **2** [I, T] to become or to make sth smaller in size or amount: *The tumour had shrunk to the size of a pea.* ◊ *The market for their products is shrinking.* ◊ ~ sth *The internet in a sense has shrunk the world.* ⇒ see also SHRUNKEN **3** [I] + adv./prep. to move back or away from sth because you are frightened or shocked SYN cower: *He shrank back against the wall as he heard them approaching.*
IDM a ˌshrinking ˈviolet (humorous) a very shy person
PHRV ˈshrink from sth (used especially in negative sentences) to be unwilling to do sth that is difficult or unpleasant: *We made it clear to them that we would not shrink from confrontation.* ◊ **shrink from doing sth** *They did not shrink from doing what was right.*
- noun (informal, humorous) a PSYCHIATRIST or psychologist

**shrink·age** /ˈʃrɪŋkɪdʒ/ noun [U] the process of becoming smaller in size; the amount by which sth becomes smaller: *the shrinkage of heavy industry* ◊ *She bought a slightly larger size to allow for shrinkage.*

**ˈshrink-wrapped** adj. wrapped tightly in a layer of thin plastic

**shrivel** /ˈʃrɪvl/ verb (-ll-, US -l-) [I, T] to become or make sth dry and WRINKLED as a result of heat, cold or being old: ~ (up) *The leaves on the plant had shrivelled up from lack of water.* ◊ ~ sth (up) *The hot weather had shrivelled the grapes in every vineyard.* ▶ **shriv·elled** adj.: *a shrivelled old man*

**shroom** /ʃruːm, ʃrʊm/ (informal, especially NAmE) (also **magic mushroom** BrE or becoming old-fashioned, NAmE) noun a type of MUSHROOM that has an effect like some drugs and that may make people who eat it HALLUCINATE (= see things that are not there) ▶ **shroom** verb [I]: *Joe was shrooming last night and has a killer headache today.*

**shroud** /ʃraʊd/ noun, verb
- noun **1** a piece of cloth that a dead person's body is wrapped in before it is buried **2** ~ of sth (literary) a thing that covers, surrounds or hides sth: *The organization is cloaked in a shroud of secrecy.* ◊ *a shroud of smoke*
- verb [usually passive] **1** ~ sth in sth (of DARKNESS, clouds, cloth, etc.) to cover or hide sth: *The city was shrouded in mist.* **2** ~ sth in sth to hide information or keep it secret and mysterious: *His family background is shrouded in mystery.*

**Shrove Tuesday** /ˌʃrəʊv ˈtjuːzdeɪ, -di; NAmE ˈtuːz-/ noun [U, C] (in the Christian Church) the day before the beginning of Lent ⇒ compare MARDI GRAS, PANCAKE DAY ⇒ see also ASH WEDNESDAY

**shrub** /ʃrʌb/ noun a large plant that is smaller than a tree and that has several STEMS of wood coming from the ground SYN bush

**shrub·bery** /ˈʃrʌbəri/ noun [C, U] (pl. **-ies**) an area planted with shrubs

**shrubby** /ˈʃrʌbi/ adj. (of plants) like a shrub

**shrug** /ʃrʌɡ/ verb, noun
- verb (**-gg-**) [I, T, no passive] to raise your shoulders and then drop them to show that you do not know or care about sth: *Sam shrugged and said nothing.* ◊ ~ sth *'I don't know,' Anna replied, shrugging her shoulders.*
PHRV ˌshrug sth↔ˈoff/aˈside to treat sth as if it is not important SYN dismiss: *Shrugging off her injury, she played on.* ◊ *He shrugged aside suggestions that he resign.* ˌshrug sb/sth↔ˈoff/aˈway to push sb/sth back or away with your shoulders: *Kevin shrugged off his jacket.* ◊ *She shrugged him away angrily.*
- noun **1** [usually sing.] an act of raising your shoulders and then dropping them to show that you do not know or care about sth: *Andy gave a shrug. 'It doesn't matter.'* **2** a very short jacket, usually made of wool, that is open at the front and worn by women

**shrunk** /ʃrʌŋk/ past tense, past part. of SHRINK

**shrunk·en** /ˈʃrʌŋkən/ adj. [usually before noun] that has become smaller (and less attractive) SYN wizened: *a shrunken old woman*

**shtetl** /ˈʃtetl/ noun a small Jewish town or village in eastern Europe in the past

**shtick** (also **schtick**) /ʃtɪk/ noun [U, sing.] (especially NAmE) **1** a style of humour that is typical of a particular performer **2** a particular ability that sb has

**shtum** (also **schtum**) /ʃtʊm/ noun [U]
IDM ˌkeep/ˌstay ˈshtum (BrE, informal) to not speak: *Police have appealed for witnesses, but it seems the locals are keeping shtum.*

**shuck** /ʃʌk/ noun, verb
- noun (NAmE) the outer layer of a nut, plant, etc. or an OYSTER or a CLAM
- verb ~ sth (NAmE) to remove the shell or covering of nuts, SHELLFISH, etc.

**shucks** /ʃʌks/ exclamation (NAmE, old-fashioned, informal) used to show that you are embarrassed or disappointed

**shud·der** /ˈʃʌdə(r)/ verb, noun
- verb **1** [I] to shake because you are cold or frightened, or because of a strong feeling: *Just thinking about the accident makes me shudder.* ◊ ~ with sth *Alone in the car, she shuddered with fear.* ◊ ~ at sth *I shuddered at the thought of all the trouble I'd caused.* ◊ ~ to do sth *I shudder to think how much this is all going to cost* (= I don't want to think about it because it is too unpleasant). **2** [I] (of a vehicle, machine, etc.) to shake very hard: *The bus shuddered to a halt.*
- noun [usually sing.] **1** a shaking movement you make because you are cold or have a feeling of fear or horror: *a shudder of fear* ◊ *She gave an involuntary shudder.* **2** a

# shuffle

strong shaking movement: *The elevator rose with a shudder.*

**shuf·fle** /ˈʃʌfl/ *verb, noun*
- *verb* **1** [I] + *adv./prep.* to walk slowly without lifting your feet completely off the ground: *He shuffled across the room to the window.* ◊ *The line shuffled forward a little.* **2** [T, I] ~ (sth) to move from one foot to another, especially because you are bored, nervous or embarrassed: *Jenny shuffled her feet and blushed with shame.* **3** [T, I] ~(sth) to mix cards up in a PACK of PLAYING CARDS before playing a game: *Shuffle the cards and deal out seven to each player.* ⊃ WORDFINDER NOTE at CARD **4** [T] ~sth to move paper or things into different positions or a different order: *I shuffled the documents on my desk.*
- *noun* [usually sing.] **1** a slow walk in which you take small steps and do not lift your feet completely off the ground **2** the act of mixing cards before a card game: *Give the cards a good shuffle.* **3** a type of dancing in which you take small steps and do not lift your feet completely off the ground **4** = RESHUFFLE

**IDM** **lose sb/sth in the 'shuffle** [usually passive] (*NAmE*) to not notice sb/sth or pay attention to sb/sth because of a confusing situation: *Middle children tend to get lost in the shuffle.* **on 'shuffle** (of pieces of music stored on a music player or music app) not in any special order: *I use my phone's music app on shuffle.*

**shuffle-board** /ˈʃʌflbɔːd; *NAmE* -bɔːrd/ *noun* [U] a game in which players use long sticks to push discs towards spaces with numbers on a board

**shuka** /ˈʃuːkə/ *EAfrE* /ˈʃuka/ *noun* (*EAfrE*) a BLANKET (= a large thick piece of cloth), often red with a pattern of squares on it, worn by Maasai people

**shun** /ʃʌn/ *verb* (-nn-) ~sb/sth to avoid sb/sth: *They were both shunned by their families when they remarried.* ◊ *an actor who shuns publicity*

**shunt** /ʃʌnt/ *verb, noun*
- *verb* **1** ~sth to move a train or a coach of a train from one track to another **2** ~sb/sth + *adv./prep.* (*usually disapproving*) to move sb/sth to a different place, especially a less important one: *John was shunted sideways to a job in sales.*
- *noun* **1** (*BrE, informal*) a road accident in which one vehicle crashes into the back of another **2** (*medical*) a small tube put in your body in a medical operation to allow the blood or other FLUID to flow from one place to another

**shush** /ʃʊʃ/ *exclamation, verb*
- *exclamation* used to tell sb to be quiet
- *verb* ~ sb to tell sb to be quiet, especially by saying 'shush', or by putting your finger against your lips: *Lyn shushed the children.*

**shut** /ʃʌt/ *verb, adj.*
- *verb* (shut·ting, shut, shut) **1** [T, I] to close sth; to become closed: *The window won't shut.* ◊ *The doors open and shut automatically.* ◊ ~sth *Philip went into his room and shut the door behind him.* ◊ *I can't shut my suitcase—it's too full.* ◊ *She shut her eyes and fell asleep immediately.* **2** [I, T] (*BrE*) when a shop, restaurant, etc. **shuts** or when sb **shuts** it, it stops being open for business and you cannot go into it: *The bank shuts at 4.* ◊ ~sth *We decided to shut the cafe early as there were no customers.* ⊃ note at CLOSE¹

**IDM** **shut your 'mouth/'face!** (*slang*) a rude way of telling sb to be quiet or stop talking **shut up 'shop** (*BrE, informal*) to close a business permanently or to stop working for the day ⊃ more at DOOR, EAR, EYE *n.*, MOUTH *n.*
**PHRV** **shut sb/sth⇔a'way** to put sb/sth in a place where other people cannot see or find them **shut yourself a'way** to go somewhere where you will be completely alone **shut 'down** (of a factory, shop, etc. or a machine) to stop opening for business; to stop working ⊃ related noun SHUTDOWN **shut sth⇔'down** to stop a factory, shop, etc. from opening for business; to stop a machine from working: *The computer system will be shut down over the weekend.* ⊃ related noun SHUTDOWN **shut sb/ yourself 'in (sth)** to put sb in a room and keep them there; to go to a room and stay there: *She shut the dog in the shed while she prepared the barbecue.* **'shut sth in sth** to close a door, LID, etc. on sth, in a way that is painful or means that the item cannot be moved: *Sam shut his finger in the car door.* **shut 'off** (of a machine, tool, etc.) to stop working: *The engines shut off automatically in an emergency.* **shut sth⇔'off 1** to stop a machine, tool, etc. from working **2** to stop a supply of gas, water, etc. from flowing or reaching a place: *A valve immediately shuts off the gas when the lid is closed.* **shut yourself 'off (from sth)** to avoid seeing people or having contact with anyone: *Martin shut himself off from the world to write his book.* **shut sb/ sth 'off from sth** to separate sb/sth from sth: *Bosnia is shut off from the Adriatic by the mountains.* **shut sb/ sth⇔'out (of sth) 1** to prevent sb/sth from entering a place: *Mum, Ben keeps shutting me out of the bedroom!* ◊ *sunglasses that shut out 99 per cent of the sun's harmful rays* **2** to not allow a person to share or be part of your thoughts; to stop yourself from having particular feelings: *I wanted to shut John out of my life for ever.* ◊ *She learned to shut out her angry feelings.* ◊ *If you shut me out, how can I help you?* **shut 'up** (*informal*) to stop talking (often used as an order or a rude way of telling sb to stop talking): *Just shut up and listen!* ◊ *Will you tell Mike to shut up?* ◊ *When they'd finally shut up, I started again.* **shut sb 'up** to make sb stop talking **SYN** silence: *She kicked Anne under the table to shut her up.* **shut sth⇔'up** to close a room, house, etc. **shut sb/sth 'up (in sth)** to keep sb/sth in a place and prevent them from going anywhere: *They shut him up in jail.*

- *adj.* [not before noun] **1** not open **SYN** closed: *The door was shut.* ◊ *She slammed the door shut.* ◊ *Keep your eyes shut.* **2** (*BrE*) not open for business **SYN** closed: *Unfortunately the bank is shut now.* ◊ *The swimming pool has been shut for a decade.*

**shut·down** /ˈʃʌtdaʊn/ *noun* the act of closing a factory or business or stopping a large machine from working, either temporarily or permanently: *factory shutdowns* ◊ *the nuclear reactor's emergency shutdown procedures*

**'shut-eye** *noun* [U] (*informal*) sleep

**'shut-in** *noun* (*NAmE*) a person who cannot leave their home very easily because they are ill or DISABLED

**shut·out** /ˈʃʌtaʊt/ *noun* (*NAmE*) a game in which one team prevents the other from scoring

**shut·ter** /ˈʃʌtə(r)/ *noun* **1** [usually pl.] one of a pair of wooden or metal covers that can be closed over the outside of a window to keep out light or protect the windows from damage: *to open/close the shutters* ◊ (*BrE, figurative*) *More than 70000 shopkeepers have been forced to put up the shutters* (= close down their businesses) *in the past year.* **2** the part of a camera that opens to allow light to pass through the LENS when you take a photograph
**IDM** **bring/ put down the 'shutters** to stop letting sb know what your thoughts or feelings are; to stop letting yourself think about sth

**shut·ter·bug** /ˈʃʌtəbʌɡ; *NAmE* -tərb-/ *noun* (*NAmE, informal*) a person who likes to take a lot of photographs

**shut·tered** /ˈʃʌtəd; *NAmE* -tərd/ *adj.* with the shutters closed; with shutters fitted

**'shutter speed** (*also* **speed**) *noun* the time taken by a camera SHUTTER to open and close

**shut·tle** /ˈʃʌtl/ *noun, verb*
- *noun* **1** a plane, bus or train that travels regularly between two places: *a shuttle service between London and Edinburgh* **2** = SPACE SHUTTLE **3** a pointed tool used in making cloth to pull a THREAD backwards and forwards over the other THREADS that pass along the length of the cloth
- *verb* **1** [I] ~ (between A and B) to travel between two places frequently: *Her childhood was spent shuttling between her mother and father.* **2** [T] ~sb (+ *adv./prep.*) to carry people between two places that are close, making regular journeys between the two places: *A bus shuttles passengers back and forth from the station to the terminal.*

**shuttle·cock** /ˈʃʌtlkɒk; *NAmE* -kɑːk/ *noun* (*NAmE also* **bir·die**) *noun* the object that players hit backwards and forwards in the game of BADMINTON

**shuttle diplomacy** noun [U] international talks in which people travel between two or more countries in order to talk to the different governments involved

**shut·tler** /ˈʃʌtlə(r)/ noun (IndE) a person who plays BADMINTON

**shwa** = SCHWA

**shy** ⓘ B1 /ʃaɪ/ adj., verb
■ adj. (**shyer**, **shy·est**) **1** ⓘ B1 (of people) nervous or embarrassed about meeting and speaking to other people SYN **timid**: *He is not exactly the shy and retiring type.* ◊ *Don't be shy—come and say hello.* ◊ *She was too shy to ask anyone for help.* ◊ *As a teenager I was painfully shy.* ◊ *~around/with sb She's very shy with adults.* **2** ⓘ B1 showing that sb is nervous or embarrassed about meeting and speaking to other people: *a shy smile* **3** (of animals) easily frightened and not willing to come near people: *The panda is a shy creature.* **4** [not before noun] (used especially in negative sentences) afraid of doing sth or being involved in sth: *~of/about sth The band has never been shy of publicity.* ◊ *~of/about doing sth He disliked her and had never been shy about saying so.* **5** [not before noun] *~(of sth)* (especially NAmE, informal) not having quite the amount that is needed to be sth or to reach a particular figure: *We are still two players shy (of a full team).* ◊ *He died before Christmas, only a month shy of his 90th birthday.* **6 -shy** (in compounds) avoiding or not liking the thing mentioned: *camera-shy* (= not liking to be photographed) ◊ *He's always been work-shy.* ▶ **shyly** adv. **shy·ness** noun [U] IDM see FIGHT v., ONCE adv.
■ verb (**shies**, **shy·ing**, **shied**, **shied**) /ʃaɪd/ [I] *~(at sth)* (especially of a horse) to turn away with a sudden movement because it is afraid or surprised: *My horse shied at the unfamiliar noise.*
PHRV **shy aˈway (from sth)** to avoid doing sth because you are nervous or frightened: *Hugh never shied away from his responsibilities.* ◊ *~from doing sth The newspapers have shied away from investigating the story.*

**shy·ster** /ˈʃaɪstə(r)/ noun (informal, especially NAmE) a dishonest person, especially a lawyer

**SI** /ˌes ˈaɪ/ abbr. International System (used to describe units of measurement; from French 'Système International'): *SI units*

**Siamese cat** /ˌsaɪəmiːz ˈkæt/ (also **Siam·ese** /ˌsaɪəˈmiːz/) noun a cat with short pale fur and a brown face, ears, tail and feet

**Siamese ˈtwin** noun (old-fashioned, offensive) an old-fashioned term for CONJOINED TWIN that is now considered offensive

**sib** /sɪb/ noun (biology) a brother or sister

**sibi·lant** /ˈsɪbɪlənt/ adj., noun
■ adj. (formal or literary) making a 's' or 'sh' sound: *the sibilant sound of whispering*
■ noun (phonetics) a sibilant sound made in speech, such as /s/ and /z/ in the English words *sip* and *zip*

**sib·ling** ⓘ+ B2 /ˈsɪblɪŋ/ noun (formal or specialist) a brother or sister: *squabbles between siblings* ◊ **sibling rivalry** (= competition between brothers and sisters)

**sic** /sɪk/ adv., verb
■ adv. (from Latin) written after a word that you have copied from somewhere, to show that you know that the word is wrongly spelled or wrong in some other way: *In the letter to parents it said: 'The school is proud of it's [sic] record of excellence'.*
■ verb (**-cc-**) *~sb* (NAmE, informal) to attack sb: *Sic him, Duke!* (= said to a dog)
PHRV **ˈsic sth on sb** (NAmE, informal) to tell a dog to attack sb

**sick** ⓘ A1 /sɪk/ adj., noun, verb
■ adj.
• ILL **1** ⓘ A1 physically or mentally ill: *a sick child* ◊ *Peter has been off sick* (= away from work because he is ill) *for two weeks.* ◊ *Emma has just called in sick* (= phoned to say she will not be coming to work because she is ill). ◊ (BrE) *Britain's workers went sick* (= did not go to work because they were ill) *for a record number of days last year.* ◊ (NAmE) *I can't afford to get sick* (= become ill). ◊ *They became sick after eating contaminated food.*
• WANTING TO VOMIT **2** ⓘ A1 [not usually before noun] feeling that you want to VOMIT: *Mum, I feel sick!* ◊ *If you eat any more cake you'll make yourself sick.* ◊ *a sick feeling in your stomach*
• -SICK **3** (in compounds) feeling sick as a result of travelling on a ship, plane, etc: *seasick* ◊ *airsick* ◊ *carsick* ◊ *travel-sick*
• BORED **4** ⓘ B2 (informal) bored with or annoyed about sth that has been happening for a long time, and wanting it to stop: *~of sb/sth I'm sick of the way you've treated me.* ◊ *I'm sick and tired of your moaning.* ◊ *I'm sick to death of all of you!* ◊ *~of (sb) doing sth We're sick of waiting around like this.*
• CRUEL/STRANGE **5** (informal) (especially of humour) dealing with physical or mental pain, disease or death in a cruel way that some people think is offensive: *a sick joke* ◊ *That's really sick.* **6** (informal) getting pleasure from doing strange or cruel things: *a sick mind* ◊ *People think I'm sick for having a rat as a pet.* ◊ *We live in a sick society.*
• GOOD **7** (slang) very good, a lot of fun, etc: *I love that song—it's sick!* ⊃ see also HOMESICK, LOVESICK
IDM **be ˈsick** (especially BrE) to bring food from your stomach back out through your mouth SYN **vomit**: *I was sick three times in the night.* ◊ *She had been violently sick.* **be worried ˈsick; be ˈsick with worry** to be extremely worried: *Where have you been? I've been worried sick about you.* **fall ˈsick** (also old-fashioned **take ˈsick**) (formal) to become sick **make sb ˈsick** to make sb angry or full of horror: *His hypocrisy makes me sick.* **(as) sick as a ˈdog** (informal) feeling very sick; VOMITING a lot **(as) sick as a ˈparrot** (BrE, humorous) very disappointed **sick at ˈheart** (formal) very unhappy or disappointed **sick to your ˈstomach 1** feeling very angry or worried: *Nora turned sick to her stomach on hearing this news.* **2** feeling that you want to VOMIT
■ noun
• VOMIT **1** [U] (BrE, informal) food that you bring back up from your stomach through your mouth SYN **vomit**
• ILL PEOPLE **2 the sick** [pl.] people who are sick: *All the sick and wounded were evacuated.*
■ verb
PHRV **ˌsick sth↔ˈup** (BrE, informal) to bring sth up from the stomach back out through your mouth SYN **vomit**

**ˈsick bag** noun a paper bag on a boat or plane into which you can VOMIT

**ˈsick·bay** /ˈsɪkbeɪ/ noun a room or rooms, for example on a ship or in a school, with beds for people who are ill

**ˈsick·bed** /ˈsɪkbed/ noun [sing.] the bed on which a person who is ill is lying: *The president left his sickbed to attend the ceremony.*

**ˈsick day** noun a day on which an employee is away from work because of illness, but still receives pay

**sick·en** /ˈsɪkən/ verb (BrE) **1** [T] *~sb* to make sb feel very shocked and angry SYN **disgust**, **nauseate 2** [I] to become ill: (old-fashioned) *The baby sickened and died before his first birthday.* ◊ (BrE) *Faye hasn't eaten all day—she must be sickening for something.*

**sick·en·ing** /ˈsɪkənɪŋ/ adj. **1** making you feel shocked or full of horror SYN **nauseating**, **repulsive**: *the sickening stench of burnt flesh* **2** [usually before noun] making you afraid that sb has been badly hurt or that sth has been broken: *Her head hit the ground with a sickening thud.* **3** (informal) making you feel JEALOUS or annoyed because you wish you had sth that sb else has: *'She's off to the Bahamas for a month.' 'How sickening!'* ▶ **sick·en·ing·ly** adv.

**sickie** /ˈsɪki/ noun (BrE, informal) a day when you say that you are ill and cannot go to work when it is not really true: *to pull/throw/chuck a sickie*

**sickle** /ˈsɪkl/ noun a tool with a curved BLADE (= cutting edge) and a short handle, used for cutting grass, etc.
⊃ see also HAMMER AND SICKLE

**'sick leave** *noun* [U] permission to be away from work because of illness; the period of time spent away from work: *on ~ to be on sick leave*

**ˌsickle cell aˈnaemia** (*BrE*) (*NAmE* **ˌsickle cell aˈnemia**) (*also* **ˈsickle cell disease**) *noun* [U] a serious form of ANAEMIA (= a disease of the blood) that is found mostly in people of African family origins, and which is passed down from parents to children

**sick·ly** /ˈsɪkli/ *adj.* (**sick·lier**, **ˌsick·li·est**) **1** often ill: *He was a sickly child.* **2** not looking healthy and strong SYN **frail**: *She looked pale and sickly.* ◊ *sickly plants* **3** that makes you feel sick, especially because it is too sweet or full of false emotion: *a sickly sweet smell* ◊ *She gave me a sickly smile.* **4** (of colours) unpleasant to look at: *a sickly green colour*

**sick·ness** /ˈsɪknəs/ *noun* **1** [U] illness; bad health: *She's been off work because of sickness.* ◊ *insurance against sickness and unemployment* ⇒ SYNONYMS at ILLNESS **2** [U, C, usually sing.] a particular type of illness or disease: *travel/radiation sickness* ⇒ *see also* ALTITUDE SICKNESS, DECOMPRESSION SICKNESS, MOTION SICKNESS, SLEEPING SICKNESS **3** [U] (*especially BrE*) the feeling that you are likely to VOMIT (= bring food back up from the stomach to the mouth); the fact of VOMITING SYN **nausea**: *symptoms include sickness and diarrhoea* ◊ *The sickness passed off after a while.* ⇒ *see also* MORNING SICKNESS **4** [sing.] a feeling of being very sad, disappointed or full of horror

**ˈsickness benefit** *noun* [U] (*BrE*) money paid by the government to people who are away from work because of illness ⇒ *compare* SICK PAY

**sicko** /ˈsɪkəʊ/ *noun* (*pl.* **-os**) (*informal, especially NAmE*) a person who gets pleasure from doing strange and cruel things: *child molesters and other sickos*

**ˈsick pay** *noun* [U] pay given to an employee who is away from work because of illness ⇒ *compare* SICKNESS BENEFIT

**sick·room** /ˈsɪkruːm, -rʊm/ *noun* a room in which a person who is ill is lying in bed

**side** 🛈 A2 /saɪd/ *noun*, *verb*
■ **noun**
- **LEFT/RIGHT 1** A2 [C, usually sing.] either of the two halves of a surface, an object or an area that is divided by an imaginary central line: *the right side of the brain* ◊ *satellite links to the other side of the world* ◊ *on the ... ~ (of sth) They drive on the left-hand side of the road in Japan.* ◊ *She was on the far side of the room.* ◊ *They crossed from one side of London to the other.* ◊ *Keep on your side of the bed!* **2** A2 [C, usually sing.] a position or an area to the left or right of sth: *He crossed the bridge to the other side of the river.* ◊ *on a/the ~ (of sth) There is a large window on either side of the front door.* ◊ *people on both sides of the Atlantic* ◊ *She saw James standing on the other side of the fence.* ◊ *She tilted her head to one side.*
- **NOT TOP OR BOTTOM 3** A2 [C] one of the flat surfaces of sth that is not the top or bottom, front or back: *on the ~ (of sth) Write your name on the side of the box.* ◊ *There's a scratch on the side of my car.* ◊ *Now lay the jar on its side.* ◊ *at the ~ (of sth) The kitchen door is at the side of the house.* ◊ *a side door/window/panel* **4** A2 [C] the VERTICAL or sloping surface around sth, but not the top or bottom of it: *A path went up the side of the hill.* ◊ *We could see sheep grazing on the side of the mountain.* ⇒ *see also* HILLSIDE, MOUNTAINSIDE
- **EDGE 5** A2 [C] a part near the edge of sth; an area just beyond the edge of sth: *The stream flows into the south side of the lake.* ◊ *on the ~ of sth She sat on the side of the bed.* ◊ *at the ~ of sth A van was parked at the side of the road.* ⇒ *see also* BEDSIDE, FIRESIDE, RINGSIDE, RIVERSIDE, ROADSIDE, SEASIDE
- **OF BODY 6** A2 [C, usually sing.] either the right or left part of a person's body, from the ARMPIT (= where the arm joins the body) to the HIP (= where the leg joins the body): *I've got a stitch in my side* (= a sudden pain from running or laughing). ◊ *on your ~ He was lying on his side.*
- **OF STH FLAT AND THIN 7** A2 [C] either of two surfaces of sth flat and thin, such as paper or cloth: *The upper side of the leaf was a much darker green.* ◊ *on a/the ~ (of sth) Write on one side of the paper only.* ⇒ *see also* A-SIDE, B-SIDE
- **PAGE 8** [C] the amount of writing needed to fill one side of a sheet of paper: *He told us not to write more than three sides.*
- **MATHEMATICS 9** A2 [C] any of the flat surfaces of a solid object: *A cube has six sides.* **10** A2 [C] any of the lines that form a flat shape such as a square or TRIANGLE: *a shape with five sides* ◊ *The farm buildings form three sides of a square.* ⇒ *picture at* POLYGON
- **-SIDED 11** used in adjectives to state the number or type of sides: *a six-sided object* ◊ *a glass-sided container*
- **NEAR TO SB/STH 12** B1 [sing.] a place or position very near to sb/sth: *at/by sb's/sth's ~ Her husband stood at her side.* ◊ *She was glad to have him by her side.*
- **IN WAR/ARGUMENT 13** B2 [C] one of the two or more people or groups taking part in an argument, war, etc: *Both sides agreed to restore diplomatic relations.* ◊ *At some point during the war he seems to have changed sides.* ◊ *on the ... ~ to be on the winning/losing side* **14** B2 [C] one of the opinions, attitudes, or positions held by sb in an argument, a business arrangement, etc: *We heard both sides of the argument.* ◊ *I just want you to hear my side of the story first.* ◊ *One side of the debate is articulated best by France and Germany.*
- **ASPECT 15** B2 [C] a particular aspect of sth, especially a situation or a person's character: *These poems reveal her gentle side.* ◊ *It's interesting to see another side of a story that is so well known.* ◊ *It's good you can see the funny side of the situation.* ◊ *I'll take care of that side of things.* ⇒ *see also* FLIP SIDE, SUNNY SIDE
- **FEELING THAT YOU ARE BETTER 16** [U] (*especially in negative sentences*) (*BrE, informal*) a feeling that you are better than other people: *There was no side to him at all.*
- **SPORTS TEAM 17** [C] a sports team: *The French have a very strong side.* ◊ *We were on the winning/losing side.* ◊ *the home side*
- **OF FAMILY 18** [C] the part of your family that people belong to who are related either to your mother or to your father: *a cousin on my father's side* (= a child of my father's brother or sister)
- **FOOD 19** [C] (*NAmE, informal*) = SIDE DISH: *Your dinner comes with a choice of two sides.*
- **MEAT 20** [C] **a ~ of beef/bacon**, etc. one of the two halves of an animal that has been killed for meat
- **TV CHANNEL 21** [C] (*old-fashioned, BrE, informal*) a television channel: *What's on the other side?*

IDM **be on sb's side** to support and agree with sb: *I'm definitely on your side in this.* ◊ *Whose side are you on anyway?* **come down on ˈone side of the fence or the ˈother** to choose between two possible choices **from ˈside to ˈside** moving to the left and then to the right and then back again: *He shook his head slowly from side to side.* ◊ *The ship rolled from side to side.* **get on the right/wrong ˈside of sb** to make sb pleased with you/annoyed with you **have sth on your ˈside** to have sth as an advantage that will make it more likely that you will achieve sth **let the ˈside down** (*especially BrE*) to fail to give your friends, family, etc. the help and support they expect, or to behave in a way that makes them disappointed **not leave sb's ˈside** to stay with sb, especially in order to take care of them **on/from all ˈsides | on/from every ˈside** in or from all directions; everywhere: *We realized we were surrounded on all sides.* ◊ *Disaster threatens on every side.* **on the ˈbig, ˈsmall, ˈhigh, etc. side** (*informal*) slightly too big, small, high, etc: *These shoes are a little on the tight side.* **on/to one ˈside 1** out of your way: *I left my bags on one side.* **2** to be dealt with later: *I put his complaint to one side until I had more time.* ◊ *Leaving that to one side for a moment, are there any other questions?* **on the ˈright/ˈwrong side of ˈ40, ˈ50, etc.** (*informal*) younger or older than 40, 50, etc. years of age **on the ˈside** (*informal*) **1** in addition to your main job: *a mechanic who buys and sells cars on the side* **2** secretly or illegally: *He's married but he has a girlfriend on the side.* **3** (*especially NAmE*) (of food in a restaurant) served at the same time as the main part of the meal, but on a separate plate **the other side of the ˈcoin** the aspect of a situation that is the opposite of or contrasts with the one you have been talking about **side by side 1** close together and facing in the same direction: *There were two children ahead, walking side by side.* **2** together, without any difficulties: *We have been using both systems, side by side, for two years.* ◇ *The two communities exist happily side by side.* **side of the 'fence** (*NAmE also* **side of the 'aisle**) used to refer to either of two opposite opinions on an issue: *The two countries are often on opposite sides of the fence when it comes to climate change.* ◇ *There are arguments on both sides of the aisle.* **take 'sides** to express support for sb in an argument: *She didn't think it was wise to take sides in their argument.* **take/draw sb to one 'side** to speak to sb in private, especially in order to warn or tell them about sth **this side of ...** before a particular time, event, age, etc: *They aren't likely to arrive this side of midnight.* ⊃ more at BED *n*., BIT, BRIGHT *adj*., CREDIT *n*., ERR, GRASS *n*., KNOW *v*., LAUGH *v*., RIGHT *adj*., SAFE *adj*., SPLIT *v*., THORN, TIME *n*., TWO, WRONG *adj*.

■ *verb*

**PHRV** **'side with sb (against sb/sth)** to support one person or group in an argument against sb else: *The kids always sided with their mother against me.*

**side·bar** /'saɪdbɑː(r)/ *noun* **1** a short article in a newspaper or magazine that is printed next to a main article, and gives extra information **2** a narrow area on the side of a computer screen or a WEB PAGE that is separate from the main part of the page **3** (*especially NAmE*) an issue, event, action, etc. that is less important than the main one: *The promoter explained free concerts as a sidebar to the festival.* **4** (*also* **sidebar 'conference**) (*US*) (in a court of law) a discussion between the judge and the lawyers that the JURY cannot hear

**side·board** /'saɪdbɔːd; *NAmE* -bɔːrd/ *noun* **1** (*NAmE also* **buf·fet**) a piece of furniture in a DINING ROOM for putting food on before it is served, with DRAWERS in it for storing knives, forks, etc. **2** (*BrE*) [*usually pl.*] = SIDEBURN

**side·burn** /'saɪdbɜːn; *NAmE* -bɜːrn/ (*BrE also* **side·board**) *noun* [*usually pl.*] hair that grows down the sides of a man's face in front of his ears

**side·car** /'saɪdkɑː(r)/ *noun* a small vehicle attached to the side of a motorcycle in which a passenger can ride

**'side dish** (*NAmE*, *informal* **side**) *noun* a small amount of food, for example a salad, served with the main course of a meal **SYN** **side order**

**'side effect** *noun* [*usually pl.*] **1** an extra and usually bad effect that a drug has on you, as well as curing illness or pain **2** an unexpected result of a situation or course of action that happens as well as the result you were aiming for

**'side-foot** *verb* ~ **sth** to kick a ball with the inside part of your foot

**'side issue** *noun* an issue that is less important than the main issue, and may take attention away from it

**'side-kick** /'saɪdkɪk/ *noun* (*informal*) a person who helps another more important or more intelligent person: *Batman and his young sidekick Robin*

**side·light** /'saɪdlaɪt/ *noun* **1** ~ **(on sb/sth)** a piece of information, usually given by accident or in connection with another subject, that helps you to understand sb/sth **2** (*BrE*) either of a pair of small lights at the front of a vehicle

**side·line** /'saɪdlaɪn/ *noun*, *verb*

■ *noun* **1** [C] an activity that you do as well as your main job in order to earn extra money **2** **sidelines** [*pl.*] the lines along the two long sides of a sports field, tennis COURT, etc. that mark the outer edges; the area just outside these: *The coach stood on the sidelines yelling instructions to the players.* **IDM** **on/from the 'sidelines** watching sth but not actually involved in it: *He was content to watch from the sidelines as his wife built up a successful business empire.*

■ *verb* [*usually passive*] **1** to prevent sb from playing in a team, especially because of an injury: **be sidelined (by sth)** *The player has been sidelined by a knee injury.* **2** to prevent sb from having an important part in sth that other

1445 **sidewinder**

people are doing: **be sidelined (by sb/sth)** *The vice-president is increasingly being sidelined.*

**side·long** /'saɪdlɒŋ; *NAmE* -lɔːŋ/ *adj.* [only before noun] (of a look) out of the corner of your eye, especially in a way that is secret or shows that you do not approve of sb/sth: *She cast a sidelong glance at Eric to see if he had noticed her blunder.* ▶ **side·long** *adv.*: *She looked sidelong at him.*

**'side note** *noun* a spoken or written comment that provides additional, but not essential, information to the subject that is being discussed **SYN** **aside**: *An interesting side note is that covers of the song also became big hits online.*

**side-'on** *adv.* (*BrE*) coming from the side rather than from the front or back: *The car hit us side-on.*

**'side order** *noun* a small amount of food ordered in a restaurant to go with the main dish, but served separately **SYN** **side dish**: *a side order of fries*

**'side plate** *noun* a small plate used for bread or other food that goes with a meal

**sid·er·eal** /saɪ'dɪəriəl; *NAmE* -'dɪr-/ *adj.* (*astronomy*) related to the stars that are far away, not the sun or planets

**'side road** *noun* a smaller and less important road leading off a main road

**'side-saddle** *adv.* if you ride a horse **side-saddle**, you ride with both your legs on the same side of the horse

**'side salad** *noun* a salad served with the main course of a meal

**side·show** /'saɪdʃəʊ/ *noun* **1** a separate small show or attraction at a FAIR or CIRCUS where you pay to see a performance or take part in a game **2** an activity or event that is much less important than the main activity or event

**'side-splitting** *adj.* (*informal*) extremely funny; making people laugh a lot: *side-splitting anecdotes* ▶ **'side-splittingly** *adv.*: *side-splittingly funny*

**'side-step** /'saɪdstep/ *verb* (**-pp-**) **1** [T] ~ **sth** to avoid answering a question or dealing with a problem: *Did you notice how she neatly sidestepped the question?* **2** [T, I] ~ **(sth)** to avoid sth, for example being hit, by stepping to one side: *He cleverly sidestepped the tackle.*

**'side street** *noun* a less important street leading off a road in a town

**side·swipe** /'saɪdswaɪp/ *noun* **1** (*NAmE*) a hit from the side: *a sideswipe by a truck* **2** ~ **(at sb/sth)** (*informal*) a critical comment made about sb/sth while you are talking about sb/sth completely different: *it was a good speech, but he couldn't resist taking a sideswipe at his opponent.* ▶ **side·swipe** *verb* ~ **sb/sth** (*NAmE*): *The bus sideswiped two parked cars.*

**'side·track** /'saɪdtræk/ *verb* [*usually passive*] ~ **sb (into doing sth)** to make sb start to talk about or do sth that is different from the main thing that they are supposed to be talking about or doing **SYN** **distract**: *I was supposed to be writing a letter but I'm afraid I got sidetracked.*

**'side view** *noun* a view of sth from the side: *The picture shows a side view of the house.*

**side·walk** /'saɪdwɔːk/ (*NAmE*) (*BrE* **pave·ment**) *noun* a flat part at the side of a road for people to walk on

**'sidewalk artist** (*NAmE*) (*BrE* **pavement artist**) *noun* an artist who draws pictures in CHALK on the SIDEWALK, hoping to get money from people who pass

**side·ways** /'saɪdweɪz/ *adv.* **1** to, towards or from the side: *He looked sideways at her.* ◇ *The truck skidded sideways across the road.* ◇ (*figurative*) *He has been moved sideways* (= moved to another job at the same level as before, not higher or lower). **2** with one side facing forwards: *She sat sideways on the chair.* ▶ **side·ways** *adj.*: *She slid him a sideways glance.* ◇ *a sideways move* **IDM** see KNOCK *v*.

**side·wind·er** /'saɪdwaɪndə(r)/ *noun* a poisonous North American snake that moves sideways across the desert by throwing its body in an S shape

# siding

**sid·ing** /ˈsaɪdɪŋ/ noun **1** [C] a short track next to a main railway line, where trains can stand when they are not being used **2** [U] (NAmE) material used to cover and protect the outside walls of buildings

**sidle** /ˈsaɪdl/ verb [I] **+ adv./prep.** to walk somewhere in a shy or uncertain way, as if you do not want to be noticed: *She sidled up to me and whispered something in my ear.*

**SIDS** /sɪdz, ˌes aɪ diː ˈes/ noun [U] the sudden death while sleeping of a baby that appears to be healthy (the abbreviation for 'sudden infant death syndrome') **SYN** **cot death**

**siege** /siːdʒ/ noun **1** a military operation in which an army tries to capture a town by surrounding it and stopping the supply of food, etc. to the people inside: *the siege of Troy ⋄ The siege was finally lifted (= ended) after six months. ⋄ The police placed the city centre under a virtual **state of siege** (= it was hard to get in or out).* **2** a situation in which the police surround a building where people are living or hiding, in order to make them come out ⊃ see also BESIEGE **IDM** **lay ˈsiege to sth 1** to begin a siege of a town, building, etc. **2** to surround a building, especially in order to speak to or question the person or people living or working there **under ˈsiege 1** surrounded by an army or the police in a siege **2** being criticized all the time or put under pressure by problems, questions, etc.

**ˈsiege mentality** noun [sing., U] a feeling that you are surrounded by enemies and must protect yourself

**si·enna** /siˈenə/ noun [U] a type of dark yellow or red CLAY used for giving colour to paints, etc.; a dark yellow or red colour

**si·erra** /siˈerə/ noun (especially in place names) a long range of steep mountains with sharp points, especially in Spain and America: *the Sierra Nevada*

**si·esta** /siˈestə/ noun a rest or sleep taken in the early afternoon, especially in hot countries: *to have/take a siesta* ⊃ compare NAP

**sieve** /sɪv/ noun, verb
■ noun a tool for separating solids from liquids or larger solids from smaller solids, made of a wire or plastic net attached to a ring. The liquid or small pieces pass through the net but the larger pieces do not.
**IDM** **have a memory/mind like a ˈsieve** (informal) to have a very bad memory; to forget things easily
■ verb ~ sth to put sth through a sieve

**sift** /sɪft/ verb **1** [T] ~ sth to put flour or some other fine substance through a SIEVE/SIFTER: *Sift the flour into a bowl.* **2** [T, I] to examine sth very carefully in order to decide what is important or useful or to find sth important: ~ sth *We will sift every scrap of evidence.* ⋄ ~ **through sth** *Crash investigators have been sifting through the wreckage of the aircraft.* **3** [T] ~ sth (out) from sth to separate sth from a group of things: *She looked quickly through the papers, sifting out from the pile anything that looked interesting.*
**PHRV** **ˌsift sth↔ˈout 1** to remove sth that you do not want from a substance by putting it through a SIEVE: *Put the flour through a sieve to sift out the lumps.* **2** to separate sth, usually sth that you do not want, from a group of things: *We need to sift out the applications that have no chance of succeeding.*

**sift·er** /ˈsɪftə(r)/ noun **1** (NAmE) a small SIEVE used for sifting flour **2** a container with a lot of small holes in the top, used for shaking flour or sugar onto things: *a sugar sifter*

**sigh** /saɪ/ verb, noun
■ verb **1** [I] to take and then let out a long deep breath that can be heard, to show that you are disappointed, sad, tired, etc: *He sighed deeply at the thought.* ⋄ ~ **with sth** *She sighed with relief that it was all over.* **2** [T] **+ speech** to say sth with a sigh: *'Oh well, better luck next time,' she sighed.* **3** [I] (literary) (especially of the wind) to make a sound like a sigh
■ noun an act or the sound of sighing: *to give/heave/let out a sigh ⋄ a deep sigh ⋄ 'I'll wait,' he said with a sigh. ⋄ We all breathed a sigh of relief when it was over.*

---

**sight** /saɪt/ noun, verb
■ noun
• ABILITY TO SEE **1** [U] the ability to see **SYN** **eyesight**: *to lose your sight (= to become blind) ⋄ She has very good sight. ⋄ The disease has affected her sight. ⋄ He has very little sight in his right eye.*
• ACT OF SEEING **2** [U] the act of seeing sb/sth: ~ **of sb/sth (doing sth)** *She kept sight of him in her mirror. ⋄ She caught sight of a car in the distance. ⋄ **at the ~ (of sb/sth)** I have been known to faint at the sight of blood. ⋄ **on ~** The soldiers were given orders to shoot on sight (= as soon as they saw sb).*
• HOW FAR YOU CAN SEE **3** [U] the area or distance within which sb can see or sth can be seen: **in ~** *There was no one in sight. ⋄ The end is in sight (= will happen soon). ⋄ **in ~ of sb/sth** At last we came in sight of a few houses. ⋄ **within ~** They marched on and by the following afternoon the enemy was within sight. ⋄ **within ~ of sb/sth** *He sprinted ahead as they came within sight of the finishing line.* ⋄ **out of ~** Leave any valuables in your car out of sight. ⋄ Keep out of sight (= stay where you cannot be seen). ⋄ **out of sb's ~** She never lets her daughter out of her sight (= always keeps her where she can see her). ⋄ **Get out of my sight!** (= Go away!) ⋄ The boat disappeared from sight.* ⊃ see also LINE OF SIGHT, SHORT SIGHT
• WHAT YOU CAN SEE **4** [C] a thing that you see or can see: *Roadside stalls are a **common sight** in the city. ⋄ The museum attempts to recreate the **sights and sounds** of wartime Britain. ⋄ He was a sorry sight, soaked to the skin and shivering. ⋄ The bird is now a **rare sight** in this country.* ⊃ SYNONYMS at VIEW
• INTERESTING PLACES **5** **sights** [pl.] the interesting places, especially in a town or city, that are often visited by tourists: *We're going to Paris for the weekend to **see the sights**.*

▼ SYNONYMS

**sight**
**view** • **vision**

These are all words for the area or distance that you can see from a particular position.

**sight** the area or distance that you can see from a particular position: *He looked up the street, but there was no one in sight. ⋄ Leave any valuables in your car out of sight.*

**view** (rather formal) the area or distance that you can see from a particular position: *The lake soon came into view.*

**vision** the area that you can see from a particular position: *The couple moved outside her field of vision (= total area you can see from a particular position).*

SIGHT, VIEW OR VISION?
• **View** is more literary than **sight** or **vision**. It is the only word for talking about how well you can see: *I didn't have a good sight/vision of the stage.* **Vision** must always be used with a possessive pronoun: *my/his/her, etc. (field of) vision.* It is not used with the prepositions *in*, *into* and *out of* that are very frequent with **sight** and **view**: *There was nobody in vision. ⋄ A tall figure came into vision.*

PATTERNS
• in/out of sight/view
• in/within sight/view of sth
• to come into/disappear from sight/view/sb's vision
• to come in sight/view of sb/sth
• to block sb's view/vision
• sb's line of sight/vision
• sb's field of view/vision

▼ HOMOPHONES

**sight** • **site** /saɪt/
• **sight** noun: *She would never forget the sight of Machu Picchu appearing out of the mist.*
• **site** noun: *Follow this link to reach the official site.*
• **site** verb: *The French government had plans to site a third major airport for Paris at Chaulnes.*

- **SILLY/UNTIDY PERSON 6 a sight** [sing.] (*informal, especially BrE*) a person or thing that looks silly, untidy, unpleasant, etc: *She looks a sight in that hat!*
- **ON GUN/TELESCOPE 7** [C, usually pl.] a device that you look through to aim a gun, etc. or to look at sth through a TELESCOPE, etc: *He had the deer in his sights now.* ◇ (*figurative*) *Even as a young actress, she always had Hollywood firmly in her sights* (= as her final goal). ⊃ see also SECOND SIGHT

**IDM** **at first ˈsight 1** when you first begin to consider sth: *At first sight, it may look like a generous offer, but always read the small print.* **2** when you see sb/sth for the first time: *It was love at first sight* (= we fell in love the first time we saw each other). **hate, be sick of, etc. the ˈsight of sb/sth** (*informal*) to hate, etc. sb/sth very much: *I can't stand the sight of him!* **in the sight of sb/in sb's sight** (*formal*) in sb's opinion: *We are all equal in the sight of God.* **lose ˈsight of sb/sth 1** to become no longer able to see sb/sth: *They finally lost sight of land.* **2** to stop considering sth; to forget sth: *We must not lose sight of our original aim.* **out of ˈsight, out of ˈmind** (*saying*) used to say sb will quickly be forgotten when they are no longer with you **raise/lower your ˈsights** to expect more/less from a situation **set your sights on sth/on doing sth** to decide that you want sth and to try very hard to get it: *She's set her sights on getting into Harvard.* **a (damn, etc.) sight better, etc.** | **a (damn, etc.) sight too good, etc.** (*informal*) very much better; much too good, etc: *She's done a damn sight better than I have.* ◇ *It's worth a damn sight more than I thought.* **a ˈsight for sore ˈeyes** (*informal*) a person or thing that you are pleased to see; something that is very pleasant to look at **sight unˈseen** if you buy sth **sight unseen**, you do not have an opportunity to see it before you buy it ⊃ more at HEAVE v., KNOW v., NOWHERE, PRETTY *adj*.

■ **verb** ~ **sth** (*formal*) to suddenly see sth, especially sth you have been looking for: *After twelve days at sea, they sighted land.*

**sight·ed** /ˈsaɪtɪd/ *adj.* **1** able to see; not blind: *the blind parents of sighted children* **2 -sighted** (in compounds) able to see in the way mentioned: *partially sighted* ◇ *short-sighted* ◇ *long-sighted*

**sight·ing** /ˈsaɪtɪŋ/ *noun* an occasion when sb sees sb/sth, especially sth unusual or sth that lasts for only a short time: *a reported sighting of the Loch Ness monster*

**sight·less** /ˈsaɪtləs/ *adj.* (*literary*) unable to see SYN **blind**: *The statue stared down at them with sightless eyes.*

**ˈsight-line** *noun* = LINE OF SIGHT

**ˈsight-read** /ˈsaɪt riːd/ *verb* [I, T] ~ **(sth)** to play or sing written music when you see it for the first time, without practising it first ▶ **ˈsight-reader** *noun* **ˈsight-reading** *noun* [U]

**sight·see·ing** /ˈsaɪtsiːɪŋ/ *noun* [U] the activity of visiting interesting buildings and places as a tourist: *to go sightseeing* ◇ *Did you have a chance to do any sightseeing?* ◇ *a sightseeing tour of the city* ⊃ WORDFINDER NOTE at TOURIST ▶ **ˈsight-see** *verb* [I] (only used in the progressive tenses) **ˈsight-seer** *noun* SYN **tourist**: *Oxford attracts large numbers of sightseers.*

**sigma** /ˈsɪɡmə/ *noun* the 18th letter of the Greek alphabet (Σ, σ)

## sign 🔊 A2 S /saɪn/ *noun, verb*

■ **noun**
- **SHOWING STH 1** 🔊 A2 [C, U] an event, an action, a fact, etc. that shows that sth exists, is happening or may happen in the future SYN **indication**: *a clear/visible sign* ◇ *an encouraging sign* ◇ *The fact that he didn't say 'no' immediately is a good sign.* ◇ *If I had noticed the warning signs, none of this would have happened.* ◇ *~ of sb/sth This move will be seen as a sign of weakness.* ◇ *Bankers say they can definitely detect signs of a recovery.* ◇ *There was no sign of life in the house* (= there seemed to be nobody there). ◇ *~ of (sb/sth) doing sth The gloomy weather shows no sign of improving.* ◇ *~ (that) … If an interview is too easy, it's a sure sign that you haven't got the job.*
- **FOR INFORMATION/WARNING 2** 🔊 B1 [C] a piece of paper, wood or metal that has writing or a picture on it that gives you information, instructions, a warning, etc: *to put up/*

1447 **sign**

*post a sign* ◇ *a street/stop sign* ◇ *The sign on the wall said 'Now wash your hands'.* ◇ *Follow the signs for the city centre.* ⊃ picture at IDEOGRAM ⊃ see also LAWN SIGN, ROAD SIGN
- **MOVEMENT/SOUND 3** 🔊 B1 [C] a movement or sound that you make to tell sb sth: *He gave a thumbs-up sign* (= to show approval/agreement). ◇ **as a ~ of sth** *He gave a slight bow as a sign of respect.* ⊃ see also V-SIGN
- **SYMBOL 4** 🔊 B1 [C] a mark used to represent sth, especially in mathematics: *a plus/minus sign (+/−)* ◇ *a dollar/pound sign ($/£)* ◇ **~ for sth** *the sign for 'square root'* ⊃ see also CALL SIGN, EQUALS SIGN, POUND SIGN
- **STAR SIGN 5** [C] (*informal*) = STAR SIGN: *What sign are you?*

**IDM** **a ˌsign of the ˈtimes** something that you feel shows what things are like now, especially how bad they are

▼ **SYNONYMS**

**sign**

indication • symptom • symbol • indicator • signal

These are all words for an event, an action or a fact that shows that sth exists, is happening or may happen in the future.

**sign** an event, an action or a fact that shows that sth exists, is happening or may happen in the future: *Headaches may be a sign of stress.*

**indication** (*rather formal*) a remark or sign that shows that sth is happening or what sb is thinking or feeling: *They gave no indication as to how the work should be done.*

**SIGN OR INDICATION?**

An **indication** often comes in the form of sth that sb says; a **sign** is usually sth that happens or sth that sb does.

**symptom** a change in your body or mind that shows that you are not healthy; a sign that sth exists, especially sth bad: *Symptoms include a sore throat.* ◇ *The rise in inflation was just one symptom of the poor state of the economy.*

**symbol** a person, an object or an event that represents a more general quality or situation: *The dove is a universal symbol of peace.*

**indicator** (*rather formal*) a sign that shows you what sth is like or how a situation is changing: *the economic indicators*

**signal** an event, an action or a fact that shows that sth exists, is happening or may happen in the future: *Chest pains can be a warning signal of heart problems.*

**SIGN OR SIGNAL?**

- **Signal** is often used to talk about an event, action or fact that suggests to sb that they should do sth. **Sign** is not usually used in this way: *Reducing prison sentences would send the wrong signs to criminals.*

**PATTERNS**

- a(n) sign/indication/symptom/symbol/indicator/signal **of** sth
- a(n) sign/indication/symptom/indicator/signal **that …**
- a **clear** sign/indication/symptom/symbol/indicator/signal
- an **obvious** sign/indication/symptom/symbol/indicator
- an **early** sign/indication/symptom/indicator/signal
- an **outward** sign/indication/symbol
- to **give** a(n) sign/indication/signal

■ **verb**
- **YOUR NAME 1** 🔊 B1 [I, T] to write your name on a document, letter, etc. to show that you have written it, that you agree with what it says, or that it is real: *Sign here, please.* ◇ **~ sth** *to sign an agreement/a deal/a contract* ◇ *to sign a document/statement/declaration/form* ◇ *Sign your name here, please.* ◇ *You haven't signed the letter.* ◇ *The treaty was signed on 24 March.* ◇ **~ yourself + noun** *He signed himself 'Jimmy'.*
- **CONTRACT 2** [T, I] to arrange for sb, for example a sports player or musician, to sign a contract agreeing to work for your company; to sign a contract agreeing to work for a company: **~ sb** *United have just signed a new goalie.* ◇ *to*

# signage

*sign a player* ◊ *~for sth He signed for United yesterday.* ◊ *~with sth The band signed with Virgin Records.* ◊ *~(sb) to sth She was the first musician signed to the new record label.*
- **MAKE MOVEMENT/SOUND** **3** [I, T] **~ (to / for sb) (to do sth)** | *~ that* … to make a request or tell sb to do sth by using a sign, especially a hand movement **SYN** **signal**: *The hotel manager signed to the porter to pick up my case.*
- **FOR DEAF PERSON** **4** [I, T] to use sign language to communicate with sb: *She learnt to sign to help her deaf child.* ◊ *~ sth An increasing number of plays are now being signed.*
▶ **sign·er** *noun*: *the signers of the petition* ◊ *signers communicating information to deaf people*

**IDM** **signed and 'sealed** | **signed, sealed and de'livered** definite, because all the legal documents have been signed **sign on the dotted 'line** (*informal*) to sign a document to show that you have agreed to buy sth or do sth: *Just sign on the dotted line and the car is yours.* ⊃ more at **PLEDGE** *n*. **PHR V** **sign sth↔a'way** to lose your rights or property by signing a document **sign for sth** to sign a document to show that you have received sth **sign 'in/'out** | **sign sb↔'in/'out** to write your/sb's name when you arrive at or leave an office, a club, etc: *All visitors must sign in on arrival.* ◊ *You must sign guests out when they leave the club.* **sign 'off** **1** (*BrE*) to end a letter: *She signed off with 'Yours, Janet'.* **2** to end a broadcast by saying goodbye or playing a piece of music **sign sth↔'off** to give your formal approval to sth, by signing your name **sign 'off on sth** (*NAmE, informal*) to express your approval of sth formally and definitely: *The president hasn't signed off on this report.* **sign 'on** (*BrE, informal*) to sign a form stating that you are an unemployed person so that you can receive payment from the government **sign 'on/'up** | **sign sb↔'on/'up** to sign a form or contract which says that you agree to do a job or become a soldier; to persuade sb to sign a form or contract like this **SYN** **enlist**: *He signed on for five years in the army.* ◊ *The company has signed up three top models for the fashion show.* **sign sth↔'over (to sb)** to give your rights or property to sb else by signing a document: *She has signed the house over to her daughter.* **sign 'up (for sth)** to arrange to do a course of study by adding your name to the list of people doing it **sign 'up to sth** **1** (*BrE*) to commit yourself to a project or course of action, especially one that you have agreed with a group of other people, countries or organizations: *How many countries have signed up to the Paris agreement on climate change?* **2** **sign up to do sth** to agree to take part in sth: *We have about 100 people signed up to help so far.*

**sign·age** /ˈsaɪnɪdʒ/ *noun* [U] (*formal*) signs, especially ones that give instructions or directions to the public

## sig·nal ❶ B1 /ˈsɪɡnəl/ *noun, verb, adj.*

■ *noun* **1** B1 a movement or sound that you make to give sb information, instructions, a warning, etc. **SYN** **sign**: *a danger/warning/distress signal* ◊ *~ (for sb) to do sth The siren was a signal for everyone to leave the building.* ◊ *When I give the signal, run!* ◊ (*NAmE*) *All I get is a busy signal when I dial his number* (= his phone is being used). ◊ *hand signals* (= movements that CYCLISTS make with their hands to tell other people that they are going to stop, turn, etc.) ⊃ see also **SMOKE SIGNAL**, **TURN SIGNAL** **2** B1 a piece of equipment that uses different coloured lights to tell drivers to go slower, stop, etc., used especially on railways and roads: *traffic signals* ◊ *a stop signal* **3** B2 a series of electrical waves that carry sounds, pictures or messages, for example to a radio, television or mobile phone: *radio signals* ◊ *a digital signal* ◊ *I couldn't get a signal on my phone.* ◊ *The signal is received by three different antennas at slightly different times.* ◊ *The satellite is used for transmitting signals around the world.* ◊ *~ from sth The signal from the transmitter seems to have been boosted.* ⊃ see also **TIME SIGNAL** **4** B2 an event, an action, a fact, etc. that shows that sth exists or is likely to happen **SYN** **indication**: *~ (that)* … *The rise in inflation is a clear signal that the government's policies are not working.* ◊ *~ of sth Chest pains can be a warning signal of heart problems.* ◊ *Reducing prison sentences would send the wrong signals to criminals.* ⊃ **SYNONYMS** at **SIGN**

■ *verb* (**-ll-**, *US* **-l-**) **1** B1 [I, T] to make a movement or sound to give sb a message, an order, etc: *Don't fire until I signal.* ◊ *~ (to sb) (for sth) He signalled to the waiter for the bill.* ◊ *~ to / for sb to do sth He signalled to us to join him.* ◊ *~ sb to do sth She signalled him to follow.* ◊ *~ sth The referee signalled a foul.* ◊ *~ (that)* … *She signalled (that) it was time to leave.* ◊ *~ which, what, etc* … *You must signal which way you are going to turn.* **2** [I, T] to show that your vehicle is going to change direction, by using lights or your arm **SYN** **indicate**: *Did you signal before you turned right?* ◊ *~ sth to signal left/right* ◊ *~ (that)* … *I signalled that I was going to turn left.* **3** [T] *~ sth* to be a sign that sth exists or is likely to happen **SYN** **indicate**: *This announcement signalled a clear change of policy.* ◊ *The scandal surely signals the end of his political career.* **4** [T] to do sth to make your feelings or opinions known: *~ sth He signalled his discontent by refusing to vote.* ◊ *~ (that)* … *She has signalled (that) she is willing to stand as a candidate.*

■ *adj.* [only before noun] (*formal*) important, clear and definite: *a signal honour* ▶ **sig·nal·ly** /-nəli/ *adv.*: *They have signally failed to keep their election promises.*

**'signal box** *noun* (*BrE*) a building next to a railway from which RAIL signals are operated

**sig·nal·man** /ˈsɪɡnəlmən/ *noun* (*pl.* **-men** /-mən/) (*also* **sig·nal·ler**, *US* **sig·nal·er** /ˈsɪɡnələ(r)/) **1** a person whose job is operating signals on a railway **2** a person trained to give and receive signals in the army or NAVY

**signal-to-'noise ratio** *noun* **1** (*specialist*) the strength of an electronic signal that you want to receive, compared to the strength of the signals that you do not want **2** a measure of how much useful information you receive, compared to information which is not useful

**sig·na·tory** /ˈsɪɡnətri; *NAmE* -tɔːri/ *noun* (*pl.* **-ies**) *~ (to / of sth)* (*formal*) a person, a country or an organization that has signed an official agreement: *a signatory of the Declaration of Independence* ◊ *Many countries are signatories to/of the Berne Convention.*

**sig·na·ture** B2+ B2 /ˈsɪɡnətʃə(r)/ *noun* **1** B2+ B2 [C] your name as you usually write it, for example at the end of a letter: *Someone had forged her signature on the cheque.* ◊ *They collected 10000 signatures for their petition.* ◊ *He was attacked for having put his signature to the deal.* ⊃ see also **ELECTRONIC SIGNATURE** **2** B2+ C1 [U] (*formal*) the act of signing sth: *Two copies of the contract will be sent to you for signature.* **3** B2+ C1 [C, usually sing.] a particular quality that makes sth different from other similar things and makes it easy to recognize: *Bright colours are his signature.* ⊃ see also **DIGITAL SIGNATURE**, **KEY SIGNATURE**, **TIME SIGNATURE**

**'signature tune** *noun* (*BrE*) a short tune played at the beginning and end of a particular television or radio programme, or one that is connected with a particular performer ⊃ compare **THEME MUSIC**

**sign·board** /ˈsaɪnbɔːd; *NAmE* -bɔːrd/ *noun* a piece of wood that has some information on it, such as a name, and is displayed outside a shop, hotel, etc.

**sig·net ring** /ˈsɪɡnət rɪŋ/ *noun* a ring with a design cut into it, that you wear on your finger

**sig·nifi·cance** B2+ B2 ❶ /sɪɡˈnɪfɪkəns/ *noun* [U, C] **1** B2+ B2 the importance of sth, especially when this has an effect on what happens in the future: *a decision of major political significance* ◊ *The new drug has great significance for the treatment of the disease.* ◊ *They discussed the statistical significance of the results.* **2** B2+ C1 the meaning of sth: *She couldn't grasp the full significance of what he had said.* ◊ *Do these symbols have any particular significance?* ⊃ compare **INSIGNIFICANCE**

## sig·nifi·cant ❶ B2 ❶ /sɪɡˈnɪfɪkənt/ *adj.* **1** B2

large or important enough to have an effect or to be noticed: *There are no significant differences between the two groups of students.* ◊ *Your work has shown a significant improvement.* ◊ *a significant increase/decrease/reduction/loss* ◊ *a significant amount/number/part/portion* ◊ *The results of the experiment are not statistically significant.* ◊ *The drug has had no significant effect on stopping the*

| æ cat | ɑː father | e bed | ɜː fur | ə about | ɪ sit | iː see | i happy | ɒ got (*BrE*) | ɔː saw | ʌ cup | ʊ put | uː too |

spread of the disease. ◊ **it is ~that ...** *It is significant that girls generally do better in examinations than boys.* ⊃ compare INSIGNIFICANT **2** [B2] having a particular meaning: *The fact that her remarks were leaked to the media in advance is highly significant.* **3** [usually before noun] having a special or secret meaning that is not understood by everyone SYN **meaningful**: *a significant look/smile*

### sig·nifi·cant·ly [B2] /sɪɡˈnɪfɪkəntli/ adv.

**1** [B2] in a way that is large or important enough to have an effect on sth or to be noticed: *significantly higher/lower/larger/smaller* ◊ *The two sets of figures are not significantly different.* ◊ *to differ/vary/change significantly* ◊ *Profits have increased significantly over the past few years.* **2** [B2] in a way that has a particular meaning: *Significantly, he did not deny that there might be an election.* **3** in a way that has a special or secret meaning: *She paused significantly before she answered.*

**sig·nificant ˈother** *noun* (*often humorous*) your husband, wife, partner or sb that you have a special relationship with

**sig·ni·fi·ca·tion** /ˌsɪɡnɪfɪˈkeɪʃn/ *noun* [U, C] (*formal or linguistics*) the exact meaning of sth, especially a word or phrase

**sig·ni·fied** /ˈsɪɡnɪfaɪd/ *noun* (*linguistics*) the meaning expressed by a LINGUISTIC sign, rather than its form ⊃ compare SIGNIFIER

**sig·ni·fier** /ˈsɪɡnɪfaɪə(r)/ *noun* (*linguistics*) the form of a LINGUISTIC sign, for example its sound or its printed form, rather than the meaning it expresses ⊃ compare SIGNIFIED

**sig·nify** /ˈsɪɡnɪfaɪ/ *verb* (**sig·ni·fies**, **sig·ni·fy·ing**, **sig·ni·fied**, **sig·ni·fied**) (*formal*) **1** [T] to be a sign of sth SYN **mean**: ~ **sth** *This decision signified a radical change in their policies.* ◊ *~that ... This mark signifies that the products conform to an approved standard.* ◊ *The white belt signifies that he's an absolute beginner.* **2** [T] to do sth to make your feelings, intentions, etc. known: ~ **sth** *She signified her approval with a smile.* ◊ *~that ... He nodded to signify that he agreed.* **3** [I] (usually used in questions or negative sentences) to be important or to matter: *His presence no longer signified.*

**sign·ing** /ˈsaɪnɪŋ/ *noun* **1** [U] the act of writing your name at the end of an official document to show that you accept it: *the signing of the Treaty of Rome* **2** [C] (*BrE*) a person who has just signed a contract to join a particular sports team or record or film company **3** [U] the act of making an official contract that arranges for sb to join a sports team or a record or film company **4** [U] the act of using sign language: *the use of signing in classrooms*

**ˈsign language** *noun* [U, C] a system of communicating using hand movements rather than spoken words, as used by people who cannot hear

**ˈsign-off** *noun* [usually sing.] **1** the ending of a letter or broadcast: *He ended each broadcast with his trademark sign-off.* **2** ~ **(on sth)** formal approval that sb has given to sth by signing their name: *We still need the CEO's sign-off on the report.*

**ˈsign·post** /ˈsaɪnpəʊst/ *noun*, *verb*
- *noun* a sign at the side of a road giving information about the direction and distance of places: *Follow the signposts to the superstore.* ◊ (*figurative*) *The chapter headings are useful signposts to the content of the book.* ⊃ WORDFINDER NOTE at ROAD
- *verb* (*BrE*) **1** [usually passive] ~ **sth** to show a road, place, etc. with signposts: *The route is well signposted.* **2** ~ **sth** to show clearly the way that an argument, a speech, etc. will develop: *You need to signpost for the reader the various points you are going to make.* ▸ **sign·post·ing** *noun* [U]

**ˈsign-writer** /ˈsaɪnraɪtə(r)/ (*also* **ˈsign painter**) *noun* a person who paints signs and advertisements for shops and businesses ▸ **ˈsign-writing** *noun* [U]

**Sikh** /siːk/ *noun* a member of a religion (called **Sikhism**) that developed in Punjab in the late 15th century and is based on a belief that there is only one God ▸ **Sikh** *adj.*

**sil·age** /ˈsaɪlɪdʒ/ *noun* [U] grass or other green crops that are stored without being dried and are used to feed farm animals in winter

### si·lence [B2] /ˈsaɪləns/ noun, verb, exclamation

- **noun 1** [U] a complete lack of noise or sound SYN **quiet**: *Their footsteps echoed in the silence.* ◊ *A scream broke the silence of the night.* ◊ *I need absolute silence when I'm working.* **2** [B2] [C, U] a situation when nobody is speaking: *an embarrassed/awkward/uncomfortable silence* ◊ *a moment's stunned silence* ◊ *I got used to his long silences.* ◊ *They finished their meal in total silence.* ◊ *She lapsed into silence again.* ◊ *There was a deafening silence* (= one that is very noticeable). ◊ *a two-minute silence in honour of those who had died* **3** [U, sing.] a situation in which sb refuses to talk about sth or to answer questions: *She broke her public silence in a TV interview.* ◊ *~ (on sth) The company's silence on the subject has been taken as an admission of guilt.* ◊ *the right to silence* (= the legal right not to say anything when you are arrested) ◊ *There is a conspiracy of silence about what is happening* (= everyone has agreed not to discuss it). **4** [U] a situation in which people do not communicate with each other by letter or phone: *The phone call came after months of silence.*
IDM **silence is ˈgolden** (*saying*) it is often best not to say anything ⊃ more at HEAVY *adj.*, PREGNANT
- *verb* **1** ~ **sb/sth** to make sb/sth stop speaking or making a noise: *She silenced him with a glare.* ◊ *Our bombs silenced the enemy's guns* (= they destroyed them). **2** ~ **sb/sth** to make sb stop expressing opinions that are opposed to yours: *All protest had been silenced.* ◊ *Her recent achievements have silenced her critics.*
- *exclamation* (*formal*) used to tell people to be quiet: *Silence in court!*

**si·len·cer** /ˈsaɪlənsə(r)/ *noun* **1** (*BrE*) (*NAmE* **muffler**) a device that is fixed to the EXHAUST of a vehicle in order to reduce the amount of noise that the engine makes **2** a device that is fixed to the end of a gun in order to reduce the amount of noise that it makes when it is fired

### si·lent [B1] /ˈsaɪlənt/ adj. 1 [B1] where there is little or no sound; making little or no sound SYN **quiet**: *At last the traffic fell silent.* ◊ *The streets were silent and deserted.* **2** [B1] (of a person) not speaking: *to remain/stay/keep silent* ◊ *As the curtain rose, the audience fell silent.* ◊ *He gave me the silent treatment* (= did not speak to me because he was angry). ◊ *Half the room went silent and turned to see what was happening.* **3** [B1] [only before noun] not expressed with words or sound: *a silent prayer/protest* ◊ *They nodded in silent agreement.* **4** (of a letter in a word) written but not pronounced: *The 'b' in 'lamb' is silent.* **5** [only before noun] (of old films/movies) with pictures but no sound: *a silent film/movie* ◊ *stars of the silent screen* **6** [only before noun] (especially of a man) not talking very much SYN **quiet**: *He's the strong silent type.* **7** ~ **(on/about sth)** not giving information about sth; refusing to speak about sth: *The report is strangely silent on this issue.* ◊ *the right to remain silent* (= the legal right not to say anything when you are arrested)

**si·lent·ly** /ˈsaɪləntli/ *adv.* **1** without speaking: *They marched silently through the streets.* **2** without making any or much sound SYN **quietly**: *She crept silently out of the room.* **3** without using words or sounds to express sth: *She prayed silently.* ◊ *He silently agreed with much of what she had said.*
IDM **sit/stand silently ˈby** to do or say nothing to help sb or deal with a difficult situation

**the ˌsilent maˈjority** *noun* [sing. + sing./pl. v.] the large number of people in a country who think the same as each other, but do not express their views publicly

**ˌsilent ˈpartner** (*NAmE*) (*BrE* **ˌsleeping ˈpartner**) *noun* a person who has put money into a business company but who is not actually involved in running it

### sil·hou·ette /ˌsɪluˈet/ noun, verb

- *noun* **1** [C, U] the dark outline or shape of a person or an object that you see against a light background: *the silhouette of chimneys and towers* ◊ **in ~** *The mountains stood out in silhouette.* **2** [C] the shape of a person's body or of an object: *The dress is fitted to give you a flattering silhouette.*

# silica 1450

**3** [C] a picture that shows sb/sth as a black shape against a light background, especially one that shows the side view of a person's face
- **verb** [usually passive] to make sth appear as a silhouette: **be silhouetted (against sth)** *A figure stood in the doorway, silhouetted against the light.*

**sil·i·ca** /ˈsɪlɪkə/ *noun* [U] (*symb.* $SiO_2$) a chemical containing silicon found in sand and in rocks such as QUARTZ, used in making glass and CEMENT

**ˈsilica gel** *noun* [U] a substance made from silica in the form of grains, which keeps things dry by taking in water

**sili·cate** /ˈsɪlɪkeɪt, -kət/ *noun* [C, U] **1** (*chemistry*) any COMPOUND containing SILICON and OXYGEN: *aluminium silicate* **2** a mineral that contains silica. There are many different silicates and they form a large part of the earth's CRUST.

**sili·con** /ˈsɪlɪkən/ *noun* [U] (*symb.* Si) a chemical element. Silicon exists as a grey solid or as a brown powder and is found in rocks and sand. It is used in making glass and TRANSISTORS.

**ˌsilicon ˈchip** *noun* a very small piece of silicon used to carry a complicated electronic CIRCUIT

**sili·cone** /ˈsɪlɪkəʊn/ *noun* [U] a chemical containing silicon. There are several different types of silicone, used to make paint, artificial rubber, VARNISH, etc.: *a silicone breast implant*

**ˌSilicon ˈValley** *noun* [U] the area in California where there are many companies connected with the computer and ELECTRONICS industries, sometimes used to refer to any area where there are a lot of computer companies

**sili·cosis** /ˌsɪlɪˈkəʊsɪs/ *noun* [U] (*medical*) a serious lung disease caused by breathing in dust containing SILICA

**silk** B2 /sɪlk/ *noun* **1** B2 [U] fine soft THREAD produced by silkworms: *The caterpillar spins the silk around its entire body.* **2** [U, C] a type of fine smooth cloth made from silk THREAD; a piece of this cloth: *a silk dress/blouse/scarf/tie/sari* ◊ *made of pure silk* ◊ *Her skin was as smooth as silk.* **3** [U] THREAD made of silk used for SEWING **4 silks** [pl.] clothes made of silk, especially the coloured shirts worn by people riding horses in a race (= JOCKEYS) **5** [C] (*BrE, law*) a type of lawyer who represents the government (= a KING'S COUNSEL/QUEEN'S COUNSEL): *to take silk* (= to become this type of lawyer)
- IDM **(you can't) make a silk purse out of a sow's ear** (you won't) succeed in making sth good out of material that does not seem very good at all

**silk·en** /ˈsɪlkən/ *adj.* (*literary*) **1** [usually before noun] soft, smooth and shiny like silk: *silken hair* **2** [usually before noun] smooth and gentle: *her silken voice* **3** [only before noun] made of silk: *silken ribbons*

**silk·worm** /ˈsɪlkwɜːm; *NAmE* -wɜːrm/ *noun* a CATERPILLAR (= a small creature like a WORM with legs) that produces silk THREAD

**silky** /ˈsɪlki/ *adj.* (**silk·ier, silki·est**) **1** soft, smooth and shiny like silk: *silky fur* **2** [usually before noun] smooth and gentle: *He spoke in a silky tone.* **3** made of silk or cloth that looks like silk: *a silky dress* ▶ **silk·ily** /-kəli/ *adv.*: *'How have I changed?' he asked silkily.* **silki·ness** *noun* [U] **silky** *adv.*: *The leaves are grey and silky smooth.*

**sill** /sɪl/ *noun* **1** = WINDOWSILL **2** a piece of metal that forms part of the frame of a vehicle below the doors

**silly** B1 /ˈsɪli/ *adj., noun*
- *adj.* (**sil·lier, sil·liest**) **1** B1 showing a lack of thought, understanding, or judgement SYN **foolish**: *a silly idea/question/name* ◊ *That was a silly thing to do!* ◊ *It sounds silly, I know, but think about it.* ◊ *Her work is full of silly mistakes.* ◊ *'I can walk home.' 'Don't be silly—it's much too far!'* ◊ **it is ~ (of sb) to do sth** *It would have been silly to pretend that I wasn't upset.* ◊ *It would be silly of me to say no.* **2** B1 stupid or embarrassing, especially in a way that is more typical of a child than an adult SYN **ridiculous**: *a silly sense of humour* ◊ *a silly game* ◊ *He would never dance in case he looked silly.* ◊ *I feel silly in these clothes.* ◊ *She had a silly grin on her face.* **3** B1 not practical or serious: *We had to wear these silly little hats.* ◊ *Why worry about a silly thing like that?* ▶ **silli·ness** *noun* [U]
- IDM **drink, laugh, shout, etc. yourself ˈsilly** (*informal*) to drink, laugh, shout, etc. so much that you cannot behave in a sensible way **play ˌsilly ˈbuggers** (*BrE, informal*) to behave in a stupid and annoying way ⊃ more at BORED, GAME *n*.
- *noun* (*BrE also* **silly ˈbilly**) [sing.] (*informal*) often used when speaking to children to say that they are not behaving in a sensible way: *No, silly, those aren't your shoes!*

**the ˌsilly ˈseason** *noun* [sing.] (*BrE*) the time, usually in the summer, when newspapers are full of unimportant stories because there is little serious news

**silo** /ˈsaɪləʊ/ *noun* (*pl.* **-os**) **1** a tall tower on a farm used for storing grain, etc. **2** an underground place where nuclear weapons or dangerous substances are kept **3** an underground place where SILAGE is made and stored **4** a system, process, department, etc. that operates separately or is thought of as separate from others: *Some departments have become silos and no longer communicate regularly with one another.* ◊ *In some countries, the economy and foreign policy are considered in separate silos.*

**silt** /sɪlt/ *noun, verb*
- *noun* [U] sand, mud, etc. that is carried by flowing water and is left at the mouth of a river or in a HARBOUR ▶ **silty** *adj.*: *silty soils*
- *verb*
- PHRV **ˌsilt sth↔ˈup** | **ˌsilt ˈup** to block sth with silt; to become blocked with silt: *Sand has silted up the river delta.* ◊ *The harbour has now silted up.*

**sil·ver** A2 /ˈsɪlvə(r)/ *noun, adj., verb*
- *noun* **1** A2 [U] (*symb.* Ag) a chemical element. Silver is shiny, grey-white PRECIOUS METAL used for making coins, jewellery, beautiful objects, etc.: *a silver ring/chain* ◊ *made of solid silver* ⊃ see also STERLING SILVER **2** A2 [U] a shiny grey-white colour: *There was a streak of silver in her hair.* ⊃ see also SILVERY **3** [U] dishes, beautiful objects, etc. that are made of silver: *Thieves stole £5000 worth of silver.* **4** [U] coins that are made of silver or a metal that looks like silver: *I need £2 in silver for the parking meter.* **5** [U, C] = SILVER MEDAL: *She won silver in last year's championships.* ◊ *The team won two silvers and a bronze.*
- IDM **on a ˌsilver ˈplatter** if you are given sth **on a silver platter**, you do not have to do much to get it: *These rich kids expect to have it all handed to them on a silver platter.* ⊃ more at BORN *v.*, CLOUD *n.*, CROSS *v.*
- *adj.* shiny grey-white in colour: *a silver car* ◊ *silver hair* ⊃ see also SILVERY
- *verb* **1** [usually passive] **~ sth** to cover the surface of sth with a thin layer of silver or sth that looks like silver **2 ~ sth** (*especially literary*) to make sth become bright like silver: *Moonlight was silvering the countryside.*

**ˌsilver anniˈversary** *noun* (*especially US*) **1** (*also* **ˌsilver ˈwedding anniversary** *BrE, NAmE*) (*BrE* **ˌsilver ˈwedding**) the 25th anniversary of a wedding **2** (*BrE* **ˌsilver ˈjubilee**) the 25th anniversary of an important event; a celebration of sth that began 25 years ago

**sil·ver·back** /ˈsɪlvəbæk; *NAmE* -vərb-/ *noun* a male adult GORILLA with white or silver hair across its back

**ˌsilver ˈband** *noun* (*BrE*) a BRASS BAND which uses silver-coloured instruments

**ˌsilver ˈbirch** *noun* [C, U] a tree with smooth, very pale grey or white BARK and thin branches, that grows in northern countries

**ˌsilver ˈbullet** (*also* **ˌmagic ˈbullet**) *noun* [usually sing.] a fast and effective solution to a serious problem: *Having a mentor is exciting but it's not a silver bullet for success.*

**ˌsilver ˈdollar** *noun* (*NAmE*) a large silver coin used in the past that was worth one dollar, sometimes used now to describe the size of sth: *a spider as big as a silver dollar*

**sil·ver·fish** /ˈsɪlvəfɪʃ; *NAmE* -vərf-/ *noun* (*pl.* **sil·ver·fish**) a small silver insect without wings that lives in houses and that can cause damage to materials such as cloth and paper

**silver ˈjubilee** (BrE) (US ˌsilver anniˈversary) noun [usually sing.] the 25th anniversary of an important event; a celebration of sth that began 25 years ago: *the silver jubilee of the Queen's accession* ◊ *The college celebrated its silver jubilee last year.* ⊃ compare DIAMOND JUBILEE, GOLDEN JUBILEE

**silver ˈmedal** noun [C] (*also* **silˈver** [U, C]) a MEDAL that is given to the person or the team that wins the second prize in a race or competition: *an Olympic silver medal winner* ⊃ compare BRONZE MEDAL, GOLD MEDAL ▶ **silver ˈmedalˌlist** (BrE) (NAmE ˌsilver ˈmedalist) noun: *He's an Olympic silver medallist.*

**silver ˈpaper** noun [U] (BrE) very thin, shiny sheets of ALUMINIUM that are used for wrapping chocolate, etc.

**silver ˈplate** noun [U] metal that is covered with a thin layer of silver; objects that are made of this metal ▶ **silver-ˈplated** adj.

**the ˌsilver ˈscreen** noun [sing.] (*old-fashioned*) the film industry

**sil·ver·smith** /ˈsɪlvəsmɪθ; NAmE -vərs-/ noun a person who makes, repairs or sells articles made of silver

**silver ˈsurfer** noun (*informal*) an old person who spends a lot of time using the internet

**silver ˈtongue** noun (*formal*) great skill at persuading people to do or to believe what you say ▶ **silver-ˈtongued** adj.

**sil·ver·ware** /ˈsɪlvəweə(r); NAmE -vərwer/ noun [U] **1** objects that are made of or covered with silver, especially knives, forks, dishes, etc. that are used for eating and serving food: *a piece of silverware* **2** (*also* **flat·ware**) (*both NAmE*) (*also* **cut·lery** *especially in BrE*) knives, forks and spoons, used for eating and serving food **3** (BrE, *informal*) a silver cup that you win in a sports competition ⓢⓨⓝ **trophy**

**silver ˈwedding** (BrE) (US ˌsilver anniˈversary) (*also* ˌsilver ˈwedding anniversary US, BrE) noun the 25th anniversary of a wedding: *They celebrated their silver wedding in May.* ⊃ compare DIAMOND WEDDING, GOLDEN WEDDING, RUBY WEDDING

**sil·very** /ˈsɪlvəri/ adj. [usually before noun] **1** shiny like silver; having the colour of silver: *silvery light* ◊ *a silvery grey colour* **2** (*literary*) (especially of a voice) having a pleasant musical sound

**sim** /sɪm/ noun (*informal*) a computer or video game that SIMULATES (= artificially creates the feeling of experiencing) an activity such as flying an aircraft or playing a sport

**SIM card** /ˈsɪm kɑːd; NAmE kɑːrd/ noun a plastic card inside a mobile phone that stores information to identify the phone and the person using it (the abbreviation for 'subscriber identification module')

**sim·ian** /ˈsɪmiən/ adj. (*specialist*) like a monkey or an ape; connected with monkeys or apes

**simi·lar** ⓣ Ⓐ1 ⓞ /ˈsɪmələ(r)/ adj. like sb/sth but not exactly the same: *We have very similar interests.* ◊ *The experiment was repeated, with similar results.* ◊ *I came across a similar situation last year.* ◊ *The brothers look very similar.* ◊ *~ to sb/sth My teaching style is similar to that of most other teachers.* ◊ *~ in sth The two houses are similar in size.* ⓞⓟⓟ **different, dissimilar**

**simi·lar·ity** ⓣ Ⓑ1 ⓦ /ˌsɪməˈlærəti/ noun (pl. **-ies**) **1** Ⓑ1 [U, sing.] the state of being similar to sb/sth but not exactly the same ⓢⓨⓝ **resemblance**: *~ between A and B The report highlights the similarity between the two groups.* ◊ *~ to sb/sth She bears a striking similarity to her mother.* ◊ *~ in sth There is some similarity in the way they sing.* ◊ *~ with sb/sth In this work we can observe the stylistic similarity with Beethoven.* ◊ *The results also showed the similarity of the two groups.* **2** Ⓑ1 [C] a feature that things or people have that makes them like each other ⓢⓨⓝ **resemblance**: *~ between A and B a study of the similarities and differences between the two countries* ◊ *~ in/of sth similarities in/of style* ◊ *~ to/with sb/sth The karate bout has many similarities to a boxing match.* ⓞⓟⓟ **difference, dissimilarity**

1451 **simple**

**simi·lar·ly** ⓣ Ⓑ1 ⓦ /ˈsɪmələli; NAmE -lərli/ adv. **1** Ⓑ1 in almost the same way: *It is a little cheaper than other similarly sized cars.* **2** Ⓑ1 used to say that two facts, actions, statements, etc. are like each other: *The United States won most of the track and field events. Similarly, in swimming, the top three places went to Americans.*

▼ **LANGUAGE BANK**

**similarly**
Making comparisons

• *This chart **provides a comparison of** the ways that teenage boys and girls in the UK spend their free time.*
• *In many cases, the results for boys and girls are virtually **the same/identical**.*
• *In many cases, the results for boys are virtually **the same as/identical to** the results for girls.*
• ***Both** boys **and** girls spend the bulk of their free time with friends.*
• *Most of the boys do more than two hours of sport a week, **as do** many of the girls.*
• ***Like** many of the girls, most of the boys spend a large part of their free time using the internet.*
• *The girls particularly enjoy using social networking websites. **Similarly**, nearly all the boys said they spent at least two to three hours a week on these sites.*

⊃ LANGUAGE BANK at CONTRAST, ILLUSTRATE, PROPORTION, SURPRISING

**sim·ile** /ˈsɪməli/ noun [C, U] (*specialist*) a word or phrase that compares sth to sth else, using the words *like* or *as*, for example *a face like a mask* or *as white as snow*; the use of such words and phrases ⊃ compare METAPHOR

**si·mili·tude** /sɪˈmɪlɪtjuːd; NAmE -tuːd/ noun [U] (*formal*) **~ (between A and B)** | **~ (to sb/sth)** the state of being similar to sth: *the similitude between humans and gorillas*

**sim·mer** /ˈsɪmə(r)/ verb, noun
■ verb **1** [T, I] **~ (sth)** to cook sth by keeping it almost at boiling point; to be cooked in this way: *Simmer the sauce gently for 10 minutes.* ◊ *Leave the soup to simmer.* **2** [I] **~ (with sth)** to be filled with a strong feeling, especially anger, which you have difficulty controlling ⓢⓨⓝ **seethe**: *She was still simmering with resentment.* ◊ *Anger simmered inside him.* **3** [I] (of an argument, a disagreement, etc.) to develop for a period of time without any real anger or violence being shown: *This argument has been simmering for months.*
ⓟⓗⓡⓥ ˌsimmer ˈdown (*informal*) to become calm after a period of anger or excitement: *I left him alone until he simmered down.*
■ noun [sing.] the state when sth is almost boiling: *Bring the sauce to a simmer and cook for 5 minutes.*

**Simon says** /ˌsaɪmən ˈsez/ noun [U] a children's game in which players should only do what a person says if he/she says 'Simon says …' at the beginning of the instruction

**sim·pat·ico** /sɪmˈpætɪkəʊ/ adj. (*informal*, *from Spanish*) **1** (of a person) pleasant; easy to like **2** (of a person) with similar interests and ideas to yours ⓢⓨⓝ **compatible**

**sim·per** /ˈsɪmpə(r)/ verb [I, T] to smile in a silly and annoying way: *a silly simpering girl* ◊ *+ speech 'You're such a darling,' she simpered.* ▶ **sim·per** noun [sing.] **sim·per·ing·ly** /-pərɪŋli/ adv.

**sim·ple** ⓣ Ⓐ2 ⓞ /ˈsɪmpl/ adj. (**sim·pler**, **sim·plest**)
ⓗⓔⓛⓟ You can also use **more simple** and **most simple**.
• EASY **1** Ⓐ2 not complicated; easy to understand or do ⓢⓨⓝ **easy**: *a simple solution/explanation/question/task/example* ◊ *~ for sb/sth You will soon see that what once seemed impossible is now simple for you.* ◊ *sth is ~ (for sb) to do This machine is very simple to use.* ◊ *it is ~ (for sb) to do sth It's too simple to blame the lack of manufacturing jobs on the last government.* ◊ *Give the necessary information but keep it simple.*
• BASIC/PLAIN **2** Ⓑ1 basic or plain without anything extra or unnecessary: *simple but elegant clothes* ◊ *We had a simple meal of soup and bread.* ◊ *The simple things in life*

are often the best. ◇ He was pleased to live **the simple life** and enjoy nature around him. **OPP fancy**
- **FOR EMPHASIS 3** [B2] used before a noun to emphasize that it is exactly that and nothing else: *We cannot ignore* **the simple fact that** *the country cannot sustain the current level of economic growth.* ◇ *The* **simple truth** *is that we just can't afford it.* ◇ *It's a* **simple matter** *of giving them enough to eat.* ◇ *I had to do it* **for the simple reason that** (= because) *I couldn't trust anyone else.* ⇨ **SYNONYMS** at PLAIN
- **WITH FEW PARTS 4** [B2] [usually before noun] consisting of only a few parts; not complicated in structure: *simple forms of life, for example amoebas* ◇ *a simple machine* ◇ *(grammar) a* **simple sentence** (= one with only one verb) ◇ *a* **simple model** *of a business market*
- **ORDINARY 5** [only before noun] (of a person) ordinary; not special: *I'm a simple country girl.*
- **NOT INTELLIGENT 6** [not usually before noun] (of a person) not very intelligent; not mentally normal: *He's not mad—just a little simple.*
- **GRAMMAR 7** used to describe the present or past tense of a verb that is formed without using an auxiliary verb, as in *She loves him* (= the simple present tense) or *He arrived late* (= the simple past tense) ⇨ see also SIMPLY **IDM** see PURE

**simple 'fracture** *noun* an injury when a bone in your body is broken but does not come through the skin ⇨ compare COMPOUND FRACTURE

**simple 'interest** *noun* [U] (*finance*) interest that is paid only on the original amount of money that you invested, and not on any interest that it has earned ⇨ compare COMPOUND INTEREST

**simple-'minded** *adj.* (*disapproving*) not intelligent; not able to understand how complicated things are: *a simple-minded person* ◇ *a simple-minded approach*

**simple-ton** /ˈsɪmpltən/ *noun* (*old-fashioned*) a person who is not very intelligent and can be tricked easily

**sim-plex** /ˈsɪmpleks/ *noun* (*linguistics*) a simple word that is not made of other words ⇨ compare COMPOUND

**sim-pli-city** /sɪmˈplɪsəti/ *noun* (*pl.* **-ies**) **1** [U] the quality of being easy to understand or use: *the relative simplicity of the new PC* ◇ **For the sake of simplicity**, *let's divide the discussion into two parts.* **2** [U] (*approving*) the quality of being natural and plain: *the simplicity of the architecture* ◇ *the simplicity of country living* **3** [C, usually pl.] an aspect of sth that is easy, natural or plain: *the simplicities of our old way of life*
**IDM** **be sim'plicity it'self** to be very easy or plain

**sim-pli-fi-ca-tion** /ˌsɪmplɪfɪˈkeɪʃn/ *noun* **1** [U, sing.] the process of making sth easier to do or understand: *Complaints have led to (a) simplification of the rules.* **2** [C] the thing that results when you make a problem, statement, system, etc. easier to understand or do: *A number of simplifications have been made to the taxation system.* ⇨ compare OVERSIMPLIFICATION

**sim-plify** W /ˈsɪmplɪfaɪ/ *verb* (**sim-pli-fies, sim-pli-fy-ing, sim-pli-fied, sim-pli-fied**) ~ **sth** to make sth easier to do or understand: *The application forms have now been simplified.* ◇ *I hope his appointment will* **simplify matters.** ◇ *a simplified version of the story for young children*

**sim-plis-tic** /sɪmˈplɪstɪk/ *adj.* (*disapproving*) making a problem, situation, etc. seem less difficult or complicated than it really is ▶ **sim-plis-tic-al-ly** /-kli/ *adv.*

**sim-ply** /ˈsɪmpli/ *adv.* **1** used to emphasize how easy or basic sth is **SYN just**: *This is not to suggest we* **simply ignore** *the problem.* ◇ *She says that the company was* **simply trying** *to protect its business.* ◇ *Simply add hot water and stir.* ◇ *Fame is often* **simply a matter of** *being in the right place at the right time.* **2** in a way that is easy to understand: *The book explains grammar simply and clearly.* ◇ *Anyway,* **to put it simply**, *we still owe them £2000.* **3** in a way that is natural and plain: *The rooms are simply furnished.* ◇ *They live simply* (= they do not spend much money). **4** used to emphasize a statement **SYN absolutely**: *You simply must see the play.* ◇ *The view is simply wonderful!* ◇ *That is* **simply not true!** ◇ *I haven't seen her for simply ages.* **5** used to introduce a summary or an explanation of sth that has been said or done: *I don't want to be rude,* **it's simply that** *we have to be careful who we give this information to.* ◇ *He was loud, vulgar and arrogant—quite simply the rudest man I've ever met!*

**sim-sim** /ˈsiːmsɪm/ *EAfrE* /ˈsɪmsɪm/ *noun* [U] (*EAfrE*) an East African word for SESAME (= a type of plant whose seeds and their oil are used in cooking)

**simu-la-crum** /ˌsɪmjuˈleɪkrəm/ *noun* (*pl.* **simu-lacra** /-krə/) (*formal*) something that looks like sb/sth else or that is made to look like sb/sth else **SYN copy**

**simu-late** /ˈsɪmjuleɪt/ *verb* **1** ~ **sth** to create particular conditions that exist in real life using computers, models, etc., usually for study or training purposes: *Computer software can be used to simulate conditions on the seabed.* **2** ~ **sth** to be made to look like sth else: *a gas heater that simulates a coal fire* **3** ~ **sth** to pretend that you have a particular feeling **SYN feign**: *I tried to simulate surprise at the news.*

**simu-lated** /ˈsɪmjuleɪtɪd/ *adj.* [only before noun] not real, but made to look, feel, etc. like the real thing: *simulated leather* ◇ *'How wonderful!' she said with simulated enthusiasm.* ◇ *The experiments were carried out under simulated examination conditions.*

**simu-la-tion** /ˌsɪmjuˈleɪʃn/ *noun* **1** [C, U] a situation in which a particular set of conditions is created artificially in order to study or experience sth that could exist in reality: *a computer simulation of how the planet functions* ◇ *a simulation model* **2** [U] the act of pretending that sth is real when it is not: *the simulation of concern*

**simu-la-tor** /ˈsɪmjuleɪtə(r)/ *noun* a piece of equipment that artificially creates a particular set of conditions in order to train sb to deal with a situation that they may experience in reality ⇨ see also FLIGHT SIMULATOR

**sim-ul-cast** /ˈsɪmlkɑːst; *NAmE* ˈsaɪmlkæst/ *noun* a programme, often recording a live event, that is broadcast on two or more television channels, radio channels, internet sites, etc., or using two or more of these types of medium at the same time: *You can either watch live coverage of the event on television or listen to the radio simulcast.* ▶ **sim-ul-cast** *verb* (**sim-ul-cast, sim-ul-cast**) ~ **sth**: *The show will be simulcast on television and the internet.*

**sim-ul-tan-eous** W /ˌsɪmlˈteɪniəs; *NAmE* ˌsaɪml-/ *adj.* happening or done at the same time as sth else: *There were several simultaneous attacks by the rebels.* ◇ **simultaneous translation** ▶ **sim-ul-tan-eity** /ˌsɪmltəˈneɪəti; *NAmE* ˌsaɪmltəˈniː-/ *noun* [U]

**simul,taneous e'quations** *noun* [pl.] (*mathematics*) EQUATIONS involving two or more unknown quantities that have the same values in each equation

**sim-ul-tan-eous-ly** W /ˌsɪmlˈteɪniəsli; *NAmE* ˌsaɪml-/ *adv.* at the same time as sth else: *The game will be broadcast simultaneously on TV and radio.* ◇ ~ **with sth** *The slowdown of the US economy occurred simultaneously with a downturn in Europe.* ⇨ LANGUAGE BANK at PROCESS¹

**sin** /sɪn/ *noun, verb, abbr.*
- *noun* **1** [C] an offence against God or against a religious or moral law: *to* **commit a sin** ◇ *Confess your sins to God and he will forgive you.* ◇ *God* **forgives our sins.** ◇ *The Bible says that stealing is a sin.* ⇨ see also DEADLY SIN, MORTAL SIN, ORIGINAL SIN **2** [U] the act of breaking a religious or moral law: *a life of sin* ⇨ see also SINFUL, SINNER **3** [C, usually sing.] (*informal*) an action that people think is very bad: *It's a sin to waste taxpayers' money like that.* ⇨ see also CARDINAL SIN
**IDM** **be/do sth for your sins** (especially *BrE, informal, humorous*) used to say that sth that sb does is like a punishment: *She works with us in Accounts, for her sins!* **(as) miserable/ugly as 'sin** (*informal*) used to emphasize that sb is very unhappy or ugly ⇨ more at LIVE¹, MULTITUDE
- *verb* [I] (**-nn-**) to break a religious or moral law: *Forgive me, Lord, for I have sinned.* ◇ ~ **against sb/sth** *He was more sinned against than sinning* (= although he did wrong, other people treated him even worse).
- *abbr.* (*mathematics*) SINE

**'sin bin** noun (informal) (in some sports, for example ICE HOCKEY) a place away from the playing area where the REFEREE sends a player who has broken the rules for a period of time before they are allowed to come back into the game

**since** 🛈 **A2** /sɪns/ prep., conj., adv.
■ prep. **1** 🔊 (used with the present perfect or past perfect tense) from a time in the past until a later past time, or until now: *She's been off work since Tuesday.* ◇ *We've lived here since 2006.* ◇ *I haven't eaten since breakfast.* ◇ *He's been working in a bank since leaving school.* ◇ *Since the party she had only spoken to him once.* ◇ *'They've split up.' 'Since when?'* ◇ *That was years ago. I've changed jobs since then.* **HELP** Use **for**, not **since**, with a period of time: *I've been learning English for five years.* ◇ *I've been learning English since five years.* **2 ~ when?** used when you are showing that you are angry about sth: *Since when did he ever listen to me?*
■ conj. **1** 🔊 (used with the present perfect, past perfect or simple present tense in the main clause) from an event in the past until a later past event, or until now: *Cath hasn't phoned since she went to Berlin.* ◇ *It was the first time I'd had visitors since I'd moved to London.* ◇ *It's twenty years since I've seen her.* ◇ *How long is it since we last went to the theatre?* ◇ *She had been worrying ever since the letter arrived.* **2** 🔊 **B2** because; as: *We thought that, since we were in the area, we'd stop by and see them.*
■ adv. (used with the present perfect or past perfect tense) **1** 🔊 **B1** from a time in the past until a later past time, or until now: *She went for a run on Monday and has not been seen since.* ◇ *She moved to Pakistan in 1997 and has been living in Lahore ever since.* ◇ *The health of the British people was better at the end of the Second World War than at any time before or since.* **2** 🔊 **B1** at a time after a particular time in the past: *The song topped the charts in 1957 and has since become a rock and roll classic.*

**sin·cere** 🛈 **B2** /sɪnˈsɪə(r); NAmE -ˈsɪr/ adj. (superlative **sin·cerest**, no comparative) **1** 🔊 **B2** (of feelings, beliefs or behaviour) showing what you really think or feel **SYN** genuine: *a sincere apology* ◇ *sincere regret* ◇ *Please accept our sincere thanks.* ◇ *We offer our sincere sympathy to the two families.* **2** 🔊 **B2** (of a person) saying only what you really think or feel **SYN** honest: *He seemed sincere enough when he said he wanted to help.* ◇ *~ in sth She is never completely sincere in what she says about people.* **OPP** insincere ▶ **sin·cer·ity** /sɪnˈserəti/ noun [U]: *She spoke with total sincerity.* ◇ *I can say in all sincerity that I knew nothing of these plans.*

**sin·cere·ly** /sɪnˈsɪəli; NAmE -ˈsɪrli/ adv. in a way that shows what you really feel or think about sb/sth: *I sincerely believe that this is the right decision.* ◇ *'I won't let you down.' 'I sincerely hope not.'* **IDM Yours sincerely** (NAmE **Sincerely (yours)**) (formal) used at the end of a formal letter before you sign your name, when you have addressed sb by their name

**Sindhi** /ˈsɪndi/ noun [U] a language spoken in Sind in Pakistan and in western India

**sine** /saɪn/ noun (abbr. **sin**) (mathematics) the RATIO of the length of the side opposite one of the angles in a RIGHT-ANGLED TRIANGLE that are less than 90° to the length of the longest side ⊃ compare COSINE, TANGENT

**sine·cure** /ˈsaɪnɪkjʊə(r), ˈsɪ-; NAmE ˈsaɪnɪkjʊr/ noun (formal) a job that you are paid for even though it involves little or no work

**sine die** /ˌsaɪni ˈdaɪi:, ˌsaɪneɪ ˈdi:eɪ/ adv. (from Latin, formal, law) without a future date being arranged: *The case was adjourned sine die.*

**sine qua non** /ˌsaɪneɪ kwɑː ˈnəʊn; NAmE ˈnoʊn/ noun [sing.] **~ (of/for sth)** (from Latin, formal) something that is essential before you can achieve sth else

**sinew** /ˈsɪnjuː/ noun **1** [C, U] a strong band of TISSUE in the body that joins a muscle to a bone **2** [usually pl.] (literary) a source of strength or power **IDM** see STRAIN v.

**sinewy** /ˈsɪnjuːi/ adj. (of a person or an animal) having a thin body and strong muscles **SYN** wiry

---

1453 **single**

**sin·ful** /ˈsɪnfl/ adj. (formal) morally wrong or evil **SYN** immoral: *sinful thoughts* ◇ *It is sinful to lie.* ◇ (informal) *It's sinful to waste good food!* ▶ **sin·ful·ly** /-fəli/ adv. **sin·ful·ness** noun [U]

**sing** 🛈 **A1** /sɪŋ/ verb (**sang** /sæŋ/, **sung** /sʌŋ/) **1** 🔊 **A1** [I, T] to make musical sounds with your voice in the form of a song or tune: *I always wanted to be on stage, singing and dancing.* ◇ *He was dancing around and singing at the top of his voice* (= very loudly). ◇ **~ to sb** *He was singing softly to the baby.* ◇ **~ sth** *to sing a hymn/an anthem* ◇ *Now I'd like to sing a song by the Beatles.* ◇ **~ sth to sb** *Will you sing a song to us?* ◇ **~ sb sth** *Will you sing us a song?*

**WORDFINDER** beat, harmony, melody, note, rhythm, tempo, tone, vocal

**2** 🔊 **B1** [I] (of birds) to make high musical sounds: *The birds were singing outside my window.* **3** [I] (+ adv./prep.) to make a high ringing sound like a WHISTLE (= a small metal or plastic tube that you blow to make a loud high sound): *Bullets sang past my ears.* ▶ **sing** noun [sing.]: *Let's have a sing.* **IDM sing a different 'tune** to change your opinion about sb/sth or your attitude towards sb/sth **sing from the same 'hymn/'song sheet** (BrE, informal) to show that you are in agreement with each other by saying the same things in public **sing sb's 'praises** to praise sb very highly: *She's always singing his praises.* ⊃ more at FAT adj. **PHRV sing aˈlong (with sb/sth) | ˌsing aˈlong (to sth)** to sing together with sb who is already singing or while a record, radio, or musical instrument is playing: *Do sing along if you know the words.* ⊃ related noun SINGALONG **ˈsing of sth** (old-fashioned or formal) to mention sth in a song or a poem, especially to praise it **ˌsing ˈout** to sing or say sth clearly and loudly: *A voice suddenly sang out above the rest.* **ˌsing ˈup** (BrE) (NAmE **ˌsing ˈout**) to sing more loudly: *Sing up, let's hear you.*

**sing·along** /ˈsɪŋəlɒŋ; NAmE -lɔːŋ/ (BrE also **ˈsing-song**) noun an informal occasion at which people sing songs together

**singe** /sɪndʒ/ verb [T, I] (**singe·ing**, **singed**, **singed**) **~ (sth)** to burn the surface of sth slightly, usually by mistake; to be burnt in this way: *He singed his hair as he tried to light his cigarette.* ◇ *the smell of singeing fur* ⊃ SYNONYMS at BURN

**sing·er** 🛈 **A1** /ˈsɪŋə(r)/ noun a person who sings, or whose job is singing, especially in public: *a pop/country/folk singer* ◇ *an opera singer* ◇ *the band's lead singer* ⊃ see also CAROL SINGER, FOLK SINGER, PLAYBACK SINGER, PRAISE SINGER, TORCH SINGER

**sing·ing** 🛈 **A2** /ˈsɪŋɪŋ/ noun [U] the activity of making musical sounds with your voice: *the beautiful singing of birds* ◇ *the singing of hymns/songs/carols* ◇ *choral singing* ◇ *There was singing and dancing all night.* ◇ *She has a beautiful singing voice.*

**sin·gle** 🛈 **A2** 🔊 /ˈsɪŋɡl/ adj., noun, verb
■ adj.
• ONE **1** 🔊 **A2** [only before noun] only one: *He sent her a single red rose.* ◇ *a single-sex school* (= for boys only or for girls only) ◇ *We won by a single point.* ◇ *They cloned a lamb from a single cell taken from an adult sheep.* ◇ *the European single currency, the euro* ◇ (BrE) *a single honours degree* (= for which you study only one subject)
• FOR ONE PERSON **2** 🔊 **A2** [only before noun] intended to be used by only one person: *a single room* ⊃ compare DOUBLE ⊃ see also SINGLE BED
• NOT MARRIED **3** 🔊 **A2** (of a person) not married or having a romantic relationship with sb: *a single person/woman/man* ◇ *a single mother/father* ◇ *Are you still single?* ◇ *to remain/stay single* ⊃ see also SINGLE PARENT
• TICKET **4** 🔊 **A2** [only before noun] (BrE) (also **one-way** NAmE, BrE) *a single ticket, etc. can be used for travelling to a place but not back again: a single ticket* ◇ *How much is the single fare to Glasgow?* ⊃ compare RETURN (7)
• FOR EMPHASIS **5** 🔊 **B2** [only before noun] used to emphasize that you are referring to one particular person or thing on

# single bed

its own: *We eat rice **every single** day.* ◊ *Every single one of her so-called friends had turned their backs on her.* ◊ *I couldn't understand a **single word** she said!* **IDM** see FILE *n.*, GLANCE *n.*, GO *n.*

■ **noun**
- TICKET **1** [C] (*BrE*) a ticket that allows you to travel to a place but not back again: *How much is a single to York?* ⇒ compare RETURN
- ROOM **2** [C] a room in a hotel, etc. for one person: *Singles are available from £50 per night.* ⇒ compare DOUBLE
- UNMARRIED PEOPLE **3 singles** [pl.] people who are not married and do not have a romantic relationship with sb else: *They organize parties for singles.* ◊ *a singles bar/club*
- MUSIC **4** [C] a piece of recorded music, usually popular music, that consists of one song; a CD that a single is recorded on: *The band releases its new single next week.* ⇒ compare ALBUM
- MONEY **5** [C] (*NAmE*) a note that is worth one dollar ⇒ compare DOUBLE
- IN SPORT **6 singles** [U + sing./pl. v.] (especially in tennis) a game when only one player plays against one other; a series of two or more of these games: *the women's singles champion* ◊ *the first round of the men's singles* ◊ *a singles match* ◊ *She's won three singles titles this year.* ⇒ compare DOUBLE **7** [C] (in CRICKET) a hit from which a player scores one RUN (= point) **8** [C] (in baseball) a hit that only allows the player to run to FIRST BASE

■ **verb**
**PHRV** ˌsingle sb/sth↔ˈout (for sth/as sb/sth) to choose sb/sth from a group for special attention: *She was singled out for criticism.* ◊ *He was singled out as the outstanding performer of the games.*

**ˌsingle ˈbed** noun (*NAmE* also **ˈtwin bed**) a bed big enough for one person

**ˌsingle-ˈbreasted** adj. (of a jacket or coat) having only one row of buttons that fasten in the middle ⇒ compare DOUBLE-BREASTED

**ˌsingle ˈcombat** noun [U] fighting between two people, usually with weapons

**ˌsingle ˈcream** noun (*BrE*) (*NAmE* **light ˈcream**) noun [U] thin cream that is used in cooking and for pouring over food ⇒ compare DOUBLE CREAM

**ˌsingle-ˈdecker** noun a bus with only one level ⇒ compare DOUBLE-DECKER

**ˌsingle ˈfigures** noun [pl.] a number that is less than ten: *Inflation is down to single figures.* ◊ *The number of people who fail each year is now in single figures.*

**ˌsingle-ˈhanded** adv. on your own with nobody helping you **SYN** alone: *to sail around the world single-handed* ▶ **ˌsingle-ˈhanded** adj.: *a single-handed voyage* **ˌsingle-ˈhandedly** adv.

**ˌsingle ˈmarket** noun [usually sing.] (*economics*) a group of countries that have few or no controls or limits on the movement of goods, money and people between the members of the group

**ˌsingle-ˈminded** adj. only thinking about one particular aim or goal because you are determined to achieve sth: *the single-minded pursuit of power* ◊ *She is very single-minded about her career.* ▶ **ˌsingle-ˈmindedly** adv. **ˌsingle-ˈmindedness** noun [U].

**single·ness** /ˈsɪŋɡlnəs/ noun [U] **1** ~ **of purpose** the ability to think about one particular aim or goal because you are determined to succeed **2** the state of not being married or having a partner

**ˌsingle ˈparent** (*BrE also* **lone ˈparent**) noun a person who takes care of their child or children without a husband, wife or partner: *a single-parent family*

**sin·glet** /ˈsɪŋɡlət/ noun (*BrE*) a piece of clothing without arms, worn under or instead of a shirt; a similar piece of clothing worn by runners, etc. ⇒ compare VEST

**single·ton** /ˈsɪŋɡltən/ noun **1** a single item of the kind that you are talking about **2** a person who is not married or in a romantic relationship **3** a person or an animal that is not a twin, etc.

**ˌsingle ˌtransˈferable ˈvote** noun [sing.] (*politics*) a system for electing representatives in which a person's vote can be given to their second or third choice if their first choice is defeated, or if their first choice wins with more votes than they need

**ˌsingle-ˈuse** adj. [only before noun] made to be used once only and then thrown away: *disposable single-use cameras*

**sin·gly** /ˈsɪŋɡli/ adv. alone; one at a time **SYN** individually: *The stamps are available singly or in books of ten.* ◊ *Guests arrived singly or in groups.*

**ˈsing-song** noun, adj.
■ noun **1** [C] (*BrE*) = SINGALONG **2** [sing.] a way of speaking in which a person's voice keeps rising and falling
■ adj. [only before noun] a **sing-song** voice keeps rising and falling

**sin·gu·lar** /ˈsɪŋɡjələ(r)/ noun, adj.
■ noun [sing.] (*grammar*) a form of a noun or verb that refers to one person or thing: *The singular of 'bacteria' is 'bacterium'.* ◊ *The verb should be in the singular.* ⇒ compare PLURAL ⇒ WORDFINDER NOTE at GRAMMAR
■ adj. **1** (*grammar*) connected with or having the singular form: *a singular noun/verb/ending* **2** (*formal*) very great or obvious **SYN** outstanding: *landscape of singular beauty* **3** (*literary*) unusual; strange **SYN** eccentric: *a singular style of dress*

**sin·gu·lar·ity** /ˌsɪŋɡjuˈlærəti/ noun [U] (*formal*) the quality of sth that makes it unusual or strange

**sin·gu·lar·ly** /ˈsɪŋɡjələli; *NAmE* -lərli/ adv. (*formal*) very; in an unusual way: *singularly beautiful* ◊ *He chose a singularly inappropriate moment to make his request.*

**Sin·hal·ese** /ˌsɪnhəˈliːz/ noun (*pl.* **Sin·hal·ese**) **1** [C] a member of a race of people living in Sri Lanka **2** [U] the language of the Sinhalese ▶ **Sin·hal·ese** adj.

**sin·is·ter** /ˈsɪnɪstə(r)/ adj. seeming evil or dangerous; making you think sth bad will happen: *There was something cold and sinister about him.* ◊ *There is another, more sinister, possibility.*

**sink** /sɪŋk/ verb, noun, adj.
■ verb (**sank** /sæŋk/, **sunk** /sʌŋk/, *less frequent* **sunk**, **sunk**)
- IN WATER/MUD, ETC. **1** [I] to go down below the surface or towards the bottom of a liquid or soft substance: *The ship sank to the bottom of the sea.* ◊ *We're sinking!* ◊ ~ **into** sth *The wheels started to sink into the mud.*
- BOAT **2** [T] ~ sth to damage a boat or ship so that it goes below the surface of the sea, etc: *The battleship was sunk by a torpedo.*
- FALL/SIT DOWN **3** [I] + adv./prep. (of a person) to move downwards, especially by falling or sitting down **SYN** collapse: *I sank into an armchair.* ◊ *She sank back into her seat, exhausted.* ◊ *The old man had sunk to his knees.*
- MOVE DOWNWARDS **4** [I] (of an object) to move slowly downwards: *The sun was sinking in the west.* ◊ *The foundations of the building are starting to sink.*
- BECOME WEAKER **5** [I] to decrease in amount, volume, strength, etc: *The pound has sunk to its lowest recorded level against the dollar.* ◊ *He is clearly sinking fast* (= getting weaker quickly and will soon die).
- OF VOICE **6** [I] to become quieter **SYN** fade: *Her voice sank to a whisper.*
- DIG IN GROUND **7** [T] ~ sth to make a deep hole in the ground **SYN** drill: *to sink a well/shaft/mine* **8** [T] ~ sth (+ adv./prep.) to place sth in the ground by digging: *to sink a post into the ground* ⇒ see also SUNKEN
- PREVENT SUCCESS **9** [T] ~ sth/sb (*informal*) to prevent sb or sb's plans from succeeding: *I think I've just sunk my chances of getting the job.* ◊ *If the car breaks down, we'll be sunk* (= have serious problems).
- BALL **10** [T] ~ sth to hit a ball into a hole in golf or SNOOKER: *He sank a 12-foot putt to win the match.*
- ALCOHOL **11** [T] ~ sth (*BrE, informal*) to drink sth quickly, especially a large amount of alcohol

**IDM** be ˈsunk in sth to be in a state of unhappiness or deep thought: *They just sat there, sunk in thought.* **(like ˈrats) deserting/leaving a ˈsinking ˈship** (*humorous,* *disapproving*) used to talk about people who leave an organization, a company, etc. that is having difficulties, without caring about the people who are left **sink your ˈdifferences** to agree to forget about your DISAGREEMENTS **a/that ˈsinking feeling** (*informal*) an unpleasant feeling that you get when you realize that sth bad has happened or is going to happen **ˌsink or ˈswim** to be in a situation where you will either succeed by your own efforts or fail completely: *The new students were just left to sink or swim.* **ˌsink so ˈlow** | **ˌsink to ˈsth** to have such low moral standards that you do sth very bad: *Stealing from your friends? How could you sink so low?* ◇ *I can't believe that anyone would sink to such depths.* ⇨ more at HEART *n.*, LOW *n.*

PHR V **ˌsink ˈin 1** (of words, an event, etc.) to be fully understood or realized: *He paused to allow his words to sink in.* ◇ *The full scale of the disaster has yet to sink in.* **2** (*also* ˌsink ˈinto sth) (of liquids) to go down into another substance through the surface: *The rain sank into the dry ground.* **ˈsink into sth** to go gradually into a less active, happy or pleasant state: *She sank into a deep sleep.* ◇ *He sank deeper into depression.* **ˌsink ˈinto sth** | **ˌsink sth ˈinto sth** to go, or to make sth sharp go, deep into sth solid: *I felt her nails sink into my wrist.* ◇ *The dog sank its teeth into my leg* (= bit it). **ˌsink sth ˈinto sth** to spend a lot of money on a business or an activity, for example in order to make money from it in the future: *We sank all our savings into the venture.*

■ *noun* **1** a large open container in a kitchen that has TAPS to supply water and that you use for washing dishes in: *Don't just leave your dirty plates in the sink!* ◇ *I felt chained to the kitchen sink* (= I had to spend all my time doing jobs in the house). ⇨ picture at PLUG **2** (*especially NAmE*) = WASH-BASIN IDM see KITCHEN

■ *adj.* [only before noun] (*BrE*) located in a poor area where social conditions are bad: *the misery of life in sink estates* ◇ *a sink school*

**sink·er** /ˈsɪŋkə(r)/ *noun* a weight that is attached to a FISH-ING LINE or net to keep it under the water IDM see HOOK *n.*

**sink·hole** /ˈsɪŋkhəʊl/ *noun* (*geology*) a large hole in the ground that a river flows into, created over a long period of time by water that has fallen as rain

**sin·ner** /ˈsɪnə(r)/ *noun* (*formal*) a person who has committed a SIN or SINS (= broken God's law)

**Sinn Fein** /ˌʃɪn ˈfeɪn/ *noun* [U + sing./pl. v.] an Irish political party that wants Northern Ireland and the Republic of Ireland to become one country

**Sino-** /ˈsaɪnəʊ/ *combining form* (in nouns and adjectives) Chinese: *Sino-Japanese relations*

**sinu·ous** /ˈsɪnjuəs/ *adj.* (*literary*) turning while moving, in an attractive way; having many curves: *a sinuous movement* ◇ *the sinuous grace of a cat* ◇ *the sinuous course of the river*
▶ **sinu·ous·ly** *adv.*

**sinus** /ˈsaɪnəs/ *noun* any of the hollow spaces in the bones of the head that are connected to the inside of the nose: *blocked sinuses*

**si·nus·itis** /ˌsaɪnəˈsaɪtɪs/ *noun* [U] the painful SWELLING of the sinuses

**-sion** ⇨ -ION

**Sioux** /suː/ *noun* (*pl.* Sioux) a member of a Native American people from the northern central region of the US

**sip** /sɪp/ *verb, noun*
■ *verb* [I, T] (-pp-) to drink sth, taking a very small amount each time: ~ **(at sth)** *She sat there, sipping at her tea.* ◇ ~ **sth** *He slowly sipped his wine.*
■ *noun* a very small amount of a drink that you take into your mouth: *to have/take a sip of water*

**si·phon** (*also* sy·phon) /ˈsaɪfn/ *noun, verb*
■ *noun* a tube that is used to move liquid from one container down into another, lower container ⇨ see also SODA SIPHON
■ *verb* **1** ~ **sth (+ adv./prep.)** to move a liquid from one container to another, using a siphon: *I siphoned the gasoline out of the car into a can.* ◇ *The waste liquid needs to be siphoned off.* **2** ~ **sth (+ adv./prep.)** (*informal*) to remove money from one place and move it to another,

especially dishonestly or illegally SYN *divert*: *She has been accused of siphoning off thousands of pounds from the company into her own bank account.*

**ˈsippy cup** /ˈsɪpi kʌp/ *noun* (*NAmE, AustralE, informal*) a cup with a LID (= cover) and small SPOUT (= tube) so that a baby can drink liquid from it

**sir** ❶ A2 /sɜː(r), sə(r)/ *noun* **1** A2 used as a polite way of addressing a man whose name you do not know, for example in a shop or restaurant: *Good morning, sir. Can I help you?* ◇ *Are you ready to order, sir?* ◇ *'Thank you very much.' 'You're welcome, sir. Have a nice day.'* ⇨ compare MA'AM ⇨ see also MADAM **2** A2 **Dear Sir/Sirs** used at the beginning of a formal business letter when you do not know the name of the man or people that you are dealing with: *Dear Sir/Sirs* ◇ *Dear Sir or Madam* **3** A2 **Sir** a title that is used before the first name of a man who has received one of the highest British honours (= a KNIGHT), or before the first name of a BARONET: *Sir Paul McCartney* ◇ *Thank you, Sir Paul.* ⇨ compare LADY **4** A2 used as a form of address to a man in a position of authority, especially in the armed forces: *'Report to me tomorrow, corporal!' 'Yes, sir!'* **5** (*BrE*) used as a form of address by children in school to a male teacher: *Please, sir, can I open a window?* ⇨ compare MISS
IDM **ˌno ˈsir!** | **ˌno siˈree!** (*informal, especially NAmE*) certainly not: *We will never allow that to happen! No sir!* **ˌyes ˈsir!** | **ˌyes siˈree!** (*informal, especially NAmE*) used to emphasize that sth is true: *That's a fine car you have. Yes sir!*

**sire** /ˈsaɪə(r)/ *noun, verb*
■ *noun* **1** (*specialist*) the male parent of an animal, especially a horse ⇨ compare DAM **2** (*old use*) a word that people used when they addressed a king
■ *verb* **1** ~ **sth** to be the male parent of an animal, especially a horse **2** ~ **sth** (*old-fashioned or humorous*) to become the father of a child

**siree** (*also* sir·ree) /səˈriː/ *exclamation* (*NAmE, informal*) used for emphasis, especially after 'yes' or 'no': *He's not going to do it, no siree.*

**siren** /ˈsaɪrən/ *noun* **1** a device that makes a long loud sound as a signal or warning: *an air-raid siren* ◇ *A police car raced past with its siren wailing.* **2** (in ancient Greek stories) any of a group of sea creatures that were part woman and part bird, or part woman and part fish, whose beautiful singing made sailors sail towards them into rocks or dangerous waters **3** a woman who is very attractive or beautiful but also dangerous **4** ~ **voices/song/call** (*literary*) the TEMPTATION to do sth that seems very attractive but that will have bad results: *The government must resist the siren voices calling for tax cuts.*

**sir·loin** /ˈsɜːlɔɪn; *NAmE* ˈsɜːrl-/ (*also* **sirloin ˈsteak**) *noun* [U, C] good quality beef that is cut from a cow's back

**si·rocco** (*also* sci·rocco) /sɪˈrɒkəʊ; *NAmE* -ˈrɑːk-/ *noun* (*pl.* -os) a hot wind that blows from Africa into southern Europe

**sis** /sɪs/ *noun* (*informal*) sister (used when you are speaking to her)

**sisal** /ˈsaɪsl/ *noun* [U] strong FIBRES made from the leaves of a tropical plant also called sisal, used for making rope, floor COVERINGS, etc.

**sissy** (*BrE also* cissy) /ˈsɪsi/ *noun* (*pl.* -ies) (*informal, disapproving*) a boy that other men or boys laugh at because they think he is weak or frightened, or only interested in the sort of things girls like SYN *wimp* ▶ **sissy** *adj.*

**sis·ter** ❶ A1 /ˈsɪstə(r)/ *noun* **1** A1 a girl or woman who has the same mother and father as another person: *an older/a younger sister* ◇ (*informal*) *a big/little sister* ◇ (*informal*) *a kid sister* ◇ *My twin sister* ◇ *We're sisters.* ◇ *the Brontë sisters—Charlotte, Emily and Anne* ◇ *My best friend has been like a sister to me* (= very close). ⇨ see also COUSIN SISTER, HALF-SISTER, STEPSISTER **2** used for talking to or about other members of a women's organization or other women who have the same ideas, purpose, etc. as

# sister city

yourself: *They supported their sisters in the dispute.* **3 Sister** (*BrE*) a senior female nurse who is in charge of a hospital WARD ⇨ see also CHARGE NURSE **4 Sister** a female member of a religious group, especially a NUN: *Sister Mary* ◇ *the Sisters of Charity* **5** (in the US) a member of a SORORITY (= a club for a group of female students at a college or university) **6** (*NAmE, informal*) used by black people as a form of address for a black woman **7** (usually used as an adjective) a thing that belongs to the same type or group as sth else: *our sister company in Italy* ◇ *a sister ship*

**ˌsister ˈcity** (*NAmE*) (*BrE* ˌtwin ˈtown) *noun* one of two towns or cities in different countries that have a special relationship with each other: *Okayama is San Jose's sister city in Japan.*

**sis·ter·hood** /ˈsɪstəhʊd; *NAmE* -stərh-/ *noun* **1** [U] the close relationship of trust between women who share ideas and aims **2** [C + sing./pl. v.] a group of women who live in a community together, especially a religious one

**ˈsister-in-law** *noun* (*pl.* sisters-in-law) the sister of your husband or wife; your brother's or sister's wife; the wife of your husband's or wife's brother or sister ⇨ compare BROTHER-IN-LAW

**sis·ter·ly** /ˈsɪstəli; *NAmE* -stərli/ *adj.* typical of or like a sister: *She gave him a sisterly kiss.*

**Sisy·phean** /ˌsɪsɪˈfiːən/ *adj.* (of a task) impossible to complete ORIGIN From the Greek myth in which **Sisyphus** was punished for the bad things he had done in his life with the never-ending task of rolling a large stone to the top of a hill, from which it always rolled down again.

**sit** 🛈 A1 /sɪt/ *verb* (**sit·ting**, **sat**, **sat** /sæt/)
- **ON CHAIR, ETC. 1 A1** [I] to rest your weight on your bottom with your back straight, for example on/in a chair: *She sat and stared at the letter in front of her.* ◇ *+ adv./prep. May I sit here?* ◇ *Don't just sit there—do something!* ◇ *Just sit still!* ◇ *The children were all sitting quietly and listening.* ◇ ~ **doing sth** *He just sits there watching the television.* ⇨ see also SIT DOWN **2** [T] ~ **sb + adv./prep.** to put sb in a sitting position: *He lifted the child and sat her on the wall.*
- **OF THINGS 3** [I] to be in a particular place: *+ adv./prep. A large bus was sitting outside.* ◇ *The pot was sitting in a pool of water.* ◇ *The jacket sat beautifully on her shoulders* (= fitted well). ◇ *+ adj. The box sat unopened on the shelf.*
- **HAVE OFFICIAL POSITION 4** [I] to have an official position as sth or as a member of sth: ~ **as sth** *He was sitting as a temporary judge.* ◇ *They both sat as MPs in the House of Commons.* ◇ ~ **in/on sth** *She sat on a number of committees.* ◇ ~ **for sth** *For years he sat for Henley* (= was the MP for that CONSTITUENCY).
- **OF PARLIAMENT, ETC. 5** [I] (of a parliament, committee, court of law, etc.) to meet in order to do official business: *Parliament sits for less than six months of the year.*
- **EXAM 6** [T, I] (*rather formal*) to do an exam (*BrE*): ~ **sth** *Candidates will sit the examinations in June.* ◇ *Most of the students sit at least 5 GCSEs.* ◇ (*especially NAmE*) ~ **for sth** *He was about to sit for his entrance exam.*
- **OF BIRD 7** [I] (*+ adv./prep.*) to rest on a branch, etc. or to stay on a NEST to keep the eggs warm
- **OF DOG 8** [I] to sit on its bottom with its front legs straight: *Rover! Sit!*
- **TAKE CARE OF CHILDREN 9** [I] ~ **(for sb)** = BABYSIT: *Who's sitting for you?* ⇨ see also HOUSE-SIT

IDM **be ˌsitting ˈpretty** (*informal*) to be in a good situation, especially when others are not **sit at sb's ˈfeet** to admire sb very much, especially a teacher or sb from whom you try to learn **sit comˈfortably, ˈeasily, ˈwell, etc. (with sth)** to seem right, natural, suitable, etc. in a particular place or situation: *His views did not sit comfortably with the management line.* **sit in ˈjudgement (on/over/upon sb)** to decide whether sb's behaviour is right or wrong, especially when you have no right to do this: *How dare you sit in judgement on me?* **sit on the ˈfence** to avoid becoming involved in deciding or influencing sth: *He tends to sit on the fence at meetings.* **ˌsit ˈtight 1** to stay where you are rather than moving away or changing position: *We sat tight and waited to be rescued.* **2** to stay in the same situation, without changing your mind or taking any action: *Shareholders are being advised to sit tight until the crisis passes.* ⇨ more at BOLT *adv.*, LAUREL, SILENTLY

PHRV **ˌsit aˈround/aˈbout** (*often disapproving*) to spend time doing nothing very useful: *I'm far too busy to sit around here.* ◇ **sit around/about doing sth** *He just sits around watching TV.* **ˌsit ˈback 1** to sit on sth, usually a chair, in a relaxed position: *He sat back in his chair and started to read.* **2** to relax, especially by not getting too involved in or anxious about sth: *She's not the kind of person who can sit back and let others do all the work.* **ˌsit ˈby** to take no action to stop sth bad or wrong from happening: *We cannot just sit by and watch this tragedy happen.* **ˌsit ˈdown** A1 | **ˌsit yourˈself ˈdown** A1 to move from a standing position to a sitting position: *Please sit down.* ◇ *He sat down on the bed.* ◇ *They sat down to consider the problem.* ◇ *Come in and sit yourselves down.* **ˌsit ˈdown and do sth** to give sth time and attention in order to try to solve a problem or achieve sth: *This is something that we should sit down and discuss as a team.* **ˈsit for sb/sth** [no passive] to be a model for an artist or a photographer: *to sit for your portrait* ◇ *She sat for Augustus John.* **ˌsit ˈin for sb** to do sb's job or perform their duties while they are away, sick, etc. SYN **stand in (for sb)** **ˌsit ˈin on sth** to attend a meeting, class, etc. in order to listen to or learn from it rather than to take an active part **ˈsit on sth** (*informal*) to have received a letter, report, etc. from sb and then not replied or taken any action relating to it: *They have been sitting on my application for a month now.* **ˌsit sth↔ˈout 1** to stay in a place and wait for sth unpleasant or boring to finish: *We sat out the storm in a cafe.* **2** to not take part in a dance, game or other activity **ˌsit ˈthrough sth** to stay until the end of a performance, speech, meeting, etc. that you think is boring or too long: *We had to sit through nearly two hours of speeches.* **ˌsit ˈup 1** to be or move yourself into a sitting position, rather than lying down or leaning back: *Sit up straight—don't slouch.* **2** to not go to bed until later than usual: *We sat up half the night,*

---

▼ **SYNONYMS**

**sit**

sit down • be seated • take a seat • perch

These words all mean to rest your weight on your bottom with your back straight, for example on a chair.

**sit** to rest your weight on your bottom with your back straight, for example on a chair: *May I sit here?* ◇ *Sit still, will you?* NOTE **Sit** is usually used with an adverb or prepositional phrase to show where or how sb sits, but sometimes another phrase or clause is used to show what sb does while they are sitting: *We sat talking for hours.*

**sit down/sit yourself down** to move from a standing position to a sitting position: *Please sit down.* ◇ *Come in and sit yourselves down.*

**be seated** (*formal*) to be sitting: *She was seated at the head of the table.* NOTE **Be seated** is often used as a formal way of inviting sb to sit down: *Please be seated.*

**take a seat** to sit down NOTE **Take a seat** is used especially as a polite way of inviting sb to sit down: *Please take a seat.*

**perch** (*rather informal*) to sit on sth, especially on the edge of sth: *She perched herself on the edge of the bed.* NOTE **Perch** is always used with an adverb or prepositional phrase to show where sb is perching.

PATTERNS
- to sit/sit down/be seated/take a seat/perch **on** sth
- to sit/sit down/be seated/take a seat **in** sth

---

▼ **GRAMMAR POINT**

**sit**
- You can use **on**, **in** and **at** with **sit**. You **sit on** a chair, a step, the edge of the table, etc. You **sit in** an armchair. If you are **sitting at** a table, desk, etc. you are sitting on a chair close to it, usually so that you can eat a meal, do some work, etc.

---

🔹 Oxford 3000 | 🔹 Oxford 5000 | A1 A2 B1 B2 C1 CEFR level | PHRV phrasal verb(s) | IDM idiom(s)

talking. **sit 'up (and do sth)** (*informal*) to start to pay careful attention to what is happening, being said, etc: *The proposal had made his clients sit up and take notice.* **sit sb 'up** to move sb into a sitting position after they have been lying down

**sitar** /sɪˈtɑː(r), ˈsɪtɑː(r)/ *noun* a musical instrument from South Asia like a guitar, with a long neck and two sets of metal strings

**sit·com** /ˈsɪtkɒm; *NAmE* -kɑːm/ *noun* (*also formal* ˌsituation ˈcomedy) *noun* [C, U] a regular comedy programme on television that shows the same characters in different funny situations ⇒ WORDFINDER NOTE at PROGRAMME

**ˈsit-down** *noun* [sing.] (*BrE, informal*) a rest while sitting in a chair: *I need a cup of tea and a sit-down.* ▶ **ˈsit-down** *adj.* [only before noun]: *a sit-down protest* (= in which people sit down to block a road or the entrance to a building until people listen to their demands) ◇ *a sit-down meal for 50 wedding guests* (= served to people sitting at tables)

**site** 🌐 A2 W /saɪt/ *noun, verb*
■ *noun* **1** A2 a place where a building, town, etc. was, is or will be located: *the site of a sixteenth-century abbey* ◇ *A site has been chosen for the new school.* ◇ **on a~** *Nothing can be built on this site.* ◇ **on~** *All the materials on site so that work can start immediately.* ⇒ SYNONYMS at PLACE ⇒ WORDFINDER NOTE at CONSTRUCTION ⇒ see also BUILDING SITE, CONSTRUCTION SITE, WORLD HERITAGE SITE **2** a place where sth has happened: *the site of the battle* ◇ *an archaeological site* ◇ *The president is to visit the crash site later today.* ◇ **the ~ of sth** *People laid flowers at the site of the accident.* ⇒ see also BOMB SITE **3** A2 a place that is used for a particular activity: *a caravan site* ⇒ see also CAMPSITE **4** A2 a place connected to the internet, where a company or an organization, or an individual person, puts information: *online dating sites* ◇ *Here are some links to other useful sites.* ◇ *For more information, visit the festival's official site.* ◇ **on a~** *She regularly posts music reviews on an online music site.* ⇒ HOMOPHONES at SIGHT ⇒ see also COMPARISON SITE, FAN SITE, MIRROR SITE, WEBSITE
■ *verb* [usually passive] to build or place sth in a particular position: **be sited + adv./prep.** *The castle is magnificently sited high up on a cliff.* ◇ *There was a meeting to discuss the siting of the new school.* ⇒ HOMOPHONES at SIGHT

**ˈsit-in** *noun* a protest in which a group of workers, students, etc. refuse to leave their factory, college, etc. until people listen to their demands: *to hold/stage a sit-in*

**sit·ter** /ˈsɪtə(r)/ *noun* **1** a person who sits or stands somewhere so that sb can paint a picture of them or photograph them **2** (*especially NAmE*) = BABYSITTER **3** (*BrE, informal*) (in football (soccer)) an easy chance to score a goal

**sit·ting** /ˈsɪtɪŋ/ *noun* **1** a period of time during which a court or a parliament deals with its business **2** a time when a meal is served in a hotel, etc. to a number of people at the same time: *A hundred people can be served at one sitting* (= at the same time). **3** a period of time that a person spends sitting and doing an activity: *I read the book in one sitting.* **4** a period of time when sb sits or stands to have their picture painted or be photographed

**ˌsitting ˈduck** (*also* ˌsitting ˈtarget) *noun* a person or thing that has no protection against attack

**ˈsitting room** *noun* (*BrE*) = LIVING ROOM

**situ** ⇒ IN SITU

**situ·ate** /ˈsɪtʃueɪt/ *verb* (*formal*) **1** ~ **sth + adv./prep.** to build or place sth in a particular position **2** ~ **sth + adv./prep.** to consider how an idea, event, etc. is related to other things that influence your view of it: *Let me try and situate the events in their historical context.*

**situ·ated** 🌐 C1 /ˈsɪtʃueɪtɪd/ *adj.* [not usually before noun] (*formal*) **1** 🌐 C1 in a particular place or position: *My bedroom was situated on the top floor of the house.* ◇ *The hotel is beautifully situated in a quiet spot near the river.* ◇ *All the best theatres and restaurants are situated within a few minutes' walk of each other.* HELP *You can use situated before a noun if you also use an adverb: a conveniently situated hotel* **2** (of a person, an organization, etc.) in a particular situation or in particular circumstances: *Small*

1457 **sit-up**

businesses *are well situated to benefit from the single market.*

**situ·ation** 🌐 A1 ⓞ /ˌsɪtʃuˈeɪʃn/ *noun* **1** A1 all the circumstances and things that are happening at a particular time and in a particular place: *the present economic/financial/political situation* ◇ *There is no doubt that the current situation is very serious.* ◇ **in a~** *We are now in a difficult situation.* ◇ *We have all been in similar embarrassing situations.* ◇ **~where/in which …** *You could get into a situation where you have to decide immediately.* ◇ **in sb's ~** *In your situation, I would look for another job.* ◇ *He could see no way out of the situation.* ◇ *I thought she handled the situation well.* ◇ *What can we do to improve the situation?* **2** (*formal*) the kind of location that a building or town has: *The town is in a delightful situation in a wide green valley.* **3** (*old-fashioned or formal*) a job: *Situations Vacant* (= the title of the section in a newspaper where jobs are advertised) ▶ **situ·ation·al** /-ʃənl/ *adj.* IDM see SAVE *v.*

▼ SYNONYMS

**situation**
circumstances • position • conditions • things • the case • state of affairs
These are all words for the conditions and facts that are connected with and affect the way things are.
**situation** all the things that are happening at a particular time and in a particular place: *the present economic situation*
**circumstances** the facts that are connected with and affect a situation, an event or an action; the conditions of a person's life, especially the money they have: *The ship sank in mysterious circumstances.*
**position** the situation that sb is in, especially when it affects what they can and cannot do: *She felt she was in a position of power.*
**conditions** the circumstances in which people live, work or do things; the physical situation that affects how sth happens: *We were forced to work outside in freezing conditions.*
CIRCUMSTANCES OR CONDITIONS?
**Circumstances** refers to sb's financial situation; **conditions** are things such as the quality and amount of food or shelter they have. The **circumstances** that affect an event are the facts surrounding it; the **conditions** that affect it are usually physical ones, such as the weather.
**things** (*rather informal*) the general situation, as it affects sb: *Hi, Jane! How are things?* ◇ *Think things over before you decide.*
**the case** the true situation: *If that is the case* (= if the situation described is true), *we need more staff.*
**state of affairs** a situation: *How did this unhappy state of affairs come about?*
SITUATION OR STATE OF AFFAIRS?
● **State of affairs** is mostly used with *this*. It is also used with adjectives describing how good or bad a situation is, such as *happy, sorry, shocking, sad* and *unhappy*, as well as those relating to time, such as *present* and *current*. **Situation** is much more frequent and is used in a wider variety of contexts.
PATTERNS
● **in** (a) particular situation / circumstances / position / state of affairs
● the / sb's **economic/financial/social** situation / circumstances / position / conditions
● (a/an) **happy/unhappy** situation / circumstances / position / state of affairs
● to **look at/review** the situation / the circumstances / the conditions / things

ˌsituation ˈcomedy *noun* [C, U] (*formal*) = SITCOM

**ˈsit-up** (*also* **crunch**) *noun* an exercise for making your stomach muscles strong, in which you lie on your back

# six

on the floor and raise the top part of your body to a sitting position ⊃ picture at PRESS-UP

**six** ⓘ A1 /sɪks/ number **1** ⓘ A1 **6** HELP There are examples of how to use numbers at the entry for **five**. **2** noun (in CRICKET) a hit that scores six RUNS (= points)

IDM **at ˌsixes and ˈsevens** (informal) in a confused state; not well organized **be ˌsix feet ˈunder** (informal) to be dead and buried in the ground **hit/knock sb for ˈsix** (BrE) to affect sb very deeply **it's six of ˌone and half a ˌdozen of the ˈother** (saying) used to say that there is not much real difference between two possible choices

**the ˌSix ˈCounties** noun [pl.] a way of referring to Northern Ireland, used especially by people who want the whole of Ireland to be one country

**sixer** /ˈsɪksə(r)/ noun (especially IndE) (in CRICKET) a hit that scores six RUNS (= points) SYN **six**

**six-figure** adj. [only before noun] used to describe a number that is 100000 or more: *a six-figure salary*

**six-fold** /ˈsɪksfəʊld/ adj., adv. ⊃ -FOLD

**ˈsix-gun** noun = SIX-SHOOTER

**ˈsix-pack** noun **1** a set of six bottles or cans sold together, especially of beer **2** (informal) stomach muscles that are very strong and that you can see clearly across sb's stomach

**six-pence** /ˈsɪkspəns/ noun a British coin in use until 1971, worth six old pence

**ˈsix-shooter** (also **ˈsix-gun**) noun (especially NAmE) a small gun that holds six bullets

**six-teen** ⓘ A1 /ˌsɪksˈtiːn/ number **16** ▸ **six-teenth** /-ˈtiːnθ/ ordinal number, noun

**ˌsixˈteenth note** (NAmE) (BrE **semi-quaver**) noun (*music*) a note that lasts half as long as an EIGHTH NOTE ⊃ picture at MUSIC

**sixth** /sɪksθ/ ordinal number, noun
▪ ordinal number 6th HELP There are examples of how to use ordinal numbers at the entry for **fifth**.
▪ noun each of six equal parts of sth

**ˈsixth form** noun [usually sing.] (BrE) the two final years at school for students between the ages of 16 and 18 who are preparing to take A LEVELS (= advanced level exams): *Sue is in the sixth form now.*

**ˈsixth-form college** noun (in England, Wales and Northern Ireland) a school for students over the age of 16

**ˈsixth-former** noun (BrE) a student who is in the sixth form at school

**ˌsixth ˈsense** noun [sing.] a special ability to know sth without using any of the five senses that include sight, touch, etc: *My sixth sense told me to stay here and wait.*

**sixty** ⓘ A1 /ˈsɪksti/ **1** A1 number **60 2** noun **the sixties** [pl.] numbers, years or temperatures from 60 to 69 ▸ **six-ti-eth** /-əθ/ ordinal number, noun HELP There are examples of how to use ordinal numbers at the entry for **fifth**.

IDM **in your ˈsixties** between the ages of 60 and 69

**the ˌsixty-four thousand dollar ˈquestion** noun (*informal*) the thing that people most want to know, or that is most important ORIGIN From the name of a US television show which gave prizes of money to people who answered questions correctly. The correct answer to the last question was worth $64000.

**size** ⓘ A2 ⓦ /saɪz/ noun, verb
▪ noun
• HOW LARGE/SMALL **1** ⓘ A2 [U, C] how large or small a person or thing is: *population/sample/group/class size* ◊ *She has almost doubled the size of her investments.* ◊ *an area the size of* (= the same size as) *Wales* ◊ *discussions about increasing the size of the army* ◊ *The company is reducing the size of its workforce.* ◊ *He was about the same size as me.* ◊ *Dogs come in all shapes and sizes.* **2** ⓘ A2 [U] **~ of sth** the large amount or extent of sth: *You should have seen the size of their house!* ◊ *The sheer size of the potential market excites investors.*
• OF CLOTHES/SHOES/GOODS **3** ⓘ A2 [C, U] one of a number of standard measurements in which clothes, shoes and other goods are made and sold: *The jacket was the wrong size.* ◊ *It's not my size.* ◊ **in sb's ~** *They didn't have the jacket in my size.* ◊ *The hats are made in three sizes: small, medium and large.* ◊ *Do you have these shoes in (a) size 5?* ◊ *She takes (a) size 5 in shoes.* ◊ *What size do you take?* ◊ *She's a size 12 in clothes.* ◊ *I need a bigger/smaller size.* ◊ **for ~** *Try this one for size* (= to see if it is the correct size). ◊ *The glass can be cut to size* (= cut to the exact measurements) *for you.* HELP To ask about the size of something, you usually say: *How big?* You use: *What size?* to ask about something that is produced in fixed measurements.
• -SIZED/-SIZE **4** (in adjectives) having the size mentioned: *a medium-sized house* ◊ *Cut it into bite-size pieces.* ⊃ see also FULL-SIZE, KING-SIZE, LEGAL-SIZE, LIFE-SIZE, MAN-SIZED, PINT-SIZED, PLUS-SIZE
• STICKY SUBSTANCE **5** [U] a sticky substance that is used for making material stiff or for preparing walls for WALLPAPER

IDM **cut sb down to ˈsize** to show sb that they are not as important as they think they are **that's about the ˈsize of it** (*informal*) that's how the situation seems to be: *'So they won't pay up?' 'That's about the size of it.'*
▪ verb
• GIVE SIZE **1** [usually passive] to mark the size of sth; to give a size to sth: **be sized (in sth)** *The screws are sized in millimetres.*
• CHANGE SIZE **2** [usually passive] to change the size of sth: **be sized** *The fonts can be sized according to what effect you want.*
• MAKE STICKY **3 ~ sth** to cover sth with a sticky substance called SIZE

PHR V **ˌsize sb/sthˈup** (*informal*) to form a judgement or an opinion about sb/sth SYN **sum up**: *She knew that he was looking at her, sizing her up.* ◊ *He sized up the situation very quickly.*

**size-able** (also **siz-able**) /ˈsaɪzəbl/ adj. fairly large SYN considerable: *The town has a sizeable Sikh population.*

**ˌsize ˈzero** noun [U, C] (in the US) the smallest size for women's clothes, used to describe women who are extremely thin: *size zero models and celebrities* ◊ *She is a size zero.*

**siz-zle** /ˈsɪzl/ verb **1** [I] to make the sound of food frying in hot oil: *sizzling sausages* **2** [I] to be very exciting, especially in a sexual way: *The screen sizzles whenever she appears on it.* ▸ **siz-zle** noun [sing., U]

**siz-zling** /ˈsɪzlɪŋ/ adj. **1** very hot: *sizzling summer temperatures* **2** very exciting: *a sizzling love affair*

**sjam-bok** /ˈʃæmbɒk; NAmE -baːk/ noun (SAfrE) a long, stiff WHIP made of leather

**ska** /skɑː/ noun [U] a type of fast popular music with strong rhythms, developed in Jamaica in the 1960s and that developed into REGGAE

**skank** /skæŋk/ noun (*informal, especially NAmE*) an unpleasant person

**skanky** /ˈskæŋki/ adj. (*informal, especially NAmE*) very unpleasant

**skate** /skeɪt/ verb, noun
▪ verb **1** [I, T] to move on skates (usually referring to ICE SKATING, if no other information is given): *Can you skate?* ◊ *It was so cold that we were able to go skating on the lake.* ◊ **~ sth** *He skated an exciting programme at the American Championships.* ⊃ see also ICE-SKATE, ROLLER SKATE **2** [I] to ride on a SKATEBOARD IDM see THIN adj.

PHR V **ˌskate ˈover sth** to avoid talking about or considering a difficult subject: *He politely skated over the issue.*
▪ noun **1 =** ICE SKATE, ROLLER SKATE: *a pair of skates* ⊃ see also IN-LINE SKATE **2** (*pl.* **skate** or **skates**) a large flat sea fish that can be eaten

IDM **ˌget/put your ˈskates on** (BrE, *informal*) used to tell sb to hurry: *Get your skates on or you'll miss the bus.*

**skate-board** /ˈskeɪtbɔːd; NAmE -bɔːrd/ noun a short narrow board with small wheels at each end, which you stand on and ride as a sport: *a skateboard park/ramp*

▶ **skate·board** verb [I] **skate·board·er** noun **skate·board·ing** noun [U]: *a skateboarding magazine*

**skate·park** /'skeɪtpɑːk; NAmE -pɑːrk/ noun an area built for people to use skateboards, with slopes, curves, etc.

**skater** /'skeɪtə(r)/ noun **1** a person who skates for pleasure or as a sport: *a figure/speed skater* ⊃ see also ICE SKATER **2** = SKATEBOARDER: *Extreme skaters perform jumps, spins, flips, etc.*

**skat·ing** /'skeɪtɪŋ/ noun [U] **1** (also **ice skating**) the sport or activity of moving on ice on SKATES: *to go skating* ⊃ see also FIGURE SKATING, SPEED SKATING **2** = ROLLER SKATING **IDM** see THIN adj.

**'skating rink** (also **rink**) noun **1** = ICE RINK **2** an area or a building where you can ROLLER SKATE

**skeet·er** /'skiːtə(r)/ noun (NAmE, informal, humorous) = MOSQUITO

**skeet shooting** /'skiːt ʃuːtɪŋ/ (NAmE) (BrE **clay 'pigeon shooting**) noun a sport in which a disc of baked clay is thrown into the air for people to shoot at

**skein** /skeɪn/ noun a long piece of wool, THREAD or YARN that is loosely tied together

**skel·etal** /'skelɪtl/ adj. **1** (specialist) connected with the skeleton of a person or an animal **2** looking like a skeleton: *skeletal figures dressed in rags* **3** that exists only in a basic form, as an outline: *He has written only a skeletal plot for the book so far.*

**skeletal 'muscle** noun [C, U] a muscle that connects different bones and works to make parts of the body like the arms, legs, etc. move

**skel·eton** /'skelɪtn/ noun **1** [C] the structure of bones that supports the body of a person or an animal; a model of this structure: *The human skeleton consists of 206 bones.* ◇ *a dinosaur skeleton* ⊃ VISUAL VOCAB page V1 **2** [C] (informal) a very thin person or animal **3** [C, usually sing.] the main structure that supports a building, etc. **SYN** framework: *Only the concrete skeleton of the factory remained.* **4** [C, usually sing.] the basic outline of a plan, piece of writing, etc. to which more details can be added later: *Examples were used to flesh out the skeleton of the argument.* **5** [sing.] ~ **staff, crew, etc.** the smallest number of people, etc. that you need to do sth: *There will only be a skeleton staff on duty over the holiday.* ◇ *We managed to operate a skeleton bus service during the strike.* **6** [C] (sport) a type of SLEDGE (= a vehicle for sliding over ice) for racing, used by one person lying on their front with their feet pointing backwards **7** [U] the sport or event of racing down a special track of ice on a skeleton (6): *Canada won gold and silver in the skeleton.*
**IDM** **a skeleton in the 'cupboard** (BrE) (also **a skeleton in the 'closet** NAmE, BrE) (informal) something SHOCKING, embarrassing, etc. that has happened to you or your family in the past that you want to keep secret

**'skeleton key** noun a key that will open several different locks

**skelm** /skelm/ noun (SAfrE) a person that you believe is a criminal or that you do not trust

**skep·tic** (NAmE) (BrE **scep·tic**) /'skeptɪk/ noun a person who usually doubts that claims or statements are true, especially those that other people believe in

**skep·tical** (NAmE) (BrE **scep·tical**) /'skeptɪkl/ adj. ~ **(about/of sth)** having doubts that a claim or statement is true or that sth will happen: *I am skeptical about his chances of winning.* ◇ *The public remain skeptical of these claims.* ◇ *She looked highly skeptical.* ▶ **skep·tic·al·ly** (NAmE) (BrE **scep·tic·al·ly**) /-kli/ adv.

**skep·ti·cism** (NAmE) (BrE **scep·ti·cism**) /'skeptɪsɪzəm/ noun [U, sing.] an attitude of doubting that claims or statements are true or that sth will happen: *Such claims should be regarded with a certain amount of skepticism.*

**sketch** /sketʃ/ noun, verb
▪ noun **1** a simple picture that is drawn quickly and does not have many details: *The artist is making sketches for his next painting.* ◇ *She drew a sketch map of the area to*

---

1459 **skid**

*show us the way.* ⊃ SYNONYMS at PICTURE **2** a short funny scene on television, in the theatre, etc: *The drama group did a sketch about a couple buying a new car.* ⊃ WORDFINDER NOTE at COMEDY **3** a short report or story that gives only basic details about sth: *a biographical sketch of the prime minister* ⊃ see also THUMBNAIL SKETCH
▪ verb **1** [T, I] ~ **(sb/sth)** to make a quick drawing of sb/sth: *He quickly sketched the view from the window.* **2** [T] ~ **sth (out)** to give a general description of sth, giving only the basic facts **SYN** outline: *She sketched out her plan for tackling the problem.*
**PHR V** **sketch sth↔in** to give more information or details about sth

**sketch·book** /'sketʃbʊk/ (also **sketch pad**) noun a book of sheets of paper for drawing on

**sketchy** /'sketʃi/ adj. (**sketch·ier, sketchi·est**) **1** not complete or detailed and therefore not very useful **SYN** rough: *He gave us a very sketchy account of his visit.* ◇ *sketchy notes* **2** (NAmE, informal) that people consider to be dishonest or bad: *a sketchy neighborhood* ▶ **sketch·ily** /-tʃəli/ adv. **sketchi·ness** noun [U]

**skew** /skjuː/ verb **1** [T] ~ **sth** to change or influence sth with the result that it is not accurate, fair, normal, etc: *to skew the statistics* **2** [I] + **adv./prep.** (BrE) to move or lie at an angle, especially in a position that is not normal: *The ball skewed off at a right angle.*

**skew·bald** /'skjuːbɔːld/ adj. (of a horse) with areas on it of white and another colour, usually not black ⊃ compare PIEBALD ▶ **skew·bald** noun: *He was riding a skewbald.*

**skewed** /skjuːd/ adj. **1** (of information) not accurate or correct **SYN** distorted: *skewed statistics* **2** ~ **(towards sb/sth)** directed towards a particular group, place, etc. in a way that may not be accurate or fair: *The book is heavily skewed towards American readers.* **3** not straight or level: *The car had ended up skewed across the road.* ⊃ see also ASKEW

**skew·er** /'skjuːə(r)/ noun, verb
▪ noun a long thin pointed piece of metal or wood that is pushed through pieces of meat, vegetables, etc. to hold them together while they are cooking, or used to test whether sth is completely cooked
▪ verb ~ **sth** to push a skewer or other thin pointed object through sth

**ski** /skiː/ noun, adj., verb
▪ noun (pl. **skis**) **1** one of a pair of long narrow pieces of wood, metal or plastic that you attach to boots so that you can move smoothly over snow: *a pair of skis* ◇ **on skis** *The children go to school on skis.* **2** = WATERSKI
▪ adj. [only before noun] connected with the sport of skiing: *a ski resort* ◇ *the ski slopes*
▪ verb (**ski·ing, skied, skied**) **1** [I] to move over snow on skis, especially as a sport: *Our children want to learn to ski.* ◇ *We ski in the winter and sail in the summer.* **2** **go skiing** [I] to spend time skiing for pleasure: *We went skiing in France in March.* ⊃ see also SKIING, WATERSKI verb

**skid** /skɪd/ verb, noun
▪ verb [I] (**-dd-**) (+ **adv./prep.**) (usually of a vehicle) to slide forward or to one side in a way that shows a loss of control: *The car skidded on the ice and went straight into the wall.* ◇ *The taxi skidded to a halt just in time.* ◇ *Her foot skidded on the wet floor and she fell heavily.*
▪ noun **1** the movement of a vehicle when it suddenly slides to one side because you have lost control of it: *The motorbike went into a skid.* ◇ *The skid marks on the road showed how fast the car had been travelling.* **2** a part that is on the bottom of some aircraft, next to the wheels, and is used for landing: *the skids of a helicopter*
**IDM** **be on the 'skids** (informal) to be in a bad situation that will get worse **put the 'skids under sb/sth** (informal) to stop sb/sth from being successful or making progress

**skid row** noun [U] (informal, especially NAmE) used to describe the poorest part of a town, the sort of place where people who have no home or job and who drink too much alcohol live: *to be on skid row*

**skier** /ˈskiːə(r)/ noun a person who skis

**skies** /skaɪz/ pl. of SKY

**skiff** /skɪf/ noun a small light boat for ROWING or sailing, usually for one person

**skif·fle** /ˈskɪfl/ noun a type of music popular in the 1950s, that was a mixture of jazz and FOLK MUSIC

**ski·ing** A2 /ˈskiːɪŋ/ noun [U] the sport or activity of moving over snow on skis: *to go skiing* ◊ *downhill skiing* ◊ *a skiing holiday/vacation/trip* ⊃ see also CROSS-COUNTRY SKIING, HELI-SKIING, JET-SKIING

**ski jump** noun a very steep artificial slope that ends suddenly and that is covered with snow. People ski down the slope, jump off the end and see how far they can travel through the air before landing. ▶ **ˈski jumper** noun **ˈski jumping** noun [U]: *Is ski jumping an Olympic sport?* ◊ *the Swiss ski-jumping team*

**skil·ful** (US **skill·ful**) /ˈskɪlfl/ adj. **1** (of a person) good at doing sth, especially sth that needs a particular ability or special training SYN accomplished: *a skilful player/performer/teacher* **2** made or done very well SYN professional: *Thanks to her skilful handling of the affair, the problem was averted.* ▶ **skil·ful·ly** (US **skillfully**) /-fəli/ adv.

**ski lift** noun a machine for taking SKIERS up a slope so that they can then ski down

**skill** A1 /skɪl/ noun **1** A1 [U] the ability to do sth well: *The job requires skill and an eye for detail.* ◊ **~in/at (doing) sth** *What made him remarkable as a photographer was his skill in capturing the moment.* ◊ **with~** *She plays the part with great skill.* **2** A1 [C] a particular ability or type of ability: *communication/language/leadership skills* ◊ *practical/technical skills* ◊ *He had poor social skills and often offended people.* ◊ *You'll learn basic skills like reading a compass and setting up camp.* ◊ **~as sth** *She wants to develop her skills as a writer.* ◊ **~to do sth** *He lacks the necessary skills to run a farm.* ⊃ see also LIFE SKILL, PEOPLE SKILLS

**skilled** B2 /skɪld/ adj. **1** B2 having enough ability, experience and knowledge to be able to do sth well: *a skilled engineer/negotiator/craftsman* ◊ *a shortage of skilled labour* (= people who have had training in a skill) ◊ **~in/at sth/doing sth** *She is highly skilled at dealing with difficult customers.* ⊃ see also SEMI-SKILLED **2** B2 (of a job) needing special abilities or training SYN expert: *Furniture-making is very skilled work.* OPP unskilled ⊃ WORD-FINDER NOTE at WORK

**skil·let** /ˈskɪlɪt/ noun (NAmE) = FRYING PAN

**skill·ful** (US) = SKILFUL

**ˈskill set** noun a person's range of skills or abilities

**skim** /skɪm/ verb (-mm-) **1** [T] to remove fat, cream, etc. from the surface of a liquid: **~sth off/from sth** *Skim the scum off the jam and let it cool.* ◊ **~sth** *Skim the jam and let it cool.* **2** [I, T, no passive] to move quickly and lightly over a surface, not touching it or only touching it occasionally; to make sth do this: **~along/over, etc. sth** *We watched the birds skimming over the lake.* ◊ **~sth** *The speedboat took off, skimming the waves.* ◊ (figurative) *This report has barely skimmed the surface of the subject.* ◊ **~sth across, over, etc. sth** (BrE) *Small boys were skimming stones across the water.* ⊃ see also SKIP verb **3** [I, T] to read sth quickly in order to find a particular point or the main points: **~through/over sth** *He skimmed through the article trying to find his name.* ◊ **~sth** *I always skim the financial section of the newspaper.* **4** [T] **~sth (from sth)** (informal) to steal small amounts of money frequently over a period of time **5** [I, T] **~(sth)** to illegally copy electronic information from a credit card in order to use it without the owner's permission
PHRV **ˌskim sth↔ˈoff** to take for yourself the best part of sth, often in an unfair way

**ˌskimmed ˈmilk** (BrE) (also **ˌskim ˈmilk** NAmE, BrE) noun [U] milk that contains less fat than normal because the cream has been removed from it ⊃ compare SEMI-SKIMMED, WHOLE MILK

**skimp** /skɪmp/ verb [I] **~(on sth)** to try to spend less time, money, etc. on sth that is really needed: *Older people should not skimp on food or heating.*

**skimpy** /ˈskɪmpi/ adj. (**skimp·ier, skimp·i·est**) **1** (of clothes) very small and not covering much of your body: *a skimpy dress* **2** (disapproving) not large enough in amount or size: *a skimpy meal* ◊ *They provided only skimpy details.*

**skin** A2 /skɪn/ noun, verb
■ noun
• ON BODY **1** A2 [U, C] the layer of TISSUE that covers the body: *to have dark/pale skin* ◊ *skin cancer* ◊ *She said she was treated unfairly because of the colour of her skin.* ◊ *skin colour/tone* ⊃ see also FORESKIN, REDSKIN
• -SKINNED **2** (in adjectives) having the type of skin mentioned: *dark-skinned* ◊ *fair-skinned* ⊃ see also THICK-SKINNED, THIN-SKINNED
• OF DEAD ANIMAL **3** A2 [C, U] (often in compounds) the skin of a dead animal with or without its fur, used for making leather, etc: *The skins are removed and laid out to dry.* ◊ *animal skins*
• OF FRUIT/VEGETABLES **4** A2 [C, U] the outer layer of some fruits and vegetables: *Remove the skins by soaking the tomatoes in hot water.* ◊ *a chemical found in the skin of grapes* ⊃ compare PEEL, RIND, ZEST ⊃ VISUAL VOCAB page V4 ⊃ see also BANANA SKIN
• OF SAUSAGE **5** [C, U] the thin outer layer of a SAUSAGE: *Prick the skins before grilling.*
• ON LIQUIDS **6** [C, U] the thin layer that forms on the surface of some liquids, especially when they become cold after being heated: *A skin had formed on the top of the milk.*
• OUTSIDE LAYER **7** [C] a layer that covers the outside of sth: *the outer skin of the earth* ◊ *the metal skin of the aircraft* **8** [C] a special cover for any small electronic device that you can carry with you: *You can create your own custom skin for your iPod.*
• IN A COMPUTER PROGRAM **9** [C] (computing) the INTERFACE of a computer program (= the way a computer program presents information on screen), that the user can change as they wish
IDM **by the ˌskin of your ˈteeth** (informal) if you do sth **by the skin of your teeth**, you only just manage to do it **get under sb's ˈskin** (informal) to annoy sb: *Don't let him get under your skin.* **have got sb under your ˈskin** (informal) to be extremely attracted to sb **it's no skin off ˈmy, ˈyour, ˈhis, etc. nose** (informal) used to say that sb is not upset or annoyed about sth because it does not affect them in a bad way **make your ˈskin crawl** to make you feel afraid or full of horror **(nothing but/all/only) skin and ˈbone** (informal) extremely thin in a way that is not attractive or healthy ⊃ more at JUMP v., SAVE v., THICK adj., THIN adj.
■ verb (-nn-)
• ANIMAL/FRUIT/VEGETABLE **1** **~sth** to take the skin off an animal, a fruit or a vegetable: *You'll need four ripe tomatoes, skinned and chopped.*
• PART OF BODY **2** **~sth** to rub the skin off part of your body by accident: *He skinned his knees climbing down the tree.* **3** (computing) **~sth** to change the way that a computer program presents information on the screen to suit your particular needs IDM see EYE n., WAY n.
PHRV **ˌskin ˈup** (BrE, informal) to make a cigarette containing MARIJUANA

**ˈskin care** /ˈskɪnkeə(r); NAmE -ker/ noun [U] the use of creams and special products to look after your skin

**skin-ˈdeep** adj. [not usually before noun] (of a feeling or an attitude) not as important or strongly felt as it appears to be SYN superficial IDM see BEAUTY

**skin·der** (also **skin·ner**) /ˈskɪnə(r)/ noun, verb (SAfrE, informal)
■ noun [U] conversation about other people's private lives, often including details which may not be true: *They talk a lot of skinder.*

---

æ cat | ɑː father | e bed | ɜː fur | ə about | ɪ sit | iː see | i happy | ɒ got (BrE) | ɔː saw | ʌ cup | ʊ put | uː too

**skin-flint** /ˈskɪnflɪnt/ noun (informal, disapproving) a person who does not like spending money SYN miser

**skin graft** noun a medical operation in which healthy skin is taken from one part of sb's body and placed on another part to replace skin that has been burned or damaged; a piece of skin that is moved in this way

**skin·head** /ˈskɪnhed/ noun a young person with very short hair, especially one who is violent, aggressive and RACIST

**skink** /skɪŋk/ noun a LIZARD with short legs or with no legs

**skin·ner** = SKINDER

**skinny** /ˈskɪni/ adj., noun
- adj. (**skin·ni·er**, **skin·ni·est**) **1** (informal, usually disapproving) very thin, especially in a way that you find unpleasant or ugly: *skinny legs* **2** (of clothes) designed to fit closely to the body: *skinny jeans* **3** (informal) low in fat: *a skinny latte*
- noun [U] **the ~ (on sb/sth)** (NAmE, informal) information about sb/sth, especially details that are not generally known: *This book gives you the skinny on Hollywood.*

**skinny-dipping** noun [U] (informal) swimming without any clothes on

**skint** /skɪnt/ adj. [not usually before noun] (BrE, informal) having no money

**skin·tight** /ˌskɪnˈtaɪt/ adj. (of clothes) fitting very closely to the body

**skip** /skɪp/ verb, noun
- verb (-pp-)
  - **MOVE WITH JUMPS 1** [I] (+ adv./prep.) to move forwards lightly and quickly making a little jump with each step: *She skipped happily along beside me.*
  - **JUMP OVER ROPE 2** [I] (BrE) (NAmE **jump rope**, **skip rope** [T]) to jump over a rope which is held at both ends by yourself or by two other people and is passed again and again over your head and under your feet: *The girls were skipping in the playground.* ◊ *She likes to skip rope as a warm-up.*
  - **NOT DO STH 3** [T] ~ **sth** to not do sth that you usually do or should do: *I often skip breakfast altogether.* ◊ *(especially NAmE) She decided to skip class that afternoon.* **4** [T, I] to leave out sth that would normally be the next thing that you would do, read, etc.: ~ **sth** *You can skip the next chapter if you have covered the topic in class.* ◊ ~ **over sth** *I skipped over the last part of the book.* ◊ ~ **to sth** *I suggest we skip to the last item on the agenda.*
  - **CHANGE QUICKLY 5** [I] + adv./prep. to move from one place to another or from one subject to another very quickly: *She kept skipping from one topic of conversation to another.*
  - **LEAVE SECRETLY 6** [T] ~ **sth** (informal) to leave a place secretly or suddenly: *The bombers skipped the country shortly after the blast.*
  - **STONES 7** (BrE also **skim**) [T] ~ **sth (across, over, etc. sth)** to make a flat stone jump across the surface of water: *The boys were skipping stones across the pond.*
  - IDM **'skip it** (informal) used to tell sb hurriedly that you do not want to talk about sth or repeat what you have said: *'What were you saying?' 'Oh, skip it!'* ⇒ more at BAIL n., HEART n.
  - PHRV **skip 'off/'out** to leave secretly or suddenly **'skip 'out on sb** (NAmE) to leave sb, especially when they need you
- noun
  - **MOVEMENT 1** a skipping movement: *She gave a skip and a jump and was off down the street.*
  - **CONTAINER FOR WASTE 2** (BrE) (NAmE **Dumpster**™) a large open container for putting old, broken building materials, rubbish, etc. in. The skip is then loaded on a lorry and taken away.

**ski-plane** noun a plane with two parts like skis fixed to the bottom so that it can land on snow or ice

**ski pole** (BrE also **ski stick**) noun a stick used to push yourself forward while skiing

---

1461 **skolly**

**skip·per** /ˈskɪpə(r)/ noun, verb
- noun **1** the captain of a small ship or fishing boat **2** (informal, especially BrE) the captain of a sports team
- verb ~ **sth** to be the captain of a boat, sports team, etc.: *to skipper a yacht* ◊ *(especially BrE) He skippered the team to victory.*

**'skipping rope** (BrE) (NAmE **'jump rope**) noun a piece of rope, usually with a handle at each end, that you hold, turn over your head and then jump over, for fun or to keep fit

**skir·mish** /ˈskɜːmɪʃ; NAmE ˈskɜːrm-/ noun, verb
- noun **1** a short fight between small groups of soldiers, etc., especially one that is not planned **2** a short argument, especially between political opponents
- verb [I] to take part in a short fight or argument ▶ **skir·mish·er** noun **skir·mish·ing** noun [U]: *There are reports of skirmishing along the border.*

**skirt** ⓘ A1 /skɜːt; NAmE skɜːrt/ noun, verb
- noun **1** A1 [C] a piece of clothing for a woman or girl that hangs from the middle part of the body: *a short/long/pleated/denim skirt* ⇒ see also GRASS SKIRT, MINISKIRT, PENCIL SKIRT **2** [C] (also **skirts** [pl.]) the part of a dress, coat, etc. that hangs below the middle part of the body **3** [C] an outer layer that covers and protects the base of a vehicle or machine: *the rubber skirt around the bottom of a hovercraft*
- verb **1** [T, I] to be or go around the edge of sth: ~ **sth** *They followed the road that skirted the lake.* ◊ ~ **around/round sth** *I skirted around the field and crossed the bridge.* **2** [T, I] to avoid talking about a subject, especially because it is difficult or embarrassing: ~ **sth** *He carefully skirted the issue of where they would live.* ◊ ~ **around/round sth** *She tactfully skirted around the subject of money.*

**'skirting board** (BrE) (NAmE **base·board**) noun [C, U] (BrE also **skirt·ing** [U]) a narrow piece of wood that is fixed along the bottom of the walls in a house

**'ski run** (also **run**) noun a track that is marked on a slope that you ski down

**skit** /skɪt/ noun ~ **(on sth)** a short piece of humorous writing or a performance that makes fun of sb/sth by copying them: *a skit on daytime TV programmes*

**skit·ter** /ˈskɪtə(r)/ verb [I] + adv./prep. to run or move very quickly and lightly

**skit·tish** /ˈskɪtɪʃ/ adj. **1** (of horses) easily excited or frightened and therefore difficult to control **2** (of people) not very serious and with ideas and feelings that keep changing **3** (especially NAmE, business) likely to change suddenly: *skittish financial markets* ▶ **skit·tish·ly** adv. **skit·tish·ness** noun [U]

**skit·tle** /ˈskɪtl/ noun **1** [C] a wooden or plastic object used in the game of skittles **2 skittles** [U] (in Britain) a game in which players roll a ball at nine skittles and try to knock over as many of them as possible ⇒ compare TENPIN BOWLING

**skive** /skaɪv/ verb [I, T] (BrE, informal) to avoid work or school by staying away or leaving early SYN **bunk off**: *'Where's Tom?' 'Skiving as usual.'* ◊ ~ **off** *She always skives off early on Fridays.* ◊ ~ **sth** *I skived the last lecture.* ▶ **skiver** noun

**skivvy** /ˈskɪvi/ noun, verb
- noun (pl. **-ies**) **1** [C] (BrE, informal) a servant, usually female, who does all the dirty or boring jobs in a house: *He treats his wife like a skivvy.* **2 Skiv·vies**™ [pl.] (NAmE, informal) underwear, especially men's underwear
- verb [I] (BrE, informal) (**skiv·vies**, **skivvy·ing**, **skiv·vied**, **skiv·vied**) to do dirty or boring jobs

**skolly** /ˈskɒli; NAmE ˈskɑːli/ SAfrE /ˈskɔːli/ noun (pl. **-ies**) (SAfrE, informal) a young person who commits crimes or behaves badly

# skua

**skua** /ˈskjuːə/ noun a large brown bird that lives near the sea. It eats fish, which it sometimes takes from other birds.

**skul·dug·gery** (also **skull·dug·gery**) /skʌlˈdʌɡəri/ noun [U] (old-fashioned or humorous) dishonest behaviour or activities

**skulk** /skʌlk/ verb [I] + adv./prep. (disapproving) to hide or move around secretly, especially when you are planning sth bad: *There was someone skulking behind the bushes.*

**skull** /skʌl/ noun **1** the bone structure that forms the head and surrounds and protects the brain **SYN** cranium: *a fractured skull* ⇒ VISUAL VOCAB page V1 **2** (informal) the head or the brain: *Her skull was crammed with too many thoughts.* ◊ (informal) *When will he get it into his thick skull that I never want to see him again!*

**skull and ˈcrossbones** noun [sing.] a picture of a human skull above two crossed bones, used in the past on the flags of PIRATE ships, and now used as a warning on containers with dangerous substances inside

**skull·cap** /ˈskʌlkæp/ noun a small round cap worn on top of the head, especially by male Jewish and Catholic BISHOPS, CARDINALS, etc. ⇒ see also YARMULKE

**skull·dug·gery** = SKULDUGGERY

**skunk** /skʌŋk/ (NAmE also **pole·cat**) noun **1** [C] a small black and white North American animal that can produce a strong unpleasant smell to defend itself when it is attacked **2** [U] (slang) = SKUNKWEED **IDM** see DRUNK adj.

**skunk·weed** /ˈskʌŋkwiːd/ (also slang **skunk**) noun [U] a strong type of CANNABIS

**sky** /skaɪ/ noun, verb
■ noun [C, U] (pl. **skies**) the space above the earth that you can see when you look up, where clouds and the sun, moon and stars appear **HELP** You usually say **the sky**. When **sky** is used with an adjective, use **a ... sky**. You can also use the plural form **skies**, especially when you are thinking about the great extent of the sky.: *The sky suddenly went dark and it started to rain.* ◊ **in the ~** *What's that in the sky?* ◊ *the night sky* ◊ *a land of blue skies and sunshine* ◊ *Clear skies could well mean temperatures plummeting tonight.* ◊ **under a ~** *A crowd had gathered in the square under an overcast sky.* ◊ **~ over/above sth** *The skies above London were ablaze with a spectacular firework display.* ⇒ see also BLUE-SKY
**IDM** **the sky's the ˈlimit** (informal) there is no limit to what sb can achieve, earn, do, etc: *With a talent like his, the sky's the limit.* ⇒ more at GREAT adj., PIE, PRAISE v.
■ verb (**skies, sky·ing, skied, skied**) ~ sth to hit a ball very high into the air: *She skied her tee shot.*

**sky-ˈblue** adj. bright blue in colour, like the sky on a clear day ▶ **sky ˈblue** noun [U]

**sky·box** /ˈskaɪbɒks/; NAmE -bɑːks/ noun (NAmE) an area of expensive seats, separated from other areas, high up in a sports ground

**sky·div·ing** /ˈskaɪdaɪvɪŋ/ noun [U] a sport in which you jump from a plane and fall for as long as you safely can before opening your PARACHUTE: *to go skydiving* ▶ **sky·diver** noun

**sky-ˈhigh** adj. very high; too high: *His confidence is still sky-high.* ◊ *sky-high interest rates* ▶ **sky-ˈhigh** adv.: *After the election, prices went sky-high.*

**sky·lark** /ˈskaɪlɑːk/; NAmE -lɑːrk/ noun a small bird that sings while it flies high up in the sky

**sky·light** /ˈskaɪlaɪt/ noun a small window in a roof

**sky·line** /ˈskaɪlaɪn/ noun the outline of buildings, trees, hills, etc. seen against the sky: *the New York skyline*

**Skype**™ /skaɪp/ noun, verb
■ noun [U] a phone system that works by direct communication between users' computers on the internet, often using WEBCAMS so the callers can see each other: *Broadcasters are using Skype for interviews.* ⇒ see also VoIP
■ verb [T, I] to speak (with sb) using Skype: *~ sb I'll Skype you later.* ◊ *~ (with sb) She Skypes with her grandchildren.*

**sky·rocket** /ˈskaɪrɒkɪt/; NAmE -rɑːk-/ verb [I] (of prices, etc.) to rise quickly to a very high level

**sky·scraper** /ˈskaɪskreɪpə(r)/ noun a very tall building in a city

**sky·wards** /ˈskaɪwədz/; NAmE -wərdz/ (also **sky·ward**) adv. towards the sky; up into the sky: *She pointed skywards.* ◊ *The rocket soared skywards.*

**SLA** /ˌes el ˈeɪ/ abbr. (linguistics) SECOND LANGUAGE ACQUISITION

**slab** /slæb/ noun **1** a thick flat piece of stone, wood or other hard material: *a slab of marble/concrete* ◊ *The road was paved with smooth stone slabs.* ◊ *paving slabs* ◊ *a dead body on the slab* (= on a table in a MORTUARY) **2** a thick, flat slice or piece of sth: *a slab of chocolate* ◊ *slabs of meat*

**slack** /slæk/ adj., noun, verb
■ adj. (**slack·er, slack·est**) **1** not stretched tight **SYN** loose: *She was staring into space, her mouth slack.* ◊ *The rope suddenly went slack.* ◊ *slack muscles* **2** (of business) not having many customers or sales; not busy: *a slack period* **3** (disapproving) not putting enough care, attention or energy into sth and so not doing it well enough: *He's been very slack in his work lately.* ◊ *Discipline in the classroom is very slack.* ▶ **slack·ly** adv.: *Her arms hung slackly by her sides.* **slack·ness** noun [U]
■ noun [U] ⇒ see also SLACKS **1** the part of a rope, etc. that is hanging loosely: *There's too much slack in the tow rope.* **2** people, money or space that should be used more fully in an organization: *There's very little slack in the budget.* **3** very small pieces of coal
**IDM** **cut sb some ˈslack** (informal) to be less critical of sb or less strict with them: *Hey, cut him some slack! He's doing his best!* **take up the ˈslack** **1** to improve the way money or people are used in an organization **2** to pull on a rope, etc. until it is tight
■ verb [I] to work less hard than you usually do or should do **PHRV** **slack ˈoff (on sth)** to do sth more slowly or with less energy than before

**slack·en** /ˈslækən/ verb **1** [I, T] to gradually become, or to make sth become, slower, less active, etc. **SYN** relax: *~ (off) We've been really busy, but things are starting to slacken off now.* ◊ *~ sth She slackened her pace a little* (= walked a little more slowly). **2** [I, T] to become, or to make sth become, less tight **SYN** loosen: *His grip slackened and she pulled away from him.* ◊ *~ sth He slackened the ropes slightly.*

**slack·er** /ˈslækə(r)/ noun (informal, disapproving) a person who is lazy and avoids work

**ˈslack-jawed** adj. having your mouth open because you are shocked or confused: *a bunch of slack-jawed idiots*

**slacks** /slæks/ noun [pl.] (old-fashioned or NAmE, formal) trousers for men or women, that are not part of a suit: *a pair of slacks*

**slag** /slæɡ/ noun, verb
■ noun **1** [U] the waste material that remains after metal has been removed from rock **2** [C] (BrE, slang, offensive) an offensive word for a woman, used to suggest that she has a lot of sexual partners
■ verb (**-gg-**)
**PHRV** **slag sb↔ˈoff** (BrE, informal) to say cruel or critical things about sb: *I hate the way he's always slagging off his colleagues.*

**slag·ging** /ˈslæɡɪŋ/ (also **slagging-ˈoff**) noun (informal) the act of speaking to or about sb/sth in a critical and offensive way: *He got a slagging from bloggers about his recent comments.*

**slain** /sleɪn/ past part. of SLAY

**slake** /sleɪk/ verb (literary) **1** ~ your thirst to drink so that you no longer feel thirsty **SYN** quench **2** ~ sth to satisfy a desire

**sla·lom** /ˈslɑːləm/ *noun* a race for people on skis or in CANOES along a winding course marked by POLES

**slam** /slæm/ *verb, noun*
- *verb* (-mm-) **1** [I, T] to shut, or to make sth shut, with a lot of force, making a loud noise SYN **bang**: *I heard the door slam behind him.* ◊ *+ adj. A window slammed shut in the wind.* ◊ *~ sth He stormed out of the house, slamming the door as he left.* ◊ *~ sth + adj. She slammed the lid shut.* ◊ *+ adv./prep. She slammed out of the room* (= went out and slammed the door behind her). **2** [T] *~ sth + adv./prep.* to put, push or throw sth into a particular place or position with a lot of force: *She slammed down the phone angrily.* ◊ *He slammed on the brakes* (= stopped the car very suddenly). **3** [I, T] to crash into sth with a lot of force; to make sb/sth crash into sth with a lot of force: *+ adv./prep. The car skidded and slammed into a tree.* ◊ *~ sb/sth + adv./prep. The force of the explosion slammed me against the wall.* ⊃ SYNONYMS at CRASH **4** [T] *~ sb/sth* (used especially in newspapers) to criticize sb/sth very strongly IDM ▸ see DOOR
- *noun* [usually sing.] **1** an act of slamming sth; the noise of sth being slammed: *She gave the door a good hard slam.* **2** a competition in which people perform their poems to an audience, which chooses a winner ⊃ see also GRAND SLAM, SPOKEN WORD (2)

**ˈslam dunk** *noun* **1** (in basketball) the act of jumping up and putting the ball through the net with a lot of force **2** (*NAmE, informal*) something that is certain to be successful: *Politically, this issue is a slam dunk for the party.*

**ˈslam-dunk** *verb* [T, I] *~(sth)* (in basketball) to jump up and put the ball through the net with a lot of force

**the ˈslam·mer** /ðə ˈslæmə(r)/ *noun* [sing.] (*slang*) prison

**slan·der** /ˈslɑːndə(r); *NAmE* ˈslæn-/ *noun, verb*
- *noun* [C, U] a false spoken statement intended to damage the good opinion people have of sb; the legal offence of making this kind of statement: *a vicious slander on the company's good name* ◊ *He's suing them for slander.* ⊃ compare LIBEL ▸ **slan·der·ous** *adj.*: *a slanderous remark*
- *verb ~ sb/sth* to make a false spoken statement about sb that is intended to damage the good opinion that people have of them: *He angrily accused the investigators of slandering both him and his family.* ⊃ compare LIBEL

**slang** /slæŋ/ *noun* [U] very informal words and expressions that are more common in spoken language, especially used by a particular group of people, for example, children, criminals, soldiers, etc: *teenage slang* ◊ *a slang word/expression/term* ⊃ see also RHYMING SLANG

**ˈslanging match** *noun* (*BrE, informal*) an angry argument in which people make offensive remarks to each other ⊃ compare SHOUTING MATCH

**slant** /slɑːnt; *NAmE* slænt/ *verb, noun*
- *verb* **1** [I, T] to slope or to make sth slope in a particular direction or at a particular angle: *+ adv./prep.* (*literary*) *The sun slanted through the window.* ◊ *~ sth + adv./prep. Slant your skis a little more to the left.* **2** [T] *~ sth (+ adv./prep.)* (sometimes disapproving) to present information based on a particular way of thinking, especially in an unfair way: *The findings of the report had been slanted in favour of the manufacturers.*
- *noun* **1** a sloping position: *at a ~ The sofa faced the fire at a slant.* ◊ *on the ~ Cut the flower stems on the slant.* **2** *~(on sth/sb)* a way of thinking about sth, especially one that shows support for a particular opinion or point of view: *She put a new slant on the play.*

**slant·ed** /ˈslɑːntɪd; *NAmE* ˈslæn-/ *adj.* **1** sloping in one direction: *The house had a low, slanted roof.* **2** *~(towards sth)* tending to be in favour of one person or thing in a way that may be unfair to others: *a slanted view of events*

**slant·ing** /ˈslɑːntɪŋ; *NAmE* ˈslæn-/ *adj.* not straight or level; sloping: *slanting eyes/handwriting/rain*

**slap** /slæp/ *verb, noun, adv.*
- *verb* (-pp-) **1** [T] *~ sb/sth (+ adv./prep.)* to hit sb/sth with the flat part of your hand SYN **smack**: *She slapped his face hard.* ◊ *She slapped him hard across the face.* ◊ *'Congratulations!' he said, slapping me on the back.* **2** [T] *~ sth + adv./prep.* to put sth on a surface in a quick,

---

1463 **slat**

careless and often noisy way, especially because you are angry: *He slapped the newspaper down on the desk.* ◊ *She slapped a $10 bill into my hand.* **3** [I] *+ adv./prep.* to hit against sth with the noise of sb being slapped: *The water slapped against the side of the boat.*

PHRV **ˌslap sb aˈround** (*also* **ˌslap sb aˈbout** *especially in BrE*) (*informal*) to hit sb regularly or often: *Her ex-husband used to slap her around.* **ˌslap sth/sb↔ˈdown** (*informal*) to criticize sb in an unfair way, often in public, so that they feel embarrassed or less confident **ˈslap sth on sb/sth** (*informal*) to order, especially in a sudden or an unfair way, that sth must happen or sb must do sth: *The company slapped a ban on using email or the staff.* **ˌslap sth ˈon sth** (*informal*) to increase the price of sth suddenly: *They've slapped 50p on the price of a pack of cigarettes.* **ˌslap sth ˈon sth** | **ˌslap sth↔ˈon** to spread sth on a surface in a quick, careless way: *Just slap some paint on the walls and it'll look fine.* ◊ *I'd better slap some make-up on before I go out.*

- *noun* **1** [C] the action of hitting sb/sth with the flat part of your hand: *She gave him a slap across the face.* ◊ *He gave me a hearty slap on the back.* **2** [sing.] the noise made by hitting sb/sth with the flat part of your hand; a similar noise made by sth else: *the gentle slap of water against the shore* **3** [U] (*BrE, informal*) = MAKE-UP (1)

IDM **ˌslap and ˈtickle** (*BrE, old-fashioned, informal*) enthusiastic kissing and CUDDLING between lovers **a ˌslap in the ˈface** an action that seems to be intended as a deliberate way of offending and showing lack of respect for sb **a ˌslap on the ˈwrist** (*informal*) a warning or mild punishment

- *adv.* (*also* **ˌslap ˈbang**) (*informal*) **1** straight, and with great force: *Storming out of her room, she went slap into Luke.* **2** exactly: *Their apartment is slap bang in the middle of town.*

**slap·dash** /ˈslæpdæʃ/ *adj.* done, or doing sth, too quickly and carelessly: *She has a very slapdash approach to keeping accounts.* ◊ *a slapdash piece of writing*

**slap·per** /ˈslæpə(r)/ *noun* (*BrE, slang*) an offensive word for a woman, used to suggest that she has a lot of sexual partners

**slap·stick** /ˈslæpstɪk/ *noun* [U] the type of humour that is based on simple actions, for example people hitting each other, falling down, etc. ⊃ WORDFINDER NOTE at COMEDY

**ˈslap-up** *adj.* [only before noun] (*BrE, informal*) (of a meal) large and very good

**slash** /slæʃ/ *verb, noun*
- *verb* **1** [T, I] to make a long cut with a sharp object, especially in a violent way SYN **slit**: *~ sth Someone had slashed the tyres on my car.* ◊ *She tried to kill herself by slashing her wrists.* ◊ *We had to slash our way through the undergrowth with sticks.* ◊ *~ at sb/sth He slashed wildly at me with a knife.* **2** [T] *~ sth* (*informal*) (often used in newspapers) to reduce sth by a large amount: *to slash spending/prices/costs* ◊ *The workforce has been slashed by half.* ⊃ SYNONYMS at CUT
- *noun* **1** [C] a sharp movement made with a knife, etc. in order to cut sb/sth **2** [C] a long narrow wound or cut: *a slash across his right cheek* ◊ (*figurative*) *Her mouth was a slash of red lipstick.* **3** [C] (*BrE also* **obˈlique**) the symbol (/) used to show alternatives, as in *lunch and/or dinner* and 4/5 *people* and to write FRACTIONS, as in ¾ ⊃ WORDFINDER NOTE at KEYBOARD ⊃ see also BACKSLASH, FORWARD SLASH **4** *a slash* [sing.] (*BrE, slang*) an act of URINATING: *He's just nipped out to have a slash.*

**ˌslash-and-ˈburn** *adj.* **1** relating to a method of farming in which existing plants, crops, etc. are cut down and burned before new seeds are planted: *slash-and-burn agriculture* **2** aggressive and causing a lot of harm or damage

**slash·er** /ˈslæʃə(r)/ *noun* (*also* **ˈslasher film**, **ˈslasher movie**) *noun* a frightening film, in which an unknown person kills a lot of people

**slat** /slæt/ *noun* **1** one of a series of thin flat pieces of wood, metal or plastic, used in furniture, fences, etc. **2** (*specialist*) a part of the wing of an aircraft, on the front of the wing,

# slate

that can be moved up or down to control movement in either direction ⊃ compare FLAP (5)

**slate** /sleɪt/ noun, verb
- noun 1 [U] a type of dark grey stone that splits easily into thin flat layers: *a slate quarry* ◊ *The sea was the colour of slate.* 2 [C] a small thin piece of slate, used for covering roofs: *A loose slate had fallen from the roof.* 3 [C] (NAmE) a list of the candidates in an election: *a slate of candidates* ◊ *the Democratic slate* 4 [C] a small sheet of slate in a wooden frame, used in the past in schools for children to write on IDM see BLANK adj., CLEAN adj., WIPE v.
- verb 1 ~ sb/sth (for sth) (BrE) to criticize sb/sth, especially in a newspaper: *to slate a book/play/writer* 2 [usually passive] to plan that sth will happen at a particular time in the future: **be slated for sth** *The houses were first slated for demolition five years ago.* ◊ **be slated to do sth** *The new store is slated to open in spring.* 3 [usually passive] (especially NAmE, informal) to suggest or choose sb for a job, position, etc: **be slated for sth** *I was told that I was being slated for promotion.* ◊ **be slated to do sth** *He is slated to play the lead in the new musical.*

**slated** /ˈsleɪtɪd/ adj. covered with pieces of SLATE: *a slated roof*

**slather** /ˈslæðə(r)/ verb ~ sth on | ~ sth on/over sth | ~ sth with/in sth to cover sth with a thick layer of a substance: *I slathered on some sun cream.* ◊ *hot dogs slathered with mustard*

**slat·ted** /ˈslætɪd/ adj. [usually before noun] made of slats (= thin pieces of wood): *slatted blinds*

**slaugh·ter** /ˈslɔːtə(r)/ noun, verb
- noun [U] 1 the killing of animals for their meat: *cows taken for slaughter* 2 the cruel killing of large numbers of people at one time, especially in a war SYN **massacre**: *the wholesale slaughter of innocent people* IDM see LAMB n.
- verb [often passive] 1 ~ sth to kill an animal, usually for its meat SYN **butcher** 2 ~ sb/sth to kill a large number of people or animals violently SYN **massacre**: *Men, women and children were slaughtered and villages destroyed.* 3 ~ sb/sth (informal) to defeat sb/sth by a large number of points in a sports game, competition, etc: *We were slaughtered 10–1 by the home team.*

**slaugh·ter·house** /ˈslɔːtəhaʊs/; NAmE -tərh-/ noun (BrE also **ab·at·toir**) a building where animals are killed for food

**Slav** /slɑːv/ noun a member of any of the races of people of central and eastern Europe who speak Slavic languages

**slave** /sleɪv/ noun, verb
- noun 1 a person who is owned by another person and is forced to work for them: *A former slave, he graduated from Claflin University in South Carolina.* ⊃ WORDFINDER NOTE at FREEDOM 2 a person who is so strongly influenced by sth that they cannot live without it, or cannot make their own decisions: **~ of sth** *We are slaves of the motor car.* ◊ **~ to sth** *Sue's a slave to fashion.* 3 (specialist) a device that is directly controlled by another one
- verb [I] ~ (away) (at sth) to work very hard: *I've been slaving away all day trying to get this work finished.* ◊ *I haven't got time to spend hours slaving over a hot stove* (= doing a lot of cooking).

**'slave-driver** noun (disapproving) a person who makes people work extremely hard SYN **tyrant**

**slave 'labour** (US slave 'labor) noun [U] 1 work that is done by slaves; the slaves who do the work: *Huge palaces were built by slave labour.* 2 (informal) work that is very hard and very badly paid: *I left because the job was just slave labour.*

**slaver¹** /ˈslævə(r)/ verb [I] (usually of an animal) to let SALIVA (= the liquid produced in the mouth) run out of the mouth, especially when hungry or excited: *slavering dogs*

**slaver²** /ˈsleɪvə(r)/ noun 1 (in the past) a person who bought and sold slaves 2 a ship that was used in the past for carrying slaves

**slav·ery** /ˈsleɪvəri/ noun [U] 1 the state of being a slave: *to be sold into slavery* 2 the practice of having slaves: *the abolition of slavery* OPP **freedom**

**'slave trade** noun [sing.] the buying and selling of people as slaves, especially in the 17th–19th centuries

**Slav·ic** /ˈslɑːvɪk/ (also **Slav·on·ic**) adj. of or connected with Slavs or their languages, which include Russian, Polish, Czech and a number of other languages

**slav·ish** /ˈsleɪvɪʃ/ adj. (disapproving) following or copying sb/sth exactly without having any original thought at all: *a slavish adherence to the rules* ▶ **slav·ish·ly** adv.

**Sla·von·ic** /sləˈvɒnɪk; NAmE -ˈvɑːn-/ adj. = SLAVIC

**slaw** /slɔː/ noun [U] (especially NAmE) = COLESLAW

**slay** /sleɪ/ verb (slew /sluː/, slain /sleɪn/) 1 ~ sb/sth (old-fashioned or literary) to kill sb/sth in a war or a fight: *St George slew the dragon.* 2 ~ sb (especially NAmE) (used especially in newspapers) to murder sb: *Two passengers were slain by the hijackers.* 3 ~ sb (old-fashioned, informal, especially NAmE) to have a strong effect on sb, especially to make them laugh: *Those old movies still slay me!* ▶ **slay·ing** noun (especially NAmE): *the drug-related slayings of five people*

**sleaze** /sliːz/ noun 1 [U] dishonest or IMMORAL behaviour, especially by politicians or business people: *allegations of sleaze* ◊ *The candidate was seriously damaged by the sleaze factor.* 2 [U] behaviour or conditions that are unpleasant and not socially acceptable, especially because sex is involved: *the sleaze of a town that was once a naval base* 3 (also **sleaze·bag** /ˈsliːzbæɡ/, **sleaze·ball** /ˈsliːzbɔːl/ especially in NAmE) [C] a person who is not honest or moral

**sleazy** /ˈsliːzi/ adj. (**sleaz·ier**, **sleazi·est**) (informal) 1 (of a place) dirty, unpleasant and not socially acceptable, especially because sex is involved SYN **disreputable**: *a sleazy bar* 2 (of people) IMMORAL or unpleasant: *a sleazy reporter* ▶ **sleazi·ness** noun [U]

**sleb** /sleb/ noun (informal) = CELEBRITY (1)

**sled** /sled/ (especially NAmE) noun, verb
- noun = SLEDGE ⊃ compare SLEIGH, TOBOGGAN
- verb (-dd-) = SLEDGE ▶ **sled·ding** /ˈsledɪŋ/ noun [U]

sledge/sled

sleigh

**sledge** /sledʒ/ (BrE) (also **sled** especially in NAmE) noun, verb
- noun a vehicle for travelling over snow and ice, with long narrow pieces of wood or metal instead of wheels. Larger sledges are pulled by horses or dogs and smaller ones are used for going down hills as a sport or for pleasure. ⊃ compare SLEIGH, TOBOGGAN
- verb [I] to ride on a sledge: *We were hoping we could go sledging.*

**sledge·hammer** /ˈsledʒhæmə(r)/ noun a large heavy tool with a long handle and a metal block at one end, used for breaking rocks, etc. IDM **use a sledgehammer to crack a 'nut** to use more force than is necessary

**sledg·ing** /ˈsledʒɪŋ/ noun [U] 1 (BrE) (NAmE **sledding**) the activity of riding on a sledge: *to go sledging* 2 (in CRICKET) offensive remarks made to players in the other team in order to destroy their concentration ⊃ compare TRASH TALK

**sleek** /sliːk/ *adj.*, *verb*
■ *adj.* (**sleek·er**, **sleek·est**) **1** (*approving*) smooth and shiny **SYN** **glossy**: *sleek black hair* ◇ *the sleek dark head of a seal* **2** (*approving*) having an attractive smooth shape: *a sleek yacht* ◇ *the sleek lines of the new car* **3** (*often disapproving*) (of a person) looking rich, and dressed in smart and expensive clothes: *a sleek and ambitious politician* ▸ **sleek·ly** *adv.* **sleek·ness** *noun* [U]
■ *verb* ~ *sth* (**back/down**) to make sth, especially hair, smooth and shiny: *His glossy hair was sleeked back over his ears.*

**sleep** ⓘ A1 /sliːp/ *verb*, *noun*
■ *verb* (**slept**, **slept** /slept/) **1** ⓘ A1 [I] to rest with your eyes closed and your mind and body not active: *Let her sleep— it'll do her good.* ◇ + *adv./prep.* *to sleep well* ◇ *to sleep deeply/soundly/peacefully/badly* ◇ *I couldn't sleep because of the noise.* ◇ *I can't sleep at night and I'm stressed all the time.* ◇ *It was nice to sleep in my own bed again.* ◇ *He told me I could sleep on the floor at his place.* ◇ *I slept at my sister's house last night* (= stayed the night there). ◇ *We both slept right through* (= were not woken up by) *the storm.* ◇ *We sometimes sleep late at the weekends* (= until late in the morning). **HELP** It is more common to say that somebody **is asleep** than to say that somebody **is sleeping**. **Sleep** can only be used in the passive with a preposition such as **in** or **on**: *It was clear her bed hadn't been slept in.*

**WORDFINDER** doze, dream, drowsy, insomnia, oversleep, REM, sedative, soporific, tired

**2** [T, no passive] ~ *sb* to have enough beds for a particular number of people: *The apartment sleeps six.* ◇ *The hotel sleeps 120 guests.*
**IDM** **let sleeping dogs 'lie** (*saying*) to avoid mentioning a subject or sth that happened in the past, in order to avoid any problems or arguments **sleep like a 'log/'baby** (*informal*) to sleep very well **sleep 'tight** (*informal*) used especially to children before they go to bed to say that you hope they sleep well: *Goodnight, sleep tight!* ⊃ more at EASY *adv.*, ROUGH *adv.*, WINK *n.*
**PHRV** **,sleep a'round** (*informal*, *disapproving*) to have sex with a lot of different people **,sleep 'in** to sleep until after the time you usually get up in the morning **,sleep sth↔'off** to get better after sth, especially drinking too much alcohol, by sleeping: *Let's leave him to sleep it off.* **'sleep on sth** (*informal*) to delay making a decision about sth until the next day, so that you have time to think about it: *Could I sleep on it and let you know tomorrow?* **,sleep 'over** to stay the night at sb else's home: *It's very late now—why don't you sleep over?* ◇ *Can I sleep over at my friend's house?* ⊃ related noun SLEEPOVER **,sleep to'gether** | **,sleep with sb** (*informal*) to have sex with sb, especially sb you are not married to: *I know he's going out with her, but I don't think they're sleeping together.* ◇ *Everyone knows she sleeps with the boss.*

■ *noun* **1** ⓘ A2 [U] the natural state of rest in which your eyes are closed, your body is not active, and your mind is not conscious: *I need to get some sleep.* ◇ *I didn't get much sleep last night.* ◇ *Can you give me something to help me get to sleep* (= start sleeping)? ◇ *Go to sleep—it's late.* ◇ *Try to go back to sleep.* ◇ **in your ~** *He cried out in his sleep.* ◇ *Anxiety can be caused by lack of sleep.* ◇ *I only got about five hours' sleep.* **2** ⓘ A2 [sing.] a period of sleep: *Did you have a good sleep?* ◇ *Ros fell into a deep sleep.* ◇ *I'll feel better after a good night's sleep* (= a night when I sleep well). **3** [U] (*informal*) the substance that sometimes forms in the corners of your eyes after you have been sleeping
**IDM** **be able to do sth in your 'sleep** (*informal*) to be able to do sth very easily because you have done it many times before **,go to 'sleep** (*informal*) if part of your body **goes to sleep**, you lose the sense of feeling in it, usually because it has been in the same position for too long **not lose 'sleep/ lose no 'sleep over sth** to not worry much about sth: *It's not worth losing sleep over.* **put sb to 'sleep** (*informal*) to make sb unconscious before an operation by using drugs (called an ANAESTHETIC) **put sth to 'sleep** to kill a sick or injured animal by giving it drugs so that it dies without pain. People say 'put to sleep' to avoid saying 'kill'. ⊃ more at WINK *n.*

▼ SYNONYMS

**sleep**
doze • nap • snooze
These words all mean to rest with your eyes closed and your mind and body not active.
**sleep** to rest with your eyes shut and your mind and body not active: *Did you sleep well?* ◇ *I couldn't sleep last night.* **NOTE** It is more usual to say that sb **is asleep** than that they **are sleeping**; but if you use an adverb to say how they are sleeping, use **sleeping**: *'What's Ashley doing?' 'Sh! She's asleep.'* ◇ *The baby was sleeping peacefully.* ◇ ~~*The baby was asleep peacefully.*~~
**doze** to sleep lightly, waking up easily, often when you are not in bed: *He was dozing in front of the TV.*
**nap** to sleep for a short time, especially during the day.
**snooze** (*informal*) to sleep lightly for a short time, especially during the day and usually not in bed: *My brother was snoozing on the sofa.*
PATTERNS
• to sleep / doze **lightly / fitfully**
• to doze / snooze **gently**

**sleep·er** /'sliːpə(r)/ *noun* **1** (used with an adjective) a person who sleeps in a particular way: *a heavy/light/sound sleeper* ⊃ see also ROUGH SLEEPER **2** a person who is asleep: *Only the snores of the sleepers broke the silence of the house.* **3** a night train with beds for passengers on it: *the London–Edinburgh sleeper* **4** = SLEEPING CAR **5** (*BrE*) (*NAmE* **tie**) one of the heavy pieces of wood or CONCRETE (= a hard building material) on which the RAILS (= metal bars) on a railway track are laid **6** (*informal*, *especially NAmE*) a film, play or book that for a long time is not very successful and then is suddenly a success **7** (*also* **'sleeper agent**) a SPY who is sent to live in a country as a normal citizen and is not used until much later **8** (*BrE*) a ring or piece of metal that you wear in an ear that has been PIERCED (= had a hole made in it) to keep the hole from closing

**'sleeping bag** *noun* a thick warm bag that you use for sleeping in, for example when you are camping

**,Sleeping 'Beauty** *noun* used to refer to sb who has been asleep for a long time: *OK, Sleeping Beauty, time to get up.* **ORIGIN** From the European fairy tale about a beautiful girl who sleeps for a hundred years and is woken up when a prince kisses her.

**'sleeping car** (*also* **sleep·er**) *noun* a coach on a train with beds for people to sleep in

**,sleeping 'partner** (*BrE*) (*NAmE* **silent 'partner**) *noun* a person who has put money into a business company but who is not actually involved in running it

**'sleeping pill** (*BrE also* **'sleeping tablet**) *noun* a PILL (= tablet) containing a drug that helps you to sleep

**'sleeping sickness** *noun* [U] a tropical disease carried by the TSETSE FLY that causes a feeling of wanting to go to sleep and usually causes death

**sleep·less** /'sliːpləs/ *adj.* **1** [only before noun] without sleep: *I've had a few sleepless nights recently.* **2** [not before noun] not able to sleep: *She lay sleepless until dawn.* ▸ **sleep·less·ly** *adv.* **sleep·less·ness** *noun* [U] **SYN** **insomnia**: *to suffer from sleeplessness*

**sleep·over** /'sliːpəʊvə(r)/ (*NAmE also* **'slumber party**) *noun* a party for children or young people when a group of them spend the night at one house

**sleep·walk** /'sliːpwɔːk/ *verb* [I] to walk around while you are asleep ▸ **sleep·walk·er** (*also formal* **som·nam·bu·list**) *noun*

**sleepy** /'sliːpi/ *adj.* (**sleepi·er**, **sleepi·est**) **1** needing sleep; ready to go to sleep **SYN** **drowsy**: *a sleepy child* ◇ *He had begun to feel sleepy.* ◇ *The heat and the wine made her sleepy.* **2** (of places) quiet and where nothing much happens: *a sleepy little town* ▸ **sleep·ily** /-pɪli/ *adv.*: *She yawned sleepily.* **sleepi·ness** *noun* [U]

# sleet

**sleet** /sliːt/ noun, verb
- noun [U] a mixture of rain and snow ⏵ WORDFINDER NOTE at SNOW
- verb [I] when **it is sleeting**, a mixture of rain and snow is falling from the sky

**sleeve** /sliːv/ noun **1** a part of a piece of clothing that covers all or part of your arm: *a dress with short/long sleeves* ◇ *Dan rolled up his sleeves and washed his hands.* ⏵ see also SHIRTSLEEVE **2** -**sleeved** (in adjectives) having sleeves of the type mentioned: *a short-sleeved shirt* **3** (*also* **jacket** *especially in NAmE*) a stiff paper cover for a record: *a colourful sleeve design* **4** a tube that covers a part of a machine to protect it ▸ **sleeve·less** *adj.*: *a sleeveless dress*
- IDM **have/keep sth up your ˈsleeve** to keep a plan or an idea secret until you need to use it ⏵ more at ACE *n.*, CARD *n.*, LAUGH *v.*, ROLL *v.*, TRICK *n.*, WEAR *v.*

ˈ**sleeve note** *noun* (*BrE, becoming old-fashioned*) = LINER NOTE

**sleigh** /sleɪ/ *noun* a SLEDGE (= a vehicle that slides over snow), especially one pulled by horses: *a sleigh ride* ⏵ picture at SLEDGE

**sleight of hand** /ˌslaɪt əv ˈhænd/ *noun* [U] **1** (*also formal* **le·ger·de·main**) movements of your hand that are done with skill so that other people cannot see them: *The trick is done simply by sleight of hand.* **2** the fact of tricking people in a clever way: *Last year's profits were more the result of financial sleight of hand than genuine growth.*

**slen·der** /ˈslendə(r)/ *adj.* (**slen·der·er, slen·der·est**) HELP You can also use **more slender** and **most slender. 1** (*approving*) (of people or their bodies) thin in an attractive way SYN **slim**: *her slender figure* ◇ *long, slender fingers* **2** thin or narrow: *a glass with a slender stem* **3** small in amount or size and hardly enough: *to win by a slender margin/majority* ◇ *people of slender means* (= with little money) ◇ *Australia held a slender 1–0 lead at half-time.* ▸ **slen·der·ness** *noun* [U]

**slept** /slept/ *past tense, past part.* of SLEEP

**sleuth** /sluːθ/ *noun* (*old-fashioned or humorous*) a person who investigates crimes SYN **detective**: *an amateur sleuth*

**sleuth·ing** /ˈsluːθɪŋ/ *noun* [U] (*old-fashioned or humorous*) the act of investigating a crime or mysterious event: *to do some private sleuthing*

**slew** /sluː/ *verb, noun*
- *verb* [I, T] **1** (especially of a vehicle) to turn or slide suddenly in another direction; to make a vehicle do this: + **adv./prep.** *The car skidded and slewed sideways.* ◇ ~ **sth** + **adv./prep.** *He slewed the motorbike over as they hit the freeway.* **2** *past tense* of SLAY
- *noun* [sing.] ~ **of sth** (*informal, especially NAmE*) a large number or amount of sth

**slice** ⏵ B1 /slaɪs/ *noun, verb*
- *noun* **1** ⏵ B1 a thin flat piece of bread, meat, cheese, etc. that has been cut off a larger piece; a piece of cake that has been cut from a larger cake: *Cut the meat into thin slices.* ◇ ~ **of sth** *a slice of bread/pie* ◇ *a slice of toast/cake/pizza* **2** (*informal*) a part or share of sth: *Our firm is well placed to grab a large slice of the market.* **3** a kitchen UTENSIL (= tool) that you use to lift and serve pieces of food: *a cake slice* ⏵ see also FISH SLICE **4** (*sport*) (in golf, tennis, etc.) a shot that makes the ball go to one side rather than straight ahead, while turning round and round
- IDM **a ˈslice of ˈlife** a film, play or book that gives a very realistic view of ordinary life ⏵ more at ACTION *n.*, CAKE *n.*, PIE
- *verb* **1** ⏵ B1 [T] ~ **sth (up)** to cut sth into slices: *to slice (up) onions* ◇ *Slice the cucumber thinly.* ◇ *sliced bread* **2** [I, T] to cut sth easily with or as if with a sharp knife: + **adv./prep.** *He accidentally sliced through his finger.* ◇ *A piece of glass sliced into his shoulder.* ◇ (*figurative*) *Her speech sliced through all the confusion surrounding the situation.* ◇ ~ **sth** (+ **adj.**) *He sliced the fruit open.* **3** [T] ~ **sth** (*sport*) to hit a ball so that it turns round and round and does not move in the expected direction: *He managed to slice a shot over the net.* **4** [T] ~ **sth** (in golf) to hit the ball so that it flies away in a curve to the right (if you are RIGHT-HANDED) or left (if you are LEFT-HANDED), when you do not mean to **5** [T] ~ **sth** (*NAmE, informal*) to reduce sth by a large amount: *The new tax has sliced annual bonuses by 30 percent.*
- IDM ˌ**slice and ˈdice (sth)** (*computing*) to divide information into small parts in order to study it more closely or to see it in different ways: *The software lets you slice and dice the data and display it in different formats.* ⏵ more at WAY *n.*
- PHRV ˌ**slice sth**↔ˈ**off/a**ˈ**way** | ˌ**slice sth**ˈ**off sth** to cut sth from a larger piece: *Slice a piece off.* ◇ (*figurative*) *He sliced two seconds off the world record.*

ˌ**sliced** ˈ**bread** *noun* [U] bread that is already cut into slices before it is sold: *a loaf of sliced bread*
- IDM **the best thing since sliced ˈbread** (*informal*) if you say that sth is **the best thing since sliced bread**, you think it is extremely good, interesting, etc.

**slick** /slɪk/ *adj., noun, verb*
- *adj.* (**slick·er, slick·est**) **1** (*sometimes disapproving*) done or made in a way that is clever and efficient but often does not seem to be sincere or lacks important ideas: *a slick advertising campaign* ◇ *a slick performance* **2** (*sometimes disapproving*) speaking very easily and smoothly but in a way that does not seem sincere SYN **glib**: *slick TV presenters* ◇ *a slick salesman* **3** done quickly and smoothly SYN **skilful**: *The crowd enjoyed the team's slick passing.* ◇ *a slick gear change* **4** smooth and difficult to hold or move on SYN **slippery**: *The roads were slick with rain.* ▸ **slick·ly** *adv.*: *The magazine is slickly produced.* **slick·ness** *noun* [U]
- *noun* **1** (*also* **oil slick**) an area of oil that is floating on the surface of the sea **2** a small area of sth wet and shiny: *a slick of sweat*
- *verb* [usually passive] to make hair very flat and smooth by putting oil, water, etc. on it: **be slicked** + **adv./prep.** *His hair was slicked back/down with gel.*

**slick·er** /ˈslɪkə(r)/ *noun* (*NAmE*) a long loose coat that keeps you dry in the rain ⏵ see also CITY SLICKER

**slide** ⏵ B2 S /slaɪd/ *verb, noun*
- *verb* (**slid, slid** /slɪd/)
- • MOVE SMOOTHLY/QUIETLY **1** ⏵ B2 [I, T] to move easily over a smooth or wet surface; to make sth move in this way: *As I turned left on a bend, my car started to slide.* ◇ + **adv./prep.** *We slid down the grassy slope.* ◇ ~ **sth** + **adv./prep.** *She slid her hand along the rail.* ◇ ~ (**sth**) + **adj.** *The automatic doors slid open.* **2** [I, T] to move quickly and quietly, for example in order not to be noticed; to make sth move in this way SYN **slip**: + **adv./prep.** *He slid into bed.* ◇ *She slid out while no one was looking.* ◇ ~ **sth** + **adv./prep.** *The man slid the money quickly into his pocket.*
- • BECOME LOWER/WORSE **3** [I] ~ (**from** …) (**to** …) to become gradually lower or of less value: *Shares slid to a 10-year low.* **4** [I] ~ (**down/into/towards sth**) to move gradually into a worse situation: *The industry has slid into decline.* ◇ *They were sliding towards bankruptcy.* ◇ *He got depressed and began to **let things slide*** (= failed to give things the attention they needed).
- *noun*
- • COMPUTERS **1** ⏵ B2 [C] one page of an electronic presentation, that may contain text and images, that is usually viewed on a computer screen or projected onto a larger screen: *I'm still working on the slides for my presentation.*
- • ON ICE **2** [sing.] a long, smooth movement on ice or a smooth surface SYN **skid**: *Her car went into a slide.*
- • BECOMING LOWER/WORSE **3** [C, usually sing.] a change to a lower or worse condition: *a downward slide in the price of oil* ◇ *the team's slide down the table* ◇ *talks to prevent a slide into civil war* ◇ *The economy is **on the slide*** (= getting worse).
- • FOR CHILDREN **4** [C] a structure with a steep slope that children use for sliding down: *to go down the slide*
- • FALL OF ROCK **5** [C] a sudden fall of a large amount of rock or earth down a hill SYN **landslide**: *I was afraid of starting a slide of loose stones.*

- **PHOTOGRAPH 6** [C] a small piece of film held in a frame that can be shown on a screen when you shine a light through it SYN **transparency**: *a talk with colour slides*
- **FOR MICROSCOPE 7** [C] a small piece of glass that sth is placed on so that it can be looked at under a MICROSCOPE
- **PART OF MUSICAL INSTRUMENT 8** [C] a part of a musical instrument or other device that slides backwards and forwards
- **FOR HAIR 9** [C] (*BrE*) = HAIRSLIDE

**'slide projector** *noun* a piece of equipment for displaying SLIDES (= small pieces of film held in frames) on a screen ⇨ compare DATA PROJECTOR, OVERHEAD PROJECTOR

**slider** /ˈslaɪdə(r)/ *noun* **1** a device for controlling sth such as the volume of a radio, which you slide up and down or from side to side **2** (*computing*) an ICON that you can slide up and down or from side to side with the mouse **3** a FRESHWATER TURTLE from North America

**'slide rule** *noun* (in the past) a long, narrow instrument like a RULER, with a middle part that slides backwards and forwards, used for calculating numbers

**'slide show** (*also* **slide-show**) *noun* **1** (*computing*) a piece of software that shows a number of images on a computer screen in a particular order: *a slideshow presentation* **2** a number of slides (= small pieces of film held in frames) shown to an audience using a SLIDE PROJECTOR, often during a lecture

**sliding 'door** *noun* a door that slides across an opening rather than moving away from it

**sliding 'scale** *noun* a system in which the rate at which sth is paid varies according to particular conditions: *Fees are calculated on a sliding scale according to income* (= richer people pay more).

**slight** ⓘ B2 /slaɪt/ *adj., noun, verb*
- *adj.* (**slight·er, slight·est**) **1** ⓘ B2 very small in degree: *a slight increase/change/difference* ◇ *a slight variation/improvement/advantage* ◇ *It won't make the slightest bit of difference* ◇ *She takes offence at the slightest thing* (= is very easily offended). ◇ *There was **not the slightest** hint of trouble.* **2** small and thin in size: *a slight woman* **3** (*formal*) not deserving serious attention: *This is a very slight novel.*
- IDM **not in the 'slightest** not at all: *He didn't seem to mind in the slightest.*
- *noun* ~ (**on sb / sth**) an act or a remark that criticizes sth or offends sb SYN **insult**: *Nick took her comment as a slight on his abilities as a manager.*
- *verb* [usually passive] to treat sb rudely or without respect SYN **insult**: **be / feel slighted** *She felt slighted because she hadn't been invited.* ▸ **slight·ing** *adj.* [only before noun]: *slighting remarks*

**slight·ly** ⓘ B1 ⓢ /ˈslaɪtli/ *adv.* **1** ⓘ B1 a little: *a slightly different version* ◇ *slightly higher/lower/larger/smaller* ◇ *She earns slightly less than $100 000 a year.* ◇ *She smiled slightly, as if she were hiding something.* **2** a slightly built person is small and thin

**slim** /slɪm/ *adj., verb, noun*
- *adj.* (**slim·mer, slim·mest**) **1** (*approving*) (of a person) thin, in a way that is attractive: *a slim figure/body/waist* ◇ *She was tall and slim.* ◇ *How do you manage to stay so slim?* ◇ (*figurative*) *Many companies are a lot slimmer than they used to be* (= have fewer workers). **2** thinner than usual: *a slim volume of poetry* **3** not as big as you would like or expect SYN **small**: *a slim chance of success* ◇ *The party was returned to power with a slim majority.* ⇨ see also SLIMMER, SLIMMING ▸ **slim·ness** *noun* [U]
- *verb* [I] (usually used in the progressive tenses) (*BrE*) (**-mm-**) to try to become thinner, for example by eating less SYN **diet**: *You can still eat breakfast when you are slimming.*
- PHR V **slim 'down** to become thinner, for example as a result of eating less **slim 'down | slim sth↔'down** to make a company or an organization smaller, by reducing the number of jobs in it; to be made smaller in this way: *They're restructuring and slimming down the workforce.* ◇ *The industry may have to slim down even further.* ◇ *the new, slimmed-down company* ⇨ see also SLIMMING
- *noun* [U] an African word for AIDS

**slime** /slaɪm/ *noun* [U] any unpleasant thick slimy substance: *The pond was full of mud and green slime.* ⇨ see also SLIMY

**slime·ball** /ˈslaɪmbɔːl/ (*also* **slime·bag** /ˈslaɪmbæɡ/) *noun* (*informal*) an extremely unpleasant or horrible person

**slim·line** /ˈslɪmlaɪn/ *adj.* [only before noun] **1** smaller or thinner in design than usual: *a slimline phone* **2** (*BrE*) (of a drink) containing very little sugar: *slimline tonic water*

**slim·mer** /ˈslɪmə(r)/ *noun* (*BrE*) a person who is trying to lose weight: *a calorie-controlled diet for slimmers* ⇨ see also SLIM *verb*

**slim·ming** /ˈslɪmɪŋ/ *noun* [U] (*BrE*) the practice of trying to lose weight: *a slimming club* ⇨ see also SLIM *verb*

**slimy** /ˈslaɪmi/ *adj.* (**slimi·er, slimi·est**) **1** like or covered with SLIME: *thick, slimy mud* ◇ *The walls were black, cold and slimy.* **2** (*informal, disapproving*) (of a person or their manner) polite and extremely friendly in a way that is not sincere or honest

**sling** /slɪŋ/ *verb, noun*
- *verb* (**slung, slung** /slʌŋ/) **1** (especially *BrE, informal*) to throw sth somewhere in a careless way SYN **chuck**: ~ **sth + adv. / prep.** *Don't just sling your clothes on the floor.* ◇ ~ **sb sth** *Sling me an apple, will you?* ⇨ see also MUD-SLINGING **2** [often passive] ~ **sth + adv. / prep.** to put sth somewhere where it hangs loosely: *Her bag was slung over her shoulder.* ◇ *We slung a hammock between two trees.* **3** [often passive] ~ **sb + adv. / prep.** (*informal*) to put sb somewhere by force; to make sb leave somewhere: *They were slung out of the club for fighting.*
- IDM **sling your 'hook** (*BrE, informal*) (used especially in orders) to go away
- PHR V **sling 'off at sb** (*AustralE, NZE, informal*) to laugh at sb in an unkind way
- *noun* **1** a band of cloth that is tied around a person's neck and used to support a broken or injured arm: **in a** ~ *He had his arm in a sling.* **2** a device consisting of a band, ropes, etc. for holding and lifting heavy objects: *The engine was lifted in a sling of steel rope.* **3** a device like a bag for carrying a baby on your back or in front of you **4** (in the past) a simple weapon made from a band of leather, etc., used for throwing stones SYN **catapult**

**sling·back** /ˈslɪŋbæk/ *noun* a woman's shoe that is open at the back with a narrow piece of leather, etc. around the heel

**sling·shot** /ˈslɪŋʃɒt; *NAmE* -ʃɑːt/ (*NAmE*) (*BrE* **cata·pult**) *noun* a stick that has the shape of a Y with a rubber band attached to it, used by children for shooting stones ⇨ picture at CATAPULT

**slink** /slɪŋk/ *verb* [I] (**slunk, slunk** /slʌŋk/) + **adv. / prep.** to move somewhere very quietly and slowly, especially because you are ashamed or do not want to be seen SYN **creep**: *John was trying to slink into the house by the back door.* ◇ *The dog howled and slunk away.*

**slinky** /ˈslɪŋki/ *adj.* (**slink·ier, slinki·est**) **1** (of a woman's clothes) fitting closely to the body in a sexually attractive way **2** (of movement or sound) smooth and slow, often in a way that is sexually attractive

**slip** ⓘ B2 /slɪp/ *verb, noun*
- *verb* (**-pp-**)
- **SLIDE / FALL 1** ⓘ B2 [I] to slide a short distance by accident so that you fall or nearly fall: *She slipped and landed flat on her back.* ◇ ~ **on sth** *He slipped on a bar of soap in the shower room.*
- **OUT OF POSITION 2** ⓘ B2 [I] to slide out of position or out of your hand: *My hand slipped as I was slicing the bread and I cut myself.* ◇ + **adv. / prep.** *His hat had slipped over one eye.* ◇ *The child slipped from his grasp and ran off.* ◇ (*figurative*) *She was careful not to let her control slip.*
- **GO / PUT QUICKLY 3** ⓘ B2 [I] + **adv. / prep.** to go somewhere quickly and quietly, especially without being noticed SYN **creep**: *She slipped out of the house before the others were awake.* ◇ *A guard was posted at the door, in case*

anyone tried to slip in. ⋄ (*figurative*) *She knew that time was slipping away.* **4** [T] to put sth somewhere quickly, quietly or secretly: *~ sth + adv./prep. Anna slipped her hand into his.* ⋄ *I managed to slip a few jokes into my speech.* ⋄ *He slipped the ring onto her finger.* ⋄ **~ sth to sb** *They'd slipped some money to the guards.* ⋄ *~ sb sth They'd slipped the guards some money.*
- **BECOME WORSE 5** [I] to fall to a lower level; to become worse: *Standards have slipped in the last few years.* ⋄ *Already the Conservatives are slipping in the polls.*
- **INTO DIFFICULT SITUATION 6** [I] **+ adv./prep.** to pass into a particular state or situation, especially a difficult or unpleasant one: *He began to slip into debt.* ⋄ *The patient had slipped into a coma.* ⋄ *We seem to have slipped behind schedule.*
- **CLOTHES ON/OFF 7** [I, T] to put clothes on or to take them off quickly and easily: **+ adv./prep.** *to slip into/out of a dress* ⋄ *~ sth + adv./prep. to slip your shoes on/off* ⋄ *He slipped a coat over his sweatshirt.*
- **GET FREE 8** [T, I] to get free; to make sth/sb/yourself free from sth: **~ sth** *The ship had slipped its moorings in the night.* ⋄ **~(sth) + adj.** *The animal had slipped free and escaped.*

**IDM** **let sth 'slip** to give sb information that is supposed to be secret: *I happened to let it slip that he had given me £1000 for the car.* ⋄ *She tried not to let slip what she knew.* **let sth 'slip (through your fingers)** to miss or fail to use an opportunity: *Don't let the chance to work abroad slip through your fingers.* **slip your 'mind** if sth **slips your mind**, you forget it or forget to do it **slip one 'over on sb** (*informal*) to trick sb **slip through the 'net** (*also* **fall/slip through the 'cracks**) when sb/sth **slips through the net**, an organization or a system fails to find them and deal with them: *We tried to contact all former students, but one or two slipped through the net.* ⇒ more at GEAR *n.*, TONGUE *n.*

**PHRV** **slip a'way** to stop existing; to disappear or die: *Their support gradually slipped away.* **slip 'out** when sth **slips out**, you say it without really intending to: *I'm sorry I said that. It just slipped out.* **slip 'up** (*informal*) to make a careless mistake: *We can't afford to slip up.* ⇒ related noun SLIP-UP

■ *noun*
- **SMALL MISTAKE 1** a small mistake, usually made by being careless or not paying attention: *He recited the whole poem without making a single slip.* ⇒ SYNONYMS at MISTAKE ⇒ see also FREUDIAN SLIP
- **PIECE OF PAPER 2** a small piece of paper, especially one for writing on or with sth printed on it: *I wrote it down on a slip of paper.* ⋄ *a betting slip* ⇒ see also PAYSLIP, PINK SLIP, SALES SLIP
- **ACT OF SLIPPING 3** an act of slipping: *One slip and you could fall to your death.*
- **CLOTHING 4** a piece of women's underwear like a thin dress or skirt, worn under a dress
- **IN CRICKET 5** a player who stands behind and to one side of the BATSMAN and tries to catch the ball; the position on the field where this player stands

**IDM** **give sb the 'slip** (*informal*) to get away from sb who is following or running after you **a 'slip of a boy, girl, etc.** (*old-fashioned*) a small or thin, usually young, person **a slip of the 'pen/'tongue** a small mistake in what you write or say: *Did I call you Richard? Sorry, Robert, just a slip of the tongue.* **there's many a 'slip 'twixt cup and 'lip** (*saying*) nothing is completely certain until it really happens because things can easily go wrong

**slip·case** /ˈslɪpkeɪs/ *noun* a stiff cover that a book or other object fits into

**slip·cover** /ˈslɪpkʌvə(r)/ (*NAmE*) (*BrE* **loose 'cover**) *noun* a cover for a chair, etc. that you can take off, for example to wash it

**slip-on** *noun* a shoe that you can slide your feet into without having to tie LACES: *a pair of slip-ons* ⋄ *slip-on shoes*

**slip·page** /ˈslɪpɪdʒ/ *noun* [U, C, usually sing.] **1** failure to achieve an aim or complete a task by a particular date **2** a slight or slow steady fall in the amount, value, etc. of sth

**slip·per** /ˈslɪpə(r)/ *noun* a loose, soft shoe that you wear in the house: *a pair of slippers*

**slip·pery** /ˈslɪpəri/ *adj.* **1** (*also informal* **slippy**) difficult to hold or to stand or move on, because it is smooth, wet or POLISHED: *slippery like a fish* ⋄ *In places the path can be wet and slippery.* ⋄ *His hand was slippery with sweat.* **2** (*informal*) (of a person) that you cannot trust: *Don't believe what he says—he's a slippery customer* (= person). **3** (*informal*) (of a situation, subject, problem, etc.) difficult to deal with and that you have to think about carefully: *Freedom is a slippery concept* (= because its meaning changes according to your point of view).
**IDM** **the/a slippery 'slope** a course of action that is difficult to stop once it has begun, and can lead to serious problems or disaster

**slippy** /ˈslɪpi/ *adj.* (**slip·pier**, **slip·pi·est**) (*informal*) = SLIPPERY

**'slip road** (*BrE*) (*NAmE* **ramp**) *noun* a road used for driving onto or off a major road such as a MOTORWAY or INTERSTATE ⇒ compare ACCESS ROAD

**slip·shod** /ˈslɪpʃɒd; *NAmE* -ʃɑːd/ *adj.* done without care; doing things without care **SYN** **careless**

**slip·stream** /ˈslɪpstriːm/ *noun* [sing.] the stream of air behind a vehicle that is moving very fast

**'slip-up** *noun* (*informal*) a careless mistake

**slip·way** /ˈslɪpweɪ/ *noun* a sloping track leading down to water, on which ships are built or pulled up out of the water for repairs, or from which they are launched

**slit** /slɪt/ *noun*, *verb*
■ *noun* a long, narrow cut or opening: *a long skirt with a slit up the side* ⋄ *His eyes narrowed into slits.*
■ *verb* (**slit·ting**, **slit**, **slit**) to make a long, narrow cut or opening in sth: **~ sth** *Slit the roll with a sharp knife.* ⋄ *The child's throat had been slit.* ⋄ *Her skirt was slit at both sides* (= designed with an opening at the bottom on each side). ⋄ **~ sth + adj.** *He slit open the envelope and took out the letter.*

**slither** /ˈslɪðə(r)/ *verb* **1** [I] **+ adv./prep.** to move smoothly over a surface, like a snake **SYN** **glide**: *The snake slithered away as we approached.* **2 + adv./prep.** to move somewhere without much control, for example because the ground is steep or wet **SYN** **slide**: *We slithered down the slope to the road.* ⋄ *They were slithering around on the ice.*

**slith·ery** /ˈslɪðəri/ *adj.* difficult to hold or stand on because it is wet or smooth; moving in a slithering way

**sliver** /ˈslɪvə(r)/ *noun* a small or thin piece of sth that is cut or broken off from a larger piece: *slivers of glass* ⋄ (*figurative*) *A sliver of light showed under the door.*

**slob** /slɒb; *NAmE* slɑːb/ *noun*, *verb*
■ *noun* (*informal*, *disapproving*) a person who is lazy and dirty or untidy: *Get out of bed, you fat slob!*
■ *verb* (**-bb-**)
**PHRV** **slob a'round/'out** (*BrE*, *informal*) to spend time being lazy and doing nothing

**slob·ber** /ˈslɒbə(r); *NAmE* ˈslɑːb-/ *verb* [I] to let SALIVA come out of your mouth **SYN** **dribble**
**PHRV** **'slobber over sb/sth** (*informal*, *disapproving*) to show how much you like or want sb/sth without any control or respect for yourself

**sloe** /sləʊ/ *noun* a bitter wild fruit like a small PLUM that grows on a bush called a BLACKTHORN

**slog** /slɒɡ; *NAmE* slɑːɡ/ *verb*, *noun*
■ *verb* (**-gg-**) (*informal*) **1** [I, T] to work hard and steadily at sth, especially sth that takes a long time and is boring or difficult: **~(away) (at sth)** *He's been slogging away at that piece of music for weeks.* ⋄ **~(through sth)** *The teacher made us slog through long lists of vocabulary.* ⋄ **~ your way through sth** *She slogged her way through four piles of ironing.* **2** [I, T] to walk or travel somewhere steadily, with great effort or difficulty: **+ adv./prep.** *I've been slogging around the streets of London all day.* ⋄ **~ your way through sth** *He started to slog his way through the undergrowth.* **3** [T, I] **~(sth) (+ adv./prep.)** to hit a ball very hard but often without skill
**IDM** **slog it 'out** (*BrE*, *informal*) to fight or compete in order to prove who is the strongest, the best, etc. ⇒ more at GUT *n.*

■ **noun** [U, C, usually sing.] (*informal*) a period of hard work or effort: *Writing the book took ten months of hard slog.* ◊ *It was a long slog to the top of the mountain.*

**slo·gan** /ˈsləʊɡən/ (*also informal* **tag line**) *noun* a word or phrase that is easy to remember, used for example by a political party or in advertising to attract people's attention or to suggest an idea quickly: *an advertising slogan* ◊ *a campaign slogan* ◊ *The crowd began chanting anti-government slogans.*

**slo·gan·eer·ing** /ˌsləʊɡəˈnɪərɪŋ/; *NAmE* -ˈnɪr-/ *noun* [U] (*disapproving*) the use of slogans in advertisements, by politicians, etc.

**slo-mo** /ˈsləʊ məʊ/ *noun* [U] (*informal*) = SLOW MOTION

**sloop** /sluːp/ *noun* a small sailing ship with one MAST (= a post to support the sails)

**slop** /slɒp/; *NAmE* slɑːp/ *verb, noun*
■ *verb* (**-pp-**) **1** [I] + **adv./prep.** (of a liquid) to move around in a container, often so that some liquid comes out over the edge: *Water was slopping around in the bottom of the boat.* ◊ *As he put the glass down the beer slopped over onto the table.* **2** [T] ~ **sth (+ adv./prep.)** to make liquid or food come out of a container in an untidy way SYN spill: *He got out of the bath, slopping water over the sides.* ◊ *She slopped some beans onto a plate.*
■ *noun* [U] (*also* **slops** [pl.]) **1** waste food, sometimes fed to animals **2** liquid or partly liquid waste, for example URINE or dirty water from baths: *a slop bucket*

**slope** /sləʊp/ *noun, verb*
■ *noun* **1** [C] a surface or piece of land that slopes (= is higher at one end than the other) SYN **incline**: **on a ~** *The town is built on a slope.* ◊ *Down the slope and beyond the road lay the Pacific Ocean.* **2** [C, usually pl.] an area of land that is part of a mountain or hill: ~ **of sth** *the eastern slopes of the Andes* ◊ *ski slopes* ◊ *He spends all winter on the slopes (= skiing).* ⊃ WORDFINDER NOTE at MOUNTAIN **3** [sing., U] the amount by which sth slopes: *a steep slope* ◊ *a gentle slope* ◊ ~ **of sth** *a slope of 45 degrees*
IDM see SLIPPERY
■ *verb* **1** [I] (of a horizontal surface) to be at an angle so that it is higher at one end than the other: *a sloping roof* ◊ **+ adv./prep.** *The garden slopes away towards the river.* **2** [I] (of sth VERTICAL) to be at an angle rather than going straight up or straight across: *It was a very old house with sloping walls.* ◊ **+ adv./prep.** *His handwriting slopes backwards.*
PHRV **ˌslope ˈoff** (*BrE, informal*) to go somewhere quietly, especially in order to avoid sth/sb SYN **slink**: *They got bored waiting for him and sloped off.*

**sloppy** /ˈslɒpi/; *NAmE* ˈslɑːpi/ *adj.* (**slop·pier, slop·pi·est**) **1** that shows a lack of care, thought or effort: *sloppy thinking* ◊ *Your work is sloppy.* ◊ *a sloppy worker* **2** (of clothes) loose and without much shape SYN **baggy**: *a sloppy T-shirt* **3** (*informal, especially BrE*) romantic in a silly or embarrassing way: *a sloppy love story* **4** containing too much liquid: *Don't make the mixture too sloppy.* ◊ (*informal*) *She gave him a big sloppy kiss.* ▶ **slop·pily** /-pɪli/ *adv.*: *a sloppily run department* **slop·pi·ness** *noun* [U]: *There is no excuse for sloppiness in your work.*

**sloppy joe** /ˌslɒpi ˈdʒəʊ/; *NAmE* ˌslɑːp-/ *noun* (*NAmE*) meat that has been cut into very small pieces, served in a spicy tomato sauce inside a BUN (= bread roll)

**slosh** /slɒʃ/; *NAmE* slɑːʃ/ *verb* (*informal*) **1** [I] + **adv./prep.** (of liquid) to move around making a lot of noise or coming out over the edge of sth: *The water was sloshing around under our feet.* ◊ *Some of the paint sloshed out of the can.* **2** [T] ~ **sth + adv./prep.** to make liquid move in a noisy way; to use liquid carelessly: *The children were sloshing water everywhere.* ◊ *She sloshed coffee into the mugs.* **3** [I] + **adv./prep.** to walk noisily in water or mud: *We all sloshed around in the puddles.*
PHRV ˌslosh aˈround/aˈbout (*BrE, informal*) (especially of money) to be available or present in large quantities

**sloshed** /slɒʃt/; *NAmE* slɑːʃt/ *adj.* (*informal*) drunk

**slot** /slɒt/; *NAmE* slɑːt/ *noun, verb*
■ *noun* **1** a long, narrow opening, into which you put or fit sth: *to put some coins in the slot* ⊃ see also MAIL SLOT **2** a position, a time or an opportunity for sb/sth, for example in a list, a programme of events or a series of broadcasts: *He has a regular slot on the late-night programme.* ◊ *Their album has occupied the Number One slot for the past six weeks.* ◊ *the airport's take-off and landing slots*
■ *verb* [T, I] (**-tt-**) to put sth into a space that is available or designed for it; to fit into such a space: ~ **sth + adv./prep.** *The bed comes in sections that can be quickly slotted together.* ◊ **+ adv./prep.** *The dishwasher slots neatly between the cupboards.* IDM see PLACE *n.*
PHRV ˌslot sb/sth↔ˈin to manage to find a position, a time or an opportunity for sb/sth: *I can slot you in between 3 and 4.* ◊ *We slotted in some extra lessons before the exam.*

**sloth** /sləʊθ/ *noun* **1** [C] an animal that lives in trees in tropical parts of America and moves very slowly **2** [U] (*formal*) the bad habit of being lazy and unwilling to work

**sloth·ful** /ˈsləʊθfl/ *adj.* (*formal*) lazy

**ˈslot machine** *noun* **1** (*BrE*) a machine with an opening for coins, used for selling things such as bars of chocolate **2** (*especially NAmE*) (*also* **one-armed ˈbandit** *NAmE, BrE*) (*BrE also* **fruit machine**) (*AustralE* **poker machine**) a machine that you put coins into to play a game in which you win money if particular pictures appear together on the screen; a similar game, played online

**slot·ted** /ˈslɒtɪd/; *NAmE* ˈslɑːt-/ *adj.* [usually before noun] (*specialist*) **1** having a SLOT or SLOTS in it **2** (of a screw) having a SLOT in it rather than a cross shape ⊃ compare PHILLIPS

**ˌslotted ˈspoon** *noun* a large spoon with holes in it for taking pieces of solid food out of liquid

**slouch** /slaʊtʃ/ *verb, noun*
■ *verb* [I] (+ **adv./prep.**) to stand, sit or move in a lazy way, often with your shoulders and head bent forward: *Sit up straight. Don't slouch.*
■ *noun* [usually sing.] a way of standing or sitting in which your shoulders are not straight, so that you look tired or lazy
IDM be no ˈslouch (*informal*) to be very good at sth or quick to do sth: *She's no slouch on the guitar.*

**slouchy** /ˈslaʊtʃi/ *adj.* (**slouch·ier, slouchi·est**) **1** (*disapproving*) holding your body in a lazy way, often with your shoulders and head bent forward: *his slouchy posture* **2** (*approving*) (of clothes) without a definite outline; not stiff: *The slouchy suede boots look great with slim pants.*

**slough**[1] /slʌf/ *verb* to lose a layer of dead skin, etc: ~ **sth** *a snake sloughing its skin* ◊ ~ **sth off** *Slough off dead skin cells by using a facial scrub.*
PHRV ˌslough sth↔ˈoff (*formal*) to get rid of sth that you no longer want: *Responsibilities are not sloughed off so easily.*

**slough**[2] /slaʊ; *NAmE* sluː, slaʊ/ *noun* (*literary*) **1** [sing.] ~ **of misery, despair, etc.** a state of being sad with no hope **2** [C] a very soft wet area of land

**sloven·ly** /ˈslʌvnli/ *adj.* careless, untidy or dirty in appearance or habits: *He grew lazy and slovenly in his habits.* ▶ **sloven·li·ness** *noun* [U]

**slow** /sləʊ/ *adj., verb, adv.*
■ *adj.* (**slow·er, slow·est**)
• NOT FAST **1** not moving, acting or done quickly; taking a long time; not fast: *a slow pace/speed* ◊ *Average earnings are rising at their slowest rate for 20 years.* ◊ *Progress was slower than expected.* ◊ *The country is experiencing slow but steady economic growth.* ◊ *Collecting data is a painfully slow process.* ◊ *Oh you're so slow; come on, hurry up!* ◊ *The slow movement opens with a cello solo.* ◊ *For the third game in a row City made a slow start.* **2** not going or allowing you to go at a fast speed: *I missed the fast train and had to get the slow one (= the one that stops at all the stations).*
• WITH DELAY **3** hesitating to do sth or not doing sth immediately: ~ **to do sth** *She wasn't slow to realize what was going on.* ◊ ~ **in doing sth** *Some insurance companies are particularly slow in processing claims.* ◊ ~ **doing sth** *They were very slow paying me.*

- **NOT CLEVER 4** not quick to learn; finding things hard to understand: *He's the slowest in the class.*
- **NOT BUSY 5** not very busy; containing little action ⓢⓨⓝ **sluggish**: *Sales are slow* (= not many goods are being sold).
- **WATCH/CLOCK 6** [not before noun] showing a time earlier than the correct time: *My watch is five minutes slow* (= it shows 1.45 when it is 1.50).
- **IN PHOTOGRAPHY 7** slow film is not very sensitive to light
▶ **slow·ness** *noun* [U]: *There was impatience over the slowness of reform.*
ⓘⓓⓜ **do a slow ˈburn** (*NAmE, informal*) to slowly get angry ⇨ more at MARK *n.*, UPTAKE

■ *verb* ⓑ1 [I, T] to go or to make sth/sb go at a slower speed or be less active: *Economic growth has slowed a little.* ⋄ ~ **down** *The car slowed down as it approached the junction.* ⋄ *indications that the US economy is slowing down* ⋄ *You must slow down* (= work less hard) *or you'll make yourself ill.* ⋄ ~ **up** *The game slowed up a little in the second half.* ⋄ ~ **sb/sth** *Economic data for last month shows steps taken by the government are* **slowing growth.** ⋄ ~ **sb/sth down/up** *The ice on the roads was slowing us down.* ⇨ see also SLOWDOWN

■ *adv.* (**slow·er, slow·est**) (used especially in the comparative and superlative forms, or in compounds) at a slow speed ⓢⓨⓝ **slowly**: *Could you go a little slower?* ⋄ *slow-drying paint* ⋄ *slow-moving traffic* ⋄ (*NAmE*) *Drive slow!*
ⓘⓓⓜ **go ˈslow (on sth)** to show less enthusiasm for achieving sth: *The government is going slow on tax reforms.* ⇨ see also GO-SLOW

▼ **WHICH WORD?**

### slow / slowly

- **Slowly** is the usual adverb from the adjective **slow**. **Slow** is sometimes used as an adverb in informal language, on road signs, etc. It can also be used to form compounds: *Slow. Major road ahead.* ⋄ *a slow-acting drug* In the comparative both **slower** and **more slowly** are used: *Can you speak slower/more slowly?*

ˈ**slow cooker** *noun* an electric pot used for cooking meat and vegetables slowly in liquid

ˈ**slow·down** /ˈsləʊdaʊn/ *noun* **1** a reduction in speed or activity: *a slowdown in economic growth* **2** (*NAmE*) (*BrE* ˈ**go-slow**) a protest that workers make by doing their work more slowly than usual ⇨ compare WORK-TO-RULE

ˈ**slow ˈfood** *noun* [U] traditional food and ways of producing, cooking and eating it ⇨ compare FAST FOOD

ˈ**slow lane** *noun* [sing.] the part of a major road such as a MOTORWAY or INTERSTATE where vehicles drive slowest
ⓘⓓⓜ **in the ˈslow lane** not making progress as fast as other people, countries, companies, etc.

**slow·ly** ⓘ ⒶⒶ2 /ˈsləʊli/ *adv.* at a slow speed; not quickly: *to move/walk/turn slowly* ⋄ *Please could you speak more slowly?* ⋄ *Don't rush into a decision. Take it slowly.* ⋄ *'I don't really know,' Anna said slowly.* ⋄ *Slowly things began to improve.* ⋄ *The film starts slowly, introducing each of the characters and establishing their relationships.* ⇨ note at SLOW
ⓘⓓⓜ ˈ**slowly but ˈsurely** making slow but definite progress: *We'll get there slowly but surely.*

ˈ**slow ˈmotion** (*also* *informal* **slo-mo**) *noun* [U] (in a film or on television) the method of showing action at a much slower speed than it happened in real life: **in ~** *Some scenes were filmed in slow motion.* ⋄ *a slow-motion replay*

ˈ**slow-ˈwitted** *adj.* not able to think quickly; slow to learn or understand things ⓞⓟⓟ **quick-witted**

**SLR** /ˌes el ˈɑː(r)/ *abbr.* single-lens reflex (used to describe a camera in which there is only one LENS which both forms the image on the film and provides the image in the VIEWFINDER)

**sludge** /slʌdʒ/ *noun* [U] **1** thick, soft, wet mud or a substance that looks like it ⓢⓨⓝ **slime**: *There was some sludge at the bottom of the tank.* **2** industrial or human waste that has been treated: *industrial sludge* ⋄ *the use of sewage sludge as a fertilizer on farm land*

**slug** /slʌɡ/ *noun, verb*
■ *noun* **1** a small, soft creature, like a SNAIL without a shell, that moves very slowly and often eats garden plants ⇨ VISUAL VOCAB page V3 **2** (*informal*) a small amount of a strong alcoholic drink: *He took another slug of whisky.* **3** (*especially NAmE, informal*) a bullet **4** (*NAmE, informal*) a piece of metal like a coin in shape used to get things from machines, etc., sometimes illegally
■ *verb* (**-gg-**) **1** ~ **sb** (*informal*) to hit sb hard, especially with your closed hand **2** ~ **sth** (in baseball) to hit the ball hard
ⓘⓓⓜ ˈ**slug it ˈout** to fight or compete until it is clear who has won

**slug·fest** /ˈslʌɡfest/ *noun* (*especially NAmE, informal*) an angry argument in which people shout offensive remarks at each other: *The battle between the two Democrats is turning into a nasty little slugfest.*

**slug·ger** /ˈslʌɡə(r)/ *noun* (*NAmE, informal*) **1** (in baseball) a player who hits the ball, especially one who hits it very hard and for long distances **2** (*approving*) used when speaking to or about sb, especially a young boy, who tries really hard at sth, and that you like: *Hang in there, slugger. You can do it!*

**slug·gish** /ˈslʌɡɪʃ/ *adj.* moving, reacting or working more slowly than normal: *sluggish traffic* ⋄ *a sluggish economy* ⋄ *the sluggish black waters of the canal* ⋄ *He felt very heavy and sluggish after the meal.* ▶ **slug·gish·ly** *adv.* **slug·gish·ness** *noun* [U]

**sluice** /sluːs/ *noun, verb*
■ *noun* (*also* ˈ**sluice gate**) a sliding gate or other device for controlling the flow of water out of or into a CANAL, etc.
■ *verb* **1** [T] ~ **sth (down/out)** | ~ **sth (with sth)** to wash sth with a stream of water: *The ship's crew was sluicing down the deck.* **2** [I] + *adv./prep.* (of water) to flow somewhere in large quantities

**slum** /slʌm/ *noun, verb*
■ *noun* an area of a city that is very poor and where the houses are dirty and in bad condition: *a slum area* ⋄ *city/urban slums* ⋄ *She was brought up in the slums of Leeds.* ⇨ WORDFINDER NOTE at CITY
■ *verb* [I] (*usually* **be slumming**) (*informal*) (**-mm-**) to spend time in places or conditions that are much worse than those you are used to: *There are plenty of ways you can cut costs on your trip without slumming.*
ⓘⓓⓜ ˈ**slum it** (*often humorous*) to accept conditions that are worse than those you are used to: *Several businessmen had to slum it in economy class.*

**slum·ber** /ˈslʌmbə(r)/ *noun, verb*
■ *noun* [U, C, usually pl.] (*literary*) sleep; a time when sb is sleeping: *She fell into a deep and peaceful slumber.*
■ *verb* [I] (*literary*) to sleep

ˈ**slumber party** *noun* (*NAmE*) = SLEEPOVER

**slum·lord** /ˈslʌmlɔːd; *NAmE* -lɔːrd/ *noun* (*NAmE, informal*) a person who owns houses or apartments in a poor area and who charges very high rent for them even though they are in bad condition

**slump** /slʌmp/ *verb, noun*
■ *verb* **1** [I] to fall in price, value, number, etc., suddenly and by a large amount ⓢⓨⓝ **drop**: *Sales have slumped this year.* ⋄ ~ **by sth** *Profits slumped by over 50 per cent.* ⋄ ~ **(from sth) (to sth)** *The paper's circulation has slumped to 90 000.* ⇨ WORDFINDER NOTE at TREND **2** [I] + *adv./prep.* to sit or fall down heavily: *The old man slumped down in his chair.* ⋄ *She slumped to her knees.*
■ *noun* **1** ~ **(in sth)** a sudden fall in sales, prices, the value of sth, etc. ⓢⓨⓝ **decline**: *a slump in profits* **2** a period when a country's economy or a business is doing very badly: *the slump of the 1930s* ⋄ *The toy industry is in a slump.* ⇨ compare BOOM

**slumped** /slʌmpt/ *adj.* [not usually before noun] ~ **(against/over sth)** sitting with your body leaning forward, for example because you are asleep or unconscious: *The driver was slumped exhausted over the wheel.*

**slung** /slʌŋ/ *past tense, past part.* of SLING

**slunk** /slʌŋk/ *past tense, past part.* of SLINK

**slur** /slɜː(r)/ *verb, noun*
- *verb* (-rr-) **1** ~ **sth | + speech** to pronounce words in a way that is not clear so that they run into each other, usually because you are drunk or tired: *She had drunk too much and her speech was slurred.* **2** ~ **sth** (*music*) to play or sing a group of two or more musical notes so that each one runs smoothly into the next **3** ~ **sb/sth** to harm sb's reputation by making unfair or false statements about them
- *noun* **1** ~ **(on sb/sth)** an unfair remark about sb/sth that may damage other people's opinion of them **SYN** **insult**: *She had dared to cast a slur on his character.* ◊ (*especially NAmE*) *The crowd started throwing bottles and shouting racial slurs.* **2** (*music*) a curved sign used to show that two or more notes are to be played smoothly and without a break ⇒ picture at MUSIC

**slurp** /slɜːp; *NAmE* slɜːrp/ *verb* [T, I] (*informal*) to make a loud noise while you are drinking sth; to make a noise like this: ~ **sth** *He was slurping his tea.* ◊ ~ **(from sth)** *She slurped noisily from her cup.* ◊ *The water slurped in the tank.*
▶ **slurp** *noun* [usually sing.]: *She took a slurp from her mug.*

**slurry** /ˈslʌri; *NAmE* ˈslɜːri/ *noun* [U] a thick liquid consisting of water mixed with animal waste, CLAY, coal dust or CEMENT

**slush** /slʌʃ/ *noun* [U] **1** partly melted snow that is usually dirty: *In the city the clean white snow had turned to grey slush.* ⇒ **WORDFINDER NOTE** at SNOW **2** (*informal, disapproving*) stories, films or feelings that are considered to be silly and without value because they are too emotional and romantic ▶ **slushy** *adj.*: *slushy pavements* ◊ *slushy romantic fiction*

**ˈslush fund** *noun* (*disapproving*) a sum of money kept for illegal purposes, especially in politics

**slut** /slʌt/ *noun* (*disapproving, offensive*) **1** a woman who has many sexual partners **2** a woman who is very untidy or lazy ▶ **sluttish** /ˈslʌtɪʃ/ *adj.*

**sly** /slaɪ/ *adj.* **1** (*disapproving*) acting or done in a secret or dishonest way, often intending to trick people **SYN** **cunning**: *a sly political move* ◊ (*humorous*) *You sly old devil! How long have you known?* **2** [usually before noun] suggesting that you know sth secret that other people do not know **SYN** **knowing**: *a sly smile/grin* ▶ **slyly** *adv.*: *He glanced at her slyly.* **slyness** *noun* [U]
**IDM** **on the ˈsly** secretly; not wanting other people to discover what you are doing: *He has to visit them on the sly.*

**smack** /smæk/ *verb, noun, adv.*
- *verb* **1** [T] ~ **sb/sth** (*especially BrE*) to hit sb with your open hand or an object, especially as a punishment: *I think it's wrong to smack children.* ⇒ compare SPANK **2** [T] ~ **sth** + **adv./prep.** to put sth somewhere with a lot of force so that it makes a loud noise **SYN** **bang**: *She smacked her hand down on the table.* ◊ *He smacked a fist into the palm of his hand.* **3** [I] + **adv./prep.** to hit against sth with a lot of force **SYN** **crash**: *Two players accidentally smacked into each other.* **IDM** see LIP
**PHRV** **ˈsmack of sth** to seem to contain or involve a particular unpleasant quality: *Her behaviour smacks of hypocrisy.* ◊ *Today's announcement smacks of a government cover-up.*
- *noun* **1** [C] (*especially BrE*) a sharp hit given with your open hand, especially to a child as a punishment: *You'll get a smack on your backside if you're not careful.* **2** [C] (*informal*) a hard hit given with a closed hand **SYN** **punch**: *a smack on the jaw* **3** [C, usually sing.] a short loud sound: *She closed the ledger with a smack.* **4** [C] (*informal*) a loud kiss: *a smack on the lips/cheek* **5** [U] (*slang*) the drug HEROIN: *smack addicts* **6** [C] (*BrE*) a small fishing boat
- *adv.* (*informal*) (*NAmE also* **ˈsmack-dab**) exactly or directly in a place: *It landed smack in the middle of the carpet.* **2** with sudden, violent force, often making a loud noise: *The car drove smack into a brick wall.*

**smacker** /ˈsmækə(r)/ *noun* **1** (*informal*) a loud kiss **2** (*slang*) a British pound or US dollar

**smacking** /ˈsmækɪŋ/ *noun* [sing., U] (*especially BrE*) an act of hitting sb, especially a child, several times with your open hand, as a punishment: *He gave both of the children a good smacking.* ◊ *We don't approve of smacking.*

---

**small** /smɔːl/ *adj., adv., noun*
- *adj.* (**smaller, smallest**)
- • **NOT LARGE 1** not large in size, number, degree, amount, etc.: *a small town/village/community* ◊ *A much smaller number of students passed than I had expected.* ◊ *a small amount/percentage/sample* ◊ *a small group/minority* ◊ *Because of the small size of the sample, findings cannot be generalized.* ◊ *They're having a relatively small wedding.* ◊ ~ **for sb/sth** *That dress is too small for you.* **2** (*abbr.* **S**) used to describe one size in a range of sizes of clothes, food, products used in the house, etc: *The T-shirts come in small, medium and large.* ◊ *This is too big—have you got a small one?* **3** not as big as sth else of the same kind: *the small intestine*
- • **YOUNG 4** young: *They have three small children.* ◊ *We travelled around a lot when I was small.* ◊ *As a small boy he had spent most of his time with his grandparents.*
- • **NOT IMPORTANT 5** slight; not important: *I made only a few small changes to the report.* ◊ *She noticed several small errors in his work.* ◊ *Everything had been planned down to the smallest detail.* ◊ *It was no small achievement getting her to agree to the deal.*
- • **BUSINESS 6** [usually before noun] not doing business on a very large scale: *small companies/firms* ◊ *The government is planning to give more help to small businesses.*
- • **LETTERS 7** [usually before noun] not written or printed as capitals: *Should I write 'god' with a small 'g' or a capital?* ◊ *She's a socialist with a small 's'* (= she has socialist ideas but is not a member of a SOCIALIST party).
- • **NOT MUCH 8** [only before noun] (used with uncountable nouns) little; not much: *The government has small cause for optimism.* ◊ *They have small hope of succeeding.*
▶ **smallness** *noun* [U]
**IDM** **be grateful/thankful for small ˈmercies** to be happy that a situation that is bad is not as bad as it could have been: *Well, at least you weren't hurt. I suppose we should be grateful for small mercies.* **it's a ˌsmall ˈworld** (*saying*) used to express your surprise when you meet sb you know in an unexpected place, or when you are talking to sb and find out that you both know the same person **look/feel ˈsmall** to look or feel stupid, weak, ashamed, etc. ⇒ more at BIG *adj.*, GREAT *adj.*, HOUR, STILL *adj.*, SWEAT *v.*, WAY *n.*, WONDER *n.*
- *adv.* (**smaller, smallest**) **1** into small pieces: *Chop the cabbage up small.* **2** in a small size: *You can fit it all in if you write very small.*
- *noun* **1 the ~ of sb/sb's back** [sing.] the lower part of the back where it curves in ⇒ VISUAL VOCAB page V1 **2 smalls** [pl.] (*old-fashioned, BrE, informal*) small items of clothing, especially underwear

**ˈsmall ad** *noun* [usually pl.] (*BrE*) = CLASSIFIED ADVERTISEMENT

**ˈsmall arms** *noun* [pl.] small light weapons that you can carry in your hands

**ˌsmall ˈbeer** (*BrE*) (*NAmE* **ˌsmall poˈtatoes**) *noun* [U] (*informal*) a person or thing that has no great importance or value, especially when compared with sb/sth else

**ˈsmall-bore** *adj.* **1** a small-bore gun is narrow inside **2** (*informal, especially NAmE*) not important: *small-bore issues*

**ˌsmall ˈcapitals** (*also* **ˌsmall ˈcaps**) *noun* [pl.] (*specialist*) capital letters which are the same height as LOWER-CASE letters

**ˌsmall ˈchange** *noun* [U] **1** coins of low value: *Have you got any small change for the car park?* **2** something that is of little value when compared with sth else

**ˌsmall ˈclaims court** *noun* a local court which deals with cases involving small amounts of money

**ˌsmall ˈfortune** *noun* [usually sing.] (*informal*) a lot of money: *That holiday cost me a small fortune.*

**ˈsmall fry** *noun* [U + sing./pl. v.] (*informal*) ~ **(to sb/sth)** people or things that are not considered important compared with sb/sth else: *That's small fry to her.* ◊ *People like us are small fry to such a large business.*

---

s see | t tea | v van | w wet | z zoo | ʃ shoe | ʒ vision | tʃ chain | dʒ jam | θ thin | ð this | ŋ sing

# smallholder

**small·hold·er** /ˈsmɔːlhəʊldə(r)/ noun (BrE) a person who owns or rents a small piece of land for farming

**small·hold·ing** /ˈsmɔːlhəʊldɪŋ/ noun a small piece of land used for farming

**small·ish** /ˈsmɔːlɪʃ/ adj. fairly small: *a smallish town*

**small-ˈminded** adj. (disapproving) having fixed opinions and ways of doing things and not willing to change them or consider other people's opinions or feelings; interested in small problems and details and not in things which are really important **SYN** intolerant, petty ▶ **ˈsmall-ˈminded·ness** noun [U]

**small poˈtatoes** (NAmE) (BrE **ˌsmall ˈbeer**) noun [U] (informal) a person or thing that has no great importance or value, especially when compared with sb/sth else

**small·pox** /ˈsmɔːlpɒks/ NAmE -pɑːks/ noun [U] (in the past) a serious disease that caused a high temperature, left permanent marks on the skin and often caused death

**the ˈsmall print** (BrE) (NAmE **the ˌfine ˈprint**) noun [U] the important details of an agreement or a legal document that are usually printed in small type and are therefore easy to miss: *Read all the small print before signing.*

**small-ˈscale** adj. 1 (of an organization, activity, etc.) not large in size or extent; limited in what it does: *small-scale farming* ◇ *a small-scale study of couples in second marriages* 2 (of maps, drawings, etc.) drawn to a small scale so that not many details are shown **OPP** large-scale

**the ˌsmall ˈscreen** noun [sing.] television (when contrasted with cinema): *This will be the film's first showing on the small screen.* ◇ *his first small-screen role*

**ˈsmall talk** noun [U] polite conversation about subjects that are ordinary or unimportant, especially at social occasions

**ˈsmall-time** adj. [only before noun] (informal, disapproving) (often of criminals) not very important or successful **SYN** petty: *a small-time crook* ⇨ compare BIG TIME

**ˈsmall-town** adj. [only before noun] 1 (disapproving) not showing much interest in new ideas or what is happening outside your own environment **SYN** narrow-minded: *small-town values* 2 connected with a small town: *small-town America* (= people who live in small towns in America)

**smarmy** /ˈsmɑːmi/ NAmE /ˈsmɑːrmi/ adj. (**smarm·ier**, **smarmi·est**) (informal, disapproving) too polite in a way that is not sincere **SYN** smooth: *a smarmy salesman*

**smart** ⓘ B1 /smɑːt; NAmE smɑːrt/ adj., verb

■ adj. (smart·er, smart·est)

• CLEAN/NEAT 1 ⓘ B1 (especially BrE) (of people) looking clean and neat; well dressed in fashionable and/or formal clothes: *You look very smart in that suit.* 2 ⓘ B1 (especially BrE) (of clothes, etc.) clean, neat and looking new and attractive: *a smart suit* ◇ *They were wearing their smartest clothes.*
• INTELLIGENT 3 ⓘ B1 (especially NAmE) intelligent: *He is obviously a smart guy.* ◇ *Why do smart people do such stupid things?* ◇ *That was a smart career move.* ◇ *OK, I admit it was not the smartest thing I ever did* (= it was a stupid thing to do) ⇨ SYNONYMS at INTELLIGENT ⇨ see also SMARTS
• COMPUTER-CONTROLLED 4 (of a device) controlled by a computer, so that it appears to act in an intelligent way: *smart bombs* ◇ *This smart washing machine will dispense an optimal amount of water for the load.*
• FASHIONABLE 5 connected with fashionable, rich people: *smart restaurants* ◇ *She mixes with the smart set* (= fashionable, rich people).
• QUICK 6 (of a movement, etc.) quick and usually done with force **SYN** brisk: *He was struck with a smart crack on the head.* ◇ *We set off at a smart pace.* ▶ **ˈsmart·ly** adv.: *smartly dressed* ◇ *He ran off pretty smartly* (= quickly and suddenly). **ˈsmart·ness** noun [U]

■ verb 1 [I] ~ (from sth) to feel a sharp pain in a part of your body: *His eyes were smarting from the smoke.* 2 [I] ~ (from/over sth) to feel upset about a criticism, failure, etc: *They are still smarting from the 4–0 defeat last week.*

**ˌsmart ˈalec** (BrE) (NAmE usually **ˌsmart ˈaleck**) /ˈsmɑːt ælɪk; NAmE ˈsmɑːrt/ (also **ˈsmarty-pants**) (BrE also offensive **ˈsmart-arse**) (NAmE also offensive **ˈsmart-ass**) noun (informal, disapproving) a person who thinks they are very clever and likes to show people this in an annoying way

**ˈsmart bomb** noun a weapon controlled by an electronic device that is intended to cause damage to the target while avoiding damage to other people, buildings, etc. that are in the area

**ˈsmart card** noun a small plastic card on which information is stored in electronic form ⇨ see also CHIP CARD

**smart·en** /ˈsmɑːtn; NAmE ˈsmɑːrtn/ verb **PHRV** **ˌsmarten sb/sthˈup**, **ˌsmarten (yourself) ˈup** (especially BrE) to make yourself, another person or a place look neater or more attractive: *The hotel has been smartened up by the new owners.*

**the ˌsmart ˈmoney** noun [U] 1 money that is invested or bet by people who have expert knowledge: *It seems the smart money is no longer in insurance* (= is no longer being invested in insurance companies). 2 used to give the opinion of people who have expert knowledge of sth: *The smart money says that he's likely to withdraw from the leadership campaign.* ◇ *The smart money is on him for the best actor award.*

**smart·phone** ⓘ A2 /ˈsmɑːtfəʊn; NAmE ˈsmɑːrt-/ noun a mobile phone that also has some of the functions of a computer, for example the facility to use apps and the internet: *You can use your smartphone to access the internet.* ⇨ compare FEATURE PHONE

**smarts** /smɑːts; NAmE smɑːrts/ noun [U] (NAmE, informal) intelligence: *She made it to the top on her smarts.*

**ˈsmart speaker** noun an electronic speaker that is connected to the internet and is controlled by spoken commands

**ˈsmart·watch** /ˈsmɑːtwɒtʃ; NAmE ˈsmɑːrtwɑːtʃ/ noun a small COMPUTING device that you wear on your WRIST

**ˈsmarty-pants** noun = SMART ALEC

**smash** ⓘ C1 /smæʃ/ verb, noun

■ verb
• BREAK 1 ⓘ+ C1 [T, I] ~ (sth) to break sth, or to be broken, violently and noisily into many pieces: *Several windows had been smashed.* ◇ *He smashed the radio to pieces.* ◇ *The glass bowl smashed into a thousand pieces.*
• HIT VERY HARD 2 ⓘ+ C1 [I, T] to move with a lot of force against sth solid; to make sth do this: + adv./prep. *the sound of waves smashing against the rocks* ◇ *The car smashed into a tree.* ◇ + adv./prep. *Mark smashed his fist down on the desk.* ⇨ SYNONYMS at CRASH 3 ⓘ+ C1 [T, I] to hit sth very hard and break it, in order to get through it: ~sth + adv./prep. *They had to smash holes in the ice.* ◇ *The elephant smashed its way through the trees.* ◇ ~sth + adj. *We had to smash the door open.* ◇ + adv./prep. *They had smashed through a glass door to get in.* 4 [T] ~sth/sb (+ adv./prep.) to hit sth/sb very hard **SYN** slam: *He smashed the ball into the goal.*
• BREAK RECORD 5 [T] ~a record to break a record by a large amount: *She has smashed the world record.*
• DESTROY/DEFEAT 6 [T] ~sth/sb to destroy, defeat or put an end to sth/sb: *Police say they have smashed a major drugs ring.*
• CRASH VEHICLE 7 [T] ~sth (up) to crash a vehicle: *He's smashed (up) his new car.* ⇨ SYNONYMS at CRASH
• IN TENNIS, ETC. 8 [T] ~sth to hit a high ball downwards and very hard over the net
**IDM** **ˌsmash ˈit** (informal) to do sth very well or be very successful **SYN** crush it: *After all that training, I'm sure he'll smash it in the competition tonight.*
**PHRV** **ˌsmash sth↔ˈdown** to make sth fall down by hitting it hard and breaking it: *The police had to smash the door down.* **ˌsmash sthˈin** to make a hole in sth by hitting it with a lot of force: *Vandals had smashed the door in.* ◇ (informal) *I wanted to smash his face in* (= hit him hard in the face). **ˌsmash sth↔ˈup** to destroy sth deliberately: *Youths had broken into the bar and smashed the place up.*

■ noun
- **ACT OF BREAKING 1** [sing.] an act of breaking sth noisily into pieces; the sound this makes: *The cup hit the floor with a smash.*
- **VEHICLE CRASH 2** [C] (*BrE*) an accident in which a vehicle hits another vehicle: *a car smash*
- **IN TENNIS, ETC. 3** [C] a way of hitting the ball downwards and very hard
- **SONG/MOVIE/PLAY 4** (*also* **smash 'hit**) [C] a song, film or play that is very popular: *her latest chart smash*

**smash-and-'grab** *adj.* [only before noun] (*BrE*) relating to the act of stealing from a shop by breaking a window and taking the goods you can see or reach easily: *a smash-and-grab raid*

**smashed** /smæʃt/ *adj.* [not before noun] (*slang*) very drunk

**smash·er** /ˈsmæʃə(r)/ *noun* (*old-fashioned, BrE, informal*) a very good or attractive person or thing

**smash·ing** /ˈsmæʃɪŋ/ *adj.* (*BrE, old-fashioned, informal*) very good or pleasant SYN **great**: *We had a smashing time.*

**smat·ter·ing** /ˈsmætərɪŋ/ *noun* [sing.] **~(of sth)** a small amount of sth, especially knowledge of a language: *He only has a smattering of French.*

**smear** /smɪə(r); *NAmE* smɪr/ *verb, noun*
■ *verb* **1** [T] to spread an OILY or soft substance over a surface in a rough or careless way SYN **daub**: **~ sth on/over sth** *The children had smeared mud on the walls.* ⋄ **~ sth with sth** *The children had smeared the walls with mud.* **2** [T, usually passive] to make sth dirty or GREASY: **(be) smeared** *His glasses were smeared.* ⋄ *smeared windows* **3** [T] **~ sb/sth** to damage sb's reputation by saying unpleasant things about them that are not true SYN **slander**: *The story was an attempt to smear the party leader.* **4** [T, usually passive, I] to rub writing, a drawing, etc. so that it is no longer clear; to become not clear in this way SYN **smudge**: **be smeared** *The last few words of the letter were smeared.*
■ *noun* **1** an OILY or dirty mark: *a smear of jam* ⮕ SYNONYMS at MARK **2** a story that is not true about sb that is intended to damage their reputation, especially in politics: *He was the victim of a smear campaign.* **3** (*BrE*) = SMEAR TEST ⮕ see also CERVICAL SMEAR, PAP SMEAR

**'smear test** (*also* **smear, cervical 'smear**) (*all BrE*) (*NAmE* **'Pap smear**) *noun* a medical test in which a very small amount of TISSUE from a woman's CERVIX is removed and examined for cancer cells

**smell** ❶ A2 /smel/ *verb, noun*
■ *verb* (**smelled, smelled**) (*BrE also* **smelt, smelt** /smelt/) **1** A2 *linking verb* to have a particular smell: **+ adj.** *The room smelt damp.* ⋄ *Dinner smells good.* ⋄ *a bunch of sweet-smelling flowers* ⋄ **~ of sth** *His breath smelt of garlic.* ⋄ **~ like sth** *What does the perfume smell like?* **2** A2 [T, no passive] (not used in the progressive tenses; often with *can* or *could*) to notice or recognize a particular smell: **~ sth** *I was watching television when I smelled smoke.* ⋄ *The dog had smelt a rabbit.* ⋄ *I could smell alcohol on his breath.* ⋄ **~ sth doing sth** *Can you smell something burning?* ⋄ **~ (that)…** *I could smell that something was burning.* **3** [I, T] **~ (sth)** (not used in the progressive tenses; often with *can* or *could*) to be able to notice and recognize smells: *I can't smell because I've got a bad cold.* **4** A2 [T] **~ sth** (not usually used in the passive) to put your nose near sth and breathe in so that you can discover or identify its smell SYN **sniff**: *Smell this and tell me what you think it is.* ⋄ *I bent down to smell the flowers.* **5** A2 [I] (not used in the progressive tenses) to have an unpleasant smell: *Does my breath smell?* ⋄ *He hadn't washed for days and was beginning to smell.* ⋄ **+ adj.** *It smells awful in here.* **6** [T, no passive] **~ sth** to feel that sth exists or is going to happen: *He smelt danger.* ⋄ *I can smell trouble.*
IDM **come up/out of sth smelling of 'roses** (*informal*) to still have a good reputation, even though you have been involved in sth that might have given people a bad opinion of you **smell a 'rat** (*informal*) to suspect that sth is wrong about a situation ⮕ *more at* ROSE *n.*, WAKE *v.*
PHRV **smell sb/sth ↔ 'out 1** to be aware of fear, danger, trouble, etc. in a situation: *He could always smell out fear.* **2** to find sth by smelling: *dogs trained to smell out drugs*

■ *noun* **1** A2 [C, U] the quality of sth that people and animals sense through their noses: *a sweet/pleasant smell* ⋄ **~ of sth** *a faint/strong smell of garlic* ⋄ *an acrid smell of smoke* ⋄ *There was a smell of burning in the air.* **2** A2 [sing.] an unpleasant smell: *What's that smell?* ⋄ *Yuk! What a smell!* **3** B1 [U] the ability to sense things with the nose: *Dogs have a very good **sense of smell**.* ⋄ *Taste and smell are closely connected.* **4** [C] the act of smelling sth SYN **sniff**: *He took one smell of the liquid and his eyes began to water.*
IDM *see* SWEET *adj.*

▼ **VOCABULARY BUILDING**

**Smells**

**Describing smells**

These adjectives describe pleasant smells:
- **scented** candles
- **aromatic** oils
- **fragrant** perfume
- **sweet-smelling** flowers

To describe unpleasant smells you can use:
- **smelly** cheese
- **stinking** fish
- **musty** old books
- **acrid** smoke

**Types of smell**

Pleasant smells:
- the rich **aroma** of fresh coffee
- a herb with a delicate **fragrance**
- a rose's sweet **perfume**
- the **scent** of wild flowers

Unpleasant smells:
- nasty household **odours**
- the **stench** of rotting meat
- the **stink** of stale sweat
- the **reek** of beer and tobacco

**'smelling salts** *noun* [pl.] a chemical with a very strong smell, kept in a small bottle, used especially in the past for putting under the nose of a person who has become unconscious

**smelly** /ˈsmeli/ *adj.* (**smell·ier, smelli·est**) (*informal*) having an unpleasant smell: *smelly feet*

**smelt** /smelt/ *verb* **1 ~ sth** to heat and melt ORE (= rock that contains metal) in order to obtain the metal it contains: *a method of smelting iron* **2** *past tense, past part.* of SMELL

**smelt·er** /ˈsmeltə(r)/ *noun* a piece of equipment for smelting metal

**smidgen** (*also* **smidg·eon, smidg·in**) /ˈsmɪdʒən/ (*also* **smidge** /smɪdʒ/) *noun* [sing.] **~ (of sth)** (*informal*) a small piece or amount of sth: *'Sugar?' 'Just a smidgen.'*

**smile** ❶ A2 /smaɪl/ *verb, noun*
■ *verb* **1** A2 [I] to make a smile appear on your face: *to smile slightly/broadly* ⋄ *Looking up from my book, I saw Monica's smiling face.* ⋄ **~ at sb/sth** *She smiled at him and he smiled back.* ⋄ *I had to smile at (= was amused by) his optimism.* ⋄ **~ with/in sth** *He smiled with relief.* **2** [T] to say or express sth with a smile: **~ sth** *She smiled her thanks.* ⋄ **+ speech** *'Perfect,' he smiled.* **3** [T, no passive] **~ sth** to give a smile of a particular type: *to smile a small smile* ⋄ *She smiled a smile of dry amusement.* IDM *see* EAR
PHRV **'smile on sb/sth** (*formal*) if luck, etc. **smiles on** you, you are lucky or successful

■ *noun* **1** A2 the expression that you have on your face when you are happy or you think sth is funny, in which the corners of your mouth turn upwards: **with a ~** *'Oh, hello,' he said, with a smile.* ⋄ *'Well, that's life,' she said with a **wry smile**.* ⋄ *He gave a weak smile as she approached.* ⋄ *He had a huge smile on his face.* ⋄ *Here's a story that is guaranteed to put a smile on your face.*
IDM **all 'smiles** looking very happy, especially soon after you have been looking worried or sad: *Twelve hours later she was all smiles again.* ⮕ *more at* WIPE *v.*

**smiley** /ˈsmaɪli/ *adj., noun*
■ *adj.* (*informal*) smiling; cheerful: *He's a happy, smiley baby.*

# smilingly

**noun** (pl. **smileys** or **smilies**) **1** a simple picture of a smiling face that is drawn as a circle with two eyes and a curved mouth **2** a simple picture or series of keyboard symbols :-) that is used, for example, in email or text messages to show the feelings of the person sending the message ⊃ compare EMOTICON

**smil·ing·ly** /ˈsmaɪlɪŋli/ *adv.* with a smile or smiles

**smirk** /smɜːk; *NAmE* smɜːrk/ *verb* [I] to smile in a silly or unpleasant way that shows that you are pleased with yourself, know sth that other people do not know, etc: *It was hard not to smirk.* ◇ *He smirked unpleasantly when we told him the bad news.* ⊃ **WORDFINDER NOTE** at EXPRESSION
▶ **smirk** *noun: She had a self-satisfied smirk on her face.*

**smite** /smaɪt/ *verb* (**smote** /sməʊt/, **smit·ten** /ˈsmɪtn/) (*old use* or *literary*) **1** ~ **sb/sth** to hit sb/sth hard; to attack or punish sb **2** ~ **sb/sth** to have a great effect on sb, especially an unpleasant or serious one ⊃ see also SMITTEN

**smith** /smɪθ/ *noun* = BLACKSMITH ⊃ see also GOLDSMITH, GUNSMITH, LOCKSMITH, SILVERSMITH

**smith·er·eens** /ˌsmɪðəˈriːnz/ *noun* [pl.]
**IDM** **smash, blow, etc. sth to smithe·reens** (*informal*) to destroy sth completely by breaking it into small pieces

**smithy** /ˈsmɪði; *NAmE* ˈsmɪθi/ *noun* (pl. **-ies**) a place where a BLACKSMITH works

**smit·ten** /ˈsmɪtn/ *adj., verb*
■ *adj.* [not usually before noun] **1** ~ **(with / by sb / sth)** (*especially humorous*) suddenly feeling that you are in love with sb: *From the moment they met, he was completely smitten by her.* **2** ~ **with / by sth** severely affected by a feeling, disease, etc.
■ *verb past part.* of SMITE

**smock** /smɒk; *NAmE* smɑːk/ *noun* **1** a loose, comfortable piece of clothing like a long shirt, worn especially by women **2** a long, loose piece of clothing worn over other clothes to protect them from dirt, etc: *an artist's smock*

**smock·ing** /ˈsmɒkɪŋ; *NAmE* ˈsmɑːk-/ *noun* [U] decoration on clothing consisting of very small, tight folds that are SEWN together

**smog** /smɒg; *NAmE* smɑːg/ *noun* [U, C] a form of air pollution that is or looks like a mixture of smoke and FOG, especially in cities: *attempts to reduce smog caused by traffic fumes* ▶ **smoggy** *adj.*

**smoke** ❶ **A2** /sməʊk/ *noun, verb*
■ *noun* **1** ❶ **A2** [U] the grey, white or black gas that is produced by sth burning: *cigarette/tobacco smoke* ◇ *Plumes of black smoke could be seen rising from the area.* ◇ *The explosion sent a huge cloud of smoke into the sky.* ◇ *The majority of people who die in fires die of smoke inhalation.* ⊃ see also SECOND-HAND SMOKE **2** ❓ **B1** [C, usually sing.] (*informal*) an act of smoking a cigarette: *He's in the back garden having a smoke.* **3 the Smoke** [sing.] (*BrE, informal*) = BIG SMOKE
**IDM** **go up in ˈsmoke 1** to be completely burnt: *The whole house went up in smoke.* **2** if your plans, hopes, etc. go up in smoke, they fail completely **(there is) no smoke without ˈfire** (*BrE*) (*NAmE* **where there's smoke, there's ˈfire**) (*saying*) used to say that if sth bad is being said about sb/sth, it usually has some truth in it **smoke and ˈmirrors** the fact of hiding the truth with information that is not important or relevant: *There's a lot of smoke and mirrors in the financing of this film.* **a smoke-filled ˈroom** (*disapproving*) a decision that people describe as being made in **a smoke-filled room** is made by a small group of people at a private meeting, rather than in an open and DEMOCRATIC way ⊃ more at BLOW *v.*
■ *verb* **1** ❓ **B1** [T, I] to take smoke from a cigarette, pipe, etc. into your mouth and let it out again: *Do you mind if I smoke?* ◇ ~ **sth** *He was smoking a large cigar.* ◇ *How many cigarettes do you smoke a day?* **2** ❓ **A2** [I] to use cigarettes, etc. in this way as a habit: *Do you smoke?* ◇ *She smokes heavily.* ⊃ see also CHAIN-SMOKE **3** [I] to produce smoke: *smoking factory chimneys* ◇ *the smoking remains of burnt-out cars* ◇ *This fireplace smokes badly* (= sends smoke into the room instead of up the CHIMNEY). **4** [T, usually passive] to preserve meat or fish by hanging it in smoke from wood fires to give it a special taste: **be smoked** *The ham is cured, then lightly smoked.* ◇ *smoked salmon*
**PHRV** **smoke sb/sth↔ˈout 1** to force sb/sth to come out of a place by filling it with smoke: *to smoke out wasps from a nest* **2** to take action to discover where sb is hiding or to make a secret publicly known: *The police are determined to smoke out the leaders of the gang.*

**ˈsmoke alarm** (*also* **ˈsmoke detector**) *noun* a device that makes a loud noise if smoke is in the air to warn you of a fire

**ˈsmoke bomb** *noun* a bomb that produces clouds of smoke when it explodes

**ˌsmoke-ˈfree** *adj.* free from cigarette smoke; where smoking is not allowed: *a smoke-free working environment*

**ˈsmoke·house** /ˈsməʊkhaʊs/ *noun* (*especially NAmE*) a place where food is preserved using smoke from wood fires

**smoke·less** /ˈsməʊkləs/ *adj.* [usually before noun] **1** able to burn without producing smoke: *smokeless fuels* **2** free from smoke: *a smokeless zone* (= where smoke from factories or houses is not allowed)

**smoker** /ˈsməʊkə(r)/ *noun* a person who smokes TOBACCO regularly: *a heavy smoker* (= sb who smokes a lot) ◇ *a smoker's cough* ◇ *a cigarette/cigar/pipe smoker* **OPP** **non-smoker** ⊃ see also CHAIN-SMOKER

**ˈsmoke·screen** /ˈsməʊkskriːn/ *noun* **1** something that you do or say in order to hide what you are really doing or intending **2** a cloud of smoke used to hide soldiers, ships, etc. during a battle

**ˈsmoke shop** *noun* (*NAmE*) a shop selling cigarettes, TOBACCO, etc.

**ˈsmoke signal** *noun* [usually pl.] **1** a signal that is sent to sb who is far away, using smoke **2** a sign of what sb is thinking or doing

**ˈsmoke·stack** /ˈsməʊkstæk/ *noun* (*especially NAmE*) **1** a tall CHIMNEY that takes away smoke from factories **2** (*also* **funnel**) a metal CHIMNEY, for example on a ship or an engine, through which smoke comes out

**smok·ing** ❶ **A2** /ˈsməʊkɪŋ/ *noun* [U] the activity or habit of smoking cigarettes, etc: *No Smoking* (= for example, on a notice) ◇ *He's trying to give up smoking.* ◇ *the harmful effects of cigarette smoking* ◇ *the introduction of the smoking ban in pubs, restaurants, and hotels* ⊃ compare NON-SMOKING ⊃ see also PASSIVE SMOKING

**ˈsmoking ceremony** *noun* (*AustralE*) (in Aboriginal culture) a ceremony in which smoke is used for RITUAL purposes, especially after death

**ˈsmoking gun** *noun* [sing.] (*informal*) something that seems to prove that sb has done sth wrong or illegal: *This memo could be the smoking gun that investigators have been looking for.*

**ˈsmoking jacket** *noun* a man's comfortable jacket worn in the past, often made of VELVET

**smoko** /ˈsməʊkəʊ/ *noun* (pl. **-os**) (*AustralE, NZE, informal*) a rest from work, for example to smoke a cigarette

**smoky** /ˈsməʊki/ *adj.* (**smoki·er, smoki·est**) **1** full of smoke: *a smoky atmosphere* ◇ *a smoky pub* **2** producing a lot of smoke: *a smoky fire* **3** tasting or smelling like smoke: *a smoky flavour* **4** having the colour or appearance of smoke: *smoky blue glass* **OPP** **clear**

**smol·der** (*US*) = SMOULDER

**smooch** /smuːtʃ/ *verb* [I] (*informal*) to kiss and hold sb closely, especially when you are dancing slowly

**smooth** ❶ **B1** /smuːð/ *adj., verb*
■ *adj.* (**smooth·er, smooth·est**)
▶ FLAT/EVEN **1** ❓ **B1** completely flat and even, without any rough areas or holes: *the smooth surface of the metal* ◇ *a lotion to make your skin feel soft and smooth* ◇ *a paint that gives a smooth, silky finish* ◇ *Over the years, the stone steps had worn smooth.* **OPP** **rough**

- **WITHOUT SOLID PIECES 2** [T] **B1** (of a liquid mixture) without any solid pieces: *Mix the flour with the milk to form a smooth paste.*
- **WITHOUT PROBLEMS 3** [T] **B2** happening or continuing without any problems: *They are introducing new measures to ensure the* **smooth running** *of the business.* ◊ *a fairly* **smooth transition** *to democracy*
- **MOVEMENT 4** [T] **B2** even and regular, without sudden stops and starts: *The car's improved suspension gives you a smoother ride.* ◊ *The plane made a smooth landing.* ◊ *She swung herself over the gate in one smooth movement.*
- **MAN 5** (*often disapproving*) (of people, especially men, and their behaviour) very polite and pleasant, but in a way that is often not very sincere **SYN** smarmy: *I don't like him. He's far too smooth for me.* ◊ *He's something of a* **smooth operator.**
- **DRINK/TASTE 6** pleasant and not bitter: *This coffee has a smooth, rich taste.*
- **VOICE/MUSIC 7** nice to hear, and without any rough or unpleasant sounds ▶ **smooth·ness** *noun* [U]: *the smoothness of her skin* ◊ *They admired the smoothness and efficiency with which the business was run.* **IDM** see ROUGH *n.*
**IDM** **be smooth / clear ˈsailing** (*NAmE*) = BE PLAIN SAILING at PLAIN *adj.*
- *verb* **1** to make sth smooth: *~ sth (back / down / out) He smoothed his hair back.* ◊ *She was smoothing out the creases in her skirt.* ◊ *~ sth + adj. He took the letter and smoothed it flat on the table.* **2** *~ sth on / into / over sth* to put a layer of a soft substance over a surface: *Smooth the icing over the top of the cake.* **3** *~ sth* to make it easier for sth to happen
**IDM** **smooth the ˈpath / ˈway** to make it easier for sb/sth to develop or make progress: *These negotiations are intended to smooth the path to a peace treaty.* **smooth (sb's) ruffled ˈfeathers** to make sb feel less angry or offended
**PHR V** **ˌsmooth sth↔aˈway / ˈout** to make problems or difficulties disappear **ˌsmooth sth↔ˈover** to make problems or difficulties seem less important or serious, especially by talking to people: *She spoke to both sides in the dispute in an attempt to smooth things over.*

**smoothie** /ˈsmuːði/ *noun* **1** a thick, smooth drink made of fruit and/or vegetables mixed with milk, ice cream, YOGURT or fruit juice **2** (*informal*) a man who dresses well and talks very politely and confidently but who is often not honest or sincere

**smooth·ly** /ˈsmuːðli/ *adv.* **1** in an even way, without suddenly stopping and starting again: *Traffic is now flowing smoothly again.* ◊ *The engine was running smoothly.* **2** without problems or difficulties: *The interview* **went smoothly.** ◊ *My job is to see that everything* **runs smoothly. 3** in a calm or confident way: *'Would you like to come this way?' he said smoothly.* **4** in a way that produces a smooth surface or mixture: *The colours blend smoothly together.*

**ˌsmooth ˈmuscle** *noun* [U] (*anatomy*) the type of muscle found in the organs inside the body, that is not under conscious control

**ˌsmooth-ˈtalking** *adj.* (*usually disapproving*) talking very politely and confidently, especially to persuade sb to do sth, but in a way that may not be honest or sincere

**s'more** /smɔː(r)/ *noun* (*NAmE*) a cooked MARSHMALLOW eaten with chocolate between two GRAHAM CRACKERS (= a type of biscuit) that is traditionally cooked over a fire when camping

**smor·gas·bord** /ˈsmɔːɡəsbɔːd; *NAmE* ˈsmɔːrɡəsbɔːrd/ *noun* [U, sing.] (*from Swedish*) a meal at which you serve yourself from a large range of hot and cold dishes ⊃ compare BUFFET¹ (1)

**smote** /sməʊt/ *past tense of* SMITE

**smother** /ˈsmʌðə(r)/ *verb* **1** *~ sb (with sth)* to kill sb by covering their face so that they cannot breathe **SYN** suffocate: *He smothered the baby with a pillow.* **2** *~ sth / sb with / in sth* to cover sth/sb thickly or with too much of sth: *a rich dessert smothered in cream* ◊ *She smothered him with kisses.* **3** *~ sth* to prevent sth from developing or being expressed **SYN** stifle: *to smother a yawn / giggle / grin* ◊ *The voices of the opposition were effectively smothered.* **4** *~ sb* to give sb too much love or protection so that they feel that their freedom is limited: *Her husband was very loving, but she felt smothered.* **5** *~ sth* to make a fire stop burning by covering it with sth: *He tried to smother the flames with a blanket.*

**smoul·der** (*US* **smol·der**) /ˈsməʊldə(r)/ *verb* **1** [I] to burn slowly without a flame: *The bonfire was still smouldering the next day.* ◊ *a smouldering cigarette* ◊ (*figurative*) *The feud smouldered on for years.* **2** [I] (*formal*) to be filled with a strong emotion that you do not fully express **SYN** burn: *~ (with sth) His eyes smouldered with anger.* ◊ *~ (in sth) Anger smouldered in his eyes.*

**SMS** /ˌes em ˈes/ *noun, verb*
- *noun* **1** [U] a system for sending short written messages from one mobile phone to another (the abbreviation for 'short message service') **2** [C] a message sent by SMS **SYN** text, text message: *I'm trying to send an SMS.*
- *verb* [T, I] *~ (sb)* to send a message to sb by SMS **SYN** text, text message: *He SMSed me every day.* ◊ *If you have any comments, just email or SMS.* ◊ *She spends her time chatting and SMSing.*

**smudge** /smʌdʒ/ *noun, verb*
- *noun* a dirty mark with no clear shape **SYN** smear: *a smudge of lipstick on a cup*
- *verb* **1** [T, I] *~ (sth)* to touch or rub sth, especially wet INK or paint, so that it is no longer clear; to become not clear in this way: *He had smudged his signature on his sleeve.* ◊ *Tears had smudged her mascara.* ◊ *Her lipstick had smudged.* **2** [T] *~ sth* to make a dirty mark on a surface **SYN** smear: *The mirror was smudged with fingerprints.*

**smudgy** /ˈsmʌdʒi/ *adj.* **1** with dirty marks on **2** (of a picture, writing, etc.) with edges that are not clear **SYN** blurred

**smug** /smʌɡ/ *adj.* (*disapproving*) looking or feeling too pleased about sth you have done or achieved **SYN** complacent: *a smug expression / smile / face, etc.* ◊ *What are you looking so smug about?* ▶ **smug·ly** *adv.* **smug·ness** *noun* [U]

**smug·gle** /ˈsmʌɡl/ *verb* *~ sth / sb (+ adv. / prep.)* to take, send or bring goods or people secretly and illegally into or out of a country, etc.: *They were caught smuggling diamonds into the country.* ◊ *He managed to smuggle a gun into the prison.* ◊ *smuggled drugs*

**smug·gler** /ˈsmʌɡlə(r)/ *noun* a person who takes goods into or out of a country illegally ⊃ see also PEOPLE SMUGGLER

**smug·gling** /ˈsmʌɡlɪŋ/ *noun* [U] the crime of taking, sending or bringing goods secretly and illegally into or out of a country: *drug smuggling* ⊃ see also PEOPLE SMUGGLING

**smut** /smʌt/ *noun* **1** [U] (*informal*) stories, pictures or comments about sex that deal with it in a way that some people find offensive **2** [U, C] dirt, ASH, etc. that causes a black mark on sth; a black mark made by this

**smutty** /ˈsmʌti/ *adj.* [*usually before noun*] (**smut·tier, smut·ti·est**) (*informal*) (of stories, pictures and comments) dealing with sex in a way that some people find offensive: *smutty jokes*

**snack** /snæk/ *noun, verb*
- *noun* **1** (*informal*) a small meal or amount of food, usually eaten in a hurry: *a mid-morning snack* ◊ *I only have time for a snack at lunchtime.* ◊ *Do you serve bar snacks?* ◊ *a snack lunch* **2** (*AustralE, informal*) a thing that is easy to do: *It'll be a snack.*
- *verb* [I] *~ (on sth)* to eat snacks between or instead of main meals: *It's healthier to snack on fruit rather than chocolate.*

**ˈsnack bar** *noun* a place where you can buy a small quick meal, such as a sandwich

**snaf·fle** /ˈsnæfl/ *verb* *~ sth* (*BrE, informal*) to take sth quickly for yourself, especially before anyone else has had the time or opportunity

**snafu** /snæˈfuː/ *noun* [sing.] (*NAmE, informal*) a situation in which nothing happens as planned: *It was another bureaucratic snafu.*

---
ⓞ Oxford Phrasal Academic Lexicon (OPAL) written and spoken word lists | Ⓦ OPAL written word list | Ⓢ OPAL spoken word list

# snag

**snag** /snæɡ/ *noun, verb*
- *noun* **1** (*informal*) a problem or difficulty, especially one that is small, hidden or unexpected **SYN difficulty**: *There is just one small snag—where is the money coming from? ◊ Let me know if you run into any snags.* **2** an object or a part of an object that is rough or sharp and may cut sth **3** (*AustralE, NZE, informal*) a SAUSAGE
- *verb* (-gg-) **1** [T, I] to catch or tear sth on sth rough or sharp; to become caught or torn in this way: *~ sth on/in sth I snagged my sweater on the wire fence. ◊ ~ sth The fence snagged my sweater. ◊ ~ (on/in sth) The nets snagged on some rocks.* **2** [T] *~ sth (from sb)* (*NAmE, informal*) to succeed in getting sth quickly, often before other people: *I snagged a ride from Joe.*

**snail** /sneɪl/ *noun* a small, soft creature with a hard, round shell on its back, that moves very slowly and often eats garden plants. Some types of snail can be eaten. ⊃ VISUAL VOCAB page V3
- **IDM at a 'snail's pace** very slowly

**'snail mail** *noun* [U] (*informal, humorous*) used to describe the system of sending letters by ordinary mail, contrasted with the speed of sending email

**snake** ⓘ A1 /sneɪk/ *noun, verb*
- *noun* A1 a REPTILE with a very long thin body and no legs. There are many types of snake, some of which are poisonous: *a snake coiled up in the grass ◊ Venomous snakes spit and hiss when they are cornered.* ⊃ see also GARTER SNAKE, GRASS SNAKE
- **IDM a 'snake (in the 'grass)** (*disapproving*) a person who pretends to be your friend but who cannot be trusted
- *verb* [I, T] to move like a snake, in long TWISTING curves; to go in a particular direction in long TWISTING curves **SYN meander**: *+ adv./prep. The road snaked away into the distance. ◊ ~ its way + adv./prep. The procession snaked its way through narrow streets.*

**snake-bite** /'sneɪkbaɪt/ *noun* [C, U] **1** a wound that you get when a poisonous snake bites you **2** an alcoholic drink made of equal parts of beer and CIDER

**'snake charmer** *noun* a person who seems to be able to control snakes and make them move by playing music to them, in order to entertain people

**'snake eyes** *noun* [pl.] (*informal*) a result in a game when you throw two DICE and both show one DOT (= small round mark)

**'snake oil** *noun* [U] (*especially NAmE, informal*) something, for example medicine, that sb tries to sell you, but that is not effective or useful: *a snake oil salesman*

**'snake pit** *noun* **1** a hole in the ground in which snakes are kept **2** a place that is extremely unpleasant or dangerous: *I thought the club would be glamorous, but it was a snake pit.*

**,snakes and 'ladders** *noun* [U] (*BrE*) a children's game played on a special board with pictures of snakes and LADDERS on it. Players move their pieces up the ladders to go forward and down the snakes to go back. ⊃ compare CHUTES AND LADDERS™

**snake·skin** /'sneɪkskɪn/ *noun* [U] the skin of a snake, used for making expensive shoes, bags, etc.

**snaky** /'sneɪki/ *adj.* (**snaki·er, snaki·est**) (*AustralE, NZE, informal*) angry: *What are you snaky about?*

**snap** ⓘ+ C1 /snæp/ *verb, noun, adj., exclamation*
- *verb* (-pp-)
- • BREAK **1** ⓘ+ C1 [T, I] to break sth suddenly with a sharp noise; to be broken in this way: *~ sth The wind had snapped the tree in two. ◊ ~ sth off (sth) He snapped a twig off a bush. ◊ ~ (off) Suddenly, the rope snapped. ◊ The branch she was standing on must have snapped off.*
- • TAKE PHOTOGRAPH **2** ⓘ+ C1 [T, I] (*informal*) to take a photograph: *~ sth A passing tourist snapped the incident. ◊ ~ (away) She seemed oblivious to the crowds of photographers snapping away.*
- • OPEN/CLOSE/MOVE INTO POSITION **3** [I, T] to move, or to move sth, into a particular position quickly, especially with a sudden sharp noise: *+ adj. The lid snapped shut. ◊ His eyes snapped open. ◊ + adv./prep. He snapped to attention and saluted. ◊ ~ sth + adj. She snapped the bag shut.*
- • SPEAK IMPATIENTLY **4** [T, I] to speak or say sth in an impatient, usually angry, voice: *+ speech 'Don't just stand there,' she snapped. ◊ ~ (at sb) I was tempted to snap back angrily at him. ◊ ~ sth He snapped a reply.*
- • OF ANIMAL **5** [I] *~ (at sb/sth)* to try to bite sb/sth **SYN nip**: *The dogs snarled and snapped at our heels.*
- • LOSE CONTROL **6** [I] to suddenly be unable to control your feelings any longer because the situation has become too difficult: *My patience finally snapped. ◊ When he said that, something snapped inside her. ◊ And that did it. I snapped.*
- • FASTEN CLOTHING **7** [I, T] *~ (sth)* (*NAmE*) to fasten a piece of clothing with a snap
- • IN AMERICAN FOOTBALL **8** [T] *~ sth* (*sport*) (in AMERICAN FOOTBALL) to start play by passing the ball back between your legs
- **IDM snap your 'fingers** to make a sharp noise by moving your second or third finger quickly against your THUMB, to attract sb's attention, or to mark the beat of music, for example ,**snap 'out of it/sth** | ,**snap sb 'out of it/sth** [no passive] (*informal*) to make an effort to stop feeling unhappy or depressed; to help sb to stop feeling unhappy: *You've been depressed for weeks. It's time you snapped out of it.* ,**snap 'to it** (*informal*) used, especially in orders, to tell sb to start working harder or more quickly ⊃ more at HEAD *n.*
- **PHRV ,snap sth↔'out** to say sth in a sharp unpleasant way: *The sergeant snapped out an order.* ,**snap sth↔'up** [often passive] (*informal*) to buy or obtain sth quickly because it is cheap or you want it very much: *All the best bargains were snapped up within hours. ◊ (figurative) She's been snapped up by Hollywood to star in two major movies.*
- *noun*
- • SHARP NOISE **1** [C] a sudden sharp noise, especially one made by sth closing or breaking: *She closed her purse with a snap. ◊ the snap of a twig*
- • PHOTOGRAPH **2** (*also* **snap-shot**) [C] a photograph, especially one taken quickly: *holiday snaps*
- • CARD GAME **3** Snap [U] a card game in which players take turns to put cards down and try to be the first to call out 'snap' when two similar cards are put down together
- • FASTENER **4** (*NAmE*) (*BrE* '**press stud, pop-per**) a type of button used for fastening clothes, consisting of two metal or plastic sections that can be pressed together ⊃ see also COLD SNAP, SUGAR SNAP
- **IDM be a 'snap** (*NAmE, informal*) to be very easy to do: *This job's a snap.*
- *adj.* [only before noun] made or done quickly and without careful thought or preparation: *It was a snap decision. ◊ They held a snap election.*
- *exclamation* **1** you say **snap!** in the card game called 'Snap' when two cards that are the same are put down **2** (*BrE, informal*) people say **snap!** to show that they are surprised when two things are the same: *Snap! I've just bought curtains exactly like those.*

**Snap·chat**™ /'snæptʃæt/ *noun* [U] a SOCIAL MEDIA service that allows you to send or share photos, short videos and messages. Photos, etc. sent or shared using this service disappear from view after a short time.

**snap·dragon** /'snæpdræɡən/ *noun* a small garden plant with red, white, yellow or pink flowers that open and shut like a mouth when pressed

**snap·per** /'snæpə(r)/ *noun* **1** [C, U] a fish that lives in warm seas and is used for food **2** [C] (*informal, BrE*) a photographer, especially one who takes pictures of famous people for newspapers and magazines

**snappy** /'snæpi/ *adj.* (**snap-pier, snap-pi-est**) **1** (of a remark, title, etc.) clever or funny and short: *a snappy slogan ◊ a snappy answer* **2** [usually before noun] (*informal*) attractive and fashionable: *a snappy outfit ◊ She's a snappy dresser.* **3** (of people or their behaviour) tending to speak to people in an angry, impatient way **4** lively; quick: *a snappy tune* ▸ **snap·pily** /-pəli/ *adv.*: *He summarized the speech snappily. ◊ snappily dressed ◊ 'What?' she asked snappily.* **snap·pi·ness** *noun* [U]

**IDM** **make it ˈsnappy** (*informal*) used to tell sb to do sth quickly or to hurry

**snap·shot** /ˈsnæpʃɒt; *NAmE* -ʃɑːt/ *noun* **1** = SNAP: *snapshots of the children* ⊃ SYNONYMS at PHOTOGRAPH **2** [usually sing.] a short description or a small amount of information that gives you an idea of what sth is like

**snare** /sneə(r); *NAmE* sner/ *noun*, *verb*
▪ *noun* **1** a device used for catching small animals and birds, especially one that holds their leg so that they cannot escape **SYN** **trap** **2** (*formal*) a situation which seems attractive but is unpleasant and difficult to escape from **3** the metal strings that are stretched across the bottom of a snare drum
▪ *verb* ~ sth/sb to catch sth, especially an animal, in a snare **SYN** **trap**: *to snare a rabbit* ◊ (*figurative*) *Her one thought was to snare a rich husband.* ◊ (*figurative*) *He found himself snared in a web of intrigue.*

ˈ**snare drum** *noun* a small drum with metal strings across one side that make a continuous sound when the drum is hit

**snarf** /snɑːf; *NAmE* snɑːrf/ *verb* ~ sth (*especially NAmE, informal*) to eat or drink sth very quickly or in a way that people think is GREEDY: *The kids snarfed all the cookies.*

**snark** /snɑːk; *NAmE* snɑːrk/ *verb*, *noun* (*NAmE, informal*)
▪ *verb* [I] ~ (at/about/on sb/sth) to criticize sb/sth in an indirect and very unkind way: *There's plenty to snark about in the article.*
▪ *noun* [U, C] very critical comments, made in an indirect way; a comment of this type

**snarky** /ˈsnɑːki; *NAmE* ˈsnɑːrki/ *adj.* (**snark·i·er**, **snarki·est**) (*especially NAmE, informal*) criticizing sb in an unkind way: *a snarky remark*

**snarl** /snɑːl; *NAmE* snɑːrl/ *verb*, *noun*
▪ *verb* **1** [I] ~ (at sb/sth) (of dogs, etc.) to show the teeth and make a deep angry noise in the throat: *The dog snarled at us.* **2** [T, I] to speak in a rough, low, angry voice: + speech (at sb) *'Get out of here!' he snarled.* ◊ ~ (sth) (at sb) *She snarled abuse at anyone who happened to walk past.*
**PHRV** ˌ**snarl ˈup** | ˌ**snarl sth**↔**ˈup** **1** to involve sb/sth in a situation that stops their movement or progress; to become involved in a situation like this: *The accident snarled up the traffic all day.* **2** to become caught or TWISTED; to make sth do this: *The sheets kept getting snarled up.*
▪ *noun* **1** [usually sing.] a deep sound that an animal makes when it is angry and shows its teeth: *The dog bared its teeth in a snarl.* **2** [usually sing.] an act of speaking in a rough, low, angry voice; the sound you make when you are angry, in pain, etc: *a snarl of hate* **3** (*informal*) something that has become TWISTED in an untidy way: *She used conditioner to remove the snarls from her hair.*

**snatch** /snætʃ/ *verb*, *noun*
▪ *verb* **1** [T, I] to take sth quickly and often rudely or roughly **SYN** **grab**: ~ sth (+ adv./prep.) *She managed to snatch the gun from his hand.* ◊ *Gordon snatched up his jacket and left the room.* ◊ (+ adv./prep.) *Hey, you kids! Don't all snatch!* **2** [T] ~ sb/sth (from sb/sth) to take sb/sth away from a person or place, especially by force **SYN** **steal**: *The raiders snatched $100 from the cash register.* ◊ *The baby was snatched from its parents' car.* **3** [T] ~ sth to take or get sth quickly, especially because you do not have much time: *I managed to snatch an hour's sleep.* ◊ *The team snatched a dramatic victory in the last minute of the game.*
**IDM** ˌ**snatch ˈvictory from the jaws of deˈfeat** to win sth even though it seemed up until the last moment that you would lose **HELP** The idiom is often reversed for humorous effect to show that a person or team were expected to win, but then lost at the last moment, snatching defeat from the jaws of victory.
**PHRV** ˈ**snatch at sth** **1** to try to take hold of sth with your hands: *He snatched at the steering wheel but I pushed him away.* **2** to take an opportunity to do sth: *We snatched at every moment we could be together.*
▪ *noun* **1** a very small part of a conversation or some music that you hear **SYN** **snippet**: *a snatch of music* ◊ *I only caught snatches of the conversation.* **2** an act of moving your hand very quickly to take or steal sth: *a bag snatch* ◊

1477 **sneeze**

*to make a snatch at sth* **3** (*taboo, slang*) an offensive word for a woman's outer sex organs
**IDM** **in ˈsnatches** for short periods rather than continuously: *Sleep came to him in brief snatches.*

**snatch·er** /ˈsnætʃə(r)/ *noun* (often in compounds) a person who takes sth quickly with their hand and steals it: *a purse snatcher*

**snazzy** /ˈsnæzi/ *adj.* (**snaz·zier**, **snaz·zi·est**) (*informal*) (of clothes, cars, etc.) fashionable, bright and modern, and attracting your attention **SYN** **jazzy**, **smart**: *a snazzy tie*

**sneak** /sniːk/ *verb*, *noun*, *adj.*
▪ *verb* **HELP** The usual past form is **sneaked**, but **snuck** is now very common in informal speech in *NAmE*, and some people use it in *BrE* too. However, many people think that it is not correct and it should not be used in formal writing. **1** [I] + adv./prep. to go somewhere secretly, trying to avoid being seen **SYN** **creep**: *I sneaked up the stairs.* **2** [T] to do sth or take sb/sth somewhere secretly, often without permission: ~ sth *We sneaked a look at her diary.* ◊ *If the gate is open, you can sneak a peek at the gardens.* ◊ ~ **sth to sb** *I managed to sneak a note to him.* ◊ ~ **sb sth** *I managed to sneak him a note.* **3** [T] ~ sth (*informal*) to secretly take sth that is small or unimportant **SYN** **pinch**: *I sneaked a cake when they were out of the room.* **4** [I] ~ (on sb) (to sb) (*old-fashioned, BrE, disapproving*) to tell an adult that another child has done sth wrong, especially in order to cause trouble **SYN** **snitch**: *Did you sneak on me to the teacher?*
**PHRV** ˌ**sneak ˈup (on sb/sth)** to move towards sb very quietly so that they do not see or hear you until you reach them: *He sneaked up on his sister and shouted 'Boo!'*
▪ *noun* (*old-fashioned, disapproving*) a person, especially a child, who tells sb about sth wrong that another person has done **SYN** **snitch**
▪ *adj.* [only before noun] done without any warning: *a sneak attack*

**sneak·er** /ˈsniːkə(r)/ *noun* (*also* ˈ**gym shoe**) (*both NAmE*) (*BrE* ˈ**train·er**, ˈ**training shoe**) *noun* [usually pl.] a shoe that you wear for sports or as informal clothing: *He wore old jeans and a pair of sneakers.*

**sneak·ing** /ˈsniːkɪŋ/ *adj.* [only before noun] if you have a **sneaking** feeling for sb or about sth, you do not want to admit it to other people, because you feel embarrassed, or you are not sure that this feeling is right: *She had always had a sneaking affection for him.* ◊ *I have a sneaking suspicion that she knows more than she's telling us.*

ˌ**sneak ˈpeek** *noun* (*informal*) an opportunity to have a quick look at sth such as a film before it is officially available: *Watch a sneak peek of Pam and Frankie's first night out in our online video.*

ˌ**sneak ˈpreview** *noun* an opportunity to see sth before it is officially shown to the public

**sneaky** /ˈsniːki/ *adj.* (**sneak·ier**, **sneaki·est**) (*informal*) behaving in a secret and sometimes dishonest or unpleasant way **SYN** **crafty**: *That was a sneaky trick!* ▸ **sneak·ily** /-kɪli/ *adv.*

**sneer** /snɪə(r); *NAmE* snɪr/ *verb*, *noun*
▪ *verb* [I, T] to show that you have no respect for sb by the expression on your face or by the way you speak **SYN** **mock**: ~ (at sb/sth) *He sneered at people who liked pop music.* ◊ *a sneering comment* ◊ + speech *'You? A writer?' she sneered.* ⊃ WORDFINDER NOTE at EXPRESSION ▸ **sneer·ing·ly** /ˈsnɪərɪŋli; *NAmE* ˈsnɪr-/ *adv.*
▪ *noun* [usually sing.] an unpleasant look, smile or comment that shows you do not respect sb/sth: *A faint sneer of satisfaction crossed her face.*

**sneeze** /sniːz/ *verb*, *noun*
▪ *verb* [I] to have air come suddenly and noisily out through your nose and mouth in a way that you cannot control, for example because you have a cold: *I've been sneezing all morning.*
**IDM** **not to be ˈsneezed/ˈsniffed at** (*informal*) good enough to be accepted or considered seriously: *In those days, $20 was not a sum to be sneezed at.*

# snicker

■ *noun* the act of sneezing or the noise you make when you sneeze: *coughs and sneezes* ◇ *She gave a violent sneeze.*

**snicker** /'snɪkə(r)/ *(especially NAmE)* (*also especially BrE* **snigger**) *verb* [I] ~ **(at sb/sth)** to laugh in a quiet unpleasant way, especially at sth rude or at sb's problems or mistakes **SYN** titter ▶ **snicker** *noun*

**snide** /snaɪd/ *adj.* (*informal*) criticizing sb/sth in an unkind and indirect way: *snide comments/remarks* ▶ **snide·ly** *adv.*

**sniff** /snɪf/ *verb, noun*

■ *verb* 1 [I] to breathe air in through your nose in a way that makes a sound, especially when you are crying, have a cold, etc: *We all had colds and couldn't stop sniffing and sneezing.* 2 [T, I] to breathe air in through the nose in order to discover or enjoy the smell of sth **SYN** smell: ~ *sth sniffing the fresh morning air* ◇ *to sniff glue* ◇ ~ **(at sth)** *The dog sniffed at my shoes.* ⇨ see also GLUE-SNIFFING 3 [T, I] + **speech** | ~ **(sth)** to say sth in a way that shows that you are annoyed, unhappy or not satisfied or that you do not approve of sb/sth: *'It's hardly what I'd call elegant,' she sniffed.*

**IDM** **not to be 'sniffed / 'sneezed at** (*informal*) good enough to be accepted or considered seriously: *In those days, $20 was not a sum to be sniffed at.*

**PHRV** **sniff a'round** (*BrE also* **sniff 'round**) (*informal*) to try to find out information about sb/sth, especially secret information: *We don't want journalists sniffing around.* **sniff a'round sb** (*BrE also* **sniff 'round sb**) [no passive] (*especially BrE*) to try to get sb as a sexual partner, an employee, etc: *Hollywood agents have been sniffing around him.* **'sniff at sth** to show no interest in or respect for sth ,**sniff sb/sth↔'out** 1 to discover or find sb/sth by using your sense of smell: *The dogs are trained to sniff out drugs.* 2 (*informal*) to discover or find sb/sth by looking or investigating: *Journalists are good at sniffing out a scandal.*

■ *noun* 1 [C] an act or the sound of sniffing: *She took a deep sniff of the perfume.* ◇ *My mother gave a sniff of disapproval.* ◇ *His sobs soon turned to sniffs.* 2 [sing.] ~ **of sth** an idea of what sth is like or that sth is going to happen: *The sniff of power went to his head.* ◇ *They make threats but back down at the first sniff of trouble.* 3 [sing.] ~ **of sth** a small chance of sth: *She didn't get even a sniff at a medal.*

**IDM** **have a (good) sniff a'round** to examine a place carefully

**'sniffer dog** *noun* (*informal, especially BrE*) a dog that is trained to find drugs or EXPLOSIVES by smell

**snif·fle** /'snɪfl/ *verb, noun*

■ *verb* [I, T] (+ **speech**) to sniff or keep sniffing, especially because you are crying or have a cold

■ *noun* 1 an act or the sound of sniffling: *After a while, her sniffles died away.* 2 **the sniffles** [pl.] a slight cold: *to get/have the sniffles*

**sniffy** /'snɪfi/ *adj.* ~ **(about sth)** (*informal*) not approving of sth/sb because you think they are not good enough for you

**snif·ter** /'snɪftə(r)/ *noun* 1 (*especially NAmE*) a large glass used for drinking BRANDY 2 (*old-fashioned, BrE, informal*) a small amount of a strong alcoholic drink

**snig·ger** /'snɪɡə(r)/ *verb, noun*

■ *verb* (*especially BrE*) (*also* **snicker** *NAmE, BrE*) [I, T] ~ **(at sb/sth)** | + **speech** to laugh in a quiet unpleasant way, especially at sth rude or at sb's problems or mistakes **SYN** **titter**: *What are you sniggering at?*

■ *noun* (*especially NAmE*) (*also* **snicker** *NAmE, BrE*) a quiet unpleasant laugh, especially at sth rude or at sb's problems or mistakes **SYN** **titter**

**snip** /snɪp/ *verb, noun*

■ *verb* [T, I] (-**pp**-) to cut sth with SCISSORS using short quick movements: ~ *sth Snip a tiny hole in the paper.* ◇ ~ **(at/through sth)** *She snipped at the loose threads hanging down.*

**PHRV** **snip sth↔'off** to remove sth by cutting it with SCISSORS in short quick movements

■ *noun* 1 [C] an act of cutting sth with SCISSORS; the sound that this makes: *Make a series of small snips along the edge of the fabric.* ◇ *Snip, snip, went the scissors.* 2 **snips** [pl.] a tool like large SCISSORS, used for cutting metal 3 **a snip** [sing.] (*BrE, informal*) a thing that is cheap and good value **SYN** **bargain**: *It's a snip at only £25.*

**snipe** /snaɪp/ *verb, noun*

■ *verb* 1 [I] ~ **(at sb/sth)** to shoot at sb from a hiding place, usually from a distance: *Gunmen continued to snipe at people leaving their homes to find food.* 2 [I] ~ **(at sb)** to criticize sb in an unpleasant way ▶ **snip·ing** *noun* [U]: *Aid workers remain in the area despite continuous sniping.*

■ *noun* (*pl.* **snipe**) a bird with a long straight BEAK that lives on wet ground

**sniper** /'snaɪpə(r)/ *noun* a person who shoots at sb from a hidden position

**snip·pet** /'snɪpɪt/ *noun* 1 a small piece of information or news: *Have you got any interesting snippets for me?* ◇ *a snippet of information* 2 a short piece of a conversation, piece of music, etc. **SYN** **snatch, extract**

**snippy** /'snɪpi/ *adj.* (**snip·pier**, **snip·pi·est**) (*NAmE, informal*) rude; not showing respect

**snit** /snɪt/ *noun*

**IDM** **be in a 'snit** (*NAmE*) to be in a bad mood and refuse to speak to anybody for a time because you are angry about sth

**snitch** /snɪtʃ/ *verb* [I] ~ **(on sb) (to sb)** (*informal, disapproving*) to tell a parent, teacher, etc. about sth wrong that another child has done **SYN** **sneak**: *Johnnie snitched on me to his mom.* ▶ **snitch** *noun*: *You little snitch! I'll never tell you anything again!*

**snivel** /'snɪvl/ *verb* (-**ll**-, *US* -**l**-) [I] to cry and complain in a way that people think is annoying **SYN** **whine**

**sniv·el·ling** (*US* **sniv·el·ing**) /'snɪvlɪŋ/ *adj.* [only before noun] (*disapproving*) tending to cry or complain a lot in a way that annoys people: *What a snivelling little brat!*

**snob** /snɒb; *NAmE* snɑːb/ *noun* (*disapproving*) 1 a person who admires people in the higher social classes too much and has no respect for people in the lower social classes: *She's such a snob!* 2 a person who thinks they are much better than other people because they are intelligent or like things that many people do not like: *an intellectual snob* ◇ *a food/wine snob* ◇ *There is a snob value in driving the latest model.*

**snob·bery** /'snɒbəri; *NAmE* 'snɑːb-/ *noun* [U] (*disapproving*) the attitudes and behaviour of people who are snobs: *intellectual snobbery* ⇨ see also INVERTED SNOBBERY

**snob·bish** /'snɒbɪʃ; *NAmE* 'snɑːb-/ (*also informal* **snobby** /'snɒbi; *NAmE* 'snɑːbi/) *adj.* (*disapproving*) thinking that having a high social class is very important; feeling that you are better than other people because you are more intelligent or like things that many people do not like ▶ **snob·bish·ness** *noun* [U]

**snog** /snɒɡ; *NAmE* snɑːɡ/ *verb* [I, T] (-**gg**-) (*BrE, informal*) (of two people) to kiss each other, especially for a long time: *They were snogging on the sofa.* ◇ ~ **sb** *I caught him snogging my friend.* ▶ **snog** *noun* [sing.]

**snood** /snuːd/ *noun* a net or bag worn over the hair at the back of a woman's head for decoration

**snook** /snuːk/ *noun* **IDM** see COCK *v.*

**snook·er** /'snuːkə(r)/ *noun, verb*

■ *noun* 1 [U] a game for two people played on a long table covered with green cloth. Players use CUES (= long sticks) to hit a white ball against other balls (15 red and 6 of other colours) in order to get the coloured balls into pockets at the edge of the table, in a particular set order: *to play snooker* ◇ *a game of snooker* ◇ *a snooker hall/player/table* ⇨ compare BILLIARDS, POOL 2 [C] a position in snooker in which one player has made it very difficult for the opponent to play a shot within the rules

■ *verb* [usually passive] 1 ~ **sb** (in the game of snooker) to have your opponent in a snooker 2 ~ **sb/sth** (*BrE, informal*) to make it impossible for sb to do sth, especially sth they want to do: *Any plans I'd had for the weekend were by now well and truly snookered.* 3 ~ **sb** (*NAmE, informal*) to cheat or trick sb

**snoop** /snuːp/ *verb, noun*

■ *verb* [I] (*informal, disapproving*) to find out private things about sb, especially by looking secretly around a place:

~ **(around/round sth)** *Someone's been snooping around my apartment.* ◇ ~ **(on sb)** *journalists snooping on politicians*
- **noun 1** (also **snoop·er** /ˈsnuːpə(r)/) [C] a person who looks around a place secretly to find out private things about sb **2** [sing.] a secret look around a place: *He had a snoop around her office.*

**snooty** /ˈsnuːti/ *adj.* (**snoot·ier**, **snooti·est**) (also *informal* **snotty**) (*disapproving*) treating people as if they are not as good or as important as you **SYN** **snobbish** ▶ **snoot·ily** /-ɪli/ *adv.* **snooti·ness** *noun* [U]

**snooze** /snuːz/ *verb*, *noun*
- *verb* [I] (*informal*) to have a short, light sleep, especially during the day and usually not in bed: *My brother was snoozing on the sofa.* ⊃ **SYNONYMS** at **SLEEP**
- *noun* **1** [C, usually sing.] (*informal*) a short, light sleep, especially during the day and usually not in bed: *I often have a snooze after lunch.* **2** [U] (also **snooze button** [C]) a control on a clock or phone that you press when you wake up, so that you can sleep a little longer and be woken up again after a short time: *I pressed snooze and drifted off again.*

**snore** /snɔː(r)/ *verb*, *noun*
- *verb* [I] to breathe noisily through your nose and mouth while you are asleep: *I could hear Paul snoring in the next room.* ▶ **snorer** *noun* **snor·ing** *noun* [U]: *loud snoring*
- *noun* noisy breathing while you are asleep: *She lay awake listening to his snores.*

**snor·kel** /ˈsnɔːkl/; *NAmE* ˈsnɔːrkl/ *noun* a tube that you can breathe air through when you are swimming under the surface of the water ▶ **snor·kel** *verb* (-**ll-**, *US* -**l-**) [I]

**snor·kel·ling** (*US* **snor·kel·ing**) /ˈsnɔːkəlɪŋ/; *NAmE* ˈsnɔːrk-/ *noun* [U] the sport or activity of swimming UNDERWATER with a snorkel: *to go snorkelling*

**snort** /snɔːt/; *NAmE* snɔːrt/ *verb*, *noun*
- *verb* **1** [I, T] to make a loud sound by breathing air out noisily through your nose, especially to show that you are angry or think sth is silly: *The horse snorted and tossed its head.* ◇ ~ **with sth** *to snort with laughter* ◇ ~ **in sth** *She snorted in disgust.* ◇ + **speech** *'You!' he snorted contemptuously.* **2** [T] ~ **sth** to take drugs by breathing them in through the nose: *to snort cocaine*
- *noun* **1** a loud sound that you make by breathing air out noisily through your nose, especially to show that you are angry or think sth is silly: *to give a snort* ◇ *a snort of disgust* ◇ *I could hear the snort and stamp of a horse.* **2** a small amount of a drug that is breathed in through the nose; an act of taking a drug in this way: *to take a snort of cocaine*

**snot** /snɒt/; *NAmE* snɑːt/ *noun* (*informal*) a word that some people find offensive, used to describe the liquid substance (= MUCUS) that is produced in the nose

**snotty** /ˈsnɒti/; *NAmE* ˈsnɑːti/ *adj.* (**snot·tier**, **snot·ti·est**) (also **snotty-nosed**) (*informal*) **1** = SNOOTY **2** full of or covered in snot: *a snotty nose* ◇ *snotty kids*

**snout** /snaʊt/ *noun* the long nose and area around the mouth of some types of animal, such as a pig ⊃ compare MUZZLE ⊃ **VISUAL VOCAB** page V2 **2** (*informal*, *humorous*) a person's nose **3** a part of sth that sticks out at the front: *the snout of a pistol* **IDM** see TROUGH

# snow  🔊 **A1** /snəʊ/ *noun*, *verb*
- *noun* **1** 🔊 **A1** [U] small soft white pieces (called FLAKES) of frozen water that fall from the sky in cold weather; this substance when it is lying on the ground: *Snow was falling heavily.* ◇ *The snow was beginning to melt.* ◇ *Heavy snow is expected tomorrow.* ◇ *We got over 100 inches of snow last winter.* ◇ *There was almost a foot of snow on the ground.* ◇ *The snow didn't settle* (= stay on the ground). ◇ *Her skin was as white as snow.*

| **WORDFINDER** avalanche, blizzard, drift, flurry, hail, icicle, sleet, slush, thaw |
|---|

**2 snows** [pl.] (*literary*) an amount of snow that falls in one particular place or at one particular time: *the first snows of winter* ◇ *the snows of Everest*
**IDM** **as clean, pure, etc. as the driven ˈsnow** extremely clean, pure, etc.
- *verb* **1** 🔊 **A1** [I] when **it snows**, snow falls from the sky: *It's been snowing heavily all day.* **2** [T] ~ **sb** (*NAmE*, *informal*) to impress sb a lot by the things you say, especially if these are not true or not sincere: *He really snowed me with all his talk of buying a Porsche.*
**IDM** **be snowed ˈin/ˈup** to be unable to leave a place because of heavy snow **be snowed ˈunder (with sth)** to have more things, especially work, than you feel able to deal with: *I'd love to come but I'm completely snowed under at the moment.* **be snowed ˈup** (especially of a road) to be blocked with snow

**snow·ball** /ˈsnəʊbɔːl/ *noun*, *verb*
- *noun* **1** [C] a ball that you make out of snow to throw at sb/sth in a game: *a snowball fight* **2** [sing.] (often used as an adjective) a situation that develops more and more quickly as it continues: *All this publicity has had a snowball effect on the sales of their latest album.* **3** [C] a drink that is a mixture of LEMONADE and a LIQUEUR (= a strong, sweet alcoholic drink) made with eggs
**IDM** **not have a ˈsnowball's chance in ˈhell** (*informal*) to have no chance at all
- *verb* [I] if a problem, a plan, an activity, etc. **snowballs**, it quickly becomes much bigger, more serious, more important, etc.

**snow·bird** /ˈsnəʊbɜːd/; *NAmE* -bɜːrd/ *noun* (*NAmE*, *informal*) a person who spends the winter in a warmer climate, especially an old person from the north of the US, or from Canada, who spends the winter in the south

**snow·blow·er** /ˈsnəʊbləʊə(r)/ *noun* a machine that removes snow from roads or paths by blowing it to one side

**snow·board** /ˈsnəʊbɔːd/; *NAmE* -bɔːrd/ *noun* a long wide board that a person stands on to move over snow in the sport of snowboarding

**snow·board·ing** /ˈsnəʊbɔːdɪŋ/; *NAmE* -bɔːrd-/ *noun* [U] the sport of moving over snow on a snowboard: *to go snowboarding* ◇ *Snowboarding is a popular sport at the winter Olympics.* ▶ **snow·board·er** *noun*

**snow·bound** /ˈsnəʊbaʊnd/ *adj.* **1** (of a person or vehicle) stuck in a particular place and unable to move because a lot of snow has fallen **2** (of a road or building) that you cannot use or reach because a lot of snow has fallen

**ˈsnow-capped** *adj.* (*literary*) (of mountains and hills) covered with snow on top

**ˈsnow chains** *noun* [pl.] chains that are put on the wheels of a car so that it can drive over snow

**ˈsnow-covered** (also *literary* **ˈsnow-clad**) *adj.* [usually before noun] covered with snow: *snow-covered fields*

**ˈsnow day** *noun* a day when schools and/or businesses are closed because there is too much snow for people to be able to get to school or work

**snow·drift** /ˈsnəʊdrɪft/ *noun* a deep pile of snow that has been blown together by the wind

**snow·drop** /ˈsnəʊdrɒp/; *NAmE* -drɑːp/ *noun* a small white flower that appears in early spring

**snow·fall** /ˈsnəʊfɔːl/ *noun* [C, U] an occasion when snow falls; the amount of snow that falls in a particular place in a period of time: *a heavy/light snowfall* ◇ *an area of low snowfall* ◇ *What is the average annual snowfall for this state?*

**snow·field** /ˈsnəʊfiːld/ *noun* a large area that is always covered with snow, for example in the mountains

**snow·flake** /ˈsnəʊfleɪk/ *noun* **1** a small soft piece of frozen water that falls from the sky as snow **2** (*informal*, *disapproving*) a person who believes they have special qualities and should receive special treatment; a person who is too sensitive to criticism and easily upset: *These little snowflakes will soon discover that life doesn't come with trigger warnings.*

**the ˈsnow line** /ðə ˈsnəʊ laɪn/ *noun* [sing.] the level on mountains above which snow never melts completely

# snowman

**snow·man** /ˈsnəʊmæn/ noun (pl. **-men** /-men/) a figure like a person that people, especially children, make out of snow for fun

**snow·mobile** /ˈsnəʊməbiːl; NAmE -moʊb-/ (also **ski-mobile**) noun a vehicle that can move over snow and ice easily

**ˈsnow pea** (NAmE) (BrE **mange-tout**) noun [usually pl.] a type of very small PEA that grows in long, flat green PODS that are cooked and eaten whole

**snow·plough** (BrE) (NAmE **snow·plow**) /ˈsnəʊplaʊ/ noun, verb
- noun a vehicle or machine for cleaning snow from roads or railways
- verb [I] to bring the two points of your skis together, in order to go slower or stop

**snow·shoe** /ˈsnəʊʃuː/ noun one of a pair of flat frames that you attach to the bottom of your shoes so that you can walk on deep snow without sinking in

**snow·slide** /ˈsnəʊslaɪd/ noun (NAmE) = AVALANCHE

**snow·storm** /ˈsnəʊstɔːm; NAmE -stɔːrm/ noun a very heavy fall of snow, usually with a strong wind

**snow-ˈwhite** adj. pure white in colour: *snow-white sheets*

**snowy** /ˈsnəʊi/ adj. (**snow·ier, snowi·est**) **1** [usually before noun] covered with snow: *snowy fields* **2** (of a period of time) when a lot of snow falls: *a snowy weekend* **3** (*literary*) very white, like new snow: *snowy hair*

**SNP** /ˌes en ˈpiː/ abbr. SCOTTISH NATIONAL PARTY

**Snr** abbr. = SR

**snub** /snʌb/ verb, noun, adj.
- verb (-bb-) **1** ~ sb to show a lack of respect for sb, especially by ignoring them when you meet SYN **cold-shoulder**: *I tried to be friendly, but she snubbed me completely.* **2** ~ sth to refuse to attend or accept sth, for example as a protest SYN **boycott**: *All the country's leading players snubbed the tournament.*
- noun ~ (to sb) an action or a comment that is deliberately rude in order to show sb that you do not like or respect them SYN **insult**: *Her refusal to attend the dinner is being seen as a deliberate snub to the president.*
- adj. [only before noun] (of a nose) short, flat and turned up at the end ▶ **snub-ˈnosed** adj.: *a snub-nosed child ◊ a snub-nosed revolver* (= with a short BARREL)

**snuck** /snʌk/ past tense, past part. of SNEAK

**snuff** /snʌf/ verb, noun
- verb **1** [T] ~ sth (out) to stop a small flame from burning, especially by pressing it between your fingers or covering it with sth SYN **extinguish 2** [I, T] ~ (sth) (of an animal) to smell sth by breathing in noisily through the nose: *The dogs were snuffing gently at my feet.*
- IDM **ˈsnuff it** (BrE, slang, humorous) to die
- PHRV **snuff sth ↔ ˈout** to stop or destroy sth completely: *An innocent child's life has been snuffed out by this senseless shooting.*
- noun [U] TOBACCO in the form of a powder that people take by breathing it into their noses
- IDM **up to ˈsnuff** (NAmE) (BrE **up to the ˈmark**) as good as it/they should be SYN **up to scratch**

**ˈsnuff·box** /ˈsnʌfbɒks; NAmE -bɑːks/ noun a small, usually decorated, box for holding snuff

**snuf·fle** /ˈsnʌfl/ verb, noun
- verb **1** [I, T] (+ **speech**) to breathe noisily because you have a cold or you are crying SYN **sniff**: *I could hear the child snuffling in her sleep.* **2** [I] ~ (**about/around**) if an animal **snuffles**, it breathes noisily through its nose, especially while it is smelling sth
- noun (also less frequent **snuff·ling**) an act or the sound of snuffling: *The silence was broken only by the snuffles of the dogs. ◊ His breath came in snuffles.*
- IDM **get, have, etc. the ˈsnuffles** (*informal*) to get/have a cold

**ˈsnuff movie** noun a film that shows a real murder, intended as entertainment

**snug** /snʌɡ/ adj., noun
- adj. **1** warm, comfortable and protected, especially from the cold SYN **cosy**: *a snug little house ◊ I spent the afternoon snug and warm in bed.* **2** fitting sb/sth closely: *The elastic at the waist gives a nice snug fit.* ▶ **snug·ly** adv.: *I left the children tucked up snugly in bed. ◊ The lid should fit snugly.* **snug·ness** noun [U]
- noun (BrE) a small comfortable room in a pub, with seats for only a few people

**snug·gle** /ˈsnʌɡl/ verb [I, T] to get into, or to put sb/sth into, a warm comfortable position, especially close to sb: + **adv./prep.** *The child snuggled up to her mother. ◊ He snuggled down under the bedclothes. ◊ She snuggled closer. ◊ ~ sth + adv./prep. He snuggled his head onto her shoulder.*

**So.** abbr. (NAmE) south; southern

**so** /səʊ/ adv., conj., noun
- adv. **1** to such a great degree: *Why has it taken so long? ◊ That wasn't so bad, was it? ◊ ~ ... (that) ... She spoke so quietly (that) I could hardly hear her. ◊ What is it that's so important it can't wait five minutes? ◊ ~ ... as to do sth I'm not so stupid as to believe that.* ⊃ HOMOPHONES at SOW¹ **2** very; extremely: *I was pleased that so many people turned up. ◊ We have so much to do. ◊ It's so good to have you back. ◊ We've worked so hard to get to this point. ◊ They came so close to winning. ◊ Their attitude is so very English.* **3** **not ~ ... (as ...)** (used in comparisons) not to the same degree: *I haven't enjoyed myself so much for a long time. ◊ It wasn't so good as last time. ◊ It's not so easy as you'd think. ◊ He was not so quick a learner as his brother. ◊ It's not so much a hobby as a career* (= more like a career than a hobby). ◊ (*disapproving*) *Off she went without so much as* (= without even) *a 'goodbye'.* **4** used to show the size, amount or number of sth: *The fish was about so big* (= said when using your hands to show the size). *◊ There are only so many* (= only a limited number of) *hours in a day.* **5** used to refer back to sth that has already been mentioned: *'Is he coming?' 'I hope so.' ◊ 'Did they mind?' 'I don't think so.' ◊ If she notices, she never says so. ◊ I might be away next week. If so, I won't be able to see you. ◊ We are very busy—so much so that we won't be able to take time off this year. ◊ Programs are expensive, and even more so if you have to keep altering them. ◊ I hear that you're a writer—is that so* (= is that true)? *◊ George is going to help me, or so he says* (= that is what he says but I am not sure if I believe him). *◊ They asked me to call them and I did so* (= I called). *◊ She leaked the story to the media and, in so doing, helped bring down the president.* **6** also: *Times have changed and so have I. ◊ 'I prefer the first version.' 'So do we.'* HELP You cannot use **so** with negative verbs. Use **neither** or **either**: *'I'm not hungry.' 'Neither am I/I'm not very hungry either.'* **7** used to agree that sth is true, especially when you are surprised: *'You were there, too.' 'So I was—I'd forgotten.' ◊ 'There's another one.' 'So there is.'* **8** (*informal*) used, often with a negative, before adjectives and noun phrases to emphasize sth that you are saying: *He is so not the right person for you. ◊ That is so not cool.* **9** (*informal*) used, especially by children, to say that what sb says is not the case and the opposite is true: *'You're not telling the truth, are you?' 'I am, so!'* **10** used when you are showing sb how to do sth or telling them how sth happened: *Stand with your arms out, so. ◊* (*literary*) *So it was that he finally returned home.*
- IDM **and ˈso forth** (also **and ˈso on** (**and ˈso forth**)) used at the end of a list to show that it continues in the same way: *We discussed everything—when to go, what to see and so on.* **(all) the ˈmore so because ...** used to give an important extra reason why sth is true: *His achievement is remarkable; all the more so because he had no help at all.* **... or ˈso** used after a number, an amount, etc. to show that it is not exact: *There were twenty or so* (= about twenty) *people there. ◊ We stayed for an hour or so.* **ˈso as to do sth** with the intention of doing sth: *We went early so as to get good seats.* **ˈso be it** (*formal*) used to show that you accept sth and will not try to change it or cannot change it: *If he doesn't want to be involved, then so be it.* **ˈso much for ˈsth 1** used to show that you have finished talking about sth: *So much for the situation in*

Germany. Now we turn our attention to France. **2** (*informal*) used to suggest that sth has not been successful or useful: *So much for that idea!* **so … that** (*formal*) in such a way that: *The programme has been so organized that none of the talks overlap.*

■ **conj. 1** A1 used to show the reason for sth: *It was still painful, so I went to see a doctor.* **2** A2 **~ (that) …** used to show the purpose of sth: *But I gave you a map so you wouldn't get lost!* ◇ *She worked hard so that everything would be ready in time.* **3** B1 **~ (that) …** used to show the result of sth: *Nothing more was heard from him so that we began to wonder if he was dead.* **4** A1 (*informal*) used to introduce a comment or a question: *So, let's see. What do we need to take?* ◇ *So, what have you been doing today?* **5** A2 used to introduce the next part of a story: *So after shouting and screaming for an hour she walked out in tears.* **6** B1 (*informal*) used to show that you think sth is not important, especially after sb has criticized you for it: *So I had a couple of drinks on the way home. What's wrong with that?* ◇ *'You've been smoking again.' 'So?'* **7** (*informal*) used when you are making a final statement: *So, that's it for today.* **8** (*informal*) used in questions to refer to sth that has just been said: *So there's nothing we can do about it?* ◇ *'I've just got back from a trip to Rome.' 'So, how was it?'* **9** (*informal*) used to introduce an answer to a question, an explanation or a statement: *So, I've been working on a new project.* **10** used when stating that two events, situations, etc. are similar: *Just as large companies are having to cut back, so small businesses are being forced to close.* IDM **so what?** (*informal*) used to show that you think sth is not important, especially after sb has criticized you for it: *'He's fifteen years younger than you!' 'So what?'* ◇ *So what if nobody else agrees with me?*
■ **noun** = SOH

**soak** B1+ C1 /səʊk/ *verb, noun*
■ **verb 1** B1+ C1 [T, I] to put sth in liquid for a time so that it becomes completely wet; to become completely wet in this way: **~ sth (in sth)** *I usually soak the beans overnight.* ◇ *If you soak the tablecloth before you wash it, the stains should come out.* ◇ **~ (in sth)** *Leave the apricots to soak for 20 minutes.* ◇ *I'm going to go and soak in the bath.* **2** B1+ C1 [T] **~ sb/sth** to make sb/sth completely wet SYN **drench**: *A sudden shower of rain soaked the spectators.* **3** [I] (of a liquid) to enter or pass through sth: **~ through sth** *Blood had soaked through the bandage.* ◇ **~ into sth** *Water dripped off the table and soaked into the carpet.* **4** [T] **~ sb** (*informal*) to obtain a lot of money from sb by making them pay very high taxes or prices: *He was accused of soaking his clients.* PHRV **soak sth↔off/out** to remove sth by leaving it in water **soak sth↔up 1** to take in and hold liquid: *Use a cloth to soak up some of the excess water.* **2** to experience sth good or pleasant with your senses, your body or your mind: *We were just sitting soaking up the atmosphere.*
■ **noun** (*also* **soak·ing**) [sing.] **1** an act of leaving sth in a liquid for a period of time; an act of making sb/sth wet: *Give the shirt a good soak before you wash it.* **2** (*informal*) a period of time spent in a bath

**soaked** /səʊkt/ *adj.* **1** [not usually before noun] **~ (with sth)** very wet SYN **drench**: *He woke up soaked with sweat.* ◇ *You're soaked through!* (= completely wet) ◇ *They were soaked to the skin/bone* (= completely wet). ◇ *You'll get soaked if you go out in this rain.* ◇ *Your clothes are soaked!* ⇒ SYNONYMS at WET **2 -soaked** used with nouns to form adjectives describing sth that is made completely wet with the thing mentioned: *a blood-soaked cloth* ◇ *rain-soaked clothing*

**soak·ing** /ˈsəʊkɪŋ/ (*also* **soaking ˈwet**) *adj.* completely wet SYN **sopping**: *That coat is soaking—take it off.* ◇ *We arrived home soaking wet.*

**so-and-so** /ˈsəʊ ən səʊ/ *noun* (*pl.* **so-and-sos**) (*informal*) **1** [usually sing.] used to refer to a person, thing, etc. when you do not know their name or when you are talking in a general way: *What would you say to Mrs So-and-so who has called to complain about a noisy neighbour?* **2** an annoying or unpleasant person. People sometimes say **so-and-so** to avoid using an offensive word: *He's an ungrateful so-and-so.*

**soap** A2 /səʊp/ *noun, verb*

1481 **sobering**

■ **noun 1** A2 [U, C] a substance that you use with water for washing your body: *Wash the affected area with soap and water.* ◇ *a bar/cake of soap* ◇ *soap bubbles* **2** [C] (*informal*) = SOAP OPERA: *soaps on TV* ◇ *She's a US soap star.*
■ **verb ~ yourself/sb/sth** to rub yourself/sb/sth with soap

**soap-box** /ˈsəʊpbɒks; *NAmE* -bɑːks/ *noun* a small temporary platform that sb stands on to make a speech in a public place, usually outdoors
IDM **get/be on your ˈsoapbox** (*informal*) to express the strong opinions that you have about a particular subject

**soapie** /ˈsəʊpi/ *noun* (*AustralE*, *SAfrE*, *informal*) a SOAP OPERA

**soap ˈopera** (*also informal* **soap**) *noun* [C, U] a story about the lives and problems of a group of people that is broadcast every day or several times a week on television or radio

**ˈsoap powder** *noun* [U, C] (*BrE*) a powder made from soap and other substances that you use for washing your clothes, especially in a machine

**soap·stone** /ˈsəʊpstəʊn/ *noun* [U] a type of soft stone that feels like soap, used for making attractive objects

**soap-suds** /ˈsəʊpsʌdz/ *noun* [pl.] = SUDS (1)

**soapy** /ˈsəʊpi/ *adj.* [usually before noun] **1** full of soap; covered with soap **2** tasting or feeling like soap

**soar** B2+ C1 /sɔː(r)/ *verb* **1** B2+ C1 [I] if the value, amount or level of sth **soars**, it rises very quickly SYN **rocket**: *soaring costs/prices/temperatures* ◇ *Unemployment has soared to 18 per cent.* **2** B2+ C1 [I] **~ (up) (into sth)** to rise quickly and smoothly up into the air: *The rocket soared (up) into the air.* ◇ (*figurative*) *Her spirits soared* (= she became very happy and excited). **3** B2+ C1 [I] to fly very high in the air or remain high in the air: *an eagle soaring high above the cliffs* **4** [I] to be very high or tall: *soaring mountains* ◇ *The building soared above us.* **5** [I] when music **soars**, it becomes higher or louder: *soaring strings*

▼ **HOMOPHONES**

**soar · sore** /sɔː(r)/

● **soar** *verb*: *Fuel prices are set to soar.*
● **sore** *adj.*: *My eyes are sore from staring at a screen for too long.*

**soar·away** /ˈsɔːrəweɪ/ *adj.* [only before noun] (*BrE*) (especially of success) very great; growing very quickly

**SOB** /ˌes əʊ ˈbiː/ *noun* (*slang*, *especially NAmE*) = SON OF A BITCH

**sob** /sɒb; *NAmE* sɑːb/ *verb, noun*
■ **verb** (**-bb-**) **1** [I] to cry noisily, taking sudden, sharp breaths: *I heard a child sobbing loudly.* ◇ *He started to sob uncontrollably.* **2** [T] to say sth while you are crying: **+ speech** *'I hate him,'* she sobbed. ◇ **~ sth (out)** *He sobbed out his troubles.*
IDM **sob your ˈheart out** to cry noisily for a long time because you are very sad
■ **noun** an act or the sound of sobbing: *He gave a deep sob.* ◇ *Her body was racked* (= shaken) *with sobs.*

**sober** /ˈsəʊbə(r)/ *adj., verb*
■ **adj. 1** [not usually before noun] not drunk (= not affected by alcohol): *I promised him that I'd stay sober tonight.* ◇ *He was as sober as a judge* (= completely sober). **2** (of people and their behaviour) serious and sensible: *a sober assessment of the situation* ◇ *He is honest, sober and hard-working.* ◇ *On sober reflection* (= after some serious thought), *I don't think I really need a car after all.* **3** (of colours or clothes) plain and not bright: *a sober grey suit* ▸ **sober·ly** *adv.* IDM see STONE COLD
■ **verb** [T, I] **~ (sb)** to make sb behave or think in a more serious and sensible way; to become more serious and sensible: *The bad news sobered us for a while.* ◇ *He suddenly sobered.*
PHRV **ˌsober ˈup**/**ˌsober sb ˈup** to become or to make sb no longer drunk: *Stay here with us until you've sobered up.*

**sober·ing** /ˈsəʊbərɪŋ/ *adj.* making you feel serious and think carefully: *a sobering effect/experience/thought* ◇ **it is ~ to do sth** *It is sobering to realize that this is not a new problem.*

---

O Oxford Phrasal Academic Lexicon (OPAL) written and spoken word lists | W OPAL written word list | S OPAL spoken word list

# sobriety

**so·bri·ety** /səˈbraɪəti/ *noun* [U] (*formal*) **1** the state of being sober (= not being drunk) **OPP** **insobriety** **2** the fact of being sensible and serious

**so·bri·quet** /ˈsəʊbrɪkeɪ/ (*also* **sou·bri·quet**) *noun* (*formal*) an informal name or title that you give sb/sth **SYN** **nickname**

**ˈsob story** *noun* (*informal*, *disapproving*) a story that sb tells you just to make you feel sorry for them, especially one that does not have that effect or is not true

**Soc.** *abbr.* (in writing) SOCIETY: *Royal Geographical Soc.*

**soca** /ˈsəʊkə/ *noun* [U] a type of dance music, originally from the Caribbean, which mixes SOUL and CALYPSO

**so-ˈcalled** ?+ B2 O *adj.* **1** ?+ B2 [only before noun] used to show that you do not think that the word or phrase that is being used to describe sb/sth is appropriate: *the opinion of a so-called 'expert'* ◊ *How have these so-called improvements helped the local community?* **2** [usually before noun] used to introduce the word that people usually use to describe sth: *artists from the so-called 'School of London'*

**soc·cer** O A2 /ˈsɒkə(r)/; NAmE ˈsɑːkər/ (*BrE also* **foot-ball**) *noun* [U] a game played by two teams of 11 players, using a round ball which players kick up and down the playing field. Teams try to kick the ball into the other team's goal. **HELP** Soccer is the usual word for this sport in NAmE; in BrE the usual word is **football**, although **soccer** is also used. **Soccer** is short for *Association football*, a formal term sometimes used in (*BrE*): *I played soccer when I was younger.* ◊ *a soccer team/club/player/fan*

**ˈsoccer mom** *noun* (*NAmE*, *informal*) a mother who spends a lot of time taking her children to activities such as sports and music lessons, used as a way of referring to a typical mother from the MIDDLE CLASSES: *a soccer mom with a minivan full of kids*

**so·ci·able** /ˈsəʊʃəbl/ (*also less frequent* **so·cial**) *adj.* (of people) enjoying spending time with other people **SYN** **gregarious**: *She's a sociable child who'll talk to anyone.* ◊ *I'm not feeling very sociable this evening.* ◊ *We had a very sociable weekend* (= we did a lot of things with other people). **OPP** **unsociable** ⊃ compare ANTISOCIAL ▶ **so·ci·abil·ity** /ˌsəʊʃəˈbɪləti/ *noun* [U] **so·ci·ably** /ˈsəʊʃəbli/ *adv.*

**so·cial** O A2 O /ˈsəʊʃl/ *adj.*, *noun*
- *adj.*
- ACTIVITIES WITH OTHERS **1** ?A2 [only before noun] connected with activities in which people meet each other for pleasure: *a busy social life* ◊ *Team sports help to develop a child's social skills* (= the ability to talk easily to other people and do things in a group). ◊ *Social events and training days are arranged for all the staff.* ◊ *Join a social club to make new friends.*
- CONNECTED WITH SOCIETY **2** ?B1 [only before noun] connected with society and the way it is organized: *social issues/problems/reforms* ◊ *a call for social and economic change* ◊ *He fought for social justice and civil rights.* ◊ *the social welfare system* **3** ?B1 [only before noun] connected with your position in society: *social class/status* ◊ *social mobility* (= the movement of people from one social class to another)
- ANIMALS **4** [only before noun] (*specialist*) living naturally in groups, rather than alone
- FRIENDLY **5** = SOCIABLE ▶ **so·cial·ly** /-ʃəli/ *adv.*: *The reforms will bring benefits, socially and politically.* ◊ *This type of behaviour is no longer socially acceptable.* ◊ *a socially disadvantaged family* (= one that is poor and from a low social class) ◊ *We meet at work, but never socially.* ◊ *Carnivores are usually socially complex mammals.*
- *noun* **1 socials** [pl.] a way of referring to all sb's SOCIAL MEDIA websites and software programs: *Don't forget to check the band's socials to hear about future tour dates.* **2** [C] (*old-fashioned*) a party that is organized by a group or club: *a church social*

**ˌsocial ˈbookmarking** *noun* [U] (*computing*) a way of BOOKMARKING (= storing and labelling) the addresses of pages on the internet, using a special service that enables you to make them available to other internet users

**ˌsocial ˈcapital** *noun* [U] the networks of relationships among people who live and work in a particular society that enable the society to exist and be successful: *The middle-class kid, whose dad knows the company director, is said to have more social capital.*

**ˌsocial ˈclimber** *noun* (*disapproving*) a person who tries to improve their position in society by becoming friendly with people who belong to a higher social class

**ˌsocial ˈconscience** *noun* [sing., U] the state of being aware of the problems that affect a lot of people in society, such as being poor or having no home, and wanting to do sth to help these people

**ˌsocial ˈcontract** (*also* **ˌsocial ˈcompact**) *noun* [sing.] the agreement among citizens to behave in a way that benefits everybody that forms the basis of society

**ˌsocial deˈmocracy** *noun* [U, C] a political system that combines the principles of SOCIALISM with the greater personal freedom of DEMOCRACY; a country that has this political system of government ▶ **ˌsocial ˈdemocrat** *noun* **ˌsocial demoˈcratic** *adj.* [only before noun]

**ˌsocial engiˈneering** *noun* [U] the attempt to change society and to deal with social problems according to particular political beliefs, for example by changing the law

**ˈsocial fund** *noun* [usually sing.] a sum of money that can be used to help people who have financial, family or other social problems

**ˌsocial ˈgaming** *noun* [U] the activity of playing computer games that are run through SOCIAL MEDIA ▶ **ˌsocial ˈgamer** *noun*

**ˌsocial ˈhousing** *noun* [U] (in the UK) houses or flats that are provided by a local council or another organization for people on low incomes to buy or rent at a low price ⊃ compare AFFORDABLE HOUSING, PUBLIC HOUSING

**so·cial·ism** /ˈsəʊʃəlɪzəm/ *noun* [U] a set of political and economic theories based on the belief that everyone has an equal right to a share of a country's wealth and that the government should own and control the main industries ⊃ compare CAPITALISM, COMMUNISM, SOCIAL DEMOCRACY ⊃ WORDFINDER NOTE at CAPITALISM

**so·cial·ist** ?+ C1 /ˈsəʊʃəlɪst/ *adj.*, *noun*
- *adj.* [usually before noun] **1** ?+ C1 connected with socialism: *socialist beliefs* **2** ?+ C1 governed by or belonging to a party that believes in socialism: *a socialist country* ◊ *the ruling Socialist Party*
- *noun* a person who believes in or supports socialism; a member of a political party that believes in socialism

**so·cial·is·tic** /ˌsəʊʃəˈlɪstɪk/ *adj.* [usually before noun] (*often disapproving*) having some of the features of socialism

**ˌsocialist ˈrealism** *noun* [U] a theory that was put into practice in some COMMUNIST countries, especially in the Soviet Union under Stalin, that art, music and literature should be used to show people the principles of a SOCIALIST society and encourage them to support it

**so·cial·ite** /ˈsəʊʃəlaɪt/ *noun* (*sometimes disapproving*) a person who goes to a lot of fashionable parties and is often written about in the newspapers, etc.

**so·cial·iza·tion** (*BrE also* **-isa·tion**) /ˌsəʊʃəlaɪˈzeɪʃn; NAmE -ləˈz-/ *noun* [U] (*formal*) the process by which sb, especially a child, learns to behave in a way that is acceptable in their society

**so·cial·ize** (*BrE also* **-ise**) /ˈsəʊʃəlaɪz/ *verb* **1** [I] ~ (**with sb**) to meet and spend time with people in a friendly way, in order to enjoy yourself **SYN** **mix**: *I enjoy socializing with the other students.* ◊ *Maybe you should socialize more.* **2** [T, often passive] ~ **sb (to do sth)** (*formal*) to teach people to behave in ways that are acceptable to their society: *The family has the important function of socializing children.* **3** [T, usually passive] ~ **sth** to organize sth according to the principles of SOCIALISM

**ˌsocialized ˈmedicine** *noun* [U] (*US*) medical and hospital care provided by the government for everyone by paying for it with public taxes

**ˌsocial ˈmedia** *noun* [U, pl.] websites and software programs used for SOCIAL NETWORKING: *social media sites*

such as Facebook and Twitter ⇒ **WORDFINDER NOTE** at **WEBSITE**

**social 'network** noun **1** a social media site or application through which users can communicate with each other by adding information, messages, images, etc. **2** a network of social connections and personal relationships between people: *People in the region usually have a broad social network.*

**social 'networking** noun [U] communication with people who share your interests using a website or other service on the internet: *a social networking site*

**social psy'chology** noun [U] the study of people's behaviour, attitudes, etc. in society ▶ **social psy'chologist** noun

**social 'science** noun **1** [U] (*also* **social 'studies** [pl.]) the study of people in society **2** [C] a particular subject connected with the study of people in society, for example geography, ECONOMICS or SOCIOLOGY

**social 'scientist** noun a person who studies social science

**social 'secretary** noun the person who organizes social activities for an organization or for another person

**social se'curity** noun [U] **1** (*also* **bene·fits** [C, usually pl., U]) (*both BrE*) (*also* **wel·fare** *especially in NAmE*) money that the government pays regularly to people who are poor, unemployed, sick, etc: *to live on social security* ⋄ *social security payments* **2 Social Security** (in the US) a system in which people pay money regularly to the government when they are working and receive payments from the government when they are unable to work, especially when they are sick or too old to work ⇒ compare NATIONAL INSURANCE

**Social Se'curity number** noun (*abbr.* **SSN**) (in the US) an official identity number that everyone is given when they are born

**social 'services** noun [pl.] a system that is organized by the local government to help people who have financial or family problems; the department or the people who provide this help: *a leaflet on the range of social services available* ⋄ *the local social services department*

**social 'software** noun [U] computer software that enables users to communicate and share data

**social 'studies** noun [pl.] = SOCIAL SCIENCE (1)

**social 'work** noun [U] paid work that involves giving help and advice to people living in the community who have financial or family problems

**social worker** noun a person whose job is social work

**so·ci·etal** W /səˈsaɪətl/ adj. [only before noun] (*specialist*) connected with society and the way it is organized

**so·ci·ety** 🔑 A2 /səˈsaɪəti/ noun (pl. -ies) **1** A2 [U] people in general, living together in communities: *She believes that the arts benefit society as a whole.* ⋄ *Racism exists at all levels of society.* ⋄ **in ~** *They carried out research into the roles of men and women in today's society.* ⇒ **WORDFINDER NOTE** at EQUAL

**WORDFINDER** civil rights, class, conform, convention, culture, custom, elite, equality, outsider

**2** A2 [C, U] a particular community of people who share the same customs, laws, etc: *modern industrial societies* ⋄ *demand created by a consumer society* ⋄ *They were discussing the problems of Western society.* ⋄ **in a ~** *We live in a society that is obsessed with how people look.* **3** B1 [C] (*abbr.* **Soc.**) (especially in names) a group of people who join together for a particular purpose: *a member of the drama society* ⋄ *the American Society of Newspaper Editors* ⇒ **WORDFINDER NOTE** at CLUB ⇒ see also BUILDING SOCIETY, FRIENDLY SOCIETY **4** [U] the group of people in a country who are fashionable, rich and powerful: *Their daughter married into high society.* ⋄ *a society wedding* **5** [U] (*formal*) the state of being with other people **SYN company**: *He was a solitary man who avoided the society of others.*

**socio-** /ˈsəʊsiəʊ; *BrE also* ˈsəʊsiˌə; *NAmE also* -ˈɑː/ combining form (in nouns, adjectives and adverbs) connected with society or the study of society: *socio-economic* ⋄ *sociolinguistics*

**so·cio-cul·tural** /ˌsəʊsiəʊˈkʌltʃərəl/ adj. relating to society and culture

**socio-eco'nomic** adj. relating to society and economics: *people from different socio-economic backgrounds*

**socio·lin·guis·tics** /ˌsəʊsiəʊlɪŋˈɡwɪstɪks/ noun [U] the study of the way language is affected by differences in social class, region, sex, etc. ▶ **socio·lin·guis·tic** /-ˈɡwɪstɪk/ adj.

**soci·olo·gist** /ˌsəʊsiˈɒlədʒɪst; *NAmE* -ˈɑːl-/ noun a person who studies sociology

**soci·ology** /ˌsəʊsiˈɒlədʒi; *NAmE* -ˈɑːl-/ noun [U] the scientific study of the nature and development of society and social behaviour ▶ **socio·logic·al** /ˌsəʊsiəˈlɒdʒɪkl; *NAmE* -ˈlɑːdʒ-/ adj.: *sociological theories* **socio·logic·al·ly** /-kli/ adv.

**socio·path** /ˈsəʊsiəʊpæθ/ noun a person who has a mental illness and who behaves in an aggressive or dangerous way towards other people

**socio-pol·it·ic·al** /ˌsəʊsiəʊpəˈlɪtɪkl/ adj. relating to society and politics

**sock** 🔑 A2 /sɒk; *NAmE* sɑːk/ noun, verb
■ noun **1** A2 a piece of clothing that is worn over the foot, ankle and lower part of the leg, especially inside a shoe: *a pair of socks* ⇒ see also ANKLE SOCK **2** (*informal*) a hard hit, especially with the FIST: *He gave him a sock on the jaw.*
IDM **blow/knock sb's 'socks off** (*informal*) to surprise or impress sb very much | **put a sock in it** (*old-fashioned, BrE, informal*) used to tell sb to stop talking or making a noise ⇒ more at PULL v.
■ verb ~ **sb** (*informal*) to hit sb hard: *She got angry and socked him in the mouth.* ⋄ (*figurative*) *The banks are socking customers with higher charges.*
IDM **'sock it to sb** (*informal or humorous*) to do sth or tell sb sth in a strong and effective way: *Go in there and sock it to 'em!*
PHRV **sock sth↔a'way** (*NAmE*) to save money

**socket** /ˈsɒkɪt; *NAmE* ˈsɑːk-/ noun **1** (*BrE also* **power point**) (*NAmE also* **out·let, re·cep·tacle**) a device in a wall that you put a PLUG into in order to connect electrical equipment to the power supply of a building: *a wall socket* ⇒ picture at PLUG **2** a device on a piece of electrical equipment that you can fix a PLUG, a light BULB, etc. into: *an aerial socket on the television* **3** a curved hollow space in the surface of sth that another part fits into or moves around in: *His eyes bulged in their sockets.*

**sock puppet** noun **1** a type of PUPPET, made from a sock, that you put over your hand **2** a person whose actions are controlled by another: *He accused the politician of being a capitalist sock puppet.* **3** a false online identity, usually created by a person or group in order to promote their own opinions: *He created sock puppets to write positive comments about his blog posts.* ▶ **sock puppetry** noun [U]

**sod** /sɒd; *NAmE* sɑːd/ noun, verb
■ noun **1** (*BrE, taboo, slang*) used to refer to a person, especially a man, that you are annoyed with or think is unpleasant: *You stupid sod!* **2** (*BrE, taboo, slang*) used with an adjective to refer to a person, especially a man: *The poor old sod got the sack yesterday.* ⋄ *You lucky sod!* HELP You can use words like **man**, **boy**, **devil** or **thing** instead. **3** (*BrE, taboo, slang*) a thing that is difficult or causes problems: *It was a real sod of a job.* **4** [usually sing.] (*formal or literary*) a layer of earth with grass growing on it; a piece of this that has been removed: *under the sod* (= in your grave)
■ verb (only used in orders) (**-dd-**) ~ **sth** (*BrE, taboo, slang*) a swear word that many people find offensive, used when sb is annoyed about sth or to show that they do not care about sth: *Sod this car! It's always breaking down.* ⋄ *Oh, sod it! I'm not doing any more.* IDM see LARK n.

# soda

**PHRV**  **,sod 'off** (*BrE*, *taboo*, *slang*) (usually used in orders) to go away: *Sod off, the pair of you!*

**soda** /ˈsəʊdə/ *noun* **1** [U, C] = SODA WATER: *a Scotch and soda* **2** (*also old-fashioned* **'soda pop**) (*both NAmE*) [U, C] a sweet FIZZY drink (= a drink with bubbles) made with SODA WATER, a fruit taste and sometimes ice cream: *He had an ice cream soda.* ⇨ see also CREAM SODA **3** [U] a chemical substance in common use that is a COMPOUND of SODIUM ⇨ see also BAKING SODA, BICARBONATE OF SODA, CAUSTIC SODA, SODIUM BICARBONATE, SODIUM CARBONATE, WASHING SODA

**'soda bread** *noun* [U] bread that rises because of SODIUM BICARBONATE that is added instead of YEAST (popular in Ireland)

**'soda fountain** *noun* (*NAmE*) **1** (*BrE* **'soda siphon**) a bottle containing SODA WATER or another drink, with a device that you press to pour the drink and put bubbles into it **2** (*old-fashioned*) a type of bar where you can buy sodas to drink, ICE CREAMS, etc.

**,sod 'all** *noun* [U] (*BrE*, *taboo*, *slang*) a phrase that some people find offensive, used to mean 'none at all' or 'nothing at all'

**'soda pop** *noun* [U, C] (*NAmE*, *old-fashioned*) = SODA (3)

**'soda siphon** (*BrE*) (*NAmE* **'soda fountain**) *noun* a bottle containing soda water or another drink, with a device that you press to pour the drink and put bubbles into it

**'soda water** (*also* **soda**) *noun* **1** [U] FIZZY water (= water with bubbles) used as a drink on its own or to mix with alcoholic drinks or fruit juice (originally made with SODIUM BICARBONATE) **2** [C] a glass of soda water

**sod·den** /ˈsɒdn; *NAmE* ˈsɑːdn/ *adj.* **1** extremely wet **SYN** soaked: *sodden grass* **2** **-sodden** extremely wet with the thing mentioned: *a rain-sodden jacket*

**sod·ding** /ˈsɒdɪŋ; *NAmE* ˈsɑːd-/ *adj.* [only before noun] (*BrE*, *taboo*, *slang*) a swear word that many people find offensive, used to emphasize a comment or an angry statement: *I couldn't understand a sodding thing!*

**so·dium** /ˈsəʊdiəm/ *noun* [U] (*symb.* **Na**) a chemical element. Sodium is a soft silver-white metal that is found naturally only in COMPOUNDS, such as salt.

**,sodium bi'carbonate** (*also* **bi,carbonate of 'soda**, **'baking soda**) (*also informal* **bi·carb**) *noun* [U] (*symb.* **NaHCO₃**) a chemical in the form of a white powder that DISSOLVES in water and is used in baking to make cakes, etc. rise and become light, and in making FIZZY drinks and some medicines

**,sodium 'carbonate** (*also* **'washing soda**) *noun* [U] (*symb.* **Na₂CO₃**) a chemical in the form of white CRYSTALS or powder that DISSOLVES in water and is used in making glass, soap and paper, and for making water soft

**,sodium 'chloride** *noun* [U] (*symb.* **NaCl**) common salt (a chemical made up of SODIUM and CHLORINE)

**Sodom and Gom·or·rah** /ˌsɒdəm ən gəˈmɒrə; *NAmE* ˌsɑːdəm ən gəˈmɔːrə/ *noun* [sing.] a place that is full of people behaving in a sexually IMMORAL way: *The village had a reputation as a latter-day Sodom and Gomorrah.* **ORIGIN** From the names of two cities in the Bible which were destroyed by God to punish the people for their sexually immoral behaviour.

**sod·om·ite** /ˈsɒdəmaɪt; *NAmE* ˈsɑːd-/ *noun* (*old-fashioned*, *formal*) a person who practises sodomy

**sod·om·ize** (*BrE also* **-ise**) /ˈsɒdəmaɪz; *NAmE* ˈsɑːd-/ *verb* ~ **sb** (*disapproving*) to have ANAL sex with sb

**sod·omy** /ˈsɒdəmi; *NAmE* ˈsɑːd-/ *noun* [U] a sexual act in which a man puts his PENIS in sb's, especially another man's, ANUS

**Sod's 'Law** *noun* [U] (*BrE*, *humorous*) the fact that things tend to happen in just the way that you do not want, and in a way that is not useful: *We always play better when we are not being recorded—but that's Sod's Law, isn't it?* ◊ *It was Sod's Law—the only day he could manage was the day I couldn't miss work.*

**sofa** /ˈsəʊfə/ *noun* a long comfortable seat with a back and arms, for two or more people to sit on **SYN** settee, couch

**'sofa bed** *noun* a sofa that can be folded out to form a bed

**soft** ❶ **A2** /sɒft; *NAmE* sɔːft/ *adj.* (**soft·er**, **soft·est**)
- **NOT HARD 1** ❶ **A2** changing shape easily when pressed; not stiff or hard: *soft margarine* ◊ *soft feather pillows* ◊ *The grass was soft and springy.* **2** ❶ **B1** less hard than average: *soft rocks such as limestone* ◊ *soft cheeses* **OPP** hard
- **NOT ROUGH 3** ❶ **B1** smooth and pleasant to touch: *soft skin* **OPP** rough
- **WITHOUT ANGLES/EDGES 4** not having sharp angles or hard edges: *This season's fashions focus on warm tones and soft lines.* ◊ *The moon's pale light cast soft shadows.*
- **LIGHT/COLOURS 5** [usually before noun] not too bright, in a way that is pleasant and relaxing to the eyes: *a soft pink* ◊ *the soft glow of candlelight* **OPP** harsh
- **RAIN/WIND 6** not strong or violent **SYN** light: *A soft breeze rustled the trees.*
- **SOUNDS 7** not loud, and usually pleasant and gentle **SYN** quiet: *soft background music* ◊ *a soft voice*
- **KIND 8** kind and showing sympathy; easily affected by other people's pain and problems: *Julia's soft heart was touched by his grief.* **OPP** hard
- **NOT STRICT 9** (*usually disapproving*) not strict or severe; not strict or severe enough **SYN** lenient: ~ (**on sb**/**sth**) *The government is not becoming soft on crime.* ◊ ~ (**with sb**) *If you're too soft with these kids they'll never respect you.* **OPP** tough
- **CRAZY 10** (*informal*, *disapproving*) stupid or crazy: *He must be going soft in the head.*
- **NOT BRAVE/TOUGH ENOUGH 11** (*informal*, *disapproving*) not brave enough; wanting to be safe and comfortable: *Stay in a hotel? Don't be so soft. I want to camp out under the stars.*
- **TOO EASY 12** (*disapproving*) not involving much work; too easy and comfortable: *They had got too used to the soft life at home.* **OPP** hard
- **WATER 13** not containing mineral salts and therefore good for washing: *You won't need much soap—the water here is very soft.* **OPP** hard
- **DRINK 14** not alcoholic: *soft beverages* ◊ *'What would you like to drink?' 'Oh, something soft—I'm driving.'*
- **CONSONANTS 15** (*phonetics*) not sounding hard, for example 'c' in *city* and 'g' in *general* **OPP** hard ▶ **soft·ness** *noun* [U, sing.]: *the softness of her skin* ◊ *the softness of the water* ⇨ see also SOFTLY

**IDM** **have a soft 'spot for sb/sth** (*also IndE* **have a soft 'corner for sb/sth**) (*informal*) to like sb/sth: *She's always had a soft spot for you.* ⇨ more at OPTION *n.*, TOUCH *n.*

**soft·ball** /ˈsɒftbɔːl; *NAmE* ˈsɔːft-/ *noun* **1** [U] a game similar to baseball but played on a smaller field with a larger, softer ball **2** [C] the ball used in softball

**,soft-'boiled** *adj.* (of eggs) boiled for a short time so that the YOLK is still soft or liquid ⇨ compare HARD-BOILED

**'soft-core** *adj.* [usually before noun] showing or describing sexual activity without being too detailed or shocking people ⇨ compare HARD-CORE

**,soft 'drink** *noun* a cold drink that does not contain alcohol ⇨ compare HARD (11)

**,soft 'drug** *noun* an illegal drug, such as CANNABIS, that some people take for pleasure, that is not considered very harmful or likely to cause ADDICTION ⇨ compare HARD DRUG

**soft·en** /ˈsɒfn; *NAmE* ˈsɔːfn/ *verb* **1** [I, T] to become, or to make sth softer: *Fry the onions until they soften.* ◊ ~ **sth** *a lotion to soften the skin* ◊ *Linseed oil will soften stiff leather.* **2** [I, T] ~ (**sth**) to become or to make sth less bright, rough or strong: *Trees soften the outline of the house.* **3** [I, T] to become or to make sb/sth more kind or friendly and less severe or critical: *She felt herself softening towards him.* ◊ *His face softened as he looked at his son.* ◊ ~ **sb**/**sth** *She softened her tone a little.* **4** [T] ~ **sth** to reduce the force or the unpleasant effects of sth **SYN** cushion: *Airbags are designed to soften the impact of a car crash.* **IDM** see BLOW *n.*

---

æ cat | ɑː father | e bed | ɜː fur | ə about | ɪ sit | iː see | i happy | ɒ got (*BrE*) | ɔː saw | ʌ cup | ʊ put | uː too

**PHR V** **soften sb↔up** (*informal*) **1** to try to persuade sb to do sth for you by being very nice to them before you ask them: *Potential customers are softened up with free gifts before the sales talk.* **2** to make an enemy weaker and easier to attack

**soft·en·er** /ˈsɒfnə(r); NAmE ˈsɔːf-/ noun **1** [C] a device that is used with chemicals to make hard water soft: *a water softener* **2** [U, C] a substance that you add when washing clothes to make them feel soft

**ˌsoft ˈfocus** noun [U] a method of producing a photograph so that the edges of the image are not clear, in order to make it look more romantic and attractive

**ˌsoft ˈfruit** noun [C, U] small fruits without large seeds or hard skin, such as STRAWBERRIES or CURRANTS

**ˌsoft ˈfurnishings** noun [pl.] (*BrE*) CUSHIONS, curtains and other things made from cloth that are found in a house

**ˌsoft-ˈhearted** adj. kind and emotional **SYN** **kind-hearted** **OPP** **hard-hearted**

**soft·ie** (*also* **softy**) /ˈsɒfti; NAmE ˈsɔːf-/ noun (pl. **-ies**) (*informal*) a kind or emotional person: *There's no need to be afraid of him—he's a big softie.*

**ˈsoft launch** noun (*business*) the activity or occasion of making a product or service available in a limited way, in advance of a full LAUNCH: *A soft launch in selected markets showed us what was working well.* ▶ **ˈsoft-launch** verb ~ sth

**soft·ly** /ˈsɒftli; NAmE ˈsɔːft-/ adv. **1** in a pleasant and gentle way; in a way that is not loud or violent: *'I missed you,' he said softly.* ◊ *She closed the door softly behind her.* **2** in a way that is not too bright but is pleasant and relaxing to the eyes: *The room was softly lit by a lamp.* **3** without sharp angles or hard edges: *a softly tailored suit*

**ˌsoftly-ˈsoftly** adj. (*BrE, informal*) (of a way of doing sth) careful and patient, with no sudden actions: *The police used a softly-softly approach with him.*

**ˌsoftly-ˈspoken** adj. = SOFT-SPOKEN

**ˌsoft ˈporn** noun [U] films, books, pictures, etc. that show or describe sexual activity in a way that is sexually exciting but not in a very detailed or violent way ⊃ compare HARD PORN

**ˌsoft ˈpower** noun [U] a way of dealing with other countries that involves using economic and cultural influence to persuade them to do things, rather than military power: *The country's soft power and growing economy allow it to dominate the region.*

**ˌsoft ˈsell** noun [sing.] a method of selling that involves persuading sb to buy sth rather than using pressure or aggressive methods ⊃ compare HARD SELL

**ˌsoft ˈskills** noun [pl.] personal qualities that enable you to communicate well with other people: *Candidates should demonstrate soft skills, such as team work, enthusiasm and emotional intelligence.*

**ˌsoft-ˈspoken** (*also less frequent* **ˌsoftly-ˈspoken**) adj. having a gentle and quiet voice

**ˌsoft ˈtarget** noun a person or thing that it is very easy to attack

**ˌsoft ˈtissue** noun [U, C] (*anatomy*) the parts of the body that are not bone, for example the skin and muscles

**ˈsoft-top** noun a type of car that has a soft roof that can be folded down or removed; the roof of such a car ⊃ see also CONVERTIBLE noun

**ˌsoft ˈtoy** (*BrE*) (*NAmE usually* **ˌstuffed ˈanimal**) (*also* **ˌstuffed ˈtoy** *BrE and NAmE*) noun a toy in the shape of an animal, made of cloth and filled with a soft substance

**soft·ware** 🔑 **B1** 🅦 /ˈsɒftweə(r); NAmE ˈsɔːftwer/ noun [U] the programs used by a computer for doing particular jobs: *This is a very clever piece of software.* ◊ *download/install/run software* ◊ *You will need to be able to use basic office software.* ◊ *The company has developed its own voice-recognition software.* ◊ *a software developer/company/engineer* ⊃ compare HARDWARE ⊃ see also SOCIAL SOFTWARE ⊃ WORDFINDER NOTE at PROGRAM

**WORDFINDER** animation, application, authoring, beta version, configure, demo, install, interactive, spreadsheet

1485 **solace**

**ˌsoftware enˈgineer** noun a person who designs, develops and maintains computer software

**ˈsoftware package** noun (*computing*) = PACKAGE (5)

**soft·wood** /ˈsɒftwʊd; NAmE ˈsɔːft-/ noun [U, C] wood from trees such as PINE, that is cheap to produce and can be cut easily ⊃ compare HARDWOOD

**softy** = SOFTIE

**soggy** /ˈsɒgi; NAmE ˈsɑːgi/ adj. (**sog·gier**, **sog·gi·est**) wet and soft, usually in a way that is unpleasant: *We squelched over the soggy ground.* ◊ *soggy bread*

**soh** (*also* **so**) /səʊ/ (*also* **sol**) noun (*music*) the fifth note of a MAJOR SCALE

**soil** 🔑 **B1** /sɔɪl/ noun, verb
■ noun [U, C] **1** 🅑 **B1** the top layer of the earth in which plants, trees, etc. grow: *instruments for measuring soil moisture* ◊ *soil erosion* ◊ *the study of rocks and soils* **2** (*literary*) a country; an area of land: *It was the first time I had set foot on African soil.* ◊ *He was the first Canadian to win on home/native soil* (= in Canada).
■ verb [often passive] ~ sth (*formal*) to make sth dirty: *soiled linen* ◊ (*figurative*) *I don't want you soiling your hands with this sort of work* (= doing sth unpleasant or wrong). ⊃ see also SHOP-SOILED

▼ **SYNONYMS**

**soil**
mud • dust • clay • land • earth • dirt • ground

These are all words for the top layer of the earth in which plants grow.

**soil** the top layer of the earth in which plants grow: *Plant the seedlings in damp soil.*

**mud** wet soil that is soft and sticky: *The car wheels got stuck in the mud.*

**dust** a fine powder that consists of very small pieces of rock, earth, etc: *A cloud of dust rose as the truck set off.*

**clay** a type of heavy sticky soil that becomes hard when it is baked and is used to make things such as pots and bricks: *The tiles are made of clay.*

**land** an area of ground, especially of a particular type: *an area of rich, fertile land*

**earth** the substance that plants grow in **NOTE** Earth is often used about the soil found in gardens or used for gardening: *She put some earth into the pot.*

**dirt** (*especially NAmE*) soil, especially loose soil: *Pack the dirt firmly around the plants.*

**ground** an area of soil: *The car got stuck in the muddy ground.* ◊ *They drove across miles of rough, stony ground.* **NOTE** Ground is not used for loose soil: *a handful of dry ground*

PATTERNS
- good/rich soil/land/earth
- fertile/infertile soil/land/ground
- to **dig** the soil/mud/clay/land/earth/ground
- to **cultivate** the soil/land/ground

**ˈsoil science** noun [U] the study of soil, for example the study of its structure or characteristics

**soirée** /ˈswɑːreɪ; NAmE swɑːˈreɪ/ noun (*from French, formal*) a formal party in the evening, especially at sb's home

**so·journ** /ˈsɒdʒən; NAmE ˈsoʊdʒɜːrn/ noun (*literary*) a temporary stay in a place away from your home ▶ **so·journ** verb [I] + adv./prep.

**sol** /sɒl; NAmE soʊl/ noun = SOH

**sol·ace** /ˈsɒləs; NAmE ˈsɑːl-/ noun [U, sing.] (*formal*) a feeling of emotional comfort when you are sad or disappointed; a person or thing that makes you feel better or happier when you are sad or disappointed **SYN** **comfort**: *He sought solace in the whisky bottle.* ◊ *She turned to Rob for solace.* ◊ *His grandchildren were a solace in his old age.* ▶ **soˈlace**

# solar

*verb* ~ sb (*literary*): *She smiled, as though solaced by the memory.*

**solar** 🔑 B2 /ˈsəʊlə(r)/ *adj.* [only before noun] **1** 🔑 B2 of or connected with the sun: *solar radiation* ◇ *a solar eclipse* ⊃ WORDFINDER NOTE at SUN **2** 🔑 B2 using the sun's energy: *solar heating* ◇ *a satellite telephone with solar-powered batteries* ⊃ WORDFINDER NOTE at ENERGY

ˌsolar ˈcell *noun* a device that receives light and heat energy from the sun and changes it into electricity

ˈsolar cooker *noun* (*IndE*) a container for cooking food that uses heat from the sun

ˌsolar ˈenergy *noun* [U] **1** energy given out by the sun in the form of heat and light **2** = SOLAR POWER

ˌsolar ˈfarm *noun* an area of land on which there are a lot of solar panels for producing electricity

**sol·ar·ium** /səˈleəriəm; *NAmE* -ˈler-/ *noun* a room whose walls are mainly made of glass, or which has special lamps, where people go to get a SUNTAN (= make their skin go brown) using light from the sun or artificial light

ˌsolar ˈpanel *noun* a piece of equipment, often on the roof of a building, that uses light and heat energy from the sun to produce hot water and electricity

ˌsolar ˈplexus /ˌsəʊlə ˈpleksəs; *NAmE* -lər/ *noun* [sing.] **1** (*anatomy*) a system of nerves at the base of the stomach **2** (*informal*) the part of the body at the front of the body, below the RIBS: *a painful punch in the solar plexus*

ˌsolar ˈpower (*also* ˌsolar ˈenergy) *noun* [U] energy obtained from the light and heat from the sun, used to produce electricity

ˈsolar system *noun* **1 the solar system** [sing.] the sun and all the planets that move around it **2** [C] any group of planets that all move around the same star

ˌsolar ˈyear *noun* the time it takes the earth to go around the sun once, approximately 365¼ days

**sold** /səʊld/ *past tense, past part.* of SELL

**sol·der** /ˈsəʊldə(r), ˈsɒl-; *NAmE* ˈsɑːd-/ *noun, verb*
- *noun* [U] a mixture of metals that is heated and melted and then used to join metals, wires, etc. together
- *verb* ~ sth (to/onto sth) | ~ (A and B together) to join pieces of metal or wire with solder

ˈsoldering iron *noun* a tool that is heated and used for joining metals and wires by soldering them

**sol·dier** 🔑 A2 /ˈsəʊldʒə(r)/ *noun, verb*
- *noun* 🔑 A2 a member of an army, especially one who is not an officer: *They visited the graves of US soldiers killed in the First World War.* ◇ *soldiers in uniform* ◇ *soldiers on duty* ⊃ see also FOOT SOLDIER, PRIVATE SOLDIER
- *verb*
  PHRV ˌsoldier ˈon to continue with what you are doing or trying to achieve, especially when this is difficult or unpleasant

**sol·dier·ing** /ˈsəʊldʒərɪŋ/ *noun* [U] the life or activity of being a soldier

**sol·dier·ly** /ˈsəʊldʒəli; *NAmE* -dʒərli/ *adj.* typical of a good soldier

ˌsoldier of ˈfortune *noun* a person who fights for any country or person who will pay them SYN mercenary

**sol·diery** /ˈsəʊldʒəri/ *noun* [U + sing./pl. v.] (*old-fashioned*) a group of soldiers, especially of a particular kind

ˌsold ˈout *adj.* **1** if a concert, match, etc. is **sold out**, there are no more tickets available for it **2** if a shop is **sold out** of a product, it has no more of it left to sell

**sole** 🔑 C1 /səʊl/ *adj., noun, verb*
- *adj.* [only before noun] **1** 🔑 C1 only; single: *the sole surviving member of the family* ◇ *My sole reason for coming here was to see you.* ◇ *This is the sole means of access to the building.* **2** 🔑 C1 belonging to one person or group; not shared: *She has sole responsibility for the project.* ◇ *the sole owner*
- *noun* **1** [C] the bottom surface of the foot: *The hot sand burned the soles of their feet.* ⊃ VISUAL VOCAB page V1 **2** [C] the bottom part of a shoe or sock, not including the heel: *leather soles* ⊃ compare HEEL **3 -soled** (in adjectives) having the type of soles mentioned: *rubber-soled shoes* **4** [U, C] (*pl.* **sole**) a flat sea fish that is used for food
- *verb* [usually passive] ~ sth to repair a shoe by replacing the sole

▼ HOMOPHONES

**sole • soul** /səʊl/
- **sole** *adj.*: *John Dashwood is the sole male heir, so inherits the entire estate.*
- **sole** *noun*: *Many jazz shoes come with a rubber sole.*
- **soul** *noun*: *Deep in her soul she knew she had to return to her country.*

**sol·ecism** /ˈsɒlɪsɪzəm; *NAmE* ˈsɑːl-/ *noun* (*formal*) **1** a mistake in the use of language in speech or writing **2** an example of bad manners or unacceptable behaviour

**sole·ly** 🔑 C1 /ˈsəʊlli/ *adv.* only; not involving sb/sth else: *She was motivated solely by self-interest.* ◇ *Selection is based solely on merit.* ◇ *He became solely responsible for the firm.*

**sol·emn** /ˈsɒləm; *NAmE* ˈsɑːl-/ *adj.* **1** (of a person) not happy or smiling SYN serious: *Her face grew solemn.* ◇ *a solemn expression* OPP cheerful **2** done, said, etc. in a very serious and sincere way: *a solemn oath/undertaking/vow*, etc. **3** (of a religious ceremony or formal occasion) performed in a serious way: *a solemn ritual* ▶ **sol·emn·ly** *adv.*: *He nodded solemnly.* ◇ *She solemnly promised not to say a word to anyone about it.* ◇ *The choir walked solemnly past.*

**sol·em·nity** /səˈlemnəti/ *noun* **1** [U] the quality of being solemn: *He was smiling, but his eyes retained a look of solemnity.* ◇ *He was buried with great pomp and solemnity.* **2 solemnities** [pl.] (*formal*) formal things that people do at a serious event or occasion: *to observe the solemnities of the occasion*

**sol·em·nize** (*BrE also* **-ise**) /ˈsɒləmnaɪz; *NAmE* ˈsɑːl-/ *verb* ~ sth (*formal*) to perform a religious ceremony, especially a marriage

**so·len·oid** /ˈsəʊlənɔɪd; *BrE also* ˈsɒl-; *NAmE also* ˈsɑːl-/ *noun* (*physics*) a piece of wire, wound into circles, which acts as a MAGNET when carrying an electric current

**sol-fa** /ˌsɒl ˈfɑː; *NAmE* ˌsəʊl/ (*also* ˌtonic ˈsol-fa) *noun* [U] (*music*) a system of naming the notes of the SCALE, used in teaching singing

**so·licit** /səˈlɪsɪt/ *verb* **1** [T, I] (*formal*) to ask sb for sth, such as support, money or information; to try to get sth or persuade sb to do sth: ~ sth (from sb) *They were planning to solicit funds from a number of organizations.* ◇ ~ sb (for sth) *Historians and critics are solicited for their opinions.* ◇ ~ (for sth) *to solicit for money* ◇ ~ sb to do sth *Volunteers are being solicited to assist with the project.* **2** [I, T] ~ (sb) (of a PROSTITUTE) to offer to have sex with people in return for money: *Prostitutes solicited openly in the streets.* ◇ *the crime of soliciting* ▶ **so·lici·ta·tion** /səˌlɪsɪˈteɪʃn/ *noun* [U, C] (*especially NAmE*): *the solicitation of money for election funds*

**so·licit·or** 🔑 C1 /səˈlɪsɪtə(r)/ *noun* **1** 🔑 C1 (*BrE*) a lawyer who prepares legal documents, for example for the sale of land or buildings, advises people on legal matters, and can speak for them in some courts of law ⊃ note at LAWYER **2** (*NAmE*) a person whose job is to visit or phone people and try to sell them sth **3** (*NAmE*) the most senior legal officer of a city, town or government department

**so·licitor ˈgeneral** *noun* (*pl.* **solicitors general**) a senior legal officer in England and Wales or the US, next in rank below the ATTORNEY GENERAL

**so·lici·tous** /səˈlɪsɪtəs/ *adj.* (*formal*) being very concerned for sb and wanting to make sure that they are comfortable, well or happy SYN attentive ▶ **so·lici·tous·ly** *adv.* (*formal*)

**so·lic·i·tude** /səˈlɪsɪtjuːd; NAmE -tuːd/ noun [U] ~ (for sb/ sth) (formal) anxious care for sb's comfort, health or happiness: *I was touched by his solicitude for the boy.*

**solids**

cylinder — vertex
cone — edge
cube — face
sphere
pyramid
prism
tetrahedron
octahedron

**solid** ⓘ B1 /ˈsɒlɪd; NAmE ˈsɑːl-/ adj., noun
■ adj.
• NOT LIQUID/GAS **1** B1 hard; not in the form of a liquid or gas: *The boat bumped against a solid object.* ◇ *She had refused all solid food.* ◇ *the collection and disposal of solid waste* ◇ *It was so cold that the stream had frozen solid.* ◇ *The boiler uses solid fuel* (= for example, coal).
• WITHOUT HOLES OR SPACES **2** B1 having no holes or spaces inside; not hollow: *They were drilling through solid rock.* ◇ *The stores are packed solid* (= very full and crowded) *at this time of year.* **3** (of a line) without spaces; continuous: *The national boundary is shown on the map as a solid line.* ⊃ compare BROKEN (4), DOTTED LINE
• MATERIAL **4** B1 [only before noun] made completely of the material mentioned (that is, the material is not only on the surface): *a solid gold bracelet*
• STRONG **5** strong and made well: *These chains seem fairly solid.*
• RELIABLE **6** that you can rely on; having a strong basis: *As yet, they have no solid evidence.* ◇ *This provided a solid foundation for their marriage.* ◇ *The Irish team were solid as a rock in defence.*
• GOOD BUT NOT SPECIAL **7** definitely good and steady but perhaps not excellent or special: *Both leading actors put in a solid performance.* ◇ *He's a good solid player.*
• PERIOD OF TIME **8** (informal) without a break; continuous: *The essay represents a solid week's work.* ◇ *It rained for two hours solid this afternoon.*
• COLOUR **9** of the colour mentioned and no other colour: *One cat is black and white, the other solid black.*
• SHAPE **10** (geometry) a shape that is **solid** has length, WIDTH and height and is not flat: *A cube is a solid figure.*
• IN AGREEMENT **11** in complete agreement; agreed on by everyone: *The strike was solid, supported by all the members.* ⊃ see also ROCK SOLID IDM see GROUND n.
■ noun
• NOT LIQUID/GAS **1** B1 a substance or an object that is solid, not a liquid or a gas: *liquids and solids* ◇ **on solids** *The baby is not yet on solids* (= eating solid food).
• SHAPE **2** (geometry) a shape that has length, WIDTH and height, such as a CUBE

**soli·dar·ity** /ˌsɒlɪˈdærəti; NAmE ˌsɑːl-/ noun [U] support by one person or group of people for another because they share feelings, opinions, aims, etc: *community solidarity* ◇ ~ **with sb** *to express/show solidarity with fellow students* ◇ *Demonstrations were held as a gesture of solidarity with the hunger strikers.*

**so·lid·ify** /səˈlɪdɪfaɪ/ verb (**so·lidi·fies**, **so·lidi·fy·ing**, **so·lidi·fied**, **so·lidi·fied**) **1** [I, T] ~ **(into sth)** | ~ **(sth)** to become solid; to make sb solid: *The mixture will solidify into toffee.* ◇ *solidified lava* **2** [I, T] (formal) (of ideas, etc.) to become or to make sth become more definite and less likely to change: ~ **(into sth)** *Vague objections to the system solidified into firm opposition.* ◇ ~ **sth** *They solidified their position as Britain's top band.* ▸ **so·lidi·fi·ca·tion** /səˌlɪdɪfɪˈkeɪʃn/ noun [U]

1487 **soluble**

**sol·id·ity** /səˈlɪdəti/ noun [U] the quality or state of being solid: *the strength and solidity of Romanesque architecture* ◇ *Her writings have extraordinary depth and solidity.* ◇ *the solidity of his support for his staff*

**sol·id·ly** /ˈsɒlɪdli; NAmE ˈsɑːl-/ adv. **1** in a strong way: *a large, solidly-built house* ◇ *He stood solidly in my path.* **2** continuously; without stopping: *It rained solidly for three hours.* **3** agreeing with or supporting sb/sth completely: *The state is solidly Republican.*

**ˌsolid-ˈstate** adj. (specialist) using or containing solid SEMICONDUCTORS: *a solid-state radio*

**so·lilo·quy** /səˈlɪləkwi/ noun [C, U] (pl. **-ies**) a speech in a play in which a character, who is alone on the stage, speaks his or her thoughts; the act of speaking thoughts in this way: *Hamlet's famous soliloquy, 'To be or not to be …'* ◇ *the playwright's use of soliloquy* ⊃ compare MONOLOGUE ⊃ WORDFINDER NOTE at DRAMA ▸ **so·lilo·quize** (BrE also **-ise**) /-kwaɪz/ verb [I]

**sol·ip·sism** /ˈsɒlɪpsɪzəm; NAmE ˈsɑːl-/ noun [U] (philosophy) the theory that only the SELF exists or can be known ▸ **sol·ip·sis·tic** /ˌsɒlɪpˈsɪstɪk; NAmE ˌsɑːl-/ adj.

**soli·taire** /ˌsɒlɪˈteə(r); NAmE ˈsɑːlətər/ noun **1** [U] (BrE) a game for one person in which you remove pieces from their places on a special board after moving other pieces over them. The aim is to finish with only one piece left on the board. **2** (NAmE) (BrE **pa·tience**) [U] a card game for only one player **3** [C] a single PRECIOUS STONE; a piece of jewellery with a single precious stone in it

**soli·tary** /ˈsɒlətri; NAmE ˈsɑːləteri/ adj., noun
■ adj. **1** [usually before noun] done alone; without other people: *She enjoys long solitary walks.* ◇ *He led a solitary life.* **2** (of a person or an animal) enjoying being alone; frequently spending time alone: *He was a solitary child.* ◇ *Tigers are solitary animals.* **3** (of a person, thing or place) alone, with no other people or things around SYN **single**: *a solitary farm* ◇ *A solitary light burned dimly in the hall.* **4** [usually before noun] (especially in negative sentences and questions) only one SYN **single**: *There was not a solitary shred of evidence* (= none at all). ▸ **soli·tari·ness** noun [U]
■ noun (pl. **-ies**) **1** [U] (informal) = SOLITARY CONFINEMENT **2** [C] (formal) a person who chooses to live alone

**solitary conˈfinement** (also informal **soli·tary**) noun [U] a punishment in which a prisoner is kept alone in a separate cell: *to be in solitary confinement*

**soli·tude** /ˈsɒlɪtjuːd; NAmE ˈsɑːlətuːd/ noun [U] the state of being alone, especially when you find this pleasant SYN **privacy**: *She longed for peace and solitude.*

**solo** C1 /ˈsəʊləʊ/ adj., noun
■ adj. [only before noun] **1** C1 done by one person alone, without anyone helping them: *his first solo flight* ◇ *a solo effort* **2** C1 connected with or played as a musical solo: *a solo artist* (= for example a singer who sings on their own, not as part of a group) ◇ *a piece for solo violin* ▸ **solo** adv.: *She wanted to fly solo across the Atlantic.* ◇ *After three years with the band he decided to go solo.*
■ noun (pl. **-os**) **1** C1 a piece of music, dance or entertainment performed by only one person: *a guitar solo* ⊃ compare DUET **2** a flight in which the pilot flies alone without an instructor (= teacher)

**solo·ist** /ˈsəʊləʊɪst/ noun a person who plays an instrument or performs alone ⊃ WORDFINDER NOTE at CONCERT

**Solo·mon** /ˈsɒləmən; NAmE ˈsɑːl-/ noun [sing.] used to talk about a very wise person: *In this job you need to exhibit the wisdom of Solomon.* ORIGIN From Solomon in the Bible, a king of Israel who was famous for being wise.

**sol·stice** /ˈsɒlstɪs; NAmE ˈsɑːl-/ noun either of the two times of the year at which the sun reaches its highest or lowest point in the sky in the middle of the day, marked by the longest and shortest days: *the summer/winter solstice* ⊃ WORDFINDER NOTE at SUN

**sol·uble** /ˈsɒljəbl; NAmE ˈsɑːl-/ adj. **1** that can be DISSOLVED (= mixed with a liquid until it forms part of that liquid) in a liquid: *soluble aspirin* ◇ ~ **in sth** *Glucose is soluble in water.*

---

ⓞ Oxford Phrasal Academic Lexicon (OPAL) written and spoken word lists | Ⓦ OPAL written word list | Ⓢ OPAL spoken word list

# solution

◊ *The paint is water-soluble.* **2** (*formal*) (of a problem) that can be solved **OPP** **insoluble** ▶ **solu·bil·ity** /ˌsɒljuˈbɪləti; *NAmE* ˌsɑː-l-/ *noun* [U]

**so·lu·tion** 🔊 **A2** 🔊 /səˈluːʃn/ *noun* **1** **A2** [C] a way of solving a problem or dealing with a difficult situation **SYN answer**: *Attempts to find a solution have failed.* ◊ *to propose/offer/provide/develop a solution* ◊ *It was decided that the only solution was for him to leave the company.* ◊ *~ to sth There's no simple solution to this problem.* **2** **A2** [C] *~* (**to sth**) an answer to a PUZZLE or to a problem in mathematics: *The solution to last week's quiz is on page 81.* **3** [C, U] a liquid in which sth is DISSOLVED (= mixed in so that it forms part of the liquid): *an alkaline solution* ◊ *saline solution* ◊ **in** *~ carbon dioxide in solution* ⊃ **WORDFINDER NOTE** at **CHEMISTRY** **4** [U] the process of DISSOLVING a solid or gas in a liquid: *the solution of glucose in water*

**solve** 🔊 **A2** 🔊 /sɒlv; *NAmE* sɑːlv/ *verb* **1** **A2** *~* **sth** to find a way of dealing with a problem or difficult situation: *Attempts are being made to solve the problem of waste disposal.* **2** **A2** *~* **sth** to find the correct answer or explanation for sth: *to solve an equation/a puzzle* ◊ *to solve a crime/mystery* ▶ **solv·able** *adj.*: *These problems are all solvable.*

**solv·ency** /ˈsɒlvənsi; *NAmE* ˈsɑːl-/ *noun* [U] the state of not being in debt (= not owing money)

**solv·ent** /ˈsɒlvənt; *NAmE* ˈsɑːl-/ *noun, adj.*
- *noun* [U, C] a substance, especially a liquid, that can DISSOLVE (= remove or destroy by a chemical process) another substance
- *adj.* **1** [not usually before noun] having enough money to pay your debts; not in debt **OPP insolvent 2** (*specialist*) able to DISSOLVE another substance, or be DISSOLVED in another substance: *Lead is more solvent in acidic water.*

**solv·er** /ˈsɒlvə(r); *NAmE* ˈsɑːl-/ *noun* a person who finds an answer to a problem or a difficult situation: *She's a good problem solver.*

**som·bre** (*US* **som·ber**) /ˈsɒmbə(r); *NAmE* ˈsɑːm-/ *adj.* **1** dark in colour **SYN drab**: *dressed in sombre shades of grey and black* **2** sad and serious **SYN melancholy**: *Paul was in a sombre mood.* ◊ *The year ended on a sombre note.* ▶ **sombre·ly** (*US* **som·ber·ly**) *adv.* **sombre·ness** (*US* **som·ber·ness**) *noun* [U]

**som·brero** /sɒmˈbreərəʊ; *NAmE* sɑːmˈbrer-/ *noun* (*pl.* **-os**) a Mexican hat for men that is tall with a very wide BRIM, turned up at the edges

**some** 🔊 **A1** /sʌm/ *det., pron., adv.*
- *det.* **1** **A1** /səm, *strong form* sʌm/ used with uncountable nouns or plural countable nouns to mean 'an amount of' or 'a number of', when the amount or number is not given: *There's still some wine in the bottle.* ◊ *Have some more vegetables.* **HELP** In negative sentences and questions **any** is usually used instead of 'some': *I don't want any more vegetables.* ◊ *Is there any wine left?* However, **some** is used in questions that expect a positive reply: *Would you like some milk in your coffee?* ◊ *Didn't you borrow some books of mine?* **2** **A1** used to refer to certain members of a group or certain types of a thing, but not all of them: *Some people find this more difficult than others.* ◊ *I like some modern music (= but not all of it).* **3** **B1** a large number or amount of sth: *It was with some surprise that I heard the news.* ◊ *We've known each other for some years now.* ◊ *We're going to be working together for some time (= a long time).* **4** **B1** a small amount or number of sth: *There is some hope that things will improve.* **5** **B1** used with singular nouns to refer to a person, place, thing or time that is not known or not identified: *There must be some mistake.* ◊ *He's in some kind of trouble.* ◊ *She won a competition in some newspaper or other.* ◊ *I'll see you again some time, I'm sure.* **6** (*informal, sometimes ironic*) used to express a positive or negative opinion about sb/sth: *That was some party!* ◊ *Some expert you are! You know even less than me.*
- *pron.* **1** **A1** *~* (**of sb/sth**) used to refer to an amount of sth or a number of people or things when the amount or number is not given: *Some disapprove of the idea.* ◊ *You'll find some in the drawer.* ◊ *Here are some of our suggestions.* **HELP** In negative sentences and questions **any** is usually used instead of 'some': *I don't want any.* ◊ *Do you have any of the larger ones?* However, **some** is used in questions that expect a positive reply: *Would you like some?* ◊ *Weren't you looking for some of those?* **2** **A1** *~* (**of sb/sth**) a part of the whole number or amount being considered: *All these students are good, but some work harder than others.* ◊ *Some of the music was weird.*

**IDM** ... **and ˈthen some** (*informal*) and a lot more than that: *We got our money's worth and then some.*
- *adv.* **1** used before numbers to mean 'approximately': *Some thirty people attended the funeral.* **2** (*NAmE, informal*) to some degree: *He needs feeding up some.* ◊ *'Are you finding the work any easier?' 'Some.'*

**-some** /səm/ *suffix* **1** (in adjectives) producing; likely to: *fearsome* ◊ *quarrelsome* **2** (in nouns) a group of the number mentioned: *a foursome*

**some·body** 🔊 **A1** /ˈsʌmbədi/ *pron.* = **SOMEONE**: *Somebody should have told me.* ◊ *She thinks she's really somebody in that car.* ⊃ compare **ANYBODY**, **EVERYBODY**, **NOBODY**

**ˈsome day** (*also* **some-day**) *adv.* at some time in the future: *Some day he'll be famous.*

**some·how** 🔊 **B2** 🔊 /ˈsʌmhaʊ/ *adv.* **1** **B2** (*also NAmE, informal* **some·way**, **some·ways**) in a way that is not known or certain: *We must stop him from seeing her somehow.* ◊ *Somehow or other I must get a new job.* **2** **B2** for a reason that you do not know or understand: *Somehow, I don't feel I can trust him.* ◊ *She looked different somehow.*

**some·one** 🔊 **A1** /ˈsʌmwʌn/ (*also* **some·body**) *pron.* **1** **A1** a person who is not known or mentioned by name: *There's someone at the door.* ◊ *Someone's left their bag behind.* ◊ *It's time for someone new (= a new person) to take over.* ◊ *It couldn't have been me—it must have been someone else (= a different person).* ◊ *Should we call a doctor or someone?* **HELP** The difference between **someone** and **anyone** is the same as the difference between **some** and **any**. Look at the notes there. **2** an important person: *He was a small-time lawyer keen to be someone.* ⊃ compare **NOBODY**

**some·place** /ˈsʌmpleɪs/ *adv., pron.* (*NAmE*) = **SOMEWHERE**: *It has to go someplace.* ◊ *Can't you do that someplace else?* ◊ *We need to find someplace to live.*

**som·er·sault** /ˈsʌməsɔːlt; *NAmE* -mərs-/ *noun, verb*
- *noun* a movement in which sb turns over completely, with their feet over their head, on the ground or in the air: *to do/turn a somersault* ◊ *He turned back somersaults.* ◊ (*figurative*) *Her heart did a complete somersault when she saw him.*
- *verb* [I] (+ *adv./prep.*) to turn over completely in the air: *The car hit the kerb and somersaulted into the air.*

**some·thing** 🔊 **A1** /ˈsʌmθɪŋ/ *pron., adv.*
- *pron.* **1** **A1** a thing that is not known or mentioned by name: *We stopped for something to eat.* ◊ *Give me something to do.* ◊ *There's something wrong with the TV.* ◊ *There's something about this place that frightens me.* ◊ *Don't just stand there. Do something!* ◊ *His name is Alan something (= I don't know his other name).* ◊ *She's a professor of something or other (= I'm not sure what) at Leeds.* ◊ *He's something in (= has a job connected with) television.* ◊ *The car hit a tree or something.* ◊ *I could just eat a little something.* **HELP** The difference between **something** and **anything** is the same as the difference between **some** and **any**. Look at the notes there. **2** **B1** (*informal*) a thing that is thought to be important or worth taking notice of: *There's something in (= some truth or some fact or opinion worth considering in) what he says.* ◊ *It's quite something (= a thing that you should feel happy about) to have a job at all these days.* ◊ *We should finish by tomorrow.' 'That's something (= a good thing), anyway.'* **3** **B1** (*informal*) used to show that a description or an amount, etc. is not exact: *She called at something after ten o'clock.* ◊ *a new comedy aimed at thirty-somethings (= people between thirty and forty years old)* ◊ *It tastes something like melon.* ◊ *They pay nine pounds an hour. Something like that.* ◊ *She found herself something of a (= to some degree a) celebrity.* ◊ *The*

*programme's* **something to do with** (= in some way about) *the environment.* ◇ *He gave her a wry look,* **something between** *amusement and regret.*

**IDM** **'make something of yourself** to be successful in life **something 'else** **1** a different thing; another thing: *He said something else that I thought was interesting.* **2** (*informal*) a person, a thing or an event that is much better than others of a similar type: *I've seen some fine players, but she's something else.*

■ *adv.* (*non-standard*) used with an adjective to emphasize a statement: *She was swearing something terrible.*

**some·time** ⁺ B2 /'sʌmtaɪm/ *adv., adj.*

■ *adv.* ⁺ B2 (*also* **some time**) at a time that you do not know exactly or has not yet been decided: *I saw him sometime last summer.* ◇ *We must get together sometime.*

■ *adj.* [only before noun] (*formal*) **1** used to refer to what sb used to be: *Thomas Atkins, sometime vicar of this parish* **2** (*NAmE*) used to refer to what sb does occasionally: *a sometime contributor to this magazine*

**some·times** ❶ A1 S /'sʌmtaɪmz/ *adv.* occasionally rather than all of the time: *Sometimes I go by car.* ◇ *He sometimes writes to me.* ◇ *I like to be on my own sometimes.*

**some·way** /'sʌmweɪ/ (*also* **someways** /'sʌmweɪz/) *adv.* (*NAmE, informal*) = SOMEHOW

**some·what** ❶ B2 /'sʌmwɒt; *NAmE* -wʌt/ *adv.* (*rather formal*) to some degree **SYN** **rather**: *somewhat different/similar* ◇ *I was somewhat surprised to see him.* ◇ *The situation has changed somewhat since we last met.*

**some·where** ❶ A2 /'sʌmweə(r); *NAmE* -wer/ (*NAmE also* **some·place**) *adv., pron.*

■ *adv.* ⁺ A2 in, at or to a place that you do not know or do not mention by name: *I read somewhere that she refuses to do interviews.* ◇ *Can we go somewhere warm?* ◇ *I've already looked there—it must be somewhere else.* ◇ *He went to school in York or somewhere* (= I'm not sure where). ◇ *They live somewhere or other in France.* **HELP** The difference between **somewhere** and **anywhere** is the same as the difference between **some** and **any**. Look at the notes there.

**IDM** **'get somewhere** (*informal*) to make progress in what you are doing **somewhere around, between, etc. sth** approximately the number or amount mentioned: *It cost somewhere around two thousand dollars.*

■ *pron.* ⁺ A2 a place that you do not know or do not mention by name: *We need to find somewhere to live.* ◇ *I know somewhere we can go.* **HELP** The difference between **somewhere** and **anywhere** is the same as the difference between **some** and **any**. Look at the notes there.

**som·mer** /'sɒmə(r); *NAmE* 'sɑːm-/ *SAfrE* ['sɔːm] *adv.* (*SAfrE, informal*) just; simply: *He sommer hit me without saying anything.*

**som·nam·bu·list** /sɒm'næmbjəlɪst; *NAmE* sɑːm-/ *noun* (*formal*) = SLEEPWALKER ▶ **som·nam·bu·lism** /-lɪzəm/ *noun* [U]

**som·no·lent** /'sɒmnələnt; *NAmE* 'sɑːm-/ *adj.* (*formal*) **1** almost asleep: *a somnolent cat* ◇ (*figurative*) *a somnolent town* **2** making you feel tired: *a somnolent Sunday afternoon* ▶ **som·no·lence** /-ləns/ *noun* [U]

**son** ❶ A1 /sʌn/ *noun* **1** ⁺ A1 [C] a person's male child: *their four-year-old son* ◇ *my teenage/eldest son* ◇ *her young/baby son* ◇ *We have two sons and a daughter.* ⇒ HOMOPHONES at SUN **2** [sing.] (*informal*) a friendly form of address that is used by an older man to a young man or boy: *Well, son, how can I help you?* **3** [C] (*literary*) a man who belongs to a particular place or country, etc: *one of France's most famous sons* **4 my son** [C] (*formal*) used by a priest to address a boy or man **5 the Son** [sing.] Jesus Christ as the second member of the TRINITY: *the Father, the Son and the Holy Spirit*

**IDM** see FATHER *n.,* FAVOURITE *adj.,* PRODIGAL

**sonar** /'səʊnɑː(r); *NAmE* 'soʊ-/ *noun* [U] equipment or a system for finding objects UNDERWATER using sound waves ⇒ compare RADAR

1489 **soon**

**son·ata** /sə'nɑːtə/ *noun* a piece of music for one instrument or for one instrument and a piano, usually divided into three or four parts

**song** ❶ A1 /sɒŋ; *NAmE* sɔːŋ/ *noun* **1** ⁺ A1 [C] a short piece of music with words that you sing: *a love/pop/rock song* ◇ *We sang a song together.* ◇ *the theme song to the hit TV show* ◇ *to write/record/perform/play a song* ⇒ see also FOLK SONG, SING-SONG, SWANSONG, TORCH SONG **2** ⁺ B2 [U] songs in general; music for singing: *The story is told through song and dance.* ◇ *Suddenly he burst into song* (= started to sing). ⇒ see also PLAINSONG **3** [U, C] the musical sounds that birds make: *the song of the blackbird*

**IDM** **for a 'song** (*informal*) very cheaply; at a low price **on 'song** (*informal*) working or performing well **a song and 'dance (about sth)** **1** (*BrE, informal, disapproving*) if you make a **song and dance** about sth, you complain or talk about it too much when this is not necessary **2** [C] (*NAmE, informal*) a long explanation about sth, or excuse for sth ⇒ more at SING

**song·bird** /'sɒŋbɜːd; *NAmE* 'sɔːŋbɜːrd/ *noun* a bird that has a musical call, for example a BLACKBIRD or THRUSH

**song·book** /'sɒŋbʊk; *NAmE* 'sɔːŋ-/ *noun* a book containing the music and words of different songs

**song·ster** /'sɒŋstə(r); *NAmE* 'sɔːŋ-/ *noun* (*old-fashioned*) a word sometimes used in newspapers to mean 'singer'

**song·stress** /'sɒŋstrəs; *NAmE* 'sɔːŋ-/ *noun* a word sometimes used in newspapers to mean 'a woman singer'

**song·writer** /'sɒŋraɪtə(r); *NAmE* 'sɔːŋ-/ *noun* a person who writes the words and usually also the music for songs: *singer-songwriter Ed Sheeran*

**song·writ·ing** /'sɒŋraɪtɪŋ; *NAmE* 'sɔːŋ-/ *noun* [U] the process of writing songs

**sonic** /'sɒnɪk; *NAmE* 'sɑːn-/ *adj.* (*specialist*) connected with sound or the speed of sound: *sonic waves*

**sonic 'boom** *noun* the EXPLOSIVE sound that is made when an aircraft travels faster than the speed of sound

**'son-in-law** *noun* (*pl.* **sons-in-law**) the husband of your daughter or son ⇒ compare DAUGHTER-IN-LAW

**son·net** /'sɒnɪt; *NAmE* 'sɑːn-/ *noun* a poem that has 14 lines, each containing 10 syllables, and a fixed pattern of RHYME: *Shakespeare's sonnets*

**sonny** /'sʌni/ *noun* [sing.] (*old-fashioned*) a word used by an older person to address a young man or boy

**son of a 'bitch** *noun* (*pl.* **sons of 'bitches**) (*also* **SOB** *especially in NAmE*) (*taboo, slang*) an offensive word for a person that you think is bad or very unpleasant: *I'll kill that son of a bitch when I get my hands on him!*

**son of a 'gun** *noun* (*pl.* **sons of 'guns**) (*NAmE, informal*) **1** a person or thing that you are annoyed with: *My car's at the shop—the son of a gun broke down again.* **2** used to express the fact that you are surprised or annoyed: *Well, son of a gun—and I thought the old guy couldn't dance!* **3** (*old-fashioned*) used by a man to address or talk about a male friend that he admires and likes: *Frank, you old son of a gun—I haven't seen you for months.*

**sono·gram** /'sɒnəgræm; *BrE also* 'sɒn-; *NAmE also* 'sɑːn-/ *noun* (*NAmE*) an image of what is inside sb's body that is produced using a special machine: *a sonogram of her developing baby* ⇒ compare ULTRASOUND

**son·or·ous** /'sɒnərəs; *NAmE* 'sɑːn-/ *adj.* (*formal*) having a pleasant full deep sound: *a sonorous voice* ▶ **son·or·ity** /sə'nɒrəti; *NAmE* -'nɔːr-/ *noun* [U, C]: *the rich sonority of the bass* **son·or·ous·ly** *adv.*

**sook** /suːk, sʊk/ *noun* (*AustralE, NZE, CanE, informal*) **1** a person who is not brave **SYN** **coward, crybaby** **2** a young cow that has been fed from a bottle, but by its mother

**soon** ❶ A1 /suːn/ *adv.* (**soon·er, soon·est**) **1** ⁺ A1 in a short time from now; a short time after sth else has happened: *She sold the house soon after her husband died.* ◇ *Soon afterwards, he joined a youth theatre group.* ◇ *I'd love to meet up again sometime soon.* ◇ *I soon realized the*

# soot

mistake. ◇ See you soon! 2 🔊 A1 early; quickly: *How soon can you get here?* ◇ *We'll deliver the goods as soon as we can.* ◇ *Please send it as soon as possible.* ◇ *Do you really have to go so soon?* ◇ *It's too soon to say what caused this.* ◇ *Next Monday is the soonest we can deliver.* ◇ *The sooner we set off, the sooner we will arrive.* ◇ *All too soon the party was over.* ⊃ see also ASAP

**IDM** **I, etc. would sooner do sth (than do sth else)** to prefer to do sth (than do sth else): *She'd sooner share a house with other students than live at home with her parents.* **no sooner said than 'done** used to say that sth was, or will be, done immediately **no sooner … than …** used to say that sth happens immediately after sth else: *No sooner had she said it than she burst into tears.* ⊃ note at HARDLY **the sooner the 'better** very soon; as soon as possible: *'When shall I tell him?' 'The sooner the better.'* **sooner or 'later** at some time in the future, even if you are not sure exactly when: *Sooner or later you will have to make a decision.* **sooner rather than 'later** after a short time rather than after a long time: *We urged them to sort out the problem sooner rather than later.* ⊃ more at ANY TIME, JUST *adv.*, SAY *v.*

**soot** /sʊt/ *noun* [U] black powder that is produced when wood, coal, etc. is burnt ⊃ see also SOOTY

**soothe** /suːð/ *verb* 1 ~ **sb** to make sb who is anxious, upset, etc. feel calmer **SYN** **calm**: *The music soothed her for a while.* 2 ~ **sth** to make a TENSE or painful part of your body feel more comfortable **SYN** **relieve**: *This should soothe the pain.* ◇ *Take a warm bath to soothe tense, tired muscles.* ▸ **sooth·ing** *adj.*: *a soothing voice/lotion* **sooth·ing·ly** *adv.*: *'There's no need to worry,' he said soothingly.*
**PHRV** **'soothe sth↔away** to remove a pain or an unpleasant feeling

**sooth·say·er** /ˈsuːθseɪə(r)/ *noun* (*old use*) a person who is believed to be able to tell what will happen in the future

**sooty** /ˈsʊti/ *adj.* 1 covered with SOOT 2 of the colour of SOOT

**sop** /sɒp/ *NAmE* sɑːp/ *noun* [usually sing.] ~ **(to sb/sth)** a small, not very important, thing that is offered to sb who is angry or disappointed in order to make them feel better

**soph·ist** /ˈsɒfɪst/ *NAmE* ˈsɑːf-/ *noun* 1 a teacher of philosophy in ancient Greece, especially one with an attitude of doubting that statements are true 2 a person who uses clever but wrong arguments

**so·phis·ti·cate** /səˈfɪstɪkət/ *noun* (*formal*) a sophisticated person

**so·phis·ti·cated** 🔊 B2 /səˈfɪstɪkeɪtɪd/ *adj.* 1 🔊 B2 (of a machine, system, etc.) clever and complicated in the way that it works or is presented: *highly sophisticated computer systems* ◇ *Medical techniques are becoming more sophisticated all the time.* 2 🔊 C1 having a lot of experience of the world and knowing about fashion, culture and other things that people think are socially important: *the sophisticated pleasures of city life* ◇ *Mark is a smart and sophisticated young man.* ⊃ compare NAIVE 3 🔊 C1 (of a person) able to understand difficult or complicated ideas: *a sophisticated audience* **OPP** **unsophisticated** ▸ **so·phis·ti·ca·tion** /səˌfɪstɪˈkeɪʃn/ *noun* [U]: *There was an air of sophistication about her.* ◇ *the increasing power and sophistication of computers*

**soph·is·try** /ˈsɒfɪstri/ *NAmE* ˈsɑːf-/ *noun* (*pl.* **-ies**) (*formal*) 1 [U] the use of clever arguments to persuade people that sth is true when it is really false 2 [C] a reason or an explanation that tries to show that sth is true when it is really false

**sopho·more** /ˈsɒfəmɔː(r)/ *NAmE* ˈsɑːf-/ *noun* (*US*) 1 a student in the second year of a course of study at a college or university 2 a HIGH SCHOOL student in the 10th grade ⊃ compare FRESHMAN, JUNIOR, SENIOR

**sopho·mor·ic** /ˌsɒfəˈmɔːrɪk/ *NAmE* ˌsɑːf-/ *adj.* (*NAmE*) showing a lack of MATURITY (= the ability to behave in a sensible, adult manner): *sophomoric jokes*

**sop·or·if·ic** /ˌsɒpəˈrɪfɪk; *NAmE* ˌsɑːp-/ *adj.* (*formal*) making you want to go to sleep: *the soporific effect of the sun* ⊃ WORDFINDER NOTE at SLEEP

**sop·ping** /ˈsɒpɪŋ; *NAmE* ˈsɑːp-/ (*also* **sopping 'wet**) *adj.* (*informal*) very wet **SYN** **soaking**

**soppy** /ˈsɒpi; *NAmE* ˈsɑːpi/ *adj.* (**sop·pier, sop·pi·est**) (*especially BrE*) (*NAmE usually* **sappy**) (*informal*) silly and SENTIMENTAL; full of unnecessary emotion: *soppy love songs*

**sop·rano** /səˈprɑːnəʊ; *NAmE* -ˈpræn-, -ˈprɑːn-/ *noun, adj.*
■ *noun* (*pl.* **-os** /-nəʊz/) 1 [C] a singing voice with the highest range for a woman or boy; a singer with a soprano voice ⊃ compare ALTO, MEZZO-SOPRANO, TREBLE 2 [sing.] a musical part written for a soprano voice
■ *adj.* [only before noun] (of a musical instrument) with the highest range of notes in its group: *a soprano saxophone* ⊃ compare ALTO, BASS¹, TENOR

**sor·bet** /ˈsɔːbeɪ; *NAmE* ˈsɔːrbət/ (*BrE also* **water ice**) *noun* [C, U] a sweet frozen food made from sugar, water and fruit juice, often eaten as a DESSERT

**sor·cer·er** /ˈsɔːsərə(r); *NAmE* ˈsɔːrs-/ *noun* (in stories) a man with magic powers, who is helped by evil spirits

**sor·cer·ess** /ˈsɔːsərəs; *NAmE* ˈsɔːrs-/ *noun* (in stories) a woman with magic powers, who is helped by evil spirits

**sor·cery** /ˈsɔːsəri; *NAmE* ˈsɔːrs-/ *noun* [U] magic that uses evil spirits **SYN** **black magic**

**sor·did** /ˈsɔːdɪd; *NAmE* ˈsɔːrd-/ *adj.* 1 not moral or honest: *It was a shock to discover the truth about his sordid past.* ◇ *I didn't want to hear the sordid details of their relationship.* 2 very dirty and unpleasant **SYN** **squalid**: *people living in sordid conditions*

**sore** /sɔː(r)/ *adj., noun*
■ *adj.* 1 if a part of your body is **sore**, it is painful, and often red, especially because of infection or because a muscle has been used too much: *to have a sore throat* ◇ *His feet were sore after the walk.* ◇ *My stomach is still sore (= painful) after the operation.* ⊃ HOMOPHONES at SOAR ⊃ SYNONYMS at PAINFUL ⊃ WORDFINDER NOTE at HURT 2 [not before noun] ~ **(at sb/about sth)** (*informal, especially NAmE*) upset and angry, especially because you have been treated unfairly **SYN** **annoyed**: *He was still sore at me for telling him he couldn't sing.* ▸ **sore·ness** *noun* [U]: *an ointment to reduce soreness and swelling*
**IDM** **a sore 'point** a subject that makes you feel angry or upset when it is mentioned: *It's a sore point with Sue's parents that the children have not been baptized yet.* **stand/stick out like a sore 'thumb** to be very easy to notice in an unpleasant way ⊃ more at BEAR *n.*, SIGHT *n.*
■ *noun* a painful, often red, place on your body where there is a wound or an infection **SYN** **wound**¹: *open sores* ⊃ see also BEDSORE, COLD SORE

**sore·ly** /ˈsɔːli; *NAmE* ˈsɔːrli/ *adv.* seriously; very much: *I was sorely tempted to complain, but I didn't.* ◇ *If you don't come to the reunion you'll be sorely missed.*

**sor·ghum** /ˈsɔːɡəm; *NAmE* ˈsɔːrɡ-/ *noun* [U] very small grain grown as food in tropical countries; the plant that produces this grain

**sor·or·ity** /səˈrɒrəti; *NAmE* -ˈrɔːr-/ *noun* (*pl.* **-ies**) (*NAmE*) a club for a group of women students at an American college or university ⊃ compare FRATERNITY

**sor·rel** /ˈsɒrəl; *NAmE* ˈsɔːr-/ *noun* [U] a plant with leaves that taste bitter and are used in salads or in making soup or sauces

**sor·row** /ˈsɒrəʊ; *NAmE* ˈsɔːr-/ *noun, verb*
■ *noun* 1 [U] ~ **(at/for/over sth)** (*rather formal*) a feeling of being very sad because sth very bad has happened **SYN** **grief**: *He expressed his sorrow at the news of her death.* ◇ *They said that the decision was made more in sorrow than in anger.* 2 [C] a very sad event or situation: *the joys and sorrows of childhood*
■ *verb* [I] (*literary*) to have or express very sad feelings: *the sorrowing relatives*

**sor·row·ful** /ˈsɒrəʊfl; *NAmE* ˈsɑːr-/ *adj.* (*literary*) very sad: *her sorrowful eyes* ▸ **sor·row·ful·ly** /-fəli/ *adv.*

---

| æ cat | ɑː father | e bed | ɜː fur | ə about | ɪ sit | i: see | i happy | ɒ got (*BrE*) | ɔː saw | ʌ cup | ʊ put | uː too |

**sorry** /ˈsɒri; NAmE ˈsɑːri/ adj., exclamation

■ **adj.** (sor·rier, sor·ri·est) **HELP** You can also use **more sorry** and **most sorry**. **1** [not before noun] feeling sad and ashamed about sth that has been done: **~ about sth** *We're very sorry about the damage to your car.* ◊ **~ for (doing) sth** *He says he's really sorry for taking the car without asking.* ◊ **~(that)…** *She was sorry that she'd lost her temper.* ◊ *If you say you're sorry we'll forgive you.*

**WORDFINDER** amends, apologize, ashamed, embarrassed, forgive, regret, remorse, repent, sympathy

**2** [not before noun] feeling sad and showing sympathy: **~(that)…** *I'm sorry that your husband lost his job.* ◊ *I'm sorry to hear that your father's in hospital again.* ◊ **~ about sb/sth** *No one is sorrier than I am about what happened.* ⇒ EXPRESS YOURSELF at SYMPATHY **3** [not before noun] feeling disappointed about sth and wishing you had done sth different or had not done sth: **~(that)…** *She was sorry that she'd lost contact with Mary.* ◊ *You'll be sorry if I catch you!* ◊ **~ to do sth** *I was genuinely sorry to be leaving college.* **4** [only before noun] very sad or bad, especially making you feel PITY or DISAPPROVAL: *The business is in a sorry state.* ◊ *They were a sorry sight when they eventually got off the boat.*

**IDM** **be/feel ˈsorry for sb** to be sad or feel sympathy for sb: *He decided to help Jan as he felt sorry for her.* **feel ˈsorry for yourself** (*informal*, *disapproving*) to feel unhappy; to be sad about yourself because you are suffering: *Stop feeling sorry for yourself and think about other people for a change.* **I'm ˈsorry** used when you are apologizing for sth: *I'm sorry, I forgot.* ◊ *Oh, I'm sorry. Have I taken the one you wanted?* ◊ *I'm sorry. I can't make it tomorrow.* **2** used for disagreeing with sb or politely saying 'no': *I'm sorry, I don't agree.* ◊ *I'm sorry, I'd rather you didn't go.* **3** used for introducing bad news: *I'm sorry to have to tell you you've failed.* **I'm ˈsorry to ˈsay** used for saying that sth is disappointing: *He didn't accept the job, I'm sorry to say.* ⇒ more at SAFE *adj.*

■ **exclamation 1** used when you are APOLOGIZING for sth: *Sorry I'm late!* ◊ *Did I stand on your foot? Sorry!* ◊ *Sorry to bother you, but could I speak to you for a moment?* ◊ *Sorry, we don't allow dogs in the house.* ◊ *He didn't even say sorry.* **2** (*especially BrE*) used for asking sb to repeat sth that you have not heard clearly: *Sorry? Could you repeat the question?* **3** used for correcting yourself when you have said sth wrong: *Take the first turning, sorry, the third turning on the right.*

▼ **EXPRESS YOURSELF**

**Apologizing**

When you have caused a problem for somebody, they are less likely to be very angry if you can make a polite apology:
- *I'm so/terribly/very sorry I'm late.*
- *I do apologize. I'll get you another cup.*
- *I must apologize for keeping you waiting.* (*BrE*)
- *We would like to apologize on behalf of the management.*
- *We would like to offer/Please accept our apologies for the inconvenience.*

Responses:
- *That's all right/OK.*
- *No problem.*
- *Don't worry about it.*
- *It's fine, really.*

**sort** /sɔːt; NAmE sɔːrt/ noun, verb

■ **noun 1** [C] a group or type of people or things that are similar in a particular way **SYN kind**: **~ of sb/sth** *'What sort of music do you like?' 'Oh, all sorts.'* ◊ *This sort of problem is quite common./These sorts of problems are quite common.* ◊ *He's the sort of person who only cares about money.* ◊ *The sort/sorts of people who are having large families in the US and Ireland are very similar.* ◊ *For dessert there's a fruit pie of some sort* (= you are not sure what kind). ◊ *Most people went on training courses of one sort or another* (= of various types) *last year.* ◊ (*informal*) *There were snacks—peanuts, olives, that sort of thing.* ◊ (*informal*) *There are all sorts of activities* (= many different ones) *for kids at the campsite.* ◊ (*informal*) *What sort of price did you want to pay?* (= approximately how much) ◊ (*informal*) *What sort of time do you call this?* (= I'm very angry that you have come so late.) ⇒ note at KIND **2** [C, usually sing.] (*informal, especially BrE*) a particular type of person: *My brother would never cheat on his wife; he's not that sort.* **3** [sing.] (*computing*) the process of putting data in a particular order: *to do a sort*

**IDM** **it takes all sorts (to make a world)** (*saying*) used to say that you think sb's behaviour is very strange or unusual but that everyone is different and likes different things **of ˈsorts** (*informal*) used when you are saying that sth is not a good example of a particular type of thing: *He offered us an apology of sorts.* **out of ˈsorts** (*especially BrE*) ill or upset: *She was tired and out of sorts by the time she arrived home.* **sort of** (*also* **sorta**) (*informal*) to some extent but in a way that you cannot easily describe: *She sort of pretends that she doesn't really care.* ◊ *'Do you understand?' 'Sort of.'* **a/some sort of sth** (*informal*) used for describing sth in a not very exact way: *I had a sort of feeling that he wouldn't come.* ◊ *She was jumping around like some sort of kangaroo.* ⇒ more at KIND *n.*

■ **verb 1** to arrange things in groups or in a particular order according to their type, etc.; to separate things of one type from others: **~ sth** *I started at the bottom, answering phones and sorting the mail.* ◊ **~ sth into sth** *The computer sorts the words into alphabetical order.* ◊ **~ sth from sth** *Women and children sorted the ore from the rock.* ◊ **~ sth by sth** *Events are sorted by date and category.* ⇒ see also SORT STH↔OUT, SORT STH OUT **2** [often passive] **~ sth** (*especially BrE, informal*) to deal with a problem successfully or organize sth/sb properly: *I'm really busy—can you sort it?* ◊ *Everything's now been sorted.* ⇒ compare SORTED **IDM** see MAN *n.*, SHEEP, WHEAT

**PHRV** **ˌsort itself ˈout** (of a problem) to stop being a problem without anyone having to take action: *It will all sort itself out in the end.* **ˌsort sth↔ˈout 1** (*informal*) to organize the contents of sth; to tidy sth: *The cupboards need sorting out.* **2** to organize sth successfully: *If you're going to the bus station, can you sort out the tickets for tomorrow?* **ˌsort sth↔ˈout (from sth)** to separate sth from a larger group: *Could you sort out the toys that can be thrown away?* ⇒ related noun SORT-OUT **ˌsort sth/sb/yourself ˈout** (*especially BrE*) to deal with sb's/your own problems successfully: *If you can wait a moment, I'll sort it all out for you.* ◊ *You load up the car and I'll sort the kids out.* **ˌsort sb↔ˈout** (*BrE, informal*) to deal with sb who is causing trouble, etc. especially by punishing or attacking them: *Wait till I get my hands on him—I'll soon sort him out!* **ˈsort through sth (for sth)** to look through a number of things, either in order to find sth or to put them in order: *I sorted through my paperwork.* ◊ *She sorted through her suitcase for something to wear.*

**ˈsort code** (*BrE*) (*US* **ˈrouting number**) *noun* a number that is used to identify a particular bank

**sort·ed** /ˈsɔːtɪd; NAmE ˈsɔːrt-/ *adj.* [not before noun] (*BrE, informal*) completed, solved or organized: *Don't worry. We'll soon have this sorted.* ◊ *It's our problem. We'll get it sorted.* ◊ *It's all sorted.* ◊ *It's time you got yourself sorted.* ⇒ compare SORT *v.* (2)

**sor·tie** /ˈsɔːti; NAmE ˈsɔːrti/ *noun* **1** a flight that is made by an aircraft during military operations; an attack made by soldiers **SYN raid 2** a short trip away from your home or the place where you are **SYN foray 3** an effort that you make to do or join sth new **SYN foray**: *His first sortie into politics was unsuccessful.*

**ˈsorting office** *noun* (*BrE*) a place where mail is sorted before being delivered

**ˈsort-out** *noun* [usually sing.] (*BrE, informal*) an act of arranging or organizing the contents of sth in a tidy or neat way and removing things you do not want

**SOS** /ˌes əʊ ˈes; NAmE ˌes oʊ ˈes/ *noun* [sing.] **1** a signal or message that a ship or plane sends when it needs help immediately: *to send an SOS* ◊ *an SOS message* **2** a serious request for immediate help: *We've received an SOS from the area asking for food parcels.* ⊃ see also MAYDAY

**so·sa·tie** /səˈsɑːti/ *noun* (SAfrE) small pieces of meat or vegetables that are cooked on a stick, usually over an open fire SYN **kebab**

**so-'so** *adj.* (*informal*) not particularly good or bad; average: *'How are you feeling today?' 'So-so.'* ▶ **so-'so** *adv.*: *I only did so-so in the exam.*

**sotto voce** /ˌsɒtəʊ ˈvəʊtʃi/ NAmE /ˌsɑːt-/ *adv.* (*from Italian, formal*) in a quiet voice so that not everyone can hear ▶ **sotto voce** *adj.*

**sou·bri·quet** /ˈsuːbrɪkeɪ/ *noun* = SOBRIQUET

**souf·flé** /ˈsuːfleɪ/ NAmE suːˈfleɪ/ *noun* [C, U] a dish made from egg whites, milk and flour mixed together to make it light, with cheese, fruit, etc. added and baked until it rises: *a cheese soufflé*

**sought** /sɔːt/ past tense, past part. of SEEK

**'sought after** *adj.* wanted by many people, because it is of very good quality or difficult to get or to find: *This design is the most sought after.* ◊ *a much sought-after actress*

**souk** /suːk/ *noun* a market in an Arab country

**soul** ❶ ₁ ₂ /səʊl/ *noun*
- **SPIRIT OF PERSON 1** ₁ ₂ [C] the spiritual part of a person, believed to exist after death: *He believed his immortal soul was in peril.* ◊ *The howling wind sounded like the wailing of lost souls (= the spirits of dead people who are not in heaven).*
- **INNER CHARACTER 2** ₂ [C] a person's inner character, containing their true thoughts and feelings: *in sb's ~* ◊ *There was a feeling of restlessness deep in her soul.* ◊ HOMOPHONES at SOLE
- **SPIRITUAL/MORAL/ARTISTIC QUALITIES 3** ₂ [sing.] the spiritual and moral qualities of humans in general SYN **psyche**: *the dark side of the human soul* **4** [U] strong and good human feeling, especially that gives a work of art its quality or enables sb to recognize and enjoy that quality: *It was a very polished performance, but it lacked soul.* **5** [sing.] *the ~ of sth* a perfect example of a good quality: *He is the soul of discretion.*
- **PERSON 6** [C] (*becoming old-fashioned*) a person of a particular type: *She's lost all her money, poor soul.* ◊ *You're a brave soul.* **7** [C] (*especially in negative sentences*) a person: *There wasn't a soul in sight (= nobody was in sight).* ◊ *Don't tell a soul (= do not tell anyone).* ◊ (*literary*) *a village of 300 souls (= with 300 people living there)*
- **MUSIC 8** (also **'soul music**) [U] a type of music that expresses strong emotions, made popular by African American musicians: *a soul singer*

IDM **good for the 'soul** (*humorous*) good for you, even if it seems unpleasant: *'Want a ride?' 'No thanks. Walking is good for the soul.'* ⊃ more at BARE *v.*, BODY, GOD, HEART *n.*, LIFE, SELL *v.*

**'soul-destroy·ing** *adj.* (of a job or task) very boring, because it has to be repeated many times or because there will never be any improvement

**'soul food** *noun* [U] the type of food that was traditionally eaten by black people in the southern US

**soul·ful** /ˈsəʊlfl/ *adj.* expressing deep feelings, especially feelings of love or being sad: *soulful eyes* ◊ *a soulful song* ▶ **soul·ful·ly** /-fəli/ *adv.* **soul·ful·ness** *noun* [U]

**soul·less** /ˈsəʊlləs/ *adj.* **1** (of things and places) not having any attractive or interesting qualities that make people feel happy SYN **depressing**: *They live in soulless concrete blocks.* **2** (of a person) not able to feel emotions

**soul·mate** /ˈsəʊlmeɪt/ *noun* a person that you have a special friendship with because you understand each other's feelings and interests

**'soul music** *noun* [U] = SOUL (8)

**'soul-searching** *noun* [U] the careful examination of your thoughts and feelings, for example in order to reach the correct decision or solution to sth

**sound** ❶ A1 /saʊnd/ *noun, verb, adj., adv.*

■ *noun*
- **STH YOU HEAR 1** ₁ A1 [C] something that you can hear SYN **noise**: *a loud/soft/faint sound* ◊ *a buzzing/hissing/popping sound* ◊ *He crept into the house trying not to make a sound.* ◊ *~of sb/sth (doing sth) She heard the sound of footsteps outside.* ◊ *The sound of children playing in the garden woke me.* **2** ₂ A1 [U] continuous rapid movements (called VIBRATIONS) that travel through air or water and can be heard when they reach a person's or an animal's ear: *Sound travels more slowly than light.* ⊃ note at NOISE
- **FROM TELEVISION/RADIO 3** ₂ A1 [U] what you can hear coming from a television, radio, etc., or as part of a film: *Could you turn the sound up/down?* ◊ *The sound quality of the tapes was excellent.* ⊃ see also SURROUND SOUND
- **OF MUSICIANS 4** [C, U] the effect that is produced by the music of a particular singer or group of musicians: *I like their sound.*
- **IMPRESSION 5** ₂ B1 [sing.] *the ~ of sth* the idea or impression that you get of sb/sth from what sb says or what you read: *They had a wonderful time by the sound of it.* ◊ *From the sound of things you were lucky to find him.* ◊ *They're consulting a lawyer? I don't like the sound of that.*
- **WATER 6** [C] (often in place names) a narrow passage of water that joins two larger areas of water SYN **strait**

IDM **like, etc. the sound of your own 'voice** (*disapproving*) to like talking a lot or too much, usually without wanting to listen to other people **within (the) sound of sth** (*BrE*) near enough to be able to hear sth: *a house within sound of the sea*

■ *verb* (not usually used in the progressive tenses)
- **GIVE IMPRESSION 1** ₁ A1 linking verb to give a particular impression when heard or read about: *+ adj. to sound good/great/right/interesting* ◊ *His voice sounded strange on the phone.* ◊ *The economy went into recession and taxpayers ended up footing the bill. Sound familiar (= does that sound familiar)?* ◊ *I'm about to say something which sounds a bit strange.* ◊ *+ noun She sounds just the person we need for the job.* ◊ *~ like sb/sth The pioneering technique sounds like something out of a science fiction film.* ◊ *~ as if/as though … I hope I don't sound as if/as though I'm criticizing you.* HELP *In spoken English people often use like instead of as if or as though, especially in NAmE, but this is not considered correct in written BrE.*
- **-SOUNDING 2** (in adjectives) giving the impression of having a particular sound: *an Italian-sounding name* ◊ *fine-sounding words*
- **PRODUCE SOUND 3** [I, T] to produce a sound; to make sth such as a musical instrument produce a sound: *The bell sounded for the end of the class.* ◊ (*BrE*) *~ sth Passing motorists sounded their horns in support.*
- **GIVE WARNING/SIGNAL 4** ₂ B2 [T] *~ sth* to give a signal such as a warning by making a sound: *When I saw the smoke, I tried to sound the alarm.* ◊ (*figurative*) *Scientists have sounded a note of caution on the technique.* ◊ *Leaving him out of the team may sound the death knell for our chances of winning (= signal the end of our chances).*
- **PRONOUNCE 5** [T] *~ sth* (*specialist*) to pronounce sth: *You don't sound the 'b' in the word 'comb'.*
- **MEASURE DEPTH 6** [T, I] *~ (sth)* (*specialist*) to measure the depth of the sea or a lake by using a line with a weight attached, or an electronic instrument

IDM **(it) sounds like a 'plan (to 'me)** (*especially NAmE*) used to agree to a suggestion that you think is good ⊃ more at NOTE *n.*, SUSPICIOUSLY

PHRV **sound 'off (about sth)** (*informal, disapproving*) to express your opinions loudly or in an aggressive way **sound sb↔'out (about/on sth)** | **sound sth↔'out** to try to find out from sb what they think about sth, often in an indirect way: *I wanted to sound him out about a job.* ◊ *They decided to sound out her interest in the project.*

■ *adj.* (sound·er, sound·est)
- **RELIABLE 1** ₂ C1 sensible; that you can rely on and that will probably give good results: *a person of sound judgement* ◊ *He gave me some very sound advice.* ◊ *This gives the design team a sound basis for their work.* ◊ *The proposal makes sound commercial sense.* ◊ *Their policies are environmentally sound.* OPP **unsound**

- **DETAILED/COMPLETE 2** [only before noun] good, detailed and complete: *a sound knowledge/understanding of sth* ◊ *He has a sound grasp of the issues.*
- **NOT DAMAGED/HURT 3** in good condition; not damaged, hurt, etc: *We arrived home safe and sound.* ◊ *to be of sound mind* (= not mentally ill) ◊ *The house needs attention but the roof is sound.* **OPP unsound**
- **SLEEP 4** [usually before noun] deep and peaceful: *to have a sound night's sleep* ◊ *to be a sound sleeper*
- **GOOD, BUT NOT EXCELLENT 5** good and accurate, but not excellent: *a sound piece of writing* ◊ *a sound tennis player*
- **PHYSICAL PUNISHMENT 6** severe: *to give sb a sound beating*
▶ **sound·ness** noun [U]: *soundness of judgement* ◊ *financial soundness* ◊ *the soundness of the building's foundations* ⊃ see also SOUNDLY
**IDM (as) sound as a 'bell** (*informal*) in perfect condition
■ *adv.* ~ *asleep* very deeply asleep

**the ˈsound barrier** *noun* [sing.] the point at which an aircraft's speed is the same as the speed of sound, causing reduced control, a very loud noise (called a SONIC BOOM) and various other effects: *to break the sound barrier* (= to travel faster than the speed of sound)

**ˈsound bite** *noun* a short phrase or sentence taken from a longer speech, especially a speech made by a politician, that is considered to be particularly effective or appropriate and so gets repeated in the media

**ˈsound card** *noun* (*computing*) a device that can be put into a computer to allow the use of sound with MULTIMEDIA software

**sound·check** /ˈsaʊndtʃek/ *noun* a process of checking that the equipment used for recording music, or for playing music at a concert, is working correctly and producing sound of a good quality

**ˈsound effect** *noun* [usually pl.] a sound that is made artificially, for example the sound of the wind or a battle, and used in a film, play, computer game, etc. to make it more realistic ⊃ WORDFINDER NOTE at FILM

**ˈsound engineer** *noun* a person who works in a recording or broadcasting studio and whose job is to control the levels and balance of sound

**sound·ing** /ˈsaʊndɪŋ/ *noun* **1 soundings** [pl.] careful questions that are asked in order to find out people's opinions about sth: *They will take soundings among party members.* ◊ *What do your soundings show?* **2** [C, usually pl.] a measurement that is made to find out how deep water is: *They took soundings along the canal.*

**ˈsounding board** *noun* a person or group of people that you discuss your ideas with before you make them known or reach a decision

**sound·less** /ˈsaʊndləs/ *adj.* without making any sound; silent: *Her lips parted in a soundless scream.* ▶ **sound·less·ly** *adv.*

**sound·ly** /ˈsaʊndli/ *adv.* **1** if you sleep **soundly**, you sleep very well and very deeply **2** in a way that is sensible or can be relied on: *a soundly based conclusion* **3** completely and by a large amount: *The team was soundly defeated.* **4** strongly: *These houses are soundly built.* **5** very well, but not in an excellent way: *He played soundly throughout the first half of the match.* **6** (of physical punishment) severely: *He was soundly beaten by his mother.*

**sound·proof** /ˈsaʊndpruːf/ (*also* **sound·proofed**) *adj.* made so that sound cannot pass through it or into it: *a soundproof room* ▶ **sound·proof** *verb* ~ *sth*

**ˈsound stage** *noun* a platform or a special area where sound can be recorded, for example for a film

**ˈsound system** *noun* equipment for playing recorded or live music and for making it louder

**sound·track** /ˈsaʊndtræk/ *noun* **1** all the music, speech and sounds that are recorded for a film: *The soundtrack of 'Casablanca' took weeks to edit.* **2** some of the music, and sometimes some speech, from a film or musical that is released on CD, the internet, etc. for people to buy: *I've just bought the soundtrack of the latest Miyazaki movie.*

**ˈsound wave** *noun* a VIBRATION in the air, in water, etc. that we hear as sound

1493 **source code**

**soup** /suːp/ *noun, verb*
■ *noun* [U, C] a liquid food made by boiling meat, vegetables, etc. in water, often eaten as the first course of a meal: *a bowl/cup of soup* ◊ *chicken/vegetable/tomato soup* ◊ *a soup spoon/bowl/plate* ◊ (*BrE*) *a tin/packet of soup* ◊ (*NAmE*) *a can/package of soup* ⊃ see also ALPHABET SOUP
**IDM from ˌsoup to ˈnuts** (*NAmE, informal*) from beginning to end: *She told me the whole story from soup to nuts.* **in the ˈsoup** (*informal*) in trouble: *We're all in the soup now.*
■ *verb*
**PHRV ˌsoup sth↔ˈup** (*informal*) to make changes to sth such as a car or computer, so that it is more powerful or exciting than before

**ˈsoup kitchen** *noun* a place where people who have no money can get soup and other food free

**soupy** /ˈsuːpi/ *adj.* **1** similar to soup: *a soupy stew* **2** (of the air) warm, wet and unpleasant **3** (*informal*) emotional in a way that is EXAGGERATED and embarrassing

**sour** /ˈsaʊə(r)/ *adj., verb*
■ *adj.* **1** having a taste like that of a lemon or of fruit that is not ready to eat: *sour apples* ◊ *a sour flavour* **OPP sweet** ⊃ SYNONYMS at BITTER ⊃ WORDFINDER NOTE at TASTE ⊃ see also SWEET-AND-SOUR **2** (especially of milk) having an unpleasant taste or smell because it is not fresh: *to turn/go sour* ⊃ SYNONYMS at BITTER **3** (of people) not cheerful; unfriendly and unpleasant: *a sour and disillusioned woman* ◊ *a sour face* ◊ *The meeting ended on a sour note with several people walking out.* ▶ **sour·ly** *adv.*: *'Who asked you?' he said sourly.* **sour·ness** *noun* [U]
**IDM ˌgo/turn ˈsour** to stop being pleasant or working properly: *Their relationship soon went sour.* **ˌsour ˈgrapes** (*saying*) used to show that you think sb is JEALOUS and is pretending that sth is not important: *He said he didn't want the job anyway, but that's just sour grapes.*
■ *verb* **1** [I, T] (of relationships, attitudes, people, etc.) to change so that they become less pleasant or friendly than before; to make sth do this: *The atmosphere at the house soured.* ◊ ~ *sth The disagreement over trade tariffs has soured relations between the two countries.* **2** [I, T] ~ **(sth)** if milk **sours** or if sth **sours** it, it becomes sour and has an unpleasant taste or smell

**source** /sɔːs; *NAmE* sɔːrs/ *noun, verb*
■ *noun* **1** a place, person or thing that you get sth from: *renewable energy sources* ◊ ~ *of sth Your local library will be a useful source of information.* ◊ *What is their main source of income?* ◊ **from a** ~ *Funding came from a wide variety of sources.* **2** [usually pl.] a person, book or document that provides information, especially for study, a piece of written work or news: *He refused to name his sources.* ◊ *Intelligence sources say they now believe he is dead.* ◊ **from a** ~ *This information comes from a very reliable source.* ◊ **according to a** ~ *According to industry sources, these prices are likely to rise.* ◊ *source material* ⊃ see also PRIMARY SOURCE, SECONDARY SOURCE **3** ~ **(of sth)** a person or thing that causes or provides sth: *The Irish landscape has long been a source of inspiration to artists.* ◊ *a potential source of conflict* **4** the place where a river or stream starts: *the source of the Nile* ⊃ WORDFINDER NOTE at RIVER
**IDM at ˈsource** at the place or the point that sth comes from or begins: *Is your salary taxed at source* (= by your employer)?
■ *verb* ~ *sth (from ...)* (*business*) to get sth from a particular place: *We source all the meat sold in our stores from British farms.* ⊃ see also OUTSOURCE

**source·book** /ˈsɔːsbʊk; *NAmE* ˈsɔːrs-/ *noun* a collection of texts on a particular subject, used especially as an introduction to the subject

**ˈsource code** *noun* [U] (*computing*) a computer program written in text form that must be translated into another form, such as MACHINE CODE, before it can run on a computer

---

Oxford Phrasal Academic Lexicon (OPAL) written and spoken word lists | OPAL written word list | OPAL spoken word list

**sour cream** (*BrE* also **soured 'cream**) *noun* [U] cream that has been made no longer fresh by adding bacteria to it, used in cooking

**sour·dough** /ˈsaʊədəʊ; *NAmE* -dər-/ *noun* [U] DOUGH (= a mixture of flour and water) that is left to FERMENT so that it has a SOUR taste, used for making bread; bread made with this DOUGH

**sour·puss** /ˈsaʊəpʊs; *NAmE* -ərp-/ *noun* (*informal*) a person who is not cheerful or pleasant

## south 🔑 A1 /saʊθ/ *noun, adj., adv.*

■ *noun* [U, sing.] (*abbr.* **S, So.**) **1** 🔑 A1 usually **the south** the direction that is on your right when you watch the sun rise; one of the four main points of the COMPASS: *Which way is south?* ◊ *warmer weather coming from the south* ◊ **to the~(of...)** *He lives to the south of* (= further south than) *the city.* ⊃ compare EAST, NORTH, WEST ⊃ picture at COMPASS **2** 🔑 A1 **the south, the South** the southern part of a country, a region or the world: *birds flying to the south for the winter* ◊ **in the~** *Houses are less expensive in the North than in the South* (= of the country). ◊ *They bought a villa in the South of France.* **3** **the South** the southern states of the US ⊃ see also DEEP SOUTH **4** **the South** (*also* **the ˌGlobal ˈSouth**) the poorer countries in the southern half of the world: *the vast informal economies of the Global South*

■ *adj.* (*abbr.* **S, So.**) [only before noun] **1** 🔑 A1 in or towards the south: *South Wales* ◊ *They live on the south coast.* **2** a **south wind** blows from the south: *A mild south wind blew all day.* ⊃ compare SOUTHERLY

■ *adv.* **1** 🔑 A1 towards the south: *This room faces south.* ◊ *a train heading south* **2** **~ of sth** nearer to the south than sth: *They live ten miles south of Bristol.* **3** **~ of sth** (*informal, NAmE* or *finance*) less or lower than sth: *The drug is achieving revenues just south of $1 billion per quarter.* OPP **north**
**IDM** **down ˈsouth** (*informal*) to or in the south of a country: *They've gone to live down south.*

**south·bound** /ˈsaʊθbaʊnd/ *adj.* travelling or leading towards the south: *southbound traffic* ◊ (*BrE*) *the southbound carriageway of the motorway*

**the ˌSouth-ˈEast** *noun* [sing.] (*BrE*) the south-eastern part of England which is the richest part of the country and has the highest population

**south-ˈeast** *noun* (*usually* **the south-east**) [sing.] (*abbr.* **SE**) the direction or region at an equal distance between south and east ⊃ picture at COMPASS ▶ **south-ˈeast** *adv., adj.*

**south-ˈeaster·ly** *adj.* **1** [only before noun] in or towards the south-east **2** [usually before noun] (of winds) blowing from the south-east

**south-ˈeastern** *adj.* [only before noun] (*abbr.* **SE**) connected with the south-east

**south-ˈeastwards** (*especially BrE*) (*also* **south-ˈeastward** *especially in NAmE*) *adv.* towards the south-east ▶ **south-ˈeastward** *adj.*

**south·er·ly** /ˈsʌðəli; *NAmE* -ðərli/ *adj., noun*
■ *adj.* **1** [only before noun] in or towards the south: *travelling in a southerly direction* **2** [usually before noun] (of winds) blowing from the south: *a warm southerly breeze* ⊃ compare SOUTH
■ *noun* (*pl.* **-ies**) a wind that blows from the south

## south·ern 🔑 B1 (*also* **Southern**) /ˈsʌðən; *NAmE* -ðərn/ *adj.* (*abbr.* **S**) [usually before noun] located in the south or facing south; connected with or typical of the south part of the world or a region: *the southern slopes of the mountains* ◊ *southern Spain* ◊ *a southern accent* ◊ *the southern part of the region*

**ˌsouthern ˈbelle** *noun* (*old-fashioned, NAmE*) a young attractive woman from the southern US

**the ˌSouthern ˈCross** *noun* [sing.] a group of stars in the shape of a cross that can be seen from the southern HEMISPHERE

**south·ern·er** /ˈsʌðənə(r); *NAmE* -ðərn-/ *noun* a person who comes from or lives in the southern part of a country

**the ˌSouthern ˈLights** *noun* [pl.] (*also* **aur·ora aus·tra·lis** [sing.]) bands of coloured light that are sometimes seen in the sky at night in the most southern countries of the world

**south·ern·most** /ˈsʌðənməʊst; *NAmE* -ðərn-/ *adj.* [usually before noun] furthest south: *the southernmost part of the island*

**south·paw** /ˈsaʊθpɔː/ *noun* (*informal, especially NAmE*) a person who prefers to use their left hand rather than their right, especially in a sport such as BOXING

**the ˌSouth ˈPole** *noun* [sing.] the point of the earth that is furthest south

**south-south-ˈeast** *noun* [sing.] (*abbr.* **SSE**) the direction at an equal distance between south and south-east ▶ **south-south-ˈeast** *adv.*

**south-south-ˈwest** *noun* [sing.] (*abbr.* **SSW**) the direction at an equal distance between south and south-west ▶ **south-south-ˈwest** *adv.*

**south·wards** /ˈsaʊθwədz; *NAmE* -wərdz/ (*especially BrE*) (*also* **south·ward** *especially in NAmE*) *adv.* towards the south: *to turn southwards* ▶ **south·ward** *adj.*: *in a southward direction*

**south-ˈwest** *noun* (*usually* **the south-west**) [sing.] (*abbr.* **SW**) the direction or region at an equal distance between south and west ⊃ picture at COMPASS ▶ **south-ˈwest** *adv., adj.*

**south-ˈwester·ly** *adj.* **1** [only before noun] in or towards the south-west **2** [usually before noun] (of winds) blowing from the south-west

**south-ˈwestern** *adj.* [only before noun] (*abbr.* **SW**) connected with the south-west

**south-ˈwestwards** (*especially BrE*) (*also* **south-ˈwestward** *especially in NAmE*) *adv.* towards the south-west ▶ **south-ˈwestward** *adj.*

**sou·ve·nir** /ˌsuːvəˈnɪə(r); *NAmE* -ˈnɪr; ˈsuːvənɪr/ *noun* a thing that you buy and/or keep to remind yourself of a place, an occasion or a holiday; something that you bring back for other people when you have been on holiday **SYN** **memento**: *I bought the ring as a souvenir of Greece.* ◊ *a souvenir shop*

**souv·la·ki** /suːˈvlɑːki/ *noun* [U, C] a Greek dish consisting of pieces of meat cooked on sticks

**souˈ'wester** /ˌsaʊˈwestə(r)/ *noun* **1** a hat made of shiny material that keeps out the rain, with a long wide piece at the back to protect the neck **2** a strong wind or storm coming from the south-west

**sov·er·eign** /ˈsɒvrɪn; *NAmE* ˈsɑːv-/ *noun, adj.*
■ *noun* **1** (*formal*) a king or queen **2** an old British gold coin worth one pound
■ *adj.* (*formal*) **1** [only before noun] (of a country or state) free to govern itself; completely independent **SYN** **autonomous** **2** having complete power or the greatest power in the country: *a sovereign ruler*

**sov·er·eign·ty** 🔑 C1 /ˈsɒvrənti; *NAmE* ˈsɑːv-/ *noun* [U] (*formal*) **1** 🔑 C1 **~ (over sth)** complete power to govern a country: *The country claimed sovereignty over the island.* ◊ *the sovereignty of Parliament* ◊ (*figurative*) *the idea of consumer sovereignty* **2** 🔑 C1 the state of being a country with freedom to govern itself: *The declaration proclaimed the full sovereignty of the republic.*

**So·viet** /ˈsəʊviət, ˈsɒv-; *NAmE* ˈsəʊviet, ˈsɑːviet/ *adj.* [usually before noun] connected with the former USSR

**so·viet** /ˈsəʊviət, ˈsɒv-; *NAmE* ˈsəʊviet, ˈsɑːviet/ *noun* **1** [C] an elected local, district or national council in the former USSR **2** **the Soviets** [pl.] (*especially NAmE*) the people of the former USSR

**sow**¹ /səʊ/ *verb* ⊃ see also SOW² (**sowed, sown** /səʊn/, **sowed, sowed**) **1** [T, I] to plant or spread seeds in or on the ground: **~(sth)** *Sow the seeds in rows.* ◊ *Water well after sowing.* ◊ **~sth with sth** *The fields around had been sown with wheat.* **2** [T] **~sth (in sth)** to introduce or spread feelings or ideas, especially ones that cause trouble: *to sow doubt in sb's mind* ◊ *to sow confusion*
**IDM** **sow the ˈseeds of sth** to start the process that leads to a particular situation or result **sow (your) wild ˈoats** (of

young men) to go through a period of wild behaviour while young, especially having a lot of romantic or sexual relationships ⇒ more at REAP

▼ HOMOPHONES

sew • so • sow /səʊ/
- **sew** *verb*: You should sew that hole up before it gets any bigger.
- **so** *adv*.: It is unsurprising that the Beatles were so successful.
- **sow** *verb*: Why would farmers want to sow GM seeds?

**sow²** /saʊ/ *noun* a female pig ⇒ compare BOAR, HOG ⇒ see also SOW¹ IDM see SILK

**sower** /'saʊə(r)/ *noun* a person or machine that puts seeds in the ground

**soya** /'sɔɪə/ (*BrE*) (*NAmE* **soy** /sɔɪ/) *noun* [U] the plant on which soya beans grow; the food obtained from soya beans: *a soya crop ◊ soya flour*

**'soya bean** (*BrE*) (*NAmE* **'soy·bean** /'sɔɪbiːn/) *noun* a type of bean, originally from south-east Asia, that is used instead of meat or animal PROTEIN in some types of food

**'soya milk** (*BrE*) (*NAmE* **'soy milk**) *noun* [U] a liquid made from soya beans, used instead of milk

**soy sauce** /ˌsɔɪ 'sɔːs/ (*also* ˌsoya 'sauce) *noun* [U] a thin dark brown sauce that is made from soya beans and tastes of salt, used in Chinese and Japanese cooking

**soz** /sɒz; *NAmE* sɑːz/ *exclamation* (*BrE*, *informal*) (especially in text messages, on SOCIAL MEDIA, etc.) sorry: *Soz, I forgot.*

**soz·zled** /'sɒzld; *NAmE* 'sɑːz-/ *adj*. (*BrE*, *slang*) very drunk

**spa** /spɑː/ *noun* **1** a place where water with minerals in it, which is considered to be good for your health, comes up naturally out of the ground; the name given to a town that has such a place and where there are, or were, places where people could drink the water: *Leamington Spa* ◊ *a spa town ◊ spa waters* **2** (*also* ˈhealth spa) a place where people can relax and receive health and beauty treatments, with, for example STEAM baths and exercise equipment: *a superb spa, which includes sauna, Turkish bath and fitness rooms* **3** (*especially NAmE*) = JACUZZI

**space** ⓘ A1 ⓞ /speɪs/ *noun*, *verb*

■ *noun*
- OUTSIDE EARTH'S ATMOSPHERE **1** ⓘ A1 (*also* ˌouter 'space) [U] the area outside the earth's atmosphere where all the other planets and stars are: *in~ the first woman in space ◊ the possibility of visitors from outer space ◊ space exploration/travel* ⇒ WORDFINDER NOTE at UNIVERSE

WORDFINDER astronaut, countdown, dock, launch, mission, orbit, rocket, satellite, weightless

- EMPTY AREA **2** ⓘ A1 [C] an area or a place that is empty: *an empty space* ◊ *a space two metres by three metres* ◊ *a parking space* ◊ *in/into a~ We were crowded together in a confined space.* ◊ ~**between A and B** *Put it in the space between the table and the wall.* ◊ **for sth** *I'll clear a space for your books.* **3** ⓘ A2 [U] an amount of an area or of a place that is empty or that is available for use SYN **room**: *floor/shelf space* ◊ *We must make good use of the available space.* ◊ *That desk takes up too much space.* ◊ *There is very little storage space in the department.* ◊ ~**for sth** *This creates space for a bigger table.* ◊ *disk/memory space* (= on a computer or device) **4** ⓘ B1 [C, U] a place, especially a room or a building, that can be used for a particular purpose: *The venue is a great space for music.* ◊ *various gallery and exhibition spaces* ◊ *to rent/lease (a) space* ◊ *He was sharing office space with a lawyer.* ⇒ see also SAFE SPACE **5** ⓘ A2 [U] the quality of being large and empty, allowing you to move freely SYN **spaciousness**: *The room has been furnished and decorated to give a feeling of space.* **6** ⓘ A2 [C, U] a large area of land that has no buildings on it: *the wide open spaces of the Canadian prairies* ◊ *Green space is important in the urban environment.* ⇒ SYNONYMS at LAND
- PERIOD OF TIME **7** [C, usually *sing*.] a period of time: *Leave a space of two weeks between appointments.* ◊ **in the ~of sth** *Forty-four people died in the space of five days.* ◊ *They had achieved a lot* **in a short space of time**.
- IN WRITING/PRINTING **8** [U, C] the part of a line, page or document that is empty: *Don't waste space by leaving a wide margin.* ◊ *There was not enough space to print all the letters we received.* ◊ *Leave a space after the comma.*
- FREEDOM **9** [U] the freedom and the time to think or do what you want to: *She was upset and needed space.* ◊ *You have to give teenagers plenty of space.* ⇒ see also BREATHING SPACE
- WHERE THINGS EXIST/MOVE **10** [U] the whole area in which all things exist and move: *It is quite possible that space and time are finite.*
- TYPE OF BUSINESS **11** [U] (*informal, business*) an area of business in which a person or an organization operates: *His investments have focused on the healthcare space.*

IDM **look/stare/gaze into 'space** to look straight in front of you without looking at a particular thing, usually because you are thinking about sth ⇒ more at PLACE *n*., WASTE *n*., WATCH *v*.

■ *verb* [often *passive*] ~ **sth** (+ *adv.* / *prep.*) to arrange things so that they have regular spaces between them: *evenly spaced plants* ◊ *a row of* **closely spaced** *dots* ◊ *Space the posts about a metre apart.*

PHRV ˌspace 'out (*informal, especially NAmE*) to take no notice of what is happening around you, especially as a result of taking drugs ⇒ see also SPACED OUT **ˌspace sth↔'out** to arrange things with a wide space between them: *The houses are spaced out in this area of town.*

**'space-age** *adj*. [usually before noun] (*informal*) (especially of design or technology) very modern and advanced: *a space-age kitchen*

**'space bar** *noun* a bar on the keyboard of a computer or TYPEWRITER that you press to make spaces between words ⇒ WORDFINDER NOTE at KEYBOARD

**'space cadet** *noun* (*slang*) a person who behaves strangely and often forgets things, as though he or she is using drugs

**'space capsule** (*also* **ˈcap·sule**) *noun* the part of a spacecraft in which people travel and that often separates from the main ROCKET

**'space·craft** /'speɪskrɑːft; *NAmE* -kræft/ *noun* (*pl.* **spacecraft**) a vehicle that travels in space

**ˌspaced 'out** (*also* **ˈspacey**) *adj*. (*informal*) not completely conscious of what is happening around you, often because of taking drugs

**'space heater** *noun* (*NAmE*) an electric device for heating a room

**'space·man** /'speɪsmæn/ *noun* (*pl.* **-men** /-men/) **1** (*informal*) a man who travels into space; an ASTRONAUT **2** (in stories) a creature that visits the earth from another planet SYN **alien** ⇒ see also SPACEWOMAN

**'space probe** *noun* = PROBE

**the 'space race** *noun* [*sing*.] competition between the US and the Soviet Union in the 1950s and 60s to be the first to explore space

**'space·ship** /'speɪsʃɪp/ *noun* a vehicle that travels in space, carrying people

**'space shuttle** (*also* **ˈshut·tle**) *noun* a SPACECRAFT designed to make repeated journeys, for example between the earth and a space station

**'space station** *noun* a large structure that is sent into space and remains above the earth as a base for people working and travelling in space

**'space·suit** /'speɪssuːt/ *noun* a special suit that covers the whole body and has a supply of air, allowing sb to survive and move around in space

**'space-time** *noun* [U] (*physics*) the universe considered as a CONTINUUM with four measurements—length, WIDTH, depth and time—inside which any event or physical object is located

**'space·walk** /'speɪswɔːk/ *noun* a period of time that an ASTRONAUT spends in space outside a SPACECRAFT

| s see | t tea | v van | w wet | z zoo | ʃ shoe | ʒ vision | tʃ chain | dʒ jam | θ thin | ð this | ŋ sing |

# spacewoman 1496

**space·woman** /ˈspeɪswʊmən/ noun (pl. -women /-wɪmɪn/) a woman who travels into space; an ASTRONAUT

**spacey** /ˈspeɪsi/ adj. = SPACED OUT

**spa·cial** = SPATIAL

**spa·cing** /ˈspeɪsɪŋ/ noun [U] **1** the amount of space that is left between things, especially between the words or lines printed on a page: *single/double spacing* (= with one or two lines left between lines of type) **2** the amount of time that is left between things happening

**spa·cious** /ˈspeɪʃəs/ adj. (approving) (of a room or building) large and with plenty of space for people to move around in ⟨SYN⟩ **roomy** ▶ **spa·cious·ly** adv. **spa·cious·ness** noun [U]: *White walls can give a feeling of spaciousness.*

**spade** /speɪd/ noun **1** [C] a garden tool with a broad metal part and a long handle, used for digging: *Turn the soil over with a spade.* ◊ (BrE) *The children took their buckets and spades to the beach.* ⊃ compare SHOVEL **2 spades** [pl., U] one of the four SUITS (= sets) in a PACK of cards. The cards have a black design with shapes like pointed leaves with short STEMS: *the five/queen/ace of spades* **3** [C] one card from the SUIT called spades: *You must play a spade if you have one.* **4** [C] (taboo, slang) an offensive word for a black person ⟨IDM⟩ **in ˈspades** (informal) in large amounts or to a great degree: *He'd got his revenge now, and in spades.* ⊃ more at CALL v.

**spade·work** /ˈspeɪdwɜːk; NAmE -wɜːrk/ noun [U] the hard work that has to be done in order to prepare for sth

**spa·ghetti** /spəˈɡeti/ noun [U] PASTA in the shape of long thin pieces that look like string when they are cooked

**spa·ghetti bol·ognese** (also **spa·ghetti bol·ognaise**) /spəˌɡeti bɒləˈneɪz; NAmE bəʊl-/ (especially BrE, informal **spag bol** /ˌspæɡ ˈbɒl; NAmE ˈbɑːl/) noun [U, C] a dish of spaghetti with a sauce of meat, tomatoes, etc.

**spaˌghetti ˈwestern** noun a film about COWBOYS, made in Europe by Italian companies

**spake** /speɪk/ (old use) past tense of SPEAK

**spam** ⚡+ ⟨C1⟩ /spæm/ noun, verb
- noun [U] **1** ⚡+ ⟨C1⟩ (informal, disapproving) advertising material sent by email to people who have not asked for it: *to send/block spam* ◊ *I get thousands of spam emails each month.* ⊃ compare JUNK MAIL **2 Spam™** cooked meat that has been cut up in very small pieces that are pressed together in a container, usually sold in cans and served cold in slices
- verb (-mm-) ~ sb/sth to send the same message to large numbers of internet users who have not requested the information: *Some companies will keep spamming you until you change your email address.* ◊ *Some idiot has been spamming my blog with comments.*

**spam·ming** /ˈspæmɪŋ/ noun [U] (informal) the practice of sending mail, especially advertising material, through the internet to a large number of people who have not asked for it ▶ **spam·mer** /-mə(r)/ noun

**spammy** /ˈspæmi/ adj. (**spam·mier**, **spam·mi·est**) (informal) connected with or full of internet spam: *spammy websites/blogs/links*

**span** ⚡+ ⟨C1⟩ /spæn/ verb, noun, adj.
- verb (-nn-) **1** ⚡+ ⟨C1⟩ ~ sth to last all through a period of time or to cover the whole of it: *His acting career spanned 55 years.* ◊ *Family photos spanning five generations were stolen.* **2** ⚡+ ⟨C1⟩ ~ sth to include a large area or a lot of things: *The operation, which spanned nine countries, resulted in 200 arrests.* **3** ⚡+ ⟨C1⟩ ~ sth to stretch right across sth, from one side to the other ⟨SYN⟩ **cross**: *a series of bridges spanning the river*
- noun **1** ⚡+ ⟨C1⟩ the length of time that sth lasts or is able to continue: *I worked with him over a span of six years.* ◊ *The project must be completed within a specific time span.* ◊ *Small children have a short attention span.* ⊃ see also LIFESPAN **2** ~ (of sth) a range or variety of sth: *Managers have a wide span of control.* ◊ *These forests cover a broad span of latitudes.* **3** the part of a bridge or an ARCH between one support and another: *The bridge crosses the river in a single span.* **4** the measurement of sth from one side to the other: *The kite has a span of 1.5 metres.* ⊃ see also WINGSPAN
- adj. ⟨IDM⟩ see SPICK

**span·dex** /ˈspændeks/ noun = LYCRA™

**span·gle** /ˈspæŋɡl/ verb, noun
- verb [usually passive] ~ sth (with sth) to cover or to decorate sth with small pieces of sth shiny ⊃ see also STAR-SPANGLED BANNER
- noun a small piece of shiny metal or plastic used to decorate clothes ⟨SYN⟩ **sequin**

**Spang·lish** /ˈspæŋɡlɪʃ/ noun [U] (informal) language which is a mixture of Spanish and English, especially a type of Spanish that includes many English words

**span·iel** /ˈspænjəl/ noun a dog with large soft ears that hang down. There are several types of spaniel.

**Span·ish** /ˈspænɪʃ/ adj., noun
- adj. from or connected with Spain
- noun [U] the language of Spain, Mexico and most countries in Central and South America

**Spanish ˈmoss** noun [U] a tropical American plant that has long, thin grey leaves and that grows over trees

**spank** /spæŋk/ verb ~ sb/sth to hit sb, especially a child, several times on their bottom as a punishment ⊃ compare SMACK ▶ **spank** noun

**spank·ing** /ˈspæŋkɪŋ/ noun, adv., adj.
- noun [C, U] a series of hits on the bottom, given to sb, especially a child, as a punishment: *to give sb a spanking* ◊ *I don't agree with spanking.*
- adv. (informal) when you say that sth is **spanking** new, etc. you are emphasizing that it is very new, etc.
- adj. [only before noun] (informal) very fast, good or impressive: *The horse set off at a spanking pace.*

**span·ner** /ˈspænə(r)/ (BrE) (also **wrench** NAmE, BrE) noun a metal tool with an end with a special shape for holding and turning NUTS and BOLTS (= small metal rings and pins that hold things together) ⊃ compare ADJUSTABLE SPANNER

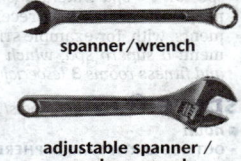
spanner/wrench

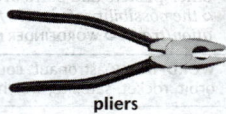
adjustable spanner / monkey wrench

⟨IDM⟩ **(throw) a ˈspanner in the works** (BrE) (NAmE **(throw) a (ˈmonkey) ˈwrench in the works**) (to cause) a delay or problem with sth that sb is planning or doing

pliers

**spar** /spɑː(r)/ verb, noun
- verb (-rr-) **1** [I] ~ (with sb) to make the movements used in BOXING, either in training or to test the speed of your opponent's reaction **2** [I] ~ (with sb) to argue with sb, usually in a friendly way
- noun **1** a strong POLE used to support the sails, etc. on a ship **2** a structure that supports the wing of an aircraft

**spare** ⚡+ ⟨B2⟩ /speə(r); NAmE sper/ adj., verb, noun
- adj.
- • TIME **1** ⚡+ ⟨B2⟩ available to do what you want with rather than work: *He's studying music in his spare time.* ◊ *I haven't had a spare moment this morning.*
- • NOT USED/NEEDED **2** ⚡+ ⟨B2⟩ [usually before noun] that is not being used or is not needed at the present time: *We've got a spare bedroom, if you'd like to stay.* ◊ *I'm afraid I haven't got any spare cash.* ◊ *Are there any tickets going spare* (= are there any available, not being used by sb else)?
- • EXTRA **3** ⚡+ ⟨B2⟩ [only before noun] kept in case you need to replace the one you usually use; extra: *a spare key/tyre* ◊ *Take some spare clothes in case you get wet.*
- • PERSON **4** thin, and usually quite tall
⟨IDM⟩ **go ˈspare** (BrE, informal) to become very angry or upset

æ cat | ɑː father | e bed | ɜː fur | ə about | ɪ sit | iː see | i happy | ɒ got (BrE) | ɔː saw | ʌ cup | ʊ put | uː too

■ **verb**
- TIME/MONEY/ROOM/THOUGHT, ETC. **1** [T] C1 to make sth such as time or money available to sb or for sth, especially when it requires an effort for you to do this: ~ **sth/sb** *I'd love to have a break, but I can't spare the time just now.* ◊ ~ **sth/sb to do sth** *Could you spare one of your staff to help us out?* ◊ ~ **sth/sb for sb/sth** *We can only spare one room for you.* ◊ *You should spare a thought for* (= think about) *the person who cleans up after you.* ◊ ~ **sb** *Surely you can spare me a few minutes?*
- SAVE SB PAIN/TROUBLE **2** [T] C1 to save sb/yourself from having to go through an unpleasant experience: ~ **sb/yourself sth** *He wanted to spare his mother any anxiety.* ◊ *Please spare me* (= do not tell me) *the gruesome details.* ◊ *You could have spared yourself an unnecessary trip by phoning in advance.* ◊ ~ **sb/yourself from sth** *She was spared from the ordeal of appearing in court.*
- NOT HARM/DAMAGE **3** [T] C1 (*formal*) to allow sb/sth to escape harm, damage or death, especially when others do not escape it: ~ **sb/sth (from sth)** *They killed the men but spared the children.* ◊ *She begged them to spare her life.* ◊ *During the bombing only one house was spared* (= was not hit by a bomb). ◊ ~ **sb/sth sth** *Hong Kong was spared a direct hit, but the storm still brought heavy rains and powerful winds.*
- NO EFFORT/EXPENSE, ETC. **4** [T] C1 ~ **no effort, expense, etc.** to do everything possible to achieve sth or to do sth well without trying to limit the time or money involved: *He spared no effort to make her happy again.* ◊ *No expense was spared in furnishing the new office.*
- WORK HARD **5 not ~ yourself** to work as hard as possible
IDM **spare sb's 'blushes** (*BrE*) to save sb from an embarrassing situation **spare sb's 'feelings** to be careful not to do or say anything that might upset sb **to 'spare** if you have time, money, etc. **to spare**, you have more than you need: *I've got absolutely no money to spare this month.* ◊ *We arrived at the airport with five minutes to spare.*
■ **noun 1** an extra thing that you keep in case you need to replace the one you usually use (used especially about a tyre of a car): *to get the spare out of the boot/trunk* ◊ *I've lost my key and I haven't got a spare.* **2** **spares** [pl.] (*especially BrE*) = SPARE PART: *It can be difficult to get spares for some older makes of car.*

**spare 'part** *noun* [usually pl.] a new part that you buy to replace an old or broken part of a car, machine, etc.

**spare 'rib** *noun* a RIB of PORK (= meat from a pig) with most of the meat cut off: *barbecued spare ribs*

**spare 'tyre** (*BrE*) (*NAmE* **spare 'tire**) *noun* **1** an extra wheel for a car **2** (*humorous*) a large area of too much fat around the middle part of sb's body

**spar·ing** /ˈspeərɪŋ; *NAmE* ˈsper-/ *adj.* careful to use or give only a little of sth: *Doctors now advise only sparing use of such creams.* ◊ ~ **with sth** *He was always sparing with his praise.* ▶ **spar·ing·ly** *adv.*: *Use the cream very sparingly.*

**spark** [A2] /spɑːk; *NAmE* spɑːrk/ *verb, noun*
■ **verb 1** [+] [T] C1 to cause sth to start or develop, especially suddenly: ~ **sth** *The proposal would spark a storm of protest around the country.* ◊ *Winds brought down power lines, sparking a fire.* ◊ ~ **sth off** *The riots were sparked off by the arrest of a local leader.* **2** [I] to produce small flashes of fire or electricity: *a sparking, crackling fire* ◊ (*figurative*) *The game suddenly sparked to life.*
PHRV **spark 'up sth** to begin a conversation, an argument, a friendship, etc., often suddenly: *I tried to spark up a conversation with her.*
■ **noun 1** [C] a very small burning piece of material that is produced by sth that is burning or by hitting two hard substances together: *A shower of sparks flew up the chimney.* **2** [C] a small flash of light produced by an electric current: *sparks from a faulty light switch* ◊ *A spark ignites the fuel in a car engine.* **3** [C, usually sing.] ~ **of sth** a small amount of a particular quality or feeling SYN **glimmer**: *a spark of hope* **4** [U, sing.] a special quality of energy, intelligence or enthusiasm that makes sb very clever, funny, etc: *As a writer he seemed to lack creative spark.* **5** [C] an action or event that causes sth important to develop, especially trouble or violence: *the sparks of revolution* **6** [C, usually pl.] feelings of anger or excitement between

people: *Sparks flew at the meeting* (= there was a lot of argument). IDM see BRIGHT *adj.*

**spar·kle** /ˈspɑːkl; *NAmE* ˈspɑːrkl/ *verb, noun*
■ **verb 1** [I] ~ **(with sth)** to shine brightly with small flashes of light: *sparkling eyes* ◊ *Her jewellery sparkled in the candlelight.* ⊃ note at SHINE **2** [I] ~ **(with sth)** to be full of life, enthusiasm or humour: *He always sparkles at parties.*
■ **noun** [C, U] **1** a series of flashes of light produced by light hitting a shiny surface: *the sparkle of glass* ◊ (*figurative*) *There was a sparkle of excitement in her eyes.* **2** the quality of being lively and original: *The performance lacked sparkle.*

**spark·ler** /ˈspɑːklə(r); *NAmE* ˈspɑːrk-/ *noun* a type of small FIREWORK that you hold in your hand and light. It burns with many bright SPARKS.

**spark·ling** /ˈspɑːklɪŋ; *NAmE* ˈspɑːrk-/ *adj.* **1** (*also less frequent, informal* **sparkly** /ˈspɑːkli; *NAmE* ˈspɑːrk-/) shining and flashing with light: *the calm and sparkling waters of the lake* ◊ *sparkling blue eyes* **2** (of drinks) containing bubbles of gas SYN **fizzy**: *a sparkling wine* ◊ *sparkling mineral water* **3** interesting and funny: *a sparkling conversation/personality* **4** excellent; of very good quality SYN **brilliant**: *The champion was in sparkling form.*

**'spark plug** (*also* **plug**) (*BrE also* **'sparking plug**) *noun* a part in a car engine that produces a SPARK (= a flash of electricity) which makes the fuel burn and starts the engine

**sparky** /ˈspɑːki; *NAmE* ˈspɑːrki/ *adj.* (**spark·ier**, **sparki·est**) (*BrE, informal*) full of life; interesting and funny: *a sparky personality*

**'sparring partner** *noun* **1** a person that you regularly have friendly arguments or discussions with **2** (in BOXING) a person that a BOXER regularly practises with

**spar·row** /ˈspærəʊ/ *noun* a small brown and grey bird, common in many parts of the world

**'sparrow·hawk** /ˈspærəʊhɔːk/ *noun* a small BIRD OF PREY (= a bird that kills other creatures for food) of the HAWK family

**sparse** /spɑːs; *NAmE* spɑːrs/ *adj.* (**sparser**, **spars·est**) only present in small amounts or numbers and often spread over a large area: *the sparse population of the islands* ◊ *Vegetation becomes sparse higher up the mountains.* ◊ *The information available on the subject is sparse.* ▶ **sparse·ly** *adv.*: *a sparsely populated area* **sparse·ness** *noun* [U]

**spar·tan** /ˈspɑːtn; *NAmE* ˈspɑːrtn/ *adj.* (of conditions) simple or severe; without anything that makes life easier or more pleasant ORIGIN From **Sparta**, a powerful city in ancient Greece, where the people were not interested in comfort or luxury. OPP **luxurious**

**spasm** /ˈspæzəm/ *noun* **1** [C, U] a sudden and often painful contracting of a muscle, which you cannot control: *a muscle spasm* ◊ *The injection sent his leg into spasm.* **2** [C] ~ **(of sth)** a sudden strong feeling or reaction that lasts for a short time: *a spasm of anxiety/anger/coughing/pain, etc.*

**spas·mod·ic** /spæzˈmɒdɪk; *NAmE* -ˈmɑːd-/ *adj.* **1** happening suddenly for short periods of time; not regular or continuous: *There was spasmodic fighting in the area yesterday.* **2** (*specialist*) caused by your muscles becoming tight in a way that you cannot control: *spasmodic movements* ▶ **spas·mod·ic·al·ly** /-kli/ *adv.*

**spas·tic** /ˈspæstɪk/ *adj.* **1** (*medical* or *old-fashioned*) having or caused by CEREBRAL PALSY, an illness which makes it difficult for sb to control their muscles and movements. Using this word is now often considered offensive: *spastic children* ◊ *spastic reactions* **2** (*informal*) an offensive word, sometimes used by children to mean 'stupid' ▶ **spas·tic** *noun*

**spat** /spæt/ *noun, verb*
■ **noun 1** (*informal*) a short argument about sth unimportant **2** [usually pl.] a piece of cloth that covers the ankle, worn in the past by men over the shoe and fastened with buttons at the side
■ **verb** past tense, past part. of SPIT

**spate** /speɪt/ noun [usually sing.] ~ of sth a large number of things, which are usually unpleasant, that happen suddenly within a short period of time: *The bombing was the latest in a spate of terrorist attacks.*
**IDM** **in (full) ˈspate** (*especially BrE*) (of a river) containing more water and flowing more strongly than usual: *After heavy rain, the river was in spate.* ◊ (*figurative*) *Celia was in full spate* (= completely involved in talking and not likely to stop or able to be interrupted).

**spa·tial** **W** (*also* **spa·cial**) /ˈspeɪʃl/ *adj.* (*formal or specialist*) relating to space and the position, size, shape, etc. of things in it: *changes taking place in the spatial distribution of the population* ◊ *the development of a child's spatial awareness* (= the ability to judge the positions and sizes of objects) ▶ **spa·tial·ly** (*also* **spa·cial·ly**) /-ʃəli/ *adv.*

**spat·ter** /ˈspætə(r)/ *verb, noun*
■ *verb* **1** [T, often passive] to cover sb/sth with drops of liquid, dirt, etc., especially by accident **SYN** splash: ~ sb/sth *blood-spattered walls* ◊ ~ sb/sth with sth *As the bus passed, it spattered us with mud.* ◊ ~ sth on/over sb/sth *Oil was spattered on the floor.* **2** [I] + *adv./prep.* (of liquid) to fall on a surface in drops, often noisily: *We heard the rain spattering on the roof.*
■ *noun* (*also* **spat·ter·ing**) [sing.] ~ (of sth) a number of drops of a liquid or small amounts of sth that hit a surface; the noise this makes: *a spatter of rain against the window* ◊ *a spattering of blood* ◊ (*figurative*) *a spatter of applause*

**spat·ula** /ˈspætʃələ/ *noun* **1** a tool with a broad flat part that is not sharp, used for mixing and spreading things, especially in cooking and painting **2** (*NAmE*) (*BrE* **ˈfish slice**) a kitchen UTENSIL that has a broad flat part with narrow holes in it, attached to a long handle, used for turning and lifting food when cooking **3** (*BrE*) (*NAmE* **ˈtongue depressor**) a thin flat instrument that doctors use for pressing the tongue down when they are examining sb's throat

**spawn** /spɔːn/ *verb, noun*
■ *verb* **1** [I, T] ~ (sth) (of fish, frogs, etc.) to lay eggs **2** [T] ~ sth (*often disapproving*) to cause sth to develop or be produced: *The band's album spawned a string of hit singles.*
■ *noun* [U] a soft substance containing the eggs of fish, frogs etc. ➔ see also FROGSPAWN

**spay** /speɪ/ *verb* ~ sth (*specialist*) to remove the OVARIES of a female animal, to prevent it from producing young: *Have you had your cat spayed?*

**spaza** /ˈspɑːzə/ *noun* (*SAfrE*) a small shop that sb operates from their home, selling food, drinks, cigarettes, etc. to local people, especially in a TOWNSHIP

**speak** **①** **A1** /spiːk/
*verb* (**spoke** /spəʊk/, **spoken** /ˈspəʊkən/)
• **HAVE CONVERSATION 1** **A1** [I] to talk to sb about sth; to have a conversation with sb: ~ **to sb** *The President refused to speak to reporters.* ◊ ~ **(to sb) about sth/sb** *I've spoken to the manager about it.* ◊ (*especially NAmE*) ~ **with sb (about sth/sb)** *Can I speak with you for a minute?* ◊ *'Do you know him?' 'Not to speak to.'* (= I recognize him but do not really know him) ◊ *'Can I speak to Susan?' 'Speaking.'* (= at the beginning of a phone conversation) ◊ *I saw her in the street but we didn't speak.* ➔ SYNONYMS at TALK
• **USE VOICE 2** **A1** [I] to use your voice to say sth: *The illness left him unable to speak.* ◊ *Please speak more slowly.* ◊ *Without speaking, she stood up and went out.* ◊ *He speaks with a Scottish accent.* ◊ *She has a beautiful speaking voice.*
• **A LANGUAGE 3** **A1** [T] (not used in the progressive tenses) ~ sth to be able to use a particular language: *to speak several languages* ◊ *to speak a little Urdu* ◊ *Do you speak English?* **4** **A1** [T, I] to use a particular language to express yourself: ~ sth *What language is it they're speaking?* ◊ ~ **in sth** *Would you prefer it if we spoke in German?*

**WORD FAMILY**
**speak** *verb*
**speaker** *noun*
**speech** *noun*
**spoken** *adj.* (≠ unspoken)

• **-SPEAKING 5** (in adjectives) speaking the language mentioned: *French-speaking Canada* ◊ *non-English-speaking students*
• **MENTION/DESCRIBE 6** **A2** [I] ~ **of/about sth/sb** to mention or describe sth/sb: *She still speaks about him with great affection.* ◊ *Witnesses spoke of a great ball of flame.* ◊ *Speaking of travelling,* (= referring back to a subject just mentioned) *are you going anywhere exciting this year?* ➔ note at MENTION
• **MAKE SPEECH 7** **A2** [I] to make a speech to an audience: + *adv./prep. I hate speaking in public.* ◊ *He was invited to speak at a conference.* ◊ ~ **(to sb) (about sth)** *Professor Todd spoke to the group about her research.* ◊ *She spoke in favour of the new tax.* ◊ *He has a number of speaking engagements this week.* ➔ **WORDFINDER NOTE** at DEBATE
• **SAY/STATE 8** [T] ~ sth to say or state sth: *She was clearly speaking the truth.* ◊ *He spoke the final words of the play.*
**IDM** **be on ˈspeaking terms (with sb) | be ˈspeaking (to sb)** to be willing to be polite or friendly towards sb, especially after an argument: *She's not been on speaking terms with her uncle for years.* ◊ *Are they speaking to each other again yet?* **ˈgenerally, ˈbroadly, ˈroughly, ˈrelatively, etc. ˈspeaking** used to show that what you are saying is true in a general, etc. way: *Generally speaking, the more you pay, the more you get.* ◊ *There are, broadly speaking, two ways of doing this.* ◊ *Personally speaking, I've always preferred Italian food.* ➔ **LANGUAGE BANK** at GENERALLY **no.../ˈnothing to ˈspeak of** such a small amount that it is not worth mentioning: *They've got no friends to speak of.* ◊ *She's saved a little money but nothing to speak of.* **ˌso to ˈspeak** used to emphasize that you are expressing sth in an unusual or humorous way: *They were all very similar. All cut from the same cloth, so to speak.* **speak for itˈself/themˈselves** to be so easy to see and understand that you do not need to say anything else about it/them: *Her success speaks for itself.* **speak for myˈself/herˈself/himˈself, etc.** to express what you think or want yourself, rather than sb else doing it for you: *I'm quite capable of speaking for myself, thank you!* **speak for yourˈself** (*informal*) used to tell sb that a general statement they have just made is not true of you: *'We didn't play very well.' 'Speak for yourself!'* (= I think that I played well.) **speaking as sth** used to say that you are the type of person mentioned and are expressing your opinion from that point of view: *Speaking as a parent, I'm very concerned about standards in education.* **speak your ˈmind** to say exactly what you think, in a very direct way **speak out of ˈturn** to say sth when you should not, for example because it is not the right time or you are not the right person to say it **speak ˈvolumes (about/for sth/sb)** to tell you a lot about sth/sb, without the need for words **speak ˈwell/ˈill of sb** (*formal*) to say good or bad things about sb ➔ more at ACTION *n.*, DEVIL, FACT, ILL *adv.*, LANGUAGE, MANNER, STRICTLY, TURN *n.*
**PHRV** **ˈspeak for sb** to state the views or wishes of a person or a group; to act as a representative for sb **ˈspeak of sth** (*formal*) to be evidence that sth exists or is present: *Everything here speaks of perfect good taste.* **speak ˈout (against sth)** to state your opinions publicly, especially in opposition to sth and in a way that takes courage ➔ see also OUTSPOKEN **ˈspeak to sb (about sth)** (*informal*) to talk to sb in a serious way about sth wrong they have done, to try to stop them doing it again **ˈspeak to sth/sb** to attract or interest sb/sth: *The story spoke to him directly.* ◊ *It's a design that speaks to the senses.* **ˈspeak to sth 1** to discuss or comment on a topic, problem or situation: *The show wants to speak to real issues affecting young people.* **2** to be evidence that sth exists or is true: *The number of cleaning firms speaks to the fact that cleaning is considered an important service.* **speak ˈup** usually used in orders to tell sb to speak more loudly: *Please speak up—we can't hear you at the back.* **speak ˈup (for sb/sth)** to say what you think clearly and freely, especially in order to support or defend sb/sth

**-speak** /spiːk/ *combining form* (in nouns) (*informal, often disapproving*) the language used by a particular group of people, especially when it is difficult for other people to understand or they find it annoying: *management-speak* ◊ *Visitors to websites don't want to read marketing-speak.*

**speak·easy** /ˈspiːkiːzi/ noun (pl. -ies) a place in the US where people could buy alcohol illegally, at the time in the 1920s and 1930s when it was illegal to make or sell alcohol

**speak·er** 🔵 **A2** /ˈspiːkə(r)/ noun **1** **A2** a person who gives a talk or makes a speech: *He was a guest speaker at the conference.* ◊ *a keynote speaker at the Republican convention* ⇒ WORDFINDER NOTE at CONFERENCE **2** **A2** a person who speaks a particular language: *English speakers* ◊ *~ of sth a fluent speaker of German* ⇒ see also NATIVE SPEAKER **3** **A2** a person who is or was speaking: *I looked around to see who the speaker was.* **4** **B2** the part of a radio, computer or piece of musical equipment that the sound comes out of: *The car had a powerful sound system with four speakers.* ⇒ see also LOUDSPEAKER, SMART SPEAKER **5** **(the) Speaker** the title of the person whose job is to control the discussions in a parliament: *the Speaker of the House of Commons/Representatives*

▼ **SYNONYMS**

**speaker**
communicator • gossip • talker

These are all words for a person who talks or who is talking, especially in a particular way.

**speaker** a person who is or was speaking; a person who speaks a particular language: *I looked around to see who the speaker was.* ◊ *a fluent Arabic speaker*

**communicator** (*rather formal*) a person who is able to describe their ideas and feelings clearly to others: *The ideal candidate will be an effective communicator.*

**gossip** (*disapproving*) a person who enjoys talking about other people's private lives: *Myra is a dear, but she's also a terrible gossip.*

**talker** a person who talks in a particular way or who talks a lot: *He's a very persuasive talker.* ◊ *She's a (great) talker* (= she talks a lot).

**SPEAKER OR TALKER?**
- **Talker** is used when you are talking about how much sb talks or how well they talk. It is not used for the person who is or was talking: *I looked round to see who the talker was.* You can say that sb is *a good/persuasive speaker* but that means that they are good at making speeches. If you mean that they speak well in conversation, use **talker**.

**PATTERNS**
- a good/great speaker/communicator/talker
- an effective/excellent speaker/communicator

**speak·er·phone** /ˈspiːkəfəʊn; NAmE -kɑːrf-/ noun a phone that can be used without being held, because it contains a MICROPHONE and a LOUDSPEAKER

**spear** /spɪə(r); NAmE spɪr/ noun, verb
■ noun **1** a weapon with a long wooden handle and a sharp metal point used for fighting, hunting and fishing in the past ⇒ picture at SWORD **2** the long pointed STEM of some plants ⇒ VISUAL VOCAB page V5
■ verb ~ sth/sb to throw or push a spear or other pointed object through sth/sb: *They were standing in the river spearing fish.* ◊ *She speared an olive with her fork.*

**spear·head** /ˈspɪəhed; NAmE ˈspɪrh-/ noun, verb
■ noun [usually sing.] a person or group that begins an activity or leads an attack against sb/sth
■ verb ~ sth to begin an activity or lead an attack against sb/sth: *He is spearheading a campaign for a new stadium in the town.*

**spear·mint** /ˈspɪəmɪnt; NAmE ˈspɪrm-/ noun [U] a type of MINT used especially in making sweets and TOOTHPASTE: *spearmint chewing gum* ⇒ compare PEPPERMINT

**spec** /spek/ noun, verb
■ noun [C] (NAmE also **specs** [pl.]) a detailed description of sth, especially the design and materials needed to produce sth: *We want the machine manufactured to our own spec.* ⇒ see also SPECIFICATION

IDM **on ˈspec** (*informal*) when you do sth **on spec**, you are trying to achieve sth without organizing it in advance, but hoping you will be lucky
■ verb [usually passive] (-cc-) to design and make sth to a particular standard: **be specced** *The camera is well specced for the price.*

**spe·cial** 🔵 **A1** /ˈspeʃl/ adj., noun
■ adj. **1** **A1** [usually before noun] not ordinary or usual; different from what is normal SYN **exceptional**: *The school will only allow this in special circumstances.* ◊ *An application has been filed for special leave to appeal in the High Court.* ◊ *There is something special about this place.* **2** **A1** more important than others; deserving or getting more attention than usual: *What are your special interests?* ◊ *Our special guest on next week's show will be …* ◊ *a special occasion* ◊ *What makes him special as a director is his obvious intelligence.* **3** **A1** organized or intended for a particular purpose: *British special forces were employed on stealth operations.* ◊ *a special event/report/team* **4** **A2** used by or intended for one particular person or group of people: *She has a special way of smiling.* ◊ *He enlivens his lectures with his own special brand of humour.* **5** **A2** [only before noun] better or more than usual: *As an only child she got special attention.* ◊ *Special thanks are due to the many volunteers who helped organize fund-raising events.* ⇒ compare ESPECIAL
■ noun **1** something that is not usually available but is provided for a particular purpose or on one occasion: *an election-night special on television* ◊ *The menu changes regularly and there are daily specials to choose from.* **2** (*informal, especially NAmE*) a price for a particular product in a shop or restaurant that is lower than usual: *There's a special on coffee this week.*
IDM **on ˈspecial** (*especially NAmE*) on sale at a lower price for a short period of time: *The chocolates were on special at my local store.*

ˌspecial ˈagent noun a detective who works for the national government in the US, for example for the FBI

ˌSpecial ˈBranch noun [U + sing./pl. v.] (*also* **the Special Branch** [sing. + sing./pl. v.]) the department of the British police force that deals with the defence of the country against political crimes and TERRORISM

ˌspecial ˈconstable noun (in the UK) a person who is not a professional police officer but who is trained to help the police force, especially during an emergency

ˌspecial deˈlivery noun [U] a service that delivers a letter, etc. faster than normal

ˌspecial eˈdition noun a version of a product that has extra material or features that do not appear in the standard version

ˌspecial eduˈcation noun [U] the education of children who have physical or learning problems

ˌspecial efˈfects (*also* **SFX**) noun [pl.] unusual or exciting pieces of action in films or television programmes, that are created by computers or clever photography to show things that do not normally exist or happen

ˌspecial ˈinterest group (*also* **special interest**) noun (*especially NAmE*) a group of people who work together to achieve sth that they are particularly interested in, especially by putting pressure on the government, etc.

**spe·cial·ism** /ˈspeʃəlɪzəm/ noun **1** [C] an area of study or work that sb SPECIALIZES in: *a business degree with a specialism in computing* ◊ *Dr Crane's specialism is tropical diseases.* **2** [U] the fact of SPECIALIZING in a particular subject

**spe·cial·ist** 🔵 **B2** 🔊 /ˈspeʃəlɪst/ noun, adj.
■ noun **1** **B2** a person who is an expert in a particular area of work or study: *~ in sth a specialist in Japanese history* **2** **B2** a doctor who has SPECIALIZED in a particular area of medicine: *You need to see a specialist.* ◊ *a cancer/fertility specialist* ⇒ compare GENERALIST ⇒ WORDFINDER NOTE at DOCTOR

**WORDFINDER** cardiologist, dermatologist, gynaecologist, neurologist, obstetrician, ophthalmologist, paediatrician, psychiatrist, radiologist

---

🔵 Oxford Phrasal Academic Lexicon (OPAL) written and spoken word lists  |  🔵 OPAL written word list  |  🔊 OPAL spoken word list

# speciality

■ **adj.** [only before noun] having or involving expert knowledge of a particular area of work, study or medicine: *specialist knowledge/training/skills* ◊ *The patient should be transferred to a specialist unit.*

**spe·ci·al·ity** /ˌspeʃiˈæləti/ (*BrE*) (also **spe·cial·ty** *NAmE, BrE*) *noun* (*pl.* **-ies**) **1** a type of food or product that a restaurant or place is famous for because it is so good: *Seafood is a speciality on the island.* ◊ *local specialities* ⊃ **WORDFINDER NOTE** at RESTAURANT **2** an area of work or study that sb gives most of their attention to and knows a lot about; sth that sb is good at: *My speciality is international tax law.*

**spe·cial·ize** (*BrE also* **-ise**) /ˈspeʃəlaɪz/ *verb* [I] to become an expert in a particular area of work, study or business; to spend more time on one area of work, etc. than on others: *Many students prefer not to specialize too soon.* ◊ *~ in sth He specialized in criminal law.* ◊ *The shop specializes in hand-made chocolates.* ▶ **spe·cial·iza·tion**, **-isa·tion** /ˌspeʃəlaɪˈzeɪʃn; *NAmE* -ləˈz-/ *noun* [U, C]

**spe·cial·ized** (*BrE also* **-ised**) /ˈspeʃəlaɪzd/ *adj.* designed or developed for a particular purpose or area of knowledge: *specialized equipment/skills* ◊ *Our industry is quite specialized.*

**special 'licence** *noun* (*BrE*) a licence allowing two people to get married at a time or place that is not usually allowed

**spe·cial·ly** /ˈspeʃəli/ *adv.* **1** for a particular purpose, person, etc: *The ring was specially made for her.* ◊ *a specially designed diet plan* ◊ *We came specially to see you.* **2** (*informal*) more than usual or more than other things: *It will be hard to work today—specially when it's so warm and sunny outside.* ◊ *I hate homework. Specially history.* ⊃ note at ESPECIALLY

**special 'needs** *noun* [pl.] (*especially BrE*) needs that a person has because of mental or physical problems: *She teaches children with special needs.*

**special 'offer** *noun* [C, U] a product that is sold at less than its usual price, especially in order to persuade people to buy it; the act of offering goods in this way: *Shop around for special offers.* ◊ *~ on sth a special offer on perfume* ◊ *on ~ French wine is on special offer this week.*

**special ope'ration** *noun* [usually pl.] a military mission that uses specially trained soldiers or special equipment, especially one that is done in secret or uses unusual TACTICS: *special operations forces*

**special 'pleading** *noun* [U] trying to persuade sb about sth by mentioning only the arguments that support your opinion and ignoring the arguments that do not support it

**special 'school** *noun* a school for children who have physical or learning problems

**spe·cialty** /ˈspeʃəlti/ *noun* (*pl.* **-ies**) (*especially NAmE or medical*) = SPECIALITY: *regional specialties* ◊ *specialty stores* ◊ *Her specialty is taxation law.* ◊ *Doctors training for general practice must complete programmes in a number of specialties, including paediatrics.*

**spe·cies** /ˈspiːʃiːz/ *noun* (*pl.* **spe·cies**) a group into which animals, plants, etc. that are able to have sex with each other and produce healthy young are divided, smaller than a GENUS and identified by a Latin name: *a conservation area for endangered species* ◊ *plant/animal/bird/fish species* ◊ *~ of sth a native species of fish* ⊃ **WORDFINDER NOTE** at GREEN ⊃ **VISUAL VOCAB** page V3

**spe·cif·ic** /spəˈsɪfɪk/ *adj.* **1** [usually before noun] connected with one particular thing only **SYN** **particular**: *specific needs/requirements* ◊ *patients who suffer from a specific type of cancer* ◊ *The money was collected for a specific purpose.* **2** detailed and exact **SYN** **precise**: *specific information/details/examples/questions* ◊ *'I'd like your help tomorrow.' 'Can you be more specific (= tell me exactly what you want)?'* **3** *~ (to sth)* (*formal*) existing only in one place or limited to one thing **SYN** **peculiar**: *a belief that is specific to this part of Africa*

**spe·cif·ic·al·ly** /spəˈsɪfɪkli/ *adv.* **1** connected with or intended for one particular thing only: *liquid vitamins specifically designed for children* ◊ *the development of new treatments that specifically target cancer cells* **2** in a detailed and exact way: *She had specifically asked him to keep her updated on the investigation.* ◊ *The agreement specifically mentions the lifting of sanctions.* **3** used when you want to add more detailed and exact information: *The newspaper, or more specifically, the editor, was taken to court for publishing the photographs.*

**spe·ci·fi·ca·tion** /ˌspesɪfɪˈkeɪʃn/ *noun* [C, U] a detailed description of how sth is, or should be, designed or made: *the technical specifications of the new model* (= of car) ◊ *The house has been built exactly to our specifications.* ◊ *The office was furnished to a high specification.*

**spe cific 'gravity** *noun* [U] = RELATIVE DENSITY

**spe·ci·fi·city** /ˌspesɪˈfɪsəti/ *noun* [U, C] (*pl.* **-ies**) (*formal*) the quality of being specific

**spe·cif·ics** /spəˈsɪfɪks/ *noun* [pl.] the details of a subject that you need to think about or discuss: *Okay, that's the broad plan—let's get down to the specifics.*

**spe·cify** /ˈspesɪfaɪ/ *verb* (**speci·fies**, **speci·fy·ing**, **speci·fied**, **speci·fied**) to state sth, especially by giving an exact measurement, time, exact instructions, etc: *~ sth Remember to specify your size when ordering clothes.* ◊ *~ who, what, etc … The contract clearly specifies who can operate the machinery.* ◊ *~ that … The regulations specify that calculators may not be used in the examination.* ▶ **spe·ci·fi·able** /-əbl/ *adj.*

**speci·men** /ˈspesɪmən/ *noun* **1** a small amount of sth that shows what the rest of it is like **SYN** **sample**: *Astronauts have brought back specimens of rock from the moon.* **2** a single example of sth, especially an animal or a plant: *The aquarium has some interesting specimens of unusual tropical fish.* ◊ (*humorous*) *They were fine specimens of British youth!* ⊃ **SYNONYMS** at EXAMPLE **3** a small quantity of blood, URINE, etc. that is taken from sb and tested by a doctor: *to provide/take a specimen*

**spe·cious** /ˈspiːʃəs/ *adj.* (*formal*) seeming right or true but actually wrong or false **SYN** **misleading**: *a specious argument*

**speck** /spek/ *noun* a very small spot; a small piece of dirt, etc: *The ship was now just a speck in the distance.* ◊ *specks of dust* ⊃ **SYNONYMS** at MARK

**speckle** /ˈspekl/ *noun* [usually pl.] a small coloured mark or spot on a background of a different colour ⊃ **WORDFINDER NOTE** at PATTERN

**speck·led** /ˈspekld/ *adj.* covered with small marks or spots **SYN** **flecked**

**specs** /speks/ *noun* [pl.] **1** (*especially BrE, informal*) = GLASSES: *I need a new pair of specs.* **2** (*NAmE*) = SPEC

**spec·tacle** /ˈspektəkl/ *noun* **1** **spectacles** [pl.] (*formal*) = GLASSES: *a pair of spectacles* ◊ *a spectacle case* (= to put your spectacles in) **2** [C, U] a performance or an event that is very impressive and exciting to look at: *The carnival parade was a magnificent spectacle.* **3** [C] a sight or view that is very impressive to look at: *The sunset was a stunning spectacle.* **4** [sing.] an unusual or surprising sight or situation that attracts a lot of attention: *I remember the sad spectacle of her standing in her wedding dress, covered in mud.*
**IDM** **make a 'spectacle of yourself** to draw attention to yourself by behaving or dressing in a silly way in public

**spec·tacu·lar** /spekˈtækjələ(r)/ *adj., noun*

■ *adj.* very impressive **SYN** **breathtaking**: *spectacular scenery* ◊ *It was a spectacular achievement on their part.* ◊ *The special effects were quite spectacular.* ▶ **spec·tacu·lar·ly** *adv.*: *It has been a spectacularly successful year.*

■ *noun* an impressive show or performance: *a Christmas TV spectacular*

**spec·tate** /spekˈteɪt/ *verb* [I] to watch sth, especially a sports event

**spec·ta·tor** /spek'teɪtə(r); NAmE 'spekteɪtər/ noun a person who is watching an event, especially a sports event: *The new football stadium will hold 75000 spectators.* ⊃ WORDFINDER NOTE at SPORT

**spec·ta·tor sport** noun a sport that many people watch; a sport that is interesting to watch

**spec·tra** /'spektrə/ pl. of SPECTRUM

**spec·tral** /'spektrəl/ adj. **1** (*literary*) like a ghost; connected with a ghost **2** (*specialist*) connected with a SPECTRUM: *spectral bands*

**spec·tre** (US **spec·ter**) /'spektə(r)/ noun **1** ~ (of sth) something unpleasant that people are afraid might happen in the future: *The country is haunted by the spectre of civil war.* ◇ *These weeks of drought have once again* **raised the spectre** *of widespread famine.* **2** (*literary*) a ghost: *Was he a spectre returning to haunt her?*

**spec·trom·eter** /spek'trɒmɪtə(r); NAmE -'trɑːm-/ noun (*specialist*) a piece of equipment for measuring the WAVELENGTHS of SPECTRA

**spec·tro·scope** /'spektrəskəʊp/ noun (*specialist*) a piece of equipment for forming and looking at SPECTRA ▶ **spec·troscop·ic** /ˌspektrə'skɒpɪk; NAmE -'skɑːp-/ adj.: *spectroscopic analysis*

**spec·tros·copy** /spek'trɒskəpi; NAmE -'trɑːs-/ noun [U] (*chemistry, physics*) the study of forming and looking at SPECTRA using spectrometers, spectroscopes, etc.

**spec·trum** /'spektrəm/ noun (*pl.* **spec·tra** /-trə/) **1** a band of coloured lights in order of their WAVELENGTHS, as seen in a RAINBOW and into which light may be separated: *A spectrum is formed by a ray of light passing through a prism.* ◇ *Red and violet are at opposite ends of the spectrum.* **2** a range of sound waves or several other types of wave: *the* **electromagnetic/radio/sound spectrum 3** [usually sing.] a complete or wide range of related qualities, ideas, etc: *a broad spectrum of interests* ◇ *We shall hear views from across the political spectrum.*

**specu·late** /'spekjuleɪt/ verb **1** ~ (about/on/as to sth) to form an opinion about sth without knowing all the details or facts: *We all speculated about the reasons for her resignation.* ◇ ~ *why, how, etc ... It is useless to speculate why he did it.* ◇ ~ *that ... We can speculate that the stone circles were used in some sort of pagan ceremony.* **2** [I] ~ (in/on sth) to buy goods, property, shares, etc, hoping to make a profit when you sell them, but with the risk of losing money: *He likes to speculate on the stock market.*

▼ **EXPRESS YOURSELF**

**Speculating**

In some exams, you have to talk about what you can see in a picture and speculate about the situation or a wider issue prompted by the picture. These are ways of saying what you think might be the case:
- *I think it's* **likely that** *these people know each other.*
- *I* **imagine** *she's his wife.*
- *They* **might/may/could** *be related.* (BrE or formal, NAmE)
- *I* **would think/imagine/guess** *they've been waiting for some time.* (BrE)
- *I* **guess** *that the car has broken down.* (NAmE)
- *I think this has* **probably** *happened before.*
- **It looks to me as though** *the woman is very angry.*
- **Perhaps/Probably/Possibly/It may be that/Maybe** *there has been an accident.* (BrE or formal, NAmE)

**specu·la·tion** /ˌspekju'leɪʃn/ noun [U, C] **1** the act of forming opinions about what has happened or what might happen without knowing all the facts: *His private life is the subject of much speculation.* ◇ ~ *that ... There was widespread speculation that she was going to resign.* ◇ ~ *about/over sth Today's announcement ends months of speculation about the company's future.* ◇ *She dismissed the newspaper reports as* **pure speculation**. ◇ *Our speculations proved right.* **2** ~ (in sth) the activity of buying and selling goods or shares in a company in

the hope of making a profit, but with the risk of losing money

**specu·la·tive** /'spekjələtɪv; NAmE also -leɪt-/ adj. **1** based on guessing or on opinions that have been formed without knowing all the facts **2** showing that you are trying to guess sth: *She cast a speculative look at Kate.* **3** (of business activity) done in the hope of making a profit but involving the risk of losing money ▶ **specu·la·tive·ly** adv.

**specu·la·tor** /'spekjuleɪtə(r)/ noun a person who buys and sells goods or shares in a company in the hope of making a profit: *property speculators*

**specu·lum** /'spekjələm/ noun (*medical*) a metal instrument that is used to make a hole or tube in the body wider so it can be examined

**sped** /sped/ past tense, past part. of SPEED

**speech** /spiːtʃ/ noun **1** [C] a formal talk that a person gives to an audience: *Several people* **made speeches** *at the wedding.* ◇ ~ **on/about sth** *to* **give/deliver a speech** *on human rights* ◇ *in a* ~ *In his* **acceptance speech**, *the actor thanked his family.* **2** [U] the language used when speaking; the fact of speaking rather than writing: *in* ~ *This expression is used mainly in speech, not in writing.* ◇ *a defence of* **free speech** (= the right to say openly what you think) ◇ *speech sounds* ⊃ see also DIRECT SPEECH, HATE SPEECH, REPORTED SPEECH, TEXT-TO-SPEECH **3** [U] the ability to speak: *I seemed to have lost the power of speech.* ◇ *a* **speech impediment 4** [U] the way in which a particular person speaks: *Her speech was slurred—she was clearly drunk.* **5** [C] a group of lines that an actor speaks in a play in the theatre: *She has the longest speech in the play.* ⊃ WORDFINDER NOTE at DRAMA ⊃ see also FIGURE OF SPEECH, PART OF SPEECH

▼ **SYNONYMS**

**speech**

lecture • address • talk • sermon

These are all words for a talk given to an audience.

**speech** a formal talk given to an audience: *Several people made speeches at the wedding.*

**lecture** a talk given to a group of people to tell them about a particular subject, often as part of a university or college course: *a lecture on the Roman army* ◇ *a course/series of lectures*

**address** a formal speech given to an audience: *a televised presidential address*

**SPEECH OR ADDRESS?**

A **speech** can be given on a public or private occasion; an **address** is always public: *He gave an address at the wedding.*

**talk** a fairly informal session in which sb tells a group of people about a subject: *She gave an interesting talk on her visit to China.*

**sermon** a talk on a moral or religious subject, usually given by a religious leader during a service: *to preach a sermon*

**PATTERNS**
- a **long/short** speech/lecture/address/talk/sermon
- a **keynote** speech/lecture/address
- to **write/prepare/give/deliver/hear** a(n) speech/lecture/address/talk/sermon
- to **attend/go to** a lecture/talk

**ˈspeech act** noun (*linguistics*) something that sb says, considered as an action, for example 'I forgive you'

**ˈspeech bubble** noun a circle around the words that sb says in a cartoon

**ˈspeech community** noun all the people who speak a particular language or variety of a language: *the Kodava speech community in India* ◇ *speech communities such as high school students or hip hop fans*

# speechifying

**speech·ify·ing** /ˈspiːtʃɪfaɪɪŋ/ *noun* [U] (*informal, disapproving*) the act of making speeches in a very formal way, trying to sound important

**speech·less** /ˈspiːtʃləs/ *adj.* not able to speak, especially because you are extremely angry or surprised: *Laura was speechless with rage.* ▶ **speech·less·ly** *adv.* **speech·less·ness** *noun* [U]

**ˈspeech recognition** (*also* **ˈvoice recognition**) *noun* [U] technology that allows a computer to understand spoken words

**ˈspeech synthesis** *noun* [U] the production of spoken language from written language by a computer

**ˈspeech ˌtherapy** *noun* [U] special treatment to help people who have problems in speaking clearly, for example in pronouncing particular sounds ▶ **ˈspeech ˌtherapist** *noun*

**ˈspeech-writer** *noun* a person whose job is to write speeches for a politician or public figure

**speed** 🅞 A2 /spiːd/ *noun, verb*

■ *noun*
• RATE OF MOVEMENT/ACTION **1** 🅞 A2 [C, U] the rate at which sb/sth moves or travels: **at … ~** at *high/low/full/top speed* ◇ *The five-door version has a maximum speed of 130 mph.* ◇ *a fast/slow speed* ◇ *London traffic moves at an average speed of 11 mph.* ◇ **~ of sth** *travelling at the speed of light/sound* ◇ *The missile reaches speeds of 5 800 kilometres per hour.* ◇ **at breakneck speed** (= fast in a way that is dangerous) Ⅎ see also AIRSPEED, GROUND SPEED, WARP SPEED **2** 🅞 A2 [C, U] the rate at which sth happens or is done: *the processing speed of the computer* ◇ **at a ~** *This course is designed so that students can progress at their own speed.* ◇ **~ of sth** *We aim to increase the speed of delivery* (= how quickly goods are sent). Ⅎ see also CLOCK SPEED **3** 🅞 A2 [U] the quality of being quick or rapid: *The Kenyan runner put on a sudden burst of speed over the last 50 metres.* ◇ *She was overtaken by the speed of events* (= things happened more quickly than she expected). ◇ **at ~** (*formal*) *A car flashed past them at speed* (= fast).
• IN PHOTOGRAPHY **4** [C] a measurement of how sensitive film for cameras, etc. is to light **5** [C] = SHUTTER SPEED
• ON BICYCLE/CAR **6** [C] (especially in compounds) a GEAR on a bicycle, in a car, etc: *a four-speed gearbox* ◇ *a ten-speed mountain bike.* Ⅎ WORDFINDER NOTE at CYCLING
• DRUG **7** [U] (*informal*) an illegal AMPHETAMINE drug that is taken to give feelings of excitement and energy
**IDM** **ˌfull ˈspeed/ˌsteam aˈhead** with as much speed or energy as possible **ˌup to ˈspeed (on sth) 1** (of a person, company, etc.) performing at an expected rate or level: *the cost of bringing the chosen schools up to speed* **2** (of a person) having the most recent and accurate information or knowledge: *Are you up to speed yet on the latest developments?* Ⅎ more at HASTE, TURN *n.*

■ *verb* (**speed·ed, speed·ed**) **HELP** In senses 1 and 2 **sped** is also used for the past tense and past participle.
• MOVE/HAPPEN QUICKLY **1** 🅞 B2 [I] + **adv./prep.** to move along quickly: *They sped off to get help.* **2** [T] **~ sb/sth + adv./prep.** (*formal*) to take sb/sth somewhere very quickly, especially in a vehicle: *The cab speeded them into the centre of the city.* **3** [T] **~ sth** (*formal*) to make sth happen more quickly: *The drugs will speed her recovery.*
• DRIVE TOO FAST **4** 🅞 B2 [I] (usually used in the progressive tenses) to drive faster than the speed that is legally allowed: *The police caught him speeding.*
**PHRV** **ˌspeed ˈup** | **ˌspeed sth↔ˈup** to move or happen faster; to make sth move or happen faster: *The train soon speeded up.* ◇ *Can you try and speed things up a bit?*

**speed·boat** /ˈspiːdbəʊt/ *noun* a boat with a motor that can travel very fast

**ˈspeed breaker** *noun* (*IndE*) a SPEED HUMP

**ˈspeed camera** *noun* (*BrE*) a machine which takes pictures of vehicles that are being driven faster than the legal limit. The pictures are then used as evidence so that the drivers can be punished.

**ˈspeed dating** *noun* [U] meeting people at an event organized for single people who want to begin a romantic relationship, where you are allowed to spend only a few minutes talking to one person before you have to move on to meet the next person

**ˈspeed dial** *noun* [U] a feature on a phone that allows numbers to be stored so that they can be called by pressing a single key: **on ~** *He's my best friend—I have him on speed dial.* ▶ **ˈspeed-dial** *verb* [I, T] (**-ll-**, *NAmE* **-l-**) **~ (sb/sth)**

**ˈspeed hump** (*especially BrE*) (*NAmE usually* **ˈspeed bump**) *noun* a raised area across a road that is put there to make traffic go slower Ⅎ WORDFINDER NOTE at TRAFFIC

**speed·ing** /ˈspiːdɪŋ/ *noun* [U] the traffic offence of driving faster than the legal limit

**ˈspeed limit** *noun* the highest speed at which you can legally drive on a particular road: *You should always keep to the speed limit.* ◇ **to break/exceed the speed limit** ◇ *The road has a 30 mph speed limit.*

**speedo** /ˈspiːdəʊ/ *noun* (*pl.* **-os**) **1** (*BrE, informal*) = SPEEDOMETER **2** **Speedo™** [usually pl.] a SWIMMING COSTUME, especially a style of tight TRUNKS for men and boys: *a pair of Speedos*

**speed·om·eter** /spiːˈdɒmɪtə(r); *NAmE* -ˈdɑːm-/ (*BrE also informal* **speedo**) *noun* an instrument in a vehicle which shows how fast the vehicle is going

**speed-read** /ˈspiːd riːd/ *verb* [I, T] **~ (sth)** to read sth very quickly, paying attention to the general meaning of sentences and phrases rather than to every word ▶ **ˈspeed-reading** *noun* [U]

**ˈspeed skating** *noun* [U] the sport of SKATING on ice as fast as possible Ⅎ compare FIGURE SKATING

**speed·ster** /ˈspiːdstə(r)/ *noun* (*informal*) **1** a person who drives a vehicle very fast **2** a machine or vehicle that works well at high speeds

**ˈspeed trap** (*BrE also* **ˈradar trap**) *noun* a place on a road where police use special equipment to catch drivers who are going faster than the legal limit

**speed·way** /ˈspiːdweɪ/ *noun* **1** [U] (*BrE*) the sport of racing motorcycles on a special track **2** [C] (*NAmE*) a special track for racing cars or motorcycles on

**speedy** /ˈspiːdi/ *adj.* (**speedi·er, speedi·est**) **1** happening or done quickly or without delay **SYN** **rapid**: *We wish you a speedy recovery* (= from an illness or injury). ◇ *a speedy reply* **2** moving or working very quickly: *speedy computers* Ⅎ note at FAST ▶ **speed·ily** *adv.*: *All enquiries will be dealt with as speedily as possible.*

**spele·olo·gist** /ˌspiːliˈɒlədʒɪst; *NAmE* -ˈɑːl-/ *noun* a scientist who studies CAVES or a person who goes into caves as a sport Ⅎ compare CAVER, POTHOLER (1), SPELUNKER (1) ▶ **spele·ology** /-dʒi/ *noun* [U]

**spell** 🅞 A1 /spel/ *verb, noun*

■ *verb* (**spelt, spelt** /spelt/ *or* **spelled, spelled**) **1** 🅞 A1 [T] **~ sth** to say or write the letters of a word in the correct order: *How do you spell your surname?* ◇ *You've spelt my name wrong.* ◇ **~ sth with sth** *I thought her name was Catherine, but it's Kathryn spelt with a 'K'.* **2** 🅞 A1 [I] to form words correctly from individual letters: *I've never been able to spell.* Ⅎ see also MISSPELL **3** 🅞 A1 [T] **~ sth** (of letters of a word) to form words when they are put together in a particular order: *C—A—T spells 'cat'.* **4** [T] **~ sth (for sb/sth)** to have sth, usually sth bad, as a result; to mean sth, usually sth bad: *The crop failure spelt disaster for many farmers.* **5** [T] **~ sb** (*NAmE, informal*) to replace for a short time sb who is doing a particular activity so that they can rest: *Carter will be here in an hour to spell you.*
**PHRV** **ˌspell sth↔ˈout 1** to explain sth in a simple, clear way: *You know what I mean—I'm sure I don't need to spell it out.* ◇ **spell out why, what, etc …** *Let me spell out why we need more money.* **2** to say or write the letters of a word in the right order: *Could you spell that name out again?*

■ *noun* **1** 🅞 C1 [C] a short period of time during which sth lasts: *a spell of warm weather* ◇ *a dry/cold spell* ◇ *There will be rain at first, with sunny spells later.* ◇ *She went to the doctor complaining of dizzy spells.* **2** 🅞 C1 [C] a period of time doing sth or working somewhere: *She had a spell as a singer before becoming an actress.* ◊ *I spent a **brief spell** on the Washington Post.* **3** [C] words that are thought to have magic power or to make a piece of magic work; a piece of magic that happens when sb says these magic words SYN **enchantment**: *a magic spell* ◊ *a book of spells* ◊ *The wizard recited a spell.* ◊ *to **cast/put a spell on sb*** ◊ ***under a~*** *to be under a spell* (= affected by magic) **4** [sing.] a quality that a person or thing has that makes them so attractive or interesting that they have a strong influence on you SYN **charm**: *I completely **fell under her spell**.* IDM see WEAVE v.

**spell·bind·ing** /ˈspelbaɪndɪŋ/ *adj.* holding your attention completely SYN **enthralling**: *a spellbinding performance*

**spell·bound** /ˈspelbaʊnd/ *adj.* [not usually before noun] with your attention completely held by what you are listening to or watching: *a storyteller who can hold audiences spellbound*

**spell·check** /ˈspeltʃek/ *verb* ~ **sth** to use a computer program to check your writing to see if your spelling is correct ▶ **spell·check** *noun* = SPELLCHECKER

**spell·check·er** /ˈspeltʃekə(r)/ (*also* **spell·check**) *noun* a computer program that checks your writing to see if your spelling is correct

**spell·er** /ˈspelə(r)/ *noun* if sb is a **good/bad speller**, they find it easy/difficult to spell words correctly

**spell·ing** /ˈspelɪŋ/ *noun* **1** [U] the act of forming words correctly from individual letters; the ability to do this: *the differences between British and American spelling* ◊ *My spelling is terrible.* ◊ *a spelling mistake/error* **2** [C] the way that a particular word is written: *a list of difficult spellings* ⇒ WORDFINDER NOTE at WORD

**'spelling bee** *noun* a competition in which people have to spell words

**spelt** /spelt/ *past tense, past part.* of SPELL

**spe·lunk·ing** /spəˈlʌŋkɪŋ/ (NAmE) (*especially BrE* **cav·ing**, *BrE* **pot·hol·ing**) *noun* [U] the sport or activity of going into CAVES under the ground ▶ **spe·lunk·er** (NAmE) (*especially BrE* **caver**, *BrE* **pot·holer**) *noun*

**spend** /spend/ *verb, noun*
■ *verb* (**spent, spent** /spent/) **1** [T, I] to give money to pay for goods, services, etc: *~sth I've spent all my money already.* ◊ *~sth on (doing) sth She spent £100 on a new dress.* ◊ *~sth doing sth The company has spent thousands of pounds updating their computer systems.* ◊ *I just can't seem to stop spending.* **2** [T] to use time for a particular purpose; to pass time: *~sth + adv./prep. We spent the day at the beach.* ◊ *I like to **spend time** with my friends.* ◊ *~sth on sth How long did you spend on your homework?* ◊ *~sth doing sth They spent the whole night talking.* ◊ *spend hours/days/months/years doing sth* ◊ *~sth in doing sth Most of her life was spent in caring for others.* **3** [T, often passive] to use energy, effort, etc., especially until it has all been used: *~sth on sth She spends too much effort on things that don't matter.* ◊ *~itself The storm had finally spent itself.* ⇒ see also SPENT
IDM **spend the 'night with sb 1** to stay with sb for a night: *My daughter's spending the night with a friend.* **2** (*also* **spend the 'night together**) to stay with sb for a night and have sex with them **spend a 'penny** (*old-fashioned, BrE*) people say 'spend a penny' to avoid saying 'use the toilet'
■ *noun* [sing.] (*informal*) the amount of money spent for a particular purpose or over a particular length of time: *The average spend at the cafe is £10 a head.*

**spend·er** /ˈspendə(r)/ *noun* a person who spends money in the particular way mentioned: *a big spender* (= who spends a lot of money)

**spend·ing** /ˈspendɪŋ/ *noun* [U] the amount of money that is spent by a government, an organization or a person: *to increase/cut/reduce spending* ◊ *government/federal spending* ◊ *defence/military spending* ◊ *~on sth More spending on education was promised.* ◊ *He went on a **spending spree** with his father's credit card.* ◊ *The government then had to impose severe **spending cuts**.* ◊ *Balancing the budget will mean significant **cuts in spending**.* ⇒ SYNONYMS at COST ⇒ see also PUBLIC SPENDING

**'spending money** *noun* [U] money that you can spend on personal things for pleasure or entertainment

**spend·thrift** /ˈspendθrɪft/ *noun* (*disapproving*) a person who spends too much money or who wastes money ▶ **spend·thrift** *adj.* [usually before noun]: *spendthrift governments*

**spendy** /ˈspendi/ *adj.* (**spend·ier, spendi·est**) (*informal*)
**1** expensive: *It's a really fun restaurant but a bit spendy.*
**2** spending a lot of money: *He's spendy—he buys luxury cars new.*

**spent** /spent/ *adj., verb*
■ *adj.* **1** [usually before noun] that has been used, so that it cannot be used again: *spent matches* **2** (*formal*) very tired SYN **exhausted**: *After the gruelling test, he felt totally spent.*
IDM **a spent 'force** a person or group that no longer has any power or influence
■ *verb past tense, past part.* of SPEND

**sperm** /spɜːm; NAmE spɜːrm/ *noun* (*pl.* **sperm** *or* **sperms**) **1** [C] a cell that is produced by the sex organs of a male and that can combine with a female egg to produce young: *He has a **low sperm count*** (= very few live male cells). **2** [U] the liquid that is produced by the male sex organs that contains these cells SYN **semen**

**sperm·ato·zoon** /ˌspɜːmətəˈzəʊən; NAmE ˌspɜːrm-/ *noun* (*pl.* **sperm·ato·zoa** /-ˈzəʊə/) (*biology*) a sperm

**'sperm bank** *noun* a place where sperm is kept and then used to help women become pregnant artificially

**spermi·cide** /ˈspɜːmɪsaɪd; NAmE ˈspɜːrm-/ *noun* [U, C] a substance that kills sperm, used during sex to prevent the woman from becoming pregnant ▶ **spermi·cidal** /ˌspɜːmɪˈsaɪdl; NAmE ˌspɜːrm-/ *adj.* [only before noun]

**'sperm whale** *noun* a large WHALE that is hunted for its oil and fat ⇒ VISUAL VOCAB page V2

**spew** /spjuː/ *verb* **1** [I, T] to flow out quickly, or to make sth flow out quickly, in large amounts: *+ adv./prep. Flames spewed from the aircraft's engine.* ◊ *~sth + adv./prep. Massive chimneys were spewing out smoke.* **2** [I, T] (*BrE, informal*) to VOMIT (= bring food from the stomach back out through the mouth): *~(up) He spewed up on the pavement.* ◊ *~sth (up) She spewed up the entire meal.*

**SPF** /ˌes piː ˈef/ *abbr.* sun protection factor (a number that tells you how much protection a particular cream or liquid gives you from the harmful effects of the sun)

**sphere** /sfɪə(r); NAmE sfɪr/ *noun* **1** (*geometry*) a solid figure that is completely round, with every point on its surface at an equal distance from the centre: *The Earth is not a perfect sphere.* ⇒ picture at SOLID **2** any object that is completely round, for example a ball **3** an area of activity, influence or interest; a particular section of society SYN **domain**: *the political sphere* ◊ *This area was formerly within the **sphere of influence** of the US.* ◊ *He and I moved in totally different social spheres.* **4 -sphere** (in nouns) a region that surrounds a planet, especially the earth: *ionosphere* ◊ *atmosphere*

**spher·ic·al** /ˈsferɪkl; NAmE ˈsfɪr-, ˈsfer-/ *adj.* like a sphere in shape SYN **round** ▶ **spher·ic·al·ly** /-kli/ *adv.*

**spher·oid** /ˈsfɪərɔɪd; NAmE ˈsfɪr-/ *noun* (*specialist*) a solid object that is approximately the same shape as a sphere

**sphinc·ter** /ˈsfɪŋktə(r)/ *noun* (*anatomy*) a ring of muscle that surrounds an opening in the body and can become tight to close it: *the anal sphincter*

**sphinx** /sfɪŋks/ *noun* (*often* **the Sphinx**) an ancient Egyptian stone statue of a creature with a human head and the body of a lion lying down. In ancient Greek stories the Sphinx spoke in RIDDLES.

**spice** /spaɪs/ *noun, verb*
■ *noun* **1** [C, U] one of the various types of powder or seed that come from plants and are used in cooking. Spices have a strong taste and smell: *common spices such as ginger and cinnamon* ◊ *a spice jar* ⇒ VISUAL VOCAB page

**spick** 1504

V8 **2** [U] extra interest or excitement: *We need an exciting trip to add some spice to our lives.* **3** [U] a powerful illegal SYNTHETIC (= artificial) drug that some people smoke for the physical and mental effects that it has on them: *spice, known as the 'zombie' drug.* IDM see VARIETY
- **verb 1** ~ sth (up) (with sth) to add spice to food in order to give it more taste **2** ~ sth (up) (with sth) to add interest or excitement to sth: *He exaggerated the details to spice up the story.*

**spick** /spɪk/ adj.
IDM ˌspick and ˈspan (also ˌspic and ˈspan) [not usually before noun] neat and clean: *Their house is always spick and span.*

**spicy** B1 /ˈspaɪsi/ adj. (spi·ci·er, spici·est) **1** B1 (of food) having a strong taste because spices have been added to it SYN hot: *I don't like spicy food.* ⇨ WORDFINDER NOTE at TASTE **2** (*informal*) (of a story, piece of news, etc.) exciting and making you feel slightly shocked ▸ **spici·ness** noun [U]

**spi·der** A2 /ˈspaɪdə(r)/ noun a small creature with eight thin legs. Many spiders SPIN webs to catch insects for food: *a poisonous spider* ⇨ VISUAL VOCAB page V3

**ˈspider monkey** noun a South American monkey with very long arms and legs and a long PREHENSILE tail ⇨ VISUAL VOCAB page V2

**ˈspider's web** (*especially BrE*) (also **spider-web** /ˈspaɪdə-web; NAmE -dərw-/ *especially in NAmE*) (also **web**) noun a fine net of THREAD made by a spider to catch insects: (*figurative*) *to be caught in a spider's web of confusion* ⇨ see also COBWEB

**spi·dery** /ˈspaɪdəri/ adj. long and thin, like the legs of a spider: *spidery fingers* ◊ *spidery writing* (= consisting of thin lines that are not very clear)

**spied** /spaɪd/ past tense, past part. of SPY

**spiel** /ʃpiːl, spiːl/ noun (*informal, usually disapproving*) a speech that sb has used many times that is intended to persuade you to believe sth or buy sth

**spies** /spaɪz/ **1** pl. of SPY **2** third person of SPY

**spiff** /spɪf/ verb
PHRV ˌspiff ˈup | ˌspiff sb/sth↔ˈup (NAmE, informal) to make yourself/sb/sth look neat and attractive

**spiffy** /ˈspɪfi/ adj. (spiffi·er, spiffi·est) (NAmE, informal) attractive and fashionable

**spig·ot** /ˈspɪɡət/ noun **1** (*specialist*) a device in a TAP that controls the flow of liquid from a container **2** (US) any TAP, especially one outdoors

**spike** /spaɪk/ noun, verb
- **noun 1** [C] a thin object with a sharp point, especially a pointed piece of metal, wood, etc.: *a row of iron spikes on a wall* ◊ *Her hair stood up in spikes.* **2** [C, usually pl.] a metal point attached to the SOLE of a sports shoe to prevent you from slipping while running ⇨ compare CLEAT **3** spikes [pl.] shoes fitted with these metal spikes, used for running: *a pair of spikes* **4** [C] a long pointed group of flowers that grow together on a single STEM **5** [C, usually sing.] a sudden large increase in sth: *a spike in oil prices*
- **verb 1** [T] ~ sb/sth (on sth) to push a sharp piece of metal, wood, etc. into sb/sth; to injure sth on a sharp point SYN stab **2** [T] ~ sth (with sth) to add alcohol, poison or a drug to sb's drink or food without them knowing: *He gave her a drink spiked with tranquillizers.* ◊ (*figurative*) *Her words were spiked with malice.* **3** [T] ~ sth to reject sth that a person has written or said; to prevent sth from happening or being made public: *The article was spiked for fear of legal action against the newspaper.* **4** [I] ~ (to sth) (*especially NAmE*) to rise quickly and reach a high value: *The US dollar spiked to a three-month high.*
IDM ˌspike sb's ˈguns (BrE) to cause the plans of an opponent to fail

**spiked** /spaɪkt/ adj. with one or more spikes: *spiked running shoes* ◊ *short spiked hair*

**spiky** /ˈspaɪki/ adj. (spiki·er, spiki·est) **1** having sharp points: *spiky plants, such as cacti* **2** (of hair) sticking straight up from the head **3** (BrE) (of people) easily annoyed or offended ▸ **spiki·ness** noun [U]

**spill** B2 /spɪl/ verb, noun
- **verb** (spilled, spilled or spilt, spilt /spɪlt/) **1** B2 [I, T] (especially of liquid) to flow over the edge of a container by accident; to make liquid do this: *Water had spilled out of the bucket onto the floor.* ◊ (*figurative*) *Light spilled from the windows.* ◊ ~ sth *He startled her and made her spill her drink.* ◊ *Thousands of gallons of crude oil were spilled into the ocean.* **2** [I] + adv./prep. (of people) to come out of a place in large numbers and spread out: *The doors opened and people spilled into the street.*
IDM ˌspill the ˈbeans (*informal*) to tell sb sth that should be kept secret or private **spill (sb's) ˈblood** (*formal* or *literary*) to kill or wound sb **spill your ˈguts (to sb)** (NAmE, *informal*) to tell sb everything you know or feel about sth, because you are upset ⇨ more at CRY v.
PHRV ˌspill sth↔ˈout | ˌspill ˈout to tell sb all about a problem etc. very quickly; to come out quickly: *Has she been spilling out her troubles to you again?* ◊ *When he started to speak, the words just spilled out.* ˌspill ˈover (into sth) **1** to fill a container and go over the edge: *She filled the glass so full that the water spilled over.* ◊ (*figurative*) *Her emotions suddenly spilled over.* **2** to start in one area and then affect other areas: *Unrest has spilt over into areas outside the city.* ⇨ related noun OVERSPILL, SPILLOVER
- **noun 1** [C] (also *formal* **spill·age** [U, C]) an act of letting a liquid come or fall out of a container; the amount of liquid that comes or falls out: *Many seabirds died as a result of the oil spill.* ◊ *I wiped up the coffee spills on the table.* **2** [C] a long match, or a thin piece of TWISTED paper, used for lighting fires, oil lamps, etc. **3** [C, usually sing.] a fall, especially from a bicycle or a boat: *to take a spill* IDM see THRILL n.

**spill·age** /ˈspɪlɪdʒ/ noun [U, C] (*formal*) = SPILL: *Put the bottle in a plastic bag in case of spillage.*

**spill·over** /ˈspɪləʊvə(r)/ noun [C, U] **1** something that is too much or too large for the place where it starts, and spreads to other places: *A second room was needed for the spillover of staff and reporters.* **2** the results or the effects of sth that have spread to other situations or places

**spill·way** /ˈspɪlweɪ/ noun (*specialist*) a passage for the extra water from a DAM (= a wall across a river that holds water back)

**spin** C1 /spɪn/ verb, noun
- **verb** (spin·ning, spun, spun /spʌn/)
- TURN ROUND QUICKLY **1** C1 [I, T] to turn round and round quickly; to make sth do this: (+ adv./prep.) *The plane was spinning out of control.* ◊ *a spinning ice skater* ◊ *My head is spinning* (= I feel as if my head is going round and I can't balance). ◊ ~ round/around *The dancers spun round and round.* ◊ ~ sth (round/around) *to spin a ball/coin/wheel* **2** C1 [I, T] ~ (sb) round/around | + adv./prep. to turn round quickly once; to make sb do this: *He spun around to face her.*
- MAKE THREAD **3** [I, T] to make THREAD from wool, cotton, silk, etc. by TWISTING it: *She sat by the window spinning.* ◊ ~ sth *to spin and knit wool* ◊ ~ A into B *spinning silk into thread* ◊ ~ B from A *spinning thread from silk*
- OF SPIDER/SILKWORM **4** [T] ~ sth to produce THREAD from its body to make a web or COCOON: *a spider spinning a web*
- DRIVE/TRAVEL QUICKLY **5** [I] + adv./prep. to drive or travel quickly: *They went spinning along the roads on their bikes.*
- DRY CLOTHES **6** [T] ~ sth to remove the water from clothes that have just been washed, in a SPIN DRYER
- PRESENT INFORMATION **7** [T] ~ sth (as sth) to present information or a situation in a particular way, especially one that makes you or your ideas seem good: *An aide was already spinning the senator's defeat as 'almost as good as an outright win'.*
IDM ˌspin (sb) a ˈyarn, ˈtale, etc. to try to make sb believe a long story that is not true ⇨ more at HEAD n., HEEL n.
PHRV ˌspin ˈoff (from sth) | ˌspin sth↔ˈoff (from sth) to happen or to produce sth as a new or unexpected result of sth that already exists: *products spinning off from favourite*

books ◊ related noun SPIN-OFF **ˌspin sth↔ˈoff** (*business, especially NAmE*) to form a new company from parts of an existing one: *The transportation operation will be spun off into a separate company.* **ˌspin sth↔ˈout** to make sth last as long as possible
■ noun
- FAST TURNING MOVEMENT **1** 💡+ B1 [C, U] a very fast turning movement: *the earth's spin ◊ the spin of a wheel ◊ Give the washing a short spin.* **2** [C, usually sing.] if an aircraft goes into a **spin**, it falls and turns round rapidly ⊃ see also FLAT SPIN
- IN CAR **3** [C] (*informal, becoming old-fashioned*) a short ride in a car for pleasure: *Let's go for a spin.*
- IN TENNIS/CRICKET **4** [U] the way you make a ball turn very fast when you throw it or hit it: *She puts a lot of spin on the ball.* ◊ *a spin bowler* (= in CRICKET, a BOWLER who uses spin) ⊃ see also TOPSPIN
- ON INFORMATION **5** [sing., U] (*informal*) a way of presenting information or a situation in a particular way, especially one that makes you or your ideas seem good: *Politicians put their own spin on the economic situation.*
IDM **in a (flat) ˈspin** very confused, worried or excited: *Her resignation put her colleagues in a spin.*

**spina bifˈiˈda** /ˌspaɪnə ˈbɪfɪdə/ *noun* [U] a medical condition in which some bones in the SPINE have not developed normally at birth, often causing PARALYSIS (= loss of control or feeling) in the legs

**spinˈach** /ˈspɪnɪtʃ, -ɪdʒ/ *noun* [U] a vegetable with large, dark-green leaves that are cooked or eaten in salads

**spinal** /ˈspaɪnl/ *adj.* [usually before noun] (*specialist*) connected with the SPINE (= the long bone in the back): *spinal injuries*

**ˈspinal ˈcolumn** *noun* the SPINE

**ˈspinal ˈcord** *noun* the mass of nerves inside the SPINE that connects all parts of the body to the brain ⊃ VISUAL VOCAB page V1

**ˈspinal ˈtap** *noun* [C] (*NAmE*) (*also* **ˈlumbar ˈpuncture** [C, U] *BrE and NAmE*) (*medical*) a medical procedure in which liquid is removed from the lower part of the SPINE with a hollow needle, usually in order to DIAGNOSE a medical problem (= identify what it is)

**spinˈdle** /ˈspɪndl/ *noun* **1** a long straight part that turns in a machine, or that another part of the machine turns around **2** a thin pointed piece of wood used for SPINNING wool into THREAD by hand

**spindly** /ˈspɪndli/ *adj.* (*informal, often disapproving*) very long and thin and not strong: *spindly legs*

**ˈspin ˈdoctor** *noun* (*informal*) a person whose job is to present information to the public about a politician, an organization, etc. in the way that seems most positive

**spine** 💡+ C1 /spaɪn/ *noun* **1** 💡+ C1 the row of small bones that are connected together down the middle of the back SYN **backbone**: *A shiver went down my spine.* ⊃ VISUAL VOCAB page V1 **2** the central feature of sth or the main source of its strength: *These speeches form the spine of his election campaign.* **3** strength of character **4** any of the sharp, pointed parts like needles on some plants and animals: *Porcupines use their spines to protect themselves.* ⊃ see also SPINY **5** the narrow part of the cover of a book that the pages are joined to

**ˈspine-chilling** *adj.* (of a book, film, etc.) frightening in an exciting way ▶ **ˈspine-chiller** *noun*

**spineˈless** /ˈspaɪnləs/ *adj.* **1** (*disapproving*) (of people) weak and easily frightened **2** (of animals) having no SPINE (= the long bone in the back) **3** (of animals or plants) having no SPINES (= sharp parts like needles)

**ˈspine-tingling** *adj.* (of an event, a piece of music, etc.) pleasant or fun because it is very exciting or frightening

**spinˈnaker** /ˈspɪnəkə(r)/ *noun* a large extra sail on a racing YACHT that you use when the wind is coming from behind

**spinˈner** /ˈspɪnə(r)/ *noun* **1** (IN CRICKET) a BOWLER who uses SPIN when throwing the ball **2** a person who SPINS wool into THREAD **3** a device that turns round and round, used on a fishing line to attract fish

**spinˈney** /ˈspɪni/ *noun* (*BrE*) a small area of trees SYN **copse**

**spinˈning** /ˈspɪnɪŋ/ *noun* [U] **1** the art or the process of TWISTING wool, etc. to make THREAD **2** Spinning™ a type of exercise performed on an EXERCISE BIKE, usually in a class

**ˈspinning ˈwheel** *noun* a simple machine that people used in their homes in the past for TWISTING wool, etc. It has a large wheel operated with the foot.

**ˈspin-off** *noun* **1** ~ **(from/of sth)** an unexpected but useful result of an activity that is designed to produce sth else: *commercial spin-offs from medical research* **2** ~ **(from/of sth)** a book, a film, a television programme, or an object that is based on a book, film or television series that has been very successful: *The TV comedy series is a spin-off of the original movie.* ◊ *spin-off merchandise from the latest Disney movie*

**spinˈster** /ˈspɪnstə(r)/ *noun* (*old-fashioned, often disapproving*) a woman who is not married, especially an older woman who is not likely to marry HELP This word should not now be used to mean simply a woman who is not married. ⊃ compare BACHELOR ▶ **spinˈsterˈhood** /ˈspɪnstəhʊd/ *NAmE* -stərh-/ *noun* [U]: *For most women, marriage used to bring a higher status than spinsterhood.*

**spiny** /ˈspaɪni/ *adj.* (of animals or plants) having sharp points like needles ⊃ see also SPINE

**ˈspiny ˈanteater** *noun* = ECHIDNA

**spiral** /ˈspaɪrəl/ *noun, adj., verb*
■ noun **1** a shape or design, consisting of a continuous curved line that winds around a central point, with each curve further away from the centre: *The birds circled in a slow spiral above the house.* **2** a continuous harmful increase or decrease in sth, that gradually gets faster and faster: *the destructive spiral of violence in the inner cities* ◊ *measures to control the inflationary spiral* ◊ *the* **upward/downward spiral** *of sales*

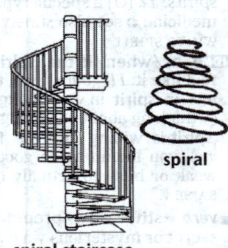
spiral staircase

■ adj. moving in a continuous curve that winds around a central point: *A snail's shell is spiral in form.* ▶ **spirˈalˈly** /-rəli/ *adv.*
■ verb (-ll-, *NAmE usually* -l-) **1** [I] (+ **adv./prep.**) to move in continuous circles, going upwards or downwards: *The plane spiralled down to the ground.* **2** [I] to increase rapidly: *the spiralling cost of healthcare* ◊ + **adv./prep.** *Prices are spiralling out of control.*
PHRV **spiral ˈdown/ˈdownward/ˈdownwards** to decrease rapidly **spiral ˈup/ˈupward/ˈupwards** to increase rapidly

**ˈspiral-ˈbound** *adj.* (of a book) held together by wire which is wound through holes along one edge

**ˈspiral ˈstaircase** *noun* a set of stairs that go upwards in a curve around a central post ⊃ picture at SPIRAL

**spire** /ˈspaɪə(r)/ *noun* a tall pointed structure on the top of a building, especially a church

**spirit** 🌐 B1 /ˈspɪrɪt/ *noun, verb*
■ noun
- MIND/FEELINGS/CHARACTER **1** 💡+ B1 [U, C] the part of a person that includes their mind, feelings and character rather than their body: *the power of the human spirit to overcome difficulties* **2** **spirits** [pl.] a person's feelings or state of mind: *They were all in good spirits as they set out.* ◊ *You must try and keep your spirits up* (= stay cheerful). ◊ *a song that never fails to lift my spirits* ◊ *My spirits sank at the prospect of starting all over again.* **3** [C] (always with an adjective) a person of the type mentioned: *a brave*

# spirited

*spirit* ◇ **kindred spirits** (= people who like the same things as you) ◇ see also FREE SPIRIT
- **COURAGE/ENERGY 4** [B2] [U] courage, energy or DETERMINATION: *Show a little fighting spirit.* ◇ *They took away his freedom and broke his spirit.* ◇ **with~** *Although the team lost, they played with tremendous spirit.*
- **FEELINGS OF SUPPORT 5** [B2] [U, sing.] feelings of support towards a group, team or society: *There's not much community spirit around here.* ◇ see also PUBLIC SPIRIT, TEAM SPIRIT
- **TYPICAL QUALITY 6** [B2] [sing.] the typical or most important quality or mood of sth: **~ of sth** *The exhibition captures the spirit of the age/times.*
- **ATTITUDE 7** [sing.] a state of mind or mood; an attitude: *We approached the situation in the wrong spirit.* ◇ *'OK, I'll try'. 'That's the spirit* (= the right attitude).*' ◇ *The party went well because everyone entered into the spirit of things.* ◇ see also PARTY SPIRIT
- **REAL MEANING 8** [U] the real or intended meaning or purpose of sth: *Obey the spirit, not the letter* (= the narrow meaning of the words) *of the law.*
- **SOUL 9** [B2] [C] the soul thought of as separate from the body and believed to live on after death; a ghost: *It was believed that people could be possessed by evil spirits.* ◇ *a message from the spirit world* ◇ see also HOLY SPIRIT
- **IMAGINARY CREATURE 10** [C] (*old-fashioned*) an imaginary creature with magic powers, for example, a FAIRY or an ELF
- **ALCOHOL 11** [B2] [C, usually pl.] (*especially BrE*) a strong alcoholic drink: *I don't drink whisky or brandy or any other spirits.* **12** [U] a special type of alcohol used in industry or medicine ◇ see also METHYLATED SPIRIT, SURGICAL SPIRIT, WHITE SPIRIT

**IDM** **as/when/if the spirit ˈmoves you** as/when/if you feel like it: *I'll go for a run this evening, if the spirit moves me.* **in ˈspirit** in your thoughts: *I shall be with you in spirit* (= thinking about you though not with you physically). **the ˈspirit is ˈwilling (but the ˈflesh is ˈweak)** (*humorous, saying*) you intend to do good things but you are too lazy, weak or busy to actually do them ◇ more at FIGHTING, RAISE v.

■ *verb* **~ sth + adv./prep.** to take sb/sth away in a quick, secret or mysterious way: *After the concert, the band was spirited away before their fans could get near them.*

**spir·it·ed** /ˈspɪrɪtɪd/ *adj.* [usually before noun] full of energy, courage or DETERMINATION: *a spirited young woman* ◇ *a spirited discussion* ◇ *She put up a spirited defence in the final game.* ◇ compare DISPIRITED ◇ see also FREE-SPIRITED, HIGH-SPIRITED, PUBLIC-SPIRITED ▶ **spir·it·ed·ly** *adv.*

**spir·it·less** /ˈspɪrɪtləs/ *adj.* (*formal*) without energy or enthusiasm

**ˈspirit level** (*also* **level**) *noun* a device used to test whether a surface is level, consisting of a glass tube partly filled with liquid with a bubble of air inside. The position of the bubble indicates whether the surface is level. ◇ picture at PLANE

**spir·it·ual** ❶ [B2] /ˈspɪrɪtʃuəl/ *adj., noun*
■ *adj.* [usually before noun] **1** [B2] connected with the human spirit, rather than the body or physical things: *His music leads us on a spiritual journey.* ◇ *the human capacity for spiritual growth* ◇ *a lack of spiritual values in the modern world* ◇ *We're concerned about your spiritual welfare.* **OPP** material **2** [B2] connected with religion: *a spiritual leader* ◇ compare TEMPORAL ▶ **spir·it·ual·ly** /-əli/ *adv.: a spiritually uplifting book*
**IDM** **your spiritual ˈhome** the place where you are happiest, especially a country where you feel you belong more than in your own country because you share the ideas and attitudes of the people who live there
■ *noun* (*also* **ˌNegro ˈspiritual**) a religious song of the type originally sung by black slaves in America

**spir·it·ual·ism** /ˈspɪrɪtʃuəlɪzəm/ *noun* [U] the belief that people who have died can send messages to living people, usually through a MEDIUM (= a person who has special powers)

**spir·it·ual·ist** /ˈspɪrɪtʃuəlɪst/ *noun* a person who believes that people who have died can send messages to living people

**spir·it·u·al·ity** /ˌspɪrɪtʃuˈæləti/ *noun* [U] the quality of being connected with religion or the human spirit

**spir·it·u·al·ized** (*BrE also* **-ised**) /ˈspɪrɪtʃuəlaɪzd/ *adj.* (*formal*) raised to a spiritual level: *She tends to have intense, spiritualized friendships.*

**spit** /spɪt/ *verb, noun*
■ *verb* (**spit·ting, spat, spat** /spæt/ **HELP** **spit** is also sometimes used for the past tense and past participle, especially in NAmE)
- **FROM MOUTH 1** [T] to force liquid, food, etc. out of your mouth: **~ sth (out)** *She took a mouthful of food and then suddenly spat it out.* ◇ **~ sth (from sth)** *He was spitting blood from a badly cut lip.* **2** [I] to force SALIVA (= the liquid that is produced in the mouth) out of your mouth, often as a sign of anger or lack of respect: *He coughed and spat.* ◇ **~ at/on/in sb/sth** *The prisoners were spat on by their guards.* ◇ *She spat in his face and went out.*
- **SAY STH ANGRILY 3** [T] to say sth in an angry or aggressive way: **+ speech** *'You liar!' she spat.* ◇ **~ sth (at sb)** *He was dragged out of the court, spitting abuse at the judge and jury.*
- **OF AN ANIMAL 4** [I] to make a short angry sound: *Snakes spit and hiss when they are cornered.*
- **OF STH COOKING/BURNING 5** [I] to make a noise and throw out fat, SPARKS, etc.: *sausages spitting in the frying pan* ◇ *The logs on the fire crackled and spat.*
- **RAIN 6** [I] (*informal*) (only used in the progressive tenses) when **it is spitting**, it is raining lightly

**IDM** **spit it ˈout** (*informal*) usually used in orders to tell sb to say sth when they seem frightened or unwilling to speak: *If you've got something to say, spit it out!* **spit ˈvenom/ˈblood** to show that you are very angry; to speak in an angry way ◇ more at DISTANCE n.
**PHRV** **spit ˈup** (*NAmE, informal*) (especially of a baby) to VOMIT (= bring food from the stomach back out through the mouth)

■ *noun*
- **IN/FROM MOUTH 1** [U] the liquid that is produced in your mouth **SYN** **saliva 2** [C, usually sing.] the act of spitting liquid or food out of your mouth
- **PIECE OF LAND 3** [C] a long, thin piece of land that sticks out into the sea, a lake, etc.
- **FOR COOKING MEAT 4** [C] a long, thin, straight piece of metal that you put through meat to hold and turn it while you cook it over a fire

**IDM** **ˌspit and ˈpolish** (*informal*) careful and complete cleaning and POLISHING of sth

**spite** [B2] [B2] /spaɪt/ *noun, verb*
■ *noun* [B2] [U] a feeling of wanting to hurt or upset sb **SYN** malice: **out of ~** *I'm sure he only said it out of spite.*
**IDM** **in ˈspite of sth** [B2] [B2] if you say that sb did sth **in spite of** a fact, you mean it is surprising that that fact did not prevent them from doing it **SYN** despite: *In spite of his age, he still leads an active life.* ◇ *They went swimming in spite of all the danger signs.* ◇ *English became the official language for business in spite of the fact that the population was largely Chinese.* ◇ LANGUAGE BANK at HOWEVER **in ˈspite of yourself** if you do sth **in spite of yourself**, you do it although you did not intend or expect to: *He fell asleep, in spite of himself.*
■ *verb* (only used in the infinitive with *to*) **~ sb** to deliberately annoy or upset sb: *They're playing the music so loud just to spite us.* **IDM** see NOSE *n.*

**spite·ful** /ˈspaɪtfl/ *adj.* behaving in an unkind way in order to hurt or upset sb **SYN** malicious: *a spiteful child* ◇ *He made some very spiteful remarks to me.* ▶ **spite·ful·ly** /-fəli/ *adv.: 'I don't need you,' she said spitefully.* **spite·ful·ness** *noun* [U]

**ˈspit-roast** *verb* **~ sth** to cook meat on a SPIT

**ˈspitting ˈimage** *noun*
**IDM** **be the spitting image of sb** to look exactly like sb else: *She's the spitting image of her mother.*

**spit·tle** /ˈspɪtl/ *noun* [U] (*old-fashioned*) the liquid that forms in the mouth **SYN** saliva, spit

**spiv** /spɪv/ noun (old-fashioned, BrE, slang, disapproving) a man who makes his money by being dishonest in business, especially one who dresses in a way that makes people believe he is rich and successful

**splash** /splæʃ/ verb, noun
- verb **1** [I] + adv./prep. (of liquid) to fall noisily onto a surface: *Water splashed onto the floor.* ◊ *Rain splashed against the windows.* **2** [T] to make sb/sth wet by making water, mud, etc. fall on them/it: ~ sth on/onto/over sb/sth *He splashed cold water on his face.* ◊ ~ sb/sth with sth *He splashed his face with cold water.* ◊ *My clothes were splashed with mud.* ◊ ~ sb/sth *Stop splashing me!* **3** [I] (+ adv./prep.) to move through water making drops fly everywhere: *The kids were splashing through the puddles.* ◊ *People were having fun in the pool, swimming or just splashing around.* **4** [T] ~ sth with sth [usually passive] to decorate sth with areas of bright colour, not in a regular pattern: *The walls were splashed with patches of blue and purple.*
- **PHRV** **ˈsplash sth across/over sth** to put a photograph, news story, etc. in a place where it will be easily noticed **ˌsplash ˈdown** (of a SPACECRAFT) to land in the sea or ocean ⊃ related noun SPLASHDOWN **ˌsplash ˈout (on sth)** | **ˌsplash sth↔ˈout (on/for sth)** (BrE, informal) to spend a lot of money on sth: *We're going to splash out and buy a new car.* ◊ *He splashed out hundreds of pounds on designer clothes.*
- noun **1** [C] the sound of sth hitting liquid or of liquid hitting sth: *We heard the splash when she fell into the pool.* **2** [C] a small amount of liquid that falls onto sth; the mark that this makes: *splashes of water on the floor* ◊ *dark splashes of mud on her skirt* **3** [C] a small area of bright colour or light that contrasts with the colours around it: *These flowers will give a splash of colour throughout the summer.* ⊃ WORDFINDER NOTE at PATTERN **4** [sing.] (informal) a small amount of liquid that you add to a drink: *coffee with just a splash of milk* ⊃ compare DASH **5** [sing.] an article in a newspaper, etc. that is intended to attract a lot of attention
- **IDM** **make, cause, etc. a ˈsplash** (informal) to do sth in a way that attracts a lot of attention or causes a lot of excitement

**splash·back** /ˈsplæʃbæk/ noun (BrE) a surface behind a sink or cooker which protects the wall from liquids

**splash·down** /ˈsplæʃdaʊn/ noun [C, U] a landing of a SPACECRAFT in the sea

**splashy** /ˈsplæʃi/ adj. (**splash·i·er**, **splashi·est**) (especially NAmE) bright and very easy to notice

**splat** /splæt/ noun [sing.] (informal) the sound made by sth wet hitting a surface with force: *The tomato hit the wall with a splat.* ▶ **splat** adv.: *The omelette fell splat onto the floor.*

**splat·ter** /ˈsplætə(r)/ verb **1** [I] (+ adv./prep.) (of large drops of liquid) to fall or hit sth noisily: *Heavy rain splattered on the roof.* **2** [T, I] to drop or throw water, paint, mud, etc. on sb/sth; to get sb/sth wet or dirty by landing on them in large drops: ~ sb/sth (+ adv./prep.) *The walls were splattered with blood.* ◊ + adv./prep. *Coffee had splattered across the front of his shirt.*

**splay** /spleɪ/ verb [T, I] ~ (sth) (out) to make fingers, legs, etc. become further apart from each other or spread out; to be spread out wide apart: *She lay on the bed, her arms and legs splayed out.* ◊ *His long fingers splayed across her back.*

**spleen** /spliːn/ noun **1** [C] a small organ near the stomach that controls the quality of the blood cells: *a ruptured spleen* ⊃ VISUAL VOCAB page V1 **2** [U] (literary) anger: *He vented his spleen* (= shouted in an angry way) *on the assembled crowd.* ⊃ see also SPLENETIC

**splen·did** /ˈsplendɪd/ adj., exclamation
- adj. (especially BrE) **1** very impressive; very beautiful: *splendid scenery* ◊ *The hotel stands in splendid isolation, surrounded by moorland.* **2** (old-fashioned) excellent; very good **SYN** great: *What a splendid idea!* ◊ *We've all had a splendid time.* ▶ **splen·did·ly** adv.: *You all played splendidly.*

- exclamation (old-fashioned, especially BrE) used to show that you approve of sth, or are pleased: *You're both coming? Splendid!*

**splen·dour** (US **splen·dor**) /ˈsplendə(r)/ noun **1** [U] grand and impressive beauty **SYN** grandeur: *a view of Rheims Cathedral, in all its splendour* ◊ *The palace has been restored to its former splendour.* **2** **splendours** [pl.] the beautiful and impressive features or qualities of sth, especially a place: *the splendours of Rome* (= its fine buildings, etc.)

**splen·et·ic** /spləˈnetɪk/ adj. (formal) often annoyed and angry

**splice** /splaɪs/ verb, noun
- verb **1** ~ sth (together) to join the ends of two pieces of rope by TWISTING them together **2** ~ sth (together) to join the ends of two pieces of film, tape, etc. by sticking them together
- **IDM** **get ˈspliced** (old-fashioned, BrE, informal) to get married
- noun the place where two pieces of film, tape, rope, etc. have been joined

**spliff** /splɪf/ noun (BrE, slang) a cigarette containing CANNABIS

**splint** /splɪnt/ noun a long piece of wood or metal that is tied to a broken arm or leg to keep it still and in the right position

**splin·ter** /ˈsplɪntə(r)/ noun, verb
- noun a small, thin, sharp piece of wood, metal, glass, etc. that has broken off a larger piece **SYN** shard
- verb **1** [I, T] (of wood, glass, stone, etc.) to break, or to make sth break, into small, thin, sharp pieces **SYN** shatter: *The mirror cracked but did not splinter.* ◊ ~ sth *The impact splintered the wood.* **2** [I] (of a group of people) to divide into smaller groups that are no longer connected; to separate from a larger group: *The party began to splinter.* ◊ ~ (off) (from sth) *Several firms have splintered off from the original company.*

**ˈsplinter group** noun a small group of people that has separated from a larger one, especially in politics

**split** /splɪt/ verb, noun
- verb (**split·ting**, **split**, **split**)
- • DIVIDE **1** [T, I] to divide, or to make sth divide, into two or more parts: ~ sth *He was a member of the team that split the atom in 1932.* ◊ ~ sth into sth *She split the class into groups of four.* ◊ *If the nail you use is too big, there's a chance that the wood will split.* ⊃ see also SPLIT SB UP **2** [T] to divide sth into two or more parts and share it between different people, activities, etc.: ~ sth (with sb) *She split the money she won with her brother.* ◊ ~ sth between A and B *His time is split between the London and Paris offices.* ⊃ see also SPLIT SB UP **3** [I, T] to divide, or to make a group of people divide, into smaller groups that have very different opinions: ~ on/over sth *The committee split over government subsidies.* ◊ ~ sth *His candidacy split the Republican vote.*
- • TEAR **4** [I, T] to tear, or to make sth tear, along a straight line: *Her dress had split along the seam.* ◊ ~ sth *Don't tell me you've split another pair of pants!* ◊ ~ (sth) open *The cushion split open and sent feathers everywhere.*
- • CUT **5** [T] to cut sb's skin and make it BLEED: ~ sth open *She split her head open on the cupboard door.* ◊ ~ sth *How did you split your lip?*
- • END RELATIONSHIP **6** [I] (informal) to leave sb and stop having a relationship with them: ~ (with sb) *The singer split with his wife last June.* ◊ ~ (from sb) *She intends to split from the band at the end of the tour.* ⊃ see also SPLIT UP (WITH SB)
- • LEAVE **7** [I] (old-fashioned, informal) to leave a place quickly: *Let's split!*
- **IDM** **ˌsplit the ˈdifference** (when discussing a price, etc.) to agree on an amount that is at an equal distance between the two amounts that have been suggested **ˌsplit ˈhairs** to pay too much attention in an argument to differences that are very small and not important **ˌsplit an ˈinfinitive** to place an adverb between 'to' and the infinitive of a verb,

# split end

for example to say 'to strongly deny the report'. Some people consider this to be bad English style. **split your 'sides (laughing/with laughter)** to laugh a lot at sb/sth **split the 'ticket** (*US, politics*) to vote for candidates from more than one party ⊃ more at MIDDLE *n.*
**PHR V** ˌsplit aˈway/ˈoff (from sth) | ˌsplit sth↔aˈway/ ˈoff (from sth) to separate from, or to separate sth from, a larger object or group: *A rebel faction has split away from the main group.* ◇ *The storm split a branch off from the main trunk.* ˌsplit on sb (to sb) (*BrE, informal*) to tell sb in authority about sth wrong, dishonest, etc. that sb else has done: *Don't worry—he won't split on us.* ˌsplit ˈup (with sb) to stop having a relationship with sb: *My parents split up last year.* ◇ *She's split up with her boyfriend.* ˌsplit sb ˈup to make two people stop having a relationship with each other: *My friend is doing her best to split us up.* ˌsplit sb ˈup | ˌsplit ˈup to divide a group of people into smaller parts; to become divided up in this way: *We were split up into groups to discuss the question.* ◇ *Let's split up now and meet again at lunchtime.* ˌsplit sth↔ˈup to divide sth into smaller parts: *The day was split up into 6 one-hour sessions.*
- **noun**
- DISAGREEMENT **1** [C] an argument or DISAGREEMENT that divides a group of people or makes sb separate from sb else: *~ in/within sth a damaging split within the party leadership* ◇ *~ with/between sth the years following his bitter split with his wife* ◇ *~ between A and B There have been reports of a split between the Prime Minister and the Cabinet.*
- TEAR/HOLE **2** [C] a long opening made when sth tears: *~ in sth There's a big split in the tent.*
- DIVISION **3** [*sing.*] a division between two or more things; one of the parts that sth is divided into: *He demanded a 50–50 split in the profits.*
- BODY POSITION **4 the splits** [*pl.*] (*US also* **split** [*sing.*]) a position in which you stretch your legs flat across the floor in opposite directions with the rest of your body sitting straight up: *a gymnast doing the splits* ⊃ see also BANANA SPLIT

ˌsplit ˈend *noun* a hair on your head that has divided into parts at the end because it is dry or in poor condition

ˌsplit inˈfinitive *noun* (*grammar*) the form of the verb with 'to', with an adverb placed between 'to' and the verb, as in *She seems to really like it.* Some people consider this to be bad English style.

ˌsplit-ˈlevel *adj.* (of a room, floor, etc.) having parts at different levels

ˌsplit ˈpea *noun* (*usually pl.*) a type of dried PEA, split into halves

ˌsplit ˈscreen *noun* a way of displaying two or more pictures or pieces of information at the same time on a television, cinema or computer screen ▶ ˌsplit-ˈscreen *adj.* [*only before noun*]: *a movie with several split-screen sequences*

ˌsplit ˈsecond *noun* a very short moment of time: **for a ~** *Their eyes met for a split second.*

ˌsplit-ˈsecond *adj.* [*only before noun*] done very quickly or very accurately: *She had to make a split-second decision.* ◇ *The success of the raid depended on split-second timing.*

ˌsplit ˈshift *noun* two separate periods of time that you spend working in a single day, with several hours between them: *I work split shifts in a busy restaurant.*

ˈsplit·ting /ˈsplɪtɪŋ/ *adj.* [*only before noun*] if you have a **splitting headache**, you have a very bad pain in your head

splodge /splɒdʒ; *NAmE* splɑːdʒ/ (*BrE*) (*also* splotch /splɒtʃ; *NAmE* splɑːtʃ/ *NAmE, BrE*) *noun* a large mark or spot of INK, paint, mud, etc., a small area of colour or light

splosh /splɒʃ; *NAmE* splɑːʃ/ *verb, noun* (*BrE, informal*)
- **verb** [I] + *adv./prep.* to move through water, making soft sounds: *Children were sploshing about in the pool.*
- **noun 1** the soft sound of sth moving through or falling into water **2** a small amount of liquid that moves through the air

splurge /splɜːdʒ; *NAmE* splɜːrdʒ/ *noun, verb*
- **noun** [*usually sing.*] (*informal*) an act of spending a lot of money on sth that you do not really need
- **verb** [T, I] **~ (sth) (out) (on sth)** (*informal*) to spend a lot of money on sth that you do not really need

splut·ter /ˈsplʌtə(r)/ *verb, noun*
- **verb 1** [T, I] to speak quickly and with difficulty, making soft SPITTING sounds, because you are angry or embarrassed SYN sputter: + *speech* (*informal*) *'But, but … you can't!' she spluttered.* ◇ **~ (with sth)** *Her father spluttered with indignation.* **2** [I] to make a series of short EXPLOSIVE sounds SYN sputter: *The firework spluttered and went out.* ◇ *She fled from the blaze, coughing and spluttering.*
- **noun** a short EXPLOSIVE sound: *The car started with a loud splutter.*

spoil **B2** /spɔɪl/ *verb, noun*
- **verb** (spoiled, spoiled /spɔɪld/ (*BrE also* spoilt, spoilt /spɔɪlt/) **1** [T] **~ sth** to change sth good into sth bad, unpleasant, etc. SYN ruin: *Our camping trip was spoilt by bad weather.* ◇ *Don't let him spoil your evening.* ◇ *The tall buildings have spoiled the view.* ◇ *Don't eat too many nuts —you'll spoil your appetite* (= will no longer be hungry at the proper time to eat). **2** [T] **~ sb** to give a child everything that they ask for and not enough discipline in a way that has a bad effect on their character and behaviour SYN overindulge: *She spoils those kids of hers.* **3** [T] **~ sb/yourself** to make sb/yourself happy by doing sth special: *Why not spoil yourself with a weekend in a top hotel?* ◇ *He really spoiled me on my birthday.* **4** [I] (of food) to become bad so that it can no longer be eaten SYN go off **5** [T] **~ sth** to mark a BALLOT PAPER in a way that is not correct so the vote does not count, especially as a form of protest
  **IDM** be ˈspoiling for a ˈfight to want to fight with sb very much ⊃ more at COOK *n.*
- **noun 1 the spoils** [*pl.*] (*formal or literary*) goods taken from a place by thieves or by an army that has won a battle or war **2 spoils** [*pl.*] the profits or advantages that sb gets from being successful: *the spoils of high office* **3** [U] (*specialist*) waste material that is brought up when a hole is dug, etc.

spoil·age /ˈspɔɪlɪdʒ/ *noun* [U] (*specialist*) the DECAY (= the process of being destroyed) of food which means that it can no longer be used

spoil·er /ˈspɔɪlə(r)/ *noun* **1** a part of an aircraft's wing that can be raised in order to interrupt the flow of air over it and so slow the aircraft's speed **2** a raised part on a fast car that prevents it from being lifted off the road when travelling very fast **3** (*especially NAmE*) a candidate for a political office who is unlikely to win but who may get enough votes to prevent one of the main candidates from winning **4** a person or thing that intends or is intended to stop sb/sth being successful **5** information that you are given about what is going to happen in a film, television series, etc. before it is shown to the public: *In the final episode (spoiler alert) he gets shot.* ◇ *Warning: this review contains spoilers.* **6** a news story, book, etc. that is produced very quickly in order to take attention away from one produced by a competitor that appears at the same time

spoil·sport /ˈspɔɪlspɔːt; *NAmE* -spɔːrt/ *noun* (*informal*) a person who stops other people from having fun, for example by not taking part in an activity or by trying to prevent other people from doing it: *Don't be such a spoilsport!*

spoilt /spɔɪlt/ (*BrE*) (*also* spoiled /spɔɪld/ *NAmE, BrE*) *adj.* (of a child) rude and badly behaved because they are given everything they ask for and not enough discipline: *a spoiled brat* ◇ *He's spoilt rotten* (= a lot).
**IDM** be spoilt for ˈchoice (*BrE*) to have such a lot of things to choose from that it is very difficult to make a decision

spoke /spəʊk; *NAmE* spoʊk/ *noun, verb*
- **noun** one of the thin bars or long, straight pieces of metal that connect the centre of a wheel to its outer edge, for example on a bicycle
**IDM** put a ˈspoke in sb's ˈwheel (*BrE*) to prevent sb from putting their plans into operation
- **verb** past tense of SPEAK

**spoken** 🔊 B1 /ˈspəʊkən/ adj. **1** B1 involving speaking rather than writing; expressed in speech rather than in writing: *spoken English* ◇ *The spoken language differs considerably from the written language.* **2** (following an adverb) speaking in the way mentioned: *a quietly spoken man* ➲ see also OUTSPOKEN, PLAIN-SPOKEN, SOFT-SPOKEN, WELL SPOKEN

▼ **SYNONYMS**

**spoken**
oral • vocal

These words all describe producing language using the voice, rather than writing.

**spoken** (of language) produced using the voice; said rather than written: *an exam in spoken English*

**oral** [usually before noun] spoken rather than written: *There will be a test of both oral and written French.*

**SPOKEN OR ORAL?**
Both of these words can be used to refer to language skills and the communication of information: *spoken/oral French* ◇ *a spoken/oral presentation.* In these cases **oral** is slightly more technical than **spoken**. **Oral** but not **spoken** can also be used with words such as *tradition, culture* and *legends* to talk about the way in which people pass stories down from one generation to the next, and in legal contexts followed by words such as *evidence* and *hearing.*

**vocal** [usually before noun] connected with the voice: *vocal music* ◇ *the vocal organs* (= the tongue, lips, etc.) NOTE **Vocal** is used to talk about the ability to produce sounds using the voice, and is often used in musical contexts when referring to singing.

**PATTERNS**
- spoken/oral **French/English/Japanese**, etc.
- spoken/oral **language skills**

ˌspoken ˈfor adj. [not before noun] already claimed or being kept for sb: *I'm afraid you can't sit there—those seats are spoken for.* ◇ (*old-fashioned*) *Liza is already spoken for* (= she is already married or has a partner).

ˌspoken ˈword noun **1 the spoken word** [sing.] language expressed in speech, rather than being written or sung **2** [U] a type of poetry that is spoken ALOUD and performed to an audience: *Sounding the Spider is a day of spoken word and live music from local artists.* ➲ see also SLAM *noun* (2)

**spokes·man** ?+ B2 /ˈspəʊksmən/, **spokes·woman** ?+ B2 /ˈspəʊkswʊmən/ *noun* (*pl.* **-men** /-mən/, **-women** /-wɪmɪn/) a person who speaks for a group or an organization: *a police spokesman* ◇ **~ for sb/sth** *A spokeswoman for the government denied the rumours.* ➲ note at GENDER

**spokes·per·son** ?+ B2 /ˈspəʊkspɜːsn; NAmE -pɜːrsn/ *noun* (*pl.* **-per·sons** or **-people**) **~ (for sb/sth)** a person who speaks for a group or an organization

**sponge** /spʌndʒ/ *noun*, *verb*
■ *noun* **1** [C] a piece of artificial or natural material that is soft and light and full of holes and can hold water easily, used for washing or cleaning: (*figurative*) *His mind was like a sponge, ready to absorb anything.* **2** [U] artificial sponge used for filling furniture, CUSHIONS, etc. **3** [C] a simple sea creature with a light body full of holes, from which natural sponge is obtained **4** [C, U] (*BrE*) = SPONGE CAKE or SPONGE PUDDING: *a chocolate sponge* ➲ see also VICTORIA SPONGE
■ *verb* **1** [T] **~ sb/yourself/sth (down)** to wash sb/yourself/sth with a wet cloth or SPONGE SYN **wipe**: *She sponged his hot face.* ◇ *Take your jacket off and I'll sponge it down with water.* **2** [T] **~ sth + adv./prep.** to remove sth using a wet cloth or SPONGE SYN **wash**: *We tried to sponge the blood off my shirt.* **3** [I] **~ (off/on sb)** (*informal, disapproving*) to get money, food, etc. regularly from other people without doing anything for them or offering to pay SYN **scrounge**: *He spent his life sponging off his relatives.*

ˈsponge bag *noun* (*also* ˈtoilet bag, ˈwash bag) (*all BrE*) (*NAmE* ˈtoiletry bag) *noun* a small bag for holding your soap, TOOTHBRUSH, etc. when you are travelling

ˈsponge cake (*BrE also* **sponge**) *noun* [C, U] a light cake made from eggs, sugar and flour, with or without fat

ˈsponge ˈpudding (*also* **sponge**) *noun* [U, C] (*BrE*) a hot DESSERT (= a sweet dish) like a sponge cake that usually has jam or fruit on top

**spon·ger** /ˈspʌndʒə(r)/ *noun* (*informal*) a person who gets money, food, etc. from other people without doing anything for them or offering to pay

**spongi·form** /ˈspʌndʒɪfɔːm; NAmE -fɔːrm/ *adj.* (*specialist*) having or relating to a structure with holes in it like a SPONGE ➲ see also BSE

**spongy** /ˈspʌndʒi/ *adj.* (**spon·gi·er**, **spon·gi·est**) soft and able to hold water easily like a SPONGE SYN **springy**: *spongy moss* ◇ *The ground was soft and spongy.* ◇ *The bread had a spongy texture.* ▶ **spon·gi·ness** *noun* [U]

**spon·sor** 🔊 B2 /ˈspɒnsə(r); NAmE ˈspɑːn-/ *verb*, *noun*
■ *verb* **1** ?+ B2 **~ sth** (of a company, etc.) to pay the costs of a particular event, programme, etc. as a way of advertising: *Sports events are no longer sponsored by the tobacco industry.* **2** ?+ B2 to agree to give sb money for a charity if they complete a particular task: **~ sb** *They got their granny and aunts and other people to sponsor them.* ◇ **~ sb for sth/to do sth** *Will you sponsor me for a charity walk I'm doing?* **3** ?+ B2 to support sb by paying for their training or education: **~ sb (through sth)** *The corporation is sponsoring several athletes and teams here in the US.* **4** ?+ B2 **~ sth** to provide money for a particular activity: *The group has been accused of sponsoring terrorism.* **5** **~ sth** to arrange for sth official to take place: *The US is sponsoring negotiations between the two sides.* **6** **~ sth** to introduce a proposal for a new law, etc: *The bill was sponsored by a Labour MP.*
■ *noun* **1** ?+ B2 a person or company that pays for a radio or television programme, or for a concert or sporting event, usually in return for advertising: *The programme is funded by a number of corporate sponsors.* **2** ?+ B2 a person who agrees to give sb money for a charity if that person succeeds in completing a particular activity: **~ for sth** *I'm collecting sponsors for next week's charity run.* **3** ?+ B2 a person or company that supports sb by paying for their training or education: *Each student's tuition was paid by an individual sponsor.* **4** a person, a group, an organization, etc. that provides money for an activity: *the list of state sponsors of terrorism* **5** a person who introduces and supports a proposal for a new law, etc: *the sponsor of the new immigration bill* **6** a person who agrees to be officially responsible for another person **7** a person who presents a child for Christian BAPTISM or CONFIRMATION SYN **godparent**

**spon·sor·ship** ?+ B2 /ˈspɒnsəʃɪp; NAmE ˈspɑːnsərʃ-/ *noun* **1** ?+ B2 [U, C] financial support from a sponsor: *a $50 million sponsorship deal* ◇ *The project needs to raise £8 million in sponsorship.* ◇ **~ for sb/sth** *We need to find sponsorships for the expedition.* **2** ?+ B2 [U] the act of supporting a person, organization or activity, especially financially: *Two million pounds were raised through sponsorship.* **3** [U] the act of introducing a proposal for a new law: *the senator's sponsorship of the job training legislation*

**spon·tan·eity** /ˌspɒntəˈneɪəti; NAmE ˌspɑːn-/ *noun* [U] the quality of being spontaneous

**spon·tan·eous** /spɒnˈteɪniəs; NAmE spɑːn-/ *adj.* **1** not planned but done because you suddenly want to do it: *a spontaneous offer of help* ◇ *The audience burst into spontaneous applause.* **2** often doing things without planning to, because you suddenly want to do them: *Jo's a cheerful, spontaneous person, always ready for some fun.* **3** (*specialist*) happening naturally, without being made to happen: *spontaneous remission of the disease* **4** done naturally, without being forced, practised or organized in advance: *a recording of spontaneous speech* ◇ *a wonderfully spontaneous performance of the piece* ▶ **spon·tan·eous·ly** *adv.*: *We spontaneously started to dance.* ◇ *The bleeding often stops spontaneously.*

# spontaneous combustion 1510

**spon‚taneous com'bustion** *noun* [U] the burning of a mineral or vegetable substance caused by chemical changes inside it and not by fire or heat from outside

**spoof** /spuːf/ *noun*, *verb*
- *noun* ~ **(on sth)** (*informal*) a humorous copy of a film, TV programme, etc. that EXAGGERATES its main features: *It's a spoof on horror movies.*
- *verb* **1** ~ **sth** to copy a film, TV programme, etc. in a humorous way by EXAGGERATING its main features: *It is a movie that spoofs other movies.* ⊃ WORDFINDER NOTE at COMEDY **2** ~ **sth** to send an email that appears to come from sb else's email address: *Someone has been spoofing my address.* ▶ **spoof·ing** *noun* [U]

**spook** /spuːk/ *noun*, *verb*
- *noun* (*informal*) **1** a ghost: *a castle haunted by spooks* **2** (*especially NAmE*) a SPY: *a CIA spook*
- *verb* [T, usually passive, I] (*especially NAmE, informal*) to frighten a person or an animal; to become frightened: **be spooked (by sb/sth)** *We were spooked by the strange noises and lights.* ◇ ~ **at sth** *The horse spooked at the siren.*

**spooky** /ˈspuːki/ *adj.* (**spook·ier, spooki·est**) HELP You can also use **more spooky** and **most spooky**. (*informal*) strange and frightening SYN **creepy**: *a spooky old house* ◇ *I was just thinking about her when she phoned. Spooky!*

**spool** /spuːl/ *noun*, *verb*
- *noun* (*especially NAmE*) = REEL: *a spool of thread*
- *verb* **1** [T] ~ **sth + adv./prep.** to wind sth onto or off a spool **2** [T, I] ~ **(sth)** (*computing*) to move data and store it for a short time, for example on a disk, especially before it is printed

**spoon** ⓘ A2 /spuːn/ *noun*, *verb*
- *noun* **1** A2 a tool that has a handle with a shallow bowl at the end, used for mixing, serving and eating food: *a plastic/metal spoon* ◇ *a soup spoon* ⊃ see also DESSERTSPOON, EGG-AND-SPOON RACE, GREASY SPOON, MEASURING SPOON, SLOTTED SPOON, TABLESPOON, TEASPOON, WOODEN SPOON **2** = SPOONFUL IDM see BORN *v.*
- *verb* ~ **sth + adv./prep.** to lift and move food with a spoon: *She spooned the sauce over the chicken pieces.*

**spoon·bill** /ˈspuːnbɪl/ *noun* a large bird with long legs, a long neck and a BEAK that is wide and flat at the end

**'spoon-feed** *verb* **1** [often passive] (*disapproving*) to teach people sth in a way that gives them too much help and does not make them think for themselves: ~ **sb (with sth)** *The students here do not expect to be spoon-fed.* ◇ ~ **sth to sb** *They had information spoon-fed to them.* **2** ~ **sb** to feed sb, especially a baby, with a spoon

**spoon·ful** /ˈspuːnfʊl/ (*also* **spoon**) *noun* the amount that a spoon can hold: *two spoonfuls of sugar*

**spoor** /spɔː(r); *NAmE* spʊr/ *noun* [sing.] a track or smell that a wild animal leaves as it travels

**spor·ad·ic** /spəˈrædɪk/ *adj.* happening only occasionally or at INTERVALS that are not regular SYN **intermittent**: *sporadic fighting/gunfire/violence* ◇ *sporadic outbreaks of the disease* ▶ **spor·ad·ic·al·ly** /-kli/ *adv.*: *She attended lectures only sporadically.* ◇ *Fighting continued sporadically for two months.*

**spore** /spɔː(r)/ *noun* (*biology*) one of the very small cells that are produced by some plants and that develop into new plants: *Ferns, mosses and fungi spread by means of spores.*

**spor·ran** /ˈspɒrən; *NAmE* ˈspɑːr-/ *noun* a flat bag, usually made of leather or fur, that is worn by men in front of the KILT as part of the Scottish national dress

**sport** ⓘ A1 /spɔːt; *NAmE* spɔːrt/ *noun*, *verb*
- *noun* **1** A1 [U] (*BrE*) (*NAmE* **sports** [pl.]) activity that you do for pleasure and that needs physical effort or skill, usually done in a special area and according to fixed rules: *There are excellent facilities for sport and recreation.* ◇ *I'm not interested in sport.* ◇ (*BrE*) *Do you do any sport?* ◇ (*NAmE*) *Do you play any sports?* HELP When talking about sport or sports in general, the form is usually the uncountable **sport** in (*BrE*) and the plural **sports** in (*NAmE*). However, before another noun the plural form **sports** is used in both (*BrE*) and (*NAmE*): *a radio station for sports fans* ◇ *a sports stadium/club/hall* ⊃ WORDFINDER NOTE at FIT

WORDFINDER athlete, champion, compete, fixture, match, record, spectator, stadium, tournament

**2** A1 [C] a particular form of sport: *What's your favourite sport?* ◇ *a team sport* ⊃ see also BLOOD SPORT, CONTACT SPORT, EXTREME SPORT, FIELD SPORTS, MOTORSPORT, SPECTATOR SPORT, WINTER SPORTS **3** [C] (*AustralE, NZE, informal*) used as a friendly way of addressing sb, especially a man: *Good on you, sport!* **4** [U] (*old-fashioned*) pleasure or fun: **in** ~ *The comments were only made in sport.* ◇ **to make sport of** (= to joke about) *sb/sth*
IDM **be a (good) 'sport** (*informal*) to be generous, cheerful and pleasant, especially in a difficult situation or when you have lost a game: *She's a good sport.* ◇ *Go on, be a sport* (= used when asking sb to help you).
- *verb* **1** [T] ~ **sth** to have or wear sth in a proud way SYN **wear**: *to sport a beard* ◇ *She was sporting a T-shirt with the company's logo on it.* **2** [I] + adv./prep. (*literary*) to play in a happy and lively way

**'sport coat** *noun* (*NAmE*) = SPORTS JACKET

**sport·ing** ⓘ B2 /ˈspɔːtɪŋ; *NAmE* ˈspɔːrt-/ *adj.* **1** B2 [only before noun] connected with sports: *a major sporting event* ◇ *a range of sporting activities* ◇ *His main sporting interests are golf and tennis.* ◇ (*NAmE*) *a store selling sporting goods* **2** (*especially BrE*) fair and generous in your treatment of other people, especially in a game or sport OPP **unsporting** ▶ **sport·ing·ly** *adv.*: *He sportingly agreed to play the point again.*
IDM **a sporting 'chance** a reasonable chance of success

**'sports car** (*US also* **'sport car**) *noun* a low, fast car, often with a roof that can be folded back

**'sports·cast** /ˈspɔːtskɑːst; *NAmE* ˈspɔːrtskæst/ *noun* (*NAmE*) a television or radio broadcast of sports news or a sports event

**'sports·cast·er** /ˈspɔːtskɑːstə(r); *NAmE* ˈspɔːrtskæs-/ *noun* (*NAmE*) a person who introduces and presents a sportscast

**'sports centre** (*US* **'sports center**) *noun* a building where the public can go to play many different kinds of sports, swim, etc.

**'sports day** (*BrE*) (*NAmE* **'field day**) *noun* a special day at school when there are no classes and children compete in sports events

**'sports drink** *noun* a type of cold drink that contains sugar and other ingredients that help you to get back energy lost through exercise

**'sports jacket** (*NAmE also* **'sport jacket**, **'sport coat**, **'sports coat**) *noun* a man's jacket that is like a suit jacket, worn on informal occasions

**sports·man** /ˈspɔːtsmən; *NAmE* ˈspɔːrts-/, **sports·woman** /ˈspɔːtswʊmən; *NAmE* ˈspɔːrts-/ *noun* (*pl.* **-men** /-mən/, **-women** /-wɪmɪn/) (*especially BrE*) a person who plays a lot of sport, especially as a professional SYN **athlete**: *a keen sportswoman* ◇ *He is one of this country's top professional sportsmen.* ⊃ note at GENDER

**sports·man·like** /ˈspɔːtsmənlaɪk; *NAmE* ˈspɔːrts-/ *adj.* behaving in a fair, generous and polite way, especially when playing a sport or game: *a sportsmanlike attitude* OPP **unsportsmanlike**

**sports·man·ship** /ˈspɔːtsmənʃɪp; *NAmE* ˈspɔːrts-/ *noun* [U] (*approving*) fair, generous and polite behaviour, especially when playing a sport or game ⊃ compare GAMESMANSHIP

**'sports medicine** *noun* [U] a branch of medicine that deals with injuries and health problems caused by playing sports

**sports·per·son** /ˈspɔːtspɜːsn; NAmE ˈspɔːrtspɜːrsn/ noun (pl. **-persons** or **-people**) (especially BrE) a person who plays a lot of sport, especially as a professional SYN **athlete**

**sports·wear** /ˈspɔːtsweə(r); NAmE ˈspɔːrtswer/ noun [U] **1** (especially BrE) clothes that are worn for playing sports, or in informal situations **2** (especially NAmE) clothes that are worn in informal situations

**sports·woman** noun (pl. **sports·women**) (especially BrE) ⊃ SPORTSMAN

**sport uˈtility vehicle** noun (abbr. **SUV**) (especially NAmE) a type of large car, often with FOUR-WHEEL DRIVE and made originally for travelling over rough ground

**sporty** /ˈspɔːti; NAmE ˈspɔːrti/ adj. (**sport·ier**, **sporti·est**) (informal) **1** (especially BrE) liking or good at sport: *I'm not very sporty.* **2** (of clothes) bright, attractive and informal; looking suitable for wearing for sports: *a sporty cotton top* **3** (of cars) fast and attractive: *a sporty Mercedes*

**spot** 🅞 B1 /spɒt; NAmE spɑːt/ noun, verb, adj.
■ noun
• SMALL MARK **1** 🅘 B1 a small round area that has a different colour or feels different from the surface it is on: *Which has spots, the leopard or the tiger?* ◊ *The male bird has a red spot on its beak.* ◊ (BrE) *She was wearing a black skirt with white spots.* ⊃ SYNONYMS at PATCH ⊃ WORDFINDER NOTE at PATTERN ⊃ see also BEAUTY SPOT, SUNSPOT **2** B1 [usually pl.] a small mark or LUMP on a person's skin, sometimes with a yellow head to it: *The baby's whole body was covered in small red spots.* ◊ *He had a large spot on his nose.* ⊃ compare PIMPLE, RASH, ZIT **3** a small dirty mark on sth: *His jacket was covered with spots of mud.* ◊ *rust spots* ⊃ SYNONYMS at MARK
• PLACE **4** B1 a particular area or place: *a quiet/secluded/lonely spot* ◊ *This is a favourite spot for walkers and climbers.* ◊ *I won't drive around for 20 minutes looking for a parking spot.* ◊ *He was exhausted and just wanted to find a spot to sleep.* ⊃ SYNONYMS at PLACE ⊃ see also BEAUTY SPOT (1), BLACK SPOT, BLIND SPOT, HOTSPOT, NIGHTSPOT, PENALTY SPOT, SWEET SPOT, TROUBLE SPOT
• FEATURE OF SB/STH **5** a small feature or part of sb/sth with a particular quality: *He usually wears a hat to hide his bald spot.* ◊ (figurative) *She knew his **weak spot** where Steve was concerned.*
• SMALL AMOUNT **6** [usually sing.] **~of sth** (BrE, informal) a small amount of sth SYN **bit**: *He's in a spot of trouble.* **7** [usually pl.] **~(of sth)** a small amount of a liquid: *I felt a few spots of rain.*
• PART OF SHOW **8** a part of a television, radio, club or theatre show that is given to a particular person or type of entertainment: *a guest/solo spot*
• IN COMPETITION **9** a position in a competition, event or team: *two teams battling for (the) top spot*
• LIGHT **10** (informal) = SPOTLIGHT ⊃ see also HIGH SPOT
IDM **glued / riveted / rooted to the ˈspot** not able to move, for example because you are frightened or surprised **in a (tight) ˈspot / ˈcorner** (informal) in a difficult situation **on the ˈspot 1** immediately: *He answered the question on the spot.* ◊ *an on-the-spot parking fine* **2** at the actual place where sth is happening: *An ambulance was on the spot within minutes.* ◊ *an on-the-spot report* **3** (NAmE also **in ˈplace**) in one exact place, without moving in any direction: *Running on the spot is good exercise.* **put sb on the ˈspot** to make sb feel uncomfortable or embarrassed by asking them a difficult question: *The interviewer's questions really put him on the spot.* ⊃ more at BRIGHT adj., HIT v., KNOCK v., LEOPARD, SOFT
■ verb (-tt-) **1** 🅘 B2 (not used in the progressive tenses) to see or notice a person or thing, especially suddenly or when it is not easy to do so: **~sb/sth** *Can you spot the difference between these two pictures?* ◊ *She's always quick to spot an opportunity.* ◊ *I finally spotted my friend in the crowd.* ◊ **~sb/sth doing sth** *Neighbours spotted smoke coming out of the house.* ◊ **~that…** *No one spotted that the gun was a fake.* ◊ **~what, where, etc…** *I soon spotted what the mistake was.* ⊃ SYNONYMS at SEE ⊃ see also SPOTTER **2 ~sb/sth sth** (NAmE, sport) to give your opponent or the other team an advantage: *We spotted the opposing team two goals.*
IDM **be ˌspotted with sth** to be covered with small round marks of sth: *His shirt was spotted with oil.*
■ adj. [only before noun] (business) connected with a system of buying and selling things where goods are delivered and paid for immediately after sale: *spot prices*

**ˈspot check** noun a check that is made suddenly and without warning on a few things or people chosen from a group to see that everything is as it should be: *to carry out random spot checks on vehicles*

**ˈspot-fixing** noun [U] (BrE, sport) (especially in CRICKET) the act of deciding in a way that is not honest what the result of a particular part of a game will be before it is played ⊃ compare MATCH-FIXING

**ˈspot kick** noun (BrE) = PENALTY KICK

**spot·less** /ˈspɒtləs; NAmE ˈspɑːt-/ adj. perfectly clean SYN **immaculate**: *a spotless white shirt* ◊ *She keeps the house spotless.* ◊ (figurative) *He has a spotless record so far.*
▸ **spot·less·ly** adv.: *spotlessly clean*

**spot·light** 🅠+ C1 /ˈspɒtlaɪt; NAmE ˈspɑːt-/ noun, verb
■ noun **1** 🅠+ C1 (also informal **spot**) [C] a light with a single, very bright BEAM that can be directed at a particular place or person, especially a performer on the stage: *The room was lit by spotlights.* **2** 🅠+ C1 **the spotlight** [U] the area of light that is made by a spotlight: **in the ~** *She stood alone on stage in the spotlight.* **3** 🅠+ C1 **the spotlight** [U] attention from newspapers, television and the public: **in the ~** *Unemployment is once again in the spotlight.* ◊ **under the ~** *The issue will come under the spotlight when parliament reassembles.* ◊ *The report has **turned the spotlight on** the startling rise in street crime.*
■ verb (**spot·lit**, **spot·lit** /-lɪt/) HELP Especially in sense 2, **spotlighted** is also used for the past tense and past participle. **1 ~sth** to shine a spotlight on sb/sth: *a spotlit stage* **2 ~sth** to give special attention to a problem, situation, etc. so that people notice it SYN **highlight**: *The programme spotlights financial problems in the health service.*

bulb

**ˌspot ˈon** adj. [not before noun] (BrE, informal) exactly right: *His assessment of the situation was spot on.*

**spot·ted** /ˈspɒtɪd; NAmE ˈspɑːt-/ (also **spotty**) adj. **1** (of cloth, etc.) having a regular pattern of small DOTS (= small round marks) on it: *a black and white spotted dress* **2** having marks on it, sometimes in a pattern: *a leopard's spotted coat*

**spot·ter** /ˈspɒtə(r); NAmE ˈspɑːt-/ noun **1** (especially in compounds) a person who looks for a particular type of thing or person, as a hobby or job: *a talent spotter* (= sb who visits clubs and theatres looking for new performers) ⊃ see also TRAINSPOTTER **2** (also **ˈspotter plane**) a plane used for finding out what an enemy is doing

**spotty** /ˈspɒti; NAmE ˈspɑːti/ adj. (**spot·tier**, **spot·ti·est**) **1** (BrE, usually disapproving) (of a person) having a lot of spots on the skin SYN **pimply**: *a spotty adolescent* ◊ *a spotty face* **2** (NAmE) = PATCHY (2) **3** = SPOTTED: *a spotty dress*

**spouse** 🅠+ C1 /spaʊs, spaʊz/ noun (formal or law) a husband or wife ▸ **spou·sal** /ˈspaʊzl, ˈspaʊsl/ adj. [only before noun] (formal): *spousal consent* ◊ *spousal abuse*

**spout** /spaʊt/ noun, verb
■ noun **1** a pipe or tube on a container through which you can pour liquid out: *the spout of a teapot* **2** a stream of liquid coming out of somewhere with great force SYN **fountain**
IDM **be / go up the ˈspout** (BrE, slang) to be/go wrong; to fail to work or be successful: *Well, that's my holiday plans gone up the spout!*
■ verb **1** [T, I] to send out sth, especially a liquid, in a stream with great force; to come out of sth in this way SYN **pour**: **~sth (from sth)** *The wound was still spouting blood.* ◊ **~from / out of sth** *Clear water spouted from the fountains.* **2** [I] (of a WHALE) to send out a stream of water from a hole in its head **3** [I, T] (informal, disapproving) to speak a lot about sth; to repeat sth in a boring or annoying way: **~(off / on) (about sth)** *He's always spouting off about being*

# sprain

**sprain** /spreɪn/ verb ~ sth to injure a JOINT in your body, especially your WRIST or ankle, by suddenly TWISTING it: *I stumbled and sprained my ankle.* ⇨ SYNONYMS at INJURE
▶ **sprain** noun: *a bad ankle sprain*

**sprang** /spræŋ/ past tense of SPRING

**sprat** /spræt/ noun a very small European sea fish that is used for food

**sprawl** /sprɔːl/ verb, noun
■ verb **1** [I] (+ adv. / prep.) to sit, lie or fall with your arms and legs spread out in a relaxed or careless way: *He was sprawling in an armchair in front of the TV.* ◊ *Something hit her and sent her sprawling to the ground.* ◊ *I tripped and went sprawling.* **2** [I] + adv. / prep. to spread in an untidy way; to cover a large area: *The town sprawled along the side of the lake.*
■ noun [U, C, usually sing.] a large area covered with buildings that spreads from the city into the countryside in an ugly way: *attempts to control the fast-growing* **urban sprawl** ◊ *a sprawl of buildings*

**sprawled** /sprɔːld/ adj. sitting or lying with your arms and legs spread out in a relaxed or careless way: *He was lying sprawled in an armchair, watching TV.*

**sprawl·ing** /ˈsprɔːlɪŋ/ adj. [only before noun] spreading in an untidy way: *a modern sprawling town*

**spray** /spreɪ/ noun, verb
■ noun **1** [U, C] very small drops of a liquid that are sent through the air, for example by the wind: *sea spray* ◊ *A cloud of fine spray came up from the waterfall.* ◊ *(figurative) a spray of machine-gun bullets* **2** [U, C] (especially in compounds) a substance that is forced out of a container such as an AEROSOL, in very small drops: *a can of insect spray* (= used to kill insects) ◊ *body spray* ⇨ see also HAIRSPRAY, PEPPER SPRAY **3** [C] a device or container, for example an AEROSOL, that you use to apply liquid in fine drops: *a throat spray* **4** [C] an act of applying liquid to sth in very small drops: *I gave the plants a quick spray.* **5** [C] a small branch of a tree or plant, with its leaves and flowers or BERRIES, that you use for decoration **SYN** sprig **6** [C] an attractive arrangement of flowers or jewellery, that you wear: *a spray of orchids*
■ verb **1** [T, I] to cover sb/sth with very small drops of a liquid that are forced out of a container or sent through the air: ~ (sth) (on/onto/over sb/sth) *Spray the conditioner onto your wet hair.* ◊ *Champagne sprayed everywhere.* ◊ ~ sb/sth (with sth) *The crops are regularly sprayed with pesticide.* ◊ ~ sth + adj. *She's had the car sprayed blue.* **2** [T, I] to cover sb/sth with a lot of small things with a lot of force: ~ sb/sth with sth *The gunman sprayed the building with bullets.* ◊ + adv. / prep. *Pieces of glass sprayed all over the room.* **3** [I] (especially of a male cat) to leave small amounts of URINE to mark its own area

**ˈspray can** noun a small metal container that has paint in it under pressure and that you use to spray paint onto sth

**spray·er** /ˈspreɪə(r)/ noun a piece of equipment used for SPRAYING liquid, especially paint or a substance used to kill insects that damage crops: *a paint/crop sprayer*

**ˈspray-on** adj. [only before noun] (*especially BrE*) that you can SPRAY onto sth/sb from a special container: *a spray-on water repellent for shoes*

**ˈspray paint** noun [U] paint that is kept in a container under pressure and that you can SPRAY onto sth ▶ **ˈspray-paint** verb [often passive]: ~ A (with B) | ~ B (on A) *The walls were spray-painted with graffiti.*

**ˈspray tan** noun an artificial SUNTAN, produced by SPRAYING the skin with small drops of liquid that contain special chemicals; the process of SPRAYING the skin in this way: *to get a spray tan* ▶ **ˈspray-tanned** adj. **ˈspray tanning** noun [U]

# spread

**spread** /spred/ verb, noun
■ verb (spread, spread)
• AMONG PEOPLE **1** [I, T] to affect or make sth affect, be known by, or be used by more and more people: *The news had spread and was causing great excitement.* ◊ + adv. / prep. *Use of computers spread rapidly during that period.* ◊ ~ sth *Someone's been spreading rumours about you.* ◊ *He's using his rap music to spread the message that violence is wrong.* ◊ *The disease is spread by mosquitoes.* ⇨ WORDFINDER NOTE at DISEASE
• COVER LARGE AREA **2** [I, T] to cover, or to make sth cover, a larger and larger area: *There is no evidence that the cancer has spread.* ◊ + adv. / prep. *The fire rapidly spread to adjoining buildings.* ◊ *A smile spread slowly across her face.* ◊ ~ sth *A strong wind spread the flames.* **3** [I, T] ~ sb/sth to cause sb/sth to be in a number of different places: *Seeds and pollen are spread by the wind.* ◊ *We have 10000 members spread all over the country.* **4** [I] ~ (out) + adv. / prep. to cover a large area: *The valley spread out beneath us.*
• SOFT LAYER **5** [T, I] to put a layer of a substance onto the surface of sth; to be able to be put onto a surface: ~ sth *They spread manure in both spring and autumn.* ◊ ~ (A on/over B) to spread butter on pieces of toast ◊ ~ (B with A) *pieces of toast spread with butter*
• OPEN/ARRANGE **6** [T] to open sth that has been folded so that it covers a larger area than before: ~ sth (out) *The bird spread its wings.* ◊ ~ sth (out) on/over sth *They spread a cloth on the table.* ◊ *Sue spread the map out on the floor.* **7** [T] to arrange objects so that they cover a large area and can be seen easily: ~ sth (out) (on/over sth) *Papers had been spread out on the desk.* **8** [T] to place the THUMB and a finger of one hand on the screen of an electronic device such as a mobile phone or small computer and move them apart to make the image on the screen larger, as though it is closer: *Re-size the text by using the pinch and spread gestures on the screen.* ⇨ see also PINCH verb (3)
• ARMS/LEGS **9** [T] ~ sth (out) to move your arms, legs, fingers, etc. far apart from each other: *She spread her arms and the child ran towards her.*
• DIVIDE/SHARE **10** [T] to separate sth into parts and divide them between different times or different people: ~ sth *Why not pay monthly and spread the cost of your car insurance?* ◊ ~ sth (out) (over sth) *A series of five interviews will be spread over two days.* ◊ ~ sth between sb/sth *We attempted to spread the workload between the departments.*
**IDM** **spread like ˈwildfire** (of news, etc.) to become known by more and more people very quickly **spread your ˈnet** to consider a wide range of possibilities or cover a large area, especially to try to find sb/sth: *They have spread their net far and wide in the search for a new team coach.* **spread your ˈwings** to become more independent and confident and try new activities, etc. **spread the ˈword** to tell people about sth: *I'm always trying to spread the word about healthy eating.* **spread yourself too ˈthin** to try to do so many different things at the same time that you do not do any of them well
**PHR V** **ˌspread ˈout** | **ˌspread yourself ˈout 1** to stretch your body or arrange your things over a large area: *There's more room to spread out in first class.* ◊ *Do you have to spread yourself out all over the sofa?* **2** to separate from other people in a group, to cover a larger area: *The searchers spread out to cover the area faster.*
■ noun
• INCREASE **1** [U] an increase in the amount or number of sth that there is, or in the area that is affected by sth: *measures to halt the spread of the disease* ◊ to *prevent/stop the spread of sth* ⇨ see also MIDDLE-AGE SPREAD
• RANGE/VARIETY **2** [C, usually sing.] ~ (of sth/sb) a range or variety of things or people: *a broad spread of opinions*
• ON BREAD **3** [C, U] a soft food that you put on bread: *Use a low-fat spread instead of butter.* ◊ *cheese spread*
• AREA COVERED **4** [C, usually sing.] ~ (of sth) the area that sth exists in or happens in: *The company has a good geographical spread of hotels in this country.* **5** [C, usually sing.] ~ (of sth) how wide sth is or the area that sth covers: *The bird's wings have a spread of nearly a metre.*

- **IN NEWSPAPER/MAGAZINE 6** [C] an article or advertisement in a newspaper or magazine, especially one that covers two opposite pages: *The story continued with a double-page spread on the inside pages.* ⇒ see also CENTRE SPREAD
- **MEAL 7** [C] (*informal*) a large meal, especially one that is prepared for a special occasion: *They had laid on a huge spread for the party.*
- **OF LAND/WATER 8** [C, usually sing.] ~**(of sth)** (*NAmE*) an area of land or water: *a vast spread of water* ◊ *They have a huge spread in California* (= a large farm or RANCH).
- **FINANCE 9** [U] the difference between two rates or prices
- **ON BED 10** [C] (*NAmE*) = BEDSPREAD

**ˌspread ˈbetting** *noun* [U] a type of BETTING in which you bet money on whether you think the predicted outcome is too high or too low. The amount of money you win or lose depends on the extent to which you are right or wrong. ▶ **ˌspread ˈbet** *noun*

**spread·er** /ˈspredə(r)/ *noun* a device or machine that spreads things: *a muck spreader*

**spread·sheet** /ˈspredʃiːt/ *noun* a computer program that is used, for example, when doing financial or project planning. You enter data in rows and columns and the program calculates costs, etc. from it. The individual documents are also called spreadsheets. ⇒ **WORDFINDER NOTE** at SOFTWARE

**spree** /spriː/ *noun* **1** a short period of time that you spend doing one particular activity that you enjoy, but often too much of it: *a shopping/spending spree* ◊ *He's out on a spree.* **2** (used especially in newspapers) a period of activity, especially criminal activity: *to go on a killing spree*

**sprig** /sprɪɡ/ *noun* a small STEM with leaves on it from a plant or bush, used in cooking or as a decoration: *a sprig of parsley/holly/heather*

**spright·ly** /ˈspraɪtli/ (*also less frequent* **spry**) *adj.* (especially of older people) full of life and energy **SYN** **lively**: *a sprightly 80-year-old* ⇒ **WORDFINDER NOTE** at OLD ▶ **spright·li·ness** *noun* [U]

**spring**

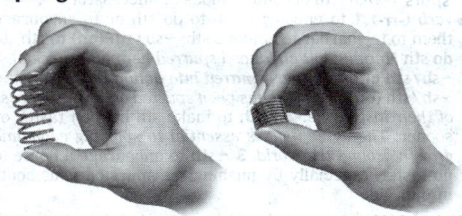

**spring** ⓘ A1 /sprɪŋ/ *noun, verb*
■ *noun*
- **SEASON 1** A1 [U, C] the season between winter and summer when plants begin to grow: *The following spring, the three artists travelled to California.* ◊ *in (the)~ flowers that bloom in (the) spring* ◊ *The birds arrive in late spring and leave again in early autumn.* ◊ *He was born in the spring of 1944.*
- **WATER 2** [C] a place where water comes naturally to the surface from under the ground: *a mountain spring* ◊ *The area is noted for its hot springs and geysers.* ◊ *spring water*
- **WIRE 3** [C] a TWISTED piece of wire that can be pushed, pressed or pulled but which always returns to its original shape or position afterwards: *bed springs* **4** [U] the ability of a spring to return to its original position: *The mattress has lost its spring.*
- **CHEERFUL QUALITY 5** [U, sing.] a cheerful, lively quality: *She walked along with a spring in her step.*
- **SUDDEN JUMP 6** [C] a quick sudden jump upwards or forwards: *With a spring, the cat leapt on to the table.* **IDM** see JOY

■ *verb* (**sprang** /spræŋ/, **sprung** /sprʌŋ/) (*NAmE also* **sprung**)
- **JUMP/MOVE SUDDENLY 1** B2 [I] (of a person or an animal) to move suddenly and with one quick movement in a particular direction **SYN** **leap**: *The cat crouched ready to spring.* ◊ **+ adv./prep.** *He turned off the alarm and sprang out of bed.* ◊ *Everyone sprang to their feet* (= stood up suddenly) *when the principal walked in.* ◊ (*figurative*) *to spring to sb's defence/assistance* (= to quickly defend or help sb) **2** B2 [I] (of an object) to move suddenly and violently: **+ adv./prep.** *The branch sprang back and hit him in the face.* ◊ **+ adj.** *She turned the key and the lid sprang open.*
- **SURPRISE 3** [T] to do sth, ask sth or say sth that sb is not expecting: ~**sth** *She sprang a surprise by winning the tournament.* ◊ ~ **sth on sb** *I'm sorry to spring it on you, but I've been offered another job.*
- **APPEAR SUDDENLY 4** [I] **+ adv./prep.** to appear or come somewhere suddenly: *Tears sprang to her eyes.*
- **FREE PRISONER 5** [T] ~**sb** (*informal*) to help a prisoner to escape: *Plans to spring the hostages have failed.*

**IDM** **ˌspring into ˈaction** | **ˌspring into/to ˈlife** (of a person, machine, etc.) to suddenly start working or doing sth: *'Let's go!' he said, springing into action.* ◊ *The town springs to life* (= becomes busy) *during the carnival.* **ˌspring a ˈleak** (of a boat or container) to develop a hole through which water or another liquid can pass **ˌspring a ˈtrap 1** to make a TRAP for catching animals close suddenly **2** to try to trick sb into doing or saying sth; to succeed in this ⇒ more at HOPE *n.*, MIND *n.*
**PHR V** **ˈspring for sth** (*NAmE*, *informal*) to pay for sth for sb else: *I'll spring for the drinks tonight.* **ˈspring from sth** (*formal*) to be caused by sth; to start from sth: *The idea for the novel sprang from a trip to India.* **ˈspring from …** (*informal*) to appear suddenly and unexpectedly from a particular place: *Where on earth did you spring from?* **ˌspring ˈup** to appear or develop quickly and/or suddenly

**spring·board** /ˈsprɪŋbɔːd; *NAmE* -bɔːrd/ *noun* **1** a strong board that you jump on and use to help you jump high in DIVING and GYMNASTICS **2** ~**(for/to sth)** something that helps you start an activity, especially by giving you ideas: *The document provided a springboard for a lot of useful discussion.* ▶ **ˈspring·board** *verb* [I, T]: ~**(sth) (into sth)** *The company expects that this strategic move would allow it to springboard into the US market.*

**spring·bok** /ˈsprɪŋbɒk; *NAmE* -bɑːk/ *noun* **1** [C] a small ANTELOPE from southern Africa that can jump high into the air **2** **Springboks** [pl.] the name of the South African national rugby team

**ˌspring ˈbreak** *noun* (*NAmE*) a week's holiday for school and college students in March or April

**ˌspring ˈchicken** *noun*
**IDM** **be no ˌspring ˈchicken** (*humorous*) to be no longer young

**ˌspring-ˈclean** *verb* [T, I] ~**(sth)** to clean a house, room, etc. carefully and completely, including the parts you do not usually clean: *Fran decided to spring-clean the apartment.* ▶ **ˌspring ˈclean** *noun* [sing.] (*BrE*): *The place needed a good spring clean before we could move in.* **ˌspring ˈcleaning** *noun* [U]

**ˌspring-ˈloaded** *adj.* containing a metal spring that presses one part against another

**ˌspring ˈonion** (*BrE*) (*NAmE* **ˌgreen ˈonion**, **ˈscal·lion**) *noun* a type of small onion with a long green STEM and leaves. Spring onions are often eaten raw in salads. ⇒ **VISUAL VOCAB** page V5

**ˌspring ˈroll** (*especially BrE*) *noun* a type of Chinese food consisting of a tube of thin PASTRY, filled with vegetables and/or meat and fried until it is hard and dry ⇒ see also EGG ROLL

**ˌspring ˈtide** *noun* a TIDE in which there is a very great rise and fall of the sea, and which happens near the new moon and the full moon each month

**spring·time** /ˈsprɪŋtaɪm/ *noun* [U] the season of spring: **in (the) ~** *a visit to Holland in (the) springtime*

**springy** /ˈsprɪŋi/ *adj.* (**ˈspring·ier**, **ˈspring·i·est**) **1** returning quickly to its original shape after being pushed, pulled, stretched, etc: *We walked across the springy grass.* **2** full of energy and confidence: *She's 73, but hasn't lost that youthful, springy step.*

# sprinkle 1514

**sprin·kle** /ˈsprɪŋkl/ *verb, noun*
- *verb* **1** [T] to shake small pieces of sth or drops of a liquid on sth: *~ A on/onto/over B Sprinkle chocolate on top of the cake.* ◊ *She sprinkled sugar over the strawberries.* ◊ *~ B with A She sprinkled the strawberries with sugar.* **2** [T, usually passive] *~ sth with sth* to include a few of sth in sth else SYN **strew**: *His poems are sprinkled with quotations from ancient Greek.* **3** [I] (*NAmE*) if **it sprinkles**, it rains lightly SYN **drizzle**: *It's only sprinkling. We can still go out.*
- *noun* **1** [usually sing.] = SPRINKLING: *Add a sprinkle of cheese and serve.* **2** (*especially NAmE*) light rain: *We've only had a few sprinkles (of rain) recently.*

**sprin·kler** /ˈsprɪŋklə(r)/ *noun* **1** a device with holes in that is used to SPRAY water in drops onto plants, soil or grass **2** a device inside a building that SPRAYS out water if it detects a rise in temperature because of a fire

**sprin·kles** /ˈsprɪŋklz/ (*especially NAmE*) (*BrE usually* **hundreds and ˈthousands**) *noun* [pl.] extremely small pieces of coloured sugar, used to decorate cakes, etc.

**sprin·kling** /ˈsprɪŋklɪŋ/ (*also* **sprin·kle**) *noun* [usually sing.] *~(of sth/sb)* a small amount of a substance that is dropped somewhere, or a number of things or people that are spread or included somewhere: *Add a sprinkling of pepper.* ◊ *Most were men, but there was also a sprinkling of young women.*

**sprint** /sprɪnt/ *verb, noun*
- *verb* [I, T] to run or swim a short distance very fast: *+ adv./prep. He sprinted for the line.* ◊ *Three runners sprinted past.* ◊ *She jumped out of the car and sprinted for the front door.* ◊ *~ sth I sprinted the last few metres.*
- *noun* a race in which the people taking part run, swim, etc. very fast over a short distance: *a 100-metre sprint* ◊ *the world sprint champion* **2** [usually sing.] a short period of running, swimming, etc. very fast: *a sprint for the line* ◊ *a sprint for the bus* ◊ *She won in a sprint finish.* ▶ **sprint·er** *noun*

**sprite** /spraɪt/ *noun* (in stories) a small creature with magic powers, especially one that likes playing tricks

**spritz** /sprɪts/ *verb ~ sth* to SPRAY very small drops of liquid on sth quickly: *Lightly spritz your hair with water.* ▶ **spritz** *noun*

**spritz·er** /ˈsprɪtsə(r)/ *noun* a drink made with wine (usually white) mixed with either SODA WATER or SPARKLING mineral water (= with bubbles in it): *a white wine spritzer*

**sprocket** /ˈsprɒkɪt/ *NAmE* ˈsprɑːk-/ *noun* **1** (*also* **ˈsprocket wheel**) a wheel with a row of teeth around the edge that connect with the holes of a bicycle chain or with holes in a film, etc. in order to turn it **2** one of the teeth on such a wheel

*sprocket wheel*

*sprocket*

*sprocket*

**sprog** /sprɒg/ *NAmE* sprɑːg/ *noun* (*BrE, informal, humorous*) a child or baby

**sprout** /spraʊt/ *verb, noun*
- *verb* **1** [I] (of plants or seeds) to produce new leaves or BUDS; to start to grow: *new leaves sprouting from the trees* ◊ *The seeds will sprout in a few days.* **2** [I, T] to appear; to develop sth, especially in large numbers: *Hundreds of mushrooms had sprouted up overnight.* ◊ *~ sth The town has sprouted shopping malls, discos and nightclubs in recent years.* **3** [T, I] to start to grow sth; to start to grow on sb/sth: *~ sth Tim has sprouted a beard since we last saw him.* ◊ *~ from sth Hair sprouted from his chest.*
- *noun* **1** = BRUSSELS SPROUT **2** a new part growing on a plant

**spruce** /spruːs/ *noun, verb, adj.*
- *noun* **1** [C, U] an EVERGREEN forest tree with leaves like needles **2** [U] the soft wood of the spruce, used, for example, in making paper
- *verb*
  PHRV **ˌspruce ˈup** | **ˌspruce sb/sth/yourself↔ˈup** to make sb/sth/yourself clean and neat: *She spruced up for the interview.* ◊ *The city is sprucing up its museums and galleries.*
- *adj.* (of people or places) neat and clean in appearance

**spruit** /spreɪt/ *SAfrE* [sprœyt] *noun* (*SAfrE*) a stream, sometimes one that only flows when there has been a lot of rain

**sprung** /sprʌŋ/ *adj., verb*
- *adj.* fitted with metal springs: *a sprung mattress*
- *verb* past tense, past part. of SPRING

**spry** /spraɪ/ *adj.* = SPRIGHTLY

**spud** /spʌd/ *noun* (*especially BrE, informal*) a potato

**spun** /spʌn/ *past part.* of SPIN

**spunk** /spʌŋk/ *noun* **1** [U] (*informal*) courage; DETERMINATION **2** [U] (*BrE, taboo, slang*) SEMEN **3** [C] (*AustralE, informal*) a sexually attractive person

**spunky** /ˈspʌŋki/ *adj.* (**spunk·ier, spunki·est**) (*informal*) **1** brave and determined; full of enthusiasm: *She is bright, tough and spunky.* **2** (*AustralE, informal*) sexually attractive: *a top babe with a spunky boyfriend*

**spur** /spɜː(r)/ *noun, verb*
- *noun* **1** a sharp pointed object that riders sometimes wear on the heels of their boots and use to encourage their horse to go faster **2** [usually sing.] *~ (to/for sth)* a fact or an event that makes you want to do sth better or more quickly SYN **motivation**: *His speech was a powerful spur to action.* **3** an area of high ground that sticks out from a mountain or hill **4** a road or a railway track that leads from the main road or line
  IDM **on the spur of the ˈmoment** suddenly, without planning in advance: *I phoned him up on the spur of the moment.* ◊ *a spur-of-the-moment decision* **win/earn your ˈspurs** (*formal*) to become famous or successful
- *verb* (**-rr-**) **1** to encourage sb to do sth or to encourage them to try harder to achieve sth: *~ sb/sth (on) to sth/to do sth Her difficult childhood spurred her on to succeed.* ◊ *~ sb/sth into sth I was spurred into action by the letter.* ◊ *~ sb/sth (on) The band has been spurred on by the success of their last single.* **2** *~ sth* to make sth happen faster or sooner: *The agreement is essential to spurring economic growth around the world.* **3** *~ sth* to encourage a horse to go faster, especially by pushing the spurs on your boots into its side

**spuri·ous** /ˈspjʊəriəs/ *NAmE* ˈspjʊr-/ *adj.* **1** false, although seeming to be real or true: *He had managed to create the entirely spurious impression that the company was thriving.* **2** based on false ideas or ways of thinking: *a spurious argument* ▶ **spuri·ous·ly** *adv.*

**spurn** /spɜːn/ *NAmE* spɜːrn/ *verb ~ sb/sth* (*formal or literary*) to reject or refuse sb/sth, especially in a proud way SYN **shun**: *Eve spurned Mark's invitation.* ◊ *a spurned lover*

**spurt** /spɜːt/ *NAmE* spɜːrt/ *verb, noun*
- *verb* **1** [I, T] (of liquid or flames) to BURST out or pour out suddenly; to produce sudden, powerful streams of liquid or flames: *~ (from sth) Blood was spurting from her nose.* ◊ *~ out (of/from sth) Red and yellow flames spurted out of the fire.* ◊ *~ sth Her nose was spurting blood.* ◊ *~ sth + adv./prep. The volcano spurted clouds of steam and ash high into the air.* **2** [I] + *adv./prep.* to increase your speed for a short time to get somewhere faster: *She spurted past me to get to the line first.*
- *noun* **1** an amount of liquid or flames that comes out of somewhere with great force: *a great spurt of blood* **2** a sudden increase in speed, effort, activity or emotion for a short period of time: *You'd better put on a spurt* (= hurry up) *if you want to finish that work today.* ◊ *Babies get very hungry during growth spurts.* ◊ *a sudden spurt of anger*
  IDM **in ˈspurts** in short periods of great activity, powerful movement, etc., rather than in a steady, continuous way: *The water came out of the tap in spurts.*

æ cat | ɑː father | e bed | ɜː fur | ə about | ɪ sit | iː see | i happy | ɒ got (*BrE*) | ɔː saw | ʌ cup | ʊ put | uː too

**sput·nik** /ˈspʌtnɪk, ˈspʊt-/ noun (from Russian) a satellite of the type that was put into space by the Soviet Union

**sput·ter** /ˈspʌtə(r)/ verb **1** [I] if an engine, a lamp or a fire **sputters**, it makes a series of short EXPLOSIVE sounds **SYN** splutter: *sputtering fireworks* **2** [T] + speech | ~ sth to speak quickly and with difficulty, making soft SPITTING sounds, because you are angry or shocked **SYN** splutter: '*W-What?' sputtered Anna.*

**spu·tum** /ˈspjuːtəm/ noun [U] (medical) liquid from the throat or lungs, especially when it is COUGHED up (= forced up from the lungs, etc.) because of disease: *blood in the sputum*

**spy** /spaɪ/ noun, verb
- noun (pl. **spies**) a person who tries to get secret information about another country, organization or person, especially sb who is employed by a government or the police: *He was denounced as a foreign spy.* ◇ *a police spy* ◇ *a spy plane/satellite* (= used to watch the activities of the enemy) ◇ *Video spy cameras are being used in public places.*
- verb (**spies**, **spy·ing**, **spied**, **spied**) **1** [I] to collect secret information about another country, organization or person: *He spied for his government for more than ten years.* **2** [T] ~ sb/sth (literary or formal) to suddenly see or notice sb/sth: *In the distance we spied the Pacific for the first time.*
**IDM** ˌspy out the ˈland to collect information before deciding what to do
**PHR V** ˈspy on sb/sth to watch sb/sth secretly: *Have you been spying on me?* ˌspy sth↔ˈout to get information about sth

**spy·glass** /ˈspaɪɡlɑːs; NAmE -ɡlæs/ noun a small TELESCOPE

**spy·hole** /ˈspaɪhəʊl/ noun a small hole in a door that you can look through to see who is on the other side before opening the door

**spy·master** /ˈspaɪmɑːstə(r); NAmE -mæs-/ noun a person who controls a group of spies

**spy·ware** /ˈspaɪweə(r); NAmE -wer/ noun [U] software that enables sb to obtain secret information about sb else and their computer activities without their knowledge or permission: *Hackers can install spyware to get all your passwords.* ⊃ see also MALWARE

**Sq.** abbr. (used in written addresses) SQUARE: *6 Hanover Sq.*

**sq** (also **sq.** especially in NAmE) abbr. (in measurements) square: *10 sq cm*

**squab·ble** /ˈskwɒbl; NAmE ˈskwɑːbl/ verb [I] ~ (with sb) (about/over sth) to argue noisily about sth that is not very important **SYN** bicker: *My sisters were squabbling over what to watch on TV.* ▸ **squab·ble** noun: *family squabbles* ◇ *There were endless squabbles over who should sit where.*

**squad** /skwɒd; NAmE skwɑːd/ noun [C + sing./pl. v.] **1** a section of a police force that deals with a particular type of crime: *the drugs/fraud/bomb/riot squad* ⊃ see also FLYING SQUAD, FRAUD SQUAD **2** (in sport) a group of players, runners, etc. from which a team is chosen for a particular game or match: *the Olympic/national squad* ◇ *They still have not named their squad for the World Cup qualifier.* **3** a small group of soldiers working or being trained together: *an elite combat squad* ⊃ see also FIRING SQUAD **4** a group of people who have a particular task ⊃ see also DEATH SQUAD, HIT SQUAD

**ˈsquad car** noun a police car

**squad·die** /ˈskwɒdi; NAmE ˈskwɑːdi/ noun (BrE, informal) a new soldier; a soldier of low rank

**squad·ron** /ˈskwɒdrən; NAmE ˈskwɑːd-/ noun [C + sing./pl. v.] a group of military aircraft or ships forming a section of a military force: *a bomber/fighter squadron*

**ˈsquadron ˈleader** noun an officer of high rank in the British AIR FORCE

**squal·id** /ˈskwɒlɪd; NAmE ˈskwɑːl-/ adj. (disapproving) **1** (of places and living conditions) very dirty and unpleasant **SYN** filthy: *squalid housing* ◇ *squalid, overcrowded refugee camps* **2** (of situations or activities) involving low moral standards or dishonest behaviour **SYN** sordid: *It was a squalid affair involving prostitutes and drugs.*

1515 **square**

**squall** /skwɔːl/ noun, verb
- noun a sudden strong and violent wind, often with rain or snow during a storm ⊃ WORDFINDER NOTE at RAIN
- verb [I] (usually used in the progressive tenses) (disapproving) to cry very loudly and noisily: *squalling kids*

**squally** /ˈskwɔːli/ adj. (of weather) involving sudden, violent and strong winds: *squally showers*

**squalor** /ˈskwɒlə(r); NAmE ˈskwɑːl-/ noun [U] dirty and unpleasant conditions: *the poverty and squalor of the slums* ◇ **in ~** *He had lost his job and was living in squalor.*

**squan·der** /ˈskwɒndə(r); NAmE ˈskwɑːn-/ verb ~ sth (on sb/sth) to waste money, time, etc. in a stupid or careless way: *He squandered all his money on gambling.*

**square** /skweə(r); NAmE skwer/ adj., noun, verb, adv.
- adj.
- SHAPE **1** having four straight equal sides and four angles of 90°: *a square room* ⊃ picture at PARALLELOGRAM **2** forming an angle of 90° exactly or approximately: *The book had rounded, not square, corners.* ◇ *square shoulders* ◇ *He had a firm, square jaw.*
- MEASUREMENT **3** (abbr. **sq**) used after a number to give a measurement of area: *an area of 36 square metres/feet/miles/kilometres/inches* **4** used after a unit of measurement to say that sth measures the same amount on each of four sides: *a carpet four metres square*
- BROAD/SOLID **5** used to describe sth that is broad or that looks solid in shape: *a man of square build* ⊃ see also FOUR-SQUARE
- LEVEL **6** [not before noun] ~ (with sth) level with sth or PARALLEL to sth: *tables arranged square with the wall*
- WITH MONEY **7** (informal) if two people are **square**, neither of them owes money to the other: *Here's the £10 I owe you —now we're square.*
- IN SPORT **8** ~ (with sb) if two teams are **square**, they have the same number of points: *The teams were all square at half-time.*
- FAIR/HONEST **9** fair or honest, especially in business matters: *a square deal* ◇ *Are you being square with me?*
- IN AGREEMENT **10** ~ with sth in agreement with sth: *That isn't quite square with what you said yesterday.*
- BORING **11** (old-fashioned, informal, disapproving) (of a person) considered to be boring, for example because they are old-fashioned or work too hard at school
**IDM** a square ˈmeal a good meal that satisfies your HUNGER: *He looks as though he hasn't had a square meal for weeks.* a square ˈpeg (in a round ˈhole) (informal) a person who does not feel happy or comfortable in a particular situation, or who is not suitable for it
- noun
- SHAPE **1** [C] a shape with four straight sides of equal length and four angles of 90°; a piece of sth that has this shape: *First break the chocolate into squares.* ◇ *The floor was tiled in squares of grey and white marble.* ⊃ see also SET SQUARE, T-SQUARE
- IN TOWN **2** [C] an open area in a town, usually with four sides, surrounded by buildings: *The hotel is just off the main square.* ◇ *the town/central/public/market square* **3** **Square** [sing.] (abbr. **Sq.**) (used in addresses): *They live at 95 Russell Square.*
- MATHEMATICS **4** [C] the number obtained when you multiply a number by itself: *The square of 7 is 49.*
- BORING PERSON **5** [C] (old-fashioned, informal, disapproving) a person who is considered to be boring, for example because they are old-fashioned or because they work too hard at school
**IDM** back to square ˈone a return to the situation you were in at the beginning of a project, task, etc., because you have made no real progress: *If this suggestion isn't accepted, we'll be back to square one.*
- verb
- SHAPE **1** ~ sth (off) to make sth have straight edges and corners: *The boat was rounded at the front but squared off at the back.*
- MATHEMATICS **2** [usually passive] ~ sth to multiply a number by itself: *Three squared is written* $3^2$. ◇ *Four squared equals 16.*

# square bracket

- **SHOULDERS 3** ~ **yourself / your shoulders** to make your back and shoulders straight to show you are ready or determined to do sth: *Bruno squared himself to face the waiting journalists.*
- **IN SPORT 4** ~ **sth** (*especially BrE*) to make the number of points you have scored in a game or competition equal to those of your opponents: *His goal squared the game 1–1.*
- **PAY MONEY 5** ~ **sb** (*informal*) to pay money to sb in order to get their help: *They must have squared the mayor before they got their plan underway.*

**IDM** **square the ˈcircle** to do sth that is considered to be impossible

**PHR V** **ˌsquare sth↔aˈway** [usually passive] (*NAmE*) to put sth in order; to finish sth completely **ˌsquare ˈoff (against sb)** (*NAmE*) to fight or prepare to fight sb **ˌsquare ˈup (to sb/sth) 1** to face a difficult situation and deal with it in a determined way **2** to face sb as if you are going to fight them **ˌsquare ˈup (with sb)** to pay money that you owe: *Can I leave you to square up with the waiter?* **ˈsquare sth with sth** | **ˈsquare with sth** to make two ideas, facts or situations agree or combine well with each other; to agree or be consistent with another idea, fact or situation: *The interests of farmers need to be squared with those of consumers.* ◊ *How can you square this with your conscience?* ◊ *Your theory does not square with the facts.* **ˈsquare sth with sb** to ask permission or check with sb that they approve of what you want to do: *I think I'll be able to come, but I'll square it with my parents first.*

- *adv.* (only used *after* the verb) directly; not at an angle **SYN** **squarely**: *I looked her square in the face.* **IDM** see FAIR *adv.*

**ˈsquare bracket** (*especially BrE*) (*NAmE usually* **bracket**) *noun* [usually pl.] either of a pair of marks, [ ], placed at the beginning and end of extra information in a text, especially comments made by an editor

**squared** /skweəd; *NAmE* skwerd/ *adj.* marked with squares; divided into squares: *squared paper*

**ˈsquare dance** *noun* **1** a traditional dance from the US in which groups of four couples dance together, starting the dance by facing each other in a square **2** a social event at which people dance square dances

**square·ly** /ˈskweəli; *NAmE* ˈskwerli/ *adv.* (usually used *after* the verb) **1** directly; not at an angle or to one side: *She looked at me squarely in the eye.* ◊ *He stood squarely in front of them, blocking the entrance.* ◊ (*figurative*) *We must meet the challenge squarely* (= not try to avoid it). **2** directly or exactly; without doubt: *The responsibility for the crisis rests squarely on the government.* **IDM** see FAIRLY

**the ˌSquare ˈMile** *noun* [sing.] (*BrE, informal*) a name used for the City of London, where there are many banks and financial businesses

**ˌsquare ˈroot** *noun* (*mathematics*) a number which when multiplied by itself produces a particular number: *The square root of 64 (√64) is 8 (8×8=64).* ⊃ compare CUBE ROOT

**squar·ish** /ˈskweərɪʃ; *NAmE* ˈskwer-/ *adj.* almost square in shape

**squash** /skwɒʃ; *NAmE* skwɑːʃ/ *verb, noun*
- *verb* **1** [T] to press sth so that it becomes soft, damaged or flat, or changes shape: ~ **sth/sb** *The tomatoes at the bottom of the bag had been squashed.* ◊ ~ **sth against sth** *He squashed his nose against the window.* ◊ ~ **sth + adj.** *Squash your cans flat before recycling.* ⊃ picture at SQUEEZE **2** [I, T] to push sb/sth or yourself into a space that is too small: ~ **sth + adv./prep.** *We all squashed into the back of the car.* ◊ ~ **sb/sth + adv./prep.** *How many people are they going to try and squash into this bus?* ◊ *She was squashed between the door and the table.* **3** [T] ~ **sth** to stop sth from continuing; to destroy sth because it is a problem for you **SYN** **quash**: *to squash a plan/an idea/a revolt* ◊ *If parents don't answer children's questions, their natural curiosity will be squashed.* ◊ *The statement was an attempt to squash the rumours.*

**PHR V** **ˌsquash ˈup (against sb/sth)** | **ˌsquash sb/sth↔ˈup (against sb/sth)** to move so close to sb/sth

else that it is uncomfortable: *We squashed up to make room for Sue.* ◊ *I was squashed up against the wall.*
- *noun* **1** (*also formal* **squash rackets**) [U] a game for two players, played in a COURT surrounded by four walls, using RACKETS and a small rubber ball: *a squash court* ◊ *to play squash* **2** [U, C] (*BrE*) a drink made with fruit juice, sugar and water: *a glass of orange/lemon squash* ◊ *Two orange squashes, please.* **3** [C, U] (*pl.* **squash** or **squashes**) a type of vegetable that grows on the ground. **Winter squash** have hard skin and are orange inside. **Summer squash** have soft yellow or green skin and are white inside. ⊃ VISUAL VOCAB page V5 **4** [sing.] (*informal*) if sth is a **squash**, there is hardly enough room for everything or everyone to fit into a small space: *It's a real squash with six of us in the car.*

**squat** /skwɒt; *NAmE* skwɑːt/ *verb, noun, adj.*
- *verb* (**-tt-**) **1** [I] ~ (**down**) to sit on your heels with your knees bent up close to your body **2** [I, T] ~ (**sth**) to live in a building or on land which is not yours, without the owner's permission: *They ended up squatting in the empty houses on Oxford Road.* ⊃ WORDFINDER NOTE at HOME
- *noun* **1** (*especially BrE*) a building that people are living in without permission and without paying rent: *to live in a squat* **2** a squatting position of the body
- *adj.* short and wide or fat, in a way that is not attractive: *a squat tower* ◊ *a squat muscular man with a shaven head*

**squat·ter** /ˈskwɒtə(r); *NAmE* ˈskwɑːt-/ *noun* a person who is living in a building or on land without permission and without paying rent

**ˈsquatter camp** *noun* (*SAfrE*) an urban area where people live in SHACKS (= small buildings made of CARDBOARD, wood or IRON SHEETS that residents have built themselves)

**squaw** /skwɔː/ *noun* (*old use*) a word for a Native American woman that is now often considered offensive

**squawk** /skwɔːk/ *verb* **1** [I] (of birds) to make a loud sharp sound: *The parrot squawked and flew away.* **2** [T, I] (+ **speech**) to speak or make a noise in a loud, sharp voice because you are angry, surprised, etc: *'You did what?!' she squawked.* ▸ **squawk** *noun*: *The bird gave a startled squawk.* ◊ *a squawk of protest*

**squeak** /skwiːk/ *verb, noun*
- *verb* **1** [I] to make a short high sound that is not very loud: *My new shoes squeak.* ◊ *The mouse ran away, squeaking with fear.* ◊ *One wheel makes a horrible squeaking noise.* **2** [T, I] (+ **speech**) to speak in a very high voice, especially when you are nervous or excited: *'Let go of me!' he squeaked nervously.* **3** [I] + **adv./prep.** to only just manage to win sth, pass a test, etc: *We squeaked into the final with a goal in the last minute.*
- *noun* a short, high call or sound, that is not usually very loud

**squeak·er** /ˈskwiːkə(r)/ *noun* (*informal, especially NAmE*) a competition or election won by only a small amount or likely to be won by only a small amount

**squeaky** /ˈskwiːki/ *adj.* (**squeak·ier**, **squeaki·est**) making a short, high sound; squeaking: *squeaky floorboards* ◊ *a high squeaky voice*

**ˌsqueaky ˈclean** *adj.* (*informal*) **1** completely clean, and therefore attractive: *squeaky clean hair* **2** morally correct in every way; that cannot be criticized

**squeal** /skwiːl/ *verb, noun*
- *verb* **1** [I] to make a long, high sound: *The pigs were squealing.* ◊ *The car squealed to a halt.* ◊ *Children were running around squealing with excitement.* **2** [T, I] (+ **speech**) to speak in a very high voice, especially when you are excited or nervous: *'Don't!' she squealed.* **3** [I] ~ (**on sb**) (*informal, disapproving*) to give information, especially to the police, about sth illegal that sb has done
- *noun* a long high call or sound: *a squeal of pain* ◊ *a squeal of delight* ◊ *He stopped with a squeal of brakes.*

**squeam·ish** /ˈskwiːmɪʃ/ *adj.* **1** easily upset, or made to feel sick by unpleasant sights or situations, especially when the sight of blood is involved **2** not wanting to do sth that might be considered dishonest or wrong **3** **the squeamish** *noun* [pl.] people who are squeamish: *This movie is not for the squeamish.* ▸ **squeam·ish·ness** *noun* [U]

**squee·gee** /ˈskwiːdʒi/ noun **1** a tool with a rubber edge and a handle, used for removing water from smooth surfaces such as windows ⇒ picture at MOP **2** (also **ˈsqueegee mop**) a tool for washing floors, that has a long handle with two thick pieces of soft material at the end, which may be pressed together using a device attached to the handle ⇒ picture at MOP

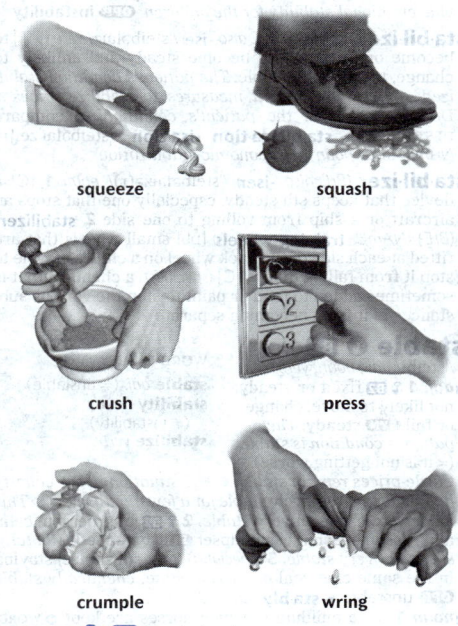

squeeze    squash
crush    press
crumple    wring

**squeeze** ⓘ+ⒸⓅ /skwiːz/ verb, noun
■ verb
- **PRESS WITH FINGERS 1** ⓘ+ⒸⓅ [T, I] ~ (sth) to press sth, especially with your fingers: *to squeeze a tube of toothpaste* ◊ *to squeeze the trigger of a gun* (= to fire it) ◊ *He squeezed her hand and smiled at her.* ◊ *Just take hold of the tube and squeeze.*
- **GET LIQUID OUT 2** ⓘ+ⒸⓅ [T] to get liquid out of sth by pressing or TWISTING it hard: ~ sth out of/from sth *to squeeze the juice from a lemon* ◊ *(figurative) She felt as if every drop of emotion had been squeezed from her.* ◊ ~ sth (out) *He took off his wet clothes and squeezed the water out.* ◊ *freshly squeezed orange juice* ◊ ~ sth + adj. *Soak the cloth in warm water and then squeeze it dry.*
- **INTO/THROUGH SMALL SPACE 3** ⓘ+ⒸⓅ [T, I] to force sb/sth/ yourself into or through a small space: ~ sb/sth into, through, etc. sth *We managed to squeeze six people into the car.* ◊ *(figurative) We managed to squeeze a lot into a week* (= we did a lot of different things). ◊ ~ into, through, etc. sth *to squeeze into a tight dress* ◊ *to squeeze through a gap in the hedge* ◊ ~ through, in, past, etc. *If you move forward a little, I can squeeze past.*
- **THREATEN 4** [T] ~ sb (for sth) (*informal*) to get sb by putting pressure on sb, threatening them, etc: *He's squeezing me for £500.*
- **LIMIT MONEY 5** [T] ~ sb/sth to strictly limit or reduce the amount of money that sb/sth has or can use: *High interest rates have squeezed the industry hard.*
▪ IDM ˌsqueeze sb ˈdry to get as much money, information, etc. out of sb as you can
▪ PHR V ˌsqueeze sb/sth↔ˈin to give time to sb/sth, although you are very busy: *If you come this afternoon the doctor will try to squeeze you in.* ˌsqueeze sb/ sth↔ˈout (of sth) to prevent sb/sth from continuing to do sth or be in business: *Supermarkets are squeezing out small shops.* ˌsqueeze sth ˈout of/ˈfrom sb to get sth by putting pressure on sb, threatening them, etc: *to squeeze a confession from a suspect* ˌsqueeze ˈup (against sb/sth) | ˌsqueeze sb↔ˈup (against sb/sth) to move close to sb/sth so that you are pressed against them/it: *There'll be enough room if we all squeeze up a little.* ◊ *I sat squeezed up against the wall.*
■ noun
- **PRESSING WITH FINGERS 1** [C, usually sing.] an act of pressing sth, usually with your hands: *He gave my hand a little squeeze.* ◊ *Give the tube another squeeze.*
- **OF LIQUID 2** [C] a small amount of liquid that is produced by pressing sth: *a squeeze of lemon juice*
- **IN SMALL SPACE 3** [sing.] a situation where it is almost impossible for a number of people or things to fit into a small or limited space: *It was a tight squeeze but we finally got everything into the case.* ◊ **at a~** *We can get six in the car at a squeeze.*
- **REDUCTION IN MONEY 4** [C, usually sing.] a reduction in the amount of money, jobs, etc. available; a difficult situation caused by this: *We're really feeling the squeeze since I lost my job.* ◊ ~ **on sth** *a squeeze on profits* ◊ *a credit squeeze*
- **BOYFRIEND/GIRLFRIEND 5** [sing.] (*especially NAmE, informal*) a boyfriend or girlfriend: *Who's his main squeeze?*
▪ IDM put the ˈsqueeze on sb (to do sth) (*informal*) to put pressure on sb to act in a particular way; to make a situation difficult for sb

**squeezy** /ˈskwiːzi/ adj. (of a container) that you have to press hard to force out the contents: *a squeezy bottle*

**squelch** /skweltʃ/ verb **1** [I] (+ adv./prep.) to make a quiet sound by pressing sth soft and wet: *The mud squelched as I walked through it.* ◊ *Her wet shoes squelched at every step.* ◊ *We squelched across the muddy field.* **2** [T] ~ sth (*NAmE*) to stop sth from growing, increasing or developing ⓢⓨⓝ **quash**, **scuash**: *to squelch a rumor* ◊ *to squelch dissent/competition.* ▶ **squelch** noun [usually sing.]: *He pulled his foot out of the mud with a squelch.* **squelchy** adj.: *squelchy ground*

**squib** /skwɪb/ noun a small FIREWORK ▪ IDM see DAMP adj.

**squid** /skwɪd/ noun [C, U] (pl. **squid** or **squids**) a sea creature that has a long soft body, eight arms and two TENTACLES (= long thin parts like arms) around its mouth, and that is sometimes used for food

**squidgy** /ˈskwɪdʒi/ adj. (**squidgi·er**, **squidgi·est**) (*especially BrE, informal*) soft and wet, and easily SQUASHED

**squig·gle** /ˈskwɪɡl/ noun a line, for example in sb's HANDWRITING, that is drawn or written in a careless way with curves and waves in it: *Are these dots and squiggles supposed to be your signature?* ▶ **squig·gly** /-gli/ adj.

**squil·lion** /ˈskwɪljən/ noun (*informal, often humorous*) a very large number: *a squillion-dollar budget*

**squint** /skwɪnt/ verb, noun
■ verb **1** [I, T] to look at sth with your eyes partly shut in order to keep out bright light or to see better: *to squint into the sun* ◊ *She was squinting through the keyhole.* ◊ *He squinted at the letter in his hand.* ◊ ~ sth *When he squinted his eyes, he could just make out a house in the distance.* **2** [I] (*BrE*) (of an eye) to look in a different direction from the other eye: *His left eye squints a little.* **3** [I] to have eyes that look in different directions
■ noun **1** [C, usually sing.] a condition of the eye muscles which causes each eye to look in a different direction: *He was born with a squint.* **2** [sing.] (*BrE, informal*) a short look: *Have a squint at this.*

**squire** /ˈskwaɪə(r)/ noun **1** (also **Squire**) (in the past in England) a man of high social status who owned most of the land in a particular country area **2** **Squire** (*BrE, informal or humorous*) used by a man as a friendly way of addressing another man: *What can I get you Squire?* **3** (in the past) a young man who was an assistant to a KNIGHT before becoming a knight himself

**squirm** /skwɜːm; NAmE skwɜːrm/ verb **1** [I] to move around a lot making small TWISTING movements, because you are nervous, uncomfortable, etc. ⓢⓨⓝ **wriggle**: (+ adv./prep.) *The children were squirming restlessly in their seats.* ◊ + adj. *Someone grabbed him but he managed to squirm free.* **2** [I] to feel very embarrassed or ashamed: *It made*

# squirrel 1518

him *squirm* to think how badly he'd messed up the interview.

**squir·rel** /ˈskwɪrəl; *NAmE* ˈskwɜːr-/ *noun, verb*
- *noun* a small animal with a long, thick tail and red, grey or black fur. Squirrels eat nuts and live in trees. ◊ VISUAL VOCAB page V2 ⇨ see also FLYING SQUIRREL, GROUND SQUIRREL
- *verb* (-ll-, *US* -l-)
  PHRV **squirrel sth↔aˈway** to hide or store sth so that it can be used later: *She had money squirrelled away in various bank accounts.*

**squir·rel·ly** /ˈskwɪrəli; *NAmE* ˈskwɜːr-/ *adj.* (*NAmE, informal*) **1** unable to keep still or be quiet: *squirrelly kids* **2** crazy

**squirt** /skwɜːt; *NAmE* skwɜːrt/ *verb, noun*
- *verb* **1** [T, I] to force liquid, gas, etc. in a thin, fast stream through a narrow opening; to be forced out of a narrow opening in this way SYN **spurt**: ~ **sth (+ adv./prep.)** *The snake can squirt poison from a distance of a metre.* ◊ *I desperately squirted water on the flames.* ◊ **(+ adv./prep.)** *When I cut the lemon, juice squirted in my eye.* **2** [T] to hit sb/sth with a stream of water, gas, etc. SYN **spray**: ~ **sb/sth (with sth)** *The children were squirting each other with water from the hose.* ◊ ~ **sth (at sb)** *He squirted a water pistol at me* (= made the water come out of it).
- *noun* **1** a thin, fast stream of liquid that comes out of a small opening SYN **spray**: *a squirt of perfume* **2** (*informal, disapproving*) a word used to refer to sb short, young or unimportant that you do not like or that you find annoying

**ˈsquirt gun** *noun* (*NAmE*) = WATER PISTOL

**squish** /skwɪʃ/ *verb* (*informal*) **1** [I, T] ~ **(sth)** if sth soft squishes or is squished, it is pushed out of shape when it is pressed **2** [I] to make a quiet sound by pressing sth soft and wet

**squishy** /ˈskwɪʃi/ *adj.* (**squish·ier**, **squishi·est**) (*informal*) soft and wet

**Sr** (also **Snr**) (both *BrE*) (also **Sr.** *NAmE, BrE*) *abbr.* SENIOR ⇨ compare JR

**Sri Srimati** = SHRI, SHRIMATI

**SS** *abbr.* **1** SAINTS: *SS Philip and James* **2** /ˌes ˈes/ STEAMSHIP: *the SS Titanic*

**SSN** /ˌes es ˈen/ *abbr.* SOCIAL SECURITY NUMBER

**St** *abbr.* **1** (*BrE*) (also **St.** *NAmE, BrE*) (used in written addresses) Street: *Fleet St* **2** **St.** (*NAmE*) State **3** (also **St.** especially in *NAmE*) SAINT

**st** (*BrE*) (also **st.** *NAmE, BrE*) *abbr.* STONE (a British measurement of weight): *9st 2lb*

**stab** /stæb/ *verb, noun*
- *verb* (-bb-) **1** ~ **sb/sth** [T] to push a sharp, pointed object, especially a knife, into sb, killing or injuring them: *He was stabbed to death in a racist attack.* ◊ *She stabbed him in the arm with a screwdriver.* **2** [T, I] to make a short, aggressive or violent movement with a finger or pointed object SYN **jab, prod**: ~ **sth (at/into/through sth)** *He stabbed his finger angrily at my chest.* ◊ ~ **sb/sth (with sth)** *She stabbed the air with her fork.* ◊ ~ **at/into/through sth**: (figurative) *The pain stabbed at his chest.*
  IDM **stab sb in the ˈback** to do or say sth that harms sb who trusts you SYN **betray**
- *noun* **1** an act of stabbing or trying to stab sb/sth; a wound caused by stabbing: *He received several stabs in the chest.* ◊ *She died of a single stab wound to the heart.* **2** a sudden sharp pain or unpleasant feeling: *She felt a sudden stab of pain in the chest.* ◊ *a stab of guilt/fear/pity/jealousy,* etc. **3** (usually sing.) (*informal*) an attempt to do sth: ~ **(at sth)** *He found the test difficult but nevertheless made a good stab at it.* ◊ ~ **(at doing sth)** *Countless people have had a stab at solving the riddle.*
  IDM **a stab in the ˈback** (*informal*) an act that harms sb, done by a person they thought was a friend ⇨ more at DARK *n.*

**stab·bing** /ˈstæbɪŋ/ *noun, adj.*
- *noun* an occasion when a person is stabbed with a knife or other pointed object: *a fatal stabbing*
- *adj.* [usually before noun] (of pain) very sharp, sudden and strong

**sta·bil·ity** /stəˈbɪləti/ *noun* [U] the quality or state of being steady and not changing or being upset in any way (= the quality of being stable): *political/economic/social stability* ◊ *the stability of the dollar on the world's money markets* ◊ *Being back with their family should provide emotional stability for the children.* OPP **instability**

**sta·bil·ize** (*BrE* also **-ise**) /ˈsteɪbəlaɪz/ *verb* [I, T] to become or to make sth become steady and unlikely to change; to make sth stable: *The patient's condition stabilized.* ◊ ~ **sth** *government measures to stabilize prices* ◊ *Doctors stabilized the patient's condition.* ⇨ compare DESTABILIZE ▶ **sta·bil·iza·tion**, **-isa·tion** /ˌsteɪbəlaɪˈzeɪʃn; *NAmE* -ləˈz-/ *noun* [U]: *economic stabilization*

**sta·bil·izer** (*BrE* also **-iser**) /ˈsteɪbəlaɪzə(r)/ *noun* **1** [C] a device that keeps sth steady, especially one that stops an aircraft or a ship from rolling to one side **2 stabilizers** (*BrE*) (*NAmE* **ˈtraining wheels**) [pl.] small wheels that are fitted at each side of the back wheel on a child's bicycle to stop it from falling over **3** [C] (*specialist*) a chemical that is sometimes added to food or paint to stop the various substances in it from becoming separate

**stable** 0⃝ **B2** ⚪
/ˈsteɪbl/ *adj., noun, verb*

| WORD FAMILY |
|---|
| **stable** *adj.* (≠ unstable) |
| **stability** *noun* |
| (≠ instability) |
| **stabilize** *verb* |

- *adj.* **1** **B2** fixed or steady; not likely to move, change or fail SYN **steady**: *The patient's condition is stable* (= it is not getting worse). ◊ *Cattle prices remain stable.* ◊ *The situation in the country has remained relatively stable for a few months now.* ◊ *This ladder doesn't seem very stable.* **2** **B2** (of a person) calm and reasonable; not easily upset SYN **balanced**: *Mentally, she is not very stable.* **3** (*specialist*) (of a substance) staying in the same chemical or ATOMIC state: *chemically stable* OPP **unstable** ▶ **staˈbly** /-bli/ *adv.*
- *noun* **1** [C] a building in which horses are kept ⇨ WORDFINDER NOTE at HORSE ⇨ see also LIVERY STABLE **2** (*BrE* also **stables**) [C + sing./pl. v.] an organization that keeps horses for a particular purpose: (*BrE*) *a riding/racing stables* ◊ *His stables are near Oxford.* **3** [C] a group of RACEHORSES owned or trained by the same person: *There have been just three winners from his stable this season.* **4** [sing.] a group of people who work or trained in the same place; a group of products made by the same company: *actors from the same stable* ◊ *the latest printer from the Epson stable*
  IDM **close, lock,** etc. **the stable door after the horse has ˈbolted** (*BrE*) (*NAmE* **close, lock,** etc. **the barn door after the horse has eˈscaped**) to try to prevent or avoid loss or damage when it is already too late to do so
- *verb* ~ **sth** to put or keep a horse in a stable: *Where do you stable your pony?*

**ˈstable boy**, **ˈstable girl** (*BrE* also **ˈstable lad**) *noun* a person who works in a stable

**stable·mate** /ˈsteɪblmeɪt/ *noun* **1** a horse, especially a racing horse, from the same stable as another horse **2** (also **ˈstable companion**) a person or product from the same organization as another person or product: *the VW corporate stablemate, Audi*

**stab·ling** /ˈsteɪblɪŋ/ *noun* [U] buildings or space where horses can be kept

**stac·cato** /stəˈkɑːtəʊ/ *adj., adv.* **1** (*music, from Italian*) with each note played separately in order to produce short, sharp sounds: *staccato sounds* ◊ *The notes are played staccato.* OPP **legato** **2** with short, sharp sounds or movements: *a peculiar staccato voice* ◊ *staccato bursts of gunfire*

**stack** /stæk/ *noun, verb*
- *noun* **1** [C] ~ **(of sth)** a pile of sth, usually neatly arranged: *a stack of books* ⇨ see also HAYSTACK **2** [C] ~ **(of sth)** (*informal, especially BrE*) a large number or amount of sth; a lot of sth: *stacks of money* ◊ *There's a stack of unopened mail waiting for you at the house.* ◊ *I've got stacks of work to do.* **3** [C] a tall CHIMNEY, especially on a factory ⇨ see also

CHIMNEY STACK, SMOKESTACK **4 the stacks** [pl.] the part of a library, sometimes not open to the public, where books that are not often needed are stored **5** [C] (*computing*) a way of storing information in a computer in which the most recently stored item is the first to be RETRIEVED (= found or got back) **6** [C] (*geology*) a tall thin part of a CLIFF that has been separated from the land and stands on its own in the sea **IDM** SEE BLOW *v*.

■ *verb* **1** [T, I] to arrange objects neatly in a pile; to be arranged in this way: **~(sth)** *to stack boxes* ◊ *Do these chairs stack?* ◊ *stacking chairs* ◊ **~sth (up) (+ adv./prep.)** *logs stacked up against a wall* **2** [T] **~sth (with sth)** to fill sth with piles of things: *They were busy stacking the shelves with goods.* **3** [I, T] **~(sth) (up)** if aircraft **stack (up)** or **are stacked (up)** over an airport, there are several flying around waiting for their turn to land **IDM** ˌstack it (*informal*) to fall over or off sth, especially in a way that makes you look silly and makes other people laugh: *I tried a spin on the ice and stacked it.* **PHRV** ˌstack ˈup **1** to keep increasing in quantity until there is a large pile, a long line, etc: *Cars quickly stacked up behind the bus.* **2** (used especially in questions or in negatives) to compare with sb/sth else; to be as good as sb/sth else **SYN** measure up (to sth/sb): *Let's try him in the job and see how he stacks up.* ◊ **stack up against sb/sth** *A mobile home simply doesn't stack up against a traditional house.* **3** (used especially in negatives) to seem reasonable; to make sense: *That can't be right. It just doesn't stack up.*

**stacked** /stækt/ *adj.* [not usually before noun] if a surface is **stacked with** objects, there are large numbers or piles of them on it: *a table stacked with glasses* **IDM** **the cards/odds are stacked aˈgainst you** you are unlikely to succeed because the conditions are not good for you **the cards/odds are stacked in your ˈfavour** you are likely to succeed because the conditions are good and you have an advantage

**staˈdium** **❶** **B1** /ˈsteɪdiəm/ *noun* (*pl.* **staˈdiums** or **staˈdia** /-diə/) a large sports ground surrounded by rows of seats and usually other buildings: *a football/sports stadium* ◊ *plans to build a new stadium* ➔ WORDFINDER NOTE at SPORT

**staff** **❶** **B1** /stɑːf; *NAmE* stæf/ *noun, verb*
■ *noun* **1** [C, usually sing., U] all the workers employed in an organization considered as a group: *medical/nursing/teaching/coaching staff* ◊ *female staff members* ◊ (*BrE*) *part-time members of staff* ◊ *to employ/recruit/hire/train staff* ◊ *We are suffering from an IT staff shortage.* ◊ *staff training* ◊ *a staff meeting* ◊ (*especially BrE*) *on the* **~** *a reporter on the staff of 'The Times'* ➔ see also GROUND STAFF **2** [sing.] (*NAmE* the) the people who work at a school, college or university, but who do not teach students: *students, faculty and staff* **3** [C + sing./pl. v.] a group of senior army officers who help a commanding officer: *a staff officer* ➔ see also CHIEF OF STAFF, GENERAL STAFF **4** [C] (*old-fashioned* or *formal*) a long stick used as a support when walking or climbing, as a weapon, or as a symbol of authority **5** [C] (*especially NAmE*) (*pl.* **staves**) (*also* **stave**) (*music*) a set of five lines on which music is written **IDM** **the ˌstaff of ˈlife** (*literary*) a basic food, especially bread
■ *verb* [T, often passive] **~sth** to work in an institution, a company, etc.; to provide people to work there: *The advice centre is staffed entirely by volunteers.* ◊ *The charity provided money to staff and equip two hospitals.* ◊ *a fully staffed department* ➔ see also OVERSTAFFED, SHORT-STAFFED, UNDERSTAFFED ▸ **ˈstaffing** *noun* [U]: *staffing levels*

**staffer** /ˈstɑːfə(r); *NAmE* ˈstæf-/ *noun* (*NAmE*) a member of staff in a big organization

**ˈstaff nurse** *noun* (in the UK) a qualified hospital nurse

**ˈstaff officer** *noun* a military officer who helps an officer of very high rank or who works at a military HEADQUARTERS or a government department

**ˈstaffroom** /ˈstɑːfruːm, -rʊm; *NAmE* ˈstæf-/ *noun* (*BrE*) a room in a school where teachers can go when they are not teaching

1519 **stage**

▼ **GRAMMAR POINT**

**staff**
● In *BrE* **staff** (sense 1) can be singular: *a staff of ten* (= a group of ten people) or plural: *I have ten staff working for me.* If it is the subject of a verb, this verb is plural: *The staff in this shop are very helpful.*
● In *NAmE* **staff** (senses 1 and 2) can only be singular: *a staff of ten* (but not: *ten staff*): *The staff in this store is very helpful.*
● The plural form **staffs** is less frequent but is used in both *BrE* and *NAmE* to refer to more than one group of people: *the senator and his staff* (singular) ◊ *senators and their staffs* (plural).

**ˈstaff ˈsergeant** *noun* a member of the army or the US AIR FORCE just above the rank of a SERGEANT: *Staff Sergeant Bob Woods*

**ˈstaff writer** *noun* a person whose job is to write stories, articles, etc. for a newspaper, magazine, radio or television company. A **staff writer** is employed by one particular organization and works in one of their offices. ➔ compare JOURNALIST (1)

**stag** /stæɡ/ *noun* a male DEER ➔ compare BUCK, DOE, HART **IDM** **go ˈstag** (*NAmE*, *old-fashioned*, *informal*) (of a man) to go to a party without a partner

**stage** **❶** **A2** /steɪdʒ/ *noun, verb*
■ *noun*
● PERIOD/STATE **1** **A2** [C] a period or state that sth/sb passes through while developing or making progress: *at...~ I can't make a decision at this stage.* ◊ *At one stage it looked as though they would win.* ◊ *The product is at the design stage.* ◊ **in ...~** *This technology is still in its early stages.* ◊ **~ in sth** *She's reached a crucial stage in her career.* ◊ **~ of (doing) sth** *The children are at various stages of development.*
● PART OF PROCESS **2** **B1** [C] a separate part that a process, etc. is divided into **SYN** phase: *We did the first stage of the trip by train.* ◊ **in stages** *The pay increase will be introduced in stages* (= not all at once). ◊ *We can take the argument one stage further.* ➔ LANGUAGE BANK at PROCESS¹
● THEATRE **3** **B1** [C] a raised area, usually in a theatre, etc. where actors, dancers, etc. perform: **on~** *There were more than 50 people on stage in one scene.* ◊ **off~** *Half the band walked off stage.* ◊ **onto the~** *The audience threw flowers onto the stage.* ◊ *The main character then takes the stage* (= comes onto it). ➔ see also BACKSTAGE, OFFSTAGE, ONSTAGE, SOUND STAGE ➔ WORDFINDER NOTE at THEATRE

| WORDFINDER backdrop, costume, curtain, footlights, prop, proscenium, scenery, set, the wings |
|---|

**4** **B2** (*often* **the stage**) [sing.] the theatre and the world of acting as a form of entertainment: **on the~** *His parents didn't want him to go on the stage* (= to be an actor). ◊ *She was a popular star of stage and screen* (= theatre and cinema/movies). ◊ *a stage play/musical/show*
● IN POLITICS **5** [sing.] an area of activity where important things happen, especially in politics: *She was forced to the centre of the political stage.* ◊ *The country is now a major player on the world stage.* ➔ see also CENTRE STAGE
● CARRIAGE **6** [C] (*old-fashioned*, *informal*) = STAGECOACH ➔ see also LANDING STAGE
**IDM** **set the ˈstage for sth** to make it possible for sth to happen; to make sth likely to happen
■ *verb* **1** **B2** **~sth** to organize and present a play or an event for people to see: *to stage a play/an event/an exhibition* ◊ *The local theatre group is staging a production of 'Hamlet'.* ◊ *Birmingham has bid to stage the next national athletics championships.* **2** **B2** **~sth** to organize and take part in action that needs careful planning, especially as a public protest: *to stage a protest/demonstration/rally* ◊ *Generals staged a coup in 1964, beginning 21 years of military dictatorship.* **3** **~sth** to make sth happen: *The dollar staged a recovery earlier today.* ◊ *After five years in retirement, he staged a comeback to international tennis.*

| s see | t tea | v van | w wet | z zoo | ʃ shoe | ʒ vision | tʃ chain | dʒ jam | θ thin | ð this | ŋ sing |

# stagecoach

**stage·coach** /ˈsteɪdʒkəʊtʃ/ noun a large CARRIAGE pulled by horses that was used in the past to carry passengers, and often mail, along a regular route

**stage·craft** /ˈsteɪdʒkrɑːft; NAmE -kræft/ noun [U] skill in presenting plays in a theatre

**stage direction** noun a note in the text of a play telling actors when to come on to or leave the stage, what actions to perform, etc.

**ˌstage ˈdoor** noun the entrance at the back of a theatre used by actors, staff, etc.

**ˈstage fright** noun [U] nervous feelings felt by performers before they appear in front of an audience

**stage·hand** /ˈsteɪdʒhænd/ noun a person whose job is to help move SCENERY, etc. in a theatre, to prepare the stage for the next play or the next part of a play

**ˌstage ˈleft** adv. on the left side of a stage in a theatre, as seen by an actor facing the audience

**stage-ˈmanage** verb 1 ~ sth to act as stage manager for a performance in a theatre 2 ~ sth to arrange and carefully plan an event that the public will see, especially in order to give a particular impression

**ˌstage ˈmanager** noun the person who is responsible for the stage, lights, SCENERY, etc. during the performance of a play in a theatre ⊃ WORDFINDER NOTE at PERFORMANCE

**ˈstage name** noun a name that an actor uses instead of his or her real name

**ˌstage ˈright** adv. on the right side of a stage in a theatre, as seen by an actor facing the audience

**stagey** = STAGY

**stag·fla·tion** /stæɡˈfleɪʃn/ noun [U] an economic situation where there is high INFLATION (= prices rising continuously) but no increase in the jobs that are available or in business activity

**stag·ger** /ˈstæɡə(r)/ verb 1 [I, T] to walk with weak unsteady steps, as if you are about to fall SYN totter: (+ adv./prep.) *The injured woman staggered to her feet.* ◇ *He staggered home, drunk.* ◇ *We seem to stagger from one crisis to the next.* ◇ *(figurative) The company is staggering under the weight of a £10m debt.* ◇ ~ sth *I managed to stagger the last few steps.* 2 [T] to shock or surprise sb very much SYN amaze: ~ sb *Her remarks staggered me.* ◇ it staggers sb that… *It staggers me that the government is doing nothing about it.* 3 [T] ~ sth to arrange for events that would normally happen at the same time to start or happen at different times: *There were so many runners that they had to stagger the start.* ▶ **stag·ger** noun: *to walk with a stagger*

**stag·gered** /ˈstæɡəd; NAmE -ɡərd/ adj. 1 [not before noun] ~ (at/by sth) | ~ (to hear, learn, see, etc.) very surprised and shocked at sth you are told or at sth that happens SYN amazed: *I was staggered at the amount of money the ring cost.* 2 arranged in such a way that not everything happens at the same time: *staggered working hours* (= people start and finish at different times)

**stag·ger·ing** /ˈstæɡərɪŋ/ adj. *(rather informal)* so great, SHOCKING or surprising that it is difficult to believe SYN astounding ▶ **stag·ger·ing·ly** adv.: *staggeringly beautiful/expensive*

**sta·ging** /ˈsteɪdʒɪŋ/ noun 1 [C, U] the way in which a play is produced and presented on stage: *a modern staging of 'King Lear'* 2 [U] a temporary platform used for standing or working on

**ˈstaging area** noun 1 an area where soldiers and equipment are gathered before a military operation: *a staging area for training exercises* 2 a place where people gather to organize an activity or a trip: *The church was used as a staging area for the flood relief effort.*

**ˈstaging post** noun a place where people, planes, ships, etc. regularly stop during a long journey

**stag·nant** /ˈstæɡnənt/ adj. 1 stagnant water or air is not moving and therefore smells unpleasant 2 not developing, growing or changing SYN static: *a stagnant economy*

**stag·nate** /stæɡˈneɪt; NAmE ˈstæɡneɪt/ verb 1 [I] to stop developing or making progress: *Profits have stagnated.* ◇ *I feel I'm stagnating in this job.* 2 [I] to be or become stagnant: *The water in the pond was stagnating.* ▶ **stag·na·tion** /stæɡˈneɪʃn/ noun [U]: *a period of economic stagnation*

**ˈstag night** noun [usually sing.] 1 *(BrE)* the night before a man's wedding, often spent with his male friends 2 *(BrE)* (also **ˈstag party** *BrE, NAmE*) *(NAmE* **bachelor party**) a party that a man has with his male friends just before he gets married ⊃ compare HEN PARTY ⊃ WORDFINDER NOTE at WEDDING

**stagy** (also **stagey**) /ˈsteɪdʒi/ adj. not natural, as if it is being acted by sb in a play

**staid** /steɪd/ adj. not fun or interesting; boring and old-fashioned

**stain** /steɪn/ verb, noun
■ verb 1 [T, I] to leave a mark that is difficult to remove on sth; to be marked in this way: ~ (sth) (with sth) *I hope it doesn't stain the carpet.* ◇ *This carpet stains easily.* ◇ ~ sth + adj. *The juice from the berries stained their fingers red.* 2 [T] to change the colour of sth using a coloured liquid: ~ sth *to stain wood* ◇ *Stain the specimen before looking at it under the microscope.* ◇ ~ sth + adj. *They stained the floors dark brown.* 3 [T] ~ sth *(formal)* to damage the opinion that people have of sth: *The events had stained the city's reputation unfairly.*
■ noun 1 [C] a dirty mark on sth, that is difficult to remove: *a blood/coffee/an ink stain* ◇ **stubborn stains** (= that are very difficult to remove) ◇ *How can I get this stain out?* ◇ *The carpet has been treated so that it is* **stain-resistant** (= it does not stain easily). ⊃ SYNONYMS at MARK 2 [U, C] a liquid used for changing the colour of wood or cloth 3 [sing.] a ~ on sth *(formal)* something that damages a person's reputation, so that people think badly of them

**stained** /steɪnd/ adj. (often in compounds) covered with stains or marked with a stain: *My dress was stained.* ◇ *paint-stained jeans* ⊃ SYNONYMS at DIRTY ⊃ see also TEAR-STAINED

**ˌstained ˈglass** noun [U] pieces of coloured glass that are put together to make windows showing pictures or special designs, especially in churches

**ˌstain·less ˈsteel** /ˌsteɪnləs ˈstiːl/ noun [U] a type of steel that does not RUST (= change colour)

**stair** /steə(r); NAmE ster/ noun 1 **stairs** [pl.] a set of steps built between two floors inside a building: *We had to carry the piano up three flights of stairs.* ◇ *He climbed the stairs to his bedroom.* ◇ **up/down the ~** *The children ran up the stairs.* ◇ **on the ~** *He remembered passing her on the stairs.* ◇ **at the bottom/top of the stairs** ⊃ see also DOWNSTAIRS noun, UPSTAIRS noun 2 [C] one of the steps in a set of stairs: *How many stairs are there up to the second floor?* ⊃ picture at STAIRCASE 3 [sing.] *(literary)* = STAIRCASE: *The house had a panelled hall and a fine oak stair.* ▶ **stair** adj. [only before noun]: *the stair carpet*
IDM **below ˈstairs** *(BrE, old-fashioned)* in the part of a house where the servants lived in the past

**stair·case** /ˈsteəkeɪs; NAmE ˈsterk-/ noun a set of stairs inside a building including the BANISTERS (= posts and bars that are fixed at the side): *a marble/stone/wooden staircase* ⊃ see also SPIRAL STAIRCASE

**stair·lift** /ˈsteəlɪft; NAmE ˈsterl-/ noun a piece of equipment in the form of a seat that sb can sit on to be moved up and down stairs, used by people who find it difficult to walk up and down stairs without help, especially in their own home

**stair·way** /ˈsteəweɪ; NAmE ˈsterw-/ noun a set of stairs inside or outside a building

**stair·well** /ˈsteəwel; NAmE ˈsterw-/ noun [usually sing.] the space in a building in which the stairs are built

**stake** /steɪk/ noun, verb
■ noun 1 [C] money that sb invests in a company: *a 20 per cent stake in the business* 2 [sing.] ~ **in sth** a part or share in a business, plan, etc. that will bring you money or other benefits if it succeeds: *She has a personal stake in the success of the play.* ◇ *Many young people no longer feel they have a stake in society.* 3 [C] something that you risk

### staircase

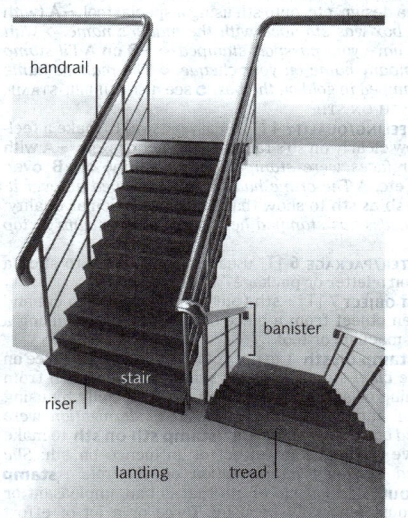

handrail, banister, stair, riser, landing, tread

losing, especially money, when you try to predict the result of a race, game, etc., or when you are involved in an activity that can succeed or fail: *How much was the stake* (= how much did you bet)? ◇ *They were playing cards for high stakes* (= a lot of money). ⇒ **WORDFINDER NOTE** at GAMBLING **4** [C] a wooden or metal post that is pointed at one end and pushed into the ground in order to support sth, mark a particular place, etc. **5 the stake** [sing.] a wooden post that sb could be tied to in former times before being burnt to death (= killed by fire) as a punishment: *Joan of Arc was burnt at the stake.* **6 stakes** [pl.] the money that is paid to the winners in horse racing **7 stakes** [U] used in the names of some horse races
**IDM** **at ˈstake** that can be won or lost, depending on the success of a particular action: *We cannot afford to take risks when people's lives are at stake.* ◇ *The prize at stake is a place in the final.* **go to the ˈstake over/for sth** to be prepared to do anything in order to defend your opinions or beliefs **in the … stakes** used to say how much of a particular quality a person has, as if they were in a competition in which some people are more successful than others: *John doesn't do too well in the personality stakes.* ⇒ more at UP v.
▪ **verb 1** ~ **sth (on sth)** to risk money or sth important on the result of sth **SYN** bet: *He staked £25 on the favourite* (= for example, in horse racing). ◇ *She staked her political career on tax reform, and lost.* ◇ *That's him over there—I'd stake my life on it* (= I am completely confident). **2** ~ **sth (up)** to support sth with a stake: *to stake newly planted trees*
**IDM** **stake (out) a/your ˈclaim (to/for/on sth)** to say or show publicly that you think sth should be yours: *Adams staked his claim for a place in the Olympic team with his easy win yesterday.*
**PHR V** **ˌstake sth↔ˈout 1** to clearly mark the limits of sth that you claim is yours **2** to state your opinion, position, etc. on sth very clearly: *The president staked out his position on the issue.* **3** to watch a place secretly, especially for signs of illegal activity: *Detectives had been staking out the house for several weeks.* ⇒ related noun STAKE-OUT

**stake·hold·er** /ˈsteɪkhəʊldə(r)/ *noun* **1** a person or company that is involved in a particular organization, project, system, etc., especially because they have invested money in it: *The government has said it wants to create a stakeholder economy in which all members of society feel that they have an interest in its success.* **2** a person who holds all the bets placed on a game or race and who pays the money to the winner

**ˈstake-out** *noun* a situation in which police watch a building secretly to find evidence of illegal activities

**stal·ac·tite** /ˈstæləktaɪt; *NAmE* stəˈlæktaɪt/ *noun* a long pointed piece of rock hanging down from the roof of a CAVE (= a hollow place underground), formed over a long period of time as water containing LIME runs off the roof ⇒ compare STALAGMITE

**stal·ag·mite** /ˈstæləgmaɪt; *NAmE* stəˈlægmaɪt/ *noun* a piece of rock pointing upwards from the floor of a CAVE (= a hollow place underground), that is formed over a long period of time from drops of water containing LIME that fall from the roof ⇒ compare STALACTITE

**stale** /steɪl/ *adj.* **1** (of food, especially bread and cake) no longer fresh and therefore unpleasant to eat **2** (of air, smoke, etc.) no longer fresh; smelling unpleasant: *stale cigarette smoke* ◇ *stale sweat* **3** something that is **stale** has been said or done too many times before and is no longer interesting or exciting: *stale jokes* ◇ *Their marriage had gone stale.* **4** a person who is **stale** has done the same thing for too long and so is unable to do it well or produce any new ideas: *After ten years in the job, she felt stale and needed a change.* ▸ **stale·ness** *noun* [U]

**stale·mate** /ˈsteɪlmeɪt/ *noun* **1** [U, C, usually sing.] a DISAGREEMENT or a situation in a competition in which neither side is able to win or make any progress **SYN** impasse: *The talks ended in (a) stalemate.* **2** [U, sing.] (in CHESS) a situation in which a player cannot successfully move any of their pieces and the game ends without a winner ⇒ compare CHECKMATE

**stalk** /stɔːk/ *noun, verb*
▪ *noun* **1** a thin STEM that supports a leaf, flower or fruit and joins it to another part of the plant or tree; the main STEM of a plant: *flowers on long stalks* ◇ *celery stalks* ◇ *He ate the apple, stalk and all.* ⇒ **VISUAL VOCAB** pages V4, V7 **2** a long, thin structure that supports sth, especially an organ in some animals, and joins it on to another part: *Crabs have eyes on stalks.*
▪ *verb* **1** [T, I] ~ **(sth/sb)** to move slowly and quietly towards an animal or a person, in order to kill, catch or harm it or them: *The lion was stalking a zebra.* ◇ *He stalked his victim as she walked home, before attacking and robbing her.* **2** [T] ~ **sb** to illegally follow and watch sb over a long period of time, in a way that is annoying or frightening: *She claimed that he had been stalking her over a period of three years.* **3** [I] + **adv./prep.** to walk in an angry or proud way: *He stalked off without a word.* **4** [T, I] ~ **(sth)** to move through a place in an unpleasant or THREATENING way: *The gunmen stalked the building, looking for victims.* ◇ (*figurative*) *Fear stalks the streets of the city at night.*

**stalk·er** /ˈstɔːkə(r)/ *noun* **1** a person who follows and watches another person over a long period of time in a way that is annoying or frightening **2** a person who follows an animal quietly and slowly, especially in order to kill or capture it

**stalk·ing** /ˈstɔːkɪŋ/ *noun* [U] the crime of following and watching sb over a long period of time in a way that is annoying or frightening

**ˈstalking horse** *noun* [sing.] **1** a person or thing that is used to hide the real purpose of a particular course of action **2** a politician who competes against the leader of their party in order to see how much support the leader has; a stronger candidate can then compete against the leader more seriously

**stall** /stɔːl/ *noun, verb*
▪ *noun* **1** [C] a table or small shop with an open front that people sell things from, especially at a market **SYN** stand: *a market stall* ⇒ see also BOOKSTALL **2** [C] a section inside a farm building that is large enough for one animal to be kept in **3** [C] (*especially NAmE*) a small area in a room, surrounded by glass, walls, etc., that contains a shower or toilet: *a bathroom stall* **4 the stalls** (*also* **the ˈorchestra stalls**) (*both BrE*) [pl.] (*NAmE* **the orchestra** [sing.]) the seats that are nearest to the stage in a theatre: *the front row of the stalls* ⇒ **WORDFINDER NOTE** at THEATRE **5** [C, usually pl.] the seats at the front of a church where the CHOIR (= singers) and priests sit **6** [C, usually sing.] a situation in which a vehicle's engine suddenly stops

# stallholder 1522

because it is not getting enough power **7** [C, usually sing.] a situation in which an aircraft loses speed and goes steeply downwards
- **verb 1** [I, T] (of a vehicle or an engine) to stop suddenly because of a lack of power or speed; to make a vehicle or an engine do this: *The car stalled and refused to start again.* ◇ **~sth** *I stalled the car three times during my driving test.* **2** [I] **~(on/over sth)** to try to avoid doing sth or answering a question so that you have more time: *They are still stalling on the deal.* ◇ *'What do you mean?' she asked, stalling for time.* **3** [T] **~sb** to make sb wait so that you have more time to do sth: *See if you can stall her while I finish searching her office.* **4** [T, I] **~(sth)** to stop sth from happening until a later date; to stop making progress: *attempts to revive the stalled peace plan* ◇ *Discussions have once again stalled.*

**stall·hold·er** /ˈstɔːlhəʊldə(r)/ *noun* (*BrE*) a person who sells things from a stall in a market, etc.

**stal·lion** /ˈstæliən/ *noun* a fully grown male horse, especially one that is used for BREEDING (= producing young) ⊃ compare COLT, GELDING, MARE

**stal·wart** /ˈstɔːlwət; *NAmE* -wərt/ *noun, adj.*
- *noun* **~ (of sth)** a LOYAL supporter who does a lot of work for an organization, especially a political party
- *adj.* [usually before noun] **1** always showing support and able to be relied on, even in a difficult situation **SYN** faithful: *stalwart supporters* **2** (*formal*) physically strong

**sta·men** /ˈsteɪmən/ *noun* (*specialist*) a small, thin male part in the middle of a flower that produces POLLEN and is made up of a STALK supporting an ANTHER. The centre of each flower usually has several stamens. ⊃ VISUAL VOCAB page V7

**stam·ina** /ˈstæmɪnə/ *noun* [U] the physical or mental strength that enables you to do sth difficult for long periods of time: *It takes a lot of stamina to run a marathon.* ⊃ WORDFINDER NOTE at FIT

**stam·mer** /ˈstæmə(r)/ *verb, noun*
- *verb* [I, T] to speak with difficulty, repeating sounds or words and often stopping, before saying things correctly **SYN** stutter: *Many children stammer but grow out of it.* ◇ *+ speech 'W-w-what?' he stammered.* ◇ **~sth (out)** *She was barely able to stammer out a description of her attacker.*
  ▸ **stam·mer·er** *noun*
- *noun* [sing.] a problem that sb has in speaking in which they repeat sounds or words or often stop, before saying things correctly

**stamp** ❶ A2 /stæmp/ *noun, verb*
- *noun*
  - **ON LETTER/PACKAGE 1** A2 (*also formal* **ˈpostage stamp**) [C] a small piece of paper with a design on it that you buy and stick on an ENVELOPE or a package before you post it: *a 67p stamp* ◇ *Could I have three first-class stamps, please?* ◇ *He has been collecting stamps since he was eight.* ◇ *a stamp album* ⊃ see also FOOD STAMP
  - **PRINTING TOOL 2** [C] a tool for printing the date or a design or mark onto a surface: *a date stamp* ⊃ see also RUBBER STAMP
  - **PRINTED DESIGN/WORDS 3** [C] a design or words made by stamping sth onto a surface: *The passports, with the visa stamps, were waiting at the embassy.* ◇ (*figurative*) *The project has the government's stamp of approval.*
  - **CHARACTER/QUALITY 4** [sing.] **~ (of sth)** (*formal*) the mark or sign of a particular quality or person: *All his work bears the stamp of authority.* **5** [sing.] (*formal*) a kind or class, especially of people: *men of a different stamp*
  - **OF FOOT 6** [sing.] an act or sound of stamping the foot: *The stamp of hoofs alerted Isabel.*
- *verb*
  - **FOOT 1** [T, I] **~(sth)** to put your foot down heavily and noisily on the ground: *I tried stamping my feet to keep warm.* ◇ *Sam stamped his foot in anger.* ◇ *The audience were stamping and cheering.*
  - **WALK 2** [I] **+ adv./prep.** to walk with loud heavy steps **SYN** stomp: *She turned and stamped out of the room.*
  - **PRINT DESIGN/WORDS 3** [T, often passive] to print letters, words, a design, etc. onto sth using a special tool: **~A (with B)** *The box was stamped with the maker's name.* ◇ *Wait here to have your passport stamped.* ◇ **~B on A** *I'll stamp the company name on your cheque.* ◇ *The maker's name was stamped in gold on the box.* ⊃ see also RUBBER-STAMP, STAMP STH ON STH
  - **SHOW FEELING/QUALITY 4** [T, usually passive] to make a feeling show clearly on sb's face, in their actions, etc.: **~A with B** *Their faces were stamped with hostility.* ◇ **~B over, across, etc. A** *The crime had revenge stamped all over it.* **5** [T] **~sb as sth** to show that sb has a particular quality: *Her success has stamped her as one of the country's top riders.*
  - **ON LETTER/PACKAGE 6** [T, usually passive] **~sth** to stick a stamp on a letter or package
  - **CUT OUT OBJECT 7** [T] **~sth (out) (of/from sth)** to cut and shape an object from a piece of metal or plastic using a special machine or tool

**PHRV** ˈstamp on sth **1** to put your foot down with force on sth: *The child stamped on the spider.* **2** to stop sth from happening or stop sb from doing sth, especially by using force or authority: *All attempts at modernization were stamped on by senior officials.* ˈstamp sth on sth to make sth have an important effect or influence on sth: *She stamped her own interpretation on the role.* ˈstamp sth↔out **1** to get rid of sth that is bad, unpleasant or dangerous, especially by using force or a lot of effort **SYN** eliminate: *to stamp out racism* **2** to put out a fire by bringing your foot down heavily on it

**ˈstamp collecting** *noun* [U] the hobby of collecting stamps from different countries ⊃ compare PHILATELY
  ▸ **ˈstamp collector** *noun*

**ˈstamp duty** *noun* [U] a tax in the UK on some legal documents

**ˌstamped adˈdressed ˈenvelope** *noun* (*abbr. sae*) (*BrE*) an ENVELOPE on which you have written your name and address and put a stamp so that sb else can use it to send sth to you: *Please enclose a stamped addressed envelope to get your test results.*

**stam·pede** /stæmˈpiːd/ *noun, verb*
- *noun* [C, usually sing.] **1** a situation in which a group of people or large animals such as horses suddenly start running in the same direction, especially because they are frightened or excited: *A stampede broke out when the doors opened.* **2** a situation in which a lot of people are trying to do or achieve the same thing at the same time: *Falling interest rates has led to a stampede to buy property.*
- *verb* **1** [I, T] **~(sth)** (of large animals or people) to run in a stampede; to make animals do this: *a herd of stampeding elephants* ◇ *A huge bunch of kids came stampeding down the corridor.* **2** [T, usually passive] **~sb (into sth/into doing sth)** to make sb rush into doing sth without giving them time to think about it: *I refuse to be stampeded into making any hasty decisions.*

**ˈstamping ground** (*NAmE also* **ˈstomping ground**) *noun* (*informal*) a place that sb likes and where they often go **SYN** haunt

**stance** ❷ B2 /stæns; *BrE also* stɑːns/ *noun* **1** ❷ B2 **~(on sth)** the opinions that sb has about sth and expresses publicly **SYN** position: *What is the newspaper's stance on the war?* **2** the way in which sb stands, especially when playing a sport

**stanch** /stɑːntʃ/ *verb* (*especially NAmE*) = STAUNCH

**stan·chion** /ˈstæntʃən, ˈstɑːn-/ *noun* (*formal*) a long thin VERTICAL piece of wood or metal used to support sth

**stand** ❶ A1 /stænd/ *verb, noun*
- *verb* (**stood**, **stood** /stʊd/)
  - **ON FEET/BE VERTICAL 1** A1 [I] to be on your feet; to be in a VERTICAL position: *She was too weak to stand.* ◇ **+ adv./prep.** *a bird standing on one leg* ◇ *Don't just stand there—do something!* ◇ *We all stood around in the corridor waiting.* ◇ *to stand on your head/hands* (= to be upside down, balancing on your head/hands) ◇ **+ adj.** *Stand still while I take your photo.* ◇ **~ doing sth** *We stood talking for a few minutes.*

## stand

▼ SYNONYMS

**stand**
get up • stand up • rise • get to your feet • be on your feet

These words all mean to be in a vertical position with your weight on your feet, or to put yourself in this position.

**stand** to be in an vertical position with your weight on your feet: *She was too weak to stand.* ◊ *Stand still when I'm talking to you!* NOTE **Stand** is usually used with an adverb or prepositional phrase to show where or how sb stands, but sometimes another phrase or clause is used to show what sb does while they are standing: *We stood talking for a few minutes.* ◊ *He stood and looked out to sea.*

**get up** to get into a standing position from a sitting, kneeling or lying position: *Please don't get up!*

**stand up** to be in a standing position; to stand after sitting: *Stand up straight!* ◊ *Everyone would stand up when the teacher entered the classroom.*

**STAND, GET UP OR STAND UP?**
**Stand** usually means 'to be in a standing position' but can also mean 'to get into a standing position'. **Stand up** can be used with either of these meanings, but its use is more limited: it is used especially when sb tells sb or a group of people to stand. **Get up** is the most frequent way of saying 'get into a standing position', and this can be from a sitting, kneeling or lying position; if you **stand up**, this is nearly always after sitting, especially on a chair. If you want to tell sb politely that they do not need to move from their chair, use **get up**: *Please don't stand up!*

**rise** (*formal*) to get into a standing position from a sitting, kneeling or lying position: *Would you all rise, please, to welcome our visiting speaker.*

**get to your feet** to stand up after sitting, kneeling or lying: *I helped her to get to her feet.*

**be on your feet** to be standing up: *I've been on my feet all day.*

◊ *After the earthquake, only a few houses were left standing.* **2** A1 [I] to get up onto your feet from another position: *Everyone stood when the president came in.* ◊ *~ up We stood up in order to get a better view.*
- PUT UPRIGHT **3** [T] *~ sth/sb + adv./prep.* to put sth/sb in a VERTICAL position somewhere: *Stand the ladder up against the wall.* ◊ *I stood the little girl on a chair so that she could see.*
- DISLIKE **4** A2 [T, no passive] (not used in the progressive tenses) used especially in negative sentences and questions to emphasize that you do not like sb/sth SYN **bear**: *~ sb/sth I can't stand his brother.* ◊ *I can't stand the sight of blood.* ◊ *I can't stand it when you do that.* ◊ *~ doing sth She couldn't stand being kept waiting.* ◊ *~ sb/sth doing sth I can't stand people interrupting all the time.* ⊃ SYNONYMS at HATE
- SURVIVE TREATMENT **5** B2 [T] *~ sth* used especially with *can/could* or *will* to say that sb/sth can survive sth or can TOLERATE sth without being hurt or damaged: *His heart won't stand the strain much longer.* ◊ *Modern plastics can stand very high and very low temperatures.*
- BE IN PLACE/CONDITION **6** B2 [I] + *adv./prep.* to be in a particular place: *The castle stands on the site of an ancient battlefield.* ◊ *An old oak tree once stood here.* **7** B2 [I] to be in a particular condition or situation: + *adj. The house stood empty for a long time.* ◊ *You never know where you stand with her—one minute she's friendly, the next she'll hardly speak to you.* ◊ *As things stand, there is little chance of a quick settlement of the dispute.*
- IN ELECTION **8** B2 [I] (*especially BrE*) (*NAmE usually* run) [I] to be a candidate in an election: *~ for sth He stood for election in Colchester.* ◊ *~ as sth She stood unsuccessfully as a candidate in the local elections.*
- BE AT HEIGHT/LEVEL **9** [I] + *noun* (not used in the progressive tenses) to be a particular height: *The tower stands 30 metres high.* **10** [I] *~ at sth* to be at a particular level, amount, height, etc: *Interest rates stand at 3 per cent.* ◊ *The world record then stood at 6.59 metres.*

1523

- OF CAR/TRAIN, ETC. **11** [I] + *adv./prep.* to be in a particular place, especially while waiting to go somewhere: *The train standing at platform 3 is for London, Victoria.*
- OF LIQUID/MIXTURE **12** [I] to remain still, without moving or being moved: *Mix the batter and let it stand for twenty minutes.* ◊ *standing pools of rainwater*
- OFFER/DECISION **13** [I] if an offer, a decision, etc. made earlier **stands**, it is still available or relevant or still exists: *My offer still stands.* ◊ *The world record stood for 20 years.*
- BE LIKELY TO DO STH **14** [I] *~ to do sth* to be in a situation where you are likely to do sth: *You stand to make a lot from this deal.*
- HAVE OPINION **15** [I] *~ (on sth)* to have a particular attitude or opinion about sth or towards sb: *Where do you stand on private education?*
- BUY DRINK/MEAL **16** [T, no passive] to buy a drink or meal for sb: *~ sth He stood drinks all round.* ◊ *~ sb sth She was kind enough to stand us a meal.* HELP Idioms containing **stand** are at the entries for the nouns and adjectives in the idioms, for example **stand on ceremony** is at **ceremony**.

PHR V ▸ **stand a'part from sb/sth** to be obviously different from sb/sth: *The brand's originality makes it stand apart from other brands.*
**,stand a'side 1** to move to one side: *She stood aside to let us pass.* **2** to not get involved in sth: *Don't stand aside and let others do all the work.* **3** to stop doing a job so sb else can do it
**,stand 'back (from sth) 1** to move back from a place: *The police ordered the crowd to stand back.* **2** to be located away from sth: *The house stands back from the road.* **3** to think about a situation as if you are not involved in it: *It's time to stand back and look at your career so far.*
**,stand be'tween sb/sth** to prevent sb from getting or achieving sth: *Only one game stood between him and victory.*
**,stand 'by 1** to be present while sth bad is happening but not do anything to stop it: *How can you stand by and see him accused of something he didn't do?* ⊃ related noun BYSTANDER **2** to be ready for action: *The troops are standing by.* ⊃ related noun STANDBY '**stand by sb** to help sb or be friends with them, even in difficult situations: *her famous song, 'Stand by your man'* '**stand by sth** to still believe or agree with sth you said, decided or agreed earlier: *She still stands by every word she said.*
**,stand 'down 1 stand down (as sth)** to leave a job or position: *He stood down to make way for someone younger.* **2** (of a witness) to leave the WITNESS BOX in court after giving evidence
'**stand for sth** [no passive] **1** (not used in the progressive tenses) to be an abbreviation or symbol of sth: *'The book's by T.C. Smith.' 'What does the 'T.C.' stand for?'* **2** to support or represent sth: *I hated the organization and all it stood for* (= the ideas that it supported). **3 not stand for sth** to not let sb do sth or sth happen: *I'm not standing for it any longer.*
**,stand 'in (for sb)** to take sb's place SYN **deputize**: *My assistant will stand in for me while I'm away.* ⊃ related noun STAND-IN
**,stand 'out (as sth)** to be much better or more important than sb/sth: *Four points stand out as being more important than the rest.* ⊃ see also OUTSTANDING **,stand 'out (from/against sth)** to be easily seen or noticed: *The lettering stood out well against the dark background.* ◊ *She's the sort of person who stands out in a crowd.*
'**stand over sb** be near sb and watch them: *I don't like you standing over me while I'm cooking.*
**,stand 'up** A1 **1** A1 to get up onto your feet: *The children stood up when the teacher walked into the room.* **2** A1 to be on your feet: *There were no seats left so I had to stand up.* ◊ *You'll look taller if you stand up straight.*
**,stand sb 'up** (*informal*) to deliberately not meet sb you have arranged to meet, especially sb you are having a romantic relationship with: *I've been stood up!* **,stand 'up for sb/sth** to support or defend sb/sth: *Always stand up for your friends.* ◊ *You must stand up for your rights.* ◊ *She had learnt to stand up for herself.* **,stand 'up (to sth)** to remain true, relevant or acceptable even when tested,

# stand-alone

examined closely, etc: *His argument simply doesn't stand up to close scrutiny.* ◇ *I'm afraid this document will never stand up in a court of law.* **stand ˈup to sb** to resist sb; to not accept bad treatment from sb without complaining: *It was brave of her to stand up to those bullies.* **stand ˈup to sth** (of materials, products, etc.) to remain in good condition despite rough treatment SYN **withstand**: *The carpet is designed to stand up to a lot of wear and tear.*

■ noun
- **OPINION** **1** ⚡ B2 [usually sing.] an attitude towards sth or an opinion that you make clear to people: *He has avoided taking a firm stand.* ◇ *~ on sth He was criticized for his tough stand on immigration.* ◇ *~ against sth I admire their principled stand against the war.*
- **DEFENCE** **2** ⚡ B2 [usually sing.] a strong effort to defend yourself or your opinion about sth: *They are willing to take a stand and defend what they believe in.* ◇ *~ against sth We must make a stand against job losses.* ◇ *the rebels' desperate last stand*
- **FOR SHOWING/HOLDING STH** **3** ⚡ B2 a table or structure that goods are sold from, especially in the street or at a market SYN **stall**: *a lemonade/hot dog/newspaper stand* ⇨ see also NEWS STAND **4** ⚡ B2 (especially BrE) a table or a VERTICAL structure where things are displayed or advertised, for example at an exhibition: *a display/an exhibition stand* **5** (often in compounds) a piece of equipment or furniture that you use for holding a particular type of thing: *a bicycle/microphone/cake stand* ⇨ see also MUSIC STAND, NIGHTSTAND
- **AT SPORTS GROUND** **6** a large sloping structure at a stadium with rows where people sit or stand to watch the game ⇨ see also BANDSTAND, GRANDSTAND
- **IN COURT** **7** [usually sing.] = WITNESS BOX: *He took the stand as the first witness.*
- **IN CRICKET** **8** [usually sing.] the period of time in which two people who are BATTING (= hitting the ball) play together and score points: *Clinch and Harris shared an opening stand of 69.*
- **FOR TAXIS/BUSES, ETC.** **9** a place where taxis, buses, etc. park while they are waiting for passengers ⇨ compare TAXI RANK ⇨ see also BUS STAND
- **OF PLANTS/TREES** **10** ~ (of sth) (*specialist*) a group of plants or trees of one kind: *a stand of pines*
- **OF LAND** **11** (SAfrE) a piece of land that you can buy and use for building a house, etc. on: *A developer bought the land and divided it into stands.* ⇨ see also HANDSTAND, ONE-NIGHT STAND

**ˈstand-alone** *adj.* [usually before noun] (especially of a computer) able to be operated on its own without being connected to a larger system

**stand·ard** ⓘ B1 ⓞ /ˈstændəd; NAmE -dərd/ *noun, adj.*

■ noun
- **LEVEL OF QUALITY** **1** ⚡ B1 [C, U] a level of quality, especially one that people think is acceptable: *a fall in living standards* ◇ *Who sets the standard for water quality?* ◇ *A number of Britain's beaches fail to meet European standards of cleanliness.* ◇ *to improve/raise standards* ◇ *He failed to reach the minimum standard and did not qualify.* ◇ *We aim to maintain high standards of customer care.* ◇ *The standard of this year's applications is very low.* ◇ *Her work is not up to standard* (= of a good enough standard). ⇨ see also STANDARD OF LIVING, SUBSTANDARD **2** ⚡ B1 [C, usually pl.] a level of quality that is normal or acceptable for a particular person or in a particular situation: *You'd better lower your standards if you want to find somewhere cheap to live.* ◇ *by ... standards It was a simple meal by Eddie's standards.* ◇ *The equipment is slow and heavy by modern standards.*
- **LEVEL OF BEHAVIOUR** **3** ⚡ B2 **standards** [pl.] a level of behaviour that sb considers to be morally acceptable: *a man of high moral standards* ◇ *Some people have no standards.* ⇨ see also DOUBLE STANDARD
- **UNIT OF MEASUREMENT** **4** [C] a unit of measurement that is officially used; an official rule used when producing sth: *a reduction in the weight standard of silver coins* ◇ *industry standards* ⇨ see also GOLD STANDARD
- **FLAG** **5** [C] a flag that is used during official ceremonies, especially one connected with a particular military group
- **SONG** **6** [C] a song that has been recorded by many different singers

■ *adj.*
- **AVERAGE/NORMAL** **1** ⚡ B1 average or normal rather than having special or unusual features: *the standard rate of tax* (= paid by everyone) ◇ *It is standard practice to search visitors as they enter the building.* ◇ *Touch screens are now a standard feature on most devices.* ◇ *The format of the show is fairly standard.* ◇ *as~ Front airbags come as standard on all models.* ⇨ see also BOG-STANDARD
- **SIZE/MEASUREMENT** **2** ⚡ B1 following a particular standard set, for example, by an industry: *standard sizes of clothes* ◇ *Our charges are standard throughout the country.*
- **BOOK/WRITER** **3** [only before noun] read by most people who are studying a particular subject
- **LANGUAGE** **4** [usually before noun] (of spelling, pronunciation, grammar, etc.) believed to be correct and used by most people: *Standard English* ⇨ compare NON-STANDARD, SUBSTANDARD

**ˈstandard-bearer** *noun* a leader in a political group or campaign

**ˈstandard deˈduction** *noun* [usually sing.] (*US*) a fixed amount of money that you can earn free of tax

**ˈstandard deviˈation** *noun* (*statistics*) the amount by which measurements in a set vary from the average for the set

**ˈstandard ˈerror** *noun* (*statistics*) a method of measuring how accurate an estimate is

**ˈStandard Grade** *noun* (in Scotland) an exam that was taken in a particular subject at a lower level than HIGHERS. Standard Grades were usually taken in a number of different subjects at the age of 16. They were replaced by NQs in 2014.

**ˈstandard ˈissue** *noun* [U] the basic equipment that is given to all the members of a particular group, especially in the army, NAVY, etc: *CS gas has been standard issue in the police force for some time.* ▶ **ˈstandard-ˈissue** *adj.* [only before noun]: *standard-issue body armour* ◇ (*figurative*) *It's a standard-issue action movie.*

**stand·ard·ize** (*BrE also* **-ise**) /ˈstændədaɪz; NAmE -dərd-/ *verb* ~ **sth** to make objects or activities of the same type have the same features or qualities; to make sth standard: *a standardized contract/design/test* ▶ **ˌstand·ard·izˈa·tion**, **-isˈa·tion** /ˌstændədaɪˈzeɪʃn; NAmE -dərdəˈz-/ *noun* [U]: *the standardization of components*

**ˈstandard lamp** (*BrE*) (*also* **ˈfloor lamp** *NAmE, BrE*) *noun* a tall lamp that stands on the floor

**ˈstandard of ˈliving** *noun* (*pl.* **standards of living**) the amount of money and level of comfort that a particular person or group has ⇨ compare QUALITY OF LIFE

**ˈstandard time** *noun* [U] the official time of a country or an area

**stand·by** /ˈstændbaɪ/ *noun, adj.*

■ *noun* (*pl.* **stand-bys**) a person or thing that can always be used if needed, for example if sb/sth else is not available or if there is an emergency: *I always keep a pizza in the freezer as a standby.* ◇ *a standby electricity generator*

IDM **on ˈstandby 1** ready to do sth immediately if needed or asked: *The emergency services were put on standby after a bomb warning.* **2** ready to travel or go somewhere if a ticket or sth that is needed suddenly becomes available: *He was put on standby for the flight to New York.*

■ *adj.* [only before noun] a **standby** ticket for a flight, concert, etc. cannot be bought in advance and is only available a very short time before the plane leaves or the performance starts

**ˈstand-down** *noun* [U, C] a period when people, especially soldiers, relax after a period of duty or danger

**ˈstand-in** *noun* **1** a person who does sb's job for a short time when they are not available **2** a person who replaces an actor in some scenes in a film, especially dangerous ones

**stand·ing** /ˈstændɪŋ/ adj., noun
- **adj.** [only before noun] **1** done from a position in which you are standing rather than sitting or running: *a standing jump/start* ◊ *The speaker got a standing ovation* (= people stood up to clap after the speech). **2** existing or arranged permanently, not formed or made for a particular situation: *a standing army* ◊ (*BrE*) *a standing charge* (= an amount of money that you pay regularly in order to use a service, such as gas or water) ◊ *a standing committee* ◊ *It's a standing joke* (= something that a group of people regularly laugh at). ◊ *We have a standing invitation to visit them anytime.* ⊃ see also FREE-STANDING
- **noun 1** [U] the position or reputation of sb/sth within a group of people or in an organization **SYN** status: *the high/low standing of politicians with the public* **2** [U] the period of time that sth has existed: *a friendship of many years' standing* ⊃ see also LONG-STANDING **3 standings** [pl.] a list of people, teams, etc. showing their positions in a sports competition

**ˌstanding ˈorder** *noun* **1** [C, U] (*BrE*) an instruction that you give to your bank to pay sb a fixed amount of money from your account on the same day each week/month, etc. ⊃ compare BANKER'S ORDER, DIRECT DEBIT **2** [C, U] **~ (for sth)** an order for sth that is repeated every week, month, etc. **3** [C] **~ (to do sth)** a military order that must always be obeyed **4** [C] a rule that says how a parliament, committee, etc. should operate

**ˈstanding room** *noun* [U] space for people to stand in, especially in a theatre, sports ground, etc: *standing room for 12000 supporters* ◊ *It was standing room only at the concert* (= all the seats were sold).

**ˈstanding stone** *noun* a tall stone that was shaped and put in position by PREHISTORIC people in western Europe

**ˈstanding water** *noun* [U] an area of water that is not moving, usually one that smells bad and is not good to drink: *Mosquitoes can breed in standing water.*

**stand-off** *noun* **~ (between A and B)** a situation in which no agreement can be reached **SYN** deadlock

**ˌstand-off ˈhalf** (*also* **ˌfly ˈhalf**) *noun* (in rugby) a player who plays behind the SCRUM HALF

**stand-offish** /ˌstænd ˈɒfɪʃ; *NAmE* ˈɔːf-/ *adj.* (*informal*) not friendly towards other people **SYN** aloof

**stand-out** /ˈstændaʊt/ *noun* (*informal*) a person or thing that is very easy to notice because they are or it is better, more impressive, etc. than others in a group ▶ **stand-out** *adj.* [only before noun]: *the standout track on this album*

**stand-pipe** /ˈstændpaɪp/ *noun* a pipe that is connected to a public water supply and used to provide water outside a building

**stand-point** /ˈstændpɔɪnt/ *noun* [usually sing.] an opinion or a way of thinking about ideas or situations **SYN** perspective: *a political/theoretical standpoint* ◊ **from a ... ~** *We must approach the problem from a different standpoint.* ◊ **from the ~ of sb** *He is writing from the standpoint of someone who knows what life is like in prison.*

**St ˈAndrew's Day** /snt ˈændruːz deɪ; *NAmE* seɪnt/ *noun* 30 November, a Christian festival of the national SAINT of Scotland

**stand·still** /ˈstændstɪl/ *noun* [sing.] a situation in which all activity or movement has stopped **SYN** halt: *The security alert brought the airport to a standstill.* ◊ **at a ~** *Traffic in the northbound lane is at a complete standstill.*

**ˈstand-up** *adj., noun*
- **adj.** [only before noun] **1 stand-up** comedy consists of one person standing in front of an audience and telling jokes **2** (*especially BrE*) a **stand-up** row (= argument) or fight is one in which people shout loudly at each other or are violent towards each other **3** worn, used, etc. in a VERTICAL position: *a stand-up collar* **4** held, used, etc. while standing up: *a stand-up meeting* ◊ *a stand-up desk*
- **noun 1** [U] stand-up comedy: *When did you start doing stand-up?* **2** [C] a person who performs stand-up comedy: *She started out as a stand-up.*

**stank** /stæŋk/ past tense of STINK

**Stan·ley knife™** /ˈstænli naɪf/ *noun* (*BrE*) a very sharp knife with a short BLADE in the shape of a TRIANGLE that can be replaced

**stanza** /ˈstænzə/ *noun* (*specialist*) a group of lines in a repeated pattern that form a unit in some types of poem **SYN** verse ⊃ WORDFINDER NOTE at POETRY

**staphylo·coc·cus** /ˌstæfɪləˈkɒkəs; *NAmE* -ˈkɑːk-/ *noun* (*pl.* **staphylo·cocci** /-kaɪ/) (*medical*) a type of bacteria that can cause infections in some parts of the body such as the skin and eyes

**staple** /ˈsteɪpl/ *adj., noun, verb*
- **adj.** [only before noun] forming a basic, large or important part of sth: *The staple crop is rice.* ◊ *Jeans are a staple part of everyone's wardrobe.*
- **noun 1** a small piece of wire that is used in a device called a STAPLER and is pushed through pieces of paper and bent over at the ends in order to fasten the pieces of paper together **2** a small piece of metal in the shape of a U that is hit into wooden surfaces using a HAMMER, used especially for holding electrical wires in place **3** a basic type of food that is used a lot: *Aid workers helped distribute corn, milk and other staples.* ⊃ WORDFINDER NOTE at CROP **4** something that is produced by a country and is important for its economy: *Rubber became the staple of the Malayan economy.* **5 ~ (of sth)** a large or important part of sth: *Royal gossip is a staple of the tabloid press.*
- **verb ~ sth + adv./prep.** to attach one thing to another using a staple or staples: *Staple the invoice to the receipt.* ◊ *Staple the invoice and the receipt together.*

**ˈstaple ˈdiet** *noun* [usually sing.] **1 ~ (of sth)** the food that a person or an animal normally eats: *a staple diet of meat and potatoes* ◊ *Bamboo is the panda's staple diet.* **2 ~ (of sth)** something that is used a lot: *Sex and violence seem to be the staple diet of television drama.*

**ˈstaple gun** *noun* a device for fixing paper to walls, etc. using staples

**stap·ler** /ˈsteɪplə(r)/ *noun* a small device used for putting staples into paper, etc.

**ˈstaple remover** *noun* a small device used for removing staples from paper, etc.

**star** /stɑː(r)/ *noun, verb*
- **noun**
- • **IN SKY 1** [C] a large ball of burning gas in space that we see as a point of light in the sky at night: *There was a big moon and hundreds of stars were shining overhead.* ◊ *Sirius is the brightest star in the sky.* ◊ **under the stars** *We camped out under the stars.* ⊃ see also DARK STAR, FALLING STAR, LODESTAR, POLE STAR, SHOOTING STAR, STARRY
- • **SHAPE 2** [C] an object, a decoration, a mark, etc., usually with five or six points, whose shape represents a star: *a horse with a white star on its forehead* ◊ *a sheriff's star* ◊ *I've put a star by the names of the girls in the class.* ◊ *Liz deserves a gold star for all her hard work.* ◊ *a four-star general*
- • **MARK OF QUALITY 3** [C, usually sing.] a mark that represents a star and tells you how good sth is, especially a hotel or restaurant: *three-/four-/five-star hotels* ◊ *What star rating does this restaurant have?*
- • **PERFORMER 4** [C] a famous and excellent singer, performer, sports player, etc: *pop/rock/Hollywood/TV stars* ◊ *a football/tennis/sports star* ◊ *She acts well but she hasn't got star quality.* ◊ *Get used to her face as she is a rising star.* ◊ *She's a former child star.* ⊃ WORDFINDER NOTE at ACTOR ⊃ see also ALL-STAR, CO-STAR *noun* (1), FILM STAR, MEGA-STAR, MOVIE STAR, SUPERSTAR **5** [C] a person who has the main part, or one of the main parts, in a film, play, etc: *The star of the show was a young Italian singer.* ◊ *The show has plenty of guest stars appearing each week.* ⊃ see also STAR TURN
- • **BEST OF GROUP 6** [C] (often used before another noun) a person or thing that is the best of a group: *a star student* ◊ *Paula is the star of the class.* ◊ *He was the star performer at the championships.* ◊ *The monkey was the star attraction* (= the best or most popular act) *at the show.*

# star anise

- **HELPFUL PERSON 7** [C, usually sing.] (*informal*) used to show that you feel very grateful for sth that sb has done or that you think they are wonderful: *Thanks! You're a star!*
- **INFLUENCE ON SB'S FUTURE 8 stars** [pl.] a description of what sb thinks is going to happen to sb in the future, based on the position of the stars and planets when they were born ▶ **SYN** **horoscope**: *Do you read your stars in the paper?*
- **IDM** **see 'stars** (*informal*) to see flashes of light in front of your eyes, usually because you have been hit on the head ˈ**stars in your eyes** if sb has **stars in their eyes**, they have dreams of becoming famous, especially as an actor, singer, etc. ⇒ more at REACH v., THANK
- **verb** (-rr-)
- **PERFORM IN MOVIE/PLAY 1** ⓘ **A2** [I] ~ **(with / opposite sb) (in sth)** to have one of the main parts in a film, play, etc: *She starred opposite Cary Grant in 'Bringing up Baby'.* ◇ *No one has yet been chosen for the starring role* (= the main part).
  **2** ⓘ [T, no passive] ~ **sb** if a film, play, etc. **stars** sb, that person has one of the main parts: *a movie starring Jennifer Lawrence and Chris Pratt* ⇒ see also CO-STAR verb
- **MARK WITH SYMBOL 3** [T, usually passive] to put a symbol with a shape like a star (= an ASTERISK) next to a word, etc. in order to make people notice it: *be starred Treat all the sections that have been starred as priority.*

**star ˈanise** *noun* [U, C] a small fruit in the shape of a star, used in cooking as a SPICE ⇒ VISUAL VOCAB page V8

**star·board** /ˈstɑːbəd; NAmE ˈstɑːrbərd/ *noun* [U] the side of a ship or an aircraft that is on the right when you are facing forward ⇒ compare PORT

**star·burst** /ˈstɑːbɜːst; NAmE ˈstɑːrbɜːrst/ *noun* a bright light in the shape of a star, or a shape that looks like a star exploding

**starch** /stɑːtʃ; NAmE stɑːrtʃ/ *noun, verb*
- *noun* **1** [U, C] a white CARBOHYDRATE food substance found in potatoes, flour, rice, etc.; food containing this: *There's too much starch in your diet.* ◇ *You need to cut down on starches.* **2** [U] starch prepared in powder form or as a SPRAY and used for making clothes, sheets, etc. stiff
- *verb* [usually passive] ~ **sth** to make clothes, sheets, etc. stiff using starch: *a starched white shirt*

**starchy** /ˈstɑːtʃi; NAmE ˈstɑːrtʃi/ *adj.* **1** (of food) containing a lot of starch **2** (*informal, disapproving*) (of a person or their behaviour) very formal; not friendly or relaxed

ˈ**star-crossed** *adj.* (*literary*) not able to be happy because of bad luck or FATE: *Shakespeare's star-crossed lovers, Romeo and Juliet*

**star·dom** /ˈstɑːdəm; NAmE ˈstɑːrd-/ *noun* [U] the state of being famous as an actor, a singer, etc: *The group is being tipped for stardom* (= people say they will be famous). ◇ *She shot to stardom in a Broadway musical.*

**star·dust** /ˈstɑːdʌst; NAmE ˈstɑːrd-/ *noun* [U] a magic quality that some famous people with a great natural ability seem to have

**stare** ⓘ **B2** /steə(r); NAmE ster/ *verb, noun*
- *verb* ⓘ **B2** [I] to look at sb/sth for a long time: *I screamed and everyone stared.* ◇ ~ **at sb/sth** *I stared blankly at the paper in front of me.* ◇ *He sat staring into space* (= looking at nothing).
- **IDM** **be staring sb in the ˈface** **1** used to describe sth that you have failed to see, even though it was obvious and should have been easy to see: *The answer was staring us in the face but we never saw it until it was too late.* **2** to be certain to happen: *Defeat was staring them in the face.* **be staring sth in the ˈface** to be unable to avoid sth: *They were staring defeat in the face.*
- **PHRV** ˌ**stare sb ˈout** (*BrE*) (*also* ˌ**stare sb ˈdown** *NAmE, BrE*) to look into sb's eyes for a long time until they feel embarrassed and are forced to look a way
- *noun* an act of looking at sb/sth for a long time, especially in a way that is unfriendly or that shows surprise: *She gave him a blank stare.* ⇒ SYNONYMS at LOOK

**star·fish** /ˈstɑːfɪʃ; NAmE ˈstɑːrf-/ *noun* (*pl.* **star·fish**) a flat sea creature in the shape of a star with five arms

---

▼ **SYNONYMS**

**stare**
**gaze • peer • glare**
These words all mean to look at sb/sth for a long time.

**stare** to look at sb/sth for a long time, especially with surprise or fear, or because you are thinking: *I screamed and everyone stared.*

**gaze** (*rather formal*) to look steadily at sb/sth for a long time, especially with surprise or love, or because you are thinking: *We all gazed at Marco in amazement.*

**peer** to look closely or carefully at sth, especially when you cannot see it clearly

**glare** to look angrily at sb/sth for a long time: *I looked at her and she glared stonily back.*

**PATTERNS**
- to stare / gaze / peer / glare **at** sb/sth
- to stare / gaze / peer / glare **suspiciously**
- to stare / gaze / peer **anxiously / intently**
- to stare / gaze / glare **wildly / fiercely**

---

**star·gazer** /ˈstɑːɡeɪzə(r); NAmE ˈstɑːrɡ-/ *noun* (*informal*) a person who studies ASTROLOGY or ASTRONOMY ▶ **star·gaz·ing** *noun* [U]

**stark** ⓘ **C1** /stɑːk; NAmE stɑːrk/ *adj., adv.*
- *adj.* (**stark·er, stark·est**) **HELP** You can also use **more stark** and **most stark**. **1** ⓘ **C1** unpleasant; real, and impossible to avoid ▶ **SYN** **bleak**: *The author paints a stark picture of life in a prison camp.* ◇ *a stark choice* ◇ *The remains of the building stand as a stark reminder of the fire.* ◇ *He now faces the stark reality of life in prison.* ⇒ SYNONYMS at PLAIN **2** ⓘ **C1** very different from sth in a way that is easy to see ▶ **SYN** **clear**: *stark differences* ◇ *Social divisions in the city are stark.* ◇ *The good weather was in stark contrast to the storms of previous weeks.* **3** looking severe and without any colour or decoration: *I think white would be too stark for the bedroom.* ◇ *The hills stood stark against the winter sky.* **4** [only before noun] complete and total ▶ **SYN** **utter**: *The children watched in stark terror.* ▶ **stark·ly** *adv.*: *The interior is starkly simple.* ◇ *The lighthouse stood out starkly against the dark sky.* ◇ *We are starkly aware of the risks.* **stark·ness** *noun* [U]
- *adv.* ~ **naked** wearing no clothes **IDM** see RAVING *adv.*

**stark·ers** /ˈstɑːkəz; NAmE ˈstɑːrkərz/ *adj.* [not before noun] (*BrE, informal*) not wearing any clothes ▶ **SYN** **naked**

**star·less** /ˈstɑːləs; NAmE ˈstɑːrl-/ *adj.* with no stars in the sky: *a starless night*

**star·let** /ˈstɑːlət; NAmE ˈstɑːrl-/ *noun* (*old-fashioned, sometimes disapproving*) a young woman actor who plays small parts and hopes to become famous: *Hollywood starlets of the 1940s*

**star·light** /ˈstɑːlaɪt; NAmE ˈstɑːrl-/ *noun* [U] light from the stars: *We walked home by starlight.*

**star·ling** /ˈstɑːlɪŋ; NAmE ˈstɑːrl-/ *noun* a common bird with dark shiny feathers and a noisy call

**star·lit** /ˈstɑːlɪt; NAmE ˈstɑːrl-/ *adj.* with light from the stars: *a starlit night*

**Star of David** /ˌstɑːr əv ˈdeɪvɪd/ *noun* (*pl.* **Stars of David**) a star with six points that is used as a symbol of Judaism and the state of Israel

**starry** /ˈstɑːri/ *adj.* [usually before noun] **1** (of the sky) full of stars: *a beautiful starry night* **2** looking like a star: *starry flowers* **3** (of eyes) shining like stars

ˌ**starry-ˈeyed** *adj.* (*informal*) full of emotion, hopes or dreams about sb/sth in a way that is not realistic

**the ˌStars and ˈStripes** *noun* [sing.] the national flag of the US

**star·ship** /ˈstɑːʃɪp; NAmE ˈstɑːrʃ-/ *noun* (in SCIENCE FICTION) a large SPACECRAFT in which people or other creatures travel through space

---

æ cat | ɑː father | e bed | ɜː fur | ə about | ɪ sit | iː see | i happy | ɒ got (*BrE*) | ɔː saw | ʌ cup | ʊ put | uː too

**star sign** (also informal **sign**) noun one of the twelve signs of the ZODIAC: 'What's your star sign?' 'Aquarius.'

**the ˌStar-ˌSpangled ˈBanner** noun [sing.] the national ANTHEM (= song) of the US

**ˈstar-struck** adj. very impressed by famous people such as actors, football players, etc.

**ˈstar-studded** adj. including many famous performers: a star-studded cast

## start ❶ A1 /stɑːt; NAmE stɑːrt/ verb, noun

■ verb

- DOING STH **1** A1 [T, I] to begin doing or using sth: **~(sth)** I start work at nine. ◇ He's just started a new job. ◇ The kids start school next week. ◇ I only started (= began to read) this book yesterday. ◇ We need to start (= begin using) a new jar of coffee. ◇ It's a long story. Where shall I start? ◇ Can you start (= a new job) on Monday? ◇ **~to do sth** It started to rain. ◇ I was starting to feel tired. ◇ **~doing sth** She started laughing. ◇ **~on sth** It's time you started on your homework. ◇ **~by doing sth** Let's start by reviewing what we did last week. ⇨ EXPRESS YOURSELF at OPEN ⇨ note at BEGIN
- HAPPENING **2** A1 [I, T] to begin happening; to make sth begin happening: Work is due to start this weekend. ◇ Have you any idea where the rumour started? ◇ **~sth** Who started the fire? ◇ Do you **start the day** with a good breakfast? ◇ You're always trying to start an argument. ◇ **~sb/sth doing sth** The news started me thinking.
- MACHINE/VEHICLE **3** A1 [T, I] **~(sth)** when you **start** a machine or a vehicle or it **starts**, it begins to operate: Start the engines! ◇ I can't get the car started. ◇ The car won't start. ⇨ see also JUMP-START, KICK-START, PUSH-START
- EXISTING **4** A1 [I, T] to begin to exist; to make sth begin to exist: **~(up)** There are a lot of small businesses starting up in that area. ◇ **~sth** She started a business while she was still at school. ◇ They want to **start a family** (= to have children). ◇ **~sth up** He decided to start up his own film festival.
- FROM PLACE/LEVEL/IN PARTICULAR WAY **5** A2 [I] to begin from a particular place, amount or situation; to begin in a particular way: **+ adv./prep.** The trail starts just outside the town. ◇ Hotel prices start at €80 for a double room. ◇ A sentence always **starts with** a capital letter. ◇ The evening started badly when the speaker failed to turn up. ◇ **+ adj.** The best professional musicians **start young. 6** B1 [I, T] to begin, or to begin sth such as a career, in a particular way that changed later: **~as sth** She started as a secretary but ended up running the department. ◇ **~out/off (as sth)** The company started out with 30 employees. ◇ **~sth (as sth)** He **started life** as a teacher before turning to journalism.
- JOURNEY **7** [I] **~(out)** to begin a journey; to leave SYN **set off, set out**: What time are we starting tomorrow?
- GOING/WALKING **8** [I] **+ adv./prep.** to begin to move in a particular direction: I started after her (= began to follow her) to tell her the news. ◇ He started for the door, but I blocked his way.
- MOVE SUDDENLY **9** [I] to move suddenly and quickly because you are surprised or afraid SYN **jump**: The sudden noise made her start.

IDM **ˌdon't ˈstart | ˌdon't you ˈstart** (informal) used to tell sb not to complain or be critical: Don't start! I told you I'd be late. **ˌget ˈstarted** to begin doing sth: It's nearly ten o'clock. Let's get started. **ˌstart ˈsomething** (informal) to cause trouble **to ˈstart with 1** used when you are giving the first and most important reason for sth: To start with it's much too expensive… **2** at the beginning: The club had only six members to start with. ◇ I'll have melon to start with. ◇ She wasn't keen on the idea to start with. **you, he, she, etc. ˈstarted it** (informal) used to blame sb for beginning a fight or an argument: 'Stop fighting, you two!' 'He started it!' ⇨ more at BALL n., FOOT n.

PHR V **ˌstart ˈback** to begin to return somewhere **ˌstart ˈoff 1** to begin to move: The horse started off at a steady trot. **2** to begin happening; to begin doing sth: The discussion started off mildly enough. **3** to begin by doing or being sth: Let's start off with some gentle exercises. ◇ We started off by introducing ourselves. ◇ **+ adj.** The leaves start off green but turn red later. ◇ **start off doing sth** I started off working quite hard, but it didn't last. **ˌstart sth↔ˈoff** to

1527 **start**

▼ SYNONYMS

**start**
begin • start off • kick off • commence • open
These words are all used to talk about things happening from the beginning, or people doing the first part of sth.

**start** to begin to happen or exist; to begin in a particular way or from a particular point: When does the class start?

**begin** to start to happen or exist; to start in a particular way or from a particular point; to start speaking: When does the concert begin?

START OR BEGIN?
There is not much difference in meaning between these words. **Start** is more frequent in spoken English and in business contexts; **begin** is more frequent in written English and is often used when you are describing a series of events: The story begins on the island of Corfu. **Start** is not used to mean 'begin speaking': ~~'Ladies and gentlemen,' he started.~~

**start off** (rather informal) to start happening or doing sth; to start by doing or being sth: The discussion started off mildly enough.

**kick off** (informal) to start an event or activity, especially in a particular way; (of an event, activity, etc.) to start, especially in a particular way: Tom will kick off with a few comments. ◇ The festival kicks off on Monday, September 13.

**commence** (formal) to start happening: The meeting is scheduled to commence at noon.

**open** to start an event or activity in a particular way; (of an event, a film or a book) to start, especially in a particular way: The story opens with a murder.

PATTERNS
- to start/begin/start off/kick off/commence/open **with** sth
- to start/begin/start off/kick off/commence/open **by** doing sth
- to start/begin/start off/commence **as** sth
- a **campaign/season/meeting** starts/begins/starts off/kicks off/commences/opens
- a **film/book** starts/begins/starts off/opens

begin doing sth; to make sth begin: Let's start off the discussion by defining what we mean by 'software architecture'. **ˌstart sb ˈoff (on sth) 1** [no passive] to make sb begin doing sth: What started her off on that crazy idea? ◇ Don't say anything to her—you'll start her off again (= make her get angry). ◇ **start sb off doing sth** Kevin started us all off laughing. **2** to help sb begin doing sth: My mother started me off on the piano when I was three. ◇ **start sb off doing sth** His father started him off farming. **ˌstart ˈon sb** [no passive] to attack sb physically or with words **ˌstart ˈon at sb (about sth) | ˌstart ˈon (at sb) about sth** (informal) to begin to complain about sth or criticize sb: She started on at me again about getting some new clothes. ◇ Don't start on about him not having a job. **ˌstart ˈout 1** to begin to do sth, especially in business or work; to start out in business ◇ She started out on her legal career in 2001. **2** to have a particular intention when you begin sth: **start out to do sth** I started out to write a short story, but it soon developed into a novel. **ˌstart ˈover** (especially NAmE) to begin again: She wasn't happy with our work and made us start over. **ˌstart ˈup | ˌstart sth↔ˈup** to begin working, happening, etc.; to make sb do this: I heard his car start up. ◇ Start up the engines! ⇨ see also START-UP

■ noun

- BEGINNING **1** A2 [C, usually sing.] the point at which sth begins: They haven't won since the start of the season. ◇ **at the ~ (of sth)** Things didn't look too hopeful at the start of the year. ◇ **from the ~** We've had problems right from the start. ◇ The trip was a disaster from start to finish. ◇ **a … ~ to sth** a perfect start to the day ◇ The campaign is off to a promising start. **2** B2 [C, usually sing.] the act or process of beginning sth: We need to get an early **start** in the morning. ◇ **~ on sth** I'll paint the ceiling if you **make a start** on the

# starter

walls. ◇ She's moving abroad to make a **fresh start** (= to begin a new life). ◇ It's not much, but **it's a start** (= sth useful has been done, although there is a lot more still to do). ⇨ see also FALSE START, KICK-START noun, PUSH-START
- OPPORTUNITY **3** [C, usually sing.] the opportunity that you are given to begin sth in a successful way: *Many critics got their start writing for this magazine.* ◇ **~ in sth** *They worked hard to give their children a good* **start in life**. ◇ *The job gave him his* **start in journalism**.
- IN RACE **4 the start** [sing.] the place where a race begins: *The runners lined up at the start.* **5** [C, usually sing.] an amount of time or distance that sb has as an advantage over other people at the beginning of a race: *I gave the younger children a start.* ◇ **~ on sb** *She went into the second round with a five-minute start on the rest of the cyclists.* ⇨ see also HEAD START **6** [C, usually pl.] (*sport*) a race or competition that sb has taken part in: *She has been beaten only once in six starts.*
- SUDDEN MOVEMENT **7** [C, usually sing.] an act of moving your body quickly and suddenly because you are surprised, afraid, etc: *You gave me quite a start!* ◇ **with a ~** *She woke from the dream with a start.*

**IDM** **by/in fits and 'starts | in 'stops and 'starts** frequently starting and stopping again; not continuously: *Because of other commitments I can only write my book in fits and starts.* **for a 'start** (*informal*) used to emphasize the first of a list of reasons, opinions, etc: *I'm not working there—for a start, it's too far to travel.* ⇨ more at FLYING START

**start-er** /ˈstɑːtə(r); NAmE ˈstɑːrt-/ noun **1** (*especially BrE*) (*NAmE usually* **ap·pe·tizer**) a small dish of food that is served before the main course of a meal ⇨ compare HORS D'OEUVRE **2** a person, horse, car, etc. that is in a race at the beginning: *Only 8 of the 28 starters completed the course.* ⇨ compare NON-STARTER **3** a person who gives the signal for a race to start **4** a device used for starting the engine of a vehicle **5** a person who begins doing a particular activity in the way mentioned: *He was a* **late starter** *in the theatre* (= older than most people when they start). ◇ *a* **slow starter** ⇨ see also SELF-STARTER **6** (often used as an adjective) something that is intended to be used by sb who is starting to do sth: *a starter home* (= a small home for sb who is buying property for the first time) ◇ *a starter kit/pack* ⇨ see also FIRE STARTER

**IDM** **for 'starters** (*informal*) used to emphasize the first of a list of reasons, opinions, etc., or to say what happens first **under starter's 'orders** (of a runner, rider, etc.) waiting for a signal to start a race

**'starting blocks** (*also* **the blocks**) *noun* [pl.] the two blocks on the ground that runners push their feet against at the beginning of a race

**'starting gate** *noun* a barrier that is raised to let horses or dogs start running in a race

**'starting grid** *noun* = GRID (5)

**'starting point** *noun* **1 ~ (for sth)** a thing, an idea or a set of facts that can be used to begin a discussion or process: *The article served as a useful starting point for our discussion.* **2** the place where you begin a journey

**'starting price** *noun* the final ODDS that are given for a horse or dog just before a race begins

**star·tle** /ˈstɑːtl; NAmE ˈstɑːrtl/ verb to surprise sb suddenly in a way that slightly shocks or frightens them: **~ sb/sth** *I didn't mean to startle you.* ◇ *The explosion startled the horse.* ◇ *I was startled by her question.* ◇ **it startles sb to do sth** *It startled me to find her sitting in my office.* ⇨ SYNONYMS AT SURPRISE ▶ **star·tled** *adj.*: *She looked at him with startled eyes.* ◇ *He looked startled.* ◇ *She jumped back like a startled rabbit.*

**start·ling** /ˈstɑːtlɪŋ; NAmE ˈstɑːrt-/ adj. **1** extremely unusual and surprising: *a startling discovery* **2** (of a colour) extremely bright: *startling blue eyes* ▶ **start·ling·ly** *adv.*

**'start-up** *adj., noun*
- *adj.* [only before noun] connected with starting a new business or project: *start-up costs*
- *noun* a company that is just beginning to operate

**star 'turn** *noun* [usually sing.] the main performer or person who provides entertainment in a show

**star·va·tion** /stɑːˈveɪʃn; NAmE stɑːrv-/ noun [U] the state in which sb suffers or dies because they have no food: *to die of/from starvation* ◇ *Millions will* **face starvation** *next year as a result of the drought.* ◇ *a starvation diet* (= one in which you do not have much to eat) ◇ *They were on* **starvation wages** (= extremely low wages).

**starve** /stɑːv; NAmE stɑːrv/ verb **1** [I, T] to suffer or die because you do not have enough food to eat; to make sb suffer or die in this way: *The animals were left* **to starve to death**. ◇ *pictures of starving children* ◇ *The new job doesn't pay as much but we won't starve!* ◇ **~ sb/yourself** *She's starving herself to try to lose weight.* **2 -starved** (in adjectives) not having sth that you need: *supply-starved rebels* ⇨ see also CASH-STARVED
**IDM** **be 'starving (for sth)** (*also* **be 'starved** *especially in NAmE*) (*informal*) to feel very hungry: *When's the food coming? I'm starving!*
**PHRV** **starve sb into sth/into doing sth** to force sb to do sth by not allowing them to get any food or money **starve sb/sth of sth** (*NAmE also* **starve sb/sth for sth**) [usually passive] to not give or have sth that is needed: *I felt starved of intelligent conversation.* ◇ *The department has been starved of resources.* **starve sb↔ out (of sth)** to force sb to leave a particular building or area by not allowing them to get any food

**stash** /stæʃ/ *verb, noun*
- *verb* **~ sth + adv./prep.** (*informal*) to store sth in a safe or secret place: *She has a fortune* **stashed away** *in various bank accounts.*
- *noun* [usually sing.] (*informal*) an amount of sth that is kept secretly: *a stash of money*

**sta·sis** /ˈsteɪsɪs/ noun [U, C] (*pl.* **sta·ses** /ˈsteɪsiːz/) (*formal*) a situation in which there is no change or development

**stat** /stæt/ noun (*informal*) = STATISTIC

**state** /steɪt/ noun, adj., verb
- *noun*
- COUNTRY **1** (*also* **State**) [C] a country considered as an organized political community controlled by one government: *the Baltic States* ◇ *European Union* **member states** ⇨ note at COUNTRY ⇨ see also CITY STATE, CLIENT STATE, FAILED STATE, HEAD OF STATE, NATION STATE, POLICE STATE, WELFARE STATE
- PART OF COUNTRY **2** (*also* **State**) [C] (*abbr.* **St.**) an organized political community forming part of a country: *the states of Victoria and Western Australia* ◇ *the southern states of the US* ◇ *She decided to return to her* **home state** *of Ohio.* ⇨ see also SWING STATE
- GOVERNMENT **3** (*also* **the State**) [U, sing.] the government of a country: *matters/affairs of state* ◇ *people who are financially dependent on the state* ◇ *a state-owned company* ◇ *They wish to limit the power of the State.*
- CONDITION OF SB/STH **4** [C] the mental, emotional or physical condition that a person or thing is in: *a confused mental state* ◇ **~ of sth** *a confused state of mind* ◇ *The government has* **declared a state of emergency** *in the flooded regions.* ◇ *Given the* **current state of knowledge**, *it will take years to find a solution.* ◇ **a ... ~ (of sth)** *The building is in a bad state of repair* (= needs to be repaired). ◇ **in a ... ~ to do sth** *You're not in a fit state to drive.* ◇ (*BrE, informal*) *Look at the state of you! You can't go out looking like that.* ⇨ note at CONDITION
- OFFICIAL CEREMONY **5** [U] the formal ceremonies connected with high levels of government or with kings and queens: **in ~** *The president was driven in state through the streets.*
- THE US **6 the States** [pl.] (*informal*) the United States of America: *I've never been to the States.*

**IDM** **be in/get into a 'state** (*informal, especially BrE*) **1** to be/become excited or anxious: *She was in a real state about her exams.* **2** to be dirty or untidy: *What a state this place is in!* **in a state of 'grace** (in the Roman Catholic Church) having been forgiven by God for the wrong or evil things you have done **a state of af'fairs** a situation: *This state of affairs can no longer be ignored.* ⇨ SYNONYMS AT SITUATION **the state of 'play 1** the stage that has been

reached in a process, etc. which has not yet been completed: *What is the current state of play in the peace talks?* **2** (*especially BrE*) the score in a sports match, especially in CRICKET
- **adj.** (*also* **State**) [only before noun]
- GOVERNMENT **1** B1 provided or controlled by the government of a country: *state officials/agencies* ◊ *state education* ◊ *families dependent on state benefits* (= in Britain, money given by the government to people who are poor) ◊ *state secrets* (= information that could be harmful to a country if it were discovered by an enemy)
- PART OF COUNTRY **2** B1 provided or controlled by a particular state of a country, especially in the US: *the state government/legislature* ◊ *California state law* ◊ *a state prison/hospital/university* ◊ *state police/troopers* ◊ *a state tax*
- OFFICIAL **3** connected with the leader of a country attending an official ceremony: *The queen is on a state visit to Berlin.* ◊ *the state opening of Parliament* ◊ *the state apartments* (= used for official ceremonies)
- **verb** B1 to formally write or say sth, especially in a careful and clear way: ~ **sth** *He has already stated his intention to run for election.* ◊ *The facts are **clearly stated** in the report.* ◊ *There is no need to **state the obvious** (= to say sth that everyone already knows).* ◊ ~ **how, what, etc…** *State clearly how many tickets you require.* ◊ ~ **that…** *He stated categorically that he knew nothing about the deal.* ◊ **it is stated that…** *It was stated that standards at the hospital were dropping.* ◊ **sth/sb is stated to be/have sth** *The contract was stated to be invalid.* ⊃ SYNONYMS at DECLARE **2** [usually passive] ~ **sth** to fix or announce the details of sth, especially on a written document: *This is not one of their stated aims.* ◊ *You must arrive at the time stated.* ◊ *Do not exceed the stated dose* (= of medicine).

**state ˈcapture** *noun* [U] (*SAfrE, disapproving*) the fact of sb using their personal or professional status in order to influence political decisions to their advantage

**ˈstate·craft** /ˈsteɪtkrɑːft; *NAmE* -kræft/ *noun* [U] skill in managing state and political affairs

**the ˈState Department** *noun* [sing.] the US government department of foreign affairs

**ˌstate eduˈcation** (*especially BrE*) (*NAmE usually* **public education**) *noun* [U] education in schools, colleges and universities provided by the government: *the state education system*

**ˈstate·hood** /ˈsteɪthʊd/ *noun* [U] **1** the fact of being an independent country and of having the rights and powers of a country **2** the condition of being one of the states within a country such as the US or Australia: *West Virginia was granted statehood in 1863.*

**ˈstate house** *noun* [usually sing.] (in the US) a building in which a state LEGISLATURE (= parliament) meets

**ˈstate·less** /ˈsteɪtləs/ *adj.* not officially a citizen of any country ▸ **ˈstate·less·ness** *noun* [U]

**ˈstate·let** /ˈsteɪtlət/ *noun* a small state (= country), especially one that is formed when a larger state breaks up

**ˈstate ˈline** *noun* the border between two states in the US: *the Nevada-California state line*

**ˈstate·ly** /ˈsteɪtli/ *adj.* **1** impressive in size, appearance or manner SYN **majestic**: *an avenue of stately chestnut trees* ◊ *a tall, stately woman* **2** slow and formal: *a stately dance* ◊ *The procession made its stately progress through the streets of the city.* ▸ **ˈstate·li·ness** *noun* [U]

**ˌstately ˈhome** *noun* (*BrE*) a large, impressive house of historical interest, especially one that the public may visit

**ˈstate·ment** 🔵 A1 Ⓦ /ˈsteɪtmənt/ *noun, verb*
- **noun 1** A1 [C] something that you say or write that gives information or an opinion: *Are the following statements true or false?* ◊ *Is that a statement or a question?* **2** B1 [C] a formal or official account of facts or opinions SYN **declaration**: *a joint/a written/an official statement* ◊ *A government spokesperson **made a statement** to the press.* ◊ ~ **on/about sth** *The government will **issue a statement** on the policy change today.* ◊ *He gave a statement* (= a written account of facts about a crime, used in court if legal action

1529 **states attorney**

follows) *in which he said he saw two men.* ⊃ see also MISSION STATEMENT, PERSONAL STATEMENT **3** [C] a printed record of money paid, received, etc: *The directors are responsible for preparing the company's financial statements.* ◊ *My bank sends me monthly statements.* ⊃ WORDFINDER NOTE at BANK ⊃ see also BANK STATEMENT **4** [C, usually sing.] a clear expression of an opinion or attitude that you make through your actions or appearance: *The play makes a strong political statement.* ◊ ~ **about sb/sth** *The way you dress makes a statement about you.* ⊃ see also FASHION STATEMENT **5** [C] (in England and Wales) an official report on a child's special needs made by a local education authority: *a statement of special educational needs* **6** [U] (*formal*) the act of stating or expressing sth in words SYN **expression**: *When writing instructions, clarity of statement is the most important thing.*
- **verb** [often passive] ~ **sb** (in England and Wales) to officially decide and report that a child has special needs for his or her education: *statemented children*

▼ SYNONYMS

**statement**
comment • announcement • remark • declaration • observation

These are all words for sth that you say or write, especially sth that gives information or an opinion.

**statement** something that you say or write that gives information or an opinion, often in a formal way: *A government spokesperson made a statement to the press.*

**comment** something that you say or write that gives an opinion on sth or is a response to a question about a particular situation: *She made helpful comments on my work.*

**announcement** a spoken or written statement that informs people about sth: *the announcement of a peace agreement*

**remark** something that you say or write that gives an opinion or thought about sb/sth: *He made a number of rude remarks about the food.*

**declaration** (*rather formal*) an official or formal statement, especially one that states an intention, belief or feeling, or that gives information: *the declaration of war*

**observation** (*rather formal*) a comment, especially one based on sth you have seen, heard or read: *He began by making a few general observations about the report.*

COMMENT, REMARK OR OBSERVATION?
- A **comment** can be official or private. A **remark** can be made in public or private but is always unofficial and the speaker may not have considered it carefully. An **observation** is unofficial but is usually more considered than a remark.

PATTERNS
- a(n) statement/comment/announcement/remark/ declaration/observation **about** sth
- a(n) statement/comment/observation **on** sth
- a(n) **public/official** statement/comment/ announcement/declaration
- to **make** a(n) statement/comment/announcement/ remark/declaration/observation
- to **issue** a(n) statement/announcement/declaration

**ˌstate of ˈsiege** *noun* a situation in which the government limits people's freedom to enter or leave a city, town or building

**ˌstate of the ˈart** *adj.* using the most modern or advanced techniques or methods; as good as it can be at the present time: *The system was state of the art.* ◊ *a state-of-the-art system*

**ˈstate·room** /ˈsteɪtruːm, -rʊm/ *noun* **1** a private room on a large ship **2** a room used by important government members, members of a royal family, etc. on formal occasions

**ˈstate's atˈtorney** *noun* (in the US) a lawyer who represents a state in a court

Ⓞ Oxford Phrasal Academic Lexicon (OPAL) written and spoken word lists | Ⓦ OPAL written word list | Ⓢ OPAL spoken word list

**state school** *noun* **1** (*BrE*) (*NAmE* **public school**) a school that is paid for by the government and provides free education ⊃ compare ACADEMY (5), FREE SCHOOL, PRIVATE SCHOOL, PUBLIC SCHOOL **2** (*NAmE*) = STATE UNIVERSITY

**state's evidence** *noun* [U] (*law*) (in the US) if a criminal **turns state's evidence**, he or she gives evidence against the people who committed a crime with him or her

**state-side** /ˈsteɪtsaɪd/ *adj., adv.* (*US, informal*) connected with the US; in or towards the US (used when the person speaking is not in the US): *When are you next planning a trip stateside?*

**states-man** /ˈsteɪtsmən/, **states-woman** /ˈsteɪtswʊmən/ *noun* (*pl.* **-men** /-mən/ or **-women** /-wɪmɪn/) a wise, experienced and respected political leader: *the party's elder statesman*

**states-man-like** /ˈsteɪtsmənlaɪk/ *adj.* having or showing the qualities and abilities of a statesman: *He was commended for his statesmanlike handling of the crisis.*

**states-man-ship** /ˈsteɪtsmənʃɪp/ *noun* [U] skill in managing state affairs

**states-per-son** /ˈsteɪtspɜːsn; *NAmE* -pɜːrsn/ *noun* (*pl.* **-people**) a wise, experienced and respected political leader

**states' rights** *noun* [pl.] (in the US) the rights of each state in relation to the national government, such as the right to make some laws and to have its own police force

**state trooper** (*also* **troop-er**) *noun* (in the US) a member of a State police force: *Scores of police and state troopers tried to clear the streets.*

**state uni'versity** (*NAmE also* **state school**) *noun* a university that is managed by a state of the US

**state-wide** /ˈsteɪtwaɪd/ *adj., adv.* happening or existing in all parts of a state of the US: *a statewide election* ⋄ *She won 10 per cent of the vote statewide.*

**static** /ˈstætɪk/ *adj., noun*
■ *adj.* **1** not moving, changing or developing: *Prices on the stock market, which have been static, are now rising again.* ⋄ *a static population level* **2** (*physics*) (of a force) acting as a weight but not producing movement: *static pressure* OPP **dynamic**
■ *noun* [U] **1** noise or other effects that interrupt radio or television signals and are caused by particular conditions in the atmosphere **2** = STATIC ELECTRICITY **3 statics** the science that deals with the forces that balance each other to keep objects in a state of rest ⊃ compare DYNAMIC **4** (*NAmE, informal*) angry or critical comments or behaviour

**static e'lectricity** (*also* **static**) *noun* [U] electricity that gathers on or in an object that is not a CONDUCTOR of electricity

**sta-tin** /ˈstætɪn; *NAmE* ˈstætn/ *noun* a drug that people take to lower the level of CHOLESTEROL (= a substance in the body that can cause heart disease) in their blood. There are several types of statin.

**sta-tion** ❶ A1 /ˈsteɪʃn/ *noun, verb*
■ *noun*
• FOR TRAINS/BUSES **1** A1 a place where trains stop so that passengers can get on and off; the buildings connected with this: *the main station* ⋄ *Euston Station* ⋄ *a train station* ⋄ (*BrE also*) *a railway station* ⋄ (*BrE*) *a tube/an underground station* ⋄ (*NAmE*) *a subway station* ⋄ *at a ~ I get off at the next station.* ⊃ WORDFINDER NOTE at TRAIN **2** A1 (usually in compounds) a place where buses stop; the buildings connected with this: *a bus station* ⋄ (*BrE also*) *a coach station* ⊃ see also BUS STATION HELP In Britain, the word **station** on its own usually refers to the train station: *Can you tell me the way to the station?* In the US it is usual to say which station you are talking about: *the train station* ⋄ *the Greyhound Bus station*
• FOR WORK/SERVICE **3** A2 (usually in compounds) a place or building where a service is organized and provided or a special type of work is done: *a police station* ⋄ (*BrE*) *a petrol station* ⋄ (*NAmE*) *a gas station* ⋄ *a pollution monitoring station* ⋄ *an agricultural research station* ⊃ see also FIRE STA-TION, POLLING STATION, POWER STATION, SERVICE STATION, SPACE STATION, WEATHER STATION
• RADIO/TV COMPANY **4** A2 (often in compounds) a radio or television company and the programmes it broadcasts: *a local radio/television/TV station* ⋄ *He tuned to another station.* ⋄ *The station broadcasts 24 hours a day.* ⊃ WORDFINDER NOTE at RADIO
• SOCIAL POSITION **5** (*old-fashioned or formal*) your social position: **above your ~** *She was definitely getting ideas above her station.*
• POSITION **6** a place where sb has to wait and watch or be ready to do work if needed: *You are not to leave your station without permission.* ⊃ see also DOCKING STATION
• LARGE FARM **7** (usually in compounds) a large sheep or cattle farm in Australia or New Zealand
• FOR SOLDIERS, SAILORS **8** a small base for the army or NAVY; the people living in it: *a naval station* ⊃ see also ACTION STATIONS, HILL STATION, WAY STATION IDM see PANIC *n.*
■ *verb*
• ARMED FORCES **1** [often passive] **~ sb + adv./prep.** to send sb, especially from one of the armed forces, to work in a place for a period of time: *troops stationed abroad*
• GO TO POSITION **2 ~ sb/yourself + adv./prep.** (*formal*) to go somewhere and stand or sit there, especially to wait for sth; to send sb somewhere to do this: *She stationed herself at the window to await his return.*

**'station agent** (*US*) (*BrE* **sta-tion-mas-ter**) *noun* a person in charge of a train station

**sta-tion-ary** /ˈsteɪʃnri; *NAmE* -ʃəneri/ *adj.* **1** not moving; not intended to be moved: *I remained stationary.* ⋄ *The car collided with a stationary vehicle.* ⋄ *a stationary exercise bike* OPP **mobile** ⊃ HOMOPHONES at STATIONERY **2** not changing in condition or quantity SYN **static**: *a stationary population*

**sta-tion-er** /ˈsteɪʃənə(r)/ *noun* (*especially BrE*) **1** a person who owns or manages a shop selling stationery **2 sta-tioner's** (*pl.* **stationers**) a shop that sells stationery: *Is there a stationer's near here?*

**sta-tion-ery** /ˈsteɪʃnri; *NAmE* -ʃəneri/ *noun* [U] **1** materials for writing and for using in an office, for example paper, pens and ENVELOPES **2** special paper for writing letters on ⊃ WORDFINDER NOTE at STORE

▼ HOMOPHONES

**stationary • stationery** /ˈsteɪʃnri; *NAmE* -ʃəneri/
• **stationary** *adj.*: *The traffic was completely stationary.*
• **stationery** *noun*: *You can find coloured pens and pencils in the stationery cupboard.*

**'station house** *noun* (*NAmE*) = POLICE STATION

**sta-tion-master** /ˈsteɪʃnmɑːstə(r); *NAmE* -mæs-/ (*US also* **'station agent**) *noun* a person in charge of a train station

**'station wagon** (*NAmE*) (*BrE* **e'state car, es'tate**) *noun* a car with a lot of space behind the back seats and a door at the back for loading large items

**stat-ism** /ˈsteɪtɪzəm/ *noun* [U] a political system in which the central government controls social and economic affairs ▶ **stat-ist** /ˈsteɪtɪst/ *adj., noun*

**stat-is-tic** ❶ B1 W /stəˈtɪstɪk/ *noun* **1** B1 **statistics** (*also informal* **stats**) [pl.] a collection of information shown in numbers: *crime statistics* ⋄ *Statistics show that far more people are able to ride a bicycle than can drive a car.* **according to ~** *According to official statistics, the disease killed over 500 people.* ⋄ **~ on sth** *He should read some of the statistics on economic growth.* ⊃ see also VITAL STATIS-TICS **2** B1 **statistics** (*also informal* **stats**) [U] the science of collecting and analysing statistics: *There is a compulsory course in statistics.* **3** B1 (*also informal* **stat**) [C] a piece of information shown in numbers: *An important statistic is that 94 per cent of crime relates to property.* ⋄ *I felt I was no longer being treated as a person but as a statistic.*

**stat-is-tic-al** ❶ B+ C1 W /stəˈtɪstɪkl/ *adj.* connected with or based on statistics: *statistical analysis* ▶ **stat-is-tic-al-ly** /-kli/ *adv.*: *The difference between the two samples was not statistically significant.*

**stat·is·ti·cian** /ˌstætɪˈstɪʃn/ noun a person who studies or works with statistics

**sta·tive** /ˈsteɪtɪv/ adj. (linguistics) (of verbs) describing a state rather than an action. **Stative** verbs (for example *be, seem, understand, like, own*) are not usually used in the progressive tenses. ⊃ compare DYNAMIC

**stats** /stæts/ noun (informal) = STATISTICS

**stat sheet** noun (NAmE) a piece of paper or a document which gives details of sth in the form of numbers, especially of a team's or a player's performance

**statu·ary** /ˈstætʃuəri; NAmE -tʃueri/ noun [U] (formal) a collection of marble statuary

**statue** ❶ B1 /ˈstætʃuː/ noun a figure of a person or an animal in stone, metal, etc., usually the same size as in real life or larger: *a bronze/marble statue* ◊ *a statue of Apollo*

**statu·esque** /ˌstætʃuˈesk/ adj. (formal) (usually of a woman) tall and beautiful in an impressive way; like a statue SYN **imposing**

**statu·ette** /ˌstætʃuˈet/ noun a small statue

**stat·ure** /ˈstætʃə(r)/ noun [U] (formal) **1** the importance and respect that a person has because of their ability and achievements: *an actress of considerable stature* ◊ *The orchestra has grown in stature.* **2** a person's height: *a woman of short stature* ◊ *He is small in stature.*

**sta·tus** ❶ B2 Ⓦ /ˈsteɪtəs; NAmE also ˈstæt-/ noun **1** ❷ B2 [U, C, usually sing.] the legal position of a person, group or country: *They were granted refugee status.* ◊ *The party was denied legal status.* **2** ❷ B2 [U, C, usually sing.] the social or professional position of sb/sth in relation to others: *She achieved celebrity status overnight.* ◊ *Women are only asking to be given equal status with men.* ◊ *to have a high social status* ◊ *low status jobs* **3** ❷ B2 [U] high rank or social position: *The job brings with it status and a high income.* **4** ❷ B2 [U, C, usually sing.] the level of importance that is given to sth: *the high status accorded to science in our culture* **5** [U] the situation at a particular time during a process: *What is the current status of our application for funds?* ◊ *She updated her Facebook status to 'in a relationship'.*

**ˈstatus bar** noun (computing) an area that you see along the bottom of your computer screen that gives you information about the program that you are using or the document that you are working on

**status quo** /ˌsteɪtəs ˈkwəʊ; NAmE also ˌstæt-/ noun [sing.] (from Latin) the situation as it is now, or as it was before a recent change: *to defend/restore the status quo* ◊ *conservatives who want to maintain the status quo*

**ˈstatus symbol** noun a possession that people think shows their high social status and wealth: *Exotic pets are the latest status symbol.*

**stat·ute** /ˈstætʃuːt/ noun **1** [C, U] a law that is passed by a parliament, council, etc. and formally written down: **in a** ~ *Penalties are laid down in the statute.* ◊ **by** ~ *Corporal punishment was banned by statute in 1987.* ◊ **under** ~ *These rights existed at common law, rather than under statute.* **2** [C] a formal rule of an organization or institution: **under a** ~ *Under the statutes of the university they had no power to dismiss him.*

**ˈstatute book** noun a collection of all the laws made by a government: **on the** ~ *It's not yet on the statute book* (= it has not yet become law).

**ˈstatute law** noun [U] all the written laws of a parliament, etc. as a group ⊃ compare CASE LAW, COMMON LAW

**ˈstatute of limiˈtations** noun (law) the legal limit on the period of time within which action can be taken on a crime or other legal question

**statu·tory** /ˈstætʃətri; NAmE -tɔːri/ adj. [usually before noun] fixed by law; that must be done by law: *The authority failed to carry out its statutory duties.* ◊ *When you buy foods you have certain statutory rights.* ▶ **statu·tor·ily** /ˈstætʃətrəli; NAmE ˌstætʃəˈtɔːrəli/ adv.

**statutory ˈholiday** noun (CanE) a public holiday that is fixed by law

1531 **stay**

**statutory ˈinstrument** noun (law) a law or other rule which has legal status

**statutory ˈrape** noun [U] (NAmE, law) the crime of having sex with sb who is not legally old enough

**staunch** /stɔːntʃ/ adj., verb

■ *adj.* (**staunch·er, staunch·est**) HELP You can also use **more staunch** and **most staunch**. always showing strong support in your opinions and attitude SYN **faithful**: *a staunch supporter of the monarchy* ◊ *one of the president's staunchest allies* ◊ *a staunch Catholic* ▶ **staunch·ly** adv.: *She staunchly defended the new policy.* ◊ *The family was staunchly Protestant.* **staunch·ness** noun [U]

■ *verb* (also **stanch** especially in NAmE) ~ **sth** (formal) to stop the flow of sth, especially blood

**stave** /steɪv/ noun, verb

■ *noun* **1** a strong stick or piece of wood, especially for POLE: *fence staves* **2** (also **staff**) (music) a set of five lines on which music is written ⊃ picture at MUSIC

■ *verb* (**staved, staved** or **stove, stove** /stəʊv/)
PHRV **stave sth↔ˈin** to break or damage sth by pushing it or hitting it from the outside: *The side of the boat was staved in when it hit the rocks.* **stave sth↔ˈoff** (**staved, staved**) to prevent sth bad from affecting you for a period of time; to delay sth: *to stave off hunger*

**stay** ❶ A1 /steɪ/ verb, noun

■ *verb* **1** ❷ A1 [I] to continue to be in a particular place for a period of time without moving away: **+ adv./prep.** *Stay there and don't move!* ◊ *to stay in bed* ◊ *She stayed at home* (= did not go out to work) *while the children were young.* ◊ (*NAmE* also) **stay home** *We ended up staying for dinner.* ◊ *Can you stay behind after the others have gone and help me clear up?* ◊ *My hat won't stay on!* ⊃ *I can't stay long.* ◊ 'Do you want a drink?' 'No, thanks, I can't stay.' ◊ **~ to do sth** *We stayed to see what would happen.* ◊ **~ doing sth** *They stayed talking until well into the night.* HELP In spoken English **stay** can be used with **and** plus another verb, instead of with **to** and the infinitive, to show purpose or to tell somebody what to do: **~ and do sth** *I'll stay and help you.* ◊ *Can you stay and keep an eye on the baby?* **2** ❷ A1 [I] to live in a place temporarily as a guest or visitor: *My sister's coming to stay next week.* ◊ **+ adv./prep.** *We found out we were staying in the same hotel.* ◊ *He's staying with friends this weekend.* ◊ **+ noun** *I stayed three nights at my cousin's house.* HELP In Indian, Scottish and South African English **stay** can mean 'to live in a place permanently': *Where do you stay* (= where do you live)? **3** ❷ A1 [I] to continue to be in a particular state or situation SYN **remain**: **+ adj.** *I can't stay awake any longer.* ◊ *The store stays open late on Thursdays.* ◊ *to stay healthy/alive/calm/silent/safe* ◊ **+ adv./prep.** *I don't know why they stay together* (= remain married or in a relationship). ◊ *Inflation stayed below 4 per cent last month.* ◊ **+ noun** *We promised to stay friends for ever.*

IDM **be here to ˈstay** | **have come to ˈstay** to now be accepted or used by most people and therefore a permanent part of our lives: *It looks like televised trials are here to stay.* **ˈstay!** used to tell a dog not to move **stay the ˈcourse** to continue doing sth until it has finished or been completed, even though it is difficult: *Very few of the trainees have stayed the course.* **stay your ˈhand** (*old-fashioned* or *literary*) to stop yourself from doing sth; to prevent you from doing sth **stay the ˈnight** (*especially BrE*) to sleep at sb's house for one night: *You can always stay the night at our house.* **stay ˈput** (*informal*) if sb/sth **stays put**, they continue to be in the place where they are or where they have been put ⊃ more at CLEAR adv., LOOSE adj., SHAPE n.

PHRV **stay aˈround** (*informal*) to not leave somewhere: *I'll stay around in case you need me.* **stay aˈway (from sb/sth)** to not go near a particular person or place: *I want you to stay away from my daughter.* **stay ˈin** to not go out or to remain indoors: *I feel like staying in tonight.* **stay ˈon** to continue studying, working, etc. somewhere for longer than expected or after other people have left **stay ˈout 1** to continue to be outdoors or away from your house at night **2** (of workers) to continue to be on strike **stay ˈout of sth 1** to not become involved in sth that you have no connection with **2** to avoid sth: *to stay out of trouble* **stay**

# stay-at-home

**'over** to sleep at sb's house for one night **stay 'up** to go to bed later than usual: *You've got school tomorrow. I don't want you staying up late.*

- **noun 1** a period of staying; a visit: *I enjoyed my stay in Prague.* ◊ *an overnight stay* ⊃ see also LONG-STAY, SHORT-STAY **2** a rope or wire that supports a ship's MAST, a POLE, etc. ⊃ see also MAINSTAY

**IDM** **a ,stay of exe'cution** (*law*) a delay in following the order of a court: *to grant a stay of execution*

**'stay-at-home** *noun, adj.*
- **noun** (*informal, often disapproving*) a person who rarely goes out or does anything exciting
- **adj.** a stay-at-home mother or father is one who stays at home to take care of their children instead of going out to work

**stay·ca·tion** /steɪˈkeɪʃn/ *noun* a holiday that you spend at or near your home

**stay·er** /ˈsteɪə(r)/ *noun* (*BrE*) a person or an animal, especially a horse, with the ability to keep going in a race or competition that needs a lot of effort

**'staying power** *noun* [U] the ability or strength to continue doing sth that is difficult or makes you tired until it is finished **SYN** stamina

**St Bernard** /snt ˈbɜːnəd; *NAmE* seɪnt bərˈnɑːrd/ *noun* a large strong dog, originally from Switzerland, where it was trained to help find people who were lost in the snow

**St Chris·to·pher** /snt ˈkrɪstəfə(r); *NAmE* seɪnt/ *noun* a small MEDAL with a picture of St Christopher (the PATRON SAINT of travellers) on it, that some people wear or carry with them when they go on a journey because they believe it will protect them from danger

**STD** /ˌes tiː ˈdiː/ *noun* a disease that is passed from one person to another during sexual activity (the abbreviation for 'sexually transmitted disease')

**St David's Day** /snt ˈdeɪvɪdz deɪ; *NAmE* seɪnt/ *noun* 1 March, a Christian festival of the national SAINT of Wales, when many Welsh people wear a DAFFODIL

**stead** /sted/ *noun*
**IDM** **in sb's/sth's 'stead** (*formal*) instead of sb/sth: *Foxton was dismissed and John Smith was appointed in his stead.* **stand sb in good 'stead** to be useful or helpful to sb when needed: *Your languages will stand you in good stead when it comes to finding a job.*

**stead·fast** /ˈstedfɑːst; *NAmE* -fæst/ *adj.* (*literary, approving*) not changing in your attitudes or aims **SYN** firm: *steadfast loyalty* ◊ *~ in sth He remained steadfast in his determination to bring the killers to justice.* ▶ **stead·fast·ly** *adv.* **stead·fast·ness** *noun* [U]

**stead·ily** /ˈstedəli/ *adv.* **1** gradually and in an even and regular way: *The company's exports have been increasing steadily.* ◊ *The situation got steadily worse.* **2** without changing or being interrupted: *He looked at her steadily.* ◊ *The rain fell steadily.*

**steady** /ˈstedi/ *adj., verb, adv., exclamation*
- **adj.** (stead·ier, steadi·est) **1** developing, growing, etc. gradually and in an even and regular way **SYN** constant: *five years of steady economic growth* ◊ *a steady decline/increase in numbers* ◊ *We are making slow but steady progress.* ◊ *The castle receives a steady stream of visitors.* **2** not changing and not interrupted **SYN** regular: *His breathing was steady.* ◊ *a steady job/income* ◊ *She drove at a steady 50 mph.* ◊ *They set off at a steady pace.* ◊ *a steady boyfriend/girlfriend* (= with whom you have a serious relationship or one that has lasted a long time) **3** fixed in a place or position, supported or balanced; controlled and not shaking or likely to fall down: *He held the boat steady as she got in.* ◊ *I met his steady gaze.* ◊ *Such fine work requires a good eye and a steady hand.* **OPP** unsteady **4** (of a person) sensible; who can be relied on ▶ **steadi·ness** *noun* [U]
**IDM** **(as) steady as a 'rock** extremely steady and calm; that you can rely on ⊃ more at READY *adj.*

- **verb** (stead·ies, steady·ing, stead·ied, stead·ied) **1** [T, I] ~ (yourself/sb/sth) to stop yourself/sb/sth from moving, shaking or falling; to stop moving, shaking or falling: *She steadied herself against the wall.* ◊ *The lift rocked slightly, steadied, and the doors opened.* **2** [I] to stop changing and become regular again: *Her heartbeat steadied.* ◊ *~against sth The pound steadied against the dollar.* **3** [T] ~ sb/sth to make sb/sth calm: *He took a few deep breaths to steady his nerves.*
- **adv.** in a way that is steady and does not change or shake: *In trading today the dollar held steady against the yen.*
**IDM** **go 'steady (with sb)** (*old-fashioned, informal*) to have a romantic or sexual relationship with sb, in which you see the other person regularly
- **exclamation** (*informal*) **1** ~ **on** (*becoming old-fashioned*) used to tell sb to be careful about what they are saying or doing, for example because it is extreme or not appropriate: *Steady on! You can't say things like that about somebody you've never met.* **2** used to tell sb to be careful: *Steady! Don't fall off.*

**steak** /steɪk/ *noun* **1** (also less frequent **beef·steak**) [U, C] a thick slice of good quality beef: *fillet/rump/sirloin steak* ◊ *How would you like your steak done?* ◊ *a steak knife* (= one with a special blade for eating steak with) **2** [U, C] a thick slice of any type of meat: *pork steak* ◊ *a gammon steak* **3** [U] (often in compounds) beef that is not of the best quality, often sold in small pieces and used in PIES, STEWS, etc: *braising/stewing steak* ◊ *a steak and kidney pie* **4** [C] a large thick piece of fish: *a cod steak*

**steak·house** /ˈsteɪkhaʊs/ *noun* a restaurant that serves mainly steak

**steak tar·tare** /ˌsteɪk tɑːˈtɑː(r); *NAmE* tɑːrˈt-/ *noun* [U, C] (*from French*) a dish made with raw beef cut up into very small pieces and mixed with raw eggs

**steal** /stiːl/ *verb, noun*
- **verb** (**stole** /stəʊl/, **stolen** /ˈstəʊlən/) **1** [I, T] to take sth from a person, shop, etc. without permission and without intending to return it or pay for it: *~ from sb/sth We found out he'd been stealing from us for years.* ◊ *~ sth My wallet was stolen.* ◊ *I had my wallet stolen.* ◊ *~ sth from sb/sth He stole a car from the parking lot of a mall.* ◊ *It's a crime to handle stolen goods.* ◊ (*figurative*) *to steal sb's ideas* ◊ (*figurative*) *They accused the president of stealing the election* (= winning it by cheating). ⊃ HOMOPHONES at STEEL **2** [I] + *adv./prep.* to move secretly and quietly so that other people do not notice you **SYN** creep: *She stole out of the room so as not to wake the baby.* ◊ (*figurative*) *A chill stole over her body.* **3** [T] ~ sth (in baseball) to run to the next BASE before another player from your team hits the ball, so that you are closer to scoring: *He tried to steal second base but was out.*
**IDM** **steal a 'glance/'look (at sb/sth)** to look at sb/sth quickly so that nobody sees you doing it **steal sb's 'heart** (*literary*) to make sb fall in love with you **steal a 'kiss (from sb)** (*literary*) to kiss sb suddenly or secretly **steal a 'march (on sb)** [no passive] to gain an advantage over sb by doing sth before them **steal the 'show** [no passive] to attract more attention and praise than other people in a particular situation: *As always, the children stole the show.* **steal sb's 'thunder** to get the attention, success, etc. that sb else was expecting, usually by saying or doing what they had intended to say or do
- **noun** (*NAmE*) (in baseball) the act of running to another BASE while the PITCHER is throwing the ball
**IDM** **be a 'steal** (*informal*) to be for sale at an unexpectedly low price: *This suit is a steal at $80.*

**stealth** /stelθ/ *noun, adj.*
- **noun** [U] the fact of doing sth in a quiet or secret way: *The government was accused of trying to introduce the tax by stealth.* ◊ *Lions rely on stealth when hunting.*
- **adj.** [only before noun] (of an aircraft) designed in a way that makes it difficult to be discovered by RADAR: *a stealth bomber*

**'stealth tax** *noun* (*BrE, disapproving*) a tax that is collected in a way that is not very obvious, so people are less aware that they are paying it

---

| æ cat | ɑː father | e bed | ɜː fur | ə about | ɪ sit | iː see | i happy | ɒ got (*BrE*) | ɔː saw | ʌ cup | ʊ put | uː too |

**stealthy** /ˈstelθi/ *adj.* (**stealth·ier, stealthi·est**) doing things quietly and secretly; done quietly and secretly: *a stealthy animal* ◊ *a stealthy movement* ▶ **stealth·ily** /-θɪli/ *adv.*

**steam** /stiːm/ *noun, verb*
■ *noun* [U] 1 the hot gas that water changes into when it boils: *Steam rose from the boiling kettle.* 2 the power that is produced from steam under pressure, used to operate engines, machines, etc: *the introduction of steam in the 18th century* ◊ *steam power* ◊ *the steam age* ◊ *a steam train/engine* 3 very small drops of water that form in the air or on cold surfaces when warm air suddenly cools **SYN** **condensation**: *She wiped the steam from her glasses.*
**IDM** ▶ **blow / let off ˈsteam** (*informal*) to get rid of your energy, anger or strong emotions by doing sth active or noisy **full speed / steam aˈhead** | **(at) full ˈsteam** with as much speed or energy as possible **get, etc. somewhere under your own ˈsteam** (*informal*) to go somewhere without help from other people **get up / pick up ˈsteam** 1 (*informal*) to become gradually more powerful, active, etc: *His election campaign is beginning to get up steam.* 2 (of a vehicle) to increase speed gradually **run out of ˈsteam** (*informal*) to lose energy and enthusiasm and stop doing sth, or do it less well
■ *verb* 1 [I] to send out steam: *a mug of steaming hot coffee* 2 [T, I] ~ (sth) to place food over boiling water so that it cooks in the steam; to be cooked in this way: *steamed fish* 3 [I] + *adv./prep.* (of a boat, ship, etc.) to move using the power produced by steam: *The boat steamed across the lake.* 4 [I] + *adv./prep.* (especially of a person) to go somewhere very quickly: *He spotted her steaming down the corridor towards him.* ◊ (*figurative*) *The company is steaming ahead with its investment programme.*
**IDM** **be / get (all) steamed ˈup (about / over sth)** (*NAmE* also **be ˈsteamed (about sth)**) (*informal*) to be/become very angry or excited about sth
**PHRV** **ˌsteam sth↔ˈoff** | **ˌsteam sth ˈoff sth** to remove one piece of paper from another using steam to make the GLUE that is holding them together softer **ˌsteam sth↔ˈopen** to open an ENVELOPE using steam to make the GLUE softer **ˌsteam ˈup** | **ˌsteam sth↔ˈup** to become, or to make sth become, covered with steam: *As he walked in, his glasses steamed up.*

**steam·boat** /ˈstiːmbəʊt/ *noun* a boat driven by STEAM, used especially in the past on rivers and along coasts

**steam·er** /ˈstiːmə(r)/ *noun* 1 a boat or ship driven by STEAM ⮕ see also PADDLE STEAMER 2 a metal container with small holes in it, that is placed over a pan of boiling water in order to cook food in the STEAM

**steam·ing** /ˈstiːmɪŋ/ *adj., noun*
■ *adj.* 1 (*informal*) very angry 2 (*also* **ˌsteaming ˈhot**) very hot
■ *noun* [U] (*informal*) a crime in which a group of thieves move quickly through a crowded public place, stealing things as they go

**steam·roll·er** /ˈstiːmrəʊlə(r)/ *noun, verb*
■ *noun* a large slow vehicle with a heavy ROLLER, used for making roads flat
■ *verb* (*NAmE usually* **ˈsteam roll**) [T, I] to defeat sb or force them to do sth, using your power or authority: ~ *sb/sth* (+ *adv./prep.*) *The team steamrollered their way to victory.* ◊ + *adv./prep. He simply steamrollered over all opposition.*

**steam·ship** /ˈstiːmʃɪp/ *noun* (*abbr.* **SS**) a ship driven by STEAM

**steamy** /ˈstiːmi/ *adj.* (**steam·ier, steami·est**) 1 full of STEAM; covered with STEAM: *a steamy bathroom* ◊ *steamy windows* ◊ *the steamy heat of Tokyo* 2 (*informal*) sexually exciting **SYN** **erotic**

**steed** /stiːd/ *noun* (*literary or humorous*) a horse to ride on

**steel** /stiːl/ *noun, verb*
■ *noun* 1 [U] a strong, hard metal that is made of a mixture of iron and CARBON: *the iron and steel industry* ◊ *The frame is made of steel.* ◊ *Small steel plates were attached to the front and back of the bone.* ⮕ see also CHROME STEEL, CHROMIUM STEEL, MILD STEEL, STAINLESS STEEL 2 [U] the industry that produces steel: *steel workers* ◊ *The factories and steel mills have now almost disappeared.* 3 [C] a long, thin, straight piece of steel with a rough surface, used for rubbing knives on to make them sharp 4 [U] (*old use or literary*) weapons that are used for fighting: *the clash of steel*
**IDM** **of ˈsteel** having a quality like steel, especially a strong, cold or hard quality: *She felt a hand of steel* (= a strong, firm hand) *on her arm.* ◊ *You need a cool head and nerves of steel* (= great courage). ◊ *There was a hint of steel in his voice* (= he sounded cold and firm).
■ *verb* to prepare yourself to deal with sth unpleasant: ~ **yourself (for / against sth)** *As she waited, she steeled herself for disappointment.* ◊ ~ **yourself to do sth** *He steeled himself to tell them the truth.*

▼ **HOMOPHONES**

**steal • steel** /stiːl/
• **steal** *verb*: *Lock your bike up so that nobody can steal it.*
• **steel** *noun*: *The best kitchen knives are made from stainless steel.*
• **steel** *verb*: *They had to steel themselves to watch their cherished work being destroyed.*

**ˌsteel ˈband** *noun* a group of musicians who play music on drums that are made from empty metal oil containers. Steel bands originally came from the West Indies.

**ˌsteel ˈdrum** (*also* **ˌsteel ˈpan**) *noun* a musical instrument used in West Indian music, made from a metal oil container which is hit in different places with two sticks to produce different notes

**ˌsteel ˈwool** (*BrE also* **ˌwire ˈwool**) *noun* [U] a mass of fine steel THREADS that you use for cleaning pots and pans, making surfaces smooth, etc.

**steel·work·er** /ˈstiːlwɜːkə(r); *NAmE* -wɜːrk-/ *noun* a person who works in a place where steel is made

**steel·works** /ˈstiːlwɜːks; *NAmE* -wɜːrks/ *noun* (*pl.* **steel·works**) [C + *sing./pl. v.*] a factory where steel is made

**steely** /ˈstiːli/ *adj.* (**steel·ier, steeli·est**) 1 (of a person's character or behaviour) strong, hard and unfriendly: *a cold, steely voice* ◊ *a look of steely determination* 2 like steel in colour: *steely blue eyes* ▶ **steeli·ness** *noun* [U]

**steep** /stiːp/ *adj., verb*
■ *adj.* (**steep·er, steep·est**) 1 (of a slope, hill, etc.) rising or falling quickly, not gradually: *a steep hill/slope* ◊ *a steep climb/descent/drop* ◊ *a steep flight of stairs* 2 [usually before noun] (of a rise or fall in an amount) sudden and very big **SYN** **sharp**: *a steep decline in the birth rate* ◊ *a steep rise in unemployment* 3 (*informal*) (of a price or demand) too much; unreasonable **SYN** **expensive**: *£4 for a cup of coffee seems a little steep to me.* ▶ **steep·ly** *adv.: a steeply sloping roof* ◊ *The path climbed steeply upwards.* ◊ *Prices rose steeply.* **steep·ness** *noun* [U]
■ *verb* [T, I] ~ (sth) (in sth) if you steep food in a liquid or leave it to steep, you put it in the liquid and leave it for some time so that it becomes soft and takes in the taste of the liquid
**IDM** **be ˈsteeped in sth** (*formal*) to have a lot of a particular quality: *a city steeped in history*
**PHRV** **ˈsteep yourself in sth** (*formal*) to spend a lot of time thinking or learning about sth: *They spent a month steeping themselves in Chinese culture.*

**steep·en** /ˈstiːpən/ *verb* [I, T] ~ (sth) to become or to make sth become steeper: *After a mile, the slope steepened.*

**steeple** /ˈstiːpl/ *noun* a tall pointed tower on the roof of a church, often with a SPIRE on it

**steeple·chase** /ˈstiːpltʃeɪs/ (*also* **chase**) *noun* 1 a long race in which horses have to jump over fences, water, etc. ⮕ compare FLAT RACING 2 a long race in which people run and jump over gates and water, etc. around a track

**steeple·chaser** /ˈstiːpltʃeɪsə(r)/ *noun* a horse or a person that takes part in steeplechases

# steer

**steer** /stɪə(r); NAmE stɪr/ verb, noun
- **verb 1** [T, I] ~ (sth/sb) (+ adv./prep.) to control the direction in which a boat, car, etc. moves: *He steered the boat into the harbour.* ◊ *(figurative)* *He took her arm and steered her towards the door.* ◊ *You row and I'll steer.* **2** [T, I] ~ (sth) (+ adv./prep.) (of a boat, car, etc.) to move in a particular direction: *The ship steered a course between the islands.* ◊ *The ship steered into port.* **3** [T] ~ sth + adv./prep. to take control of a situation and influence the way in which it develops: *He managed to steer the conversation away from his divorce.* ◊ *She steered the team to victory.* ◊ *The skill is in steering a middle course between the two extremes.* **IDM** see CLEAR adv.
- **noun 1** [sing.] (*BrE, informal*) a piece of advice or information that helps you do sth or avoid a problem: *Can anyone give me a steer on this?* **2** [C] a BULL (= a male cow) that has been CASTRATED (= had part of its sex organs removed), kept for its meat ⊃ compare BULLOCK, OX

**steer·age** /ˈstɪərɪdʒ; NAmE ˈstɪr-/ noun [U] (in the past) the part of a ship where passengers with the cheapest tickets used to travel

**steer·ing** /ˈstɪərɪŋ; NAmE ˈstɪr-/ noun [U] the equipment in a vehicle that you use to control the direction it goes in ⊃ see also POWER STEERING

**ˈsteering column** noun the part of a car or other vehicle that the STEERING WHEEL is fitted on

**ˈsteering committee** (*also* **ˈsteering group**) noun a group of people that a government or an organization chooses to direct an activity and to decide how it will be done

**ˈsteering wheel** noun the wheel that the driver turns to control the direction that a vehicle goes in

**stego·saur** /ˈstegəsɔː(r)/ (*also* **stego·saurus** /ˌstegəˈsɔːrəs/) noun a DINOSAUR with a small head, four legs and two rows of SPIKES along its back

**stein** /staɪn/ noun (from German) a large decorated cup for drinking beer, usually made of EARTHENWARE and often with a LID (= cover)

**stel·lar** /ˈstelə(r)/ adj. [usually before noun] **1** (*specialist*) connected with the stars ⊃ compare INTERSTELLAR **2** (*informal*) excellent: *a stellar performance*

**STEM** /stem/ abbr. science, technology, engineering and mathematics (used to refer to these subjects as a group in the context of education and jobs): *We need to encourage more girls to enrol on STEM courses.*

**stem** /stem/ noun, verb
- **noun 1** the main long, thin part of a plant above the ground from which the leaves or flowers grow; a smaller part that grows from this and supports flowers or leaves ⊃ VISUAL VOCAB page V7 **2** the long, thin part of a wine glass between the bowl and the base **3** the thin tube of a TOBACCO pipe **4 -stemmed** (in adjectives) having one or more stems of the type mentioned: *a long-stemmed rose* **5** (*grammar*) the main part of a word that stays the same when endings are added to it: *'Writ' is the stem of the forms 'writes', 'writing' and 'written'.*
  **IDM from stem to stern** all the way from the front of a ship to the back
- **verb** (-mm-) ~ sth to stop sth that is flowing from spreading or increasing: *The cut was bandaged to stem the bleeding.* ◊ *They discussed ways of stemming the flow of smuggled drugs.* ◊ *The government had failed to stem the tide of factory closures.*
  **PHRV stem from sth** (not used in the progressive tenses) to be the result of sth ⊃ LANGUAGE BANK at BECAUSE OF

**ˈstem cell** noun a basic type of cell which can divide and develop into cells with particular functions. All the different kinds of cells in the human body develop from stem cells.

**stench** /stentʃ/ noun [sing.] a strong, very unpleasant smell **SYN** reek: *an overpowering stench of rotting fish* ◊ *(figurative) The stench of treachery hung in the air.*

**sten·cil** /ˈstensl/ noun, verb
- **noun** a thin piece of metal, plastic or card with a design cut out of it, that you put onto a surface and paint over so that the design is left on the surface; the pattern or design that is produced in this way
- **verb** [T, I] (-ll-, *NAmE also* -l-) ~ (sth) to make letters or a design on sth using a stencil

**steno** /ˈstenəʊ/ noun (*pl.* -os) (*NAmE, informal*) **1** [C] = STENOGRAPHER **2** [U] = STENOGRAPHY

**sten·og·raph·er** /stəˈnɒɡrəfə(r); NAmE -ˈnɑːɡ-/ (*also informal* **steno**) noun (*especially NAmE*) a person whose job is to write down what sb else says, using a quick system of signs or abbreviations

**sten·og·raphy** /stəˈnɒɡrəfi; NAmE -ˈnɑːɡ-/ (*also informal* **steno**) noun [U] (*NAmE*) = SHORTHAND

**stent** /stent/ noun (*medical*) a small support that is put inside a BLOOD VESSEL (= tube) in the body, in order to keep the blood vessel open enough for blood to flow through

**sten·tor·ian** /stenˈtɔːriən/ adj. (*formal*) (of a voice) loud and powerful

**step** /step/ noun, verb
- **noun**
- • **IN SERIES/PROCESS 1** [C] one of a series of things that you do in order to achieve sth: *We are taking steps to prevent pollution.* ◊ *It's a big step giving up your job and moving halfway across the world.* ◊ *a necessary/an important/a positive step* ◊ *~ toward(s) sth This was a first step towards a united Europe.* ◊ *This won't solve the problem but it's a step in the right direction.* ◊ *The new drug represents a major step forward in the treatment of the disease.* ⊃ SYNONYMS at ACTION ⊃ see also BABY STEP **2** [C] one of a series of things that sb does or that happen, which forms part of a process **SYN** stage: *Having completed the first stage, you can move on to step 2.* ◊ *I'd like to take this idea a step further.* ◊ *This was a big step up* (= to a better position) *in his career.* ◊ *I'll explain it to you step by step.* ◊ *a step-by-step guide to building your own home*
- • **MOVEMENT/SOUND 3** [C] the act of lifting your foot and putting it down in order to walk or move somewhere; the sound this makes: *a baby's first steps* ◊ *He took a step towards the door.* ◊ *We heard steps outside.* ⊃ see also FOOTSTEP, GOOSE-STEP
- • **DISTANCE 4** [C] the distance that you cover when you take a step: *It's only a few steps further.* ◊ *He turned around and retraced his steps* (= went back the way he had come). ◊ *She moved a step closer to me.* ◊ *(figurative) The hotel is only a short step* (= a short distance) *from the beach.*
- • **STAIR 5** [C] a surface that you put your foot on in order to walk to a higher or lower level, especially one of a series: *She was sitting on the bottom step of the staircase.* ◊ *We walked down some stone steps to the beach.* ◊ *A short flight of steps led up to the door.* ⊃ see also DOORSTEP noun, NAUGHTY STEP
- • **IN DANCE 6** [C, usually pl.] a series of movements that you make with your feet and which form a dance ⊃ WORDFINDER NOTE at DANCE ⊃ see also QUICKSTEP, TWO-STEP
- • **WAY OF WALKING 7** [C, usually sing.] the way that sb walks: *He walked with a quick light step.*
- • **EXERCISE 8** [U] (often in compounds) a type of exercise that you do by stepping on and off a raised piece of equipment: *step aerobics* ◊ *a step class*
- • **LADDER 9** **steps** [pl.] (*BrE*) a STEPLADDER: *a pair of steps* ◊ *We need the steps to get into the attic.*
- • **IN MUSIC 10** [C] (*NAmE*) the INTERVAL between two notes that are next to each other in a SCALE ⊃ compare SEMITONE, TONE ⊃ see also HALF STEP, WHOLE STEP

**IDM break ˈstep** to change the way you are walking so that you do not walk in the same rhythm as the people you are walking or MARCHING with **fall into ˈstep (beside/with sb)** to change the way you are walking so that you start walking in the same rhythm as the person you are walking with: *He caught her up and fell into step beside her.* **in/out of ˈstep (with sb/sth) 1** putting your feet on the ground in the right/wrong way, according to the rhythm of the music or the people you are moving with **2** having ideas that are the same as or different from other people's: *She was out of step with her colleagues.* **mind/watch your**

**step 1** to walk carefully **2** to behave in a careful and sensible way **one step forward, two steps back** (*saying*) used to say that every time you make progress, sth bad happens that means that the situation is worse than before **a/one step ahead (of sb/sth)** when you are **one step ahead** of sb/sth, you manage to avoid them or to achieve sth more quickly than they do **a/one step at a time** when you do sth **one step at a time** you do it slowly and gradually
- **verb** B2 (**-pp-**) [I] + *adv./prep.* to lift your foot and move it in a particular direction or put it on or in sth; to move a short distance: *to step on/off a bus* ◊ *I stepped forward when my name was called out.* ◊ *She stepped aside to let them pass.* ◊ *We stepped carefully over the broken glass.* ◊ *I turned around quickly and stepped on his toes.* ◊ (*figurative*) *Going into the hotel is like stepping back in time.*

**IDM** **step into the ˈbreach** to do sb's job or work when they are suddenly or unexpectedly unable to do it **step into sb's ˈshoes** to continue a job or the work that sb else has started **ˈstep on it** (*informal*) used especially in orders to tell sb to drive faster **step on sb's ˈtoes** (*NAmE, informal*) = TREAD ON SB'S TOES at TREAD *v.* **step out of ˈline | be/get out of ˈline** to behave badly or break the rules **step up to the ˈplate** (especially *NAmE*) to do what is necessary in order to benefit from an opportunity or deal with a crisis: *It's important for world leaders to step up to the plate and honor their commitments on global warming.*

**PHRV** **ˌstep aˈside/ˈdown** to leave an important job or position and let sb else take your place **ˌstep ˈback (from sth)** to think about a situation calmly, as if you are not involved in it yourself: *We are learning to step back from ourselves and identify our strengths and weaknesses.* **ˌstep ˈforward** to offer to help sb or give information **ˌstep ˈin** to help sb in a difficult situation or an argument: *A local businessman stepped in with a large donation for the school.* ◊ *The team coach was forced to step in to stop the two athletes from coming to blows.* **ˌstep ˈout** (especially *NAmE*) to go out: *I'm just going to step out for a few minutes.* **ˌstep ˈup** to come forward: *She stepped up to receive her prize.* ◊ (*figurative*) *Employers have stepped up to help bridge the gap between education and work.* **ˌstep sth↔ˈup** to increase the amount, speed, etc. of sth: *He has stepped up his training to prepare for the race.* ◊ *If he wants to win this election, he really needs to **step it up** (= put in more effort).*

**step-** /step/ *combining form* (in nouns) related as a result of one parent marrying again: *stepmother*

**ˈstep-brother** /ˈstepbrʌðə(r)/ *noun* the son from an earlier marriage of your STEPMOTHER or STEPFATHER ⊃ compare HALF-BROTHER

**ˈstep change** *noun* [usually sing.] (*BrE*) a big change or improvement in sth: *His speech called for a step change in attitudes to the environment in the 21st century.*

**ˈstep-child** /ˈsteptʃaɪld/ *noun* (*pl.* **step-chil-dren** /ˈsteptʃɪldrən/) a child that your husband or wife has from an earlier marriage to another person

**ˈstep-daugh-ter** /ˈstepdɔːtə(r)/ *noun* a daughter that your husband or wife has from an earlier marriage to another person

**ˈstep-fam-ily** /ˈstepfæməli/ *noun* (*pl.* **-ies**) the family that is formed when sb marries a person who already has children ⊃ WORDFINDER NOTE at FAMILY

**ˈstep-father** /ˈstepfɑːðə(r)/ *noun* the man who is married to your mother but who is not your real father

**ˈStep-ford wife** /ˈstepfəd waɪf; *NAmE* -fərd/ *noun* a woman who does not behave or think in an independent way, always following the accepted rules of society and obeying her husband without thinking: *She's gradually turning into a Stepford wife.* **ORIGIN** From the title of the book and film *The Stepford Wives*, in which a group of women who behave in this way are in fact robots.

**ˈstep-lad-der** /ˈsteplædə(r)/ *noun* a short LADDER that is made of two parts, one with steps, that are joined together at the top, so that it can stand on its own or be folded flat for carrying or storing ⊃ picture at LADDER

**ˈstep-mother** /ˈstepmʌðə(r)/ *noun* the woman who is married to your father but who is not your real mother

**ˈstep-ney** /ˈstepni/ *noun* (*IndE*) a SPARE wheel for a car

**ˈstep-parent** *noun* a stepmother or stepfather

**steppe** /step/ *noun* [C, usually pl., U] a large area of land with grass but few trees, especially in south-east Europe and Siberia: *the vast Russian steppes*

**ˈstepping stone** *noun* **1** one of a line of flat stones that you step on in order to cross a stream or river **2** something that allows you to make progress or begin to achieve sth: *a stepping stone to a more lucrative career*

**ˈstep-sis-ter** /ˈstepsɪstə(r)/ *noun* the daughter from an earlier marriage of your STEPMOTHER or STEPFATHER ⊃ compare HALF-SISTER

**ˈstep-son** /ˈstepsʌn/ *noun* a son that your husband or wife has from an earlier marriage to another person

**ˈstep-wise** /ˈstepwaɪz/ *adj.* **1** in a series of steps, rather than continuously **2** (*music*) (of a MELODY) moving in a way that uses only the notes that are next to each other in a SCALE

**-ster** /stə(r)/ *suffix* (in nouns) a person who is connected with or has the quality of: *gangster* ◊ *youngster*

**stereo** /ˈsteriəʊ/ *noun* (*pl.* **-os**) **1** [U] the system for playing recorded music, speech, etc. in which the sound is directed through two channels: *in ~ to broadcast in stereo* **2** (*also* **ˈstereo system**) [C] a machine that plays CDs, etc., sometimes with a radio, that has two separate SPEAKERS so that you hear different sounds from each: *a car/personal stereo* ⊃ compare MONO ▶ **stereo** (*also formal* **stereo-phon-ic**) *adj.* [only before noun]: *stereo sound*

**stereo-scop-ic** /ˌsteriəˈskɒpɪk; *NAmE* -ˈskɑːp-/ *adj.* **1** (specialist) able to see how long, wide and deep objects are, as humans do: *stereoscopic vision* **2** (of a picture, photograph, etc.) that is made so that you see how long, wide and deep the objects in it are when you use a special machine SYN **three-D**

**stereo-type** B2+ C1 /ˈsteriətaɪp/ *noun, verb*
- **noun** B2+ C1 a fixed idea or image that many people have of a particular type of person or thing, but which is often not true in reality: *cultural/gender/racial stereotypes* ◊ *He doesn't conform to the usual stereotype of the businessman with a dark suit and briefcase.* ▶ **stereo-typ-ical** /ˌsteriəˈtɪpɪkl/ *adj.*: *the stereotypical image of feminine behaviour* **stereo-typ-ical-ly** /-kli/ *adv.*
- **verb** [often passive] to form a fixed idea about a person or thing which may not really be true: *~sb Children from certain backgrounds tend to be stereotyped by their teachers.* ◊ *~sb as sth Why are professors stereotyped as absent-minded?* ▶ **stereo-typed** *adj.*: *a play full of stereotyped characters* **stereo-typ-ing** *noun* [U]: *sexual stereotyping*

**ster-ile** /ˈsteraɪl; *NAmE* -rəl/ *adj.* **1** (of humans or animals) not able to produce children or young animals SYN **infertile** ⊃ compare FERTILE **2** completely clean and free from bacteria: *sterile bandages* ◊ *sterile water* **3** (of a discussion, an argument, etc.) not producing any useful result SYN **fruitless**: *a sterile debate* **4** not having individual personality, imagination or new ideas: *The room felt cold and sterile.* ◊ *He felt creatively and emotionally sterile.* **5** (of land) not good enough to produce crops ▶ **ster-il-ity** /stəˈrɪləti/ *noun* [U]: *The disease can cause sterility in men and women.* ◊ *the meaningless sterility of statistics* ◊ *She contemplated the sterility of her existence.*

**ster-il-ize** (*BrE also* **-ise**) /ˈsterəlaɪz/ *verb* **1** [often passive] *~sth* to kill the bacteria in or on sth: *to sterilize surgical instruments* ◊ *sterilized milk/water* **2** [usually passive] *~sb/sth* to make a person or an animal unable to have babies, especially by removing or blocking their sex organs ▶ **ster-il-iza-tion**, **-isa-tion** /ˌsterəlaɪˈzeɪʃn; *NAmE* -ləˈz-/ *noun* [U, C]

**ster-il-izer** (*BrE also* **-iser**) /ˈsterəlaɪzə(r)/ *noun* a machine or piece of equipment that you use to make objects or substances completely clean and free from bacteria

# sterling 1536

**ster·ling** /ˈstɜːlɪŋ; NAmE ˈstɜːrl-/ noun, adj.
- noun [U] the money system of the UK, based on the pound: *the value of sterling* ◊ *You can be paid in pounds sterling or American dollars.*
- adj. [usually before noun] (*formal*) of excellent quality: *He has done sterling work on the finance committee.*

**ˌsterling ˈsilver** noun [U] silver of a particular standard of PURITY

**stern** /stɜːn; NAmE stɜːrn/ adj., noun
- adj. (**ˈstern·er**, **ˈstern·est**) **1** serious and often showing that you do not approve of sb/sth; expecting sb to obey you **SYN** strict: *a stern face/expression/look* ◊ *a stern warning* ◊ *Her voice was stern.* ◊ *The police are planning sterner measures to combat crime.* **2** serious and difficult: *We face stern opposition.* ▶ **ˈstern·ly** adv. **ˈstern·ness** /ˈstɜːnnəs; NAmE ˈstɜːrn-/ noun [U]
  **IDM** **be made of sterner ˈstuff** to have a stronger character and to be more determined in dealing with problems than other people
- noun the back end of a ship or boat ⸺ compare BOW¹, POOP
  **IDM** see STEM n.

**ster·num** /ˈstɜːnəm; NAmE ˈstɜːrn-/ noun (pl. **ster·nums** or **sterna** /-nə/) (*anatomy*) the BREASTBONE ⸺ VISUAL VOCAB page V1

**ster·oid** /ˈsterɔɪd; BrE also ˈstɪər-; NAmE also ˈstɪr-/ noun a chemical substance produced naturally in the body. There are several different steroids and they can be used to treat various diseases and are also sometimes used illegally by people playing sports to improve their performance.

**stetho·scope** /ˈsteθəskəʊp/ noun an instrument that a doctor uses to listen to sb's heart and breathing

**stet·son** (*BrE*) (*NAmE* **Stetson™**) /ˈstetsn/ noun a tall hat with a wide BRIM, worn especially by American COWBOYS

**steve·dore** /ˈstiːvədɔː(r)/ noun a person whose job is moving goods on and off ships, especially one with responsibility for loading ships ⸺ compare DOCKER

**stew** /stjuː; NAmE stuː/ noun, verb
- noun [U, C] a dish of meat and/or vegetables cooked slowly in liquid in a container that has a LID (= cover): *beef stew and dumplings* ◊ *I'm making a stew for lunch.*
  **IDM** **get (yourself)/be in a ˈstew (about/over sth)** (*informal*) to become/feel very anxious or upset about sth
- verb **1** [T, I] ~ (**sth**) to cook sth slowly in liquid in a closed dish; (of food) to be cooked in this way: *stewed apples* ◊ *The meat needs to stew for two hours.* ⸺ see also STEWED **2** [I] (+ adv./prep.) to think or worry about sth: *I've been stewing over the problem for a while.* ◊ *Leave him to stew.*
  **IDM** **let sb stew in their own ˈjuice** (*informal*) to leave sb to worry and suffer the unpleasant effects of their own actions

**stew·ard** /ˈstjuːəd; NAmE ˈstuːərd/ noun **1** a man whose job is to take care of passengers on a ship, an aircraft or a train and who brings them meals, etc. **2** a person who helps at a large public event, for example a race or public meeting, by keeping order, showing people where to go, etc. **SYN** **marshal** **3** a person whose job is to arrange for the supply of food to a college, club, etc. ⸺ see also SHOP STEWARD **4** a person employed to manage another person's property, especially a large house or land **5** a person whose responsibility it is to take care of sth: *Farmers pride themselves on being stewards of the countryside.*

**stew·ard·ess** /ˌstjuːəˈdes, ˈstjuːədes; NAmE ˈstuːərdəs/ noun **1** (*old-fashioned*) a female FLIGHT ATTENDANT **2** a woman whose job is to take care of the passengers on a ship or train ⸺ note at GENDER

**stew·ard·ship** /ˈstjuːədʃɪp; NAmE ˈstuːərd-/ noun [U] (*formal*) the act of taking care of or managing sth, for example property, an organization, money or valuable objects: *The organization certainly prospered under his stewardship.*

**stewed** /stjuːd; NAmE stuːd/ adj. (of tea) tasting too strong and bitter because it has been left in the pot too long

**St ˈGeorge's Day** /snt ˈdʒɔːdʒɪz deɪ; NAmE seɪnt ˈdʒɔːrdʒ-/ noun 23 April, the day of the national SAINT of England

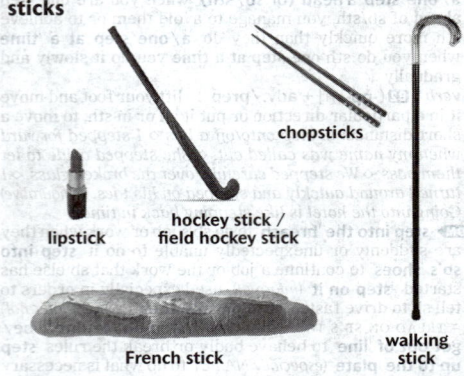

sticks
chopsticks
lipstick
hockey stick / field hockey stick
French stick
walking stick

**STI** /ˌes tiː ˈaɪ/ noun an infection that is passed from one person to another during sexual activity (the abbreviation for 'sexually transmitted infection')

**stick** ❶ **B1** /stɪk/ verb, noun

- verb (**stuck**, **stuck** /stʌk/)
- • **ATTACH 1** **B1** [T, I] to fix sth to sth else, usually with a sticky substance; to become fixed to sth in this way: ~ **sth** + **adv./prep.** *He stuck a stamp on the envelope.* ◊ *We used glue to stick the broken pieces together.* ◊ *I stuck the photos into an album.* ◊ (+ **adv./prep.**) *Her wet clothes were sticking to her body.* ◊ *The glue's useless—the pieces just won't stick.*
- • **BECOME FIXED 2** **B1** [I] to become fixed in one position and impossible to move **SYN** **jam**: *This drawer keeps sticking.* ◊ ~ **in sth** *The key has stuck in the lock.*
- • **PUSH STH IN 3** **B1** [T, I] to push sth, usually a sharp object, into sth; to be pushed into sth: ~ **sth** + **adv./prep.** *The nurse stuck the needle into my arm.* ◊ *Don't stick your fingers through the bars of the cage.* ◊ + **adv./prep.** *I found a nail sticking in the tyre.*
- • **PUT 4** **B1** [T] ~ **sth** + **adv./prep.** (*informal*) to put sth in a place, especially quickly or carelessly: *Stick your bags down there.* ◊ *He stuck his hands in his pockets and strolled off.* ◊ *Can you stick this on the noticeboard?* ◊ *Peter stuck his head around the door and said, 'Coffee, anyone?'* ◊ (*informal*) *Stick 'em up!* (= Put your hands above your head —I have a gun!) **5** [T] **sb can stick sth** (*informal*) used to say in a rude and angry way that you are not interested in what sb has, offers, does, etc.: *I got sick of my boss's moaning and told him he could stick the job.*
- • **DIFFICULT SITUATION 6** [T] (*BrE, informal*) (usually used in negative sentences and questions) to accept a difficult or unpleasant situation or person **SYN** **stand**: ~ **sth/sb** *I don't know how you stick that job.* ◊ ~ **doing sth** *John can't stick living with his parents.*
- • **BECOME ACCEPTED 7** [I] to become accepted: *The police couldn't make the charges stick* (= show them to be true). ◊ *His friends called him Bart and the name has stuck* (= has become the name that everyone calls him).
- • **IN CARD GAMES 8** [I] (in some card games) to say that you will not take any more cards ⸺ see also STUCK
  **IDM** **stick in your ˈhead/ˈmind** (of a memory, an image, etc.) to be remembered for a long time: *One of her paintings in particular sticks in my mind.* **stick in your ˈthroat/ˈcraw** (*informal*) **1** (of words) to be difficult or impossible to say **2** (of a situation) to be difficult or impossible to accept; to make you angry **stick your ˈneck out** (*informal*) to do or say sth when there is a risk that you may be wrong **stick to your ˈguns** (*informal*) to refuse to change your mind about sth even when other people are trying to persuade you that you are wrong ⸺ more at BOOT n., FINGER n., KNIFE n., MILE n., MUD, OAR, SORE adj., TELL
  **PHRV** **stick aˈround** (*informal*) to stay in a place, waiting for sth to happen or for sb to arrive: *Stick around; we'll need you to help us later.* **ˈstick at sth** to continue to work in a serious and determined way to achieve sth: *If you want to play an instrument well, you've got to stick at it.*

b bad | d did | f fall | g get | h hat | j yes | k cat | l leg | m man | n now | p pen | r red

**'stick by sb** [no passive] to continue to support sb, especially in a difficult situation **'stick by sth** [no passive] to do what you promised or planned to do: *They stuck by their decision.* **,stick sth↔'down** (*informal*) to write sth somewhere: *I think I'll stick my name down on the list.* **,stick 'out** to be easily seen or noticed SYN **stand out (from/against sth)**: *They wrote the notice in big red letters so that it would stick out.* **,stick 'out (of sth)** | **,stick sth↔'out (of sth)** to be further out than sth else or to come through a hole; to push sth further out than sth else or through a hole: *His ears stick out.* ◊ *She stuck her tongue out at me.* ◊ *Don't stick your arm out of the car window.* **,stick it/sth 'out** (*informal*) to continue doing sth to the end, even when it is difficult or boring: *She didn't like the course but she stuck it out to get the certificate.* **,stick 'out for sth** (*informal*) to refuse to give up until you get what you need or want: *They are sticking out for a higher pay rise.* **'stick to sth 1** B2 to continue doing sth despite difficulties: *She finds it impossible to stick to a diet.* **2** to continue doing or using sth and not want to change it: *Let's stick to the original plan.* ◊ *'Shall we meet on Friday this week?' 'No, let's stick to Saturday.'* ◊ *She stuck to her story.* **,stick to'gether** (*informal*) (of people) to stay together and support each other **,stick 'up** to point upwards or be above a surface: *The branch was sticking up out of the water.* **,stick 'up for sb/yourself/sth** [no passive] (*informal*) to support or defend sb/yourself/sth: *Stick up for what you believe.* ◊ *She taught her children to stick up for themselves at school.* ◊ *Don't worry—I'll stick up for you.* **'stick with sb/sth** [no passive] (*informal*) **1** to stay close to sb so that they can help you **2** to continue with sth or continue doing sth: *They decided to stick with their original plan.*

■ *noun*
- FROM TREE **1** B1 [C] a thin piece of wood that has fallen or been broken from a tree: *We collected dry sticks to start a fire.* ◊ *He said he was beaten with a stick.* ◊ *Her arms and legs were like sticks* (= very thin).
- FOR WALKING **2** [C] (*especially BrE*) = WALKING STICK: *He walks with a stick these days, but he still gets about.* ⊃ see also WHITE STICK
- IN SPORT **3** [C] a long, thin object that is used in some sports to hit or control the ball: *a hockey stick*
- LONG THIN PIECE **4** B1 [C] (often in compounds) ~ (of sth) a long, thin piece of sth: *a stick of dynamite* ◊ *carrot/cinnamon/celery sticks* ◊ (*NAmE*) *a stick of butter* ⊃ see also FISH STICK, FRENCH STICK **5** [C] (often in compounds) a thin piece of wood or plastic that you use for a particular purpose: *pieces of pineapple on sticks* ◊ *I used a selfie stick to take the picture.*
- CONTAINER OF GLUE **6** [C] a quantity of a substance, such as solid GLUE (= a sticky substance), that is sold in a small container with round ends and straight sides, and can be pushed further out of the container as it is used ⊃ see also LIPSTICK
- IN PLANE/VEHICLE **7** [C] (*especially NAmE, informal*) a stick with a handle in a plane that is used to control direction or height ⊃ see also JOYSTICK **8** [C] (*especially NAmE, informal*) a handle used to change the GEARS of a vehicle ⊃ see also GEAR LEVER, STICK SHIFT
- FOR ORCHESTRA **9** [C] a BATON, used by the person who CONDUCTS an ORCHESTRA
- CRITICISM **10** [U] (*BrE, informal*) criticism or severe words: *The referee got a lot of stick from the home fans.*
- COUNTRY AREAS **11** the sticks [pl.] (*informal, usually disapproving*) country areas, a long way from cities: *We live out in the sticks.*
- PERSON **12** [C] (*BrE, old-fashioned, informal*) a person: *He's not such a bad old stick.* HELP There are many other compounds ending in stick. You will find them at their place in the alphabet. ⊃ see also NON-STICK IDM see BEAT v., BIG adj., CARROT, CLEFT adj., SHORT adj., UP v., WRONG adj.

**stick·er** /'stɪkə(r)/ *noun* a sticky label with a picture or message on it, that you stick onto sth: *bumper stickers* (= on cars) ◊ *a sticker album* (= to collect stickers in) ⊃ SYNONYMS at LABEL

**'sticker price** *noun* (*NAmE*) the price that is marked on sth, especially a car

**'sticker shock** *noun* [U] (*NAmE*) the unpleasant feeling that people experience when they find that sth is much more expensive than they expected

**'stick figure** *noun* a picture of a person drawn only with thin lines for the arms and legs, a circle for the head, etc.

stick figures
stick man  stick woman

**'sticking plaster** *noun* (*BrE*) = PLASTER

**'sticking point** *noun* something that people do not agree on and that prevents progress in a discussion: *This was one of the major sticking points in the negotiations.*

**'stick insect** *noun* a large insect with a long thin body that looks like a stick

**'stickle·back** /'stɪklbæk/ *noun* a small FRESHWATER fish with sharp points on its back

**stick·ler** /'stɪklə(r)/ *noun* ~ (for sth) a person who thinks that a particular quality or type of behaviour is very important and expects other people to think and behave in the same way: *a stickler for punctuality*

**'stick-on** *adj.* [only before noun] (of an object) with GLUE on one side so that it sticks to sth: *stick-on labels*

**'stick shift** *noun* (*NAmE, informal*) **1** (*NAmE also* **gear·shift**) (*BrE* **'gear lever**, **'gear·stick**) a handle used to change the GEARS of a vehicle **2** (*BrE* **man·ual**) a vehicle that has a stick shift ⊃ compare AUTOMATIC

**'stick-up** *noun* (*especially NAmE, informal*) = HOLD-UP: *This is a stick-up!*

**sticky** ⊙ B2 /'stɪki/ *adj., noun*
■ *adj.* (**stick·ier, sticki·est**) **1** B2 made of or covered in a substance that sticks to things that touch it: *sticky fingers covered in jam* ◊ *There's a dish of mango with sweet sticky rice.* **2** (of paper, labels, etc.) with GLUE (= a sticky substance) on one side so that you can stick it to a surface **3** (*informal*) (of the weather) hot and slightly wet **4** (*informal*) (of a person) feeling hot and uncomfortable SYN **sweaty 5** (*informal*) difficult or unpleasant: *a sticky situation* **6** (*computing*) (of a website) so interesting and well organized that the people who visit it stay there for a long time ▶ **stick·ily** /-kɪli/ *adv.* **sticki·ness** *noun* [U] IDM **have sticky 'fingers** (*informal*) to be likely to steal sth **a sticky 'wicket** (*BrE, informal*) a difficult situation ⊃ more at END n.
■ *noun* (*pl.* **-ies**) (*also* **'sticky note**) a small piece of sticky paper that you use for writing a note on, and that can be easily removed ⊃ compare POST-IT™

**'sticky tape** *noun* [U] (*BrE*) = SELLOTAPE™

**stiff** ⊙ B2 /stɪf/ *adj., adv., noun, verb*
■ *adj.* (**stiff·er, stiff·est**)
- DIFFICULT TO BEND/MOVE **1** B2 difficult to bend or move: *stiff cardboard* ◊ *a stiff brush* ◊ *The windows were stiff and she couldn't get them open.*
- MUSCLES **2** when a person or a part of their body is stiff, their muscles hurt when they move them: *I'm really stiff after that bike ride yesterday.* ◊ *I've got a stiff neck.*
- MIXTURE **3** thick; difficult to STIR (= move around with a spoon): *Whisk the egg whites until stiff.*
- DIFFICULT/SEVERE **4** more difficult or severe than usual: *It was a stiff climb to the top of the hill.* ◊ *The company faces stiff competition from its rivals.* ◊ *The new proposals have met with stiff opposition.* ◊ *Firms face stiff penalties for breaking the rules.* ◊ *a stiff breeze/wind* (= one that blows strongly)
- NOT FRIENDLY **5** (of a person or their behaviour) not friendly or relaxed: *The speech he made to welcome them was stiff and formal.*
- PRICE **6** (*informal*) costing a lot or too much: *There's a stiff $30 entrance fee to the exhibition.*

# stiff-arm

- **ALCOHOLIC DRINK** 7 [only before noun] strong; containing a lot of alcohol: *a stiff whisky* ▶ **stiff·ly** *adv.* **stiff·ness** *noun* [U]: *pain and stiffness in her legs*
**IDM** **(keep) a stiff upper 'lip** to keep calm and hide your feelings when you are in pain or in a difficult situation
- *adv.* **1** (*informal*) very much; to an extreme degree: *be bored/scared/worried stiff* **2** *frozen* ~ (of wet material) very cold and hard because the water has become ice: *The clothes on the washing line were frozen stiff.* ◇ (*figurative*) *I came home from the game frozen stiff* (= very cold).
- *noun* (*slang*) the body of a dead person
- *verb* ~ **sb** (*NAmE*, *informal*) to cheat sb or not pay them what you owe them, especially by not leaving any money as a tip

**stiff-'arm** *verb* (*NAmE*) = STRAIGHT-ARM

**stiff·en** /ˈstɪfn/ *verb* **1** [I, T] to make yourself or part of your body straight and still, especially because you are angry or frightened: ~ **(with sth)** *She stiffened with fear.* ◇ ~ **sth (with sth)** *I stiffened my back and faced him.* **2** [I, T] (of part of the body) to become, or to make sth become, difficult to bend or move: ~ **(up)** *My muscles had stiffened up after the climb.* ◇ ~ **sth** *stiffened muscles* **3** [T, I] ~ **(sth)** to make an attitude or idea stronger or more powerful; to become stronger **SYN** **strengthen**: *The threat of punishment has only stiffened their resolve* (= made them even more determined to do sth). **4** [T] ~ **sth (with sth)** to make sth, such as cloth, hard and unable to bend

**stifle** /ˈstaɪfl/ *verb* **1** [T] ~ **sth** to prevent sth from happening; to prevent a feeling from being expressed **SYN** **suppress**: *She managed to stifle a yawn.* ◇ *They hope the new rules will not stifle creativity.* ◇ *The government failed to stifle the unrest.* **2** [I, T] to feel unable to breathe, or to make sb unable to breathe, because it is too hot and/or there is no fresh air **SYN** **suffocate**: *I felt I was stifling in the airless room.* ▶ ~ **sb** *Most of the victims were stifled by the fumes.* ▶ **sti·fling** /-flɪŋ/ *adj.*: *a stifling room* ◇ '*It's stifling in here—can we open a window?*' ◇ *At 25, she found family life stifling.* **sti·fling·ly** *adv.*: *The room was stiflingly hot.*

**stigma** /ˈstɪɡmə/ *noun* **1** [U, C, usually sing.] negative feelings that people have about particular circumstances or characteristics that sb may have: *the social stigma of alcoholism* ◇ *There is no longer any stigma attached to being divorced.* **2** [C] (*biology*) the part in the middle of a flower where POLLEN is received ⇒ VISUAL VOCAB page V7

**stig·mata** /stɪɡˈmɑːtə, ˈstɪɡmətə/ *noun* [pl.] marks that look like the wounds made by nails on the body of Jesus Christ, believed by some Christians to have appeared as holy marks on the bodies of some SAINTS

**stig·ma·tize** (*BrE also* -**ise**) /ˈstɪɡmətaɪz/ *verb* [usually passive] ~ **sb/sth** (*formal*) to treat sb in a way that makes them feel that they are very bad or unimportant ▶ **stig·ma·tiza·tion**, **-isa·tion** /ˌstɪɡmətaɪˈzeɪʃn; *NAmE* -təˈz-/ *noun* [U]

 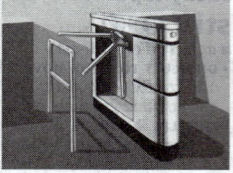
stile — turnstile

**stile** /staɪl/ *noun* a set of steps that help people climb over a fence or gate in a field, etc.

**stil·etto** /stɪˈletəʊ/ *noun* (*pl.* -**os** or -**oes**) **1** (*also* **stiletto 'heel**) (*especially BrE*) a woman's shoe with a very high narrow heel; the heel on such a shoe **2** a small knife with a narrow pointed BLADE (= cutting edge)

**still** 🔑 **A1** /stɪl/ *adv.*, *adj.*, *noun*, *verb*
- *adv.* **1** 🔑 **A1** continuing until a particular point in time and not finishing: *I am very happy that you all are still alive and well.* ◇ *Tickets are still available for the 8 o'clock perform-*

*ance.* ◇ *He's still very young and has a lot to learn.* ◇ *She still has a chance to win the title.* ◇ *If you still need help next week, contact me.* **2** 🔑 **B1** despite what has just been said: *The weather was cold and wet. Still, we had a great time.* ◇ *I know it's not rational, but I still feel terribly guilty.* **3** used for making a comparison stronger: *The next day was warmer still.* ◇ *If you can manage to get two tickets that's better still.* **4** ~ **more** / **another** even more: *There was still more bad news to come.* **IDM** *see* EARLY *adv.*, LESS *adv.*
- *adj.* **1** 🔑 **B1** not moving; calm and quiet: *still water* ◇ *Keep still while I brush your hair.* ◇ *The kids found it hard to stay still.* ◇ *Can't you sit still?* ◇ *We stayed in a village where time has stood still* (= life has not changed for many years). **2** [not before noun] a **still** photograph or image does not move, in contrast to a moving image from a film or video **3** with no wind: *a still summer's day* ◇ *the still night air* **4** (*BrE*) (of a drink) not containing bubbles of gas; not FIZZY: *still mineral water*
**IDM** **the still of the 'night** (*literary*) the time during the night when it is quiet and calm **a/the still small 'voice** (*literary*) the voice of God or your CONSCIENCE, that tells you to do what is morally right **still waters run 'deep** (*saying*) a person who seems to be quiet or shy may surprise you by knowing a lot or having deep feelings
- *noun* **1** a photograph of a scene from a film or video: *a publicity still from his new movie* **2** a piece of equipment that is used for making strong alcoholic drinks: *a whisky still* ⇒ *see also* DISTIL
- *verb* [I, T] (*literary*) to become calm and quiet; to make sth calm and quiet: *The wind stilled.* ◇ ~ **sb/sth** *She spoke quietly to still the frightened child.* ◇ (*figurative*) *to still sb's doubts/fears*

**still·birth** /ˈstɪlbɜːθ; *NAmE* -bɜːrθ/ *noun* [C, U] a birth in which the baby is born dead

**still·born** /ˈstɪlbɔːn; *NAmE* -bɔːrn/ *adj.* **1** born dead: *a stillborn baby* **2** not successful; not developing

**still 'life** *noun* [U, C] (*pl.* **still lifes**) the art of painting or drawing arrangements of objects such as flowers, fruit, etc.; a painting, etc. like this

**still·ness** /ˈstɪlnəs/ *noun* [U] the quality of being quiet and not moving: *The sound of footsteps on the path broke the stillness.*

**stilt** /stɪlt/ *noun* [usually pl.] **1** one of a set of posts that support a building so that it is high above the ground or water **2** one of two long pieces of wood that have a step on the side that you can stand on, so that you can walk above the ground: *a circus performer on stilts*

**stilt·ed** /ˈstɪltɪd/ *adj.* (*disapproving*) (of a way of speaking or writing) not natural or relaxed; too formal: *We made stilted conversation for a few moments.* ▶ **stilt·ed·ly** *adv.*

**Stil·ton**™ /ˈstɪltən/ *noun* [U, C] a type of English cheese with blue lines of MOULD running through it and a strong taste

**stimu·lant** /ˈstɪmjələnt/ *noun* (*formal*) **1** a drug or substance that makes you feel more active and gives you more energy: *Coffee and tea are mild stimulants.* **2** ~ **(to sth)** an event or activity that encourages more activity

**stimu·late** 🔑+ **B2** 🌐 /ˈstɪmjuleɪt/ *verb* **1** 🔑+ **B2** ~ **sth** to make sth develop or become more active; to encourage sth: *The exhibition has stimulated interest in her work.* ◇ *The article can be used to stimulate discussion among students.* **2** 🔑+ **C1** to make sb interested and excited about sth: ~ **sb** *Parents should give children books that stimulate them.* ◇ *Both men and women are stimulated by erotic photos* (= sexually). ◇ ~ **sb to do sth** *The conference stimulated him to study the subject in more depth.* **3** ~ **sth** (*specialist*) to make a part of the body function: *The women were given fertility drugs to stimulate the ovaries.* ▶ **stimu·la·tion** /ˌstɪmjuˈleɪʃn/ *noun* [U]: *sensory/intellectual/sexual/visual/physical stimulation*

**stimu·lat·ing** /ˈstɪmjuleɪtɪŋ/ *adj.* **1** full of interesting or exciting ideas; making people feel enthusiastic **SYN** **inspiring**: *a stimulating discussion* ◇ *a stimulating teacher* ⇒ SYNONYMS *at* INTERESTING **2** making you feel more active and healthy: *shower gel containing plant extracts that have a stimulating effect on the skin*

**stim·u·lus** /ˈstɪmjələs/ noun (pl. **stim·u·li** /-laɪ/) **1** [usually sing.] ~ (to/for sth) | ~ (for sb) (to do sth) something that helps sb/sth to develop better or more quickly: *Books provide children with ideas and a stimulus for play.* ◇ *The new tax laws should act as a stimulus to exports.* **2** something that produces a reaction in a human, an animal or a plant: *sensory/verbal/visual stimuli* ◇ *The animals were conditioned to respond to auditory stimuli* (= sounds).

**sting** /stɪŋ/ verb, noun
- **verb** (**stung**, **stung** /stʌŋ/) **1** [T, I] ~ (sb/sth) (of an insect or plant) to touch your skin or make a very small hole in it so that you feel a sharp pain: *I was stung on the arm by a wasp.* ◇ *Be careful of the nettles—they sting!* **2** [I, T] to feel, or to make sb feel, a sharp pain in a part of their body: *I put some antiseptic on the cut and it stung for a moment.* ◇ *My eyes were stinging from the smoke.* ◇ *sth Tears stung her eyes.* ⊃ SYNONYMS at HURT **3** [T] to make sb feel angry or upset: ~ sb *He was stung by their criticism.* ◇ *They launched a stinging attack on the government.* ◇ ~ sb to/ into sth *Their cruel remarks stung her into action.* ◇ ~ sb into doing sth *He was stung into answering in his defence.* **4** [T, often passive] ~ sb (for sth) (informal) to charge sb more money than they expected; to charge sb who did not expect to pay: *I got stung for a £100 meal.*
- **noun 1** (NAmE also **sting·er**) [C] the sharp pointed part of an insect or creature that can go into the skin leaving a small, painful and sometimes poisonous wound: *the sting of a bee* ◇ *The scorpion has a sting in its tail.* ⊃ VISUAL VOCAB page V3 **2** [C] a wound that is made when an insect, a creature or a plant stings you: *A wasp or bee sting is painful but not necessarily serious.* **3** [C, U] any sharp pain in your body or mind: *the sting of salt in a wound* ◇ *He smiled at her, trying to take the sting out of his words* (= trying to make the situation less painful or difficult). **4** [C] a clever secret plan by the police to catch criminals: *a sting operation to catch heroin dealers in Detroit* **5** [C] (especially NAmE) a clever plan by criminals to cheat people out of a lot of money

IDM **a ˈsting in the ˈtail** (informal) an unpleasant feature that comes at the end of a story, an event, etc. and makes it less good, successful, etc.

**ˈstinging nettle** noun = NETTLE

**ˈsting·ray** /ˈstɪŋreɪ/ noun a large, wide, flat sea fish that has a long tail with a sharp sting in it that can cause serious wounds

**stingy** /ˈstɪndʒi/ adj. (**stin·gier**, **stin·gi·est**) (informal) not given or giving willingly; not generous, especially with money SYN **mean**: *You're stingy!* (= not willing to spend money) ◇ *Don't be so stingy with the cream!* ▶ **stin·gi·ness** noun [U]

**stink** /stɪŋk/ verb, noun
- **verb** (**stank** /stæŋk/, **stunk** /stʌŋk/ or **stunk**, **stunk**) (informal) **1** [I] ~ (of sth) to have a strong, unpleasant smell SYN **reek**: *Her breath stank of garlic.* ◇ *It stinks of smoke in here.* **2** [I] ~ (of sth) to seem very bad, unpleasant or dishonest: *The whole business stank of corruption.* ◇ *'What do you think of the idea?' 'I think it stinks.'*
PHRV **ˌstink sth↔ˈout** to fill a place with a strong, unpleasant smell
- **noun** (informal) **1** [C, usually sing.] a very unpleasant smell SYN **reek**: *the stink of sweat and urine* **2** [sing.] a lot of trouble and anger about sth: *The whole business caused quite a stink.* ◇ *We'll kick up a stink* (= complain a lot and cause trouble) *if they try to close the school down.*

**ˈstink bomb** noun a container that produces a very bad smell when it is broken. Stink bombs are used for playing tricks on people.

**stink·er** /ˈstɪŋkə(r)/ noun (informal) a person or thing that is very unpleasant or difficult

**stink·ing** /ˈstɪŋkɪŋ/ adj., adv.
- **adj. 1** having a very strong, unpleasant smell: *I was pushed into a filthy, stinking room.* **2** [only before noun] (informal, especially BrE) very bad or unpleasant: *I've got a stinking cold.* **3** [only before noun] (BrE, informal) showing a lot of anger: *I wrote them a stinking letter to complain.*
- **adv.** (informal, usually disapproving) extremely: *They must be stinking rich.*

**stinky** /ˈstɪŋki/ adj. (**stink·ier**, **stink·iest**) (informal) **1** having an extremely bad smell **2** extremely unpleasant or bad

**stint** /stɪnt/ noun, verb
- **noun** (+ adv./prep.) a period of time that you spend working somewhere or doing a particular activity: *He did a stint abroad early in his career.* ◇ *a two-year stint in the Navy*
- **verb** [I, T] (usually used in negative sentences) to provide or use only a small amount of sth: ~ (on sth) *She never stints on the food at her parties.* ◇ ~ yourself *We don't need to stint ourselves—have some more!* ⊃ see also UNSTINTING

**sti·pend** /ˈstaɪpend/ noun (formal) an amount of money that is paid regularly to sb, especially a priest, as wages or money to live on: *a monthly stipend* ◇ (especially NAmE) *a summer internship with a small stipend*

**stip·ple** /ˈstɪpl/ verb (often passive) ~ sth (specialist) to paint or draw sth using small marks ▶ **stip·pling** /-plɪŋ/ noun [U]

**stipu·late** /ˈstɪpjuleɪt/ verb (formal) to state clearly and definitely that sth must be done, or how it must be done SYN **specify**: ~ sth *A delivery date is stipulated in the contract.* ◇ ~ that … *The job advertisement stipulates that the applicant must have three years' experience.* ◇ ~ what, how, etc… *The policy stipulates what form of consent is required.* ▶ **stipu·la·tion** /ˌstɪpjuˈleɪʃn/ noun [C, U]: *The only stipulation is that the topic you choose must be related to your studies.*

**stir** /stɜː(r)/ verb, noun
- **verb** (-rr-)
- MIX **1** [T] to move a liquid or substance around, using a spoon or sth similar, in order to mix it completely: ~ sth *She stirred her tea.* ◇ ~ sth into sth *The vegetables are stirred into the rice while it is hot.* ◇ ~ sth in *Stir in the milk until the sauce thickens.* ⊃ SYNONYMS at MIX
- MOVE **2** [I, T] to move, or to make sth move, slightly: *She heard the baby stir in the next room.* ◇ ~ sth/sb *A slight breeze was stirring the branches.* ◇ *A noise stirred me from sleep.* **3** [I, T] to move, or to make sb move, in order to do sth: *You haven't stirred from that chair all evening!* ◇ ~ yourself/sb *Come on, stir yourself. You're late!* ◇ ~ sb into/to sth *Their complaints have finally stirred him into action.*
- FEELINGS **4** [T] to make sb excited or make them feel sth strongly: ~ sth *a book that really stirs the imagination* ◇ ~ sb (to sth) *She was stirred by his sad story.* **5** [I] (of a feeling or a mood) to begin to be felt: *A feeling of guilt began to stir in her.*
- CAUSE TROUBLE **6** [T, I] ~ (it) (BrE, informal, disapproving) to try to cause trouble: *You're just stirring it!* ⊃ see also STIRRER

IDM **stir the ˈblood** to make sb excited **stir your ˈstumps** (old-fashioned, BrE, informal) to begin to move; to hurry
PHRV **ˌstir sb↔ˈup** to encourage sb to do sth; to make sb feel they must do sth ˌ**stir sth↔ˈup 1** to make people feel strong emotions: *to stir up hatred* **2** to try to cause arguments or problems: *to stir up a debate* ◇ *Whenever he's around, he always manages to stir up trouble.* ◇ *We've got enough problems without you trying to stir things up.* **3** to make sth move around in water or air: *The wind stirred up a lot of dust.*
- **noun 1** [sing.] excitement, anger or shock that is felt by a number of people SYN **commotion**: *Her resignation caused quite a stir.* **2** [C, usually sing.] the action of stirring sth: *Could you give the rice a stir?*

**ˈstir-fry** verb, noun
- **verb** ~ sth to cook thin pieces of vegetables or meat quickly by moving them around with a spoon or etc. in very hot oil: *stir-fried chicken*
- **noun** (pl. **-ies**) a hot dish made by stir-frying small pieces of meat, fish and/or vegetables

**stir·rer** /ˈstɜːrə(r)/ noun (BrE, informal, disapproving) a person who likes causing trouble, especially between other people, by spreading secrets

# stirring

**stir·ring** /ˈstɜːrɪŋ/ *noun, adj.*
- *noun* ~ (of sth) the beginning of a feeling, an idea or a development: *She felt a stirring of anger.*
- *adj.* [usually before noun] causing strong feelings; exciting: *a stirring performance* ◊ *stirring memories*

**stir·rup** /ˈstɪrəp/ *noun* one of the metal rings that hang down on each side of a horse's SADDLE, used to support the rider's foot ⊃ WORDFINDER NOTE at HORSE

**stitch** /stɪtʃ/ *noun, verb*
- *noun* **1** [C] one of the small lines of THREAD that you can see on a piece of cloth after it has been SEWN; the action that produces this: *Try to keep the stitches small and straight.* ⊃ WORDFINDER NOTE at SEW **2** [C] one of the small circles of wool that you make around the needle when you are KNITTING (= making clothing out of wool with two long needles): *to drop a stitch* (= to lose one that you have made) **3** [C, U] (especially in compounds) a particular style of SEWING or KNITTING that you use to make the pattern you want: *chain stitch* **4** [C] a short piece of THREAD, etc. that doctors use to SEW the edges of a wound together: *The cut needed eight stitches.* ⊃ WORDFINDER NOTE at OPERATION **5** [C, usually sing.] a sudden pain in the side of your body, usually caused by running or laughing: *Can we slow down? I've got a stitch.*
  - **IDM** **in ˈstitches** (*informal*) laughing a lot: *The play had us in stitches.* **not have a stitch ˈon | not be wearing a ˈstitch** (*informal*) to be wearing no clothes **a stitch in ˈtime (saves ˈnine)** (*saying*) it is better to deal with sth immediately because if you wait it may become worse or more difficult and cause extra work
- *verb* **1** [often passive] to use a needle and THREAD to repair, join, or decorate pieces of cloth **SYN** **be stitched** (+ *adv./prep.*) *Her wedding dress was stitched by hand.* ◊ (*figurative*) *An agreement was hastily stitched together* (= made very quickly). **2** ~ sth (up) to SEW the edges of a wound together: *The cut will need to be stitched.*
  - **PHRV** **stitch sb↔ˈup** (*BrE, informal*) to cheat sb or put them in a position where they seem guilty of sth they have not done **stitch sth↔ˈup 1** to use a needle and THREAD to join things together **2** (*informal*) to arrange or complete sth: *to stitch up a deal* ◊ *They think they have the US market stitched up.*

**stitch·ing** /ˈstɪtʃɪŋ/ *noun* [U] a row of stitches

**ˈstitch-up** *noun* (*BrE, informal*) a situation in which sb deliberately cheats you or causes you to be wrongly blamed for sth

**St John's Wort** /snt ˌdʒɒnz ˈwɜːt; *NAmE* seɪnt ˌdʒɑːnz ˈwɜːrt/ *noun* [U, C] a HERB with yellow flowers, used in medicines

**stoat** /stəʊt/ *noun* a small wild animal with a long body and brown fur that, in northern areas, turns white in winter. The white fur is called ERMINE.

**stock** 🔑 B2 Ⓦ /stɒk; *NAmE* stɑːk/ *noun, verb, adj.*
- *noun*
  - • SUPPLY **1** 🔑 B2 [U, C] a supply of goods that is available for sale in a shop: *We have a fast turnover of stock.* ◊ *That particular model is not currently in stock.* ◊ **out of ~** *I'm afraid we're temporarily out of stock.* ◊ **~ of sth** *We don't carry a large stock of pine furniture.* **2** 🔑 B2 [C] a supply of sth that is available for use: *declining fish stocks in the oceans* ◊ *a country's housing stock* (= all the houses available for living in) ◊ **~ of sth** *She's built up a good stock of teaching materials over the years.*
  - • FINANCE **3** [U] the value of the shares in a company that have been sold **4** [C, usually pl.] a share that sb has bought in a company or business: *stock prices* ◊ *to buy/sell/trade stocks* ◊ (*BrE*) *to invest in stocks and shares* ◊ (*NAmE*) *to invest in stocks and bonds* ⊃ compare SHARE **5** [U, C] (*BrE*) money that is lent to a government at a fixed rate of interest; an official document that gives details of this: *government stock*
  - • FARM ANIMALS **6** [U] farm animals, such as cows and sheep, that are kept for their meat, wool, etc: *breeding stock* ⊃ see also LIVESTOCK
  - • FAMILY/ANCESTORS **7** [U] **of farming, noble, French**, etc. ~ having the type of family or ANCESTORS mentioned **SYN** descent
  - • FOOD **8** [U, C] a liquid made by cooking bones, meat, etc. in water, used for making soups and sauces: *vegetable stock*
  - • FOR PUNISHMENT **9 stocks** [pl.] a wooden structure with holes for the feet, used in the past to lock criminals in as a form of punishment, especially in a public place ⊃ compare PILLORY
  - • RESPECT **10** [U] (*formal*) the degree to which sb is respected or liked by other people: *Their stock is high/low.*
  - • OF GUN **11** [C] the part of a gun that you hold against your shoulder when firing it
  - • PLANT **12** [U, C] a garden plant with brightly coloured flowers with a sweet smell
  - • THEATRE **13** [C] (*NAmE*) = STOCK COMPANY ⊃ see also LAUGHING STOCK, ROLLING STOCK
  - **IDM** **on the ˈstocks** in the process of being made, built or prepared: *Our new model is already on the stocks and will be available in the spring.* **put ˈstock in sth** (especially *NAmE*) to have a particular amount of belief in sth: *She no longer puts much stock in their claims.* **take ˈstock (of sth)** to stop and think carefully about the way in which a particular situation is developing in order to decide what to do next ⊃ more at LOCK *n.* ⊃ see also STOCKTAKING
- *verb* **1** ~ sth (of a shop) to keep a supply of a particular type of goods to sell: *Do you stock green tea?* **2** [often passive] ~ sth (with sth) to fill sth with food, books, etc: *The pond was well stocked with fish.* ◊ *a well-stocked library*
  - **PHRV** **stock sth↔ˈup** to fill sth with goods, food, etc: *We need to stock up the freezer.* **stock ˈup (on/with sth)** to buy a lot of sth so that you can use it later: *We ought to stock up on sun cream before our trip.*
- *adj.* [only before noun] **1** (*disapproving*) a **stock** excuse, answer, etc. is one that is often used because it is easy and convenient, but that is not very original: *'No comment,' was the actor's stock response.* **2** usually available for sale in a shop **SYN** standard: *stock sizes*

**stock·ade** /stɒˈkeɪd; *NAmE* stɑːˈk-/ *noun* a line or wall of strong wooden posts built to defend a place

**stock·broker** /ˈstɒkbrəʊkə(r); *NAmE* ˈstɑːk-/ (*also* **broker**) *noun* a person or an organization that buys and sells shares for other people

**stock·brok·ing** /ˈstɒkbrəʊkɪŋ; *NAmE* ˈstɑːk-/ *noun* [U] the work of a stockbroker

**ˈstock car** *noun* an ordinary car that has been made stronger for use in stock-car racing

**ˈstock-car racing** *noun* [U] (*BrE*) (*NAmE* **demolition derby**) [C]) a type of race in which the competing cars are allowed to hit each other

**ˈstock company** *noun* (*NAmE*) **1** a company owned by people who have shares in it **2** (*also* **stock**) a theatre company that does several different plays in a season; a REPERTORY company

**ˈstock exchange** *noun* [usually sing.] a place where shares in companies are bought and sold; all of the business activity involved in doing this: *the London Stock Exchange* ◊ *to lose money on the stock exchange*

**stock·hold·er** /ˈstɒkhəʊldə(r); *NAmE* ˈstɑːk-/ *noun* (especially *NAmE*) a person who owns STOCKS and shares in a business **SYN** shareholder

**ˈstock index** *noun* [usually sing.] (*NAmE*) = SHARE INDEX

**stock·ing** /ˈstɒkɪŋ; *NAmE* ˈstɑːk-/ *noun* **1** either of a pair of thin pieces of clothing that fit closely over a woman's legs and feet: *a pair of silk stockings* ⊃ compare TIGHTS ⊃ see also BODY STOCKING **2** = CHRISTMAS STOCKING
- **IDM** **in your ˌstocking(ed) ˈfeet** wearing socks or stockings but not shoes

**ˈstocking filler** (*BrE*) (*NAmE* **ˈstocking stuffer**) *noun* a small present that is put in a CHRISTMAS STOCKING

**ˌstock-in-ˈtrade** *noun* [U] a person's **stock-in-trade** is sth that they do, say or use very often or too often: *Famous people and their private lives are the stock-in-trade of the popular newspapers.*

**stock·ist** /ˈstɒkɪst; NAmE ˈstɑːk-/ noun (BrE) a shop or company that sells a particular product or type of goods **SYN** retailer

**stock·man** /ˈstɒkmən; NAmE ˈstɑːk-/ noun (pl. -men /-mən/) **1** a man whose job is to take care of farm animals **2** (NAmE) a man who owns farm animals **3** (NAmE) a man who is in charge of the goods in a WAREHOUSE, etc.

**ˈstock market** (also **mar·ket**) noun the business of buying and selling shares in companies and the place where this happens; a STOCK EXCHANGE: *to make money on the stock market* ◊ *a stock market crash* (= when prices of shares fall suddenly and people lose money)

**ˈstock option** (NAmE) (BrE **ˈshare option**) noun a right given to employees to buy shares in their company at a fixed price

**stock·pile** /ˈstɒkpaɪl; NAmE ˈstɑːk-/ noun, verb
- noun a large supply of sth that is kept to be used in the future if necessary: *the world's stockpile of nuclear weapons*
- verb ~ sth to collect and keep a large supply of sth

**stock·room** /ˈstɒkruːm, -rʊm; NAmE ˈstɑːk-/ noun a room for storing things in a shop, an office, etc.

**stock·tak·ing** /ˈstɒkteɪkɪŋ; NAmE ˈstɑːk-/ noun [U] **1** (especially BrE) the process of making a list of all the goods in a shop or business ⊃ compare INVENTORY **2** the process of thinking carefully about your own situation or position

**stocky** /ˈstɒki; NAmE ˈstɑːki/ adj. (**stock·ier**, **stocki·est**) (of a person) short, with a strong, solid body **SYN** thickset
▶ **stock·ily** adv.

**stock·yard** /ˈstɒkjɑːd; NAmE ˈstɑːkjɑːrd/ noun a place where farm animals are kept for a short time before they are sold at a market

**stodgy** /ˈstɒdʒi; NAmE ˈstɑːdʒi/ adj. (especially BrE, informal, usually disapproving) **1** (of food) heavy and making you feel very full **2** serious and boring; not exciting

**stoep** /stuːp, stʊp/ noun (SAfrE) a raised area outside the door of a house, with a roof over it, where you can sit and relax, eat meals, etc.

**stoic** /ˈstəʊɪk/ noun a person who is able to suffer pain or trouble without complaining or showing what they are feeling ▶ **stoic** (also **sto·ic·al** /-ɪkl/) adj.: *her stoic endurance* ◊ *his stoical acceptance of death* **sto·ic·al·ly** /-kli/ adv. **ORIGIN** From the **Stoics**, a group of ancient Greek philosophers, who believed that wise people should not allow themselves to be affected by painful or pleasant experiences.

**sto·icism** /ˈstəʊɪsɪzəm/ noun [U] (formal) the fact of not complaining or showing what you are feeling when you are suffering: *She endured her long illness with stoicism.*

**stoke** /stəʊk/ verb **1** ~ sth (up) (with sth) to add fuel to a fire, etc.: *to stoke up a fire with more coal* ◊ *to stoke a furnace* **2** ~ sth (up) to make people feel sth more strongly: *to stoke up envy* **3** ~ sth (up) to make sth increase or develop more quickly: *They were accused of stoking the crisis.*
**PHRV** **ˌstoke ˈup (on/with sth)** (informal) to eat or drink a lot of sth, especially so that you do not feel hungry later: *Stoke up for the day on a good breakfast.*

**stoked** /stəʊkt/ adj. (especially NAmE, informal) excited and pleased about sth: *I'm really stoked that they chose me for the team.*

**stoker** /ˈstəʊkə(r)/ noun a person whose job is to add coal or other fuel to a fire, etc., especially on a ship or a STEAM train

**stok·vel** /ˈstɒkfel; NAmE ˈstɑːk-; SAfrE [ˈstɔkfel]/ noun (SAfrE) a group of people who agree to pay regular amounts of money and take turns to receive all or part of what is collected

**stole** /stəʊl/ noun, verb
- noun a piece of clothing consisting of a wide band of cloth or fur, worn by a woman around the shoulders; a similar piece of clothing worn by a priest
- verb past tense of STEAL

**stolen** /ˈstəʊlən/ verb past part. of STEAL

---

**stolid** /ˈstɒlɪd; NAmE ˈstɑːl-/ adj. (usually disapproving) not showing much emotion or interest; remaining always the same and not reacting or changing ▶ **stol·id·ly** adv. **stol·id·ity** /stəˈlɪdəti/ noun [U]

**stoma** /ˈstəʊmə/ noun (pl. **stomas** or **sto·mata** /-mətə/) **1** (biology) a tiny PORE (= hole) in the outer layer of a plant's leaf or STEM **2** (biology) a small opening like a mouth, in some animals **3** (medical) an artificial opening made in an organ of the body, especially in the COLON or TRACHEA

**stom·ach** 🔵 **A2** /ˈstʌmək/ noun, verb
- noun **1** 🔸 **A2** the organ inside the body where food goes when you eat it: *stomach pains/cramps* ◊ *an upset stomach* ◊ (BrE also) *a stomach upset* ◊ *It's not a good idea to drink* (= alcohol) *on an empty stomach* (= without having eaten anything). ⊃ VISUAL VOCAB page V1 ⊃ see also TUMMY **2** 🔸 **A2** the front part of the body below the chest: *The attacker kicked him in the stomach.* ◊ *Lie on your stomach with your arms by your side.*
**IDM** **have no ˈstomach for sth 1** to not want to eat sth: *She had no stomach for the leftover stew.* **2** to not have the desire or courage to do sth: *They had no stomach for a fight.* **turn your ˈstomach** to make you feel upset, sick or full of horror: *Pictures of the burnt corpses turned my stomach.* ⊃ more at BUTTERFLY, EYE n., PIT n., PUMP v., SICK adj., STRONG
- verb (especially in negative sentences or questions) **1** ~ sth to approve of sth and be able to enjoy it; to enjoy being with a person: *I can't stomach violent films.* ◊ *I find him very hard to stomach.* **2** ~ sth to be able to eat sth without feeling sick: *She couldn't stomach any breakfast.*

**ˈstomach ache** noun [C, U] pain in or near your stomach

**ˈstomach-churning** (also **ˈstomach-turning**) adj. making you feel that you want to VOMIT because it is so horrible: *The team daily faces stomach-churning crime scenes.*

**stomp** /stɒmp; NAmE stɑːmp/ verb [I] + adv./prep. (informal) to walk, dance, or move with heavy steps: *She stomped angrily out of the office.*

**stom·pie** /ˈstɒmpi; NAmE ˈstɑːm-; SAfrE [ˈstɔmpi]/ noun (SAfrE, informal) a cigarette that has been partly smoked; the end of a cigarette that is thrown away after it has been smoked

**ˈstomping ground** noun (NAmE, informal) = STAMPING GROUND

**stone** 🔵 **A2** /stəʊn/ noun, verb
- noun
• HARD SUBSTANCE **1** 🔸 **A2** [U] (often used before nouns or in compounds) a hard solid mineral substance that is found in the ground, often used for building: *Most of the houses are built of stone.* ◊ *stone walls* ◊ *a stone floor/bridge/carving/pillar/slab* ◊ *a brick and stone building* ⊃ see also DRY-STONE WALL, LIMESTONE, SANDSTONE, SOAPSTONE **2** 🔸 **A2** [C] (especially BrE) a small piece of rock of any shape: *a pile of stones* ◊ *Some children were throwing stones into the lake.* ⊃ see also HAILSTONE, PHILOSOPHER'S STONE **3** 🔸 **A2** [C] (usually in compounds) a piece of stone shaped for a particular purpose: *These words are carved on the stone beside his grave.* ⊃ see also CORNERSTONE, FOUNDATION STONE, GRAVESTONE, HEADSTONE, LODESTONE, MILLSTONE, PAVING STONE, STANDING STONE, STEPPING STONE, TOMBSTONE
• JEWEL **4** [C] = PRECIOUS STONE
• IN FRUIT **5** [C] (especially BrE) (NAmE usually **pit**) a hard shell containing the nut or seed in the middle of some types of fruit: *cherry/peach stones* ⊃ VISUAL VOCAB page V4
• IN BODY **6** [C] (often in compounds) a small piece of hard material that can form in the BLADDER or KIDNEY and cause pain: *kidney stones* ⊃ see also GALLSTONE
• MEASUREMENT OF WEIGHT **7** [C] (pl. **stone**) (abbr. **st**) (in the UK) a unit for measuring weight, equal to 6.35 KILOGRAMS or 14 pounds: *He weighs over 15 stone.* ◊ *She's trying to lose a stone.*
**IDM** **ˌcarved/ˌset in ˈstone** (of a decision, plan, etc.) unable to be changed: *People should remember that our proposals aren't set in stone.* **ˌleave no ˌstone unˈturned** to try every

**the Stone Age** 1542

possible course of action in order to find or achieve sth **a 'stone's throw** a very short distance away: *We live just a stone's throw from here.* ◊ *The hotel is within a stone's throw of the beach.* ⊃ more at BLOOD *n.*, HEART *n.*, KILL *v.*, PEOPLE *n.*, ROLL *v.*

■ *verb* [usually passive]
- **THROW STONES 1** to throw stones at sb/sth: **be stoned** *Shops were looted and vehicles stoned.* ◊ *to be stoned to death* (= as a punishment)
- **FRUIT 2** (*BrE*) (also **pit** *NAmE, BrE*) ~ **sth** to remove the stone from the inside of a fruit: *stoned black olives*

**the 'Stone Age** *noun* [sing.] the very early period of human history when tools and weapons were made of stone: (*figurative*) *My dad's taste in music is from the Stone Age* (= very old-fashioned). ▶ **'stone-age** *adj.* [only before noun]: (*figurative*) *stone-age* (= very out-of-date) *computers*

**stone 'circle** *noun* a circle of large, tall stones set in the ground from PREHISTORIC times, thought to have been used for religious or other ceremonies

**stone 'cold** *adj.* completely cold, when it should be warm or hot: *The soup was stone cold.*
**IDM** **stone-cold 'sober** having drunk no alcohol at all

**stoned** /stəʊnd/ *adj.* [not usually before noun] (*informal*) not behaving or thinking normally because of the effects of a drug such as MARIJUANA or alcohol

**stone 'dead** *adj.* completely dead or completely destroyed

**stone-'faced** *adj.* (*especially NAmE*) = STONY-FACED

**stone·mason** /ˈstəʊnmeɪsn/ *noun* a person whose job is cutting and preparing stone for buildings

**stone·wall** /ˈstəʊnwɔːl/ *verb* [T, I] ~ **(sb/sth)** (especially in politics) to delay a discussion or decision by refusing to answer questions or by talking a lot

**stone·ware** /ˈstəʊnweə(r); *NAmE* -wer/ *noun* [U] pots, dishes, etc. made from CLAY that contains a small amount of the hard stone called FLINT

**stone·work** /ˈstəʊnwɜːk; *NAmE* -wɜːrk/ *noun* [U] the parts of a building that are made of stone

**stonk·ing** /ˈstɒŋkɪŋ; *NAmE* ˈstɑːŋ-/ *adj.* [usually before noun] (*BrE, informal*) extremely large or impressive

**stony** /ˈstəʊni/ *adj.* (**stoni·er**, **stoni·est**) **1** having a lot of stones on it or in it: *stony soil* **2** showing a lack of feeling or sympathy **SYN** **cold**: *They listened to him in stony silence.*
**IDM** **fall on stony 'ground** to fail to produce the result or the effect that you hope for; to have little success **stony 'broke** (*BrE*) = FLAT BROKE at FLAT *adv.*

**stony-'faced** (also **stone-'faced** especially in *NAmE*) *adj.* not showing any friendly feelings

**stood** /stʊd/ *past tense, past part.* of STAND

**stooge** /stuːdʒ/ *noun* **1** (*informal, usually disapproving*) a person who is used by sb to do things that are unpleasant or dishonest **2** a performer in a show whose role is to appear silly so that the other performers can make jokes about him or her

**stool** /stuːl/ *noun* **1** (often in compounds) a seat with legs but with nothing to support your back or arms: *a bar stool* ◊ *a piano stool* **2** (*medical*) a piece of solid waste from your body **IDM** see TWO

**stoop** /stuːp/ *verb, noun*
■ *verb* **1** [I] ~ **(down)** to bend your body forwards and downwards: *She stooped down to pick up the child.* ◊ *The doorway was so low that he had to stoop.* **2** [I] to stand or walk with your head and shoulders bent forwards: *He tends to stoop because he's so tall.*
**IDM** **stoop so 'low (as to do sth)** (*formal*) to drop your moral standards far enough to do sth bad or unpleasant: *She was unwilling to believe anyone would stoop so low as to steal a ring from a dead woman's finger.* ⊃ more at LOW *n.*
**PHRV** **'stoop to sth** to drop your moral standards to do sth bad or unpleasant: *You surely don't think I'd stoop to that!* ◊ *stoop to doing sth I didn't think he'd stoop to cheating.*

■ *noun* **1** [sing.] if sb has a **stoop**, their shoulders are always bent forward **2** [C] (*NAmE*) a raised area outside the door of a house with steps leading up to it

**stooped** /stuːpt/ *adj.* **1** standing or walking with your head and shoulders bent forwards **2** **stooped shoulders** are bent forwards

**stop** ⓘ **A1** /stɒp; *NAmE* stɑːp/ *verb, noun*
■ *verb* (-pp-)
- **NOT MOVE 1 A1** [I, T] to no longer move; to make sb/sth no longer move: *The car stopped at the traffic lights.* ◊ ~ **sb/sth** *He was stopped by the police for speeding.*
- **NOT CONTINUE 2 A1** [I, T] to no longer continue to do sth; to make sb/sth no longer do sth: *Can't you just stop?* ◊ ~ **doing sth** *That phone never stops ringing!* ◊ *She criticizes everyone and the trouble is, she doesn't know when to stop.* ◊ ~ **sb/sth** *Stop me* (= make me stop talking) *if I'm boring you.* ◊ *Stop it! You're hurting me.* ◊ ~ **what …** *Mike immediately stopped what he was doing.* **HELP** Notice the difference between **stop doing sth** and **stop to do sth**: *We stopped taking pictures* means 'We were no longer taking pictures.'; *We stopped to take pictures* means 'We stopped what we were doing so that we could start taking pictures.' ⊃ EXPRESS YOURSELF at INTERRUPT
- **END 3 A1** [I, T] to end or finish; to make sth end or finish: *When is this fighting going to stop?* ◊ *The bus service stops at midnight.* ◊ ~ **doing sth** *Has it stopped raining yet?* ◊ ~ **sth** *Doctors couldn't stop the bleeding.* ◊ *The referee was forced to stop the game because of heavy snow.*
- **PREVENT 4 A2** [T] to prevent sb from doing sth; to prevent sth from happening: ~ **sb/sth** *I want to go and you can't stop me.* ◊ *efforts to stop the spread of the disease* ◊ *There's no stopping us now* (= nothing can prevent us from achieving what we want to achieve). ◊ ~ **sb/sth (from) doing sth** *You can't stop people (from) saying what they think.* ◊ *There's nothing to stop you from accepting the offer.*
- **FOR SHORT TIME 5 A2** [I] to end an activity for a short time in order to do sth: ~ **for sth** *I'm hungry. Let's stop for lunch.* ◊ ~ **to do sth** *We stopped to admire the scenery.* ◊ *People just don't stop to think about the consequences.* **HELP** In spoken English, **stop** can be used with **and** plus another verb, instead of with **to** and the infinitive, to show purpose: *He stopped and bought some flowers.* ◊ *Let's stop and look at the map.*
- **NOT FUNCTION 6 A2** [I, T] to no longer be working or functioning; to make sth be no longer working or functioning: *Why has the engine stopped?* ◊ *I felt as if my heart had stopped.* ◊ ~ **sth** *Can you stop the printer once it's started?*
- **STAY 7** [I] (*BrE, informal*) to stay somewhere for a short time, especially at sb's house: *I'm not stopping. I just came to give you this message.* ◊ ~ **for sth** *Can you stop for tea?*
- **MONEY 8** [T] to prevent money from being paid: ~ **sth** *to stop a cheque* (= tell the bank not to pay it) ◊ ~ **sth from sth** (*BrE*) *Dad threatened to stop £1 a week from our pocket money if we didn't clean our rooms.*
- **CLOSE HOLE 9** [T] ~ **sth (up) (with sth)** to block, fill or close a hole, an opening, etc: *Stop up the other end of the tube, will you?* ◊ *I stopped my ears but still heard her cry out.*
**IDM** **stop at 'nothing** to be willing to do anything to get what you want, even if it is dishonest or wrong **stop the 'clock** to stop measuring time in a game or an activity that has a time limit **stop 'short** | **stop sb 'short** to suddenly stop, or make sb suddenly stop, doing sth: *He stopped short when he heard his name.* **stop short of sth/of doing sth** to be unwilling to do sth because it may involve a risk, but to nearly do it: *She stopped short of calling the president a liar.* ⊃ more at TRACK *n.*
**PHRV** **stop 'by (sth)** to make a short visit somewhere: *I'll stop by this evening for a chat.* ◊ *Could you stop by the store on the way home for some bread?* **stop 'in** (*BrE, informal*) to stay at home rather than go out **stop 'off (at/in …)** to make a short visit somewhere during a trip in order to do sth: *We stopped off at a hotel for the night.* **stop 'out** (*BrE, informal*) to stay out late at night **stop 'over (at/in …)** to stay somewhere for a short time during a long journey: *I wanted to stop over in India on the way to Australia.* ⊃ related noun STOPOVER **stop 'up** (*BrE, informal*) to stay up late

■ **noun**
- OF BUS/TRAIN **1** 🔑 **A1** a place where a bus or train stops regularly for passengers to get on or off: *I get off at the next stop.* ◇ *Is this your stop?* ⇒ see also BUS STOP, PIT STOP, TRUCK STOP
- ACT OF STOPPING **2** 🔑 **B1** an act of stopping or stopping sth; the state of being stopped: *The trip included an overnight stop in Brussels.* ◇ *We made several stops along the way.* ◇ *She brought the car to a stop.* ◇ *Work has temporarily come to a stop while the funding is reviewed.* ◇ *It is time to put a stop to the violence.* ⇒ see also NON-STOP, WHISTLE-STOP
- PUNCTUATION **3** (*BrE*) = FULL STOP
- MUSIC **4** a row of pipes on an organ that produce the different sounds **5** a handle on an organ that the player pushes in or pulls out to control the sound produced by the pipes
- PHONETICS **6** a speech sound made by stopping the flow of air coming out of the mouth and then suddenly releasing it, for example /p/, /k/, /t/ ⇒ see also GLOTTAL STOP ⇒ see also TAB STOP **IDM** see FULL STOP *n.*, PULL *v.*, START *n.*

**stop·cock** /ˈstɒpkɒk; *NAmE* ˈstɑːpkɑːk/ (*also* **cock**) *noun* a TAP that controls the flow of liquid or gas through a pipe

**stop·gap** /ˈstɒpɡæp; *NAmE* ˈstɑːp-/ *noun* something that you use or do for a short time while you are looking for sth better: *The arrangement was only intended as a stopgap.* ◇ *a stopgap measure*

**ˌstop-ˈgo** (*especially BrE*) (*especially NAmE* ˌ**stop-and-ˈgo**) *adj.* [usually before noun] (*disapproving*) **1** starting and then stopping: *stop-go driving in heavy traffic* **2** used to describe the policy of first limiting and then encouraging economic activity and growth: *the damaging stop-go economic cycle*

**ˈstop light** *noun* [C] **1** (*BrE*) a red TRAFFIC LIGHT **2** (*also* **stoplights** [pl.]) (*NAmE*) = TRAFFIC LIGHT **3** (*NAmE*) = BRAKE LIGHT

**stop·over** /ˈstɒpəʊvə(r); *NAmE* ˈstɑːp-/ (*NAmE also* **layover**) *noun* a short stay somewhere between two parts of a journey: *We had a two-day stopover in Fiji on the way to Australia.*

**stop·page** /ˈstɒpɪdʒ; *NAmE* ˈstɑːp-/ *noun* **1** [C] a situation in which people stop working as part of a protest or strike **2** [C] (*sport*) a situation in which a game is interrupted for a particular reason: *Play resumed quickly after the stoppage.* ◇ *stoppage time* (= added on at the end of the game if there have been stoppages) **3** [C] a situation in which sth does not move forward or is blocked: *a stoppage of blood to the heart* **4** **stoppages** [pl.] (*BrE, old-fashioned, formal*) an amount of money that an employer takes from people's wages for tax and other payments

**stop·per** /ˈstɒpə(r); *NAmE* ˈstɑːp-/ (*NAmE also* **plug**) *noun* an object that fits into the top of a bottle to close it ⇒ see also BARBECUE STOPPER, CONVERSATION STOPPER, SHOW-STOPPER ▶ **stop·per** *verb* ~ **sth**

**ˈstop street** *noun* (*SAfrE*) a place where one road joins or crosses another at which there is a sign indicating that vehicles must stop before continuing

**stop·watch** /ˈstɒpwɒtʃ; *NAmE* ˈstɑːpwɑːtʃ/ *noun* a watch that you can stop and start by pressing buttons, in order to time a race, etc. accurately, or an app on a phone that can perform the same function

**stor·age** 🔑+ **C1** /ˈstɔːrɪdʒ/ *noun* [U] **1** 🔑+ **C1** the process of keeping sth in a particular place until it is needed; the space where things can be kept: *tables that fold flat for storage* ◇ *There's a lot of storage space in the loft.* ◇ *food storage facilities* ◇ *We need more storage now.* ⇒ see also COLD STORAGE **2** 🔑+ (*computing*) the process of keeping information, etc. on a computer; the way it is kept: *the storage and retrieval of information* ◇ *data storage* **3** 🔑+ **C1** the process of paying to keep furniture, etc. in a special building until you want it: **in** ~ *When we moved we had to put our furniture in storage for a while.* ⇒ see also SELF-STORAGE

**ˈstorage battery** (*NAmE*) (*BrE* **ac·cu·mu·la·tor**) *noun* a large battery that you can fill with electrical power (= that you can RECHARGE)

1543 **storey**

**store** 🔑 **A2** w /stɔː(r)/ *noun, verb*
■ **noun 1** 🔑 **A2** [C] a large shop that sells many different types of goods: *It's available at London's three biggest stores.* ⇒ see also BOTTLE STORE, CHAIN STORE, DEPARTMENT STORE, LIQUOR STORE ⇒ **WORDFINDER NOTE** at SHOP

**WORDFINDER** appliances, cookware, fashion, furnishings, hardware, linen, lingerie, menswear, stationery

**2** 🔑 **A2** [C] (*NAmE*) a shop, large or small: *I'm going to the store.* ◇ *His father opened a small grocery store.* ◇ *Retail stores across Europe were reporting no stock left of the game.* ⇒ see also CONSIGNMENT SHOP, CONVENIENCE STORE, GENERAL STORE **3** 🔑 **A2** (in compounds) a website that sells things: *an online store* ◇ *You can get it on the app store.* **4** [C] a quantity or supply of sth that you have and use: *her secret store of chocolate* ◇ *a vast store of knowledge* **5** **stores** [pl.] goods of a particular kind or for a particular purpose: *medical stores* **6** [C] (*often* **stores**) a place where goods of a particular kind are kept: *a grain store* ◇ *weapons stores* ⇒ see also COLD STORE

**IDM** **in store (for sb)** waiting to happen to sb: *We don't know what life holds in store for us.* ◇ *If she had known what lay in store for her, she would never have agreed to go.* ◇ *They think it'll be easy but they have a surprise in store.* **set/put (great, etc.) store by sth** to consider sth to be important: *She sets great store by her appearance.* ◇ *It is unwise to put too much store by these statistics.* ⇒ more at MIND *v.*
■ **verb 1** 🔑 **B1** to put sth somewhere and keep it there to use later: ~ **sth** *We do not have adequate space to store these documents.* ◇ ~ **sth away/up** *animals storing up food for the winter* ◇ ~ **sth + adv./prep.** *You can store coffee beans in the freezer to keep them fresh.* **2** 🔑 **B1** to keep information or facts in a computer or in your brain: ~ **sth** *to store data/information* ◇ ~ **sth + adv./prep.** *Digital music files can be stored on your computer.*

**PHR V** **ˌstore sth ↔ ˈup** to not deal with problems when you have them, especially when this causes problems later: *By ignoring your feelings you are only storing up trouble for yourself.* ◇ *They have stored up big problems for the future.*

**ˌstore-ˈbought** (*NAmE*) (*BrE* **ˌshop-ˈbought**) *adj.* [only before noun] bought from a shop and not made at home: *store-bought cookies*

**ˈstore-brand** (*US*) (*BrE* **ˌown-ˈbrand**, **ˌown-ˈlabel**) *adj.* used to describe goods that are marked with the name of the shop in which they are sold rather than with the name of the company that produced them

**ˈstore card** *noun* a card that a particular shop provides for regular customers so that they can use it to buy goods that they will pay for later ⇒ compare CREDIT CARD ⇒ **WORDFINDER NOTE** at BUY

**store·front** /ˈstɔːfrʌnt; *NAmE* ˈstɔːrf-/ *noun* **1** (*BrE* **ˈshop-front**) the outside of a shop that faces the street **2** a room at the front of a shop: *They run their business from a small storefront.* ◇ *a storefront office* ◇ *a place on the internet where you can buy goods and services: Welcome to our online storefront.*

**store·house** /ˈstɔːhaʊs; *NAmE* ˈstɔːrh-/ *noun* **1** a building where things are stored **SYN** warehouse **2** ~ **of information, knowledge, etc.** a place or thing that has or contains a lot of information

**store·keep·er** /ˈstɔːkiːpə(r); *NAmE* ˈstɔːrk-/ *noun* (*especially NAmE*) = SHOPKEEPER

**store·room** /ˈstɔːruːm, -rʊm/ *noun* a room used for storing things

**ˈstore window** (*NAmE*) (*BrE* **ˌshop ˈwindow**) (*also* **window**) *noun* the glass at the front of a shop and the area behind it where goods are shown to the public

**storey** (*US* **story**) /ˈstɔːri/ *noun* (*pl.* **storeys**, *US* **stories**) **1** a level of a building; a floor: *the upper/lower storey of the house* ◇ *a single-storey/two-storey building* ⇒ see also MULTI-STOREY at MULTI-STOREY CAR PARK **2** **-storeyed**

# storied

**storeyed** (*BrE*) (*US* **-storied**) (in adjectives) (of a building) having the number of levels mentioned: *a four-storeyed building*

▼ **HOMOPHONES**

**storey • story** /ˈstɔːri/
- **storey** *noun*: *There are splendid views from the tenth storey.*
- **story** *noun*: *It's not real—it's just a story.*

▼ **WHICH WORD?**

**storey / floor**
- You use **storey** (*BrE*) / **story** (*US*) mainly when you are talking about the number of levels a building has: *a five-storey house* ◇ *The office building is five storeys high.*
- **Floor** is used mainly to talk about which particular level in the building someone lives on, goes to, etc: *His office is on the fifth floor.*
- ⊃ note at FLOOR

**sto·ried** /ˈstɔːrid/ *adj.* (*NAmE*) **1** [only before noun] mentioned in stories; famous; well known: *the rock star's storied career* **2 -storied** = -STOREYED

**stork** /stɔːk; *NAmE* stɔːrk/ *noun* a large black and white bird with a long BEAK and neck and long legs, that lives near water but often builds its NEST on the top of a high building. There is a tradition that says that it is storks that bring people their new babies.

**storm** ❶ A2 /stɔːm; *NAmE* stɔːrm/ *noun, verb*
■ *noun* **1** ⚡ A2 very bad weather with strong winds and rain, and often THUNDER and LIGHTNING: *fierce/heavy/severe/violent storms* ◇ *Her home was hit by two tropical storms.* ◇ *Off on the horizon, dark grey storm clouds gathered.* ◇ *storm damage* ⊃ note at RAIN **2** ⚡ A2 (in compounds) very bad weather of the type mentioned: *She had to brave an ice storm to get to the interview.* ⊃ see also DUST STORM, ELECTRICAL STORM, RAINSTORM, SANDSTORM, SNOWSTORM, THUNDERSTORM **3** ~ **(of sth)** a situation in which a lot of people suddenly express very strong feelings about sth: *a storm of protest* ◇ *A political storm is brewing over the prime minister's comments.* ◇ *The footballer has been at the centre of a media storm after remarks he made on the radio caused controversy.* ⊃ see also PERFECT STORM **4** ~ **of sth** a sudden loud noise that is caused by emotion or excitement SYN *roar*: *a storm of applause* ⊃ see also BRAINSTORM
**IDM** **cook, dance, etc. up a ˈstorm** (*informal*) to do sth with great energy and enthusiasm: *Leonie was in the kitchen, cooking up a storm for her friends.* **a storm in a ˈteacup** (*BrE*) (*NAmE* **a tempest in a ˈteapot**) a lot of anger or worry about sth that is not important **take sth/sb by ˈstorm 1** to be extremely successful very quickly in a particular place or among particular people: *The play took London by storm.* **2** to attack a place suddenly and capture it ⊃ more at CALM *n.*, PORT *n.*
■ *verb* **1** [T, I] to suddenly attack a place: *~ sth Police stormed the building and captured the gunman.* ◇ *~ into sth Soldiers stormed into the city at dawn.* **2** [I] + *adv./prep.* to go somewhere quickly and in an angry, noisy way: *She stormed into my office waving a newspaper.* ◇ *He burst into tears and stormed off.* **3** [T] + *speech* to say sth in a loud angry way: *'Don't you know who I am?' she stormed.*

**ˈstorm cloud** *noun* [usually pl.] a dark cloud that you see when bad weather is coming: (*figurative*) *The storm clouds of revolution were gathering.*

**storm·ing** /ˈstɔːmɪŋ; *NAmE* ˈstɔːrm-/ *adj.* [only before noun] (*BrE*) (of a performance) very impressive; done with a lot of energy: *Arsenal scored three late goals in a storming finish.*

**ˈstorm surge** *noun* [C, U] an unusual rise in the level of the sea near the coast, caused by wind from a severe storm

**ˈstorm trooper** *noun* a soldier who is specially trained for violent attacks, especially one in Nazi Germany in the 1930s and 1940s

**ˈstorm water** *noun* [U] water covering the ground in large quantities because of heavy rain

**stormy** /ˈstɔːmi; *NAmE* ˈstɔːrmi/ *adj.* (**storm·ier**, **stormi·est**) **1** with strong winds and heavy rain or snow: *a dark and stormy night* ◇ *stormy weather* ◇ *stormy seas* (= with big waves) **2** full of strong feelings and angry arguments: *a stormy debate* ◇ *a stormy relationship*

**story** ❶ A1 S /ˈstɔːri/ *noun* (*pl.* **-ies**) **1** A1 a description of events and people that the writer or speaker has invented in order to entertain people: *a tragic love story* ◇ *adventure/detective stories* ◇ *a bedtime story* ◇ *Shall I tell you a story?* ◇ *He read the children a story.* ◇ **~ about/of sb/sth** *a story about time travel* ◇ **in the ~** *What are the key events in the story?* ⊃ HOMOPHONES at STOREY ⊃ see also FAIRY STORY at FAIRY TALE, GHOST STORY, HORROR STORY (1), SHORT STORY

**WORDFINDER** comic, far-fetched, gripping, historical, mannered, moving, rambling, readable, tragic

**2** ⚡ A2 (also **ˈstory·line**) the series of events in a book, film, play, etc. SYN *plot*: *Her novels always have the same basic story.* **3** ⚡ A2 an account of past events or of how sth has developed: *The film is based on a true story.* ◇ **~ of sth/sb** *He told us the story of his life.* ◇ **~ behind sth/sb** *Every piece of art has an interesting story behind it.* **4** ⚡ B1 an account, often spoken, of what happened to sb or of how sth happened: *The police didn't believe her story.* ◇ *I suspected he hadn't told us the whole story.* ◇ **~ about sth/sb** *We must stick to our story about the accident.* ◇ **~ of sth/sb** *It's a story of courage.* ◇ *I can't decide until I've heard both sides of the story.* ◇ *Many years later I returned to Africa but that's another story* (= I am not going to talk about it now). ⊃ SYNONYMS at REPORT ⊃ see also COCK AND BULL STORY, COVER STORY (2), HARD-LUCK STORY, HORROR STORY (2), LIFE STORY, SOB STORY, SUCCESS STORY, TALL STORY **5** ⚡ B1 a report in a newspaper, magazine or news broadcast: *a front-page story* ◇ *Now for a summary of tonight's main news stories.* ◇ *Let's check the top stories right now.* ⊃ see also COVER STORY (1), LEAD STORY **6** (*informal*) something that sb says which is not true: *She knew the child had been telling stories again.* **7** (*US*) = STOREY
**IDM** **the story goes (that) … | so the story goes** used to describe sth that people are saying although it may not be correct: *He never saw him again—or so the story goes.* **that's the ˈstory of my ˈlife** (*informal*) when you say that's the story of my life about a bad experience you have had, you mean you have had many similar experiences ⊃ more at LIKELY *adj.*, LONG *adj.*, OLD *adj.*, PITCH *v.*, TELL

**story·board** /ˈstɔːribɔːd; *NAmE* -bɔːrd/ *noun* a series of drawings or pictures that show the outline of the story of a film, etc. ▸ **ˈstory·board** *verb* **~ sth** **ˈstory·board·ing** *noun* [U]: *the storyboarding process*

**story·book** /ˈstɔːribʊk/ *noun* a book of stories for children: *a picture in a storybook* ◇ *storybook characters* ◇ *storybook adventures* (= like the ones in stories for children)

**story·line** /ˈstɔːrilaɪn/ *noun* the basic story in a novel, play, film, etc. SYN *plot* ⊃ WORDFINDER NOTE at PLOT

**story·tell·er** /ˈstɔːritelə(r)/ *noun* a person who tells or writes stories ▸ **ˈstory·tell·ing** *noun* [U]

**stout** /staʊt/ *adj., noun*
■ *adj.* (**stout·er**, **stout·est**) **1** (of a person) rather fat SYN *plump* **2** [usually before noun] strong and thick: *a stout pair of shoes* **3** [usually before noun] brave and determined: *He put up a stout defence in court.* ▸ **ˈstout·ly** *adv.*: *He was tall and stoutly built.* ◇ *'I disagree,' said Polly stoutly.* **ˈstout·ness** *noun* [U]
■ *noun* [U, C] strong dark beer made with MALT or BARLEY

**stove** /stəʊv/ *noun, verb*
■ *noun* **1** a piece of equipment that can burn various fuels and is used for heating rooms: *a gas/wood-burning stove* **2** (*BrE also* **cook·er**) (*NAmE also* **range**) a large piece of equipment for cooking food, containing an oven and gas or electric rings on top: *She put a pan of water on the stove.* ◇ *Most people don't want to spend hours slaving over a hot stove* (= cooking).
■ *verb* past tense, past part. of STAVE

**stove-top** /ˈstəʊvtɒp; NAmE -tɑːp/ (NAmE) (BrE **hob**) noun the top part of a cooker where food is cooked in pans; a similar surface that is built into a kitchen unit and is separate from the oven: *stovetop cooking*

**stow** /stəʊ/ verb ~ **sth (away) (in sth)** to put sth in a safe place: *She found a seat, stowed her backpack and sat down.*
**PHR V** **stow aˈway** to hide in a ship, plane, etc. in order to travel secretly ⊃ related noun STOWAWAY

**stow-age** /ˈstəʊɪdʒ/ noun [U] space provided for stowing things away, in a boat or a plane

**stow-away** /ˈstəʊəweɪ/ noun a person who hides in a ship or plane before it leaves, in order to travel without paying or being seen

**St Patˈrick's Day** /snt ˈpætrɪks deɪ; NAmE seɪnt/ noun 17 March, a Christian festival of the national SAINT of Ireland, when many Irish people wear a SHAMROCK

**strad-dle** /ˈstrædl/ verb **1** ~ **sth/sb** to sit or stand with one of your legs on either side of sb/sth: *He swung his leg over the motorcycle, straddling it easily.* **2** ~ **sth** to cross, or exist on both sides of, a river, a road or an area of land: *The mountains straddle the French-Swiss border.* **3** ~ **sth** to exist within, or include, different periods of time, activities or groups of people: *a writer who straddles two cultures*

**strafe** /streɪf; BrE also strɑːf/ verb ~ **sth** to attack a place with bullets or bombs from an aircraft flying low

**strag-gle** /ˈstrægl/ verb **1** [I] (+ *adv./prep.*) to grow, spread or move in an untidy way in different directions: *The town straggled to an end and the fields began.* **2** [I] (+ *adv./prep.*) to move slowly behind a group of people that you are with so that you become separated from them: *On the way the kids straggled behind us.*

**strag-gler** /ˈstræɡlə(r)/ noun [usually pl.] a person or an animal that is among the last or the slowest in a group to do sth, for example, to finish a race or leave a place

**strag-gly** /ˈstræɡli/ adj. growing or hanging in a way that does not look tidy or attractive: *a thin woman with grey, straggly hair*

## straight ⓘ **A2** /streɪt/ adv., adj., noun

■ **adv. (straight-er, straight-est)**
- **NOT IN CURVE 1** **A2** not in a curve or at an angle; in a straight line: *Keep straight on for two miles.* ◇ *Can you stretch your arms out straighter?* ◇ *He was too tired to walk straight.* ◇ *I can't shoot straight* (= accurately). ◇ *She looked me straight in the eye.* ⊃ picture at LINE
- **IMMEDIATELY 2** **A2** by a direct route; immediately: *Come straight home after school.* ◇ *I was so tired I went straight to bed.* ◇ *She went straight from college to a top job.* ◇ **~ after sth** *I'm going to the library straight after the class.* ◇ *I'll come straight to the point—your work isn't good enough.*
- **IN LEVEL/CORRECT POSITION 3** **A2** in or into a level or VERTICAL position; in or into the correct position: *Sit up straight!* ◇ *She pulled her hat straight.*
- **HONESTLY 4** honestly and directly: *I told him straight that I didn't like him.* ◇ *Are you playing straight with me?*
- **CONTINUOUSLY 5** continuously without being interrupted: *They had been working for 16 hours straight.*
**IDM** **go ˈstraight** (*informal*) to stop being a criminal and live an honest life **play it ˈstraight** to be honest and not try to trick sb **straight aˈway** immediately; without delay **SYN** **at once**: *I'll do it straight away.* **straight from the ˈshoulder** if you say sth **straight from the shoulder**, you are being very honest and direct, even if what you are saying is critical **straight ˈoff/ˈout** (*informal*) without hesitating: *She asked him straight off what he thought about it all.* **straight ˈup** (*BrE, informal, becoming old-fashioned*) used to ask if what sb has said is true or to emphasize that what you have said is true: *I saw it—straight up!* ⊃ more at HIT *v.*, HORSE *n.*, THINK *v.*

■ **adj. (straight-er, straight-est)**
- **WITHOUT CURVES 1** **A2** without a bend or curve; going in one direction only: *a straight road* ◇ *long, straight hair* (= not curly) ◇ *a boat sailing in a straight line* ◇ *straight-backed chairs*
- **IN LEVEL/CORRECT POSITION 2** **B1** positioned in the correct way; level, VERTICAL or PARALLEL to sth: *Is my tie straight?*
- **CLOTHING 3** not fitting close to the body and not curving away from the body: *a straight skirt*
- **AIM/BLOW 4** going directly to the correct place: *a straight punch to the face*
- **CLEAN/NEAT 5** [not usually before noun] clean and neat, with everything in the correct place: *It took hours to get the house straight.*
- **HONEST 6** honest and direct: *a straight answer to a straight question* ◇ **~ with sb** *I don't think you're being straight with me.* ◇ *It's time for some straight talking.* ⊃ SYNONYMS at HONEST
- **CHOICE 7** [only before noun] simple; involving only two clear choices: *It was a straight choice between taking the job and staying out of work.* ◇ (*3rE*) *The election was a straight fight between the two main parties.*
- **ACTOR/PLAY 8** [only before noun] (of an actor or a play) not connected with comedy or musical theatre, but with serious theatre
- **WITHOUT BEING INTERRUPTED 9** [only before noun] one after another in a series that is not interrupted **SYN** **consecutive**: *The team has had five straight wins.*
- **ALCOHOLIC DRINK 10** (*BrE also* **neat**) not mixed with water or anything else
- **NORMAL/BORING 11** (*informal*) you can use **straight** to describe a person who is normal and ordinary, but who you consider boring
- **SEX 12** (*informal*) HETEROSEXUAL **OPP** gay ▶ **straight-ness** noun [U]
**IDM** **get sth ˈstraight** to make a situation clear; to make sure that you or sb else understands the situation: *Let's get this straight—you really had no idea where he was?* **put/ set sb ˈstraight (about/on sth)** to correct sb's mistake; to make sure that sb knows the correct facts when they have had the wrong idea or impression **the ˌstraight and ˈnarrow** (*informal*) the honest and morally acceptable way of living: *His wife is trying to keep him on the straight and narrow.* **(earn/get) straight ˈA's** (*especially NAmE*) (to get) the best grades in all your classes: *a straight A student* **a straight ˈface** if you keep a **straight face**, you do not laugh or smile, although you find sth funny ⊃ see also STRAIGHT-FACED ⊃ more at RAMROD, RECORD *n.*

■ **noun**
- **SEX 1** (*informal*) a person who has sexual relationships with people of the opposite sex, rather than the same sex: *gays and straights*
- **OF ROAD/TRACK 2** (*NAmE also* **straight-away**) a straight part of a RACETRACK or road ⊃ see also HOME STRAIGHT

**straight-ˈarm** (*also* **stiff-ˈarm**) (*both NAmE*) (*BrE* **hand sb ⇌ ˈoff**) verb ~ **sb** (in sport) to push away a player who is trying to stop you, with your arm straight

**straight-away** /ˌstreɪtəˈweɪ/ adv., noun
■ **adv.** (*also* **straight away**) immediately; without delay
■ **noun** (*NAmE*) = STRAIGHT (2)

**ˈstraight edge** noun a narrow piece of wood, metal or plastic with a straight edge used for drawing accurate straight lines, or checking them

**straight-en** /ˈstreɪtn/ verb **1** [T, I] to become straight; to make sth straight: **~ sth (out)** *I straightened my tie and walked in.* ◇ **~ (out)** *The road bends here then straightens out.* **2** [T, I] to make your body straight without bending any part of it: **~ sth** *He stood up and straightened his shoulders.* ◇ **~ sth/yourself up** *I even straightened myself up to answer the question.* ◇ **~ (up)** *Straighten up slowly, then repeat the exercise ten times.*
**PHR V** **straighten sb ⇌ ˈout** to help sb to deal with problems or understand a confused situation **straighten sth ⇌ ˈout** to deal with a confused situation by organizing things that are causing problems: *I need time to straighten out my finances.* **straighten sth ⇌ ˈup** to make sth neat and tidy

**straight-en-er** /ˈstreɪtnə(r)/ noun **1 straighteners** [pl.] = HAIR STRAIGHTENERS **2** any substance that you can use to make your hair straight: *chemical straighteners*

**straight-faced** *adj.* without laughing or smiling, even if you find sth funny

**straight·for·ward** /streɪtˈfɔːwəd; NAmE -ˈfɔːrwərd/ *adj.* **1** easy to do or to understand; not complicated SYN easy: *a straightforward process* ◇ *It's quite straightforward to get here.* **2** (of a person or their behaviour) honest and open; not trying to trick sb or hide sth ▸ **straight·for·ward·ly** *adv.*: *Let me put it more straightforwardly.* **straight·for·ward·ness** *noun* [U]

**straight·jacket** *noun* = STRAITJACKET

**straight-laced** = STRAIT-LACED

**straight man** *noun* a person in a show whose role is to provide the main person with opportunities to make jokes

**straight 'shooter** *noun* (*especially NAmE*, *informal*) a person who is honest and direct: *He's a straight shooter who will tell you exactly what he thinks.*

**strain** /streɪn/ *noun*, *verb*

■ *noun*
- **PRESSURE 1** [U, C] pressure on a system or relationship because great demands are being placed on it: *The transport service cannot cope with the strain of so many additional passengers.* ◇ *under~ Their marriage is under great strain at the moment.* ◇ *on sth These repayments are putting a strain on our finances.* ⇒ SYNONYMS at PRESSURE **2** [C, U] mental pressure or worry felt by sb because they have too much to do or manage; sth that causes this pressure: *You will learn to cope with the stresses and strains of public life.* ◇ *I found it a strain having to concentrate for so long.* ◇ *Relax, and let us take the strain* (= do things for you). ◇ *under~ Television newsreaders come under enormous strain.* **3** [U, C] the pressure that is put on sth when a physical force stretches, pushes, or pulls it: *under the~ The rope broke under the strain.* ◇ *~on sth You should try not to place too much strain on muscles and joints.* ◇ *The ground here cannot take the strain of a large building.* ◇ *The cable has a 140kg breaking strain* (= it will break when it is stretched or pulled by a force greater than this).
- **INJURY 4** [C, U] an injury to a part of your body, such as a muscle, that is caused by using it too much or by TWISTING it: *a calf/groin/leg strain* ◇ *muscle strain*
- **TYPE OF PLANT/ANIMAL/DISEASE 5** [C] a particular type of plant or animal, or of a disease caused by bacteria, etc: *a new strain of mosquitoes resistant to the poison* ◇ *This is only one of the many strains of the disease.*
- **IN SB'S CHARACTER 6** [C, usually sing.] a particular feature of the character of a person or group, or a quality in their manner SYN streak: *He had a definite strain of snobbery in him.*
- **OF MUSIC 7** [C, usually pl.] (*formal*) the sound of music being played or sung: *She could hear the strains of Mozart through the window.* IDM see CREAK *v.*

■ *verb*
- **INJURE 1** [T] *~sth/yourself* to injure yourself or part of your body by making it work too hard: *to strain a muscle* ⇒ SYNONYMS at INJURE
- **MAKE EFFORT 2** [T, I] to make an effort to do sth, using all your mental or physical strength: *~sth to do sth I strained my ears* (= listened very hard) *to catch what they were saying.* ◇ *~sth Necks were strained for a glimpse of the stranger.* ◇ *to do sth People were straining to see what was going on.* ◇ *~(sth) (for sth) He burst to the surface, straining for air.* ◇ *Bend gently to the left without straining.*
- **STRETCH TO LIMIT 3** [T] *~sth* to try to make sth do more than it is able to do: *The sudden influx of visitors is straining hotels in the town to the limit.* ◇ *His constant complaints were straining our patience.* ◇ *The dispute has strained relations between the two countries* (= made them difficult).
- **PUSH/PULL HARD 4** [I] *+ adv./prep.* to push hard against sth; to pull hard on sth: *She strained against the ropes that held her.* ◇ *The dogs were straining at the leash, eager to get to the park.*
- **SEPARATE SOLID FROM LIQUID 5** [T] to pour food, etc. through sth with very small holes in it, for example a SIEVE, in order to separate the solid part from the liquid part: *~sth Use a colander to strain the vegetables.* ◇ *~sth off Strain off any excess liquid.*

IDM **strain at the 'leash** (*informal*) to want to do sth very much: *Like all youngsters, he's straining at the leash to leave home.* **strain every 'nerve/'sinew (to do sth)** to try as hard as you can to do sth

**strained** /streɪnd/ *adj.* **1** showing the effects of worry or pressure SYN tense: *Her face looked strained and weary.* ◇ *He spoke in a low, strained voice.* **2** (of a situation) not relaxed or friendly SYN tense: *There was a strained atmosphere throughout the meeting.* ◇ *Relations between the two families are strained.* **3** not natural; produced by a deliberate effort SYN forced: *She gave a strained laugh.*

**strain·er** /ˈstreɪnə(r)/ *noun* a kitchen UTENSIL (= a tool) with a lot of small holes in it, used for separating solids from liquids: *a tea-strainer*

**strait** /streɪt/ *noun* **1** (*also* **straits**) [pl.] (*especially in the names of places*) a narrow passage of water that connects two seas or large areas of water: *the Strait(s) of Gibraltar* **2 straits** [pl.] a very difficult situation especially because of lack of money: *The factory is in dire straits.* ◇ *She found herself in desperate financial straits.*

**strait·ened** /ˈstreɪtnd/ *adj.* [only before noun] (*formal*) without enough money or as much money as there was before: *The family of eight was living in straitened circumstances.*

**strait·jacket** (*also* **straight·jacket**) /ˈstreɪtdʒækɪt/ *noun* **1** a piece of clothing like a jacket with long arms which are tied to prevent the person wearing it from behaving violently. Straitjackets are sometimes used to control people who are mentally ill. **2** (*disapproving*) a thing that stops sth from growing or developing: *The government has been caught in the straitjacket of debt.*

**strait-laced** (*also* **straight-laced**) *adj.* (*disapproving*) having strict or old-fashioned ideas about people's moral behaviour

**strand** /strænd/ *noun*, *verb*

■ *noun* **1** a single thin piece of THREAD, wire, hair, etc: *a strand of wool* ◇ *a few strands of dark hair* ◇ *She wore a single strand of pearls around her neck.* **2** one of the different parts of an idea, a plan, a story, etc: *We heard every strand of political opinion.* ◇ *The author draws the different strands of the plot together in the final chapter.* **3** (*literary or IrishE*) the land along the edge of the sea or ocean, or of a lake or river

■ *verb* [usually passive] **1** *~sb* to leave sb in a place from which they have no way of leaving: *The strike left hundreds of tourists stranded at the airport.* **2** *~sth* to make a boat, fish, WHALE, etc. be left on land and unable to return to the water: *The ship was stranded on a sandbank.*

**strange** /streɪndʒ/ *adj.* (**stran·ger**, **stran·gest**) **1** unusual or surprising, especially in a way that is difficult to understand: *A strange thing happened this morning.* ◇ *He had a strange feeling that he had seen her somewhere before.* ◇ *This may seem strange but it's the truth.* ◇ *~(that)... It's strange (that) we haven't heard from him.* ◇ *~how... It's strange how childhood impressions linger.* ◇ *That's strange—the front door's open.* ◇ *There was something strange about her eyes.* **2** not familiar because you have not been there before or met the person before: *a strange city* ◇ *to wake up in a strange bed* ◇ *Never accept lifts from strange men.* ◇ *~to sb At first the place was strange to me.* ▸ **strange·ness** *noun* [U] IDM **feel 'strange** to not feel comfortable in a situation; to have an unpleasant physical feeling: *She felt strange sitting at her father's desk.* ◇ *It was terribly hot and I started to feel strange.* ⇒ more at FUNNY, TRUTH

**strange·ly** /ˈstreɪndʒli/ *adv.* in an unusual or surprising way: *She's been acting very strangely lately.* ◇ *The house was strangely quiet.* ◇ *strangely shaped rocks* ◇ *Strangely enough, I don't feel at all nervous.*

**stran·ger** /ˈstreɪndʒə(r)/ *noun* **1** a person that you do not know: *There was a complete stranger sitting at my desk.* ◇ *We've told our daughter not to speak to strangers.* ◇ *~to sb She remained a stranger to me.* **2** a person who is in a place that they have not been in before:

Sorry, I don't know where the bank is. I'm a stranger here myself. ◇ ~ **to** ... He must have been a stranger to the town. **IDM** **be no/a ˈstranger to sth** (formal) to be familiar/not familiar with sth because you have/have not experienced it many times before: He is no stranger to controversy.

**stran·gle** /ˈstræŋgl/ verb **1** ~ **sb** to kill sb by pressing their throat and neck hard, especially with your fingers: to strangle sb to death ◇ The victim had been strangled with a scarf. **2** ~ **sth** to prevent sth from growing or developing: The current monetary policy is strangling the economy.

**stran·gled** /ˈstræŋgld/ adj. (of a sound, sb's voice, etc.) not clear because it stops before it has completely finished: There was a strangled cry from the other room.

**strangle·hold** /ˈstræŋglhəʊld/ noun [sing.] **1** a strong hold around sb's neck that makes it difficult for them to breathe **2** ~ **(on sth)** complete control over sth that makes it impossible for it to grow or develop well: The company now had a stranglehold on the market.

**stran·gler** /ˈstræŋglə(r)/ noun a person who kills sb by pressing their throat hard

**stran·gu·lated** /ˈstræŋgjuleɪtɪd/ adj. **1** (medical) (of a part of the body) made so narrow by pressure that blood etc. cannot pass through it **2** (formal) (of a voice) sounding as though the throat is being pressed hard, usually because of fear or worry: He gave a strangulated squawk.

**stran·gu·la·tion** /ˌstræŋgjuˈleɪʃn/ noun [U] **1** the act of killing sb by pressing their throat hard; the state of being killed in this way: to die of slow strangulation **2** (disapproving) the act of preventing sth from growing or developing: the strangulation of the human spirit

**strap** /stræp/ noun, verb
- **noun** a narrow piece of leather, cloth or other material that is used to fasten sth, keep sth in place, carry sth or hold onto sth: the shoulder straps of her dress ◇ a watch with a leather strap
- **verb** (-pp-) **1** ~ **sb/sth + adv./prep.** to fasten sb/sth in place using a strap or straps: He strapped the knife to his leg. ◇ Everything had to be strapped down to stop it from sliding around. ◇ Are you strapped in (= wearing a seat belt in a car, plane, etc.)? **2** ~ **sth (up)** to wrap long, narrow pieces of material around a wound or an injured part of the body **SYN** **bandage**: I have to keep my leg strapped up for six weeks.

**strap·less** /ˈstræpləs/ adj. (especially of a dress or BRA) without straps

**strapped** /stræpt/ adj. ~ **(for cash, funds, etc.)** (informal) having little or not enough money

**strap·ping** /ˈstræpɪŋ/ adj. [only before noun] (informal) (of people) big, tall and strong: a strapping lad

**strappy** /ˈstræpi/ adj. (**strap·pier**, **strap·pi·est**) (informal) (of shoes or clothes) having straps: white strappy sandals

**strata** /ˈstrɑːtə; NAmE ˈstreɪtə/ pl. of STRATUM

**strata·gem** /ˈstrætədʒəm/ noun (formal) a trick or plan that you use to gain an advantage or to trick an opponent

**stra·tegic** **?**+ **C1** /strəˈtiːdʒɪk/ (also less frequent **stra·teg·ic·al** /strəˈtiːdʒɪkl/) adj. [usually before noun] **1** **?**+ **C1** done as part of a plan that is meant to achieve a particular purpose or to gain an advantage: strategic planning ◇ a strategic decision to sell off part of the business ◇ Cameras were set up at strategic points (= in places where they would be most effective) along the route. ⇨ compare TACTICAL (1) **2** **?**+ **C1** connected with getting an advantage in a war or other military situation: Malta was of vital strategic importance during the war. **3** (of weapons, especially nuclear weapons) intended to be fired at an enemy's country rather than used in a battle ⇨ compare TACTICAL (3) ▶ **stra·teg·ic·al·ly** /-kli/ adv.: a strategically placed microphone ◇ a strategically important target

**strat·egist** /ˈstrætədʒɪst/ noun a person who shows skill at planning things, especially military activities

**strat·egy** **1** **A2** **O** /ˈstrætədʒi/ noun (pl. **-ies**) **1** **?**+ **A2** [C] a plan that is intended to achieve a particular purpose: the government's economic strategy ◇ We need to devise **an effective long-term strategy**. ◇ **to adopt/implement/pursue a strategy** ◇ ~ **for doing sth** to develop a strategy for dealing with unemployment ◇ ~ **to do sth** It's all part of an overall strategy to gain promotion. ⇨ see also EXIT STRATEGY **2** **?** **B2** [U] the process of planning sth or putting a plan into operation: marketing strategy **3** **?** **B2** [U, C] the skill of planning the movements of armies in a battle or war; an example of doing this: military strategy ◇ defence strategies ⇨ compare TACTIC

**strati·fi·ca·tion** /ˌstrætɪfɪˈkeɪʃn/ noun [U] (specialist) the division of sth into different layers or groups: social stratification

**strat·ify** /ˈstrætɪfaɪ/ verb [usually passive] (**strati·fies**, **strati·fy·ing**, **strati·fied**, **strati·fied**) ~ **sth** (formal or specialist) to arrange sth in layers or STRATA: a highly stratified society ◇ stratified rock

**the strato·sphere** /ðə ˈstrætəsfɪə(r); NAmE -sfɪr/ noun [sing.] the layer of the earth's atmosphere between about 10 and 50 kilometres above the surface of the earth ⇨ compare IONOSPHERE ▶ **strato·spher·ic** /ˌstrætəˈsferɪk; NAmE -ˈsfɪr-, -ˈsfer-/ adj.: stratospheric clouds **IDM** **in/into the ˈstratosphere** (informal) at or to an extremely high level: The technology boom sent share prices into the stratosphere.

**stra·tum** /ˈstrɑːtəm; NAmE ˈstreɪt-/ noun (pl. **strata** /ˈstrɑːtə; NAmE ˈstreɪtə/) **1** (geology) a layer or set of layers of rock, earth, etc. **2** (formal) a class in a society: people from all social strata

**straw** /strɔː/ noun **1** [U] STEMS of WHEAT or other grain plants that have been cut and dried. Straw is used for making MATS, hats, etc., for packing things to protect them, and as food for animals or for them to sleep on: a mattress filled with straw ◇ a straw hat ⇨ compare HAY **2** [C] a single STEM or piece of straw: He was leaning over the gate chewing on a straw. **3** (also **ˈdrinking straw**) a thin tube of plastic or paper that you drink a liquid through **IDM** **clutch/grasp at ˈstraws** to try all possible means to find a solution or some hope in a difficult or unpleasant situation, even though this seems very unlikely **the last/final ˈstraw** | **the straw that breaks the camel's ˈback** the last in a series of bad events, etc. that makes it impossible for you to accept a situation any longer **a straw in the ˈwind** (BrE) a small sign of what might happen in the future ⇨ more at BRICK n., DRAW v.

**straw·berry** /ˈstrɔːbəri; NAmE -beri/ noun (pl. **-ies**) a soft red fruit with very small yellow seeds on the surface, that grows on a low plant: strawberries and cream ◇ strawberry plants ⇨ VISUAL VOCAB page V4

**ˌstrawberry ˈblonde** (also **ˌstrawberry ˈblond**) adj. (of hair) between blonde and red in colour

**ˈstraw man** noun a weak imaginary opponent or argument that is set up in order to be defeated easily

**ˌstraw ˈpoll** (NAmE also **ˌstraw ˈvote**) noun an occasion when a number of people are asked in an informal way to give their opinion about sth or to say how they are likely to vote in an election

**stray** /streɪ/ verb, adj., noun
- **verb 1** [I] **(+ adv./prep.)** to move away from the place where you should be, without intending to: He strayed into the path of an oncoming car. ◇ Her eyes kept straying over to the clock on the wall. **2** [I] **(+ adv./prep.)** to begin to think about or discuss a different subject from the one you should be thinking about or discussing: My mind kept straying back to our last talk together. ◇ We seem to be straying from the main theme of the debate. **3** [I] (of a person who is married or in a relationship) to have a sexual relationship with sb who is not your usual partner
- **adj.** [only before noun] **1** (of animals normally kept as pets) away from home and lost; having no home: stray dogs **2** separated from other things or people of the same kind: A civilian was killed by a stray bullet. ◇ a few stray hairs
- **noun 1** an animal that has got lost or separated from its owner or that has no owner **2** a person or thing that is not in the right place or is separated from others of the same kind ⇨ see also WAIF

**O** Oxford Phrasal Academic Lexicon (OPAL) written and spoken word lists | **W** OPAL written word list | **S** OPAL spoken word list

# streak

**streak** /striːk/ *noun, verb*
- *noun* **1** a long, thin mark or line that is a different colour from the surface it is on: *streaks of grey in her hair* ◇ *dirty streaks on the window* ⮕ SYNONYMS at MARK ⮕ WORDFINDER NOTE at PATTERN **2** a part of a person's character, especially an unpleasant part: *a ruthless/vicious/mean streak* ◇ *a streak of cruelty* **3** a series of successes or failures, especially in a sport or in GAMBLING: *a streak of good luck* ◇ *to hit* (= have) *a winning streak* ◇ *to be on a winning/losing streak* ◇ *a lucky/unlucky streak* ⮕ WORDFINDER NOTE at GAMBLING
- *verb* **1** [T] to mark or cover sth with streaks: ~ *sth Tears streaked her face.* ◇ *She's had her hair streaked* (= had special chemicals put on her hair so that it has attractive coloured lines in it). ◇ ~ *sth with sth His face was streaked with mud.* **2** [I] + *adv./prep.* to move very fast in a particular direction SYN **speed**: *A car pulled out and streaked off down the road.* **3** [I] (+ *adv./prep.*) (*informal*) to run through a public place with no clothes on as a way of getting attention

**streak·er** /ˈstriːkə(r)/ *noun* a person who runs through a public place with no clothes on as a way of getting attention

**streaky** /ˈstriːki/ *adj.* marked with lines of a different colour: *streaky blonde hair* ◇ *The wallpaper was streaky with grease.* ◇ (*BrE*) **streaky bacon** (= with layers of fat in it)

**stream** 🔊 B2 /striːm/ *noun, verb*
- *noun* **1** 🔊 B2 a small, narrow river: *a mountain stream* ⮕ see also DOWNSTREAM, UPSTREAM **2** 🔊 B2 ~ (**of sth**) a continuous flow of liquid or gas: *A stream of blood flowed from the wound.* ⮕ see also BLOODSTREAM, GULF STREAM, JET STREAM **3** 🔊 B2 a continuous flow of people or vehicles: ~ **of sth/sb** *I've had a steady stream of visitors.* ◇ **in a** ~ *Cars filed past in an endless stream.* **4** 🔊 B2 a continuous supply of sth; a large number of things that happen one after the other: *By licensing their works, artists can create an ongoing revenue stream.* ◇ ~ **of sth** *The agency provided me with a steady stream of work.* ⮕ see also REVENUE STREAM **5** (*computing*) a continuous flow of video or sound sent over the internet; a continuous flow of computer data or instructions: *You can listen to the live audio stream.* **6** (*especially BrE*) a group of students of the same age and level of ability in some schools: *She was put into the fast stream.*
- IDM **be/come on ˈstream** to be in operation or available: *The new computer system comes on stream next month.*
- *verb* **1** [I, T] (of liquid or gas) to move or pour out in a continuous flow; to produce a continuous flow of liquid or gas: (+ *adv./prep.*) *Tears streamed down his face.* ◇ *a streaming cold* (= with a lot of liquid coming from the nose) ◇ ~ **with sth** *Her head was streaming with blood.* ◇ ~ **from sth** *Blood was streaming from her head.* ◇ *Black smoke streamed from the exhaust.* ◇ ~ **sth** *The exhaust streamed black smoke.* **2** [I] + *adv./prep.* (of people or things) to move somewhere in large numbers, one after the other: *People streamed across the bridge.* **3** [I] + *adv./prep.* to move freely, especially in the wind or water: *Her scarf streamed behind her.* **4** (*especially BrE*) (*NAmE usually* **track**) [T, usually passive] (in schools) to put school students into groups according to their ability: **be streamed (for sth)** *Pupils are streamed for French and maths.* **5** [T] ~ **sth** (*computing*) to play video or sound on a computer by receiving it as a continuous stream, from the internet for example, rather than needing to wait until the whole of the material has been downloaded

**stream·er** /ˈstriːmə(r)/ *noun* **1** a long, narrow piece of coloured paper, used to decorate a place for a party or other celebration **2** a long, narrow piece of cloth or other material

**stream·ing** /ˈstriːmɪŋ/ *noun* [U] **1** (*also* **band·ing**) (*both BrE*) the policy of dividing school students into groups of the same ability: *Streaming within comprehensive schools is common practice.* **2** a method of sending or receiving data, especially video, over a computer network: *digital streaming*

**stream·line** /ˈstriːmlaɪn/ *verb* [usually passive] **1** ~ **sth** to give sth a smooth, even shape so that it can move quickly and easily through air or water: *The cars all have a new streamlined design.* **2** ~ **sth** to make a system, an organization, etc. work better, especially in a way that saves money: *The production process is to be streamlined.*

**stream of ˈconsciousness** *noun* [U] a continuous flow of ideas, thoughts, and feelings, as they are experienced by a person; a style of writing that expresses this without using the usual methods of description and conversation

**street** 🔊 ❶ A1 /striːt/ *noun, adj.*
- *noun* **1** 🔊 A1 [C] (*abbr.* **St, st**) a public road in a city or town that has houses and buildings on one side or both sides: **along/down/up the** ~ *I was just walking along the street when it happened.* ◇ **across the** ~ *The bank is just across the street.* ◇ **in the** ~ *He is used to being recognized in the street.* ◇ *It's not safe to walk the streets at night.* ◇ *the town's narrow cobbled streets* ◇ *92nd Street* ◇ *10 Downing Street* ◇ *You can find these shops on every street corner.* ⮕ note at ROAD ⮕ see also BACKSTREET *noun*, CROSS STREET, HIGH STREET, MAIN STREET, SIDE STREET, STOP STREET **2** [sing.] the ideas and opinions of ordinary people, especially people who live in cities, which are considered important: *The feeling I get from the street is that we have a good chance of winning this election.* ◇ *The word on the street is that it's not going to happen.* ⮕ see also GRUB STREET
- IDM **(out) on/onto the ˈstreets/ˈstreet** 🔊 B1 (*informal*) without a home; outside, not in a house or other building: *the problems of young people living on the streets* ◇ *If it had been left to me I would have put him out on the street long ago.* **on/walking the ˈstreets** working as a PROSTITUTE **ˈstreets ahead (of sb/sth)** (*BrE, informal*) much better or more advanced than sb/sth else: *a country that is streets ahead in the control of environmental pollution* **the streets are ˌpaved with ˈgold** (*saying*) used to say that it seems easy to make money in a place **(right) up your ˈstreet** (*especially BrE*) (*NAmE usually* **(right) up your ˈalley**) (*informal*) very suitable for you because it is sth that you know a lot about or are very interested in: *This job seems right up your street.* ⮕ more at EASY *adj.*, MAN *n.*
- *adj.* **1** [only before noun] working, living or taking place on the streets of a city; based on the daily life of ordinary people in cities: *street vendors selling fruit, snacks and local handicrafts* ◇ *street kids* ◇ *angry street protests/demonstrations* ◇ *street sports such as skateboarding and skating* ◇ *street culture/dance/law* **2** showing or connected with the attitude and way of life of fashionable young people in cities: *London street style* ◇ *You're not very street in those old trainers.*

**street·car** /ˈstriːtkɑː(r)/ (*also* **trol·ley**) (*both US*) (*BrE* **tram, tram·car**) *noun* a vehicle driven by electricity, that runs on RAILS along the streets of a town and carries passengers

**ˈstreet child** *noun* a child who has no home and lives in poverty on the streets of a town or city: *a charity that helps street children*

**ˈstreet clothes** *noun* [pl.] (*NAmE*) ordinary clothes that people wear in public: *She took off her uniform and changed into street clothes.*

**ˈstreet cred** (*also* **cred**) (*informal*) (*also less frequent* **ˈstreet credibility**) *noun* [U] a quality that makes sb acceptable to young people, especially those who live in cities and have experienced the problems of real life: *Those clothes do nothing for your street cred.*

**ˈstreet furniture** *noun* [U] (*specialist*) equipment such as road signs, street lights, etc. placed at the side of a road

**ˈstreet light** (*also* **ˈstreet lamp**) *noun* a light at the top of a tall post in the street ⮕ compare LAMP POST

**ˈstreet party** *noun* (*especially BrE*) an outdoor party, usually held on a street that has been closed to traffic, for all the people who live on the street or in the neighbourhood ⮕ compare BLOCK PARTY

**ˈstreet people** *noun* (*especially NAmE*) people who have no home and who live outside in a town SYN **homeless**

**street·scape** /ˈstriːtskeɪp/ noun the appearance or a picture of a street or area of streets

**ˈstreet-smart** adj. (NAmE) = STREETWISE ⇒ compare BOOK-SMART

**ˈstreet smarts** noun [pl.] (NAmE, informal) the knowledge and experience that is needed to deal with the difficulties and dangers of life in a big city

**ˈstreet theatre** (BrE) (NAmE **ˈstreet theater**) noun [U] plays or other performances that are done in the street

**ˈstreet value** noun [usually sing.] a price for which sth that is illegal or has been obtained illegally can be sold: *drugs with a street value of over £1 million*

**street·wear** /ˈstriːtweə(r); NAmE -wer/ noun [U] informal clothes of a style worn by young people in cities, especially those who are fans of a particular type of music, sport, culture, etc.

**street·wise** /ˈstriːtwaɪz/ (NAmE also **ˈstreet-smart**) adj. (informal) having the knowledge and experience that is needed to deal with the difficulties and dangers of life in a big city

**strength** ⓘ B1 ⓞ /streŋθ/ noun
- BEING PHYSICALLY STRONG **1** ʔ+ B1 [U, sing.] the quality of being physically strong: *He pushed against the rock with all his strength.* ◊ *It may take a few weeks for you to build up your strength again.* ◊ *He had a physical strength that matched his outward appearance.* ◊ *~ to do sth She didn't have the strength to walk any further.* **OPP** weakness **2** ʔ B1 [U] the ability that sth has to resist force or hold heavy weights without breaking or being damaged: *the strength of a rope* ⇒ see also INDUSTRIAL-STRENGTH
- BEING BRAVE **3** ʔ B2 [U, sing.] the quality of being brave and determined in a difficult situation: *During this ordeal he was able to draw strength from his faith.* ◊ *She has a remarkable* **inner strength**. ◊ *You have shown great* **strength of character**. **OPP** weakness
- POWER/INFLUENCE **4** ʔ B2 [U] the power and influence that sb/sth has: *Political power depends upon economic strength.* ◊ *Their superior military strength gives them a huge advantage.* ◊ *to negotiate from* **a position of strength** ◊ *The rally was intended to be* **a show of strength** *by the socialists.* **OPP** weakness
- OF OPINION/FEELING **5** ʔ B2 [U] how strong or deeply felt an opinion or a feeling is: *the strength of public opinion* ◊ *This view has recently gathered strength* (= become stronger or more widely held). ◊ *I was surprised by the strength of her feelings.*
- ADVANTAGE **6** ʔ B2 [C] a quality or an ability that a person or thing has that gives them an advantage: *The ability to keep calm is one of her many strengths.* ◊ *the* **strengths and weaknesses** *of an argument* **OPP** weakness
- OF NATURAL FORCE **7** ʔ B2 [U] how strong a natural force or a signal is: *the strength of the sun* ◊ *wind strength* ◊ *the strength and direction of the tide*
- OF TASTE/SUBSTANCE **8** [U, C] how strong a particular taste or substance is: *Add more curry powder depending on the strength required.* ◊ *a range of beers with different strengths* (= with different amounts of alcohol in them)
- OF CURRENCY **9** [U] *~ (of sth) (against sth)* how strong a country's currency is in relation to other countries' currencies: *the relative strength of the euro against the dollar* **OPP** weakness
- NUMBER IN GROUP **10** [U] the number of people in a group, a team or an organization: *The strength of the workforce is about to be doubled from 3000 to 6000.* ◊ *The team will be back* **at full strength** (= with all the best players) *for the next match.* ◊ **in** *~ The protesters turned out in strength* (= in large numbers). ◊ **under/below** *~ These cuts have left the local police force under strength* (= with fewer members than it needs).

**IDM** **go from ˈstrength to ˈstrength** to become more and more successful: *Since her appointment the department has gone from strength to strength.* **on the strength of sth** because sb has been influenced or persuaded by sth: *I got the job on the strength of your recommendation.* **strength in ˈdepth** the quality of being strong because you have a great variety of good people, ideas, etc. that can contribute to the success of sth: *The French team does not have the strength in depth that the Australians have.* **there's strength in ˈnumbers** *(saying)* being in a group gives you more power: *There's strength in numbers, so encourage your friends and family to join us.* ⇒ more at TOWER *n.*

**strength·en** ʔ+ B2 Ⓦ /ˈstreŋθən/ verb **1** ʔ+ B2 [I, T] to become more powerful or effective; to make sb/sth more powerful or effective: *Her position in the party has strengthened in recent weeks.* ◊ *~ sb/sth The move is clearly intended to strengthen the president's position as head of state.* ◊ *The new evidence will strengthen their case.* ◊ *The new manager has strengthened the side by bringing in several younger players.* **2** ʔ+ B2 [T] *~ sb/sth* to become physically stronger: *The exercises are designed to strengthen your stomach muscles.* ◊ *Repairs are necessary to strengthen the bridge.* **3** ʔ+ B2 [T, I] *~ (sth)* to make a feeling, an opinion or a relationship stronger; to become stronger: *This temporary setback merely strengthened her resolve.* ◊ *His determination only strengthened in the face of this opposition.* **4** ʔ+ B2 [I] (of a natural force) to become stronger: *The wind had strengthened overnight.* **5** ʔ+ B2 [I, T] (of a country's currency or economy) to become stronger; to make a currency or an economy stronger: *~ (against sth) Yesterday the pound strengthened against the dollar.* ◊ *~ sth The measures should help create jobs and strengthen the economy.* **OPP** weaken

**strenu·ous** /ˈstrenjuəs/ adj. **1** needing great effort and energy **SYN** arduous: *a strenuous climb* ◊ *Avoid strenuous exercise immediately after a meal.* ◊ *How about a stroll in the park? Nothing too strenuous.* **2** determined and showing great energy: *The ship went down although strenuous efforts were made to save it.* ▸ **strenu·ous·ly** *adv.*: *He still works out strenuously every morning.* ◊ *The government strenuously denies the allegations.*

**strep throat** /strep ˈθrəʊt/ noun (NAmE, informal) an infection of the throat

**strepto·coc·cus** /ˌstreptəˈkɒkəs; NAmE -ˈkɑːk-/ noun (*pl.* **strepto·cocci** /-kaɪ/) (*medical*) a type of bacteria, some types of which can cause serious infections and illnesses

**stress** ⓘ A2 ⓞ /stres/ noun, verb
■ noun
- MENTAL PRESSURE **1** ʔ A2 [U, C] pressure or worry caused by the problems in sb's life: *emotional/mental stress* ◊ *to suffer from stress* ◊ *to relieve/reduce/alleviate stress* ◊ **under** *~ Things can easily go wrong when people are under stress.* ◊ *The incident has caused enormous stress and anxiety to my family.* ◊ *She failed to withstand the stresses and strains of public life.* ◊ *stress-related illnesses* ◊ **stress management** (= dealing with stress) ⇒ SYNONYMS at PRESSURE ⇒ see also POST-TRAUMATIC STRESS DISORDER
- PHYSICAL PRESSURE **2** ʔ B2 [U, C] physical pressure put on sth that can damage it or make it lose its shape: *~ on sth When you have an injury you start putting stress on other parts of your body.* ◊ *a* **stress fracture** *of the foot* (= one caused by such pressure)
- ON WORD/SYLLABLE **3** ʔ A2 [U, C] (*phonetics*) an extra force used when pronouncing a particular word or syllable: *We worked on pronunciation, stress and intonation.* ◊ *~ on sth There's a stress on the second syllable.* ⇒ compare INTONATION ⇒ WORDFINDER NOTE at PRONUNCIATION ⇒ see also PRIMARY STRESS, SECONDARY STRESS
- EMPHASIS **4** [U] *~ (on sth)* special importance given to sth: *She lays great stress on punctuality.* ◊ *I think the company places too much stress on cost and not enough on quality.*
- IN MUSIC **5** [U, C] extra force used when making a particular sound in music
- ILLNESS **6** [U] illness caused by difficult physical conditions: *Those most vulnerable to heat stress are the elderly.*

■ verb
- WORD/SYLLABLE **1** ʔ A2 [T] *~ sth* to give extra force to a word or syllable when saying it: *You stress the first syllable in 'happiness'.*
- EMPHASIZE **2** ʔ B2 [T] to emphasize a fact, an idea, etc.: *~ sth He stressed the importance of a good education.* ◊ *~ that… I must stress that everything I've told you is strictly*

# stressed

*confidential.* ◊ **+ speech** 'There is,' Johnson stressed, 'no real alternative.' ◊ **it is stressed that ...** It must be stressed that this disease is very rare. ◊ **~ how, what, etc.** I cannot stress too much how important this is.
- **WORRY 3** [B2] [I, T] to become or make sb become too anxious or tired to be able to relax: *~ out* I try not to stress out when things go wrong. ◊ *~ sb (out)* Driving in cities really stresses me (out).

▼ **SYNONYMS**

**stress**
**emphasize**

These words both mean to give extra force to a syllable, word or phrase when you are saying it.

**stress** to give extra force to a word or syllable when saying it: *You stress the first syllable in 'happiness'.*
**emphasize** to give extra force to a word or phrase when saying it, especially to show that it is important: *'Let nothing ... nothing,' he emphasized the word, 'tempt you.'*

**stressed** /strest/ *adj.* **1** (*also informal* **stressed 'out**) [not before noun] too anxious and tired to be able to relax **2** (of a syllable) pronounced with emphasis [OPP] **unstressed**

**stress·ful** /ˈstresfl/ *adj.* causing a lot of worry: *a stressful job* ◊ *It was a stressful time for all of us.*

**'stress mark** *noun* the symbols ' and ˌ used to show where the stress is placed on a particular word or syllable ⇒ see also PRIMARY STRESS, SECONDARY STRESS

**stretch** ⓘ [B2] /stretʃ/ *verb, noun*

■ *verb*
- **MAKE/BECOME BIGGER/LOOSER 1** [B2] [T, I] *~ (sth)* to make sth longer, wider or looser, for example by pulling it; to become longer, etc. in this way: *Is there any way of stretching shoes?* ◊ *This sweater has stretched.* **2** [I] (of cloth) to be able to be bigger or longer when you pull it and return to its original shape when you stop: *The jeans stretch to provide a perfect fit.*
- **PULL TIGHT 3** [B2] [T] to pull sth so that it is smooth and tight: *~ sth (+ adv./prep.) Stretch the fabric tightly over the frame.* ◊ *~ sth + adj. Make sure that the rope is stretched tight.*
- **YOUR BODY 4** [B2] [I, T] to put your arms or legs out straight and contract your muscles: *He stretched and yawned lazily.* ◊ *~ sth The exercises are designed to stretch and tone your leg muscles.*
- **REACH WITH ARM 5** [B2] [I, T] to put out an arm or a leg in order to reach sth: *+ adv./prep. She stretched across the table for the butter.* ◊ *~ sth + adv./prep. I stretched out a hand and picked up the book.*
- **OVER AREA 6** [B2] [I] *+ adv./prep.* to spread over an area of land [SYN] **extend**: *Fields and hills stretched out as far as we could see.*
- **OVER TIME 7** [I] *+ adv./prep.* to continue over a period of time: *The town's history stretches back to before 1500.* ◊ *The talks look set to stretch into a second week.*
- **MONEY/SUPPLIES/TIME 8** [I] *~ (to sth)* (used in negative sentences and questions about an amount of money) to be enough to buy or pay for sth: *I need a new car, but my savings won't stretch to it.* **9** [T] *~ sb/ sth* to make use of a lot of your money, supplies, time, etc: *The influx of refugees has stretched the country's resources to the limit.* ◊ *We can't take on any more work—we're fully stretched as it is.*
- **THE LEAD 10** [T] *~ the lead (to sth)* to increase your lead over sb in a game or competition: *A minute later, Kelly stretched their lead to eight points.*
- **SB'S SKILL/INTELLIGENCE 11** [T] *~ sb/sth* to make use of all sb's skill, intelligence, etc: *I need a job that will stretch me.*
- **TRUTH/BELIEF 12** [T] *~ sth* to use sth in a way that would not normally be considered fair, acceptable, etc: *He admitted that he had maybe stretched the truth a little (= not been completely honest).* ◊ *The play's plot stretches credulity to the limit.*

[IDM] **stretch your 'legs** (*informal*) to go for a short walk after sitting for some time: *It was good to get out of the car and stretch our legs.* **stretch a 'point** to allow or do sth that is not usually acceptable, especially because of a particular situation ⇒ more at RULE *n*.

[PHRV] **stretch 'out | stretch yourself 'out** to lie down, usually in order to relax or sleep: *He stretched himself out on the sofa and fell asleep.*

■ *noun*
- **AREA OF LAND/WATER 1** [B2] [C] *~ (of sth)* an area of land or water, especially a long one: *a particularly dangerous stretch of road* ◊ *There are tailbacks along a 10-mile stretch of the motorway.* ◊ *an unspoilt stretch of coastline*
- **PERIOD OF TIME 2** [C] a continuous period of time [SYN] **spell**: *They worked in four-hour stretches.* ◊ *at a ~ She used to read for hours at a stretch (= without stopping).* **3** [C, usually sing.] (*informal*) a period of time that sb spends in prison: *He did a ten-year stretch for fraud.*
- **OF BODY 4** [C, U] an act of stretching out your arms or legs or your body and pulling the muscles tight; the state of being stretched: *We got out of the car and had a good stretch.* ◊ *Only do these more difficult stretches when you are warmed up.* ◊ *Stay in this position and feel the stretch in your legs.*
- **OF FABRIC 5** [U] the ability to be made longer or wider without breaking or tearing: *You need a material with plenty of stretch in it.* ◊ *stretch jeans*
- **ON RACETRACK 6** [C, usually sing.] a straight part at the end of a racing track [SYN] **straight**: *the finishing/home stretch* ◊ (*figurative*) *The campaign has entered its final stretch.*

[IDM] **at full 'stretch** using as much energy as possible, or the greatest possible amount of supplies: *Fire crews have been operating at full stretch.* **not by any stretch of the imagination | by no stretch of the imagination** used to say strongly that sth is not true, even if you try to imagine or believe it: *She could not, by any stretch of the imagination, be called beautiful.*

**stretch·er** /ˈstretʃə(r)/ *noun, verb*

■ *noun* a long piece of strong cloth with a POLE on each side, used for carrying sb who is sick or injured and who cannot walk: *He was carried off on a stretcher.* ◊ *stretcher cases (= people too badly injured to be able to walk)* ⇒ WORDFINDER NOTE at ACCIDENT
■ *verb* [usually passive] *~ sb + adv./prep.* to carry sb somewhere on a stretcher: *He was stretchered off the pitch with a broken leg.*

**'stretcher-bearer** *noun* a person who helps to carry a stretcher, especially in a war or when there is a very serious accident

**stretch 'limo** (*also formal* **stretch limouˈsine**) *noun* a very large car that has been made longer so that it can have extra seats

**'stretch marks** *noun* [pl.] the marks that are left on a person's skin after it has been stretched, particularly after a woman has been pregnant

**stretchy** /ˈstretʃi/ *adj.* (**stretch·ier, stretchi·est**) that can easily be made longer or wider without tearing or breaking: *stretchy fabric*

**strew** /struː/ *verb* (**strewed, strewed** *or* **strewed, strewn** /struːn/) **1** [usually passive] to cover a surface with things [SYN] **scatter**: *~ A on, over, across, etc.* B *Clothes were strewn across the floor.* ◊ *~ B with A The floor was strewn with clothes.* ◊ (*figurative*) *The way ahead is strewn with difficulties.* **2** *~ sth* to be spread or lying over a surface: *Leaves strewed the path.*

**stri·ation** /straɪˈeɪʃn/ *noun* [usually pl.] (*specialist*) a pattern of lines on sth ▶ **stri·ated** /straɪˈeɪtɪd; *NAmE* ˈstraɪeɪtɪd/ *adj.*: *striated muscle fibre* ◊ *striated rock*

**stricken** /ˈstrɪkən/ *adj.* (*formal*) **1** seriously affected by an unpleasant feeling or disease or by a difficult situation: *She raised her stricken face and begged for help.* ◊ *We went to the aid of the stricken boat.* ◊ *~ with/by sth Whole villages were stricken with the disease.* ◊ *He was stricken by a heart attack on his fiftieth birthday.* **2** (in compounds) seriously affected by the thing mentioned: *poverty-stricken families* ⇒ see also CONSCIENCE-STRICKEN, GRIEF-STRICKEN, HORROR-STRICKEN at HORROR-STRUCK, PANIC-STRICKEN, POVERTY-STRICKEN

**strict** /strɪkt/ *adj.* (**strict·er**, **strict·est**) **1** that must be obeyed exactly: *strict rules/regulations* ◊ *The head teacher imposed very strict discipline.* ◊ *She's on a very strict diet.* ◊ *He told me in the strictest confidence* (= on the understanding that I would tell nobody else). **2** demanding that rules, especially rules about behaviour, should be obeyed: *a strict teacher/parent/disciplinarian* ◊ *I had a very strict upbringing.* ◊ **~ about sth** *She's very strict about things like homework.* ◊ **~ with sb** *They were always very strict with their children.* **3** obeying the rules of a particular religion, belief, etc. exactly: *a strict Muslim* ◊ *a strict vegetarian* **4** [usually before noun] very exact and clearly defined: *It wasn't illegal in the strict sense (of the word).* ◊ *They insisted on their strict legal rights.* ▸ **strict·ness** *noun* [U]

**strict·ly** /ˈstrɪktli/ *adv.* **1** with a lot of control and rules that must be obeyed: *She was brought up very strictly.* ◊ *The industry is strictly regulated.* **2** used to emphasize that sth happens or must happen in all circumstances **SYN** **absolutely**: *Smoking is strictly forbidden.* ◊ *My letter is, of course, strictly private and confidential.* **3** in all details; exactly: *This is not strictly true.* **4** used to emphasize that sth only applies to one particular person, thing or situation **SYN** **purely**: *We'll look at the problem from a strictly legal point of view.* ◊ *I know we're friends, but this is strictly business.*
**IDM** **ˌstrictly ˈspeaking** if you are using words or rules in their exact or correct sense: *Strictly speaking, the book is not a novel, but a short story.*

**stric·ture** /ˈstrɪktʃə(r)/ *noun* (*formal*) **1** [usually pl.] **~ (on sb/sth)** a severe criticism, especially of sb's behaviour **2 ~ (against/on sth)** a rule or situation that limits your behaviour **SYN** **restriction**: *strictures against civil servants expressing political opinions*

**stride** /straɪd/ *verb, noun*
▪ *verb* [I] (not used in the perfect tenses) (**strode** /strəʊd/) + *adv./prep.* to walk with long steps in a particular direction: *We strode across the snowy fields.* ◊ *She came striding along to meet me.*
▪ *noun* **1** one long step; the distance covered by a step **SYN** **pace**¹: *He crossed the room in two strides.* ◊ *I was gaining on the other runners with every stride.* **2** your way of walking or running: *his familiar purposeful stride* ◊ *She did not slow her stride until she was face to face with us.* **3** an improvement in the way sth is developing: *We're making great strides in the search for a cure.* **4 strides** [pl.] (*AustralE, informal*) trousers
**IDM** **get into your ˈstride** (*BrE*) (*NAmE* **hit (your) ˈstride**) to begin to do sth with confidence and at a good speed after a slow uncertain start **put sb off their ˈstride** to make sb take their attention off what they are doing and stop doing it so well **(match sb) ˈstride for ˈstride** to keep doing sth as well as sb else, even though they keep making it harder for you **take sth in your ˈstride** (*BrE*) (*NAmE* **take sth in ˈstride**) to accept and deal with sth difficult without letting it worry you too much **without breaking ˈstride** (especially *NAmE*) without stopping what you are doing

**stri·dent** /ˈstraɪdnt/ *adj.* **1** having a loud, rough and unpleasant sound: *a strident voice* ◊ *strident music* **2** aggressive and determined: *He is a strident advocate of nuclear power.* ◊ *strident criticism* ▸ **stri·dency** /-dənsi/ *noun* [U] **stri·dent·ly** *adv.*

**strife** /straɪf/ *noun* **1** [U] (*formal* or *literary*) anger or violence between two people or groups of people who disagree **SYN** **conflict**: *civil strife* ◊ *The country was torn apart by strife.* **2** (*AustralE, NZE*) trouble or difficulty of any kind

**strike** /straɪk/ *verb, noun*
▪ *verb* (**struck**, **struck** /strʌk/)
• HIT SB/STH **1** [T, I] (*formal*) to hit sb/sth hard or with force: ~**sb/sth** *The ship struck a rock.* ◊ *The child ran into the road and was struck by a car.* ◊ *The tree was struck by lightning.* ◊ **~sb/sth + adv./prep.** *He fell, striking his head on the edge of the table.* ◊ **against sth** *The oar struck against something hard.* ⊃ SYNONYMS at HIT **2** [T] **~sb/sth** (*formal*) to hit sb/sth with your hand or a weapon:

# strike

*She struck him in the face.* ◊ *He struck the table with his fist.* ◊ *Who struck the first blow* (= started the fight)?
• KICK/HIT BALL **3** [T] **~ sth (+ adv./prep.)** (*formal*) to hit or kick a ball, etc: *He walked up to the penalty spot and struck the ball firmly into the back of the net.*
• ATTACK **4** [I] to attack sb/sth, especially suddenly: *The lion crouched ready to strike.* ◊ *Police fear that the killer may strike again.*
• OF DISASTER/DISEASE **5** [I, T] to happen suddenly and have a harmful or damaging effect on sb/sth: *Disaster struck again when their best player was injured.* ◊ **~sb/sth** *The area was struck by an outbreak of cholera.*
• THOUGHT/IDEA/IMPRESSION **6** [T] (not used in the progressive tenses) (of a thought or an idea) to come into sb's mind suddenly: **~sb** *An awful thought has just struck me.* ◊ *I was struck by her resemblance to my aunt.* ◊ **it strikes sb how, what, etc.** *It suddenly struck me how we could improve the situation.* **7** [T] to give sb a particular impression: **~sb** *Another part of his comment struck me.* ◊ **~sb as sth** *His reaction struck me as odd.* ◊ *How does the idea strike you?* ◊ **it strikes sb that …** *It strikes me that nobody is really in favour of the changes.*
• OF WORKERS **8** [I] to refuse to work because of an argument over pay or conditions: *Over 100000 civil servants are set to strike on Tuesday.* ◊ **~ over sth** *Drivers are threatening to strike over pay.* ⊃ WORDFINDER NOTE at UNION
• OF LIGHT **9** [T] **~sth** to fall on a surface: *The windows sparkled as the sun struck the glass.*
• DUMB/DEAF/BLIND **10** [T] **~ sb + adj.** [usually passive] to put sb suddenly into a particular state: *to be struck dumb/deaf/blind*
• MATCH **11** [T, I] **~(sth)** to rub sth such as a match against a surface so that it produces a flame; to produce a flame when rubbed against a rough surface: *to strike a match on a wall* ◊ *The sword struck sparks off the stone floor.* ◊ *The matches were damp and he couldn't make them strike.*
• OF CLOCK **12** [I, T] to show the time by making a ringing noise, etc. **SYN** **chime**: *Did you hear the clock strike?* ◊ **~sth** *The clock has just struck three.*
• MAKE SOUND **13** [T] **~ sth** to produce a musical note, sound, etc. by pressing a key or hitting sth: *to strike a chord on the piano*
• GOLD/OIL, ETC. **14** [T] **~ sth** to discover gold, oil, etc. by digging or DRILLING: *They had struck oil!*
• GO WITH PURPOSE **15** [I] **~ + adv./prep.** to go somewhere with great energy or purpose: *We left the road and struck off across the fields.* ◊ *He struck out* (= started swimming) *towards the shore.*
**IDM** **be ˈstruck by/on/with sb/sth** (*informal*) to be impressed or interested by sb/sth; to like sb/sth very much: *I was struck by her youth and enthusiasm.* ◊ *We're not very struck on that new restaurant.* **strike a ˈbalance (between A and B)** to manage to find a way of being fair to two things that are opposed to each other; to find an acceptable position that is between two things: *We need to strike a balance between these conflicting interests.* **strike a ˈbargain/ˈdeal (with sb/sth)** to make an agreement with sb in which both sides have an advantage **strike a ˈblow for/against/at sth** to do sth in support of/against a belief, principle, etc: *He felt that they had struck a blow for democracy.* **strike ˈfear, etc. into sb/sb's heart** (*formal*) to make sb be afraid, etc. **strike ˈgold** to find or do sth that brings you a lot of success or money: *He has struck gold with his latest novel.* **strike it ˈrich** (*informal*) to get a lot of money, especially suddenly or unexpectedly **strike (it) ˈlucky** (*informal*) to have good luck **strike a ˈnerve (with sb)** to have a strong effect: *His work strikes a nerve with people who are attracted to nostalgia.* ◊ *It seems I struck a nerve with my last post about cell phones.* ◊ *Nissan may well strike a popular nerve here.* **strike a ˈpose/an ˈattitude** to hold your body in a particular way to create a particular impression **strike while the iron is ˈhot** (*saying*) to make use of an opportunity immediately **ORIGIN** This expression refers to a blacksmith making a shoe for a horse. The blacksmith has to strike/hammer the iron while it is hot enough to bend into the shape of the shoe. **within ˈstriking distance (of sth)** near enough to be

reached or attacked easily; near enough to reach or attack sth easily: *The beach is within striking distance.* ◊ *The cat was now within striking distance of the duck.* ⇒ more at CHORD, HARD *adj.*, HOME *adv.*, LIGHTNING *n.*, NOTE *n.*, PAY DIRT, WOODWORK

**PHRV** **ˈstrike at sb/sth** **1** to try to hit sb/sth, especially with a weapon: *He struck at me repeatedly with a stick.* **2** to cause damage or have a serious effect on sb/sth: *to strike at the root of the problem* ◊ *criticisms that strike at the heart of the party's policies* **ˌstrike ˈback (at/against sb)** to try to harm sb in return for an attack or injury you have received **ˌstrike sb ˈdown** [usually passive] **1** (of a disease, etc.) to make sb seriously ill; to kill sb: *He was struck down by cancer at the age of thirty.* **2** to hit sb very hard, so that they fall to the ground **ˌstrike sth ↔ ˈdown** (*especially NAmE*) to decide that a law is illegal and should not apply: *The Supreme Court struck down a Texas state law.* **ˌstrike sth ↔ ˈoff** to remove sth with a hard hit; to cut sth off: *He struck off the rotten branches with an axe.* **ˌstrike sb/sth ˈoff (sth)** (*also* **ˌstrike sb/sth ˈfrom sth**) to remove sb/sth's name from sth, such as the list of members of a professional group: *Strike her name off the list.* ◊ *The doctor was struck off* (= not allowed to continue to work as a doctor) *for incompetence.* **ˌstrike ˈout** **1** to start being independent: *I knew it was time I struck out on my own.* **2** (*NAmE, informal*) to fail or be unsuccessful: *The movie struck out and didn't win a single Oscar.* **ˌstrike ˈout (at sb/sth)** **1** to aim a sudden violent hit at sb/sth: *He lost his temper and struck out wildly.* **2** to criticize sb/sth, especially in a public speech or in a book or newspaper: *In a recent article she strikes out at her critics.* **ˌstrike ˈout** | **ˌstrike sb ↔ ˈout** (in baseball) to fail to hit the ball three times and therefore not be allowed to continue hitting; to make sb do this ⇒ related noun STRIKEOUT **ˌstrike sth ↔ ˈout/ˈthrough** to remove sth by drawing a line through it **SYN** cross sth out/through: *The editor struck out the whole paragraph.* **ˌstrike ˈup (with sb)** | **ˌstrike ˈup sth** (of a band, an ORCHESTRA, etc.) to begin to play a piece of music: *The orchestra struck up and the curtain rose.* ◊ *The band struck up a waltz.* **ˌstrike ˈup sth (with sb)** to begin a friendship, a relationship, a conversation, etc: *He would often strike up conversations with complete strangers.*

■ *noun*
- OF WORKERS **1** B2 a period of time when an organized group of employees of a company stops working because of an argument over pay or conditions: *the miners'/firefighters'/teachers' strike* ◊ *a strike by teachers* ◊ *a one-day strike* ◊ *Air traffic controllers are threatening to go on strike.* ◊ *Half the workforce are now (out) on strike.* ◊ *The train drivers have voted to **take strike action**.* ◊ *The student union has called for a **rent strike** (= a refusal to pay rent as a protest).* ⇒ see also GENERAL STRIKE, HUNGER STRIKE
- ATTACK **2** B2 a military attack, especially by aircraft dropping bombs: *They decided to launch a **pre-emptive strike**.* ◊ **~ against sb/sth** *Diplomatic efforts have averted a military strike against the country.* ⇒ see also AIR STRIKE, FIRST STRIKE
- HITTING/KICKING **3** (*usually sing.*) an act of hitting or kicking sth/sb: *His spectacular strike in the second half made the score 2–0.* ⇒ see also BIRD STRIKE, LIGHTNING *noun*
- IN BASEBALL **4** an unsuccessful attempt to hit the ball
- IN BOWLING **5** a situation in TENPIN BOWLING when a player knocks down all the pins with the first ball
- DISCOVERY OF OIL **6** [usually *sing.*] a sudden discovery of sth valuable, especially oil
- BAD THING/ACTION **7** **~ (against sb/sth)** (*NAmE*) a bad thing or action that damages sb/sth's reputation: *The amount of fuel that this car uses is a big strike against it.*

**IDM** **ˌthree ˌstrikes and you're ˈout** | **the ˌthree ˈstrikes rule** used to describe a law that says that people who commit three crimes will go straight to prison **ORIGIN** From baseball, in which a batter who misses the ball three times is out.

**ˈstrike-breaker** *noun* a person who continues to work while other employees are on strike; a person who is

employed to replace people who are on strike ⇒ compare BLACKLEG ▸ **ˈstrike-breaking** *noun* [U]

**ˈstrike force** *noun* [C + *sing./pl. v.*] a military or police force that is ready to act quickly when necessary

**ˈstrike-out** /ˈstraɪkaʊt/ *noun* (in baseball) a situation in which the player who is supposed to be hitting the ball has to stop because he or she has tried to hit the ball three times and failed

**striker** /ˈstraɪkə(r)/ *noun* **1** a worker who has stopped working because of argument over pay or conditions **2** (in football (soccer)) a player whose main job is to attack and try to score goals

**ˈstrike rate** *noun* [usually *sing.*] (*sport*) the number of times a player is successful in relation to the number of times they try to score or win

**ˈstrike zone** *noun* (in baseball) the area between a BATTER'S upper arms and their knees, to which the ball must be PITCHED

**strik·ing** ? C1 /ˈstraɪkɪŋ/ *adj.* **1** ? C1 interesting and unusual enough to attract attention **SYN** marked: *a striking feature* ◊ *She bears **a striking resemblance** to her older sister.* ◊ ***In striking contrast*** *to their brothers, the girls were both intelligent and charming.* ⇒ LANGUAGE BANK at SURPRISING **2** ? C1 very attractive, often in an unusual way **SYN** stunning: *striking good looks* ▸ **strik·ing·ly** *adv.*: *The two polls produced strikingly different results.* ◊ *She is strikingly beautiful.*

**Strim·mer™** /ˈstrɪmə(r)/ *noun* (*BrE*) an electric garden tool held in the hands and used for cutting grass that is difficult to cut with a larger machine

**Strine** /straɪn/ (*also* **strine**) *noun* (*informal*) **1** [U] Australian English, especially when spoken in an informal way and with a strong ACCENT (= a way of pronouncing the words of a language) **2** [C] an Australian ▸ **Strine** *adj.*: *a Strine accent*

**string** ? B1 /strɪŋ/ *noun, verb, adj.*

■ *noun*
- FOR TYING/FASTENING **1** ? B1 [U, C] long, thin material used for tying things together, made of several THREADS that have been TWISTED together; a piece of string used to fasten or pull sth or keep sth in place: *a piece/length/ball of string* ◊ *He wrapped the package in brown paper and tied it with string.* ◊ *The key is hanging on a string by the door.* ⇒ picture at ROPE ⇒ see also DRAWSTRING, G-STRING, PURSE STRINGS
- THINGS JOINED **2** [C] a set or series of things that are joined together, for example on a string: *a string of pearls* ◊ *The molecules join together to form long strings.*
- SERIES **3** [C] **~ of sth** a series of things or people that come closely one after another: *The band had a string of hits in the nineties.* ◊ *He owns a string of racing stables.*
- COMPUTING **4** [C] a series of characters (= letters, numbers, etc.): *to key in/enter a **search string***
- MUSICAL INSTRUMENTS **5** [C] a tightly stretched piece of wire, NYLON, or CATGUT on a musical instrument, that produces a musical note when the instrument is played ⇒ picture at BRIDGE **6** **strings** [*pl.*] the group of musical instruments in an ORCHESTRA that have strings, for example VIOLINS; the people who play them: *The opening theme is taken up by the strings.* ⇒ compare BRASS, PERCUSSION, WOODWIND
- ON TENNIS RACKET **7** [C] any of the tightly stretched pieces of NYLON or natural GUT in a RACKET, used for hitting balls in tennis and some other sports
- CONDITIONS **8** **strings** [*pl.*] special conditions or limits: *Major loans like these always come with strings.* ◊ *It's a business proposition, pure and simple. **No strings attached**.*

**IDM** **have another string/more strings to your bow** (*BrE*) to have more than one skill or plan that you can use if you need to ⇒ more at APRON, LONG *adj.*, PULL *v.*

■ *verb* (**strung, strung** /strʌŋ/)
- HANG DECORATION **1** to hang or tie sth in place, especially as decoration: **~ sth + adv./prep.** *We strung paper lanterns up in the trees.* ◊ **~ A on, along, in, etc. B** *Flags were strung out along the route.* ◊ **~ B with A** *The route was strung with flags.*

- **JOIN THINGS** 2 ~ sth + adv./prep. to put a series of small objects on string, etc.; to join things together with string, etc. **SYN** thread: *She had strung the shells on a silver chain.* ◇ *(figurative) carbon atoms strung together to form giant molecules*
- **RACKET/MUSICAL INSTRUMENT** 3 ~ sth to put a string or strings on a RACKET or musical instrument ⊃ see also HIGHLY STRUNG

**PHRV** **string sb a'long** *(informal)* to allow sb to believe sth that is not true, for example that you love them, intend to help them, etc: *She has no intention of giving you a divorce; she's just stringing you along.* **string a'long (with sb)** *(BrE, informal)* to go somewhere with sb, especially because you have nothing else to do **string sth↔'out** to make sth last longer than expected or necessary: *They seem determined to string the talks out for an indefinite period.* ⊃ see also STRUNG OUT **string sth↔to'gether** to combine words or phrases to form sentences: *I can barely string two words together in Japanese.* **string sb↔'up** *(informal)* to kill sb by hanging them, especially illegally

■ *adj.* [only before noun]
- **MUSICAL INSTRUMENT** 1 consisting of musical instruments that have strings; connected with these musical instruments: *a string quartet* ◇ *a string player*
- **MADE OF STRING** 2 made of string or sth like string: *a string bag/vest*

**string 'bean** *noun* 1 *(BrE)* = RUNNER BEAN 2 *(NAmE)* = GREEN BEAN

**'stringed instrument** *noun* any musical instrument with strings that you play with your fingers or with a BOW

**strin·gent** /ˈstrɪndʒənt/ *adj. (formal)* 1 (of a law, rule, regulation, etc.) very strict and that must be obeyed: *stringent air quality regulations* 2 (of financial conditions) difficult and with very strict controls because there is not much money: *the government's stringent economic policies*
▸ **strin·gency** /-dʒənsi/ *noun* [U]: *a period of financial stringency* **strin·gent·ly** *adv.*: *The rules are stringently enforced.*

**string·er** /ˈstrɪŋə(r)/ *noun* a journalist who is not on the regular staff of a newspaper, but who often supplies stories for it ▸ **WORDFINDER NOTE** at JOURNALIST

**stringy** /ˈstrɪŋi/ *adj. (disapproving)* 1 (of hair) long and thin and looking as if it has not been washed 2 (of food) containing long thin pieces like string and difficult to CHEW: *tough, stringy meat* 3 (of a person or part of their body) thin so that you can see the muscles: *a stringy neck*

**strip** /strɪp/ *noun, verb*

■ *noun*
- **LONG, NARROW PIECE** 1 a long narrow piece of paper, metal, cloth, etc: *a strip of material* ◇ *Cut the meat into strips.* ⊃ see also MAGNETIC STRIP, MÖBIUS STRIP, RUMBLE STRIP 2 a long narrow area of land, sea, etc: *the Gaza Strip* ◇ *The islands are separated by a narrow strip of water.* ⊃ see also AIRSTRIP, LANDING STRIP, NATURE STRIP
- **OF SPORTS TEAM** 3 [usually sing.] *(BrE) (NAmE* **uniform**) the uniform that is worn by the members of a sports team when they are playing: *Juventus in their famous black and white strip* ◇ *the team's away strip* (= that they use when playing games away from home)
- **TAKING CLOTHES OFF** 4 [usually sing.] an act of taking your clothes off, especially in a sexually exciting way and in front of an audience: *to do a strip* ◇ *a strip show* ⊃ see also STRIPTEASE
- **STREET** 5 *(NAmE)* a street that has many shops, stores, restaurants, etc. along it: *Sunset Strip*
- **PICTURE STORY** 6 *(NAmE)* = COMIC STRIP **IDM** see TEAR¹ *v.*

■ *verb* (-pp-)
- **TAKE OFF CLOTHES** 1 [I, T] to take off all or most of your clothes or another person's clothes **SYN** undress: *I stripped and washed myself all over.* ◇ ~ down to sth *She stripped down to her underwear.* ◇ ~ (sth) off *We stripped off and ran down to the water.* ◇ ~ sb (to sth) *He stood there stripped to the waist* (= he had no clothes on the upper part of his body). ◇ ~ sb + adj. *He was stripped naked and left in a cell.* 2 [I] to take off your clothes as a form of entertainment; to perform a STRIPTEASE
- **REMOVE LAYER** 3 [T] to remove a layer from sth, especially so that it is completely exposed: ~ sth (off) *Strip off all the existing paint.* ◇ *After the guests had gone, I stripped all the beds* (= removed all the sheets in order to wash them). ◇ ~ A off/from B *Deer had stripped all the bark off the tree.* ◇ ~ B of A *Deer had stripped the tree of its bark.*
- **REMOVE EVERYTHING** 4 [T] to remove all the things from a place and leave it empty: ~ sth (out) *We had to strip out all the old wiring and start again.* ◇ ~ sth away *First, you need to strip away all the old plaster.* ◇ *(figurative) The movie aims to strip away the lies surrounding Kennedy's life.* ◇ ~ sth + adj. *Thieves had stripped the house bare.*
- **MACHINE** 5 [T] ~ sth (down) to separate a machine, etc. into parts so that they can be cleaned or repaired **SYN** dismantle: *They taught us how to strip down a car engine and put it back together again.*
- **PUNISHMENT** 6 [T] ~ sb of sth to take away property or honours from sb, as a punishment: *He was disgraced and stripped of his title.*

**strip car'toon** *(also* **car·toon**) *noun (BrE)* = COMIC STRIP

**'strip club** *(also* **'strip joint** *especially in NAmE) noun* a club where people go to watch performers take their clothes off in a sexually exciting way

**stripe** /straɪp/ *noun* 1 a long narrow line of colour, that is a different colour from the areas next to it: *a zebra's black and white stripes* ◇ *a white tablecloth with red stripes* ⊃ **WORDFINDER NOTE** at PATTERN ⊃ see also PINSTRIPE, STARS AND STRIPES 2 a narrow piece of cloth, often in the shape of a V, that is worn on the uniform of a soldier or police officer to show their rank 3 *(especially NAmE)* a type, category or opinion: *politicians of every stripe* ◇ *commentators of all political stripes* ◇ *She's an educator of a very different stripe.*

**striped** /straɪpt/ *(also BrE, informal* **stripy**, **stripey**) *adj.* marked with a pattern of stripes: *a striped shirt* ◇ *a blue and white striped jacket*

**stripey** *(also* **stripy**) /ˈstraɪpi/ *adj. (BrE, informal)* = STRIPED

**strip·ling** /ˈstrɪplɪŋ/ *noun (old-fashioned* or *humorous)* a young man who is older than a boy but who does not seem to be a real man yet

**'strip mall** *noun (NAmE)* a line of shops and restaurants next to a main road

**stripped-'down** *adj.* [usually before noun] 1 keeping only the most basic or essential features, with everything else removed: *a stripped-down version of the song* 2 (of a machine or vehicle) taken to pieces, with all the parts removed

**strip·per** /ˈstrɪpə(r)/ *noun* 1 [C] a performer who takes his or her clothes off in a sexually exciting way in front of an audience: *a male stripper* 2 [U, C] (especially in compounds) a substance or tool that is used for removing paint, etc. from sth: *paint stripper*

**'strip search** *noun* an act of searching a person for illegal drugs, weapons, etc., for example at an airport or in a prison, after they have been made to take off all their clothes ▸ **'strip-search** *verb* ~ sb

**strip·tease** /ˈstrɪptiːz/ *noun* [C, U] a form of entertainment, for example in a bar or club, when a performer removes his or her clothes in a sexually exciting way, usually to music, in front of an audience

**stripy** *(also* **stripey**) /ˈstraɪpi/ *adj. (BrE, informal)* = STRIPED: *a stripy jumper*

**strive** /straɪv/ *verb* (**strove** /strəʊv/, **striven** /ˈstrɪvn/ or *less frequent* **strived**, **strived**) [I] *(formal)* to try very hard to achieve sth: *We encourage all members to strive for the highest standards.* ◇ ~ against sth *striving against corruption* ◇ ~ to do sth *Newspaper editors all strive to be first with a story.* ▸ **striv·ing** *noun* [U, sing.]: *our striving for perfection*

**strobe** /strəʊb/ *(also* **'strobe light**) *noun* a bright light that flashes rapidly on and off

# strobing

**strob·ing** /ˈstrəʊbɪŋ/ noun [U] (specialist) the effect, sometimes seen in the lines and STRIPES in a television picture, of sudden movements or flashing

**strode** /strəʊd/ past tense of STRIDE

**stroke** /strəʊk/ noun, verb

■ noun

- **HITTING MOVEMENT 1** [C] an act of hitting a ball, for example with a BAT or RACKET: *What a beautiful stroke!* ◇ *He won by two strokes* (= in golf, by taking two fewer strokes than his opponent). **2** [C] a single movement of the arm when hitting sb/sth: *His punishment was six strokes of the cane.*
- **ACTION 3** [C] ~ (of sth) a single successful action or event: *Your idea was a stroke of genius.* ◇ *It was a stroke of luck that I found you here.* ◇ *It was a bold stroke to reveal the identity of the murderer on the first page.* ◇ *She never does a stroke (of work)* (= never does any work). ⇒ see also MASTERSTROKE
- **ILLNESS 4** [C, U] a sudden serious illness when a blood VESSEL (= tube) in the brain BURSTS (= breaks open) or is blocked, which can cause death or the loss of the ability to move or to speak clearly: *to have/suffer a stroke* ◇ *The stroke left him partly paralysed.* ◇ *Smoking increases the risk of stroke.*
- **IN SWIMMING/ROWING 5** [C] any of a series of repeated movements in swimming or ROWING: *She took a few more strokes to reach the bank.* ⇒ WORDFINDER NOTE at SWIMMING **6** [C] (often in compounds) a style of swimming: *Butterfly is the only stroke I can't do.* ⇒ see also BACKSTROKE, BREASTSTROKE **7** [C] the person who sets the speed at which everyone in a boat ROWS
- **GENTLE TOUCH 8** [C, usually sing.] (*especially BrE*) an act of moving your hand gently over a surface, usually several times: *He gave the cat a stroke.*
- **OF PEN/BRUSH 9** [C] a mark made by moving a pen, brush, etc. once across a surface: *to paint with fine brush strokes* ◇ *At the stroke of a pen* (= by signing sth) *they removed thousands of people from the welfare system.*
- **OF CLOCK 10** [C] each of the sounds made by a clock or bell giving the hours: *At the first stroke it will be 9 o'clock exactly.* ◇ *on the stroke of three* (= at 3 o'clock exactly)

IDM **at a (single) ˈstroke | at one ˈstroke** with a single immediate action: *They threatened to cancel the whole project at a stroke.* **put sb off their ˈstroke** (*BrE*) to make sb make a mistake or hesitate in what they are doing

■ verb

- **TOUCH GENTLY 1** ~ sth (*especially BrE*) to move your hand gently and slowly over an animal's fur or hair: *He's a beautiful dog. Can I stroke him?* ⇒ see also PET **2** ~ sth/sb (+ adv./prep.) to move your hand gently over a surface, sb's hair, etc: *He stroked her hair affectionately.*
- **MOVE STH GENTLY 3** ~ sth + adv./prep. to move sth somewhere with a gentle movement: *She stroked away his tears.* ◇ *He stroked the ball between the posts.*
- **BE NICE TO SB 4** ~ sb (*especially NAmE, informal*) to be very nice to sb, especially to get them to do what you want

**ˈstroke play** (also **ˈmedal play**) noun [U] a way of playing golf in which your score depends on the number of times you hit the ball in the whole game, rather than on the number of holes that you win ⇒ compare MATCH PLAY

**stroll** /strəʊl/ verb, noun

■ verb [I] (+ adv./prep.) to walk somewhere in a slow relaxed way: *People were strolling along the beach.*

■ noun a slow relaxed walk: *We went for a stroll in the park.*

**stroll·er** /ˈstrəʊlə(r)/ noun **1** a person who is enjoying a slow relaxed walk **2** (*NAmE*) (*BrE* **push-chair**) (also **buggy** *BrE and NAmE*) a small folding seat on wheels in which a small child sits and is pushed along ⇒ picture at PUSHCHAIR

**strong** /strɒŋ/; *NAmE* strɔːŋ/ adj. (**strong·er** /ˈstrɒŋɡə(r)/; *NAmE* ˈstrɔːŋ-/, **strong·est** /-ɡɪst/)

| WORD FAMILY |
|---|
| **strong** adj. |
| **strongly** adv. |
| **strength** noun |
| **strengthen** verb |

- **HAVING PHYSICAL POWER 1** (of people, animals, etc.) having a lot of physical power so that you can lift heavy weights, do hard physical work, etc: *He's strong enough to lift a car!* ◇ *strong muscles* ◇ *She wasn't a strong swimmer* (= she could not swim well). **2** (of a natural or physical force) having great power: *Stay indoors in the middle of the day, when the sun is strongest.* ◇ *a strong wind* ◇ *a strong magnet/current* **3** having a powerful effect on the body or mind: *a strong drug* ◇ *His imagery made a strong impression on the critics.*
- **HAVING POWER OVER PEOPLE 4** having a lot of power or influence: *a strong leader* ◇ *What the country needs right now is a strong government.* **5 the strong** [pl.] people who are rich or powerful
- **HARD TO RESIST/DEFEAT/ATTACK 6** (of an argument, evidence, etc.) difficult to attack or criticize: *There is strong evidence of a link between exercise and a healthy heart.* ◇ *You have a strong case for getting your job back.* **7** very powerful and difficult for people to fight against or defeat: *a strong team* ◇ *The proposal aroused strong opposition.* ◇ *The temptation to tell her everything was very strong.*
- **OPINION/BELIEF/FEELING 8** (of an opinion, a belief, or a feeling) very powerful: *strong support for the government* ◇ *People have strong feelings about this issue.* **9** [only before noun] (of a person) holding an opinion or a belief very seriously SYN **firm**: *a strong supporter of the government*
- **EASY TO SEE/HEAR/FEEL/SMELL 10** easy to see, hear, feel or smell; very great or intense: *a strong smell* ◇ *a strong feeling of nausea* ◇ *a strong voice* (= loud) ◇ *strong colours* ◇ *a face with strong features* (= large and easy to notice) ◇ *She spoke with a strong Australian accent.* ◇ *He was under strong pressure to resign.*
- **FOOD 11** having a lot of taste: *strong cheese* OPP **mild**
- **DRINKS 12** containing a lot of a substance: *strong black coffee*
- **NOT EASILY BROKEN 13** (of objects) not easily broken or damaged; made well: *The box looks strong enough.*
- **NOT EASILY UPSET 14** not easily upset or frightened; not easily influenced by other people: *You need strong nerves to ride a bike in London.* ◇ *Every child needs to develop a strong sense of identity.* ◇ *It's difficult, I know. But be strong!* ⇒ see also HEADSTRONG, STRONG-MINDED, STRONG-WILLED
- **LIKELY TO SUCCEED 15** likely to succeed or happen: *a strong candidate for the job* ◇ *You're in a strong position to negotiate a deal.*
- **DIFFICULT TO DESTROY 16** having existed for a long time and functioning well; difficult to destroy: *a strong marriage* ◇ *The college has strong links with local industry.* ◇ *I know that their relationship is growing stronger every day.*
- **BUSINESS 17** (of prices, an economy, etc.) having a value that is high or increasing: *The country is currently experiencing particularly strong economic growth.* ◇ *The euro is getting stronger against the dollar.* **18** (of a business or an industry) in a safe financial position: *Their catering business remained strong despite the recession.*
- **GOOD AT STH 19** good at sth; done well: *The play has a very strong cast.* ◇ *The actors give extremely strong performances.* ◇ *Mathematics was never my strong point* (= I was never very good at it).
- **NUMBER 20** great in number: *There was a strong police presence at the demonstration.* **21** used after numbers to show the size of a group: *a 5000-strong crowd* ◇ *The crowd was 5000 strong.*
- **HEALTHY 22** (of a person) not easily affected by disease; healthy: *These vitamins are meant to keep you healthy and strong.* ⇒ SYNONYMS at WELL
- **WORDS 23** (of words or language) having a lot of force, often causing offence to people: *The movie has been criticized for strong language* (= swearing).
- **GRAMMAR 24** [usually before noun] (of a verb) forming the past tense and past participle by changing a vowel, not by adding a regular ending, for example *sing, sang, sung*
- **PHONETICS 25** [usually before noun] used to describe the way some words are pronounced when they have stress. For example, the strong form of *and* is /ænd/. OPP **weak**

IDM **be a bit ˈstrong** (*BrE, informal*) used to say that you think what sb has said is unfair or too critical **be ˈstrong**

**on sth 1** to be good at sth: *I'm not very strong on dates* (= I can't remember the dates of important events). **2** to have a lot of sth: *The report was strong on criticism, but short on practical suggestions.* **be sb's ˈstrong suit** to be a subject that sb knows a lot about: *I'm afraid geography is not my strong suit.* **come on ˈstrong** (*informal*) to make your feelings clear in an aggressive way, especially your sexual feelings towards sb **going ˈstrong** (*informal*) to continue to be healthy, active or successful: *My grandmother is 90 and still going strong.* **ˌhave a ˌstrong ˈstomach** to be able to see or do unpleasant things without feeling sick or upset ⊃ more at CARD *n.*

**ˈstrong-arm** *adj.* [only before noun] (*disapproving*) using threats or violence in order to make people do what you want: *to use strong-arm tactics against your political opponents*

**ˈstrong force** *noun* (*physics*) one of the four FUNDAMENTAL FORCES in the universe, which holds the parts of the NUCLEUS of an ATOM together ⊃ see also ELECTROMAGNETISM, GRAVITY, WEAK FORCE

**strong·hold** /ˈstrɒŋhəʊld; *NAmE* ˈstrɔːŋ-/ *noun* **1** an area in which there is a lot of support for a particular belief or group of people, especially a political party: *a Republican stronghold/a stronghold of Republicanism* **2** a castle or a place that is strongly built and difficult to attack **3** an area where there are a large number of a particular type of animal: *This valley is one of the last strongholds of the Siberian tiger.*

**strong·ly** ❶ **B1** ⓦ /ˈstrɒŋli; *NAmE* ˈstrɔːŋ-/ *adv.* **1** **B1** in a way that shows definite and serious opinions or beliefs: *He was strongly opposed to the idea.* ◊ *This is an issue I feel strongly about.* ◊ *to strongly agree/disagree* **2** **B1** to a great degree or extent: *These conclusions are strongly supported by a recent study.* ◊ *Interest is already very high and advance booking is strongly recommended.* ◊ *She was strongly influenced by his views.* **3** in a way that is easy to notice: *The room smelt strongly of polish.* **4** with a lot of power or force: *a light shining strongly* ◊ *The market rebounded strongly in the second half of the year.* **5** in a way that means sth cannot be easily broken or damaged: *a strongly built boat*

**strong·man** /ˈstrɒŋmæn; *NAmE* ˈstrɔːŋ-/ *noun* (*pl.* -men /-men/) **1** a leader who uses threats or violence to rule a country **2** a physically very strong man, especially sb who performs in a CIRCUS

**ˌstrong-ˈminded** *adj.* having strong opinions that are not easily influenced by what other people think or say **SYN** determined

**ˈstrong·room** /ˈstrɒŋruːm, -rʊm; *NAmE* ˈstrɔːŋ-/ *noun* a room, for example in a bank, with thick walls and a strong, solid door, where valuable items are kept

**ˌstrong ˈsafety** *noun* (in AMERICAN FOOTBALL) a defending player who plays opposite the attacking team's strongest side

**ˌstrong-ˈwilled** *adj.* determined to do what you want to do, even if other people advise you not to

**stron·tium** /ˈstrɒntiəm, ˈstrɒnʃi-; *NAmE* ˈstrɑːntiəm, ˈstrɑːnʃi-/ *noun* [U] (*symb.* **Sr**) a chemical element. Strontium is a soft, silver-white metal.

**strop** /strɒp; *NAmE* strɑːp/ *noun* [sing.] (*BrE, informal*) a very bad mood when you are annoyed about sth: *Don't get in a strop—I'm only a few minutes late.*

**strop·py** /ˈstrɒpi; *NAmE* ˈstrɑːpi/ *adj.* (**strop·pier, strop·piest**) (*BrE, informal*) (of a person) easily annoyed and difficult to deal with: *Don't get stroppy with me—it isn't my fault!*

**strove** /strəʊv/ *past tense* of STRIVE

**struck** /strʌk/ *past tense, past part.* of STRIKE

**struc·tural** ❷+ **C1** ⓦ /ˈstrʌktʃərəl/ *adj.* [usually before noun] connected with the way in which sth is built or organized: *Storms have caused structural damage to hundreds of homes.* ◊ *structural changes in society* ▸ **struc·tur·al·ly** /ˈstrʌktʃərəli/ *adv.*: *The building is structurally sound.* ◊ *The languages are structurally different.*

# 1555 struggle

**ˌstructural engiˈneer** *noun* a person whose job is to plan large buildings, bridges, etc.

**struc·tur·al·ism** /ˈstrʌktʃərəlɪzəm/ *noun* [U] (in literature, language and social science) a theory that considers any text as a structure whose various parts only have meaning when they are considered in relation to each other ⊃ compare DECONSTRUCTION ▸ **struc·tur·al·ist** *noun, adj.*: *a structuralist approach*

**struc·ture** ❶ **A2** ⓞ /ˈstrʌktʃə(r)/ *noun, verb*
▪ *noun* **1** **A2** [U, C] the way in which the parts of sth are connected together, arranged or organized; a particular arrangement of parts: *the structure of the building* ◊ *changes in the economic structure of society* ◊ *Bees have a complex social structure.* ◊ *the grammatical structures of a language* ◊ *the structure of proteins/DNA* **2** **B2** [C] a thing that is made of several parts, especially a building: *a stone/brick/wooden structure* ⊃ SYNONYMS at BUILDING **3** **B2** [U, C] the state of being well organized or planned with all the parts linked together; a careful plan: *Your essay needs (a) structure.*
▪ *verb* **B2** [often passive] to arrange or organize sth into a system or pattern: *~ sth How well does the teacher structure the lessons?* ◊ *Make use of the toys in structured group activities.* ◊ *~ sth around sth The exhibition is structured around the themes of work and leisure.*

▼ **SYNONYMS**

**structure**
framework • form • composition • construction • fabric
These are all words for the way the different parts of sth combine together or the way that sth has been made.

**structure** the way in which the parts of sth are connected together or arranged; a particular arrangement of parts: *the structure of the building/human body* ◊ *the social structure of society* ◊ *the grammatical structures of a language* ◊ *a salary structure*

**framework** a set of beliefs, ideas or rules that forms the basis of a system or society: *The report provides a framework for further research.*

**form** [U] the arrangement of parts in a whole, especially in a work of art or piece of writing: *As a photographer, shape and form were more important to him than colour.*

**composition** [U] (*rather formal*) the different parts or people that combine to form sth; the way in which they combine: *recent changes in the composition of the workforce*

**construction** [U] the way that sth has been built or made: *ships of steel construction*

**fabric** (*rather formal*) the basic structure of a society or an organization that enables it to function successfully: *This is a trend which threatens the very fabric of society.*

**PATTERNS**
- the **basic** structure/framework/form/composition/construction/fabric of sth
- a **simple**/**complex** structure/framework/form
- the **economic**/**political**/**social** structure/framework/composition/fabric of sth
- the **chemical**/**genetic** structure/composition of sth

**stru·del** /ˈstruːdl/ *noun* [U, C] (*from German*) a cake made from pieces of fruit, especially apple, rolled in thin PASTRY and baked

**strug·gle** ❶ **B2** /ˈstrʌɡl/ *verb, noun*
▪ *verb* **1** **B2** [I] to try very hard to do sth when it is difficult or when there are a lot of problems: *~ for sth Shona struggled for breath.* ◊ *~ to do sth The firm is struggling to cope with the demand for its products.* ◊ *Local workers were still struggling to find employment.* ◊ *Most social enterprises struggle to survive.* **2** **B2** [I] + *adv./prep.* to move somewhere or do sth with difficulty: *I struggled up the hill with the heavy bags.* ◊ *Paul struggled out of his wheelchair.* **3** **B2** [I] to fight against sb/sth in order to prevent a bad situation or result: *~ against sb/sth He struggled against*

# strum

*cancer for two years.* ◊ **with sb/sth** *I have been* **struggling with injury for a couple of years* 4 [I] to fight sb or try to get away from them: *I struggled and screamed for help.* ◊ **with sb** *James was hit in the mouth as he struggled with the raiders.* ◊ *+ adj. How did she manage to* **struggle free**? 5 [I] **~ (with sb) (for sth)** to compete or argue with sb/sth, especially in order to get sth: *rival leaders struggling for power*

**PHRV** **struggle a'long/'on** to continue despite problems
- **noun 1** [C] a hard fight in which people try to obtain or achieve sth, especially sth that sb else does not have them to have: *Marx wrote about the class struggle.* ◊ **~ for sth** *a struggle for independence* ◊ **~ against sth** *They took up the struggle against racism.* ◊ **~ with sth** *her struggle with cancer* ◊ **~ (with sb) (to do sth)** *He is engaged in a bitter struggle with his rival to get control of the company.* ◊ **~ between A and B** *an ongoing power struggle between president and prime minister* ◊ *She will not give up her children without a struggle.* ⊃ SYNONYMS at CAMPAIGN **2** [C] a physical fight between two people or groups of people, especially when one of them is trying to escape, or to get sth from the other: **~ with sb** *He was involved in a struggle with the police.* ◊ **~ against sth** *The group supported the* **armed struggle** *against the dictator.* ⊃ SYNONYMS at FIGHT **3** [sing.] something that is difficult for you to do or achieve **SYN** **effort**: **~ to do sth** *It was a real struggle to be ready on time.*

**strum** /strʌm/ *verb* [I, T] (**-mm-**) **~ (on)** sth to play a guitar or similar instrument by moving your fingers up and down across the strings: *As she sang she strummed on a guitar.*

**strung** /strʌŋ/ *past tense, past part.* of STRING

**strung 'out** *adj.* [not before noun] **1** spread out in a line: *a group of riders strung out along the beach* **2** **~ (on sth)** (*slang*) strongly affected by an illegal drug such as HEROIN

**strung 'up** *adj.* [not before noun] (*BrE, informal*) very nervous, worried or excited

**strut** /strʌt/ *verb, noun*
- *verb* [I] (**-tt-**) to walk proudly with your head up and chest out to show that you think you are important: *The players strutted and posed for the cameras.*
**IDM** **strut your 'stuff** (*informal*) to proudly show your ability, especially at dancing or performing
- *noun* **1** a long, thin piece of wood or metal used to support or make part of a vehicle or building stronger **2** [sing.] (*disapproving*) an act of walking in a proud and confident way

**strych·nine** /ˈstrɪkniːn/ *noun* [U] a poisonous substance used in very small amounts as a medicine

**stub** /stʌb/ *noun, verb*
- *noun* **1** a short piece of a cigarette, pencil, etc. that is left when the rest of it has been used **2** the small part of a ticket, CHEQUE, etc. that you keep as a record when you have given the main part to sb
- *verb* (**-bb-**) **~ your toe (against/on sth)** to hurt your toe by accident by hitting it against sth hard
**PHRV** **stub sth↔'out** to stop a cigarette, etc. from burning by pressing the end against sth hard

**stub·ble** /ˈstʌbl/ *noun* [U] **1** the lower short, stiff part of the STEMS of crops such as WHEAT that are left in the ground after the top part has been cut and collected **2** the short, stiff hairs that grow on a man's face when he has not SHAVED recently ▶ **stub·bly** /-bli/ *adj.*

**stub·born** /ˈstʌbən/; *NAmE* -bərn/ *adj.* **1** (*often disapproving*) determined not to change your opinion or attitude **SYN** **obstinate**: *He was too stubborn to admit that he was wrong.* ◊ *She can be* **as stubborn as a mule** (= extremely stubborn). ◊ *stubborn pride* ◊ *a stubborn resistance to change* ◊ *a stubborn refusal to listen* **2** (*usually before noun*) difficult to get rid of or deal with **SYN** **persistent**: *a stubborn cough/stain* ◊ *a stubborn problem* ▶ **stub·born·ly** *adv.*: *She stubbornly refused to pay.* ◊ *Unemployment remains stubbornly high.* **stub·born·ness** /ˈstʌbənnəs/; *NAmE* -bərn-/ *noun* [U]

**stubby** /ˈstʌbi/ *adj., noun*
- *adj.* (*usually before noun*) (**stub·bier, stub·bi·est**) short and thick: *stubby fingers*
- *noun* (*pl.* **-ies**) (*AustralE, NZE*) **1** [C] (*informal*) a small, fat bottle of beer usually holding 0.375 LITRES **2** **Stubbies**™ [pl.] a pair of short trousers for men

**stucco** /ˈstʌkəʊ/ *noun* [U] a type of PLASTER that is used for covering ceilings and the outside walls of buildings ▶ **stuccoed** *adj.*: *a stuccoed wall*

**stuck** /stʌk/ *adj., verb*
- *adj.* [not before noun] **1** unable to move or to be moved: *The wheels were stuck in the mud.* ◊ *This drawer keeps getting stuck.* ◊ *She got the key stuck in the lock.* ◊ *I can't get out—I'm stuck.* **2** in an unpleasant situation or place that you cannot escape from: *We were stuck in traffic for over an hour.* ◊ *I hate being stuck at home all day.* **3** **~ (on sth)** unable to answer or understand sth: *I got stuck on the first question.* ◊ *I'll help you if you're stuck.* **4** **~ (for sth)** not knowing what to do in a particular situation: *If you're stuck for something to do tonight, come out with us.* ◊ *I've never known him to be stuck for words before.* **5** **~ with sb/sth** (*informal*) unable to get rid of sb/sth that you do not want: *I was stuck with him for the whole journey.*
**IDM** **get stuck 'in | get stuck 'into sth** (*BrE, informal*) to start doing sth in an enthusiastic way, especially to start eating ⊃ more at BROKEN *adj.*, GROOVE, ROCK *n.*, TIME WARP
- *verb past tense, past part.* of STICK

**stuck-'up** *adj.* (*informal, disapproving*) thinking that you are more important than other people and behaving in an unfriendly way towards them **SYN** **snobbish**

**stud** /stʌd/ *noun* **1** [C] a small piece of jewellery with a part that is pushed through a hole in your ear, nose, etc: *diamond studs* **2** [C] a small, round piece of metal that is attached to the surface of sth, especially for decoration: *a leather jacket with studs on the back* **3** [C, usually pl.] (*BrE*) one of several small metal or plastic objects that are fixed to the bottom part of a FOOTBALL BOOT or sports shoe ⊃ compare CLEAT **4** [C] a small metal object used in the past for fastening a COLLAR onto a shirt ⊃ see also PRESS STUD **5** [C, U] an animal, especially a horse, that is kept for BREEDING (= producing young); a place where animals, especially horses, are kept for breeding: *a stud farm* ◊ *The horse has been retired from racing and* **put out to stud** (= kept for breeding). **6** [C] (*informal*) a man who has many sexual partners and who is thought to be sexually attractive

**stud·ded** /ˈstʌdɪd/ *adj.* **1** decorated with small raised pieces of metal: *a studded leather belt* **2** **~ with sth** having a lot of sth on or in it: *The sky was clear and studded with stars.* ◊ *an essay studded with quotations* ⊃ see also STAR-STUDDED ▶ **stud** *verb* (**-dd-**): **~ sth** *Stars studded the sky.*

**stu·dent** /ˈstjuːdnt; *NAmE* ˈstuː-/ *noun* **1** a person who is studying at a university or college: *a college/university student* ◊ *a graduate student* ◊ *a medical/law student* ◊ *international students* (= who come to study from other countries) ◊ *She's a student at Oxford.* ◊ *a student loan* (= money lent to students to pay for their studies) ◊ *He is here on a student visa.* ◊ *a student nurse/teacher* ⊃ see also MATURE STUDENT, SUMMER STUDENT, TRANSFER STUDENT **2** a person who is studying at a school, especially a SECONDARY SCHOOL: *a 15-year-old high school student* ⊃ compare PUPIL ⊃ see also A STUDENT **3** **~ of sth** (*formal*) a person who is very interested in a particular subject: *a keen student of human nature*

**student 'body** *noun* all the students in a high school or college: *The university has a student body of just over 30000.*

**student 'council** *noun* [C, U] (*NAmE*) a STUDENT GOVERNMENT, especially in a high school: *She served on the student council for four years.*

**student 'government** *noun* [C, U] (*NAmE*) an elected group of students who plan activities and deal with various student issues, especially at a college or university: *He's the faculty adviser to the student government.* ⊃ compare STUDENT COUNCIL

### ▼ MORE ABOUT...
**students**
- A **student** is a person who is studying at a school, college, university, etc.
- An **undergraduate** is a student who is studying for their first degree at a university or college.
- In *BrE*, a **graduate** is a person who has completed a first degree at a university or college. In *NAmE* **graduate** is usually used with another noun and can also apply to a person who has finished high school: *a high school graduate* ◊ *a graduate student*.
- A **postgraduate** is a person who has finished a first degree and is doing advanced study or research. This is the usual term in *BrE*, but it is formal in *NAmE* and **graduate student** is usually used instead.

### ▼ SYNONYMS
**student**
pupil • schoolboy/schoolchild/schoolgirl

These are all words for a child who attends school.

**student** a person who is studying in a school, especially an older child: *Students are required to be in school by 8.30.* ◊ *Any high school student could tell you the answer.*

**pupil** (*BrE*) a person who is being taught, especially a child in a school: *The school has over 850 pupils.* **NOTE** Pupil is used only in *BrE* and is starting to become old-fashioned. Student is often preferred, especially by teachers and other people involved in education, and especially when talking about older children.

**schoolboy/schoolgirl/schoolchild** a boy, girl or child who attends school: *Since she was a schoolgirl she had dreamed of going on the stage.* **NOTE** These words emphasize the age of the children or this period in their lives; they are less often used to talk about teaching and learning: *an able schoolboy/schoolgirl/schoolchild*

PATTERNS
- a(n) good/bright/able/brilliant/star/outstanding student/pupil
- a naughty schoolboy/schoolgirl/schoolchild
- a disruptive student/pupil
- a(n) ex-/former student/pupil
- a school student/pupil
- to teach students/pupils/schoolboys/schoolgirls/schoolchildren

**stu·dent·ship** /ˈstjuːdəntʃɪp; *NAmE* ˈstuː-/ *noun* (*BrE*) one of a small number of places that a university gives to students who wish to continue studying or to do research after they have finished their degree; an amount of money that is given to a student who wins one of these places

**students' union** (also **student union**) *noun* **1** a building where students at a university or college can go to meet socially **2** (*BrE*) an association of students at a particular university or college, interested and involved in students' rights, living conditions, etc.

**student teaching** (*US*) (*BrE* **teaching practice**) *noun* [U] the part of a course for people who are training to become teachers which involves teaching classes of students

**stud·ied** /ˈstʌdid/ *adj.* [only before noun] (*formal*) deliberate and carefully planned: *She introduced herself with studied casualness.*

**stu·dio** 🔊 **B1** /ˈstjuːdiəʊ; *NAmE* ˈstuː-/ *noun* (*pl.* **-os**) **1** **B1** a room where radio or television programmes are recorded and broadcast from, or where music is recorded: *a television/recording studio* ◊ *a studio audience* (= one in a studio, that can be seen or heard as a programme is broadcast) **2** **B1** a place where films are made or produced: *a movie/film studio* **3** **B1** a company that makes films: *She works for a major Hollywood studio.* ◊ *a film/movie studio* **4** **B1** a room where an artist works: *I wanted to turn the room into an artist's studio.* **5** a place where dancing is taught or where dancers practise: *a dance stu-*

dio **6** (*BrE* also **studio flat**) (*NAmE* also **studio apartment**) a small flat with one main room for living and sleeping in and usually a kitchen and bathroom

**stu·di·ous** /ˈstjuːdiəs; *NAmE* ˈstuː-/ *adj.* spending a lot of time studying or reading **SYN** **scholarly**: *a studious young man*

**stu·di·ous·ly** /ˈstjuːdiəsli; *NAmE* ˈstuː-/ *adv.* in a way that is carefully planned and deliberate: *He studiously avoided answering the question.*

## study 🔊 **A1** 🔊 /ˈstʌdi/ *noun*, *verb*

■ *noun* (*pl.* **-ies**)
- **ACTIVITY OF LEARNING 1** **A1** [U] the activity of learning or gaining knowledge, either from books or by examining things in the world: *a room set aside for private study* ◊ *academic/literary/scientific study* ◊ *It is important to develop good study skills.* ◊ *Physiology is the study of how living things work.* ⊃ see also **SELF-STUDY**

**WORDFINDER** course, distance learning, education, exam, further education, graduate, higher education, qualification, tertiary

**2** **A1** **studies** [pl.] (often used with a possessive) (*formal*) a particular person's learning activities, for example at a college or university: *to continue your studies*
- **ACADEMIC SUBJECT 3** **A2** **studies** [U + sing./pl. v.] used in the names of some academic subjects: *business/media/American studies*
- **RESEARCH 4** **B1** [C] a piece of research that examines a subject or question in detail: *to conduct/undertake a study* ◊ *~ of sth a detailed study of how animals adapt to their environment* ◊ *This study shows/finds/suggests that...* ◊ *the results/findings of a study* ◊ *in a~ the methods used in the present study* ◊ *according to a~ According to a recent study published in the Journal of Sleep Research...* ⊃ **WORDFINDER NOTE** at **SCIENCE** ⊃ see also **CASE STUDY**
**5** **B1** [C] an academic book or article on a particular topic: *a study of Jane Austen's novels* **6** **B1** [U] the act of considering or examining sth in detail: *These proposals deserve careful study.*
- **ROOM 7** **B1** [C] a room, especially in sb's home, used for reading and writing
- **ART 8** [C] a drawing or painting of sth, especially one done for practice or before doing a larger picture: *a study of Chartres Cathedral* ◊ *a nude study*
- **CHARACTER 9** [C] the act of showing or describing sb/sth in literature or another art form, especially a character or an aspect of behaviour: *The novel is a character study of a city and its people.*
- **MUSIC 10** (also **étude**) [C] a piece of music designed to give a player practice in technical skills
- **PERFECT EXAMPLE 11** [sing.] *~ (in sth)* (*formal*) a perfect example of sth: *His face was a study in concentration.*
**IDM** see **BROWN** *adj.*

■ *verb* (**stud·ies**, **study·ing**, **stud·ied**, **stud·ied**)
- **LEARN 1** **A1** [T, I] to spend time learning about a subject by reading, going to college, etc: *He sat up very late that night, studying.* ◊ *~ sth How long have you been studying English?* ◊ *~ for sth Don't disturb Jane, she's studying for her exams.* ◊ *~ (sth) at... She studied at New College, Oxford.* ◊ *~ (sth) under sb a composer who studied music under Nadia Boulanger* (= was taught music by Nadia Boulanger) ◊ *~ to do/be sth Nina is studying to be an architect.*
- **EXAMINE CAREFULLY 2** **B1** [T] to watch or to look at sb/sth carefully in order to find out sth: *~ sth for sth Scientists are studying photographs of the planet for signs of life.* ◊ *~ sth He studied her face thoughtfully.* ◊ *Fran was studying the menu.* **3** **B1** [T] to examine sth carefully in order to understand it: *~ sth We will study the report carefully before making a decision.* ◊ *~ how, what, etc... The group will study how the region coped with the loss of thousands of jobs.* ⊃ **SYNONYMS** at **EXAMINE**

**study hall** *noun* [U] (*NAmE*) a period of time during the school day when students study quietly on their own, usually with a teacher present

# stuff

**stuff** ⓘ B1 /stʌf/ noun, verb

■ noun [U] **1** B1 (informal) used to refer to a substance, material, group of objects, etc. when you do not know the name, when the name is not important or when it is obvious what you are talking about: *What's all that sticky stuff on the carpet?* ◇ *The chairs were covered in some sort of plastic stuff.* ◇ *I don't know how you can eat that stuff!* ◇ *They sell stationery and stuff (like that).* ◇ *Where's all my stuff (= my possessions)?* ◇ *Could you move all that stuff off the table?* ⊃ SYNONYMS at THING ⊃ see also FOODSTUFF **2** B2 (informal) used to refer in a general way to things that people do, say, think, etc: *There's still a lot of cool stuff happening in Manchester.* ◇ *I've got loads of stuff to do today.* ◇ *I like reading and stuff.* ◇ *The band did some great stuff on their first album.* ◇ *This is all good stuff. Well done!* ◇ *I don't believe in all that stuff about ghosts.* **3** ~ (of sth) (formal or literary) the most important feature of sth; something that sth else is based on or is made from: *The trip was magical; the stuff of which dreams are made.* ◇ *Parades and marches were the very stuff of politics in the region.* ◇ *Let's see what stuff you're made of (= what sort of person you are).* ⊃ see also HOT STUFF

IDM **do your 'stuff** (informal) to do what you are good at or what you have been trained to do: *Some members of the team are just not doing their stuff (= doing as well as they should).* ◇ *(figurative) The medicine has clearly done its stuff.* **not give a 'stuff** (BrE, slang) to not care at all about sth ,**stuff and 'nonsense** (old-fashioned, informal) used to say that sth is stupid or not true ⊃ more at KID n., KNOW v., STERN adj., STRUT v., SWEAT v.

■ verb **1** B2 to fill a space or container tightly with sth: ~ A with B *She had 500 envelopes to stuff with leaflets.* ◇ ~ B in, into, under A *She had 500 leaflets to stuff into envelopes.* ◇ ~ sth *The fridge is stuffed to bursting.* ◇ ~ sth + adj. *All the drawers were stuffed full of letters and papers.* **2** B2 ~ sth + adv./prep. to push sth quickly and carelessly into a small space SYN **shove**: *She stuffed the money under a cushion.* ◇ *His hands were stuffed in his pockets.* **3** ~ sth to fill a vegetable, chicken, etc. with another type of food: *Are you going to stuff the turkey?* ◇ *stuffed peppers* **4** (informal) to eat a lot of food or too much food; to give sb a lot or too much to eat: ~ **sb/yourself** *He sat at the table stuffing himself.* ◇ ~ **sb/yourself with sth** *Don't stuff the kids with chocolate before their dinner.* ◇ ~ **your face** *We stuffed our faces at the party.* **5** [usually passive] to fill the dead body of an animal with material and preserve it, so that it keeps its original shape and appearance: **have sth/be stuffed** *They had had their pet dog stuffed.*

IDM **get 'stuffed** (BrE, informal) used to tell sb in a rude and angry way to go away, or that you do not want sth ˈ**stuff it** (informal) used to show that you have changed your mind about sth or do not care about sth: *I didn't want a part in the play, then I thought—stuff it—why not?* ˈ**you, etc. can stuff sth** (informal) used to tell sb in a rude and angry way that you do not want sth: *I told them they could stuff their job.*

**stuffed** /stʌft/ adj. [not before noun] (informal) having eaten so much that you cannot eat anything else SYN **full**

ˌ**stuffed 'animal** noun **1** (especially NAmE) (BrE usually ˌ**soft 'toy**) (also ˌ**stuffed 'toy** BrE and NAmE) a toy in the shape of an animal, made of cloth and filled with a soft substance **2** a dead animal that has been stuffed: *stuffed animals in glass cases*

ˌ**stuffed 'up** adj. if you are **stuffed up**, your nose is blocked and you are not able to breathe easily

**stuff·ing** /ˈstʌfɪŋ/ noun [U] **1** (NAmE also **dress·ing**) a mixture of food such as bread, onions and HERBS, cut into very small pieces and placed inside a chicken, etc. before it is cooked **2** soft material used to fill CUSHIONS, toys, etc. SYN **filling** IDM see KNOCK v.

**stuffy** /ˈstʌfi/ adj. (**stuffi·er**, **stuffi·est**) **1** (of a building, room, etc.) warm in an unpleasant way and without enough fresh air: *a stuffy room* ◇ *It gets very hot and stuffy in here in summer.* **2** (informal, disapproving) very serious, formal, boring or old-fashioned: *a stuffy, formal family* ◇ *plain, stuffy clothes* **3** (especially NAmE) if you have a stuffy nose, your nose is blocked because you have a cold ▶ **stuffi·ness** noun [U]

**stul·ti·fy·ing** /ˈstʌltɪfaɪɪŋ/ adj. (formal) making you feel very bored and unable to think of new ideas: *the stultifying effects of work that never varies* ▶ **stul·tify** verb (**stul·ti·fies**, **stul·ti·fy·ing**, **stul·ti·fied**, **stul·ti·fied**) ~ **sb/sth** **stul·ti·fy·ing·ly** adv.

**stum·ble** ⓘ+ C1 /ˈstʌmbl/ verb **1** ⓘ+ C1 [I] to hit your foot against sth while you are walking or running and almost fall SYN **trip**: *The child stumbled and fell.* ◇ ~ **over/on sth** *I stumbled over a rock.* **2** [I] + adv./prep. to walk or move in an unsteady way: *We were stumbling around in the dark looking for a candle.* **3** [I] ~ **(over/through sth)** to make a mistake or mistakes and stop while you are speaking, reading to sb or playing music: *In her nervousness she stumbled over her words.* ◇ *I stumbled through the piano piece with difficulty.* ▶ **stum·ble** noun

PHRV ˈ**stumble across/on/upon sth/sb** to discover sth/sb unexpectedly: *Police have stumbled across a huge drugs ring.* ˈ**stumble into sth** to become involved in sth by chance: *I stumbled into acting when I left college.*

ˈ**stumbling block** noun ~ **(to sth)** | ~ **(to doing sth)** something that causes problems and prevents you from achieving your aim SYN **obstacle**

**stump** /stʌmp/ noun, verb

■ noun **1** [C] the bottom part of a tree left in the ground after the rest has fallen or been cut down **2** [C] the end of sth or the part that is left after the main part has been cut, broken off or worn away: *the stump of a pencil* **3** [C] the short part of sb's leg or arm that is left after the rest has been cut off **4** [C, usually pl.] (in CRICKET) one of the set of three wooden sticks (called **the stumps**) that stand in the ground and form the WICKET **5** *usually* **the stump** [sing.] (informal, especially NAmE) the fact of a politician going to different places before an election and trying to get people's support by making speeches: **on the ~** *politicians on the stump* ◇ *The senator gave his standard stump speech.* IDM see STIR v.

■ verb **1** [T, usually passive] ~ **sb** (informal) to ask sb a question that is too difficult for them to answer or give them a problem that they cannot solve SYN **baffle**: *I'm stumped. I don't know how they got here before us.* **2** [I] + adv./prep. to walk in a noisy, heavy way, especially because you are angry or upset SYN **stomp**: *He stumped off, muttering under his breath.* **3** [I, T] + adv./prep. | ~ **sth** (NAmE) to travel around making political speeches, especially before an election: *He stumped (around) the country trying to build up support.* **4** [T] ~ **sb** (in CRICKET) (of a WICKETKEEPER) to put a BATSMAN out of the game by knocking off either of the BAILS (= the two pieces of wood that bridge the stumps) with the ball, when he or she is out of the area in which the ball can be hit, but not running

PHRV ˌ**stump 'up (for sth)** | ˌ**stump 'up sth (for sth)** (BrE, informal) to pay money for sth SYN **cough up**: *We were asked to stump up for the repairs.* ◇ *Who is going to stump up the extra money?*

**stumpy** /ˈstʌmpi/ adj. (disapproving) short and thick SYN **stubby**: *stumpy fingers* ◇ *a stumpy tail*

**stun** ⓘ+ C1 /stʌn/ verb (**-nn-**) **1** ⓘ+ C1 ~ **sb/sth** to make a person or an animal unconscious for a short time, especially by hitting them on the head SYN **knock out**: *The fall stunned me for a moment.* ◇ *The animals are stunned before slaughter.* **2** ⓘ+ C1 ~ **sb** to surprise or shock sb so much that they cannot think clearly or speak SYN **astound**: *Her words stunned me—I had no idea she felt that way.* **3** SYNONYMS at SURPRISE **3** ~ **sb** to impress sb very much SYN **amaze**: *They were stunned by the view from the summit.* ▶ **stunned** adj.: *She was too stunned to speak.* ◇ *There was a stunned silence when I told them the news.*

**stung** /stʌŋ/ past tense, past part. of STING

ˈ**stun grenade** noun a small bomb that shocks people so that they cannot do anything, without seriously injuring them

ˈ**stun gun** noun a weapon that makes a person or an animal unconscious or unable to move for a short time, usually by giving them a small electric shock

**stunk** /stʌŋk/ past part. of STINK

**stun·ner** /'stʌnə(r)/ noun (informal) **1** a person (especially a woman) or a thing that is very attractive or exciting to look at **2** something, such as a piece of news, that surprises or shocks you very much

**stun·ning** /'stʌnɪŋ/ adj. (rather informal) **1** extremely attractive or impressive SYN **beautiful**: *You look absolutely stunning!* ◊ *a stunning view of the lake* **2** that surprises or shocks you very much: *He suffered a stunning defeat in the election.* ▶ **stun·ning·ly** adv.: *stunningly beautiful* ◊ *a stunningly simple idea*

**stunt** /stʌnt/ noun, verb
- noun **1** a dangerous and difficult action that sb does to entertain people, especially as part of a film: *He did all his own stunts.* ◊ *a stunt pilot* **2** (*sometimes disapproving*) something that is done in order to attract people's attention: *a publicity stunt* **3** (*informal*) a stupid or dangerous act: *I've had enough of her childish stunts.* ◊ *Don't you ever pull a stunt like that again!*
- verb ~ sb/sth to prevent sb/sth from growing or developing as much as they/it should: *The constant winds had stunted the growth of plants and bushes.* ◊ *His illness had not stunted his creativity.*

**stunt·ed** /'stʌntɪd/ adj. that has not been able to grow or develop as much as it should: *stunted trees* ◊ *the stunted lives of children deprived of education*

**stunt·man** /'stʌntmæn/, **stunt·woman** /'stʌntwʊmən/ noun (pl. -men /-men/, -women /-wɪmɪn/) a person whose job is to do dangerous things in place of an actor in a film, etc.; a person who does dangerous things in order to entertain people ⇨ WORDFINDER NOTE at ACTOR

**stu·pefy** /'stju:pɪfaɪ; NAmE 'stu:-/ verb [often passive] (stu·pe·fies, stu·pe·fy·ing, stu·pe·fied, stu·pe·fied) ~ sb to surprise or shock sb; to make sb unable to think clearly: *He was stupefied by the amount they had spent.* ◊ *She was stupefied with cold.* ▶ **stu·pe·fac·tion** /ˌstju:pɪ'fækʃn; NAmE ˌstu:-/ noun [U]

**stu·pe·fy·ing** /'stju:pɪfaɪɪŋ; NAmE 'stu:-/ adj. **1** making you unable to think clearly: *stupefying boredom* **2** that surprises or shocks you very much ▶ **stu·pe·fy·ing·ly** adv.: *The party was stupefyingly dull.*

**stu·pen·dous** /stju:'pendəs; NAmE stu:-/ adj. (rather informal) extremely large or impressive, especially greater or better than you expect SYN **staggering**: *stupendous achievements* ◊ *stupendous costs* ▶ **stu·pen·dous·ly** adv.

**stu·pid** /'stju:pɪd; NAmE 'stu:-/ adj., noun
- adj. (stu·pid·er, stu·pid·est) HELP more stupid and most stupid are also common **1** showing a lack of thought or good judgement SYN **foolish**, **silly**: *a stupid mistake/question/idea* ◊ *It was a pretty stupid thing to do.* ◊ *I was stupid enough to believe him.* ◊ *It was stupid of you to get involved.* **2** (*disapproving*) (of a person) slow to learn or understand things; not clever or intelligent: *He'll manage—he isn't stupid.* ◊ *Forgetting my notes made me look stupid.* ◊ *She always makes me feel really stupid.* **3** [only before noun] (*informal*) used to emphasize that you are annoyed with sb/sth: *I can't get the stupid thing open!* ◊ *Get your stupid feet off the chair!* ▶ **stu·pid·ly** adv.: *I stupidly agreed to lend him the money.* ◊ *Todd stared stupidly at the screen.*
- noun [sing.] (*informal*, *sometimes offensive*) if you call sb **stupid**, you are telling them that you think they are not being very intelligent: *Yes, stupid, it's you I'm talking to!*

**stu·pid·ity** /stju:'pɪdəti; NAmE stu:-/ noun (pl. -ies) **1** [U, C, usually pl.] behaviour that shows a lack of thought or good judgement: *I couldn't believe my own stupidity.* ◊ *the errors and stupidities of youth* **2** [U] the state or quality of being slow to learn and not clever or intelligent

**stu·por** /'stju:pə(r); NAmE 'stu:-/ noun [sing., U] a state in which you are unable to think, hear, etc. clearly, especially because you have drunk too much alcohol, taken drugs or had a shock: *He drank himself into a stupor.* ◊ *a drunken stupor*

**sturdy** /'stɜ:di; NAmE 'stɜ:rdi/ adj. (stur·dier, stur·di·est) **1** (of an object) strong and not easily damaged SYN **robust**: *a sturdy pair of boots* ◊ *a sturdy table* **2** [usually before noun] (of people and animals, or their bodies) physically strong and healthy: *a man of sturdy build* ◊ *sturdy legs* ◊ *a* sturdy breed of cattle **3** not easily influenced or changed by other people SYN **firm**, **determined**: *The village has always maintained a sturdy independence.* ▶ **stur·dily** /-dɪli/ adv.: *The boat was sturdily made.* ◊ *a sturdily built young man* ◊ *a sturdily independent community* **stur·di·ness** noun [U]

**stur·geon** /'stɜ:dʒən; NAmE 'stɜ:rdʒ-/ noun [C, U] (pl. sturgeon or stur·geons) a large sea and FRESHWATER fish that lives in northern regions. Sturgeon are used for food and the eggs (called CAVIAR) are also eaten.

**stut·ter** /'stʌtə(r)/ verb, noun
- verb **1** [T, I] to have difficulty speaking because you cannot stop yourself from repeating the first sound of some words several times SYN **stammer**: + *speech* '*W-w-what?*' *he stuttered.* ◊ ~ (sth) *I managed to stutter a reply.* **2** [I] (of a vehicle or an engine) to move or start with difficulty, making short sharp noises or movements: *The car stuttered along in first gear.*
- noun [sing.] a speech problem in which a person finds it difficult to say the first sound of a word and repeats it several times: *He had a terrible stutter.*

**St 'Valentine's Day** noun the day (14 February), when people send a card to the person that they love, sometimes without signing their name on it

**sty** /staɪ/ noun **1** (pl. **sties**) **2** (*also* **stye**) (pl. **sties** or **styes**) an infection of the EYELID (= the skin above or below the eye) which makes it red and painful

**style** /staɪl/ noun, verb
- noun
  - WAY STH IS DONE **1** [C, U] the particular way in which sth is done: *a wide range of musical styles* ◊ *different learning/management styles* ◊ ~ of sth *a style of management* ◊ *His aggressive style of play sometimes gets him in trouble.* ◊ *I like your style* (= I like the way you do things). ◊ *Caution was not her style* (= not the way she usually behaved). ◊ *I'm surprised he rides a motorbike—I'd have thought big cars were more his style* (= what suited him). ⇨ see also LIFESTYLE
  - DESIGN OF CLOTHES/HAIR **2** [C] a particular design of sth, especially clothes: *We stock a wide variety of styles and sizes.* ◊ *Have you thought about having your hair in a shorter style?* ⇨ see also HAIRSTYLE **3** [U] the quality of being fashionable in the clothes that you wear: *style-conscious teenagers* ◊ **in ~** *Short skirts are back in style* (= fashionable).
  - BEING ATTRACTIVE **4** [U] the quality of being attractive and made or done to a high standard: *The hotel has been redecorated but it's lost a lot of its style.*
  - OF BOOK/PAINTING/BUILDING **5** [C, U] the features of a book, painting, building, etc. that make it typical of a particular author, artist, historical period, etc: ~ **(of sth)** *a style of architecture* ◊ *The film has a unique visual style.* ◊ **in the ~ of sb/sth** *a parody written in the style of Molière*
  - USE OF LANGUAGE **6** [U, C] the correct use of language: *It's not considered good style to start a sentence with 'but'.*
  - -STYLE **7** (in adjectives) having the type of style mentioned: *Italian-style gardens* ◊ *a buffet-style breakfast* ⇨ see also OLD-STYLE
  - IN A PLANT **8** (*biology*) the long, thin part of a flower that carries the STIGMA ⇨ VISUAL VOCAB page V7
  - IDM **in (great, grand, etc.) style** in an impressive way: *She always celebrates her birthday in style.* ◊ *He won the championship in great style.* ⇨ more at CRAMP *v.*
- verb
  - CLOTHES/HAIR, ETC. **1** ~ sth to design, make or shape sth in a particular way: *an elegantly styled jacket* ◊ *He'd had his hair styled at an expensive salon.*
  - GIVE NAME/TITLE **2** ~ sb/sth/yourself + noun (*formal*) to give sb/sth/yourself a particular name or title: *He styled himself Major Carter.*
  - PHRV **'style sth/yourself on sth/sb** to copy the style, manner or appearance of sb/sth SYN **model**: *a coffee bar styled on a Parisian cafe* ◊ *He styled himself on Elvis Presley.*

**'style sheet** noun (*computing*) a file which is used for creating documents in a particular style

# styli

**sty·li** /ˈstaɪlaɪ/ *pl.* of STYLUS

**styl·ing** /ˈstaɪlɪŋ/ *noun* [U] **1** the act of cutting and/or shaping hair in a particular style: *styling gel* **2** the way in which sth is designed: *The car has been criticized for its outdated body styling.*

**styl·ish** /ˈstaɪlɪʃ/ *adj.* (*approving*) fashionable and attractive **SYN** **classy**: *his stylish wife ◇ a stylish restaurant ◇ It was a stylish performance by both artists.* ▶ **styl·ish·ly** *adv.* **styl·ish·ness** *noun* [U]

**styl·ist** /ˈstaɪlɪst/ *noun* **1** (*also* **hair·styl·ist**) a person whose job is cutting and shaping people's hair **2** a person who designs fashionable clothes or advises people on fashion **3** a writer who takes great care to write or says sth in a beautiful or unusual way **4** a person whose job is to create or design a particular style or image for a product, a person, an advertisement, etc. **5** (*in sport or music*) a person who performs with style

**styl·is·tic** /staɪˈlɪstɪk/ *adj.* [only before noun] connected with the style an artist uses in a particular piece of art, writing or music: *stylistic analysis ◇ stylistic features* ▶ **styl·is·tic·al·ly** /-kli/ *adv.*

**styl·is·tics** /staɪˈlɪstɪks/ *noun* [U] (*linguistics*) the study of style and the methods used in written language

**styl·ized** (*BrE also* **-ised**) /ˈstaɪlaɪzd/ *adj.* drawn, written, etc. in a way that is not natural or realistic: *a stylized drawing of a house ◇ the highly stylized form of acting in Japanese theatre* ▶ **styl·iza·tion**, **-isa·tion** /ˌstaɪlaɪˈzeɪʃn; *NAmE* -ləˈz-/ *noun* [U]

**sty·lus** /ˈstaɪləs/ *noun* (*pl.* **sty·luses** *or* **sty·li** /-laɪ/) **1** a device on a RECORD PLAYER that looks like a small needle and is placed on the record in order to play it **2** (*computing*) a special pen used to write text or draw an image on a special computer screen

**sty·mie** /ˈstaɪmi/ *verb* (**sty·mie·ing**, **sty·my·ing**, **sty·mied**, **sty·mied**) ~ **sb/sth** (*informal*) to prevent sb from doing sth that they have planned or want to do; to prevent sth from happening **SYN** **foil**

**Styro·foam™** /ˈstaɪrəfəʊm/ *noun* (*especially NAmE*) = POLYSTYRENE: *Styrofoam cups*

**suave** /swɑːv/ *adj.* (*especially of a man*) confident, attractive and polite, sometimes in a way that does not seem sincere ▶ **suave·ly** *adv.*

**sub** /sʌb/ *noun, verb*
- *noun* (*informal*) **1** = SUBMARINE **2** a SUBSTITUTE who replaces another player in a team: *He came on as sub.* **3** (*BrE*) a SUBSCRIPTION (= money that you pay regularly when you are a member of a club, etc.) **4** (*BrE*) a SUBEDITOR **5** (*NAmE*) a SUBSTITUTE TEACHER
- *verb* **1** [T] ~ **sb** to replace a sports player with another player during a game **SYN** **substitute**: *He was subbed after just five minutes because of a knee injury.* **2** [I] ~ (**for sb**) to do sb else's job for them for a short time **SYN** **substitute 3** [T] ~ **sth for sth** to use sth instead of sth else, especially instead of the thing you would normally use **SYN** **substitute**: *For a lower-calorie version of the recipe, try subbing milk for cream.* **4** [T] ~ **sb sth** (*BrE, informal*) to lend sb money for a short time: *Could you sub me £50 till next week?*

**sub-** /sʌb/ *prefix* **1** (in nouns and adjectives) below; less than: *sub-zero temperatures ◇ a subtropical* (= almost tropical) *climate ◇ substandard* **2** (in nouns and adjectives) under: *subway ◇ submarine* **3** (in verbs and nouns) a smaller part of sth: *subdivide ◇ subset*

**sub·al·tern** /ˈsʌbltən; *NAmE* səˈbɔːltərn/ *noun* any officer in the British army who is lower in rank than a captain

**sub·atom·ic** /ˌsʌbəˈtɒmɪk; *NAmE* -ˈtɑːm-/ *adj.* [usually before noun] (*physics*) smaller than, or found in, an ATOM

**ˌsubatomic ˈparticle** *noun* (*physics*) a very small piece of MATTER, such as an ELECTRON or a PROTON, that is smaller than an ATOM ⊃ compare ELEMENTARY PARTICLE

**sub·clause** /ˈsʌbklɔːz/ *noun* (*law*) one of the parts of a clause (= section) in a legal document

**sub·com·mit·tee** /ˈsʌbkəmɪti/ *noun* [C + sing./pl. v.] a smaller committee formed from a main committee in order to study a particular subject in more detail

**sub·com·pact** /ˌsʌbˈkɒmpækt; *NAmE* -ˈkɑːm-/ *noun* (*NAmE*) a small car, smaller than a COMPACT

**sub·con·scious** /ˌsʌbˈkɒnʃəs; *NAmE* -ˈkɑːn-/ *adj., noun*
- *adj.* [usually before noun] connected with feelings that influence your behaviour even though you are not aware of them: *subconscious desires ◇ the subconscious mind* ⊃ compare CONSCIOUS, UNCONSCIOUS ▶ **sub·con·scious·ly** *adv.*: *Subconsciously, she was looking for the father she had never known.*
- *noun* **the/your subconscious** [sing.] the part of your mind that contains feelings that you are not aware of ⊃ compare UNCONSCIOUS

**sub·con·tin·ent** /ˌsʌbˈkɒntɪnənt; *NAmE* -ˈkɑːn-/ *noun* [usually sing.] a large land mass that forms part of a continent, especially the part of Asia that includes India, Pakistan and Bangladesh: *the Indian subcontinent*

**sub·con·tract** *verb, noun*
- *verb* /ˌsʌbkənˈtrækt; *NAmE* ˌsʌbˈkɑːntrækt/ to pay a person or company to do some of the work that you have been given a contract to do: ~ **sth (to sb/sth)** *We subcontracted the work to a small engineering firm.* ◇ ~ **sb/sth (to do sth)** *We subcontracted a small engineering firm to do the work.* ▶ **sub·con·tract·ing** *noun* [U]
- *noun* /ˌsʌbˈkɒntrækt; *NAmE* -ˈkɑːn-/ a contract to do part of the work that has been given to another person or company

**sub·con·tract·or** /ˌsʌbkənˈtræktə(r); *NAmE* ˌsʌbˈkɑːntræktər/ *noun* a person or company that does part of the work given to another person or company

**sub·cul·ture** /ˈsʌbkʌltʃə(r)/ *noun* (*sometimes disapproving*) the behaviour and beliefs of a particular group of people in society that are different from those of most people: *the criminal/drug/youth subculture*

**sub·cu·ta·ne·ous** /ˌsʌbkjuˈteɪniəs/ *adj.* [usually before noun] (*specialist*) under the skin: *a subcutaneous injection* ▶ **sub·cu·ta·ne·ous·ly** *adv.*

**sub·dir·ec·tory** /ˈsʌbdərektəri, -daɪr-/ *noun* (*pl.* **-ies**) (*computing*) a DIRECTORY (= list of files or programs) which is inside another directory

**sub·div·ide** /ˌsʌbdɪˈvaɪd, ˌsʌbdɪˈvaɪd/ *verb* [T, often passive, I] ~ (**sth**) (**into sth**) to divide sth into smaller parts; to be divided into smaller parts

**sub·div·ision** *noun* **1** /ˌsʌbdɪˈvɪʒn/ [U] the act of dividing a part of sth into smaller parts **2** [C] one of the smaller parts into which a part of sth has been divided: *a police subdivision* (= the area covered by one particular police force) ◇ *subdivisions within the Hindu caste system* **3** /ˈsʌbdɪvɪʒn/ [C] (*NAmE*) an area of land that has been divided up for building houses on

**sub·due** /səbˈdjuː; *NAmE* -ˈduː/ *verb* (*rather formal*) **1** ~ **sb/sth** to bring sb/sth under control, especially by using force **SYN** **defeat**: *Troops were called in to subdue the rebels.* **2** ~ **sth** to calm or control your feelings **SYN** **suppress**: *Julia had to subdue an urge to stroke his hair.*

**sub·dued** /səbˈdjuːd; *NAmE* -ˈduːd/ *adj.* **1** (of a person) unusually quiet, and possibly unhappy: *He seemed a bit subdued to me. ◇ She was in a subdued mood. ◇ The reception was a subdued affair.* **2** (of light or colours) not very bright: *subdued lighting* **3** (of sounds) not very loud: *a subdued conversation* **4** (of business activity) not very busy; with not much activity: *a period of subdued trading*

**sub·editor** /ˈsʌbedɪtə(r)/ (*also informal* **sub**) *noun* (*BrE*) a person whose job is to check and make changes to the text of a newspaper or magazine before it is printed ▶ **sub·edit** *verb* [I, T] ~ (**sth**)

**sub·group** /ˈsʌbɡruːp/ *noun* a smaller group made up of members of a larger group

**sub·head·ing** /ˈsʌbhedɪŋ/ *noun* a title given to any of the sections into which a longer piece of writing has been divided

**sub·human** /ˌsʌbˈhjuːmən/ *adj.* (*disapproving*) **1** (of a person or their behaviour) so cruel or bad that they do not deserve to be called human: *subhuman behaviour* ⊃ compare INHUMAN, SUPERHUMAN **2** not fit for humans: *They were living in subhuman conditions.*

## sub·ject ⓘ A1 ○ *noun, adj., verb*

■ *noun* /ˈsʌbdʒɪkt, -dʒekt/
- OF CONVERSATION/BOOK **1** A1 a thing or person that is being discussed, described or dealt with: *~ of sth Walker's work has been the subject of much debate.* ◊ *a subject of discussion/conversation* ◊ *Nelson Mandela is the subject of a new biography.* ◊ **on a/the~** *books on many different subjects* ◊ *I have nothing more to say on the subject.* ◊ **on the ~ of sth** *a magazine article on the subject of space travel* ◊ *How did we get onto the subject of marriage?* ◊ *I wish you'd change the subject* (= talk about sth else). ◊ *The university runs a wide range of research programmes in different subject areas.*
- AT SCHOOL/COLLEGE **2** A1 an area of knowledge studied in a school, college, etc: *Biology is my favourite subject.* ◊ *The college offers a wide range of subjects.*
- OF PICTURE/PHOTOGRAPH **3** a person or thing that is the main feature of a picture or photograph, or that a work of art is based on: *Focus the camera on the subject.* ◊ *Classical landscapes were a popular subject with many 18th century painters.*
- OF EXPERIMENT **4** a person or thing being used to study sth, especially in an experiment: *We need male subjects between the ages of 18 and 25 for the experiment.*
- GRAMMAR **5** a noun, noun phrase or pronoun representing the person or thing that performs the action of the verb (*I* in *I sat down*.), about which sth is stated (*the house in the house is very old*) or, in a passive sentence, that is affected by the action of the verb (*the tree in the tree was blown down in the storm*) ⊃ compare OBJECT, PREDICATE ⊃ WORDFINDER NOTE at GRAMMAR
- OF COUNTRY **6** a person who belongs to a particular country, especially one with a king or queen: *a British subject* ⊃ compare CITIZEN (1)

■ *adj.* /ˈsʌbdʒɪkt, -dʒekt/ (*formal*) **1** B2 ~ **to sth** likely to be affected by sth, especially sth bad: *At this stage these are proposals and are still subject to change.* **2** B2 ~ **to sth** depending on sth in order to be completed or agreed: *The article is ready to publish, subject to your approval.* ◊ *The offer is subject to certain conditions.* **3** B2 ~ **to sth/sb** under the authority of sth/sb: *As a diplomat, he is not subject to local laws.* **4** [only before noun] controlled by the government of another country: *subject peoples*

■ *verb* /səbˈdʒekt/ ~ **sth (to sth)** (*formal*) to bring a country or group of people under your control, especially by using force: *The Roman Empire subjected most of Europe to its rule.* ▶ **sub·jec·tion** /-ˈdʒekʃn/ *noun* [U]

**PHRV** **sub·ject sb/sth to sth** [often passive] to make sb/sth experience, suffer or be affected by sth, usually sth unpleasant: *to be subjected to ridicule* ◊ *The city was subjected to heavy bombing.* ◊ *The defence lawyers claimed that the prisoners had been subjected to cruel and degrading treatment.*

**sub·ject·ive** Ⓦ /səbˈdʒektɪv/ *adj.* **1** based on your own ideas or opinions rather than facts and therefore sometimes unfair: *a highly subjective point of view* ◊ *Everyone's opinion is bound to be subjective.* OPP objective **2** (of ideas, feelings or experiences) existing in sb's mind rather than in the outside world OPP objective **3** [only before noun] (*grammar*) the **subjective** case is the one which is used for the subject of a sentence ▶ **sub·ject·ive·ly** *adv.*: *People who are less subjectively involved are better judges.* ◊ *subjectively perceived changes* **sub·ject·iv·ity** /ˌsʌbdʒekˈtɪvəti/ *noun* [U]: *There is an element of subjectivity in her criticism.*

**sub·ject·iv·ism** /səbˈdʒektɪvɪzəm/ *noun* [U] (*philosophy*) the theory that all knowledge and moral values are subjective rather than based on truth that actually exists in the real world

ˈ**subject line** *noun* the line of text at the start of an email that says what it is about; the space where this is written: *Please include your customer reference number in the subject line of the email.*

ˈ**subject matter** *noun* [U] the ideas or information contained in a book, speech, painting, etc: *The artist was revo-*lutionary in both subject matter and technique.* ◊ *She's searching for subject matter for her new book.*

**sub ˈju·dice** /ˌsʌb ˈdʒuːdəsi; *NAmE also* ˈjuːdəkeɪ/ *adj.* [not usually before noun] (*from Latin, law*) if a legal case is **sub judice**, it is still being discussed in court and it is therefore illegal for anyone to talk about it in newspapers, etc.

**sub·ju·gate** /ˈsʌbdʒugeɪt/ *verb* [usually passive] (*formal*) to defeat sb/sth; to gain control over sb/sth: **be subjugated (to sth)** *Her personal ambitions had been subjugated to* (= considered less important than) *the needs of her family.* ◊ *a subjugated race* ▶ **sub·ju·ga·tion** /ˌsʌbdʒuˈɡeɪʃn/ *noun* [U] (*formal*): *the subjugation of Ireland by England*

**sub·junct·ive** /səbˈdʒʌŋktɪv/ *noun* (*grammar*) the form (or MOOD) of a verb that expresses wishes, possibility or UNCERTAINTY; a verb in this form: *The verb is in the subjunctive.* ◊ *In 'I wish I were taller', 'were' is a subjunctive.* ▶ **sub·junct·ive** *adj.*: *the subjunctive mood*

**sub·let** /ˌsʌbˈlet/ (*also* **sub-lease** /ˌsʌbˈliːs/; *especially in NAmE*) *verb* [T, I] (**sub·let·ting**, **sub·let**, **sub·let**) ~ **(sth) (to sb)** to rent to sb else all or part of a property that you rent from the owner

**sub·lim·ate** /ˈsʌblɪmeɪt/ *verb* ~ **sth** (*psychology*) to direct your energy, especially sexual energy, to socially acceptable activities such as work, exercise, art, etc. SYN channel ▶ **sub·lim·ation** /ˌsʌblɪˈmeɪʃn/ *noun* [U]

**sub·lime** /səˈblaɪm/ *adj., noun*

■ *adj.* **1** of very high quality or great beauty: *sublime beauty* ◊ *a sublime combination of flavours* **2** (*formal, often disapproving*) (of a person's behaviour or attitudes) extreme, especially in a way that shows they are not aware of what they are doing or are not concerned about what happens because of it: *the sublime confidence of youth* ▶ **sub·lime·ly** *adv.*: *sublimely beautiful* ◊ *She was sublimely unaware of the trouble she had caused.* **sub·lim·ity** /-ˈblɪməti/ *noun* [U]

■ *noun* **the sublime** [sing.] something that is sublime: *He transforms the most ordinary subject into the sublime.*

**IDM** **from the sublime to the ri'diculous** used to describe a situation in which sth serious, important or of high quality is followed by sth silly, unimportant or of poor quality

**sub·lim·inal** /ˌsʌbˈlɪmɪnl/ *adj.* affecting your mind even though you are not aware of it: *subliminal advertising* ▶ **sub·lim·in·al·ly** /-nəli/ *adv.*

**sub·list** /ˈsʌblɪst/ *noun* a list that includes some of the items from a longer list: *The list is made up of five sublists, each containing 200 items.*

ˌ**sub·ma'chine gun** *noun* a light MACHINE GUN that you can hold in your hands to fire

**sub·mar·ine** /ˌsʌbməˈriːn; ˈsʌbməriːn/ *noun, adj.*

■ *noun* (*also informal* **sub**) **1** a ship that can travel UNDERWATER: *a nuclear submarine* ◊ *a submarine base* ⊃ WORDFINDER NOTE at NAVY **2** (*also* **submarine ˈsandwich, hero**) (*all NAmE*) a long bread roll split open along its length and filled with various types of food

■ *adj.* [only before noun] (*specialist*) existing or located under the sea: *submarine plant life* ◊ *submarine cables*

**sub·mar·in·er** /ˌsʌbˈmærɪnə(r); *NAmE also* ˌsʌbməˈriːnər/ *noun* a sailor who works on a submarine

**sub·merge** /səbˈmɜːdʒ; *NAmE* -ˈmɜːrdʒ/ *verb* **1** [I, T] to go under the surface of water or liquid; to put sth or make sth go under the surface of water or liquid: *The submarine had had time to submerge before the warship could approach.* ◊ **be submerged (by sth)** *The fields had been submerged by floodwater.* ◊ *Her submerged car was discovered in the river by police divers.* **2** [T] ~ **sth** to hide ideas, feelings, opinions, etc. completely: *Doubts that had been submerged in her mind suddenly resurfaced.* ▶ **sub·mer·sion** /səbˈmɜːʃn; *NAmE* -ˈmɜːrʒn/ *noun* [U]

**sub·mers·ible** /səbˈmɜːsəbl; *NAmE* -ˈmɜːrs-/ *adj., noun*

■ *adj.* (*NAmE also* **sub·merg·ible** /səbˈmɜːdʒəbl; *NAmE* -ˈmɜːrdʒ-/) that can be used UNDERWATER: *a submersible camera*

■ *noun* a SUBMARINE (= a ship that can travel UNDERWATER) that goes UNDERWATER for short periods

# submission

**sub·mis·sion** /səbˈmɪʃn/ noun **1** [U] the act of accepting that sb has defeated you and that you must obey them SYN **surrender**: *a gesture of submission* ◊ *to beat/force/starve sb into submission* **2** [U, C] the act of giving a document, proposal, etc. to sb in authority so that they can study or consider it; the document, etc. that you give: *When is the final date for the submission of proposals?* ◊ *~ to sb/sth They prepared a report for submission to the council.* ◊ *The deadline is 1 October and late submissions will not be marked.* **3** [C] (*law*) a statement that is made to a judge in court: *All parties will have the opportunity to make submissions relating to this case.*

**sub·mis·sive** /səbˈmɪsɪv/ adj. too willing to accept sb else's authority and willing to obey them without questioning anything they want you to do: *He expected his daughters to be meek and submissive.* ◊ *She followed him like a submissive child.* OPP **assertive** ▸ **sub·mis·sive·ly** adv.: *'You're right and I was wrong,' he said submissively.* **sub·mis·sive·ness** noun [U]

**sub·mit** /səbˈmɪt/ verb (-tt-) **1** [T] to give a document, proposal, etc. to sb in authority so that they can study or consider it: *~ sth to submit an application/a claim/a proposal* ◊ *sth to sb/sth She submitted her report to the committee.* ⊃ WORDFINDER NOTE at COMPETITION **2** [I, T] (*formal*) to accept the authority, control or greater strength of sb/sth; to agree to sth because of this SYN **give in (to sb/sth)**, **yield**: *~ to sb/sth She refused to submit to threats.* ◊ *~ yourself to sb/sth He submitted himself to a search by the guards.* **3** [T] *~ that* … (*law* or *formal*) to say or suggest sth: *Counsel for the defence submitted that the evidence was inadmissible.*

**sub·nor·mal** /ˌsʌbˈnɔːml; NAmE -ˈnɔːrml/ adj. **1** (*specialist*) lower than normal: *subnormal temperatures* **2** (*sometimes offensive*) having less than the normal level of intelligence: *educationally subnormal children*

**sub·opti·mal** /ˌsʌbˈɒptɪməl; NAmE -ˈɑːp-/ adj. of less than the best standard or quality: *Some breeders keep their animals in suboptimal conditions.* ◊ *A score of 6 is optimal; 5 or less is suboptimal.* ⊃ compare OPTIMAL ▸ **sub·opti·mal·ly** adv.

**sub·or·din·ate** adj., noun, verb
■ adj. /səˈbɔːdɪnət; NAmE -ˈbɔːrd-/ **1** *~ (to sb)* having less power or authority than sb else in a group or an organization: *In some societies women are still subordinate to men.* **2** *~ (to sth)* less important than sth else SYN **secondary**: *All other issues are subordinate to this one.*
■ noun /səˈbɔːdɪnət; NAmE -ˈbɔːrd-/ a person who has a position with less authority and power than sb else in an organization SYN **inferior**: *the relationship between subordinates and superiors*
■ verb /səˈbɔːdɪneɪt; NAmE -ˈbɔːrd-/ [often passive] (*formal*) to treat sb/sth as less important than sb/sth else: **be subordinated (to sb/sth)** *Safety considerations were subordinated to commercial interests.* ▸ **sub·or·din·ation** /səˌbɔːdɪˈneɪʃn; NAmE -ˌbɔːrd-/ noun [U]

**su·bordinate ˈclause** (also **deˌpendent ˈclause**) noun (*grammar*) a group of words that is not a sentence but adds information to the main part of a sentence, for example *when it rang* in *She answered the phone when it rang.* ⊃ compare COORDINATE CLAUSE, MAIN CLAUSE

**suˌbordinating conˈjunction** noun (*grammar*) a word that begins a subordinate clause, for example 'although' or 'because' ⊃ compare COORDINATING CONJUNCTION

**sub·orn** /səˈbɔːn; NAmE -ˈbɔːrn/ verb *~ sb* (*law*) to pay or persuade sb to do sth illegal, especially to tell lies in court: *to suborn a witness*

**sub·par** /ˌsʌbˈpɑː(r)/ adj. (especially NAmE) below a level of quality that is usual or expected: *a subpar performance*

**sub·plot** /ˈsʌbplɒt; NAmE -plɑːt/ noun a series of events in a play, novel, etc. that is separate from but linked to the main story

**sub·poena** /səˈpiːnə/ noun, verb
■ noun (*law*) a written order to attend court as a witness to give evidence
■ verb *~ sb (to do sth)* (*law*) to order sb to attend court and give evidence as a witness: *The court subpoenaed her to appear as a witness.*

**ˌsub-ˈpost office** noun (*BrE*) a small local post office

**ˌsub-ˈprime** (*BrE*) (*NAmE* **subprime**) adj. (*finance*) connected with the practice of lending money to sb who is likely to have difficulty paying it back: *a sub-prime loan/mortgage* ◊ *subprime lenders/borrowers*

**sub·rou·tine** /ˈsʌbruːtiːn/ (also **sub·pro·gram** /ˈsʌbprəʊɡræm/) noun (*computing*) a set of instructions which perform a task within a program

**sub-Saharan** /ˌsʌb səˈhɑːrən/ adj. [only before noun] from or relating to areas in Africa that are south of the Sahara Desert: *sub-Saharan Africa*

**sub·scribe** /səbˈskraɪb/ verb **1** [I] *~ (to sth)* to pay an amount of money regularly in order to receive or use sth: *Which journals does the library subscribe to?* ◊ *We subscribe to several sports channels* (= on TV). **2** [I] *~ (to sth)* to arrange to have regular access to an electronic information service or other internet service: *He subscribed to a newsgroup* (= on the internet). ◊ *To hear the full interview, subscribe to the free National Geographic News podcast.* **3** [I] *~ (to sth)* to pay money regularly to be a member of an organization or to support a charity: *He subscribes regularly to Amnesty International.* **4** [I] *~ (for sth)* (*finance*) to apply to buy shares in a company ⊃ see also OVERSUBSCRIBED **5** [T, usually passive] *~ sth* to apply to take part in an activity, use a service, etc: *The tour of Edinburgh is fully subscribed.*
PHRV **subˈscribe to sth** (*formal*) to agree with or support an opinion, a theory, etc. SYN **believe in sth**: *The authorities no longer subscribe to the view that disabled people are unsuitable as teachers.*

**sub·scriber** /səbˈskraɪbə(r)/ noun **1** a person who pays money, usually once a year, to receive regular copies of a magazine or newspaper or have access to it online: *subscribers to 'New Scientist'* **2** a person who pays to receive a service: *subscribers to cable television* **3** a person who gives money regularly to help the work of an organization such as a charity: *subscribers to Oxfam*

**sub·script** /ˈsʌbskrɪpt/ noun **1** a letter, number or symbol that is written or printed below the normal line of writing or printing: *A subscript is used for secondary stress.* ◊ *The subscript 'B' designates 'Brown'.* ⊃ compare SUPERSCRIPT **2** (*computing*) a symbol, sometimes written as a subscript, used in a computer program to identify one part of an ARRAY ▸ **sub·script** adj. [only before noun]

**sub·scrip·tion** /səbˈskrɪpʃn/ noun [C, U] **1** an amount of money that you pay regularly to receive a service, be a member of a club, support a charity or receive regular copies of a newspaper or magazine; the act of paying this money: *an annual subscription* ◊ *~ to/for sth a subscription to Netflix* ◊ *a monthly subscription to Oxfam* ◊ *to take out a subscription to 'Newsweek'* ◊ *to cancel/renew a subscription* ◊ *by ~ Copies are available by subscription.* ⊃ WORDFINDER NOTE at CLUB **2** the act of people paying money for sth to be done: *A statue in his memory was erected by public subscription.* ⊃ SYNONYMS at PAYMENT

**sub·sec·tion** /ˈsʌbsekʃn/ noun a part of a section, especially of a legal document ⊃ WORDFINDER NOTE at DOCUMENT

**sub·se·quent** /ˈsʌbsɪkwənt/ adj. [only before noun] (*formal*) happening or coming after sth else: *subsequent generations* ◊ *Subsequent events confirmed our doubts.* ◊ *Developments on this issue will be dealt with in a subsequent report.* OPP **previous**

**sub·se·quent·ly** /ˈsʌbsɪkwəntli/ adv. (*formal*) afterwards; later; after sth else has happened: *The original interview notes were subsequently lost.* ◊ *Subsequently, new guidelines were issued to all employees.*

**ˈsubsequent to** prep. (*formal*) after; following: *There have been further developments subsequent to our meeting.*

**sub·ser·vi·ent** /səbˈsɜːviənt; NAmE -ˈsɜːrv-/ adj. **1** *~ (to sb/sth)* (*disapproving*) too willing to obey other people: *The press was accused of being subservient to the* government. ◇ *Women were expected to take subservient roles.* **2** ~ **(to sth)** (*formal*) less important than sth else: *The needs of individuals were subservient to those of the group as a whole.* ▶ **sub·ser·vi·ence** /-əns/ *noun* [U]

**sub·set** /ˈsʌbset/ *noun* (*specialist*) a smaller group of people or things formed from the members of a larger group

**sub·side** /səbˈsaɪd/ *verb* **1** [I] to become calmer, quieter or less intense: *She waited nervously for his anger to subside.* ◇ *I took an aspirin and the pain gradually subsided.* **2** [I] (of water) to go back to a normal level: *The flood waters gradually subsided.* **3** [I] (of land or a building) to sink to a lower level; to sink lower into the ground: *Weak foundations caused the house to subside.*

**sub·sid·ence** /səbˈsaɪdns, ˈsʌbsɪdns/ *noun* [U] the process by which an area of land sinks to a lower level than normal, or by which a building sinks into the ground

**sub·sidi·ar·ity** /səbˌsɪdiˈærəti, ˌsʌbsɪ-/ *noun* [U] the principle that a central authority should not be very powerful, and should only control things which cannot be controlled by local organizations

**sub·sid·iary** /səbˈsɪdiəri; *NAmE* -dieri/ *adj., noun*
■ *adj.* **1** ~ **(to sth)** connected with sth but less important than it **SYN** **additional**: *subsidiary information* ◇ *a subsidiary matter* ◇ (*BrE*) *I'm taking history as a subsidiary subject* (= one that is not studied in as great depth as a main subject). **2** (of a business company) owned or controlled by another company
■ *noun* (*pl.* **-ies**) a business company that is owned or controlled by another larger company

**sub·sid·ize** (*BrE also* **-ise**) /ˈsʌbsɪdaɪz/ *verb* ~ **sb/sth** to give money to sb or an organization to help pay for sth; to give a subsidy **SYN** **fund**: *The housing projects are subsidized by the government.* ◇ *She's not prepared to subsidize his gambling any longer.* ▶ **sub·sid·iz·ation, -isa·tion** /ˌsʌbsɪdaɪˈzeɪʃn; *NAmE* -dəˈz-/ *noun* [U]

**sub·sidy** /ˈsʌbsədi/ *noun* [C, U] (*pl.* **-ies**) money that is paid by a government or an organization to reduce the costs of services or of producing goods so that their prices can be kept low: *agricultural subsidies* ◇ *to reduce the level of subsidy*

**sub·sist** /səbˈsɪst/ *verb* [I] ~ **(on sth)** to manage to stay alive, especially with limited food or money: *Old people often subsist on very small incomes.*

**sub·sist·ence** /səbˈsɪstəns/ *noun* [U] the state of having just enough money or food to stay alive: *Many families are living below the level of subsistence.* ◇ *to live below (the) subsistence level* ◇ *They had no visible means of subsistence.* ◇ *subsistence agriculture/farming* (= growing enough only to live on, not to sell) ◇ *subsistence crops* ◇ *He worked a 16-hour day for a subsistence wage* (= enough money to buy only basic items).

**sub·soil** /ˈsʌbsɔɪl/ *noun* [U] the layer of soil between the surface of the ground and the hard rock below it ⇒ compare **TOPSOIL**

**sub·son·ic** /ˌsʌbˈsɒnɪk; *NAmE* -ˈsɑːn-/ *adj.* less than the speed of sound; flying at less than the speed of sound ⇒ compare **SUPERSONIC**

**sub·spe·cies** /ˈsʌbspiːʃiːz/ *noun* (*pl.* **sub·spe·cies**) a group into which animals, plants, etc. that have similar characteristics are divided, smaller than a species

**sub·stance** /ˈsʌbstəns/ *noun* **1** [C] a type of solid, liquid or gas that has particular qualities: *a sticky substance* ◇ *a chemical/radioactive/hazardous substance* ◇ *Some frogs produce toxic substances in their skin.* **2** [C] a drug, especially an illegal one: *banned/illegal/controlled substances* ◇ *substance use* **3** [U] the quality of being based on facts or the truth: *The commission's report gives substance to these allegations.* ◇ *There is some substance in what he says.* ◇ *without* ~ *It was malicious gossip, completely without substance.* **4** [U] the most important or main part of sth: *the* ~ *of sth Love and guilt form the substance of his new book.* ◇ *in* ~ *I agreed with what she said in substance, though not with every detail.* **5** [U] (*formal*) importance **SYN** **significance**: *of* ~ *matters of substance* ◇ *Nothing of any substance was achieved in the meeting.*

1563 **substructure**

**IDM** **a man/woman of ˈsubstance** (*formal*) a rich and powerful man or woman

**ˈsubstance abuse** *noun* [U] the habit of taking too much of a harmful drug or drinking too much alcohol: *a treatment centre for substance abuse*

**sub·stand·ard** /ˌsʌbˈstændəd; *NAmE* -dərd/ *adj.* not as good as normal; not acceptable **SYN** **inferior**: *substandard goods*

**sub·stan·tial** /səbˈstænʃl/ *adj.* **1** large in amount, value or importance **SYN** **considerable**: *substantial sums of money* ◇ *a substantial change* ◇ *Substantial numbers of people support the reforms.* ◇ *He ate a substantial breakfast.* **2** [usually before noun] (*formal*) large and solid; strongly built: *a substantial house*

**sub·stan·tial·ly** /səbˈstænʃəli/ *adv.* **1** very much; a lot **SYN** **considerably**: *The costs have increased substantially.* ◇ *The plane was substantially damaged in the crash.* **2** (*formal*) mainly; in most details, even if not completely: *What she says is substantially true.*

**sub·stan·ti·ate** /səbˈstænʃieɪt/ *verb* ~ **sth** (*formal*) to provide information or evidence to prove that sth is true: *The results of the tests substantiated his claims.* ▶ **sub·stan·ti·ation** /səbˌstænʃiˈeɪʃn/ *noun* [U]

**sub·stan·tive** /səbˈstæntɪv, ˈsʌbstəntɪv; *NAmE* ˈsʌbstəntɪv/ *adj., noun*
■ *adj.* (*formal*) dealing with real, important or serious matters: *substantive issues* ◇ *The report concluded that no substantive changes were necessary.*
■ *noun* (*old-fashioned, grammar*) a noun

**sub·sta·tion** /ˈsʌbsteɪʃn/ *noun* a place where the strength of electric power from a **POWER STATION** is reduced before it is passed on to homes and businesses

**sub·sti·tute** /ˈsʌbstɪtjuːt; *NAmE* -tuːt/ *noun, verb*
■ *noun* **1** a person or thing that you use or have instead of the one you normally use or have: *a meat substitute* ◇ *a substitute family* ◇ ~ **for sb/sth** *Paul's father only saw him as a substitute for his dead brother.* ◇ *The course teaches you the theory but there's no substitute for practical experience.* ◇ *The local bus service was a poor substitute for their car.* **2** (*also informal* **sub**) a player who replaces another player in a sports game: *He was brought on as (a) substitute after half-time.*
■ *verb* [I, T] to take the place of sb/sth else; to use sb/sth instead of sb/sth else: ~ **for sb/sth** *Nothing can substitute for the advice your doctor is able to give you.* ◇ ~ **A for B** *Margarine can be substituted for butter in this recipe.* ◇ ~ **B with/by A** *Butter can be substituted with margarine in this recipe.* ◇ ~ **sb/sth** *Kane was substituted in the second half after a knee injury* (= sb else played instead of Kane in the second half). **HELP** When **for**, **with** or **by** are not used, as in the last example, it can be difficult to tell whether the person or thing mentioned is being used, or has been replaced by somebody or something else. The context will usually make this clear.

**ˌsubstitute ˈteacher** (*also informal* **sub**) (*both NAmE*) (*BrE* **ˈsupply teacher**) *noun* a teacher employed to do the work of another teacher who is absent because of illness, etc.

**sub·sti·tu·tion** /ˌsʌbstɪˈtjuːʃn; *NAmE* -ˈtuː-/ *noun* [U, C] an act of using one person or thing in the place of another: *Two substitutions were made during the game.* ◇ ~ **of A for B** *the substitution of low-fat spreads for butter* ◇ ~ **of B with A** *the substitution of butter with low-fat spreads*

**sub·strate** /ˈsʌbstreɪt/ *noun* (*specialist*) a substance or layer which is under sth or on which sth happens, for example the surface on which a living thing grows and feeds

**sub·stra·tum** /ˈsʌbstrɑːtəm; *NAmE* -streɪt-/ *noun* (*pl.* **sub·strata** /ˈsʌbstrɑːtə; *NAmE* -streɪtə/) (*specialist*) a layer of sth, especially rock or soil, that is below another layer

**sub·struc·ture** /ˈsʌbstrʌktʃə(r)/ *noun* a base or structure that is below another structure and that supports it: *a substructure of timber piles* ◇ (*figurative*) *the substructure of national culture* ⇒ compare **SUPERSTRUCTURE**

**sub·sume** /səbˈsjuːm; *NAmE* -ˈsuːm/ *verb* [often passive] (*formal*) to include sth in a particular group and not consider it separately: *be subsumed* (+ *adv./prep.*) *All these different ideas can be subsumed under just two broad categories.*

**sub·tend** /səbˈtend/ *verb* ~ **sth** (*geometry*) (of a line or CHORD) to be opposite to an ARC or angle

**sub·ter·fuge** /ˈsʌbtəfjuːdʒ; *NAmE* -tərf-/ *noun* [U, C] (*formal*) a secret, usually dishonest, way of behaving

**sub·ter·ra·nean** /ˌsʌbtəˈreɪniən/ *adj.* [usually before noun] (*formal*) under the ground: *a subterranean cave*

**sub·text** /ˈsʌbtekst/ *noun* a hidden meaning or theme in a piece of writing or conversation

**sub·title** /ˈsʌbtaɪtl/ *noun, verb*
- *noun* **1** [usually pl.] words that translate what is said in a film into a different language and appear on the screen at the bottom. Subtitles are also used, especially on television, to help DEAF people (= people who cannot hear well): *a Polish film with English subtitles* ◇ *Is the movie dubbed or are there subtitles?* ⊃ compare SURTITLES **2** a second title of a book that appears after the main title and gives more information
- *verb* [usually passive] to give a subtitle or subtitles to a book, film, etc.: ~ **sth** *a Spanish film subtitled in English* ◇ ~ **sth + noun** *The book is subtitled 'New language for new times'.* ⊃ compare DUB

**sub·tle** ʔ+ C1 /ˈsʌtl/ *adj.* (**sub·tler** /-tələr/, **sub·tlest** /-təlɪst/) HELP **more subtle** is also common ʔ+ C1 (*often approving*) not very obvious or easy to notice: *subtle colours/flavours/smells, etc.* ◇ *There are subtle differences between the two versions.* ◇ *She's been dropping subtle hints about what she'd like as a present.* **2** ʔ+ C1 behaving or organized in a clever way, and using indirect methods, in order to achieve sth: *I decided to try a more subtle approach.* ◇ *a subtle plan* ◇ *a subtle use of lighting in the play* **3** good at noticing and understanding things: *The job required a subtle mind.* ▸ **subtly** /-təli/ *adv.*: *Her version of events is subtly different from what actually happened.* ◇ *Not very subtly, he raised the subject of money.*

**subtle·ty** /ˈsʌtlti/ *noun* (*pl.* **-ies**) **1** [U] the quality of being subtle: *It's a thrilling movie even though it lacks subtlety.* **2** [C, usually pl.] the small but important details or aspects of sth: *the subtleties of language*

**sub·total** /ˈsʌbtəʊtl/ *noun* the total of a set of numbers which is then added to other totals to give a final number

**sub·tract** /səbˈtrækt/ *verb* [T, I] ~ **(sth) (from sth)** to take a number or an amount away from another number or amount SYN TAKE: *6 subtracted from 9 is 3* OPP ADD ▸ **sub·trac·tion** /-ˈtrækʃn/ *noun* [U, C] ⊃ compare ADDITION

**sub·trop·ic·al** /ˌsʌbˈtrɒpɪkl; *NAmE* -ˈtrɑːp-/ (*also* ˌsemi-ˈtropical) *adj.* in or connected with regions that are near tropical parts of the world

**sub·urb** ʔ+ B2 /ˈsʌbɜːb; *NAmE* -ɜːrb/ *noun* (*also NAmE, informal* **the burbs**) an area where people live that is outside the centre of a city: *a suburb of London* ◇ *a London suburb* ◇ **in the suburbs** *They live in the suburbs.* ⊃ WORDFINDER NOTE at CITY

**sub·ur·ban** ʔ+ C1 /səˈbɜːbən; *NAmE* -ˈbɜːrb-/ *adj.* **1** ʔ+ C1 [usually before noun] in or connected with a suburb: *suburban areas* ◇ *a suburban street* ◇ *life in suburban London* ⊃ WORDFINDER NOTE at LOCATION **2** (*disapproving*) boring and ordinary: *a suburban lifestyle*

**sub·ur·ban·ite** /səˈbɜːbənaɪt; *NAmE* -ˈbɜːrb-/ *noun* (*often disapproving*) a person who lives in the SUBURBS of a city

**sub·ur·bia** /səˈbɜːbiə; *NAmE* -ˈbɜːrb-/ *noun* [U] (*often disapproving*) the SUBURBS and the way of life, attitudes, etc. of the people who live there

**sub·ven·tion** /səbˈvenʃn/ *noun* (*formal*) an amount of money that is given by a government, etc. to help an organization

**sub·ver·sive** /səbˈvɜːsɪv; *NAmE* -ˈvɜːrs-/ *adj.* trying or likely to destroy or damage a government or political system by attacking it secretly or indirectly SYN SEDITIOUS ▸ **sub-**

**ver·sive** *noun*: *He was a known political subversive.* **sub·ver·sive·ly** *adv.* **sub·ver·sive·ness** *noun* [U]

**sub·vert** /səbˈvɜːt; *NAmE* -ˈvɜːrt/ *verb* (*formal*) **1** [T, I] ~ **(sth)** to try to destroy the authority of a political, religious, etc. system by attacking it secretly or indirectly SYN UNDERMINE **2** [T] ~ **sth** to challenge sb's ideas or expectations and make them consider the opposite SYN UNDERMINE ▸ **sub·ver·sion** /səbˈvɜːʃn; *NAmE* -ˈvɜːrʒn/ *noun* [U]

**sub·way** /ˈsʌbweɪ/ *noun* **1** (*NAmE*) an underground railway system in a city: *the New York subway* ◇ *a subway station/train* ◇ *a downtown subway stop* ◇ *to ride/take the subway* ⊃ note at UNDERGROUND **2** (*BrE*) a path that goes under a road, etc. which people can use to cross to the other side SYN UNDERPASS

**sub·woof·er** /ˈsʌbwʊfə(r), -wuːf-; *NAmE* -wuːf-/ *noun* (*specialist*) a part of a LOUDSPEAKER that produces very low sounds

**sub-ˈzero** *adj.* [usually before noun] (of temperatures) below zero

**suc·ceed** ⓘ A2 /səkˈsiːd/ *verb* **1** ʔ+ A2 [I] to achieve sth that you have been trying to do or get; to have the result or effect that was intended: *Our plan succeeded.* ◇ ~ **in doing sth** *He succeeded in getting a place at art school.* ◇ *I tried to discuss it with her but only succeeded in making her angry* (= I failed and did the opposite of what I intended). OPP FAIL ⊃ see also SUCCESS **2** ʔ+ A2 [I] to be successful in your job, earning money, power, respect, etc: *You will have to work hard if you are to succeed.* ◇ **in sth** *She doesn't have the ruthlessness required to succeed in business.* ◇ ~ **as sth** *He had hoped to succeed as a violinist.* ⊃ see also SUCCESS **3** [T] ~ **sb/sth** to come next after sb/sth and take their/its place or position SYN FOLLOW: *Who succeeded Kennedy as President?* ◇ *Their early success was succeeded by a period of miserable failure.* ◇ *Strands of DNA are reproduced through succeeding generations.* ⊃ see also SUCCESSION **4** [I] ~ **(to sth)** to gain the right to a title, property, etc. when sb dies: *She succeeded to the throne* (= became queen) *in 1558.* ⊃ see also SUCCESSION IDM **ˌnothing succeeds like sucˈcess** (*saying*) when you are successful in one area of your life, it often leads to success in other areas

**suc·cess** ⓘ A1 /səkˈses/ *noun* **1** ʔ+ A1 [U] the fact that you have achieved sth that you want and have been trying to do or get: *to achieve/enjoy success* ◇ ~ **in doing sth** *I didn't have much success in finding a job.* ◇ **without** ~ *I tried a second time, but without success.* ◇ *Confidence is the key to success.* ◇ *Their plan will probably meet with little success.* **2** ʔ+ A2 [U] the fact of becoming rich or famous or of getting a high social position: *What's the secret of your success?* ◇ *They didn't have much success in life.* ◇ *She was surprised by the book's success* (= that it had sold a lot of copies). **3** ʔ+ A2 [C] a person or thing that has achieved a good result and been successful: *The party was a great success.* ◇ *The book proved a huge commercial success.* ◇ *He was determined to make a success of the business.* ◇ ~ **as sth** *She wasn't a success as a teacher.* OPP FAILURE IDM see ROARING, SUCCEED, SWEET *adj.*

**suc·cess·ful** ⓘ A2 W /səkˈsesfl/ *adj.* **1** ʔ+ A2 achieving your aims or what was intended: *We congratulated them on the successful completion of the project.* ◇ ~ **in (doing) sth** *He's always been highly successful in his work.* ◇ ~ **at (doing) sth** *I wasn't very successful at keeping the news secret.* **2** ʔ+ A2 having become popular and/or made a lot of money: *The play was very successful on Broadway.* ◇ *a successful actor/businessman* ◇ *She has had a long and successful career in television.* OPP UNSUCCESSFUL

**suc·cess·ful·ly** ⓘ B1 W /səkˈsesfəli/ *adv.* in a way that achieves your aims or what was intended: *She had already successfully completed these courses.* ◇ *Companies have to be able to compete successfully in international markets.*

**suc·ces·sion** ʔ+ C1 /səkˈseʃn/ *noun* **1** ʔ+ C1 [C, usually sing.] a number of people or things that follow each other in time or order SYN SERIES: *a succession of visitors* ◇ *He's been hit by a succession of injuries since he joined the*

▼ SYNONYMS

### successful
**profitable · commercial · lucrative · economic**

These words all describe sb/sth that is making or is likely to make money.

**successful** making a lot of money, especially by being popular: *The play was very successful on Broadway.* ◇ *The company has had another successful year.*

**profitable** making a profit: *a highly profitable business*

**commercial** [only before noun] making or intended to make a profit: *The movie was not a commercial success* (= made no profit).

**lucrative** (of business or work) producing or paying a large amount of money; making a large profit: *They do a lot of business in lucrative overseas markets.*

**economic** (often used in negative sentences) (of a process, business or activity) producing enough profit to continue: *Small local shops stop being economic when a supermarket opens up nearby.*

**PATTERNS**
- a successful/profitable/lucrative **business**
- a successful/profitable/lucrative **year**
- a(n) commercial/economic **success**

---

team. ◇ **in~** *She has won the award for the third year in succession.* ◇ *They had three children* **in quick succession.** ◇ *The gunman fired three times* **in rapid succession.** **2** [U] the regular pattern of one thing following another thing: *the succession of the seasons* **3** [U] the act of taking over an official position or title; the right to take over an official position or title, especially to become the king or queen of a country: **in~to sb/sth** *He became chairman in succession to Bernard Allen.* ◇ *She's third* **in order of succession to the throne.** ⊃ see also SUCCEED

**suc'cession planning** *noun* [U] (*business*) the process of training and preparing employees in a company or an organization so that there will always be sb to replace a senior manager who leaves

**suc·ces·sive** ?+ C1 /səkˈsesɪv/ *adj.* [only before noun] following immediately one after the other SYN **consecutive**: *This was their fourth successive win.* ◇ *Successive governments have tried to tackle the problem.* ▶ **suc·ces·sive·ly** *adv.*: *This concept has been applied successively to painting, architecture and sculpture.*

**suc·ces·sor** ?+ C1 /səkˈsesə(r)/ *noun* ~ **(to sb/sth)** a person or thing that comes after sb/sth else and takes their/its place: *Who's the likely successor to him as party leader?* ◇ *Their latest release is a* **worthy successor** *to their popular debut album.* ⊃ compare PREDECESSOR

**suc'cess story** *noun* a person or thing that is very successful

**suc·cinct** /səkˈsɪŋkt/ *adj.* (*approving*) expressed clearly and in a few words SYN **concise**: *Keep your answers as succinct as possible.* ◇ *a succinct explanation* ▶ **suc·cinct·ly** *adv.*: *You put that very succinctly.* **suc·cinct·ness** *noun* [U]

**suc·cour** (*US* **suc·cor**) /ˈsʌkə(r)/ *noun, verb*
- **noun** [U] (*literary*) help that you give to sb who is suffering or having problems
- **verb ~sb** (*literary*) to help sb who is suffering or having problems

**suc·cu·bus** /ˈsʌkjʊbəs/ *noun* (*pl.* **suc·cu·bi** /-baɪ/) (*literary*) a female evil spirit, supposed to have sex with a sleeping man ⊃ compare INCUBUS

**suc·cu·lent** /ˈsʌkjələnt/ *adj., noun*
- **adj. 1** (*approving*) (of fruit, vegetables and meat) containing a lot of juice and tasting good SYN **juicy**: *a succulent pear/steak* **2** (*specialist*) (of plants) having leaves and STEMS that are thick and contain a lot of water ▶ **suc·cu·lence** /-ləns/ *noun* [U]
- **noun** (*specialist*) any plant with leaves and STEMS that are thick and contain a lot of water, for example a CACTUS

**suc·cumb** /səˈkʌm/ *verb* (*formal*) **1** [I] to not be able to fight an attack, a TEMPTATION, etc: *The town succumbed after a*

---

1565 **sucker**

*short siege.* ◇ **~to sth** *He finally succumbed to Lucy's charms and agreed to her request.* **2** [I] **~(to sth)** to die from the effect of a disease or an injury: *His career was cut short when he succumbed to cancer.*

**such** ❶ A2 ⓞ /sʌtʃ/ *det., pron.* **1** ? A2 used to emphasize the great degree of sth: *This issue was of such importance that we could not afford to ignore it.* ◇ **~a/an…** *Why are you in such a hurry?* ◇ *It's such a beautiful day!* ◇ **~is sth that…** (*formal*) *Such is the elegance of this typeface that it is still a favourite of designers.* **2** ? B1 of the type already mentioned: *They had been invited to a Hindu wedding and were not sure what happened on such occasions.* ◇ *He said he didn't have time or made* **some** *such excuse.* ◇ *She longed to find somebody who understood her problems, and in him she thought she had found such a person.* ◇ *We were second-class citizens and they treated us* **as such.** ◇ *Accountants were boring. Such* (= that) *was her opinion before meeting Ian!* **3** ? B1 of the type that you are just going to mention: *There is* **no such thing** *as a free lunch.* ◇ *Such advice as he was given* (= it was not very much) *has proved almost worthless.* ◇ *The knot was fastened* **in such a way that** *it was impossible to undo.* ◇ *The damage was such that it would cost thousands to repair.*

IDM **…and such** and similar things or people: *The centre offers activities like canoeing and sailing and such.* **as 'such** as the word is usually understood; in the exact sense of the word: *The new job is not a promotion as such, but it has good prospects.* '*Well, did they offer it to you?*' '*No, not as such, but they said I had a good chance.*' **such as 1** ? A1 for example: *Wild flowers such as primroses are becoming rare.* ◇ '*There are loads of things to do.*' '*Such as?*' (= give me an example) **2** of a kind that; like: *Opportunities such as this did not come every day.* ⊃ LANGUAGE BANK at E.G. **such as it 'is/they 'are** used to say that there is not much of sth or that it is of poor quality: *The food, such as it was, was served at nine o'clock.*

**'such-and-such** *pron., det.* (*informal*) used for referring to sth without saying exactly what it is: *Always say at the start of an application that you're applying for such-and-such a job because…*

**such·like** /ˈsʌtʃlaɪk/ *pron.* things of the type mentioned: *You can buy brushes, paint, varnish and suchlike there.*
▶ **suchlike** *det.*: *food, drink, clothing and suchlike provisions*

**suck** ?+ C1 /sʌk/ *verb, noun*
- **verb 1** ?+ C1 [T] **~sth (+ adv./prep.)** to take liquid, air, etc. into your mouth by using the muscles of your lips: *to suck the juice from an orange* ◇ *She was noisily sucking up milk through a straw.* **2** ?+ C1 [I, T] to keep sth in your mouth and pull on it with your lips and tongue: **~at/on sth** *The baby sucked at its mother's breast.* ◇ *She sucked on a mint.* ◇ **~sth** *She sucked a mint.* ◇ *Stop sucking your thumb!* **3** ?+ C1 [T] to take liquid, air, etc. out of sth: **~sth + adv./prep.** *The pump sucks air out through the valve.* ◇ **~sth + adj.** *Greenfly can literally suck a plant dry.* **4** ?+ C1 [T] **~sb/sth + adv./prep.** to pull sb/sth with great force in a particular direction: *The canoe was sucked down into the whirlpool.* **5 sth sucks** [I] (*slang*) used to say that sth is very bad: *Their new album sucks.* ⊃ compare ROCK
IDM **suck it and 'see** (*BrE, informal*) used to say that the only way to know if sth is suitable is to try it **suck it 'up** (*especially NAmE, informal*) to accept sth bad and deal with it well, controlling your emotions ⊃ more at DRY *adj.,* TEACH
PHRV **suck sb 'in** | **suck sb 'into sth** [usually passive] to involve sb in an activity or a situation, especially one they do not want to be involved in **suck 'up (to sb)** (*informal, disapproving*) to try to please sb in authority by praising them too much, helping them, etc., in order to gain some advantage for yourself
- **noun** [usually sing.] an act of sucking

**suck·er** /ˈsʌkə(r)/ *noun, verb*
- **noun 1** (*informal*) a person who is easily tricked or persuaded to do sth: *She always said the lottery was for suckers.* **2** **~for sb/sth** (*informal*) a person who cannot

---

Ⓞ Oxford Phrasal Academic Lexicon (OPAL) written and spoken word lists | Ⓦ OPAL written word list | Ⓢ OPAL spoken word list

# sucker punch

resist sb/sth or likes sb/sth very much: *I've always been a sucker for men with green eyes.* **3** a special organ on the body of some animals that enables them to stick to a surface ⇒ VISUAL VOCAB page V3 **4** a disc like a cup in shape, usually made of rubber or plastic, that sticks to a surface when you press it against it **5** a part of a tree or bush that grows from the roots rather than from the main STEM or the branches and can form a new tree or bush **6** (*NAmE, slang*) used to refer in a general way to a person or thing, especially for emphasis: *The pilot said, 'I don't know how I got the sucker down safely.'* **7** (*NAmE, informal*) = LOLLIPOP
■ *verb*
**PHRV** ˌsucker sb ˈinto sth/into ˈdoing sth (*NAmE, informal*) to use sb's lack of knowledge or experience to persuade them to do sth that they do not really want to do: *I was suckered into helping.*

**ˈsucker punch** *noun* (*informal*) a hard hit that the person who receives it is not expecting ▶ **ˈsucker punch** *verb* ~ **sb**

**suckle** /ˈsʌkl/ *verb* **1** [T] ~ **sb/sth** (of a woman or female animal) to feed a baby or young animal with milk from the breast or UDDER: *a cow suckling her calves* ◊ (*old-fashioned*) *a mother suckling a baby* **2** [I] (of a baby or young animal) to drink milk from its mother's breast or UDDER

**suck·ling** /ˈsʌklɪŋ/ *noun* (*old-fashioned*) a baby or young animal that is still drinking milk from its mother **IDM** see MOUTH *n.*

**ˈsuckling pig** *noun* [U, C] a young pig still taking milk from its mother that is cooked and eaten

**sucky** /ˈsʌki/ *adj.* (**suck·ier**, **sucki·est**) (*NAmE, informal*) very bad or unpleasant: *a really sucky job*

**su·crose** /ˈsuːkrəʊz, -krəʊs; *NAmE* -krəs, -krəʊz/ *noun* [U] (*chemistry*) the form of sugar that is obtained from SUGAR CANE and SUGAR BEET

**suc·tion** /ˈsʌkʃn/ *noun* [U] the process of removing air or liquid from a space or container so that sth else can be taken into it or so that two surfaces can stick together: *Vacuum cleaners work by suction.* ◊ *a suction pump/pad*
▶ **suc·tion** *verb* ~ **sth** (*specialist*)

**sud·den** /ˈsʌdn/ *adj.* happening or done quickly and unexpectedly: *News of his sudden and unexpected death came as a great shock.* ◊ *a sudden change in temperature* ◊ *It was only decided yesterday. It's all been very sudden.* ▶ **sud·den·ness** /-dnnəs/ *noun* [U]
**IDM** ˌall of a ˈsudden quickly and unexpectedly: *All of a sudden someone grabbed me around the neck.*

**ˌsudden ˈdeath** *noun* [U] a way of deciding the winner of a game when the scores are equal at the end. The players or teams continue playing and the game ends as soon as one of them gains the lead: *a sudden-death play-off in golf*

**ˌsudden infant ˈdeath syndrome** *noun* [U] (*abbr.* SIDS) the sudden death while sleeping of a baby that appears to be healthy **SYN** **cot death**

**sud·den·ly** /ˈsʌdənli/ *adv.* quickly and unexpectedly: *I suddenly realized what I had to do.* ◊ *I suddenly became aware of just how late it was.* ◊ *She took ill and died suddenly at her home.*

**su·doku** /suˈdəʊkuː; *BrE* also -ˈdɒku:/ *noun* [C, U] a number PUZZLE with nine squares, each containing nine smaller squares, in which you have to put the numbers one to nine so that a number appears only once in each of the nine squares and in each row of nine across and down the puzzle: *He passes the time doing sudokus.*

sudoku

**suds** /sʌdz/ *noun* **1** (*also* ˈsoap-suds) [pl.] a mass of very small bubbles that forms on top of water that has soap in it **SYN** **lather**: *She was up to her elbows in suds.* **2** [U] (*old-fashioned, NAmE, informal*) beer

**sue** /suː/ *verb* **1** [T, I] to make a claim against a person or an organization in court about sth that they have said or done to harm you: *They threatened to sue if the work was not completed.* ◊ ~ **(sb/sth) (for sth)** *to sue sb for breach of contract* ◊ *to sue sb for $10 million* (= in order to get money from sb) ◊ *to sue sb for damages* **2** [I] ~ **for sth** (*formal*) to formally ask for sth, especially in court: *to sue for divorce* ◊ *The rebels were forced to sue for peace.*

**suede** /sweɪd/ *noun* [U] soft leather with a surface like VELVET on one side, used especially for making clothes and shoes: *a suede jacket*

**suet** /ˈsuːɪt/ *noun* [U] hard fat from around the KIDNEYS of cows, sheep, etc., used in cooking: *suet pudding* (= one made using suet)

**suf·fer** /ˈsʌfə(r)/ *verb* **1** [I] to be badly affected by a disease, pain, sad feelings, a lack of sth, etc: *I hate to see animals suffering.* ◊ *The country has suffered greatly at the hands of its corrupt government.* ◊ ~ **from sth** *to suffer from a disorder/a disease/an illness/a condition* ◊ *patients suffering from depression/cancer* ◊ *The economy is still suffering badly from a lack of demand.* ◊ ~ **for sth** *He made a rash decision and now he is suffering for it.* **2** [T] ~ **sth** to experience sth unpleasant, such as injury, defeat or loss: *to suffer a stroke/heart attack* ◊ *Victims suffered severe injuries in the accident.* ◊ *The company suffered huge losses in the last financial year.* ◊ *Crops suffered serious damage as a result of the floods.* ◊ *The party suffered a humiliating defeat in the general election.* **3** [I] to become worse: *His school work is suffering because of family problems.*
**IDM** ˌnot suffer fools ˈgladly to be very impatient with people that you think are stupid

**suf·fer·ance** /ˈsʌfrəns/ *noun* [U]
**IDM** on ˈsufferance if you do sth **on sufferance**, sb allows you to do it although they do not really want you to: *He's only staying here on sufferance.*

**suf·fer·er** /ˈsʌfərə(r)/ *noun* a person who suffers, especially sb who is suffering from a disease: *cancer sufferers* ◊ *She received many letters of support from fellow sufferers.*

**suf·fer·ing** /ˈsʌfərɪŋ/ *noun* **1** [U] physical or mental pain: *Death finally brought an end to her suffering.* ◊ *This war has caused widespread human suffering.* **2** **sufferings** [pl.] feelings of pain and unhappiness: *The hospice aims to ease the sufferings of the dying.*

**suf·fice** /səˈfaɪs/ *verb* [I] (*formal*) (not used in the progressive tenses) to be enough for sb/sth: *Generally a brief note or a phone call will suffice.* ◊ ~ **to do sth** *One example will suffice to illustrate the point.*
**IDM** sufˌfice (it) to ˈsay (that)… used to suggest that although you could say more, what you do say will be enough to explain what you mean

**suf·fi·ciency** /səˈfɪʃnsi/ *noun* [sing.] ~ **(of sth)** (*formal*) an amount of sth that is enough for a particular purpose

**suf·fi·cient** /səˈfɪʃnt/ *adj.* enough for a particular purpose; as much as you need: *Allow sufficient time to get there.* ◊ ~ **to do sth** *These reasons are not sufficient to justify the ban.* ◊ ~ **for sth/sb** *Is £100 sufficient for your expenses?* **OPP** **insufficient** ⇒ see also SELF-SUFFICIENT

**suf·fi·cient·ly** /səˈfɪʃntli/ *adv.* enough for a particular purpose; as much as you need: *The following day she felt sufficiently well to go to work.* ◊ *By 1995, bald eagles had recovered sufficiently to be removed from the endangered list.* **OPP** **insufficiently**

**suf·fix** /ˈsʌfɪks/ *noun* (*grammar*) a letter or group of letters added to the end of a word to make another word, such as *-ly* in *quickly* or *-ness* in *sadness* ⇒ compare AFFIX, PREFIX

**suf·fo·cate** /ˈsʌfəkeɪt/ *verb* [I, T] to die because there is no air to breathe; to kill sb by not letting them breathe air: *Many dogs have suffocated in hot cars.* ◊ ~ **sb/sth** *The couple were suffocated by fumes from a faulty gas fire.* ◊ *He put the pillow over her face and suffocated her.* ◊ (*figurative*) *She felt suffocated by all the rules and regulations.*
▶ **suf·fo·ca·tion** /ˌsʌfəˈkeɪʃn/ *noun* [U]: *to die of suffocation*

**suf·fo·cat·ing** /ˈsʌfəkeɪtɪŋ/ adj. **1** making it difficult to breathe normally SYN **stifling**: *The afternoon heat was suffocating.* ◇ *it is~ Can I open a window? It's suffocating in here!* **2** limiting what sb/sth can do: *Some marriages can sometimes feel suffocating.*

**suf·fra·gan** /ˈsʌfrəgən/ (also ˌsuffragan ˈbishop) noun a BISHOP who is an assistant to a bishop of a particular DIOCESE

**suf·frage** /ˈsʌfrɪdʒ/ noun [U] the right to vote in political elections: *universal suffrage* (= the right of all adults to vote) ◇ *women's suffrage*

**suf·fra·gette** /ˌsʌfrəˈdʒet/ noun a member of a group of women who, in the UK and the US in the early part of the 20th century, worked to get the right for women to vote in political elections ⊃ compare SUFFRAGIST

**suf·fra·gist** /ˈsʌfrədʒɪst/ noun (especially in the past) a person who campaigns for a group of people who do not have the right to vote in elections, in order to get this right for them ⊃ compare SUFFRAGETTE

**suf·fuse** /səˈfjuːz/ verb [often passive] ~ sb/sth (with sth) (literary) (especially of a colour, light or feeling) to spread all over or through sb/sth: *Her face was suffused with colour.* ◇ *Colour suffused her face.*

**Sufi** /ˈsuːfi/ noun a member of a Muslim group who try to become united with God through prayer and MEDITATION and by living a very simple, strict life ▶ **Suf·ism** /-fɪzəm/ noun [U]

**su·fur·ia** /suːˈfuːriə/ EAfrE [sufuˈria] noun (EAfrE) a metal pot used for cooking

**sugar** ⓘ A1 /ˈʃʊɡə(r)/ noun, verb, exclamation
■ noun **1** [U] a sweet substance, often in the form of white or brown CRYSTALS, made from the juices of various plants, used in cooking or to make tea, coffee, etc. sweeter: *Do you take sugar* (= have it in your tea, coffee, etc.)? ◇ *This juice contains no added sugar.* ◇ *a sugar bowl* ⊃ see also BARLEY SUGAR, BROWN SUGAR, CANE SUGAR, CASTER SUGAR, GRANULATED SUGAR, ICING SUGAR **2** [C] the amount of sugar that a small spoon can hold or that is contained in a small CUBE, added to tea, coffee, etc: *How many sugars do you take in coffee?* **3** [C, usually pl.] (specialist) any of various sweet substances that are found naturally in plants, fruit, etc: *fruit sugars* ⊃ see also BLOOD SUGAR **4** [U] (informal, especially NAmE) a way of addressing sb that you like or love: *See you later, sugar.*
■ verb ~ sth to add sugar to sth; to cover sth in sugar IDM see PILL n.
■ exclamation used to show that you are annoyed when you do sth stupid or when sth goes wrong (to avoid saying 'shit'): *Oh sugar! I've forgotten my book!*

ˈsugar beet noun [U] a plant with a large round root, from which sugar is made

ˈsugar cane noun [U] a tall tropical plant with thick STEMS from which sugar is made

ˈsugar-coat verb ~ sth to do sth that makes an unpleasant situation seem less unpleasant

ˈsugar-ˌcoated adj. **1** covered with sugar **2** (disapproving) made to seem attractive, in a way that tricks people: *a sugar-coated promise*

ˈsugar cube (especially NAmE) (BrE also ˈsugar lump) noun a small CUBE of sugar, used in cups of tea or coffee

ˈsugar daddy noun (informal) a rich older man who gives presents and money to a much younger woman, usually in return for sex

ˌsugar-ˈfree adj. not containing any sugar: *sugar-free yogurt*

ˈsugar·ing /ˈʃʊɡərɪŋ/ noun [U] **1** a way of removing hair from your skin using a mixture of sugar and water **2** the process of boiling juice from a MAPLE tree until it becomes sugar

ˈsugar lump (also informal lump) (both BrE) (also ˈsugar cube NAmE, BrE) noun a small CUBE of sugar, used in cups of tea or coffee

ˈsugar·plum /ˈʃʊɡəplʌm; NAmE -gərp-/ noun (especially NAmE) a small round sweet

1567 **suggestion**

ˈsugar snap (also ˌsugar snap ˈpea, ˈsugar pea) noun a type of PEA which is eaten while still in its POD

**sug·ary** /ˈʃʊɡəri/ adj. **1** containing sugar; tasting of sugar: *sugary snacks* **2** (disapproving) seeming too full of emotion in a way that is not sincere SYN **sentimental**: *a sugary smile* ◇ *sugary pop songs*

**sug·gest** ⓘ A2 ⓞ /səˈdʒest; NAmE also səɡˈdʒ-/ verb **1** A2 to put forward an idea or a plan for other people to think about SYN **propose**: ~ sth (to sb) *I'd like to suggest a different explanation for the company's decline.* ◇ *~ itself (to sb) A solution immediately suggested itself to me* (= I immediately thought of a solution). ◇ *~ (that) ... I strongly suggest (that) you don't get involved.* ◇ *~ doing sth I suggested going in my car.* ◇ *it is suggested that ... It has been suggested that bright children take their exams early.* ◇ +speech *'We could go for a drive,' Nate suggested hopefully.* ⊃ LANGUAGE BANK at ARGUE **2** A2 to tell sb about a suitable person, thing, method, etc. for a particular job or purpose SYN **recommend**: ~ sb/sth for sth *Who would you suggest for the job?* ◇ ~ sb/sth as sth *She suggested Paris as a good place for the conference.* ◇ ~ sb/sth *Can you suggest a better way of doing it?* HELP You cannot 'suggest somebody something': *Can you suggest me a better way of doing it?* ◇ *~ how, what, etc … Can you suggest how I might contact him?* **3** B2 to put an idea into sb's mind; to make sb think that sth is true SYN **indicate**: ~ (that) … *All the evidence suggests (that) he stole the money.* ◇ *~ sth Recent studies suggest the possibility of a cure for the disease.* ◇ *Some believe that organic foods offer no health benefits, but this research suggests otherwise.* ◇ *~ sth to sb What do these results suggest to you?* **4** B2 to state sth indirectly SYN **imply**: ~ (that) … *Are you suggesting (that) I'm lazy?* ◇ *~ sth I would never suggest such a thing.*

▼ **EXPRESS YOURSELF**
**Making suggestions**
There are various ways of putting forward your suggestions:
• **How about** going out for a walk on Saturday?
• **Shall we** ask Sarah to come along? (BrE or formal, NAmE)
• **Should we** ask Sarah to come along? (especially NAmE)
• **We could** go a bit earlier and have a drink first, **if you like**.
• **What do you think of the idea** of sending this to the Research Department?
• **Why don't you** try calling his landline?
• **Why not just** wait until they come back?
• **Why not simply** explain your problem to them and see what they say? (BrE or formal, NAmE)

**sug·gest·ible** /səˈdʒestəbl; NAmE also səɡˈdʒ-/ adj. easily influenced by other people: *He was young and highly suggestible.*

**sug·ges·tion** ⓘ A2 /səˈdʒestʃən; NAmE also səɡˈdʒ-/ noun **1** A2 [C] an idea or a plan that you mention for sb else to think about: *Can I make a suggestion?* ◇ *Do you have any suggestions?* ◇ *to offer/reject a suggestion* ◇ *~ for sth The report offers suggestions for improvement to policy.* ◇ *~ about/on sth We welcome any comments and suggestions on these proposals.* ◇ *~ that … He agreed with my suggestion that we should change the date.* ◇ *We are open to suggestions* (= willing to listen to ideas from other people). ◇ *We need to get it there by four. Any suggestions?* **2** B2 [U, C, usually sing.] a reason to think that sth, especially sth bad, is true SYN **hint**: *~ of sth A spokesman dismissed any suggestion of a boardroom rift.* ◇ *~ that … There was no suggestion that he was doing anything illegal.* **3** [U] putting an idea into people's minds by connecting it with other ideas: *Most advertisements work through suggestion.* ◇ *the power of suggestion* **4** [C, usua sing.] (formal or literary) a slight amount or sign of sth SYN **trace**: *She looked at me with just a suggestion of a smile.*
IDM **at/on sb's sug'gestion** because sb suggested it: *At his suggestion, I bought the more expensive printer.*

# suggestive

**sug·gest·ive** /səˈdʒestɪv; NAmE also səɡˈdʒ-/ adj. **1** ~ (of sth) reminding you of sth or making you think about sth: *music that is suggestive of warm summer days* **2** making people think about sex: *suggestive jokes* ▶ **sug·gest·ive·ly** adv.: *He leered suggestively.*

**sui·cidal** /ˌsuːɪˈsaɪdl/ adj. **1** people who are **suicidal** feel that they want to kill themselves: *On bad days I even felt suicidal.* ◊ *suicidal tendencies* **2** very dangerous and likely to lead to the person's own death; likely to cause them very serious problems or disaster: *a suicidal leap into the swollen river* ◊ *it is~to do sth It would be suicidal to risk going out in this weather.* ◊ *~for sb/sth The new economic policies could prove suicidal for the party.* ▶ **sui·cid·al·ly** /-dəli/ adv.: *suicidally depressed*

**sui·cide** /ˈsuːɪsaɪd/ noun **1** [U, C] the act of killing yourself deliberately: *to commit suicide* ◊ *an attempted suicide* (= one in which the person survives) ◊ *a suicide bomber* (= who expects to die while trying to kill other people with a bomb) ⇨ see also ASSISTED SUICIDE **2** [U] a course of action that is likely to destroy your career, position in society, etc: *It would have been political suicide for him to challenge the allegations in court.* **3** [C] (*formal*) a person who commits suicide

**'suicide pact** noun an agreement between two or more people to kill themselves at the same time

**sui gen·eris** /ˌsuːiː ˈdʒenərɪs, ˌsuːaɪ-/ adj. (*from Latin, formal*) different from all other people or things SYN **unique**

**suit** /suːt/ noun, verb
■ noun **1** a set of clothes made of the same cloth, including a jacket and trousers or a skirt: *a business suit* ◊ *They won't let you into the restaurant without a suit and tie.* ◊ *a two-/three-piece suit* (= of two/three pieces of clothing) ⇨ see also DINNER SUIT, JOGGING SUIT, JUMPSUIT, LEISURE SUIT, LOUNGE SUIT, MORNING SUIT, SWEATSUIT, TRACKSUIT, TROUSER SUIT **2** a set of clothing worn for a particular activity: *a diving suit* ◊ *a suit of armour* ⇨ see also BATHING SUIT, BOILER SUIT, PRESSURE SUIT, SPACESUIT, SWIMSUIT, WETSUIT **3** any of the four sets that form a PACK of cards: *The suits are called hearts, clubs, diamonds and spades.* ⇨ WORDFINDER NOTE at CARD **4** = LAWSUIT: *to file/bring a suit against sb* ◊ *a divorce suit* ⇨ see also PATERNITY SUIT **5** [usually pl.] (*informal*) a person with an important job as a manager in a company or organization, especially one who is thought to work mainly with financial matters or to have a lot of influence
IDM see BIRTHDAY, FOLLOW, STRONG
■ verb [no passive] (not used in the progressive tenses) **1** to be convenient or useful for sb: *~ sb/sth If we met at two, would that suit you?* ◊ *If you want to go by bus, that suits me fine.* ◊ *Customers will be offered solutions that best suit their needs.* ◊ *it suits sb to do sth It suits me to start work at a later time.* **2** *~ sb* (especially of clothes, colours, etc.) to make you look attractive: *Blue suits you. You should wear it more often.* ◊ *I don't think this coat really suits me.* **3** *~ sb/sth* (*especially BrE*) (usually used in negative sentences) to be right or good for sb/sth: *This hot weather doesn't suit me.*
IDM **suit your/sb's 'book** (*BrE, informal*) to be convenient or useful for you/sb **suit sb down to the 'ground** (*BrE, informal*) to be very convenient or acceptable for sb: *This job suits me down to the ground.* **suit your'self** (*informal*) **1** to do exactly what you would like: *I choose my assignments to suit myself.* **2** usually used in orders to tell sb to do what they want, even though it annoys you: *'I think I'll stay in this evening.' 'Suit yourself!'*
PHRV **'suit sth to sth/sb** to make sth appropriate for sth/sb: *He can suit his conversation to whoever he is with.*

**suit·able** /ˈsuːtəbl/ adj. right or appropriate for a particular purpose or occasion: *a suitable candidate* ◊ *a suitable habitat/location/site* ◊ *~ for sth/sb This programme is not suitable for children.* ◊ *a suitable place for a picnic* ◊ *~ to do sth I don't have anything suitable to wear for the party.* OPP **unsuitable** ▶ **suit·abil·ity** /ˌsuːtəˈbɪləti/ noun [U]: *There is no doubt about her suitability for the job.*

**suit·ably** /ˈsuːtəbli/ adv. **1** in a way that is right or appropriate for a particular purpose or occasion: *I am not really suitably dressed for a party.* ◊ *suitably qualified candidates* **2** showing the feelings, etc. that you would expect in a particular situation: *He was suitably impressed when I told him I'd won.*

**suit·case** /ˈsuːtkeɪs/ (*also* **case**) noun a case with flat sides and a handle, used for carrying clothes, etc. when you are travelling: *to pack/unpack a suitcase*

**suite** /swiːt/ noun **1** a set of rooms, especially in a hotel: *a hotel/private/honeymoon suite* ◊ *a suite of rooms/offices* ⇨ WORDFINDER NOTE at HOTEL ⇨ see also EN SUITE **2** a set of matching pieces of furniture: *a bathroom/bedroom suite* ◊ (*BrE*) *a three-piece suite with two armchairs and a sofa* **3** a piece of music made up of three or more related parts, for example pieces from an OPERA: *Stravinsky's Firebird Suite* **4** (*computing*) a set of related computer programs: *a suite of software development tools*

▼ **HOMOPHONES**

**suite** • **sweet** /swiːt/

- **suite** *noun*: *She booked a hotel suite overlooking Central Park.*
- **sweet** *adj*.: *Add some honey to make it sweet.*
- **sweet** *noun*: *Suck this sweet—it might soothe your throat.*

**suit·ed** /ˈsuːtɪd/ adj. [not before noun] **1** right or appropriate for sb/sth: *~ (to sb/sth) She was ideally suited to the part of Eva Perón.* ◊ *This diet is suited to anyone who wants to lose weight fast.* ◊ *~ (for sb/sth) He is not really suited for a teaching career.* OPP **unsuited 2** if two people are **suited** or **well suited**, they are likely to make a good couple: *Jo and I are very well suited.* ◊ *~ to sb They were not suited to one another.* OPP **unsuited 3** wearing a suit, or a suit of the type mentioned: *sober-suited city businessmen*
IDM **suited and 'booted** (*BrE, informal*) dressed in very smart clothes and shoes

**suit·ing** /ˈsuːtɪŋ/ noun [U] cloth made especially of wool, used for making suits: *men's suiting*

**suitor** /ˈsuːtə(r)/ noun **1** (*old-fashioned*) a man who wants to marry a particular woman **2** (*business*) a company that wants to buy another company

**su·kuma·wiki** /ˌsuːkuməˈwiːki/ EAfrE [sukumaˈwiːki] (*also* **su·kuma wiki**) noun [U] (*EAfrE*) a vegetable with dark green leaves that are cooked; KALE: *a meal of ugali and sukuma-wiki*

**sul·fate, sul·fide, sul·fur, sul·fur·ic acid** (*US*) = SULPHATE, SULPHIDE, SULPHUR, SULPHURIC ACID

**sulk** /sʌlk/ verb, noun
■ verb [I] (*disapproving*) to look angry and refuse to speak or smile because you want people to know that you are upset about sth: *He went off to sulk in his room.*
■ noun (*BrE also* **the sulks** [pl.]) a period of not speaking and being unpleasant because you are angry about sth: *in a ~ Jo was in a sulk upstairs.* ◊ *to have the sulks*

**sulky** /ˈsʌlki/ adj. (*disapproving*) in a bad mood or not speaking because you are angry about sth: *Sarah had looked sulky all morning.* ◊ *a sulky child* ⇨ WORDFINDER NOTE at YOUNG ▶ **sulk·ily** /-kɪli/ adv. **sulki·ness** noun [U]

**sul·len** /ˈsʌlən/ adj. (*disapproving*) **1** in a bad mood and not speaking, either on a particular occasion or because it is part of your character: *Bob looked pale and sullen.* ◊ *She gave him a sullen glare.* ◊ *sullen teenagers* **2** (*literary*) (of the sky or weather) dark and unpleasant ▶ **sul·len·ly** adv. **sul·len·ness** /-lənnəs/ noun [U]

**sully** /ˈsʌli/ verb (**sul·lies, sully·ing, sul·lied, sul·lied**) (*formal or literary*) **1** *~ sth* to damage or reduce the value of sth **2** *~ sth* to make sth dirty

**sul·phate** (*US* **sul·fate**) /ˈsʌlfeɪt/ noun [C, U] (*chemistry*) a COMPOUND of SULPHURIC ACID and a chemical element: *copper sulphate* ⇨ note at SULPHUR

**sul·phide** (US **sul·fide**) /ˈsʌlfaɪd/ noun [C, U] (chemistry) a COMPOUND of sulphur and another chemical element ⊃ note at SULPHUR

**sul·phur** (US **sul·fur**) /ˈsʌlfə(r)/ noun [U] (symb. **S**) a chemical element. Sulphur is a pale yellow substance that produces a strong unpleasant smell when it burns and is used in medicine and industry. **HELP** The spelling **sulfur** has been adopted by the International Union of Pure and Applied Chemistry and by the Royal Society of Chemistry in the UK. However, **sulphur** still remains the usual spelling in British, Irish, South African and Indian English. Both spellings are used in Canadian, Australian and New Zealand English.
▸ **sul·phur·ous** (US **sul·fur·ous**) /-fərəs/ adj.: sulphurous fumes

**sulphur di'oxide** (US **sulfur di'oxide**) noun [U] (symb. $SO_2$) a poisonous gas with a strong smell, that is used in industry and causes air pollution ⊃ note at SULPHUR

**sul·phur·ic acid** (US **sul·fur·ic acid**) /sʌlˌfjʊərɪk ˈæsɪd; NAmE -ˌfjʊr-/ noun [U] (symb. $H_2SO_4$) a strong, clear ACID ⊃ note at SULPHUR

**sul·tan** /ˈsʌltən/ noun the title given to Muslim rulers in some countries: the Sultan of Brunei

**sul·tana** /sʌlˈtɑːnə; NAmE -ˈtænə/ noun **1** (BrE) (NAmE **golden 'raisin**) a small dried GRAPE without seeds, used in cakes, etc. **2** the wife, mother, sister or daughter of a sultan

**sul·tan·ate** /ˈsʌltəneɪt/ noun **1** the rank or position of a SULTAN **2** an area of land that is ruled over by a SULTAN: the Sultanate of Oman **3** the period of time during which sb is a SULTAN

**sul·try** /ˈsʌltri/ adj. (**sul·trier**, **sul·tri·est**) **1** (of the weather or air) very hot and uncomfortable **SYN** **muggy**: a sultry summer afternoon **2** (of a woman or her appearance) sexually attractive; seeming to have strong sexual feelings **SYN** **sexy**: a sultry smile ◇ a sultry singer ▸ **sul·tri·ness** noun [U]

**sum** 🔵 **B2** ⊙ /sʌm/ noun, verb
▪ noun **1** 🔵 **B2** [C] ~ (of sth) an amount of money: You will be fined the sum of £200. ◇ a **large sum** of money ◇ a six-figure sum ◇ Huge sums have been invested in this project. ⊃ see also CAPITAL SUM, LUMP SUM **2** [C, usually sing.] ~ (of sth) the number you get when you add two or more numbers together: The sum of 7 and 12 is 19. **3** (also **sum 'total** [sing.] **the ~ of sth** all of sth, especially when you think that it is not very much: This is the sum of my achievements so far. **4** [C] a simple problem that involves calculating numbers: to **do a sum** in your head ◇ I was good at sums at school. ◇ If I've got my sums right, I should be able to afford the rent. ⊃ see also DIM SUM
**IDM** **be greater/more than the ˌsum of its ˈparts** to be better or more effective as a group than you would think just by looking at the individual members of the group **in 'sum** (formal) used to introduce a short statement of the main points of a discussion, speech, etc.
▪ verb (**-mm-**)
**PHRV** **ˌsum ˈup** | **ˌsum sth↔ˈup 1** 🔵 **B2** to state the main points of sth in a short and clear form **SYN** **summarize**: To sum up, there are three main ways of tackling the problem… ◇ **sum up what…** Can I just sum up what we've agreed so far? ⊃ LANGUAGE BANK at CONCLUSION **2** (of a judge) to give a summary of the main facts and arguments in a legal case, near the end of a trial ⊃ related noun SUMMING-UP **ˌsum sb/sth↔ˈup 1** to describe or show the most typical characteristics of sb/sth, especially in a few words: Totally lazy—that just about sums him up. **2** to form or express an opinion of sb/sth **SYN** **size up**: She quickly summed up the situation and took control. ⊃ related noun SUMMING-UP

**summa cum laude** /ˌsʊmə kʊm ˈlɔːdi, ˈlaʊdeɪ/ adv., adj. (from Latin) (in the US) at the highest level of achievement that students can reach when they finish their studies at college: He graduated summa cum laude from Harvard. ⊃ compare CUM LAUDE, MAGNA CUM LAUDE

**sum·mar·ize** 🔵 **B1** 🌐 (BrE also **-ise**) /ˈsʌməraɪz/ verb [T, I] ~(sth) to give a summary of sth: This essay briefly summarizes some of our approaches. ◇ The results of the research are summarized at the end of the chapter. ⊃

To summarize, the main conclusions are as follows…
⊃ LANGUAGE BANK at CONCLUSION

**sum·mary** 🔵 **B1** ⊙ /ˈsʌməri/ noun, adj.
▪ noun 🔵 **B1** (pl. **-ies**) a short statement that gives only the main points of sth, not the details: **~ of sth** The following is a summary of our conclusions. ◇ What follows is a **brief summary** of the findings. ◇ He has **provided a useful summary** of the main categories. ◇ **in ~** In summary, this was a disappointing performance. ⊃ see also EXECUTIVE SUMMARY
▪ adj. [only before noun] **1** (formal) giving only the main points of sth, not the details: a summary financial statement ◇ I made a summary report for the records. **2** (sometimes disapproving) done immediately, without paying attention to the normal process that should be followed: summary justice/execution ◇ a summary judgement ▸ **sum·mar·ily** /ˈsʌməreli; NAmE səˈmerəli/ adv.: to be summarily dismissed/executed

**sum·mat** /ˈsʌmət/ noun (NEngE, non-standard) a way of writing a spoken form of 'something'

**sum·ma·tion** /sʌˈmeɪʃn/ noun **1** [usually sing.] (formal) a summary of what has been done or said: What he said was a fair summation of the discussion. **2** (formal) a collection of different parts that forms a complete account or impression of sb/sth: The exhibition presents a summation of the artist's career. **3** (NAmE, law) a final speech that a lawyer makes near the end of a trial in court, after all the evidence has been given

**sum·mer** 🔵 **A1** /ˈsʌmə(r)/ noun [U, C] the warmest season of the year, coming between spring and autumn: **in the ~** We're going away in the summer. ◇ in the summer of 2019 ◇ this/next/last summer ◇ **in ~** It's very hot here in summer. ◇ late/early summer ◇ **during the ~** during the long hot summer ◇ **over the ~** I managed to get six weeks' work over the summer. ◇ a summer's day ◇ The house is now open to the public during the **summer months**. ◇ the **summer holidays/vacation/break** ◇ We're at the height of **summer travel season**. ⊃ see also INDIAN SUMMER **IDM** see SWALLOW n.

**'summer camp** noun [C, U] = CAMP (2)

**'summer house** noun **1** a small building in a garden for sitting in in good weather **2** (also **'summer home**) (NAmE) a house that sb lives in only during the summer

**'summer school** noun [C, U] courses that are held in the summer at a university or college or, in the US, at a school

**'summer student** noun (CanE) a student, especially a university student, who is working at a job for the summer

**sum·mer·time** /ˈsʌmətaɪm; NAmE -mərt-/ noun [U] the season of summer: It's beautiful here in (the) summertime.

**'summer time** (BrE) (NAmE ˌdaylight ˈsaving time) noun [U] the period during which in some countries the clocks are put forward one hour, so that it is light for an extra hour in the evening

**sum·mery** /ˈsʌməri/ adj. typical of or suitable for the summer: summery weather ◇ a light summery dress **OPP** **wintry**

**summing-'up** noun (pl. **summings-up**) **1** a speech that the judge makes near the end of a trial in court, in which he or she reminds the JURY about the evidence and the most important points in the case before the JURY makes its decision **2** an occasion when sb states the main points of an argument, etc.

**sum·mit** 🔵 **C1** /ˈsʌmɪt/ noun **1** 🔵 **C1** the highest point of sth, especially the top of a mountain: We reached the summit at noon. ◇ This path leads to the summit. ◇ (figurative) the summit of his career ⊃ WORDFINDER NOTE at MOUNTAIN **2** 🔵 **C1** an official meeting or series of meetings between the leaders of two or more governments at which they discuss important matters: a summit in Moscow ◇ a summit conference

**sum·mon** /ˈsʌmən/ verb **1** ~ **sb (to do sth)** (formal) to order sb to appear in court **SYN** **summons**: He was summoned to

# summons

appear before the magistrates. **2** ~ **sb (to sth)** | ~ **sb to do sth** (*formal*) to order sb to come to you: *In May 1688 he was urgently summoned to London.* ◊ *She summoned the waiter.* **3** ~ **sth** (*formal*) to call for or try to obtain sth: *to summon assistance/help/reinforcements* **4** ~ **sth** (*formal*) to arrange an official meeting **SYN** **convene**: *to summon a meeting* **5** ~ **sth (up)** to make an effort to produce a particular quality in yourself, especially when you find it difficult **SYN** **muster**: *She was trying to summon up the courage to leave him.* ◊ *I couldn't even summon the energy to get out of bed.*

**PHRV** **summon sth↔ˈup** to make a feeling, an idea, a memory, etc. come into your mind **SYN** **evoke**: *The book summoned up memories of my childhood.*

**sum·mons** /ˈsʌmənz/ *noun, verb*
- *noun* (*pl.* **sum·monses** /-mənzɪz/) **1** (*NAmE also* **cit·ation**) an order to appear in court: *to issue a summons against sb* ◊ *The police have been unable to serve a summons on him.* ◊ *She received a summons to appear in court the following week.* **2** an order to come and see sb: *to obey a royal summons*
- *verb* to order sb to appear in court **SYN** **summon**: ~ **sb (for sth)** *She was summonsed for speeding.* ◊ ~ **sb to do sth** *He was summonsed to appear in court.*

**sumo** /ˈsuːməʊ/ (*also* **sumo ˈwrestling**) *noun* [U] a Japanese style of WRESTLING, in which the people taking part are extremely large: *a sumo wrestler*

**sump** /sʌmp/ *noun* **1** a hole or hollow area in which liquid waste collects **2** (*NAmE also* **ˈoil pan**) the place under an engine that holds the engine oil

**sump·tu·ous** /ˈsʌmptʃuəs/ *adj.* (*formal*) very expensive and looking very impressive: *a sumptuous meal* ◊ *We dined in sumptuous surroundings.* ▶ **sump·tu·ous·ly** *adv.* **sump·tu·ous·ness** *noun* [U]

**sum ˈtotal** *noun* [*sing.*] (*sometimes disapproving*) the whole of sth; everything: *A photo, a book of poems and a gold ring —this was the sum total of his possessions.*

**Sun.** *abbr.* (*in writing*) Sunday

**sun** 🔑 **A1** /sʌn/ *noun, verb*
- *noun* **1** 🔑 **A1** **the sun, the Sun** [*sing.*] the star that shines in the sky during the day and gives the earth heat and light: *The sun was shining and birds were singing.* ◊ *the sun's rays* ◊ *The sun rises highest in the sky during the summer.* ◊ *the rising/setting sun*

**WORDFINDER** daylight, eclipse, equinox, ray, rise, solar, solstice, twilight, the universe

**2** **A1** (*usually* **the sun**) [*sing.*, U] the light and heat from the sun **SYN** **sunshine**: *the warmth of the afternoon sun* ◊ *The sun was blazing hot.* ◊ **in the ~** *We sat in the sun.* ◊ *They've booked a holiday in the sun* (= in a place where it is warm and the sun shines a lot). ◊ **out of the ~** *We did our best to keep out of the sun.* ◊ *Her face had obviously* **caught the sun** (= become red or brown) *on holiday.* ◊ *I was driving westwards and I* **had the sun in my eyes** (= the sun was shining in my eyes). ⊃ *see also* SUNNY **3** [C] (*specialist*) any star around which planets move

**IDM** **under the ˈsun** used to emphasize that you are talking about a very large number of things: *We talked about everything under the sun.* **with the ˈsun** when the sun rises or sets: *I get up with the sun.* ⊃ *more at* HAY, PLACE *n.*
- *verb* (**-nn-**) ~ **yourself** to sit or lie in a place where the sun is shining on you: *We lay sunning ourselves on the deck.*

▼ **HOMOPHONES**

**son** • **sun** /sʌn/
- **son** *noun*: *Their youngest son is still living at home.*
- **sun** *noun*: *Let's go for a picnic while the sun is shining!*

**sun-baked** *adj.* **1** made hard and dry by the heat of the sun: *sun-baked earth* **2** receiving a lot of light and heat from the sun: *sun-baked beaches*

**sun·bathe** /ˈsʌnbeɪð/ *verb* [I] to sit or lie in the sun, especially in order to go brown (get a SUNTAN) ⊃ *note at* BATH

**sun·beam** /ˈsʌnbiːm/ *noun* a stream of light from the sun

**sun·bed** /ˈsʌnbed/ *noun* a bed for lying on under a SUN-LAMP ⊃ *compare* SUNLOUNGER

**sun·block** /ˈsʌnblɒk; *NAmE* -blɑːk/ *noun* [U, C] a cream that you put on your skin to protect it from the harmful effects of the sun

**sun·burn** /ˈsʌnbɜːn; *NAmE* -bɜːrn/ *noun* [U] the condition of having painful red skin because you have spent too much time in the sun ⊃ *compare* SUNTAN

**sun·burned** /ˈsʌnbɜːnd; *NAmE* -bɜːrnd/ (*also* **sun·burnt** /ˈsʌnbɜːnt; *NAmE* -bɜːrnt/) *adj.* **1** suffering from sunburn: *Her shoulders were badly sunburned.* **2** (*BrE*) (of a person or of skin) having an attractive brown colour from being in the sun **SYN** **tanned**: *She looked fit and sunburned.*

**sun·burst** /ˈsʌnbɜːst; *NAmE* -bɜːrst/ *noun* an occasion when the sun appears from behind the clouds and sends out bright streams of light

**ˈsun cream** *noun* [U, C] (*especially BrE*) cream that you put on your skin to protect it from the harmful effects of the sun ⊃ *compare* SUNSCREEN

**sun·dae** /ˈsʌndeɪ, -di/ *noun* a cold DESSERT (= a sweet dish) of ice cream covered with a sweet sauce, nuts, pieces of fruit, etc., usually served in a tall glass

**Sun·day** 🔑 **A1** /ˈsʌndeɪ, -di/ *noun* (*abbr.* **Sun.**) **1** 🔑 **A1** [C, U] the day of the week after Saturday and before Monday, thought of as either the first or the last day of the week **HELP** To see how **Sunday** is used, look at the examples at **Monday**. **ORIGIN** From the Old English for 'day of the sun', translated from Latin *dies solis.* **2** [C, usually *pl.*] (*BrE, informal*) a newspaper published on a Sunday

**IDM** **your Sunday ˈbest** (*informal, humorous*) your best clothes ⊃ *more at* MONTH

**ˈSunday school** *noun* [C, U] a class that is organized by a church or SYNAGOGUE where children can go for a short time on Sundays to learn about the Christian or Jewish religion ⊃ *compare* RELIGIOUS SCHOOL (1)

**ˈsun deck** *noun* the part of a ship where passengers can sit to enjoy the sun, or a similar area next to a restaurant or swimming pool

**sun·der** /ˈsʌndə(r)/ *verb* ~ **sth/sb (from sth/sb)** (*formal or literary*) to split or break sth/sb apart, especially by force ⊃ *see also* ASUNDER

**sun·dial** /ˈsʌndaɪəl/ *noun* a device used outdoors, especially in the past, for telling the time when the sun is shining. A pointed piece of metal throws a shadow on a flat surface that is marked with the hours like a clock, and the shadow moves around as the sun moves across the sky.

sundial

**sun·down** /ˈsʌndaʊn/ *noun* [U] (*especially NAmE*) the time when the sun goes down and night begins **SYN** **sunset**

**ˈsun-drenched** *adj.* [only before noun] (*approving*) having a lot of hot sun: *sun-drenched Mediterranean beaches*

**sun·dress** /ˈsʌndres/ *noun* a dress that does not cover the arms, neck or shoulders, worn in hot weather

**ˈsun-dried** *adj.* [only before noun] (*especially of food*) dried naturally by the heat of the sun: *sun-dried tomatoes*

**sun·dries** /ˈsʌndriz/ *noun* [*pl.*] various items, especially small ones, that are not important enough to be named separately

**sun·dry** /ˈsʌndri/ *adj.* [only before noun] (*formal*) various; not important enough to be named separately: *a watch, a diary and sundry other items*

**IDM** **all and ˈsundry** (*informal*) everyone, not just a few special people: *She was known to all and sundry as Bella.* ◊ *The club is open to all and sundry.*

**sun·flower** /ˈsʌnflaʊə(r)/ *noun* a very tall plant with large yellow flowers, grown in gardens or for its seeds and their oil that are used in cooking: *sunflower oil* ⊃ VISUAL VOCAB page V7

**sung** /sʌŋ/ *past part.* of SING

**sun·glasses** /ˈsʌŋglɑːsɪz; NAmE -glæs-/ (also informal **shades**) noun [pl.] a pair of glasses with dark glass in them that you wear to protect your eyes from bright light from the sun: *a pair of sunglasses* ⇒ see also DARK GLASSES

**sun hat** noun a hat worn to protect the head and neck from the sun

**sunk** /sʌŋk/ past part. of SINK

**sunk·en** /ˈsʌŋkən/ adj. **1** [only before noun] that has fallen to the bottom of the sea or the ocean, or of a lake or river: *a sunken ship* ◇ *sunken treasure* **2** (of eyes or cheeks) hollow and deep as a result of disease, getting old, or not having enough food **3** [only before noun] at a lower level than the area around: *a sunken garden*

**sun-kissed** adj. [usually before noun] made warm or brown by the sun: *sun-kissed bodies on the beach*

**sun lamp** /ˈsʌnlæmp/ noun a lamp that produces ULTRAVIOLET light that has the same effect as the sun and can turn the skin brown

**sun·less** /ˈsʌnləs/ adj. without any sun; receiving no light from the sun SYN gloomy: *a sunless day* OPP sunny

**sun·light** /ˈsʌnlaɪt/ noun [U] the light from the sun: *a ray/pool of sunlight* ◇ *shafts of bright sunlight* ◇ *The morning sunlight flooded into the room.*

**sun·lit** /ˈsʌnlɪt/ adj. [usually before noun] receiving light from the sun: *sunlit streets*

**sun lounge** (BrE) (also **sun-room** NAmE, BrE) noun a room with large windows, and often a glass roof, that lets in a lot of light

**sun·loun·ger** /ˈsʌnlaʊndʒə(r)/ noun (BrE) a chair with a long seat that supports your legs, used for sitting or lying on in the sun ⇒ compare LOUNGER, SUNBED

**Sunni** /ˈsʊni, ˈsʌni/ noun (pl. **Sunni** or **Sun·nis**) **1** [U] one of the two main branches of the Islamic religion ⇒ compare SHIA **2** [C] a member of the Sunni branch of Islam ⇒ compare SHIITE ▶ **Sun·nite** /-naɪt/ adj. [usually before noun]

**sun·nies** /ˈsʌniz/ noun [pl.] (AustralE, NZE, informal) SUNGLASSES

**sunny** /ˈsʌni/ adj. (**sun·ni·er**, **sun·ni·est**) **1** with a lot of bright light from the sun: *a sunny day* ◇ *sunny weather* ◇ *The outlook for the weekend is hot and sunny.* ◇ *a sunny garden* ◇ *Italy was at its sunniest.* **2** cheerful and happy: *a sunny disposition*

**sunny side** noun the side of sth that receives most light from the sun: (figurative) *the sunny side of life* (= the more cheerful aspects of life)
IDM **sunny side ˈup** (NAmE) (of an egg) fried on one side only

**sun·rise** /ˈsʌnraɪz/ noun **1** [U] the time when the sun first appears in the sky in the morning : **at ~** *We got up at sunrise.* ⇒ compare DAWN **2** [C, usually sing.] the colours in the part of the sky where the sun first appears in the morning: *the pinks and yellows of the sunrise*

**sun·roof** /ˈsʌnruːf/ noun (pl. **-roofs**) a part of the roof of a car that you can open to let air and light in

**sun·room** /ˈsʌnruːm, -rʊm/ noun (especially NAmE) (BrE also **sun lounge**) noun a room with large windows, and often a glass roof, that lets in a lot of light

**sun·screen** /ˈsʌnskriːn/ noun [C, U] a cream or liquid that you put on your skin to protect it from the harmful effects of the sun: *a high factor* (= strong) *sunscreen*

**sun·set** /ˈsʌnset/ noun, adj., verb
- noun **1** [U] the time when the sun goes down and night begins: **at ~** *Every evening at sunset the flag was lowered.* **2** [C] the colours in the part of the sky where the sun slowly goes down in the evening: *a spectacular sunset* **3** [C] a fixed period of time after which a law or the effect of a law will end: *There is a five-year sunset on the new tax.*
- adj. [only before noun] **1** used to describe a colour that is like one of the colours in a sunset: *sunset yellow* **2** used to describe sth that is near its end, or that happens at the end of sth: *This is his sunset tour after fifty years as a singer.* **3** (of a law or the effect of a law) designed to end or to end

1571

sth after a fixed period of time: *a two-year sunset clause in the new law*
- verb [I, T] (**-tt-**) **~ (sth)** (of a law or the effect of a law) to end or to end sth after a fixed period of time: *The tax relief will sunset after a year.*

**ˈsunset provision** (also **ˈsunset clause**) noun (law) part of a law, a rule or an agreement that states that it will no longer apply from a particular date

**sun·shade** /ˈsʌnʃeɪd/ noun **1** a light umbrella or other object such as an AWNING, that is used to protect people from hot sun: *a child's buggy fitted with a sunshade* ⇒ compare PARASOL **2 sunshades** [pl.] a pair of dark glasses that you wear to protect your eyes from bright light from the sun, especially ones that fix on to your ordinary glasses

**sun·shine** /ˈsʌnʃaɪn/ noun [U] **1** the light and heat of the sun: *the warm spring sunshine* **2** (informal) happiness: *She brought sunshine into our dull lives.* **3** (BrE, informal) used for addressing sb in a friendly, or sometimes a rude way: *Hello, sunshine!* ◇ *Look, sunshine, who do you think you're talking to?* IDM see RAY

**ˈsunshine law** noun (US) a law that forces government organizations to make certain types of information available to the public

**sun·spot** /ˈsʌnspɒt; NAmE -spɑːt/ noun a dark area that sometimes appears on the sun's surface

**sun·stroke** /ˈsʌnstrəʊk/ noun [U] an illness with a high temperature, weakness, headache, etc. caused by too much direct sun, especially on the head ⇒ compare HEATSTROKE

**sun·tan** /ˈsʌntæn/ noun [usually sing.] = TAN: *Where have you been to get that suntan?* ⇒ compare SUNBURN ▶ **sun·tan** adj. [only before noun]: *suntan oil* **sun·tanned** adj. = TANNED: *a suntanned face*

**sun·trap** /ˈsʌntræp/ noun a place that is sheltered from the wind and gets a lot of sun

**sun·up** /ˈsʌnʌp/ noun [U] (especially NAmE) the time when the sun rises and day begins

**sup** /sʌp/ verb [I, T] (**-pp-**) **~ (sth)** (NEngE or old-fashioned) to drink sth, especially in small amounts ▶ **sup** noun

**super** /ˈsuːpə(r)/ adj., adv., noun
- adj. (informal, becoming old-fashioned) extremely good: *a super meal* ◇ *We had a super time in Italy.* ◇ *She was super* (= very kind) *when I was having problems.*
- adv. (informal) especially; particularly: *He's been super understanding.*
- noun **1** (BrE, informal) a SUPERINTENDENT in the police **2** (NAmE) a SUPERINTENDENT of a building

**super-** /ˈsuːpə(r)/ combining form **1** (in adjectives, adverbs and nouns) extremely; more or better than normal: *super-rich* ◇ *superhuman* ◇ *superglue* **2** (in nouns and verbs) above; over: *superstructure* ◇ *superimpose*

**super·abun·dance** /ˌsuːpərəˈbʌndəns/ noun [sing., U] (formal) much more than enough of sth ▶ **super·abun·dant** /-dənt/ adj.

**super·annu·ated** /ˌsuːpərˈænjueɪtɪd/ adj. [usually before noun] (formal or humorous) (of people or things) too old for work or to be used for their original purpose: *superannuated rock stars*

**super·annu·ation** /ˌsuːpərˌænjuˈeɪʃn/ noun [U] (especially BrE) a pension that you get, usually from your employer, when you stop working when you are old and that you pay for while you are working; the money that you pay for this

**su·perb** /suːˈpɜːb; NAmE -ˈpɜːrb/ adj. excellent; of very good quality: *a superb player* ◇ *The car's in superb condition.* ◇ *His performance was absolutely superb.* ◇ *You look superb.* ⇒ SYNONYMS at EXCELLENT ▶ **su·perb·ly** adv.: *a superbly illustrated book* ◇ *She plays superbly.*

**the ˈSuper Bowl™** noun an AMERICAN FOOTBALL game played every year to decide the winner of the National Football League

# superbug 1572

**super·bug** /ˈsuːpəbʌg/ *NAmE* -bɜːrb-/ *noun* a type of bacteria that cannot easily be killed by ANTIBIOTICS ⊃ see also MRSA

**super·center** (*US*) (*BrE* **super·centre**) /ˈsuːpəsentə(r); *NAmE* -pərs-/ *noun* (especially US) a very large store, especially a supermarket that also sells lots of other goods

**super·charged** /ˈsuːpətʃɑːdʒd; *NAmE* -pərtʃɑːrdʒd/ *adj.* **1** (of an engine) powerful because it is supplied with air or fuel at a pressure that is higher than normal **2** (*informal*) stronger, more powerful or more effective than usual: *supercharged words, like 'terrorism' or 'fascism'* ▶ **super·charge** *verb* ~ *sth* **super·char·ger** *noun*: *VW's supercharger for its 16-valve engine*

**super·cili·ous** /ˌsuːpəˈsɪliəs; *NAmE* -pərˈs-/ *adj.* (*disapproving*) behaving towards other people as if you think you are better than they are SYN **superior** ▶ **super·cili·ous·ly** *adv.* **super·cili·ous·ness** *noun* [U]

**super·com·puter** /ˈsuːpəkəmpjuːtə(r); *NAmE* -pərk-/ *noun* a powerful computer with a large amount of memory and a very fast CENTRAL PROCESSING UNIT

**super·con·duct·iv·ity** /ˌsuːpəˌkɒndʌkˈtɪvəti; *NAmE* -pərˌkɑːn-/ *noun* [U] (*physics*) the property (= characteristic) of some substances at very low temperatures to let electricity flow with no RESISTANCE

**super·con·duct·or** /ˈsuːpəkəndʌktə(r); *NAmE* -pərk-/ *noun* (*physics*) a substance that has superconductivity

**super·con·tin·ent** /ˈsuːpəkɒntɪnənt; *NAmE* -pərkɑːn-/ *noun* (*geology*) any of the very large areas of land, for example Gondwana or Laurasia, that existed millions of years ago

**super-duper** /ˌsuːpə ˈduːpə(r); *NAmE* ˌsuːpər-/ *adj.* (*old-fashioned, informal*) excellent

**super·ego** /ˌsuːpərˈiːgəʊ/ *noun* [usually sing.] (*pl.* **-os**) (*psychology*) the part of the mind that makes you aware of right and wrong and makes you feel guilty if you do wrong ⊃ compare EGO, ID

**super·fast** /ˈsuːpəfɑːst; *NAmE* -pərfæst/ *adj.* extremely fast: *a superfast broadband connection*

**super·fi·cial** /ˌsuːpəˈfɪʃl; *NAmE* -pərˈf-/ *adj.* **1** (often disapproving) not studying or looking at sth carefully or completely; seeing only what is obvious: *a superficial analysis* ◇ *The book shows only a superficial understanding of the historical context.* **2** appearing to be true, real or important until you look at it more carefully: *superficial differences/similarities* ◇ *When you first meet her, she gives a superficial impression of warmth and friendliness.* **3** (of a wound or damage) only affecting the surface and therefore not serious: *a superficial injury* ◇ *superficial burns* **4** (*disapproving*) not serious or important and not having any depth of understanding or feeling SYN **shallow**: *a superficial friendship* ◇ *The guests engaged in superficial chatter.* ◇ *She's so superficial!* **5** (*specialist*) of or on the surface of sth: *superficial veins* ◇ *a superficial deposit of acidic soils* ▶ **super·fici·al·ity** /ˌsuːpəˌfɪʃiˈæləti; *NAmE* -pərˌf-/ *noun* [U] **super·fi·cial·ly** /ˌsuːpəˈfɪʃli; *NAmE* -pərˈf-/ *adv.*

**super·fine** /ˈsuːpəfaɪn; *NAmE* -pərf-/ *adj.* (*specialist*) **1** extremely light or thin; made of extremely small pieces: *superfine fibres* ◇ *superfine powder* **2** of extremely good quality: *superfine cloth*

**su·per·flu·ous** /suːˈpɜːfluəs; *NAmE* -ˈpɜːrf-/ *adj.* (*formal*) unnecessary or more than you need or want: *She gave him a look that made words superfluous.* ▶ **su·per·flu·ity** /ˌsuːpəˈfluːəti; *NAmE* -pərˈf-/ *noun* [U, sing.] (*formal*) **su·per·flu·ous·ly** *adv.*

**super·food** /ˈsuːpəfuːd; *NAmE* -pərf-/ *noun* a type of food that some people think is very good for you and helps to prevent disease: *the health benefits of so-called superfoods*

**Super·fund** /ˈsuːpəfʌnd; *NAmE* -pərf-/ *noun* [U, sing.] (*US*) a US government program for finding and cleaning up places where dangerous waste has been thrown away; The area has been designated as a Superfund site.

**super·glue** /ˈsuːpəgluː; *NAmE* -pərg-/ *noun* [U] a very strong GLUE that sticks strongly and is used in small quantities for repairing things

**super·grass** /ˈsuːpəgrɑːs; *NAmE* -pərgræs/ *noun* (*BrE, informal*) a criminal who informs the police about the activities of a large number of other criminals, usually in order to get a less severe punishment ⊃ compare GRASS

**super·group** /ˈsuːpəgruːp; *NAmE* -pərg-/ *noun* a very successful and very famous band that plays rock music, especially one whose members have already become famous in other bands

**super·heated** /ˌsuːpəˈhiːtɪd; *NAmE* -pərˈh-/ *adj.* (*physics*) **1** (of a liquid) that has been heated under pressure above its boiling point without becoming a gas **2** (of a gas) that has been heated above its temperature of SATURATION (= below which it becomes a liquid)

**super·heavy·weight** /ˌsuːpəˈheviweɪt; *NAmE* -pərˈh-/ *noun* [U, C] a weight above HEAVYWEIGHT in BOXING and other sports, in BOXING usually 91 KILOGRAMS or more; a BOXER or other competitor in this class

**super·hero** /ˈsuːpəhɪərəʊ; *NAmE* -pərhɪr-/ *noun* (*pl.* **-oes**) a character in a story, film, etc. who has unusual strength or power and uses it to help people; a real person who has done sth unusually brave to help sb OPP **supervillain**

**super·high·way** /ˈsuːpəhaɪweɪ; *NAmE* -pərh-/ *noun* (*NAmE, old-fashioned*) = INTERSTATE

**super·human** /ˌsuːpəˈhjuːmən; *NAmE* -pərˈh-/ *adj.* having much greater power, knowledge, etc. than is normal SYN **heroic**: *superhuman strength* ◇ *It took an almost superhuman effort to contain his anger.* ⊃ compare SUBHUMAN

**super·im·pose** /ˌsuːpərɪmˈpəʊz/ *verb* **1** ~ *sth* (**on**/**onto** *sth*) to put one image on top of another so that the two can be seen combined: *A diagram of the new road layout was superimposed on a map of the city.* **2** ~ *sth* (**on**/**onto** *sth*) to add some of the qualities of one system or pattern to another one in order to produce sth that combines the qualities of both: *She has tried to superimpose her own attitudes onto this ancient story.* ▶ **super·im·pos·ition** /ˌsuːpərˌɪmpəˈzɪʃn/ *noun* [U]

**super·in·tend** /ˌsuːpərɪnˈtend/ *verb* ~ *sth* (*formal*) to be in charge of sth and make sure that everything is working, being done, etc. as it should be SYN **supervise** ▶ **super·in·tend·ence** /-ˈtendəns/ *noun* [U]

**super·in·tend·ent** /ˌsuːpərɪnˈtendənt/ *noun* **1** a person who has a lot of authority and manages and controls an activity, a place, a group of workers, etc.: *a park superintendent* ◇ *the superintendent of schools in Dallas* **2** (*abbr.* **Supt**) (in the UK) a police officer just above the rank of CHIEF INSPECTOR: *Superintendent Livesey* **3** (*abbr.* **Supt.**) (in the US) the head of a police department **4** (*NAmE*) a person whose job is to be in charge of a building and make small repairs, etc. to it

**su·per·ior** /suːˈpɪəriə(r); *NAmE* -ˈpɪr-/ *adj., noun*
■ *adj.* **1** better in quality than sb/sth else; greater than sb/sth else: *vastly superior* ◇ *superior intelligence* ◇ *Liverpool were clearly the superior team.* ◇ ~ **to sb/sth** *This model is technically superior to its competitors.* ◇ *The enemy won because of their superior numbers* (= there were more of them). OPP **inferior 2** [only before noun] higher in rank, importance or position: *my superior officer* ◇ *superior status* ◇ *a superior court of law* OPP **inferior 3** (*disapproving*) showing by your behaviour that you think you are better than others SYN **arrogant**: *a superior manner* ◇ *He always looks so superior.* **4** (used especially in advertisements) of very good quality; better than other similar things: *superior apartments*
■ *noun* **1** a person of higher rank, status or position: *your social superiors* ◇ *He's my immediate superior* (= the person directly above me). ◇ *I'm going to complain to your superiors.* OPP **inferior 2** used in titles for the head of a religious community: *Mother Superior*

**su·per·ior·ity** /suːˌpɪəriˈɒrəti; *NAmE* -ˌpɪriˈɔːr-/ *noun* [U] **1** the state or quality of being better, more powerful, greater, etc. than others: *to have naval/air superiority* (= more ships/planes than the enemy) ◇ ~ **in sth** *We should make use of our superiority in numbers.* ◇ ~ **to/over sth/sb**

*the company's clear technological superiority over its rivals* **2** behaviour that shows that you think you are better than other people: *an air of superiority* **OPP inferiority**

**su,peri'ority complex** *noun* a feeling that you are better or more important than other people, often as a way of hiding your feelings of failure

**su·per·la·tive** /suːˈpɜːlətɪv; NAmE -ˈpɜːrl-/ *adj., noun*
■ *adj.* **1** excellent **SYN first-rate**: *a superlative performance* **2** (*grammar*) relating to adjectives or adverbs that express the highest degree of sth, for example *best, worst, slowest* and *most difficult* ⊃ compare COMPARATIVE ▶ **su·per·la·tive·ly** *adv.*
■ *noun* (*grammar*) the form of an adjective or adverb that expresses the highest degree of sth: *It's hard to find enough superlatives to describe this book.* ⊃ compare COMPARATIVE

**super·man** /ˈsuːpəmæn; NAmE -pərm-/ *noun* (*pl.* **-men** /-men/) a man who is unusually strong or intelligent or who can do sth extremely well ⊃ compare SUPERWOMAN

**super·mar·ket** ❶ **A1** /ˈsuːpəmɑːkɪt; NAmE -pərmɑːrk-/ (NAmE also **grocery store**) *noun* a large shop that sells food, drinks and goods used in the home. People choose what they want from the shelves and pay for it as they leave: *It is the fifth largest supermarket chain in the UK.*

**super·max** /ˈsuːpəmæks; NAmE -pərm-/ *noun* (*especially* NAmE) a maximum security prison, intended for very dangerous prisoners

**super·model** /ˈsuːpəmɒdl; NAmE -pərmɑːdl/ *noun* a very famous and highly paid fashion model

**super·moon** /ˈsuːpəmuːn; NAmE -pərm-/ *noun* an occasion on which the moon appears particularly large in the sky because it is at its closest point to the earth

**super·nat·ural** /ˌsuːpəˈnætʃrəl; NAmE -pərˈn-/ *adj.* **1** that cannot be explained by the laws of science and that seems to involve gods or magic **SYN paranormal**: *supernatural powers* ◊ *supernatural strength* ⊃ compare NATURAL **2 the supernatural** *noun* [sing.] events, forces or powers that cannot be explained by the laws of science and that seem to involve gods or magic **SYN the paranormal**: *a belief in the supernatural* ▶ **super·nat·ur·al·ly** /-rəli/ *adv.*

**super·nova** /ˈsuːpənəʊvə; NAmE -pərn-/ *noun* (*pl.* **super·novae** /-viː/ or **super·novas**) (*astronomy*) a star that suddenly becomes much brighter because it is exploding ⊃ compare NOVA

**super·numer·ary** /ˌsuːpəˈnjuːmərəri; NAmE -pərˈnuːməreri/ *adj.* (*formal*) more than you normally need; extra

**super·pose** /ˌsuːpəˈpəʊz; NAmE -ˈpoʊz/ *verb* (*formal or specialist*) ~ *sth* to put sth on or above sth else: *They had superposed a picture of his head onto someone else's body.* ▶ **super·pos·ition** /ˌsuːpəpəˈzɪʃn; NAmE -pərp-/ *noun* [U, C]

**super·power** /ˈsuːpəpaʊə(r); NAmE -pərp-/ *noun* **1** one of the countries in the world that has very great military or economic power and a lot of influence, for example the US **2** (*in films and stories*) a special power or ability that sb has, especially a SUPERHERO

**super·script** /ˈsuːpəskrɪpt; NAmE -pərs-/ *noun* (*specialist*) a number, letter or symbol that is written or printed above the normal line of writing or printing ⊃ compare SUBSCRIPT ▶ **super·script** *adj.* [only before noun]

**super·sede** /ˌsuːpəˈsiːd; NAmE -pərˈs-/ *verb* [often passive] to take the place of sth/sb that is considered to be old-fashioned or no longer the best available: **be superseded (by sth)** *The theory has been superseded by more recent research.*

**super·size** /ˈsuːpəsaɪz; NAmE -pərs-/ *adj., verb*
■ *adj.* (*also* **super·sized**) bigger than normal: *supersize portions of fries* ◊ *supersized clothing*
■ *verb* [T, I] ~ **(sb/sth)** to make sth/sb bigger; to become bigger: *We are being supersized into obesity* (= made very fat) *by the fast food industry.* ◊ *TV ads encourage kids to supersize.*

**super·sonic** /ˌsuːpəˈsɒnɪk; NAmE -pərˈsɑːn-/ *adj.* faster than the speed of sound: *a supersonic aircraft* ◊ *supersonic flight* ⊃ compare SUBSONIC

**super·star** /ˈsuːpəstɑː(r); NAmE -pərs-/ *noun* a very famous performer, for example an actor, a singer or a sports player

**super·state** /ˈsuːpəsteɪt; NAmE -pərs-/ *noun* a very powerful state, especially one that is formed by several nations joining or working together: *the European superstate*

**super·sti·tion** /ˌsuːpəˈstɪʃn; NAmE -pərˈs-/ *noun* [U, C] (*often disapproving*) the belief that particular events happen in a way that cannot be explained by reason or science; the belief that particular events bring good or bad luck: *According to superstition, breaking a mirror brings bad luck.* ⊃ WORDFINDER NOTE at LUCK

**super·sti·tious** /ˌsuːpəˈstɪʃəs; NAmE -pərˈs-/ *adj.* believing in superstitions: *superstitious beliefs* ◊ *I'm superstitious about the number 13.* ▶ **super·sti·tious·ly** *adv.*

**super·store** /ˈsuːpəstɔː(r); NAmE -pərs-/ *noun* a very large supermarket or a large shop that sells a wide variety of one type of goods: *a computer superstore*

**super·struc·ture** /ˈsuːpəstrʌktʃə(r); NAmE -pərs-/ *noun* **1** a structure that is built on top of sth, for example the upper parts of a ship or the part of a building above the ground ⊃ compare SUBSTRUCTURE **2** (*formal*) the systems and beliefs in a society that have developed from more simple ones

**super·tank·er** /ˈsuːpətæŋkə(r); NAmE -pərt-/ *noun* a very large ship for carrying oil, etc.

**Super 'Tuesday** *noun* [sing.] (*informal*) a day on which several US states hold PRIMARY elections

**super·vene** /ˌsuːpəˈviːn; NAmE -pərˈv-/ *verb* [I] (*formal*) to happen, especially unexpectedly, and have a powerful effect on the existing situation

**super·vil·lain** /ˈsuːpəvɪlən; NAmE -pərv-/ *noun* a very bad character in a story, especially one with magic powers **OPP superhero**

**super·vise** ⚹+ **C1** /ˈsuːpəvaɪz; NAmE -pərv-/ *verb* [T, I] to be in charge of sb/sth and make sure that everything is done correctly, safely, etc: ~ **(sb/sth)** *to supervise building work* ◊ *Who is supervising?* ◊ ~ **sb doing sth** *She supervised the children playing near the pool.* ⊃ see also UNSUPERVISED

**super·vi·sion** ⚹+ **C1** /ˌsuːpəˈvɪʒn; NAmE -pərˈv-/ *noun* **1** ⚹+ **C1** [U] the work or activity involved in being in charge of sb/sth and making sure that everything is done correctly, safely, etc: *Very young children should not be left to play without supervision.* ◊ **under ~** *The drug should only be used under medical supervision.* **2** [C] a meeting between a student and their TUTOR or supervisor that involves teaching and discussion of the student's work **SYN tutorial**: *I have weekly supervisions.*

**super'vision order** *noun* (*law*) in the UK, an order made by a court which says that the local government or a PROBATION OFFICER must be responsible for a child, help them and check that they behave well

**super·visor** ⚹+ **C1** /ˈsuːpəvaɪzə(r); NAmE -pərv-/ *noun* a person who supervises sb/sth: *I have a meeting with my supervisor about my research topic.* ▶ **super·vis·ory** /ˌsuːpəˈvaɪzəri; NAmE -pərˈv-/ *adj.*: *She has a supervisory role on the project.*

**super·woman** /ˈsuːpəwʊmən; NAmE -pərw-/ *noun* (*pl.* **-women** /-wɪmɪn/) a woman who is unusually strong or intelligent or who can do sth extremely well, especially a woman who has a successful career and also takes care of her home and family ⊃ compare SUPERMAN

**su·pine** /ˈsuːpaɪn; BrE also ˈsjuː-/ *adj.* (*formal*) **1** lying flat on your back: *a supine position* ⊃ compare PRONE, PROSTRATE (1) **2** (*disapproving*) not willing to act or disagree with sb because you are lazy or morally weak ▶ **su·pine·ly** *adv.*

**sup·per** /ˈsʌpə(r)/ *noun* [U, C] the last meal of the day, either a main meal, usually smaller and less formal than dinner, or a SNACK eaten before you go to bed: *I'll do my homework after supper.* ◊ *What's for supper?* ◊ *We'll have an early supper tonight.* ⊃ compare TEA (6) ⊃ note at MEAL

# supplant

**sup·plant** /səˈplɑːnt; *NAmE* -ˈplænt/ *verb* ~ **sb/sth** (*formal*) to take the place of sb/sth (especially sb/sth older or less modern) **SYN** **replace**

**sup·ple** /ˈsʌpl/ *adj.* **1** able to bend and move parts of your body easily into different positions: *her slim, supple body* ◊ *These exercises will help to keep you supple.* **2** soft and able to bend easily without starting to split: *Moisturizing cream helps to keep your skin soft and supple.* ▸ **supple·ness** *noun* [U]

**sup·ple·ment** noun, verb
- *noun* /ˈsʌplɪmənt/ **1** a thing that is added to sth else to improve or complete it: *vitamin/dietary supplements* (= vitamins and other foods eaten in addition to what you usually eat) ◊ ~ **to sth** *Industrial sponsorship is a supplement to government funding.* **2** an extra separate section, often in the form of a magazine, that is sold with a newspaper: *the Sunday colour supplements* ⇒ **WORDFINDER NOTE** at **NEWSPAPER 3** ~ **(to sth)** a book or a section at the end of a book that gives extra information or deals with a special subject: *the supplement to the Oxford English Dictionary* **4** (*BrE*) an amount of money that you pay for an extra service or item, especially in addition to the basic cost of a holiday **SYN** **surcharge**: ~ **(for sth)** *There is a £10 supplement for a single room.* ◊ **at/for a** ~ *Safety deposit boxes are available at a supplement.*
- *verb* /ˈsʌplɪment/ to add sth to sth in order to improve it or make it more complete: ~ **sth with sth** *a diet supplemented with vitamin pills* ◊ ~ **sth** *He supplements his income by giving private lessons.* ▸ **sup·ple·men·ta·tion** /ˌsʌplɪmenˈteɪʃn/ *noun* [U]

**sup·ple·men·tary** /ˌsʌplɪˈmentri/ (*especially BrE*) (*NAmE* usually **sup·ple·men·tal** /ˌsʌplɪˈmentl/) *adj.* provided in addition to sth else in order to improve or complete it **SYN** **additional**: *supplementary information*

**sup·pli·cant** /ˈsʌplɪkənt/ (also **sup·pli·ant** /ˈsʌpliənt/) *noun* (*formal*) a person who asks for sth in a HUMBLE way, especially from God or a powerful person

**sup·pli·ca·tion** /ˌsʌplɪˈkeɪʃn/ *noun* [U, C] (*formal*) the act of asking for sth with a very HUMBLE request or prayer: *She knelt in supplication.*

**sup·plier** /səˈplaɪə(r)/ *noun* a person or company that supplies goods: *a leading supplier of computers in the UK*

**sup·ply** /səˈplaɪ/ *noun, verb*
- *noun* **1** [C] an amount of sth that is provided or available to be used: *Advances in agriculture increased the food supply.* ◊ *Demand for skilled labour outstrips supply.* ◊ *We cannot guarantee adequate supplies of raw materials.* ⇒ see also **MONEY SUPPLY 2 supplies** [pl.] the things such as food, medicines, fuel, etc. that are needed by a group of people, for example an army or expedition: *Our supplies were running out.* ◊ *food and medical supplies for refugees* **3** [U] the act of supplying sth; the fact of receiving sth that is being supplied: *the electricity/energy/gas supply* ◊ *The storm disrupted the town's power supply.* ◊ *A stroke is caused by disruption to the blood supply to the brain.* ◊ *the supply of goods and services* ⇒ see also **WATER SUPPLY** **IDM** **SHORT** *adj.*
- *verb* (**sup·plies, sup·ply·ing, sup·plied, sup·plied**) to provide sb/sth with sth that they need or want, especially in large quantities: ~ **sth to sb/sth** *The company supplied sports equipment to schools.* ◊ ~ **sb/sth with sth** *The company supplied schools with sports equipment.* ◊ ~ **sb/sth** *The well stopped supplying water for the village many years ago.* ◊ *foods supplying our daily vitamin needs* ◊ *This information was kindly supplied by the manufacturer.*

**sup·ply and deˈmand** *noun* [U] (*economics*) the relationship between the amount of goods or services that are available and the amount that people want to buy, especially when this controls prices

**supˈply chain** *noun* [usually sing.] (*business*) the series of processes involved in the production and supply of goods, from when they are first made, grown, etc. until they are bought or used ⇒ **WORDFINDER NOTE** at **INDUSTRY**

**supˈply line** *noun* a route along which food, equipment, etc. is transported to an army during a war

**supˈply-side** *adj.* [only before noun] (*economics*) connected with the policy of reducing taxes in order to encourage economic growth

**supˈply teacher** (*BrE*) (*NAmE* **ˈsubstitute ˈteacher**) *noun* a teacher employed to do the work of another teacher who is away because of illness, etc.

**sup·port** /səˈpɔːt; *NAmE* -ˈpɔːrt/ *verb, noun*
- *verb*
  - ENCOURAGE/GIVE HELP **1** to help or encourage sb/sth by saying or showing that you agree with them/it **SYN** **back**: ~ **sb/sth** *to support an idea/a view* ◊ *Efforts to reduce waste are strongly supported by environmental groups.* ◊ *If you raise it at the meeting, I'll support you.* ◊ ~ **sb/sth in sth** *The government supported the unions in their demand for a minimum wage.* **2** ~ **sb** to give or be ready to give help to sb if they need it: *an organization that supports people with AIDS* ◊ *The company will support customers in Europe* (= solve their problems with a product).
  - SPORTS TEAM **3** ~ **sb/sth** (*BrE*) to like a particular sports team, watch their games, etc: *Which team do you support?*
  - PROVIDE MONEY, ETC. **4** ~ **sth** to help or encourage sth to be successful by giving it money **SYN** **sponsor**: *The project was supported by grants from various charities.* ◊ *A number of famous actors actively supported the campaign.* **5** ~ **sb/sth/yourself** to provide everything necessary, especially money, so that sb/sth can live or exist: *He struggles to support his family.* ◊ *She supported herself through college by working as a waitress in a local bar.* ◊ *The atmosphere of Mars could not support life.*
  - HELP PROVE STH **6** ~ **sth** to help to show that sth is true **SYN** **corroborate**: *Current data support this hypothesis.* ◊ *There is no evidence to support his claims.* ⇒ **LANGUAGE BANK** at **EVIDENCE**
  - HOLD IN POSITION **7** ~ **sb/sth** to hold sb/sth in position; to prevent sb/sth from falling: *a platform supported by concrete pillars* ◊ *Support the baby's head when you hold it.*
  - POP/ROCK CONCERT **8** ~ **sb/sth** (of a band or singer) to perform at a pop or rock concert before the main performer: *They were supported by a local Liverpool band.* ⇒ **WORDFINDER NOTE** at **CONCERT**
  - COMPUTER **9** ~ **sth** (of a computer or computer system) to allow a particular program, language or device to be used with it: *This digital audio player supports multiple formats.*
- *noun*
  - APPROVAL **1** [U] approval that you give to sb/sth because you want them to be successful: ~ **for sth** *There is strong public support for the policy.* ◊ *His ideas are gaining popular support* (= the support of many people). ◊ *to provide/offer support* ◊ *I intend to lend my full support to the campaign.* ◊ **to win/gain sb's support** ◊ ~ **from sb/sth** *The policy has broad support from industry.* ◊ **in ~ of sth** *Only a few people spoke in support of the proposal.* ⇒ see also **AIR SUPPORT**
  - MONEY **2** [U] ~ **(from sb/sth)** money or goods that you give to sb/sth in order to help them: *They received no financial support from the government.* ⇒ see also **CHILD SUPPORT, INCOME SUPPORT**
  - HELP **3** [U] sympathy and help that you give to sb who is in a difficult or unhappy situation: *Her family and friends have given her lots of support.* ◊ *Thank you for all your messages of support at this difficult time.* ◊ *support staff/services* ⇒ see also **LIFE SUPPORT, LIFE SUPPORT MACHINE, MORAL SUPPORT, VICTIM SUPPORT**
  - PROOF **4** [U] evidence that helps to show that sth is true or correct: ~ **for sth** *The statistics offer further support for our theory.* ◊ **in ~ of sth** *There is little evidence in support of this hypothesis.*
  - HOLDING IN POSITION **5** [C] a thing that holds sth and prevents it from falling: *The supports under the bridge were starting to bend.* ◊ (*figurative*) *When my father died, Jim was a real support.* **6** [U] the act of holding sth in position or preventing it from falling: **for ~** *She held on to his arm for support.* ◊ **without ~** *After the operation he couldn't walk without support.* **7** [C] something you wear

to hold an injured or weak part of your body in position: *a knee/back support*
- **POP/ROCK CONCERT** 8 [U] a band or singer who performs in a pop or rock concert before the main performer: *The support (act) has yet to be confirmed.*
- **TECHNICAL HELP** 9 [U] technical help that a company gives to customers using their computers or other products: *There is a lack of decent home user support.* ⇒ see also TECHNICAL SUPPORT

**sup·port·er** 🔊 B1 /səˈpɔːtə(r); NAmE -ˈpɔːrt-/ noun
1 🔊 B1 a person who supports a political party, an idea, etc: *a strong/loyal/staunch/ardent supporter* ◇ *Labour supporters* 2 🔊 B1 (BrE) a person who supports a particular sports team SYN fan: *I'm an Arsenal supporter.*

**sup·port group** noun a group of people who meet to help each other with a particular problem: *a support group for single parents*

**sup·port·ing** /səˈpɔːtɪŋ/; NAmE -ˈpɔːrt-/ adj. [only before noun] 1 a supporting actor in a play or film has an important part but not the leading one: *The movie featured Robert Lindsay in a supporting role.* 2 (formal) helping to show that sth is true: *There was a wealth of supporting evidence.* 3 carrying the weight of sth: *a supporting wall*

**sup·port·ive** 🔊+ C1 /səˈpɔːtɪv; NAmE -ˈpɔːrt-/ adj. encouraging sb or giving them help or sympathy: *a supportive family* ◇ *She was very supportive during my father's illness.*

**sup·pose** 🔊 A2 🔊 /səˈpəʊz/ verb 1 🔊 A2 [I, T] to think or believe that sth is true or possible (based on the knowledge that you have): *Getting a visa isn't as simple as you might suppose.* ◇ *Prices will go up, I suppose.* ◇ ~(that)... *I don't suppose for a minute that he'll agree* (= I'm sure that he won't). ◇ *Why do you suppose he resigned?* ◇ *There is no reason to suppose she's lying.* ◇ *I suppose you think it's funny, do you?* (= showing anger). HELP 'That' is nearly always left out, especially in speech.: ~ sb/sth (to be/have) sth (formal) *She had supposed him (to be) very rich.* 2 🔊 A2 [I, T] used to make a statement, request or suggestion less direct or less strong: *I could take you in the car, I suppose* (= but I don't really want to). ◇ *'Can I borrow the car?' 'I suppose so'* (= Yes, but I'm not happy about it). ◇ ~(that)... *I don't suppose (that) I could have a look at your newspaper, could I?* ◇ *Suppose we take a later train?* 3 🔊 B2 [T] to pretend that sth is true; to imagine what would happen if sth were true: ~(that)... *Suppose flights are fully booked on that day—which other day could we go?* ◇ *Let us suppose, for example, that you are married with two children.* ◇ ~ sth (formal) *The theory supposes the existence of life on other planets.* ◇ ~ sb/sth (to be/have) sth (formal) *Suppose him (to be) dead—what then?*
**IDM** **be supposed to do/be sth** 1 🔊 B1 to be expected or required to do/be sth according to a rule, a custom, an arrangement, etc: *What am I supposed to do?* ◇ *You're supposed to buy a ticket, but not many people do.* ◇ *I thought we were supposed to be paid today.* ◇ *The engine doesn't sound like it's supposed to.* ◇ *How was I supposed to know you were waiting for me?* ◇ *Yes and no.' 'What is that supposed to mean?'* (= showing that you are annoyed) ⇒ EXPRESS YOURSELF at HAVE TO 2 🔊 B2 to be generally believed or expected to be/do sth: *I haven't seen it myself, but it's supposed to be a great movie.* ◇ *This combination of qualities is generally supposed to be extremely rare.* **not be supposed to do sth** to not be allowed to do sth: *You're not supposed to walk on the grass.*

**sup·posed** /səˈpəʊzd, -ˈpəʊzɪd/ adj. [only before noun] used to show that you think that a claim, statement or way of describing sb/sth is not true or correct, although it is generally believed to be SYN alleged: *This is the opinion of the supposed experts.* ◇ *When did this supposed accident happen?*

**sup·posed·ly** 🔊+ C1 /səˈpəʊzɪdli/ adv. according to what is generally thought or believed but not known for certain SYN allegedly: *The novel is supposedly based on a true story.*

**sup·pos·ing** /səˈpəʊzɪŋ/ conj. ~(that) used to ask sb to pretend that sth is true or to imagine that sth will happen:

*Supposing (that) you are wrong, what will you do then?* ◇ *But supposing he sees us?*

**sup·pos·ition** /ˌsʌpəˈzɪʃn/ noun (formal) 1 [C] ~(that...) an idea that you think is true although you may not be able to prove it SYN assumption: *The police are working on the supposition that he was murdered.* 2 [U] the act of believing or claiming that sth is true even though it cannot be proved: *The report is based entirely on supposition.*

**sup·posi·tory** /səˈpɒzɪtri; NAmE -ˈpɑːzətɔːri/ noun (pl. -ies) a small piece of solid medicine that is placed in the RECTUM or VAGINA and left to DISSOLVE gradually

**sup·press** 🔊+ C1 /səˈpres/ verb 1 🔊+ C1 ~ sth (usually disapproving) (of a government, ruler, etc.) to put an end, often by force, to a group or an activity that is believed to threaten authority SYN quash: *The rebellion was brutally suppressed.* 2 🔊+ C1 ~ sth (usually disapproving) to prevent sth from being published or made known: *The police were accused of suppressing vital evidence.* 3 🔊+ C1 ~ sth to prevent yourself from having or expressing a feeling or an emotion: *to suppress a smile* ◇ *She was unable to suppress her anger.* 4 🔊+ C1 ~ sth to prevent sth from growing, developing or continuing: *drugs that suppress the appetite*

**sup·pres·sant** /səˈpresnt/ noun a drug that is used to prevent one of the body's functions from working normally: *an appetite suppressant*

**sup·pres·sion** /səˈpreʃn/ noun [U] the act of suppressing sth: *the suppression of a rebellion* ◇ *the suppression of emotion*

**sup·pres·sor** /səˈpresə(r)/ noun a thing or person that SUPPRESSES sb/sth: *the body's pain suppressors*

**supra·nation·al** /ˌsuːprəˈnæʃnəl/ adj. (formal) involving more than one country

**su·prema·cist** /suːˈpreməsɪst/ noun a person who believes that their own race is better than others and should be in power: *a white supremacist*

**su·prem·acy** /suːˈpreməsi/ noun [U] a position in which you have more power, authority or status than anyone else: *the battle for supremacy in the region* ◇ *~ over sb/sth The company has established total supremacy over its rivals.* ⇒ see also WHITE SUPREMACY

**su·preme** 🔊+ C1 /suːˈpriːm/ adj. [usually before noun] 1 🔊+ C1 highest in rank or position: *the Supreme Commander of the armed forces* ◇ *the supreme champion* ◇ *It is an event in which she reigns supreme.* 2 🔊+ C1 very great or the greatest in degree: *to make the supreme sacrifice* (= die for what you believe in) ◇ *a supreme effort* ◇ *She smiled with supreme confidence.*

**the Supreme Being** noun [sing.] (formal) God

**the Supreme Court** (also high court) noun [sing.] the highest court in a country or state

**su·preme·ly** /suːˈpriːmli/ adv. extremely: *supremely confident* ◇ *They managed it all supremely well.*

**su·premo** /suːˈpriːməʊ/ noun (pl. -os) (BrE, informal) a person who has the most power or authority in a particular business or activity: *the world football supremo, Gianni Infantino*

**Supt** (also Supt. especially in NAmE) abbr. (in the police force) SUPERINTENDENT: *Chief Supt Pauline Clark*

**sura** (also surah) /ˈsʊərə; NAmE ˈsʊrə/ noun a chapter or section of the Koran

**sur·charge** /ˈsɜːtʃɑːdʒ; NAmE ˈsɜːrtʃɑːrdʒ/ noun, verb
■ noun ~(on sth) an extra amount of money that you must pay in addition to the usual price SYN supplement
■ verb ~ sb (sth) to make sb pay a surcharge: *We were surcharged £50 for travelling on a Friday.*

**sure** 🔊 A1 /ʃʊə(r), ʃɔː(r); NAmE ʃʊr/ adj., adv.
■ adj. (surer, surest) HELP You can also use more sure and most sure, especially in sense 1. 1 🔊 A1 [not before noun] confident that you know sth or that you are right SYN certain: *'Is that John over there?' 'I'm not sure'.* ◇ ~(that)... *I'm pretty sure (that) he'll agree.* ◇ *Are you sure you don't mind?* ◇ ~ of sth *I hope you are sure of your facts.* ◇ ~ about

# sure-fire

## ▼ SYNONYMS

**sure**

confident · convinced · certain · positive · clear

These words all describe sb who knows without doubt that sth is true or will happen.

**sure** [not before noun] without any doubt that you are right, that sth is true, that you will get sth or that sth will happen: *'Is that John over there?' 'I'm not sure.'* ◊ *Are you sure about that?* ◊ *England must win this game to be sure of qualifying.* **NOTE** **Sure** is often used in negative statements and questions, because there is some doubt or worry over the matter. If there is no doubt, people often say *quite sure*: *I'm quite sure (that) I left my bag here* (= I have no doubt about it).

**confident** completely sure that sth will happen in the way that you want or expect: *I'm quite confident that you'll get the job.* ◊ *The team feels confident of winning.* **NOTE** **Confident** is a stronger and more definite word than **sure** and is more often used in positive statements, when you feel no worry.

**convinced** [not before noun] completely sure that sth is true or right, especially because the evidence seems to prove it or sb else has persuaded you to believe it: *I'm convinced that she's innocent.*

**certain** [not usually before noun] sure that you are right or that sth is true: *Are you absolutely certain about this?*

### SURE OR CERTAIN?

Like **sure**, **certain** is often used in negative statements and questions. It is slightly more formal than **sure**; **sure** is more frequent, especially in spoken English.

**positive** [not before noun] (*rather informal*) completely sure that sth is true: *She was positive that he'd been there.* ◊ *'Are you sure?' 'Positive.'*

**clear** (often used in negative statements and questions) having no doubt or confusion about sth: *My memory isn't really clear on that point.*

### PATTERNS

- sure / confident / convinced / certain / positive / clear about sth
- sure / confident / convinced / certain of sth
- sure / confident / convinced / certain / positive / clear that …
- sure / certain / clear who / what / how, etc.
- to **feel** sure / confident / convinced / certain / positive
- **quite** / **absolutely** / **completely** / **fairly** / **pretty** sure / confident / convinced / certain / positive / clear
- **not altogether** sure / confident / convinced / certain / clear

sth *Are you sure about that?* ◊ *not ~ how, whether, etc …* *Ask me if you're not sure how to do it.* ◊ *I'm not sure whether I should tell you this.* ◊ *not exactly / entirely / absolutely / really sure* **OPP** **unsure** **2** **B1** [not before noun] certain that you will receive sth or that sth will happen: **~ of sth** *You're always sure of a warm welcome there.* ◊ **~ of doing sth** *England must win this game to be sure of qualifying for the World Cup.* **3** **B1** **~ to do sth** certain to do sth or to happen: *The exhibition is sure to be popular.* ◊ *It's sure to rain.* ⇨ SYNONYMS at CERTAIN **4** [usually before noun] that can be trusted or relied on: *It's* **a sure sign** *of economic recovery.* ◊ *There's only one sure way to do it.* ◊ *He is a* **sure bet** *for the presidential nomination* (= certain to succeed). ⇨ SYNONYMS at CERTAIN **5** [usually before noun] steady and confident: *We admired her sure touch at the keyboard.* **IDM** **be sure to do sth** used to tell sb to do sth: *Be sure to give your family my regards.* **HELP** In spoken English **and** plus another verb can be used instead of **to** and the infinitive: *Be sure and call me tomorrow.* **for ˈsure** (*informal*) without doubt: *No one knows for sure what happened.* ◊ *I think he'll be back on Monday, but I can't say for sure.* ◊ *One thing is for sure—it's not going to be easy.* ◊ (*NAmE*) *'Will you be there?' 'For sure.'* **make ˈsure (of sth / that …)** **1** **A2** to do sth in order to be certain that sth else happens: *Make sure (that) no one finds out about this.* ◊ *They* scored another goal and made sure of victory. ◊ *Our staff will do their best to make sure you enjoy your vis* **2** **A2** to check that sth is true or has been done: *She looked around to make sure that she was alone.* ◊ *I think the door's locked, but I'll just go and make sure.* **ˈsure of yourself** (*sometimes disapproving*) very confident: *She seems very sure of herself.* **sure ˈthing** (*informal, especially NAmE*) used to say 'yes' to a suggestion or request: *'Are you coming?' 'Sure thing.'* **to be ˈsure** (*formal*) used to admit that sth is true: *He is intelligent, to be sure, but he's also very lazy.* ⇨ more at BET n.

- **adv.** (*informal, especially NAmE*) **1** **A2** used to say 'yes' to sb: *'Will you open the wine?' 'Sure, where is it?'* ◊ *Did it hurt? Sure it hurt.* **2** used to emphasize sth that you are saying: *Boy, it sure is hot.* ◊ *'Amazing view'. 'Sure is.'* ◊ *I sure hope you are right about that.* ◊ *That song* **sure as hell** *sounds familiar.* **3** used to reply to sb who has just thanked you for sth: *'Thanks for the ride.' 'Sure—anytime.'*

**IDM** **(as) sure as ˈeggs is ˈeggs** (*old-fashioned, BrE, informal*) used to say that sth is definitely true **ˌsure eˈnough** used to say that sth happened as expected: *I said he'd forget, and sure enough he did.*

**ˈsure-fire** *adj.* [only before noun] (*informal*) certain to be successful or to happen as you expect: *a sure-fire success*

**ˌsure-ˈfooted** *adj.* **1** not likely to fall when walking or climbing on rough ground **2** confident and unlikely to make mistakes, especially in difficult situations

**sure·ly** ❶ **B1** /ˈʃʊəli, ˈʃɔːli; *NAmE* ˈʃʊrli/ *adv.* **1** **B1** used to show that you are almost certain of what you are saying and want other people to agree with you: *Surely we should do something about it?* ◊ *It's surely only a matter of time before he is found, isn't it?* **2** **B1** used with a negative to show that sth surprises you and you do not want to believe it: *Surely you don't think I was responsible for this?* ◊ *'They're getting married.' 'Surely not!'* ◊ *They won't go, surely?* **3** (*formal*) without doubt; certainly: *He knew that if help did not arrive soon they would surely die.* **4** (*old-fashioned, NAmE, informal*) used to say 'yes' to sb or to agree to sth **IDM** see SLOWLY

### ▼ WHICH WORD?

**surely / certainly**

- You use **surely**, especially in *BrE*, to show that you are almost certain about what you are saying and you want other people to agree with you: *Surely this can't be right?* **Surely** in negative sentences shows that something surprises you and you do not want to believe it: *You're surely not thinking of going, are you?*
- **Certainly** usually means 'without doubt' or 'definitely', and is used to show that you strongly believe something or to emphasize that something is really true: *I'll certainly remember this trip!* In informal *NAmE* this would be: *I'll sure remember this trip!*
- Compare: *The meal was certainly too expensive* (= there is no doubt about it) and *The meal was surely too expensive?* (= that is my opinion. Don't you agree?).
- In formal language only, **surely** can be used to mean 'without doubt': *This will surely end in disaster.*

⇨ note at COURSE, SURE

**sure·ness** /ˈʃʊənəs, ˈʃɔːn-; *NAmE* ˈʃʊrn-/ *noun* [U] the quality of being confident and steady; not hesitating or doubting: *an artist's sureness of touch* ◊ *her sureness that she had done the right thing*

**surety** /ˈʃʊərəti, ˈʃɔːr-; *NAmE* ˈʃʊr-/ *noun* [C, U] (*pl.* **-ies**) (*law*) **1** money given as a promise that you will pay a debt, appear in court, etc: *She was granted bail with a surety of $500.* **2** a person who accepts responsibility if sb else does not pay a debt, appear in court, etc: *to act as surety for sb*

**surf** /sɜːf; *NAmE* sɜːrf/ *noun, verb*

- *noun* **1** [U] large waves in the sea or ocean, and the white FOAM that they produce as they fall on the beach, on rocks, etc: *the sound of surf breaking on the beach* ⇨ WORDFINDER NOTE at SEA **2** [*sing.*] an act of going SURFING: *He decided to go for a surf near Fremantle.* ◊ *Sydney, surf capital of the world* (= where the sport of surfing is very popular)

- **verb 1** (*often* go 'surfing) [I, T] ~ (sth) to take part in the sport of riding on waves on a SURFBOARD **2** [T] ~ the Net / internet to use the internet: *I was surfing the Net looking for information on Indian music.*

**sur·face** 🔑 B1 /ˈsɜːfɪs; NAmE ˈsɜːrf-/ *noun, verb*
- *noun* **1** 🔑 B1 [C] the outside or top layer of sth: *We need a flat, smooth surface to play the game on.* ◊ *an uneven road surface* ◊ *a broad leaf with a large surface area* **2** 🔑 B1 [C, usually sing.] the top layer of an area of water or land: *the earth's surface* ◊ **on the ~ (of sth)** *These plants float on the surface of the water.* ◊ **below / beneath / under the ~ (of sth)** *We could see fish swimming just below the surface.* **3** 🔑 B2 [C] the flat upper part of a piece of furniture, that is used for working on: *She's cleaned all the kitchen surfaces.* **4** [sing.] the outer appearance of a person, thing or situation; the qualities that you see or notice, that are not hidden: **below / beneath / under the ~ (of sth)** *Rage bubbled just below the surface of his mind.*
- **IDM** **on the 'surface** when not thought about deeply or carefully and completely; when not looked at carefully: *It seems like a good idea on the surface but there are sure to be problems.* ◊ *On the surface, he appeared unchanged.* ⇒ more at SCRATCH *v.*
- *verb* **1** [I] to come up to the surface of water **SYN emerge**: *The ducks dived and surfaced again several metres away.* **2** [I] to suddenly appear or become obvious after having been hidden for a while **SYN emerge**: *Doubts began to surface.* ◊ *She surfaced again years later in London.* **3** [I] (*informal*) to wake up or get up after being asleep: *He finally surfaced around noon.* **4** [T] ~ sth to put a surface on a road, path, etc.

'**surface mail** *noun* [U] letters, etc. carried by road, railway or sea, not by air

'**surface structure** *noun* (*grammar*) the structure of a well-formed sentence in a language, rather than its UNDERLYING form ⇒ compare DEEP STRUCTURE

'**surface tension** *noun* [U] (*specialist*) the property (= characteristic) of liquids by which they form a layer at their surface, and which makes sure that this surface covers as small an area as possible

'**surface-to-'air** *adj.* [only before noun] (especially of MISSILES) fired from the ground or from ships and aimed at aircraft

'**surface-to-'surface** *adj.* [only before noun] (especially of MISSILES) fired from the ground or from ships and aimed at another point on the ground or a ship

**sur·fac·tant** /sɜːˈfæktənt; NAmE sɜːrˈf-/ *noun* [C, U] (*specialist*) a substance that reduces the SURFACE TENSION of a liquid, often forming bubbles in the liquid

'**surf and 'turf** = SURF 'N' TURF

'**surf·board** /ˈsɜːfbɔːd; NAmE ˈsɜːrfbɔːrd/ (*also* **board**) *noun* a long narrow board used for SURFING

**sur·feit** /ˈsɜːfɪt; NAmE ˈsɜːrf-/ *noun* [usually sing.] ~ (of sth) (*formal*) an amount that is too large **SYN excess**

**surf·er** /ˈsɜːfə(r); NAmE ˈsɜːrf-/ *noun* **1** a person who goes SURFING **2** (*informal*) a person who spends a lot of time using the internet ⇒ see also SILVER SURFER

**surf·ing** /ˈsɜːfɪŋ; NAmE ˈsɜːrf-/ *noun* [U] **1** the sport of riding on waves while standing on a narrow board called a SURFBOARD: *to go surfing* **2** the activity of looking at different things on the internet in order to find sth interesting

'**surf 'lifesaver** *noun* (AustralE, NZE) = LIFEGUARD

'**surf 'n' 'turf** (*also* '**surf and 'turf**) *noun* [U] (*especially* NAmE) SEAFOOD and STEAK served together as a meal

**surge** 🔑 C1 /sɜːdʒ; NAmE sɜːrdʒ/ *noun, verb*
- *noun* **1** 🔑 C1 ~ (of sth) a sudden increase of a strong feeling **SYN rush**: *She felt a sudden surge of anger.* ◊ *a surge of excitement* ⇒ see also UPSURGE **2** 🔑 C1 a sudden increase in the amount or number of sth: ~ **in sth** *a surge in consumer spending* ◊ *We are having trouble keeping up with the recent surge in demand.* ◊ ~ **of sth** *After an initial surge of interest, there has been little call for our services.* ⇒ see also UPSURGE **3** 🔑 C1 a sudden, strong movement forward or upwards: *a tidal surge* ◊ *A surge of people poured through the gates.* ⇒ see also STORM SURGE **4** 🔑 C1 a sudden increase in the flow of electrical power through a

system: *An electrical surge damaged the computer's disk drive.* ◊ *The National Grid was hit by a huge power surge.*
- *verb* **1** 🔑 C1 [I] + *adv. / prep.* to move quickly and with force in a particular direction: *The gates opened and the crowd surged forward.* ◊ *Flood waters surged into their homes.* **2** 🔑 C1 [I] (+ *adv. / prep.*) to fill sb with a strong feeling **SYN sweep**: *Relief surged through her.* **3** 🔑 C1 [I] (of prices, profits, etc.) to suddenly increase in value: *Share prices surged.* ⇒ related noun UPSURGE **4** [I] (of the flow of electrical power) to increase suddenly

**sur·geon** 🔑+ /ˈsɜːdʒən; NAmE ˈsɜːrdʒ-/ *noun* a doctor who is trained to perform surgery (= medical operations that involve cutting open a person's body): *a brain / heart surgeon* ⇒ compare PHYSICIAN ⇒ **WORDFINDER NOTE** at DOCTOR ⇒ see also DENTAL SURGEON, PLASTIC SURGEON, TREE SURGEON, VETERINARY SURGEON

'**Surgeon 'General** *noun* (*pl.* **Surgeons General**) (in the US) the head of a public health service or of a medical service in the armed forces: *Surgeon General's warning: cigarette smoking causes cancer*

**sur·gery** 🔑 B2 /ˈsɜːdʒəri; NAmE ˈsɜːrdʒ-/ *noun* (*pl.* **-ies**) **1** 🔑 B2 [U] medical treatment of injuries or diseases that involves cutting open a person's body and often removing or replacing some parts; the branch of medicine connected with this treatment: *major / minor surgery* ◊ *to undergo heart / knee / shoulder surgery* ◊ *She's a specialist in reconstructive and cosmetic surgery.* **HELP** In formal or American English the countable form can be used: *She had three surgeries over ten days.* ⇒ **WORDFINDER NOTE** at OPERATION ⇒ see also BRAIN SURGERY, KEYHOLE SURGERY, OPEN-HEART SURGERY, PLASTIC SURGERY, TREE SURGERY **2** 🔑 B2 [C] (BrE) (NAmE **office**) a place where a doctor, dentist or VET sees patients: *a doctor's / dentist's / vet's surgery* **3** [U, C] (BrE) the time during which a doctor, dentist or VET is available to see patients: *morning / afternoon / evening surgery* ◊ *surgery hours* ◊ *Is there a surgery this evening?* **4** [C] (BrE) a time when people can meet their Member of Parliament to ask questions and get help: *a constituency surgery*

**sur·gi·cal** 🔑+ C1 /ˈsɜːdʒɪkl; NAmE ˈsɜːrdʒ-/ *adj.* [only before noun] used in or connected with surgery: *surgical procedures* ◊ *a surgical ward* (= for patients having operations)
▸ **sur·gi·cal·ly** /-kli/ *adv.*: *The lumps will need to be surgically removed.*

'**surgical 'spirit** (BrE) (NAmE '**rubbing 'alcohol**) *noun* [U] a clear liquid, consisting mainly of alcohol, used for cleaning wounds, etc.

**surly** /ˈsɜːli; NAmE ˈsɜːrli/ *adj.* (**sur·lier**, **sur·li·est**) unfriendly and rude: *a surly youth* ▸ **sur·li·ness** *noun* [U]

**sur·mise** *verb, noun*
- *verb* /səˈmaɪz; NAmE sərˈm-/ ~ (that) … | ~ what, where, etc … | ~ sth | + speech (*formal*) to guess or suppose sth using the evidence you have, without definitely knowing **SYN conjecture**: *From the looks on their faces, I surmised that they had had an argument.*
- *noun* /ˈsɜːmaɪz; NAmE ˈsɜːrm-/ [U, C, usually sing.] (*formal*) a guess based on some facts that you know already: *This is pure surmise on my part.*

**sur·mount** /səˈmaʊnt; NAmE sərˈm-/ *verb* (*formal*) **1** ~ sth to deal successfully with a difficulty **SYN overcome**: *She was well aware of the difficulties that had to be surmounted.* **2** [usually passive] ~ sth to be placed on top of sth: *a high column surmounted by a statue*

**sur·name** /ˈsɜːneɪm; NAmE ˈsɜːrn-/ *noun* (especially BrE) a name shared by all the members of a family (written last in English names) ⇒ compare FAMILY NAME, LAST NAME

**sur·pass** /səˈpɑːs; NAmE sərˈpæs/ *verb* (*formal*) to do or be better than sb / sth: ~ **sth / sb** *He hopes one day to surpass the world record.* ◊ *Its success has surpassed all expectations.* ◊ ~ **yourself** *Her cooking was always good, but this time she had surpassed herself* (= done better than her own high standards).

**sur·plice** /ˈsɜːpləs; NAmE ˈsɜːrp-/ *noun* a loose white piece of clothing with wide SLEEVES (= parts covering the arms)

# surplus

worn by priests and singers in the CHOIR during church services

**sur·plus** 🔊 **C1** /ˈsɜːpləs; NAmE ˈsɜːrplʌs/ noun, adj.
- **noun** [C, U] **1** 🔊 **C1** an amount that is extra or more than you need: *food surpluses* ◊ *in ~ Wheat was in surplus that year.* **2** 🔊 **C1** the amount by which the amount of money received is greater than the amount of money spent: *a surplus of £400 million* ◊ *in ~ The balance of payments was in surplus last year* (= the value of exports was greater than the value of imports). ⊃ compare DEFICIT ⊃ see also TRADE SURPLUS
- **adj.** more than is needed or used: *surplus cash* ◊ *Surplus grain is being sold for export.* ◊ **~to** *sth These items are surplus to requirements* (= not needed).

**sur·prise** 🔊 **A2** /səˈpraɪz; NAmE sərˈp-/ noun, verb
- **noun 1** 🔊 **A2** [C] an event, a piece of news, etc. that is unexpected or that happens suddenly: *What a nice surprise!* ◊ *I have a surprise for you!* ◊ *It comes as no surprise to learn that they broke their promises.* ◊ *Her letter came as a complete surprise.* ◊ *'The appointment came as a pleasant surprise to me,' she says.* ◊ *The announcements came as something of a surprise to them.* ◊ *There are lots of surprises in store for visitors to the gallery.* ◊ *He was there on a surprise visit to the troops.* **2** 🔊 **A2** [U, C] a feeling caused by sth happening suddenly or unexpectedly: *a look of surprise* ◊ *in~ She looked up in surprise.* ◊ **~at** *sth He gasped with surprise at her strength.* ◊ **~at seeing, hearing,** etc. *They couldn't conceal their surprise at seeing us together.* ◊ *I got a surprise when I saw the bill.* ◊ **to sb's ~** *To everyone's surprise, the plan succeeded.* ◊ **Much to my surprise,** *I passed.* ◊ *Imagine our surprise when he walked into the room!* **3** [U] the use of methods that cause feelings

▼ SYNONYMS
### surprise
startle • amaze • stun • astonish • take sb aback • astound

These words all mean to make sb feel surprised.

- **surprise** to give sb the feeling that you get when sth happens that you do not expect or do not understand, or sth that you do expect does not happen; to make sb feel surprised: *The outcome didn't surprise me at all.*
- **startle** to surprise sb suddenly in a way that slightly shocks or frightens them: *Sorry, I didn't mean to startle you.* ◊ *The explosion startled the horse.*
- **amaze** to surprise sb very much: *Just the huge size of the place amazed her.*
- **stun** (*rather informal*) (often in newspapers) to surprise or shock sb so much that they cannot think clearly or speak
- **astonish** to surprise sb very much: *The news astonished everyone.*

AMAZE OR ASTONISH?
These two words have the same meaning and in most cases you can use either. If you are talking about sth that both surprises you and makes you feel ashamed, use **astonish**: *He was astonished by his own stupidity.*

- **take sb aback** [usually passive] (especially of sth negative) to surprise or shock sb: *We were rather taken aback by her hostile reaction.*
- **astound** to surprise or shock sb very much: *His arrogance astounded her.*

PATTERNS
- It surprises sb / startles sb / amazes sb / stuns sb / astonishes sb / takes sb aback / astounds sb
- to surprise / startle / amaze / stun / astonish / astound sb that …
- to surprise / amaze sb what / how …
- to surprise / startle / amaze / stun / astonish / astound sb to know / find / learn / see / hear …
- to be surprised / startled / stunned into (doing) sth

of surprise: *A successful campaign should have an element of surprise.*

IDM ▶ **sur·prise, sur·prise** (*informal*) **1** (ironic, often disapproving) used to show that sth is not a surprise to you, as you could easily have predicted that it would happen or be true: *One of the candidates was the manager's niece, and, surprise, surprise, she got the job.* **2** used when giving sb a surprise: *Surprise, surprise! Look who's here!* **take sb by sur·prise** to happen unexpectedly so that sb is slightly shocked; to surprise sb: *His frankness took her by surprise.* **take sb / sth by sur·prise** to attack or capture sb/sth unexpectedly or without warning: *The police took the burglars by surprise.*

- **verb 1** 🔊 **A2** to make sb feel surprised: **~sb** *It wouldn't surprise me if they got married soon.* ◊ **~sb how, what** *It's always surprised me how popular he is.* ◊ **it surprises sb that …** *It surprises me that you've never sung professionally.* ◊ **it surprises sb to do sth** *Would it surprise you to know that I'm thinking of leaving?* **2** **~sb** to attack, discover, etc., sb suddenly and unexpectedly: *The army attacked at night to surprise the rebels.* ◊ *We arrived home early and surprised a burglar trying to break in.*

**sur·prised** 🔊 **A2** /səˈpraɪzd; NAmE sərˈp-/ adj. feeling or showing surprise: *She looked surprised when I told her.* ◊ **~at / by sb/sth** *I was surprised at how quickly she agreed.* ◊ *I'm surprised at you, behaving like that in front of the kids.* ◊ **~to see, hear, learn, discover, find** *They were surprised to find that he'd already left.* ◊ **~(that) …** *You shouldn't be surprised (that) he didn't come.* ◊ *Don't be surprised if I pretend not to recognize you.* ◊ *'Will she cancel the party?' 'I wouldn't be surprised.'* ◊ *He was pleasantly surprised to discover that he was no longer afraid.* ⊃ compare UNSURPRISED

**sur·pris·ing** 🔊 **A2** /səˈpraɪzɪŋ; NAmE sərˈp-/ adj. causing surprise: *It's not surprising (that) they lost.* ◊ *The frequency of such bad weather is hardly surprising given how far north we are.* ◊ **a surprising number of people came.** ▶ **sur·pris·ing·ly** adv.: *She looked surprisingly well.* ◊ *Surprisingly, he agreed straight away.* ◊ *Not surprisingly on such a hot day, the beach was crowded.*

▼ LANGUAGE BANK
### surprising
Highlighting interesting data
- **What is surprising** about these results **is that** boys are more likely to be left-handed than girls.
- **Surprisingly**, boys are more likely to be left-handed than girls.
- **Interestingly**, even when both parents are left-handed, there is still only a 26 per cent chance of their children being left-handed.
- **One of the most interesting** findings is that only 2 per cent of the left-handers surveyed have two left-handed parents.
- **It is interesting to note that** people are more likely to be left-handed if their mother is left-handed than if their father is.
- **The most striking** feature of these results **is that** left-handed mothers are more likely to have left-handed children.

⊃ LANGUAGE BANK at CONTRAST, EMPHASIS, ILLUSTRATE, SIMILARLY

**sur·real** /səˈrɪəl/ (*also less frequent* **sur·real·is·tic**) adj. very strange; more like a dream than reality, with ideas and images mixed together in a strange way

**sur·real·ism** /səˈrɪəlɪzəm/ noun [U] a 20th century style and movement in art and literature in which images and events that are not connected are put together in a strange or impossible way, like a dream, to try to express what is happening deep in the mind ▶ **sur·real·ist** adj. [usually before noun]: *a surrealist painter/painting* **sur·real·ist** noun: *the surrealist Salvador Dali*

**sur·real·is·tic** /ˌsɜːrɪəˈlɪstɪk/ adj. **1** = SURREAL **2** connected with surrealism: *a surrealistic painting*

**sur·ren·der** /səˈrendə(r)/ verb, noun
- **verb 1** [I, T] to admit that you have been defeated and want to stop fighting; to allow yourself to be caught, taken prisoner, etc. **SYN** give in (to sb/sth): ~(to sb) *The rebel soldiers were forced to surrender.* ◊ ~ **yourself (to sb)** *The hijackers eventually surrendered themselves to the police.* ⇨ WORDFINDER NOTE at PEACE **2** (*formal*) to give up sth/sb when you are forced to **SYN** relinquish: ~ sth/sb to sb *He agreed to surrender all claims to the property.* ◊ *They surrendered their guns to the police.* ◊ ~ sth/sb *The defendant was released to await trial but had to surrender her passport.*

**PHRV** sur'render to sth | sur'render yourself to sth (*formal*) to stop trying to prevent yourself from having a feeling, habit, etc. and allow it to control what you do: *He finally surrendered to his craving for drugs.*

- **noun** [U, sing.] **1** ~(to sb/sth) an act of admitting that you have been defeated and want to stop fighting: *They demanded (an) unconditional surrender.* **2** ~(to sth) the fact of allowing yourself to be controlled by sth: *They accused the government of a surrender to business interests.* **3** ~of sth (to sb) an act of giving sth to sb else even though you do not want to, especially after a battle, etc: *They insisted on the immediate surrender of all weapons.*

**sur·rep·ti·tious** /ˌsʌrəpˈtɪʃəs; NAmE ˌsɜːr-/ adj. done secretly or quickly, in the hope that other people will not notice **SYN** furtive: *She sneaked a surreptitious glance at her watch.* ▸ **sur·rep·ti·tious·ly** adv.

**sur·ro·gacy** /ˈsʌrəgəsi; NAmE ˈsɜːr-/ noun [U] the practice of giving birth to a baby for another person or couple, usually because they are unable to have babies themselves

**sur·ro·gate** /ˈsʌrəgət; NAmE ˈsɜːr-/ adj. (*formal*) used to describe a person or thing that takes the place of, or is used instead of, sb/sth else: *She saw him as a sort of surrogate father.* ▸ **sur·ro·gate** noun

**ˌsurrogate ˈmother** noun a woman who gives birth to a baby for another person or couple, usually because they are unable to have babies themselves ⇨ WORDFINDER NOTE at FAMILY

**sur·round** /səˈraʊnd/ verb, noun
- **verb 1** to be all around sth/sb: ~ sth/sb *Tall trees surround the lake.* ◊ *the membranes surrounding the brain* ◊ **be surrounded by sth** *The garden is surrounded by a wall.* ◊ *As a child I was surrounded by love and kindness.* **2** to move into position all around sb/sth, especially so as to prevent them from escaping; to move sb/sth into position in this way: ~ sb/sth *Police surrounded the building.* ◊ ~ sb/sth with sb/sth *They've surrounded the building with police.* **3** ~ sth/sb to be closely connected with sth/sb: *publicity surrounding the divorce* **4** ~ **yourself with sb/sth** to choose to have particular people or things near you all the time: *I like to surround myself with beautiful things.*
- **noun** a border or an area around the edge of sth, especially one that is decorated

**sur·round·ing** /səˈraʊndɪŋ/ adj. [only before noun] that is near or around sth: *Oxford and the surrounding area* ◊ *From the top of the hill you can see all the surrounding countryside.*

**sur·round·ings** /səˈraʊndɪŋz/ noun [pl.] everything that is around or near sb/sth **SYN** environment: *to work in pleasant surroundings* ◊ *The buildings have been designed to blend in with their surroundings.* ⇨ SYNONYMS at ENVIRONMENT

**surˈround sound** noun [U] a system for REPRODUCING sound using several SPEAKERS (= the pieces of equipment that the sound comes out of) placed around the person listening in order to produce a more realistic sound

**sur·tax** /ˈsɜːtæks; NAmE ˈsɜːrt-/ noun [U] a tax charged at a higher rate than the normal rate, on income above a particular level

**sur·titles** (NAmE **Sur·titles™**) /ˈsɜːtaɪtlz; NAmE ˈsɜːrt-/ noun [pl.] words that appear on a screen above or next to the stage to show or translate into a different language what is being sung in an OPERA, or spoken in a play in the theatre ⇨ compare SUBTITLE (1) ⇨ WORDFINDER NOTE at OPERA

---

1579 **survive**

**sur·veil·lance** /sɜːˈveɪləns; NAmE sɜːrˈv-/ noun [U] the act of carefully watching a person suspected of a crime or a place where a crime may be committed **SYN** observation: *The police are keeping the suspects under constant surveillance.* ◊ *surveillance cameras/ equipment*

**sur·vey** noun, verb
- **noun** /ˈsɜːveɪ; NAmE ˈsɜːrv-/ **1** an investigation of the opinions, behaviour, etc. of a particular group of people, which is usually done by asking them questions: *A recent survey showed 75 per cent of those questioned were in favour of the plan.* ◊ *The survey revealed/found that …* ◊ *to conduct/carry out/do/complete a survey* **2** the act of examining and recording the measurements, features, etc. of an area of land in order to make a map or plan of it: *an aerial survey* (= made by taking photographs from an aircraft) ◊ *a geological survey* **3** (*BrE*) an examination of the condition of a house, etc., usually done for sb who is thinking of buying it **4** a general study, view or description of sth: *a comprehensive survey of modern music*
- **verb** /səˈveɪ; NAmE sərˈv-/ **1** ~ sth to look carefully at the whole of sth, especially in order to get a general impression of it **SYN** inspect: *The next morning we surveyed the damage caused by the fire.* ◊ *He surveyed himself in the mirror before going out.* **2** ~ sth to study and give a general description of sth: *This chapter briefly surveys the current state of European politics.* **3** ~ sb/sth to investigate the opinions or behaviour of a group of people by asking them a series of questions **SYN** interview: *We surveyed 500 smokers and found that over three quarters would like to give up.* **4** ~ sth to measure and record the features of an area of land, for example in order to make a map or in preparation for building **5** ~ sth (*BrE*) to examine a building to make sure it is in good condition

**ˈsurvey course** noun (*NAmE*) a college course that gives an introduction to a subject for people who are thinking about studying it further

**sur·vey·or** /səˈveɪə(r); NAmE sərˈv-/ noun **1** a person whose job is to examine and record the details of a piece of land **2** (*BrE*) a person whose job is to examine a building to make sure it is in good condition, usually done for sb who is thinking of buying it ⇨ see also QUANTITY SURVEYOR

**sur·viv·able** /səˈvaɪvəbl; NAmE sərˈv-/ adj. (of an accident or experience) able to be survived: *a severe but survivable chest injury*

**sur·vival** /səˈvaɪvl; NAmE sərˈv-/ noun **1** [U] the state of continuing to live or exist, often despite difficulty or danger: *the struggle/battle/fight for survival* ◊ *His only chance of survival was a heart transplant.* ◊ *Exporting is necessary for our economic survival.* **2** [C] ~(from sth) something that has continued to exist from an earlier time **SYN** relic: *The ceremony is a survival from pre-Christian times.*

**IDM** **the surˌvival of the ˈfittest** the principle that only the people or things that are best adapted to their environment will continue to exist

**sur·vival·ist** /səˈvaɪvəlɪst; NAmE sərˈv-/ noun a person who prepares for a dangerous or unpleasant situation such as a war by learning how to survive outdoors, practising how to use weapons, storing food, etc. ▸ **sur·vival·ism** /-lɪzəm/ noun [U]

**surˈvival kit** noun a set of emergency equipment, including food, medical supplies and tools

**sur·vive** /səˈvaɪv; NAmE sərˈv-/ verb **1** [I] to continue to live or exist: *She was the last surviving member of the family.* ◊ *Of the six people injured in the crash, only two survived.* ◊ *Many of these teachers are struggling to survive financially.* ◊ (*humorous*) *'How are you these days?' 'Oh, surviving.'* ◊ *Don't worry, it's only a scratch—you'll survive.* ◊ ~ **from sth** *Some strange customs have survived from earlier times.* ◊ ~ **on sth** *I can't survive on £40 a week* (= it is not enough for my basic needs). ◊ ~ **as sth** *He survived as party leader until his second election defeat.*

# survivor

**2** [B1] [T] to continue to live or exist despite a dangerous event or time: ~ **sth** *Her 5-year-old son miraculously survived the crash.* ◊ *He only* **survived the attack** *because he was wearing body armour.* ◊ ~ **sth + adj.** *Few buildings survived the war intact.* **3** [T] ~ **sb/sth** to live or exist longer than sb/sth SYN **outlive**: *She survived her husband by ten years.* ◊ *He is survived by his wife and two sons* (= he has just died but they are still alive).

**sur·vi·vor** [B2] /səˈvaɪvə(r); NAmE sərˈv-/ *noun* a person who continues to live, especially despite being nearly killed or experiencing great danger or difficulty: *the sole/only survivor of the massacre* ◊ *The plane crashed in an area of dense jungle. There were no survivors.* ◊ *There are only a few survivors from the original team* (= members who remain in it while others have been replaced). ◊ *She'll cope. She's one of life's great survivors* (= sb who deals very well with difficult situations).

**sus** = SUSS

**sus·cep·ti·bil·ity** /səˌseptəˈbɪləti/ *noun* (*pl.* **-ies**) **1** [U, sing.] ~ **(to sth)** the state of being very likely to be influenced, harmed or affected by sth: *susceptibility to disease* **2 susceptibilities** [pl.] a person's feelings that are likely to be easily hurt SYN **sensibility**: *It was all carried out without any consideration for the susceptibilities of the bereaved family.*

**sus·cep·tible** /səˈseptəbl/ *adj.* **1** [not usually before noun] ~ **(to sth)** very likely to be influenced, harmed or affected by sth: *He's highly susceptible to flattery.* ◊ *Some of these plants are more susceptible to frost damage than others.* ◊ *Salt intake may lead to raised blood pressure in susceptible adults.* **2** easily influenced by feelings and emotions SYN **impressionable**: *She was both charming and susceptible.* **3** ~ **(of sth)** (*formal*) allowing sth; capable of sth: *Is this situation not susceptible of improvement by legislation?*

**sushi** /ˈsuːʃi/ *noun* [U] a Japanese dish of small cakes of cold cooked rice, with VINEGAR added and served with raw fish, etc. on top: *a sushi bar/restaurant*

**sus·pect** [B2] *verb, noun, adj.*

WORD FAMILY
**suspect** *verb*
**suspected** *adj.*
**suspicion** *noun*
**suspicious** *adj.*
**suspiciously** *adv.*
**suspect** *noun, adj.*

- *verb* /səˈspekt/ (not used in the progressive tenses) **1** [B2] [T, I] to have an idea that sth is probably true or likely to happen, especially sth bad, but without having definite proof: *As I had suspected all along, he was not a real policeman.* ◊ ~ **sth** *If you suspect a gas leak, do not strike a match or even turn on an electric light.* ◊ ~ **(that)** … *I began to suspect (that) they were trying to get rid of me.* ◊ *I strongly suspect (that) this whole story is fictional.* ◊ **it is suspected that** … *It was suspected that the drugs had been brought into the country by boat.* ◊ ~ **sb/sth to be/have sth** *The suspected him to be an impostor.* **2** [B2] [T] to have an idea that sb is guilty of sth, without having definite proof: ~ **sb/sth of sth** *He resigned after being suspected of theft.* ◊ ~ **sb/sth of doing sth** *The drug is suspected of causing over 200 deaths.* ◊ ~ **sb/sth** *Whom do the police suspect?* **3** [T] ~ **sth** to feel that sth is not completely right, legal or honest, without having any proof; to not trust sb/sth: *I suspected her motives in offering to help.* ▶ **sus·pected** *adj.*: *a suspected broken arm* ◊ *suspected tax evasion* ◊ *suspected terrorists*

- *noun* [B2] /ˈsʌspekt/ a person who is suspected of a crime or of having done sth wrong: *a murder suspect* ◊ *He is the prime suspect in the case.* IDM see USUAL

- *adj.* /ˈsʌspekt/ **1** that may be false and that cannot be relied on SYN **questionable**: *Some of the evidence they produced was highly suspect.* **2** that you suspect to be dangerous or illegal SYN **suspicious**: *a suspect package* (= one that may contain drugs, a bomb, etc.)

**sus·pend** [B2] /səˈspend/ *verb* **1** [B2] [often passive] (*formal*) to hang sth from sth else: **be suspended from sth** *A lamp was suspended from the ceiling.* ◊ **be suspended by/on sth** *Her body was found suspended by a rope.*

**2** [C1] ~ **sth** to officially stop sth for a time; to prevent sth from being active, used, etc. for a time: *Production has been suspended while safety checks are carried out.* ◊ *The constitution was suspended as the fighting grew worse.* ◊ *In the theatre we willingly* **suspend disbelief** (= temporarily believe that the characters, etc. are real). **3** [C1] ~ **sth** to officially delay sth; to arrange for sth to happen later than planned: *The introduction of the new system has been suspended until next year.* ◊ *to suspend judgement* (= delay forming or expressing an opinion) **4** [C1] [usually passive] to officially prevent sb from doing their job, going to school, etc. for a time, as a punishment or while a complaint against them is investigated: **be suspended** *The police officer was suspended while the complaint was investigated.* **5 be suspended in sth** (*specialist*) to float in liquid or air without moving ⇒ see also SUSPENSION

**suˌspended aniˈmation** *noun* [U] **1** the state of being alive but not conscious or active **2** a feeling that you cannot do anything because you are waiting for sth to happen

**suˌspended ˈsentence** *noun* a punishment given to a criminal in court that means that they will only go to prison if they commit another crime within a particular period of time

**sus·pend·er** /səˈspendə(r)/ *noun* **1** [C, usually pl.] (*BrE*) (*NAmE* **garter**) a piece of ELASTIC attached to a belt and fastened to the top of a STOCKING to hold it up **2 suspenders** (*NAmE*) (*BrE* **braces**) [pl.] long narrow pieces of cloth, leather, etc. for holding trousers up. They are fastened to the top of the trousers at the front and back and passed over the shoulders.

**suˈspender belt** *noun* (*BrE*) (*NAmE* ˈ**garter belt**) a piece of women's underwear like a belt, worn around the middle part of the body, used for holding STOCKINGS up

**sus·pense** /səˈspens/ *noun* [U] a feeling of worry or excitement that you have when you feel that sth is going to happen, sb is going to tell you some news, etc: *a tale of mystery and suspense* ◊ *Don't* **keep us in suspense.** *Tell us what happened!* ◊ *I couldn't bear the suspense a moment longer.*

**sus·pen·sion** [C1] /səˈspenʃn/ *noun* **1** [C1] [U, C] ~ **(from sth)** the act of officially removing sb from their job, school, team, etc. for a period of time, usually as a punishment: *suspension from school* ◊ *The two players are appealing against their suspensions.* **2** [C1] [U, sing.] the act of delaying sth for a period of time, until a decision has been taken: *These events have led to the suspension of talks.* **3** [U, C] the system of springs, etc. by which a vehicle is supported on its wheels and that makes it more comfortable to ride in when the road surface is not even **4** [C, U] (*specialist*) a liquid with very small pieces of solid matter floating in it; the state of such a liquid ⇒ see also SUSPEND

**suˈspension bridge** *noun* a bridge that hangs from steel cables that are supported by towers at each end

**sus·pi·cion** [C1] /səˈspɪʃn/ *noun* **1** [C1] [U, C] a feeling that sb has done sth wrong, illegal or dishonest, even though you have no proof: *They drove away slowly to avoid arousing suspicion.* ◊ **on-** *or* **of sth** *He was arrested on suspicion of murder.* ◊ **~ that** … *I have* **a sneaking suspicion** *that she's not telling the truth.* ◊ *My* **suspicions were confirmed** *when police raided the property.* ⇒ see also SUSPECT *noun* **2** [C] ~ **(that** …**)** a feeling or belief that sth is true, even though you have no proof: *I have a horrible suspicion that we've come to the wrong station.* **3** [U, C] the feeling that you cannot trust sb/sth: *Their offer was greeted with some suspicion.* **4** [sing.] ~ **of sth** (*formal*) a small amount of sth SYN **hint**: *His mouth quivered in the suspicion of a smile.*

IDM **above/beyond suˈspicion** too good, honest, etc. to have done sth wrong, illegal or dishonest: *Nobody who was near the scene of the crime is above suspicion.* **under suˈspicion (of sth)** suspected of doing sth wrong, illegal or dishonest: *The whole family is currently under suspicion of her murder.* ◊ *A number of doctors* **came under suspicion** *of unethical behaviour.* ⇒ more at FINGER *n.*

**sus·pi·cious** /səˈspɪʃəs/ *adj.* **1** ~ (of / about sb / sth) feeling that sb has done sth wrong, illegal or dishonest, without having any proof: *They became suspicious of his behaviour and contacted the police.* ◊ *a suspicious look* ◊ *You have a very suspicious mind* (= you always think that people are behaving in an illegal or dishonest way). **2** making you feel that sth is wrong, illegal or dishonest: *Didn't you notice anything suspicious in his behaviour?* ◊ *She died in suspicious circumstances.* ◊ *Police are not treating the fire as suspicious.* ◊ *It was all very suspicious.* **3** ~ (of sb / sth) not willing or able to trust sb / sth SYN **sceptical**: *I was suspicious of his motives.* ◊ *Many were suspicious of reform.* ⊃ see also SUSPECT *adj.*

**sus·pi·cious·ly** /səˈspɪʃəsli/ *adv.* **1** in a way that shows you think sb has done sth wrong, illegal or dishonest: *The man looked at her suspiciously.* **2** in a way that makes people think sth wrong, illegal or dishonest is happening: *Let me know if you see anyone acting suspiciously.* **3** in a way that shows you think there may be sth wrong with sth: *She eyed the fish on her plate suspiciously.*
IDM **look / sound suspiciously like sth** (*often humorous*) to be very similar to sth: *Their latest single sounds suspiciously like the last one.*

**suss** (*also* **sus**) /sʌs/ *verb* [T, I] ~ (sb / sth) (out) | ~ that … | ~ what, how, etc … (*informal*) to realize sth; to understand the important things about sb / sth: *I think I've got him sussed* (= now I understand him). ◊ *He cheated on her for years, but she never sussed.* ◊ *If you want to succeed in business you have to suss out the competition.*

**sussed** /sʌst/ *adj.* (*BrE, informal*) knowing what you need to know about the situations and people around you, so that you are not easily tricked and are able to take care of yourself

**sus·tain** /səˈsteɪn/ *verb* **1** ~ sb / sth to provide enough of what sb / sth needs in order to live or exist: *Which planets can sustain life?* ◊ *The love and support of his family sustained him during his time in prison.* **2** ~ sth to make sth continue for some time without becoming less SYN **maintain**: *She managed to sustain everyone's interest until the end of her speech.* **3** ~ sth (*formal*) to experience sth bad SYN **suffer**: *to sustain damage / an injury / a defeat* ◊ *The company sustained losses of millions of dollars.* **4** ~ sth to provide evidence to support an opinion, a theory, etc. SYN **uphold**: *The evidence is not detailed enough to sustain his argument.* **5** ~ sth (*formal*) to support a weight without breaking or falling SYN **bear**: *The ice will not sustain your weight.* **6** ~ sth (*law*) to decide that a claim, etc. is true or legally VALID **uphold**: *The court sustained his claim that the contract was illegal.* ◊ *Objection sustained!* (= said by a judge when a lawyer makes an OBJECTION in court)

**sus·tain·able** /səˈsteɪnəbl/ *adj.* **1** ~ involving the use of natural products and energy in a way that does not harm the environment: *sustainable forest management* ◊ *an environmentally sustainable society* ⊃ WORDFINDER NOTE at GREEN **2** ~ that can continue or be continued for a long time: *sustainable economic growth* OPP **unsustainable** ▸ **sus·tain·abil·ity** /səˌsteɪnəˈbɪləti/ *noun* [U] **sus·tain·ably** /səˈsteɪnəbli/ *adv.*

**sus·tained** /səˈsteɪnd/ *adj.* continuing for a period of time without becoming less: *a period of sustained economic growth* ◊ *a sustained attack*

**sus·ten·ance** /ˈsʌstənəns/ *noun* [U] (*formal*) **1** the food and drink that people, animals and plants need to live and stay healthy: *There's not much sustenance in a bowl of soup.* ◊ (*figurative*) *Arguing would only give further sustenance to his allegations.* **2** ~ (of sth) the process of making sth continue to exist: *Elections are essential for the sustenance of parliamentary democracy.*

**sutra** /ˈsuːtrə/ *noun* **1** a rule or statement in Sanskrit literature, or a set of rules **2** a Buddhist or Jainist holy text

**sut·tee** = SATI

**su·ture** /ˈsuːtʃə(r)/ *noun, verb*
■ *noun* (*medical*) a STITCH or stitches made when SEWING up a wound, especially after an operation
■ *verb* ~ sth (*medical*) to SEW up a wound

**SUV** /ˌes juː ˈviː/ *noun* SPORT UTILITY VEHICLE

**su·zer·ainty** /ˈsuːzərənti, -reɪn-/ *noun* [U] (*formal*) the right of a country to rule over another country

**svelte** /svelt, sfelt/ *adj.* (*approving*) (of a person, especially a woman) thin and attractive

**Sven·gali** /svenˈɡɑːli/ *noun* a person who has the power to control another person's mind, make them do bad things, etc. ORIGIN From the name of a character in George du Maurier's novel *Trilby*.

**SW** *abbr.* **1** (*especially BrE*) SHORT WAVE: *SW and LW radio* **2** south-west; south-western: *SW Australia*

**swab** /swɒb; *NAmE* swɑːb/ *noun, verb*
■ *noun* **1** a piece of soft material used by a doctor, nurse, etc. for cleaning wounds or taking a sample from sb's body for testing **2** an act of taking a sample from sb's body, with a swab: *to take a throat swab* ⊃ WORDFINDER NOTE at EXAMINE
■ *verb* (-bb-) **1** ~ sth to clean or remove liquid from a wound, etc., using a swab **2** ~ sth (down) to clean or wash a floor, surface, etc. using water and a cloth, etc.

**swad·dle** /ˈswɒdl; *NAmE* ˈswɑːdl/ *verb* ~ sb / sth to wrap sb / sth, especially a baby, tightly in clothes or a piece of cloth

**swa·deshi** /swəˈdeɪʃi/ *adj.* (*IndE*) made in India from materials that have also been produced in India

**swag** /swæɡ/ *noun* **1** [U] (*old-fashioned, informal*) goods that have been stolen SYN **loot** **2** [U] (*informal*) products given away free, especially at a marketing event: *Everyone who attends gets a swag bag and a T-shirt.* **3** [C, usually pl.] cloth that is hung in large curved folds as decoration, especially above a window **4** [C] (*AustralE, NZE*) a pack of things tied or wrapped together and carried by a traveller **5** [C] (*AustralE, NZE, informal*) a large number, amount or variety of sth: *The novel has won a swag of awards.* **6** [C, usually pl.] a bunch of flowers or fruit that is CARVED onto walls, etc. as decoration **7** [U] (*informal, approving*) a confident attitude that you admire: *This guy's got some serious swag.*

**swag·ger** /ˈswæɡə(r)/ *verb, noun*
■ *verb* [I] (+ *adv. / prep.*) (*usually disapproving*) to walk in an extremely proud and confident way SYN **strut**
■ *noun* [sing.] (*disapproving*) a way of walking or behaving that seems too confident

**Swa·hili** /swəˈhiːli, swɑːˈh-/ *noun* [U] = KISWAHILI

**swain** /sweɪn/ *noun* (*old use* or *humorous*) a young man who is in love

**swal·low** /ˈswɒləʊ; *NAmE* ˈswɑːl-/ *verb, noun*
■ *verb*
• **FOOD / DRINK 1** [T, I] to make food, drink, etc. go down your throat into your stomach: ~ (sth) *Always chew food well before swallowing it.* ◊ *I had a sore throat and it hurt to swallow.* ◊ ~ sth + *adj.* *The pills should be swallowed whole.*
• **MOVE THROAT MUSCLES 2** [I] to move the muscles of your throat as if you were swallowing sth, especially because you are nervous: *She swallowed hard and told him the bad news.*
• **COMPLETELY COVER 3** [T, *often passive*] to take sb / sth in or completely cover them / it so that they / it cannot be seen or exist separately any longer: ~ sb / sth *I watched her walk down the road until she was swallowed by the darkness.* ◊ ~ sb / sth up *Large areas of countryside have been swallowed up by towns.*
• **USE UP MONEY 4** [T] ~ sb / sth (up) to use up sth completely, especially an amount of money: *Most of my salary gets swallowed (up) by the rent and bills.*
• **BELIEVE 5** [T] to accept that sth is true; to believe sth: ~ sth *I found her excuse very hard to swallow.* ◊ ~ sth + *adj.* *He told her a pack of lies, but she swallowed it whole.*
• **FEELINGS 6** [T] ~ sth to hide your feelings: *to swallow your doubts* ◊ *You're going to have to swallow your pride and ask for your job back.*

# swam

- **ACCEPT INSULTS** 7 [T] ~ sth to accept offensive remarks, criticisms, etc. without complaining or protesting: *I was surprised that he just sat there and swallowed all their remarks.* IDM see BITTER adj.
- *noun*
- **BIRD** 1 a small bird, with long pointed wings and a tail with two points, that MIGRATES (= moves from one part of the world to another according to the season)
- **OF FOOD/DRINK** 2 an act of swallowing; an amount of food or drink that is swallowed at one time
- IDM **one ˌswallow doesn't make a ˈsummer** (*saying*) you must not take too seriously a small sign that sth is happening or will happen in the future, because the situation could change

**swam** /swæm/ *past tense of* SWIM

**swa·mi** /ˈswɑːmi/ *noun* (also used as a title) a Hindu religious teacher: *Swami Vivekananda*

**swamp** /swɒmp; *NAmE* swɑːmp/ *noun, verb*
- *noun* [C, U] an area of ground that is very wet or covered with water and in which plants, trees, etc. are growing SYN marsh: *tropical swamps* ▸ **swampy** *adj.*: *swampy ground*
- *verb* [often passive] 1 to make sb have more of sth than they can deal with SYN inundate: *~ sb/sth with sth The department was swamped with job applications.* ◇ *~ sb/sth In summer visitors swamp the island.* 2 ~ sth to fill or cover sth with a lot of water SYN engulf: *The little boat was swamped by the waves.*

**swamp·land** /ˈswɒmplænd; *NAmE* ˈswɑːm-/ *noun* [U, pl.] a large area of SWAMP

**swan** /swɒn; *NAmE* swɑːn/ *noun, verb*
- *noun* a large bird that is usually white and has a long, thin neck. Swans live on or near water.
- *verb* [I] (-nn-) + **adv./prep.** (*informal, disapproving*) to go around enjoying yourself in a way that annoys other people or makes them JEALOUS: *They've gone swanning off to Paris for the weekend.*

**swanky** /ˈswæŋki/ (**swankˌier, swankiˌest**) (*especially BrE*) (also **swank** *especially in NAmE*) *adj.* (*informal, approving*) fashionable and expensive in a way that is intended to impress people: *a swanky new hotel*

**ˈswan-song** /ˈswɒnsɒŋ; *NAmE* ˈswɑːnsɔːŋ/ *noun* [sing.] the last piece of work produced by an artist, a musician, etc. or the last performance by an actor, athlete, etc.

**swap** (*also* **swop**) /swɒp; *NAmE* swɑːp/ *verb, noun*
- *verb* (-pp-) 1 [I, T] to give sth to sb and receive sth in exchange: *~ (sth) (with sb) I've finished this magazine. Can I swap with you?* ◇ *~ sth for sth I swapped my red scarf for her blue one.* ◇ *~ sth Can we swap places? I can't see the screen.* ◇ *We spent the evening in the pub swapping stories (= telling each other stories) about our travels.* 2 [I] *~(over)* to start doing sb else's job, etc. while they do yours: *I'll drive there and then we'll swap over on the way back.* 3 [T] (*especially BrE*) to replace one person or thing with another: *~ sb/sth (for sb/sth) I think I'll swap this sweater for one in another colour.* ◇ *~ sb/sth (over) I'm going to swap you over. Mike will go first and Jon will go second.* IDM see PLACE *n.*
- *noun* 1 [usually sing.] an act of exchanging one thing or person for another: *Let's do a swap. You work Friday night and I'll do Saturday.* 2 a thing or person that has been exchanged for another: *Most of my football stickers are swaps.*

**ˈswap meet** *noun* (*especially NAmE*) an occasion at which people buy and sell or exchange items that interest them: *a swap meet for collectors of Star Trek memorabilia*

**sward** /swɔːd; *NAmE* swɔːrd/ *noun* [C, U] (*literary*) an area of grass

**swarm** /swɔːm; *NAmE* swɔːrm/ *noun, verb*
- *noun* 1 ~ **(of sth)** a large group of insects, especially bees, moving together in the same direction: *a swarm of bees/locusts/flies* 2 a large group of people, especially when they are all moving quickly in the same direction SYN **horde**
- *verb* 1 [I] + **adv./prep.** (*often disapproving*) (of people, animals, etc.) to move around in a large group: *Tourists were swarming all over the island.* 2 (of bees and other flying insects) to move around together in a large group, looking for a place to live
- PHRV **ˈswarm with sb/sth** to be full of people or things: *The capital city is swarming with police.*

**swar·thy** /ˈswɔːði; *NAmE* ˈswɔːrði/ *adj.* (especially of a person or their face) having dark skin

**swash** /swɒʃ; *NAmE* swɑːʃ/ *noun* [sing.] (*specialist*) the flow of water up the beach after a wave has BROKEN

**swash·buck·ling** /ˈswɒʃbʌklɪŋ; *NAmE* ˈswɑːʃ-/ *adj.* [only before noun] (especially of films/movies) set in the past and full of action, adventure, fighting with SWORDS, etc.: *a swashbuckling tale of adventure on the high seas* ◇ *the swashbuckling hero of Hollywood epics*

**swas·tika** /ˈswɒstɪkə; *NAmE* ˈswɑːs-/ *noun* an ancient symbol in the form of a cross with its ends bent at an angle of 90°, used in the 20th century as the symbol of the German Nazi party

**swat** /swɒt; *NAmE* swɑːt/ *verb* (-tt-) ~ sth to hit sth, especially an insect, using your hand or a flat object ▸ **swat** *noun*

**swatch** /swɒtʃ; *NAmE* swɑːtʃ/ *noun* a small piece of cloth used to show people what a larger piece would look or feel like

**swathe** /sweɪð/ *noun, verb*
- *noun* (also **swath** /swɒθ; *NAmE* swɑːθ/) (*formal*) 1 a long piece of land, especially one on which the plants or crops have been cut: *The combine had cut a swathe around the edge of the field.* ◇ *Development has affected vast swathes of our countryside.* 2 a large piece or area of sth: *The mountains rose above a swathe of thick cloud.*
- IDM **cut a ˈswathe through sth** (of a person, fire, etc.) to pass through a particular area destroying a large part of it
- *verb* [usually passive] (*formal*) to wrap or cover sb/sth in sth: *(be) swathed in sth He was lying on the hospital bed, swathed in bandages.*

**SWAT team** /ˈswɒt tiːm; *NAmE* ˈswɑːt/ *noun* (especially US) a group of police officers who are especially trained to deal with violent situations. SWAT stands for 'Special Weapons and Tactics'.

**sway** /sweɪ/ *verb, noun*
- *verb* 1 [I, T] to move slowly from side to side; to move sth in this way: (+ **adv./prep.**) *The branches were swaying in the wind.* ◇ *Vicky swayed and fell.* ◇ *~ sth (+ **adv./prep.**) They danced rhythmically, swaying their hips to the music.* 2 [T, often passive] ~ **sb** to persuade sb to believe sth or do sth SYN **influence**: *He's easily swayed.* ◇ *She wasn't swayed by his good looks or his clever talk.*
- *noun* [U] 1 movement from side to side 2 (*literary*) power or influence over sb: *Rebel forces hold sway over much of the island.* ◇ *He was quick to exploit those who fell under his sway.*

**swear** B2 /sweə(r); *NAmE* swer/ *verb* (**swore** /swɔː(r); *NAmE* swɔːr/, **sworn** /swɔːn; *NAmE* swɔːrn/) 1 [I] to use rude or offensive language, usually because you are angry: *She fell over and swore loudly.* ◇ *~ at sb/sth Why did you let him swear at you like that?* 2 B2 [T, no passive] to make a serious promise to do sth SYN **vow**: *~ sth He swore revenge on the man who had killed his father.* ◇ *~ (that)... I solemnly swear (that) it will never happen again.* ◇ *~ to do sth She made him swear not to tell anyone.* 3 B2 [T] to promise that you are telling the truth: *~ (that)... She swore (that) she'd never seen him before.* ◇ *I could have sworn (= I am sure) I heard the phone ring.* ◇ *~ to sb/on sth (that)... I swear to God I had nothing to do with it.* 4 B2 [I, T] to make a public or official promise, especially in court: *~ on sth Witnesses were required to swear on the Bible.* ◇ *~ that... Are you willing to stand up in court and swear that you don't recognize him?* ◇ *~ to do sth Remember, you have sworn to tell the truth.* ◇ *~ sth Barons had to swear an oath of allegiance to the king.* 5 [T] *~ sb to secrecy/silence* to make sb promise not to tell sth to anyone: *Everyone was sworn to secrecy about what had happened.* ⊃ see also SWORN

**IDM** **swear ˈblind** (*informal*) to say that sth is definitely true **swear like a ˈtrooper** (*old-fashioned*, *BrE*) to often use very rude or offensive language
**PHR V** **ˈswear by sb/sth 1** to name sb/sth to show that you are making a serious promise: *I swear by almighty God that I will tell the truth.* **2** (not used in the progressive tenses) to be certain that sth is good or useful: *She swears by meditation as a way of relieving stress.* **ˌswear sb↔ˈin** | **ˌswear sb ˈinto sth** [often passive] to formally introduce a new public official or leader at a special ceremony at which they promise to perform their duties well and show strong support for the organization or country: *He was sworn in as president.* ⋄ *The new prime minister was sworn into office.* ⊃ related noun SWEARING-IN **ˌswear ˈoff sth** (*informal*) to promise that you will not do or use sth again: *I decided to swear off burgers forever.* **ˈswear to sth** (*informal*) to say that sth is definitely true: *I think I put the keys back in the drawer, but I couldn't swear to it* (= I'm not completely sure).

**swear·ing** /ˈsweərɪŋ; *NAmE* -swer-/ *noun* [U] rude or offensive language: *I was shocked at the swearing.*

**swearing-ˈin** *noun* [U, sing.] a special ceremony at which a new public official or leader promises to perform their duties well and show strong support for the organization or country: *the swearing-in of the new president*

**ˈswear word** *noun* a rude or offensive word, used, for example, to express anger **SYN** **expletive**

**sweat** /swet/ *noun*, *verb*
■ *noun*
- **LIQUID ON SKIN 1** [U] drops of liquid that appear on the surface of your skin when you are hot, ill or afraid **SYN** **perspiration**: *beads of sweat* ⋄ *She wiped the sweat from her face.* ⋄ *By the end of the match, the sweat was pouring off him.* ⊃ see also SWEATY **2** [usually sing.] the state of being covered with sweat: *I woke up in a sweat.* ⋄ *She completed the routine without even* ***working up a sweat****.* ⋄ *He* ***breaks out in a sweat*** *just at the thought of flying.* ⋄ *He started having night sweats.* ⊃ see also COLD SWEAT
- **HARD WORK 3** [U] hard work or effort (*informal*): *Growing your own vegetables sounds like a lot of sweat.* ⋄ (*literary*) *She achieved success* ***by the sweat of her brow*** (= by working very hard).
- **CLOTHES 4 sweats** [pl.] (*informal*, *especially NAmE*) a SWEAT-SUIT or SWEATPANTS: *I hung around the house all day in my sweats.*

**IDM** **be/get in a ˈsweat (about sth)** to be/become anxious or frightened about sth **break ˈsweat** (*BrE*) (*NAmE* **break a ˈsweat**) (*informal*) to use a lot of physical effort: *He hardly needed to break sweat to reach the final.* **no ˈsweat** (*informal*) used to tell sb that sth is not difficult or a problem when they thank you or ask you to do sth: *'Thanks for everything.' 'Hey, no sweat!'* ⊃ more at BLOOD *n.*

■ *verb*
- **PRODUCE LIQUID ON SKIN/SURFACE 1** [I, T] when you **sweat**, drops of liquid appear on the surface of your skin, for example when you are hot, ill or afraid **SYN** **perspire**: *to sweat heavily* ⋄ ~**sth** *He was sweating buckets* (= a lot). **2** [I] if sth **sweats**, the liquid that is contained in it appears on its surface: *The cheese was beginning to sweat.*
- **WORK HARD 3** [I] ~ **(over sth)** to work hard at sth: *Are you still sweating over that report?*
- **WORRY 4** [I] (*informal*) to worry or feel nervous about sth: *They really made me sweat during the interview.*
- **HEAT FOOD 5** [T, I] ~ **(sth)** (*BrE*) if you **sweat** meat or vegetables or let them **sweat**, you heat them slowly with a little fat in a pan that is covered with a LID

**IDM** **don't ˈsweat it** (*NAmE*, *informal*) used to tell sb to stop worrying about sth **don't sweat the ˈsmall stuff** (*NAmE*, *informal*) used to tell sb not to worry about small details or things that are not important **sweat ˈblood** (*informal*) to work very hard ⊃ more at GUT *n.*
**PHR V** **ˌsweat sth↔ˈoff** to lose weight by doing a lot of hard exercise to make yourself sweat **ˌsweat it ˈout** (*informal*) to be waiting for sth difficult or unpleasant to end, and being worried about it

**sweat·band** /ˈswetbænd/ *noun* a band of cloth worn around the head or WRIST that prevents SWEAT from going into the eyes or onto the hands

**sweat·er** 🔊 **A1** /ˈswetə(r)/ *noun* a piece of clothing for the upper part of the body, made of wool or cotton, with long SLEEVES **SYN** **jumper**: *She wore jeans and a sweater.*

**sweat·pants** /ˈswetpænts/ (*also informal* **sweats**) *noun* [pl.] (*especially NAmE*) loose, warm trousers, usually made of thick cotton and worn for relaxing or playing sports in

**sweat·shirt** /ˈswetʃɜːt; *NAmE* -ʃɜːrt/ *noun* a piece of clothing for the upper part of the body, with long SLEEVES, usually made of thick cotton and often worn for sports

**sweat·shop** /ˈswetʃɒp; *NAmE* -ʃɑːp/ *noun* (*disapproving*) a place where people work for low wages in poor conditions ⊃ WORDFINDER NOTE at POOR

**sweat·suit** /ˈswetsuːt/ *noun* (*also informal* **sweats** [pl.]) (*both NAmE*) a sweatshirt and sweatpants worn together, for relaxing or playing sports in

**sweaty** /ˈsweti/ *adj.* (**sweat·ier**, **sweati·est**) **1** covered or wet with SWEAT: *sweaty feet* ⋄ *He felt all hot and sweaty.* **2** [only before noun] making you become hot and covered with SWEAT: *It was sweaty work, under the hot sun.*

**swede** /swiːd/ (*BrE*) (*NAmE* **ru·ta·baga**) (*ScotE* **tur·nip**) *noun* [C, U] a large round yellow root vegetable ⊃ VISUAL VOCAB page V5

**sweep** 🔊 **B2** /swiːp/ *verb*, *noun*
■ *verb* (**swept**, **swept** /swept/)
- **WITH BRUSH OR HAND 1** 🔊 **B2** [T, I] to clean a room, surface, etc. using a BROOM (= a type of brush on a long handle): ~**(sth)** *to sweep the floor* ⋄ ~**up** *Don't just stand around—grab a broom and sweep up.* ⋄ ~**sth + adj.** *The showroom had been emptied and swept clean.* **2** 🔊 **B2** [T] ~**sth + adv./prep.** to remove sth from a surface using a brush, your hand, etc: *She swept the crumbs into the wastebasket.* ⋄ *He swept the leaves up into a pile.*
- **MOVE QUICKLY/WITH FORCE 3** [T] ~**sb/sth + adv./prep.** to move or push sb/sth suddenly and with a lot of force: *The little boat was swept out to sea.* ⋄ *She let herself be swept along by the crowd.* **4** [I, T] (of weather, fire, etc.) to move suddenly and/or with force over an area or in a particular direction: **+ adv./prep.** *Rain swept in through the broken windows.* ⋄ ~**sth** *Strong winds regularly sweep the islands.*
- **OF A PERSON 5** [I] **+ adv./prep.** to move quickly and/or smoothly, especially in a way that impresses or is intended to impress other people: *Without another word she swept out of the room.* ⋄ (*figurative*) *He swept into the lead with an almost perfect performance.* **6** [T] ~**sth + adv./prep.** to move sth, especially your hand or arm, quickly and smoothly in a particular direction: *He rushed to greet her, sweeping his arms wide.*
- **OF FEELINGS 7** [T] **+ adv./prep.** to suddenly affect sb strongly: *A wave of tiredness swept over her.* ⋄ *Memories came sweeping back.*
- **OF IDEAS/FASHIONS 8** [I, T] to spread quickly: **+ adv./prep.** *Rumours of his resignation swept through the company.* ⋄ ~**sth** *the latest craze sweeping the nation*
- **LOOK/MOVE OVER AREA 9** [I, T] to move over an area, especially in order to look for sth: **+ adv./prep.** *His eyes swept around the room.* ⋄ ~**sth** *Searchlights swept the sky.*
- **TOUCH SURFACE 10** [T] ~**sth** to move, or move sth, over a surface, touching it lightly: *Her dress swept the ground as she walked.*
- **HAIR 11** [T] ~**sth + adv./prep.** to brush, COMB, etc. your hair in a particular direction: *Her hair was swept back from her face.*
- **OF LANDSCAPE 12** [I] **+ adv./prep.** to form a long, smooth curve: *The hotel gardens sweep down to the beach.*
- **IN SPORT 13** [T] ~**sth** (*NAmE*) to win all the games in a series of games against another team or all the parts of a contest: *The Blue Jays have a chance to sweep the series.* ⋄ *New Jersey swept Detroit last season.*

**IDM** **sweep the ˈboard** to win all the prizes, etc. in a competition **ˌsweep sb off their ˈfeet** to make sb fall suddenly and deeply in love with you **sweep (sb) to ˈpower** to win an election by a large number of votes; to make sb win an election with a large number of votes **sweep to ˈvictory**

# sweeper

to win a contest easily **sweep sth under the ˈcarpet** (*NAmE also* **sweep sth under the ˈrug**) to try to stop people from finding out about sth wrong, illegal, embarrassing, etc. that has happened or that you have done **PHRV** **ˌsweep sb aˈlong/aˈway/up** [usually passive] to make sb very interested or involved in sth, especially in a way that makes them forget everything else: *They were swept along by the force of their emotions.* **ˌsweep sth↔aˈside** to ignore sth completely: *All their advice was swept aside.* **ˌsweep sth↔aˈway** to get rid of sth completely: *Any doubts had long since been swept away.* **ˌsweep sth↔ˈout** to remove all the dust, dirt, etc. from a room or building using a brush **ˌsweep sb↔ˈup** to lift sb up with a sudden smooth movement: *He swept her up into his arms.*

■ **noun**
- **WITH BRUSH** **1** [C, usually sing.] an act of cleaning a room, surface, etc. using a BROOM: *Give the room a good sweep.*
- **CURVING MOVEMENT** **2** [C] a smooth curving movement: *He indicated the door with a sweep of his arm.*
- **LANDSCAPE** **3** [C, usually sing.] a long, often curved, piece of road, river, coast, etc: *the broad sweep of white cliffs around the bay*
- **RANGE** **4** [U] the range of an idea, a piece of writing, etc. that considers many different things: *Her book covers the long sweep of the country's history.*
- **MOVEMENT/SEARCH OVER AREA** **5** [C] a movement over an area, for example in order to search for sth or attack sth: *The rescue helicopter made another sweep over the bay.*
- **CHIMNEY** **6** [C] = CHIMNEY SWEEP
- **GAMBLING** **7** [C] (*NAmE also* **sweeps**) (*informal*) = SWEEPSTAKE
- **IN SPORT** **8** [C] (*NAmE*) a series of games that a team wins against another team; the fact of winning all the parts of a contest: *a World Series sweep*
- **TELEVISION** **9** **the sweeps** [pl.] (*NAmE*) a time when television companies examine their programmes to find out which ones are the most popular, especially in order to calculate advertising rates **IDM** see CLEAN *adj.*

**sweep·er** /ˈswiːpə(r)/ *noun* **1** a person whose job is to sweep sth: *a road sweeper* **2** a thing that sweeps sth: *a carpet sweeper* ⇒ see also MINESWEEPER **3** (in football (soccer)) a player who plays behind the other defending players in order to try and stop anyone who passes them

**sweep·ing** /ˈswiːpɪŋ/ *adj.* **1** [usually before noun] having an important effect on a large part of sth: *sweeping reforms/changes* ◊ *Security forces were given sweeping powers to search homes.* **2** [usually before noun] (*disapproving*) too general and failing to think about or understand particular examples: *a sweeping generalization/statement* **3** ~**victory** a victory by a large number of votes, etc. **4** [only before noun] forming a curved shape: *a sweeping gesture* (= with your hand or arm) ◊ *a sweeping staircase*

**sweep·stake** /ˈswiːpsteɪk/ (*also informal* **sweep**) (*NAmE also* **sweep·stakes**, *informal* **sweeps**) *noun* a type of BETTING in which the winner gets all the money bet by everyone else

**sweet** **🅐🅐** /swiːt/ *adj., noun*

■ **adj. (sweet·er, sweet·est)**
- **FOOD/DRINK** **1** **🅐🅐** containing, or tasting as if it contains, a lot of sugar: *a cup of hot sweet tea* ◊ *sweet food* ◊ *I had a craving for something sweet.* ◊ *This wine is too sweet for me.* **OPP** sour ⇒ compare BITTER, SALTY ⇒ HOMOPHONES at SUITE ⇒ WORDFINDER NOTE at TASTE
- **SMELL** **2** having a pleasant smell **SYN** **fragrant**: *a sweet-smelling rose* ◊ *The air was sweet with incense.*
- **SOUND** **3** having a pleasant sound: *a sweet voice*
- **PURE** **4** pleasant and not containing any harmful substances: *the sweet air of a mountain village*
- **SATISFYING** **5** making you feel happy and/or satisfied: *Goodnight. Sweet dreams.* ◊ *I can't tell you how sweet this victory is.*
- **ATTRACTIVE** **6** (*especially BrE*) (*especially of children or small things*) attractive **SYN** **cute**: *His sister's a sweet young thing.* ◊ *You look sweet in this photograph.* ◊ *We stayed in a sweet little hotel on the seafront.*

- **KIND** **7** having or showing a kind character: *She gave him her sweetest smile.* ◊ **it is ~ of sb to do sth** *It was sweet of them to offer to help.*
- **GOOD** **8** **Sweet!** (*especially NAmE, informal*) used to show that you approve of sth: *Free tickets? Sweet!*

**IDM** **be ˈsweet on sb** (*old-fashioned, informal*) to like sb very much in a romantic way **have a sweet ˈtooth** (*informal*) to like food that contains a lot of sugar **in your ˈown sweet ˈtime/ˈway** how and when you want to, even though this might annoy other people: *He always does the work, but in his own sweet time.* **keep sb ˈsweet** (*informal*) to say or do pleasant things in order to keep sb in a good mood so that they will agree to do sth for you **she's ˈsweet** (*AustralE, NZE, informal*) everything is all right **sweet ˈnothings** romantic words: *to whisper sweet nothings in sb's ear* **the sweet smell of sucˈcess** (*informal*) the pleasant feeling of being successful ⇒ more at HOME *n.*, ROSE *n.*, SHORT *adj.*

■ **noun**
- **FOOD** **1** **🅐🅐** [C] (*BrE*) a small piece of sweet food, usually made with sugar and/or chocolate and eaten between meals **SYN** **candy**: *a packet of sweets* ◊ *a sweet shop* ⇒ HOMOPHONES at SUITE ⇒ see also BOILED SWEET **2** [C, U] (*BrE*) a sweet dish eaten at the end of a meal **SYN** **afters, dessert, pudding**: *I haven't made a sweet today.* ◊ *Would you like some more sweet?*
- **PERSON** **3** [U] (*old-fashioned*) a way of addressing sb that you like or love: *Don't you worry, my sweet.*

**ˌsweet-and-ˈsour** *adj.* [only before noun] (of food) cooked in a sauce that contains sugar and VINEGAR or lemon: *Chinese sweet-and-sour pork*

**sweet·bread** /ˈswiːtbred/ *noun* [usually pl.] the THYMUS (= an organ in the neck) or the PANCREAS (= an organ near the stomach) of a young cow or sheep, eaten as food

**sweet·corn** /ˈswiːtkɔːn; *NAmE* -kɔːrn/ (*NAmE also* **corn**) *noun* [U] the yellow seeds of a type of MAIZE plant, also called sweetcorn, which grow on thick STEMS and are cooked and eaten as a vegetable: *(BrE) tinned sweetcorn* ⇒ VISUAL VOCAB page V5 ⇒ see also CORN ON THE COB

**sweet·en** /ˈswiːtn/ *verb* **1** ~**sth** to make food or drinks taste sweeter by adding sugar, etc. **2** ~**sb (up)** (*informal*) to try to make sb more willing to help you, agree to sth, etc. by giving them money, praising them, etc. **3** ~**sth** to make sth more pleasant or acceptable **IDM** see PILL *n.*

**sweet·en·er** /ˈswiːtnə(r)/ *noun* **1** [U, C] a substance used to make food or drink taste sweeter, used instead of sugar: *artificial sweetener(s)* **2** [C] (*informal*) something that is given to sb in order to persuade them to do sth, especially when this is done in a secret or dishonest way

**sweet·heart** /ˈswiːthɑːt; *NAmE* -hɑːrt/ *noun* **1** [sing.] (*informal*) used to address sb in a kind and loving way: *Do you want a drink, sweetheart?* **2** [C] (*becoming old-fashioned*) a person with whom sb is having a romantic relationship: *They were childhood sweethearts.*

**sweet·ie** /ˈswiːti/ *noun* (*informal*) **1** [C] (*BrE*) a child's word for a sweet **2** [C] a person who is kind and easy to like: *He's a real sweetie.* **3** [sing.] used to address sb in a kind and loving way

**sweet·ly** /ˈswiːtli/ *adv.* **1** in a pleasant way: *She smiled sweetly at him.* **2** in a way that smells sweet: *a sweetly scented flower* **3** in a way that is without difficulties or problems: *Everything went sweetly and according to plan.* ◊ *He headed the ball sweetly into the back of the net.*

**sweet·meat** /ˈswiːtmiːt/ *noun* (*old use*) a sweet; any food preserved in sugar

**sweet·ness** /ˈswiːtnəs/ *noun* [U] **1** the quality of being pleasant: *a smile of great sweetness* **2** the quality of tasting or smelling sweet: *The air was filled with the sweetness of mimosa.* **IDM** **be (all) ˌsweetness and ˈlight** **1** (of a person) to be pleasant, friendly and polite **2** (of a situation) to be fun and easy to deal with

**ˌsweet ˈpea** *noun* a climbing garden plant with pale flowers that have a sweet smell ⇒ VISUAL VOCAB page V7

**sweet ˈpepper** (*BrE* also **pep·per**) (*NAmE* also **ˈbell pep·per**) *noun* a hollow red, usually red, green or yellow, eaten as a vegetable either raw or cooked

**ˌsweet poˈtato** *noun* [C, U] a root vegetable that looks like a red potato, but that is yellow inside and tastes sweet ⇒ VISUAL VOCAB page V5

**ˈsweet spot** *noun* **1** the area on a BAT, RACKET or CLUB that hits the ball in the most effective way **2** a location or combination of characteristics that produces the best results: *This series aims to hit a sweet spot between romantic comedy and thriller.*

**ˈsweet-talk** *verb* ~ sb (into sth / into doing sth) (*disapproving*) to try to persuade sb to do sth by praising them and telling them things they like to hear: *I can't believe you let him sweet-talk you into working for him!* ▸ **ˈsweet talk** *noun* [U]

**swell** /swel/ *verb, noun, adj.*
■ *verb* (**swelled** /sweld/, **swol·len** /ˈswəʊlən/, **swelled**, **swelled**) **1** [I] ~ (**up**) to become bigger or rounder: *Her arm was beginning to swell up where the bee had stung her.* ⇒ WORDFINDER NOTE at HURT **2** [I, T] to go out or make sth go out in a curved shape: ~ (**out**) *The sails swelled (out) in the wind.* ◇ ~ **sth** (**out**) *The wind swelled (out) the sails.* **3** [T, I] to increase or make sth increase in number or size: ~ **sth** (**to sth**) *Last year's profits were swelled by a fall in production costs.* ◇ *We are looking for more volunteers to swell the ranks* (= increase the number) *of those already helping.* ◇ ~ (**to sth**) *Membership has swelled to over 20000.* OPP **shrink** **4** [I] (of a sound) to become louder: *The cheering swelled through the hall.* **5** [C] [I] ~ (**with sth**) to be filled with a strong emotion: *to swell with pride* ▸ see also SWOLLEN
■ *noun* **1** [C, usually sing.] the movement of the sea when it rises and falls without the waves breaking: *The boat was caught in a heavy* (= strong) *swell.* **2** [sing.] (*formal*) the curved shape of sth, especially a part of the body: *the firm swell of her breasts* **3** [sing.] a situation in which sth increases in size, number, strength, etc.: *a growing swell of support* ◇ *a swell of pride* ⇒ see also GROUNDSWELL **4** [sing.] (of music or noise) a slow steady increase in the volume of sth SYN **crescendo** **5** [C] (*old-fashioned, informal*) an important or fashionable person
■ *adj.* (*old-fashioned, NAmE, informal*) very good, a lot of fun, etc: *We had a swell time.*

**swell·ing** /ˈsweliŋ/ *noun* **1** [U] the condition of being larger or rounder than normal (= of being SWOLLEN): *Use ice to reduce the swelling.* **2** [C] a place on your body that has become larger or rounder than normal as the result of an illness or injury: *The fall left her with a painful swelling above her eye.*

**swel·ter** /ˈsweltə(r)/ *verb* [I] to be very hot in a way that makes you feel uncomfortable: *Passengers sweltered in temperatures of over 90°F.* ▸ **swel·ter·ing** *adj.* SYN **stifling**: *sweltering heat* **swel·ter·ing·ly** *adv.*: *swelteringly hot*

**swept** /swept/ *past, past part.* of SWEEP

**swerve** /swɜːv; *NAmE* swɜːrv/ *verb* [I] (especially of a vehicle) to change direction suddenly, especially in order to avoid hitting sb/sth: *She swerved sharply to avoid a cyclist.* ◇ *The bus suddenly swerved into his path.* ◇ *The ball swerved into the net.* ▸ **swerve** *noun*

**swift** /swɪft/ *adj., noun*
■ *adj.* (**swift·er, swift·est**) **1** happening or done quickly and immediately; doing sth quickly: *swift action* ◇ *a swift decision* ◇ ~ **to do sth** *The White House was swift to deny the rumours.* **2** moving very quickly; able to move very quickly: *a swift current* ◇ *a swift runner* ⇒ note at FAST ▸ **swift·ly** *adv.*: *She moved swiftly to the rescue.* **swift·ness** *noun* [U]
■ *noun* a small bird with long, narrow wings, similar to a SWALLOW

**swig** /swɪɡ/ *verb* (**-gg-**) ~ **sth** (*informal*) to take a quick drink of sth, especially alcohol: *They sat around swigging beer from bottles.* ▸ **swig** *noun*: *She took a swig of wine.*

**swill** /swɪl/ *verb, noun*
■ *verb* **1** [T] ~ **sth** (**out/down**) (*especially BrE*) to clean sth by pouring large amounts of water in, on or through it SYN **rinse**: *She swilled the glasses with clean water.* **2** [T] ~ **sth** (**down**) (*informal*) to drink sth quickly and/or in large quantities **3** [T, I] to move, or to make a liquid move, in a particular direction or around a particular place: ~ **sth + adv./prep.** *He swilled the juice around in his glass.* ◇ + **adv./prep.** *Water swilled around in the bottom of the boat.*
■ *noun* **1** (*also* **pig·swill**) [U] a mixture of waste food and water that is given to pigs to eat **2** [U] (*informal*) drink or food that is unpleasant or of a poor quality **3** [C, usually sing.] (*informal*) a large amount of a drink that you take into your mouth: *He had a quick swill of wine.*

**swim** ❶ A1 /swɪm/ *verb, noun*
■ *verb* (**swim·ming, swam** /swæm/, **swum** /swʌm/) **1** [I, T] (of a person or animal) to move through water by moving your arms and legs, without touching the bottom: *I can't swim.* ◇ *The boys swam across the lake.* ◇ *I've only just learned to swim.* ◇ ~ **sth** *Can you swim backstroke yet?* ◇ *How long will it take her to swim the Channel?* ⇒ note at BATH **2** ❶ A1 [I] **go swimming** to spend time swimming for pleasure: *I go swimming twice a week.* **3** ❶ A1 [I] (of a fish, etc.) to move through or across water: *Sharks must swim or die.* ◇ ~ **+ adv./prep.** *A shoal of fish swam past.* **4** [I] (*usually* **be swimming**) to be covered with a lot of liquid: ~ (**in sth**) *The main course was swimming in oil.* ◇ ~ (**with sth**) *Her eyes were swimming with tears.* **5** [I] (of objects, etc.) to seem to be moving around, especially when you are ill or drunk: *The pages swam before her eyes.* **6** [I] to feel confused and/or as if everything is turning round and round: *His head swam and he swayed dizzily.* IDM see SINK *v.*
■ *noun* **1** ❶ B1 [sing.] a period of time during which you swim: *Let's go for a swim.* **2** (*especially NAmE*) (in compounds) related to or used for swimming: *a swim meet* (= a swimming competition between teams) ◇ *swim trunks*
IDM **in the ˈswim (of things)** (*informal*) involved in things that are happening in society or in a particular situation

**swim·mer** /ˈswɪmə(r)/ *noun* a person who can swim; a person who is swimming: *a good/strong swimmer* ◇ *They watched the swimmers splashing through the water.* ◇ *a shallow pool for non-swimmers*

**swim·ming** ❶ A1 /ˈswɪmɪŋ/ *noun* [U] the sport or activity of swimming: *Swimming is a good form of exercise.*

**WORDFINDER** armband, dive, flipper, float, goggles, length, paddle, stroke

**ˈswimming bath** *noun* [usually pl.] (*old-fashioned, BrE*) a public swimming pool inside a building

**ˈswimming cap** (*also* **ˈswimming hat**) (*both BrE*) (*also* **ˈbathing cap** *NAmE, BrE*) *noun* a soft rubber or plastic cap that fits closely over your head to keep your hair dry while you are swimming

**ˈswimming costume** *noun* (*BrE*) = SWIMSUIT

**swim·ming·ly** /ˈswɪmɪŋli/ *adv.* (*informal*) without any problems or difficulties: *We hope everything will go swimmingly.*

**ˈswimming pool** (*also* **pool**) *noun* **1** an area of water that has been created for people to swim in: *an indoor/outdoor swimming pool* ◇ *a heated swimming pool* ◇ *an open-air swimming pool* **2** the building that contains a public swimming pool: *She trained five times a week at her local swimming pool.*

**ˈswimming trunks** (*also* **trunks**) (*NAmE also* **ˈswim trunks**) *noun* [pl.] a piece of clothing covering the lower part of the body and sometimes the top part of the legs, worn by men and boys for swimming: *a pair of swimming trunks* ⇒ picture at TRUNK

**swim·suit** /ˈswɪmsuːt/ *noun* (*BrE also* **ˈswimming costume**) (*also* **ˈbathing suit** *NAmE* or *old-fashioned*) a piece of clothing worn for swimming, especially the type worn by women and girls

**swim·wear** /ˈswɪmweə(r); *NAmE* -wer/ *noun* [U] clothing that you wear for swimming

# swindle

**swin·dle** /ˈswɪndl/ *verb, noun*

■ *verb* to cheat sb in order to get sth, especially money, from them: *~ sb (out of sth) They swindled him out of hundreds of dollars.* ◊ *~sth (out of sb) They swindled hundreds of dollars out of him.* ► **swind·ler** /ˈswɪndlə(r)/ *noun* **SYN** conman

■ *noun* [usually sing.] a situation in which sb uses dishonest or illegal methods in order to get money from a company, another person, etc. **SYN** **con**: *an insurance swindle*

**swine** /swaɪn/ *noun* (*pl.* **swines** or **swine**) **1** [C] (*informal*) an unpleasant person: *He's an arrogant little swine!* **2** [C] (*BrE, informal*) a difficult or unpleasant thing or task: *The car can be a swine to start.* **3** **swine** [pl.] (*old use* or *specialist*) pigs: *a herd of swine* ◊ *swine fever* (= a disease of pigs) **IDM** see PEARL

**'swine flu** *noun* [U] **1** a serious illness that affects pigs **2** a serious illness spread between humans, that is GENETICALLY similar to swine flu in pigs, and that in some cases causes death

**swing** /swɪŋ/ *verb, noun*

■ *verb* (**swung, swung** /swʌŋ/)
- HANG AND MOVE **1** [I, T] to move backwards or forwards or from side to side while hanging from a fixed point; to make sth do this: *His arms swung as he walked.* ◊ *As he pushed her, she swung higher and higher* (= while sitting on a swing). ◊ *~from sth A set of keys swung from her belt.* ◊ *~sth He sat on the stool, swinging his legs.* **2** [I, T] to move from one place to another by holding sth that is fixed and pulling yourself along, up, etc: *+ adv./prep. The gunshot sent monkeys swinging away through the trees.* ◊ *~yourself + adv./prep. He swung himself out of the car.*
- MOVE IN CURVE **3** [I, T] to move or make sth move with a wide curved movement: *+ adv./prep. A line of cars swung out of the palace gates.* ◊ *~sth + adv./prep. He swung his legs over the side of the bed.* ◊ *+ adj. The door swung open.* ◊ *~sth + adj. She swung the door open.*
- CHANGE OPINION/MOOD **4** [I, T] to change or make sb/sth change from one opinion, mood, etc. to another: *~(from A) (to B) The state has swung from Republican to Democrat.* ◊ *~(between A and B) His emotions swung between fear and curiosity.* ◊ *The game could swing either way* (= either side could win it). ◊ *~sb/sth (to sth) I managed to swing them round to my point of view.*
- TURN QUICKLY **5** [I, T] to turn or change direction suddenly; to make sth do this: *The bus swung sharply to the left.* ◊ *~sth + adv./prep. He swung the camera around to face the opposite direction.*
- TRY TO HIT **6** [I, T] to try to hit sb/sth: *~at sb/sth She swung at me with the iron bar.* ◊ *~sth (at sb/sth) He swung another punch in my direction.*
- DO/GET STH **7** [T] (*informal*) to succeed in getting or achieving sth, sometimes in a slightly dishonest way: *~sth We're trying to swing it so that we can travel on the same flight.* ◊ *~sb sth Is there any chance of you swinging us a couple of tickets?*
- OF MUSIC **8** [I] to have a strong rhythm
- OF PARTY **9** [I] (*informal*) if a party, etc. **is swinging**, there are a lot of people there having a good time

**IDM** **swing the 'balance** = TIP THE BALANCE/SCALES at TIP *v.* **swing both 'ways** (*informal*) to be BISEXUAL (= sexually attracted to both men and women) **swing for the 'fences** (*NAmE*) to really try to achieve sth great, even when it is not reasonable to expect to be so successful: *entrepreneurs who think big and swing for the fences* **swing into 'action** to start doing sth quickly and with a lot of energy **swing the 'lead** (*old-fashioned, BrE, informal*) (usually used in the progressive tenses) to pretend to be ill when in fact you are not, especially to avoid work: *I don't think there's anything wrong with her—she's just swinging the lead.* **ORIGIN** The lead was a weight at the bottom of a line that sailors used to measure how deep water was when the ship was near land. 'Swinging the lead' was thought to be an easy task, and came to mean avoiding hard work. ⊃ more at ROOM *n.*

**PHRV** **,swing 'by | ,swing by sth** (*NAmE, informal*) to visit a place or person for a short time **SYN** **drop by/in**: *I'll swing by your house on the way home from work.*

■ *noun*
- MOVEMENT **1** [C] a swinging movement or rhythm: *He took a wild swing at the ball.* ◊ *the swing of her hips*
- OF OPINION/MOOD **2** [C] a change from one opinion or situation to another; the amount by which this changes: *He is liable to abrupt mood swings* (= for example from being very happy to being very sad). ◊ *Voting showed a 10 per cent swing to Labour.*
- HANGING SEAT **3** [C] a seat for swinging on, hung from above on ropes or chains: *The kids were playing on the swings.*
- IN GOLF **4** [sing.] the swinging movement you make with your arms and body when you hit the ball in the game of golf: *I need to work on my swing.*
- MUSIC **5** [U] a type of jazz with a smooth rhythm, played especially by big dance bands in the 1930s
- JOURNEY **6** [sing.] (*NAmE*) a quick journey, especially one made by a politician, in which sb visits several different places in a short time: *a three-day campaign swing through California*

**IDM** **get in/into the 'swing (of sth)** (*informal*) to get used to an activity or a situation and become fully involved in it **go with a 'swing** (*BrE*) **1** (of a party or an activity) to be lively and fun **2** (of music) to have a strong rhythm **in full 'swing** having reached a very lively level: *When we arrived the party was already in full swing.* **,swings and 'roundabouts** (*BrE, informal*) used to say that there are advantages and disadvantages whatever decision you make: *If you earn more, you pay more in tax, so it's all swings and roundabouts.*

**'swing bridge** *noun* a bridge that can be moved to one side to allow tall ships to pass

**,swing 'door** (*BrE*) (*NAmE* **,swinging 'door**) *noun* a door that you can open in either direction and that closes itself when you stop holding it open

**swinge·ing** /ˈswɪndʒɪŋ/ *adj.* [usually before noun] (*BrE*) **1** large and likely to cause people problems, especially financial problems: *swingeing cuts in benefits* ◊ *swingeing tax increases* **2** extremely critical of sb/sth: *a swingeing attack on government policy*

**swing·er** /ˈswɪŋə(r)/ *noun* (*old-fashioned, informal*) **1** a person who is fashionable and has an active social life **2** a person who takes part in group sex or exchanging sexual partners

**swing·ing** /ˈswɪŋɪŋ/ *adj.* [usually before noun] (*old-fashioned, informal*) lively and fashionable

**,swinging 'door** (*NAmE*) (*BrE* **,swing 'door**) *noun* a door that you can open in either direction and that closes itself when you stop holding it open

**,swing 'state** *noun* (*politics*) (in an election for president in the US) a state where none of the candidates can be certain of getting the most support ⊃ WORDFINDER NOTE at CONGRESS

**,swing 'vote** *noun* [C, sing.] (*especially US*) the votes of people who do not always vote for the same political party and have not decided which party to vote for in an election ⊃ WORDFINDER NOTE at DEMOCRACY

**,swing 'voter** (*NAmE*) (*BrE* **,floating 'voter**) *noun* a person who does not always vote for the same political party or who has not decided which party to vote for in an election

**swipe** /swaɪp/ *verb, noun*

■ *verb* **1** [I, T] ~(at) sb/sth to hit or try to hit sb/sth with your hand or an object by moving your arm with a wide, curved movement: *He swiped at the ball and missed.* **2** [T] ~sth (*informal*) to steal sth **SYN** **pinch** **3** [T] ~sth to pass a plastic card, such as a credit card, through a special machine that is able to read the information that is stored on it **4** [I, T] ~(sth) (on/across sth) to move your finger quickly across the screen of an electronic device such as a mobile phone or small computer in order to move text, pictures, etc. or give commands: *Switch on the phone and swipe your finger across the screen to unlock it.*

■ *noun* (*informal*) **1** ~(at sb/sth) an act of hitting or trying to hit sb/sth by moving your arm or sth that you are holding with a wide, curved movement: *She took a swipe at him with her umbrella.* **2** ~ **(at sb/sth)** an act of criticizing sb/sth: *He used the interview to take a swipe at his critics.*

**'swipe card** *noun* a special plastic card with information recorded on it that can be read by an electronic device: *Access to the building is by swipe card only.* ⊃ see also KEY CARD

**swirl** /swɜːl; NAmE swɜːrl/ *verb, noun*
- *verb* [I, T] to move around quickly in a circle; to make sth do this: **(+ adv./prep.)** *The water swirled down the drain.* ◇ *A long skirt swirled around her ankles.* ◇ *swirling mists* ◇ ~ **sth (+ adv./prep.)** *He took a mouthful of water and swirled it around his mouth.*
- *noun* **1** the movement of sth that TWISTS and turns in different directions and at different speeds **2** a pattern or an object that TWISTS in circles

**swish** /swɪʃ/ *verb, noun, adj.*
- *verb* [I, T] to move quickly through the air in a way that makes a soft sound; to make sth do this: **(+ adv./prep.)** *A large car swished past them and turned into the embassy gates.* ◇ *The pony's tail swished.* ◇ ~ **sth (+ adv./prep.)** *The pony swished its tail.* ◇ *She swished her racket aggressively through the air.*
- *noun* [sing.] the movement or soft sound made by sth moving quickly, especially through the air
- *adj.* (BrE, *informal*) looking expensive and fashionable **SYN** smart: *a swish restaurant*

**Swiss** /swɪs/ *adj., noun*
- *adj.* from or connected with Switzerland
- *noun* (*pl.* **Swiss**) a person from Switzerland

**Swiss 'Army knife™** *noun* a small knife with several different BLADES (= cutting parts) and tools such as SCISSORS, that fold into the handle

**Swiss 'chard** *noun* [U] = CHARD

**Swiss 'cheese** *noun* [U, C] any hard cheese with holes in it

**Swiss 'roll** (BrE) (NAmE **jelly roll**) *noun* a thin flat cake that is spread with jam, etc. and rolled up

**switch** 0̶ **B1** /swɪtʃ/ *verb, noun*
- *verb* **1** ? **B1** [I, T] to change or make sth change from one thing to another: ~ **(over) (from sth) (to sth)** *We're in the process of switching over to a new system of invoicing.* ◇ ~ **between A and B** *Press these two keys to switch between documents on screen.* ◇ ~ **sth (over) (from sth) (to sth)** *The meeting has been switched to next week.* ◇ *He switched sides halfway through the debate.* **2** [T] to exchange one thing for another **SYN** swap: ~ **sth** *The dates of the last two exams have been switched.* ◇ ~ **sth over/around/round** *I see you've switched the furniture around* (= changed its position). ◇ ~ **sth with sth** *Do you think she'll notice if I switch my glass with hers?* **3** [I, T] to do sb else's job for a short time or work during different hours so that they can do your job or work during your usual hours **SYN** swap: ~ **(with sb)** *I can't work next weekend—will you switch with me?* ◇ ~ **sth (with sb)** *Have you been able to switch your shift with anyone?* ◇ ~ **(sth) (over/around/round)** *Can we switch our shifts around?*
- **PHRV** **switch 'off** (*informal*) to stop thinking about sth or paying attention to sth: *When I hear the word 'football' I switch off* (= because I am not interested in it). ◇ *The only time he really switches off* (= stops thinking about work, etc.) *is when we're on vacation.* **switch 'off/on** | **switch sth↔'off/'on** to turn a light, machine, etc. off/on by pressing a button or switch: *Please switch the lights off as you leave.* ◇ *How do you switch this thing on?* **switch 'over** | **switch sth↔'over** (BrE) to change stations on a radio or television
- *noun* **1** ? **B2** a small device that you press or move up and down in order to turn a light or piece of electrical equipment on and off: *a light switch* ◇ *an on-off switch* ◇ *He flipped a switch and the lights came on.* ◇ *to flick/press a switch* ◇ *to throw a switch* (= to move a large switch) ◇ *That was in the days before electricity was available at the flick of a switch* (= by simply pressing a switch). ⊃ **WORDFINDER NOTE** at ELECTRICITY ⊃ see also DIMMER SWITCH, DIP SWITCH, KILL SWITCH, TOGGLE SWITCH **2** a change from one thing to another, especially when this is

1587 **swop**

sudden and complete: *a policy switch* ◇ ~ **in/of sth** *a switch of priorities* ◇ ~ **from A to B** *She made the switch from full-time to part-time work when her first child was born.* **3** (NAmE) the POINTS on a railway line **IDM** see ASLEEP

**switch·back** /'swɪtʃbæk/ *noun* **1** a road or railway track that has many sharp bends as it goes up a steep hill, or one that rises and falls steeply many times **2** (NAmE) a 180 degree bend in a road that is going up a steep hill **SYN** hairpin bend **3** (BrE, *old-fashioned*) = ROLLER COASTER

**switch·blade** /'swɪtʃbleɪd/ (*especially NAmE*) (BrE *also* **'flick knife**) *noun* a knife with a BLADE (= sharp metal cutting part) inside the handle that jumps out quickly when a button is pressed

**switch·board** /'swɪtʃbɔːd; NAmE -bɔːrd/ *noun* the central part of a phone system used by a company, etc., where phone calls are answered and PUT THROUGH (= connected) to the appropriate person or department; the people who work this equipment: *a switchboard operator* ◇ *Call the switchboard and ask for extension 410.* ◇ *Hundreds of fans jammed the switchboard for over an hour.*

**switched 'on** *adj.* **1** ~ **(to sth)** aware of new things that are happening: *We're trying to get people switched on to the benefits of healthy eating.* ◇ *an organization for switched-on young people* **2** made to feel interested and excited: *People get really switched on by this music.*

**'switch-hitter** *noun* (in baseball) a player who can hit with the BAT on either side of their body

**switch·over** /'swɪtʃəʊvə(r)/ *noun* a change from one system, method, policy, etc. to another: *a switchover from petrol and diesel to electric cars*

**swivel** /'swɪvl/ *noun, verb*
- *noun* (often used as an adjective) a device used to connect two parts of an object together, allowing one part to turn around without moving the other: *a swivel chair* (= one on which the seat turns around without moving the base)
- *verb* (-**ll**-, US -**l**-) **1** [T, I] ~ **(sth) (+ adv./prep.)** to turn or make sth turn around a fixed central point **SYN** spin: *She swivelled the chair around to face them.* **2** [I, T] ~ **(sth) (+ adv./prep.)** to turn or move your body, eyes or head around quickly to face another direction **SYN** swing: *He swivelled around to look at her.*

**swizz** (*also* **swiz**) /swɪz/ *noun* [usually sing.] (BrE, *informal*) something unfair or disappointing: *What a swizz!*

**swol·len** /'swəʊlən/ *adj., verb*
- *adj.* **1** (of a part of the body) larger than normal, especially as a result of a disease or an injury: *swollen glands* ◇ *Her eyes were red and swollen from crying.* **2** (of a river) containing more water than normal
- *verb* past part. of SWELL

**swoon** /swuːn/ *verb* **1** [I] ~ **(over sb)** to feel very excited, emotional, etc. about sb that you think is sexually attractive: *He's used to having women swooning over him.* **2** [I] (*old-fashioned*) to become unconscious **SYN** faint ▶ **swoon** *noun* [sing.] (*old-fashioned*): *to go into a swoon*

**swoop** /swuːp/ *verb, noun*
- *verb* **1** [I] ~ **(+ adv./prep.)** (of a bird or plane) to fly quickly and suddenly downwards, especially in order to attack sb/sth **SYN** dive: *The aircraft swooped down over the buildings.* **2** [I] ~ **(on sb/sth)** (especially of police or soldiers) to visit or attack sb/sth suddenly and without warning
- *noun* **1** an act of moving suddenly and quickly downwards through the air, as a bird does **SYN** dive **2** ~ **(on sth/sb)** an act of arriving somewhere or attacking sth/sb in a way that is sudden and unexpected **SYN** raid: *Large quantities of drugs were found during a police swoop on the star's New York home.* **IDM** see FELL *adj.*

**swoosh** /swuːʃ/ *verb* [I] + **adv./prep.** to move quickly through the air in a way that makes a sound: *Cars and trucks swooshed past.* ▶ **swoosh** *noun* [sing.].

**swop** = SWAP

# sword

**sword** /sɔːd; NAmE sɔːrd/ noun a weapon with a long metal BLADE (= sharp cutting part) and a handle: *to draw/sheathe a sword* (= to take it out of/put it into its cover) **IDM** **put sb to the ˈsword** (*old-fashioned* or *literary*) to kill sb with a sword **a/the sword of ˈDamocles** (*literary*) a bad or unpleasant thing that might happen to you at any time and that makes you feel worried or frightened **ORIGIN** From the legend in which Damocles had to sit at a meal at the court of Dionysius with a sword hanging by a single hair above his head. He had praised Dionysius' happiness, and Dionysius wanted him to understand how quickly happiness can be lost. **turn swords into ˈploughshares** (*literary*) to stop fighting and return to peaceful activities ⊃ more at CROSS v., DOUBLE-EDGED, PEN n.

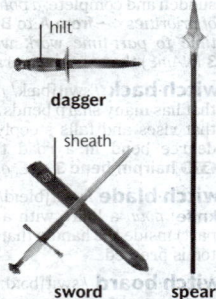

hilt — dagger — sheath — sword — spear

**sword·fish** /ˈsɔːdfɪʃ; NAmE ˈsɔːrd-/ noun [C, U] (pl. **sword·fish**) a large sea fish with a very long, thin, pointed upper JAW

**sword·play** /ˈsɔːdpleɪ; NAmE ˈsɔːrd-/ noun [U] the sport or skill of FENCING

**swords·man** /ˈsɔːdzmən; NAmE ˈsɔːrdz-/ noun (pl. **-men** /-mən/) (usually used with an adjective) a person who fights with a SWORD: *a fine swordsman*

**swords·man·ship** /ˈsɔːdzmənʃɪp; NAmE ˈsɔːrdz-/ noun [U] skill in fighting with a SWORD

**swore** /swɔː(r)/ past tense of SWEAR

**sworn** /swɔːn; NAmE swɔːrn/ adj., verb
■ **adj.** [only before noun] **1** made after you have promised to tell the truth, especially in court: *a sworn statement* **2** ~**enemies** people, countries, etc. that are determined to hate each other
■ **verb** past part. of SWEAR

**swot** /swɒt; NAmE swɑːt/ noun, verb
■ **noun** (*BrE*) (*US* **grind**) (*informal, disapproving*) a person who spends too much time studying
■ **verb** [I] (-tt-) ~ **(for sth)** (*BrE, informal*) to study very hard, especially in order to prepare for an exam **PHRV** **ˌswot sth↔ˈup** | **ˌswot ˈup on sth** (*BrE, informal*) to study a particular subject very hard, especially in order to prepare for an exam: *Make sure you swot up on the company before the interview.*

**SWOT analysis** /ˈswɒt ənæləsɪs; NAmE ˈswɑːt-/ noun a study done by an organization in order to find its strengths and weaknesses, and what problems or opportunities it should deal with. **SWOT** is formed from the initial letters of 'strengths', 'weaknesses', 'opportunities' and 'threats'.

**swum** /swʌm/ past part. of SWIM

**swung** /swʌŋ/ past tense, past part. of SWING

**syb·ar·it·ic** /ˌsɪbəˈrɪtɪk/ adj. [usually before noun] (*formal*) connected with a desire for pleasure: *his sybaritic lifestyle*

**syca·more** /ˈsɪkəmɔː(r)/ noun **1** [C, U] (*especially BrE*) a European tree of the MAPLE family, with leaves that have five points and seeds that are like pairs of wings ⊃ VISUAL VOCAB page V6 **2** [C] (*especially NAmE*) an American PLANE TREE **3** [U] the valuable hard wood of the European sycamore

**syco·phant** /ˈsɪkəfænt/ noun (*formal, disapproving*) a person who praises important or powerful people too much and in a way that is not sincere, especially in order to get sth from them ▶ **syco·phancy** /-fənsi/ noun [U] **syco·phan·tic** /ˌsɪkəˈfæntɪk/ adj.: *a sycophantic review*

**syl·lab·ic** /sɪˈlæbɪk/ adj. (*phonetics*) **1** based on syllables: *syllabic stress* **2** (of a consonant) forming a whole syllable, for example /l/ in *settle*

**syl·lable** /ˈsɪləbl/ noun any of the units into which a word is divided, containing a vowel sound and usually one or more consonants: *a word with two syllables* ◇ *a two-syllable word* ◇ *'Potato' is stressed on the second syllable.* **IDM** see WORD n.

**syl·la·bus** /ˈsɪləbəs/ noun (pl. **syl·la·buses** or less frequent **syl·labi** /-baɪ/) a list of the topics, books, etc. that students should study in a particular subject at school or college: **on the** ~ *American history will be on the syllabus next term.* ⊃ compare CURRICULUM

**syl·lo·gism** /ˈsɪlədʒɪzəm/ noun (*specialist*) a way of arguing in which two statements are used to prove that a third statement is true, for example: 'All humans must die; I am a human; therefore I must die.' ▶ **syl·lo·gist·ic** /ˌsɪləˈdʒɪstɪk/ adj. [only before noun]

**sylph** /sɪlf/ noun **1** an imaginary spirit **2** a girl or woman who is thin and attractive

**syl·van** /ˈsɪlvən/ adj. (*literary*) connected with forests and trees

**sym·bi·osis** /ˌsɪmbaɪˈəʊsɪs; NAmE -ˈoʊsɪs/ noun [U, C] (pl. **sym·bi·oses** /-ˈəʊsiːz/) **1** (*biology*) the relationship between two different living creatures that live close together and depend on each other in particular ways, each getting particular benefits from the other **2** a relationship between people, companies, etc. that is to the advantage of both ▶ **sym·bi·ot·ic** /ˌsɪmbaɪˈɒtɪk; NAmE -ˈɑːt-/ adj.: *a symbiotic relationship* **sym·bi·ot·ic·al·ly** /-kli/ adv.

**sym·bol** /ˈsɪmbl/ noun **1** a person, an object, an event, etc. that represents a more general quality or situation: *The vase is decorated with religious symbols.* ◇ ~ **of sth** *The new school stands as a symbol of hope for a better future.* ⊃ HOMOPHONES at CYMBAL ⊃ SYNONYMS at SIGN **2** ~ **(for sth)** a sign, number, letter, etc. that has a fixed meaning, especially in science, mathematics and music: *the mathematical symbol for infinity* ⊃ see also SEX SYMBOL, STATUS SYMBOL

**sym·bol·ic** /sɪmˈbɒlɪk; NAmE -ˈbɑːl-/ adj. containing symbols, or being used as a symbol: *The ceremony has a deep symbolic meaning.* ◇ *The new regulations are largely symbolic* (= they will not have any real effect). ◇ ~ **of sth** *The dove is symbolic of peace.* ▶ **sym·bol·ic·al·ly** /-kli/ adv.: *a symbolically significant gesture*

**sym·bol·ism** /ˈsɪmbəlɪzəm/ noun [U] the use of symbols to represent ideas, especially in art and literature ▶ **sym·bol·ist** /-lɪst/ adj., noun: *the symbolist poet Rimbaud*

**sym·bol·ize** (*BrE also* **-ise**) /ˈsɪmbəlaɪz/ verb ~**sth** to be a symbol of sth **SYN** **represent**: *The use of light and dark symbolizes good and evil.* ◇ *He came to symbolize his country's struggle for independence.*

**sym·met·rical** /sɪˈmetrɪkl/ (*also* **sym·met·ric** /sɪˈmetrɪk/) adj. (of a body, a design, an object, etc.) having two halves, parts or sides that are the same in size and shape: *a symmetrical pattern* **OPP** **asymmetric** ▶ **sym·met·ric·al·ly** /-kli/ adv.

**sym·metry** /ˈsɪmətri/ noun [U] **1** the exact match in size and shape between two halves, parts or sides of sth: *the perfect symmetry of the garden design* ⊃ picture at AXIS **2** the quality of being very similar or equal: *the increasing symmetry between men's and women's jobs*

**sym·pa·thet·ic** /ˌsɪmpəˈθetɪk/ adj. **1** kind to sb who is hurt or sad; showing that you understand and care about their problems: *a sympathetic listener* ◇ ~ **to/towards sb** *I did not feel at all sympathetic towards Kate.* ◇ *I'm here if you need a sympathetic ear* (= sb to talk to about your problems). **2** showing that you approve of sb/sth or that you share their views and are willing to support them: *He was speaking to a highly sympathetic audience.* ◇ ~ **to/towards sb/sth** *to be sympathetic to the party's aims* **3** (of a person) easy to like: *a sympathetic character in a novel* ◇ *I don't find her a very sympathetic person.* **OPP** **unsympathetic** ▶ **sym·pa·thet·ic·al·ly** /-kli/ adv.: *to smile at sb sympathetically* ◇ *We hope this application will be treated sympathetically* (= it will be approved).

**sym·pa·thize** (*BrE also* **-ise**) /ˈsɪmpəθaɪz/ verb **1** [I, T] ~ **(with sb/sth)** | + **speech** to feel sorry for sb; to show that you understand and feel sorry about sb's problems: *I find it very hard to sympathize with him.* **2** [I] **~ with sb/sth** to support sb/sth: *He has never really sympathized with the aims of Animal Rights activists.*

**sym·pa·thizer** (*BrE also* **-iser**) /ˈsɪmpəθaɪzə(r)/ *noun* a person who supports or approves of sb's ideas, especially a political cause or party: *communist sympathizers*

**sym·pa·thy** ❶ **B2** /ˈsɪmpəθi/ *noun* (*pl.* **-ies**) **1** ❓ **B2** [U, C, *usually pl.*] the feeling of being sorry for sb; showing that you understand and care about sb's problems: **~ for sb** *to express/feel sympathy for sb* ◊ *I have no sympathy for Jan—it's all her own fault.* ◊ *Our heartfelt sympathy goes out to the victims of the war.* ◊ **out of~for sb** *Shops were closed out of sympathy for the victims.* ◊ (*formal*) *May we offer our deepest sympathies on the death of your wife.* ◊ (*formal*) *I would like to extend our sincere sympathies to his family at this sad time.* ⊃ **WORDFINDER NOTE** at SORRY **2** [U, C, *usually pl.*] the act of showing support for or approval of an idea, a cause, an organization, etc: **in ~ with sb/sth** *The seamen went on strike in sympathy with* (= to show their support for) *the dockers.* ◊ *Her sympathies lie with the anti-abortion lobby.* **3** [U] friendship and understanding between people who have similar opinions or interests: *There was no personal sympathy between them.*

**IDM** **in ˈsympathy with sth** happening because sth else has happened: *Share prices slipped in sympathy with the German market.* **out of ˈsympathy with sb/sth** not agreeing with or not wanting to support sb/sth

▼ EXPRESS YOURSELF
**Expressing sympathy**
If someone is ill, or something bad has happened to them, you can show them that you are sorry:
• *I'm sorry you're not well. I hope you feel better soon.*
• *I am sorry to hear that.*
• *That's bad luck.*
• *How awful for you.*
• *I'm sorry for your loss* (when sb has died).

**sym·phony** /ˈsɪmfəni/ *noun* (*pl.* **-ies**) a long, complicated piece of music for a large ORCHESTRA, in three or four main parts (called MOVEMENTS): *Beethoven's Fifth Symphony* ▸ **sym·phon·ic** /sɪmˈfɒnɪk; *NAmE* -ˈfɑːn-/ *adj.*: *Mozart's symphonic works*

**ˈsymphony orchestra** *noun* a large ORCHESTRA that plays classical music: *the Boston Symphony Orchestra*

**sym·po·sium** /sɪmˈpəʊziəm/ *noun* (*pl.* **sym·po·sia** /-ziə/ *or* **sym·po·siums**) **~ (on sth)** a meeting at which experts have discussions about a particular subject; a small conference

**symp·tom** ❶ **B1** /ˈsɪmptəm/ *noun* **1** ❓ **B1** a change in your body or mind that shows that you are not healthy: *Symptoms include a headache and sore throat.* ◊ **~ of sth** *experience symptoms of anxiety and depression* ◊ *to show/develop symptoms of illness* ◊ *to relieve/alleviate symptoms* ⊃ **WORDFINDER NOTE** at EXAMINE **2** ❓ **B2** **~ (of sth)** a sign that sth exists, especially sth bad **SYN** **indication**: *The rise in inflation was just one symptom of the poor state of the economy.* ⊃ **SYNONYMS** at SIGN

**symp·tom·at·ic** /ˌsɪmptəˈmætɪk/ *adj.* being a sign of an illness or a problem: *a symptomatic infection* ◊ **~ of sth** *These disagreements are symptomatic of the tensions within the party.*

**syn·aes·the·sia** (*also* **syn·es·the·sia**) /ˌsɪnəsˈθiːziə; *NAmE* -ˈθiːʒə/ *noun* [U] (*biology*) the fact of experiencing some things in a different way from most other people, for example experiencing colours as sounds, experiencing shapes as tastes, or feeling sth in one part of the body when a different part is STIMULATED

**syna·gogue** /ˈsɪnəɡɒɡ; *NAmE* -ɡɑːɡ/ *noun* a building where Jews meet for religious WORSHIP and teaching

**syn·apse** /ˈsaɪnæps, ˈsɪ-/ *noun* (*biology*) a connection between two nerve cells ▸ **syn·ap·tic** /saɪˈnæptɪk, sɪ-/ *adj.*: *the synaptic membranes*

1589

# syndrome

**sync** (*also* **synch**) /sɪŋk/ *noun, verb* (*informal*)
■ *noun*
**IDM** **in ˈsync** **1** moving or working at exactly the same time and speed as sb/sth else: *The soundtrack is not in sync with the picture.* **2** in agreement with sb/sth; working well with sb/sth: *His opinions were in sync with those of his colleagues.* **out of ˈsync** **1** not moving or working at exactly the same time and speed as sb/sth else **2** not in agreement with sb/sth; not working well with sb/sth ⊃ *see also* LIP-SYNC, SYNCHRONIZATION
■ *verb* [T, I] = SYNCHRONIZE: **~ sth (up) (to/with sth)** *The live music isn't synced to the visuals.* ◊ **~ sth + adv./prep.** *How do I sync email across all my devices?* ◊ **~ (up) with/to sth** *Bluetooth technology enables a cell phone to sync with a car's stereo speaker.* ⊃ *see also* LIP-SYNC

**syn·chron·icity** /ˌsɪŋkrəˈnɪsəti/ *noun* [U] (*specialist*) the fact of two or more things happening at exactly the same time

**syn·chron·ize** (*BrE also* **-ise**) /ˈsɪŋkrənaɪz/ (*also informal* **sync, synch**) *verb* **1** [I, T] to happen at the same time or to move at the same speed as sth; to make sth do this: **~ (with sth)** *The sound track did not synchronize with the action.* ◊ **~ sth (with sth)** *Let's synchronize our watches* (= make them show exactly the same time). **2** [T] to link data files between one computer or mobile device and another so that the information in the files on both machines is the same: **~ sth (between A and B)** *You can use the technology to synchronize data between computers.* ◊ **~ sth (with sth)** *The phone lets you synchronize your calendar and contacts with your PC.* ▸ **syn·chron·iza·tion** (*also* **-isa·tion**) /ˌsɪŋkrənaɪˈzeɪʃn; *NAmE* -nəˈz-/ (*also informal* **sync**) *noun* [U]

**ˌsynchronized ˈswimming** (*BrE also* **-ised**) *noun* [U] a sport in which groups of SWIMMERS move in patterns in the water to music

**syn·chron·ous** /ˈsɪŋkrənəs/ *adj.* (*specialist*) happening or existing at the same time

**syn·cline** /ˈsɪŋklaɪn/ *noun* (*geology*) an area of ground where layers of rock in the earth's surface have been folded into a curve that is lower in the middle than at the ends ⊃ *compare* ANTICLINE

**syn·co·pated** /ˈsɪŋkəpeɪtɪd/ *adj.* (*music*) in *syncopated* rhythm the strong BEATS are made weak and the weak BEATS are made strong ▸ **syn·co·pa·tion** /ˌsɪŋkəˈpeɪʃn/ *noun* [U]

**syn·cre·tism** /ˈsɪŋkrətɪzəm/ *noun* [U] **1** (*specialist*) the mixing of different religions, philosophies or ideas **2** (*linguistics*) the mixing of different forms of the same word during the development of a language

**syn·dic·al·ism** /ˈsɪndɪkəlɪzəm/ *noun* [U] the belief that factories, businesses, etc. should be owned and managed by all the people who work in them

**syn·dic·al·ist** /ˈsɪndɪkəlɪst/ *noun* a person who believes in syndicalism ▸ **syn·dic·al·ist** *adj.*

**syn·di·cate** *noun, verb*
■ *noun* /ˈsɪndɪkət/ a group of people or companies who work together and help each other in order to achieve a particular aim
■ *verb* /ˈsɪndɪkeɪt/ [usually passive] to sell an article, a photograph, a television programme, etc. to several different newspapers, etc: **be syndicated** *His column is syndicated throughout the world.* ▸ **syn·di·ca·tion** /ˌsɪndɪˈkeɪʃn/ *noun* [U]

**syn·drome** ❓ **C1** /ˈsɪndrəʊm/ *noun* **1** ❓ **C1** a set of physical conditions that show you have a particular disease or medical problem: *PMS or premenstrual syndrome* ◊ *This syndrome is associated with frequent coughing.* ⊃ *see also* AIDS, ASPERGER'S SYNDROME, CARPAL TUNNEL SYNDROME, CHRONIC FATIGUE SYNDROME, DOWN'S SYNDROME, FETAL ALCOHOL SYNDROME, IRRITABLE BOWEL SYNDROME, LOCKED-IN SYNDROME, POSTVIRAL SYNDROME, TOURETTE'S SYNDROME, TOXIC SHOCK SYNDROME **2** a set of opinions or a way of behaving that is typical of a particular type of person, attitude or social problem: *With teenagers, be*

# synecdoche

prepared for the 'Me, me, me!' syndrome (= they think of themselves first).

**syn·ec·doche** /sɪˈnɛkdəki/ noun [U, C] (specialist) a word or phrase in which a part of sth is used to represent a whole, or a whole is used to represent a part of sth. For example, in 'Australia lost by two goals', *Australia* is used to represent the Australian team.

**syn·ergy** /ˈsɪnədʒi/ NAmE -nərdʒi/ noun [U, C] (pl. **-ies**) (specialist) the extra energy, power, success, etc. that is achieved by two or more people, companies or elements working together, instead of on their own ▶ **syn·er·gis·tic** /ˌsɪnəˈdʒɪstɪk/ NAmE -nərˈ-/ adj. **syn·er·gis·tic·al·ly** /-kli/ adv.

**synod** /ˈsɪnəd; BrE also -ɒd/ noun an official meeting of Church members to discuss religious matters and make important decisions

**syno·nym** /ˈsɪnənɪm/ noun a word or expression that has the same or nearly the same meaning as another in the same language: *'Big' and 'large' are synonyms.* ⊃ compare ANTONYM ⊃ WORDFINDER NOTE at WORD

**syn·onym·ous** /sɪˈnɒnɪməs; NAmE -ˈnɑːn-/ adj. **1** (of words or expressions) having the same, or nearly the same, meaning **2** ~ (with sth) so closely connected with sth that the two things appear to be the same: *Wealth is not necessarily synonymous with happiness.* ▶ **syn·onym·ous·ly** adv.

**syn·onymy** /sɪˈnɒnɪmi; NAmE -ˈnɑːn-/ noun [U] (linguistics) the fact of two or more words or expressions having the same meaning

**syn·op·sis** /sɪˈnɒpsɪs; NAmE -ˈnɑːp-/ noun (pl. **syn·op·ses** /sɪˈnɒpsiːz; NAmE -ˈnɑːp-/) a summary of a piece of writing, a play, etc. ▶ **syn·op·tic** /sɪˈnɒptɪk; NAmE -ˈnɑːp-/ adj. (formal)

**syn·ovial** /saɪˈnəʊviəl, sɪ-; NAmE sɪ-/ adj. (biology) (of a part of the body ) having a MEMBRANE (= a piece of very thin skin) containing liquid between the bones, which allows the JOINT to move freely

**syn·tac·tic** /sɪnˈtæktɪk/ adj. (linguistics) connected with SYNTAX ▶ **syn·tac·tic·al·ly** /-kli/ adv.: *to be syntactically correct*

**syn·tax** /ˈsɪntæks/ noun [U] **1** (linguistics) the way that words and phrases are put together to form sentences in a language; the rules of grammar for this ⊃ compare MORPHOLOGY **2** (computing) the rules that state how words and phrases must be used in a computer language

**synth** /sɪnθ/ noun (informal) = SYNTHESIZER

**syn·the·sis** /ˈsɪnθəsɪs/ noun (pl. **syn·the·ses** /-θəsiːz/) **1** [U, C] the act of combining separate ideas, beliefs, styles, etc.; a mixture or combination of ideas, beliefs, styles, etc.: ~ **of A with B** *the synthesis of art with everyday life* ◊ ~ **of A and B** *a synthesis of traditional and modern values* **2** [U] (specialist) the natural chemical production of a substance in animals and plants: *protein synthesis* **3** [U] (specialist) the artificial production of a substance that is present naturally in animals and plants: *the synthesis of penicillin* **4** [U] (specialist) the production of sounds, music or speech by electronic means ⊃ see also SPEECH SYNTHESIS

**syn·the·size** (BrE also **-ise**) /ˈsɪnθəsaɪz/ verb **1** ~ **sth** (specialist) to produce a substance by means of chemical or BIOLOGICAL processes **2** ~ **sth** to produce sounds, music or speech using electronic equipment **3** ~ **sth** to combine separate ideas, beliefs, styles, etc: *Students learn to synthesize information and search for what is relevant.*

**syn·the·sizer** (BrE also **-iser**) /ˈsɪnθəsaɪzə(r)/ (also informal **synth**) noun an electronic machine for producing different sounds. Synthesizers are used as musical instruments, especially for copying the sounds of other instruments, and for copying speech sounds: *a speech synthesizer* ⊃ compare KEYBOARD

**syn·thet·ic** /sɪnˈθetɪk/ adj., noun

■ adj. artificial; made by combining chemical substances rather than being produced naturally by plants or animals

**SYN** man-made: *synthetic drugs/fabrics* ◊ *synthetic dyes* ⊃ SYNONYMS at ARTIFICIAL ▶ **syn·thet·ic·al·ly** /-kli/ adv.
■ noun an artificial substance or material: *cotton fabrics and synthetics*

**'synth-pop** noun [U] a type of pop music that uses synthesizers and other electronic instruments

**syph·ilis** /ˈsɪfɪlɪs/ noun [U] a disease that gets worse over a period of time, spreading from the sexual organs to the skin, bones, muscles and brain. It is caught by having sex with a person who already has the disease. ▶ **syph·il·it·ic** /ˌsɪfɪˈlɪtɪk/ adj.

**sy·phon** = SIPHON

**syr·inge** /sɪˈrɪndʒ/ noun, verb
■ noun **1** (also **hypo·der·mic**, **hypodermic sy'ringe**) a plastic or glass tube with a long hollow needle that is used for putting drugs, etc. into a person's body or for taking a small amount of blood from a person **2** a plastic or glass tube with a rubber part at the end, used for taking liquid in and then pushing it out
■ verb ~ **sth** to clean sb's ear, a wound, etc. by SPRAYING liquid into it with a SYRINGE: *I had my ears syringed.*

**syrup** /ˈsɪrəp/ noun [U, C] **1** a sweet liquid made from sugar and water, often used in cans of fruit: *pears in syrup* **2** any thick sweet liquid made with sugar, used especially as a sauce ⊃ see also CORN SYRUP, GOLDEN SYRUP, MAPLE SYRUP

**syr·upy** /ˈsɪrəpi/ adj. **1** thick and sticky like syrup; containing syrup **2** (disapproving) extremely emotional and romantic and therefore unpleasant; too SENTIMENTAL: *a syrupy romantic novel*

**sys·tem** ⓘ A2 ◎ /ˈsɪstəm/ noun **1** A2 [C] an organized set of ideas or theories or a particular way of doing sth: *reform of the country's education system* ◊ *the criminal justice system* ◊ *the healthcare system* ◊ *the legal/financial/political system* ◊ ~ **for doing sth** *Systems are in place for dealing with complaints.* ◊ ~ **of sth** *a system of government* ⊃ WORDFINDER NOTE at GOVERNMENT ⊃ see also BINARY, HONOR SYSTEM, IMPERIAL (2), METRIC SYSTEM, VALUE SYSTEM **2** [C] a group of things, pieces of equipment, etc. that are connected or work together: *They installed a security system but it failed.* ◊ *How does the system work?* ⊃ see also ECOSYSTEM, PUBLIC ADDRESS SYSTEM, SOLAR SYSTEM, SOUND SYSTEM **3** B1 [C] a set of computer equipment and programs that are used together: *to develop/design a new system* ⊃ see also DISTRIBUTED SYSTEM, EXPERT SYSTEM, OPERATING SYSTEM **4** B1 [C] a human or an animal body, or a part of it, when it is being thought of as the organs and processes that make it function: *Wait until the drugs have passed through your system.* ◊ *the male reproductive system* ⊃ see also CENTRAL NERVOUS SYSTEM, DIGESTIVE SYSTEM, IMMUNE SYSTEM, LIMBIC SYSTEM, NERVOUS SYSTEM **5** **the system** [sing.] (informal, usually disapproving) the rules or people that control a country or an organization, especially when they seem to be unfair because you cannot change them: *You can't beat the system* (= you must accept it). ◊ *You have to learn how to work the system if you want to succeed.*

**IDM** **get sth out of your 'system** (informal) to do sth so that you no longer feel a very strong emotion or have a strong desire: *I was very angry with him, but now I feel I've got it out of my system.*

**sys·tem·at·ic** ⓘ C1 Ⓦ /ˌsɪstəˈmætɪk/ adj. [usually before noun] done according to a system or plan, in a complete, efficient or determined way: *a systematic approach to solving the problem* ◊ *a systematic attempt to destroy the organization* ◊ *The prisoner was subjected to systematic torture.* OPP unsystematic ▶ **sys·tem·at·ic·al·ly** /-kli/ adv.: *The search was carried out systematically.*

**sys·tem·atize** (BrE also **-ise**) /ˈsɪstəmətaɪz/ verb ~ **sth** (formal) to arrange sth according to a system SYN organize ▶ **sys·tem·atiza·tion**, **-isa·tion** /ˌsɪstəmətaɪˈzeɪʃn; NAmE -tə'z-/ noun [U]

**sys·tem·ic** /sɪˈstiːmɪk, -ˈstem-; NAmE -ˈstem-/ adj. (specialist) **1** affecting or connected with the whole of sth, especially the human body or a society: *a systemic disease* ◊ *systemic racism in society* **2** systemic chemicals or drugs that are used to treat diseases in plants or animals enter the body of the plant or animal and spread to all parts of it: *systemic weedkillers* ▶ **sys·tem·ic·al·ly** /-kli/ *adv.*

**ˈsystem operator** (*also* **ˈsystems operator**) *noun* (*computing*) a person who manages a computer system or electronic communication service

**ˈsystems ˈanalyst** *noun* a person whose job is to analyse the needs of a business company or an organization and then design processes for working efficiently using computer programs ▶ **systems aˈnalysis** *noun* [U]

**ˈsystem unit** *noun* (*computing*) the main part of a computer, separate from the keyboard, mouse and monitor, that contains the unit that controls all the other parts of the system

**sys·tole** /ˈsɪstəli/ *noun* [U, C] (*medical*) the stage of the heart's rhythm when the heart PUMPS blood ⊃ compare DIASTOLE ▶ **sys·tol·ic** /ˌsɪˈstɒlɪk; *NAmE* -ˈstɑːl-/ *adj.*

# T t

**T** (*also* **t**) /tiː/ *noun* [C, U] (*pl.* **Ts**, **T's**, **t's** /tiːz/) the 20th letter of the English alphabet: *'Tin' begins with (a) T/'T'.* ⇒ see also T-BONE STEAK, T-JUNCTION, T-SHIRT, T-SQUARE
**IDM** **to a ˈT/ˈtee** (*informal*) used to say that sth is exactly right for sb, succeeds in doing sth in exactly the right way, etc: *Her new job suits her to a T.* ◇ *The novel captures the feeling of the pre-war period to a T.* ⇒ more at DOT v.

**TA** /ˌtiː ˈeɪ/ *noun* **1** (*BrE*) TERRITORIAL ARMY **2** TEACHING ASSISTANT

**ta** /tɑː/ *exclamation* (*BrE*, *informal*) thank you

**taa·rab** /ˈtæræb/ *EAfrE* [ˈtɑːrab] *noun* [U] (*EAfrE*) a type of music that is popular in East Africa, especially along the coast, and that is influenced by Arabian and Indian music

**tab** /tæb/ *noun*, *verb*
■ *noun* **1** a small piece of paper, cloth, metal, etc. that sticks out from the edge of sth, and that is used to give information about it, or to hold it, fasten it, etc: *Insert tab A into slot 1* (= for example to make a model, box, etc.). **2** = TAB STOP **3** (*NAmE*) = PULL TAB **4** a bill for goods you receive but pay for later, especially for food or drinks in a restaurant or bar; the price or cost of sth: *a bar tab* ◇ *Can I put it on my tab?* ◇ *The tab for the meeting could be $3000.* **5** (*informal*) a small solid piece of an illegal drug: *a tab of Ecstasy*
**IDM** **keep (close) tabs on sb/sth** (*informal*) to watch sb/sth carefully in order to know what is happening so that you can control a particular situation: *It's not always possible to keep tabs on everyone's movements.* ⇒ more at PICK v.
■ *verb* (**-bb-**) **1** ~ **sb (as) sth** (*especially NAmE*) to say that sb is suitable for a particular job or role or describe them in a particular way: *He has been tabbed by many people as a future champion.* **2** ~ **sth** to use the TAB KEY when you are using a keyboard

**tab·ard** /ˈtæbəd, -bɑːd; *NAmE* -bərd, -bɑːrd/ *noun* a simple piece of clothing consisting of back and front sections without arms, and a hole for the head

**Tab·asco™** /təˈbæskəʊ/ *noun* [U] a red spicy sauce made from PEPPERS

**tabby** /ˈtæbi/ *noun* (*pl.* **-ies**) (*also* ˈ**tabby cat**) a cat with brown or grey fur marked with dark lines or spots

**tab·er·nacle** /ˈtæbənækl; *NAmE* -bərn-/ *noun* **1** [C] a place of WORSHIP for some groups of Christians: *a Mormon tabernacle* **2** **the tabernacle** [sing.] a small place of WORSHIP that could be moved, used by the Jews in ancient times when they were travelling in the desert

ˈ**tab key** (*also* **tab**, *formal* **tabu·la·tor**) *noun* a button on a keyboard that you use to move to a certain fixed position in a line of a document that you are typing

**tabla** /ˈtæblə; *NAmE* ˈtɑːb-/ *noun* a pair of small drums played with the hands and used in South Asian music, usually to go with other instruments

**table** 🔑 **A1** /ˈteɪbl/ *noun*, *verb*
■ *noun*
• FURNITURE **1** 🔑 **A1** a piece of furniture that consists of a flat top supported by legs: *at a/the~ We sat at a round table in the corner.* ◇ *around/round a/the~ They were sitting around the kitchen table.* ◇ *A table for two, please* (= in a restaurant). ◇ *I'd like to book a table for dinner tonight* (= in a restaurant). ◇ *to set the table* (*BrE also* **to lay the table** (= to put the plates, knives, etc. on it for a meal)) ◇ *to clear the table* (= take away the dirty plates, etc. at the end of a meal) ◇ *a pool/billiard/snooker table* **HELP** There are many compounds ending in **table**. You will find them at their place in the alphabet.
• PEOPLE **2** the people sitting at a table for a meal or to play cards, etc: *He kept the whole table entertained with his jokes.* ⇒ see also ROUND-TABLE
• LIST OF FACTS/NUMBERS **3** 🔑 **A2** a list of facts or numbers arranged in a special order, usually in rows and columns: *a table of contents* (= a list of the main points or information in a book, usually at the front of the book) ◇ *The table below shows how prices have changed over the past 20 years.* ⇒ see also PERIODIC TABLE
• IN SPORT **4** a list of sports teams, countries, schools, etc. that shows their position in a competition, etc: *If Arsenal win this game they'll go to the top of the table.* ◇ *United are second in the table.* ⇒ see also LEAGUE TABLE
• MATHEMATICS **5** = MULTIPLICATION TABLE: *Do you know your six times table?* ⇒ see also TURNTABLE, WATER TABLE
**IDM** **bring sth to the ˈparty/ˈtable** to contribute sth useful to a discussion, project, etc: *What Hislop brought to the table was real commitment and energy.* **come to the ˈtable** to join formal discussions about sth: *Different countries come to the table with differing expectations about what they can achieve.* **off the ˈtable** if a topic is **off the table** at a formal discussion, people are not willing or allowed to discuss it: *Some issues were so controversial they were taken off the table.* **on the ˈtable 1** (of a plan, suggestion, etc.) offered to people so that they can consider or discuss it: *Management have put several new proposals on the table.* **2** (*NAmE*) (of a plan, suggestion, etc.) not going to be discussed or considered until a future date **turn the ˈtables (on sb)** to change a situation so that you are now in a stronger position than the person who used to be in a stronger position than you ⇒ more at CARD *n.*, DRINK *v.*, WAIT *v.*
■ *verb* **1** ~ **sth** (*BrE*) to present sth formally for discussion: *They have tabled a motion for debate at the next Party Conference.* **2** ~ **sth** (*NAmE*) to leave an idea, a proposal, etc. to be discussed at a later date: *They voted to table the proposal until the following meeting.*

**tab·leau** /ˈtæbləʊ/ *noun* (*pl.* **tab·leaux** /ˈtæbləʊ, -bləʊz/) **1** a scene showing, for example, events and people from history, that is presented by a group of actors who do not move or speak: *The procession included a tableau of the Battle of Hastings.* ◇ (*figurative*) *She stood at the door observing the peaceful domestic tableau around the fire.* **2** a work of art, especially a set of statues, showing a group of people, animals, etc.

**table·cloth** /ˈteɪblklɒθ; *NAmE* -klɔːθ/ *noun* a cloth that you use for covering a table, especially when you have a meal

**table d'hôte** /ˌtɑːbl ˈdəʊt/ *noun* [U] (*from French*) a system in a restaurant of offering meals at a fixed price with only a limited number of dishes to choose from: *The restaurant offers both table d'hôte and à la carte.* ◇ *the table d'hôte menu*

ˈ**table ˈfootball** (*BrE*) (*NAmE* ˈ**foos·ball** /ˈfuːzbɔːl; *BrE also* ˈfuːsb-/) *noun* [U] an indoor game for two people or teams, played by moving rows of small models of football (soccer) players in order to move a ball on a board that has marks like a football (soccer) field

ˈ**table lamp** *noun* a small lamp that you can put on a table, etc.

**table·land** /ˈteɪbllænd/ *noun* a large area of high flat land **SYN** plateau

ˈ**table linen** *noun* [U] the cloths that you use during a meal, for example TABLECLOTHS and NAPKINS

ˈ**table manners** *noun* [pl.] the behaviour that is considered correct while you are having a meal at a table with other people

ˈ**table napkin** *noun* = NAPKIN

**table·spoon** /ˈteɪblspuːn/ *noun* **1** a large spoon, used especially for serving food **2** (*also* **table·spoon·ful** /ˈteɪblspuːnfʊl/) (*abbr.* **tbsp**) the amount a tablespoon can hold: *Add two tablespoons of water.*

**tab·let** 🔑 **A2** /ˈtæblət/ *noun* **1** 🔑 **A2** (*also* **Tablet PC™**) a small computer that is easy to carry, with a large TOUCH SCREEN and usually without a physical keyboard: *The company has launched its latest 10-inch tablet.* **2** **B1** (*especially BrE*) a small round solid piece of medicine that you SWALLOW **SYN** pill: *Take two tablets with water before meals.* **3** an amount of a substance in a small, round, solid piece:

| æ cat | ɑː father | e bed | ɜː fur | ə about | ɪ sit | iː see | i happy | ɒ got (*BrE*) | ɔː saw | ʌ cup | ʊ put | uː too |

water purification tablets **4** a flat piece of stone that has words written on it, especially one that has been fixed to a wall in memory of an important person or event **SYN** **plaque**: *(figurative)* *We can be very flexible—our entry requirements are not set in tablets of stone* (= they can be changed). **5** **~ of soap** *(old-fashioned, formal)* a piece of soap **6** *(NAmE)* a number of pieces of paper for writing or drawing on, that are fastened together at one edge

**ˈtable tennis** *(BrE, informal* **ˈping-pong***) (NAmE* **ˈPing-Pong™***) noun* [U] a game played like tennis with BATS and a small plastic ball on a table with a net across it

**ˈtable-top** /ˈteɪbltɒp; *NAmE* -tɑːp/ *noun* the top or the surface of a table ▶ **table-top** *adj.* [only before noun]: *a tabletop machine* (= that can be used on a table) ◇ *(BrE) a tabletop sale* (= where goods for sale are displayed on tables)

**Tablet PC™** /ˌtæblət ˌpiː ˈsiː/ *noun* = TABLET (1)

**ˈtable-ware** /ˈteɪblweə(r); *NAmE* -wer/ *noun* [U] the word used in shops, etc. for items that you use for meals, such as plates, glasses, knives and forks

**ˈtable wine** *noun* [U, C] a fairly cheap wine, suitable for drinking with meals

**tab·loid** /ˈtæblɔɪd/ *noun* **1** a newspaper with small pages (usually half the size of those in larger papers) ⊃ compare BROADSHEET **2** *(sometimes disapproving)* a newspaper of this size with short articles and a lot of pictures and stories about famous people, often thought of as less serious than other newspapers: *The story made the front page in all the tabloids.* ⊃ compare QUALITY NEWSPAPER ▶ **tab·loid** *adj.* [only before noun]: *a serious paper in a new tabloid format* ◇ *tabloid journalists* ◇ *a tabloid newspaper* ◇ *the tabloid press*

**taboo** /təˈbuː/ *noun (pl.* **ta·boos***)* **1** ~ **(against / on sth)** a cultural or religious custom that does not allow people to do, use or talk about a particular thing as people find it offensive or embarrassing: *an incest taboo* ◇ *a taboo on working on a Sunday* ◇ *to break/violate a taboo* ◇ *Death is one of the great taboos in our culture.* **2** ~ **(against / on sth)** a general agreement not to do sth or talk about sth: *The subject is still a taboo in our family.* ▶ **taboo** *adj.*: *in the days when sex was a taboo subject*

**taˈboo word** *noun* a word that many people consider offensive or shocks them, for example because it refers to sex, the body or people's race

**ˈtab stop** *(also* **tab***) noun* a fixed position in a line of a document that you are typing that shows where a piece of text or a column of figures, etc. will begin

**tabu·lar** /ˈtæbjələ(r)/ *adj.* [usually before noun] presented or arranged in a TABLE (= in rows and columns): *tabular data* ◇ *The results are presented in tabular form.*

**tab·ula rasa** /ˌtæbjələ ˈrɑːzə/ *noun (pl.* **tab·ulae rasae** /ˌtæbjəliː ˈrɑːziː/*) (from Latin, formal)* **1** a situation in which there are no fixed ideas about how sth should develop **2** the human mind as it is at birth, with no ideas or thoughts in it

**tabu·late** /ˈtæbjuleɪt/ *verb* ~ **sth** to arrange facts or figures in columns or lists so that they can be read easily ▶ **tabu·la·tion** /ˌtæbjuˈleɪʃn/ *noun* [U, C]

**tabu·la·tor** /ˈtæbjuleɪtə(r)/ *noun* = TAB KEY

**tach·om·eter** /tæˈkɒmɪtə(r); *NAmE* -ˈkɑːm-/ *noun* a device that measures the rate that sth turns and is used to measure the speed of an engine in a vehicle

**tacit** /ˈtæsɪt/ *adj.* [usually before noun] that is suggested indirectly or understood, rather than said in words: *tacit approval/support/knowledge* ◇ *By tacit agreement, the subject was never mentioned again.* ▶ **tacit·ly** *adv.*

**taci·turn** /ˈtæsɪtɜːn; *NAmE* -tɜːrn/ *adj. (formal)* tending not to say very much, in a way that seems unfriendly ▶ **taci·turn·ity** /ˌtæsɪˈtɜːnəti; *NAmE* -ˈtɜːrn-/ *noun* [U]

**tack** /tæk/ *noun, verb*
■ *noun* **1** [U, sing.] the way in which you deal with a particular situation; the direction of your words or thoughts: *a complete change of tack* ◇ *It was a brave decision to change tack in the middle of the project.* ◇ *When threats failed, she* decided to *try/take a different tack.* ◇ *His thoughts wandered off on another tack.* **2** [C, U] *(specialist)* the direction that a boat with sails takes as it sails at an angle to the wind in order to fill its sails: *They were sailing on (a)* **port/starboard tack** (= with the wind coming from the left/right side). **3** [C] a small nail with a sharp point and a flat head, used especially for fixing a carpet to the floor: *a carpet tack* ⊃ compare NAIL **4** [C] *(NAmE)* = THUMBTACK ⊃ see also BLU-TACK **5** [C] a long, loose STITCH used for holding pieces of cloth together temporarily, before you SEW them finally ⊃ WORDFINDER NOTE at SEW **6** [U] *(specialist)* the equipment that you need for riding a horse, such as a SADDLE and BRIDLE ⊃ WORDFINDER NOTE at HORSE **IDM** see BRASS
■ *verb* **1** [T] ~ **sth + adv. / prep.** to fasten sth in place with a tack or tacks **SYN** **nail**: *The carpet was tacked to the floor.* **2** [T] ~ **sth (+ adv. / prep.)** to fasten pieces of cloth together temporarily with long, loose STITCHES before SEWING them finally **3** [I] *(specialist)* to change the direction of a sailing boat by turning the front of the boat into and through the wind, so that the wind blows onto the sails from the opposite side; to do this several times in order to travel in the direction that the wind is coming from ⊃ compare GYBE
**PHRV** **tack sth↔ˈon** | **tack sth ˈonto sth** *(informal)* to add sth to sth that already exists, especially in a careless way: *The poems were tacked on at the end of the book.*

**tackie** *(also* **tak·kie***)* /ˈtæki/ *noun (SAfrE)* **1** a shoe with a rubber SOLE (= the bottom part), worn when dressing informally or for taking part in sports ⊃ compare TRAINER **2** *(informal)* a tyre on a car, etc.

**tackle** ʔ+ B2 /ˈtækl/ *verb, noun*
■ *verb* **1** ʔ+ B2 [T] ~ **sth** to make a determined effort to deal with a difficult problem or situation: *The government is determined to tackle inflation.* **2** ʔ- C1 ~ **sb (about sth)** to speak to sb about a problem or difficult situation **SYN** **confront**: *I tackled him about the money he owed me.* **3** ʔ+ C1 [T, I] ~ **(sb)** (in football (soccer), hockey, etc.) to try and take the ball from an opponent: *He was tackled just outside the penalty area.* **4** ʔ+ C1 [I, T] ~ **(sb)** (in rugby or AMERICAN FOOTBALL) to make an opponent fall to the ground in order to stop them running **5** [T] ~ **sb** to deal with sb who is violent or threatening you: *He tackled a masked intruder at his home.*
■ *noun* **1** ʔ+ C1 [C] an act of trying to take the ball from an opponent in football (soccer), hockey, etc.; an act of knocking sb to the ground, for example in rugby or AMERICAN FOOTBALL **2** [C] *(NAmE)* (in AMERICAN FOOTBALL) a player whose job is to stop opponents by knocking them to the ground **3** [U] the equipment used to do a particular sport or activity, especially fishing ⊃ see also BLOCK AND TACKLE, FISHING TACKLE **4** [U] *(BrE, slang)* a man's sexual organs

**tack·ler** /ˈtæklə(r)/ *noun (BrE)* a player who tries to TACKLE an opponent in some sports

**tacky** /ˈtæki/ *adj.* (**tack·ier**, **tacki·est**) **1** *(informal)* cheap, badly made and/or not in good taste: *tacky souvenirs* ◇ *The movie had a really tacky ending.* **2** (of paint, glue, etc.) not dry and therefore slightly sticky ▶ **tacki·ness** *noun* [U]

**taco** /ˈtækəʊ; *NAmE* ˈtɑːk-/ *noun (pl.* **-os***) (from Spanish)* a type of Mexican food consisting of a fried PANCAKE that is folded over and filled with meat, beans, etc.

**tact** /tækt/ *noun* [U] the ability to deal with difficult or embarrassing situations carefully and without doing or saying anything that will annoy or upset other people **SYN** **sensitivity**: *Settling the dispute required great tact and diplomacy.* ◇ *She is not exactly known for her tact.*

**tact·ful** /ˈtæktfl/ *adj.* careful not to say or do anything that will annoy or upset other people **SYN** **diplomatic**: *That wasn't a very tactful thing to say!* ◇ *I tried to find a tactful way of telling her the truth.* **OPP** **tactless** ▶ **tact·ful·ly** /-fəli/ *adv.*: *a tactfully worded reply* ◇ *I tactfully suggested he should see a doctor.*

**tac·tic** ʔ+ C1 /ˈtæktɪk/ *noun* **1** ʔ+ C1 [C, usually pl.] the particular method you use to achieve sth: *They tried all kinds*

# tactical

of tactics to get us to go. ◇ This was just the latest in a series of **delaying tactics**. ◇ The manager discussed tactics with his team. ◇ Confrontation is not always the best tactic. ◇ It's time to try a change of tactic. **2 tactics** [pl.] the art of moving soldiers and military equipment around during a battle or war in order to use them in the most effective way ⮕ compare STRATEGY ⮕ **WORDFINDER NOTE** at ARMY

**tac·tic·al** /ˈtæktɪkl/ adj. **1** [usually before noun] connected with the particular method you use to achieve sth: *tactical planning* ◇ *to have a tactical advantage* ◇ *Telling your boss you were looking for a new job was a tactical error* (= it was the wrong thing to do at that time). ⮕ compare STRATEGIC (1) **2** [usually before noun] carefully planned in order to achieve a particular aim: *a tactical decision* ⮕ see also TACTICAL VOTING **3** [only before noun] (especially of weapons) used or having an effect over short distances or for a short time: *tactical weapons/missiles* ⮕ compare STRATEGIC (3) **4** [only before noun] connected with military tactics: *He was given tactical command of the operation.* ▸ **tac·tic·al·ly** /-kli/ adv.: *At the time, it was tactically the right thing to do.* ◇ *The enemy was tactically superior.*

**ˌtactical ˈvoting** noun [U] (BrE) the act of voting for a particular person or political party, not because you support them, but in order to prevent sb else from being elected

**tac·ti·cian** /tækˈtɪʃn/ noun a person who is very clever at planning the best way to achieve sth

**tact·ile** /ˈtæktaɪl; NAmE -tl/ adj. [usually before noun] connected with the sense of touch; using your sense of touch: *tactile stimuli* ◇ *visual and tactile communication* ◇ *tactile fabric* (= pleasant to touch) ◇ *tactile maps* (= that you can touch and feel) ◇ *He's a very tactile man* (= he enjoys touching people).

**tact·less** /ˈtæktləs/ adj. saying or doing things that are likely to annoy or to upset other people **SYN** insensitive: *a tactless remark* ◇ *It was tactless of you to comment on his hair!* **OPP** tactful ▸ **tact·less·ly** adv. **tact·less·ness** noun [U]

**tad** /tæd/ noun **a tad** [sing.] (informal) a very small amount: *Could you turn the sound down just a tad?* ▸ **a tad** adv.: *It's a tad too expensive for me.*

**tad·pole** /ˈtædpəʊl/ (NAmE also **polli·wog**) noun a small creature with a large head and a small tail, that lives in water and is the young form of a frog, TOAD, etc. ⮕ **VISUAL VOCAB** page V3

**tae kwon do** /ˌtaɪ ˌkwɒn ˈdəʊ; NAmE ˌkwɑːn/ noun a Korean system of fighting without weapons, similar to KARATE

**taf·feta** /ˈtæfɪtə/ noun a type of stiff, shiny cloth made from silk or a similar material, used especially for making dresses

**Taffy** /ˈtæfi/ noun (pl. **-ies**) (also **Taff** /tæf/) (BrE, informal, often offensive) a person from Wales

**taffy** /ˈtæfi/ noun (pl. **-ies**) [U, C] (NAmE) a type of soft sweet made of brown sugar boiled until it is very thick and given different shapes and colours

**tag** /tæg/ noun, verb
- noun **1** [C] (often in compounds) a small piece of paper, cloth, plastic, etc. attached to sth to identify it or give information about it: *He put name tags on all his shirts.* ◇ *a gift tag* (= tied to a present) ⮕ SYNONYMS at LABEL ⮕ see also DOG TAG, NAME TAG, PRICE TAG **2** [C] an electronic device that can be attached to a person, animal or object so that police, researchers, etc. know where the person, etc. is: *The police use electronic tags to monitor the whereabouts of young offenders on probation.* **3** [C, usually sing.] a name or phrase that is used to describe a person or thing in some way: *They are finally ready to drop the tag 'the new Beatles'.* ◇ *The 'lucky' tag stuck for years.* **4** [C] (linguistics) a word or phrase that is added to a sentence for emphasis, for example *I do* in *Yes, I do* ⮕ see also QUESTION TAG **5** [C] (computing) a set of letters or symbols that are put before and after a piece of text or data in order to

identify it or show that it is to be treated in a particular way **6** [C] a short quotation or saying in a foreign language: *the Latin tag 'Si vis pacem, para bellum.'* (= if you want peace, prepare for war) **7** (BrE also **tig**) [U] a children's game in which one child runs after the others and tries to touch one of them **8** [C] a symbol or name used by a GRAFFITI writer and painted in a public place
- verb (-gg-) **1** ~ sth/sb to fasten a tag onto sth/sb: *Each animal was tagged with a number for identification.* **2** ~ sb/sth to attach an electronic device to a person, animal or object so that the police, researchers, etc. know where the person, etc. is ⮕ see also ELECTRONIC TAGGING **3** ~ sb/sth as sth to give sb/sth a name that describes what they are or do **SYN** label: *The country no longer wanted to be tagged as a Third World nation.* **4** ~ sth (computing) to add a set of letters or symbols to a piece of text or data in order to identify it or to show that it is to be treated in a particular way **5** ~ sb/sth to add a link to various users' profiles from a photo on a SOCIAL MEDIA website: *If you upload a photo, people can tag the people in it.* ◇ *The site lets you tag and share photographs.* **6** ~ sth to leave a name or mark on a piece of GRAFFITI to show who made it
**PHRV** **tag aˈlong (behind/with sb)** to go somewhere with sb, especially when you have not been asked or invited | **tag sth↔ˈon** | **tag sth ˈonto sth** to add sth to the end of sth that already exists, especially in a careless way: *An apology was tagged onto the end of the letter.*

**Taga·log** /təˈɡɑːlɒɡ; NAmE -lɔːɡ/ noun [U] the national language spoken in the Philippine islands

**tag·ger** /ˈtæɡə(r)/ noun **1** a person who writes or paints GRAFFITI in a public place, using a special symbol or name **2** (computing) a piece of software that adds tags to a piece of text or data

**ta·gine** (also **ta·jine**) /təˈʒiːn, -ˈdʒiːn/ noun **1** [C, U] a hot dish, originally from North Africa, made with meat and vegetables, cooked with liquid and SPICES in a closed container **2** [C] a container made of CLAY, with a pointed LID (= cover), for cooking and serving tagine, originally used in North Africa

**taglia·telle** /ˌtæljəˈteli; NAmE ˌtɑːl-/ noun [U] (from Italian) PASTA in the shape of long flat pieces

**ˈtag line** noun (informal) **1** (NAmE) = PUNCHLINE **2** = SLOGAN

**ˈtag question** noun (grammar) = QUESTION TAG

**ˈtag team** noun **1** a team of two WRESTLERS who take turns to fight in the same match **2** (informal, especially NAmE) two people working or performing together: *The show used a tag team of interviewers.*

**ta·hini** /təˈhiːni/ (also **ta·hina** /təˈhiːnə/) noun [U] a thick mixture made with CRUSHED (= pressed and broken) SESAME seeds, eaten in the Middle East

**t'ai chi ch'uan** /ˌtaɪ tʃiː ˈtʃwɑːn/ (also **ˌt'ai ˈchi**) noun [U] (from Chinese) a Chinese MARTIAL ART and system of exercises consisting of sets of very slow movements

**taiga** /ˈtaɪɡə/ noun [sing., U] forest that grows in wet ground in far northern regions of the earth: *the Siberian taiga*

**tail** /teɪl/ noun, verb
- noun
- OF BIRD/ANIMAL/FISH **1** [C] the part that sticks out at the back of the body of a bird, an animal or a fish, which the animal can move from side to side or up and down: *The dog ran up, wagging its tail.* ◇ *The male has beautiful tail feathers.* ⮕ HOMOPHONES at TALE ⮕ **VISUAL VOCAB** page V2 ⮕ see also PONYTAIL
- -TAILED **2** (in adjectives) having the type of tail mentioned: *a white-tailed eagle*
- OF PLANE/SPACECRAFT **3** [C] the back part of a plane, SPACECRAFT, etc.
- BACK/END OF STH **4** [C] ~ (of sth) a part of sth that sticks out at the back like a tail: *the tail of a kite* **5** [C] ~ (of sth) the last part of sth that is moving away from you: *the tail of the procession* ⮕ see also TAIL END
- JACKET **6 tails** [pl.] (informal) = TAILCOAT: *The men all wore top hat and tails.* ⮕ compare DINNER JACKET, MORNING COAT ⮕ see also COAT-TAILS

- **SIDE OF COIN 7 tails** [U] the side of a coin that does not have a picture of the head of a person on it, used as one choice when a coin is TOSSED to decide sth ⊃ compare HEADS
- **PERSON WHO FOLLOWS SB 8** [C] (*informal*) a person who is sent to follow sb secretly and find out information about where that person goes, what they do, etc: *The police have put a tail on him.* ▶ **tail·less** *adj.*: *Manx cats are tailless.*

**IDM** **on sb's 'tail** (*informal*) following behind sb very closely, especially in a car **the tail (is) wagging the 'dog** used to describe a situation in which the most important aspect is being influenced and controlled by sb/sth that is not as important **turn 'tail** to run away from a fight or dangerous situation **with your tail between your 'legs** (*informal*) feeling ashamed or unhappy because you have been defeated or punished ⊃ more at CHASE *v.*, HEAD *n.*, NOSE *n.*, STING *n.*

- **verb** ~ **sb** to follow sb closely, especially in order to watch where they go and what they do **SYN** **shadow**: *A private detective had been tailing them for several weeks.* ⊃ HOMOPHONES at TALE **IDM** see TOP *v.*

**PHR V** **,tail a'way/'off** (*especially BrE*) to become smaller or weaker: *The number of tourists tails off in October.* ◊ *'But why…?' Her voice tailed away.* **,tail 'back** (of traffic) to form a tailback

**tail·back** /ˈteɪlbæk/ *noun* **1** [C] (*BrE*) a long line of traffic that is moving slowly or not moving at all, because sth is blocking the road ⊃ WORDFINDER NOTE at TRAFFIC **2** [C, U] = HALF BACK

**tail·board** /ˈteɪlbɔːd; *NAmE* -bɔːrd/ *noun* = TAILGATE

**tail·bone** /ˈteɪlbəʊn/ *noun* the small bone at the bottom of the SPINE **SYN** **coccyx** ⊃ VISUAL VOCAB page V1

**tail·coat** /ˈteɪlkəʊt/ *noun* [C] (*also informal* **tails** [pl.]) a long jacket divided at the back below the WAIST into two pieces that become narrower at the bottom, worn by men at very formal events ⊃ compare DINNER JACKET

**,tail 'end** *noun* [sing.] the very last part of sth: *the tail end of the queue*

**tail·gate** /ˈteɪlɡeɪt/ *noun, verb*
- *noun* **1** (*also* **tail·board**) a door at the back of a lorry that opens downwards and that you can open or remove when you are loading or unloading the vehicle **2** the door that opens upwards at the back of a car (called a HATCHBACK) that has three or five doors
- *verb* **1** [I, T] ~ **(sb/sth)** (*informal*) to drive too closely behind another vehicle **2** [I] (*NAmE*) to eat food and drinks outdoors, served from the tailgate of a car

**'tailgate party** *noun* (*NAmE*) a party held by a group of fans in a PARKING LOT before a sports event

**'tail light** *noun* a red light at the back of a car, bicycle or train

**tailor** /ˈteɪlə(r)/ *noun, verb*
- *noun* a person whose job is to make men's clothes, especially sb who makes suits, etc. for individual customers
- *verb* to make or adapt sth for a particular purpose, a particular person, etc.: ~ **sth to/for sb/sth** *Special programmes of study are tailored to the needs of specific groups.* ◊ ~ **sth to do sth** *Most travel agents are prepared to tailor travel arrangements to meet individual requirements.*

**tailored** /ˈteɪləd; *NAmE* -lərd/ *adj.* [usually before noun] **1** (of clothes) made to fit well or closely: *a tailored jacket* **2** made for a particular person or purpose **SYN** **tailor-made**

**tailor·ing** /ˈteɪlərɪŋ/ *noun* [U] **1** the style or the way in which a suit, jacket, etc. is made: *Clever tailoring can flatter your figure.* **2** the job of making men's clothes

**,tailor-'made** *adj.* **1** ~ **(for sb/sth)** | ~ **(to sth/to do sth)** made for a particular person or purpose, and therefore very suitable: *a tailor-made course of study* ◊ *a trip tailor-made just for you* ◊ *She seems tailor-made for the job* (= perfectly suited for it). **2** (of clothes) made by a TAILOR for a particular person **SYN** **bespoke**: *a tailor-made suit*

**tail·piece** /ˈteɪlpiːs/ *noun* **1** ~ **(to sth)** a part that you add to the end of a piece of writing to make it longer or complete **2** (*music*) a piece of wood that the lower ends of the strings of some musical instruments are attached to

**tail·pipe** /ˈteɪlpaɪp/ *noun* (*especially NAmE*) = EXHAUST PIPE

**tail·plane** /ˈteɪlpleɪn/ *noun* a small wing at the back of an aircraft

**tail·spin** /ˈteɪlspɪn/ *noun* [sing.] **1** a situation in which a pilot loses control of an aircraft and it turns round and round as it falls quickly towards the ground, with the back making larger circles than the front **2** a situation that suddenly becomes much worse and is not under control: *Following the announcement, share prices went into a tailspin.*

**tail·wind** /ˈteɪlwɪnd/ *noun* a wind that blows from behind a moving vehicle, a runner, etc. ⊃ compare HEADWIND

**taint** /teɪnt/ *verb, noun*
- *verb* [often passive] (*formal*) to damage or harm the quality of sth or the opinion that people have of sb/sth: **be tainted (with/by sth)** *The administration was tainted with scandal.* ▶ **taint·ed** *adj.*: *tainted drinking water*
- *noun* [usually sing.] (*formal*) the effect of sth bad or unpleasant that damages or harms the quality of sb/sth: *to be free from the taint of corruption*

**ta·jine** = TAGINE

**take** ❶ **A1** /teɪk/ *verb, noun*
- *verb* (**took** /tʊk/, **taken** /ˈteɪkən/).
- **CARRY/LEAD 1** **A1** [T] to carry or move sth from one place to another: ~ **sth** *Remember to take your coat when you leave.* ◊ ~ **sth with you** *I forgot to take my bag with me when I got off the bus.* ◊ ~ **sb sth** *Shall I take my host family a gift?* ◊ ~ **sth to sb/sth** *Can you take my suit to the dry-cleaner's?* ◊ ~ **sth for sb/sth** *Don't forget to take a present for Catherine's new baby.* **2** **A1** [T] to go with sb from one place to another, especially to guide or lead them: ~ **sb** *It's too far to walk—I'll take you by car.* ◊ ~ **sb to sth** *A boy took us to our room.* ◊ ~ **sb doing sth** *I'm taking the kids swimming later.* ◊ ~ **sb to do sth** *The boys were taken to see their grandparents most weekends.* **3** **B1** [T] ~ **sb/sth + adv./prep.** to make sb/sth go from one level, situation, etc. to another: *Her energy and talent took her to the top of her profession.* ◊ *The new loan takes the total debt to $100000.* ◊ *I'd like to take my argument a stage further.* ◊ *He believes he has the skills to take the club forward.* ◊ *We'll take the matter forward at our next meeting* (= discuss it further).
- **TIME 4** **A1** [T, no passive, I] to need or require a particular amount of time: ~ **sth** *The process took about a year.* ◊ ~ **sth to do sth** *It takes about half an hour to get to the airport.* ◊ *That cut is taking a long time to heal.* ◊ ~ **sb to do sth** *It took her three hours to repair her bike.* ◊ ~ **sth for sb to do sth** *It'll take time* (= take a long time) *for her to recover from the illness.* ◊ ~ **+ adv.** *I need a shower—I won't take long.* ⊃ note at LAST[1]
- **PHOTOGRAPH 5** **A1** [T] to photograph sb/sth: ~ **sth** *to take a picture/photo/shot of sb/sth* ◊ *to have your picture/photo taken*
- **TRANSPORT/ROAD 6** **A1** [T] ~ **sth** to use a form of transport, a road, a path, etc. to go to a place: *to take the bus/train* ◊ *Take the second road on the right.* ◊ *It's more interesting to take the coast road.*
- **REACH AND HOLD 7** **A2** [T] ~ **sb/sth** to put your hands or arms around sb/sth and hold them/it; to reach for sb/sth and hold them/it: *I passed him the rope and he took it.* ◊ *Can you take* (= hold) *the baby for a moment?* ◊ *He took her hand/took her by the hand* (= held her hand, for example to lead her somewhere). ◊ *She took the child in her arms and kissed him.*
- **REMOVE 8** **A2** [T] ~ **sth/sb + adv./prep.** to remove sth/sb from a place or a person: *Will you take your books off the table?* ◊ *The sign must be taken down.* ◊ *He took some keys out of his pocket.* ◊ *My name had been taken off the list.* ◊ *She was playing with a knife, so I took it away from her.* ◊ (*informal*) *She was playing with a knife, so I took it off her.* ◊ (*figurative*) *The new sports centre will take the pressure off the old one.* **9** **A2** [T] ~ **sth** to remove sth without permission or by mistake: *Someone has taken my scarf.* ◊ (*figurative*) *The storms took the lives of 50 people.* **10** **B1** [T] to get sth from a particular source: ~ **sth from sth** *The scientists are taking water samples from the river.* ◊ *The machine*

---

*Oxford Phrasal Academic Lexicon (OPAL) written and spoken word lists* | **W** OPAL written word list | **S** OPAL spoken word list

# take

## ▼ SYNONYMS

**take**
lead • escort • drive • show • walk • guide • usher • direct

These words all mean to go with sb from one place to another.

**take** to go with sb from one place to another, for example in order to show them sth or to show them the way to a place: *It's too far to walk—I'll take you by car.*

**lead** to go with or go in front of sb in order to show them the way or to make them go in the right direction: *Firefighters led the survivors to safety.*

**escort** to go with sb in order to protect or guard them or to show them the way: *The president arrived, escorted by twelve bodyguards.*

**drive** to take sb somewhere in a car, taxi, etc: *My mother drove us to the airport.*

**show** to take sb to a particular place, in the right direction, or along the correct route: *The attendant showed us to our seats.*

**walk** to go somewhere with sb on foot, especially in order to make sure that they get there safely; to take an animal, especially a dog, for a walk or make an animal walk somewhere: *He always walked her home.* ◊ *Have you walked the dog yet today?*

**guide** to show sb the way to a place, often by going with them; to show sb a place that you know well: *She guided us through the busy streets.* ◊ *We were guided around the museums.*

**usher** (*rather formal*) to politely take or show sb where they should go, especially within a building: *She ushered her guests to their seats.*

**direct** (*rather formal*) to tell or show sb how to get somewhere or where to go: *A young woman directed them to the station.*

### PATTERNS
- to take / lead / escort / drive / show / walk / guide / usher / direct sb **to / out of / into** sth
- to take / lead / escort / drive / show / walk / guide sb **around / round**
- to take / lead / escort / drive / walk sb **home**
- to take / lead / escort / guide sb **to safety**
- to lead / show **the way**

takes its name from its inventor. ◊ ~ **sth out of sth** *Part of her article is taken straight (= copied) out of my book.*
- **SEAT** **11** [A2] [T] ~ **sth** to sit down in or use a chair, etc: *Are these seats taken?* ◊ *Come in; take a seat.* ⊃ SYNONYMS at SIT
- **EAT/DRINK** **12** [A2] [T] ~ **sth** to eat, drink, etc. sth: *Do you take sugar in your coffee?* ◊ *The doctor has given me some medicine to take for my cough.* ◊ *He started taking drugs (= illegal drugs) at college.*
- **WRITE DOWN** **13** [A2] [T] ~ **sth** to find out and record sth; to write sth down: *The police officer took my name and address.* ◊ *Did you take notes in the class?*
- **EXAM** **14** [T] ~ **sth** to do an exam or a test: *When did you take your driving test?*
- **STUDY** **15** [A2] [T] ~ **sth** to study a subject at school, college, etc: *She is planning to take a course in web design.* ◊ *How many subjects are you taking this year?*
- **ACTION** **16** [B1] [T] to use a particular course of action in order to deal with or achieve sth: *We need to take a different approach to the problem.* ◊ *The government is taking action to combat drug abuse.* **17** [B1] [T] ~ **sth** used with nouns to say that sb is doing sth, performing an action, etc: *to take a look* ◊ *to take a break* ◊ *to take a shot at sb/sth* ◊ *to take a bath/shower/wash* ◊ *to take a deep breath* ◊ (*BrE*) *We will take a decision on the matter next week.* ◊ *Experts have urged ministers to take the necessary steps to resolve the issue.*
- **MEASUREMENT** **18** [B1] [T] ~ **sth** to test or measure sth: *to take sb's temperature* ◊ *I need to have my blood pressure taken.*

- **CAPTURE** **19** [B1] [T] to capture a place or person; to get control of sth: ~ **sth** *The rebels succeeded in taking the town.* ◊ *The state has taken control of the company.* ◊ ~ **sth from sb** *The militants took the city from government forces.* ◊ ~ **sb + noun** *The rebels took him prisoner.*
- **CHOOSE/BUY** **20** [B1] [T] ~ **sth** to choose, buy or rent sth: *I'll take the grey jacket.* ◊ *We took a room at the hotel for two nights.* **21** [T] ~ **sth** (*formal*) to buy a newspaper or magazine regularly: *We take the 'Express'.*
- **ACCEPT/RECEIVE** **22** [A2] [T] (not usually used in the progressive tenses or in the passive) ~ **sth** to accept or receive sth: *If they offer me the job, I'll take it.* ◊ *She was accused of taking bribes.* ◊ *I'll take the call in my office.* ◊ *I take full responsibility for my actions.* ◊ *Why should I take the blame for somebody else's mistakes?* ◊ *If you take my advice you'll have nothing more to do with him.* ◊ *Will you take $10 for the book (= will you sell it for $10)?* ◊ *The store took (= sold goods worth) $100 000 last week.* **23** [T] ~ **sth** to act in response to an opportunity: *When the bus stopped for fuel, we took the opportunity to get something to eat.* ◊ *England failed to take their chances and had to settle for a draw.* ◊ *He isn't afraid to take risks.* **24** [T] (not usually used in the progressive tenses) ~ **sb** to accept sb as a customer, patient, etc: *The school doesn't take boys (= only has girls).* ◊ *The dentist can't take any new patients.* **25** [T] (not usually used in the progressive tenses) ~ **sth** to experience or be affected by sth: *The school took the full force of the explosion.* ◊ *Can the ropes take the strain (= not break)?* ◊ *The team took a terrible beating.* **26** [B2] [T, no passive] (not usually used in the progressive tenses) ~ **sth** to be able to bear sth: *I don't think I can take much more of this heat.* ◊ *I find his attitude a little hard to take.* **27** [B2] [T] ~ **sth/sb + adv./prep.** to react to sth/sb in a particular way: *He took the criticism surprisingly well.* ◊ *These threats are not to be taken lightly.* ◊ *I wish you'd take me seriously.*
- **CONSIDER** **28** [B2] [T] (not used in the progressive tenses) to understand or consider sth in a particular way: ~ **sth** *How am I supposed to take that remark?* ◊ *Taken overall, the project was a success.* ◊ ~ **sth as sth** *She took what he said as a compliment.* ◊ ~ **sth to do sth** *What did you take his comments to mean?* **29** [T] (not used in the progressive tenses) to consider sb/sth to be sb/sth, especially when you are wrong: ~ **sb/sth for sb/sth** *Even the experts took the painting for a genuine Van Gogh.* ◊ *Of course I didn't do it! What do you take me for (= what sort of person do you think I am)?* ◊ ~ **sb/sth to be sb/sth** *I took the man with him to be his father.*
- **HAVE FEELING/OPINION** **30** [B2] [T] (not usually used in the progressive tenses) ~ **sth** to have a particular feeling, opinion or attitude: *My parents always took an interest in my hobbies.* ◊ *Don't take offence (= be offended) at what I said.* ◊ *I took a dislike to him.* ◊ *He takes the view that children are responsible for their own actions.*
- **MATHEMATICS** **31** [T] (not used in the progressive tenses) to reduce one number by the value of another SYN **subtract**: ~ **A (away) (from B)** *Take 5 from 12 and you're left with 7.* ◊ **B ~ away A** (*informal*) *80 take away 5 is 75.*
- **GIVE EXAMPLE** **32** [T] ~ **sb/sth** used to introduce sb/sth as an example: *Lots of couples have problems in the first year of marriage. Take Ann and Paul.*
- **FORM/POSITION** **33** [T] ~ **sth** to have or start to have a particular form, position or state: *Our next class will take the form of a debate.* ◊ *The new president takes office in January.* ◊ *The home side had a chance to take the lead.*
- **NEED** **34** [T, no passive] to need or require sth in order to happen or be done: ~ **sb/sth to do sth** *It only takes one careless driver to cause an accident.* ◊ *It doesn't take much to make her angry.* ◊ ~ **sth** (*informal*) *He didn't take much persuading (= he was easily persuaded).* **35** [T, no passive] (not used in the progressive tenses) ~ **sth** (of machines, etc.) to use sth in order to work: *The buses have been adapted to take biofuel.*
- **SIZE OF SHOES/CLOTHES** **36** [T, no passive] (not used in the progressive tenses) ~ **sth** to wear a particular size in shoes or clothes: *What size shoes do you take?*
- **HOLD/CONTAIN** **37** [T, no passive] (not used in the progressive tenses) ~ **sth/sb** to have enough space for sth/sb; to be able to hold or contain a particular quantity: *The bus can take 60 passengers.* ◊ *The tank takes 50 litres.*

- **TEACH/LEAD** **38** [T] ~ **sb (for sth)** | ~ **sth** to be the teacher or leader in a class or a religious service: *The head teacher usually takes us for French.*
- **GO OVER/AROUND** **39** [T] ~ **sth (+ adv./prep.)** to go over or around sth: *The horse took the first fence well.* ◊ *He takes bends much too fast.*
- **IN SPORTS** **40** [T] ~ **sth** (of a player in a sports game) to kick or throw the ball from a fixed or agreed position: *to take a penalty/free kick/corner*
- **VOTE/SURVEY** **41** [T] ~ **sth** to use a particular method to find out people's opinions: *to take a vote/poll/survey*
- **BE SUCCESSFUL** **42** [I] to be successful; to work: *The skin graft failed to take.*
- **GRAMMAR** **43** [T] (not used in the progressive tenses) ~ **sth** (of verbs, nouns, etc.) to have or require sth when used in a sentence or other structure: *The verb 'rely' takes the preposition 'on'.*

**IDM HELP** Most idioms containing **take** are at the entries for the nouns and adjectives in the idioms, for example **take the biscuit** is at **biscuit**. ˌsb can ˈtake it or ˈleave it **1** used to say that you do not care if sb accepts or rejects your offer **2** used to say that sb does not have a strong opinion about sth: *Dancing? I can take it or leave it.* ˌhave (got) what it ˈtakes (*informal*) to have the qualities, ability, etc. needed to be successful ˌI, ˌyou, ˌetc. ˌcan't take sb ˈanywhere (*informal, often humorous*) used to say that you cannot trust sb to behave well in public ˌtake sth as it ˈcomes | ˌtake sb as they ˈcome to accept sth/sb without wishing it/them to be different or without thinking about it/them very much in advance: *She takes life as it comes.* ˈtake it (that …) to suppose; to assume: *I take it you won't be coming to the party?* ˌtake it from ˈme (that …) (*informal*) used to emphasize that what you are going to say is the truth: *Take it from me—he'll be a millionaire before he's 30.* ˌtake it on/upon yourself to do sth to decide to do sth without asking permission or advice ˌtake it/a ˌlot ˈout of sb (*informal*) to make sb physically or mentally tired: *Looking after small children really takes it out of you.* ˌtake ˌsome/a ˈlot of ˈdoing (*informal*) to need a lot of effort or time; to be very difficult to do ˈtake ˈthat! (*informal*) used as an exclamation when you are hitting sb or attacking them in some other way

**PHRV** ˌtake sb aˈback [usually passive] to shock or surprise sb very much: *Brendan was taken aback by her sudden question.*
ˈtake after sb [no passive] **1** (not used in the progressive tenses) to look or behave like an older member of your family, especially your mother or father: *Your daughter doesn't take after you at all.* **2** (*NAmE, informal*) to follow sb quickly: *I'm afraid that if I started running the man would take after me.*
ˌtake aˈgainst sb/sth [no passive] (*old-fashioned, BrE*) to start not liking sb/sth for no clear reason
ˌtake sb/sth↔aˈpart (*informal*) **1** to defeat sb easily in a game or competition **2** to criticize sb/sth severely ˌtake sth↔aˈpart to separate a machine or piece of equipment into the different parts that it is made of **SYN** **dismantle**
ˌtake sth↔aˈway **1** to make a feeling, pain, etc. disappear: *I was given some pills to take away the pain.* **2** (*BrE*) (*NAmE* ˌtake sth↔ˈout*) to buy cooked food at a restaurant and carry it away to eat, for example at home: *Two burgers to take away, please.* ⊃ related noun **TAKE-AWAY, TAKEOUT** ˌtake aˈway from sth | ˌtake sth aˈway from sth [no passive] to make the effort or value of sth seem less **SYN** **detract**: *I don't want to take away from his achievements, but he couldn't have done it without my help.*
ˌtake sb↔ˈback to allow sb, such as your husband, wife or partner, to come home after they have left because of a problem ˌtake sb ˈback (to …) to make sb remember sth: *The smell of the sea took him back to his childhood.* ˌtake sth↔ˈback **1** if you take sth back to a shop, or a shop takes sth back, you return sth that you have bought there, for example because it is the wrong size or does not work **2** to admit that sth you said was wrong or that you should not have said it: *OK, I take it all back!*
ˌtake sth↔ˈdown **1** to remove a structure, especially by separating it into pieces: *to take down a tent* **2** to pull down a piece of clothing worn on the lower part of the body without completely removing it: *to take down your trousers/pants* **3** to write sth down: *Reporters took down every word of his speech.* **4** to remove sth from the internet or a website: *The webmaster will decide whether to take down the web page or make the required changes.*
ˌtake sb↔ˈin **1** to allow sb to stay in your home: *to take in lodgers* ◊ *He was homeless, so we took him in.* **2** (of the police) to take sb to a police station in order to ask them questions: *Police have taken a man in for questioning following the attacks.* **3** [often passive] to make sb believe sth that is not true **SYN** **deceive**: *Don't be taken in by his charm—he's ruthless.* ⊃ **SYNONYMS** at **CHEAT** ˌtake sth↔ˈin **1** to **ABSORB** sth into the body, for example by breathing or **SWALLOWING**: *Fish take in oxygen through their gills.* ⊃ related noun **INTAKE** **2** to make a piece of clothing narrower or tighter **OPP** **let out** **3** [no passive] to include or cover sth: *The tour takes in six European capitals.* **4** [no passive] to go to see or visit sth such as a film: *I generally take in a show when I'm in New York.* **5** to take notice of sth with your eyes: *He took in every detail of her appearance.* **6** to understand or remember sth that you hear or read: *Halfway through the chapter I realized I hadn't taken anything in.*
ˌtake ˈoff **1** [A2] (of an aircraft, etc.) to leave the ground and begin to fly: *The plane took off an hour late.* ⊃ related noun **TAKE-OFF** **OPP** **land** **2** (*informal*) to leave a place, especially in a hurry: *When he saw me coming he took off in the opposite direction.* **3** (of an idea, a product, etc.) to become successful or popular very quickly or suddenly: *The new magazine has really taken off.* ˌtake sb↔ˈoff **1** to copy sb's voice, actions or manner in a humorous way **SYN** **impersonate** **2** (in sports, entertainment, etc.) to make sb stop playing, acting, etc. and leave the field or the stage: *He was taken off after twenty minutes.* ˌtake sth↔ˈoff **1** [A2] to remove sth, especially a piece of clothing from your/sb's body: *to take off your coat* ◊ *He took off my wet boots and made me sit by the fire.* **OPP** **put sth on** **2** to have a period of time as a break from work: *I've decided to take a few days off next week.* **3** [often passive] to stop a public service, television programme, performances of a show, etc: *The show was taken off because of poor audience figures.* **4** to remove some of sb's hair, part of sb's body, etc: *The hairdresser asked me how much she should take off.* ◊ *The explosion nearly took his arm off.* ˌtake yourself/sb ˈoff (to …) (*informal*) to leave a place; to make sb leave a place ˌtake sb ˈoff sth [often passive] to remove sb from sth such as a job, position, piece of equipment, etc: *The officer leading the investigation has been taken off the case.* ◊ *After three days she was taken off the ventilator.* ˌtake sth ˈoff sth to remove an amount of money or a number of marks, points, etc. in order to reduce the total: *The manager took $10 off the bill.* ◊ *That experience took ten years off my life* (= made me feel ten years older).
ˌtake sb↔ˈon **1** (especially *BrE*) to employ sb: *to take on new staff* ◊ *She was taken on as a trainee.* **2** [no passive] to play sb in a game or contest; to fight against sb: *to take somebody on at tennis* ◊ *The rebels took on the entire Roman army.* ˌtake sth↔ˈon [no passive] to begin to have a particular quality, appearance, etc: *The chameleon can take on the colours of its background.* ◊ *His voice took on a more serious tone.* ˌtake sth/sb↔ˈon **1** [B1] to decide to do sth; to agree to be responsible for sth/sb: *I can't take on any extra work.* ◊ *We're not taking on any new clients at present.* **2** (of a bus, plane or ship) to allow sb/sth to enter: *The bus stopped to take on more passengers.* ◊ *The ship took on more fuel at Freetown.*
ˌtake sb↔ˈout to go to a restaurant, theatre, club, etc. with sb you have invited ˌtake sb/sth↔ˈout (*informal*) to kill sb or destroy sth: *They took out two enemy bombers.* ˌtake sth↔ˈout **1** to remove sth from inside sb's body, especially a part of it: *How many teeth did the dentist take out?* **2** to obtain an official document or service: *to take out an insurance policy/a mortgage/a loan* ◊ *to take out an ad in a newspaper* **3** (*NAmE*) (*BrE* ˌtake sth↔aˈway) to buy cooked food at a restaurant and carry it away to eat, for example at home ⊃ related noun **TAKEAWAY, TAKEOUT** ˌtake sth↔ˈout (against sb) to start legal action against

# takeaway

sb by means of an official document: *The police have taken out a summons against the driver of the car.* ,take sth↔'out (of sth) to obtain money by removing it from your bank account ,take sth 'out of sth to remove an amount of money from a larger amount, especially as a payment: *The fine will be taken out of your wages.* ,take it/sth 'out on sb to behave in an unpleasant way towards sb because you feel angry, disappointed, etc., although it is not their fault: *OK, so you had a bad day. Don't take it out on me.* ◇ *She tended to take her frustrations out on her family.* ,take sb 'out of himself/herself to make sb forget their worries and become less concerned with their own thoughts and situation
,take 'over (from sth) to become bigger or more important than sth else; to replace sth: *Try not to let negative thoughts take over.* ◇ *It has been suggested that mammals took over from dinosaurs 65 million years ago.* ,take 'over (from sb) | ,take sth↔'over (from sb) 1 B1 to begin to have control of or responsibility for sth, especially in place of sb else: *Paul's daughter took over the job in 2017.* 2 to gain control of a political party, a country, etc: *The army is threatening to take over if civil unrest continues.* ,take sth↔'over to gain control of a business, a company, etc., especially by buying shares: *CBS Records was taken over by Sony.* ⊃ related noun TAKEOVER
,take sb 'through sth to help sb learn or become familiar with sth, for example by talking about each part in turn: *The director took us through the play scene by scene.*
'take to sth [no passive] 1 to go away to a place, especially to escape from danger: *The rebels took to the hills.* 2 to begin to do sth as a habit: **take to doing sth** *I've taken to waking up very early.* 3 to develop an ability for sth: *She took to tennis as if she'd been playing all her life.* 'take to sb/sth [no passive] to start liking sb/sth: *I took to my new boss immediately.* ◇ *He hasn't taken to his new school.*
,take 'up to continue, especially starting after sb/sth else has finished: *The band's new album takes up where their last one left off.* ,take 'up sth ? B1 to fill or use an amount of space or time: *The table takes up too much room.* ◇ *I won't take up any more of your time.* ,take sth↔'up 1 ? B1 to learn or start to do sth, especially for pleasure: *They've taken up golf.* ◇ *She has taken up* (= started to learn to play) *the oboe.* 2 to start or begin sth such as a job: *He takes up his duties next week.* 3 to join in singing or saying sth: *to take up the chorus* ◇ *Their protests were later taken up by other groups.* 4 to continue sth that sb else has not finished, or that has not been mentioned for some time: *She took up the story where Tim had left off.* ◇ *I'd like to take up the point you raised earlier.* 5 to move into a particular position: *I took up my position by the door.* 6 to accept sth that is offered or available: *to take up a challenge* ◇ *She took up his offer of a drink.* 7 to make sth such as a piece of clothing shorter: *This skirt needs taking up.* OPP **let sth down** ,take 'up with sb (*informal*) to begin to be friendly with sb, especially sb with a bad reputation ,take sb 'up on sth 1 to question sb about sth, because you do not agree with them: *I must take you up on that point.* 2 (*informal*) to accept an offer, a bet, etc. from sb: *Thanks for the invitation—we'll take you up on it some time.* ,take sth 'up with sb to speak or write to sb about sth that they may be able to deal with or help you with: *They decided to take the matter up with their MP.* be ,taken 'up with sth/sb to be giving all your time and energy to sth/sb
be 'taken with sth/sb to find sb/sth attractive or interesting: *We were all very taken with his girlfriend.* ◇ *I think he's quite taken with the idea.*

■ **noun** 1 a scene or part of a film that is filmed at one time without stopping the camera: *We managed to get it right in just two takes.* 2 [usually sing.] (*informal*) an amount of money that sb receives, especially the money that is earned by a business during a particular period of time SYN **takings**: *How much is my share of the take?* 3 **~ on sth** (*informal*) the particular opinion or idea that sb has about sth: *What's his take on the plan?* ◇ *a new take on the Romeo and Juliet story* (= a way of presenting it) ⊃ see also DOUBLE TAKE

IDM **be on the 'take** (*informal*) to accept money from sb for helping them in a dishonest or illegal way

**take-away** /'teɪkəweɪ/ *noun* 1 (*BrE*) (*NAmE* 'take-out) (*also* 'carry-out *US, ScotE*) a restaurant that cooks and sells food that you take away and eat somewhere else 2 (*BrE*) (*NAmE* 'take-out) (*also* 'carry-out *US, ScotE*) a meal that you buy at this type of restaurant: *Let's have a takeaway tonight.* 3 an important fact, point or idea to be remembered from a talk, meeting or event

**take-down** /'teɪkdaʊn/ *noun* 1 a move in which a WRESTLER quickly gets his/her opponent down to the floor from a standing position 2 (*informal*) an arrest or unexpected visit by the police

**'take-home pay** *noun* [U] the amount of money that you earn after you have paid tax, etc.

**'take-off** *noun* 1 [U, C] the moment at which an aircraft leaves the ground and starts to fly: *The plane is ready for take-off.* ◇ *take-off speed* ◇ (*figurative*) *The local economy is poised for take-off.* OPP **landing** ⊃ WORDFINDER NOTE at PLANE 2 [C, U] the moment when your feet leave the ground when you jump 3 [C] if you do a **take-off** of sb, you copy the way they speak or behave, in a humorous way to entertain people ⊃ WORDFINDER NOTE at COMEDY

**take-out** /'teɪkaʊt/ *noun* (*NAmE*) = TAKEAWAY

**take-over** /'teɪkəʊvə(r)/ *noun* [C, U] 1 an act of taking control of a company by buying most of its shares: *a take-over bid for the company* ⊃ WORDFINDER NOTE at DEAL 2 an act of taking control of a country, an area or a political organization by force

**taker** /'teɪkə(r)/ *noun* 1 [usually pl.] a person who is willing to accept sth that is being offered: *They won't find many takers for the house at that price.* 2 (often in compounds) a person who takes sth: *drug takers* ◇ *It is better to be a giver than a taker.* ⊃ see also HOSTAGE TAKER

**'take-up** *noun* [U, sing.] the rate at which people accept sth that is offered or made available to them: *a low take-up of government benefits*

**tak·ings** /'teɪkɪŋz/ *noun* [pl.] (*BrE*) the amount of money that a shop, theatre, etc. receives from selling goods or tickets over a particular period of time: *The box office takings are up on last week.*

**tak·kie** = TACKIE

**tala** /'tɑːlə/ *noun* a traditional pattern of rhythm in classical Indian music

**tal·cum pow·der** /'tælkəm paʊdə(r)/ (*also informal* **talc** /tælk/) *noun* [U] a fine soft powder, usually with a pleasant smell, that you put on your skin to make it feel smooth and dry

**tale** ❶ B2 /teɪl/ *noun* 1 ? B2 **~ (of sth)** a story created using the imagination, especially one that is full of action and adventure: *The story is a classic tale of love and betrayal.* ⊃ see also FAIRY TALE, FOLK TALE 2 ? B2 **~ (of sth)** an exciting spoken description of an event, which may not be completely true: *I love listening to his tales of life at sea.* ◇ *The team's **tale of woe** continued on Saturday* (= they lost another match). ◇ *Her experiences provide a **cautionary tale*** (= a warning) *for us all.* ⊃ see also TELLTALE *noun* IDM ⊃ see OLD, TELL

▼ **HOMOPHONES**

**tail** • **tale** /teɪl/

- **tail** *noun*: *The peacock fans out its magnificent tail to attract females.*
- **tail** *verb*: *A spy is sent to tail the family and find out everything they do.*
- **tale** *noun*: *She told the children the tale of the tortoise and the hare.*

**tal·ent** ❶ B1 /'tælənt/ *noun* 1 ? B1 [U, C] a natural ability to do sth well: *The festival showcases the talent of young musicians.* ◇ *to possess/have exceptional musical talent* ◇ *a man of many talents* ◇ **~ for (doing) sth** *She displayed her talent for comedy at the event.* ◇ *a talent contest/competition* (= in which people perform, to show how well they can sing, dance, etc.) 2 ? B2 [U, C] people or a person with a natural ability to do sth well: *to nurture/ develop young talent* ◊ *He is a great talent.* **3** [U] (*BrE, slang*) people who are sexually attractive: *He likes to spend his time chatting up the local talent.*

**tal·ent·ed** ⓘ B1 /ˈtæləntɪd/ *adj.* having a natural ability to do sth well: *a talented player/musician/artist*

ˈtalent scout (*also* scout, ˈtalent spotter) *noun* a person whose job is to find people who are good at singing, acting, sport, etc. in order to give them work

ˈtalent show *noun* a show or event, for example on television or in a school, in which people compete to show how well they can sing, dance, play a musical instrument, entertain by telling funny jokes or stories, etc.

**tal·is·man** /ˈtælɪzmən/ *noun* an object that is thought to have magic powers and to bring good luck ⊃ WORDFINDER NOTE at LUCK

**talk** ⓘ A1 Ⓢ /tɔːk/ *verb, noun*
■ *verb*
- **SPEAK TO SB 1** ⓘ A1 [I, T] to say things; to speak in order to give information or to express feelings, ideas, etc: *Stop talking and listen!* ◊ *We talked on the phone for over an hour.* ◊ ~ *to sb Who were you talking to just now?* ◊ *Ann and Joe aren't talking to each other right now* (= they refuse to speak to each other because they have argued). ◊ ~ **with sb** *We looked around the school and talked with the principal.* ◊ ~ **about sb/sth** *They talk a lot about the inspiration for their music.* ◊ *What are you talking about?* (= used when you are surprised, annoyed and/or worried by sth that sb has just said) ◊ *I don't know what you're talking about* (= used to say that you did not do sth that sb has accused you of). ◊ ~ **to/with sb about sb/sth** *She started talking loudly to her friends about the film they'd just seen.* ◊ ~ **of (doing) sth** *Mary is talking of looking for another job.* ⊃ WORDFINDER NOTE at CONFERENCE
- **DISCUSS 2** ⓘ A1 [I, T] to discuss sth, usually sth serious or important: *This situation can't go on. We need to talk.* ◊ *The two sides in the dispute are finally willing to talk.* ◊ ~ **to/ with sb** *Talk with your doctor before radically changing your diet.* ◊ ~ **(to/with sb) about sth** *We want to talk to people about this issue.* ◊ ~ **sth** *to talk politics*
- **SAY WORDS 3** ⓘ A1 [I, T] to say words in a language: *The baby is just starting to talk.* ◊ ~ **in sth** *We couldn't understand them because they were talking in Chinese.* ◊ ~ **sth** *Are they talking Swedish or Danish?*
- **SENSE/NONSENSE 4** [T] ~ **sth** to say things that are/are not sensible: *She talks a lot of sense.* ◊ (*BrE*) *You're talking rubbish!* ◊ *See if you can talk some sense into him* (= persuade him to be sensible).
- **FOR EMPHASIS 5** [T] **be talking sth** (*informal*) used to emphasize an amount of money, how serious sth is, etc: *We're talking £500 for three hours' work.*
- **ABOUT PRIVATE LIFE 6** [I] to talk about a person's private life SYN **gossip**: *Don't phone me at work—people will talk.*
- **GIVE INFORMATION 7** [I] to give information to sb, especially unwillingly: *The police questioned him but he refused to talk.*

IDM ▶ **look who's ˈtalking** | **ˈyou can/can't talk** | **you're a ˈfine one to talk** (*informal*) used to tell sb that they should not criticize sb else for sth because they do the same things too: *'George is so careless with money.' 'Look who's talking!'* **now you're ˈtalking** (*informal*) used when you like what sb has suggested very much ˈtalk about… (*informal*) used to emphasize sth: *Talk about mean! She didn't even buy me a card.* talk ˈdirty (*informal*) to talk to sb about sex in order to make them sexually excited talk a good ˈgame to talk in a way that sounds convincing, but may not be sincere talking of sb/sth (*informal, especially BrE*) used when you are going to say more about a subject that has already been mentioned: *Talking of Sue, I met her new boyfriend last week.* talk ˈshop (*usually disapproving*) to talk about your work with the people you work with, especially when you are also with other people who are not connected with or interested in it talk the ˈtalk (*informal, sometimes disapproving*) to be able to talk in a confident way that makes people think you are good at what you do: *You can talk the talk, but can you walk the walk?* (= can you act in a way that matches your words?) talk

1599

**talk**

through your ˈhat (*old-fashioned, informal*) to say silly things while you are talking about a subject you do not understand talk ˈtough (on sth) (*informal, especially NAmE*) to tell people very strongly what you want talk ˈturkey (*informal, especially NAmE*) to talk about sth seriously talk your way ˈout of sth/of doing sth to make excuses and give reasons for not doing sth; to manage to get yourself out of a difficult situation: *I managed to talk my way out of having to give a speech.* ˈyou can/can't talk (*informal*) = LOOK WHO'S TALKING v. you're a ˈfine one to talk (*informal*) = LOOK WHO'S TALKING v. ⊃ more at DEVIL, KNOW v., LANGUAGE, MONEY, SENSE *n*., TURN *n*.

PHRV ▶ talk aˈround sth (*BrE also* talk ˈround sth) to talk about sth in a general way without dealing with the most important parts of it ˌtalk ˈat sb to speak to sb without listening to what they say in reply ˌtalk ˈback (to sb) to answer sb rudely, especially sb in authority SYN answer back ⊃ related noun BACK TALK ˌtalk sb/sth↔ˈdown to help a pilot of a plane to land by giving instructions from the ground ˌtalk sth↔ˈdown to make sth seem less important or successful than it really is: *You shouldn't talk down your own achievements.* ˌtalk ˈdown to sb to speak to sb as if they were less important or intelligent than you ˌtalk sb/yourself ˈinto/ˈout of sth to persuade sb/yourself to do/not to do sth: *I didn't want to move abroad but Bill talked me into it.* ◊ talk sb/yourself into/out of doing sth *She tried to talk him out of leaving.* ˌtalk sth↔ˈout to discuss sth carefully and completely in order to make a decision, solve a problem, etc. ˌtalk sth↔ˈover (with sb) to discuss sth carefully and completely, especially in

▼ SYNONYMS

**talk**
discuss • speak • communicate • debate • consult

These words all mean to share news, information, ideas or feelings with another person or other people, especially by talking with them.

**talk** to speak in order to give information, express feelings or share ideas: *We talked on the phone for over an hour.*

**discuss** (*rather formal*) to talk and share ideas on a subject or problem with other people, especially in order to decide sth: *Have you discussed the problem with anyone?* NOTE You cannot say 'discuss about sth': *I'm not prepared to discuss about this on the phone.*

**speak** to talk to sb about sth; to have a conversation with sb: *I've spoken to the manager about it.* ◊ *'Can I speak to Susan?' 'Speaking.'* (= at the beginning of a phone conversation)

TALK OR SPEAK?
**Speak** can suggest a more formal level of communication than **talk**. You **speak** to sb about sth to try to achieve a particular goal or to tell them to do sth. You **talk** to sb in order to be friendly or to ask their advice: *Have you talked to your parents about the problems you're having?* ◊ *I've spoken to Ed about it and he's promised not to let it happen again.*

**communicate** (*rather formal*) to exchange information or ideas with sb: *We only communicate by email.* ◊ *Dolphins use sound to communicate with each other.* NOTE **Communicate** is often used when the speaker wants to draw attention to the means of communication used.

**debate** to discuss sth, especially formally, before making a decision or finding a solution: *Politicians will be debating the bill later this week.*

**consult** (*rather formal*) to discuss sth with sb in order to get their permission for sth, or to help you make a decision: *You shouldn't have done it without consulting me.*

PATTERNS
- to talk/discuss sth/speak/communicate/debate/ consult **with** sb
- to talk/speak **to** sb
- to talk/speak to sb/consult sb **about** sth
- to talk/speak **of** sth

# talkative

order to reach an agreement or make a decision: *You'll find it helpful to talk things over with a friend.* **talk 'round sth** (*BrE*) = TALK AROUND STH **talk sb 'round (to sth)** (*BrE*) to persuade sb to accept sth or agree to sth: *We finally managed to talk them round to our way of thinking.* **talk sb 'through sth** to explain to sb how sth works so that they can do it or understand it: *Can you talk me through the various investment options?* **talk sth ↔ 'through** to discuss sth carefully and completely until you are sure you understand it **talk sb/sth/yourself 'up** to describe sb/sth/yourself in a way that makes them/it/you sound better than they really are

■ **noun**
- **SPEECH 1** [C] a speech or lecture on a particular subject: *I went to several interesting talks at the conference.* ◇ *~on/about sth She gave a talk on her visit to China.* ⊃ SYNONYMS at SPEECH
- **CONVERSATION 2** [C] a conversation or discussion: *She looked worried so we had a talk.* ◇ *~(with sb) (about sth) I had a long talk with my boss about my career prospects.* ⊃ SYNONYMS at DISCUSSION
- **FORMAL DISCUSSIONS 3** **talks** [pl.] formal discussions between governments or organizations: *peace/trade talks* ◇ *to hold talks* ◇ *with sb/sth The delegation arrived for talks with their government.* ◇ *in~with sb/sth He is currently in talks with two football clubs.* ◇ *~between A and B Talks between management and workers broke down over the issue of holiday pay.* ◇ *~on/over sth Leaders will resume talks on the trade deal next month.* ◇ *A further round of talks will be needed if the dispute is to be resolved.*
- **WORDS WITHOUT ACTIONS 4** [U] (*informal*) words that are spoken, but without the necessary facts or actions to support them: *It's just talk. He'd never carry out his threats.* ◇ *Don't pay any attention to her—she's all talk.*
- **STORIES/RUMOURS 5** [U] *~(of sth/of doing sth)* | *~(that ...)* stories that suggest a particular thing might be true or might happen in the future: *She dismissed the stories of her resignation as newspaper talk.* ◇ *There was talk in Washington of sending in troops.*
- **TOPIC/WAY OF SPEAKING 6** [U] (often in compounds) a topic of conversation or a way of speaking: *business talk* ◇ *She said it was just girl talk that a man wouldn't understand.* ◇ *The book teaches you how to understand Spanish street talk* (= slang). ◇ *It was tough talk, coming from a man who had begun the year in a hospital bed.* ⊃ see also BABY TALK, BACK TALK, PEP TALK, SHOP TALK, SMALL TALK, SWEET TALK, TRASH TALK

**IDM** **the talk of sth** the person or thing that everyone is talking about in a particular place: *Overnight, she became the talk of the town* (= very famous). ◆ more at FIGHTING

**talka·tive** /ˈtɔːkətɪv/ *adj.* liking to talk a lot: *He's not very talkative, is he?* ◇ *She was in a talkative mood.*

**'talk·back** /ˈtɔːkbæk/ *noun* [U] (*specialist*) a system that allows people working in a recording or broadcasting studio to talk to each other without their voices being recorded or heard on the radio

**talk·er** /ˈtɔːkə(r)/ *noun* a person who talks in a particular way or who talks a lot: *a brilliant talker* ◇ *She's a (great) talker* (= she talks a lot). ◇ *He's more a talker than a doer* (= he talks instead of doing things). ⊃ SYNONYMS at SPEAKER **IDM** see FAST *adj.*

**talkie** /ˈtɔːki/ *noun* [usually pl.] (*especially NAmE, old-fashioned*) a film that has sounds and not just pictures ⊃ see also WALKIE-TALKIE

**ˌtalking 'head** *noun* (*informal*) a person on television who talks straight to the camera and is seen close up: *The election broadcast consisted largely of talking heads.*

**'talking point** *noun* **1** (*BrE*) a subject that is talked about or discussed by many people: *The judge's decision became a legal talking point.* **2** (*NAmE*) an item that sb will speak about at a meeting, often one that supports a particular argument

**'talking shop** *noun* (*BrE, disapproving*) a place where there is a lot of discussion and argument but no action is taken

**ˈtalking-to** *noun* [sing.] (*informal*) an act of talking seriously to sb to tell them they have done sth wrong: *to give sb a good talking-to*

**ˈtalk radio** *noun* [U] radio programmes in which sb discusses a particular subject with people who phone the radio station to give their opinions

**ˈtalk show** *noun* **1** (*BrE also* **ˈchat show**) a television or radio programme in which famous people are asked questions and talk in an informal way about their work and opinions on various topics: *a talk-show host* **2** a television or radio programme in which a PRESENTER introduces a particular topic which is then discussed by the audience

**ˈtalk time** *noun* [U] the amount of time that a mobile phone can be used for calls without needing more power or more payments

**talky** /ˈtɔːki/ *adj.* (*informal*) **1** (of a film, play or book) containing a lot of talk or conversation: *The film is brilliantly animated, but it's overly talky and suffers from painfully slow pacing.* **2** (about a person) liking to talk a lot **SYN** talkative

**tall** /tɔːl/ *adj.* (**tall·er**, **tall·est**) **1** (of a person, building, tree, etc.) having a greater than average height: *She's tall and thin.* ◇ *the tallest building in the world* ◇ *a tall glass of iced tea* ◇ *He's grown taller since I last saw him.* **OPP** short **2** used to describe or ask about the height of sb/sth: *How tall are you?* ◇ *He's six feet tall and weighs 200 pounds.* ⊃ note at HIGH ▸ **ˈtall-ness** *noun* [U]

**IDM** **be a tall ˈorder** (*informal*) to be very difficult to do **stand ˈtall** (*especially NAmE*) to show that you are proud and able to deal with anything ⊃ more at OAK, WALK *v.*

**tal·low** /ˈtæləʊ/ *noun* [U] animal fat used for making CANDLES, soap, etc.

**ˌtall ˈstory** (*especially BrE*) (*NAmE usually* **ˌtall ˈtale**) *noun* a story that is difficult to believe because what it describes seems EXAGGERATED and not likely to be true

**tally** /ˈtæli/ *noun, verb*
■ *noun* (*pl.* **-ies**) a record of the number or amount of sth, especially one that you can keep adding to: *He hopes to improve on his tally of three goals in the past nine games.* ◇ *Keep a tally of how much you spend while you're away.*
■ *verb* (**tal·lies**, **tally·ing**, **tal·lied**, **tal·lied**) **1** [I] *~(with sth)* to be the same as or to match another person's account of sth, another set of figures, etc. **SYN** match up (with sth): *Her report of what happened tallied exactly with the story of another witness.* **2** [T] *~sth (up)* to calculate the total number, cost, etc. of sth

**the Tal·mud** /ðə ˈtælmʊd; *NAmE also* ˈtɑːl-/ *noun* [sing.] a collection of ancient writings on Jewish law and traditions ▸ **Tal·mud·ic** /ˌtælˈmʊdɪk, -ˈmjuːd-; *NAmE also* ˌtɑːlˈmʊdɪk, -ˈmjuːd-/ *adj.*

**talon** /ˈtælən/ *noun* a long, sharp, curved nail on the feet of some birds, especially BIRDS OF PREY (= birds that kill other creatures for food) ⊃ VISUAL VOCAB page V2

**taluk** /ˈtɑːlʊk/ (*also* **taluka** /ˈtɑːlʊkɑː/) *noun* (in some countries in South Asia) a smaller division of a district that governs itself

**tam·ale** /təˈmɑːli, -leɪ/ *noun* a Mexican dish of meat or beans and CORNMEAL that is wrapped and cooked in CORN HUSKS

**tam·ar·ind** /ˈtæmərɪnd/ *noun* a tropical tree that produces fruit, also called tamarinds, that are often preserved and used in Asian cooking

**tam·bour·ine** /ˌtæmbəˈriːn/ *noun* a musical instrument that has a round wooden frame, sometimes covered with plastic or skin, with metal discs around the edge. To play it you shake it or hit it with your hand.

**tame** /teɪm/ *adj., verb*
■ *adj.* (**tamer**, **tam·est**) **1** (of animals, birds, etc.) not afraid of people, and used to living with them **OPP** wild **2** (*informal*) not interesting or exciting: *You'll find life here pretty tame after New York.* **3** (*informal*) (of a person) willing to do what other people ask: *I have a tame doctor who'll always give me a sick note when I want a day off.* ▸ **tame·ly** *adv.* **tame·ness** *noun* [U]

- **verb 1** ~**sth** to make an animal, bird, etc. not afraid of people and used to living with them: *Lions can never be completely tamed.* **2** ~**sth** to make an emotion, an organization, a situation, etc., less powerful or easier to control: *She made strenuous efforts to tame her anger.*

**tamer** /ˈteɪmə(r)/ noun (usually in compounds) a person who trains wild animals: *a lion-tamer*

**Tamil** /ˈtæmɪl/ noun **1** [C] a member of a race of people living in Tamil Nadu in southern India and in Sri Lanka **2** [U] the language of the Tamils ▶ **Tamil** adj.

**tam·oxi·fen** /təˈmɒksɪfen; NAmE -ˈmɑːk-/ noun [U] (medical) a drug that is especially used to treat breast cancer

**tamp** /tæmp/ verb ~**sth (down)** to press sth down hard, especially into a closed space

**Tam·pax™** /ˈtæmpæks/ noun [C, U] (pl. **Tam·pax**) a type of TAMPON

**tam·per** /ˈtæmpə(r)/ verb
**PHRV** ˈ**tamper with sth** to make changes to sth without permission, especially in order to damage it **SYN** **interfere with**: *Someone had obviously tampered with the brakes of my car.* ⇨ see also WITNESS TAMPERING

**ˈtamper-proof** adj. something that is **tamper-proof** is specially designed so that it cannot be easily changed or damaged: *a tamper-proof identity card*

**tamp·ing** /ˈtæmpɪŋ/ adj. (WelshE, informal) very angry

**tam·pon** /ˈtæmpɒn; NAmE -pɑːn/ noun a piece of cotton material with a special shape that a woman puts inside her VAGINA to hold blood during her PERIOD ⇨ compare SANITARY TOWEL

**tan** /tæn/ verb, noun, adj., abbr.
- **verb** (-nn-) **1** [I, T] ~**(sb/sth)** if a person or their skin tans or is tanned, they become brown as a result of spending time in the sun **2** [T] ~**sth** to make animal skin into leather by treating it with chemicals **IDM** see HIDE *n.*
- **noun 1** [U] a yellow-brown colour **2** (also **sun·tan**) [C] the brown colour that sb with pale skin goes when they have been in the sun: *to get a tan* ⇨ see also SPRAY TAN
- **adj.** yellow-brown in colour
- **abbr.** (mathematics) TANGENT

**tan·dem** /ˈtændəm/ noun a bicycle for two riders, one behind the other ⇨ WORDFINDER NOTE at CYCLING
**IDM** in ˈtandem (with sb/sth) if sb/sth works or happens in tandem with sb/sth else, they work together or happen at the same time

**tan·doori** /tænˈduəri; NAmE tɑːnˈdʊri/ noun [U] (often used as an adjective) a method of cooking meat on a long straight piece of metal (called a SPIT) in a CLAY oven called a **tandoor** /tænˈdʊə(r); NAmE tɑːnˈdʊr/, originally used in South Asia: *tandoori chicken* ◊ *a tandoori restaurant*

**tang** /tæŋ/ noun [usually sing.] a strong sharp taste or smell: *the tang of lemons* ▶ **tangy** /ˈtæŋi/ adj.: *a refreshing tangy lemon flavour*

**tan·gent** /ˈtændʒənt/ noun **1** (geometry) a straight line that touches the outside of a curve but does not cross it ⇨ picture at CIRCLE **2** (abbr. **tan**) (mathematics) the RATIO of the length of the side opposite to an angle in a RIGHT-ANGLED TRIANGLE to the length of the side next to it ⇨ compare COSINE, SINE
**IDM** ˌfly/ˌgo off at a ˈtangent (BrE) (NAmE ˌgo off on a ˈtangent) (informal) to suddenly start saying or doing sth that does not seem to be connected to what has gone before

**tan·gen·tial** /tænˈdʒenʃl/ adj. **1** (formal) having only a slight or indirect connection with sth: *a tangential argument* **2** (geometry) of or along a tangent ▶ **tan·gen·tial·ly** /-ʃəli/ adv.

**tan·ger·ine** /ˌtændʒəˈriːn; NAmE ˈtændʒəriːn/ noun **1** [C] a type of small sweet orange with loose skin that comes off easily **2** [U] a deep orange-yellow colour ▶ **tan·ger·ine** adj.: *a tangerine evening gown*

**tangi** /ˈtæŋi/ noun (NZE) a Maori FUNERAL (= ceremony for a dead person), or meal that is held after the ceremony

---

1601 **tannin**

**tan·gible** /ˈtændʒəbl/ adj. **1** [usually before noun] that can be clearly seen to exist: *tangible benefits/improvements/results, etc.* ◊ *tangible assets* (= a company's buildings, machinery, etc.) **2** that you can touch or feel: *The tension between them was almost tangible.* **OPP** intangible ▶ **tan·gibly** /-bli/ adv.

**tan·gle** /ˈtæŋɡl/ noun, verb
- **noun 1** a TWISTED mass of THREADS, hair, etc. that cannot be easily separated: *a tangle of branches* ◊ *Her hair was a mass of tangles.* **2** a lack of order; a confused state: *His financial affairs are in a tangle.* **3** (informal) a DISAGREEMENT or fight
- **verb** [T, I] ~**(sth) up** to TWIST sth into an untidy mass; to become TWISTED in this way: *She had tangled up the sheets on the bed as she lay tossing and turning.*
**PHRV** ˈ**tangle with sb/sth** to become involved in an argument or a fight with sb/sth

**tan·gled** /ˈtæŋɡld/ adj. **1** TWISTED together in an untidy way: *tangled hair/bed clothes* **2** complicated, and not easy to understand: *tangled financial affairs*

**tango** /ˈtæŋɡəʊ/ noun, verb
- **noun** (pl. **-os**) a fast South American dance with a strong beat, in which two people hold each other closely; a piece of music for this dance
- **verb** (**tango·ing**, **tan·goed**, **tan·goed**) [I] to dance the tango
**IDM** **it takes ˌtwo to ˈtango** (informal) used to say that two people or groups, and not just one, are responsible for sth that has happened (usually sth bad)

**tank** /tæŋk/ noun, verb
- **noun 1** a large container for holding liquid or gas: *a fuel/water/storage tank* ◊ *a fish tank* (= for keeping fish in) ◊ (NAmE) *the gas tank* ⇨ see also FLOTATION TANK, SEPTIC TANK, THINK TANK **2** (also **tank·ful** /ˈtæŋkfʊl/) ~**(of sth)** the contents of a tank or the amount it will hold: *We drove there and back on one tank of fuel.* **3** a military vehicle covered with strong metal and armed with guns. It can travel over very rough ground using wheels that move inside metal belts. **4** (*IndE*) an artificial pool, lake or RESERVOIR ⇨ see also DRUNK TANK
- **verb 1** [I] (especially NAmE) (of a company or a product) to fail completely: *The company's shares tanked on Wall Street.* **2** [T, I] ~**(sth)** (NAmE, sport) to lose a game, especially deliberately: *She was accused of tanking the match.*
**PHRV** ˌtank ˈup | ˌtank sth ˈup (NAmE) (also ˌfill ˈup, ˌfill sth⇿ˈup BrE and NAmE) to fill a car with gas: *He tanked up and drove off.* ◊ *We stopped to tank the car up.*

**tank·ard** /ˈtæŋkəd; NAmE -kərd/ noun a large, usually metal, cup with a handle, that is used for drinking beer from

**ˌtanked ˈup** (BrE) (NAmE **tanked**) adj. (informal) very drunk

**ˈtank engine** noun a STEAM engine that carries its own fuel and water inside, rather than using another small truck

**tank·er** /ˈtæŋkə(r)/ noun a ship or lorry that carries oil, gas or petrol in large quantities: *an oil tanker* ⇨ see also SUPERTANKER

**ˈtank top** noun **1** (BrE) a sweater without arms **2** (NAmE) a piece of clothing like a T-shirt without arms

**tanned** /tænd/ (also **sun-tanned**) adj. having a brown skin colour as a result of being in the sun

**tan·ner** /ˈtænə(r)/ noun a person whose job is to TAN animal skins to make leather

**tan·nery** /ˈtænəri/ noun (pl. **-ies**) a place where animal skins are TANNED and made into leather

**tan·nie** /ˈtæni/ SAfrE [ˈteni] noun (SAfrE, informal) **1** an aunt; a friendly form of address for a woman who is older than you **2** (sometimes disapproving) a woman, especially one with old-fashioned views or tastes

**tan·nin** /ˈtænɪn/ (also ˌtannic ˈacid) noun [U] a yellow or brown substance found in the BARK of some trees and the fruit of many plants, which is present in wine and tea and used in making leather ▶ **tan·nic** /ˈtænɪk/ adj.

---

**Oxford Phrasal Academic Lexicon (OPAL) written and spoken word lists** | **OPAL written word list** | **OPAL spoken word list**

# Tannoy

**Tan·noy**™ /ˈtænɔɪ/ *noun* (*BrE*) a system with LOUDSPEAKERS used for giving information in a public place: *to make an announcement over the Tannoy*

**tan·tal·ize** (*BrE also* **-ise**) /ˈtæntəlaɪz/ *verb* ~ **sb** to make you want sth that you cannot have or do ▶ **tan·tal·iz·ing, -is·ing** *adj.*: *The tantalizing aroma of fresh coffee wafted towards them.* ◇ *a tantalizing glimpse of the future* **tan·tal·iz·ing·ly, -is·ing·ly** *adv.*: *The branch was tantalizingly out of reach.*

**tan·ta·lum** /ˈtæntələm/ *noun* [U] (*symb.* **Ta**) a chemical element. Tantalum is a hard silver-grey metal used in the production of electronic parts and of metal plates and pins for connecting broken bones.

**tan·ta·mount** /ˈtæntəmaʊnt/ *adj.* ~ **to sth** (*formal*) having the same bad effect as sth else: *If he resigned it would be tantamount to admitting that he was guilty.*

**tan·tra** /ˈtæntrə/ *noun* **1** [C] an ancient Hindu or Buddhist text **2** [U] behaviour based on these texts, including prayer and MEDITATION ▶ **tan·tric** /-trɪk/ *adj.* [*usually before noun*]

**tan·trum** /ˈtæntrəm/ *noun* a sudden short period of angry, unreasonable behaviour, especially in a child: *to have/throw a tantrum* ◇ *Children often have temper tantrums at the age of two or thereabouts.*

**Taoi·seach** /ˈtiːʃəx/ *noun* the Prime Minister of the Irish Republic

**Tao·ism** /ˈdaʊɪzəm, ˈtaʊ-/ *noun* [U] a Chinese philosophy based on the writings of Lao-tzu ▶ **Tao·ist** /-ɪst/ *noun, adj.*

**tap** /tæp/ *verb, noun*

■ *verb* (**-pp-**) **1** [I, T] to hit sb/sth quickly and lightly: ~ (**away**) (**at sth**) *Someone tapped at the door.* ◇ *He was busy tapping away at his computer.* ◇ ~ **sb/sth** *Ralph tapped me on the shoulder.* ◇ *Tap the icon to open the app.* **2** [T, I] ~ (**sth**) if you **tap** your fingers, feet, etc. or they **tap**, you hit them gently against a table, the floor, etc., for example to the rhythm of music: *He kept tapping his fingers on the table.* ◇ *The music set everyone's feet tapping.* **3** [T, I] to make use of a source of energy, knowledge, etc. that already exists: ~ **sth** *We need to tap the expertise of the people we already have.* ◇ ~ **into sth** *The movie seems to tap into a general sentimentality about animals.* **4** ~ **sth** (*especially BrE*) to fit a device to a phone so that sb's calls can be listened to secretly: *He was convinced his phone was being tapped.* ⊃ *see also* WIRETAPPING **5** [T] ~ **sth** to cut into a tree in order to get liquid from it **6** [T, *usually passive*] ~ **sb** (*NAmE*) to choose sb to do a particular job: *Richards has been tapped to replace the retiring chairperson.* **7** [T] ~ **sth** (*phonetics*) to produce a TAP (6) **SYN** **flap**
**PHRV** ▶ **ˈtap sb for sth** (*BrE, informal*) to persuade sb to give you sth, especially money **tap sth↔in** to put information, numbers, letters, etc. into a machine by pressing buttons: *Tap in your PIN number.* **tap sth↔out 1** to hit a surface gently to the rhythm of music: *She tapped out the beat on the table.* **2** to write sth using a computer or a mobile phone: *I tapped out a text message to Mandy.*

■ *noun* **1** (*especially BrE*) (*NAmE usually* **fau·cet**) [C] a device for controlling the flow of water from a pipe into a bath or SINK: *bath taps* ◇ *the hot/cold tap* (= the tap that hot/cold water comes out of) ◇ *Turn the tap on/off.* ◇ *Don't leave the tap running.* ◇ *the sound of a dripping tap* ⊃ *see also* TAP WATER **2** [C] a device for controlling the flow of liquid or gas from a pipe or container: *a gas tap* ◇ *beer taps* ⊃ *see also* SPINAL TAP **3** [C] a light hit with your hand or fingers: ~ **on sth** *He felt a tap on his shoulder and turned round.* ◇ **at sth** *a tap at the door* **4** [C] an act of fitting a device to a phone so that sb's phone calls can be listened to secretly: *a phone tap* **5** [U] = TAPDANCING **6** (*also* **flap**) [C] (*phonetics*) a speech sound that is produced by striking the tongue quickly and lightly against the part of the mouth behind the upper front teeth. The 't' in *later* in American English is an example of a tap.
**IDM** **on ˈtap 1** available to be used at any time: *We have this sort of information on tap.* **2** beer that is **on tap** is in a BARREL with a tap on it **3** (*NAmE*) something that is **on tap** is being discussed or prepared and will happen soon

**tapas** /ˈtæpəs, -pæs/ *noun* [*pl.*] (*from Spanish*) small amounts of a variety of Spanish dishes, served with drinks in a bar

**ˈtap dance** *noun* [U, C] a style of dancing in which you tap the rhythm of the music with your feet, wearing special shoes with pieces of metal on the heels and toes ▶ **ˈtap dancer** *noun* **ˈtap-dancing** (*also* **tap**) *noun* [U]

**tape** /teɪp/ *noun, verb*

■ *noun* **1** [U] a long, narrow piece of material with a sticky substance on one side that is used for sticking things together: *adhesive/sticky tape* ⊃ *see also* DUCT TAPE, MASKING TAPE, SCOTCH TAPE™, SELLOTAPE™, STICKY TAPE **2** [U] a long, thin piece of MAGNETIC material, used for recording sounds, pictures or information, especially before digital technology became available: *on* ~ *Twenty years ago he was caught on tape in a very embarrassing situation.* ⊃ *see also* AUDIO TAPE, MAGNETIC TAPE, VIDEOTAPE *noun* **3** [C] a CASSETTE that contains sounds, or sounds and pictures, that have been recorded: *a blank tape* (= a tape with nothing recorded on it) **4** [C, U] a narrow piece of material that is used for tying things together or as a label: *The papers were in a pile, tied together with a tape.* ⊃ *see also* RED TAPE, TICKER TAPE **5** [C] a long, thin piece of material that is stretched across the place where a race will finish or used to mark off an area: *the finishing tape* ◇ *Police tape cordoned off the street in front of the house.* **6** [C] = TAPE MEASURE ⊃ *see also* MEASURING TAPE

■ *verb* **1** ~ **sb/sth** to record sb/sth on MAGNETIC tape using a special machine: *Private conversations between the two had been taped and sent to a newspaper.* **2** ~ **sth** (**up**) to fasten sth by sticking or tying it with tape: *Put it in a box and tape it up securely.* **3** ~ **sth** + *adv./prep.* to stick sth onto sth else using sticky tape: *Someone had taped a message on the door.* **4** ~ **sth** (**up**) (*NAmE*) to tie a BANDAGE (= a piece of cloth) around an injury or a wound: *That's a nasty cut—come on, we'll get it all taped up.*
**IDM** **have (got) sb/sth ˈtaped** (*BrE, informal*) to understand sb/sth completely and to have learned how to deal with them/it successfully: *He can't fool me—I've got him taped.*

**ˈtape measure** (*also* **tape**, **ˈmeasuring tape**) *noun* a long, thin piece of plastic, cloth or flexible metal that has measurements marked on it and is used for measuring the length or height of sth

**taper** /ˈteɪpə(r)/ *verb, noun*

■ *verb* [I, T] to become gradually narrower; to make sth become gradually narrower: *The tail tapered to a rounded tip.* ◇ ~ **sth** *The pots are wide at the base and tapered at the top.*
**PHRV** **ˈtaper off** to become gradually less in number, amount, degree, etc: *The number of applicants for teaching posts has tapered off.* **ˈtaper sth↔off** to make sth become gradually less in number, amount, degree, etc: *They are gradually tapering off production of the older models.*

■ *noun* **1** a long, thin piece of wood, paper, etc. that is used for lighting fires or lamps **2** a long, thin CANDLE **3** [*usually sing.*] the way that sth gradually decreases in size, becoming thinner

**ˈtape-record** *verb* ~ **sth** to record sth on tape: *a tape-recorded interview*

**ˈtape recorder** *noun* a machine that is used for recording and playing sounds on tape

**ˈtape recording** *noun* something that has been recorded on tape: *a tape recording of the interview*

**tape·script** /ˈteɪpskrɪpt/ *noun* the printed text of a recording of speech

**tap·es·try** /ˈtæpəstri/ *noun* [C, U] (*pl.* **-ies**) a picture or pattern that is made by WEAVING coloured wool onto heavy cloth; the art of doing this: *medieval tapestries* ◇ *tapestry cushions* ◇ *crafts such as embroidery and tapestry* ▶ **tap·es·tried** *adj.* [*only before noun*]: *tapestried walls*

**tape·worm** /ˈteɪpwɜːm; *NAmE* -wɜːrm/ *noun* a long, flat WORM that can live in the INTESTINES of animals and humans and can cause illness

**tap-in** *noun* (in sport) an easy, light hit of the ball into the goal or hole from a close position: *The pass left Tevez with a simple tap-in.*

**tapi·oca** /ˌtæpiˈəʊkə/ *noun* [U] hard white grains obtained from the CASSAVA plant, often cooked with milk to make a DESSERT (= a sweet dish)

**tapir** /ˈteɪpə(r)/ *noun* an animal like a pig with a long nose, that lives in Central and South America and south-east Asia

**tap ˈpenalty** *noun* (in rugby) a situation where a player is allowed a free kick of the ball because the other team has broken a rule, and chooses to touch it lightly with the foot then immediately pick it up

**tap·root** /ˈtæpruːt/ *noun* the main root of a plant that grows straight downwards and produces smaller side roots

**ˈtap water** *noun* [U] water supplied through pipes to TAPS in a building: *Is the tap water safe to drink?*

**tar** /tɑː(r)/ *noun, verb*
■ *noun* [U] **1** a thick, sticky black liquid that becomes hard when cold. Tar is obtained from coal and is used especially in making roads. ⊃ see also COAL TAR **2** a substance similar to tar that is formed when TOBACCO is burned: *low-tar cigarettes*
■ *verb* (**-rr-**) ~ **sth** to cover sth with tar: *a tarred road*
IDM **be tarred with the same ˈbrush (as sb)** to be thought to have the same faults, etc. as sb else **tar and ˈfeather sb** to put tar on sb then cover them with feathers, as a punishment

**ta-ra** /tə ˈrɑː/ *exclamation* (*especially* NEngE, *informal*) goodbye: *Margaret said ta-ra and left.*

**ta·ran·tula** /təˈræntʃələ/ *noun* a large poisonous spider covered with hair that lives in Central and South America

**tardy** /ˈtɑːdi; NAmE ˈtɑːrdi/ *adj.* ~ **(in doing sth)** (*formal*) slow to act, move or happen; late in happening or arriving: *The law is often tardy in reacting to changing attitudes.* ◊ *people who are tardy in paying their bills* ◊ (*NAmE*) *to be tardy for school* ▶ **tar·dily** /-dɪli/ *adv.* **tar·di·ness** *noun* [U]

**tar·get** ⓘ A2 ⓞ /ˈtɑːɡɪt; NAmE ˈtɑːrɡ-/ *noun, verb*
■ *noun* **1** ⓘ A2 a result that you try to achieve: *to meet/hit a target* ◊ *The firm is on track to achieve its growth target for the year.* ◊ *The university will reach its target of 5000 students next September.* ◊ *The department has missed its sales target for the third month running.* ◊ *Set yourself targets that you can reasonably hope to achieve.* ◊ **on~** *The new sports complex is on target to open in June.* ◊ *a target audience/market* (= the particular audience, area etc. that a product, programme, etc. is aimed at) **2** ⓘ B1 an object, a person or a place that people aim at when attacking: *They attacked military and civilian targets.* ◊ ~ **for sb/sth** *Doors and windows are an easy target for burglars.* ◊ *It's a prime target* (= an obvious target) *for terrorist attacks.* ◊ ~ **of sth** (*figurative*) *He's become the target of a lot of criticism recently.* **3** an object that people practise shooting at, especially a round board with circles on it: *to aim at a target* ◊ *to hit/miss the target* ◊ *target practice*
■ *verb* (**tar·get·ing, tar·get·ed, tar·get·ed**) [*often passive*]
**1** ⓘ B2 to aim an attack or a criticism at sb/sth: ~ **sb/sth** *He accused the group of deliberately targeting civilians.* ◊ ~ **sth at sb/sth** *The criticism was targeted chiefly at the managing director.* **2** to try to have an effect on a particular group of people or particular thing: ~ **sb/sth** *Filmmakers are increasingly targeting international markets.* ◊ ~ **sth at/on sb** *The campaign is specifically targeted at children.* ◊ ~ **sth for sth** *This hospital has been targeted for additional funding.* ▶ **tar·get·ed** *adj.*: *strategically targeted attacks* ◊ *Emails are scanned for keywords in order to deliver targeted advertising.*

**ˈtarget language** *noun* (*linguistics*) **1** (*also* **ˈobject language**) a language into which a text is being translated **2** a foreign language that sb is learning

**tar·iff** /ˈtærɪf/ *noun* **1** a tax that is paid on goods coming into or going out of a country ⊃ SYNONYMS at TAX ⊃ WORDFINDER NOTE at TRADE **2** a list of fixed prices that are charged by a hotel or restaurant for rooms, meals, etc., or by a company for a particular service: *mobile-phone tariffs* **3** (*BrE, law*) a level of punishment for sb who has been found guilty of a crime

**Tar·mac**™ /ˈtɑːmæk; NAmE ˈtɑːrm-/ *noun* [U] **1** (*also less frequent* **tar·mac·adam** /ˌtɑːməˈkædəm; NAmE ˌtɑːrm-/) (NAmE *also* **ˈblacktop**) a black material used for making road surfaces, that consists of small stones mixed with TAR **2 the tarmac** an area with a Tarmac surface, especially at an airport: *Three planes were standing on the tarmac, waiting to take off.*

**tar·mac** /ˈtɑːmæk; NAmE ˈtɑːrm-/ *verb* (**-ck-**) (*BrE*) ~ **sth** to cover a surface with Tarmac™: *tarmacked roads*

**tarn** /tɑːn; NAmE tɑːrn/ *noun* a small lake in the mountains

**tar·na·tion** /tɑːˈneɪʃn; NAmE tɑːrˈn-/ *exclamation* (*old-fashioned, especially* NAmE) a word that people use to show that they are annoyed with sb/sth

**tar·nish** /ˈtɑːnɪʃ; NAmE ˈtɑːrn-/ *verb, noun*
■ *verb* **1** [I, T] if metal **tarnishes** or sth **tarnishes** it, it no longer looks bright and shiny: *The mirrors had tarnished with age.* ◊ ~ **sth** *The silver candlesticks were tarnished and dusty.* **2** [T, *often passive*] to damage the good opinion people have of sb/sth SYN **taint**: *be tarnished Reputations can be easily tarnished.* ◊ *He hopes to improve the newspaper's somewhat tarnished public image.*
■ *noun* [*sing., U*] a thin layer on the surface of a metal that makes it look darker and less bright

**tarot** /ˈtærəʊ/ *noun* [*sing., U*] a set of special cards with pictures on them, used for telling sb what will happen to them in the future

**tar·paulin** /tɑːˈpɔːlɪn; NAmE tɑːrˈp-/ (*also* NAmE, *informal* **tarp**) *noun* [C, U] a large sheet made of heavy WATERPROOF material, used to cover things with and to keep rain off

---

## SYNONYMS

### target
**objective • goal • object • end**

These are all words for sth that you are trying to achieve.

**target** a result that you try to achieve: *Set yourself targets that you can reasonably hope to achieve.* ◊ *attainment targets in schools*

**objective** (*rather formal*) something that you are trying to achieve: *What is the main objective of this project?*

**goal** something that you hope to achieve: *He continued to pursue his goal of becoming an actor.*

**TARGET, OBJECTIVE OR GOAL?**
A **target** is usually officially recorded in some way, for example by an employer or by a government committee. It is often specific, and in the form of figures, such as number of sales or exam passes, or a date. People often set their own **objectives**: these are things that they wish to achieve, often as part of a project or a talk they are giving. **Goals** are often long-term, and relate to people's life and career plans or the long-term plans of a company or organization.

**object** the purpose of sth; sth that you plan to achieve: *The object is to educate people about road safety.*

**end** something that you plan to achieve: *He joined the society for political ends.* ◊ *That's only OK if you believe that the end justifies the means* (= bad methods of doing sth are acceptable if the final result is good). NOTE **End** is usually used in the plural or in particular fixed expressions.

**PATTERNS**
- to work **towards** a(n) target/objective/goal
- a(n) **ambitious/major/long-term/short-term/future** target/objective/goal
- **economic/financial/business** targets/objectives/goals
- to **set/agree on/identify/reach/meet/exceed** a(n) target/objective/goal
- to **achieve** a(n) target/objective/goal/end

# tarragon

**tar·ra·gon** /ˈtærəɡən/ noun [U] a plant with leaves that have a strong taste and are used in cooking as a HERB ⊃ VISUAL VOCAB page V8

**tarry** /ˈtæri/ verb (**tar·ries**, **tarry·ing**, **tar·ried**, **tar·ried**) [I] (*old use* or *literary*) to stay in a place, especially when you ought to leave; to delay coming to or going from a place **SYN** linger

**tar·sal** /ˈtɑːsl; NAmE ˈtɑːrsl/ noun (*anatomy*) one of the small bones in the ankle and upper foot ⊃ VISUAL VOCAB page V1

**tart** /tɑːt; NAmE tɑːrt/ noun, adj., verb
- noun **1** [C, U] an open PIE filled with sweet food such as fruit: *a strawberry tart* ⊃ compare FLAN, QUICHE **2** [C] (*BrE*, *informal*, *disapproving*) a woman who you think behaves or dresses in a way that is intended to attract sexual attention ⊃ see also TARTY **3** [C] (*slang*) a PROSTITUTE
- adj. **1** having a bitter, sharp taste that may be pleasant or unpleasant: *tart apples* ⊃ WORDFINDER NOTE at TASTE **2** [usually before noun] (of remarks, etc.) quick and unkind **SYN** sharp: *a tart reply* ▸ **tart·ly** adv.: *'Too late!' said my mother tartly.* **tart·ness** noun [U]
- verb
**PHRV** **tart yourself ˈup** (*informal*) (especially of a woman) to make yourself more attractive by putting on nice clothes, jewellery, MAKE-UP, etc. **ˌtart sth↔ˈup** (*informal*) to decorate or improve the appearance of sth, often in a way that other people do not think is attractive

**tar·tan** /ˈtɑːtn; NAmE ˈtɑːrtn/ noun **1** [U, C] a pattern of squares and lines of different colours and widths that cross each other at an angle of 90°, used especially on cloth, and originally from Scotland: *a tartan rug* **2** [C] a tartan pattern connected with a particular group of families (= a CLAN) in Scotland: *the MacLeod tartan* **3** [U] cloth, especially made of wool, that has a tartan pattern ⊃ compare PLAID

**tar·tar** /ˈtɑːtə(r); NAmE ˈtɑːrt-/ noun **1** [U] a hard substance that forms on teeth **2** [C] (*old-fashioned*) a person in a position of authority who is strict and easily made angry

**ˌtartare ˈsauce** (NAmE **ˌtar·tar ˈsauce**) /ˌtɑːtə ˈsɔːs; NAmE ˌtɑːrtər/ noun [U] a thick cold white sauce made from MAYONNAISE, onions and CAPERS, usually eaten with fish

**tarty** /ˈtɑːti; NAmE ˈtɑːrti/ adj. (*disapproving*) (of a woman) dressing or behaving in a way that is intended to attract sexual attention

**Tar·zan** /ˈtɑːzæn; NAmE ˈtɑːrzæn/ noun a man with a very strong body **ORIGIN** From the novel *Tarzan of the Apes* by Edgar Rice Burroughs about a man who lived with wild animals.

**Taser™** /ˈteɪzə(r)/ noun a gun that fires DARTS that give a person a small electric shock and make them unable to move for a short time ▸ **Taser** (also **tase** /teɪz/) verb ~ sb

**task** ❶ A2 ○ /tɑːsk; NAmE tæsk/ noun, verb
- noun **1** ❷ A2 a piece of work that sb has to do, especially a hard or unpleasant one: *to accomplish/perform/undertake/complete a task* ◊ *a difficult/a daunting/an impossible task* ◊ *Getting hold of this information was no easy task* (= was difficult). ◊ *a thankless task* (= an unpleasant one that nobody wants to do and nobody thanks you for doing) ◊ *The first task for the new leader is to focus on the economy.* ◊ *~ of (doing) sth Detectives are now faced with the task of identifying the body.* ◊ *We should stop chatting and get back to the task at hand.* **2** ❷ A2 an activity that is designed to help achieve a particular learning goal, especially in language teaching: *Look at the diagram and then do the task below.* ◊ *task-based learning*
**IDM** **take sb to ˈtask (for/over sth)** to criticize sb strongly for sth they have done
- verb [usually passive] (*formal*) to give sb a task to do: **be tasked with sth** *NATO troops were tasked with keeping the peace.*

---

▼ **SYNONYMS**

**task**
duties • mission • job • chore
These are all words for a piece of work that sb has to do.
**task** a piece of work that sb has to do, especially a difficult or unpleasant one: *Our first task will be to set up a communications system.*
**duties** tasks that are part of your job: *Your duties will include setting up a new computer system.*
**mission** an important official job that a person or group of people is given to do, especially when they are sent to another country: *They undertook a fact-finding mission in the region.*
**job** a piece of work that sb has to do: *I've got various jobs around the house to do.*

**TASK OR JOB?**
A **task** may be more difficult than a **job** and require you to think carefully about how you are going to do it. A **job** may be sth small that is one of several jobs that you have to do, especially in the home; or a **job** can be sth that takes a long time and is boring or needs a lot of patience.
**chore** a task that you have to do regularly, especially one that you do in the home and find unpleasant or boring: *household chores*

**PATTERNS**
- the task/mission/job/chore of (doing) sth
- (a) **daily/day-to-day** task/duties/job/chore
- (a) **routine** task/duties/mission/job/chore
- (a/an) **easy/difficult** task/mission/job
- (a) **household/domestic** task/duties/job/chore
- to **do** a task/a job/the chores
- to **finish** a task/a mission/a job/the chores
- to **give** sb a task/their duties/a mission/a job/a chore

---

**ˈtask force** noun **1** a military force that is brought together and sent to a particular place **2** a group of people who are brought together to deal with a particular problem

**task·mas·ter** /ˈtɑːskmɑːstə(r); NAmE ˈtæskmæs-/ noun a person who gives other people work to do, often work that is difficult: *She was a hard taskmaster.*

**tas·sel** /ˈtæsl/ noun a bunch of THREADS that are tied together at one end and hang from CUSHIONS, curtains, clothes, etc. as a decoration

**tas·selled** (*BrE*) (*US* **tas·seled**) /ˈtæsld/ adj. decorated with tassels

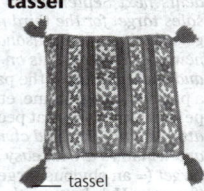
tassel

**taste** ❶ A2 /teɪst/ noun, verb
- noun
- **OF FOOD AND DRINK 1** ❷ A2 [C, U] the particular quality that different foods and drinks have that allows you to recognize them when you put them in your mouth: *a sweet/salty/bitter/sour taste* ◊ *I don't like the taste of olives.* ◊ *This dish has an unusual combination of tastes and textures.* ◊ *The soup has very little taste.* ⊃ WORDFINDER NOTE at EAT

**WORDFINDER** bitter, bland, hot, pungent, savoury, sour, spicy, sweet, tart

- **SENSE 2** ❷ A2 [U] the sense you have that allows you to recognize different foods and drinks when you put them in your mouth: *I've lost my sense of taste.*
- **SMALL QUANTITY 3** [C, usually sing.] a small quantity of food or drink that you try in order to see what it is like: *Just have a taste of this cheese.*
- **SHORT EXPERIENCE 4** [sing.] a short experience of sth: *This was my first taste of live theatre.* ◊ *Although we didn't know it, this incident was a taste of things to come.*

- **ABILITY TO CHOOSE WELL** 5 [U] a person's ability to choose things that people recognize as being of good quality or appropriate: *~ in sth He has very good taste in music.* ◇ *They've got more money than taste.*
- **WHAT YOU LIKE** 6 [C, U] what a person likes or prefers: *You can adapt the recipe to suit your personal taste.* ◇ **~ for sth** *That trip gave me a taste for foreign travel.* ◇ **~ in sth** *He has very expensive taste in clothes.* ◇ **to sb's ~** *Modern art is not to everyone's taste.*

**IDM** **be in bad, poor, the worst possible, etc. ˈtaste** to be offensive and not at all appropriate: *Most of his jokes were in very poor taste.* **be in good, the best possible, etc. ˈtaste** to be appropriate and not at all offensive **leave a bad / nasty ˈtaste in the mouth** (of events or experiences) to make you feel upset or ashamed afterwards **to ˈtaste** in the quantity that is needed to make sth taste the way you prefer: *Add salt and pepper to taste.* ⇒ more at ACCOUNT *v.*, ACQUIRE, MEDICINE

- **verb** (not usually used in the progressive tenses)
- **HAVE TASTE** 1 linking verb to have a particular taste: **+ adj.** *to taste good/delicious/sweet* ◇ **~ like sth** *This drink tastes like sherry.* ◇ **~ of sth** *The ice tasted of mint.* ⇒ note at WANT 2 **-tasting** (in adjectives) having a particular taste: *foul-tasting medicine*
- **RECOGNIZE TASTE** 3 [T] **~ sth** (often used with *can* or *could*) to be able to recognize tastes in food and drink: *You can taste the garlic in this stew.*
- **TEST TASTE** 4 [T] **~ sth** to test the taste of sth by eating or drinking a small amount of it **try**: *Taste it and see if you think there's enough salt in it.*
- **EAT/DRINK** 5 [T] **~ sth** to eat or drink food or liquid: *That's the best ice cream I've ever tasted.*
- **HAVE SHORT EXPERIENCE** 6 [T] **~ sth** to have a short experience of sth, especially sth that you want more of: *He had tasted freedom only to lose it again.*

**ˈtaste bud** *noun* [usually pl.] one of the small structures on the tongue that allow you to recognize the different tastes of food and drink

**taste·ful** /ˈteɪstfl/ *adj.* (especially of clothes, furniture, decorations, etc.) attractive and of good quality and showing that the person who chose them can recognize good things ▶ **taste·ful·ly** /-fəli/ *adv.*: *The bedroom was tastefully furnished.*

**taste·less** /ˈteɪstləs/ *adj.* **1** having little or no taste: *tasteless soup* **2** offensive and not appropriate: *tasteless jokes* **3** showing a lack of the ability to choose things that people recognize as attractive and of good quality ▶ **taste·less·ly** *adv.* **taste·less·ness** *noun* [U]

**taster** /ˈteɪstə(r)/ *noun* **1** a person whose job is to judge the quality of wine, tea, etc. by tasting it **2** (*informal, especially BrE*) a small example of sth for you to try in order to see if you would like more of it

**-tastic** /ˈtæstɪk/ *suffix* (in adjectives) (*BrE, informal*) used to emphasize that sb/sth of a particular type is extremely good: *We have a toptastic line-up of stars for you tonight.* ◇ *Try this new choctastic recipe!*

**tast·ing** /ˈteɪstɪŋ/ *noun* an event at which people can try different kinds of food and drink, especially wine, in small quantities: *a wine tasting*

**tasty** /ˈteɪsti/ *adj.* (**tasti·er, tasti·est**) **1** (*approving*) having a strong and pleasant taste when it is eaten: *a tasty meal* ◇ *something tasty to eat* **2** (*BrE, informal, sometimes offensive*) a word that some men use about women that they think are sexually attractive ▶ **tasti·ness** *noun* [U]

**tat** /tæt/ *noun* [U] (*BrE, informal*) goods that are cheap and of low quality ⇒ see also TIT FOR TAT

**tat·ami** /təˈtɑːmi/ *noun* (*pl.* **tat·ami**) (*also* **taˈtami mat**) (*from Japanese*) a traditional Japanese MAT made from dried RUSHES and used to cover a floor

**tater** /ˈteɪtə(r)/ *noun* [usually pl.] (*informal*) a potato

**tat·tered** /ˈtætəd; *NAmE* -tərd/ *adj.* old and torn; in bad condition: *tattered clothes* ◇ (*figurative*) *tattered relationships* ◇ (*figurative*) *the hotel's tattered reputation*

**tat·ters** /ˈtætəz; *NAmE* -tərz/ *noun* [pl.] clothes or pieces of cloth that are badly torn

**IDM** **in tatters** **1** torn in many places: *His clothes were in tatters.* **2** damaged too badly to be saved **SYN in shreds**: *Her reputation was in tatters.* ◇ *The government's education policy lies in tatters.*

**tat·tie** /ˈtæti/ *noun* (*ScotE, informal*) a potato

**tat·tle** /ˈtætl/ *verb* [I] **~ (on sb) (to sb)** (*informal, disapproving, especially NAmE*) to tell sb, especially sb in authority, about sth bad that sb else has done **SYN tell on sb**

**tat·tle·tale** /ˈtætlteɪl/ (*NAmE*) (*BrE* **tell-tale**) *noun* (*informal, disapproving*) a child who tells an adult what another child has done wrong

**tat·too** /təˈtuː; *NAmE* tæˈtuː/ *noun, verb*
- **noun** (*pl.* **-oos**) **1** a picture or design that is marked permanently on a person's skin by making small holes in the skin with a needle and filling them with coloured INK: *His arms were covered in tattoos.* **2** (*especially BrE*) an outdoor show by members of the armed forces that includes MARCHING, music and military exercises **3** [usually sing.] a rapid and continuous series of hits, especially on a drum as a military signal
- **verb** to mark sb's skin with a tattoo: **~ A on B** *He had a heart tattooed on his shoulder.* ◇ **~ B (with A)** *His shoulder was tattooed with a heart.*

**tat·too·ist** /təˈtuːɪst; *NAmE* tæˈt-/ *noun* a person who draws tattoos on people's skin, as a job

**tatty** /ˈtæti/ *adj.* (*informal, especially BrE*) (**tat·tier, tat·ti·est**) in a bad condition: that has been used a lot or has not been cared for well **SYN shabby**: *a tatty carpet*

**tau** /tɔː, taʊ/ *noun* the 19th letter of the Greek alphabet (Τ, τ)

**taught** /tɔːt/ *past tense, past part.* of TEACH

**taunt** /tɔːnt/ *verb, noun*
- **verb** **~ sb** to try to make sb angry or upset by saying unkind things about them, laughing at their failures, etc: *The other kids continually taunted him about his size.*
- **noun** an offensive or unkind remark that is intended to make sb angry or upset: *Black players often had to endure racist taunts.*

**taupe** /təʊp/ *noun* [U] a grey-brown colour ▶ **taupe** *adj.*

**taur·ine** /ˈtɔːriːn/ *noun* [U] a substance that is sometimes used in drinks that are designed to make you feel more active

**Taurus** /ˈtɔːrəs/ *noun* **1** [U] the second sign of the ZODIAC, the BULL **2** [sing.] a person born when the sun is in this sign, that is between 21 April and 21 May ▶ **Taur·ean** /-riən/ *noun, adj.*

**taut** /tɔːt/ *adj.* **1** stretched tightly: *Keep the rope taut.* **2** showing that you are anxious or TENSE: *Her face was taut and pale.* **3** (of a person or their body) with hard muscles; not fat: *His body was solid and ˈtaut.* **4** (of a piece of writing, etc.) carefully written with no unnecessary parts in it ▶ **taut·ly** *adv.* **taut·ness** *noun* [U]

**taut·en** /ˈtɔːtn/ *verb* [I, T] **~ (sth)** to become taut; to make sth taut

**tau·tol·ogy** /tɔːˈtɒlədʒi; *NAmE* -ˈtɑːl-/ *noun* [U, C] a statement in which you say the same thing twice in different words, when this is unnecessary, for example 'They spoke in turn, one after the other.' ▶ **tauto·logic·al** /ˌtɔːtəˈlɒdʒɪkl; *NAmE* -ˈlɑːdʒ-/ *adj.* **tau·tolo·gous** /tɔːˈtɒləgəs; *NAmE* -ˈtɑːl-/ *adj.*

**tav·ern** /ˈtævən; *NAmE* -vərn/ *noun* (*old use or literary*) a pub or an INN

**taw·dry** /ˈtɔːdri/ *adj.* (*disapproving*) **1** intended to be bright and attractive but cheap and of low quality: *tawdry jewellery* **2** involving low moral standards; extremely unpleasant or offensive: *a tawdry affair* ▶ **taw·dri·ness** *noun* [U]

**tawny** /ˈtɔːni/ *adj.* brown-yellow in colour: *the lion's tawny mane*

**tax** /tæks/ *noun, verb*
- **noun** [C, U] money that you have to pay to the government so that it can pay for public services. People pay tax according to their income and businesses pay tax

# taxable

according to their profits. Tax is also often paid on goods and services: *to pay your taxes* ◇ *to raise/cut taxes* ◇ *~ on sth a 20% tax on income* ◇ *in~ to pay over £1000 in tax* ◇ *before/after~ profits before/after tax* ◇ *tax increases/cuts* ◇ *an increase in tax rates* ⊃ WORDFINDER NOTE at PAY **HELP** There are many compounds ending in **tax**. You will find them at their place in the alphabet.

■ **verb 1** ⓘ **B1** to put a tax on sb/sth; to make sb pay tax: *~ sb/sth His declared aim was to tax the rich.* ◇ *Cigarettes are heavily taxed by the government.* ◇ **be taxed on sth** *You will be taxed on all your income.* **2** *~ sth* (*BrE*) to pay tax on a vehicle so that you may use it on the roads: *The car is taxed until July.* **3** *~ sb/sth* to need a great amount of physical or mental effort: *The questions did not tax me.* ◇ *The problem is currently taxing the brains of the nation's experts* (= making them think very hard).
**PHRV** ˈtax sb with sth (*formal*) to accuse sb of doing sth wrong: *I taxed him with avoiding his responsibility as a parent.*

▼ SYNONYMS

**tax**
duty • customs • tariff • rates
These are all words for money that you have to pay to the government.
**tax** money that you have to pay to the government so that it can pay for public services: *income tax* ◇ *tax cuts*
**duty** a tax that you pay on things that you buy, especially those that you bring into a country: *The company has to pay customs duties on all imports.*
**customs** tax that is paid when goods are brought in from other countries
**tariff** a tax that is paid on goods coming into or going out of a country, often in order to protect industry from cheap imports: *A general tariff was imposed on foreign imports.*
**rates** (in Britain) a tax paid by businesses to a local authority for land and buildings that they use, and in the past also paid by anyone who owned a house: *Business rates are very high in the city centre.*

PATTERNS
- (a) tax/duty/tariff/rates **on** sth
- to pay an amount of money **in** tax/duty/customs/rates
- to **pay** (a) tax/duty/customs/tariff/rates
- to **collect** taxes/duties/rates
- to **increase/raise/reduce** taxes/duty/tariffs/rates
- to **cut** taxes/duties/rates
- to **impose** a tax/duty/tariff
- to **put** a tax/duty **on** sth

ˈtax·able /ˈtæksəbl/ *adj.* (of money) that you have to pay tax on: *taxable income*

tax·ˈa·tion /tækˈseɪʃn/ *noun* [U] **1** money that has to be paid as taxes: *to reduce taxation* **2** the system of collecting money by taxes: *changes in the taxation structure*

ˈtax aˌvoidance *noun* [U] ways of paying only the smallest amount of tax that you legally have to ⊃ compare TAX EVASION

ˈtax ˌbracket (*BrE* also ˈtax band) *noun* a range of different incomes on which the same rate of tax must be paid: *There are three tax brackets—20 per cent, 40 per cent and 45 per cent.*

ˈtax ˌbreak *noun* a special advantage or reduction in taxes that the government gives to particular people or organizations

ˈtax colˌlector *noun* a person whose job is collecting the tax that people must pay on the money they earn

ˈtax ˌcredit *noun* **1** money that is taken off your total tax bill **2** money provided by the government to people who need financial help, especially if they have children or are on a low income

tax-deˈduct·ible *adj.* (of costs) that can be taken off your income before the amount of tax that you have to pay is calculated

tax-deˈferred *adj.* (*NAmE*) that you only pay tax on later: *a tax-deferred savings plan*

ˈtax ˌdodge *noun* (*informal*) a way of paying less tax, legally or illegally ▶ ˈtax ˌdodger *noun*

ˈtax eˌvasion *noun* [U] the crime of deliberately not paying all the taxes that you should pay ⊃ compare TAX AVOIDANCE

tax-eˈxempt *adj.* that is not taxed: *tax-exempt savings*

ˈtax ˌexile *noun* a rich person who has left their own country and gone to live in a place where the taxes are lower

tax-ˈfree *adj.* (of money, goods, etc.) that you do not have to pay tax on: *a tax-free allowance* ▶ tax-ˈfree *adv.*

ˈtax ˌhaven *noun* a place where taxes are low and where people choose to live or officially register their companies because taxes are higher in their own countries

**taxi** ❶ **A1** /ˈtæksi/ *noun, verb*
■ *noun* **1** **A1** (*also* **cab**, **ˈtaxi cab**) a car with a driver that you pay to take you somewhere. Taxis usually have METERS that show how much money you have to pay: *We took a taxi to the airport.* ◇ *to call/hail/catch/get a taxi* ◇ *by ~ I came home by taxi.* ◇ *a taxi driver* **2** (in some places in Africa) a small bus with a driver that you pay to take you somewhere. Taxis usually have fixed routes and stop wherever passengers need to get on or off. ⊃ see also DALADALA, MATATU
■ *verb* (**taxi·ing**, **tax·ied**, **tax·ied**) [I] (of a plane) to move slowly along the ground before taking off or after landing

taxi·der·mist /ˈtæksɪdɜːmɪst; *NAmE* -dɜːrm-/ *noun* a person who does taxidermy as a job or interest

taxi·dermy /ˈtæksɪdɜːmi; *NAmE* -dɜːrmi/ *noun* [U] the art of STUFFING dead animals, birds and fish with a special material so that they look like living ones and can be displayed

tax·ing /ˈtæksɪŋ/ *adj.* needing a great amount of physical or mental effort **SYN** demanding: *a taxing job* ◇ *This shouldn't be too taxing for you.* ⊃ SYNONYMS at DIFFICULT

ˈtax inˌspector *noun* (*BrE*) = INSPECTOR OF TAXES

ˈtaxi rank (*BrE*) (*also* ˈtaxi stand *NAmE*, *BrE*) *noun* a place where taxis park while they are waiting for passengers

ˈtaxi·way /ˈtæksiweɪ/ *noun* the hard path that a plane uses as it moves to and from the RUNWAY (= the hard surface where planes take off and land)

tax·man /ˈtæksmæn/ *noun* (*pl.* -men /-men/) **1 the taxman** [sing.] (*informal*) a way of referring to the government department that is responsible for collecting taxes: *He had been cheating the taxman for years.* **2** [C] a person whose job is to collect taxes

tax·ono·mist /tækˈsɒnəmɪst; *NAmE* -ˈsɑːn-/ *noun* a person who studies or has skill in taxonomy

tax·on·omy /tækˈsɒnəmi; *NAmE* -ˈsɑːn-/ *noun* (*pl.* **-ies**) **1** [U] the scientific process of CLASSIFYING things (= arranging them into groups): *plant taxonomy* ⊃ VISUAL VOCAB page V3 **2** [C] a particular system of CLASSIFYING things ⊃ WORDFINDER NOTE at BREED ▶ taxo·nom·ic /ˌtæksəˈnɒmɪk; *NAmE* -ˈnɑːm-/ *adj.*

tax·pay·er ⓘ+ **C1** /ˈtækspeɪə(r)/ *noun* a person who pays tax to the government, especially on the money that they earn: *Hundreds of thousands of pounds of taxpayers' money* (= money paid in taxes) *have been spent on the project.*

ˈtax reˌlief (*also* reˈlief) *noun* [U] a reduction in the amount of tax you have to pay

ˈtax reˌturn *noun* an official document in which you give details of your income so that the government can calculate how much tax you have to pay

ˈtax ˌshelter *noun* a way of using or investing money so that you can legally avoid paying tax on it

ˈtax ˌyear *noun* (*BrE*) = FINANCIAL YEAR

**TB** noun, abbr.
- **noun** /ˌtiː ˈbiː/ [U] a serious disease, caused by bacteria, in which SWELLINGS appear on the lungs and other parts of the body (the abbreviation for 'tuberculosis')
- **abbr.** (in writing) TERABYTE

**Tb** abbr. (in writing) TERABIT

**TBA** /ˌtiː biː ˈeɪ/ abbr. (used in notices about events) to be announced: *party with live band (TBA)*

**T-bar** noun **1** (also **T-bar lift**) a machine that pulls two people up a mountain on skis together **2** a piece of leather, etc. in the shape of a T on a shoe

**TBC** /ˌtiː biː ˈsiː/ abbr. (used in notices about events) to be confirmed: *The four-day course will run from March 8–11 (TBC).*

**TBH** (also **tbh**) /ˌtiː biː ˈeɪtʃ/ abbr. (informal) (used in text messages, on SOCIAL MEDIA, etc. to say that this is what you really think) to be honest: *I don't know anything about it, TBH.*

**T-bill** abbr. (NAmE, informal) = TREASURY BILL

**T-bone ˈsteak** noun a thick slice of beef containing a bone in the shape of a T

**tbsp** (also **tbs**) abbr. (pl. **tbsp** or **tbsps**) TABLESPOON: *Add 3 tbsp sugar.*

**TCO** /ˌtiː siː ˈəʊ/ abbr. (business) total cost of ownership (an estimate of all the direct and indirect costs involved in having and operating a product or system)

**TCP / IP** /ˌtiː siː ˌpiː aɪ ˈpiː/ abbr. (computing) transmission control protocol/internet protocol (a system that controls the connection of computers to the internet)

**TD** /ˌtiː ˈdiː/ noun a member of the LOWER HOUSE of the parliament of the Republic of Ireland (the abbreviation for 'Teachta Dála', which means 'Member of the Dáil')

**te** (BrE) (NAmE **ti**) /tiː/ noun (music) the 7th note of a MAJOR SCALE

**tea** 🔑 A1 /tiː/ noun **1** A1 [U, C] the dried leaves (called TEA LEAVES) of the tea bush: *a packet of tea ◊ a blend of different teas* (= types of tea) ⇒ see also GREEN TEA **2** A1 [U, C] a hot drink made by pouring boiling water onto tea leaves. It may be drunk with milk or lemon and/or sugar added: *a cup of tea ◊ A pot of tea for two, please. ◊ Would you like tea or coffee? ◊ I don't drink tea.* ⇒ see also BUBBLE TEA **3** A1 [C] a cup of tea: *Two teas, please.* **4** [U, C] a hot drink made by pouring boiling water onto the leaves of other plants: *camomile/mint/herbal tea* ⇒ see also BEEF TEA **5** [U, C] (BrE) the name used by some people in the UK for the cooked meal eaten in the evening, especially when it is eaten early in the evening: *You can have your tea as soon as you come home from school.* ⇒ compare DINNER, SUPPER **6** [U, C] (BrE) a light meal eaten in the afternoon or early evening, usually with sandwiches and/or biscuits and cakes and with tea to drink ⇒ note at MEAL ⇒ see also CREAM TEA, HIGH TEA IDM see CUP n. IDM see CUP n.

**ˈtea-bag** /ˈtiːbæɡ/ noun a small, thin paper bag containing tea leaves, which you pour boiling water onto in order to make tea

**ˈtea break** noun (BrE) a short period of time when people stop working and drink tea, coffee, etc.

**tea·cake** /ˈtiːkeɪk/ noun a small, flat, round cake made of a bread-like mixture, usually containing dried fruit: *toasted teacakes*

**ˈtea ceremony** noun a Japanese ceremony in which tea is served and drunk according to complicated rules

**teach** 🔑 A1 S /tiːtʃ/ verb (**taught, taught** /tɔːt/) **1** A1 [I, T] to give lessons to students in a school, college, university, etc.; to help sb learn sth by giving information about it: *She teaches at our local school.* ◊ ~ **sth** *I'll be teaching history and sociology next term.* ◊ (NAmE) to **teach school** (= teach in a school) ◊ ~ **sth to sb** *He teaches English to advanced students.* ◊ ~ **sb (sth)** *He teaches them English.* ◊ ~ **sb about sth** *Schools should teach children about healthy eating.* **2** A1 [T] to show sb how to do sth so that they will be able to do it themselves: ~ **sb to do sth** *Could you teach me to do that?* ◊ ~ **sb how, what, etc …** *My father* taught me how to ride a bike. **3** A1 [T] to make sb feel or think in a different way: ~ **sb to do sth** *She taught me to be less critical of other people.* ◊ ~ **(sb) that …** *My parents taught me that honesty was always the best policy.* ◊ ~ **sb sth** *Our experience as refugees taught us many valuable lessons.* **4** [T, no passive] (informal) to persuade sb not to do sth again by making them suffer so much that they are afraid to do it: ~ **sb to do sth** *Lost all your money? That'll teach you to gamble.* ◊ *I'll teach you to call* (= punish you for calling) *me a liar!* ◊ ~ **sb sth** *The accident taught me a lesson I'll never forget.*
IDM **teach your grandmother to ˈsuck ˈeggs** (BrE, informal) to tell or show sb how to do sth that they can already do well, and probably better than you can **(you ˈcan't) teach an old dog new ˈtricks** (saying) (you cannot) successfully make people change their ideas, methods of work, etc., when they have had them for a long time **teach to the ˈtest** to teach students only what is necessary in order to pass a particular test, rather than help them develop a range of skills

▼ **VOCABULARY BUILDING**

**Teach and teachers**

**Verbs**
- **teach**: *John teaches French at the local school.* ◊ *She taught me how to change a tyre.*
- **educate**: *Our priority is to educate people about the dangers of drugs.*
- **instruct**: *Members of staff should be instructed in the use of fire equipment.*
- **train**: *She's a trained midwife.* ◊ *He's training the British Olympic swimming team.*
- **coach**: *He's the best football player I've ever coached.* ◊ (BrE) *She coaches some of the local children in maths.*
- **tutor**: (NAmE) *She tutors some of the local children in math.*

**Nouns**
- **teacher**: *school/college teachers*
- **instructor**: *a swimming/science instructor*
- **trainer**: *a horse trainer* ◊ *Do you have a personal trainer?*
- **coach**: *a football coach*
- **tutor**: *tutors working with migrant children*

**teach·able** /ˈtiːtʃəbl/ adj. **1** (of a subject) that can be taught **2** (of a person) able to learn by being taught

**teach·er** 🔑 A1 S /ˈtiːtʃə(r)/ noun a person whose job is teaching, especially in a school: *an English/a science teacher ◊ primary/elementary school teachers ◊ There is a growing need for qualified teachers of Business English.* ⇒ note at TEACH

**ˈteacher training** noun [U] the process of teaching or learning the skills you need to be a teacher in a school
▶ **ˈteacher ˈtrainer** noun: *experienced teachers and teacher trainers*

**ˈteach-in** noun an informal lecture and discussion on a subject of public interest

**teach·ing** 🔑 A2 /ˈtiːtʃɪŋ/ noun **1** A2 [U] the work of a teacher: *She wants to go into teaching* (= make it a career). ◊ *the teaching profession* ◊ *traditional/innovative teaching methods* **2** B2 [U, C, usually pl.] the ideas of a particular person or group, especially about politics, religion or society, that are taught to other people: *views that go against traditional Catholic teaching ◊ the teachings of Lenin*

**ˈteaching assistant** noun (abbr. **TA**) **1** a person who is not a qualified teacher who helps a teacher in a school **2** (NAmE) (also **ˈteaching fellow** BrE and NAmE) a graduate student who teaches UNDERGRADUATE classes at a university or college, takes discussion or practical classes, marks written work, etc.

**ˈteaching practice** (BrE) (NAmE **student ˈteaching**) noun [U] the part of a course for people who are training to become teachers that involves teaching classes of students

○ Oxford Phrasal Academic Lexicon (OPAL) written and spoken word lists | W OPAL written word list | S OPAL spoken word list

**tea cloth** noun (BrE) = TEA TOWEL

**tea-cup** /ˈtiːkʌp/ noun a cup in which tea is served IDM see STORM n.

**tea dance** noun a social event held in the afternoon, especially in the past, at which people dance, drink tea, and eat a small meal

**tea-house** /ˈtiːhaʊs/ noun a Chinese or Japanese restaurant where tea is served, often as part of a special ceremony

**teak** /tiːk/ noun [U] the strong hard wood of a tall Asian tree, used especially for making furniture

**teal** /tiːl/ noun **1** [C] (pl. teal) a small wild DUCK **2** [U] (especially NAmE) a blue-green colour

**tea leaf** noun a small piece of a dried leaf of the tea bush; used especially in the plural to describe what is left at the bottom of a cup or pot after the tea has been made

**team** ⓘ A1 /tiːm/ noun, verb
- noun [C + sing./pl. v.] **1** A1 a group of people who play a particular game or sport against another group of people: *a football/basketball/soccer team* ◊ *They play volleyball for the national team.* ◊ (BrE) *Whose team are you in?* ◊ (NAmE) *Whose team are you on?* ◊ *The team is/are not playing very well this season.* ⊃ see also A-TEAM, DREAM TEAM, TAG TEAM **2** A1 a group of people who work together at a particular job: *a team member/leader* ◊ *a member of the senior management team* ◊ *She leads a research team of twenty scientists.* ◊ *He joined the legal team five years ago.* ◊ ~ of sb *A team of experts has/have been called in to investigate.* ◊ as a ~ *We're learning to work together as a team.* ⊃ see also CRASH TEAM, SWAT TEAM **3** two or more animals that are used together to pull a CART, etc.
IDM ,take one for the ˈteam (informal) to give up sth that is important to you or to do sth that is unpleasant in order to benefit your friends or colleagues: *Sometimes you have to take one for the team.*
- verb [usually passive] ~ sb/sth (with sb/sth) to put two or more things or people together in order to do sth or to achieve a particular effect: *He was teamed with his brother in the doubles.*
PHRV ,team ˈup (with sb) to join with another person or group in order to do sth together ,team sb/sth ˈup (with sb) to put two or more people or things together in order to do sth or to achieve a particular effect

**ˈteam building** noun [U] the process of encouraging a group of people to work well together as a team by having them take part in activities and games: *team-building activities/exercises/skills*

**ˌteam ˈhandball** noun [U] (US) = HANDBALL

**team·mate** /ˈtiːmmeɪt/ noun a member of the same team or group as yourself

**ˌteam ˈplayer** noun (approving) a person who is good at working as a member of a team, usually in their job

**ˌteam ˈspirit** noun [U] (approving) the quality of being willing to work together with other people as part of a team

**team·ster** /ˈtiːmstə(r)/ noun (NAmE) a person whose job is driving a truck SYN trucker

**team·work** /ˈtiːmwɜːk; NAmE -wɜːrk/ noun [U] the activity of working well together as a team: *She stressed the importance of good teamwork.* ▶ **team·work·ing** noun [U]: *effective teamworking and problem-solving* ◊ *teamworking skills*

**ˈtea party** noun a social event at which people eat cake, drink tea, etc. in the afternoon

**tea·pot** /ˈtiːpɒt; NAmE -pɑːt/ noun a container with a SPOUT, a handle and a LID (= cover), used for making and serving tea IDM see TEMPEST

**tear¹** ⓘ B2 /teə(r); NAmE ter/ verb, noun ⊃ see also TEAR²
- verb (tore /tɔː(r)/, torn /tɔːn; NAmE tɔːrn/)
- DAMAGE **1** B2 [T, I] to damage sth by pulling it apart or into pieces or by cutting it on sth sharp; to become damaged in this way SYN rip: ~ sth + adv./prep. *I tore my jeans on the fence.* ◊ *I tore a hole in my jeans.* ◊ *He tore the letter in two.* ◊ ~ (sth) *His clothes were badly torn.* ◊ *Careful—the fabric tears very easily.* ◊ ~ sth + adj. *I tore the package open.* **2** [T] ~ sth in sth to make a hole in sth by force SYN rip: *The blast tore a hole in the wall.*
- REMOVE FROM STH/SB **3** B2 [T] ~ sth + adv./prep. to remove sth from sth else by pulling it roughly or violently SYN rip: *The storm nearly tore the roof off.* ◊ *I tore another sheet from the pad.* ◊ *He tore his clothes off* (= took them off quickly and carelessly) *and dived into the lake.* **4** [T] to pull yourself/sb away by force from sb/sth that is holding you or them: ~ yourself/sb from sb/sth *She tore herself from his grasp.* ◊ ~ yourself/sb + adj. *He tore himself free.*
- INJURE MUSCLE **5** [T] ~ sth to injure a muscle, etc. by stretching it too much: *a torn ligament/muscle*
- MOVE QUICKLY **6** [I] + adv./prep. to move somewhere very quickly or in an excited way: *He tore off down the street.* ◊ *A truck tore past the gates.*
- -TORN **7** (in adjectives) very badly affected or damaged by sth: *to bring peace to a strife-torn country* ◊ *a strike-torn industry* ⊃ see also WAR-TORN
IDM be torn (between A and B) to be unable to decide or choose between two people, things or feelings: *I was torn between my parents and my friend.* ˌtear sb/sth aˈpart, to ˈshreds, ˈbits, etc. (also ˌtear sb/sth↔ˈup) to destroy or defeat sb/sth completely or criticize them or it severely: *We tore the other team apart in the second half.* ◊ *The critics tore his last movie to shreds.* ˌtear at your ˈheart | ˌtear your ˈheart out (formal) to strongly affect you in an emotional way ˌtear your ˈhair (out) (informal) to show that you are very angry or anxious about sth: *She's keeping very calm—anyone else would be tearing their hair out.* (be in) a ˌtearing ˈhurry/ˈrush (especially BrE) (to be) in a very great hurry ˌtear sb ˈoff a strip | ˌtear a ˈstrip off sb (BrE, informal) to speak angrily to sb who has done sth wrong ˌthat's ˈtorn it (BrE, informal) used to say that sth has happened to cause your plans to fail ⊃ more at HEART n., LIMB, PIECE n.
PHRV ˌtear sb↔aˈpart/ˈup to make sb feel very unhappy or worried SYN rip sb apart: *It tears me apart to think I might have hurt her feelings.* ˌtear sth↔aˈpart **1** to destroy sth violently, especially by pulling it to pieces: *The dogs tore the fox apart.* **2** to make people in a country, an organization or other place fight or argue with each other: *Racial strife is tearing our country apart.* **3** to search a place, making it look untidy and causing damage SYN rip sth apart: *They tore the room apart, looking for money.* ˌtear at sth to pull or cut sth violently so that it tears: *He tore at the meat with his bare hands.* ˌtear yourself aˈway (from sth) | ˌtear sth aˈway (from sth) to leave somewhere even though you would prefer to stay there; to take sth away from somewhere: *Dinner's ready, if you can tear yourself away from the TV.* ◊ *She was unable to tear her eyes away from him* (= could not stop looking at him). ˌtear sth↔ˈdown to pull or knock down a building, wall, etc. SYN demolish ˌtear ˈinto sb/sth **1** to attack sb/sth physically or with words: *She tore into him with claims of failure and lies.* **2** to start doing sth with a lot of energy: *They tore into their food as if they were starving.* ˌtear sb↔ˈup = TEAR SB/STH APART, TO SHREDS, BITS, ETC. ˌtear sth↔ˈup to destroy a document, etc. by tearing it into pieces SYN rip sth up: *She tore up all the letters he had sent her.* ◊ (figurative) *He accused the leader of tearing up the party's manifesto* (= of ignoring it).
- noun B2 a hole that has been made in sth by tearing: *This sheet has a tear in it.* IDM see WEAR n.

**tear²** ⓘ B2 /tɪə(r); NAmE tɪr/ noun [usually pl.] ⊃ see also TEAR¹ a drop of liquid that comes out of your eye when you cry: *A tear rolled down his face.* ◊ *I shed a tear* (= cried a little) *during the final episode of the show.* ◊ in tears *She left the room in tears* (= crying). ◊ *He suddenly burst into tears* (= began to cry). ◊ tears of sth *He was crying tears of joy.* ◊ *The memory brought a tear to her eye* (= made her cry). ◊ *As he listened to the music, his eyes filled with tears.* ◊ *Their story will move you to tears* (= make you cry). ◊ *They reduced her to tears* (= made her cry, especially by being cruel or unkind). ◊ *Most of the audience was on the verge of tears* (= very close to crying). ◊ *I was close to tears as I told them the news.* ◊ *Desperately* *she fought back the tears* (= tried not to cry). ◇ *The tears welled up* (= appeared and started to flow) *in his eyes.* ◇ *We were in floods of tears* (= crying a lot) *at the end of the film.* ▶ **teary** /ˈtɪəri; NAmE ˈtɪri/ *adj.*: *teary eyes* ◇ *a teary smile/goodbye* IDM see BLOOD *n.*, BORED, CROCODILE, END *v.*

**tear·away** /ˈteərəweɪ; NAmE ˈter-/ *noun* (*BrE*, *informal*) a young person who is difficult to control and often does stupid, dangerous and/or illegal things ⇒ WORDFINDER NOTE at YOUNG

**tear·drop** /ˈtɪədrɒp; NAmE ˈtɪrdrɑːp/ *noun* a single tear that comes from your eye

**tear duct** /ˈtɪə dʌkt; NAmE ˈtɪr/ *noun* a tube through which tears pass from the tear GLANDS to the eye, or from the eye to the nose

**tear·ful** /ˈtɪəfl; NAmE ˈtɪrfl/ *adj.* **1** (of a person) crying, or about to cry: *She suddenly became very tearful.* **2** (of an event, etc.) at which people feel emotional and cry: *a tearful farewell* ▶ **tear·ful·ly** /-fəli/ *adv.* **tear·ful·ness** *noun* [U]

**tear gas** /ˈtɪə ɡæs; NAmE ˈtɪr/ *noun* [U] a gas that makes your eyes STING (= hurt) and fill with tears, used by the police or army to control crowds

**tear-jerker** /ˈtɪə dʒɜːkə(r); NAmE ˈtɪr dʒɜːrk-/ *noun* (*informal*) a film, story, etc. that is designed to make people feel sad SYN weepy

ˈ**tea room** (*BrE also* ˈ**tea shop**) *noun* a restaurant in which tea, coffee, cakes and sandwiches are served

**tear-stained** /ˈtɪə steɪnd; NAmE ˈtɪr/ *adj.* (especially of sb's face or cheeks) wet with tears

**tease** /tiːz/ *verb*, *noun*
■ *verb* **1** [I, T] to laugh at sb and make jokes about them, either in a friendly way or in order to annoy them or make them embarrassed: *Don't get upset—I was only teasing.* ◇ *~sb I used to get teased about my name.* ◇ *~(sb) + speech 'You're not scared, are you?' she teased him.* **2** [T] ~ *sth* to annoy an animal, especially by touching it, pulling its tail, etc. **3** [I, T] ~(sb) (*disapproving*) to make sb sexually excited, especially when you do not intend to have sex with them **4** [T] ~ *sb* (with sth) to make sb want sth or become excited about sth by showing or offering them just a small part of it; to make sb want more of sth: *Spring is here and we have already been teased with a glimpse of summer.* ◇ *There are tempting menus to tease the taste buds.* **5** [T] ~ *sth* (+ *adv./prep.*) to pull sth gently apart into separate pieces: *to tease wool into strands* **6** (*NAmE*) (*BrE* **back·comb**) [T] ~ *sth* to COMB your hair in the opposite direction to the way it grows so that it looks thicker
PHRV **tease sth⇿out 1** to remove KNOTS from hair, wool, etc. by gently pulling or brushing it **2** to spend time trying to find out information or the meaning of sth, especially when this is complicated or difficult: *The teacher helped them tease out the meaning of the poem.*
■ *noun* [*usually sing.*] **1** a person who likes to play tricks and jokes on other people, especially by telling them sth that is not true or by not telling them sth that they want to know **2** an act that is intended as a trick or joke **3** (*disapproving*) a person who pretends to be attracted to sb, makes them sexually excited and then refuses to have sex with them

**teas·er** /ˈtiːzə(r)/ *noun* **1** (*informal*) a difficult problem or question ⇒ see also BRAIN-TEASER **2** (*also* ˈ**teaser ad**) an advertisement for a product that does not mention the name of the product or say much about it but is intended to make people interested and likely to pay attention to later advertisements ⇒ see also COCK-TEASER, EVE-TEASER

ˈ**tea set** (*also* ˈ**tea service**) *noun* a set consisting of a TEAPOT, sugar bowl, cups, plates, etc., used for serving tea

ˈ**tea shop** *noun* (*BrE*) = TEA ROOM

**teas·ing·ly** /ˈtiːzɪŋli/ *adv.* **1** in a way that is intended to make sb feel embarrassed, annoyed, etc. **2** in a way that suggests sth and makes sb want to know more **3** in a way that is intended to make sb sexually excited

**tea·spoon** /ˈtiːspuːn/ *noun* **1** a small spoon for putting sugar into tea and other drinks **2** (*also* ˈ**tea·spoon·ful** /ˈtiːspuːnfʊl/) (*abbr.* **tsp**) the amount a teaspoon can hold: *Add two teaspoons of salt.*

**teat** /tiːt/ *noun* **1** (*BrE*) (*NAmE* ˈ**nip·ple**) the rubber part at the end of a baby's bottle that the baby SUCKS on with its lips and tongue in order to get milk, etc. from the bottle **2** one of the parts of a female animal's body that the young animals drink milk from

**tea·time** /ˈtiːtaɪm/ *noun* [U] (*BrE*) the time during the afternoon or early evening when people have the meal called tea

ˈ**tea towel** (*also* ˈ**tea cloth**) (*both BrE*) (*NAmE* ˈ**dish·towel**) *noun* a small towel used for drying cups, plates, knives, etc. after they have been washed

ˈ**tea tree** *noun* a small Australian and New Zealand tree. The oil from its leaves can be used to treat wounds and skin problems.

**tebi·bit** /ˈtebibɪt/ *noun* (*abbr.* **Tib**) (*computing*) = TERABIT (2)

**tebi·byte** /ˈtebibaɪt/ *noun* (*abbr.* **TB**) (*computing*) = TERABYTE (2)

**tech** /tek/ *noun* **1** = TECHNOLOGY: *tech companies* ⇒ see also EDTECH, FINTECH, HIGH-TECH, LOW-TECH **2** (*BrE*, *informal*) = TECHNICAL COLLEGE **3** (*informal*) = TECHNICIAN (1)

**techie** (*also* **techy**) /ˈteki/ *noun* (*pl.* -**ies**) (*informal*) a person who is expert in or enthusiastic about technology, especially computers ▶ **techie** (*also* **techy**) *adj.*: *How techie are you?*

**tech·ne·tium** /tekˈniːʃiəm/ *noun* [U] (*symb.* **Tc**) a chemical element. Technetium is found naturally as a product of URANIUM or made artificially from MOLYBDENUM.

**tech·nical** ❶ B1 ⓞ /ˈteknɪkl/ *adj.* **1** B1 [*usually before noun*] connected with the practical use of machines, methods, etc. in science and industry: *We offer free technical support for those buying our software.* ◇ *The organization provides technical assistance to farmers.* ◇ *technical skills/expertise.* **2** ？B1 [*usually before noun*] connected with the skills needed for a particular job, sport, art, etc: *She doesn't possess the technical ability to perform the song well.* **3** B1 connected with a particular subject and therefore difficult to understand if you do not know about that subject: *A lot of the discussions were highly technical.* ◇ *The article is full of technical terms.* **4** [*only before noun*] connected with the details of a law or set of rules: *Their lawyers spent days arguing over technical details.*

ˌ**technical ˈcollege** (*NAmE also* ˌ**technical ˈschool**) (*also BrE*, *informal* **tech**) *noun* a college where students can study mainly practical subjects

ˌ**technical ˈfoul** *noun* (in basketball) an act of breaking certain rules of the game, especially ones relating to fair play

ˌ**technical ˈhitch** *noun* a temporary problem or difficulty, especially one caused by a machine or a piece of equipment

**tech·ni·cal·ity** /ˌteknɪˈkæləti/ *noun* (*pl.* -**ies**) **1 technical·ities** [*pl.*] the small details of how to do sth or how sth works **2** a small detail in a law or set of rules, especially one that does not seem fair: *She was released on a technicality* (= because of a small detail in the law).

ˌ**technical ˈknockout** *noun* (in BOXING) a victory when the opponent is still standing but is unable to continue fighting

**tech·nic·al·ly** /ˈteknɪkli/ *adv.* **1** according to the exact meaning, facts etc: *Technically (speaking), the two countries are still at war.* ◇ *It is still technically possible for them to win* (= but it seems unlikely). **2** in a way that is connected with the skills needed for a particular job, sport, art, etc: *As a musician, she is technically accomplished.* **3** in a way that is connected with the practical use of machines, methods, etc. in science and industry: *a technically advanced society* ◇ *In those days recording sound was not technically possible.*

ˌ**technical ˈschool** *noun* (*NAmE*) = TECHNICAL COLLEGE

ˌ**technical sup ˈport** (*also informal* ˈ**tech support**) *noun* **1** [U] technical help that a company gives to customers using their computers or other products: *All our software* licences include technical support. **2** [U + sing./pl. v.] a department in a company that provides technical help to its workers or customers: *I called tech support and they fixed it.*

**tech·ni·cian** /tekˈnɪʃn/ *noun* **1** (*also* **tech**) a person whose job is keeping a particular type of equipment or machine in good condition: *laboratory technicians* **2** a person who shows skill at the technical aspects of an art, a sport, etc.

**Tech·ni·color™** /ˈteknɪkʌlə(r)/ *noun* [U] a process of producing colour film, as used in cinema films

**tech·ni·col·our** (*US* **tech·ni·color**) /ˈteknɪkʌlə(r)/ *noun* [U] (*informal*) the state of having many bright colours: *The rooms were painted in glorious technicolour.*

**tech·ni·kon** /ˈteknɪkɒn; *NAmE* -kɑːn/ *SAfrE* /ˈteknɪkən/ (*also informal* **tech**) *noun* (*SAfrE*) a type of college or university that teaches mainly practical subjects

**tech·nique** 🔑 **B1** ○ /tekˈniːk/ *noun* **1** 🔑 **B1** [C] a particular way of doing sth, especially one in which you have to learn special skills: *management techniques* ◇ *Researchers used advanced techniques to analyse the brain scans.* ◇ *~ for doing sth Teachers learn various techniques for dealing with problem students.* **2** 🔑 **B1** [U, sing.] the skill with which sb is able to do sth practical: *The artist spent years perfecting his technique.*

**techno** /ˈteknəʊ/ *noun* [U] a type of fast, electronic dance music, typically with little or no singing

**techno-** /teknəʊ, teknə; *BrE also* teknɒ; *NAmE also* tekˈnɑː/ *combining form* (in nouns, adjectives and adverbs) connected with technology: *technophobe* (= a person who is afraid of technology)

**tech·noc·racy** /tekˈnɒkrəsi; *NAmE* -ˈnɑːk-/ *noun* [U, C] (*pl.* -**ies**) a social or political system in which people with scientific knowledge have a lot of power

**techno·crat** /ˈteknəkræt/ *noun* an expert in science, engineering, etc. who has a lot of power in politics and/or industry ▶ **techno·crat·ic** /ˌteknəˈkrætɪk/ *adj.* [usually before noun]

**techno·logic·al** 🔑+ **B2** **W** /ˌteknəˈlɒdʒɪkl; *NAmE* -ˈlɑːdʒ-/ *adj.* [usually before noun] connected with technology: *technological advances* ◇ *technological change* ◇ *a major technological breakthrough* ▶ **techno·logic·al·ly** /-kli/ *adv.*: *technologically advanced countries*

**tech·nolo·gist** /tekˈnɒlədʒɪst; *NAmE* -ˈnɑːl-/ *noun* an expert in technology

**tech·nol·ogy** 🔑 **A2** ○ /tekˈnɒlədʒi; *NAmE* -ˈnɑːl-/ *noun* (*pl.* -**ies**) **1** 🔑 **A2** [U, C] scientific knowledge used in practical ways in industry, for example in designing new machines: *science and technology* ◇ *advances in communications technology* ◇ *advanced/modern technology* ◇ *to develop and use new technologies* ◇ *the use of the latest digital technology to create a virtual world* ⊃ *see also* INFORMATION TECHNOLOGY **2** 🔑 **A2** [U] machines or equipment designed using technology: *The scheme provides access to advanced computer technology in the classroom.* ⊃ *see also* HIGH TECHNOLOGY, INTERMEDIATE TECHNOLOGY

**techno·phile** /ˈteknəʊfaɪl/ *noun* a person who is enthusiastic about new technology

**techno·phobe** /ˈteknəʊfəʊb/ *noun* a person who is afraid of, dislikes or avoids new technology

**tech-'savvy** *adj.* (*informal*) having a good knowledge and understanding of modern technology, especially computers: *the tech-savvy younger generation*

**'tech support** *noun* [U] (*informal*) = TECHNICAL SUPPORT

**techy** = TECHIE

**tec·ton·ic** /tekˈtɒnɪk; *NAmE* -ˈtɑːn-/ *adj.* [only before noun] (*geology*) relating to the structure of the earth's surface ⊃ *see also* PLATE TECTONICS

**teddy bear** /ˈtedi beə(r); *NAmE* ber/ (*also* **teddy** *pl.* -**ies**) *noun* a soft toy bear

**te·di·ous** /ˈtiːdiəs/ *adj.* lasting or taking too long and not interesting **SYN** **boring**: *The journey soon became tedious.* ◇ *We had to listen to the tedious details of his operation.* ⊃ SYNONYMS *at* BORING ▶ **te·di·ous·ly** *adv.* **te·di·ous·ness** *noun* [U]

**te·dium** /ˈtiːdiəm/ *noun* [U] the fact of being boring **SYN** **boredom**: *She longed for something to relieve the tedium of everyday life.*

**tee** /tiː/ *noun, verb*
■ *noun* **1** a flat area on a GOLF COURSE from which players hit the ball: *to drive off from the first tee* ◇ *a tee shot* **2** a small piece of plastic or wood that you stick in the ground to support a golf ball before you hit it IDM see T
■ *verb* (**teed**, **teed**)
PHRV ▶ **tee 'off** to hit a golf ball from a tee, especially at the start of a match **tee sb↔'off** (*NAmE*, *informal*) to make sb angry or annoyed **tee sth↔'up** | **tee 'up** to prepare to hit a golf ball by placing it on a tee

**teed off** /ˌtiːd ˈɒf; *NAmE* ˈɔːf/ *adj.* (*NAmE*, *informal*) annoyed or angry

**tee-hee** /ˌtiː ˈhiː/ *exclamation* used to represent the sound of a quiet laugh

**teem** /tiːm/ *verb* [I] (*usually* **be teeming**) (of rain) to fall heavily **SYN** **pour**: *The rain was teeming down.* ◇ *It was teeming with rain.*
PHRV ▶ **'teem with sth** (*usually* **be 'teeming with sth**) to be full of people, animals, etc. moving around: *The streets were teeming with tourists.* ◇ *a river teeming with fish*

**teem·ing** /ˈtiːmɪŋ/ *adj.* present in large numbers; full of people, animals, etc. that are moving around: *teeming insects* ◇ *the teeming streets of the city*

**teen·age** 🔑 **A2** /ˈtiːneɪdʒ/ (*also informal* **teen** especially in NAmE) *adj.* [usually before noun] between 13 and 19 years old; connected with people of this age: *a teenage girl/boy* ◇ *teenage angst* ◇ *teenage pregnancy* ◇ *teen magazines* ⊃ WORDFINDER NOTE *at* AGE

**teen-aged** /ˈtiːneɪdʒd/ *adj.* between 13 and 19 years old: *They have two teenaged daughters.*

**teen·ager** 🔑 **A1** /ˈtiːneɪdʒə(r)/ (*also informal* **teen** especially in NAmE) *noun* a person who is between 13 and 19 years old: *a magazine aimed at teenagers* ◇ *She's just acting like a normal teenager.* ⊃ WORDFINDER NOTE *at* YOUNG

**teens** 🔑+ **B2** /tiːnz/ *noun* [pl.] the years of a person's life when they are between 13 and 19 years old: **in your ~** *She began writing poetry in her teens.* ◇ *to be in your early/late teens*

**teeny** /ˈtiːni/ *adj.* (*informal*) (**teen·ier**, **teeni·est**) **1** (*also* **teeny-weeny** /ˌtiːni ˈwiːni/, **teensy** /ˈtiːnzi/, **teensy-weensy** /ˌtiːnzi ˈwiːnzi/) very small **SYN** **tiny** **2** connected with people between 13 and 19 years old: *teeny magazines*

**teeny·bop·per** /ˈtiːnibɒpə(r); *NAmE* -bɑːp-/ *noun* (*old-fashioned, informal*) a young girl between the ages of about 10 and 13, who is very interested in pop music, fashionable clothes, etc.

**tee·pee** = TEPEE

**'tee shirt** = T-SHIRT

**tee·ter** /ˈtiːtə(r)/ *verb* [I] to stand or move in an unsteady way so that you look as if you are going to fall: *She teetered after him in her high-heeled shoes.*
IDM ▶ **teeter on the 'brink/'edge of sth** to be very close to a very unpleasant or dangerous situation: *The country is teetering on the brink of civil war.*

**'teeter-totter** *noun* (*NAmE*) = SEE-SAW

**teeth** /tiːθ/ *pl. of* TOOTH

**teethe** /tiːð/ *verb* [I] when a baby **is teething**, its first teeth are starting to grow ⊃ WORDFINDER NOTE *at* BABY

**'teething problems** (*BrE also* **'teething troubles**) *noun* [pl.] small problems that a company, product, system, etc. has at the beginning: *Despite a few teething problems, the car has been a great success.*

**tee·total** /ˌtiːˈtəʊtl/ *adj.* never drinking alcohol: *He's strictly teetotal.* ▶ **tee·total·ism** *noun* [U]

**tee·total·ler** (*BrE*) (*US* **tee·total·er**) /ˌtiːˈtəʊtlə(r)/ *noun* a person who does not drink alcohol

**TEFL** /ˈtefl/ abbr. (BrE) teaching English as a foreign language

**Tef·lon™** /ˈteflɒn; NAmE -lɑːn/ noun, adj.
- noun [U] a substance used especially to cover the inside of cooking pans, that stops food from sticking to them
- adj. (especially of a politician) still having a good reputation after making a mistake or doing sth that is not legal: *The Teflon Prime Minister has survived another crisis.*

**tel.** (also **Tel.**) abbr. (in writing) telephone number

**telco** /ˈtelkəʊ/ noun (pl. **-os**) (used especially in newspapers) a TELECOMMUNICATIONS company: *Telcos were struggling to make money from broadband services.*

**tele-** /teli, telɪ, təˈle/ combining form (in nouns, verbs, adjectives and adverbs) **1** over a long distance; far: *telepathy* ◊ *telescopic* **2** connected with television: *teletext* **3** done using a telephone: *telesales*

**tele·cast** /ˈtelikɑːst; NAmE -kæst/ noun (especially NAmE) a broadcast on television ▶ **tele·cast** verb (**tele·cast**, **tele·cast**) [usually passive]: ~ *sth The event will be telecast simultaneously to nearly 150 cities.* **tele·cast·er** noun

**tele·com·mu·ni·ca·tion** /ˌtelikəˌmjuːnɪˈkeɪʃn/ (also informal **tele·com** /ˈtelikɒm; NAmE -kɑːm/) noun **1 telecommunications**, informal **tele·coms** [U] the technology of sending signals, images and messages over long distances by radio, phone, television, satellite, etc: *technological developments in telecommunications* ◊ *the telecommunications industry* **2** [U] communication over long distances by radio, phone, television, satellite, etc: *a telecommunication company* **3** [C] (formal) a message sent over a long distance by radio, phone, etc.

**tele·com·mut·ing** /ˌtelikəˈmjuːtɪŋ/ (BrE also **tele·work·ing**) noun [U] the practice of working from home, making use of the internet, email and phone ▶ **tele·com·mute** (BrE also **tele·work**) verb [I] **tele·com·muter** (BrE also **tele·worker**) noun

**tele·con·fer·ence** /ˈtelikɒnfrəns; NAmE -kɑːn-/ noun a conference or discussion at which members are in different places and speak to each other using phone, internet and video connections ▶ **tele·con·fer·ence** verb [I] **tele·con·fer·enc·ing** /-frənsɪŋ/ noun [U]

**tele·film** /ˈtelifɪlm/ noun a film that is made specially to be shown on television

**tele·gen·ic** /ˌtelɪˈdʒenɪk/ adj. a **telegenic** person looks good on television

**tele·gram** /ˈteligræm/ noun a message sent by TELEGRAPH and then printed and given to sb

**tele·graph** /ˈteligrɑːf; NAmE -græf/ noun, verb
- noun [U] a method of sending messages over long distances, using wires that carry electrical signals
- verb **1** [I, T] ~ **(sth)** to send a message by telegraph **2** [T] ~ **sth** to make it clear to people what you are going to do, often without intending to

**tele·graph·ic** /ˌtelɪˈɡræfɪk/ adj. connected with sending messages by telegraph

**ˈtelegraph pole** (BrE) (NAmE **ˈtelephone post**) noun a tall, straight piece of wood used for carrying phone or telegraph wires high above the ground

**tel·eg·raphy** /təˈleɡrəfi/ noun [U] the process of sending messages by telegraph

**tele·kin·esis** /ˌtelikɪˈniːsɪs, -kaɪ-/ noun [U] the SUPPOSED ability to move objects without touching them, using mental powers

**tele·mark** /ˈtelimɑːk; NAmE -mɑːrk/ noun [U] (in skiing or SKI JUMPING) a style of turning or landing with one ski forward and bent knees

**tele·mar·ket·ing** /ˈtelimɑːkɪtɪŋ; NAmE -mɑːrk-/ (BrE also **tele·sales** /-seɪlz/) noun [U] a method of selling things and taking orders for sales by phone

**tele·mat·ics** /ˌtelɪˈmætɪks/ noun [U] the use or study of technology that allows information to be sent over long distances using computers

**tel·em·etry** /təˈlemətri/ noun [U] (specialist) the process of using special equipment to send, receive and measure scientific data over long distances

1611 **teleprompter**

**tele·ology** /ˌtiːliˈɒlədʒi; NAmE -ˈɑːl-/ noun [U, sing.] (philosophy) the theory that events and developments are meant to achieve a purpose and happen because of that ▶ **teleo·logic·al** /ˌtiːliəˈlɒdʒɪkl; NAmE -ˈlɑːdʒ-/ adj.

**tele·path·ic** /ˌtelɪˈpæθɪk/ adj. **1** using telepathy: *telepathic communication* **2** (of a person) able to communicate by telepathy: *How do I know what he's thinking? I'm not telepathic!* ▶ **tele·path·ic·al·ly** /-kli/ adv.

**tel·ep·athy** /təˈlepəθi/ noun [U] the direct communication of thoughts or feelings from one person to another without using speech, writing, or any other normal method

**tele·phone** 🔊 A1 /ˈtelɪfəʊn/ noun, verb
- noun (rather formal) (also **phone**) **1** A1 [C, U] a system for talking to sb else over long distances, using wires or radio; a machine used for this: *The telephone rang and Pat answered it.* ◊ *I need to make a telephone call.* ◊ *over the ~ You can reserve seats over the telephone.* ◊ *by ~ Can I get in touch by telephone?* **2** A1 [C] the part of the phone that you hold in your hand and speak into: *I picked up the telephone and called some people I knew.* SYN **handset, receiver**
- IDM **be on the ˈtelephone 1** to be using the phone: *He's on the telephone at the moment.* ◊ *You're wanted (= sb wants to speak to you) on the telephone.* **2** (BrE, old-fashioned) to have a phone in your home or place of work: *We were not on the telephone at the cottage.* HELP This expression became old-fashioned when mobile phones came into use. These days we would say: 'We don't have a landline at the cottage.'
- verb A1 (especially BrE, formal) (also **phone** especially in BrE) (also **call** BrE and NAmE) [I, T] to speak to sb by phone: *Please write or telephone for details.* ◊ *He telephoned to say he'd be late.* ◊ *~ sb/sth I was about to telephone the police.* ◊ *You can telephone your order 24 hours a day.* ⊃ note at PHONE

**ˈtelephone booth** noun = PHONE BOOTH

**ˈtelephone box** noun (BrE) = PHONE BOX

**ˈtelephone call** noun (formal) = CALL (1)

**ˈtelephone directory** (also **ˈphone book**, **ˈtelephone book**) noun a book that lists the names, addresses and phone numbers of people in a particular area: *to look up a number in the telephone directory*

**ˈtelephone exchange** (also **exchange**) noun a place where phone calls are connected so that people can speak to each other

**ˈtelephone number** (also **ˈphone number**) noun the number of a particular phone, that you use when you make a call to it

**ˈtelephone pole** (NAmE) (BrE **ˈtelegraph pole**) noun a tall, straight piece of wood used for carrying phone or telegraph wires high above the ground

**ˈtelephone tapping** noun [U] (rather formal) = PHONE TAPPING

**tel·eph·on·ist** /təˈlefənɪst/ noun (BrE, old-fashioned) = OPERATOR (3)

**tel·eph·ony** /təˈlefəni/ noun [U] the process of sending messages and signals by telephone

**tele·photo lens** /ˌtelifəʊtəʊ ˈlenz/ noun a camera LENS that produces a large image of an object that is far away and allows you to take photographs of it

**tele·port** /ˈtelipɔːt; NAmE -pɔːrt/ verb [I, T] ~ **(sb/sth)** (usually in SCIENCE FICTION) to move sb/sth immediately from one place to another a distance away, using special equipment; to be moved in this way: *The search party was teleported down to the planet's surface.* ▶ **tele·por·ta·tion** /ˌtelipɔːˈteɪʃn; NAmE -pɔːrt-/ noun [U]

**tele·prompt·er** /ˈteliprɒmptə(r); NAmE -prɑːmp-/ (especially NAmE) (BrE also **Auto·cue™**) noun a device used by people who are speaking in public, especially on television, that displays the words that they have to say

# telesales

**tele·sales** /ˈteliseɪlz/ (*BrE*) (*also* **tele·mar·ket·ing** *NAmE, BrE*) *noun* [U] a method of selling things and taking orders for sales by phone

**tele·scope** /ˈteliskəʊp/ *noun, verb*
- *noun* a piece of equipment like a tube in shape, containing LENSES, that you look through to make objects that are far away appear larger and nearer: *to look at the stars through a telescope* ⊃ see also RADIO TELESCOPE ⊃ picture at BINOCULARS
- *verb* **1** [I, T] ~ **(sth)** to become shorter, or make sth shorter, by sliding sections inside one another **2** [T] ~ **sth (into sth)** to reduce sth so that it happens in less time: *Three episodes have been telescoped into a single programme.*

**tele·scop·ic** /ˌteliˈskɒpɪk; *NAmE* -ˈskɑːp-/ *adj.* **1** connected with or using a telescope; making things look larger as a telescope does: *a rifle with a telescopic sight* **2** made of sections that can slide into each other to make the object longer or shorter: *a telescopic aerial* ▸ **tele·scop·ic·al·ly** /-kli/ *adv.*

**tele·thon** /ˈteləθɒn; *NAmE* -θɑːn/ *noun* a very long television show, broadcast to raise money for charity ⊃ WORDFINDER NOTE at CHARITY

**tele·van·gel·ist** /ˌteliˈvændʒəlɪst/ *noun* (especially in the US) a person who appears regularly on television to try to persuade people to become Christians and to give money ▸ **tele·van·gel·ism** /-lɪzəm/ *noun* [U]

**tele·vise** /ˈtelɪvaɪz/ *verb* [usually passive] ~ **sth** to broadcast sth on television: *a televised debate* ◇ *to televise a novel* ◇ *The speech will be televised live.*

**tele·vi·sion** 🛈 A1 /ˈtelɪvɪʒn/ *noun* (*also* **TV**) **1** 📖 A1 (*also* **television set**) (*also BrE, informal* **telly**) [C] a piece of electrical equipment with a screen on which you can watch programmes with moving pictures and sounds: *a widescreen/flat-screen/plasma television* ◇ *to turn the television on/off* ◇ *The series first appeared on television screens in 2017.* **2** 📖 A1 (*also BrE, informal* **telly**) [U] the programmes broadcast on television: *We don't do much in the evenings except watch television.* ⊃ WORDFINDER NOTE at PROGRAMME ⊃ see also PUBLIC TELEVISION **3** 📖 A1 [U] the system, process or business of broadcasting television programmes: *satellite/terrestrial/digital/network television* ◇ *in~ I'd like to work in television* (= for a television company). ◇ *a television show/series/programme/broadcast* ◇ *a television drama/documentary/interview/commercial* ◇ *a television company/presenter/station/channel* ⊃ see also CABLE TELEVISION, CLOSED-CIRCUIT TELEVISION, DIGITAL TELEVISION
- **IDM** **on (the) ˈtelevision** (*also informal* **on TV**) (*also BrE, informal* **on (the) ˈtelly**) 📖 A1 being broadcast by television; appearing in a television programme: *What's on television tonight?* ◇ *Is there anything good on the telly tonight?* ◇ *It was on TV yesterday.* ◇ *Millions watched the events on live television.* ◇ *I recognize you. Aren't you on television?*

**tele·vis·ual** /ˌteliˈvɪʒuəl/ *adj.* relating to or suitable for television: *a major televisual event*

**tele·work·ing** /ˈteliwɜːkɪŋ; *NAmE* -wɜːrk-/ (*BrE*) (*also* **tele·com·mut·ing** *BrE and NAmE*) *noun* [U] the practice of working from home, making use of the internet, email and phone ▸ **tele·worker** *noun* = TELECOMMUTER

**tell** 🛈 A1 /tel/ *verb* (**told**, **told** /təʊld/)
- **GIVE INFORMATION 1** 📖 A1 [T] (of a person) to give information to sb by speaking or writing: ~ **sth to sb** *He told the news to everybody he saw.* ◇ ~ **sb sth** *He told everybody he saw the news.* ◇ *Did she tell you her name?* ◇ *What did I tell you?* (= you should have listened to my advice) ◇ ~ **sb about sth** *Why wasn't I told about the accident?* ◇ ~ **sb/yourself (that)** … *They've told us (that) they're not coming.* ◇ *I kept telling myself (that) everything was OK.* ◇ *Are you telling me you didn't have any help with this?* (= I don't believe what you have said) ◇ ~ **sb where, what, etc** … *Tell me where you live.* ◇ ~ **sb + speech** *'I'm ready to go now,'* he told her. ⊃ note at SAY ⊃ EXPRESS YOURSELF at INFORMATION **2** 📖 A1 [T] (of some writing, an instrument, a sign, etc.) to give information about sth: ~ **sb sth** *The advertisement told us very little about the product.* ◇ ~ **sb how, where, etc** … *This gauge tells you how much fuel you have left.* ◇ ~ **sb (that)** … *The sound of his breathing told her (that) he was asleep.*
- **EXPRESS IN WORDS 3** 📖 A1 [T] to express sth in words: ~ **sth to** *tell stories/jokes/lies* ◇ *Are you sure you're telling the truth?* ◇ ~ **sb how, what, etc** … *I can't tell you how happy I am.* ◇ ~ **sb sth** *We'd go fishing and she'd tell me stories.*
- **SECRET 4** [I] (*informal*) to let sb know a secret: *Promise you won't tell.* ◇ *'Who are you going out with tonight?' 'That would be telling!'* (= it's a secret)
- **ORDER 5** 📖 A1 [T] to order or advise sb to do sth: ~ **sb/yourself to do sth** *He was told to sit down and wait.* ◇ *There was a sign telling motorists to slow down.* ◇ *I kept telling myself to keep calm.* ◇ ~ **sb sth** *Do what I tell you.* ◇ ~ **sb Children must do as they're told.* ◇ ~ **sb what, when, etc** … *Don't tell me what to do!* ◇ ~ **sb (that)** … *The doctor told me (that) I should eat less fat.* ⊃ SYNONYMS at ORDER ⊃ note at SAY
- **KNOW/JUDGE 6** 📖 B2 [I, T] (not used in the progressive tenses) to know, see or judge sth correctly: *I think he's happy. It's hard to tell.* ◇ *As far as I can tell, she's enjoying the course.* ◇ *'That's not an original.' 'How can you tell?'* ◇ ~ **(that)** … *I could tell (that) he was angry from his expression.* ◇ ~ **how, if, etc** … *The only way to tell if you like something is by trying it.*
- **DISTINGUISH 7** 📖 B2 [T] (not used in the progressive tenses or in the passive) to recognize the difference between one thing or person and another: ~ **sth** *It was hard to tell the difference between the two versions.* ◇ ~ **A from B** *Can you tell Tom from his twin brother?* ◇ ~ **A and B apart** *It's difficult to tell them apart.* ◇ ~ **which, what, etc** … *The kittens look exactly alike—how can you tell which is which?*
- **HAVE EFFECT 8** [I] ~ **(on sb)** to have an effect on sb/sth, especially a bad one: *The strain was beginning to tell on the rescue team.*

**IDM** **all ˈtold** with all people, etc. counted and included: *There are 52 people coming, all told.* **don't ˈtell me** (*informal*) used to say that you know or can guess what sb is going to say, especially because it is typical of them: *Don't tell me you were late again!* **I/I'll ˈtell you ˈwhat** (*informal*) used to introduce a suggestion: *I'll tell you what—let's stay in instead.* **I tell a ˈlie** (*BrE, informal*) used to say that sth you have just said is not true or correct: *We first met in 2006, no, I tell a lie, it was 2007.* **I ˈtell you** | **I can ˈtell you** | **I'm ˈtelling you** (*informal*) used to emphasize what you are saying, especially when it is surprising or difficult to believe: *It isn't cheap, I can tell you!* ◇ *I'm telling you, that's exactly what she said.* **I ˈtold you (so)** (*informal*) used when sth bad has happened, to remind sb that you warned them about it and they did not listen to you **live, etc. to ˈtell the ˈtale** to survive a difficult or dangerous experience so that you can tell others what really happened **tell a ˈdifferent story/tale** to give some information that is different from what you expect or have been told **tell its own tale/story** to explain itself, without needing any further explanation or comment: *Her face told its own story.* **ˈtell me** (*informal*) used to introduce a question: *Tell me, have you had lunch yet?* **tell me about it** (*informal*) used to say that you understand what sb is talking about and have had the same experience: *'I get so annoyed with Steve!' 'Tell me about it. He drives me crazy.'* **tell me aˈnother!** (*informal*) used to tell sb that you do not believe what they have said **tell ˈtales (about sth/on sb)** to tell sb about sth that another person has done wrong ⊃ related noun TELLTALE **tell the ˈtime** (*BrE*) (*NAmE* **tell ˈtime**) to read the time from a clock, etc: *She's only five—she hasn't learnt to tell the time yet.* **tell sb where to get ˈoff/where they can get ˈoff** (*BrE, informal*) to make it clear to sb that you will no longer accept their bad behaviour **tell sb where to ˈput/ˈstick sth** | **tell sb what they can ˈdo with sth** (*informal*) to make it clear to sb that you are angry and are rejecting what they are offering you **there's no ˈtelling** used to say that it is impossible to know what happened or will happen: *There's no telling how they'll react.* **to tell (you) the ˈtruth** (*informal*) used when admitting sth: *To tell the truth, I fell asleep in the middle of her talk.* **you can never ˈtell** | **you never can ˈtell** (*saying*) you can never be sure, for example because things are not always what they appear to be **you're telling 'me!** (*informal*) I completely agree with you ⊃ more at HEAR, KISS *v.*, LITTLE *adj.*, THING, TIME *n.*, TRUTH

**PHRV** **tell a'gainst sb** (*BrE, formal*) to be a disadvantage to sb: *Her lack of experience told against her.* **'tell of sth** (*formal or literary*) to make sth known; to give an account of sth: *notices telling of the proposed job cuts* **tell sb↔'off (for sth/for doing sth)** (*informal*) to speak angrily to sb for doing sth wrong **SYN** scold: *I told the boys off for making so much noise.* ◊ *Did you get told off?* **'tell on sb** (*informal*) to tell a person in authority about sth bad that sb has done: *Promise not to tell on me!*

▼ **EXPRESS YOURSELF**

**Telling somebody to do something**
- *Could you* wait here for a moment, *please?*
- *Would you* come through now?/*You can* come through now.
- *Can you* send it up to my room, *please?*
- *Just* sign here for me, please.
- *I need you to* finish the report by Friday.
- *Everyone has to* use the side entrance this week.
- *You have to* sign these reports before submitting them.

**'tell-all** *adj.* [only before noun] (of a book, an interview in a newspaper or magazine, etc.) in which sb, usually sb famous, admits sth that may shock people: *a tell-all book/memoir/autobiography*

**tell·er** /ˈtelə(r)/ *noun* **1** (*especially NAmE*) a person who works in a bank, receiving and paying out money from and to customers **2** (*NAmE*) a machine that pays out money from a person's bank account **SYN** ATM, **cash machine** **3** a person whose job is to count votes, especially in a parliament **4** (*usually in compounds*) a person who tells stories, etc: *a foul-mouthed teller of lies* ⊃ see also FORTUNE TELLER, STORYTELLER

**tell·ing** /ˈtelɪŋ/ *adj.* **1** having a strong or important effect; effective: *a telling argument* **2** showing effectively what sb/sth is really like, but often without intending to: *The number of homeless people is a telling comment on the state of society.* ▶ **tell·ing·ly** *adv.*

**tell·tale** /ˈtelteɪl/ *adj., noun*
- *adj.* [only before noun] showing that sth exists or has happened: *telltale clues/marks/signs/sounds* ◊ *The telltale smell of cigarettes told her that he had been in the room.*
- *noun* (*BrE*) (*NAmE* **tat·tle·tale**) (*informal, disapproving*) a child who tells an adult what another child has done wrong

**tel·lur·ium** /teˈljʊəriəm; *NAmE* -ˈlʊr-/ *noun* [U] (*symb.* Te) a chemical element. Tellurium is a shiny, silver-white substance that breaks easily, found in SULPHIDE ORES.

**telly** /ˈteli/ *noun* (*pl.* **-ies**) (*BrE, informal*) **1** [C] a television set **SYN** TV: *He spends most evenings just sitting in front of the telly.* **2** [U] the programmes broadcast on television **SYN** TV: *daytime telly* ◊ *I don't want to watch telly.* ◊ on ~ *Is there anything good on telly?*

**Tel·ugu** /ˈteləɡuː/ *noun* [U] a language spoken in Andhra Pradesh in south-east India

**tem·blor** /ˈtemblə(r)/ *noun* (*NAmE*) an earthquake (= a sudden, violent shaking of the earth's surface)

**tem·er·ity** /təˈmerəti/ *noun* [U] (*formal*) extremely confident behaviour that people are likely to consider rude: *He had the temerity to call me a liar!*

**temp** /temp/ *noun, verb, abbr.*
- *noun* a temporary employee in an office
- *verb* [I] (*informal*) to do a temporary job or a series of temporary jobs: *I've been temping for an employment agency.*
- *abbr.* (*also* **temp.** *especially in NAmE*) temperature: *max temp 17°C*

**tem·peh** /ˈtempeɪ/ *noun* [U] an Indonesian dish made from FERMENTED SOYA BEANS

**tem·per** /ˈtempə(r)/ *noun, verb*
- *noun* **1** [C, usually sing., U] if sb has a **temper**, they become angry very easily: *to have a fiery/hot/violent temper* ◊ *He must learn to control his temper.* ◊ *After an hour of waiting, tempers began to fray* (= people began to get angry). **2** [C, usually sing., U] a short period of feeling very angry: *in a ~*

---

**tempest**

*She says awful things when she's in a temper.* ◊ *to fly into a temper* ◊ *She broke the plates in a fit of temper.* **3** [C] the way that you are feeling at a particular time **SYN** mood: *in a ...~ Come back when you're in a better temper.* ◊ *to be in a bad/foul temper* **4** -**tempered** (*in adjectives*) having a particular type of temper: *good-/bad-tempered* ◊ *a sweet-tempered child*

**IDM** **have a quick/short 'temper** to become angry easily ⊃ see also SHORT-TEMPERED **lose/keep your 'temper (with sb)** to fail/manage to control your anger: *She lost her temper with a customer and shouted at him.* ◊ *I struggle to keep my temper with the kids when they misbehave.*

- *verb* [usually passive] **1** (*formal*) to make sth less severe by adding sth that has the opposite effect: **be tempered with sth** *Justice must be tempered with mercy.* **2** (*specialist*) to make metal as hard as it needs to be by heating and then cooling it: **be tempered** *The blade is hardened and tempered so that it resists damage.*

**tem·pera** /ˈtempərə/ *noun* [U] (*art*) a kind of paint in which the colour is mixed with egg and water; a method of painting that uses this kind of paint

**tem·pera·ment** /ˈtemprəmənt/ *noun* **1** [C, U] a person's or an animal's nature as shown in the way they behave or react to situations or people: *to have an artistic temperament* ◊ *a horse with an excellent temperament* ◊ *She's a dreamer and a romantic by temperament.* **2** [U] the fact of tending to get emotional and excited very easily and behave in an unreasonable way: *an actor given to displays of temperament*

**tem·pera·men·tal** /ˌtemprəˈmentl/ *adj.* **1** (*usually disapproving*) tending to become angry, excited or upset easily, and to behave in an unreasonable way: *You never know what to expect with her. She's so temperamental.* ◊ (*figurative*) *The printer's being temperamental this morning.* **2** connected with sb's nature and personality: *They are firm friends in spite of temperamental differences.* ▶ **tem·pera·men·tal·ly** /-təli/ *adv.*: *I'm temperamentally unsuited to this job.*

**tem·per·ance** /ˈtempərəns/ *noun* [U] **1** (*old-fashioned*) the practice of not drinking alcohol because of your moral or religious beliefs **2** (*formal*) the practice of controlling your behaviour, the amount you eat, etc., so that it is always reasonable **SYN** moderation

**tem·per·ate** /ˈtempərət/ *adj.* **1** [usually before noun] (*specialist*) (of a climate or region) having a mild temperature without extremes of heat or cold **2** (*formal*) behaving in a calm way and with control **OPP** intemperate ▶ **tem·per·ate·ly** *adv.*

**'temperate zone** *noun* [C, usually sing.] (*specialist*) an area of the earth that is not near the EQUATOR or the South or North Pole

**tem·pera·ture** /ˈtemprətʃə(r); *NAmE also* -tʃʊr/ *noun* [C, U] (*abbr.* **temp**) **1** the measurement in degrees of how hot or cold a thing or place is: *high/low temperatures* ◊ *cold/warm temperatures* ◊ *a drop/rise in temperature* ◊ *The temperature has risen (by) five degrees.* ◊ *Some places have had temperatures in the 40s* (= over 40° CENTIGRADE). ◊ **at a ~** *Chemical reactions take place more slowly at low temperatures.* ⊃ see also ROOM TEMPERATURE **2** the measurement of how hot sb's body is: *to take sb's temperature* (= measure the temperature of sb's body using a special instrument) ◊ (*BrE*) *Does he have a temperature* (= is it higher than normal, because of illness)? ◊ *He's in bed with a temperature of 40°.* ◊ *When your body temperature rises, your body tries to compensate.* **HELP** In NAmE you can *take sb's temperature* but in the other examples the word **fever** is used. ⊃ compare FEVER

**IDM** **raise/lower the 'temperature** to increase/decrease the amount of excitement, emotion, etc. in a situation: *His angry refusal to agree raised the temperature of the meeting.*

**tem·pest** /ˈtempɪst/ *noun* (*formal or literary*) a violent storm **IDM** **a tempest in a 'teapot** (*NAmE*) (*BrE* **a storm in a 'teacup**) a lot of anger or worry about sth that is not important

# tempestuous

**tem·pes·tu·ous** /tem'pestʃuəs/ adj. **1** (formal) full of extreme emotions SYN **stormy**: *a tempestuous relationship* **2** (formal or literary) caused by or affected by a violent storm SYN **stormy**: *tempestuous seas*

**tem·plate** /'templeɪt; NAmE -plət/ noun **1** a shape cut out of a hard material, used as a model for producing exactly the same shape many times in another material **2** a thing that is used as a model for producing other similar examples: *If you need to write a lot of similar letters, set up a template on your computer.*

**tem·ple** B2 /'templ/ noun **1** C1 a building used for religious WORSHIP, especially in religions other than Christianity: *the Temple of Diana at Ephesus ◊ a Buddhist/Hindu/Sikh temple ◊* (NAmE) *to go to temple* (= to a service in a SYNAGOGUE, where Jews worship) **2** each of the flat parts at the sides of the head, at the same level as the eyes and higher: *He had black hair, greying at the temples.*

**Tempo**™ /'tempəʊ/ noun (pl. -os) (IndE) a vehicle with three wheels, used to deliver goods

**tempo** /'tempəʊ/ noun [C, U] (pl. -os) **1** (pl. **tempi** /-piː/) the speed or rhythm of a piece of music: *a slow/fast tempo ◊ It's a difficult piece, with numerous changes of tempo.* ⊃ WORDFINDER NOTE at SING **2** the speed of any movement or activity SYN **pace**¹: *the increasing tempo of life in Western society*

**tem·poral** /'tempərəl/ adj. **1** (formal) connected with the real physical world, not spiritual matters: *Although spiritual leader of millions of people, the Pope has no temporal power.* **2** (formal) connected with or limited by time: *a universe which has spatial and temporal dimensions* **3** (anatomy) near the TEMPLE(S) at the side of the head: *the right temporal lobe of the brain*

**tem·por·ar·ily** C1 B2 /'temprərəli; NAmE ˌtempə'rerəli/ adv. in a way that lasts or is intended to last or be used only for a short time; in a way that is not permanent: *We regret this service is temporarily unavailable. ◊ The company announced that it would be temporarily closing the factory because of the global downturn.* OPP **permanently**

**tem·por·ary** ⓘ B2 /'temprəri; NAmE -pəreri/ adj. lasting or intended to last or be used only for a short time; not permanent: *to hire temporary workers ◊ They had to move into temporary accommodation. ◊ Volunteers built temporary shelters for the survivors. ◊ temporary relief from pain ◊ More than half the staff are temporary.* OPP **permanent** ⊃ WORDFINDER NOTE at WORK ▶ **tem·por·ari·ness** noun [U]

**tem·por·ize** (BrE also **-ise**) /'tempəraɪz/ verb [I] (formal) to delay making a decision or giving a definite answer, in order to gain time

**tempt** C1 /tempt/ verb **1** C1 to attract sb or make sb want to do or have sth, even if they know it is wrong: *~sb I was tempted by the dessert menu. ◊ Don't tempt thieves by leaving valuables clearly visible. ◊ ~sb into (doing) sth He was tempted into a life of crime. ◊ ~sb to do sth I was tempted to take the day off.* **2** C1 to persuade or try to persuade sb to do sth that you want them to do, for example by offering them sth: *~sb (into sth/into doing sth) How can we tempt young people into engineering? ◊ ~sb to do sth Nothing would tempt me to live here.* IDM **tempt ˈfate/ˈprovidence** to do sth too confidently in a way that might mean that your good luck will come to an end

**temp·ta·tion** /temp'teɪʃn/ noun **1** [C, U] the desire to do or have sth that you know is bad or wrong: *the temptation of easy profits ◊ to give way to/yield to temptation ◊ I couldn't resist the temptation to open the letter. ◊ Don't put temptation in her way by offering her a cigarette.* **2** [C] a thing that makes sb want to do or have sth that they know is bad or wrong: *An expensive bicycle is a temptation to thieves.*

**tempt·er** /'temptə(r)/ noun a person who tries to persuade sb to do sth, especially sth bad or wrong

**tempt·ing** /'temptɪŋ/ adj. something that is **tempting** is attractive, and makes people want to have it, do it, etc: *It was a tempting offer. ◊ That cake looks very tempting. ◊ It's tempting to speculate about what might have happened.* ▶ **tempt·ing·ly** adv.

**temp·tress** /'temptrəs/ noun (old-fashioned or humorous) a woman who TEMPTS sb, especially one who deliberately makes a man want to have sex with her

**tem·pura** /'tempərə; BrE also tem'pʊərə; NAmE also tem'pʊrə/ noun [U, C] a Japanese dish consisting of pieces of vegetables or fish that have been fried in BATTER (= a mixture of flour, egg and water)

**ten** ⓘ A1 /ten/ number **10** HELP There are examples of how to use numbers at the entry for **five**.
IDM **ˌten out of ˈten (for sth)** (BrE, often ironic) used to say that sb has guessed sth correctly or done sth very well: *Not brilliant, Robyn, but I'll give you ten out of ten for effort.* **ˌten to ˈone** (informal) very probably: *Ten to one he'll be late.* ⊃ more at PENNY

**ten·able** /'tenəbl/ adj. **1** (of a theory, an opinion, etc.) easy to defend against attack or criticism: *a tenable position ◊ The old idea that this work was not suitable for women was no longer tenable.* OPP **untenable 2** [not before noun] (of a job, position, etc., especially in a university) that can be held for a particular period of time: *The lectureship is tenable for a period of three years.*

**ten·acious** /tə'neɪʃəs/ adj. (formal) **1** that does not stop holding sth or give up sth easily; determined: *a tenacious grip ◊ She's a tenacious woman. She never gives up. ◊ The party has kept its tenacious hold on power for more than twenty years.* **2** continuing to exist, have influence, etc. for longer than you might expect SYN **persistent**: *a tenacious illness* ▶ **ten·acious·ly** adv.: *Though seriously ill, he still clings tenaciously to life.* **ten·acity** /tə'næsəti/ noun [U]: *They competed with skill and tenacity.*

**ten·ancy** /'tenənsi/ noun (pl. -ies) **1** [C] a period of time that you rent a house, land, etc. for: *a three-month tenancy ◊ a tenancy agreement* **2** [C, U] the right to live or work in a building or on land that you rent: *They had taken over the tenancy of the farm.*

**ten·ant** C1 /'tenənt/ noun, verb
■ noun C1 a person who pays rent for the use of a room, building, land, etc. to the person who owns it: *They had evicted their tenants for non-payment of rent. ◊ The decorating was done by a previous tenant. ◊ tenant farmers* (= ones who do not own their own farms) ⊃ WORDFINDER NOTE at HOME
■ verb [usually passive] **~sth** to live or work in a place as a tenant: *a tenanted farm*

**tench** /tentʃ/ noun (pl. **tench**) a European FRESHWATER fish

**tend** ⓘ B1 ⓞ /tend/ verb **1** B1 [I] **~to do sth** to be likely to do sth or to happen in a particular way because this is what often or usually happens: *When I'm tired, I tend to make mistakes. ◊ It tends to get very cold here in the winter. ◊ People tend to think that the problem will never affect them. ◊ I tend to agree with many of the points you make.* ⊃ LANGUAGE BANK at GENERALLY **2** [I] **~(to/towards sth)** to take a particular direction or often have a particular quality: *His views tend towards the extreme. ◊ Prices have tended downwards over recent years.* **3** [T, I] to care for sb/sth: *~sb/sth a shepherd tending his sheep ◊ Doctors and nurses tended the injured. ◊ well-tended gardens ◊ ~to sb/sth Ambulance crews were tending to the injured.* **4** [T] **~sth** (NAmE) to serve customers in a store, bar, etc: *He had a job tending bar in San Francisco.*

**ten·dency** C1 B2 ⓞ /'tendənsi/ noun (pl. -ies) **1** C1 B2 [C] if sb/sth has a particular **tendency**, they are likely to behave or act in a particular way: *to display artistic tendencies ◊ ~to do sth I have a tendency to talk too much when I'm nervous. ◊ ~for sb/sth to do sth There is a tendency for this disease to run in families. ◊ ~to/towards sth She has a strong natural tendency towards caution.* **2** C1 B2 [C] a new custom that is starting to develop SYN **trend**: *~(for sb/sth) (to do sth) There's a growing tendency for women to marry later. ◊ ~to/towards sth Industry showed a tendency towards increasingly centralized*

b **b**ad | d **d**id | f **f**all | g **g**et | h **h**at | j **y**es | k **c**at | l **l**eg | m **m**an | n **n**ow | p **p**en | r **r**ed

administration. **3** [C + sing./pl. v.] (*BrE*) a group within a larger political group, whose views are more extreme than those of the rest of the group

**ten·den·tious** /ten'denʃəs/ *adj.* (*formal, usually disapproving*) (of a speech, piece of writing, theory, etc.) expressing a strong opinion that people are likely to disagree with **SYN** controversial ▸ **ten·den·tious·ly** *adv.* **SYN** controversially **ten·den·tious·ness** *noun* [U]

**ten·der** ⓘ+ **C1** /'tendə(r)/ *adj., noun, verb*
- *adj.* (**ten·der·er, ten·der·est**) **HELP** *more tender* and *most tender* are also common **1** ⓘ+ **C1** kind, gentle and loving: *tender words* ◇ *What he needs now is a lot of* **tender loving care** (= sympathetic treatment). ◇ see also TLC **2** ⓘ+ **C1** (of food) easy to bite through and cut: *This meat is extremely tender.* **OPP tough** ⊃ WORDFINDER NOTE at CRISP **3** (of part of the body) painful when you touch it **SYN** sore **4** easily hurt or damaged **SYN** delicate: *tender young plants* ▸ **ten·der·ly** *adv.* **ten·der·ness** *noun* [U]
- **IDM at a ˌtender ˈage | at the tender age of …** used in connection with sb who is still young and does not have much experience: *He left home at the tender age of 15.* ◇ *She shouldn't be having to deal with problems like this at such a tender age.*
- *noun* **1** a formal offer to supply goods or do work at a stated price **SYN** bid¹: *Cleaning services have been put out to tender* (= companies have been asked to make offers to supply these services). ◇ *a competitive tender* **2** a truck attached to a STEAM engine, carrying fuel and water **3** a small boat, used for carrying people or goods between a larger boat and land ⊃ see also LEGAL TENDER
- *verb* **1** [I] ~ **(for sth)** to make a formal offer to supply goods or do work at a stated price: *Local firms were invited to tender for the building contract.* **2** [T] ~ **sth (to sb)** (*formal*) to offer or give sth to sb: *He has tendered his resignation to the prime minister.*

**ten·der·foot** /'tendəfʊt; *NAmE* -dərf-/ *noun* (*pl.* **ten·der·feet** or **ten·der·foots**) (*NAmE, informal*) a person who is new to sth and not experienced **SYN** greenhorn

**ten·der·ize** (*BrE also* **-ise**) /'tendəraɪz/ *verb* ~ **sth** to make meat softer and easier to cut and eat by preparing it in a particular way

**ten·der·loin** /'tendəlɔɪn; *NAmE* -dərl-/ *noun* [U] good quality meat from the back or side of a cow or pig

**ten·din·itis** (*also* **ten·don·itis**) /ˌtendə'naɪtɪs/ *noun* [U] pain and SWELLING in a TENDON of the body: *tendinitis of the shoulder*

**ten·don** /'tendən/ *noun* a strong band of TISSUE in the body that joins a muscle to a bone

**ten·dril** /'tendrəl/ *noun* **1** a thin, curly STEM that grows from a climbing plant. A plant uses tendrils to attach itself to a wall or other support. ⊃ VISUAL VOCAB page V7 **2** (*literary*) a thin, curly piece of sth such as hair

**tene·ment** /'tenəmənt/ *noun* a large building divided into flats, especially in a poor area of a city: *a tenement block*

**tenet** /'tenɪt/ *noun* (*formal*) one of the principles or beliefs that a theory or larger set of beliefs is based on: *one of the basic/central tenets of Christianity*

**ten·fold** /'tenfəʊld/ *adj., adv.* ⊃ -FOLD

**ten·ner** /'tenə(r)/ *noun* (*BrE, informal*) £10 or a ten pound note: *You can have it for a tenner.*

**ten·nis** ⓘ **A1** /'tenɪs/ *noun* [U] a game in which two or four players use RACKETS to hit a ball backwards and forwards across a net on a specially marked court: *to play tennis* ◇ *a tennis player/court/ball* ⊃ see also LAWN TENNIS, TABLE TENNIS

**ˌtennis ˈelbow** *noun* [U] painful SWELLING of the ELBOW caused by TWISTING the arm too often

**ˈtennis racket** (*also* **ˈtennis racquet**) *noun* the RACKET that you use when you play tennis

**ˈtennis shoe** (*NAmE also* **ˈathˈletic shoe**) *noun* a sports shoe that is made of strong cotton cloth or leather

**tenon** /'tenən/ *noun* (*specialist*) an end of a piece of wood that has been cut to fit into a MORTISE so that the two are held together

**tenor** /'tenə(r)/ *noun, adj.*
- *noun* **1** [C] a man's singing voice with a range just below the lowest woman's voice; a man with a tenor voice ⊃ compare ALTO, BARITONE, BASS¹, COUNTERTENOR **2** [sing.] a musical part written for a tenor voice **3** [sing.] **the ~of sth** (*formal*) the general character or meaning of sth: *I was encouraged by the general tenor of his remarks.*
- *adj.* [only before noun] (of a musical instrument) with a range of notes similar to that of a tenor voice: *a tenor saxophone* ⊃ compare ALTO, BASS¹, SOPRANO

**ˌten pence ˈpiece** (*also* **10p** /ˌten 'piː/) *noun* a British coin worth ten pence: *Have you got a ten pence piece?*

**ten·pin** /'tenpɪn/ *noun* **1** [C] any of the ten objects like bottles in shape that players try to knock over in the game of TENPIN BOWLING ⊃ compare SKITTLE (1) **2 tenpins** [U] (*NAmE*) = TENPIN BOWLING

**ˌtenpin ˈbowling** (*NAmE also* **ten·pins**) *noun* [U] a game in which players try to knock over tenpins by rolling a heavy ball at them, played indoors, especially in a BOWLING ALLEY ⊃ compare SKITTLES

**tense** /tens/ *adj., noun, verb*
- *adj.* **1** (of a person) nervous or worried, and unable to relax: *He's a very tense person.* ◇ *She sounded tense and angry.* **2** (of a situation, an event, a period of time, etc.) in which people have strong feelings such as worry, anger, etc. that often cannot be expressed openly: *I spent a tense few weeks waiting for the results of the tests.* ◇ *The atmosphere in the meeting was getting more and more tense.* **3** (of a muscle or other part of the body) tight rather than relaxed: *A massage will relax those tense muscles.* **4** (of wire, etc.) stretched tightly **SYN** taut **5** (*phonetics*) (of a speech sound) produced with the muscles of the speech organs stretched tight **OPP** lax ▸ **tense·ly** *adv.* **tense·ness** *noun* [U]
- *noun* (*grammar*) any of the forms of a verb that may be used to show the time of the action or state expressed by the verb: *the past/present/future tense* ⊃ WORDFINDER NOTE at GRAMMAR
- *verb* [T, I] if you **tense** your muscles, or you or your muscles **tense**, they become tight and stiff, especially because you are not relaxed: **~ sth/yourself (up)** *She tensed her muscles in anticipation of the blow.* ◇ *He tensed himself, listening to see if anyone had followed him.* ◇ **~ (up)** *His muscles tensed as he got ready to run.* ◇ *She tensed, hearing the strange noise again.*
- **IDM be/get tensed ˈup** to become or feel nervous or worried so that you cannot relax

**ten·sile** /'tensaɪl; *NAmE* -sl/ *adj.* (*specialist*) **1** [only before noun] used to describe the extent to which sth can stretch without breaking: *the tensile strength of rope* **2** that can be drawn out or stretched: *tensile cable*

**ten·sion** ⓘ+ **B2** **W** /'tenʃn/ *noun, verb*
- *noun* **1** ⓘ+ **B2** [U, C, usually pl.] a situation in which people do not trust each other, or feel unfriendly towards each other, and that may cause them to attack each other: *There is mounting tension along the border.* ◇ *international/racial/political tensions* ◇ **~ between A and B** *The incident has further increased tension between the two countries.* **2** ⓘ+ **B2** [C, U] ~ **(between A and B)** a situation in which the fact that there are different needs or interests causes difficulties: *There is often a tension between the aims of the company and the wishes of the employees.* **3** ⓘ+ **B2** [U] a feeling of worry and stress that makes it impossible to relax: *nervous tension* ◇ *We laughed and that helped ease the tension.* ⊃ SYNONYMS at PRESSURE **4** ⓘ+ **B2** [U] the feeling of fear and excitement that is created by a writer or a film director: *dramatic tension* ◇ *As the movie progresses the tension builds.* ⊃ WORDFINDER NOTE at PLOT **5** ⓘ+ **C1** [U] the state of being stretched tight; the extent to which sth is stretched tight: *muscular tension* ◇ *Adjust the string tension of your tennis racket to suit your style of playing.* ⊃ see also SURFACE TENSION
- *verb* ~ **sth** (*specialist*) to make a wire, sail, etc. tight and stretched

**ten·sor** /ˈtensə(r), -sɔː(r)/ *noun* (*anatomy*) a muscle that TIGHTENS or stretches part of the body

**tent**

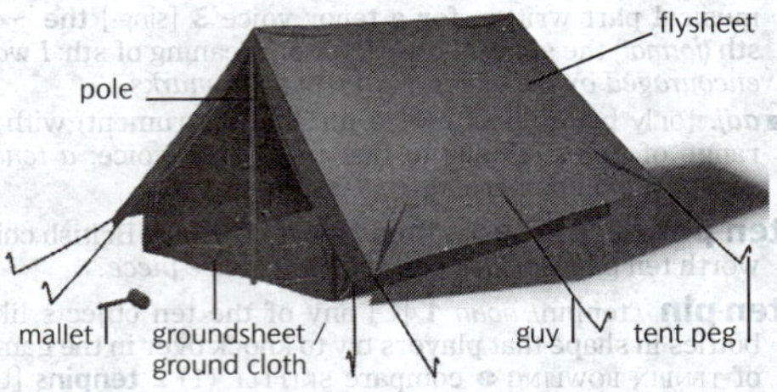


**tent** ⓘ **B1** /tent/ *noun* a shelter made of a large sheet of CANVAS, NYLON, etc. that is supported by POLES and ropes fixed to the ground, and is used especially for camping: *to **put up/take down a tent** ◇ to **pitch** (= put up) **a tent** ◇ Food will be served in the hospitality tent* (= for example at an outdoor show). ➲ see also BIG TENT

**ten·tacle** /ˈtentəkl/ *noun* **1** [C] a long, thin part of the body of some creatures, such as SQUID, used for feeling or holding things, for moving or for getting food ➲ VISUAL VOCAB page V3 **2 tentacles** [pl.] (*usually disapproving*) the influence that a large place, organization or system has and that is hard to avoid: *The tentacles of satellite television are spreading even wider.*

**ten·ta·tive** /ˈtentətɪv/ *adj.* **1** (of an arrangement, agreement, etc.) not definite or certain because you may want to change it later: *We made a **tentative arrangement** to meet on Friday. ◇ tentative conclusions* **2** not behaving or done with confidence SYN **hesitant**: *a tentative greeting ◇ I'm taking the first **tentative steps** towards fitness.* ▶ **ten·ta·tive·ly** *adv.* **ten·ta·tive·ness** *noun* [U]

**tent·ed** /ˈtentɪd/ *adj.* consisting of tents; like a tent: *a tented village*

**ten·ter·hooks** /ˈtentəhʊks; *NAmE* -tərh-/ *noun* [pl.]
IDM **(be) on ˈtenterhooks** (*NAmE also* **be on ˌpins and ˈneedles**) (to be) very anxious or excited while you are waiting to find out sth or see what will happen: *I've been on tenterhooks all week waiting for the results.* ORIGIN From **tenterhook**, a hook that in the past was used to keep material stretched on a drying frame during manufacture.

T

**tenth** /tenθ/ *ordinal number, noun*
■ ***ordinal number*** 10th HELP There are examples of how to use ordinal numbers at the entry for **fifth**.
■ ***noun*** each of ten equal parts of sth IDM see POSSESSION

**ˈtent peg** *noun* = PEG (2) ➲ picture at PEG, TENT

**tenu·ous** /ˈtenjuəs/ *adj.* **1** so weak or uncertain that it hardly exists: *a tenuous hold on life ◇ His links with the organization turned out to be, at best, tenuous.* **2** extremely thin and easily broken ▶ **tenu·ous·ly** *adv.*

**ten·ure** 🔑+ **C1** /ˈtenjə(r)/ *noun* [U] **1** 🔑+ **C1** the period of time when sb holds an important job, especially a political one; the act of holding an important job: *his four-year tenure as president ◇ She had a long tenure of office.* **2** the right to stay permanently in your job, especially as a teacher at a university: *It's still extremely difficult to get tenure.* **3** the legal right to live in a house or use a piece of land

**ten·ured** /ˈtenjəd; *NAmE* -jərd/ *adj.* [usually before noun] **1** (of an official job) that you can keep permanently: *a tenured post* **2** (of a person, especially a teacher at a university) having the right to keep their job permanently: *a tenured professor*

**tepee** (*also* **tee·pee**) /ˈtiːpiː/ *noun* a type of tall tent like a CONE in shape, used by Native Americans in the past ➲ see also WIGWAM

**tepid** /ˈtepɪd/ *adj.* **1** slightly warm, sometimes in a way that is not pleasant SYN **lukewarm**: *tepid tea ◇ a tepid bath* ➲ SYNONYMS at COLD **2** not enthusiastic SYN **lukewarm**: *The play was greeted with tepid applause.*

**te·quila** /təˈkiːlə/ *noun* **1** [U, C] a strong alcoholic drink made in Mexico from a tropical plant **2** [C] a glass of tequila

**tera-** /terə/ *combining form* (*specialist*) (in nouns; used in units of measurement) **1** $10^{12}$, or 1000000000000 **2** $2^{40}$, or 1099511627776

**tera·bit** /ˈterəbɪt/ *noun* (*abbr.* **Tb**) (*computing*) **1** a unit of computer memory or data, equal to one million million, or $10^{12}$ (= 1000000000000) BITS **2** (*also* **tebi·bit**) a unit of computer memory or data, equal to $2^{40}$ (= 1099511627 776) BITS

**tera·byte** /ˈterəbaɪt/ *noun* (*abbr.* **TB**) (*computing*) **1** a unit of computer memory or data, equal to one million million, or $10^{12}$ (= 1000000000000) BYTES **2** (*also* **tebi·byte**) a unit of computer memory or data, equal to $2^{40}$ (= 1099511627 776) BYTES

**ter·cen·ten·ary** /ˌtɜːsenˈtiːnəri; *NAmE* ˌtɜːrsenˈten-/ *noun* (*pl.* **-ies**) the 300th anniversary of sth: *the tercentenary of the school's foundation ◇ tercentenary celebrations*

**teri·yaki** /ˌteriˈæki; *NAmE* -ˈjɑːki/ *noun* [U, C] a Japanese dish consisting of meat or fish that has been left in a sweet sauce and then cooked

**term** ⓘ **A2** ⓞ /tɜːm; *NAmE* tɜːrm/ *noun, verb*
■ ***noun*** ➲ see also TERMS **1** 🔑 **A2** [C] a word or phrase used as the name of sth, especially one connected with a particular type of language: *a technical/legal/generic term ◇ William Gibson **coined the term*** (= invented the term) *'cyberspace' in 1984. ◇* **~for sth** *'Old man' is a slang term for 'father'.* ➲ see also SEARCH TERM ➲ SYNONYMS at WORD ➲ LANGUAGE BANK at DEFINE **2** 🔑 **B1** (*NAmE also* **tri·mes·ter**) [C, U] (especially in the UK) one of the three periods in the year during which classes are held in schools, universities, etc: *the spring/summer/autumn/fall term ◇* (*BrE*) *It's nearly the **end of term**. ◇* (*NAmE*) *It's nearly the **end of the term**.* ➲ see also HALF-TERM, SEMESTER, TERMLY, TERM TIME **3** 🔑 **B2** [C] a period of time for which sth lasts; a fixed or limited time: *during the president's first **term of/in office** ◇* **~as sth** *a term as president/mayor/governor/prime minister ◇* **~of sth** *He was sentenced to a **prison/jail term** of 25 years for the offence. ◇ She served a five-year **term** of **imprisonment**. ◇ The contract was for a **fixed term** of five years.* ➲ see also FIXED-TERM **4** [sing.] (*formal*) the end of a particular period of time, especially one for which sth is expected to last: *His life had reached its natural term. ◇* (*medical*) *The pregnancy went to **full term*** (= lasted the normal length of time). ➲ see also FULL-TERM **5** [C] (*mathematics*) each of the various parts in a series, an EQUATION, etc.
IDM **in the ˈlong/ˈshort/ˈmedium term** used to describe what will happen a long, short, etc. time in the future: *Such a development seems unlikely, at least in the short term* (= it will not happen for quite a long time). ➲ see also LONG-TERM, MEDIUM-TERM, SHORT-TERM
■ ***verb*** 🔑 **B2** [often passive] (*formal*) to use a particular name or word to describe sb/sth: **~sb/sth + noun/adj.** *At his age, he can hardly be termed young. ◇* **~sb/sth as sth** *Her condition would be more accurately termed as 'chronic fatigue'.*

**ter·min·al** 🔑+ **B2** /ˈtɜːmɪnl; *NAmE* ˈtɜːrm-/ *noun, adj.*
■ ***noun*** **1** 🔑+ **B2** a building or set of buildings at an airport where passengers arrive and leave: *A second terminal was opened last year.* ➲ WORDFINDER NOTE at AIRPORT ➲ see also AIR TERMINAL **2** 🔑+ **B2** a place, building or set of buildings where journeys by train, bus or boat begin or end: *a **railway/bus/ferry terminal*** **3** 🔑+ **C1** (*computing*) a piece of equipment, usually consisting of a keyboard and a screen that joins the user to a central computer system **4** (*specialist*) a point at which connections can be made in an electric CIRCUIT: *a **positive/negative terminal***
■ ***adj.*** **1** 🔑+ **C1** (of an illness or a disease) that cannot be cured and will lead to death, often slowly: *He has terminal lung cancer. ◇ The illness is usually terminal. ◇* (*figurative*) *She's suffering from terminal* (= very great) *boredom.* ➲ WORDFINDER NOTE at HEALTH **2** 🔑+ **C1** (of a person) suffering from an illness that cannot be cured and will lead to death: *a terminal patient* **3** 🔑+ **C1** certain to get worse and come to

an end: *The industry is **in terminal decline**.* **4** [only before noun] (*formal* or *specialist*) at the end of sth: *a terminal branch of a tree* ◊ *terminal examinations* (= at the end of a course, etc.) ▶ **ter·min·al·ly** /-nəli/ *adv.*: *a hospice for the terminally ill* ◊ *a terminally dull film*

**ter·min·ate** ʕ+ **C1** /ˈtɜːmɪneɪt; NAmE ˈtɜːrm-/ *verb* (*formal*) **1** ʕ+ **C1** [I, T] to end; to make sth end: *Your contract of employment terminates in December.* ◊ *~ sth The agreement was terminated immediately.* ◊ *to terminate a pregnancy* (= to perform or have an ABORTION) **2** [I] (of a bus or train) to end a journey: *This train terminates at London Victoria.* **OPP** originate

**ter·min·ation** /ˌtɜːmɪˈneɪʃn; NAmE ˌtɜːrm-/ *noun* **1** [U, C] (*formal*) the act of ending sth; the end of sth: *Failure to comply with these conditions will result in termination of the contract.* **2** [C] (*medical*) a medical operation to end a PREGNANCY at an early stage **SYN** abortion

**ter·min·ology** W /ˌtɜːmɪˈnɒlədʒi; NAmE ˌtɜːrmɪˈnɑːl-/ *noun* [U, C] (*pl.* **-ies**) the set of technical words or expressions used in a particular subject: *medical terminology* ◊ *The disagreement arose over a different use of terminology.* ➔ SYNONYMS at LANGUAGE ▶ **ter·min·ologic·al** /ˌtɜːmɪnəˈlɒdʒɪkl; NAmE ˌtɜːrmɪnəˈlɑːdʒ-/ *adj.*

**ter·minus** /ˈtɜːmɪnəs; NAmE ˈtɜːrm-/ *noun* (*pl.* **ter·mini** /-naɪ/) the last station at the end of a railway line or the last stop on a bus route

**ter·mite** /ˈtɜːmaɪt; NAmE ˈtɜːrm-/ *noun* an insect that lives in organized groups, mainly in hot countries. Termites do a lot of damage by eating the wood of trees and buildings: *a termite colony*

**term·ly** /ˈtɜːmli; NAmE ˈtɜːrm-/ *adj.* (*BrE*) happening each term in a school, college, etc: *termly reports*

**ˈterm paper** *noun* ~ (**on sth**) (in an American school or college) a long piece of written work that a student does on a subject that is part of a course of study

**terms** ʕ+ **B2** O /tɜːmz; NAmE tɜːrmz/ *noun* [pl.] **1** ʕ+ **B2** the conditions that people offer, demand or accept when they make an agreement, an arrangement or a contract: *peace terms* ◊ *They failed to agree on the terms of a settlement.* ◊ *These are the **terms and conditions** of your employment.* ◊ **under the ~ of sth** *Under the terms of the agreement, their funding of the project will continue until 2025.* **2** ʕ+ **C1** conditions that you agree to when you buy, sell, or pay for sth; a price or cost: *to buy sth **on easy terms*** (= paying for it over a long period) ◊ *My terms are £20 a lesson.* **3** ʕ+ **C1** a way of expressing yourself or of saying sth: *We wish to protest in the **strongest possible terms*** (= to say we are very angry). ◊ *I'll try to explain in simple terms.* ◊ *The letter was brief, and couched in very polite terms.* ➔ SYNONYMS at LANGUAGE 
**IDM** **be on good, friendly, bad, etc. ˈterms (with sb)** to have a good, friendly, etc. relationship with sb: *I had no idea that you and he were on such intimate terms* (= were such close friends). ◊ *He is still on excellent terms with his ex-wife.* ◊ *I'm **on first-name terms** with my boss now* (= we call each other by our first names). **come to ˈterms (with sb)** to reach an agreement with sb; to find a way of living or working together **come to ˈterms with sth** to accept sth unpleasant by learning to deal with it: *She is still coming to terms with her son's death.* **in terms of ˈsth** ʕ **B1** | **in ... terms** ʕ **B1** used to show what aspect of a subject you are talking about or how you are thinking about it: *The job is great in terms of salary, but it has its disadvantages.* ◊ *What does this mean in terms of cost?* ◊ *In practical terms this law may be difficult to enforce.* ◊ *The decision was disastrous in political terms.* ◊ *He's talking in terms of starting a completely new career.* **on your own ˈterms** | **on sb's ˈterms** according to the conditions that you or sb else decides: *I'll only take the job on my own terms.* ◊ *I'm not doing it on your terms.* ➔ more at CONTRADICTION, EQUAL *adj.*, SPEAK, UNCERTAIN

**terms of ˈreference** *noun* [pl.] the limits that are set on what an official committee or report has been asked to do: *The matter, they decided, lay outside the commission's terms of reference.*

**ˈterm time** *noun* [U] (*BrE*) the period of time when classes are held at a school, college, or university, as opposed to the holidays: *I never went out in the evenings during term time.* ▶ **ˈterm-time** *adj.* [only before noun]: *Please give your term-time address.*

**tern** /tɜːn; NAmE tɜːrn/ *noun* a bird with long pointed wings and a tail with two points that lives near the sea

**ter·race** /ˈterəs/ *noun* **1** [C] (*BrE*) (often in the names of streets) a continuous row of similar houses that are joined together in one block: *12 Albert Terrace* **2** [C] a flat, hard area, especially outside a house or restaurant, where you can sit, eat and enjoy the sun: *a sun terrace* ◊ *a roof terrace* ◊ *All rooms have a balcony or terrace.* ➔ see also PATIO **3 terraces** [pl.] (*BrE*) (at some football (soccer) grounds, especially in the past) the wide steps where people stand to watch the game **4** [C] one of a series of flat areas of ground that are cut into the side of a hill like steps so that crops can be grown there

**ter·raced** /ˈterəst/ *adj.* [usually before noun] **1** (*BrE*) used to describe houses that form part of a terrace, or streets with houses in terraces: *a terraced cottage* ◊ *terraced housing* ◊ *terraced streets* **2** (of a slope or the side of a hill) having a series of flat areas of ground like steps cut into it

**ˌterraced ˈhouse** (*also less frequent* **ˌterrace ˈhouse**) (*both BrE*) (*NAmE* **ˈrow house, ˈtown·house**) *noun* a house that is one of a row of houses that are joined together on each side

**ter·ra·cing** /ˈterəsɪŋ/ *noun* [U] **1** (*BrE*) (at some football (soccer) grounds, especially in the past) an area with wide steps where people can stand to watch the game **2** a slope or the side of a hill that has had flat areas like steps cut into it

**terra·cotta** /ˌterəˈkɒtə; NAmE -ˈkɑːtə/ *noun* [U] **1** red-brown CLAY that has been baked but not GLAZED, used for making pots, etc. **2** a red-brown colour

**terra ˈfirma** /ˌterə ˈfɜːmə; NAmE ˈfɜːrmə/ *noun* [U] (*from Latin, usually humorous*) safe dry land, as contrasted with water or air **SYN** dry land: *After two days at sea, it was good to be back on terra firma again.*

**terra·form** /ˈterəfɔːm; NAmE -fɔːrm/ *verb* ~ **sth** to make a planet more like Earth, so that people can live on it

**ter·rain** ʕ+ **C1** /təˈreɪn/ *noun* [C, U] used to refer to an area of land when you are mentioning its natural features, for example, if it is rough, flat, etc: *difficult/rough/mountainous terrain* ➔ SYNONYMS at COUNTRY ➔ see also ALL-TERRAIN ▶ WORDFINDER NOTE at EXPLORE

**terra·pin** /ˈterəpɪn/ *noun* a small TURTLE (= a REPTILE with a hard round shell), that lives in warm rivers and lakes in North America ➔ compare TORTOISE

**ter·rar·ium** /təˈreəriəm; NAmE -ˈrer-/ *noun* a glass container for growing plants in or for keeping small animals such as snakes or insects in

**ter·res·trial** /təˈrestriəl/ *adj.* **1** (*specialist*) (of animals and plants) living on the land or on the ground, rather than in water, in trees or in the air **2** connected with the planet Earth: *terrestrial life* ➔ compare CELESTIAL, EXTRATERRESTRIAL **3** (of television and broadcasting systems) operating by using equipment on the surface of the earth, rather than sending the signal via a satellite

**ter·rible** ◆ **A1** /ˈterəbl/ *adj.* **1** ʕ **A1** very unpleasant; making you feel very unhappy, upset or frightened: *a terrible experience* ◊ *What terrible news!* ◊ *I've just had a terrible thought.* ➔ note on page 1618 **2** ʕ **A1** causing great harm or injury; very serious: *a terrible accident* ◊ *He had suffered terrible injuries.* **3** ʕ **A1** [not before noun] unhappy or ill: *I feel terrible—I think I'll go to bed.* **4** ʕ **A1** (*informal*) of very bad quality; very bad: *a terrible meal* ◊ *Your driving is terrible!* **5** ʕ **A1** [only before noun] used to show the great extent or degree of sth bad: *a terrible mistake* ◊ *to be in terrible pain* ◊ *The room was in a terrible mess.* ◊ (*informal*) *I had a terrible job* (= it was very difficult) *to persuade her to come.*

**ter·ribly** ʕ+ **B2** /ˈterəbli/ *adv.* **1** ʕ+ **B2** (*especially BrE*) very: *I'm terribly sorry—did I hurt you?* ◊ *It's terribly important*

# terrier

## SYNONYMS

**terrible**
awful • horrible • dreadful • vile • horrendous
These words all describe sth that is very unpleasant.

**terrible** very bad or unpleasant; making you feel unhappy, frightened, upset, ill, guilty or disapproving: *What terrible news!* ◊ *That's a terrible thing to say!*

**awful** (*rather informal*) very bad or unpleasant; used to describe sth that you do not like or that makes you feel depressed, ill, guilty or disapproving: *That's an awful colour.* ◊ *The weather last summer was awful.*

**horrible** (*rather informal*) very unpleasant; used to describe sth that you do not like: *The coffee tasted horrible.*

**dreadful** (*especially BrE, rather informal*) very bad or unpleasant; used to describe sth that you do not like or that you disapprove of: *What dreadful weather!*

**vile** (*informal*) extremely bad or unpleasant: *There was a vile smell coming from the room.* ◊ *He was in a vile mood.*

**horrendous** (*rather informal*) extremely unpleasant and unacceptable: *The traffic around the city was horrendous.*

PATTERNS
- terrible / awful / horrible / dreadful for sb
- a(n) terrible / awful / horrible / dreadful / vile thing
- a(n) terrible / awful / horrible / vile smell
- terrible / awful / horrible / dreadful / vile / horrendous conditions
- terrible / awful / horrible / dreadful / vile weather
- terrible / awful / dreadful news

for parents to be consistent. **2** very much; very badly: *I miss him terribly.* ◊ *They suffered terribly when their son was killed.* ◊ *The experiment went terribly wrong.*

**ter·rier** /ˈteriə(r)/ *noun* a small active dog. There are many types of terrier. ⊃ see also BULL TERRIER, PIT BULL TERRIER, SCOTTISH TERRIER, YORKSHIRE TERRIER

**ter·rif·ic** /təˈrɪfɪk/ *adj.* **1** (*informal*) excellent; wonderful: *I feel absolutely terrific today!* ◊ *She's doing a terrific job.* ⊃ SYNONYMS at GREAT **2** (*informal*) very large; very great: *I've got a terrific amount of work to do.* ◊ *We drove along at a terrific speed.*

**ter·rif·ic·al·ly** /təˈrɪfɪkli/ *adv.* (*informal*) extremely (usually used about positive qualities): *terrifically exciting*

**ter·ri·fied** /ˈterɪfaɪd/ *adj.* very frightened: *~ (of sb/sth)* to *be terrified of spiders* ◊ *~ (of doing sth) I'm terrified of losing you.* ◊ *~ (that …) He was terrified (that) he would fall.* ◊ *~ (at sth) She was terrified at the thought of being alone.* ⊃ SYNONYMS at AFRAID see WIT

**ter·rify** /ˈterɪfaɪ/ *verb* (**ter·ri·fies**, **ter·ri·fy·ing**, **ter·ri·fied**, **ter·ri·fied**) *~ sb* to make sb feel extremely frightened: *~ sb Flying terrifies her.* ⊃ SYNONYMS at FRIGHTEN ▶ **ter·ri·fy·ing** *adj.*: *It was a terrifying experience.* **ter·ri·fy·ing·ly** *adv.*

**ter·rine** /teˈriːn/ *noun* [U, C] a soft mixture of meat or fish, etc. cut into small pieces, pressed into a container and served cold, especially in slices as the first course of a meal

**Ter·ri·tor·ial** /ˌterəˈtɔːriəl/ *noun* (in the UK) a member of the Territorial Army

**ter·ri·tor·ial** /ˌterəˈtɔːriəl/ *adj.* **1** [usually before noun] connected with the land or sea that is owned by a particular country: *territorial disputes* ◊ *Both countries feel they have territorial claims to* (= have a right to own) *the islands.* **2** (of animals, birds, etc.) guarding and defending an area of land that they believe to be their own: *territorial instincts* ◊ *Cats are very territorial.* ▶ **ter·ri·tori·al·ity** /ˌterəˌtɔːriˈæləti/ *noun* [U]: *the instinctive territoriality of some animals* **ter·ri·tori·al·ly** /ˌterəˈtɔːriəli/ *adv.*: *The country was trying to expand territorially.*

**the Territorial Army** *noun* [sing. + sing. / pl. v.] (*abbr.* TA) (in the UK) a military force of people who are not professional soldiers but who train as soldiers in their free time, now called the Army Reserve

**territorial ˈwaters** *noun* [pl.] the parts of a sea or an ocean that are near a country's coast and are legally under its control

**ter·ri·tory** /ˈterətri; NAmE -tɔːri/ *noun* (*pl.* -**ies**)
**1** [C, U] land that is under the control of a particular country or political leader: *enemy/disputed/foreign territory* ◊ *occupied territories* ◊ *They have refused to allow UN troops to be stationed in their territory.* ⊃ WORDFINDER NOTE at CONFLICT **2** [C, U] an area that one person, group, animal, etc. considers as their own and defends against others who try to enter it: *Blackbirds will defend their territory against intruders.* **3** [C, usually sing.] an area of activity, especially one that is familiar/unfamiliar or sb's particular responsibility: *This type of work is uncharted territory for us.* ◊ *Legal problems are Andy's territory.* **4** [C, U] an area of a town, country, etc. that sb has responsibility for in their work or another activity: *Our representatives cover a very large territory.* **5** [U] a particular type of land: *unexplored territory* ⊃ WORDFINDER NOTE at EXPLORE **6** (*also* **Territory**) [C] a country or an area that is part of the US, Australia or Canada but is not a state or PROVINCE: *Guam and American Samoa are US territories.*
**IDM** **come / go with the ˈterritory** to be a normal and accepted part of a particular job, situation, etc: *She has to work late most days, but in her kind of job that goes with the territory.* ⊃ more at NEUTRAL *adj.*

**ter·ror** /ˈterə(r)/ *noun* **1** [U, sing.] a feeling of extreme fear: *a feeling of sheer/pure terror* ◊ *Her eyes were wild with terror.* ◊ *in ~ People fled from the explosion in terror.* ◊ *He lives in terror of* (= is constantly afraid of) *losing his job.* ◊ *Some women have a terror of losing control in the birth process.* ◊ (*literary*) *The very name of the enemy struck terror into their hearts.* ⊃ SYNONYMS at FEAR **2** [C] a person, situation or thing that makes you very afraid: *These street gangs have become the terror of the neighbourhood.* ◊ *The terrors of the night were past.* ◊ (*literary*) *Death holds no terrors for* (= does not frighten or worry) *me.* **3** [U] violent action or the threat of violent action that is intended to cause fear, usually for political purposes **SYN** **terrorism**: *a campaign of terror* ◊ *terror tactics/groups* ⊃ see also REIGN OF TERROR **4** [C] (*informal*) a person (usually a child) or an animal that causes you trouble or is difficult to control: *Their kids are real little terrors.*

**ter·ror·ism** /ˈterərɪzəm/ *noun* [U] the use of violent action in order to achieve political aims or to force a government to act: *an act of terrorism* ⊃ WORDFINDER NOTE at ATTACK

**ter·ror·ist** /ˈterərɪst/ *noun* a person who takes part in terrorism: *The terrorists are threatening to blow up the plane.* ◊ *a terrorist attack/bomb/group*

**ter·ror·ize** (*BrE also* -**ise**) /ˈterəraɪz/ *verb* to frighten and threaten people so that they will not oppose sth or will do as they are told: *~ sb drug dealers terrorizing the neighbourhood* ◊ *~ sb into doing sth People were terrorized into leaving their homes.*

**terry** /ˈteri/ *noun* [U] a type of soft cotton cloth that has a surface covered with raised LOOPS of THREAD, used especially for making towels **SYN** **towelling**

**terse** /tɜːs; NAmE tɜːrs/ *adj.* using few words and often not seeming polite or friendly: *a terse style* ◊ *The president issued a terse statement denying the charges.* ▶ **terse·ly** *adv.* **terse·ness** *noun* [U]

**ter·tiary** /ˈtɜːʃəri; NAmE ˈtɜːrʃieri/ *adj.* third in order, rank or importance: *the tertiary sector* (= the area of industry that deals with services) ⊃ compare PRIMARY, SECONDARY ⊃ WORDFINDER NOTE at STUDY

**ˈtertiary college** *noun* (in Britain) a college that provides education for people aged 16 and older, but that is not a university

**tertiary eduˈcation** *noun* [U] (*BrE*) education for people above school age, including college, university and training courses for particular jobs ⊃ compare FURTHER EDUCATION, HIGHER EDUCATION

**TESL** /ˈtesl/ *abbr.* teaching English as a second language

**TESOL** /ˈtiːsɒl, ˈtes-; *NAmE* -sɑːl/ *abbr.* **1** teaching English to speakers of other languages **2** (*NAmE*) teachers of English to speakers of other languages (an organization of teachers)

**test** ⓘ A1 ⓞ /test/ *noun, verb*

■ *noun*
- **OF KNOWLEDGE/ABILITY 1** A1 an examination of sb's knowledge or ability, consisting of questions for them to answer or activities for them to perform: *an IQ/a fitness test* ◊ *~ on sth a test on irregular verbs* ◊ *~ in sth Students take standardized tests in English and maths.* ◊ (*BrE also*) **to do a test** ◊ **to pass/fail a test** ◊ **in a ~** (*BrE*) *a good mark in the test* ◊ **on a~** (*NAmE*) *a good score on the test* ⊃ note at EXAM ⊃ see also DRIVING TEST
- **OF HEALTH 2** A2 a medical examination to discover what is wrong with you or to check the condition of your health: *The hospital is doing some tests.* ◊ *~ for sth screening tests for cancer* ◊ *Three athletes were sent home after failing drugs tests.* ◊ *negative/positive test results* ⊃ see also BLOOD TEST, BREATH TEST ⊃ **WORDFINDER NOTE** at EXAMINE
- **OF MACHINE/PRODUCT, ETC. 3** A2 an experiment to discover whether or how well sth works, or to find out more information about it: *the results of laboratory tests* ◊ *to conduct a nuclear test* ◊ *Tests have shown high levels of pollutants in the water.* ◊ *I'll run a diagnostic test to determine why the server keeps crashing.* ⊃ see also ACID TEST, ALPHA TEST, BETA TEST, BLIND TEST, FIELD TEST, MEANS TEST, ROAD TEST
- **OF STRENGTH, ETC. 4** a situation or an event that shows how good, strong, etc. sb/sth is: *The local elections will be a good test of the government's popularity.*
- **IN CRICKET, ETC. 5 Test** = TEST MATCH

IDM **put sb/sth to the ˈtest** to put sb/sth in a situation that will show what their or its true qualities are: *His theories have never really been put to the test.* **stand the test of ˈtime** to prove to be good, popular, etc. over a long period of time ⊃ more at TEACH

■ *verb*
- **KNOWLEDGE/ABILITY 1** A1 [T, I] to find out how much sb knows, or what they can do by asking them questions or giving them activities to perform: *~ sb (on/in sth) Children are tested on core subjects at age 11.* ◊ *We test all students in English and maths.* ◊ *~ sth Applicants' skills, ability and knowledge are tested before job offers are made.* **2** [I] *~ well/badly* to perform well/badly in a test of knowledge or ability: *students who tested well in reading*
- **HEALTH 3** A2 [T, I] to examine the blood, a part of the body, etc. to find out what is wrong with a person, or to check the condition of their health: *~ sb/sth to test sb's eyesight/hearing* ◊ *~ sb/sth for sth The doctor tested him for hepatitis.* ◊ *~ + adj. (for sth) to test positive/negative (for sth)*
- **MACHINE/PRODUCT/THEORY, ETC. 4** A2 [T] to use or try a machine, substance, idea, etc. to find out how well it works or to find out more information about it: *~ sth Test your brakes regularly.* ◊ *~ sth on sb/sth Our beauty products are not tested on animals.* ◊ *~ sth out The chef uses his family to test out new ideas for the restaurant menu.* ◊ *~ sth for sth The software has been tested for viruses.* ◊ *~ sth against sth Researchers are now testing the hypothesis against available data.* ⊃ see also ALPHA-TEST, BETA-TEST, FIELD-TEST, ROAD-TEST **5** [I] *~ well/badly* (of a machine or product) to perform well/badly in a test of how well it works: *The ad had tested badly with consumers.*
- **STRENGTH, ETC. 6** [T] *~ sb/sth* to be difficult and therefore need all your strength, ability, etc: *The long climb tested our fitness and stamina.* ⊃ see also TESTING

IDM **test the ˈwaters** to find out what the situation is before doing sth or making a decision ⊃ more at TRIED *adj.*

**test·able** /ˈtestəbl/ *adj.* that can be tested: *testable hypotheses*

**tes·ta·ment** /ˈtestəmənt/ *noun* (*formal*) **1** [C, usually sing., U] *~ (to sth)* a thing that shows that sth else exists or is true SYN **testimony**: *The new model is a testament to the skill and dedication of the workforce.* **2** [C] = WILL (3): *This is the last will and testament of …* ⊃ see also NEW TESTAMENT, OLD TESTAMENT

**test ban** *noun* an agreement between countries to stop testing nuclear weapons: *a test ban treaty*

**ˈtest bed** *noun* a piece of equipment used for testing new machines, especially aircraft engines: (*figurative*) *The country is an ideal test bed for emerging technologies.*

**ˈtest case** *noun* a legal case or other situation whose result will be used as an example when decisions are being made on similar cases in the future

**ˈtest drive** *noun* an occasion when you drive a vehicle that you are thinking of buying so that you can see how well it works and if you like it ▶ **test-drive** *verb* *~ sth*

**test·er** /ˈtestə(r)/ *noun* **1** a person or thing that tests sth: *testers of new software* **2** a small container of a product, such as PERFUME, that you can try in a shop to see if you like it

**tes·tes** /ˈtestiːz/ *pl.* of TESTIS

**ˈtest flight** *noun* a flight during which an aircraft or part of its equipment is tested

**tes·ti·cle** /ˈtestɪkl/ *noun* either of the two organs that produce SPERM, located in a bag of skin below the PENIS ▶ **tes·ticu·lar** /teˈstɪkjələ(r)/ *adj.* [only before noun]: *testicular cancer*

**test·ify** ？+ C1 /ˈtestɪfaɪ/ *verb* (**testi·fies, testi·fy·ing, testi·fied, testi·fied**) **1** ？+ C1 [I, T] to make a statement that sth happened or that sth is true, especially as a witness in court: *~ against sb/sth She refused to testify against her husband.* ◊ *~ for sb/sth There are several witnesses who will testify for the defence.* ◊ *~ about sth He was summoned to testify before a grand jury about his role in the affair.* ◊ *~ to sth/to doing sth Evans testified to receiving $200 000 in bribes.* ◊ *~ (that) … He testified (that) he was at the theatre at the time of the murder.* ◊ *+ speech 'I was approached by a man I did not recognize,' she testified.* **2** [T] *~ (that) …* (*formal*) to say that you believe sth is true because you have evidence of it: *Too many young people are unable to write or spell well, as employers will testify.* **3** [I] (*especially NAmE*) to express your belief in God publicly

PHRV **ˈtestify to sth** (*formal*) to show or be evidence that sth is true SYN **evidence**: *The film testifies to the courage of ordinary people during the war.*

**tes·ti·mo·nial** /ˌtestɪˈməʊniəl/ *noun* **1** a formal written statement, often by a former employer, about sb's abilities, qualities and character; a formal written statement about the quality of sth: *a glowing testimonial* ◊ *The catalogue is full of testimonials from satisfied customers.* **2** a thing that you give or do to show that you admire and appreciate sb: *a testimonial game* (= to raise money for a particular player)

**tes·ti·mony** ？+ C1 /ˈtestɪməni; *NAmE* -məʊni/ *noun* (*pl.* -**ies**) **1** ？+ C1 [U, sing.] *~ (to sth)* (*formal*) a thing that shows that sth else exists or is true SYN **testament**: *This increase in exports bears testimony to the successes of industry.* ◊ *The pyramids are an eloquent testimony to the ancient Egyptians' engineering skills.* **2** ？+ C1 [C, U] a formal written or spoken statement saying what you know to be true, usually in court: *a sworn testimony* ◊ *Can I refuse to give testimony?*

**test·ing** ？+ B2 /ˈtestɪŋ/ *noun, adj.*

■ *noun* ？+ B2 [U] the activity of testing sb/sth in order to find sth out, see if it works, etc: *nuclear testing* ◊ *testing and assessment in education*

■ *adj.* (of a problem or situation) difficult to deal with and needing particular strength or abilities

**ˈtesting ground** *noun* **1** a place or situation used for testing new ideas and methods to see if they work **2** a place used for testing machines, etc. to see if they work correctly: *a piece of land in use as a tank testing ground*

**tes·tis** /ˈtestɪs/ *noun* (*pl.* **tes·tes** /ˈtestiːz/) (*anatomy*) a TESTICLE

**Test match** (*also* **Test**) *noun* a CRICKET or rugby match played between the teams of two different countries, usually as part of a series of matches on a tour

# testosterone

**tes·tos·ter·one** /teˈstɒstərəʊn; NAmE -ˈstɑːs-/ noun a HORMONE (= chemical substance produced in the body) that causes men to develop the physical and sexual features that are characteristic of the male body ⊃ compare OESTROGEN, PROGESTERONE

**'test pilot** noun a pilot whose job is to fly new aircraft in order to test their performance

**'test run** noun = TRIAL RUN

**'test tube** noun a small glass tube, closed at one end, that is used in scientific experiments

**'test-tube baby** noun a baby that grows from an egg that is FERTILIZED outside the mother's body and then put back inside to continue developing normally ⊃ see also IN VITRO

**testy** /ˈtesti/ adj. easily annoyed SYN irritable ▸ **test·ily** /-stɪli/ adv.: 'Leave me alone,' she said testily.

**tet·anus** /ˈtetnəs/ noun [U] a disease in which the muscles, especially the JAW muscles, become stiff, caused by bacteria entering the body through cuts or wounds

**tetchy** /ˈtetʃi/ adj. (informal) easily annoyed SYN irritable ▸ **tetch·ily** /-tʃɪli/ adv.

**tête-à-tête** /ˌteɪt ɑː ˈteɪt/ noun (from French) a private conversation between two people

**tether** /ˈteðə(r)/ verb, noun
- verb 1 ~ sth (to sth) to tie an animal to a post so that it cannot move very far 2 ~ sth (to sth) to use a smartphone to connect a computer to the internet ▸ **tether·ing** noun [U]
- noun a rope or chain used to tie an animal to sth, allowing it to move around in a small area IDM see END n.

**tetra·he·dron** /ˌtetrəˈhiːdrən/ noun (geometry) a solid shape with four flat sides that are TRIANGLES ⊃ picture at SOLID

**tet·ral·ogy** /teˈtrælədʒi/ noun (pl. -ies) a group of four books, films, etc. that have the same subject or characters

**Tetra Pak**™ /ˈtetrə pæk/ noun a type of thick card and plastic container in which milk or other drinks are sold

**Teut·on·ic** /tjuːˈtɒnɪk; NAmE tuːˈtɑːn-/ adj. [usually before noun] (often disapproving) showing qualities considered typical of German people: The preparations were made with Teutonic thoroughness.

**Tex-Mex** /ˌteks ˈmeks/ adj. [only before noun] connected with the variety of Mexican cooking, music, etc. that is found in Texas and the south-west part of the US

**text** 🔊 A1 O /tekst/ noun, verb
- noun 1 🔊 A1 [U] any form of written material: a computer that can process text ◊ printed text ⊃ see also PLAIN TEXT 2 🔊 A1 [C] a piece of writing that you have to answer questions about in an exam or a lesson SYN passage: Read the text carefully and then answer the questions. 3 A1 (also **'text message**) [C] a written message that you send using a mobile phone: She sent me a text to say she would be late. 4 A1 [U] the main printed part of a book or magazine, not the notes, pictures, etc.: My job is to lay out the text and graphics on the page. 5 A1 [C] the written form of a speech, a play, an article, etc.: The newspaper had printed the full text of the president's speech. 6 A1 [C] a book, play, etc., especially one that is being studied: a literary text ◊ sacred/religious/ancient texts ◊ (BrE) 'Macbeth' is a set text (= a book that students must study for their exam) this year. 7 [C] (NAmE) = TEXTBOOK: medical texts 8 [C] a sentence or short passage from the Bible that is read out and discussed by sb, especially during a religious service
- verb 🔊 A2 (also less frequent **text-message**) [T, I] to send sb a written message using a mobile phone SYN SMS: ~(sb) Text me when you're on your way. ◊ Kids seem to be texting non-stop these days. ◊ ~ sb sth I'll text you the final score.

**text·book** 🔊 B2 S /ˈtekstbʊk/ noun, adj.
- noun 🔊 B2 (NAmE also **text**) a book that teaches a particular subject and that is used especially in schools and colleges: a school/medical/history textbook
- adj. [only before noun] used to describe sth that is done exactly as it should be done, in the best possible way: a textbook example of how the game should be played

**'text editor** noun (computing) a system or program that allows you to make changes to text

**texter** /ˈtekstə(r)/ noun a person who sends text messages

**tex·tile** /ˈtekstaɪl/ noun 1 [C] any type of cloth made by WEAVING or KNITTING: a factory producing a range of textiles ◊ the textile industry ◊ a textile designer ⊃ note at FABRIC 2 **textiles** [pl.] the industry that makes cloth

**text·ing** /ˈtekstɪŋ/ (also less frequent **'text-messaging**) noun [U] the act of sending written messages using a mobile phone

**'text message** noun = TEXT (3): Send a text message to this number to vote. ▸ **'text-message** (also more frequent **text**) verb [T, I]: ~ (sb) (sth) I text-messaged him to say we were waiting in the pub. **'text-messaging** (also more frequent **text·ing**) noun [U]

**text-to-'speech** noun (abbr. TTS) [U] (computing) a computer program that changes text into spoken language: text-to-speech software

**text·ual** /ˈtekstʃuəl/ adj. [usually before noun] connected with or contained in a text: textual analysis ◊ textual errors

**tex·tural** /ˈtekstʃərəl/ adj. (specialist) relating to texture: the textural characteristics of the rocks

**tex·ture** 🔊+ C1 /ˈtekstʃə(r)/ noun [C, U] 1 🔊+ C1 the way a surface, substance or piece of cloth feels when you touch it, for example how rough, smooth, hard or soft it is: the soft texture of velvet ◊ She uses a variety of different colours and textures in her wall hangings. 2 🔊+ C1 the way food or drink tastes or feels in your mouth, for example whether it is rough, smooth, light, heavy, etc: The two cheeses were very different in both taste and texture. 3 the way that different parts of a piece of music or literature are combined to create a final impression: the rich texture of the symphony

**tex·tured** /ˈtekstʃəd; NAmE -tʃərd/ adj. with a surface that is not smooth, but has a particular texture: textured wallpaper

**TFT** /ˌtiː ef ˈtiː/ noun a piece of technology used to make flat screens for computers, mobile phones, etc. (the abbreviation for 'thin film transistor'): a 17 in. TFT screen

**TGIF** /ˌtiː dʒiː aɪ ˈef/ abbr. (informal) thank God it's Friday (used to say that you are glad the working week is nearly over): TGIF! I for one am looking forward to the weekend.

**-th** /θ/ suffix 1 (in ordinal numbers): sixth ◊ fifteenth ◊ hundredth 2 (in nouns) the action or process of: growth

**thali** /ˈtɑːli/ noun (IndE) 1 a metal plate on which food is served 2 a set meal at a restaurant

**thal·ido·mide** /θəˈlɪdəmaɪd/ noun [U] a SEDATIVE drug that was used until the 1960s, when it was discovered that, if given to pregnant women, it prevented some babies from developing normal arms and legs

**thal·lium** /ˈθæliəm/ noun [U] (symb. Tl) a chemical element. Thallium is a soft silver-white metal whose COMPOUNDS are very poisonous.

**than** 🔊 O A1 /ðən, strong form ðæn/ prep., conj. 1 🔊 A1 used to introduce the second part of a comparison: I'm older than her. ◊ There was more whisky in it than soda. ◊ He loves me more than you do. ◊ It was much better than I'd expected. ◊ You should know better than to behave like that. ◊ I'd rather email than phone, if that's OK by you. 2 **more/less/fewer, etc.** ~ used for comparing amounts, numbers, distances, etc: It never takes more than an hour. ◊ It's less than a mile to the beach. ◊ There were fewer than twenty people there. 3 used in expressions showing that one thing happens straight after another: No sooner had I sat down **than** there was a loud knock on the door. ◊ Hardly had we arrived **than** the problems started. IDM see OTHER

**thang** /θæŋ/ noun (NAmE, informal) a way of saying or writing the word 'thing', that represents the pronunciation of the southern US

**thank** ⓘ A1 /θæŋk/ verb to tell sb that you are grateful for sth: **~ sb for sth** *I must write and thank Mary for the present.* ◊ *In his speech, he thanked everyone for all their hard work.* ◊ **~ sb for doing sth** *She said goodbye and thanked us for coming.* ◊ **~ sb** *There's no need to thank me —I enjoyed doing it.*
IDM **have sb/sth to thank (for sth)** used when you are saying who or what is responsible for sth: *I have my parents to thank for my success.* **I'll thank you for sth/to do sth** (*formal*) used to tell sb that you are annoyed and do not want them to do sth: *I'll thank you to mind your own business.* **thank 'God / 'goodness / 'heaven(s) (for sth)** used to say that you are pleased about sth: *Thank God you're safe!* ◊ *'Thank goodness for that!' she said with a sigh of relief.* ◊ *Thank heavens I've found my keys.* HELP Some people find this use of **God** offensive. **thank your lucky 'stars** to feel very grateful and lucky about sth **sb won't 'thank you for sth** used to say that sb will not be pleased or will be annoyed about sth: *John won't thank you for interfering.*

▼ **EXPRESS YOURSELF**

**Thanking somebody for something**

When someone gives you something, or does something for you, you often want to say more than just a brief 'thank you':
- *Thank you very much. It's very kind of you. / You really shouldn't have.*
- *Thank you so much for coming. It was really nice to see you.*
- *I'm very grateful.*
- *I do appreciate your help.*

Responses:
- *That's all right.*
- *Don't mention it.*
- *No problem.*
- *My pleasure.*
- *I'm glad I could help.*

**thank·ful** /'θæŋkfl/ *adj.* [not usually before noun] pleased about sth good that has happened, or that sth bad has not happened: **~ (to do sth)** *I was thankful to see they'd all arrived safely.* ◊ **~ for sth** *He wasn't badly hurt—that's something to be thankful for.* ◊ **~ (that)** ... *I was thankful that he hadn't been hurt.* IDM see SMALL *adj.*

**thank·ful·ly** B+ C1 /'θæŋkfəli/ *adv.* 1 B+ C1 used to show that you are pleased that sth good has happened or that sth bad has been avoided SYN **fortunately**: *There was a fire in the building, but thankfully no one was hurt.* 2 B+ C1 in a pleased or grateful way: *I accepted the invitation thankfully.*

**thank·less** /'θæŋkləs/ *adj.* unpleasant or difficult to do and unlikely to bring you any rewards or thanks from anyone: *Sometimes being a mother and a housewife felt like a thankless task.*

**thanks** ⓘ A1 /θæŋks/ *exclamation, noun*
▪ *exclamation* ⊃ see also THANK YOU *exclamation* 1 A1 used to show that you are grateful to sb for sth they have done: *'How are you?' 'Fine, thanks* (= thanks for asking).*' ◊ **~ for doing sth** *Thanks for lending me the money.* ◊ **~ for sth** *Many thanks for your support.* 2 A1 a polite way of accepting sth that sb has offered you: *'Would you like a coffee?' 'Oh, thanks.'* ◊ *'Here's the change.' 'Thanks very much.'* 3 A1 **no thanks** a polite way of refusing sth that sb has offered you: *'Would you like some more?' 'No thanks.'*
▪ *noun* A1 [pl.] words or actions that show that you are grateful to sb for sth SYN **gratitude**: **~ (to sb) (for sth)** *How can I ever express my thanks to you for all you've done?* ◊ *We extend our thanks to Mary, who is stepping down as chair after serving for three years.* ◊ *Sincere thanks go to Alex.* ⊃ see also VOTE OF THANKS
IDM **no thanks to sb/sth** despite sb/sth; with no help from sb/sth: *We managed to get it finished in the end—no thanks to him* (= he didn't help). **thanks a lot** 1 used to show that you are very grateful to sb for sth they have done: *Thanks a lot for all you've done.* 2 (*ironic*) used to show that you are annoyed that sb has done sth because it causes trouble or difficulty for you: *'I'm afraid I've finished all the milk.' 'Well, thanks a lot!'* **thanks to sb / sth** B1 (*sometimes ironic*) used to say that sth has happened because of sb/sth: *It was all a great success—thanks to a lot of hard work.* ◊ (*ironic*) *Everyone knows about it now, thanks to you!*

**thanks·giv·ing** /ˌθæŋks'gɪvɪŋ/ *noun* 1 **Thanksgiving (Day)** [U, C] a public holiday in the US (on the fourth Thursday in November) and in Canada (on the second Monday in October), originally to give thanks to God for the HARVEST and for health: *We always eat turkey on Thanksgiving.* ◊ *Are you going home for Thanksgiving?* ⊃ compare HARVEST FESTIVAL 2 [U] (*formal*) the expression of thanks to God

**'thank you** *exclamation, noun*
▪ *exclamation* ⊃ see also THANKS *exclamation* 1 used to show that you are grateful to sb for sth they have done: **~ (for sth)** *Thank you for your letter.* ◊ **~ (for doing sth)** *Thank you very much for sending the photos.* 2 a polite way of accepting sth that sb has offered you: *'Would you like some help with that?' 'Oh, thank you.'* 3 **no thank you** a polite way of refusing sth that sb has offered you: *'Would you like some more cake?' 'No thank you.'* 4 used at the end of a sentence to tell sb clearly that you do not need their help or advice: *'Shall I do that?' 'I can do it myself, thank you.'*
▪ *noun* [usually sing.] **~ (to sb) (for sth)** an act, a gift, a comment, etc. intended to thank sb for sth they have done: *The actor sent a big thank you to all his fans for their letters of support.* ◊ *She took the money without so much as a thank you.* ◊ *a thank-you letter*

**thanx** /θæŋks/ *exclamation* (*informal, non-standard*) an informal way of writing 'thanks', for example in an email or text to a friend: *Thanx for your help!* HELP You should not write this form in formal or standard writing. ⊃ compare THX

**that** ⓘ A1 *det., pron., conj., adv.*
▪ *det.* /ðæt/ (*pl.* **those** /ðəʊz/) 1 A1 used for referring to a person or thing that is not near the speaker or as near to the speaker as another: *Look at that man over there.* ◊ *How much are those apples at the back?* 2 A1 used for referring to sb/sth that has already been mentioned or is already known about: *I was living with my parents at that time.* ◊ *That incident changed their lives.* ◊ *Have you forgotten about that money I lent you last week?* ◊ *That dress of hers is too short.*
▪ *pron.* /ðæt/ (*pl.* **those** /ðəʊz/) 1 A1 used for referring to a person or thing that is not near the speaker or as near to the speaker as another: *Who's that?* ◊ *That's Peter over there.* ◊ (*BrE*) *Hello. Is that Jo?* (= when speaking on the phone) HELP In NAmE say *Is this Jo?* ◊ *That's a nice dress.* ◊ *Those look riper than these.* 2 A1 used for referring to sb/sth that has already been mentioned, or is already known about: *What can I do about that?* ◊ *Do you remember when we went to Norway? That was a good trip.* ◊ *That's exactly what I think.* 3 B1 (*formal*) used for referring to people or things of a particular type: *Those present were in favour of change.* ◊ *There are those who say* (= some people say) *she should not have got the job.* ◊ *Salaries are higher here than those in my country.* 4 A1 /ðət, ðæt/ (*pl.* **that**) used as a relative pronoun to introduce a part of a sentence which refers to the person, thing or time you have been talking about: *Where's the letter that came yesterday?* ◊ *Who was it that won the US Open?* ◊ *The watch (that) you gave me keeps perfect time.* ◊ *The people (that) I spoke to were very helpful.* ◊ *It's the best novel (that) I've ever read.* ◊ *We moved here the year (that) my mother died.* HELP In spoken and informal written English **that** is nearly always left out when it is not the subject of the verb.
IDM **and (all) 'that** (*BrE, informal*) and everything else connected with an activity, a situation, etc. SYN **and so forth**: *Did you bring the contract and (all) that?* **that is (to say)** B2 used to say what sth means or to give more information: *He's a local government administrator, that is to say a civil servant.* ◊ *You'll find her very helpful—if she's not too busy, that is.* ⊃ LANGUAGE BANK at I.E. **that's 'it** (*informal*) 1 B1 used to say that sb is right, or is doing sth right: *No, the other one... that's it.* ◊ *That's it, carry on!* 2 B1 used to say that sth is finished, or that no more can be done:

# thatch

*That's it, the fire's out now.* ◊ *That's it for now, but if I get any news I'll let you know.* ◊ *A week to go, and that's it!* **3** used to say that you will not accept sth any longer: *That's it, I've had enough!* **4** used to talk about the reason for sth: *So that's it—the fuse had gone.* ◊ *You don't love me any more, is that it?* **that's 'that** (*informal*) used to say that your decision cannot be changed: *Well I'm not going, and that's that.*

■ **conj.** /ðət, ðæt/ **1** used after some verbs, adjectives and nouns to introduce a new part of the sentence: *She said (that) the story was true.* ◊ *It's possible (that) he has not received the letter.* ◊ *The fact (that) he's older than me is not relevant.* **HELP** In spoken and informal written English **that** is usually left out after reporting verbs and adjectives. It is less often left out after nouns. ⊃ see also GIVEN THAT **2** **so … that …** used to express a result: *She was so tired (that) she couldn't think straight.* **HELP** In informal English **that** is often left out. **3** (*literary*) used for expressing a hope or a wish: *Oh that I could see him again!*

■ **adv.** /ðæt/ **1** to such a degree; so: *I can't walk that far* (= as far as that). ◊ *If only it were that simple.* **2** used when saying how much or showing how long, big, etc. sth is with your hands: *It's about that long.* **3** **not (all) ~** not very, or not as much as has been said: *It isn't all that cold.* ◊ *It's not quite that easy.* ◊ *There aren't that many people here.* **4** (*BrE, informal*) used to emphasize how much: *I was that scared I didn't know what to do.*

## thatch /θætʃ/ noun, verb

■ **noun 1** [U, C] dried STRAW, REEDS, etc. used for making a roof; a roof made of this material: *a roof made of thatch* ◊ *The thatch was badly damaged in the storm.* **2** [sing.] **~(of hair)** (*informal*) thick hair on sb's head

■ **verb ~ sth** to cover the roof of a building with thatch ▸ **thatched** *adj.*: *They live in a thatched cottage.*

## thaw /θɔː/ verb, noun

■ **verb 1** [I] **~ (out)** (of ice and snow) to turn back into water after being frozen SYN melt OPP freeze ⊃ WORDFINDER NOTE at SNOW **2** [I] when **it thaws** or **is thawing**, the weather becomes warm enough to melt snow and ice: *It's starting to thaw.* **3** [I, T] **~ (sth) (out)** to become, or to let frozen food become, soft or liquid ready for cooking ⊃ compare DEFROST, DE-ICE, UNFREEZE: *Leave the meat to thaw completely before cooking.* **4** [I, T] **~ (sth) (out)** to become, or make sth become, a normal temperature after being very cold: *I could feel my ears and toes start to thaw out.* **5** [I] **~ (out)** to become more friendly and less formal: *Relations between the two countries thawed a little after the talks.*

■ **noun 1** [C, usually sing.] a period of warmer weather following a long cold period, causing snow and ice to melt **2** [sing.] **~ (in sth)** a situation in which the relations between two enemy countries become more friendly

## the /ðə, before vowels ði, strong form ðiː/ definite article

**1** used to refer to sb/sth that has already been mentioned or is easily understood: *There were three questions. The first two were relatively easy but the third one was hard.* ◊ *There was an accident here yesterday. A car hit a tree and the driver was killed.* ◊ *The heat was getting to be too much for me.* ◊ *The nights are getting longer.* **2** used to refer to sb/sth that is the only, normal or obvious one of their kind: *the Mona Lisa* ◊ *the Nile* ◊ *the Queen* ◊ *What's the matter?* ◊ *The phone rang.* ◊ *I patted her on the back.* ◊ *How's the (= your) baby?* **3** used when explaining which person or thing you mean: *the house at the end of the street* ◊ *The people I met there were very friendly.* ◊ *It was the best day of my life.* ◊ *You're the third person to ask me that.* ◊ *Friday the thirteenth* ◊ *Alexander the Great* **4** used to refer to a thing in general rather than a particular example: *He taught himself to play the violin.* ◊ *The dolphin is an intelligent animal.* ◊ *They placed the African elephant on their endangered list.* ◊ *I heard it on the radio.* ◊ *I'm usually out during the day.* **5** used with adjectives to refer to a thing or a group of people described by the adjective: *With him, you should always expect the unexpected.* ◊ *the unemployed* ◊ *the* 

*French* **6** used before the plural of sb's last name to refer to a whole family or a married couple: *Don't forget to invite the Jordans.* **7** used with a unit of measurement to mean 'every': *My car does forty miles to the gallon.* ◊ *You get paid by the hour.* **8** enough of sth for a particular purpose: *I wanted it but I didn't have the money.* **9** used with a unit of time to mean 'the present': *Why not have the dish of the day?* ◊ *She's flavour of the month with him.* **10** /ðiː/ used, stressing *the*, to show that the person or thing referred to is famous or important: *Sheryl Crow? Not* the *Sheryl Crow?* ◊ *At that time London was* the *place to be.*
**IDM** **the more, less, etc…, the more, less, etc…** used to show that two things change to the same degree: *The more she thought about it, the more depressed she became.* ◊ *The less said about the whole thing, the happier I'll be.*

## the·a·tre (*US* theater) /ˈθɪətə(r); *NAmE* ˈθiːə-/ noun

**1** [C] a building or an outdoor area where plays and similar types of entertainment are performed: *Broadway theatres* ◊ *an open-air theatre* ◊ *How often do you go to the theatre?* ⊃ see also COMMUNITY THEATER (2), LECTURE THEATRE

**WORDFINDER** artistic director, auditorium, balcony, box office, circle, director, foyer, stage, the stalls

**2** (also **ˈmovie theater**) (both *NAmE*) (*BrE* **cin·ema**) [C] a building in which films are shown: *They arrived at the movie theater a few minutes later.* **3** [U] plays considered as entertainment: *an evening of live music and theatre* ◊ *current ideas about what makes good theatre* (= what makes good entertainment when performed) ◊ *We're huge fans of* **musical theatre**. ⊃ see also FRINGE THEATRE, STREET THEATRE **4** [U] (also **the theatre** [sing.]) the work of writing, producing and acting in plays: *I want to work in theatre.* ◊ *a theatre troupe/company* ⊃ see also COMMUNITY THEATER (1) **5** [C, U] (*BrE*) = OPERATING THEATRE: *a theatre sister* (= a nurse who helps during operations) **in ~** *He's still in theatre.* **6** [C, usually sing.] **~(of war/operations)** (*formal*) the place in which a war or fighting takes place

## the·atre·goer (*US* theater·goer) /ˈθɪətəɡəʊə(r); *NAmE* ˈθiːətərɡ-/ (also **play-goer**) noun a person who goes regularly to the theatre ▸ **ˈtheatre-going** (*US* **ˈtheater-going**) *adj.* [only before noun]: *the theatre-going public*

## the·at·ric·al /θiˈætrɪkl/ adj. 1 [only before noun] connected with the theatre: *a theatrical agent* **2** (*often disapproving*) (of behaviour) deliberately attracting attention or creating a particular effect in a way that seems false: *a theatrical gesture* ▸ **the·at·ric·al·ly** /-kli/ *adv.*

## the·at·ric·al·ity /θiˌætrɪˈkæləti/ noun [U] the EXAGGERATED quality of sth that is intended to attract attention or create a particular effect

## the·at·ric·als /θiˈætrɪklz/ noun [pl.] **1** performances of plays: *amateur theatricals* **2** (also **the·at·rics** /θiˈætrɪks/; *especially in NAmE*) behaviour that is EXAGGERATED and emotional in order to attract attention

## thee /ðiː/ pron. (*old use* or *dialect*) a word meaning 'you', used when talking to only one person who is the object of the verb: *We beseech thee, O Lord.* ⊃ compare THOU

## theft /θeft/ noun [U, C] **~ (of sth)** the crime of stealing sth from a person or place: *car theft* ◊ *Police are investigating the theft of computers from the company's offices.* ⊃ compare BURGLARY, ROBBERY ⊃ see also GRAND THEFT, IDENTITY THEFT, THIEF

## their /ðeə(r); *NAmE* ðer/ det. (the possessive form of *they*) **1** of or belonging to people, animals or things that have already been mentioned or are easily identified: *Their parties are always fun.* ◊ *Which is their house?* **2** used instead of *his* or *her* to refer to a person whose sex is not mentioned or not known: *If anyone calls, ask for their number so I can call them back.* ⊃ note at GENDER

**theirs** /ðeəz; NAmE ðerz/ pron. (the possessive form of *they*) of or belonging to them: *Theirs are the children with very fair hair.* ◊ *It's a favourite game of theirs.*

**the·ism** /ˈθiːɪzəm/ noun [U] belief in the existence of God or gods OPP **atheism**

**them** /ðəm, strong form ðem/ pron. (the object form of *they*) **1** used when referring to people, animals or things as the object of a verb or preposition, or after the verb *be*: *Tell them the news.* ◊ *What are you doing with those matches? Give them to me.* ◊ *Did you eat all of them?* ◊ *It's them.* **2** used instead of *him* or *her* to refer to a person whose sex is not mentioned or not known: *If anyone comes in before I get back, ask them to wait.*

**the·mat·ic** /θɪˈmætɪk, θiː'm-/ adj. [usually before noun] connected with the theme or themes of sth: *the thematic structure of a text* ▶ **the·mat·ic·al·ly** /-kli/ adv.: *The books have been grouped thematically.*

**theme** /θiːm/ noun, adj.
■ noun **1** the subject or main idea in a talk, piece of writing or work of art: *the central/main/key/major theme* ◊ *Births are a recurring theme in Leigh's work.* ◊ *Hot temperatures were a common theme over the past couple of weeks.* ◊ *~ of sth The stories are all variations on the theme of unhappy marriage.* **2** (*music*) a short tune that is repeated or developed in a piece of music **3** = THEME MUSIC: *the theme from 'The Godfather'* **4** (NAmE, old-fashioned) a short piece of writing on a particular subject, done for school **5** (*linguistics*) the part of a sentence or clause that contains information that is not new to the reader or audience
■ adj. (BrE) *~ pub/bar/restaurant, etc.* a pub, bar, etc. that is designed to reflect a particular subject or period of history: *an Irish theme pub*

**themed** /θiːmd/ adj. [usually before noun] (BrE) (of an event or a place of entertainment) designed to reflect a particular subject or period of history: *a themed restaurant*

**ˈtheme music** noun [U] (*also* **theme**, **ˈtheme song**, **ˈtheme tune** [C]) music that is played at the beginning and end and/or is often repeated in a film, television programme, etc. ⊃ compare SIGNATURE TUNE

**ˈtheme park** noun a large park where people go to enjoy themselves, for example by riding on large machines such as ROLLER COASTERS, and where much of the entertainment is connected with one subject or idea: *a western-style theme park*

**them·self** /ðəmˈself/ pron. (the reflexive form of *they*) used instead of *himself* or *herself* to refer to a person whose sex is not mentioned or not known: *Does anyone here consider themself a good cook?* HELP *Although* **themself** *is fairly common, especially in spoken English, many people think it is not correct.*

**them·selves** /ðəmˈselvz/ pron. **1** (the reflexive form of *they*) used when people or animals performing an action are also affected by it: *They seemed to be enjoying themselves.* ◊ *The children were arguing amongst themselves.* ◊ *They've bought themselves a new car.* **2** used instead of *himself* or *herself* to refer to a person whose sex is not mentioned or not known: *There wasn't anyone who hadn't enjoyed themselves.* HELP *Although this use of* **themselves** *is fairly common, especially in spoken English, many people think it is not correct.* **3** used to emphasize *they* or a plural subject: *They themselves had had a similar experience.* ◊ *Don and Julie paid for it themselves.*
IDM **(all) by themˈselves 1** alone; without anyone else: *They wanted to spend the evening by themselves.* **2** without help: *They did the cooking by themselves.* **(all) to themˈselves** for only them to have or use; not shared with others

**then** /ðen/ adv., adj.
■ adv. **1** used to refer to a particular time in the past or future: *Life was harder then because neither of us had a job.* ◊ *Things were very different* ***back then***. ◊ *She grew up in Zimbabwe, or Rhodesia as it was then.* ◊ *I saw them at Christmas but haven't heard a thing* ***since then***. ◊ *I've been invited too, so I'll see you then.* ◊ *There's a room free in Bob's house next week but you can stay with us* ***until then***. ◊ *Call again next week. They should have reached a decision* ***by then***. ◊ ***Just then*** (= at that moment) *there was a knock at the door.* ◊ *She left in 1984 and* ***from then on*** *he lived alone.* ◊ *I took one look at the car and offered to buy it* ***there and then/then and there*** (= immediately). **2** used to introduce the next item in a series of actions, events, instructions, etc: *He drank a glass of whisky, then another and then another.* ◊ *First cook the onions, then add the mushrooms.* ◊ *We lived in France and then Italy before coming back to England.* ⊃ LANGUAGE BANK at PROCESS¹ **3** used to show the logical result of a particular statement or situation: *If you miss that train then you'll have to get a taxi.* ◊ *'My wife's got a job in Glasgow.' 'I take it you'll be moving, then.'* ◊ *'You haven't done anything to upset me.' 'So what's wrong, then?'* ◊ *Why don't you hire a car? Then you'll be able to visit more of the area.* **4** used to introduce additional information: *She's been very busy at work* ***and then*** *there was all that trouble with her son.* **5** (*formal*) used to introduce a summary of sth that has just been said: *These, then, are the main areas of concern.* **6** used to show the beginning or end of a conversation, statement, etc: *Right then, where do you want the table to go?* ◊ *'I really have to go.' 'OK. Bye, then.'* ◊ *OK then, I think we've just about covered everything on the agenda.*
IDM **...and ˈthen some** (*informal*) used to emphasize the large amount or number of sth, and to say that you have not mentioned everything: *There are Indian, Chinese, Mexican, Thai restaurants... and then some!* **but ˈthen** | **then aˈgain** | **but then aˈgain** (*informal*) used to introduce additional information or information that contrasts with sth that has just been said: *She was early, but then again, she always is.* ◊ *'So you might accept their offer?' 'Yes, then again I might not.'* ⊃ more at NOW *adv.*
■ adj. [only before noun] used to describe sb who had a particular title, job, etc. at the time in the past that is being discussed: *That decision was taken by the then president.*

**thence** /ðens/ adv. (*old use or formal*) from that place; following that: *They made their way from Spain to France and thence to England.* ◊ *He was promoted to manager, thence to a partnership in the firm.*

**thence·forth** /ˌðensˈfɔːθ; NAmE -ˈfɔːrθ/ (*also* **thence·forward** /ˌðensˈfɔːwəd; NAmE -ˈfɔːrwərd/) adv. (*old use or formal*) starting from that time

**theo-** /θiːəʊ, θiːə; BrE also θiːɒ; NAmE also θiːɑː/ combining form (in nouns, adjectives and adverbs) connected with God or a god

**the·oc·racy** /θiˈɒkrəsi; NAmE -ˈɑːk-/ noun (pl. -ies) **1** [U] government of a country by religious leaders **2** [C] a country that is governed by religious leaders ▶ **theo·crat·ic** /ˌθiːəˈkrætɪk/ adj.: *theocratic rule*

**theo·lo·gian** /ˌθiːəˈləʊdʒən/ noun a person who studies theology

**the·ology** /θiˈɒlədʒi; NAmE -ˈɑːl-/ noun (pl. -ies) **1** [U] the study of religion and beliefs: *a degree in theology* ◊ *a theology student* **2** [C] a set of religious beliefs: *the theologies of the East* ⊃ see also LIBERATION THEOLOGY ▶ **theo·logic·al** /ˌθiːəˈlɒdʒɪkl; NAmE -ˈlɑːdʒ-/ adj. (BrE): *a theological college* ◊ (NAmE) *a theological seminary* **theo·logic·al·ly** /-kli/ adv.

**the·orem** /ˈθɪərəm; NAmE ˈθiːə-, ˈθɪr-/ noun (*specialist*) a rule or principle, especially in mathematics, that can be proved to be true

**the·or·et·ic·al** /ˌθɪəˈretɪkl; NAmE ˌθiːə-/ adj. [usually before noun] **1** connected with the ideas and principles on which a particular subject is based, rather than with practice and experiment: *a theoretical approach* ◊ *theoretical physics* ◊ *The first year provides students with a sound theoretical basis for later study.* OPP **experimental, practical 2** that could possibly exist, happen or be true, although this is unlikely: *It's a theoretical possibility.* ▶ **the·or·et·ic·al·ly** /-kli/ adv.: *theoretically sound conclusions* ◊ *It is theoretically possible for him to overrule their decision, but highly unlikely.*

# theorist

**the·or·ist** /ˈθɪərɪst; NAmE ˈθiːə-, ˈθɪr-/ (also **the·or·et·ician** /ˌθɪərəˈtɪʃn; NAmE ˌθiːə-, ˌθɪr-/) noun a person who develops ideas and principles about a particular subject in order to explain why things happen or exist

**the·or·ize** (BrE also **-ise**) /ˈθɪəraɪz; NAmE ˈθiːə-, ˈθɪr-/ verb [I, T] ~ (about/on sth) | ~ sth | ~ that … to suggest facts and ideas to explain sth; to form a theory or theories about sth: *The study theorizes about the role of dreams in peoples' lives.* ▶ **the·or·iz·ing, -is·ing** noun [U]

**the·ory** /ˈθɪəri; NAmE ˈθiːəri, ˈθɪri/ noun (pl. **-ies**) **1** [C, U] a formal set of ideas that is intended to explain why sth happens or exists: *~ of sth the theory of evolution/relativity* ◊ *scientific/economic theory* ◊ *~ about/on sth He developed a new theory about the cause of stomach ulcers.* ◊ **according to a~** *According to the theory of relativity, nothing can travel faster than light.* ⇨ see also CHAOS THEORY, CRITICAL THEORY, GAME THEORY, GRAND UNIFIED THEORY, INFORMATION THEORY, QUANTUM THEORY **2** [U] the principles on which a particular subject is based: *the theory and practice of language teaching* **3** [C] an opinion or idea that sb believes is true but that is not proved: *~ about/on sth Theories abound* (= people have lots of different ideas) *about what happened.* ◊ *~ that … I don't subscribe to the theory that all Hollywood audiences want a happy ending.*
IDM **in ˈtheory** used to say that a particular statement is supposed to be true but may in fact be wrong: *In theory, these machines should last for ten years or more.* ◊ *That sounds fine in theory, but have you really thought it through?*

**thera·peut·ic** /ˌθerəˈpjuːtɪk/ adj. **1** [usually before noun] helping to treat an illness: *the therapeutic benefits of herbs* **2** helping you to relax: *Painting can be very therapeutic.* ▶ **thera·peut·ic·al·ly** /-kli/ adv.

**thera·peut·ics** /ˌθerəˈpjuːtɪks/ noun [U] the branch of medicine that deals with the treatment of diseases

**ther·ap·ist** /ˈθerəpɪst/ noun **1** (especially in compounds) a specialist who treats a particular type of illness or problem, or who uses a particular type of treatment: *a speech therapist* ◊ *a beauty therapist* ⇨ see also OCCUPATIONAL THERAPIST, PHYSICAL THERAPIST, PHYSIO-THERAPIST **2** = PSYCHOTHERAPIST

**ther·apy** /ˈθerəpi/ noun (pl. **-ies**) **1** [U, C] the treatment of a physical problem or an illness: *He is receiving therapy for cancer.* ◊ *Most leukaemia patients undergo some sort of drug therapy* (= treatment using drugs). ◊ *alternative/complementary therapies* (= treatments that do not use traditional drugs) ⇨ see also CHEMO-THERAPY, GENE THERAPY, HORMONE REPLACEMENT THERAPY, OCCUPATIONAL THERAPY, PHYSICAL THERAPY, PHYSIOTHERAPY, RADIOTHERAPY, SPEECH THERAPY **2** [U] = PSYCHOTHERAPY: **in~** *She's in therapy.* ◊ *a therapy group/session* ⇨ see also ART THERAPY, AVERSION THERAPY, ELECTROCONVULSIVE THERAPY, GROUP THERAPY, RETAIL THERAPY, SHOCK THERAPY

**there** /ðeə(r); NAmE ðer/ adv., exclamation
■ adv. **1** /weak form ðə(r); BrE strong form ðeə(r); NAmE strong form ðer/ **there is, are, was, were, etc.** used to show that sth exists or happens: *There's a restaurant around the corner.* ◊ *There are two people waiting outside.* ◊ *Has there been an accident?* ◊ *I don't want there to be any misunderstanding.* ◊ *There seemed to be no doubt about it.* ◊ *There comes a point where you give up.* ◊ *There remains the problem of finance.* ◊ *There used to be a cinema here.* ◊ (informal) *There's only four days left.* ◊ (literary) *There once was a poor farmer who had four sons.* **2** in, at or to that place or position: *We went on to Paris and stayed there eleven days.* ◊ *I hope we get there in time.* ◊ *It's there, right in front of you!* ◊ *There it is—just behind the chair.* ◊ *We're almost there* (= we have almost arrived). ◊ *Hello, is Bob there please?* (= used when calling sb on the phone) ◊ **prep. +~** *'Have you seen my pen?' 'Yes, it's over there.'* ◊ *There are a lot of people back there* (= behind) *waiting to get in.* ◊ *I'm not going in there—it's freezing!* ◊ *I left in 2008 and I haven't been back there since.* ◊ *Can I get there and back in a day?* ◊ *I took one look at the car and offered to buy it there a then/then and there* (= immediately). **3** existing or available: *I went to see if my old school was still there.* ◊ *This is the most exciting technology out there today.* **4** at that point (in a story, an argument, etc.): *'I feel …' There she stopped.* ◊ *I don't agree with you there.* **5** used to attract sb's attention: *Hello, there!* ◊ *You there! Come back!* ◊ *There you are! I've been looking for you everywhere.* **6** used to attract sb's attention to a particular person, thing or fact: *There's the statue I was telling you about.* ◊ *That woman there is the boss's wife.* ◊ *There goes the last bus* (= we've just missed it). ◊ *There goes the phone* (= it's ringing). ◊ (humorous) *There goes my career!* (= my career is ruined) ◊ *So, there you have it: that's how it all started.* **7** ~ **to do sth** used to show the role of a person or thing in a situation: *The fact is, they're there to make money.*
IDM **ˌbeen ˈthere, ˌdone ˈthat** (informal) used to show that you think a place or an activity is not very interesting or impressive because you have already experienced it: *Not Spain again! Been there, done that, got the T-shirt.* **be ˈthere for sb** to be available if sb wants to talk to you or if they need help: *You know I'll always be there for you.* **by ˈthere** (WelshE) there; to there: *He's over by there.* **ˌhave been there beˈfore** (informal) to know all about a situation because you have experienced it **ˌnot all ˈthere** (informal) not very intelligent, especially because of mental illness **ˌso ˈthere!** (informal) used to show that you are determined not to change your attitude or opinion: *Well, you can't have it, so there!* **ˌthere it ˈis** (informal) that is the situation: *It's crazy, I know, but there it is.* **ˌthere or thereˈabouts** (BrE, informal) used to say that sth is very good, even if it is not perfect: *At the end of the tournament, he'll be there or thereabouts* (= he may not win, but he will be one of the best players). **ˈthere's a good boy, girl, dog, etc.** (informal) used to praise or encourage small children or animals: *Finish your lunch, there's a good boy.* **ˈthere's lovely, nice, etc.** (WelshE) used to say that sth has a particular quality **ˌthere's ˈsth for you** (informal) used to say that sth is a very good example of sth: *She visited him every day he was in the hospital. There's devotion for you.* ◊ (ironic) *He didn't even say thank you. There's gratitude for you!* **ˈthere, ˈthere!** (informal) used to persuade a small child to stop crying or being upset: *There, there! Never mind, you'll soon feel better.* **ˌthere you ˈare** (also **ˌthere you ˈgo**) (informal) **1** used when giving sb a thing they want or have asked for: *There you are—that'll be £3.80, please.* ◊ *OK, there you go.* **2** used when explaining or showing sth to sb: *You switch on, push in the DVD and there you are!* ◊ *There you are! I told you it was easy!* **3** used when you are talking about sth that happens in a typical way or about a situation that cannot be changed: *There you go—that's what they're like.* ◊ *I know it's not ideal but there you go …* **ˌthere you go aˈgain** (informal) used to criticize sb when they behave in a way that is typical of them: *There you go again—jumping to conclusions.* ⇨ more at HERE adv.
■ exclamation **1** used to show that you are satisfied that you were right about sth or to show that sth annoys you: *There now! What did I tell you?* (= you can see that I was right) ◊ *There! That didn't hurt too much, did it?* **2** used to show that sth annoys you: *There! You've gone and woken the baby!*

**there·abouts** /ˌðeərəˈbaʊts; NAmE ˌðer-/ adv. (usually used after *or*) **1** near the place mentioned: *He comes from Leeds or thereabouts.* **2** used to say that a particular number, quantity, time, etc. is not exact: *They paid $100000 or thereabouts for the house.* IDM see THERE adv.

**there·after** /ˌðeərˈɑːftə(r); NAmE ˌðerˈæf-/ adv. (formal) after the time or event mentioned: *She married at 17 and gave birth to her first child shortly thereafter.* ⇨ compare HEREAFTER

**there·by** /ˌðeəˈbaɪ; NAmE ˌðerˈb-/ adv. (formal) used to introduce the result of the action or situation mentioned: *Regular exercise strengthens the heart, thereby reducing the risk of heart attack.*

**there·fore** /ˈðeəfɔː(r); NAmE ˈðerf-/ adv. used to introduce the logical result of sth that has just been mentioned: *He's only 17 and therefore not eligible to vote.* ◊ *There is still much to discuss. We shall, therefore, return to this item at our next meeting.*

> ▼ **LANGUAGE BANK**
>
> **therefore**
>
> Ways of saying 'For this reason …'
>
> - *Today's children eat more junk food and get less exercise than previous generations of children. It is not surprising, **therefore**, that rates of childhood obesity are on the increase.*
> - *Children who grow up on a diet of junk food find it difficult to change this habit later in life. It is essential, **therefore**, that parents encourage healthy eating from an early age.*
> - *Children who grow up on a diet of junk food find it difficult to change this habit later in life. **For this reason, / This is why** it is essential that children eat healthily from an early age.*
> - *Eating habits formed in childhood tend to continue into adult life. **Thus**, the best way to prevent heart disease among adults is to encourage healthy eating from an early age.*
> - *Eating habits formed in childhood tend to continue into adult life, **hence** the importance of encouraging healthy eating from an early age.*
>
> ⊃ LANGUAGE BANK at BECAUSE OF, CAUSE, CONSEQUENTLY, EMPHASIS, VITAL

**there·from** /ˌðeəˈfrɒm/; *NAmE* ˌðerˈfrʌm/ *adv.* (*formal or law*) from the thing mentioned: *The committee will examine the agreement and any problems arising therefrom.*

**there·in** /ˌðeərˈɪn/; *NAmE* ˌðerˈ-/ *adv.* (*law or formal*) in the place, object, document, etc. mentioned: *The insurance policy covers the building and any fixtures contained therein.*
▪ **IDM** **therein lies …** used to emphasize the result or consequence of a particular situation: *He works extremely hard and therein lies the key to his success.*

**there·of** /ˌðeərˈɒv/; *NAmE* ˌðerˈʌv/ *adv.* (*law or formal*) of the thing mentioned: *Is the property or any part thereof used for commercial activity?*

**there·on** /ˌðeərˈɒn/; *NAmE* ˌðerˈɑːn/ *adv.* (*law or formal*) on the thing mentioned: *a meeting to discuss the annual accounts and the auditors' report thereon*

**there's** /ðeəz/; *NAmE* ðerz/ *short form* **1** there is **2** there has

**there·to** /ˌðeəˈtuː/; *NAmE* ˌðerˈtuː/ *adv.* (*law or formal*) to the thing mentioned: *The lease entitles the holder to use the buildings and any land attached thereto.*

**there·under** /ˌðeərˈʌndə(r)/; *NAmE* ˌðer-/ *adv.* (*law or formal*) under the thing mentioned: *This savings plan is only available under the Finance Act 1990 and any regulations made thereunder.*

**there·upon** /ˌðeərəˈpɒn/; *NAmE* ˌðerəˈpɑːn/ *adv.* (*formal*) **1** immediately after the situation mentioned; as a direct result of the situation mentioned: *The audience thereupon rose cheering to their feet.* **2** on the thing mentioned: *a large notice with black letters printed thereupon*

**there·with** /ˌðeəˈwɪð, -ˈwɪθ/; *NAmE* ˌðerˈw-/ *adv.* (*old use or formal*) **1** with or in the thing mentioned **2** soon or immediately after that

**ther·mal** /ˈθɜːml/; *NAmE* ˈθɜːrml/ *adj.*, *noun*
▪ *adj.* [only before noun] **1** (*specialist*) connected with heat: *thermal energy* **2** (of clothing) designed to keep you warm by preventing heat from escaping from the body: *thermal underwear* **3** (of streams, lakes, etc.) in which the water has been naturally heated by the earth: *thermal springs*
▸ **ther·mal·ly** /-məli/ *adv.*
▪ *noun* **1** [C] a rising current of warm air used, for example, by a GLIDER to gain height **2** **thermals** [pl.] (*especially BrE*) warm underwear that prevents heat from escaping from the body

**thermal ˈimaging** *noun* [U] (*specialist*) the process of producing an image of sth or finding out where sth is, using the heat that comes from it: *Rescue teams are using thermal imaging to locate survivors of the earthquake.*

**thermo-** /θɜːməʊ, θɜːmə, θɜːˈmɒ/; *NAmE* θɜːrməʊ, θɜːrmə, θɜːrˈmɑː/ *combining form* (in nouns, adjectives and adverbs) connected with heat: *thermonuclear* ◊ *thermometer*

**thermo·dynam·ics** /ˌθɜːməʊdaɪˈnæmɪks/; *NAmE* ˌθɜːrm-/ *noun* [U] the science that deals with the relations between heat and other forms of energy: *the laws of thermodynamics* ▸ **thermo·dynam·ic** *adj.*

**therm·om·eter** /θəˈmɒmɪtə(r)/; *NAmE* θərˈmɑːm-/ *noun* an instrument used for measuring the temperature of the air, a person's body, etc: *a thermometer reading*

**thermo·nuclear** /ˌθɜːməʊˈnjuːkliə(r)/; *NAmE* ˌθɜːrməʊˈnuː-/ *adj.* connected with nuclear reactions that only happen at very high temperatures

**thermo·plas·tic** /ˌθɜːməʊˈplæstɪk/; *NAmE* ˌθɜːrm-/ *noun* [U] (*specialist*) a plastic material that can be easily shaped and bent when it is heated, and that becomes hard when it is cooled

**Ther·mos**™ /ˈθɜːməs/; *NAmE* ˈθɜːrm-/ (*BrE* also **ˈThermos flask**) (*NAmE* also **ˈThermos bottle**) *noun* a particular kind of VACUUM FLASK (= a container like a bottle with double walls with a VACUUM between them, used for keeping liquids hot or cold) ⊃ compare FLASK

**thermo·stat** /ˈθɜːməstæt/; *NAmE* ˈθɜːrm-/ *noun* a device that measures and controls the temperature of a machine or room, by switching the heating or cooling system on and off as necessary ▸ **thermo·stat·ic** /ˌθɜːməˈstætɪk/; *NAmE* ˌθɜːrm-/ *adj.* [only before noun] **thermo·stat·ic·al·ly** /-kli/ *adv.*

**the·saurus** /θɪˈsɔːrəs/ *noun* (pl. **the·sauri** /-raɪ/ or **the·saur·uses**) a book that lists words in groups that have similar meanings

**these** /ðiːz/ ⊃ THIS *det.*

**thesis** ⚡+ B2 /ˈθiːsɪs/ *noun* (pl. **theses** /ˈθiːsiːz/) **1** ⚡+ B2 ~ (on sth) a long piece of writing completed by a student as part of a university degree, based on their own research: *Students must submit a thesis on an agreed subject within four years.* **2** ⚡+ C1 ~ (that …) a statement or an opinion that is discussed in a logical way and presented with evidence in order to prove that it is true: *The basic thesis of the book is fairly simple.*

**thes·pian** /ˈθespiən/ *noun* (*often humorous*) an actor ▸ **thes·pian** *adj.*

**theta** /ˈθiːtə/; *NAmE* ˈθeɪtə/ *noun* the 8th letter of the Greek alphabet (Θ, θ)

**they** ⓞ A1 /ðeɪ/ *pron.* (used as the subject of a verb) **1** A1 people, animals or things that have already been mentioned or are easily identified: *'Where are John and Liz?' 'They went for a walk.'* ◊ *They* (= the things you are carrying) *go on the bottom shelf.* **2** ⚡ A2 used instead of *he* or *she* to refer to a person whose sex is not mentioned or not known: *If anyone arrives late they'll have to wait outside.* ⊃ note at GENDER **3** ⚡ A2 people in general: *The rest, as they say, is history.* **4** ⚡ A2 people in authority or experts: *They cut my water off.* ◊ *They now say that red wine is good for you.*

**they'd** /ðeɪd/ *short form* **1** they had ▪ HELP **They'd** is only used when *had* is an auxiliary verb: *They'd just left school.* When *had* is the main verb, use the full form: *I'm glad they had a good time.* ◊ ~~I'm glad they'd a good time.~~ **2** they would

**they'll** /ðeɪl/ *short form* they will

**they're** /ðeə(r)/; *NAmE* ðer, *weak form* ðər/ *short form* they are

**they've** /ðeɪv/ *short form* they have ▪ HELP **They've** is usually only used when *have* is an auxiliary verb: *They've just got here.* When *have* is the main verb, use the full form: *They have two children.* ◊ ~~They've two children.~~

**thia·mine** (also **thia·min**) /ˈθaɪəmɪn, -miːn/ *noun* [U] a vitamin of the B group, found in grains, beans and LIVER

**thick** ⓞ A1 /θɪk/ *adj.*, *noun*, *adv.*
▪ *adj.* (**thick·er**, **thick·est**)
• **DISTANCE BETWEEN SIDES 1** ⚡ A2 having a larger distance between opposite sides or surfaces than other similar

# thicken

objects or than normal: *a thick slice of bread* ◊ *a thick book* (= one that has a lot of pages) ◊ *a thick coat* (= one made of heavy cloth) ◊ *thick fingers* ◊ *Everything was covered with a thick layer of dust.* **2** ⓘ **A2** used to ask about or state the distance between opposite sides or surfaces: *How thick are the walls?* ◊ *They're two feet thick.*
- **HAIR/FUR/TREES 3** ⓘ **B1** growing closely together in large amounts or numbers: *thick dark hair* ◊ *a thick forest*
- **LIQUID 4** ⓘ **B1** not flowing very easily: *thick soup* ◊ *The effect will be ruined if the paint is too thick.*
- **FOG/SMOKE/AIR 5** ⓘ **B1** difficult to see through; difficult to breathe in: *The plane crashed in thick fog.* ◊ *thick smoke* ◊ *~ with sth The air was thick with dust.* ◊ (*figurative*) *The atmosphere was thick with tension.*
- **WITH LARGE NUMBER/AMOUNT 6** *~ with sb/sth* having a large number of people or a large amount of sth in one place: *The beach was thick with sunbathers.*
- **STUPID 7** (*informal, disapproving*) (of a person) slow to learn or understand things **SYN** **stupid**: *Are you thick, or what?*
- **ACCENT 8** (*sometimes disapproving*) easily recognized as being from a particular country or area **SYN** **strong**: *a thick Brooklyn accent*
- **VOICE 9** *~ (with sth)* deep and not as clear as normal, especially because of illness or emotion: *His voice was thick with emotion.*
- **FRIENDLY WITH SB 10** *~ (with sb)* (*informal*) very friendly with sb, especially in a way that makes other people suspect that sth wrong, illegal or dishonest is involved in the situation: *You seem to be very thick with the boss!* ⇒ see also **THICKLY, THICKNESS**

**IDM** **give sb/get a thick 'ear** (*BrE, informal*) to hit sb/be hit on the head as a punishment **(as) thick as 'thieves** (*informal*) (of two or more people) very friendly, especially in a way that makes other people suspect that sth wrong, illegal or dishonest is involved in the situation **(as) thick as two short 'planks** (*BrE, informal*) (of a person) very stupid **a thick 'head** (*informal*) a physical condition in which your head is painful or you cannot think clearly as a result of an illness or of drinking too much alcohol **your thick 'head** (*informal*) used to show that you are annoyed that sb does not understand sth: *When will you get it into your thick head that I don't want to see you again!* **a ,thick 'skin** the ability to accept criticism, offensive remarks, etc. without becoming upset **OPP** **a thin skin** ⇒ see also **THICK-SKINNED** ⇒ more at **BLOOD** *n.*, **GROUND** *n.*

■ *noun* [U]
**IDM** **in the 'thick of sth** involved in the busiest or most active part of sth **through ,thick and 'thin** even when there are problems or difficulties: *He's supported the team for over ten years through thick and thin.*

■ *adv.* (**thick·er, thick·est**) in a way that produces a wide piece or deep layer of sth: *Make sure you cut the bread nice and thick.*
**IDM** **lay it on 'thick** (*informal*) to talk about sb/sth in a way that makes them or it seem much better or much worse than they really are; to **EXAGGERATE** sth: *Praise them when necessary, but don't lay it on too thick.* **thick and 'fast** quickly and in large quantities: *Questions were coming at them thick and fast.*

**thick·en** /ˈθɪkən/ *verb* [I, T] to become thicker; to make sth thicker: *Stir until the sauce has thickened.* ◊ *It was a dangerous journey through thickening fog.* ◊ *~ sth Thicken the stew with flour.* **IDM** see **PLOT** *n.*

**thick·en·er** /ˈθɪkənə(r)/ *noun* a substance used to make a liquid thicker: *paint thickeners*

**thick·et** /ˈθɪkɪt/ *noun* **1** a group of bushes or small trees growing closely together **2** a large number of things that are not easy to understand or separate

**thick·ly** /ˈθɪkli/ *adv.* **1** in a way that produces a wide piece or deep layer of sth: *thickly sliced bread* ◊ *Apply the paint thickly in even strokes.* **2** *~ wooded, populated, etc.* having a lot of trees, people, etc. close together **3** in a deep voice that is not as clear as normal, especially because of illness or emotion

**thick·ness** /ˈθɪknəs/ *noun* **1** [U, C] the size of sth between opposite surfaces or sides **SYN** **width**: *Use wood of at least 12 mm thickness.* ◊ *The board is available in four thicknesses.* **2** [C] *~ (of sth)* a layer of sth: *The jacket was lined with a double thickness* (= two layers) *of fabric.*

**thick·set** /ˌθɪkˈset/ *adj.* (especially of a man) having a strong, heavy body

**thick-'skinned** *adj.* **1** (of a person) not easily upset by criticism or unkind comments **2** (of fruit) having a thick skin **OPP** **thin-skinned**

**thief** ⓘ **A2** /θiːf/ *noun* (*pl.* **thieves** /θiːvz/) a person who steals sth from another person or place: *a car/jewel thief* ◊ *Thieves stole £70 000 worth of jewellery from his home.* ⇒ see also **THEFT** **IDM** see **HONOUR** *n.*, **THICK** *adj.*

**thiev·ery** /ˈθiːvəri/ *noun* [U] (*formal*) the crime of stealing things: *Burglary and petty thievery are common.*

**thiev·ing** /ˈθiːvɪŋ/ *noun* [U] (*informal*) the act of stealing things ▶ **thiev·ing** *adj.* (*informal*): *You've no right to take that, you thieving swine!*

**thigh** /θaɪ/ *noun* **1** the top part of the leg between the knee and the **HIP** (= where the leg joins the body) ⇒ **VISUAL VOCAB** page V1 **2** the top part of the leg of a chicken, etc., cooked and eaten

**'thigh bone** *noun* the large, thick bone in the top part of the leg between the **HIP** and the knee **SYN** **femur** ⇒ **VISUAL VOCAB** page V1

**thim·ble** /ˈθɪmbl/ *noun* a small metal or plastic object that you wear on the end of your finger to protect it when **SEWING**

**thin** ⓘ **A2** /θɪn/ *adj., adv., verb*
■ *adj.* (**thin·ner, thin·nest**)
- **NOT THICK 1** ⓘ **A2** having a smaller distance between opposite sides or surfaces than other similar objects or than normal: *Cut the vegetables into thin strips.* ◊ *A number of thin cracks appeared in the wall.* ◊ *The body was hidden beneath a thin layer of soil.* ◊ *a thin blouse* (= of light cloth) ⇒ see also **PAPER-THIN, RAZOR-THIN, WAFER-THIN** ⇒ note at **NARROW**
- **NOT FAT 2** ⓘ **A2** (*sometimes disapproving*) (of a person or part of the body) not covered with much fat or muscle: *He was tall and thin, with dark hair.* ◊ *She was looking pale and thin.* ◊ *He is as thin as a rake* (= very thin). ◊ *thin legs*
- **HAIR 3** ⓘ **B1** not growing closely together or in large amounts: *thin grey hair*
- **LIQUID 4** ⓘ **B1** containing more liquid than is normal or expected **SYN** **runny**: *The sauce was thin and tasteless.*
- **SMOKE 5** fairly easy to see through: *They fought their way through where the smoke was thinner.*
- **AIR 6** containing less **OXYGEN** than normal
- **SOUND 7** (*disapproving*) high and weak: *Her thin voice trailed off into silence.*
- **SMILE 8** not sincere or enthusiastic: *He gave a thin smile.*
- **LIGHT 9** not very bright: *the thin grey light of dawn*
- **POOR QUALITY 10** of poor quality; without an important quality: *a thin excuse* (= one that people are not likely to believe) ◊ *Their arguments all sound a little thin to me.*
▶ **thin·ness** /ˈθɪnəs/ *noun* [U] ⇒ see also **THINLY**

**IDM** **be skating/walking on thin 'ice** to be taking a risk **disappear, vanish, etc. into thin 'air** to disappear suddenly in a mysterious way **have a thin 'time (of it)** (*BrE, informal*) to have many problems or difficulties to deal with; to not be successful **out of thin 'air** from nowhere or nothing, as if by magic **the thin end of the 'wedge** (*especially BrE*) an event or action that is the beginning of sth more serious and/or unpleasant **a ,thin 'skin** the lack of ability to accept criticism, offensive remarks, etc. without becoming upset **OPP** **a thick skin** ⇒ see also **THIN-SKINNED** ⇒ more at **GROUND** *n.*, **LINE** *n.*, **SPREAD** *v.*, **THICK** *n.*, **TOP** *n.*, **WEAR** *v.*

■ *adv.* (**thin·ner, thin·nest**) in a way that produces a thin piece or layer of sth: *Don't spread it too thin.* ◊ *I like my bread sliced thin.*

■ *verb* (**-nn-**)
- **LIQUID 1** [T] *~ sth (down) (with sth)* to make a liquid less thick or strong by adding water or another substance: *Thin the paint with water.*
- **OF HAIR 2** [I] to become less thick: *a middle-aged man with thinning hair*

- **BECOME LESS THICK 3** [I, T] to become less thick or fewer in number; to make sth less thick or fewer, for example by removing some things or people: *The clouds thinned and the moon shone through.* ◇ **~ out** *The crowd had thinned out and only a few people were left.* ◇ **~ sth (out)** *Thin out the seedlings to about 10cm apart.*

▼ **VOCABULARY BUILDING**

### Saying that somebody is thin

**Thin** is the most usual word: *Steve is tall and thin and has brown hair.* It is sometimes used with a negative meaning: *Mother looked thin and tired after her long illness.*

The following words all express praise or admiration:
- **Slim** means pleasantly thin. It is often used to describe women who have controlled their weight by diet or exercise: *She has a beautifully slim figure.*
- A **slender** girl or woman is thin and graceful.
- A **lean** man is thin and fit.
- **Willowy** describes a woman who is attractively tall and thin.

The following words are more negative in their meaning:
- **Skinny** means very thin, often in a way that is not attractive: *a skinny little kid.*
- **Bony** describes parts of the body when they are so thin that the bones can be seen: *the old man's bony hands.*
- **Scrawny** suggests that a person is thin, weak and not attractive: *a scrawny old woman.*
- **Gaunt** describes a person who is a little too thin and looks sad or ill.
- **Underweight** is used in medical contexts to describe people who are too thin because they are ill or have not had enough food: *Women who smoke risk giving birth to underweight babies.*
- **Emaciated** describes a serious condition resulting from illness or not enough food.
- **Anorexic** is a medical term, but is also used informally to describe somebody, especially a girl or woman, who is so thin that you are worried about them.

It is more acceptable to talk to somebody about how thin or slim they are than about how fat they are. ⇨ note at FAT

**thine** /ðaɪn/ *pron., det. (old use)*
- *pron.* a word meaning 'yours', used when talking to only one person
- *det.* the form of *thy* that is used before a vowel or 'h', meaning 'your'

**thing** ❼ 🅰🅱 ⓢ /θɪŋ/ *noun*
- **OBJECT 1** 🅱 🅰🅱 [C] an object whose name you do not use because you do not need to or want to, or because you do not know it: *Can you pass me that thing over there?* ◇ *She's very fond of sweet things* (= sweet foods). ◇ *He's just bought one of those exercise things.* ◇ *Turn that thing off while I'm talking to you!* **2** 🅱 🅰🅱 [C] an object that is not alive in the way that people and plants are: *Don't treat her like that—she's a person, not a thing!* ◇ *He's good at making things with his hands.* ◇ *She took no interest in the people and things around her.* ◇ *Books may one day become* **a thing of the past** (= something that no longer exists).
- **POSSESSIONS/EQUIPMENT 3** 🅱 🅰🅱 **things** [pl.] *(rather informal)* objects, clothing or tools that belong to sb or are used for a particular purpose: *Shall I help you pack your things?* ◇ *Bring your swimming things with you.* ◇ *I'll just clear away the breakfast things.* ◇ *Put your things* (= coat, etc.) *on and let's go.*
- **FACT/EVENT/SITUATION/ACTION 4** 🅱 🅰🅱 [C] a fact, an event, a situation or an action; what sb says or thinks: *They talked about many things, like books, music and films.* ◇ *Bad things happen to good people.* ◇ *I've got lots of* **things to do** *today.* ◇ *He has things on his mind.* ◇ *The most* **important thing** *in life is to have fun!* ◇ *She said* **the first thing** *that came into her head.* ◇ *He found* **the whole thing** (= the situation) *very boring.* ◇ **Among other things,** *I have to deal with mail and keep the accounts.* ◇ *I like camping, climbing and* **that sort of thing.** ◇ *There's* **no such thing as** *a typical day in this job.* ◇ **One thing is for sure**—*it will be a memorable evening!* **5** 🅱 🅰🅱 **things** [pl.] *(rather informal)* the general situation, as it affects sb: *Things haven't gone entirely to plan.* ◇ *(informal) Hi, Jane!* **How are things?** ◇ **As things stand** *at present, he seems certain to win.* ◇ **All things considered** (= considering all the difficulties or problems), *she's done very well.* ◇ *They're trying to* **change things** *for the better.* ◇ **Things have changed** *over the last few years.* ⇨ SYNONYMS at SITUATION
- **QUALITY/CONCEPT 6** 🅱 🅰🅱 [C] a quality or a concept: *Reality and truth are* **not the same thing.** ◇ *The two of them have one thing in common*—*they never give up.* ◇ *The* **good thing** *about this job is all the travelling.*
- **WHAT IS NEEDED/RIGHT 7** 🅱 🅰🅱 🅰🅱 [C, usually sing.] what is needed or socially acceptable: *You need something to cheer you up*—*I know just the thing!* ◇ *to say the right/wrong thing* ◇ **The best thing** *to do is to apologize.*
- **SOMETHING IMPORTANT 8 a thing** [sing.] *(informal, humorous)* used to say that sth is important or real: *I don't understand why these corny films are still a thing in 2020.* ◇ *I'm not sure that 'modular techno music' is really a thing.*
- **ANYTHING 9 a thing** [sing.] used with negatives to mean 'anything' in order to emphasize what you are saying: *I haven't got a thing to wear!* ◇ *There wasn't a thing we could do to help.* ◇ *Ignore what he said*—*it* **doesn't mean a thing.**
- **THINGS OF PARTICULAR TYPE 10 things** [pl.] *(formal)* (followed by an adjective) all that can be described in a particular way: *She loves all things Japanese.*
- **CREATURE 11** [C] (used with an adjective) a living creature: *All living things are composed of cells.*
- **PERSON/ANIMAL 12** [C] (with an adjective) *(informal)* used to talk to or about a person or an animal, to show how you feel about them: *You silly thing!* ◇ *You must be starving, you poor things.* ◇ *The cat's very ill, poor old thing.* ⇨ see also BRIGHT YOUNG THING, YOUNG THING

**IDM** **A is ˈone thing, B is aˈnother** | **it's ˈone thing to do A, it's aˈnother thing to do B** B is very different from A, for example it is more difficult, serious or important: *Romance is one thing; marriage is quite another.* ◇ *It's one thing to tease your sister, but it's another to hit her.* **ˌall / ˌother things being ˈequal** if the conditions stay the same; if other conditions are the same: *All things being equal, we should finish the job tomorrow.* **and ˈthings (ˌlike ˈthat)** *(informal)* used when you do not want to complete a list: *She likes nice clothes and things like that.* ◇ *I've been busy shopping and things.* **be ˌall things to ˌall ˈmen / ˈpeople 1** (of people) to please everyone by changing your attitudes or opinions to suit different people **2** (of things) to be understood or used in different ways by different people **be a ˈgood thing (that) …** to be lucky that …: *It's a good thing we got here early.* **be no bad ˈthing (that) …** used to say that although sth seems to be bad, it could have good results: *We didn't want the press to get hold of the story, but it might be no bad thing.* **be onto a good ˈthing** to have found a job, situation or style of life that is pleasant or easy **be ˈseeing / ˈhearing things** *(informal, humorous)* to imagine that you can see or hear sth that is in fact not there **come to / be the same ˈthing** to have the same result or meaning **do your own ˈthing** *(informal)* to do what you want to do or what interests you, without thinking about other people; to be independent **ˈdo things to sb** *(informal)* to have a powerful emotional effect on sb: *That song just does things to me.* **first / ˌlast ˈthing** early in the morning / late in the evening: *I need the report on my desk first thing Monday morning.* **first things ˈfirst** *(often humorous)* the most important matters must be dealt with first: *We have a lot to discuss, but, first things first, let's have a cup of coffee!* **for ˈone thing** used to introduce one of two or more reasons for doing sth: *'Why don't you get a car?' 'Well, for one thing, I can't drive!'* **have a ˈthing about sb/ sth** *(informal)* to have a strong like or dislike of sb/sth in a way that seems strange or unreasonable: *She has a thing about men with beards.* **have a ˈthing for sb/sth** *(informal)* to be sexually attracted to sb; to like sth very much: *Liz has always had a thing for guys in bands.* **it isn't my, his, etc. ˈthing** *(informal)* it isn't sth that you really enjoy or are interested in **it's a … thing** *(informal)* it is sth that only a particular group understands: *You wouldn't know what it means*—*it's a girl thing.* **know / tell sb a ˈthing or ˌtwo (about sb/sth)** *(informal)* to know / tell sb some

# thingummy

useful, interesting or surprising information about sb/sth: *She's been married five times, so she knows a thing or two about men!* **make a (big) 'thing of/about sth** (*informal*) to make sth seem more important than it really is **not know, etc. the first thing a'bout sth/sb** to know nothing at all about sth/sb **not ,quite the 'thing 1** not considered socially acceptable: *It wouldn't be quite the thing to turn up in running gear.* **2** (*old-fashioned*) not healthy or normal **(just) one of those 'things** used to say that you do not want to discuss or think about sth bad or unpleasant that has happened, but just accept it: *It wasn't your fault. It was just one of those things.* **one (damned/damn) thing after a'nother** (*informal*) used to complain that a lot of unpleasant things keep happening to you **,one thing leads to a'nother** used to suggest that the way one event or action leads to others is so obvious that it does not need to be stated: *He offered me a ride home one night, and, well, one thing led to another and now we're married!* **there's only ,one thing 'for it** there is only one possible course of action **,these 'things are sent to 'try us** (*saying*) used to say that you should accept an unpleasant situation or event because you cannot change it **the (whole) … thing** (*informal*) a situation or an activity of the type mentioned: *She really didn't want to be involved in the whole family thing.* **the ,thing 'is** (*informal*) used to introduce an important fact, reason or explanation: *I'm sorry my assignment isn't finished. The thing is, I've had a lot of other work this week.* **the ,thing (about/with sth/sb) 'is** used to introduce a problem about sth/sb: *The thing with Karl is, he's always late.* **,things that go ,bump in the 'night** (*informal, humorous*) used to refer to ghosts and other SUPERNATURAL things that cannot be explained **,too 'much of a good thing** used to say that, although sth is pleasant, you do not want to have too much of it ⇒ more at CHANCE *n.*, CLOSE² *adj.*, CLOSE² *adv.*, DAY, DECENT, DONE *adj.*, EASY *adv.*, NATURE, NEAR *adj.*, ONLY *adj.*, OVERDO, PUSH *v.*, REAL *adj.*, SCHEME *n.*, SHAPE *n.*, SURE *adj.*, TURN *v.*, WAY *n.*, WORK *v.*

▼ **VOCABULARY BUILDING**
### Other words for thing

Instead of using the word **thing**, try to use more precise and interesting words, especially in formal written English.
- **aspect**: *That was the most puzzling aspect of the situation.* (…*the most puzzling thing about*…)
- **attribute**: *Curiosity is an essential attribute for a journalist.* (…*an essential thing for a journalist to have.*)
- **characteristic**: *This bird has several interesting characteristics.* (*There are several interesting things about this bird.*)
- **detail**: *I want to know every detail of what happened.* (…*everything about*…)
- **feature**: *Noise is a familiar feature of city life.* (…*a familiar thing in city life.*)
- **issue**: *She has campaigned on many controversial issues.* (…*many controversial things.*)
- **matter**: *We have several important matters to deal with at this meeting.* (…*several important things*…)
- **point**: *That's a very interesting point you made.* (…*a very interesting thing you said.*)
- **subject**: *The book covers a number of subjects.* (…*a number of things.*)
- **topic**: *We discussed a wide range of topics.* (…*a wide range of things.*)
- **trait**: *Her generosity is one of her most attractive traits.* (…*one of the most attractive things about her.*)
- Don't use **thing** after an adjective when the adjective can be used on its own: *Having your own computer is very useful.* ◊ *Having your own computer is a very useful thing.*
- It is often more natural to use words like **something**, **anything**, etc. instead of **thing**: *I have something important to tell you.* ◊ *I have an important thing to tell you.* ◊ *Do you want anything else?* ◊ *Do you want any other thing?*
- It is more natural to say **a lot**, **a great deal**, **much**, etc. rather than **many things**: *I have so much to tell you.* ◊ *I have so many things to tell you.* ◊ *She knows a lot about basketball.* ◊ *She knows many things about basketball.*

▼ **SYNONYMS**
### things

stuff • property • possessions • junk • belongings • goods • valuables

These are all words for objects or items, especially ones that you own or have with you at a particular time.

**things** (*rather informal*) objects, clothing or tools that you own or that are used for a particular purpose: *Shall I help you pack your things?* ◊ *Bring your swimming things.*

**stuff** [U] (*informal*) used to refer to a group of objects when you do not know their names, when the names are not important or when it is obvious what you are talking about: *Where's all my stuff?*

**property** [U] (*rather formal*) a thing or things that are owned by sb: *This building is government property.* ◊ *Be careful not to damage other people's property.*

**possessions** things that you own, especially sth that can be moved: *Prisoners were allowed no personal possessions except letters and photographs.*

**junk** [U] things that are considered useless or of little value: *I've cleared out all that old junk from the attic.*

**belongings** possessions that can be moved, especially ones that you have with you at a particular time: *Please make sure you have all your belongings with you when leaving the plane.*

**goods** (*specialist* or *rather formal*) possessions that can be moved: *He was found guilty of* **handling stolen goods***.*

**valuables** things that are worth a lot of money, especially small personal things such as jewellery or cameras: *Never leave cash or other valuables lying around.*

**PATTERNS**
- **personal** things/stuff/property/possessions/belongings
- to **collect/gather/pack** (up) your things/stuff/possessions/belongings
- to **search** sb's/your/the things/stuff/property/belongings
- to **go through** sb's/your/the things/stuff/belongings

**thing·ummy** /ˈθɪŋəmi/ (also **thingy** /ˈθɪŋi/) *noun* (*pl.* **-ies**) (*informal*) used to refer to a person or thing whose name you do not know or have forgotten, or that you do not want to mention: *It's one of those thingummies for keeping papers together.* ◊ *Is thingummy going to be there? You know, that woman from the Sales Department?*

# think ⓘ A1 /θɪŋk/ *verb*, *noun*

■ **verb** (**thought, thought** /θɔːt/)
- **HAVE OPINION/BELIEF 1** A1 [T, I] (not usually used in the progressive tenses) to have a particular idea or opinion about sth/sb; to believe sth: **~ (that)** … *Do you really think (that) he'll win?* ◊ *I thought I heard a scream.* ◊ *I didn't think people were allowed to park here.* ◊ *Am I right in thinking that you used to live here?* ◊ *I think this is their house, but I'm not sure.* ◊ *He ought to resign, I think.* ◊ *That's my opinion, but you might* **think otherwise** (= have a different opinion). ◊ *We'll need about 20 chairs,* **I should think***.* ◊ *I can't help thinking (that) things could have been different.* ◊ **it is thought that** … *It was once thought that the sun travelled around the earth.* ◊ **~ sth** *Well, I like it. What do you think?* ◊ **~ sth about/of sth** *What did you think about the idea?* ◊ **~ so** *'Is he any good?' 'I don't think so.'* ◊ **~ sb/sth + noun/adj.** *I think it highly unlikely that I'll get the job.* ◊ **be thought to be sb/sth** *He's thought to be one of the richest men in Europe.* ◊ **~ of sb/sth as sb/sth** *I think of this place as my home.* ⇒ EXPRESS YOURSELF at SPECULATE ⇒ LANGUAGE BANK at ACCORDING TO, OPINION ⇒ note at WANT ⇒ see also WELL THOUGHT OF
- **USE MIND 2** A1 [I, T] to use your mind to consider sth, to form connected ideas, to try to solve problems, etc: *Are animals able to think?* ◊ *Let me think* (= give me time before I answer). ◊ *I'm sorry,* **I wasn't thinking** (= said when you have upset or offended sb accidentally). ◊ **~ about sth** *I can't tell you now—I'll have to* **think about it***.* ◊ *The government needs to* **think carefully** *about the issues raised.* ◊ *All he ever thinks about is money.* ◊ **~ what, how, etc** … *He was trying to think what to do.* **3** A1 [T] (usually used in

the progressive tenses) to have ideas, words or images in your mind: **~sth** *You're very quiet. What are you thinking?* ◊ **~what, how, etc** ... *I was just thinking what a long way it is.* ◊ **+ speech** *'I must be crazy,' she thought.*
- **IMAGINE 4** [T, no passive, I] to form an idea of sth; to imagine sth: **~where, how, etc** ... *We couldn't think where you'd gone.* ◊ *Just think how nice it would be to see them again.* ◊ **~(that)** ... *I like to think (that) he would help if I needed it.* ◊ **~(sth)** *If I'm home late, my mother always thinks the worst.* ◊ *Just think—we'll be lying on the beach this time tomorrow.* ◊ *Try to **think yourself into** the role.*
⊃ SYNONYMS at IMAGINE
- **EXPECT 5** [T] to expect sth: **~(that)** ... *I never thought (that) I'd see her again.* ◊ *The job took longer than we thought.* ◊ *You'd think she'd have been grateful for my help (= but she wasn't).* ◊ **~to do sth** (*formal*) *Who would have thought to find you here?*
- **IN A PARTICULAR WAY 6** [I, T] (*informal*) [no passive] to think in a particular way or on a particular subject: **+ adj**. *Let's think positive.* ◊ *You need to **think big** (= aim to achieve a lot).* ◊ **~sth** *If you want to make money, you've got to think money.*
- **SHOWING ANGER/SURPRISE 7** [T] **~(that)** ... used in questions to show that you are angry or surprised: *What do you think you're doing?*
- **BEING LESS DEFINITE/MORE POLITE 8** [T, I] used to make sth you say sound less definite or more polite: **~(that)** ... *I thought we could go out tonight.* ◊ *Twenty guests are enough, I would have thought.* ◊ *Do you **think** you could open the window?* ◊ **so** *'You've made a mistake.' 'I don't think so.'*
- **INTEND 9** [T, I] **~(that ...)** to intend sth; to have a plan about sth: *I think I'll go for a swim.* ◊ *I'm thinking in terms of about 70 guests at the wedding.*
- **REMEMBER 10** [T] to remember sth; to have sth come into your mind: **~to do sth** *I didn't think (= it did not occur to me) to tell her.* ◊ **~where, what, etc** ... *I can't think where I put the keys.*

**IDM** **come to ˈthink of it** used when you suddenly remember sth or realize that it might be important: *Come to think of it, he did mention seeing you.* **I ˈdon't ˈthink so** (*informal*) used to say very strongly that you do not agree with sth, or that sth is not possible: *Me? Fail? I don't think so.* **if/when you ˈthink about it** used to draw attention to a fact that is not obvious or has not previously been mentioned: *It was a difficult situation, when you think about it.* **I ˈthought as much** that is what I expected or suspected: *'He said he'd forgotten.' 'I thought as much.'* **think aˈgain** to consider a situation again and perhaps change your idea or intention **think aˈloud/out ˈloud** to say what your thoughts are as you have them **think (the) ˈbetter of sb** to have a higher opinion of sb: *She has behaved appallingly—I must say I thought better of her.* **think ˈbetter of it/of doing sth** to decide not to do sth after thinking further about it **SYN** **reconsider**: *Rosie was about to protest but thought better of it.* **think for yourˈself** to form your own opinions and make decisions without depending on others **think ˈnothing ˈof it** (*formal*) used as a polite response when sb has said sorry to you or thanked you **think ˈnothing of sth/of doing sth** to consider an activity to be normal and not particularly unusual or difficult: *She thinks nothing of walking thirty miles a day.* **think on your ˈfeet** to be able to think and react to things very quickly and effectively without any preparation **think out of the ˈbox** to think about sth, or how to do sth, in a way that is new, different or shows imagination **ˈthink straight** (used especially in negative sentences) to think in a clear or logical way **think ˈtwice about sth/about doing sth** to think carefully before deciding to do sth: *You should think twice about employing someone you've never met.* **think the ˈworld, ˈhighly, a ˈlot, ˈpoorly, ˈlittle, etc. of sb/sth** to have a very good, poor, etc. opinion of sb/sth: *He thinks the world of his daughter.* ◊ *I don't think much of her idea.* **to ˈthink (that ...)** used to show that you are surprised or shocked by sth: *To think that my mother wrote all those books and I never knew!* ⊃ more at FIT *adj.*, GREAT *adj.*, ILL *adv.*, LET *v.*, LIKE *v.*, OWN *v.*

**PHR V** **ˈthink about/of sb/sth 1** to consider sb/sth when you are doing or planning sth: *Don't you ever think about other people?* **2** to consider doing sth **SYN** **contemplate**: *She's thinking of changing her job.* **ˌthink aˈhead (to sth)** to think about a future event or situation and plan for it **ˌthink ˈback (to sth)** to think about sth that happened in the past: *I keep thinking back to the day I arrived here.* **ˈthink of sth/sb 1** to have an image or idea of sth/sb in your mind: *When I said that I wasn't thinking of anyone in particular.* **2** to create an idea in your imagination: *Can anybody think of a way to raise money?* ◊ *'What shall we do now?' 'I'll think of something.'* ◊ *Have you thought of a name for the baby yet?* **3** [no passive] (used especially with *can*) to remember sth/sb: *I can think of at least three occasions when he arrived late.* ◊ *I can't think of her name at the moment.* **ˈthink of sth** to imagine an actual or a possible situation: *Just think of the expense!* **think of doing sth** *I couldn't think of letting you take the blame (= I would not allow that to happen).* **ˌthink sth ↔ ˈout** to consider or plan sth carefully: *Are you sure you've thought it out properly?* ◊ *It's a very well-thought-out plan.* **ˌthink sth ↔ ˈover** to consider sth carefully, especially before reaching a decision: *He'd like more time to think things over.* **ˌthink sth ↔ ˈthrough** to consider a problem or a possible course of action fully **ˌthink sth ↔ ˈup** (*informal*) to create sth in your mind **SYN** **devise, invent**: *Can't you think up a better excuse than that?*

■ **noun** [sing.] ⊃ compare THOUGHT
**IDM** **have a ˈthink (about sth)** (*informal*) to think carefully about sth in order to make a decision about it: *I'll have a think and let you know tomorrow.* **you've got another ˈthink ˈcoming** (*informal*) used to tell sb that they are wrong about sth and must change their plans or opinions

▼ **SYNONYMS**

**think**
**believe • feel • reckon • be under the impression**
These words all mean to have an idea that sth is true or possible or to have a particular opinion about sb/sth.

**think** to have an idea that sth is true or possible, although you are not completely certain; to have a particular opinion about sb/sth: *Do you think (that) they'll come?* ◊ *Well, I like it. What do you think?*

**believe** to have an idea that sth is true or possible, although you are not completely certain; to have a particular opinion about sb/sth: *Police believe (that) the man may be armed.*

THINK OR BELIEVE?
When you are expressing an idea that you have or that sb has of what is true or possible, **believe** is more formal than **think**. It is used especially for talking about ideas that other people have; **think** is used more often for talking about your own ideas: *Police believe ... ◊ I think ...* When you are expressing an opinion, **believe** is stronger than **think** and is used especially for matters of principle; **think** is used more for practical matters or matters of personal taste.

**feel** to have a particular opinion about sth that has happened or about what you/sb ought to do: *We all felt (that) we were unlucky to lose.*

**reckon** (*informal*) to think that sth is true or possible: *I reckon (that) I'm going to get that job.*

**be under the impression that ...** to have an idea that sth is true: *I was under the impression that the work had already been completed.*

PATTERNS
- to think/believe/feel/reckon/be under the impression that ...
- It is thought/believed/reckoned that ...
- to be thought/believed/felt/reckoned to be sth
- to think/believe/feel sth about sb/sth
- to sincerely/honestly/seriously/mistakenly think/believe/feel

# thinkable

### ▼ EXPRESS YOURSELF
**Asking for somebody's opinion and involving others in a conversation**

In a meeting or a discussion you may need to find out what other people think. In some exams, you have to show that you can control the conversation by asking for contributions from the examiner.
- I would say it's OK in the city, but not in the country. **What do you think?**
- My feeling is that we could improve our performance. **Do you agree with that?**
- **What would you say** if we waited another month?
- **What about you?** Do you cycle?
- Which place **do you think** is more dangerous?
- The traffic's going faster there, **isn't it?/don't you think?**
- **Would you say that** traffic's going faster there?
- So this would be a better option, **right?** (*NAmE, informal*)

**think·able** /ˈθɪŋkəbl/ *adj.* [not before noun] that you can imagine as a possibility: *Such an idea was scarcely thinkable ten years ago.* **OPP** unthinkable

**think·er** /ˈθɪŋkə(r)/ *noun* **1** a person who thinks seriously, and often writes about important things, such as philosophy or science: *Einstein was one of the greatest thinkers of the 20th century.* **2** a person who thinks in a particular way: *a clear thinker*

**think·ing** /ˈθɪŋkɪŋ/ *noun, adj.*
■ *noun* [U] **1** the process of thinking about sth: *I had to do some quick thinking.* ◇ *creative thinking* ◇ see also CRITICAL THINKING, LATERAL THINKING, WISHFUL THINKING **2** ideas or opinions about sth: *What is the current thinking on this question?* ◇ *the ~ behind sth She explained the thinking behind the campaign.* **IDM** see WAY *n.*
■ *adj.* [only before noun] intelligent and able to think seriously about things: *the thinking woman's magazine*

**ˈthinking cap** *noun*
**IDM** **put your ˈthinking cap on** (*informal*) to try to solve a problem by thinking about it

**ˈthink tank** *noun* a group of experts who provide advice and ideas on political, social or economic issues

**thin·ly** /ˈθɪnli/ *adv.* **1** in a way that produces a thin piece or layer of sth: *Slice the potatoes thinly.* **2** with only a few things or people spread over a place so that there is a lot of space between them: *a thinly populated area* **3** in a way that is not sincere or enthusiastic: *She smiled thinly.* **4** in a way that does not hide the truth very well **SYN** *barely*: *The novel is a thinly disguised autobiography.*

**thin·ner** /ˈθɪnə(r)/ *noun* [U, C] a substance that is added to paint, VARNISH, etc. to make it less thick

**thin-ˈskinned** *adj.* **1** easily upset by criticism or offensive remarks **2** (of fruit) having a thin skin **OPP** thick-skinned

**third** /θɜːd/ *NAmE* θɜːrd/ *ordinal number, noun*
■ *ordinal number* 3rd **HELP** There are examples of how to use ordinal numbers at the entry for **fifth**.
**IDM** **third time ˈlucky** (*US* **third time is the ˈcharm**) used when you have failed to do sth twice and hope that you will succeed the third time
■ *noun* **1** each of three equal parts of sth: *He divided the money into thirds.* ◇ *~of sth Over a third of sales were made over the internet.* ◇ LANGUAGE BANK at PROPORTION **2** ~ (in sth) the lowest standard of degree given by a British university ◇ compare FIRST, SECOND¹

**the ˌthird ˈage** *noun* [sing.] (*BrE*) the period of your life between MIDDLE AGE and OLD AGE, when you are still active

**ˌthird ˈbase** *noun* [sing.] (in baseball) the third of the four positions that players must reach in order to score points; the position of the player on the defending team near third base

**ˌthird ˈclass** *noun* **1** [U, sing.] (especially in the past) the cheapest and least comfortable part of a train, ship, etc. **2** [U] (in the US) the class of mail used for sending advertisements, etc. **3** [U, sing.] the lowest standard of HONOURS degree given by a British university

**ˌthird-ˈclass** *adj.* **1** (especially in the past) connected with the cheapest and least comfortable way of travelling on a train, ship, etc. **2** (in the US) connected with the class of mail used to send advertisements, etc. **3** [only before noun] used to describe the lowest standard of degree given by a British university **4** (*disapproving*) (of people) less important than other people: *They are treated as third-class citizens.* ▶ **ˌthird ˈclass** *adv.*: *to travel third class*

**ˌthird deˈgree** *noun* [sing.]
**IDM** **give sb the ˌthird deˈgree** (*informal*) to question sb for a long time and in a careful and detailed way; to use threats or violence to get information from sb

**ˌthird-deˈgree** *adj.* **1** ~ **burns** burns of the most serious kind, affecting TISSUE below the skin **2** (*NAmE*) ~ **murder, assault, robbery, etc.** murder, etc. of the least serious of three kinds ◇ compare FIRST-DEGREE, SECOND-DEGREE

**ˌthird-geneˈration** *adj.* (*abbr.* 3G) used to describe technology that was developed to send data to mobile phones, etc. at much higher speeds than were possible with previous SECOND-GENERATION mobile phone technology

**third·ly** /ˈθɜːdli/ *NAmE* ˈθɜːrd-/ *adv.* used to introduce the third of a list of points you want to make in a speech or piece of writing: *Thirdly, I would like to say that …*

**ˌthird ˈparty** *noun* (*law or formal*) a person who is involved in a situation in addition to the two main people involved

**ˌthird-party inˈsurance** *noun* [U] insurance that COVERS (= protects) you if you injure sb or damage sb's property

**the ˌthird ˈperson** *noun* [sing.] **1** (*grammar*) a set of pronouns and verb forms used by a speaker to refer to other people and things: *'They are'* is the third person plural of the verb 'to be'. **2** a way of writing a novel in which the NARRATOR (= person telling the story) is not involved in the story but knows everything about it and tells the story using third person forms: *in ~ The story is told in the third person.* ◇ compare FIRST PERSON, SECOND PERSON

**ˌthird-ˈrate** *adj.* of very poor quality **SYN** *inferior*: *a third-rate actor*

**the ˌthird ˈsector** *noun* [sing.] (*economics*) the part of an economy or a society that includes organizations that do not belong to the government and do not make a profit: *The forum was aimed at key business leaders from across the private, public and third sectors in the region.* ◇ see also PRIVATE SECTOR, PUBLIC SECTOR

**ˌthird-ˈstring** *adj.* [only before noun] (*NAmE*) (usually of a player on a sports team) only used very occasionally when sb/sth else is not available: *a third-string quarterback*

**ˌthird ˈway** *noun* [sing.] a course of action or political policy that is between two extreme positions

**the ˌThird ˈWorld** *noun* [sing.] a way of referring to the poor or developing countries of Africa, Asia and Latin America, which is sometimes considered offensive: *the causes of poverty and injustice in the Third World* ◇ *Third-World debt* ◇ compare FIRST WORLD

**thirst** /θɜːst/ *NAmE* θɜːrst/ *noun, verb*
■ *noun* **1** [U, sing.] the feeling of needing or wanting a drink: *He quenched his thirst with a long drink of cold water.* ◇ *She woke up with a raging thirst and a headache.* **2** [U] the state of not having enough water to drink: *Thousands are dying of thirst.* **3** [sing.] ~ **(for sth)** a strong desire for sth **SYN** *craving*: *a thirst for knowledge*
■ *verb* [I] (*old use*) to be thirsty
**PHRV** **ˈthirst for sth** (*literary*) to feel a strong desire for sth **SYN** *crave*: *She thirsted for power.*

**thirsty** /ˈθɜːsti/ *NAmE* ˈθɜːrs-/ *adj.* (**thirst·ier**, **thirsti·est**) **1** needing or wanting to drink: *We were hungry and thirsty.* ◇ *Digging is thirsty work* (= makes you thirsty). **2** ~ **for sth** having a strong desire for sth **SYN** *hungry*: *He is thirsty for power.* **3** (of plants, fields, etc.) dry; in need of water ▶ **thirst·ily** /-stɪli/ *adv.*: *Paul drank thirstily.*

**thir·teen** /ˌθɜːˈtiːn; NAmE ˌθɜːrˈt-/ number 13
▶ **thir·teenth** /-ˈtiːnθ/ ordinal number, noun

**thir·teenth cheque** noun (SAfrE) an annual payment equal to one month's salary that is paid at the end of the year

**thirty** /ˈθɜːti; NAmE ˈθɜːrti/ 1 number 30 2 noun **the thirties** [pl.] numbers, years or temperatures from 30 to 39 ▶ **thir·ti·eth** /-əθ/ ordinal number, noun **HELP** There are examples of how to use ordinal numbers at the entry for **fifth**.
**IDM** **in your ˈthirties** between the ages of 30 and 39

**this** /ðɪs/ det., pron., adv.
■ det., pron. (pl. **these** /ðiːz/) 1 used to refer to a particular person, thing or event that is close to you, especially compared with another: *How long have you been living in this country?* ◇ *Well, make up your mind. Which do you want? This one or that one?* ◇ *I think you'll find these more comfortable than those.* ◇ *Is this your bag?* 2 used to refer to sth/sb that has already been mentioned: *There was a court case resulting from this incident.* ◇ *The boy was afraid and the dog had sensed this.* ◇ *What's this I hear about you getting married?* 3 used for introducing sb/yourself: *Hello, this is Carlos Diaz (= on the phone).* ◇ (NAmE) *Is this Maria? (= on the phone)* ◇ (BrE) *Is that Maria?* ◇ *Jo, this is Kate (= when you are introducing them).* ◇ *This is the captain speaking.* 4 used for showing sb to sth or calling sb's attention to sth: *Do it like this (= in the way I am showing you).* ◇ *Listen to this.* 5 used with periods of time related to the present: *this week/month/year* ◇ *I saw her this morning (= today in the morning).* ◇ *Do you want me to come this Tuesday (= Tuesday of this week) or next Tuesday?* ◇ *Do it this minute (= now).* ◇ *He never comes to see me these days (= now, as compared with the past).* 6 ~ **sth of sb's** (informal) used to refer to sb/sth that is connected with a person, especially when you have a particular attitude towards it or them: *These new friends of hers are supposed to be very rich.* 7 (informal) used when you are telling a story or telling sb about sth: *There was this strange man sitting next to me on the plane.* ◇ *I've been getting these pains in my chest.*
**IDM** ˌthis and ˈthat | ˌthis, ˈthat and the ˈother (informal) various things or activities: *'What did you talk about?' 'Oh, this and that.'*
■ adv. to this degree; so: *It's about this high (= as high as I am showing you with my hands).* ◇ *I didn't think we'd get this far.*

**this·tle** /ˈθɪsl/ noun a wild plant with leaves with sharp points and purple, yellow or white flowers made up of a mass of narrow PETALS pointing upwards. The thistle is the national symbol of Scotland. ⊃ VISUAL VOCAB page V7

**thistle·down** /ˈθɪsldaʊn/ noun [U] a very light, soft substance that contains thistle seeds and is blown from thistle plants by the wind

**thith·er** /ˈðɪðə(r)/ adv. (old use) to or towards that place
**IDM** see HITHER

**tho'** /ðəʊ/ adv. an informal spelling of 'though'

**thong** /θɒŋ/ noun 1 a narrow piece of leather that is used to fasten sth or as a WHIP 2 a pair of women's KNICKERS or men's UNDERPANTS that has only a very narrow piece of cloth, like a string, at the back 3 (NAmE, AustralE, NZE) = FLIP-FLOP

**thorax** /ˈθɔːræks/ noun (pl. **thor·axes** or **thor·aces** /-rəsiːz/) 1 (anatomy) the part of the body that is surrounded by the RIBS, between the neck and the WAIST 2 the middle section of an insect's body, to which the legs and wings are attached ⊃ VISUAL VOCAB page V3 ▶ **thor·acic** /θɔːˈræsɪk/ adj. [only before noun]

**thor·ium** /ˈθɔːriəm/ noun [U] (symb. **Th**) a chemical element. Thorium is a white RADIOACTIVE metal used as a source of nuclear energy.

**thorn** /θɔːn; NAmE θɔːrn/ noun 1 a small sharp, pointed part on the STEM of some plants, such as ROSES ⊃ VISUAL VOCAB page V7 2 a tree or bush that has thorns ⊃ see also BLACKTHORN, HAWTHORN 3 the letter that was used in Old English and Icelandic to represent the sounds /θ/ and /ð/ and later written as *th*

---

1631 **thought**

**IDM** **a thorn in sb's ˈflesh/ˈside** a person or thing that repeatedly annoys sb or stops them from doing sth

**thorny** /ˈθɔːni; NAmE ˈθɔːrni/ adj. (**thorn·ier**, **thorni·est**) 1 [usually before noun] causing difficulty or DISAGREEMENT **SYN** **knotty**: *a thorny question/issue/problem* 2 having thorns: *a thorny bush*

**thor·ough** /ˈθʌrə; NAmE ˈθɜːrəʊ/ adj. 1 done completely; with great attention to detail: *a thorough knowledge of the subject* ◇ *The police carried out a thorough investigation.* 2 [not usually before noun] (of a person) doing things very carefully and with great attention to detail: *She's very thorough and conscientious.* 3 (BrE, informal) used to emphasize how bad or annoying sb/sth is **SYN** **complete**: *Everything was in a thorough mess.* ▶ **thor·ough·ness** noun [U]: *I was impressed by the thoroughness of the report.* ◇ *I admire his thoroughness.*

**thor·ough·bred** /ˈθʌrəbred; NAmE ˈθɜːrəʊb-/ noun an animal, especially a horse, of high quality, that has parents that are both of the same type ⊃ WORDFINDER NOTE at HORSE
▶ **thor·ough·bred** adj.: *a thoroughbred mare*

**thor·ough·fare** /ˈθʌrəfeə(r); NAmE ˈθɜːrəʊfer/ noun a public road or street used by traffic, especially a main road in a city or town

**thor·ough·going** /ˌθʌrəˈɡəʊɪŋ; NAmE ˌθɜːrəʊˈɡ-/ adj. [only before noun] 1 very careful and complete; looking at every detail: *a thoroughgoing revision of the text* 2 complete: *a thoroughgoing commitment to change*

**thor·ough·ly** /ˈθʌrəli; NAmE ˈθɜːrə-/ adv. 1 very much; completely: *We thoroughly enjoyed ourselves.* ◇ *I'm thoroughly confused.* ◇ *a thoroughly professional performance* 2 completely and with great attention to detail: *Wash the fruit thoroughly before use.* ◇ *The work had not been done very thoroughly.*

**those** /ðəʊz/ ⊃ THAT det.

**thou** /ðaʊ/ pron. (old use or dialect) a word meaning 'you', used when talking to only one person who is the subject of the verb ⊃ compare THEE

**though** /ðəʊ/ conj., adv.
■ conj. 1 despite the fact that **SYN** **although**: *Anne was fond of Tim, though he often annoyed her.* ◇ *Though she gave no sign, I was sure she had seen me.* ◇ *His clothes, though old and worn, looked clean and of good quality.* ◇ *Strange though it may sound, I was pleased it was over.* 2 used to add a fact or an opinion that makes the previous statement less strong or less important: *They're very different, though they did seem to get on well when they met.* ◇ *He'll probably say no, though it's worth asking.* ⊃ note at ALTHOUGH **IDM** see as *conj.*, EVEN adv.
■ adv. used especially at the end of a sentence or clause to add a fact or an opinion that makes the previous statement less strong or less important: *Our team lost. It was a good game though.* ◇ *'Have you ever been to Australia?' 'No. I'd like to, though.'* ⊃ note at ALTHOUGH

**thought** /θɔːt/ noun
• STH YOU THINK 1 [C] something that you think of or remember: *~ of doing sth I couldn't bear the thought of waiting any longer.* ◇ *~ of sth/sb (doing sth) The very thought of it makes me feel sick.* ◇ *~ (that) ... She was struck by the sudden thought that he might already have left.* ◇ *~ on/about sth Thank you for sharing your thoughts on this topic.* ◇ *I've just had a thought (= an idea).* ◇ *Would Mark be able to help? It's just a thought.* ◇ *'Why don't you try the other key?' 'That's a thought!'*
• MIND/IDEAS 2 **thoughts** [pl.] a person's mind and all the ideas that they have in it when they are thinking: *This is the time of year when our thoughts turn to summer holidays.* ◇ **in sb's thoughts** *You are always in my thoughts.*
• PROCESS/ACT OF THINKING 3 [U] the act of thinking seriously and carefully about sth **consideration**: *I've given the matter careful thought.* ◇ *We need to put some thought into how to solve this problem.* 4 [U] the power or process of thinking: *A good teacher encourages independence of thought.* ◇ *She was lost in thought (= concentrating*

# thoughtful

so much on her thoughts that she was not aware of her surroundings).
- **CARE/WORRY** **5** [C] ~ (for sb/sth) a feeling of care or worry: *Spare a thought for those without enough to eat this winter.* ◊ ***Don't give it another thought*** (= to tell sb not to worry after they have said they are sorry). ◊ *It's the thought that counts* (= used to say that sb has been very kind even if they have only done or given sth small or unimportant).
- **INTENTION** **6** [U, C] an intention or a hope of doing sth: ~ (of doing sth) *She had given up all thought of changing her job.* ◊ ~ (of sth) *He acted with no thoughts of personal gain.*
- **IN POLITICS/SCIENCE, ETC.** **7** [U] ideas in politics, science, etc. connected with a particular person, group or period of history: *feminist thought* ⊃ see also THINK *noun*

**IDM** **have ˌsecond ˈthoughts** to change your opinion after thinking about sth again **on ˈsecond thoughts** (*BrE*) (*NAmE* **on ˈsecond thought**) used to say that you have changed your opinion: *I'll wait here. No, on second thoughts, I'll come with you.* **without a second ˈthought** immediately; without stopping to think about sth further: *He dived in after her without a second thought.* ⊃ more at COLLECT *v.*, FOOD, PAUSE *n.*, PENNY, PERISH, SCHOOL *n.*, TRAIN *n.*, WISH *n.*

**thoughtˑful** /ˈθɔːtfl/ *adj.* **1** quiet, because you are thinking: *He looked thoughtful.* ◊ *They sat in thoughtful silence.* **2** ~ (of sb) (to do sth) (*approving*) showing that you think about and care for other people **SYN** **conˑsiderate, kind**: *It was very thoughtful of you to send the flowers.* **3** showing signs of careful thought: *a player who has a thoughtful approach to the game* ▸ **thoughtˈfulˑly** /-fəli/ *adv.*: *Martin looked at her thoughtfully.* ◊ *She used the towel thoughtfully provided by her host.* **thoughtˈfulˑness** *noun* [U]

**ˈthought leader** *noun* a person whose views on a subject are important and have a strong influence: *She is one of the key thought leaders in our business.*

**ˈthought leadership** *noun* [U] the practice of developing important new ways of thinking that influence others: *This company provides thought leadership and innovation in the area of alternative energy.*

**thoughtˑless** /ˈθɔːtləs/ *adj.* (*disapproving*) not caring about the possible effects of your words or actions on other people **SYN** **inconsiderate**: *a thoughtless remark* ▸ **thoughtˈlessˑly** *adv.* **thoughtˈlessˑness** *noun* [U]

**ˈthought police** *noun* [pl.] a group of people who are seen as trying to control people's ideas and stop them from having their own opinions

**ˈthought-provokˑing** *adj.* making people think seriously about a particular subject or issue: *a brilliant and thought-provoking play*

**thouˑsand** /ˈθaʊznd/ *number* (*abbr.* **K**) **1** 1000 **HELP** You say **a, one, two, etc. thousand** without a final 's' on 'thousand'. **Thousands (of …)** can be used if there is no number or quantity before it. Always use a plural verb with **thousand** or **thousands**, except when an amount of money is mentioned: *Four thousand (people) are expected to attend.* ◊ *Two thousand (pounds) was withdrawn from the account.* **2 a thousand** or **thousands (of …)** (*usually informal*) a large number: *There were thousands of people there.* **3 the thousands** the numbers from 1000 to 9999: *The cost ran into the thousands.* **HELP** There are more examples of how to use numbers at the entry for **hundred**. **IDM** see BAT *v.*

**thouˑsandth** /ˈθaʊznθ/ *ordinal number, noun*
- *ordinal number* 1000th: *the city's thousandth anniversary*
- *noun* each of one thousand parts of sth: *a/one thousandth of a second*

**thrall** /θrɔːl/ *noun*
**IDM** **in (sb's/sth's) ˈthrall** | **in ˈthrall to sb/sth** (*literary*) controlled or strongly influenced by sb/sth

**thrash** /θræʃ/ *verb, noun*
- *verb* **1** [T] ~ **sb/sth** to hit a person or an animal many times with a stick, etc. as a punishment **SYN** **beat** **2** [I, T] to move or make sth move in a way that is violent or shows

a loss of control: ~ **(about/around)** *Someone was thrashing around in the water, obviously in trouble.* ◊ ~ **sth (about/around)** *A whale was thrashing the water with its tail.* ◊ *She thrashed her head from side to side.* **3** [T] ~ **sb/sth** (*informal, especially BrE*) to defeat sb very easily in a game: *Scotland thrashed England 5–1.* ⊃ compare WHIP
**PHR V** **thrash sth↔ˈout** (*informal*) to discuss a situation or problem carefully and completely in order to decide sth
- *noun* **1** a type of loud rock music **2** [C] (*old-fashioned, informal*) a party with music and dancing

**thrashˑing** /ˈθræʃɪŋ/ *noun* **1** an act of hitting a person or an animal very hard, especially with a stick: *to give sb/get a thrashing* **2** (*informal*) a severe defeat in a game

**thread** /θred/ *noun, verb*
- *noun* **1** [U, C] a thin string of cotton, wool, silk, etc. used for SEWING or making cloth: *a needle and thread* ◊ *a robe embroidered with gold thread* ◊ *the delicate threads of a spider's web* ⊃ picture at ROPE ⊃ WORDFINDER NOTE at SEW **2** [C] an idea or a feature that is part of sth greater; an idea that connects the different parts of sth: *A common thread runs through these discussions.* ◊ *The author skilfully draws together the different threads of the plot.* ◊ *I lost the thread of the argument* (= I could no longer follow it). **3** [C] ~ **(of sth)** a long, thin line of sth: *A thread of light emerged from the keyhole.* **4** [C] (*computing*) a series of connected messages on email, social media, etc. that have been sent by different people **5** [C] the raised line that runs around the length of a SCREW and that allows it to be fixed in place by TWISTING ⊃ picture at NAIL **6 threads** [pl.] (*NAmE, old-fashioned, informal*) clothes **IDM** see HANG *v.*, PICK *v.*
- *verb* **1** [T] ~ **sth (+ adv./prep.)** to pass sth long and thin, especially thread, through a narrow opening or hole: *to thread a needle (with cotton)* ◊ *to thread cotton through a needle* ◊ *A tiny wire is threaded through a vein to the heart.* **2** [I, T] to move or make sth move through a narrow space, avoiding things that are in the way **SYN** **pick your way**: + **adv./prep.** *The waiters threaded between the crowded tables.* ◊ ~ **your way + adv./prep.** *It took me a long time to thread my way through the crowd.* **3** [T] ~ **sth (onto sth)** to join two or more objects together by passing sth long and thin through them: *to thread beads (onto a string)* **4** [T] ~ **sth** to pass film, tape, string, etc. through parts of a piece of equipment so that it is ready to use **5** [T, usually passive] ~ **sth (with sth)** to SEW or TWIST a particular type of thread into sth: *a robe threaded with gold and silver*

**threadˑbare** /ˈθredbeə(r); *NAmE* -ber/ *adj.* **1** (of cloth, clothing, etc.) old and thin because it has been used a lot: *a threadbare carpet* **2** (of an argument, excuse, etc.) that does not have much effect, especially because it has been used too much

**threadˑed** /ˈθredɪd/ *adj.* (*specialist*) (of a SCREW, etc.) having a THREAD (5)

**threadˑworm** /ˈθredwɜːm; *NAmE* -wɜːrm/ *noun* a small, thin WORM that lives in the INTESTINES of humans and animals

**threat** /θret/ *noun* **1** [C, U] a statement in which you tell sb that you will punish or harm them, especially if they do not do what you want: ~ **against sb/sth** *to make threats against sb* ◊ ~ **to do sth** *She is prepared to carry out her threat to resign.* ◊ *He received death threats from right-wing groups.* **2** ~ **of sth** crimes involving violence or the threat of violence **2** [U, C, usually sing.] the possibility of trouble, danger or disaster: **under ~ (from sb/sth)** *These ancient woodlands are under threat from new road developments.* ◊ ~ **of sth** *There is a real threat of war.* **3** [C, usually sing.] a person or thing that is likely to cause trouble, danger, etc.: **to sb/sth** *Drugs pose a major threat to our society.* ◊ *We're facing a very strong terrorist threat.*

**threatˑen** /ˈθretn/ *verb* [T] to say that you will cause trouble, hurt sb, etc. if you do not get what you want: ~ **sb/sth** *They broke my windows and threatened me.* ◊ ~ **sb with sth** *The attacker threatened them with a gun.* ◊ ~ **sth** *The threatened strike has been called off.* ◊ ~ **to do sth** *The hijackers threatened to kill one passenger every hour if their demands were not met.* ◊ ~ **that …** *They* *threatened that passengers would be killed.* ◊ ~ + **speech** '*I'm going to kill him!*' *she threatened.* **2** [I, T] to seem likely to happen or cause sth unpleasant: *A storm was threatening.* ◊ **~ to do sth** *This dispute threatens to split the party.* ◊ **~ sth** *The clouds threatened rain.* ◊ **~ sth with sth** *Many species are now threatened with extinction.* **3** [T] **~ sth** to be a danger to sth **SYN** **endanger, at risk**: *Pollution is threatening marine life.*

**threat·en·ing** /ˈθretnɪŋ/ *adj.* **1** expressing a threat of harm or violence **SYN** **menacing**: *threatening letters* ◊ *threatening behaviour* **2** (of the sky, clouds, etc.) showing that bad weather is likely: *The sky was dark and threatening.* ▸ **threat·en·ing·ly** *adv.*: *He glared at her threateningly.*

**three** ⓘ A1 /θriː/ *number* 3 HELP There are examples of how to use numbers at the entry for **five**.
IDM **the three ˈRs** (*old-fashioned*) reading, writing and ARITHMETIC, thought to be the most important parts of a child's education ⇒ more at **TWO**

**ˌthree-ˈcornered** *adj.* [usually before noun] **1** having three corners: *a three-cornered hat* **2** involving three people or groups: *a three-cornered contest*

**ˌthree-ˈD** (*also* **3D**) *noun* [U] the quality of having, or appearing to have, length, WIDTH and depth (= three DIMENSIONS): *These glasses allow you to see the film in three-D.* ▸ **ˌthree-ˈD** (*also* **3D**) *adj.*: *a three-D image*

**ˈthree-day eˈventing** *noun* [U] = EVENTING

**ˌthree-diˈmensional** *adj.* having, or appearing to have, length, WIDTH and depth: *three-dimensional objects*

**three·fold** /ˈθriːfəʊld/ *adj., adv.* ⇒ -FOLD

**three ˈfourths** *noun* [pl.] (*US*) = THREE QUARTERS

**ˌthree-ˈpeat** *noun* (*NAmE, informal*) (used especially in newspapers) an occasion when a person or team wins a competition for the third time, especially in sport ▸ **ˌthree-ˈpeat** *verb* [I]

**ˌthree-ˈpiece** *adj.* [only before noun] consisting of three separate parts or pieces: *a three-piece suit* (= a set of clothes consisting of trousers, a jacket and a WAISTCOAT) ◊ (*BrE*) *a three-piece suite* (= a set of three pieces of furniture, usually a SOFA and two ARMCHAIRS)

**ˌthree-point ˈturn** *noun* a method of turning a car in a small space so that it faces in the opposite direction, by driving forwards, then backwards, then forwards again, in a series of curves

**ˌthree-ˈquarter** *adj.* [only before noun] used to describe sth that is three quarters of the usual size: *a three-quarter length coat*

**three ˈquarters** (*US also* **three ˈfourths**) *noun* **~ (of sth)** three of the four equal parts into which sth may be divided: *three quarters of an hour*

**three·some** /ˈθriːsəm/ *noun* **1** [C + sing./pl. v.] a group of three people **2** [C] an occasion when three people have sex together

**ˈthree-star** *adj.* [usually before noun] **1** having three stars in a system that measures quality. The highest standard is usually represented by four or five stars: *a three-star hotel* **2** (in the US) having the third-highest military rank, and wearing uniform that has three stars on it: *a three-star general*

**ˌthree-ˈway** *adj.* [only before noun] happening or working in three ways or directions, or between three people: *a three-way switch* ◊ *a three-way discussion*

**thresh** /θreʃ/ *verb* **1** [T] **~ sth** to separate grains of rice, WHEAT, etc. from the rest of the plant using a machine or, especially in the past, by hitting it with a special tool **2** [I, T] **~ (sth)** to move or make sth move in a way that is violent or shows a loss of control **SYN** **thrash** ▸ **thresh·ing** *noun* [U]: *a threshing machine*

**thresh·old** /ˈθreʃhəʊld/ *noun* **1** the floor or ground at the bottom of a DOORWAY, considered as the entrance to a building or room: *He stepped across the threshold.* ◊ **on the ~** *She stood hesitating on the threshold.* **2** the level at which sth starts to happen or have an effect: *He has a low boredom threshold* (= he gets bored easily). ◊ *I have a high pain threshold* (= I can suffer a lot of pain before I start to react). ◊ *My earnings are just above the tax threshold* (= more than the amount at which you start paying tax). **3** [usually sing.] the point just before a new situation, period of life, etc. begins: **on the ~ of sth** *She felt as though she was on the threshold of a new life.*

**threw** /θruː/ *past tense* of **THROW** ⇒ **HOMOPHONES** at **THROUGH**

**thrice** /θraɪs/ *adv.* (*old use or formal*) three times

**thrift** /θrɪft/ *noun* [U] **1** (*approving*) the habit of saving money and spending it carefully so that none is wasted ⇒ see also **SPENDTHRIFT** **2** a wild plant with bright pink flowers that grows by the sea

**ˈthrift shop** (*also* **ˈthrift store**) (*both NAmE*) (*BrE* **ˈcharity shop**) *noun* a shop that sells clothes and other goods given by people to raise money for a charity

**thrifty** /ˈθrɪfti/ *adj.* (*approving*) careful about spending money and not wasting things **SYN** **frugal**

**thrill** /θrɪl/ *noun, verb*
■ *noun* **1** a strong feeling of excitement or pleasure; an experience that gives you this feeling: **~ (to do sth)** *It gave me a big thrill to meet my favourite author in person.* ◊ **~ (of doing sth)** *the thrill of catching a really big fish* ◊ *She gets an obvious thrill out of performing.* ⇒ **WORDFINDER NOTE** at **ADVENTURE** **2** a sudden, strong feeling that produces a physical effect: *A thrill of alarm ran through him.*
IDM **(the) thrills and ˈspills** (*informal*) the excitement that is involved in dangerous activities, especially sports
■ *verb* **~ sb** to cause sb to feel very pleased or excited: *This band has thrilled audiences all over the world.* ◊ *I was thrilled by your news.*
PHRV **ˈthrill to sth** (*formal*) to feel very excited at sth

**thrilled** /θrɪld/ *adj.* very excited and pleased: '*Are you pleased?*' '*I'm thrilled.*' ◊ **~ about/at/with sth** *He was thrilled at the prospect of seeing them again.* ◊ **~ to do sth** *I was thrilled to be invited.* ◊ **~ that …** (*BrE*) *She was thrilled to bits* (= extremely pleased) *that he'd been offered the job.* ⇒ **SYNONYMS** at **GLAD**

**thrill·er** /ˈθrɪlə(r)/ *noun* a book, play or film with an exciting story, especially one about crime or SPYING

**thrill·ing** /ˈθrɪlɪŋ/ *adj.* exciting and a lot of fun: *a thrilling experience/finish* ⇒ **SYNONYMS** at **EXCITING** ▸ **thrill·ing·ly** *adv.*

**ˈthrill ride** *noun* a ride at an AMUSEMENT PARK that makes you feel very excited and frightened at the same time

**thrive** /θraɪv/ *verb* [I] to become, and continue to be, successful, strong, healthy, etc. **SYN** **flourish**: *New businesses thrive in this area.* ◊ *These animals rarely thrive in captivity.* ▸ **thriv·ing** *adj.*: *a thriving industry*
PHRV **ˈthrive on sth** to enjoy sth or be successful at sth, especially sth that other people would not like: *He thrives on hard work.*

**throat** ⓘ B1 /θrəʊt/ *noun* **1** a passage in the neck through which food and air pass on their way into the body; the front part of the neck: *a sore throat* ◊ *A sob caught in his throat.* ◊ *He held the knife to her throat.* ◊ *Their throats had been cut.* ⇒ see also **STREP THROAT** **2 -throated** (in adjectives) having the colour of throat mentioned; making a sound in the **throat** of the type mentioned: *a blue-throated macaw* ◊ *a deep-throated roar* ⇒ see also **CUT-THROAT**
IDM **be at each other's ˈthroats** (*informal*) (of two or more people, groups, etc.) to be fighting or arguing with each other **cut your own ˈthroat** to do sth that is likely to harm you, especially when you are angry and trying to harm sb else **force/thrust/ram sth down sb's ˈthroat** (*informal*) to try to force sb to listen to and accept your opinions in a way that they find annoying ⇒ more at **CLEAR** *v.*, **FROG**, **JUMP** *v.*, **LUMP** *n.*, **STICK** *v.*

**throaty** /ˈθrəʊti/ *adj.* sounding low and rough: *a throaty laugh* ◊ *the throaty roar of the engines* ▸ **throat·ily** /-tɪli/ *adv.*

# throb

**throb** /θrɒb; NAmE θrɑːb/ verb, noun
- **verb** (**-bb-**) **1** [I] ~ (with sth) (of a part of the body) to feel a series of regular painful movements: *His head throbbed painfully.* ◊ *My feet were throbbing after the long walk home.* ⊃ SYNONYMS at HURT **2** [I] to beat or sound with a strong, regular rhythm **SYN** **pulsate**: *The ship's engines throbbed quietly.* ◊ *a throbbing drumbeat* ◊ *The blood was throbbing in my veins.* ◊ ~ with sth (*figurative*) *His voice was throbbing with emotion.*
- **noun** (*also* **throb·bing**) **1** [sing.] a feeling of pain that you experience as a series of strong beats: *My headache faded to a dull throb.* **2** [C, usually sing.] a strong, regular beat: *the throb of the machines* ⊃ see also HEART-THROB

**throes** /θrəʊz/ noun [pl.] violent pains, especially at the moment of death: *The creature went into its death throes.*
**IDM** **in the throes of sth / of doing sth** in the middle of an activity, especially a difficult or complicated one: *The country was in the throes of revolutionary change.*

**throm·bosis** /θrɒmˈbəʊsɪs/ NAmE θrɑːm-/ noun [C, U] (*pl.* **throm·boses** /-ˈbəʊsiːz/) (*medical*) a serious condition caused by a blood CLOT (= a thick mass of blood) forming in a blood VESSEL (= tube) or in the heart ⊃ see also CORONARY THROMBOSIS, DEEP VEIN THROMBOSIS

**throne** /θrəʊn/ noun **1** [C] a special chair used by a king or queen to sit on at ceremonies **2 the throne** [sing.] the position of being a king or queen: *Queen Elizabeth came/succeeded to the throne in 1952.* ◊ **on the~** *when Henry VIII was on the throne* (= was king) ⊃ WORDFINDER NOTE at KING
**IDM** see POWER *n.*

**throng** /θrɒŋ; NAmE θrɔːŋ/ noun, verb
- **noun** (*literary*) a crowd of people: *We pushed our way through the throng.*
- **verb** [I, T] (*literary*) to go somewhere or be present somewhere in large numbers: + **adv./prep.** *The children thronged into the hall.* ◊ **~ to do sth** *People are thronging to see his new play.* ◊ **~ sth** *Crowds thronged the stores.*
**PHRV** **ˈthrong with sb/sth | be ˈthronged with sb/sth** to be full of people, cars, etc: *The cafes were thronging with students.* ◊ *The streets were thronged with people.*

**throt·tle** /ˈθrɒtl; NAmE ˈθrɑːtl/ verb, noun
- **verb** ~ sb to attack or kill sb by pressing their throat in order to stop them from breathing **SYN** **strangle**: *He throttled the guard with his bare hands.* ◊ (*humorous*) *I like her, although I could cheerfully throttle her at times* (= because she is annoying). ◊ (*figurative*) *The city is being throttled by traffic.*
**PHRV** **ˌthrottle (sth) ˈback/ˈdown/ˈup** to control the supply of fuel or power to an engine in order to reduce/increase the speed of a vehicle: *I throttled back as we approached the runway.*
- **noun** a device that controls the amount of fuel that goes into the engine of a vehicle, for example the ACCELERATOR in a car
**IDM** **at full ˈthrottle** as fast as possible; with as much power or energy as possible: *He drove along at full throttle.* ◊ *The campaign is continuing to run at full throttle.*

**through** /θruː/ prep., adv., adj.
- **prep. HELP** For the special uses of **through** in phrasal verbs, look at the entries for the verbs. For example **get through sth** is in the phrasal verb section at **get**. **1** from one end or side of sth/sb to the other: *The burglar got in through the window.* ◊ *The bullet went straight through him.* ◊ *Her knees had gone through* (= made holes in) *her jeans.* ◊ *The sand ran through* (= between) *my fingers.* ◊ *The path led through the trees to the river.* ◊ *The doctor pushed his way through the crowd.* ◊ *The Charles River flows through Boston.* ◊ *The flood was too deep to drive through.* **2** **see, hear, etc. ~ sth** to see, hear, etc. sth from the other side of an object or a substance: *I couldn't hear their conversation through the wall.* ◊ *He could just make out three people through the mist.* **3** from the beginning to the end of an activity, a situation or a period of time: *The children are too young to sit through a concert.* ◊ *He will not live through the night.* ◊ *I'm halfway through* (= reading) *her second novel.* **4** past a barrier, stage or test: *Go through this gate, and you'll see the house on your left.* ◊ *He drove through a red light* (= passed it when he should have stopped). ◊ *First I have to get through the exams.* ◊ *The bill had a difficult passage through Parliament.* ◊ *I'd never have got through it all* (= a difficult situation) *without you.* **5** (*also informal* **thru**) (*both NAmE*) until, and including: *We'll be in New York Tuesday through Friday.* ⊃ note at INCLUSIVE **6** by means of; because of: *You can only achieve success through hard work.* ◊ *It was through him* (= as a result of his help) *that I got the job.* ◊ *The accident happened through no fault of mine.*
- **adv. HELP** For the special uses of **through** in phrasal verbs, look at the entries for the verbs. For example **carry sth through** is in the phrasal verb section at **carry**. **1** from one end or side of sth to the other: *Put the coffee in the filter and let the water run through.* ◊ *The tyre's flat—the nail has gone right through.* ◊ *The onlookers stood aside to let the paramedics through.* **2** from the beginning to the end of a thing or period of time: *Don't tell me how it ends—I haven't read it all the way through yet.* ◊ *I expect I'll struggle through until payday.* **3** past a barrier, stage or test: *The lights were red but he drove straight through.* ◊ *Our team is through to* (= has reached) *the semi-finals.* **4** travelling through a place without stopping or without people having to get off one train and onto another: '*Did you stop in Oxford on the way?*' '*No, we drove straight through.*' ◊ *This train goes straight through to York.* **5** connected by phone: *Ask to be put through to me personally.* ◊ *I tried to call you but I couldn't get through.* **6** used after an adjective to mean 'completely': *We got wet through.*
**IDM** **through and ˈthrough** completely; in every way: *He's British through and through.*
- **adj. 1** [only before noun] **through** traffic travels from one side of a place to the other without stopping **2** [only before noun] a **through** train takes you to the final place you want to get to and you do not have to get off and get on another train **3** [only before noun] a **through** road or route is open at both ends and allows traffic to travel from one end to the other: *The village lies on a busy through road.* ◊ **No through road** (= the road is closed at one end). **4** [not before noun] **~(with sth/sb)** (*especially NAmE*) used to show that you have finished using sth or have ended a relationship with sb: *Are you through with that newspaper?* ◊ *Todd and I are through.*

▼ HOMOPHONES

**threw** • **through** /θruː/
- **threw** *verb* (*past tense of* THROW): *He threw a stone at the window.*
- **through** *prep.*: *Just go through this tunnel and then it's on the right.*
- **through** *adv.*: *You can do it—you're three-quarters of the way through already!*
- **through** *adj.*: *It's not a through road so it's quite quiet.*

**through·out** /θruːˈaʊt/ prep., adv. **1** in or into every part of sth: *They export their products to markets throughout the world.* ◊ *The house was painted white throughout.* **2** during the whole period of time of sth: *The museum is open daily throughout the year.* ◊ *The ceremony lasted two hours and we had to stand throughout.*

**through·put** /ˈθruːpʊt/ noun [U, C, usually sing.] (*specialist*) the amount of work that is done, or the number of people that are dealt with, in a particular period of time

**through·way** = THRUWAY

**throw** /θrəʊ/ verb, noun
- **verb** (**threw** /θruː/, **thrown** /θrəʊn/)
- • WITH HAND **1** [T, I] to send sth from your hand through the air by moving your hand or arm quickly: *Practise throwing and catching.* ◊ **~ sth** *Who threw that rock?* ◊ **~ sth + adv./prep.** *Stop throwing stones at the window!* ◊ **~ sth to sb** *Don't throw it to him; give it to him!* ◊ **~ sb sth** *Can you throw me that towel?* ⊃ HOMOPHONES at THROUGH
- • PUT CARELESSLY **2** [T] **~ sth + adv./prep.** to put sth in a particular place quickly and carelessly: *Just throw your bag down over there.*

- **MOVE WITH FORCE** 3 ⟨B1⟩ [T] to move sth/sb suddenly and with force: ~ **sth/sb + adv./prep.** *The boat was thrown onto the rocks.* ◊ ~ **sth/sb + adj.** *I threw open the windows to let the smoke out.*
- **PART OF BODY** 4 ⟨B1⟩ [T] ~ **sth/yourself + adv./prep.** to move your body or part of it quickly or suddenly: *He threw back his head and roared with laughter.* ◊ *I ran up and threw my arms around him.* ◊ *Jenny threw herself onto the bed.*
- **MAKE SB FALL** 5 [T] ~ **sb** to make sb fall quickly or violently to the ground: *Two riders were thrown* (= off their horses) *in the second race.*
- **INTO PARTICULAR STATE** 6 [T, usually passive] to make sb/sth be in a particular state: **be thrown out of sth** *Hundreds were thrown out of work.* ◊ **be thrown into sth** *The future of the project has been thrown into doubt.*
- **DIRECT STH AT SB/STH** 7 [T] ~ **sth on/at sb/sth** to direct sth at sb/sth: *to throw doubt on the verdict* ◊ *to throw the blame on someone* ◊ *to throw accusations at someone* ◊ *He threw the question back at me* (= expected me to answer it myself).
- **UPSET** 8 [T] ~ **sb** (*informal*) to make sb feel upset, confused, or surprised: *The news of her death really threw me.*
- **DICE** 9 [T] ~ **sth** to roll a DICE or let it fall after shaking it; to obtain a particular number in this way: *Throw the dice!* ◊ *He threw three sixes in a row.*
- **CLAY POT** 10 [T] ~ **sth** (*specialist*) to make a CLAY pot, dish, etc. on a POTTER'S WHEEL: *a hand-thrown vase*
- **LIGHT/SHADE** 11 [T] ~ **sth (+ adv./prep.)** to send light or shade onto sth: *The trees threw long shadows across the lawn.*
- **YOUR VOICE** 12 [T] ~ **your voice** to make your voice sound as if it is coming from another person or place ⟨SYN⟩ **project**
- **A PUNCH** 13 [T] ~ **a punch** to hit sb with your FIST
- **SWITCH/HANDLE** 14 [T] ~ **a switch** to move a switch to operate sth
- **ANGRY BEHAVIOUR** 15 [T] ~ **sth** to have a sudden period of angry behaviour, violent emotion, etc.: *She'll throw a fit if she finds out.* ◊ *Children often throw tantrums at this age.*
- **A PARTY** 16 [T] ~ **a party** (*informal*) to give a party
- **IN SPORTS/COMPETITIONS** 17 [T] ~ **sth** (*informal*) to deliberately lose a game or contest that you should have won: *He was accused of having thrown the game.* ⟨HELP⟩ Idioms containing **throw** are at the entries for the nouns and adjectives in the idioms, for example **throw your hat into the ring** is at **hat**.

⟨PHRV⟩ ,throw sth↔a'side to reject sth such as an attitude, a way of life, etc. 'throw yourself at sth/sb 1 to rush violently at sth/sb 2 (*informal*, *disapproving*) (usually of a woman) to be too enthusiastic in trying to attract a sexual partner ,throw sth↔a'way 1 ⟨?⟩ ⟨A2⟩ (*also* ,throw sth↔'out*) to get rid of sth that you no longer want: *I don't need that—you can throw it away.* ◊ *That old chair should be thrown away.* 2 to fail to make use of sth; to waste sth: *to throw away an opportunity* ⊃ see also THROWAWAY ,throw sth 'back at sb to remind sb of sth they have said or done in the past, especially to upset or annoy them ,throw sb 'back on sth [usually passive] to force sb to rely on sth because nothing else is available: *There was no TV so we were thrown back on our own resources* (= had to entertain ourselves). ,throw sth↔'in to include sth with what you are selling or offering, without increasing the price: *You can have the piano for $200, and I'll throw in the stool as well.* 2 to add a remark to a conversation: *Jack threw in the odd encouraging comment.* ,throw yourself/sth 'into sth to begin to do sth with energy and enthusiasm ,throw sth/sb↔'off 1 to manage to get rid of sth/sb that is making you suffer, annoying you, etc: *to throw off a cold/your worries/your pursuers* 2 to take off a piece of clothing quickly and carelessly: *She entered the room and threw off her wet coat.* ,throw sth↔'on to put on a piece of clothing quickly and carelessly: *She just threw on the first skirt she found.* ,throw sth↔'open (to sb) 1 to allow people to enter or visit a place where they could not go before 2 to allow people to discuss sth, take part in a competition, etc: *The debate will be thrown open to the audience.* ,throw sb↔'out (of …) to force sb to leave a place: *You'll be thrown out if you don't pay the rent.* ,throw

,throw sth↔'out 1 to say sth in a way that suggests you have not given it a lot of thought: *to throw out a suggestion* 2 to decide not to accept a proposal, an idea, etc. 3 = THROW STH AWAY 4 to produce smoke, light, heat, etc.: *a small fire that threw out a lot of heat* 5 to confuse sth or make it wrong: *Our calculations of the cost of our trip were thrown out by changes in the exchange rate.* ,throw sb 'over (*old-fashioned*) to stop being friends with sb or having a romantic relationship with them ,throw sb↔to'gether [often passive] to bring people into contact with each other, often unexpectedly: *Fate had thrown them together.* ,throw sth↔to'gether to make or produce sth in a hurry: *I threw together a quick meal.* ,throw 'up (*informal*) to VOMIT ⟨SYN⟩ **be sick** *The smell made me want to throw up.* ,throw sth↔'up (*informal*) 1 to VOMIT food ⟨SYN⟩ **sick sth up**: *The baby's thrown up her dinner.* 2 to make people notice sth: *Her research has thrown up some interesting facts.* 3 to build sth suddenly or in a hurry: *They're throwing up new housing estates all over the place.* 4 to leave your job: *to throw up your career*

■ *noun* 1 the act of throwing sth, especially a ball or DICE: *a well-aimed throw* ◊ *It's your throw* (= it's your turn to throw the dice). ◊ *He threw me to the ground with a judo throw.* 2 the distance that sth is thrown: *a javelin throw of 57 metres* 3 a loose cloth cover that can be placed over a SOFA, etc.

⟨IDM⟩ **$100, £50, etc. a 'throw** (*informal*) used to say how much items cost each: *The tickets for the dinner were £50 a throw.* ⊃ more at STONE *n.*

▼ SYNONYMS

**throw**

toss • hurl • fling • chuck • lob • bowl • pitch

These words all mean to send sth from your hand through the air.

**throw** to send sth from your hand or hands through the air: *Some kids were throwing stones at the window.* ◊ *She threw the ball and he caught it.*

**toss** to throw sth lightly or carelessly: *She tossed her jacket onto the bed.*

**hurl** to throw sth violently in a particular direction: *Rioters hurled a brick through the car's windscreen.*

**fling** to throw sb/sth somewhere with a lot of force, especially because you are angry or in a hurry: *She flung the letter down onto the table.*

**chuck** (*especially* BrE, *informal*) to throw sth carelessly: *I chucked him the keys.*

**lob** (*informal*) to throw sth so that it goes high through the air: *They were lobbing stones over the wall.*

**bowl** (in cricket) to throw the ball to the batsman

**pitch** (in baseball) to throw the ball to the batter

PATTERNS

- to throw / toss / hurl / fling / chuck / lob / bowl / pitch sth **at/to** sb / sth
- to throw / toss / fling / chuck sth **aside** / **away**
- to throw / toss / hurl / fling / chuck / lob / bowl / pitch a **ball**
- to throw / toss / hurl / fling / chuck **stones** / **rocks** / **a brick**
- to throw / toss / hurl / fling sth **angrily**
- to throw / toss sth **casually** / **carelessly**

**throw·away** /ˈθrəʊəweɪ/ *adj.* [only before noun] 1 ~ **line / remark / comment** something you say quickly without careful thought, sometimes in order to be funny: *She was very upset at what to him was just a throwaway remark.* 2 (of goods, etc.) produced cheaply and intended to be thrown away after use ⟨SYN⟩ **disposable**: *throwaway products* ◊ *We live in a throwaway society* (= a society in which things are not made to last a long time).

**throw·back** /ˈθrəʊbæk/ *noun* [usually sing.] ~ **(to sth)** a person or thing that is similar to sb/sth that existed in the past: *The car's design is a throwback to the 1960s.*

**throw·er** /ˈθrəʊə(r)/ *noun* a person who throws sth: *a discus thrower* ⊃ see also FLAMETHROWER

# throw-in

**throw-in** *noun* (in football (soccer) and rugby) the act of throwing the ball back onto the playing field after it has gone outside the area

**thrown** /θrəʊn/ *past part.* of THROW

**throw pillow** (NAmE) (BrE **scatter cushion**) *noun* a small CUSHION that can be placed on furniture, on the floor, etc. for decoration

**thru** (NAmE, *informal*) = THROUGH (5)

**thrush** /θrʌʃ/ *noun* **1** [C] a bird with a brown back and brown spots on its chest: *a song thrush* **2** [U] a disease that affects the mouth and throat **3** [U] (BrE) (NAmE **yeast infection**) a disease that affects the VAGINA

**thrust** /θrʌst/ *verb*, *noun*
- *verb* (**thrust**, **thrust**) **1** [T, I] to push sth/sb suddenly or violently in a particular direction; to move quickly and suddenly in a particular direction: *~sth/sb/yourself + adv./prep. He thrust the baby into my arms and ran off.* ◊ *She thrust her hands deep into her pockets.* ◊ (*figurative*) *He tends to thrust himself forward too much.* ◊ *+adv./prep. She thrust past him angrily and left.* **2** [I, T] *~(at sb)* (**with sth**) | *~(sth at sb)* to make a sudden, strong forward movement at sb with a weapon, etc: *He thrust at me with a knife.* ◊ *a thrusting movement* **IDM** see THROAT
- **PHRV** **thrust sth ↔ a'side** to refuse to listen to sb's complaints, comments, etc: *All our objections were thrust aside.* **'thrust sth/sb on/upon sb** [*usually passive*] to force sb to accept or deal with sth/sb that they do not want: *She was annoyed at having three extra guests suddenly thrust on her.*
- *noun* **1** the thrust [*sing.*] the main point of an argument, a policy, etc: *The thrust of his argument was that change was needed.* **2** [C] a sudden, strong movement that pushes sth/sb forward: *He killed her with a thrust of the knife.* **3** [U] (*specialist*) the force that is produced by an engine to push a plane, ROCKET, etc. forward **IDM** see CUT *n.*

**thrust·er** /ˈθrʌstə(r)/ *noun* a small engine used to provide extra force, especially on a SPACECRAFT

**thru·way** (*also* **through·way**) /ˈθruːweɪ/ *noun* (NAmE) used in the names of some FREEWAYS (= important roads across or between states): *the New York State Thruway*

**thud** /θʌd/ *noun*, *verb*
- *noun* a sound like the one that is made when a heavy object hits sth else: *His head hit the floor with a dull thud.*
- *verb* (**-dd-**) **1** [I, T] *~(sth) + adv./prep.* to fall or hit sth with a low, heavy sound: *His arrow thudded into the target.* **2** [I] (*literary*) (especially of the heart) to beat strongly

**thug** /θʌɡ/ *noun* a violent person, especially a criminal: *a gang of thugs* ▸ **thug·gish** /ˈθʌɡɪʃ/ *adj.*: *thuggish brutality*

**thug·gery** /ˈθʌɡəri/ *noun* [U] (*formal*) violent, usually criminal, behaviour

**thumb** /θʌm/ *noun*, *verb*
- *noun* **1** the short, thick finger at the side of the hand, slightly apart from the other four: *She still sucks her thumb when she's worried.* ⊃ see also GREEN THUMB **2** the part of a glove that covers the THUMB: *There's a hole in the thumb.*
- **IDM** **be all (fingers and) 'thumbs** to be AWKWARD with your hands so that you drop things or are unable to do sth **hold 'thumbs** (SAfrE) to hope that your plans will be successful or that sth will take place in the way that you want it to: *Let's hold thumbs that you get the job.* **thumbs 'up/'down** (*informal*) used to show that sth has been accepted/rejected or that it is/is not a success: *Their proposals were given the thumbs down.* ◊ *It looks like their thumbs up for their latest album.* **ORIGIN** In contests in ancient Rome the public put their thumbs up if they wanted a gladiator to live, and down if they wanted him to be killed. **under sb's 'thumb** (*informal*) (of a person) completely controlled by sb ⊃ more at RULE *n.*, SORE *adj.*, TWIDDLE *v.*
- *verb* **1** [I, T] to make a signal with your thumb to passing drivers to ask them to stop and take you somewhere: *+adv./prep. He had thumbed all across Europe.* ◊ (BrE) *~a lift We managed to thumb a lift with a lorry driver.* ◊ (NAmE) *~a ride We managed to thumb a ride with a truck driver.* **2** [T] *~sth (+ adv./prep.)* to touch or move sth with your thumb: *She thumbed off the safety catch of her pistol.* ⊃ see also WELL THUMBED
- **IDM** **thumb your 'nose at sb/sth** (*informal*) to make a rude sign with your thumb on your nose; to show that you have no respect for sb/sth: *The company just thumbs its nose at the legislation on pollution.*
- **PHRV** **'thumb through sth** to turn the pages of a book quickly in order to get a general idea of what is in it

**'thumb drive** *noun* (NAmE) = FLASH DRIVE

**thumb·nail** /ˈθʌmneɪl/ *noun* **1** the nail on the THUMB **2** (*also* **thumbnail 'image**) (*computing*) a very small picture on a computer screen that shows you what a larger picture looks like, or what a page of a document will look like when you print it

**thumbnail 'sketch** *noun* a short description of sth, giving only the main details

**'thumb piano** (*also* **sansa**, **mbira**) *noun* an African musical instrument consisting of a row of narrow metal pieces, that you play with your fingers and THUMBS

**thumb·print** /ˈθʌmprɪnt/ *noun* the mark made by the pattern of lines on the inner part of the top of a person's THUMB

**thumb·screw** /ˈθʌmskruː/ *noun* an instrument that was used in the past for TORTURING people by pressing on and breaking their THUMBS

**thumb·suck** /ˈθʌmsʌk/ *noun* [C, *usually sing.*, U] (SAfrE, *informal*, *often disapproving*) a guess or an estimate: *Their sales projections are a total thumbsuck.*

**thumb·tack** /ˈθʌmtæk/ *noun* (*also* **tack**) (*both* NAmE) (BrE **drawing pin**) *noun* a short pin with a large round, flat head, used especially for fastening paper to a board or wall

**thump** /θʌmp/ *verb*, *noun*
- *verb* **1** [T, I] *~(sb/sth) (+ adv./prep.)* to hit sb/sth hard, especially with your closed hand: *He thumped the table angrily.* ◊ *She couldn't get her breath and had to be thumped on the back.* ◊ (*informal*) *I'll thump you if you say that again.* ◊ (*informal*, *figurative*) *He thumped out a tune (= played it very loudly) on the piano.* **2** [I, T] to fall on or hit a surface hard, with a loud sound; to make sth do this: *+adv./prep. A bird thumped against the window.* ◊ *~sth + adv./prep. He thumped the report down on my desk.* **3** [I] to beat strongly: *My heart was thumping with excitement.* ⊃ see also TUB-THUMPING
- *noun* **1** the sound of sth heavy hitting the ground or another object: *There was a thump as the truck hit the bank.* **2** (*informal*) an act of hitting sb/sth hard: *She gave him a thump on the back.*

**thump·ing** /ˈθʌmpɪŋ/ *adj.* [*only before noun*] (*informal*) very big **SYN** **huge**: *a thumping majority* ▸ **thump·ing** *adv.* (BrE): *He told us a thumping great lie.*

**thun·der** /ˈθʌndə(r)/ *noun*, *verb*
- *noun* [U] **1** the loud noise that you hear after a flash of LIGHTNING, during a storm: *the rumble of distant thunder* ◊ *a clap/crash/roll of thunder* ◊ *Thunder crashed in the sky.* **2** a loud noise like thunder: *the thunder of horses' hooves* **IDM** see FACE *n.*, STEAL *v.*
- *verb* **1** [I] when **it thunders**, there is a loud noise in the sky during a storm **2** [I] to make a very loud, deep noise **SYN** **roar**: *A voice thundered in my ear.* ◊ *thundering traffic* **3** [I] *+adv./prep.* to move very fast and with a loud deep noise **SYN** **roar**: *Heavy trucks kept thundering past.* **4** [T] *~sth + adv./prep.* (*informal*) (especially in sport) to make sth move somewhere very fast: *Essien thundered the ball past the goalie.* **5** [I, T] (*literary*) to shout, complain, etc. very loudly and angrily: *~(sth) He thundered against the evils of television.* ◊ *+speech 'Sit still!' he thundered.*

**thun·der·bolt** /ˈθʌndəbəʊlt; NAmE -dərb-/ *noun* a flash of LIGHTNING that comes at the same time as the noise of THUNDER and that hits sth: (*figurative*) *The news hit them like a thunderbolt (= was very shocking).*

**thun·der·clap** /ˈθʌndəklæp; NAmE -dərk-/ *noun* a loud crash made by THUNDER

**thun·der·cloud** /ˈθʌndəklaʊd; NAmE -dərk-/ noun a large dark cloud that produces THUNDER and LIGHTNING during a storm

**thun·der·ous** /ˈθʌndərəs/ adj. (formal) **1** very loud **SYN** **deafening**: *thunderous applause* **2** looking very angry: *his thunderous expression* ▶ **thun·der·ous·ly** adv.

**thun·der·storm** /ˈθʌndəstɔːm; NAmE -dərstɔːrm/ noun a storm with THUNDER and LIGHTNING and usually very heavy rain

**thun·der·struck** /ˈθʌndəstrʌk; NAmE -dərs-/ adj. [not usually before noun] extremely surprised and shocked **SYN** **amazed**

**thun·dery** /ˈθʌndəri/ adj. (of weather) with THUNDER; suggesting that THUNDER is likely

**Thurs·day** 🛈 **A1** /ˈθɜːzdeɪ, -di; NAmE ˈθɜːrz-/ noun [C, U] (abbr. **Thur.**, **Thurs.**) the day of the week after Wednesday and before Friday **HELP** To see how **Thursday** is used, look at the examples at **Monday**. **ORIGIN** From the Old English for 'day of thunder', translated from Latin *Jovis dies* 'Jupiter's day'. Jupiter was the god associated with thunder.

**thus** 🛈 **B2** 🇼 /ðʌs/ adv. (formal) **1** **B2** in this way; like this: *Many scholars have argued thus. ◇ The universities have expanded, thus allowing many more people the chance of higher education.* **2** 🇼 **B2** as a result of sth just mentioned **SYN** **hence**, **therefore**: *He is the eldest son and thus heir to the title. ◇ We do not own the building. Thus, it would be impossible for us to make any major changes to it.* ⸺ LANGUAGE BANK at THEREFORE **IDM** see FAR adv.

**thwack** /θwæk/ verb ~ sb/sth to hit sb/sth hard, making a short, loud sound ▶ **thwack** noun: *the thwack of bat on ball*

**thwart** /θwɔːt; NAmE θwɔːrt/ verb [often passive] (formal) to prevent sb from doing what they want to do **SYN** **frustrate**: *~ sth to thwart sb's plans ◇ be thwarted in sth She was thwarted in her attempt to take control of the party.*

**thx** (also **tx**) abbr. (in writing) (informal) thanks; thank you (used, for example, in text messages or TWEETS): *Thx for the info, everyone!*

**thy** /ðaɪ/ det. (old use) a word meaning 'your', used when talking to only one person: *Honour thy father and thy mother.* **HELP** Before a vowel sound, the form is **thine** /ðaɪn/.

**thyme** /taɪm/ noun [U] a plant with small leaves that have a sweet smell and are used in cooking as a HERB ⸺ VISUAL VOCAB page V8

**thy·mus** /ˈθaɪməs/ (also **ˈthymus gland**) noun (anatomy) an organ in the neck that produces LYMPHOCYTES (= cells to fight infection)

**thy·roid** /ˈθaɪrɔɪd/ (also **ˈthyroid gland**) noun (anatomy) a small organ at the front of the neck that produces HORMONES that control the way in which the body grows and functions

**thy·self** /ðaɪˈself/ pron. (old use or dialect) a word meaning 'yourself', used when talking to only one person

**ti** (NAmE) (BrE **te**) /tiː/ noun (music) the 7th note of a MAJOR SCALE

**tiara** /tiˈɑːrə/ noun a piece of jewellery like a small CROWN decorated with PRECIOUS STONES, worn by a woman, for example a princess, on formal occasions

**TiB** abbr. (in writing) TEBIBYTE

**Tib** abbr. (in writing) TEBIBIT

**tibia** /ˈtɪbiə/ noun (pl. **tib·iae** /-bii:/) (anatomy) the SHIN BONE ⸺ VISUAL VOCAB page V1 ⸺ see also FIBULA

**tic** /tɪk/ noun a sudden, quick movement of a muscle, especially in your face or head, that you cannot control

**tick** /tɪk/ verb, noun
■ verb **1** [I] (of a clock, etc.) to make short, light, regular repeated sounds to mark time passing: *In the silence we could hear the clock ticking. ◇ a ticking bomb ◇ ~away While we waited the taxi's meter kept ticking away.* **2** [T] (BrE) (NAmE **check**) ~ sth to put a mark (✓) next to an item on a list, an answer, etc: *Please tick the appropriate box. ◇ Tick 'yes' or 'no' to each question. ◇ I've ticked the names of the people who have paid.*

1637 **ticket**

**IDM** **ˌtick all the/sb's ˈboxes** (BrE, informal) to do exactly the right things to please sb: *This is a movie that ticks all the boxes.* **what makes sb ˈtick** what makes sb behave in the way that they do: *I've never really understood what makes her tick.* ⸺ more at CLOCK n.
**PHRV** **ˌtick aˈway/ˈby/ˈpast** (of time) to pass: *I had to get to the airport by two, and the minutes were ticking away.* **ˌtick sth⇔aˈway** (of a clock, etc.) to mark the time as it passes: *The clock ticked away the minutes.* **ˌtick sb⇔ˈoff 1** (BrE, old-fashioned, informal) to speak angrily to sb, especially a child, because they have done sth wrong **SYN** **tell sb off** ⸺ related noun TICKING OFF **2** (NAmE, informal) to make sb angry or annoyed: *It really ticked me off when he said I was late.* **ˌtick ˈoff/ˌtick ˈoff** (BrE) (NAmE **check sb/sth ˈoff**) to put a mark (✓) next to a name or an item on a list to show that sth has been dealt with. **ˌtick ˈover** (BrE) (usually used in the progressive tenses) **1** (of an engine) to run slowly while the vehicle is not moving **SYN** **idle** **2** (of a business, a system, an activity, etc.) to keep working slowly without producing or achieving much: *Just keep things ticking over while I'm away.*
■ noun **1** [C] (BrE) (NAmE **ˈcheck mark**, **check**) a mark (✓) put next to a sum or an item on a list, usually to show that it has been checked or done or is correct: *Put a tick in the appropriate box if you would like further information about any of our products.* ⸺ compare CROSS, X **2** [C] a very small creature that bites humans and animals and drinks their blood. There are several types of tick, some of which can carry diseases: *a tick bite* ⸺ VISUAL VOCAB page V3 **3** (also **ˈtick·ing**) [U] a short, light, regularly repeated sound, especially that of a clock or watch: *The only sound was the soft tick of the clock.* **4** [C] (BrE, informal) a moment: *Hang on a tick! ◇ I'll be with you in two ticks.*
**IDM** **on ˈtick** (BrE, old-fashioned, informal) on credit: *Can I have these on tick?*

**ˈtick-box** /ˈtɪkbɒks; NAmE -bɑːks/ noun (BrE) = CHECKBOX

**tick·er** /ˈtɪkə(r)/ noun **1** = NEWS TICKER **2** (old-fashioned, informal) a person's heart

**ˈticker tape** noun [U] (especially NAmE) (in the past) long, narrow pieces of paper with information, for example STOCK MARKET prices, printed on them by a special TELEGRAPH machine: *a ticker-tape parade in the streets of New York* (= an occasion when people throw pieces of paper as part of a celebration, for example in honour of a famous person)

**ticket** 🛈 **A1** /ˈtɪkɪt/ noun, verb
■ noun **1** **A1** a printed piece of paper, or a message or image received on your phone or computer, that gives you the right to travel on a particular bus, train, etc. or to go into a theatre, etc: *a plane/bus/train ticket ◇ an airline ticket ◇ ~for/to sth free tickets to the show ◇ a ticket office ◇ (figurative) She hoped that getting this job would finally be her ticket to success.* ⸺ picture at LABEL ⸺ see also ALL-TICKET, E-TICKET, MEAL TICKET, RETURN TICKET, SEASON TICKET **2** **A1** a printed piece of paper with a number or numbers on it, that you buy in order to have the chance of winning a prize if the number or numbers are later chosen: *a lottery/raffle ticket ◇ There are three winning tickets.* **3** a label that is attached to sth in a shop giving details of its price, size, etc. ⸺ see also BIG-TICKET **4** an official notice that orders you to pay a FINE because you have done sth illegal while driving or parking your car **SYN** **fine**: *a speeding ticket* ⸺ see also PARKING TICKET **5** [usually sing.] (especially NAmE) a list of candidates that are supported by a particular political party in an election: *She ran for office on the Democratic ticket.* ⸺ see also DREAM TICKET
**IDM** **be ˈtickets** (SAfrE, informal) be the end: *It's tickets for the team that loses.* **just the ˈticket** (BrE also **just the ˈjob**) (informal, approving) exactly what is needed in a particular situation **ˌthat's the ˈticket** (old-fashioned, informal) used to say that sth is just what is needed or that everything is just right ⸺ more at SPLIT v.
■ verb [usually passive] **1** (specialist) to produce and sell tickets for an event, a trip, etc.; to give sb a ticket: **be ticketed** *Passengers can now be ticketed electronically.*

*Oxford Phrasal Academic Lexicon (OPAL) written and spoken word lists* | 🇼 OPAL written word list | 🇸 OPAL spoken word list

# ticketed

**2** (*especially NAmE*) to give sb an official notice that orders them to pay a FINE because they have done sth illegal while driving or parking a car: **be ticketed** *Park illegally, and you're likely to be ticketed.*

**tick·et·ed** /ˈtɪkɪtɪd/ *adj.* [usually before noun] a **ticketed** event is one for which you need a ticket to get in: *The museum holds both free and ticketed events.*
- IDM **be ˈticketed for sth** (*especially NAmE*) to be intended for a particular purpose

**tick·et·ing** /ˈtɪkɪtɪŋ/ *noun* [U] the process of producing and selling tickets: *ticketing systems*

**ˈticket tout** *noun* (*BrE*) = TOUT

**tick·ing** /ˈtɪkɪŋ/ *noun* [U] a type of strong cotton cloth that is often marked with a pattern of lines, used especially for making MATTRESS and PILLOW covers

**ˌticking ˈoff** *noun* [sing.] (*BrE, old-fashioned, informal*) the act of telling sb that they have done sth to make you angry: *She gave the boys a severe ticking off.*

**tickle** /ˈtɪkl/ *verb, noun*
- *verb* **1** [T, I] ~ **(sb/sth)** to move your fingers on a sensitive part of sb's body in a way that makes them laugh: *The bigger girls used to chase me and tickle me.* ◊ *Stop tickling!* **2** [T, I] ~ **(sth)** to produce a slightly uncomfortable feeling in a sensitive part of the body; to have a feeling like this: *His beard was tickling her cheek.* ◊ *My throat tickles.* ◊ *a tickling cough* **3** [T] to please and interest sb: ~ **sb/sth** *to tickle sb's imagination* ◊ ~ **sb to do sth** *I was tickled to discover that we'd both done the same thing.*
- IDM **be tickled ˈpink** (*informal*) to be very pleased **ˈtickle sb's ˈfancy** (*informal*) to please sb: *See if any of these tickle your fancy.*
- *noun* [usually sing.] **1** an act of tickling sb: *She gave the child a little tickle.* **2** a slightly uncomfortable feeling in a part of your body: *to have a tickle in your throat* (= that makes you want to cough) IDM see SLAP *n.*

**tick·lish** /ˈtɪklɪʃ/ *adj.* **1** (of a person) sensitive to being tickled: *Are you ticklish?* **2** (*informal*) (of a situation or problem) difficult to deal with, and possibly embarrassing SYN awkward **3** (of a cough) that makes your throat painful: *a dry ticklish cough*

**tick-tock** /ˌtɪk ˈtɒk; *NAmE* -ˈtɑːk/ *noun* [usually sing.] used to describe the sound of a large clock TICKING

**tic-tac-toe** (*also* **tick-tack-toe**) /ˌtɪk tæk ˈtəʊ/ (*NAmE*) (*BrE* **ˌnoughts and ˈcrosses**) *noun* [U] a simple game in which two players take turns to write Os or Xs in a set of nine squares. The first player to complete a row of three Os or three Xs is the winner.

**tidal** /ˈtaɪdl/ *adj.* connected with TIDES (= the regular rise and fall of the sea): *tidal forces/energy* ◊ *a tidal river*

**ˈtidal wave** *noun* **1** a very large ocean wave that is caused by a storm or an earthquake, and that destroys things when it reaches the land ⊃ compare TSUNAMI **2** ~ **(of sth)** a sudden increase in a particular feeling, activity or type of behaviour: *a tidal wave of crime*

**tid·bit** /ˈtɪdbɪt/ (*NAmE*) (*BrE* **tit·bit**) *noun* a small special piece of food SYN morsel

**tid·dler** /ˈtɪdlə(r)/ *noun* (*BrE, informal*) a very small fish

**tid·dly** /ˈtɪdli/ *adj.* (*BrE, informal*) **1** slightly drunk **2** very small SYN tiny

**tiddly·winks** /ˈtɪdliwɪŋks/ *noun* [U] a game in which players try to make small plastic discs jump into a cup by pressing them on the edge with a larger disc

**tide** /taɪd/ *noun, verb*
- *noun* **1** [C, U] a regular rise and fall in the level of the sea, caused by the pull of the moon and sun; the flow of water that happens as the sea rises and falls: *the ebb and flow of the tide* ◊ *The tide is in/out.* ◊ *Is the tide coming in or going out?* ◊ *The body was washed up on the beach by the tide.* ⊃ WORDFINDER NOTE at COAST ⊃ see also FLOOD TIDE, HIGH TIDE, LOW TIDE, NEAP TIDE, SPRING TIDE **2** [C, usually sing.] the direction in which the opinion of a large number of people seems to be moving: *It takes courage to speak out against the tide of opinion.* **3** [C, usually sing.] a large amount of sth unpleasant that is increasing and is difficult to control: *There is anxiety about the rising tide of crime.* **4** [sing.] ~ **of sth** a feeling that you suddenly have that gets stronger and stronger: *A tide of rage surged through her.* **5** **-tide** [sing.] (*old use*) (in compounds) a time or season of the year: *Christmastide*
- IDM **go, swim, etc. with/against the ˈtide** to agree with/oppose the attitudes or opinions that most other people have **the ˈtide turned** | **turn the ˈtide** used to say that there is a change in sb's luck or in how successful they are being
- *verb*
- PHRV **ˌtide sb ˈover (sth)** [no passive] to help sb during a difficult period by providing what they need: *Can you lend me some money to tide me over until I get paid?*

▼ **HOMOPHONES**

**tide • tied** /taɪd/

- **tide** *noun*: *We'll swim back to the beach before the tide turns.*
- **tide** *verb*: *Short-term loans are designed to tide borrowers over until their next payday.*
- **tied** *verb* (past tense, past participle of TIE): *She tied her hair up with ribbon.*

**tide·line** /ˈtaɪdlaɪn/ *noun* a line left or reached by the sea when the tide is at its highest point

**tide·mark** /ˈtaɪdmɑːk; *NAmE* -mɑːrk/ *noun* **1** a line that is made by the sea on a beach at the highest point that the sea reaches **2** (*BrE, informal*) a line that is left around the inside of a bath by dirty water

**ˈtide pool** (*NAmE*) (*BrE* **ˈrock pool**) *noun* a small amount of water that collects between the rocks by the sea

**tide·water** /ˈtaɪdwɔːtə(r)/ *noun* **1** [C] (*NAmE*) an area of land at or near the coast **2** [U, C] water that is brought by the TIDE

**tid·ings** /ˈtaɪdɪŋz/ *noun* [pl.] (*old-fashioned* or *humorous*) news: *I am the bearer of good tidings.* ◊ *He brought glad tidings.*

**tidy** /ˈtaɪdi/ *adj., verb, noun*
- *adj.* (**tidi·er**, **tidi·est**) **1** (*especially BrE*) arranged neatly and with everything in order: *a tidy desk* ◊ *She keeps her flat very tidy.* ◊ *I like everything to be neat and tidy.* OPP untidy **2** (*especially BrE*) keeping things neat and in order: *I'm a tidy person.* ◊ *tidy habits* OPP untidy **3** [only before noun] (*informal*) a **tidy** amount of money is fairly large SYN considerable: *It must have cost a tidy sum.* ◊ *a tidy profit* ▸ **tidi·ly** /-dɪli/ *adv.*: *The room was very tidily arranged.* **tidi·ness** *noun* [U]
- *verb* (I, T] (**tidies**, **tidy·ing**, **tidied**, **tidied**) (*especially BrE*) to make sth look neat by putting things in the place where they belong: *I spent all morning cleaning and tidying.* ◊ ~ **sth** *to tidy a room*
- PHRV **ˌtidy sth↔aˈway** (*BrE*) to put things in the place where they belong, especially where they cannot be seen, so that a room appears tidy **ˌtidy ˈup** (*especially BrE*) to make sth look neat by putting things in the place where they belong: *When you cook, could you please tidy up after yourself.* **ˌtidy sth/yourˈself ˈup** (*especially BrE*) to make sth/yourself look neat and tidy: *I need to tidy the place up a bit.* **ˌtidy sth↔ˈup** (*especially BrE*) to arrange or deal with sth so that it is well or correctly finished: *I tidied up the report before handing it in.*
- *noun* (*pl.* **-ies**) (*BrE*) (*especially in compounds*) a container for putting small objects in, in order to keep a place tidy: *a desk tidy*

**tie** /taɪ/ *verb, noun*
- *verb* (**ties, tying, tied, tied**)
- • FASTEN WITH STRING/ROPE **1** ~ **sth** [T] to attach or hold two or more things together using string, rope, etc.; to fasten sb/sth with string, rope, etc: ~ **sth + adv./prep.** *She tied the newspapers in a bundle.* ◊ *He had to tie her hands together.* ◊ *They tied him to a chair with cable.* ◊ *I tie back my hair when I'm cooking.* ◊ ~ **sth** *Shall I tie the package or tape it?* ⊃ HOMOPHONES at TIDE **2** [T] ~ **sth + adv./**

**prep.** to fasten sth to or around sth else: *She tied a label on to the suitcase.* **3** [T] ~ **sth** to make a knot in a piece of string, rope, etc: *to tie a ribbon* ◇ *Can you help me tie my tie?* ◇ ~ **sth up** *Tie up your shoelaces!* ◇ ~ **sth in sth** *I tied a knot in the rope.* **4** [I] (+ *adv./prep.*) to be closed or fastened with a KNOT, etc: *The skirt ties at the waist.*
- **CONNECT/LINK 5** [T, usually passive] to connect or link sb/sth closely with sb/sth else: **be tied (to sth/sb)** *Pay increases are tied to inflation.* ◇ *Their company's future is closely tied to our own.*
- **LIMIT 6** [T, usually passive] to limit sb's freedom to act and make them unable to do everything they want: **be tied (by sth)** *to be tied by a contract* ◇ **be tied to sth** *I want to work but I'm tied to the house with the baby.* ◇ **be tied to doing sth** *I don't want to be tied to coming home at a particular time.*
- **IN GAME/COMPETITION 7** [I, T] (of two teams, etc.) to have the same number of points **SYN draw**: ~ **(with sb)** *England tied 2–2 with Germany in the first round.* ◇ ~ **for sth** *They tied for second place.* ◇ ~ **sth** *The scores are tied at 3–3.* ◇ *Last night's vote was tied.*
- **MUSIC 8** [T] ~ **sth** (in written music) to join notes with a tie ⊃ see also TONGUE-TIED

**IDM** **tie sb/yourself (up) in ˈknots** (*informal*) to become or make sb very confused **tie the ˈknot** (*informal*) to get married ⊃ more at APRON, HAND *n.*

**PHRV** **tie sb ˈdown (to sth/to doing sth)** to limit sb's freedom, for example by making them accept particular conditions or by keeping them busy: *Kids tie you down, don't they?* ◇ *I don't want to tie myself down to coming back on a particular date.* **tie ˈin (with sth)** to match or agree with sth: *This evidence ties in closely with what we already know.* **tie ˈin (with sth)** | **tie sth↔ˈin (with sth)** to link sth or be linked to sth; to happen, or arrange for sth to happen, at the same time as sth else: *The concert will tie in with the festival of dance taking place the same weekend.* ⊃ related noun TIE-IN **tie sth↔ˈoff** to put a KNOT in the end of sth; to close sth with string, THREAD, etc: *to tie off a rope* ◇ *to tie off an artery* **tie ˈup** | **tie sth↔ˈup 1** to attach a boat to a fixed object with a rope: *We tied up alongside the quay.* ◇ *We tied the boat up.* **2** to close with a KNOT; to be closed or fastened with a knot: *to tie up a garbage bag* **tie sb↔ˈup 1** to tie sb's arms and legs tightly so that they cannot move or escape: *The gang tied up a security guard.* **2** [usually passive] to keep sb busy so that they have no time for other things: *I'm tied up in a meeting until 3.* **tie sth↔ˈup 1** to attach an animal to sth with a rope, chain, etc: *He left his dog tied up to a tree.* **2** [usually passive] to connect or link sth to sth else: *Her behaviour is tied up with her feelings of guilt.* ⊃ related noun TIE-UP **3 be tied up in sth** (of money) to be invested so that it is not easily available for use: *Most of the capital is tied up in property.* **4** to deal with all the final details of sth: *We are hoping to tie up the deal by tomorrow.* ◇ *I went into the office for an hour to* **tie up any loose ends** (= finish remaining small jobs).

■ *noun*
- **CLOTHES 1** A2 (*NAmE also* **neck-tie**) a long, narrow piece of cloth worn around the neck, especially by men, with a KNOT in front: *He was dressed impeccably in a suit and tie.* ◇ *They prefer their employees to wear a shirt and tie.* ⊃ see also BLACK TIE, BOLO TIE, BOW TIE, WHITE TIE
- **FOR FASTENING 2** a piece of string or wire used for fastening or tying sth: *ties for closing plastic bags*
- **CONNECTION 3** B2 [usually pl.] a strong connection between people or organizations: *diplomatic/economic/bilateral ties* ◇ ~ **with/between/to sb/sth** *The firm has close ties with an American corporation.* ◇ *Both sides agreed to* **strengthen** *political ties.* ◇ *They* **severed** *ties after a dispute.*
- **LIMIT 4** a thing that limits sb's freedom of action: *He was still a young man and he did not want any ties.*
- **IN GAME/COMPETITION 5** a situation in a game or competition when two or more players have the same score: *The match ended in a tie.* ⊃ compare DRAW **6** (*BrE*) a sports match, especially a football (soccer) match, that is part of a larger competition: *the first leg of the tie between Leeds and Roma* ⊃ see also CUP TIE
- **MUSIC 7** a curved line written over two notes of the same PITCH (= how high or low a note is) to show that they are to be played or sung as one note ⊃ picture at MUSIC
- **ON RAILWAY 8** (*NAmE*) (*BrE* **sleep-er**) one of the heavy pieces of wood or CONCRETE on which the RAILS (= metal bars) on a railway track are laid

**tie-break** /ˈtaɪbreɪk/ (*BrE*) (*NAmE* **tie-break-er**) *noun* (in tennis) a period of extra play to decide who is the winner of a SET when both players have won six games

**tie-break-er** /ˈtaɪbreɪkə(r)/ *noun* **1** (*NAmE*) = TIEBREAK **2** an extra question in a competition to decide who is the winner when two or more of those taking part have equal scores ⊃ WORDFINDER NOTE at COMPETITION

**tied** /taɪd/ *adj.* [only before noun] (*BrE*) (of a house) rented to sb on the condition that they work for the owner: *a tied cottage on a farm*

**ˈtie-dye** *verb* ~ **sth** to make patterns on cloth by tying KNOTS in it or tying string around it before you put it in a DYE, so that some parts receive more colour than others

**ˈtie-in** *noun* a product such as a book or toy that is connected with a new film, television programme, etc.

**tier** /tɪə(r); *NAmE* tɪr/ *noun* **1** a row or layer of sth that has several rows or layers placed one above the other: *a wedding cake with three tiers* ◇ **in tiers** *The seating is arranged in tiers.* **2** one of several levels in an organization or a system: *We have introduced an extra tier of administration.* ◇ *a two-tier system of management*

**tiered** /tɪəd; *NAmE* tɪrd/ *adj.* **1** arranged in tiers: *tiered seating* **2 -tiered** (in compounds) having the number of tiers mentioned: *a two-tiered system*

**ˈtie-up** *noun* **1** ~ **(with sb/sth)** (*BrE*) an agreement between two companies to join together: *They're negotiating a tie-up with Ford.* **2** ~ **(between A and B)** (*BrE*) a connection between two or more things: *a tie-up between politics and economics* **3** (*especially NAmE*) a situation in which sth stops working or moving forward: *a traffic tie-up*

**TIFF** /tɪf/ *noun* [U, C] (*computing*) a form in which images can be stored and shown on a computer; an image created in this form (the abbreviation for 'tagged image file format')

**tiff** /tɪf/ *noun* (*informal*) a slight argument between close friends or two people who love each other: *to have a tiff with sb*

**tif-fin** /ˈtɪfɪn/ *noun* [U] (*old-fashioned* or *IndE*) a small meal, especially lunch

**ˈtiffin carrier** *noun* (*especially IndE*) a set of shallow metal food containers that fit on top of each other and that are attached together using a metal frame with a fastening device

**tig** /tɪg/ *noun* [U] (*BrE*) = TAG

**tiger** /ˈtaɪgə(r)/ *noun* a large wild animal of the cat family that has orange fur with black STRIPES (= narrow lines) and lives in parts of Asia: *She fought like a tiger to be able to keep her children.* ⊃ compare TIGRESS ⊃ see also PAPER TIGER

**tight** ● B1 /taɪt/ *adj., adv.*
■ *adj.* (**tight·er**, **tight·est**)
- **FIRM 1** B1 held or fixed in position securely; difficult to move, open or separate: *He kept a tight grip on her arm.* ◇ *She twisted her hair into a tight knot.* ◇ *The screw was so tight that it wouldn't move.*
- **CLOTHES 2** B1 fitting closely to your body and sometimes uncomfortable: *She was wearing a tight pair of jeans.* ◇ *These shoes are much too tight.* ◇ *The new sweater was a tight fit.* **OPP loose** ⊃ see also SKINTIGHT
- **MONEY/TIME 3** B2 difficult to manage with because there is not enough: *We have a very tight budget.* ◇ *The president has a tight schedule today.*
- **CONTROL 4** B2 very strict and hard to resist, avoid, etc: *to keep tight control over sth* ◇ *Dozens of streets are being closed and security is tight.*
- **STRETCHED 5** stretched or pulled so that it cannot stretch much further: *The rope was stretched tight.*

# tighten

- **CLOSE TOGETHER** 6 [usually before noun] with things or people packed closely together, leaving little space between them: *There was a tight group of people around the speaker.* ◊ *With six of us in the car it was **a tight squeeze**.*
- **EXPRESSION/VOICE** 7 looking or sounding anxious, upset or angry: *'I'm sorry,' she said, with a tight smile.* ⇒ see also UPTIGHT
- **PART OF BODY** 8 feeling painful or uncomfortable because of illness or emotion **SYN** constricted: *He complained of having a tight chest.* ◊ *Her throat felt tight, just looking at her baby.*
- **RELATIONSHIP** 9 having a close relationship with sb else or with other people: *It was a tight community and newcomers were not welcome.* ⇒ see also TIGHT-KNIT
- **BEND/CURVE** 10 curving suddenly rather than gradually: *The driver slowed down at a tight bend in the road.* ◊ *The plane flew around in a tight circle.*
- **CONTEST/RACE** 11 with runners, teams, etc. that seem to be equally good **SYN** close²: *a tight race*
- **NOT GENEROUS** 12 (*informal, disapproving*) not wanting to spend much money; not generous **SYN** mean: *He's very tight with his money.*
- **DRUNK** 13 [not usually before noun] (*old-fashioned, informal*) drunk **SYN** tipsy
- **-TIGHT** 14 (in compounds) not allowing the substance mentioned to enter: *measures to make your home weathertight* ⇒ see also AIRTIGHT, WATERTIGHT ▶ **tight·ness** noun [U]
- **IDM** **keep a tight 'rein on sb/sth** to control sb/sth carefully or strictly **run a tight 'ship** to organize sth in a very efficient way, controlling other people very closely ⇒ more at SPOT n.
- ■ *adv.* (tight·er, tight·est) closely and strongly; tightly: *Hold tight!* ◊ *My suitcase was packed tight.* ◊ *His fists were clenched tight.* **IDM** see SIT, SLEEP v.

> **WHICH WORD?**
> 
> **tight / tightly**
> - **Tight** and **tightly** are both adverbs that come from the adjective **tight**. They have the same meaning, but **tight** is often used instead of **tightly** after a verb, especially in informal language, and in compounds: *packed tight* ◊ *a tight-fitting lid*. Before a past participle **tightly** is used: *clusters of tightly packed flowers*.

**tight·en** /ˈtaɪtn/ verb 1 [I, T] to become or make sth become tight or tighter: ~(up) *The rope holding the boat suddenly tightened and shook.* ◊ *His mouth tightened into a thin line.* ◊ ~sth (up) *to tighten a lid/screw/rope/knot* ◊ *She tightened her grip on his arm.* ◊ *The nuts weren't properly tightened and the wheel came off.* 2 [T] ~sth to make sth become stricter: *to tighten security* **OPP** loosen

**IDM** **tighten your 'belt** to spend less money because there is less available ⇒ SYNONYMS at SAVE
**PHRV** **tighten 'up (on sth) | tighten sth↔'up** to become stricter or more careful; to make sth become stricter: *The police are tightening up on under-age drinking.* ◊ *The regional government has tightened up the country's lax planning laws.*

**tight 'end** noun (in AMERICAN FOOTBALL) an attacking player who plays close to the TACKLE

**tight-'fisted** adj. not willing to spend or give much money **SYN** mean, stingy

**tight-'fitting** adj. that fits very tightly or closely **SYN** close-fitting: *a tight-fitting skirt*

**tight-'knit** (also **tightly 'knit**) adj. (of a family or community) with all the members having strong, friendly relationships with one another: *a tight-knit mining community*

**tight-'lipped** adj. 1 not willing to talk about sth 2 keeping your lips pressed together, especially because you are angry about sth

**tight·ly** /ˈtaɪtli/ adv. 1 in a way that is very strict and hard to resist, avoid, etc: *The project's finances are tightly con-*trolled. 2 securely in position; in a way that is difficult to move, open or separate: *Her eyes were tightly closed.* ◊ *I held on tightly to her arm.* 3 close together; leaving little or no space between: *a tightly packed crowd of tourists* ⇒ note at TIGHT

**tight·rope** /ˈtaɪtrəʊp/ noun a rope or wire that is stretched tightly high above the ground and that performers walk along, especially in a CIRCUS: *a tightrope walker*
**IDM** **tread/walk a 'tightrope** to be in a difficult situation in which you do not have much freedom of action and need to be extremely careful about what you do

**tights** /taɪts/ noun [pl.] 1 (*BrE*) (*NAmE* **panty-hose**) a piece of clothing made of very thin cloth that fits closely over a woman's HIPS, legs and feet: *a pair of tights* ⇒ compare STOCKING 2 a piece of clothing similar to tights but made of thicker cloth, worn especially by dancers

**ti·gress** /ˈtaɪɡrəs/ noun a female TIGER

**tik** /tɪk/ noun [U] (*SAfrE, informal*) the drug METHAMPHETAMINE, especially in the form of very small CRYSTALS **SYN** meth

**tike** = TYKE

**tikka** /ˈtiːkə, ˈtɪkə; NAmE ˈtɪkə/ noun [U, C] a spicy South Asian dish consisting of pieces of meat or vegetables that have been left in a sauce and then cooked: *chicken tikka*

**til, 'til** /tɪl/ ⇒ UNTIL

**tilak** /ˈtɪlæk/ noun a mark on the FOREHEAD of a Hindu, worn as a religious symbol or for decoration

**til·apia** /tɪˈlæpiə, -ˈleɪp-; NAmE -ˈlɑːp-/ noun (*pl.* **til·apia** or **til·apias**) [C, U] a FRESHWATER fish found in hot countries that is used for food

**tilde** /ˈtɪldə/ noun 1 the mark (~) placed over letters in some languages and some vowels in the International Phonetic Alphabet to show how they should be pronounced, as in *España*, *São Paulo* and /pɒʃ/ (*penchant*) 2 the mark (~), used in this dictionary in some parts of an entry to represent the word in blue type at the top of the entry

**tile** /taɪl/ noun, verb
■ noun 1 a flat, usually square, piece of baked CLAY, carpet or other material that is used in rows for covering walls and floors: *ceramic floor tiles* ◊ *carpet tiles* 2 a piece of baked CLAY that is used in rows for covering roofs 3 any of the small flat pieces that are used in particular board games **IDM** see NIGHT
■ verb 1 ~sth to cover a surface with tiles: *a tiled bathroom* 2 ~sth (*computing*) to arrange several windows on a computer screen so that they fill the screen but do not cover each other

**til·er** /ˈtaɪlə(r)/ noun a person whose job is to lay tiles

**til·ing** /ˈtaɪlɪŋ/ noun [U] 1 an area covered with tiles 2 the work of covering a floor, wall, etc. with tiles

**till** /tɪl/ conj., prep., noun, verb
■ conj., prep. until: *We're open till 6 o'clock.* ◊ *Can't you wait till we get home?* ◊ *Just wait till you see it. It's great.* **HELP** Till is generally felt to be more informal than until and is used much less often in writing. At the beginning of a sentence, **until** is usually used.
■ noun 1 (*BrE*) = CASH REGISTER 2 (*BrE, informal*) the place where you pay for goods in a large shop: *Please pay at the till.* ◊ *a long queue at the till* 3 (*especially NAmE*) the DRAWER where the money is put in a CASH REGISTER ⇒ WORDFINDER NOTE at SHOP **IDM** see FINGER n.
■ verb ~sth (*old use*) to prepare and use land for growing crops

**till·age** /ˈtɪlɪdʒ/ noun [U] (*old-fashioned*) 1 the process of preparing and using land for growing crops 2 land that is used for growing crops

**till·er** /ˈtɪlə(r)/ noun a bar that is used to turn the RUDDER of a small boat in order to control the direction in which it moves ⇒ compare HELM

**tilt** /tɪlt/ verb, noun
■ verb 1 [I, T] to move, or make sth move, into a position with one side or end higher than the other **SYN** tip:

**(+ adv./prep.)** *Suddenly the boat tilted to one side.* ◊ *The seat tilts forward, when you press this lever.* ◊ **~ sth (+ adv./ prep.)** *His hat was tilted slightly at an angle.* ◊ *She tilted her head back and looked up at me with a smile.* **2** [T, I] **~ (sth/sb) (in favour of/away from sth/sb)** to make sth/ sb change slightly so that one particular opinion, person, etc. is preferred or more likely to succeed than another; to change in this way: *The conditions may **tilt the balance** in favour of the Kenyan runners.* ◊ *Popular opinion has **tilted in favour** of the socialists.*
**IDM** **tilt at ˈwindmills** to waste your energy attacking imaginary enemies **ORIGIN** From Cervantes' novel *Don Quixote*, in which the hero thought that the windmills he saw were giants and tried to fight them.
**PHRV** **ˈtilt at sb/sth** (*BrE*) to attack sb/sth in speech or writing **ˈtilt at sth** (*BrE*) to try to win sth: *He was tilting at the top prize.*
■ **noun 1** [C, usually sing., U] a position in which one end or side of sth is higher than the other; an act of tilting sth to one side: *The table is at a slight tilt.* ◊ *He answered with a tilt of his head.* **2** [C] (*BrE*) an attempt to win sth or defeat sb: *She aims to **have a tilt** at the world championship next year.*
**IDM** **(at) full ˈtilt/ˈpelt** as fast as possible

**tim·ber** /ˈtɪmbə(r)/ *noun* **1** [U] trees that are grown to be used in building or for making things: *the timber industry* **2** [U] (*especially BrE*) (*also* **lum·ber** *especially in NAmE*) wood that is prepared for use in building, etc: *houses built of timber* **3** [C, usually pl.] a long heavy piece of wood used in building a house or ship: *roof timbers* **4 Timber!** used to warn people that a tree that has been cut is about to fall

**tim·bered** /ˈtɪmbəd; *NAmE* -bərd/ *adj.* built of timbers; with a FRAMEWORK of timbers ⇒ see also HALF-TIMBERED

**timbre** /ˈtæmbə(r)/ *noun* (*formal*) the quality of sound that is produced by a particular voice or musical instrument

**Tim·buktu** (*also* **Tim·buctoo**) /ˌtɪmbʌkˈtuː/ *noun* a place that is very far away **ORIGIN** From the name of a town in northern Mali.

**time** /taɪm/ *noun, verb*
■ *noun* ⇒ see also TIMES
• **MINUTES/HOURS/YEARS, ETC. 1** [U] what is measured in minutes, hours, days, etc: *time and space* ◊ **in ~** *A visit to the museum will take you **back in time** to the 1930s.* ◊ **At this point in time**, *it seems unlikely that he will write any more books.* ◊ **over ~** *Perceptions change over time* (= as time passes). ◊ *As time goes on I love this city more and more.* ⇒ see also FATHER TIME **2** [U] the time shown on a clock in minutes and hours: *What time is it/What's the time?* ◊ *Do you have the time?* ◊ (*BrE*) *What time do you make it?* ◊ (*NAmE*) *What time do you have?* ◊ *The time is now half past ten.* ◊ (*BrE*) *Can she **tell the time** yet* (= say what time it is by looking at a clock)? ◊ (*NAmE*) *Can she **tell time** yet?* ◊ *My watch **keeps perfect time** (= always shows the correct time).* ◊ *Look at the time! We'll be late.* ◊ *This time tomorrow I'll be in Canada.* **3** [U] the time measured in a particular part of the world: *6 o'clock local time* ◊ *We're two hours behind Central European Time.* ⇒ see also STANDARD TIME, SUMMER TIME **4** [U, C] the time when sth happens or when sth should happen: *What time do you finish work?* ◊ *A computer screen shows arrival and departure times.* ◊ **~ to do sth** *I think it's time to go to bed.* ◊ **~ for sth** *It's time for lunch.* ◊ **~ (that)** … *It's time the kids were in bed.* ◊ **by the ~ (that)** … *By the time you get there the meeting will be over.* ◊ **at a …~** *Have I called at a bad time? Shall I call back later?* ◊ **at the ~** *I didn't realize it at the time, but that was the best day of my life.* ◊ *The promotion came at just the **right time** for me.* ◊ *You'll feel differently about it **when the time comes*** (= when it happens). ⇒ see also ANY TIME, CLOSING TIME, CRUNCH TIME, DRIVE TIME, GAME-TIME, NIGHT-TIME, OPENING TIME
• **PERIOD 5** [U] an amount of time; the amount of time available to work, rest, etc: *I can't go with you—I don't have time.* ◊ *He **spends a lot of his time** working.* ◊ **~ for sth** *Do you have time for a chat?* ◊ **~ to do sth** *Allow plenty of time to get to the airport.* ◊ *It **takes time** to make changes in the law.* ◊ *She plans to study overseas for an extended period of time.* ◊ **free/spare time** ◊ *Don't **waste any more***

*time!* ◊ *What a **waste of time!*** ◊ *Time's running out for them to complete the project.* ◊ *Time's up—have you worked out the answer yet?* ◊ *He never takes any **time off*** (= time spent not working). ◊ *Jane's worked here for some time* (= for a fairly long period of time). ◊ *Do it now please—not in three hours' time* (= three hours from now). ⇒ see also REACTION TIME, RESPONSE TIME, SCREEN TIME **6** **a time** [sing.] a period of time, either long or short, during which you do sth or sth happens: *His injuries will **take a long time** to heal.* ◊ **for a~** *I lived in Egypt for a time.* ◊ *The early morning is the best **time of day**.* ◊ *Her parents died a long **time ago**.* ◊ **At one time** (= at a period of time in the past) *Emily was my best friend.* ◊ *Mr Curtis was the manager **in my time*** (= when I was working there). **7** [U, pl.] a period of history connected with particular events or experiences in people's lives: **at the~ of sth** *The movie is set at the time of the Russian Revolution.* ◊ **in … time(s)** *the politician who promised 'peace in our time'* ◊ *The business was successful, even during difficult times.* ◊ *Times are hard for the unemployed.* ◊ *Times have changed since Grandma was young.* ⇒ see also OLD-TIME
• **OCCASION/EVENT 8** [C] an occasion when you do sth or when sth happens: *Every time I hear that song I feel happy.* ◊ *Next time you're here let's have lunch together.* ◊ *He failed his driving test three times.* ◊ *He's determined to pass this time.* ◊ *When was the **last time** you saw her?* ◊ *I see her two or three **times a week**.* ◊ *How many times* (= how often) *do I have to tell you not to do that?* ◊ (*especially NAmE*) *I remember **one time*** (= once) *we had to abandon our car in the snow.* ◊ (*formal*) **At no time** *did I give my consent to the plan.* **HELP** To talk about the first or the last time you do sth, use **the first/last time (that) I** …: *This is the first time (that) I've been to London.* ◊ ~~*This is the first time for me to go to London.*~~ ◊ *That was the last time (that) I saw her.* **9** [C] an event or occasion that you experience in a particular way: *Did you **have a good time** in Spain?* ◊ *They're **having a hard time** dealing with her illness.*
• **FOR RACE 10** [C, U] how long sb takes to run a race or complete an event: *The winner's time was 11.6 seconds.* ◊ *She completed the 500 metres **in record time*** (= faster than any previous runner). ◊ *one of the fastest times ever*
• **IN MUSIC 11** [U] the number of BEATS (= units of rhythm) in a BAR of music: *This piece is in four-four time.* ◊ *a slow waltz time* ◊ *The conductor **beat time** with a baton.* **12** [U] the correct speed and rhythm of a piece of music: **in~ sth** *Try and dance in time to the music* (= with the same speed and rhythm). ◊ *Clap your hands to **keep time*** (= sing or move with the correct speed and rhythm). ◊ **in/out of~** *to play in/out of time* (= follow/not follow the correct speed and rhythm) ◊ *He always plays in perfect time.* ⇒ see also BIG TIME *noun*, SMALL-TIME

**IDM** **(and) about ˈtime (ˈtoo) | (and) not before ˈtime** used to say that sth should have happened before now **against ˈtime** if you do sth **against** time, you do it as fast as you can because you do not have much time: *They're working against time to try and get people out of the rubble alive.* **ahead of/behind ˈtime** earlier/later than was expected: *We finished 15 minutes **ahead of time**.* **ahead of your ˈtime** having advanced or new ideas that other people use or copy later **all the ˈtime | the whole ˈtime 1** during the whole of a particular period of time: *The letter was in my pocket all the time* (= while I was looking for it). **2** very often; repeatedly: *She leaves the lights on all the time.* **at all ˈtimes** always: *Our representatives are ready to help you at all times.* **at the ˈbest of times** even when the circumstances are very good: *He's never very happy at the best of times—he'll be much worse now!* **at the same ˈtime 1** at one time; together: *She was laughing and crying at the same time.* **2** used to introduce a fact that is different and must be considered: *You have to be firm, but at the same time you should try and be sympathetic.* **at a ˈtime** separately or in groups of two, three, etc. on each occasion: *We had to go and see the principal one at a time.* ◊ *She ran up the stairs two at a time.* **at ˈmy, ˈyour, ˈhis, etc. time of life** at the age you are (especially when you are not young): *Eyesight doesn't get any better at my time of life.* **at ˈtimes** sometimes: *He can be really*

# time bomb 1642

bad-tempered at times. **before my, your, his, etc. ˈtime 1** happening before you were born or can remember or before you lived, worked, etc. somewhere: *'Were you taught by Professor Pascal?' 'No, he was before my time.'* **2** before the usual time in sb's life when sth happens ⓢʏɴ **prematurely**: *She got old before her time.* **behind the ˈtimes** old-fashioned in your ideas, methods, etc. **do ˈtime** (*informal*) to spend time in prison **every ˈtime** whenever there is a choice: *I don't really like cities—give me the countryside every time.* **for the time ˈbeing** for a short period of time but not permanently: *You can leave your suitcase here for the time being.* **from ˌtime to ˈtime** occasionally but not regularly: *She has to work at weekends from time to time.* **have a lot of time for sb/sth** (*informal, especially BrE*) to like and be interested in sb/sth **have no time for sb/sth | not have much time for sb/sth** (*informal*) to dislike sb/sth: *I have no time for lazy people like Steve.* **have the ˌtime of your ˈlife** (*informal*) to enjoy yourself very much **have time on your ˈhands | have time to ˈkill** (*informal*) to have nothing to do or not be busy **in good ˈtime** early; with enough time so that you are not in a hurry **(all) in good ˈtime** (*informal*) used to say that sth will be done or will happen at the appropriate time and not before: *Be patient, Emily! All in good time.* **in (less than/next to) ˈno time** so soon or so quickly that it is surprising: *The kids will be leaving home in no time.* **in ˈtime** after a period of time when a situation has changed ⓢʏɴ **eventually**: *They learned to accept their stepmother in time.* **in ˈtime (for sth/to do sth)** ⓡ B1 not late; with enough time to be able to do sth: *Will we be in time for the six o'clock train? ◊ The ambulance got there just in time (= to save sb's life).* **in your own (good) ˈtime** (*informal*) when you are ready and not sooner: *Don't hassle him! He'll do it in his own good time.* **in your own ˈtime** in your free time and not when you usually work or study **it's a bout/high ˈtime** (*informal*) used to say that you think sb should do sth soon: *It's about time you cleaned your room!* **keep up/move with the ˈtimes** to change and develop your ideas, way of working, etc. so that you do what is modern and what is expected **make good, etc. ˈtime** to complete a journey quickly: *We made excellent time and arrived in Spain in two days.* **ˈmany a time | ˈmany's the time (that) …** (*old-fashioned*) many times; frequently **(the) next, first, second, etc. time ˈround** on the next, first, etc. occasion that the same thing happens: *He repeated none of the errors he'd made first time round.* ◊ *This time round it was not so easy.* **ˌnine times out of ˈten | ˌninety-nine times out of a ˈhundred** used to say that sth is usually true or almost always happens: *Nine times out of ten she gives the right answer.* **(and) not before ˈtime = (AND) ABOUT TIME (TOO)** *n.* **not give sb the ˌtime of ˈday** to refuse to speak to sb because you do not like or respect them: *Since the success of her novel, people shake her hand who once wouldn't have given her the time of day.* **(there is) no time like the ˈpresent** (*saying*) now is the best time to do sth, not in the future **of all ˈtime** that has ever existed: *Many rated him the best singer of all time.* ⊃ see also ALL-TIME **on ˈtime** ⓡ A2 at the arranged or correct time; not late: *The train arrived right on time.* **play for ˈtime** to find or create reasons why sth has to be delayed, often so you have longer to prepare for it: *His legal team, clearly playing for time, sought to have the case heard a month later.* **take your ˈtime (over sth) | take your ˈtime to do sth/doing sth 1** to use as much time as you need without hurrying: *There's no rush—take your time.* **2** used to say you think sb is late or is too slow in doing sth: *You certainly took your time getting here!* **take time ˈout** to spend some time away from your usual work or activity in order to rest or do sth else instead: *She is taking time out from her music career for a year.* ⊃ SYNONYMS at REST **there's a first time for everything** (*saying, humorous*) the fact that sth has not happened before does not mean that it will never happen **ˌtime after ˈtime | ˌtime and (ˌtime) aˈgain** often; on many or all occasions: *You will get a perfect result time after time if you follow these instructions.* **time and a ˈhalf** one and a half times the usual rate of pay ⊃ see also DOUBLE TIME **time ˈflies** (*saying*) time seems to pass very quickly: *How time flies! I've got to go now.* ◊ *Time has flown since the holiday began.* ⓞʀɪɢɪɴ This phrase is a translation of the Latin 'tempus fugit'. **time is ˈmoney** (*saying*) time is valuable, and should not be wasted **time is on your ˈside** used to say that sb can wait for sth to happen or can wait before doing sth **time ˈwas (when) …** (*old-fashioned*) used to say that sth used to happen in the past **time (alone) will ˈtell | only time will ˈtell** (*saying*) used to say that you will have to wait for some time to find out the result of a situation: *Only time will tell if the treatment has been successful.* **the whole ˈtime = ALL THE TIME** *n.* ⊃ more at BEAT *v.*, BIDE, BORROW, BUY *v.*, CALL *v.*, COURSE *n.*, DAY, DEVIL, EASY *adj.*, FORTH, FULLNESS, GAIN *v.*, GIVE *v.*, HARD *adj.*, HIGH *adj.*, KILL *v.*, LONG *adj.*, LOST *adj.*, LUCK *n.*, MARK *v.*, MATTER *n.*, NICK *n.*, NINETY, OLD, OLDEN, ONCE *adv.*, PASS *v.*, RACE *n.*, RIGHT *adj.*, SIGN *n.*, STITCH *n.*, SWEET *adj.*, THIN *adj.*, THIRD ordinal number, WHALE

■ verb
- **MEASURE TIME 1** ⓡ B2 to measure how long it takes for sth to happen or for sb to do sth: *~ sth (at sth) The winner was timed at 20.4 seconds.* ◊ *~ how long … Time how long it takes you to run ten laps.*
- **ARRANGE TIME 2** ⓡ B2 [often passive] to arrange to do sth or arrange for sth to happen at a particular time: *~ sth for sth She timed her arrival for shortly after 3.* ◊ *be … timed Their visit was perfectly timed.* ◊ *~ sth + adv. If we time it right, we should miss the traffic.* ◊ *be timed to do sth The announcement of her new role was timed to coincide with the launch of her latest book.*
- **IN SPORT 3** *~ sth* to hit or kick a ball at a particular moment in a sports game: *She timed the pass perfectly.* ◊ *a beautifully timed shot* ⊃ see also ILL-TIMED, MISTIME, TIMING, WELL TIMED

ᴘʜʀᴠ **ˌtime ˈout | ˌtime sth ˈout** (of a computer program or task) to turn off, or turn sth off, after a particular length of time even if the user has not finished: *My satellite connection timed out—it was so frustrating.*

**ˈtime bomb** *noun* **1** a bomb that can be set to explode at a particular time **2** a situation that is likely to cause serious problems in the future: *Rising unemployment is a political time bomb for the government.*

**ˈtime capsule** *noun* a container that is filled with objects that people think are typical of the time they are living in. It is buried so that it can be discovered by people in the future.

**ˈtime card** *noun* (*especially NAmE*) a piece of card on which the number of hours that sb has worked are recorded, usually by a machine

**ˈtime clock** *noun* a special clock that records the exact time that sb starts and finishes work

**time-conˈsum·ing** *adj.* taking or needing a lot of time: *a difficult and time-consuming process*

**ˈtime frame** *noun* the length of time that is used or available for sth

**ˌtime-ˈhonoured** (*US* **-honored**) *adj.* respected because it has been used or done for a long time: *They showed their approval in the time-honoured way (= by clapping, for example).*

**ˈtime·keep·er** /ˈtaɪmkiːpə(r)/ *noun* a person who records the time that is spent doing sth, for example at work or at a sports event

ɪᴅᴍ **be a good/bad ˈtimekeeper** to be regularly on time/late for work

**ˈtime·keep·ing** /ˈtaɪmkiːpɪŋ/ *noun* [U] **1** a person's ability to arrive in time for things, especially work **2** the activity of recording the time sth takes

**ˈtime lag** (*also* **lag**, **ˈtime lapse**) *noun* the period of time between two connected events: *There is a long time lag between when I do the work and when I get paid.*

**ˈtime-lapse** *adj.* [only before noun] (of photography) using a method in which a series of individual pictures of a process are shown together so that sth that really happens very slowly is shown as happening very quickly: *a time-lapse sequence of a flower opening*

**ˈtime·less** /ˈtaɪmləs/ *adj.* (*formal*) **1** not appearing to be affected by the process of time passing or by changes in fashion: *her timeless beauty* **2** existing or continuing forever **SYN** **unending**: *timeless eternity* ▶ **time·less·ly** *adv.* **time·less·ness** *noun* [U]

**'time limit** *noun* the length of time within which you must do or complete sth: *We have to set a time limit for the work.* ◇ *The work must be completed within a certain time limit.*

**time·line** /'taɪmlaɪn/ *noun* **1** a HORIZONTAL line that is used to represent time, with the past towards the left and the future towards the right **2** a list of all sb's SOCIAL MEDIA activity on a particular website or software program in the order in which it happened, with the most recent activity shown at the beginning of the list

**'time lock** *noun* **1** a lock with a device that prevents it from being opened until a particular time **2** (*computing*) part of a program that stops the program operating after a particular time

**time·ly** ?+ **C1** /'taɪmli/ *adj.* happening at exactly the right time **SYN** **opportune**: *A nasty incident was prevented by the timely arrival of the police.* ◇ *This has been a timely reminder to us all.* **OPP** **untimely** ▶ **time·li·ness** *noun* [U]

**'time machine** *noun* (in SCIENCE FICTION stories) a machine that enables you to travel in time to the past or the future

**time·out** /'taɪmaʊt/ *noun* **1** [C, U] a break in play during a sports game, especially one that a coach asks for in order to give new instructions to the team: *New coach Steve Kerr called (a) timeout and his team responded.* **2** [C] (*computing*) an occasion when a process or program stops after a particular amount of time because it has not worked successfully

**time·pass** /'taɪmpɑːs; *NAmE* -pæs/ *noun* [U] (*IndE*) the action of spending time doing sth, especially sth that has no aim or is not very useful: *She wants to have a career rather than just a few years of timepass.* ▶ **time·pass** *adj.* [only before noun]: *It's a good timepass film.*

**time·piece** /'taɪmpiːs/ *noun* (*old-fashioned* or *formal*) a clock or watch

**'time-poor** *adj.* having very little or no free time because you work all the time: *time-poor business owners* ⊃ compare CASH-RICH

**timer** /'taɪmə(r)/ *noun* (often in compounds) a device that is used to measure the time that sth takes; a device that starts or stops a machine working at a particular time: *an oven timer* ⊃ see also FIRST-TIMER, FULL-TIMER, OLD-TIMER, PART-TIMER, TWO-TIMER

**'time-release** *adj.* [usually before noun] releasing an active substance, for example a drug, a little at a time

**times** /taɪmz/ *prep., noun, verb*
- *prep.* multiplied by: *Five times two is/equals ten (5×2=10).*
- *noun* [pl.] used in comparisons to show how much more, better, etc. sth is than sth else: *three times as long as sth* ◇ *three times longer than sth* ◇ *three times the length of sth* ⊃ LANGUAGE BANK at PROPORTION
- *verb* ~ sth (by sth) (*informal*) to multiply a number: *You times the six by four to get twenty-four.*

**'time-saving** *adj.* [usually before noun] that reduces the amount of time it takes to do sth: *time-saving devices*

**time·scale** /'taɪmskeɪl/ *noun* the period of time that it takes for sth to happen or be completed: *What's the timescale for the project?*

**'time-server** *noun* (*disapproving*) a person who does as little work as possible in their job because they are just waiting until they leave for another job or retire ▶ **'time-serving** *adj., noun* [U]

**time·share** /'taɪmʃeə(r); *NAmE* -ʃer/ *noun* **1** (*also* **'time-sharing**) [U] an arrangement in which several people own a holiday home together and each uses it at a different time of the year: *timeshare apartments* **2** [C] a holiday home you own in this way: *They have a timeshare in Florida.*

**'time sheet** *noun* a piece of paper or electronic document on which the number of hours that sb has worked are recorded

**'time signal** *noun* a sound or sounds that show the exact time of day, especially a series of short, high sounds that are broadcast on the radio

**'time signature** *noun* (*music*) a sign at the start of a piece of music, usually in the form of numbers, showing the number of BEATS (= units of rhythm) in each BAR ⊃ picture at MUSIC

**'time span** *noun* a period of time: *These changes have occurred over a long time span.*

**times 'table** *noun* (*informal*) = MULTIPLICATION TABLE

**time·stamp** /'taɪmstæmp/ *noun, verb*
- *noun* a mark or record that shows when sth happened, especially a digital record of when sth was done in a computer or other electronic system: *Every message you send has a location and timestamp on it.*
- *verb* ~ sth to mark sth with a record that shows when sth happened, especially a digital record of when sth was done in a computer or other electronic system

**time·table** /'taɪmteɪbl/ *noun, verb*
- *noun* **1** (*especially BrE*) (*NAmE usually* **sched·ule**) a chart showing the times at which trains, buses and planes leave and arrive: *a bus/train timetable* **2** (*BrE*) (*NAmE* **sched·ule**) a chart or plan of the classes that a student or teacher has in school each week: *We have a new timetable each term.* ◇ *Sport is no longer so important in the school timetable* (= all the subjects that are taught at schools). **3** a plan of when you expect or hope particular events to happen **SYN** **schedule**: *I have a busy timetable this week* (= I have planned to do many things). ◇ *The government has set out its timetable for the peace talks.*
- *verb* [usually passive] (*BrE*) to arrange for sth to take place at a particular time **SYN** **schedule**: *be timetabled (for sth) A series of discussion groups have been timetabled for the afternoons.* ▶ **time·tab·ling** /-bəlɪŋ/ *noun* [U]

**'time trial** *noun* (in cycle racing and some other sports) a race in which the people who are taking part race on their own in as fast a time as possible, instead of racing against each other at the same time

**'time warp** *noun* an imaginary situation, described for example in SCIENCE FICTION, in which it is possible for people or things from the past or the future to move to the present
**IDM** **be (stuck) in a 'time warp** not having changed at all from a time in the past although everything else has

**'time-wasting** *noun* [U] (*disapproving*) **1** the act of wasting time **2** (*BrE*) (in sport) the act of playing more slowly towards the end of a game to prevent the other team from scoring ⊃ compare RUN DOWN / OUT THE CLOCK ▶ **'time-waster** *noun*

**'time-worn** *adj.* old and used a lot, and therefore damaged, or no longer useful or interesting

**'time zone** *noun* one of the 24 areas that the world is divided into, each with its own time that is one hour earlier than that of the time zone immediately to the east

**timid** /'tɪmɪd/ *adj.* shy and nervous; not brave: *He stopped in the doorway, too timid to go in.* ◇ *They've been rather timid in the changes they've made* (= they've been afraid to make any big changes). ◇ *a timid voice* ▶ **tim·id·ity** /tɪ'mɪdəti/ *noun* [U] **tim·id·ly** /'tɪmɪdli/ *adv.*

**tim·ing** ?+ **B2** /'taɪmɪŋ/ *noun* **1** ?+ **B2** [U, C] the act of choosing when sth happens; a particular point or period of time when sth happens or is planned: *The timing of the decision was a complete surprise.* ◇ *Please check your flight timings carefully.* **2** ?+ **B2** [U] the skill of doing sth at exactly the right time: *an actor with a great sense of comic timing* ◇ *Your timing is perfect. I was just about to call you.* **3** [U] the repeated rhythm of sth; the skill of producing this: *She played the piano confidently but her timing was not good.* **4** [U] (*specialist*) the rate at which an electric SPARK is produced in a vehicle's engine in order to make it work

**tim·or·ous** /'tɪmərəs/ *adj.* (*literary* or *formal*) nervous and easily frightened **SYN** **timid** ▶ **tim·or·ous·ly** *adv.*

# timpani

**tim·pani** /ˈtɪmpəni/ (also informal **timps** /tɪmps/) noun [pl.] a set of large metal drums (also called KETTLEDRUMS) in an ORCHESTRA ▸ **tim·pan·ist** /ˈtɪmpənɪst/ noun

**tin** ⓘ B1 /tɪn/ noun 1 ⓘ B1 [C] (BrE) (also **tin can**, **can** NAmE, BrE) a metal container in which food is sold; the contents of one of these containers: *Open the tin and drain the tuna.* ◇ **~ of sth** *a tin of beans/soup* 2 ⓘ B1 [C] (BrE) (also **can** NAmE, BrE) a metal container with a LID (= cover), in the shape of a CYLINDER, in which paint, GLUE , etc. is sold and stored; the contents of one of these containers: **~ of sth** *a tin of varnish* ◇ *The bedroom needed three tins of paint* (= in order to paint it). 3 [C] a metal container with a LID (= cover) used for keeping food in: *a biscuit/cake/cookie tin* 4 [C] (BrE) (NAmE **pan**) a metal container used for cooking food in: *a cake tin* 5 ⓘ B2 [U] (symb. **Sn**) a chemical element. Tin is a soft silver-white metal that is often mixed with other metals or used to cover them to prevent them from RUSTING: *a tin mine* ◇ *a tin box*
▸ IDM **(it) does (e̱xactly) what it says on the ˈtin** (informal, saying) used to say that sth is as good or effective as it claims to be, or that it really does what it claims to do. This expression is especially used when you are comparing advertisements with actual products: *I paid £150 for this camera and am more than happy with it. It does exactly what it says on the tin!* ⇨ more at CAT

**tin ˈcan** noun = TIN (1)

**tinc·ture** /ˈtɪŋktʃə(r)/ noun [C, U] (specialist) a substance DISSOLVED in alcohol for use as a medicine

**tin·der** /ˈtɪndə(r)/ noun [U] dry material, especially wood or grass, that burns easily and can be used to light a fire: *The fire started late Saturday in tinder-dry grass near the Snake River.*

**tin·der·box** /ˈtɪndəbɒks; NAmE -dɑːrbɑːks/ noun 1 a box containing dry material, used in the past for lighting a fire 2 (formal) a situation that is likely to become dangerous

**tine** /taɪn/ noun (specialist) any of the points or sharp parts of, for example, a fork or the ANTLERS of a DEER

**tin·foil** /ˈtɪnfɔɪl/ noun [U] = FOIL (1)

**tinge** /tɪndʒ/ verb, noun
▪ verb [usually passive] 1 **~ sth (with sth)** to add a small amount of colour to sth: *white petals tinged with blue* 2 **~ sth (with sth)** to add a small amount of a particular emotion or quality to sth: *a look of surprise tinged with disapproval*
▪ noun [usually sing.] a small amount of a colour, feeling or quality: *to feel a tinge of envy* ◇ *There was a faint pink tinge to the sky.* ⇨ SYNONYMS at COLOUR

**tin·gle** /ˈtɪŋgl/ verb, noun
▪ verb 1 [I] (of a part of your body) to feel as if a lot of small sharp points are pushing into it: *The cold air made her face tingle.* ◇ *a tingling sensation* ⇨ SYNONYMS at HURT 2 [I] **~ with sth** to feel an emotion strongly: *She was still tingling with excitement.*
▪ noun [usually sing.] (also **ting·ling** /ˈtɪŋglɪŋ/ [sing., U]) 1 a slight uncomfortable feeling in a part of your body 2 an exciting or uncomfortable feeling of emotion: *to feel a tingle of excitement*

**tin·gly** /ˈtɪŋgli/ adj. causing or experiencing a slight feeling of tingling: *a tingly sensation*

**tin·ker** /ˈtɪŋkə(r)/ noun, verb
▪ noun (in the past) a person who travelled from place to place, selling or repairing things
▪ verb [I] **~ (with sth)** to make small changes to sth in order to repair or improve it, especially in a way that may not be helpful

**tin·kle** /ˈtɪŋkl/ noun, verb
▪ noun [usually sing.] 1 (also **tink·ling** /ˈtɪŋklɪŋ/ [sing., U]) a light, high ringing sound: *the tinkle of glass breaking* 2 (BrE, old-fashioned, informal) a phone call 3 (informal) an act of URINATING: *to have a tinkle*

▪ verb [I, T] **~ (sth)** to make a series of light, high ringing sounds; to make sth produce this sound: *A bell tinkled as the door opened.* ◇ *tinkling laughter*

**tinned** /tɪnd/ (BrE) (also **canned** NAmE, BrE) adj. (of food) preserved in a can: *tinned fruit*

**tin·nitus** /ˈtɪnɪtəs/ noun [U] (medical) an unpleasant condition in which sb hears ringing in their ears

**tinny** /ˈtɪni/ adj., noun
▪ adj. (especially BrE, disapproving) 1 having a high, thin sound like small pieces of metal hitting each other 2 having a taste like metal: *The beer tasted tinny.*
▪ noun (also **tin·nie**) (pl. **-ies**) (AustralE, NZE, informal) a can of beer

**ˈtin opener** (BrE) (also **ˈcan opener** NAmE, BrE) noun a kitchen UTENSIL (= a tool) for opening tins of food

**tin·plate** /ˈtɪnpleɪt/ noun [U] a metal material made from iron and steel and covered with a layer of tin

**tin·pot** /ˈtɪnpɒt; NAmE -pɑːt/ adj. [only before noun] (disapproving) (especially of a leader or government) not important and of little worth or use: *a tinpot dictator*

**tin·sel** /ˈtɪnsl/ noun [U] long, thin pieces of shiny material like metal, used as decorations, especially at Christmas

**Tin·sel·town** /ˈtɪnsltaʊn/ noun [U] (informal) a way of referring to Hollywood in California, the centre of the US movie industry

**tint** /tɪnt/ noun, verb
▪ noun 1 a shade or small amount of a particular colour; a small amount of colour covering a surface: *leaves with red and gold autumn tints* ◇ *the brownish tint of an old photo* ⇨ SYNONYMS at COLOUR 2 an artificial colour used to change the colour of your hair; the act of colouring the hair with a tint: *a blond tint* ◇ *to have a tint*
▪ verb 1 [usually passive] **~ sth (with sth)** to add a small amount of colour to sth 2 **~ sth** to change the colour of sb's hair with a tint ▸ **tint·ed** adj.: *tinted glasses*

**T-intersection** (NAmE) (BrE **ˈT-junction**) noun a place where one road joins another but does not cross it, so that the roads form the shape of the letter T

**ˈtin whistle** (also **ˈpenny whistle**) noun a simple musical instrument like a short pipe with six holes, that you play by blowing

**tiny** ⓘ B1 /ˈtaɪni/ adj. (**tini·er**, **tini·est**) very small in size or amount: *We come from a tiny little town in upstate New York.* ◇ *Only a tiny minority hold such extreme views.*
▸ IDM see PATTERN n.

**-tion** ⇨ -ION

**tip** ⓘ A2 /tɪp/ noun, verb
▪ noun
• ADVICE 1 ⓘ A2 a small piece of advice about sth practical SYN **hint**: **~ on/for doing sth** *handy tips for buying a computer* ◇ **~ on/for sth** *useful tips on how to save money* 2 (informal) a secret or expert piece of advice about what the result of a competition, etc. is likely to be, especially about which horse is likely to win a race: *a hot tip for the big race* 3 (NAmE) (also **ˈtip-off** especially in BrE) (informal) secret information that sb gives, for example to the police, to warn them about an illegal activity that is going to happen or has happened: *The man was arrested after an anonymous tip.*
• EXTRA MONEY 4 ⓘ B1 a small amount of extra money that you give to sb, for example sb who serves you in a restaurant: *to leave a tip* ◇ *He gave the waiter a generous tip.*
• END OF STH 5 the thin, pointed end of sth: *the tips of your fingers* ◇ *the tip of your nose* ◇ *the northern tip of the island* ⇨ see also FINGERTIP 6 a small part that fits on or over the end of sth: *a walking stick with a rubber tip* ⇨ see also FELT-TIP PEN, Q-TIP™
• FOR RUBBISH 7 (BrE) a place where you can take rubbish and leave it
• UNTIDY PLACE 8 (BrE, informal, disapproving) an untidy place SYN **dump**: *Their flat is a tip!* ⇨ see also HAT TIP
▸ IDM **on the tip of your ˈtongue** if a word or name is **on the tip of your tongue**, you are sure that you know it but you

cannot remember it **the tip of the ˈiceberg** only a small part of a much larger problem
- **verb** (**-pp-**)
- • GIVE EXTRA MONEY **1** ⓘ B1 [I, T] to give sb an extra amount of money to thank them for sth they have done for you as part of their job: *Americans were always welcome because they tended to tip heavily.* ◇ **~sb** *Did you remember to tip the waiter?* ◇ **~sb sth** *She tipped the porter a dollar.*
- • LEAN/POUR/PUSH AT AN ANGLE **2** [I, T] to move so that one end or side is higher than the other; to move sth into this position SYN **tilt**. (**+ adv./prep.**) *The boat tipped to one side.* ◇ *The seat tips forward to allow passengers into the back.* ◇ **~sth (+ adv./prep.)** *She tipped her head back and laughed loudly.* **3** [T] **~sth/sb + adv./prep.** to make sth/sb come out of a container or its/their position by holding or lifting it/them at an angle: *She tipped the dirty water down the drain.* ◇ *The bus stopped abruptly, nearly tipping me out of my seat.* **4** [T] **~sth + adv./prep.** to touch sth lightly so that it moves in a particular direction: *The goalkeeper just managed to tip the ball over the crossbar.*
- • LEAVE RUBBISH **5** [I, T] **~(sth)** (*BrE*) to leave rubbish somewhere outdoors in order to get rid of it: *'No tipping.'* (= for example, on a notice) ⊃ see also FLY-TIP
- • PREDICT SUCCESS **6** [T, usually passive] (*especially BrE*) to say in advance that sb/sth will be successful: **be tipped for sth** *The band is being tipped for the top.* ◇ **be tipped as sth** *The senator has been tipped by many as a future president.* ◇ **be tipped to do sth** *The actor is tipped to win an Oscar for his performance.*
- • COVER END **7** [T, usually passive] to cover the end or edge of sth with a colour, a substance, etc: **be tipped with sth** *The wings are tipped with yellow.*

IDM ▶ **it is/was ˈtipping (it) down** (*BrE*) it is/was raining heavily **tip the ˈbalance/ˈscales** (*also* **swing the ˈbalance**) to affect the result of sth in one way rather than another: *In an interview, smart presentation can tip the scales in your favour.* **tip your ˈhand** (*NAmE*) (*BrE* **show your ˈhand/ˈcards**) to make your plans or intentions known **tip the scales at sth** to weigh a particular amount: *He tipped the scales at just over 80 kilos.* **tip the ˈwink** | **tip the ˈwink to sb** (*BrE, informal*) to give sb secret information that they can use to gain an advantage for themselves ⊃ more at HAT

PHRV ▶ ˌtip sb↔ˈoff (about sth) (*informal*) to warn sb about sth that is going to happen or has happened, especially sth illegal: *Three men were arrested after police were tipped off about the raid.* ◇ **tip sb off that … ** *They were tipped off that he might be living in Wales.* ⊃ related noun TIP-OFF ˌtip ˈup/ˈover | ˌtip sth ↔ ˈup/ˈover to fall or turn over; to make sth do this: *The mug tipped over, spilling hot coffee everywhere.* ◇ *We'll have to tip the sofa up to get it through the door.*

**ˈtip-off** *noun* (*especially BrE*) (*NAmE usually* **tip**) (*informal*) secret information that sb gives, for example to the police, to warn them about an illegal activity that is going to happen or has happened: *The man was arrested after an anonymous tip-off.*

**tip·per** /ˈtɪpə(r)/ *noun* **1** (used with an adjective) a person who gives sb a tip (= a small amount of extra money to thank them for doing sth as part of their job) of the size mentioned: *She says that Americans are usually big tippers.* **2** (*also* **ˈtipper lorry/truck**) a lorry with a container part that can be moved into a sloping position so that its load can slide off at the back

**ˈtipping point** *noun* the point at which the number of small changes over a period of time reaches a level where a further small change has a sudden and very great effect on a system or leads to an idea suddenly spreading quickly among a large number of people

**tip·ple** /ˈtɪpl/ *noun, verb*
- **noun** [usually sing.] (*especially BrE, informal*) an alcoholic drink: *His favourite tipple was rum and lemon.*
- **verb** [I, T] **~(sth)** (*especially BrE, informal*) to drink alcohol ▶ **tip·pler** /-plə(r)/ *noun*

**tip·ster** /ˈtɪpstə(r)/ *noun* **1** a person who tells you, often in exchange for money, which horse is likely to win a race, so that you can bet on it and win money **2** (*especially NAmE*) a

---

**1645**      **tissue**

person who gives information to the police about a crime or criminal

**tipsy** /ˈtɪpsi/ *adj.* (*informal*) slightly drunk SYN **tight**

**tip·toe** /ˈtɪptəʊ/ *noun, verb*
- **noun**
IDM **on ˈtiptoe/ˈtiptoes** standing or walking on the front part of your foot, with your heels off the ground, in order to make yourself taller or to move very quietly: *She had to stand on tiptoe to reach the top shelf.* ◇ *We crept around on tiptoes so as not to disturb him.*
- **verb** [I] (**+ adv./prep.**) to walk using the front parts of your feet only, so that other people cannot hear you: *I tiptoed over to the window.*

**ˈtip-ˈtop** *adj.* (*usually before noun*) (*informal*) excellent: *The house is in tip-top condition.*

**ˈtip-up** *adj.* (of a seat) moving up into a VERTICAL position when nobody is sitting on it

**tir·ade** /taɪˈreɪd; *NAmE* ˈtaɪreɪd/ *noun* **~(against sb/sth)** a long angry speech criticizing sb/sth or accusing sb of sth: *She launched into a tirade of abuse against politicians.*

**tira·misu** /ˌtɪrəməˈsuː; *NAmE* -rəˈmiːsuː/ *noun* [U, C] (*from Italian*) an Italian DESSERT (= sweet dish) made from layers of cake with coffee, chocolate and MASCARPONE cheese

**tire** /ˈtaɪə(r)/ *verb, noun*
- **verb** [I, T] **~(sb)** to become tired and feel as if you want to sleep or rest; to make sb feel this way: *Her legs were beginning to tire.* ◇ *Walking even a short distance tires him.*
IDM **never tire of doing sth** to do sth a lot, especially in a way that annoys people: *He went to Harvard—as he never tires of reminding us.*
PHRV ˈ**tire of sth/sb** to become bored with sth/sb or begin to enjoy it/them less: *They soon tired of the beach and went for a walk.* ˌ**tire sb/yourˈself out** to make sb/yourself feel very tired ⊃ see also TIRED
- **noun** (*NAmE*) (*BrE* **tyre**) a thick rubber ring that fits around the edge of a wheel of a car, bicycle, etc: *a front/rear tire* ◇ *to pump up a tire* ◇ *a flat tire* ◇ *Someone had slashed the tires on her car.* ◇ *Remember to check your tire pressure regularly.* ⊃ see also SPARE TYRE

**tired** ⓘ A1 /ˈtaɪəd; *NAmE* -ərd/ *adj.* **1** A1 feeling that you would like to sleep or rest; needing rest SYN **weary**: *to be/look/feel tired* ◇ *They were cold, hungry and tired out* (= very tired). ◇ *He still felt really tired and wanted to stay in bed.* ◇ **~from (doing) sth** *I'm still a bit tired from the journey.* ⊃ WORDFINDER NOTE at SLEEP **2** ⓘ A2 feeling that you have had enough of sb/sth because you no longer find them/it interesting or because they make you angry or unhappy: **~of sb/sth** *I'm sick and tired of all the arguments.* ◇ **~of (sb) doing sth** *She was tired of hearing about their trip to India.* **3** boring because it is too familiar or has been used too much: *He always comes out with the same tired old jokes.* ▶ **tired·ly** *adv.*: *He shook his head tiredly.* **tired·ness** *noun* [U] ⊃ see also DOG-TIRED

**ˈtire iron** *noun* (*NAmE*) a metal tool for taking tires off wheels

**tire·less** /ˈtaɪələs; *NAmE* -ərl-/ *adj.* (*approving*) putting a lot of hard work and energy into sth over a long period of time SYN **indefatigable**: *a tireless campaigner for human rights* ▶ **tire·less·ly** *adv.*

**tire·some** /ˈtaɪəsəm; *NAmE* -ərs-/ *adj.* making you feel annoyed SYN **annoying**: *Buying a house can be a very tiresome business.* ◇ *The children were being very tiresome.* ▶ **tire·some·ly** *adv.*

**tir·ing** /ˈtaɪərɪŋ/ *adj.* making you feel the need to sleep or rest SYN **exhausting**: *It had been a long, tiring day.*

**'tis** /tɪz/ *short form* (*old use*) it is

**tis·sue** ⓘ B2 /ˈtɪʃuː/ *noun* **1** ⓘ B2 [C] a piece of soft paper, used especially as a HANDKERCHIEF: *a box of tissues* ◇ *He wiped his nose on a tissue.* **2** ⓘ C1 [U] (*also* **tissues** [pl.]) a collection of cells that form the different parts of humans, animals and plants: *muscle/brain/lung tissue* ◇ *scar tissue* ⊃ see also SOFT TISSUE **3** (*also* **ˈtissue paper**) [U] very thin

# Titan

paper used for wrapping and packing things that break easily
**IDM** **a ˌtissue of ˈlies** (*literary*) a story, an excuse, etc. that is full of lies

**tit** /tɪt/ *noun* **1** [usually pl.] (*also* **titty**) (*taboo, slang*) a woman's breast or NIPPLE **2** (*BrE, slang*) a stupid person **3** a small European bird. There are several types of tit: *a great tit* ⇨ see also BLUE TIT

**Titan** (*also* **titan**) /ˈtaɪtn/ *noun* (*formal*) a person who is very large, strong, intelligent or important ORIGIN From the Titans, who in Greek mythology were the older gods who were defeated in a battle with Zeus.

**ti·tan·ic** /taɪˈtænɪk/ *adj.* (*formal*) very large, important, strong or difficult: *a titanic struggle between good and evil*

**ti·tan·ium** /tɪˈteɪniəm, taɪ-/ *noun* [U] (*symb.* **Ti**) a chemical element. Titanium is a silver-white metal used in making various strong, light materials.

**tit·bit** /ˈtɪtbɪt/ (*BrE*) (*NAmE* **tid·bit**) *noun* **1** a small special piece of food SYN **morsel 2** a small but interesting piece of news SYN **snippet**: *titbits of gossip*

**titch** /tɪtʃ/ *noun* (*BrE, informal, often humorous*) used as a way of talking about or addressing a very small person

**titchy** /ˈtɪtʃi/ *adj.* (*BrE, informal*) very small

**ˌtit for ˈtat** *noun* [U] a situation in which you do sth bad to sb because they have done the same to you: *the routine tit for tat when countries expel each other's envoys* ◊ *tit-for-tat assassinations by rival gangs*

**tithe** /taɪð/ *noun* **1** (in the past) a tenth of the goods that sb produced or the money that they earned, that was paid as a tax to support the Church **2** (in some Christian Churches today) a tenth of a person's income, that they give to the Church

**tit·il·late** /ˈtɪtɪleɪt/ *verb* [I, T] (*often disapproving*) to cause sb to be interested or excited, especially in a sexual way: *titillating pictures* ▸ **~ sth** *a story intended to titillate the imagination of the public* ▸ **tit·il·la·tion** /ˌtɪtɪˈleɪʃn/ *noun* [U]

**title** ❶ A1 **S** /ˈtaɪtl/ *noun*, *verb*
■ *noun* **1** A1 [C] the name of a book, poem, painting, piece of music, etc: *What's title of her new book?* ◊ *under a~ His poems were published under the title of 'Love and Reason'.* ◊ *the title track from their latest CD* (= the song with the same title as the disc) ⇨ see also WORKING TITLE ⇨ WORDFINDER NOTE at BOOK **2** [C] a particular book or magazine: *The company publishes twenty new titles a year.* **3** B1 [C] a word in front of a person's name to show their rank or profession, whether or not they are married, etc: *The present duke inherited the title from his father.* ◊ *Give your name and title* (= Mr, Miss, Ms, Dr, etc.). ⇨ note at NAME **4** B1 [C] a name that describes a job: *What is your name and job title?* **5** [C] the position of being the winner of a competition, especially a sports competition: *She has won three world titles.* ◊ *the world heavyweight title* ◊ *the league/division/national title* **6** [U, sing.] **~ (to sth/to do sth)** (*law*) the legal right to own sth, especially land or property; the document that shows you have this right
■ *verb* B2 [usually passive] to give a book, piece of music, etc. a particular name: **be titled** … *Their first album was titled 'Made in Valmez'.*

**ˈtitle bar** *noun* (*computing*) a bar at the top of a computer screen, which shows the name of the program and file that is on the screen

**titled** /ˈtaɪtld/ *adj.* having a title such as Lord, LADY, etc. ⇨ see also SELF-TITLED

**ˈtitle deed** *noun* [usually pl.] a legal document proving that sb is the owner of a particular house, etc.

**ˈtitle-holder** *noun* **1** a person or team that has defeated all the other people or teams taking part in an important competition: *the current Olympic title-holder* **2** (*specialist, NAmE*) the legal owner of sth

**ˈtitle page** *noun* a page at the front of a book that has the title and the author's name on it

**titl·ist** /ˈtaɪtlɪst/ *noun* (*NAmE*) a person who has won a sports title: *a heavyweight titlist*

**ti·trate** /taɪˈtreɪt, tɪ-/ *verb* **~ sth** (*chemistry*) to find out how much of a particular substance is in a liquid by measuring how much of another substance is needed to react with it ▸ **ti·tra·tion** /-ˈtreɪʃn/ *noun* [U]

**tit·ter** /ˈtɪtə(r)/ *verb* [I] to laugh quietly, especially in a nervous or embarrassed way SYN **giggle** ▸ **tit·ter** *noun*

**tittle-tattle** /ˈtɪtl ˌtætl/ *noun* [U] (*informal, disapproving*) unimportant talk, usually not true, about other people and their lives SYN **gossip**

**titty** /ˈtɪti/ *noun* (*pl.* **-ies**) (*taboo, slang*) = TIT (1)

**titu·lar** /ˈtɪtjələ(r); *NAmE* -tʃə-/ *adj.* [only before noun] **1** (*formal*) having a particular title or status but no real power or authority SYN **nominal**: *the titular head of state* **2** the titular character of a book, play, film, etc. is the one mentioned in the title SYN **eponymous**

**tix** /tɪks/ *noun* [pl.] (*especially NAmE, informal*) tickets: *We got tix for the game tomorrow.*

**tizzy** /ˈtɪzi/ (*also* **tizz** /tɪz/) *noun* [sing.] (*informal*) a state of nervous excitement or worry: *She was in a real tizzy before the meeting.*

**tjant·ing tool** /ˈtʃæntɪŋ tuːl/ *noun* (*EAfrE*) a tool like a pen used in BATIK (= a method of printing patterns on cloth using hot WAX)

**ˈT-junction** (*BrE*) (*NAmE* **ˌT-ˈintersection**) *noun* a place where one road joins another but does not cross it, so that the roads form the shape of the letter T

**TLC** /ˌtiː el ˈsiː/ *noun* [U] (*informal*) care that you give sb to make them feel better (the abbreviation for 'tender loving care'): *What he needs now is just rest and a lot of TLC.*

**Tlin·git** /ˈtlɪŋɡɪt/ *noun* (*pl.* **Tlin·git** or **Tlin·gits**) a member of a Native American people, many of whom live in the US state of Alaska

**TM** /ˌtiː ˈem/ *abbr.* **1** TRADEMARK **2** (*US* **T.M.**) TRANSCENDENTAL MEDITATION

**TMI** (*also* **tmi**) /ˌtiː em ˈaɪ/ *abbr.* (*informal*) too much information (used to say that sb has given some personal information that is embarrassing): *I needed to go to the bathroom very badly—sorry, TMI!*

**TNT** /ˌtiː en ˈtiː/ *noun* [U] a powerful EXPLOSIVE

**to** ❶ A1 /tə, before vowels tu, strong form tuː/ *prep.*, *infinitive marker*, *adv.*
■ *prep.* HELP For the special uses of **to** in phrasal verbs, look at the entries for the verbs. For example **see to sth** is in the phrasal verb section at **see**. **1** A1 in the direction of sth; towards sth: *I walked to the office.* ◊ *It fell to the ground.* ◊ *It was on the way to the station.* ◊ *He's going to Paris.* ◊ *my first visit to Africa* ◊ *He pointed to something on the opposite bank.* ◊ *Her childhood was spent travelling from place to place.* **2** A1 **as far as sth**: *The meadows lead down to the river.* ◊ *Her hair fell to her waist.* **3** A1 **~ the sth (of sth)** located in the direction mentioned from sth: *Place the cursor to the left of the first word.* ◊ *There are mountains to the north.* **4** A1 used to show the person or thing that receives sth: *He gave it to his sister.* ◊ *I'll explain to you where everything goes.* ◊ *I am deeply grateful to my parents.* ◊ *Who did she address the letter to?* ◊ (*formal*) *To whom did she address the letter?* **5** A1 used to show the end or limit of a range or period of time: *a drop in profits from $105 million to around $75 million* ◊ *I'd say he was 25 to 30 years old* (= approximately 25 or 30 years old). ◊ *I like all kinds of music from opera to reggae.* ◊ *We only work from Monday to Friday.* ◊ *I watched the programme from beginning to end.* **6** A1 before the start of sth: *How long is it to lunch?* ◊ (*especially BrE*) *It's five to ten* (= five minutes before ten o'clock). **7** A1 reaching a particular state: *The vegetables were cooked to perfection.* ◊ *He tore the letter to pieces.* ◊ *She sang the baby to sleep.* ◊ *The letter reduced her to tears* (= made her cry). ◊ *His expression changed from amazement to joy.* **8** A1 used to show the person or thing that is affected by an action: *She is devoted to her family.* ◊ *What have you done to your hair?* **9** A1 used to show that two things are attached or connected: *Attach this rope to the front of the car.* **10** A1 used to show a

relationship between one person or thing and another: *She's married to an Italian.* ◊ *the Japanese ambassador to France* ◊ *the key to the door* ◊ *the solution to this problem* **11** 🔑 **A1** directed towards; in connection with: *It was a threat to world peace.* ◊ *She made a reference to her recent book.* **12** 🔑 **A1** used to introduce the second part of a comparison or RATIO: *I prefer walking to climbing.* ◊ *The industry today is nothing to what it once was.* ◊ *We won by six goals to three.* **13** 🔑 **B1** used to show a quantity or rate: *There are 2.54 centimetres to an inch.* ◊ *This car does 30 miles to the gallon.* ⊃ compare PER **14** 🔑 **B1** in honour of sb/sth: *a monument to the soldiers who died in the war* ◊ *Let's drink to Julia and her new job.* **15** 🔑 **A1** used to show sb's attitude or reaction to sth: *His music isn't really to my taste.* ◊ *To her astonishment, he smiled.* **16** 🔑 **B1** used to show what sb's opinion or feeling about sth is: *It sounded like crying to me.* **17** while sth else is happening or being done: *He left the stage to prolonged applause.* **18** used after verbs of movement to mean 'with the intention of giving sth': *People rushed to her rescue and picked her up.*

■ **infinitive marker** HELP **To** is often used before the base form of a verb to show that the verb is in the infinitive. The infinitive is used after many verbs and also after many nouns and adjectives. **1** 🔑 **A1** used to show purpose or intention: *I set out to buy food.* ◊ *I am going to tell you a story.* ◊ *She was determined to do well.* ◊ *His aim was to become president.* ◊ *To be honest with you, I don't remember what he said.* **2** 🔑 **A1** used to show the result of sth: *She managed to escape.* ◊ *It was too hot to go out.* ◊ *He couldn't get close enough to see.* **3** 🔑 **A1** used to show the cause of sth: *I'm sorry to hear that.* **4** 🔑 **A1** used to show an action that you want or are advised to do: *I'd love to go to France this summer.* ◊ *The leaflet explains how to apply for a place.* ◊ *I don't know what to say.* HELP **To** can also be used without a following verb when the missing verb is easy to understand: *He asked her to come but she said she didn't want to.* **5** 🔑 **A1** used to show sth that is known or reported about a particular person or thing: *The house was said to be haunted.* **6** 🔑 **A1** used to show that one action immediately follows another: *I reached the station only to find that my train had already left.* **7 am, is, are, was, were ~** used to show that you must or should do sth: *You are not to talk during the exam.* ◊ *She was to be here at 8.30 but she didn't arrive.*

■ ***adv.*** /tu:/ (usually of a door) in or into a closed position: *Push the door to.*

IDM **,to and 'fro** backwards and forwards: *She rocked the baby to and fro.* ⊃ see also TOING AND FROING at TOING

**toad** /təʊd/ *noun* **1** a small animal like a frog but with a drier and less smooth skin, that lives on land but BREEDS (= produces young) in water (= is an AMPHIBIAN) ⊃ VISUAL VOCAB page V3 **2** (*informal, disapproving*) an unpleasant person

**toad·stool** /ˈtəʊdstuːl/ *noun* a FUNGUS with a round flat or curved head and a short STEM. Many types of toadstool are poisonous. ⊃ compare MUSHROOM

**toady** /ˈtəʊdi/ *noun, verb*

■ ***noun*** (*pl.* **-ies**) (*informal, disapproving*) a person who is too kind or shows too much respect towards sb more important in order to gain their favour or help SYN sycophant

■ ***verb*** [I] (**toad·ies, toady·ing, toad·ied, toad·ied**) **~ (to sb)** (*disapproving*) to treat sb more important with special respect or kind treatment in order to gain their favour or help

**toast** /təʊst/ *noun, verb*

■ ***noun*** **1** [U] slices of bread that have been made brown and dry by heating them on both sides in a toaster or under a GRILL: *cheese on toast* ◊ *a piece of toast* ◊ *two* **slices/rounds** *of toast* ⊃ see also FRENCH TOAST **2** [C] **~ (to sb/sth)** the act of a group of people wishing sb happiness, success, etc. by drinking a glass of sth, especially alcohol, at the same time: *I'd like to* **propose a toast** *to the bride and groom.* ◊ *The committee* **drank a toast** *to the new project.* **3** [sing.] **the ~ of …** a person who is praised by a lot of people in a particular place because of sth that they have done well: *The performance made her the toast of the festival.*

IDM **be ˈtoast** (*informal*) to be likely to die or be destroyed; to be in serious trouble: *One mistake and you're toast.* ⊃ more at DRINK *v.*

■ ***verb*** **1** [T] **~ sb/sth** to lift a glass of wine, etc. in the air and drink it at the same time as other people in order to wish sb/sth success, happiness, etc: *The happy couple were toasted in champagne.* ◊ *We toasted the success of the new company.* **2** [T, I] **~(sth)** to make sth, especially bread, turn brown by heating it in a toaster or close to heat; to turn brown in this way: *a toasted sandwich* ◊ *Place under a hot grill until the nuts have toasted.* **3** [T] **~ sth** to warm a part of your body by placing it near a fire

**toast·er** /ˈtəʊstə(r)/ *noun* an electrical machine for making toast

**toastie** /ˈtəʊsti/ *noun* (*BrE*) a sandwich that has been TOASTED

**toasty** /ˈtəʊsti/ *adj.* (*especially NAmE*) warm and comfortable

**to·bacco** 🔑+ **C1** /təˈbækəʊ/ *noun* [U, C] (*pl.* **-os**) the dried leaves of the tobacco plant that are used for making cigarettes, smoking in a pipe, etc: *The government imposed a ban on tobacco advertising* (= the advertising of cigarettes and all other forms of tobacco).

**to·bac·con·ist** /təˈbækənɪst/ *noun* **1** a person who owns, manages or works in a shop selling cigarettes, tobacco for pipes, etc. **2 to·bac·con·ist's** (*pl.* **to·bac·con·ists**) a shop that sells cigarettes, tobacco, etc: *There's a tobacconist's on the corner.*

**to·bog·gan** /təˈbɒɡən/ *NAmE* -ˈbɑːɡ-/ *noun, verb*

■ ***noun*** a long, light, narrow SLEDGE (= a vehicle that slides over snow) sometimes curved up in front, used for sliding down slopes

■ ***verb*** [I] to travel down a slope on snow or ice using a toboggan ▸ **to·bog·gan·ing** *noun* [U]

**toc·cata** /təˈkɑːtə/ *noun* a piece of music for a keyboard instrument that includes difficult passages designed to show the player's skill

**today** 🔑 **A1** /təˈdeɪ/ *adv., noun*

■ ***adv.*** **1** 🔑 **A1** on this day: *I've got a piano lesson later today.* ◊ *The exams start a* **week today/today week** (= one week from now). **2** 🔑 **A1** at the present period SYN **nowadays**: *Young people today face a very difficult future at work.*

■ ***noun*** [U] **1** 🔑 **A1** this day: *Today is her tenth birthday.* ◊ *The review is in today's paper.* ◊ *I'm leaving a week from today.* **2** 🔑 **A1** the present period of time: *The film is about growing up in* **today's** *world.* ◊ **of ~** *the youth of today*

**tod·dle** /ˈtɒdl/; *NAmE* ˈtɑːdl/ *verb* **1** [I] when a young child who has just learnt to walk **toddles**, he/she walks with short, unsteady steps **2** [I] **+ adv./prep.** (*informal*) to walk or go somewhere: *She toddles down to the park most afternoons.* ◊ *I locked the door and then toddled off to bed.*

**tod·dler** /ˈtɒdlə(r)/; *NAmE* ˈtɑːd-/ *noun* a child who has only recently learnt to walk

**toddy** /ˈtɒdi/; *NAmE* ˈtɑːdi/ *noun* [C, U] (*pl.* **-ies**) a drink made with strong alcohol, sugar, hot water and sometimes SPICES

**to-do** /tə ˈduː/ *noun* [sing.] (*informal, becoming old-fashioned*) unnecessary excitement or anger about sth SYN **fuss**: *What a to-do!*

**to-ˈdo list** *noun* a list of tasks that you have to do: *on your ~ A marathon has been on my to-do list for 20 years.*

**toe** 🔑 **B1** /təʊ/ *noun, verb*

■ ***noun*** **1** 🔑 **B1** one of the five small parts that stick out from the foot; any similar part on the foot of an animal or bird: *the* **big/little toe** (= the largest/smallest toe) ◊ *Can you* **touch your toes**? (= by bending over while keeping your legs straight) ◊ **on your toes** *She stood on her toes and kissed him.* ⊃ HOMOPHONES at TOW ⊃ VISUAL VOCAB page V1 **2** 🔑 **B1** the part of a sock, shoe, etc. that covers the toes: *He kicked the earth with the toe of his boot.* **3 -toed** (in adjectives) having the type or number of toes mentioned: *open-toed sandals* ◊ *a three-toed sloth*

# toecap

**IDM** **keep sb on their ˈtoes** to make sure that sb is ready to deal with anything that might happen by doing things that they are not expecting: *Surprise visits help to keep the staff on their toes.* **make sb's ˈtoes curl** to make sb feel embarrassed or uncomfortable ⇒ see also TOE-CURLING ⇒ more at DIG v., DIP v., HEAD n., STEP v., TOP n., TREAD v.
■ *verb*
**IDM** **toe the (party) ˈline** (*NAmE also* **toe the ˈmark**) to say or do what sb in authority tells you to say or do, even if you do not share the same opinions, etc: *MPs rarely fail to toe the party line.*

**toe·cap** /ˈtəʊkæp/ *noun* a piece of metal or leather that covers the front part of a shoe or boot to make it stronger

**ˈtoe-curling** *adj.* (*informal*) extremely embarrassing because of being very bad or silly ▶ **ˈtoe-curlingly** *adv.*: *a toe-curlingly awful movie*

**TOEFL™** /ˈtəʊfl/ *noun* a test of a person's level of English that is taken in order to go to a university in the US (the abbreviation for 'Test of English as a Foreign Language')

**toe·hold** /ˈtəʊhəʊld/ *noun* **1** a position in a place or an activity that you hope will lead to more power or success: *The firm is anxious to gain a toehold in Europe.* **2** a very small hole or space on a ROCK FACE, just big enough to put your foot in when you are climbing

**TOEIC™** /ˈtəʊɪk/ *noun* [U] a test that measures your ability to read and understand English if it is not your first language (the abbreviation for 'Test of English for International Communication')

**toe·nail** /ˈtəʊneɪl/ *noun* the nail on a toe ⇒ VISUAL VOCAB page V1

**ˈtoe-tapping** *adj.* (*informal*) (of music) lively and making you want to move your feet

**toe-to-ˈtoe** *adj.* = HEAD-TO-HEAD ▶ **toe-to-ˈtoe** *adv.*: *Democratic leaders are going toe-to-toe with the president.*

**toff** /tɒf/ *noun* (*BrE, informal*) a way of referring to sb from a high social class that shows that you do not approve of them

**tof·fee** /ˈtɒfi/ *NAmE* /ˈtɑːfi/ *noun* [U, C] a sticky sweet made by heating sugar, butter and water together and allowing it to cool
**IDM** **can't do sth for ˈtoffee** (*BrE, old-fashioned, informal*) if sb **can't do sth for toffee**, they are very bad at doing it: *He can't dance for toffee!*

**ˈtoffee apple** (*BrE*) (*NAmE* **ˈcandy apple**) *noun* an apple covered with a thin layer of hard toffee and fixed on a stick

**tofu** /ˈtəʊfuː/ (*also* **ˈbean curd**) *noun* [U] a soft white substance that is made from SOYA and used in cooking, often instead of meat

**tog** /tɒɡ/; *NAmE* /tɑːɡ/ *noun, verb*
■ *noun* **1 togs** [pl.] (*informal, becoming old-fashioned*) clothes, especially ones that you wear for a particular purpose: *running togs* **2** (*BrE*) a unit for measuring how warm bed covers such as DUVETS are
■ *verb* (-gg-)
**IDM** **be ˌtogged ˈout/ˈup (in sth)** (*informal*) to be wearing clothes for a particular activity or occasion: *They were all togged up in their skiing gear.*

**toga** /ˈtəʊɡə/ *noun* a loose outer piece of clothing worn by the citizens of ancient Rome

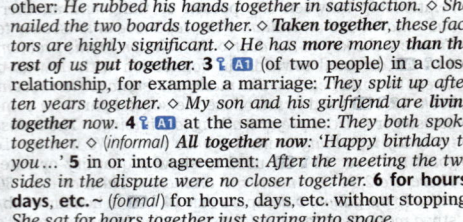
toga

**to·gether** ● A1 ⓢ /təˈɡeðə(r)/ *adv., adj.*
■ *adv.* **HELP** For the special uses of **together** in phrasal verbs, look at the entries for the verbs. For example **pull yourself together** is in the phrasal verb section at **pull**. **1** A1 with or near to sb/sth else; with each other: *We grew up together.* ◇ *Get all the ingredients together before you start cooking.* ◇ *Stay close together—I don't want anyone to get lost.* ◇ *Do you want to get together* (= meet) *again next week?* **2** A1 so that two or more things touch or are joined to or combined with each other: *He rubbed his hands together in satisfaction.* ◇ *She nailed the two boards together.* ◇ **Taken together**, these factors are highly significant. ◇ *He has more money than the rest of us put together.* **3** A1 (of two people) in a close relationship, for example a marriage: *They split up after ten years together.* ◇ *My son and his girlfriend are living together now.* **4** A1 at the same time: *They both spoke together.* ◇ (*informal*) **All together now**: 'Happy birthday to you…' **5** in or into agreement: *After the meeting the two sides in the dispute were no closer together.* **6 for hours, days, etc.** ~ (*formal*) for hours, days, etc. without stopping: *She sat for hours together just staring into space.*
**IDM** **toˌgether ˈwith 1** B1 including: *Together with the Johnsons, there were 12 of us in the villa.* **2** B1 in addition to; as well as: *Our meal arrived, together with a bottle of red wine.*
■ *adj.* (*informal, approving*) (of a person) well organized and confident: *He's incredibly together for someone so young.*

**to·gether·ness** /təˈɡeðənəs/; *NAmE* -ðərn-/ *noun* [U] the happy feeling you have when you are with people you like, especially family and friends

**tog·gle** /ˈtɒɡl/; *NAmE* /ˈtɑːɡl/ *noun, verb*
■ *noun* **1** a short piece of wood, plastic, etc. that is put through a LOOP of THREAD to fasten sth, such as a coat or bag, instead of a button **2** (*also* **ˈtoggle switch**) (*computing*) a key on a computer that you press to change from one style or operation to another, and back again
■ *verb* [I, T] (*computing*) to press a key or set of keys on a computer keyboard in order to turn a feature on or off, or to move from one program, etc. to another: ~ (**between A and B**) *He toggled between the two windows.* ◇ ~ **sth** *This key toggles various views of the data.* ⇒ WORDFINDER NOTE at COMMAND

**ˈtoggle switch** *noun* **1** an electrical switch that you move up and down or backwards and forwards **2** (*computing*) = TOGGLE

**toil** /tɔɪl/ *verb, noun*
■ *verb* (*formal*) **1** [I] to work very hard and/or for a long time, usually doing hard physical work **SYN** **slave** **2** [I] + *adv./prep.* to move slowly and with difficulty **SYN** **slog**: *They toiled up the hill in the blazing sun.* ▶ **toil·er** *noun*
■ *noun* [U] (*formal or literary*) hard, unpleasant work that makes you very tired: *a life of hardship and toil* ⇒ see also TOILS

**toi·let** ● A1 /ˈtɔɪlət/ *noun* **1** A1 [C] a large bowl attached to a pipe that you sit on or stand over when you get rid of waste matter from your body: *Have you flushed the toilet?* ◇ (*BrE*) *I need to go to the toilet* (= use the toilet). ◇ *a toilet seat* ◇ *Do you need the toilet?* ◇ *The girl asked if she could use the toilet.* **2** A1 (*BrE*) (*NAmE* **ˈbath·room**) [C] a room containing a toilet: *Every flat has its own bathroom and toilet.* **3** A1 (*BrE*) [C] (*also* **toi·lets** [pl.]) a room or small building containing several toilets, each in a separate smaller room: *Could you tell me where the ladies' toilet is, please?* ◇ *a disabled toilet* (= for disabled people) **4** [U] (*old-fashioned*) the process of washing and dressing yourself, arranging your hair, etc.

---

▼ **BRITISH/AMERICAN**

**toilet / bathroom**

• In *BrE*, but not in *NAmE*, the room that has a toilet in it is usually referred to as the **toilet**. This room in people's houses can also be called the **lavatory**, or informally, the **loo**. An extra downstairs toilet in a house can be called the **cloakroom**. In public places, especially on signs, the words **toilets**, **Gents** (for men's toilets) or **Ladies** (for women's toilets) are used for a room or small building containing several toilets. You might also see **WC** or **Public Conveniences** on some signs.

• In *NAmE* the room that contains a toilet is called the **bathroom**, never the **toilet**. A room with a toilet in a public place can also be called a **restroom**, **ladies' room**, **women's room** or **men's room**. **Washroom** is also used, especially in Canada.

---

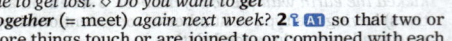

**'toilet bag** *noun* (*BrE*) = SPONGE BAG

**'toilet paper** (also **'toilet tissue**) *noun* [U] thin, soft paper used for cleaning yourself after you have used the toilet: *a roll of toilet paper*

**toi·let·ries** /'tɔɪlətriz/ *noun* [pl.] things such as soap or TOOTHPASTE that you use for washing, cleaning your teeth, etc.

**'toilet roll** *noun* (*BrE*) a roll of toilet paper

**'toiletry bag** (*NAmE*) (*BrE* **'sponge bag**, **'toilet bag**, **'wash-bag**) *noun* a small bag for holding your soap, TOOTHBRUSH, etc. when you are travelling

**'toilet-train** *verb* [usually passive] ~ **sb** to teach a small child to use the toilet ▶ **'toilet-trained** *adj.* **'toilet-training** *noun* [U]

**'toilet water** *noun* [U] a kind of PERFUME (= a pleasant-smelling liquid for the skin) that contains a lot of water and does not smell very strong **SYN** eau de toilette

**toils** /tɔɪlz/ *noun* [pl.] (*formal or literary*) if you are caught in **the toils** of an unpleasant feeling or situation, you cannot escape from it **SYN** snare

**toing** /'tuːɪŋ/ *noun*
**IDM** **toing and 'froing 1** movement or travel backwards and forwards between two or more places: *All this toing and froing between London and New York takes it out of him.* **2** a lot of unnecessary or repeated activity or discussion: *After a great deal of toing and froing, I decided not to change jobs after all.*

**toke** /təʊk/ *noun* (*informal*) an act of breathing in smoke from a cigarette containing MARIJUANA ▶ **toke** *verb* [I]

**token** /'təʊkən/ *noun, adj.*
■ *noun* **1** a round piece of metal or plastic used instead of money to operate some machines or as a form of payment: *a parking token* **2** (*BrE*) a piece of paper that you pay for and that sb can exchange for sth in a shop: *a £20 book/record/gift token* **3** a piece of paper that you can collect when you buy a particular product and then exchange for sth: *Collect six tokens for a free T-shirt.* **4** something that is a symbol of a feeling, a fact, an event, etc. **SYN** expression, mark: *Please accept this small gift as a token of our gratitude.*
**IDM** **by the same 'token** for the same reasons: *The penalty for failure will be high. But, by the same token, the rewards for success will be great.*
■ *adj.* [only before noun] **1** involving very little effort or feeling and intended only as a way of showing other people that you think sb/sth is important, when really you are not sincere: *The government has only made a token gesture towards helping the unemployed.* ◊ *There was one token woman on the committee* (= so that people could not complain there were no women on the committee). **2** (of a small amount of money) that you pay or charge sb only as a symbol, because a payment is expected **SYN** nominal: *We charge only a token fee for use of the facilities.*

**token·ism** /'təʊkənɪzəm/ *noun* [U] (*disapproving*) the fact of doing sth only in order to do what the law requires or to satisfy a particular group of people, but not in a way that is really sincere: *Appointing one woman to the otherwise all-male staff could look like tokenism.*

**to·kol·oshe** /'tɒkɒlɒʃ; *NAmE* 'tɑːkəlɑːʃ/ *SAfrE* /'tɒkələʃe/ *noun* (*SAfrE*) an evil imaginary creature that some people believe can harm you while you are sleeping

**Tok Pisin** /ˌtɒk 'pɪzən, 'pɪsən; *NAmE* ˌtɑːk/ (also **Pidgin**) *noun* [U] a CREOLE language based on English, used in Papua New Guinea

**told** /təʊld/ *past tense, past part.* of TELL

**tol·er·able** /'tɒlərəbl; *NAmE* 'tɑːl-/ *adj.* (*formal*) **1** fairly good, but not of the best quality **SYN** reasonable: *a tolerable degree of success* **2** that you can accept or bear, although unpleasant or painful **SYN** bearable: *At times, the heat was barely tolerable.* **OPP** intolerable ▶ **tol·er·ably** /-bli/ *adv.*: *He plays the piano tolerably (well).*

**tol·er·ance** /'tɒlərəns; *NAmE* 'tɑːl-/ *noun* **1** [U] ~ (**of/for sb/sth**) the quality of being willing to accept or TOLERATE sb/sth, especially opinions or behaviour that you may not agree with, or people who are not like you: *She had no tolerance for jokes of any kind.* ◊ *religious tolerance* ◊ *a reputation for tolerance towards refugees* ⊃ see also ZERO TOLERANCE **OPP** intolerance **2** [C, U] ~ (**to sth**) the ability to suffer sth, especially pain, difficult conditions, etc. without being harmed: *tolerance to cold* ◊ *Tolerance to alcohol decreases with age.* **3** [C, U] (*specialist*) the amount by which the measurement of a value can vary without causing problems: *They were working to a tolerance of 0.0001 of a centimetre.*

**tol·er·ant** /'tɒlərənt; *NAmE* 'tɑːl-/ *adj.* **1** ~ (**of/towards sb/sth**) able to accept what other people say or do even if you do not agree with it: *He has a very tolerant attitude towards other religions.* **2** ~ (**of sth**) (of plants, animals or machines) able to survive or operate in difficult conditions: *The plants are tolerant of frost.* **OPP** intolerant ▶ **tol·er·ant·ly** *adv.*

**tol·er·ate** /'tɒləreɪt; *NAmE* 'tɑːl-/ *verb* **1** to allow sb to do sth that you do not agree with or like **SYN** put up with sb/sth: ~ **sth** *Their relationship was tolerated but not encouraged.* ◊ *This sort of behaviour will not be tolerated.* ◊ ~ (**sb/sth**) **doing/being/having sth** *She refused to tolerate being called a liar.* **2** ~ **sb/sth** to accept sb/sth that is annoying, unpleasant, etc. without complaining **SYN** put up with sb/sth: *There is a limit to what one person can tolerate.* ◊ *I don't know how you tolerate that noise!* **3** ~ **sth** to be able to be affected by a drug, difficult conditions, etc. without being harmed: *She tolerated the chemotherapy well.* ◊ *Few plants will tolerate sudden changes in temperature.*

**tol·er·ation** /ˌtɒlə'reɪʃn; *NAmE* ˌtɑːl-/ *noun* [U] the fact of being willing to allow sth that you do not like or agree with to happen or continue **SYN** tolerance: *religious toleration*

**toll** /təʊl/ *noun, verb*
■ *noun* **1** [C] money that you pay to use a particular road or bridge: *motorway tolls* ◊ *a toll bridge* ⊃ SYNONYMS at RATE ⊃ WORDFINDER NOTE at TRAFFIC ⊃ see also E-TOLL **2** [C, usually sing.] the amount of damage or the number of deaths and injuries that are caused in a particular war, disaster, etc: *the war's growing casualty toll* ⊃ see also DEATH TOLL **3** [sing.] the sound of a bell ringing with slow, regular sounds **4** [C] (*NAmE*) a charge for a phone call that is calculated at a higher rate than a local call
**IDM** **take a heavy 'toll (on sb/sth) | take its 'toll (on sb/sth)** to have a bad effect on sb/sth; to cause a lot of damage, deaths, pain, etc: *Illness had taken a heavy toll on her.* ◊ *The recession is taking its toll on the housing markets.*
■ *verb* [I, T] when a bell **tolls** or sb **tolls** it, it is rung slowly many times, especially as a sign that sb has died: ~ (**for sb**) *The Abbey bell tolled for those killed in the war.* ◊ ~ **sth** *The bell tolled the hour.* ◊ (*figurative*) *The revolution tolled the death knell* (= signalled the end) *for the Russian monarchy.*

**'toll·booth** /'təʊlbuːð; *NAmE* -buːθ/ *noun* a small building by the side of a road where you pay to drive on a road, go over a bridge, etc.

**'toll-free** *adj.* (*NAmE*) (of a phone call to an organization or a service) that you do not have to pay for: *a toll-free number* ⊃ see also FREEPHONE

**'toll gate** (also **'toll-gate**) *noun* a gate across a road where you stop and pay to drive on a road, go over a bridge, etc: *Vehicles had to wait for up to 20 minutes at the toll gates.*

**'toll plaza** *noun* a row of TOLLBOOTHS across a road

**'toll road** (also **'toll-road**) (*NAmE* **'toll·way** /'təʊlweɪ/, **turn·pike**) *noun* a road that drivers must pay to use

**Tom** /tɒm; *NAmE* tɑːm/ *noun*
**IDM** **any/every Tom, Dick or 'Harry** (*usually disapproving*) any ordinary person rather than the people you know or people who have special skills or qualities: *We don't want any Tom, Dick or Harry using the club bar.*

**tom** /tɒm; *NAmE* tɑːm/ *noun* = TOMCAT

**toma·hawk** /'tɒməhɔːk; *NAmE* 'tɑːm-/ *noun* a light AXE used by Native Americans

**to·mato** /tə'mɑːtəʊ; *NAmE* -'meɪt-/ *noun* [C, U] (*pl.* **-oes**) a soft fruit with a lot of juice and shiny red skin

# tomato ketchup

that is eaten as a vegetable either raw or cooked: *a bacon, lettuce, and tomato sandwich* ◊ *sliced/chopped tomatoes* ◊ *tomato plants* ⊃ VISUAL VOCAB page V5 ⊃ see also CHERRY TOMATO, PLUM TOMATO

**to·mato 'ketchup** *noun* [U] = KETCHUP

**tomb** /tuːm/ *noun* a large GRAVE (= where a dead person is buried), especially one built of stone above or below the ground

**tom·bola** /tɒmˈbəʊlə; *NAmE* tɑːm-/ *noun* [U, C] (*BrE*) a game in which you buy tickets with numbers on them. If the number on your ticket is the same as the number on one of the prizes, you win the prize.

**tom·boy** /ˈtɒmbɔɪ; *NAmE* ˈtɑːm-/ *noun* a young girl who enjoys activities and games that are traditionally considered to be for boys

**tomb·stone** /ˈtuːmstəʊn/ *noun* a large, flat stone that lies over a GRAVE (= where a dead person is buried) or stands at one end, that shows the name, age, etc. of the person buried there ⊃ compare GRAVESTONE, HEADSTONE

**tom·cat** /ˈtɒmkæt; *NAmE* ˈtɑːm-/ (*also* **tom**) *noun* a male cat

**tome** /təʊm/ *noun* (*formal*) a large, heavy book, especially one dealing with a serious topic

**tom·fool·ery** /tɒmˈfuːləri; *NAmE* tɑːm-/ *noun* [U] (*old-fashioned*) silly behaviour SYN **foolishness**

**Tommy** /ˈtɒmi; *NAmE* ˈtɑːmi/ *noun* (*old use, informal*) a British soldier

**'tommy gun** *noun* a type of SUB-MACHINE GUN

**tom·og·raphy** /təˈmɒɡrəfi; *NAmE* -ˈmɑːɡ-/ *noun* [U] a way of producing an image of the inside of the human body or a solid object using X-RAYS or ULTRASOUND

**to·mor·row** 🔊 A1 /təˈmɒrəʊ; *NAmE* -ˈmɑːr-/ *adv., noun*

■ *adv.* 🔊 A1 on or during the day after today: *I'm off now. See you tomorrow.* ◊ *She's leaving tomorrow.* ◊ (*especially BrE*) *They arrive a week tomorrow/tomorrow week* (= after a week, starting from tomorrow). IDM see JAM *n.*

■ *noun* [U] 1 🔊 A1 the day after today: *Today is Tuesday, so tomorrow is Wednesday.* ◊ *tomorrow afternoon/morning/night/evening* ◊ *I'll see you the day after tomorrow.* ◊ *The announcement will appear in tomorrow's newspapers.* ◊ *I want it done by tomorrow.* 2 🔊 A2 the future: *Who knows what changes tomorrow may bring?* ◊ *Tomorrow's workers will have to be more adaptable.*

IDM **do sth as if / like there's no to'morrow** to do sth a lot or as though you do not care what effects it will have: *I ate as if there was no tomorrow.* ◊ *She spends money like there's no tomorrow.*

**tom-tom** *noun, verb*

■ *noun* 1 a medium-sized drum that may be part of a DRUM KIT 2 a drum, often played with the hands, especially in Asian or Native American cultures

■ *verb* ~ **(about)** *sth* (*IndE*) to make sth known or to talk about it in a way that shows that you are too proud of it

**ton** 🔊+ B2 /tʌn/ *noun* 1 🔊+ B2 [C] (*pl.* **tons** *or* **ton**) a unit for measuring weight, in the UK 2240 pounds ('**long ton**') and in the US 2000 pounds ('**short ton**'): (*informal*) *What have you got in this bag? It weighs a ton* (= is very heavy). ⊃ compare TONNE 2 [C] a unit for measuring the size of a ship. 1 ton is equal to 100 CUBIC feet. 3 🔊+ B2 **tons** [pl.] (*informal*) a lot: *They've got tons of money.* ◊ *I've still got tons to do.* 4 **a / the ton** (*BrE, informal*) 100, especially when connected with a speed of 100 miles per hour: *He was caught doing a ton.* IDM **like a ton of 'bricks** (*informal*) very heavily; very severely: *Disappointment hit her like a ton of bricks.* ◊ *They came down on him like a ton of bricks* (= criticized him very severely).

**tonal** /ˈtəʊnl/ *adj.* 1 (*specialist*) relating to tones of sound or colour 2 (*music*) having a particular KEY OPP **atonal**
▶ **tonal·ly** /-nəli/ *adv.*

**ton·al·ity** /təʊˈnæləti/ *noun* (*pl.* **-ies**) (*music*) the quality of a piece of music that depends on the KEY in which it is written

**tone** 🔊 B2 /təʊn/ *noun, verb*

■ *noun*
• OF VOICE 1 🔊 [C] the quality of sb's voice, especially expressing a particular emotion: *speaking in hushed/low/clipped/measured, etc. tones* ◊ *a conversational tone* ◊ *a tone of surprise* ◊ *Don't speak to me in that tone of voice* (= in that unpleasant way). ◊ *There's not need to take that tone* (= speak critically or rudely) *with me—it's not my fault we're late.*
• CHARACTER/ATMOSPHERE 2 🔊 B2 [sing.] the general character and attitude of sth such as a piece of writing, or the atmosphere of an event: *The overall tone of the book is gently nostalgic.* ◊ *She set the tone for the meeting with a firm statement of company policy.* ◊ *Trust you to lower the tone of the conversation* (= for example by telling a rude joke). ◊ *in ~ The article was moderate in tone and presented both sides of the case.*
• OF SOUND 3 🔊 B2 [C] the quality of a sound, especially the sound of a musical instrument or one produced by electronic equipment: *the full rich tone of the trumpet* ◊ *the volume and tone controls on a car stereo*
• COLOUR 4 [C] a shade of a colour: *a carpet in warm tones of brown and orange*
• OF MUSCLES/SKIN 5 [U] how strong and tight your muscles or skin are: *how to improve your muscle/skin tone*
• ON PHONE 6 [C] a sound heard on a phone line (*BrE*): *the dialling tone* ◊ (*NAmE*) *the dial tone* ◊ *Please speak after the tone* (= for example as an instruction on an answering machine). ⊃ see also RINGTONE
• IN MUSIC 7 (*BrE*) (*US* **whole step**) [C] one of the five longer INTERVALS in a musical SCALE, for example the INTERVAL between C and D or between E and F♯ ⊃ compare SEMITONE, STEP ⊃ WORDFINDER NOTE at SING
• PHONETICS 8 [C] the PITCH (= how high or low a sound is) of a syllable in speaking: *a rising/falling tone* 9 a particular PITCH pattern on a syllable in languages such as Chinese, that can be used to recognize the difference in meanings ⊃ WORDFINDER NOTE at PRONUNCIATION
• -TONED 10 (in adjectives) having the type of tone mentioned: *a bright-toned soprano* ◊ *olive-toned skin*

■ *verb*
• MUSCLES/SKIN 1 [T] ~ *sth* (**up**) to make your muscles, skin, etc. tighter and stronger: *Massage will help to tone up loose skin under the chin.* ◊ *a beautifully toned body*
• COLOUR 2 [I] ~ (**in**) (**with** *sth*) (*BrE*) to match the colour of sth: *The beige of his jacket toned (in) with the cream shirt.*
PHRV **tone** *sth* ↔ **'down** 1 to make a speech, an opinion, etc. less extreme or offensive: *The language of the article will have to be toned down for the mass market.* 2 to make a colour less bright

**tone-'deaf** *adj.* unable to hear the difference between musical notes

**'tone language** *noun* a language in which differences in TONE can change the meaning of words

**tone·less** /ˈtəʊnləs/ *adj.* (of a voice, etc.) not expressing any emotion or interest ▶ **tone·less·ly** *adv.*

**'tone poem** *noun* a piece of music that is intended to describe a place or express an idea

**toner** /ˈtəʊnə(r)/ *noun* [U, C] 1 a type of INK (= coloured liquid) used in machines that print or PHOTOCOPY 2 a liquid or cream used for making the skin on your face tighter and smoother

**tongs** /tɒŋz; *NAmE* tɑːŋz/ *noun* [pl.] 1 a tool with two long parts that are joined at one end, used for picking up and holding things: *a pair of tongs* 2 (*also* '**curling tongs**') (both *BrE*) (*NAmE* '**curling iron**) [C] a tool that is heated and used to CURL hair
IDM see HAMMER *n.*

**tongue** 🔊 B1 /tʌŋ/ *noun, verb*

■ *noun* 1 🔊 B1 [C] the soft part in the mouth that moves around, used for tasting, SWALLOWING, speaking, etc: *He clicked his tongue to attract their attention.* ◊ *She ran her tongue over her lips.* ◊ *It's very rude to stick your tongue out*

at people. ⇒ VISUAL VOCAB page V1 **2** [U, C] the tongue of some animals, cooked and eaten: *a slice of ox tongue* **3** [C] (*formal* or *literary*) a language: *None of the tribes speak the same tongue.* ◊ *I tried speaking to her in her native tongue.* ⇒ see also MOTHER TONGUE **4** [sing.] a particular way of speaking: *He has a sharp tongue.* ◊ (*formal*) *I'll thank you to keep a civil tongue in your head* (= speak politely). ⇒ see also SILVER TONGUE **5 -tongued** (in adjectives) speaking in the way mentioned: *sharp-tongued* **6** [C] a long, narrow piece of leather under the LACES on a shoe **7** [C] ~ **(of sth)** (*literary*) something that is long and narrow and like a tongue in shape: *a tongue of flame*
IDM **get your ˈtongue around/round sth** to pronounce a difficult word correctly **ˌhold your ˈtongue/ˈpeace** (*old-fashioned*) to say nothing although you would like to give your opinion **ˌroll/ˌslip/ˌtrip off the ˈtongue** to be easy to say or pronounce: *It's not a name that exactly trips off the tongue, is it?* **ˌset ˈtongues wagging | ˈtongues are wagging** (*informal*) to cause people to start talking/people are talking about sb's private affairs **ˌwith your ˈtongue in your ˈcheek | ˌwith tongue in ˈcheek** if you say sth **with your tongue in your cheek**, you are not being serious and mean it as a joke ⇒ more at BITE *v.*, FIND *v.*, LOOSE *adj.*, LOOSEN, SLIP *n.*, TIP *n.*, WATCH *v.*
- *verb* **1** ~ sth to stop the flow of air into a wind instrument with your tongue in order to make a note **2** ~ sth to LICK sth with your tongue

**ˈtongue depressor** (*NAmE*) (*BrE* **ˈspatˌula**) *noun* a thin, flat instrument that doctors use for pressing the tongue down when they are examining sb's throat

**ˌtongue-in-ˈcheek** *adj.* not intended seriously; done or said as a joke: *a tongue-in-cheek remark* ▶ **ˌtongue-in-ˈcheek** *adv.*: *The offer was made almost tongue-in-cheek.*

**ˈtongue-tied** *adj.* not able to speak because you are shy or nervous

**ˈtongue-twister** *noun* a word or phrase that is difficult to say quickly or correctly, such as 'She sells sea shells on the seashore.'

**tonic** /ˈtɒnɪk; *NAmE* ˈtɑːn-/ *noun* **1** (*also* **ˈtonic water**) [U, C] a clear FIZZY drink (= with bubbles in it) with a slightly bitter taste, that is often mixed with a strong alcoholic drink, especially GIN or VODKA: *a gin and tonic* **2** [C] a medicine that makes you feel stronger and healthier, taken especially when you feel tired: *herbal tonics* **3** [C, U] a liquid that you put on your hair or skin in order to make it healthier: *skin tonic* **4** [C, usually *sing.*] (*old-fashioned*) anything that makes people feel healthier or happier: *The weekend break was just the tonic I needed.* **5** [C] (*music*) the first note of a SCALE of eight notes

**ˌtonic solˈfa** *noun* [U] (*music*) = SOL-FA

**toˈnight** 🔊 A1 /təˈnaɪt/ *adv., noun*
- *adv.* A1 on or during the evening or night of today: *Will you have dinner with me tonight?* ◊ *It's cold tonight.*
- *noun* A1 [U] the evening or night of today: *Here are tonight's football results.* ◊ *Tonight will be cloudy.*

**ˈtonˌnage** /ˈtʌnɪdʒ/ *noun* [U, C] **1** the size of a ship or the amount it can carry, expressed in TONS or tonnes **2** the total amount that sth weighs

**tonne** 🔊+ B2 /tʌn/ (*pl.* **tonnes** *or* **tonne**) (*also* **ˌmetric ˈton**) *noun* a unit for measuring weight, equal to 1000 KILOGRAMS: *a record grain harvest of 236m tonnes* ◊ *a 17-tonne truck* ⇒ compare TON

**tonˌsil** /ˈtɒnsl; *NAmE* ˈtɑːn-/ *noun* either of the two small organs at the sides of the throat, near the base of the tongue: *I've had my tonsils out* (= removed). ⇒ VISUAL VOCAB page V1

**ˌtonˌsilˈlecˌtomy** /ˌtɒnsəˈlektəmi; *NAmE* ˌtɑːn-/ *noun* (*pl.* **-ies**) (*medical*) a medical operation to remove the TONSILS

**ˌtonˌsilˈlitis** /ˌtɒnsəˈlaɪtɪs; *NAmE* ˌtɑːn-/ *noun* [U] an infection of the tonsils in which they become SWOLLEN (= larger than normal) and painful

**Tony** /ˈtəʊni/ *noun* (*pl.* **Tonys**) an award given in the US for achievement in the theatre

**tony** /ˈtəʊni/ *adj.* (*NAmE, informal, becoming old-fashioned*) fashionable and expensive

1651

**too** 🔊 A1 /tuː/ *adv.* **1** A1 used before adjectives and adverbs to say that sth is more than is good, necessary, possible, etc: *He's far too young to go on his own.* ◊ *She was much too big to be carried.* ◊ *This is too large a helping for me/This helping is too large for me.* ◊ *It's **too late** to do anything about it now.* ◊ *Accidents like this happen **all too*** (= much too) *often.* ◊ *You can never have **too many** friends.* **2** A1 (usually placed at the end of a clause) also; as well: *Can I come too?* ◊ *When I've finished painting the bathroom, I'm going to do the kitchen too.* ◊ note at ALSO ⇒ see also ME-TOO **3** A2 very: *I'm not too sure if this is right.* ◊ *I'm just going out—I won't be too long.* ◊ *Mary will be **only too** glad to help.* **4** used to comment on sth that makes a situation worse: *She broke her leg last week—and on her birthday too!* **5** used to emphasize sth, especially your anger, surprise or agreement with sth: *'He did apologize eventually.' 'I should think so too!'* ◊ *'She gave me the money.' 'About time too!'*
IDM **be ˌtoo ˈmuch (for sb)** to need more skill or strength than you have; to be more difficult, annoying, etc. than you can bear ⇒ more at RIGHT *adv.*

**took** /tʊk/ *past tense of* TAKE

**tool** 🔊 A2 W /tuːl/ *noun, verb*
- *noun* **1** A2 an instrument such as a HAMMER, SCREWDRIVER, SAW, etc. that you hold in your hand and use for making things, repairing things, etc: *garden tools* ◊ *a cutting tool* ◊ *power tools* (= using electricity) ◊ *Always select the right tool for the job.* ⇒ see also MACHINE TOOL **2** A2 a thing that helps you to do your job or to achieve sth: *research tools like questionnaires* ◊ *a useful/valuable tool* ◊ *Some of them carried the guns which were the **tools of their trade*** (= the things they needed to do their job). **3** a person who is used or controlled by another person or group: *The prime minister was an unwitting tool of the president.* **4** (*taboo, slang*) a PENIS IDM ⇒ see DOWN *v.*, SHARP *adj.*
- *verb* [I] + *adv./prep.* (*NAmE, informal*) to drive around in a vehicle
PHRV **ˌtool ˈup** | **ˌtool sb/sth ↔ ˈup** (*specialist*) to get or provide sb/sth with the equipment, etc. that is necessary to do or produce sth: *The factory is not tooled up to produce this type of engine.*

**ˈtoolˌbar** /ˈtuːlbɑː(r)/ *noun* (*computing*) a row of symbols (= ICONS) on a computer screen, smartphone, etc. that show the different things that you can do with a particular program

**ˈtoolˌbox** /ˈtuːlbɒks; *NAmE* -bɑːks/ *noun* a box with a LID (= cover) for keeping tools in

**tooled** /tuːld/ *adj.* (of leather) decorated with patterns made with a special heated tool

**ˈtoolˌkit** /ˈtuːlkɪt/ *noun* **1** a set of tools in a box or bag **2** (*computing*) a set of software tools **3** the things that you need in order to achieve sth

**ˈtoolˌtip** /ˈtuːltɪp/ *noun* (*computing*) a message that appears when you move a CURSOR over an image, a symbol, a link, etc. on a computer screen: *Moving your mouse over an icon displays a tooltip explaining its function.*

**toonie** /ˈtuːni/ *noun* (*CanE*) the Canadian two-dollar coin

**toot** /tuːt/ *noun, verb*
- *noun* a short, high sound made by a car HORN or a WHISTLE: *She gave a sharp toot on her horn.*
- *verb* [I, T] (*especially BrE*) when a car HORN **toots** or you toot it, it makes a short, high sound: *the sound of horns tooting* ◊ ~ **sth** *Toot your horn to let them know we're here.* IDM ⇒ see HORN *n.*

**tooth** 🔊 A1 /tuːθ/ *noun* (*pl.* **teeth** /tiːθ/) **1** A1 any of the hard white structures in the mouth used for biting food: *I've just **had a tooth out** at the dentist's.* ◊ *to brush/ clean your teeth* ◊ *tooth decay* ◊ *She answered through*

# toothache 1652

clenched teeth (= opening her mouth only a little because of anger). ◊ *The cat sank its teeth into his finger.* ⇨ see also BUCK TEETH, FALSE TEETH, MILK TOOTH, WISDOM TOOTH **2** a narrow, pointed part that sticks out of an object: *the teeth on a saw* ⇨ see also FINE-TOOTH COMB

**IDM** **cut your teeth on sth** to do sth that gives you your first experience of a particular type of work **cut a 'tooth** (of a baby) to grow a new tooth **get your 'teeth into sth** (*informal*) to put a lot of effort and enthusiasm into sth that is difficult enough to keep you interested: *Choose an essay topic that you can really get your teeth into.* **have 'teeth** (*informal*) (of an organization, a law, etc.) to be powerful and effective **in the teeth of sth** **1** despite problems, opposition, etc: *The new policy was adopted in the teeth of fierce criticism.* **2** in the direction that a strong wind is coming from: *They crossed the bay in the teeth of a howling gale.* **set sb's 'teeth on edge** (of a sound or taste) to make sb feel physically uncomfortable: *Just the sound of her voice sets my teeth on edge.* ⇨ more at ARMED, BARE v., BIT, EYE n., EYE TEETH, FIGHT v., GNASH, GRIT v., HELL, KICK v., KICK n., LIE² v., LONG adj., PULL v., RED adj., SKIN n., SWEET adj.

**tooth·ache** /ˈtuːθeɪk/ *noun* [U, C, usually sing.] **a pain in your teeth or in one tooth**: (*BrE*) *I've got toothache.* ◊ (*NAmE*, *BrE*) *I've got a toothache.*

**tooth·brush** /ˈtuːθbrʌʃ/ *noun* a small brush for cleaning your teeth

**toothed** /tuːθt, tuːðd/ *adj.* [only before noun] **1** (*specialist*) having teeth: *a toothed whale* **2 -toothed** (in compounds) having the type of teeth mentioned: *a gap-toothed smile*

**the 'tooth fairy** *noun* [sing.] an imaginary creature that is said to take away a tooth that a small child leaves near his or her bed at night and to leave a coin there in its place

**tooth·less** /ˈtuːθləs/ *adj.* **1** having no teeth: *a toothless old man* ◊ *She gave us a toothless grin.* **2** having no power or authority

**tooth·paste** /ˈtuːθpeɪst/ *noun* [U, C] a substance that you put on a brush and use to clean your teeth: *a tube of toothpaste* ◊ *fluoride toothpastes*

**tooth·pick** /ˈtuːθpɪk/ *noun* a short pointed piece of wood or plastic used for removing bits of food from between the teeth

**tooth·some** /ˈtuːθsəm/ *adj.* (*humorous*) (of food) tasting good **SYN** tasty

**toothy** /ˈtuːθi/ *adj.* a **toothy** smile shows a lot of teeth

**too·tle** /ˈtuːtl/ *verb* (*informal*) **1** [I] + *adv./prep.* to walk, drive, etc. somewhere without hurrying **2** [I, T] ~ (sth) to produce a series of notes by blowing into a musical instrument

**toot·sies** /ˈtʊtsiz/ *noun* [pl.] (*informal*) (used by or when speaking to young children) toes or feet

**top** **❶** **A2** /tɒp; *NAmE* tɑːp/ *noun, adj., verb*

■ *noun*

- **HIGHEST POINT** **1 A2** [C] the highest part or point of sth: *at the ~ of sth She was standing at the top of the stairs.* ◊ *The title is right at the top of the page.* ◊ *at the ~ Write your name at the top.* ◊ *to the ~ He filled my glass to the top.* ◊ *to the ~ of sth We climbed to the very top of the hill.* ◊ *on the ~ (of sth) Snow was falling on the mountain tops.* ◊ *I was out of breath when I reached the top.* ⇨ see also ROOFTOP, TREETOP
- **UPPER SURFACE** **2 A2** [C] the upper flat surface of sth: *Can you polish the top of the table?* ⇨ see also DESKTOP (2), HARDTOP, SOFT-TOP, TABLETOP
- **CLOTHING** **3 A2** [C] a piece of clothing worn on the upper part of the body: *I need a top to go with this skirt.* ◊ *a tracksuit/bikini/pyjama top* ⇨ see also CROP TOP, TANK TOP
- **OF PEN/BOTTLE** **4 A2** [C] a thing that you put on the end of sth to close it: *Where's the top of this pen?* ◊ *a bottle with a screw top* ⇨ SYNONYMS at LID

- **HIGHEST RANK** **5 B1** the top [sing.] the highest or most important rank or position: *at the ~ of sth They finished the season at the top of the league.* ◊ *We have a lot of things to do, but packing is at the top of the list.* ◊ *at the ~ The company needs to make a change at the top.* ◊ *to the ~ (of sth) She is determined to make it to the top (= achieve fame or success).* ◊ *I would not have gone into boxing if I didn't think I could reach the top.*
- **FURTHEST POINT** **6** [sing.] the ~ of sth the end of a street, table, etc. that is furthest away from you or from where you usually come to it: *I'll meet you at the top of Thorpe Street.*
- **LEAVES OF PLANT** **7** [C, usually pl.] the leaves of a plant that is grown mainly for its root: *Remove the green tops from the carrots.*
- **AMOUNT OF MONEY/TIME** **8** tops [pl.] (*informal*) used after an amount of money, time, etc. to show that it is the highest, longest, etc. possible: *It couldn't have cost more than £50, tops.* ◊ *It'll take a couple of hours, tops.*
- **BEST** **9** tops [pl.] (*old-fashioned*, *informal*) a person or thing of the best quality: *Among sports superstars she's (the) tops.* ◊ *In the survey the Brits come out tops for humour.*
- **TOY** **10** [C] a child's toy that turns round on a point when it is moved very quickly by hand or by a string: *She was so confused—her mind was spinning like a top.* ⇨ see also BIG TOP

**IDM** **at the top of the 'tree** in the highest position or rank in a profession or career **at the top of your 'voice** as loudly as possible: *She was screaming at the top of her voice.* **come out on 'top** to win a contest or an argument: *In most boardroom disputes he tends to come out on top.* **from top to 'bottom** going to every part of a place in a very careful way: *We cleaned the house from top to bottom.* **from top to 'toe** completely; all over: *She was dressed in green from top to toe.* **get on top of sb** to be too much for sb to manage or deal with: *All this extra work is getting on top of him.* **get on 'top of sth** to manage to control or deal with sth: *How will I ever get on top of all this work?* **off the top of your 'head** (*informal*) just guessing or using your memory, without taking time to think carefully or check the facts: *I can't remember the name off the top of my head, but I can look it up for you.* **on 'top** **1** on the highest point or surface: *a cake with cream on top* ◊ *Stand on top and look down.* **2** in a leading position or in control: *She remained on top for the rest of the match.* **3** in addition: *Look, here's 30 dollars, and I'll buy you lunch on top.* **on top of sth/sb** **A2** on, over or covering sth/sb: *Books were piled on top of one another.* ◊ *Many people were crushed when the building collapsed on top of them.* **2 B2** in addition to sth: *He gets commission on top of his salary.* ◊ *On top of everything else, my car's been stolen.* **3** very close to sth/sb: *We were all living on top of each other in that tiny apartment.* **4** in control of a situation: *Do you think he's really on top of his job?* **on top of the 'world** very happy or proud **over the 'top** (*abbr.* **OTT**) (*especially BrE*, *informal*) done with too much acting, emotion or effort: *His performance is completely over the top.* ◊ *an over-the-top reaction* **take sth from the 'top** (*informal*) to go back to the beginning of a song, piece of music, etc. and repeat it: *OK, everybody, let's take it from the top.* **thin/bald on 'top** (*informal*) with little or no hair on the head: *He's starting to get a little thin on top (= he's losing his hair).* **up 'top** (*BrE*, *informal*) used to talk about a person's intelligence: *He hasn't got much up top (= he isn't very intelligent).* ⇨ more at BLOW v., HEAP n., PILE n.

■ *adj.* [usually before noun] **1 A2** highest in position: *He lives on the top floor.* ◊ *She kept her passport in the top drawer.* **2 B1** highest in rank, degree or importance: *He's one of the top players in the country.* ◊ *She got the top job.* ◊ *top officials/executives/aides* ◊ *He finished top in the exam.* ◊ *They're top of the league.* ◊ *The club can claim top spot in the league with a victory.* ◊ *He was City's top scorer last season.* ◊ *Welfare reform is a top priority for the government.* ◊ *The car was travelling at top speed.* **3** (*BrE*, *informal*) very good: *He's a top bloke.*

■ *verb* (-pp-)

- **BE MORE** **1 C1** ~ sth to be higher than a particular amount: *Worldwide sales look set to top $1 billion.*

- **BE THE BEST** 2 ⟨+ C1⟩ ~ **sth** to be in the highest position on a list because you are the most successful, important, etc.: *The band topped the charts for five weeks with their first single.*
- **PUT ON TOP** 3 ⟨+ C1⟩ [usually passive] to put sth on the top of sth else: **be topped by/with sth** *The chapel was topped by a dome of white marble.* ◊ *fruit salad topped with cream*
- **SAY/DO STH BETTER** 4 ~ **sth** to say or do sth that is better, funnier, more impressive, etc. than sth that sb else has said or done in the past: *I'm afraid the other company has topped your offer* (= offered more money).
- **KILL YOURSELF** 5 ~ **yourself** (*BrE, informal*) to kill yourself deliberately
- **CLIMB HILL** 6 ~ **sth** (*literary*) to reach the highest point of a hill, etc.

**IDM** **to top/cap it 'all** (*informal*) used to introduce the final piece of information that is worse than the other bad things that you have just mentioned ,**top and 'tail sth** (*BrE*) to cut the top and bottom parts off fruit and vegetables to prepare them to be cooked or eaten

**PHRV** ,**top sth↔'off (with sth)** to complete sth successfully by doing or adding one final thing ,**top 'out (at sth)** if sth **tops out** at a particular price, speed, etc. it does not rise any higher: *Inflation topped out at 12 per cent.* ,**top 'up** to get more of sth, especially fuel or credit on an account for a mobile phone, etc.: *If you run out of credit on your electricity meter, you need to top up.* ◊ *Some hybrid vehicles take a long time to top up.* ◊ *Get extra minutes when you top up.* ,**top sth↔'up** (*especially BrE*) **1** to fill a container that already has some liquid in it with more liquid: *Top the car up with oil before you set off.* ◊ *Top the oil up before you set off.* **2** to increase the amount of sth to the level you want or need: *She relies on tips to top up her wages.* ◊ (*BrE*) *I need to top up my mobile phone* (= pay more money so you can make more calls). ⊃ related noun TOP-UP ,**top sb 'up** (*especially BrE*) to fill sb's glass or cup with sth more to drink: *Can I top you up?* ⊃ related noun TOP-UP

**topaz** /'təʊpæz/ *noun* [C, U] a clear yellow SEMI-PRECIOUS stone: *a topaz ring*

,**top 'brass** *noun* [U + sing./pl. v.] (*informal*) = BRASS (5)

,**top-'class** *adj.* of the highest quality or standard: *a top-class performance*

**top·coat** /'tɒpkəʊt; NAmE 'tɑːp-/ *noun* **1** the last layer of paint put on a surface ⊃ compare UNDERCOAT **2** (*old-fashioned*) an OVERCOAT

,**top 'dog** *noun* [usually sing.] (*informal*) a person, group or country that is better than all the others, especially in a situation that involves competition

,**top 'dollar** *noun*
**IDM** **pay, earn, charge, etc. top 'dollar** (*informal*) pay, earn, charge, etc. a lot of money: *If you want the best, you have to pay top dollar.* ◊ *We can help you get top dollar when you sell your house.*

,**top-'down** *adj.* **1** (of a plan, project, etc.) starting with a general idea to which details are added later ⊃ compare BOTTOM-UP **2** starting from or involving the people who have higher positions in an organization: *a top-down management style*

,**top 'drawer** *noun* [sing.] if sb/sth is out of **the top drawer**, they are of the highest social class or of the highest quality ▸ ,**top-'drawer** *adj.*

**topee** = TOPI

,**top-'end** *adj.* [only before noun] among the best, most expensive, etc. examples of sth: *Many people are upgrading their mobiles to top-end models.*

,**top 'flight** *adj.* of the highest quality, rank or level ⊃ see also IN THE FIRST / TOP FLIGHT at FLIGHT *noun*

,**top 'gear** *noun* [U] **1** the highest GEAR in a vehicle: **in/into ~** *They cruised along in top gear.* **2** (*informal*) the highest level of activity or success: **in/into ~** *Her career is moving into top gear.*

,**top-'grossing** *adj.* [only before noun] earning more money than other similar things or people: *the top-grossing movie of 2013*

# topple

,**top 'hat** (*also informal* **top·per**) *noun* a man's tall black or grey hat, worn with formal clothes on very formal occasions

,**top-'heavy** *adj.* **1** too heavy at the top and therefore likely to fall **2** (of an organization) having too many senior staff compared to the number of workers

**topi** (*also* **topee**) /'təʊpi; NAmE *also* təʊ'piː/ *noun* a light, hard hat worn to give protection from the sun in very hot countries

**topi·ary** /'təʊpiəri; NAmE -pieri/ *noun* [U] the art of cutting bushes into shapes such as birds or animals

**topic** ⓘ **A1** ⓞ /'tɒpɪk; NAmE 'tɑːp-/ *noun* a subject that you talk, write or learn about: *The main topic of conversation was Tom's new girlfriend.* ◊ *to cover/discuss/address a topic* ◊ *a range/variety of topics* ◊ *Hot topics* (= that are being discussed a lot) *for discussion included global warming and pollution of the oceans.*

**IDM** **off 'topic** not appropriate or relevant to the situation: *That comment is completely off topic.* ◊ *He keeps veering off topic.* **on 'topic** appropriate or relevant to the situation: *Keep the text short and on topic.* ◊ *Let's get back on topic.*

**top·ic·al** /'tɒpɪkl; NAmE 'tɑːp-/ *adj.* **1** connected with sth that is happening or of interest at the present time: *a topical joke/reference* ◊ *topical events* **2** (*medical*) connected with, or put directly on, a part of the body ▸ **top·ic·al·ity** /,tɒpɪ'kæləti; NAmE ,tɑːp-/ *noun* [U. sing.]

**top·knot** /'tɒpnɒt; NAmE 'tɑːpnɑːt/ *noun* a way of arranging your hair in which it is tied up on the top of your head

**top·less** /'tɒpləs; NAmE 'tɑːp-/ *adj.* (of a woman) not wearing any clothes on the upper part of the body so that her breasts are not covered: *a topless model* ◊ *a topless bar* (= where the female staff are topless) ▸ **top·less** *adv.*: *to sunbathe topless*

,**top-'level** *adj.* [only before noun] involving the most important or best people in a company, an organization or a sport: *a top-level meeting* ◊ *top-level tennis*

,**top 'line** *noun* (*business*) the information that appears first in a company's accounts, showing its total income before taxes, costs, etc. have been taken off: *Analysts were encouraged by the company's strong top line for the quarter.* ⊃ compare BOTTOM LINE (2)

,**top-'line** *adj.* [only before noun] **1** (*business*) relating to the line that appears first in a company's accounts and shows its total income before taxes, costs, etc. have been taken off: *Their impressive top-line growth didn't generate any profits.* **2** (*informal*) of the highest quality: *a top-line act*

**top·most** /'tɒpməʊst; NAmE 'tɑːp-/ *adj.* [only before noun] (*formal*) highest: *the topmost branches of the tree*

,**top-'notch** *adj.* (*informal*) excellent; of the highest quality

,**top of the 'range** (*BrE*) (*NAmE* ,**top of the 'line**) *adj.* [usually before noun] used to describe the most expensive of a group of similar products: *Our equipment is top of the range.* ◊ *our top-of-the-range model*

**top·og·raphy** /tə'pɒgrəfi; NAmE -'pɑːg-/ *noun* [U] (*specialist*) the physical features of an area of land, especially the position of its rivers, mountains, etc.; the study of these features: *a map showing the topography of the island* ▸ **topo·graph·ic·al** /,tɒpə'græfɪkl; NAmE ,tɑːp-/ (*also* **topo·graph·ic** /-fɪk/) *adj.*: *a topographical map/feature* **topo·graph·ic·al·ly** /-kli/ *adv.*

**top·ology** /tə'pɒlədʒi; NAmE -'pɑːl-/ *noun* [U, C] (*specialist*) the way the parts of sth are arranged and related: *The Canadian banking topology is relatively flat, with a few large banks controlling the entire market.*

**top·per** /'tɒpə(r); NAmE 'tɑːp-/ *noun* (*informal*) **1** = TOP HAT **2** (*IndE*) a student who gets the highest results in the class

**top·ping** /'tɒpɪŋ; NAmE 'tɑːp-/ *noun* [C, U] a layer of food that you put on top of a dish, cake, etc. to add taste or to make it look nice

**top·ple** /'tɒpl; NAmE 'tɑːpl/ *verb* **1** [I, T] to become unsteady and fall down; to make sth do this: **+ adv./prep.**

# top-ranking

The pile of books toppled over. ◊ ~ sb/sth + adv./prep. He brushed past, toppling her from her stool. **2** [T] ~ sb/sth to make sb lose their position of power or authority **SYN** **overthrow**: *a plot to topple the President*

**top-ˈranking** *adj.* [only before noun] of the highest rank, status or importance in an organization, a sport, etc.

**top-ˈrated** *adj.* [only before noun] most popular with the public: *a top-rated TV show*

**top ˈsecret** *adj.* that must be kept completely secret, especially from other governments: *This information has been classified top secret.* ◊ *top-secret documents*

**top-ˈshelf** *adj.* [only before noun] **1** (BrE) including pictures of NAKED people and/or sexual acts: *top-shelf magazines/DVDs* **2** (*especially* NAmE) of the highest class: *It is a top-shelf law firm.*

**top·side** /ˈtɒpsaɪd; NAmE ˈtɑːp-/ *noun* [U] (BrE) a piece of beef that is cut from the upper part of the leg

**top·soil** /ˈtɒpsɔɪl; NAmE ˈtɑːp-/ *noun* [U] the layer of soil nearest the surface of the ground ⇒ compare SUBSOIL

**top·spin** /ˈtɒpspɪn; NAmE ˈtɑːp-/ *noun* [U] (*sport*) the action of making a ball turn round and forward fast by hitting it or throwing it in a special way

**topsy-turvy** /ˌtɒpsi ˈtɜːvi; NAmE ˌtɑːpsi ˈtɜːrvi/ *adj.* (*informal*) in a state in which nothing is certain and everything is very confused: *Everything's topsy-turvy in my life at the moment.*

**top ˈtable** (BrE) (NAmE **head ˈtable**) *noun* the table at which the most important guests sit at a formal dinner

**top ˈten** *noun* [C + sing./pl. v.] **1** **the top ten** the ten pop songs or albums that have sold the most in a particular week **2** a list of the ten best or most popular things in a particular category: *in the/sb's ~ It's a good movie but it isn't in my top ten.*

**top-up** *noun* (BrE) **1** a payment that you make to increase the amount of money, etc. to the level that is needed: *a phone top-up* (= to buy more time for calls) ◊ *Students will have to pay top-up fees* (= fees that are above the basic level). **2** (*informal*) an amount of a drink that you add to a cup or glass in order to fill it again: *Can I give anyone a top-up?*

**toque** /təʊk/ *noun* **1** a woman's small hat (*CanE*) a close-fitting hat made of wool, sometimes with a ball of wool on the top

**tor** /tɔː(r)/ *noun* a small hill with rocks at the top, especially in parts of south-west England

**Torah** /ˈtɔːrə; BrE also /ˈrɑː/ *noun* [usually sing., U] (*usually* **the Torah**) (in Judaism) the law of God as given to Moses and recorded in the first five books of the Bible

**torch** /tɔːtʃ; NAmE tɔːrtʃ/ *noun, verb*
■ *noun* **1** (BrE) (*also* **flash-light** NAmE, BrE) a small electric lamp that you can hold in your hand and carry with you: *Shine the torch on the lock while I try to get the key in.* **2** (NAmE) = BLOWTORCH **3** a long stick that has material at one end that is set on fire and that people carry to give light: *a flaming torch* ◊ *the Olympic torch*
**IDM** **put sth to the ˈtorch** (*literary*) to set fire to sth deliberately ⇒ more at CARRY
■ *verb* ~ sth (*informal*) to set fire to a building or vehicle deliberately in order to destroy it

**torch·bear·er** /ˈtɔːtʃbeərə(r); NAmE ˈtɔːrtʃber-/ *noun* **1** a person who carries a torch, for example at the Olympic Games: *She was a torchbearer at the Rio Olympics in 2016.* **2** ~(for sth) a person who leads other people, or sets an example, in working towards a particular goal: *She became a torchbearer for civil rights.*

**torch·light** /ˈtɔːtʃlaɪt; NAmE ˈtɔːrtʃ-/ *noun* [U] the light that is produced by an electric torch or by burning torches

**torch song** *noun* a type of sad romantic song about feelings of love for a person who does not share those feelings ▶ **torch singer** *noun*

**tore** /tɔː(r)/ *past tense* of TEAR¹

**tor·ment** *noun, verb*
■ *noun* /ˈtɔːment; NAmE ˈtɔːrm-/ [U, C] (*formal*) extreme pain, especially mental pain; a person or thing that causes this **SYN** **anguish**: *She suffered years of mental torment after her son's death.* ◊ *in ~ the cries of a man in torment*
■ *verb* /tɔːˈment; NAmE tɔːrˈm-/ **1** ~ sb (*formal*) to make sb suffer very much **SYN** **plague**: *He was tormented by feelings of insecurity.* **2** ~ sb/sth to annoy a person or an animal in a cruel way **SYN** **torture**

**tor·ment·or** /tɔːˈmentə(r); NAmE tɔːrˈm-/ *noun* (*formal*) a person who causes sb to suffer

**torn** /tɔːn; NAmE tɔːrn/ *past part.* of TEAR¹

**tor·nado** /tɔːˈneɪdəʊ; NAmE tɔːrˈn-/ *noun* (*pl.* **-oes** or **-os**) a violent storm with very strong winds that move in a circle. There is often also a long cloud that is narrower at the bottom than the top. ⇒ WORDFINDER NOTE at DISASTER

**tor·pedo** /tɔːˈpiːdəʊ; NAmE tɔːrˈ-/ *noun, verb*
■ *noun* (*pl.* **-oes**) a long, narrow bomb that is fired under the water from a ship or SUBMARINE and that explodes when it hits a ship, etc. ⇒ WORDFINDER NOTE at NAVY
■ *verb* (**tor·pe·does, tor·pe·do·ing, tor·pe·doed, tor·pe·doed**) **1** ~ sth to attack a ship or make it sink using a torpedo **2** ~ sth (*informal*) to completely destroy the possibility that sth could succeed: *Her comments had torpedoed the deal.*

**tor·pid** /ˈtɔːpɪd; NAmE ˈtɔːrp-/ *adj.* (*formal*) not active; with no energy or enthusiasm **SYN** **lethargic**

**tor·por** /ˈtɔːpə(r); NAmE ˈtɔːrp-/ *noun* [U, sing.] (*formal*) the state of not being active and having no energy or enthusiasm **SYN** **lethargy**: *In the heat they sank into a state of torpor.*

**torque** /tɔːk; NAmE tɔːrk/ *noun* [U] (*specialist*) a TWISTING force that causes machines, etc. to ROTATE (= turn around)

**tor·rent** /ˈtɒrənt; NAmE ˈtɔːr-/ *noun* **1** a large amount of water moving very quickly: *After the winter rains, the stream becomes a raging torrent.* ◊ **in torrents** *The rain was coming down in torrents.* **2** a large amount of sth that comes suddenly and violently **SYN** **deluge**: *a torrent of abuse/criticism*

**tor·ren·tial** /təˈrenʃl/ *adj.* (of rain) falling in large amounts

**tor·rid** /ˈtɒrɪd; NAmE ˈtɔːr-/ *adj.* [usually before noun] **1** full of strong emotions, especially connected with sex and love **SYN** **passionate**: *a torrid love affair* **2** (*formal*) (of a climate or country) very hot or dry: *a torrid summer* **3** (BrE) very difficult: *They face a torrid time in tonight's game.*

**tor·sion** /ˈtɔːʃn; NAmE ˈtɔːrʃn/ *noun* [U] (*specialist*) the action of TWISTING sth, especially one end of sth while the other end is held fixed

**torso** /ˈtɔːsəʊ; NAmE ˈtɔːrs-/ *noun* (*pl.* **-os**) **1** the main part of the body, not including the head, arms or legs **SYN** **trunk** **2** a statue of a torso

**tort** /tɔːt; NAmE tɔːrt/ *noun* [C, U] (*law*) something wrong that sb does to sb else that is not criminal, but that can lead to action in a CIVIL court

**torte** /ˈtɔːtə, tɔːt; NAmE ˈtɔːrtə, tɔːrt/ *noun* [C, U] a large cake filled with a mixture of cream, chocolate, fruit, etc.

**tor·tilla** /tɔːˈtiːə; NAmE tɔːrˈt-/ *noun* (from Spanish) **1** a thin Mexican PANCAKE made with CORN (MAIZE) flour or WHEAT flour, usually eaten hot and filled with meat, cheese, etc. **2** a Spanish dish made with eggs and potatoes fried together

**torˈtilla chip** *noun* a small flat hard piece of food, often like a TRIANGLE in shape, made from MAIZE

**tor·toise** /ˈtɔːtəs; NAmE ˈtɔːrt-/ *noun* a REPTILE with a hard round shell, that lives on land and moves very slowly. It can pull its head and legs into its shell. ⇒ VISUAL VOCAB page V3 ⇒ compare TERRAPIN, TURTLE

**tor·toise·shell** /ˈtɔːtəʃel, -təs-; NAmE ˈtɔːrt-/ *noun* **1** [U] the hard shell of a TURTLE, especially the type with orange and brown marks, used for making COMBS, jewellery, etc. **2** (NAmE also **ˈcalico cat**) [C] a cat with black, brown, orange and white fur **3** [C] a BUTTERFLY with orange and brown marks on its wings

**tor·tu·ous** /ˈtɔːtʃuəs; NAmE ˈtɔːrtʃ-/ *adj.* [usually before noun] (*formal*) **1** (*usually disapproving*) not simple and direct;

long, complicated and difficult to understand **SYN** **convoluted**: *tortuous language* ◊ *the long, tortuous process of negotiating peace* **2** (of a road, path, etc.) full of bends **SYN** **winding** ▶ **tor·tu·ous·ly** adv.

**tor·ture** /ˈtɔːtʃə(r); NAmE ˈtɔːrtʃ-/ noun, verb
■ noun [U, C] **1** the act of causing sb severe pain in order to punish them or make them say or do sth: *Many of the refugees have suffered torture.* ◊ *the use of torture* ◊ **under** ~ *His confessions were made under torture.* ◊ *I heard stories of gruesome tortures in prisons.* **2** (*informal*) mental or physical pain; sth that causes this: *The interview was sheer torture from start to finish.*
■ verb [often passive] **1** to hurt sb physically or mentally in order to punish them or make them tell you sth: ~ **sb** *Many of the rebels were captured and tortured by secret police.* ◊ ~ **sb into doing sth** *He was tortured into giving them the information.* **2** ~ **sb** to make sb feel extremely unhappy or anxious **SYN** **torment**: *He spent his life tortured by the memories of his childhood.* ▶ **tor·turer** /ˈtɔːtʃərə(r); NAmE ˈtɔːrtʃ-/ noun

**tor·tured** /ˈtɔːtʃəd; NAmE ˈtɔːrtʃərd/ adj. [only before noun] suffering severely; involving a lot of pain and difficulty: *a tortured mind*

**Tory** /ˈtɔːri/ noun (pl. **-ies**) (informal) a member or supporter of the British Conservative party: *The Tories* (= the Tory party) *lost the election.* ▶ **Tory** adj. [usually before noun]: *the Tory party* ◊ *Tory policies* **Tory·ism** noun [U]

**tosh** /tɒʃ; NAmE tɑːʃ/ noun [U] (BrE, old-fashioned, informal) ideas, statements or beliefs that you think are silly or not true **SYN** **nonsense**, **rubbish**

**toss** /tɒs; NAmE tɔːs/ verb, noun
■ verb
• **THROW** **1** [T] to throw sth lightly or carelessly: ~ **sth + adv./prep.** *I tossed the book aside and got up.* ◊ ~ **sth to sb** *He tossed the ball to Anna.* ◊ ~ **sb sth** *He tossed Anna the ball.* ⊃ SYNONYMS at THROW
• **COIN** **2** [T, I] to throw a coin in the air in order to decide sth, especially by guessing which side is facing upwards when it lands **SYN** **flip**: ~ **sth** *Let's toss a coin.* ◊ ~ **(sb) for sth** (*especially BrE*) *There's only one ticket left—I'll toss you for it.* ◊ ~ **up (for sth)** (*BrE*) *We tossed up to see who went first.* ◊ ~ **up between A and B** (*BrE, figurative*) *He had to toss up between* (= decide between) *paying the rent or buying food.* ⊃ related noun TOSS-UP
• **YOUR HEAD** **3** [T] ~ **sth** to move your head suddenly upwards, especially to show that you are annoyed or impatient: *She just tossed her head and walked off.*
• **SIDE TO SIDE/UP AND DOWN** **4** [I, T] to move or make sb/sth move from side to side or up and down: *Branches were tossing in the wind.* ◊ *I couldn't sleep but kept tossing and turning in bed all night.* ◊ ~ **sb/sth** *Our boat was being tossed by the huge waves.*
• **IN COOKING** **5** [T] ~ **sth** to shake or turn food in order to cover it with oil, butter, etc: *Drain the pasta and toss it in melted butter.* **6** [T] ~ **a pancake** (*BrE*) to throw a PANCAKE upwards so that it turns over in the air and lands back in the FRYING PAN *so you can fry the other side*
**PHRV** **toss ˈoff** | **toss sb/ˈyourself ˈoff** (BrE, taboo, slang) to give yourself sexual pleasure by rubbing your sex organs; to give sb sexual pleasure by rubbing their sex organs **SYN** **masturbate** ˌtoss **sth**↔**ˈoff** (BrE, informal) to produce sth quickly and without much thought or effort
■ noun [usually sing.]
• **OF COIN** **1** an act of throwing a coin in the air in order to decide sth: *The final result was decided on/by the toss of a coin.* ◊ **to win/lose the toss** (= to guess correctly/wrongly which side of a coin will face upwards when it lands on the ground after it has been thrown in the air)
• **OF HEAD** **2** ~ **of your head** an act of moving your head suddenly upwards, especially to show that you are annoyed or impatient: *She dismissed the question with a toss of her head.*
**IDM** **not give a ˈtoss (about sb/sth)** (BrE, slang) to not care at all about sb/sth ⊃ more at ARGUE

**toss·er** /ˈtɒsə(r); NAmE ˈtɔːs-/ noun (BrE, slang) a stupid or unpleasant person

**ˈtoss-up** noun [sing.] (informal) a situation in which either of two choices, results, etc. is equally possible: *'Have you decided on the colour yet?' 'It's **a toss-up** between the blue and the green.'*

**tot** /tɒt; NAmE tɑːt/ noun, verb
■ noun **1** (informal) a very young child **2** (especially BrE) a small amount of a strong alcoholic drink in a glass
■ verb (-tt-)
**PHRV** ˌtot **sth**↔**ˈup** (especially BrE, informal) to add together several numbers or amounts in order to calculate the total **SYN** **add up**

**total** /ˈtəʊtl/ adj., noun, verb
■ adj. [usually before noun] **1** being the amount or number after everyone or everything is counted or added together: *Their total cost was $18000.* ◊ *This brought the total number of accidents so far this year to 113.* ◊ *The club has a total membership of 300.* **2** used when you are emphasizing sth, to mean 'to the greatest degree possible' **SYN** **complete**: *The room was in total darkness.* ◊ *They wanted a total ban on handguns.* ◊ *The evening was a total disaster.* ◊ *I can't believe you'd tell a total stranger about it!*
■ noun the amount you get when you add several numbers or amounts together; the final number of people or things when they have all been counted: **a ~ of sth** *You got 47 points on the written examination and 18 on the oral, making a total of 65.* ◊ **Out of a total of 15 games, they only won 2.* ◊ **in ~** *The repairs came to over £500 in total* (= including everything). ◊ *The number of employees has tripled, bringing the total to 400.* ⊃ see also GRAND TOTAL, RUNNING TOTAL, SUM TOTAL
■ verb (**-ll-**, *US* **-l-**) **1** ~ **sth** to reach a particular total: *Imports totalled $1.5 billion last year.* **2** ~ **sth/sb (up)** to add up the numbers of sth/sb and get a total: *Each student's points were totalled and entered in a list.* **3** ~ **sth** (*especially NAmE, informal*) to damage a car very badly, so that it is not worth repairing it ⊃ see also WRITE OFF

**to·tali·tar·ian** /ˌtəʊtæliˈteəriən; NAmE -ˈter-/ adj. (*disapproving*) (of a country or system of government) in which there is only one political party, which has complete power and control over the people ▶ **to·tali·tar·ian·ism** noun [U]

**to·tal·ity** /təʊˈtæləti/ noun [C, U] (formal) the state of being complete or whole; the whole number or amount: *The seriousness of the situation is difficult to appreciate **in its totality**.*

**to·tal·ly** /ˈtəʊtəli/ adv. completely: *They come from totally different cultures.* ◊ *This behaviour is totally unacceptable.* ◊ *He totally ignored us.* ◊ (*especially NAmE, informal*) *'She's so cute!' 'Totally!'* (= I agree) ◊ (*informal*) *It's a totally awesome experience.*

**tote** /təʊt/ noun, verb
■ noun **1** (also **the Tote**) [sing.] a system of BETTING on horses in which the total amount of money that is bet on each race is divided among the people who bet on the winners **2** (also **ˈtote bag**) [C] (especially NAmE) a large bag for carrying things with you
■ verb **1** ~ **sth** (especially NAmE, informal) to carry sth, especially sth heavy: *We arrived, toting our bags and suitcases.* **2** **-toting** (in adjectives) carrying the thing mentioned: *gun-toting soldiers*

**totem** /ˈtəʊtəm/ noun an animal or other natural object that is chosen and respected as a special symbol of a community or family, especially among Native Americans; an image of this animal, etc. ▶ **to·tem·ic** /təʊˈtemɪk/ adj.: *totemic animals*

**ˈtotem pole** noun **1** a tall, straight piece of wood that has symbols and pictures (called TOTEMS) CARVED or painted on it, traditionally made by Native Americans **2** (NAmE, informal) a range of different levels in an organization, etc: *I didn't want to be **low man on the totem pole** for ever.*

**t'other** /ˈtʌðə(r)/ adj., pron. (BrE, dialect) the other: *I saw it t'other day.* ◊ *They were talking of this, that and t'other.*

**toto** ⊃ IN TOTO

# totter

**tot·ter** /ˈtɒtə(r); NAmE ˈtɑːt-/ verb **1** [I] (+ adv./prep.) to walk or move with weak, unsteady steps, especially because you are drunk or ill **SYN** stagger **2** [I] to be weak and seem likely to fall: *the tottering walls of the castle* ◊ *(figurative) a tottering dictatorship*

**totty** /ˈtɒti; NAmE ˈtɑːti/ noun [U] (BrE, slang) sexually attractive women (an expression used by men, and usually offensive to women)

**tou·can** /ˈtuːkæn/ noun a tropical American bird that is black with some areas of very bright feathers, and that has a very large BEAK

**touch** ⓘ A2 /tʌtʃ/ verb, noun

■ verb
- **WITH HAND/PART OF BODY 1** A2 [T] ~ sb/sth to put your hand or another part of your body onto sb/sth: *Don't touch that plate—it's hot!* ◊ *Can you touch your toes?* (= bend and reach them with your hands) ◊ ~ **sb on sth** *I touched him lightly on the arm.* ◊ ~ **sb/sth with sth** *Do not touch anything with your bare hands.* ◊ *(figurative) I must do some more work on that article—I haven't touched it all week.*
- **NO SPACE BETWEEN 2** A2 [I, T] (of two or more things, surfaces, etc.) to be or come so close together that there is no space between: *Make sure the wires don't touch.* ◊ ~ **sth** *Don't let your coat touch the wet paint.* ◊ *His coat was so long it was almost touching the floor.*
- **MOVE STH/HIT SB 3** B1 [T] (often in negative sentences) ~ **sth/sb** to move sth, especially in such a way that you damage it; to hit or harm sb: *I told you not to touch my things.* ◊ *He said I kicked him, but I never touched him!*
- **AFFECT SB/STH 4** B2 [T] to make sb feel upset or emotional: ~ **sb/sth (to do sth)** *Her story touched us all deeply.* **5** [T] ~ **sb/sth** (old-fashioned or formal) to affect sb/sth: *These are issues that touch us all.*
- **EAT/DRINK/USE 6** [T] (usually in negative sentences) ~ **sth** to eat, drink or use sth: *You've hardly touched your food.* ◊ *He hasn't touched the money his aunt left him.*
- **EQUAL SB 7** [T] (usually in negative sentences) ~ **sb** to be as good as sb in skill, quality, etc: *No one can touch him when it comes to interior design.*
- **REACH LEVEL 8** [T] ~ **sth** to reach a particular level, etc: *The speedometer was touching 90.*
- **BE INVOLVED WITH 9** [T] ~ **sth/sb** to become connected with or work with a situation or person: *Everything she touches turns to disaster.* ◊ *His last two movies have been complete flops and now no studio will touch him.*
- **OF SMILE 10** [T] ~ **sth** to be seen on sb's face for a short time: *A smile touched the corners of his mouth.*

IDM **be touched with sth** to have a small amount of a particular quality: *His hair was touched with grey.* **not touch sb/sth with a ˈbargepole** (BrE) (NAmE **not touch sb/sth with a ten-foot ˈpole**) (informal) to refuse to get involved with sb/sth or in a particular situation **ˈtouch ˈbase (with sb)** (informal) to make contact with sb again **ˈtouch ˈbottom 1** to reach the ground at the bottom of an area of water **2** to reach the worst possible state or condition **ˈtouch ˈwood** (BrE) (NAmE **knock on ˈwood**) (saying) used when talking about your previous good luck or your hopes for the future, to avoid bringing bad luck: *I've been playing for over 20 years and never had an accident—touch wood!* ⊃ more at CHORD, DISTANCE n., FORELOCK, HAIR, NERVE n., RAW n.

PHR V **touch ˈdown 1** (of a plane, SPACECRAFT, etc.) to make contact with the ground as it lands: *The helicopter touched down on the helipad.* ⊃ related noun TOUCHDOWN **2** (of a TORNADO) to make contact with the ground: *Tornadoes touched down in Alabama and Louisiana.* **3** (in rugby) to score a TRY by putting the ball on the ground behind the other team's GOAL LINE ⊃ related noun TOUCH-DOWN **ˈtouch sb for sth** (informal) to persuade sb to give or lend you sth, especially money **ˌtouch sthˌoff** to make sth begin, especially a difficult or violent situation **ˈtouch on/upon sth** to mention or deal with a subject in only a few words, without going into detail: *In his speech he was only able to touch on a few aspects of the problem.* **ˌtouch sbˌup** (BrE, informal) to touch sb sexually, usually in a way that is not expected or welcome **SYN** grope **ˌtouch sthˌup** to improve sth by changing or adding to it slightly: *She was busy touching up her make-up in the mirror.*

■ noun
- **SENSE 1** B1 [U] the sense that enables you to be aware of things and what they are like when you put your hands and fingers on them: **by ~** *They had to identify various materials by touch.*
- **WITH HAND/PART OF BODY 2** B1 [C, usually sing.] an act of putting your hand or another part of your body onto sb/sth: *The gentle touch of his hand on her shoulder made her jump.* ◊ **at the ~ of sth** *All this information is readily available at the touch of a button* (= by simply pressing a button). ◊ **at sb's ~** *The door swung open at his touch.*
- **WAY STH FEELS 3** [sing.] the way that sth feels when you put your hand or fingers on it or when it comes into contact with your body: *material with a smooth silky touch* ◊ *He could not bear the touch of clothing on his sunburnt skin.* ◊ **to the ~** *The body was cold to the touch.*
- **SMALL DETAIL 4** [C] a small detail that is added to sth in order to improve it or make it complete: *Meeting them at the airport was a nice touch.* ⊃ see also FINISHING TOUCH
- **WAY OF DOING STH 5** [sing.] a way or style of doing sth: *She prefers to answer any fan mail herself for a more personal touch.* ◊ *Computer graphics will give your presentation the professional touch.* ◊ *He couldn't find his magic touch with the ball today* (= he didn't play well). ◊ *This meal is awful. I think I'm losing my touch* (= my ability to do sth). ⊃ see also MIDAS TOUCH
- **SMALL AMOUNT 6** [C, usually sing.] ~ **of sth** a very small amount **SYN** trace: *There was a touch of sarcasm in her voice.*
- **SLIGHTLY 7 a touch** [sing.] slightly; a little: *The music was a touch too loud for my liking.*
- **IN FOOTBALL/RUGBY 8** [U] the area outside the lines that mark the sides of the playing field: **into ~** *He kicked the ball into touch.*

IDM **be, get, keep, stay, etc. in ˈtouch (with sb)** B1 to communicate with sb, especially by writing to them or phoning them: *Are you still in touch with your friends from college?* ◊ *Thanks for showing us your products—we'll be in touch.* ◊ *I'm trying to get in touch with Jane. Do you have her number?* ◊ *Let's keep in touch.* ◊ *I'll put you in touch with someone in your area.* **be, keep, etc. in ˈtouch (with sth)** to know what is happening in a particular subject or area: *It is important to keep in touch with the latest research.* **be out of ˈtouch (with sb)** to no longer communicate with sb, so that you no longer know what is happening to them **be, become, etc. out of ˈtouch (with sth)** to not know or understand what is happening in a particular subject or area: *Unfortunately, the people making the decisions are out of touch with the real world.* **an easy/a soft ˈtouch** (informal) a person that you can easily persuade to do sth, especially to give you money: *Unfortunately, my father is no soft touch.* **lose ˈtouch (with sb/sth) 1** to no longer have any contact with sb/sth: *I've lost touch with all my old friends.* **2** to no longer understand sth, especially how ordinary people feel ⊃ more at COMMON adj., KICK v., LIGHT adj.

**touch-and-ˈgo** adj. [not usually before noun] (informal) used to say that the result of a situation is uncertain and that there is a possibility that sth bad or unpleasant will happen: *She's fine now, but it was touch-and-go for a while* (= there was a possibility that she might die).

**touch·down** /ˈtʌtʃdaʊn/ noun **1** [C, U] the moment when a plane or SPACECRAFT lands **SYN** landing **2** [C] (in rugby) an act of scoring points by putting the ball down on the area of ground behind the other team's GOAL LINE **SYN** try **3** [C] (in AMERICAN FOOTBALL) an act of scoring points by crossing the other team's GOAL LINE while carrying the ball, or receiving the ball when you are over the other team's GOAL LINE

**tou·ché** /ˈtuːʃeɪ; NAmE tuːˈʃeɪ/ exclamation (from French) used during an argument or a discussion to show that you accept that sb has answered your comment in a clever way and has gained an advantage by making a good point

**touched** /tʌtʃt/ adj. [not before noun] **1** feeling happy and grateful because of sth kind that sb has done; feeling emotional about sth: ~(by sth) *She was touched by their warm welcome.* ◊ *She was touched by the plight of the refugees.* ◊ *~(that ...) I was touched that he still remembered me.* **2** (*old-fashioned, informal*) slightly crazy

**touch football** *noun* [U] (*NAmE*) a type of AMERICAN FOOTBALL in which touching is used instead of TACKLING ⊃ compare FLAG FOOTBALL

**touch·ing** /ˈtʌtʃɪŋ/ *adj.* causing feelings of sympathy; making you feel sad or emotional SYN **moving**: *It was a touching story that moved many of us to tears.* ▸ **touch·ing·ly** *adv.*

**touch judge** *noun* (in rugby) a LINESMAN

**touch·less** /ˈtʌtʃləs/ *adj.* used to describe technology that allows you to give instructions by making movements rather than by touching any part: *Hand dryers are available with push button or touchless automatic operation.*

**touch·line** /ˈtʌtʃlaɪn/ *noun* a line that marks the side of the playing field in football (soccer), rugby, etc.

**touch·pad** /ˈtʌtʃpæd/ (*also* **track·pad**) *noun* (*computing*) a device that you touch in different places in order to operate a program

**touch·paper** /ˈtʌtʃpeɪpə(r)/ *noun* a piece of paper that burns slowly, that you light in order to start a FIREWORK burning

**touch point** (*also* **touch-point**) *noun* **1** a place or situation in which a business has contact with its customers: *We need to provide a consistent experience for customers, not only online but at every touch point.* **2** something that you already know that helps you understand a situation or explain sth to sb SYN **point of reference**: *Music has always been a cultural touch point.*

**touch·screen** /ˈtʌtʃskriːn/ *noun* a screen on a computer, phone, etc. that allows you to give instructions to the device by touching areas on it

**touch-ˈsensitive** *adj.* (especially of a phone or computer screen) allowing you to give instructions to the device by touching areas on it: *The system has a touch-sensitive control panel.*

**touch·stone** /ˈtʌtʃstəʊn/ *noun* [usually sing.] ~(of/for sth) (*formal*) something that provides a standard against which other things are compared and/or judged: *the touchstone for quality*

**touch-type** *verb* [I] to type without having to look at the keys of a TYPEWRITER or keyboard

**touch-up** *noun* a quick improvement made to the appearance or condition of sth: *My lipstick needed a touch-up.*

**touchy** /ˈtʌtʃi/ *adj.* (**touch·i·er**, **touch·i·est**) **1** [not usually before noun] ~(about sth) (of a person) easily upset or offended SYN **sensitive**: *He's a little touchy about his weight.* **2** [usually before noun] (of a subject) that may upset or offend people and should therefore be dealt with carefully SYN **delicate, sensitive** ▸ **touchi·ness** *noun* [U]

**touchy-ˈfeely** *adj.* (*informal, usually disapproving*) expressing emotions too openly

**tough** ❶ B2 /tʌf/ *adj., noun, verb*
■ *adj.* (**tough·er, tough·est**)
• DIFFICULT **1** B2 having or causing problems or difficulties: *a tough childhood* ◊ *a tough decision/question/choice/challenge* ◊ *She's been having a tough time of it* (= a lot of problems) *lately.* ◊ *It can be tough trying to juggle a career and a family.* ◊ *~on sb Puberty can be tough on kids.*
• STRICT **2** B2 demanding that particular rules be obeyed and showing a lack of sympathy for any problems that this may cause: *~with sb/sth It's about time teachers started to get tough with bullies.* ◊ *~on sb/sth Politicians believe they have to be tough on crime.* ◊ *tough new anti-terror measures* OPP **soft**
• STRONG **3** B2 strong enough to deal successfully with difficult conditions or situations: *a tough breed of cattle* ◊ *He's not tough enough for a career in sales.* ◊ *She's a tough cookie/customer* (= sb who knows what they want and is not easily influenced by other people). **4** B2 (of a person) physically strong and likely to be violent: *You think you're so tough, don't you?* ◊ *He plays the tough guy in the movie.*

# Tourette's syndrome

• VIOLENT **5** B2 (of a place or area) with a lot of crime or violence: *She grew up in a tough neighbourhood.*
• MEAT **6** B2 difficult to cut or bite on: *The meat was a bit tough.* OPP **tender** ⊃ WORDFINDER NOTE at CRISP
• NOT EASILY DAMAGED **7** not easily cut, broken, torn, etc.: *a tough pair of shoes* ◊ *The reptile's skin is tough and scaly.*
• NOT LUCKY **8** ~(on sb) (*informal*) unlucky for sb in a way that seems unfair: *It was tough on her being dropped from the team like that.* ◊ (*ironic*) *'I can't get it finished in time.' 'Tough!'* (= I don't feel sorry about it.)' ▸ **toughˈly** *adv.* **toughˈness** *noun* [U]
IDM **(as) tough as ˈboots** | **(as) tough as ˈnails** (*informal*) very strong and able to deal successfully with difficult conditions or situations **tough ˈluck** (*informal*) **1** used to show sympathy for sb that sth bad that has happened to: *'I failed by one point.' 'That's tough luck.'* **2** (*ironic*) used to show that you do not feel sorry for sb who has a problem: *'If you take the car, I won't be able to go out.' 'Tough luck!'* ⊃ more at ACT *n.*, GOING *n.*, HANG *v.*, NUT *n.*, TALK *v.*
■ *noun* (*old-fashioned, informal*) a person who regularly uses violence against other people
■ *verb*
PHR V **tough sth↔ˈout** to stay strong and determined in a difficult situation: *You're just going to have to tough it out.*

**tough·en** /ˈtʌfn/ *verb* **1** [T, I] ~(sth) (up) to become or make sth stronger, so that it is not easily cut, broken, etc: *toughened glass* **2** [T] ~sth (up) to make sth such as laws or rules stricter: *The government is considering toughening up the law on censorship.* **3** [T] ~sb (up) to make sb stronger and more able to deal with difficult situations

**tough·ie** /ˈtʌfi/ *noun* (*informal*) **1** a person who is determined and not easily frightened **2** a very difficult choice or question

**tough ˈlove** *noun* [U] the fact of helping sb who has problems by dealing with them in a strict way because you believe it is good for them

**tough-ˈminded** *adj.* dealing with problems and situations in a determined way without being influenced by emotions SYN **hard-headed**

**tou·pee** /ˈtuːpeɪ; *NAmE* tuːˈpeɪ/ (*also informal, humorous* **rug**) *noun* a small section of artificial hair, worn by a man to cover an area of his head where hair no longer grows

**tour** ❶ A2 /tʊə(r), tɔː(r); *NAmE* tʊr/ *noun, verb*
■ *noun* **1** ❶ A2 a journey made for pleasure during which several different towns, countries, etc. are visited: *a walking/sightseeing/bus tour* ◊ *~of/round/around sth a coach tour of northern France* ◊ *a tour operator* (= a person or company that organizes tours) ⊃ SYNONYMS at TRIP ⊃ see also GRAND TOUR, PACKAGE TOUR, WHISTLE-STOP **2** ❶ A2 an act of walking around a town, building, etc. in order to visit it: *We were given a guided tour* (= by sb who knows about the place) *of the palace.* ◊ *a virtual tour* (= shown on a computer) *of the Taj Mahal* ◊ *a tour of inspection* (= an official visit of a factory, classroom, etc. made by sb whose job is to check that everything is working as expected) **3** ❶ A2 an official series of visits made to different places by a sports team, an ORCHESTRA, an important person, etc.: *The band is currently on a nine-day tour of France.* ◊ *on ~ The band is on tour in France.* ◊ *a tour bus* ◊ *The prince will visit Boston on the last leg* (= part) *of his American tour.* **4** = TOUR OF DUTY: *He served tours all over the world during his 35-year career.*
■ *verb* ❶ B1 [T, I] to travel around a place, for example on holiday, or to perform, to advertise sth, etc: *~sth He toured America with his one-man show.* ◊ *(+ adv./prep.) We spent four weeks touring around Europe.* ◊ *She is currently touring with her new band.* ◊ *He no longer tours.*

**tour de force** /ˌtʊə də ˈfɔːs; *NAmE* ˌtʊr də ˈfɔːrs/ *noun* (*pl.* **tours de force** /ˌtʊə də ˈfɔːs; *NAmE* ˌtʊr də ˈfɔːrs/) (from French) a performance or achievement that shows a lot of skill: *a cinematic tour de force*

**Tour·ette's syn·drome** /ˌtʊˈrets ˈsɪndrəʊm; *NAmE* tʊˈr-/ *noun* [U] (*medical*) a DISORDER of the nerves in which a person makes a lot of small movements and sounds that they cannot control, including using swear words

# tourism

**tour·ism** ⓘ [A2] /ˈtʊərɪzəm, ˈtɔːr-; NAmE ˈtʊr-/ noun [U] the business activity connected with providing accommodation, services and entertainment for people who are visiting a place for pleasure: *The area is heavily dependent on tourism.* ◊ *the tourism industry* ⇒ see also HEALTH TOURISM, MEDICAL TOURISM

**tour·ist** ⓘ [A1] /ˈtʊərɪst, ˈtɔːr-; NAmE ˈtʊr-/ noun **1** [A1] a person who is travelling or visiting a place for pleasure: *busloads of foreign tourists* ◊ *a popular tourist attraction/destination/resort* ◊ *the tourist industry/sector* ◊ *The island attracts tourists from all over the world.* ⇒ WORDFINDER NOTE at HOLIDAY

> WORDFINDER abroad, backpack, border, guide, passport, resort, sightseeing, travel, visa

**2** (*BrE*) a member of a sports team that is playing a series of official games in a foreign country

**ˈtourist class** noun [U] the cheapest type of ticket or accommodation that is available on a plane or ship or in a hotel

**ˈtourist trap** noun (*informal, disapproving*) a place that attracts a lot of tourists and where food, drink, entertainment, etc. is more expensive than normal

**tour·isty** /ˈtʊərɪsti, ˈtɔːr-; NAmE ˈtʊr-/ adj. (*informal, disapproving*) attracting or designed to attract a lot of tourists: *Jersey is the most touristy of the islands.* ◊ *a shop full of touristy souvenirs*

**tour·na·ment** [+] [B2] /ˈtʊənəmənt, ˈtɔːn-; NAmE ˈtʊrn-/ noun **1** [+] [B2] (NAmE, less frequent **tour·ney**) a sports competition involving a number of teams or players who take part in different games and must leave the competition if they lose. The competition continues until there is only the winner left: *a golf/tennis/soccer/chess tournament* ⇒ WORDFINDER NOTE at SPORT **2** a competition in the Middle Ages between KNIGHTS on HORSEBACK fighting to show courage and skill

**tour·ney** /ˈtʊəni; NAmE ˈtʊrni/ noun (NAmE) = TOURNAMENT (1)

**tour·ni·quet** /ˈtʊənɪkeɪ; NAmE ˈtɜːrnəkət/ noun a piece of cloth, etc. that is tied tightly around an arm or a leg to stop the loss of blood from a wound

**ˌtour of ˈduty** (*also* tour) noun (*pl.* tours of duty) a period of time when sb is serving in the ARMED FORCES or as a DIPLOMAT in a particular place: *She has served two tours of duty overseas.* ◊ **on a ~** *He was wounded while on a tour of duty.*

**tou·sle** /ˈtaʊzl/ verb [usually passive] **~ sth** to make sb's hair untidy ▶ **tou·sled** adj.: *a boy with blue eyes and tousled hair*

**tout** /taʊt/ verb, noun
■ verb **1** [T, often passive] to try to persuade people that sb/sth is important or valuable by praising them/it: **be touted (as sth)** *She's being touted as the next leader of the party.* **2** [I, T] (*especially BrE*) to try to persuade people to buy your goods or services, especially by going to them and asking them directly: **~ (for sth)** *the problem of unlicensed taxi drivers touting for business at airports* ◊ **~ sth** *He's busy touting his client's latest book around London publishers.* **3** [T] (*BrE*) (NAmE **scalp**) **~ sth** to sell tickets for a popular event illegally, at a price that is higher than the official price, especially outside a theatre, stadium, etc.
■ noun (*also* **ˈticket tout**) (*both BrE*) (NAmE **ˈscalp·er**) a person who buys tickets for concerts, sports events, etc. and then sells them to other people at a higher price

**tow** /təʊ/ verb, noun
■ verb **1** **~ sth (+ adv./prep.)** to pull a car, boat, etc. behind another vehicle, using a rope or chain: *Our car was towed away by the police.* ⇒ SYNONYMS at PULL **2** **~ sb (+ adv./prep.)** (of a person) to pull sb along behind you: *Vicky was towing Rosa along by the hand.*
■ noun [sing.] an act of one vehicle pulling another vehicle using a rope or chain: *The car broke down and we had to get somebody to give us a tow.* ◊ *a tow truck*

[IDM] **in tow 1** (*informal*) if you have sb **in tow**, they are with you and following closely behind: *She turned up with her mother in tow.* **2** if a ship is taken **in tow**, it is pulled by another ship

▼ HOMOPHONES

**toe • tow** /təʊ/
● **toe** noun: *He stepped on my toe while we were dancing!*
● **tow** verb: *Luckily, a truck came to tow our car to safety.*

**to·wards** ⓘ [A2] /təˈwɔːdz; NAmE tɔːrdz/ (*also* **to·ward** /təˈwɔːd; NAmE tɔːrd/ *especially in NAmE*) prep. **1** [A2] in the direction of sb/sth: *They were heading towards the German border.* ◊ *She had her back towards me.* **2** [+] [A2] getting closer to achieving sth: *This is a first step towards political union.* **3** [+] [A2] close or closer to a point in time: *towards the end of April* **4** [+] [A2] in relation to sb/sth: *He was warm and tender towards her.* ◊ *our attitude towards death* **5** with the aim of obtaining sth, or helping sb to obtain sth: *The money will go towards a new school building* (= will help pay for it).

**towel** ⓘ [A2] /ˈtaʊəl/ noun, verb
■ noun [A2] a piece of cloth or paper used for drying things, especially your body: *Help yourself to a clean towel.* ◊ *a hand/bath towel* (= a small/large towel) ◊ *a beach towel* (= a large towel used for lying on in the sun) ⇒ see also PAPER TOWEL, SANITARY TOWEL, TEA TOWEL
[IDM] **throw in the ˈtowel** (*informal*) to admit that you have been defeated and stop trying
■ verb (-ll-, NAmE also -l-) **~ yourself/sb/sth (down)** to dry yourself/sb/sth with a towel

**tow·el·ling** (*BrE*) (*US* **tow·el·ing**) /ˈtaʊəlɪŋ/ noun [U] a type of soft cotton cloth that has a surface covered with raised LOOPS of THREAD, used especially for making towels [SYN] **terry**: *a towelling bathrobe*

**ˈtowel rail** (*BrE*) (NAmE **ˈtowel rack**) noun a bar or frame for hanging towels on in a bathroom

**tower** ⓘ [A2] /ˈtaʊə(r)/ noun, verb
■ noun **1** [A2] a tall narrow building or part of a building, especially of a church or castle: *a bell tower* ◊ *the Eiffel Tower* ◊ *The castle is rectangular in shape, with a tower at each corner.* ⇒ see also CLOCK TOWER, CONNING TOWER, CONTROL TOWER, COOLING TOWER, IVORY TOWER, WATCHTOWER, WATER TOWER **2** (often in compounds) a tall structure used for sending television or radio signals: *a television tower* **3** (usually in compounds) a tall piece of furniture used for storing things: *a CD tower*
[IDM] **a ˌtower of ˈstrength** a person that you can rely on to help, protect and comfort you when you are in trouble
■ verb
[PHR V] **ˌtower ˈover/aˈbove sb/sth 1** to be much higher or taller than the people or things that are near: *The cliffs towered above them.* ◊ *He towered over his classmates.* **2** to be much better than others in ability, quality, etc: *She towers over other dancers of her generation.*

**ˈtower block** noun (*BrE*) a very tall block of flats or offices

**tower·ing** /ˈtaʊərɪŋ/ adj. [only before noun] **1** extremely tall or high and therefore impressive: *towering cliffs* **2** of extremely high quality: *a towering performance* **3** (of emotions) extremely strong: *a towering rage*

**tow·line** /ˈtəʊlaɪn/ noun = TOW ROPE

**town** ⓘ [A1] /taʊn/ noun **1** [+] [A1] [C, U] a place with many houses, shops, etc. where people live and work. It is larger than a village but smaller than a city: *The nearest town is ten miles away.* ◊ *a university/seaside/market town* ◊ **in a ~** *I live in a small town.* ◊ *They live in a rough part of town.* [HELP] You will find compounds ending in **town** at their place in the alphabet. **2 the town** [sing.] the people who live in a particular town: *The whole town is talking about it.* **3** [+] [A1] [U] the area of a town where most of the shops and businesses are: **in ~** *Mum's in town doing some shopping.* ⇒ see also DOWNTOWN, MIDTOWN, OUT-OF-TOWN (1),

UPTOWN **4** [U] (*especially NAmE*) a particular town where sb lives and works or one that has just been referred to: **in~** *I'll be in town next week if you want to meet.* ◊ **out of~** *He married a girl from out of town.* ⊃ see also OUT-OF-TOWN (2) **5** [sing., U] life in towns or cities as opposed to life in the country: *Pollution is just one of the disadvantages of living in the town.* ⊃ WORDFINDER NOTE at CITY

**IDM** ▶ **go to 'town (on sth)** (*informal*) to do sth with a lot of energy, enthusiasm, etc., especially by spending a lot of money **(out) on the 'town** (*informal*) visiting restaurants, clubs, theatres, etc. for entertainment, especially at night: *a night on the town* ◊ *How about going out on the town tonight?* ⊃ more at GAME *n.*, MAN *n.*, PAINT *v.*

**town and 'gown** *noun* [U] the relationship between the people who live permanently in a town where there is a university and the members of the university

**town 'centre** *noun* (*BrE*) the main part of a town, where the shops are: *in the town centre* ◊ *a town-centre car park* ⊃ compare DOWNTOWN

**town 'clerk** *noun* **1** (*NAmE*) a public officer in charge of the records of a town **2** (*BrE*) in the past, the person who was the secretary of, and gave legal advice to, the local government of a town

**town 'crier** (*also* **crier**) *noun* (in the past) a person whose job was to walk through a town shouting news, official announcements, etc.

**townee** = TOWNIE (1)

**town 'hall** *noun* a building containing local government offices and, in the UK, usually a hall for public meetings, concerts, etc.

**'town house** *noun* **1** a house in a town owned by sb who also has a house in the country **2** a tall, narrow house in a town that is part of a row of similar houses: *an elegant Georgian town house* **3** (*usually* **townhouse**) (*NAmE*) = ROW HOUSE

**townie** /'taʊni/ *noun* (*disapproving*) **1** (*also* **townee**) a person who lives in or comes much from a town or city, especially sb who does not know much about life in the countryside **2** (*NAmE*) a person who lives in a town with a college or university but does not attend it or work at it

**town 'meeting** *noun* a meeting when people in a town come together to discuss problems that affect the town and to give their opinions on various issues

**town 'planner** *noun* = PLANNER

**town 'planning** (*also* **plan·ning**, *NAmE also* **city 'plan·ning**) *noun* [U] the control of the development of towns and their buildings, roads, etc. so that they can be pleasant and convenient places for people to live in; the subject that studies this

**town·scape** /'taʊnskeɪp/ *noun* **1** what you see when you look at a town, for example from a distance: *an industrial townscape* **2** (*specialist*) a picture of a town ⊃ compare LANDSCAPE, SEASCAPE

**town·ship** /'taʊnʃɪp/ *noun* **1** (in South Africa in the past) a town or part of a town that black people had to live in, and where only black people lived **2** (in the US or Canada) a division of a county that is a unit of local government

**towns·people** /'taʊnzpiːpl/ (*also* **towns·folk** /'taʊnsfəʊk/) *noun* [pl.] people who live in towns, not in the countryside; the people who live in a particular town

**tow·path** /'təʊpɑːθ; *NAmE* -pæθ/ *noun* a path along the bank of a river or CANAL, that was used in the past by horses pulling boats (called NARROWBOATS)

**'tow rope** (*also* **tow-line**) *noun* a rope that is used for pulling sth along, especially a vehicle

**'tow truck** (*especially NAmE*) (*BrE usually* **breakdown truck**) *noun* a truck that is used for taking cars away to be repaired when they have had a breakdown

**tox·ae·mia** (*BrE*) (*NAmE* **tox·emia**) /tɒkˈsiːmiə; *NAmE* tɑːk-/ *noun* [U] (*medical*) infection of the blood by harmful bacteria **SYN** **blood poisoning**

---

**toxic** /'tɒksɪk; *NAmE* 'tɑːk-/ *adj.* **1** containing poison; poisonous: *toxic chemicals/fumes/gases/substances* ◊ *to dispose of toxic waste* ◊ *Many pesticides are highly toxic.* ◊ **~to sb/sth** *This chemical is toxic to many forms of life.* **OPP** **non-toxic** ⊃ WORDFINDER NOTE at GREEN **2** **~debt/loan/asset/investment** a level of debt or high-risk investment that causes very serious problems for a bank or other financial institution **3** (*informal, disapproving*) (of a person, relationship or situation) very unpleasant, especially in the way sb likes to control and influence other people in a dishonest way: *I felt trapped in this toxic relationship.* ◊ *The political situation is highly toxic.*

**tox·icity** /tɒkˈsɪsəti; *NAmE* tɑːk-/ *noun* [U] (*specialist*) the fact of being poisonous; the extent to which sth is poisonous: *substances with high levels of toxicity*

**toxi·col·ogy** /ˌtɒksɪˈkɒlədʒi; *NAmE* ˌtɑːksɪˈkɑːl-/ *noun* [U] the scientific study of poisons ▶ **toxi·co·logical** /ˌtɒksɪkəˈlɒdʒɪkl; *NAmE* ˌtɑːksɪkəˈlɑːdʒ-/ *adj.* **toxi·colo·gist** /ˌtɒksɪˈkɒlədʒɪst; *NAmE* ˌtɑːksɪˈkɑːl-/ *noun*

**toxic 'shock syndrome** *noun* [U] a serious illness in women caused by harmful bacteria in the VAGINA, connected with the use of TAMPONS

**toxin** /'tɒksɪn; *NAmE* 'tɑːk-/ *noun* a poisonous substance, especially one that is produced by bacteria in plants and animals

**toxo·plas·mo·sis** /ˌtɒksəʊplæzˈməʊsɪs; *NAmE* ˌtɑːk-/ *noun* [U] (*medical*) a disease that can be dangerous to a baby while it is still in its mother's body, caught from bacteria in meat, soil or animal FAECES

**toy** /tɔɪ/ *noun, adj., verb*

■ *noun* **1** an object for children to play with: *cuddly/stuffed toys* ◊ *The children were playing happily with their toys.* ⊃ see also SOFT TOY **2** an object that you have for fun or pleasure rather than for a serious purpose **SYN** **plaything**: *executive toys* ◊ *His latest toy is the electric drill he bought last week.* ⊃ see also BOY TOY

■ *adj.* [only before noun] **1** made as a copy of a particular thing and used for playing with: *a toy car* ◊ *toy soldiers* **2** (of a dog) of a very small type: *a toy poodle*

■ *verb*

**PHR V** **'toy with sth 1** to consider an idea or a plan, but not very seriously and not for a long time **SYN** **flirt with**: *I did briefly toy with the idea of living in France.* **2** to play with sth and move it around carelessly or without thinking: *He kept toying nervously with his pen.* ◊ *She hardly ate a thing, just toyed with a piece of cheese on her plate.*

**'toy boy** *noun* (*BrE*) (*NAmE* **boy toy**) (*informal, humorous*) a man in a sexual relationship who is much younger than his partner

**toyi-toyi** /ˈtɔɪ tɔɪ/ *noun* [U] (*SAfrE*) a type of dance or MARCH, used as a form of protest, in which you repeatedly move one leg up and down followed by the other

**trace** /treɪs/ *verb, noun*

■ *verb* **1** **~sb/sth (to sth)** to find or discover sb/sth by looking carefully for them/it **SYN** **track down**: *We finally traced him to an address in Chicago.* **2** **~sth (back) (to sth)** to find the origin or cause of sth: *She could trace her family tree back to the 16th century.* ◊ *The leak was eventually traced to a broken seal.* ◊ *The police traced the call* (= used special electronic equipment to find out who made the phone call) *to her ex-husband's number.* **3** **~sth (from sth) (to sth)** to describe a process or the development of sth: *Her book traces the town's history from Saxon times to the present day.* **4** **~sth (out)** to draw a line or lines on a surface: *She traced a line in the sand.* **5** **~sth** to follow the shape or outline of sth: *He traced the route on the map.* ◊ *A tear traced a path down her cheek.* **6** **~sth** to copy a map, drawing, etc. by drawing on TRACING PAPER (= paper that you can see through) placed over it

■ *noun* **1** [C, U] a mark, an object or a sign that shows that sb/sth existed or was present: *It's exciting to discover traces of earlier civilizations.* ◊ *Police searched the area*

# traceable

but found **no trace** of the escaped prisoners. ◊ *Years of living in England had eliminated* **all trace** *of her American accent.* ◊ **without (a)~** *The ship had vanished without (a) trace.* **2** ~ **of sth** [C] a very small amount of sth: *The post-mortem revealed traces of poison in his stomach.* ◊ *She spoke without a trace of bitterness.* **3** [C] (*specialist*) a line or pattern on paper or a screen that shows information that is found by a machine: *The trace showed a normal heart rhythm.* **4** [C] ~ **on sb/sth** a search to find out information about the identity of sb/sth, especially what number a phone call was made from: *The police ran a trace on the call.* **5** [C, usually pl.] one of the two long pieces of leather that fasten a CARRIAGE or CART to the horse that pulls it **IDM** see KICK *v.*

**trace·able** /ˈtreɪsəbl/ *adj.* ~ **(to sb/sth)** if sth is **traceable**, you can find out where it came from, where it has gone, when it began or what its cause was: *Most telephone calls are traceable.*

**ˈtrace element** *noun* **1** a chemical substance that is found in very small amounts **2** a chemical substance that living things, especially plants, need only in very small amounts to be able to grow well

**tracer** /ˈtreɪsə(r)/ *noun* **1** a bullet or SHELL (= a kind of bomb) that leaves a line of smoke or flame behind it **2** (*specialist*) a RADIOACTIVE substance that can be seen in the human body and is used to find out what is happening inside the body

**trachea** /trəˈkiːə/; *NAmE* ˈtreɪkiə/ *noun* (*pl.* **trach·eas** or **trach·eae** /trəˈkiːiː/; *NAmE* ˈtreɪkiː/) (*anatomy*) the tube in the body that carries air from the throat to the lungs **SYN** windpipe ⊃ VISUAL VOCAB page V1

**trache·ot·omy** /ˌtrækiˈɒtəmi/; *NAmE* ˌtreɪkiˈɑːt-/ (*also* **trache·ost·omy** /ˌtrækiˈɒstəmi/; *NAmE* ˌtreɪkiˈɑːs-/) *noun* (*pl.* **-ies**) (*medical*) a medical operation to cut a hole in sb's trachea so that they can breathe

**tra·cing** /ˈtreɪsɪŋ/ *noun* a copy of a map, drawing, etc. that you make by drawing on a piece of TRANSPARENT paper (= that you can see through) that is placed on top of it

**ˈtracing paper** *noun* [U] strong TRANSPARENT paper (= that you can see through) that is placed on top of a drawing, etc. so that you can follow the lines with a pen or pencil in order to make a copy of it

**track** ⓘ [A2] /træk/ *noun, verb*
■ *noun*
- FOR TRAIN **1** [A2] [C, U] RAILS (= metal bars) that a train moves along: *railway/railroad tracks* ◊ *India has thousands of miles of track.* ⊃ WORDFINDER NOTE at TRAIN **2** [A2] [C] (*NAmE*) a track with a number at a train station that a train arrives at or leaves from: *The train for Chicago is on track 9.* ⊃ note at PLATFORM
- FOR RACES **3** [A2] [C] a piece of ground with a special surface for people, cars, etc. to have races or to drive on: *a race track* ◊ *a Formula One Grand Prix track* (= for motor racing) ⊃ see also DIRT TRACK (2) **4** [U] (*NAmE*) the sport of running on a track: *He loves sports and participates in track and basketball.*
- ROUGH PATH **5** [B1] [C] a rough path or road, usually one that has not been built but that has been made by people walking there: *a muddy track through the forest*
- MARKS ON GROUND **6** [B1] [C, usually pl.] marks left by a person, an animal or a moving vehicle: *We followed the bear's tracks in the snow.* ◊ *tyre tracks*
- DIRECTION/COURSE **7** [C] the path or direction that sb/sth is moving in: *He switched tracks and went back to college.* ◊ **on the ~ of sb/sth** *Police are on the track of* (= searching for) *the thieves.* ⊃ see also FAST TRACK, ONE-TRACK MIND
- RECORDING **8** [B1] [C] a recording of one song or piece of music: *a track from their latest album* **9** [C] part of a computer disk or tape that music or information can be recorded on: *a sixteen track recording studio* ◊ *She sang on the backing track.* **10** (especially in compounds) the SOUNDTRACK of a film or video: *The film is available with French and Spanish audio tracks.*
- FOR CURTAIN **11** [C] a long, thin, straight piece of metal, wood or plastic that a curtain hangs from and moves along
- ON LARGE VEHICLE **12** [C] a continuous belt of metal plates around the wheels of a large vehicle such as a BULLDOZER that allows it to move over the ground ⊃ see also INSIDE TRACK

**IDM** **back on ˈtrack** going in the right direction again after a mistake, failure, etc: *I tried to get my life back on track after my divorce.* **be ˌon ˈtrack** to be doing the right thing in order to achieve a particular result: *Curtis is on track for the gold medal.* **keep/lose ˈtrack of sb/sth** to have/ not have information about what is happening or where sb/sth is: *Bank statements help you keep track of where your money is going.* ◊ *I lost all track of time* (= forgot what time it was). **make ˈtracks** (*informal*) to leave a place, especially to go home **on the right/wrong ˈtrack** thinking or behaving in the right/wrong way **stop/halt sb in their ˈtracks** | **stop/halt/freeze in your ˈtracks** to suddenly make sb stop by frightening or surprising them; to suddenly stop because sth has frightened or surprised you: *The question stopped Alice in her tracks.* ⊃ more at BEAT *v.*, COVER *v.*, HOT *adj.*, WRONG *adj.*

■ *verb*
- FOLLOW **1** [B2] [T, I] to find sb/sth by following the marks, signs, information, etc., that they have left behind them: ~ **sb/sth** *hunters tracking and shooting bears* **2** [B2] [T] ~ **sb/sth** | ~ **where, how, etc …** to follow the movements of sb/sth, especially by using special electronic equipment: *We continued tracking the plane on our radar.* **3** [B2] [T] ~ **sb/sth** | ~ **where, how, etc …** to follow the progress or development of sb/sth: *The research project involves tracking the careers of 400 graduates.* ⊃ see also FAST-TRACK
- OF CAMERA **4** [I] + *adv./prep.* to move in relation to the thing that is being filmed: *The camera eventually tracked away.*
- SCHOOL STUDENTS **5** [T] (*NAmE*) = STREAM (4)
- LEAVE MARKS **6** [T] ~ **sth** (+ *adv./prep.*) (*especially NAmE*) to leave dirty marks behind you as you walk: *Don't track mud on my clean floor.*
- OF A STATISTIC, NUMBER, ETC. **7** [I] to stay at the same level for a period of time: *Annual employment growth is tracking at 2%.*

**PHRV** **ˌtrack sb/sthˈdown** to find sb/sth after searching in several different places **SYN** **trace**: *The police have so far failed to track down the attacker.*

**ˌtrack and ˈfield** (*NAmE*) (*BrE* **athˈletics**) *noun* sports such as running, jumping and throwing that people compete in

**track·ball** /ˈtrækbɔːl/ (*also* **roller-ball**) *noun* (*computing*) a device containing a ball that is used instead of a mouse to move the CURSOR around the screen

**track·er** /ˈtrækə(r)/ *noun* **1** a person who can find people or wild animals by following the marks that they leave on the ground **2** a device that follows and records the movements of sb/sth: *Electronic trackers show how far the animals range in search of food.* ⊃ see also FITNESS TRACKER

**ˈtrack event** *noun* [usually pl.] a sports event that is a race run on a track, rather than jumping or throwing sth ⊃ compare FIELD EVENT

**ˌtrackless ˈtrolley** (*US*) (*BrE* **ˈtrolley-bus**) *noun* a bus driven by electricity from a cable above the street

**ˈtrack list** /ˈtræklɪst/ *noun* a list of songs or pieces of music in the order in which they appear on a recording

**ˈtrack pad** /ˈtrækpæd/ *noun* = TOUCHPAD

**ˈtrack record** *noun* all the past achievements, successes or failures of a person or an organization: *He has a proven track record in marketing.*

**track·suit** /ˈtræksuːt/ (*also* **jogging suit**) *noun* a warm, loose pair of trousers and matching jacket worn for sports practice or as informal clothes

**tract** /trækt/ *noun* **1** (*biology*) a system of connected organs or TISSUES along which materials or messages pass: *the digestive tract* ◊ *a nerve tract* **2** an area of land, especially a large one **SYN** **stretch**: *vast tracts of forest* **3** (*sometimes disapproving*) a short piece of writing, especially on a religious, moral or political subject, that is intended to influence people's ideas

**tract·able** /ˈtræktəbl/ *adj.* (*formal*) easy to deal with or control **SYN** **manageable** **OPP** **intractable** ▶ **tract·abil·ity** /ˌtræktəˈbɪləti/ *noun* [U]

**trac·tion** /ˈtrækʃn/ *noun* [U] **1** the action of pulling sth along a surface; the power that is used for doing this **2** a way of treating a broken bone in your body that involves using special equipment to pull the bone gradually back into its correct place: **in~** *He spent six weeks in traction after he broke his leg.* **3** the force that stops sth, for example the wheels of a vehicle, from sliding on the ground **4** the extent to which an idea, a product, etc. becomes popular or gains support: *The president's message is gaining traction among undecided voters.*

**ˈtraction engine** *noun* a vehicle, driven by STEAM or DIESEL oil, used in the past for pulling heavy loads

**trac·tor** /ˈtræktə(r)/ *noun* **1** a powerful vehicle with two large and two smaller wheels, used especially for pulling farm machines ⇒ WORDFINDER NOTE at FARM **2** (*NAmE*) the front part of a tractor-trailer, where the driver sits

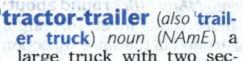
tractor

**ˈtractor-trailer** (*also* **ˈtrailer truck**) *noun* (*NAmE*) a large truck with two sections, one in front where the driver sits and one behind for carrying goods. The sections are connected by a flexible JOINT so that the tractor-trailer can turn corners more easily. ⇒ *see also* ARTICULATED

**trad** /træd/ (*also less frequent* ˌtrad ˈjazz) (*both BrE*) *noun* [U] traditional jazz in the style of the 1920s, with free playing (= IMPROVISATION) against a background of fixed rhythms and combinations of notes ⇒ *see also* DIXIELAND

**trad·able** (*also* **trade·able**) /ˈtreɪdəbl/ *adj.* (*specialist*) that you can easily buy and sell or exchange for money or goods **SYN** **marketable**

**trade** 🅞 🅱🅵 /treɪd/ *noun, verb*
▪ *noun* **1** 🅸 🅱🅵 [U] the activity of buying and selling or of exchanging goods or services between people or countries: *international/foreign/global/world trade* ◊ **~in sth** *the international trade in oil* ◊ *the arms/drugs trade* ◊ *The Senate has approved a trade agreement with Latin American nations.* ⇒ *see also* BALANCE OF TRADE, FAIR TRADE, FREE TRADE

  **WORDFINDER** boom, business, commerce, embargo, import, market, monopoly, sanction, tariff

**2** 🅸 🅱🅵 [C] a particular type of business: *the building/food/tourist trade* ◊ **in the … ~** *He works in the retail trade* (= selling goods in shops/stores). ⇒ *see also* SLAVE TRADE **3 the trade** [sing. + sing./pl. v.] a particular area of business and the people or companies that are connected with it: *They offer discounts to the trade* (= to people who are working in the same business). ◊ *a trade magazine/journal* ⇒ *see also* STOCK-IN-TRADE **4** 🅸 🅱🅵 [U, C] the amount of goods or services that you sell **SYN** **business**: *Trade was very good last month.* **5** 🅸 🅱🅵 [U, C] a job, especially one that involves working with your hands and that requires special training and skills: **by~** *He was a carpenter by trade.* ◊ *When she leaves school, she wants to learn a trade.* ◊ *She was surrounded by the tools of her trade* (= everything she needs to do her job). ⇒ SYNONYMS at WORK
**IDM** *see* JACK *n.*, PLY *v.*, ROARING, TRICK *n.*
▪ *verb* **1** 🅱🅵 [I, T] to buy and sell things: **~(in sth) (with sb)** *The firm openly traded in arms.* ◊ *Early explorers traded directly with the Indians.* ◊ *trading partners* (= countries that you trade with) ◊ **~sth (with sb)** *Our products are now traded worldwide.* **2** [I] to exist and operate as a business or company: *The firm has now ceased trading.* ◊ **~as sb/sth** *They traded as 'Walker and Son'.* **3** [I, T] **~(sth)** to be bought and sold, or to buy and sell sth, on a STOCK EXCHANGE: *Shares were trading at under half their usual*

1661 **trade unionist**

*value.* **4** [T] to exchange sth that you have for sth that sb else has: **~(sb) sth** *to trade secrets/insults/jokes* ◊ **~sth for sth** *She traded her posters for his CD.* ◊ **~sth with sb** *I wouldn't mind trading places with her for a day.*
**PHRV** ˌtrade ˈat sth (*US*) to buy goods or shop at a particular store ˌtrade ˈdown to spend less money on things than you used to: *Shoppers are trading down and looking for bargains.* ˌtrade sth↔ˈin to give sth used as part of the payment for sth new: *He traded in his old car for a new Mercedes.* ⇒ *related noun* TRADE-IN ˌtrade sth↔ˈoff (aˈgainst/for sth) to balance two things or situations that are opposed to each other: *They were attempting to trade off inflation against unemployment.* ⇒ *related noun* TRADE-OFF ˈtrade on sth (*disapproving*) to use sth to your own advantage, especially in an unfair way **SYN** **exploit**: *They trade on people's insecurity to sell them insurance.* ˌtrade ˈup **1** to sell sth in order to buy sth more expensive: *We're going to trade up to a larger house.* **2** to give sth you have used as part of the payment for sth more expensive

**ˈtrade balance** *noun* = BALANCE OF TRADE

**ˈtrade deficit** (*also* **ˈtrade gap**) *noun* [usually sing.] a situation in which the value of a country's imports is greater than the value of its exports

**ˈtrade fair** (*also* **ˈtrade show**) *noun* an event at which many different companies show and sell their products

**ˈtrade-in** *noun* a method of buying sth by giving a used item as part of the payment for a new one; the used item itself: *the trade-in value of a car* ◊ *Do you have a trade-in?* ⇒ *see also* PART EXCHANGE

**trade·mark** 🅸+ 🅲🅵 /ˈtreɪdmɑːk; *NAmE* -mɑːrk/ *noun, verb*
▪ *noun* **1** 🅸+ 🅲🅵 (*abbr.* **TM**) a name, symbol or design that a company uses for its products and that cannot be used by anyone else: *'Big Mac' is McDonald's best-known trademark.* **2** 🅸+ 🅲🅵 a special way of behaving or dressing that is typical of sb and that makes them easily recognized: *Attention to detail is Anthea's trademark.*
▪ *verb* to register sth as a trademark: *They have trademarked the name in the US and the UK.*

**ˈtrade name** *noun* **1** = BRAND NAME **2** a name that is taken and used by a company for business purposes

**ˈtrade-off** *noun* **~(between sth and sth)** the act of balancing two things that are opposed to each other: *a trade-off between increased production and a reduction in quality*

**trader** /ˈtreɪdə(r)/ *noun* a person who buys and sells things as a job: *small/independent/local traders* ◊ *bond/currency traders*

**ˈtrade route** *noun* (in the past) the route that people buying and selling goods used to take across land or sea

**ˈtrade school** *noun* (*NAmE*) a school where students go to learn a trade

**ˌtrade ˈsecret** *noun* a secret piece of information that is known only by the people at a particular company: *The recipe for their drink is a closely guarded trade secret.*

**ˈtrade show** *noun* = TRADE FAIR

**trades·man** /ˈtreɪdzmən/ *noun* (*pl.* **-men** /-mən/) **1** a person whose job involves going to houses to sell or deliver goods **2** (*especially BrE*) a person who sells goods, especially in a shop **SYN** **shopkeeper** **3** a person whose job involves training and special skills, for example a CARPENTER

**trades·people** /ˈtreɪdzpiːpl/ *noun* [pl.] **1** people whose job involves selling goods or services, especially people who own a shop **2** people whose job involves training and special skills, for example CARPENTERS

**the ˌTrades ˈUnion ˈCongress** *noun* [sing.] = TUC

**ˌtrade ˈsurplus** *noun* a situation in which the value of a country's exports is greater than the value of its imports

**ˌtrade ˈunion** (*BrE also* **ˌtrades ˈunion**) *noun* = UNION
▶ **ˌtrade ˈunionism** *noun* [U]: *the history of trade unionism*

**ˌtrade ˈunionist** (*also* **ˌtrades ˈunionist**, **ˈunion·ist**) *noun* a member of a trade union

**trade-up** noun a sale of an object in order to buy sth similar but better and more expensive

**trade winds** noun [pl.] strong winds that blow all the time towards the EQUATOR and then to the west

**trad·ing** /ˈtreɪdɪŋ/ noun [U] the activity of buying and selling things: *new laws on Sunday trading* (= shops being open on Sundays) ◊ *Supermarkets everywhere reported excellent trading in the run-up to Christmas.* ◊ *Shares worth $8 million changed hands during a day of hectic trading.* ⇒ see also CARBON TRADING, DAY TRADING, EMISSIONS TRADING, HORSE-TRADING, INSIDER TRADING

**trading card** noun (especially in NAmE) one of a set of cards, often showing sports players or other famous people on them, that children collect and exchange with one another

**trading estate** noun (BrE) an area of land, often on the edge of a city or town, where there are a number of businesses and small factories ⇒ compare INDUSTRIAL ESTATE

**trading floor** noun (especially in the past) an area in a STOCK EXCHANGE or bank where shares and other SECURITIES are bought and sold

**trading post** noun a small place in an area that is a long way from any town, used as a centre for buying and selling goods (especially in North America in the past)

**trad·i·tion** /trəˈdɪʃn/ noun [C, U] a belief, custom or way of doing sth that has existed for a long time among a particular group of people; a set of these beliefs or customs: *religious/cultural/ancient traditions* ◊ *a ~ of sth The company has a long tradition of fine design.* ◊ *The British are said to love tradition* (= to want to do things in the way they have always been done). ◊ *They broke with tradition* (= did things differently) *and got married quietly.* ◊ *by ~ By tradition, children play tricks on 1 April.* ◊ *according to ~ According to tradition, a tree grew on this spot.* ◊ *There's a tradition in our family that we have a party on New Year's Eve.* ◊ *in the ~ of sb He's a politician in the tradition of* (= similar in style to) *Kennedy.*

**trad·i·tion·al** /trəˈdɪʃənl/ adj. **1** being part of the beliefs, customs or way of life of a particular group of people, that have not changed for a long time: *traditional dress/music/art/culture/dance* ◊ *It's traditional in America to eat turkey on Thanksgiving Day.* **2** (sometimes disapproving) following older methods and ideas rather than modern or different ones SYN conventional: *a traditional method/way of doing sth* ◊ *Their marriage is very traditional.* ▶ **trad·i·tion·al·ly** /-nəli/ adv.: *The festival is traditionally held in May.* ◊ *Housework has traditionally been regarded as women's work.*

**trad·i·tion·al·ism** /trəˈdɪʃənəlɪzəm/ noun [U] the belief that customs and traditions are more important for a society than modern ideas

**trad·i·tion·al·ist** /trəˈdɪʃənəlɪst/ noun a person who prefers tradition to modern ideas or ways of doing things ▶ **trad·i·tion·al·ist** adj.

**tra·ditional ˈmedicine** noun [U, C] medical treatment that is based on the ancient beliefs and practices from a particular culture: *a key ingredient in traditional medicine* ⇒ compare ALTERNATIVE MEDICINE, COMPLEMENTARY MEDICINE, CONVENTIONAL (3)

**trad ˈjazz** noun [U] = TRAD

**tra·duce** /trəˈdjuːs; NAmE -ˈduːs/ verb ~ sb (formal) to say things about sb that are unpleasant or not true SYN slander

**traf·fic** /ˈtræfɪk/ noun, verb
■ noun [U] **1** the vehicles that are on a road at a particular time: *There's always a lot of traffic at this time of day.* ◊ *heavy/rush-hour traffic* ◊ *in ~ They were stuck in traffic and missed their flight.* ◊ *a plan to reduce traffic congestion* ◊ *She was badly injured in a road traffic accident.* ◊ *The delay is due simply to the volume of traffic.* ⇒ WORDFINDER NOTE at CAR

WORDFINDER clamp, cone, contraflow, pedestrian, roadworks, speed hump, tailback, toll, zebra crossing

**2** the movement of ships, trains, aircraft, etc. along a particular route: *transatlantic traffic* ⇒ see also AIR TRAFFIC CONTROL **3** the movement of people or goods from one place to another: *commuter/freight/passenger traffic* ◊ *the traffic of goods between one country and another* **4** the movement of messages and signals through an electronic communication system: *the computer servers that manage global internet traffic* ◊ *web/network traffic* **5** ~ (in sth) illegal trade in sth: *the traffic in firearms*
■ verb (-ck-) **1** [T, I, usually passive] ~ (in) sb to move people illegally, especially in order to make them work in bad conditions without proper payment: *The women had been trafficked and forced into prostitution.* ◊ *The cartel is now trafficking in illegal immigrants.* **2** [T, I] ~ (in) sth to buy and sell sth illegally: *Smugglers were trafficking arms across the border to the rebels.* ◊ *to traffic in drugs* ▶ **traf·fick·er** noun: *a drugs trafficker* ⇒ see also HUMAN TRAFFICKER **traf·fick·ing** noun [U]: *drug trafficking* ⇒ see also HUMAN TRAFFICKING, PEOPLE TRAFFICKING

**traffic calming** noun [U] (BrE) ways of making roads safer, especially for people who are walking or riding bicycles, by building raised areas, etc. to make cars go more slowly

**traffic circle** (also **ro·tary**) (both NAmE) (BrE **round·about**) noun a place where two or more roads meet, forming a circle that all traffic must go around in the same direction

**traffic cone** noun = CONE (3)

**traffic island** (BrE also **island**, **ref·uge**) noun an area in the middle of a road where you can stand and wait for cars to go past until it is safe for you to cross

**traffic jam** noun a long line of vehicles on a road that cannot move or that can only move very slowly: *We were stuck in a traffic jam.*

**traffic light** noun [C] (also **traffic lights** [pl.]) (NAmE also **stop·lights** [pl.]) a set of lights that controls the traffic on a road. The red, orange and green lights show when you must stop and when you can go: *Turn left at the traffic lights.*

**traffic warden** noun (BrE) a person whose job is to check that people do not park their cars in the wrong place or for longer than is allowed, and to place tickets on vehicles that are parked illegally to make the owners pay a FINE

**tra·gedian** /trəˈdʒiːdiən/ noun (formal) **1** a person who writes tragedies for the theatre **2** an actor in tragedies

**tra·gedy** /ˈtrædʒədi/ noun [C, U] (pl. -ies) **1** a very sad event or situation, especially one that involves death: *It's a tragedy that she died so young.* ◊ *Tragedy struck the family when their son was hit by a car and killed.* ◊ *The whole affair ended in tragedy.* **2** a serious play with a sad ending, especially one in which the main character dies; plays of this type: *Shakespeare's tragedies* ◊ *Greek tragedy* ⇒ compare COMEDY

**tra·gic** /ˈtrædʒɪk/ adj. **1** making you feel very sad, usually because sb has died or suffered a lot: *He was killed in a tragic accident at the age of 24.* ◊ *Cuts in the health service could have tragic consequences for patients.* ◊ *It would be tragic if her talent remained unrecognized.* **2** [only before noun] connected with tragedy (= the style of literature): *a tragic actor/hero* ▶ WORDFINDER NOTE at STORY ▶ **tra·gic·al·ly** /-kli/ adv.: *Tragically, his wife was killed in a car accident.* ◊ *He died tragically young.*

**tragi·com·edy** /ˌtrædʒiˈkɒmədi; NAmE -ˈkɑːm-/ noun [C, U] (pl. -ies) **1** a play that is both funny and sad; plays of this type **2** an event or a situation that is both funny and sad ▶ **tragi·com·ic** /-mɪk/ adj.

**trail** /treɪl/ noun, verb
■ noun **1** ~ a long line or series of marks that is left by sb/sth: *a trail of blood* ◊ *tourists who leave a trail of litter everywhere they go* ◊ *The hurricane left a trail of destruction behind it.* **2** a track, sign or smell that is left behind and can be followed, especially in hunting: *The hounds were following the fox's trail.* ◊ **on the ~ of sb/sth**

The police are still on the trail of the escaped prisoner. ◇ Fortunately the **trail was still warm** (= clear and easy to follow). ◇ The **trail had gone cold.** ⇨ **WORDFINDER NOTE** at HUNT ⇨ see also VAPOUR TRAIL **3** a path through the countryside: *a trail through the forest* ⇨ see also NATIONAL TRAIL, NATURE TRAIL **4** a route that is followed for a particular purpose: *a tourist trail* (= of famous buildings) ◇ *politicians on the campaign trail* (= travelling around to attract support) ⇨ see also AUDIT TRAIL, PAPER TRAIL **IDM** see BLAZE v., HIT v., HOT adj.

■ **verb 1** [T, I] to pull sth behind sb/sth, usually along the ground; to be pulled along in this way: *~sth A jeep trailing a cloud of dust was speeding in my direction.* ◇ *I trailed my hand in the water as the boat moved along.* (+ **adv./prep.**) *The bride's dress trailed behind her.* **2** [I] + **adv./prep.** to walk slowly because you are tired or bored, especially behind sb else; to go from one place to another without enthusiasm: *The kids trailed around after us while we shopped for clothes.* **3** [I, T] (used especially in the progressive tenses) to be losing a game or other contest: *United were trailing 2–0 at half-time.* ◇ *~by sth We were trailing by five points.* ◇ *~in sth This country is still trailing badly in scientific research.* ◇ *~sb/sth The Conservatives are trailing Labour in the opinion polls.* **4** [T] *~sb/sth* to follow sb/sth by looking for signs that show you where they have been: *The police trailed Dale for days.* **5** [I] to grow or hang downwards over sth or along the ground; to move downwards over sth: *trailing plants* ◇ *He had tears trailing down his cheeks.* **6** [T] *~sth* to advertise a film, TV programme, etc. in advance: *It was trailed heavily as the Big Film of the New Year.*

**PHRV** ˌtrail aˈway/ˈoff (of sb's speech) to become gradually quieter and then stop: *His voice trailed away to nothing.* ◇ **+ speech** *'I only hope...', she trailed off.*

ˈtrail bike noun a bicycle or light motorcycle that can be used on rough ground

ˈtrail·blazer /ˈtreɪlbleɪzə(r)/ noun a person who is the first to do or discover sth and so makes it possible for others to follow ⇨ compare BLAZE A TRAIL ▶ **ˈtrail·blaz·ing** adj. [usually before noun]: *trailblazing scientific research*

**trail·er** /ˈtreɪlə(r)/ noun **1** a truck, or a container with wheels, that is pulled by another vehicle: *a car towing a trailer with a boat on it* ⇨ see also HORSE TRAILER, SEMI-TRAILER, TRACTOR-TRAILER **2** (NAmE) (BrE ˌmobile ˈhome) a vehicle without an engine, that can be pulled by a car or truck or used as a home or an office when it is parked: *a trailer park* (= an area where trailers are parked and used as homes) **3** (NAmE) (also ˌmobile ˈhome especially in NAmE) a small building for people to live in that is made in a factory and moved to a permanent place **4** (especially BrE) (NAmE usually **preview**) a series of short scenes from a film or television programme, shown in advance to advertise it ⇨ SYNONYMS at ADVERTISEMENT

ˈtrailer trash noun [U] (NAmE, informal, offensive) a way of referring to poor white people from a low social class

ˈtrailer truck noun (NAmE) = TRACTOR-TRAILER

ˈtrailing ˈedge noun (specialist) the back edge of sth moving, especially an aircraft wing

**train** /treɪn/ noun, verb

■ **noun 1** a number of connected coaches or trucks, pulled by an engine or powered by a motor in each one, taking people and goods from one place to another: *to get on/off a train* ◇ *by~ I like travelling by train.* ◇ *a passenger/commuter train* ◇ *a train journey/driver/operator* ◇ *Basel's main train station* ◇ *He boarded the train in Kansas City.* ⇨ see also BULLET TRAIN, FREIGHT TRAIN, GHOST TRAIN, GRAVY TRAIN, ROAD TRAIN, WAGON TRAIN

> **WORDFINDER** aisle, buffet, carriage, connection, locomotive, luggage rack, platform, station, track

**2** a number of people or animals moving in a line: *a camel train* **3** [usually sing.] a series of events or actions that are connected: *His death set in motion a train of events that led* to the outbreak of war. **4** the part of a long formal dress that spreads out on the floor behind the person wearing it **IDM** ˌbring sth in its ˈtrain (*formal*) to have sth as a result: *Unemployment brings great difficulties in its train.* ˌin sb's ˈtrain (*formal*) following behind sb: *In the train of the rich and famous came the journalists.* ˌset sth in ˈtrain (*formal*) to prepare or start sth: *That telephone call set in train a whole series of events.* **a train of ˈthought** the connected series of thoughts that are in your head at a particular time: *The phone ringing interrupted my train of thought.*

■ **verb 1** [T, I] to teach a person or an animal the skills for a particular job or activity; to be taught in this way: *~sb/sth highly trained professionals* ◇ *~sb/sth to do sth They train dogs to sniff out drugs.* ◇ *~(sb) as/in/for sth He trained as a teacher before becoming an actor.* ◇ *All members of the team have trained in first aid.* ◇ *~to do/be sth Sue is training to be a doctor.* ⇨ see also POTTY-TRAIN, TOILET-TRAIN **2** [I, T] to prepare yourself for a particular activity, especially a sport, by doing a lot of exercise; to prepare a person or an animal in this way: *~for sth athletes training for the Olympics* ◇ *~sb/sth (for sth) She trains horses.* ◇ *The athletes will be trained for all events.* **3** [T] to develop a natural ability or quality so that it improves: *~sth An expert with a trained eye will spot the difference immediately.* ◇ *~sth to do sth You can train your mind to think positively.* **4** [T] *~sth (around/along/up, etc.)* to make a plant grow in a particular direction: *Roses had been trained around the door.* **5** [T] *~sth at/on sb/sth* to aim a gun, camera, light, etc. at sb/sth

**train·ee** /ˌtreɪˈniː/ noun a person who is being taught how to do a particular job: *a management trainee* ◇ *a trainee teacher*

**train·er** /ˈtreɪnə(r)/ noun **1** (also **ˈtraining shoe**) (both BrE) (NAmE **ˈsneak·er, ˈgym shoe**) [usually pl.] a shoe that you wear for sports or as informal clothing: *a pair of trainers* **2** a person who teaches people or animals to perform a particular job or skill well, or to do a particular sport: *teacher trainers* ◇ *a racehorse trainer* ◇ *Her trainer had decided she shouldn't run in the race.* ⇨ see also PERSONAL TRAINER, TEACHER TRAINER

**train·ing** /ˈtreɪnɪŋ/ noun [U] **1** ~ **(in sth/in doing sth)** the process of learning the skills that you need to do a job: *staff training* ◇ *Few candidates had received any training in management.* ◇ *a training course/session/programme*

> **WORDFINDER** apprentice, certificate, coaching, college, course, intern, probation, qualify, work experience

**2** the process of preparing to take part in a sports competition by doing physical exercise: *in ~ (for sth) She is currently in training for the New York City marathon.*

ˈtraining camp noun a place where people live temporarily while they develop their skills, for example in a sport or fighting

ˈtraining college noun (BrE) a college that trains people for a job or profession: *a police training college*

ˈtraining ground noun **1** (BrE) a place where people go to get fit and practise the skills necessary for the sport that they play **2** a place where soldiers go to practise the skills necessary for fighting in a war **3** a place that provides the chance to learn the skills necessary for a job or an activity: *Paris was the traditional training ground for artists in the early twentieth century.*

ˈtraining shoe noun (BrE) = TRAINER (1)

ˈtraining wheels (NAmE) (BrE ˈsta·bil·izers) noun [pl.] small wheels that are fitted at each side of the back wheel on a child's bicycle to stop it from falling over

ˈtrain set noun a toy train, together with the track that it runs on, a toy station, etc.

**train·spot·ter** /ˈtreɪnspɒtə(r); NAmE -spɑːt-/ noun (BrE) **1** a person who collects the numbers of railway engines

# train wreck

as a hobby **2** (*disapproving*) a person who is interested in the details of a subject that other people think are boring ▶ **ˈtrain-spot-ting** *noun* [U]

**ˈtrain wreck** *noun* **1** an accident in which a train crashes into sth else or comes off the track **2** (*informal*) a situation, a person's life, etc. that people find extremely interesting because it lacks order, is very bad or is unsuccessful: *She gives a train wreck of a performance in the movie.* ◊ *This guy is a train wreck.* ⊃ compare CAR CRASH (2)

**traipse** /treɪps/ *verb* [I] + *adv./prep.* (*informal*) to walk somewhere slowly when you are tired and unwilling

**trait** /treɪt/ *noun* a particular quality in your personality: *personality traits* ⊃ WORDFINDER NOTE at CHARACTER

**trai·tor** /ˈtreɪtə(r)/ *noun* ~ (to sb/sth) a person who gives away secrets about their friends, their country, etc: *He was seen as a traitor to the socialist cause.* ◊ *She denied that she had turned traitor* (= become a traitor).

**trai·tor·ous** /ˈtreɪtərəs/ *adj.* (*formal*) giving away secrets about your friends, your country, etc. ▶ **trai·tor·ous·ly** *adv.*

**tra·jec·tory** /trəˈdʒektəri/ *noun* (*pl.* -ies) *noun* (*specialist*) the curved path of sth that has been fired, hit or thrown into the air: *a missile's trajectory* ◊ (*figurative*) *My career seemed to be on a downward trajectory.*

**tram** /træm/ *noun* (*also* **tram-car** /ˈtræmkɑː(r)/) (*both BrE*) (*US* **street-car, trol·ley**) *noun* a vehicle driven by electricity, that runs on RAILS along the streets of a town and carries passengers: *a tram route*

**tram-lines** /ˈtræmlaɪnz/ *noun* [pl.] **1** the RAILS in the street that trams run on **2** (*BrE, informal*) the pair of straight lines on a tennis or BADMINTON COURT that mark the extra area that is used when four people are playing ⊃ compare ALLEY (2)

**tram·mel** /ˈtræml/ *verb* [often passive] (-ll-, *US* -l-) ~ sb/sth (*formal*) to limit sb's freedom of movement or activity SYN **restrict** ⊃ compare UNTRAMMELLED

**tramp** /træmp/ *noun, verb*
- *noun* **1** (*also* **hobo**) [C] a person with no home or job who travels from place to place, usually asking people in the street for food or money **2** [sing.] **the ~ of sth** the sound of sb's heavy steps: *the tramp of marching feet* **3** [C, usually sing.] a long walk SYN **trek**: *We had a long tramp home.* **4** (*NAmE, old-fashioned, disapproving*) a woman who has many sexual partners
- *verb* (*also NAmE, informal* **tromp**) [I, T] to walk with heavy or noisy steps, especially for a long time: (+ *adv./prep.*) *We tramped across the wet grass to look at the statue.* ◊ *the sound of tramping feet* ◊ **~ sth** *She's been tramping the streets looking for a job.*

**tramp·ing** /ˈtræmpɪŋ/ *noun* [U] (*NZE*) the activity of going for long walks over rough country, carrying all the food and equipment that you need ▶ **tramp·er** *noun*

**tram·ple** /ˈtræmpl/ *verb* [T, I] to step heavily on sb/sth so that you damage or harm them/it with your feet: **~ sb/sth** *People were trampled underfoot in the rush for the exit.* ◊ *He was trampled to death by a runaway horse.* ◊ **~ sb/sth down** *The campers had trampled the corn down.* ◊ **~ on/over sth** *Don't trample on the flowers!* **2** [I] **~ (on/over) sb/sth** to ignore sb's feelings or rights and treat them as if they are not important: *The government is trampling on the views of ordinary people.*

**tram·po·line** /ˈtræmpəliːn/ *noun, verb*
- *noun* a piece of equipment that is used in GYMNASTICS for doing jumps in the air. It consists of a sheet of strong material that is attached by springs to a frame.
- *verb* [I] to jump on a trampoline ▶ **tram·po·lin·ing** *noun* [U]

**tram·way** /ˈtræmweɪ/ *noun* the RAILS that form the route for a TRAM

**trance** /trɑːns; *NAmE* træns/ *noun* **1** [C] a state in which sb seems to be asleep but is aware of what is said to them, for example if they are HYPNOTIZED: *to go/fall into a trance* **2** [C] a state in which you are thinking so much about sth that you do not notice what is happening around you SYN **daze** **3** (*also* **ˈtrance music**) [U] a type of electronic dance music with HYPNOTIC rhythms and sounds

**tranche** /trɑːnʃ/ *noun* (*BrE, finance*) one of the parts into which an amount of money or a number of shares in a company is divided

**tranny** (*also* **tran·nie**) /ˈtræni/ *noun* (*pl.* -ies) (*informal*) **1** (*offensive*) a TRANSSEXUAL or TRANSVESTITE **2** (*especially BrE*) a TRANSISTOR radio **3** a TRANSPARENCY

**tran·quil** /ˈtræŋkwɪl/ *adj.* (*formal*) quiet and peaceful SYN **serene**: *a tranquil scene* ◊ *the tranquil waters of the lake* ◊ *She led a tranquil life in the country.* ▶ **tran·quil·lity** (*NAmE also* **tran·quil·ity**) /træŋˈkwɪləti/ *noun* [U] **tran·quil·ly** /ˈtræŋkwɪli/ *adv.*

**tran·quil·lize** (*also* -ise) (*both BrE*) (*NAmE* **tran·quil·ize**) /ˈtræŋkwəlaɪz/ *verb* ~ sb/sth to make a person or an animal calm or unconscious, especially by giving them a drug (= a TRANQUILLIZER)

**tran·quil·lizer** (*also* -iser) (*both BrE*) (*NAmE* **tran·quil·izer**) /ˈtræŋkwəlaɪzə(r)/ *noun* a drug used to reduce ANXIETY (= worry and stress): *She's on* (= regularly takes) *tranquillizers.*

**trans** /trænz/ *adj.* short for TRANSSEXUAL or TRANSGENDER: *They campaign for rights for lesbian, gay, bi and trans people.*

**trans-** /trænz, træns/ *prefix* **1** (in adjectives) across; beyond: *transatlantic* ◊ *transcontinental* **2** (in verbs) into another place or state: *transplant* ◊ *transform*

**trans·act** /trænˈzækt/ *verb* [T, I] ~ (sth) (with sb) (*formal*) to do business with a person or an organization: *There are new rules about how they transact business with customers.*

**trans·ac·tion** /trænˈzækʃn/ *noun* **1** [C] ~ (between A and B) a piece of business that is done between people, especially an act of buying or selling SYN **deal**: *financial transactions between companies* ◊ *commercial transactions* **2** [U] **~ of sth** (*formal*) the process of doing sth: *the transaction of government business*

**trans·ac·tion·al** /trænˈzækʃənl/ *adj.* **1** relating to the process of buying or selling: *The team processes transactional data, such as records of purchases.* **2** relating to communication between people: *Their relationship is more transactional than emotional.*

**trans·at·lan·tic** /ˌtrænzətˈlæntɪk/ *adj.* [only before noun] **1** crossing the Atlantic Ocean: *a transatlantic flight* **2** connected with countries on both sides of the Atlantic Ocean: *a transatlantic alliance* **3** on or from the other side of the Atlantic Ocean: *to speak with a transatlantic accent*

**trans·ceiver** /trænˈsiːvə(r)/ *noun* a radio that can both send and receive messages

**trans·cend** /trænˈsend/ *verb* ~ sth (*formal*) to be or go beyond the usual limits of sth SYN **exceed**

**trans·cend·ent** /trænˈsendənt/ *adj.* (*formal*) going beyond the usual limits; extremely great ▶ **trans·cend·ence** /-dəns/ *noun* [U]: *the transcendence of God*

**trans·cen·den·tal** /ˌtrænsenˈdentl/ *adj.* [usually before noun] going beyond the usual limits of human knowledge, experience or reason, especially in a religious or spiritual way: *a transcendental experience*

**ˌtranscenˈdental mediˈtation** (*BrE*) (*NAmE* **Transcenˈdental Meditation™**) *noun* [U] (*abbr.* **TM**) a method of making yourself calm by thinking deeply in silence and repeating a special phrase to yourself many times

**trans·con·tin·en·tal** /ˌtrænzˌkɒntɪˈnentl; *NAmE* -ˌkɑːn-/ *adj.* crossing a continent: *a transcontinental railway/ railroad*

**tran·scribe** /trænˈskraɪb/ *verb* **1** to record thoughts, speech or data in a written form, or in a different written form from the original: **~ sth** *Clerks transcribe everything that is said in court.* ◊ *The interview was recorded and then transcribed.* ◊ **~ sth into sth** *How many official documents have been transcribed into Braille for blind people?* **2** **~ sth** (*specialist*) to show the sounds of speech using a special

PHONETIC alphabet **3** ~ **sth (for sth)** to write a piece of music in a different form so that it can be played by a different musical instrument or sung by a different voice: *a piano piece transcribed for the guitar*

**tran·script** /ˈtrænskrɪpt/ *noun* **1** (*also* **tran·scription**) a written or printed copy of words that have been spoken: *a transcript of the interview* **2** (*especially NAmE*) an official record of a student's work that shows the courses they have taken and the grades they have achieved

**tran·scrip·tion** /trænˈskrɪpʃn/ *noun* **1** [U] the act or process of representing sth in a written or printed form: *errors made in transcription* ⋄ *phonetic transcription* **2** [C] = TRANSCRIPT: *The full transcription of the interview is attached.* **3** [C] something that is represented in writing: *This dictionary gives phonetic transcriptions of all headwords.* **4** [C] a change in the written form of a piece of music so that it can be played on a different instrument or sung by a different voice

**trans·ducer** /trænzˈdjuːsə(r)/; *NAmE* -ˈduː-/ *noun* (*specialist*) a device for producing an electrical signal from another form of energy such as pressure

**tran·sept** /ˈtrænsept/ *noun* (*architecture*) either of the two wide parts of a church in the shape of a cross, that are built at RIGHT ANGLES to the main central part ⊃ compare NAVE

**tran·sex·ual** = TRANSSEXUAL

**trans-fatty ˈacid** (*also* **trans-fat**) *noun* [C, U] a type of fat produced when oils are changed by a chemical process into solids, for example to make MARGARINE. Trans-fatty acids are believed to encourage the harmful development of CHOLESTEROL: *foods that are low in trans-fatty acids* ⊃ see also MONOUNSATURATED FAT, POLYUNSATURATED FAT, SATURATED FAT, UNSATURATED FAT

**trans·fer** *verb, noun*

■ *verb* /trænsˈfɜː(r)/ (**-rr-**)
- ▸ TO NEW PLACE **1** [I, T] to move from one place to another; to move sth/sb from one place to another: ~ **(from sth) (to sth)** *The film studio is transferring to Hollywood.* ⋄ (*especially NAmE*) *If I spend a semester in Madrid, will my credits transfer?* ⋄ ~ **sth/sb (from sth) (to sth)** *How can I transfer money from my bank account to his?* ⋄ ~ **sth into/onto sth** *She transferred the sauce into a china jug.* ⋄ ~ **sth between A and B** *The honeybee transfers pollen between flowers.*
- ▸ TO NEW JOB/SCHOOL/SITUATION **2** [I, T] to move from one job, school, situation, etc. to another; to arrange for sb to move: ~ **(from sth) (to sth)** *Children usually transfer to secondary school at 11 or 12.* ⋄ *He transferred to UCLA after his freshman year.* ⋄ ~ **sb (from sth) (to sth)** *Some employees are being transferred from the sales department.*
- ▸ TO NEW VEHICLE **3** [I, T] to change to a different vehicle during a journey; to arrange for sb to change to a different vehicle during a journey: ~ **(from sth) (to sth)** *It was a relief, after transferring from ship to ship, to just sit and relax.* ⋄ *I transferred at Bahrain for a flight to Singapore.* ⋄ ~ **sb (from sth) (to sth)** *Passengers are transferred from the airport to the hotel by taxi.*
- ▸ INFORMATION/MUSIC, ETC. **4** [T, I] to copy information, music, an idea, etc. from one method of recording or presenting it to another; to be recorded or presented in a different way: ~ **sth (from sth) (to sth)** *You can transfer data to a memory stick in a few seconds.* ⋄ ~ **(from sth) (to sth)** *The novel does not transfer well to the movies.*
- ▸ FEELING/DISEASE/POWER **5** [T] ~ **sth (from …) (to …)** if you transfer a feeling, a disease, or a power, etc. from one person to another, the second person has it, often instead of the first: *Joe had already transferred his affections from Lisa to Cleo.* ⋄ *This disease is sometimes transferred from mother to baby* (= so that the baby has it as well as the mother).
- ▸ PROPERTY **6** [T] ~ **sth (to sb)** to officially arrange for sth to belong to sb else or for sb else to control sth **SYN** **sign over**: *He transferred the property to his son.*
- ▸ IN SPORT **7** [I, T] (*especially BrE*) to move, or to move sb, to a different sports team, especially a professional football

(soccer) team: ~ **(from …) (to …)** *He transferred to Everton for £60 million.* ⋄ ~ **sb (from …) (to …)** *He was transferred from Spurs to Arsenal for a huge fee.*
- ▸ PHONE CALL **8** [T] ~ **sth/sb (to sth)** to send a phone call that you have received to another phone number: *I'll just transfer you to customer service.*

■ *noun* /ˈtrænsfɜː(r)/
- ▸ CHANGE OF PLACE/JOB/SITUATION **1** [U, C] the act of moving sb/sth from one place, group or job to another; an occasion when this happens: *electronic data transfer* ⋄ ~ **of sth** *After the election there was a swift transfer of power.* ⋄ ~ **(of sth) (from sth) (to sth)** *He has asked for a transfer to the company's Paris branch.* ⋄ ~ **(of sth) between sb/sth** *the transfer of property between private buyers* ⊃ see also CASH TRANSFER, MONEY TRANSFER
- ▸ CHANGE OF VEHICLE **2** [U, C] an act of changing to a different place, vehicle or route when you are travelling: *The transfer from the airport to the hotel is included in the price.*
- ▸ TRAIN/BUS TICKET **3** [C] (*NAmE*) a ticket that allows a passenger to continue their journey on another bus or train
- ▸ IN SPORT **4** [U, C] the act of moving a sports player from one club or team to another: *It was the first goal he had scored since his transfer from Chelsea.* ⋄ *a transfer fee* ⋄ *to be on the transfer list* (= available to join another club)
- ▸ PICTURE **5** [C] (*especially BrE*) (*NAmE usually* **decal**) a picture or design that can be removed from a piece of paper and stuck onto a surface, for example by being pressed or heated
- ▸ PSYCHOLOGY **6** [U] (*psychology*) the process of using behaviour that has already been learnt in one situation in a new situation

**trans·fer·able** /trænsˈfɜːrəbl/ *adj.* that can be moved from one place, person or use to another: *This ticket is not transferable* (= it may only be used by the person who has bought it). ⋄ *We aim to provide our students with transferable skills* (= that can be used in different jobs). ▸ **trans·fer·abil·ity** /ˌtrænsˌfɜːrəˈbɪləti/ *noun* [U]

**trans·fer·ence** /ˈtrænsfərəns; *NAmE* trænsˈfɜːrəns/ *noun* [U] (*specialist or formal*) the process of moving sth from one place, person or use to another: *the transference of heat from the liquid to the container*

**trans·fer·ral** /trænsˈfɜːrəl/ *noun* [U] the action of transferring sth or sb

**ˈtransfer student** *noun* (*NAmE*) a student at a college or university who has completed classes at another college or university after leaving high school

**trans·fig·ure** /trænsˈfɪɡə(r); *NAmE* -ˈfɪɡjər/ *verb* [often passive] ~ **sb/sth** (*literary*) to change the appearance of a person or thing so that they look more beautiful ▸ **trans·fig·ur·ation** /ˌtrænsˌfɪɡəˈreɪʃn; *NAmE* -ˌfɪɡjə-/ *noun* [U, sing.]

**trans·fix** /trænsˈfɪks/ *verb* [usually passive] ~ **sb** to make sb unable to move because they are afraid, surprised, etc. **SYN** **paralyse**: *Luisa stood transfixed with shock.*

**trans·form** *verb* **1** ~ **(sth/sb) (from sth) (into sth)** to change the form of sth; to change in form **SYN** **convert**: *The photochemical reactions transform the light into electrical impulses.* ⋄ *I am convinced that the electric power industry is transforming.* **2** [T, I] to completely change the appearance or character of sth/sb, especially so that it is better; to completely change in appearance or character: ~ **sth/sb/yourself (from sth) (into sth)** | ~ **sth/sb/yourself** *A new colour scheme will transform your bedroom.* ⋄ *It was an event that would transform my life.* ⋄ ~ **(from sth) (into/to sth)** *The surface of the lake has completely transformed from bright green to blood red.*

**trans·form·ation** /ˌtrænsfəˈmeɪʃn; *NAmE* -fɔːrˈm-/ *noun* **1** [C, U] a complete change in sb/sth: *The way in which we work has undergone a complete transformation in the past decade.* ⋄ *What a transformation! You look great.* ⋄ ~ **(from sth) (to/into sth)** *the country's transformation from dictatorship to democracy* **2** [U] (in South Africa) the process of making institutions and

# transformer 1666

organizations more DEMOCRATIC: *a lack of transformation in the private sector* ▶ **trans·form·a·tion·al** /-ʃənl/ *adj.*

**trans·form·er** /ˌtrænsˈfɔːmə(r); *NAmE* -ˈfɔːrm-/ *noun* a device for reducing or increasing the VOLTAGE of an electric power supply, usually to allow a particular piece of electrical equipment to be used

**trans·fu·sion** /trænsˈfjuːʒn/ *noun* [C, U] **1** = BLOOD TRANSFUSION **2** ~ **of sth** the act of investing extra money in a place or an activity that needs it: *The project badly needs a transfusion of cash.* ▶ **trans·fuse** /-ˈfjuːz/ *verb*: ~ **sth (into sb/sth)** *to transfuse blood into a patient*

**trans·gen·der** /trænzˈdʒendə(r)/ (*also* **trans**, **trans·gendered** /trænzˈdʒendəd; *NAmE* -dərd/) *adj.* describing or relating to people whose sense of GENDER IDENTITY does not match their BIOLOGICAL sex or does not easily fit in with the usual division between male and female: *transgender issues* ⊃ compare INTERSEX

**trans·gen·ic** /trænzˈdʒenɪk/ *adj., noun* (biology)
■ *adj.* (of a plant or an animal) having GENETIC material introduced from another type of plant or animal SYN **genetically modified**: *transgenic crops* ▶ **trans·gen·ic·ally** /-kli/ *adv.*
■ *noun* **1 trans·gen·ics** [U] the study or practice of creating transgenic plants or animals **2** [C] a transgenic plant or animal

**trans·gress** /trænzˈɡres/ *verb* [T, I] ~ **(sth)** (*formal*) to go beyond the limit of what is morally or legally acceptable ▶ **trans·gres·sion** /-ˈɡreʃn/ *noun* [C, U] **trans·gres·sor** *noun*

**tran·si·ent** /ˈtrænziənt; *NAmE* ˈtrænʃnt/ *adj., noun*
■ *adj.* (*formal*) **1** continuing for only a short time SYN **fleeting**, **temporary**: *the transient nature of speech* **2** staying or working in a place for only a short time, before moving on: *a city with a large transient population* (= of students, temporary workers, etc.) ▶ **tran·si·ence** /ˈtrænziəns; *NAmE* ˈtrænʃns/ *noun* [U]: *the transience of human life*
■ *noun* (*especially NAmE*) a person who stays or works in a place for only a short time, before moving on

**tran·sis·tor** /trænˈzɪstə(r)/ *noun* **1** a small electronic device used in computers, radios, televisions, etc. for controlling an electric current as it passes along a CIRCUIT **2** (*also* **tran`sistor `radio**) (*also informal* **tranny** *especially in BrE*) a small radio with transistors

**Transit™** /ˈtrænzɪt/ (*also* ˈ**Transit van**) *noun* (*BrE*) a type of large van that is used for delivering goods, carrying equipment, etc.

**tran·sit** 🔑+ C1 /ˈtrænzɪt/ *noun, verb*
■ *noun* **1** 🔑+ C1 [U] the process of being moved or carried from one place to another: *The cost includes transit.* ◇ *in ~ goods damaged in transit* ◇ *transit times* **2** 🔑+ C1 [U, C, usually sing.] the act of going through a place on the way to somewhere else: *the transit lounge at Vienna airport* ◇ *a transit visa* (= one that allows a person to pass through a country but not to stay there) **3** 🔑+ C1 [U] (*NAmE*) the system of buses, trains, etc. that people use to travel from one place to another: *the city's mass/public transit system*
■ *verb* [T, I] ~ **(sth)** to pass across or through an area: *The ship is currently transiting the Gulf of Mexico.*

ˈ**transit camp** *noun* a camp that provides temporary accommodation for REFUGEES

**tran·si·tion** 🔑 B2 W /trænˈzɪʃn/ *noun, verb*
■ *noun* 🔑 B2 [U, C] the process or a period of changing from one state or condition to another: ~ **(from sth) (to/into sth)** *the transition from school to full-time work* ◇ *He will remain head of state during the period of transition to democracy.* ◇ ~ **between A and B** *We need to ensure a smooth transition between the old system and the new one.* ◇ *in ~ This course is useful for students who are in transition from one training programme to another.*
■ *verb* [I, T] to change or to make sth change from one state or condition to another: *They transitioned from print journalism to the digital world.* ◇ ~ **sb/sth** *They decided to transition the farm to organic.* ▶ **tran·si·tion·al** /-ʃənl/ *adj.*: *a transitional period* ◇ *a transitional government*

**tran`sition ˈmetal** (*also* **tran`sition ˈelement**) *noun* (*chemistry*) one of the group of metals in the centre of the PERIODIC TABLE (= a list of all the chemical elements) that form coloured COMPOUNDS and often act as CATALYSTS (= substances that make chemical reactions happen faster)

**tran·si·tive** /ˈtrænzətɪv/ *adj.* (*grammar*) (of verbs) used with a DIRECT OBJECT: *In 'She wrote a letter', the verb 'wrote' is transitive and the word 'letter' is the direct object.* OPP **intransitive** ▶ **tran·si·tive·ly** *adv.*: *The verb is being used transitively.*

**tran·si·tiv·ity** /ˌtrænzəˈtɪvəti/ *noun* [U] (*grammar*) the fact of a particular verb being either TRANSITIVE or INTRANSITIVE

**tran·si·tory** /ˈtrænzətri; *NAmE* -tɔːri/ *adj.* (*formal*) continuing for only a short time SYN **fleeting**, **temporary**: *the transitory nature of his happiness*

**trans·late** 🔑 B1 /trænzˈleɪt/ *verb* **1** 🔑 B1 [T, I] to express the meaning of speech or writing in a different language: ~ **sth (from sth) (into sth)** *He translated the letter into English.* ◇ *Her books have been translated into 24 languages.* ◇ *This chapter was translated from the French by Oliver Breen.* ◇ ~ **sth as sth** *'Suisse' had been wrongly translated as 'Sweden'.* ◇ ~ **(from sth) (into sth)** *My work involves translating from German.* ◇ *I don't speak Greek so Dina offered to translate for me.* ⊃ WORDFINDER NOTE at LANGUAGE **2** 🔑 B1 [I] to be changed from one language to another: *Most poetry does not translate well.* ◇ ~ **as sth** *The Welsh name translates as 'Land's End'.* **3** [T, I] to change sth into a different form; to lead to a particular result: ~ **sth (into sth)** *It's time to translate words into action.* ◇ **into sth** *I hope all the hard work will translate into profits.* **4** [T, I] ~ **(sth) (as sth)** to understand sth in a particular way or give sth a particular meaning SYN **interpret**: *the various words and gestures that we translate as love*

**trans·la·tion** 🔑 B1 /trænzˈleɪʃn/ *noun* **1** 🔑 B1 [U] the process of changing sth that is written or spoken into another language: ~ **(from sth) (into sth)** *He specializes in translation from Danish into English.* ◇ ~ **(into sth)** *The poems do not survive the translation into English.* ◇ *in ~ The book loses something in translation.* ◇ *The irony is lost in translation.* **2** 🔑 B1 [C, U] a text or word that has been changed from one language into another: ~ **of sth** *The usual translation of 'glasnost' is 'openness'.* ◇ *a copy of Dryden's translation of the Aeneid* ◇ *a rough translation* (= not translating everything exactly) ◇ *a literal translation* (= following the original words exactly) ◇ *a free translation* (= not following the original words exactly) ◇ *in ~ I have only read Tolstoy in translation.* **3** [U] ~ **(of sth) into sth** the process of changing sth into a different form: *the translation of theory into practice*

**trans·la·tor** /trænzˈleɪtə(r)/ *noun* a person who translates writing or speech into a different language, especially as a job: *She works as a translator of technical texts.* ⊃ compare INTERPRETER

**trans·lit·er·ate** /trænzˈlɪtəreɪt/ *verb* ~ **sth (into/as sth)** (*specialist*) to write words or letters using letters of a different alphabet or language ▶ **trans·lit·er·ation** /ˌtrænzˌlɪtəˈreɪʃn/ *noun* [C, U]

**trans·lu·cent** /trænzˈluːsnt/ *adj.* (*formal*) allowing light to pass through but not completely clear ▶ **trans·lu·cence** /-sns/ (*also* **trans·lu·cency** /-snsi/) *noun* [U]

**trans·mi·gra·tion** /ˌtrænzmaɪˈɡreɪʃn/ *noun* [U] the process of a person's soul passing into another body after death

**trans·mis·sion** 🔑+ C1 W /trænzˈmɪʃn/ *noun* (*formal*) **1** 🔑+ C1 [U] the act or process of passing sth from one person, place or thing to another SYN **transfer**: *the transmission of the disease* ◇ *the risk of transmission* **2** 🔑+ C1 [U] the act or process of sending out an electronic signal or message or of broadcasting a radio or television programme: *the transmission of computer data along telephone lines* ◇ *a break in transmission* (= of a radio or television broadcast) *due to a technical fault* **3** 🔑+ C1 [C] a radio or television message or broadcast: *a live transmission from Sydney* **4** [U, C] the system in a vehicle by which power is passed from the engine to the wheels ⊃ see also AUTOMATIC TRANSMISSION

**trans·mit** ʵ+ B2 Ⓦ /trænzˈmɪt/ verb (-tt-) 1 ʵ+ B2 [T, I] ~ (sth) (from …) (to …) to send an electronic signal, radio or television broadcast, etc: *signals transmitted from a satellite* ◊ *The ceremony was transmitted live by satellite to over fifty countries.* ◊ *a short-wave radio that can transmit as well as receive* 2 ʵ+ C1 [T] (*formal*) to pass from one person to another **SYN** transfer: ~ *sth sexually transmitted diseases* ◊ ~ **sth to sb** *Parents can unwittingly transmit their own fears to their children.* 3 [T] ~ **sth** (*specialist*) to allow heat, light, sound, etc. to pass through **SYN conduct**

**trans·mit·ter** /trænzˈmɪtə(r)/ noun 1 a piece of equipment used for sending electronic signals, especially radio or television signals ⊃ compare RECEIVER 2 ~ **of sth** (*formal*) a person or thing that transmits sth from one person or thing to another: *Emphasis was placed on the school as a transmitter of moral values.*

**trans·mog·ri·fy** /ˌtrænzˈmɒɡrɪfaɪ; NAmE -ˈmɑːɡ-/ verb (**trans·mog·ri·fies**, **trans·mog·ri·fy·ing**, **trans·mog·ri·fied**, **trans·mog·ri·fied**) ~ **sb/sth** (*often humorous*) to change sth completely, especially in a surprising way **SYN** transform ▶ **trans·mog·ri·fi·ca·tion** /ˌtrænzˌmɒɡrɪfɪˈkeɪʃn; NAmE -ˌmɑːɡ-/ noun [U]

**trans·mute** /trænzˈmjuːt/ verb [T, I] ~ (**sth**) (**into sth**) (*formal*) to change, or make sth change, into sth different **SYN transform**: *It was once thought that lead could be transmuted into gold.* ▶ **trans·mu·ta·tion** /ˌtrænzmjuːˈteɪʃn/ noun [C, U]

**trans·nation·al** /ˌtrænzˈnæʃnəl/ adj. (*business*) existing in or involving different countries: *transnational corporations*

**tran·som** /ˈtrænsəm/ noun 1 a bar of wood or stone across the top of a door or window 2 (NAmE) = FANLIGHT

**trans·par·ency** ʵ+ C1 /trænsˈpærənsi/ noun (pl. -**ies**) 1 ʵ+ C1 [U] the quality of sth, such as a situation or an argument, that makes it easy to understand: *a need for greater transparency in legal documents* ◊ *The police reforms will ensure greater transparency and accountability.* 2 [U] the quality of sth, such as glass, that allows you to see through it 3 (*also informal* **tranny**) [C] a picture printed on a piece of film, usually in a frame, that can be shown on a screen by shining light through the film **SYN slide**: *an overhead transparency* (= used with an OVERHEAD PROJECTOR) 4 [U] the quality in sth, such as an excuse or a lie, that allows sb to see the truth easily: *They were shocked by the transparency of his lies.*

**trans·par·ent** ʵ+ C1 /trænsˈpærənt/ adj. 1 ʵ+ C1 (of glass, plastic, etc.) allowing you to see through it: *The insect's wings are almost transparent.* **OPP opaque** 2 (especially of an excuse, a lie, etc.) that you can easily see is false; allowing you to see the truth easily **SYN obvious**: *a transparent attempt to buy votes* ◊ *Am I that transparent?* (= are my intentions that obvious?) 3 (of language, information, etc.) easy to understand: *a campaign to make official documents more transparent* **OPP opaque** ▶ **trans·par·ent·ly** adv.: *transparently obvious*

**tran·spir·ation** /ˌtrænspɪˈreɪʃn/ noun [U] (*biology*) the process of water passing out from the surface of a plant or leaf ⊃ compare PERSPIRATION

**tran·spire** /trænˈspaɪə(r)/ verb (*formal*) 1 [T] (not usually used in the progressive tenses) ~ **that …** *if* **it transpires that** sth has happened or is true, it is known or has been shown to be true: *It transpired that the gang had had a contact inside the bank.* ◊ *This story, it later transpired, was untrue.* 2 [I] to happen: *You're meeting him tomorrow? Let me know what transpires.* 3 [I, T] ~ (**sth**) (*biology*) when plants or leaves **transpire**, water passes out from their surface

**trans·plant** verb, noun
■ verb /trænsˈplɑːnt; NAmE -ˈplænt/ 1 ~ **sth** (**from sb/sth**) (**into sb/sth**) to take an organ, skin, etc. from one person, animal, part of the body, etc. and put it into or onto another: *Surgeons have successfully transplanted a liver into a four-year-old boy.* ◊ *Patients often reject transplanted organs.* ⊃ compare IMPLANT 2 ~ **sth** to move a growing plant and plant it somewhere else 3 ~ **sb/sth** (**from …**) (**to / into …**) (*formal*) to move sb/sth to a different place or environment: *Japanese production methods have been transplanted into some British factories.* ▶ **trans·plan·ta·tion** /ˌtrænsplɑːnˈteɪʃn; NAmE -plæn-/ noun [U]: *liver transplantation* ◊ *the transplantation of entire communities overseas*
■ noun /ˈtrænsplɑːnt; NAmE -plænt/ 1 [C, U] a medical operation in which a damaged organ, etc. is replaced with one from another person: *to have a heart transplant* ◊ *a transplant operation* ◊ *a shortage of suitable kidneys for transplant* ⊃ WORDFINDER NOTE at OPERATION 2 [C] an organ, etc. that is used in a transplant operation: *There is always a chance that the body will reject the transplant.* ⊃ compare IMPLANT

**tran·spon·der** /trænˈspɒndə(r); NAmE -ˈspɑːn-/ noun (*specialist*) a device that receives a radio signal and then sends out a different signal in reply

**trans·port** Ⓞ A2 Ⓦ noun, verb
■ noun /ˈtrænspɔːt; NAmE -spɔːrt/ 1 ʵ A2 (*especially BrE*) (NAmE *usually* **trans·por·ta·tion**) [U] a system for carrying people or goods from one place to another using vehicles, roads, etc: *air/freight/road transport* ◊ *the government's transport policy* ⊃ see also PUBLIC TRANSPORT 2 ʵ A2 (BrE) (NAmE **trans·por·ta·tion**) [U] a vehicle or method of travel: *Applicants must have their own transport.* ◊ *Transport to and from the airport is included in the price.* ◊ **a means/ mode/form of transport** 3 ʵ B1 (*especially BrE*) (*also* **trans·por·ta·tion** NAmE, BrE) [U] the activity or business of carrying goods from one place to another using lorries, trains, etc: *The goods were damaged during transport.* ◊ *controls on the transport of nuclear waste* 4 [C] a ship, plane or lorry used for carrying soldiers, supplies, etc. from one place to another 5 **transports** [pl.] ~ **of sth** (*literary*) strong feelings and emotions: *to be in transports of delight*
■ verb /trænˈspɔːt; NAmE -ˈspɔːrt/ 1 ʵ B1 ~ **sth/sb** to take sth/ sb from one place to another in a vehicle: *to transport goods/passengers* ◊ ~ **sth/sb + adv./prep.** *He collapsed and was immediately transported to hospital.* 2 ~ **sth** (+ *adv./prep.*) to move sth somewhere by means of a natural process **SYN carry**: *The seeds are transported by the wind.* ◊ *Blood transports oxygen around the body.* 3 ~ **sb** (+ *adv./prep.*) to make sb feel that they are in a different place, time or situation: *The book transports you to another world.* 4 ~ **sb** (+ *adv./prep.*) (in the past) to send sb to a far away place as a punishment: *British convicts were transported to Australia for life.*

**trans·port·able** /trænˈspɔːtəbl; NAmE -ˈspɔːrt-/ adj. [not usually before noun] that can be carried or moved from one place to another, especially by a vehicle

**trans·por·ta·tion** ʵ+ B2 Ⓦ /ˌtrænspɔːˈteɪʃn; NAmE -spər't-/ noun [U] 1 ʵ+ B2 (*especially NAmE*) = TRANSPORT: *public transportation* (= the system of buses, trains, etc. provided for people to travel from one place to another) ◊ *the transportation industry* ◊ *The city is providing free transportation to the stadium from downtown.* ◊ *the transportation of heavy loads* ◊ **transportation costs** 2 (in the past) the act of sending criminals to a place that is far away as a form of punishment

**ˈtransport cafe** noun (BrE) a cafe at the side of a main road that serves cheap food and is used mainly by lorry drivers ⊃ compare TRUCK STOP

**trans·port·er** /trænˈspɔːtə(r); NAmE -ˈspɔːrt-/ noun a large vehicle used for carrying heavy objects, for example other vehicles: *a car transporter*

**trans·pose** /trænˈspəʊz/ verb [often passive] 1 ~ **sth** (*formal*) to change the order of two or more things **SYN reverse** 2 ~ **sth** (**from sth**) (**to sth**) (*formal*) to move or change sth to a different place or environment or into a different form **SYN transfer**: *The director transposes Shakespeare's play from 16th century Venice to present-day England.* 3 ~ **sth** (*music*) to write or play a piece of

# transsexual

music or a series of notes in a different key ▶ **trans·pos·ition** /ˌtrænspəˈzɪʃn/ noun [C, U]

**trans·sex·ual** (also **tran·sex·ual**) /trænzˈsekʃuəl/ noun a person whose sense of GENDER IDENTITY does not match their BIOLOGICAL sex, especially one who has a medical operation to change their sexual organs

**tran·sub·stan·ti·ation** /ˌtrænsəbˌstænʃiˈeɪʃn/ noun [U] the belief that the bread and wine of the COMMUNION service become the actual body and blood of Jesus Christ after they have been BLESSED, even though they still look like bread and wine

**trans·verse** /ˈtrænzvɜːs; NAmE -vɜːrs/ adj. [usually before noun] (specialist) placed across sth SYN **diagonal**: A transverse bar joins the two posts.

**trans·vest·ite** /trænzˈvestaɪt/ noun a person, especially a man, who enjoys dressing as a member of the opposite sex ▶ **trans·vest·ism** /-tɪzəm/ noun [U]

**trap** B2 /træp/ noun, verb
■ noun
• FOR ANIMALS **1** B2 a piece of equipment for catching animals: *a fox with its leg in a trap* ◇ *A trap was laid, with fresh bait.* ⇒ see also MOUSETRAP
• TRICK **2** B2 a clever plan designed to trick sb, either by capturing them or by making them do or say sth that they did not mean to do or say: *She had set a trap for him and he had walked straight into it.* ⇒ see also BOOBY TRAP, SPEED TRAP, TOURIST TRAP
• BAD SITUATION **3** C1 [usually sing.] an unpleasant situation from which it is hard to escape: *the unemployment trap* ◇ *Some women see marriage as a trap.* ⇒ see also DEATH TRAP, FIRE TRAP, POVERTY TRAP
• CARRIAGE **4** a light CARRIAGE with two wheels, pulled by a horse: *a pony and trap*
• MOUTH **5** (slang) mouth SYN **gob**: *Shut your trap!* (= a rude way of telling sb to be quiet) ◇ *to keep your trap shut* (= to not tell a secret)
• FOR RACING DOG **6** a CAGE from which a GREYHOUND (= a type of dog) is let out at the start of a race
• IN GOLF **7** (especially NAmE) = BUNKER
IDM **to fall into/avoid the trap of doing sth** to do/avoid doing sth that is a mistake but that seems at first to be a good idea: *Parents often fall into the trap of trying to do everything for their children.* ⇒ more at SPRING v.

■ verb (-pp-)
• IN DANGEROUS/BAD SITUATION **1** B2 [usually passive] to put sb in a dangerous place that they cannot get out of: **be trapped** *Help! I'm trapped!* ◇ **be trapped by sth** *We became trapped by the rising floodwater.* ◇ **be trapped + adv./prep.** *They were trapped in the burning building.* **2** B2 [usually passive] to keep sb in a bad situation that they want to get out of but cannot: **be trapped + adv./prep.** *He was trapped in an unhappy marriage.* ◇ *I feel trapped in my job.*
• PART OF BODY/CLOTHING **2** B2 ~ **sth (+ adv./prep.)** to have part of your body, your clothing, etc. held in a place so tightly that you cannot remove it and it may be injured or damaged: *I trapped my coat in the car door.* ◇ *The pain was caused by a trapped nerve.*
• CATCH **4** B2 ~ **sb/sth (+ adv./prep.)** to force sb/sth into a place or situation that they cannot escape from, especially in order to catch them: *The escaped prisoners were eventually trapped in an underground garage and recaptured.* **5** C1 ~ **sth** to catch an animal in a trap: *Raccoons used to be trapped for their fur.* **6** C1 ~ **sth** to catch or keep sth in a place and prevent it from escaping, especially so that you can use it: *Solar panels trap energy from the sun.*
• TRICK **7** C1 ~ **sb (into sth/into doing sth)** to trick sb into sth: *He felt he had been trapped into accepting the terms of the contract.*

**trap·door** /ˈtræpdɔː(r)/ noun a small door in a floor or ceiling

**trap·eze** /trəˈpiːz; NAmE træˈp-/ noun a wooden or metal bar hanging from two pieces of rope high above the ground, used especially by CIRCUS performers: *a trapeze artist*

**tra·pez·ium** /trəˈpiːziəm/ noun (pl. **tra·pez·iums** or **tra·pezia** /-ziə/) (geometry) **1** (BrE) (NAmE **trap·ez·oid**) a flat shape with four straight sides, one pair of opposite sides being PARALLEL (= the same distance apart at every point) and the other pair not PARALLEL **2** (NAmE **trap·ez·oid**) a flat shape with four straight sides, none of which are PARALLEL (= the same distance apart at every point)

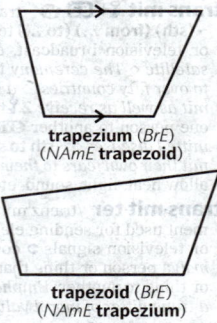

trapezium (BrE)
(NAmE **trapezoid**)

trapezoid (BrE)
(NAmE **trapezium**)

**trap·ez·oid** /ˈtræpəzɔɪd/ noun (geometry) **1** (BrE) (NAmE **tra·pez·ium**) a flat shape with four straight sides, none of which are PARALLEL (= the same distance apart at every point) ⇒ picture at TRAPEZIUM **2** (NAmE) (BrE **tra·pez·ium**) a flat shape with four straight sides, one pair of opposite sides being PARALLEL (= the same distance apart at every point) and the other pair not PARALLEL ⇒ picture at TRAPEZIUM

**trap·per** /ˈtræpə(r)/ noun a person who traps and kills animals, especially for their fur

**trap·pings** /ˈtræpɪŋz/ noun [pl.] ~ **(of sth)** (formal, especially disapproving) the possessions, clothes, etc. that are connected with a particular situation, job or social position: *They enjoyed all the trappings of wealth.*

**Trap·pist** /ˈtræpɪst/ adj. belonging to a group of MONKS who have very strict rules, including a rule that they must not speak ▶ **Trap·pist** noun

**trash** /træʃ/ noun, verb
■ noun **1** [U] (NAmE) things that you throw away because you no longer want or need them ⇒ note at RUBBISH ⇒ see also GARBAGE **2** (informal, disapproving) objects, writing, ideas, etc. that you think are of poor quality: *What's this trash you're watching?* ◇ (especially BrE) *He's talking trash* (= nonsense). **3** (NAmE, informal) an offensive word used to describe people that you do not respect ⇒ see also TRAILER TRASH, WHITE TRASH

■ verb (informal) **1** ~ **sth** to damage or destroy sth: *The band was famous for trashing hotel rooms.* **2** ~ **sth/sb** to criticize sth/sb very strongly: *Several journalists attempted to trash his reputation.* **3** ~ **sth** (NAmE) to throw away sth that you do not want: *I'm leaving my old toys here—if you don't want them, just trash them.*

**'trash can** noun (NAmE) **1** (BrE **'litter bin**) a container for people to put rubbish in, in the street or in a public building **2** = GARBAGE CAN

**'trash talk** (also **'trash talking**) noun [U] (NAmE, informal) a way of talking that is intended to make sb, especially an opponent, feel less confident ⇒ compare SLEDGING

**trashy** /ˈtræʃi/ adj. (informal) (**trash·ier**, **trashi·est**) of poor quality; with no value SYN **rubbishy**: *trashy TV shows*

**trat·toria** /ˌtrætəˈriːə; NAmE ˌtrɑːt-/ noun (from Italian) an Italian restaurant serving simple food

**trauma** C1 /ˈtrɔːmə; NAmE also ˈtraʊmə/ noun **1** C1 [U] (psychology) a mental condition caused by severe shock, especially when the harmful effects last for a long time **2** C1 [C, U] an unpleasant experience that makes you feel upset and/or anxious: *She felt exhausted after the traumas of recent weeks.* **3** [U, C] (medical) an injury: *The patient suffered severe brain trauma.*

**trau·mat·ic** /trɔːˈmætɪk; NAmE trəˈm-/ adj. **1** extremely unpleasant and causing you to feel upset and/or anxious: *a traumatic experience* ◇ *Divorce can be traumatic for everyone involved.* **2** [only before noun] (psychology or medical) connected with or caused by trauma: *traumatic amnesia* ⇒ see also POST-TRAUMATIC STRESS DISORDER
▶ **trau·mat·ic·al·ly** /-kli/ adv.

**trau·ma·tize** (*BrE* also **-ise**) /ˈtrɔːmətaɪz; *NAmE* also ˈtraʊm-/ *verb* [usually passive] **~ sb** to shock and upset sb very much, often making them unable to think or work normally

**trav·ail** /ˈtræveɪl, trəˈveɪl/ *noun* [U, pl.] (*old use* or *literary*) an unpleasant experience or situation that involves a lot of hard work, difficulties and/or pain

**travel** 🔵 **A1** /ˈtrævl/ *verb, noun*
■ *verb* (**-ll-**, *US* **-l-**) **1** **A1** [I, T] to go from one place to another, especially over a long distance: *I go to bed early if I'm travelling the next day.* ◊ **+ adv./prep.** *to travel around the world* ◊ *I love travelling by train.* ◊ *We always travel first class.* ◊ *We travelled to California for the wedding.* ◊ *When I finished college I **went travelling** for six months* (= spent time visiting different places). ◊ **~ sth** *As a journalist, she has **travelled the world**.* ◊ *I travel 40 miles to work every day.* **2** **A1** [I] **+ adv./prep.** to go or move at a particular speed, in a particular direction, or a particular distance: *to travel at 50 miles an hour* ◊ *Messages travel along the spine from the nerve endings to the brain.* ◊ *News travels fast these days.* **3** [I] (of food, wine, an object, etc.) to be still in good condition after a long journey: *Some wines do not travel well.* **4** [I] to go fast: *Their car can really travel!* **5** [I] (in basketball) to take more than three steps while you are holding the ball, without BOUNCING it on the ground, which is against the rules of the game
**IDM** **travel ˈlight** to take very little with you when you go on a trip
■ *noun* **1** **A1** [U] the act or activity of travelling: *air/rail/space travel* ◊ *travel expenses* ◊ *The job involves a considerable amount of foreign travel.* ◊ *the travel industry* ◊ *travel sickness* ◊ *a travel bag/clock* (= for use when travelling) ◊ *The pass allows **unlimited travel** on all public transport in the city.* ⊃ WORDFINDER NOTE at HOLIDAY **2** **A2** **travels** [pl.] time spent travelling, especially in foreign countries and for pleasure: **~ + adv./prep.** *The novel is based on his travels in India.* ◊ **on your ~** *When are you off on your travels* (= going travelling)?

ˈtravel agency *noun* a company that arranges travel and/or accommodation for people going on a holiday or journey

ˈtravel agent *noun* **1** a person or business whose job is to make arrangements for people wanting to travel, for example buying tickets or arranging hotel rooms **2 ˈtravel agent's** (*pl.* **ˈtravel agents**) a shop where you can go to arrange a holiday, etc: *He works in a travel agent's.* ⊃ see also TRAVEL AGENCY

**trav·elled** (*US* **trav·eled**) /ˈtrævld/ *adj.* (usually in compounds) **1** (of a person) having travelled the amount mentioned: *a much-travelled man* **2** (of a road, etc.) used the amount mentioned: *The path was steeper and less travelled than the previous one.*

**trav·el·ler** 🔵 **A2** (*US* **trav·el·er**) /ˈtrævələ(r)/ *noun*
**1** **A2** a person who is travelling or who often travels: *She is a frequent traveller to Belgium.* ◊ *leisure/business travellers* ⊃ see also FELLOW TRAVELLER **2** (*BrE*) a person who does not live in one place but travels around, especially as part of a group: *New Age travellers* **HELP** *Traveller* is used especially to talk about travelling people of Irish origin, but is also used as a word for all travelling people, including people from the ROMANI community. ⊃ compare GYPSY

**trav·el·ling** (*US* **trav·el·ing**) /ˈtrævəlɪŋ/ *adj., noun*
■ *adj.* [only before noun] **1** going from place to place: *a travelling circus/exhibition/performer, etc.* ◊ *the travelling public* ◊ (*BrE*) **travelling people** (= people who have no fixed home, especially those living in a community that moves from place to place, also known as 'travellers') **2** used when you travel: *a travelling clock*
■ *noun* [U] the act of travelling: *The job requires a lot of travelling.* ◊ *a **travelling companion***

ˈtravelling ˈsalesman (*US* ˌtraveling ˈsalesman) *noun* (*old-fashioned*) = SALES REP

**trav·el·ogue** (*NAmE* also **trav·elog**) /ˈtrævəlɒg; *NAmE* -lɔːg/ *noun* a film, broadcast or piece of writing about travel

**ˈtravel-sick** *adj.* (*BrE*) feeling sick because you are travelling in a vehicle ▸ **ˈtravel sickness** (*BrE*) (also **motion sickness** *NAmE, BrE*) *noun* [U]

**tra·verse** *verb, noun*
■ *verb* /trəˈvɜːs; *NAmE* -ˈvɜːrs/ **~ sth** (*formal*) to cross an area of land or water
■ *noun* /ˈtrævɜːs; *NAmE* -vɜːrs/ (*specialist*) (in mountain climbing) an act of moving SIDEWAYS across a steep slope, not climbing up or down it; a place where this is possible or necessary

**trav·esty** /ˈtrævəsti/ *noun* (*pl.* **-ies**) **~ (of sth)** something that does not have the qualities or values that it should have, and as a result is often considered wrong or offensive **SYN** **parody**: *The trial was a **travesty of justice**.*

**trawl** /trɔːl/ *verb, noun*
■ *verb* **1** [T, I] to search through a large amount of information or a large number of people, places, etc. looking for a particular thing or person: **~ sth (for sth/sb)** *She trawled the shops for bargains.* ◊ **~ (through sth) (for sth/sb)** *The police are trawling through their files for similar cases.* **2** [I] **~ (for sth)** to fish for sth by pulling a large net with a wide opening through the water ⊃ WORDFINDER NOTE at FISHING
■ *noun* **1** a search through a large amount of information, documents, etc: *A quick trawl through the newspapers yielded five suitable job adverts.* **2** (also **ˈtrawl net**) a large net with a wide opening, that is dragged along the bottom of the sea by a boat in order to catch fish

**trawl·er** /ˈtrɔːlə(r)/ *noun* a fishing boat that uses large nets that it drags through the sea behind it

**tray** /treɪ/ *noun* **1** a flat piece of wood, metal or plastic with raised edges, used for carrying or holding things, especially food: *He brought her breakfast in bed on a tray.* ◊ *She came in with a tray of drinks.* ◊ *a tea tray* **2** (often in compounds) a shallow plastic box, used for various purposes: *a seed tray* (= for planting seeds in) ◊ *a cat's litter tray* ◊ *an ice tray* (= for making ice cubes) ⊃ see also BAKING TRAY at BAKING SHEET, IN TRAY, OUT TRAY

**treach·er·ous** /ˈtretʃərəs/ *adj.* **1** that cannot be trusted; intending to harm you **SYN** **deceitful**: *He was weak, cowardly and treacherous.* ◊ *lying, treacherous words* **2** dangerous, especially when seeming safe: *The ice on the roads made driving conditions treacherous.* ▸ **treach·er·ous·ly** *adv.*

**treach·ery** /ˈtretʃəri/ *noun* [U, C] (*pl.* **-ies**) behaviour that involves hurting sb who trusts you, for example by telling their secrets to other people; an example of this: *an act of treachery*

**trea·cle** /ˈtriːkl/ *noun* [U] (*BrE*) **1** (*NAmE* **mo·las·ses**) a thick black, sweet, sticky liquid produced when sugar is REFINED (= made pure), used in cooking **2** = GOLDEN SYRUP

**trea·cly** /ˈtriːkli/ *adj.* **1** (*BrE*) like treacle: *a treacly brown liquid* **2** expressing feelings of love in a way that seems false or EXAGGERATED: *treacly music*

**tread** /tred/ *verb, noun*
■ *verb* (**trod** /trɒd; *NAmE* trɑːd/, **trod·den** /ˈtrɒdn; *NAmE* ˈtrɑːdn/ or **trod**) **1** [I] **+ adv./prep.** (*especially BrE*) to put your foot down while you are stepping or walking: *Ouch! You trod on my toe!* ◊ *Careful you don't tread in that puddle.* **2** [T] **~ sth (+ adv./prep.)** to move, push or press sth with your feet **SYN** **trample**: *Don't tread ash into the carpet!* ◊ *The wine is still made by treading grapes in the traditional way.* **3** [T, I] **~ (sth)** (*formal* or *literary*) to walk somewhere: *Few people had trod this path before.* ◊ *He was treading quietly and cautiously.*
**IDM** **tread ˈcarefully, ˈwarily, etc.** to be very careful about what you do or say: *The government will have to tread very carefully in handling this issue.* **tread a difficult, dangerous, solitary, etc. ˈpath** to choose and follow a particular way of life, way of doing sth, etc: *A restaurant has to tread the tricky path between maintaining quality and keeping prices down.* **tread on sb's ˈheels** to follow sb closely **tread on sb's ˈtoes** (*especially BrE*) (*NAmE usually* **step on sb's ˈtoes**) (*informal*) to offend or annoy sb, especially

# treadle

by getting involved in sth that is their responsibility
**,tread 'water 1** to keep yourself in the same place in deep water by moving your arms and legs **2** to make no progress while you are waiting for sth to happen ⊃ more at FOOL *n.*, LINE *n.*, TIGHTROPE
- *noun* **1** [sing.] the way that sb walks; the sound that sb makes when they walk: *I heard his heavy tread on the stairs.* **2** [C, U] the raised pattern on the surface of a tyre on a vehicle: *The tyres were worn below the legal limit of 1.6 mm of tread.* **3** [C] the upper surface of a step or stair ⊃ picture at STAIRCASE ⊃ compare RISER

**treadle** /ˈtredl/ *noun* (especially in the past) a device worked by the foot to operate a machine

**tread·mill** /ˈtredmɪl/ *noun* **1** [sing.] work or a way of life that is boring or makes you tired because it involves always doing the same things: *I'd like to escape the office treadmill.* **2** [C] (especially in the past) a large wheel turned by the weight of people or animals walking on steps around its inside edge, and used to operate machines **3** [C] an exercise machine that has a moving surface that you can walk or run on while remaining in the same place ⊃ picture at EXERCISE BIKE

**trea·son** /ˈtriːzn/ (*also* **high 'treason**) *noun* [U] the crime of doing sth that could cause danger to your country, such as helping its enemies during a war ▶ **treas·on·able** /-zənəbl/ *adj.*: *a treasonable act*

**treas·ure** 🔑+ 🄱🄱 /ˈtreʒə(r)/ *noun, verb*
- *noun* **1** 🔑+ 🄱🄱 [U] a collection of valuable things such as gold, silver and jewellery: *buried treasure* ◊ *a pirate's treasure chest* **2** 🔑+ 🄱🄱 [C, usually pl.] a highly valued object: *the priceless art treasures of the Uffizi Gallery* **3** [sing.] a person who is much loved or valued
- *verb* ~ **sth** to have or keep sth that you value and that is extremely valuable to you SYN **cherish**: *I treasure his friendship.* ◊ *This ring is my most treasured possession.*

**'treasure house** *noun* a place that contains many valuable or interesting things: *The area is a treasure house of archaeological relics.*

**'treasure hunt** *noun* a game in which players try to find a hidden prize by answering a series of questions that have been left in different places

**treas·urer** /ˈtreʒərə(r)/ *noun* a person who is responsible for the money and accounts of a club or an organization ⊃ WORDFINDER NOTE at CLUB

**'treasure trove** *noun* **1** [U, C, usually sing.] valuable things that are found hidden and whose owner is unknown **2** [C, usually sing.] a place, book, etc. containing many useful or beautiful things

**treas·ury** /ˈtreʒəri/ *noun* (*pl.* **-ies**) **1** the Treasury [sing. + sing. / pl. v.] (in the UK, the US and some other countries) the government department that controls public money **2** [C] a place in a castle, etc. where valuable things are stored

**'treasury bill** (*also informal* **'T-bill**) *noun* a type of investment sold by the US government in which a fixed amount of money is paid back on a certain date

**treat** 🔑 🄱🄱 ⦿ /triːt/ *verb, noun*
- *verb*
- **BEHAVE TOWARDS SB/STH 1** 🔑 🄱🄱 to behave in a particular way towards sb/sth: ~ **sb/sth (with sth)** *to treat people with respect* ◊ ~ **sb/sth like sth** *My parents still treat me like a child.* ◊ ~ **sb/sth as sth** *He was treated as a hero on his release from prison.*
- **CONSIDER 2** 🔑 🄱🄱 ~ **sth as sth** to consider sth in a particular way: *I decided to treat his remark as a joke.* **3** 🔑 🄱🄱 to deal with or discuss sth in a particular way: ~ **sth + adv. / prep.** *The question is treated in more detail in the next chapter.* ◊ ~ **sth as sth** *All cases involving children are treated as urgent.*
- **ILLNESS / INJURY 4** 🔑 🄱🄱 to give medical care or attention to a person, an illness, an injury, etc.: ~ **sb (for sth) (with sth)** *She was treated for sunstroke.* ◊ ~ **sth (with sth)** *to treat a disease / a condition / cancer*

- **USE CHEMICAL 5** 🔑 🄱🄱 to use a chemical substance or process to clean, preserve, etc. sth: ~ **sth (with sth)** *to treat crops with insecticide* ◊ *wood treated with preservative*
- **PAY FOR STH PLEASANT 6** ~ **sb / yourself (to sth)** to pay for sth that sb/you will enjoy and that you do not usually have or do: *She treated him to lunch.* ◊ *Don't worry about the cost—I'll treat you.* ◊ *I'm going to treat myself to a new pair of shoes.* ▶ **treat·able** *adj.*: *a treatable infection*
- IDM **treat sb like 'dirt** (*informal*) to treat sb with no respect at all
- PHR V **'treat sb to sth** [often passive] to entertain sb with sth special: *The crowd were treated to a superb display of tennis.*
- *noun* something very pleasant that sb can enjoy, especially sth that you give sb or do for them: *When I was young chocolate was a treat.* ◊ **as a ~** *We took the kids to the zoo as a special treat.* ◊ **in for a ~** *You've never been to this area before? Then you're in for a real treat.* ◊ *Let's go out for lunch—my treat* (= I will pay). ⊃ SYNONYMS at PLEASURE
- IDM **a 'treat** (*BrE, informal*) extremely well or good: *His idea worked a treat* (= was successful). ⊃ more at TRICK *n.*

**trea·tise** /ˈtriːtɪs; *BrE also* -tɪz/ *noun* ~ **(on sth)** (*formal*) a long and serious piece of writing on a particular subject

**treat·ment** 🔑 🄱🄱 ⦿ /ˈtriːtmənt/ *noun* **1** 🔑 🄱🄱 [U, C] something that is done to cure an illness or injury, or to make sb look and feel good: ~ **for sth** *He is receiving treatment for shock.* ◊ *to seek / undergo treatment* ◊ *She is responding well to treatment.* ◊ *to require hospital / medical treatment* ◊ *There are various treatments available for this condition.* ◊ *Guests at the health spa receive a range of beauty treatments.* ⊃ WORDFINDER NOTE at HEALTH

> **WORDFINDER** acupuncture, chiropractor, complementary medicine, herbalism, holistic, homeopathy, hypnotist, massage, reflexology

**2** 🔑 🄱🄱 [U] a way of behaving towards or dealing with a person or thing: *the brutal treatment of political prisoners* ◊ *Certain city areas have been singled out for special treatment.* **3** [U, C] a way of dealing with or discussing a subject, work of art, etc: *Shakespeare's treatment of madness in 'King Lear'* **4** [U, C] a process by which sth is cleaned, or protected against sth: *a sewage treatment plant* ◊ ~ **for sth** *an effective treatment for dry rot*

**treaty** 🔑+ 🄲🄱 /ˈtriːti/ *noun* (*pl.* **-ies**) a formal agreement between two or more countries: *the Treaty of Rome* ◊ *a peace treaty* ◊ *to draw up / sign / ratify a treaty* ◊ *Under the terms of the treaty, La Rochelle was ceded to the English.* ⊃ WORDFINDER NOTE at ALLY

**treble** /ˈtrebl/ *noun, verb, det., adj.*
- *noun* **1** [U] the high tones or part in music or a sound system: *to turn up the treble on the stereo* ⊃ compare BASS¹ **2** [C] a child's high voice; a boy who sings with a treble voice ⊃ compare SOPRANO **3** [sing.] a musical part written for a treble voice **4** [sing.] (*BrE*) three successes in a row: *The victory completed a treble for the horse's owner.*
- *verb* [I, T] to become, or to make sth, three times as much or as many SYN **triple**: *Cases of food poisoning have trebled in the last two years.* ◊ ~ **sth** *He trebled his earnings in two years.*
- *det.* [usually before noun] three times as much or as many: *Capital expenditure was treble the 2013 level.*
- *adj.* [only before noun] high in tone: *a treble voice* ◊ *the* **treble clef** (= the symbol in music showing that the notes following it are high) ⊃ picture at MUSIC ⊃ compare BASS¹

**tree** 🔑 🄰🄱 /triː/ *noun* a tall plant that can live a long time. Trees have a thick central wooden TRUNK from which branches grow, usually with leaves on them: *an oak / olive / apple tree* ◊ *to plant a tree* ◊ *to chop / cut down / fell a tree* ◊ *They took a seat on a fallen tree trunk in the middle of a small clearing.* ⊃ compare BUSH, SHRUB ⊃ see also BAY TREE, CHRISTMAS TREE, FAMILY TREE, GUM TREE, PLANE TREE, TEA TREE ⊃ VISUAL VOCAB page V6
- IDM **be out of your 'tree** (*informal*) to be behaving in a crazy or stupid way, perhaps because of drugs or alcohol ⊃ more at APPLE, BARK *v.*, FOREST, GROW, TOP *n.*, WOOD

---

æ cat | ɑː father | e bed | ɜː fur | ə about | ɪ sit | iː see | i happy | ɒ got (*BrE*) | ɔː saw | ʌ cup | ʊ put | uː too

**tree house** *noun* a structure built in the branches of a tree, usually for children to play on

**tree hugger** *noun* (*informal, usually disapproving*) a person who cares very much about the environment and tries to protect it

**tree·less** /ˈtriːləs/ *adj.* without trees: *a treeless plain*

**tree·line** /ˈtriːlaɪn/ (*also* **tree line**) *noun* [sing.] a level of land, for example on a mountain, above which trees will not grow

**tree surgeon** (*also formal* **ar·bor·ist**) *noun* a person whose job is treating trees that are damaged or have a disease, especially by cutting off branches, to try to preserve them ▶ **tree surgery** *noun* [U]

**tree·top** /ˈtriːtɒp; *NAmE* -tɑːp/ *noun* [usually pl.] the branches at the top of a tree: *birds nesting in the treetops*

**tre·foil** /ˈtrefɔɪl, ˈtriːf-/ *noun* **1** (*specialist*) a plant whose leaves are divided into three similar parts, for example CLOVER **2** a decoration or a design like a trefoil leaf in shape

**trek** /trek/ *noun, verb*
- *noun* **1** a long, hard walk lasting several days or weeks, especially in the mountains **2** (*informal*) a long walk SYN **tramp**: *It's a long trek into town.*
- *verb* (**-kk-**) **1** [I] (**+ adv./prep.**) (*informal*) to make a long or difficult journey, especially on foot: *I hate having to trek up that hill with all the groceries.* **2** (*also* **go trekking**) [I, T] to spend time walking, especially in mountains and for pleasure and interest: (**+ adv./prep.**) *We went trekking in Nepal.* ◇ *During the expedition, they trekked ten to thirteen hours a day.* ◇ **~ sth** *He spent the summer trekking the Taurus mountains.* ⊃ see also PONY-TREKKING

**trel·lis** /ˈtrelɪs/ *noun* [C, U] a light frame made of long, narrow pieces of wood that cross each other, used to support climbing plants

**trem·ble** /ˈtrembl/ *verb, noun*
- *verb* **1** [I] **~ (with sth)** to shake in a way that you cannot control, especially because you are very nervous, excited, frightened, etc: *My legs were trembling with fear.* ◇ *Her voice trembled with excitement.* ◇ *He opened the letter with trembling hands.* **2** [I] to shake slightly SYN **quiver**: *leaves trembling in the breeze* **3** [I] to be very worried or frightened: *I trembled at the thought of having to make a speech.*
- *noun* [C, usually sing.] (*also* **trem·bling** /ˈtremblɪŋ/ [C, U]) a feeling, movement or sound of trembling: *a tremble of fear* ◇ *She tried to control the trembling in her legs.*

**tre·men·dous** /trəˈmendəs/ *adj.* **1** very great SYN **huge**: *a tremendous explosion* ◇ *A tremendous amount of work has gone into the project.* **2** extremely good SYN **remarkable**: *It was a tremendous experience.* ▶ **tre·men·dous·ly** *adv.*: *tremendously exciting*

**trem·olo** /ˈtreməloʊ/ *noun* (*pl.* **-os**) (*music, from Italian*) a special effect in singing or playing a musical instrument made by repeating the same note or two notes very quickly

**tremor** /ˈtremə(r)/ *noun* **1** a small earthquake in which the ground shakes slightly: *an earth tremor* **2** a slight shaking movement in a part of your body caused, for example, by cold or fear SYN **quiver**: *There was a slight tremor in his voice.*

**tremu·lous** /ˈtremjələs/ *adj.* (*literary*) shaking slightly because you are nervous; causing you to shake slightly SYN **trembling**: *a tremulous voice* ◇ *He was in a state of tremulous excitement.* ▶ **tremu·lous·ly** *adv.*

**trench** /trentʃ/ *noun* **1** a long, deep hole dug in the ground, for example for carrying away water **2** a long, deep hole dug in the ground in which soldiers can be protected from enemy attacks (for example in northern France and Belgium in the First World War): *life in the trenches* ◇ *trench warfare* **3** (*also* **ocean trench**) a long, deep, narrow hole in the ocean floor

**tren·chant** /ˈtrentʃənt/ *adj.* (*formal*) (of criticism, remarks, etc.) expressed strongly and effectively, in a clear way SYN **incisive** ▶ **tren·chant·ly** *adv.*

1671 **trial**

**trench coat** *noun* a long, loose coat, worn especially to keep off rain, with a belt and pockets in the style of a military coat

**trend** /trend/ *noun, verb*
- *noun* B1 a general direction in which a situation is changing or developing: *fashion/market trends* ◇ **~ towards sth** *There is a growing trend towards later retirement.* ◇ **~ in sth** *The article discusses current trends in language teaching* ◇ *a downward/an upward trend in sales* ◇ *You seem to have set* (= started) *a new trend.* ◇ *This trend is being reversed* (= is going in the opposite direction). ◇ *One region is attempting to* **buck** (= oppose or resist) *the trend of economic decline.* ◇ *The underlying trend of inflation is still upwards.* ◇ **on ~** *Linen is on trend* (= fashionable) *again this summer.* ⊃ see also ON-TREND ⊃ LANGUAGE BANK at FALL

**WORDFINDER** boom, decline, dip, fluctuate, level off/out, peak, plateau, plummet, slump

- *verb* [I] (used especially in the progressive tenses) **1** to change or develop in a general direction: *Prices have been trending upwards.* **2** (of a topic) to be discussed a lot on SOCIAL MEDIA within a short period of time: *See what's trending on Twitter in your local area right now.*

**trend·ing** /ˈtrendɪŋ/ *adj.* being discussed a lot on SOCIAL MEDIA: *It's in the top ten trending topics on Twitter right now.*

**trend·set·ter** /ˈtrendsetə(r)/ *noun* (*often approving*) a person who starts a new fashion or makes it popular ▶ **trend·set·ting** *adj.* [only before noun]

**trendy** /ˈtrendi/ *adj., noun*
- *adj.* (**trend·ier, trendi·est**) (*informal*) very fashionable: *trendy clothes* ▶ **trend·ily** /-dəli/ *adv.* **trendi·ness** *noun* [U]
- *noun* (*pl.* **-ies**) (*BrE, informal, usually disapproving*) a trendy person: *young trendies from art college*

**trepi·da·tion** /ˌtrepɪˈdeɪʃn/ *noun* [U] (*formal*) great worry or fear about sth unpleasant that may happen

**tres·pass** /ˈtrespəs; *NAmE* -pæs/ *verb, noun*
- *verb* **1** [I] **~ (on sth)** to enter land or a building that you do not have permission or the right to enter: *He told me I was trespassing on private land.* **2** [I] (*old use*) to do sth wrong
PHRV **trespass on sth** (*formal*) to make unfair use of sb's time, help, etc. SYN **encroach on**: *I mustn't trespass on your time any longer.*
- *noun* **1** [U, C] the act or crime of entering land or a building that you do not have permission or the right to enter **2** [C] (*old use*) something that you do that is morally wrong SYN **sin**

**tres·pass·er** /ˈtrespəsə(r); *NAmE* -pæs-/ *noun* a person who goes onto sb's land without their permission: *The notice read: 'Trespassers will be prosecuted.'*

**tresses** /ˈtresɪz/ *noun* [pl.] (*literary*) a woman's long hair SYN **locks**

**tres·tle** /ˈtresl/ *noun* a wooden or metal structure with two pairs of sloping legs. Trestles are used in pairs to support a flat surface, for example the top of a table.

**trey** /treɪ/ *noun* (in basketball) a shot that scores three points

**tri-** /traɪ/ *combining form* (in nouns and adjectives) three; having three: *tricycle* ◇ *triangular*

**tri·ad** /ˈtraɪæd/ *noun* **1** (*formal*) a group of three related people or things **2** (*also* **Triad**) a Chinese secret organization involved in criminal activity

**tri·age** /ˈtriːɑːʒ/ *noun* [U] (in a hospital) the process of deciding how seriously ill or injured a person is, so that the most serious cases can be treated first

**trial** /ˈtraɪəl/ *noun, verb*
- *noun*
- LAW **1** B2 [U, C] a formal examination of evidence in court by a judge and often a JURY, to decide if sb accused of a crime is guilty or not: *a murder/criminal trial* ◇ **on ~** *He's on trial for murder.* ◇ *She will stand trial/go on trial for*

# trial balloon

fraud. ◊ *He was facing trial on a murder charge.* ◊ *The men were arrested but not brought to trial.* ◊ *She is awaiting trial on corruption charges.* ◊ *He did not receive a fair trial.* ◊ *the right to trial by jury* ⇨ see also SHOW TRIAL ⇨ WORDFINDER NOTE at LAW

**WORDFINDER** accuse, appeal, counsel, defendant, evidence, justice, offence, plea, prosecution

- **TEST 2** [C, U] the process of testing the ability, quality or performance of sb/sth, especially before you make a final decision about them: *a clinical/field/randomized/controlled trial* ◊ *to conduct a trial* ◊ *She agreed to employ me for a trial period.* ◊ *on~ We had the machine on trial for a week.* ◊ *The system was introduced on a trial basis for one month.*
- **IN SPORT 3** [C, usually pl.] (*NAmE also* **try-out**) a competition or series of tests to find the best players for a sports team or an important event: *Olympic trials* ⇨ see also TIME TRIAL
- **FOR ANIMALS 4** [C, usually pl.] an event at which animals compete or perform: *horse trials*
- **DIFFICULT EXPERIENCE 5** [C] an experience or a person that causes difficulties for sb: *the trials and tribulations of married life* ◊ ~**to sb** *She was a sore trial to her family at times.*
- **IDM** **trial and ˈerror** the process of solving a problem by trying various methods until you find a method that is successful: *Children learn to use computer programs by trial and error.*

■ **verb** [T, I] (**-ll-**, *NAmE* **-l-**) ~ (sth) (*BrE*) to test the ability, quality or performance of sth to see if it will be effective or successful

**ˈtrial balloon** *noun* (*especially NAmE*) something that you say or do to find out what people think about a course of action before you take it

**ˈtrial ˈrun** (*also* **ˈtest run**) *noun* a test of how well sth new works, so that you can see if any changes are necessary

### triangles

scalene triangle

equilateral triangle

isosceles triangle

right-angled/right triangle

hypotenuse

right angle

**tri·angle** /ˈtraɪæŋgl/ *noun* **1** a flat shape with three straight sides and three angles; a thing in the shape of a triangle: *Cut the sandwiches into triangles.* ⇨ see also EQUILATERAL TRIANGLE, ISOSCELES TRIANGLE, RIGHT-ANGLED TRIANGLE, SCALENE TRIANGLE **2** a simple musical instrument that consists of a long piece of metal bent into the shape of a triangle, that you hit with another piece of metal **3** a situation involving three people in a complicated relationship: *the romantic triangle at the centre of the novel* ⇨ see also LOVE TRIANGLE **4** (*NAmE*) (*BrE* **ˈset square**) an instrument for drawing straight lines and angles, made from a flat piece of plastic or metal in the shape of a triangle with one angle of 90°

**tri·angu·lar** /traɪˈæŋɡjələ(r)/ *adj.* **1** like a triangle in shape **2** involving three people or groups: *a triangular contest in an election*

**tri·angu·la·tion** /traɪˌæŋɡjuˈleɪʃn/ *noun* [U] (*specialist*) a method of finding out distance and position, usually on a map, by measuring the distance between two fixed points and then measuring the angle from each of these to the third point

**triˌanguˈlation point** *noun* = TRIG POINT

**tri·ath·lete** /traɪˈæθliːt/ *noun* a person who competes in a triathlon

**tri·ath·lon** /traɪˈæθlən/ *noun* a sporting event in which people compete in three different sports, usually swimming, cycling and running ⇨ compare BIATHLON, DECATHLON, HEPTATHLON, PENTATHLON

**tri·bal** /ˈtraɪbl/ *adj., noun*
■ *adj.* [usually before noun] connected with a tribe or tribes: *tribal art* ◊ *tribal leaders*
■ *noun* a member of a tribe, especially in South Asia

**tri·bal·ism** /ˈtraɪbəlɪzəm/ *noun* [U] **1** behaviour, attitudes, etc. that are based on supporting and being LOYAL to a tribe or other social group **2** the state of being organized in a tribe or tribes

**tribe** /traɪb/ *noun* **1** (*sometimes offensive*) (in developing countries) a group of people of the same race, and with the same customs, language, religion, etc., living in a particular area and often having one leader known as a chief: *tribes living in remote areas of the Amazonian rainforest* **2** (*usually disapproving*) a group or class of people, especially of one profession: *He had a sudden outburst against the whole tribe of actors.* **3** (*biology*) a group of related animals or plants: *a tribe of cats* **4** (*informal or humorous*) a large family: *One or two of the grandchildren will be there, but not the whole tribe.*

**tribes·man** /ˈtraɪbzmən/, **tribes·woman** /ˈtraɪbzwʊmən/ *noun* (*pl.* **-men** /-mən/, **-women** /-wɪmɪn/) a member of a tribe

**tribes·people** /ˈtraɪbzpiːpl/ *noun* [pl.] the people who belong to a particular tribe

**tribu·la·tion** /ˌtrɪbjuˈleɪʃn/ *noun* [C, U] (*literary or humorous*) great trouble, difficulty or mental pain: *the tribulations of modern life*

**tri·bu·nal** /traɪˈbjuːnl/ *noun* [C + sing./pl. v.] a type of court with the authority to deal with a particular problem or DISAGREEMENT: *an international war crimes tribunal* ◊ *a military tribunal* ⇨ see also EMPLOYMENT TRIBUNAL, INDUSTRIAL TRIBUNAL

**trib·une** /ˈtrɪbjuːn/ *noun* an official elected by the people in ancient Rome to defend their rights; a popular leader

**tribu·tary** /ˈtrɪbjətri; *NAmE* -teri/ *noun* (*pl.* **-ies**) a river or stream that flows into a larger river or a lake ⇨ WORDFINDER NOTE at RIVER

**trib·ute** /ˈtrɪbjuːt/ *noun* **1** [U, C] ~ (to sb) an act, a statement or a gift that is intended to show your love or respect, especially for a dead person: *At her funeral her oldest friend paid tribute to her life and work.* ◊ *This book is a fitting tribute to the bravery of the pioneers.* ◊ *floral tributes* (= gifts of flowers at a funeral) **2** [sing.] ~ **to sth/sb** showing the good effects or influence of sth/sb: *His recovery is a tribute to the doctors' skill.* **3** [U, C] (especially in the past) money given by one country or political leader to another, especially in return for protection or for not being attacked

**ˈtribute band** *noun* a group of musicians who play the music of a famous band and copy the way they look and sound

**trice** /traɪs/ *noun*
**IDM** **in a ˈtrice** very quickly or suddenly **SYN** **instant**: *He was gone in a trice.*

**tri·ceps** /ˈtraɪseps/ *noun* (*pl.* **tri·ceps**) the large muscle at the back of the top part of the arm ⇨ compare BICEPS

**tri·cera·tops** /traɪˈserətɒps; *NAmE* -tɑːps/ *noun* (*pl.* **tri·cera·tops** *or* **tri·cera·topses**) a large DINOSAUR with two large HORNS and one small HORN on its very large head

**trick** /trɪk/ *noun, verb, adj.*
■ *noun*
- **STH TO CHEAT SB 1** something that you do to make sb believe sth that is not true, or to annoy sb as a joke: *The kids are always playing tricks on their teacher.* ⇨ see also CONFIDENCE TRICK, DIRTY TRICK

- **STH CONFUSING 2** [B1] something that confuses you so that you see, understand, remember, etc. things in the wrong way: *One of the problems of old age is that your memory can start to **play tricks** on you.* ◇ *Was there somebody standing there or was it a trick of the light?*
- **ENTERTAINMENT 3** [B1] a clever action that sb/sth performs as a way of entertaining people: *He amused the kids with conjuring tricks.* ◇ *a magic trick* ⊃ see also HAT-TRICK, ONE-TRICK PONY
- **GOOD METHOD 4** [usually sing.] a way of doing sth that works well; a good method: *The trick is to pick the animal up by the back of its neck.* ◇ *He used the old trick of attacking in order to defend himself.*
- **IN CARD GAMES 5** the cards that you play or win in a single part of a card game: *I won six tricks in a row.*

**IDM** **a bag/box of ˈtricks** (*informal*) a set of methods or equipment that sb can use **be up to your (old) ˈtricks** (*informal*, *disapproving*) to be behaving in the same bad way as before **do the ˈtrick** (*informal*) to succeed in solving a problem or achieving a particular result: *I don't know what it was that did the trick, but I am definitely feeling much better.* **every trick in the ˈbook** every available method, whether it is honest or not: *He'll try every trick in the book to stop you from winning.* **have a ˈtrick, some more ˈtricks, etc. up your ˈsleeve** to have an idea, some plans, etc. that you keep ready to use if it becomes necessary **ˌtrick or ˈtreat** said by children who visit people's houses at Halloween and threaten to play tricks on people who do not give them sweets **the ˌtricks of the ˈtrade** the clever ways of doing things, known and used by people who do a particular job or activity **ˌturn a ˈtrick** (*NAmE*, *slang*) to have sex with sb for money ⊃ more at MISS *v*., TEACH

- **verb** [B1] to make sb believe sth which is not true, especially in order to cheat them: **~ sb** *I'd been tricked and I felt stupid.* ◇ **~ your way + adv./prep.** *He managed to trick his way past the security guards.* ⊃ SYNONYMS at CHEAT

**PHRV** **ˌtrick sb ˈinto sth/into doing sth** to make sb do sth by means of a trick: *He tricked me into lending him £100.* **ˌtrick sb ˈout of sth** to get sth from sb by means of a trick: *She was tricked out of her life savings.* **ˌtrick sb/sth↔ˈout (in/with sth)** (*literary*) to dress or decorate sb/sth in a way that attracts attention

- **adj.** [only before noun] 1 intended to trick sb: *It was a **trick question*** (= one to which the answer seems easy but actually is not). ◇ *It's all done using **trick photography*** (= photography that uses clever techniques to show things that do not actually exist or are impossible). **2** (*NAmE*) (of part of the body) weak and not working well: *a trick knee*

**trick·ery** /ˈtrɪkəri/ *noun* [U] the use of dishonest methods to trick people in order to achieve what you want **SYN** **deception**

**trickle** /ˈtrɪkl/ *verb, noun*
- **verb 1** [I, T] to flow, or to make sth flow, slowly in a thin stream: **(+ adv./prep.)** *Tears were trickling down her cheeks.* ◇ **~ sth (+ adv./prep.)** *Trickle some oil over the salad.* **2** [I, T] **~ (sth) + adv./prep.** to go, or to make sth go, somewhere slowly or gradually: *People began trickling into the hall.* ◇ *News is starting to trickle out.*
**PHRV** **ˌtrickle ˈdown** (especially of money) to spread from rich to poor people through the economic system of a country
- **noun 1** a small amount of liquid, flowing slowly **2** [usually sing.] **~ (of sth)** a small amount or number of sth, coming or going slowly: *a steady trickle of visitors*

**trickle-down** *noun* [U] the theory that if the richest people in society become richer, this will have a good effect on poorer people as well, for example by creating more jobs

**trick·ster** /ˈtrɪkstə(r)/ *noun* (*disapproving*) a person who tricks or cheats people

**tricksy** /ˈtrɪksi/ *adj.* (*informal*, *usually disapproving*) using ideas and methods that are intended to be clever but are too complicated

**tricky** /ˈtrɪki/ *adj.* (**trick·ier**, **tricki·est**) (*rather informal*) **1** difficult to do or deal with: *a tricky situation* ◇ *Getting it to fit exactly is a **tricky** business.* ◇ *The equipment can be tricky to install.* **2** (of people) clever but likely to trick you **SYN** **crafty**

**tri-col·our** (*US* **tri-color**) /ˈtrɪkələ(r); *NAmE* ˈtraɪkʌl-/ *noun* [C] a flag that has three bands of different colours, especially the French and Irish national flags

**tri·cycle** /ˈtraɪsɪkl/ (*also informal* **trike**) *noun* a vehicle similar to a bicycle, but with one wheel at the front and two at the back

**tri·dent** /ˈtraɪdnt/ *noun* a weapon used in the past that looks like a long fork with three points

**tried** /traɪd/ *adj., verb*
- **adj.**
**IDM** **ˌtried and ˈtested/ˈtrusted** (*BrE*) (*NAmE* **ˌtried and ˈtrue**) that you have used or relied on in the past successfully: *a tried-and-tested method for solving the problem*
- **verb** *past tense, past part.* of TRY

**tri·en·nial** /traɪˈeniəl/ *adj.* happening every three years

**trier** /ˈtraɪə(r)/ *noun* a person who tries very hard at what they are doing and does their best

**tries** /traɪz/ **1** *third person* of TRY **2** *pl.* of TRY

**trifle** /ˈtraɪfl/ *noun, verb*
- **noun 1** [C, U] (*BrE*) a cold DESSERT (= a sweet dish) made from cake and fruit with layers of JELLY, CUSTARD and cream **2 a ˈtrifle** [sing.] (used as an adverb) (*formal*) slightly: *She seemed a trifle anxious.* **3** [C] (*formal*) something that is not valuable or important: *$1000 is a mere trifle to her.*
- **verb**
**PHRV** **ˈtrifle with sb/sth** (*formal*) (used especially in negative sentences) to treat sb/sth without real respect: *He is not a person to be trifled with.* ◇ *You should not trifle with someone's affections.*

**trif·ling** /ˈtraɪflɪŋ/ *adj.* (*formal*) small and not important **SYN** **trivial**: *trifling details*

**trig·ger** [B2] /ˈtrɪɡə(r)/ *verb, noun*
- **verb 1** [B2] **~ sth (off)** to make sth happen suddenly **SYN** **set off**: *Nuts can trigger off a violent allergic reaction.* **2** [B2] **~ sth** to cause a device to start functioning **SYN** **set off**: *to trigger an alarm*
- **noun 1** [C1] the part of a gun that you press in order to fire it: *to **pull/squeeze the trigger*** ◇ *He kept his finger on the trigger.* **2** [C1] **~ (for sth)** | **~ (to sth/to do sth)** something that is the cause of a particular reaction or development, especially a bad one: *The trigger for the strike was the closure of yet another factory.*

**ˈtrigger-happy** *adj.* (*informal*, *disapproving*) too willing and quick to use violence, especially with guns

**ˈtrigger warning** *noun* a statement at the start of a piece of writing, video, etc. that warns readers or viewers that it contains material that may upset them

**trig·onom·etry** /ˌtrɪɡəˈnɒmətri; *NAmE* -ˈnɑːm-/ *noun* [U] the type of mathematics that deals with the relationship between the sides and angles of TRIANGLES ⊃ WORDFINDER NOTE at MATHS ▶ **trig·ono·met·ric** /ˌtrɪɡənəˈmetrɪk/ (*also* **trig·ono·met·ric·al** /-trɪkl/) *adj.*

**ˈtrig point** /ˈtrɪɡ pɔɪnt/ (*also* **triˌanguˈlation point**) *noun* (*specialist*) a position on a high place used as a REFERENCE POINT, especially by people who make and use maps. It is usually marked on the ground by a short stone PILLAR.

**trike** /traɪk/ *noun* (*informal*) = TRICYCLE

**tri·lat·eral** /ˌtraɪˈlætərəl/ *adj.* involving three groups of people or three countries: *trilateral talks* ⊃ compare BILATERAL, MULTILATERAL, UNILATERAL

**trilby** /ˈtrɪlbi/ *noun* (*pl.* **-ies**) (*especially BrE*) a man's soft hat with a narrow BRIM and the top part pushed in from front to back

**tri·lin·gual** /ˌtraɪˈlɪŋɡwəl/ *adj.* **1** able to speak three languages equally well: *He is trilingual in English, Spanish and Danish.* **2** using three languages; written in three languages: *trilingual education* ◇ *a trilingual menu*

**trill** /trɪl/ *noun, verb*
- **noun 1** a repeated short, high sound made, for example, by sb's voice or by a bird **2** (*music*) the sound made when

# trillion

two notes next to each other in the musical SCALE are played or sung quickly several times one after the other **3** (also **roll**) (*phonetics*) a sound, usually a /r/, produced by making the tongue VIBRATE against a part of the mouth
- **verb 1** [I] to make repeated short, high sounds SYN **warble**: *A phone trilled on the desk.* ◊ *The canary was trilling away happily.* **2** [T] **+ speech** to say sth in a high, cheerful voice SYN **warble**: *'How wonderful!' she trilled.* **3** [T] ~ **sth** (*phonetics*) to pronounce a /r/ sound by making a trill ⊃ compare ROLL

**tril·lion** /ˈtrɪljən/ *number* **1** 1000000000000; one million million HELP You say **a, one, two, several,** etc. **trillion** without a final 's' on 'trillion'. **Trillions (of…)** can be used if there is no number or quantity before it. Always use a plural verb with **trillion** or **trillions**. **2** **a trillion** or **trillions (of…)** (*informal*) a very large amount HELP There are more examples of how to use numbers at the entry for **hundred**. **3** (*old-fashioned, BrE*) one million million million; 1000000000000000000

**tri·lo·bite** /ˈtraɪləbaɪt; *NAmE* -ləb-/ *noun* a small sea creature that lived millions of years ago and is now a FOSSIL

**tril·ogy** /ˈtrɪlədʒi/ *noun* (*pl.* **-ies**) a group of three books, films, etc. that have the same subject or characters

**trim** /trɪm/ *verb, noun, adj.*
- **verb** (**-mm-**) **1** ~ **sth** to make sth neater, smaller, better, etc., by cutting parts from it: *to trim your hair* ◊ *to trim a hedge (back)* ◊ (*figurative*) *The training budget had been trimmed by £10000.* **2** to cut away unnecessary parts from sth: ~ **sth (off sth)** *Trim any excess fat off the meat.* ◊ ~ **sth away/off** *Trim away the lower leaves.* **3** [usually passive] ~ **sth (with sth)** to decorate sth, especially around its edges: *gloves trimmed with fur*
- IDM **trim your ˈsails 1** to arrange the sails of a boat to suit the wind so that the boat moves faster **2** to reduce your costs
- PHRV **trim ˈdown** | **trim sth↔ˈdown** to become smaller in size; to make sth smaller: *Using the diet he's trimmed down from 90 kilos to 70.*
- **noun 1** [C, usually sing.] an act of cutting a small amount off sth, especially hair: *a wash and trim* ◊ *The hedge needs a trim.* **2** [U, sing.] material that is used to decorate clothes, furniture, cars, etc., especially along the edges, by being a different colour, etc: *The car is available with black or red trim* (= the colour of the seats). ◊ *a blue jacket with a white trim*
- IDM **in (good, etc.) ˈtrim** (*informal*) in good condition or order: *He keeps in trim by running every day.* ◊ *The team need to get in trim for the coming season.*
- **adj. 1** (of a person) looking thin, healthy and attractive: *She has kept very trim.* ◊ *a trim figure* **2** neat and well cared for SYN **well kept**: *a trim garden*

**tri·maran** /ˈtraɪməræn/ *noun* a fast sailing boat like a CATAMARAN, but with three HULLS instead of two

**tri·mes·ter** /traɪˈmestə(r)/ *noun* **1** (*medical*) a period of three months during the time when a woman is pregnant: *the first trimester of pregnancy* **2** (*NAmE*) = TERM: *The school year is divided into three trimesters.* ⊃ compare SEMESTER

**trim·mer** /ˈtrɪmə(r)/ *noun* a machine for cutting the edges of bushes, grass and HEDGES: *a hedge trimmer*

**trim·ming** /ˈtrɪmɪŋ/ *noun* **1** **trimmings** (*NAmE* also **fix·ings**) [pl.] the extra things that it is traditional to have for a special meal or occasion: *a splendid feast of turkey with all the trimmings* **2** **trimmings** [pl.] the small pieces of sth that are left when you have cut sth: *hedge trimmings* **3** [U, C, usually pl.] material that is used to decorate sth, for example along its edges: *a white blouse with blue trimming*

**trin·ity** /ˈtrɪnəti/ *noun* [sing.] **1 the Trinity** (in Christianity) the union of Father, Son and HOLY SPIRIT as one God **2** (*formal*) a group of three people or things

**trin·ket** /ˈtrɪŋkɪt/ *noun* a piece of jewellery or small attractive object that is not worth much money

**trio** /ˈtriːəʊ/ *noun* (*pl.* **-os**) **1** [C + sing./pl. v.] a group of three people or things: *A trio of English runners featured in the women's 1500 metres.* ⊃ compare DUO **2** [C + sing./pl. v.] a group of three musicians or singers who play or sing together **3** [C] a piece of music for three musicians or singers: *a trio for piano, oboe and bassoon* ⊃ compare DUET

**trip** /trɪp/ *noun, verb*
- **noun 1** a journey to a place and back again, especially a short one for pleasure or a particular purpose: *Did you have a good trip?* ◊ *We went on a trip to the mountains.* ◊ *a boat/coach/bus trip* ◊ *a business/school/shopping trip* ◊ *They took a trip down the river.* ◊ *We had to make several trips to bring all the equipment over.* ⊃ see also DAY TRIP, EGO TRIP, FIELD TRIP, ROAD TRIP, ROUND TRIP **2** (*slang*) the experience that sb has if they take a powerful drug that affects the mind and makes them imagine things: *an acid (= LSD) trip* **3** an act of falling or nearly falling down, because you hit your foot against sth IDM see GUILT *n.*, MEMORY LANE
- **verb** (**-pp-**) **1** [I] to catch your foot on sth and fall or almost fall: *She tripped and fell.* ◊ ~ **over/on sth** *Someone will trip over that cable.* ◊ ~ **over/up** *Be careful you don't trip up on the step.* **2** [T] ~ **sb** (also **trip sb ˈup**) to catch sb's foot and make them fall or almost fall: *As I passed, he stuck out a leg and tried to trip me up.* **3** [I] **+ adv./prep.** (*literary*) to walk, run or dance with quick light steps: *She said goodbye and tripped off along the road.* **4** [T] ~ **sth** to release a switch, etc. or to operate sth by doing so: *to trip a switch* ◊ *Any intruders will trip the alarm.* **5** [I] (*informal*) to be under the influence of a drug that makes you HALLUCINATE IDM see TONGUE *n.*

▼ **SYNONYMS**

**trip**
journey • tour • expedition • excursion • outing • day out

These are all words for an act of travelling to a place.

**trip** an act of travelling from one place to another, and usually back again: *a business trip* ◊ *a five-minute trip by taxi*

**journey** an act of travelling from one place to another, especially when they are a long way apart: *a long and difficult journey across the mountains*

**TRIP OR JOURNEY?**
A **trip** usually involves you going to a place and back again; a **journey** is usually one-way. A **trip** is often shorter than a **journey**, although it does not have to be: *a trip to New York* ◊ *a round-the-world trip*. It is often short in time, even if it is long in distance. **Journey** is more often used when the travelling takes a long time and is difficult. In North American English **journey** is not used for short trips: (*BrE*) *Don't use the car for short journeys.*

**tour** a journey made for pleasure during which several different places are visited: *a tour of Bavaria*

**expedition** an organized journey with a particular purpose, especially to find out about a place that is not well known: *the first expedition to the South Pole*

**excursion** a short trip made for pleasure, especially one that has been organized for a group of people: *We went on an all-day excursion to the island.*

**outing** a short trip made for pleasure or education, usually with a group of people and lasting no more than a day: *The children were on a day's outing from school.*

**day out** a trip to somewhere for a day, especially for pleasure: *We had a day out at the beach.*

**PATTERNS**
- a(n) **foreign/overseas** trip/journey/tour/expedition
- a **bus/coach/train/rail** trip/journey/tour
- to **go on** a(n) trip/journey/tour/expedition/excursion/outing/day out
- to **set out/off on** a(n) trip/journey/tour/expedition/excursion
- to **make** a(n) trip/journey/tour/expedition/excursion

**PHR V** **trip up | trip sb ↔ up** to make a mistake; to deliberately make sb do this: *Read the questions carefully, because the examiners sometimes try to trip you up.*

**tri·par·tite** /traɪˈpɑːtaɪt; NAmE -ˈpɑːrt-/ adj. [usually before noun] (formal) having three parts or involving three people, groups, etc.

**tripe** /traɪp/ noun [U] **1** the LINING of a cow's or pig's stomach, eaten as food **2** (old-fashioned, informal) something that sb says or writes that you think is silly or not true, or not of good quality **SYN** **garbage, nonsense, rubbish**.

**triple** /ˈtrɪpl/ adj., verb
■ adj. **1** [only before noun] having three parts or involving three people or groups: *a triple heart bypass operation* ◊ *a triple alliance* ◊ *They're showing a **triple bill** of horror movies* (= three horror movies one after the other). **2** [not before noun] three times as much or as many as sth: *The amount of alcohol in his blood was triple the legal maximum.* ◊ *Its population is about triple that of Venice.* ▶ **triply** /-pli/ adv.
■ verb [I, T] to become, or to make sth, three times as much or as many **SYN** **treble**: *Output should triple by next year.* ◊ *~ sth The company recently tripled the size of its operation.*

**the ˈtriple jump** noun [sing.] a sporting event in which people try to jump as far forward as possible with three jumps. The first jump lands on one foot, the second on the other and the third on both feet.

**trip·let** /ˈtrɪplət/ noun **1** one of three children born at the same time to the same mother **2** (music) a group of three equal notes to be played or sung in the time usually taken to play or sing two of the same kind

**trip·li·cate** /ˈtrɪplɪkət/ noun
**IDM** **in ˈtriplicate 1** done three times: *Each sample was tested in triplicate.* **2** (of a document) copied twice, so that there are three copies in total ⊃ compare DUPLICATE

**tri·pod** /ˈtraɪpɒd; NAmE -pɑːd/ noun a support with three legs for a camera, TELESCOPE, etc.

**trip·per** /ˈtrɪpə(r)/ noun (BrE) a person who is visiting a place for a short time for pleasure: *a day tripper*

**trip·tych** /ˈtrɪptɪk/ noun (specialist) a picture that is painted or CARVED on three pieces of wood placed side by side, especially one over an ALTAR in a church

**trip·wire** /ˈtrɪpwaɪə(r)/ noun a wire that is stretched close to the ground as part of a device for catching sb/sth if they touch it

**tri·shaw** /ˈtraɪʃɔː/ noun a light vehicle with three wheels and PEDALS, used in south-east Asia to carry passengers

**trite** /traɪt/ adj. (of a remark, an opinion, etc.) boring because it has been expressed so many times before; not original **SYN** **banal** ▶ **trite·ly** adv. **trite·ness** noun [U]

**tri·tium** /ˈtrɪtiəm/ noun [U] (symb. T) an ISOTOPE (= a different form) of hydrogen with a mass that is three times that of the usual isotope

**tri·umph** ₂⁺ **C1** /ˈtraɪʌmf/ noun, verb
■ noun **1** ₂⁺ **C1** [C, U] a great success, achievement or victory: *one of the greatest triumphs of modern science* ◊ *~ over sb/sth It was a personal triumph over her old rival.* **2** ₂⁺ **C1** [U] the feeling of great pleasure or joy that you get from a great success or victory: *a shout of triumph* ◊ *in ~ The winning team returned home in triumph.* **3** ₂⁺ **C1** [sing.] **a ~ (of sth)** an excellent example of how successful sth can be: *Her arrest was a triumph of international cooperation.*
■ verb [I] **~ (over sb/sth)** to defeat sb/sth; to be successful: *As is usual in this kind of movie, good triumphs over evil in the end.* ◊ *France triumphed 3–0 in the final.*

**tri·umph·al** /traɪˈʌmfl/ adj. [usually before noun] done or made in order to celebrate a great success or victory

**tri·umph·al·ism** /traɪˈʌmfəlɪzəm/ noun [U] (disapproving) behaviour that celebrates a victory or success in a way that is too proud and intended to upset the people you have defeated ▶ **tri·umph·al·ist** /-lɪst/ adj.

**tri·umph·ant** /traɪˈʌmfənt/ adj. **1** very successful in a way that causes great pleasure: *They emerged triumphant in the September election.* **2** showing great pleasure or joy about a victory or success: *a triumphant smile* ▶ **tri·umph·ant·ly** adv.

**tri·um·vir·ate** /traɪˈʌmvərət/ noun (formal) a group of three powerful people or groups who control sth together

**trivia** /ˈtrɪviə/ noun [U] **1** unimportant matters, details or information: *We spent the whole evening discussing domestic trivia.* **2** (usually in compounds) facts about many subjects that are used in a game to test people's knowledge: *a trivia quiz*

**triv·ial** /ˈtrɪviəl/ adj. not important or serious; not worth considering: *a trivial detail* ◊ *I know it sounds trivial, but I'm worried about it.* ◊ *I'll try to fix it—but it's not trivial* (= it may be difficult to fix). ▶ **triv·ial·ly** /-əli/ adv.

**triv·ial·ity** /ˌtrɪviˈæləti/ noun (pl. **-ies**) (disapproving) **1** [C] a matter that is not important: *I don't want to waste time on trivialities.* **2** [U] the state of being unimportant or of dealing with unimportant things: *His speech was one of great triviality.*

**triv·ial·ize** (BrE also **-ise**) /ˈtrɪviəlaɪz/ verb ~ **sth** (usually disapproving) to make sth seem less important, serious, difficult, etc. than it really is ▶ **triv·ial·iza·tion, -isa·tion** /ˌtrɪviəlaɪˈzeɪʃn; NAmE -ləˈz-/ noun [U]

**trod** /trɒd; NAmE trɑːd/ past tense of TREAD

**trod·den** /ˈtrɒdn; NAmE ˈtrɑːdn/ past part. of TREAD

**trog·lo·dyte** /ˈtrɒɡlədaɪt; NAmE ˈtrɑːɡ-/ noun a person living in a CAVE, especially in PREHISTORIC times **SYN** **cave dweller**

**troika** /ˈtrɔɪkə/ noun (formal) a group of three politicians, organizations or countries working together

**Tro·jan** /ˈtrəʊdʒən/ noun, adj. a person from the ancient city of Troy in Asia Minor
**IDM** **work like a ˈTrojan** (old-fashioned) to work very hard

**Trojan ˈhorse** noun **1** a person or thing that is used to trick an enemy in order to achieve a secret purpose **2** (computing) a computer program that seems to be helpful but that is, in fact, designed to destroy data, etc. **ORIGIN** From the story in which the ancient Greeks hid inside a hollow wooden statue of a horse in order to enter the city of their enemies, Troy.

**troll** /trɒl, trəʊl; NAmE trəʊl/ noun, verb
■ noun **1** (in Scandinavian stories) a creature that looks like an ugly person. Some trolls are very large and evil, others are small and friendly but like to trick people. **2** (informal) a message to a discussion group on the internet that sb deliberately sends to make other people angry; a person who sends a message like this
■ verb **1** [I] **~ (for sth)** (especially NAmE) to catch fish by pulling a line with BAIT on it through the water behind a boat **2** [T, I] (informal) to search for or try to get sth: ~ **sth** *He trolled the internet for advice on the disease.* ◊ *~ for sth Both candidates have been trolling for votes.* **3** [I, T] **~ (sb/sth)** to write false or offensive messages on the internet in order to make other people angry

**trol·ley** /ˈtrɒli; NAmE ˈtrɑːli/ noun **1** (BrE) (NAmE **cart**) a small vehicle with wheels that can be pushed or pulled along and is used for carrying things: *a shopping/supermarket/luggage trolley* **2** (BrE) (US **cart, wagon**) a small table on very small wheels, used for carrying or serving food or drink: *a drinks trolley* ◊ *a tea trolley* **3** (US) = STREETCAR ⊃ see also TRACKLESS TROLLEY

shopping trolley/cart

**IDM** **off your ˈtrolley** (BrE, informal) crazy; stupid

**trol·ley·bus** /ˈtrɒlibʌs; NAmE ˈtrɑːl-/ (BrE) (US **trackless ˈtrolley**) noun a bus driven by electricity from a cable above the street

**'trolley car** noun (US, old-fashioned) = STREETCAR

**trol·lop** /ˈtrɒləp/ NAmE /ˈtrɑːl-/ noun (old-fashioned, offensive) **1** a woman who has many sexual partners **2** a woman who is very untidy

**trom·bone** /trɒmˈbəʊn; NAmE trɑːm-/ noun a large BRASS musical instrument that you blow into, with a sliding tube used to change the note

**trom·bon·ist** /trɒmˈbəʊnɪst; NAmE trɑːm-/ noun a person who plays the trombone

**tromp** /trɒmp; NAmE trɑːmp/ verb (NAmE, informal) = TRAMP

**trompe l'œil** /ˌtrɒmp ˈlɔɪ; NAmE ˌtrɑːmp/ noun (pl. **trompe l'œils** /ˌtrɒmp ˈlɔɪ; NAmE ˌtrɑːmp/) (from French) a painting or design intended to make the person looking at it think that it is a real object

**troop** ʔ+ B2 /truːp/ noun, verb
- noun **1** ʔ+ B2 **troops** [pl.] soldiers, especially in large groups: *They announced the withdrawal of 12 000 troops from the area.* ◇ *The president decided to* **send in the troops**. ◇ *Russian troops* **2** [C] one group of soldiers, especially in tanks or on horses: (figurative) *A troop of guests was moving towards the house.* **3** [C] a local group of SCOUTS ▶ **troop** adj. [only before noun]: *troop movements* (= of soldiers)
- verb [I] (used with a plural subject) + **adv./prep.** to walk somewhere together as a group: *After lunch we all trooped down to the beach.*

**troop·er** /ˈtruːpə(r)/ noun **1** a soldier of low rank in the part of an army that uses tanks or horses **2** (NAmE) = STATE TROOPER IDM see SWEAR

**'troop·ship** /ˈtruːpʃɪp/ noun a ship used for transporting soldiers

**trope** /trəʊp/ noun (specialist) **1** a word or phrase that is used in a way that is different from its usual meaning in order to create a particular mental image or effect. METAPHORS and SIMILES are tropes. **2** a theme that is important or repeated in literature, films, etc: *the trope of the mad scientist in horror movies*

**troph·ic** /ˈtrəʊfɪk; BrE also ˈtrɒf-/ adj. (biology) **1** relating to feeding, and to the food necessary for growth **2** (of a HORMONE or its effect) causing the release of another HORMONE or other substance into the blood

**trophy** ʔ+ C1 /ˈtrəʊfi/ noun, adj.
- noun (pl. **-ies**) **1** ʔ+ C1 an object such as a silver cup that is given as a prize for winning a competition ⊃ picture at MEDAL **2** *Trophy* used in the names of some competitions and races in which a trophy is given to the winner **3** an object that you keep to show that you were successful in sth, especially hunting or war
- adj. [only before noun] ~**building/art/girlfriend, etc.** (informal, disapproving) an impressive or beautiful thing or person that you have in order to make other people admire you: *We don't need a trophy building for our business.*

**'trophy wife** noun (informal, disapproving) a young attractive woman who is married to an older person and thought of as a trophy (= sth that shows that you are successful and impresses other people)

**trop·ic** /ˈtrɒpɪk; NAmE ˈtrɑːp-/ noun **1** [C, usually sing.] one of the two imaginary lines drawn around the world 23° 26′ north (**the Tropic of 'Cancer**) or south (**the Tropic of 'Capricorn**) of the EQUATOR ⊃ WORDFINDER NOTE at EARTH **2 the tropics** [pl.] the area between the two tropics, which is the hottest part of the world

**trop·ic·al** ❶ B2 /ˈtrɒpɪkl; NAmE ˈtrɑːp-/ adj. (usually before noun) coming from, found in or typical of the tropics: *tropical fish/birds/fruit* ◇ *Tropical storms battered the Gulf Coast all week.* ◇ *a lush tropical forest* ⊃ WORDFINDER NOTE at CLIMATE ⊃ VISUAL VOCAB page V4

**the tropo·sphere** /ðə ˈtrɒpəsfɪə(r); NAmE ˈtrəʊpəsfɪr, ˈtrɑːp-/ noun [sing.] (specialist) the lowest layer of the earth's atmosphere, between the surface of the earth and about 6–10 kilometres above the surface

**trot** /trɒt; NAmE trɑːt/ verb, noun
- verb (**-tt-**) **1** [I] (of a horse or its rider) to move forward at a speed that is faster than a walk and slower than a CANTER **2** [T] ~ **sth** (+ **adv./prep.**) to ride a horse in this way: *She trotted her pony around the field.* **3** [I] + **adv./prep.** (of a person or an animal) to run or walk fast, taking short, quick steps: *The children trotted into the room.* **4** [I] + **adv./prep.** (informal) to walk or go somewhere: *The guide led the way and we trotted along behind him.* IDM see HOT adj.
- PHR V **trot sth**↔**'out** (informal, disapproving) to give the same excuses, facts, explanations, etc. for sth that have often been used before: *They trotted out the same old excuses for the lack of jobs in the area.*
- noun **1** [sing.] a trotting speed, taking short, quick steps: *The horse slowed to a trot.* ◇ *The girl* **broke into a trot** and disappeared around the corner. **2** [C] a period of trotting IDM **on the 'trot** (BrE, informal) **1** one after the other SYN succession: *They've now won three games on the trot.* **2** busy all the time: *I've been on the trot all day.*

**troth** /trəʊθ; NAmE trɑːθ/ noun IDM see PLIGHT v.

**trot·ter** /ˈtrɒtə(r); NAmE ˈtrɑːt-/ noun **1** a pig's foot, especially when cooked and eaten as food **2** a horse that has been trained to TROT fast in races

**trou·ba·dour** /ˈtruːbədɔː(r)/ noun (literary) a writer and performer of songs or poetry (after the French travelling performers of the eleventh to thirteenth centuries)

**trouble** ❶ A2 /ˈtrʌbl/ noun, verb
- noun
- PROBLEM/WORRY **1** ʔ A2 [U, C] a problem, worry, difficulty, etc. or a situation causing this: *We* **have trouble** *getting staff.* ◇ *to* **make/cause/spell trouble** *for sb* ◇ ~ **with sb/sth** *The* **trouble with you is** *you don't really want to work.* ◇ *We've never* **had much trouble with** *vandals around here.* ◇ *Her trouble is she's incapable of making a decision.* ◇ *The* **trouble is** (= what is difficult is) *there aren't any trains at that time.* ◇ *The only trouble is we won't be here then.* ◇ *No, I don't know his number—I have quite enough trouble remembering my own.* ◇ *financial troubles* ◇ *Our troubles aren't over yet.* ⊃ see also TEETHING TROUBLES at TEETHING PROBLEMS
- DIFFICULT/VIOLENT SITUATION **2** ʔ A2 [U] a situation in which you can be criticized or punished: **in** ~ *If I don't get this finished in time, I'll be in trouble.* ◇ *We're in* **deep/serious trouble** ◇ **in** ~ **with sb** *He's in trouble with the police.* ◇ *My brother was always* **getting me into trouble** *with my parents.* **3** ʔ B1 [U] a situation that is difficult or dangerous: *The company* **ran into trouble** *early on, when a major order was cancelled.* ◇ *A yachtsman* **got into trouble** *off the coast and had to be rescued.* **4** ʔ B1 [U] an angry or violent situation: *The police were expecting trouble after the match.* ◇ *If you're not in by midnight, there'll be trouble* (= I'll be very angry). ◇ *He had to throw out a few drunks who were* **causing trouble** *in the bar.*
- ILLNESS/PAIN **5** ʔ B1 [U] illness or pain: *back trouble* ◇ *I've been having trouble with my knee.* ⊃ SYNONYMS at ILLNESS
- WITH MACHINE **6** ʔ B1 [U] something that is wrong with a machine, vehicle, etc: *mechanical trouble*
- EXTRA EFFORT **7** ʔ B2 [U] extra effort or work SYN **bother**: *I don't want to* **put you to a lot of trouble**. ◇ *I'll get it if you like, that will* **save you the trouble** *of going out.* ◇ *Making your own yogurt is* **more trouble than it's worth**. ◇ *She went* **to a lot of trouble** *to find the book for me.* ◇ *Nothing is ever* **too much trouble** *for her* (= she's always ready to help). ◇ *I can call back later—it's* **no trouble** (= I don't mind). ◇ *I hope the children weren't* **too much trouble**. ◇ *It is worth* **taking the trouble** *to read the introduction.*
- IN NORTHERN IRELAND **8 the Troubles** [pl.] the time of political and social problems in Northern Ireland, especially after 1968, when there was violence between Catholics and Protestants
- IDM **get sb into 'trouble** (old-fashioned) to make a woman who is not married pregnant **give (sb) (some, no, any, etc.) 'trouble** to cause problems or difficulties: *My back's been giving me a lot of trouble lately.* ◇ *The children didn't give me any trouble at all when we were out.* **look for 'trouble** to behave in a way that is likely to cause an argument, violence, etc: *Drunken youths hang around outside*

looking for trouble. **take trouble over/with sth** | **take trouble doing/to do sth** to try hard to do sth well: *They take a lot of trouble to find the right person for the right job.* **take the trouble to do sth** to do sth even though it involves effort or difficulty ⓢⓨⓝ **effort**: *She didn't even take the trouble to find out how to spell my name.* **a trouble shared is a trouble 'halved** (*saying*) if you talk to sb about your problems and worries, instead of keeping them to yourself, they seem less serious ⊃ more at ASK *v.*

■ **verb**
- MAKE SB WORRIED **1** ⓘ ⒷⒶ [T] ~ **sb** to make sb worried or upset: *He was **deeply troubled** by the allegations.*
- INTERRUPT **2** [T] (often used in polite requests) to interrupt sb because you want to ask them sth ⓢⓨⓝ **bother**: ~ **sb Sorry to trouble you, but could you tell me the time?** ◇ ~ **sb with sth** *I don't want to trouble the doctor with such a small problem.* ◇ (*formal*) ~ **sb to do sth** *Could I trouble you to open the window, please?*
- MAKE EFFORT **3** [I] ~ **to do sth** (*formal*) (usually used in negative sentences) to make an effort to do sth ⓢⓨⓝ **bother**: *He rushed into the room without troubling to knock.*
- CAUSE PAIN **4** [T] ~ **sb** (of a medical problem) to cause pain: *My back's been troubling me again.*

**troubled** ⓘ+ ⒸⒷ /ˈtrʌbld/ *adj.* **1** ⓘ+ ⒸⒷ (of a person) worried and anxious: *She looked into his troubled face.* **2** ⓘ+ ⒸⒷ (of a place, situation or time) having a lot of problems: *a troubled marriage* ◇ *We live in **troubled times**.* ⓘⒹⓜ see POUR

**trouble-maker** /ˈtrʌblmeɪkə(r)/ *noun* a person who often causes trouble, especially by involving others in arguments or encouraging them to complain about people in authority

**trouble-shoot** /ˈtrʌblʃuːt/ *verb* **1** [I, T] ~ **(sth)** to analyse and solve serious problems for a company or other organization **2** [I, T] ~ **(sth)** (*computing*) to identify and correct faults in a computer system ▶ **trouble-shoot-ing** *noun* [U]

**trouble-shoot-er** /ˈtrʌblʃuːtə(r)/ *noun* a person who helps to solve problems in a company or an organization

**trouble-some** /ˈtrʌblsəm/ *adj.* causing trouble, pain, etc. over a long period of time ⓢⓨⓝ **annoying, irritating**: *a troublesome cough/child/problem*

**'trouble spot** *noun* a place or country where trouble often happens, especially violence or war

**trough** /trɒf; *NAmE* trɔːf/ *noun* **1** a long, narrow open container for animals to eat or drink from **2** (*specialist*) a long narrow region of low air pressure between two regions of higher pressure ⊃ compare RIDGE **3** a period of time when the level of sth is low, especially a time when a business or the economy is not growing: *There have been **peaks and troughs** in the long-term trend of unemployment.* **4** a low area between two waves in the sea, or two hills

ⓘⒹⓜ **get/have your nose/snout in the trough** (*BrE, informal, disapproving*) if you say that people have their noses **in the trough**, you mean that they are trying to get a lot of money for themselves

**trounce** /traʊns/ *verb* ~ **sb** (*formal*) to defeat sb completely: *Brazil trounced Italy 5–1 in the final.*

**troupe** /truːp/ *noun* [C + sing./pl. v.] a group of actors, singers, etc. who work together

**trouper** /ˈtruːpə(r)/ *noun* (*informal*) an actor or other person who has a lot of experience and who you can depend on

**trou-ser** /ˈtraʊzə(r)/ *verb* ~ **sth** (*BrE, informal*) to take or earn an amount of money ⓢⓨⓝ **pocket**

**trou-sers** ⓘ Ⓐ⒈ /ˈtraʊzəz; *NAmE* -zərz/ (*especially BrE*) (*NAmE usually* **pants**) *noun* [pl.] a piece of clothing that covers the lower body and is divided into two parts to cover each leg separately: *a pair of grey trousers* ◇ *Doug was wearing black trousers and a blue shirt.* ◇ *baggy/tight/cropped trousers* ▶ **trou-ser** *adj.* [only before noun]: *trouser pockets* ⓘⒹⓜ see CATCH *v.*, WEAR *v.*, ⓘⒹⓜ see CATCH *v.*

**'trouser suit** (*BrE*) (*NAmE* **pant-suit**) *noun* a woman's suit of jacket and trousers

**trous-seau** /ˈtruːsəʊ/ *noun* (*pl.* **trous-seaus** or **trous-seaux** /-səʊz/) (*old-fashioned*) the clothes and other possessions collected by a woman who is soon going to get married, to begin her married life with

**trout** /traʊt/ *noun* **1** [C, U] (*pl.* **trout**) a common FRESHWATER fish that is used for food. There are several types of trout: *rainbow trout* ◇ *trout fishing* ◇ *Shall we have trout for dinner?* ⊃ VISUAL VOCAB page V2 **2** [C, usually sing.] (*usually* **old 'trout**) (*informal, disapproving*) an annoying or angry old woman

**trove** /trəʊv/ *noun* ⊃ TREASURE TROVE

**trowel** /ˈtraʊəl/ *noun* **1** a small garden tool with a curved metal part for lifting plants and digging holes **2** a small tool with a flat metal part, used in building for spreading CEMENT or PLASTER

ⓘⒹⓜ **lay it on with a 'trowel** (*informal*) to talk about sb/sth in a way that makes them or it seem much better or much worse than they really are; to EXAGGERATE sth: *He was laying the flattery on with a trowel.*

**troy** /trɔɪ/ *noun* [U] a system for measuring PRECIOUS METALS and PRECIOUS STONES

**tru-ancy** /ˈtruːənsi/ *noun* [U] the practice of staying away from school without permission

**tru-ant** /ˈtruːənt/ *noun* a child who stays away from school without permission ▶ **tru-ant** *verb* [I]: *A number of pupils have been truanting regularly.*

ⓘⒹⓜ **play 'truant** (*BrE*) (*NAmE, old-fashioned, informal* **play 'hooky**) to stay away from school without permission ⊃ see also BUNK OFF at BUNK, SKIVE

**truce** /truːs/ *noun* an agreement between enemies or opponents to stop fighting for an agreed period of time; the period of time that this lasts: *to call/break a truce* ⊃ WORDFINDER NOTE at PEACE

**truck** ⓘ Ⓐ⒉ /trʌk/ *noun, verb*
■ *noun* **1** ⓘ Ⓐ⒉ (*especially NAmE*) (*BrE usually* **lorry**) a large vehicle for carrying heavy loads by road: *a truck driver* **2** ⓘ ⒷⒶ (*BrE*) (*NAmE* **car**) an open railway vehicle for carrying goods or animals: *a cattle truck* **3** ⓘ ⒷⒶ a vehicle that is open at the back, used for carrying goods, soldiers, animals, etc.: *a delivery/farm truck* ⊃ see also BREAKDOWN TRUCK, DUMP TRUCK, DUMPER TRUCK, FORKLIFT TRUCK, GARBAGE TRUCK, MONSTER TRUCK, PICKUP TRUCK at PICKUP *noun*, SALT TRUCK, TOW TRUCK **4** a vehicle for carrying things, that is pulled or pushed by hand

ⓘⒹⓜ **have/want no truck with sb/sth** (*formal*) to refuse to deal with sb; to refuse to accept or consider sth: *We in this party will have no truck with illegal organizations.*

■ *verb* ~ **sth (+ adv./prep.)** (*especially NAmE*) to take sth somewhere by truck ▶ **truck-ing** *noun* [U]: *trucking companies*

**truck-er** /ˈtrʌkə(r)/ *noun* (*especially NAmE*) a person whose job is driving a truck

**'truck farm** (*NAmE*) (*BrE* **market 'garden**) *noun* a type of farm where vegetables and fruit are grown for sale ▶ **'truck farmer** *noun* **'truck farming** *noun* [U]

**truck-load** /ˈtrʌkləʊd/ *noun* ~ **(of sb/sth)** the amount of sb/sth that fills a truck (often used to express the fact that an amount is large)

**'truck stop** *noun* (*NAmE*) a place at the side of a main road where truck drivers can stop for a time and can rest, get sth to eat, etc. ⊃ compare TRANSPORT CAFE

**trucu-lent** /ˈtrʌkjələnt/ *adj.* (*formal, disapproving*) tending to argue or become angry; slightly aggressive ▶ **trucu-lence** /-ləns/ *noun* [U] **trucu-lent-ly** *adv.*

**trudge** /trʌdʒ/ *verb, noun*
■ *verb* [I] to walk slowly or with heavy steps, because you are tired or carrying sth heavy: + **noun** *He trudged the last two miles to the town.* ◇ + **adv./prep.** *The men trudged up the hill, laden with supplies.*
■ *noun* [sing.] a long walk that makes you tired

# true

**true** /truː/ adj., adv., noun

**WORD FAMILY**
true adj. (≠ untrue)
truth noun
truthful adj. (≠ untruthful)
truthfully adv.
truly adv.

■ **adj. (truer, tru·est)**
- **CORRECT 1** connected with facts rather than things that have been invented or guessed: *Indicate whether the following statements are true or false.* ◊ *All the rumours turned out to be true.* ◊ *be ~ (that) … Is it true she's leaving?* ◊ *That's not strictly (= completely) true.* ◊ *The novel is based on a true story.* ◊ *~ for sb/sth Unfortunately, these findings do not hold true (= are not valid) for women and children.* ◊ *~ of sb/sth The music is dull and uninspiring, and the same is true of the acting.* **OPP untrue**
- **REAL 2** real or exact, especially when this is different from how sth seems: *the true face of war (= what it is really like rather than what people think it is like)* ◊ *This project demonstrates the true value of teamwork.* ◊ *I did not realize the true nature of their relationship.* **3** [usually before noun] having the qualities or characteristics of the thing mentioned: *It was true love between them.* ◊ *He's a true gentleman.* ◊ *The painting is a masterpiece in the truest sense of the word.*
- **ADMITTING FACT 4** used to admit that a particular fact or statement is correct, although you think that sth else is more important: *~ (that) … It's true that he could do the job, but would he fit in with the rest of the team?* ◊ *'We could get it cheaper.' 'True, but would it be as good?'* ➔ **LANGUAGE BANK at NEVERTHELESS**
- **LOYAL 5** showing respect and support for a particular person or belief in a way that does not change, even in different situations: *a true friend* ◊ *~ to sb/sth She has always been true to herself (= done what she thought was good, right, etc.).* ◊ *He was true to his word (= did what he promised to do).*
- **ACCURATE 6** *~ (to sth)* being an accurate version or copy of sth: *The movie is not true to the book.* **7** [not usually before noun] (*old-fashioned or literary*) straight and accurate: *His aim was true (= he hit the target).*

**IDM** **come ˈtrue** (of a hope, wish, etc.) to become reality: *Winning the medal was like a dream come true.* **too good to be ˈtrue** used to say that you cannot believe that sth is as good as it seems: *'I'm afraid you were quoted the wrong price.' 'I thought it was too good to be true.'* **your true ˈcolours** (*often disapproving*) your real character, rather than the one that you usually allow other people to see **true to ˈform** used to say that sb is behaving in the way that you expect them to behave, especially when this is annoying **true to ˈlife** (of a book, film, etc.) seeming real rather than invented ➔ more at **RING**² v., **TRIED** adj.

■ **adv.** (*old-fashioned or literary*)
- **STRAIGHT 1** in a direct line: *The arrow flew straight and true to the target.*
- **CORRECTLY 2** *speak ~* to tell the truth: *He had spoken truer than he knew.*

■ **noun**

**IDM** **out of ˈtrue** if an object is *out of true*, it is not straight or in the correct position

**true-ˈblue** adj. **1** (*BrE*) strongly supporting the British Conservative Party: *true-blue Tory voters* **2** (*especially NAmE*) being a strong supporter of a particular person, group, principle, etc.; being a typical example of sth: *a true-blue Californian*

**ˌtrue ˈcrime** noun [U] a genre of book, film, etc. that examines or tells the story of a real crime

**true-ˈlife** adj. [only before noun] a *true-life* story is one that actually happened rather than one that has been invented

**ˌtrue ˈnorth** noun [U] north according to the earth's AXIS (= the imaginary line through the earth's centre from north to south) ➔ compare **MAGNETIC NORTH**

**truf·fle** /ˈtrʌfl/ noun **1** an expensive type of FUNGUS that grows underground, used in cooking **2** a soft round sweet made of chocolate

---

▼ **SYNONYMS**

**true**
right • correct

These words all describe sth that cannot be doubted as fact and includes no mistakes.

**true** connected with facts rather than things that have been invented or guessed: *Are the following statements true or false?* ◊ *Is it true (that) she's leaving?*

**right** that is true and cannot be doubted as a fact: *I got about half the answers right.* ◊ *What's the right time?*

**correct** right according to the facts and without any mistakes: *Only one of the answers is correct.* ◊ *Check that all the details are correct.*

**RIGHT OR CORRECT?**
- **Correct** is more formal than **right** and is more likely to be used in official or formal instructions or documents.

**PATTERNS**
- right/correct **about** sb/sth
- the true/right/correct **answer**
- the right/correct **time**

---

**tru·ism** /ˈtruːɪzəm/ noun a statement that is clearly true and does not therefore add anything interesting or important to a discussion

**truly** /ˈtruːli/ adv. **1** used to emphasize that a particular statement, feeling, etc. is sincere or real: *She truly believes that none of this is her fault.* **2** used to emphasize a particular quality: *The results are truly amazing.* **3** used to emphasize that a particular description is accurate or correct: *a truly democratic system of government* ◊ (*informal*) *Well, really and truly, things were better than expected.*

**IDM** **yours ˈtruly 1 Yours Truly** (*NAmE, formal*) used at the end of a formal letter before you sign your name **2** (*informal, often humorous*) I/me: *Steve came first, Robin second, and yours truly came last.* ➔ more at **WELL** adv.

**trump** /trʌmp/ noun, verb

■ **noun 1** (also **ˈtrump card**) [C] (in some card games) a card that belongs to the SUIT (= one of the four sets in a PACK of cards) that has been chosen for a particular game to have a higher value than the other three suits: *I played a trump and won the trick.* **2 trumps** [U + sing./pl. v.] (in some card games) the SUIT that has been chosen for a particular game to have a higher value than the other three suits: *What's trumps?* ◊ *Clubs are trumps.* ➔ **WORDFINDER NOTE at CARD**

**IDM** **ˌcome up/ˌturn up ˈtrumps** to do what is necessary to make a particular situation successful, especially when this is sudden or unexpected: *I didn't honestly think he'd pass the exam but he came up trumps on the day.*

■ **verb 1** *~ sth (with sth)* (in some card games) to play a trump card that beats sb else's card **2** *~ sth/sb* to beat sth that sb says or does by saying or doing sth even better

**PHRV** **ˌtrump sth↔ˈup** to make up a false story about sb/sth, especially accusing them of doing sth wrong: *He accused his opponent of trumping up the charge for political reasons.*

**ˈtrump card** noun **1** = **TRUMP 2** something that gives you an advantage over other people, especially when they do not know what it is and you are able to use it to surprise them

**ˌtrumped-ˈup** adj. (of a story about sb/sth) falsely accusing them of doing sth wrong: *She was arrested on a trumped-up charge.*

**trum·pet** /ˈtrʌmpɪt/ noun, verb

■ **noun 1** a BRASS musical instrument made of a curved metal tube that you blow into, with three VALVES for changing the note **2** a thing like a trumpet in shape, especially the open flower of a DAFFODIL ➔ **VISUAL VOCAB page V7** **IDM** see **BLOW** v.

■ **verb 1** [T] to talk or write about sth publicly in a proud or enthusiastic way: ~ **sth** *to trumpet somebody's achievements* ◊ ~ **sth as sth** *Their marriage was trumpeted as the wedding of the year.* **2** [I] (especially of an elephant) to make a loud noise

**trum·pet·er** /ˈtrʌmpɪtə(r)/ *noun* a person who plays the trumpet

**trun·cate** /trʌŋˈkeɪt; *NAmE* ˈtrʌŋkeɪt/ *verb* [usually passive] ~ **sth** (*formal*) to make sth shorter, especially by cutting off the top or end: *My article was published in truncated form.* ▸ **trun·ca·tion** /trʌŋˈkeɪʃn/ *noun* [U, C]

**trun·cheon** /ˈtrʌntʃən/ *noun* (*especially BrE*) = BATON (1)

**trun·dle** /ˈtrʌndl/ *verb* **1** [I, T] ~ **(sth) + adv./prep.** to move or roll somewhere slowly and noisily; to move sth with wheels slowly and noisily, especially sth heavy: *A train trundled across the bridge.* **2** [I] + **adv./prep.** (of a person) to walk slowly with heavy steps

**PHR V** **trundle sth↔ˈout** (*especially BrE, disapproving*) to mention or do sth that you have often mentioned or done before: *A long list of reasons was trundled out to justify their demands.*

**trunks**

trunk of a tree    elephant's trunk    swimming trunks

**trunk** /trʌŋk/ *noun* **1** [C] the thick main STEM of a tree, that the branches grow from ⇨ VISUAL VOCAB page V6 **2** (*NAmE*) (*BrE* **boot**) [C] the space at the back of a car that you put bags, cases, etc. in **3** [C] the long nose of an elephant ⇨ VISUAL VOCAB page V2 **4** **trunks** [pl.] = SWIMMING TRUNKS **5** [C] a large, strong box with a LID (= cover), used for storing or transporting clothes, books, etc. **6** [C, usually sing.] the main part of the human body apart from the head, arms and legs ⇨ see also TORSO

**ˈtrunk road** *noun* (*BrE*) an important main road

**truss** /trʌs/ *noun, verb*
■ *noun* **1** a special belt with a thick piece of material, worn by sb suffering from a HERNIA in order to support the muscles **2** a frame made of pieces of wood or metal used to support a roof, bridge, etc.
■ *verb* **1** ~ **sb/sth (up)** to tie up sb's arms and legs so that they cannot move **2** ~ **sth** to tie the legs and wings of a chicken, etc. before it is cooked

**trust** 🅞 🅱🟰 🅢 /trʌst/ *noun, verb*
■ *noun* **1** 🅱🟰 [U] ~ **(in sb/sth)** the belief that sb/sth is good, sincere, honest, etc. and will not try to harm or trick you: *Our partnership is based on trust.* ◊ *It has taken years to earn their trust.* ◊ ~ **in sb/sth** *Her trust in him was unfounded.* ◊ *If you put your trust in me, I will not let you down.* ◊ *She will not betray your trust* (= do sth that you have asked her not to do). ◊ *He was appointed to a position of trust* (= a job involving a lot of responsibility, because people trust him). ◊ *This is a serious breach of trust.* **2** 🅱🟰 [U] ~ **(in sth)** the belief that sth is true or correct or that you can rely on it: *We place so much trust in computers that it gets a little scary.* ◊ *Public trust in science is harmed by inaccurate journalism.* **3** [C, U] (*law*) an arrangement by which an organization or a group of people has legal control of money or property that has been given to sb, usually until that person reaches a particular age; an amount of money or property that is controlled in this way: *He set up a trust for his children.* ◊ *The money will be held in trust until she is 18.* ◊ *Our fees depend on the value of the trust.* ⇨ see also BLIND TRUST, UNIT TRUST **4** [C] (*law*) an organization or a group of people that invests money that is given or lent to it and uses the profits to help a charity: *a charitable trust* **5** [C] (*especially NAmE, business*) a group of companies that work together illegally to reduce competition, control prices, etc: *anti-trust laws*
**IDM** **in sb's ˈtrust** | **in the trust of sb** being taken care of by sb: *The family pet was left in the trust of a neighbour.* **take sth on ˈtrust** to believe what sb says even though you do not have any proof or evidence to show that it is true

■ *verb* **1** 🅱🟰 to have confidence in sb; to believe that sb is good, sincere, honest, etc: ~ **sb** *She trusts Alan implicitly.* ◊ *He has shown that he can't be trusted.* ◊ *a trusted adviser/friend* ◊ ~ **sb to do sth** *You can trust me not to tell anyone.* **2** 🅱🟰 to believe that sth is true or correct or that you can rely on it: ~ **sth** *He trusted her judgement.* ◊ ~ **what…** *Don't trust what the newspapers say.* **3** ~ **(that)…** (*formal*) to hope and expect that sth is true: *I trust (that) you have no objections to our proposals?*
**IDM** **not trust sb an ˈinch** to not trust sb at all **trust ˈyou, ˈhim, ˈher, etc. (to do sth)** (*informal*) used when sb does or says sth that you think is typical of them: *Trust John to forget Sue's birthday!* ⇨ more at TRIED *adj.*
**PHR V** **ˈtrust in sb/sth** (*formal*) to have confidence in sb/sth; to believe that sb/sth is good and can be relied on: *She needs to trust more in her own abilities.* **ˈtrust to sth** [no passive] to put your confidence in sth such as luck, chance, etc. because there is nothing else to help you: *I stumbled along in the dark, trusting to luck to find the right door.* **ˈtrust sb with sth/sb** to give sth/sb to a person to take care of because you believe they would be very careful with it/them: *I'd trust her with my life.*

▼ **SYNONYMS**

**trust**

depend on sb/sth • rely on sb/sth • count on sb/sth • believe in sb

These words all mean to believe that sb/sth will do what you hope or expect of them or that what they tell you is correct or true.

**trust** to believe that sb is good, honest, sincere, etc. and that they will do what you expect of them or do the right thing; to believe that sth is true or correct: *You can trust me not to tell anyone.* ◊ *Don't trust what you read on the internet!*

**depend on/upon sb/sth** (often used with *can/cannot/could/could not*) to trust sb/sth to do what you expect or want, to do the right thing, or to be true or correct: *He was the sort of person you could depend on.* ◊ *Can you depend on her version of what happened?*

**rely on/upon sb/sth** (used especially with *can/cannot/could/could not* and *should/should not*) to trust sb/sth to do what you expect or want, or to be honest, correct or good enough: *Can I rely on you to keep this secret?* ◊ *You can't rely on any figures you get from them.*

**TRUST, DEPEND OR RELY ON/UPON SB/STH?**
You can **trust** a person but not a thing or system. You can **trust** sb's *judgement* or *advice*, but not their support. You can **depend on** sb's *support*, but not their judgement or advice. **Rely on/upon sb/sth** is used especially with *you can/could* or *you should* to give advice or a promise: *I don't really rely on his judgement.* ◊ *You can't really rely on his judgement.*

**count on sb/sth** (often used with *can/cannot/could/could not*) to be sure that sb will do what you need them to do, or that sth will happen as you want it to happen: *I'm counting on you to help me.* ◊ *We can't count on the good weather lasting.*

**believe in sb** to feel that you can trust sb and/or that they will be successful: *They need a leader they can believe in.*

PATTERNS
- to trust/depend on/rely on/count on sb/sth **to do sth**
- to trust/believe **in** sb/sth
- to trust/rely on **sb's advice/judgement**
- to depend on/rely on/count on **sb's support**
- to **completely** trust/depend on/rely on/believe in sb/sth

🅞 Oxford Phrasal Academic Lexicon (OPAL) written and spoken word lists    |    🅦 OPAL written word list    |    🅢 OPAL spoken word list

# trustee

**trust·ee** ?+ C1 /trʌˈstiː/ noun **1** ?+ C1 a person or an organization that has control of money or property that has been put into a TRUST for sb: *The bank will act as trustees for the estate until the child is 18.* **2** ?+ C1 a member of a group of people that controls the financial affairs and decides the policy of a charity or other organization: *the board of trustees*

**trustee·ship** /trʌˈstiːʃɪp/ noun (U, C] **1** the job of being a trustee **2** the responsibility for governing a particular region, given to a country by the United Nations Organization; a region that is governed by another country in this way

**'trust fund** noun money that is controlled for sb by an organization or a group of people

**trust·ing** /ˈtrʌstɪŋ/ adj. tending to believe that other people are good, honest, etc.: *If you're too trusting, other people will take advantage of you.* ▶ **trust·ing·ly** adv.

**trust·worthy** /ˈtrʌstwɜːði; NAmE -wɜːrði/ adj. that you can rely on to be good, honest, sincere, etc. SYN **reliable** ▶ **trust·worthi·ness** noun [U]

**trusty** /ˈtrʌsti/ adj., noun
- adj. [only before noun] (*old use or humorous*) that you have had a long time and have always been able to rely on SYN **reliable**: *a trusty friend* ◊ *She spent years touring Europe with her trusty old camera.*
- noun (pl. **-ies**) (informal) a prisoner who is given special advantages because of good behaviour

**truth** ? B1 /truːθ/ noun (pl. **truths** /truːðz/) **1** ? B1 the **truth** [sing.] the true facts about sth, rather than the things that have been invented or guessed: *Do you think she's telling the truth?* ◊ *We are determined to get at (= discover) the truth.* ◊ **the ~ is (that) ...** *The truth is that there are no easy answers.* ◊ **The truth of the matter is** *we can't afford to keep all the staff on.* ◊ **the ~ about sth** *I don't think you are telling me the whole truth about what happened.* **2** ? B1 [U] the quality or state of being based on fact: *There is no truth in the rumours.* ◊ *There is not a grain of truth in what she says.* OPP **falsity** ⇒ see also POST-TRUTH **3** [C] a fact that is believed by most people to be true: *universal truths* ◊ *She was forced to face up to a few unwelcome truths about her family.* ⇒ compare UNTRUTH ⇒ see also HALF-TRUTH, HOME TRUTH
IDM **if (the) truth be ˈknown/ˈtold** used to tell sb the true facts about a situation, especially when these are not known by other people **in ˈtruth** (formal) used to emphasize the true facts about a situation: *She laughed and chatted but was, in truth, not having much fun.* **nothing could be further from the ˈtruth** used to say that a fact or comment is completely false **to tell (you) the ˈtruth** (informal) used when admitting sth: *To tell you the truth, I'll be glad to get home.* **truth is stranger than ˈfiction** (saying) used to say that things that actually happen are often more surprising than stories that are invented **(the) ˌtruth will ˈout** (saying) used to say that people will find out the true facts about a situation even if you try to keep them secret ⇒ more at BEND v., ECONOMICAL, MOMENT

**truth·ful** /ˈtruːθfl/ adj. **1** ~ (about sth) (of a person) saying only what is true SYN **honest**: *They were less than truthful about their part in the crime.* ◊ *Are you being completely truthful with me?* **2** (of a statement) giving the true facts about sth: *a truthful answer* OPP **untruthful** ▶ **truth·ful·ly** /-fəli/ adv.: *She answered all their questions truthfully.* **truth·ful·ness** noun [U]

**try** ? A1 S /traɪ/ verb, noun
- verb (**tries**, **try·ing**, **tried**, **tried**) **1** ? A1 [I, T] to make an attempt or effort to do or get sth: *I don't know if I can come but I'll try.* ◊ **~ to do sth** *What are you trying to do?* ◊ *I tried hard not to laugh.* ◊ *I was just trying to help!* ◊ **~ your best/hardest (to do sth)** *She tried her best to solve the problem.* ◊ **~ doing sth** *I tried calling them but there was no answer.* ◊ *Please try again later.* HELP In spoken English **try and** can be used with another verb, instead of **try to** and the infinitive: *I'll try and get you a new one tomorrow.* ◊ *Try and finish quickly.* In this structure, only the form **try** can be used, not **tries**, **trying** or **tried**. **2** ? A1 [T] to use, do or test sth in order to see if it is good, suitable, etc.: **~ sth** *Have you tried this new coffee? It's very good.* ◊ *'Would you like to try some raw fish?' 'Why not? I'll try anything once!'* ◊ *I'd like to try something new.* ◊ *Have you ever tried windsurfing?* ◊ **Try these shoes for size**—*they should fit you.* ◊ *She tried the door, but it was locked.* ◊ **~ doing sth** *John isn't here. Try phoning his mobile.* **3** [T] (often passive) to examine evidence in court and decide whether sb is innocent or guilty: **~ sb (for sth)** *He was tried for murder.* ◊ **~ sth** *The case was tried before a jury.*
IDM **not for want/lack of ˈtrying** used to say that although sb has not succeeded in sth, they have tried very hard: *They haven't won a game yet, but it isn't for want of trying.* **try your ˈhand (at sth)** to do sth such as an activity or a sport for the first time **try it ˈon (with sb)** (BrE, informal, disapproving) **1** to behave badly towards sb or try to get sth from them, even though you know this will make them angry: *Children often try it on with new teachers.* **2** to try to start a sexual relationship with sb **try your ˈluck (at sth)** to do sth that involves risk or luck, hoping to succeed: *My grandparents emigrated to Canada to try their luck there.* **try sb's ˈpatience** to make sb feel impatient ⇒ more at DAMNEDEST, LEVEL adj., THING
PHRV **ˈtry for sth** to make an attempt to get or win sth **ˌtry sth↔ˈon** to put on a piece of clothing to see if it fits and how it looks: *Try the shoes on before you buy them.* **ˌtry ˈout for sth** (especially NAmE) to compete for a position or place in sth, or to be a member of a team: *She's trying out for the school play.* ⇒ related noun TRYOUT **ˌtry sb/sth↔ˈout (on sb)** to test or use sb/sth in order to see how good or effective they are: *They're trying out a new presenter for the show.* ⇒ related noun TRYOUT
- noun (pl. **tries**) **1** ? B2 [usually sing.] an act of trying to do sth SYN **attempt**: *I doubt they'll be able to help but it's worth a try (= worth asking them).* ◊ **~ (at sth/at doing sth)** *Why don't you have a try at convincing him?* ◊ (NAmE) *The US negotiators decided to make another try at reaching a settlement.* ◊ (informal) *'What's that behind you?' 'Nice try (= at making me turn round), but you'll have to do better than that!'* **2** ? B2 [usually sing.] an act of trying sth new or different to see if it is good, suitable, etc.: *I don't think I'll be any good at tennis, but I'll give it a try.* **3** (in rugby) an act of scoring points by touching the ground behind your opponents' GOAL LINE with the ball: *to score a try*

**try·ing** /ˈtraɪɪŋ/ adj. annoying or difficult to deal with: *These are trying times for all of us.*

**try·out** /ˈtraɪaʊt/ noun **1** an act of testing how good or effective sb/sth is before deciding whether to use them/it in the future **2** (NAmE) (BrE **trial**) a competition or series of tests to find the best players for a sports team or an important event

**tryst** /trɪst/ noun (literary or humorous) a secret romantic meeting between two people

**tsar** (also **tzar**, **czar**) /zɑː(r)/ noun **1** the EMPEROR of Russia in the past: *Tsar Nicholas II* **2** (in compounds) (informal) an official whose job is to advise the government on policy in a particular area: (BrE) *a drugs tsar* ◊ (NAmE) *a drug tsar*

**tsar·ina** (also **tzar·ina**, **czar·ina**) /zɑːˈriːnə/ noun the EMPRESS of Russia in the past

**tsar·ism** (also **tzar·ism**, **czar·ism**) /ˈzɑːrɪzəm/ noun [U] the Russian system of government by a tsar, which existed before 1917 ▶ **tsar·ist** (also **tzar·ist**, **czar·ist**) noun, adj.

**ˈtsetse fly** /ˈtsetsi flaɪ/ noun an African fly that bites humans and animals and drinks their blood and can spread a disease called SLEEPING SICKNESS

**T-shirt** ? A1 (also **tee shirt**) noun an informal shirt, usually with short SLEEVES (= arms) no COLLAR or buttons, or just a few buttons at the top: *He was wearing a faded pair of blue jeans and an old T-shirt.*

**tsk tsk** exclamation used in writing to represent the sound you make with your tongue when you think that something is bad: *So you were out drinking again last night were you? Tsk tsk!*

**tsotsi** /ˈtsɒtsi; *NAmE* ˈtsɑːt-/ *SAfrE* [ˈtsɔtsi] *noun* (*SAfrE*) a young black criminal

**Tsotsi·taal** /ˈtsɒtsitɑːl; *NAmE* ˈtsɑːt-/ *SAfrE* [ˈtsɔtsitɑːl] *noun* [U] (*SAfrE*) a simple form of language that includes words from Afrikaans and African languages, used especially between young black people in cities or TOWNSHIPS

**tsp** *abbr.* (*pl.* **tsp** or **tsps**) TEASPOON: *1 tsp chilli powder*

**T-square** *noun* a plastic or metal instrument in the shape of a T for drawing or measuring RIGHT ANGLES (= of 90°)

**tsu·nami** /tsuːˈnɑːmi/ *noun* (*from Japanese*) an extremely large wave in the sea caused, for example, by an earthquake: *A tsunami early warning system was set up in Hawaii.* ⇒ compare TIDAL WAVE ⇒ **WORDFINDER NOTE** at DISASTER

**TTS** /ˌtiː tiː ˈes; *NAmE* ˌtiː ˈes/ *abbr.* (*computing*) = TEXT-TO-SPEECH: *a TTS package*

**TTYL** (*also* **ttyl**) /ˌtiː tiː waɪ ˈel/ *abbr.* (*informal*) (used when ending a message to sb on SOCIAL MEDIA, etc.) talk to you later: *OK, I've gotta fly. Bye. TTYL.*

**tub** /tʌb/ *noun* **1** a large round container without a LID (= cover), used for washing clothes in, growing plants in, etc: *There were tubs of flowers on the balcony.* **2** a small, wide plastic or paper container with a LID (= cover), used for food, etc: *a tub of margarine* **3** (*especially NAmE, informal*) = BATHTUB: *They found her lying in the tub.* ⇒ see also HOT TUB

**tuba** /ˈtjuːbə; *NAmE* ˈtuː-/ *noun* a large BRASS musical instrument that you play by blowing, and that produces low notes

**tubal** /ˈtjuːbl; *NAmE* ˈtuː-/ *adj.* (*medical*) connected with the FALLOPIAN TUBES: *a tubal pregnancy*

**tubby** /ˈtʌbi/ *adj.* (*informal*) (of a person) short and slightly fat SYN stout

**tube** /tjuːb; *NAmE* tuːb/ *noun*
- PIPE **1** [C] a long, hollow pipe made of metal, plastic, rubber, etc., through which liquids or gases move from one place to another: *He had to be fed through a feeding tube for several months.* ⇒ see also CATHODE RAY TUBE, TEST TUBE **2** [C] a hollow object in the shape of a pipe or tube: *the cardboard tube from the centre of a toilet roll* ⇒ see also INNER TUBE
- CONTAINER **3** [C] a long, narrow container made of soft metal or plastic, with a LID (= cover), used for holding thick liquids that can be forced out of it by pressing: *~(of sth) a tube of toothpaste* **4** (*AustralE, informal*) a can of beer: *a tube of lager*
- PART OF BODY **5** [C] a part inside the body that is like a tube in shape and through which air, liquid, etc. passes: *bronchial tubes* ⇒ see also FALLOPIAN TUBE
- UNDERGROUND RAILWAY **6** (*also* **The Tube**™) [sing.] (*BrE*) the underground railway system in London: *on the ~ I often travel on the tube* ◇ *by ~ We came by tube.* ◇ *a tube station/train* ⇒ note at UNDERGROUND
- TELEVISION **7 the tube** [sing.] (*NAmE, informal*) the television
- IN EAR **8** (*NAmE*) (*BrE* **grom·met**) [C] a small tube placed in a child's ear in order to DRAIN liquid from it when there is an infection

IDM **go down the 'tube/'tubes** (*informal*) (of a plan, company, situation, etc.) to fail: *The education system is going down the tubes.*

**'tube light** *noun* (*IndE*) a FLUORESCENT light in the shape of a tube

**tuber** /ˈtjuːbə(r); *NAmE* ˈtuː-/ *noun* the short, thick, round part of an underground STEM or root of some plants, such as potatoes, which stores food and from which new plants grow ▸ **tu·ber·ous** *adj.*

**tu·ber·cle** /ˈtjuːbəkl; *NAmE* ˈtuːbərkl/ *noun* **1** (*anatomy, biology*) a small round part, especially on a bone or on the surface of an animal or plant **2** (*medical*) a small SWOLLEN (= larger than normal) area in the lung caused by TUBERCULOSIS

**tu·ber·cu·losis** /tjuːˌbɜːkjuˈləʊsɪs; *NAmE* tuːˌbɜːrkjəˈl-/ *noun* [U] (*abbr.* **TB**) a serious disease, caused by bacteria, in which SWELLINGS appear on the lungs and other parts of the body ▸ **tu·ber·cu·lar** /tjuːˈbɜːkjələ(r); *NAmE* tuːˈbɜːrk-/ *adj.*: *a tubercular infection*

**'tube top** (*NAmE*) (*BrE* **'boob tube**) *noun* a piece of women's clothing that is made of cloth that stretches and covers the chest

**'tube well** *noun* a pipe with holes in the sides near the end, that is put into the ground and used with a PUMP operated by hand to bring water up from under the ground

**tub·ing** /ˈtjuːbɪŋ; *NAmE* ˈtuː-/ *noun* [U] metal, plastic, etc. in the shape of a tube: *a length of copper tubing*

**'tub-thumping** *noun* [U] (*BrE, disapproving*) the act of giving your opinions about sth in a loud and aggressive way ▸ **'tub-thumping** *adj.* [only before noun]

**tu·bu·lar** /ˈtjuːbjələ(r); *NAmE* ˈtuː-/ *adj.* **1** made of tubes or of parts that are like tubes in shape: *a tubular metal chair* **2** like a tube in shape

**tubular 'bells** *noun* [pl.] a musical instrument that sounds like a set of bells, consisting of a row of hanging metal tubes that are hit with a stick

**TUC** /ˌtiː juː ˈsiː/ *abbr.* Trades Union Congress (an organization to which many British trade unions belong)

**tuck** /tʌk/ *verb, noun*
■ *verb* **1** ~ **sth + adv./prep.** to push, fold or turn the ends or edges of clothes, paper, etc. so that they are held in place or look neat: *She tucked up her skirt and waded into the river.* ◇ *The sheets should be tucked in neatly* (= around the bed). ◇ *Tuck the flap of the envelope in.* **2** ~ **sth + adv./prep.** to put sth into a small space, especially to hide it or keep it safe or comfortable: *She tucked her hair (up) under her cap.* ◇ *He sat with his legs tucked up under him.* ◇ *The letter had been tucked under a pile of papers.* **3** ~ **sth + adv./prep.** to cover sb with sth so that they are warm and comfortable: *She tucked a blanket around his legs.*
PHRV **tuck sth⇿a'way 1** be tucked away to be located in a quiet place, where not many people go: *The shop is tucked away down a backstreet.* **2** to hide sth somewhere or keep it in a safe place: *She kept his letters tucked away in a drawer.* ◇ *They have thousands of pounds tucked away in a savings account.* **3** (*BrE, informal*) to eat a lot of food **tuck sb 'in/'up** to make sb feel comfortable in bed by pulling the covers up around them: *I tucked the children in and said goodnight.* **tuck 'in | tuck 'into sth** (*BrE, informal*) to eat a lot of food, especially when it is done quickly and with enthusiasm: *Come on, tuck in everyone!* ◇ *He was tucking into a huge plateful of pasta.*
■ *noun* **1** [C] a fold that is SEWN into a piece of clothing or cloth, either for decoration or to change the shape of it **2** [C] (*informal*) a medical operation in which skin and/or fat is removed to make sb look younger or thinner **3** [U] (*BrE, old-fashioned, informal*) food, especially sweets, etc. eaten by children at school

**tuck·er** /ˈtʌkə(r)/ *noun* [U] (*AustralE, NZE, informal*) food

**Tudor** /ˈtjuːdə(r); *NAmE* ˈtuː-/ *adj.* connected with the time when kings and queens from the Tudor family ruled England (1485–1603): *Tudor architecture*

**Tues·day** /ˈtjuːzdeɪ, -di; *NAmE* ˈtuːz-/ *noun* [C, U] (*abbr.* **Tue., Tues.**) the day of the week after Monday and before Wednesday HELP To see how **Tuesday** is used, look at the examples at **Monday**. ORIGIN Originally translated from the Latin for 'day of Mars' *dies Marti* and named after the Germanic god *Tiw*.

**tuft** /tʌft/ *noun* ~ **(of sth)** a number of pieces of hair, grass, etc. growing or held closely together at the base

**tuft·ed** /ˈtʌftɪd/ *adj.* [usually before noun] having a tuft or tufts; growing in tufts: *a tufted carpet* ◇ *a tufted duck*

**tug** /tʌɡ/ *verb, noun*
■ *verb* (-gg-) **1** [I, T] to pull sth hard, often several times: ~ (at/on sth) *She tugged at his sleeve to get his attention.* ◊ ~ sth *The baby was tugging her hair.* ◊ ~ sth + adj. *He tugged the door open.* **2** [T] ~ sth/sb + adv./prep. to pull sth/sb hard in a particular direction: *He tugged the hat down over his head.* ⇒ SYNONYMS at PULL IDM see FORELOCK
■ *noun* **1** (*also* **tug·boat** /'tʌɡbəʊt/) a small powerful boat for pulling ships, especially into a HARBOUR or up a river **2** a sudden, hard pull: *I felt a tug at my sleeve.* ◊ *She gave her sister's hair a sharp tug.* **3** [usually sing.] a sudden, strong emotional feeling: *a tug of attraction*

**'tug of 'war** *noun* [sing., U] **1** a sporting event in which two teams pull at opposite ends of a rope until one team drags the other over a line on the ground **2** a situation in which two people or groups try very hard to get or keep the same thing

**tu·ition** /tju'ɪʃn/; *NAmE* tu-/ *noun* [U] **1** ~ (in sth) (*formal*) the act of teaching sth, especially to one person or to people in small groups: *She received private tuition in French.* **2** (*also* **tu'ition fees** [pl.]) the money that you pay to be taught, especially in a college or university: *He won't be able to finish his education unless someone pays his tuition.*

**tuk-tuk** (*also* **tuk tuk**) /'tʊk tʊk/ *noun* (in some countries) a vehicle with three wheels and an engine, typically with open sides, that is used as a taxi

**tu·lip** /'tju:lɪp/; *NAmE* 'tu:-/ *noun* a large, brightly coloured spring flower, like a cup in shape, on a tall STEM ⇒ VISUAL VOCAB page V7

**tulle** /tju:l/; *NAmE* tu:l/ *noun* [U] a type of soft, fine cloth made of silk, cotton or NYLON and full of very small holes, used especially for making VEILS and dresses

**tum** /tʌm/ *noun* (*BrE, informal*) a person's stomach or the area around the stomach

**tum·ble** /'tʌmbl/ *verb, noun*
■ *verb* **1** [I, T] ~ (sb/sth) + adv./prep. to fall downwards, often hitting the ground several times, but usually without serious injury; to make sb/sth fall in this way: *He slipped and tumbled down the stairs.* **2** [I] ~ (down) to fall suddenly and in a dramatic way: *The scaffolding came tumbling down.* ◊ (*figurative*) *World records tumbled at the last Olympics.* ⇒ see also TUMBLEDOWN **3** [I] to fall rapidly in value or amount: *The price of oil is still tumbling.* **4** [I] + adv./prep. to move or fall somewhere in a relaxed or noisy way, or with a lack of control: *A group of noisy children tumbled out of the bus.* ◊ *Thick golden curls tumbled down over her shoulders.* **5** [I] to perform ACROBATICS on the floor, especially SOMERSAULTS (= a jump in which you turn over completely in the air)
PHR V **'tumble to sth/sb** (*BrE, informal*) to suddenly understand sth or be aware of sth
■ *noun* **1** [C, usually sing.] a sudden fall: *The jockey took a nasty tumble at the third fence.* ◊ *Share prices took a sharp tumble following news of the merger.* ⇒ see also ROUGH AND TUMBLE **2** [sing.] ~ (of sth) an untidy group of things: *a tumble of blond curls*

**tumble·down** /'tʌmbldaʊn/ *adj.* [usually before noun] (of a building) old and in a poor condition so that it looks as if it is falling down SYN dilapidated

**'tumble 'dryer** (*also* **'tumble 'drier**) (*both BrE*) *noun* a machine that uses hot air to dry clothes after they have been washed

**tum·bler** /'tʌmblə(r)/ *noun* **1** a glass for drinking out of, with a flat bottom, straight sides and no handle or STEM **2** (*also* **tum·bler·ful** /'tʌmbləful/; *NAmE* -blərf-/) the amount held by a tumbler **3** (*old-fashioned*) an ACROBAT who performs SOMERSAULTS (= a jump in which you turn over completely in the air)

**tumble·weed** /'tʌmblwi:d/ *noun* [U] a plant that grows like a bush in the desert areas of North America and Australia. In the autumn, it breaks off just above the ground and is blown around like a ball by the wind.

**tu·mes·cent** /tju:'mesnt; *NAmE* tu:-/ *adj.* (*formal*) (especially of parts of the body) larger than normal, especially as a result of sexual excitement SYN swollen ▸ **tu·mes·cence** /-sns/ *noun* [U]

**tummy** /'tʌmi/ *noun* (*pl.* -ies) (*informal*) (used especially by children or when speaking to children) the stomach or the area around the stomach: *Mum, my tummy hurts.* ◊ *to have (a) tummy ache* ◊ *a tummy bug/upset* (= an illness when you feel sick or VOMIT)

**'tummy button** *noun* (*BrE, informal*) = NAVEL

**tu·mour** (*US* **tu·mor**) /'tju:mə(r); *NAmE* 'tu:-/ *noun* a mass of cells growing in or on a part of the body where they should not, usually causing medical problems: *a brain tumour* ◊ *a benign/malignant* (= harmless/harmful) *tumour*

**tu·mult** /'tju:mʌlt; *NAmE* 'tu:-/ *noun* [U, C, usually sing.] (*formal*) **1** a confused situation in which there is usually a lot of noise and excitement, often involving large numbers of people **2** a state in which your thoughts or feelings are confused

**tu·mul·tu·ous** /tju:'mʌltʃuəs; *NAmE* tu:-/ *adj.* [usually before noun] **1** very loud; involving strong feelings, especially feelings of approval: *tumultuous applause* ◊ *a tumultuous reception/welcome* **2** involving many difficulties and a lot of change and often violence SYN tempestuous: *the tumultuous years of the English Civil War*

**tun** /tʌn/ *noun* (*old-fashioned*) a large, round wooden container for beer, wine, etc. SYN barrel

**tuna** /'tju:nə; *NAmE* 'tu:-/ *noun* [C, U] (*pl.* **tuna** *or* **tunas**) (*also* **'tuna fish**) (*BrE also, less frequent* **tunny**) a large sea fish that is used for food: *fishing for tuna* ◊ *tuna steaks* ◊ *a tin/can of tuna in vegetable oil*

**tun·dra** /'tʌndrə/ *noun* [U] the large, flat Arctic regions of northern Europe, Asia and North America where no trees grow and where the soil below the surface of the ground is always frozen

**tune** /tju:n; *NAmE* tu:n/ *noun, verb*
■ *noun* a series of musical notes that are sung or played in a particular order to form a piece of music: *to hum/sing/whistle/play a tune* ◊ *I don't know the title but I recognize the tune.* ◊ *It was a catchy tune* (= easy to remember). ◊ **to the ~ of sth** *a football song sung to the tune of* (= using the tune of) *'When the saints go marching in'.* ⇒ see also SIGNATURE TUNE, THEME TUNE at THEME MUSIC
IDM **be in/out of 'tune** to be/not be singing or playing the correct musical notes to sound pleasant: *None of them could sing in tune.* ◊ *The piano is out of tune.* **be in/out of 'tune (with sb/sth)** to be/not be in agreement with sb/sth; to have/not have the same opinions, feelings, interests, etc. as sb/sth: *These proposals are perfectly in tune with our own thoughts on the subject.* ◊ *The President is out of tune with public opinion.* **to the tune of sth** (*informal*) used to emphasize how much money sth has cost: *The hotel has been refurbished to the tune of a million dollars.* ⇒ more at CALL *v.*, CHANGE *v.*, DANCE *v.*, MARCH *v.*, PAY *v.*, SING
■ *verb* **1** ~ sth to make changes to a musical instrument so that it plays at the correct PITCH: *to tune a guitar* **2** ~ sth to make changes to an engine so that it runs smoothly and as well as possible **3** [usually passive] to change the controls on a radio or television so that you can receive a particular programme or channel: **be tuned (in) (to sth)** *The radio was tuned (in) to the BBC World Service.* ◊ (*informal*) *Stay tuned for the news coming up next.* **4** ~ sth (to sth) to prepare or change sth so that it is suitable for a particular situation: *His speech was tuned to what the audience wanted to hear.*
PHR V **,tune 'in (to sth)** to listen to a radio programme or watch a television programme **,tune 'in to sb/sth** to become aware of other people's thoughts and feelings, etc. **,tune 'out | ,tune sb/sth↔'out** to stop listening to sth: *When she started talking about her job, he just tuned out.* **,tune 'up | ,tune sth↔'up** to make changes to a

musical instrument so that it plays at the correct PITCH: *The orchestra was tuning up as we entered the hall.*

**tuned 'in** *adj.* [not before noun] **~ (to sth)** aware of what is happening in a particular situation: *The resort is tuned in to the tastes of young and old alike.*

**tune·ful** /'tjuːnfl; *NAmE* 'tuːn-/ *adj.* having a pleasant tune or sound OPP **tuneless** ▶ **tune·ful·ly** /-fəli/ *adv.* **tune·ful·ness** *noun* [U]

**tune·less** /'tjuːnləs; *NAmE* 'tuːn-/ *adj.* not having a pleasant tune or sound OPP **tuneful** ▶ **tune·less·ly** *adv.*

**tuner** /'tjuːnə(r); *NAmE* 'tuː-/ *noun* **1** (especially in compounds) a person who TUNES musical instruments, especially pianos **2** the part of a radio, television, etc. that you move in order to change the signal and receive the radio or television station that you want **3** an electronic device that receives a radio signal and sends it to an AMPLIFIER so that it can be heard

**tung·sten** /'tʌŋstən/ *noun* [U] (*symb.* **W**) a chemical element. Tungsten is a very hard silver-grey metal, used especially in making steel and in FILAMENTS for LIGHT BULBS.

**tunic** /'tjuːnɪk; *NAmE* 'tuː-/ *noun* **1** a loose piece of clothing covering the body down to the knees, usually without arms, as worn in ancient Greece and Rome **2** a piece of women's clothing like a tunic, that reaches to the HIPS (= where the legs join the body) and is worn over trousers or a skirt **3** (*BrE*) a tightly fitting jacket worn as part of a uniform by police officers, soldiers, etc.

**'tuning fork** *noun* a small metal instrument with two long parts joined together at one end, that produces a particular musical note when you hit it and is used in TUNING musical instruments

**'tuning peg** *noun* = PEG (4) ⊃ picture at PEG

**tun·nel** 🔑 B2 /'tʌnl/ *noun, verb*
- *noun* **1** B2 a passage built underground, for example to allow a road or railway to go through a hill, under a river, etc: *a railway/railroad tunnel* ◊ *the Channel Tunnel* ⊃ see also WIND TUNNEL **2** an underground passage made by an animal or natural processes IDM see LIGHT *n.*
- *verb* [I, T] (-ll-, *NAmE also* -l-) to dig a tunnel under or through the ground: *The engineers had to tunnel through solid rock.* ◊ **~ your way + *adv./prep.*** *The rescuers tunnelled their way in to the trapped miners.*

**tunnel 'vision** *noun* [U] **1** (*medical*) a condition in which sb can only see things that are straight ahead of them **2** (*disapproving*) a lack of ability to see or understand all the aspects of a situation, an argument, etc. instead of just one part of it

**tunny** /'tʌni/ *noun* (*pl.* tunny) (*BrE*) = TUNA

**tup·pence** (*also* **two-pence**) /'tʌpəns/ *noun* [U] (*BrE, informal*) the sum of two pence
IDM **not care/give 'tuppence for sb/sth** (*BrE, informal*) to think that sb/sth is not important or that they have no value

**tup·penny** /'tʌpəni/ *adj.* [only before noun] (*BrE, informal*) = TWOPENNY

**Tup·per·ware™** /'tʌpəweə(r); *NAmE* -pərwer/ *noun* [U] plastic containers used mainly for storing food

**tur·ban** /'tɜːbən; *NAmE* 'tɜːrb-/ *noun* **turban** **1** a long piece of cloth wound tightly around the head, worn, for example, by Muslim or Sikh men **2** a woman's hat that looks like a turban ▶ **tur·baned** *adj.*: *turbaned Sikhs*

**tur·bid** /'tɜːbɪd; *NAmE* 'tɜːrb-/ *adj.* (*formal*) (of liquid) full of mud, dirt, etc. so that you cannot see through it SYN **muddy** ▶ **tur·bid·ity** /tɜː'bɪdəti; *NAmE* tɜːr'b-/ *noun* [U]

**tur·bine** /'tɜːbaɪn; *NAmE* 'tɜːrb-/ *noun* a machine or part of a machine that produces continuous turning power from a fast-moving flow of a liquid or gas, using a set of VANES attached to a

turban

wheel or ROTOR: *Gas turbines can be used to generate electricity.* ⊃ see also WIND TURBINE

**turbo-charged** /'tɜːbəʊtʃɑːdʒd; *NAmE* 'tɜːrboʊtʃɑːrdʒd/ *adj.* **1** (of an engine) fitted with a turbocharger **2** (*informal*) stronger, more powerful or more effective than usual: *turbocharged business growth* ▶ **turbo-charge** *verb* **~ sth**

**turbo-char·ger** /'tɜːbəʊtʃɑːdʒə(r); *NAmE* 'tɜːrboʊtʃɑːrdʒ-/ (*also* **turbo** *pl.* **-os**) *noun* a system driven by a turbine that gets its power from an engine's EXHAUST gases. It sends the mixture of petrol and air into the engine at high pressure, making it more powerful.

**turbo·jet** /'tɜːbəʊdʒet; *NAmE* 'tɜːrb-/ *noun* **1** a TURBINE engine that produces forward movement by forcing out a stream of hot air and gas behind it **2** a plane that gets its power from this type of engine

**turbo·prop** /'tɜːbəʊprɒp; *NAmE* 'tɜːrboʊprɑːp/ *noun* **1** a TURBINE engine that produces forward movement by turning a PROPELLER (= a set of BLADES that turn round and round) **2** a plane that gets its power from this type of engine

**tur·bot** /'tɜːbət; *NAmE* 'tɜːrb-/ *noun* [C, U] (*pl.* **tur·bot** or **tur·bots**) a large, flat European sea fish that is used for food

**tur·bu·lence** /'tɜːbjələns; *NAmE* 'tɜːrb-/ *noun* [U] **1** a situation in which there is a lot of sudden change, trouble, argument and sometimes violence SYN **upheaval** **2** a series of sudden and violent changes in the direction that air or water is moving in: *We experienced severe turbulence during the flight.*

**tur·bu·lent** /'tɜːbjələnt; *NAmE* 'tɜːrb-/ *adj.* [usually before noun] **1** in which there is a lot of sudden change, trouble, argument and sometimes violence: *a short and turbulent career in politics* ◊ *a turbulent part of the world* **2** (of air or water) changing direction suddenly and violently: *The aircraft is designed to withstand turbulent conditions.* ◊ *a turbulent sea/storm* (= caused by turbulent water/air) **3** (of people) noisy and/or difficult to control SYN **unruly**: *a turbulent crowd*

**turd** /tɜːd; *NAmE* tɜːrd/ *noun* (*offensive, slang*) **1** a piece of solid waste from the BOWELS: *dog turds* **2** an offensive word for an unpleasant person

**tur·een** /tjʊ'riːn; *NAmE* tə'r-/ *noun* a large, deep dish with a LID (= cover), used for serving vegetables or soup

**turf** /tɜːf; *NAmE* tɜːrf/ *noun, verb*
- *noun* (*pl.* **turfs** or **turves** /tɜːvz; *NAmE* tɜːrvz/) **1** [U, C] short grass and the surface layer of soil that is held together by its roots; a piece of this that has been cut from the ground and is used especially for making LAWNS (= the area of grass in a garden): *newly laid turf* ◊ (*especially BrE*) *the hallowed turf of Wimbledon, etc.* (= the grass used for playing a sport on) ⊃ see also SURF AND TURF, SURF 'N' TURF **2** [U, C] PEAT that is cut to be used as fuel; a piece of this **3** **the turf** [sing.] the sport of horse racing **4** [U] (*informal*) the place where sb lives and/or works, especially when they think of it as their own: *He feels more confident on home turf.*
- *verb* **~ sth** to cover an area of ground with turf
PHRV **turf sb 'out (of sth)** | **turf sb 'off (sth)** (*BrE, informal*) to make sb leave a place, an organization, etc. SYN **throw sb out**: *He was turfed out of the party.* ◊ *The boys were turfed off the bus.*

**'turf accountant** *noun* (*BrE, formal*) = BOOKMAKER

**'turf war** *noun* a violent situation between two groups of people who disagree about who should control a particular area, activity or business: *a vicious turf war between rival gangs of drug dealers*

**tur·gid** /'tɜːdʒɪd; *NAmE* 'tɜːrdʒ-/ *adj.* (*formal*) **1** (of language, writing, etc.) boring, complicated and difficult to understand **2** SWOLLEN; containing more water than usual: *the turgid waters of the Thames*

**tur·key** /'tɜːki; *NAmE* 'tɜːrki/ *noun* (*pl.* **-eys**) **1** [C] a large bird that is often kept for its meat, eaten especially at

# Turkish

Christmas in the UK and at Thanksgiving in the US ⇒ **VISUAL VOCAB** page V2 **2** [U] meat from a turkey: *roast turkey* **3** [C] (*NAmE, informal*) a failure: *His latest movie is a real turkey.* **4** [C] (*NAmE, informal*) a stupid person who is not useful to anyone ⇒ see also COLD TURKEY **IDM** see TALK v.

**Turk·ish** /ˈtɜːkɪʃ; *NAmE* ˈtɜːrk-/ *adj., noun*
- *adj.* from or connected with Turkey
- *noun* [U] the language of Turkey

**Turkish ˈbath** *noun* a type of bath in which you sit in a room full of hot STEAM, have a MASSAGE and then a cold shower or bath; a building where this treatment takes place

**Turkish ˈcoffee** *noun* [U, C] very strong, usually very sweet, black coffee, served with coffee GROUNDS in it

**Turkish deˈlight** *noun* [U, C] a sweet made from a substance like JELLY with a fruit taste and covered with fine white sugar

**tur·meric** /ˈtɜːmərɪk; *NAmE* ˈtɜːrm-/ *noun* [U] a yellow powder made from the root of an Asian plant, used in cooking as a SPICE, especially in CURRY ⇒ **VISUAL VOCAB** page V8

**tur·moil** /ˈtɜːmɔɪl; *NAmE* ˈtɜːrm-/ *noun* [U, sing.] a state of great worry in which everything is confused and nothing is certain **SYN** confusion: *emotional/mental/political turmoil* ◊ *His statement threw the court into turmoil.* ◊ *Her mind was in (a) turmoil.*

**turn** ⓘ **A1** /tɜːn; *NAmE* tɜːrn/ *verb, noun*
- *verb*
- **MOVE ROUND 1** **A1** [I, T] to move or make sth move around a central point: *The wheels of the car began to turn.* ◊ *I can't get the screw to turn.* ◊ ~**sth (+ adv./prep.)** *He turned the key in the lock.* ◊ *She turned the wheel sharply to the left.*
- **CHANGE POSITION/DIRECTION 2** **A1** [I, T] to move your body or part of your body so as to face or start moving in a different direction: *We turned and headed for home.* ◊ ~**to do sth** *She turned to look at me.* ◊ **+ adv./prep.** *He turned back to his work.* ◊ *I turned away and looked out of the window.* ◊ ~**sth (+ adv./prep.)** *He turned his back to the wall.* ◊ *She turned her head away.* ⇒ see also TURN OVER **3** **A1** [T] ~**sth + adv./prep.** to move sth so that it is in a different position or facing a different direction: *She turned the chair on its side to repair it.* ◊ *Turn the sweater inside out before you wash it.* ⇒ see also TURN STH OVER **4** **A1** [I, T] to change the direction you are moving or travelling in; to make sth change the direction it is moving in: ~**into sth** *He turned into a narrow street.* ◊ ~**left/right** *Turn left at the traffic lights.* ◊ ~**sth** *The man turned the corner and disappeared.* ◊ ~**sth into sth** *I turned the car into the car park.* **5** **A1** [I] **(+ adv./prep.)** (of a road or river) to bend or curve in a particular direction: *The road turns to the left after the church.*
- **PAGE 6** **A1** [T, I] if you **turn** a page of a book or magazine, you move it so that you can read the next page: ~**sth** *He sat turning the pages idly.* ◊ ~**to sth** *Turn to p.23.*
- **BECOME 7** **A2** linking verb to change into a particular state or condition; to make sth do this: **+ adj.** *The leaves were turning brown.* ◊ *The weather has turned cold.* ◊ *He turned nasty when we refused to give him the money.* ◊ *He decided to turn professional.* ◊ ~**sth + adj.** *The heat turned the milk sour.* ◊ **+ noun** *She turned a deathly shade of white when she heard the news.* ◊ *He's a lawyer turned politician* (= he used to be a lawyer but is now a politician).
- **AIM/POINT 8** [T, I] to aim or point sth in a particular direction: ~**sth on sb/sth/yourself** *Police turned water cannon on the rioters.* ◊ *He turned the gun on himself.* ◊ ~**sth to sb/sth/yourself** *She looked at him then turned her attention back to me.* ◊ ~**to sb/sth/yourself** *His thoughts turned to his dead wife.*
- **OF TIDE IN SEA 9** [I] to start to come in or go out: *The tide is turning—we'd better get back.*
- **LET SB/STH GO 10** [T] to make or let sb/sth go into a particular place or state: ~**sth + adv./prep.** *They turned the horse into the field.* ◊ ~**sth + adj.** *to turn the dogs loose*
- **FOLD 11** [T] ~**sth + adv./prep.** to fold sth in a particular way: *She turned down the blankets and climbed into bed.* ◊ *He turned up the collar of his coat and hurried out into the rain.*
- **CARTWHEEL/SOMERSAULT 12** [T, no passive] ~**sth** to perform a movement by moving your body in a circle: *to turn cartwheels/somersaults*
- **GAME 13** [I, T] ~**(sth) (around)** if a game **turns** or sb **turns** it, it changes the way it is developing so that a different person or team starts to win
- **AGE/TIME 14** linking verb (not used in the progressive tenses) **+ noun** to reach or pass a particular age or time: *She turns 21 in June.* ◊ *It's turned midnight.*
- **STOMACH 15** [I, T] ~**(your stomach)** when your stomach **turns** or sth **turns** your stomach, you feel as though you will VOMIT
- **WOOD 16** [T] ~**sth** (*specialist*) to shape sth on a LATHE: *to turn a chair leg* ◊ *turned boxes and bowls*

**IDM** **HELP** Most idioms containing **turn** are at the entries for the nouns and adjectives in the idioms, for example **not turn a hair** is at **hair**. **as it/things turned ˈout** as was shown or proved by later events: *I didn't need my umbrella, as it turned out* (= because it didn't rain). **be well, badly, etc. turned ˈout** to be well, badly, etc. dressed **turn round/around and do sth** (*informal*) used to report what sb says or does, when this is surprising or annoying: *How could she turn round and say that, after all I've done for her?*

**PHRV** **turn aˈgainst sb** | **turn sb aˈgainst sb** to stop or make sb stop being friendly towards sb: *She turned against her old friend.* ◊ *After the divorce he tried to turn the children against their mother.*
**turn aˈround** | **turn sb/sth aˈround** (*also* **turn ˈround, turn sb/sth ˈround** *especially in BrE*) to change position or direction so as to face the other way; to make sb/sth do this: *Turn around and let me look at your back.* ◊ *I turned my chair around to face the fire.* **turn aˈround** | **turn sth↔aˈround** (*also* **turn ˈround, turn sth↔ˈround** *especially in BrE*) if a business, economy, etc. **turns around** or sb **turns it around**, it starts being successful after it has been unsuccessful for a time ⇒ related noun TURNAROUND
**turn sb↔aˈway (from sth)** to refuse to allow sb to enter a place: *Hundreds of people were turned away from the stadium* (= because it was full). ◊ *They had nowhere to stay so I couldn't turn them away.*
**turn ˈback** | **turn sb/sth↔ˈback** to return the way you have come; to make sb/sth do this: *The weather became so bad that they had to turn back.* ◊ (*figurative*) *We said we would do it—there can be no turning back.* ◊ *Our car was turned back at the border.* ⇒ SYNONYMS at RETURN
**turn sb/sth↔ˈdown** to reject or refuse to consider an offer, a proposal, etc. or the person who makes it: *Why did she turn down your invitation?* ◊ *He has been turned down for ten jobs so far.* ◊ *He asked her to marry him but she turned him down.* **turn sth↔ˈdown** to reduce the noise, heat, etc. produced by a piece of equipment by moving its controls: *Please turn the volume down.* ◊ **+ adj.** *He turned the lights down low.*
**turn ˈin 1** to face the centre or move towards the centre in a curve: *Her feet turn in.* **2** (*old-fashioned*) to go to bed **turn sb↔ˈin** (*informal*) to take sb to the police or sb in authority because they have committed a crime: *She threatened to turn him in to the police.* ◊ *He decided to turn himself in.* **turn sth↔ˈin 1** to give back sth that you no longer need: *You must turn in your pass when you leave the building.* **2** (*especially NAmE*) to give sth to sb in authority: *They turned in a petition with 80000 signatures.* ◊ *I haven't even turned in Monday's work yet.* **3** to achieve a score, performance, profit, etc: *The champion turned in a superb performance to retain her title.* **turn ˈin on yourself** to become too interested in your own problems and stop communicating with others
**turn (from sth) ˈinto sth** **B2** to become sth: *Our dream holiday turned into a nightmare.* ◊ *In one year she turned from a problem child into a model student.* **turn sb/sth (from sth) ˈinto sth** to make sb/sth become sth: *Ten years of prison had turned him into an old man.* ◊ *The prince was turned into a frog by the witch.*
**turn ˈoff** (*informal*) to stop listening to or thinking about sb/sth: *I couldn't understand the lecture so I just turned off.*

**turn ˈoff** | **turn ˈoff sth** [no passive] to leave a road in order to travel on another: *Is this where we turn off?* ◊ *The jet began to turn off the main runway.* **turn sb↔ˈoff 1** to make sb feel bored or not interested: *People had been turned off by both candidates in the election.* **2** to stop sb feeling sexually attracted; to make sb have a strong feeling of dislike ⊃ related noun TURN-OFF **turn sth↔ˈoff ⓘ A2** to stop the flow of electricity, gas, water, etc. by moving a switch, button, etc: *to turn off the light* ◊ *Please turn the television off before you go to bed.*

**ˈturn on sb** to attack sb suddenly and unexpectedly: *The dogs suddenly turned on each other.* ◊ *Why are you all turning on me* (= criticizing or blaming me)? **ˈturn on sth** [no passive] **1** to depend on sth: *Much turns on the outcome of the current peace talks.* **2** to have sth as its main topic: *The discussion turned on the need to raise standards.* **turn sb↔ˈon** (*informal*) to make sb excited or interested, especially sexually: *Jazz has never really turned me on.* ◊ *She gets turned on by men in uniform.* ⊃ related noun TURN-ON **turn sb ˈon (to sth)** (*informal*) to make sb become interested in sth or to use sth for the first time: *He turned her on to jazz.* **turn sth↔ˈon ⓘ A2** to start the flow of electricity, gas, water, etc. by moving a switch, button, etc: *to turn on the heating* ◊ *I'll turn the television on.* ◊ (*figurative*) *He really knows how to* **turn on the charm** (= suddenly become pleasant and attractive).

**ˌturn ˈout 1 ⓘ B1** to be discovered to be; to prove to be: **turn out that …** *It turned out that she was a friend of my sister.* ◊ **turn out to be/have sth** *The job turned out to be harder than we thought.* ◊ *The house they had offered us turned out to be a tiny apartment.* **2** (used with an adverb or adjective, or in questions with *how*) to happen in a particular way; to develop or end in a particular way: *Despite our worries everything turned out well.* ◊ *You never know how your children will turn out.* ◊ **+ adj.** *If the day turns out wet, we may have to change our plans.* **3** to be present at an event: *A vast crowd turned out to watch the procession.* ⊃ related noun TURNOUT **4** to point away from the centre: *Her toes turn out.* **turn sb/sth↔ˈout** to produce sb/sth: *The factory turns out 900 cars a week.* **turn sb ˈout (of/from sth)** to force sb to leave a place **turn sth↔ˈout 1** to switch a light or a source of heat off: *Remember to turn out the lights when you go to bed.* **2** (*BrE*) to clean sth carefully and completely by removing the contents and organizing them again: *to turn out the attic* **3** to empty sth, especially your pockets **4** to make sth point away from the centre: *She turned her toes out.*

**ˌturn ˈover 1** to change position so that the other side is facing towards the outside or the top: *If you turn over you might find it easier to get to sleep.* ◊ *The car skidded and turned over.* ◊ (*figurative*) *The smell made my stomach turn over* (= made me feel sick). **2** (of an engine) to start or to continue to run **3** to change to another channel when you are watching television **ˌturn ˈover sth** to do business worth a particular amount of money in a particular period of time: *The company turns over £3.5 million a year.* ⊃ related noun TURNOVER **turn sth↔ˈover 1** to make sth change position so that the other side is facing towards the outside or the top: *Brown the meat on one side, then turn it over and brown the other side.* **2** to think about sth carefully: *She kept turning over the events of the day in her mind.* **3** (of a shop) to sell goods and replace them: *A supermarket will turn over its stock very rapidly.* ⊃ related noun TURNOVER **4** (*informal*) to steal from a place: *Burglars had turned the house over.* **5** to make an engine start running **turn sb↔ˈover to sb** to deliver sb to the control or care of sb else, especially sb in authority: *Customs officials turned the man over to the police.* **turn sth↔ˈover to sb** to give the control of sth to sb: *He turned the business over to his daughter.* **turn sth↔ˈover to sth** to change the use or function of sth: *The factory was turned over to the manufacture of aircraft parts.*

**ˌturn ˈround** | **ˌturn sb/sth ˈround** (*especially BrE*) = TURN AROUND

**ˈturn to sb/sth** to go to sb/sth for help, advice, etc: *She has nobody she can turn to.*

**ˌturn ˈup 1** to be found, especially by chance, after being lost: *Don't worry about the letter — I'm sure it'll turn up.* **2** (of a person) to arrive: *We arranged to meet at 7.30, but* she never turned up. **3** (of an opportunity) to happen, especially by chance: *He's still hoping something* (= for example, a job or a piece of luck) *will turn up.* ⊃ related noun TURN-UP **ˌturn sth↔ˈup 1 ⓘ B1** to increase the sound, heat, etc. of a piece of equipment: *Could you turn the TV up?* ◊ **+ adj.** *The music was turned up loud.* **2** (*BrE*) to make a piece of clothing shorter by folding and SEWING it up at the bottom **OPP** **let sth ˈdown** ⊃ related noun TURN-UP **3** to find sth: *Our efforts to trace him turned up nothing.*

■ *noun* [C]

• **TIME 1 ⓘ A1** the time when sb in a group of people should or is allowed to do sth: *When it's your turn, take another card.* ◊ *Please* **wait your turn**. ◊ **sb's ~ to do sth** *Whose turn is it to cook?* ◊ *Steve took a turn driving while I slept.*
• **OF ROAD/VEHICLE 2 ⓘ A2** a change in direction in a vehicle: *Make a left/right turn into West Street.* ⊃ see also THREE-POINT TURN, U-TURN **3** (*especially AmE*) (*BrE usually* **turning**) a place where a road leads away from the one you are travelling on: *Take the next turn on the right.* ◊ *He took a wrong turn and ended up on the coast road.* **4** a bend or corner in a road: *a lane full of twists and turns*
• **MOVEMENT 5 ⓘ B1** an act of turning sb/sth around: *Give the handle a few turns.*
• **CHANGE 6** an unusual or unexpected change in what is happening: *a surprising* **turn of events** ◊ *His health has* **taken a turn for the worse** (= suddenly got worse). ◊ *Events took a dramatic turn in the weeks that followed.* ◊ **by turns** *The book is, by turns, funny and very sad.* ⊃ see also ABOUT-TURN
• **PERFORMANCE 7** a short performance or piece of entertainment such as a song, etc: *Everyone got up on stage to do a turn.* ⊃ see also STAR TURN
• **WALK 8** (*old-fashioned*) a short walk: *We took a turn around the park.*
• **ILLNESS 9** (*old-fashioned*) a feeling of illness: *a funny turn* (= a feeling that you may faint)

**IDM** **at every ˈturn** everywhere or every time you try and do sth: *At every turn I met with disappointment.* **ˌdone to a ˈturn** cooked for exactly the right amount of time **ˌgive sb a ˈturn** (*old-fashioned*) to frighten or shock sb **(ˌdo sb) a good ˈturn** (to do) sth that helps sb: *Well, that's my good turn for the day.* **in ˈturn ⓘ B2** one after the other in a particular order: *The children called out their names in turn.* **2** as a result of sth in a series of events: *Increased production will, in turn, lead to increased profits.* **ˌone good turn deserves aˈnother** (*saying*) you should help sb who has helped you **on the ˈturn** (*especially BrE*) going to change **out of ˈturn** if you do sth **out of turn**, you do it when you are not supposed to be the next person to do sth: *Batista had batted out of turn.* **ˌspeak/talk out of ˈturn** to say sth that you should not because it is the wrong situation or because it offends sb **take ˈturns (doing sth/in doing sth/to do sth)** (*BrE also* **take it in ˈturns**) if people **take turns** or **take it in turns** to do sth, they do it one after the other to make sure it is done fairly: *The male and female birds take turns in sitting on the eggs.* ◊ *We take it in turns to do the housework.* **the ˌturn of the ˈcentury/ˈyear** the time when a new century/year starts: *It was built at the turn of the century.* **a ˌturn of ˈmind** a particular way of thinking about things **a ˌturn of ˈphrase** a particular way of describing sth **a ˌturn of the ˈscrew** an extra amount of pressure, CRUELTY, etc. added to a situation that is already difficult to bear or understand **a ˌturn of ˈspeed** a sudden increase in your speed or rate of progress; the ability to suddenly increase your speed: *He put on an impressive turn of speed in the last lap.* ⊃ more at SERVE *v.*

**turn·about** /ˈtɜːnəbaʊt; *NAmE* ˈtɜːrn-/ *noun* [sing.] **~ (in sth)** a sudden and complete change in sb/sth **SYN** **reversal**

**turn·around** /ˈtɜːnəraʊnd; *NAmE* ˈtɜːrn-/ (*BrE also* **turn-round**) *noun* [usually sing.] **1** the amount of time it takes to unload a ship or plane at the end of one journey and load it again for the next one: *Budget airlines rely on very fast turnaround times.* **2 ~ (between A and B)** the amount of time it takes to do a piece of work that you have been given and return it: *Customers want a quick turnaround*

# turncoat

between order and delivery. **3** a situation in which sth changes from bad to good: *a turnaround in the economy* **4** a complete change in sb's opinion, behaviour, etc.

**turn·coat** /ˈtɜːnkəʊt; NAmE ˈtɜːrn-/ noun (*disapproving*) a person who leaves one political party, religious group, etc. to join one that has very different views

**turn·ing** /ˈtɜːnɪŋ; NAmE ˈtɜːrn-/ (*BrE*) (also **turn** *especially in NAmE*) *noun* a place where a road leads away from the one you are travelling on: *Take the first turning on the right.* ◊ *I think we must have taken a wrong turning somewhere.*

ˈ**turning circle** *noun* the smallest circle that a vehicle can turn around in

ˈ**turning point** *noun* ~ **(in sth)** the time when an important change takes place, usually with the result that a situation improves: *The promotion marked a turning point in her career.*

**tur·nip** /ˈtɜːnɪp; NAmE ˈtɜːrn-/ *noun* [C, U] **1** a round white, or white and purple, root vegetable ⇨ VISUAL VOCAB page V5 **2** (*ScotE*) = SWEDE ⇨ VISUAL VOCAB page V5

**turn·key** /ˈtɜːnki; NAmE ˈtɜːrn-/ *adj.* (especially of computer systems) complete and ready to use immediately

ˈ**turn-off** *noun* **1** a place where a road leads away from another larger or more important road: *We missed the turn-off for the airport.* **2** [usually sing.] (*informal*) a person or thing that people find boring or not attractive: *The city's crime rate is a serious turn-off to potential investors.* ◊ *I find beards a real turn-off.*

ˈ**turn-on** *noun* [usually sing.] (*informal*) a person or thing that people find sexually exciting

**turn·out** /ˈtɜːnaʊt; NAmE ˈtɜːrn-/ *noun* [C, usually sing., U] **1** the number of people who attend a particular event: *This year's festival attracted a record turnout.* **2** the number of people who vote in a particular election: *a high/low/poor turnout* ◊ *a 60% turnout of voters*

**turn·over** /ˈtɜːnəʊvə(r); NAmE ˈtɜːrn-/ *noun* **1** [C, usually sing., U] ~ **(of sth)** the total amount of goods or services sold by a company during a particular period of time: *an annual turnover of $75 million* ◊ *a fall in turnover* **2** [sing.] ~ **(of sb)** the rate at which employees leave a company and are replaced by other people: *a high turnover of staff* **3** [sing.] ~ **(of sth)** the rate at which goods are sold in a shop and replaced by others: *a fast turnover of stock* **4** [C] a small PIE in the shape of a TRIANGLE or half a circle, filled with fruit or jam

**turn·pike** /ˈtɜːnpaɪk; NAmE ˈtɜːrn-/ (also **pike**) (both NAmE) *noun* a wide road, where traffic can travel fast for long distances and that drivers must pay a TOLL to use

**turn·round** /ˈtɜːnraʊnd; NAmE ˈtɜːrn-/ *noun* (*BrE*) = TURNAROUND

ˈ**turn signal** (NAmE) (BrE **in·di·ca·tor**) (also informal **blink·er** NAmE, BrE) *noun* a light on a vehicle that flashes to show that the vehicle is going to turn left or right

**turn·stile** /ˈtɜːnstaɪl; NAmE ˈtɜːrn-/ *noun* a gate at the entrance to a public building, stadium, etc. that turns in a circle when pushed, allowing one person to go through at a time ⇨ picture at STILE

**turn·table** /ˈtɜːnteɪbl; NAmE ˈtɜːrn-/ *noun* **1** the round surface on a RECORD PLAYER that you place the record on to be played **2** a large, round surface that is able to move in a circle and onto which a railway engine is driven in order to turn it to go in the opposite direction

ˈ**turn-up** *noun* (*BrE*) **1** (*NAmE* **cuff**) [C] the bottom of the leg of a pair of trousers that has been folded over on the outside **2** [sing.] (*informal*) something surprising or unexpected that happens: *He actually offered to help? That's a turn-up for the books!*

**tur·pen·tine** /ˈtɜːpəntaɪn; NAmE ˈtɜːrp-/ (also informal **turps** /tɜːps; NAmE tɜːrps/) *noun* [U] a clear liquid with a strong smell, used especially for making paint thinner and for cleaning paint from brushes and clothes

**tur·pi·tude** /ˈtɜːpɪtjuːd; NAmE ˈtɜːrpɪtuːd/ *noun* [U] (*formal*) very bad behaviour SYN **wickedness**

**tur·quoise** /ˈtɜːkwɔɪz; NAmE ˈtɜːrkwɔɪz/ *noun* **1** [C, U] a blue or blue-green SEMI-PRECIOUS stone: *a turquoise brooch* **2** [U] a blue-green colour ▸ **tur·quoise** *adj.*: *a turquoise dress*

**tur·ret** /ˈtʌrət; NAmE ˈtɜːr-/ *noun* **1** a small tower on top of a wall or building, especially a castle **2** a small metal tower on a ship, plane or TANK that can usually turn around and from which guns are fired

**tur·ret·ed** /ˈtʌrətɪd; NAmE ˈtɜːr-/ *adj.* [usually before noun] having one or more turrets

**tur·tle** /ˈtɜːtl; NAmE ˈtɜːrtl/ *noun* **1** (NAmE also ˈ**sea turtle**) a large REPTILE with a hard round shell that lives in the sea ⇨ VISUAL VOCAB page V3 **2** (*NAmE*, *informal*) any REPTILE with a large shell, for example a TORTOISE or TERRAPIN IDM **turn ˈturtle** (of a boat) to turn over completely while sailing

ˈ**turtle dove** *noun* a wild DOVE (= a type of bird) with a pleasant soft call, thought to be a very loving bird

**turtle·neck** /ˈtɜːtlnek; NAmE ˈtɜːrt-/ *noun* **1** (also ˈ**turtle-neck sweater**) a sweater with a high part fitting closely around the neck **2** (*NAmE*) (*BrE* ˈ**polo neck**) a high, round COLLAR made when the neck of a piece of clothing is folded over; a piece of clothing with a turtleneck

**turves** /tɜːvz; NAmE tɜːrvz/ *pl.* of TURF

**tusk** /tʌsk/ *noun* either of the long, curved teeth that stick out of the mouth of elephants and some other animals ⇨ VISUAL VOCAB page V2 ⇨ see also IVORY

**tus·sle** /ˈtʌsl/ *noun*, *verb*
▪ *noun* ~ **(for / over sth)** a short struggle, fight or argument especially in order to get sth: *He was injured during a tussle for the ball.*
▪ *verb* [I] ~ **(with sb / sth)** to fight or compete with sb/sth, especially in order to get sth: *The children were tussling with one another for the ball.*

**tus·sock** /ˈtʌsək/ *noun* a small area of grass that is longer and thicker than the grass around it ▸ **tus·socky** *adj.*: *tussocky grass*

**tut** /tʌt/ (also **tut-ˈtut**) *exclamation*, *noun* used as the written or spoken way of showing the sound that people make when they think sth is bad: *Tut-tut, I expected better of you.* ◊ *tuts of disapproval* ▸ **tut** (also ˌ**tut-ˈtut**) *verb* (**-tt-**) [I]: *He tut-tutted under his breath.*

**tutee** /tjuːˈtiː; NAmE tuː-/ *noun* a person who is taught or given advice by a TUTOR

**tu·tel·age** /ˈtjuːtəlɪdʒ; NAmE ˈtuː-/ *noun* [U] (*formal*) **1** the teaching and instruction that one person gives to another SYN **tuition 2** the state of being protected or controlled by another person, organization or country: *parental tutelage*

**tutor** /ˈtjuːtə(r); NAmE ˈtuː-/ *noun*, *verb*
▪ *noun* **1** a private teacher, especially one who teaches an individual student or a very small group **2** (*especially BrE*) a teacher whose job is to pay special attention to the studies or health, etc. of a student or a group of students: *his history tutor* ◊ *He was my personal tutor at university.* ◊ *She's in my tutor group at school.* **3** (*NAmE*) a teacher, especially one who teaches adults or who has a special role in a school or college: *a part-time adult education tutor* **4** (*NAmE*) an assistant LECTURER in a college **5** a book of instruction in a particular subject, especially music: *a violin tutor*
▪ *verb* **1** [T] ~ **sb (in sth)** to be a tutor to an individual student or a small group; to teach sb, especially privately: *He tutors students in mathematics.* **2** [I] to work as a tutor: *Her work was divided between tutoring and research.*

**tu·tor·ial** /tjuːˈtɔːriəl; NAmE tuː-/ *noun*, *adj.*
▪ *noun* **1** a period of teaching in a university that involves discussion between an individual student or a small group of students and a tutor ⇨ WORDFINDER NOTE at UNIVERSITY

ic
**2** a short book or computer program that gives information on a particular subject or explains how sth is done: *An online tutorial is provided.*
- *adj.* connected with the work of a tutor: *tutorial staff* ◇ *(BrE) a tutorial college* (= a private school that prepares students for exams)

**tutti-frutti** /ˌtuːti ˈfruːti/ *noun* [U] a type of ice cream that contains pieces of fruit of various kinds

**tutu** /ˈtuːtuː/ *noun* a BALLET dancer's skirt made of many layers of material. Tutus may be either short and stiff, sticking out from the middle part of the body, or long and like a bell in shape.

**tux·edo** /tʌkˈsiːdəʊ/ *noun* (*pl.* **-os**) (*also informal* **tux** /tʌks/) (*especially NAmE*) **1** (*BrE usually* **'dinner suit**) a black or white jacket and trousers, worn with a BOW TIE at formal occasions in the evening **2** (*also* **'dinner jacket**) a black or white jacket worn with a BOW TIE at formal occasions in the evening ORIGIN From Tuxedo Park in New York, where it was first worn.

**TV** 🔑 A1 /ˌtiː ˈviː/ *noun* [C, U] television: *We spent the evening watching TV.* ◇ *on ~* ◇ *What's on TV tonight?* ◇ *We're buying a new TV with the money.* ◇ *Almost all homes have at least one TV set.* ◇ *a TV show/programme/series* ◇ *cable/satellite TV* ◇ *She's a highly paid TV presenter.* ⊃ *see also* PAY TV

**TV 'dinner** *noun* a meal that you can buy already cooked and prepared, that you only have to heat up before you can eat it

**twad·dle** /ˈtwɒdl; *NAmE* ˈtwɑːdl/ *noun* [U] (*old-fashioned, informal*) something that has been said or written that you think is stupid and not true SYN **nonsense**

**twain** /tweɪn/ *number* (*old use*) two
IDM ▶ **never the ˌtwain shall 'meet** (*saying*) used to say that two things are so different that they cannot exist together

**twang** /twæŋ/ *noun, verb*
- *noun* [usually sing.] **1** used to describe a way of speaking, usually one that is typical of a particular area and especially one in which the sounds are produced through the nose as well as the mouth **2** a sound that is made when a tight string, especially on a musical instrument, is pulled and released
- *verb* [I, T] to make a sound like a tight wire or string being pulled and released; to make sth do this: *The bed springs twanged.* ◇ *~ sth Someone was twanging a guitar in the next room.*

**'twas** /twɒz; *NAmE* twʌz/ *abbr.* (*literary*) it was

**twat** /twæt, twɒt; *NAmE* twɑːt/ *noun* (*taboo, slang, especially BrE*) **1** an offensive word for an unpleasant or stupid person **2** an offensive word for the outer female sex organs

**tweak** /twiːk/ *verb, noun*
- *verb* **1** *~ sth* to pull or TWIST sth suddenly: *She tweaked his ear playfully.* **2** *~ sth* to make slight changes to a machine, system, etc. to improve it: *I think you'll have to tweak these pictures a little before you show them to the boss.*
- *noun* **1** a sharp pull or TWIST: *She gave his ear a tweak.* **2** a slight change that you make to a machine, system, etc. to improve it

**twee** /twiː/ *adj.* (*BrE, informal, disapproving*) very pretty, in a way that you find unpleasant and silly; appearing SENTIMENTAL: *The room was decorated with twee little pictures of animals.*

**tweed** /twiːd/ *noun* **1** [U] a type of thick, rough cloth made of wool that has small spots of different coloured THREAD in it: *a tweed jacket* **2** **tweeds** [pl.] clothes made of tweed

**tweedy** /ˈtwiːdi/ *adj.* **1** made of or looking like tweed: *a tweedy jacket* **2** (*BrE, informal, often disapproving*) used to describe the sort of person who often wears tweeds and therefore shows that they belong to the social class of rich people who live in the country

**tween** /twiːn/ *noun* (*also* **tween-ager** /ˈtwiːneɪdʒə(r)/, *especially BrE* **tween-er**) /ˈtwiːnə(r)/ *noun* (*informal*) a child between the ages of about 10 and 12 SYN **pre-teen**

**tween·er** /ˈtwiːnə(r)/ *noun* (*informal*) **1** (*especially BrE*) = TWEEN **2** (*NAmE*) a person or thing that is between two categories, classes or age groups: *The film is a tweener, neither indie nor mainstream.*

**tweet** /twiːt/ *noun, verb*
- *noun* **1** a message sent using the Twitter SOCIAL MEDIA service **2** the short, high sound made by a small bird
- *verb* **1** (*also less frequent* **twitter**) [I, T] to send a message or picture using the Twitter SOCIAL MEDIA service: *~ about sth She's always tweeting about environmental issues.* ◇ *~ sth He tweeted a picture of himself with fans at the rally.* **2** [I] = TWITTER (1)

**tweet·able** /ˈtwiːtəbl/ *adj.* suitable to send out as a message on the Twitter SOCIAL MEDIA service: *I'll give you the tweetable summary of the plan.*

**tweet·er** /ˈtwiːtə(r)/ *noun* a LOUDSPEAKER through which the high notes in a SOUND SYSTEM are heard ⊃ *compare* WOOFER

**tweez·ers** /ˈtwiːzəz; *NAmE* -zərz/ *noun* [pl.] a small tool with two long, thin parts joined together at one end, used for picking up very small things or for pulling out hairs: *a pair of tweezers*

**Twelfth 'Night** *noun* [U] **1** January 6th, the day of the Christian festival of EPIPHANY **2** the evening of January 5th, the day before EPIPHANY, which traditionally marks the end of Christmas celebrations

**twelve** 🔑 A1 /twelv/ *number* 12 HELP There are examples of how to use numbers at the entry for **five**.
▶ **twelfth** /twelfθ/ *ordinal number, noun* HELP There are examples of how to use ordinal numbers at the entry for **fifth**.

**twenty** 🔑 A1 /ˈtwenti/ **1** A1 *number* 20 HELP There are examples of how to use numbers at the entry for **five**. **2** *noun* **the twenties** [pl.] numbers, years or temperatures from 20 to 29 ▶ **twen·ti·eth** /-əθ/ *ordinal number, noun* HELP There are examples of how to use ordinal numbers at the entry for **fifth**.
IDM **in your 'twenties** between the ages of 20 and 29

**twenty-'first** *noun* [sing.] (*especially BrE*) a person's 21st birthday and the celebrations for this occasion

**twenty-four 'seven** (*also* **24/7**) *adv.* (*informal*) twenty-four hours a day, seven days a week (used to mean 'all the time'): *He's on duty twenty-four seven.*

**twenty 'pence** (*also* **twenty pence 'piece**, **20p** /ˌtwenti ˈpiː/) *noun* a British coin worth 20 pence: *You need two 20ps for the machine.*

**twenty-twenty 'vision** (*also* **20/20 vision**) *noun* [U] the ability to see with the CLARITY of a normal, healthy, young adult human

**'twere** /twɜː(r)/ *abbr.* (*old use*) it were

**twerk** /twɜːk; *NAmE* twɜːrk/ *verb* [I] (*informal*) to dance to popular music with the body bent low and the HIPS moving forwards and backwards ▶ **twerk·ing** *noun* [U]

**twerp** /twɜːp; *NAmE* twɜːrp/ *noun* (*old-fashioned, informal*) a stupid or annoying person

**twice** 🔑 A1 /twaɪs/ *adv.* **1** A1 two times; on two occasions: *I don't know him well; I've only met him twice.* ◇ *The cows are milked twice daily.* ◇ *The cows are milked twice a day.* **2** B1 double in quantity, rate, etc: *an area twice the size of Wales* ◇ *Cats sleep twice as much as people.* ◇ *At 56 he's twice her age.*
IDM ▶ **twice 'over** not just once but twice: *There was enough of the drug in her stomach to kill her twice over.* ⊃ *more at* LIGHTNING *n.*, ONCE *adv.*, THINK *v.*

**twid·dle** /ˈtwɪdl/ *verb, noun*
- *verb* [I, T] to TWIST or turn sth with your fingers often because you are nervous or bored: *~ with sth He twiddled with the radio knob until he found the right programme.* ◇ *~ sth She was twiddling the ring on her finger.*

# twig

**IDM** **twiddle your ˈthumbs 1** to move your THUMBS around each other with your fingers joined together **2** to do nothing while you are waiting for sth to happen
■ *noun* **1** a TWIST or turn: *a twiddle of the knob* **2** a feature of a pattern, piece of music, etc. that decorates it: *twiddles on the clarinet*

**twig** /twɪɡ/ *noun*, *verb*
■ *noun* a small, very thin branch that grows out of a larger branch on a bush or tree⇨ VISUAL VOCAB page V6
■ *verb* (-gg-) [I, T] ~ (to sth) | ~ what … | ~ (that) … (*BrE*, *informal*) to suddenly understand or realize sth: *Haven't you twigged yet?* ◇ *~ what* … *I finally twigged what he meant.*

**twi·light** /ˈtwaɪlaɪt/ *noun* [U] **1** the small amount of light or the period of time at the end of the day after the sun has gone down: **in the ~** *It was hard to see him clearly in the twilight.* ◇ **at ~** *We went for a walk along the beach at twilight.* ⇨ compare DUSK⇨ WORDFINDER NOTE at SUN **2** the final stage of sth when it becomes weaker or less important than it was: *She was in the twilight of her career by then.* ◇ *He spent his twilight years* (= the last years of his life) *living with his daughter in Bristol.*
**IDM** **a/the twilight world (of sth) | the ˈtwilight zone** a state in which things are strange, mysterious or secret; a state that exists on the dividing line between two things: *the twilight world of the occult* ◇ *the twilight zone between living and merely existing*

**twill** /twɪl/ *noun* [U] a type of strong cloth that is made in a particular way to produce a surface of raised DIAGONAL lines: *a cotton twill skirt*

**ˈtwill** /twɪl/ *abbr.* (*old use*) it will

**twin** ⓘ A2 /twɪn/ *noun*, *verb*, *adj*.
■ *noun* **1** ⓘ A2 one of two children born at the same time to the same mother: *She's expecting twins.* ⇨ see also CONJOINED TWIN, FRATERNAL TWIN, IDENTICAL TWIN, SIAMESE TWIN **2** one of two similar things that make a pair
■ *adj.* [only before noun] **1** ⓘ A2 used to describe one of a pair of children who are twins: *a twin brother/sister* ◇ *twin daughters/sons* **2** used to describe two things that are used as a pair: *a ship with twin propellers* **3** used to describe two things that are connected, or present or happening at the same time: *The prison service has the twin goals of punishment and rehabilitation.*
■ *verb* (-nn-) **1** [usually passive] ~ sth (with sth) to make a close relationship between two towns or areas: *Oxford is twinned with Bonn in Germany.* **2** ~ sth (with sth) to join two people or things closely together: *The opera twins the themes of love and death.*

**ˈtwin bed** *noun* **1** [usually pl.] one of a pair of single beds in a room: *Would you prefer twin beds or a double?* **2** (*NAmE*) (*BrE* **single bed**) a bed big enough for one person: *sheets to fit a twin bed*

**ˌtwin-ˈbedded** *adj.* (of a room in a hotel, etc.) having two single beds in it

**ˌtwin ˈbedroom** *noun* a room in a hotel, etc. that has two single beds

**twine** /twaɪn/ *noun*, *verb*
■ *noun* [U] strong string that has two or more STRANDS (= single thin pieces of string) TWISTED together
■ *verb* [I, T] ~ (sth) around/round/through/in sth to wind or TWIST around sth; to make sth do this: *ivy twining around a tree trunk* ◇ *She twined her arms around my neck.*

**ˌtwin-ˈengined** *adj.* (of an aircraft) having two engines

**twinge** /twɪndʒ/ *noun* **1** a sudden short feeling of pain: *He felt a twinge in his knee.* **2** **~ (of sth)** a sudden short feeling of an unpleasant emotion: *a twinge of disappointment*

**twin·kle** /ˈtwɪŋkl/ *verb*, *noun*
■ *verb* **1** [I] to shine with a light that keeps changing from bright to pale to bright again: *Stars twinkled in the sky.* ◇ *twinkling lights in the distance* ⇨ SYNONYMS at SHINE **2** [I] ~(with sth) | ~(at sb) if your eyes **twinkle**, you have a bright expression because you are happy or excited: *twinkling blue eyes* ◇ *Her eyes twinkled with merriment.*
■ *noun* [sing.] **1** an expression in your eyes that shows you are happy or pleased about sth: *He looked at me with a twinkle in his eye.* **2** a small light that keeps changing from bright to pale to bright again: *the twinkle of stars* ◇ *the twinkle of the harbour lights in the distance*

**twink·ling** /ˈtwɪŋklɪŋ/ *noun* [sing.] (*old-fashioned*, *informal*) a very short time
**IDM** **in the ˌtwinkling of an ˈeye** very quickly **SYN** instant

**ˈtwin-set** /ˈtwɪnset/ *noun* a woman's matching sweater and CARDIGAN that are designed to be worn together

**ˌtwin ˈtown** (*BrE*) (*NAmE* **ˌsister ˈcity**) *noun* one of two towns or cities in different countries that have a special relationship with each other: *a visit to Lyon, Birmingham's twin town in France*

**twirl** /twɜːl; *NAmE* twɜːrl/ *verb*, *noun*
■ *verb* **1** [I, T] **~ (sb) (around/round)** to move or dance round and round; to make sb do this: *She twirled around in front of the mirror.* ◇ *He held her hand and twirled her around.* **2** [T] **~ sth (around/about)** to make sth turn quickly and lightly round and round **SYN** spin: *He twirled his hat in his hand.* ◇ *She sat twirling the stem of the glass in her fingers.* **3** [T] **~ sth** to turn sth round and round with your fingers: *He kept twirling his moustache.*
■ *noun* the action of a person turning around in a circle once: *Kate did a twirl in her new dress.*

**twist** ⓘ C1 /twɪst/ *verb*, *noun*
■ *verb*
- **BEND INTO SHAPE 1** ⓘ C1 [T] **~ sth (into sth)** to bend or turn sth into a particular shape: *Twist the wire to form a circle.* **2** ⓘ C1 [T, I] to bend or turn sth into a shape or position that is not normal or natural; to be bent or turned in this way: **~ sth (+ adv./prep.)** *He grabbed me and twisted my arm behind my back.* ◇ **+ adv./prep.** *Her face twisted in anger.*
- **TURN BODY 3** ⓘ C1 [T, I] to turn part of your body around while the rest stays still: **~ sth (+ adv./prep.)** *He twisted his head around to look at her.* ◇ **+ adv./prep.** *She twisted in her chair when I called her name.* **4** ⓘ C1 [I, T] to turn your body with quick, sharp movements and change direction often: *I twisted and turned to avoid being caught.* ◇ **+ adv./prep.** *She tried unsuccessfully to twist free.* ◇ **~ sth/yourself (+ adv./prep.)** *He managed to twist himself round in the restricted space.*
- **TURN WITH HAND 5** ⓘ C1 [T] **~ sth (+ adv./prep.)** to turn sth around in a circle with your hand: *Twist the knob to the left to open the door.* ◇ *Nervously I twisted the ring on my finger.*
- **OF ROADS/RIVERS 6** ⓘ C1 [I] to bend and change direction often: *The road twists and turns along the coast.* ◇ *narrow twisting streets* ◇ *a twisting staircase*
- **INJURE PART OF BODY 7** ⓘ C1 [T] **~ sth** to injure part of your body, especially your ankle, WRIST or knee, bending it in an uncomfortable way: *She fell and twisted her ankle.*
- **WIND AROUND 8** ⓘ C1 [T] **~ sth (+ adv./prep.)** to wind sth around or through an object: *She twisted a scarf around her head.* ◇ *The telephone cable has got twisted* (= wound around itself). **9** ⓘ C1 [I] **~ (round/around sth)** to move or grow by winding around sth: *A snake was twisting around his arm.*
- **FACTS 10** [T] **~ sth** to deliberately change the meaning of what sb has said, or to present facts in a particular way, in order to benefit yourself or harm sb else **SYN** misrepresent: *You always twist everything I say.* ◇ *The newspaper was accused of twisting the facts.*
- **STRINGS 11** [T] **~ sth (into sth)** to turn or wind strings, etc. together to make sth longer or thicker: *They had twisted the sheets into a rope and escaped by climbing down it.*
**IDM** **twist sb's ˈarm** (*informal*) to persuade or force sb to do sth ⇨ more at KNIFE *n*., LITTLE FINGER
**PHR V** **twist sth↔ˈoff** to turn and pull sth with your hand to remove it from sth: *I twisted off the lid and looked inside.* ◇ *a twist-off top*

---

æ cat | ɑː father | e bed | ɜː fur | ə about | ɪ sit | iː see | i happy | ɒ got (*BrE*) | ɔː saw | ʌ cup | ʊ put | uː too

■ noun
- **ACTION OF TURNING** **1** [C] the action of turning sth with your hand, or of turning a part of your body: *She gave the lid another twist and it came off.* ◊ *He gave a shy smile and a little twist of his head.*
- **UNEXPECTED CHANGE** **2** [C] an unexpected change or development in a story or situation: *the twists and turns of his political career* ◊ *The story has taken another twist.* ◊ *The disappearance of a vital witness added a* **new twist** *to the case.* ◊ *By a curious* **twist of fate** *we met again only a week or so later.* ⇨ WORDFINDER NOTE at PLOT
- **IN ROAD/RIVER** **3** [C] a sharp bend in a road or river: *The car followed the* **twists and turns** *of the mountain road.*
- **SHAPE** **4** [C] a thing that has been twisted into a particular shape: *mineral water with a twist of lemon*
- **DANCE** **5 the twist** [sing.] a fast dance that was popular in the 1960s, in which you twist from side to side

IDM **round the bend / twist** (*especially BrE, informal*) crazy: *She's gone completely round the twist.* ⇨ more at KNICKERS

**twist·ed** /ˈtwɪstɪd/ *adj.*
**1** turned around on itself so that the original shape is lost: *After the crash the car was a mass of twisted metal.* ◊ *a twisted ankle (= injured by being turned suddenly)* ◊ *She gave a small twisted smile.* **2** (of a person's mind or behaviour) not normal; strange in an unpleasant way: *Her experiences had left her bitter and twisted.*

twisted      bent

**twist·er** /ˈtwɪstə(r)/ *noun* (*NAmE, informal*) a violent storm with very strong winds that move in circles SYN **tornado**

**twisty** /ˈtwɪsti/ *adj.* (especially of a road) having many bends or turns SYN **winding**, **zigzag**

**twit** /twɪt/ *noun* (*especially BrE, informal*) a silly or annoying person

**twitch** /twɪtʃ/ *verb, noun*
■ *verb* **1** [I, I] **~(sth)** if a part of your body **twitches**, or if you **twitch** it, it makes a sudden, quick movement, sometimes one that you cannot control: *Her lips twitched with amusement.* ◊ *The cats watched each other, their tails twitching.* **2** [T, I] **~(sth)** to give sth a short, sharp pull; to be pulled in this way: *He twitched the package out of my hands.* ◊ *The curtains twitched as she rang the bell.*
■ *noun* a sudden, quick movement that you cannot control in one of your muscles: *She has a twitch in her left eye.* ◊ *a nervous twitch* **2** a sudden, quick movement or feeling: *He greeted us with a mere twitch of his head.* ◊ *At that moment she felt the first twitch of anxiety.*

**twitchy** /ˈtwɪtʃi/ *adj.* (*informal*) **1** nervous or anxious about sth SYN **jittery 2** making sudden, quick movements

**Twit·ter**™ /ˈtwɪtə(r)/ *noun* [U] a SOCIAL MEDIA service that allows you to send out short messages about what you are doing or thinking, that people can access on the internet or on their mobile phones ⇨ compare MICROBLOGGING, TWEET

**twit·ter** /ˈtwɪtə(r)/ *verb, noun*
■ *verb* **1** (*also* **tweet**) [I] when birds **twitter**, they make a series of short, high sounds **2** [I, T] **~(on) (about sb/sth)** | **+ speech** (*especially BrE*) to talk quickly in a high, excited voice, especially about sth that is not very important **3** [I, T] **~(sth)** = TWEET (1)
■ *noun* [sing.] **1** (*also* **twit·ter·ing**) a series of short, high sounds that birds make **2** (*informal*) a state of nervous excitement **3** = TWEET (1)

**Twit·ter·verse** /ˈtwɪtəvɜːs; *NAmE* -vɜːrs/ (*usually* **the Twit·ter·verse**) (*also* **the Twit·ter·sphere**) /ðə ˈtwɪtəsfɪə(r); *NAmE* -sfɪr/ *noun* [sing.] (*informal*) all the messages that are sent using the Twitter SOCIAL MEDIA service, viewed as a network of people communicating with each other

**'twixt** /twɪkst/ *prep.* (*old use*) between IDM see SLIP *n.*

**two** /tuː/ *number* **2** HELP There are examples of how to use numbers at the entry for **five**.
IDM **a ˈday, ˈmoment, ˈpound, etc. or two** one or a few days, moments, pounds, etc.: *May I borrow it for a day or two?* **fall between two ˈstools** (*BrE*) to fail to be or to get either of two choices, both of which would have been acceptable **in ˈtwo** in or into two pieces or halves: *He broke the bar of chocolate in two and gave me half.* **in ˌtwos and ˈthrees** two or three at a time; in small numbers: *People arrived in twos and threes.* **it takes two to do sth** (*saying*) one person cannot be completely responsible for sth: *You can't put all the blame on him. It takes two to make a marriage.* **not have two cents, pennies, brain cells, etc. to rub toˈgether** (*informal*) to be very poor, stupid, etc. **put ˌtwo and ˌtwo toˈgether** to guess the truth from what you see, hear, etc: *He's inclined to put two and two together and make five (= reaches the wrong conclusion from what he sees, hears, etc.).* **that makes ˌtwo of us** (*informal*) I am in the same position or I agree with you: *'I'm tired.' 'That makes two of us!'* **two ˌsides of the same ˈcoin** used to talk about two ways of looking at the same situation ⇨ more at MIND *n.*, PENNY, SHAKE *n.*, TANGO *v.*

**ˈtwo-bit** *adj.* [only before noun] (*especially NAmE, informal*) not good or important: *She wanted to be more than just a two-bit secretary.*

**two ˈbits** *noun* [pl.] (*NAmE, old-fashioned, informal*) 25 cents

**two-diˈmen·sion·al** *adj.* **1** flat; having only two DIMENSIONS: *a two-dimensional drawing* **2** (especially of characters in fiction) having no depth; not seeming like real people: *The novel was criticized for its two-dimensional characters.*

**two-ˈedged** *adj.* = DOUBLE-EDGED

**two-ˈfaced** *adj.* (*informal, disapproving*) not sincere; not acting in a way that supports what you say that you believe; saying different things to different people about a particular subject SYN **hypocritical**

**two ˈfingers** *noun* [pl.] (*BrE, informal*) a sign that you make by holding up your hand with the inside part facing towards you and making a V-shape with your first and second fingers (used as a way of being rude to other people): *I gave him the two fingers.* ⇨ compare V-SIGN

**two·fold** /ˈtuːfəʊld/ *adj.* (*formal*) **1** consisting of two parts: *The problem was twofold.* **2** twice as much or as many: *a twofold increase in demand* ▶ **two·fold** *adv.*: *Her original investment has increased twofold.*

**two-ˈhanded** *adj.* using or needing both hands: *a two-handed backhand (= in tennis)* ◊ *a two-handed catch*

**two-ˈhander** *noun* (*especially BrE*) a play that is written for only two actors

**two ˈpence** (*also* **ˌtwo pence ˈpiece**, **2p** /ˌtuː ˈpiː/) *noun* a British coin worth two pence

**two·pence** /ˈtʌpəns/ *noun* (*BrE*) = TUPPENCE

**two·penny** (*also informal* **tup·penny**) /ˈtʌpəni; *NAmE also* ˈtuːpeni/ *adj.* (*BrE*) costing or worth two old pence: *a two-penny stamp*

**ˈtwo-piece** *noun* a set of clothes consisting of two matching pieces of clothing, for example a skirt and jacket or trousers and a jacket ▶ **two-piece** *adj.* [only before noun]: *a two-piece suit*

**ˈtwo-ply** *adj.* (of wool, cloth, paper or other material) with two THREADS or layers

**two-ˈseater** *noun* a vehicle, an aircraft or a piece of furniture with seats for two people

**two·some** /ˈtuːsəm/ *noun* a group of two people who do sth together SYN **pair**

**ˈtwo-star** *adj.* [usually before noun] **1** having two stars in a system that measures quality. The highest standard is usually represented by four or five stars: *a two-star hotel* **2** (in the US) having the fourth-highest military rank, and wearing uniform that has two stars on it

**two-step** *noun* a dance with long, sliding steps; the music for this dance

**two-stroke** *adj.* (of an engine or vehicle) with a PISTON that makes two movements, one up and one down, in each power CYCLE ⊃ compare FOUR-STROKE

**two-time** *verb* ~ **sb** (*informal*) to not be FAITHFUL to a person you have a relationship with, especially a sexual one, by having a secret relationship with sb else at the same time: *Are you sure he's not two-timing you?* ▶ **'two-timer** *noun*

**'two-tone** *adj.* [only before noun] having two different colours or sounds

**'twould** /twʊd/ *abbr.* (*old use*) it would

**two-,up two-'down** *noun* (*BrE, informal*) a house with two rooms on the bottom floor and two bedrooms upstairs

**two-way** *adj.* [usually before noun] **1** moving in two different directions; allowing sth to move in two different directions: *two-way traffic* ◊ *two-way trade* ◊ *a two-way switch* (= that allows electric current to be turned on or off from either of two points) **2** (of communication between people) needing equal effort from both people or groups involved: *Friendship is a two-way process.* **3** (of radio equipment, etc.) used both for sending and receiving signals

**two-way 'mirror** (*also* ,one-way 'mirror) *noun* a piece of glass that is a mirror on one side, but that you can see through from the other

**ty·coon** /taɪˈkuːn/ *noun* a person who is successful in business or industry and has become rich and powerful: *a business/property/media tycoon*

**tying** /ˈtaɪɪŋ/ *pres. part.* of TIE

**tyke** (*also* **tike**) /taɪk/ *noun* (*informal*) **1** a small child, especially one who behaves badly **2** (*BrE*) a person from Yorkshire

**type** 🔊 A1 ◐ /taɪp/ *noun, verb*
■ *noun* **1** A1 [C] a class or group of people or things that share particular qualities or features and are part of a larger group; a kind or sort: *a rare blood type* ◊ *~of sth Bungalows are a type of house.* ◊ *What type of car do you drive?* ◊ *There are three main types of contract(s).* ◊ *I think the same type of thing could happen here.* ◊ *I am not the type of person who gives up easily.* ◊ *He grew up listening to different types of music.* ◊ *I love this type of book.* ◊ *I love these types of books.* ◊ *of this/its~ It is the first car of its type to have this design feature.* **2** [sing.] (*informal*) a person of a particular character, with particular features, etc: *She's the artistic type.* ◊ *He's not the type to be unfaithful.* ◊ *She's not my type* (= not the kind of person I am usually attracted to). **3** **-type** (in adjectives) having the qualities or features of the group, person or thing mentioned: *a police-type badge* ◊ *a continental-type cafe* **4** [U] letters that are printed or typed: *The type was too small for me to read.* ◊ *The important words are in bold type.*
■ *verb* **1** B1 [I, T] to write sth using a computer keyboard or TYPEWRITER: *How fast can you type?* ◊ *typing errors* ◊ *~sth I typed my name and password.* ◊ *~sth in Type (in) the file-name, then press 'Return'.* ◊ *~sth out/up Have you typed up that report yet?* **2** [T] *~sb/sth* (*specialist*) to find out the group or class that a person or thing belongs to: *Blood samples were taken from patients for typing.*

**type·cast** /ˈtaɪpkɑːst; *NAmE* -kæst/ *verb* [usually passive] (**type·cast, type·cast**) ~ **sb** (**as sth**) if an actor is typecast, he or she is always given the same kind of character to play: *She didn't want to be typecast as a dumb blonde.*

**type·face** /ˈtaɪpfeɪs/ *noun* a set of letters, numbers, etc. of a particular design, used in printing: *I'd like the heading to be in a different typeface from the text.*

**type·script** /ˈtaɪpskrɪpt/ *noun* [C, U] a copy of a text or document that has been typed

**type·set·ter** /ˈtaɪpsetə(r)/ *noun* a person, machine or company that prepares a book, etc. for printing ▶ **type·set** *verb* (**type·set·ting, type·set, type·set**): *~sth Pages can now be typeset on screen.* **type·set·ting** *noun* [U]: *computerized typesetting*

**type·writer** /ˈtaɪpraɪtə(r)/ *noun* a machine that produces writing similar to print. It has keys that you press to make metal letters or signs hit a piece of paper through a long, narrow piece of cloth covered with INK (= coloured liquid). ⊃ see also TYPIST

**type·writ·ing** /ˈtaɪpraɪtɪŋ/ *noun* [U] = TYPING

**type·writ·ten** /ˈtaɪprɪtn/ *adj.* written using a typewriter or computer

**ty·phoid** /ˈtaɪfɔɪd/ (*also less frequent* **,typhoid 'fever**) *noun* [U] a serious disease that causes a high temperature, red spots on the chest and severe pain in the BOWELS, and sometimes causes death: *a typhoid epidemic*

**ty·phoon** /taɪˈfuːn/ *noun* a violent tropical storm with very strong winds ⊃ compare CYCLONE, HURRICANE

**ty·phus** /ˈtaɪfəs/ *noun* [U] a serious disease that causes a high temperature, headaches, purple marks on the body and often death

**typ·ical** 🔊 A2 ◐ /ˈtɪpɪkl/ *adj.* **1** A2 having the usual qualities or features of a particular type of person, thing or group SYN **representative**: *a typical Italian cafe* ◊ *This is a typical example of Roman pottery.* ◊ *~of sb/sth This meal is typical of local cookery.* ◊ *The weather at the moment is not typical for July.* OPP **atypical** ⚓ A2 [usually before noun] happening in the usual way; showing what sth is usually like SYN **normal**: *A typical working day for me begins at 7.30.* OPP **untypical** **3** B1 (*often disapproving*) behaving in the way that you expect: *He spoke with typical enthusiasm.* ◊ *~of sb/sth It was typical of her to forget.* ◊ (*informal*) *She's late again—typical!*

**typ·ic·al·ly** 🔊 B1 ◐ /ˈtɪpɪkli/ *adv.* **1** B1 used to say that sth usually happens in the way that you are stating: *The standard chips are typically used for databases and other business software.* ◊ *Generating solar power has typically involved higher capital costs.* **2** B1 in a way that shows the usual qualities or features of a particular type of person, thing or group: *typically American hospitality* ◊ *Mothers typically worry about their children.* **3** B1 in the way that you expect sb/sth to behave: *Typically, she couldn't find her keys.* ◊ *He was typically modest about his achievements.*

**typ·ify** /ˈtɪpɪfaɪ/ *verb* (**typi·fies, typi·fy·ing, typi·fied, typi·fied**) (not usually used in the progressive tenses) **1** ~ **sth** to be a typical example of sth: *clothes that typify the 1960s* ◊ *the new style of politician, typified by the Prime Minister* **2** ~ **sth** to be a typical feature of sth: *the haunting guitar melodies that typify the band's music*

**typ·ing** /ˈtaɪpɪŋ/ (*also less frequent* **type·writ·ing**) *noun* [U] **1** the activity or job of using a TYPEWRITER or computer to write sth: *to do the typing* ◊ *typing errors* ◊ *a typing pool* (= a group of people who share a company's typing work) **2** writing that has been done on a TYPEWRITER or computer

**typ·ist** /ˈtaɪpɪst/ *noun* **1** a person who works in an office typing letters, etc. **2** a person who uses a TYPEWRITER or computer keyboard: *I'm quite a fast typist.*

**typo** /ˈtaɪpəʊ/ *noun* (*pl.* **-os**) (*informal*) a small mistake in a typed or printed text

**typ·og·raph·er** /taɪˈpɒɡrəfə(r); *NAmE* -ˈpɑːɡ-/ *noun* a person who has skill in typography

**typ·og·raphy** /taɪˈpɒɡrəfi; *NAmE* -ˈpɑːɡ-/ *noun* [U] the art or work of preparing books, etc. for printing, especially of designing how text will appear when it is printed ▶ **typo·graph·ic·al** /ˌtaɪpəˈɡræfɪkl/ (*also* **typo·graph·ic** /-fɪk/) *adj.*: *a typographical error* ◊ *typographic design* **typo·graph·ic·al·ly** /-kli/ *adv.*

**typ·ology** /taɪˈpɒlədʒi; *NAmE* -ˈpɑːl-/ *noun* (*pl.* **-ies**) (*specialist*) a system of dividing things into different types

**tyr·an·nical** /tɪˈrænɪkl/ (*also formal* **tyr·an·nous** /ˈtɪrənəs/) *adj.* using power or authority over people in an unfair and cruel way SYN **autocratic, dictatorial**: *a tyrannical* government ◇ *He was brought up by a cruel and tyrannical father.*

**tyr·an·nize** (*BrE also* **-ise**) /ˈtɪrənaɪz/ *verb* [T, I] to use your power to treat sb in a cruel or unfair way: **~ sb/sth** *a father tyrannizing his children* ◇ **~ over sb/sth** *a political leader who tyrannizes over his people* ⊃ see also TYRANT

**tyr·an·no·saurus** /tɪˌrænəˈsɔːrəs, taɪ-/ (*also* **tyr·an·no·saur** /tɪˈrænəsɔː(r), taɪ-/) *noun* a very large DINOSAUR that stood on two legs, had large, powerful JAWS and two short front legs

**tyr·anny** /ˈtɪrəni/ *noun* [U, C] (*pl.* **-ies**) **1** unfair or cruel use of power or authority: *a victim of oppression and tyranny* ◇ *The children had no protection against the tyranny of their father.* ◇ *the tyrannies of Nazi rule* ◇ (*figurative*) *These days it seems we must all submit to the tyranny of the motor car.* **2** the rule of a tyrant; a country under this rule **SYN** **dictatorship**: *Any political system refusing to allow dissent becomes a tyranny.*

**tyr·ant** /ˈtaɪrənt/ *noun* a person who has complete power in a country and uses it in a cruel and unfair way **SYN** **dictator**: *The country was ruled by a succession of tyrants.* ◇ (*figurative*) *His boss is a complete tyrant.*

**tyre** ❶ **B1** (*BrE*) (*NAmE* **tire**) /ˈtaɪə(r)/ *noun* a thick rubber ring that fits around the edge of a wheel of a car, bicycle, etc: *a front/rear tyre* ◇ *to pump up a tyre* ◇ *a flat tyre* ◇ *Someone had slashed the tyres on her car.* ◇ *Remember to check your tyre pressure regularly.* ⊃ see also SPARE TYRE **IDM** see KICK *v.*

**tyro** /ˈtaɪrəʊ/ *noun* (*pl.* **-os**) a person who has little or no experience of sth or is beginning to learn sth **SYN** **novice**

**tzar, tzar·ina, tzar·ism, tzar·ist** = TSAR, TSARINA, TSARISM, TSARIST

# U u

**U** /juː/ *noun, abbr.*
- *noun* (also **u**) [C, U] (*pl.* **Us, U's, u's** /juːz/) the 21st letter of the English alphabet: *'Under' begins with (a) U/'U'.* ⇒ see also U-BOAT, U-TURN
- *abbr.* (*BrE*) universal (the label of a film that is suitable for anyone including children): *Aladdin, certificate U* ⇒ compare PG

**UAV** /ˌjuː eɪ ˈviː/ *noun* an aircraft without a pilot, controlled from the ground or by a computer on board (the abbreviation for 'unmanned aerial vehicle') **SYN** **drone**

**ˈU-bend** *noun* a section of pipe with a shape like a U, especially one that carries away used water

**uber-** (also **über-**) /ˈuːbə(r)/ *combining form* (from German, *informal*) (in nouns and adjectives) of the greatest or best kind; to a very large degree: *His girlfriend was a real uber-babe, with long blonde hair and a big smile.* ◊ *This stylish new restaurant is futuristic and uber-cool.*

**ubi·qui·tous** /juːˈbɪkwɪtəs/ *adj.* [usually before noun] (*formal or humorous*) seeming to be everywhere or in several places at the same time; very common: *the ubiquitous bicycles of university towns* ◊ *the ubiquitous movie star, Tom Hanks* ▸ **ubi·qui·tous·ly** *adv.* **ubi·quity** /-kwəti/ *noun* [U]: *the ubiquity of the mass media*

**ˈU-boat** *noun* a German SUBMARINE (= a ship that can travel UNDERWATER)

**u·buntu** /ʊˈbʊntuː/ *SAfrE* [ʊˈbʊntʊ] *noun* [U] (*SAfrE*) the idea that people are not only individuals but live in a community and must share things and care for each other: *The concept of ubuntu involves deep concern for others and having sound morals.* ◊ *The rekindling of the spirit of Ubuntu will restore tolerance and dialogue.*

**u.c.** *abbr.* (in writing) UPPER CASE

**UCAS** /ˈjuːkæs/ *abbr.* (in the UK) Universities and Colleges Admissions Service (an official organization that deals with applications to study at universities and colleges)

**udder** /ˈʌdə(r)/ *noun* an organ like a bag in shape that produces milk and hangs under the body of a cow, GOAT, etc.

**UEFA** /juːˈeɪfə/ *abbr.* Union of European Football Associations

**UFO** (also **ufo**) /ˌjuː ef ˈəʊ; ˈjuːfəʊ/ *noun* (*pl.* **UFOs** or **ufos**) a strange object that some people claim to have seen in the sky and believe is a SPACECRAFT from another planet (the abbreviation for 'unidentified flying object') ⇒ compare FLYING SAUCER

**ugali** /uːˈɡɑːli/ *EAfrE* [uˈɡali] *noun* [U] (*EAfrE*) a type of food made with flour from MAIZE or MILLET, usually eaten with meat or vegetable STEW

**UGC** /ˌjuː dʒiː ˈsiː/ *abbr.* user-generated content (any data or media created by individual users of a website and available for others to use): *Consumers between 25 and 54 years old were the biggest content drivers, contributing 70% of all UGC.*

**ugh** (also **urgh**) /ɜː, ʊx/ *exclamation* the way of writing the sound that people make when they think that sth is horrible: *Ugh! How can you eat that stuff?*

**Ugli™** /ˈʌɡli/ (also **Ugli fruit**) *noun* a large CITRUS fruit with a rough, yellow-orange skin, that is sweet inside and has a lot of juice

**ugly** 🔑 B1 /ˈʌɡli/ *adj.* (**ug·lier, ug·li·est**) **1** 🔑 B1 unpleasant to look at **SYN** **unattractive**: *an ugly face* ◊ *an ugly building* **2** 🔑 B2 (of an event, a situation, etc.) unpleasant or dangerous; involving threats or violence: *an ugly incident/scene* ◊ *A fight started and things got pretty ugly.* ▸ **ugli·ness** *noun* [U] **IDM** see HEAD *n.*, SIN *n.*

**ˌugly ˈduckling** *noun* a person or thing that at first does not seem attractive or likely to succeed but that later becomes successful or much admired **ORIGIN** From the title of a story by Hans Christian Andersen, in which a young swan thinks it is an ugly young duck until it grows up into a beautiful adult swan.

**uh** /ʌ, ɜː/ *exclamation* the way of writing the sound that people make when they are not sure about sth, when they do not hear or understand sth you have said, or when they want you to agree with what they have said: *Uh, yeah, I guess so.* ◊ *'Are you ready yet?' 'Uh? Oh. Yes.'* ◊ *We can discuss this another time, uh?*

**UHF** /ˌjuː eɪtʃ ˈef/ *abbr.* ultra-high frequency (a range of radio waves used for high-quality radio and television broadcasting)

**uh-huh** /ʌ ˈhʌ/ *exclamation* the way of writing the sound that people make when they understand or agree with what you have said, when they want you to continue or when they are answering 'Yes': *'Did you read my note?' 'Uh-huh.'*

**uh-oh** /ˈʌ əʊ/ (also **oh-oh**) *exclamation* the way of writing the sound that people make when they want to say that they have done sth wrong or that they think there will be trouble: *Uh-oh. I forgot to write that letter.* ◊ *Uh-oh! Turn the TV off. Here comes Dad!*

**UHT** /ˌjuː eɪtʃ ˈtiː/ *abbr.* (*BrE*) ultra heat treated. UHT milk has been heated to a very high temperature in order to make it last for a long time.

**uh-uh** /ˈʌ ʌ/ *exclamation* the way of writing the sound that people make when they are answering 'No' to a question

**UI** /ˌjuː ˈaɪ/ *abbr.* (*computing*) user interface (the way a computer gives information to a user or receives instructions from a user)

**uja·maa** /uːˈdʒɑːmɑː/ *EAfrE* [uˈdʒamaː] *noun* [U] (*EAfrE*) (in Tanzania) SOCIALISM

**UK** (also **U.K.** especially in US) /ˌjuː ˈkeɪ/ *abbr.* UNITED KINGDOM

**UK garage** /ˌjuː keɪ ˈɡærɪdʒ; *NAmE* ɡəˈrɑːdʒ/ *noun* [U] = GARAGE (4)

**uku·lele** /ˌjuːkəˈleɪli/ (also *informal* **uke** /juːk/) *noun* a musical instrument with four strings, like a small guitar

ukulele

**ulcer** /ˈʌlsə(r)/ *noun* a painful area on the outside of the body or on the surface of an organ inside the body that may BLEED or produce a poisonous substance: *a stomach ulcer* ⇒ see also PEPTIC ULCER

**ul·cer·ate** /ˈʌlsəreɪt/ *verb* [I, T, usually passive] ~ **(sth)** (*medical*) to become, or make sth become, covered with ulcers ▸ **ul·cer·ation** /ˌʌlsəˈreɪʃn/ *noun* [U, C]

**ulna** /ˈʌlnə/ *noun* (*pl.* **ulnae** /-niː/) (*anatomy*) the longer bone of the two bones in the lower part of the arm between the ELBOW and the WRIST, on the side opposite the THUMB ⇒ see also RADIUS (3) ⇒ VISUAL VOCAB page V1

**ul·ter·ior** /ʌlˈtɪəriə(r); *NAmE* -ˈtɪr-/ *adj.* [only before noun] (of a reason for doing sth) that sb keeps hidden and does not admit: *She must have some* ***ulterior motive*** *for being nice to me—what does she really want?*

**ul·tim·ate** 🔑+ B2 🌐 /ˈʌltɪmət/ *adj., noun*
- *adj.* [only before noun] **1** 🔑+ B2 happening at the end of a long process **SYN** **final**: *our ultimate goal/aim/objective/target* ◊ *We will accept ultimate responsibility for whatever happens.* ◊ *The ultimate decision lies with the parents.* **2** 🔑+ B2 most extreme; best, worst, greatest, most important, etc.: *This race will be the ultimate test of your skill.* ◊ *Silk sheets are the ultimate luxury.* **3** from which sth originally comes **SYN** **basic, fundamental**: *the ultimate truths of philosophy and science*
- *noun* [sing.] **the ~ in sth** (*informal*) the best, most advanced, greatest, etc. of its kind: *the ultimate in modern design*

**ˌUltimate ˈFighting™** (also **exˌtreme ˈfighting**) *noun* [U] a sport that combines different styles of fighting such as BOXING, WRESTLING and MARTIAL ARTS and in which there are not many rules

**ul·ti·mate·ly** 🔊 B2 W /ˈʌltɪmətli/ adv. **1** B2 in the end; finally: *A poor diet will ultimately lead to illness.* ◇ *He is ultimately responsible for the actions of the rebels he leads* **2** at the most basic and important level: *All life depends ultimately on oxygen.* ◇ *Ultimately, however, films come down to their stories and characters.*

**ul·ti·ma·tum** /ˌʌltɪˈmeɪtəm/ noun (pl. **ul·ti·ma·tums** or **ul·ti·ma·ta** /-tə/) a final warning to a person or country that if they do not do what you ask, you will use force or take action against them: *to issue an ultimatum*

**ultra** /ˈʌltrə/ noun a person who holds extreme views, especially in politics

**ultra-** /ˈʌltrə/ prefix (in adjectives and nouns) extremely; beyond a particular limit: *ultra-modern* ◇ *ultraviolet* ⇒ compare INFRA-

**ultra-high ˈfrequency** noun [U] = UHF

**ultra·light** /ˈʌltrəlaɪt/ (NAmE) (BrE **micro·light**) noun a very small light aircraft for one or two people

**ultra·mar·ine** /ˌʌltrəməˈriːn/ noun [U] a bright blue colour

**ultra·short** /ˌʌltrəˈʃɔːt; NAmE -ˈʃɔːrt/ adj. (of radio waves) having a very short WAVELENGTH (shorter than 10 metres), with a frequency greater than 30 MEGAHERTZ ⇒ compare LONG WAVE, MEDIUM WAVE, SHORT WAVE

**ultra·son·ic** /ˌʌltrəˈsɒnɪk; NAmE -ˈsɑːn-/ adj. [usually before noun] (of sounds) higher than humans can hear: *ultrasonic waves*

**ultra·sound** /ˈʌltrəsaʊnd/ noun **1** [U] sound that is higher than humans can hear **2** [U, C] a medical process that produces an image of what is inside your body: *Ultrasound showed she was expecting twins.* ⇒ WORDFINDER NOTE at EXAMINE

**ultra·vio·let** /ˌʌltrəˈvaɪələt/ (abbr. **UV**) adj. [usually before noun] (physics) of or using ELECTROMAGNETIC waves that are just shorter than those of VIOLET light in the SPECTRUM and that cannot be seen: *ultraviolet rays* (= that cause the skin to go darker) ◇ *an ultraviolet lamp* ⇒ compare INFRARED

**ulu·late** /ˈʌljuleɪt, ˈjuːl-/ verb [I] (literary) to give a long, loud call SYN wail ▶ **ulu·la·tion** /ˌʌljuˈleɪʃn, ˌjuːl-/ noun [U, C]

**um** /ʌm, əm/ exclamation the way of writing the sound that people make when they hesitate, or do not know what to say next: *Um, I'm not sure how to ask you this…*

**umami** /uːˈmɑːmi/ noun [U] a taste found in some foods that is neither sweet, SOUR, bitter nor SALTY: *Tomatoes have lots of umami.*

**umber** /ˈʌmbə(r)/ noun [U] a dark brown or yellow-brown colour used in paints

**um·bil·ical cord** /ʌmˈbɪlɪkl kɔːd; NAmE kɔːrd/ noun a long piece of TISSUE that connects a baby to its mother before it is born and is cut at the moment of birth ⇒ WORDFINDER NOTE at BIRTH

**um·bil·icus** /ʌmˈbɪlɪkəs, ˌʌmbɪˈlaɪkəs/ noun (pl. **um·bil·ici** /ʌmˈbɪlɪsaɪ, -lɪkaɪ, ˌʌmbɪˈlaɪsaɪ, -ˈlaɪkaɪ/ or **um·bil·icuses**) (specialist) the NAVEL

**umbra** /ˈʌmbrə/ noun (pl. **um·bras** or **um·brae** /-briː/) (specialist) **1** the darkest part of a shadow **2** the area on the earth or the moon that is the darkest during an ECLIPSE ⇒ compare PENUMBRA

**um·brage** /ˈʌmbrɪdʒ/ noun
IDM ▶ **take ˈumbrage (at sth)** (formal or humorous) to feel offended, hurt or upset by sth, often without a good reason SYN **offence**

**um·brella** 🔊 A1 /ʌmˈbrelə/ noun **1** A1 (also BrE, informal **brolly**) an object with a round folding frame of long, straight pieces of metal covered with material, that you use to protect yourself from the rain or from hot sun: *to carry/hold an umbrella* ◇ *colourful beach umbrellas* ⇒ compare PARASOL, SUNSHADE **2** a thing that contains or includes many different parts or elements: **under the ~ of sth** *Many previously separate groups are now operating under the umbrella of a single authority.* ◇ *an umbrella organization/group/fund* ◇ *'Contact sports' is an umbrella term for a variety of different sports.* **3** a country or system that protects people

**um·faan** /ʊmˈfɑːn/ noun (pl. **um·faans** or **ba·fana** /bəˈfɑːnə/) (SAfrE) **1** a young black man who is not married **2** a young black boy

**um·laut** /ˈʊmlaʊt/ noun the mark placed over a vowel in some languages to show how it should be pronounced, as over the *u* in the German word *für* ⇒ compare ACUTE ACCENT, CIRCUMFLEX, GRAVE², TILDE

**um·pire** /ˈʌmpaɪə(r)/ noun, verb
▪ noun (also NAmE, informal **ump** /ʌmp/) (in sports such as tennis and baseball ) a person whose job is to watch a game and make sure that rules are not broken ⇒ compare REFEREE
▪ verb [I, T] to act as an umpire: *We need someone to umpire.* ◇ *~ sth to umpire a game of baseball*

**ump·teen** /ˌʌmpˈtiːn/ det. (informal) very many: *I've told this story umpteen times.* ▶ **ump·teen** pron.: *Umpteen of them all arrived at once.* **ump·teenth** /-ˈtiːnθ/ det.: *'This is crazy,' she told herself for the umpteenth time* (= she had done it many times before).

**UN** (also **U.N.** especially in US) /ˌjuː ˈen/ abbr. United Nations (an association of many countries that aims to help economic and social conditions improve and to solve political problems in the world in a peaceful way): *the UN Security Council* ◇ *a UN peacekeeping plan*

**un-** /ʌn/ prefix **1** (in adjectives, adverbs and nouns) not; the opposite of: *unable* ◇ *unconsciously* ◇ *untruth* **2** (in verbs that describe the opposite of a process): *unlock* ◇ *undo*

**'un** /ən/ pron. (BrE, informal) a way of saying or writing 'one': *That was a good 'un.* ◇ *The little 'uns* (= the small children) *couldn't keep up.*

**un·abashed** /ˌʌnəˈbæʃt/ adj. not ashamed, embarrassed or affected by people's negative opinions, when other people would be OPP **abashed** ▶ **un·abashed·ly** /-ˈbæʃɪdli/ adv.

**un·abated** /ˌʌnəˈbeɪtɪd/ adj. [not usually before noun] (formal) without becoming any less strong: *The rain continued unabated.*

**un·able** 🔊 B1 /ʌnˈeɪbl/ adj. [not before noun] **~ to do sth** (rather formal) not having the skill, strength, time, knowledge, etc. to do sth: *a former soldier who has been unable to find work since the war ended* ◇ *They have been unable or unwilling to resolve the conflict.* OPP **able**

**un·abridged** /ˌʌnəˈbrɪdʒd/ adj. (of a novel, play, speech, etc.) complete, without being made shorter in any way OPP **abridged**

**un·accept·able** 🔊 B2 /ˌʌnəkˈseptəbl/ adj. so bad that you think it should not be allowed: *Such behaviour is totally unacceptable in a civilized society.* ◇ *Noise from the factory has reached an unacceptable level.* OPP **acceptable** ▶ **un·accept·ably** /-bli/ adv.: *unacceptably high levels of unemployment*

**un·accom·pan·ied** /ˌʌnəˈkʌmpənid/ adj. **1** (formal) without a person going together with sb/sth: *No unaccompanied children allowed.* ◇ *unaccompanied luggage/baggage* (= travelling separately from its owner) **2** (music) performed without anyone else playing or singing at the same time: *a sonata for unaccompanied violin* **3** (formal) **~ by sth** not together with a particular thing: *Mere words, unaccompanied by any violence, cannot amount to an assault.*

**un·account·able** /ˌʌnəˈkaʊntəbl/ adj. (formal) **1** impossible to understand or explain SYN **inexplicable**: *For some unaccountable reason, the letter never arrived.* **2 ~ (to sb/sth)** not having to explain or give reasons for your actions to anyone: *Too many government departments are unaccountable to the general public.* OPP **accountable**

**un·account·ably** /ˌʌnəˈkaʊntəbli/ adv. (formal) in a way that is very difficult to explain; without any obvious reason SYN **inexplicably**: *He has been unaccountably delayed.*

**un·account·ed for** /ˌʌnəˈkaʊntɪd fɔː(r)/ adj. [not before noun] **1** a person or thing that is **unaccounted for** cannot be found and people do not know what has happened to them or it: *At least 300 civilians are unaccounted for after the bombing raids.* **2** not explained: *In the story he gave the police, half an hour was left unaccounted for.*

**un·accus·tomed** /ˌʌnəˈkʌstəmd/ adj. (formal) **1 ~ to sth / to doing sth** not in the habit of doing sth; not used to sth: *He was unaccustomed to hard work.* ◇ *I am unaccustomed to being told what to do.* **2** [usually before noun] not usual, normal or familiar: *The unaccustomed heat made him weary.* **OPP** accustomed

**un·achiev·able** /ˌʌnəˈtʃiːvəbl/ adj. that you cannot manage to reach or obtain: *unachievable goals* **OPP** achievable

**un·acknow·ledged** /ˌʌnəkˈnɒlɪdʒd; *NAmE* -ˈnɑːl-/ adj. **1** not receiving the thanks or praise that is deserved: *Her contribution to the research went largely unacknowledged.* **2** that people do not admit as existing or true; that people are not aware of: *unacknowledged feelings* **3** not publicly or officially recognized: *the unacknowledged leader of the group*

**un·ac·quaint·ed** /ˌʌnəˈkweɪntɪd/ adj. **~ (with sth / sb)** (formal) not familiar with sth/sb; having no experience of sth: *visitors unacquainted with local customs* **OPP** acquainted

**un·ad·just·ed** /ˌʌnəˈdʒʌstɪd/ adj. (statistics) (of figures) not changed according to particular facts or circumstances; not ADJUSTED: *Unadjusted figures which do not take tourism into account showed that unemployment fell in July.*

**un·adorned** /ˌʌnəˈdɔːnd; *NAmE* -ˈdɔːrnd/ adj. (formal) without any decoration **SYN** simple: *The walls were plain and unadorned.*

**un·adul·ter·ated** /ˌʌnəˈdʌltəreɪtɪd/ adj. **1** [usually before noun] you use **unadulterated** to emphasize that sth is complete or total **SYN** undiluted: *For me, the holiday was sheer unadulterated pleasure.* **2** not mixed with other substances; not ADULTERATED **SYN** pure: *unadulterated foods*

**un·ad·ven·tur·ous** /ˌʌnədˈventʃərəs/ adj. not willing to take risks or try new and exciting things **SYN** cautious **OPP** adventurous

**un·affect·ed** /ˌʌnəˈfektɪd/ adj. **1 ~ (by sth)** not changed or influenced by sth; not affected by sth: *People's rights are unaffected by the new law.* ◇ *Some members of the family may remain unaffected by the disease.* **2** (approving) (of a person or their behaviour) natural and sincere **OPP** affected

**un·affili·ated** /ˌʌnəˈfɪlieɪtɪd/ adj. **~ (with sth)** not belonging to or connected with a political party or a large organization **SYN** independent **OPP** affiliated

**un·afford·able** /ˌʌnəˈfɔːdəbl; *NAmE* -ˈfɔːrd-/ adj. costing so much that people do not have enough money to pay for it: *Health insurance is now unaffordable for many people.* **OPP** affordable

**un·afraid** /ˌʌnəˈfreɪd/ adj. [not before noun] (formal) not afraid or nervous; not worried about what might happen: **~ (of sth)** *She was unafraid of conflict.* ◇ **~ (to do sth)** *He's unafraid to speak his mind.*

**un·aid·ed** /ʌnˈeɪdɪd/ adj., adv. (formal) without help from anyone or anything: *He can now walk unaided.*

**un·ali·en·able** /ʌnˈeɪliənəbl/ adj. (formal) = INALIENABLE

**un·alloyed** /ˌʌnəˈlɔɪd/ adj. (formal) not mixed with anything else, such as negative feelings **SYN** pure: *unalloyed joy*

**un·alter·able** /ʌnˈɔːltərəbl/ adj. (formal) that cannot be changed **SYN** immutable: *the unalterable laws of the universe*

**un·altered** /ʌnˈɔːltəd; *NAmE* -tərd/ adj. that has not changed or been changed: *This practice has remained unaltered for centuries.*

**un·am·bigu·ous** /ˌʌnæmˈbɪɡjuəs/ adj. clear in meaning; that can only be understood in one way: *an unambiguous statement* ◇ *The message was clear and unambiguous—'Get out!'* **OPP** ambiguous ▸ **un·am·bigu·ous·ly** adv.

**un·am·bi·tious** /ˌʌnæmˈbɪʃəs/ adj. **1** (of a person) not interested in becoming successful, rich, powerful, etc. **2** not involving a lot of effort, time, money, etc. or anything new: *an unambitious plan* **OPP** ambitious

**un-A·mer·i·can** adj. against American values or interests

**unan·im·ity** /ˌjuːnəˈnɪməti/ noun [U] complete agreement about sth among a group of people

**unani·mous** /juˈnænɪməs/ adj. **1** if a decision or an opinion is **unanimous**, it is agreed or shared by everyone in a group: *a unanimous vote* ◇ *unanimous support* ◇ *The decision was not unanimous.* **2 ~ (in sth)** if a group of people are **unanimous**, they all agree about sth: *Local people are unanimous in their opposition to the proposed new road.* ▸ **unani·mous·ly** adv.: *The motion was passed unanimously.*

**un·announced** /ˌʌnəˈnaʊnst/ adj. happening without anyone being told or warned in advance: *She just turned up unannounced on my doorstep.* ◇ *an unannounced increase in bus fares*

**un·answer·able** /ʌnˈɑːnsərəbl; *NAmE* -ˈæn-/ adj. **1** an **unanswerable** argument, etc. is one that nobody can question or disagree with **SYN** irrefutable: *They presented an unanswerable case for more investment.* **2** an **unanswerable** question is one that has no answer or that you cannot answer

**un·answered** /ʌnˈɑːnsəd; *NAmE* -ˈænsərd/ adj. **1** (of a question, problem, etc.) that has not been answered: *Many questions about the crime remain unanswered.* **2** (of a letter, phone call, etc.) that has not been replied to: *unanswered letters*

**un·antici·pated** /ˌʌnænˈtɪsɪpeɪtɪd/ adj. (formal) that you have not expected or predicted: *unanticipated costs* **OPP** anticipated

**un·apolo·get·ic** /ˌʌnəpɒləˈdʒetɪk; *NAmE* -ˌpɑːl-/ adj. not saying that you are sorry about sth, even in situations in which other people might expect you to **OPP** apologetic ▸ **un·apolo·get·ic·al·ly** /-kli/ adv.

**un·appeal·ing** /ˌʌnəˈpiːlɪŋ/ adj. not attractive or pleasant: *The room was painted in an unappealing shade of brown.* ◇ *The prospect of studying for another five years was distinctly unappealing.* **OPP** appealing

**un·appe·tiz·ing** (*BrE also* -is·ing) /ʌnˈæpɪtaɪzɪŋ/ adj. (of food) unpleasant to eat; looking as if it will be unpleasant to eat **OPP** appetizing

**un·appre·ci·ated** /ˌʌnəˈpriːʃieɪtɪd/ adj. [not usually before noun] not having your work or your qualities recognized and enjoyed by other people; not appreciated: *He was in a job where he felt unappreciated and undervalued.*

**un·approach·able** /ˌʌnəˈprəʊtʃəbl/ adj. (of a person) not friendly or easy to talk to: *Neighbours described the man as being difficult and unapproachable.* **OPP** approachable

**un·argu·able** /ʌnˈɑːɡjuəbl; *NAmE* -ˈɑːrɡju-/ adj. (formal) that nobody can disagree with: *unarguable proof* ⇨ compare ARGUABLE ▸ **un·argu·ably** /-bli/ adv.: *She is unarguably one of the country's finest athletes.*

**un·armed** /ʌnˈɑːmd; *NAmE* -ˈɑːrmd/ adj. **1** not carrying a weapon: *unarmed civilians* **2** not involving the use of weapons: *The soldiers were trained in unarmed combat.* **OPP** armed

**un·ashamed** /ˌʌnəˈʃeɪmd/ adj. not feeling ashamed or embarrassed about sth, especially when people might expect you to ⇨ compare ASHAMED ▸ **un·ashamed·ly** /-ˈʃeɪmɪdli/ adv.: *She wept unashamedly.* ◇ *an unashamedly sentimental song*

**un·asked** /ʌnˈɑːskt; *NAmE* -ˈæskt/ adj. **1** an **unasked** question is one that you have not asked even though you would like to know the answer **2** without being invited or asked: *He came to the party unasked.* ◇ *She brought him, unasked, the relevant file.*

**unˈasked-for** adj. that has not been asked for or requested: *unasked-for advice*

**un·assail·able** /ˌʌnəˈseɪləbl/ adj. (formal) that cannot be destroyed, defeated or questioned: *The party now has an* *unassailable lead.* ◇ *Their ten-point lead puts the team in an almost unassailable position.*

**un·assigned** /ˌʌnəˈsaɪnd/ *adj.* not given to or reserved for any particular person or purpose

**un·assist·ed** /ˌʌnəˈsɪstɪd/ *adj.* not helped by anyone or anything **SYN** **unaided**: *She could not move unassisted.*

**un·assum·ing** /ˌʌnəˈsjuːmɪŋ; *NAmE* -ˈsuː-/ *adj.* (*approving*) not wanting to draw attention to yourself or to your abilities or status **SYN** **modest**

**un·attached** /ˌʌnəˈtætʃt/ *adj.* **1** not married or involved in a romantic relationship **SYN** **single**: *He was still unattached at the age of 34.* **2** not connected with or belonging to a particular group or organization ⇒ compare ATTACHED

**un·attain·able** /ˌʌnəˈteɪnəbl/ *adj.* impossible to achieve or reach: *an unattainable goal* **OPP** **attainable**

**un·attend·ed** /ˌʌnəˈtendɪd/ *adj.* (*formal*) without the owner present; not being watched or cared for: *unattended vehicles* ◇ *Never leave young children unattended.*

**un·attract·ive** /ˌʌnəˈtræktɪv/ *adj.* **1** not attractive or pleasant to look at: *an unattractive brown colour* **2** not good, interesting or pleasant: *one of the unattractive aspects of the free market economy* **OPP** **attractive** ▸ **un·attract·ive·ly** *adv.*

**un·author·ized** (*BrE also* **-ised**) /ʌnˈɔːθəraɪzd/ *adj.* without official permission: *No access for unauthorized personnel.* **OPP** **authorized**

**un·avail·able** /ˌʌnəˈveɪləbl/ *adj.* [not usually before noun] **1** ~ (to sb/sth) that cannot be obtained: *Such luxuries are unavailable to ordinary people.* **2** not able or not willing to see, meet or talk to sb: *The minister was unavailable for comment.* **OPP** **available** ▸ **un·avail·abil·ity** /ˌʌnəveɪləˈbɪləti/ *noun* [U]

**un·avail·ing** /ˌʌnəˈveɪlɪŋ/ *adj.* (*formal*) without success **SYN** **unsuccessful**: *Their efforts were unavailing.*

**un·avoid·able** /ˌʌnəˈvɔɪdəbl/ *adj.* impossible to avoid or prevent: *unavoidable delays* **OPP** **avoidable** ▸ **un·avoid·ably** /-bli/ *adv.*: *I was unavoidably delayed.*

**un·aware** /ˌʌnəˈweə(r); *NAmE* -ˈwer/ *adj.* [not before noun] not knowing or realizing that sth is happening or that sth exists: *~ of sth He was completely unaware of the whole affair.* ◇ *~ that … She was unaware that I could see her.* **OPP** **aware** ▸ **un·aware·ness** *noun* [U]

**un·awares** /ˌʌnəˈweəz; *NAmE* -ˈwerz/ *adv.* **1** when not expected: *The camera had caught me unawares.* ◇ *The announcement took me unawares.* ◇ *She came upon him unawares when he was searching her room.* **2** (*formal*) without noticing or realizing: *He slipped unawares into sleep.*

**un·bal·ance** /ʌnˈbæləns/ *verb* **1** ~ sth to make sth no longer balanced, for example by giving too much importance to one part of it **2** ~ sb/sth to make sb/sth unsteady so that they are likely to fall down **3** ~ sb to make sb slightly crazy or mentally ill

**un·bal·anced** /ʌnˈbælənst/ *adj.* **1** [not usually before noun] (of a person) slightly crazy; mentally ill **2** [usually before noun] giving too much or too little importance to one part or aspect of sth: *an unbalanced article* ◇ *an unbalanced diet*

**un·bear·able** /ʌnˈbeərəbl; *NAmE* -ˈber-/ *adj.* too painful, annoying or unpleasant to deal with or accept **SYN** **intolerable**: *The heat was becoming unbearable.* ◇ *unbearable pain* ◇ *He's been unbearable since he won that prize.* **OPP** **bearable** ▸ **un·bear·ably** /-bli/ *adv.*: *unbearably hot*

**un·beat·able** /ʌnˈbiːtəbl/ *adj.* **1** (of a team, player, etc.) impossible to defeat **SYN** **invincible** **2** (of prices, value, etc.) impossible to improve: *unbeatable offers*

**un·beat·en** /ʌnˈbiːtn/ *adj.* (*sport*) not having been defeated: *The team are unbeaten in their last four games.* ◇ *They will be putting their unbeaten record to the test next Saturday.*

**un·be·com·ing** /ˌʌnbɪˈkʌmɪŋ/ *adj.* (*formal*) **1** not suiting a particular person **SYN** **unflattering**: *She was wearing an unbecoming shade of purple.* **2** ~ (to/of sb) not appropriate or acceptable **SYN** **inappropriate**: *He was accused of conduct unbecoming to an officer.* **OPP** **becoming**

**un·be·fit·ting** /ˌʌnbɪˈfɪtɪŋ/ *adj.* ~ (of/for/to sb/sth) (*formal*) not suitable or good enough for sb/sth: *His behaviour is unbefitting of a university professor.* ◇ *The amount of litter in the streets is unbefitting for a historic city.*

**un·be·known** /ˌʌnbɪˈnəʊn/ (*also less frequent* **un·be·knownst** /ˌʌnbɪˈnəʊnst/) *adj.* ~ to sb (*formal*) without the person mentioned knowing: *Unbeknown to her they had organized a surprise party.*

**un·be·lief** /ˌʌnbɪˈliːf/ *noun* [U] (*formal*) lack of belief, or the state of not believing, especially in God, a religion, etc. ⇒ compare BELIEF, DISBELIEF

**un·believ·able** /ˌʌnbɪˈliːvəbl/ *adj.* **1** (*informal*) used to emphasize how good, bad or extreme sth is **SYN** **incredible**: *We had an unbelievable (= very good) time in Paris.* ◇ *Conditions in the prison camp were unbelievable (= very bad).* ◇ *The cold was unbelievable (= it was extremely cold).* ◇ *It's unbelievable that (= very shocking) they have permitted this trial to go ahead.* **2** very difficult to believe and unlikely to be true **SYN** **incredible**: *I found the whole story bizarre, not to say unbelievable.* ▸ **un·believ·ably** *adv.*: *unbelievably bad/good* ◇ *Unbelievably it actually works.*

**un·believer** /ˌʌnbɪˈliːvə(r)/ *noun* (*formal*) a person who does not believe, especially in God, a religion, etc. **OPP** **believer**

**un·believ·ing** /ˌʌnbɪˈliːvɪŋ/ *adj.* (*formal*) feeling or showing that you do not believe sb/sth: *She stared at us with unbelieving eyes.* ◇ *He gazed at the letter, unbelieving.*

**un·bend** /ʌnˈbend/ *verb* (**un·bent**, **un·bent** /-ˈbent/) **1** [I] to relax and become less strict or formal in your behaviour or attitude **2** [T, I] ~ (sth) to make sth that was bent become straight; to become straight

**un·bend·ing** /ʌnˈbendɪŋ/ *adj.* (*often disapproving*) unwilling to change your opinions, decisions, etc. **SYN** **inflexible**

**un·biased** /ʌnˈbaɪəst/ *adj.* fair and not influenced by your own or sb else's opinions, desires, etc. **SYN** **impartial**: *unbiased advice* ◇ *an unbiased judge* **OPP** **biased**

**un·bid·den** /ʌnˈbɪdn/ *adj.* (*literary*) (usually used after the verb) without being asked, invited or expected **SYN** **unasked**: *He walked into the room unbidden.*

**un·bleached** /ʌnˈbliːtʃt/ *adj.* not made whiter by the use of chemicals; not bleached: *unbleached flour*

**un·blem·ished** /ʌnˈblemɪʃt/ *adj.* (*formal*) not SPOILED, damaged or marked in any way: *He had an unblemished reputation.* ◇ *her pale unblemished skin*

**un·blink·ing** /ʌnˈblɪŋkɪŋ/ *adj.* (*formal*) if sb has an **unblinking stare** or looks with **unblinking eyes**, they look very steadily at sth and do not BLINK ▸ **un·blink·ing·ly** *adv.*

**un·block** /ʌnˈblɒk; *NAmE* -ˈblɑːk/ *verb* **1** ~ sth to clean sth, for example a pipe, by removing sth that is blocking it **2** ~ sth to make it possible to use a mobile phone again after it has been stopped from working as a security measure ⇒ compare UNLOCK (3)

**un·born** /ʌnˈbɔːn; *NAmE* -ˈbɔːrn/ *adj.* [usually before noun] not yet born: *her unborn baby*

**un·bound·ed** /ʌnˈbaʊndɪd/ *adj.* (*formal*) having, or seeming to have, no limits **SYN** **boundless**, **infinite**: *her unbounded energy*

**un·bowed** /ʌnˈbaʊd/ *adj.* (*literary*) not defeated or not ready to accept defeat: *The losing team left the field bloody but unbowed.*

**un·brand·ed** /ʌnˈbrændɪd/ *adj.* (of a product) that does not have a brand name: *The website sells cheap, unbranded clothes and accessories.* **OPP** **branded**

**un·break·able** /ʌnˈbreɪkəbl/ *adj.* impossible to break **SYN** **indestructible**: *This new material is virtually unbreakable.* **OPP** **breakable**

**un·bridge·able** /ʌnˈbrɪdʒəbl/ *adj.* an **unbridgeable** gap or difference between two people or groups or their opinions is one that cannot be closed or made less wide

**un·bridled** /ʌnˈbraɪdld/ *adj.* [usually before noun] (*literary*) lacking control and therefore extreme: *unbridled passion*

# unbroken

**un·bro·ken** /ʌnˈbrəʊkən/ *adj.* **1** not interrupted in any way: *a single unbroken line* ◊ *30 years of virtually unbroken peace* ◊ *my first night of unbroken sleep since the baby was born* **2** (of a record in a sport, etc.) that has not been improved on: *His long jump record remained unbroken for 25 years.*

**un·buckle** /ʌnˈbʌkl/ *verb* ~ sth to open the BUCKLE of a belt, shoe, etc.

**un·bur·den** /ʌnˈbɜːdn; *NAmE* -ˈbɜːrdn/ *verb* (*formal*) **1** ~ yourself / sth (of sth) (to sb) to talk to sb about your problems or sth you have been worrying about, so that you feel less anxious: *She needed to unburden herself to somebody.* **2** ~ sb / sth (of sth) to take sth that causes a lot of work or worry away from sb/sth OPP **burden**

**un·but·ton** /ʌnˈbʌtn/ *verb* ~ sth to open the buttons on a piece of clothing: *He unbuttoned his shirt.* OPP **button (up)**

**un·but·toned** /ʌnˈbʌtnd/ *adj.* informal and relaxed: *Staff respond well to her unbuttoned style of management.*

**un·called for** /ʌnˈkɔːld fɔː(r)/ *adj.* (of behaviour or remarks) not fair or appropriate SYN **unnecessary**: *His comments were uncalled for.* ◊ *uncalled-for comments*

**un·canny** /ʌnˈkæni/ *adj.* strange and difficult to explain SYN **weird**: *I had an uncanny feeling I was being watched.* ◊ *It was uncanny really, almost as if she knew what I was thinking.* ▶ **un·can·nily** /-nɪli/ *adv.*: *He looked uncannily like someone I knew.*

**un·cared for** /ʌnˈkeəd fɔː(r); *NAmE* -ˈkerd/ *adj.* not taken care of SYN **neglected**: *The garden looked uncared for.* ◊ *an uncared-for garden*

**un·car·ing** /ʌnˈkeərɪŋ; *NAmE* -ˈker-/ *adj.* (*disapproving*) not showing sympathy about the problems or pain of other people SYN **callous** OPP **caring**

**un·ceas·ing** /ʌnˈsiːsɪŋ/ *adj.* (*formal*) continuing all the time SYN **incessant**: *unceasing efforts* ◊ *Planes passed overhead with unceasing regularity.* ▶ **un·ceas·ing·ly** *adv.*: *Snow fell unceasingly.*

**un·cen·sored** /ʌnˈsensəd; *NAmE* -sərd/ *adj.* (of a report, film, etc.) not having had parts removed that are not considered suitable for the public): *an uncensored newspaper article*

**un·cere·mo·ni·ous** /ˌʌnserəˈməʊniəs/ *adj.* (*formal*) done roughly and rudely: *He was bundled out of the room with unceremonious haste.* ⊃ compare CEREMONIOUS

**un·cere·mo·ni·ous·ly** /ˌʌnserəˈməʊniəsli/ *adv.* (*formal*) in a rough or rude way, without caring about a person's feelings: *They dumped his belongings unceremoniously on the floor.*

**un·cer·tain** /ʌnˈsɜːtn; *NAmE* -ˈsɜːrtn/ *adj.* **1** [not before noun] ~ (about / of sth) feeling doubt about sth; not sure: *They're both uncertain about what to do.* ◊ *I'm still uncertain of my feelings for him.* OPP **certain** ⊃ EXPRESS YOURSELF at CERTAIN **2** likely to change, especially in a negative or unpleasant way: *Our future looks uncertain.* ◊ *a man of uncertain temper* **3** not definite or decided SYN **unclear**: *It is uncertain what his role in the company will be.* **4** not confident SYN **hesitant**: *The baby took its first uncertain steps.*
IDM **in no un·certain ˈterms** clearly and strongly: *I told him what I thought of him in no uncertain terms.*

**un·cer·tain·ly** /ʌnˈsɜːtnli; *NAmE* -ˈsɜːrt-/ *adv.* without confidence SYN **hesitantly**: *They smiled uncertainly at one another.*

**un·cer·tainty** /ʌnˈsɜːtnti; *NAmE* -ˈsɜːrt-/ *noun* (*pl.* -ies) **1** [U] the state of being uncertain: *There is considerable uncertainty about the company's future.* ◊ *He had an air of uncertainty about him.* **2** [C] something that you cannot be sure about; a situation that makes you not be or feel certain: *life's uncertainties* ◊ *the uncertainties of war*

**un·chal·lenge·able** /ʌnˈtʃælɪndʒəbl/ *adj.* that cannot be questioned or argued with; that cannot be challenged: *unchallengeable evidence*

**un·chal·lenged** /ʌnˈtʃælɪndʒd/ *adj.* **1** not doubted; accepted without question; not challenged: *She could not allow such a claim to go unchallenged.* **2** (of a ruler or leader, or their position) not opposed by anyone: *He is in a position of unchallenged authority.* **3** without being stopped and asked to explain who you are, what you are doing, etc: *I walked into the building unchallenged.*

**un·change·able** /ʌnˈtʃeɪndʒəbl/ *adj.* that cannot be changed: *unchangeable laws* ⊃ compare CHANGEABLE

**un·changed** /ʌnˈtʃeɪndʒd/ *adj.* [not usually before noun] that has stayed the same and not changed: *My opinion remains unchanged.*

**un·chang·ing** /ʌnˈtʃeɪndʒɪŋ/ *adj.* that always stays the same and does not change: *unchanging truths*

**un·char·ac·ter·is·tic** /ˌʌnkærəktəˈrɪstɪk/ *adj.* ~ (of sb) not typical of sb; not the way sb usually behaves: *The remark was quite uncharacteristic of her.* OPP **characteristic** ▶ **un·char·ac·ter·is·tic·al·ly** /-kli/ *adv.*: *The children had been uncharacteristically quiet.*

**un·char·it·able** /ʌnˈtʃærɪtəbl/ *adj.* (*disapproving*) unkind and unfair in the way that you judge people: *uncharitable thoughts* OPP **charitable** ▶ **un·char·it·ably** /-bli/ *adv.*

**un·chart·ed** /ʌnˈtʃɑːtɪd; *NAmE* -ˈtʃɑːrt-/ *adj.* [usually before noun] not marked on a map; that has not been visited or investigated before: *The ship hit an uncharted rock.* ◊ *They set off into the country's uncharted interior.* ◊ (*figurative*) *The party is sailing in uncharted waters* (= a situation it has not been in before). ◊ (*figurative*) *I was moving into uncharted territory* (= a completely new experience) *with this relationship.*

**un·check** /ʌnˈtʃek/ *verb* [T] to remove a mark (✓) from a box on an electronic form to show that you do not want sth

**un·checked** /ʌnˈtʃekt/ *adj.* if sth harmful is unchecked, it is not stopped from getting worse SYN **uncontrolled**: *The fire was allowed to burn unchecked.* ◊ *The rise in violent crime must not go unchecked.* ◊ *The plant will soon choke ponds and waterways if left unchecked.*

**un·chris·tian** /ʌnˈkrɪstʃən/ *adj.* (*disapproving*) not showing the qualities you expect of a Christian; not kind or thinking about other people's feelings OPP **Christian**

**un·civil** /ʌnˈsɪvl/ *adj.* (*formal*) not polite OPP **civil** ⊃ see also INCIVILITY

**un·civ·il·ized** (*BrE also* **-ised**) /ʌnˈsɪvəlaɪzd/ *adj.* (*disapproving*) **1** (of people or their behaviour) not behaving in a way that is acceptable according to social or moral standards **2** (of people or places) not having developed a modern culture and way of life: *I have worked in the wildest and most uncivilized parts of the world.* OPP **civilized**

**un·claimed** /ʌnˈkleɪmd/ *adj.* that nobody has claimed as belonging to them or being owed to them

**un·clas·si·fied** /ʌnˈklæsɪfaɪd/ *adj.* **1** (of documents, information, etc.) not officially secret; available to everyone OPP **classified 2** (*specialist*) that has not been CLASSIFIED as being the member of a particular group: (*BrE*) *A high proportion of candidates get low or unclassified grades* (= their work is not good enough to receive a grade). **3** (*BrE*) (of a road) not large or important enough to be given a number

**uncle** /ˈʌŋkl/ *noun* **1** the brother of your mother or father; the husband of your aunt: *Uncle Ian* ◊ *I'm going to visit my uncle.* ◊ *a maternal/paternal uncle* (= related through the mother's/father's side of the family) **2** used by children, with a first name, to address a man who is a close friend of their parents **3** (*IndE, SEAsianE*) used as a polite way of addressing or referring to an older man HELP In this meaning, say *Paul uncle*, not: *Uncle Paul.* If you want to sound especially polite, you can say *uncleji* /ˈʌŋkldʒi/. IDM see BOB

**un·clean** /ʌnˈkliːn/ *adj.* **1** (*formal*) dirty and therefore likely to cause disease: *unclean water* OPP **clean 2** considered to be bad, IMMORAL or not pure in a religious way, and therefore not to be touched, eaten, etc. SYN **impure**: *unclean thoughts* ◊ *unclean food*

**un·clear** /ʌnˈklɪə(r); *NAmE* -ˈklɪr/ *adj.* **1** not clear or definite; difficult to understand or be sure about: *His* motives are unclear. ◊ It is unclear whether there is any damage. ◊ Your diagrams are unclear. **2** ~(about sth) | ~(as to sth) not fully understanding sth **SYN** **uncertain**: *I'm unclear about what you want me to do.*

**Uncle Sam** /ˌʌŋkl ˈsæm/ *noun* (*informal*) a way of referring to the United States of America or the US government (sometimes shown as a tall man with a white BEARD and a tall hat): *He owed $20000 in tax to Uncle Sam.*

**Uncle Tom** /ˌʌŋkl ˈtɒm; *NAmE* ˈtɑːm/ *noun* (*taboo, offensive*) sometimes used in the past to refer to a black man who wants to please or serve white people **ORIGIN** From a character in the novel *Uncle Tom's Cabin* by Harriet Beecher Stowe.

**un·clog** /ˌʌnˈklɒɡ; *NAmE* -ˈklɑːɡ/ *verb* (**-gg-**) ~ **sth** to clear sth, for example a pipe, by removing sth that is blocking it **OPP** **clog, clog (up)**

**un·clothed** /ˌʌnˈkləʊðd; *NAmE* -ˈkloʊðd/ *adj. (formal)* not wearing any clothes **SYN** **naked** **OPP** **clothed**

**un·clut·tered** /ˌʌnˈklʌtəd; *NAmE* -tərd/ *adj. (approving)* not containing too many objects, details or unnecessary items **SYN** **tidy** **OPP** **cluttered**

**un·coil** /ˌʌnˈkɔɪl/ *verb* [I, T] to become or make sth straight after it has been wound or TWISTED round in a circle: *The snake slowly uncoiled.* ◊ *to uncoil a rope*

**un·combed** /ˌʌnˈkəʊmd; *NAmE* -ˈkoʊmd/ *adj.* (of hair) that has not been brushed or COMBED; very untidy

**un·com·fort·able** ❶ B1 /ʌnˈkʌmftəbl; *BrE also* -ˈkʌmfət-; *NAmE also* -ˈkʌmfərt-/ *adj.* **1** B1 (of clothes, furniture, etc.) not letting you feel physically comfortable; unpleasant to wear, sit on, etc: *uncomfortable shoes* ◊ ~ **to do sth** *The headphones can be uncomfortable to wear.* **OPP** **comfortable** **2** B1 not feeling physically relaxed, warm, etc.: *I was sitting in an extremely uncomfortable position.* ◊ **it is** ~ **to do sth** *It was uncomfortable to walk for long periods of time.* **OPP** **comfortable** **3** B2 anxious, embarrassed or afraid and unable to relax; making you feel like this: *He looked distinctly uncomfortable when the subject was mentioned.* ◊ ~ **with sth** *She felt uncomfortable with the way George looked at her.* ◊ ~ **about (doing) sth** *She was always a little uncomfortable about being photographed.* **OPP** **comfortable** **4** unpleasant or difficult to deal with: *an uncomfortable fact* ◊ *I had the uncomfortable feeling that it was my fault.*

**un·com·fort·ably** /ʌnˈkʌmftəbli; *BrE also* -ˈkʌmfət-; *NAmE also* -ˈkʌmfərt-/ *adv.* **1** in a way that makes you feel anxious or embarrassed; in a way that shows you are anxious or embarrassed: *I became uncomfortably aware that no one else was laughing.* ◊ *Her comment was uncomfortably close to the truth.* ◊ *He shifted uncomfortably in his seat when I mentioned money.* **2** in a way that is not physically comfortable: *I was feeling uncomfortably hot.* ◊ *She perched uncomfortably on the edge of the table.*

**un·com·mit·ted** /ˌʌnkəˈmɪtɪd/ *adj.* ~ **(to sb/sth)** not having given or promised support to a particular person, group, belief, action, etc: *The party needs to canvass the uncommitted voters.* ⊃ compare **COMMITTED**

**un·com·mon** /ʌnˈkɒmən; *NAmE* -ˈkɑːm-/ *adj.* **1** not existing in large numbers or in many places **SYN** **unusual, rare**: *an uncommon occurrence* ◊ *Side effects from the drug are uncommon.* ◊ *It is* **not uncommon** *for college students to live at home.* ◊ *Red squirrels are uncommon in England.* **OPP** **common** **2** *(formal or literary)* unusually large in degree or amount; great **SYN** **remarkable**: *She showed uncommon pleasure at his arrival.*

**un·com·mon·ly** /ʌnˈkɒmənli; *NAmE* -ˈkɑːm-/ *adv. (formal)* **1** to an unusual degree; extremely: *an uncommonly gifted child* **2** not often; not usually: *Not uncommonly, there is a great deal of rain in August.*

**un·com·mu·ni·ca·tive** /ˌʌnkəˈmjuːnɪkətɪv/ *adj. (disapproving)* (of a person) not willing to talk to other people or give opinions **SYN** **taciturn** **OPP** **communicative**

**un·com·peti·tive** /ˌʌnkəmˈpetətɪv/ *adj. (business)* not cheaper or better than others and therefore not able to compete equally: *an uncompetitive industry* ◊ *uncompetitive prices* **OPP** **competitive**

1697 **unconscious**

**un·com·plain·ing** /ˌʌnkəmˈpleɪnɪŋ/ *adj. (approving)* not saying that you are unhappy about a difficult or unpleasant situation; not saying that you are in pain ▸ **un·com·plain·ing·ly** *adv.*

**un·com·pleted** /ˌʌnkəmˈpliːtɪd/ *adj.* that has not been finished: *an uncompleted project*

**un·com·pli·cated** /ʌnˈkɒmplɪkeɪtɪd; *NAmE* -ˈkɑːm-/ *adj.* simple; without any difficulty or worry **SYN** **straightforward**: *an easygoing, uncomplicated young man* ◊ *Why can't I have an uncomplicated life?* **OPP** **complicated**

**un·com·pli·men·tary** /ʌnˌkɒmplɪˈmentri; *NAmE* -ˌkɑːm-/ *adj.* rude or showing a lack of respect: *uncomplimentary remarks* ⊃ compare **COMPLIMENTARY**

**un·com·pre·hend·ing** /ˌʌnkɒmprɪˈhendɪŋ; *NAmE* -ˌkɑːm-/ *adj. (formal)* (of a person) not understanding a situation or what is happening ▸ **un·com·pre·hend·ing·ly** *adv.*: *She looked at him uncomprehendingly.*

**un·com·prom·is·ing** /ʌnˈkɒmprəmaɪzɪŋ; *NAmE* -ˈkɑːm-/ *adj.* unwilling to change your opinions or behaviour: *an uncompromising attitude* ◊ *He has a reputation for being tough and uncompromising.* ▸ **un·com·prom·is·ing·ly** *adv.*

**un·con·cealed** /ˌʌnkənˈsiːld/ *adj.* [usually before noun] (of an emotion, etc.) that you do not try to hide **SYN** **obvious**: *unconcealed curiosity*

**un·con·cern** /ˌʌnkənˈsɜːn; *NAmE* -ˈsɜːrn/ *noun* [U] *(formal)* a lack of care, interest or worry about sth that other people would care about **SYN** **indifference**: *She received the news with apparent unconcern.* ⊃ compare **CONCERN**

**un·con·cerned** /ˌʌnkənˈsɜːnd; *NAmE* -ˈsɜːrnd/ *adj.* **1** ~ **(about/by sth)** not worried or anxious about sth because you feel it does not affect you or is not important: *He drove on, apparently unconcerned about the noise the engine was making.* **2** ~ **(with sb/sth)** not interested in sth: *Young people are often unconcerned with political issues.* **OPP** **concerned** ▸ **un·con·cern·ed·ly** /ˌʌnkənˈsɜːnɪdli; *NAmE* -ˈsɜːrn-/ *adv.*

**un·con·di·tion·al** /ˌʌnkənˈdɪʃənl/ *adj.* without any conditions or limits: *the unconditional surrender of military forces* ◊ *She gave her children unconditional love.* **OPP** **conditional** ▸ **un·con·di·tion·al·ly** /-nəli/ *adv.*

**un·con·di·tioned** /ˌʌnkənˈdɪʃnd/ *adj. (psychology)* (of behaviour) not trained or influenced by experience; natural: *an unconditioned response*

**un·con·fined** /ˌʌnkənˈfaɪnd/ *adj. (formal)* not limited in space, range or amount: *The animals have unconfined access to pasture.* ◊ *When the news came through joy was unconfined.*

**un·con·firmed** /ˌʌnkənˈfɜːmd; *NAmE* -ˈfɜːrmd/ *adj.* that has not yet been proved to be true or confirmed: *unconfirmed rumours* ◊ *Unconfirmed reports said that at least six people had been killed.*

**un·con·gen·ial** /ˌʌnkənˈdʒiːniəl/ *adj. (formal)* **1** (of a person) not friendly or pleasant to be with: *uncongenial company* **2** ~ **(to sb)** (of a place, job, etc.) not pleasant; not making you feel relaxed; not suitable for your personality: *an uncongenial atmosphere* **3** ~ **(to sth)** not suitable for sth; not encouraging sth: *The religious climate at the time was uncongenial to new ideas.* **OPP** **congenial**

**un·con·nect·ed** /ˌʌnkəˈnektɪd/ *adj.* not related or connected in any way: *The two crimes are apparently unconnected.* ◊ ~ **with/to sth** *My resignation was totally unconnected with recent events.*

**un·con·quer·able** /ʌnˈkɒŋkərəbl; *NAmE* -ˈkɑːŋ-/ *adj.* too strong to be defeated or changed **SYN** **invincible**

**un·con·scion·able** /ʌnˈkɒnʃənəbl; *NAmE* -ˈkɑːn-/ *adj.* [usually before noun] *(formal)* **1** (of an action, etc.) so bad, IMMORAL, etc. that it should make you feel ashamed **2** *(often humorous)* too great, large, long, etc. **SYN** **excessive**

**un·con·scious** ❶ B2 /ʌnˈkɒnʃəs; *NAmE* -ˈkɑːn-/ *adj., noun*

■ *adj.* **1** ⁇ B2 in a state like sleep because of an injury or illness, and not able to use your senses: *They found him*

○ Oxford Phrasal Academic Lexicon (OPAL) written and spoken word lists | Ⓦ OPAL written word list | Ⓢ OPAL spoken word list

# unconsciously

lying unconscious on the floor. ◊ *She was knocked unconscious.* **2** ⚑ B2 (of feelings, thoughts, etc.) existing or happening without you realizing or being aware; not deliberate: *unconscious desires* ◊ *Freud sought to unlock the workings of the unconscious mind.* ⊃ compare SUBCONSCIOUS **3** ⚑ B2 **~ of sb/sth** not aware of sb/sth; not noticing sth; not conscious SYN oblivious: *She is unconscious of the effect she has on people.* ◊ *He was quite unconscious of the danger.* OPP conscious
- *noun* **the unconscious** [sing.] (*psychology*) the part of a person's mind with thoughts, feelings, etc. that they are not aware of and cannot control but that can sometimes be understood by studying their behaviour or dreams ⊃ compare SUBCONSCIOUS

**un·con·scious·ly** /ʌnˈkɒnʃəsli; *NAmE* -ˈkɑːn-/ *adv.* without being aware: *Perhaps, unconsciously, I've done something to offend her.* OPP **consciously**

**un·con·scious·ness** /ʌnˈkɒnʃəsnəs; *NAmE* -ˈkɑːn-/ *noun* [U] a state like sleep caused by injury or illness, when you are unable to use your senses: *He had lapsed into unconsciousness.*

**un·con·sid·ered** /ˌʌnkənˈsɪdəd; *NAmE* -dərd/ *adj.* (*formal*) not thought about, or not thought about with enough care: *I came to regret my unconsidered remarks.*

**un·con·sti·tu·tion·al** /ˌʌnˌkɒnstɪˈtjuːʃənl; *NAmE* -ˌkɑːnstɪˈtuː-/ *adj.* not allowed by the CONSTITUTION of a country, a political system or an organization OPP **constitutional**
▸ **un·con·sti·tu·tion·al·ly** /-nəli/ *adv.*

**un·con·strained** /ˌʌnkənˈstreɪnd/ *adj.* (*formal*) not limited in amount, extent, etc: *unconstrained growth* ⊃ see also CONSTRAIN

**un·con·tam·in·ated** /ˌʌnkənˈtæmɪneɪtɪd/ *adj.* not harmed by sth (for example, dangerous or dirty substances): *uncontaminated water* OPP **contaminate**

**un·con·test·ed** /ˌʌnkənˈtestɪd/ *adj.* without any opposition or argument: *an uncontested election/divorce* ◊ *These claims have not gone uncontested.*

**un·con·trol·lable** /ˌʌnkənˈtrəʊləbl/ *adj.* that you cannot control or prevent: *an uncontrollable temper* ◊ *uncontrollable bleeding* ◊ *I had an uncontrollable urge to laugh.* ◊ *The ball was uncontrollable.* ◊ *He's an uncontrollable child* (= he behaves very badly and cannot be controlled). ▸ **un·con·trol·lably** /-bli/ *adv.*: *She began shaking uncontrollably.*

**un·con·trolled** /ˌʌnkənˈtrəʊld/ *adj.* **1** (of emotions, behaviour, etc.) that sb cannot control or stop: *uncontrolled anger* ◊ *The thoughts rushed into my mind uncontrolled.* **2** that is not limited or managed by law or rules: *the uncontrolled growth of cities* ◊ *uncontrolled dumping of toxic waste* ⊃ compare CONTROLLED

**un·con·tro·ver·sial** /ˌʌnˌkɒntrəˈvɜːʃl; *NAmE* ˌkɑːntrəˈvɜːrʃl/ *adj.* not causing, or not likely to cause, people to disagree: *an uncontroversial opinion* ◊ *He chose an uncontroversial topic for his speech.* OPP **controversial** ⊃ compare NON-CONTROVERSIAL

**un·con·ven·tion·al** /ˌʌnkənˈvenʃənl/ *adj.* not following what is done or considered normal or acceptable by most people; different and interesting SYN **unorthodox**: *an unconventional approach to the problem* ◊ *unconventional views* OPP **conventional** ▸ **un·con·ven·tion·al·ity** /ˌʌnkənˌvenʃəˈnæləti/ *noun* [U] **un·con·ven·tion·al·ly** /ˌʌnkənˈvenʃənəli/ *adv.*

**un·con·vinced** /ˌʌnkənˈvɪnst/ *adj.* not believing or not certain about sth despite what you have been told: **~ (of sth)** *I remain unconvinced of the need for change.* ◊ **~ (by sth)** *She seemed unconvinced by their promises.* ◊ **~ (that …)** *The jury were unconvinced that he was innocent.* OPP **convinced**

**un·con·vin·cing** /ˌʌnkənˈvɪnsɪŋ/ *adj.* not seeming true or real; not making you believe that sth is true: *I find the characters in the book very unconvincing.* ◊ *She managed a weak, unconvincing smile.* OPP **convincing** ▸ **un·con·vin·cing·ly** *adv.*

**un·cooked** /ˌʌnˈkʊkt/ *adj.* not cooked SYN **raw**: *Eat plenty of uncooked fruit and vegetables.*

**un·cool** /ˌʌnˈkuːl/ *adj.* (*informal*) not considered acceptable by fashionable young people OPP **cool**

**un·co·opera·tive** /ˌʌnkəʊˈɒpərətɪv; *NAmE* -ˈɑːp-/ *adj.* not willing to be helpful to other people or do what they ask SYN **unhelpful** OPP **cooperative**

**un·co·or·din·ated** /ˌʌnkəʊˈɔːdɪneɪtɪd; *NAmE* -ˈɔːrd-/ *adj.* **1** if a person is **uncoordinated**, they are not able to control their movements well, and are therefore not very good at some sports and physical activities **2** (of movements or parts of the body) having no control; not moving smoothly or together **3** (of plans, projects, etc.) not well organized; with no thought for how the different parts work together

**un·cork** /ʌnˈkɔːk; *NAmE* -ˈkɔːrk/ *verb* **~ sth** to open a bottle by removing the CORK from the top OPP **cork**

**un·cor·rob·or·ated** /ˌʌnkəˈrɒbəreɪtɪd; *NAmE* -ˈrɑːb-/ *adj.* (of a statement or claim) not supported by any other evidence; not having been CORROBORATED SYN **unconfirmed**

**un·count·able** /ʌnˈkaʊntəbl/ *adj.* (*grammar*) a noun that is **uncountable** cannot be made plural or used with *a* or *an*, for example *water*, *bread* and *information* OPP **countable** ⊃ compare COUNTLESS

**un·count noun** /ˈʌnkaʊnt naʊn/ *noun* (*grammar*) an uncountable noun OPP **count noun**

**un·couple** /ʌnˈkʌpl/ *verb* **~ sth (from sth)** to remove the connection between two vehicles, two parts of a train, etc.

**un·couth** /ʌnˈkuːθ/ *adj.* (of a person or their behaviour) rude or socially unacceptable SYN **coarse**: *uncouth laughter* ◊ *an uncouth young man*

**un·cover** /ʌnˈkʌvə(r)/ *verb* **1** **~ sth** to remove sth that is covering sth: *Uncover the pan and let the soup simmer.* **2** **~ sth** to discover sth that was previously hidden or secret: *Police have uncovered a plot to kidnap the President's son.*

**un·covered** /ʌnˈkʌvəd; *NAmE* -vərd/ *adj.* not covered by anything: *His head was uncovered.*

**un·crit·ic·al** /ʌnˈkrɪtɪkl/ *adj.* (*usually disapproving*) not willing to criticize sb/sth or to judge whether sb/sth is right or wrong: *Her uncritical acceptance of everything I said began to irritate me.* OPP **critical** ▸ **un·crit·ic·al·ly** /-kli/ *adv.*

**un·crowd·ed** /ʌnˈkraʊdɪd/ *adj.* not full of people: *The beach was pleasantly uncrowded.* OPP **crowded**

**un·crowned** /ʌnˈkraʊnd/ *adj.* (of a king or queen) not yet CROWNED (= had a CROWN officially placed on their head as a sign of royal power)
IDM **the uncrowned ˈking/ˈqueen (of sth)** the person considered to be the best, most famous or successful in a particular place or area of activity

**unc·tion** /ˈʌŋkʃn/ *noun* [U] **1** the act of pouring oil on sb's head or another part of their body as part of an important religious ceremony **2** (*formal*, *disapproving*) behaviour or speech that is not sincere and that expresses too much praise of sb

**unc·tu·ous** /ˈʌŋktʃuəs/ *adj.* (*formal*, *disapproving*) friendly or giving praise in a way that is not sincere and that is therefore unpleasant ▸ **unc·tu·ous·ly** *adv.*

**un·culti·vated** /ʌnˈkʌltɪveɪtɪd/ *adj.* (of land) not used for growing crops OPP **cultivated**

**un·cul·tured** /ʌnˈkʌltʃəd; *NAmE* -tʃərd/ *adj.* (of people) not well educated; not able to understand or enjoy art, literature, etc. OPP **cultured**

**un·cut** /ˌʌnˈkʌt/ *adj.* **1** left to grow; not cut short: *The uncut grass came up to her waist.* **2** (of a book, film, etc.) left in its complete form; without any parts removed; not CENSORED: *the original uncut version* **3** (of a PRECIOUS STONE) not given a shape by cutting: *uncut diamonds*

**un·dam·aged** /ʌnˈdæmɪdʒd/ *adj.* not damaged, harmed or made less good: *There was a slight collision but my car was undamaged.* ◊ *He emerged from the court case with his reputation undamaged.*

**un·dated** /ʌnˈdeɪtɪd/ *adj.* **1** without a date written or printed on it: *an undated letter* **2** of which the date is not known: *undated archaeological remains* ⊃ compare DATED

**un·daunt·ed** /ˌʌnˈdɔːntɪd/ *adj.* [not usually before noun] (*formal*) still enthusiastic and determined, despite difficulties, danger, etc. **SYN** **undeterred**: *He seemed undaunted by all the opposition to his idea.*

**un·dead** /ˌʌnˈded/ *adj.* **1** (in stories) dead, but still able to move, act and (in some cases) think and speak. VAMPIRES and ZOMBIES *are undead.* **2** **the undead** *noun* [pl.] creatures who are undead: *In this game, players have to battle a vast army of the undead.* ⊃ compare LIVING DEAD

**un·de·cid·ed** /ˌʌndɪˈsaɪdɪd/ *adj.* [not usually before noun] **1** not having made a decision about sb/sth: *~ (about sb/sth) I'm still undecided (about) who to vote for.* ◊ *~ (as to sth) He was undecided as to what to do next.* **2** not having been decided: *The venue for the World Cup remains undecided.* ⊃ compare DECIDED

**un·de·clared** /ˌʌndɪˈkleəd; *NAmE* -ˈklerd/ *adj.* not admitted to; not stated in an open way; not having been declared: *No income should remain undeclared.* ◊ *Undeclared goods* (= that the customs are not told about) *may be confiscated.*

**un·de·feat·ed** /ˌʌndɪˈfiːtɪd/ *adj.* (especially in sport) not having lost or been defeated: *They are undefeated in 13 games.* ◊ *the undefeated world champion*

**un·de·fend·ed** /ˌʌndɪˈfendɪd/ *adj.* **1** not protected or guarded **SYN** **unprotected**: *undefended borders* **2** if a case in court is **undefended**, no defence is made against it

**un·de·fined** /ˌʌndɪˈfaɪnd/ *adj.* not made clear or definite: *The money was lent for an undefined period of time.*

**un·de·mand·ing** /ˌʌndɪˈmɑːndɪŋ; *NAmE* -ˈmæn-/ *adj.* **1** not needing a lot of effort or thought: *an undemanding job* **2** (*approving*) (of a person) not asking for a lot of attention or action from other people **OPP** **demanding**

**un·demo·crat·ic** /ˌʌndeməˈkrætɪk/ *adj.* against or not acting according to the principles of DEMOCRACY: *undemocratic decisions* ◊ *an undemocratic regime* **OPP** **democratic** ▸ **un·demo·crat·ic·al·ly** /-kli/ *adv.*: *an undemocratically elected government* ◊ *He was accused of acting undemocratically.*

**un·deni·able** /ˌʌndɪˈnaɪəbl/ *adj.* true or certain; that cannot be denied **SYN** **indisputable**: *He had undeniable charm.* ◊ *It is an undeniable fact that crime is increasing.* **OPP** **deniable** ▸ **un·deni·ably** /-bli/ *adv.*: *undeniably impressive*

**under** **⊙** **A1** /ˈʌndə(r)/ *prep., adv., adj.*
■ *prep.* **1 A1** in, to or through a position that is below sth: *Have you looked under the bed?* ◊ *She placed the ladder under* (= just lower than) *the window.* ◊ *The dog squeezed under the gate and ran into the road.* **2 A1** below the surface of sth; covered by sth: *The boat lay under several feet of water.* **3 A1** less than; younger than: *an annual income of under £10000* ◊ *I'm actually in the film for just under two minutes.* ◊ *Nobody under 18 is allowed to buy alcohol.* **4 B1** affected by sth: *The wall collapsed under the strain.* ◊ *I've been feeling under stress lately.* ◊ *I'm under no illusions about what hard work this will be.* ◊ *You'll be under anaesthetic, so you won't feel a thing.* **5 B2** used to say who or what controls, governs or manages sb/sth: *The country is now under martial law.* ◊ *The coinage was reformed under Elizabeth I* (= when she was queen). ◊ *She has a staff of 19 working under her.* ◊ *Under its new conductor, the orchestra has established an international reputation.* **6 B2** according to an agreement, a law or a system: *A man was detained under the Mental Health Act.* ◊ *Under the terms of the lease you had no right to sublet the property.* ◊ *Is the television still under guarantee?* **7 B2** experiencing a particular process: *The hotel is still under construction.* ◊ *The matter is under investigation.* **8** using a particular name: *She also wrote under the pseudonym of Barbara Vine.* **9** found in a particular part of a book, list, etc: *If it's not under 'sports', try looking under 'games'.*
■ *adv.* **1 A1** below sth: *He pulled up the covers and crawled under.* **2 A1** below the surface of water: *She took a deep breath and stayed under for more than a minute.* ◊ *The boat was going under fast.* **3 A1** less; younger: *prices of ten dollars and under* ◊ *children aged 12 and under* **4** in or into an unconscious state: *He felt himself going under.*

1699 **undercurrent**

■ *adj.* [only before noun] lower: *the under layer* ◊ *the under surface of a leaf* ⊃ compare UNDERNEATH

**under-** /ˈʌndə(r)/ *prefix* **1** (in nouns and adjectives) below: *undergrowth* ◊ *undercoat* **2** (in nouns) lower in age or rank: *the under-fives* ◊ *an undergraduate* **3** (in adjectives and verbs) not enough: *underripe* ◊ *undercooked*

**under·achieve** /ˌʌndərəˈtʃiːv/ *verb* [I] to do less well than you could do, especially in school work ▸ **under·achieve·ment** *noun* [U] **under·achiev·er** *noun*

**under·age** /ˈʌndəreɪdʒ/ *adj.* [only before noun] done by people who are too young by law: *underage drinking* ⊃ see also AGE *noun*

**under·arm** /ˈʌndərɑːm; *NAmE* -ɑːrm/ *adj., adv.*
■ *adj.* **1** [only before noun] connected with a person's ARMPIT: *underarm hair/deodorant/sweating* **2** an **underarm** throw of a ball is done with your hand kept below the level of your shoulder ⊃ compare OVERARM
■ *adv.* if you throw, etc. **underarm**, you throw keeping your hand below the level of your shoulder ⊃ compare OVERARM

**under·belly** /ˈʌndəbeli/ *noun* [sing.] **1** the soft part of an animal on the UNDERSIDE of its body **2** the weakest part of sth that is most easily attacked: *The trade deficit remains the* ***soft underbelly*** *of the US economy.* **3** an unpleasant or criminal part of society that is usually hidden: *He became familiar with the* ***dark underbelly*** *of life in the city.*

**under·bid** /ˌʌndəˈbɪd; *NAmE* -dər-/ *verb* (**under·bid·ding**, **under·bid**, **under·bid**) ~ **sb/sth** to make a lower BID (= offer) than sb else, for example when trying to win a contract

**under·brush** /ˈʌndəbrʌʃ; *NAmE* -dər-/ (*NAmE*) (also **under·growth** *BrE, NAmE*) *noun* [U] a mass of bushes and plants that grow close together under trees in woods and forests

**under·car·riage** /ˈʌndəkærɪdʒ; *NAmE* -dər-/ (also **land·ing gear**) *noun* the part of an aircraft, including the wheels, that supports it when it is on the ground

**under·charge** /ˌʌndəˈtʃɑːdʒ; *NAmE* -dərˈtʃɑːrdʒ/ *verb* [I, T] ~ **(sb) (for sth)** to charge too little for sth, usually by mistake **OPP** **overcharge**

**under·class** /ˈʌndəklɑːs; *NAmE* -dərklæs/ *noun* [sing.] a social class that is very poor and has no status: *The long-term unemployed are becoming a new underclass.*

**under·class·man** /ˌʌndəˈklɑːsmən; *NAmE* -dərˈklæs-/, **under·class·woman** /ˌʌndəˈklɑːswʊmən; *NAmE* -dərˈklæs-/ *noun* (*pl.* **-men** /-mən/, **-women** /-wɪmɪn/) (in the US) a student in the first or second year of HIGH SCHOOL or college ⊃ compare UPPERCLASSMAN

**under·clothes** /ˈʌndəkləʊðz; *NAmE* -dərk-/ *noun* [pl.] (also **under·cloth·ing** /ˈʌndəkləʊðɪŋ; *NAmE* -dərk-/ [U]) (*formal*) = UNDERWEAR

**under·coat** /ˈʌndəkəʊt; *NAmE* -dərk-/ *noun* [C, U] a layer of paint under the final layer; the paint used for this ⊃ compare TOPCOAT

**under·cook** /ˌʌndəˈkʊk; *NAmE* -dərk-/ *verb* [usually passive] ~ **sth** to not cook sth for long enough, with the result that it is not ready to eat

**under·count** /ˌʌndəˈkaʊnt; *NAmE* -dərk-/ *verb* (*especially NAmE*) ~ **sb/sth** to count fewer than the actual number of people or things in a particular group: *The census undercounts low-income people and children.*

**under·cover** /ˌʌndəˈkʌvə(r); *NAmE* -dərk-/ *adj.* [usually before noun] working or done secretly in order to find out information for the police, a government, etc: *an undercover agent* ◊ *an undercover operation/investigation* ⊃ WORDFINDER NOTE at POLICE ▸ **under·cover** *adv.*: *The illegal payments were discovered by a journalist working undercover.*

**under·cur·rent** /ˈʌndəkʌrənt; *NAmE* -dərkɜːr-/ *noun* ~ **(of sth)** a feeling, especially a negative one, that is hidden but

# undercut

whose effects are felt SYN **undertone**: *I detect an undercurrent of resentment towards the new proposals.*

**under·cut** *verb, noun*
- *verb* /ˌʌndəˈkʌt/ *NAmE* -dər'k-/ (**under·cut·ting, under·cut, under·cut**) **1** ~ **sb/sth** to sell goods or services at a lower price than your competitors: *to undercut sb's prices* ◇ *We were able to undercut our European rivals by 5%.* **2** ~ **sb/sth** to make sb/sth weaker or less likely to be effective SYN **undermine**: *Some members of the board were trying to undercut the chairman's authority.*
- *noun* /ˈʌndəkʌt/ *NAmE* -dərk-/ a way of cutting sb's hair in which the hair is left quite long on top but the hair on the lower part of the head is cut much shorter

**under·devel·oped** /ˌʌndədɪˈveləpt/ *NAmE* -dərd-/ *adj.* (of a country, society, etc.) having few industries and a low standard of living ⊃ compare DEVELOPED, DEVELOPING, UNDEVELOPED **HELP** 'A **developing country**' is now the usual expression. ▶ **under·devel·op·ment** /-ləpmənt/ *noun* [U]

**under·dog** /ˈʌndədɒɡ/ *NAmE* -dərdɔːɡ/ *noun* a person, team, country, etc. that is thought to be in a weaker position than others and therefore not likely to be successful, win a competition, etc: *Before the game we were definitely the underdogs.* ◇ *In politics, he was a champion of the underdog* (= always fought for the rights of weaker people).

**under·done** /ˌʌndəˈdʌn/ *NAmE* -dərˈd-/ *adj.* not cooked enough ⊃ compare WELL DONE, OVERDO (3)

**under·dressed** /ˌʌndəˈdrest/ *NAmE* -dərˈd-/ *adj.* (*usually disapproving*) wearing clothes that are too informal for a particular occasion OPP **overdressed**

**under·employed** /ˌʌndərɪmˈplɔɪd/ *adj.* not having enough work to do; not having work that makes full use of your skills and abilities

**under·esti·mate** *verb, noun*
- *verb* /ˌʌndərˈestɪmeɪt/ **1** to think or guess that the amount, cost or size of sth is smaller than it really is: ~ **sth** *to underestimate the cost of the project* ◇ ~ **what, how, etc** ... *We underestimated how long it would take.* **2** to not realize how good, strong, determined, difficult, etc. sb/sth really is: ~ **sb/sth** *Never underestimate your opponent.* ◇ ~ **what, how, etc** ... *Don't underestimate how difficult this is going to be.* OPP **overestimate** ⊃ compare UNDERRATE
- *noun* /ˌʌndərˈestɪmət/ (*also* **under·esti·ma·tion** /ˌʌndərˌestɪˈmeɪʃn/ [C, U]) an estimate about the size, cost, etc. of sth that is too low: *My guess of 400 proved to be a serious underestimate.* OPP **overestimate**

**under·expose** /ˌʌndərɪkˈspəʊz/ *verb* [usually passive] ~ **sth** to allow too little light to reach the film when you take a photograph OPP **overexpose**

**under·fed** /ˌʌndəˈfed/ *NAmE* -dərˈf-/ *adj.* having had too little food to eat SYN **malnourished** OPP **overfed**

**under·floor** /ˌʌndəˈflɔː(r)/ *NAmE* -dərˈf-/ *adj.* [only before noun] placed under the floor: *underfloor heating*

**under·foot** /ˌʌndəˈfʊt/ *NAmE* -dərˈf-/ *adv.* under your feet; on the ground where you are walking: *The ground was dry and firm underfoot.* ◇ *I was nearly trampled underfoot by the crowd of people rushing for the door.*

**under·fund·ed** /ˌʌndəˈfʌndɪd/ *NAmE* -dərˈf-/ *adj.* (of an organization, a project, etc.) not having enough money to spend, with the result that it cannot function well: *seriously/chronically underfunded*

**under·gar·ment** /ˈʌndəɡɑːmənt/ *NAmE* -dərɡɑːrm-/ *noun* (*old-fashioned* or *formal*) a piece of underwear

**under·go** ?+ B2 W /ˌʌndəˈɡəʊ/ *NAmE* -dərˈɡ-/ *verb* (**under·goes** /-ˈɡəʊz/, **under·went** /-ˈwent/, **under·gone** /-ˈɡɒn/ *NAmE* -ˈɡɔːn/) ~ **sth** to experience sth, especially a change or sth unpleasant: *to undergo tests/trials/repairs* ◇ *My mother underwent major surgery last year.* ◇ *Some children undergo a complete transformation when they become teenagers.*

**under·gradu·ate** ?+ C1 /ˌʌndəˈɡrædʒuət/ *NAmE* -dərˈɡ-/ (*also informal* **under·grad** /ˈʌndəɡræd/ *NAmE* -dərɡ-/) *noun* a university or college student who is study-ing for their first degree: *a first-year undergraduate* ◇ *an undergraduate course/student/degree* ⊃ note at STUDENT

**under·ground** ?+ A2 *adj., adv., noun*
- *adj.* /ˌʌndəˈɡraʊnd/ *NAmE* -dərˈɡ-/ [only before noun] **1** ?+ A2 under the surface of the ground: *an underground bunker/tunnel* ◇ *underground parking* ⊃ compare OVERGROUND **2** operating secretly and often illegally, especially against a government: *an underground resistance movement*
- *adv.* /ˌʌndəˈɡraʊnd/ *NAmE* -dərˈɡ-/ **1** ?+ A2 under the surface of the ground: *Rescuers found victims trapped several feet underground.* ◇ *animals that live underground* **2** in or into a secret place in order to hide from the police, the government, etc: *He went underground to avoid arrest.*
- *noun* /ˈʌndəɡraʊnd/ *NAmE* -dərɡ-/ **1** (*often* **the Underground**) (*BrE*) (*NAmE* **sub·way**) [sing.] an underground railway system in a city: *underground stations* ◇ *the London Underground* ◇ *I always travel by underground.* ⊃ compare METRO, TUBE **2** **the underground** [sing. + sing./pl. v.] a secret political organization, usually working against the government of a country **3** (*IndE*) a person who works against the government as a member of a secret political organization

▼ **BRITISH/AMERICAN**

### underground / subway / metro / tube

- A city's underground railway system is usually called the **underground** (often **the Underground**) in *BrE* and the **subway** in *NAmE*. Speakers of *BrE* also use **subway** for systems in American cities and **metro** for systems in other European countries. **The Metro** is the name for the systems in Paris and Washington, D.C. London's system is often called **the Tube**.

**the underground eˈconomy** (*NAmE*) (*BrE* **the black eˈconomy**) *noun* [sing.] business activity or work that is done without the knowledge of the government or other officials so that people avoid paying tax on the money they earn

**under·growth** /ˈʌndəɡrəʊθ/ *NAmE* -dərɡ-/ (*BrE*) (*NAmE also* **under·brush**) *noun* [U] a mass of bushes and plants that grow close together under trees in woods and forests: *They used their knives to clear a path through the dense undergrowth.* ◇ *The murder weapon was found concealed in undergrowth.* ⊃ compare OVERGROWTH

**under·hand** /ˌʌndəˈhænd/ *NAmE* -dərˈh-/ (*also less frequent* **under·hand·ed** /ˌʌndəˈhændɪd/ *NAmE* -dərˈh-/) *adj.* (*disapproving*) secret and dishonest: *I would never have expected her to behave in such an underhand way.*

**under·in·sured** /ˌʌndərɪnˈʃʊəd/ -ˈʃɔːd/ *NAmE* -ˈʃʊrd/ *adj.* not having enough insurance protection

**under·lay** /ˈʌndəleɪ/ *NAmE* -dərl-/ *noun* [U, C] a layer of thick material placed under a carpet to protect it

**under·lie** /ˌʌndəˈlaɪ/ *NAmE* -dərˈl-/ *verb* [no passive] (**under·lying, under·lay** /-ˈleɪ/, **under·lain** /-ˈleɪn/) ~ **sth** (*formal*) to be the basis or cause of sth: *These ideas underlie much of his work.* ◇ *It is a principle that underlies all the party's policies.* ⊃ see also UNDERLYING

**under·line** /ˌʌndəˈlaɪn/ *NAmE* -dərˈl-/ (*also* **under·score** *especially in NAmE*) *verb* **1** ~ **sth** to draw or print a line under a word, sentence, etc. **2** to emphasize or show that sth is important or true: ~ **sth** *The report underlines the importance of pre-school education.* ◇ ~ **how, what, etc** ... *Her question underlined how little she understood him.* ◇ ~ **that** ... *The report underlined that the project enjoyed considerable support in both countries.* ◇ **it is underlined that** ... *It should be underlined that these are only preliminary findings.*

**under·ling** /ˈʌndəlɪŋ/ *NAmE* -dərl-/ *noun* (*disapproving*) a person with a lower rank or status SYN **minion**

**under·lying** ?+ C1 O /ˌʌndəˈlaɪɪŋ/ *NAmE* -dərˈl-/ *adj.* [only before noun] **1** ?+ C1 important in a situation but not always easily noticed or stated clearly: *The underlying assumption is that the amount of money available is limited.* ◇ *Unemployment may be an underlying cause of the rising crime rate.* **2** existing under the surface of sth else: *the underlying rock formation* ⊃ see also UNDERLIE

**under·manned** /ˌʌndəˈmænd; *NAmE* -dərˈm-/ *adj.* (of a hospital, factory, etc.) not having enough people working in order to be able to function well **SYN** **understaffed**

**under·mine** /ˌʌndəˈmaɪn; *NAmE* -dərˈm-/ *verb* **1** ~ **sth/sb** to make sth, especially sb's confidence or authority, gradually weaker or less effective: *Our confidence in the team has been seriously undermined by their recent defeats.* ◊ *This crisis has undermined his position.* ◊ *It's all a plot to undermine me.* **2** ~ **sth** to make sth weaker at the base, for example by digging under it

**under·neath** /ˌʌndəˈniːθ; *NAmE* -dərˈn-/ *prep., adv., noun*
■ *prep., adv.* **1** under or below sth else, especially when it is hidden or covered by the thing on top: *The coin rolled underneath the piano.* ◊ *This jacket's too big, even with a sweater underneath.* **2** used to talk about sb's real feelings or character, as opposed to the way they seem to be: *Underneath her cool exterior she was really very frightened.* ◊ *He seems bad-tempered, but he's very soft-hearted underneath.*
■ *noun* **the underneath** [sing.] the lower surface or part of sth: *She pulled the drawer out and examined the underneath carefully.*

**under·nour·ished** /ˌʌndəˈnʌrɪʃt; *NAmE* -dərˈnɜːr-/ *adj.* in bad health because of a lack of food or a lack of the right type of food **SYN** **malnourished**: *severely undernourished children* ▶ **under·nour·ish·ment** /-rɪʃmənt/ *noun* [U]

**under·paid** /ˌʌndəˈpeɪd; *NAmE* -dərˈp-/ *adj.* not paid enough for the work you do: *Nurses complain of being overworked and underpaid.*

**under·pants** /ˈʌndəpænts; *NAmE* -dərp-/ *noun* [pl.] **1** (*also informal* **pants**) (*BrE*) a piece of men's underwear worn under their trousers **2** (*NAmE*) a piece of underwear worn by men or women under trousers, a skirt, etc.

**under·pass** /ˈʌndəpɑːs; *NAmE* -dərpæs/ *noun* a road or path that goes under another road or railway track ⊃ compare **OVERPASS**

**under·pay** /ˌʌndəˈpeɪ; *NAmE* -dərˈp-/ *verb* [usually passive] (**under·paid**, **under·paid** /-ˈpeɪd/) ~ **sb** to pay sb too little money, especially for their work **OPP** **overpay** ▶ **under·pay·ment** *noun* [U, C]

**under·per·form** /ˌʌndəpəˈfɔːm; *NAmE* -dərpərˈfɔːrm/ *verb* [I] to not be as successful as was expected

**under·pin** /ˌʌndəˈpɪn; *NAmE* -dərˈp-/ *verb* (**-nn-**) **1** ~ **sth** (*formal*) to support or form the basis of an argument, a claim, etc: *The report is underpinned by extensive research.* **2** ~ **sth** (*specialist*) to support a wall and make it stronger by putting metal, CONCRETE (= a hard building material), etc. under it ▶ **under·pin·ning** *noun* [C, U]

**under·play** /ˌʌndəˈpleɪ; *NAmE* -dərˈp-/ *verb* ~ **sth** (*especially BrE*) to make sth seem less important than it really is **SYN** **downplay**, **play down**: *I think she's underplaying the significance of the report.* **OPP** **overplay**

**under·pre·pared** /ˌʌndəprɪˈpeəd; *NAmE* -dərprɪˈperd/ *adj.* not having done enough preparation for sth you have to do

**under·priced** /ˌʌndəˈpraɪst; *NAmE* -dərˈp-/ *adj.* something that is **underpriced** is sold at a price that is too low and less than its real value

**under·priv·il·eged** /ˌʌndəˈprɪvəlɪdʒd; *NAmE* -dərˈp-/ *adj.* **1** [usually before noun] having less money and fewer opportunities than most people in society **SYN** **disadvantaged**: *underprivileged sections of the community* ◊ *educationally/socially underprivileged groups* ⊃ compare **PRIVILEGED** **2** **the underprivileged** *noun* [pl.] people who are underprivileged

**under·rate** /ˌʌndəˈreɪt/ *verb* ~ **sb/sth** to not recognize how good, important, etc. sb/sth really is: *He's seriously underrated as a writer.* ◊ *an underrated movie* ⊃ compare **OVERRATE**, **UNDERESTIMATE**

**under·re·hearsed** /ˌʌndərɪˈhɜːst; *NAmE* -rɪˈhɜːrst/ *adj.* (of a play or other performance) that has not been prepared and practised enough

**under-repre·sent·ed** /ˌʌndə ˌreprɪˈzentɪd/ *adj.* not having as many representatives as would be expected or needed: *Women are under-represented at senior levels in business.*

1701 **understand**

**under-re·sourced** *adj.* not provided with as much money or as many staff, materials, etc. as are needed: *Nurses are overstretched and the hospital is seriously under-resourced.*

**under·score** *verb, noun*
■ *verb* /ˌʌndəˈskɔː(r); *NAmE* -dərˈs-/ (*especially NAmE*) = **UNDERLINE**
■ *noun* /ˈʌndəskɔː(r); *NAmE* -dərs-/ (*computing*) the symbol ( _ ) that is used to draw a line between letters or words, especially in computer commands and internet addresses

**under·sea** /ˈʌndəsiː; *NAmE* -dərsiː/ *adj.* [only before noun] found, used or happening below the surface of the sea: *undersea cables/earthquakes*

**under·sec·re·tary** /ˌʌndəˈsekrətri; *NAmE* ˌʌndərsekrəˈteri/ *noun* (*pl.* **-ies**) **1** (in the UK) a senior CIVIL SERVANT in charge of one part of a government department ⊃ compare **PERMANENT UNDERSECRETARY** **2** (in the UK) a junior minister who works for the minister in charge of a government department **3** (in the US) an official of high rank in a government department, directly below a member of a CABINET

**under·sell** /ˌʌndəˈsel; *NAmE* -dərˈs-/ *verb* (**un·der·sold**, **un·der·sold** /-ˈsəʊld/) **1** ~ **sth** to sell goods or services at a lower price than your competitors **2** ~ **sth** to sell sth at a price lower than its real value **3** ~ **sb/sth/yourself** to make people think that sb/sth is/you are not as good or as interesting as they/you really are: *Don't undersell yourself at the interview.*

**under·served** /ˌʌndəˈsɜːvd; *NAmE* -dərˈsɜːrvd/ *adj.* (of an area or group of people) not getting enough help, products or services: *improving access to healthcare in underserved areas*

**under·shirt** /ˈʌndəʃɜːt; *NAmE* -dərʃɜːrt/ (*NAmE*) (*BrE* **vest**) *noun* a piece of underwear worn under a shirt, etc. next to the skin ⊃ compare **SINGLET**

**under·shoot** /ˌʌndəˈʃuːt; *NAmE* -dərˈʃ-/ *verb* (**under·shot**, **under·shot** /-ˈʃɒt; *NAmE* -ˈʃɑːt/) **1** [I, T] ~ **(sth)** to fail to reach the intended level, target, etc. **2** [I, T] ~ **(sth)** (of an aircraft) to land before reaching the RUNWAY ▶ **under·shoot** /ˈʌndəʃuːt; *NAmE* -dərʃ-/ *noun*

**under·shorts** /ˈʌndəʃɔːts; *NAmE* -dərʃɔːrts/ *noun* [pl.] (*NAmE*) UNDERPANTS that are worn by men

**under·side** /ˈʌndəsaɪd; *NAmE* -dərs-/ *noun* the bottom or lower side or surface of sth **SYN** **bottom**

**the under·signed** /ði ˌʌndəˈsaɪnd; *NAmE* -dərˈs-/ *noun* (*pl.* **the under·signed**) (*formal*) the person who has signed that particular document: *We, the undersigned, agree to …*

**under·sized** /ˌʌndəˈsaɪzd; *NAmE* -dərˈs-/ *adj.* not as big as normal

**under·sold** /ˌʌndəˈsəʊld; *NAmE* -dərˈs-/ *past tense, past part.* of **UNDERSELL**

**under·spend** /ˌʌndəˈspend; *NAmE* -dərˈs-/ *verb* (**under·spent**, **under·spent** /-ˈspent/) [I, T] to not spend enough money on sth, especially when money has been made available for sth but still not spent: ~ **(on sth)** *The inquiry found that the company had seriously underspent on safety equipment.* ◊ ~ **sth** *We've underspent our budget this year.* ▶ **under·spend** /ˈʌndəspend; *NAmE* -dərs-/ *noun* [sing.] (*BrE*): *a £1 million underspend*

**under·staffed** /ˌʌndəˈstɑːft; *NAmE* -dərˈstæft/ *adj.* [not usually before noun] not having enough people working and therefore not able to function well **SYN** **undermanned** **OPP** **overstaffed**

**under·stand** /ˌʌndəˈstænd; *NAmE* -dərˈs-/ *verb* (**under·stood**, **under·stood** /-ˈstʊd/) (not usually used in the progressive tenses)
• **MEANING** **1** [T, I] to know or realize the meaning of words, a language, what sb says, etc: ~ **(sth)** *Can you understand*

**WORD FAMILY**
**understand** *verb* (≠ misunderstand)
**understandable** *adj.*
**misunderstood** *adj.*
**understanding** *adj., noun* (≠ misunderstanding)

# understandable

French? ◊ Do you understand the instructions? ◊ She didn't understand the form she was signing. ◊ I'm not sure that I understand. Go over it again. ◊ I don't want you doing that again. Do you understand? ◊ **~ what ...** I don't understand what he's saying. ⇨ EXPRESS YOURSELF at EXPLAIN ⇨ note at WANT
- **HOW STH WORKS/HAPPENS 2** [A1] [T] to know or realize how or why sth happens, how it works or why it is important: **~ sth** Doctors still don't understand much about the disease. ◊ No one is answering the phone—I can't understand it. ◊ **~ why, what, etc ...** I could never understand why she was fired. ◊ **~ sb/sth doing sth** I just can't understand him taking the money. ◊ **~ that ...** He was the first to understand that we live in a knowledge economy.
- **KNOW SB 3** [T, I] to know sb's character, how they feel and why they behave in the way they do: **~ sb** Nobody understands me. ◊ He doesn't understand women at all. ◊ **~ what, how, etc ...** They understand what I have been through. ◊ **~ (that ...)** I quite understand that you need some time alone. ◊ If you want to leave early, I'm sure he'll understand. ◊ **~ sb doing sth** I quite understand you needing some time alone.
- **THINK/BELIEVE 4** [T] (*formal*) to think or believe that sth is true because you have been told that it is: **~ (that) ...** I understand (that) you wish to see the manager. ◊ Am I to understand that you refuse? ◊ **~ sb/sth to be/have sth** The Prime Minister is understood to have been extremely angry about the report. ◊ **it is understood that ...** It is understood that the band are working on their next album.
- **BE AGREED 5** [T] **it is understood that ...** to agree sth with sb without it needing to be said: I thought it was understood that my expenses would be paid.
- **MISSING WORD 6** [T, usually passive] **~ sth** to realize that a word in a phrase or sentence is not expressed and to supply it in your mind: In the sentence 'I can't drive', the object 'a car' is understood.

**IDM** **make yourself under'stood** to make your meaning clear, especially in another language: He doesn't speak much Japanese but he can make himself understood. ⇨ more at GIVE v.

**under·stand·able** /ˌʌndəˈstændəbl; *NAmE* -dərˈs-/ *adj.*
**1** (of behaviour, feelings, reactions, etc.) seeming normal and reasonable in a particular situation **SYN** natural: *Their attitude is perfectly understandable.* ◊ *It was an understandable mistake to make.* **2** (of language, documents, etc.) easy to understand **SYN** comprehensible: *Warning notices must be readily understandable.*

**under·stand·ably** /ˌʌndəˈstændəbli; *NAmE* -dərˈs-/ *adv.* in a way that seems normal and reasonable in a particular situation **SYN** naturally: *They were understandably disappointed with the result.*

## under·stand·ing [A2] /ˌʌndəˈstændɪŋ; *NAmE* -dərˈs-/ *noun, adj.*

- *noun* **1** [A2] [U, sing.] **~ (of sth)** the knowledge that sb has about a particular subject or situation: *Students will gain a broad understanding of the workings of Parliament.* ◊ *a deep/clear understanding of sth* ◊ *Unions said her comments showed a complete lack of understanding of what the civil service does.* **2** [B1] [U, sing.] the ability to understand why people behave in a particular way and to forgive them when they do sth wrong: *Organizers of the rally say they want to promote understanding, tolerance and open-mindedness* ◊ *These efforts would foster mutual understanding and respect for different values.* **3** [B2] [C, usually sing.] an informal agreement: **~ about sth** *We finally came to an understanding about what hours we would work.* ◊ **~ that ...** *We have this understanding that nobody talks about work over lunch.* **4** [B2] [U, C] **~ (of sth)** the particular way in which sb understands sth **SYN** interpretation: *My understanding of the situation is different* ◊ *It was our understanding that you had already been informed.* ◊ *The statement is open to various understandings.*

**IDM** **on the understanding that ...** (*formal*) used to introduce a condition that must be agreed before sth else can happen: *They agreed to the changes on the understanding that they would be introduced gradually.*

- *adj.* showing sympathy for other people's problems and being willing to forgive them when they do sth wrong **SYN** sympathetic: *She has very understanding parents.*
▶ **under·stand·ing·ly** *adv.*

**under·state** /ˌʌndəˈsteɪt; *NAmE* -dərˈs-/ *verb* **~ sth** to state that sth is smaller, less important or less serious than it really is: *It would be a mistake to understate the seriousness of the problem.* **OPP** overstate

**under·stated** /ˌʌndəˈsteɪtɪd; *NAmE* -dərˈs-/ *adj.* (*approving*) if a style, colour, etc. is **understated**, it is attractive in a way that is not too obvious **SYN** subtle

**under·state·ment** /ˈʌndəsteɪtmənt; *NAmE* -dərs-/ *noun*
**1** [C] a statement that makes sth seem less important, impressive, serious, etc. than it really is: *To say we were pleased is an understatement (= we were extremely pleased).* ◊ *'These figures are a bit disappointing.' 'That's got to be the understatement of the year.'* **2** [U] the practice of making things seem less impressive, important, serious, etc. than they really are: *typical English understatement* ◊ *He always goes for subtlety and understatement in his movies.* **OPP** overstatement

**under·stood** /ˌʌndəˈstʊd; *NAmE* -dərˈs-/ *past tense, past part.* of UNDERSTAND

**under·storey** (*NAmE* **under·story** *pl.* -stories) /ˈʌndəstɔːri; *NAmE* -dərs-/ *noun* (*specialist*) a layer of plants, bushes, etc. that is found below the main CANOPY of a forest (= the top leaves and branches of the trees that form a thick layer)

---

## SYNONYMS

### understand
see • get • follow • grasp • comprehend

These words all mean to know or realize sth, for example why sth happens, how sth works or what sth means.

**understand** to know or realize the meaning of words, a language, what sb says, etc; to know or realize how or why sth happens, how it works or why it is important: *I don't understand the instructions.* ◊ *Doctors still don't understand much about the disease.*

**see** to understand what is happening, what sb is saying, how sth works or how important sth is: *'It opens like this.' 'Oh, I see.'* ◊ *Oh yes, I see what you mean.*

**get** (*informal*) to understand a joke, what sb is trying to tell you, or a situation that they are trying to describe: *She didn't get the joke.* ◊ *I don't get you.*

**follow** to understand an explanation, a story or the meaning of sth: *Sorry—I don't quite follow.* ◊ *The plot is almost impossible to follow.*

**grasp** to come to understand a fact, an idea or how to do sth: *They failed to grasp the importance of his words.*

**UNDERSTAND OR GRASP?**
You can use **understand** or **grasp** for the action of realizing the meaning or importance of sth for the first time: *It's a difficult concept for children to understand/grasp.* Only **understand** can be used to talk about languages, words or writing: *I don't grasp French/the instructions.*

**comprehend** (often used in negative statements) (*formal*) to understand a fact, idea or reason: *The concept of infinity is almost impossible for the human mind to comprehend.*

**PATTERNS**
- to understand/see/get/follow/grasp/comprehend what/why/how ...
- to understand/see/grasp/comprehend that ...
- to understand/see/get/grasp **the point/idea** (of sth)
- to be **easy/difficult/hard** to understand/see/follow/grasp/comprehend
- to **fully** understand/see/grasp/comprehend sth

**under·study** /ˈʌndəstʌdi; NAmE -dərs-/ noun, verb
- noun (pl. **-ies**) ~ **(to sb)** an actor who learns the part of another actor in a play so that they can play that part if necessary ⊃ **WORDFINDER NOTE** at ACTOR
- verb (**under·stud·ies**, **under·study·ing**, **under·stud·ied**, **under·stud·ied**) ~ **sb/sth** to learn a part in a play as an understudy; to act as an understudy to sb

**under·take** 🔒+ B2 Ⓦ /ˌʌndəˈteɪk; NAmE -dərˈt-/ verb (**under·took** /-ˈtʊk/, **under·taken** /-ˈteɪkən/) (formal) **1** 🔒+ B2 ~ **sth** to make yourself responsible for sth and start doing it: *to undertake a task/project* ◊ *University professors both teach and undertake research.* ◊ *The company has announced that it will undertake a full investigation into the accident.* **2** 🔒+ C1 ~ **to do sth** | ~ **that…** to agree or promise that you will do sth: *He undertook to finish the job by Friday.*

**under·taker** /ˈʌndəteɪkə(r); NAmE -dərt-/ (also formal **'funeral director**) (NAmE also **mor·ti·cian**) noun a person whose job is to prepare the bodies of dead people to be buried or CREMATED, and to arrange FUNERALS

**under·tak·ing** Ⓦ /ˌʌndəˈteɪkɪŋ; NAmE -dərˈt-/ noun **1** [C] a task or project, especially one that is important and/or difficult **SYN venture**: *He is interested in buying the club as a commercial undertaking.* ◊ *In those days, the trip across country was a dangerous undertaking.* **2** [C] (formal) an agreement or a promise to do sth: ~ **(to do sth)** *a government undertaking to spend more on education* ◊ ~ **(that…)** *The landlord gave a written undertaking that the repairs would be carried out.* **3** [U] /ˈʌndəteɪkɪŋ; NAmE -dərt-/ the business of an undertaker

**under-the-ˈcounter** adj. (informal) (of goods or payments) bought or made secretly and sometimes illegally ⊃ see also UNDER THE COUNTER at COUNTER noun

**under·tone** /ˈʌndətəʊn; NAmE -dərt-/ noun ~ **(of sth)** a feeling, quality or meaning that is not expressed directly but can still be understood from what sb says or does **SYN undercurrent**: *His soft words contained an undertone of warning.* ◊ *The play does not have the political undertones of the novel.* ⊃ compare OVERTONE
**IDM in an 'undertone | in 'undertones** in a quiet voice

**under·took** /ˌʌndəˈtʊk; NAmE -dərˈt-/ past tense of UNDERTAKE

**under·tow** /ˈʌndətəʊ; NAmE -dərt-/ noun [usually sing.] **1** a current in the sea or ocean that moves in the opposite direction to the water near the surface: *The children were carried out to sea by the strong undertow.* **2** ~ **(of sth)** a feeling or quality that influences people in a particular situation even though they may not really be aware of it

**under·trial** /ˈʌndətraɪəl; NAmE -dərt-/ noun (IndE) a person who has been charged with a crime: *The undertrials will appear in court next week.*

**under·used** /ˌʌndəˈjuːzd; NAmE -dərˈj-/ (also formal **under·utilˌized**) adj. not used as much as it could or should be
▶ **under-use** /-ˈjuːs/ (also formal **under·util·iza·tion**) noun [U]

**under·util·ized** (BrE also **-ised**) /ˌʌndəˈjuːtəlaɪzd; NAmE -dərˈj-/ adj. (formal) = UNDERUSED ▶ **under·util·iza·tion**, **-isa·tion** /ˌʌndəˌjuːtəlaɪˈzeɪʃn; NAmE -dərˌjuːtələˈz-/ noun [U] (formal) = UNDERUSE

**under·value** /ˌʌndəˈvæljuː; NAmE -dərˈv-/ verb [usually passive] **1** ~ **sb/sth** to not recognize how good, valuable or important sb/sth really is: *Education is currently undervalued in this country.* **2** ~ **sth** to state that the financial value of sth is lower than it really is: *He believes his house has been undervalued.* **OPP overvalue**

**under·water** /ˌʌndəˈwɔːtə(r); NAmE -dərˈw-/ adj. [only before noun] found, used or happening below the surface of water: *an underwater camera/photographer* ◊ *an underwater cave/volcano/mountain* ▶ **under·water** adv.: *Take a deep breath and see how long you can stay underwater.*

**under·way** /ˌʌndəˈweɪ; NAmE -dərˈw-/ adj. [not before noun] = UNDER WAY

**under·wear** 🔒 B1 /ˈʌndəweə(r); NAmE -dərwer/ noun [U] (also formal **under·clothes**, **under·cloth·ing**) clothes that you wear under other clothes and next to the skin: *I never wear underwear.*

1703 **undifferentiated**

**under·weight** /ˌʌndəˈweɪt; NAmE -dərˈw-/ adj. (especially of a person) weighing less than the normal or expected weight: *She is a few pounds underweight for* (= in relation to) *her height.* **OPP overweight**

**under·went** /ˌʌndəˈwent; NAmE -dərˈw-/ past tense of UNDERGO

**under·whelmed** /ˌʌndəˈwelmd; NAmE -dərˈw-/ adj. (informal, humorous) not impressed with or excited about sth at all: *We were distinctly underwhelmed by the director's speech.* ⊃ compare OVERWHELM

**under·whelm·ing** /ˌʌndəˈwelmɪŋ; NAmE -dərˈw-/ adj. (informal, humorous) not impressing or exciting you at all: *the contrast between his overwhelming guitar-playing and his underwhelming singing*

**under·world** /ˈʌndəwɜːld; NAmE -dərwɜːrld/ noun [sing.] **1** the people and activities involved in crime in a particular place: *the criminal underworld* ◊ *the Glasgow underworld* **2 the underworld** (in MYTHS and LEGENDS, for example those of ancient Greece) the place under the earth where people are believed to go when they die

**under·write** /ˌʌndəˈraɪt; NAmE -dərˈr-/ verb (**under·wrote** /-ˈrəʊt/, **under·writ·ten** /-ˈrɪtn/) (specialist) **1** ~ **sth** to accept financial responsibility for an activity so that you will pay for special costs or for losses it may make **2** ~ **sth** to accept responsibility for an insurance policy so that you will pay money in case loss or damage happens ⊃ **WORDFINDER NOTE** at INSURANCE **3** ~ **sth** to agree to buy shares that are not bought by the public when new shares are offered for sale

**under·writer** /ˈʌndəraɪtə(r); NAmE -dərr-/ noun **1** a person or organization that underwrites insurance policies, especially for ships **2** a person whose job is to estimate the risks involved in a particular activity and decide how much sb must pay for insurance

**un·deserved** /ˌʌndɪˈzɜːvd; NAmE -ˈzɜːrvd/ adj. that sb does not deserve and therefore unfair: *The criticism was totally undeserved.* ◊ *an undeserved victory* ▶ **un·deserv·ed·ly** /ˌʌndɪˈzɜːvɪdli; NAmE -ˈzɜːrv-/ adv.

**un·deserv·ing** /ˌʌndɪˈzɜːvɪŋ; NAmE -ˈzɜːrv-/ adj. ~ **(of sth)** (formal) not deserving to have or receive sth: *He was undeserving of her affections.* **OPP deserving**

**un·desir·able** /ˌʌndɪˈzaɪərəbl; NAmE -ˈzaɪr-/ adj., noun
- adj. not wanted or approved of; likely to cause trouble or problems: *undesirable consequences/effects* ◊ *It would be highly undesirable to increase class sizes further.* ◊ *prostitution and other undesirable practices* **OPP desirable**
▶ **un·desir·ably** /-bli/ adv.
- noun [usually pl.] a person who is not wanted in a particular place, especially because they are considered dangerous or criminal: *He's been mixing with drug addicts and other undesirables.*

**un·detect·able** /ˌʌndɪˈtektəbl/ adj. impossible to see or find: *The sound is virtually undetectable to the human ear.* **OPP detectable**

**un·detect·ed** /ˌʌndɪˈtektɪd/ adj. not noticed by anyone: *How could anyone break into the palace undetected?* ◊ *The disease often goes/remains undetected for many years.*

**un·deterred** /ˌʌndɪˈtɜːd; NAmE -ˈtɜːrd/ adj. if sb is **undeterred** by sth, they do not allow it to stop them from doing sth

**un·devel·oped** /ˌʌndɪˈveləpt/ adj. **1** (of land) not used for farming, industry, building, etc. **2** (of a country) not having modern industries, and with a low standard of living **HELP** 'A **developing** country' is now the usual expression. **3** not grown to full size: *undeveloped limbs* ⊃ compare UNDERDEVELOPED

**un·did** /ʌnˈdɪd/ past tense of UNDO

**un·dies** /ˈʌndiz/ noun [pl.] (informal) underwear

**un·dif·fer·en·ti·ated** /ˌʌndɪfəˈrenʃiətɪd/ adj. having parts that you cannot see a difference between; not split into different parts or sections: *a view of society as an undifferentiated whole* ◊ *an undifferentiated target audience*

---

Ⓞ Oxford Phrasal Academic Lexicon (OPAL) written and spoken word lists | Ⓦ OPAL written word list | Ⓢ OPAL spoken word list

# undignified

**un·dig·ni·fied** /ʌnˈdɪɡnɪfaɪd/ *adj.* causing you to look silly and to lose the respect of other people: *There was an undignified scramble for the best seats.* **OPP** **dignified**

**un·diluted** /ˌʌndaɪˈluːtɪd/ *adj.* **1** (of a liquid) not made weaker by having water added to it; not having been DILUTED **2** (of a feeling or quality) not mixed or combined with anything and therefore very strong **SYN** **unadulterated**

**un·dimin·ished** /ˌʌndɪˈmɪnɪʃt/ *adj.* that has not become smaller or weaker: *They continued with undiminished enthusiasm.*

**un·dis·cip·lined** /ʌnˈdɪsəplɪnd/ *adj.* not having enough control or organization; behaving badly **OPP** **disciplined**

**un·dis·closed** /ˌʌndɪsˈkləʊzd/ *adj.* not made known or told to anyone; not having been DISCLOSED: *He was paid an undisclosed sum.*

**un·dis·cov·ered** /ˌʌndɪˈskʌvəd/; *NAmE* -vərd/ *adj.* that has not been found or noticed; that has not been discovered: *a previously undiscovered talent*

**un·dis·guised** /ˌʌndɪsˈɡaɪzd/ *adj.* (especially of a feeling) that you do not try to hide from other people; not DISGUISED: *a look of undisguised admiration*

**un·dis·puted** /ˌʌndɪˈspjuːtɪd/ *adj.* **1** that cannot be questioned or proved to be false; that cannot be DISPUTED **SYN** **irrefutable**: *undisputed facts* **2** that everyone accepts or recognizes: *the undisputed champion of the world*

**un·dis·tin·guished** /ˌʌndɪˈstɪŋɡwɪʃt/ *adj.* not very interesting, successful or attractive: *an undistinguished career* **OPP** **distinguished**

**un·dis·turbed** /ˌʌndɪˈstɜːbd/; *NAmE* -ˈstɜːrbd/ *adj.* **1** [not usually before noun] not moved or touched by anyone or anything **SYN** **untouched**: *The treasure had lain undisturbed for centuries.* **2** not interrupted by anyone **SYN** **uninterrupted**: *She succeeded in working undisturbed for a few hours.* **3** [not usually before noun] ~ (by sth) not affected or upset by sth **SYN** **unconcerned**: *He seemed undisturbed by the news of her death.* ⊃ compare DISTURBED

**un·div·ided** /ˌʌndɪˈvaɪdɪd/ *adj.* **1** not split into smaller parts; not divided: *an undivided Church* **2** [usually before noun] total; complete; not divided: *undivided loyalty* ◊ *You must be prepared to give the job your undivided attention.*

**undo** /ʌnˈduː/ *verb* (un·does /-ˈdʌz/, un·did /-ˈdɪd/, un·done /-ˈdʌn/) **1** ~ sth to open sth that is fastened, tied or wrapped: *to undo a button/knot/zip* ◊ *to undo a jacket/shirt* ◊ *I undid the package and took out the books.* **OPP** **do up** **2** ~ sth to cancel the effect of sth: *He undid most of the good work of the previous manager.* ◊ *It's not too late to try and undo some of the damage.* ◊ UNDO (= a command on a computer that cancels the previous action) **3** [usually passive] ~ sb/sth (*formal*) to make sb/sth fail: *The team was undone by the speed and strength of their opponents.*

**un·dock** /ʌnˈdɒk/; *NAmE* -ˈdɑːk/ *verb* ~ sth (*computing*) to remove a computer from a DOCKING STATION **OPP** **dock**

**un·docu·ment·ed** /ʌnˈdɒkjumentɪd/; *NAmE* -ˈdɑːk-/ *adj.* **1** not supported by written evidence: *undocumented accusations* **2** not having the necessary documents, especially permission to live and work in a foreign country: *undocumented immigrants*

**un·do·ing** /ʌnˈduːɪŋ/ *noun* [sing.] the reason why sb fails at sth or is unsuccessful in life **SYN** **downfall**: *That one mistake was his undoing.*

**un·done** /ʌnˈdʌn/ *adj.* [not usually before noun] **1** (especially of clothing) not fastened or tied: *Her blouse had come undone.* **2** (especially of work) not finished: *Most of the work had been left undone.* **3** (*old use*) (of a person) defeated and without any hope for the future

**un·doubt·ed** /ʌnˈdaʊtɪd/ *adj.* [usually before noun] used to emphasize that sth exists or is definitely true **SYN** **indubitable**: *She has an undoubted talent as an organizer.*

**un·doubt·ed·ly** /ʌnˈdaʊtɪdli/ *adv.* used to emphasize that sth exists or is definitely true **SYN** **indubitably**: *There is undoubtedly a great deal of truth in what he says.*

**un·dreamed-of** /ʌnˈdriːmd ɒv/; *NAmE* ʌv/ (*also* **un·dreamt-of** /ʌnˈdremt ɒv/; *NAmE* ʌv/ *especially in BrE*) *a* much more or much better than you thought was possible: *undreamed-of success*

**un·dress** /ʌnˈdres/ *verb*, *noun*
■ *verb* [I, T] to take off your clothes; to remove sb else's clothes: *She undressed and got into bed.* ◊ ~ sb to undress a child ◊ *He got undressed in a small cubicle next to the pool.* **OPP** **dress**
■ *noun* [U] (*formal*) the fact of sb wearing no, or few, clothes: *He appeared at the window in a state of undress.*

**un·dressed** /ʌnˈdrest/ *adj.* [not usually before noun] not wearing any clothes: *She began to get undressed* (= remove her clothes). **OPP** **dressed**

**un·drink·able** /ʌnˈdrɪŋkəbl/ *adj.* not good or pure enough to drink **OPP** **drinkable**

**undue** /ʌnˈdjuː/; *NAmE* -ˈduː/ *adj.* [only before noun] (*formal*) more than you think is reasonable or necessary **SYN** **excessive**: *They are taking undue advantage of the situation.* ◊ *The work should be carried out without undue delay.* ◊ *We did not want to put any undue pressure on them.* ⊃ compare DUE

**un·du·late** /ˈʌndʒəleɪt/ *verb* [I] (*formal*) to go or move gently up and down like waves: *The countryside undulates pleasantly.* ⊃ WORDFINDER NOTE at LANDSCAPE

**un·du·lat·ing** /ˈʌndʒəleɪtɪŋ/ *adj.* having a shape like a wave or moving like a wave: *undulating countryside/fields/terrain/ground* ◊ *undulating flight/movement/motion*

**un·du·la·tion** /ˌʌndʒəˈleɪʃn/ *noun* [C, U] a smooth, curving shape or movement like a series of waves

**un·duly** /ʌnˈdjuːli/; *NAmE* -ˈduː-/ *adv.* (*formal*) more than you think is reasonable or necessary **SYN** **excessively**: *He did not sound unduly worried at the prospect.* ◊ *The levels of pollution in this area are unduly high.* ◊ *The thought did not disturb her unduly.* ⊃ compare DULY

**un·dying** /ʌnˈdaɪɪŋ/ *adj.* [only before noun] lasting forever **SYN** **eternal**: *undying love*

**un·earned** /ʌnˈɜːnd/; *NAmE* -ˈɜːrnd/ *adj.* [usually before noun] used to describe money that you receive but do not earn by working: *Declare all unearned income.*

**un·earth** /ʌnˈɜːθ/; *NAmE* -ˈɜːrθ/ *verb* **1** ~ sth to find sth in the ground by digging **SYN** **dig up**: *to unearth buried treasures* **2** ~ sth to find or discover sth by chance or after searching for it **SYN** **dig up**: *I unearthed my old diaries when we moved house.* ◊ *The newspaper has unearthed some disturbing facts.*

**un·earth·ly** /ʌnˈɜːθli/; *NAmE* -ˈɜːrθ-/ *adj.* [usually before noun] very strange; not natural and therefore frightening: *an unearthly cry* ◊ *an unearthly light*
**IDM** **at an unearthly 'hour** (*informal*) very early, especially when this is annoying: *The job involved getting up at some unearthly hour to catch the first train.*

**un·ease** /ʌnˈiːz/ (*also* **un·easi·ness** /ʌnˈiːzinəs/) *noun* [U, sing.] the feeling of being worried or unhappy about sth **SYN** **anxiety**: *a deep feeling/sense of unease* ◊ *There was a growing unease about their involvement in the war.* ◊ *He was unable to hide his unease at the way the situation was developing.*

**un·easy** /ʌnˈiːzi/ *adj.* **1** feeling worried or unhappy about a particular situation, especially because you think that sth bad or unpleasant may happen or because you are not sure that what you are doing is right **SYN** **anxious**: *an uneasy laugh* ◊ ~ about sth *He was beginning to feel distinctly uneasy about their visit.* ◊ ~ about doing sth *She felt uneasy about leaving the children with them.* ⊃ SYNONYMS at WORRIED **2** not certain to last; not safe or settled: *an uneasy peace* ◊ *The two sides eventually reached an uneasy compromise.* **3** that does not enable you to relax or feel comfortable: *She woke from an uneasy sleep to find the house empty.* **4** used to describe a mixture of two things, feelings, etc. that do not go well together: *an uneasy mix of humour and violence* ◊ *Old farmhouses and new villas stood together in uneasy proximity.* ▶ **un·eas·ily** /-zɪli/ *adv.*: *I wondered uneasily what he was thinking.* ◊ *She* shifted uneasily in her chair. ◇ His socialist views **sit uneasily** with his huge fortune.

**un·eat·able** /ʌnˈiːtəbl/ *adj.* (of food) not good enough to be eaten ⊃ see also INEDIBLE

**un·eat·en** /ʌnˈiːtn/ *adj.* not eaten: *Bill put the uneaten food away.*

**un·eco·nom·ic** /ˌʌniːkəˈnɒmɪk, -ˌek-; *NAmE* -ˈnɑːm-/ *adj.* **1** (of a business, factory, etc.) not making a profit **SYN** **unprofitable**: *uneconomic industries* **OPP** **economic** **2** = UNECONOMICAL

**un·eco·nom·ic·al** /ˌʌniːkəˈnɒmɪkl, -ˌek-; *NAmE* -ˈnɑːm-/ (*also* **un·eco·nom·ic**) *adj.* **~ (to do sth)** using too much time or money, or too many materials, and therefore not likely to make a profit: *It soon proved uneconomical to stay open 24 hours a day.* **OPP** **economical**

**un·edi·fy·ing** /ʌnˈedɪfaɪɪŋ/ *adj.* (*formal, especially BrE*) unpleasant in a way that causes DISAPPROVAL: *the unedifying sight of the two party leaders screeching at each other* ⊃ compare EDIFYING

**un·edu·cated** /ʌnˈedʒukeɪtɪd/ *adj.* having had little or no formal education at a school; showing a lack of education: *an uneducated workforce* ◇ *an uneducated point of view* ⊃ compare EDUCATED

**un·elect·ed** /ˌʌnɪˈlektɪd/ *adj.* not having been chosen by people in an election: *unelected bureaucrats*

**un·emo·tion·al** /ˌʌnɪˈməʊʃənl/ *adj.* not showing your feelings: *an unemotional speech* ◇ *She seemed very cool and unemotional.* **OPP** **emotional** ▶ **un·emo·tion·al·ly** /-nəli/ *adv.*

**un·em·ploy·able** /ˌʌnɪmˈplɔɪəbl/ *adj.* not having the skills or qualities that you need to get a job **OPP** **employable**

**un·em·ployed** ⓘ B1 /ˌʌnɪmˈplɔɪd/ *adj.* without a job although able to work **SYN** **jobless**: *How long have you been unemployed?* ◇ *unemployed workers/people* ▶ **the un·em·ployed** *noun* [pl.]: *a programme to get the long-term unemployed back to work* ◇ *I've joined the ranks of the unemployed* (= I've lost my job).

**un·em·ploy·ment** ⓘ B1 /ˌʌnɪmˈplɔɪmənt/ *noun* [U] **1** ⓘ B1 the fact of a number of people not having a job; the number of people without a job: *an area of high/low unemployment* ◇ *rising unemployment* ◇ *It was a time of mass unemployment.* ◇ *Government schemes to combat youth unemployment* ◇ *the level/rate of unemployment* ◇ *The unemployment rate rose to 4.7 per cent.* **2** ⓘ B1 the state of not having a job: *Thousands of young people are facing long-term unemployment.* ⊃ compare EMPLOYMENT **3** (*US*) = UNEMPLOYMENT BENEFIT: *Since losing his job, Mike has been collecting unemployment.* ⊃ WORDFINDER NOTE at POOR

**un·em·ployment benefit** (*BrE*) (*US* **un·em·ployment compen·sation, un·em·ployment**) *noun* [U] (*also* **un·em·ployment benefits** [pl.] *BrE and NAmE*) money paid by the government to sb who is unemployed: *people on* (= receiving) *unemployment benefit* ◇ *Applications for unemployment benefits dropped last month.* ⊃ see also JOBSEEKER'S ALLOWANCE

**un·en·cum·bered** /ˌʌnɪnˈkʌmbəd; *NAmE* -bərd/ *adj.* **1** not having or carrying anything heavy or anything that makes you go more slowly **2** (*law*) (of property) not having any debts left to be paid

**un·end·ing** /ʌnˈendɪŋ/ *adj.* seeming to last forever: *a seemingly unending supply of money*

**un·en·dur·able** /ˌʌnɪnˈdjʊərəbl; *NAmE* -ˈdʊr-/ *adj.* (*formal*) too bad, unpleasant, etc. to bear **SYN** **unbearable**: *unendurable pain*

**un·envi·able** /ʌnˈenviəbl/ *adj.* [usually before noun] difficult or unpleasant; that you would not want to have: *She was given the unenviable task of informing the losers.* **OPP** **enviable**

**un·equal** /ʌnˈiːkwəl/ *adj.* **1** [usually before noun] in which people are treated in different ways or have different advantages in a way that seems unfair **SYN** **unfair**: *an unequal distribution of wealth* ◇ *an unequal contest* **2 ~ (in sth)** different in size, amount, etc: *The sleeves are unequal in length.* ◇ *The rooms upstairs are of unequal size.*

1705 **unexpurgated**

**3 ~ to sth** (*formal*) not capable of doing sth: *She felt unequal to the task she had set herself.* **OPP** **equal** ▶ **un·equal·ly** /-kwəli/ *adv.*

**un·equalled** (*US* **un·equaled**) /ʌnˈiːkwəld/ *adj.* better than all others **SYN** **unparalleled**: *an unequalled record of success*

**un·equivo·cal** /ˌʌnɪˈkwɪvəkl/ *adj.* (*formal*) expressing your opinion or intention very clearly and strongly **SYN** **unambiguous**: *an unequivocal rejection* ◇ *The answer was an unequivocal 'no'.* **OPP** **equivocal** ⊃ SYNONYMS at PLAIN ▶ **un·equivo·cal·ly** /-kəli/ *adv.*

**un·err·ing** /ʌnˈɜːrɪŋ/ *adj.* always right or accurate **SYN** **unfailing**: *She had an unerring instinct for a good business deal.* ▶ **un·err·ing·ly** *adv.*

**UNESCO** (*also* **Unesco**) /juːˈneskəʊ/ *abbr.* United Nations Educational, Scientific and Cultural Organization

**un·eth·ic·al** /ʌnˈeθɪkl/ *adj.* not morally acceptable: *unethical behaviour* **OPP** **ethical** ▶ **un·eth·ic·al·ly** /-kli/ *adv.*

**un·even** /ʌnˈiːvn/ *adj.* **1** not level, smooth or flat: *The floor felt uneven under his feet.* **OPP** **even 2** not following a regular pattern; not having a regular size and shape **SYN** **irregular**: *Her breathing was quick and uneven.* ◇ *uneven teeth* **OPP** **even 3** not having the same quality in all parts: *an uneven performance* (= with some good parts and some bad parts) **4** (of a contest or match) in which one group, team or player is much better than the other **SYN** **unequal** **OPP** **even 5** organized in a way that is not regular and/or fair **SYN** **unequal**: *an uneven distribution of resources* **OPP** **even** ▶ **un·even·ly** *adv.* **un·even·ness** /-vnnəs/ *noun* [U]

**un·even 'bars** (*BrE also* **asymmetric 'bars**) *noun* [pl.] two bars on posts of different heights that are used by women for doing GYMNASTIC exercises on

**un·event·ful** /ˌʌnɪˈventfl/ *adj.* in which nothing interesting, unusual or exciting happens: *an uneventful life* **OPP** **eventful** ▶ **un·event·ful·ly** /-fəli/ *adv.*: *The day passed uneventfully.*

**un·ex·cep·tion·able** /ˌʌnɪkˈsepʃənəbl/ *adj.* **1** (*formal*) not giving any reason for criticism: *a man of unexceptionable character* **2** (*informal*) not very new or exciting

**un·ex·cep·tion·al** /ˌʌnɪkˈsepʃənl/ *adj.* not interesting or unusual **SYN** **unremarkable** ⊃ compare EXCEPTIONAL

**un·ex·cit·ing** /ˌʌnɪkˈsaɪtɪŋ/ *adj.* not interesting; boring **OPP** **exciting**

**un·ex·pect·ed** ⓘ B2 /ˌʌnɪkˈspektɪd/ *adj.* if sth is unexpected, it surprises you because you were not expecting it: *Things took an unexpected turn.* ◇ *an unexpected death* ◇ *The news was disappointing but not unexpected.* ▶ **the unexpected** *noun* [sing.]: *Police officers must be prepared for the unexpected.* **un·ex·pect·ed·ly** *adv.*: *They had arrived unexpectedly.* ◇ *an unexpectedly large bill* ◇ *The plane was unexpectedly delayed.* ◇ *Not unexpectedly, most local business depends on tourism.* **un·ex·pect·ed·ness** *noun* [U] ⊃ compare EXPECT, EXPECTED

**un·ex·pired** /ˌʌnɪkˈspaɪəd; *NAmE* -ərd/ *adj.* [usually before noun] (of an agreement or a period of time) still legally acceptable or current; not yet having come to an end or EXPIRED

**un·ex·plained** /ˌʌnɪkˈspleɪnd/ *adj.* for which the reason or cause is not known; that has not been explained: *an unexplained mystery* ◇ *He died in unexplained circumstances.*

**un·ex·ploded** /ˌʌnɪkˈspləʊdɪd/ *adj.* [only before noun] (of a bomb, etc.) that has not yet exploded

**un·ex·plored** /ˌʌnɪkˈsplɔːd; *NAmE* -ˈsplɔːrd/ *adj.* **1** (of a country or an area of land) that nobody has investigated or put on a map; that has not been explored **2** (of an idea, a theory, etc.) that has not yet been examined or discussed carefully and completely

**un·ex·pressed** /ˌʌnɪkˈsprest/ *adj.* (of a thought, a feeling or an idea) not shown or made known in words, looks or actions; not expressed

**un·ex·pur·gated** /ˌʌnˈekspəɡeɪtɪd; *NAmE* -pərɡ-/ *adj.* (of a text) complete and containing all the original material,

# unfailing

even if it is considered offensive: *This is the full unexpurgated version of the diaries.*

**un·fail·ing** /ʌnˈfeɪlɪŋ/ *adj.* that you can rely on to always be there and always be the same: *unfailing support* ◊ *She fought the disease with unfailing good humour.* ▶ **un·fail·ing·ly** *adv.*: *unfailingly loyal/polite*

**un·fair** 🅘 B1 /ˌʌnˈfeə(r); NAmE -ˈfer/ *adj.* not right or fair according to a set of rules or principles; not treating people equally SYN **unjust**: *They had been given an unfair advantage.* ◊ *We hope the authorities will move to end such unfair practices.* ◊ *unfair dismissal* (= a situation in which sb is illegally dismissed from their job) ◊ *It's so unfair!* ◊ *~ on sb I was working really long hours, which was unfair on my wife and my kids.* ◊ *it is ~ (to/on sb) (to do sth) It would be unfair not to let you have a choice.* ◊ *it is ~ for sb to do sth Most Americans think it is unfair for the government to take more than 25% of anyone's income in taxes.* ◊ *it is ~ that… They say it's grossly unfair that consumers are having to pay more now.* OPP **fair** ▶ **un·fair·ly** *adv.*: *She claims to have been unfairly dismissed.* ◊ *The tests discriminate unfairly against older people.* **un·fair·ness** *noun* [U]

**un·faith·ful** /ʌnˈfeɪθfl/ *adj.* ~ (to sb) having sex with sb who is not your husband, wife or usual partner: *Have you ever been unfaithful to him?* OPP **faithful** ▶ **un·faith·ful·ness** *noun* [U]

**un·famil·iar** /ˌʌnfəˈmɪliə(r)/ *adj.* **1** that you do not know or recognize: *She felt uneasy in the unfamiliar surroundings.* ◊ *~ to sb Please highlight any terms that are unfamiliar to you.* **2** *~ with sth* not having any knowledge or experience of sth: *an introductory course for students who are unfamiliar with computers* OPP **familiar** ▶ **un·famil·iar·ity** /ˌʌnfəˌmɪliˈærəti/ *noun* [U]

**un·fash·ion·able** /ʌnˈfæʃnəbl/ *adj.* not popular or fashionable at a particular time: *an unfashionable part of London* ◊ *unfashionable ideas* OPP **fashionable** ▶ **un·fash·ion·ably** /-bli/ *adv.*: *a man with unfashionably long hair*

**un·fas·ten** /ʌnˈfɑːsn; NAmE -ˈfæsn/ *verb* ~ **sth** to open sth that is fastened: *to unfasten a belt/button, etc.* OPP **fasten**

**un·fath·om·able** /ʌnˈfæðəməbl/ *adj.* (*formal*) **1** too strange or difficult to be understood: *an unfathomable mystery* **2** if sb has an **unfathomable** expression, it is impossible to know what they are thinking

**un·favour·able** (*US* **un·favor·able**) /ʌnˈfeɪvərəbl/ *adj.* (*formal*) **1** ~ (for/to sth) (of conditions, situations, etc.) not good and likely to cause problems or make sth more difficult: *The conditions were unfavourable for agriculture.* ◊ *an unfavourable exchange rate* **2** showing that you do not approve of or like sb/sth: *an unfavourable comment* ◊ *The documentary presents him in a very unfavourable light.* ◊ *an unfavourable comparison* (= one that makes one thing seem much worse than another) OPP **favourable** ▶ **un·favour·ably** (*US* **un·favor·ably**) /-bli/ *adv.*: *In this respect, Britain compares unfavourably with other European countries.*

**un·fazed** /ʌnˈfeɪzd/ *adj.* (*informal*) not worried or surprised by sth unexpected that happens OPP **fazed**

**un·feas·ible** /ʌnˈfiːzəbl/ *adj.* not possible to do or achieve OPP **feasible**

**un·feel·ing** /ʌnˈfiːlɪŋ/ *adj.* not showing care or sympathy for other people

**un·feigned** /ʌnˈfeɪnd/ *adj.* (*formal*) real and sincere SYN **genuine**: *unfeigned admiration*

**un·fenced** /ʌnˈfenst/ *adj.* (of a road or piece of land) without fences next to or around it

**un·fet·tered** /ʌnˈfetəd; NAmE -tərd/ *adj.* (*formal*) not limited in any way: *an unfettered free market*

**un·filled** /ʌnˈfɪld/ *adj.* **1** if a job or position is **unfilled**, nobody has been chosen for it: *There are thousands of unfilled vacancies in the nation's schools.* **2** (especially NAmE) if an order for goods is **unfilled**, the goods have not been supplied

**un·fin·ished** /ʌnˈfɪnɪʃt/ *adj.* not complete; not finished: *We have some unfinished business to settle.*

**unfit** /ʌnˈfɪt/ *adj.* **1** not of an acceptable standard; not suitable: ~ **(for sth)** *The housing was unfit for human habitation.* ◊ *The food on offer was unfit for human consumption.* ◊ *~ to eat, drink, live in, etc. This water is unfit to drink.* ◊ *Most of the buildings are unfit to live in.* ◊ *~ to do sth They described him as unfit to govern.* ◊ (*specialist*) *Many of the houses were condemned as unfit.* ◊ (*specialist*) *The court claims she is an unfit mother.* **2** not capable of doing sth, for example because of illness: *~ for sth He's still unfit for work.* ◊ *~ to do sth The company's doctor found that she was unfit to carry out her normal work.* **3** (*especially BrE*) (of a person) not in good physical condition; not fit, because you have not taken exercise: *The captain is still unfit and will miss tonight's game.* OPP **fit** ▶ **un·fit·ness** *noun* [U]

**un·flag·ging** /ʌnˈflæɡɪŋ/ *adj.* [usually before noun] remaining strong; not becoming weak or tired SYN **tireless**: *unflagging energy*

**un·flap·pable** /ʌnˈflæpəbl/ *adj.* (*informal*) able to stay calm in a difficult situation SYN **imperturbable**

**un·flat·ter·ing** /ʌnˈflætərɪŋ/ *adj.* making sb/sth seem worse or less attractive than they really are: *an unflattering dress* ◊ *unflattering comments* OPP **flattering**

**un·flinch·ing** /ʌnˈflɪntʃɪŋ/ *adj.* remaining strong and determined, even in a difficult or dangerous situation SYN **steadfast**: *unflinching loyalty* ◊ *an unflinching stare* ▶ **un·flinch·ing·ly** *adv.* ⊃ see also **FLINCH**

**un·focused** (also **un·focussed**) /ʌnˈfəʊkəst/ *adj.* **1** (especially of eyes) not looking at a particular thing or person; not having been focused: *an unfocused look* **2** (of plans, work, etc.) not having a clear aim or purpose; not well organized or clear: *The research is too unfocused to have any significant impact.* ◊ *unfocused questions/discussions*

**un·fold** B2+ B2 /ʌnˈfəʊld/ *verb* **1** B2+ B2 [T, I] ~ **(sth)** to spread open or flat sth that has previously been folded; to become open and flat: *to unfold a map* ◊ *She unfolded her arms.* OPP **fold 2** B2+ C1 [I, T] to be gradually made known; to gradually make sth known to other people: *The audience watched as the story unfolded before their eyes.* ◊ *~ sth (to sb) She unfolded her tale to us.*

**un·follow** /ʌnˈfɒləʊ; NAmE -ˈfɑːl-/ *verb* [T, I] to decide to stop receiving messages from a particular person, group, etc. on a social media service by removing them from the list of people you receive messages from

**un·forced** /ʌnˈfɔːst; NAmE -ˈfɔːrst/ *adj.* **1** (especially in sports) an **unforced** error is one that you make by playing badly, not because your opponent has caused you to make a mistake by playing well **2** natural; done without effort: *unforced humour*

**un·fore·see·able** /ˌʌnfɔːˈsiːəbl; NAmE -ˈfɔːrs-/ *adj.* that you cannot predict or FORESEE: *Building a dam here could have unforeseeable consequences for the environment.* OPP **foreseeable**

**un·fore·seen** /ˌʌnfɔːˈsiːn; NAmE -ˈfɔːr-/ *adj.* that you did not expect to happen SYN **unexpected**: *unforeseen delays/problems* ◊ *The project was running late owing to unforeseen circumstances.* ⊃ compare **FORESEE**

**un·for·get·table** /ˌʌnfəˈɡetəbl; NAmE -fərˈɡ-/ *adj.* if sth is **unforgettable**, you cannot forget it, usually because it is so beautiful, interesting, pleasant, etc. SYN **memorable** ⊃ compare **FORGETTABLE**

**un·for·giv·able** /ˌʌnfəˈɡɪvəbl; NAmE -fərˈɡ-/ *adj.* if sb's behaviour is **unforgivable**, it is so bad or unacceptable that you cannot forgive the person SYN **inexcusable** OPP **forgivable** ▶ **un·for·giv·ably** /-bli/ *adv.*

**un·for·giv·ing** /ˌʌnfəˈɡɪvɪŋ; NAmE -fərˈɡ-/ *adj.* **1** (of a person) unwilling to forgive other people when they have done sth wrong OPP **forgiving 2** (of a place, situation, etc.) unpleasant and causing difficulties for people

**un·formed** /ʌnˈfɔːmd; NAmE -ˈfɔːrmd/ *adj.* (*formal*) not fully developed: *unformed ideas*

**un·forth·com·ing** /ˌʌnfɔːˈθkʌmɪŋ/; *NAmE* -fɔːrθ-/ *adj.* not wanting to help or give information about sth **SYN** **reticent**: *He was very unforthcoming about what had happened.* **OPP** **forthcoming**

**un·for·tu·nate** /ʌnˈfɔːtʃənət; *NAmE* -ˈfɔːrtʃ-/ *adj., noun*
■ *adj.* **1** having bad luck; caused by bad luck **SYN** **unlucky**: *He was unfortunate to lose in the final round.* ◇ *It was an unfortunate accident.* **OPP** **fortunate** **2** (*formal*) if you say that a situation is **unfortunate**, you wish that it had not happened or that it had been different **SYN** **regrettable**: *She described the decision as 'unfortunate'.* ◇ *It was unfortunate that he couldn't speak English.* ◇ *You're putting me in a most unfortunate position.* ⇒ LANGUAGE BANK *at* IMPERSONAL **3** embarrassing and/or offensive: *It was an unfortunate choice of words.*
■ *noun* (*literary*) a person who does not have much luck, money, etc: *one of life's unfortunates*

**un·for·tu·nate·ly** /ʌnˈfɔːtʃənətli; *NAmE* -ˈfɔːrtʃ-/ *adv.* used to say that a particular situation or fact makes you sad or disappointed, or gets you into a difficult position **SYN** **regrettably**: *Unfortunately, I won't be able to attend the meeting.* ◇ *I can't make it, unfortunately.* ◇ *~ for sb/sth Unfortunately for him, the police had been informed and were waiting outside.* ◇ *It won't be finished for a few weeks. Unfortunately!* **OPP** **fortunately**

**un·found·ed** /ʌnˈfaʊndɪd/ *adj.* not based on reason or fact: *unfounded allegations/rumours, etc.* ◇ *Speculation about a divorce proved totally unfounded.*

**un·freeze** /ʌnˈfriːz/ *verb* (**un·froze** /-ˈfrəʊz/, **un·frozen** /-ˈfrəʊzn/) **1** [T, I] *~ (sth)* if you **unfreeze** sth that has been frozen or very cold, or it **unfreezes**, it melts or warms until it reaches a normal temperature ⇒ compare DEFROST, DE-ICE, THAW **2** [T] *~ sth* to remove official controls on money or an economy: *The party plans to unfreeze some of the cash held by local government.* **OPP** **freeze**

**un·friend** /ʌnˈfrend/ (*also* **de-friend**) *verb* [T, I] *~ (sb)* (*informal*) to remove sb from a list of friends or contacts on SOCIAL MEDIA: *If a Facebook friend suddenly becomes your boss, do you unfriend them?* ◇ *Young adults are more likely to unfriend.*

**un·friend·ly** /ʌnˈfrendli/ *adj.* not kind or pleasant to sb: *an unfriendly atmosphere* ◇ *~ (to/towards sb) There's no need to be so unfriendly towards them.* ◇ *the use of environmentally unfriendly products* (= that harm the environment) **OPP** **friendly** ▶ **un·friend·li·ness** *noun* [U]

**un·ful·filled** /ˌʌnfʊlˈfɪld/ *adj.* **1** (of a need, wish, etc.) that has not been satisfied or achieved: *unfulfilled ambitions/hopes/promises, etc.* **2** if a person feels **unfulfilled**, they feel that they could achieve more in their life or work **OPP** **fulfilled**

**un·ful·fil·ling** /ˌʌnfʊlˈfɪlɪŋ/ *adj.* not causing sb to feel satisfied and useful: *an unfulfilling job*

**un·fund·ed** /ʌnˈfʌndɪd/ *adj.* not provided with money or funds; not funded: *The new education programme remains unfunded.*

**un·funny** /ʌnˈfʌni/ *adj.* not funny, especially when sth is supposed to be funny: *The show was deeply unfunny.*

**un·furl** /ʌnˈfɜːl; *NAmE* -ˈfɜːrl/ *verb* [I, T] when sth that is CURLED or rolled tightly **unfurls**, or you **unfurl** it, it opens: *The leaves slowly unfurled.* ◇ *~ sth to unfurl a flag*

**un·fur·nished** /ʌnˈfɜːnɪʃt; *NAmE* -ˈfɜːrn-/ *adj.* without furniture: *We rented an unfurnished apartment.* **OPP** **furnished**

**unga** /ˈʊŋɡə/ *EAfrE* [ˈʊŋɡa] *noun* [U] (*EAfrE*) flour made from MAIZE, used to make UGALI

**un·gain·ly** /ʌnˈɡeɪnli/ *adj.* moving in a way that is not smooth or attractive **SYN** **awkward**: *He was a tall, ungainly boy of 18.*

**un·gen·tle·man·ly** /ʌnˈdʒentlmənli/ *adj.* (of a man's behaviour) not polite or pleasant; not acceptable **OPP** **gentlemanly**

**un·glam·or·ous** /ʌnˈɡlæmərəs/ *adj.* not attractive or exciting: *an unglamorous job* **OPP** **glamorous**

**un·glued** /ʌnˈɡluːd/ *adj.*
**IDM** **come un·glued** (*NAmE, informal*) **1** to become very upset **2** if a plan, etc. **comes unglued**, it does not work successfully

**un·god·ly** /ʌnˈɡɒdli; *NAmE* -ˈɡɑːd-/ *adj.* (*old-fashioned*) not showing respect for God; evil **OPP** **godly**
**IDM** **at an ungodly ˈhour** (*informal*) very early or very late and therefore annoying

**un·gov·ern·able** /ʌnˈɡʌvənəbl; *NAmE* -vərn-/ *adj.* **1** (of a country, region, etc.) impossible to govern or control **2** (*formal*) (of a person's feelings) impossible to control **SYN** **uncontrollable**: *ungovernable rage*

**un·gra·cious** /ʌnˈɡreɪʃəs/ *adj.* (*formal*) not polite or friendly, especially towards sb who is being kind to you **OPP** **gracious** ▶ **un·gra·cious·ly** *adv.*

**un·gram·mat·ical** /ˌʌnɡrəˈmætɪkl/ *adj.* not following the rules of grammar **OPP** **grammatical**

**un·grate·ful** /ʌnˈɡreɪtfl/ *adj.* not showing or expressing thanks for sth that sb has done for you or given to you **OPP** **grateful** ▶ **un·grate·ful·ly** /-fəli/ *adv.*

**un·guard·ed** /ʌnˈɡɑːdɪd; *NAmE* -ɡɑːrd-/ *adj.* **1** not protected or watched: *The museum was unguarded at night.* ◇ *an unguarded fire* (= that has nothing to stop people from burning themselves on it) **2** (of a remark, look, etc.) said or done carelessly, at a time when you are not thinking about the effects of your words or are not paying attention: *an unguarded remark* ◇ *It was something I'd let out in an unguarded moment.* ⇒ compare GUARDED

**un·gu·late** /ˈʌŋɡjələt, -ɡjuleɪt/ *noun* (*specialist*) any animal that has HOOFS, such as a cow or horse

**un·hap·pily** /ʌnˈhæpɪli/ *adv.* **1** in an unhappy way: *He sighed unhappily.* **2** used to say that a particular situation or fact makes you sad or disappointed **SYN** **unfortunately**: *Unhappily, such good luck is rare.* ◇ *His wife, unhappily, died five years ago.* **OPP** **happily**

**un·happy** /ʌnˈhæpi/ *adj.* (**un·hap·pier**, **un·happi·est**) **HELP** **more unhappy** and **most unhappy** are also common **1** not happy; sad: *to feel/look/seem/sound/become unhappy* ◇ *an unhappy marriage/childhood* ◇ *I didn't realize but he was deeply unhappy at that time.* **2** not pleased or satisfied with sb/sth: *~ about/at (doing) sth He was unhappy at being left out of the team.* ◇ *~ with sb/sth They were unhappy with their accommodation.* **3** (*formal*) not suitable **SYN** **unfortunate**: *an unhappy coincidence* ◇ *It was an unhappy choice of words.* ▶ **un·happi·ness** *noun* [U]

**un·harmed** /ʌnˈhɑːmd; *NAmE* -ˈhɑːrmd/ *adj.* [not usually before noun] not injured or damaged; not harmed

**UNHCR** /ˌjuː en ˌeɪtʃ siː ˈɑː(r)/ *abbr.* United Nations High Commission for Refugees (an organization whose function is to help and protect REFUGEES)

**un·healthy** /ʌnˈhelθi/ *adj.* **1** not having good health; showing a lack of good health: *They looked poor and unhealthy.* ◇ *unhealthy skin* ◇ *His eyeballs were an unhealthy yellow.* **2** harmful to your health; likely to make you ill: *unhealthy living conditions* ◇ *an unhealthy diet/lifestyle* **3** not normal and likely to be harmful **SYN** **unwholesome**: *He had an unhealthy interest in disease and death.* **OPP** **healthy** ▶ **un·health·ily** /-θɪli/ *adv.* **un·health·i·ness** *noun* [U]: *the unhealthiness of suppressing emotions*

**un·heard** /ʌnˈhɜːd; *NAmE* -ˈhɜːrd/ *adj.* **1** that nobody pays attention to: *Their protests went unheard.* **2** not listened to or heard: *a previously unheard tape of their conversations*

**un·ˈheard-of** *adj.* that has never been known or done; very unusual: *He'd dyed his hair, which was almost unheard-of in the 1960s.* ◇ *It is almost unheard-of for a new band to be offered such a deal.*

**un·heat·ed** /ʌnˈhiːtɪd/ *adj.* having no form of heating: *an unheated bathroom* **OPP** **heated**

**un·heed·ed** /ʌnˈhiːdɪd/ *adj.* (*formal*) that is heard, seen or noticed but then ignored: *Her warning went unheeded.* ⇒ compare HEED

# unhelpful

**un·help·ful** /ʌnˈhelpfl/ *adj.* not helpful or useful; not willing to help sb: *an unhelpful response* ◊ *The taxi driver was being very unhelpful.* **OPP** helpful ▶ **un·help·ful·ly** /-fəli/ *adv.*

**un·her·ald·ed** /ʌnˈherəldɪd/ *adj.* (*formal*) not previously mentioned; happening without any warning

**un·hesi·tat·ing** /ʌnˈhezɪteɪtɪŋ/ *adj.* done or given immediately and confidently: *He gave an unhesitating 'yes' when asked if he would go through the experience again.* ▶ **un·hesi·tat·ing·ly** *adv.*

**un·hin·dered** /ʌnˈhɪndəd; *NAmE* -dərd/ *adj.* without anything stopping or preventing the progress of sb/sth: *She had unhindered access to the files.* ◊ *He was able to pass unhindered through several military checkpoints.* ⊃ see also HINDER

**un·hinge** /ʌnˈhɪndʒ/ *verb* [usually passive] ~ **sb/sth** to make sb mentally ill

**un·holy** /ʌnˈhəʊli/ *adj.* **1** dangerous; likely to be harmful: *an unholy alliance between the medical profession and the pharmaceutical industry* **2** not respecting the laws of a religion **OPP** holy **3** [only before noun] (*informal*) used to emphasize how bad sth is: *She wondered how she had got into this unholy mess.*

**un·hook** /ʌnˈhʊk/ *verb* ~ **sth (from sth)** to remove sth from a HOOK, to UNFASTEN the HOOKS on clothes, etc: *He unhooked his coat from the door.* ◊ *She unhooked her bra.*

**un·hur·ried** /ʌnˈhʌrid; *NAmE* -ˈhɜːr-/ *adj.* (*formal*) relaxed and calm; not done too quickly **OPP** hurried ▶ **un·hur·ried·ly** *adv.*: *Lynn walked unhurriedly into the kitchen.*

**un·hurt** /ʌnˈhɜːt; *NAmE* -ˈhɜːrt/ *adj.* [not before noun] not injured or harmed **SYN** unharmed: *He escaped from the crash unhurt.* **OPP** hurt

**un·hygien·ic** /ˌʌnhaɪˈdʒiːnɪk; *NAmE* -ˈdʒen-, -ˈdʒiːn-/ *adj.* not clean and therefore likely to cause disease or infection **OPP** hygienic

**uni** /ˈjuːni/ *noun* (*BrE, AustralE, informal*) university: *friends from uni* ◊ **at ~** *Where were you at uni?*

**uni-** /ˈjuːni/ *combining form* (in nouns, adjectives and adverbs) one; having one: *uniform* ◊ *unilaterally*

**uni·cam·eral** /ˌjuːnɪˈkæmərəl/ *adj.* (*specialist*) (of a parliament) that has only one main LEGISLATIVE (= law-making) body

**UNICEF** /ˈjuːnɪsef/ *abbr.* United Nations Children's Fund (an organization within the United Nations that helps to take care of the health and education of children all over the world)

**uni·cel·lu·lar** /ˌjuːnɪˈseljələ(r)/ *adj.* (*biology*) (of a living thing) consisting of only one cell: *unicellular organisms*

**uni·corn** /ˈjuːnɪkɔːn; *NAmE* -kɔːrn/ *noun* (in stories) an animal like a white horse with a long straight HORN on its head

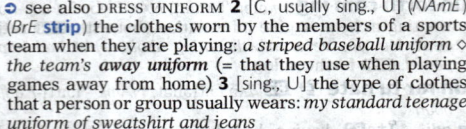
unicorn
horn

**uni·cycle** /ˈjuːnɪsaɪkl/ *noun* a vehicle that is similar to a bicycle but that has only one wheel

**un·iden·ti·fi·able** /ˌʌnaɪˈdentɪfaɪəbl/ *adj.* impossible to identify: *He had an unidentifiable accent.* ◊ *Many of the bodies were unidentifiable except by dental records.* **OPP** identifiable

**un·iden·ti·fied** /ˌʌnaɪˈdentɪfaɪd/ *adj.* not recognized or known; not identified: *an unidentified virus* ◊ *The painting was sold to an unidentified American dealer* (= his or her name was not given).

**uni·form** /ˈjuːnɪfɔːm; *NAmE* -fɔːrm/ *noun, adj.*
■ *noun* **1** [C, U] the special set of clothes worn by all members of an organization or a group at work, or by children at school: *The hat is part of the school uniform.* ◊ *a military uniform* ◊ *Do you have to wear uniform?* ◊ **in (a) ~** *He was dressed in the uniform of a Royal Navy officer.* ⊃ see also DRESS UNIFORM **2** [C, usually sing., U] (*NAmE*) (*BrE* **strip**) the clothes worn by the members of a sports team when they are playing: *a striped baseball uniform* ◊ *the team's away uniform* (= that they use when playing games away from home) **3** [sing., U] the type of clothes that a person or group usually wears: *my standard teenage uniform of sweatshirt and jeans*
■ *adj.* not varying; the same in all parts and at all times: *uniform rates of pay* ◊ *The walls were a uniform grey.* ◊ *Growth has not been uniform across the country.* ◊ *uniform lines of terraced houses* (= they all looked the same) ▶ **uni·form·ity** /ˌjuːnɪˈfɔːməti; *NAmE* -ˈfɔːrm-/ *noun* [U, sing.]: *They tried to ensure uniformity across the different departments.* ◊ *the drab uniformity of the houses* **uni·form·ly** /ˈjuːnɪfɔːmli; *NAmE* -fɔːrm-/ *adv.*: *The principles were applied uniformly across all the departments.* ◊ *The quality is uniformly high.* ◊ *Pressure must be uniformly distributed over the whole surface.*

**uni·formed** /ˈjuːnɪfɔːmd; *NAmE* -fɔːrmd/ *adj.* wearing a uniform: *a uniformed chauffeur*

**unify** /ˈjuːnɪfaɪ/ *verb* (**uni·fies**, **uni·fy·ing**, **uni·fied**, **uni·fied**) ~ **sth** to join people, things, parts of a country, etc. together so that they form a single unit: *The new leader hopes to unify the country.* ◊ *the task of unifying Europe* ◊ *a unified transport system* ▶ **uni·fi·ca·tion** /ˌjuːnɪfɪˈkeɪʃn/ *noun* [U]: *the unification of Germany*

**uni·lat·eral** /ˌjuːnɪˈlætrəl/ *adj.* (of an action or decision) done by or affecting only one person, group or country involved in a situation without the agreement of the others: *a unilateral decision* ◊ *a unilateral declaration of independence* ◊ *They were forced to take unilateral action.* ◊ *They had campaigned vigorously for unilateral nuclear disarmament* (= when one country gets rid of its nuclear weapons without waiting for other countries to do the same). ⊃ compare BILATERAL, MULTILATERAL, TRILATERAL ▶ **uni·lat·eral·ly** /-trəli/ *adv.*

**uni·lat·eral·ism** /ˌjuːnɪˈlætrəlɪzəm/ *noun* [U] belief in or support of unilateral action, especially the policy of getting rid of nuclear weapons without waiting for other countries to do the same ▶ **uni·lat·eral·ist** *noun*: *the defeat of the unilateralists on nuclear disarmament* **uni·lat·eral·ist** *adj.*: *unilateralist defence policy*

**un·imagin·able** /ˌʌnɪˈmædʒɪnəbl/ *adj.* (*formal*) impossible to think of or to believe exists; impossible to imagine: *unimaginable wealth* ◊ *This level of success would have been unimaginable just last year.* **OPP** imaginable ▶ **un·imagin·ably** /-bli/ *adv.*

**un·imagina·tive** /ˌʌnɪˈmædʒɪnətɪv/ *adj.* not having any original or new ideas **SYN** dull: *an unimaginative solution to a problem* ◊ *a boring unimaginative man* **OPP** imaginative

**un·imagined** /ˌʌnɪˈmædʒɪnd/ *adj.* that you had not imagined or thought of as possible: *new and unimagined freedom* ◊ *Things could change in ways that are unimagined.*

**un·im·paired** /ˌʌnɪmˈpeəd; *NAmE* -ˈperd/ *adj.* (*formal*) not damaged or made less good: *Although he's ninety, his mental faculties remain unimpaired.* **OPP** impaired

**un·im·peach·able** /ˌʌnɪmˈpiːtʃəbl/ *adj.* (*formal, approving*) that you cannot doubt or question: *evidence from an unimpeachable source*

**un·im·peded** /ˌʌnɪmˈpiːdɪd/ *adj.* (*formal*) with nothing blocking or stopping sb/sth: *an unimpeded view of the bay* ◊ *free and unimpeded trade*

**un·im·port·ant** /ˌʌnɪmˈpɔːtnt; *NAmE* -ˈpɔːrt-/ *adj.* not important: *unimportant details* ◊ *relatively/comparatively unimportant* ◊ *They dismissed the problem as unimportant.* ◊ *This consideration was not unimportant.* ◊ *I was just a young girl from a small town and I felt very unimportant.* ▶ **un·im·port·ance** /ˌʌnɪmˈpɔːtns; *NAmE* -ˈpɔːrt-/ *noun* [U]

**un·im·pressed** /ˌʌnɪmˈprest/ *adj.* ~ **(by/with sb/sth)** not thinking that sb/sth is particularly good, interesting, etc.; not impressed by sb/sth

**un·im·pres·sive** /ˌʌnɪmˈpresɪv/ *adj.* ordinary; not special in any way: *His academic record was unimpressive.* **OPP** impressive

**un·im·proved** /ˌʌnɪmˈpruːvd/ adj. (especially NAmE) **1** (of land) that has not been changed in a way that would make it more useful, for example by putting buildings on it: *The property is unimproved.* **2** (of sb's medical condition or health) not showing an improvement: *The patient's condition remains unimproved.*

**un·in·cor·por·ated** /ˌʌnɪnˈkɔːpəreɪtɪd; NAmE -ˈkɔːrp-/ adj. (NAmE) (of an area of land) not part of a particular city or town: *an unincorporated community governed by the county*

**un·in·forma·tive** /ˌʌnɪnˈfɔːmətɪv; NAmE -ˈfɔːrm-/ adj. not giving enough information: *The reports of the explosion were brief and uninformative.* **OPP** **informative**

**un·in·formed** /ˌʌnɪnˈfɔːmd; NAmE -ˈfɔːrmd/ adj. having or showing a lack of knowledge or information about sth: *an uninformed comment/criticism* ◇ **~ about sth** *The public is generally uninformed about these diseases.* **OPP** **informed**

**un·in·hab·it·able** /ˌʌnɪnˈhæbɪtəbl/ adj. not fit to live in; impossible to live in: *The building was totally uninhabitable.* **OPP** **habitable**

**un·in·hab·it·ed** /ˌʌnɪnˈhæbɪtɪd/ adj. with no people living there; not INHABITED: *an uninhabited island*

**un·in·hib·it·ed** /ˌʌnɪnˈhɪbɪtɪd/ adj. behaving or expressing yourself freely without worrying about what other people think **SYN** **unrestrained**: *uninhibited dancing* **OPP** **inhibited**

**the un·in·iti·ated** /ði ˌʌnɪˈnɪʃieɪtɪd/ noun [pl.] people who have no special knowledge or experience of sth: *To the uninitiated the system seems too complicated.* ▶ **un·initi·ated** adj.

**un·in·jured** /ʌnˈɪndʒəd; NAmE -dʒərd/ adj. [not usually before noun] not hurt or injured in any way **SYN** **unhurt**: *They escaped from the crash uninjured.*

**un·in·spired** /ˌʌnɪnˈspaɪəd; NAmE -ərd/ adj. not original or exciting **SYN** **dull** **OPP** **inspired**

**un·in·spir·ing** /ˌʌnɪnˈspaɪərɪŋ/ adj. not making people interested or excited: *The view from the window was uninspiring.* **OPP** **inspiring**

**un·in·stall** /ˌʌnɪnˈstɔːl/ verb ~ **sth** (computing) to remove a program from a computer: *Uninstall any programs that you no longer need.*

**un·in·sur·able** /ˌʌnɪnˈʃʊərəbl, -ˈʃɔːr-; NAmE -ˈʃʊr-/ adj. a person or thing that is **uninsurable** cannot be given insurance because there is too much risk

**un·in·sured** /ˌʌnɪnˈʃʊəd, -ˈʃɔːd; NAmE -ˈʃʊrd/ adj. not having insurance; not covered by insurance: *an uninsured driver* ◇ *an uninsured claim*

**un·in·tel·li·gent** /ˌʌnɪnˈtelɪdʒənt/ adj. not intelligent: *He was not unintelligent, but he was lazy.*

**un·in·tel·li·gible** /ˌʌnɪnˈtelɪdʒəbl/ adj. impossible to understand **SYN** **incomprehensible**: *She turned away and muttered something unintelligible.* ◇ **~ to sb** *A lot of the jargon they use is unintelligible to outsiders.* **OPP** **intelligible** ▶ **un·in·tel·li·gibly** /-bli/ adv.

**un·in·tend·ed** /ˌʌnɪnˈtendɪd/ adj. an **unintended** effect, result or meaning is one that you did not plan or intend to happen

**un·in·ten·tion·al** /ˌʌnɪnˈtenʃənl/ adj. not done deliberately, but happening by accident: *Perhaps I misled you, but it was quite unintentional* (= I did not mean to). **OPP** **intentional** ▶ **un·in·ten·tion·al·ly** /-ʃənəli/ adv.: *They had unintentionally provided wrong information.*

**un·in·ter·est·ed** /ʌnˈɪntrəstɪd, -trest-/ adj. ~ **(in sb/sth)** not interested; not wanting to know about sb/sth: *He was totally uninterested in sport.* ◇ *She seemed cold and uninterested.* ⊃ note at INTERESTED

**un·in·ter·est·ing** /ʌnˈɪntrəstɪŋ, -trest-/ adj. not attracting your attention or interest; not interesting ⊃ note at INTERESTED

**un·in·ter·rupt·ed** /ˌʌnˌɪntəˈrʌptɪd/ adj. not stopped or blocked by anything; continuous and not interrupted: *We had an uninterrupted view of the stage.* ◇ *eight hours of uninterrupted sleep* ◇ *We managed to eat our meal uninterrupted by phone calls.*

**un·in·vited** /ˌʌnɪnˈvaɪtɪd/ adj. doing sth or going somewhere when you have not been asked or invited to, especially when sb does not want you to: *uninvited guests at a party* ◇ *He turned up uninvited.*

**un·in·vit·ing** /ˌʌnɪnˈvaɪtɪŋ/ adj. not attractive or pleasant: *The water looked cold and uninviting.* **OPP** **inviting**

**un·in·volved** /ˌʌnɪnˈvɒlvd; NAmE -ˈvɑːlvd/ adj. ~ **(in/with sth)** not taking part in sth; not connected with sb/sth, especially on an emotional level: *My mum was distant and cold and very uninvolved in my life.* **OPP** **involved**

**union** **O** **B1** /ˈjuːniən/ noun **1** **B1** (BrE also **trade ˈunion**, **ˌtrades ˈunion**) (NAmE also **ˈlabor ˌunion**) [C] an organization of workers, usually in a particular industry, that exists to protect their interests, improve conditions of work, etc: *I've joined the union.* ◇ *Teachers' unions in England are demanding the same improvements as in Scotland.* ◇ *a union leader/official/representative/activist*

> **WORDFINDER** ballot, closed shop, collective bargaining, industrial action, labour, picket, protest, representative, strike

**2** [C] an association or a club for people or organizations with the same interest: *the Scottish Rugby Union* ⊃ see also CREDIT UNION, STUDENTS' UNION (2) **3** **B1** [C] a group of states or countries that have the same central government or that agree to work together: *the former Soviet Union* ◇ *the European Union* ⊃ see also CUSTOMS UNION **4 Union** [sing.] the US (used especially at the time of the Civil War): *the Union and the Confederacy* ◇ *the State of the Union address by the President* **5** **B1** [U, sing.] the act of joining two or more things together; the state of being joined together: *a meeting to discuss economic and currency union* ◇ **~ with sth** *Northern Ireland's union with Britain* ◇ **~ between A and B** *the union between mainland Tanzania and the Zanzibar Island* **6** [C] (old-fashioned or formal) a marriage: *Their union was blessed with six children.*

**union·ist** /ˈjuːniənɪst/ noun **1** = TRADE UNIONIST **2 Unionist** a person who believes that Northern Ireland should stay part of the United Kingdom **3 Unionist** a supporter of the Union during the Civil War in the US ▶ **union·ism**, **Unionism** noun [U]

**union·ize** (BrE also **-ise**) /ˈjuːniənaɪz/ verb [T, I] ~ **(sb/sth)** to organize people to become members of a trade union; to become a member of a trade union: *a unionized workforce* ◇ *They were forbidden to unionize.* ▶ **union·iza·tion**, **-isa·tion** /ˌjuːniənaɪˈzeɪʃn; NAmE -nəˈz-/ noun [U]

**the ˌUnion ˈJack** noun [sing.] the name for the national flag of the United Kingdom

**unique** **O** **B2** **W** /juˈniːk/ adj. **1** **B2** being the only one of its kind: *Everyone's fingerprints are unique.* **HELP** You can use **absolutely**, **totally** or **almost** with **unique** in this meaning. **2** **B2** very special or unusual: *The preview offers a unique opportunity to see the show without the crowds.* ◇ *This house has many unique features, including a 45-foot-long outdoor swimming pool.* ◇ *He approaches problems in his own unique way.* **HELP** You can use **more**, **very**, etc. with **unique** in this meaning. **3** **B2** belonging to or connected with one particular person, place or thing: **~ to sb/sth** *an atmosphere that is unique to New York* ◇ *The koala is unique to Australia.* ▶ **unique·ly** adv.: *Her past experience made her uniquely suited to lead the campaign.* ◇ *The UK, uniquely, has not had to face the problem of mass unemployment.* ◇ *He was a uniquely gifted teacher.* **unique·ness** noun [U]: *The author stresses the uniqueness of the individual.*

**uni·sex** /ˈjuːnɪseks/ adj. intended for or used by both men and women: *a unisex hair salon* ◇ *unisex jeans*

**uni·son** /ˈjuːnɪsn/ noun
**IDM** **in ˈunison (with sb/sth)** **1** if people do or say sth **in unison**, they all do it at the same time **2** if people or

# unit

organizations are working **in unison**, they are working together, because they agree with each other **3** (*music*) if singers or musicians sing or play **in unison**, they sing or play notes at the same PITCH or at one or more OCTAVES apart

**unit⁰** A2 ⓞ /ˈjuːnɪt/ *noun*
- SINGLE THING **1** A2 a single thing, person or group that is complete by itself but can also form part of sth larger: *After 1946 the British Government treated the four territorial divisions as a* **single unit**. ◇ *The basic* **unit** *of society is the family.* **2** (*business*) a single item of the type of product that a company sells: *The game's selling price was $15 per unit.* ◇ *What's the* **unit cost**?
- IN TEXTBOOK **3** A2 one of the parts into which a TEXTBOOK or a series of lessons is divided: *Each unit of the course that we completed felt like a real achievement.*
- GROUP OF PEOPLE **4** B2 a group of people who work or live together, especially for a particular purpose: *army/military/combat/police units* ◇ *a special unit of the FBI*
- IN HOSPITAL **5** B2 a department, especially in a hospital, that provides a particular type of care or treatment: *the intensive care unit* ◇ *a maternity unit*
- FURNITURE **6** B2 a piece of furniture, especially a cupboard, that fits with and matches others of the same type: *a fitted kitchen with white units* ◇ *floor/wall units* ◇ *bedroom/kitchen units*
- MEASUREMENT **7** B2 a fixed quantity, etc. that is used as a standard measurement: *a unit of measurement* ◇ *Women are advised not to drink more than fourteen units of alcohol per week.* ◇ **per**~ *Electricity is ten pence per unit.*
- SMALL MACHINE **8** a small machine that has a particular purpose or is part of a larger machine: *a waste disposal unit* ◇ *the central processing unit of a computer*
- FLAT/PART OF BUILDING **9** (*formal*) a single flat, house or section in a building or group of buildings: *a housing/residential unit* ◇ (*AustralE, NZE*) *The site is being redeveloped for 62 home units.* ◇ *a retail/business unit* ◇ *an industrial unit*
- NUMBER **10** any whole number from 0 to 9: *a column for the tens and a column for the units*

**Uni·tar·ian** /ˌjuːnɪˈteəriən; *NAmE* -ˈter-/ *noun* a member of a Christian Church that does not believe in the TRINITY and has no formal teachings ▶ **Uni·tar·ian** *adj.* **Uni·tar·ian·ism** *noun* [U]

**uni·tary** /ˈjuːnətri; *NAmE* -teri/ *adj.* **1** (*specialist*) (of a country or an organization) consisting of a number of areas or groups that are joined together and are controlled by one government or group: *a single unitary state* ◇ (*BrE*) *a* **unitary authority** (= a type of local council, introduced in some areas from 1995 to replace existing local governments that consisted of county and district councils) **2** (*formal*) single; forming one unit

**unite** + B2 /juˈnaɪt/ *verb* **1** + B2 [I] to join together with other people in order to do sth as a group: *Nationalist parties united to oppose the government's plans.* ◇ ~ **in sth** *Local resident groups have* **united in opposition** *to the plan.* ◇ ~ **in doing sth** *We will unite in fighting crime.* ◇ ~ **behind/against sb/sth** *Will they unite behind the new leader?* **2** + B2 [T, I] to make people or things join together to form a unit; to join together: ~ **(sb/sth)** *A special bond unites our two countries.* ◇ *His aim was to unite Italy.* ◇ *The two countries united in 1887.* ◇ ~ **(sb/sth)** **(with sb/sth)** *She unites keen business skills with a charming personality.*

**united⁰** A2 /juˈnaɪtɪd/ *adj.* **1** A2 (of countries) joined together as a political unit or by shared aims: *the United States of America* ◇ *efforts to build a united Europe* **2** B1 (of people or groups) in agreement and working together: *We need to become a more united team.* ◇ ~ **in (doing) sth** *They are united in their opposition to the plan.* ◇ ~ **by sth** *The various religious and ethnic groupings were united by their desire to end British rule.* **3** used in the names of some teams and companies: *Manchester United* ◇ *United Biscuits*

**IDM** ► **form, present, etc. a united ˈfront** to show people that all members of a group have the same opinion about things: *The prime minister stressed the need to present a united front.*

**the Uˌnited ˈKingdom** *noun* [sing.] (*abbr.* **(the) UK**) England, Scotland, Wales and Northern Ireland (considered as a political unit)

**the Uˌnited ˈNations** *noun* [sing. + sing./pl. v.] (*abbr.* **(the) UN**) an association of many countries that aims to improve economic and social conditions and to solve political problems in the world in a peaceful way

**the Uˌnited Nations Seˈcurity Council** *noun* = SECURITY COUNCIL

**the Uˌnited ˈStates (of America)** /ðə juːˌnaɪtɪd ˈsteɪts əv əˈmerɪkə/ *noun* (*abbr.* **(the) US, (the) USA**) a large country in North America consisting of 50 states and the District of Columbia **HELP** Although **United States** is sometimes found with a plural verb after it, this is quite rare and it is much more common to use a singular verb. ⊃ note at AMERICAN

**ˌunit ˈtrust** (*BrE*) (*NAmE* **ˈmutual fund**) *noun* a company that offers a service to people by investing their money in various different businesses

**unity** + B2 /ˈjuːnəti/ *noun* (*pl.* **-ies**) **1** + B2 [U, sing.] the state of being in agreement and working together; the state of being joined together to form one unit: *European unity* ◇ *a plea for unity within the party* ◇ *unity of purpose* OPP **disunity 2** + C1 [U] (in art, design, etc.) the quality of looking or being complete in a natural and attractive way: *The design lacks unity.* **3** [C] (*specialist*) (in literature and theatre) any of the principles of classical or NEOCLASSICAL theatre that limit the action of a play to a single story, day and place: *the unities of action, time and place* **4** [sing.] (*formal*) a single thing that may consist of a number of different parts: *If society is to exist as a unity, its members must have shared values.* **5** [U] (*mathematics*) the number one

**Univ.** *abbr.* (in writing) University

**uni·ver·sal** + B2 Ⓦ /ˌjuːnɪˈvɜːsl; *NAmE* -ˈvɜːrsl/ *adj.* **1** + B2 done by or involving all the people in the world or in a particular group: *Such problems are a universal feature of old age.* ◇ *Agreement on this issue is almost universal.* ◇ **universal ˈsuffrage** (= the right of all the people in a country to vote) **2** + B2 true or right at all times and in all places: *universal facts about human nature* ▶ **uni·ver·sal·ity** /ˌjuːnɪvɜːˈsæləti; *NAmE* -vɜːrˈs-/ *noun*: *the universality of religious experience*

**Uniˌversal Coˈordinated ˈTime** *noun* = UTC

**Universal ˈCredit** *noun* [U] (in the UK) money paid by the state to people who need financial help to pay for housing, the care of children, the cost of living while unemployed, etc. It consists of a single monthly payment to cover all these needs, instead of separate smaller payments for each area of need.

**uni·ver·sal·ly** /ˌjuːnɪˈvɜːsəli; *NAmE* -ˈvɜːrs-/ *adv.* **1** by everyone: *to be universally accepted* **2** everywhere or in every situation: *This treatment is not universally available.* ◇ *The theory does not apply universally.*

**Uniˌversal ˈTime Coˈordinated** *noun* = UTC

**uni·verse⁰** B2 /ˈjuːnɪvɜːs; *NAmE* -vɜːrs/ *noun* **1** B2 **the universe** [sing.] the whole of space and everything in it, including the earth, the planets and the stars: *in the* ~ *Could there be intelligent life elsewhere in the universe?* ⊃ WORDFINDER NOTE at SUN

**WORDFINDER** asteroid, astronomy, comet, constellation, cosmic, galaxy, meteorite, orbit, space

**2** [C] a system of stars, planets, etc. in space outside our own: *The idea of a* **parallel universe** *is hard to grasp.* ◇ (*figurative*) *He lives in a little universe of his own.* **3** [sing.] a particular area of experience or activity: *the moral universe*

**uni·ver·sity⁰** A1 Ⓢ /ˌjuːnɪˈvɜːsəti; *NAmE* -ˈvɜːrs-/ *noun* [C, U] (*pl.* **-ies**) (*abbr.* **Univ.**) an institution at the highest level of education where you can study for a degree or do research: *Is there a university in this town?* ◊ *Ohio State University* ◊ **at a/the~** *She studied at the University of Chicago.* ◊ (*BrE*) **at~** *Both their children are at university.* ◊ (*BrE*) *He's hoping to* **go to university** *next year.* ◊ **a university student/lecturer/professor** ◊ **a university degree/course** ⊃ note at COLLEGE ⊃ see also DEEMED UNIVERSITY, STATE UNIVERSITY

> **WORDFINDER** degree, dissertation, education, graduate, hall of residence, lecture, major, seminar, tutorial

**IDM** **the university of 'life** (*informal*) the experience of life thought of as giving sb an education, instead of the person gaining formal qualifications: *a degree from the university of life*

**Unix™** /ˈjuːnɪks/ *noun* [U] (*computing*) the original version and basis of many computer OPERATING SYSTEMS in use today (for example, LINUX)

**un·just** /ˌʌnˈdʒʌst/ *adj.* not deserved or fair: *an unjust law* **OPP** **just** ▸ **un·just·ly** *adv.*: *She felt that she had been unjustly treated.*

**un·jus·ti·fi·able** /ˌʌnˈdʒʌstɪfaɪəbl, ˌʌnˌdʒʌstɪˈfaɪəbl/ *adj.* (of an action) impossible to excuse or accept because there is no good reason for it **SYN** **indefensible**: *an unjustifiable delay* **OPP** **justifiable** ▸ **un·jus·ti·fi·ably** /-bli/ *adv.*

**un·jus·ti·fied** /ˌʌnˈdʒʌstɪfaɪd/ *adj.* not fair or necessary **SYN** **unwarranted**: *The criticism was wholly unjustified.* **OPP** **justified**

**un·kempt** /ˌʌnˈkempt/ *adj.* (*formal*) (especially of sb's hair or general appearance) not well cared for; not neat or tidy **SYN** **dishevelled**: *greasy, unkempt hair*

**un·kind** /ˌʌnˈkaɪnd/ *adj.* ~ **(to sb/sth) (to do sth)** not pleasant or friendly; slightly cruel: *an unkind remark* ◊ *He was never actually unkind to them.* ◊ *It would be unkind to go without him.* **OPP** **kind** ▸ **un·kind·ly** *adv.*: *'That's your problem,' she remarked unkindly.* **un·kind·ness** *noun* [U]

**un·know·able** /ʌnˈnəʊəbl/ *adj.* (*formal*) that cannot be known: *a distant, unknowable divine power*

**un·know·ing** /ʌnˈnəʊɪŋ/ *adj.* [usually before noun] (*formal*) not aware of what you are doing or what is happening: *He was the unknowing cause of all the misunderstanding.* ⊃ compare KNOWING ▸ **un·know·ing·ly** *adv.*: *She had unknowingly broken the rules.*

**un·known** 🔵 **B2** /ʌnˈnəʊn/ *adj., noun*

- *adj.* **1** 🔵 **B2** not known or identified: *A previously unknown group claimed responsibility for the bombing.* ◊ *He was trying,* **for some unknown reason***, to count the stars.* ◊ *The man's identity* **remains unknown**. **2** 🔵 **B2** (of people) not famous or well known: *She was then still* **relatively unknown**. ◊ *The author is* **virtually unknown** *outside Poland.* **3** 🔵 **B2** never happening or existing: *~* **in** *… The disease is as yet unknown in Europe* (= there have been no cases there). ◊ *it* **is** *~* **for sb/sth to do sth** *It was* **not unknown** *for people to have to wait several hours* (= it happened sometimes).
  **IDM** **an unknown 'quantity** a person or thing whose qualities or abilities are not yet known **unknown to sb** without the person mentioned being aware of it: *Unknown to me, he had already signed the agreement.*
- *noun* **1** **the unknown** [sing.] places or things that are not known about: *a journey into the unknown* ◊ *a fear of the unknown* **2** [C] a person who is not well known: *A young unknown played the leading role.* **3** [C] a fact or an influence that is not known: *There are so many unknowns in the proposal.* **4** [C] (*mathematics*) a quantity that does not have a known value: *X and Y in the equation are both unknowns.*

**the ˌUnknown ˈSoldier** *noun* [sing.] a soldier who has been killed in a war, whose body has not been identified, and who is buried in special ceremony. The **Unknown Soldier** is a symbol for all the soldiers killed in a particular war or in wars generally: *the tomb of the Unknown Soldier*

**un·laden** /ˌʌnˈleɪdn/ *adj.* (*specialist*) (of a vehicle) not loaded: *a vehicle with an unladen weight of 3000 kg* ⊃ compare LADEN

**un·law·ful** /ʌnˈlɔːfl/ *adj.* (*formal*) not allowed by the law **SYN** **illegal** **OPP** **lawful** ▸ **un·law·ful·ly** /-fəli/ *adv.*

---

1711 **unlimited**

**unˌlawful ˈkilling** *noun* (*law*) a murder, or other killing that is considered a crime, for example when a person dies because sb is careless: *The two police officers were accused of unlawful killing.*

**un·lead·ed** /ˌʌnˈledɪd/ *adj.* (of petrol) not containing LEAD and therefore less harmful to the environment **OPP** **leaded** ▸ **un·lead·ed** *noun* [U]: *Unleaded is cheaper than diesel.*

**un·learn** /ˌʌnˈlɜːn; NAmE -ˈlɜːrn/ *verb* **~ sth** to deliberately forget sth that you have learned, especially sth bad or wrong: *You'll have to unlearn all the bad habits you learned with your last piano teacher.*

**un·leash** /ʌnˈliːʃ/ *verb* **~ sth (on/upon sb/sth)** to suddenly let a strong force, emotion, etc. be felt or have an effect: *The government's proposals unleashed a storm of protest in the press.*

**un·leav·ened** /ˌʌnˈlevnd/ *adj.* (of bread) made without any YEAST, or other substance that would cause the bread to rise, and therefore flat ⊃ see also LEAVEN *verb*

**un·less** 🔵 **B1** /ənˈles/ *conj.* **1** 🔵 **B1** used to say that sth can only happen or be true in a particular situation: *You won't get paid for time off unless you have a doctor's note.* ◊ *I won't tell them—not unless you say I can.* ◊ *Unless I'm mistaken, she was back at work yesterday.* ◊ *He hasn't got any hobbies—unless you call watching TV a hobby.* **2** 🔵 **B1** used to give the only situation in which sth will not happen or be true: *I sleep with the window open unless it's really cold.* ◊ *Unless something unexpected happens, I'll see you tomorrow.* ◊ *Have a cup of tea—unless you'd prefer a cold drink?* **HELP** *Unless* is used to talk about a situation that could happen, or something that could be true, in the future. If you know that something has not happened or that sth is not true, use *if … not*: *If you weren't always in such a hurry* (= but you are), *your work would be much better.* ◊ ~~*Your work would be much better unless you were always in such a hurry.*~~

**un·let·tered** /ʌnˈletəd; NAmE -tərd/ *adj.* (*formal*) unable to read

**un·licensed** /ʌnˈlaɪsnst/ *adj.* without a licence: *an unlicensed vehicle* **OPP** **licensed**

**un·like** 🔵 **B1** /ʌnˈlaɪk/ *prep., adj., verb*

- *prep.* **1** 🔵 **B1** different from a particular person or thing: *Music is quite unlike any other art form.* ◊ *The sound was* **not unlike** *that of birds singing.* **2** 🔵 **B1** used to contrast sb/sth with another person or thing: *Unlike most systems, this one is very easy to install.* ⊃ LANGUAGE BANK at CONTRAST **3** 🔵 **B2** not typical of sb/sth: *It's very unlike him to be so late.* **OPP** **like**
- *adj.* [not before noun] (of two people or things) different from each other: *They are both teachers. Otherwise they are quite unlike.* ⊃ compare ALIKE, LIKE
- *verb* [T] (*informal*) ~ **sth** to show, by clicking a special button, that you disagree with sth on SOCIAL MEDIA, a news website, a blog, etc. ⊃ compare UNFRIEND

**un·like·able** (especially in *BrE*) (also **un·lik·able** especially in *NAmE*) /ʌnˈlaɪkəbl/ *adj.* not easy to like: *She's adept at playing unlikeable characters.* **OPP** **likeable**

**un·like·ly** 🔵 **B1** ⓦ /ʌnˈlaɪkli/ *adj.* (**un·like·lier, un·likeli·est**) **HELP** **more unlikely** and **most unlikely** are the usual forms **1** 🔵 **B1** not likely to happen; not PROBABLE: ~ **to do sth** *The project seemed unlikely to succeed.* ◊ **it is** ~ **(that …)** *It was highly unlikely that the gunshot wound was self-inflicted.* ◊ **In the unlikely event of** *a problem arising, please contact the hotel manager.* ⊃ EXPRESS YOURSELF at LIKELY **2** [only before noun] not the person, thing or place that you would normally think of or expect: *He seems a most unlikely candidate for the job.* ◊ *They have built hotels in the most unlikely places.* **3** [only before noun] difficult to believe **SYN** **implausible**: *She gave me an unlikely explanation for her behaviour.* **OPP** **likely** ▸ **un·like·li·hood** *noun* [U] **un·like·li·ness** *noun* [U]

**un·lim·it·ed** /ʌnˈlɪmɪtɪd/ *adj.* as much or as many as is possible; not limited in any way: *The ticket gives you unlimited travel for seven days.* ◊ *You will be allowed*

# unlined

*unlimited access to the files.* ◊ *The possibilities are unlimited.*

**un·lined** /ˌʌnˈlaɪnd/ *adj.* **1** not marked with lines: *unlined paper/skin* **2** (of a piece of clothing, etc.) made without an extra layer of cloth on the inside **OPP** **lined**

**un·list·ed** /ˌʌnˈlɪstɪd/ *adj.* **1** not on a published list, especially of STOCK EXCHANGE prices: *an unlisted company* **2** (of a phone number) not listed in the public phone book or online DIRECTORY, at the request of the owner of the phone. *The phone company will not give unlisted numbers to people who ask for them.*

**un·lit** /ˌʌnˈlɪt/ *adj.* **1** dark because there are no lights or the lights are not switched on: *an unlit passage* **2** not yet burning: *an unlit cigarette* **OPP** **lighted**

**un·load** /ˌʌnˈləʊd/ *verb* **1** [T, I] to remove things from a vehicle or ship after it has taken them somewhere: *~ sth from sth Everyone helped to unload the luggage from the car.* ◊ *~(sth) This isn't a suitable place to unload the van.* ◊ *The truck driver was waiting to unload.* **OPP** **load** **2** [T] *~sth* to remove the contents of sth after you have finished using it **OPP** **load** **3** [T] *~sth/sb (on/onto sb)* (*informal*) to pass the responsibility for sb/sth to sb else; to tell sb about your problems and worries: *It's his problem, not something he should unload onto you.* **4** [T] *~sth (on/onto sb/sth)* (*informal*) to get rid of or sell sth, especially sth illegal or of bad quality: *They want to unload their shares at the right price.*

**un·lock** /ˌʌnˈlɒk/ *NAmE* -ˈlɑːk/ *verb* **1** *~sth* to open the lock of a door, window, etc., usually using a key: *to unlock the door* **OPP** **lock** **2** *~sth* to discover sth and let it be known: *The divers hoped to unlock some of the secrets of the seabed.* **3** *~sth* to enable a mobile phone to use any network rather than only one particular one: *Have an old phone lying around? Unlock it and keep it as a spare.* **4** *~sth* to use a code or PASSWORD to get access to more data or features on a computer or phone, or in a computer game: *Players complete goals, unlock new levels and progress through the game.*

**un·locked** /ˌʌnˈlɒkt; *NAmE* -ˈlɑːkt/ *adj.* not locked: *Don't leave your desk unlocked.*

**un·looked for** /ˌʌnˈlʊkt fə(r)/ *adj.* (*formal*) not expected: *unlooked-for developments*

**un·loved** /ˌʌnˈlʌvd/ *adj.* (*formal*) not loved by anyone: *unloved children*

**un·love·ly** /ˌʌnˈlʌvli/ *adj.* (*formal*) not attractive: *an unlovely building*

**un·luck·ily** /ˌʌnˈlʌkɪli/ *adv.* unfortunately; as a result of bad luck: *He was injured in the first game and unluckily missed the final.* **OPP** **luckily**

**un·lucky** /ˌʌnˈlʌki/ *adj.* (**un·luck·ier, un·lucki·est**) **HELP** You can also use **more unlucky** and **most unlucky**. **1** *~(to do sth)* having bad luck or happening because of bad luck; not lucky **SYN** **unfortunate**: *He was very unlucky not to win.* ◊ *By some unlucky chance, her name was left off the list.* **2** *~(to do sth)* causing bad luck: *Some people think it's unlucky to walk under a ladder.* ◊ *Thirteen is often considered an unlucky number.* **OPP** **lucky**

**un·made** /ˌʌnˈmeɪd/ *adj.* **1** an **unmade** bed is not ready for sleeping in because the sheets, etc. have not been arranged neatly **2** (*BrE*) an **unmade** road does not have a hard, smooth surface

**un·man·age·able** /ˌʌnˈmænɪdʒəbl/ *adj.* difficult or impossible to control or deal with **OPP** **manageable**

**un·man·ly** /ˌʌnˈmænli/ *adj.* (*formal*) not having the qualities that are admired or expected in a man **OPP** **manly**

**un·manned** /ˌʌnˈmænd/ *adj.* if a machine, a vehicle, a place or an activity is **unmanned**, it does not have or need a person to control or operate it: *an unmanned spacecraft* ◊ *an unmanned Mars mission* **OPP** **manned**

**un·marked** /ˌʌnˈmɑːkt; *NAmE* -ˈmɑːrkt/ *adj.* **1** without a sign or words to show what or where sth is: *an unmarked police car* ◊ *He was buried in an unmarked grave.* ⊃ compare MARKED **2** (*especially BrE*) (of a player in a team game, especially football (soccer)) with no player from the other team staying close to prevent them from getting the ball: *He headed the ball to the unmarked Gray.* **3** (*linguistics*) (of a word or form of a word) not showing any particular feature or style, such as being formal or informal **OPP** **marked**

**un·mar·ried** /ˌʌnˈmærid/ *adj.* not married **SYN** **single**: *an unmarried mother*

**un·mask** /ˌʌnˈmɑːsk; *NAmE* -ˈmæsk/ *verb* *~sb/sth* to show the true character of sb, or a hidden truth about sth **SYN** **expose**: *to unmask a spy*

**un·matched** /ˌʌnˈmætʃt/ *adj.* *~(by sb/sth)* (*formal*) better than all others: *He had a talent unmatched by any other politician of this century.*

**un·mem·or·able** /ˌʌnˈmemərəbl/ *adj.* that cannot be remembered because it was not special **OPP** **memorable**

**un·men·tion·able** /ˌʌnˈmenʃənəbl/ *adj.* [usually before noun] too SHOCKING or embarrassing to be mentioned or spoken about: *an unmentionable disease*

**un·met** /ˌʌnˈmet/ *adj.* (*formal*) (of needs, etc.) not satisfied: *a report on the unmet needs of elderly people*

**un·mind·ful** /ˌʌnˈmaɪndfl/ *adj.* *~of sb/sth* (*formal*) not giving thought or attention to sb/sth **OPP** **mindful**

**un·miss·able** /ˌʌnˈmɪsəbl/ *adj.* that you must not miss because it is so good: *an unmissable opportunity*

**un·mis·tak·able** (*also less frequent* **un·mis·take·able**) /ˌʌnmɪˈsteɪkəbl/ *adj.* that cannot be mistaken for sb/sth else: *Her accent was unmistakable.* ◊ *the unmistakable sound of gunfire* ▶ **un·mis·tak·ably** (*also less frequent* **un·mis·take·ably**) /-bli/ *adv.*: *His accent was unmistakably British.*

**un·miti·gated** /ˌʌnˈmɪtɪɡeɪtɪd/ *adj.* [only before noun] used to mean 'complete', usually when describing sth bad **SYN** **absolute**: *The evening was an unmitigated disaster.* ⊃ see also MITIGATE

**un·modi·fied** /ˌʌnˈmɒdɪfaɪd; *NAmE* -ˈmɑːd-/ *adj.* not changed in any way; not modified

**un·mol·est·ed** /ˌʌnməˈlestɪd/ *adj.* [not usually before noun] (*formal*) not attacked or DISTURBED by sb; not prevented from doing sth

**un·moti·vated** /ˌʌnˈməʊtɪveɪtɪd/ *adj.* **1** not having interest in or enthusiasm for sth, especially work or study: *unmotivated students* **2** without a reason or MOTIVE: *an unmotivated attack* **OPP** **motivate**

**un·moved** /ˌʌnˈmuːvd/ *adj.* *~(by sth)* not feeling sympathy or not feeling sad, especially in a situation where it would be normal to do so: *Alice seemed totally unmoved by the whole experience.* ◊ *She pleaded with him but he remained unmoved.*

**un·mov·ing** /ˌʌnˈmuːvɪŋ/ *adj.* (*formal*) not moving: *He stood, unmoving, in the shadows.*

**un·music·al** /ˌʌnˈmjuːzɪkl/ *adj.* **1** (of a sound) unpleasant to listen to: *His voice was harsh and unmusical.* **2** (of a person) unable to play or enjoy music **OPP** **musical**

**un·named** /ˌʌnˈneɪmd/ *adj.* whose name is not given or not known: *information from an unnamed source* ◊ *Two casualties, as yet unnamed, are still in the local hospital.*

**un·nat·ural** /ˌʌnˈnætʃrəl/ *adj.* **1** different from what is normal or expected, or from what is generally accepted as being right: *It seems unnatural for a child to spend so much time alone.* ◊ *There was an unnatural silence and then a scream.* ◊ *unnatural sexual practices* ◊ *He gave an unnatural smile* (= that did not seem genuine). **2** different from anything in nature: *Her leg was bent at an unnatural angle.* ◊ *an unnatural death* (= one, not from natural causes) **OPP** **natural** ▶ **un·nat·ural·ly** /-rəli/ *adv.*: *She was, not unnaturally, very surprised at the news.* ◊ *His eyes were unnaturally bright.*

**un·neces·sary** 🔵 **B1** /ʌnˈnesəsəri; *NAmE* -seri/ *adj.* **1** 🔵 **B1** not needed; more than is needed **SYN** **unjustified**: *They were found guilty of causing unnecessary suffering to animals.* ◊ *All this fuss is totally unnecessary.* ◊ *it is ~(for sb/sth) to do sth It was unnecessary to carry out more stringent safety testing.* **OPP** **necessary 2** (of remarks, etc.) not needed in the situation and likely to be offensive **SYN** uncalled for: *That last comment was a little unnecessary, wasn't it?* ▶ **un·neces·sar·ily** /ˌʌnˈnesəsərəli; *NAmE* ˌʌnˌnesəˈserəli/ *adv*: *There's no point worrying him unnecessarily.* ◇ *unnecessarily complicated instructions*

**un·nerve** /ʌnˈnɜːv; *NAmE* -ˈnɜːrv/ *verb* ~ **sb** to make sb feel nervous or frightened or lose confidence: *His silence unnerved us.* ◇ *She appeared strained and a little unnerved.* ▶ **un·nerv·ing** *adj*. **un·nerv·ing·ly** *adv*.

**un·noticed** /ʌnˈnəʊtɪst/ *adj*. [not before noun] not seen or noticed: *His kindness did not go unnoticed by his staff.*

**un·num·bered** /ˌʌnˈnʌmbəd; *NAmE* -bərd/ *adj*. not marked with a number; not numbered: *unnumbered seats*

**UNO** /ˈjuː en ˈəʊ, ˈjuːnəʊ/ *abbr*. United Nations Organization ⊃ see also UNITED NATIONS

**un·ob·jec·tion·able** /ˌʌnəbˈdʒekʃənəbl/ *adj*. (*formal*) (of an idea, etc.) that you can accept or agree with **SYN** acceptable

**un·ob·served** /ˌʌnəbˈzɜːvd; *NAmE* -ˈzɜːrvd/ *adj*. without being seen: *It's not easy for somebody to get into the building unobserved.*

**un·ob·tain·able** /ˌʌnəbˈteɪnəbl/ *adj*. [not usually before noun] that cannot be obtained **OPP** obtainable

**un·ob·tru·sive** /ˌʌnəbˈtruːsɪv/ *adj*. (*formal*, *often approving*) not attracting unnecessary attention: *The service at the hotel is efficient and unobtrusive.* **OPP** obtrusive ▶ **un·ob·tru·sive·ly** *adv*.: *Dora slipped unobtrusively in through the back door.*

**un·occu·pied** /ʌnˈɒkjupaɪd; *NAmE* -ˈɑːk-/ *adj*. **1** empty, with nobody living there or using it: *an unoccupied house* ◇ *I sat down at the nearest unoccupied table.* **2** (of a region or country) not controlled by foreign soldiers: *unoccupied territory* **OPP** occupied

**un·offi·cial** /ˌʌnəˈfɪʃl/ *adj*. [usually before noun] **1** that does not have permission or approval from sb in authority: *an unofficial agreement/strike* ◇ *Unofficial estimates put the figure at over two million.* **2** that is not part of sb's official business: *The former president paid an unofficial visit to China.* **OPP** official ▶ **un·offi·cial·ly** /-ʃəli/ *adv*.

**un·opened** /ʌnˈəʊpənd/ *adj*. not opened yet: *The letter was returned unopened.*

**un·opposed** /ˌʌnəˈpəʊzd/ *adj*. [not usually before noun] not opposed or stopped by anyone: *The party leader was re-elected unopposed.*

**un·organ·ized** (*BrE also* **-ised**) /ʌnˈɔːɡənaɪzd; *NAmE* -ˈɔːrɡ-/ *adj*. **1** (of workers) without a trade union or other organization to represent or support them **2** = DISORGANIZED **3** not having been organized: *unorganized data* ⊃ compare ORGANIZED

**un·ortho·dox** /ʌnˈɔːθədɒks; *NAmE* -ˈɔːrθədɑːks/ *adj*. different from what is usual or accepted: *unorthodox methods* **OPP** orthodox ⊃ compare HETERODOX

**un·pack** /ʌnˈpæk/ *verb* **1** [T, I] ~ **(sth)** to take things out of a bag, case, etc.: *I unpacked my bags as soon as I arrived.* ◇ *She unpacked all the clothes she needed and left the rest in the case.* ◇ *She went to her room to unpack.* **OPP** pack **2** [T] ~ **sth** to separate sth into parts so that it is easier to understand: *to unpack a theory*

**un·paid** /ˌʌnˈpeɪd/ *adj*. **1** not yet paid: *unpaid bills* **2** done or taken without payment: *unpaid work* ◇ *unpaid leave* **OPP** paid **3** (of people) not receiving payment for work that they do: *unpaid volunteers/labour* **OPP** paid

**un·pal·at·able** /ʌnˈpælətəbl/ *adj*. **1** ~ **(to sb)** (of facts, ideas, etc.) unpleasant and not easy to accept **SYN** distasteful: *Only then did I learn the unpalatable truth.* **2** ~ **(to sb)** not pleasant to taste: *unpalatable food* **OPP** palatable

**un·par·al·leled** /ʌnˈpærəleld/ *adj*. (*formal*) used to emphasize that sth is bigger, better or worse than anything else like it **SYN** unequalled: *It was an unparalleled opportunity to develop her career.* ◇ *The book has enjoyed a success unparalleled in recent publishing history.* ⊃ compare PARALLEL

1713 **unpremeditated**

**un·par·don·able** /ʌnˈpɑːdnəbl; *NAmE* -ˈpɑːrd-/ *adj*. that cannot be forgiven or excused **SYN** unforgivable, inexcusable **OPP** pardonable

**un·par·lia·men·tary** /ˌʌnˌpɑːləˈmentri; *NAmE* -ˌpɑːrl-/ *adj*. against the accepted rules of behaviour in a parliament: *unparliamentary language*

**un·pat·ri·ot·ic** /ˌʌnˌpætriˈɒtɪk, -ˌpeɪt-; *NAmE* -ˌpeɪtriˈɑːt-/ *adj*. not supporting your own country **OPP** patriotic

**un·paved** /ˌʌnˈpeɪvd/ *adj*. (of a road) not covered with a hard, smooth surface; not PAVED: *Roads are often dusty and unpaved.* ◇ *an unpaved dirt track*

**un·per·turbed** /ˌʌnpəˈtɜːbd; *NAmE* -pərˈtɜːrbd/ *adj*. not worried or anxious: *She seemed unperturbed by the news.* **OPP** perturbed

**un·pick** /ˌʌnˈpɪk/ *verb* ~ **sth** to take out STITCHES from a piece of SEWING or KNITTING

**un·placed** /ˌʌnˈpleɪst/ *adj*. (*BrE*) not one of the first three to finish in a race or competition

**un·planned** /ˌʌnˈplænd/ *adj*. not planned in advance: *an unplanned pregnancy*

**un·play·able** /ʌnˈpleɪəbl/ *adj*. (*especially BrE*) **1** not able to be played; impossible to play on or with: *The two coaches decided the pitch was unplayable so the match was cancelled.* ⊃ compare PLAYABLE **2** (of a SPORTSPERSON or team) playing so well that it is impossible to beat them: *When they're good, they're unplayable.*

**un·pleas·ant** ⊕ **B1** /ʌnˈpleznt/ *adj*. **1 ?** **B1** not pleasant or comfortable **SYN** disagreeable: *an unpleasant experience/surprise/task* ◇ ~ **(for sb) to do sth** *The minerals in the water made it unpleasant to drink.* **2 ?** **B1** not kind, friendly or polite: ~ **to sb** *He was very unpleasant to me.* ◇ ~ **about sb/sth** *You don't have to be so unpleasant about it. I said I was sorry.* **OPP** pleasant ▶ **un·pleas·ant·ly** *adv*.: *The drink is very sweet, but not unpleasantly so.* ◇ *He laughed unpleasantly.*

**un·pleas·ant·ness** /ʌnˈplezntnəs/ *noun* [U] bad feeling or arguments between people

**un·plug** /ˌʌnˈplʌɡ/ *verb* (**-gg-**) ~ **sth** to remove the PLUG of a piece of electrical equipment from the electricity supply: *Unplug the TV before you go on holiday.* **OPP** plug in

**Un·plugged**™ /ˌʌnˈplʌɡd/ *adj*. (sometimes after noun) (of pop or ROCK music or musicians) performed or performing with ACOUSTIC rather than electric instruments: *an Unplugged concert* ◇ *Bob Dylan Unplugged*

**un·pol·luted** /ˌʌnpəˈluːtɪd/ *adj*. that has not been POLLUTED (= made dirty by harmful substances)

**un·popu·lar** /ʌnˈpɒpjələ(r); *NAmE* -ˈpɑːp-/ *adj*. not liked or enjoyed by a person, a group or people in general: *an unpopular choice* ◇ *an unpopular government* ◇ ~ **with/among sb** *The proposed increase in income tax proved deeply unpopular with the electorate.* **OPP** popular ▶ **un·popu·lar·ity** /ˌʌnˌpɒpjuˈlærəti; *NAmE* -ˌpɑːp-/ *noun* [U]: *the growing unpopularity of the military regime*

**un·pre·ced·ent·ed ?+** **C1** /ʌnˈpresɪdentɪd/ *adj*. that has never happened, been done or been known before: *The situation is unprecedented in modern times.* ▶ **un·pre·ced·ent·ed·ly** *adv*.: *a period of unprecedentedly high food prices*

**un·pre·dict·able** /ˌʌnprɪˈdɪktəbl/ *adj*. **1** that cannot be predicted because it changes a lot or depends on too many different things: *unpredictable weather* ◇ *The result is entirely unpredictable.* **2** if a person is **unpredictable**, you cannot predict how they will behave in a particular situation **OPP** predictable ▶ **un·pre·dict·abil·ity** /ˌʌnprɪˌdɪktəˈbɪləti/ *noun* [U]: *the unpredictability of the English weather* **un·pre·dict·ably** /ˌʌnprɪˈdɪktəbli/ *adv*.

**un·pre·ju·diced** /ʌnˈpredʒədɪst/ *adj*. not influenced by an unreasonable fear or dislike of sth/sb; willing to consider different ideas and opinions **OPP** prejudiced

**un·pre·medi·tated** /ˌʌnpriːˈmedɪteɪtɪd/ *adj*. (*formal*) (of a crime or bad action) not planned in advance **OPP** premeditated

# unprepared

**un·pre·pared** /ˌʌnprɪˈpeəd; *NAmE* -ˈperd/ *adj.* **1** ~ **(for sth)** not ready or not expecting sth: *She was totally unprepared for his response.* **2** ~ **(to do sth)** (*formal*) not willing to do sth: *She was unprepared to accept that her marriage was over.* **OPP** **prepared**

**un·pre·pos·sess·ing** /ˌʌnˌpriːpəˈzesɪŋ/ *adj.* (*formal*) not attractive; not making a good or strong impression **SYN** **unattractive** ⇨ compare **PREPOSSESSING**

**un·pre·ten·tious** /ˌʌnprɪˈtenʃəs/ *adj.* (*approving*) not trying to appear more special, intelligent, important, etc. than you really are/it really is **OPP** **pretentious**

**un·prin·cipled** /ʌnˈprɪnsəpld/ *adj.* (*formal*) without moral principles **SYN** **dishonest** **OPP** **principled**

**un·print·able** /ʌnˈprɪntəbl/ *adj.* (of words or comments) too offensive or SHOCKING to be printed and read by people **OPP** **printable**

**un·prob·lem·at·ic** /ˌʌnˌprɒbləˈmætɪk; *NAmE* -ˌprɑːb-/ (*also less frequent* **un·prob·lem·at·ic·al** /ˌʌnˌprɒbləˈmætɪkl; *NAmE* -ˌprɑːb-/) *adj.* not having or causing problems **OPP** **problematic** ▸ **un·prob·lem·at·ic·al·ly** /-kli/ *adv.*

**un·pro·duct·ive** /ˌʌnprəˈdʌktɪv/ *adj.* not producing very much; not producing good results: *unproductive land* ◊ *a three-hour meeting that was totally unproductive* ◊ *I've had a very unproductive day.* **OPP** **productive** ▸ **un·pro·duct·ive·ly** *adv.*

**un·pro·fes·sion·al** /ˌʌnprəˈfeʃənl/ *adj.* not reaching the standard expected in a particular profession: *She was found guilty of unprofessional conduct.* **OPP** **professional** ⇨ compare **NON-PROFESSIONAL** ▸ **un·pro·fes·sion·al·ly** /-nəli/ *adv.*

**un·prof·it·able** /ʌnˈprɒfɪtəbl; *NAmE* -ˈprɑːf-/ *adj.* **1** not making any financial profit: *unprofitable companies* **2** (*formal*) not bringing any advantage **OPP** **profitable** ▸ **un·prof·it·ably** /-bli/ *adv.*

**un·prom·is·ing** /ʌnˈprɒmɪsɪŋ; *NAmE* -ˈprɑːm-/ *adj.* not likely to be successful or show good results **OPP** **promising**

**un·prompt·ed** /ʌnˈprɒmptɪd; *NAmE* -ˈprɑːmp-/ *adj.* said or done without sb asking you to say or do it: *Quite unprompted, Sam started telling us exactly what had happened that night.* ⇨ see also **PROMPT** *verb*

**un·pro·nounce·able** /ˌʌnprəˈnaʊnsəbl/ *adj.* (of a word, especially a name) too difficult to pronounce **OPP** **pronounceable**

**un·pro·tect·ed** /ˌʌnprəˈtektɪd/ *adj.* **1** not protected against being hurt or damaged **2** not covered to prevent it from causing damage or injury: *Machinery was often unprotected and accidents were frequent.* **3** (of sex) done without using a CONDOM

**un·proven** /ˌʌnˈpruːvn/ *adj.* not proved or tested: *unproven theories* ⇨ compare **PROVEN**

**un·pro·voked** /ˌʌnprəˈvəʊkt/ *adj.* (especially of an attack) not caused by anything the person being attacked has said or done: *a vicious and unprovoked attack* ◊ *Her angry outburst was totally unprovoked.* ⇨ see also **PROVOKE**

**un·pub·lished** /ʌnˈpʌblɪʃt/ *adj.* not published: *an unpublished novel*

**un·pun·ished** /ʌnˈpʌnɪʃt/ *adj.* not punished: *He promised that the murder would not go unpunished.*

**un·quali·fied** /ʌnˈkwɒlɪfaɪd; *NAmE* -ˈkwɑːl-/ *adj.* **1** not having the right knowledge, experience or qualifications to do sth: *an unqualified instructor* ◊ ~ **to do sth** *I feel unqualified to comment on the subject.* ◊ ~ **for sth** *He was totally unqualified for his job as a senior manager.* **2** [*usually before noun*] complete; not limited by any negative qualities: *The event was not an unqualified success.* ◊ *I gave her my unqualified support.* **OPP** **qualified**

**un·quench·able** /ʌnˈkwentʃəbl/ *adj.* (*formal*) that cannot be satisfied: *He had an unquenchable thirst for life.* ⇨ see also **QUENCH**

**un·ques·tion·able** /ʌnˈkwestʃənəbl/ *adj.* (*formal*) that cannot be doubted: *a man of unquestionable honesty* **OPP** **questionable** ▸ **un·ques·tion·ably** /-bli/ *adv.*: *It was unquestionably a step in the right direction.*

**un·ques·tioned** /ʌnˈkwestʃənd/ *adj.* (*formal*) **1** so obvious that it cannot be doubted: *His courage remains unquestioned.* **2** accepted as right or true without really being considered: *an unquestioned assumption*

**un·ques·tion·ing** /ʌnˈkwestʃənɪŋ/ *adj.* (*formal*) done or given without asking questions, expressing doubt, etc: *unquestioning obedience* ▸ **un·ques·tion·ing·ly** *adv.*

**un·quiet** /ʌnˈkwaɪət/ *adj.* [*usually before noun*] (*literary*) not calm; anxious and RESTLESS

**un·quote** /ʌnˈkwəʊt/ *noun* **IDM** see **QUOTE** *v.*

**un·rated** /ʌnˈreɪtɪd/ *adj.* (*especially NAmE*) an **unrated** movie has not been given a RATING (= a letter or number that shows which groups of people it is suitable for), usually because it contains a high level of sex and/or violence

**un·ravel** /ʌnˈrævl/ *verb* (-ll-, *US* -l-) **1** [T, I] ~ **(sth)** if you **unravel** THREADS that are TWISTED, WOVEN or KNITTED, or if they **unravel**, they become separated: *I unravelled the string and wound it into a ball.* **2** [I] (of a system, plan, relationship, etc.) to start to fail or no longer stay together as a whole **3** [T, I] ~ **(sth)** to explain sth that is difficult to understand or is mysterious; to become clearer or easier to understand: *The discovery will help scientists unravel the mystery of the Ice Age.*

**un·read** /ʌnˈred/ *adj.* (of a book, etc.) that has not been read: *a pile of unread newspapers*

**un·read·able** /ʌnˈriːdəbl/ *adj.* **1** (of a book, etc.) too boring or difficult to be worth reading **2** = **ILLEGIBLE** **3** if sb's face or expression is **unreadable**, you cannot tell what they are thinking or feeling **4** (*computing*) (of a computer file, disk, etc.) containing information that a computer is not able to read

**un·real** /ʌnˈrɪəl; *NAmE* -ˈriːəl/ *adj.* **1** so strange that it is more like a dream than reality: *The party began to take on an unreal, almost nightmarish quality.* **2** not related to reality **SYN** **unrealistic**: *Many people have unreal expectations of what marriage will be like.* **3** (*informal*) used to say that you like sth very much or that sth surprises you: *'That's unreal!' she laughed.* ▸ **un·real·ity** /ˌʌnriˈæləti/ *noun* [U]

**un·real·is·tic** /ˌʌnrɪəˈlɪstɪk; *NAmE* -riːə-/ *adj.* not showing or accepting things as they are: *unrealistic expectations* ◊ *It is unrealistic to expect them to be able to solve the problem immediately.* **OPP** **realistic** ▸ **un·real·is·tic·al·ly** /-kli/ *adv.*: *These prices are unrealistically high.*

**un·real·ized** (*BrE also* **-ised**) /ʌnˈrɪəlaɪzd; *BrE also* -ˈriːə-/ *adj.* **1** not achieved or created: *an unrealized ambition* ◊ *Their potential is unrealized.* **2** (*finance*) not sold or changed into the form of money: *unrealized assets*

**un·rea·son·able** /ʌnˈriːznəbl/ *adj.* not fair; expecting too much: *The job was beginning to make unreasonable demands on his free time.* ◊ *The fees they charge are not unreasonable.* ◊ *He was being totally unreasonable about it.* ◊ **it is ~ to do sth** *It would be unreasonable to expect somebody to come at such short notice.* **OPP** **reasonable** ▸ **un·rea·son·able·ness** *noun* [U] **un·rea·son·ably** /-bli/ *adv.*

**un·rea·son·ing** /ʌnˈriːzənɪŋ/ *adj.* [*usually before noun*] (*formal*) not based on facts or reason **SYN** **irrational**: *unreasoning fear*

**un·rec·og·niz·able** (*BrE also* **-is·able**) /ˌʌnrekəɡˈnaɪzəbl; *BrE also* ʌnˈrekəɡnaɪ-/ *adj.* (of a person or thing) so changed or damaged that you do not recognize them or it: *He was unrecognizable without his beard.* **OPP** **recognizable**

**un·rec·og·nized** (*BrE also* **-ised**) /ʌnˈrekəɡnaɪzd/ *adj.* **1** that people are not aware of or do not realize is important: *The problem of ageism in the workplace often goes unrecognized.* **2** (of a person) not having received the praise and notice they deserve for sth that they have done or achieved

**un·re·con·struct·ed** /ˌʌnriːkənˈstrʌktɪd/ *adj.* [*only before noun*] (*disapproving*) (of people and their beliefs) not having changed, although general opinion on these matters has changed

**un·re·cord·ed** /ˌʌnrɪˈkɔːdɪd; NAmE -ˈkɔːrd-/ adj. not written down or recorded: *Many crimes go unrecorded.*

**un·re·fined** /ˌʌnrɪˈfaɪnd/ adj. **1** (of a substance) not separated from the other substances that it is combined with in its natural form: *unrefined sugar* **2** (of a person or their behaviour) not polite or educated **OPP** **refined**

**un·re·gis·tered** /ˌʌnˈredʒɪstəd; NAmE -stərd/ adj. not listed in an official or public record; not registered: *a high number of unregistered births ◊ unregistered firearms*

**un·regu·lated** /ˌʌnˈreɡjuleɪtɪd/ adj. not controlled by laws or regulations

**un·re·lated** ⓦ /ˌʌnrɪˈleɪtɪd/ adj. **1** not connected; not related to sth else **SYN** **unconnected**: *The two events were totally unrelated. ◊ ~ to sth In my free time I like to do things that are unrelated to my work.* **2** (of people, animals, etc.) not belonging to the same family **OPP** **related**

**un·re·lent·ing** /ˌʌnrɪˈlentɪŋ/ adj. (formal) **1** (of an unpleasant situation) not stopping or becoming less severe **SYN** **relentless**: *unrelenting pressure ◊ The heat was unrelenting.* **2** if a person is **unrelenting**, they continue with sth without considering the feelings of other people **SYN** **relentless**: *She is one of the president's most unrelenting critics.* ▶ **un·re·lent·ing·ly** adv.

**un·re·li·able** /ˌʌnrɪˈlaɪəbl/ adj. that cannot be trusted or depended on: *The trains are notoriously unreliable. ◊ The judge found that she was an unreliable witness.* **OPP** **reliable** ▶ **un·re·li·abil·ity** /ˌʌnrɪˌlaɪəˈbɪləti/ noun [U]: *the unreliability of some statistics*

**un·re·lieved** /ˌʌnrɪˈliːvd/ adj. (formal) (of an unpleasant situation) continuing without changing

**un·re·mark·able** /ˌʌnrɪˈmɑːkəbl; NAmE -ˈmɑːrk-/ adj. ordinary; not special in any way: *an unremarkable life* **OPP** **remarkable**

**un·re·marked** /ˌʌnrɪˈmɑːkt; NAmE -ˈmɑːrkt/ adj. (formal) not noticed: *His absence went unremarked.*

**un·re·mit·ting** /ˌʌnrɪˈmɪtɪŋ/ adj. (formal) never stopping: *unremitting hostility* ▶ **un·re·mit·ting·ly** adv.: *unremittingly gloomy weather*

**un·re·peat·able** /ˌʌnrɪˈpiːtəbl/ adj. **1** too offensive or SHOCKING to be repeated: *He called me several unrepeatable names.* **2** that cannot be repeated or done again: *an unrepeatable experience* **OPP** **repeatable**

**un·re·pent·ant** /ˌʌnrɪˈpentənt/ adj. showing no shame about your actions or beliefs **OPP** **repentant** ▶ **un·re·pent·ant·ly** adv.

**un·re·port·ed** /ˌʌnrɪˈpɔːtɪd; NAmE -ˈpɔːrt-/ adj. not reported to the police or sb in authority or to the public: *Many cases of bullying go unreported.*

**un·rep·re·sen·ta·tive** /ˌʌnˌreprɪˈzentətɪv/ adj. ~ (of sb/sth) not typical of a group of people or things and therefore not useful as a source of information about that group **SYN** **untypical**: *an unrepresentative sample* **OPP** **representative**

**un·re·quit·ed** /ˌʌnrɪˈkwaɪtɪd/ adj. (formal) (of love) not returned by the person that you love ⊃ compare REQUITE

**un·re·served** /ˌʌnrɪˈzɜːvd; NAmE -ˈzɜːrvd/ adj. **1** (of seats in a theatre, etc.) not paid for in advance; not kept for the use of a particular person **2** (formal) complete and without any doubts: *He offered us his unreserved apologies.*

**un·re·served·ly** /ˌʌnrɪˈzɜːvɪdli; NAmE -ˈzɜːrv-/ adv. completely; without hesitating or having any doubts: *We apologize unreservedly for any offence we have caused.*

**un·re·solved** /ˌʌnrɪˈzɒlvd; NAmE -ˈzɑːlvd/ adj. (formal) (of a problem or question) not yet solved or answered; not having been resolved

**un·re·spon·sive** /ˌʌnrɪˈspɒnsɪv; NAmE -ˈspɑːn-/ adj. (formal) not reacting to sb/sth; not giving the response that you would expect or hope for: *If the person is unconscious or unresponsive, dial 999. ◊ ~ to sth a politician who is unresponsive to the mood of the country* **OPP** **responsive**

**un·rest** /ʌnˈrest/ noun [U] a political situation in which people are angry and likely to protest or fight: *industrial/civil/social/political/popular unrest ◊ There is growing unrest in the south of the country.*

**un·re·strained** /ˌʌnrɪˈstreɪnd/ adj. (formal) not controlled; not having been RESTRAINED: *unrestrained greed/joy*

**un·re·strict·ed** /ˌʌnrɪˈstrɪktɪd/ adj. not limited or controlled in any way **SYN** **unlimited**: *We have unrestricted access to all the facilities.* **OPP** **restricted**

**un·re·ward·ed** /ˌʌnrɪˈwɔːdɪd; NAmE -ˈwɔːrd-/ adj. not receiving the success that you are trying to achieve: *Real talent often goes unrewarded.*

**un·re·ward·ing** /ˌʌnrɪˈwɔːdɪŋ; NAmE -ˈwɔːrd-/ adj. (of an activity, etc.) not bringing feelings of pleasure or achievement **OPP** **rewarding**

**un·ripe** /ʌnˈraɪp/ adj. not yet ready to eat: *unripe fruit* **OPP** **ripe**

**un·rivalled** (especially BrE) (NAmE usually **un·rivaled**) /ʌnˈraɪvld/ adj. (formal) better or greater than any other **SYN** **unsurpassed**

**un·roll** /ʌnˈrəʊl/ verb **1** [T, I] ~ (sth) if you unroll paper, cloth, etc. that was in a roll or if it unrolls, it opens and becomes flat: *We unrolled our sleeping bags.* ⊃ compare ROLL **2** [I] (of events) to happen one after another in a series: *We watched the events unroll before the cameras.*

**un·ruf·fled** /ʌnˈrʌfld/ adj. (of a person) calm **SYN** **unperturbed**: *He remained unruffled by their accusations.*

**un·ruly** /ʌnˈruːli/ adj. difficult to control or manage **SYN** **disorderly**: *an unruly class ◊ unruly behaviour ◊ unruly hair (= difficult to keep looking neat)* ▶ **un·ru·li·ness** noun [U]

**un·safe** /ʌnˈseɪf/ adj. **1** (of a thing, a place or an activity) not safe; dangerous: *The roof was declared unsafe. ◊ It was considered unsafe to release the prisoners. ◊ unsafe sex (= for example, sex without a CONDOM)* **2** (of people) in danger of being harmed: *He felt unsafe and alone.* **3** (BrE, law) (of a decision in a court of law) based on evidence that may be false or is not good enough: *Their convictions were declared unsafe.* **OPP** **safe**

**un·said** /ʌnˈsed/ adj. [not before noun] thought but not spoken: *Some things are better left unsaid.*

**un·sale·able** (also **un·sal·able**) /ʌnˈseɪləbl/ adj. that cannot be sold, because it is not good enough or because nobody wants to buy it **OPP** **saleable**

**un·salt·ed** /ʌnˈsɔːltɪd; BrE also -ˈsɒl-/ adj. (especially of food) without added salt: *unsalted butter*

**un·sani·tary** /ʌnˈsænətri; NAmE -teri/ adj. (especially NAmE) = INSANITARY

**un·sat·is·fac·tory** /ˌʌnˌsætɪsˈfæktəri/ adj. not good enough **SYN** **inadequate, unacceptable** **OPP** **satisfactory** ▶ **un·sat·is·fac·tor·ily** /-rəli/ adv.

**un·sat·is·fied** /ʌnˈsætɪsfaɪd/ adj. **1** (of a need, demand, etc.) not dealt with **2** (of a person) not having got what you hoped; not having had enough of sth ⊃ compare DISSATISFIED, SATISFIED

**un·sat·is·fy·ing** /ʌnˈsætɪsfaɪɪŋ/ adj. not making you feel satisfied **OPP** **satisfying**: *a shallow, unsatisfying relationship*

**un·sat·ur·ated** /ʌnˈsætʃəreɪtɪd 'fæt/ noun [U, C] a type of fat found in nuts, seeds and vegetable oils that does not encourage the harmful development of CHOLESTEROL: *Avocados are high in unsaturated fat.* ⊃ see also MONOUNSATURATED FAT, POLYUNSATURATED FAT, SATURATED FAT, TRANS-FATTY ACID

**un·savoury** (US **un·savory**) /ʌnˈseɪvəri/ adj. unpleasant or offensive; not considered morally acceptable: *an unsavoury incident ◊ Her friends are all pretty unsavoury characters.*

**un·scathed** /ʌnˈskeɪðd/ adj. [not before noun] not hurt **SYN** **unharmed**: *The hostages emerged from their ordeal unscathed.*

---

Ⓞ Oxford Phrasal Academic Lexicon (OPAL) written and spoken word lists | Ⓦ OPAL written word list | Ⓢ OPAL spoken word list

**un·sched·uled** /ˌʌnˈʃedjuːld/ *NAmE* -ˈskedʒuːld/ *adj.* that was not planned in advance **SYN** **unplanned**: *an unscheduled stop*

**un·sci·en·tif·ic** /ˌʌnˌsaɪənˈtɪfɪk/ *adj.* (*often disapproving*) not scientific; not done in a careful, logical way: *an unscientific approach to a problem* ⊃ compare NON-SCIENTIFIC

**un·scram·ble** /ˌʌnˈskræmbl/ *verb* **1** ~ sth to change a word, message, television signal, etc. that has been sent in a code so that it can be read or understood **OPP** **scramble** **2** ~ sth to arrange sth that is confused or in the wrong order in a clear, correct way

**un·screw** /ˌʌnˈskruː/ *verb* **1** [T, I] ~ (sth) to remove sth by TWISTING or turning it; to be removed in this way: *I can't unscrew the lid of this jar.* **2** [T] ~ sth to take the SCREWS out of sth: *You'll have to unscrew the handles to paint the door.*

**un·script·ed** /ˌʌnˈskrɪptɪd/ *adj.* (of a speech, broadcast, etc.) not written or prepared in detail in advance **OPP** **scripted**

**un·scru·pu·lous** /ˌʌnˈskruːpjələs/ *adj.* without moral principles; not honest or fair **SYN** **unprincipled**: *unscrupulous methods* **OPP** **scrupulous** ▶ **un·scru·pu·lous·ly** *adv.* **un·scru·pu·lous·ness** *noun* [U]

**un·sea·son·able** /ˌʌnˈsiːznəbl/ *adj.* unusual for the time of year: *unseasonable weather* **OPP** **seasonable** ▶ **un·sea·son·ably** /-bli/ *adv.*: *unseasonably warm*

**un·sea·son·al** /ˌʌnˈsiːzənl/ *adj.* not typical of or not suitable for the time of year: *unseasonal weather* **OPP** **seasonal**

**un·seat** /ˌʌnˈsiːt/ *verb* **1** ~ sb to remove sb from a position of power **2** ~ sb to make sb fall off a horse or bicycle: *The horse unseated its rider at the first fence.*

**un·secured** /ˌʌnsɪˈkjʊəd/ *NAmE* -ˈkjʊrd/ *adj.* **1** if a debt or loan is **unsecured**, a person has arranged it without legally agreeing to give sb valuable property if they cannot pay the money back: *an unsecured personal loan of £15000* ⊃ see also SECURITY (6) **2** (of a person or company) having given sb a loan without SECURITY (= an agreement that they will give you valuable property if they cannot pay the money back): *unsecured creditors* **3** not locked, guarded or protected: *unsecured windows*

**un·seed·ed** /ˌʌnˈsiːdɪd/ *adj.* not chosen as a SEED (= one of the players expected to do well) in a sports competition, especially in tennis: *unseeded players* **OPP** **seeded**

**un·see·ing** /ˌʌnˈsiːɪŋ/ *adj.* (*literary*) not noticing or really looking at anything although your eyes are open ▶ **un·see·ing·ly** *adv.*: *They stared unseeingly at the wreckage.*

**un·seem·ly** /ˌʌnˈsiːmli/ *adj.* (*old-fashioned* or *formal*) (of behaviour, etc.) not polite or suitable for a particular situation **SYN** **improper** **OPP** **seemly**

**un·seen** /ˌʌnˈsiːn/ *adj.* **1** that cannot be seen; that is not seen: *unseen forces* ◇ *He was killed by a single shot from an unseen soldier.* ◇ *I managed to slip out of the room unseen.* **2** not previously seen: *unseen dangers* ◇ *The exam consists of an essay and an unseen translation.* **IDM** see SIGHT *n.*

**un·self-con·scious** /ˌʌnselfˈkɒnʃəs/ *NAmE* -ˈkɑːn-/ *adj.* not worried about or aware of what other people think of you **OPP** **self-conscious** ▶ **un·self-con·scious·ly** *adv.*

**un·self·ish** /ˌʌnˈselfɪʃ/ *adj.* giving more time or importance to other people's needs, wishes, etc. than to your own **SYN** **selfless**: *unselfish motives* **OPP** **selfish** ▶ **un·self·ish·ly** *adv.* **un·self·ish·ness** *noun* [U]

**un·sen·ti·men·tal** /ˌʌnˌsentɪˈmentl/ *adj.* not having or expressing emotions such as love or sympathy; not allowing such emotions to influence what you do **OPP** **sentimental**

**un·ser·vice·able** /ˌʌnˈsɜːvɪsəbl/ *NAmE* -ˈsɜːrv-/ *adj.* not suitable to be used **OPP** **serviceable**

**un·set·tle** /ˌʌnˈsetl/ *verb* ~ sb to make sb feel upset or worried, especially because a situation has changed: *Changing schools might unsettle the kids.*

**un·set·tled** /ˌʌnˈsetld/ *adj.* **1** (of a situation) that may change; making people uncertain about what might happen: *These were difficult and unsettled times.* ◇ *The weather has been very unsettled* (= it has changed a lot). **2** not calm or relaxed: *They all felt restless and unsettled.* **3** (of an argument, etc.) that continues without any agreement being reached **SYN** **unresolved** **4** (of a bill, etc.) not yet paid

**un·set·tling** /ˌʌnˈsetlɪŋ/ *adj.* making you feel upset, nervous or worried

**un·shaded** /ˌʌnˈʃeɪdɪd/ *adj.* (of a source of light) without a SHADE or other type of cover: *an unshaded light bulb*

**un·shak·able** (also **un·shake·able**) /ˌʌnˈʃeɪkəbl/ *adj.* (of a feeling or an attitude) that cannot be changed or destroyed **SYN** **firm**

**un·shaken** /ˌʌnˈʃeɪkən/ *adj.* ~ (in sth) not having changed a particular feeling or attitude: *They remain unshaken in their loyalty.*

**un·shaven** /ˌʌnˈʃeɪvn/ *adj.* not having been SHAVED or been SHAVED recently: *He looked pale and unshaven.* ◇ *his unshaven face* ⊃ compare SHAVEN

**un·sight·ly** /ˌʌnˈsaɪtli/ *adj.* not pleasant to look at **SYN** **ugly**

**un·signed** /ˌʌnˈsaɪnd/ *adj.* **1** not having been signed by sb; without a SIGNATURE: *an unsigned letter to the editor* **2** not having a contract with a company or team: *an unsigned band/player*

**un·skilled** /ˌʌnˈskɪld/ *adj.* not having or needing special skills or training: *unskilled manual workers* ◇ *unskilled work* **OPP** **skilled**

**un·smil·ing** /ˌʌnˈsmaɪlɪŋ/ *adj.* (*formal*) not smiling; looking unfriendly: *His eyes were hard and unsmiling.* ▶ **un·smil·ing·ly** *adv.*

**un·soci·able** /ˌʌnˈsəʊʃəbl/ *adj.* **1** not enjoying the company of other people; not friendly **OPP** **sociable** **2** = UNSOCIAL

**un·social** /ˌʌnˈsəʊʃl/ (also less frequent **un·soci·able**) (*BrE*) *adj.* outside the normal times of working: *I work long and unsocial hours.*

**un·sold** /ˌʌnˈsəʊld/ *adj.* not bought by anyone: *Many of the houses remain unsold.*

**un·soli·cit·ed** /ˌʌnsəˈlɪsɪtɪd/ *adj.* not asked for and sometimes not wanted: *unsolicited advice*

**un·solved** /ˌʌnˈsɒlvd/ *NAmE* -ˈsɑːlvd/ *adj.* not having been solved: *an unsolved murder/mystery/problem*

**un·sophis·ti·cated** /ˌʌnsəˈfɪstɪkeɪtɪd/ *adj.* **1** not having or showing much experience of the world and social situations: *unsophisticated tastes* **2** simple and basic; not complicated **SYN** **crude**: *unsophisticated equipment* **OPP** **sophisticated**

**un·sorted** /ˌʌnˈsɔːtɪd/ *NAmE* -ˈsɔːrt-/ *adj.* not sorted, or not arranged in any particular order: *a pile of unsorted papers*

**un·sound** /ˌʌnˈsaʊnd/ *adj.* **1** (of a building, etc.) in poor condition; weak and likely to fall down: *The roof is structurally unsound.* **2** not acceptable; not based on reliable evidence: *ideologically unsound* ◇ *This line of argument is unsound.* **3** containing mistakes; that cannot rely on **SYN** **unreliable**: *The methods used were unsound.* **OPP** **sound** ▶ **un·sound·ness** *noun* [U]
**IDM** **of unsound mind** (*law*) not responsible for your actions because of a mental illness

**un·spar·ing** /ˌʌnˈspeərɪŋ/ *NAmE* -ˈsper-/ *adj.* **1** ~ (in sth) (*formal*) not caring about people's feelings: *She is unsparing in her criticism.* ◇ *an unsparing portrait of life in the slums* **2** giving or given generously: *He won his mother's unsparing approval.* ⊃ compare SPARING ▶ **un·spar·ing·ly** *adv.*

**un·speak·able** /ˌʌnˈspiːkəbl/ *adj.* (*literary, usually disapproving*) that cannot be described in words, usually because it is so bad **SYN** **indescribable** ▶ **un·speak·ably** /-bli/ *adv.*

**un·speci·fied** /ˌʌnˈspesɪfaɪd/ *adj.* not stated clearly or definitely; not having been SPECIFIED: *The story takes place at an unspecified date.*

**un·spec·tacu·lar** /ˌʌnspekˈtækjələ(r)/ *adj.* not exciting or special: *He had a steady but unspectacular career.*

**un·spoiled** /ˌʌnˈspɔɪld/ (*BrE also* **un·spoilt** /ˌʌnˈspɔɪlt/) *adj.* (*approving*) **1** (of a place) beautiful because it has not been changed or built on **2** (of a person) not made unpleasant, badly behaved, etc. by being praised too much **OPP** **spoil**

**un·spoken** /ˌʌnˈspəʊkən/ *adj.* (*formal*) not stated; not said in words but understood or agreed between people **SYN** **unstated**: *an unspoken assumption* ◇ *Something unspoken hung in the air between them.*

**un·sport·ing** /ˌʌnˈspɔːtɪŋ; *NAmE* -ˈspɔːrt-/ *adj.* (*disapproving*) not fair or generous in your behaviour or treatment of others, especially of an opponent in a game **OPP** **sporting**

**un·sports·man·like** /ˌʌnˈspɔːtsmənlaɪk; *NAmE* -ˈspɔːrts-/ *adj.* (*disapproving*) not behaving in a fair, generous and polite way, especially when playing a sport or game: *unsportsmanlike conduct* **OPP** **sportsmanlike**

**un·stable** **W** /ˌʌnˈsteɪbl/ *adj.* **1** likely to change suddenly **SYN** **volatile**: *The political situation remains highly unstable.* **2** if people are **unstable**, their behaviour and emotions change often and suddenly because their minds are upset **3** likely to move or fall **4** (*specialist*) (of a substance) not staying in the same chemical or ATOMIC state: *chemically unstable* **OPP** **stable** ⊃ see also INSTABILITY

**un·stated** /ˌʌnˈsteɪtɪd/ *adj.* (*formal*) not stated; not said in words but understood or agreed between people **SYN** **unspoken**: *Their reasoning was based on a set of unstated assumptions.*

**un·steady** /ˌʌnˈstedi/ *adj.* **1** not completely in control of your movements so that you might fall: *She is still a little unsteady on her feet after the operation.* **2** shaking or moving in a way that lacks control: *an unsteady hand* **OPP** **steady** ▶ **un·stead·ily** /-dəli/ *adv.* **un·steadi·ness** *noun* [U]

**un·stint·ing** /ˌʌnˈstɪntɪŋ/ *adj.* given or giving generously: *unstinting support* ◇ **~in sth** *They were unstinting in their praise.* ▶ **un·stint·ing·ly** *adv.*

**un·stop·pable** /ˌʌnˈstɒpəbl; *NAmE* -ˈstɑːp-/ *adj.* that cannot be stopped or prevented: *an unstoppable rise in prices* ◇ *On form, the team was simply unstoppable.*

**un·stressed** /ˌʌnˈstrest/ *adj.* (*phonetics*) (of a syllable) pronounced without emphasis **OPP** **stressed**

**un·struc·tured** /ˌʌnˈstrʌktʃəd; *NAmE* -tʃərd/ *adj.* without structure or organization

**un·stuck** /ˌʌnˈstʌk/ *adj.*
**IDM** **come un·stuck 1** to become separated from sth it was stuck or fastened to: *The flap of the envelope had come unstuck.* **2** (*BrE, informal*) (of a person, plan, etc.) to fail completely, with bad results

**un·sub·scribe** /ˌʌnsəbˈskraɪb/ *verb* [I, T] **~(from sth)** | **~sb/sth** (*computing*) to remove your/sb's email address from an internet MAILING LIST ⊃ WORDFINDER NOTE at WEB

**un·sub·stan·ti·ated** /ˌʌnsəbˈstænʃieɪtɪd/ *adj.* (*formal*) not proved to be true by evidence **SYN** **unsupported**: *an unsubstantiated claim/rumour, etc.*

**un·suc·cess·ful** /ˌʌnsəkˈsesfl/ *adj.* not successful; not achieving what you wanted to: *His efforts to get a job proved unsuccessful.* ◇ *They were unsuccessful in meeting their objectives for the year.* ◇ *She made several unsuccessful attempts to see him.* **OPP** **successful** ▶ **un·suc·cess·ful·ly** /-fəli/ *adv.*

**un·suit·able** /ˌʌnˈsuːtəbl/ *adj.* **~(for sb/sth)** not right or appropriate for a particular person, purpose or occasion: *He was wearing shoes that were totally unsuitable for climbing.* **OPP** **suitable** ▶ **un·suit·abil·ity** /ˌʌnsuːtəˈbɪləti/ *noun* [U] **un·suit·ably** /ˌʌnˈsuːtəbli/ *adv.*: *They were unsuitably dressed for the occasion.*

**un·suit·ed** /ˌʌnˈsuːtɪd/ *adj.* **1 ~(to/for sth)** | **~(to do sth)** not having the right or necessary qualities for sth: *He is unsuited to academic work.* ◇ *She was totally unsuited for the job.* **2** if two people are **unsuited** to each other, they do not have the same interests, etc. and are therefore not likely to make a good couple **OPP** **suited**

**un·sul·lied** /ˌʌnˈsʌlid/ *adj.* (*literary*) not made less good by anything; still pure and in the original state **SYN** **unspoiled**

**un·sung** /ˌʌnˈsʌŋ/ *adj.* [usually before noun] (*formal*) not praised or famous but deserving to be: *the unsung heroes of the war*

**un·super·vised** /ˌʌnˈsuːpəvaɪzd; *NAmE* -pərv-/ *adj.* without being watched; without sb responsible for ensuring that things are safe and correct: *There are many dangers in a house for an unsupervised child.* ◇ *Young children should not be left unsupervised in the playground.*

**un·sup·port·ed** /ˌʌnsəˈpɔːtɪd; *NAmE* -ˈpɔːrt-/ *adj.* **1** (of a statement, etc.) not proved to be true by evidence **SYN** **unsubstantiated**: *Their claims are unsupported by research findings.* **2** not helped or paid for by sb/sth else: *She has brought up three children unsupported.* **3** not physically supported: *Sections of the structure have been left unsupported.*

**un·sure** /ˌʌnˈʃʊə(r), -ˈʃɔː(r); *NAmE* -ˈʃʊr/ *adj.* [not before noun] **1** not certain of sth; having doubts: **~about/of sth** *There were a lot of things I was unsure about.* ◇ **~how, what, etc ...** *I was unsure how to reply to this question.* ◇ **~of how, what, etc ...** *He was unsure of what to do next.* ◇ **~as to how, what, etc ...** *They were unsure as to what the next move should be.* **2 ~(of yourself)** not having enough confidence in yourself: *Like many women, deep down she was unsure of herself.* **OPP** **sure**

**un·sur·passed** /ˌʌnsəˈpɑːst; *NAmE* -sərˈpæst/ *adj.* (*formal*) better or greater than any other **SYN** **unrivalled**

**un·sur·prised** /ˌʌnsəˈpraɪzd; *NAmE* -sərˈp-/ *adj.* [not usually before noun] not surprised: *She appeared totally unsurprised at the news.*

**un·sur·pris·ing** /ˌʌnsəˈpraɪzɪŋ; *NAmE* -sərˈp-/ *adj.* not causing surprise **OPP** **surprising** ▶ **un·sur·pris·ing·ly** *adv.*: *Unsurprisingly, the plan failed.*

**un·sus·pect·ed** /ˌʌnsəˈspektɪd/ *adj.* not predicted or known; that you were not previously aware of

**un·sus·pect·ing** /ˌʌnsəˈspektɪŋ/ *adj.* [usually before noun] not suspecting that anything is wrong; not aware of danger or of sth bad: *He had crept up on his unsuspecting victim from behind.*

**un·sus·tain·able** /ˌʌnsəˈsteɪnəbl/ *adj.* that cannot be continued at the same level, rate, etc: *unsustainable growth* **OPP** **sustainable**

**un·sweet·ened** /ˌʌnˈswiːtnd/ *adj.* (of food or drinks) without sugar or a similar substance having been added

**un·swerv·ing** /ˌʌnˈswɜːvɪŋ; *NAmE* -ˈswɜːrv-/ *adj.* (*formal*) strong and not changing or becoming weaker: *unswerving loyalty/support, etc.*

**un·sym·pa·thet·ic** /ˌʌnˌsɪmpəˈθetɪk/ *adj.* **1 ~(to/ towards sb)** not feeling or showing any sympathy: *I told him about the problem but he was totally unsympathetic.* **2 ~(to/towards sth)** not in agreement with sth; not supporting an idea, aim, etc: *The government was unsympathetic to the needs of the poor.* **3** (of a person) not easy to like; unpleasant **OPP** **sympathetic** ▶ **un·sym·pa·thet·ic·al·ly** /-kli/ *adv.*: *'You've only got yourself to blame,' she said unsympathetically.*

**un·sys·tem·at·ic** /ˌʌnˌsɪstəˈmætɪk/ *adj.* not organized into a clear system **OPP** **systematic** ▶ **un·sys·tem·at·ic·al·ly** /-kli/ *adv.*

**un·taint·ed** /ˌʌnˈteɪntɪd/ *adj.* **~(by sth)** (*formal*) not damaged or harmed by sth unpleasant; not TAINTED

**un·tal·ent·ed** /ˌʌnˈtæləntɪd/ *adj.* without a natural ability to do sth well **OPP** **talented**

**un·tamed** /ˌʌnˈteɪmd/ *adj.* allowed to remain in a wild state; not changed, controlled or influenced by anyone; not TAMED

**un·tan·gle** /ˌʌnˈtæŋgl/ *verb* **1 ~sth (from sth)** to separate pieces of string, hair, wire, etc. that have become TWISTED or have KNOTS in them **2 ~sth** to make sth that is complicated or confusing easier to deal with or understand

**un·tapped** /ˌʌnˈtæpt/ *adj.* available but not yet used: *untapped reserves of oil*

# untenable

**un·ten·a·ble** /ʌnˈtenəbl/ *adj.* (*formal*) (of a theory, position, etc.) that cannot be defended against attack or criticism: *His position had become untenable and he was forced to resign.* **OPP** tenable

**un·test·ed** /ʌnˈtestɪd/ *adj.* not tested; of unknown quality or value

**un·think·able** /ʌnˈθɪŋkəbl/ *adj.* it is ~ (for sb/sth) (to do sth) | it is ~ (that …) impossible to imagine or accept **SYN** inconceivable: *It was unthinkable that she could be dead.* **OPP** thinkable ▶ **the un·think·able** *noun* [sing.]: *Suddenly the unthinkable happened and he drew out a gun.* ◊ *The time has come to think the unthinkable* (= consider possibilities that used to be unacceptable).

**un·think·ing** /ʌnˈθɪŋkɪŋ/ *adj.* (*formal*) not thinking about the effects of what you do or say **SYN** thoughtless ▶ **un·think·ing·ly** *adv.*

**un·tidy** /ʌnˈtaɪdi/ *adj.* (**un·tidi·er**, **un·tidi·est**) **1** not neat or well arranged; not in order: *an untidy desk* ◊ *untidy hair* **2** (of a person) not keeping things neat or well organized: *Why do you have to be so untidy?* **OPP** tidy ▶ **un·tidi·ly** /-dɪli/ *adv.* **un·tidi·ness** *noun* [U]

**untie** /ʌnˈtaɪ/ *verb* ~ sth to separate the pieces of string, rope, etc. that form a KNOT in sth; to remove the string, rope, etc. from sth that is tied: *to untie a knot* ◊ *I quickly untied the package and peeped inside.* ◊ *He untied the rope and pushed the boat into the water.*

**until** ❶ **A1** /ənˈtɪl/ *conj.*, *prep.* (also informal **till**, **til**, **'til**) up to the point in time or the event mentioned: *Let's wait until the rain stops.* ◊ *Until she spoke I hadn't realized her wasn't English.* ◊ *You're not going out until you've finished this.* ◊ *Until now I have always lived alone.* ◊ *They moved here in 2009. Until then they'd always been in the London area.* ◊ *He continued working up until his death.* ◊ *The street is full of traffic from morning till night.* ◊ *You can stay on the bus until London* (= until you reach London).

**un·time·ly** /ʌnˈtaɪmli/ *adj.* (*formal*) **1** [usually before noun] happening too soon or sooner than is normal or expected **SYN** premature: *She met a tragic and untimely death at 25.* **2** happening at a time or in a situation that is not suitable **SYN** ill-timed: *His interruption was untimely.* **OPP** timely

**un·tir·ing** /ʌnˈtaɪərɪŋ/ *adj.* (*approving*) continuing to do sth for a long period of time with a lot of effort and/or enthusiasm **SYN** tireless

**un·titled** /ʌnˈtaɪtld/ *adj.* (of a work of art) without a title

**unto** /ˈʌntə, before vowels -tu/ *prep.* (*old use*) **1** to or towards sb/sth: *The angel appeared unto him in a dream.* **2** until a particular time or event: *The knights swore loyalty unto death.*

**un·told** /ʌnˈtəʊld/ *adj.* **1** [only before noun] used to emphasize how large, great, unpleasant, etc. sth is **SYN** immeasurable: *untold misery/wealth* ◊ *These gases cause untold damage to the environment.* **2** (of a story) not told to anyone

**un·touch·able** /ʌnˈtʌtʃəbl/ *adj.*, *noun*

■ *adj.* **1** a person who is **untouchable** is in a position where they are unlikely to be punished or criticized: *Given his political connections, he thought he was untouchable.* **2** that cannot be touched or changed by other people: *The department's budget is untouchable.* **3** (in India in the past) belonging to or connected with the Hindu social class (or CASTE) that was considered by other classes to be the lowest

■ *noun* often **Untouchable** (in India in the past) a member of a Hindu social class (or CASTE) that was considered by other classes to be the lowest

**un·touched** /ʌnˈtʌtʃt/ *adj.* [not usually before noun] **1** ~ (by sth) not affected by sth, especially sth bad or unpleasant; not damaged: *The area has remained relatively untouched by commercial development.* **2** (of food or drink) not eaten or drunk: *She left her meal untouched.* **3** not changed in any way: *The final clause in the contract will be left untouched.*

**un·to·ward** /ˌʌntəˈwɔːd; *NAmE* ʌnˈtɔːrd/ *adj.* unusual and unexpected, and usually unpleasant: *That's the plan—unless anything untoward happens.* ◊ *He had noticed nothing untoward.*

**un·trained** /ˌʌnˈtreɪnd/ *adj.* ~ (in sth) not trained to perform a particular job or skill; without formal training in sth: *untrained in keyboard skills* ◊ *untrained teachers* ◊ *To the untrained eye, the products look remarkably similar.*

**un·tram·melled** (US **un·tram·meled**) /ʌnˈtræmld/ *adj.* ~ (by sth) (*formal*) not limited by sth ⊃ compare TRAMMEL

**un·treat·ed** /ʌnˈtriːtɪd/ *adj.* **1** not receiving medical treatment: *If untreated, the illness can become severe.* **2** (of substances) not made safe by chemical or other treatment: *untreated sewage* **3** (of wood) not treated with substances to preserve it

**un·tried** /ʌnˈtraɪd/ *adj.* **1** without experience of doing a particular job: *She chose two untried actors for the leading roles.* **2** not yet tried or tested to discover if it works or is successful **SYN** untested: *This is a new and relatively untried procedure.*

**un·true** /ʌnˈtruː/ *adj.* **1** not true; not based on facts: *These accusations are totally untrue.* ◊ *an untrue claim* ◊ *It is untrue to say that something like this could never happen again.* **2** ~ (to sb/sth) (*formal*) not LOYAL to sb/sth; doing sth that hurts or damages sb/sth **SYN** unfaithful: *If he agreed to their demands, he would have to be untrue to his own principles.* **OPP** true

**un·trust·worthy** /ʌnˈtrʌstwɜːði; *NAmE* -wɜːrði/ *adj.* that cannot be trusted **OPP** trustworthy

**un·truth** /ʌnˈtruːθ/ *noun* (*pl.* **un·truths** /ʌnˈtruːðz, -ˈtruːθs/) **1** [C] (*formal*) a lie. People often say 'untruth' to avoid saying 'lie'. ⊃ compare TRUTH **2** [U] the state of being false

**un·truth·ful** /ʌnˈtruːθfl/ *adj.* saying things that you know are not true **OPP** truthful ▶ **un·truth·ful·ly** /-fəli/ *adv.*

**un·turned** /ʌnˈtɜːnd; *NAmE* -ˈtɜːrnd/ *adj.* **IDM** see STONE *n.*

**un·tutored** /ʌnˈtjuːtəd; *NAmE* -ˈtuːtərd/ *adj.* (*formal*) not having been formally taught about sth

**un·typ·ical** /ʌnˈtɪpɪkl/ *adj.* ~ (of sb/sth) not typical: *an untypical example* ◊ *Schools in this area are quite untypical of schools in the rest of the country.* ◊ *All in all, it had been a not untypical day* (= it had been very like other days). **OPP** typical ⊃ compare ATYPICAL ▶ **un·typ·ic·al·ly** /-kli/ *adv.*

**un·usable** /ʌnˈjuːzəbl/ *adj.* in such a bad condition or of such low quality that it cannot be used **OPP** usable

**un·used**[1] /ʌnˈjuːzd/ *adj.* not being used at the moment; never having been used ⊃ compare DISUSED

**un·used**[2] /ʌnˈjuːst/ *adj.* not having much experience of sth and therefore not knowing how to deal with it; not used to sth: ~ to sth *This is an easy routine, designed for anyone who is unused to exercise.* ◊ ~ to doing sth *She was unused to talking about herself.* **OPP** used[1]

**un·usual** ❶ **A2** /ʌnˈjuːʒuəl, -ʒəl/ *adj.* **1** 💡 **A2** different from what is usual or normal **SYN** uncommon: *The case is highly unusual.* ◊ *Police then took the unusual step of publishing the names and pictures of the two suspects.* ◊ *it is ~ (for sb/sth) to do sth It's not unusual for young doctors to work a 70-hour week* (= it happens often). **2** 💡 **A2** different from other similar things and therefore interesting and attractive: *an unusual colour*

**un·usu·al·ly** /ʌnˈjuːʒuəli, -ʒə-/ *adv.* **1** used before adjectives to emphasize that a particular quality is greater than normal: *unusually high levels of radiation* ◊ *an unusually cold winter* **2** used to say that a particular situation is not normal or expected: *Unusually for him, he wore a tie.*

**un·utter·able** /ʌnˈʌtərəbl/ *adj.* [only before noun] (*formal*) used to emphasize how great a particular emotion or quality is: *unutterable sadness* ▶ **un·utter·ably** /-bli/ *adv.*

**un·var·nished** /ʌnˈvɑːnɪʃt; *NAmE* -ˈvɑːrn-/ *adj.* **1** [only before noun] (*formal*) with nothing added: *It was the plain unvarnished truth.* **2** (of wood, etc.) not covered with VARNISH

**un·vary·ing** /ʌnˈveəriɪŋ; *NAmE* -ˈver-, -ˈvær-/ *adj.* (*formal*) never changing: *an unvarying routine*

**un·veil** /ʌnˈveɪl/ verb 1 ~ sth to remove a cover or curtain from a painting, statue, etc. so that it can be seen in public for the first time: *The Queen unveiled a plaque to mark the official opening of the hospital.* 2 ~ sth to show or introduce a new plan, product, etc. to the public for the first time SYN **reveal**: *They will be unveiling their new models at the Motor Show.*

**un·vi·able** /ʌnˈvaɪəbl/ adj. that cannot be done; that is not capable of working successfully: *The airport had become financially unviable and closed in December 2019.* OPP **viable**

**un·voiced** /ʌnˈvɔɪst/ adj. 1 thought about but not expressed in words 2 (*phonetics*) (of consonants) produced without moving your VOCAL CORDS; not VOICED SYN **voiceless**: *unvoiced consonants such as 'p' and 't'*

**un·waged** /ʌnˈweɪdʒd/ adj. (*BrE*) 1 (of a person) not earning money by working OPP **waged** 2 (of work) for which you are not paid SYN **unpaid** 3 **the unwaged** *noun* [pl.] people who are unwaged

**un·want·ed** /ʌnˈwɒntɪd; *NAmE* -ˈwɑːn-/ adj. that you do not want: *unwanted advice* ◇ *It is very sad when children feel unwanted* (= feel that other people do not care about them).

**un·war·rant·ed** /ʌnˈwɒrəntɪd; *NAmE* -ˈwɔːr-/ adj. (*formal*) not reasonable or necessary; not appropriate SYN **unjustified**: *Much of the criticism was totally unwarranted.*

**un·wary** /ʌnˈweəri; *NAmE* -ˈweri/ adj. 1 [only before noun] not aware of the possible dangers or problems of a situation and therefore likely to be harmed in some way ⊃ compare WARY 2 **the unwary** *noun* [pl.] people who are unwary: *The stock market is full of traps for the unwary.*

**un·washed** /ʌnˈwɒʃt; *NAmE* -ˈwɑːʃt/ adj. not washed; dirty: *a pile of unwashed dishes* ◇ *Their clothes were dirty and their hair unwashed.*

**un·waver·ing** /ʌnˈweɪvərɪŋ/ adj. (*formal*) not changing or becoming weaker in any way: *unwavering support* ▶ **un·waver·ing·ly** adv.

**un·wed** /ʌnˈwed/ adj. (used especially in newspapers) not married SYN **unmarried**: *unwed mothers*

**un·wel·come** /ʌnˈwelkəm/ adj. not wanted: *an unwelcome visitor* ◇ *To avoid attracting unwelcome attention he kept his voice down.* OPP **welcome**

**un·wel·com·ing** /ʌnˈwelkəmɪŋ/ adj. 1 (of a person) not friendly towards sb who is visiting or arriving 2 (of a place) not attractive; looking uncomfortable to be in OPP **welcoming**

**un·well** /ʌnˈwel/ adj. [not before noun] (*rather formal*) ill: *She said she was feeling unwell and went home.* OPP **well**

**un·whole·some** /ʌnˈhəʊlsəm/ adj. 1 harmful to health; not looking healthy 2 that you consider unpleasant or not natural SYN **unhealthy** OPP **wholesome**

**un·wieldy** /ʌnˈwiːldi/ adj. 1 (of an object) difficult to move or control because of its size, shape or weight SYN **cumbersome** 2 (of a system or group of people) difficult to control or organize because it is very large or complicated

**un·will·ing** /ʌnˈwɪlɪŋ/ adj. 1 [not usually before noun] ~ (to do sth) not wanting to do sth and refusing to do it: *They are unwilling to invest any more money in the project.* ◇ *She was unable, or unwilling, to give me any further details.* 2 [only before noun] not wanting to do or be sth, but forced to by other people SYN **reluctant**: *an unwilling hero* ◇ *He became the unwilling object of her attention.* OPP **willing** ▶ **un·will·ing·ly** adv. **un·will·ing·ness** *noun* [U]

**un·wind** /ʌnˈwaɪnd/ verb (**un·wound**, **un·wound** /-ˈwaʊnd/) 1 [T, I] ~ (sth) (from sth) if sth that has been wrapped into a ball or around sth **unwinds** or you **unwind** it, it becomes, or you make it, straight, flat or loose again: *to unwind a ball of string* ◇ *He unwound his scarf from his neck.* ◇ *The bandage gradually unwound and fell off.* 2 [I] to stop worrying or thinking about problems and start to relax SYN **relax**, **wind down**: *Music helps me unwind after a busy day.*

**un·wise** /ʌnˈwaɪz/ adj. ~ (to do sth) showing a lack of good judgement SYN **foolish**: *It would be unwise to comment on the situation without knowing all the facts.* ◇ *an unwise investment* OPP **wise** ▶ **un·wise·ly** adv.: *Perhaps unwisely, I agreed to help.*

**un·wit·ting** /ʌnˈwɪtɪŋ/ adj. [only before noun] not aware of what you are doing or of the situation you are involved in: *He became an unwitting accomplice in the crime.* ◇ *She was the unwitting cause of the argument.*

**un·wit·ting·ly** /ʌnˈwɪtɪŋli/ adv. without being aware of what you are doing or the situation that you are involved in: *She had broken the law unwittingly, but still she had broken it.* OPP **wittingly**

**un·work·able** /ʌnˈwɜːkəbl; *NAmE* -ˈwɜːrk-/ adj. not practical or possible to do successfully: *an unworkable plan* ◇ *The law as it stands is unworkable.* OPP **workable**

**un·world·ly** /ʌnˈwɜːldli; *NAmE* -ˈwɜːrld-/ adj. 1 not interested in money or the things that it buys 2 having little experience of life SYN **naive** OPP **worldly** 3 having qualities that do not seem to belong to this world: *The landscape had a stark, unworldly beauty.*

**un·wor·ried** /ʌnˈwʌrid; *NAmE* -ˈwɜːr-/ adj. [not usually before noun] (*formal*) not worried; calm; relaxed: *She appeared unworried by criticism.*

**un·worthy** /ʌnˈwɜːði; *NAmE* -ˈwɜːrði/ adj. (*formal*) 1 ~ (of sth) not having the necessary qualities to deserve sth, especially respect: *He considered himself unworthy of the honour they had bestowed on him.* OPP **worthy** 2 ~ (of sb) not acceptable from sb, especially sb who has an important job or high social position SYN **unbefitting**: *Such opinions are unworthy of educated people.* ▶ **un·worthi·ness** *noun* [U]: *feelings of unworthiness*

**un·wound** /ʌnˈwaʊnd/ *past tense, past part.* of UNWIND

**un·wrap** /ʌnˈræp/ verb (**-pp-**) ~ sth to take off the paper, etc. that covers or protects sth: *Don't unwrap your present until your birthday.* OPP **wrap up**

**un·writ·ten** /ʌnˈrɪtn/ adj. 1 ~ **law**, **rule**, **agreement**, etc. a law, etc. that everyone knows about and accepts even though it has not been made official: *an unwritten understanding that nobody leaves before five o'clock* 2 (of a book, etc.) not yet written: *The photographs were to be included in his as yet unwritten autobiography.*

**un·yield·ing** /ʌnˈjiːldɪŋ/ adj. (*formal*) 1 if a person is **unyielding**, they are not easily influenced and they are unlikely to change their mind SYN **inflexible** 2 an **unyielding** substance or object does not bend or break when pressure is put on it

**un·zip** /ʌnˈzɪp/ verb (**-pp-**) 1 [T, I] ~ (sth) if you **unzip** a piece of clothing, a bag, etc., or if it **unzips**, you open the ZIP that fastens it SYN **zip up** 2 [T] ~ sth (*computing*) to return a file to its original size after it has been COMPRESSED (= made smaller) SYN **decompress** OPP **zip**

# up

**up** /ʌp/ adv., prep., adj., verb, noun

■ adv. HELP For the special uses of **up** in phrasal verbs, look at the entries for the verbs. For example **break up** is in the phrasal verb section at **break**. 1 towards or in a higher position: *He jumped up from his chair.* ◇ *Your mum said you were up here* (= upstairs). ◇ *The sun was already up* (= had risen) *when they set off.* ◇ *They live up in the mountains.* ◇ *It didn't take long to put the tent up.* ◇ *You look nice with your hair up* (= arranged on top of or at the back of your head). ◇ *Lay the cards face up* (= facing upwards) *on the table.* ◇ *Up you come!* (= said when lifting a child) 2 to or at a higher level: *She turned the volume up.* ◇ *Prices are still going up* (= rising). ◇ *United were 3-1 up at half-time.* ◇ *The wind is getting up* (= blowing more strongly). ◇ *Sales are well up on last year.* ⊃ LANGUAGE BANK at INCREASE 3 to the place where sb/sth is: *A car drove up and he got in.* ◇ *She went straight up to the door and knocked loudly.* 4 out of bed: *I stayed up late* (= did not go to bed until late) *last night.* ◇ (*BrE*) *He's up and about again after his illness.* 5 to or at an important place, especially a large city: *We're going up to New York for the day.* ◇ (*BrE, formal*) *His son's up at Oxford* (= Oxford University). 6 to a place in the north of a country; further north than somewhere else: *They've moved up north.* ◇ *We drove up to*

**up-**

*Inverness to see my father.* **7** completely: *We ate all the food up.* ◊ *The stream has dried up.* **8** so as to be finished or closed: *I have some paperwork to finish up.* ◊ *Do your coat up; it's cold.* **9** into pieces or parts: *She tore the paper up.* ◊ *They've had the road up (= with the surface broken or removed) to lay some pipes.* ◊ *How shall we divide up the work?* **10** so as to be formed or brought together: *The government agreed to set up a committee of inquiry.* ◊ *She gathered up her belongings.* **11** (of a period of time) finished; over: *Time's up. Stop writing and hand in your papers.* **12** (*informal*) used to say that sth is happening, especially sth unusual or unpleasant: *I could tell **something was up** by the looks on their faces.* ◊ *What's up?* (= What is the matter?) ◊ *What's up with him?* *He looks furious.* ◊ *Is anything up? You can tell me.* **HELP** Especially in *NAmE* **What's up?** can just mean 'What's new?' or 'What's happening?' There may not be anything wrong. **13** about to happen, be discussed, etc: *Next up in our top ten is a new release by Ariana Grande.* ◊ *Up after the break we will be introducing our mystery guest!*

**IDM** **be up to sb** to be sb's duty or responsibility; to be for sb to decide: *It's not up to you to tell me how to do my job.* ◊ *Shall we eat out or stay in? It's up to you.* **not be 'up to much** (*BrE*) to be of poor quality; to not be very good: *His work isn't up to much.* **up against sth** (*informal*) facing problems or opposition: *Teachers are up against some major problems these days.* ◊ *She's really **up against it** (= in a difficult situation).* **up and 'down 1** moving upwards and downwards: *The boat bobbed up and down on the water.* **2** in one direction and then in the opposite direction: *She was pacing up and down in front of her desk.* **3** sometimes good and sometimes bad: *My relationship with him was up and down.* **4** (*NAmE*, *informal*) if you swear **up and down** that sth is true, you say that it is definitely true. **up and 'running** (of a system, for example a computer system) working; being used: *By that time the new system should be up and running.* **up before sb/sth** appearing in front of sb in authority for a judgement to be made about sth that you have done: *He came up before the local magistrate for speeding.* **up for sth 1** on offer for sth: *The house is up for sale.* **2** being considered for sth, especially as a candidate: *Two candidates are up for election.* **3** (*informal*) willing to take part in a particular activity: *We're going clubbing tonight. Are you **up for it**?* '**up there** (*informal*) among or almost the best, worst, most important, etc: *It may not have been the worst week of my life but it's up there.* ◊ *OK, it's not my absolute dream, but it's up there.* ◊ *These people can't live without the internet—it's up there with air and water.* **up to sth 1** as far as a particular number, level, etc: *I can take up to four people (= but no more than four) in my car.* ◊ *The temperature went up to 35°C.* **2** (also **up until sth**) not further or later than sth; until sth: *Read up to page 100.* ◊ *Up to now he's been very quiet.* **3** as high or as good as sth: *Her latest book isn't up to her usual standard.* **4** (also **up to doing sth**) physically or mentally capable of sth: *He's not up to the job.* ◊ *I don't feel up to going to work today.* **5** (*informal*) doing sth, especially sth bad: *What's she up to?* ◊ *What've you been up to?* ◊ *I'm sure he's **up to no good** (= doing sth bad).*

■ **prep. 1** to or in a higher position somewhere: *She climbed up the flight of steps.* ◊ *The village is further up the valley.* **2** along or further along a road or street: *We live just up the road, past the post office.* **3** towards the place where a river starts: *a cruise up the Rhine*
**IDM** **up and down sth** in one direction and then in the opposite direction along sth: *I looked up and down the corridor.* **up 'yours!** (*taboo*, *slang*) an offensive way of being rude to sb, for example because they have said sth that makes you angry

■ **adj. 1** [only before noun] directed or moving upwards: *an up stroke* ◊ *the up escalator* **2** [not before noun] (*informal*) cheerful; happy or excited: *The mood here is resolutely up.* **3** [not before noun] (of a computer system) working: *Our system should be up by this afternoon.*

■ **verb** (**-pp-**) **1** [I] **up and ...** (*informal* or *humorous*) to suddenly move or do sth unexpected: *He upped and left without telling anyone.* **2** [T] ~ **sth** to increase the price or amount of sth **SYN** **raise**: *The buyers upped their offer by £1000.*
**IDM** **up 'sticks** (*BrE*) (*NAmE* **pull up 'stakes**) (*informal*) to suddenly move from your house and go to live somewhere else ⊃ more at ANTE

■ **noun**
**IDM** **on the 'up** increasing or improving: *Business confidence is on the up.* **on the 'up and 'up** (*informal*) **1** (*BrE*) becoming more and more successful: *The club has been on the up and up since the beginning of the season.* **2** (*NAmE*) = ON THE LEVEL at LEVEL *n*.: *The offer seems to be on the up and up.* **ups and 'downs** the mixture of good and bad things in life or in a particular situation or relationship

**up-** /ʌp/ *prefix* (in adjectives, verbs and related nouns) higher; upwards; towards the top of sth: *upland* ◊ *upturned* ◊ *upgrade* ◊ *uphill*

**up-and-'coming** *adj.* likely to be successful and popular in the future: *up-and-coming young actors*

**up·beat** /ˈʌpbiːt/ *adj.* (*informal*) positive and enthusiastic; making you feel that the future will be good **SYN** **optimistic**: *The tone of the speech was upbeat.* ◊ *The meeting ended on an upbeat note.* **OPP** **downbeat**

**up·braid** /ʌpˈbreɪd/ *verb* ~ **sb (for sth/for doing sth)** (*formal*) to criticize sb or speak angrily to them because you do not approve of sth that they have said or done **SYN** **reproach**

**up·bring·ing** /ˈʌpbrɪŋɪŋ/ *noun* [sing., U] the way in which a child is cared for and taught how to behave while it is growing up: *to have had a sheltered upbringing* ◊ **by ~** *He was a Catholic by upbringing.*

**UPC** /ˌjuː piː ˈsiː/ *abbr.* (*NAmE*, *specialist*) Universal Product Code: *The Universal Product Code symbol, also known as the 'barcode', is printed on products for sale and contains information that a computer can read.*

**up-close** /ˌʌp ˈkləʊs/ *adj.* in a position very near to sth: *The highlight of the safari was having an up-close encounter with a giraffe.* ⊃ see also CLOSE¹ at CLOSE² *adv.*

**up·com·ing** /ˈʌpkʌmɪŋ/ *adj.* [only before noun] going to happen soon: *the upcoming presidential election* ◊ *a single from the band's upcoming album*

**up-'country** *adj.* [only before noun] relating to an area of a country that is not near large towns ▶ **up-'country** *adv.*

**up·cycle** /ˈʌpsaɪkl/ *verb* ~ **sth** to treat an item that has already been used in such a way that you make sth of greater quality or value than the original item: *Plastic straws have been upcycled into jewellery.* ⊃ see also RECYCLE ▶ **up·cycled** *adj.*: *This wallet is made from 98 per cent upcycled bicycle inner tubes.*

**up·date** *verb, noun*
■ **verb** /ʌpˈdeɪt/ **1** ~ **sth** to make sth more modern by adding new parts, etc: *an updated version of the app* **2** to give sb the most recent information about sth; to add the most recent information to sth **SYN** **bring up to date**: ~ **sb (on sth)** *I called the office to update them on the day's developments.* ◊ ~ **sth (with sth)** *The site tells you when the information was **last updated**.*
■ **noun** /ˈʌpdeɪt/ **1** a report or broadcast that gives the most recent information about sth; a new version of sth containing the most recent information: *They will send you regular updates by email.* ◊ **on sth** *Now let's get an update on our other big story of the day.* **2** (*computing*) the most recent improvements to a computer program that are sent to users of the program: *software updates* ◊ *How do I get myself set up to receive **automatic updates**?*

**updo** /ˈʌpduː/ *noun* (*informal*) (*pl.* **updos**) long hair that is pulled away from the face and fastened on top or at the back of the head

**up·draught** (*BrE*) (*NAmE* **up·draft**) /ˈʌpdrɑːft/ *NAmE* -dræft/ *noun* a movement of air going upwards: *hawks riding the thermal updraughts* **OPP** **downdraught**

**upend** /ʌpˈend/ *verb* ~ **sb/sth** to turn sb/sth the wrong way up or onto one end: *The bicycle lay upended in a ditch.*

**up-field** /ˌʌpˈfiːld/ *adv.* (*sport*) towards your opponent's end of the playing field

**up·front** /ˌʌpˈfrʌnt/ *adj.* **1** ~ **(about sth)** not trying to hide what you think or do SYN **honest, frank**: *He's been upfront about his intentions since the beginning.* **2** [only before noun] paid in advance, before other payments are made: *There will be an upfront fee of 4%.* ⇒ see also UP FRONT at FRONT *noun*

**up·grad·ation** /ˌʌpɡreɪˈdeɪʃn, -ɡrəˈd-/ *noun* [U] (*IndE*) the fact of UPGRADING sth: *the upgradation of civic facilities in large cities*

**up·grade** B2+ C1 *verb, noun*
- *verb* /ˌʌpˈɡreɪd; NAmE also ˈʌpɡreɪd/ **1** B2+ [T, I] to make a machine, computer system, etc. more powerful and efficient; to start using a new and better version of a machine, system, etc.: ~ *sth We are constantly upgrading our software to meet customers' needs.* ◇ ~ **(from sth) (to sth)** *customers who want to upgrade from version 4.2 to version 4.5* **2** B2+ C1 [T] ~ **sth** to improve the condition of a building, etc. in order to provide a better service: *to upgrade the town's leisure facilities* ◇ compare DOWNGRADE **3** [T, often passive] to give sb a better seat on a plane, room in a hotel, etc. than the one that they have paid for: **be upgraded (to sth)** *On the flight back, we were upgraded to business class.* **4** [T] ~ **sb (to sth)** to give sb a more important job SYN **promote**
- *noun* /ˈʌpɡreɪd/ **1** B2+ C1 ~ **(to sth)** the act of making a machine, computer system, etc. more powerful and efficient; the more powerful and efficient machine, computer system, etc: *instructions for installing an upgrade to the existing system* **2** the act of improving the condition of a building, etc. in order to provide a better service **3** the act of giving sb a better seat on a plane, room in a hotel, etc. than the one that they paid for; the seat, room, etc. itself

**up·heav·al** /ʌpˈhiːvl/ *noun* [C, U] a big change that causes a lot of worry and problems SYN **disruption**: *the latest upheavals in the education system* ◇ *I can't face the upheaval of moving house again.* ◇ *a period of emotional upheaval*

**up·hill** /ˌʌpˈhɪl/ *adj., adv.*
- *adj.* **1** sloping upwards: *an uphill climb/slope* ◇ *The last part of the race is all uphill.* OPP **downhill 2** ~ **battle, struggle, task,** etc. an argument or a struggle that is difficult to win and takes a lot of effort over a long period of time
- *adv.* towards the top of a hill or slope: *We cycled uphill for over an hour.* ◇ *The path slopes steeply uphill.* OPP **downhill**

**up·hold** B2+ C1 /ʌpˈhəʊld/ *verb* (**up·held, up·held** /-ˈheld/) **1** B2+ C1 ~ **sth** to support sth that you think is right and make sure that it continues to exist: *We have a duty to uphold the law.* **2** B2+ C1 ~ **sth** (especially of a court of law) to agree that a previous decision was correct or that a request is reasonable: *to uphold a conviction/an appeal/a complaint* ▶ **up·hold·er** *noun*: *an upholder of traditional values*

**up·hol·ster** /ʌpˈhəʊlstə(r)/ *verb* [usually passive] ~ **sth (in sth)** to cover a chair, etc. with soft material (= PADDING) and cloth or leather

**up·hol·ster·er** /ʌpˈhəʊlstərə(r)/ *noun* a person whose job is to upholster furniture

**up·hol·stery** /ʌpˈhəʊlstəri/ *noun* [U] **1** soft material that covers furniture such as ARMCHAIRS and SOFAS **2** the process or trade of UPHOLSTERING

**up·keep** /ˈʌpkiːp/ *noun* [U] **1** ~ **(of sth)** the cost or process of keeping sth in good condition SYN **maintenance**: *Tenants are responsible for the upkeep of rented property.* **2** ~ **(of sb / sth)** the cost or process of giving a child or an animal the things that they need: *He makes payments to his ex-wife for the upkeep of their children.*

**up·land** /ˈʌplənd/ *noun* [C, usually pl., U] an area of high land that is not near the coast ▶ **up·land** *adj.* [only before noun]: *upland agriculture*

**up·lift** *noun, verb*
- *noun* /ˈʌplɪft/ [U, sing.] **1** the fact of sth being raised or of sth increasing: *an uplift in sales* ◇ *an uplift bra* (= that raises the breasts) **2** a feeling of hope and happiness: *The news gave them a much needed uplift.* **3** (*geology*) the

---

1721 **the upper crust**

process or result of land being moved to a higher level by movements inside the earth
- *verb* /ʌpˈlɪft/ ~ **sb** (*formal*) to make sb feel happier or give sb more hope

**up·lift·ed** /ʌpˈlɪftɪd/ *adj.* **1** [not before noun] feeling happy and full of hope **2** (*literary*) lifted upwards: *a sea of uplifted faces*

**up·lift·ing** /ʌpˈlɪftɪŋ/ *adj.* making you feel happier or giving you more hope: *an uplifting experience/speech*

**up·link** /ˈʌplɪŋk/ *noun* (*specialist*) a communications link to a satellite

**up·load** *verb, noun*
- *verb* /ˌʌpˈləʊd/ ~ **sth** (*computing*) to send data to another computer OPP **download**
- *noun* /ˈʌpləʊd/ (*computing*) data that has been moved to a larger computer system from a smaller one OPP **download**

**up·mar·ket** /ˌʌpˈmɑːkɪt; NAmE -ˈmɑːrk-/ (*especially BrE*) (NAmE *also* **up·scale**) *adj.* [usually before noun] designed for or used by people who belong to a high social class or have a lot of money: *an upmarket restaurant* OPP **downmarket** ▶ **up·mar·ket** (*BrE*) (NAmE **up·scale**) *adv.*: *The company has been forced to move more upmarket.*

**upon** ⓘ B1 /əˈpɒn; NAmE əˈpɑːn/ *prep.* **1** B1 (*formal, especially BrE*) = ON: *The decision was based upon two considerations.* HELP *Although the word* **upon** *has the same meaning as* **on**, *it is usually used in more formal contexts or in phrases such as: once upon a time and: row upon row of seats.* **2** ... **upon** ... used to emphasize that there is a large number or amount of sth: *mile upon mile of dusty road* ◇ *thousands upon thousands of letters*
IDM **(almost) u'pon you** if sth in the future is **almost upon you**, it is going to arrive or happen very soon: *The summer season was almost upon them again.* ⇒ more at ONCE *adv.*

**upper** ⓘ B2 ⓞ /ˈʌpə(r)/ *adj., noun*
- *adj.* [only before noun] **1** B2 located above sth else, especially sth of the same type or the other of a pair: *her upper lip* ◇ *the upper floors of the building* **2** B2 at or near the top of sth: *There is an upper limit of £20000 spent on any one project.* ◇ *the upper echelons of society* ◇ *a blockage in the throat or upper airway* ◇ *the upper arm/body* ◇ *in the upper left/right corner of the painting* **3** (of a place) located away from the coast, on high ground or towards the north of an area: *the upper reaches of the river* OPP **lower¹**
IDM **gain, get, have,** etc. **the upper 'hand** to get an advantage over sb so that you are in control of a particular situation ⇒ more at STIFF *adj.*
- *noun* [usually pl.] **1** the top part of a shoe that is attached to the SOLE: *shoes with leather uppers* **2** (*informal*) a drug that makes you feel excited and full of energy ⇒ compare DOWNER
IDM **on your 'uppers** (*BrE, informal*) having very little money

**upper 'case** *noun* [U] (*specialist*) capital letters (= the large form of letters, for example A, B, C rather than a, b, c): *Headings should be in upper case.* ◇ *upper-case letters* ⇒ compare LOWER CASE

**upper 'chamber** *noun* [sing.] = UPPER HOUSE

**the upper 'class** *noun* [sing.] (*also* **the upper 'classes** [pl.]) the groups of people that are considered to have the highest social status and have more money and/or power than other people in society: *a member of the upper class/upper classes* ▶ **upper 'class** *adj.*: *Her family is very upper class.* ◇ *an upper-class accent* ⇒ compare LOWER CLASS, MIDDLE CLASS, WORKING CLASS

**upper·class·man** /ˌʌpəˈklɑːsmən; NAmE ˌʌpərˈklæs-/, **upper·class·woman** /ˌʌpəˈklɑːswʊmən; NAmE ˌʌpərˈklæs-/ *noun* (*pl.* -**men** /-mən/, -**women** /-wɪmɪn/) (in the US) a student in the last two years of HIGH SCHOOL or college ⇒ compare UNDERCLASSMAN

**the upper 'crust** *noun* [sing. + sing. / pl. v.] (*informal*) the people who belong to the highest social class SYN **aristocracy** ▶ **upper-'crust** *adj.*

---

Ⓞ Oxford Phrasal Academic Lexicon (OPAL) written and spoken word lists | Ⓦ OPAL written word list | Ⓢ OPAL spoken word list

# uppercut 1722

**upper-cut** /ˈʌpəkʌt; NAmE ˈʌpərk-/ noun (in boxing) a way of hitting sb on the CHIN (= part of the face below the mouth), in which you bend your arm and move your hand upwards

**upper ˈhouse** (also ˌupper ˈchamber) (also ˌsecond ˈchamber especially in BrE) noun [sing.] one of the parts of a parliament in countries that have a parliament that is divided into two parts. In the UK it is the House of Lords and in the US it is the Senate. ⊃ compare LOWER HOUSE

**upper-most** /ˈʌpəməʊst; NAmE ˈʌpərm-/ adj., adv.
- **adj. 1** [usually before noun] (formal) higher or nearer the top than other things: *the uppermost branches of the tree* **2** [not usually before noun] more important than other things in a particular situation: *These thoughts were uppermost in my mind.*
- **adv.** (formal) in the highest position; facing upwards: *Place the material on a flat surface, shiny side uppermost.*

**ˈupper school** noun (BrE) a school, or the classes in a school, for older students, usually between the ages of 14 and 18 ⊃ compare LOWER SCHOOL, MIDDLE SCHOOL

**up-pity** /ˈʌpəti/ adj. (old-fashioned, informal) behaving as if you are more important than you really are, especially when this means that you refuse to obey orders

**up-raised** /ˌʌpˈreɪzd/ adj. lifted upwards: *She strode towards them, her fist upraised.*

**up-right** /ˈʌpraɪt/ adj., adv., noun
- **adj. 1** (of a person) not lying down, and with the back straight rather than bent: *an upright posture* ◊ *Gradually raise your body into an upright position.* **2** placed in a VERTICAL position: *Keep the bottle upright.* ◊ *an upright freezer* (= one that is taller than it is wide) **3** (of a person) behaving in a moral and honest way SYN **upstanding**: *an upright citizen* IDM see BOLT adv.
- **adv.** in or into a straight, VERTICAL position: *She sat upright in bed.* ◊ *He managed to pull himself upright.*
- **noun 1** a long piece of wood, metal or plastic that is placed in a VERTICAL position, especially in order to support sth **2** = UPRIGHT PIANO

**up-right-ness** /ˈʌpraɪtnəs/ noun [U] behaviour or attitudes that are very moral and honest

**ˌupright piˈano** (also **upˈright**) noun a piano in which the strings are VERTICAL (= go straight up and down) ⊃ compare GRAND PIANO

**up-ris-ing** /ˈʌpraɪzɪŋ/ noun ~ **(against sth)** a situation in which a group of people join together in order to fight against the people who are in power SYN **rebellion**, **revolt**: *an armed uprising against the government* ◊ *a popular uprising* (= by the ordinary people of the country) ◊ *to crush/suppress an uprising* ⊃ WORDFINDER NOTE at PROTEST

**up-river** /ˌʌpˈrɪvə(r)/ adv. = UPSTREAM

**up-roar** /ˈʌprɔː(r)/ noun [U, sing.] **1** a situation in which people shout and make a lot of noise because they are angry or upset about sth: *The room was **in (an) uproar**.* ◊ *Her comments provoked (an) uproar from the audience.* **2** a situation in which there is a lot of public criticism and angry argument about sth that sb has said or done SYN **outcry**: *The article caused (an) uproar.*

**up-roari-ous** /ʌpˈrɔːriəs/ adj. [usually before noun] **1** in which there is a lot of noise and people laugh or shout a lot: *an uproarious party* **2** extremely funny: *an uproarious story* ► **up-roari-ous-ly** adv.: *The audience laughed uproariously.* ◊ *uproariously funny*

**up-root** /ˌʌpˈruːt/ verb [T] **1** ~ **sth** to pull a tree, plant, etc. out of the ground **2** [I, T] to leave a place where you have lived for a long time; to make sb do this: *We decided to uproot and head for Scotland.* ◊ *uproot yourself/sb* *If I accept the job, it will mean uprooting my family and moving to Italy.*

**ups-a-daisy** /ˈʊps ə deɪzi, ˈʌps/ exclamation = UPSY-DAISY

**up-scale** /ˌʌpˈskeɪl/ adj., verb
- **adj.** [usually before noun] (NAmE) (also especially BrE **upmarket**) designed for or used by people who belong to a

high social class or have a lot of money OPP **downscale** ▶ **upˈscale** (NAmE) (BrE **upˈmarket**) adv.
- **verb 1** ~ **sth** to make sth better, bigger or more powerful: *The pilot project will begin in three areas and then be upscaled to the entire state.* **2** ~ **sth** to change a product so that it will be used or bought by people who have more money or belong to a higher social class

**up-sell** /ˈʌpsel/ verb (**up-sold**, **up-sold** /-səʊld/) [I] (business) to persuade a customer to buy more products or a more expensive product than they originally intended: *You can usually upsell to about half the customers.* ▶ **upˈsell** noun: *Some of the sales team pressure customers into expensive upsells.* **up-sell-ing** noun [U] (business): *You can make great profits from upselling.*

**upset** 🔊 B1 adj., verb, noun
- **adj.** /ʌpˈset/ **1** 🔊 B1 [not before noun] unhappy or disappointed because of sth unpleasant that has happened: ~ **about/at/over (doing) sth** *There's no point getting upset about it.* ◊ ~ **(that)** … *She was upset that he had left without saying goodbye.* **2** an **upset ˈstomach** an illness in the stomach that makes you feel sick (= want to VOMIT) or have DIARRHOEA
- **verb** /ʌpˈset/ (**up-set-ting**, **upset**, **upset**) **1** 🔊 B1 to make sb/ yourself feel unhappy, anxious or annoyed SYN **distress**: ~ **sb/yourself** *This decision is likely to upset a lot of people.* ◊ **it upsets sb that** … *It upset him that nobody had bothered to tell him about it.* ◊ **it upsets sb to do sth** *It upsets me to think of her all alone in that big house.* **2** ~ **sth** to make a plan, situation, etc. go wrong: *He arrived an hour late and upset all our arrangements.* **3** ~ **sb's stomach** to make sb feel sick (= want to VOMIT) after they have eaten or drunk sth **4** ~ **sth** to make sth fall over by hitting it by accident: *She stood up suddenly, upsetting a glass of wine.*
IDM **upset the ˈapple cart** to cause problems for sb or cause their plans, arrangements, etc. to fail
- **noun** /ˈʌpset/ **1** [U] a situation in which there are problems or difficulties, especially when these are unexpected: *The company has survived the recent upset in share prices.* ◊ *His health has not been improved by all the upset at home.* **2** [C] (in a competition) a situation in which a person or team beats the person or team that was expected to win **3** [C] an illness in the stomach that makes you feel sick (= want to VOMIT) or have DIARRHOEA: *a stomach upset* **4** [U, C] the state of being unhappy, disappointed or worried because of sth unpleasant that has happened: *It had been the cause of much emotional upset.*

**up-set-ting** /ʌpˈsetɪŋ/ adj. making you feel unhappy, anxious or annoyed: *an upsetting experience*

**the up-shot** /ði ˈʌpʃɒt; NAmE -ʃɑːt/ noun [sing.] the final result of a series of events SYN **outcome**: *The upshot of it all was that he left college and got a job.*

**up-side** /ˈʌpsaɪd/ noun [sing.] the more positive aspect of a situation that is generally bad OPP **downside**

**upside ˈdown** adv. in or into a position in which the top of sth is where the bottom is normally found and the bottom is where the top is normally found: *The canoe floated upside down on the lake.* OPP **right side up** ▶ **ˌupside ˈdown** adj. [not usually before noun]: *The painting looks like it's upside down to me.*
IDM **turn sth upside ˈdown 1** to make a place untidy when looking for sth: *The police turned the whole house upside down looking for clues.* **2** to cause big changes in a person's life that upset and confuse them: *His sudden death turned her world upside down.*

**up-si-lon** /ʌpˈsaɪlən, ˈʊpsɪlɒn; NAmE ˈʊpsɪlɑːn/ noun the 20th letter of the Greek alphabet (Υ, υ)

**up-skill** /ˈʌpskɪl/ verb [T, I] ~ **(sb)** (business) to teach sb new skills; to learn new skills: *The company has invested heavily in upskilling its workforce.* ▶ **upˈskill-ing** noun [U]

**up-stage** /ˌʌpˈsteɪdʒ/ adv., adj., verb
- **adv., adj.** at or towards the back of the stage in a theatre OPP **downstage**
- **verb** ~ **sb** to say or do sth that makes people notice you more than the person that they should be interested in: *She was furious at being upstaged by her younger sister.*

**up·stairs** /ˌʌpˈsteəz; NAmE -ˈsterz/ adv., adj., noun
- **adv.** up the stairs; on or to a floor of a house or other building higher than the one that you are on: *to run/walk/head upstairs* ◊ *The cat belongs to the people who live upstairs.* ◊ *She went upstairs to get dressed.* **OPP** downstairs
- **adj.** [only before noun] on a floor of a house or other building that is higher than the one that you are on: *an upstairs room/bedroom/window/bathroom* **OPP** downstairs
- **noun** [sing.] the floor or floors in a building that are above the ground floor: *We've converted the upstairs into an office.* **OPP** downstairs

**up·stand·ing** /ˌʌpˈstændɪŋ/ adj. [usually before noun] (formal) behaving in a moral and honest way **SYN** upright: *an upstanding member of the community*
**IDM** **be upˈstanding** (BrE, formal) used in a formal situation to tell people to stand up: *Ladies and gentlemen, please be upstanding for the bride and groom.*

**up·start** /ˈʌpstɑːt; NAmE -stɑːrt/ noun (disapproving) a person who has just started in a new position or job but who behaves as if they were more important than other people, in a way that is annoying

**up·state** /ˌʌpˈsteɪt/ adv. (US) in or to a part of a state that is far from its main cities, especially a northern part: *They retired and went to live upstate.* **OPP** downstate ▶ **up·state** adj. [only before noun]: *upstate New York*

**up·stream** /ˌʌpˈstriːm/ (*also less frequent* **up·river**) adv. ~ (of/from sth) along a river, in the opposite direction to the way in which the water flows: *The nearest town is about ten miles upstream.* ◊ *upstream of/from the bridge* **OPP** downstream

**up·surge** /ˈʌpsɜːdʒ; NAmE -sɜːrdʒ/ noun [usually sing.] (formal) a sudden large increase in sth: ~ **(in sth)** *an upsurge in violent crime* ◊ ~ **(of sth)** *a recent upsurge of interest in his movies*

**up·swing** /ˈʌpswɪŋ/ noun [usually sing.] ~ **(in sth)** a situation in which sth improves or increases over a period of time **SYN** upturn: *an upswing in economic activity* ◊ *an upswing in the team's fortunes*

**upsy-daisy** /ˈʊpsi deɪzi, ˈʌp-/ (*also* **ups-a-daisy**, **oops-a-daisy**) exclamation (used to or by a young child) said when you have fallen down, dropped sth, etc. or when sb else has

**up·take** /ˈʌpteɪk/ noun [U, sing.] **1** ~ **(of sth)** the use that is made of sth that has become available: *There has been a high uptake of the free training.* **2** ~ **(of sth)** (specialist) the process by which sth is taken into a body or system; the rate at which this happens: *the uptake of oxygen by muscles*
**IDM** **be quick/ˈslow on the ˈuptake** (informal) to be quick/slow to understand sth: *Is he always this slow on the uptake?*

**up·tempo** /ˈʌptempəʊ/ adj. (especially of music) fast: *up-tempo dance tunes*

**up·tick** /ˈʌptɪk/ noun (NAmE, economics) a small increase in the level or value of sth: *The futures market is showing an uptick.* **OPP** downtick

**up·tight** /ˌʌpˈtaɪt/ adj. **1** ~ **(about sth)** (informal) anxious and/or angry about sth: *Relax! You're getting too uptight about it.* **2** ~ **(about sth)** (especially NAmE, informal) nervous about showing your feelings: *an uptight teenager*

**up·time** /ˈʌptaɪm/ noun [U] the time during which a machine, especially a computer, is working **OPP** downtime

**up to ˈdate** adj. **1** modern; fashionable: *This technology is bang up to date* (= completely modern). ◊ *up-to-date clothes* ◊ *up-to-date equipment* **2** having or including the most recent information: *We are keeping up to date with the latest developments.* ◊ **up-to-date information** ◊ *She brought him up to date with what had happened.* ⊃ see also OUT OF DATE

**up-to-the-ˈminute** adj. [usually before noun] **1** having or including the most recent information: *up-to-the-minute news* **2** modern; fashionable: *up-to-the-minute designs* ⊃ see also UP TO THE MINUTE at MINUTE¹ noun

**up·town** /ˌʌpˈtaʊn/ adv., adj. (NAmE)
- **adv.** in or to the parts of a town or city that are away from the centre, where people live: *They live in an apartment uptown.* ◊ *We walked uptown a couple of blocks until we found a cab.* ⊃ compare DOWNTOWN, MIDTOWN
- **adj.** **1** [only before noun] in, to or typical of the parts of a town or city that are away from the centre, where people live: *an uptown train* **2** typical of an area of a town or city where people have a lot of money: *uptown prices* ◊ *an uptown girl*

**up·trend** /ˈʌptrend/ noun [usually sing.] (NAmE) a situation in which business activity or performance increases or improves over a period of time **OPP** downtrend

**up·turn** /ˈʌptɜːn; NAmE -tɜːrn/ noun [usually sing.] ~ **(in sth)** a situation in which sth improves or increases over a period of time **SYN** upswing: *an upturn in the economy* ◊ *The restaurant trade is on the upturn.* **OPP** downturn

**up·turned** /ˌʌpˈtɜːnd; NAmE -ˈtɜːrnd/ adj. [usually before noun] **1** pointing or facing upwards: *an upturned nose* (= that curves upwards at the end) ◊ *She looked down at the sea of upturned faces.* **2** turned into a position in which the top part is where the bottom part normally is: *She sat on an upturned box.*

**uPVC** /ˌjuː piː viː ˈsiː/ noun [U] a strong plastic used to make window frames and pipes (the abbreviation for 'unplasticized polyvinyl chloride')

**up·vote** /ˈʌpvəʊt/ verb, noun
- **verb** [T, I] ~ **(sth)** to show that you agree with an online article or comment by using a particular ICON: *Very few people upvoted his comments.* ◊ *You can upvote, comment and always find plenty of cool stuff.* **OPP** downvote
- **noun** an act of showing that you agree with an online article or comment by using a particular ICON: *You definitely get an upvote from me.* **OPP** downvote

**up·ward** /ˈʌpwəd; NAmE -wərd/ adj. **1** pointing towards or facing a higher place: *an upward gaze* **2** increasing in amount or price: *an upward movement in property prices* **OPP** downward

**upwardly ˈmobile** adj. moving towards a higher social position, usually in which you become richer: *upwardly mobile immigrant groups* ◊ *an upwardly mobile lifestyle*
▶ **upward moˈbility** noun [U]

**up·wards** /ˈʌpwədz; NAmE -wərdz/ (*especially BrE*) (*also* **up·ward** *especially in NAmE*) adv. **1** towards a higher place or position: *Place your hands on the table with the palms facing upwards.* ◊ *We are moving upwards at an incredible speed.* **OPP** downwards **2** towards a higher amount or price: *Bad weather forced the price of fruit upwards.* ◊ *The budget has been revised upwards.* **OPP** downwards **3** ~ **of sth** more than the amount or number mentioned: *You should expect to pay upwards of £50 for a hotel room.*

**up·wind** /ˌʌpˈwɪnd/ adv., adj. in the opposite direction to the way in which the wind is blowing: *to sail upwind* ◊ *The house was upwind of the factory and its smells* (= the wind did not blow the smells towards the house). **OPP** downwind

**ur·an·ium** /juˈreɪniəm/ noun [U] (symb. **U**) a chemical element. Uranium is a heavy, silver-white, RADIOACTIVE metal, used mainly in producing nuclear energy.

**Ura·nus** /ˈjʊərənəs; NAmE ˈjʊrənəs/ noun the planet in the SOLAR SYSTEM that is 7th in order of distance from the sun

**urban** /ˈɜːbən; NAmE ˈɜːrb-/ adj. **1** [usually before noun] connected with a town or city: *urban and rural communities* ◊ *urban areas/centres* ◊ *the urban environment/landscape* ◊ *urban development* (= the process of building towns and cities or making them larger) ◊ *urban renewal/regeneration* (= the process of improving the buildings, etc. in the poor parts of a town or city) ◊ *efforts to control urban sprawl* (= the spread of city buildings into the countryside) ⊃ compare RURAL ⊃ WORDFINDER NOTE at CITY **2** [only before noun] connected with types of music such as RHYTHM AND BLUES, REGGAE, SOUL, etc. that are

ian music played by black musicians: *today's urban music scene* ◊ *urban radio shows*

**ur·bane** /ɜːˈbeɪn; NAmE ɜːrˈb-/ *adj.* (especially of a man) good at knowing what to say and how to behave in social situations; appearing relaxed and confident ▶ **ur·bane·ly** *adv.* **ur·ban·ity** /-ˈbænəti/ *noun* [U]

**ur·ban·ite** /ˈɜːbənaɪt; NAmE ˈɜːrb-/ *noun* a person who lives in a town or city

**ur·ban·ized** (*BrE also* **-ised**) /ˈɜːbənaɪzd; NAmE ˈɜːrb-/ *adj.* **1** (of an area, a country, etc.) having a lot of towns, streets, factories, etc. rather than countryside **2** (of people) living and working in towns and cities rather than in the country: *an increasingly urbanized society* ▶ **ur·ban·iza·tion, -isa·tion** /ˌɜːbənaɪˈzeɪʃn; NAmE ˌɜːrbənəˈz-/ *noun* [U]

**ˌurban ˈmyth** (*also* ˌ**urban ˈlegend**) *noun* a story about a strange event that is supposed to have happened (but did not really happen) that is often repeated and that many people believe is true

**ur·chin** /ˈɜːtʃɪn; NAmE ˈɜːrtʃ-/ *noun* **1** (*old-fashioned*) a young child who is poor and dirty, often one who has no home: *a dirty little street urchin* **2** = SEA URCHIN

**Urdu** /ˈʊədu:, ˈɜːdu:; NAmE ˈʊrdu:, ˈɜːr-/ *noun* [U] the official language of Pakistan, also widely used in India

**-ure** /ə(r)/ *suffix* (in nouns) the action, process or result of: *closure* ◊ *failure*

**urea** /jʊˈriːə/ *noun* [U] (*specialist*) a clear substance containing NITROGEN that is found especially in URINE

**ur·ethra** /jʊˈriːθrə/ *noun* (*anatomy*) the tube that carries liquid waste out of the body. In men and male animals SPERM also flows along this tube. ▶ **ur·eth·ral** /-θrəl/ *adj.* [only before noun]

**urge** ❶ B2 /ɜːdʒ; NAmE ɜːrdʒ/ *verb, noun*

■ *verb* **1** B2 to advise or try hard to persuade sb to do sth: ~ **sb to do sth** *If you ever get the chance to visit this place, I strongly urge you to do so.* ◊ ~ **that …** *The report urged that all children be taught to swim.* ◊ ~ **(sb) + speech** *'Why not give it a try?' she urged (him).* ⊃ SYNONYMS *at* RECOMMEND **2** B2 to recommend sth strongly: ~ **sth** *The situation is dangerous and the UN is urging caution.* **3** ~ **sb/sth + adv./prep.** (*formal*) to make a person or an animal move more quickly and/or in a particular direction, especially by pushing or forcing them: *He urged his horse forward.* PHR V ˌ**urge sb**↔**ˈon** to encourage sb to do sth or support them so that they do it better: *She could hear him urging her on as she ran past.*

■ *noun* a strong desire to do sth: *sexual urges* ◊ ~ **to do sth** *I had a sudden urge to hit him.*

**ur·gent** ❶+ B2 /ˈɜːdʒənt; NAmE ˈɜːrdʒ-/ *adj.* **1**+ B2 that needs to be dealt with or happen immediately SYN **pressing**: *an urgent appeal for information* ◊ *a problem that requires urgent attention* ◊ *'Can I see you for a moment?' 'Is it urgent?'* ◊ *Mark the message 'urgent', please.* ◊ *The law is* **in urgent need of** *reform.* **2** showing that you think that sth needs to be dealt with immediately: *an urgent whisper* ▶ **ur·gen·cy** /-dʒənsi/ *noun* [sing.]: *This is a matter of some urgency.* ◊ *The attack added a new urgency to the peace talks.* **ur·gent·ly** *adv.*: *New equipment is urgently needed.* ◊ *I need to speak to her urgently.* ◊ *'We must find him,' she said urgently.*

**urgh** /əx; NAmE ərx/ *exclamation* = UGH: *Urgh! There's a dead fly in my coffee!*

**ur·inal** /jʊəˈraɪnl, ˈjʊərɪnl; NAmE ˈjʊr-/ *noun* a type of toilet for men that is attached to the wall; a room or building containing urinals

**urin·ary** /ˈjʊərənəri; NAmE ˈjʊrəneri/ *adj.* [usually before noun] (*medical*) connected with URINE or the parts of the body through which it passes

**urin·ate** /ˈjʊərəneɪt; NAmE ˈjʊr-/ *verb* [I] (*formal or specialist*) to get rid of URINE from the body ▶ **urin·ation** /ˌjʊərəˈneɪʃn; NAmE ˌjʊr-/ *noun* [U]

**urine** /ˈjʊərɪn, -raɪn; NAmE ˈjʊrɪn/ (*also informal* **wee** especially *in BrE*) *noun* [U] the waste liquid that collects in the BLADDER and that you pass from your body

**URL** /ˌjuː ɑːr ˈel/ *abbr.* (*computing*) uniform/universal resource locator (typically, the address of a WORLD WIDE WEB page): ⊃ WORDFINDER NOTE *at* WEBSITE

**urn** /ɜːn; NAmE ɜːrn/ *noun* **1** a tall decorated container, especially one used for holding the ASHES of a dead person **2** a large metal container with a TAP, used for making and/or serving tea or coffee: *a tea urn*

**ur·ology** /jʊəˈrɒlədʒi; NAmE jʊˈrɑːl-/ *noun* [U] (*medical*) the scientific study of the URINARY system ▶ **uro·logic·al** /ˌjʊərəˈlɒdʒɪkl; NAmE ˌjʊrəˈlɑːdʒ-/ *adj.* **uro·lo·gist** /jʊəˈrɒlədʒɪst; NAmE jʊˈrɑːl-/ *noun*

**ur·sine** /ˈɜːsaɪn; NAmE ˈɜːrs-/ *adj.* [usually before noun] (*specialist or literary*) connected with bears; like a bear

**ur·ti·caria** /ˌɜːtɪˈkeəriə; NAmE ˌɜːrtɪˈker-/ *noun* (*medical*) [U] (*also* **hives** [U, pl.]) red spots on the skin that ITCH (= make you want to rub your skin with your nails), caused by an ALLERGIC reaction, for example to certain foods

**US** (*also* **U.S.** *especially in US*) /ˌjuː ˈes/ *abbr.* UNITED STATES (OF AMERICA): *She became a US citizen.* ◊ *the US dollar*

**us** ❶ A1 /əs, *strong form* ʌs/ *pron.* (the object form of **we**) **1** A1 used when the speaker or writer and another or others are the object of a verb or preposition, or after the verb *be*: *She gave us a picture as a wedding present.* ◊ *We'll take the dog with us.* ◊ *Hello, it's us back again.* **2** (*BrE, informal*) *me*: *Give us the newspaper, will you?*

**USA** (*also* **U.S.A.** *especially in NAmE*) /ˌjuː es ˈeɪ/ *abbr.* UNITED STATES OF AMERICA: *Do you need a visa for the USA?*

**us·able** /ˈjuːzəbl/ *adj.* that can be used; in good enough condition to be used: *How can we display this data in a usable form?* ◊ *The bike is rusty but usable.* OPP **unusable** ▶ **us·abil·ity** /ˌjuːzəˈbɪləti/ *noun* [U]: *They are improving the accessibility and usability of government websites.*

**USAF** /ˌjuː es eɪ ˈef/ *abbr.* United States Air Force

**usage** ❷+ B2 W /ˈjuːsɪdʒ, ˈjuːzɪdʒ/ *noun* **1** ❷+ B2 [U, C] the way in which words are used in a language: *current English usage* ◊ *It's not a word in common usage.* **2** ❷+ B2 [U] the fact of sth being used; how much sth is used: *land usage* ◊ *Car usage is predicted to increase.*

**USB** /ˌjuː es ˈbiː/ *abbr.* (*computing*) universal serial bus (the system for connecting other pieces of equipment to a computer): *All new PCs now have USB sockets.* ◊ *a USB port*

**ˌUSB ˈdrive** (*also informal* ˌ**USB ˈstick**) *noun* = FLASH DRIVE

**USCIS** /ˌjuː es si: aɪ ˈes/ *abbr.* United States Citizenship and Immigration Services (the US government department that deals with people from other countries who want to visit or live in the US or become a US citizen, part of the Department of Homeland Security)

**use** ❶ A1 ● *verb, noun*

■ *verb* /juːz/ (**used, used** /juːzd/) **1** ❶ A1 [T] to do sth with a machine, a method, an object, etc. for a particular purpose: ~ **sth** *Can I use the photocopier?* ◊ *He makes beer using traditional methods.* ◊ *How often do you use (= travel by) the bus?* ◊ *They were able to achieve a settlement without using military force.* ◊ *a widely used technique for assessing the strength of metals* ◊ *I have some information you may be able to use (= to get an advantage from).* ◊ ~ **sth for (doing) sth** *We used a carrot for the snowman's nose.* ◊ ~ **sth to do sth** *Police used tear gas to disperse the crowds.* ◊ ~ **sth as sth** *The building is currently being used as a warehouse.* **2** ❷ A1 [T] ~ **sth** to take a particular amount of a liquid, substance, etc. in order to achieve or make sth: *This type of heater uses a lot of electricity.* ◊ *I hope you haven't used all the milk.* **3** A1 [T] to say or write particular words or a particular type of language: ~ **sth** *The poem uses simple language.* ◊ *That's a word I never use.* ◊ *You have to use the past tense.* ◊ ~ **sth to do sth** *'Pop art' is a term* **used to** *describe a movement that began in the 1950s.* **4** [T] ~ **sb** (*disapproving*) to be kind, friendly, etc. to sb with the intention of getting an advantage for yourself from them SYN **exploit**: *Can't you see he's just using you for his own ends?* ◊ *I felt used.* **5** [T, I] ~ **(sth)** to take illegal

| æ cat | ɑː father | e bed | ɜː fur | ə about | ɪ sit | iː see | i happy | ɒ got (*BrE*) | ɔː saw | ʌ cup | ʊ put | uː too |

drugs: *Most of the inmates have used drugs at some point in their lives.* ◊ (*slang*) *She's been using since she was 13.* **IDM** **I, you, etc. could 'use sth** (*informal*) used to say that you would like to have sth very much: *I think we could all use a drink after that!* **use your 'head** (*BrE also* **use your 'loaf**) (*informal*) used to tell sb to think about sth, especially when they have asked for your opinion or said sth stupid: *'Why don't you want to see him again?' 'Oh, use your head!'* **ORIGIN** From rhyming slang, in which **loaf of bread** stands for 'head'. **PHRV** **,use sth⇿'up** to use all of sth so that there is none left: *Making soup is a good way of using up leftover vegetables.*

■ **noun** /juːs/ **1** 🔊 **A2** [U, sing.] the act of using sth; the state of being used: *A ban was imposed on the use of chemical weapons.* ◊ *You can't justify the use of military force.* ◊ *I'm not sure that this is the most valuable use of my time.* ◊ **for~ in sth** *The software is designed for use in schools.* ◊ **in ~** *The chapel was built in the 12th century and is still in use today.* ⊃ see also POINT OF USE **2** 🔊 **A2** [C, U] a purpose for which sth is used; a way in which sth is or can be used: *The plant has various medical uses.* ◊ **~for sth** *Can you find a use for this old table?* ◊ *What use is a mouse without a computer?* ⊃ see also SINGLE-USE **3** [U] **~(of sth)** the right or opportunity to use sth, for example sth that belongs to sb else: *I have the use of the car this week.* **4** [U] the ability to use your mind or body: *He lost the use of his legs* (= became unable to walk) *in an accident.* **5** [C] a particular word or phrase, used with a particular meaning: *The phrase 'all told' comes from an old use of the verb 'tell', meaning 'to count'.* **IDM** **,be no 'use (to sb)** (*also formal* **be of no 'use**) to not be useful or helpful: *You can throw those away—they're no use to anyone.* **be of 'use (to sb)** (*formal*) to be useful: *Can I be of any use* (= can I help)? **HELP** In questions, you can leave out 'of': *Is it any use to you?* **come into/go out of, etc. 'use** to start/stop being used: *When did this word come into common use?* **have its/their/your 'uses** (*informal, often humorous*) to be useful sometimes: *I know you don't like him, but he has his uses.* **have no 'use for sb** to dislike sb: *I've no use for people who don't make an effort.* **have no 'use for sth** to not need sth **it's no 'use (doing sth) | what's the 'use (of doing sth)?** used to say that there is no point in doing sth because it will not be successful or have a good result: *What's the use of worrying about it?* ◊ *It's no use—I can't persuade her.* **make 'use of sth/sb** to use sth/sb, especially in order to get an advantage: *We could make better use of our resources.* ◊ **to make effective use of technology** **put sth to good 'use** to be able to use sth for a purpose, and get an advantage from doing so: *She'll be able to put her languages to good use in her new job.*

**used¹** 🔊 **B1** Ⓢ /juːst/ *adj.* familiar with sth because you do it or experience it often: **~to (sb/sth) doing sth** *I'm not used to eating so much at lunchtime.* ◊ **~to sb/sth** *I found the job tiring at first but I soon got used to it.* ⊃ note at USED TO

**used²** 🔊 **B1** /juːzd/ *adj.* [usually before noun] **1** 🔊 **B1** that has belonged to or been used by sb else before **SYN** second-hand: *used cars* **2** that has already been used: *a used teabag*

**'used to** 🔊 **A2** /ˈjuːst tə, *before vowels and finally* tu/ *modal verb* (*negative* **didn't use to** /,dɪdnt ˈjuːs tə, *before vowels and finally* tu/, *also BrE, old-fashioned or formal* **used not to**, *short form* **usedn't to** /ˈjuːsnt tə, *before vowels and finally* tu/) used to say that sth happened continuously or frequently during a period in the past: *I used to live in London.* ◊ *That's what my father always used to say.* ◊ *I didn't use to like him much when we were at school.* ◊ *Didn't you use to have long hair?* ⊃ note at MODAL

**use·ful** 🔊 **A1** Ⓞ /ˈjuːsfl/ *adj.* **1** 🔊 **A1** that can help you to do or achieve what you want: *a useful tool* ◊ **~to sb** *He might be useful to us.* ◊ **~for sb/sth** *The mortgages are especially useful for people with fluctuating incomes.* ◊ **~for doing sth** *These plants are particularly useful for brightening up shady areas.* ◊ **it is~(for sb) to do sth** *It can be useful to write a short summary of your argument*

1725 **user interface**

▼ **GRAMMAR POINT**

**used to**
● Except in negatives and questions, the correct form is **used to**: *I used to go there every Saturday.* ◊ ~~*I use to go there every Saturday.*~~
● To form questions, use *did*: *Did she use to have long hair?* Note that the correct spelling is **use to**, not 'used to'.
● The negative form is usually **didn't use to**, but in *BrE* this is quite informal and is not usually used in writing.
● The negative form **used not to** (*rather formal*) and the question form **used you to ...?** (*old-fashioned and very formal*) are only used in *BrE*, usually in writing.

▼ **WHICH WORD?**

**used to / be used to**
● Do not confuse **used to do sth** with **be used to sth**.
● You use **used to do sth** to talk about something that happened regularly or was the case in the past, but is not now: *I used to smoke, but I gave up a couple of years ago.*
● You use **be used to (doing) sth** to talk about something that you are familiar with so that it no longer seems new or strange to you: *We're used to the noise from the traffic now.* ◊ *I'm used to getting up early.* You can also use **get used to sth**: *Don't worry—you'll soon get used to his sense of humour.* ◊ *I didn't think I could ever get used to living in a big city after living in the country.*

first. ◊ **~in (doing) sth** *These drugs are useful in the treatment of many forms of cancer.* ◊ *This information could prove useful.* **2** *Both scholars and general readers will find the book extremely useful.* **2** (*BrE informal*) good; of the right standard **SYN** **competent**: *He's a very useful player.* ▶ **use·ful·ly** /-fəli/ *adv.*: *The money could be more usefully spent on new equipment.*

**use·ful·ness** /ˈjuːsflnəs/ *noun* [U] the fact of being useful or possible to use: *There are doubts about the usefulness of these tests.* ◊ *The building has outlived its usefulness.*

**use·less** 🔊+ **B2** /ˈjuːsləs/ *adj.* **1** 🔊+ **B2** not useful; not doing or achieving what is needed or wanted: *This pen is useless.* ◊ **~to do sth** *He knew it was useless to protest.* ◊ **~doing sth** *It's useless worrying about it.* ◊ *She tried to work, but it was useless* (= she wasn't able to). **2** 🔊+ **B2** (*informal*) not very good at sth; not able to do things well: **~at (doing) sth** *I'm useless at French.* ◊ *Don't ask her to help. She's useless.* ▶ **use·less·ly** *adv.* **use·less·ness** *noun* [U]

**user** 🔊 **A2** /ˈjuːzə(r)/ *noun* **1** 🔊 **A2** a person or thing that uses sth: *road users* ◊ *The service allows users to download and read a wide collection of books for no charge.* ◊ *computer/internet/mobile phone users* ⊃ see also END USER, MULTI-USER, POWER USER **2** (*slang*) a person who uses illegal drugs

**user ex'perience** *noun* (*abbr.* **UX**) (*computing*) what it is like for sb to use a particular product such as a website, for example how easy or pleasant it is to use: *They seek to continuously improve the user experience of the games.*

**'user fee** *noun* (*NAmE*) a tax on a service that is provided for the public

**,user-'friend·ly** *adj.* easy for people who are not experts to use or understand ▶ **,user-'friend·li·ness** *noun* [U]

**,user-'generated** *adj.* connected with material on a website that has been contributed by the people who use the website: *user-generated content*

**'user group** *noun* a group of people who use a particular thing and who share information about it, especially people who share information about computers on the internet

**,user 'interface** *noun* (*abbr.* **UI**) (*computing*) the way a computer gives information to a user or receives instructions from a user: *It features an intuitive, easy-to-use user interface.*

# username 1726

**user·name** /'juːzəneɪm; NAmE -zərn-/ (also **user I'D**) noun (computing) the name you use in order to be able to use a computer program or system: *Please enter your username.*

**usher** /'ʌʃə(r)/ noun, verb
- noun **1** a person who shows people where to sit in a church, public hall, etc. **2** an official who has special responsibilities in court, for example allowing people in and out of the court **3** a friend of the couple at a wedding who helps show people to their seats ⊃ compare BEST MAN, BRIDESMAID, GROOMSMAN
- verb ~ sb + adv./prep. to take or show sb where they should go: *The secretary ushered me into his office.*
⊃ SYNONYMS at TAKE
**PHRV** **usher sth⟷ˈin** (formal) to be the beginning of sth new or to make sth new begin: *The change of management ushered in fresh ideas and policies.*

**USN** /ˌjuː es 'en/ abbr. United States Navy

**the U.S. of A.** /ðə ˌjuː ˌes əv 'eɪ/ noun [sing.] (NAmE, informal, humorous) the United States of America: *It's nice to be back in the U.S. of A.*

**USP** /ˌjuː es 'piː/ noun (business) a feature of a product or service that makes it different from all the others that are available and is a reason for people to choose it (the abbreviation for 'unique selling proposition' or 'unique selling point'): *You need to come up with a USP.*

**USPS** (also **U.S.P.S.**) /ˌjuː es piː 'es/ abbr. United States Postal Service (the service in the US that collects and delivers letters)

**USS** /ˌjuː es 'es/ abbr. United States Ship (used before the name of a ship in the US NAVY): *USS Oklahoma*

**USSR** /ˌjuː es es 'ɑː(r)/ abbr. (the former) Union of Soviet Socialist Republics

**ustad** /'uːstɑːd/ noun (IndE) an expert or a person with a special skill, especially a musician: *She learned classical music from an ustad.*

**usual** /'juːʒuəl, -ʒəl/ adj. that happens or is done most of the time or in most cases **SYN** *normal*: *This is the usual way of doing it.* ◇ *He came home later than usual.* ◇ *He didn't sound like his usual happy self.* ◇ ~ **for sb/sth** *This weather is not usual for this time of year.* ◇ **it is ~ (for sb/sth) to do sth** *It is usual to start a speech by thanking everybody for coming.* ⊃ compare UNUSUAL
**2 the usual** noun [sing.] (informal) what usually happens; what you usually have, especially the drink that you usually have
**IDM** **as ˈusual** in the same way as what happens most of the time or in most cases: *Steve, as usual, was the last to arrive.* ◇ *As usual at that hour, the place was deserted.* ◇ *Despite her problems, she carried on working as usual.* **the usual ˈsuspects** the people you would usually expect to do sth or be included in sth: *She thanked all the usual suspects in her acceptance speech: her family, the director, the cast and the crew.* ⊃ more at BUSINESS, PER

**usu·al·ly** /'juːʒuəli, -ʒə-/ adv. in the way that is usual or normal; most often: *How long does the journey usually take?* ◇ *Tension headache is not usually associated with any other symptoms.* ◇ *For Americans, 'mad' usually means 'angry'.*

**us·uri·ous** /juː'ʒʊəriəs; NAmE -'ʒʊr-/ adj. (formal) lending money at very high rates of interest

**usurp** /juː'zɜːp; NAmE -'zɜːrp/ verb ~ **sb/sth** (formal) to take sb's position and/or power without having the right to do this ▶ **usurp·ation** /ˌjuːzɜː'peɪʃn; NAmE -zɜːr'p-/ noun [U, C] **usurp·er** /juː'zɜːpə(r); NAmE -'zɜːrpər/ noun

**usury** /'juːʒəri/ noun [U] (old-fashioned, disapproving) the practice of lending money to people at unfairly high rates of interest

**UTC** /ˌjuː tiː 'siː/ abbr. Universal Time Coordinated (the time based on ATOMIC CLOCKS, used as the basis for legal time in most countries, also known as **Co·ordinated Universal Time** or **Universal Co·ordinated Time**) ⊃ compare GMT

**Utd** abbr. UNITED

**Ute** /juːt/ noun (pl. **Ute** or **Utes**) a member of a Native American people many of whom live in the US states of Colorado and Utah

**ute** /juːt/ noun (AustralE, NZE, informal) a vehicle with low sides and no roof at the back used, for example, by farmers **SYN** *pickup*

**uten·sil** /juː'tensl/ noun (formal) a tool that is used in the house: *cooking/kitchen utensils*

**uterus** /'juːtərəs/ noun (anatomy) the organ in women and female animals in which babies or young animals develop before they are born **SYN** *womb* ▶ **uter·ine** /-raɪn/ adj. [only before noun] ⊃ see also INTRAUTERINE DEVICE

**utili·tar·ian** /ˌjuːtɪlɪ'teəriən; NAmE -'ter-/ adj. **1** (formal) designed to be useful and practical rather than attractive **2** (philosophy) based on or supporting the ideas of utilitarianism

**utili·tar·ian·ism** /ˌjuːtɪlɪ'teəriənɪzəm; NAmE -'ter-/ noun [U] (philosophy) the belief that the right course of action is the one that will produce the greatest happiness of the greatest number of people

**util·ity** /juː'tɪləti/ noun, adj.
- noun (pl. **-ies**) **1** [C] a service provided for the public, for example an electricity, water or gas supply: *a privatized electricity utility* ⊃ see also PUBLIC UTILITY **2** [U] (formal) the quality of being useful **SYN** *usefulness* **3** [C] (computing) a piece of computer software that performs a particular task
- adj. [only before noun] that can be used for several different purposes: *an all-round utility player* (= one who can play equally well in several different positions in a sport) ⊃ see also SPORT UTILITY VEHICLE

**uˈtility room** noun a room, especially in a private house, that contains large pieces of equipment such as a WASHING MACHINE, FREEZER, etc.

**uˈtility vehicle** (also **uˈtility truck**) noun a small truck with low sides designed for carrying light loads

**util·ize** (BrE also **-ise**) /'juːtəlaɪz/ verb ~ **sth** (as sth) (formal) to use sth, especially for a practical purpose **SYN** *make use of*: *The Romans were the first to utilize concrete as a building material.* ◇ *The resources at our disposal could have been better utilized.* ▶ **util·iza·tion**, **-isa·tion** /ˌjuːtəlaɪ'zeɪʃn; NAmE -lə'z-/ noun [U]

**ut·most** /'ʌtməʊst/ adj., noun
- adj. (also less frequent **ut·ter·most**) [only before noun] greatest; most extreme: *This is a matter of the utmost importance.* ◇ *You should study this document with the utmost care.*
- noun [sing.] the greatest amount possible: *Our resources are strained to the utmost.* ◇ *He did his utmost* (= tried as hard as possible) *to persuade me not to go.*

**uto·pia** (also **Uto·pia**) /juː'təʊpiə/ noun [C, U] an imaginary place or state in which everything is perfect **ORIGIN** From the title of a book by Sir Thomas More, which describes a place like this.

**uto·pian** (also **Uto·pian**) /juː'təʊpiən/ adj. having a strong belief that everything can be perfect, often in a way that does not seem to be realistic or practical: *utopian ideals* ◇ *a utopian society* ▶ **uto·pian·ism** (also **Uto·pian·ism**) noun [U]

**utter** /'ʌtə(r)/ adj., verb
- adj. [only before noun] used to emphasize how complete sth is: *That's complete and utter nonsense!* ◇ *To my utter amazement she agreed.* ◇ *He felt an utter fool.*
- verb ~ **sth** (formal) to make a sound with your voice; to say sth: *to utter a cry* ◇ *She did not utter a word during lunch* (= said nothing).

**ut·ter·ance** /'ʌtərəns/ noun (formal) **1** [U] the act of expressing sth in words: *to give utterance to your thoughts* **2** [C] something that you say: *one of her few recorded public utterances*

**ut·ter·ly** /'ʌtəli; NAmE 'ʌtərli/ adv. (used for emphasis) completely: *We're so utterly different from each other.* ◇ *She utterly failed to convince them.*

**ut·ter·most** /'ʌtəməʊst; NAmE 'ʌtərm-/ adj., noun [sing.] = UTMOST

**U-turn** *noun* **1** a turn of 180° that a vehicle makes so that it can move forwards in the opposite direction: *to do/make a U-turn* **2** (*informal*) a complete change in policy or behaviour, usually one that is embarrassing

**UUP** /ˌjuː juː ˈpiː/ *abbr.* Ulster Unionist Party (a political party in Northern Ireland that wants it to remain part of the United Kingdom)

**UV** /ˌjuː ˈviː/ *abbr.* ULTRAVIOLET: *UV radiation*

**UVA** /ˌjuː viː ˈeɪ/ *noun* [U] ULTRAVIOLET RAYS that are relatively long: *UVA rays*

**UVB** /ˌjuː viː ˈbiː/ *noun* [U] ULTRAVIOLET RAYS that are relatively short: *UVB rays*

**UVC** /ˌjuː viː ˈsiː/ *noun* [U] ULTRAVIOLET RAYS that are very short and do not get through the OZONE LAYER: *UVC radiation*

**uvula** /ˈjuːvjələ/ *noun* (*pl.* **uvu·lae** /-liː/) (*anatomy*) a small, soft part of the body that hangs from the top of the inside of the mouth just above the throat ○ VISUAL VOCAB page V1

**UX** /ˌjuː ˈeks/ *abbr.* (*computing*) user experience (what it is like for sb to use a particular product such as a website, for example how easy or pleasant it is to use)

**Uzi™** /ˈuːzi/ *noun* a type of SUB-MACHINE GUN designed in Israel

# Vv

**V** /viː/ noun, abbr., symbol
- **noun** (also **v**) (pl. **Vs, V's, v's** /viːz/) **1** [C, U] the 22nd letter of the English alphabet: *'Violin' begins with (a) V/'V'.* **2** a thing like a V in shape: *Ahead was the deep V of a gorge with water pouring down it.* ⇒ see also V-NECK, V-SIGN
- **abbr.** (in writing) VOLT: *a 1.5 V battery*
- **symbol** (also **v**) the number 5 in ROMAN NUMERALS

**v** /viː/ abbr. **1** (also **vs** especially in NAmE) (in sport or in a legal case) VERSUS (= against): *England v West Indies* ◊ *the State vs Kramer* (= a case in a court of law) **2** (in writing) (BrE, informal) very: *I was v pleased to get your letter.* **3** (in writing) VIDE

**vac** /væk/ noun (BrE, informal) a university vacation

**va·can·cy** /ˈveɪkənsi/ noun (pl. **-ies**) **1** [C] a job that is available for sb to do: *job vacancies* ◊ *a temporary vacancy* ◊ *~ (for sb/sth) vacancies for bar staff* ◊ *to fill a vacancy* ⇒ SYNONYMS (= against). **2** [C] a room that is available in a hotel, etc: *I'm sorry, we have no vacancies.* ⇒ WORDFINDER NOTE at HOTEL **3** [U] (especially in noun compounds) the fact of a job or room being available: *high office vacancy rates and stagnant housing prices* **4** [U] lack of interest or ideas **SYN** **emptiness**: *the vacancy of her expression*

**va·cant** /ˈveɪkənt/ adj. **1** (of a seat, hotel room, house, etc.) empty; not being used **SYN** **unoccupied**: *vacant properties* ◊ *The seat next to him was vacant.* ◊ (especially NAmE) *a vacant lot* (= a piece of land in a city that is not being used) ⇒ compare ENGAGED, OCCUPIED **2** (formal) if a job in a company is **vacant**, nobody is doing it and it is available for sb to take: *When the post finally fell* (= became) *vacant, they offered it to Fiona.* ◊ (BrE) **Situations Vacant** (= a section in a newspaper or on a website where jobs are advertised) **3** (of a look, an expression, etc.) showing no sign that the person is thinking of anything: *a vacant look* ▶ **va·cant·ly** adv.: *to stare vacantly*

**vac·ate** /vəˈkeɪt, veɪˈk-; NAmE ˈveɪkeɪt/ verb (formal) **1** ~ sth to leave a building, seat, etc., especially so that sb else can use it: *Guests are requested to vacate their rooms by noon on the day of departure.* **2** ~ sth to leave a job, position of authority, etc. so that it is available for sb else

## va·ca·tion ❶ A1 /veɪˈkeɪʃn, vəˈk-/ noun, verb
- **noun 1** A1 (NAmE) (BrE **holi·day**) [U, C] a period of time spent travelling or resting away from home: **on** ~ *They're on vacation in Hawaii right now.* ◊ *I'm going on vacation for a couple of weeks.* ◊ *You look tired—you should take a vacation.* ◊ *We're planning a summer vacation to Europe next year.* ⇒ note at HOLIDAY **2** A2 [C] (in the UK) one of the periods of time when universities or courts of law are closed; (in the US) one of the periods of time when schools, colleges, universities or courts of law are closed: *the Christmas/Easter/summer vacation* ◊ (BrE) *the long vacation* (= the summer vacation) ⇒ see also VAC
- **verb** (NAmE) (BrE **holi·day**) [I] to spend a holiday somewhere: *They are currently vacationing in Florida.*

**va·ca·tion·er** /veɪˈkeɪʃənə(r), vəˈk-/ noun (NAmE) (BrE **holi·day-maker**) a person who is visiting a place on holiday

**vac·cin·ate** /ˈvæksɪneɪt/ verb [often passive] ~ **sb** (against sth) to give a person or an animal a vaccine, especially by INJECTING it, in order to protect them against a disease: *I was vaccinated against tetanus.* ⇒ WORDFINDER NOTE at DISEASE ⇒ compare IMMUNIZE, INOCULATE ▶ **vac·cin·ation** /ˌvæksɪˈneɪʃn/ noun [C, U]: *Make sure your vaccinations are up to date.* ◊ *vaccination against typhoid*

**vac·cine** /ˈvæksiːn; NAmE vækˈsiːn/ noun [C, U] a substance that is put into the blood and that protects the body from a disease: *a measles vaccine* ◊ *There is no vaccine against HIV infection.*

**vacil·late** /ˈvæsəleɪt/ verb [I] (formal) to keep changing your opinion or thoughts about sth, especially in a way that annoys other people **SYN** **waver** ▶ **va·cil·la·tion** /ˌvæsəˈleɪʃn/ noun [U, C]

**vacu·ity** /vəˈkjuːəti/ noun [U] (formal) lack of serious thought or purpose

**vacu·ole** /ˈvækjuəʊl/ noun **1** (biology) a small space within a cell, usually filled with liquid **2** (medical) a small hole in the TISSUE of the body, usually caused by disease

**vacu·ous** /ˈvækjuəs/ adj. (formal) showing no sign of intelligence or sensitive feelings: *a vacuous expression* ▶ **vacu·ous·ly** adv. **vacu·ous·ness** noun [U]

## vac·uum ?+ C1 /ˈvækjuːm/ noun, verb
- **noun 1** ?+ C1 [C] a space that is completely empty of all substances, including all air or other gas: *a vacuum pump* (= one that creates a vacuum) ◊ *vacuum-packed foods* (= in a package from which most of the air has been removed) **2** ?+ C1 [usually sing.] a situation in which sb/sth is missing: *His resignation has created a vacuum which cannot easily be filled.* **3** [usually sing.] the act of cleaning sth with a vacuum cleaner: *to give a room a quick vacuum*
  - **IDM** **in a ˈvacuum** existing separately from other people, events, etc. when there should be a connection: *This kind of decision cannot ever be made in a vacuum.*
- **verb** [T, I] ~ (sth) to clean sth using a vacuum cleaner **SYN** **hoover**: *Have you vacuumed the stairs?*

**ˈvacuum cleaner** (BrE also **Hoover™**) noun an electrical machine that cleans floors, carpets, etc. by SUCKING up dirt and dust ⇒ picture at BROOM

**ˈvacuum flask** (also **flask**) (both BrE) (NAmE **ˈvacuum bottle**) noun a container like a bottle with double walls with a vacuum between them, used for keeping liquids hot or cold ⇒ compare THERMOS

**vaga·bond** /ˈvæɡəbɒnd; NAmE -bɑːnd/ noun (old-fashioned, disapproving) a person who has no home or job and who travels from place to place

**va·gar·ies** /ˈveɪɡəriz/ noun [pl.] (formal) changes in sb/sth that are difficult to predict or control

**va·gina** /vəˈdʒaɪnə/ noun the passage in the body of a woman or female animal between the outer sex organs and the WOMB ▶ **va·gin·al** /-nl/ adj. **va·gin·al·ly** /-nəli/ adv.

**va·grancy** /ˈveɪɡrənsi/ noun [U] (law) the crime of living on the streets and begging (= asking for money) from people

**va·grant** /ˈveɪɡrənt/ noun (formal or law) a person who has no home or job, especially one who begs (= asks for money) from people ▶ **va·grant** adj. [only before noun]

**vague** ?+ C1 /veɪɡ/ adj. (**vaguer, vaguest**) **1** ?+ C1 not clear in a person's mind: *to have a vague impression/memory/recollection of sth* ◊ *They had only a vague idea where the place was.* **2** ?+ C1 ~ (about sth) not having or giving enough information or details about sth: *She's a little vague about her plans for next year.* ◊ *The politicians made vague promises about tax cuts.* ◊ *He was accused of being deliberately vague.* ◊ *We had only a vague description of the attacker.* **3** (of a person's behaviour) suggesting a lack of clear thought or attention **SYN** **absent-minded**: *His vague manner concealed a brilliant mind.* **4** not having a clear shape **SYN** **indistinct**: *In the darkness they could see the vague outline of a church.* ▶ **vague·ness** noun [U]

**vague·ly** /ˈveɪɡli/ adv. **1** in a way that is not detailed or exact: *a vaguely worded statement* ◊ *I can vaguely remember my first day at school.* **2** slightly: *There was something vaguely familiar about her face.* ◊ *He was vaguely aware of footsteps behind him.* **3** in a way that shows that you are not paying attention or thinking clearly: *He smiled vaguely, ignoring her questions.*

**vain** /veɪn/ adj. **1** that does not produce the result you want **SYN** **useless**: *She closed her eyes tightly in a vain attempt to hold back the tears.* ◊ *I knocked loudly in the vain hope that someone might answer.* **2** (disapproving) too proud of your own appearance, abilities or achievements **SYN** **conceited**: *She's too vain to wear glasses.* ⇒ see also VANITY
- **IDM** **in ˈvain** without success: *They tried in vain to persuade her to go.* ◊ *All our efforts were in vain.* ⇒ more at NAME *n.*

### HOMOPHONES

**vain** • **vein** /veɪn/
- **vain** *adj.*: He plunged into the icy water in a vain effort to rescue his dog.
- **vein** *noun*: A vein in her head throbbed when she was angry.

**vain·glori·ous** /ˌveɪnˈɡlɔːriəs/ *adj.* (*literary, disapproving*) too proud of your own abilities or achievements ▶ **vain·glory** /ˌveɪnˈɡlɔːri; *NAmE* ˈveɪnɡlɔːri/ *noun* [U]

**vain·ly** /ˈveɪnli/ *adv.* without success: *He shouted after them, vainly trying to attract their attention.*

**val·ance** /ˈvæləns/ *noun* **1** a narrow piece of cloth like a short curtain that hangs around the frame of a bed, under a shelf, etc. **2** (*especially NAmE*) = PELMET

**vale** /veɪl/ *noun* (*old use or literary*) (also used in modern place names) a valley: *a wooded vale* ◇ *the Vale of the White Horse*

**val·edic·tion** /ˌvælɪˈdɪkʃn/ *noun* [C, U] (*formal*) the act of saying goodbye, especially in a formal speech

**val·edic·tor·ian** /ˌvælɪdɪkˈtɔːriən/ *noun* (*NAmE*) the student who has the highest grades in a particular group of students and who gives the valedictory speech at a GRADUATION ceremony

**val·edic·tory** /ˌvælɪˈdɪktəri/ *adj.* [usually before noun] (*formal*) connected with saying goodbye, especially at a formal occasion: *a valedictory speech*

**va·lency** /ˈveɪlənsi/ *noun* [C, U] (*pl.* **-ies**) (also **va·lence** /ˈveɪləns/ *especially in NAmE*) **1** (*chemistry*) a measurement of the power of an ATOM to combine with others, by the number of ATOMS of HYDROGEN it can combine with or DISPLACE: *Carbon has a valency of 4.* ⊃ **WORDFINDER NOTE** at ATOM **2** (*linguistics*) the number of GRAMMATICAL elements that a word, especially a verb, combines with in a sentence

**val·en·tine** /ˈvæləntaɪn/ *noun* **1** (also **ˈvalentine card**, **ˈvalentine's card**) a card that you send to sb that you love on St Valentine's Day (14 February), often without putting your name on it **2** a person that you send a valentine to

**Valentine's Day** ⊃ ST VALENTINE'S DAY

**val·er·ian** /vəˈlɪəriən; *NAmE* -ˈlɪr-/ *noun* [U] a drug obtained from the root of a plant with the same name, used to make people feel calmer

**valet** *noun, verb*
- *noun* /ˈvæleɪ, -lɪt; *NAmE* also væˈleɪ/ **1** a man's personal servant who takes care of his clothes, serves his meals, etc. **2** a hotel employee whose job is to clean the clothes of hotel guests **3** (*especially NAmE*) a person who parks your car for you at a hotel or restaurant: *Do they have valet parking?*
- *verb* /ˈvæleɪt/ **1** [T] ~ sth (*BrE*) to clean a person's car carefully and completely, especially on the inside: *a car valeting service* **2** [I] to perform the duties of a valet

**Val·halla** /vælˈhælə/ *noun* [U] (in ancient Scandinavian stories) a palace in which some chosen men who had died in battle went to live with the god Odin forever

**vali·ant** /ˈvæliənt/ *adj.* (*especially literary*) very brave or determined SYN **courageous**: *valiant warriors* ◇ *She made a valiant attempt not to laugh.* ▶ **vali·ant·ly** *adv.*

**valid** ?+ B2 W /ˈvælɪd/ *adj.* **1** ?+ B2 that is legally or officially acceptable: *a valid passport* ◇ *a bus pass valid for 1 month* ◇ *They have a valid claim to compensation.* **2** ?+ B2 based on what is logical or true: *She had valid reasons for not supporting the proposals.* ◇ *The point you make is perfectly valid.* ◇ *That argument is not strictly valid in this case.* **3** ?+ B2 (*computing*) that is accepted by the system: *a valid password* OPP **invalid** ▶ **val·id·ly** *adv.*: *The contract had been validly drawn up.*

**val·id·ate** W /ˈvælɪdeɪt/ *verb* (*formal*) **1** ~ sth to prove that sth is true: *to validate a theory* ◇ *The research findings do not validate the claims made by the manufacturer.* OPP **invalidate 2** ~ sth to make sth legally recognized: *to validate a contract* OPP **invalidate 3** ~ sth to state officially that sth is useful and of an acceptable standard: *Check* that their courses have been validated by a reputable organization. **4** to recognize the value of a person or their feelings or opinions; to make sb feel valued: *~sb/sth Be sure to validate your child's feelings—don't minimize them.* ◇ *~sb/sth as sth She seemed to need his admiration to validate her as a person.* ▶ **val·id·ation** /ˌvælɪˈdeɪʃn/ *noun* [U, C]

**val·id·ity** ?+ C1 W /vəˈlɪdəti/ *noun* [U] **1** ?+ C1 the state of being legally or officially acceptable: *The period of validity of the agreement has expired.* **2** ?+ C1 the state of being logical and true: *We had doubts about the validity of their argument.*

**Val·ium**™ /ˈvæliəm/ *noun* [U] a drug used to reduce ANXIETY (= feelings of fear and worry)

**Val·kyrie** /ˈvælkəri/ *noun* (in ancient Scandinavian stories) one of the twelve female servants of the god Odin. The Valkyries selected men who had been killed in battle and took them to VALHALLA.

**val·ley** 🌐 A2 /ˈvæli/ *noun* an area of low land between two hills or mountains, often with a river flowing through it; the land that a river flows through: *in a ~* ◇ *In the valley below cows were grazing peacefully.* ◇ *the fertile soils of river valleys* ◇ *the valley floor* ◇ *the Shenandoah Valley* ⊃ **WORDFINDER NOTE** at MOUNTAIN ⊃ see also LILY OF THE VALLEY, RIFT VALLEY

**ˈValley Girl** *noun* (*NAmE, informal*) a girl from a rich family who is only interested in things like shopping, thought to be typical of one of those living in the San Fernando Valley of California

**val·our** (*US* **valor**) /ˈvælə(r)/ *noun* [U] (*literary*) great courage, especially in war SYN **bravery** ▶ **val·or·ous** /-lərəs/ *adj.* IDM see DISCRETION

**valu·able** 🌐 B1 W /ˈvæljuəbl/ *adj.* **1** ? B1 worth a lot of money: *My home is my most valuable asset.* ◇ *She claims hospitals waste valuable resources by admitting patients days before surgery.* OPP **valueless, worthless** ⊃ compare INVALUABLE, PRICELESS **2** ? B1 very useful or important: *a valuable experience/lesson* ◇ *You should gain some valuable insights into the world of business.* ◇ *~to sb/sth documents that are enormously valuable to historians*

### ▼ SYNONYMS

**valuable**

**precious** • **priceless** • **irreplaceable**

These words all describe sth that is worth a lot of money or very important to sb.

**valuable** worth a lot of money: *The thieves took three pieces of valuable jewellery.*

**precious** rare and worth a lot of money; loved or valued very much: *a precious Chinese vase, valued at half a million pounds* ◇ *precious memories of our time together*

**priceless** extremely valuable; loved or valued very much: *a priceless collection of antiques*

**irreplaceable** too valuable or special to be replaced

**PATTERNS**
- valuable/precious/priceless/irreplaceable **possessions**
- valuable/precious/priceless **antiques/jewels/jewellery**

**valu·ables** /ˈvæljuəblz/ *noun* [pl.] things that are worth a lot of money, especially small personal things such as jewellery, cameras, etc. ⊃ **SYNONYMS** at THING

**valu·ation** /ˌvæljuˈeɪʃn/ *noun* [C, U] **1** a professional judgement about how much money sth is worth; its estimated value: *Surveyors carried out a valuation of the property.* ◇ *Experts set a high valuation on the painting.* ◇ *land valuation* **2** (*formal*) a judgement about how useful or important sth is; its estimated importance: *She puts a high valuation on trust between colleagues.*

# value

**value** ⓘ **B1** ⊙
/ˈvæljuː/ noun, verb

**WORD FAMILY**
value noun, verb
valuable adj.
invaluable adj.
 (≠ valueless)
valuables noun

■ **noun**
- **HOW MUCH STH IS WORTH 1** ⓘ **B1** [U, C] how much sth is worth in money or other goods for which it can be exchanged: *to go up/rise/increase in value* ◇ *to go down/fall/decline in value* ◇ *rising property values* ◇ **to the ~ of sth** *The winner will receive a prize to the value of £1000.* ◇ **of~** *Don't leave anything of value in the car.* ◇ *Sports cars tend to hold their value well.* ⇒ SYNONYMS at PRICE ⇒ see also FACE VALUE, MARKET VALUE, STREET VALUE **2** ⓘ **B1** [U] (*especially BrE*) how much sth is worth compared with its price: *to be good/great value* (= worth the money it costs) ◇ *to be bad/poor value* (= not worth the money it costs) ◇ *Larger sizes give the best value for money.*
- **BEING USEFUL/IMPORTANT 3** ⓘ **B1** [U, sing.] the quality of being useful or important SYN **benefit**: *The value of regular exercise should not be underestimated.* ◇ *She placed a high value on loyalty.* ◇ **of ~ (to sb)** *The arrival of canals was of great value to many industries.* ◇ *to be of little/no value to sb* ◇ *This ring has great sentimental value for me.* ◇ *I suppose it has a certain novelty value* (= it's interesting because it's new). ◇ *Branding has to add value to the product.*
- **BELIEFS 4** ⓘ **B2** **values** [pl.] beliefs about what is right and wrong and what is important in life: *moral values* ◇ *a return to traditional values in education, such as firm discipline* ◇ *The school's core values include the ability to work with others.* ◇ *The young have a completely different set of values and expectations.* ⇒ see also FAMILY VALUES
- **MATHEMATICS 5** [C] the amount represented by a letter or symbol: *Let y have the value 33.* ⇒ see also PRODUCTION VALUES

■ **verb**
- **CONSIDER IMPORTANT 1** ⓘ **B2** (not used in the progressive tenses) to think that sb/sth is important: **~ sb/sth (as sth)** *I really value him as a friend.* ◇ **~ sb/sth (for sth)** *The area is valued for its vineyards.* ◇ *a valued member of staff*
- **DECIDE WORTH 2** ⓘ **B2** [usually passive] **~ sth (at sth)** to decide that sth is worth a particular amount of money: *The property has been valued at over $2 million.*

**ˌvalue ˈadded ˈtax** noun [U] (*BrE*) = VAT

**ˌvalue-ˈfree** adj. not influenced by personal opinions

**ˈvalue judgement** (also **ˈvalue judgment** *especially in NAmE*) noun [C, U] (*sometimes disapproving*) a judgement about how good or important sth is, based on personal opinions rather than facts

**ˌvalue-ˈladen** adj. influenced by personal opinions: *'Freedom fighter' is a value-laden word.*

**value·less** /ˈvæljuːləs/ adj. (*formal*) without value or worth SYN **worthless** OPP **valuable**

**valu·er** /ˈvæljuə(r)/ (*BrE*) (*NAmE* **ap·prais·er**) noun a person whose job is to examine a building, an object, etc. and say how much it is worth

**ˈvalue system** noun a set of connected principles that describe what people think is important and the correct way to behave

**valve** /vælv/ noun **1** a device for controlling the flow of a liquid or gas, letting it move in one direction only **2** (*anatomy*) a structure in the heart or in a VEIN that lets blood flow in one direction only **3** (*music*) a device in some BRASS musical instruments for changing the note

**vamp** /væmp/ noun (*old-fashioned, disapproving*) a sexually attractive woman who tries to control men

**vam·pire** /ˈvæmpaɪə(r)/ noun (in stories) a dead person who leaves their GRAVE (= where they are buried) at night to bite living people and drink their blood

**ˈvampire bat** noun a Central and South American BAT (= an animal like a mouse with wings) that bites other animals and drinks their blood

**vam·pir·ism** /ˈvæmpaɪərɪzəm/ noun [U] the behaviour or practices of VAMPIRES

**van** ⓘ **A2** /væn/ noun **1** ⓘ **A2** a covered vehicle with no side windows in its back half, usually smaller than a lorry, used for carrying goods or people: *the driver of a white van* ◇ *a police van* (= for carrying police officers or prisoners) ◇ *a delivery van* ◇ *a van driver* ⇒ see also CONVERSION VAN, FURNITURE VAN, MOVING VAN, PANEL VAN, REMOVAL VAN **2** (*NAmE*) a covered vehicle with side windows, usually smaller than a lorry, that can carry about twelve passengers **3** (*BrE*) a closed coach on a train for carrying bags, cases, etc. or mail: *a luggage van*
IDM **in the ˈvan** (*BrE, formal*) at the front or in the leading position

**van·adium** /vəˈneɪdiəm/ noun [U] (*symb.* **V**) a chemical element. Vanadium is a soft, poisonous, silvery-grey metal that is added to some types of steel to make it stronger.

**ˈvan conversion** noun (*US*) = CONVERSION VAN

**van·dal** /ˈvændl/ noun a person who deliberately destroys or damages public property

**van·dal·ism** /ˈvændəlɪzəm/ noun [U] the crime of destroying or damaging sth, especially public property, deliberately and for no good reason: *an act of vandalism*

**van·dal·ize** (*BrE also* **-ise**) /ˈvændəlaɪz/ verb [usually passive] **~ sth** to damage sth, especially public property, deliberately and for no good reason

**vane** /veɪn/ noun a flat BLADE that is moved by wind or water and is part of the machines in a WINDMILL, etc. ⇒ see also WEATHERVANE

**van·guard** /ˈvæŋɡɑːd/; *NAmE* -ɡɑːrd/ noun usually **the vanguard** [sing.] **1** the leaders of a movement in society, for example in politics, art, industry, etc: **in the ~ of sth** *The company is proud to be in the vanguard of scientific progress.* **2** the part of an army, etc. that is at the front when moving forward to attack the enemy OPP **rearguard**

**van·illa** /vəˈnɪlə/ noun, adj.
■ **noun** [U] a substance obtained from the beans of a tropical plant, also called vanilla, used to add taste to sweet foods, for example ice cream: (*BrE*) *vanilla essence* ◇ (*NAmE*) *vanilla extract* ◇ (*BrE*) *a vanilla pod* ◇ (*NAmE*) *a vanilla bean*
■ **adj. 1** tasting of vanilla: *vanilla ice cream* **2** (*informal*) ordinary; not special in any way: *The city is pretty much plain vanilla.*

**van·il·lin** /vəˈnɪlɪn/ noun [U] a strong-smelling chemical that gives VANILLA its smell

**van·ish** ⓘ **C1** /ˈvænɪʃ/ verb **1** ⓘ **C1** [I] to disappear suddenly and/or in a way that you cannot explain: *The magician vanished in a puff of smoke.* ◇ *My glasses seem to have vanished.* ◇ *He vanished without trace.* **2** ⓘ **C1** [I] to stop existing: *the vanishing woodlands of Europe* ◇ *All hopes of a peaceful settlement had now vanished.* IDM see ACT n., FACE n., THIN adj.

**ˈvanishing point** noun [usually sing.] (*specialist*) the point in the distance at which PARALLEL lines (= lines that are the same distance apart at every point) appear to meet

**van·ity** /ˈvænəti/ noun (*pl.* **-ies**) **1** [U] (*disapproving*) the fact of being too proud of your own appearance, abilities or achievements: *She had no personal vanity* (= about her appearance). ⇒ see also VAIN **2** [U] (*literary*) the fact of being unimportant, especially compared with other things that are important: *the vanity of human ambition in the face of death* **3** **vanities** [pl.] behaviour or attitudes that show people's vanity: *Politics is too often concerned only with the personal vanities of politicians.* **4** (*also* **ˈvanity table**) [C] = DRESSING TABLE

**ˈvanity unit** noun (*BrE*) a WASHBASIN fixed into a flat surface with cupboards below

**van·quish** /ˈvæŋkwɪʃ/ verb **~ sb/sth** (*literary*) to defeat sb completely in a competition, war, etc. SYN **conquer**

**the ˌvanˈquished** /ðə ˈvæŋkwɪʃt/ noun [pl.] (*literary*) people who have been completely defeated in a competition, war, etc.

**vantage point** /ˈvɑːntɪdʒ pɔɪnt; *NAmE* ˈvæn-/ (*also formal* **vantage**) noun **1** a position from which you watch sth: *The cafe was a good vantage point for watching the world go by.*

**2** a point in time or a situation from which you consider sth, especially the past: *From the vantage point of the present, the war seems to have achieved nothing.*

**vape** /veɪp/ *verb, noun*
- *verb* [I, T] (*informal*) to take VAPOUR from an E-CIGARETTE or similar device into your mouth and let it out again: *Are you allowed to vape at work?*: **~ sth** *Many smokers have started vaping e-cigarettes.*
- *noun* (*informal*) **1** an electronic device, similar to an E-CIGARETTE, that produces VAPOUR, usually containing NICOTINE, that you can take into your lungs through your mouth: *I've never tried a vape.* **2** an act of smoking an E-CIGARETTE or similar device: *I wanted to chill out and take a vape.*

**vapid** /ˈvæpɪd/ *adj.* (*formal*) not showing interest or intelligence **SYN** dull ▶ **vapidity** /vəˈpɪdəti/ *noun* [U]

**vapor** /ˈveɪpə(r)/ (*US*) = VAPOUR

**vaporize** (*BrE also* **-ise**) /ˈveɪpəraɪz/ *verb* [I, T] **~ (sth)** (*specialist*) to turn into gas; to make sth turn into gas ▶ **vaporization, -isation** /ˌveɪpəraɪˈzeɪʃn; *NAmE* -rəˈz-/ *noun* [U]

**vaporous** /ˈveɪpərəs/ *adj.* (*formal*) full of vapour; like vapour: *clouds of vaporous air*

**vapour** (*US* **vapor**) /ˈveɪpə(r)/ *noun* [C, U] a mass of very small drops of liquid in the air, for example STEAM: *water vapour*

**ˈvapour trail** (*US* **ˈvapor trail**) *noun* the white line that is left in the sky by a plane **SYN** contrail

**vapourware** (*US* **vaporware**) /ˈveɪpəweə(r); *NAmE* -pərwer/ *noun* [U] (*computing*) a piece of software or other computer product that has been advertised but is not available to buy yet, either because it is only an idea or because it is still being written or designed

**variability** /ˌveəriəˈbɪləti; *NAmE* ˌver-, ˌvær-/ *noun* [U] the fact of sth being likely to vary: *climatic variability* ◊ *a degree of variability in the exchange rate*

**variable** ?+ C1 ⊙ /ˈveəriəbl; *NAmE* ˈver-, ˈvær-/ *noun, adj.*
- *noun* ?+ C1 a situation, number or quantity that can vary or be varied: *With so many variables, it is difficult to calculate the cost.* ◊ *The temperature remained constant while pressure was a variable in the experiment.* **OPP** constant
- *adj.* **1** ?+ C1 often changing; likely to change **SYN** fluctuating: *variable temperatures* ◊ *The acting is of variable quality* (= some of it is good and some of it is bad). ⊃ compare INVARIABLE **2** ?+ C1 able to be changed: *The drill has variable speed control.* ◊ *variable lighting* ▶ **variably** /-bli/ *adv.*

**variance** W /ˈveəriəns; *NAmE* ˈver-, ˈvær-/ *noun* [U, C] (*formal*) the amount by which sth changes or is different from sth else: *variance in temperature* ◊ *a note with subtle variances of pitch*
**IDM** **at ˈvariance (with sb/sth)** (*formal*) disagreeing with or opposing sb/sth: *These conclusions are totally at variance with the evidence.*

**variant** /ˈveəriənt; *NAmE* ˈver-, ˈvær-/ *noun* **~ (of/on sth)** a thing that is a slightly different form or type of sth else: *This game is a variant of baseball.* ▶ **variant** *adj.* [only before noun]: *variant forms of spelling*

**variation** ?+ B2 ⊙ /ˌveəriˈeɪʃn; *NAmE* ˌver-/ *noun*
**1** ?+ B2 [C, U] **~ (in/of sth)** a change, especially in the amount or level of sth: *The dial records very slight variations in pressure.* ◊ *Currency exchange rates are always subject to variation.* ◊ *regional/seasonal variation* (= depending on the region or time of year) **2** ?+ B2 [C] **~ (on sth)** a thing that is different from other things in the same general group: *This soup is a spicy variation on a traditional favourite.* **3** [C] **~ (on sth)** (*music*) any of a set of short pieces of music based on a simple tune repeated in a different and more complicated form: *a set of variations on a theme by Mozart* ◊ (*figurative*) *His numerous complaints are all variations on a theme* (= all about the same thing).

**varicose vein** /ˌværɪkəʊs ˈveɪn/ *noun* a VEIN, especially one in the leg, that has become SWOLLEN (= larger than normal) and painful

**varied** ?+ C1 W /ˈveərid; *NAmE* ˈver-, ˈvær-/ *adj.* (*usually approving*) **1** ?+ C1 of many different types: *varied opinions* ◊ *a wide and varied selection of cheeses* **2** ?+ C1 not staying the same, but changing often: *He led a full and varied life.*

**variegated** /ˈveəriəɡeɪtɪd, -rɪɡ-; *NAmE* ˈverɪɡeɪtɪd/ *adj.*
**1** (*specialist*) having spots or marks of a different colour: *a plant with variegated leaves* ⊃ *VISUAL VOCAB* page V7
**2** (*formal*) consisting of many different types of thing or person

**variety** ⊙ A2 ⊙ /vəˈraɪəti/ *noun* (*pl.* **-ies**) **1** ?⊙ A2 [sing. + sing./pl. v.] **~ (of sth)** several different sorts of the same thing: *There is a wide variety of patterns to choose from.* ◊ *He resigned for a variety of reasons.* ◊ *This tool can be used in a variety of ways.* ◊ *The text consists of extracts from a variety of sources.* ◊ *articles and essays on a variety of topics* **HELP** A plural verb is needed after a/an (large, wide, etc.) variety of...: *A variety of reasons were given.* You can use a singular or a plural verb before it: *There is/are a wide variety of patterns to choose from.* **2** ?⊙ B1 [U] the quality of not being the same or not doing the same thing all the time **SYN** diversity: *It's the variety that makes my job so enjoyable.* ◊ *We all need variety in our diet.* **3** ?⊙ B1 [C] a type of a thing, for example a plant or language, that is different from the others in the same general group: *Apples come in a great many varieties.* ◊ *six different varieties of English* ◊ *a rare variety of orchid* ◊ *A typical estate in the region will grow at least three grape varieties.* ◊ *My cooking is of the 'quick and simple' variety.* **4** (*NAmE also* **vaudeville**) [U] a form of theatre or television entertainment that consists of a series of short performances, such as singing, dancing and funny acts: *a variety show/theatre*
**IDM** **variety is the spice of ˈlife** (*saying*) having a range of different experiences makes life more interesting

**vaˈriety meats** *noun* [pl.] (*US*) = OFFAL

**varifocals** /ˈveərɪfəʊklz; *NAmE* ˈver-/ *noun* [pl.] a pair of glasses in which each LENS varies in how thick it is from the upper part to the lower part. The upper part is for looking at things at a distance, and the lower part is for looking at things that are close to you. ⊃ compare BIFOCALS ▶ **varifocal** *adj.* ⊃ compare BIFOCAL

**various** ⊙ B1 ⊙ /ˈveəriəs; *NAmE* ˈver-, ˈvær-/ *adj.*
**1** ?⊙ B1 [usually before noun] several different **SYN** diverse: *various types/forms/kinds of sb/sth* ◊ *We talked about jobs, family, football and various other things.* ◊ *documentaries that explored various aspects of life in Germany* ◊ (*formal*) *His complaints were many and various.* **2** (*formal*) having many different features **SYN** diverse: *a large and various country*

**variously** /ˈveəriəsli; *NAmE* ˈver-, ˈvær-/ *adv.* (*formal*) in several different ways, usually by several different people: *He has been variously described as a hero, a genius and a bully.* ◊ *The cost has been variously estimated at between £10 million and £20 million.*

**varmint** /ˈvɑːmɪnt; *NAmE* ˈvɑːrm-/ *noun* (*especially NAmE, old-fashioned, informal*) **1** a wild animal that causes problems **2** a person, especially a child, who causes trouble

**varnish** /ˈvɑːnɪʃ; *NAmE* ˈvɑːrn-/ *noun, verb*
- *noun* [U, C] a liquid that is painted onto wood, metal, etc. and that forms a hard shiny surface that you can see through when it is dry ⊃ see also NAIL VARNISH at NAIL POLISH
- *verb* to put varnish on the surface of sth: **~ sth** *The doors are then stained and varnished.* ◊ (*BrE*) *Josie was sitting at her desk, varnishing her nails.* ◊ **~ sth + noun** (*BrE*) *Her nails were varnished a brilliant shade of red.*

**varsity** /ˈvɑːsəti; *NAmE* ˈvɑːrs-/ *noun, adj.*
- *noun* [C, U] (*pl.* **-ies**) **1** (*NAmE*) the main team that represents a college or HIGH SCHOOL, especially in sports competitions **2** (*BrE, old use or IndE or SAfrE*) university: *She's still at varsity.*
- *adj.* [only before noun] (*BrE, informal*) used when describing activities connected with the universities of Oxford and Cambridge, especially sports competitions: *the varsity match*

# vary

**vary** 🔑 B2 ⊙ /ˈveəri; NAmE ˈveri, ˈværi/ *verb*
(vary·ing, var·ied, var·ied)

**WORD FAMILY**
vary *verb*
varied *adj.*
variable *adj.*
variation *noun*
various *adj.*
variety *noun*

**1** B2 [I] (of a group of similar things) to be different from each other in size, shape, etc.: *New techniques were introduced with varying degrees of success.* ◊ *Estimates of how many civilians were killed varied widely.* ◊ *Class size varies greatly.* ◊ **~ in sth** *The students' work varies considerably in quality.* **2** B2 [I] to change or be different according to the situation: **~ with sth** *The menu varies with the season.* ◊ **~ by sth** *Cancer rates vary significantly by gender and ethnicity.* ◊ **~ from sb/sth to sb/sth** *Results can vary greatly from year to year.* ◊ **~ between A and B** *Class numbers vary between 25 and 30.* ◊ *Costs are likely to vary depending on where you live.* **3** B2 [T] **~ sth** to make changes to sth to make it slightly different: *The job enables me to vary the hours I work.* **IDM** *see* MILEAGE

**vas·cu·lar** /ˈvæskjələ(r)/ *adj.* [usually before noun] (*specialist*) of or containing VEINS (= the tubes that carry liquids around the bodies of animals and plants)

**vas def·er·ens** /ˌvæs ˈdefərenz/ *noun* (*pl.* **vasa defer·en·tia** /ˌveɪsə defəˈrenʃiə/) (*anatomy*) the tube through which SPERM pass from the TESTIS on their way out of the body

**vase** /vɑːz; NAmE veɪs, veɪz/ *noun* a container made of glass, etc., used for holding cut flowers or as an attractive object: *a vase of flowers*

**vas·ec·tomy** /vəˈsektəmi/ *noun* (*pl.* -ies) (*medical*) a medical operation to remove part of each of the tubes in a man's body that carry SPERM, after which he is not able to make a woman pregnant

**Vas·el·ine**™ /ˈvæsəliːn/ *noun* [U] a thick, soft, clear substance that is used on skin to protect it or to help a wound to get better, or as a LUBRICANT to stop surfaces from sticking together

**vaso·con·stric·tion** /ˌveɪzəʊkənˈstrɪkʃn/ *noun* [U] (*biology or medical*) a process in which BLOOD VESSELS become narrower, which tends to increase BLOOD PRESSURE

**vaso·di·la·tion** /ˌveɪzəʊdaɪˈleɪʃn/ *noun* [U] (*biology or medical*) a process in which BLOOD VESSELS become wider, which tends to reduce BLOOD PRESSURE

**vas·sal** /ˈvæsl/ *noun* **1** a man in the Middle Ages who promised to fight for and show support for a king or other powerful owner of land, in return for being given land to live on **2** a country that depends on and is controlled by another country: *a vassal state*

**vast** 🔑 B2 /vɑːst; NAmE væst/ *adj.* extremely large in area, size, amount, etc. **SYN** huge: *a vast area of forest* ◊ *a vast crowd* ◊ *In the vast majority of cases, this should not be a problem.* ◊ *They sell a vast array of products.* ◊ *a vast amount of information* ◊ *At dusk bats appear in vast numbers.* ◊ *vast quantities of food* ◊ *His business empire was vast.* ▶ **vast·ness** *noun* [U, C]: *the vastness of space*

**vast·ly** /ˈvɑːstli; NAmE ˈvæst-/ *adv.* very much: *I'm a vastly different person now.* ◊ *The quality of the training has vastly improved.*

**VAT** /ˌviː eɪ ˈtiː, væt/ *noun* [U] (*BrE*) a tax that is added to the price of goods and services (the abbreviation for 'value added tax'): *Prices include VAT.* ◊ *£27.50 + VAT*

**vat** /væt/ *noun* a large container for holding liquids, especially in industrial processes: *distilling vats* ◊ *a vat of whisky*

**the Vati·can** /ˈvætɪkən/ *noun* **1** [sing.] the group of buildings in Rome where the POPE lives and works **2** [sing. + sing./pl. v.] the centre of government of the Roman Catholic Church

**vaude·ville** /ˈvɔːdəvɪl/ *noun* **1** (*NAmE*) = VARIETY **2** (*BrE also* ˈmusic hall) a type of entertainment popular in the late nineteenth and early twentieth centuries, including singing, dancing and comedy

**ˈvaudeville ˌtheater** (*NAmE*) (*BrE* ˈmusic ˌhall) *noun* a theatre used for popular entertainment in the late nineteenth and early twentieth centuries

**vault** /vɔːlt/ *noun, verb*
■ *noun* **1** a room with thick walls and a strong door, especially in a bank, used for keeping valuable things safe **2** a room under a church or in a CEMETERY, used for burying people **3** a roof or ceiling in the form of an ARCH or a series of ARCHES **4** a jump made by vaulting ⊃ *see also* POLE VAULT
■ *verb* [I, T] to jump over an object in a single movement, using your hands or a POLE to push you: **~ over sth** *She vaulted over the gate and ran up the path.* ◊ **~ sth** *to vault a fence* ⊃ *see also* POLE VAULT

**vault·ed** /ˈvɔːltɪd/ *adj.* (*architecture*) made in the shape of an ARCH or a series of ARCHES; having a ceiling or roof of this shape: *a vaulted ceiling* ◊ *a vaulted cellar/roof*

**vault·ing** /ˈvɔːltɪŋ/ *noun* [U] (*architecture*) a pattern of ARCHES in a ceiling or roof

**ˈvaulting ˌhorse** (*also* horse) *noun* a large object with legs, and sometimes handles, that GYMNASTS use to vault over

**vaunt·ed** /ˈvɔːntɪd/ *adj.* [usually before noun] (*formal*) proudly talked about or praised as being very good, especially when this is not deserved: *Their much vaunted reforms did not materialize.*

**VC** /ˌviː ˈsiː/ *noun* [sing.] a MEDAL for special courage that is given to members of the British and Commonwealth armed forces (the abbreviation for 'Victoria Cross'): *He was awarded the VC.* ◊ *Captain Edward Bell VC*

**VCR** /ˌviː siː ˈɑː(r)/ *noun* (*especially NAmE*) a machine that was used, especially in the past, to play videos or to record programmes from a television (the abbreviation for 'video cassette recorder')

**VD** /ˌviː ˈdiː/ *abbr.* (*old-fashioned*) VENEREAL DISEASE

**veal** /viːl/ *noun* [U] meat from a CALF (= a young cow)

**vec·tor** /ˈvektə(r)/ *noun* **1** (*mathematics*) a quantity that has both size and direction: *Acceleration and velocity are both vectors.* ⊃ *compare* SCALAR **2** (*biology*) an insect, etc. that carries a particular disease from one living thing to another **3** (*specialist*) a course taken by an aircraft

**Veda** /ˈveɪdə, ˈviːdə/ *noun* any of the four collections of ancient holy texts of Hinduism

**Vedic** /ˈveɪdɪk, ˈviːd-/ *adj., noun*
■ *adj.* relating to the Vedas
■ *noun* [U] the language of the Vedas, an early form of Sanskrit

**veep** (*also* **Veep**) /viːp/ *noun* (*NAmE, informal*) VICE-PRESIDENT

**veer** /vɪə(r); NAmE vɪr/ *verb* **1** [I] **+ adv./prep.** (especially of a vehicle) to change direction suddenly **SYN** swerve: *The bus veered onto the wrong side of the road.* **2** [I] **+ adv./prep.** (of a conversation or way of behaving or thinking) to change in the way it develops: *The debate veered away from the main topic of discussion.* ◊ *His emotions veered between fear and anger.* **3** [I] **+ adv./prep.** (*specialist*) (of the wind) to change direction: *The wind veered to the west.*

**veg** /vedʒ/ *noun, verb, adj.*
■ *noun* [U, C] (*pl.* veg) (*BrE, informal*) a vegetable or vegetables: *a fruit and veg stall* ◊ *He likes the traditional meat and two veg for his main meal.*
■ *verb* (**-gg-**)
**PHRV** ˌveg ˈout (*informal*) to relax by doing sth that needs very little effort, for example watching television
■ *adj.* (*IndE, SEAsianE, informal*) **1** suitable for a person who does not eat meat or fish; not containing or serving meat or fish **SYN** vegetarian: *We have a choice of veg options.* ◊ *a veg restaurant* **2** (of a person) eating no meat or fish **SYN** vegetarian **OPP** non-veg

**vegan** /ˈviːɡən/ *noun, adj.*
■ *noun* a person who does not eat any animal products such as meat, milk or eggs or use animal products such as leather or wool
■ *adj.* using or containing no animal products: *a vegan diet*

**vegan·ism** /ˈviːɡənɪzəm/ noun [U] the practice of not eating or using any animal products, including meat, milk, leather, wool, etc: *the growing popularity of veganism*

**Vege·bur·ger**™ /ˈvedʒɪbɜːɡə(r); NAmE -bɜːrɡ-/ noun = VEGGIE BURGER

**Vege·mite**™ /ˈvedʒɪmaɪt/ noun [U] (in Australia and New Zealand) a dark substance made from YEAST, spread on bread, etc. ⇒ compare MARMITE™

**vege·table** ⓘ A1 /ˈvedʒtəbl/ noun 1 ⓘ A1 *(also informal, especially in NAmE* **veg·gie**) a plant or part of a plant that is eaten as food. Potatoes, beans and onions are all vegetables: *The children don't eat enough fresh vegetables.* ◇ **root vegetables** (= for example CARROTS) ◇ *a vegetable garden* ◇ *We grow our own vegetables.* ⇒ compare ANIMAL, FRUIT, MINERAL ⇒ see also GREEN VEGETABLE ⇒ VISUAL VOCAB page V5 **2** *(offensive)* a person who is physically alive but not capable of much mental or physical activity, for example because of an accident or illness: *Severe brain damage turned him into a vegetable.* **3** a person who has a boring life: *Since losing my job I've been a vegetable.*

**vege·tal** /ˈvedʒətl/ adj. *(formal)* connected with plants

**vege·tar·ian** /ˌvedʒəˈteəriən; NAmE -ˈter-/ *(also informal* **veg·gie**) noun a person who does not eat meat or fish: *Is she a vegetarian?* ⇒ compare HERBIVORE ⇒ see also NON-VEGETARIAN ▸ **vege·tar·ian** adj.: *Are you vegetarian?* ◇ *a vegetarian diet* (= with no meat or fish in it) ◇ *a vegetarian restaurant* (= that serves no meat or fish) **vege·tar·ian·ism** noun [U]

**vege·tate** /ˈvedʒəteɪt/ verb [I] (of a person) to spend time doing very little and feeling bored

**vege·tated** /ˈvedʒəteɪtɪd/ adj. having the amount of plant life mentioned: *a densely/sparsely vegetated area*

**vege·ta·tion** /ˌvedʒəˈteɪʃn/ noun [U] plants in general, especially the plants that are found in a particular area or environment: *The hills are covered in lush green vegetation.*

**vege·ta·tive** /ˈvedʒɪtətɪv; NAmE -teɪt-/ adj. **1** relating to plant life **2** *(medical)* (of a person) alive but showing no sign of brain activity ⇒ see also PERSISTENT VEGETATIVE STATE

**veg·gie** /ˈvedʒi/ noun *(informal)* **1** = VEGETARIAN: *He's turned veggie* (= become a vegetarian). **2** *(especially NAmE)* = VEGETABLE ▸ **veg·gie** adj.

**ˈveggie burger** *(also* **Vege·bur·ger**™) noun a BURGER made with vegetables, especially beans, instead of meat

**vehe·ment** /ˈviːəmənt/ adj. SYN forceful showing very strong feelings, especially anger SYN forceful: *a vehement denial/attack/protest, etc.* ◇ *He had been vehement in his opposition to the idea.* ▸ **vehe·mence** /-məns/ noun [U] **vehe·ment·ly** adv.: *The charge was vehemently denied.*

**ve·hicle** ⓘ A2 /ˈviːəkl; NAmE also ˈviːhɪkl/ noun **1** A2 *(rather formal)* a thing that is used for transporting people or goods from one place to another, such as a car or lorry: *motor vehicles* (= cars, buses, lorries, etc.) ◇ *Are you the driver of this vehicle?* ◇ *rows of parked vehicles* **2** ~ (for sth) something that can be used to express your ideas or feelings, or as a way of achieving sth: *Art may be used as a vehicle for propaganda.* ◇ *The play is an ideal vehicle for her talents.*

**ve·hicu·lar** /vəˈhɪkjələ(r); NAmE viːˈh-/ adj. [only before noun] *(formal)* intended for vehicles or consisting of vehicles: *vehicular access* ◇ *The road is closed to vehicular traffic.*

**veil** /veɪl/ noun, verb
■ noun **1** a piece of very thin material, worn especially by women to protect or hide the face, or as part of a hat, etc: *a bridal veil* **2** a piece of cloth worn over the head and shoulders by NUNS or Muslim women **3** [sing.] *(formal)* something that stops you from learning the truth about a situation: *Their work is carried out behind a veil of secrecy.* ◇ *It would be better to draw a veil over what happened next* (= not talk about it). **4** [sing.] *(formal)* a thin layer that stops

you from seeing sth: *The mountain tops were hidden beneath a veil of mist.*
IDM **take the ˈveil** *(old-fashioned)* to become a NUN
■ verb **1** ~ sth/yourself to cover your face with a veil **2** ~ sth *(literary)* to cover sth with sth that hides it partly or completely SYN shroud: *A fine drizzle began to veil the hills.*

**veiled** /veɪld/ adj. **1** a veiled threat, warning, etc. is not expressed directly or clearly because you do not want your meaning to be too obvious: *a thinly veiled threat* ◇ *She made a veiled reference to his past mistakes.* **2** wearing a veil: *a mysterious veiled woman*

**vein** ⓘ C1 /veɪn/ noun **1** ⓘ C1 [C] any of the tubes that carry blood from all parts of the body towards the heart: *the jugular vein* ⇒ compare ARTERY ⇒ see also DEEP VEIN THROMBOSIS, PORTAL VEIN, VARICOSE VEIN ⇒ HOMOPHONES at VAIN **2** [C] any of the very thin tubes that form the frame of a leaf or an insect's wing **3** [C] a narrow area of a different colour in some types of stone, wood and rock **4** [C] a thin layer of minerals or metal contained in rock SYN seam: *a vein of gold* **5** [sing.] ~ (of sth) an amount of a particular quality or feature in sth: *They had tapped a rich vein of information in his secretary.* **6** [sing., U] a particular style or manner: *A number of other people commented in a similar vein.* ◇ *'And that's not all,' he continued in angry vein.*

**veined** /veɪnd/ adj. having or marked with veins or thin lines: *thin blue-veined hands* ◇ *veined marble*

**Vel·cro**™ /ˈvelkrəʊ/ noun [U] a material with two different surfaces, one rough and one smooth, that stick to each other when they are pressed together, used for fastening clothes, etc.

**veld** /velt/ noun [U] (in South Africa) flat, open land with grass and no trees ⇒ compare PAMPAS, PRAIRIE, SAVANNAH, STEPPE

**vel·lum** /ˈveləm/ noun [U] **1** material made from the skin of a sheep, GOAT or CALF, used for making book covers and, in the past, for writing on **2** smooth cream-coloured paper used for writing on

**vel·oci·rap·tor** /vəˈlɒsɪræptə(r); NAmE -ˈlɑːs-/ noun a small DINOSAUR that moved fairly quickly

**vel·ocity** /vəˈlɒsəti; NAmE -ˈlɑːs-/ noun (pl. -**ies**) **1** *(specialist)* the speed of sth in a particular direction: *the velocity of light* ◇ *to gain/lose velocity* ◇ *a high-velocity rifle* **2** *(formal)* high speed: *Jaguars can move with an astonishing velocity.*

**velo·drome** /ˈveləʊdrəʊm/ noun a track or building used for cycle racing ⇒ WORDFINDER NOTE at CYCLING

**vel·our** /vəˈlʊə(r); NAmE -ˈlʊr/ noun [U] a type of silk or cotton cloth with a thick, soft surface like VELVET

**vel·vet** /ˈvelvɪt/ noun [U] a type of cloth made from silk, cotton or NYLON, with a thick, soft surface: *a velvet dress* ◇ *velvet curtains/drapes* IDM see IRON adj.

**vel·vet·een** /ˌvelvəˈtiːn/ noun [U] a type of cotton cloth that looks like VELVET but is less expensive

**vel·vety** /ˈvelvəti/ adj. pleasantly smooth and soft: *velvety skin* ◇ *a velvety red wine*

**vena cava** /ˌviːnə ˈkeɪvə/ noun (pl. **venae cavae** /ˌviːniː ˈkeɪviː/) *(anatomy)* either of the two VEINS that take blood without OXYGEN in it towards the heart

**venal** /ˈviːnl/ adj. *(formal)* prepared to do things that are not honest or moral in return for money SYN **corrupt**: *venal journalists* ▸ **ve·nal·ity** /viːˈnæləti/ noun [U]

**vend** /vend/ verb ~ sth *(formal)* to sell sth

**ven·detta** /venˈdetə/ noun **1** a long period of violence between two families or groups, in which people are murdered in return for previous murders SYN **feud 2** ~ (against sb) a long argument or campaign in which one person or group does or says things to harm another: *He has accused the media of pursuing a vendetta against him.* ◇ *She conducted a personal vendetta against me.*

**vending machine** /ˈvendɪŋ məʃiːn/ noun a machine from which you can buy cigarettes, drinks, etc. by putting coins into it

**vend·or** /ˈvendə(r)/ noun **1** a person who sells things, for example food or newspapers, usually outside on the street: *street vendors* **2** (*formal*) a company that sells a particular product: *software vendors* **3** (*law*) a person who is selling a house, etc. ⊃ compare SELLER

**ven·eer** /vəˈnɪə(r); NAmE -ˈnɪr/ noun, verb
- noun **1** [C, U] a thin layer of wood or plastic that is stuck to the surface of cheaper wood with GLUE, especially on a piece of furniture **2** [sing.] ~ (of sth) an outer appearance of a particular quality that hides the true nature of sb/sth: *Her veneer of politeness began to crack.*
- verb [usually passive] to cover the surface of sth with a veneer of wood, etc: **be veneered with/in sth** *The bed was veneered with cherrywood.*

**ven·er·able** /ˈvenərəbl/ adj. **1** [usually before noun] (*formal*) venerable people or things deserve respect because they are old, important, wise, etc: *a venerable old man* ◊ *a venerable institution* **2 the Venerable …** [only before noun] (in the Anglican Church) a title of respect used when talking about an ARCHDEACON: *the Venerable Martin Roberts* **3 the Venerable …** [only before noun] (in the Roman Catholic Church) a title given to a dead person who is very holy but who has not yet been made a SAINT

**ven·er·ate** /ˈvenəreɪt/ verb [often passive] ~ sb/sth (as sth) (*formal*) to have and show a lot of respect for sb/sth, especially sb/sth that is considered to be holy or very important SYN revere ▸ **ven·er·ation** /ˌvenəˈreɪʃn/ noun [U]: *The relics were objects of veneration.*

**ven·ereal** /vəˈnɪəriəl; NAmE -ˈnɪr-/ adj. [only before noun] relating to diseases spread by sexual contact: *a venereal infection*

**ve'nereal disease** noun [C, U] (abbr. VD) (*old-fashioned*) a disease that is caught by having sex with a person who already has the disease SYN STI

**ven·etian blind** /vəˌniːʃn ˈblaɪnd/ noun a BLIND for a window that has flat plastic or metal pieces going across it that you can turn to let in as much light as you want

**ven·geance** /ˈvendʒəns/ noun [U] (*formal*) the act of punishing or harming sb in return for what they have done to you, your family or friends SYN revenge: *a desire for vengeance* ◊ **on/upon sb** *to take vengeance on sb* ◊ *He swore vengeance on his child's killer.*
- IDM **with a 'vengeance** (*informal*) to a greater degree than is expected or usual: *She set to work with a vengeance.*

**venge·ful** /ˈvendʒfl/ adj. (*formal*) showing a desire to punish sb who has harmed you ▸ **venge·ful·ly** /-fəli/ adv.

**ve·nial** /ˈviːniəl/ adj. [usually before noun] (*formal*) (of a SIN or mistake) not very serious and therefore able to be forgiven: *a venial sin*

**ven·ison** /ˈvenɪsn/ noun [U] meat from a DEER

**Venn diagram** /ˈven daɪəɡræm/ noun (*mathematics*) a picture showing SETS (= groups of things that have a shared quality) as circles that cross over each other, to show which qualities the different sets have in common

**venom** /ˈvenəm/ noun [U] **1** the poisonous liquid that some snakes, spiders, etc. produce when they bite or STING you **2** (*formal*) a strong, bitter feeling; feelings of hate and a desire to hurt sb: *a look of pure venom* IDM see SPIT *v.*

**ven·om·ous** /ˈvenəməs/ adj. **1** (of a snake, etc.) producing venom **2** (*formal*) full of bitter feelings or hate: *a venomous look* ▸ **ven·om·ous·ly** adv.

**ven·ous** /ˈviːnəs/ adj. (*specialist*) of or contained in VEINS (= the tubes that carry liquids around the bodies of animals and plants): *venous blood*

**vent** /vent/ noun, verb
- noun **1** an opening that allows air, gas or liquid to pass out of or into a room, building, container, etc: *air/heating vents* ⊃ compare REGISTER ⊃ picture at VOLCANO **2** (*specialist*) the opening in the body of a bird, fish, REPTILE or other small animal, through which waste matter is passed out **3** a long,

# vending machine 1734

## Venn diagram

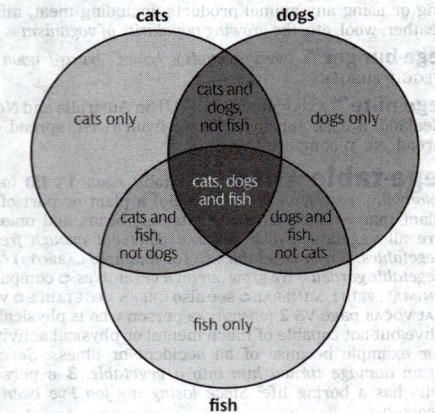

thin opening at the bottom of the back or side of a coat or jacket
- IDM **give (full) vent to sth** (*formal*) to express a feeling, especially anger, strongly: *She gave full vent to her feelings in a violent outburst.*
- verb [T, I] (*formal*) to express feelings, especially anger, strongly: ~ **sth (on sb)** *He vented his anger on the referee.* ◊ ~ **(about sth)** *She vented for two minutes about work and her boss.*

**ven·ti·late** /ˈventɪleɪt/ verb [usually passive] to allow fresh air to enter and move around a room, building, etc: **be ventilated (by sth)** *The bathroom is ventilated by means of an extractor fan.* ◊ *a well-ventilated room* ▸ **ven·ti·la·tion** /ˌventɪˈleɪʃn/ noun [U]: *a ventilation shaft* ◊ *Make sure that there is adequate ventilation in the room before using the paint.*

**ven·ti·la·tor** /ˈventɪleɪtə(r)/ noun **1** a device or an opening for letting fresh air come into a room, etc. **2** a piece of medical equipment with a PUMP that helps sb to breathe by sending air in and out of their lungs: *He was put on a ventilator.*

**ven·tral** /ˈventrəl/ adj. [only before noun] (*biology*) on or connected with the part of a fish or an animal that is under its body (or that in humans faces forward): *a fish's ventral fin* ⊃ compare DORSAL ⊃ **VISUAL VOCAB** page V2

**ven·tricle** /ˈventrɪkl/ noun (*anatomy*) **1** either of the two lower spaces in the heart that PUMP blood to the LUNGS or around the body ⊃ compare AURICLE **2** any hollow space in the body, especially one of four main hollow spaces in the brain

**ven·trilo·quism** /venˈtrɪləkwɪzəm/ noun [U] the art of speaking without moving your lips and of making it look as if your voice is coming from a PUPPET or another person ▸ **ven·trilo·quist** /-kwɪst/ noun: *Entertainment included a ventriloquist.* ◊ *a ventriloquist's dummy*

**ven·ture** /ˈventʃə(r)/ noun, verb
- noun **1** a business project or activity, especially one that involves taking risks SYN **undertaking**: *A disastrous business venture lost him thousands of dollars.* ⊃ see also JOINT VENTURE
- verb **1** [I] + adv./prep. to go somewhere even though you know that it might be dangerous or unpleasant: *They ventured nervously into the water.* ◊ *He's never ventured abroad in his life.* **2** [T] (*formal*) to say or do sth in a careful way, especially because it might upset or offend sb: ~ **sth** *She hardly dared to venture an opinion.* ◊ ~ **to do sth** *I ventured to suggest that she might have made a mistake.* ◊ **speech** *'And if I say no?' she ventured.* ◊ ~ **that …** *He ventured that the data might be flawed.* **3** [T] ~ **sth (on sth)** to risk losing sth valuable or important if you are not successful at sth SYN **gamble**: *It was wrong to venture his financial security on such a risky deal.*

**IDM** **nothing ˌventured, nothing ˈgained** (*saying*) used to say that you have to take risks if you want to achieve things and be successful
**PHR V** **ˈventure into/on sth** to do sth, even though it involves risks: *This is the first time the company has ventured into movie production.*

**ˈventure capital** *noun* [U] (*business*) money that is invested in a new company to help it develop, which may involve a lot of risk ⊃ compare WORKING CAPITAL

**venue** /ˈvenjuː/ *noun* a place where people meet for an organized event, for example a concert, sporting event or conference: *The band will be playing at 20 different venues on their UK tour.* ◊ *music/entertainment venues* ⊃ SYNONYMS at PLACE ⊃ WORDFINDER NOTE at CONCERT

**Venus** /ˈviːnəs/ *noun* the planet in the SOLAR SYSTEM that is second in order of distance from the sun, between Mercury and the Earth

**ˈVenus fly-trap** /ˌviːnəs ˈflaɪtræp/ *noun* a small CARNIVOROUS (= meat-eating) plant with leaves that catch insects by closing quickly around them

**ver·ac·ity** /vəˈræsəti/ *noun* [U] (*formal*) the quality of being true; the habit of telling the truth **SYN** **truth, truthfulness**: *They questioned the veracity of her story.*

**ver·anda** (also **ver·an·dah**) /vəˈrændə/ *noun* 1 (*especially BrE*) (*NAmE usually* **porch**) a platform with an open front and a roof, built onto the side of a house on the ground floor: *After dinner, we sat talking on the veranda.* 2 (*AustralE, NZE*) a roof over the part of the street where people walk in front of a shop **SYN** **awning**

**verb** /vɜːb; *NAmE* vɜːrb/ *noun* (*grammar*) a word or group of words that expresses an action (such as *eat*), an event (such as *happen*) or a state (such as *exist*): *regular/irregular verbs* ◊ *transitive/intransitive verbs* ⊃ see also LINKING VERB, MAIN VERB, PHRASAL VERB, PRO-VERB

**ver·bal** /ˈvɜːbl; *NAmE* ˈvɜːrbl/ *adj.* 1 relating to words: *The job applicant must have good verbal skills.* ◊ *non-verbal communication* (= expressions of the face, GESTURES, etc.) 2 spoken, not written: *a verbal agreement/warning* ◊ *verbal instructions* ⊃ compare ORAL 3 (*grammar*) relating to verbs: *a verbal noun* (= a noun formed from a verb, for example *smoking*).

**ver·bal·ize** (*BrE also* **-ise**) /ˈvɜːbəlaɪz; *NAmE* ˈvɜːrb-/ *verb* [T, I] ~**(sth)** (*formal*) to express your feelings or ideas in words: *He's a real genius but he has difficulty verbalizing his ideas.*

**ver·bal·ly** /ˈvɜːbəli; *NAmE* ˈvɜːrb-/ *adv.* in spoken words and not in writing or actions: *The company had received complaints both verbally and in writing.*

**ver·ba·tim** /vɜːˈbeɪtɪm; *NAmE* vɜːrˈb-/ *adj., adv.* exactly as spoken or written **SYN** **word for word**: *a verbatim report* ◊ *He reported the speech verbatim.*

**ver·bena** /vɜːˈbiːnə; *NAmE* vɜːrˈb-/ *noun* [U, C] a garden plant with bright flowers

**ver·bi·age** /ˈvɜːbiɪdʒ; *NAmE* ˈvɜːrb-/ *noun* [U] (*formal, disapproving*) the use of too many words, or of more difficult words than are needed, to express an idea

**ver·bose** /vɜːˈbəʊs; *NAmE* vɜːrˈb-/ *adj.* (*formal, disapproving*) using or containing more words than are needed **SYN** **long-winded**: *a verbose speaker/style* ▸ **ver·bos·ity** /vɜːˈbɒsəti; *NAmE* vɜːrˈbɑːs-/ *noun* [U]

**ver·bo·ten** /vəˈbəʊtn, fə-; *NAmE* vərˈb-, fər-/ *adj.* (*especially NAmE, from German, humorous*) not allowed: *Cake and cookies are strictly verboten in my house.*

**ver·dant** /ˈvɜːdnt; *NAmE* ˈvɜːrd-/ *adj.* (*literary*) (of grass, plants, fields, etc.) fresh and green

**ver·dict** /ˈvɜːdɪkt; *NAmE* ˈvɜːrd-/ *noun* 1 an official judgement made in court or at an INQUEST (= an official investigation into sb's death): *Has the jury reached a verdict?* ◊ *The jury returned a verdict* (= gave a verdict) *of guilty.* ◊ *The coroner recorded a verdict of accidental death.* ⊃ see also MAJORITY VERDICT, OPEN VERDICT 2 ~ a decision that you make or an opinion that you give about

1735 **verruca**

sth, after you have tested it or considered it carefully: *Well, what's your verdict?* ◊ ~ **on sth/sb** *The panel will give their verdict on the latest album releases.*

**ver·dure** /ˈvɜːdʒə(r); *NAmE* ˈvɜːrdʒ-/ *noun* [U] (*literary*) thick green plants growing in a particular place

**verge** /vɜːdʒ; *NAmE* vɜːrdʒ/ *noun, verb*
■ *noun* (*BrE*) a piece of grass at the edge of a path, road, etc: *a grass verge*
**IDM** **on/to the verge of sth/of doing sth** very near to the moment when sb does sth or sth happens: *He was on the verge of tears.* ◊ *They are on the verge of signing a new contract.*
■ *verb*
**PHR V** **ˈverge on sth** to be very close to an extreme state or condition **SYN** **border on sth**: *Some of his suggestions verged on the outrageous.*

**ver·ger** /ˈvɜːdʒə(r); *NAmE* ˈvɜːrdʒ-/ *noun* (*especially BrE*) an official whose job is to take care of the inside of a church and to perform some simple duties during church services

**ver·ify** /ˈverɪfaɪ/ *verb* (**veri·fies, veri·fy·ing, veri·fied, veri·fied**) (*formal*) 1 to check that sth is true or accurate: ~ **sth** *We have no way of verifying his story.* ◊ ~ **that** ... *Please verify that there is sufficient memory available before loading the program.* ◊ ~ **whether, what, etc** ... *I'll leave you to verify whether these claims are true.* 2 ~ **sth** | ~ **that** ... to show or say that sth is true or accurate **SYN** **confirm**: *Her version of events was verified by neighbours.* ▸ **veri·fi·able** /-əbl/ *adj.*: *a verifiable fact* **veri·fi·ca·tion** /ˌverɪfɪˈkeɪʃn/ *noun* [U]: *the verification of hypotheses*

**ver·ily** /ˈverɪli/ *adv.* (*old use*) really; truly

**veri·sim·ili·tude** /ˌverɪsɪˈmɪlɪtjuːd; *NAmE* -tuːd/ *noun* [U] (*formal*) the quality of seeming to be true or real **SYN** **authenticity**: *To add verisimilitude, the stage is covered with sand for the desert scenes.*

**ver·it·able** /ˈverɪtəbl/ *adj.* [only before noun] (*formal or humorous*) a word used to emphasize that sb/sth can be compared to sb/sth else that is more exciting, more impressive, etc. **SYN** **positive**: *The meal that followed was a veritable banquet.*

**ver·ity** /ˈverəti/ *noun* (*pl.* **-ies**) 1 [usually pl.] (*formal*) a belief or principle about life that is accepted as true: *the eternal verities of life* 2 [U] (*old use*) truth

**vermi·celli** /ˌvɜːmɪˈtʃeli; *NAmE* ˌvɜːrm-/ *noun* 1 PASTA in the shape of very thin sticks, often broken into small pieces and added to soups 2 (*BrE*) small pieces of chocolate in the shape of very thin sticks broken into small pieces, used to decorate cakes

**ver·mil·ion** /vəˈmɪliən; *NAmE* vərˈm-/ *adj.* bright red in colour ▸ **ver·mil·ion** *noun* [U]

**ver·min** /ˈvɜːmɪn; *NAmE* ˈvɜːrm-/ *noun* [pl.] 1 wild animals or birds that destroy plants or food, or attack farm animals and birds: *On farms the fox is considered vermin and treated as such.* 2 insects that live on the bodies of animals and sometimes humans: *The room was crawling with vermin.* 3 (*disapproving*) people who are very unpleasant or dangerous to society

**ver·mouth** /ˈvɜːməθ, ˈvɜːmuːθ; *NAmE* vərˈmuːθ/ *noun* [U] a strong wine, made with HERBS and SPICES to add taste, often mixed with other drinks as a COCKTAIL

**ver·nac·u·lar** /vəˈnækjələ(r); *NAmE* vərˈn-/ *noun* 1 *usually* **the vernacular** [sing.] the language spoken by ordinary people in a particular country or region 2 [U] (*specialist*) a style of architecture used for ordinary houses rather than large public buildings ▸ **ver·nacu·lar** *adj.*

**ver·nal** /ˈvɜːnl; *NAmE* ˈvɜːrnl/ *adj.* [only before noun] (*formal or literary*) connected with the season of spring: *the vernal equinox*

**ver·ruca** /vəˈruːkə/ (*BrE*) (*NAmE* **plantar wart**) *noun* a small hard spot like a WART on the bottom of the foot, which can be easily spread from person to person

**ver·sa·tile** /ˈvɜːsətaɪl; NAmE ˈvɜːrsətl/ adj. (approving) **1** (of a person) able to do many different things: *He's a versatile actor who has played a wide variety of parts.* **2** (of food, a building, etc.) having many different uses: *Eggs are easy to cook and are an extremely versatile food.* ▸ **ver·sa·til·ity** /ˌvɜːsəˈtɪləti; NAmE ˌvɜːrs-/ noun [U]: *She is a designer of extraordinary versatility.*

**verse** /vɜːs; NAmE vɜːrs/ noun **1** [U] writing that is arranged in lines, often with a regular rhythm or pattern of RHYME SYN **poetry**: *in* ~ *Most of the play is written in verse, but some of it is in prose.* ⊃ see also BLANK VERSE, FREE VERSE ⇒ WORDFINDER NOTE at POETRY **2** [C] a group of lines that form a unit in a poem or song: *a hymn with six verses* **3** *verses* [pl.] (old-fashioned) poetry: *a book of comic verses* **4** [C] any one of the short numbered divisions of a chapter in the Bible IDM see CHAPTER

**versed** /vɜːst; NAmE vɜːrst/ adj. ~ **in sth** having a lot of knowledge about sth, or skill at sth SYN **expert**, **practised**: *He was well versed in employment law.*

**ver·sion** /ˈvɜːʃn; NAmE ˈvɜːrʒn/ noun **1** a form of sth that is slightly different from an earlier form or from other forms of the same thing: ~ **of sth** *the latest version of the software package* ⋄ *an expanded version of the article* ⋄ *The original/final version is vastly superior.* ⊃ see also ALPHA VERSION, BETA VERSION **2** a film, play, piece of music, etc. that is based on a particular piece of work but is in a different form, style or language: ~ **of sth** *the film version of 'War and Peace'* ⋄ *The English version of the novel is due for publication next year.* ⊃ see also COVER VERSION **3** a description of an event from the point of view of a particular person or group of people: ~ **of what, how, etc ...** *She gave us her version of what had happened that day.* ⋄ ~ **of sth** *She agreed to give her version of events to journalists.* ⊃ SYNONYMS at REPORT

**verso** /ˈvɜːsəʊ; NAmE ˈvɜːrs-/ noun (pl. **-os**) (specialist) the page on the left side of an open book ⋄ compare RECTO

**ver·sus** /ˈvɜːsəs; NAmE ˈvɜːrs-/ prep. (abbr. **v**, **vs**) **1** (sport or law) used to show that two teams or sides are against each other: *It is France versus Brazil in the final.* ⋄ *in the case of the State versus Ford* **2** used to compare two different ideas, choices, etc: *It was the promise of better job opportunities versus the inconvenience of moving away and leaving her friends.*

**ver·tebra** /ˈvɜːtɪbrə; NAmE ˈvɜːrt-/ noun (pl. **ver·te·brae** /-breɪ, -briː/) any of the small bones that are connected together to form the BACKBONE ⊃ VISUAL VOCAB page V1 ▸ **ver·te·bral** adj. [only before noun]

**ver·te·brate** /ˈvɜːtɪbrət; NAmE ˈvɜːrt-/ noun (specialist) any animal with a BACKBONE, including all MAMMALS, birds, fish, REPTILES and AMPHIBIANS ⋄ compare INVERTEBRATE ▸ **ver·te·brate** adj.

**ver·tex** /ˈvɜːteks; NAmE ˈvɜːrt-/ noun (pl. **ver·ti·ces** /-tɪsiːz/ or **ver·texes**) **1** (geometry) a point where two lines meet to form an angle, especially the point of a TRIANGLE or CONE opposite the base ⋄ picture at SOLID **2** (specialist) the highest point or top of sth

**ver·ti·cal** /ˈvɜːtɪkl; NAmE ˈvɜːrt-/ adj., noun
- adj. **1** (of a line, pole, etc.) going straight up or down from a level surface or from top to bottom in a picture, etc: *the vertical axis of the graph* ⋄ *The cliff was almost vertical.* ⋄ *There was a vertical drop to the ocean.* ⋄ compare HORIZONTAL ⋄ picture at LINE **2** having a structure in which there are top, middle and bottom levels: *a vertical flow of communication* ▸ **ver·ti·cal·ly** /-kli/ adv.
- noun usually **the vertical** a straight line or position from top to bottom or bottom to top SYN **perpendicular**: *The wall is several degrees off the vertical.*

**vertical inteˈgration** noun [U] (business) the combination in one company of two or more stages of production normally operated by separate companies

**ver·tigin·ous** /vɜːˈtɪdʒɪnəs; NAmE vɜːrˈt-/ adj. (formal) causing a feeling of vertigo because of being very high SYN **dizzying**: *From the path there was a vertiginous drop to the valley below.*

**ver·tigo** /ˈvɜːtɪɡəʊ; NAmE ˈvɜːrt-/ noun [U] the feeling of DIZZINESS and fear, and of losing your balance, that is caused in some people when they look down from a very high place

**verve** /vɜːv; NAmE vɜːrv/ noun [U, sing.] energy, excitement or enthusiasm SYN **gusto**: *It was a performance of verve and vitality.*

**very** /ˈveri/ adv., adj.
- adv. (abbr. **v**) **1** used before adjectives, adverbs and determiners to mean 'in a high degree' or 'extremely': *Very few people know that.* ⋄ *We have very little information at present on the incident.* ⋄ *Thanks very much.* ⋄ *I'm not very* (= not at all) *impressed.* ⋄ *I'm very very grateful.* ⋄ *Things could have been so very different.* ⋄ *Australia has a very good reputation for producing high-quality grain.* ⋄ *This is a very important part of our marketing.* **2** used to emphasize a superlative adjective or before *own*: *They wanted the very best quality.* ⋄ *Be there by six at the very latest.* ⋄ *At last he had his very own car* (= belonging to him and to nobody else). **3** **the ~ same** exactly the same: *Mario said the very same thing.*
- adj. [only before noun] **1** used to emphasize that you are talking about a particular thing or person and not about another SYN **actual**: *He might be phoning her at this very moment.* ⋄ *The US initiated the deal for that very reason.* ⋄ *I'd intended to tell him that very day.* **2** used to emphasize an extreme place or time: *It happens at the very beginning of the book.* **3** used to emphasize a noun SYN **mere**: *The very nature of its business is to secretly monitor and profile internet users' habits.* ⋄ *a civil war in which the very existence of the nation is in question* IDM see EYE *n.*

> ▸ GRAMMAR POINT
>
> **very / very much**
>
> - **Very** is used with adjectives, past participles used as adjectives, and adverbs: *I am very hungry.* ⋄ *I was very pleased to get your letter.* ⋄ *You played very well.* But notice this use: *I'm very much afraid that your son may be involved in the crime.*
> - **Very** is not used with past participles that have a passive meaning. **Much**, **very much** or **greatly** (formal) are usually used instead: *Your help was very much appreciated.* ⋄ *He was much loved by everyone.* ⋄ *She was greatly admired.*
> - **Very** is used to emphasize superlative adjectives: *my very best work* ⋄ *the very youngest children.* However, with comparative adjectives **much**, **very much**, **a lot**, etc. are used: *Your work is very much better.* ⋄ *much younger children.*
> - **Very** is not used with adjectives and adverbs that already have an extreme meaning. You are more likely to use an adverb such as *absolutely*, *completely*, etc: *She was absolutely furious.* ⋄ *I'm completely exhausted.* ⋄ *You played really brilliantly.*
> - **Very** is not used with verbs. Use **very much** instead: *We enjoyed staying with you very much.*

**very high ˈfrequency** noun [U] = VHF

**ves·icle** /ˈvesɪkl/ noun **1** (biology) a small hollow structure in the body of a plant or an animal **2** (medical) a small SWELLING filled with liquid under the skin SYN **blister**

**ves·pers** /ˈvespəz; NAmE -spərz/ noun [U] the service of evening prayer in some Christian Churches ⋄ compare EVENSONG, MATINS

**ves·sel** /ˈvesl/ noun **1** a tube that carries blood through the body of a person or an animal, or liquid through the parts of a plant: *to burst/rupture a blood vessel* **2** (formal) a ship or large boat: *ocean-going vessels* ⋄ *a small fishing vessel* **3** (old use or specialist) a container used for holding liquids, such as a bowl, cup, etc: *a Bronze Age drinking vessel*

**vest** /vest/ noun, verb
- noun **1** (BrE) (NAmE **under-shirt**) a piece of underwear worn under a shirt, etc. next to the skin: *a cotton vest* ⋄ compare SINGLET **2** a special piece of clothing that covers the upper part of the body: *a bullet-proof vest* ⋄ *a*

running vest **3** (*NAmE*) (*BrE* **waistcoat**) a short piece of clothing with buttons down the front but no arms, usually worn over a shirt and under a jacket, often forming part of a man's suit
■ *verb*
**PHRV** **'vest in sb/sth** (*law*) (of power, property, etc.) to belong to sb/sth legally **'vest sth in sb** | **'vest sb with sth** [often passive] (*formal*) **1** to give sb the legal right or power to do sth: *Overall authority is vested in the Supreme Council.* ◊ *The Supreme Council is vested with overall authority.* **2** to make sb the legal owner of land or property

**‚vested 'interest** *noun* ~ **(in sth)** a personal reason for wanting sth to happen, especially because you get some advantage from it: *They have a vested interest in keeping the club as exclusive as possible.* ◊ *Vested interests* (= people with a vested interest) *are opposing the plan.*

**ves·ti·bule** /ˈvestɪbjuːl/ *noun* **1** (*formal*) an entrance hall of a large building, for example where hats and coats can be left **2** (*specialist*) a space at the end of a coach on a train that connects it with the next coach

**ves·tige** /ˈvestɪdʒ/ *noun* (*formal*) **1** a small part of sth that still exists after the rest of it has stopped existing **SYN** **trace**: *the last vestiges of the old colonial regime* **2** usually used in negative sentences, to say that not even a small amount of sth exists: *There's not a vestige of truth in the rumour.*

**ves·tig·ial** /veˈstɪdʒiəl/ *adj.* [usually before noun] (*formal* or *specialist*) that remain as the last small part of sth that used to exist: *vestigial traces of an earlier culture* ◊ *It is often possible to see the vestigial remains of rear limbs on some snakes.*

**vest·ment** /ˈvestmənt/ *noun* [usually pl.] a piece of clothing worn by a priest during church services

**ves·try** /ˈvestri/ *noun* (*pl.* **-ies**) a room in a church where a priest prepares for a service by putting on special clothes and where various objects used in WORSHIP are kept **SYN** **sacristy**

**vet** /vet/ *noun, verb*
■ *noun* **1** (*especially BrE*) (*NAmE usually* **vet·er·in·ar·ian**) (*also BrE, formal* **veterinary surgeon**) a person who has been trained in the science of animal medicine, whose job is to treat animals who are sick or injured **2** *vet's* (*pl.* **vets**) the place where a vet works: *I've got to take the dog to the vet's tomorrow.* **3** (*NAmE, informal*) = VETERAN: *a Vietnam vet*
■ *verb* (**-tt-**) **1** ~ **sb** to find out about a person's past life and career in order to decide if they are suitable for sth **SYN** **screen**: *All candidates are carefully vetted for security reasons.* ➔ see also VETTING **2** ~ **sth** to check the contents, quality, etc. of sth carefully **SYN** **screen**: *All reports are vetted before publication.*

**vetch** /vetʃ/ *noun* [U, C] a plant of the PEA family. There are several types of vetch, one of which is used as food for farm animals.

**vet·eran** /ˈvetərən/ *noun* **1** a person who has a lot of experience in a particular area or activity: *the veteran American actor, Clint Eastwood* **2** (*NAmE, informal* **vet**) a person who has been a soldier, sailor, etc. in a war: *war veterans*

**'Veterans Day** *noun* a holiday in the US on 11 November, in honour of members of the armed forces and others who have died in war ➔ see also MEMORIAL DAY, REMEMBRANCE SUNDAY

**vet·er·in·ar·ian** /ˌvetərɪˈneəriən; *NAmE* -ˈner-/ *noun* (*NAmE*) = VET (1)

**vet·er·in·ary** /ˈvetnri, -trənəri; *NAmE* -təraneri/ *adj.* [only before noun] connected with caring for the health of animals: *veterinary medicine/science*

**'veterinary surgeon** *noun* (*BrE, formal*) = VET (1)

**vet·koek** /ˈfetkʊk/ *noun* (*pl.* **vet·koek** or **vet·koeks** or **vet·koeke** /ˈfetkʊkə/) (*SAfrE*) a small cake made by frying DOUGH

**veto** /ˈviːtəʊ/ *noun, verb*
■ *noun* (*pl.* **-oes**) **1** [C, U] the right to refuse to allow sth to be done, especially the right to stop a law from being passed or a decision from being taken: *The British government used its veto to block the proposal.* ◊ *to have the* **power/ right of veto** ◊ *the use of the presidential veto* **2** [C] ~ **(on sth/on doing sth)** an occasion when sb refuses to allow sth to be done **SYN** **ban**: *For months there was a veto on employing new staff.*
■ *verb* (**ve·toes, veto·ing, ve·toed, ve·toed**) **1** ~ **sth** to stop sth from happening or being done by using your official authority (= by using your veto): *Plans for the dam have been vetoed by the Environmental Protection Agency.* **2** ~ **sth** to refuse to accept or do what sb has suggested **SYN** **rule out**: *I wanted to go camping but the others quickly vetoed that idea.*

**vet·ting** /ˈvetɪŋ/ *noun* [U, C] **1** the process of checking sth with great care: *The agreement went through a careful process of vetting by lawyers.* **2** the process of finding out everything about a person's past life and career in order to decide if they are suitable for sth: *the screening and vetting of all airport-based employees*

**vex** /veks/ *verb* ~ **sb** (*old-fashioned* or *formal*) to annoy or worry sb ▸ **vex·ing** *adj.*: *a vexing problem*

**vex·ation** /vekˈseɪʃn/ *noun* (*old-fashioned* or *formal*) **1** [U] the state of feeling upset or annoyed **2** [C] a thing that upsets or annoys you

**vex·atious** /vekˈseɪʃəs/ *adj.* (*old-fashioned* or *formal*) making you feel upset or annoyed

**vexed** /vekst/ *adj.* **1** ~ **question/issue** a problem that is difficult to deal with **SYN** **thorny**: *The conference spent days discussing the vexed question of border controls.* **2** ~ **(at/with sb/sth)** (*old-fashioned*) upset or annoyed

**VHF** /ˌviː eɪtʃ ˈef/ *abbr.* very high frequency (a range of radio waves used for high-quality broadcasting)

**via** /ˈvaɪə, ˈviːə/ *prep.* **1** through a place: *We flew home via Dubai.* **2** by means of a particular person, system, etc.: *I heard about the sale via Jane.* ◊ *The news programme came to us via satellite.*

**vi·able** /ˈvaɪəbl/ *adj.* **1** that can be done; that will be successful **SYN** **feasible**: *a viable option/proposition* ◊ *There is no viable alternative.* ◊ *to be commercially/ politically/financially/economically viable* **OPP** **unviable** **2** (*biology*) capable of developing and surviving independently: *viable organisms* ▸ **via·bil·ity** /ˌvaɪəˈbɪləti/ *noun* [U]: *There are doubts about the commercial viability of the newspaper.*

**via·duct** /ˈvaɪədʌkt/ *noun* a long, high bridge, usually with ARCHES, that carries a road or railway across a river or valley

**Vi·agra™** /vaɪˈægrə/ *noun* (*U*) a drug used to treat IMPOTENCE in men

**vial** /ˈvaɪəl/ *noun* (*especially NAmE*) = PHIAL

**vibes** /vaɪbz/ *noun* [pl.] (*informal*) **1** (*also formal* **vi·bra·tions**) (*also* **vibe** [sing.]) a mood or an atmosphere produced by a particular person, thing or place: *good/bad vibes* ◊ *The vibes weren't right.* **2** = VIBRAPHONE: *a jazzy vibes backing*

**vi·brant** /ˈvaɪbrənt/ *adj.* **1** full of life and energy **SYN** **exciting**: *a vibrant city* ◊ *Thailand is at its most vibrant during the New Year celebrations.* **2** (of colours) very bright and strong **SYN** **brilliant**: *The room was decorated in vibrant reds and yellows.* ➔ SYNONYMS at BRIGHT **3** (of music, sounds, etc.) loud and powerful: *vibrant rhythms* ▸ **vi·brancy** /-brənsi/ *noun* [U] **vi·brant·ly** *adv.*

**vi·bra·phone** /ˈvaɪbrəfəʊn/ *noun* [C] (*also informal* **vibes** [pl.]) a musical instrument used especially in jazz that has two rows of metal bars that you hit, and a motor that makes them vibrate

**vi·brate** /vaɪˈbreɪt; *NAmE* ˈvaɪbreɪt/ *verb* [I, T] to move or make sth move from side to side very quickly and with small movements: ~ **(sth)** *Every time a train went past the walls vibrated.* ◊ ~ **with sth** *The atmosphere seemed to vibrate with tension.*

**vi·bra·tion** /vaɪˈbreɪʃn/ *noun* **1** [C, U] a continuous shaking movement or feeling: *We could feel the vibrations from the*

# vibrato

trucks passing outside. ◊ a reduction in the level of vibration in the engine **2 vibrations** [pl.] (formal) = VIBES

**vi·bra·to** /vɪˈbrɑːtəʊ/ noun [U, C] (pl. -os) (music, from Italian) a shaking effect in singing or playing a musical instrument, made by rapid, slight changes in PITCH (= how high or low a sound is)

**vi·bra·tor** /vaɪˈbreɪtə(r); NAmE ˈvaɪbreɪtər/ noun an electrical device that produces a continuous shaking movement, used in MASSAGE or for sexual pleasure

**vicar** /ˈvɪkə(r)/ noun **1** (especially BrE) an Anglican priest who is in charge of a church and the district around it (called a PARISH) **2** (NAmE) a priest in the US Episcopal Church ⊃ compare CURATE¹, MINISTER, PRIEST, RECTOR

**vic·ar·age** /ˈvɪkərɪdʒ/ noun a vicar's house

**vic·ari·ous** /vɪˈkeəriəs; NAmE vaɪˈker-/ adj. [only before noun] felt or experienced by watching or reading about sb else doing sth, rather than by doing it yourself: He got a vicarious thrill out of watching his son score the winning goal. ▶ **vic·ari·ous·ly** adv.

**vice** ⓘ ⓑ /vaɪs/ noun **1** ⓘ [U] criminal activities that involve sex or drugs: plain-clothes detectives from the vice squad **2** [U, C] behaviour that is evil or IMMORAL; a quality in sb's character that is evil or immoral: The film ended most satisfactorily: vice punished and virtue rewarded. ◊ Greed is a terrible vice. ◊ (humorous) Cigarettes are my only vice. **3** (especially BrE) (NAmE usually **vise**) [C] a tool with two metal blocks that can be moved together by turning a SCREW. The vice is used to hold an object in place while work is done on it: He held my arm in a **vice-like** (= very firm) **grip**.

vice

**vice-** /vaɪs/ combining form (in nouns and related adjectives) next in rank to sb and able to represent them or act for them: vice-captain

**ˌvice ˈadmiral** noun an officer of very high rank in the NAVY

**ˌvice ˈchancellor** noun the head of a university in England, Wales and Northern Ireland, who is in charge of the work of running the university. (Compare the CHANCELLOR, who is the official head of a university but only has duties at various ceremonies.)

**ˌvice-ˈpresident** noun (abbr. **VP**) **1** the person below the president of a country in rank, who takes control of the country if the president is not able to **2** (NAmE) a person in charge of a particular part of a business company: the vice-president of sales ▶ **ˌvice-presiˈdential** adj. [usually before noun]

**vice·roy** /ˈvaɪsrɔɪ/ noun (often used as a title) (in the past) a person who was sent by a king or queen to govern a COLONY

**ˌvice ˈversa** /ˌvaɪs ˈvɜːsə; ˌvaɪsi; NAmE ˈvɜːrsə/ adv. used to say that the opposite of what you have just said is also true: You can cruise from Cairo to Aswan or vice versa (= also from Aswan to Cairo).

**vicin·ity** /vəˈsɪnəti/ usually **the vicinity** noun [usually sing.] (pl. -ies) (rather formal) the area around a particular place: **in the ~ (of sth)** Crowds gathered in the vicinity of Trafalgar Square. ◊ There is no hospital **in the immediate vicinity**.

**vi·cious** ⓘ ⓒ¹ /ˈvɪʃəs/ adj. **1** ⓒ¹ violent and cruel ⓢⓨⓝ **brutal**: a vicious attack ◊ a vicious criminal ◊ She has a vicious temper. **2** ⓘ ⓒ¹ (of animals) aggressive and dangerous: a vicious dog **3** (of an attack, criticism, etc.) full of hate and anger: She wrote me a vicious letter. **4** (informal) very bad or severe: a vicious headache ◊ a vicious spiral of rising prices ▶ **vi·cious·ly** adv. **vi·cious·ness** noun [U]: Police were shocked by the viciousness of the assault.

**ˌvicious ˈcircle** (also **ˌvicious ˈcycle**) noun [sing.] a situation in which one problem causes another problem which then makes the first problem worse ⊃ compare VIRTUOUS CIRCLE

**vi·cis·si·tude** /vɪˈsɪsɪtjuːd; NAmE -tuːd/ noun [usually pl.] (formal) one of the many changes and problems in a situation or in your life, that you have to deal with

**vic·tim** ⓘ ⓑ¹ /ˈvɪktɪm/ noun **1** ⓑ¹ a person who has been attacked, injured or killed as the result of a crime, a disease, an accident, etc: murder/rape victims ◊ She was the innocent victim of an arson attack. ◊ victims of crime/abuse/violence ◊ the alleged victim of a serious assault ◊ Several countries have pledged millions of dollars to help the victims of the tsunami. ⊃ WORDFINDER NOTE at ACCIDENT **2** ⓘ ⓑ¹ a person who has been tricked ⓢⓨⓝ **target**: They were the victims of a cruel hoax. ⊃ see also FASHION VICTIM **3** ⓘ ⓑ² a person or thing that is badly affected by a situation, a decision, etc: Schools are the latest victims of cuts in public spending. ◊ The small company became **a victim of its own success** when it could not supply all its orders on time. **4** an animal or a person that is killed and offered as a SACRIFICE: a sacrificial victim

ⓘⓓⓜ **fall ˈvictim (to sth)** (formal) to be injured, cheated, damaged or killed by sb/sth

**vic·tim·hood** /ˈvɪktɪmhʊd/ noun [U] the state of being a victim: The attacks left them with a deep sense of victimhood.

**vic·tim·ize** (BrE also **-ise**) /ˈvɪktɪmaɪz/ verb [often passive] ~ sb to make sb suffer unfairly because you do not like them, their opinions, or sth that they have done: For years the family had been victimized by racist neighbours. ◊ The union claimed that some of its members had been victimized for taking part in the strike. ▶ **vic·tim·iza·tion**, **-isa·tion** /ˌvɪktɪmaɪˈzeɪʃn; NAmE -məˈz-/ noun [U]

**vic·tim·less** /ˈvɪktɪmləs/ adj. a **victimless** crime is one in which nobody seems to suffer or be harmed

**ˈvictim supˌport** noun [U] a service provided by the police that helps people who are victims of crime

**vic·tor** /ˈvɪktə(r)/ noun (literary) the winner of a battle, competition, game, etc.

**Vic·tor·ian** /vɪkˈtɔːriən/ adj., noun

■ adj. **1** connected with the period from 1837 to 1901 in Britain when Queen Victoria was queen in the UK: Victorian architecture ◊ the Victorian age **2** having the attitudes that were typical of society during Queen Victoria's REIGN: Victorian attitudes to sex (= being easily shocked by sexual matters) ◊ She advocated a return to Victorian values (= hard work, pride in your country, etc.).

■ noun a British person who was alive during the period from 1837 to 1901, when Queen Victoria was queen

**Vicˈtoria ˌsponge** /vɪkˌtɔːriə ˈspʌndʒ/ noun [C, U] a type of SPONGE CAKE that is made with fat in the mixture

**vic·tori·ous** /vɪkˈtɔːriəs/ adj. having won a victory; that ends in victory ⓢⓨⓝ **successful**, **triumphant**: the victorious army/team ◊ **in sth** He emerged victorious in the elections. ▶ **vic·tori·ous·ly** adv.

**vic·tory** ⓘ ⓑ² /ˈvɪktəri/ noun [C, U] (pl. -ies) success in a game, an election, a war, etc: to **win a narrow victory** ◊ an election victory ◊ **~ in sth** a decisive/landslide victory in the election ◊ She is confident of victory in Saturday's final. ◊ **~ over/against sb/sth** the team's 3–2 victory over Poland ◊ **~ for sb/sth** The case is being seen as a victory for freedom of speech. ◊ a victory speech/celebration/parade ⊃ see also MORAL VICTORY, PYRRHIC VICTORY

ⓘⓓⓜ **roar, romp, sweep, etc. to ˈvictory** to win sth easily: He swept to victory in the final of the championship. ⊃ more at SNATCH v.

**vict·uals** /ˈvɪtlz/ noun [pl.] (old-fashioned) food and drink

**vi·cuña** /vɪˈkuːnjə/ noun a wild animal with a long neck and very soft wool, which lives in South America. Vicuñas are related to LLAMAS.

**vide** /ˈviːdeɪ/ (abbr. **v.**) verb **~ sth** (from Latin) used (meaning 'see') as an instruction in books to tell the reader to look at a particular book, passage, etc. for more information

**video** 🔵 **A1** /ˈvɪdiəʊ/ noun, verb
▪ **noun** (pl. **-os**) **1** 🔑 **A1** [U] a system of recording moving pictures and sound, either using a digital method of storing data or (in the past) using VIDEOTAPE: *A wedding is the perfect subject for video.* ◇ **on** ~ *The robbery was captured on video.* **2** 🔑 **A1** (also ˈ**video clip**) [C, U] a short film or recording of an event, made using digital technology and viewed on a computer, especially over the internet: *More than a million people have watched a video of the incident.* ◇ *Upload your videos and share them with friends and family online.* ◇ *This phone can store up to 20 hours of video.* **3** [C] (also ˈ**music video**) a short film made by a pop or rock band to be shown with a song when it is played on television or online **4** (also ˈ**video tape**) [U, C] a type of MAGNETIC tape used in the past for recording moving pictures and sound; a box containing this tape, also called a ˈ**video casˈsette 5** [C] a copy of a film, programme, etc. recorded on VIDEOTAPE **6** (also ˌ**video casˈsette reˌcorder**) [C] (abbr. **VCR**) (BrE) a piece of equipment used, especially in the past, to record and play films and TV programmes on video
▪ **verb 1** ~ **sb/sth** to record moving pictures and sound, either using a digital method of storing data or (in the past) using videotape: *Videoing students can be a useful teaching exercise.* **2** (also formal ˈ**video tape**) ~ **sth** (especially BrE) to record a television programme using a VCR (= video cassette recorder)

ˈ**video camera** noun a special camera for making video films ⇒ see also CAMCORDER

ˈ**video card** noun (computing) a device that allows images to be shown on a computer screen

ˈ**video-conˌferencing** /ˈvɪdiəʊkɒnfərənsɪŋ/; NAmE -kɑːn-/ noun [U] a system that enables people in different parts of the world to have a meeting by watching and listening to each other using video screens

ˈ**video diary** noun a series of video recordings made by sb over a period of time, in which they record their experiences, thoughts and feelings

ˈ**video game** noun a game in which you press buttons to control and move images on a screen

ˈ**video graph** /ˈvɪdiəʊɡrɑːf/; NAmE -ɡræf/ verb ~ **sb/sth** (IndE) to make a video recording of sb/sth **SYN** video

ˈ**video tape** /ˈvɪdiəʊteɪp/ noun, verb
▪ **noun** [U, C] = VIDEO
▪ **verb** ~ **sth** (formal) = VIDEO: *a videotaped interview*

**viˈdeshi** /vɪˈdeɪʃi/ adj., noun (IndE)
▪ **adj.** not Indian or not made in India: *Videshi fruit is more expensive than locally produced fruit.* ⇒ compare DESI
▪ **noun** a person who does not come from India

**vie** /vaɪ/ verb (**vying** /ˈvaɪɪŋ/, **vied, vied**) [I] (formal) to compete strongly with sb in order to obtain or achieve sth **SYN** compete: ~ **(with sb) (for sth)** *She was surrounded by men all vying for her attention.* ◇ *a row of restaurants vying with each other for business* ◇ ~ **(to do sth)** *Screaming fans vied to get closer to their idol.*

**view** 🔵 **A2** 🔊 /vjuː/ noun, verb
▪ **noun**
- **WHAT YOU CAN SEE 1** 🔑 **A2** [C] what you can see from a particular place or position, especially beautiful countryside: ~ **of sth** *There were magnificent views of the surrounding countryside.* ◇ ~ **from sth** *The view from the top of the tower was spectacular.* ◇ *a sea/mountain view* ◇ *I'd like a room with a view.* **2** 🔑 **B1** [U, sing.] used when you are talking about whether you can see sth or whether sth can be seen in a particular situation: *The lake soon came into view.* ◇ *The sun disappeared from view.* ◇ **in**~ *There was nobody in view.* ◇ *Sit down—you're blocking my view.* ◇ ~ **of sth** *I didn't have a good view of the stage.* ⇒ note at SIGHT ⇒ see also SIDE VIEW, REAR-VIEW MIRROR
- **OPINION 3** 🔑 **A2** [C] a personal opinion about sth; an attitude towards sth: *to have strong political views* ◇ *to express/share/support a view* ◇ ~ **on/about sth** *She and I hold opposing views on the matter.* ◇ ~ **that** … *We take the view that it would be wrong to interfere.* ◇ *My own/personal view is that …* ◇ **in sb's** ~ *In my view it was a waste of time.* ◇ *There was a frank exchange of views* (= an angry argument) *between Dr Wilson and the other members of the committee.* ⇒ **LANGUAGE BANK** at ACCORDING TO, OPINION ⇒ see also POINT OF VIEW
- **WAY OF UNDERSTANDING 4** 🔑 **B1** [sing.] ~ **(of sth)** a way of understanding or thinking about sth: *He has an optimistic view of life.* ◇ *the Christian view of the world* ◇ *The traditional view was that marriage was meant to last.* ⇒ see also WORLD VIEW
- **ONLINE 5** [C] an occasion when a video is watched online: *His performance went viral, attracting over 8 million views on YouTube.*
- **PHOTOGRAPH/PICTURE 6** [C] ~ **(of sth)** a photograph or picture that shows an interesting place or scene: *a book with views of Paris*
- **CHANCE TO SEE STH 7** [also ˈ**viewing**] [C] a special chance to see or admire sth ⇒ see also PRIVATE VIEW ⇒ see also PAGE VIEW, PAY-PER-VIEW
- **IDM** **have, etc. sth in ˈview** (formal) to have a particular aim, plan, etc. in your mind **SYN** **have sb/sth in mind**: *He wanted to make money and went abroad with this end in view.* **in full ˈview (of sb/sth)** that can be seen completely, directly in front of sb/sth: *He was shot in full view of a large crowd.* **in view of sth** (formal) considering sth: *In view of the weather, the event will now be held indoors.* **on ˈview** being shown in a public place so that people can look at it **with a view to sth/to doing sth** (formal) with the intention or hope of doing sth: *He's painting the house with a view to selling it.* ⇒ more at BIRD n., DIM adj., HEAVE v., LONG adj.
▪ **verb**
- **THINK ABOUT STH 1** 🔑 **B1** to think about sb/sth in a particular way: ~ **sb/sth + adv./prep.** *How do you view your position within the company?* ◇ ~ **sb/sth as sth** *to view sth as a threat/an opportunity* ◇ *He is widely viewed as a possible leader.* ◇ ~ **sb/sth with sth** *She viewed him with suspicion.* ⇒ **SYNONYMS** at REGARD
- **LOOK AT STH 2** 🔑 **B1** ~ **sth** (formal) to look at sth, especially when you look carefully: *People came from all over the world to view her work.* ◇ *A viewing platform gave stunning views over the valley.* ⇒ **SYNONYMS** at LOOK **3** ~ **sth** (formal) to visit a house, etc. before deciding whether to buy or rent it: *The property can only be viewed by appointment.*
- **WATCH TV, FILM/MOVIE 4** ~ **sth** (formal) to watch television, a film, etc. *The show has a viewing audience of six million* (= six million people watch it). ◇ *an opportunity to view the movie before it goes on general release* ⇒ note at LOOK

▼ **SYNONYMS**
**view**
sight · scene · panorama
These are all words for a thing that you can see, especially from a particular place.
**view** what you can see from a particular place or position, especially beautiful natural scenery: *The cottage had a delightful sea view.*
**sight** a thing that you see or can see, especially sth that is impressive or unusual: *It's a spectacular sight as the flamingos lift into the air.*
**scene** a view that you see, especially one with people and/or animals moving about and doing things: *It was a delightful rural scene.*
**panorama** a view of a wide area of land: *The tower offers a breathtaking panorama of Prague.*
**PATTERNS**
- a view/panorama of sth
- a **beautiful/breathtaking** view/sight/scene/panorama
- a **magnificent/spectacular** view/sight/panorama
- to **take in** the view/sight/scene
- to **admire** the view/sight

**viewable** /ˈvjuːəbl/ adj. that can be looked at: *The film's trailer is viewable online.*

**viewer** 🔵 **B1** 🌐 /ˈvjuːə(r)/ noun **1** 🔑 **B1** a person watching television or a video on the internet: *television/TV viewers* ◇ *Her performance has grabbed the attention of*

# viewership

100 million YouTube viewers. **2** a person who looks at or considers sth: *Some of her art is intended to shock the viewer.* ◊ *viewers of the current political scene* **3** a device for looking at SLIDES (= photographs on special film), for example a small box with a light in it

**view·er·ship** /ˈvjuːəʃɪp; *NAmE* -ərʃ-/ *noun* [usually sing.] the number or type of people who watch a particular television programme or television channel

**view·find·er** /ˈvjuːfaɪndə(r)/ *noun* the part of a camera that you look through to see the area that you are photographing

**view·point** 🎓+ B2 /ˈvjuːpɔɪnt/ *noun* **1** 🎓+ B2 a way of thinking about a subject SYN **point of view**: **from a ... ~** *Try looking at things from a different viewpoint.* ◊ *From a practical viewpoint, I'd advise you not to go.* ◊ **~on sth** *She will have her own viewpoint on the matter.* **2** 🎓+ C1 a direction or place from which you look at sth SYN **angle**: **from a ...~** *The artist has painted the scene from various viewpoints.* ⇒ see also POINT OF VIEW

**view·port** /ˈvjuːpɔːt; *NAmE* -pɔːrt/ *noun* **1** (*computing*) an area inside a frame on a screen, for viewing information **2** a window in a SPACECRAFT

**vigil** /ˈvɪdʒɪl/ *noun* [C, U] a period of time when people do not sleep, especially at night, in order to watch a sick person, say prayers, protest, etc: *His parents kept a round-the-clock vigil at his bedside.*

**vigi·lant** /ˈvɪdʒɪlənt/ *adj.* (*formal*) very careful to notice any signs of danger or trouble SYN **alert**, **watchful**: *A pilot must remain vigilant at all times.* ▸ **vigi·lance** /-ləns/ *noun* [U] SYN **watchfulness**: *She stressed the need for constant vigilance.* **vigi·lant·ly** *adv.*

**vigi·lante** /ˌvɪdʒɪˈlænti/ *noun* (*sometimes disapproving*) a member of a group of people who try to prevent crime or punish criminals in their community, especially because they think the police are not doing this ▸ **vigi·lant·ism** /-tɪzəm/ *noun* [U]

**vi·gnette** /vɪnˈjet/ *noun* (*formal*) **1** a short piece of writing or acting that clearly shows what a particular person, situation, etc. is like **2** a small picture or drawing, especially on the first page of a book

**vig·or·ous** /ˈvɪɡərəs/ *adj.* **1** very active, determined or full of energy SYN **energetic**: *a vigorous campaign against tax fraud* ◊ *a vigorous opponent of the government* ◊ *Take vigorous exercise for several hours a week.* **2** strong and healthy: *a vigorous young man* ◊ *This plant is a vigorous grower.* ▸ **vig·or·ous·ly** *adv.*

**vig·our** (*US* **vigor**) /ˈvɪɡə(r)/ *noun* [U] energy, force or enthusiasm SYN **vitality**: *He worked with renewed vigour and determination.*

**Vi·king** /ˈvaɪkɪŋ/ *noun* a member of a race of Scandinavian people who attacked and sometimes settled in parts of north-west Europe, including Britain, in the 8th to the 11th centuries

**vile** /vaɪl/ *adj.* (**viler**, **vil·est**) **1** (*informal*) extremely unpleasant or bad SYN **disgusting**: *a vile smell* ◊ *The weather was really vile most of the time.* ◊ *He was in a vile mood.* ⇒ SYNONYMS at TERRIBLE **2** (*formal*) morally bad; completely unacceptable SYN **wicked**: *the vile practice of taking hostages* ▸ **vile·ly** /ˈvaɪlli/ *adv.* **vile·ness** *noun* [U]

**vil·ify** /ˈvɪlɪfaɪ/ *verb* (**vili·fies**, **vili·fy·ing**, **vili·fied**, **vili·fied**) **~sb/sth (as sth)** | **~sb/sth (for sth/for doing sth)** (*formal*) to say or write unpleasant things about sb/sth so that other people will have a low opinion of them SYN **malign**, **revile** ▸ **vili·fi·ca·tion** /ˌvɪlɪfɪˈkeɪʃn/ *noun* [U]: *the vilification of single parents by right-wing politicians*

**villa** /ˈvɪlə/ *noun* **1** (*BrE*) a house where people stay on holiday, especially in southern Europe: *We rented a holiday villa in Spain.* **2** a house in the country with a large garden, especially in southern Europe **3** (*BrE*) a large house in a town: *a Victorian villa in North London* **4** (in Roman times) a country house or farm with land attached to it

**vil·lage** 🎓❶ A1 /ˈvɪlɪdʒ/ *noun* **1** 🎓 A1 [C] a very small town located in a country area: *We visited towns and vil-*

lages all over Spain. ◊ *a meeting in the village hall* ◊ *a remote/nearby/neighbouring village* ◊ *Residents of the village are unhappy with the bus service.* ◊ **in a/the ~** *I soon got to know everybody in the village.* ⇒ see also GLOBAL VILLAGE, MODEL VILLAGE **2 the village** [sing.] (*especially BrE*) the people who live in a village: *The whole village was invited to the party.*

**village ˈidiot** *noun* a person in a village who is thought to be stupid; a stupid person

**vil·la·ger** 🎓+ C1 /ˈvɪlɪdʒə(r)/ *noun* a person who lives in a village: *Some of the villagers have lived here all their lives.*

**vil·lain** /ˈvɪlən/ *noun* **1** the main bad character in a story, play, etc: *He often plays the part of the villain.* ⇒ WORDFINDER NOTE at CHARACTER **2** a person who is morally bad or responsible for causing trouble or harm: *the heroes and villains of the 20th century* ◊ *Industrialized nations are the real environmental villains.* **3** (*informal*) a criminal 
IDM **the ˈvillain of the piece** (*especially humorous*) the person or thing that is responsible for all the trouble in a situation

**vil·lain·ous** /ˈvɪlənəs/ *adj.* [usually before noun] (*formal*) very evil; very unpleasant

**vil·lainy** /ˈvɪləni/ *noun* IMMORAL or cruel behaviour

**vil·lus** /ˈvɪləs/ *noun* (*pl.* **villi** /ˈvɪlaɪ, -liː/) (*biology*) any one of the many small, thin parts, like fingers in shape, that stick out from some surfaces on the inside of the body (for example in the INTESTINE). Villi increase the area of these surfaces so that the body can take in substances more easily.

**vim** /vɪm/ *noun* [U] (*old-fashioned, informal*) energy

**vin·ai·grette** /ˌvɪnɪˈɡret/ *noun* [U] a mixture of oil, VINEGAR and various HERBS, etc., added to a salad SYN **French dressing**

**vin·da·loo** /ˌvɪndəˈluː/ *noun* [U, C] (*pl.* **-oos**) a very spicy Indian dish, usually containing meat or fish: *lamb vindaloo*

**vin·di·cate** /ˈvɪndɪkeɪt/ *verb* (*formal*) **1** **~ sth** to prove that sth is true or that you were right to do sth, especially when other people had a different opinion SYN **justify**: *I have every confidence that this decision will be fully vindicated.* **2** **~ sb** to prove that sb is not guilty when they have been accused of doing sth wrong or illegal; to prove that sb is right about sth: *New evidence emerged, vindicating him completely.* ▸ **vin·di·ca·tion** /ˌvɪndɪˈkeɪʃn/ *noun* [U, sing.]: *Anti-nuclear protesters regarded the Chernobyl accident as a clear vindication of their campaign.*

**vin·dic·tive** /vɪnˈdɪktɪv/ *adj.* showing a strong and unreasonable desire to harm or upset sb because you think that they have harmed you SYN **spiteful**: *He accused her of being vindictive.* ◊ *a vindictive comment* ▸ **vin·dic·tive·ly** *adv.* **vin·dic·tive·ness** *noun* [U]

**vine** /vaɪn/ *noun* **1** a climbing plant that produces GRAPES: *grapes on the vine* ◊ *vine leaves* ⇒ see also GRAPEVINE **2** any climbing plant with long, thin STEMS; one of these STEMS

**vin·egar** /ˈvɪnɪɡə(r)/ *noun* [U] a liquid with a bitter taste made from wine or MALT, used to add taste to food or to preserve it: *onions pickled in vinegar* ⇒ see also BALSAMIC VINEGAR, MALT VINEGAR, WINE VINEGAR

**vin·egary** /ˈvɪnɪɡəri/ *adj.* having a taste or smell that is typical of vinegar: *a vinegary wine*

**vine·yard** /ˈvɪnjəd; *NAmE* -jərd/ *noun* a piece of land where GRAPES are grown in order to produce wine; a business that produces wine from the GRAPES it grows in a vineyard ⇒ compare WINERY

**vino** /ˈviːnəʊ/ *noun* [U] (*informal, humorous*) wine

**vin·tage** /ˈvɪntɪdʒ/ *noun, adj.*

■ *noun* **1** the wine that was produced in a particular year or place; the year in which it was produced: *the 1999 vintage* ◊ *2005 was a particularly fine vintage.* **2** [usually sing.] the period or season of gathering GRAPES for making wine: *The vintage was later than usual.*

■ *adj.* [only before noun] **1 vintage** wine is of very good quality and has been stored for several years **2** (*BrE*) (of a vehicle) made between 1919 and 1930 and admired for its style and interest **3** typical of a period in the past and of

**vint·ner** /ˈvɪntnə(r)/ noun (old-fashioned, formal) a person whose business is buying and selling wines or a person who grows GRAPES and makes wine

**vinyl** /ˈvaɪnl/ noun [U] **1** a strong plastic that can bend easily, used for covering walls, floors and furniture, and for making book covers and, especially in the past, records **2** records made of vinyl, in contrast to CDs: *on ~ My dad still has all his old albums on vinyl.*

**viol** /ˈvaɪəl/ noun an early type of musical instrument with strings, like a VIOLIN in shape

**viola** /viˈəʊlə/ noun a musical instrument with strings, that you hold under your CHIN and play with a BOW. A viola is larger than a VIOLIN and plays lower notes: *a viola player*

**vio·late** ⚑+ C1 /ˈvaɪəleɪt/ verb **1** ⚑+ C1 ~ sth (formal) to go against or refuse to obey a law, an agreement, etc. SYN flout: *to violate international law* **2** ⚑+ C1 ~ sth (formal) to upset or not respect sb's peace, privacy, etc: *She accused the press photographers of violating her privacy.* **3** ~ sth to damage or destroy a holy or special place SYN desecrate: *to violate a grave* **4** ~ sb (literary or old-fashioned) to force sb to have sex SYN rape ▶ **vio·la·tor** /-leɪtə(r)/ noun

**vio·la·tion** ⚑+ C1 /ˌvaɪəˈleɪʃn/ noun [U, C] **1** ⚑+ C1 (formal) the act of going against or refusing to obey a law, an agreement, etc: *They were in open violation of the treaty.* **2** ⚑+ C1 (formal) the act of not respecting sb's rights, peace, privacy, etc: *gross violations of human rights* **3** the act of damaging or destroying a holy or special place SYN desecration: *This was a violation of a sacred space.* **4** (literary or old-fashioned) the act of forcing sb to have sex SYN rape

**vio·lence** 🛈 B2 W /ˈvaɪələns/ noun [U] **1** ⚑ B2 violent behaviour that is intended to hurt or kill sb: *acts/threats of violence ◊ ~against sb He condemned the protesters' use of violence against the police. ◊ domestic violence (= between family members) ◊ Why do they always have to resort to violence? ◊ Violence broke out/erupted inside the prison last night. ◊ Is there too much sex and violence on TV?* **2** ⚑ B2 physical or emotional force and energy: *The violence of her feelings surprised him.*
IDM **do violence to sth** (formal) to damage sth or have a bad effect on it: *This version of the play does violence to Shakespeare's text.*

**vio·lent** 🛈 B1 /ˈvaɪələnt/ adj. **1** ⚑ B1 involving or caused by physical force that is intended to hurt or kill sb: *violent crime/criminals ◊ violent protests/attacks/incidents ◊ Students were involved in violent clashes with the police. ◊ The crowd suddenly turned violent. ◊ ~towards/to sb He was violent towards his wife on several occasions. ◊ violent acts/behaviour* **2** ⚑ B2 showing or caused by very strong emotion: *He is prone to violent outbursts.* **3** ⚑ B2 [usually before noun] very strong and sudden SYN intense, severe: *I took a violent dislike to him. ◊ a violent storm ◊ a violent explosion ◊ a violent headache* **4** [usually before noun] (of a colour) extremely bright: *Her dress was a violent pink.*

**vio·lent·ly** /ˈvaɪələntli/ adv. **1** with great energy or strong movement, especially caused by a strong emotion such as fear or hate: *She shook her head violently. ◊ to shiver violently* **2** very strongly or severely: *He was violently sick. ◊ They are violently opposed to the idea.* **3** in a way that involves physical violence: *The crowd reacted violently.*

**vio·let** /ˈvaɪələt/ noun **1** [C] a small wild or garden plant with purple or white flowers with a sweet smell that appear in spring **2** [U] a colour between blue and purple: *dressed in violet* ▶ **vio·let** adj.: *violet eyes* IDM see SHRINK v.

**vio·lin** /ˌvaɪəˈlɪn/ noun a musical instrument with strings, which you hold under your CHIN and play with a BOW: *Brahms' violin concerto* ⊃ compare VIOLA ⊃ see also FIDDLE noun

**vio·lin·ist** /ˌvaɪəˈlɪnɪst/ noun a person who plays the violin

**vio·list** noun **1** /viˈəʊlɪst/ a person who plays the VIOLA **2** /ˈvaɪəlɪst/ a person who plays the VIOL

**vio·lon·cello** /ˌvaɪələnˈtʃeləʊ/ noun (pl. -os) (formal) = CELLO

**VIP** /ˌviː aɪ ˈpiː/ noun a famous or important person who is treated in a special way (the abbreviation for 'Very Important Person') SYN celebrity, dignitary: *the VIP lounge ◊ to get the VIP treatment*

**viper** /ˈvaɪpə(r)/ noun **1** a small poisonous snake **2** (formal) a person who harms other people

**viral** /ˈvaɪrəl/ adj. **1** like or caused by a virus: *a viral infection* **2** used to describe a piece of information, a video, an image, etc. that is sent rapidly over the internet and seen by large numbers of people within a short time: *a viral email ◊ Within 24 hours, the video went viral on YouTube and Facebook.*

**viral ˈmarketing** noun [U] a way of advertising in which information about a company's products or services is sent by email or SOCIAL MEDIA to people who then send it on by email to other people they know

**vir·gin** /ˈvɜːdʒɪn/ NAmE ˈvɜːrdʒ-/ noun, adj.
▪ noun **1** [C] a person who has never had sex **2 the (Blessed) Virgin** [sing.] the Virgin Mary, mother of Jesus Christ **3** [C] a person who has no experience of a particular activity: *a political virgin ◊ an internet virgin*
▪ adj. **1** [usually before noun] in its original pure or natural condition and not changed, touched or made less good: *virgin forest/land/territory ◊ virgin snow (= fresh and not marked)* ⊃ see also EXTRA VIRGIN **2** [only before noun] with no sexual experience: *a virgin bride ◊ the virgin birth (= the belief that Mary was a virgin before and after giving birth to Jesus)*

**vir·gin·al** /ˈvɜːdʒɪnl; NAmE ˈvɜːrdʒ-/ adj. of or like a virgin; pure and innocent: *She was dressed in virginal white.*

**vir·gin·ity** /vəˈdʒɪnəti; NAmE vərˈdʒɪn-/ noun [U] the state of being a virgin: *He lost his virginity (= had sex for the first time) when he was 18.*

**Virgo** /ˈvɜːɡəʊ; NAmE ˈvɜːrɡ-/ noun **1** [U] the 6th sign of the ZODIAC, the VIRGIN **2** [C] (pl. -os) a person born when the sun is in this sign, that is between 23 August and 23 September, approximately

**vir·id·ian** /vɪˈrɪdiən/ noun [U] (specialist) a blue-green PIGMENT used in art; the colour of this pigment

**vir·ile** /ˈvɪraɪl; NAmE -rəl/ adj. (usually approving) **1** (of men) strong and full of energy, especially sexual energy **2** having or showing the strength and energy that is considered typical of men: *a virile performance ◊ virile athleticism*

**vir·il·ity** /vəˈrɪləti/ noun [U] **1** sexual power in men: *displays of male virility ◊ a need to prove his virility* **2** strength or energy: *economic virility*

**vir·ology** /vaɪˈrɒlədʒi; NAmE -ˈrɑːl-/ noun [U] the scientific study of viruses and the diseases caused by them ▶ **vir·olo·gist** noun

**vir·tual** 🛈 B2 /ˈvɜːtʃuəl; NAmE ˈvɜːrtʃ-/ adj. [only before noun] **1** ⚑ B2 (computing) made to appear to exist by the use of computer software, for example on the internet: *a system to help programmers create virtual environments* **2** ⚑ B2 almost or very nearly the thing described, so that any slight difference is not important: *The company has a virtual monopoly in this area of trade. ◊ The economy has come to a virtual standstill. ◊ He married a virtual stranger.*

**vir·tu·al·ly** /ˈvɜːtʃuəli; NAmE ˈvɜːrtʃ-/ adv. **1** almost or very nearly, so that any slight difference is not important: *to be virtually impossible ◊ Virtually all students will be exempt from the tax. ◊ He virtually admitted he was guilty. ◊ This year's results are virtually the same as last year's.* **2** (computing) by the use of computer software that makes sth appear to exist; using VIRTUAL REALITY technology

**virtual maˈchine** noun (computing) a feature of a computer's OPERATING SYSTEM that allows multiple other

# virtual memory 1742

systems to be run on the same computer, each with its own operating environment

**virtual 'memory** (also **virtual 'storage**) noun [U] (computing) a feature of a computer's OPERATING SYSTEM that provides additional memory for applications using the computer's HARD DISK

**virtual private 'network** noun (computing) = VPN

**virtual re'ality** noun [U] (abbr. **VR**) images and sounds created by a computer that seem almost real to the user, who can INTERACT with them by using SENSORS

**virtual 'world** noun images, sounds and text used by a computer to create a world where people can communicate with each other, play games and pretend to live another life

**vir·tue** /ˈvɜːtʃuː; NAmE ˈvɜːrtʃuː/ noun **1** [U] (formal) behaviour or attitudes that show high moral standards: *He led a life of virtue.* ◊ *She was certainly no paragon of virtue* (= her moral standards were very far from perfect). **2** [C] a particular good quality or habit: *Patience is not one of her virtues, I'm afraid.* **3** [C, U] an attractive or useful quality SYN **advantage**: *The plan has the virtue of simplicity.* ◊ *He was extolling the virtues of the internet.* ◊ *They could see no virtue in discussing it further.*
IDM **by/in virtue of sth** (formal) by means of or because of sth: *She got the job by virtue of her greater experience.* **make a virtue of sth** to manage to present as a good quality sth that other people might consider to be bad: *There are artists who make a virtue of repetition.* **make a virtue of ne'cessity** to manage to gain an advantage from sth that you have to do and cannot avoid **virtue is its own re'ward** (saying) the reward for acting in a moral or correct way is the knowledge that you have done so, and you should not expect more than this, for example praise from other people or payment

**vir·tu·os·ity** /ˌvɜːtʃuˈɒsəti; NAmE ˌvɜːrtʃuˈɑːs-/ noun [U] (formal) a very high degree of skill in performing or playing: *technical virtuosity* ◊ *a performance of breathtaking virtuosity*

**vir·tu·oso** /ˌvɜːtʃuˈəʊsəʊ, -ˈəʊzəʊ; NAmE ˌvɜːrtʃ-/ noun, adj.
■ noun (pl. **vir·tu·osos** or **vir·tu·osi** /-ˈəʊsi, -ˈəʊzi/) a person who shows very great skill at doing sth, especially playing a musical instrument: *a piano virtuoso*
■ adj. [only before noun] showing extremely great skill: *a virtuoso performance* ◊ *a virtuoso pianist/player*

**vir·tu·ous** /ˈvɜːtʃuəs; NAmE ˈvɜːrtʃ-/ adj. **1** (formal) behaving in a very good and moral way; showing high moral standards SYN **irreproachable**: *a wise and virtuous man* ◊ *She lived an entirely virtuous life.* **2** (disapproving or humorous) claiming to behave better or have higher moral standards than other people: *He was feeling virtuous because he had finished and they hadn't.* ▸ **vir·tu·ous·ly** adv.

**virtuous 'circle** noun (formal) a series of events in which each one seems to increase the good effects of the previous one ⇒ compare VICIOUS CIRCLE

**viru·lent** /ˈvɪrələnt/ adj. **1** (of a disease or poison) extremely dangerous or harmful and quick to have an effect **2** (formal) showing strong negative and bitter feelings: *virulent criticism* ◊ *virulent nationalism* ▸ **viru·lence** /-ləns/ noun [U] **viru·lent·ly** adv.

**virus** /ˈvaɪrəs/ noun **1** a living thing, too small to be seen without a MICROSCOPE, that causes disease in people, animals and plants: *the flu/influenza virus* ◊ *patients known to have been infected with the virus* ⇒ WORDFINDER NOTE at DISEASE **2** (informal) a disease caused by a virus: *There's a virus going around the office.* **3** instructions that are hidden within a computer program and are designed to cause faults or destroy data: *a computer virus* ⇒ see also VIRAL

**visa** /ˈviːzə/ noun a stamp or mark put in your passport by officials of a foreign country that gives you permission to enter, pass through or leave their country: *to apply for a visa* ◊ *an entry/tourist/transit/exit visa* ⇒ WORDFINDER NOTE at HOLIDAY

**vis·age** /ˈvɪzɪdʒ/ noun (literary) a person's face

**vis-à-vis** /ˌviːz ɑː ˈviː/ prep. (from French) **1** in relation to: *Britain's role vis-à-vis the United States* **2** in comparison with: *It was felt that the company had an unfair advantage vis-à-vis smaller companies elsewhere.*

**vis·cera** /ˈvɪsərə/ noun [pl.] (anatomy) the large organs inside the body, especially the INTESTINES

**vis·ceral** /ˈvɪsərəl/ adj. **1** (literary) resulting from strong feelings rather than careful thought: *She had a visceral dislike of all things foreign.* **2** (anatomy) relating to the viscera

**vis·cose** /ˈvɪskəʊz, -skəʊs/ noun [U] (especially BrE) a chemical made from CELLULOSE, used to make FIBRES that can be used to make clothes, etc.

**vis·count** /ˈvaɪkaʊnt/ noun (in the UK) a NOBLEMAN of a rank below an EARL and above a BARON

**vis·count·cy** /ˈvaɪkaʊntsi/ noun the rank or position of a viscount

**vis·count·ess** /ˈvaɪkaʊntəs/ noun **1** a woman who has the rank of a VISCOUNT **2** the wife of a VISCOUNT

**vis·cous** /ˈvɪskəs/ adj. (specialist) (of a liquid) thick and sticky; not flowing freely ▸ **vis·cos·ity** /vɪˈskɒsəti; NAmE -ˈskɑː-/ noun [U, C] (pl. **-ies**)

**vise** (NAmE) (especially BrE **vice**) /vaɪs/ noun a tool with two metal blocks that can be moved together by turning a SCREW. The vise is used to hold an object in place while work is done on it: *He held my arm in a vise-like* (= very firm) *grip.*

**visi·bil·ity** /ˌvɪzəˈbɪləti/ noun [U] **1** how far or well you can see, especially as affected by the light or the weather: *good/poor/bad/zero visibility* ◊ *Visibility was down to about 100 metres in the fog.* ◊ *The car has excellent all-round visibility* (= you can see what is around you very easily from it). **2** the fact of attracting attention or being easy to see: *The advertisements were intended to increase the company's visibility in the marketplace* (= make people more aware of its products and services). ⇒ see also HIGH-VISIBILITY

**vis·ible** /ˈvɪzəbl/ adj. **1** that can be seen: *The house is clearly visible from the beach.* ◊ *Most stars are not visible to the naked eye.* **2** [usually before noun] that is obvious enough to be noticed SYN **obvious**: *visible benefits* ◊ *a visible police presence* ◊ *He showed no visible sign of emotion.* ◊ *She made a visible effort to control her anger.* ⇒ compare INVISIBLE

**visible mi'nority** noun (CanE) a group whose members are clearly different in race from those of the majority race in a society

**vis·ibly** /ˈvɪzəbli/ adv. in a way that is easy to see: *He was visibly shocked.* ◊ *She paled visibly at the news.*

**vi·sion** /ˈvɪʒn/ noun **1** [U] the ability to see; the area that you can see from a particular position: *to have good/perfect/poor/blurred/normal vision* ◊ *Cats have good night vision.* ◊ *Her vision was still blurry.* ◊ *The disease causes a gradual loss of peripheral vision.* ⇒ note at SIGHT ⇒ see also DOUBLE VISION, FIELD OF VISION, LINE OF VISION at LINE OF SIGHT, TUNNEL VISION, TWENTY-TWENTY VISION **2** [C] an idea or a picture in your imagination: *~ of sb/sth He had a vision of a world in which there would be no wars.* ◊ *~ of (sb/sth) doing sth I had visions of us getting hopelessly lost.* ◊ *~ for sb/sth These two men share a similar vision for the country.* **3** [C] a dream or similar experience, especially of a religious kind: **in a ~** *The idea came to her in a vision.* **4** [U] the ability to think about or plan the future with great imagination and intelligence SYN **foresight**: *She had vision and determination.* **5** [C] **a ~ (of sth)** (literary) a person of great beauty or who shows the quality mentioned: *She was a vision in white lace.* ◊ *a vision of loveliness* **6** [U] the picture on a television or cinema screen: *We apologize for the loss of vision.*

**vi·sion·ary** /ˈvɪʒənri; NAmE -ʒəneri/ adj., noun
■ adj. **1** (approving) original and showing the ability to think about or plan the future with great imagination and

intelligence: *a visionary leader* **2** relating to dreams or strange experiences, especially of a religious kind: *visionary experiences*
- **noun** (*pl.* **-ies**) (*usually approving*) a person who has the ability to think about or plan the future in a way that is intelligent and shows imagination

**visit** 🔊 **A1** /ˈvɪzɪt/ *verb, noun*
- **verb 1** **A1** [T] **~ sb/sth** to go to see a person or a place for a period of time: *My parents are coming to visit me next week.* ◇ *to visit friends/family* ◇ *It looks like a lovely place to visit.* **2** **A1** [T] **~ sth** (*computing*) to go to a website on the internet: *For more information, visit our website.* ➔ WORDFINDER NOTE at WEB **3** **A1** [I, T] to stay somewhere for a short time: *We don't live here. We're just visiting.* ◇ **~ sth** *Ships visit the island occasionally.* **4** **A1** [T] **~ sth** to make an official visit to sb, for example to perform checks or give advice: *Government inspectors are visiting schools in the area.*
- PHRV ˈ**visit sth on/upon sb/sth** (*old use*) to punish sb/sth: *The sins of the fathers are visited upon the children* (= children are blamed or suffer for what their parents have done). ˈ**visit with sb** (*NAmE*) to spend time with sb, especially talking socially: *Come and visit with me some time.*
- **noun 1** **A1** an occasion or a period of time when sb goes to see a place or person and spends time there: *a two-day/three-day visit* ◇ *the prime minister's surprise visit to the troops* ◇ *an official/state visit* ◇ **~ to sb/sth** *It's my first visit to New York.* ◇ *If you have time, pay a visit to the local museum.* ◇ *The family made a visit to England in the summer of 1923.* ◇ **~ from sb** *We had a visit from the police last night.* ➔ see also FLYING VISIT, RETURN VISIT **2** **A1** (*computing*) an occasion when sb looks at a website on the internet: **~ to sth** *Visits to our website have doubled in a year.* **3** **~ (with sb)** (*NAmE, informal*) an occasion when two or more people meet to talk in an informal way

**vis·it·ation** /ˌvɪzɪˈteɪʃn/ *noun* **1** [U] (*NAmE*) the right of a parent who is divorced or separated from his or her partner to visit a child who is living with the partner: *She is seeking more liberal visitation with her daughter.* ◇ *visitation rights* ➔ compare ACCESS **2** [C, U] **~ (of/from sb/sth)** (*formal*) an official visit, especially to check that rules are being obeyed and everything is as it should be **3** [C] **~ (of/from sb/sth)** (*formal*) an unexpected appearance of sth, for example a ghost **4** [C] **~ (of sth)** (*formal*) a disaster that is believed to be a punishment from God: *a visitation of plague*

**vis·it·ing** /ˈvɪzɪtɪŋ/ *adj.* [only before noun] a **visiting** professor or lecturer is one who is teaching for a fixed period at a particular university or college, but who normally teaches at another one

ˈ**visiting card** (*BrE*) (*NAmE* ˈ**calling card**) (*also* **card** *BrE, NAmE*) *noun* (especially in the past) a small card with your name on it that you leave with sb after, or instead of, a formal visit ➔ compare BUSINESS CARD

**vis·it·or** 🔊 **A1** /ˈvɪzɪtə(r)/ *noun* **1** **A1** a person who visits a person or place: *We've got visitors coming this weekend.* ◇ *Do you get many visitors?* ◇ *The theme park attracts 2.5 million visitors a year.* ◇ **~ sth** *She's a frequent visitor to the US.* ◇ *a visitor centre/attraction* ➔ see also HEALTH VISITOR, PRISON VISITOR **2 ~ (to sth)** (*computing*) a person who looks at a website on the internet: *How can we attract more visitors to our website?*

ˈ**visitors' book** *noun* a book in which visitors write their names, addresses and sometimes comments, for example, at a hotel or place of public interest

**visor** /ˈvaɪzə(r)/ *noun* **1** a part of a helmet that can be pulled down to protect the eyes and face **2** a curved piece of plastic, etc. worn on the head above the eyes to protect them from the sun **3** a small piece of plastic, etc. inside the front window of a car that can be pulled down to protect the driver's eyes from the sun **4** (*NAmE*) = BILL (9)

**vista** /ˈvɪstə/ *noun* **1** (*literary*) a beautiful view, for example, of the countryside, a city, etc. SYN **panorama 2** (*formal*) a range of things that might happen in the future SYN **prospect**: *This new job could open up whole new vistas for her.*

# vitamin C

**vis·ual** 🔊 **B2** **W** /ˈvɪʒuəl/ *adj., noun*
- *adj.* **B2** of or connected with seeing or sight: *the visual arts* ◇ *The building makes a tremendous visual impact.* ◇ *dramatic visual effects* ▶ **visu·al·ly** /-əli/ *adv.*: *visually handicapped/impaired* ◇ *visually exciting*
- *noun* a picture, map, piece of film, etc. used to make an article or a talk easier to understand or more interesting: *He used striking visuals to get his point across.*

ˈ**visual ˈaid** *noun* [usually pl.] a picture, video, etc. used in teaching to help people to learn or understand sth

ˈ**visual ˈfield** *noun* (*specialist*) = FIELD OF VISION

**visu·al·ize** (*BrE also* **-ise**) /ˈvɪʒuəlaɪz/ *verb* **1** to form a picture of sb/sth in your mind SYN **imagine**: **~ sb/sth/yourself (as sth)** *Try to visualize him as an old man.* ◇ **~ what, how, etc…** *I can't visualize what this room looked like before it was decorated.* ◇ **~ sb/sth/yourself doing sth** *It can help to visualize yourself making your speech clearly and confidently.* ◇ **~ doing sth** *She couldn't visualize climbing the mountain.* **2 ~ sth** (*specialist*) to make sth able to be seen by the eye: *Ultrasound is a technique that uses sound waves to visualize internal structures.* ▶ **visu·al·iza·tion**, **-isa·tion** /ˌvɪʒuəlaɪˈzeɪʃn; *NAmE* -lə'z-/ *noun* [U, C]

**vita** /ˈviːtə/ *noun* (*US*) = CURRICULUM VITAE

**vital** 🔊 **B2** /ˈvaɪtl/ *adj.* **1** **B2** necessary or essential in order for sth to succeed or exist: **~ sth** *the vitamins that are vital for health* ◇ **~ to sth** *Good financial accounts are vital to the success of any enterprise.* ◇ *Reading is of vital importance in language learning.* ◇ *The police play a vital role in our society.* ◇ **it is ~ that…** *It is vital that you keep accurate records when you are self-employed* ◇ **it is ~ (for sb/sth) to do sth** *It was vital to show that he was not afraid.* ➔ SYNONYMS at ESSENTIAL ➔ LANGUAGE BANK at EMPHASIS, IMPERSONAL **2** [only before noun] connected with or necessary for staying alive: *the vital organs* (= the brain, heart, lungs, etc.) **3** (of a person) full of energy and enthusiasm SYN **dynamic**

---

**LANGUAGE BANK**

**vital**

Saying that something is necessary

- **It is vital that** journalists can verify the accuracy of their reports.
- Journalists play a **vital/crucial** role in educating the public.
- Public trust is a **crucial** issue for all news organizations.
- The ability to write well is **essential** for any journalist.
- The internet has become an **indispensable** tool for reporters.
- In journalism, accuracy is **paramount** / …is of paramount importance.
- **It is imperative that** journalists maintain the highest possible standards of reporting.

➔ SYNONYMS at ESSENTIAL
➔ LANGUAGE BANK at EMPHASIS, IMPERSONAL

---

**vi·tal·ity** /vaɪˈtæləti/ *noun* [U] energy and enthusiasm SYN **vigour**: *She is bursting with vitality and new ideas.*

**vi·tal·ly** /ˈvaɪtəli/ *adv.* extremely; in an essential way: *Education is vitally important for the country's future.*

ˈ**vital signs** (*also* **vitals**) *noun* [pl.] (*medical*) measurements that show that sb is alive, such as the rate of their breathing, their body temperature or their HEARTBEAT

ˈ**vital sta'tistics** *noun* [pl.] **1** figures that show the number of births and deaths in a country **2** (*BrE, informal*) the measurements of a woman's chest, WAIST and HIPS

**vita·min** 🔊 **B2** /ˈvɪtəmɪn; *NAmE* ˈvaɪt-/ *noun* a natural substance found in food that is an essential part of what humans and animals need to help them grow and stay healthy. There are many different vitamins: *vitamin A/B/D/E* ◇ *The plants are an excellent source of vitamins and minerals.* ◇ *vitamin supplements*

ˌ**vitamin ˈC** (*also* ˌ**as·corbic ˈacid**) *noun* [U] a vitamin found in fruits such as oranges and lemons, and in green vegetables: *Oranges are rich in vitamin C.*

# vitiate 1744

**viti·ate** /ˈvɪʃieɪt/ verb [usually passive] ~ sth (formal) to destroy or reduce the effect of sth

**viti·cul·ture** /ˈvɪtɪkʌltʃə(r)/ noun [U] (specialist) the science or practice of growing GRAPES

**vit·re·ous** /ˈvɪtriəs/ adj. (specialist) hard, shiny and clear like glass: *vitreous enamel*

**vitreous ˈhumour** (US **vitreous ˈhumor**) noun [U] (anatomy) the clear substance inside the eye ⊃ compare AQUEOUS HUMOUR

**vit·riol** /ˈvɪtriəl/ noun [U] (formal) very cruel and bitter comments or criticism SYN **abuse**

**vit·ri·ol·ic** /ˌvɪtriˈɒlɪk; NAmE -ˈɑːl-/ adj. (formal) (of language or comments) full of anger and hate SYN **bitter**: *The newspaper launched a vitriolic attack on the president.*

**vitro** ⊃ IN VITRO

**vi·tu·per·ation** /vɪˌtjuːpəˈreɪʃn; NAmE vaɪˌtuː-/ noun [U] (formal) cruel and angry criticism SYN **abuse** ▸ **vi·tu·pera·tive** /vɪˈtjuːpərətɪv; NAmE vaɪˈtuːpəreɪt-/ adj.: *a vituperative attack*

**viva¹** /ˈviːvə/ exclamation (from Italian) used for expressing support for sb or sth: *Viva the revolution!*

**viva²** /ˈvaɪvə/ noun (BrE) = VIVA VOCE

**viv·ace** /vɪˈvɑːtʃeɪ/ noun (from Italian, music) a piece of music to be played in a quick, lively way ▸ **viv·ace** adv., adj.

**viv·acious** /vɪˈveɪʃəs/ adj. (approving) (especially of a woman) having a lively, attractive personality: *He had three pretty, vivacious daughters.* ▸ **viv·acious·ly** adv. **viv·acity** /-ˈvæsəti/ noun [U]: *He was charmed by her beauty and vivacity.*

**viv·ar·ium** /vaɪˈveəriəm, vɪ-; NAmE -ˈver-/ noun (pl. **viv·ar·ia** /-riə/) a container for keeping live animals in, especially for scientific study

**viva voce** /ˌvaɪvə ˈvəʊtʃi/ (BrE also **viva**) noun (from Latin) a spoken exam, especially in a British university

**vive la dif·fer·ence** /ˌviːv lɑː ˌdɪfəˈrɒns; NAmE -ˈrɑːns/ exclamation (from French, humorous) used to show that you think it is good that there is a difference between two people or things, especially a difference between men and women

**vivid** /ˈvɪvɪd/ adj. **1** (of memories, a description, etc.) producing very clear pictures in your mind SYN **graphic**: *vivid memories ◊ He gave a vivid account of his life as a fighter pilot.* **2** (of light, colours, etc.) very bright: *vivid blue eyes* ⊃ SYNONYMS at BRIGHT **3** (of sb's imagination) able to form pictures of ideas, situations, etc. easily in the mind ▸ **viv·idly** adv.: *I vividly remember the day we first met.* **viv·id·ness** noun [U]: *the vividness of my dream*

**vivi·sec·tion** /ˌvɪvɪˈsekʃn/ noun [U] the practice of doing experiments on live animals for medical or scientific research

**vivo** ⊃ IN VIVO

**vixen** /ˈvɪksn/ noun **1** a female FOX (= a wild animal of the dog family) **2** (old-fashioned) an unpleasant and angry woman

**viz.** /vɪz/ adv. (formal, especially BrE) used to introduce a list of things that explain sth more clearly or are given as examples SYN **namely**: *four major colleges of surgery, viz. London, Glasgow, Edinburgh and Dublin*

**viz·ier** /vɪˈzɪə(r); NAmE -ˈzɪr/ (also **wazir**) noun an important official in some Muslim countries in the past

**VLE** /ˌviː el ˈiː/ noun (BrE) a software system for teaching and learning using the internet (the abbreviation for 'virtual learning environment')

**vlei** /fleɪ/ noun [C, U] (SAfrE) an area of low land that is always soft and wet; a shallow natural pool of water

**vlog** /vlɒg; NAmE vlɑːg/ noun a blog in which most of the content is in the form of videos ▸ **vlog** verb [I, T] (-gg-): *~ (about) sth They vlog about their daily lives as a couple.* **vlog·ger** noun **vlog·ging** noun [U]

**V-mail™** noun [U] = VOICEMAIL: *He insistently calls, texts and leaves V-mail messages.*

**V-neck** noun an opening for the neck in a piece of clothing that has a shape like the letter V; a piece of clothing with a V-neck: *a V-neck sweater ◊ a navy V-neck* ▸ **ˈV-necked** adj.: *a V-necked sweater*

**VOA** /ˌviː əʊ ˈeɪ/ abbr. VOICE OF AMERICA

**vo·cabu·lary** /vəˈkæbjələri; NAmE -leri/ noun (pl. **-ies**) **1** [C, U] all the words that a person knows or uses: *to have a wide/limited vocabulary ◊ your active vocabulary (= the words that you use) ◊ your passive vocabulary (= the words that you understand but don't use) ◊ Reading will increase your vocabulary.* ⊃ SYNONYMS at LANGUAGE ⊃ see also DEFINING VOCABULARY **2** [C] all the words in a particular language: *When did the word 'bungalow' first enter the vocabulary?* ⊃ SYNONYMS at LANGUAGE **3** [U, C] the words that people use when they are talking about a particular subject: *The word has become part of advertising vocabulary.* ⊃ SYNONYMS at LANGUAGE **4** (also informal **vocab** /ˈvəʊkæb/) [C] a list of words with their meanings, especially in a book for learning a foreign language ⊃ WORDFINDER NOTE at WORD
**IDM** **not be in sb's ˈvocabulary** to not be sth that sb understands: *The word 'failure' is not in his vocabulary (= for him, failure does not exist).*

**vocal** /ˈvəʊkl/ adj., noun
■ adj. **1** [only before noun] connected with the voice: *vocal music ◊ the vocal organs (= the tongue, lips, etc.)* ⊃ SYNONYMS at SPOKEN ▸ WORDFINDER NOTE at SING **2** telling people your opinions or protesting about sth loudly and with confidence: *He has been very vocal in his criticism of the government's policy. ◊ The protesters are a small but vocal minority.*
■ noun [usually pl.] the part of a piece of music that is sung, rather than played on a musical instrument: *backing vocals ◊ In this recording Armstrong himself is on vocals.*

**ˈvocal cords** noun [pl.] the thin pieces of TISSUE in the throat that are moved by the flow of air to produce the voice

**vo·cal·ist** /ˈvəʊkəlɪst/ noun a singer, especially in a pop, rock or jazz band: *a lead/guest/backing vocalist* ⊃ compare INSTRUMENTALIST

**vo·cal·iza·tion** (BrE also **-isa·tion**) /ˌvəʊkəlaɪˈzeɪʃn; NAmE -ləˈz-/ noun (specialist) **1** [C] a word or sound that is produced by the voice: *the vocalizations of animals* **2** [U] the process of producing a word or sound with the voice

**vo·cal·ize** (BrE also **-ise**) /ˈvəʊkəlaɪz/ verb (specialist) **1** [T] ~ sth to use words to express sth SYN **articulate, express**: *Showing children pictures sometimes helps them to vocalize their ideas.* **2** [I, T] ~(sth) to say or sing sounds or words: *Your baby will begin to vocalize long before she can talk.*

**vo·cal·ly** /ˈvəʊkəli/ adv. **1** in a way that uses the voice: *to communicate vocally* **2** by speaking in a loud and confident way: *They protested vocally.*

**vo·ca·tion** /vəʊˈkeɪʃn/ noun **1** [C] a type of work or way of life that you believe is especially suitable for you SYN **calling**: *Nursing is not just a job—it's a vocation. ◊ She believes that she has found her true vocation in life. ◊ You missed your vocation—you should have been an actor.* **2** [C, U] ~(for sth) a belief that a particular type of work or way of life is especially suitable for you: *He has a vocation for teaching. ◊ She is a doctor with a strong sense of vocation.* **3** [C, U] a belief that you have been chosen by God to be a priest or NUN: *a vocation to the priesthood*

**vo·ca·tion·al** /vəʊˈkeɪʃənl/ adj. connected with the skills, knowledge, etc. that you need to have in order to do a particular job: *vocational education/qualifications/training*

**voˈcational school** noun [C, U] (in the US) a school that teaches skills that are necessary for particular jobs

**voca·tive** /ˈvɒkətɪv; NAmE ˈvɑːk-/ noun (grammar) (in some languages) the form of a noun, a pronoun or an adjective used when talking to a person or thing ⊃ compare ACCUSATIVE, DATIVE, GENITIVE, INSTRUMENTAL (2), LOCATIVE, NOMINATIVE ▸ **voca·tive** adj.: *the vocative case*

**vo·cif·er·ous** /vəˈsɪfərəs; NAmE vəʊˈs-/ adj. (formal) expressing your opinions or feelings in a loud and confident way **SYN** **strident**: *vociferous protests* ◇ *a vociferous critic of the president's stance* ▶ **vo·cif·er·ous·ly** adv.: *to complain vociferously*

**vodka** /ˈvɒdkə; NAmE ˈvɑːd-/ noun **1** [U, C] a strong, clear alcoholic drink, made from grain, originally from Russia **2** [C] a glass of vodka: *I'll have a vodka and lime.*

**vogue** /vəʊɡ/ noun [C, usually sing., U] a fashion for sth: *~ for sth the vogue for child-centred education* ◇ **in ~** *Black is in vogue again.*

**voice** ⓞ 🅰🅰 /vɔɪs/ noun, verb
■ noun
• SOUND FROM MOUTH **1** 🅰🅰 [C, U] the sound or sounds produced through the mouth by a person speaking or singing: *I could hear voices in the next room.* ◇ **in a ... ~** *to speak in a deep/soft/loud voice* ◇ *'I promise,' she said in a small voice* (= a quiet, shy voice). ◇ *to raise/lower your voice* (= to speak louder/more quietly) ◇ *Keep your voice down* (= speak quietly). ◇ *Don't take that tone of voice with me!* ◇ *Her voice shook with emotion.* ◇ *'There you are,' said a voice behind me.* ◇ *When did his voice break* (= become deep like a man's)? ◇ *He was suffering from flu and had lost his voice* (= could not speak). ◇ *She has a good singing voice.* ◇ *She was in good voice* (= singing well) *at the concert tonight.*
• -VOICED **2** (in adjectives) having a voice of the type mentioned: *low-voiced* ◇ *squeaky-voiced*
• OPINION **3** [sing.] **~ (in sth)** the right to express your opinion and influence decisions: *Employees should have a voice in the decision-making process.* **4** [C] a particular attitude, opinion or feeling that is expressed; a feeling or an opinion that you become aware of inside yourself: *He pledged that his party would listen to the voice of the people.* ◇ *Very few dissenting voices were heard on the right of the party.* ◇ *the voice of reason/sanity/conscience* ◇ *'Coward!' a tiny inner voice insisted.* **5** an organization that expresses the opinion of a particular section of society: *The Royal Society is the voice of the British science establishment.*
• GRAMMAR **6** [sing.] **the active/passive ~** the form of a verb that shows whether the subject of a sentence performs the action (*the active voice*) or is affected by it (*the passive voice*)
• PHONETICS **7** [U] sound produced by movement of the VOCAL CORDS used in the pronunciation of vowels and some consonants ⊃ see also VOICED, VOICELESS
**IDM** **give voice to sth** to express your feelings, worries, etc. **make your 'voice heard** to express your feelings, opinions, etc. in a way that makes people notice and consider them **with one 'voice** as a group; with everyone agreeing: *The various opposition parties speak with one voice on this issue.* ⊃ more at FIND v., SOUND n., STILL adj., TOP n.
■ verb
• GIVE OPINION **1** **~ sth** to tell people your feelings or opinions about sth: *to voice complaints/criticisms/doubts/objections, etc.* ◇ *A number of parents have voiced concern about their children's safety.*
• PHONETICS **2** **~ sth** to produce a sound with a movement of your VOCAL CORDS as well as your breath ⊃ compare UNVOICED, VOICELESS

**ˈvoice-activated** adj. (of an electronic device) that you can control by spoken commands: *voice-activated computers/controls*

**ˈvoice assistant** noun a computer program that can hold a conversation with sb and complete particular tasks by responding to instructions or to information that it gathers from that person's digital device: *This digital voice assistant will learn that you like to work out in the morning and what type of music you listen to.* ⊃ compare CHATBOT

**ˈvoice box** noun the area at the top of the throat that contains the VOCAL CORDS **SYN** **larynx**

**voiced** /vɔɪst/ adj. (phonetics) (of consonants) produced by moving your VOCAL CORDS. In English the consonants /b d

1745

ɡ dʒ v ð z m n ŋ l r j w/ are voiced. **OPP** **unvoiced** ⊃ WORDFINDER NOTE at PRONUNCIATION

**voice·less** /ˈvɔɪsləs/ adj. (phonetics) (of consonants) produced without moving your VOCAL CORDS. In English the consonants /p t k tʃ f θ s ʃ h/ are voiceless. **SYN** **unvoiced** **OPP** **voiced**

**voice·mail** /ˈvɔɪsmeɪl/ (also **ˈV-mail™**) noun [U] an electronic system that can store phone messages, so that sb can listen to them later ⊃ WORDFINDER NOTE at CALL

**the Voice of America** /ðə ˌvɔɪs əv əˈmerɪkə/ noun [sing.] (abbr. **VOA**) an official US government service that broadcasts news and other programmes in English and many other languages around the world

**ˈvoice-over** noun information or comments in a film, television programme, etc. that are given by a person who is not seen on the screen: *She earns a lot of money doing voice-overs for TV commercials.*

**ˈvoice recognition** noun [U] **1** technology that allows a computer to identify a voice **2** = SPEECH RECOGNITION

**void** /vɔɪd/ noun, adj., verb
■ noun [usually sing.] (formal or literary) **1** a large empty space: *Below him was nothing but a black void.* **2** a feeling of being empty, caused by the loss of sb/sth: *The void left by his mother's death was never filled.*
■ adj. **1** **~ of sth** (formal) completely without sth **SYN** **devoid**: *The sky was void of stars.* **2** (law) (of a contract, an agreement etc.) not correct or legally VALID: *The agreement was declared void.* **3** (formal) empty: *void spaces* **IDM** see NULL
■ verb **1** **~ sth** (law) to state officially that sth is no longer correct or legally VALID **SYN** **invalidate**, **nullify 2 ~ sth** (formal) to empty waste matter from the BLADDER or BOWELS

**ˈvoid deck** noun (SEAsianE) the ground floor of a block of flats, which is left empty and is usually for the use of all the people who live in the building

**voilà** /vwʌˈlɑː; NAmE vwɑːˈlɑː/ exclamation (from French) used to say 'there it is!' when you show sth to sb, or sth appears suddenly: *'Voilà!' she said, producing a pair of strappy white sandals.*

**voile** /vɔɪl/ noun [U] a type of cloth made of cotton, wool or silk that you can almost see through, used for making clothes and curtains

**VoIP** /vɔɪp/ (also **IP telephony** /ˌaɪ ˌpiː təˈlefəni/) noun [U] a phone system that allows users to make and receive calls using the internet (the abbreviation for 'voice over internet protocol')

**vol.** abbr. (in writing) VOLUME: *the Complete Works of Byron Vol. 2*

**vola·tile** /ˈvɒlətaɪl; NAmE ˈvɑːlət̬l/ adj. **1** (often disapproving) (of a person or their moods) changing easily from one mood to another: *a highly volatile personality* **2** (of a situation) likely to change suddenly; easily becoming dangerous **SYN** **unstable**: *a highly volatile situation from which riots might develop* ◇ *a volatile exchange rate* **3** (specialist) (of a substance) that changes easily into a gas: *Petrol is a volatile substance.* ▶ **vola·til·ity** /ˌvɒləˈtɪləti/; NAmE ˌvɑːl-/ noun [U]

**vol·can·ic** /vɒlˈkænɪk; NAmE vɑːl-/ adj. caused or produced by a volcano: *volcanic rocks* ◇ *volcanic eruptions* ⊃ WORDFINDER NOTE at LANDSCAPE

**vol·cano** /vɒlˈkeɪnəʊ; NAmE vɑːl-/ noun (pl. **-oes** or **-os**) a mountain with a large opening at the top through which gases and LAVA (= hot liquid rock) are forced out into the air, or have been in the past: *An active volcano may erupt at any time.* ◇ *a dormant volcano* (= one that is not active at present) ◇ *an extinct volcano* (= one that is no longer active) ⊃ picture on page 1746 ⊃ WORDFINDER NOTE at MOUNTAIN

**vol·can·ology** /ˌvɒlkəˈnɒlədʒi; NAmE ˌvɑːlkəˈnɑːl-/ (also **vul·can·ology**) noun [U] the scientific study of volcanoes

**vole** /vəʊl/ noun a small animal like a mouse or RAT that lives in fields or near rivers ⊃ see also WATER VOLE

---

ⓞ Oxford Phrasal Academic Lexicon (OPAL) written and spoken word lists | Ⓦ OPAL written word list | Ⓢ OPAL spoken word list

# volition

## volcano

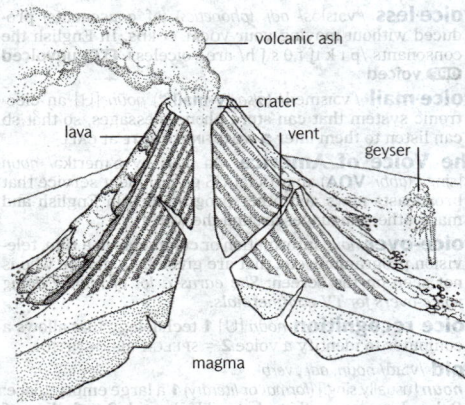

labels: volcanic ash, crater, vent, geyser, lava, magma

**vol·ition** /vəˈlɪʃn; NAmE voʊ-/ noun [U] (formal) the power to choose sth freely or to make your own decisions SYN **free will**: *They left entirely of their own volition* (= because they wanted to).

**vol·ley** /ˈvɒli; NAmE ˈvɑːli/ noun, verb
■ noun 1 (in some sports, for example tennis or football (soccer)) a hit or kick of the ball before it touches the ground: *She hit a forehand volley into the net.* ⇨ compare GROUNDSTROKE ⇨ see also HALF-VOLLEY 2 ~ (of sth) a lot of bullets, stones, etc. that are fired or thrown at the same time: *A volley of shots rang out.* ◇ *Police fired a volley over the heads of the crowd.* 3 ~ (of sth) a lot of questions, comments, offensive remarks, etc. that are directed at sb quickly one after the other SYN **torrent**: *She faced a volley of angry questions from her mother.*
■ verb [T, I] ~ (sth) (in some sports, for example tennis or football (soccer)) to hit or kick the ball before it touches the ground: *He volleyed the ball into the back of the net.*

**vol·ley·ball** /ˈvɒlibɔːl; NAmE ˈvɑːl-/ noun [U] a game in which two teams of six players use their hands to hit a large ball backwards and forwards over a high net while trying not to let the ball touch the ground on their own side ⇨ see also BEACH VOLLEYBALL

**volt** /vəʊlt; BrE also vɒlt/ noun (abbr. **V**) a unit for measuring the force of an electric current: *a high security fence with 5000 volts passing through it*

**volt·age** /ˈvəʊltɪdʒ/ noun [U, C] electrical force measured in volts: *high/low voltage*

**volte-face** /ˌvɒlt ˈfɑːs; NAmE ˌvɔːlt/ noun [sing.] (from French, formal) a complete change of opinion or plan SYN **about-turn**: *This represents a volte-face in government thinking.*

**vol·uble** /ˈvɒljəbl; NAmE ˈvɑːl-/ adj. (formal) 1 talking a lot, and with enthusiasm, about a subject: *Evelyn was very voluble on the subject of women's rights.* 2 expressed in many words and spoken quickly: *voluble protests* ▶ **vol·ubly** /-bli/ adv.

**vol·ume** /ˈvɒljuːm; NAmE ˈvɑːljəm/ noun
1 [U, C] the amount of space that an object or a substance fills; the amount of space that a container has: *~of sth How do you measure the volume of a gas?* ◇ *Patients showed an improvement in lung volume.* 2 [U, C] the amount of sth: **of sth** *the sheer volume* (= large amount) *of business* ◇ *New roads are being built to cope with the increased volume of traffic.* ◇ *Sales volumes fell 0.2% in June.* ◇ *The total volume of exports fell by 14.5 per cent.* 3 [U] the amount of sound that is produced by a television, radio, etc: *to turn the volume up/down* 4 [C] (abbr. **vol.**) a book that is part of a series of books: *an encyclopedia in 20 volumes* 5 [C] (formal) a book: *a library of over 50000 volumes* ◇ *a slim volume of poetry* 6 [C] (abbr. **vol.**) a series of different issues of the same magazine, especially all the issues for one year: '*New Scientist' volume 142, number 3* IDM see SPEAK

**vo·lu·min·ous** /vəˈluːmɪnəs/ adj. (formal) 1 (of clothing) very large; having a lot of cloth SYN **ample**: *a voluminous skirt* 2 (of a piece of writing, a book, etc.) very long and detailed 3 (of a container, piece of furniture, etc.) very large: *I sank down into a voluminous armchair.* ▶ **vo·lu·min·ous·ly** adv.

**vol·un·tar·ily** /ˈvɒləntrəli; NAmE ˌvɑːlənˈterəli/ adv. 1 willingly; without being forced: *He was not asked to leave—he went voluntarily.* 2 without payment; free: *The fund is voluntarily administered.*

**vol·un·tar·ism** /ˈvɒləntərɪzəm; NAmE ˈvɑːl-/ noun [U] (especially NAmE) = VOLUNTEERISM (2)

**vol·un·tary** /ˈvɒləntri; NAmE ˈvɑːlənteri/ adj., noun
■ adj. 1 done willingly, not because you are forced: *a voluntary agreement* ◇ *Attendance on the course is purely voluntary.* ◇ *to pay voluntary contributions into a pension fund* ◇ (*BrE*) *He took voluntary redundancy.* OPP **compulsory** 2 [usually before noun] (of work) done by people who choose to do it without being paid: *I do some voluntary work at the local hospital.* ◇ *She works there on a voluntary basis.* ◇ *voluntary services/bodies/agencies/organizations* (= organized, controlled or supported by people who choose to do this and are usually not paid) ◇ *the voluntary sector* (= organizations that are set up to help people and that do not make a profit, for example charities) ⇨ WORDFINDER NOTE at WORK 3 [only before noun] (of a person) doing a job without wanting to be paid for it: *a voluntary worker* 4 (*specialist*) (of movements of the body) that you can control OPP **involuntary**
■ noun (pl. -ies) (music) a piece of music played before, during or after a church service, usually on an organ

**Voluntary Service Overseas** noun [U] (abbr. **VSO**) a British charity that sends people with special skills, such as doctors and teachers, to work in other countries as volunteers

**vol·un·teer** /ˌvɒlənˈtɪə(r); NAmE ˌvɑːlənˈtɪr/ noun, verb
■ noun 1 a person who does a job without being paid for it: *Schools need volunteers to help children to read.* ◇ *She does volunteer work at an orphanage.* ⇨ WORDFINDER NOTE at CHARITY 2 a person who chooses to do sth without being forced to do it: *Are there any volunteers to help clear up?* ◇ *For my next trick, I'll need a volunteer from the audience.* 3 a person who chooses to join the armed forces without being forced to join ⇨ compare CONSCRIPT
■ verb 1 [I, T] to offer to do sth without being forced to do it or without getting paid for it: *~ to do sth Jill volunteered to organize a petition.* ◇ *~ for/as sth Several staff members volunteered for early retirement.* ◇ *~ sth (for/as sth) Workers volunteer their time, as no funds are available to pay professional staff.* ◇ *He volunteered his services as a driver.* 2 [T] *~ sth | + speech* to suggest sth or tell sb sth without being asked: *to volunteer advice* 3 [I] *~ (for sth)* | *~ to do sth* to join the army, etc. without being forced to: *to volunteer for military service* 4 [T] *~ sb (for/as sth)* | *~ sb to do sth* to suggest sb for a job or an activity, even though they may not want to do it: *They volunteered me for the job of interpreter.*

**vol·un·teer·ism** /ˌvɒlənˈtɪərɪzəm; NAmE ˌvɑːlənˈtɪr-/ noun [U] (especially NAmE) 1 the practice of working as a volunteer, especially in community service 2 (also **vol·un·tar·ism**) the practice of using or relying on volunteers rather than paid workers

**vo·lup·tu·ous** /vəˈlʌptʃuəs/ adj. 1 (formal) (of a woman) attractive in a sexual way with large breasts and HIPS SYN **buxom**: *a voluptuous woman* ◇ *a voluptuous body* 2 (*literary*) giving you physical pleasure SYN **sensual**: *voluptuous perfume* ▶ **vo·lup·tu·ous·ly** adv. **vo·lup·tu·ous·ness** noun [U]

**vomit** /ˈvɒmɪt; NAmE ˈvɑːm-/ verb, noun
■ verb (also informal **throw up**) [I, T] to bring food from the stomach back out through the mouth SYN **be sick**: *The smell made her want to vomit.* ◇ *~ sth up He had vomited*

up his supper. ◇ ~ sth *The injured man was vomiting blood.* ⊃ see also SICK *verb*
- **noun** [U] food from the stomach brought back out through the mouth

**voo·doo** /ˈvuːduː/ *noun* [U] a religion that is practised especially in Haiti and involves magic and WITCHCRAFT

**vor·acious** /vəˈreɪʃəs/ *adj.* (*formal*) **1** eating or wanting large amounts of food **SYN** **greedy**: *a voracious eater* ◇ *to have a voracious appetite* **2** wanting a lot of new information and knowledge **SYN** **avid**: *a voracious reader* ◇ *a boy with a voracious and undiscriminating appetite for facts* ▶ **vor·acious·ly** *adv.* **vor·acity** /-ˈræsəti/ *noun* [U]

**vor·tex** /ˈvɔːteks; NAmE ˈvɔːrt-/ *noun* (*pl.* **vor·texes** or **vor·tices** /-tɪsiːz/) **1** (*specialist*) a mass of air, water, etc. that turns round and round very fast and pulls things into its centre **SYN** **whirlpool, whirlwind** **2** (*literary*) a very powerful feeling or situation that you cannot avoid or escape from: *They were caught up in a whirling vortex of emotion.*

**vo·tary** /ˈvəʊtəri/ *noun* (*pl.* **-ies**) **~ of sb/sth** (*formal*) a person who WORSHIPS or loves sb/sth: *a votary of John Keats*

**vote** 🔸 B1 /vəʊt/ *noun, verb*
- **noun** **1** 🔸 B1 [C] a formal choice that you make in an election or at a meeting in order to choose sb or decide sth: *to win/lose votes* ◇ *You can cast your vote at the local polling station.* ◇ *He took 53% of the votes in the election.* ◇ *They've started opening the ballot boxes and counting the votes.* ⊃ WORDFINDER NOTE at DEBATE ⊃ see also ALTERNATIVE VOTE, BLOCK VOTE, CASTING VOTE, ELECTORAL VOTE, POPULAR VOTE (1), POSTAL VOTE, PROTEST VOTE (1), SINGLE TRANSFERABLE VOTE, SWING VOTE **2** 🔸 B1 [C] an occasion when a group of people vote on sth: *to win/lose a vote* ◇ *~ on sth to have/take/hold a vote on an issue* ◇ *in favour of sth We saw today a decisive vote in favour of (= for) industrial action.* ⊃ SYNONYMS at ELECTION ⊃ see also FREE VOTE **3** 🔸 B1 **the vote** [sing.] the right to vote, especially in political elections: *In Britain and the US, people get the vote at 18.* ⊃ WORDFINDER NOTE at PARLIAMENT **4** 🔸 B2 **the vote** [sing.] the total number of votes in an election: *She obtained 40% of the vote.* ◇ *The party increased their share of the vote.* ⊃ see also THE POPULAR VOTE **5** 🔸 B2 **the vote** [sing.] the vote given by a particular group of people, or for a particular party, etc: *the student vote* ◇ *the Labour vote* ⊃ see also PROTEST VOTE (2)
- **verb 1** 🔸 B1 [I, T] to show formally by marking a paper, raising your hand, using a VOTING MACHINE, etc. which person you want to win an election, or which plan or idea you support: *How did you vote at the last election?* ◇ *~ for/against sb/sth to vote for a candidate/party/bill* ◇ *~ in favour of sth Over 60% of members voted in favour of (= for) the motion.* ◇ *~ on sth We'll listen to the arguments on both sides and then vote on it.* ◇ *About 1.8 million people voted in the election.* ◇ *~ sth We voted Democrat in the last election.* ◇ *~ to do sth The board voted unanimously not to file for bankruptcy.* ◇ *Everyone over 18 has the right to vote.* ◇ *to be registered/eligible to vote* **2** 🔸 B2 [T, usually passive] **~ sb/sth + noun** to choose sb/sth for a position or an award by voting: *He was voted most promising new director.* **3** [T, usually passive] **~ sth + noun** to say that sth is good or bad: *The event was voted a great success.* **4** [T] **~ sb/yourself sth** to agree to give sb/yourself sth by voting: *The directors have just voted themselves a huge pay increase.* **5** [T] **~ (that) …** to suggest sth or support a suggestion that sb has made: *I vote (that) we go out to eat.*
**IDM** **vote with your 'feet** to show what you think about sth by going or not going somewhere: *Shoppers voted with their feet and avoided the store.*
**PHRV** **vote sb/sth↔'down** to reject or defeat sb/sth by voting for sb/sth else **vote sb 'in | vote sb 'into/'onto sth** to choose sb for a position by voting: *He was voted in as treasurer.* ◇ *She was voted onto the board of governors.* **vote sb 'out | vote sb 'out of/'off sth** to dismiss sb from a position by voting: *He was voted out of office.* **vote sth↔'through** to bring a plan, etc. into effect by voting for it: *A proposal to merge the two companies was voted through yesterday.*

**'vote bank** *noun* (*IndE*) a group of people or a community who are likely to vote for a particular political party: *The party has lost part of its traditional vote bank.*

**vote of 'confidence** *noun* [usually sing.] a formal vote to show that people support a leader, a political party, an idea, etc.

**vote of no 'confidence** *noun* [usually sing.] a formal vote to show that people do not support a leader, a political party, an idea, etc.

**vote of 'thanks** *noun* [usually sing.] a short formal speech in which you thank sb for sth and ask other people to join you in thanking them

**voter** /ˈvəʊtə(r)/ *noun* a person who votes or has the right to vote, especially in a political election: *A clear majority of voters were in favour of the motion.* ◇ *Only 60% of eligible voters actually used their vote.* ⊃ see also FLOATING VOTER, SWING VOTER

**vot·ing** 🔸 B2 /ˈvəʊtɪŋ/ *noun* [U] the action of choosing sb/sth in an election or at a meeting: *He was eliminated in the first round of voting.* ◇ *Voting will take place on May 1.* ◇ *tactical voting* ◇ *to be of voting age*

**'voting booth** *noun* (*especially NAmE*) = POLLING BOOTH

**'voting machine** *noun* a machine in which votes can be recorded AUTOMATICALLY, used, for example, in the US

**vo·tive** /ˈvəʊtɪv/ *adj.* [usually before noun] (*specialist*) presented to a god as a sign of thanks: *votive offerings*

**vouch** /vaʊtʃ/ *verb*
**PHRV** **'vouch for sb/sth** (*formal*) to say that you believe that sb will behave well and that you will be responsible for their actions: *Are you willing to vouch for him?* ◇ *I can vouch for her ability to work hard.* **'vouch for sth** (*formal*) to say that you believe that sth is true or good because you have evidence for it **SYN** **confirm**: *I was in bed with the flu. My wife can vouch for that.*

**vouch·er** /ˈvaʊtʃə(r)/ *noun* a printed piece of paper or an electronic code that can be used instead of money to pay for sth, or that allows you to pay less than the usual price of sth: *a voucher for a free meal* ◇ *a travel voucher* ◇ *This discount voucher entitles you to 10% off your next purchase.* ⊃ WORDFINDER NOTE at BUY

**vouch·safe** /ˌvaʊtʃˈseɪf/ *verb* **~ sth (to sb) | ~ sb sth | ~ that …** (*old-fashioned* or *formal*) to give, offer or tell sth to sb, especially in order to give them a special advantage: *He vouchsafed to me certain family secrets.*

**vow** 🔸 C1 /vaʊ/ *verb, noun*
- **verb** 🔸 C1 to make a formal and serious promise to do sth or a formal statement that is true: **~ to do sth** *She vowed never to speak to him again.* ◇ **~ (to sb) (that) …** *He vowed (that) he had not hurt her.* ◇ **~ sth** *They vowed eternal friendship.* ◇ **+ speech** *'I'll be back,' she vowed.*
- **noun** a formal and serious promise, especially a religious one, to do sth: *to make/take a vow* ◇ *to break/keep a vow* ◇ *to break your marriage vows* ◇ *Nuns take a vow of chastity.*

**vowel** /ˈvaʊəl/ *noun* **1** (*phonetics*) a speech sound in which the mouth is open and the tongue is not touching the top of the mouth, the teeth, etc., so that the flow of air is not limited, for example /ɑː, e, ɔː/: *vowel sounds* ◇ *Each language has a different vowel system.* **2** a letter that represents a vowel sound. In English the vowels are a, e, i, o and u. ⊃ compare CONSONANT ⊃ see also DIPHTHONG

**vox pop** /ˌvɒks ˈpɒp; NAmE vɑːks ˈpɑːp/ *noun* [C, U] (*BrE, informal*) the opinion of members of the public, especially when it is broadcast or published; the process of asking members of the public for their opinion on sth in order to broadcast or publish it: *to do a vox pop*

**voy·age** /ˈvɔɪɪdʒ/ *noun, verb*
- **noun** a long journey, especially by sea or in space: *an around-the-world voyage* ◇ *a voyage in space* ◇ *The Titanic sank on its maiden voyage (= first journey).* ◇ (*figurative*) *Going to college can be a voyage of self-discovery.* ⊃ WORDFINDER NOTE at EXPLORE
- **verb** [I] **+ adv./prep.** (*literary*) to travel, especially by sea or in space over a long distance

# voyager

**voy·ag·er** /ˈvɔɪɪdʒə(r)/ noun (old-fashioned or literary) a person who goes on a long journey, especially by sea or in space to unknown parts of the world or universe

**voy·eur** /vwaːˈɜː(r); NAmE vwɑːˈjɜːr/ noun (disapproving) **1** a person who gets pleasure from secretly watching people who are wearing no clothes or having sex **2** a person who enjoys watching the problems and private lives of others ▶ **voy·eur·ism** noun [U] **voy·eur·is·tic** /ˌvwaːjəˈrɪstɪk; NAmE ˌvwɑːjə-/ adj.: a voyeuristic interest in other people's lives

**VP** /ˌviː ˈpiː/ abbr. VICE-PRESIDENT

**VPN** /ˌviː piː ˈen/ noun (computing) a system that uses code to securely access a computer in a different location via the internet (the abbreviation for 'virtual private network')

**VR** /ˌviː ˈɑː(r)/ abbr. VIRTUAL REALITY

**vroom** /vruːm, vrʊm/ noun [U] used to represent the loud sound made by a vehicle moving very fast: *Vroom! A sports car roared past.*

**vs** abbr. (especially NAmE) (in writing) VERSUS

**V-sign** noun a sign that you make by holding up your hand and making a V-shape with your first and second fingers. When the PALM (= inside part) of your hand is facing away from you, the sign means 'victory'; when the palm is facing towards you the sign is used as a way of being rude to other people. ⇒ compare TWO FINGERS

**VSO** /ˌviː es ˈəʊ/ abbr. VOLUNTARY SERVICE OVERSEAS

**VTOL** /ˌviː tiː əʊ ˈel/ abbr. vertical take-off and landing (used to refer to an aircraft that can take off and land by going straight up or straight down)

**vul·can·ology** /ˌvʌlkəˈnɒlədʒi; NAmE -ˈnɑːl-/ noun [U] = VOLCANOLOGY

**vul·gar** /ˈvʌlɡə(r)/ adj. **1** not having or showing good taste; not polite, pleasant or well behaved SYN **coarse**, **in bad taste**: *a vulgar man* ◊ *vulgar decorations* ◊ *She found their laughter and noisy games coarse and rather vulgar.* **2** rude and likely to offend SYN **crude**: *vulgar jokes* ▶ **vul·gar·ly** adv.: *He eyed her vulgarly.*

**vul·gar·ity** /vʌlˈɡærəti/ noun [U, C] the fact of being rude or not having good taste; a rude object, picture, etc: *She was offended by the vulgarity of their jokes.* ◊ *a pornographic magazine full of vulgarities*

**the Vul·gate** /ðə ˈvʌlɡeɪt, -ɡət/ noun [sing.] the main Latin version of the Bible prepared in the late 4th century

**vul·ner·abil·ity** /ˌvʌlnərəˈbɪləti/ noun [U] ~ (of sb/sth) (to sth) the fact of being weak and easily hurt physically or emotionally: *the vulnerability of newborn babies to disease* ◊ *financial vulnerability*

**vul·ner·able** /ˈvʌlnərəbl/ adj. ~ (to sb/sth) weak and easily hurt physically or emotionally: *to be vulnerable to attack* ◊ *She looked very vulnerable standing there on her own.* ◊ *In cases of food poisoning, young children are especially vulnerable.* ◊ *The sudden resignation of the financial director put the company in a very vulnerable position.* ▶ **vul·ner·ably** /-bli/ adv.

**vul·ture** /ˈvʌltʃə(r)/ noun **1** a large bird, usually without feathers on its head or neck, that eats animals that are already dead: *vultures circling/wheeling overhead* ⇒ VISUAL VOCAB page V2 **2** a person who hopes to gain from the troubles of other people

**vulva** /ˈvʌlvə/ noun (anatomy) the outer opening of the female sex organs

**Vu·vu·zela**™ /ˌvuːvuːˈzeɪlə/ noun a long plastic instrument in the shape of a TRUMPET that makes a very loud noise when you blow it and is popular with football (soccer) fans in South Africa

**vying** /ˈvaɪɪŋ/ pres. part. of VIE

**W** /ˈdʌbljuː/ noun, abbr.
- **noun** (also **w**) [C, U] (pl. **Ws**, **W's**, **w's** /-juːz/) the 23rd letter of the English alphabet: 'Water' begins with (a) W/'W'.
- **abbr.** (in writing) **1** west; western **2** WATT: a 100W light bulb

**wacko** (also **whacko**) /ˈwækəʊ/ adj., noun
- **adj.** (especially NAmE, informal) crazy; not sensible: wacko opinions
- **noun** (pl. **-os** or **-oes**) (especially NAmE, informal) a crazy person

**wacky** (also **whacky**) /ˈwæki/ adj. (**wack·i·er**, **wacki·est**) (informal) funny in a slightly crazy way SYN **zany**: wacky ideas ◊ Some of his friends are pretty wild and wacky characters.

**wad** /wɒd; NAmE wɑːd/ noun, verb
- **noun 1** a thick pile of pieces of paper, paper money, etc. folded or rolled together: He pulled a thick wad of £10 notes out of his pocket. ◊ (BrE, slang) They had a wad/wads of money (= a large amount). **2** a mass of soft material, used for blocking sth or keeping sth in place: The nurse used a wad of cotton wool to stop the bleeding.
- **verb** (**-dd-**) **1** ~ **sth** (**up**) (especially NAmE) to fold or press sth into a tight wad **2** ~ **sth** to fill sth with soft material to make it warmer or to protect it

**wad·ding** /ˈwɒdɪŋ; NAmE ˈwɑːd-/ noun [U] soft material that you wrap around things to protect them

**wad·dle** /ˈwɒdl; NAmE ˈwɑːdl/ verb [I] (+ adv./prep.) to walk with short steps, moving your body from side to side, like a DUCK ▶ **wad·dle** noun [sing.]: She walked with a waddle.

**wade** /weɪd/ verb [I, T] to walk with an effort through sth, especially water or mud: (+ adv./prep.) He waded into the water to push the boat out. ◊ Sometimes they had to wade waist-deep through mud. ◊ ~ **sth** They waded the river at a shallow point. **2** (NAmE) (BrE **pad·dle**) [I] to walk or stand with no shoes or socks in shallow water in the sea, a lake, etc.
PHRV **wade 'in** | **wade 'into sth** (informal) to enter a fight, a discussion or an argument in an aggressive way or not very sensitive way: The police waded into the crowd with batons. ◊ You shouldn't have waded in with all those unpleasant accusations. **wade 'into sb** (informal) to attack sb with words in an angry aggressive way **wade 'through sth** [no passive] to deal with or read sth that is boring and takes a lot of time: I spent the whole day wading through the paperwork on my desk.

**wader** /ˈweɪdə(r)/ noun **1** (also **'wading bird**) [C] any of several different types of bird with long legs that feed in shallow water **2 waders** [pl.] long rubber boots that reach up to your THIGH, that you wear for standing in water, especially when fishing: a pair of waders

**wadi** /ˈwɒdi; NAmE ˈwɑːdi/ noun (in the Middle East and North Africa) a valley or channel that is dry except when it rains

**'wading pool** (NAmE) (BrE **'paddling pool**) noun a shallow swimming pool for children to play in, especially a small plastic one that you fill with water

**wafer** /ˈweɪfə(r)/ noun **1** a thin, light biscuit, often eaten with ice cream **2** a very thin round piece of special bread given by the priest during COMMUNION **3** ~ (**of sth**) a very thin piece of sth

**wafer-'thin** adj. very thin ⊃compare PAPER-THIN

**waf·fle** /ˈwɒfl; NAmE ˈwɑːfl/ noun, verb
- **noun 1** [C] a dry, flat cake with a pattern of squares on both sides, often eaten with sweet sauce, cream, etc. on top: a **waffle iron** (= for making waffles with) **2** [U] (BrE, informal) language that uses a lot of words but does not say anything important or interesting: The report is just full of waffle.
- **verb 1** [I] ~ (**on**) (**about sth**) (BrE, informal, disapproving) to talk or write using a lot of words but without saying anything interesting or important: The principal waffled on about exam results but no one was listening. **2** [I] ~ (**on/over sth**) (NAmE, informal) to be unable to decide what to do about sth or what you think about sth: The senator was accused of waffling on major issues.

**waft** /wɒft; NAmE wɑːft, wæft/ verb, noun
- **verb** [I, T] to move, or make sth move, gently through the air SYN **drift**: + adv./prep. The sound of their voices wafted across the lake. ◊ Delicious smells wafted up from the kitchen. ◊ ~ **sth** + adv./prep. The scent of the flowers was wafted along by the breeze.
- **noun** (formal) a smell or a line of smoke carried through the air: wafts of perfume/smoke

**Wag** /wæɡ/ noun (BrE, informal) one of a group of 'wives and girlfriends' of famous men, especially members of a sports team: Wags at the World Cup

**wag** /wæɡ/ verb, noun
- **verb** (**-gg-**) **1** [T, I] ~ (**sth**) if a dog wags its tail, or its tail wags, its tail moves from side to side several times **2** [T] ~ **sth** to shake your finger or your head from side to side or up and down, often because you do not approve of sth **3** [T] ~ **sth** (AustralE, NZE) to stay away from school without permission: to wag school IDM see TAIL n., TONGUE n.
- **noun 1** (especially BrE, old-fashioned) a person who enjoys making jokes SYN **joker 2** a wagging movement

**wage** ❶ B2 /weɪdʒ/ noun, verb
- **noun** ❶ B2 [sing.] (also **wages** [pl.]) a regular amount of money that you earn, usually every week or every month, for work or services: wages of £300 a week ◊ a weekly wage of £300 ◊ an hourly/a daily/a monthly wage ◊ Workers in these stores **earn a good wage**. ◊ We all hope we can find a job that pays a decent wage. ◊ Wages were paid on Fridays. ◊ There are extra benefits for people on **low wages**. ◊ low/minimum wage earners ◊ wage cuts ◊ a wage increase of 3% ◊ The staff have agreed to a voluntary **wage freeze** (= a situation in which wages are not increased for a time). ⊃ SYNONYMS at INCOME ⊃ WORDFINDER NOTE at PAY ⊃ compare SALARY ⊃ see also LIVING WAGE, MINIMUM WAGE
- **verb** to begin and continue a war, a battle, etc.: ~ **sth** The rebels have waged a guerrilla war since 2007. ◊ ~ **sth against/on sb/sth** He alleged that a press campaign was being waged against him.

**waged** /weɪdʒd/ adj. **1** (of a person) having regular paid work: waged workers **2** (of work) for which you are paid: waged employment **3 the waged** noun [pl.] people who have regular paid work OPP **unwaged**

**'wage earner** noun a person who earns money, especially a person who works for wages: We have two wage earners in the family.

**'wage gap** noun = PAY GAP

**'wage packet** noun (BrE) = PAY PACKET

**wager** /ˈweɪdʒə(r)/ noun, verb
- **noun** (old-fashioned or formal) an arrangement to risk money on the result of a particular event SYN **bet**
- **verb** (old-fashioned or formal) **1** [I, T] to bet money SYN **bet**: ~ **on sth** She always wagered on an outsider. ◊ ~ **sth** (**on sth**) to wager £50 on a horse ◊ ~ **sth/sb that** ... I had wagered a great deal of money that I would beat him. **2** [T] ~ (**that**) ... used to say that you are so confident that sth is true or will happen that you would be willing to bet money on it SYN **bet**: I'll wager that she knows more about it than she's saying.

**wag·gle** /ˈwæɡl/ verb [T, I] ~ (**sth**) (informal) to make sth move with short movements from side to side or up and down; to move in this way: Can you waggle your ears? ▶ **wag·gle** noun

**Wag·ner·ian** /vɑːɡˈnɪəriən; NAmE -ˈnɪr-/ adj. **1** related to the music of the German COMPOSER Richard Wagner; typical of this music **2** (humorous) very big or great, or in a style that is too serious or EXAGGERATED: a hangover of Wagnerian proportions

# wagon 1750

wagons / freight cars

wagon

**wagon** /ˈwægən/ noun **1** (BrE) (NAmE ˈfreight car) a railway truck for carrying goods **2** (BrE also ˈwag·gon) a vehicle with four wheels, pulled by horses or OXEN and used for carrying heavy loads ⇨ see also COVERED WAGON **3** (also cart) (both NAmE) (BrE ˈtrol·ley) a small table on very small wheels, used for carrying or serving food or drink ⇨ see also BANDWAGON, MAMMY-WAGON, STATION WAGON
**IDM** be/go on the ˈwagon (informal) to not drink alcohol, either for a short time or permanently

**ˈwagon train** noun a long line of WAGONS and horses, used by people travelling west in North America in the 19th century

**wag·tail** /ˈwægteɪl/ noun a small bird with a long tail that moves up and down when the bird is walking

**wah-wah** /ˈwɑː wɑː/ noun [U] (music) a special effect made on electric musical instruments, especially the guitar, which varies the quality of the sound

**waif** /weɪf/ noun a small, thin person, usually a child, who looks as if they do not have enough to eat: *the waifs and strays of our society* (= people with no home) ▸ **ˈwaif-like** adj.: *waif-like young girls*

**wail** /weɪl/ verb, noun
■ verb **1** [I] to make a long, loud, high noise because you are sad or in pain: *The little girl was wailing miserably.* **2** [T, I] to cry or complain about sth in a loud high voice **SYN** moan: + speech *'It's broken,' she wailed.* ◇ *~ (about sth) There's no point wailing about something that happened so long ago.* **3** [I] (of things) to make a long, loud, high sound: *Ambulances raced by with sirens wailing.* ▸ **ˈwail·ing** noun [sing., U]: *a high-pitched wailing*
■ noun a long, loud, high cry expressing pain or very sad feelings; a sound similar to this **SYN** moan: *a wail of despair* ◇ *the distant wail of sirens*

▼ **HOMOPHONES**
wail • whale /weɪl/
- **wail** verb: *The blow made him wail with pain.*
- **wail** noun: *The blood-curdling wail sent shivers down her spine.*
- **whale** noun: *The blue whale is the largest mammal on the planet.*

**waist** /weɪst/ noun **1** the area around the middle of the body between the RIBS and the HIPS, often narrower than the areas above and below: *He put his arm around her waist.* ◇ *She was paralysed from the waist down* (= in the area below her waist). ◇ *The workmen were stripped to the waist* (= wearing no clothes on the top half of their bodies). ⇨ VISUAL VOCAB page V1 **2** the part of a piece of clothing that covers the waist: *a skirt with an elasticated waist* **3** **-waisted** (in adjectives) having the type of waist mentioned: *a high-waisted dress*

**waist·band** /ˈweɪstbænd/ noun the piece of cloth that forms the waist of a piece of clothing, especially at the top of a skirt or pair of trousers: *an elasticated waistband*

▼ **HOMOPHONES**
waist • waste /weɪst/
- **waist** noun: *She wore a wide sash around her waist.*
- **waste** verb: *You can't afford to waste time by waiting.*
- **waste** noun: *Doing such a mundane job is a waste of your talent.*
- **waste** adj.: *Waste products from the process can be made into fertilizer.*

**waist·coat** /ˈweɪskəʊt; NAmE ˈweskət, ˈweɪstkəʊt/ (BrE) (NAmE vest) noun a short piece of clothing with buttons down the front but no arms, usually worn over a shirt and under a jacket, often forming part of a man's suit

**ˌwaist-ˈdeep** adj., adv. up to the middle part of the body: *The water was waist-deep.* ◇ *We waded waist-deep into the muddy water.*

**ˌwaist-ˈhigh** adj., adv. high enough to reach the middle part of the body: *waist-high grass* ◇ *The grass had grown waist-high.*

**waist·line** /ˈweɪstlaɪn/ noun **1** the amount that a person measures around the middle part of their body, used to talk about how fat or thin they are: *an expanding waistline* **2** the part of a piece of clothing where your WAIST is **SYN** waist

**wait** **A1** /weɪt/ verb, noun
■ verb **1** [I, T] to stay where you are or delay doing sth until sb/sth comes or sth happens: *I waited and waited, but the bus didn't come.* ◇ *~ + adv./prep. Have you been waiting long?* ◇ *to wait (for) hours/days/weeks/months/years* ◇ *~ for sb/sth Wait for me!* ◇ *to wait for a bus* ◇ *~ for sb/sth to do sth We're waiting for the rain to stop before we go out.* ◇ *~ to do sth Hurry up! We're waiting to go.* ◇ *~ your turn You'll just have to wait your turn* (= wait until your turn comes). ⇨ HOMOPHONES at WEIGHT **2** **A1** [I, T] to hope or watch for sth to happen, especially for a long time: *~ for sth Leeds United had waited for success for eighteen years.* ◇ *~ for sb/sth to do sth He's waiting for me to make a mistake.* ◇ *~ to do sth I've been waiting a long time to say that to her.* ◇ *~ your chance I waited my chance and slipped out when no one was looking.* **3** **A2** be waiting [I] (of things) to be ready for sb to have or use: *~ for sb There's a letter waiting for you at home.* ◇ *~ to do sth The hotel had a taxi waiting to collect us.* **4** **A2** [I] to be left to be dealt with at a later time because immediate action is not needed: *I've got some calls to make but they can wait until tomorrow.*
**IDM** an ˌaccident/a diˈsaster waiting to ˈhappen a thing or person that is very likely to cause danger or a problem in the future because of the condition it is in or the way they behave  I, they, etc. can't ˈwait/can hardly ˈwait used when you are emphasizing that sb is very excited about sth or keen to do it: *The children can't wait for Christmas to come.* ◇ *I can hardly wait to see him again.* keep sb ˈwaiting to make sb have to wait or be delayed, especially because you arrive late: *I'm sorry to have kept you waiting.* ˌwait and ˈsee used to tell sb that they must be patient and wait to find out about sth later: *We'll just have to wait and see—there's nothing we can do at the moment.* ◇ *a wait-and-see policy* ◇ *'Where are we going?' 'Wait and see!'* ˌwait at ˈtable (formal) to serve food to people, for example at a formal meal ˈwait for it (informal, especially BrE) **1** used to say that you are about to tell sb sth that is surprising: *They're off on a trip, to—wait for it—the Maldives!* **2** used to tell sb not to start doing sth yet, but to wait until you tell them ˌwait a ˈminute/ˈmoment/ˈsecond **1** to wait for a short time: *Can you wait a second while I make a call?* **2** used when you have just noticed or remembered sth, or had a sudden idea: *Wait a minute—this isn't the right key.* ˌwait on sb hand and ˈfoot (disapproving) to take care of sb's needs so well that they do not have to do anything for themselves ˌwait ˈtables (NAmE) to work serving food to people in a restaurant ˌwait ˈtill/until … (informal) **1** used to show that you are very excited about telling or showing sth to sb: *Wait till you see what I've found!* **2** used to threaten to punish sb or do sth bad to them: *Wait till I get*

my hands on him! **what are we ˈwaiting for?** (informal) used to suggest that you should all start doing what you have been discussing **what are you ˈwaiting for?** (informal) used to tell sb to do sth now rather than later: *If the car needs cleaning, what are you waiting for?* **(just) you ˈwait** used to emphasize a threat, warning or promise: *I'll be famous one day, just you wait!* ⊃ more at DUST *n.*, WING *n.*

**PHR V** ˌwait aˈround/aˈbout to stay in a place, with nothing particular to do, for example because you are expecting sth to happen or sb to arrive ˌwait beˈhind (*especially BrE*) to stay after other people have gone, especially in order to be able to speak to sb privately ˌwait ˈin (*BrE*) to stay at home because you are expecting sb to come, phone, etc. ˈwait on sb to act as a servant to sb, especially by serving food to them ˈwait on sth/sb (*informal, especially NAmE*) to wait for sth to happen before you do or decide sth: *She is waiting on the result of a blood test.* ˌwait sth↔ˈout to wait until an unpleasant event has finished: *We sheltered in a doorway to wait out the storm.* ˌwait ˈup (*NAmE*) used to ask sb to stop or go more slowly so that you can join them ˌwait ˈup (for sb) to wait for sb to come home at night before you go to bed

■ *noun* **?** **A2** [usually sing.] an act of waiting; an amount of time waited: *It took six months for the house to be finished, but it was worth the wait.* ◊ **~ for sb/sth** *We had a long wait for the bus.* ⊃ HOMOPHONES at WEIGHT **IDM** see LIE¹ *v.*

**waitˑer** **?** **A1** /ˈweɪtə(r)/ (*feminine* **waitˑress**) *noun* a person whose job is to serve customers at their tables in a restaurant, etc.: *I'll ask the waitress for the bill.* ◊ *Waiter, could you bring me some water?* ⊃ note at GENDER ⊃ WORD-FINDER NOTE at RESTAURANT ⊃ see also SERVER

**waitˑing** /ˈweɪtɪŋ/ *noun* [U] **1** the fact of staying where you are or delaying doing sth until sb/sth comes or sth happens: *No waiting* (= on a sign at the side of the road, telling vehicles that they must not stop there). **2** the job of working as a waiter or WAITRESS ⊃ see also WAITRESSING ⊃ see also CALL WAITING, LADY-IN-WAITING

ˈwaiting game *noun* [sing.] a policy of waiting to see how a situation develops before you decide how to act

ˈwaiting list *noun* a list of people who are waiting for sth such as a service or medical treatment that is not yet available: *There are no places available right now but I'll put you on a waiting list.* ◊ *There's a waiting list to join the golf club.* ◊ (*BrE*) *The government has promised to cut hospital waiting lists.*

ˈwaiting room *noun* a room where people can sit while they are waiting, for example for a bus or train, or to see a doctor or dentist

ˈwait list *noun* (*NAmE*) = WAITING LIST: *She was on a wait list for a liver transplant.*

**waitˑ-list** *verb* (*NAmE*) [usually passive] to put sb's name on a WAITING LIST: *He's been wait-listed for a football scholarship to Stanford.*

**waitˑperˑson** /ˈweɪtpɜːsn; *NAmE* -pɜːrsn/ *noun* (*pl.* **-persons**) (*NAmE*) a person whose job is to serve customers at their tables in a restaurant, etc.

**waitˑress** /ˈweɪtrəs/ *noun* ⊃ WAITER

**waitˑressˑing** /ˈweɪtrəsɪŋ/ *noun* [U] the job of being a waitress: *I did some waitressing when I was a student.*

**waitˑstaff** /ˈweɪtstɑːf; *NAmE* -stæf/ *noun* [U] (*NAmE*) the people whose job is to serve customers at their tables in a restaurant, etc.

**waive** /weɪv/ *verb* **~ sth** to choose not to demand sth in a particular case, even though you have a legal or official right to do so **SYN** forgo: *He waived his right to appeal against the verdict.*

**waivˑer** /ˈweɪvə(r)/ *noun* (*law*) a situation in which sb gives up a legal right or claim; an official document stating this

**wake** **?** **A1** /weɪk/ *verb*, *noun*

■ *verb* (woke /wəʊk/, woken /ˈwəʊkən/) **1** [I, T] to stop sleeping; to make sb stop sleeping: *I always wake early in the summer.* ◊ **~ up** *What time do you usually wake up in the morning?* ◊ **~ to sth** (*formal*) *They woke to a clear blue sky.* ◊ **~ from sth** (*formal*) *She had just woken from a deep* sleep. ◊ **~ (up) to do sth** *He woke up to find himself alone in the house.* ◊ **~ sb** *I was woken by the sound of someone moving around.* ◊ **~ sb up** *Try not to wake the baby up.* ⊃ note at AWAKE **2** [T] **~ sth** (*literary or formal*) to make sb remember sth or feel sth again: *The incident woke memories of his past sufferings.*

**IDM** ˌwake up and smell the ˈcoffee (*informal*) used to tell sb to become aware of what is really happening in a situation, especially when this is sth unpleasant **PHR V** ˌwake ˈup **?** **A1** **?** **A1** to stop sleeping: *Wake up! It's eight o'clock.* **2** to become more lively and interested: *Wake up and listen!* ⊃ see also WAKE *verb* ˌwake sb↔ˈup **1** to make sb stop sleeping: *You'll wake the whole neighbourhood with that noise!* **2** to make sb feel more lively: *A cold shower will soon wake you up.* ◊ *The class needs waking up.* ⊃ see also WAKE *verb* ˌwake ˈup to sth to become aware of sth; to realize sth: *He hasn't yet woken up to the seriousness of the situation.*

■ *noun* **1** an occasion before or after a FUNERAL when people gather to remember the dead person, traditionally held the night before the FUNERAL to watch over the body before it is buried **2** the track that a boat or ship leaves behind on the surface of the water

**IDM** in the wake of sb/sth coming after or following sb/sth: *There have been demonstrations on the streets in the wake of the recent bomb attack.* ◊ *A group of reporters followed in her wake.* ◊ *The storm left a trail of destruction in its wake.*

**wakeˑboardˑing** /ˈweɪkbɔːdɪŋ; *NAmE* -bɔːrd-/ *noun* [U] the sport of riding on a short, wide board called a **wakeboard** while being pulled along through the water by a fast boat ▶ **wakeˑboard** *verb* [I]

**wakeˑful** /ˈweɪkfl/ *adj.* (*formal*) **1** not sleeping; unable to sleep **SYN** sleepless: *He lay wakeful all night.* **2** (of a period at night) spent with little or no sleep **SYN** sleepless: *She had spent many wakeful nights worrying about him.* ▶ **wakeˑfulˑness** *noun* [U]

**wakˑen** /ˈweɪkən/ *verb* (*formal*) **1** [I, T] to wake, or make sb wake, from sleep: **~ (up)** *The child had just wakened.* ◊ **~ sb (up)** *I was wakened by a knock at the door.* ⊃ note at AWAKE **2** [T] **~ sth** to make sb remember sth or feel sth again: *The dream wakened a forgotten memory.*

ˈwake-up call *noun* **1** a phone call that you arrange to be made to you at a particular time, for example in a hotel, in order to wake you up: *I asked for a wake-up call at 6.30 a.m.* **2** an event that makes people realize that there is a problem that they need to do sth about: *These riots should be a wake-up call for the government.*

**wakeyˑ-wakey** /ˌweɪki ˈweɪki/ *exclamation* (*BrE, informal, humorous*) used to tell sb to wake up

**wakˑing** /ˈweɪkɪŋ/ *adj.* [only before noun] used to describe time when you are not asleep: *She spends all her waking hours caring for her mother.* ▶ **wakˑing** *noun* [U]: *the dreamlike state between waking and sleeping*

**walk** **?** **A1** /wɔːk/ *verb*, *noun*

■ *verb* **1 ? A1** [I, T] to move or go somewhere by putting one foot in front of the other on the ground, but without running: *The baby is just learning to walk.* ◊ *'How did you get here?' 'I walked.'* ◊ **~ + adv./prep.** *He walked slowly away from her.* ◊ *The door opened and Jane walked in.* ◊ *She missed the bus and had to walk home.* ◊ *The school is within easy walking distance of the train station.* ◊ **~ sth** *They walked the dark streets of Los Angeles.* **2 ? A1** (*also* go walking) (*both especially BrE*) [I, T] to spend time walking for pleasure: **~ + adv./prep.** *We're going walking in the mountains this summer.* ◊ *I walked across Scotland with a friend.* ◊ **~ sth** *They love walking the moors.* **3** [T] **~ sb + adv./prep.** to go somewhere with sb on foot, especially in order to make sure they get there safely: *He always walked her home.* **4** [T] **~ sth (+ adv./prep.)** to take an animal for a walk; to make an animal walk somewhere: *They walk their dogs every day.* ⊃ SYNONYMS at TAKE **5** [I] (*informal*) to disappear; to be taken away: *Lock up any valuables. Things tend to walk here* (= be stolen).

# walkable

**IDM** **run before you can ˈwalk** to do things that are difficult, without learning the basic skills first **walk the ˈbeat** (of police officers) to walk around the area that they are responsible for **walk ˈfree** to be allowed to leave court, etc., without receiving any punishment **ˈwalk it** (*informal*) **1** to go somewhere on foot instead of in a vehicle **2** (*BrE*) to easily achieve sth that you want: *It's not a difficult exam. You'll walk it!* **walk sb off their ˈfeet** (*informal*) to make sb walk so far or so fast that they are very tired **walk off the ˈjob** (*NAmE*) to stop working in order to go on strike **walk the ˈplank** (in the past) to walk along a board placed over the side of a ship and fall into the sea, as a punishment **walk the ˈstreets** to walk around the streets of a town or city: *Is it safe to walk the streets alone at night?* **walk ˈtall** to feel proud and confident **walk the ˈwalk** (*informal, approving*) to act in a way that shows people you are really good at what you do, and not just good at talking about it: *You can talk the talk but can you walk the walk?* ⇨ more at AIR *n.*, AISLE, LINE *n.*, THIN *adj.*, TIGHTROPE

**PHR V** **walk aˈway (from sb/sth)** to leave a difficult situation or relationship, etc. instead of staying and trying to deal with it **walk aˈway with sth** (*informal*) to win or obtain sth easily: *She walked away with the gold medal.* **walk ˈin on sb/sth** to enter a room when sb in there is doing sth private and does not expect you **walk ˈinto sth** (*informal*) **1** to become involved in an unpleasant situation, especially because you were not sensible enough to avoid it: *I realized I'd walked into a trap.* **2** to succeed in getting a job very easily **walk ˈinto sth/sb** to crash into sth/sb while you are walking, for example because you do not see them **walk ˈoff** to leave a person or place suddenly because you are angry or upset **walk sth↔ˈoff** to go for a walk after a meal so that you feel less full: *We walked off a heavy Sunday lunch.* **walk ˈoff with sth** (*informal*) **1** to win sth easily **2** to take sth that is not yours; to steal sth **walk ˈout** (*informal*) (of workers) to stop working in order to go on strike ⇨ related noun WALKOUT **walk ˈout (of sth)** to leave a meeting, performance, etc. suddenly, especially in order to show that you do not like or approve of it **walk ˈout (on sb)** (*informal, disapproving*) to suddenly leave sb that you are having a relationship with and that you have a responsibility for **SYN** **desert**: *How could she walk out on her kids?* **walk ˈout (on sth)** (*informal*) to stop doing sth that you have agreed to do before it is completed: *I never walk out on a job half done.* **walk (all) ˈover sb** (*informal*) **1** to treat sb badly, without considering them or their needs: *She'll always let him walk all over her.* **2** to defeat sb easily ⇨ related noun WALKOVER **walk sb ˈthrough sth** to help sb learn or become familiar with sth, by showing them each stage of the process in turn: *She walked me through a demonstration of the software.* ⇨ related noun WALK-THROUGH **walk ˈup (to sb/sth)** to walk towards sb/sth, especially in a confident way

▪ *noun* **1** 🔊 **A1** [C] a journey on foot, usually for pleasure or exercise: *Let's go for a walk.* ◊ *I like to have a walk in the evenings.* ◊ *I decided to take a walk to clear my head* ◊ *She's taken the dog for a walk.* ◊ *He set out on the long walk home.* ◊ *a ten-minute walk* ◊ *He's out for a walk with a friend.* **2** 🔊 **A2** [C] a path or route for walking, usually for pleasure; an organized event when people walk for pleasure: *I'm going on a sponsored walk to raise money for cancer research.* ◊ *a guided walk around the farm* ◊ *We wanted to do a walk for charity.* **3** [sing.] a way or style of walking; the act or speed of walking rather than running: *I recognized him by his walk.* ◊ *The horse slowed to a walk.* **4** [C] (*NAmE*) a SIDEWALK or path **5** [C] a sports event in which people compete to walk a long distance as fast as possible without running: *the 20k walk*

**IDM** **a ˌwalk in the ˈpark** (*informal*) a thing that is very easy to do or deal with: *The role isn't exactly a walk in the park.* **a walk of ˈlife** a person's job or position in society **SYN** **background**: *She has friends from all walks of life.* ⇨ more at MEMORY LANE

**walk·able** /ˈwɔːkəbl/ *adj.* **1** (of an area or a route) suitable or safe for walking: *New paths and trails have made the area more walkable.* **2 ~ (from …)** (of a destination) close enough to be easy to walk to: *The hotel is walkable from the bus station.*

**walk·about** /ˈwɔːkəbaʊt/ *noun* **1** (*BrE*) an occasion when an important person walks among ordinary people to meet and talk to them **2** (*AustralE*) a journey (originally on foot) that is made by an Australian Aboriginal in order to live in the traditional manner

**IDM** **go ˈwalkabout 1** (*informal*) to be lost or not where it/you should be: *My rucksack seems to have gone walkabout.* **2** (of an Australian Aboriginal) to go into the country away from cities and towns in order to live in the traditional manner

**walk·er** /ˈwɔːkə(r)/ *noun* **1** (*especially BrE*) a person who walks, usually for pleasure or exercise: *The coastal path is a popular route for walkers.* **2 a fast, slow, etc. ~** a person who walks fast, slow, etc. **3** (*NAmE*) (*BrE* **walking frame**, **Zimmer frame™**, *informal* **Zim·mer**) a metal frame that people use to support them when they are walking, for example people who are old or who have sth wrong with their legs: *He now needs a walker to get around.* ⇨ picture at FRAME **4** (*NAmE*) (*BrE* **baby walker**) a frame with wheels and a HARNESS that enables a baby to walk around a room, supported by the frame

**walkie-talkie** /ˌwɔːki ˈtɔːki/ *noun* (*informal*) a small radio that you can carry with you and use to send or receive messages

**ˈwalk-in** *adj.* [only before noun] **1** large enough to walk into: *a walk-in closet* **2** not arranged in advance; where you do not need to arrange a time in advance: *a walk-in interview* ◊ *a walk-in clinic*

**walk·ing** /ˈwɔːkɪŋ/ *noun, adj.*

▪ *noun* [U] **1** (*especially BrE*) the activity of going for walks in the countryside for exercise or pleasure: *to go walking* ◊ *walking boots* ◊ *a walking holiday in Scotland* **2** the sport of walking a long distance as fast as possible without running

▪ *adj.* [only before noun] (*informal*) used to describe a human or living example of the thing mentioned: *She's a walking dictionary* (= she knows a lot of words).

**ˈwalking frame** *noun* (*BrE*) = ZIMMER FRAME™

**ˈwalking stick** (*also* **stick** *especially in BrE*) *noun* a stick that you carry and use as a support when you are walking ⇨ picture at STICK

**the ˌwalking ˈwounded** *noun* [pl.] people who have been injured in a battle or an accident but who are still able to walk

**Walk·man™** /ˈwɔːkmən/ *noun* (*pl.* **-mans** /-mənz/) a type of PERSONAL STEREO

**ˈwalk-on** *adj.* ~ **part/role** used to describe a very small part in a play or film, without any words to say

**walk·out** /ˈwɔːkaʊt/ *noun* **1** a sudden strike by workers **2** the act of suddenly leaving a meeting as a protest against sth

**walk·over** /ˈwɔːkəʊvə(r)/ *noun* **1** an easy victory in a game or competition **2** a victory given to a player or team because their opponent did not take part

---

**VOCABULARY BUILDING**

**Ways of walking**

- **creep**: *He could hear someone creeping around downstairs.*
- **limp**: *One player limped off the field with a twisted ankle.*
- **pace**: *I found him in the corridor nervously pacing up and down.*
- **pad**: *She spent the morning padding about the house in her slippers.*
- **plod**: *They wearily plodded home through the rain.*
- **shuffle**: *The queue gradually shuffled forward.*
- **stagger**: *They staggered out of the pub, completely drunk.*
- **stomp**: *She stomped out of the room, slamming the door behind her.*
- **stroll**: *Families were strolling around the park.*
- **tiptoe**: *They tiptoed upstairs so they wouldn't wake the baby.*
- **trudge**: *We trudged up the hill.*

**walk-through** noun **1** an occasion when you practise a performance, etc. without an audience being present **2** a careful explanation of the details of a process

**walk-up** noun (NAmE) a tall building with stairs but no ELEVATOR; an office or apartment in such a building

**walk·way** /ˈwɔːkweɪ/ noun a passage or path for walking along, often outside and raised above the ground

**wall** 🔑 A1 /wɔːl/ noun, verb
- noun **1** 🔑 A1 a long, solid structure that rises straight up from the ground, made of stone, BRICK or CONCRETE, that surrounds, divides or protects an area of land: *to build a wall* ◇ *a brick/concrete wall* ◇ *The fields were divided by stone walls.* ⊃ see also DRYSTONE WALL, GREEN WALL, SEA WALL **2** 🔑 A1 any of the sides of a building or room: *She leaned against the wall.* ◇ **on the ~** *Colourful abstract paintings hung on the walls.* ◇ *He drilled a hole in the wall.* ⊃ see also CAVITY WALL, CLIMBING WALL, PARTY WALL **3** something that forms a barrier or stops you from making progress: *The boat struck a solid wall of water.* ◇ *The investigators were confronted by a wall of silence.* ⊃ see also FOURTH WALL **4** the outer layer of sth hollow such as an organ of the body or a cell of an animal or a plant: *the abdominal wall* ◇ *the wall of an artery* **5** a space on a SOCIAL MEDIA website where you can share messages, photos, etc. with other users
- IDM **go to the ˈwall** (*informal*) (of a company or an organization) to fail because of lack of money **off the ˈwall** (*informal*) unusual or slightly crazy: *Some of his ideas are really off the wall.* ◇ **off-the-wall ideas** **up the ˈwall** (*informal*) crazy or angry: *That noise is driving me up the wall.* ◇ *I mustn't be late or Dad will go up the wall.* **ˈwalls have ˈears** (*saying*) used to warn people to be careful what they say because other people may be listening ⊃ more at BACK n., BOUNCE v., BRICK n., FLY n., FOUR, HANDWRITING, HEAD n., HIT v., WRITING
- verb [usually passive] **~ sth** to surround an area, a town, etc. with a wall or walls: *a walled city*
- PHR V **ˌwall sth↔ˈin** [usually passive] to surround sth/sb with a wall or barrier **ˌwall sth↔ˈoff** [usually passive] to separate one place or area from another with a wall **ˌwall sb↔ˈup** [usually passive] to keep sb as a prisoner behind walls **ˌwall sth↔ˈup** [usually passive] to fill an opening with a wall, stones, etc. so that you can no longer use it

**wal·laby** /ˈwɒləbi/; NAmE /ˈwɑːl-/ noun (pl. **-ies**) an Australian animal like a small KANGAROO, that moves by jumping on its strong back legs and keeps its young in a POUCH (= a pocket of skin) on the front of the mother's body

**wal·lah** /ˈwɒlə/; NAmE /ˈwɑːlə/ noun **1** (IndE or old-fashioned, informal) a person connected with a particular job: *office wallahs* **2** (IndE) a person who was born in or lives in the country or area mentioned: *a Delhi wallah*

**wall·chart** /ˈwɔːltʃɑːt/; NAmE /ˈwɔːltʃɑːrt/ noun a large piece of paper on which there is information, fixed to a wall for people to look at

**ˈwall·cover·ing** /ˈwɔːlkʌvərɪŋ/ noun [U, C] WALLPAPER or cloth used to decorate the walls in a room

**wal·let** /ˈwɒlɪt/; NAmE /ˈwɑːl-/ noun **1** (NAmE also **bill·fold**) a small, flat, folding case made of leather or plastic used for keeping paper money and credit cards in **2** (BrE) a flat case made of leather, plastic or card for carrying documents in: *a document wallet*

**wall-eye** /ˈwɔːlaɪ/ (pl. **wall-eye**) (also **wall-eyed pike** /ˌwɔːlaɪd ˈpaɪk/) noun a North American FRESHWATER fish with large eyes

**wall·flower** /ˈwɔːlflaʊə(r)/ noun **1** a garden plant with yellow, orange or red flowers with a sweet smell that appear in late spring **2** (*informal*) a person who does not dance at a party because they do not have sb to dance with or because they are too shy

**wall·ing** /ˈwɔːlɪŋ/ noun [U] **1** material from which a wall is built: *stone walling* **2** the act or skill of building a wall or walls: *a firm that does paving and walling*

**wall-ˈmounted** adj. fixed onto a wall: *wall-mounted lights*

**wal·lop** /ˈwɒləp/; NAmE /ˈwɑːl-/ noun, verb
- noun [sing.] (*informal*) a heavy, powerful hit
- verb (*informal*) **1** **~ sb/sth** to hit sb/sth very hard SYN **thump 2 ~ sb/sth** to defeat sb completely in a contest, match, etc. SYN **thrash**: *We walloped them 6–0.*

**wal·lop·ing** /ˈwɒləpɪŋ/; NAmE /ˈwɑːl-/ noun, adj.
- noun [usually sing.] (*informal*) **1** a heavy defeat: *Our team got a real walloping last week.* **2** an act of hitting sb very hard several times, often as a punishment
- adj. [only before noun] (*informal*) very big: *They had to pay a walloping great fine.*

**wal·low** /ˈwɒləʊ/; NAmE /ˈwɑːloʊ/ verb, noun
- verb **1** [I] **~ (in sth)** (of large animals or people) to lie and roll about in water or mud, to keep cool or for pleasure: *hippos wallowing in the river* ◇ *He loves to wallow in a hot bath after a game.* **2** [I] **~ in sth** (*often disapproving*) to enjoy sth that causes you pleasure: *She wallowed in the luxury of the hotel.* ◇ **to wallow in despair/self-pity** (= to think about your unhappy feelings all the time and seem to be enjoying them)
- noun [sing.] an act of wallowing: *pigs having a wallow in the mud*

**ˈwall painting** noun a picture painted straight onto the surface of a wall

**wall·paper** /ˈwɔːlpeɪpə(r)/ noun, verb
- noun [U] **1** thick paper, often with a pattern on it, used for covering the walls and ceiling of a room: *wallpaper paste* ◇ *a roll of wallpaper* ◇ *to hang wallpaper* **2** (*computing*) the background pattern or picture that you choose to have on the screen of your computer, mobile phone, etc.
- verb (also **paper**) [T, I] **~ (sth)** to put wallpaper onto the walls of a room

**ˈWall Street** noun [U] the US financial centre and STOCK EXCHANGE in New York City (used to refer to the business that is done there): *Share prices fell on Wall Street today.* ◇ *Wall Street responded quickly to the news.*

**ˌwall-to-ˈwall** adj. [only before noun] **1** covering the floor of a room completely: *wall-to-wall carpets/carpeting* **2** (*informal*) continuous; happening or existing all the time or everywhere: *wall-to-wall TV sports coverage*

**wally** /ˈwɒli/; NAmE /ˈwɑːli/ noun (pl. **-ies**) (BrE, *informal*) a stupid person

**wal·nut** /ˈwɔːlnʌt/ noun **1** [C] the light-brown nut of the walnut tree that has a rough surface and a hard round shell in two halves ⊃ VISUAL VOCAB page V8 **2** (also **ˈwalnut tree**) [C] the tree on which walnuts grow **3** [U] the brown wood of the walnut tree, used in making furniture

**wal·rus** /ˈwɔːlrəs/ noun an animal like a large SEAL (= a sea animal with thick fur, that eats fish and lives around coasts), that has two long outer teeth called TUSKS and lives in Arctic regions

**ˌWal·ter ˈMitty** /ˌwɔːltə ˈmɪti/; NAmE /-tər-/ noun a person who imagines that their life is full of excitement and adventures when it is in fact just ordinary ORIGIN From the name of the main character in James Thurber's story *The Secret Life of Walter Mitty*.

**waltz** /wɔːls, wɔːlts/ noun, verb
- noun a dance in which two people dance together to a regular rhythm; a piece of music for this dance: *to dance a/the waltz* ◇ *a Strauss waltz*
- verb **1** [I, T] to dance a waltz: **(+ adv./prep.)** *I watched them waltzing across the floor.* ◇ **~ sb + adv./prep.** *He waltzed her around the room.* **2** [I] **~ + adv./prep.** (*informal*) to walk or go somewhere in a very confident way: *I don't like him waltzing into the house as if he owned it.* **3** [I] **~ (through sth)** to complete or achieve sth without any difficulty: *The recruits have waltzed through their training.*
- PHR V **ˌwaltz ˈoff (with sth/sb)** (*informal*) to leave a place or person in a way that is very annoying, often taking sth that is not yours: *He just waltzed off with my car!*

# WAN

**WAN** /wæn/ *noun* (*computing*) a system in which computers in different places are connected, usually over a large area (the abbreviation for 'wide area network') ⊃ compare LAN

**wan** /wɒn; *NAmE* wɑːn/ *adj.* looking pale and weak: *his grey, wan face* ◊ *She gave me a wan smile* (= showing no energy or enthusiasm). ▸ **wanly** *adv.*: *He smiled wanly.*

**wa·nan·chi** /ˌwəˈnæntʃi; *EAfrE* ˌwanaˈntʃi/ *noun* [pl.] (*EAfrE*) ordinary people; the public ⊃ see also MWANANCHI

**wand** /wɒnd; *NAmE* wɑːnd/ *noun* **1** (*also* **magic 'wand**) a straight, thin stick that is held by sb when performing magic or magic tricks: *The fairy waved her wand and the table disappeared.* ◊ *You can't expect me to just **wave a (magic) wand** and make everything all right.* **2** any object in the shape of a straight, thin stick: *a mascara wand*

**wan·der** ⭐+ B2 /ˈwɒndə(r); *NAmE* ˈwɑːn-/ *verb, noun*
▪ *verb* **1** ⭐+ B2 [I, T] to walk slowly around or to a place, often without any particular sense of purpose or direction: **+ adv./prep.** *She wandered aimlessly around the streets.* ◊ *We wandered back towards the car.* ◊ ~ **sth** *The child wandered the streets alone.* **2** ⭐+ B2 [I] to move away from the place where you ought to be or the people you are with SYN stray: ~ **away/off** *The child wandered off and got lost.* ◊ ~ **from/off sth** *They had wandered from the path into the woods.* **3** ⭐+ C1 [I] (of a person's mind or thoughts) to stop being directed on sth and to move without much control to other ideas, subjects, etc. SYN drift: *It's easy to be distracted and let your attention wander.* ◊ *Try not to let your mind wander.* ◊ ~ **away, back, to, etc. sth** *Her thoughts wandered back to her youth.* **4** ⭐+ C1 [I] (of a person's eyes) to move slowly from looking at one thing to looking at another thing or in other directions: *She let her gaze wander.* ◊ **+ adv./prep.** *His eyes wandered towards the photographs on the wall.* **5** [I] (**+ adv./prep.**) (of a road or river) to go in a curve instead of following a straight course: *The road wanders along through the hills.*
▪ *noun* [sing.] a short walk in or around a place, usually with no special purpose: *I went to the park and had a wander around.*

**wan·der·er** /ˈwɒndərə(r); *NAmE* ˈwɑːn-/ *noun* a person who keeps travelling from place to place with no permanent home

**wan·der·ings** /ˈwɒndərɪŋz; *NAmE* ˈwɑːn-/ *noun* [pl.] (*literary*) journeys from place to place, usually with no special purpose

**wan·der·lust** /ˈwɒndəlʌst; *NAmE* ˈwɑːndərl-/ *noun* [U] (*from German*) a strong desire to travel

**wane** /weɪn/ *verb, noun*
▪ *verb* **1** [I] to become gradually weaker or less important SYN **decrease, fade**: *Her enthusiasm for the whole idea was waning rapidly.* **2** [I] (of the moon) to appear slightly smaller each day after being round and full OPP **wax** IDM see WAX v.
▪ *noun* [sing.] IDM **on the 'wane** becoming smaller, less important or less common SYN **decline**: *Her popularity has been on the wane for some time.*

**wan·gle** /ˈwæŋgl/ *verb* (*informal*) to get sth that you or another person wants, but do not really have a right to have, by persuading sb or by a clever plan: ~ **sth** *She had wangled an invitation to the opening night.* ◊ ~ **sb sth** *He had wangled her a seat on the plane.*

**wank** /wæŋk/ *verb, noun*
▪ *verb* [I] (*BrE, taboo, slang*) to MASTURBATE
▪ *noun* [usually sing.] (*BrE, taboo, slang*) an act of MASTURBATION

**wank·er** /ˈwæŋkə(r)/ *noun* (*BrE, taboo, slang*) an offensive word used to refer to a man that you dislike or are angry with: *a bunch of wankers*

**wanna** /ˈwɒnə; *NAmE* ˈwɑːnə/ (*informal, non-standard*) a way of saying or writing 'want to' or 'want a' in informal speech: *I wanna go.* ◊ *Wanna drink?* (= Do you want …) HELP You should not write this form unless you are copying somebody's speech.

**wan·nabe** /ˈwɒnəbi; *NAmE* ˈwɑːn-/ *noun* (*informal, disapproving*) a person who behaves, dresses, etc. like sb famous because they want to be like them

**want** ⭐ A1 /wɒnt; *NAmE* wɑːnt/ *verb, noun*
▪ *verb* (not usually used in the progressive tenses)
• WISH **1** ⭐ A1 to have a desire or a wish for sth/sb: ~ **sb/sth** *Do you want some more tea?* ◊ *to* ***want children/kids*** ◊ *She's always wanted a large family.* ◊ *All I want is the truth.* ◊ *Thanks for the present—it's* ***just what I wanted****.* ◊ *The last thing I wanted was to upset you.* ◊ ~ **sth for sth** *What do you want for Christmas?* ◊ ~ **sb/sth as sth** *The party wants her as leader.* ◊ ~ **to do sth** *What do you want to do tomorrow?* ◊ *What* ***I really want to know*** *is why you would even think that?* ◊ *'It's time you did your homework.' 'I don't want to!'* ◊ *I just wanted to know if everything was all right.* ◊ (*informal*) *You can come too,* ***if you want****.* ◊ ~ **sb/sth to do sth** *Do you want me to help?* ◊ ***I want people to know*** *what I've done.* ◊ ~ **sb/sth doing sth** *I don't want you coming home so late.* ◊ ~ **sb/sth + adj.** *Do you want your coffee black or white?* ◊ ~ **sth from sb/sth** *What do you want from me?* ◊ ~ **sth out of sth** *I had to discover what I really wanted out of life.*
• NEED **2** ⭐ B2 (*informal*) to need sth: ~ **sth** *We'll want more furniture for the new office.* ◊ ~ **doing sth** *The plants want watering daily.* ◊ ~ **to be sth** *The cake mixture wants to be smooth and light.* ◊ ~ **to be/have sth done** *The plants want to be watered daily.* **3** [usually passive] ~ **sb (+ adv./prep.)** to need sb to be present in the place or for the purpose mentioned: *She's wanted immediately in the director's office.* ◊ *Excuse me, you're wanted on the phone.* ⊃ see also WANTED
• SHOULD/OUGHT TO **4** ~ **to do sth** (*informal*) used to give advice to sb, meaning 'should' or 'ought to': *If possible, you want to avoid alcohol.* ◊ *He wants to be more careful.* ◊ *You don't want to do it like that.*
• FEEL SEXUAL DESIRE **5** ~ **sb** to feel sexual desire for sb
• LACK **6** ~ **sth** (*formal*) to lack sth SYN **be short of**: *He doesn't want courage.*
IDM **not want to 'know (about sth)** (*informal*) to take no interest in sth because you do not care about it or it is too much trouble: *I've tried to ask her advice, but she doesn't want to know* (= about my problems). ◊ *'How much was it?' 'You don't want to know'* (= it is better if you don't know). **want 'rid of sb/sth** (*BrE, informal*) to want to be free of sb/sth that has been annoying you or that you do not want: *Are you trying to say you want rid of me?* **what do you 'want?** used to ask sb in a rude or angry way why they are there or what they want you to do ⊃ more at NONE *pron.*, TRUCK *n.*, WASTE *v.*, WAY *n.*
PHRV **'want for sth** (especially in negative sentences) (*formal*) to lack sth that you really need: *He's ensured that his children will* ***want for nothing*** (= will have everything they need). **want 'in/'out** (*informal, especially NAmE*) to want to come in or out of a place: *The dog wants in.* **want 'in | want 'in/'into sth** (*informal*) to want to be involved in sth: *He wants in on the deal.* **want 'out | want 'out of sth** (*informal*) to want to stop being involved in sth: *Jenny was fed up. She wanted out.*

▪ *noun* (*formal*)
• STH YOU NEED **1** [C, usually pl.] something that you need or want: *She spent her life pandering to the wants of her children.*
• LACK **2** [U, sing.] ~ **of sth** (*formal*) a situation in which there is not enough of sth SYN **lack**: *a want of adequate medical facilities*
• BEING POOR **3** [U] (*formal*) the state of being poor, not having food, etc: *Visitors to the slums were clearly shocked to see so many families living* ***in want****.*
IDM **for (the) want of sth** because of a lack of sth; because sth is not available: *The project failed for want of financial backing.* ◊ *We call our music 'postmodern' for the want of a better word.* **in want of sth** (*formal*) needing sth: *The present system is in want of a total review.* **not for (the) want of doing sth** used to say that if sth is not successful, it is not because of a lack of effort: *If he doesn't manage to convince them, it won't be for* ***want of trying*** (= he has tried hard).

---

æ cat | ɑː father | e bed | ɜː fur | ə about | ɪ sit | iː see | i happy | ɒ got (*BrE*) | ɔː saw | ʌ cup | ʊ put | uː too

▼ **GRAMMAR POINT**

**want / like / love / hate / think**
- These verbs belong to a group known as *stative verbs* because they describe a state rather than an action (although **think** can describe either an action or a state). Stative verbs are not usually used in the progressive tenses. However, it is becoming more common for some stative verbs to be used with progressive tenses. Stative verbs such as **want**, **like**, **love**, **hate** and **think** are sometimes used in informal language to describe a state at a particular moment, or a state that continues for a period of time: *Why are you wanting a new phone when your current one works perfectly well? ◊ What shall we do tonight? I'm thinking bowling. ◊ I'm loving the weather today!* Other stative verbs that can be used this way include **prefer**, **remember**, **taste** and **understand**.

▼ **MORE ABOUT ...**

**offers and invitations**
- **Would you like ...?** is the most usual polite question form for offers and invitations, especially in *BrE*: *Would you like a cup of coffee?*
- **Do you want ...?** is less formal and more direct. It is more common in *NAmE* than in *BrE*: *We're going to a club tonight. Do you want to come with us?*
- **Would you care ...?** is very formal and now sounds old-fashioned.

**'want ad** *noun* [usually pl.] (*NAmE*) = CLASSIFIED ADVERTISEMENT

**want·ed** /'wɒntɪd; *NAmE* 'wɑːn-/ *adj.* being searched for by the police, in connection with a crime: *He is wanted by the police in connection with the deaths of two people. ◊ Italy's most wanted man*

**want·ing** /'wɒntɪŋ; *NAmE* 'wɑːn-/ *adj.* [not before noun] (*formal*) **1** ~ (in sth) not having enough of sth SYN lacking: *The students were certainly not wanting in enthusiasm.* **2** ~ (in sth) not good enough: *This explanation is wanting in many respects. ◊ The new system was tried and found wanting.*

**wan·ton** /'wɒntən; *NAmE* 'wɑːn-/ *adj.* (*formal*) **1** [usually before noun] causing harm or damage deliberately and for no acceptable reason: *wanton destruction ◊ a wanton disregard for human life* **2** (*old-fashioned, disapproving*) (usually of a woman) behaving in an IMMORAL way; having many sexual partners ▶ **wan·ton·ly** *adv.* **wan·ton·ness** /-tənnɪs/ *noun* [U]

**wap·iti** /'wɒpɪti; *NAmE* 'wɑːp-/ *noun* (*pl.* **wap·iti**) (*NAmE also* **elk**) a very large North American DEER ⊃ picture at ELK

**war** /wɔː(r)/ *noun* **1** [U, C] a situation in which two or more countries or groups of people fight against each other over a period of time: *the Second World War ◊ the threat of (a) nuclear war ◊ to win/lose a/the war ◊ ~ between A and B the war between England and Scotland ◊ ~ with/against sb England's war with Scotland ◊ ~ on sb It was the year Britain declared war on Germany. ◊ (formal) In the Middle Ages England waged war on France. ◊ Social and political problems led to the outbreak (= the beginning) of war. ◊ Where were you living when war broke out? ◊ The government does not want to go to war (= start a war) unless all other alternatives have failed. ◊ The two countries fought a short but bloody war. ◊ My grandfather fought in the war. ◊ Her husband was killed during the war. ◊ at ~ How long have they been at war? ◊ a war hero/veteran ◊ More troops are being despatched to the war zone.* ⊃ WORDFINDER NOTE at CONFLICT ⊃ see also CIVIL WAR, COLD WAR, COUNCIL OF WAR, PHONEY WAR, POST-WAR, PRE-WAR, PRISONER OF WAR, PROXY WAR, WARRING, WORLD WAR **2** [C, U] ~ (against/on/with sb/sth) a situation in which there is aggressive competition between groups, companies, countries, etc: *the class war ◊ a trade war* ⊃ see also PRICE WAR, TURF WAR **3** [U, sing.] a fight or an effort over a long period of time to get rid of or stop sth unpleasant: *~ on sb/sth The government has declared war on drug dealers. ◊ against sb/sth We seem to be winning the war against crime.* ⊃ SYNONYMS at CAMPAIGN
IDM **have been in the wars** (*informal*) to have been injured in a fight or an accident: *You look like you've been in the wars—who gave you that black eye?* **a war of nerves** an attempt to defeat your opponents by putting pressure on them so that they lose courage or confidence **a war of words** a bitter argument over a period of time between two or more people or groups: *the political war of words over tax* ⊃ more at FAIR *adj.*

▼ **HOMOPHONES**

**war • wore** /wɔː(r)/
- **war** *noun*: *It's in memory of the soldiers who gave their lives during the war.*
- **wore** *verb* (past tense of **WEAR**): *He wore his raincoat all day, even though it was sunny.*

**war·ble** /'wɔːbl; *NAmE* 'wɔːrbl/ *verb* **1** [T, I] ~ (sth) | + **speech** (*humorous*) to sing, especially in a high voice that is not very steady: *He warbled his way through the song.* **2** [I, T] ~ (sth) (of a bird) to sing with rapidly changing notes ▶ **war·ble** *noun* [usually sing.]

**warb·ler** /'wɔːblə(r); *NAmE* 'wɔːrb-/ *noun* a small bird. There are many types of warbler, some of which have a musical call.

**'war chest** *noun* an amount of money that a government or an organization has available to spend on a particular plan, project, etc.

**'war crime** *noun* a cruel act that is committed during a war and is against the international rules of war

**'war criminal** *noun* a person who has committed war crimes

**'war cry** *noun* a word or phrase that is shouted by people fighting in a battle in order to give themselves courage and to frighten the enemy

**ward** /wɔːd; *NAmE* wɔːrd/ *noun, verb*
■ *noun* **1** a separate room or area in a hospital for people with the same type of medical condition: *a maternity/surgical/psychiatric/children's ward ◊ on the ~ He worked as a nurse on the children's ward.* ⊃ WORDFINDER NOTE at HOSPITAL **2** (in the UK) one of the areas into which a city or town is divided and which elects and is represented by a member of the local council **3** (*law*) a person, especially a child, who is under the legal protection of a court or another person (called a GUARDIAN): *The child was made a ward of court.*
■ *verb*
PHRV **ward sb/sth off** to protect or defend yourself against danger, illness, attack, etc: *to ward off criticism ◊ She put up her hands to ward him off.*

**-ward** /wəd; *NAmE* wərd/ (*also less frequent* **-wards**) *suffix* (in adjectives) in the direction of: *backward ◊ eastward ◊ homeward* ▶ **-wards** /wədz; *NAmE* wərdz/ (*also* **-ward** *especially in NAmE*) (in adverbs): *onwards ◊ forwards*

**'war dance** *noun* a dance that is performed by members of some peoples, for example before a battle or to celebrate a victory

**war·den** /'wɔːdn; *NAmE* 'wɔːrdn/ *noun* **1** a person who is responsible for taking care of a particular place and making sure that the rules are obeyed: *a forest warden ◊ (BrE) the warden of a youth hostel* ⊃ see also CHURCHWARDEN, DOG WARDEN, GAME WARDEN, TRAFFIC WARDEN **2** (*especially NAmE*) the person in charge of a prison **3** (especially in England) a title given to the head of some colleges and institutions: *the Warden of Wadham College, Oxford*

**ward·er** /'wɔːdə(r); *NAmE* 'wɔːrd-/ (*feminine* **ward·ress** /-drəs/) *noun* (*BrE*) a person who guards prisoners in a prison ⊃ compare GUARD ⊃ WORDFINDER NOTE at PRISON

**ward·robe** /'wɔːdrəʊb; *NAmE* 'wɔːrd-/ *noun* **1** a large cupboard for hanging clothes in, which is either a piece of furniture or (in British English) built into the wall: *a fitted*

# wardroom

***wardrobe*** ⇨ compare CLOSET **2** [usually sing.] the clothes that a person has: *everything you need for your summer wardrobe* **3** [usually sing.] the department in a theatre or television company that takes care of the clothes that actors wear

**ward·room** /ˈwɔːdruːm, -rʊm; NAmE ˈwɔːrd-/ *noun* a room in a ship, especially a WARSHIP, where the officers live and eat

**-wards** ⇨ -WARD

**ward·ship** /ˈwɔːdʃɪp; NAmE ˈwɔːrd-/ *noun* [U] (*law*) the fact of a child being cared for by a GUARDIAN (= a person who is not his or her parent) or of being protected by a court ⇨ see also WARD *noun*

**ware** /weə(r); NAmE wer/ *noun* **1** [U] (in compounds) objects made of the material or in the way or place mentioned: *ceramic ware* ◇ *a collection of local ware* ◇ *basketware* ⇨ see also FLATWARE, GLASSWARE, SILVERWARE **2** [U] (in compounds) objects used for the purpose or in the room mentioned: *bathroom ware* ◇ *ornamental ware* ◇ *homeware* ⇨ see also KITCHENWARE, TABLEWARE ◆ HOMOPHONES at WEAR **3 wares** [pl.] (*old-fashioned*) things that sb is selling, especially in the street or at a market: *He travelled from town to town selling his wares.*

**ware·house** ᛒ+ 🅲🅻 /ˈweəhaʊs; NAmE ˈwerh-/ *noun* a building where large quantities of goods are stored, especially before they are sent to shops to be sold ⇨ WORDFINDER NOTE at INDUSTRY

**ware·hous·ing** /ˈweəhaʊzɪŋ; NAmE ˈwerh-/ *noun* [U] the practice or business of storing things in a warehouse ⇨ see also DATA WAREHOUSING

**war·fare** ᛒ+ 🅲🅻 /ˈwɔːfeə(r); NAmE ˈwɔːrfer/ *noun* **1** ᛒ+ 🅲🅻 the activity of fighting a war, especially using particular weapons or methods: *air/naval/guerrilla warfare* ◇ *countries engaged in warfare* ⇨ see also BIOLOGICAL WARFARE, CHEMICAL WARFARE, GERM WARFARE **2** ᛒ+ 🅲🅻 the activity of competing in an aggressive way with another group, company, etc: *class/gang warfare* ◇ *The debate soon degenerated into open warfare.* ⇨ see also PSYCHOLOGICAL WARFARE

**war·farin** /ˈwɔːfərɪn; NAmE ˈwɔːrf-/ *noun* [U] a substance that is used as a poison to kill RATS and also for people as a medicine to make the blood thinner, for example in the treatment of THROMBOSIS

**ˈwar game** *noun* **1** a practice battle that is used to test military plans and equipment **2** a game or activity in which imaginary battles are fought, for example by moving models of soldiers, ships, etc. around on a table, or on a computer

**war·head** /ˈwɔːhed; NAmE ˈwɔːrh-/ *noun* the EXPLOSIVE part of a MISSILE: *nuclear warheads*

**war·horse** /ˈwɔːhɔːs; NAmE ˈwɔːrhɔːrs/ *noun* **1** (in the past) a large horse used in battle **2** (*informal*) an old soldier or politician who has a lot of experience

**wari·ly**, **wari·ness** ⇨ WARY

**war·like** /ˈwɔːlaɪk; NAmE ˈwɔːrl-/ *adj.* (*formal*) **1** aggressive and wanting to fight 🆂🆈🅽 belligerent: *a warlike nation* **2** connected with fighting wars 🆂🆈🅽 military: *warlike preparations*

**war·lock** /ˈwɔːlɒk; NAmE ˈwɔːrlɑːk/ *noun* a man who is believed to have magic powers, especially evil ones

**war·lord** /ˈwɔːlɔːd; NAmE ˈwɔːrlɔːrd/ *noun* (*disapproving*) the leader of a military group that is not official and that fights against other groups within a country or an area

**warm** 🄾 🅰🅱 /wɔːm; NAmE wɔːrm/ *adj., verb, noun, adv.*
■ *adj.* (**warm·er**, **warm·est**)
- AT PLEASANT TEMPERATURE **1** 🅰🅱 at a fairly high temperature in a way that is pleasant, rather than being hot or cold: *warm weather/temperatures/air* ◇ *Wash the blouse in warm soapy water.* ◇ *Tomorrow will be warm and sunny.* ◇ *a warm and dry spell* ◇ *Are you warm enough?* ◇ *The children jumped up and down to keep warm.*
- CLOTHES/BUILDINGS **2** 🅰🅱 keeping you warm or staying warm in cold weather: *warm clothing/clothes* ◇ *a warm pair of socks* ◇ *This sleeping bag is very warm.*
- FRIENDLY **3** 🅱🅱 showing enthusiasm, friendship or love: *Her smile was warm and friendly.* ◇ *to give sb a warm welcome/reception* ◇ *He felt a warm glow at the memory.*
- COLOURS **4** (of colours) containing red, orange or yellow, which creates a pleasant, comfortable and relaxed feeling or atmosphere: *The room was decorated in warm shades of red and orange.*
- IN GAME **5** [not before noun] used to say that sb has almost guessed the answer to sth or that they have almost found sb/sth that has been hidden: *Keep guessing—you're getting warmer.* ⇨ see also WARMTH ▶ **warm·ly** *adv.*: *They were warmly dressed in coats and scarves.* ◇ *The play was warmly received by the critics.*
■ *verb*
- MAKE/BECOME WARM **1** 🅱🅱 [T, I] to make sth/sb warm or warmer; to become warm or warmer: ~ *sth/sb/yourself Come in and warm yourself by the fire.* ◇ ~ *sth/sb/yourself up I'll warm up some milk.* ◇ *There is little doubt that the planet is warming.* ◇ ~ **up** *As the climate warms up, the ice caps will melt.*
- BECOME FRIENDLY **2** [I, T] ~ (**sb/sth**) to become more friendly, loving, etc.; to make sb feel or become more friendly, loving, etc: *The story warmed our hearts.* ⇨ see also GLOBAL WARMING, HOUSE-WARMING
- 🅸🅳🅼 **warm the ˈcockles (of sb's ˈheart)** (*BrE*) to make sb feel happy or SYMPATHETIC ◆ more at DEATH
- 🅿🅷🆁🆅 **warm ˈdown** to do gentle exercises to help your body relax after doing a particular sport or activity **ˈwarm to/towards sb** to begin to like sb: *I warmed to her immediately.* **ˈwarm to/towards sth** to become more interested in or enthusiastic about sth: *The speaker was now warming to her theme.* **warm ˈup 1** to prepare for physical exercise or a performance by doing gentle exercises or practice ⇨ related noun WARM-UP **2** (of a machine, an engine, etc.) to run for a short time in order to reach the temperature at which it will operate well **warm ˈup | warm sb/sth↔up** to become more lively or enthusiastic; to make sb/sth more lively or enthusiastic: *The party soon warmed up.* **warm sth↔up** to heat previously cooked food again for eating
■ *noun* **the warm** [sing.]
- PLACE a place where the temperature is warm: *Come inside into the warm.*
■ *adv.* (**warm·er**, **warm·est**) (*informal*) in a way that makes you feel warm 🆂🆈🅽 **warmly**: *Wrap up warm before you go outside!*

**ˈwar machine** *noun* **1** the resources that a country has available for fighting a war: *the American war machine* **2** a powerful weapon, especially an armed military vehicle such as a tank, BOMBER or SUBMARINE: *They went into battle in a heavily armed and armoured war machine.*

**warm-ˈblooded** *adj.* (of animals) having a warm blood temperature that does not change if the temperature around them changes ⇨ compare COLD-BLOODED, HOT-BLOODED

**warm·er** /ˈwɔːmə(r); NAmE ˈwɔːrm-/ *noun* (especially in compounds) a piece of clothing, a device, etc. that warms sb/sth: *a plate warmer* ⇨ see also LEG WARMER

**warm-ˈhearted** *adj.* (of a person) kind and friendly ⇨ compare COLD-HEARTED

**warm·ing** ᛒ+ 🅱🅱 /ˈwɔːmɪŋ; NAmE ˈwɔːrm-/ *noun* [U] the process of making sth, or of becoming, warm or warmer: *atmospheric warming* ⇨ see also GLOBAL WARMING ▶ **warm·ing** *adj.*: *the warming rays of the sun* ◇ *a warming drink*

**war·mon·ger** /ˈwɔːmʌŋɡə(r); NAmE ˈwɔːrmɑːŋ-/ *noun* (*disapproving*) a person, especially a politician or leader, who wants to start a war or encourages people to start a war ▶ **war·mon·ger·ing** *noun* [U] **war·mon·ger·ing** *adj.* [only before noun]

**warmth** /wɔːmθ; NAmE wɔːrmθ/ *noun* [U] **1** the state or quality of being warm, rather than hot or cold: *She felt the warmth of his arms around her.* ◇ *The animals huddled together for warmth.* ◇ *He led the child into the warmth* *and safety of the house.* **2** the state or quality of being enthusiastic and/or friendly: *They were touched by the warmth of the welcome.*

**'warm-up** *noun* [usually sing.] **1** a short practice or a series of gentle exercises that you do to prepare yourself for doing a particular sport or activity: *warm-up exercises* **2** a short performance of music, comedy, etc. that is intended to prepare the audience for the main show: *a warm-up act*

**warn** /wɔːn; *NAmE* wɔːrn/ *verb* [T, I] **1** to tell sb about sth, especially sth dangerous or unpleasant that is likely to happen, so that they can avoid it: *~ sb I tried to warn him, but he wouldn't listen.* ◇ *If you're thinking of getting a dog, be warned—they take a lot of time and money.* ◇ *~ (sb) about/ against/ of/ sth Security experts warned about the problems months ago.* ◇ *~ (sb) of/ about sth Officials warned the pilot of an anonymous threat.* ◇ *~ (sb) that ... Aid agencies have repeatedly warned that a humanitarian catastrophe is imminent.* ◇ *~ sb what, how, etc ... I had been warned what to expect.* ◇ *~ (sb) + speech 'Beware of pickpockets,' she warned (him).* ⊃ HOMOPHONES at WORN **2** [I, T] to strongly advise sb to do or not to do sth in order to avoid danger or punishment SYN **advise**: *~(sb) against/about (doing) sth The guidebook warns against walking alone at night.* ◇ *~ sb (to do sth) He warned Billy to keep away from his daughter.* **3** [T] *~ sb (for sth)* (in sport, etc.) to give sb an official warning after they have broken a rule: *The referee warned him for dangerous play.*
**PHR V** **warn sb 'off (sth)** **1** to tell sb to leave or stay away from a place or person, especially in a THREATENING way: *The farmer warned us off his land when we tried to camp there.* **2** to advise sb not to do sth or to stop doing sth: **warn sb off doing sth** *We were warned off buying the house.*

▼ EXPRESS YOURSELF

**Warning people of danger**

You may need to tell someone that they are in danger or advise them not to do something dangerous:
• *Look out! There's a car coming.*
• *Be careful. It can be quite dangerous on that path.*
• *Watch out. That's not a very safe place at night.*
• *Make sure you keep hold of your bag.*
• *I wouldn't do that if I were you.*

**warn·ing** /ˈwɔːnɪŋ; *NAmE* ˈwɔːrn-/ *noun* **1** [C, U] a statement, an event, etc. telling sb that sth bad or unpleasant may happen in the future so that they can try to avoid it: *I had absolutely no warning.* ◇ *~ against doing sth Doctors issued a warning against eating any fish caught in the river.* ◇ *The bridge collapsed without (any) warning.* ◇ *~ about sb/ sth Many people continue to ignore warnings about the dangers of sunbathing.* ◇ *~ about doing sth The report contained dire warnings about eating too much fat and salt.* ⊃ see also EARLY WARNING, GOVERNMENT HEALTH WARNING, PROFIT WARNING, TRIGGER WARNING **2** [C] a statement telling sb that they will be punished if they continue to behave in a particular way SYN **caution**: *to give sb a verbal/written/final warning* ▶ **warn·ing** *adj.* [only before noun]: *She had ignored the warning signs of trouble ahead.* ◇ *Police fired a number of warning shots.* ◇ **Warning bells began to ring** (= it was a sign that sth was wrong) *when her letters were returned unopened.*

**warp** /wɔːp; *NAmE* wɔːrp/ *verb, noun*
■ *verb* **1** [I, T] *~ (sth)* to become, or make sth become TWISTED, or bent out of its natural shape, for example because it has become too hot, too wet, etc: *The window frames had begun to warp.* **2** [T] *~ sth* to influence sb so that they begin to behave in an unacceptable way: *His judgement was warped by prejudice.*
■ *noun* **the warp** [sing.] (*specialist*) the THREADS on a LOOM (= a machine used for making cloth) that other THREADS are passed over and under in order to make cloth ⊃ compare WEFT ⊃ see also TIME WARP

**war·paint** /ˈwɔːpeɪnt; *NAmE* ˈwɔːrp-/ *noun* [U] **1** paint that some peoples, for example Native American peoples, put on their bodies and faces before fighting a battle **2** (*infor-*

*mal, humorous*) MAKE-UP, especially when it is thick or bright

**war·path** /ˈwɔːpɑːθ; *NAmE* ˈwɔːrpæθ/ *noun*
**IDM** **(be/go) on the 'warpath** (*informal*) (to be) angry and wanting to fight or punish sb

**warped** /wɔːpt; *NAmE* wɔːrpt/ *adj.* **1** (*disapproving*) (of a person) having ideas that most people think are strange or unpleasant: *a warped mind* ◇ *a warped sense of humour* **2** bent or TWISTED and not in the normal shape

**war·plane** /ˈwɔːpleɪn; *NAmE* ˈwɔːrp-/ *noun* a military plane that is designed for fighting in the air or dropping bombs ⊃ WORDFINDER NOTE at AIRCRAFT

**'warp speed** *noun* [sing.] (*informal, humorous*) a very fast speed **ORIGIN** From the US television series *Star Trek*, in which a 'warp drive' allowed space travel at speeds faster than the speed of light.

**war·rant** /ˈwɒrənt; *NAmE* ˈwɔːr-/ *noun, verb*
■ *noun* **1** [C] a legal document that is signed by a judge and gives the police authority to do sth: *an arrest warrant* ◇ *~ for sth They issued a warrant for her arrest.* ◇ *~ to do sth They had a warrant to search the house.* ⊃ see also DEATH WARRANT, SEARCH WARRANT **2** [C] *~ (for sth)* a document that gives you the right to receive money, services, etc. **3** [U] *~ (for sth/for doing sth)* (*formal*) (usually in negative sentences) an acceptable reason for doing sth: *There is no warrant for such criticism.*
■ *verb* (*formal*) to make sth necessary or appropriate in a particular situation SYN **justify**: *~ sth Further investigation is clearly warranted.* ◇ *~ (sb/sth) doing sth The situation scarcely warrants their/them being dismissed.* ⊃ see also UNWARRANTED
**IDM** **I/I'll warrant (you)** (*old-fashioned*) used to tell sb that you are sure of sth and that they can be sure of it too

**'warrant officer** *noun* a member of one of the middle ranks in the army, the British AIR FORCE and the US NAVY: *Warrant Officer Gary Owen*

**war·ranty** /ˈwɒrənti; *NAmE* ˈwɔːr-/ *noun* [C, U] (*pl.* **-ies**) a written agreement in which a company selling sth promises to repair or replace it if there is a problem within a particular period of time SYN **guarantee**: *The television comes with a full two-year warranty.* ◇ **under** *~ Is the car still under warranty?*

**war·ren** /ˈwɒrən; *NAmE* ˈwɔːr-/ *noun* = RABBIT WARREN: (*figurative*) *The offices were a warren of small rooms and passages.*

**war·ring** /ˈwɔːrɪŋ/ *adj.* [only before noun] involved in a war: *A ceasefire has been agreed by the country's three warring factions.*

**war·rior** /ˈwɒriə(r); *NAmE* ˈwɔːr-/ *noun* (*formal*) **1** (especially in the past) a person who fights in a battle or war: *a warrior nation* (= whose people are skilled in fighting) ◇ *a Zulu warrior* **2** (in compounds) (*often disapproving*) a person who leads or takes part in a campaign for a political or social cause, especially in an aggressive way that other people think is bad: *a class/culture warrior* ⊃ see also KEYBOARD WARRIOR, ROAD WARRIOR, WEEKEND WARRIOR

**war·ship** /ˈwɔːʃɪp; *NAmE* ˈwɔːrʃ-/ *noun* a ship that has weapons and that is used in war ⊃ WORDFINDER NOTE at NAVY

**wart** /wɔːt; *NAmE* wɔːrt/ *noun* **1** a small hard spot that grows on your skin and that is caused by a virus **2** (*NAmE*) = VERRUCA
**IDM** **warts and 'all** (*informal*) including all the bad or unpleasant features of sb/sth: *She still loves him, warts and all.*

**'wart·hog** /ˈwɔːthɒɡ; *NAmE* ˈwɔːrthɑːɡ/ *noun* an African wild pig with two large outer teeth called TUSKS and growths like warts on its face

**war·time** /ˈwɔːtaɪm; *NAmE* ˈwɔːrt-/ *noun* [U] the period during which a country is fighting a war: *Different rules applied in wartime.* ▶ **war·time** *adj.* [only before noun]:

# war-torn

*Fruit was a luxury in wartime Britain.* ⇨ compare PEACETIME

**ˈwar-torn** *adj.* [only before noun] a **war-torn** country or area is severely affected by the fighting that is taking place there

**warty** /ˈwɔːti; NAmE ˈwɔːrti/ *adj.* covered with WARTS ⇨ VISUAL VOCAB page V3

**ˈwar widow** *noun* a woman whose husband was killed in a war

**wary** /ˈweəri; NAmE ˈweri/ *adj.* (**wari·er**, **wari·est**) careful when dealing with sb/sth because you think that there may be a danger or problem **SYN** cautious: ~ (of sb/sth) *Be wary of strangers who offer you a ride.* ◇ ~ (of doing sth) *She was wary of getting involved with him.* ◇ *He gave her a wary look.* ◇ *The police will need to keep a wary eye on this area of town* (= watch it carefully, in case there is trouble). ⇨ compare UNWARY ▸ **wari·ly** /-rəli/ *adv.*: *The cat eyed him warily.* **wari·ness** *noun* [U, sing.]: *feelings of wariness* ◇ *There was a wariness in her tone.*

**ˈwar zone** *noun* a region in which a war is being fought

**was** /wəz; BrE strong form wɒz; NAmE strong form wʌz/ ⇨ BE *verb*

**was·abi** /wəˈsɑːbi/ *noun* [U] (*from Japanese*) a root vegetable with a strong taste like HORSERADISH, used in Japanese cooking, especially with raw fish

**wash** ⓘ **A1** /wɒʃ; NAmE wɑːʃ/ *verb, noun*

■ *verb* **1** ~ [T] to make sth/sb clean using water and usually soap: *~ sth/sb These jeans need washing.* ◇ *to wash the car* ◇ *to wash your hands/hair/face* ◇ *Wash the fruit thoroughly before eating.* ◇ *~ sth from sth She washed the blood from his face.* ◇ *~ sth/sb + adj. The potatoes are washed clean without damaging the skins.* ⇨ SYNONYMS at CLEAN **2** ~ **A1** [I, T] (*especially BrE*) to make yourself clean using water and usually soap: *By this time we were already washed and dressed.* ◇ ~ **yourself** *She was no longer able to wash herself.* **3** [I] (+ adv./prep.) (of clothes, cloth, etc.) to be able to be washed without losing colour or being damaged: *This sweater washes well.* **4** [I, T] (of water) to flow or carry sth/sb in a particular direction: **+ adv./prep.** *Water washed over the deck.* ◇ *~ sth/sb + adv./prep. Pieces of the wreckage were washed ashore.* ◇ *He was washed overboard by a huge wave.*
**IDM** **wash your ˈhands of sb/sth** to refuse to be responsible for or involved with sb/sth: *When her son was arrested again she washed her hands of him.* **sth won't/doesn't ˈwash (with sb)** used to say that sb's explanation, excuse, etc. is not true or that you/sb else will not accept it: *That excuse simply won't wash with me.* ⇨ more at DIRTY *adj.*
**PHRV** **ˌwash sb/sth⇿aˈway** (of water) to remove or carry sb/sth away to another place: *Part of the path had been washed away by the sea.* **ˌwash sth⇿ˈdown (with sth)** **1** to clean sth large or a surface with a lot of water: *Wash down the walls before painting them.* **2** to drink sth after, or at the same time as, eating sth: *For lunch we had bread and cheese, washed down with beer.* **ˌwash ˈoff** to be removed from the surface of sth or from clothes by washing: *Those grease stains won't wash off.* **ˌwash sth⇿ˈoff (sth)** to remove sth from the surface of sth or from clothes by washing: *Wash that mud off your boots before you come in.* **ˌwash ˈout** (of a dirty mark) to be removed from clothes by washing: *These ink stains won't wash out.* **ˌwash sth⇿ˈout** **1** to wash the inside of sth to remove dirt, etc: *to wash out empty bottles* **2** to remove a substance from sth by washing: *Wash the dye out with shampoo.* **3** [usually passive] (of rain) to make a game, an event, etc. end early or prevent it from starting: *The game was completely washed out.* ⇨ related noun WASHOUT **ˌwash ˈover sb 1** ⇨ **wash ˈthrough sb** (*literary*) (of a feeling) to suddenly affect sb strongly, so that they are not aware of anything else: *Waves of nausea washed over him.* **2** to happen to or around sb without affecting them: *She manages to let criticism just wash over her.* **ˌwash ˈup 1** (*BrE*) (*also* **do the ˈdishes** *NAmE, BrE*) to wash plates, glasses, etc. after a meal ⇨ related noun WASHING-UP **2** (*also* **get washed ˈup**) (*NAmE*) to wash your face and hands: *Go and get washed up.* **ˌwash sth⇿ˈup 1** (*BrE*) to wash dishes after a meal: *I didn't wash up the pans.* **2** [usually passive] (of water) to carry sth onto land: *The body was found washed up on a beach.*

■ *noun* **1** ~ **A2** [C, usually sing.] (*especially BrE*) an act of cleaning sb/sth using water and usually soap: *These towels are ready for a wash.* ◇ *I'll just have a quick wash before dinner.* ◇ *I'm doing a dark wash* (= washing all the dark clothes together). ◇ *Your shirt's in the wash* (= being washed or waiting to be washed). ◇ *My sweater shrank in the wash.* ◇ *That blouse shouldn't look like that after only two washes.* ⇨ see also CAR WASH **2** **the wash** [sing.] an area of water that has waves and is moving a lot, especially after a boat has moved through it; the sound made by this: *The dinghy was rocked by the wash of a passing ferry.* ◇ *They listened to the wash of waves on the beach.* **3** [C] a thin layer of a liquid, especially paint, that is put on a surface: *The walls were covered with a pale yellow wash.* ⇨ see also WHITEWASH *noun* **4** [C, U] a liquid containing soap, used for cleaning your skin: *an antiseptic skin wash* ⇨ see also MOUTHWASH
**IDM** **it will (all) come out in the ˈwash** (*informal*) **1** used to say that the truth about a situation will be made known at some time in the future **2** used to make sb less anxious by telling them that any problems or difficulties will be solved in the future

**wash·able** /ˈwɒʃəbl; NAmE ˈwɑːʃ-/ *adj.* **1** that can be washed without being damaged: *machine washable* (= that can be washed in a washing machine) **2** that can be removed from sth by washing it: *washable ink/paint/marker pens*

**ˈwash·bag** /ˈwɒʃbæɡ; NAmE ˈwɑːʃ-/ *noun* (*BrE*) = SPONGE BAG

**wash·basin** /ˈwɒʃbeɪsn; NAmE ˈwɑːʃ-/ (*also* **basin**) (*both especially BrE*) (*also* **sink** *NAmE, BrE*) (*also especially NAmE* **ˈwash·bowl** /ˈwɒʃbəʊl; NAmE ˈwɑːʃboʊl/) *noun* a large bowl that has TAPS and is fixed to the wall in a bathroom, used for washing your hands and face in ⇨ picture at PLUG

**wash·board** /ˈwɒʃbɔːd; NAmE ˈwɑːʃbɔːrd/ *noun* a board with a surface with RIDGES on it, used in the past for rubbing clothes on when washing them; a similar board played as a musical instrument

**wash·cloth** /ˈwɒʃklɒθ; NAmE ˈwɑːʃklɔːθ/ (*NAmE*) (*BrE* **flannel**, **ˈface-cloth**) *noun* a small piece of cloth used for washing yourself

**ˌwashed ˈout** *adj.* **1** (of cloth, clothes or colours) no longer brightly coloured, often as a result of being washed many times: *She didn't like jeans that looked too washed out.* ◇ *a pair of washed-out old jeans* ◇ *The walls were a washed-out blue colour.* **2** (of a person) pale and tired **SYN** exhausted: *He always looks washed out at the end of the week.*

**ˌwashed ˈup** *adj.* (*informal*) no longer successful and unlikely to succeed again in the future: *Her singing career was all washed up by the time she was 27.*

**wash·er** /ˈwɒʃə(r); NAmE ˈwɑːʃ-/ *noun* **1** a small flat ring made of rubber, metal or plastic placed between two surfaces, for example under a NUT to make a connection tight **2** (*informal*) a WASHING MACHINE ⇨ see also DISHWASHER

**ˈwasher-dryer** *noun* an electric machine that washes and dries clothes, etc.

**ˈwasher-up** *noun* (*BrE, informal*) a person who washes dishes

**wash·er·wom·an** /ˈwɒʃəwʊmən; NAmE ˈwɑːʃərwʊmən/ *noun* (*pl.* **-women** /-wɪmɪn/) a woman in the past whose job was to wash clothes, etc. for other people

**wash·ing** ⓘ **A2** /ˈwɒʃɪŋ; NAmE ˈwɑːʃ-/ *noun* **1** ~ **A2** [U, sing.] the act of cleaning sth using water and usually soap: *a gentle shampoo for frequent washing* ◇ *I do the washing* (= wash the clothes) *in our house.* ⇨ see also BRAINWASHING **2** ~ **B1** [U] (*BrE*) clothes, sheets, etc. that are waiting to be washed, being washed or have just been washed: *a pile of dirty washing* ◇ *Would you hang the washing out* (= hang it outside to dry)?

**ˈwashing line** *noun* (*BrE*) = CLOTHES LINE

**washing machine** noun an electric machine for washing clothes

**washing powder** noun [U] (BrE) soap or DETERGENT in the form of powder for washing clothes

**washing soda** noun [U] = SODIUM CARBONATE

**washing-up** noun [U] (BrE) **1** the act of washing plates, glasses, pans, etc. after a meal: *If you cook, I'll do the washing-up.* ◇ *a washing-up bowl* **2** the dirty plates, glasses, pans, etc. that have to be washed after a meal: *The sink was still full of last night's washing-up.*

**washing-up liquid** (BrE) (NAmE **dishwashing liquid**) noun [U] liquid soap for washing dishes, pans, etc.

**wash-out** /ˈwɒʃaʊt; NAmE ˈwɑːʃ-/ noun (informal) an event, etc. that is a complete failure, especially because of rain

**wash-room** /ˈwɒʃruːm, -rʊm; NAmE ˈwɑːʃ-/ noun (CanE or old-fashioned, US) a toilet, especially one that is in a public building

**wasn't** /ˈwɒznt; NAmE ˈwʌz-/ ⊃ BE verb

**Wasp** (also **WASP**) /wɒsp; NAmE wɑːsp/ noun (especially NAmE, usually disapproving) a white American whose family originally came from northern Europe and is therefore thought to be from the most powerful section of society (the abbreviation for 'White Anglo-Saxon Protestant'): *a privileged Wasp background*

**wasp** /wɒsp; NAmE wɑːsp/ noun a black and yellow flying insect that can STING: *a wasp sting* ◇ *a wasps' nest* ⊃ VISUAL VOCAB page V3

**wasp·ish** /ˈwɒspɪʃ; NAmE ˈwɑːs-/ adj. (formal) expressing criticism or showing that sb is annoyed ▸ **wasp·ish·ly** adv.

**wast·age** /ˈweɪstɪdʒ/ noun **1** [U, sing.] ~ (of sth) the fact of losing or destroying sth, especially because it has been used or dealt with carelessly: *It was a new production technique aimed at minimizing wastage.* **2** [U] the amount of sth that is wasted: *There is little wastage from a lean cut of meat.* **3** [U] (BrE) the loss of employees because they stop working or move to other jobs; the number of students who do not finish a particular course of study: *Half of the posts will be lost through natural wastage.* ◇ *student wastage rates*

**waste** ❶ B1 /weɪst/ noun, verb, adj.
■ noun
• NOT GOOD USE **1** B1 [U, sing.] the act of using sth in a careless or unnecessary way, causing it to be lost or destroyed: *I hate unnecessary waste.* ◇ *It seems such a waste to throw good food away.* ◇ *I hate to see good food go to waste* (= be thrown away). ◇ *~ of sth The report is critical of the department's waste of resources.* ◇ *What a waste of paper!* ⊃ HOMOPHONES at WAIST **2** B1 [sing.] ~(of sth) a situation in which it is not worth spending time, money, etc. on sth: *These meetings are a complete waste of time.* ◇ *They believe the statue is a waste of taxpayers' money.*
• MATERIALS **3** B1 [U] (also **wastes** [pl.]) materials that are no longer needed and are thrown away: *household/garden/industrial waste* ◇ *hazardous/toxic/radioactive waste* ◇ *waste disposal* (= the process of getting rid of waste) ⊃ see also NUCLEAR WASTE

| WORDFINDER drain, dump, effluent, exhaust, fly-tip, incinerator, landfill, rubbish, sewage |
|---|

**4** (also **waste 'matter**) [U] material that the body gets rid of as solid or liquid material: *The farmers use both animal and human waste as fertilizer.*
• LAND **5** **wastes** [pl.] (formal) a large area of land where there are very few people, animals or plants: *the frozen wastes of Siberia*
IDM **a waste of 'space** (informal) a person who is not useful or good at anything
■ verb
• NOT USE WELL **1** B1 to use more of sth than is necessary or useful: *~sth Stop wasting time and just get on with it!* ◇ *~sth on sth Why waste money on clothes you don't need?* ◇ *~sth (in) doing sth She wasted no time in rejecting the offer* (= she rejected it immediately). ◇ *You're wasting your time trying to explain it to him* (= because he will not understand). ⊃ HOMOPHONES at WAIST **2** B2 [usually passive] to not make good or full use of sb/sth: *~sb/sth It was a wasted opportunity.* ◇ *~sb/sth as sth You're wasted as a sales manager—you should have been an actor.* **3** ~sth (on sb/sth) to give, say, use, etc. sth good where it is not valued or used in the way that it should be: *Don't waste your sympathy on him—he got what he deserved.* ◇ *Expensive wine is wasted on me* (= because I cannot appreciate it properly).
• KILL SB **4** ~sb (informal, especially NAmE) to get rid of sb, usually by killing them
• DEFEAT SB **5** ~sb (NAmE, informal) to defeat sb very badly in a game or competition
IDM **waste your 'breath** to say sth that nobody takes any notice of **waste not, 'want not** (saying) if you never waste anything, especially food or money, you will always have it when you need it
PHR V **waste a'way** (of a person) to become thin and weak, especially because of illness ⊃ see also EMACIATED
■ adj. [usually before noun]
• MATERIALS **1** B1 no longer needed for a particular process and therefore thrown away: *the disposal of waste material* ⊃ HOMOPHONES at WAIST
• LAND **2** B1 not suitable for building or growing things on and therefore not used SYN **derelict**: *The car was found on a piece of waste ground.*
IDM **lay sth 'waste | lay 'waste (to) sth** (formal) to destroy a place completely

**waste-bas·ket** /ˈweɪstbɑːskɪt; NAmE -bæs-/ (NAmE) (BrE **waste 'paper basket**) noun a BASKET or other container for waste paper, etc. ⊃ picture at BASKET

**waste bin** noun (BrE) a container that you put rubbish in

**wasted** /ˈweɪstɪd/ adj. **1** [only before noun] (of an action) unsuccessful because it does not produce the result you wanted: *We had a wasted trip—they weren't in.* **2** too thin, especially because of illness: *thin wasted legs* **3** (slang) strongly affected by alcohol or drugs

**waste disposal unit** (also **waste disposer**) (both BrE) (NAmE **garbage dis·posal, dis·posal**) noun a machine connected to the waste pipe of a kitchen SINK, for cutting food waste into small pieces

**waste·ful** /ˈweɪstfl/ adj. using more of sth than is necessary; not saving or keeping sth that could be used: *The whole process is wasteful and inefficient.* ◇ *~of sth an engine that is wasteful of fuel* ▸ **waste·ful·ly** /-fəli/ adv. **waste·ful·ness** noun [U]

**waste·land** /ˈweɪstlænd/ noun [C, U] an area of land that cannot be used or that is no longer used for building or growing things on: *industrial wasteland* ◇ *the desert wastelands of Arizona* ◇ (figurative) *The mid 1970s are seen as a cultural wasteland for rock music.*

**waste 'paper** noun [U] paper that is not wanted and is thrown away

**waste 'paper basket** (BrE) (NAmE **waste·basket**) noun a BASKET or other container for waste paper, etc. ⊃ picture at BASKET

**waste product** noun a material or substance that has no use or value that is made while producing sth else

**waster** /ˈweɪstə(r)/ noun **1** (often in compounds) a person or thing that uses too much of sth in an unnecessary way: *He's a time-waster.* **2** (informal, disapproving) a person who is not helpful, useful or good at anything

**waste·water** /ˈweɪstwɔːtə(r)/ noun [U] used water that contains waste substances from homes, factories and farms: *municipal water and wastewater systems* ◇ *a wastewater treatment plant* ⊃ compare SEWAGE

**wast·ing** /ˈweɪstɪŋ/ adj. a **wasting** disease or illness is one that causes sb to gradually become weaker and thinner

**wast·rel** /ˈweɪstrəl/ noun (literary) a lazy person who spends their time and/or money in a careless and stupid way

**watch** ❶ A1 /wɒtʃ; NAmE wɑːtʃ/ verb, noun
■ verb **1** A1 [T, I] to look at sb/sth for a time, paying attention to what happens: *~sb/sth to watch television/TV* ◇ *to*

# watchable

*watch a film/movie/video/show/game* ◊ *~sth for sth* He watched the house for signs of activity. ◊ *~(for sth)* He watched for signs of activity in the house. ◊ 'Would you like to play?' 'No thanks—I'll just watch.' ◊ **We watched to see what would happen next.** ◊ **~ what, how, etc …** *Watch what I do, then you try.* ◊ *~ sb/sth doing sth* She watched the kids playing in the yard. ◊ *~ sb/sth do sth* They watched the bus disappear into the distance. ⊃ SYNONYMS at LOOK **2** [B1] [T] *~ sb/sth (for sb)* to take care of sb/sth for a short time: *Could you watch my bags for me while I buy a paper?* **3** [B1] (*BrE also* **mind**) [T] (*informal*) to be careful about sth: *~ sth/ yourself Watch yourself!* (= be careful, because you're in a dangerous situation) ◊ *Watch your bag—there are thieves around.* ◊ *Watch your head on the low ceiling.* ◊ *I have to watch every penny* (= be careful what I spend). ◊ *~ where, what, etc …* *Hey, watch where you're going!* **4** [B1] [T, I] to pay attention to a situation so that you notice any changes: *~ sth We're watching the situation very carefully.* ◊ *This election is being closely watched in the region.* ◊ *~ for sth We'll watch for any developments.* **5** [often passive] (often in the progressive tenses) to observe sb's activities without their knowledge, especially over a period of time: **be (being) watched** *He didn't know he was being watched by the authorities.*
**IDM** **watch your 'back** to protect yourself against danger: *She'd better watch her back if she wants to hold onto the top job.* **watch the 'clock** (*disapproving*) to be careful not to work longer than the required time; to think more about when your work will finish than about the work itself ⊃ see also CLOCK-WATCHER **a watched ,pot never 'boils** (*saying*) used to say that when you are impatient for sth to happen, time seems to pass very slowly **'watch it** (*informal*) used as a warning to sb to be careful **watch your 'mouth/'tongue** to be careful what you say in order not to offend sb or make them angry **watch this 'space** (*informal*) used in orders, to tell sb to wait for more news about sth to be announced: *I can't tell you any more right now, but watch this space.* **watch the 'time** to be sure that you know what the time is, so that you finish sth at the correct time, or are not late for sth: *I'll have to watch the time. I need to leave early today.* **watch the 'world go by** to relax and watch people in a public place: *We sat outside a cafe, watching the world go by.* ⊃ more at LANGUAGE, STEP *n.*
**PHRV** **'watch for sb/sth** to look and wait for sth to happen: *The cat was on the wall, watching for birds.* **watch 'out** (*informal*) used to warn sb about sth dangerous: *Watch out! There's a car coming!* **,watch 'out for sb/sth 1** to make an effort to be aware of what is happening, so that you will notice if anything bad or unusual happens: *The cashiers were asked to watch out for forged banknotes.* **2** to be careful of sth: *Watch out for the stairs—they're steep.* **,watch 'over sb/sth** (*formal*) to take care of sb/sth; to guard and protect sb/sth
▪ **noun 1** [B1] [C] a type of small clock that you wear on your WRIST, or (in the past) carried in your pocket: *She kept looking anxiously at her watch.* ◊ *My watch is fast/slow.* ⊃ picture at CLOCK ⊃ see also STOPWATCH, WRISTWATCH **2** [sing., U] the act of watching sb/sth carefully in case of possible danger or problems: *The police have mounted a watch outside the hotel.* ◊ *I'll keep watch while you go through his papers* (= watch and warn you if somebody is coming). ◊ *The government is keeping a close watch on how the situation develops.* ⊃ see also NEIGHBOURHOOD WATCH **3** [C, U] a fixed period of time, usually while other people are asleep, during which sb watches for any danger so that they can warn others, for example on a ship; the person or people who do this: **on~** *I go on watch in an hour.* ◊ *I'm on first watch.* ⊃ see also NIGHTWATCHMAN
**IDM** **be on the 'watch (for sb/sth)** to be looking carefully for sb/sth that you expect to see, especially in order to avoid possible danger: *Be on the watch for thieves.* ⊃ more at CLOSE² *adj.*

**watch·able** /'wɒtʃəbl; *NAmE* 'wɑːtʃ-/ *adj.* (*informal*) interesting, fun or pleasant to watch

**watch·dog** /'wɒtʃdɒɡ; *NAmE* 'wɑːtʃdɔːɡ/ *noun* **1** a person or group of people whose job is to check that companies are not doing anything illegal or ignoring people's rights: *a consumer watchdog* **2** a dog that is kept to guard a building **SYN** guard dog

**watch·er** /'wɒtʃə(r); *NAmE* 'wɑːtʃ-/ *noun* (often in compounds) a person who watches and studies sb/sth regularly: *an industry/a market watcher* ⊃ see also BIRDWATCHER, CLOCK-WATCHER

**watch·ful** /'wɒtʃfl; *NAmE* 'wɑːtʃ-/ *adj.* paying attention to what is happening in case of danger, accidents, etc: *Her expression was watchful and alert.* ◊ *His mother kept a watchful eye on him.* ◊ *The children played under the watchful eye of their teacher.* ▸ **watch·ful·ly** /-fəli/ *adv.* **watch·ful·ness** *noun* [U]

**watching 'brief** *noun* [sing.] the task of watching a group or situation to report on what is happening but without getting directly involved

**watch·maker** /'wɒtʃmeɪkə(r); *NAmE* 'wɑːtʃ-/ *noun* a person who makes and repairs watches and clocks as a job

**watch·man** /'wɒtʃmən; *NAmE* 'wɑːtʃ-/ *noun* (*pl.* **-men** /-mən/) (*old-fashioned*) a man whose job is to guard a building, for example a bank, an office building or a factory, especially at night ⊃ see also NIGHTWATCHMAN

**watch·tower** /'wɒtʃtaʊə(r); *NAmE* 'wɑːtʃ-/ *noun* a tall tower from which soldiers, etc. watch when they are guarding a place

**watch·word** /'wɒtʃwɜːd; *NAmE* 'wɑːtʃwɜːrd/ *noun* a word or phrase that expresses sb's beliefs or attitudes, or that explains what sb should do in a particular situation: *Quality is our watchword.*

# water [circle] [A1] /'wɔːtə(r)/ *noun, verb*

▪ **noun 1** [B1] [A1] [U] a liquid without colour, smell or taste that falls as rain, is in lakes, rivers and seas, and is used for drinking, washing, etc. **HELP** Water is the name given to the chemical compound of OXYGEN and HYDROGEN with the chemical symbol $H_2O$ : *a glass of water* ◊ *drinking water* ◊ *supplies of clean/fresh water* ◊ *There is hot and cold running water* (= water supplied by pipes) *in all the bedrooms.* ◊ *water pollution* ◊ *water shortages* **2** [A1] [U] an area of water, especially a lake, river, sea or ocean: *We walked down to the water's edge.* ◊ **shallow/deep water** ◊ **in the~** *It was lovely and cool in the water.* ◊ *She fell into the water.* ⊃ see also BACKWATER, BREAKWATER, DEEP-WATER, HIGH WATER, STANDING WATER **3** [A1] [U] the surface of a mass of water: **on the~** *The leaves floated on the water.* ◊ **in the ~** *I could see my reflection in the water.* ◊ **under the~** *She dived under the water.* ⊃ see also UNDERWATER **4** [A2] **waters** [pl.] the water in a particular lake, river, sea or ocean: *the grey waters of the River Clyde* ◊ *This species is found in coastal waters around the Indian Ocean.* **5 waters** [pl.] an area of sea or ocean belonging to a particular country: **in …~** *We were still in British waters.* ◊ *fishing in international waters* ⊃ see also TERRITORIAL WATERS **6 waters** [pl.] **murky, uncharted, stormy, dangerous, etc.~** used to describe a situation, usually one that is difficult, dangerous or not familiar: *The conversation got into the murky waters of jealousy and relationships.* ◊ *The government has warned of stormy waters ahead.* **HELP** There are many other compounds ending in **water**. You will find them at their place in the alphabet.
**IDM** **by 'water** (*formal*) using a boat or ship **it's (all) water under the 'bridge** used to say that sth happened in the past and is now forgotten or no longer important **like 'water** (*informal*) in large quantities: *He spends money like water.* **not hold 'water** (*informal*) if an argument, an excuse, a theory, etc. does not **hold water**, you cannot believe it **sb's 'waters break** when a pregnant woman's **waters break**, the liquid in her womb passes out of her body just before the baby is born **(like) water off a ,duck's 'back** (*informal*) used to say that sth, especially criticism, has no effect on sb: *I can't tell my son what to do; it's water off a duck's back with him.* ⊃ more at BLOOD *n.*, BLOW *v.*, CLEAR *adj.*, COLD *adj.*, DEAD *adj.*, DEEP *adj.*, DIP *v.*, DUCK *n.*, FISH *n.*, HEAD *n.*, HELL, HORSE *n.*, HOT *adj.*, PASS *v.*, POUR, STILL *adj.*, TEST *v.*, TREAD *v.*
▪ **verb 1** [B1] [T] *~sth* to pour water on plants, etc: *to water the plants/garden* **2** [I] (of the eyes) to become full of tears: *The smoke made my eyes water.* **3** [I] (of the mouth) to produce SALIVA: *The smells from the kitchen made our*

mouths water. **4** [T] ~ sth to give water to an animal to drink: *to water the horses* ◇ (*humorous*) *After a tour of the grounds, the guests were fed and watered.* **5** [T, usually passive] (*specialist*) (of a river, etc.) to provide an area of land with water: **be watered by sth** *The valley is watered by a stream.* **6** [T] ~ sth to add water to an alcoholic drink: *watered wine*

**PHRV** ,water sth↔'down **1** to make a liquid weaker by adding water **SYN** **dilute** **2** [usually passive] to change a speech, a piece of writing, etc. in order to make it less strong or offensive **SYN** **dilute**

**the 'Water Bearer** *noun* [sing.] = AQUARIUS (1)

**water-bed** /ˈwɔːtəbed; *NAmE* -tərb-/ *noun* a bed with a rubber or plastic MATTRESS that is filled with water

**water-bird** /ˈwɔːtəbɜːd; *NAmE* -tərbɜːrd/ *noun* a bird that lives near water, especially rivers or lakes, and often walks or swims in the water

**water-board-ing** /ˈwɔːtəbɔːdɪŋ; *NAmE* -tərbɔːrd-/ *noun* [U] a form of TORTURE used to try to force sb to give information by pouring water onto their face while making them lie on their back, so that they feel as if they are DROWNING

**water-borne** /ˈwɔːtəbɔːn; *NAmE* -tərbɔːrn/ *adj.* spread or carried by water: *cholera and other waterborne diseases* ◇ *waterborne goods* ⊃ compare AIRBORNE

**'water buffalo** *noun* (*pl.* **water buf-falo** or **water buf-faloes**) a large Asian animal of the cow family, used for pulling vehicles and farm equipment in tropical countries

**'water butt** (*BrE*) (*NAmE* **'rain barrel**) *noun* a large BARREL for collecting rain as it flows off a roof

**'water cannon** *noun* a machine that produces a powerful flow of water, used by the police to control crowds of people

**the 'Water Carrier** *noun* [sing.] = AQUARIUS (1)

**'water chestnut** *noun* the thick, round white root of a tropical plant that grows in water, often used in Chinese cooking

**'water closet** *noun* (*abbr.* **WC**) (*old-fashioned*) a toilet

**water-col-our** (*US* **water-color**) /ˈwɔːtəkʌlə(r); *NAmE* -tərk-/ *noun* **1** [U] (*also* **water-col-ours** [pl.]) paints that you mix with water, not oil, and use for painting pictures: **in ~** *He worked in watercolour, ink and crayon.* **2** [C] a picture painted with these paints ⊃ WORDFINDER NOTE at PAINTING

**water-col-our-ist** (*US* **water-col-or-ist**) /ˈwɔːtəkʌlərɪst; *NAmE* -tərk-/ *noun* a person who paints with watercolours

**'water-cooled** *adj.* (of machines, etc.) cooled using water

**'water cooler** *noun* **1** a machine, for example in an office, that cools water and supplies it for drinking **2** used when referring to a place where office workers talk in an informal way, for example near the water cooler: *It was a story they'd shared around the water cooler.*

**water-course** /ˈwɔːtəkɔːs; *NAmE* -tərkɔːrs/ *noun* (*specialist*) a stream or an artificial channel for water

**water-cress** /ˈwɔːtəkres; *NAmE* -tərk-/ *noun* [U] a water plant with small round green leaves and thin STEMS. It has a strong taste and is often eaten raw in salads. ⊃ VISUAL VOCAB page V5

**the 'water cycle** *noun* [usually sing.] the processes by which water passes between the earth's atmosphere, land and oceans, involving water falling from clouds as rain and snow, flowing in streams and rivers to the sea, and then returning to the atmosphere through EVAPORATION and forming clouds again

**,watered-'down** *adj.* **1** a **watered-down** speech, piece of writing, etc. is changed in order to make it less strong or offensive **2** a **watered-down** liquid is made weaker by adding water

**water-fall** /ˈwɔːtəfɔːl; *NAmE* -tərf-/ *noun* a place where a stream or river falls from a high place, for example over a CLIFF or rock ⊃ WORDFINDER NOTE at RIVER

# waterproof

**'water feature** *noun* an artificial area of water, or structure with water flowing through it, which is intended to make a garden more attractive and interesting

**'water fountain** *noun* (*NAmE*) = DRINKING FOUNTAIN

**water-fowl** /ˈwɔːtəfaʊl; *NAmE* -tərf-/ *noun* [usually pl.] (*pl.* **water-fowl**) a bird that can swim and lives near water, especially a DUCK or GOOSE

**water-front** /ˈwɔːtəfrʌnt; *NAmE* -tərf-/ *noun* [usually sing.] a part of a town or an area that is next to water, for example in a HARBOUR: *a waterfront apartment*

**'water gun** *noun* (*NAmE*) = WATER PISTOL

**water-hole** /ˈwɔːtəhəʊl; *NAmE* -tərh-/ (*also* **'water-ing hole**) *noun* a place in a hot country where animals go to drink

**'water ice** *noun* [U, C] (*BrE*) = SORBET

**'water-ing can** *noun* a metal or plastic container with a handle and a long SPOUT, used for pouring water on plants

**'water-ing hole** *noun* **1** = WATERHOLE **2** (*informal, humorous*) a bar or place where people go to drink

**water-less** /ˈwɔːtələs; *NAmE* -tərl-/ *adj.* with no water: *a waterless barren region*

**'water level** *noun* [U, C] the height that the surface of a mass of water rises or falls to, or the height it is at

**'water lily** *noun* a plant that floats on the surface of water, with large, round, flat leaves and white, yellow or pink flowers

**the 'water-line** /ðə ˈwɔːtəlaɪn; *NAmE* -tərl-/ *noun* [sing.] the level that the water reaches along the side of a ship

**water-logged** /ˈwɔːtəlɒɡd; *NAmE* -tərlɔːɡd/ *adj.* **1** (of soil, a field, etc.) so full of water that it cannot hold any more and becomes covered by a large amount of it: *They couldn't play because the pitch was waterlogged.* **2** (of a boat, etc.) so full of water that it can no longer float

**Water-loo** /ˌwɔːtəˈluː; *NAmE* -tərˈluː/ *noun* [sing.] **sb's ~** a final defeat for sb: *This was the point at which he was to meet his Waterloo.* **ORIGIN** From the battle of **Waterloo** in 1815, in which the British (under the Duke of Wellington) and the Prussians finally defeated Napoleon.

**'water main** *noun* a large underground pipe that supplies water to buildings, etc.

**water-mark** /ˈwɔːtəmɑːk; *NAmE* -tərmɑːrk/ *noun* a symbol or design in some types of paper, which can be seen when the paper is held against the light ⊃ see also HIGH-WATER MARK, LOW-WATER MARK

**water-melon** /ˈwɔːtəmelən; *NAmE* -tərm-/ *noun* [C, U] a type of large MELON, with hard, dark-green skin, that is red inside and has black seeds ⊃ VISUAL VOCAB page V4

**water-mill** /ˈwɔːtəmɪl; *NAmE* -tərm-/ *noun* a MILL next to a river in which the equipment for GRINDING grain into flour is driven by the power of the water turning a wheel

**'water moccasin** *noun* = COTTONMOUTH

**'water park** *noun* an outdoor area with swimming pools and equipment for activities involving water

**'water pistol** (*NAmE also* **'water gun**, **'squirt gun**) *noun* a toy gun that shoots water

**'water polo** *noun* [U] a game played by two teams of people swimming in a swimming pool. Players try to throw a ball into the other team's goal.

**'water power** *noun* [U] power produced by the movement of water, used to drive machines or produce electricity

**water-proof** /ˈwɔːtəpruːf; *NAmE* -tərp-/ *adj., noun, verb*
■ *adj.* that does not let water through or that cannot be damaged by water: *waterproof clothing* ◇ *a waterproof camera*
■ *noun* [usually pl.] a piece of clothing made from material that does not let water through: *You'll need waterproofs* (= a waterproof jacket and trousers).
■ *verb* ~ sth to make sth waterproof

# water rat

**ˈwater rat** *noun* = WATER VOLE

**ˈwater-repellent** *adj.* a material, etc. that is **water-repellent** is specially treated so that water runs off it rather than going into it: *a water-repellent coating*

**ˈwater-resistant** *adj.* that does not let water through easily: *a water-resistant jacket*

**water·shed** /ˈwɔːtəʃed; NAmE -tərʃ-/ *noun* **1** [C] ~ (in sth) an event or a period of time that marks an important change: *The middle decades of the 19th century marked a watershed in Russia's history.* **2** [C] a line of high land where streams on one side flow into one river, and streams on the other side flow into a different river **3 the watershed** [sing.] (in the UK) the time before which programmes that are not considered suitable for children may not be shown on television: *the 9 o'clock watershed*

**water·side** /ˈwɔːtəsaɪd; NAmE -tərs-/ *noun* [sing.] the area at the edge of a river, lake, etc: *They strolled down to the waterside.* ◇ *a waterside cafe*

**water·ski** /ˈwɔːtəskiː; NAmE -tərs-/ *verb, noun*
- *verb* [I] to ski on water while being pulled by a fast boat
  ▶ **water·ski·ing** *noun* [U]: *We snorkelled and did some waterskiing.*
- *noun* either of the pair of long, flat boards on which a person stands in order to waterski

**ˈwater softener** *noun* [U, C] a device or substance that removes particular minerals, especially CALCIUM, from water

**ˈwater sports** *noun* [pl.] sports that are done on or in water, for example sailing and WATERSKIING

**water·spout** /ˈwɔːtəspaʊt; NAmE -tərs-/ *noun* a column of water that is pulled up from the sea during a storm by a column of air that turns round and round rapidly

**ˈwater supply** *noun* [C, U] the water provided for a town, an area or a building; the act of or system for supplying water to a town, etc: *a clean/contaminated water supply* ◇ *to improve the water supply to rural villages* ◇ *Negative results are not a guarantee of a safe water supply.*

**ˈwater table** *noun* [usually sing.] (*specialist*) the level at and below which water is found in the ground

**water·tight** /ˈwɔːtətaɪt; NAmE -tərt-/ *adj.* **1** that does not allow water to get in or out: *a watertight container* **2** (of an excuse, a plan, an argument, etc.) carefully prepared so that it contains no mistakes, faults or weaknesses: *a watertight alibi* ◇ *The case has to be made watertight.*

**ˈwater tower** *noun* a tall structure with a tank of water at the top from which water is supplied to buildings in the area around it

**ˈwater vole** (*also* **ˈwater rat**) *noun* an animal like a RAT that swims and lives in a hole next to a river or lake

**water·way** /ˈwɔːtəweɪ; NAmE -tərw-/ *noun* a river, CANAL, etc. along which boats can travel: *inland waterways* ◇ *a navigable waterway*

**water·wheel** /ˈwɔːtəwiːl; NAmE -tərw-/ *noun* a wheel turned by the movement of water, used, especially in the past, to drive machines

**water·works** /ˈwɔːtəwɜːks; NAmE -tərwɜːrks/ *noun* (*pl.* **water·works**) **1** [C + sing./pl. v.] a building with machines for supplying water to an area **2** [pl.] (*informal or humorous*) the organs of the body through which URINE (= waste water) is passed
**IDM** **turn on the ˈwaterworks** (*informal, disapproving*) to start crying, especially in order to get sympathy or attention

**watery** /ˈwɔːtəri/ *adj.* **1** of or like water; containing a lot of water: *a watery fluid* ◇ *His eyes were red and watery.* ◇ (*literary*) *She was rescued from a watery grave* (= saved from DROWNING). **2** weak and/or pale: *a watery sun* ◇ *His eyes were a watery blue.* ◇ *a watery smile* (= weak and without much feeling) **3** (of food, drink, etc.) containing too much water; thin and having no taste: *watery soup*

**watt** /wɒt; NAmE wɑːt/ *noun* (*abbr.* **W**) a unit for measuring electrical power: *a 60-watt light bulb*

**watt·age** /ˈwɒtɪdʒ; NAmE ˈwɑːt-/ *noun* [U, C] (*specialist*) an amount of electrical power expressed in watts

**wat·tle** /ˈwɒtl; NAmE ˈwɑːtl/ *noun* **1** [U] sticks WOVEN together as a material for making fences, walls, etc: *walls made of* **wattle and daub** **2** [C] a piece of red skin that hangs down from the throat of a bird such as a TURKEY **3** [C, U] (*especially AustralE*) a name for various types of ACACIA tree

## wave ⓘ A2 /weɪv/ *noun, verb*

■ *noun*
- **OF WATER 1** B1 [C] a raised line of water that moves across the surface of the sea, ocean, etc: *Huge waves were breaking on the shore.* ◇ *Surfers flocked to the beach to* **ride the waves.** ◇ *the gentle sound of waves lapping* ◇ *The wind made little waves on the pond.* ◇ **in the waves** *Children were playing in the waves.* ◇ **on the waves** *Seagulls bobbed on the waves.* ⇒ WORDFINDER NOTE at SEA ⇒ see also TIDAL WAVE
- **OF HEAT/SOUND/LIGHT 2** B1 [C] the form that some types of energy such as heat, sound, light, etc. take as they move: *electromagnetic/gravity/ultrasonic waves* ⇒ picture at WAVELENGTH ⇒ see also AIRWAVES, LONG WAVE, MEDIUM WAVE, MICROWAVE *noun*, RADIO WAVE, SHOCK WAVE, SHORT WAVE, SOUND WAVE
- **MOVEMENT OF ARM/HAND/BODY 3** B1 [C] a movement of your arm and hand from side to side: **with a ~** *She declined the offer with a wave of her hand.* ◇ *He gave us a wave as the bus drove off.* **4 the wave** [sing.] (*NAmE*) (*BrE* **Mexican ˈwave**) [C] a continuous movement that looks like a wave on the sea, made by a large group of people, especially people watching a sports game, when one person after another stands up, raises their arms, and then sits down again
- **OF ACTIVITY/FEELING 5** B2 [C] a sudden increase in a particular activity or feeling: **~ of sth** *Insurgents launched a* **wave of attacks** *against the security forces.* ◇ *a wave of protests/strikes/scandals* ◇ *a wave of violence/unrest* ◇ *A wave of panic spread through the crowd.* ◇ **in waves** *Guilt and horror flooded her in waves.* ⇒ see also BRAINWAVE, CRIME WAVE, HEATWAVE
- **LARGE NUMBER 6** [C] a large number of people or things suddenly moving or appearing somewhere: *Wave after wave of aircraft passed overhead.* ⇒ see also NEW WAVE
- **IN HAIR 7** [C] if a person's hair has **a wave** or **waves**, it is not straight but slightly curly ⇒ see also PERMANENT WAVE
- **SEA 8 the waves** [pl.] (*literary*) the sea ⇒ see also WAVY
**IDM** **make ˈwaves** (*informal*) to be very active in a way that makes people notice you, and that may sometimes cause problems ⇒ more at CREST *n.*, RIDE *v.*

■ *verb*
- **MOVE HAND/ARM 1** B1 [I, T] to move your hand or arm from side to side in the air in order to attract attention, say hello, etc: *The people on the bus waved and we waved back.* ◇ **~ at/to sb** *Why did you wave at him?* ◇ **~ sth (about/around)** *The driver leaped out, waving his fist and swearing.* ◇ **~ sth at sb** *She waved her hand dismissively at the housekeeper.* ◇ **~ sb sth** *My mother was crying as I waved her goodbye.* ◇ **~ sth to sb** *My mother was crying as I waved goodbye to her.* **2** B1 [I, T] to show where sth is, show sb where to go, etc. by moving your hand in a particular direction: **~ + adv./prep.** *She waved vaguely in the direction of the house.* ◇ **~ sb/sth + adv./prep.** *'He's over there,' said Ali, waving a hand towards some trees.* ◇ *I showed my pass to the security guard and he waved me through.* **3** B1 [T] to hold sth in your hand and move it from side to side: **~ sth** *Crowds lined the route,* **waving flags and cheering.** ◇ **~ sth + adv./prep.** *'I'm rich!' she exclaimed, waving the money under his nose.*
- **MOVE FREELY 4** B1 [I] to move freely and gently, for example in the wind, while one end or side is held in position: *The flag waved in the breeze.*
- **HAIR 5** [I] to be slightly curly: *His hair waves naturally.* **6** [T] **~ sth** to make sb's hair slightly curly: *She's had her hair waved.*

**IDM** **like waving a red flag in front of a ˈbull** (NAmE) (BrE **a red rag to a ˈbull**) used to talk about sth that is likely to make sb very angry ⊃ more at FLAG n.
**PHR V** ˌwave sth↔aˈside/aˈway to not accept sth because you do not think it is necessary or important **SYN** dismiss: *My objections to the plan were waved aside.* ˌwave sth/sbˈdown to signal to a vehicle or its driver to stop by waving your hand ˌwave sb↔ˈoff to wave goodbye to sb as they are leaving

**ˈwave-band** /ˈweɪvbænd/ noun = BAND (6): *a radio set with medium and short wavebands*

**ˈwave-form** /ˈweɪvfɔːm; NAmE -fɔːrm/ noun (*physics*) a curve showing the shape of a wave at a particular time

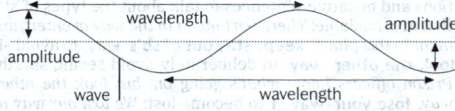

**wave-length** /ˈweɪvleŋkθ/ noun **1** the distance between two similar points on a wave of energy, such as light or sound **2** the size of a radio wave that is used by a particular radio station, etc. for sending signals or broadcasting programmes
**IDM** **be on the same ˈwavelength** | **be on sb's ˈwavelength** (*informal*) to have the same way of thinking or the same ideas or feelings as sb else

**wave-let** /ˈweɪvlət/ noun (*literary*) a small wave on the surface of a lake, the sea or the ocean

**waver** /ˈweɪvə(r)/ verb **1** [I] to be or become weak or unsteady: *His voice wavered with emotion.* ◊ *Her determination never wavered.* ◊ *She never wavered in her determination to succeed.* **2** [I] ~ **(between A and B)** | ~ **(on/over sth)** to hesitate and be unable to make a decision or choice **SYN** hesitate: *She's wavering between buying a house in the city or moving away.* **3** [I] (especially of light) to move in an unsteady way ▶ **waver·er** noun: *The strength of his argument convinced the waverers.*

**wavy** /ˈweɪvi/ adj. (wavi·er, wavi·est) having curves; not straight: *brown wavy hair* ◊ *a pattern of wavy lines* ⊃ picture at LINE

**wax** /wæks/ noun, verb
■ noun **1** a solid substance that is made from BEESWAX or from various fats and oils and used for making CANDLES, POLISH, models, etc. It becomes soft when it is heated: *styling wax for the hair* ◊ *floor wax* ◊ *wax crayons* ◊ *wax polish* ⊃ see also PARAFFIN WAX **2** a soft, sticky yellow-brown substance that is found in your ears
■ verb **1** [T] ~ **sth** to POLISH sth with wax **2** [T, usually passive] ~ **sth** to cover sth with wax: *waxed paper* ◊ *a waxed jacket* **3** [T, often passive] ~ **sth** to remove hair from a part of the body using wax: *to wax your legs/to have your legs waxed* **4** [I] (of the moon) to seem to get gradually bigger until its full form can be seen **OPP** wane **5** [I] + lyrical, eloquent, sentimental, etc. (*formal*) to become LYRICAL, etc. when speaking or writing: *He waxed lyrical on the food at the new restaurant.*
**IDM** **wax and ˈwane** (*literary*) to increase then decrease in strength, importance, etc. over a period of time

**ˈwaxed paper** (NAmE also **ˈwax paper**) noun [U] paper covered with a thin layer of wax, used to wrap food or when cooking ⊃ compare GREASEPROOF PAPER

**waxen** /ˈwæksn/ adj. **1** (*formal*) made of wax: *waxen images* **2** (*literary*) pale and looking ill: *a waxen face*

**wax·work** /ˈwækswɜːk; NAmE -wɜːrk/ noun **1** a model of a person that is made of wax **2** wax·works (*pl.* wax·works) (*especially BrE*) (NAmE *usually* ˈwax museum) a museum where you can see wax models of famous people

**waxy** /ˈwæksi/ adj. made of wax; looking or feeling like wax

**way** /weɪ/ noun, adv.
■ noun
• METHOD/STYLE **1** [C] a method, style or manner of doing sth: *I prefer to do things the easy way.* ◊ **to do sth** *I'm sure we can find a way to make this work.* ◊ *Using the subway is the only way to avoid the traffic.* ◊ ~ **of doing sth** *I'm not happy with this way of working.* ◊ ~ **(that)** ... *It's not what you say, it's the way that you say it.* ◊ *I hate the way she always criticizes me.* ◊ *I told you we should have done it my way!* ◊ **in the ...** ~ *She dresses in the same way as her sister.* ◊ *In this way, we can track the storms as they move across the ocean.* ◊ **in the ~ (that)** ... *It works in the way you'd expect.* ◊ **in a ~ that** ... *She writes in a way that is easy to understand.* ◊ *I generally get what I want one way or another* (= by some means). ⊃ see also THIRD WAY
• BEHAVIOUR **2** [C] a particular manner or style of behaviour: *in a ...* ~ *They grinned at her in a friendly way.* ◊ *It was not his way to admit that he had made a mistake.* ◊ *Don't worry, if she seems quiet—it's just her way.* **3** ways [pl.] the typical way of behaving and living of a particular group of people: *After ten years I'm used to the strange British ways.*
• ROUTE/ROAD **4** [C, usually sing.] a route or road that you take in order to reach a place: *to ask sb the way* ◊ ~ **to** ... *Can you tell me the way to Leicester Square?* ◊ ~ **from ... to ...** *the best/quickest/shortest way from A to B* ◊ *We went the long way round.* **5** [C, usually sing.] the route along which sb/sth is moving; the route that sb/sth would take if there was nothing stopping them/it: *Get out of my way! I'm in a hurry.* ◊ *Riot police with shields were blocking the demonstrators' way.* ⊃ + **adv./prep.** *We fought our way through the dense vegetation.* ◊ (*figurative*) *We will eventually find a way out of the crisis.* ⊃ see also RIGHT OF WAY **6** [C] a road, path or street for travelling along: *There's a way across the fields.* ⊃ see also FREEWAY, HIGHWAY, MOTORWAY, RAILWAY, WATERWAY **7 Way** used in the names of streets: *106 Headley Way*
• DIRECTION **8** [C, usually sing.] **which, this, that, etc.** ~ a particular direction; in a particular direction: *Which way did they go?* ◊ *We just missed a car coming the other way.* ◊ *Look both ways* (= look left and right) *before crossing the road.* ◊ *Make sure that sign's the right way up.* ◊ *The pipe could be moved a few inches either way.* ◊ *Kids were running this way and that* (= in all directions). ◊ *They decided to split the money four ways* (= between four different people). ◊ (*figurative*) *Which way* (= for which party) *are you going to vote?* ⊃ see also EACH WAY, ONE-WAY, THREE-WAY, TWO-WAY
• FOR ENTERING/LEAVING **9** [C, usually sing.] a means of going into or leaving a place, such as a door or gate: *the way in/out* ◊ *They escaped out the back way.*
• DISTANCE/TIME **10** [sing.] (*also* NAmE, *informal* ways) a distance or period of time between two points: *The museum is up on the left is the Museum of Modern Art.* ◊ *We had to go a long way before we found a place to eat.* ◊ *September was a long way off.* ◊ *You came all this way to see us?* ◊ (*figurative*) *The area's wine industry still has a way to go to full maturity.* ◊ (NAmE, *informal*) *We still have a ways to go.*
• AREA **11** [sing.] (*informal*) an area, a part of a country, etc: **over/down ...** ~ *I think he lives somewhere over Greenwich way.* ◊ **down your/my** ~ *I'll stop by and see you next time I'm down your way.*
• ASPECT **12** [C] a particular aspect of sth **SYN** respect: *I have changed in every way.* ◊ *It's been quite a day, one way and another* (= for several reasons).
• CONDITION/STATE **13** [sing.] a particular condition or state: **in a ...** ~ *The economy's in a bad way.* ◊ *I don't know how we're going to manage, the way things are.*

**IDM** **across the ˈway** (BrE also **over the ˈway**) on the other side of the street, etc: *Music blared from the open window of the house across the way.* **all the ˈway 1** (also **the whole ˈway**) during the whole journey/period of time: *She didn't speak a word to me all the way back home.* **2** completely; as much as it takes to achieve what you want: *I'm fighting him all the way.* ◊ *You can feel that the audience is with her all the way.* **along the ˈway** as you make progress with sth: *You'll learn something along the way.* **(that's/it's) always the ˈway** (*informal*) used to say that things often happen in a particular way, especially when it is not convenient **any way you ˈslice it** (NAmE, *informal*) however you choose to look at a situation **be set in your ˈways** to have habits or opinions that you have had

# way

for a long time and that you do not want to change **'be/be 'born/be 'made that way** (of a person) to behave or do things in a particular manner because it is part of your character: *It's not his fault he's so pompous—he was born that way.* **by the 'way** (also **by the 'by/'bye**) (abbr. **BTW**) (informal) used to introduce a comment or question that is not directly related to what you have been talking about: *By the way, I found that book you were looking for.* ◇ *What's the time, by the way?* ◇ *Oh by the way, if you see Jackie, tell her I'll call her this evening.* **by way of sth** by a route that includes the place mentioned SYN **via**: *The artist recently arrived in Paris from Bulgaria by way of Vienna.* ◇ *She came to TV by way of drama school.* **by way of/in the way of sth** as a form of sth; for sth; as a means of sth: *He received £600 by way of compensation from the company.* ◇ *She rolled her eyes by way of an answer and left.* **come your 'way** to happen to you by chance, or when you were not expecting it: *He took the first job that came his way.* **cut both/two 'ways** (of an action, argument, etc.) to have two opposite effects or results **either way | one way or the other** used to say that it does not matter which one of two possibilities happens, is chosen or is true: *Was it his fault or not? Either way, an explanation is due.* ◇ *We could meet today or tomorrow—I don't mind one way or the other.* **every 'which way** (informal) in all directions: *Her hair tumbled every which way.* **get into/out of the way of (doing) sth** to become used to doing sth/to lose the habit of doing sth: *The women had got into the way of going up on the deck every evening.* **get in the way of** to prevent sb from doing sth; to prevent sth from happening: *He wouldn't allow emotions to get in the way of him doing his job.* **get/have your own 'way** to get or do what you want, especially when sb has tried to stop you: *She always gets her own way in the end.* **give 'way** to break or fall down: *The pillars gave way and a section of the roof collapsed.* ◇ *Her numb leg gave way beneath her and she stumbled clumsily.* **give 'way (to sb/sth)** 1 to stop resisting sb/sth; to agree to do sth that you do not want to do: *He refused to give way on any of the points.* 2 (BrE) to allow sb/sth to be or go first: *Give way to traffic already on the roundabout.* **give way to sth** 1 to allow yourself to be very strongly affected by sth, especially an emotion: *Flinging herself on the bed, she gave way to helpless misery.* 2 to be replaced by sth: *The storm gave way to bright sunshine.* **go all the 'way (with sb)** (informal) to have full SEXUAL INTERCOURSE with sb **go a long/some way towards doing sth** to help very much/a little in achieving sth: *The new law goes a long way towards solving the problem.* **go out of your 'way (to do sth)** to make a special effort to do sth: *He would always go out of his way to be friendly towards her.* **go your own 'way** to do as you choose, especially when sb has advised you against it: *It's best to let her go her own way if you don't want a fight.* **go sb's way** 1 to travel in the same direction as sb: *I'm going your way—I'll walk with you.* 2 (of events) to go well for you; to be in your favour: *By the third round he knew the fight was going his way.* **go the way of all 'flesh** to die **have/want it 'both ways** to have or want to have the advantages of two different situations or ways of behaving that are impossible to combine: *You can't have it both ways. If you can afford to go out all the time, you can afford to pay off some of your debts.* **have it your 'own way!** (informal) used to say in an angry way that although you are not happy about sth that sb has said, you are not going to argue: *Oh OK, then. Have it your own way!* **have it/things/everything your 'own way** to have sth arranged in the way that you want, even though other people want it to be arranged differently **have a way of doing sth** used to say that sth often happens in a particular way, especially when it is out of your control: *First love affairs have a way of not working out.* **have a way with sb/sth** to be good at dealing with sb/sth: *He has a way with small children.* ◇ *She has a way with words* (= is very good at expressing herself). **have your (wicked) way with sb** (old-fashioned, humorous) to persuade sb to have sex with you **if I had my way** used to explain what you would do if you had total control over sth: *If I had my way, smoking* would be banned completely. **in a big/small way** on a large/small scale: *The new delivery service has taken off in a big way.* ◇ *Many people are investing in a small way in the stock market.* **in more ways than 'one** used to show that a statement has more than one meaning: *With the first goal he used his head in more ways than one.* **in a 'way | in one way | in some ways** to some extent; not completely: *In a way it was one of our biggest mistakes.* **in her, his, its, etc. (own) 'way** in a manner that is appropriate to or typical of a person or thing but that may seem unusual to other people: *I expect she does love you in her own way.* **in the/sb's 'way** stopping sb from moving or doing sth: *You'll have to move—you're in my way.* ◇ *I left them alone, as I felt I was in the way.* **in the way of sth** used in questions and negative sentences to talk about the types of sth that are available: *There isn't much in the way of entertainment in this place.* **keep/stay out of sb's 'way** to avoid sb **look the other 'way** to deliberately avoid seeing sb/sth: *Prison officers know what's going on, but look the other way.* **lose your 'way** 1 to become lost: *We lost our way in the dark.* 2 to forget or move away from the purpose or reason for sth: *I feel that the project has lost its way.* **make 'way (for sb/sth)** to allow sb/sth to pass; to allow sb/sth to take the place of sb/sth: *Make way for the Lord Mayor!* ◇ *Tropical forest is felled to make way for grassland.* **make your 'way (to/towards sth)** to move or get somewhere; to make progress: *Will you be able to make your own way to the airport* (= get there without help, a ride, etc.)? ◇ *Is this your plan for making your way in the world?* **my way or the 'highway** (NAmE, informal) used to say that sb else has either to agree with your opinion or to leave **(there are) no two ways a'bout it** (saying) used to show that you are certain about sth: *It was the wrong decision—there are no two ways about it.* **(there is) no 'way!** (informal) used to say that there is no possibility that you will do sth or that sth will happen: *'Do you want to help?' 'No way!' No way am I going to drive them there.* ◇ *There's no way we could afford that sort of money.* **on the/its/your 'way** 1 during the journey: *He stopped for breakfast on the way.* ◇ *She grabbed her camera and bag on her way out.* 2 going or coming: *I'd better be on my way* (= I must leave) *soon.* ◇ *The letter should be on its way to you.* 3 (of a baby) not yet born: *They've got three kids and one on the way.* **the 'other way 'round** 1 in the opposite position, direction or order: *I think it should go on the other way round.* 2 the opposite situation: *I didn't leave you. It was the other way round* (= you left me). **out of the 'way** 1 no longer stopping sb from moving or doing sth: *I moved my legs out of the way so that she could get past.* ◇ *I didn't say anything until Dad was out of the way.* 2 finished; dealt with: *Our region is poised for growth once the election is out of the way.* 3 used in negative sentences to mean 'unusual': *She had obviously noticed nothing out of the way.* ⇨ see also OUT-OF-THE-WAY. **out of your 'way** not on the route that you planned to take: *I'd love a ride home—if it's not out of your way.* **see your 'way ('clear) to doing sth/to do sth** to find that it is possible or convenient to do sth: *Small builders cannot see their way clear to take on many trainees.* **see which way the 'wind is blowing** to get an idea of what is likely to happen before deciding what to do **(not) stand in sb's 'way** to (not) prevent sb from doing sth: *If you believe you can make her happy, I won't stand in your way.* **that's the way the cookie 'crumbles** (informal) that is the situation and we cannot change it, so we must accept it **there's more than 'one way to skin a 'cat** (saying, humorous) there are many different ways to achieve sth **to 'my way of thinking** in my opinion **under 'way** (also **under·way**) having started: *Preparations are well under way for a week of special events in May.* **the way 'forward** a plan of action that is likely to be successful: *Personal electronic health records are the way forward for effective healthcare in the future.* **a way 'into sth** (also **a way 'in to sth**) something that allows you to join a group of people, an industry, etc. that is difficult to join, or to understand sth that it is difficult to understand **a/the/sb's way of life** the typical pattern of behaviour of a person or group: *the American way of life* **the way of the 'world** the way that most people behave; the way that things happen, which you cannot change: *The rich and powerful make the* *decisions—that's the way of the world.* **ways and means** the methods and materials available for doing sth: *ways and means of raising money* **way to go!** (*NAmE, informal*) used to tell sb that you are pleased about sth they have done: *Good work, guys! Way to go!* **the way to sb's heart** the way to make sb like or love you: *The way to a man's heart is through his stomach* (= by giving him good food). **work your way through college, round the world, etc.** to have a job or series of jobs while studying, travelling, etc. in order to pay for your education, etc. **work your way through sth** to do sth from beginning to end, especially when it takes a lot of time or effort: *She worked her way through the pile of documents.* **work your way up** to move regularly to a more senior position in a company: *He worked his way up from messenger boy to account executive.* ⇒ more at CHANGE *v.*, CLAW *v.*, CLEAR *v.*, DOWNHILL *adj.*, EASY *adj.*, ERROR, FAMILY *n.*, FEEL *v.*, FIND *v.*, HARD *adj.*, HARM *n.*, HEAD *n.*, KNOW *v.*, LAUGH *v.*, LIE² *v.*, LONG *adj.*, MEND *v.*, MIDDLE *adj.*, OPEN *v.*, ORDINARY, PARTING *n.*, PAVE, PAY *v.*, PICK *v.*, RUB *v.*, SEPARATE *adj.*, SHAPE *n.*, SHOW *v.*, SMOOTH *v.*, SWEET *adj.*, SWING *v.*, TALK *v.*, WELL *adv.*, WILL *n.*, WINNING, WRONG *adj.*

■ *adv.* **1** 🔢 **B2** (used with a preposition or an adverb) very far; by a large amount: *She finished the race way ahead of the other runners.* ◊ *children who are way behind in reading skills* ◊ *I must be going home; it's way past my bedtime.* ◊ *I guessed that there would be a hundred people there, but I was way out* (= wrong by a large amount). ◊ *This skirt is way too short.* **2** (used with an adjective) (*informal, especially NAmE*) very: *Things just got way difficult.* ◊ *I'm way glad to hear that.*

**IDM** **way back (in …)** a long time ago: *I first met him way back in the 80s.*

**way·farer** /ˈweɪfeərə(r)/ *NAmE* -fer-/ *noun* (*old-fashioned or literary*) a person who travels from one place to another, usually on foot

**way·lay** /ˌweɪˈleɪ/ *verb* (**way·laid, way·laid** /-ˈleɪd/) ~ **sb** to stop sb who is going somewhere, especially in order to talk to them or attack them: *I got waylaid on my way here.*

**way·mark** /ˈweɪmɑːk; *NAmE* -mɑːrk/ *noun* a mark or sign on a route in the countryside to show the way to people who are walking, etc: *Turn right where you see a waymark arrow.* ▶ **way·marked** *adj.*: *waymarked routes*

**way out** *noun* **1** (*BrE*) a door used for leaving a building **SYN** **exit 2** a way of escaping from a difficult situation: *She was in a mess and could see no way out.*

**IDM** **on the way out 1** as you are leaving **2** going out of fashion

**way-out** *adj.* (*old-fashioned, informal*) unusual or strange **SYN** **weird**: *way-out ideas*

**way·point** /ˈweɪpɔɪnt/ *noun* **1** a place where you stop during a journey **2** (*specialist*) the COORDINATES, checked by a computer, of each stage of a flight or journey by sea

**-ways** /weɪz/ *suffix* (in adjectives and adverbs) in the direction of: *lengthways* ◊ *sideways*

**the Ways and Means Committee** *noun* [sing. + sing./pl. v.] a group of members of the US House of Representatives that makes suggestions about laws concerning tax and trade in order to provide money for the US government

**way·side** /ˈweɪsaɪd/ *noun* [sing.] the area at the side of a road or path: *a wayside inn* ◊ *wild flowers growing by the wayside*

**IDM** **fall by the wayside** to fail or be unable to make progress

**way station** *noun* (*especially NAmE*) a place where people stop to eat or rest during a long journey

**way·ward** /ˈweɪwəd; *NAmE* -wərd/ *adj.* (*formal*) difficult to control **SYN** **headstrong**: *a wayward child* ◊ *wayward emotions* ▶ **way·ward·ness** *noun* [U]

**wazir** /wəˈzɪə(r); *NAmE* -ˈzɪr/ *noun* = VIZIER

**wazoo** /wæˈzuː/ *noun* (*US, slang*) a person's bottom (the part they sit on) or ANUS

**IDM** **out/up the wazoo** (*US, slang*) in large numbers or amounts

**wazungu** /wəˈzʊŋuː/ *pl.* of MZUNGU

**WC** /ˌdʌbljuː ˈsiː/ *noun* (*BrE or NAmE, old-fashioned*) (on signs and doors in public places) toilet (the abbreviation for 'water closet')

**w/c** *abbr.* (in writing) (*BrE*) week commencing (the week that begins on the date mentioned): *the schedule for w/c 19 November*

**we** 🅾 **A1** /wi; *strong form* wiː/ *pron.* (used as the subject of a verb) **1** 🔢 **A1** I and another person or other people; I and you: *We've moved to Atlanta.* ◊ *We'd* (= the company would) *like to offer you the job.* ◊ *Why don't we go and see it together?* **2** 🔢 **A2** people in general: *We should take more care of our historic buildings.* ⇒ see also ROYAL 'WE'

**weak** 🅾 **A2** /wiːk/ *adj.* (**weaker, weakest**)

• NOT PHYSICALLY STRONG **1** 🔢 **A2** not physically strong: *She is still weak after her illness.* ◊ *His legs felt weak.* ◊ ~ **with/from sth** *I was exhausted and weak with hunger.*
• LIKELY TO BREAK **2** 🔢 **A2** that cannot support a lot of weight; likely to break: *That bridge is too weak for heavy traffic.*
• WITHOUT POWER **3** 🔢 **A2** easy to influence; not having much power: *In a weak moment* (= when I was easily persuaded) *I said she could borrow the car.* ◊ *Small firms find themselves in a very weak position during a recession.* ◊ *a weak leader* ◊ *The unions have always been weak in this industry.*
• POOR/SICK PEOPLE **4 the weak** *noun* [pl.] people who are poor, sick or without power
• CURRENCY/ECONOMY **5** 🔢 **B1** not FINANCIALLY strong or successful: *A weak dollar isn't bad news for everyone.* ◊ *The economy is very weak.*
• LIQUID **6** 🔢 **B1** a weak liquid contains a lot of water: *weak tea*
• HARD TO SEE/HEAR **7** not easily seen or heard: *a weak light/signal/sound*
• NOT GOOD AT STH **8** not good at sth: *a weak team* ◊ ~ **in sth** *I was always weak in the science subjects.*
• NOT CONVINCING **9** that people are not likely to believe or be persuaded by **SYN** **unconvincing**: *weak arguments/evidence* ◊ *I enjoyed the movie but I thought the ending was very weak.*
• WITHOUT ENTHUSIASM **10** done without enthusiasm or energy: *a weak smile* ◊ *He made a weak attempt to look cheerful.*
• POINT/SPOT **11** ~ **point/spot** the part of a person's character, an argument, etc. that is easy to attack or criticize: *The team's weak points are in defence.* ◊ *He knew her weak spot where Steve was concerned.*
• GRAMMAR **12** a weak verb forms the past tense and past participle by adding a regular ending and not by changing a vowel. In English this is done by adding *-d*, *-ed* or *-t* (for example *walk, walked*).
• PHONETICS **13** (of the pronunciation of some words) used when there is no stress on the word. For example, the weak form of *and* is /ən/ or /n/, as in *fish and chips* /ˌfɪʃ ən ˈtʃɪps/. **OPP** **strong**

**IDM** **weak at the knees** (*informal*) hardly able to stand because of emotion, fear, illness, etc: *His sudden smile made her go weak at the knees.* **the weak link (in the chain)** the point at which a system or an organization is most likely to fail ⇒ more at SPIRIT *n.*

▼ **HOMOPHONES**

**weak • week** /wiːk/

• **weak** *adj.*: *He was weak with hunger.*
• **week** *noun*: *I've been waiting to hear from them for over a week.*

**weak·en** 🔢+ 🅒1 /ˈwiːkən/ *verb* **1** 🔢+ 🅒1 [T, I] ~ **(sb/sth)** to make sb/sth less strong or powerful; to become less strong or powerful: *The team has been weakened by injury.* ◊ *The new evidence weakens the case against her.* ◊ *His authority is steadily weakening.* **2** 🔢+ 🅒1 [T, I] ~ **(sth)** to make sth less physically strong; to become less physically strong: *The explosion had weakened the building's*

# weak force

foundations. ◊ She felt her legs **weaken**. **3** [I, T] to become or make sb become less determined or certain about sth: *You must not agree to do it. Don't weaken.* ◊ *~ sth Nothing could weaken his resolve to continue.* **4** [I] (of a natural force) to become less strong: *The storm eventually weakened.* **5** [I, T] (of a country's currency or economy) to become less strong; to make a currency or economy less strong: **~ (against sth)** *The dollar has weakened against the euro.* ◊ *~ sth measures that could weaken the economy* **OPP strengthen**

**weak force** *noun* (*specialist*) one of the four FUNDAMENTAL FORCES in the universe, which is produced between PARTICLES in an ATOM ⇒ see also ELECTROMAGNETISM, GRAVITY, STRONG FORCE

**weak-'kneed** *adj.* (*informal*) not having courage or strength

**weak·ling** /ˈwiːklɪŋ/ *noun* (*disapproving*) a person who is not physically strong

**weak·ly** /ˈwiːkli/ *adv.* in a weak way: *She smiled weakly at them.* ◊ *'I'm not sure about it,' he said weakly.*

**weak·ness** /ˈwiːknəs/ *noun* **1** [U] lack of physical strength: *muscle weakness* ◊ **~ in sth** *The sudden weakness in her legs made her stumble.* **OPP strength** **2** [U] lack of power, influence or strength of character: *He thought that crying was a sign of weakness.* ◊ *the underlying weakness of the coalition's position* **OPP strength 3** [C] a weak point in a system, sb's character, etc: *It's important to know your own strengths and weaknesses.* ◊ **~ in sth** *Can you spot the weakness in her argument?* **OPP strength 4** [U] **~ (of sth) (against sth)** how weak a country's currency is in relation to other countries' currencies **OPP strength 5** [C, usually sing.] **~ (for sth/sb)** difficulty in resisting sth/sb that you like very much: *He has a weakness for chocolate.*

**weal** /wiːl/ *noun* a painful, raised red mark on sb's skin where they have been hit **SYN welt**

**wealth** /welθ/ *noun* **1** [U] a large amount of money, property, etc. that a person or country owns: *the desire to gain wealth and power* ◊ *He has pledged to redistribute the country's vast oil wealth.* ◊ *Their aim is to keep taxes low enough to encourage wealth creation.* **2** [U] the state of being rich: *Good education often depends on wealth.* ◊ *The new rich elite publicly flaunted their wealth.* **3** [sing.] **~ of sth** a large amount of sth: *a wealth of information* ◊ *The new manager brings a great wealth of experience to the job.* ⇒ compare RICHNESS

**wealthy** /ˈwelθi/ *adj.* (**wealth·ier**, **wealthi·est**) **1** having a lot of money, possessions, etc. **SYN rich**: *a wealthy businessman/individual/family* ◊ *a wealthy country/nation* ◊ *The deal is about to make him a very wealthy man.* ⇒ SYNONYMS at RICH **2 the wealthy** *noun* [pl.] people who are rich

**wean** /wiːn/ *verb* **~ sb/sth (off/from/onto sth)** to gradually stop feeding a baby or young animal with its mother's milk and start feeding it with solid food
**PHRV** **ˌwean sb ˈoff/from sth** to make sb gradually stop doing or using sth: *The doctor tried to wean her off sleeping pills.* **ˈwean sb on sth** (usually passive) to make sb experience sth regularly, especially from an early age: *He was weaned on a diet of rigid discipline and duty.*

**weapon** /ˈwepən/ *noun* **1** an object such as a knife, gun, bomb, etc. that is used for fighting or attacking sb: *nuclear weapons* ◊ *a lethal/deadly weapon* ◊ *The police still haven't found the murder weapon.* ◊ *Police believed the men were carrying weapons.* ⇒ WORDFINDER NOTE at ARMY ⇒ see also BIOLOGICAL WEAPON, CHEMICAL WEAPON **2** something such as knowledge, words, actions, etc. that can be used to attack or fight against sb/sth: *Education is the only weapon to fight the spread of the disease.* ◊ *Guilt is the secret weapon for the control of children.*
**IDM** see DOUBLE-EDGED

**weap·on·ize** (*BrE also* **-ise**) /ˈwepənaɪz/ *verb* **~ sth** to make sth suitable for use to harm sb or to damage sth: *They may have weaponized quantities of anthrax.* ▸ **weap·on·iza·tion**, **-isa·tion** /ˌwepənaɪˈzeɪʃn; *NAmE* -nəˈz-/ *noun* [U]

**ˌweapon of mass deˈstruction** *noun* (*abbr.* **WMD**) a weapon such as a nuclear weapon, a CHEMICAL WEAPON or a BIOLOGICAL WEAPON that can destroy large areas and kill many people

**weap·on·ry** /ˈwepənri/ *noun* [U] all the weapons of a particular type or belonging to a particular country or group: *high-tech weaponry* ◊ *US weaponry*

**wear** /weə(r)/; *NAmE* wer/ *verb, noun*

■ *verb* (**wore** /wɔː(r)/, **worn** /wɔːn/; *NAmE* wɔːrn/)
• CLOTHING/DECORATION **1** [T] **~ sth** to have sth on your body as a piece of clothing, a decoration, etc: *He was wearing a new suit.* ◊ *Do I have to wear a tie?* ◊ *Was she wearing a seat belt?* ◊ *She never wears make-up.* ◊ *She always wears black* (= black clothes). ⇒ HOMOPHONES at WAR
• HAIR **2** [T] to have your hair in a particular style; to have a BEARD or MOUSTACHE: **~ sth + adj.** *She wears her hair long.* ◊ **~ sth** *to wear a beard*
• EXPRESSION ON FACE **3** [T] **~ sth** to have a particular expression on your face: *He wore a puzzled look on his face.* ◊ *His face wore a puzzled look.*
• DAMAGE WITH USE **4** [I, T] to become, or make sth become thinner, smoother or weaker through continuous use or rubbing: *The carpets are starting to wear.* ◊ **~ + adj.** *The sheets have worn thin.* ◊ **~ sth + adj.** *The stones have been worn smooth by the constant flow of water.* **5** [T] **~ sth + adv./prep.** to make a hole, path, etc. in sth by continuous use or rubbing: *I've worn holes in all my socks.*
• STAY IN GOOD CONDITION **6** [I] **~ well** to stay in good condition after being used for a long time: *That carpet is wearing well, isn't it?* ◊ (*figurative, humorous*) *You're wearing well —only a few grey hairs!*
• ACCEPT/ALLOW **7** [T] (usually in questions and negative sentences) **~ sth** (*BrE, informal*) to accept or allow sth, especially sth that you do not approve of
**IDM** **ˌwear your ˈheart on your ˈsleeve** to allow your feelings to be seen by other people **ˌwear ˈthin** to begin to become weaker or less acceptable: *These excuses are wearing a little thin* (= because we've heard them so many times before). **ˌwear the ˈtrousers** (*BrE*) (*NAmE* **ˌwear the ˈpants**) (*often disapproving*) (especially of a woman) to be the person in a marriage or other relationship who makes most of the decisions ⇒ more at SHOE *n.*
**PHRV** **ˌwear aˈway** | **ˌwear sth↔aˈway** to become, or make sth become, gradually thinner or smoother through continuous use or rubbing: *The inscription on the coin had worn away.* ◊ *The steps had been worn away by the feet of thousands of pilgrims.* **ˌwear ˈdown** | **ˌwear sth↔ˈdown** to become, or make sth become, gradually smaller or smoother through continuous use or rubbing: *Notice how the tread on this tyre has worn down.* **ˌwear sb/sth↔ˈdown** to make sb/sth weaker or less determined, especially by continuously attacking or putting pressure on them or it over a period of time: *Her persistence paid off and she eventually wore me down.* **ˌwear ˈoff** to gradually disappear or stop: *The effects of the drug will soon wear off.* **ˌwear ˈon** (of time) to pass, especially in a way that seems slow: *As the evening wore on, she became more and more nervous.* **ˌwear ˈout** | **ˌwear sth↔ˈout** to become, or make sth become, thin or no longer able to be used, usually because it has been used too much: *He wore out two pairs of shoes last year.* **ˌwear yourself/sb ˈout** to make yourself/sb feel very tired: *The kids have totally worn me out.* ◊ *You'll wear yourself out if you carry on working so hard.*

■ *noun* [U]
• CLOTHING **1** (usually in compounds) used especially in shops to describe clothes for a particular purpose or occasion: *casual/evening wear* ◊ *children's/ladies' wear* ⇒ see also FOOTWEAR, MENSWEAR, SPORTSWEAR, STREETWEAR, UNDERWEAR **2** the fact of wearing sth: *casual clothes for everyday wear* ◊ *These woollen suits are not designed for wear in hot climates.* ⇒ SYNONYMS at CLOTHES
• USE **3** the amount or type of use that sth has over a period of time: *You should get years of wear out of that carpet.*

• DAMAGE 4 the damage or loss of quality that is caused when sth has been used a lot: *His shoes were beginning to show signs of wear.*
IDM **wear and ˈtear** the damage to objects, furniture, property, etc. that is the result of normal use: *The insurance policy does not cover damage caused by normal wear and tear.* ⊃ more at WORSE n.

▼ **HOMOPHONES**

**ware • wear • where** /weə(r); NAmE wer/
- **ware** noun: *The products include porcelain and ceramic ware.*
- **wear** verb: *Don't wear that jacket—it's far too big!*
- **wear** noun: *Comfortable and smart, this jacket is suitable for office wear.*
- **where** adv.: *Where are you going on your next adventure?*
- **where** conj.: *He was free to go where he liked.*

**wearˈable** /ˈweərəbl/; NAmE ˈwer-/ adj., noun
■ adj. (of clothes, etc.) pleasant and comfortable to wear; suitable to be worn
■ noun [usually pl.] **1** a small COMPUTING device that you can wear, for example on your WRIST: *phones, tablets and wearables* **2** (NAmE) any item that you can wear: *knitted wearables*

**wearˈer** /ˈweərə(r); NAmE ˈwer-/ noun the person who is wearing sth; a person who usually wears the thing mentioned: *The straps can be adjusted to suit the wearer.* ◊ *contact lens wearers*

**wearˈing** /ˈweərɪŋ; NAmE ˈwer-/ adj. that makes you feel very tired mentally or physically SYN **exhausting**

**weariˈsome** /ˈwɪərisəm; NAmE ˈwɪr-/ adj. (formal) that makes you feel very bored and tired SYN **tedious**

**weary** /ˈwɪəri/; NAmE ˈwɪri/ adj., verb
■ adj. (weari·er, weari·est) **1** very tired, especially after you have been working hard or doing sth for a long time: *a weary traveller* ◊ *She suddenly felt old and weary.* ◊ *a weary sigh* **2** (*literary*) making you feel tired or bored: *a weary journey* **3** ~ **of sth/of doing sth** (*formal*) no longer interested in or enthusiastic about sth: *Students soon grow weary of listening to a parade of historical facts.* ▸ **wear·ily** /-rəli/: *He closed his eyes wearily.* **weari·ness** noun [U]
■ verb (wear·ies, weary·ing, wear·ied, wear·ied) **1** [T] ~ **sb** (*formal*) to make sb feel tired SYN **tire 2** [I] ~ **of sth/of doing sth** to lose your interest in or enthusiasm for sth SYN **tire**: *She soon wearied of his stories.*

**weasel** /ˈwiːzl/; noun, verb
■ noun a small wild animal with red-brown fur, a long thin body, and short legs. Weasels eat smaller animals.
■ verb (-ll-, NAmE -l-)
PHRV **ˌweasel ˈout (of sth)** (*especially NAmE, informal, disapproving*) to avoid doing sth that you ought to do or have promised to do: *He's now trying to weasel out of our agreement.*

**ˈweasel word** noun [usually pl.] (*informal, disapproving*) a word that has little meaning, or more than one meaning, that you use when you want to avoid saying sth in a clear or direct way

**weaˈther** 🅐 A1 /ˈweðə(r)/ noun, verb
■ noun [U] **1** A1 the condition of the atmosphere at a particular place and time, such as the temperature, and if there is wind, rain, sun, etc: *cold/hot/warm/wet/dry weather* ◊ *severe/extreme weather* ◊ *good/bad weather* ◊ *Flights have been delayed because of the inclement weather.* ◊ *Weather conditions are set to improve by Thursday.* ◊ *concerns about changing weather patterns* ◊ *We'll have the party outside, weather permitting* (= if it doesn't rain). ◊ *in …~ I'm not going out in this weather!* ◊ *Did you have good weather on your trip?* ◊ *The winter weather kept us from going out for a walk.* ⊃ HOMOPHONES at WHETHER **2** A1 **the weather** (*informal*) a report of what the weather will be like, on the radio or television, in the newspapers or online: *to listen to/watch the weather*
IDM **in all ˈweathers** in all kinds of weather, good and bad: *She goes out jogging in all weathers.* **ˌkeep a ˈweather eye on sb/sth** to watch sb/sth carefully in case you need to take action **ˌunder the ˈweather** (*informal*) if you are or feel **under the weather**, you feel slightly ill and not as well as usual ⊃ more at BRASS, HEAVY adj.
■ verb **1** [I, T] to change, or make sth change, colour or shape because of the effect of the sun, rain or wind: *This brick weathers to a warm pinkish-brown colour.* ◊ ~ **sth** *Her face was weathered by the sun.* **2** [T] ~ **sth** to come safely through a difficult period or experience: *The company just managed to weather the recession.* ◊ *She refuses to resign, intending to* **weather the storm** (= wait until the situation improves again). ⊃ HOMOPHONES at WHETHER

**ˈweather balloon** noun a BALLOON that carries instruments into the atmosphere to measure weather conditions

**ˈweather-beaten** adj. [usually before noun] (especially of a person or their skin) rough and damaged because the person spends a lot of time outside

**weaˈther·board** /ˈweðəbɔːd; NAmE -ɔːrbɔːrd/ (*also* **clap·board** *especially in NAmE*) noun one of a series of long, narrow pieces of wood, each with one edge thicker than the other. They are fixed to the outside walls of a house, going from side to side, with the bottom of one over the top of the one below, to cover the wall and protect it from rain and wind: *a weatherboard house* ▸ **weaˈther·boarded** adj. **ˈweaˈther·board·ing** noun [U]

**ˈweather centre** (*BrE*) (*US* **ˈweather bureau**) noun a place where information about the weather is collected and reports are prepared

**weaˈther·cock** /ˈweðəkɒk; NAmE -ðərkɑːk/ noun a WEATHERVANE in the shape of a male chicken (called a COCK or ROOSTER)

weathercock

**ˈweather forecast** (*also* **ˈfore·cast**) noun a description, for example on the radio or television, of what the weather will be like tomorrow or for the next few days

**weaˈther·ing** /ˈweðərɪŋ/ noun [U] the action of sun, rain or wind on rocks, making them change shape or colour

**weaˈther·man** /ˈweðəmæn; NAmE -ðərm-/ (*pl.* **-men** /-men/), **weaˈther·girl** /-ɡɜːl; NAmE -ɡɜːrl/ (*old-fashioned*) noun (*informal*) a person on radio or television whose job is describing the weather and telling people what it is going to be like

**weaˈther·proof** /ˈweðəpruːf; NAmE -ðərp-/ adj. that is not affected by weather; that protects sb/sth from wind and rain: *The finished roof should be weatherproof for years.* ◊ *a weatherproof jacket*

**ˈweather station** noun a place where weather conditions are studied and recorded

**weaˈther·vane** /ˈweðəveɪn; NAmE -ðərv-/ noun a metal object on the roof of a building that turns easily in the wind and shows which direction the wind is blowing from ⊃ see also WEATHERCOCK

**weave** 🅑+ 🅒 /wiːv/ verb, noun
■ verb (wove /wəʊv; NAmE woʊv/, woven /ˈwəʊvn; NAmE ˈwoʊvn/) HELP In sense 3 **weaved** is used for the past tense and past participle.
**1** 🅑+ 🅒 [T, I] to make cloth, a carpet, a BASKET, etc. by crossing THREADS or narrow pieces of material across, over and under each other by hand or on a machine called a LOOM: ~ **A from B** *The baskets are woven from strips of willow.* ◊ ~ **B into A** *The strips of willow are woven into baskets.* ◊ ~ **sth together** *threads woven together* ◊ ~ **(sth)** *Most spiders weave webs that are almost invisible.* ◊ *She is skilled at spinning and weaving.* **2** 🅑+ 🅒 [T] ~ **A (out of/from B)** | ~ **B (into A)** to make sth by TWISTING flowers, pieces of wood, etc. together: *She deftly wove the flowers into a garland.* **3** 🅑+ 🅒 (**weaved, weaved**) [I, T] to move along by running and changing direction continuously to

# weaver

avoid things that are in your way: + *adv./prep. She was weaving in and out of the traffic.* ◊ *The road weaves through a range of hills.* ◊ *~ your way + adv./prep. He had to weave his way through the milling crowds.* **4** [T] to put facts, events, details, etc. together to make a story or a closely connected whole: *~ (sth into) sth to weave a narrative* ◊ *~ sth together The biography weaves together the various strands of Einstein's life.*

**IDM** **weave your 'magic | weave a 'spell (over sb)** (*especially BrE*) to perform or behave in a way that is attractive or interesting, or that makes sb behave in a particular way: *Will Hegerberg be able to weave her magic against Italy on Wednesday?*

■ *noun* the way in which THREADS are arranged in a piece of cloth that has been woven; the pattern that the threads make

**weaver** /ˈwiːvə(r)/ *noun* a person whose job is weaving cloth

**weav·ing** /ˈwiːvɪŋ/ *noun* **1** [U] the activity of making cloth by WEAVING **2** [C] an article that is made by WEAVING especially one that is used for decoration

**web** 🅐 A2 /web/ *noun* **1** 🅢 A2 **the Web, the web** (*also* **the World Wide 'Web**) [sing.] a system for finding information on the internet, in which documents are connected to other documents: *to surf/browse/search the web* ◊ *on the ~ I found the information on the Web.* ◊ *a web browser/server* ⊃ see also DARK WEB

**WORDFINDER** access, blog, browse, chat, google, navigate, search engine, unsubscribe, visit

**2** [C] = SPIDER'S WEB: *A spider had spun a perfect web outside the window.* ⊃ VISUAL VOCAB page V3 **3** [C] a complicated pattern of things that are closely connected to each other: *a web of streets* ◊ *We were caught in a tangled web of relationships.* **4** [C] a piece of skin that joins the toes of some birds and animals that swim, for example DUCKS and frogs

**Web 2.0** /ˌweb tuː ˈpɔɪnt ˈəʊ/ *noun* [U] the second stage of development of the internet that allowed users to create, change and share information, for example through blogs and SOCIAL MEDIA

**web·bed** /webd/ *adj.* [only before noun] a bird or an animal (such as a DUCK or frog) that has **webbed feet** has pieces of skin between the toes ⊃ VISUAL VOCAB page V2

**web·bing** /ˈwebɪŋ/ *noun* [U] strong, narrow pieces of cloth that are used to make belts, etc., and to support the seats of chairs, etc.

**'web browser** *noun* = BROWSER (1)

**web·cam** /ˈwebkæm/ *noun* a video camera that is connected to a computer so that what it records can be seen on a website or on another computer as it happens

**web·cast** /ˈwebkɑːst; *NAmE* -kæst/ *noun* a live broadcast that is sent out on the internet

**'Web-enabled** *adj.* able to be connected to and used with the internet: *a Web-enabled interface*

**'web hosting** *noun* [U] the activity or business of providing space to store websites, access to them and other services related to them: *If you are starting your own business you can buy affordable web hosting or host your own website.* ◊ *a web hosting business/company/provider/service*

**webi·nar** /ˈwebɪnɑː(r)/ *noun* a presentation or SEMINAR (= a meeting for discussion or training) that is conducted over the internet: *Our company uses webinars to train representatives in other countries.*

**web·log** /ˈweblɒg; *NAmE* -blɔːg/ *noun* = BLOG

**web·master** /ˈwebmɑːstə(r); *NAmE* -mæs-/ *noun* a person who is responsible for particular pages of information on the World Wide Web

**'web page** *noun* a document that is connected to the World Wide Web and that anyone with an internet connection can see, usually forming part of a website: *We learned how to create and register a new web page.*

**web·site** 🅐 A1 🅦 /ˈwebsaɪt/ *noun* a set of pages on the internet, where a company or an organization, or an individual person, puts information: *For current prices please visit our website.* ◊ *The company has recently launched a new website.* ◊ *the festival's official website* ◊ *on a ~ I found this information on their website.*

**WORDFINDER** bookmark, cookie, domain, home page, hyperlink, landing page, online, social media, URL

**Wed.** (*also* **Weds.**) *abbr.* (in writing) Wednesday

**wed** /wed/ *verb* (**wed·ded, wed·ded** *or* **wed, wed**) [I, T] (not used in the progressive tenses) (*old-fashioned* or used in newspapers) to marry: *The couple plan to wed next summer.* ◊ *~ sb Rock star to wed top model* (= in a newspaper headline).

**we'd** /wiːd, wɪd/ *short form* **1** we had **HELP We'd** is only used when *had* is an auxiliary verb: *We'd just missed the bus.* When *had* is the main verb, use the full form: *We had a good time at the party.* ◊ *We'd a good time at the party.* **2** we would

**wed·ded** /ˈwedɪd/ *adj.* **1** *~* **to sth** (*formal*) if you are **wedded** to sth, you like or support it so much that you are not willing to give it up: *She's wedded to her job.* **2** [usually before noun] (*old-fashioned* or *formal*) legally married: *your lawfully wedded husband* ◊ *to live together in wedded bliss*

**wed·ding** 🅐 A2 /ˈwedɪŋ/ *noun* a marriage ceremony, and the meal or party that usually follows it: *I dreamed of having a big wedding, with all my family and friends.* ◊ *television coverage of the royal wedding* ◊ *at a ~ I met her at my brother's wedding.* ◊ *~ to sb Over 300 guests attended his wedding to the former model.* ◊ *a wedding ceremony/reception* ⊃ see also DIAMOND WEDDING, GOLDEN WEDDING, SHOTGUN WEDDING, SILVER WEDDING, WHITE WEDDING

**WORDFINDER** best man, bride, ceremony, engaged, honeymoon, marriage, propose, reception, stag night

**'wedding anniversary** *noun* the celebration every year of the date when two people were married: *Today's our wedding anniversary.*

**'wedding band** (*especially NAmE*) *noun* = WEDDING RING

**'wedding breakfast** *noun* (*BrE, formal*) a special meal after a marriage ceremony

**'wedding cake** *noun* [C, U] a special cake eaten at a wedding party, usually covered with ICING and with several layers

**'wedding dress** *noun* a dress that a woman wears at her wedding, especially a long white one

**'wedding ring** (*also* **'wedding band** *especially in NAmE*) *noun* a ring, usually in the form of a plain gold band, that is given during a marriage ceremony and worn afterwards to show that you are married

**wedge** /wedʒ/ *noun, verb*

■ *noun* **1** a piece of wood, rubber, metal, etc. with one thick end and one thin, pointed end that you use to keep a door open, to keep two things apart, or to split wood or rock: *He hammered the wedge into the crack in the stone.* **2** something that is like a wedge in shape or that is used like a wedge: *a wedge of cake/cheese* ◊ *shoes with wedge heels* **3** a shoe with a wedge heel (= one that forms a solid block with the bottom part of the shoe): *a pair of wedges* **4** a type of GOLF CLUB that has its face (= the part that you hit the ball with) at a greater angle than other types of golf club **IDM** see DRIVE *v.*, THIN *adj.*

■ *verb* **1** *~* **sth + adv./prep.** to put or force sth tightly into a narrow space, so that it cannot move easily **SYN** jam: *The boat was now wedged between the rocks.* ◊ *She wedged herself into the passenger seat.* **2** *~* **sth (+ adj.)** to make sth stay in a particular position, especially open or shut, by placing sth against it: *to wedge the door open*

**wedge issue** noun (NAmE) an important and difficult political issue, used by a political party to draw supporters away from another party

**wedgie** /ˈwedʒi/ noun (informal) an act of lifting sb up by his/her underwear, usually done as a joke

**wed·lock** /ˈwedlɒk; NAmE -lɑːk/ noun [U] (old-fashioned or law) the state of being married: **in/out of ~** children born in/out of wedlock (= whose parents are/are not married)

**Wed·nes·day** 🔊 **A1** /ˈwenzdeɪ, -di/ noun [C, U] (abbr. **Wed.**, **Weds.**) the day of the week after Tuesday and before Thursday **HELP** To see how **Wednesday** is used, look at the examples at **Monday**. **ORIGIN** Originally translated from the Latin for 'day of Mercury' *Mercurii dies* and named after the Germanic god *Odin*.

**wee** /wiː/ adj., noun, verb
■ **adj.** (informal) **1** (especially ScotE) very small in size: *a wee girl* **2** small in amount; little: *Just a wee drop of milk for me.* ◊ *I felt a wee bit guilty about it.*
**IDM** **the wee small ˈhours** (ScotE) (NAmE **the wee ˈhours**) = THE SMALL/EARLY HOURS AT HOUR
■ **noun** (also **ˈwee-wee**) (informal, especially BrE) (often used by young children or when you are talking to them) **1** [sing.] an act of passing liquid waste (called URINE) from your body: *to do/have a wee* **2** [U] = URINE: *a puddle of wee*
■ **verb** (also **ˈwee-wee**) [I] (informal, especially BrE) (often used by young children or when you are talking to them) to pass liquid waste (called URINE) from the body: *Do you need to wee?*

**weed** 🔊+ **C1** /wiːd/ noun, verb
■ **noun 1** 🔊+ **C1** [C] a wild plant growing where it is not wanted, especially among crops or garden plants: *The yard was overgrown with weeds.* **2** [U] any wild plant without flowers that grows in water and forms a green floating mass **3 the weed** [sing.] (humorous) TOBACCO or cigarettes: *I wish I could give up the weed* (= stop smoking). **4** [U] (informal) the drug CANNABIS **5** [C] (BrE, informal, disapproving) a person with a weak character or body
**IDM** **in the ˈweeds** (NAmE, informal) **1** with more problems, work or commitments than you can manage **2** too concerned with the details of sth: *I don't want to get too deep in the weeds here, but here's the short version: …*
■ **verb** [T, I] **~ (sth)** to take out weeds from the ground: *I've been weeding the flower beds.*
**PHR V** **ˌweed sth/sb↔ˈout** to remove or get rid of people or things from a group because they are not wanted or are less good than the rest

**weed·kill·er** /ˈwiːdkɪlə(r)/ noun [U, C] a substance that is used to destroy weeds

**weedy** /ˈwiːdi/ adj. (**weed·ier**, **weedi·est**) **1** (informal, disapproving) having a thin, weak body: *a weedy little man* **2** full of or covered with weeds

**week** 🔊 **A1** /wiːk/ noun (abbr. **wk**) **1** 🔊+ **A1** a period of seven days, either from Monday to Sunday or from Sunday to Saturday: *last/this/next week* ◊ *They won by two goals the previous week.* ◊ *a/per~ She works three days a week.* ◊ *He comes to see us once a week.* ◊ HOMOPHONES at WEAK **2** 🔊+ **A1** any period of seven days: *The course lasts five weeks.* ◊ **in a~** *She'll be back in a week.* ◊ **in weeks** *It hasn't rained in weeks.* ◊ **within a~** *Within a week he was dead.* ◊ **for a~** *We stayed there for a whole week.* ◊ **for weeks** *I haven't seen him for weeks.* ◊ *I will be away for a couple of weeks.* **3** 🔊 **A1** the five days other than Saturday and Sunday: **during the~** *They live in town during the week and go to the country for the weekend.* ◊ **in the~** (BrE) *I never have the time to go out in the week.* **4** 🔊+ **A1** the part of the week when you go to work: *a 35-hour week* ⤳ see also WORKING WEEK, WORKWEEK
**IDM** **today, tomorrow, Monday, etc. ˈweek** (BrE) (also **a week (from) toˈday, etc.** NAmE, BrE) seven days after the day that you mention: *I'll see you Thursday week.* **ˌweek after ˈweek** (informal) continuously for many weeks: *Week after week the drought continued.* **ˌweek by ˈweek** as the weeks pass: *Week by week he grew a little stronger.* **ˌweek in, ˌweek ˈout** happening every week: *Every Sunday, week in, week out, she goes to her parents for lunch.* **a ˌweek next/on/this ˈMonday, etc.** | **a ˌweek**

**toˈmorrow, etc.** (BrE) (also **a ˌweek from ˈMonday, etc.** NAmE, BrE) seven days after the day that you mention: *It's my birthday a week on Tuesday.* **a ˌweek ˈyesterday, last ˈMonday, etc.** (especially BrE) seven days before the day that you mention: *She started work a week yesterday.* ⤳ more at OTHER

**week·day** /ˈwiːkdeɪ/ noun any day except Saturday and Sunday: *The centre is open from 9 a.m. to 6 p.m. on weekdays.* ▸ **weekˌdays** adv.: *open weekdays from 9 a.m. to 6 p.m.*

**week·end** 🔊 **A1** /ˌwiːkˈend; NAmE ˈwiːkend/ noun, verb
■ **noun 1** 🔊 **A1** Saturday and Sunday: *this/next/last weekend* ◊ **at the~** (BrE) *The office is closed at the weekend.* ◊ **on the ~** (especially NAmE) *The office is closed on the weekend.* ◊ **on the ~ of …** *It happened on the weekend of 24 and 25 April.* ◊ **over the ~** *Are you doing anything over the weekend?* ◊ *We spent the weekend at the beach.* ◊ *Her birthday is this coming weekend.* ⤳ see also DIRTY WEEKEND, LONG WEEKEND **2** 🔊+ **A1** Saturday and Sunday, or a slightly longer period, as a holiday: *He won a weekend for two in Rome.* ◊ (BrE) *a bank holiday weekend*
■ **verb** [I] **+ adv./prep.** to spend the weekend somewhere: *They're weekending in Paris.*

**week·end·er** /ˌwiːkˈendə(r)/ noun **1** a person who visits or lives in a place only on Saturdays and Sundays **2** (AustralE, informal) a house in the country that people go to for weekends and holidays

**weekend ˈwarrior** noun (NAmE) a person who works all week, especially in an office or other indoor job, and uses the weekends to go out and do more active and/or dangerous physical activities

**week-long** adj. lasting for a week: *a week-long visit to Rome* ◊ *week-long courses*

**week·ly** 🔊+ **B2** /ˈwiːkli/ adj., noun
■ **adj.** 🔊+ **B2** [only before noun] happening, done or published once a week or every week: *weekly meetings* ◊ *a weekly magazine* ▸ **weekˌly** adv.: *Employees are paid weekly.* ◊ *The newspaper is published twice weekly.*
■ **noun** (pl. **-ies**) a newspaper or magazine that is published every week

**week·night** /ˈwiːknaɪt/ noun any night of the week except Saturday, Sunday and sometimes Friday night: *I have to stay in on weeknights.*

**weenie** /ˈwiːni/ noun (NAmE, informal) **1** (disapproving) a person who is not strong, brave or confident **SYN** wimp: *Don't be such a weenie!* **2** = FRANKFURTER **3** (slang) a word for a PENIS, used especially by children

**weeny** /ˈwiːni/ adj. (**ween·ier**, **weeni·est**) (informal) extremely small **SYN** tiny: *Weren't you just a weeny bit scared?* ⤳ see also TEENY

**weep** /wiːp/ verb, noun
■ **verb** (**wept**, **wept** /wept/) **1** [I, T] (formal or literary) to cry, usually because you are sad: *She started to weep uncontrollably.* ◊ *I could have wept* (= I was sad enough to cry) *thinking about what I'd missed.* ◊ **for/with sth** *He wept for joy.* ◊ **at/over sth** *I do not weep over his death.* ◊ **~ sth** *She wept bitter tears of disappointment.* ◊ **~ to do sth** *I wept to see him looking so sick.* ◊ **+ speech** *'I'm so unhappy!' she wept.* **2** [I] (usually used in the progressive tenses) (of a wound) to produce liquid: ◊ *His legs were covered with weeping sores* (= that had not HEALED).
■ **noun** [sing.] an act of crying: *Sometimes you feel better for a good weep.*

**weep·ing** /ˈwiːpɪŋ/ adj. [only before noun] (of some trees) with branches that hang downwards: *a weeping willow/fig/birch*

**weepy** /ˈwiːpi/ adj., noun
■ **adj.** (informal) sad and tending to cry easily: *She was feeling tired and weepy.*

# weevil

**noun** (also **weepie**) (*pl.* **-ies**) (*informal*) a sad film or play that makes you want to cry SYN **tear-jerker**

**wee·vil** /ˈwiːvl/ *noun* a small insect with a hard shell, that eats grain, nuts and other seeds and destroys crops

**ˈwee-wee** *noun, verb* = WEE

**the weft** /ðə ˈweft/ (also less frequent **the woof**) *noun* [sing.] the THREADS that are TWISTED under and over the THREADS that are held on a LOOM (= a frame or machine for making cloth) ⇨ compare WARP

**weigh** B1 /weɪ/ *verb* **1** B1 *linking verb* + **noun** to have a particular weight: *How much do you weigh* (= how heavy are you)? ⬦ *A healthy baby usually weighs 6 lbs or more.* ⬦ (*informal*) *These cases weigh a ton* (= are very heavy). **2** T ~ **sb/sth/yourself** to measure how heavy sb/sth is, usually by using SCALES: *He weighed himself on the bathroom scales.* ⬦ *She weighed the stone in her hand* (= estimated how heavy it was by holding it). **3** [T] to consider sth carefully before making a decision: ~ **sth (up)** *You must weigh up the pros and cons* (= consider the advantages and disadvantages of sth). ⬦ *She weighed up all the evidence.* ⬦ ~ **(up) sth against sth** *I weighed the benefits of the plan against the risks involved.* **4** [I] ~ **(with sb) (against sb/sth)** to have an influence on sb's opinion or the result of sth: *His past record weighs heavily against him.* **5** [T] ~ **anchor** to lift an ANCHOR out of the water and into a boat before sailing away

IDM **weigh your ˈwords** to choose your words carefully so that you say exactly what you mean

PHR V **weigh sb ˈdown** to make sb feel worried or anxious SYN **burden**: *The responsibilities of the job are weighing her down.* ⬦ *He is weighed down with guilt.* **weigh sb/sth↔down** to make sb/sth heavier so that they are not able to move easily: *I was weighed down with baggage.* **ˌweigh ˈin (at sth)** to have your weight measured, especially before a contest, race, etc: *Both boxers weighed in at several pounds below the limit.* ⇨ related noun WEIGH-IN **ˌweigh ˈin (with sth)** (*informal*) to join in a discussion, an argument, an activity, etc. by saying sth important, persuading sb, or doing sth to help: *We all weighed in with our suggestions.* ⬦ *Finally the government weighed in with financial aid.* **ˈweigh on sb/sth** to make sb worried and unhappy: *The responsibilities weigh heavily on him.* ⬦ *Something was weighing on her mind.* **weigh sth↔out** to measure an amount of sth by weight: *She weighed out a kilo of flour.* **weigh sb↔up** to form an opinion of sb by watching or talking to them

**weigh·bridge** /ˈweɪbrɪdʒ/ *noun* a machine for weighing vehicles and their loads, usually with a platform onto which the vehicle is driven

**ˈweigh-in** *noun* the occasion when the weight of a BOXER, JOCKEY, etc. is checked officially

**weight** A2 W /weɪt/ *noun, verb*

■ *noun*
- BEING HEAVY **1** A2 [U, C] how heavy sb/sth is, which can be measured in, for example, KILOGRAMS or pounds: **in** ~ *It is about 76 kilos in weight.* ⬦ **by** ~ *Bananas are sold by weight.* ⬦ *She is trying to lose weight* (= become less heavy and less fat). ⬦ *He's put on/gained weight* (= become heavier and fatter) *since he gave up smoking.* ⬦ *Body fat increases rapidly as body weight increases.* ⬦ *The point is to achieve permanent weight loss.* ⬦ *Stress can cause weight gain.* ⇨ see also BIRTHWEIGHT, OVERWEIGHT, UNDERWEIGHT **2** B1 [U] the fact of being heavy: ~ **of sb/sth** *The pillars have to support the weight of the roof.* ⬦ *I just hoped the branch would take my weight.* ⬦ **under the** ~ *He staggered a little under the weight of his backpack.* ⬦ *Don't put any weight on that ankle for at least a week.* ⇨ see also DEAD WEIGHT
- HEAVY OBJECT **3** B1 [C] an object that is heavy: *The doctor said he should not lift heavy weights.* **4** [C] an object used to keep sth in position or as part of a machine: *weights on a fishing line* ⇨ see also PAPERWEIGHT
- RESPONSIBILITY/WORRY **5** [sing.] ~ **(of sth)** a great responsibility or worry SYN **burden**: *The full weight of responsibility falls on her.* ⬦ *The news was certainly a weight off my mind.* (= I did not have to worry about it any more). ⬦ *Finally telling the truth was a great weight off my shoulders.*
- INFLUENCE/STRENGTH **6** [U] importance, influence or strength: *The many letters of support added weight to the campaign.* ⬦ *The President has now offered to lend his weight to the project.* ⬦ *Your opinion carries weight with the boss.* ⬦ *How can you ignore the sheer weight of medical opinion?* ⬦ *The weight of evidence against her is overwhelming.*
- FOR MEASURING/LIFTING **7** [C, U] a unit or system of units by which weight is measured: *tables of weights and measures* ⬦ *imperial/metric weight* **8** [C] a piece of metal that is known to weigh a particular amount and is used to measure the weight of sth, or lifted by people to improve their strength and as a sport: *a light/heavy weight* ⬦ *She lifts weights as part of her training.* ⬦ *He does a lot of weight training.*

IDM **take the weight off your feet** (*informal*) to sit down and rest, especially when you are tired: *Come and sit down and take the weight off your feet for a while.* **throw your ˈweight about/around** (*informal*) to use your position of authority or power in an aggressive way in order to achieve what you want **throw/put your weight behind sth** to use all your influence and power to support sth **weight of ˈnumbers** the combined power, strength or influence of a group: *They won the argument by sheer weight of numbers.* ⇨ more at CARRY, GROAN *v.*, PULL *v.*, PUNCH *v.*, WORTH *adj.*

■ *verb*
- ATTACH HEAVY OBJECT **1** ~ **sth (down) (with sth)** to attach a weight to sth in order to keep it in the right position or make it heavier: *The fishing nets are weighted with lead.*
- GIVE IMPORTANCE **2** [usually passive] to give different values to things to show how important you think each of them is compared with the others: **be weighted** *The results of the survey were weighted to allow for variations in the sample.* ⬦ *a weighted vote* (= one that is worth more than a single vote) ⬦ (*NAmE*) *a weighted grade* (= given at school for a course that is more advanced or harder and so has a higher value)

▼ **HOMOPHONES**

**wait • weight** /weɪt/

- **wait** *verb*: *You won't have to wait long—the next train is in five minutes.*
- **wait** *noun*: *It was an anxious wait, but finally she found out that she'd passed.*
- **weight** *noun*: *He has lost a lot of weight.*
- **weight** *verb*: *Weight the tablecloth down so that it doesn't move or blow away.*

**weight·ed** /ˈweɪtɪd/ *adj.* [not before noun] arranged in such a way that a particular person or thing has an advantage or a disadvantage SYN **biased**: ~ **towards sb/sth** *The proposal is weighted towards smaller businesses.* ⬦ ~ **against sb/sth** *Everything seemed weighted against them.* ⬦ ~ **in favour of sb/sth** *The course is heavily weighted in favour of engineering.*

**weight·ing** /ˈweɪtɪŋ/ *noun* **1** [U] (*BrE*) extra money that you get paid for working in a particular area because it is expensive to live there **2** [C, U] a value that you give to each of a number of things to show how important it is compared with the others: *Each of the factors is given a weighting on a scale of 1 to 10.* ⬦ *Each question in the exam has equal weighting.*

**weight·less** /ˈweɪtləs/ *adj.* having no weight or appearing to have no weight, for example because there is no GRAVITY: *Astronauts work in weightless conditions.* ⇨ WORDFINDER NOTE at SPACE ▶ **weight·less·ness** *noun* [U]

**weight·lift·ing** /ˈweɪtlɪftɪŋ/ *noun* [U] the sport or activity of lifting heavy weights ▶ **weight·lift·er** *noun*

**weighty** /ˈweɪti/ *adj.* (**weight·ier, weighti·est**) **1** important and serious: *weighty matters* **2** heavy: *a weighty volume/tome* ▶ **weight·ily** /-tɪli/ *adv.* **weighti·ness** *noun* [U]

**weir** /wɪə(r); NAmE wɪr/ *noun* a low wall or barrier built across a river in order to control the flow of water or change its direction

**weird** 0️⃣+ B2 /wɪəd; NAmE wɪrd/ *adj., verb*
- *adj.* (**weird·er, weird·est**) **1** 0️⃣+ B2 very strange or unusual and difficult to explain SYN **strange**: *a weird dream* ◇ *She's a really weird girl.* ◇ *He's got some weird ideas.* ◇ *It's really weird seeing yourself on television.* ◇ *the weird and wonderful creatures that live beneath the sea* **2** 0️⃣+ B2 strange in a mysterious and frightening way SYN **eerie**: *She began to make weird inhuman sounds.* ▸ **weird·ly** *adv.*: *The town was weirdly familiar.* **weird·ness** *noun* [U] IDM see FUNNY
- *verb*
  PHR V **weird sb 'out** (*informal*) to seem strange to sb and make them feel worried or uncomfortable: *The whole concept really weirds me out.*

**weirdo** /ˈwɪədəʊ; NAmE ˈwɪrd-/ *noun* (*pl.* **-os** /-dəʊz/) (*informal, disapproving*) a person who looks strange and/or behaves in a strange way

**welch** /welʃ, weltʃ/ *verb* = WELSH

**wel·come** 🔊 A1 /ˈwelkəm/ *exclamation, verb, adj., noun*
- *exclamation* 🔊 A1 used as a GREETING to tell sb that you are pleased that they are there: *Welcome home!* ◇ *~ to sth Welcome to Oxford!* ◇ *Good evening everybody. Welcome to the show!*
- *verb* **1** 🔊 A1 to say hello to sb in a friendly way when they arrive somewhere: *~ sb They were at the door to welcome us.* ◇ *to welcome a visitor/guest* ◇ *~ sb to sth It is a pleasure to welcome you to our home.* **2** 🔊 B1 to be pleased that sb has come or has joined an organization, activity, etc.: *~ sb (to/into sth) They welcomed the new volunteers with open arms* (= with enthusiasm). **3** 🔊 B1 *~ sth* to be pleased to receive or accept sth: *to welcome a decision/move* ◇ *Women's rights campaigners welcomed the news.* ◇ *I warmly welcome this announcement.*
- *adj.* **1** 🔊 A1 (of people) accepted or wanted somewhere: **+ adv./prep.** *They were anxious to make us feel welcome in their home.* ◇ *Children are always welcome at the hotel.* ◇ *Poetry Reading. Tonight at 8 p.m. Admission free. All are welcome.* **2** 🔊 B1 that you are pleased to have, receive, etc.: *Her book is a welcome addition to the literature on late Victorian Britain.* ◇ *It was a welcome return to form for the current world champion.* ◇ *Your letter was very welcome.* **3** 🔊 B1 *~ to do sth* (*informal*) used to say that you are happy for sb to do sth if they want to: *Everyone is welcome to attend, but places are limited.* **4** *~ to sth* (*informal*) used to say that you are very happy for sb to have sth because you definitely do not want it: *It's an awful job. If you want it, you're welcome to it!*
  IDM **you're 'welcome** 🔊 A2 used as a polite reply when sb thanks you for sth: *'Thanks for your help.' 'You're welcome.'*
- *noun* **1** 🔊 A2 [C, U] something that you do or say to sb when they arrive, especially sth that makes them feel you are happy to see them: *to get/receive a welcome* ◇ *Thank you for your warm welcome.* ◇ *The winners were given an enthusiastic welcome when they arrived home.* ◇ *He returned to a hero's welcome.* ◇ *~ to sth It was a nice welcome to a strange new city.* **2** [C] the way that people react to sth, which shows their opinion of it: *This new comedy deserves a warm welcome.* ◇ *The proposals were given a cautious welcome by the trade unions.*
  IDM **outstay/overstay your 'welcome** to stay somewhere as a guest longer than you are wanted

**'welcome mat** *noun*
IDM **lay, put, roll, etc. out the 'welcome mat (for sb)** (*especially NAmE*) to make sb feel welcome; to try to attract visitors, etc.

**welcome to 'country** (*also* **Welcome to 'Country**) *noun* (*AustralE*) a formal welcome to the traditional land of an Aboriginal people by one or more members of the local Aboriginal community

**wel·com·ing** /ˈwelkəmɪŋ/ *adj.* **1** friendly towards sb who is visiting or arriving: *The locals were extremely welcoming.* ◇ *She gave me a welcoming smile.* **2** (of a place) attractive and looking comfortable to be in OPP **unwelcoming**

**weld** /weld/ *verb, noun*
- *verb* **1** [T, I] to join pieces of metal together by heating their edges and pressing them together: *~ (sth) to weld a broken axle* ◇ *~ A (on) (to B) The car has had a new wing welded on.* ◇ *~ A and B (together) All the parts of the sculpture have to be welded together.* **2** [T] to make people or things join together into a strong and effective group: *~ sb/sth into sth They had welded a bunch of untrained recruits into an efficient fighting force.* ◇ *~ sth together The crisis helped to weld the party together.*
- *noun* a JOINT made by welding

**weld·er** /ˈweldə(r)/ *noun* a person whose job is welding metal

**wel·fare** 0️⃣+ B2 🔊 /ˈwelfeə(r); NAmE -fer/ *noun* [U] **1** 0️⃣+ B2 the general health, happiness and safety of a person, an animal or a group SYN **well-being**: *We are concerned about the child's welfare.* **2** 0️⃣+ B2 practical or financial help that is provided, often by the government, for people or animals that need it: *The state is still the main provider of welfare.* ◇ *child welfare* ◇ *a social welfare programme* ◇ *welfare provision/services/work* ⊃ see also CORPORATE WELFARE ⊃ WORDFINDER NOTE at CHARITY **3** 0️⃣+ B2 (*especially NAmE*) (*BrE usually* **bene·fit** [C, usually pl., U]) money that the government pays regularly to people who are poor, unemployed, sick, etc.: **on ~** *They would rather work than live on welfare.*

**welfare 'state** *noun* **1** *often* **the Welfare State** [usually sing.] a system by which the government provides a range of services to people who need them, for example medical care, money for people without work, care for old people, etc. **2** [C] a country that has such a system

**well** 🔊 A1 /wel/ *adv., adj., exclamation, noun, verb*
- *adv.* (**bet·ter** /ˈbetə(r)/, **best** /best/) **1** 🔊 A1 in a good, right or acceptable way: *They played well in the tournament.* ◇ *The team work well together.* ◇ *The conference was very well organized.* ◇ ***Well done!*** (= expressing admiration for what sb has done) ◇ *His campaign was not going well.* ◇ *These animals make very good pets if treated well* (= with kindness). ◇ *People spoke well of* (= spoke with approval of) *him.* ◇ *She took it very well* (= did not react too badly), *all things considered.* ◇ *They lived well* (= in comfort and spending a lot of money) *and were generous with their money.* **2** 🔊 A1 completely and properly: *Add the lemon juice and mix well.* ◇ *The surface must be well prepared before you start to paint.* ◇ *How well do you know Carla?* ◇ *He's well able to take care of himself.* **3** 🔊 B1 to a great extent or degree: *He was driving at well over the speed limit.* ◇ *She is well aware of the dangers.* ◇ *They are very well suited to each other.* ◇ *a well-loved tale* ◇ *The castle is well worth a visit.* ◇ (*BrE, informal*) *I was well annoyed, I can tell you.* **4** **can/could well** easily: *She could well afford to pay for it herself.* **5** **can/could/may/might well** probably: *You may well be right.* ◇ *It may well be that the train is delayed.* **6** **can/could/may/might well** with good reason: *I can't very well leave now.* ◇ *I couldn't very well refuse to help them, could I?* ◇ *'What are we doing here?' 'You may well ask* (= I don't really know either).'
  IDM **as well (as sb/sth)** 🔊 A2 in addition to sb/sth; too: *Are they coming as well?* ◇ *They sell books as well as newspapers.* ◇ *She is a talented musician as well as being a photographer.* ⊃ note at ALSO **be doing 'well** to be getting healthier after an illness; to be in good health after a birth: *Mother and baby are doing well.* **be well on the way to sth/doing sth** to have nearly achieved sth and be going to achieve it soon: *She is well on the way to recovery.* ◇ *He is well on the way to establishing himself among the top ten players in the world.* **be ˌwell ˈout of sth** (*BrE, informal*) to be lucky that you are not involved in sth unpleasant or difficult to deal with **be ˌwell 'up in sth** to know a lot about sth: *He's well up in all the latest developments.* **do 'well** to be successful: *Jack is doing very well at school.* **do 'well by sb** to treat sb generously **do 'well for yourself** to become successful or rich **do ˌwell ˈout of sth/sb** to

# well

make a profit or get money from sb/sth **do ˈwell to do sth** to be sensible or wise to do sth: *He would do well to concentrate more on his work.* ◊ *You did well to sell when the price was high.* **ˌleave / ˌlet well aˈlone** (*BrE*) (*NAmE* **ˌlet well enough aˈlone**) to not get involved in sth that you have no connection with: *When it comes to other people's arguments, it's better to leave well alone.* **(you, etc.) may / might as well be hanged / hung for a ˈsheep as (for) a ˈlamb** (*saying*) if you are going to be punished for doing sth wrong, whether it is a big or small thing, you may as well do the big thing **may / might (just) as well do sth 1** used to say that sth seems the best thing to do in the situation that you are in, although you may not really want to do it: *If no one else wants it, we might as well give it to him.* **2** used to say that there is no real difference between two things that you might do: *If you are going to have sugar, you may as well have a bar of chocolate.* **ˌwell and ˈtruly** (*informal*) completely: *By that time we were well and truly lost.* **ˌwell aˈway** (*BrE, informal*) **1** having made good progress: *If we got Terry to do that, we'd be well away.* **2** drunk or in a deep sleep **ˌwell ˈin (with sb)** (*informal*) to be good friends with sb, especially sb important: *She seems to be well in with all the right people.* ⇒ more at BLOODY[1], FUCKING, JOLLY *adv.*, KNOW *v.*, MEAN *v.*, PRETTY *adv.*

■ *adj.* (**betˑter** /ˈbetə(r)/, **best** /best/) **1** ? A1 [not usually before noun] in good health: *I don't feel very well.* ◊ *Is she well enough to travel?* ◊ *Get well soon!* (= for example, on a card) ◊ *I'm better now, thank you.* ◊ (*informal*) *He's not a well man.* **2** [not before noun] in a good state or position: *It seems that all is not well at home.* ◊ *All's well that ends well* (= used when sth has ended happily, even though you thought it might not). **3** [not before noun] **(as) ~ (to do sth)** sensible; a good idea: *It would be just as well to call and say we might be late.* ◊ (*formal*) *It would be well to start early.*

IDM ˌall very ˈwell (for sb) (to do sth) (*informal*) used to criticize or reject a remark that sb has made, especially when they were trying to make you feel happier about sth: *It's all very well for you to say it doesn't matter, but I've put a lot of work into this and I want it to be a success.* **ˌall well and ˈgood** (*informal*) quite good but not exactly what is wanted: *That's all well and good, but why didn't he call her to say so?* ⇒ more at ALIVE

■ *exclamation* **1** ? A1 used to express surprise, anger or relief: *Well, well—I would never have guessed it!* ◊ *Well, really! What a thing to say!* ◊ *Well, thank goodness that's over!* **2** A1 used to show that you accept that sth cannot be changed: *Well, it can't be helped.* ◊ *'We lost.' 'Oh, well. Better luck next time.'* **3** ? A1 used to agree to sth, rather unwillingly: *Well, I suppose I could fit you in at 3.45.* ◊ *Oh, very well, then, if you insist.* **4** A1 used when continuing a conversation after a break: *Well, as I was saying …* **5** ? A1 used to say that sth is uncertain: *'Do you want to come?' 'Well, I'm not sure.'* **6** ? A1 used to show that you are waiting for sb to say sth: *Well? Are you going to tell us or not?* **7** ? A1 used to mark the end of a conversation: *Well, I'd better be going now.* **8** used when you are stopping to consider your next words: *I think it happened, well, towards the end of last summer.* **9** used when you want to correct or change sth that you have just said: *There were thousands of people there—well, hundreds, anyway.*

IDM ˌwell I ˈnever (ˈdid)! (*old-fashioned*) used to express surprise ⇒ more at SAY *v.*

■ *noun* **1** ? + C1 a deep hole in the ground from which people obtain water. The sides of wells are usually covered with BRICK or stone and there is usually a cover or a small wall at the top of the well. **2** = OIL WELL **3** a narrow space in a building that drops down from a high to a low level, giving room for stairs or a lift, or to allow light into the building: *a light well* ⇒ see also STAIRWELL **4** (*BrE, specialist*) the space in front of the judge in a court, where the lawyers sit

■ *verb* **1** [I] **~ (up)** (of a liquid) to rise to the surface of sth and start to flow: *Tears were welling up in her eyes.* **2** [I] **~ (up)** (*literary*) (of an emotion) to become stronger: *Hate welled up inside him as he thought of the two of them together.*

---

▼ **GRAMMAR POINT**

**well**
- Compound adjectives beginning with **well** are generally written with no hyphen when they are used alone after a verb, but with a hyphen when they come before a noun: *She is well dressed.* ◊ *a well-dressed woman.* The forms without hyphens are given in the entries in the dictionary, but forms with hyphens can be seen in some example sentences.
- The comparative and superlative forms are usually formed with **better** and **best**: *better-known poets* ◊ *the best-dressed person in the room.*

▼ **SYNONYMS**

**well**
all right • OK • fine • healthy • strong • fit
These words all describe sb who is not ill and is in good health.

**well** [not usually before noun] (*rather informal*) in good health: *I'm not feeling very well.* ◊ *Is he well enough to travel?* NOTE **Well** is used especially to talk about your own health, to ask sb about their health or to make a comment on it.

**all right** [not before noun] (*rather informal*) not feeling ill; not injured: *Are you feeling all right?*

**OK** [not before noun] (*informal*) not feeling ill; not injured: *She says she's OK now, and will be back at work tomorrow.*

**ALL RIGHT OR OK?**
These words are slightly less positive than the other words in this group. They are both used in spoken English to talk about not actually being ill or injured, rather than being positively in good health. Both are rather informal but **OK** is slightly more informal than **all right**.

**fine** [not before noun] (not used in negative statements) (*rather informal*) completely well: *'How are you?' 'Fine, thanks.'* NOTE **Fine** is used especially to talk about your health, especially when sb asks you how you are. It is also used to talk about sb's health when you are talking to sb else. Unlike **well** it is not often used to ask sb about their health or make a comment on it: *Are you keeping fine?*

**healthy** in good health and not likely to become ill: *Keep healthy by exercising regularly.*

**strong** in good health and not suffering from an illness: *After a few weeks she was feeling stronger.* NOTE **Strong** is often used to talk about becoming healthy again after an illness.

**fit** (*especially BrE*) in good physical health, especially because you take regular physical exercise: *I go swimming every day in order to keep fit.*

**PATTERNS**
- all right / OK / fit **for** sth
- all right / OK / fit **to do** sth
- to **feel / look** well / all right / OK / fine / healthy / strong / fit
- to **keep (sb)** well / healthy / fit
- **perfectly** well / all right / OK / fine / healthy / fit
- **physically** well / healthy / strong / fit

**weˈll** /wiːl, wɪl/ *short form* **1** we will **2** we shall

**ˌwell adˈjusted** *adj.* (of a person) able to deal with people, problems and life in general in a normal, sensible way ⇒ compare MALADJUSTED

**ˌwell adˈvised** *adj.* [not before noun] **~ (to do sth)** acting in the most sensible way: *You would be well advised to tackle this problem urgently.* ⇒ compare ILL-ADVISED

**ˌwell apˈpointed** *adj.* (*formal*) having all the necessary equipment; having comfortable and attractive furniture, etc.

**ˌwell atˈtended** *adj.* attended by a lot of people: *a well-attended conference*

**ˌwell ˈbalanced** *adj.* **1** containing a sensible variety of the sort of things or people that are needed: *a well-balanced diet* ◊ *The team was not well balanced.* **2** (of a person or their behaviour) sensible and emotionally in control: *His response was well balanced.*

**well be'haved** *adj.* behaving in a way that other people think is polite or correct: *a well-behaved child* ◊ *The audience was surprisingly well behaved.*

**'well-being** ?+ C1 *noun* [U] general health and happiness: *emotional/physical/psychological well-being* ◊ *to have a sense of well-being*

**well 'born** *adj.* (*old-fashioned, formal*) from a rich family or a family from a high social class

**well 'bred** *adj.* (*old-fashioned, formal*) having or showing good manners; typical of a high social class: *a well-bred young lady* ◊ *She was too well bred to show her disappointment.* OPP **ill-bred**

**well 'built** *adj.* **1** (of a person) with a solid, strong body **2** (of a building or machine) strongly made

**well con'nected** *adj.* (of a person) having important or rich friends or relatives

**well 'cut** *adj.* (of clothes) made well and therefore probably expensive

**well de'fined** *adj.* easy to see or understand: *well-defined rules* ◊ *These categories are not well defined.* OPP **ill-defined**

**well de'veloped** *adj.* fully developed; fully grown: *He had a well-developed sense of his own superiority.*

**well di'sposed** *adj.* ~ **(towards/to sb/sth)** having friendly feelings towards sb or a positive attitude towards sth OPP **ill-disposed**

**well 'documented** *adj.* having a lot of written evidence to prove, support or explain it: *The problem is well documented.* ◊ *well-documented facts*

**well 'done** *adj.* (of food, especially meat) cooked completely or for a long time: *He prefers his steak well done.* ⊃ compare RARE, UNDERDONE

**well 'dressed** *adj.* wearing fashionable or expensive clothes: *This is what today's well-dressed man is wearing.*

**well 'earned** *adj.* much deserved: *a well-earned rest*

**well en'dowed** *adj.* **1** (*informal, humorous*) (of a woman) having large breasts **2** (*informal, humorous*) (of a man) having large GENITALS **3** (of an organization) having a lot of money: *well-endowed colleges*

**well e'stablished** *adj.* having a respected position, because of being successful, etc. over a long period: *a well-established firm* ◊ *He is now well established in his career.*

**well 'fed** *adj.* having plenty of good food to eat regularly: *well-fed family pets* ◊ *The animals all looked well fed and cared for.*

**well 'formed** *adj.* (*linguistics*) (of sentences) written or spoken correctly according to the rules of grammar

**well 'founded** (*also less frequent* **well 'grounded**) *adj.* having good reasons or evidence to cause or support it: *well-founded suspicions* ◊ *His fear turned out to be well founded.* OPP **ill-founded**

**well 'groomed** *adj.* (of a person) looking clean, neat and carefully dressed

**well 'grounded** *adj.* **1** ~ **in sth** having a good training in a subject or skill **2** = WELL FOUNDED

**well 'heeled** /ˌwel ˈhiːld/ *adj.* (*informal*) having a lot of money SYN **rich, wealthy**

**well 'hung** *adj.* **1** (of meat) having been left for several days before being cooked in order to improve the taste **2** (of a man) (*informal*) having a large PENIS

**well in'formed** *adj.* having or showing knowledge or information about many subjects or about one particular subject: *a well-informed decision* OPP **ill-informed**

**wel·ling·ton** /ˈwelɪŋtən/ (*also* **wellington boot**, *informal* **welly**) (*all BrE*) (*NAmE* **rubber boot**) *noun* one of a pair of long rubber boots, usually reaching almost up to the knee, that you wear to stop your feet getting wet: *a pair of wellingtons*

**well in'ten·tioned** /ˌwel ɪnˈtenʃnd/ *adj.* intending to be helpful or useful but not always succeeding very well SYN **well meaning**

**well 'kept** *adj.* **1** kept neat and in good condition: *well-kept gardens* **2** (of a secret) known only to a few people

**well 'known** *adj.* **1** known about by a lot of people SYN **famous**: *a well-known actor* ◊ *His books are not well known.* **2** (of a fact) generally known and accepted: *It is a well-known fact that caffeine is a stimulant.*

**well 'mannered** *adj.* (*formal*) having good manners SYN **polite** OPP **ill-mannered**

**well 'matched** *adj.* able to live together, play or fight each other, etc. because they are similar in character, ability, etc: *a well-matched couple* ◊ *The two teams were well matched.*

**well 'meaning** *adj.* intending to do what is right and helpful but often not succeeding SYN **well intentioned**: *a well-meaning attempt to be helpful* ◊ *He's very well meaning.*

**well 'meant** *adj.* done, said, etc. in order to be helpful but often not succeeding: *well-meant comments* ◊ *His offer was well meant.*

**well·ness** /ˈwelnəs/ *noun* [U] (*especially NAmE*) the state of being healthy, especially when you actively try to achieve this

**well-'nigh** *adv.* almost: *Defence was well-nigh impossible against such opponents.*

**well 'off** *adj.* **1** (*comparative* **better 'off**, no *superlative*) having a lot of money SYN **rich**: *a well-off family* ◊ *They are much better off than us.* ⊃ SYNONYMS at RICH **2** (**better 'off**, **best 'off**) in a good situation: *I've got my own room so I'm well off.* ◊ *Some people don't know when they're well off.* OPP **badly off**

IDM **be well 'off for sth** (*BrE*) to have enough of sth: *We're well off for jobs around here* (= there are many available).

**well 'oiled** *adj.* operating smoothly and well: *The system ran like a well-oiled machine.*

**well 'paid** *adj.* earning or providing a lot of money: *well-paid managers* ◊ *The job is very well paid.*

**well 'placed** *adj.* in a good position to do sth: ~ **for sth** *The port is well placed for European trade.* ◊ ~ **to do sth** *As a successful farmer and businessman, he is well placed to take advantage of developments in agriculture.*

**well pre'served** *adj.* not showing many signs of age; kept in good condition

**well 'read** *adj.* having read many books and therefore having gained a lot of knowledge

**well 'rounded** *adj.* **1** having a variety of experiences and abilities and a fully developed personality: *well-rounded individuals* **2** providing or showing a variety of experience, ability, etc: *a well-rounded education* **3** (of a person's body) pleasantly round in shape

**well 'run** *adj.* managed smoothly and well: *a well-run hotel*

**well 'spoken** *adj.* (*approving*) having a way of speaking that is considered educated and correct

**well·spring** /ˈwelsprɪŋ/ *noun* (*literary*) a supply or source of a particular quality, especially one that never ends

**well 'thought of** *adj.* respected, admired and liked: *Their family has always been well thought of around here.*

**well thought 'out** *adj.* carefully planned

**well 'thumbed** *adj.* a **well-thumbed** book has been read many times

**well 'timed** *adj.* done or happening at the right time or at an appropriate time SYN **timely**: *a well-timed intervention* ◊ *Your remarks were certainly well timed.* OPP **ill-timed**

**well-to-'do** *adj.* having a lot of money SYN **rich, wealthy**: *a well-to-do family* ◊ *They're very well-to-do.*

**well travelled** (BrE) (NAmE **well traveled**) adj. **1** (of a person) having travelled to many different places **2** (of a route) used by a lot of people

**well 'tried** adj. used many times before and known to be successful: *a well-tried method*

**well 'trodden** adj. (*formal*) (of a road or path) much used

**well 'turned** adj. (*formal*) expressed in an intelligent way: *a well-turned phrase*

**well used** /ˌwel ˈjuːzd/ adj. used a lot: *a well-used path*

**'well-wisher** noun a person who wants to show that they support sb and want them to be happy, successful, etc.

**well 'worn** adj. **1** worn or used a lot or for a long time: *a well-worn jacket* ◊ *Most British visitors beat a well-worn path to the same tourist areas of the US.* **2** (of a phrase, story, etc.) heard so often that it does not sound interesting any more **SYN** hackneyed

**welly** /ˈweli/ noun, verb
■ noun (*pl.* -ies) (BrE, *informal*) = WELLINGTON: *a pair of green wellies*
**IDM** **give it some 'welly** (BrE, *informal*) to use a lot of physical effort
■ verb (**wel·lies, welly·ing, wel·lied, wel·lied**) ~ **sth (+ adv. / prep.)** (BrE, *informal*) to hit or kick sth very hard: *He wellied the ball over the bar.*

**Welsh** /welʃ/ noun, adj.
■ noun **1** [U] the Celtic language of Wales: *Do you speak Welsh?* **2 the Welsh** [pl.] the people of Wales
■ adj. of or connected with Wales, its people or its language: *Welsh poetry*

**welsh** /welʃ/ (*also* **welch**) verb [I] ~ **(on sb / sth)** (*disapproving, informal*) to not do sth that you have promised to do, for example to not pay money that you owe: *'I'm not in the habit of welshing on deals,' said Don.*

**the ˌWelsh Asˈsembly** (*also the* **National Asˈsembly for ˈWales**) noun [sing.] the group of people who are elected as a government for Wales, which is to some extent independent of the UK parliament and has the power to make some laws

**ˌWelsh 'dresser** noun (BrE) = DRESSER (1)

**welt** /welt/ noun a raised red mark on the skin where sth has hit or rubbed you **SYN** weal

**wel·ter** /ˈweltə(r)/ noun [sing.] ~ **of sth** (*formal*) a large and confusing amount of sth: *a welter of information*

**wel·ter·weight** /ˈweltəweɪt/ NAmE -tərw-/ noun [U, C] a weight in BOXING and other sports, between LIGHTWEIGHT and MIDDLEWEIGHT, in BOXING usually between 60 and 67 KILOGRAMS; a BOXER or other competitor in this class: *a welterweight champion*

**wench** /wentʃ/ noun (*old use or humorous*) a young woman

**wend** /wend/ verb [T, I] ~ **(your way)** (+ **adv. / prep.**) (*old use* or *literary*) to move or travel slowly somewhere: *Leo wended his way home through the wet streets.*

**Wendy house** /ˈwendi haʊs/ noun (BrE) = PLAYHOUSE

**went** /went/ past tense of GO

**wept** /wept/ past tense, past part. of WEEP

**were** /wə(r), *strong form* wɜː(r)/ ⊃ BE verb

**we're** /wɪə(r), NAmE wɪr/ short form we are

**weren't** /wɜːnt; NAmE wɜːrnt/ short form were not

**were·wolf** /ˈweəwʊlf; NAmE ˈwerw-/ noun (*pl.* **-wolves** /-wʊlvz/) (in stories) a person who sometimes changes into a WOLF, especially at the time of the full moon

**west** ⊙ A1 /west/ noun, adj., adv.
■ noun [U, sing.] (*also* **W**) **1** 🔑 A1 *usually* **the west** the direction that you look towards to see the sun go down; one of the four main points of the COMPASS: *Which way is west?* ◊ *Rain is spreading from the west.* ◊ **to the ~ (of …)** *He lives to the west of (= further west than) the town.* ⊃ picture at COMPASS ⊃ compare EAST, NORTH, SOUTH **2** 🔑 A1 **the west, the West** the western part of a country, region or city: *The west of the country is especially popular with tourists.* ◊ *in the ~ Elsewhere in the West, wet, unsettled weather will continue until the weekend.* **3** 🔑 A1 **the West** Europe and North America, contrasted with other parts of the world: *I was born in Japan, but I've lived in the West for some years now.* **4 the West** (NAmE) the western side of the US: *the history of the American West* ⊃ see also MIDWEST, WILD WEST **5 the West** (in the past) Western Europe and North America, when contrasted with the Communist countries of Eastern Europe: *East–West relations*
■ adj. [only before noun] (*abbr.* **W**) **1** 🔑 A1 in or towards the west: *West Africa* ◊ *the west coast of Scotland* **2** **a west wind** blows from the west: *prevailing west winds* ⊃ compare WESTERLY
■ adv. **1** 🔑 A1 towards the west: *This room faces west.* **2** 🔑 A1 ~ **of sth** nearer to the west than sth: *They live five miles west of Dublin.*

**west·bound** /ˈwestbaʊnd/ adj. travelling or leading towards the west: *westbound traffic* ◊ *the westbound carriageway of the motorway*

**the ˌWest ˈCoast** noun [sing.] the states on the west coast of the US, especially California

**the ˌWest ˈEnd** noun [sing.] the western area of central London where there are many theatres, shops and hotels

**west·er·ly** /ˈwestəli; NAmE -stərli/ adj., noun
■ adj. **1** [only before noun] in or towards the west: *travelling in a westerly direction* **2** [usually before noun] (of winds) blowing from the west: *westerly gales* ⊃ compare WEST
■ noun (*pl.* -ies) a wind that blows from the west: *light westerlies*

**west·ern** ⊙ B1 /ˈwestən; NAmE -stərn/ adj., noun
■ adj. **1** [only before noun] (*abbr.* **W**) **Western** located in the west or facing west: *western Spain* ◊ *Western Europe* ◊ *the western slopes of the mountain* ◊ *all over the western hemisphere* **2** 🔑 B1 *usually* **Western** connected with the west part of the world, especially Europe and North America: *Western art* ◊ *the Western world*
■ noun a film or book about life in the western US in the nineteenth century, usually involving COWBOYS

**west·ern·er** /ˈwestənə(r); NAmE -stərn-/ noun **1** a person who comes from or lives in the western part of the world, especially Western Europe or North America **2 Westerner** a person who was born in or who lives in western Canada or the US

**west·ern·ize** (BrE *also* **-ise**) /ˈwestənaɪz; NAmE -stərn-/ verb [*usually passive*] to bring ideas or ways of life that are typical of Western Europe and North America to other countries: **be westernized (by sth)** *The islands have been westernized by the growth of tourism.* ▸ **west·ern·iza·tion, -isa·tion** noun [U] **west·ern·ized, -ised** adj.: *a westernized society*

**west·ern·most** /ˈwestənməʊst; NAmE -stərn-/ adj. located furthest west: *the westernmost tip of the island*

**the ˌWest ˈIndies** /ðə ˌwest ˈɪndiz; -diːz; NAmE -diːz/ noun [pl.] several groups of islands between the Caribbean and the Atlantic, that include the Antilles and the Bahamas ▸ **ˌWest ˈIndian** adj., **ˌWest ˈIndian** noun

**West·min·ster** /ˈwestmɪnstə(r)/ noun [U] the British parliament and government: *The rumours were still circulating at Westminster.* **ORIGIN** From the name of the part of London with the Houses of Parliament, Downing Street and many government offices.

**ˌwest-north-ˈwest** noun [sing.] (*abbr.* **WNW**) the direction at an equal distance between west and north-west ▸ **ˌwest-north-ˈwest** adv.

**the ˌWest ˈSide** noun [sing.] the western part of Manhattan in New York City, which includes Broadway and Central Park

**ˌwest-south-ˈwest** noun [sing.] (*abbr.* **WSW**) the direction at an equal distance between west and south-west ▸ **ˌwest-south-ˈwest** adv.

**west·wards** /ˈwestwədz; NAmE -wərdz/ (*especially BrE*) (*also* **west·ward** *especially in NAmE*) adv. towards the west: *to turn westwards* ▸ **west·ward** adj.: *in a westward direction*

**wet** /wet/ adj., verb, noun [A2]

■ **adj.** (**wet·ter**, **wet·test**) **1** [A2] covered with or containing liquid, especially water: *wet clothes/hair/grass* ◊ *You'll get wet* (= in the rain) *if you go out now.* ◊ *Try not to get your shoes wet.* ◊ *His face was wet with tears.* ◊ *We were all soaking wet* (= extremely wet). ◊ *Her hair was still dripping wet.* ◊ *My shirt was wet through* (= completely wet). **2** [A2] (of weather, etc.) with rain: *a spell of cold, wet weather* ◊ *a wet climate* ◊ *a wet day* ◊ *It's wet outside.* ◊ *It's going to be wet tomorrow.* ◊ *It was the wettest October for many years.* **3** [A2] (of paint, ink, etc.) not yet dry: *Keep off! Wet paint.* **4** if a child or its NAPPY is **wet**, its nappy is full of URINE **5** (*BrE*) (of a person) (*informal, disapproving*) not having a strong character [SYN] **feeble, wimpish**: *'Don't be so wet,' she laughed.* ▶ **wet·ly** adv. **wet·ness** noun [U]
[IDM] **all 'wet** (*NAmE, informal*) completely wrong (**still**) **wet behind the 'ears** (*informal, disapproving*) young and without much experience [SYN] **naive** ⊃ more at FOOT *n.*

■ **verb** (**wet·ting**, **wet**, **wet** or **wet·ting**, **wet·ted**, **wet·ted**) ~ **sth** to make sth wet: *Wet the brush slightly before putting it in the paint.*
[IDM] **wet the/your 'bed** [no passive] to URINATE in your bed by accident: *It is quite common for small children to wet their beds.* **'wet yourself** (*also* **wet your 'pants/ 'knickers**) [no passive] to URINATE in your underwear by accident

■ **noun 1 the wet** [sing.] wet weather; rain: *Come in out of the wet.* **2 the wet** [sing.] liquid, especially water: *The dog shook the wet from its coat.* **3** [C] (*BrE, disapproving*) a Conservative politician who supports MODERATE policies rather than extreme ones: *Tory wets* **4** [C] (*BrE, informal, disapproving*) a person who does not have a strong character [SYN] **wimp**

▼ **SYNONYMS**

**wet**

moist • damp • soaked • drenched • saturated

These words all describe things covered with or full of liquid, especially water.

**wet** covered with or full of liquid, especially water: *The car had skidded on the wet road.* ◊ *You'll get wet* (= in the rain) *if you go out now.*

**moist** slightly wet, often in a way that is pleasant or useful: *a lovely rich moist cake*

**damp** slightly wet, often in a way that is unpleasant: *The cottage was cold and damp.*

**soaked** (*rather informal*) very wet: *You're soaked through!* (= completely wet)

**drenched** very wet: *We were caught in the storm and came home drenched to the skin.*

**SOAKED OR DRENCHED?**

Both of these words can be used with *with* or *in*: *soaked/ drenched with/in sweat/blood*. **Soaked** but not usually **drenched** can also be used before a noun: *their soaked clothes* ◊ *their drenched clothes*

**saturated** very wet: *The ground is completely saturated: it would be pointless to plant anything.*

PATTERNS

- wet/moist/damp/soaked/drenched/saturated **with** sth
- soaked/drenched **in** sth
- sb's **coat/shirt/shoes/clothes/hair** is/are wet/damp/ soaked/drenched
- wet/moist/damp/saturated **ground/earth**
- **to get** wet/moist/damp/soaked/drenched/saturated

**wet 'blanket** noun (*informal, disapproving*) a person who is not enthusiastic about anything and who stops other people from enjoying themselves

**wet 'dream** noun **1** a sexually exciting dream that a man has that results in EJACULATION of SEMEN **2** (*informal*) something that appeals very much to a particular type of person: *The kitchen is a gourmet chef's wet dream.*

**wet·land** /'wetlənd/ noun [C, U] (*also* **wetlands** [pl.]) an area of land that is naturally wet most or all of the time: *The wetlands are home to a large variety of wildlife.* ▶ **wet·land** adj. [only before noun]: *wetland birds*

**'wet look** noun [sing.] the appearance of hair being shiny and wet, obtained by using hair GEL or by treating it with chemicals ▶ **'wet-look** adj.: *wet-look hair gel*

**'wet nurse** noun (usually in the past) a woman employed to feed another woman's baby with her own breast milk

**'wet room** noun (*BrE*) a bathroom in which the shower is not separated from the rest of the room

**wet·suit** /'wetsu:t/ noun a piece of clothing made of rubber that fits the whole body closely, worn, for example, by people swimming UNDERWATER or sailing in order to keep warm

**we've** /wi:v, weak form wiv/ short form we have [HELP] We've is usually only used when *have* is an auxiliary verb: *We've just got here.* When *have* is the main verb, use the full form: *We have two children.* ◊ *We've two children.*

**whack** /wæk/ verb, noun

■ **verb 1** ~ **sb/sth** (+ **adv./prep.**) (*informal*) to hit sb/sth very hard: *She whacked him with her handbag.* ◊ *James whacked the ball over the net.* **2** ~ **sth** + **adv./prep.** (*informal*) to put sth somewhere without much care: *Just whack your bags in the corner.* **3** ~ **sb** (*NAmE, slang*) to murder sb

■ **noun** [usually sing.] (*informal*) **1** the act of hitting sb/sth hard; the sound made by this: *He gave the ball a good whack.* ◊ *I heard the whack of the bullet hitting the wood.* **2** (*BrE*) a share of sth; an amount of sth: *Don't leave all the work to her. Everyone should do their fair whack.* ◊ *You have to pay the full whack. There are no reductions.* ◊ *He charges top whack* (= the highest amount possible).
[IDM] **out of 'whack** (*informal, especially NAmE*) **1** no longer correct or working properly: *The system is clearly out of whack.* ◊ *All the traveling had thrown my body out of whack.* **2** not agreeing with or the same as sth else: *Expectations and reality got out of whack.*

**whacked** /wækt/ (*also* **whacked 'out**) adj. [not usually before noun] (*BrE, informal*) very tired: *I'm whacked!*

**whack·ing** /'wækɪŋ/ (*also* **whacking great**) adj. (*BrE, informal*) used to emphasize how big or how much sth is [SYN] **whopping**: *a whacking great hole in the roof* ◊ *They were fined a whacking £100000.*

**whacko** = WACKO

**whacky** = WACKY

**whale** /weɪl/ noun a very large animal that lives in the sea and looks like a very large fish. There are several types of whale, some of which are hunted: *whale meat* ⊃ see also BLUE WHALE, KILLER WHALE, PILOT WHALE, SPERM WHALE ◆ HOMOPHONES at WAIL
[IDM] **have a 'whale of a time** (*informal*) to enjoy yourself very much; to have a very good time

**whale·bone** /'weɪlbəʊn/ noun [U] a thin, hard substance found in the upper JAW of some types of whale, used in the past to make some clothes stiffer

**whal·er** /'weɪlə(r)/ noun **1** a ship used for hunting whales **2** a person who hunts whales

**whal·ing** /'weɪlɪŋ/ noun [U] the activity or business of hunting and killing WHALES

**wham** /wæm/ exclamation (*informal*) **1** used to represent the sound of a sudden, loud hit: *The bombs went down— wham!—right on target.* **2** used to show that sth is unexpected has suddenly happened: *I saw him yesterday and—wham!—I realized I was still in love with him.*

**whammy** /'wæmi/ noun (*pl.* **-ies**) (*informal*) an unpleasant situation or event that causes problems for sb/sth: *With this government we've had a double whammy of tax increases and benefit cuts.* [ORIGIN] From the 1950s American cartoon *Li'l Abner*, in which one of the characters could **shoot a whammy** (put a curse on sb) by pointing a finger with one eye open, or a **double whammy** with both eyes open.

**wha·nau** /'fɑːnaʊ/ noun (*pl.* **wha·nau**) (*NZE*) a family or community of related families who live together in the same area

---

[O] Oxford Phrasal Academic Lexicon (OPAL) written and spoken word lists | [W] OPAL written word list | [S] OPAL spoken word list

# wharf 1776

**wharf** /wɔ:f; NAmE wɔ:rf/ noun (pl. **wharves** /wɔ:vz; NAmE wɔ:rvz/ or **wharfs**) a flat structure built next to the sea or a river where boats can be tied up and goods unloaded

**what** ⓘ A1 /wɒt; NAmE wʌt/ pron., det. **1** A1 used in questions to ask for particular information about sb/sth: *What is your name?* ◊ *What (= what job) does he do?* ◊ *What time is it?* ◊ *What kind of music do you like?* ⊃ compare WHICH **2** A1 the thing or things that; whatever: *What you need is a good meal.* ◊ *Nobody knows what will happen next.* ◊ *I spent what little time I had with my family.* **3** A1 used to say that you think that sth is especially good, bad, etc: *What awful weather!* ◊ *What a beautiful house!* IDM **and ˌwhat ˈnot** | **and what ˈhave you** (*informal*) and other things of the same type: *It's full of old toys, books and what not.* **ˌget/ˌgive sb what ˈfor** (*informal*) to be punished/ punish sb severely: *I'll give her what for if she does that again.* **or ˈwhat** (*informal*) **1** used to emphasize your opinion: *Is he stupid or what?* **2** used when you are not sure about sth: *I don't know if he's a teacher or what.* ◊ *Are we going now or what?* **ˈwhat?** (*informal*) **1** used when you have not heard or have not understood sth: *What? I can't hear you.* **2** used to show that you have heard sb and to ask what they want: *'Mummy!' 'What?' 'I'm thirsty.'* **3** used to express surprise or anger: *'It will cost $500.' 'What?'* ◊ *'I asked her to marry me.' 'You what?'* **ˌwhat aˈbout …?** (*informal*) **1** A1 used to make a suggestion: *What about a trip to France?* **2** A1 used to introduce sb/sth into the conversation: *What about you, Joe? Do you like football?* **ˈwhat-d'you-call-him/-her/-it/-them** | **ˈwhat's-his/ -her/-its/-their-name** used instead of a name that you cannot remember: *She's just gone out with old what-d'you- call-him.* **ˌwhat ˈfor?** for what purpose or reason?: *What is this tool for?* ◊ *What did you do that for (= why did you do that)?* ◊ *'I need to see a doctor.' 'What for?'* **ˌwhat ˈif …?** what would happen if?: *What if the train is late?* ◊ *What if she forgets to bring it?* **ˌwhat ˈof it?** (*informal*) used when admitting that sth is true, to ask why it should be considered important: *Yes, I wrote the article. What of it?* **ˌwhat's ˌall ˈthat about?** (*BrE*) (*NAmE* **ˌwhat's ˌup with ˈthat?**) used to suggest that sth you have heard is a stupid idea or does not make sense: *They dropped their best player. What's all that about?* **(ˌknow) what's ˈwhat** (*informal*) (know) what things are useful, important, etc. **ˌwhat's ˌwith sb?** (*NAmE, informal*) used to ask why sb is behaving in a strange way: *What's with you? You haven't said a word all morning.* **ˌwhat's ˌwith sth?** (*NAmE, informal*) used to ask the reason for sth: *What's with all this walking? Can't we take a cab?* **what with sth** used to list the various reasons for sth: *What with the cold weather and my bad leg, I haven't been out for weeks.* ⊃ more at COME *v.*, SAY *v.*, SO *conj.*

**what·ev·er** ⓘ B1 Ⓢ /wɒtˈevə(r); NAmE wət-/ det., pron., adv.
■ **det., pron. 1** B1 any or every; anything or everything: *Take whatever action is needed.* ◊ *Do whatever you like.* **2** B1 used when you are saying that it does not matter what sb does or what happens, because the result will be the same: *Whatever decision he made I would support it.* ◊ *You have our support, whatever you decide.* **3** (*especially BrE*) used in questions to express surprise or lack of understanding: *Whatever do you mean?* ◊ *Chocolate-flavoured carrots! Whatever next?* **4** (*informal, ironic*) used as a reply to tell sb that you do not care what happens or that you are not interested in what they are talking about: *'You should try a herbal remedy.' 'Yeah, whatever.'* **5** (*informal*) used to say that you do not mind what you do, have, etc. and that anything is acceptable: *'What would you like to do today?' 'Whatever.'* IDM **or whatˈever** (*informal*) or sth of a similar type: *It's the same in any situation: in a prison, hospital or whatever.* **whatˈever you ˈdo** used to warn sb not to do sth under any circumstances: *Don't tell Paul, whatever you do!* ⊃ more at SAY *v.*
■ **adv. 1** C1 (*also* **what·so·ever**) **no, nothing, none, etc.** ~ not at all; not of any kind: *They received no help whatever.* ◊ *'Is there any doubt about it?' 'None whatsoever.'* **2** (*informal*) used to say that it does not matter what sb does, or what happens, because the result will be the same: *We told him we'd back him whatever.*

**what·not** /ˈwɒtnɒt; NAmE ˈwʌtnɑ:t/ noun [U] **and ~** (*informal*) used when you are referring to sth, but are not being exact and do not mention its name: *It's a new firm. They make toys and whatnot.*

**WhatsApp™** /ˈwɒtsæp, ˌwɒtsˈæp; NAmE ˈwʌtsæp, ˌwʌtsˈæp/ noun, verb
■ **noun** a phone app that allows you to send messages, photos and short videos to one or more people
■ **verb** [T, I] ~ (sb) to send a message, photo or video using the WhatsApp service

**whats·it** /ˈwɒtsɪt; NAmE ˈwʌt-/ noun (*especially BrE, informal*) used when you cannot think of the word or name you want, or do not want to use a particular word: *I've got to make a whatsit for the party. That's it—a flan.*

**ˌwhat·soˈever** ⓘ C1 /ˌwɒtsəʊˈevə(r); NAmE ˌwʌt-/ adv. = WHATEVER

**wheat** ⓘ B2 /wi:t/ noun [U] a plant grown for its grain that is used to produce the flour for bread, cakes, PASTA, etc.; the grain of this plant: *wheat flour* ⊃ VISUAL VOCAB page V8 IDM **sort out/separate the ˌwheat from the ˈchaff** to recognize the difference between useful or valuable people or things and those that are not useful or have no value

**whee** /wi:/ exclamation used to express excitement

**whee·dle** /ˈwi:dl/ verb (*disapproving*) to persuade sb to give you sth or do sth by saying nice things that you do not mean SYN **coax**: **~ sth (out of sb)** *The kids can always wheedle money out of their father.* ◊ **~ sb into doing sth** *She wheedled me into lending her my new coat.* ◊ **+ speech** *'Come on, Em,' he wheedled.*

**wheel** ⓘ A2 /wi:l/ noun, verb
■ **noun**
• **ON/IN VEHICLES 1** ⓘ A2 [C] one of the round objects under a car, bicycle, bus, etc. that turns when it moves: *He braked suddenly, causing the front wheels to skid.* ◊ **on wheels** *One of the boys was pushing the other along in a little box on wheels.* ⊃ see also PADDLE WHEEL **2** B1 [C, usually sing.] the round object used for controlling the direction in which a car, etc. or ship moves: *Always keep both hands on the wheel.* ◊ **behind the ~** *Never get behind the wheel if you're too tired.* ◊ **at the ~** *A car swept past with Laura at the wheel.* ⊃ see also HELM, STEERING WHEEL **3 wheels** [pl.] (*informal*) a car: *At last he had his own wheels.*
• **IN MACHINE 4** [C] a flat, round part in a machine: *gear wheels* ⊃ see also CARTWHEEL, CATHERINE WHEEL, FERRIS WHEEL, MILL WHEEL, SPINNING WHEEL, WATERWHEEL
• **ORGANIZATION/SYSTEM 5 wheels** [pl.] **~ (of sth)** an organization or a system that seems to work like a complicated machine that is difficult to understand: *the wheels of bureaucracy/commerce/government* ◊ *It was Rob's idea. I merely set the wheels in motion (= started the process).*
• **-WHEELED 6** (in adjectives) having the number or type of wheels mentioned: *a sixteen-wheeled lorry*
• **-WHEELER 7** (in nouns) a car, bicycle, etc. with the number of wheels mentioned: *a three-wheeler*
IDM **ˌwheels within ˈwheels** a situation that is difficult to understand because it involves complicated or secret processes and decisions: *There are wheels within wheels in this organization—you never really know what is going on.* ⊃ more at ASLEEP, COG, GREASE *v.*, OIL *v.*, REINVENT, SHOULDER *n.*, SPOKE *n.*
■ **verb**
• **MOVE STH/SB WITH WHEELS 1** [T] **~sth (+ adv./prep.)** to push or pull sth that has wheels: *She wheeled her bicycle across the road.* **2** [T] **~sb/sth (+ adv./prep.)** to move sb/sth that is in or on sth that has wheels: *The nurse wheeled him along the corridor.*
• **MOVE IN CIRCLE 3** [I] **(+ adv./prep.)** to move or fly in a circle: *Birds wheeled above us in the sky.*
• **TURN QUICKLY 4** [I, T] to turn quickly or suddenly and face the opposite direction; to make sb/sth do this: **(+ adv./**

**prep.**) *She wheeled around and started running.* ◊ **~ sb/sth (+ adv./prep.)** *He wheeled his horse back to the gate.* **IDM** **ˌwheel and ˈdeal** (usually used in the progressive tenses) (*often disapproving*) to do a lot of complicated deals in business or politics, often in a dishonest way **PHRV** **ˌwheel sth↔ˈout** to show or use sth to help you do sth, even when it has often been seen or heard before: *They wheeled out the same old arguments we'd heard so many times before.*

**ˈwheel arch** *noun* a space in the body of a vehicle over a wheel, like an ARCH in shape

**wheel·bar·row** /ˈwiːlbærəʊ/ (*also* **barˈrow**) *noun* a large open container with a wheel and two handles that you use outside to carry things

**wheel·base** /ˈwiːlbeɪs/ *noun* [sing.] (*specialist*) the distance between the front and back wheels of a car or other vehicle

**wheel·chair** /ˈwiːltʃeə(r); *NAmE* -tʃer/ *noun* a special chair with wheels, used by people who cannot walk because of illness, an accident, etc: *He's been confined to a wheelchair since the accident.* ◊ *Does the hotel have wheelchair access?* ◊ *wheelchair users*

**ˈwheel clamp** *noun* (*BrE*) = CLAMP, DENVER BOOT

**wheeler-dealer** /ˌwiːlə ˈdiːlə(r); *NAmE* ˌwiːlər-/ *noun* (*informal, often disapproving*) a person who does a lot of complicated deals in business or politics, often in a dishonest way

**wheel·house** /ˈwiːlhaʊs/ *noun* **1** a small CABIN with walls and a roof on a ship where the person controlling the direction in which the ship moves stands at the wheel **2** (*NAmE*) a person's area of expert knowledge or experience: **in sb's ~** *The movie has superstar DiCaprio in a role that is right in his wheelhouse.*

**wheelie** /ˈwiːli/ *noun* (*informal*) a trick that you can do on a bicycle or motorcycle by balancing on the back wheel, with the front wheel off the ground: *to do a wheelie*

**ˈwheelie bin** *noun* (*BrE, informal*) a large container with a LID (= cover) and wheels, that you keep outside your house and use for putting rubbish in

**wheel·wright** /ˈwiːlraɪt/ *noun* a person whose job is making and repairing wheels, especially wooden ones

**wheeze** /wiːz/ *verb, noun*
■ *verb* [I, T] to breathe noisily and with difficulty: *He was coughing and wheezing all night.* ◊ **+ speech** '*I have a chest infection,*' *she wheezed.*
■ *noun* [usually sing.] **1** the high, WHISTLING sound that your chest makes when you cannot breathe easily **2** (*BrE, old-fashioned, informal*) a clever trick or plan

**wheezy** /ˈwiːzi/ *adj.* making the high, WHISTLING sound that your chest makes when you cannot breathe easily: *I'm wheezy today.* ◊ *a wheezy cough* ▶ **wheez·ily** /-zɪli/ *adv.* **wheezi·ness** *noun* [U]

**whelk** /welk/ *noun* a small SHELLFISH that can be eaten

**whelp** /welp/ *noun, verb*
■ *noun* (*specialist*) a young animal of the dog family; a PUPPY or CUB
■ *verb* [I, T] **~ (sth)** (*specialist*) (of a female dog) to give birth to a PUPPY or PUPPIES

**when** 🔊 **A1** /wen/ *adv., pron., conj.*
■ *adv.* **1** **A1** (used in questions) at what time; on what occasion: *When did you last see him?* ◊ *When can I see you?* ◊ *When* (= in what circumstances) *would such a solution be possible?* **2** **A1** used after an expression of time to mean 'at which' or 'on which': *Sunday is the only day when I can relax.* ◊ *There are times when I wonder why I do this job.* **3** **A1** at which time; on which occasion: *The last time I went to Scotland was in May, when the weather was beautiful.*
■ *pron.* **A1** *what/which time: Until when can you stay?* ◊ *'I've got a new job.' 'Since when?'*
■ *conj.* **1** **A1** at or during the time that: *I loved history when I was at school.* **2** **A1** after: *Call me when you've finished.* **3** **A1** at any time that; whenever: *Can you spare five minutes when it's convenient?* **4** **A1** just after which: *He had just drifted off to sleep when the phone rang.* **5** **B1** con-

sidering that: *How can they expect to learn anything when they never listen?* **6** although: *She claimed to be 18, when I know she's only 16.* **IDM** see AS *conj.*, IF *conj.*

**whence** /wens/ *adv.* (*old use*) from where: *They returned whence they had come.*

**when·ever** 🔊 **B1** /wenˈevə(r)/ *conj., adv.*
■ *conj.* **1** **B1** at any time that; on any occasion that: *You can ask for help whenever you need it.* **2** **B1** every time that: *Whenever she comes, she brings a friend.* ◊ *The roof leaks whenever it rains.* ◊ *We try to help whenever possible.* **3** used when the time when sth happens is not important: '*When do you need it by?*' '*Saturday or Sunday. Whenever.*' ◊ *It's not urgent—we can do it next week or whenever.*
■ *adv.* used in questions to mean 'when', expressing surprise: *Whenever did you find time to do all that cooking?*

**where** 🔊 **A1** /weə(r); *NAmE* wer/ *adv., conj.*
■ *adv.* **1** **A1** in or to what place or situation: *Where do you live?* ◊ *I wonder where they will take us to.* ◊ *Where* (= at what point) *did I go wrong in my calculations?* ◊ *Where* (= in what book, newspaper, etc.) *did you read that?* ◊ *Just where* (= to what situation or final argument) *is all this leading us?* ➔ HOMOPHONES at WEAR **2** **A1** used after words or phrases that refer to a place or situation to mean 'at, in or to which': *It's one of the few countries where people drive on the left.* **3** **A1** the place or situation in which: *We then moved to Paris, where we lived for six years.*
■ *conj.* **A1** (in) the place or situation in which: *This is where I live.* ◊ *Sit where I can see you.* ◊ *Where people were concerned, his threshold of boredom was low.* ◊ *That's where* (= the point in the argument at which) *you're wrong.* ➔ HOMOPHONES at WEAR

**where·abouts** *noun, adv.*
■ *noun* /ˈweərəbaʊts; *NAmE* ˈwer-/ [U + sing./pl. v.] the place where sb/sth is: *His whereabouts are/is still unknown.*
■ *adv.* /ˌweərəˈbaʊts; *NAmE* ˌwer-/ used to ask the general area where sb/sth is: *Whereabouts did you find it?*

**where·as** 🔊 **B2** ⊙ /ˌweərˈæz; *NAmE* ˌwer-/ *conj.*
**1** **B2** used to compare or contrast two facts: *Some of the studies show positive results, whereas others do not.* ➔ LANGUAGE BANK at CONTRAST **2** (*law*) used at the beginning of a sentence in an official document to mean 'because of the fact that …'

**where·by** 🔊 **C1** /weəˈbaɪ; *NAmE* werˈb-/ *adv.* (*formal*) by which; because of which: *They have introduced a new system whereby all employees must undergo regular training.*

**where·fore** /ˈweəfɔː(r); *NAmE* ˈwerf-/ *noun* **IDM** see WHY *n.*

**where·in** /weərˈɪn; *NAmE* werˈ-/ *adv., conj.* (*formal*) in which place, situation or thing; in what way: *Wherein lies the difference between conservatism and liberalism?*

**where·of** /weərˈɒv; *NAmE* werˈʌv/ *conj.* (*old use or humorous*) of what or which: *I know whereof I speak* (= I know a lot about what I am talking about).

**where·upon** /ˌweərəˈpɒn; *NAmE* ˌwerəˈpɑːn/ *conj.* (*formal*) and then; as a result of this: *He told her she was a liar, whereupon she walked out.*

**wher·ever** 🔊 **B2** /weərˈevə(r); *NAmE* werˈ-/ *conj., adv.*
■ *conj.* **1** **B2** in any place: *Sit wherever you like.* ◊ *He comes from Boula, wherever that may be* (= I don't know where it is). **2** **B2** in all places that **SYN** **everywhere**: *Wherever she goes, there are crowds of people waiting to see her.* **3** **B2** in all cases that **SYN** **whenever**: *Use wholegrain breakfast cereals wherever possible.* **IDM** **or wherˈever** (*informal*) or any other place: *tourists from Spain, France or wherever*
■ *adv.* used in questions to mean 'where', expressing surprise: *Wherever can he have gone to?*

**the where·withal** /ðə ˈweəwɪðɔːl; *NAmE* ˈwerw-/ *noun* [sing.] **~ (to do sth)** the money, things or skill that you need in order to be able to do sth: *They lacked the wherewithal to pay for the repairs.*

# whet   1778

**whet** /wet/ *verb* (**-tt-**) ~ **sth** to increase your desire for or interest in sth: *The book will **whet your appetite** for more of her work.*

**whether** ① B1 W /'weðə(r)/ *conj.* **1** ⓘ B1 used to express a doubt or choice between two possibilities: *He seemed undecided **whether** to go or stay.* ◊ *It remains to be seen **whether or not** this idea can be put into practice.* ◊ *I asked him **whether** he had done it all himself **or whether** someone had helped him.* ◊ *I'll see whether she's at home (= or not at home).* ◊ *It's doubtful whether there'll be any seats left.* ⊃ note at IF **2** ⓘ B1 used to show that sth is true in either of two cases: *You are entitled to a free gift whether you accept our offer of insurance or not.* ◊ *I'm going whether you like it or not.* ◊ *Whether or not we're successful, we can be sure that we did our best.*

▽ HOMOPHONES
**weather** • **whether** /'weðə(r)/
- **weather** *noun*: *Next day the weather turned cold.*
- **weather** *verb*: *Be prepared to weather a storm of criticism.*
- **whether** *conj.*: *You'll have wonderful views whether you travel by sea or by air.*

**whew** /hwju:/ *exclamation* a sound that people make to show that they are surprised or RELIEVED about sth or that they are very hot or tired: *Whew—and I thought it was serious!* ◊ *Ten grand? Whew!* ⊃ compare PHEW

**whey** /weɪ/ *noun* [U] the thin liquid that is left from milk after the solid part (called CURDS) has been removed

**which** ① A1 /wɪtʃ/ *pron., det.* **1** ⓘ A1 used in questions to ask sb to be exact about one or more people or things from a limited number: *Which is better exercise—swimming or tennis?* ◊ *Which way is the wind blowing?* HELP Use a singular verb after which if only one person or thing is meant; use a plural verb if it is more than one: *Which of the applicants **has** got the job?* (= Although there was more than one applicant, I know that only one has got the job.) ◊ *Which of the patients **have** recovered?* (= It is possible that more than one patient has recovered.) ⊃ compare WHAT ◇ HOMOPHONES at WITCH **2** ⓘ A2 used to be exact about the thing or things that you mean: *Houses **which** overlook the lake cost more.* ◊ *It was a crisis **for which** she was totally unprepared.* HELP That can be used instead of which in this meaning, but it is not used immediately after a preposition: *It was a crisis **that** she was totally unprepared for.* ◊ *It was a crisis **for that** she was totally unprepared.* **3** ⓘ A2 used to give more information about sth: *His best movie, **which** won several awards, was about the life of Gandhi.* ◊ *Your claim ought to succeed, **in which case** the damages will be substantial.* HELP That cannot be used instead of which in this meaning.
IDM **which is 'which** used to talk about recognizing the difference between one person or thing and another: *The twins are so alike I can't tell which is which.*

**which·ev·er** /wɪtʃ'evə(r)/ *det., pron.* **1** used to say what feature or quality is important in deciding sth: *Choose **whichever** brand you prefer.* ◊ *Pensions should be increased annually in line with earnings or prices, whichever is the higher.* ◊ *Whichever of you gets here first will get the prize.* **2** used to say that it does not matter which, as the result will be the same: *It takes three hours, whichever route you take.* ◊ *The situation is an awkward one, whichever way you look at it.* ◊ *Whichever they choose, we must accept their decision.*

**whiff** /wɪf/ *noun, verb*
■ *noun* [usually sing.] **1** ~ **(of sth)** a smell, especially one that you only smell for a short time: *a whiff of cigar smoke* ◊ *He caught a whiff of perfume as he leaned towards her.* **2** ~ **(of sth)** a slight sign or feeling of sth: *a whiff of danger* **3** (*NAmE*) (in golf or baseball) an unsuccessful attempt to hit the ball
■ *verb* **1** [I] (*BrE, informal*) to smell bad **2** [I] (*NAmE*) (in golf or baseball) to try without success to hit the ball

**Whig** /wɪɡ/ *noun* in Britain in the past, a member of a party that supported progress and change and that later became the Liberal Party

**while** ① A2 /waɪl/ *conj., noun, verb*
■ *conj.* (also *formal* **whilst** /waɪlst/ *especially in BrE*) **1** ⓘ A2 during the time that sth is happening; at the same time as sth else is happening SYN **when**: *We must have been burgled while we were asleep.* ◊ *Her parents died while she was still at school.* ◊ *While I was waiting at the bus stop, three buses went by in the opposite direction.* ◊ *You can go swimming while I'm having lunch.* ◊ *shoes mended while you wait* **2** ⓘ B1 used to contrast two things: *While Tom's very good at science, his brother is absolutely hopeless.* ⊃ LANGUAGE BANK at CONTRAST **3** ⓘ B2 (used at the beginning of a sentence) although; despite the fact that ...: *While I am willing to help, I do not have much time available.* ⊃ LANGUAGE BANK at NEVERTHELESS
IDM **while you're / I'm etc. 'at it** used to suggest that sb could do sth while they are doing sth else: *'I'm just going to buy some postcards.' 'Can you get me some stamps while you're at it?'*
■ *noun* ⓘ B1 [sing.] a period of time: *for a ~ I only stayed for a short while.* ◊ *after a ~ After a while John started to relax a bit.* ◊ *in a ~ I'll be back in a little while (= a short time).* ◊ *It took me a while (= a fairly long time) to realize what he meant.* IDM see ONCE *adv.*, WORTH *adj.*
■ *verb*
PHR V **while sth↔a'way** to spend time in a pleasant lazy way: *We whiled away the time reading and playing cards.*

**whim** /wɪm/ *noun* [C, U] a sudden wish to do or have sth, especially when it is sth unusual or unnecessary: *He was forced to pander to **her every whim**.* ◊ *on a ~ We bought the house on a whim.* ◊ *at the ~ of sb My duties seem to change daily at the whim of the boss.* ◊ *at ~ She hires and fires people at whim.*

**whim·per** /'wɪmpə(r)/ *verb, noun*
■ *verb* [I, T] to make low, weak crying noises; to speak in this way: *The dog whimpered softly.* ◊ + **speech** *'Don't leave me alone,' he whimpered.*
■ *noun* a low, weak sound that a person or an animal makes when they are hurt, frightened or sad

**whim·si·cal** /'wɪmzɪkl/ *adj.* unusual and not serious in a way that is either funny or annoying: *to have a whimsical sense of humour* ◊ *Much of his writing has a whimsical quality.* ▸ **whim·si·cal·ly** /-kli/ *adv.*

**whimsy** /'wɪmzi/ *noun* [U] a way of thinking or behaving or a style of doing sth that is unusual and not serious, in a way that is either funny or annoying

**whine** /waɪn/ *verb, noun*
■ *verb* **1** [I, T] (+ **speech**) | ~ **that ...** to complain in an annoying, crying voice: *Stop whining!* ◊ *'I want to go home,' whined Toby.* ⊃ SYNONYMS at COMPLAIN **2** [I] to make a long, high, unpleasant sound because you are in pain or unhappy: *The dog whined and scratched at the door.* **3** [I] (of a machine) to make a long, high, unpleasant sound ▸ **whiny** *adj.*: *a whiny voice/tone* ◊ *a whiny kid/brat*
■ *noun* [usually sing.] **1** a long, high sound that is usually unpleasant or annoying: *the steady whine of the engine* **2** a long, high sound that a child or dog makes when it is hurt or wants sth **3** a high tone of voice that you use when you complain about sth

▽ HOMOPHONES
**whine** • **wine** /waɪn/
- **whine** *verb*: *Don't whine—I'm doing everything I can to help you.*
- **whine** *noun*: *The dog let out a long whine.*
- **wine** *noun*: *Would you prefer beer, wine or a soft drink?*

**whinge** /wɪndʒ/ *verb* [I] (*pres. part.* **whinge·ing** or **whing·ing**) ~ **(about sb/sth)** (*BrE, informal, disapproving*) to complain in an annoying way: *She's always whingeing about how unfair everything is.* ▸ **whinge** *noun* **whin·ger** *noun*

**whinny** /'wɪni/ *verb* (**whin·nies, whinny·ing, whin·nied, whin·nied**) [I] (of a horse) to make a quiet NEIGH ▸ **whinny** *noun* (*pl.* **-ies**)

---

æ cat | ɑː father | e bed | ɜː fur | ə about | ɪ sit | iː see | i happy | ɒ got (*BrE*) | ɔː saw | ʌ cup | ʊ put | uː too

**whip** /wɪp/ verb, noun

- **verb** (-pp-) **1** ~ **sb/sth** to hit a person or an animal hard with a whip, as a punishment or to make them go faster or work harder **2** [I, T] to move, or make sth move, quickly and suddenly or violently in a particular direction: + *adv./prep. A branch whipped across the car window.* ◊ *Her hair whipped around her face in the wind.* ◊ ~ **sth** *The waves were being whipped by 50 mile an hour winds.* **3** [T] ~ **sth** + *adv./prep.* to remove or pull sth quickly and suddenly: *She whipped the mask off her face.* ◊ *The man whipped out a knife.* **4** [T] to mix cream, etc. very quickly until it becomes stiff: ~ **sth** *Serve the pie with whipped cream.* ◊ ~ **sth up** *Whip the egg whites up into stiff peaks.* **5** [T] ~ **sb/sth** (NAmE, informal) to defeat sb very easily in a game: *The team whipped its opponents by 35 points.* ⊃ compare THRASH **6** [T] ~ **sth** (BrE, informal) to steal sth

PHRV **whip ˈthrough sth** (informal) to do or finish sth very quickly: *We whipped through customs in ten minutes.* **ˌwhip sb/sth↔ˈup 1** to deliberately try and make people excited or feel strongly about sth SYN **rouse**: *The advertisements were designed to whip up public opinion.* ◊ *He was a speaker who could really whip up a crowd.* **2** to quickly make a meal or sth to eat: *She whipped up a delicious lunch for us in 15 minutes.*

- **noun 1** [C] a long, thin piece of rope or leather, attached to a handle, used for hitting animals or people, to make them move, or move faster, or as a punishment: *He cracked his whip and the horse leapt forward.* **2** [C] an official in a political party who is responsible for making sure that the party's MPs attend and vote in important debates in a parliament: *the chief whip* **3** [C] (BrE) a written instruction telling the MPs of a political party how to vote on a particular issue **4 the whip** [sing.] (BrE) the fact of being an MP belonging to a particular party, with the duties and rights associated with that: *He resigned the Tory whip and sat as an independent.* **5** [U, C] a sweet dish made from cream, eggs, sugar and fruit mixed together

IDM **have/hold, etc. the ˈwhip hand (over sb/sth)** to be in a position where you have power or control over sb/sth ⊃ more at CRACK v., FAIR *adj.*

**whip·lash** /ˈwɪplæʃ/ noun **1** [C, usually sing.] a hit with a whip **2** [U] = WHIPLASH INJURY: *He was very bruised and suffering from whiplash.*

**ˈwhiplash injury** noun [C, U] (also **ˈwhip-lash** [U]) a neck injury caused when your head moves forward and back suddenly, especially in a car accident

**whip·per·snap·per** /ˈwɪpəsnæpə(r); NAmE -pərs-/ noun (old-fashioned, informal) a young and unimportant person who behaves in a way that others think is too confident and rude

**whip·pet** /ˈwɪpɪt/ noun a small, thin dog, similar to a GREY-HOUND, that can run very fast and is often used for racing

**whip·ping** /ˈwɪpɪŋ/ noun [usually sing.] an act of hitting sb with a whip, as a punishment

**ˈwhipping boy** noun a person who is often blamed or punished for things other people have done

**ˈwhipping cream** noun [U] cream that becomes thicker when it is mixed quickly (= WHIPPED)

**ˈwhip-round** noun (BrE, informal) if a group of people have a **whip-round**, they all give money so they can buy sth for sb or pay for sth

**whir** (also **whirr**) /wɜː(r)/ verb, noun

- **verb** [I] (-rr-) to make a continuous, low sound like the parts of a machine moving: *The clock began to whir before striking the hour.*
- **noun** (also **whir·ring**) [usually sing.] a continuous, low sound, for example the sound made by the regular movement of a machine or the wings of a bird: *the whir of a motor* ◊ *There was a whirring of machinery.*

**whirl** /wɜːl; NAmE wɜːrl/ verb, noun

- **verb 1** [I, T] to move, or make sb/sth move, around quickly in a circle or in a particular direction SYN **spin**: (+ *adv./prep.*) *Leaves whirled in the wind.* ◊ *She whirled around to face him.* ◊ *the whirling blades of the helicopter* ◊ ~ **sb/sth** (+ *adv./prep.*) *Tom whirled her across the dance floor.* **2** [I] if your mind, thoughts, etc. **whirl**, you feel confused and

1779

**whisper**

excited and cannot think clearly SYN **reel**: *I couldn't sleep —my mind was whirling from all that had happened.* ◊ *So many thoughts whirled around in her mind.*

- **noun** [sing.] **1** a movement of sth turning round and round: *a whirl of dust* ◊ (figurative) *Her mind was in a whirl* (= in a state of confusion or excitement). **2** a number of activities or events happening one after the other: *Her life was one long whirl of parties.* ◊ *It's easy to get caught up in the social whirl.*

IDM **give sth a ˈwhirl** (informal) to try sth to see if you like it or can do it

**whirli·gig** /ˈwɜːlɪɡɪɡ; NAmE ˈwɜːrl-/ noun **1** something that is very active and always changing: *the whirligig of fashion* **2** (old-fashioned) a MERRY-GO-ROUND at a FAIRGROUND for children to ride on

**whirl·pool** /ˈwɜːlpuːl; NAmE ˈwɜːrl-/ noun **1** a place in a river or the sea where currents of water turn round and round very fast SYN **eddy**: (figurative) *She felt she was being dragged into a whirlpool of emotion.* **2** (also **ˈwhirlpool bath**) a special bath or swimming pool for relaxing in, in which the water moves in circles ⊃ see also JACUZZI

**whirl·wind** /ˈwɜːlwɪnd; NAmE ˈwɜːrl-/ noun, adj.

- **noun 1** a very strong wind that moves very fast in circles and causes a lot of damage **2** a situation or series of events where a lot of things happen very quickly: *To recover from the divorce, I threw myself into a whirlwind of activities.*
- **adj.** [only before noun] happening very fast: *a whirlwind romance* ◊ *a whirlwind tour of America*

**whirr** (especially NAmE) = WHIR

**whisk** /wɪsk/ verb, noun

- **verb 1** ~ **sth** to mix liquids, eggs, etc. into a stiff, light mass, using a fork or special tool SYN **beat**: *Whisk the egg whites until stiff.* **2** ~ **sb/sth** + *adv./prep.* to take sb/sth somewhere very quickly and suddenly: *Jamie whisked her off to Paris for the weekend.* ◊ *The waiter whisked away the plates before we had finished.*
- **noun** a kitchen UTENSIL (= a tool) for mixing eggs, etc. very fast: *an electric whisk*

**whis·ker** /ˈwɪskə(r)/ noun **1** [C] any of the long, stiff hairs that grow near the mouth of a cat, mouse, etc. **2 whiskers** [pl.] (old-fashioned or humorous) the hair growing on a man's face, especially on the sides of his face ⊃ VISUAL VOCAB page V2

IDM **be, come, etc. within a whisker of sth/doing sth** (informal) to almost do sth: *They came within a whisker of being killed.* **by a ˈwhisker** (informal) by a very small amount ⊃ more at CAT

**whis·kered** /ˈwɪskəd; NAmE -skərd/ (also **whis·kery** /ˈwɪskəri/) adj. having whiskers

**whisky** (BrE) (US, IrishE **whis·key**) /ˈwɪski/ noun (pl. **whis·kies, whis·keys**) **1** [U, C] a strong alcoholic drink made from MALTED grain. It is sometimes drunk with water and/or ice: *a bottle of whisky* ◊ *Scotch whisky* ◊ *highland whiskies* ⊃ see also BOURBON, SCOTCH **2** [C] a glass of whisky: *a whisky and soda* ◊ *Two whiskies, please.* ⊃ see also SCOTCH noun

**whis·per** /ˈwɪspə(r)/ verb, noun

- **verb 1** [I, T] to speak very quietly to sb so that other people cannot hear what you are saying SYN **murmur**: *Don't you know it's rude to whisper?* ◊ ~ **about sth** *What are you two whispering about?* ◊ ~ **(to sb) + speech** *'Can you meet me tonight?' he whispered.* ◊ ~ **sth (to sb)** *She leaned over and whispered something in his ear.* ◊ ~ **(to sb) that…** *He whispered to me that he was afraid.* **2** [T, often passive] to say or suggest sth about sb/sth in a private or secret way: **it is whispered that…** *It was whispered that he would soon die and he did.* **3** [I] (+ *adv./prep.*) (literary) (of leaves, the wind, etc.) to make a soft, quiet sound
- **noun 1** [C] a low, quiet voice or the sound it makes SYN **murmur**: **in a** ~ *'I love you,' he said in a whisper.* ◊ **in whispers** *They spoke in whispers.* ◊ (also **whis·per·ing**) (literary) a soft sound SYN **murmur**: *I could hear the whispering of the sea.* **3** a piece of news that is spread by being talked

# whispering campaign 1780

about but may not be true **SYN** **rumour**: *I've heard whispers that he's leaving.*

**'whispering campaign** *noun* an attempt to damage sb's reputation by saying unpleasant things about them and passing this information from person to person

**whist** /wɪst/ *noun* [U] a card game for two pairs of players in which each pair tries to win the most cards

**whis·tle** /ˈwɪsl/ *noun*, *verb*
- *noun* **1** a small metal or plastic tube that you blow to make a loud, high sound, used to attract attention or as a signal: *The referee finally blew the whistle to stop the game.* ⇨ see also TIN WHISTLE **2** the sound made by blowing a whistle: *He scored the winning goal just seconds before the final whistle.* **3** the sound that you make by forcing your breath out when your lips are almost closed ⇨ see also WOLF WHISTLE **4** the loud, high sound produced by air or STEAM being forced through a small opening, or by sth moving quickly through the air **5** a piece of equipment that makes a loud, high sound when air or STEAM is forced through it: *The train whistle blew as we left the station.* ◇ *a factory whistle* **IDM** see BLOW v.
- *verb* **1** [T, I] to make a high sound or a musical tune by forcing your breath out when your lips are almost closed: *~(sth) to whistle a tune* ◇ *He whistled in amazement.* ◇ *The crowd booed and whistled as the player came onto the field.* ◇ *~ to sb/sth She whistled to the dog to come back.* ◇ *~ at sb/sth Workmen whistled at her as she walked past.* **2** [I] to make a loud, high sound by blowing into a whistle: *The referee whistled for a foul.* **3** [I] (of a KETTLE or other machine) to make a loud, high sound: *The kettle began to whistle.* ◇ *The microphone was making a strange whistling sound.* **4** [I] + **adv./prep.** to move quickly, making a loud, high sound: *The wind whistled down the chimney.* ◇ *A bullet whistled past his ear.* **5** [I] (of a bird) to make a high sound

**IDM** **sb can 'whistle for sth** (*BrE*, *informal*) used to say that you are not going to give sb sth that they have asked for

**'whistle-blower** *noun* (used especially in newspapers) a person who informs people in authority or the public that the company they work for is doing sth wrong or illegal

**'whistle-stop** *adj.* [only before noun] visiting a lot of different places in a very short time: *to go on a whistle-stop tour of Europe* ◇ *politicians on a whistle-stop election campaign*

**Whit** /wɪt/ *adj.* connected with Whitsun: *Whit Monday*

**whit** /wɪt/ *noun* [sing.] (*old-fashioned*) (usually in negative sentences) a very small amount **SYN** **jot**

**IDM** **not a 'whit | not one 'whit** not at all; not the smallest amount

**white** ⓘ **A1** /waɪt/ *adj.*, *noun*
- *adj.* (**whiter**, **whit·est**) **1** **A1** having the colour of fresh snow or of milk: *a crisp white shirt* ◇ *a set of perfect white teeth* ◇ *His hair was as white as snow.* ◇ *The horse was almost pure white in colour.* **2** **A1** belonging to or connected with a race of people who have pale skin: *She writes about her experiences as a black girl in a predominantly white city.* ◇ *He grew up in a mostly white neighbourhood.* ◇ *middle-aged white men in suits* **3** **A1** (of the skin) pale because of emotion or illness: *~ with sth white with shock* ◇ *Zack's face turned white and his jaw dropped.* **4** **A2** (*BrE*) (of tea or coffee) with milk added: *Two white coffees, please.* ◇ *Do you take your coffee black or white?* ⇨ compare BLACK▸ **white·ness** *noun* [U, sing.]
- *noun* **1** **A1** [U] the colour of fresh snow or of milk: *various shades of white* ◇ *in~ She was dressed all in white.* **2** [C, usually pl.] a member of a race or people who have pale skin **3** [U, C] white wine: *Would you like red or white?* ◇ *a very dry white* **4** [C, U] the part of an egg that surrounds the YOLK (= the yellow part): *Use the whites of two eggs.* **5** [C, usually pl.] the white part of the eye: *The whites of her eyes were bloodshot.* **6** **whites** [pl.] white clothes, sheets, etc. when they are separated from coloured ones to be washed: *Don't wash whites and coloureds together.* ◇ (*NAmE*) *Don't wash whites and colors together.* **7** **whites** [pl.] white clothes worn for playing some sports:

*cricket/tennis whites* ⇨ see also FLAT WHITE **IDM** see BLACK

**IDM** **whiter than 'white** (of a person) completely honest and morally good: *The government must be seen to be whiter than white.*

**white·bait** /ˈwaɪtbeɪt/ *noun* [pl.] very small young fish of several types that are fried and eaten whole

**white 'blood cell** (also **'white cell**) (also specialist **leuco·cyte**) *noun* (*biology*) any of the clear cells in the blood that help to fight disease

**white·board** /ˈwaɪtbɔːd; *NAmE* -bɔːrd/ *noun* **1** a large board with a smooth white surface that teachers, etc. write on with special pens ⇨ compare BLACKBOARD **2** = INTERACTIVE WHITEBOARD

**'white bread** *noun* [U] bread made with WHITE FLOUR

**'white-bread** *adj.* [only before noun] (*NAmE*, *informal*) ordinary and traditional: *a white-bread town*

**'white·caps** /ˈwaɪtkæps/ (*NAmE*) (*BrE* **white 'horses**) *noun* [pl.] waves in the sea or ocean with white tops on them

**white 'chocolate** *noun* [U] a yellow-white sweet food that is made with COCOA BUTTER ⇨ compare DARK CHOCOLATE, MILK CHOCOLATE

**white 'Christmas** *noun* a Christmas during which there is snow on the ground

**white-'collar** *adj.* [usually before noun] working in an office, rather than in a factory, etc.; connected with work in offices: *white-collar workers* ◇ *a white-collar job* ◇ *white-collar crime* (= in which office workers steal from their company, etc.) ⇨ compare BLUE-COLLAR

**white 'dwarf** *noun* (*astronomy*) a small star that is near the end of its life and is very DENSE (= solid and heavy)

**white 'elephant** *noun* [usually sing.] a thing that has no use and is no longer needed, although it may have cost a lot of money: *The new office block has become an expensive white elephant.* **ORIGIN** From the story that in Siam (now Thailand) the king would give a white elephant as a present to sb that he did not like. That person would have to spend all their money on looking after the rare animal.

**white 'fish** *noun* [U, C] (*pl.* **white fish**) fish that is pale inside and used for food

**white 'flag** *noun* [usually sing.] a sign that you accept defeat and wish to stop fighting: *to raise/show/wave the white flag*

**white 'flight** *noun* [U] (*US*) a situation where white people who can afford it go to live outside the cities because they are worried about crime in city centres

**white 'flour** *noun* [U] flour made from WHEAT grains from which most of the BRAN (= outer layer) and WHEAT-GERM (= centre part) have been removed

**white 'goods** *noun* [pl.] large pieces of electrical equipment in the house, such as WASHING MACHINES, etc.

**White·hall** /ˈwaɪthɔːl/ *noun* **1** [U] a street in London where there are many government offices **2** [U + sing./pl. v.] a way of referring to the British government or the officials who work for it: *Whitehall are/is refusing to comment.*

**white 'heat** *noun* [U] the very high temperature at which metal looks white

**white 'hope** *noun* [sing.] (*informal*) a person who is expected to bring success to a team, an organization, etc: *He was once the great white hope of British boxing.*

**white 'horses** (*BrE*) (*NAmE* **white·caps**) *noun* [pl.] waves in the sea or ocean with white tops on them

**white-'hot** *adj.* **1** (of metal or sth burning) so hot that it looks white **2** very strong and intense

**the 'White House** *noun* [sing.] **1** the official home of the President of the US in Washington, DC **2** the US President and his or her officials: *The White House has issued a statement.* ◇ *White House aides*

**white 'knight** *noun* (*business*) a person or an organization that rescues a company from being bought by another company at too low a price

**white 'lie** noun a small lie, especially one that you tell to avoid hurting sb

**white 'light** noun [U] ordinary light that has no colour

**white 'meat** noun [U] **1** meat that is pale in colour when it has been cooked, such as chicken ⊃ compare RED MEAT **2** pale meat from the breast of a chicken or other bird that has been cooked ⊃ compare DARK MEAT

**whiten** /'waɪtn/ verb [I, T] to become white or whiter; to make sth white or whiter: *He gripped the wheel until his knuckles whitened.* ◊ *~sth Snow had whitened the tops of the trees.*

**white 'noise** noun [U] (*physics*) noise that contains many different sound FREQUENCIES that are equally strong, for example the noise that comes from a television or radio that is turned on but not TUNED IN

**'white-out** noun weather conditions in which there is so much snow or cloud that it is impossible to see anything

**White 'Paper** noun (in the UK) a government report that gives information about sth and explains government plans before a new law is introduced ⊃ compare GREEN PAPER

**white 'pepper** noun [U] a grey-brown powder made from dried BERRIES (called PEPPERCORNS), used to add taste to food

**white 'sauce** noun [U] a thick sauce made from butter, flour and milk **SYN** béchamel

**white 'spirit** noun [U] (*BrE*) a clear liquid made from petrol, used as a cleaning substance or to make paint thinner

**white 'stick** noun a long, thin white stick carried by blind people to help them walk around without knocking things and to show others that they are blind

**white su'premacy** noun [U] the belief that white people are better than other races and should be in power ▶ **white su'premacist** noun

**white 'tie** noun a man's white BOW TIE, also used to mean very formal evening dress for men: *dressed in white tie and tails*

**white-'tie** adj. (of social occasions) very formal, when men are expected to wear white BOW TIES and jackets with TAILS: *Is it a white-tie affair?*

**white 'trash** noun [U] (*informal, offensive*) a way of referring to poor white people, especially those living in the southern US

**white-wash** /'waɪtwɒʃ; *NAmE* -wɑːʃ/ noun, verb
■ noun **1** [U] a mixture of CHALK or LIME and water, used for painting houses and walls white **2** [U, sing.] (*disapproving*) an attempt to hide unpleasant facts about sb/sth **SYN** cover-up: *The opposition claimed the report was a whitewash.* **3** [C, usually sing.] (*especially BrE, informal*) (in sport) a victory in every game in a series: *a 7–0 whitewash* ◊ *a whitewash victory*
■ verb **1** ~sth to cover sth such as a wall with whitewash **2** ~sb/sth (*disapproving*) to try to hide unpleasant facts about sb/sth; to try to make sth seem better than it is: *His wife had wanted to whitewash his reputation after he died.* **3** ~sb (*especially BrE, informal*) (in sport) to defeat an opponent in every game in a series

**white 'water** noun [U] **1** a part of a river that looks white because the water is moving very fast over rocks: *a stretch of white water* ◊ *white-water rafting* **2** a part of the sea or ocean that looks white because it is very rough and the waves are high

**white 'wedding** noun a traditional wedding, especially in a church, at which the bride wears a white dress

**white 'wine** noun **1** [U, C] pale yellow wine: *a bottle of dry white wine* ◊ *chilled white wine* **2** [C] a glass of white wine ⊃ compare RED WINE, ROSÉ

**white 'witch** noun a person who does magic that does not harm other people

**whitey** /'waɪti/ noun (*taboo, slang*) an offensive word for a white person, used by black people

**whither** /'wɪðə(r)/ adv., conj. **1** (*old use*) where; to which: *Whither should they go?* ◊ *They did not know whither they* should go. ◊ *the place whither they were sent* **2** (*formal*) used to ask what is likely to happen to sth in the future: *Whither modern architecture?*

**whit-ing** /'waɪtɪŋ/ noun [C, U] (*pl.* **whit-ing**) a small sea fish that is white inside and used for food

**whit-ish** /'waɪtɪʃ/ adj. fairly white in colour: *a bird with a whitish throat*

**Whit-sun** /'wɪtsn/ noun [U, C] the 7th Sunday after Easter and the days close to it

**Whit 'Sunday** noun [U, C] (*BrE*) = PENTECOST

**whit-tle** /'wɪtl/ verb to form a piece of wood, etc. into a particular shape by cutting small pieces from it: *~A (from B) He whittled a simple toy from the piece of wood.* ◊ *~B (into A) He whittled the piece of wood into a simple toy.*
**PHRV** **whittle sth↔a'way** to make sth gradually decrease in value or amount **whittle sth↔'down** to reduce the size or number of sth: *I finally managed to whittle down the names on the list to only five.*

**whizz** (*especially BrE*) (*also* **whiz** *especially in NAmE*) /wɪz/ verb, noun
■ verb (*informal*) **1** [I] + adv./prep. to move very quickly, making a high, continuous sound: *A bullet whizzed past my ear.* ◊ *He whizzed down the road on his motorbike.* **2** [I] + adv./prep. to do sth very quickly: *She whizzed through the work.*
■ noun (*informal*) a person who is very good at sth: *She's a whizz at crosswords.*

**'whizz-kid** (*especially BrE*) (*NAmE usually* **'whiz-kid**) noun (*informal*) a person who is very good and successful at sth, especially at a young age: *financial whizz-kids*

**whizzy** /'wɪzi/ adj. (**whiz-zier, whiz-ziest**) (*informal*) having features that make use of advanced technology: *a game with whizzy graphics*

**WHO** /,dʌblju: eɪtʃ 'əʊ/ abbr. World Health Organization (an international organization that aims to fight and control disease)

**who** ⊙ **A1** /huː/ pron. **1** ⓘ **A1** used in questions to ask about the name, identity or function of one or more people: *Who is that woman?* ◊ *I wonder who that letter was from.* ◊ *Who are you phoning?* ◊ *Who's the money for?* **2** ⓘ **A1** used to show which person or people you mean: *The people who called yesterday want to buy the house.* ◊ *The people (who) we met in France have sent us a card.* **3** ⓘ **A2** used to give more information about sb: *Mrs Smith, who has a lot of teaching experience at junior level, will be joining the school in September.* ◊ *And then Mary, who we had been talking about earlier, walked in.* ⊃ compare WHOM
**IDM** **who am 'I, who are 'you, etc. to do sth?** used to ask what right or authority sb has to do sth: *Who are you to tell me I can't park here?* ⊃ see also WHO'S WHO

**whoa** /wəʊ/ exclamation used as a command to a horse, etc. to make it go slower, stop or stand still

**who'd** /huːd/ short form **1** who had **2** who would

**who-dun-nit** (*BrE*) (*also* **who-dun-it** *NAmE, BrE*) /,huː'dʌnɪt/ noun (*informal*) a story, play, etc. about a murder in which you do not know who did the murder until the end

**who-ever** ⓘ **B2** /huː'evə(r)/ pron. **1** ⓘ **B2** the person or people who; any person who: *Whoever says that is a liar.* ◊ *Send it to whoever is in charge of sales.* **2** ⓘ **B2** used to say that it does not matter who, since the result will be the same: *Come out of there, whoever you are.* ◊ *I don't want to see them, whoever they are.* **3** used in questions to mean 'who', expressing surprise: *Whoever heard of such a thing!*

# whole

**whole** ⊙ **A2** ⊙ /həʊl/ adj., noun, adv.
■ adj. **1** ⓘ **A2** [only before noun] full; complete: *Let's forget the whole thing.* ◊ *Jenna was my best friend in the whole world.* ◊ *It seems I've spent my whole life travelling.* ◊ *The whole family will be there.* ◊ *But that's not the whole story, is it?* ⊃ HOMOPHONES at HOLE **2** ⓘ **B2** [only before noun] used to emphasize how large or important sth is: *I'm going to be talking about a whole range of things today.* ◊ *We are going to have a whole bunch of people over tomorrow night.* ◊ *I*

# wholefood

can't afford it—that's **the whole point**. ⇨ HOMOPHONES at HOLE **3** ⓘ B2 not broken or damaged SYN **(all) in one piece**: *Owls usually swallow their prey whole* (= without biting it into small pieces). ⇨ note at HALF ▸ **whole‧ness** *noun* [U] ⇨ see also WHOLLY

IDM HELP Most idioms containing **whole** are at the entries for the nouns and verbs in the idioms, for example **go the whole hog** is at **hog**. **a ˌwhole ˈlot** (*informal*) very much; a lot: *I'm feeling a whole lot better.* **a ˈwhole lot (of sth)** (*informal*) a large number or amount: *There were a whole lot of people I didn't know.* ◊ *I lost a whole lot of money.* **the ˌwhole ˈlot** everything; all of sth: *I've sold the whole lot.* **a whole ˈnother …** (*US, non-standard*) a completely different thing: *Now that's a whole 'nother question.*

■ *noun* **1** ⓘ B1 [sing.] **the ~ of sth** all that there is of sth: *The scheme would cover the whole of the UK.* ⇨ HOMOPHONES at HOLE ⇨ note at HALF **2** ⓘ B2 [C] a thing that is complete in itself: *Four quarters make a whole.* ◊ *Taken as a whole, the image is slightly disappointing.* IDM **as a ˈwhole** ⓘ B2 as one thing or piece and not as separate parts: *Unemployment is higher in the north than in the country as a whole.* **on the ˈwhole** considering everything; in general: *On the whole, I'm in favour of the idea.*

■ *adv.* **~ new/different/other …** (*informal*) completely new/different: *It's a whole new world out here.* ◊ *That's a whole other story.*

**whole‧food** /ˈhəʊlfuːd/ *noun* [U] (*also* **whole‧foods** [pl.]) food that is considered healthy because it is in a simple form, has not been REFINED, and does not contain artificial substances

**whole‧grain** /ˈhəʊlɡreɪn/ *adj.* made with or containing whole grains, for example of WHEAT

**whole‧heart‧ed** /ˌhəʊlˈhɑːtɪd/ *NAmE* -ˈhɑːrt- /*adj.* (*approving*) complete and enthusiastic: *The plan was given wholehearted support.* ▸ **whole‧heart‧ed‧ly** *adv.*: *to agree wholeheartedly*

**whole‧meal** /ˈhəʊlmiːl/ *adj.* (*BrE*) (*also* **whole‧wheat** *NAmE*, *BrE*) *adj.* **wholemeal** bread or flour contains the whole grains of WHEAT, etc. including the HUSK

**ˈwhole milk** *noun* [U] milk from which fat has not been removed ⇨ compare SKIMMED MILK, SEMI-SKIMMED

**ˈwhole note** (*NAmE*) (*BrE* **semi‧breve**) *noun* (*music*) a note that lasts as long as four QUARTER NOTES ⇨ picture at MUSIC

**ˌwhole ˈnumber** *noun* (*mathematics*) a number that consists of one or more units, with no FRACTIONS (= parts of a number less than one)

**whole‧sale** /ˈhəʊlseɪl/ *adj.* [only before noun] **1** connected with goods that are bought and sold in large quantities, especially so they can be sold again to make a profit: *wholesale prices* ⇨ compare RETAIL¹ **2** (especially of sth bad) happening or done to a very large number of people or things: *the wholesale slaughter of innocent people* ▸ **whole‧sale** *adv.*: *We buy the building materials wholesale.* ◊ *These young people die wholesale from heroin overdoses.*

**whole‧sal‧ing** /ˈhəʊlseɪlɪŋ/ *noun* [U] the business of buying and selling goods in large quantities, especially so they can be sold again to make a profit ⇨ compare RETAILING ▸ **whole‧saler** *noun*: *fruit and vegetable wholesalers*

**whole‧some** /ˈhəʊlsəm/ *adj.* **1** good for your health: *fresh, wholesome food* **2** morally good; having a good moral influence: *It was clean wholesome fun.* OPP **unwholesome** ▸ **whole‧some‧ness** *noun* [U]

**ˈwhole step** (*US*) (*BrE* **tone**) *noun* (*music*) one of the five longer INTERVALS in a musical SCALE, for example the INTERVAL between C and D or between E and F♯

**whole‧wheat** /ˈhəʊlwiːt/ *adj.* (*BrE also* **whole‧meal**) *adj.* **wholewheat** bread or flour contains the whole grains of WHEAT, etc. including the HUSK

**who'll** /huːl/ *short form* **who will**

**whol‧ly** ⓘ+ C1 /ˈhəʊlli/ *adv.* (*formal*) completely SYN **totally**: *wholly inappropriate behaviour* ◊ *The government is not wholly to blame for the recession.*

**whom** ⓘ B2 /huːm/ *pron.* (*formal*) used instead of 'who' as the object of a verb or preposition: *Whom did they invite?* ◊ *To whom should I write?* ◊ *The author whom you criticized in your review has written a reply.* ◊ *Her mother, in whom she confided, said she would support her unconditionally.*

▼ GRAMMAR POINT

**whom**

- **Whom** is not used very often in spoken English. **Who** is usually used as the object pronoun, especially in questions: *Who did you invite to the party?*
- The use of **whom** as the pronoun after prepositions is very formal: *To whom should I address the letter?* ◊ *He asked me with whom I had discussed it.* In spoken English it is much more natural to use **who** and put the preposition at the end of the sentence: *Who should I address the letter to?* ◊ *He asked me who I had discussed it with.*
- In defining relative clauses the object pronoun **whom** is not often used. You can either use **who** or **that**, or leave out the pronoun completely: *The family (who/that/whom) I met at the airport were very kind.*
- In non-defining relative clauses **who** or, more formally, **whom** (but not *that*) is used and the pronoun cannot be left out: *Our doctor, who/whom we all liked very much, retired last week.* This pattern is not used very much in spoken English.

**whom‧ever** /huːmˈevə(r)/ (*also* **whom‧so‧ever** /ˌhuːmsəʊˈevə(r)/) *pron.* (*literary*) used instead of 'whoever' as the object of a verb or preposition: *He was free to marry whomever he chose.*

**whoop** /wuːp, wʊp/ *noun, verb*
■ *noun* a loud shout expressing joy, excitement, etc: *whoops of delight*
■ *verb* [I] to shout loudly because you are happy or excited IDM **ˌwhoop it ˈup** (*informal*) **1** to enjoy yourself very much with a noisy group of people **2** (*NAmE*) to make people excited or enthusiastic about sth

**whoo‧pee** /ˈwʊpiː/ *exclamation, noun*
■ *exclamation* /ˈwʊpiː/ (*informal*) used to express happiness: *Whoopee, we've won!*
■ *noun* /ˈwʊpi/ [U] IDM **make ˈwhoopee** (*old-fashioned, informal*) to celebrate in a noisy way

**whoop‧ing cough** /ˈhuːpɪŋ kɒf/ *NAmE* kɔːf/ (*medical* **per‧tus‧sis**) *noun* [U] a disease, especially of children, that makes them COUGH (= force air noisily through the throat) and have difficulty breathing

**whoops** /wʊps/ *exclamation* (*informal*) **1** used when sb has almost had an accident, broken sth, etc: *Whoops! Careful, you almost spilt coffee everywhere.* **2** used when you have done sth embarrassing, said sth rude by accident, told a secret, etc: *Whoops, you weren't supposed to hear that.*

**whoosh** /wʊʃ, wuːʃ/ *noun, verb*
■ *noun* [usually sing.] (*informal*) the sudden movement and sound of air or water rushing past: *a whoosh of air* ◊ *There was a whoosh as everything went up in flames.*
■ *verb* [I] + *adv./prep.* (*informal*) to move very quickly with the sound of air or water rushing

**whop‧per** /ˈwɒpə(r)/ *NAmE* ˈwɑːp- /*noun* (*informal*) **1** something that is very big for its type: *Pete has caught a whopper* (= a large fish). **2** a lie: *She's told some whoppers about her past.*

**whop‧ping** /ˈwɒpɪŋ/ *NAmE* ˈwɑːp- /(*also* **ˌwhopping ˈgreat**) *adj.* [only before noun] (*informal*) very big: *The company made a whopping 75 million dollar loss.*

**whore** /hɔː(r)/ *noun* **1** (*old-fashioned*) a female PROSTITUTE **2** (*taboo*) an offensive word used to refer to a woman who has sex with a lot of men

**who're** /'huːə(r)/ short form who are

**whore·house** /'hɔːhaʊs/ NAmE /'hɔːrh-/ noun (old-fashioned) a BROTHEL (= a place where people pay to have sex)

**whor·ing** /'hɔːrɪŋ/ noun [U] (old-fashioned) the activity of having sex with a PROSTITUTE

**whorl** /wɜːl/ NAmE /wɜːrl/ noun **1** a pattern made by a curved line that forms a rough circle, with smaller circles inside bigger ones: *the whorls on your fingertips* **2** (*specialist*) a ring of leaves, flowers, etc. around the STEM of a plant

**who's** /huːz/ short form **1** who is **2** who has

**whose** 🔑 A2 /huːz/ det., pron. **1** ? A2 used in questions to ask who sth belongs to: *Whose house is that?* ◇ *I wonder whose this is.* **2** ? B1 used to say which person or thing you mean: *He's a man whose opinion I respect.* ◇ *It's the house whose door is painted red.* **3** ? B1 used to give more information about a person or thing: *Isobel, whose brother he was, had heard the joke before.*

**who·so·ever** /ˌhuːsəʊ'evə(r)/ pron. (old use) = WHOEVER

**who's 'who** noun **1** [U] people's names, jobs, status, etc: *You'll soon find out who's who in the office.* **2** [sing.] a list or book of facts about famous people: *The list of delegates attending read like a who's who of the business world.* ORIGIN From the reference book *Who's Who*, which gives information about many well-known people and what they have done.

**who've** /huːv/ short form who have

**whup** /wʌp/ verb (-pp-) ~ sb/sth (informal, especially US) to defeat sb easily in a game, a fight, an election, etc.

**why** 🔑 A1 /waɪ/ adv., exclamation, noun

■ adv. **1** ? A1 used in questions to ask the reason for or purpose of sth: *Why were you late?* ◇ *Tell me why you did it.* ◇ *'I would like you to go.' 'Why me?'* ◇ (*informal*) *Why oh why do people keep leaving the door open?* **2** ? A1 used in questions to suggest that it is not necessary to do sth: *Why get upset just because you got one bad grade?* ◇ *Why bother to write? We'll see him tomorrow.* **3** ? A1 used to give or talk about a reason: *That's why I left so early.* ◇ *I know you did it—I just want to know why.* ◇ *The reason why the injection needs repeating every year is that the virus changes.* IDM **why 'ever** used in questions to mean 'why', expressing surprise: *Why ever didn't you tell us before?* **why 'not?** ? A2 used to make or agree to a suggestion: *Why not write to her?* ◇ *'Let's eat out.' 'Why not?'* ◇ *Why don't we go together?*

■ exclamation (old-fashioned or NAmE) used to express a feeling of being surprised, impatient, etc: *Why Jane, it's you!* ◇ *Why, it's easy—a child could do it!*

■ noun IDM **the ˌwhys and (the) 'wherefores** the reasons for sth: *I had no intention of going into the whys and the wherefores of the situation.*

▼ EXPRESS YOURSELF

**Giving reasons, justifying a choice**

In various exams, you are asked to make a choice and give reasons for it. In conversation or in a meeting, you need to explain and justify your decisions.

● **There are two main reasons** why I think it's the best option: first, there's the cost and second, the quality.
● I **think/believe** it's the right thing to do **because** it gives everyone a fair chance.
● I would choose the newer one **on the grounds that** it will last longer.
● Of the three houses, the largest one **seems to me** to be the best, because they need the room.
● My choice would be number 3, **simply because** it's the clearest design.

**WI** abbr. **1** West Indies **2** /ˌdʌblju:'aɪ/ Women's Institute (a British women's organization in which groups of women meet regularly to take part in various activities)

**Wicca** /'wɪkə/ noun [U] a modern form of WITCHCRAFT, practised as a religion ▶ **Wic·can** /-kən/ adj., noun

**wick** /wɪk/ noun, verb

---

1783 **wide**

■ noun **1** the piece of string in the centre of a CANDLE that you light so that the candle burns ⇒ picture at CANDELABRA **2** the piece of material in an oil lamp that takes in the oil and that you light so that the lamp burns
IDM **get on sb's 'wick** (*BrE, informal*) to annoy sb
■ verb ~ sth (away) (of a material) to take small drops of liquid from an area and move them away: *Wool socks wick away sweat.*

**wicked** /'wɪkɪd/ adj., noun

■ adj. (**wick·ed·er, wick·ed·est**) HELP You can also use **more wicked** and **most wicked**. **1** morally bad SYN evil: *a wicked deed* ◇ *stories about a wicked witch* **2** (*informal*) slightly bad but in a way that is funny and/or attractive SYN mischievous: *a wicked grin* ◇ *Jane has a wicked sense of humour.* **3** dangerous, harmful or powerful: *He has a wicked punch.* ◇ *a wicked-looking knife* **4** (*slang*) very good: *This song's wicked.* ▶ **wick·ed·ly** adv.: *Martin grinned wickedly.* ◇ *a wickedly funny comedy* ◇ *a wickedly sharp blade* **wick·ed·ness** noun [U]

■ noun **the wicked** [pl.] people who are wicked
IDM **(there's) no peace/rest for the 'wicked** (*usually humorous*) used when sb is complaining that they have a lot of work to do

**wicker** /'wɪkə(r)/ noun [U] thin sticks of wood TWISTED together to make BASKETS, furniture, etc: *a wicker chair*

**wicket** /'wɪkɪt/ noun **1** (in CRICKET) either of the two sets of three sticks standing in the ground (called STUMPS) with pieces of wood (called BAILS) lying across the top. The BOWLER tries to hit the wicket with the ball. **2** the area of ground between the two wickets
IDM **ˌkeep 'wicket** to act as a WICKETKEEPER ⇒ more at STICKY adj.

**wicket-keep·er** /'wɪkɪtkiːpə(r)/ (also BrE, informal **keeper**) noun (in CRICKET) a player who stands behind the WICKET in order to stop or catch the ball

wicker
wicker chair

**wide** 🔑 A2 W /waɪd/ adj., adv., noun

| WORD FAMILY |
|---|
| **wide** adj., adv. |
| **widely** adv. |
| **widen** verb |
| **width** noun |

■ adj. (**wider, wid·est**)
● FROM ONE SIDE TO THE OTHER **1** ? A2 measuring a large distance from one side to the other: *a wide river* ◇ *The river gets quite wide here.* ◇ *a jacket with wide lapels* ◇ *Her face broke into a wide grin.* OPP narrow ⇒ see also WIDTH **2** ? A2 measuring a particular distance from one side to the other: *How wide is that stream?* ◇ *It's about 2 metres wide.* ◇ *The road was just wide enough for two vehicles to pass.*
● LARGE NUMBER/AMOUNT **3** ? B1 [usually before noun] including a large number or variety of different people or things; covering a large area: *a wide range/choice/variety/selection of goods* ◇ *The company offers a wide array of services to businesses.* ◇ *Her music appeals to a wide audience.* ◇ *It's the best job in the whole wide world.* ◇ *Experts believe the project could bring positive benefits to the wider community.* ◇ *The contributors to this volume represent a wide spectrum of opinion on the subject.* ◇ *Publication on the internet makes the material accessible to a wider public for the first time.*
● DIFFERENCE/GAP **4** ? B1 very big: *The Australians won by a wide margin.*
● GENERAL **5** (only used in the comparative and superlative) general; not only looking at details: *the wider aims of the project* ◇ *We are talking about education in its widest sense.*
● EYES **6** fully open: *She stared at him with wide eyes.*
● NOT CLOSE **7** ~ (of sth) far from the point aimed at: *Her shot was wide (of the target).*
● -WIDE **8** (in adjectives and adverbs) happening or existing in the whole of a country, etc: *a nationwide search* ◇ *We need to act on a Europe-wide scale.*

# wide-angle lens 1784

**IDM** **give sb/sth a wide ˈberth** to not go too near sb/sth; to avoid sb/sth: *He gave the dog a wide berth.* **wide of the ˈmark** not accurate: *Their predictions turned out to be wide of the mark.*

■ *adv.* (**wider**, **wid·est**) as far or fully as possible: *The door was wide open.* ◇ *The championship is still wide open (= anyone could win).* ◇ *She had a fear of wide-open spaces.* ◇ *He stood with his legs wide apart.* ◇ *In a few seconds she was wide awake.* ◇ *Open your mouth wide.* **IDM** see CAST *v.*, FAR *adv.*

■ *noun* (in CRICKET) a ball that has been BOWLED (= thrown) where the BATSMAN cannot reach it

▼ **WHICH WORD?**

**wide / broad**

These adjectives are frequently used with the following nouns:

| wide ~ | broad ~ |
|---|---|
| street | shoulders |
| river | back |
| area | smile |
| range | range |
| variety | agreement |
| choice | outline |

- **Wide** is the word most commonly used to talk about something that measures a long distance from one side to the other. **Broad** is more often used to talk about parts of the body. (Although **wide** can be used with *mouth*.) It is used in more formal or written language to describe the features of the countryside, etc: *a broad river* ◇ *a broad stretch of meadowland*.
- Both **wide** and **broad** can be used to describe something that includes a large variety of different people or things: *a wide/broad range of products*. **Broad**, but not **wide**, can be used to mean 'general' or 'not detailed': *All of us are in broad agreement on this matter.*

**ˈwide-angle ˈlens** *noun* a camera LENS that can give a wider view than a normal lens

**ˈwide ˌarea ˈnetwork** *noun* = WAN

**ˈwide-ˌeyed** *adj.* **1** with your eyes fully open because of fear, surprise, etc: *She stared at him in wide-eyed amazement.* **2** having little experience and therefore very willing to believe, trust or accept sb/sth **SYN** **naive**

**wide·ly** /ˈwaɪdli/ *adv.* **1** by a lot of people; in or to many places: *The term is widely used in everyday speech.* ◇ *The idea is now widely accepted.* ◇ *There is still no word on when the service will become widely available.* ◇ *to be widely regarded/acknowledged/recognized as sb/sth* ◇ *He has travelled widely in Asia.* **2** to a large degree; a lot: *Standards vary widely.*

**widen** /ˈwaɪdn/ *verb* **1** [I, T] to become wider; to make sth wider: *Her eyes widened in surprise.* ◇ *~ into sth Here the stream widens into a river.* ◇ *~ sth They may have to widen the road to cope with the increase in traffic.* **2** [I, T] to become larger in degree or range; to make sth larger in degree or range: *the widening gap between rich and poor* ◇ *~ sth We plan to widen the scope of our existing activities by offering more language courses.* ◇ *The legislation will be widened to include all firearms.* **IDM** **ˈwiden the net** to consider or include a larger range of options or possibilities, especially when searching for sth: *It's time to widen the net in the search for a suitable candidate.*

**ˈwide-out** /ˈwaɪdaʊt/ *noun* = WIDE RECEIVER

**ˈwide-ˌranging** *adj.* including or dealing with a large number of different subjects or areas: *The commission has been given wide-ranging powers.* ◇ *a wide-ranging discussion/debate*

**ˈwide reˈceiver** (*also* **ˈwide-out**) *noun* (in AMERICAN FOOTBALL) a RECEIVER whose position is near the edge of the field

**ˈwide-screen** /ˈwaɪdskriːn/ *noun* [U] a way of presenting a film in which the image is a lot wider than it is high **SYN** **letterbox**: *a widescreen TV*

**wide·spread** /ˈwaɪdspred/ *adj.* existing or happening over a large area or among many people: *widespread damage* ◇ *The plan received widespread support throughout the country.*

**widg·eon** = WIGEON

**widget** /ˈwɪdʒɪt/ *noun* **1** (*informal*) used to refer to any small device that you do not know the name of **2** (*business*) a product that does not exist, used as an example of a typical product: *Company A produces two million widgets a year.* **3** (*computing*) a small box on a computer screen that delivers changing information, such as news items or weather reports, while the rest of the page remains the same

**widow** /ˈwɪdəʊ/ *noun*, *verb*
■ *noun* a woman whose husband or wife has died and who has not married again ⇒ see also BLACK WIDOW, GRASS WIDOW ⇒ WORDFINDER NOTE at OLD
■ *verb* **be widowed** if sb **is widowed**, their husband or wife has died: *She was widowed when she was 35.* ▶ **widowed** *adj.*: *his widowed father*

**wid·ow·er** /ˈwɪdəʊə(r)/ *noun* a man whose wife or husband has died and who has not married again

**widow·hood** /ˈwɪdəʊhʊd/ *noun* [U] the state or period of being a widow or widower

**ˈwidow's ˈpeak** *noun* hair growing in the shape of a V on sb's FOREHEAD

**width** /wɪdθ, wɪtθ/ *noun* **1** [U, C] the measurement from one side of sth to the other; how wide sth is: *The terrace runs the full width of the house.* ◇ *in ~ It's about ten metres in width.* ◇ *The carpet is available in different widths.* ⇒ picture at DIMENSION **2** [C] a piece of material of a particular width: *You'll need two widths of fabric for each curtain.* **3** [C] the distance between the two long sides of a swimming pool: *How many widths can you swim?* ⇒ compare LENGTH

**wield** /wiːld/ *verb* **1** ~ **sth** to have and use power, authority, etc: *She wields enormous power within the party.* **2** ~ **sth** to hold sth, ready to use it as a weapon or tool **SYN** **brandish**: *He was wielding a large knife.*

**wie·ner** /ˈwiːnə(r)/ *noun* (*NAmE*) **1** = FRANKFURTER **2** (*slang*) a word for a PENIS, used especially by children

**wife** /waɪf/ *noun* (*pl.* **wives** /waɪvz/) the woman that sb is married to; a married woman: *I met my wife at university.* ◇ *He wants a divorce from his estranged wife.* ◇ *He is survived by his wife Anne.* ⇒ see also FISHWIFE, HOUSEWIFE, MIDWIFE, TROPHY WIFE **IDM** see HUSBAND *n.*, OLD, WORLD

**wife·ly** /ˈwaɪfli/ *adj.* (*old-fashioned* or *humorous*) typical or expected of a wife: *wifely duties*

**ˈwife-ˌswapping** *noun* [U] (*informal*) the practice of exchanging sexual partners between a group of married couples

**Wi-Fi™** /ˈwaɪ faɪ/ *noun* [U] (*computing*) a system for connecting to the internet or sending data over computer networks using radio waves instead of wires

**wig** /wɪɡ/ *noun*, *verb*
■ *noun* a piece of artificial hair that is worn on the head, for example to hide the fact that a person is BALD, to cover sb's own hair, or by a judge and some other lawyers in some courts of law
■ *verb* (-gg-)
**PHRV** **ˈwig out** (*NAmE*, *informal*) to become very excited, very anxious or angry about sth; to go crazy

**wig·eon** (*also* **widg·eon**) /ˈwɪdʒən/ *noun* (*pl.* **wig·eon** or **wig·eons**) a type of wild DUCK

**wig·gle** /ˈwɪɡl/ *verb*, *noun*
■ *verb* [I, T] (*informal*) to move from side to side or up and down in short, quick movements; to make sth move in this way **SYN** **wriggle**: *Her bottom wiggled as she walked past.* ◇ *~ sth He removed his shoes and wiggled his toes.*
■ *noun* a small movement from side to side or up and down

---

æ cat | ɑː father | e bed | ɜː fur | ə about | ɪ sit | iː see | i happy | ɒ got (*BrE*) | ɔː saw | ʌ cup | ʊ put | uː too

**wiggle room** noun [U] (informal) the chance to change sth or to understand it in a different way: *The buyer still has some wiggle room when the deal is under contract.* ◊ *The amendment leaves no wiggle room for lawmakers.*

**wig·gly** /ˈwɪgli/ adj. (informal) (of a line) having many curves in it SYN **wavy**

**wight** /waɪt/ noun (literary or old use) **1** a ghost or other spirit **2** (especially following an adjective) a person, considered in a particular way: *a poor wight*

**wig·wam** /ˈwɪgwæm; NAmE -wɑːm/ noun a type of tent, like a DOME in shape, used by Native Americans in the past ⇒ see also TEPEE

**wiki** /ˈwɪki/ noun a website that allows any user to change or add to the information it contains: *There's a wiki page hosted by the conference where you can share ideas and information.*

**wilco** /ˈwɪlkəʊ/ exclamation people say **Wilco!** in communication by radio to show that they agree to do sth

**wild** ❶ A2 /waɪld/ adj., noun
■ adj. (**wild·er**, **wild·est**)
• ANIMALS/PLANTS **1** A2 living or growing in natural conditions; not kept in a house or on a farm: *wild animals/birds/flowers* ◊ *wild salmon* ◊ *wild mushrooms/rice* ◊ *The plants grow wild along the banks of rivers.*
• SCENERY/LAND **2** B2 in its natural state; not changed by people: *the destruction of forests and other wild lands*
• OUT OF CONTROL **3** B1 having no discipline or control: *The boy is wild and completely out of control.* ◊ *He had a wild look in his eyes.*
• FEELINGS **4** B1 full of very strong feeling: *The crowd went wild.* ◊ *It makes me wild (= very angry) to see such waste.* ◊ *Everything about her drove him wild (= made him like her very much).*
• NOT SENSIBLE **5** not carefully planned; not sensible or accurate: *He made a wild guess at the answer.* ◊ *wild accusations*
• EXCITING **6** (informal) very good, pleasant or exciting: *We had a wild time in New York.*
• ENTHUSIASTIC **7** ~ **about sb/sth** (informal) very enthusiastic about sb/sth: *She's totally wild about him.* ◊ *I'm not wild about the idea.*
• WEATHER/SEA **8** affected by storms and strong winds SYN **stormy**: *a wild night* ◊ *The sea was wild.* ▸ **wild·ness** noun [U] ⇒ see also WILDLY
IDM **beyond sb's wildest 'dreams** far more, better, etc. than you could ever have imagined or hoped for **not/never in sb's wildest 'dreams** used to say that sth has happened in a way that sb did not expect at all: *Never in my wildest dreams did I think I'd meet him again.* **run 'wild 1** to grow or develop freely without any control: *The ivy has run wild.* ◊ *Let your imagination run wild and be creative.* **2** if children or animals **run wild**, they behave as they like because nobody is controlling them **wild 'horses would not drag sb somewhere**, **make sb do sth**, **etc.** used to say that nothing would persuade sb to go somewhere or do sth they do not want to do ⇒ more at SOW¹
■ noun **1 the wild** [sing.] a natural environment that is not controlled by people: *The bird is too tame now to survive in the wild.* **2 the wilds** [pl.] areas of a country far from towns or cities, where few people live: *the wilds of Alaska* ◊ (humorous) *They live on a farm somewhere out in the wilds.*

**wild 'boar** noun = BOAR

**'wild card** noun **1** (in card games) a card that has no value of its own and takes the value of any card that the player chooses **2** (sport) an opportunity for sb to play in a competition when they have not qualified in the usual way; a player who enters a competition in this way **3** (computing) a symbol that can represent any letter or number **4** a person or thing whose behaviour or effect is difficult to predict

**wild·cat** /ˈwaɪldkæt/ adj., verb, noun
■ adj. [only before noun] **1** a **wildcat** strike happens suddenly and without the official support of a trade union **2** (of a business or project) that has not been carefully planned and that will probably not be successful; that does not follow normal standards and methods
■ verb [I] (NAmE) (-tt-) to look for oil in a place where nobody has found any yet ▸ **wild-cat·ter** noun
■ noun a type of small wild cat that lives in mountains and forests

**wilde·beest** /ˈwɪldəbiːst/ noun (pl. **wilde·beest**) (also **gnu**) a large ANTELOPE with curved HORNS: *a herd of wildebeest*

**wil·der·ness** /ˈwɪldənəs; NAmE -dərn-/ noun [usually sing.] **1** a large area of land that has never been developed or used for growing crops because it is difficult to live there: *The Antarctic is the world's last great wilderness.* ◊ (NAmE) *a wilderness area* (= one where it is not permitted to build houses or roads) ◊ (figurative) *the barren wilderness of modern life* **2** a place that people do not take care of or control: *Their garden is a wilderness of grass and weeds.* **3** a position that is no longer important, especially in politics: **in the ~** *After three years in the wilderness she was given a government post.*

**wild·fire** /ˈwaɪldfaɪə(r)/ noun a very big fire that spreads quickly and burns natural areas like woods, forests and GRASSLAND IDM ⇒ see SPREAD v.

**wild·flower** /ˈwaɪldflaʊə(r)/ (also **wild 'flower**) noun a flower growing in natural conditions, not planted by sb

**wild·fowl** /ˈwaɪldfaʊl/ noun [pl.] birds that people hunt for sport or food, especially birds that live near water such as DUCKS and GEESE

**wild 'goose chase** noun a search for sth that is impossible for you to find or that does not exist, that makes you waste a lot of time

**wild·life** ❶ B2 /ˈwaɪldlaɪf/ noun [U] animals, birds, insects, etc. that are wild and live in a natural environment: *policies designed to protect wildlife* ◊ *a wildlife habitat*

**wild·ly** /ˈwaɪldli/ adv. **1** in a way that is not controlled: *She looked wildly around for an escape.* ◊ *His heart was beating wildly.* **2** extremely; very: *The story had been wildly exaggerated.* ◊ *It is not a wildly funny play.*

**wild 'rice** noun [U] a grain that is produced by a type of North American grass and is used as food; the plant that produces this grain

**the Wild 'West** noun [sing.] the western states of the US during the years when the first Europeans were settling there, used especially when you are referring to the fact that there was not much respect for the law there

**wiles** /waɪlz/ noun [pl.] clever tricks that sb uses in order to get what they want or to make sb behave in a particular way

**wil·ful** (especially BrE) (NAmE usually **will·ful**) /ˈwɪlfl/ adj. (disapproving) **1** [usually before noun] (formal, disapproving or law) (of a bad or harmful action) done deliberately, although the person doing it knows that it is wrong: *wilful damage* **2** determined to do what you want; not caring about what other people want SYN **headstrong**: *a wilful child* ▸ **wil·ful·ly** /-fəli/ (especially BrE) (NAmE usually **will·ful·ly**) adv. **wil·ful·ness** (especially BrE) (NAmE usually **will·ful·ness**) noun [U]

**will** ❶ A1 /wɪl/ modal verb, verb, noun
■ modal verb (short form **'ll** /l/, negative **will not**, short form **won't** /wəʊnt/, pt **would** /wəd/, strong form **wʊd**/, short form **'d** /d/, negative **would not**, short form **wouldn't** /ˈwʊdnt/) **1** A1 used for talking about or predicting the future: *You'll be in time if you hurry.* ◊ *How long will you be staying in Paris?* ◊ *Fred said he'd be leaving soon.* ◊ *By next year all the money will have been spent.* ⇒ HOMOPHONES at HEEL **2** A1 used for asking sb to do sth: *Will you send this letter for me, please?* ◊ *You'll water the plants while I'm away, won't you?* ◊ *I asked him if he wouldn't mind calling later.* **3** A1 used for inviting sb to do sth: *Will you join us for lunch?* **4** A1 used for showing that sb is willing to do sth: *I'll check this letter for you, if you want.* ◊ *They won't lend us any more money.* ◊ *He wouldn't come—he said he was too busy.* ◊ *We said we would keep them.* **5** A2 used for ordering sb to do sth: *You'll do it this minute!* ◊ *Will you be quiet!* **6** B1 used for stating what you think is probably

# willful

true: *That'll be the doctor now.* ◊ *You'll have had dinner already, I suppose.* **7** 🔑 **B1** used for stating what is generally true: *If it's made of wood it will float.* ◊ *Engines won't run without lubricants.* **8** 🔑 **B1** used for stating what is true or possible in a particular case: *This jar will hold a kilo.* ◊ *The door won't open!* **9** 🔑 **B2** used for talking about habits: *She'll listen to music, alone in her room, for hours.* ◊ *He would spend hours on the telephone.* **HELP** If you put extra stress on the word **will** or **would** in this meaning, it shows that the habit annoys you: *He 'will comb his hair at the table, even though he knows I don't like it.* **10** (*IrishE, NZE*) used in questions with *I* for making offers or suggestions: *Will I call back later?* ⊃ note at MODAL, SHALL

- **verb** (*third person sing. pres. t.* **will**) [I] (only used in the simple present tense) (*old-fashioned* or *formal*) to want or like: *Call it what you will, it's still a problem.*

- **verb 1** to use the power of your mind to do sth or to make sth happen: *~ sth As a child he had thought he could fly, if he willed it enough.* ◊ *~ sb/sth to do sth She willed her eyes to stay open.* ◊ *He willed himself not to panic.* **2** *~ sth | ~ that …* (*old use*) to intend or want sth to happen: *They thought they had been victorious in battle because God had willed it.* **3** to formally give your property or possessions to sb after you have died, by means of a WILL: *~ sb sth Joe had willed them everything he possessed.* ◊ *~ sth (to sb) Joe had willed everything he possessed to them.*

- **noun 1** 🔑 **B1** [C, U] the ability to control your thoughts and actions in order to achieve what you want to do; a strong and determined desire to do sth that you want to do: *to have a strong will* ◊ *to have an iron will/a will of iron* ◊ *Her decision to continue shows great strength of will.* ◊ *The matter became a battle of wills between the king and the barons.* ◊ *~ to do sth The government lacked the political will to reform the tax system.* ◊ *In spite of what happened, he never lost the will to live.* ⊃ see also FREE WILL, GOODWILL, ILL WILL, WILLPOWER **2** 🔑 **B2** [sing.] what sb wants to happen in a particular situation: *They governed according to the will of the people.* ◊ *against sb's ~ I was forced to sign the agreement against my will.* ◊ *She always wants to impose her will on other people* (= to get what she wants). **3** 🔑 **B2** (*also formal* **tes·ta·ment**) [C] a legal document that says what is to happen to sb's money and property after they die: *I ought to make a will.* ◊ *in your ~ My father left me the house in his will.* ⊃ see also LIVING WILL **4** **-willed** (in adjectives) having the type of will mentioned: *a strong-willed young woman* ◊ *weak-willed greedy people*

**IDM** **at 'will** whenever or wherever you like: *They were able to come and go at will.* **where there's a ,will there's a 'way** (*saying*) if you really want to do sth then you will find a way of doing it **with a 'will** in a willing and enthusiastic way **with the best will in the 'world** used to say that you cannot do sth, even though you really want to: *With the best will in the world I could not describe him as a good father.*

**will·ful** (*NAmE*) = WILFUL

**wil·lie** = WILLY

**the wil·lies** /ðə ˈwɪliz/ *noun* [pl.] (*informal*) if sth **gives you the willies**, you are frightened by it or find it unpleasant

**will·ing** 🔑 **B2** /ˈwɪlɪŋ/ *adj.* **1** 🔑 **B2** [not usually before noun] *~ (to do sth)* not objecting to doing sth; having no reason for not doing sth: *Many consumers are willing to pay more for organic food* ◊ *They are willing and able to share their knowledge and experience.* **2** 🔑 **B2** [usually before noun] ready or pleased to help and not needing to be persuaded; done or given in an enthusiastic way: *a willing participant/accomplice* ◊ *a willing buyer/seller* ◊ *She's very willing.* ◊ *their willing participation in the plan* **OPP** unwilling ▶ **will·ing·ly** *adv.*: *People would willingly pay more for better services.* ◊ *'Will you help me?' 'Willingly.'* **IDM** SEE SHOW *v.,* SPIRIT *n.*

**will·ing·ness** 🔑 **C1** /ˈwɪlɪŋnəs/ *noun* [U, sing.] the quality of being happy and ready to do sth: *Success in studying depends on a willingness to learn.*

**will-o'-the-wisp** /ˌwɪl ə ðə ˈwɪsp/ *noun* [usually sing.] **1** a thing that is impossible to obtain; a person that you cannot depend on **2** a blue light that is sometimes seen at night on soft, wet ground and is caused by natural gases burning

**wil·low** /ˈwɪləʊ/ *noun* **1** [C] a tree with long, thin branches and long, thin leaves, that often grows near water ⊃ VISUAL VOCAB page V6 **2** [U] the wood of the willow tree, used especially for making CRICKET BATS

**wil·lowy** /ˈwɪləʊi/ *adj.* (*approving*) (of a person, especially a woman) tall, thin and attractive

**will·power** /ˈwɪlpaʊə(r)/ *noun* [U] the ability to control your thoughts and actions in order to achieve what you want to do

**willy** (*also* **wil·lie**) /ˈwɪli/ *noun* (*pl.* **-ies**) (*BrE, informal*) a word for a PENIS, used especially by children or when speaking to children ⊃ see also WILLIES

**willy-nilly** /ˌwɪli ˈnɪli/ *adv.* (*informal*) **1** whether you want to or not: *She was forced willy-nilly to accept the company's proposals.* **2** in a careless way without planning: *Don't use your credit card willy-nilly.*

**wilt** /wɪlt/ *verb* **1** [I] (of a plant or flower) to bend towards the ground because of the heat or a lack of water **SYN** **droop 2** [I] (*informal*) to become weak or tired or less confident **SYN** **flag**: *The spectators were wilting visibly in the hot sun.* ◊ *He was wilting under the pressure of work.* **3** **thou wilt** (*old use*) used to mean 'you will', when talking to one person

**wilt·ed** /ˈwɪltɪd/ *adj.* **wilted** vegetable leaves, for example LETTUCE leaves, have been cooked for a short time and then used in a salad

**wily** /ˈwaɪli/ *adj.* (**wili·er, wili·est**) clever at getting what you want, and willing to trick people **SYN** **cunning**: *The boss is a wily old fox.*

**wimp** /wɪmp/ *noun, verb*
- **noun** (*informal, disapproving*) a person who is not strong, brave or confident **SYN** **weed** ▶ **wimp·ish** (*also* **wimpy**) *adj.*: *wimpish behaviour*
- **verb**

**PHRV** **wimp ˈout (of sth)** (*informal, disapproving*) to not do sth that you intended to do because you are too frightened or not confident enough to do it

**win** 🔑 **A1** /wɪn/ *verb, noun*

- **verb** (**win·ning, won, won** /wʌn/) **1** 🔑 **A1** [I, T] to be the most successful in a competition, race, battle, etc: *Which team won?* ◊ *~ sth to win an election* ◊ *to win a game/race/war/battle* ◊ *She loves to win an argument.* ◊ *~ at sth to win at cards/chess* ◊ *~ (by sth) (against sb/sth) France won by six goals to two against Denmark.* **2** 🔑 **A1** [T] to get sth as the result of a competition, race, election, etc: *~ sth Britain won five gold medals.* ◊ *He won £3000 in the lottery.* ◊ *Everyone who takes part wins a small prize.* ◊ *to win an award/a title* ◊ *~ sth from sb The Conservatives won the seat from Labour in the last election.* ◊ *~ yourself/sb sth You've won yourself a trip to New York.* ⊃ HOMOPHONES at ONE **3** 🔑 **B1** [T] *~ sth* to achieve or get sth that you want, especially by your own efforts: *They are trying to win support for their proposals.* ◊ *The company has won a contract to supply books and materials to schools.* ◊ *She won the admiration of many people in her battle against cancer.* ⊃ see also NO-WIN, WINNER, WINNING, WIN-WIN

**IDM** **win (sth) hands ˈdown** (*informal*) to win sth very easily **win sb's ˈheart** to make sb love you **win or ˈlose** whether you succeed or fail: *Win or lose, we'll know we've done our best.* **you, he, etc. can't ˈwin** (*informal*) used to say that there is no acceptable way of dealing with a particular situation **you can't win them ˈall | you ˈwin some, you ˈlose some** (*informal*) used to express sympathy for sb who has been disappointed about sth **you ˈwin** (*informal*) used to agree to what sb wants after you have failed to persuade them to do or let you do sth else: *OK, you win. I'll admit I was wrong.* ⊃ more at DAY, SPUR *n.*

**PHRV** **win sb↔aˈround/ˈover (to sth)** (*also* **win sb↔ˈround (to sth)** *especially in BrE*) to get sb to change their opinion about sth and give you their support and approval: *She's against the idea but I'm sure I can win her over.* **win sth/sb↔ˈback** to get or have again sth/sb that you had before: *The party is struggling to win back voters who have been alienated by recent scandals.* **win**

**ˈout/ˈthrough** (*informal*) to be successful despite difficulties: *It won't be easy but we'll win through in the end.*
- **noun** 🔑 B1 a victory in a game, contest, etc: *two wins and three defeats* ◊ *The team are in hot form with nine **straight wins*** (= nine wins, one after another, without any losses). ◊ *They have not had a win so far this season.* ◊ **~ over/against sb** *France swept to a 6–2 win over Denmark.* ◊ (*figurative*) *The company is **scoring big wins** with new products.*

**wince** /wɪns/ *verb* [I] **~ (at sth)** to suddenly make an expression with your face that shows that you are embarrassed or feeling pain: *He winced as a sharp pain shot through his left leg.* ◊ *I still wince when I think about that stupid thing I said.* ⊃ **WORDFINDER NOTE** at EXPRESSION
▶ **wince** *noun* [usually sing.]: *a wince of pain*

**winch** /wɪntʃ/ *noun, verb*
- **noun** a machine for lifting or pulling heavy objects using a rope or chain
- **verb** **~ sb/sth + adv./prep.** to lift sb/sth up into the air using a winch

**wind¹** 🔑 A2 /wɪnd/ *noun, verb* ⊃ see also WIND²
- **noun 1** 🔑 A2 [C, U] (*also* **the wind**) air that moves quickly as a result of natural forces: **strong/high winds** ◊ **gale-force winds** ◊ *a light wind* ◊ *a north/south/east/west wind* ◊ *a chill/cold/biting wind from the north* ◊ *The **wind is blowing** from the south.* ◊ **in the ~** *The trees were swaying in the wind.* ◊ *A **gust of wind** blew my hat off.* ◊ *The weather was hot, without a **breath of wind**.* ◊ *The wall gives some protection from the **prevailing wind*** (= the direction the wind blows from most often). ◊ **wind speed/direction** ◊ *renewable energies like solar and **wind power*** ⊃ see also CROSSWIND, DOWNWIND, HEADWIND, TAILWIND, TRADE WINDS, WINDY

**WORDFINDER** breeze, buffet, calm, force, gale, gust, hurricane, prevailing, tornado

**2** (*BrE*) (*NAmE* **gas**) [U] air that you SWALLOW with food or drink; gas that is produced in your stomach or INTESTINES that makes you feel uncomfortable: *I can't eat beans—they give me wind.* ◊ *Try to bring the baby's wind up.* **3** [U] breath that you need when you do exercise or blow into a musical instrument: *I need time to get my wind back after that run.* ◊ *He kicked Gomez in the stomach, knocking the wind out of him.* ⊃ see also SECOND WIND **4** [U + sing./pl. v.] (*also* **winds** [pl.]) the group of musical instruments in an ORCHESTRA that produce sounds when you blow into them, especially WOODWIND instruments; the musicians who play those instruments: *music for wind and strings* ◊ *The wind section played beautifully.* **IDM** **break ˈwind** to release gas from your BOWELS through your ANUS **get ˈwind of sth** (*informal*) to hear about sth secret or private **get/have the ˈwind up (about sth)** (*informal*) to become/be frightened about sth **in the ˈwind** about to happen soon, although you do not know exactly how or when **like the ˈwind** very quickly **put the ˈwind up sb** (*BrE*, *informal*) to make sb frightened **take the ˈwind out of sb's sails** (*informal*) to make sb suddenly less confident or angry, especially when you do or say sth that they do not expect **a wind/the winds of ˈchange** (used especially by journalists) an event or a series of events that has started to happen and will cause important changes or results: *A wind of change was blowing through the banking world.* ⊃ more at CAUTION *n.*, FOLLOWING *adj.*, ILL *adj.*, SAIL *v.*, STRAW, WAY *n.*

- **verb 1** [usually passive] to make sb unable to breathe easily for a short time: **be winded (by sth)** *He was momentarily winded by the blow to his stomach.* **2 ~ sb** (*BrE*) to gently hit or rub a baby's back to make it BURP (= release gas from its stomach through its mouth) **SYN** **burp** ⊃ see also LONG-WINDED

**wind²** 🔑 B2 /waɪnd/ *verb* ⊃ see also WIND¹ (**wound**, **wound** /waʊnd/) **1** 🔑 B2 [I, T] (of a road, river, etc.) to have many bends and TWISTS: **~ + adv./prep.** *The path wound down to the beach.* ◊ **~ its way + adv./prep.** *The river winds its way between two meadows.* ⊃ see also WINDING **2** 🔑 B2 [T] **~ sth + adv./prep.** to wrap or TWIST sth around itself or sth else: *He wound the wool into a ball.* ◊ *Wind the bandage around your finger.* **3** 🔑 B2 [T, I] to operate a tape, film, etc. so that it moves nearer to its ending or starting position: **~ sth forward/back** *He wound the tape back to the beginning.* ◊ **~ forward/back** *Wind forward to the bit where they discover the body.* **4** [T, I] to make a clock or a machine work by turning a KNOB, handle, etc. several times; to be able to be made to work in this way: **~ sth (up)** *He had forgotten to wind his watch.* ◊ **~ up** *It was one of those old-fashioned gramophones that winds up.* ⊃ see also WIND-UP **5** [T] **~ sth** to turn a handle several times: *You operate the trapdoor by winding this handle.* ▶ **wind** *noun*: *Give the handle another couple of winds.* **IDM** see LITTLE FINGER

**PHR V** **ˌwind ˈdown 1** (of a person) to rest or relax after a period of activity or excitement **SYN** **unwind 2** (of a machine) to go slowly and then stop **ˌwind sth↔ˈdown 1** to bring a business, an activity, etc. to an end gradually over a period of time: *The government is winding down its nuclear programme.* ⊃ related noun WIND-DOWN **2** to make sth such as the window of a car move downwards by turning a handle, pressing a button, etc: *Can I wind my window down?* **ˌwind ˈup** (*informal*) (of a person) to find yourself in a particular place or situation: *I always said he would wind up in prison.* ◊ **wind up doing sth** *We eventually wound up staying in a little hotel a few miles from town.* ◊ **+ adj.** *If you take risks like that you'll wind up dead.* **ˌwind ˈup** | **ˌwind sth↔ˈup** to bring sth such as a speech or meeting to an end: *The speaker was just winding up when the door was flung open.* ◊ *If we all agree, let's wind up the discussion.* **ˌwind sb↔ˈup** (*BrE*, *informal*) to deliberately say or do sth in order to annoy sb *Calm down! Can't you see he's only winding you up?* ◊ *That can't be true! You're winding me up.* ⊃ related noun WIND-UP **ˌwind sth↔ˈup 1** to stop running a company, business, etc. and close it completely **2** to make sth such as the window of a car move upwards by turning a handle, pressing a button, etc.

**wind-bag** /ˈwɪndbæɡ/ *noun* (*informal, disapproving*) a person who talks too much, and does not say anything important or interesting

**wind-blown** /ˈwɪnd bləʊn/ *adj.* **1** carried from one place to another by the wind **2** made untidy by the wind: *wind-blown hair*

**wind-break** /ˈwɪndbreɪk/ *noun* a row of trees, a fence, etc. that provides protection from the wind

**wind-break-er** /ˈwɪndbreɪkə(r)/ (*NAmE*) (*BrE*, old-fashioned **wind-cheat-er** /ˈwɪndtʃiːtə(r)/) *noun* a jacket designed to protect you from the wind

**wind chill** /ˈwɪnd tʃɪl/ *noun* [U] the effect of low temperature combined with wind on sb/sth: *The high **wind chill factor** made it seem even colder.*

**wind chimes** /ˈwɪnd tʃaɪmz/ *noun* [pl.] a set of hanging pieces of metal, etc. that make a pleasant ringing sound in the wind

**wind-down** /ˈwaɪnd daʊn/ (*also* **winding-ˈdown**) *noun* [sing.] a slow, steady reduction in activity as sth comes to an end: *The wind-down of the company was handled very efficiently.*

**wind-er** /ˈwaɪndə(r)/ *noun* a device or a machine that winds sth, for example sth that winds a watch or the film in a camera

**wind-fall** /ˈwɪndfɔːl/ *noun* **1** an amount of money that sb/sth wins or receives unexpectedly: *The hospital got a sudden windfall of £300000.* ◊ *windfall profits* ◊ *The government imposed a **windfall tax*** (= a tax on profits to be paid once only, not every year) *on some industries.* **2** a fruit, especially an apple, that the wind has blown down from a tree

**wind farm** /ˈwɪnd fɑːm; *NAmE* fɑːrm/ *noun* an area of land on which there are a lot of WINDMILLS or WIND TURBINES for producing electricity ⊃ **WORDFINDER NOTE** at ENERGY

**wind-ing** /ˈwaɪndɪŋ/ *adj.* having a curving and TWISTING shape: *a long and winding road*

**winding-down** /ˌwaɪndɪŋ ˈdaʊn/ *noun* = WIND-DOWN

# wind instrument 1788

**wind instrument** /'wɪnd ɪnstrəmənt/ noun any musical instrument that you play by blowing ⊃ compare BRASS, WOODWIND

**wind·less** /'wɪndləs/ adj. (formal) without wind: *a windless day* OPP **windy**

**wind machine** /'wɪnd məʃiːn/ noun **1** a machine used in the theatre or in films that blows air to give the effect of wind **2** a machine used in ORCHESTRAS to produce the sound of wind

**wind·mill** /'wɪndmɪl/ noun **1** a building with equipment for GRINDING grain into flour that is driven by the power of the wind turning long arms (called SAILS) **2** a tall, thin structure with parts that turn round, used to change the power of the wind into electricity **3** (BrE) (NAmE **pin·wheel**) a toy with curved plastic parts that form the shape of a flower that turns round on the end of a stick when you blow on it IDM see TILT v.

**win·dow** ❶ A1 /'wɪndəʊ/ noun **1** ? A1 an opening in the wall or roof of a building, car, etc., usually covered with glass, that allows light and air to come in and people to see out; the glass in a window: *She looked out of the window.* ◇ *to open/close the window* ◇ *the bedroom/kitchen/car window* ◇ *a broken window* ⊃ see also BAY WINDOW, DORMER WINDOW, FRENCH WINDOW, PICTURE WINDOW, SASH WINDOW **2** ? A1 = SHOP WINDOW: **in the ~** *I saw the dress I wanted in the window.* ◇ *a window display* **3** ? B1 a small area of sth that you can see through, for example to talk to sb or read sth on the other side: *There was a long line of people at the box-office window.* ◇ *The address must be clearly visible through the window of the envelope.* **4** ? B1 (computing) an area within a frame on a computer screen, in which a particular program is operating or in which information of a particular type is shown: *to create/open a window* **5** [sing.] **~ on/into sth** a way of seeing and learning about sth: *Television is a sort of window on the world.* ◇ *It gave me an intriguing window into the way people live.* **6** a time when there is an opportunity to do sth, although it may not last long: *We now have a small window of opportunity in which to make our views known.*
IDM **fly/go out (of) the ˈwindow** (*informal*) to stop existing; to disappear completely: *As soon as the kids arrived, order went out of the window.*

**ˈwindow box** noun a long, narrow box outside a window, in which plants are grown

**ˈwindow cleaner** noun **1** (*especially BrE*) (NAmE usually **ˈwindow washer**) [C] a person whose job is to clean windows **2** [U] (*especially NAmE*) a liquid substance used for cleaning windows

**ˈwindow dressing** noun [U] **1** the art of arranging goods in shop windows in an attractive way **2** (*disapproving*) the fact of doing or saying sth in a way that creates a good impression but does not show the real facts: *The reforms are seen as window dressing.*

**ˈwindow ledge** noun = WINDOWSILL

**win·dow·less** /'wɪndəʊləs/ adj. without windows: *a tiny, windowless cell*

**win·dow·pane** /'wɪndəʊpeɪn/ noun a piece of glass in a window

**ˈwindow seat** noun **1** a seat next to a window in a plane, train or other vehicle **2** a seat below a window

**ˈwindow shade** noun (NAmE) = BLIND

**ˈwindow shopping** noun [U] the activity of looking at the goods in shop windows, usually without intending to buy anything: *to go window shopping*

**win·dow·sill** /'wɪndəʊsɪl/ (also **sill**, **ˈwindow ledge**) noun a narrow shelf below a window, either inside or outside: *Place the plants on a sunny windowsill.*

**ˈwindow washer** noun (NAmE) = WINDOW CLEANER (1)

**wind·pipe** /'wɪndpaɪp/ noun the tube in the body that carries air from the throat to the lungs SYN **trachea** ⊃ VISUAL VOCAB page V1

**wind·screen** /'wɪndskriːn/ (BrE) (NAmE **wind·shield**) noun the window across the front of a vehicle

**ˈwindscreen wiper** (BrE) (NAmE **ˈwindshield wiper**) (also **wiper** BrE, NAmE) noun a long metal part with a rubber edge that moves across a windscreen to make it clear of rain, snow, etc.

**wind·shield** /'wɪndʃiːld/ noun **1** (NAmE) (BrE **wind·screen**) the window across the front of a vehicle **2** a glass or plastic screen that provides protection from the wind, for example at the front of a motorcycle

**wind·storm** /'wɪndstɔːm; NAmE -stɔːrm/ noun (NAmE) a storm where there is very strong wind but little rain or snow

**wind·surf·er** /'wɪndsɜːfə(r); NAmE -sɜːrf-/ noun **1** (also **sail·board**) a long, narrow board with a sail, that you stand on and sail across water on **2** a person on a windsurfer

**wind·surf·ing** /'wɪndsɜːfɪŋ; NAmE -sɜːrf-/ (also **board·sail·ing**) noun [U] the sport of sailing on water standing on a windsurfer: *to go windsurfing* ▶ **wind·surf** verb [I]: *Most visitors come to sail or windsurf.*

**wind·swept** /'wɪndswept/ adj. **1** (of a place) having strong winds and little protection from them: *the windswept Atlantic coast* **2** looking as though you have been in a strong wind: *windswept hair*

**wind tunnel** /'wɪnd tʌnl/ noun a large tunnel where aircraft, etc. are tested by forcing air past them

**wind turbine** /'wɪnd tɜːbaɪn; NAmE tɜːrb-/ noun a type of modern WINDMILL used for producing electricity

**wind-up** /'waɪnd ʌp/ adj., noun
- adj. [only before noun] **1** that you operate by turning a key or handle: *an old-fashioned wind-up gramophone* **2** intended to bring sth to an end: *a wind-up speech*
- noun (BrE, informal) something that sb says or does in order to be deliberately annoying, especially as a joke

**wind·ward** /'wɪndwəd; NAmE -wərd/ adj., noun
- adj. on the side of sth from which the wind is blowing: *the windward side of the boat* OPP **leeward** ⊃ see also LEE ▶ **wind·ward** adv. OPP **leeward**
- noun [U] the side or direction from which the wind is blowing: *to sail to windward* ⊃ compare LEEWARD

**windy** /'wɪndi/ adj. (**wind·ier**, **windi·est**) **1** (of weather, etc.) with a lot of wind: *a windy day* OPP **windless 2** (of a place) getting a lot of wind: *windy hills* **3** (*informal*, *disapproving*) (of speech) involving speaking for longer than necessary and in a way that is complicated and not clear

**the ˌWindy ˈCity** noun [sing.] a name for the US city of Chicago

**wine** ❶ A1 /waɪn/ noun, verb
- noun **1** ? A1 [U, C] an alcoholic drink made from the juice of GRAPES that has been left to FERMENT. There are many different kinds of wine: *sparkling wine* ◇ *red/rosé/white wine* ◇ *a selection of fine wines* ◇ *a glass/bottle of wine* ◇ *He never drank wine, beer or spirits.* ⊃ see also RED WINE, TABLE WINE, WHITE WINE ⊃ HOMOPHONES at WHINE **2** [U, C] an alcoholic drink made from plants or fruits other than GRAPES: *elderberry/rice wine* **3** [U] (also **ˌwine ˈred**) a dark red colour
- verb
IDM **ˌwine and ˈdine (sb)** to go to restaurants, etc. and enjoy good food and drink; to entertain sb by buying them good food and drink: *The firm spent thousands wining and dining potential clients.*

**ˈwine bar** noun a bar or small restaurant where wine is the main drink available

**ˈwine cellar** (also **ˈcel·lar**) noun an underground room where wine is stored; the wine stored in this room

**wine cool·er** noun **1** /waɪn ˈkuːlə(r)/ (NAmE) a drink made with wine, fruit juice, ice and SODA WATER **2** /ˈwaɪn kuːlə(r)/ a container for putting a bottle of wine in to cool it or keep it cool

**ˈwine farm** noun (SAfrE) a VINEYARD (= a place where GRAPES are grown for making wine)

**ˈwine glass** noun a glass for drinking wine from

**wine·grow·er** /ˈwaɪnɡrəʊə(r)/ noun a person who grows GRAPES for wine

**ˈwine list** noun a list of wines available in a restaurant

**wine·maker** /ˈwaɪnmeɪkə(r)/ noun a person who produces wine ▶ **wine·mak·ing** /-kɪŋ/ noun [U]

**win·ery** /ˈwaɪnəri/ noun (pl. -ies) (especially NAmE) a place where wine is made ⊃ compare VINEYARD

**ˈwine tasting** noun **1** [C] an event at which people taste and compare a number of wines **2** [U] the activity of tasting and comparing a number of wines

**wine ˈvinegar** noun [U] VINEGAR that is made from wine rather than from grain or apples

# wing ⓘ B1 /wɪŋ/ noun, verb

■ noun
- OF BIRD/INSECT **1** B1 [C] one of the parts of the body of a bird, insect or BAT that it uses for flying: *The swan flapped its wings noisily.* ⊃ VISUAL VOCAB pages V2, V3 **2** B1 the wing of a chicken, etc. eaten as food: *We ordered the fried chicken wings.* ⊃ see also BUFFALO WINGS
- OF PLANE **3** B1 [C] one of the large, flat parts that stick out from the side of a plane and help to keep it in the air when it is flying: *Salvage teams have been able to recover part of the wing of the plane.*
- OF BUILDING **4** [C] a part of a large building that sticks out from the main part: *the east wing* ◊ *the new wing of the hospital*
- OF CAR **5** (BrE) (NAmE **fend·er**) [C] a part of a car that is above a wheel: *There was a dent in the nearside wing.*
- OF ORGANIZATION **6** [C] one section of an organization that has a particular function or whose members share the same opinions SYN **arm**: *the radical wing of the party* ◊ *the political wing of the National Resistance Army* ⊃ see also LEFT WING, RIGHT WING
- IN FOOTBALL/HOCKEY **7** [C] = WINGER ⊃ see also LEFT WING, RIGHT WING **8** [C] the far left or right side of the sports field: *He plays on the wing.*
- IN THEATRE **9** the wings [pl.] the area at either side of the stage that cannot be seen by the audience ⊃ WORDFINDER NOTE at STAGE

IDM **get your ˈwings** to pass the exams that mean you are allowed to fly a plane **(waiting) in the ˈwings** ready to take over a particular job or be used in a particular situation when needed **on a ˌwing and a ˈprayer** with only a very slight chance of success **on the ˈwing** (literary) (of a bird, insect, etc.) flying **take sb under your ˈwing** to take care of and help sb who has less experience of sth than you **take ˈwing** (literary) (of a bird, insect, etc.) to fly away: *Her imagination took wing.* ⊃ more at CLIP v., SPREAD v.

■ verb
- FLY **1** [T, I] ~ (its way) + adv./prep. (literary) to fly somewhere: *A solitary seagull winged its way across the bay.*
- GO QUICKLY **2** [T] ~ its way + adv./prep. to be sent somewhere very quickly: *An application form will be winging its way to you soon.*

IDM **ˈwing it** (informal) to do sth without planning or preparing it first SYN **improvise**: *I didn't know I'd have to make a speech—I just had to wing it.*

**ˈwing back** noun (in football (soccer)) a player who plays near the edge of the field and who both attacks and defends

**ˈwing commander** noun an officer of high rank in the British AIR FORCE: *Wing Commander Brian Moore*

**winged** /wɪŋd/ adj. **1** having wings: *winged insects* OPP **wingless 2 -winged** (in adjectives) having the number or type of wings mentioned: *a long-winged bird*

**wing·er** /ˈwɪŋə(r)/ (also **wing**) noun (sport) either of the attacking players who play towards the side of the playing area in sports such as football (soccer) or hockey

**ˈwing·less** /ˈwɪŋləs/ adj. (especially of insects) without wings OPP **winged**

**ˈwing mirror** (BrE) (NAmE **ˈside-view mirror**) noun a mirror that sticks out from the side of a vehicle and allows the driver to see behind the vehicle

**ˈwing nut** noun a NUT for holding things in place, which has parts that stick out at the sides so that you can turn it easily

**ˈwing·span** /ˈwɪŋspæn/ noun the distance between the end of one wing and the end of the other when the wings are fully stretched: *a bird with a two-foot wingspan*

**ˈwing·suit** /ˈwɪŋsuːt/ noun a piece of clothing with material between the legs and under the arms that fills with air when the user jumps from an aircraft or a high place: *wingsuit flying/flyers*

**ˈwing·tips** /ˈwɪŋtɪps/ noun [pl.] (NAmE) strong leather shoes that fasten with LACES and have an extra piece of leather with small holes in it over the toe

**wink** /wɪŋk/ verb, noun
■ verb **1** [I] ~ (at sb) to close one eye and open it again quickly, especially as a private signal to sb, or to show sth is a joke: *He winked at her and she knew he was thinking the same thing that she was.* ⊃ compare BLINK **2** [I] to shine with an unsteady light; to flash on and off SYN **blink**: *We could see the lights of the ship winking in the distance.*
PHRV **ˌwink at ˈsth** to pretend that you have not noticed sth, especially sth bad or illegal
■ noun an act of winking, especially as a signal to sb: *He gave her a knowing wink.*
IDM **not get/have a ˈwink of sleep | not sleep a ˈwink** to not be able to sleep: *I didn't get a wink of sleep last night.* ◊ *I hardly slept a wink.* ⊃ more at NOD n., NUDGE n., TIP v.

**win·kle** /ˈwɪŋkl/ noun, verb
■ noun (BrE) (also **peri·win·kle** NAmE, BrE) a small SHELLFISH, like a SNAIL, that can be eaten
■ verb (BrE, informal)
PHRV **ˌwinkle sth/sb↔ˈout (of sth)** to get sb/sth out of a place or position, especially when this is not easy to do **ˌwinkle sth ˈout of sb** to get information from sb, especially with difficulty SYN **extract**: *She always manages to winkle secrets out of people.*

**Win·ne·bago™** /ˌwɪnɪˈbeɪɡəʊ/ noun (NAmE) (pl. **Win·nebago** or **-os**) a large vehicle designed for people to live and sleep in when they are camping; a type of RV

**win·ner** ⓘ A2 /ˈwɪnə(r)/ noun **1** A2 a person, a team, an animal, etc. that wins sth: *The lucky winner gets an all-expenses-paid trip to Sydney.* ◊ *an award winner* ◊ *a medal/prize winner* ◊ *the winner of a prize/an award* ◊ *the 2018 World Cup winners* ⊃ WORDFINDER NOTE at COMPETITION **2** [usually sing.] (informal) a thing or person that is successful or likely to be successful: *I think your idea is a winner.* **onto a ~** *The design is very good. We could be onto a winner* (= we may do or produce sth successful). **3** [sing.] (sport) a goal or point that causes a team or a person to win a game: *Morgan scored the winner after 20 minutes.* ⊃ compare LOSER IDM see PICK v.

**win·ning** /ˈwɪnɪŋ/ adj. **1** [only before noun] that wins or has won sth, for example a race or competition: *the winning horse* ◊ *the winning goal* **2** [usually before noun] attractive in a way that makes other people like you: *a winning smile* ▶ **win·ning·ly** adv. IDM see CARD n.
IDM **winning ˈways** (informal) a series of victories or successes: *He'll look to continue his winning ways with a victory in Mexico on 16 February.*

**win·ning·est** /ˈwɪnɪŋɪst/ adj. (NAmE, informal) having won the most games, races or competitions: *the winningest coach in the history of the US national team*

**ˈwinning post** noun (especially BrE) a post that shows where the end of a race is: *to be first past the winning post*

# winnings 1790

**win·nings** /ˈwɪnɪŋz/ noun [pl.] money that sb wins in a competition or game or by GAMBLING

**win·now** /ˈwɪnəʊ/ verb ~ sth to blow air through grain in order to remove its outer layer (called the CHAFF)
**PHRV** **winnow sb/sth 'out (of sth)** (formal) to remove people or things from a group so that only the best ones are left **SYN** **sift**

**wino** /ˈwaɪnəʊ/ noun (pl. -os) (informal) a person who drinks a lot of cheap alcohol and who has no home

**win·some** /ˈwɪnsəm/ adj. (especially literary) (of people or their manner) pleasant and attractive **SYN** **engaging**: *a winsome smile* ▶ **win·some·ly** adv.

**win·ter** **🔊** **A1** /ˈwɪntə(r)/ noun, verb
■ noun **🔊** **A1** [U, C] the coldest season of the year, between autumn and spring: *a cold/mild/harsh winter* ◇ *a severe/hard winter* ◇ *We went to New Zealand last winter.* ◇ **in (the) ~** *Our house can be very cold in (the) winter.* ◇ *the winter months* ◇ *winter storms/weather* ◇ *a winter coat* **IDM** see DEAD n.
■ verb [I] (+ adv./prep.) to spend the winter somewhere: *Many British birds winter in Africa.* ⇨ compare OVERWINTER

**winter 'sports** noun [pl.] sports that people do on snow or ice

**win·ter·time** /ˈwɪntətaɪm/ NAmE -tərt-/ noun [U] the period of time when it is winter: *The days are shorter in (the) wintertime.*

**winter 'vomiting bug** (also **winter 'vomiting virus**) noun (BrE) = NOROVIRUS

**win·try** /ˈwɪntri/ adj. **1** typical of winter; cold: *wintry weather* ◇ *a wintry landscape* ◇ *wintry showers* (= of snow) **2** not friendly **SYN** **frosty**: *a wintry smile*

**win-'win** adj. [only before noun] (of a situation) in which there is a good result for each person or group involved: *This is a win-win situation all around.*

**wipe** **🔊+** **C1** /waɪp/ verb, noun
■ verb **1** **🔊+** **C1** to rub sth against a surface, in order to remove dirt or liquid from it; to rub a surface with a cloth, etc. in order to clean it: **~ sth (on sth)** *Please wipe your feet on the mat.* ◇ *He wiped his hands on a clean towel.* ◇ **~ sth with sth** *She was sniffing and wiping her eyes with a tissue.* ◇ **~ sth + adj.** *He wiped his plate clean with a piece of bread.* **2** **🔊+** **C1** to remove dirt, liquid, etc. from sth by using a cloth, your hand, etc: **~ sth (from/off sth)** *He wiped the sweat from his forehead.* ◇ **~ sth away/off/up** *She wiped off her make-up.* ◇ *Use that cloth to wipe up the mess.* **3** to remove information, sound, images, etc. from a computer, video, etc. **SYN** **erase**: **~ sth off (sth)** *You must have wiped off that programme I recorded.* ◇ **~ sth** *Somebody had wiped all the tapes.* **4** to deliberately forget an experience because it was unpleasant or embarrassing **SYN** **erase**: **~ sth from sth** *I tried to wipe the whole episode from my mind.* ◇ **~ sth out** *You can never wipe out the past.*
**IDM** **wipe the 'grin/'smile off your 'face** (especially in orders) to stop smiling, especially because sb else is annoyed and does not think the situation is funny: *Wipe that grin off your face and get back to work.* **wipe sb/sth off the 'face of the 'earth | wipe sth off the 'map** to destroy or remove sb/sth completely **wipe the slate 'clean** to agree to forget about past mistakes or arguments and start again with a relationship ⇨ more at FLOOR n.
**PHRV** **wipe sth↔'down** to clean a surface completely, using a wet cloth: *She took a cloth and wiped down the kitchen table.* **wipe sth off sth** to remove sth from sth: *Billions of pounds were wiped off share prices today.* **wipe 'out** (informal) to fall over, especially when you are doing a sport such as skiing or SURFING **wipe sb↔'out** (informal) to make sb extremely tired: *All that travelling has wiped her out.* ⇨ see also WIPED OUT **wipe sb/sth↔'out** [often passive] to destroy or remove sb/sth completely: *Whole villages were wiped out by the earthquake.* ◇ *Last year's profits were virtually wiped out.* ◇ *a campaign to wipe out malaria* ⇨ related noun WIPEOUT

■ noun **1** an act of cleaning sth using a cloth: *Can you give the table a quick wipe?* **2** a special piece of thin cloth or soft paper that has been treated with a liquid and that you use to clean away dirt and bacteria: *Remember to take nappies and baby wipes.* ◇ *a packet of wet wipes*

**wiped 'out** adj. [not before noun] (informal) extremely tired: *You look wiped out.*

**wipe-out** /ˈwaɪpaʊt/ noun (informal) **1** [U, C] complete failure, defeat or DESTRUCTION: *The party faces virtual wipeout in the election.* ◇ *a 5–0 wipeout* **2** [C] a fall from a SURFBOARD

**wiper** /ˈwaɪpə(r)/ noun = WINDSCREEN WIPER

**wire** **🔊** **B2** /ˈwaɪə(r)/ noun, verb
■ noun **1** **🔊** **B2** [U, C] metal in the form of thin THREAD; a piece of this: *a coil of copper wire* ◇ *wire mesh* ◇ *A high wire fence encircles the complex.* ◇ *The box was fastened with a rusty wire.* ⇨ picture at CORD ⇨ see also BARBED WIRE, CHICKEN WIRE, HIGH WIRE, RAZOR WIRE, TRIPWIRE **2** **🔊** [C, U] a piece of wire that is used to carry an electric current or signal: *electrical wires* ◇ *overhead wires* ◇ *The telephone wires had been cut.* ⇨ **WORDFINDER NOTE** at ELECTRICITY ⇨ see also HOT-WIRE **3** an electronic listening device that can be hidden on a person **4** **the wire** [sing.] a wire fence: *Three prisoners escaped by crawling under the wire.* **5** [C] (informal, especially NAmE) = TELEGRAM: *We sent a wire asking him to join us.* ⇨ see also WIRY
**IDM** **get your 'wires crossed** (informal) to become confused about what sb has said to you so that you think they meant sth else **go, come, etc. (right) down to the 'wire** (informal) if you say that a situation goes **down to the wire**, you mean that the result will not be decided or known until the very end **under the 'wire** (informal, especially NAmE) at the last possible opportunity; just in time ⇨ more at LIVE² adj., PULL v.
■ verb **1** **~ sth (up)** to connect a building, piece of equipment, etc. to an electricity supply using wires: *Make sure the plug is wired up correctly.* **2** **~ sb/sth up (to sth) | ~ sb/sth to sth** to connect sb/sth to a piece of equipment: *In the test, volunteers were wired up to brain monitors.* **3** **~ sth (for sth)** to put a special device somewhere in order to listen secretly to other people's conversations **SYN** **bug**: *The room had been wired for sound.* **4** (especially NAmE) to send sb a message by TELEGRAM: **~ sth (to sb)** *He wired the news to us.* ◇ **~ sb (sth)** *He wired us the news.* **5** to send money from one bank to another using an electronic system: **~ sth (to sb)** *The bank wired the money to her.* ◇ **~ sb sth** *The bank wired her the money.* **6** **~ sth** to join things together using wire

**wired** /ˈwaɪəd; NAmE -ərd/ adj. **1** connected to a device or computer network by wires: *wired headphones/headsets* ◇ *Wired internet connections are still useful.* **2** (of glass, material, etc.) containing wires that make it strong or stiff **3** (informal) excited or nervous; not relaxed **4** (informal, especially NAmE) under the influence of alcohol or an illegal drug

**'wire fraud** noun [U, C] FRAUD (= dishonest ways of getting money) using computers and phones

**wire·less** /ˈwaɪələs; NAmE -ərl-/ noun, adj.
■ noun **1** [U] any system of sending electronic information, such as the internet, phone signals, etc. without using wires for the receiving equipment: *a message sent by wireless* **2** [C] (especially BrE, old-fashioned) a radio: *I heard it on the wireless.*
■ adj. not using wires: *wireless communications* ▶ **wire·less·ly** adv.

**wire-pull·er** /ˈwaɪəpʊlə(r); NAmE -ərp-/ noun (NAmE) a person who is able to control or influence events without people realizing it

**'wire service** noun (especially NAmE) an organization that supplies news to newspapers and to radio and television stations

**wire·tap·ping** /ˈwaɪətæpɪŋ; NAmE -ərt-/ noun [U] the act of secretly listening to other people's phone conversations by attaching a device to the phone line ▶ **wire·tap** /-tæp/ verb (-pp-) ~ sth **wire·tap** noun: *the use of illegal wiretaps* ⇨ see also TAP verb (4), TAP noun (4)

---

æ cat | ɑː father | e bed | ɜː fur | ə about | ɪ sit | iː see | i happy | ɒ got (BrE) | ɔː saw | ʌ cup | ʊ put | uː too

**wire ˈwool** noun [U] (BrE) = STEEL WOOL

**wir·ing** /ˈwaɪərɪŋ/ noun [U] the system of wires that is used for carrying electricity around a building or machine: *to check the wiring* ◇ *a wiring diagram*

**wiry** /ˈwaɪəri/ adj. **(wiri·er, wiri·est) 1** (of a person) thin but strong **SYN** sinewy: *a wiry little man* **2** (of hair, plants, etc.) stiff and strong; like wire

**wis·dom** ?+ B2 /ˈwɪzdəm/ noun [U] **1** ?+ B2 the ability to make sensible decisions and give good advice because of the experience and knowledge that you have: *a woman of great wisdom* ◇ *words of wisdom* **2** ?+ B2 **~ of (doing) sth** how sensible sth is: *I question the wisdom of giving a child so much money.* **3** the knowledge that a society or culture has gained over a long period of time: *the collective wisdom of the Native American people*
**IDM** **conventional/received/popular ˈwisdom** the view or belief that most people hold: *Conventional wisdom has it that riots only ever happen in cities.* **in his/her/its, etc. (infinite) ˈwisdom** used when you are saying that you do not understand why sb has done sth: *The government in its wisdom has decided to support the ban.* ⊃ more at PEARL

**ˈwisdom tooth** noun any of the four large teeth at the back of the mouth that do not grow until you are an adult ⊃ compare CANINE (1), INCISOR, MOLAR, PREMOLAR

**wise** ❶ B2 /waɪz/ adj., verb
■ adj. **(wiser, wis·est) 1** ?+ B2 able to make sensible decisions and give good advice because of the experience and knowledge that you have: *a wise man* ◇ *I'm older and wiser after ten years in the business.* **2** ?+ B2 (of actions and behaviour) sensible; based on good judgement **SYN** prudent: *a wise decision/move/choice/investment* ◇ *I was grateful for her wise counsel.* ◇ **~ to do sth** *You would be wise to steer clear of the cheapest local wines.* ◇ **it is ~ (of sb) to do sth** *It was very wise to leave when you did.* ▸ **wise·ly** adv.: *She nodded wisely.* ◇ *He wisely decided to tell the truth.*
**IDM** **be none the ˈwiser | not be any the ˈwiser 1** to not understand sth, even after it has been explained to you: *I've read the instructions, but I'm still none the wiser.* **2** to not know or find out about sth bad that sb has done: *If you put the money back, no one will be any the wiser.* **be ˈwise after the eˈvent** (often disapproving) to understand sth, or realize what you should have done, only after sth has happened **be/get ˈwise to sb/sth** (informal) to become aware that sb is being dishonest: *He thought he could fool me but I got wise to him.* **put sb ˈwise (to sth)** (informal) to inform sb about sth
■ verb
**PHRV** **wise ˈup (to sth)** (informal) to become aware of the unpleasant truth about a situation

**-wise** /waɪz/ suffix (in adjectives and adverbs) **1** in the manner or direction of: *likewise* ◇ *clockwise* **2** (informal) relating to: *Things aren't too good businesswise.*

**wise·crack** /ˈwaɪzkræk/ noun (informal) a clever remark or joke ▸ **wise·crack** verb [I, T]: *He plays a wisecracking detective.* ◇ **+ speech** *'We knew you'd be back,' he wisecracked. 'Just not this soon.'*

**ˈwise guy** noun **1** (especially NAmE, informal, disapproving) a person who speaks or behaves as if they know more than other people **SYN** know-all **2** (US, slang) a member of the Mafia

**ˈwise woman** noun (old use) a woman with knowledge of traditional medicines and magic

**wish** ❶ A2 /wɪʃ/ verb, noun
■ verb **1** ? A2 [T] (not usually used in the present progressive tense) to want sth to happen or to be true even though it is unlikely or impossible: **~ (that) …** *I wish I were taller.* ◇ (BrE also) *I wish I was taller.* ◇ *I wish I hadn't eaten so much.* ◇ *'Where is he now?' 'I only wish I knew!'* ◇ *I wish you wouldn't leave your clothes all over the floor.* ◇ **~ sb/sth/yourself + adj.** *He's dead and it's no use wishing him alive again.* ◇ **~ sb/sth/yourself + adv./prep.** *She wished herself a million miles away.* **2** ? B1 [I, T] (especially BrE, formal) to want to do sth; to want sth to happen: *You may stay until morning, if you wish.* ◇ *'I'd rather not talk now.' '(Just) as you wish.'* ◇ **~ to do sth** *This course is designed for people wishing to update their computer skills.* ◇ *I wish to speak to the manager.* ◇ **~ sb sth** *She could not believe that he wished her harm.* ◇ **~ sb/sth to do sth** *He was not sure whether he wished her to stay or go.* **3** ? B1 [I] to think very hard that you want sth, especially sth that can only be achieved by good luck or magic: *If you wish really hard, maybe you'll get what you want.* ◇ **~ for sth** *It's no use wishing for the impossible.* ◇ *He has everything he could possibly wish for.* **4** ? B1 [T] to say that you hope that sb will be happy, lucky, etc.: **~ sb sth** *I wished her a happy birthday.* ◇ *Wish me luck!* ◇ **~ sb well** *We wish them both well in their retirement.*
**IDM** **I/you ˈwish!** (informal) used to say that sth is impossible or very unlikely, although you wish it were possible **SYN** if only: *'You'll have finished by tomorrow.' 'I wish!'* ◇ *A job at the BBC? You wish!*
**PHRV** **wish sth aˈway** to try to get rid of sth by wishing it did not exist **ˈwish sb/sth on sb** (informal) (used in negative sentences) to want sb to have sth unpleasant: *I wouldn't wish something like that on my worst enemy.*
■ noun **1** ? A2 **wishes** [pl.] used especially in a letter, email or card to say that you hope that sb will be happy, well or successful: *Give my good wishes to the family.* ◇ **~ for sth** *We all send our best wishes for the future.* ◇ **With best wishes** (= for example, at the end of a letter) **2** ? B1 [C] an attempt to make sth happen by thinking hard about it, especially in stories when it often happens by magic: *Throw some money in the fountain and make a wish.* ◇ *The genie granted him three wishes.* ◇ *The prince's wish came true.* **3** ? B2 [C] a desire or a feeling that you want to do sth or have sth: **~ to do sth** *She expressed a wish to be alone.* ◇ *He had no wish to start a fight.* ◇ *His dearest wish (= what he wants most of all) is to see his grandchildren again.* ◇ **~ for sth** *I can understand her wish for secrecy.* ◇ **~ that …** *It was her dying wish that I should have it.* **4** ? B2 [C] a thing that you want to have or to happen: *to carry out sb's wishes* ◇ *I'm sure that you will get your wish.* ◇ **against sb's wishes** *She married against her parents' wishes.* ⊃ see also DEATH WISH
**IDM** **if wishes were ˌhorses, beggars would/might ˈride** (saying) wishing for sth does not make it happen **your ˈwish is my comˈmand** (humorous) used to say that you are ready to do whatever sb asks you to do **the wish is father to the ˈthought** (saying) we believe a thing because we want it to be true

▼ **GRAMMAR POINT**

**wish**
- After the verb **wish** in sense 1, a past tense is always used in a *that* clause: *Do you wish (that) you had a better job?* In more formal English, especially in NAmE, many people use *were* after *I, he, she, it* instead of *was*: *I wish he were here tonight.*

**wish·bone** /ˈwɪʃbəʊn/ noun a bone in the shape of a V between the neck and breast of a chicken, DUCK, etc. When the bird is eaten, this bone is sometimes pulled apart by two people, and the person who gets the larger part can make a wish.

**wish·ful ˈthink·ing** /ˌwɪʃfl ˈθɪŋkɪŋ/ noun [U] the belief that sth that you want to happen is happening or will happen, although this is actually not true or very unlikely: *I've got a feeling that Alex likes me, but that might just be wishful thinking.*

**ˈwish·ing well** noun a WELL that people drop a coin into and make a wish

**ˈwish list** noun (informal) all the things that you would like to have, or that you would like to happen

**wishy-washy** /ˈwɪʃi wɒʃi; NAmE wɑːʃi/ adj. (informal, disapproving) **1** not having clear or definite ideas or beliefs: *a wishy-washy liberal* **2** not bright in colour: *a wishy-washy blue*

**wisp** /wɪsp/ noun **1 ~ (of sth)** a small, thin piece of hair, grass, etc. **2 ~ (of sth)** a long, thin line of smoke or cloud

**wispy** /ˈwɪspi/ adj. consisting of small, thin pieces; not thick: *wispy hair/clouds* ◇ *a wispy beard*

# wisteria

**wis·te·ri·a** /wɪˈstɪəriə; NAmE -ˈstɪr-/ (also **wis·taria** /wɪˈsteərɪə; NAmE -ˈster-/) noun [U] a climbing plant with bunches of pale purple or white flowers that hang down

**wist·ful** /ˈwɪstfl/ adj. thinking sadly about sth that you would like to have, especially sth in the past that you can no longer have: *a wistful smile* ▶ **wist·ful·ly** /-fəli/ adv.: *She sighed wistfully.* ◇ *'If only I had known you then,' he said wistfully.* ▶ **wist·ful·ness** noun [U]

**wit** /wɪt/ noun **1** [U, sing.] the ability to say or write things that are both clever and humorous: *to have a quick/sharp/dry/ready wit* ◇ *a woman of wit and intelligence* ◇ *a book full of the wit and wisdom of his 30 years in politics* **2** [C] a person who has the ability to say or write things that are both clever and humorous: *a well-known wit and raconteur* **3** **wits** [pl.] your ability to think quickly and clearly and to make good decisions: *He needed all his wits to find his way out.* ◇ *The game was a long battle of wits.* ◇ *Kate paused and gathered her wits.* ◇ *a chance to pit your wits against* (= compete with, using your intelligence) *our quiz champion* **4** -**witted** (in adjectives) having the type of intelligence mentioned: *a quick-witted group of students* **5** [U] ~ **to do sth** the intelligence or good sense to know what is the right thing to do: *At least you had the wit to ask for help.* ◇ *It should not be beyond the wit of man to resolve this dispute.* ⇒ see also WITLESS

**IDM** **be at your wits' end** (informal) to be so worried by a problem that you do not know what to do next  **be frightened/scared/terrified out of your 'wits** (also **to frighten/scare the 'wits out of sb**) to be very frightened; to frighten sb very much  **have/keep your 'wits about you** to be aware of what is happening around you and ready to think and act quickly  **to 'wit** (old-fashioned, formal) you use **to wit** when you are about to be more exact about sth that you have just referred to: *Pilot error, to wit failure to follow procedures, was the cause of the accident.* ⇒ more at LIVE¹

**witch** /wɪtʃ/ noun **1** a woman who is believed to have magic powers, especially to do evil things. In stories, she usually wears a black pointed hat and flies on a BROOMSTICK. **2** (disapproving) an ugly, unpleasant old woman **IDM** see BREW n.

### WORD FAMILY
wit noun
witty adj.
witticism noun
outwit verb

▼ **HOMOPHONES**

**which • witch** /wɪtʃ/

• **which** pron.: *Which would you prefer—chocolate cake or carrot cake?*
• **witch** noun: *He was turned into a rat by a wicked witch.*

**witch·craft** /ˈwɪtʃkrɑːft; NAmE -kræft/ noun [U] the use of magic powers, especially evil ones

**'witch doctor** noun (especially in Africa) a person who is believed to have special magic powers that can be used to make sick people well again ⇒ compare MEDICINE MAN

**'witch hazel** noun [U] a liquid that is used for treating injuries on the skin

**'witch-hunt** noun (usually disapproving) an attempt to find and punish people who hold opinions that are thought to be unacceptable or dangerous to society

**the 'witch·ing hour** noun [sing.] the time, late at night, when it is thought that magic things can happen

**with** /wɪð, wɪθ/ prep. **HELP** For the special uses of **with** in phrasal verbs, look at the entries for the verbs. For example **bear with sb/sth** is in the phrasal verb section at **bear**. **1** in the company or presence of sb/sth: *She lives with her parents.* ◇ *I have a client with me right now.* ◇ *a nice steak with a bottle of red wine* **2** having or carrying sth: *a girl with* (= who has) *red hair* ◇ *a jacket with a hood* ◇ *He looked at her with a hurt expression.* ◇ *They're both in bed with flu.* ◇ *a man with a suitcase* **3** using sth: *Cut it with a knife.* ◇ *It is treated with acid before being analysed.* **4** used to say what fills, covers, etc. sth: *The bag was stuffed with dirty clothes.* ◇ *Sprinkle the dish with salt.* **5** in opposition to sb/sth; against sb/sth: *to fight with sb* ◇ *to play tennis with sb* ◇ *at war with a neighbouring country* ◇ *I had an argument with my boss.* **6** in connection with; in the case of: *Be careful with the glasses.* ◇ *Are you pleased with the result?* ◇ *Don't be angry with her.* ◇ *With these students it's pronunciation that's the problem.* **7** used to show the way in which sb does sth: *He behaved with great dignity.* ◇ *She sleeps with the window open.* ◇ *Don't stand with your hands in your pockets.* **8** used when considering one fact in relation to another: *She won't be able to help us with all the family commitments she has.* ◇ *It's much easier compared with last time.* **9** including: *The meal with wine came to $20 each.* ◇ *With all the lesson preparation I have to do I work 12 hours a day.* **10** used to show who has possession of or responsibility for sth: *The keys are with reception.* ◇ *Leave it with me.* **11** employed by; using the services of: *She acted with a touring company for three years.* ◇ *I bank with HSBC.* **12** because of; as a result of: *She blushed with embarrassment.* ◇ *His fingers were numb with cold.* **13** because of sth and as it happens: *The shadows lengthened with the approach of sunset.* ◇ *Skill comes with practice.* **14** in the same direction as sth: *Marine mammals generally swim with the current.* **15** showing that sth/sb has been separated from sth/sb: *I could never part with this ring.* ◇ *Can we dispense with the formalities?* **16** despite sth: *With all her faults I still love her.* **17** used in exclamations: *Off to bed with you!* ◇ *Down with school!*

**IDM** **be 'with me/you** (informal) to be able to understand what sb is talking about: *Are you with me?* ◇ *I'm afraid I'm not quite with you.*  **be 'with sb (on sth)** to support sb and agree with what they say: *We're all with you on this one.*  **'with it** (informal) **1** understanding what is happening around you **SYN** alert: *You don't seem very with it today.* **2** (old-fashioned) knowing about current fashions and ideas **SYN** trendy  **with 'that** straight after that; then: *He muttered a few words of apology and with that he left.*

**with·draw** /wɪðˈdrɔː, wɪθˈd-/ verb (**with·drew** /-ˈdruː/, **with·drawn** /-ˈdrɔːn/) **1** [T] ~ **sth (from sth)** to take money out of a bank account: *With this account, you can withdraw up to £300 a day.* **2** [I, T] to move back or away from a place or situation; to make sb/sth do this **SYN** pull out (of sth): *Government troops were forced to withdraw.* ◇ ~ (**sb/sth**) (**from sth**) *Both powers withdrew their forces from the region.* ◇ *She withdrew her hand from his.* **3** [I, T] to stop taking part in an activity or being a member of an organization; to stop sb/sth from doing these things: ~ (**from sth**) *In 2016 Britain voted to withdraw from the EU.* ◇ ~ **sb/sth** (**from sth**) *The horse had been withdrawn from the race.* **4** [T] to stop giving or offering sth to sb: ~ **sth** *Workers have threatened to withdraw their labour* (= go on strike). ◇ *He withdrew his support for our campaign.* ◇ ~ **sth from sth** *The drug was withdrawn from sale after a number of people suffered serious side effects.* **5** [T] ~ **sth** (formal) to say that you no longer believe that sth you previously said is true **SYN** retract: *The newspaper withdrew the allegations the next day.* **6** [I] ~ (**from sth**) (**into sth/yourself**) to become quieter and spend less time with other people: *She's beginning to withdraw into herself.*

**with·draw·al** /wɪðˈdrɔːəl, wɪθˈd-/ noun **1** [C] ~ (**of sth**) (**from sth**) the act of taking an amount of money out of your bank account: *You can make withdrawals of up to $250 a day.* ⇒ WORDFINDER NOTE at BANK **2** [U, C] ~ (**of sth**) (**from sth**) the act of moving or taking sth away or back: *the withdrawal of support* ◇ *the withdrawal of the UN troops from the region* ◇ *the withdrawal of a product from the market* **3** [U] ~ (**from sth**) the act of no longer taking part in sth or being a member of an organization: *his withdrawal from the election* ◇ *Britain's withdrawal from the EU* **4** [U] the period of time when sb is getting used to not taking a drug that they have become ADDICTED to, and the unpleasant effects of doing this: *I got withdrawal symptoms after giving up smoking.* ⇒ WORDFINDER NOTE at DRUG **5** [C, usually sing., U] the act of saying that you no longer believe that sth that you have previously said is true SYN **retraction**: *The newspaper published a withdrawal the next day.* **6** [U] (*psychology*) the behaviour of sb who wants to be alone and does not want to communicate with other people

**with·drawn** /wɪðˈdrɔːn/ *adj.* not wanting to talk to other people; extremely quiet and shy

**wither** /ˈwɪðə(r)/ *verb* **1** [I, T] ~ **(sth)** if a plant withers or sth withers it, it dries up and dies: *The grass had withered in the warm sun.* **2** [I] ~ **(away)** to become less or weaker, especially before disappearing completely: *All our hopes just withered away.*

**withered** /ˈwɪðəd; *NAmE* -ərd/ *adj.* [usually before noun] **1** (of plants) dried up and dead SYN **shrivelled**: *withered leaves* **2** (of people) looking old because they are thin and weak and have very dry skin **3** (of parts of the body) thin and weak and not fully developed because of disease: *withered limbs*

**wither·ing** /ˈwɪðərɪŋ/ *adj.* (of a look, remark, etc.) intended to make sb feel silly or ashamed: *withering scorn* ◊ *She gave him a withering look.* ▶ **wither·ing·ly** *adv.*

**with·ers** /ˈwɪðəz; *NAmE* -ərz/ *noun* [pl.] the highest part of a horse's back, between its shoulders

**with·hold** /wɪðˈhəʊld, wɪθˈh-/ *verb* (**with·held, with·held** /-ˈheld/) ~ **sth (from sb/sth)** (*formal*) to refuse to give sth to sb SYN **keep back**: *She was accused of withholding information from the police.*

**with·ˈhold·ing tax** *noun* [C, U] (in the US) an amount of money that is taken out of sb's income as tax and paid directly to the government ⊃ compare PAY AS YOU EARN

**with·in** ⊙ B1 ⊙ /wɪˈðɪn/ *prep., adv.*
■ *prep.* **1** ? B1 before a particular period of time has passed; during a particular period of time: *You should receive a reply within seven days.* ◊ *The ambulance arrived within minutes of the call being made.* ◊ *Two elections were held within the space of a year.* **2** ? B1 not further than a particular distance from sth: *a house within a mile of the station* ◊ *Is it within walking distance?* **3** ? B1 inside the range or limits of sth: *That question is not within the scope of this talk.* ◊ *We are now within range of enemy fire.* ◊ *He finds it hard to live within his income* (= without spending more than he earns). **4** ? B1 (*formal*) inside sth/sb: *The noise seems to be coming from within the building.* ◊ *There is discontent within the farming industry.*
■ *adv.* (*formal*) inside: *Cleaner required. Apply within.* (= on a sign)

**with·out** ⊙ A1 ⊙ /wɪˈðaʊt/ *prep., adv.*
■ *prep.* **1** ? A1 not having, experiencing or showing sth: *They had gone two days without food.* ◊ *He found the place without difficulty.* ◊ *She spoke without much enthusiasm.* **2** ? A1 not in the company of sb: *Don't go without me.* **3** ? A1 not using or taking sth: *Can you see without your glasses?* ◊ *Don't go out without your coat.* **4** ? A1 not doing the action mentioned: ~ **doing sth** *He left without saying goodbye.* ◊ *You can't make an omelette without breaking eggs.* ◊ **Without wanting to criticize***, I think you could have done better.* (= used before you make a critical comment) ◊ ~ **sb doing sth** *The party was organized without her knowing anything about it.*
■ *adv.* not having or showing sth: *Do you want a room with a bath or one without?* ◊ *If there's none left we'll have to do without.* ◊ *I'm sure we'll manage without.*

**with·stand** /wɪðˈstænd, wɪθˈs-/ *verb* (**with·stood, with·stood** /-ˈstʊd/) ~ **sth** (*formal*) to be strong enough not to be hurt or damaged by extreme conditions, the use of force, etc. SYN **resist, stand up to**: *The materials used have to be able to withstand high temperatures.* ◊ *They had withstood siege, hunger and deprivation.*

**wit·less** /ˈwɪtləs/ *adj.* silly or stupid; not sensible SYN **foolish**
IDM **be scared/bored ˈwitless** (*informal*) to be extremely frightened or bored

**wit·ness** ⊙ B2 /ˈwɪtnəs/ *noun, verb*
■ *noun*
• PERSON WHO SEES STH **1** ? B2 (*also* **eye·wit·ness**) [C] a person who sees sth happen and is able to describe it to other

1793 **witness**

people: *He failed to interview a key witness.* ◊ ~ **to sth** *Police have appealed for witnesses to the accident.* ⊃ WORDFINDER NOTE at ACCIDENT
• IN COURT **2** ? B2 [C] a person who gives evidence in court: *a defence/prosecution witness* ◊ *He was hired to be an **expert witness** in the trial.*
• OF SIGNATURE **3** ? B2 [C] a person who is present when an official document is signed and who also signs it to prove that they saw this happen: *He was one of the witnesses at our wedding.*
• OF RELIGIOUS BELIEFS **4** [U] evidence of a person's strong religious beliefs, that they show by what they say and do in public ⊃ see also JEHOVAH'S WITNESS
IDM **be (a) ˈwitness to sth 1** (*formal*) to see sth take place: *He has been witness to a terrible murder.* **2** to show that sth is true; to provide evidence for sth: *His good health is a witness to the success of the treatment.* **bear/give ˈwitness (to sth)** to provide evidence of the truth of sth

▼ SYNONYMS

**witness**
observer • onlooker • passer-by • bystander • eyewitness

These are all words for a person who sees sth happen.

**witness** a person who sees sth happen and is able to describe it to other people; a person who gives evidence in a court of law: *Police have appealed for* **witnesses** *to the accident.*

**observer** a person who sees sth happen: *According to observers, the plane exploded shortly after take-off.*

**onlooker** a person who watches sth that is happening but is not involved in it: *A crowd of onlookers gathered at the scene of the crash.*

**passer-by** a person who is going past sb/sth by chance, especially when sth unexpected happens: *Police asked passers-by if they had witnessed the accident.*

**bystander** a person who is near and can see what is happening when sth such as an accident or fight takes place: *Three innocent bystanders were killed in the crossfire.*

**eyewitness** a person who has seen a crime or accident and can describe it afterwards.

PATTERNS
• a witness / an observer / an onlooker / a passer-by / a bystander / an eyewitness **sees** sth
• an observer / an onlooker / a passer-by / a bystander **witnesses** sth

■ *verb*
• SEE STH **1** ? B2 [T] ~ **sth** to see sth happen (typically a crime or an accident): *to witness an accident/a murder/an attack* ◊ *Police have appealed for anyone who witnessed the incident to contact them.* ◊ *We are now witnessing an unprecedented increase in violent crime.* ⊃ SYNONYMS at NOTICE
• OF TIME/PLACE **2** [T] ~ **sth** to be the place, period, organization, etc. in which particular events take place: *Recent years have witnessed a growing social mobility.* ◊ *The retail trade is witnessing a sharp fall in sales.*
• SIGNATURE **3** [T] ~ **sth** to be present when an official document is signed and sign it yourself to prove that you saw this happen: *to witness a signature* ⊃ WORDFINDER NOTE at DOCUMENT
• BE SIGN/PROOF **4** [I, T, usually passive] to be a sign or proof of sth: ~ **to sth** *The huge attendance figures for the exhibition witness to a healthy interest in modern art.* ◊ **as witnessed by sth** *There has been increasing interest in her life and work, as witnessed by the publication of two new biographies.* **5** [T] ~ **sth** (*formal*) used when giving an example that proves sth you have just said: *Authentic Italian cooking is very healthy—witness the low incidence of heart disease in Italy.*
• TO RELIGIOUS BELIEFS **6** [I] ~ **(to sth)** (*especially NAmE*) to speak to people about your strong religious beliefs SYN **testify**

---

⊙ Oxford Phrasal Academic Lexicon (OPAL) written and spoken word lists | ⓦ OPAL written word list | ⓢ OPAL spoken word list

# witness box

**'witness box** (*BrE*) (*NAmE* **'witness stand**) (*also* **stand** *BrE*, *NAmE*) *noun* the place in court where people stand to give evidence

**'witness tam·per·ing** (especially *BrE*) (*also* **witness inti·mi'dation** especially *NAmE*) *noun* [U] the illegal act of trying to make sb change their evidence or not give evidence in a criminal trial

**wit·ter** /ˈwɪtə(r)/ *verb* [I] ~ (**on**) (**about sth**) (*BrE*, *informal*, *usually disapproving*) to talk about sth boring and unimportant for a long time: *What's he wittering on about?*

**wit·ti·cism** /ˈwɪtɪsɪzəm/ *noun* a clever and humorous comment

**wit·ting·ly** /ˈwɪtɪŋli/ *adv.* (*formal*) in a way that shows that you are aware of what you are doing **SYN** **intentionally**: *It was clear that, wittingly or unwittingly, he had offended her.* **OPP** **unwittingly**

**witty** /ˈwɪti/ *adj.* (**wit·tier**, **wit·ti·est**) clever and humorous: *a witty speaker ◇ a witty remark* ⊃ SYNONYMS at FUNNY ▶ **wit·tily** *adv.* **wit·ti·ness** *noun* [U]

**wives** /waɪvz/ *pl.* of **WIFE**

**wiz·ard** /ˈwɪzəd; *NAmE* -zərd/ *noun* **1** (in stories) a man with magic powers **2** a person who is especially good at sth: *a computer/financial, etc. wizard* **3** (*computing*) a program that makes it easy to use another program or perform a task by giving you a series of simple choices

**wiz·ard·ry** /ˈwɪzədri; *NAmE* -zərd-/ *noun* [U] a very impressive and clever achievement; great skill: *electronic wizardry ◇ The second goal was sheer wizardry.*

**wiz·ened** /ˈwɪznd/ *adj.* looking smaller and having many folds and lines in the skin, because of being old **SYN** **shrivelled**: *a wizened little man ◇ wizened apples*

**wk** (*BrE*) (*also* **wk.** *NAmE*, *BrE*) *abbr.* (in writing) week

**WLAN** /ˌdʌbljuːˈlæn/ *abbr.* (*computing*) wireless local area network (a system for communicating by computer within a large building or group of buildings, that does not use wires) ⊃ see also **LAN**, **WAN**

**WLTM** *abbr.* (in writing) would like to meet (used in personal advertisements)

**WMD** /ˌdʌbljuː em ˈdiː/ *abbr.* WEAPON OF MASS DESTRUCTION

**w/o** *abbr.* (in writing) without

**wob·ble** /ˈwɒbl; *NAmE* ˈwɑːbl/ *verb*, *noun*

■ *verb* **1** [I, T] to move from side to side in an unsteady way; to make sth do this: *This chair wobbles. ◇ (figurative) Her voice wobbled with emotion. ◇ ~ sth Don't wobble the table — I'm trying to write.* **2** [I] **+ adv./prep.** to go in a particular direction while moving from side to side in an unsteady way: *He wobbled off on his bike.* **3** [I] to hesitate or lose confidence about doing sth: *Yesterday the president showed the first signs of wobbling over the issue.*
■ *noun* **1** [usually sing.] a slight unsteady movement from side to side: *The handlebars developed a wobble.* **2** a moment when you hesitate or lose confidence about sth: *The team is experiencing a mid-season wobble.*

**wob·bly** /ˈwɒbli; *NAmE* ˈwɑːb-/ *adj.*, *noun*

■ *adj.* (*informal*) **1** not properly fixed in place so that it moves from side to side: *a chair with a wobbly leg ◇ a wobbly tooth* **2** weak and unsteady because you are ill or tired: *He's still a bit wobbly after the operation.* **3** not certain or confident **SYN** **shaky**: *the wobbly singing of the choir ◇ The evening got off to a wobbly start.*
■ *noun* **IDM** **throw a 'wobbly** (*BrE*, *informal*) to suddenly become very angry or upset

**wodge** /wɒdʒ; *NAmE* wɑːdʒ/ *noun* ~ (**of sth**) (*BrE*, *informal*) a large piece or amount of sth: *a thick wodge of ten-pound notes*

**woe** /wəʊ/ *noun* (*old-fashioned* or *humorous*) **1** **woes** [pl.] the troubles and problems that sb has: *financial woes ◇ Thanks for listening to my woes.* **2** [U] great unhappiness **SYN** **misery**: *a tale of woe*
**IDM** **woe be'tide sb** | **'woe to sb** (*formal* or *humorous*) a phrase that is used to warn sb that there will be trouble for them if they do sth or do not do sth: *Woe betide anyone who gets in her way!* **woe is 'me!** *exclamation* (*old use* or *humorous*) a phrase that is used to say that you are very unhappy

**woe·be·gone** /ˈwəʊbɪɡɒn; *NAmE* -ɡɔːn/ *adj.* (*formal*) looking very sad **SYN** **miserable**: *a woebegone expression*

**woe·ful** /ˈwəʊfl/ *adj.* **1** [usually before noun] very bad or serious; that you DISAPPROVE of **SYN** **deplorable**: *She displayed a woeful ignorance of the rules.* **2** (*literary* or *formal*) very sad: *a woeful face ◇ woeful tales of broken romances* ▶ **woe·ful·ly** /-fəli/ *adv.*

**wog** /wɒɡ; *NAmE* wɑːɡ/ *noun* **1** (*BrE*, *taboo*, *slang*) a very offensive word for a person who does not have white skin **2** (*AustralE*, *taboo*, *slang*) an offensive word for a person from southern Europe or whose parents came from southern Europe **3** (*AustralE*, *informal*) an illness, usually one that is not very serious: *A flu wog struck.*

**wok** /wɒk; *NAmE* wɑːk/ *noun* (from Chinese) a large pan like a bowl in shape, used for cooking food, especially Chinese food

**woke** /wəʊk/ *verb*, *adj.*
■ *verb* past tense of **WAKE**
■ *adj.* (especially *NAmE*, *informal*) aware of social and political issues, especially RACISM: *We need to stay woke and keep fighting for what's right.*

**woken** /ˈwəʊkən/ *past part.* of **WAKE**

**Wolds** /wəʊldz/ *noun* [pl.] used in the names of places in England for an area of high, open land: *the Lincolnshire Wolds*

**wolf** /wʊlf/ *noun*, *verb*
■ *noun* (*pl.* **wolves** /wʊlvz/) a large wild animal of the dog family, that lives and hunts in groups: *a pack of wolves*
**IDM** **keep the 'wolf from the door** (*informal*) to have enough money to avoid going hungry; to stop sb feeling hungry **throw sb to the 'wolves** to leave sb to be roughly treated or criticized without trying to help or defend them **a wolf in sheep's 'clothing** a person who seems to be friendly or not likely to cause any harm but is really an enemy ⊃ more at **CRY** *v.*, **LONE**
■ *verb* ~ **sth** (**down**) (*informal*) to eat food very quickly, especially by putting a lot of it in your mouth at once **SYN** **gobble**

**wolf·hound** /ˈwʊlfhaʊnd/ *noun* a very large, tall dog with long hair and long legs, originally used for hunting wolves: *an Irish wolfhound*

**wolf·ish** /ˈwʊlfɪʃ/ *adj.* (especially *literary*) like a wolf: *wolfish yellow eyes ◇ (figurative) a wolfish grin* (= showing sexual interest in sb) ▶ **wolf·ish·ly** *adv.*

**'wolf whistle** *noun* a WHISTLE with a short rising note and a long falling note, made by sb, usually a man, to show that they find sb else attractive, especially sb passing in the street: *She was fed up with the builders' wolf whistles each morning.* ▶ **'wolf-whistle** *verb* [I, T] ~ (**sb**)

**wol·ver·ine** /ˈwʊlvəriːn/ *noun* a wild animal that looks similar to a small bear, with short legs, long brown hair and a long tail. Wolverines live in cold, northern areas of Europe and North America.

**wolves** /wʊlvz/ *pl.* of **WOLF**

**woman** /ˈwʊmən/ *noun* (*pl.* **women** /ˈwɪmɪn/) **1** [C] an adult female human: *a beautiful young woman ◇ a 24-year-old woman ◇ men, women and children ◇ I prefer to see a woman doctor. ◇ a women's group/movement* **2** [U] female humans in general: (*informal*) *She's all woman!* (= has qualities that are typical of women) **3** [C] (in compounds) a woman who comes from the place mentioned or whose job or interest is connected with the thing mentioned: *an Englishwoman ◇ a businesswoman ◇ a Congresswoman ◇ a horsewoman* ⊃ note at **GENDER** **4** [C] a female worker, especially one who works with her hands: *We used to have a woman to do the cleaning.* **5** [sing.] (*old-fashioned*, *offensive*) a rude way of addressing a female person in an angry or important way: *Be quiet, woman!* **6** [C] (*sometimes disapproving*) a person's wife, girlfriend or female partner: *He's got a new woman in his life.* ⊃ see also **FALLEN WOMAN**, **KEPT WOMAN**, **OTHER WOMAN**

**IDM** **be your own ˈman / ˈwoman** (*approving*) to act or think independently, not following others or being ordered: *Working for herself meant that she could be her own woman.* ⇨ more at HEART *n.*, HELL, HONEST, MAN *n.*, PART *n.*, PEOPLE, POSSESSED, SUBSTANCE, WORLD

**womanˈhood** /ˈwʊmənhʊd/ *noun* [U] (*formal*) **1** the state of being a woman, rather than a girl: *He watched his daughters grow to womanhood.* **2** women in general: *the womanhood of this country* ⇨ compare MANHOOD

**womanˈizˈing** (*BrE also* **-isˈing**) /ˈwʊmənaɪzɪŋ/ *noun* [U] (*disapproving*) behaviour in which a man has sexual relationships with many different women **SYN** **philandering** ▸ **ˈwomanˌizer**, **-iser** *noun*

**womanˈkind** /ˈwʊmənkaɪnd/ *noun* [U] (*old-fashioned, formal*) women in general ⇨ compare MANKIND

**womanˈly** /ˈwʊmənli/ *adj.* (*approving*) behaving, dressing, etc. in a way that people think is typical of or very suitable for a woman **SYN** **feminine**: *womanly qualities* ⋄ *a soft womanly figure* ▸ **ˈwomanˈliˈness** *noun* [U]

**womb** /wuːm/ *noun* the organ in women and female animals in which babies or young animals develop before they are born **SYN** **uterus** ⇨ WORDFINDER NOTE at PREGNANT

**womˈbat** /ˈwɒmbæt/; *NAmE* /ˈwɑːm-/ *noun* an Australian animal like a small bear, that carries its young in a POUCH (= a pocket of skin) on the front of the mother's body

**womenˈfolk** /ˈwɪmɪnfəʊk/ *noun* [pl.] (*formal or humorous*) all the women in a community or family, especially one that is led by men: *The male hunters brought back the food for their womenfolk to cook.* ⇨ compare MENFOLK

**ˈwomen's libeˈration** *noun* [U] (*old-fashioned*) **1** (*also informal* **ˈwomen's ˈlib** /ˌwɪmɪnz ˈlɪb/) the freedom of women to have the same legal, social and economic rights as men **2 Women's Liberation** (*also informal* **Women's Lib**) the movement that aimed to achieve equal legal, social and economic rights for women

**ˈwomen's ˈrights** *noun* [pl.] legal, social and economic rights for women that are equal to those of men

**ˈwomen's ˈroom** (*also* **ˈladies' ˈroom**) (*both NAmE*) (*BrE* **ˈladies'**) *noun* a bathroom for women in a public building or place

**ˈwomen's ˈstudies** *noun* [U + sing./pl. v.] the study of women and their role in history, literature and society: *to major in women's studies.*

**ˈwomensˈwear** /ˈwɪmɪnzweə(r)/; *NAmE* /-wer/ *noun* [U] (used especially in shops) clothes for women

**won** /wʌn/ *past tense, past part.* of WIN ⇨ HOMOPHONES at ONE

**wonˈder** 🔵 **B1** /ˈwʌndə(r)/ *verb, noun*

■ *verb* **1** 🔵 **B1** [T, I] to think about sth and try to decide what is true, what will happen, what you should do, etc: *'Why do you want to know?' 'No particular reason. I was just wondering.'* ⋄ *~ who, where, etc... I wonder who she is.* ⋄ *I was just beginning to wonder where you were.* ⋄ *You have to wonder just what he sees in her.* ⋄ *I can't help wondering whether I'm missing something here.* ⋄ + **speech** *'Where's Natasha?' he wondered aloud.* **2** 🔵 **B1** [T] *~ if, whether...* used as a polite way of asking a question or asking sb to do sth: *I wonder if you can help me.* ⋄ *I was wondering whether you'd like to come to a party.* **3** [I, T] to be very surprised by sth: *~ (at sth) She wondered at her own stupidity.* ⋄ *(BrE, informal) He's gone and left us to do all the work, I shouldn't wonder* (= I wouldn't be surprised if he had). ⋄ *~ (that)... I wonder (that) he didn't hurt himself jumping over that wall.* ⋄ *I don't wonder you're tired. You've had a busy day.*

■ *noun* **1** 🔵 **B1** [U] a feeling of surprise and pleasure that you have when you see or experience sth beautiful, unusual or unexpected **SYN** **awe**: *He retained a childlike sense of wonder.* ⋄ *in~ She gazed down in wonder at the city spread below her.* **2** 🔵 **B1** [C] something that fills you with surprise and pleasure **SYN** **marvel**: *The temple, built in 1403, is an architectural wonder.* ⋄ *of sth The Grand Canyon is one of the natural wonders of the world.* ⋄ *the wonders of modern technology* ⋄ *the Seven Wonders of the World* (= the seven most impressive structures of the ancient world) **3** [sing.]

(*informal*) a person who is very clever at doing sth; a person or thing that seems very good or effective: *Dita, you're a wonder! I would never have thought of doing that.* ⋄ *Have you seen the boy wonder play yet?* ⋄ *a new wonder drug*

**IDM** **do ˈwonders (for sb/sth)** to have a very good effect on sb/sth: *The news has done wonders for our morale.* **it's a ˈwonder (that)...** (*informal*) it is surprising or strange: *It's a wonder (that) more people weren't hurt.* **(it's) no/little/small ˈwonder (that)...** it is not surprising: *It is little wonder (that) she was so upset.* ⋄ *(informal)* *No wonder you're tired—you've been walking for hours.* **wonders will never ˈcease** (*informal, usually ironic*) a phrase used to express surprise and pleasure at sth: *'I've cleaned my room.' 'Wonders will never cease!'* **work ˈwonders** to achieve very good results: *Her new diet and exercise programme has worked wonders for her.* ⇨ more at CHINLESS, NINE

**wonˈderˈful** 🔵 **A1** /ˈwʌndəfl/; *NAmE* /-dərfl/ *adj.*
**1** 🔵 **A1** very good, pleasant or a lot of fun: *This is a wonderful opportunity to invest in new markets.* ⋄ *The builders have done a wonderful job here.* ⋄ **it ~ to do sth** *It's wonderful to see you!* ⋄ **it ~ that...** *It's so wonderful that you can all come!* **2** 🔵 **B1** **it is ~ what...** making you feel great surprise and pleasure **SYN** **remarkable**: *It's wonderful what you can do when you have to.*

▼ **SYNONYMS**

**wonderful**
lovely • delightful

These words all describe an experience, feeling or sight that gives you great pleasure.

**wonderful** that you enjoy very much; that gives you great pleasure; extremely good: *We had a wonderful time last night.* ⋄ *The weather was absolutely wonderful.*

**lovely** (*especially BrE, rather informal*) that you enjoy very much; that gives you great pleasure; very attractive: *What a lovely day!* (= the weather is very good) ⋄ *It's been lovely having you here.*

**delightful** that gives you great pleasure; very attractive: *a delightful little fishing village*

**WONDERFUL, LOVELY OR DELIGHTFUL?**

- All these words can describe times, events, places, sights, feelings and the weather. **Wonderful** can also describe a chance or ability. **Lovely** is the most frequent in spoken British English, but in North American English, both spoken and written, **wonderful** is the most frequent. **Delightful** is used especially to talk about times, events and places.

**PATTERNS**

- wonderful / lovely / delightful **weather / views / scenery**
- It's wonderful / lovely **to be / feel / find / have / know / see...**
- It would be wonderful / lovely / delightful **if...**
- It's wonderful / lovely **that...**
- That **sounds** wonderful / lovely / delightful.
- **really / quite / absolutely** wonderful / lovely / delightful

**wonˈderˈfulˈly** /ˈwʌndəfəli/; *NAmE* /-dərf-/ *adv.* (*formal*) **1** very; very well: *The hotel is wonderfully comfortable.* ⋄ *Things have worked out wonderfully (well).* **2** unusually; in a surprising way: *He's wonderfully fit for his age.*

**wonˈderˈingˈly** /ˈwʌndrɪŋli/ *adv.* (*formal*) in a way that shows great surprise: *She gazed at him wonderingly.*

**wonˈderˈland** /ˈwʌndəlænd/; *NAmE* /-dərl-/ *noun* [usually sing.] **1** an imaginary place in children's stories **2** a place that is exciting and full of beautiful and interesting things: *a winter wonderland* (= a beautiful scene with fresh snow)

**wonˈderˈment** /ˈwʌndəmənt/; *NAmE* /-dərm-/ *noun* [U] (*formal*) a feeling of pleasant surprise or wonder

**wonˈdrous** /ˈwʌndrəs/ *adj.* (*literary*) strange, beautiful and impressive **SYN** **wonderful** ▸ **ˈwonˈdrousˈly** *adv.*

**wonˈga** /ˈwɒŋɡə/; *NAmE* /ˈwɑːŋ-/ *noun* [U] (*BrE, slang*) money

# wonk

**wonk** /wɒŋk; *NAmE* wɑːŋk/ *noun* (*especially US, informal*) **1** (*disapproving*) a person who works too hard and is considered boring **2** a person who takes a great deal of interest in the details of political policy: *the President's chief economic policy wonk*

**wonky** /'wɒŋki; *NAmE* 'wɑːŋ-/ *adj.* (*informal*) not steady; not straight: *a wonky chair*

**wont** /wəʊnt; *NAmE* wɔːnt/ *adj., noun*
- *adj.* [not before noun] ~ **(to do sth)** (*old-fashioned, formal*) in the habit of doing sth **SYN** **accustomed**: *He was wont to fall asleep after supper.*
- *noun* [sing.] (*old-fashioned, formal*) something a person often does **SYN** **habit**: *She got up early, as was her wont.*

**won't** /wəʊnt/ short form will not

**won·ton** /ˌwɒnˈtɒn; *NAmE* ˈwɑːntɑːn/ *noun* (*from Chinese*) a small piece of food wrapped in DOUGH, often served in Chinese soup or as DIM SUM

**woo** /wuː/ *verb* **1** ~ **sb** to try to get the support of sb: *Voters are being wooed with promises of lower taxes.* **2** ~ **sb** (*old-fashioned*) (of a man) to try to persuade a woman to love him and marry him **SYN** **court**

**wood** ❶ **A2** /wʊd/ *noun* **1** **A2** [U, C] the hard material that the TRUNK and branches of a tree are made of; this material when it is used to build or make things with, or as a fuel: *He chopped some wood for the fire.* ◊ *a piece of wood* ◊ *a plank /block of wood* ◊ *All the furniture was made of wood.* ◊ *a wood floor* ◯ see also DEAD WOOD, HARDWOOD, SOFTWOOD, WOODEN, WOODY ◯ **VISUAL VOCAB** page V6 **2** **A2** [C] (*also* **woods** [pl.]) an area of trees, smaller than a forest: *a large wood* ◊ *a walk in the woods* ◯ see also WOODED **3** [C] a heavy wooden ball used in the game of BOWLS **4** [C] a GOLF CLUB with a large head, that was usually made of wood in the past ◯ compare IRON
**IDM** **not out of the 'woods** (*informal*) not yet free from difficulties or problems **not see the 'wood for the 'trees** (*BrE*) (*NAmE* **not see the 'forest for the 'trees**) to not see or understand the main point about sth, because you are paying too much attention to small details ◯ more at KNOCK *v.*, NECK *n.*, TOUCH *v.*

**wood·block** /'wʊdblɒk; *NAmE* -blɑːk/ *noun* **1** each of the small, flat pieces of wood that are fitted together to cover a floor: *a woodblock floor* ◯ compare PARQUET **2** a piece of wood with a pattern cut into it, used for printing

**wood·carv·ing** /'wʊdkɑːvɪŋ; *NAmE* -kɑːrv-/ *noun* [U, C] the process of shaping a piece of wood with a sharp tool; an attractive object made in this way ▶ **wood-carver** *noun*

**wood·chuck** /'wʊdtʃʌk/ (*also* **ground·hog**) *noun* a small North American animal of the SQUIRREL family

**wood·cock** /'wʊdkɒk; *NAmE* -kɑːk/ *noun* (*pl.* **wood·cock** *or* **wood·cocks**) a brown bird with a long, straight BEAK, short legs and a short tail, hunted for food or sport

**wood·cut** /'wʊdkʌt/ *noun* a print that is made from a pattern cut in a piece of wood

**wood·cut·ter** /'wʊdkʌtə(r)/ *noun* (*old-fashioned*) a person whose job is cutting down trees

**wood·ed** /'wʊdɪd/ *adj.* (of land) covered with trees ◯ **WORDFINDER NOTE** at LANDSCAPE

**wood·en** ❶ **A2** /'wʊdn/ *adj.* **1** **A2** [usually before noun] made of wood: *a wooden box/door/floor* **2** not showing enough natural expression, emotion or movement **SYN** **stiff**: *The actor playing the father was too wooden.* ▶ **wood·en·ly** *adv.*: *She speaks her lines very woodenly.* **wood·en·ness** /-dnnəs/ *noun* [U]

**wooden 'spoon** *noun* **1** a spoon made of wood, used in cooking for STIRRING and mixing **2** (*BrE, informal*) an imaginary prize for sb who comes last in a race or competition: *My team got the wooden spoon after getting all the questions wrong.*

**wood·land** /'wʊdlənd/ *noun* [U, C] (*also* **wood·lands** [pl.]) an area of land that is covered with trees: *ancient woodland* ◊ *The house is fringed by fields and woodlands.* ◊ *woodland walks*

**wood·louse** /'wʊdlaʊs/ *noun* (*pl.* **wood·lice** /-laɪs/) a small grey creature like an insect, with a hard shell, that lives in DECAYING wood or wet soil ◯ **VISUAL VOCAB** page V3

**wood·man** /'wʊdmən/ *noun* (*pl.* **-men** /-mən/) = WOODSMAN

**wood·peck·er** /'wʊdpekə(r)/ *noun* a bird with a long BEAK that it uses to make holes in trees when it is looking for insects to eat

**'wood pigeon** *noun* a bird of the PIGEON family, that lives in woods and fields rather than in cities

**wood·pile** /'wʊdpaɪl/ *noun* a pile of wood that will be used for fuel

**'wood pulp** *noun* [U] wood that has been broken into small pieces and pressed until it is soft. It is used for making paper.

**wood·shed** /'wʊdʃed/ *noun* a small building for storing wood in, especially for fuel

**woods·man** /'wʊdzmən/ (*also* **wood·man**) *noun* (*pl.* **-men** /-mən/) a person who works or lives in a forest, taking care of and sometimes cutting down trees, etc.

**woodsy** /'wʊdzi/ *adj.* (*informal, especially NAmE*) covered with trees; connected with woods

**wood·wind** /'wʊdwɪnd/ *noun* [U + sing./pl. v.] (*also* **wood·winds** [pl.]) the group of musical instruments in an ORCHESTRA that are traditionally made of wood and are played by blowing. FLUTES, CLARINETS and BASSOONS are all woodwind instruments: *the woodwind section of the orchestra* ◯ compare BRASS, PERCUSSION, STRING, WIND[1] (4), WIND INSTRUMENT

**wood·work** /'wʊdwɜːk; *NAmE* -wɜːrk/ *noun* [U] **1** things made of wood in a building or room, such as doors and stairs: *The woodwork needs painting.* **2** (*BrE*) (*also* **wood·work·ing** *NAmE, BrE*) the activity or skill of making things from wood
**IDM** **blend/fade into the 'woodwork** (*informal*) to behave in a way that does not attract any attention; to disappear or hide **come/crawl out of the 'woodwork** (*informal, disapproving*) if you say that sb **comes/crawls out of the woodwork**, you mean that they have suddenly appeared in order to express an opinion or to take advantage of a situation: *When he won the lottery, all sorts of distant relatives came out of the woodwork.* **hit/strike the 'woodwork** (*BrE, informal*) to hit the wooden frame of the goal in the game of football (soccer), instead of scoring a goal: *She hit the woodwork twice before scoring.*

**wood·worm** /'wʊdwɜːm; *NAmE* -wɜːrm/ *noun* **1** [C] a small WORM that eats wood, making a lot of small holes in it **2** [U] the damage caused by woodworms: *The beams are riddled with woodworm.*

**woody** /'wʊdi/ *adj.* **1** (of plants) having a thick, hard STEM like wood **2** covered with trees: *a woody valley* **3** having a smell like wood

**woof** /wʊf/ *exclamation, noun*
- *exclamation* (*informal*) a word used to describe the loud noise that a dog makes: *'Woof! Woof!' he barked.* ▶ **woof** *verb* [I]
- *noun* **1** [C] (*informal*) the loud noise that a dog makes **2** [sing.] = WEFT

**woof·er** /'wuːfə(r), 'wʊf-; *NAmE* 'wʊf-/ *noun* a LOUDSPEAKER through which the low notes in a SOUND SYSTEM are heard ◯ compare TWEETER

**woo hoo** /ˌwuː ˈhuː/ *exclamation* (*informal*) used when you are glad because sth happens that you enjoy: *Woo hoo! The weekend is here.*

**wool** ❶ **B1** /wʊl/ *noun* [U] **1** **B1** the soft hair that covers the body of sheep and some other animals: *Sheep were kept for their wool and meat.* **2** **B1** long, thick THREAD made from animal's wool, used for KNITTING (= making clothing with wool using two long needles or a machine): *a ball of wool* **3** **B1** cloth made from animal's wool, used for making clothes, etc: *This scarf is 100% wool.*

---

æ cat | ɑː father | e bed | ɜː fur | ə about | ɪ sit | iː see | i happy | ɒ got (*BrE*) | ɔː saw | ʌ cup | ʊ put | uː too

◊ *pure new wool* ◊ *a wool blanket/sweater* ⊃ see also COTTON WOOL, DYED IN THE WOOL, LAMBSWOOL, STEEL WOOL, WIRE WOOL **IDM** see PULL *v.*

**wool·len** (*BrE*) (*NAmE* **wool·en**) /ˈwʊlən/ *adj.* **1** [usually before noun] made of wool: *a woollen blanket* ◊ *woollen cloth* **2** [only before noun] involved in making cloth from wool: *the woollen industry*

**wool·lens** (*BrE*) (*NAmE* **wool·ens**) /ˈwʊlənz/ *noun* [pl.] clothes made of wool, especially KNITTED clothes (= made by hand using two long needles or by machine)

**wool·ly** /ˈwʊli/ *adj., noun*
■ *adj.* (*NAmE also* **wooly**) (**wool·li·er, wool·li·est**) **1** covered with wool or with hair like wool: *woolly monkeys* **2** (*informal, especially BrE*) made of wool; like wool; like wool **SYN** **woollen**: *a woolly hat* **3** (of people or their ideas, etc.) not thinking clearly; not clearly expressed **SYN** **confused**: *woolly arguments* ▸ **wool·li·ness** *noun* [U]
■ *noun* (*pl.* **-ies**) (*informal*) **1** (*BrE, becoming old-fashioned*) a piece of clothing made of wool, especially one that has been KNITTED **2** (*AustralE, NZE*) a sheep

**woozy** /ˈwuːzi/ *adj.* (*informal*) **1** feeling unsteady, confused and unable to think clearly **2** (*especially NAmE*) feeling as though you might VOMIT

**Wor·ces·ter·shire sauce** /ˌwʊstəʃə ˈsɔːs/, *NAmE* /ˈwʊstərʃɪr/ (*also* **Wor·ces·ter sauce** /ˌwʊstə ˈsɔːs/, *NAmE* /ˈwʊstər sɔːs/) *noun* [U] a dark, thin sauce made of VINEGAR, sugar and SPICES

**word** 🔊 **A1** 🔊 /wɜːd/, *NAmE* wɜːrd/ *noun, verb, exclamation*
■ *noun*
• **UNIT OF LANGUAGE 1** 🔊 **A1** [C] a single unit of language that means sth and can be spoken or written: *Do not write more than 200 words.* ◊ *Do you know the words to this song?* ◊ *~for sth What's the Spanish word for 'table'?* ◊ *He was a true friend in all senses of the word.* ◊ *Tell me what happened in your own words.* ◊ *I could hear every word they were saying.* ◊ *He couldn't find the words to thank her enough.* ◊ *Words fail me* (= I cannot express how I feel). ◊ *There are no words to say how sorry we are.* ◊ *I can't remember her exact words.* ◊ *Angry is not the word for it—I was furious.* ⊃ WORDFINDER NOTE at LANGUAGE ⊃ see also BUZZWORD, CODE WORD, FOUR-LETTER WORD, HOUSEHOLD WORD, SPOKEN WORD, SWEAR WORD

**WORDFINDER** connotation, definition, dictionary, homonym, meaning, pronunciation, spelling, synonym, vocabulary

• **STH YOU SAY 2** 🔊 **B1** [C] a thing that you say; a remark or statement: *Have a word with Pat and see what she thinks.* ◊ *Could I have a quick word with you* (= speak to you quickly)? ◊ *A word of warning: read the instructions very carefully.* ◊ *She left without a word* (= without saying anything). ◊ *I don't believe a word of his story* (= I don't believe any of it). ◊ *a man of few words* (= who doesn't talk very much) ◊ *I'd like to say a few words about future plans.* ◊ *Remember—not a word to* (= don't tell) *Peter about any of this.* ◊ *He never breathed a word of this to me.*
• **PROMISE 3** 🔊 **B2** [sing.] a promise or guarantee that you will do sth or that sth will happen or is true: *I give you my word that this won't happen again.* ◊ *I give you my word of honour* (= my sincere promise)… ◊ *We never doubted her word.* ◊ *We only have his word for it that the cheque is in the post.* ◊ *to keep your word* (= do what you promised) ◊ *He promised to help and was as good as his word* (= did what he promised). ◊ *He's a man of his word* (= he does what he promises). ◊ *I trusted her not to go back on her word* (= break her promise). ◊ *I can't prove it—you'll have to take my word for it* (= believe me).
• **INFORMATION/NEWS 4** [sing.] a piece of information or news: *There's been no word from them since before Christmas.* ◊ *She sent word that she would be late.* ◊ *If word gets out about the affair, he will have to resign.* ◊ *Word has it that she's leaving.* ◊ *The word is they've split up.* ◊ *He likes to spread the word about the importance of healthy eating.*
• **BIBLE 5 the Word** (*also* **the Word of God**) [sing.] the Bible and its teachings
**IDM** **beyond ˈwords** in a way that cannot be expressed in words: *We were bored beyond words.* **by ˌword of ˈmouth**

1797 **break word**

because people tell each other and not because they read about it: *The news spread by word of mouth.* **(right) from the word ˈgo** (*informal*) from the very beginning **(not) get a word in (ˈedgeways)** (*BrE*) (*also* **(not) get a word in (ˈedgewise)** *NAmE, BrE*) (not) to be able to say anything because sb else is speaking too much: *When Mary starts talking, no one else can get a word in edgeways.* **have a word in sb's ˈear** (*BrE*) to speak to sb privately about sth **have/exchange ˈwords (with sb) (about sth)** (*especially BrE*) to have an argument with sb: *We've had words.* ◊ *Words were exchanged.* **in ˌother ˈwords** 🔊 **B1** used to introduce an explanation of sth: *They asked him to leave—in other words he was fired.* ⊃ LANGUAGE BANK at I.E. **(not) in so/as many ˈwords** (not) in exactly the same words as sb says were used: *'Did she say she was sorry?' 'Not in so many words.'* ◊ *He didn't approve of the plan and said so in as many words.* **in a ˈword** (*informal*) used for giving a very short, usually negative, answer or comment: *'Would you like to help us?' 'In a word, no.'* **in words of one ˈsyllable** using very simple language: *Could you say that again in words of one syllable?* **the last/final ˈword (on sth)** the last comment or decision about sth: *He always has to have the last word in any argument.* **(upon) my ˈword** (*old-fashioned*) used to show that you are surprised about sth **not have a good word to ˌsay for sb / sth** (*informal*) to never say anything good about sb/sth: *Nobody had a good word to say about him.* **put in a (good) ˈword for sb** to praise sb to sb else in order to help them get a job, etc. **put ˈwords into sb's mouth** to suggest that sb has said sth when in fact they have not **say/give the ˈword** to give an order; to make a request: *Just say the word, and I'll go.* **take sb at their ˈword** to believe exactly what sb says or promises **take the ˈwords right out of sb's mouth** to say what sb else was going to say **too funny, silly, ridiculous, etc. for ˈwords** extremely funny, silly, RIDICULOUS, etc. **ˌword for ˈword** in exactly the same words or (when translated) words with exactly the same meaning: *She repeated their conversation word for word to me.* ◊ *a word-for-word translation* **sb's word is their ˈbond** somebody's promise can be relied on completely **words to that efˈfect** used to show that you are giving the general meaning of what sb has said rather than the exact words: *He*

▼ **SYNONYMS**

**word**
term • phrase • expression • idiom
These are all words for a unit of language used to express sth.

**word** a single unit of language that means sth and can be spoken or written: *Do not write more than 200 words.* ◊ *He uses a lot of long words.*

**term** (*rather formal*) a word or phrase used as the name of sth, especially one connected with a particular type of language: *technical/legal/scientific terms* ◊ *'Old man' is a slang term for 'father'.*

**phrase** a group of words that have a particular meaning when used together: *Who coined the phrase 'fake news'?*
**NOTE** In grammar, a **phrase** is a group of words without a finite verb, especially one that forms part of a sentence: 'the green car' and 'on Friday morning' are phrases.

**expression** a word or phrase: *He tends to use a lot of slang expressions that I've never heard before.*

**idiom** a group of words whose meaning is different from the meanings of the individual words: *'Let the cat out of the bag' is an idiom meaning to tell a secret by mistake.*

**PATTERNS**
• a word/term for sth
• a **new** word/term/phrase/expression
• a **technical/colloquial** word/term/phrase/expression
• a **slang** word/term/phrase
• an **idiomatic** phrase/expression
• to **use** a(n) word/term/phrase/expression/idiom
• to **coin** a(n) word/term/phrase/expression
• a(n) word/term/phrase/expression/idiom **means** sth

# word break

told me to leave—or words to that effect. ⇒ more at ACTION n., BANDY v., DIRTY WORD, EAT, FAMOUS, HANG v., LAST¹ det., LOST adj., MINCE v., MUM adj., OPERATIVE adj., PLAY n., PRINT v., WAR, WEIGH, WRITTEN adj.

■ **verb** [often passive] to write or say sth using particular words: **be worded** *How was the letter worded* (= what did it say exactly?) ▶ **word·ed** *adj.* (used with an adverb): *a carefully worded speech* ◊ *a strongly worded letter of protest*

■ **exclamation word!** (*NAmE, informal*) used to show that you accept or agree with what sb has just said

**ˈword break** (*also* **ˈword division**) *noun* (*specialist*) a point at which a word is split, or can be split, between two lines of text, if there is not enough space on the first line

**ˈword class** *noun* (*grammar*) one of the classes into which words are divided according to their grammar, such as noun, verb, adjective, etc. **SYN** **part of speech**

**word·ing** /ˈwɜːdɪŋ; *NAmE* ˈwɜːrd-/ *noun* [U, C, usually sing.] the words that are used in a piece of writing or speech, especially when they have been carefully chosen: *The wording was deliberately ambiguous.* ⇒ SYNONYMS at LANGUAGE

**word·less** /ˈwɜːdləs; *NAmE* ˈwɜːrd-/ *adj.* (*formal or literary*) **1** [usually before noun] without saying any words; silent: *a wordless cry/prayer* **2** (of people) not saying anything ▶ **ˈword·less·ly** *adv.*

**ˈword list** (*also* **ˈword·list**) *noun* a list of words or phrases that are useful or important, often on a particular topic or of a particular type: *the Oxford Learner's Word Lists*

**word·play** /ˈwɜːdpleɪ; *NAmE* ˈwɜːrd-/ *noun* [U] making jokes by using words in a clever and humorous way, especially by using a word that has two meanings, or different words that sound the same ⇒ compare PUN

**ˈword pro·cess·ing** *noun* [U] the use of a computer to create, edit and store a piece of text, usually typed in from a keyboard

**ˈword processor** *noun* a program or machine used to create, edit and store text documents, usually typed from a keyboard

**ˈword search** *noun* a game consisting of letters arranged in a square, containing several hidden words that you must find

**word·smith** /ˈwɜːdsmɪθ; *NAmE* ˈwɜːrdsmɪθ/ *noun* a person who shows skill at using words

**wordy** /ˈwɜːdi; *NAmE* ˈwɜːrdi/ *adj.* (*usually disapproving*) using too many words, especially formal ones **SYN** **verbose**: *a wordy and repetitive essay* ▶ **wordi·ness** *noun* [U]

**wore** /wɔː(r)/ past tense of WEAR ⇒ HOMOPHONES at WAR

**work** 🔑 **A1** /wɜːk; *NAmE* wɜːrk/ *verb, noun*

■ **verb**
- **DO JOB/TASK 1** 🔑 **A1** [I] to do sth that involves physical or mental effort, especially as part of a job: *I can't work if I'm cold.* ◊ *The kids always work hard at school.* ◊ **~ on sth** *The whole team is currently working on the project.* ◊ **~ at sth** *I've been working at my assignment all day.* ◊ **~ with sb** *Work with a partner to solve the problem.* ◊ *We work closely with clients to develop specific solutions.* ◊ **+ noun** *Doctors often work very long hours.* **2** 🔑 **A1** [I] to have a job: *Both my parents work.* ◊ **~ for sb/sth** *She works for an engineering company.* ◊ **~ in sth** *I've always worked in education.* ◊ **~ with sb/sth** *Do you enjoy working with children?* ◊ **~ as sth** *My son is working as a teacher.*
- **MAKE EFFORT 3** 🔑 **A1** [I] to make efforts to achieve sth: **~ for sth** *She dedicated her life to working for peace.* ◊ **~ to do sth** *The committee is working to get the prisoners freed.* ◊ **~ together (to do sth)** *The police and the public need to work together to combat crime.* **4** [T] **~ yourself / sb + adv. / prep.** to make yourself/sb work, especially very hard: *She works herself too hard.*
- **MACHINE/DEVICE/SYSTEM 5** 🔑 **A2** [I] to function; to operate: *The printer isn't working.* ◊ *How does the device actually work?* ◊ **by (doing) sth** *It works by electricity.* **6** [T] **~ sth** to make a machine, device, etc. operate: *Do you know how* 

*to work the coffee machine?* ◊ *The machine is worked by wind power.*
- **HAVE RESULT/EFFECT 7** 🔑 **B1** [I] to have the result or effect that you want: *The pills the doctor gave me aren't working.* ◊ *My plan worked, and I got them to agree.* ◊ *The system seemed to work well.* ◊ **~ on sb/sth** *His charm doesn't work on me* (= does not affect or impress me). **8** [I] to have a particular effect: **~ against sb** *Your age can work against you in this job.* ◊ **~ in sb's favour** *Speaking Italian should work in his favour.*
- **MANAGE 9** [T] **~ sth** to manage or operate sth to gain benefit from it: *to work the land* (= grow crops on it, etc.) ◊ *He works a large area* (= selling a company's goods, etc.). ◊ *You have to learn how to work the system if you want to succeed.* ◊ (*figurative*) *She was a skilful speaker who knew how to work a crowd* (= to excite them or make them feel sth strongly).
- **USE MATERIAL 10** [T] to make a material into a particular shape or form by pressing, stretching, hitting it, etc: **~ sth** *to work clay* ◊ *to work gold* ◊ **~ sth into sth** *to work the mixture into a paste* **11** [I] **~ in / with sth** (of an artist, etc.) to use a particular material to produce a picture or other item: *an artist working in oils* ◊ *a craftsman working with wool*
- **OF PART OF FACE/BODY 12** [I] (*formal*) to move violently: *He stared at me in horror, his mouth working.*
- **MOVE GRADUALLY 13** [I, T] to move or pass to a particular place or state, usually gradually: **+ adv. / prep.** *It will take a while for the drug to work out of your system.* **~ your way + adv. / prep.** (*figurative*): *He worked his way to the top of his profession.* ◊ **~ yourself/sth + adj.** *I was tied up, but managed to work myself free.* ◊ **+ adj.** *The screw had worked loose.*

**IDM** **HELP** Most idioms containing **work** are at the entries for the nouns and adjectives in the idioms, for example **work your fingers to the bone** is at **finger**. **ˈwork it / things** (*informal*) to arrange sth in a particular way, especially by being clever: *Can you work it so that we get free tickets?*

**PHRV** **ˌwork aˈround sth** to find a way of working that avoids a particular problem without actually solving the problem: *The lack of test data is a problem, but we've found a way to work around that.* ⇒ related noun WORKAROUND **ˌwork aˈround to sth/sb** (*BrE also* **ˌwork ˈround to sth/sb**) to gradually turn a conversation towards a particular topic, subject, etc: *It was some time before he worked around to what he really wanted to say.* **ˌwork at ˈsth** to make great efforts to achieve sth or do sth well: *He's working at losing weight.* ◊ *Learning to play the piano isn't easy. You have to work at it.* **ˌwork sth ˈin** | **ˌwork sth into sth 1** to try to include sth: *Can't you work a few more jokes into your speech?* **2** to add one substance to another and mix them together: *Gradually work in the butter.* **ˌwork sth↔ˈoff 1** to get rid of sth, especially a strong feeling, by using physical effort: *She worked off her anger by going for a walk.* **2** to earn money in order to be able to pay a debt: *They had a large bank loan to work off.* **ˈwork on sb** to try to persuade sb to agree to sth or to do sth: *He hasn't said he'll do it yet, but I'm working on him.* **ˈwork on sth** 🔑 **B1** to try hard to improve or achieve sth: *You need to work on your pronunciation a bit more.* 'Have you sorted out a babysitter yet?' 'No, but *I'm working on it*.' **ˌwork ˈout 1** 🔑 **A2** to train the body by physical exercise: *I work out regularly to keep fit.* ⇒ related noun WORKOUT **2** to develop in a successful way: *My first job didn't work out.* ◊ *Things have worked out quite well for us.* **ˌwork ˈout (at / to sth)** if sth **works out** at sth, you calculate that it will be a particular amount: *The restaurant bill worked out at £23 each.* ◊ **+ adj.** *It'll work out cheaper to travel by bus.* **ˌwork sb↔ˈout** (*BrE*) to understand sb's character: *I've never been able to work her out.* **ˌwork sth↔ˈout 1** 🔑 **B1** to calculate sth: *to work out the answer* **2** 🔑 **B1** (*especially BrE*) to find the answer to sth **SYN** **solve**: *to work out a problem* ◊ **work out what, where, etc...** *Can you work out what these squiggles mean?* ◊ *I couldn't work out where the music was coming from.* **3** to plan or think of sth: *I've worked out a new way of doing it.* **4** [usually passive] to remove all the coal, minerals, etc. from a mine over a period of time: *a worked-out silver mine* **ˌwork sb↔ˈover** (*slang*) to attack sb and hit them, for example to make them give you information ,work 'round to sth/sb (BrE) = WORK AROUND TO STH/SB  'work to sth to follow a plan, schedule, etc: *to work to a budget* ◇ *We're working to a very tight deadline* (= we have little time in which to do the work). ,work to'wards sth to try to reach or achieve a goal  ,work sth↔'up to develop or improve sth with some effort: *I can't work up any enthusiasm for his idea.* ◇ *She went for a long walk to work up an appetite.* ,work sb/your'self 'up (into sth) to make sb/yourself reach a state of great excitement, anger, etc: *Don't work yourself up into a state about it. It isn't worth it.* ⊃ see also WORKED UP  ,work sth 'up into sth to bring sth to a more complete or more acceptable state: *I'm working my notes up into a dissertation.* ,work 'up to sth to develop or move gradually towards sth, usually sth more exciting or extreme: *The music worked up to a rousing finale.* ◇ *I began by jogging in the park and worked up to running five miles a day.*

▪ **noun**
- **JOB/TASK 1** 🔊 **A1** [U] (used without *the*) the job that a person does especially in order to earn money **SYN** **employment**: *He started work as a security guard.* ◇ *I'm still looking for work.* ◇ *It is difficult to find work in the present economic climate.* ◇ *She's planning to return to work once the children start school.* ◇ **full-time/part-time/unpaid/voluntary work** ◇ **out of** ~ *She had been out of work* (= without a job) *for a year.* ◇ **in** ~ (BrE) *They are in work* (= have a job). ◇ *What line of work are you in* (= what type of work do you do)? ◇ **off** ~ *She's been off work* (= not going to work) *with a bad back since July.* ⊃ WORDFINDER NOTE at EMPLOY

> **WORDFINDER** administrative, freelance, managerial, manual, part-time, seasonal, skilled, temporary, voluntary

**2** 🔊 **A1** [U] (used without *the*) the place where you do your job; the time that you spend there: *I go to work at 8 o'clock.* ◇ *I was late for work again.* ◇ *I have to leave work early today.* ◇ *work colleagues* ◇ **at** ~ *The new legislation concerns health and safety at work.* ◇ **before/after** ~ *I like to go for a run after work.* **3** 🔊 **A1** [U] the duties that you have and the activities that you do as part of your job: *Police work is mainly routine.* ◇ *The accountant described his work to the sales staff.* ⊃ see also PIECEWORK, SOCIAL WORK **4** **A1** [U] tasks that need to be done: *Taking care of a baby is hard work.* ◇ *Whenever am I going to do all this work?* ◇ *There is plenty of work to be done in the garden.* ◇ *Stop talking and get on with your work.* ⊃ see also DETECTIVE WORK, HOMEWORK, SCHOOLWORK **5** [U] materials needed or used for doing work, especially books, papers, etc: *She often brings work* (= for example, files and documents) *home with her from the office.* ◇ *His work was spread all over the floor.* ⊃ see also PAPERWORK
- **EFFORT 6** 🔊 [U] the use of physical strength or mental power in order to do or make sth: *She earned her grades through sheer hard work.* ◇ ~ **on sth** *We began work on the project last year.* ◇ *Work continues on renovating the hotel.* ◇ ~ **of doing sth** *The work of building the bridge took six months.* ◇ *The art collection was his life's work.* ◇ *She set them to work painting the fence.* ⊃ see also DONKEY WORK, FIELDWORK
- **PRODUCT OF WORK 7** 🔊 **A2** [U] a thing or things that are produced as a result of work: *She's an artist whose work I really admire.* ◇ *Is this all your own work* (= did you do it without help from others)? ◇ *The book is a detailed and thorough piece of work covering all aspects of the subject.*
- **BOOK/MUSIC/ART 8** 🔊 **A2** [C] a book, piece of music, painting, etc: *the collected/complete works of Tolstoy* ◇ *works of fiction/literature* ◇ *Chopin's piano works* ⊃ compare OPUS ⊃ see also WORK OF ART
- **RESULT OF ACTION 9** [U] ~(**of sb/sth**) the result of an action; what is done by sb: *The damage is clearly the work of vandals.*
- **BUILDING/REPAIRING 10 works** [pl.] (often in compounds) activities involving building or repairing sth: *roadworks* ◇ *They expanded the shipyards and started engineering works.* ⊃ see also PUBLIC WORKS
- **FACTORY 11 works** (*pl.* **works**) [C + sing./pl. v.] (often in compounds) a place where things are made or industrial processes take place: *an engineering works* ◇ *a brickworks* ⊃ SYNONYMS at FACTORY
- **PARTS OF MACHINE 12 the works** [pl.] the moving parts of a machine, etc. **SYN** **mechanism**
- **EVERYTHING 13 the works** [pl.] (*informal*) everything: *We went to the chip shop and had the works: fish, chips, gherkins, mushy peas.*
- **PHYSICS 14** [U] the use of force to produce movement ⊃ see also JOULE

**IDM** ▶ ,all ,work and no 'play (makes ,Jack a dull 'boy) (*saying*) it is not healthy to spend all your time working; you need to relax too  at 'work 1 having an effect on sth: *She suspected that secret influences were at work.* 2 ~(**on sth**) busy doing sth: *He is still at work on the painting.* ◇ *Danger—men at work.*  get (down) to/set to 'work to begin; to make a start: *We set to work on the outside of the house* (= for example, painting it).  give sb the 'works (*informal*) to give or tell sb everything  ,good 'works kind acts to help others  go/set about your 'work to do/start to do your work: *She went cheerfully about her work.* have your 'work cut out (*informal*) to be likely to have difficulty doing sth: *You'll have your work cut out to get there by nine o'clock.*  in the 'works something that is **in the works** is being discussed, planned or prepared and will happen or exist soon **SYN** **in the pipeline**  the work of a 'moment, 'second, etc. (*formal*) a thing that takes a very short time to do ⊃ more at DAY, DIRTY *adj.*, HAND *n.*, HARD *adj.*, JOB, LIGHT *adj.*, NASTY, NICE, SHORT *adj.*, SPANNER

▼ **SYNONYMS**

**work**

employment • career • profession • occupation • trade

These are all words for the jobs that sb does in return for payment, especially over a long period of time.

**work** the job that sb does, especially in order to earn money: *It's very difficult to find work at the moment.*

**employment** (*rather formal*) work, especially when it is done to earn money; the state of being employed or the situation in which people have work: *Only half the people here are in paid employment.*

**career** the job or series of jobs that sb has in a particular area of work, usually involving more responsibility as time passes: *He had a very distinguished career in the Foreign Office.*

**profession** a type of job that needs special training or skill, especially one that needs a high level of education: *He hopes to enter the medical profession.* **NOTE** The profession is all the people who work in a particular profession: *the legal profession.* The professions are the traditional jobs that need a high level of education and training, such as being a doctor or lawyer.

**occupation** (*rather formal*) a job or profession: *Please state your name, age, and occupation.*

**trade** a job, especially one that involves working with your hands and requires special training and skills: *Carpentry is a highly skilled trade.*

**PATTERNS**
- in/out of work/employment
- (a) full-time/part-time work/employment/career/occupation
- permanent/temporary work/employment
- (a) well-paid work/employment/profession/occupation
- (a) low-paid work/employment/occupation
- to look for/seek/find work/employment/a career/an occupation
- to get/obtain/give sb/offer sb/create/generate/provide work/employment

**work·able** /ˈwɜːkəbl; *NAmE* ˈwɜːrk-/ *adj.* **1** (of a system, an idea, etc.) that can be used successfully and effectively **SYN** **practical**: *a workable plan* **2** that you can shape, spread, dig, etc. *Add more water until the dough is workable.* **3** (of a mine, etc.) that can still be used and will make a profit

**work·aday** /ˈwɜːkədeɪ; *NAmE* ˈwɜːrk-/ *adj.* [usually before noun] (*formal*) ordinary; not very interesting **SYN** **everyday**

## workaholic

**work·ahol·ic** /ˌwɜːkəˈhɒlɪk; NAmE ˌwɜːrkəˈhɑːl-/ noun (informal, usually disapproving) a person who works very hard and finds it difficult to stop working and do other things

**work·around** /ˈwɜːkəraʊnd; NAmE ˈwɜːrk-/ noun a way of working, especially with a piece of software, that avoids a particular problem but does not actually solve the problem

**work·bench** /ˈwɜːkbentʃ; NAmE ˈwɜːrk-/ (also **bench**) noun a long, heavy table used for doing practical jobs, working with tools, etc.

**work·book** /ˈwɜːkbʊk; NAmE ˈwɜːrk-/ (NAmE also **exercise book**) noun a book with exercises in it, often with spaces for students to write answers in, to help them practise what they have learnt

**work·day** /ˈwɜːkdeɪ; NAmE ˈwɜːrk-/ noun 1 (NAmE) (BrE ˈworking ˈday) the part of a day during which you work: *an 8-hour workday* 2 = WORKING DAY (2): *workday traffic*

**worked ˈup** adj. [not before noun] ~ (about sth) (informal) very excited or upset about sth: *There's no point in getting worked up about it.*

**work·er** /ˈwɜːkə(r); NAmE ˈwɜːrk-/ noun 1 (often in compounds) a person who works, especially one who does a particular kind of work: *farm/factory/office workers* ◊ *construction/health/care workers* ◊ *manual/skilled/unskilled workers* ◊ *temporary/part-time/casual workers* ◊ *seasonal migrant workers picking blueberries* ◊ *Aid workers quickly arrived at the scene of the disaster.* ⇒ see also GUEST WORKER, SANITATION WORKER, SEX WORKER, SOCIAL WORKER 2 [usually pl.] a person who is employed in a company or industry, especially sb who does physical work rather than organizing things or managing people: *Conflict between employers and workers intensified and the number of strikes rose.* ◊ *talks between workers and management* 3 (usually after an adjective) a person who works in a particular way: *a hard/fast/quick/slow worker* 4 a female bee that helps do the work of the group of bees but does not produce young ⇒ compare DRONE, QUEEN BEE **IDM** see FAST adj.

**ˌworkers' compenˈsation** (also **ˈworkers' comp**) noun [U] (NAmE, AustralE, NZE) a type of insurance that provides payments to employees who get injured or sick as a direct result of their job: *He filed a claim for workers' compensation.*

**ˈwork ethic** noun [sing.] a person's attitude to work, especially the idea that hard work is a good habit and should be rewarded: *They have a very strong work ethic.*

**ˈwork experience** noun [U] 1 the work or jobs that you have done in your life so far: *The opportunities available will depend on your previous work experience and qualifications.* 2 (BrE) a period of time that a young person, especially a student, spends working in a company as a form of training ⇒ compare INTERNSHIP ⇒ WORDFINDER NOTE at TRAINING

**work·fare** /ˈwɜːkfeə(r); NAmE ˈwɜːrkfer/ noun [U] a system in which unemployed people have to work in order to get money for food, rent, etc. from the government

**work·flow** /ˈwɜːkfləʊ; NAmE ˈwɜːrk-/ noun [C, U] the series of stages that a particular piece or type of work passes through from the beginning until it is finished; the rate at which it passes through these stages

**work·force** /ˈwɜːkfɔːs; NAmE ˈwɜːrkfɔːrs/ noun [C + sing./pl. v.] 1 all the people who work for a particular company, organization, etc. **SYN** staff: *The factory has a 1000-strong workforce.* ◊ *Two thirds of the workforce is/are women.* ⇒ WORDFINDER NOTE at FACTORY 2 all the people in a country or an area who are available for work: *A quarter of the local workforce is/are unemployed.* ⇒ WORDFINDER NOTE at EMPLOY

**work·horse** /ˈwɜːkhɔːs; NAmE ˈwɜːrkhɔːrs/ noun a person or machine that you can rely on to do hard and/or boring work

**work·house** /ˈwɜːkhaʊs; NAmE ˈwɜːrk-/ (BrE) (also **poor-house** NAmE, BrE) noun (in England and Wales in the past) a building where very poor people were sent to live and given work to do

**work·ing** /ˈwɜːkɪŋ; NAmE ˈwɜːrk-/ adj., noun

■ adj. [only before noun] 1 having a job for which you are paid **SYN** employed: *the working population* ◊ *working people/mothers/families* ⇒ see also HARD-WORKING 2 having a job that involves hard physical work rather than office work, studying, etc: *a working man* ◊ *the working masses* 3 connected with your job and the time you spend doing it: *long working hours* ◊ *poor working conditions* ◊ *I have a good working relationship with my boss.* ◊ *She spent most of her working life as a teacher.* ◊ *recent changes in working practices* 4 a **working** breakfast or lunch is one at which you discuss business 5 used as a basis for work, discussion, etc. but likely to be changed or improved in the future: *a working theory* ◊ *Have you decided on a working title for your thesis yet?* 6 if you have a **working** knowledge of sth, you can use it at a basic level 7 the **working** parts of a machine are the parts that move in order to make it function 8 a **working** majority is a small majority that is enough to enable a government to win votes in parliament and make new laws **IDM** see ORDER n.

■ noun 1 [U] the action of doing work: *More businesses now offer flexible working.* 2 [C, usually pl.] ~ (of sth) the way in which a machine, a system, an organization, etc. works: *an introduction to the workings of Congress* ◊ *the workings of the human mind* ◊ *the machine's inner workings* 3 [C, usually pl.] the parts of a mine or QUARRY where coal, metal, stone, etc. is or has been dug from the ground

**ˌworking ˈcapital** noun [U] (business) the money that is needed to run a business rather than the money that is used to buy buildings and equipment when starting the business ⇒ compare VENTURE CAPITAL

**the ˌworking ˈclass** noun [sing. + sing./pl. v.] (also **the ˌworking ˈclasses** [pl.]) the social class whose members do not have much money or power and are usually employed to do MANUAL work (= physical work using their hands): *the political party of the working class* ◊ *The working class has/have rejected them in the elections.* ⇒ compare MIDDLE CLASS, UPPER CLASS ▶ **ˌworking ˈclass** adj.: *a working-class background*

**ˌworking ˈday** noun (BrE) 1 (NAmE **work·day**) the part of a day during which you work: *I spend most of my working day sitting at a desk.* 2 (also less frequent **work·day**) a day on which you usually work or on which most people usually work: *Sunday is a normal working day for me.* ◊ *Thousands of working days were lost through strikes last year.* ◊ *Allow two working days (= not Saturday or Sunday) for delivery.*

**ˈworking girl** noun (informal) 1 (becoming old-fashioned) a PROSTITUTE. People say 'working girl' to avoid saying 'prostitute'. 2 (sometimes offensive) a woman who has a paid job

**ˌworking ˈpaper** noun 1 [C] a report written by a group of people chosen to study an aspect of law, education, health, etc. 2 **working papers** [pl.] (in the US) an official document that enables sb under 16 years old or born outside the US to have a job

**ˌworking ˈparty** (BrE) (also **ˈworking group** NAmE, BrE) noun [C + sing./pl. v.] ~ (on sth) a group of people chosen to study a particular problem or situation in order to suggest ways of dealing with it

**the ˌworking ˈpoor** noun [pl.] people who have jobs where they earn very little money: *The working poor have little choice but to take more than one job at a time.*

**ˌworking ˈtitle** noun a temporary name that is used during the production of a book, film, etc. before the actual name is chosen

**ˌworking ˈweek** (BrE) (NAmE **work·week**) noun the total amount of time that you spend at work during the week: *a 40-hour working week*

---

b **b**ad | d **d**id | f **f**all | g **g**et | h **h**at | j **y**es | k **c**at | l **l**eg | m **m**an | n **n**ow | p **p**en | r **r**ed

**work in progress** noun [C, U] (pl. **works in progress**) a project that is not yet finished and is still being added to or developed: *My essay is still a work in progress.*

**work-life balance** noun [sing.] the number of hours per week you spend working, compared with the number of hours you spend with your family, relaxing, etc: *Part-time working is often the best way to improve your work-life balance.*

**work·load** /ˈwɜːkləʊd; NAmE ˈwɜːrk-/ noun the amount of work that has to be done by a particular person or organization: *a heavy workload* ◊ *We have taken on extra staff to cope with the increased workload.*

**work·man** /ˈwɜːkmən; NAmE ˈwɜːrk-/ noun (pl. **-men** /-mən/) **1** a man who is employed to do physical work **2** (with an adjective) a person who works in the way mentioned: *a good/bad workman*

**work·man·like** /ˈwɜːkmənlaɪk; NAmE ˈwɜːrk-/ adj. done, made, etc. in a way that is careful and complete and shows skill but is not usually very original or exciting

**work·man·ship** /ˈwɜːkmənʃɪp; NAmE ˈwɜːrk-/ noun [U] the skill with which sb makes sth, especially when this affects the way it looks or works: *Our buyers insist on high standards of workmanship and materials.*

**work·mate** /ˈwɜːkmeɪt; NAmE ˈwɜːrk-/ noun (especially BrE) a person that you work with, often doing the same job, in an office, a factory, etc. **SYN** colleague

**work of ˈart** noun (pl. **works of ˈart**) **1** a painting, statue, etc: *A number of priceless works of art were stolen from the gallery.* **2** something that is attractive and made with skill: *The bride's dress was a work of art.*

**work·out** ʔ+ 🅒 /ˈwɜːkaʊt; NAmE ˈwɜːrk-/ noun a period of physical exercise that you do to keep fit: *She does a 20-minute workout every morning.* ⊃ WORDFINDER NOTE at FIT

**ˈwork permit** noun an official document that sb needs in order to work in a particular foreign country

**work·place** ʔ+ 🅑 /ˈwɜːkpleɪs; NAmE ˈwɜːrk-/ noun [C] (often **the workplace** [sing.]) the office, factory, etc. where people work: *the introduction of new technology into the workplace* ◊ *workplace safety*

**ˈwork placement** noun [U, C] (BrE) = PLACEMENT (2)

**ˈwork release** noun [U] (US) a system that allows prisoners to leave prison during the day to go to work

**work·room** /ˈwɜːkruːm, -rʊm; NAmE ˈwɜːrk-/ noun a room in which work is done, especially work that involves making things: *The jeweller has a workroom at the back of his shop.*

**works** noun ⊃ WORK noun

**ˈworks council** noun (especially BrE) a group of employees who represent all the employees at a factory, etc. in discussions with their employers over conditions of work

**work·sheet** /ˈwɜːkʃiːt; NAmE ˈwɜːrk-/ noun **1** a piece of paper or an electronic document on which there is a series of questions and exercises to be done by a student **2** a piece of paper or an electronic document on which work that has been done or has to be done is recorded

**work·shop** ʔ+ 🅑 /ˈwɜːkʃɒp; NAmE ˈwɜːrkʃɑːp/ noun **1** ʔ+ 🅑 a period of discussion and practical work on a particular subject, in which a group of people share their knowledge and experience: *a drama/poetry workshop* ⊃ WORDFINDER NOTE at CONFERENCE **2** ʔ+ 🅑 a room or building in which things are made or repaired using tools or machines: *a car repair workshop* ⊃ SYNONYMS at FACTORY

**ˈwork-shy** adj. (BrE, disapproving) unwilling to work **SYN** lazy

**work·space** /ˈwɜːkspeɪs; NAmE ˈwɜːrk-/ noun **1** [U, C] a space in which to work, especially in an office **2** [C] (computing) a place where information that is being used by one person on a computer network is stored

**work·sta·tion** /ˈwɜːksteɪʃn; NAmE ˈwɜːrk-/ noun the desk and computer at which a person works; one computer that is part of a computer network

**work·top** /ˈwɜːktɒp; NAmE ˈwɜːrktɑːp/ (also **work surface** both BrE) (NAmE **counter, counter·top**) noun a flat surface in a kitchen for preparing food on

1801

**work-to-ˈrule** noun [usually sing.] a situation in which workers refuse to do any work that is not in their contracts, in order to protest about sth ⊃ compare GO-SLOW ⊃ see also WORK TO RULE at RULE noun

**work·week** /ˈwɜːkwiːk; NAmE ˈwɜːrkwiːk/ (NAmE) (BrE **working week**) noun the total amount of time that you spend at work during the week

**world** 🅘 🅐🅰 ⊙ /wɜːld; NAmE wɜːrld/ noun
• THE EARTH/ITS PEOPLE **1** ʔ 🅐 **the world** [sing.] the earth, with all its countries, peoples and natural features: *a map of the world* ◊ *French is spoken in many parts of the world.* ◊ **in the ~** *Which is the largest city in the world?* ◊ **around/round the ~** *to sail around the world* ◊ **all over the ~** *She has been all over the world.* ◊ **throughout the ~** *Their products are sold throughout the world.* ◊ *They travelled the world for pleasure.* ◊ *a meeting of world leaders* ◊ *campaigning for world peace* ◊ *the world economy* **2** ʔ 🅐 [sing.] (in compounds) used before another noun to describe one of the most important people or things of their type in the world: *the world champion/championship/record/title* ◊ *As of October, her world ranking was No.1.* ◊ *the major world religions* **3** ʔ 🅑 [C, usually sing.] a particular part of the earth; a particular group of countries or people; a particular period of history and the people of that period: *the Arab world* ◊ *the English-speaking world* ◊ **in the …~** *farmers in the developing world* ◊ *in the modern/ancient world* ⊃ see also FIRST WORLD, NEW WORLD, OLD WORLD, THIRD WORLD
• TYPE OF LIFE **4** ʔ 🅑 [C] the people or things belonging to a particular group or connected with a particular interest, job, etc: *the animal/plant/insect world* ◊ *the business/corporate world* ◊ *She is a popular figure in the art world.* ◊ **the ~ of sth** *the world of politics/business/sport* **5** ʔ 🅑 [usually sing.] (usually used with an adjective) everything that exists of a particular kind; a particular kind of life or existence: *the natural world* (= animals, plants, minerals, etc.) ◊ *They are a couple in the real world as well as in the movie.* ◊ *The island is a world of brilliant colours and dramatic sunsets.* ◊ *They had little contact with the outside world* (= people and places that were not part of their normal life).
• SOCIETY **6** ʔ 🅑 [sing.] our society and the way people live and behave; the people in the world: *We live in a rapidly changing world.* ◊ *Young people always think they are going to change the world.* ◊ *The whole world was waiting for news of the astronauts.* ◊ *The eyes of the world are on the President* (= many people around the world are waiting to see what the President will do). **7** **the world** [sing.] a way of life where possessions and physical pleasures are important, rather than spiritual values: *monks and nuns renouncing the world* ⊃ see also OLDE WORLDE, OLD-WORLD
• PERSON'S LIFE **8** ʔ 🅑 [sing.] a person's environment, experiences, friends and family, etc: *Parents are the most important people in a child's world.* ◊ *When his wife died, his entire world was turned upside down.*
• IMAGINED ENVIRONMENT **9** ʔ 🅑 [C] an environment that is imagined or constructed, for example in a computer game: *Computer games create whole virtual worlds.* ◊ *The game comprises four separate worlds, each split into six levels.* ◊ *You're living in a fantasy world!*
• ANOTHER PLANET **10** [C] a planet like the earth: *There may be other worlds out there.*
• HUMAN EXISTENCE **11** [sing.] the state of human existence: *this world and the next* (= life on earth and existence after death)
**IDM** **be all the ˈworld to sb** to be loved by and very important to sb **the best of ˈboth worlds / ˈall possible worlds** the benefits of two or more completely different situations that you can enjoy at the same time: *If you enjoy the coast and the country, you'll get the best of both worlds on this walk.* **be ˈworlds apart** to be completely different in attitudes, opinions, etc. **come/go ˈdown / ˈup in the ˈworld** to become less/more important or successful in society **come into the ˈworld** (*literary*) to be born **do sb/ sth the ˈworld of good** to make sb feel much better; to improve sth: *A change of job would do you the world of*

# the World Bank

good. **for all the world as if / though ...** | **for all the world like sb/sth** (*formal*) exactly as if ...; exactly like sb/sth: *She behaved for all the world as if nothing unusual had happened.* ◊ *He looked for all the world like a schoolboy caught stealing apples.* **have the world at your 'feet** to be very successful and admired **how, why, etc. in the 'world** (*informal*) used to emphasize sth and to show that you are surprised or annoyed: *What in the world did they think they were doing?* **in an ideal / a perfect 'world** used to say that sth is what you would like to happen or what should happen, but you know it cannot: *In an ideal world we would be recycling and reusing everything.* **in the 'world** used to emphasize what you are saying: *There's nothing in the world I'd like more than to visit New York.* ◊ *Don't rush—we've got all the time in the world.* ◊ *You look as if you haven't got a care in the world!* **(be/live) in a world of your 'own** if you are **in a world of your own**, you are so concerned with your own thoughts that you do not notice what is happening around you **a man / woman of the 'world** a person with a lot of experience of life, who is not easily surprised or shocked **not for (all) the 'world** used to say that you would never do sth: *I wouldn't hurt you for the world.* **the ... of this world** (*informal*) used to refer to people of a particular type: *We all envy the Bill Gateses of this world* (= the people who are as rich and successful as Bill Gates). **out of this 'world** (*informal*) used to emphasize how good, beautiful, etc. sth is: *The meal was out of this world.* **see the 'world** to travel widely and gain wide experience **set the 'world on fire** (*BrE also* **set the 'world alight**) (*informal*) (usually used in negative sentences) to be very successful and admired by other people: *He's never going to set the world on fire with his paintings.* **set/put the world to 'rights** to talk about how the world could be changed to be a better place: *We stayed up all night, setting the world to rights.* **what is the world 'coming to?** used to express dislike, surprise or shock, especially at changes in people's attitudes or behaviour: *When I listen to the news these days, I sometimes wonder what the world is coming to.* **(all) the 'world and his 'wife** (*BrE, informal, humorous*) everyone; a large number of people **a 'world away (from sth)** used to emphasize how different two things are: *His new luxury mansion was a world away from the tiny house where he was born.* **the world is your 'oyster** there is no limit to the opportunities open to you **a / the 'world of difference** (*informal*) used to emphasize how much difference there is between two things: *There's a world of difference between liking someone and loving them.* **the (whole) world 'over** everywhere in the world: *People are basically the same the world over.* ⇒ more at BRAVE *adj.*, DEAD *adj.*, END *n.*, LOST *adj.*, PROMISE *v.*, SMALL *adj.*, TOP *n.*, TWILIGHT, WATCH *v.*, WAY *n.*, WILL *n.*, WORST *n.*

**the World 'Bank** *noun* [sing.] an international organization that lends money to countries who are members at times when they are in difficulty and need more money

**'world-beater** *noun* a person or thing that is better than all others ▶ **'world-beating** *adj.*

**world-'class** *adj.* as good as the best in the world: *a world-class athlete*

**the World 'Cup** *noun* (in several sports) a competition between national teams from all over the world, usually held every few years: *The next Rugby World Cup will take place in three years' time.*

**world 'English** *noun* [U] the English language, used throughout the world for international communication, including all of its regional varieties, such as Australian, Indian and South African English

**world-'famous** *adj.* known all over the world: *a world-famous scientist* ◊ *His books are world-famous.*

**World 'Heritage Site** *noun* a natural or MAN-MADE place that is recognized as having great international importance and is therefore protected by UNESCO

**world 'language** *noun* a language that is known or spoken in many countries

**world·ly** /ˈwɜːldli/ *NAmE* ˈwɜːrld-/ *adj.* (*literary*) **1** [only before noun] connected with the world in which we live rather than with spiritual things: *worldly success* ◊ *your worldly goods* (= the things that you own) **OPP** spiritual **2** having a lot of experience of life and therefore not easily shocked: *At 15, he was more worldly than his older cousins who lived in the country.* **OPP** unworldly ▶ **world·li·ness** *noun* [U]

**worldly-'wise** *adj.* having a lot of experience of life and therefore not easily shocked

**world 'music** *noun* [U] traditional music from non-Western countries, sometimes including elements of Western popular music

**world 'power** *noun* a powerful country that has a lot of influence in international politics

**the World 'Series™** *noun* a series of baseball games played every year between the winners of the American League and the National League

**world 'view** *noun* a person's way of thinking about and understanding life, which depends on their beliefs and attitudes: *Your education is bound to shape your world view.*

**world 'war** *noun* [C, U] a war that involves many countries

**World War 'One** (*also* **World War 'I**) *noun* = FIRST WORLD WAR

**World War 'Two** (*also* **World War 'II**) *noun* = SECOND WORLD WAR

**'world-weary** *adj.* (*literary*) no longer excited by life; showing this **SYN** jaded ▶ **'world-weariness** *noun* [U]

**world·wide** /ˌwɜːldˈwaɪd/ *NAmE* ˌwɜːrld-/ *adj., adv.* affecting all parts of the world: *an increase in worldwide sales* ◊ *The show has a worldwide audience of 115 million viewers.* ◊ *The company employs 28 000 people worldwide.*

**the World Wide 'Web** *noun* (*abbr.* WWW) = THE WEB: *to browse a site on the World Wide Web*

**worm** /wɜːm/ *NAmE* wɜːrm/ *noun, verb*

■ *noun* **1** [C] a long, thin creature with a soft body and no bones or legs: *birds looking for worms* ⇒ see also EARTHWORM **2** **worms** [pl.] long, thin creatures that live inside the bodies of humans or animals and can cause illness: *The dog has worms.* ⇒ see also HOOKWORM, TAPEWORM **3** [C] the young form of an insect when it looks like a short worm: *This apple is full of worms.* ⇒ see also GLOW-WORM, SILKWORM, WOODWORM **4** [C] (*computing*) a computer program that is a type of virus and that spreads across a network by copying itself **5** [C, usually sing.] (*informal, disapproving*) a person you do not like or respect, especially because they have a weak character and do not behave well towards other people

**IDM** **the worm will 'turn** (*saying*) a person who is normally quiet and does not complain will protest when the situation becomes too hard to bear ⇒ more at CAN² *n.*, EARLY *adj.*

■ *verb* **1** ~ **your way + adv. / prep.** to use a TWISTING and turning movement, especially to move through a narrow or crowded place: *She wormed her way through the crowd to the reception desk.* **2** ~ **sth** to give an animal medicine that makes worms pass out of its body in the FAECES

**PHRV** **worm your way/yourself 'into sth** (*disapproving*) to make sb like you or trust you, in order to gain some advantage for yourself **SYN** insinuate: *He managed to worm his way into her life.* **worm sth 'out of sb** (*informal*) to make sb tell you sth, by asking them questions in a clever way for a long period of time: *We eventually wormed the secret out of her.*

**worm·hole** /ˈwɜːmhəʊl; *NAmE* ˈwɜːrm-/ *noun* **1** a hole made by a worm or young insect **2** (*physics*) a possible connection between regions of SPACE-TIME that are far apart

**worm·wood** /ˈwɜːmwʊd; *NAmE* ˈwɜːrm-/ *noun* [U] a plant with a bitter taste, used in making alcoholic drinks and medicines

**wormy** /ˈwɜːmi; NAmE ˈwɜːrmi/ adj. containing worms: *a wormy apple*

**worn** /wɔːn; NAmE wɔːrn/ adj., verb
- adj. **1** [usually before noun] (of a thing) damaged or thinner than normal because it is old and has been used a lot: *an old pair of worn jeans* ◊ *The stone steps were worn and broken.* ⊃ see also WELL WORN **2** (of a person) looking very tired SYN **weary**: *She came out of the ordeal looking thin and worn.*
- verb past part. of WEAR

▼ **HOMOPHONES**

**warn · worn** /wɔːn; NAmE wɔːrn/
- **warn** verb: *I thought I should warn him about the risks involved.*
- **worn** verb (past participle of FLY): *This is the first time I've worn this suit.*
- **worn** adj.: *She was wearing a worn old leather jacket.*

**ˌworn ˈout** adj. **1** (of a thing) badly damaged and/or no longer useful because it has been used a lot: *These shoes are worn out.* ◊ *the gradual replacement of worn-out equipment* ◊ *a speech full of worn-out old clichés* **2** [not usually before noun] (of a person) looking or feeling very tired, especially as a result of hard work or physical exercise: *Can we sit down? I'm worn out.*

**wor·ried** ❶ A2 /ˈwʌrid; NAmE ˈwɜːr-/ adj. thinking about unpleasant things that have happened or that might happen and therefore feeling unhappy and afraid: *Don't look so worried!* ◊ *~ about sb/sth I'm not worried about her —she can take care of herself.* ◊ *~ about doing sth People are really worried about losing their jobs.* ◊ *~ for sb/sth He is extremely worried for her safety.* ◊ *I was worried for my family.* ◊ *~ by sth We're not too worried by these results.* ◊ *~ (that) ... The police are worried that the man may be armed.* ◊ *Where have you been? I've been worried sick (= extremely worried).* ◊ *Try not to get worried.* ◊ *His worried parents were waiting for him when he got home.*
▶ **wor·ried·ly** adv.: *He glanced worriedly at his father.*
IDM **you had me ˈworried** (informal) used to tell sb that you were worried because you had not understood what they had said correctly: *You had me worried for a moment —I thought you were going to resign!*

**wor·rier** /ˈwʌriə(r); NAmE ˈwɜːr-/ noun a person who worries a lot about unpleasant things that have happened or that might happen

**wor·ri·some** /ˈwʌrisəm; NAmE ˈwɜːr-/ adj. (especially NAmE) that makes you worry

**worry** ❶ A2 /ˈwʌri; NAmE ˈwɜːri/ verb, noun
- verb (wor·ries, worry·ing, wor·ried, wor·ried) **1** A2 [I] to keep thinking about unpleasant things that might happen or about problems that you have: *Don't worry. We have plenty of time.* ◊ *Stop worrying, Dad—it'll be fine.* ◊ *~ about sb/sth Don't worry about me. I'll be all right.* ◊ *Never mind —it's nothing to worry about.* ◊ *~ about doing sth You can stay here tonight, so you don't have to worry about walking home in the dark.* ◊ *~ over sb/sth There's no point in worrying over things you can't change.* ◊ *~ (that) ... I worry that I won't get into college.* **2** B1 [T] to make sb/yourself anxious about sth: *~ sb/yourself (about (sth/)) What worries me is how I am going to get another job.* ◊ *~ sb/yourself + adj. (about sb/sth) He's worried himself sick (= become extremely anxious) about his daughter.* ◊ *it worries sb that ... It worries me that he hasn't come home yet.* ◊ *it worries sb to do sth It worried me to think what might happen.* **3** B2 [T] to annoy or upset sb: *~ sb The noise never seems to worry her.* ◊ *~ sb with sth Don't keep worrying him with a lot of silly questions.* SYN **disturb 4** [T] *~ sth* (of a dog) to attack animals, especially sheep, by running after and/or biting them
IDM **not to ˈworry** (informal, especially BrE) it is not important; it does not matter: *Not to worry—I can soon fix it.* ◊ *Not to worry—no harm done.*
PHRV **ˈworry at sth 1** to bite sth and shake or pull sth: *Rebecca worried at her lip.* ◊ *He began to worry at the knot in the cord.* **2** to think about a problem a lot and try and find a solution
- noun (pl. -ies) **1** B1 [U] the state of worrying about sth SYN **anxiety**: *~ about sth Levels of worry about crime had fallen by a third.* ◊ *with ~ to be frantic with worry* **2** B1 [C] something that worries you: *You need have no worries— everything's been taken care of.* ◊ *~ about/over (doing) sth worries about the future* ◊ *~ for/to sb Mugging is a real worry for many old people.* ◊ *The biggest worry is that further stock market falls might dent consumer confidence.*
IDM **ˌno ˈworries!** (informal) it's not a problem; it's all right (often used as a reply when sb thanks you for sth)

**worry·ing** /ˈwʌriɪŋ; NAmE ˈwɜːr-/ adj. that makes you worry: *a worrying development* ◊ *It must be worrying for you not to know where he is.* ◊ *It is particularly worrying that nobody seems to be in charge.* ◊ *It's been a worrying time for us all.* ▶ **worry·ing·ly** adv.: *worryingly high levels of radiation* ◊ *Worryingly, the plan contains few details on how spending will be cut.*

**wors** /vɔːs; NAmE vɔːrs/ noun [U] (SAfrE) SAUSAGE

**worse** ❶ A2 /wɜːs; NAmE wɜːrs/ adj., adv., noun
- adj. (comparative of BAD) **1** B1 of poorer quality or lower standard; more unpleasant: *The weather got worse during the day.* ◊ *I've been to far worse places.* ◊ *~ than sth The film was no worse than many others he made in the 1930s.* ◊ *The interview was much worse than he had expected.* ◊ *~ than doing sth There's nothing worse than going out in the cold with wet hair.* **2** A2 more serious or severe: *They were trying to prevent an even worse tragedy.* ◊ *Don't tell*

# worsen

her that—you'll only make things worse. ◊ Never mind—it **could be worse** (= although the situation is bad, it is not as bad as it might have been). ◊ **~ than (doing) sth** *The situation was worse than he had imagined.* **3** [not before noun] more ill or unhappy: *If he gets any worse, we'll call the doctor.* ◊ **~ than ...** *He told her she'd let them down and she felt **worse than ever**.*

**IDM come off 'worse** to lose a fight, competition, etc. or suffer more compared with others **go from bad to 'worse** (of a bad condition, situation, etc.) to get even worse **worse 'luck!** (*BrE, informal*) used to show that you are disappointed about sth: *I shall have to miss the party, worse luck!* ⇒ more at BARK *n.*, FATE

- **adv.** (comparative of *badly*) **1** less well: **~ than sb/sth** *They are performing much worse than their counterparts at competitor firms.* **2** more seriously or severely: **~ than sb/sth** *It's raining worse than ever.* **3** used to introduce a statement about sth that is more serious or unpleasant than things already mentioned: *She'd lost her job. Even worse, she'd lost her house and her children, too.*

**IDM be worse 'off (than sb/sth)** to be poorer, unhappier, etc. than before or than sb else: *The increase in taxes means that we'll be £30 a month worse off than before.* **you can/could do worse than do sth** used to say that you think sth is a good idea: *If you want a safe investment, you could do a lot worse than put your money in a building society.*

- **noun** [U] more problems or bad news: *I'm afraid there is worse to come.*

**IDM be none the 'worse (for sth)** to not be harmed by sth: *The kids were none the worse for their adventure.* **the worse for 'wear** (*informal*) **1** in a poor condition because of being used a lot **2** drunk ⇒ more at BETTER *n.*, CHANGE *n.*

**wors·en** /ˈwɜːsn; NAmE ˈwɜːrsn/ *verb* [I, T] to become or make sth worse than it was before: *The political situation is steadily worsening.* ◊ *Her health has worsened considerably since we last saw her.* ◊ **~ sth** *Staff shortages have been worsened by the flu epidemic.* ▶ **wors·en·ing** /-sənɪŋ/ *noun* [sing.]: *a worsening of the international debt crisis* **worsening** *adj.*: *worsening weather conditions*

**wor·ship** /ˈwɜːʃɪp; NAmE ˈwɜːrʃ-/ *noun, verb*

- **noun 1** [U] the practice of showing respect for God or a god, by saying prayers, singing with others, etc.; a ceremony for this: *an act/a place of worship* ◊ *morning/evening worship* (= a church service in the morning/evening) ◊ *ancestor worship* **2** [U] a strong feeling of love and respect for sb/sth **SYN** adoration: *What she feels for him is akin to worship.* ⇒ see also HERO WORSHIP **3 His, Your, etc. Worship** [C] (*BrE, formal*) a polite way of addressing or referring to a MAGISTRATE or MAYOR

- **verb** (-pp-, *NAmE also* -p-) **1** [T] **~ sb/sth** to show respect for God or a god, especially by saying prayers, singing, etc. with other people in a religious building **2** [I] to go to a service in a religious building: *We worship at St Mary's.* ◊ *He worshipped at the local mosque.* **3** [T] **~ sb/sth** to love and admire sb very much, especially so much that you cannot see their faults: *She worships her children.* ◊ *He worshipped her from afar* (= he loved her but did not tell her his feelings). ◊ *She worships the ground he walks on.*

**wor·ship·ful** /ˈwɜːʃɪpfl; NAmE ˈwɜːrʃ-/ *adj.* [only before noun] **1** (*formal*) feeling or showing that you respect or admire sb/sth very much **2 Worshipful** used in the UK in the titles of some MAYORS and some groups of CRAFTSMEN: *the Worshipful Company of Goldsmiths*

**wor·ship·per** (*US* **wor·ship·er**) /ˈwɜːʃɪpə(r); NAmE ˈwɜːrʃ-/ *noun* a person who worships God or a god: *regular worshippers at St Andrew's Church* ◊ (*figurative*) *sun worshippers lying on the beach*

## worst /wɜːst; NAmE wɜːrst/ adj., adv., noun, verb

- **adj.** (superlative of *bad*) of the poorest quality or lowest standard; worse than any other person or thing of a similar kind: *What's the **worst thing** that could happen?* ◊ *What she said confirmed my **worst fears** (= proved they were right).* ◊ *This is every parent's **worst nightmare**.*

**IDM be your own worst 'enemy** to be the cause of your own problems **come off 'worst** to lose a fight, competition, etc. or suffer more compared with others

- **adv.** (superlative of *badly*) most badly or seriously: *He was voted the worst dressed celebrity.* ◊ *Manufacturing industry was worst affected by the fuel shortage.* ◊ **Worst of all**, *I lost the watch my father had given me.*

- **noun** **the worst** [sing.] the most serious or unpleasant thing that could happen; the part, situation, possibility, etc. that is worse than any other: *When they did not hear from her, they **feared the worst**.* ◊ *It doesn't matter what I say. My mother always **expects the worst**.* ◊ **the ~ of sth** *The worst of it is that I can't even be sure if they received my letter.* ◊ *Although all the votes have not yet been counted, the party **is preparing for the worst**.*

**IDM at (the) 'worst** used for saying what is the worst thing that can happen: *At the very worst, he'll have to pay a fine.* **bring out the 'worst in sb** to make sb show their worst qualities: *Pressure can bring out the worst in people.* **do your 'worst** (of a person) to do as much damage or be as unpleasant as possible: *Let them do their worst—we'll fight them every inch of the way.* **get the 'worst of it** to be defeated: *He'd been in a fight and had obviously got the worst of it.* **if the worst comes to the 'worst** (*NAmE also* **if worst comes to 'worst**) if the situation becomes too difficult or dangerous: *If the worst comes to the worst, we'll just have to sell the house.* **the worst of 'all (possible) worlds** a situation in which you have all the possible disadvantages at the same time

- **verb** [usually passive] (*old-fashioned* or *formal*) to defeat sb in a fight, a contest or an argument **SYN** get the better of: **be worsted (by sb) (in sth)** *She couldn't bear to be worsted in a fight.*

**'worst-case** *adj.* [only before noun] involving the worst situation that could happen: *In the **worst-case scenario** more than ten thousand people might be affected.*

**worst·ed** /ˈwʊstɪd; NAmE *also* ˈwɜːrs-/ *noun* [U] a type of cloth made of wool with a smooth surface, used for making clothes: *a grey worsted suit*

## worth /wɜːθ; NAmE wɜːrθ/ adj., noun

- **adj.** [not before noun] (used like a preposition, followed by a noun, pronoun or number, or by the -ing form of a verb) **1** **~ sth** having a value in money, etc: *Our house is worth about £100 000.* ◊ *How much is this painting worth?* ◊ *to be **worth a bomb/packet/fortune** (= a lot of money)* ◊ *It isn't worth much.* ⇒ SYNONYMS at PRICE **2** used to recommend the action mentioned because you think it may be useful, pleasant, etc: **~ sth** *The museum is certainly **worth a visit**.* ◊ **~ doing sth** *This idea is **well worth considering**.* ◊ *It's so unimportant it's hardly **worth mentioning**.* **3** important, good or pleasant enough to make sb feel satisfied, especially when difficulty or effort is involved: **~ sth** *Was it **worth the effort**?* ◊ *The job involves a lot of hard work but **it's worth it**.* ◊ *The trip was expensive but it was **worth every penny**.* ◊ **~ doing sth** *The film is definitely **worth seeing**.* ⇒ see also WORTHWHILE **4 ~ sth** (of a person) having money and possessions of a particular value: *He's worth £10 million.*

**IDM for all sb/it is 'worth 1** in a very determined way, with great energy and effort: *He was rowing for all he was worth.* **2** in order to get as much as you can from sb/sth: *She is milking her success for all it's worth.* **for what it's 'worth** (*informal*) used to emphasize that what you are saying is only your own opinion or suggestion and may not be very helpful: *I prefer this colour, for what it's worth.* **(the game is) not worth the 'candle** (*old-fashioned, saying*) the advantages to be gained from doing sth are not great enough, considering the effort or cost involved **not worth the paper it's 'written/'printed on** (of an agreement or official document) having no value, especially legally, or because one of the people involved has no intention of doing what they said they would **worth your/its 'salt** deserving respect, especially because you do your job well: *Any teacher worth her salt knows that.* **worth your/its weight in 'gold** very useful or valuable: *A good mechanic is worth his weight in gold.* **worth sb's 'while**

interesting or useful for sb to do: *It will be worth your while to come to the meeting.* ◊ *He'll do the job if you make it worth his while* (= pay him well). ⇒ more at BIRD *n.*, JOB
- *noun* [U] **1** **B2** **ten dollars', £40, etc. ~ of sth** an amount of sth that has the value mentioned: *The winner will receive fifty pounds' worth of books.* ◊ *The floods caused tens of millions of pounds' worth of damage.* **2 a week's, month's, etc. ~ of sth** an amount of sth that lasts a week, etc. **3** the financial, practical or moral value of sb/sth: *Their contribution was of great worth.* ◊ *The activities help children to develop a sense of their own worth.* ◊ *A good interview enables candidates to prove their worth* (= show how good they are). ◊ *a personal net worth of $10 million* ⇒ SYNONYMS at PRICE IDM see CENT, MONEY

**worth·less** /'wɜːθləs; NAmE 'wɜːrθ-/ *adj.* **1** having no practical or financial value: *Critics say his paintings are worthless.* OPP **valuable 2** (of a person) having no good qualities or useful skills: *a worthless individual* ◊ *Constant rejections made him feel worthless.* ▶ **worth·less·ness** *noun* [U]: *a sense of worthlessness*

**worth·while** **C1** /ˌwɜːθˈwaɪl/; NAmE /ˌwɜːrθ-/ *adj.* important, pleasant, interesting, etc.; worth spending time, money or effort on: *It was in aid of a worthwhile cause* (= a charity, etc.). ◊ *The smile on her face made it all worthwhile.* ◊ **~ for sb to do sth** *High prices in the UK make it worthwhile for buyers to look abroad.* ◊ **~ to do sth** *It is worthwhile to include really high-quality illustrations.* ◊ **~ doing sth** *It didn't seem worthwhile writing it all out again.* **HELP** This word can be written **worth while**, except when it is used before a noun.

**worthy** **C1** /'wɜːði; NAmE 'wɜːrði/ *adj., noun*
- *adj.* (**wor·thier, wor·thi·est**) **1** **~ (of sb/sth)** (*formal*) having the qualities that deserve sb/sth: *to be worthy of attention* ◊ *A number of the report's findings are worthy of note.* ◊ *No composer was considered worthy of the name until he had written an opera.* ◊ *a worthy champion* (= one who deserved to win) ◊ *He felt he was not worthy of her.* OPP **unworthy 2** [usually before noun] having qualities that deserve your respect or attention SYN **deserving**: *The money we raise will be going to a very worthy cause.* ◊ *a worthy member of the team* **3** having good qualities but not very interesting or exciting: *her worthy but dull husband* **4** **~ of sb/sth** typical of what a particular person or thing might do, give, etc: *He gave a speech that was worthy of Martin Luther King.* **5 -worthy** (in compounds) deserving, or suitable for, the thing mentioned: *trustworthy* ◊ *roadworthy* ▶ **wor·thily** /-ðɪli/ *adv.* **worthi·ness** *noun* [U]
- *noun* (*pl.* **-ies**) (*often humorous*) an important person: *a meeting attended by local worthies*

**wot** /wɒt; NAmE wɑːt/ (*BrE, non-standard, often humorous*) a way of writing 'what', used to show that sb is speaking very informal English: *'Wot's going on?' he shouted.*

**wotcha** /'wɒtʃə; NAmE 'wɑːtʃə/ *exclamation* (*BrE, informal*) used as a friendly way of saying hello to a person: *Wotcha Dave—thanks for coming.*

**would** **A1** /strong form wʊd, weak form wəd, əd/ *modal verb* (*short form* **'d** /d/, *negative* **would not**, *short form* **wouldn't** /'wʊdnt/) **1 ~ you …?** used in polite offers or invitations: *Would you like a sandwich?* ◊ *Would you have dinner with me on Friday?* **2** used to say what you like, love, hate, etc: **~ like, love, hate, prefer, etc. sth** *I'd love a coffee.* ◊ **~ like, etc. to do sth** *I'd be only too glad to help.* ◊ **~ like, etc. sb to do sth** *I'd hate you to think I was criticizing you.* ◊ **~ rather do sth** *I'd rather come with you.* ◊ **~ rather sb did sth** *I'd rather you came with us.* **3** **~ do sth** used as the past form of **will** when reporting what sb has said or thought: *He said he would be here at eight o'clock* (= His words were: 'I will be there at eight o'clock.'). ◊ *She asked if I would help.* ◊ *They told me that they probably wouldn't come.* **4** **~ do sth** used for talking about the result of an event that you imagine: *She'd look better with shorter hair.* ◊ *If you went to see him, he would be delighted.* ◊ *Hurry up! It would be a shame to miss the beginning of the play.* ◊ *She'd be a fool to accept it* (= if she accepted). **5** **~ have done sth** used for describing a possible action or event that did not in fact

happen, because sth else did not happen first: *If I had seen the advertisement in time, I would have applied for the job.* ◊ *They would never have met if she hadn't gone to Emma's party.* **6** **so that/in order that sb/sth ~ do sth** used for saying why sb does sth: *She burned the letters so that her husband would never read them.* **7** **wish (that) sb/ sth ~ do sth** used for saying what you want to happen: *I wish that you'd be quiet for a minute.* **8** **~ not do sth** used to show that sb/sth was not willing or refused to do sth: *She wouldn't change it, even though she knew it was wrong.* ◊ *My car wouldn't start this morning.* **9** **~ you …?** used to ask sb politely to do sth: *Would you mind leaving us alone for a few minutes?* ◊ *Would you open the door for me, please?* **10** **~ imagine, say, think, etc. (that) …** used to give opinions that you are not certain about: *I would imagine the job will take about two days.* ◊ *I'd say he was about fifty.* **11** **I would …** used to give advice: *I wouldn't have any more to drink, if I were you.* **12** **~ do sth** used for talking about things that often happened in the past SYN **used to**: *When my parents were away, my grandmother would take care of me.* ◊ *He'd always be the first to offer to help.* **13** (*usually disapproving*) used for talking about behaviour that you think is typical: *'She said it was your fault.' 'Well, she would say that, wouldn't she? She's never liked me.* **14** **~ that …** (*literary*) used to express a strong wish: *Would that he had lived to see it.* ⇒ note at MODAL, SHOULD

**would-be** /'wʊd biː/ *adj.* [only before noun] used to describe sb who is hoping to become the type of person mentioned: *a would-be actor* ◊ *advice for would-be parents*

**wound¹** **B2** /wuːnd/ *noun, verb* ⇒ see also WOUND²
- *noun* **1** **B2** an injury to part of the body, especially one in which a hole is made in the skin using a weapon: *a gunshot/stab wound* ◊ *a head/leg wound* ◊ *The nurse cleaned the wound.* ◊ *The wound healed slowly.* ◊ *He died of his wounds.* ◊ **~ to sth** *He suffered a fatal wound to the abdomen.* ⇒ see also FLESH WOUND ⇒ WORDFINDER NOTE at HURT **2** **B2** mental or emotional pain caused by sth unpleasant that has been said or done to you: *Seeing him again opened up old wounds.* ◊ *They say that time heals all wounds.* IDM see LICK *v.*, REOPEN, RUB *v.*
- *verb* [often passive] **1** **B2** **~ sb/sth** to injure part of the body, especially by making a hole in the skin using a weapon: *He had been wounded in the arm.* ◊ *The driver was seriously wounded in the shooting.* ⇒ SYNONYMS at INJURE **2** **B2** **~ sb/sth** to hurt sb's feelings: *She had been deeply wounded by his remarks.* ◊ *You wounded his pride.*

**wound²** /waʊnd/ *past tense, past part.* of WIND² ⇒ see also WOUND¹

**wound·ed** /'wuːndɪd/ *adj.* **1** injured by a weapon, for example in a war: *wounded soldiers* ◊ *seriously wounded* ◊ *There were 79 killed and 230 wounded.* **2** feeling emotional pain because of sth unpleasant that sb has said or done: *wounded pride* **3 the wounded** *noun* [pl.] people who are wounded, for example in a war

**wound·ing** /'wuːndɪŋ/ *adj.* that hurts sb's feelings: *He found her remarks deeply wounding.*

**wove** /wəʊv/ *past tense* of WEAVE

**woven** /'wəʊvn/ *past part.* of WEAVE

**wow** **A2** /waʊ/ *exclamation, verb, noun*
- *exclamation* **A2** (*also less frequent* **wowee** /ˌwaʊˈiː/) (*informal*) used to show that you are very surprised or impressed by sb/sth: *Wow! You look terrific!*
- *verb* **~ sb (with sth)** (*informal*) to impress sb very much, especially with a performance: *He wowed audiences around the country with his new show.*
- *noun* **1** [sing.] (*informal*) a great success: *Don't worry. You'll be a wow.* **2** [U] (*specialist*) slow changes in the PITCH of sound played in a sound recording ⇒ compare FLUTTER

**'wow factor** *noun* [sing.] (*informal*) the quality sth has of being very impressive or surprising to people: *If you want to sell your house quickly, it needs a wow factor.*

**wow·ser** /ˈwaʊzə(r)/ noun (AustralE, NZE, informal) **1** a person who criticizes people who are enjoying themselves **SYN** killjoy **2** a person who does not drink alcohol **SYN** teetotaller

**WPC** /ˌdʌblju: pi: ˈsi:/ noun (BrE) a woman police officer of the lowest rank (the abbreviation for 'woman police constable'): *WPC (Linda) Green*

**wpm** abbr. words per minute: *to type at 60 wpm*

**wrack** = RACK

**wraith** /reɪθ/ noun the ghost of a person that is seen a short time before or after that person dies **SYN** spectre: *a wraith-like figure* (= a very thin, pale person)

**wran·gle** /ˈræŋgl/ noun, verb
- noun ~(with sb)(over sth) | ~(between A and B) an argument that is complicated and continues over a long period of time: *a legal wrangle between the company and their suppliers* ▸ **wran·gling** /-glɪŋ/ noun [U, C]
- verb [I] ~(with sb) (over/about sth) to argue angrily and usually for a long time about sth: *They're still wrangling over the financial details.*

**wran·gler** /ˈræŋglə(r)/ noun (NAmE, informal) a COWBOY or a COWGIRL, especially one who takes care of horses

**wrap** ⓘ B2 /ræp/ verb, noun
- verb (-pp-) **1** B2 [T] to cover sth completely in paper or other material, for example when you are giving it as a present: *~sth (up) He spent the evening wrapping up the Christmas presents.* ◇ *~sth (up) in sth Each apple was wrapped in paper.* ⇨ see also GIFT-WRAP ⬥ HOMOPHONES at RAP **2** B2 [T] to cover sth/sb in material, for example in order to protect it/them: *~A (up) in B Wrap the meat in foil before you cook it.* ◇ *~yourself (up) in sth He tossed her a towel. 'Wrap yourself in that.'* ◇ *~B round/around A I wrapped a blanket around the baby.* ⇨ see also SHRINK-WRAPPED **3** B2 [T] *~sth around/round sth/sb* to put sth around sth/sb: *The nurse wrapped a bandage tightly around my ankle.* ◇ *His arms were wrapped around her waist.* **4** [T, I] (computing) to cause a word or text to be carried over to a new line as the end of the previous line is reached by the writer; to be carried over in this way: *~sth (around/round) How can I wrap the text around?* ◇ *~(around/round) The text wraps around if it is too long to fit the screen.* ⇨ compare UNWRAP
  - **IDM** **be wrapped 'up in sb/sth** to be so involved with sb/sth that you do not pay enough attention to other people or things **SYN** absorbed, engrossed ⇨ more at LITTLE FINGER
  - **PHRV** **wrap 'up | wrap it 'up** (informal) usually used as an order to tell sb to stop talking or causing trouble, etc. ˌwrap 'up | ˌwrap sb/yourself 'up to put warm clothes on sb/yourself: *She told them to wrap up warm/warmly.* ˌwrap sth↔'up (informal) to complete sth such as an agreement or a meeting in an acceptable way: *That just about wraps it up for today.*
- noun **1** [C] a piece of cloth that a woman wears around her shoulders for decoration or to keep warm, or a loose piece of clothing worn over sth else **2** [U] paper, plastic, etc. that is used for wrapping things in: *We stock a wide range of cards and gift wrap.* ⇨ see also PLASTIC WRAP ⬥ HOMOPHONES at RAP **3** [sing.] used when making a film to say that filming has finished: *Cut! That's a wrap.* **4** [C] a type of sandwich made with a cold TORTILLA rolled around meat or vegetables
  - **IDM** **under 'wraps** (informal) being kept secret until some time in the future: *Next year's collection is still being kept under wraps.*

**ˈwrap-around** adj. **1** curving or stretching round at the sides: *wrap-around sunglasses* **2** (of a piece of clothing) having one part that is pulled over to cover another part at the front and then loosely fastened: *a wrap-around skirt*

**wrap·arounds** /ˈræpəraʊndz/ noun [pl.] a pair of SUN-GLASSES that fit closely and go round the sides of the head in a curved form

**wrapped** /ræpt/ adj. (AustralE, informal) extremely pleased: *The minister declared that he was wrapped.*

**wrap·per** /ˈræpə(r)/ noun **1** a piece of paper, plastic, etc. that is wrapped around sth, especially food, when you buy it in order to protect it and keep it clean: (BrE) *sweet wrappers* ◇ (NAmE) *candy wrappers* **2** (WAfrE) a piece of cloth that is worn as an item of clothing around the lower body and legs

**wrap·ping** /ˈræpɪŋ/ noun [U] (also **wrap·pings** [pl.]) paper, plastic, etc. used for covering sth in order to protect it: *She tore the cellophane wrapping off the box.* ◇ *shrink wrapping* (= plastic designed to SHRINK around objects so that it fits them tightly) ◇ *The painting was still in its wrappings.*

**ˈwrapping paper** noun [U] coloured paper used for wrapping presents **SYN** gift wrap: *a piece/sheet/roll of wrapping paper*

**wrasse** /ræs/ noun (pl. **wrasse** or **wrasses**) a sea fish with thick lips and strong teeth

**wrath** /rɒθ; NAmE ræθ/ noun [U] (old-fashioned or formal) extreme anger: *the wrath of God* ▸ **wrath·ful** /ˈrɒθfl; NAmE ˈræθ-/ adj. **wrath·ful·ly** /-fəli/ adv.

**wreak** /ri:k/ verb *~sth (on sb/sth)* (formal) to do great damage or harm to sb/sth: *Their policies would wreak havoc on the economy.* ◇ *He swore to wreak vengeance on those who had betrayed him.*

**wreath** /ri:θ/ noun (pl. **wreaths** /ri:ðz/) **1** an arrangement of flowers and leaves, especially in the shape of a circle, placed on GRAVES, etc. as a sign of respect for sb who has died: *The Queen laid a wreath at the war memorial.* **2** an arrangement of flowers and/or leaves in the shape of a circle, traditionally hung on doors as a decoration at Christmas: *a holly wreath* **3** a circle of flowers or leaves worn on the head, and used in the past as a sign of honour: *a laurel wreath* **4** (literary) a circle of smoke, cloud, etc.

**wreathe** /ri:ð/ verb (formal) **1** [T, usually passive] to surround or cover sth: *be wreathed in/with sth The mountain tops were wreathed in mist.* ◇ (figurative) *Her face was wreathed in smiles* (= she was smiling a lot). **2** [I] + adv./prep. (literary) to move slowly and lightly, especially in circles **SYN** weave: *smoke wreathing into the sky*

**wreck** /rek/ noun, verb
- noun **1** a ship that has sunk or that has been very badly damaged ⇨ see also SHIPWRECK noun **2** a car, plane, etc. that has been very badly damaged in an accident: *Two passengers are still trapped in the wreck.* ⇨ SYNONYMS at CRASH **3** [usually sing.] (informal) a person who is in a bad physical or mental condition: *Physically, I was a total wreck.* ◇ *The interview reduced him to a nervous wreck.* **4** (informal) a vehicle, building, etc. that is in very bad condition: *The house was a wreck when we bought it.* ◇ (figurative) *They still hoped to salvage something from the wreck of their marriage.* **5** (NAmE) = CRASH: *a car/train wreck*
- verb **1** *~sth* to damage or destroy sth: *The building had been wrecked by the explosion.* ◇ *The road was littered with wrecked cars.* **2** *~sth* to cause sth to fail completely: *The weather wrecked all our plans.* ◇ *A serious injury nearly wrecked his career.* **3** [usually passive] to damage a ship so much that it sinks or can no longer sail: *be wrecked The ship was wrecked off the coast of France.* ⇨ see also SHIP-WRECK verb

**wreck·age** /ˈrekɪdʒ/ noun [U] the parts of a vehicle, building, etc. that remain after it has been badly damaged or destroyed: *A few survivors were pulled from the wreckage.* ◇ *Pieces of wreckage were found ten miles away from the scene of the explosion.* ◇ (figurative) *Could nothing be rescued from the wreckage of her dreams?*

**wrecked** /rekt/ adj. **1** [only before noun] having been wrecked: *a wrecked ship/marriage* **2** [not before noun] (BrE, slang) very drunk; not behaving or thinking normally because of the effects of an illegal drug **3** [not before noun] (informal) very tired **SYN** exhausted

**wreck·er** /ˈrekə(r)/ noun **1** a person who destroys another person's plans, relationship, etc. **2** (NAmE) a vehicle used for moving other vehicles that have been damaged in an accident

**wreck·ing ball** noun a heavy metal ball that hangs from a CRANE and is used to hit a building to make it fall down

**wren** /ren/ noun a very small brown bird

**wrench** /rentʃ/ verb, noun
- **verb 1** [T, I] to pull or TWIST sth/sb/yourself suddenly and violently SYN **jerk**: ~(sth/sb/yourself) + adv./prep. *The bag was wrenched from her grasp.* ◊ *He grabbed Ben, wrenching him away from his mother.* ◊ (*figurative*) *Guy wrenched his mind back to the present.* ◊ ~(sth/sb/yourself) + adj. *They wrenched the door open.* ◊ *She managed to wrench herself free.* **2** [T] ~sth to TWIST and injure a part of your body, especially your ankle or shoulder SYN **twist**: *She wrenched her knee when she fell.* **3** [T, I] (*formal*) to make sb feel great pain or unhappiness, especially so that they make a sound or cry: ~(sth) (from sb) *Her words wrenched a sob from her.* ◊ *a wrenching experience* ◊ ~at sth *Her words wrenched at my heart.* ⊃ see also GUT-WRENCHING
- **noun 1** (*especially NAmE*) (*BrE usually* **span·ner**) [C] a metal tool with a special shape at the end for holding and turning things, including one that can be changed to fit objects of different sizes, also called a MONKEY WRENCH or an ADJUSTABLE SPANNER ⊃ picture at SPANNER **2** [sing.] pain or unhappiness that you feel when you have to leave a person or place that you love: *Leaving home was a terrible wrench for me.* **3** [C, usually sing.] a sudden and violent TWIST or pull: *She stumbled and gave her ankle a painful wrench.*
- IDM **throw a 'wrench in/into sth** (*NAmE*) = (THROW) A SPANNER IN THE WORKS at SPANNER

**wrest** /rest/ verb
- PHRV **'wrest sth from sb/sth** (*formal*) **1** to take sth such as power or control from sb/sth with great effort: *They attempted to wrest control of the town from government forces.* **2** to take sth from sb that they do not want to give, suddenly or violently SYN **wrench**: *He wrested the gun from my grasp.*

**wres·tle** /ˈresl/ verb **1** [I, T] to fight sb by holding them and trying to throw or force them to the ground, sometimes as a sport: *As a boy he had boxed and wrestled.* ◊ ~with sb *Armed guards wrestled with the intruder.* ◊ ~sb (+ adv./prep.) *Shoppers wrestled the raider to the ground.* **2** [I, T] ~(with) sth to struggle physically to move or manage sth: *He wrestled with the controls as the plane plunged.* **3** [I] to struggle to deal with sth that is difficult SYN **battle, grapple**: ~with sth *She had spent the whole weekend wrestling with the problem.* ◊ ~to do sth *She has been wrestling to raise the money all year.*

**wrest·ler** /ˈreslə(r)/ noun a person who takes part in the sport of wrestling

**wrest·ling** /ˈreslɪŋ/ noun [U] a sport in which two people fight by holding each other and trying to throw or force their opponent to the ground

**wretch** /retʃ/ noun **1** (*literary*) a person that you feel sympathy for or are sad about: *a poor wretch* **2** (*often humorous*) an evil, unpleasant or annoying person

**wretch·ed** /ˈretʃɪd/ adj. **1** [not usually before noun] (of a person) feeling ill or unhappy: *You look wretched—what's wrong?* ◊ *I felt wretched about the way things had turned out.* **2** (*formal*) extremely bad or unpleasant SYN **awful**: *She had a wretched time of it at school.* ◊ *The animals are kept in the most wretched conditions.* **3** [usually before noun] (*formal*) making you feel sympathy or making you sad SYN **pitiful**: *She finally agreed to have the wretched animal put down.* **4** [only before noun] (*informal*) used to show that you think that sb/sth is extremely annoying: *Is it that wretched woman again?* ▶ **wretch·ed·ly** adv. **wretch·ed·ness** noun [U]

**wrig·gle** /ˈrɪɡl/ verb, noun
- **verb 1** [I, T] to TWIST and turn your body or part of it with quick, short movements SYN **wiggle**: ~(about/around) *The baby was wriggling around on my lap.* ◊ ~sth *She wriggled her toes.* **2** [I, T] to move somewhere by TWISTING and turning your body or part of it SYN **squirm**: (+ adv./prep.) *The fish wriggled out of my fingers.* ◊ + adj. *She managed to wriggle free.* ◊ ~your way/yourself + adv./prep. *They wriggled their way through the tunnel.*

# write

PHRV **wriggle 'out of sth/out of doing sth** (*informal, disapproving*) to avoid doing sth that you should do, especially by thinking of clever excuses: *He tried desperately to wriggle out of giving a clear answer.*
- **noun** [usually sing.] an act of wriggling

**wring** /rɪŋ/ verb (**wrung, wrung** /rʌŋ/) **1** ~sth (out) to TWIST and SQUEEZE wet clothes, etc. in order to get the water out of them ⊃ picture at SQUEEZE **2** ~sth if you **wring** a bird's neck, you TWIST it in order to kill the bird
- IDM **,wring sb's 'hand** to press sb's hand very hard when you shake hands ,**wring your 'hands** to hold your hands together, and TWIST and press them together in a way that shows you are anxious or upset, especially when you cannot change the situation ⊃ see also HAND-WRINGING ,**wring sb's 'neck** (*informal*) when you say that you will **wring sb's neck**, you mean that you are very angry or annoyed with them
- PHRV **'wring sth from/out of sb** to obtain sth from sb with difficulty, especially by putting pressure on them SYN **extract**

**wring·er** /ˈrɪŋə(r)/ noun = MANGLE
- IDM **go through the 'wringer** (*informal*) to have a difficult or unpleasant experience, or a series of them

**wrin·kle** /ˈrɪŋkl/ noun, verb
- **noun 1** a line or small fold in your skin, especially on your face, that forms as you get older: *There were fine wrinkles around her eyes.* **2** [usually pl.] a small fold that you do not want in a piece of cloth or paper SYN **crease**
- **verb 1** [T, I] to make the skin on your face form into lines or folds; to form lines or folds in this way: ~sth (up) *She wrinkled up her nose in distaste.* ◊ *He wrinkled his brow in concentration.* ◊ ~(up) *His face wrinkled in a grin.* **2** [I, T] ~(sth) to form raised folds or lines in an untidy way; to make sth do this: *Her stockings were wrinkling at the knees.*

**wrin·kled** /ˈrɪŋkld/ adj. (of skin, clothing, etc.) having wrinkles

**wrink·ling** /ˈrɪŋklɪŋ/ noun [U] the process by which wrinkles form in the skin

**wrink·ly** /ˈrɪŋkli/ adj., noun
- **adj.** (*informal*) (of skin, clothing, etc.) having WRINKLES
- **noun** (*pl.* **-ies**) (*BrE, informal*) an offensive word for an old person, used by younger people

**wrist** /rɪst/ noun the JOINT between the hand and the arm: *She's broken her wrist.* ◊ *He wore a copper bracelet on his wrist.* IDM see SLAP n.

**wrist·band** /ˈrɪstbænd/ noun a narrow piece of material worn around the WRIST, as a decoration, to take in SWEAT during exercise, or to show support for sth: *He was wearing an anti-racism wristband.*

**wrist·watch** /ˈrɪstwɒtʃ; *NAmE* -wɑːtʃ/ noun a watch that you wear on your WRIST HELP It is more usual just to call this a **watch**.

**writ** /rɪt/ noun, verb
- **noun** ~(for sth) (against sb) a legal document from a court telling sb to do or not to do sth: *The company has been served with a writ for breach of contract.* ◊ *We fully intend to issue a writ against the newspaper.* ⊃ see also HOLY WRIT
- **verb** (*old use*) past part. of WRITE
- IDM **,writ 'large** (*literary*) **1** easy to see or understand: *Mistrust was writ large on her face.* **2** (used after a noun) being a typical or obvious example of the thing mentioned: *This is deception writ large.*

**write** /raɪt/ verb (**wrote** /rəʊt/, **writ·ten** /ˈrɪtn/)
- **LETTERS/NUMBERS 1** [I, T] to make letters or numbers on a surface, especially using a pen or a pencil: *In some countries children don't start learning to read and write until they are six.* ◊ ~in sth *Please write in pen on both sides of the paper.* ◊ ~with sth *I haven't got anything to write with.* ◊ ~sth *Write your name at the top of the paper.* ◊ *The teacher wrote the answers on the board.* ◊ *The 'b' had been wrongly written as a 'd'.*

# write-down

- **BOOK/MUSIC/PROGRAM** 2 [A1] [T, I] to produce sth in written form so that people can read, perform or use it, etc: ~ sth *to write a novel/song/computer program* ◊ *Who was 'The Grapes of Wrath' written by?* ◊ *He hopes to write a book about his experiences one day.* ◊ *The text is very well written.* ◊ ~ **about sth** *I wanted to travel and then write about it.* ◊ ~ **for sth** *He writes for the 'New Yorker'* (= works as a writer). ◊ *No decision has been made* **at the time of writing.** ◊ ~ **sb sth** *She wrote him several poems.*

**WORDFINDER** author, book, classic, critic, drama, fiction, genre, literature, poetry

- **A LETTER/AN EMAIL** 3 [A1] [I, T] to put information, a message of good wishes, etc. in a letter or an email and send it to sb: *Bye! Don't forget to write.* ◊ *I'm writing to enquire about language courses.* ◊ ~ **to sb** *She wrote to him in France.* ◊ ~ **sth to sb** *I wrote a letter to the Publicity Department.* ◊ ~ **sb sth** *I wrote the Publicity Department a letter.* ◊ ~ **that...** *She wrote that they were all fine.* ◊ ~ **sb** (*NAmE*) *Write me while you're away.* ◊ ~ **sb that...** (*NAmE*) *He wrote me that he would be arriving Monday.* ◊ ~ **doing sth** *They wrote thanking us for the present.*
- **STATE IN WRITING** 4 [A1] [T, I] to state the information or the words mentioned: ~ **that...** *The author writes that this theory has now been disproved.* ◊ ~ **of sth** *Ancient historians wrote of a lost continent beneath the ocean.* ◊ **+ speech** *'Of all my books,' wrote Dickens, 'I like this the best.'*
- **FORM** 5 [A1] [T] to put information in the appropriate places on a form: ~ **sth (out)** *to write (out) a cheque* ◊ ~ **sb sth** *The doctor wrote her a prescription for more antibiotics.* ◊ ~ **sb out sth** *I'll write you out a receipt.*
- **COMPUTING** 6 [T, I] ~ **(sth) to/onto sth** to record data in the memory of a computer: *An error was reported when he tried to write data to the file for the first time.*
- **OF PEN/PENCIL** 7 [I] to work correctly or in the way mentioned: *This pen won't write.*

**IDM** **be written all over sb's 'face** (of a feeling) to be very obvious to other people from the expression on sb's face: *Guilt was written all over his face.* **have sth/sb written all 'over it/sb** (*informal*) to show clearly the quality mentioned or the influence of the person mentioned: *It was a performance with star quality written all over it.* ◊ *This essay has got Mike written all over it.* **nothing (much) to write 'home about** (*informal*) not especially good; ordinary **that's all she 'wrote** (*NAmE*, *informal*) used when you are stating that there is nothing more that can be said about sth or that sth is completely finished ⊃ more at WORTH *adj.*

**PHRV** **write a'way** = WRITE OFF/AWAY (TO SB/STH) (FOR STH), **write 'back (to sb)** to write sb a letter or an email replying to their letter or email **SYN** reply: *I'm afraid I never wrote back.* ◊ *She wrote back saying that she couldn't come.* **write sth↔'down** 1 to write sth on paper, especially in order to remember or record it: *Write down the address before you forget it.* 2 (*business*) to reduce the value of ASSETS when stating it in a company's accounts ⊃ related noun WRITE-DOWN **write 'in (to sb/sth) (for sth/to do sth)** to write to an organization or a company, for example to ask about sth or to express an opinion: *I'll write in for more information.* **write sb/sth↔'in** (*NAmE*, *politics*) to add an extra name to your voting paper in an election in order to be able to vote for them ⊃ related noun WRITE-IN **write sth 'into sth** to include a rule or condition in a contract or an agreement when it is made **write 'off/a'way (to sb/sth) (for sth)** to write to an organization or a company, usually in order to ask them to send you sth **SYN** send off (for sth): *I've written off for the catalogue.* **write sth↔'off** 1 (*business*) to cancel a debt; to recognize that sth is a failure, has no value, etc: *to write off a debt/an investment* 2 (*BrE*) to damage sth, especially a vehicle, so badly that it cannot be repaired or would cost more to repair than to replace ⊃ related noun WRITE-OFF ⊃ see also TOTAL *verb* **write sb/sth↔'off (as sth)** to decide that sb/sth is a failure or not worth paying any attention to **SYN** dismiss **write sth↔'out** to write sth on paper, including all the details,

especially a piece of work or an account of sth ⊃ see also WRITE (5) **write sb↔'out (of sth)** to remove a character from a regular series on television or radio **write sth↔'up** to record sth in writing in a full and complete form, often using notes that you made earlier: *to write up your notes/the minutes of a meeting* ⊃ related noun WRITE-UP

'**write-down** *noun* (*business*) a reduction in the value of ASSETS, etc.

'**write-in** *noun* (*US*) a vote for sb who is not an official candidate in an election, in which you write their name on your BALLOT PAPER

'**write-off** *noun* **1** (*BrE*) a vehicle that has been so badly damaged in an accident that cannot be repaired or would cost more to repair than to replace **2** [*sing.*] (*informal*) a period of time during which you do not achieve anything: *With meetings and phone calls, yesterday was a complete write-off.* **3** ~ **(of sth)** (*business*) an act of cancelling a debt and accepting that it will never be paid

**writer** [A1] /ˈraɪtə(r)/ *noun* 1 [A1] a person whose job is writing books, stories, articles, etc: *Who's your favourite writer?* ◊ *a travel/cookery/science fiction writer* ◊ *a freelance feature writer for 'Time' magazine* ⊃ see also STAFF WRITER 2 [A1] a person who has written a particular thing: *the writer of this letter* 3 (with an adjective) a person who forms letters in a particular way when they are writing: *a messy writer*

'**writer's block** *noun* [U] a problem that writers sometimes have when they cannot think of what to write and have no new ideas

'**writer's cramp** *noun* [U] a pain or stiff feeling in the hand caused by writing for a long time

'**write-up** *noun* an article in a newspaper or magazine in which sb writes what they think about a new book, play, product, etc.

**writhe** /raɪð/ *verb* [I] ~ **(about/around) (in/with sth)** to TWIST or move your body without stopping, often because you are in great pain: *She was writhing around on the floor in agony.* ◊ *The snake writhed and hissed.* ◊ (*figurative*) *He was writhing* (= suffering a lot) *with embarrassment.*

**writing** [A1] /ˈraɪtɪŋ/ *noun* 1 [A1] [U] the activity of writing, in contrast to reading, speaking, etc: *Our son's having problems with his reading and writing* (= at school) ◊ *a writing case* (= containing paper, pens, etc.) 2 [A1] [U] the activity of writing books, articles, etc., especially as a job: *Only later did she discover a talent for writing.* ◊ *I wanted to try out a new style of writing.* ◊ *creative writing* ◊ *feminist/travel writing* ⊃ see also SONGWRITING 3 [A1] [U] books, articles, etc. in general: *The review is a brilliant piece of writing.* 4 [A1] [U] words that have been written or painted on sth: *There was writing all over the desk.* 5 [A1] [U] the particular way in which sb forms letters when they write **SYN** handwriting: *Who's this from? I don't recognize the writing.* 6 [B1] **writings** [pl.] a group of pieces of writing, especially by a particular person or on a particular subject: *His experiences in India influenced his later writings.* ◊ ~ **on sth** *His writings on complex subjects are clear and definitive.*

**IDM** **in 'writing** in the form of a letter, document, etc. (that gives proof of sth): *All telephone reservations must be confirmed in writing.* ◊ *Could you put your complaint in writing?* ◊ *You must get it in writing.* **the 'writing is on the 'wall** | **see the 'writing on the 'wall** (*NAmE* also **the handwriting on the 'wall**) (*saying*) used when you are describing a situation in which there are signs that sth is going to have problems or that it is going to be a failure: *It is amazing that not one of them saw the writing on the wall.* **ORIGIN** From the Bible story in which strange writing appeared on a wall during a feast given by King Belshazzar, predicting Belshazzar's death and the fall of his city.

'**writing paper** *noun* [U] = NOTEPAPER

**written** [B1] /ˈrɪtn/ *adj.*, *verb*

■ *adj.* 1 [B1] [usually before noun] expressed in writing rather than in speech: *Having a written record of what I've done is very valuable.* 2 [B1] [usually before noun] (of

an exam, a piece of work, etc.) involving writing rather than speaking or practical skills: *a written test* ◊ *Students must submit one or more pieces of **written work** for assessment.* **3** B1 [only before noun] in the form of a letter, document, etc. and therefore official: *No portion of this site may be copied without express **written consent.*** ◊ *You must give **written permission** before this information can be shared.*
IDM **the ˌwritten ˈword** language expressed in writing rather than in speech: *the permanence of the written word*
■ *verb* past part. of WRITE

## wrong ◑ A1 /rɒŋ; NAmE rɔːŋ/ adj., adv., noun, verb

■ *adj.*
- **NOT CORRECT 1** ◑ A1 not right or correct: *I got all the answers wrong.* ◊ *He was driving on the **wrong side of the road.*** ◊ *You're holding the camera **the wrong way up!*** ◊ *That picture is **the wrong way round.*** ◊ *I soon realised I'd taken a **wrong turn.*** OPP right **2** ◑ A2 [not before noun] (of a person) not right about sth/sb SYN **mistaken**: *I think she lives at number 44, but I could be wrong.* ◊ *~ about sth/sb You were wrong about Tom; he's not married after all.* ◊ *~ to do sth We were wrong to assume that she'd agree.* ◊ *She would **prove him wrong** (= prove that he was wrong) whatever happened.* ◊ *(informal) **Correct me if I'm wrong** (= I may be wrong) but didn't you say you knew each other?* ◊ *(informal) If you think I'm happy, you're **dead wrong.***
- **CAUSING PROBLEMS 3** ◑ B1 [not before noun] causing problems or difficulties; not as it should be: *Is anything wrong? You look worried.* ◊ *'What's wrong?' 'Oh, nothing.'* ◊ *~ with sb/sth There's something wrong with the printer.* ◊ *I have something wrong with my foot.*
- **NOT SUITABLE 4** ◑ B1 [usually before noun] not suitable, right or what you need: *~ sth for sth He's the wrong person for the job.* ◊ *~ for sth She's simply wrong for this job.* ◊ *~ sth to do I realized that it was the wrong thing to say.* ◊ *Most people think that the country is heading **in the wrong direction.*** ◊ *It was his bad luck to be in the **wrong place at the wrong time** (= so that he got involved in trouble without intending to).*
- **NOT MORALLY RIGHT 5** ◑ B1 [not usually before noun] not morally right or honest: *This man has **done nothing wrong.*** ◊ *~ to do sth It is wrong to tell lies.* ◊ *~ of sb (to do sth) It was wrong of me to get so angry.* ◊ *~ with doing sth What's wrong with eating meat?* ◊ *~ with sth There's nothing inherently wrong with this type of nostalgia.* ◊ *~ that ... It is wrong that he should not be punished for what he did.*
▶ **ˈwrongˌness** noun [U] (formal)
IDM **from/on the ˌwrong side of the ˈtracks** from or living in a poor area or part of town **get (hold of) the ˌwrong end of the ˈstick** (*BrE, informal*) to understand sth in the wrong way **on the ˌwrong side of the ˈlaw** in trouble with the police **take sth the wrong ˈway** to be offended by a remark that was not intended to be offensive ⊃ more at BACK v., BARK v., BED n., FAR adv., FOOT n., NOTE n., RUB v., SIDE n., TRACK n.

■ *adv.* ◑ B1 (used after verbs) in a way that produces a result that is not correct or that you do not want: *My name is spelt wrong.* ◊ *The program won't load. What am I **doing wrong?*** ◊ *I was trying to apologize but it **came out wrong** (= what I said sounded wrong).* ◊ *'I thought you were going out.' 'Well you must have **thought wrong, then!*** OPP right
IDM **get sb ˈwrong** (*informal*) to not understand correctly what sb means or what they are: *Don't get me wrong (= do not be offended by what I am going to say), I think he's doing a good job, but ...* **get sth ˈwrong** (*informal*) **1** to not understand a situation correctly: *No, you've got it all wrong. She's his wife.* **2** to make a mistake with sth: *I must have got the figures wrong.* **go ˈwrong 1** ◑ B1 to make a mistake: *If you do what she tells you, you won't go far wrong.* ◊ *Where did we go wrong with those kids (= what mistakes did we make for them to behave so badly?)* **2** ◑ B1 (of a machine) to stop working correctly: *My watch keeps going wrong.* **3** ◑ B1 to experience problems or difficulties: *The relationship started to go wrong when they moved abroad.* ◊ *What else can go wrong (= what other problems are we going to have)?* **you can't go ˌbadly/terribly/ seriously ˌwrong (with sth)** (*informal*) used to say that sth will always be acceptable in a particu-

lar situation: *For a quick lunch you can't go wrong with pasta.* ⊃ more at FOOT n.

■ *noun* **1** ◑ B2 [U] behaviour that is not honest or morally acceptable: *Children must be taught the difference between **right and wrong.*** ◊ *Her son can **do no wrong** in her eyes.* **2** [C] (*formal*) an act that is not legal, honest or morally acceptable: *It is time to forgive past wrongs if progress is to be made.* OPP right
IDM **in the ˈwrong** responsible for an accident, a mistake, an argument, etc: *The motorcyclist was clearly in the wrong.* **two ˌwrongs don't make a ˈright** (*saying*) used to say that if sb does sth bad to you, the situation will not be improved by doing sth bad to them ⊃ more at RIGHT v.

■ *verb* [usually passive] (*formal*) to treat sb badly or in an unfair way: **be/feel wronged (by sb/sth)** *He felt deeply wronged by the allegations.*

▼ SYNONYMS

### wrong
false • mistaken • incorrect • inaccurate • misguided • untrue

These words all describe sth that is not right or correct, or sb who is not right about sth.

**wrong** not right or correct; (of a person) not right about sb/sth: *I got all the answers wrong.* ◊ *We were wrong to assume she'd agree.*

**false** not true or correct; wrong because it is based on sth that is not true or correct: *A whale is a fish. True or false?* ◊ *She gave false information to the insurance company.*

**mistaken** wrong in your opinion or judgement; based on a wrong opinion or bad judgement: *You're completely mistaken about Jane.*

**incorrect** (*rather formal*) wrong according to the facts; containing mistakes: *Many of the figures were incorrect.*

**inaccurate** wrong according to the facts; containing mistakes: *The report was badly researched and quite inaccurate.*

INCORRECT OR INACCURATE?

A fact, figure or spelling that is wrong is **incorrect**; information, a belief or a description based on incorrect facts can be **incorrect** or **inaccurate**; something that is produced, such as a film, report or map, that contains incorrect facts is **inaccurate**.

**misguided** wrong because you have understood or judged a situation badly: *In her misguided attempts to help, she only made the situation worse.*

**untrue** not based on facts, but invented or guessed: *These accusations are totally untrue.*

PATTERNS
- to be wrong/mistaken **about** sth
- wrong/false/mistaken/incorrect/inaccurate/untrue **information**
- a(n) false/mistaken/incorrect/inaccurate/misguided **belief**
- a(n) wrong/incorrect **answer**

▼ WHICH WORD?

### wrong / wrongly / wrongfully
- In informal language **wrong** can be used as an adverb instead of **wrongly**, when it means 'incorrectly' and comes after a verb or its object: *My name was spelt wrong.* ◊ *I'm afraid you guessed wrong.* **Wrongly** is used before a past participle or a *that* clause: *My name was wrongly spelt.* ◊ *She guessed wrongly that he was a teacher.*
- **Wrongfully** is usually used in a formal legal situation with words like *convicted, dismissed* and *imprisoned*.

**ˈwrongˌdoer** /ˈrɒŋduːə(r); NAmE ˈrɔːŋ-/ noun (formal) a person who does sth dishonest or illegal SYN **criminal, offender**

# wrongdoing 1810

**wrong·doing** /ˈrɒŋduːɪŋ; NAmE ˈrɔːŋ-/ noun [U, C] (formal) illegal or dishonest behaviour ⓢⓨⓝ **crime**

**wrong-ˈfoot** verb ~ **sb** (BrE) to put sb in a difficult or embarrassing situation by doing sth that they do not expect: *It was an attempt to wrong-foot the opposition.*

**wrong·ful** /ˈrɒŋfl; NAmE ˈrɔːŋ-/ adj. [usually before noun] (law) not fair, morally right or legal: *She decided to sue her employer for wrongful dismissal.* ▶ **wrong·ful·ly** /-fəli/ adv.: *to be wrongfully convicted/dismissed* ⊃ note at WRONG

**wrong-ˈheaded** adj. having or showing bad judgement and refusing to change your opinion or ideas: *wrong-headed beliefs*

**wrong·ly** /ˈrɒŋli; NAmE ˈrɔːŋ-/ adv. **1** in a way that is not right or correct: *He assumed, wrongly, that she did not care.* ◊ *The sentence had been wrongly translated.* ◊ *Rightly or wrongly, they felt they should have been better informed* (= I do not know whether they were right to feel this way). **2** in a way that is not fair or not morally right: *She was wrongly accused of stealing.* ◊ *They knew they had acted wrongly.* ⊃ note at WRONG

**wrote** /rəʊt/ past tense of WRITE

**wrought** /rɔːt/ verb (used only in the past tense) ~ **sth** (formal or literary) caused sth to happen, especially a change: *This century wrought major changes in our society.* ◊ *The storm wrought havoc in the south.* ⓗⓔⓛⓟ **Wrought** is an old form of the past tense of **work**.

**wrought ˈiron** noun [U] a form of iron used to make attractive fences, gates, etc: *The gates were made of wrought iron.* ◊ *wrought-iron gates* ⊃ compare CAST IRON

**WRT** (also **w.r.t.**) abbr. (in writing, especially emails, text messages, etc.) with reference to: *And WRT your last point, this is what I think:…*

**wrung** /rʌŋ/ past tense, past part. of WRING

**wry** /raɪ/ adj. [usually before noun] **1** showing that you think sth is funny but also disappointing or annoying: *'At least we got one vote,' she said with a wry smile.* ◊ *He pulled a wry face when I asked him how it had gone.* **2** funny in a way that shows IRONY: *a wry comedy about family life* ◊ *a wry comment* ◊ *wry humour* ▶ **wry·ly** adv.: *to smile wryly* **wry·ness** noun [U]

**WTO** /ˌdʌblju tiː ˈəʊ/ abbr. World Trade Organization (an international organization that encourages international trade and economic development, especially by reducing limits on trade)

**Wu** /wuː/ noun [U] a form of Chinese spoken in Jiangsu, Zhejiang and Shanghai

**wun·der·kind** /ˈwʊndəkɪnd; NAmE -dərk-/ noun (pl. **wun·der·kinds** or **wun·der·kind·er** /ˈwʊndəkɪndə(r); NAmE -dərk-/) (from German, sometimes disapproving) a person who is very successful at a young age

**wuss** /wʊs/ noun (informal) a person who is not strong or brave: *Don't be such a wuss!*

**WWW** /ˌdʌblju ˌdʌblju ˈdʌblju/ abbr. = WORLD WIDE WEB: *several useful WWW addresses*

**WYSIWYG** /ˈwɪziwɪɡ/ abbr. (computing) what you see is what you get (what you see on the computer screen is exactly the same as will be printed or displayed)

# Xx

**X** /eks/ (also **x**) noun, symbol
■ noun (pl. **Xs**, **X's**, **x's** /'eksɪz/) **1** [C, U] the 24th letter of the English alphabet: 'Xylophone' begins with (an) X/'X'. **2** [U] (mathematics) used to represent a number whose value is not mentioned: The equation is impossible for any value of x greater than 2. **3** [U] a person, a number, an influence, etc. that is not known or not named: Let's suppose X knows what Y is doing. ⊃ see also X CHROMOSOME, X-RATED, X-RAY noun
■ symbol **1** the number 10 in ROMAN NUMERALS **2** used to represent a kiss at the end of a letter, etc: Love from Kathy XXX. **3** used to show a vote for sb in an election: Write X beside the candidate of your choice. **4** used to show that a written answer is wrong ⊃ compare TICK (1) **5** used to show position, for example on a map: X marks the spot.

**'X chromosome** noun (biology) a SEX CHROMOSOME. Two X chromosomes exist in the cells of human females. In human males each cell has one X chromosome and one Y chromosome.

**xenon** /'zenɒn, 'ziːn-; NAmE -nɑːn/ noun [U] (symb. **Xe**) a chemical element. Xenon is a gas that is found in very small quantities in the air and is used in some special electric lamps.

**xeno·pho·bia** /ˌzenəˈfəʊbiə/ noun [U] (disapproving) a strong feeling of dislike or fear of people from other countries: a campaign against racism and xenophobia ▸ **xeno·pho·bic** /-bɪk/ adj.

**xeno·trans·plan·ta·tion** /ˌziːnəʊˌtrænsplɑːnˈteɪʃn; NAmE -plæn-/ noun [U] (medical) the process of taking organs from animals and putting them into humans for medical purposes

**'X factor** noun [sing.] a special quality, especially one that is essential for success and is difficult to describe: She certainly has the X factor that all great singers have.

**Xhosa** /'kəʊsə, 'kɔːsə/ noun **1** [C] a member of a race of black people who live in South Africa **2** [U] = ISIXHOSA

**xi** /saɪ, zaɪ, ksaɪ, gzaɪ/ noun the 14th letter of the Greek alphabet (Ξ, ξ)

**Xiang** (also **Hsiang**) /ʃiˈæŋ/ noun [U] a form of Chinese spoken mainly in Hunan

**-xion** ⊃ -ION

**XL** /ˌeks ˈel/ abbr. extra large (used for sizes of things, especially clothes): an XL T-shirt

**Xmas** /'krɪsməs, 'eks-/ noun [C, U] (informal) used as a short form of 'Christmas', usually in writing: A merry Xmas to all our readers!

**XML** /ˌeks em ˈel/ noun (computing) Extensible Markup Language (a system used for marking the structure of text on a computer, for example when creating website pages)

**XP** /ˌeks ˈpiː/ (also **XPs** /ˌeks ˈpiːz/) (also **EXP, Exp, EXPs, Exps**) noun [pl.] points that you earn in a computer game (the abbreviation for 'experience points'): You get XP for killing monsters and completing quests.

**'X-rated** adj. (especially of a film) that people under 18 are not allowed to see because it contains sex and/or violence

**'X-ray** noun, verb
■ noun **1** [usually pl.] a type of RADIATION that can pass through solid objects and make it possible to see inside or through them: an X-ray machine (= one that produces X-rays) **2** a photograph made by X-rays, especially one showing bones or organs in the body: a chest X-ray ◊ The doctor studied the X-rays of her lungs. ◊ to take an X-ray ⊃ WORDFINDER NOTE at EXAMINE **3** a medical examination using X-rays: I had to go for an X-ray.
■ verb ~ sth to photograph and examine bones and organs inside the body, using X-rays: He had to have his chest X-rayed.

**xylem** /'zaɪləm/ noun [U] (biology) the material in plants that carries water and minerals upwards from the root ⊃ compare PHLOEM

**xylo·phone** /'zaɪləfəʊn/ noun a musical instrument made of two rows of wooden bars of different lengths that you hit with two small sticks ⊃ compare GLOCKENSPIEL

# Y y

**Y** /waɪ/ *noun, abbr.*
- *noun* (*also* **y**) (*pl.* **Ys, Y's, y's** /waɪz/) **1** [C, U] the 25th letter of the English alphabet: *'Year' begins with (a) Y/'Y'.* **2** [U] (*mathematics*) used to represent a number whose value is not mentioned: *Can the value of y be predicted from the value of x?* **3** [U] a person, a number, an influence, etc. that is not known or not named: *Let's suppose X knows what Y is doing.* ⇨ see also Y CHROMOSOME, Y-FRONTS™
- *abbr.* **the Y** (*NAmE, informal*) YMCA, YWCA
- *symbol* the symbol for the chemical element YTTRIUM

**-y** /i/ *suffix* **1** (*also* **-ey**) (in adjectives) full of; having the quality of: *dusty* ◇ *clayey* **2** (in adjectives) tending to: *runny* ◇ *sticky* **3** (in nouns) the action or process of: *enquiry* **4** (*also* **-ie**) (in nouns, showing affection): *doggy* ◇ *daddy*

**ya** /jə/ *pron., det.* (*informal, non-standard*) used in writing as a way of showing the way people sometimes pronounce the word 'you' or 'your': *He said, 'I got something for ya.'*

**yaar** /jɑː(r)/ *noun* (*IndE, informal*) (used as a friendly way of addressing sb) a friend: *Let's go for a drink, yaar!*

**yacht** /jɒt; *NAmE* jɑːt/ (*NAmE also* **sail·boat**) *noun* a large sailing boat, often also with an engine and a place to sleep on board, used for pleasure trips and racing: *a yacht club/race* ◇ *a motor yacht* ◇ *a luxury yacht* ⇨ compare DINGHY

**yacht·ing** /ˈjɒtɪŋ; *NAmE* ˈjɑːt-/ *noun* [U] the sport or activity of sailing or racing yachts

**yachts·man** /ˈjɒtsmən; *NAmE* ˈjɑːts-/, **yachts·woman** /ˈjɒtswʊmən; *NAmE* ˈjɑːts- /məs/, /-men /-mən/, **-women** /-wɪmɪn/) a person who sails a yacht for pleasure or as a sport: *a round-the-world yachtsman*

**yack** = YAK

**yada yada yada** (*also* **yadda yadda yadda**) /ˌjædə ˌjædə ˈjædə; *NAmE* ˌjɑːdə ˌjɑːdə ˈjɑːdə/ *exclamation* (*NAmE, informal*) used when you are talking about sth to show that some of the details are not worth saying because they are not important or are boring or obvious: *His new girlfriend is attractive, funny, smart, yada yada yada.*

**yah** /jɑː/ *exclamation* **1** a way of writing 'yes' to show that the speaker has an upper-class ACCENT (= a way of pronouncing the words of a language) **2** used to show that you have a low opinion of sb/sth: *Yah, you missed!*

**yahoo** *noun, exclamation*
- *noun* /jəˈhuː; jɑːˈhuː/ (*pl.* **-oos**) (*disapproving*) a rude, noisy or violent person
- *exclamation* /jəˈhuː; jɑːˈhuː/ (*informal*) used to show that you are very happy: *Yahoo, we did it!*

**Yah·weh** /ˈjɑːweɪ/ *noun* = JEHOVAH

**yak** /jæk/ *noun, verb*
- *noun* an animal of the cow family, with long HORNS and long hair, that lives in central Asia
- *verb* (*also* **yack**) [I] (*informal, often disapproving*) (**-kk-**) to talk continuously about things that are not very serious or important: *She just kept yakking on.*

**yakka** /ˈjækə/ *noun* [U] (*AustralE, NZE, informal*) work, especially of a hard physical kind: *hard yakka*

**y'all** /jɔːl/ *pron.* = YOU-ALL

**yam** /jæm/ *noun* [C, U] the large root of a tropical plant that is cooked as a vegetable ⇨ VISUAL VOCAB page V5

**yang** /jæŋ/ *noun* [U] (*from Chinese*) (in Chinese philosophy) the bright active male principle of the universe ⇨ compare YIN

**Yank** /jæŋk/ (*also* **Yan·kee**) *noun* (*BrE, informal*) an offensive word for a person from the US; an American

**yank** /jæŋk/ *verb* [T, I] (*informal*) to pull sth/sb hard, quickly and suddenly: *~ sth/sb (+ adv./prep.) He yanked her to her feet.* ◇ *~ sth/sb + adj. I yanked the door open.* ◇ *+ adv./prep. Liz yanked at my arm.* ▶ **yank** *noun*: *She gave the rope a yank.*

**Yan·kee** /ˈjæŋki/ *noun* **1** (*NAmE*) a person who comes from or lives in any of the northern states of the US, especially New England **2** a soldier who fought for the Union (= the northern states) in the American Civil War **3** (*BrE, informal*) = YANK

**yap** /jæp/ *verb* (**-pp-**) **1** [I] ~ (at sb/sth) (especially of small dogs) to BARK a lot, making a high, sharp and usually annoying sound: *The dogs yapped at his heels.* ◇ *yapping dogs* **2** [I] (*informal*) to talk in a silly, noisy and usually annoying way ▶ **yap** *noun*

**yard** 🔑 B1 /jɑːd; *NAmE* jɑːrd/ *noun* **1** 🔑 B1 (*BrE*) (*NAmE* **gar·den**) a piece of land next to or around your house where you can grow flowers, fruit, vegetables, etc., usually with a LAWN (= an area of grass): *They have a gorgeous old oak tree in their front yard.* ⇨ see also BACKYARD (1) **2** 🔑 B2 (*BrE*) an area outside a building, usually with a hard surface and a surrounding wall: *the prison yard* ⇨ see also BACKYARD (2) **3** (usually in compounds) an area of land used for a special purpose or business: *a boat yard* **HELP** You will find other compounds ending in **yard** at their place in the alphabet. ⇨ SYNONYMS at FACTORY **4** 🔑 B1 (*abbr.* **yd**) (in Britain and North America) a unit for measuring length, equal to 3 feet (36 inches) or 0.9144 of a metre: *They still live within yards of each other.* **5** (*specialist*) a long piece of wood fastened to a MAST that supports a sail on a boat or ship ⇨ see also SCOTLAND YARD **IDM** see INCH *n.*, NINE

**yard·age** /ˈjɑːdɪdʒ; *NAmE* ˈjɑːrd-/ *noun* [C, U] (*specialist*) **1** size measured in yards or square yards **2** (in AMERICAN FOOTBALL) the number of yards that a team or player has moved forward

**'yard sale** *noun* (*NAmE*) a sale of things from sb's house, held in their yard ⇨ compare GARAGE SALE, RUMMAGE SALE

**yard·stick** /ˈjɑːdstɪk; *NAmE* ˈjɑːrd-/ *noun* **1** (*especially NAmE*) a RULER for measuring one yard **2** a standard used for judging how good or successful sth is: *a yardstick by which to measure sth* ◇ *Exam results are not the only yardstick of a school's performance.*

**yar·mulke** (*also* **yar·mulka**) /ˈjɑːmʊlkə; *NAmE* ˈjɑːrm-/ (*also* **kippa**) *noun* a small round cap worn on top of the head by Jewish men; a type of SKULLCAP

**yarn** /jɑːn; *NAmE* jɑːrn/ *noun* **1** [U, C] THREAD that has been SPUN, used for KNITTING, making cloth, etc. **2** [C] (*informal*) a long story, especially one that is EXAGGERATED or invented: *He used to spin yarns* (= tell stories) *about his time in the army.* **IDM** see PITCH *v.*

**yar·row** /ˈjærəʊ/ *noun* [U, C] a plant with flat groups of many small white or pink flowers that have a strong smell

**yatra** /ˈjɑːtrɑː/ *noun* (*IndE*) **1** a line of people or vehicles that move along slowly as part of a ceremony or a journey to a holy place, usually carried out for religious reasons **2** a tour by an official or members of a movement, etc: *Party leaders are planning on embarking on their campaign yatras later in the year.*

**yaw** /jɔː/ *verb* [I] (*specialist*) (of a ship or plane) to turn to one side, away from a straight course, in an unsteady way ▶ **yaw** *noun* [C, U]

**yawl** /jɔːl/ *noun* **1** a type of boat with sails **2** a ROWING BOAT carried on a ship

**yawn** /jɔːn/ *verb, noun*
- *verb* **1** [I] to open your mouth wide and breathe in deeply through it, usually because you are tired or bored: *He stood up, stretched and yawned.* **2** [I] (of a large hole or an empty space) to be very wide and often frightening and difficult to get across **SYN** gape: *A crevasse yawned at their feet.* ◇ (*figurative*) *There's a yawning gap between rich and poor.*
- *noun* **1** an act of yawning: *She stifled another yawn and tried hard to look interested.* **2** [usually sing.] (*informal*) a boring event, idea, etc: *The meeting was one big yawn from start to finish.*

**yay** /jeɪ/ *exclamation, adv.* (*informal, especially NAmE*)
- *exclamation* used to show that you are very pleased about sth: *I won! Yay!*

■ *adv.* **1** to this degree SYN **so**: *The fish I caught was yay big.* **2** to a high degree SYN **extremely**: *Yay good movie!*

**'Y chromosome** *noun* (*biology*) a SEX CHROMOSOME. In human males each cell has one X chromosome and one Y chromosome. In human females there is never a Y chromosome.

**yd** *abbr.* (*pl.* **yds**) YARD: *12 yds of silk*

**ye** *pron., det.*

■ *pron.* /jiː; weak form ji/ (*old use* or *dialect*) a word meaning 'you', used when talking to more than one person: *Gather ye rosebuds while ye may.* ▶ IDM see GOD

■ *det.* /jiː/ a word meaning 'the', used in the names of pubs, shops, etc. to make them seem old: *Ye Olde Starre Inn*

**yea** /jeɪ/ *adv., noun* (*old use*) yes ⊃ compare NAY

**yeah** ❶ A1 /jeə/ *exclamation* (*informal*) yes
IDM ▶ **oh 'yeah?** used when you are commenting on what sb has just said: *'We're off to France soon.' 'Oh yeah? When's that?'* ◇ *'I'm going to be rich one day.' 'Oh yeah?'* (= I don't believe you.) **yeah, 'right** used to say that you do not believe what sb has just said, disagree with it, or are not interested in it: *'You'll be fine.' 'Yeah, right.'*

**year** ❶ A1 /jɪə(r), jɜː(r); NAmE jɪr/ *noun* (*abbr.* **yr**) **1** A1 (also **calendar 'year**) [C] the period from 1 January to 31 December, that is 365 or 366 days, divided into 12 months: *Elections take place every year.* ◇ *I lost my job earlier this year.* ◇ **next/last year** ◇ *the previous/following year* ◇ *in the ~... She was born in the year 1865.* ◇ **in ... years** *in previous/later years* ◇ *The museum is open all year round* (= during the whole year). ⊃ see also LEAP YEAR, NEW YEAR **2** A1 [C] a period of twelve months, measured from any particular time: *It's exactly a year since I started working here.* ◇ *She gave up teaching three years ago.* ◇ *in the ~(of sth) in the first year of their marriage* ◇ **in ... years** *Production has declined in recent years.* ◇ *His early years were spent in San Francisco.* ◇ *the coming year* (= the next twelve months) ⊃ see also GAP YEAR, LIGHT YEAR, OFF YEAR **3** A1 [C, usually pl.] age; time of life: *He was 14 years old when it happened.* ◇ *She looks young for her years.* ◇ *They were both only 20 years of age.* ◇ *a twenty-one-year-old man* ◇ *He died in his sixtieth year.* **4** A1 [C] a period of twelve months connected with a particular activity: *the tax/fiscal year* ◇ *the school year* ⊃ see also ACADEMIC YEAR, FINANCIAL YEAR **5** A1 [C] (*especially BrE*) (at a school, etc.) a level that you stay in for one year; a student at a particular level: *in~... We started German in year seven.* ◇ *in sb's ~ She was in my year at school.* ◇ *a year-seven pupil* ◇ *The first years do French.* **6** A2 **years** [pl.] (*informal*) a long time: *It's years since we last met.* ◇ *They haven't seen each other for years and years.* ◇ **in ~** *That's the best movie I've seen in years.* ◇ **over the ~** *We've had a lot of fun over the years.*

IDM **man, woman, car, etc. of the 'year** a person or thing that people decide is the best in a particular field in a particular year **not/never in a hundred, etc. 'years** (*informal*) used to emphasize that you will/would never do sth: *I'd never have thought of that in a million years.* **put 'years on sb** to make sb feel or look older **since/from the year 'dot** (*BrE*) (*NAmE* **since/from the year 'one**) (*informal*) a very long time ago: *I've been going there every summer since the year dot.* **take 'years off sb** to make sb feel or look younger **,year after 'year** every year for many years **,year by 'year** as the years pass; each year: *Year by year their affection for each other grew stronger.* **,year in, year 'out** every year **,year of 'grace | ,year of our 'Lord** (*formal*) any particular year after the birth of Christ **,year on 'year** (used especially when talking about figures, prices, etc.) each year, compared with the last year: *Spending has increased year on year.* ◇ *a year-on-year increase in spending* ⊃ more at ADVANCED, DECLINING, DONKEY, ROAD, SEVEN, TURN *n.*

**year·book** /ˈjɪəbʊk; *NAmE* ˈjɪrb-/ *noun* **1** a book published once a year, giving details of events, etc. of the previous year, especially those connected with a particular area of activity **2** (*especially NAmE*) a book that is produced by the senior class in a school or college, containing photographs of students and details of school activities

1813 **yellow journalism**

**,year 'end** (also **,year's 'end**) *noun* [U] the end of the year: *at ~ We will discuss additional budget cuts at year end.* ▶ **'year-end** *adj.* [only before noun]: *year-end bonuses*

**year·ling** /ˈjɜːlɪŋ; *NAmE* ˈjɜːrl-/ *noun* an animal, especially a horse, between one and two years old

**,year-'long** *adj.* [only before noun] continuing for a whole year: *a year-long dispute*

**year·ly** /ˈjɪəli, ˈjɜːli; *NAmE* ˈjɪrli/ *adv.* **1** happening once a year or every year: *Pay is reviewed on a yearly basis.* **2** paid, calculated or legally in force for one year: *yearly income/interest* ▶ **year·ly** *adv.*: *The magazine is issued twice yearly* (= twice every year).

**yearn** /jɜːn; *NAmE* jɜːrn/ *verb* [I] (*literary*) to want sth very much, especially when it is very difficult to get SYN **long**: *~(for sth/sb) The people yearned for peace.* ◇ *There was a yearning look in his eyes.* ◇ *~to do sth She yearned to escape from her office job.*

**yearn·ing** /ˈjɜːnɪŋ; *NAmE* ˈjɜːrn-/ *noun* [C, U] (*formal*) a strong and emotional desire SYN **longing**: *~(for sb/sth) a yearning for a quiet life* ◇ *~to do sth She had no great yearning to go back.* ▶ **yearn·ing·ly** *adv.*

**,year-'round** *adj.* all through the year: *an island with year-round sunshine*

**yeast** /jiːst/ *noun* [U, C] a FUNGUS used in making beer and wine, or to make bread rise ▶ **yeasty** *adj.*: *a yeasty smell*

**'yeast extract** *noun* [U] a black substance made from yeast, spread on bread, etc. ⊃ see also MARMITE™, VEGEMITE™

**'yeast infection** (*NAmE*) (*BrE* **thrush**) *noun* a disease that affects the VAGINA

**yebo** /ˈjebəʊ; *SAfrE* ˈjeːbɔ/ *exclamation* (*SAfrE*, *informal*) **1** yes **2** hello: *Yebo Craig. Thanks for the email.*

**yell** ❶+ C1 /jel/ *verb, noun*
■ *verb* ❶+ C1 [I, T] to shout loudly, for example because you are angry, excited, frightened or in pain: *~(at sb/sth) He yelled at the other driver.* ◇ *~at sb to do sth She yelled at the child to get down from the wall.* ◇ *~with sth They yelled with excitement.* ◇ *~out (in sth) She yelled out in pain.* ◇ *+ speech 'Be careful!' he yelled.* ◇ *~sth (at sb/sth) The crowd yelled encouragement at the players.* ◇ *~out sth He yelled out her name.* ⊃ SYNONYMS at SHOUT

■ *noun* **1** a loud shout of pain, excitement, etc. to **let out/give a yell** ◇ *a yell of delight* **2** (*NAmE*) an organized shout of support for a team at a sports event

**yel·low** ❶ A1 /ˈjeləʊ/ *adj., noun, verb*
■ *adj.* (**yel·low·er, yel·low·est**) **1** A1 having the colour of lemons or butter: *pale yellow flowers* ◇ *a bright yellow waterproof jacket* **2** (*taboo*) an offensive word used to describe the light brown skin of people from some East Asian countries **3** (*informal*, *disapproving*) easily frightened SYN **cowardly** ▶ **yel·low·ness** *noun* [U, sing.]

■ *noun* ❶ A1 [U, C] the colour of lemons or butter: *She was dressed in yellow.* ◇ *the reds and yellows of the trees*

■ *verb* [I, T] ~(sth) to become yellow; to make sth become yellow

**,yellow 'card** *noun* (in football (soccer) and some other games) a card shown by the REFEREE to a player as a warning about bad behaviour ⊃ compare RED CARD

**,yellow 'fever** *noun* [U] a tropical disease that makes the skin turn yellow and often causes death

**,yellow 'flag** *noun* **1** a type of yellow IRIS (= a flower) that grows near water **2** a yellow flag on a ship showing that sb has or may have an INFECTIOUS disease (= one that can spread easily)

**yel·low·ish** /ˈjeləʊɪʃ/ (also *less frequent* **yel·lowy** /ˈjeləʊi/) *adj.* fairly yellow in colour: *The paper had a yellowish tinge because it was so old.*

**,yellow 'journalism** *noun* [U] (*US*) newspaper reports that are EXAGGERATED and written to shock readers ORIGIN From a comic strip *The Yellow Kid* that was printed in yellow ink to attract readers' attention.

# yellow line 1814

**,yellow 'line** *noun* (in the UK) a yellow line painted at the side of a road to show that you can only park your car there at particular times or for a short time: *double yellow lines* (= two lines that mean you cannot park there at all)

**,Yellow 'Pages™** (*BrE*) (*NAmE* **,yellow 'pages**) *noun* [pl.] (until 2019) a book with yellow pages that gave a list of companies and organizations and their phone numbers, arranged according to the type of services they offered

**,yellow 'ribbon** *noun* (in the US) a piece of yellow material that sb ties around a tree as a sign that they are thinking about sb who has gone away, especially a soldier fighting in a war, or sb taken as a HOSTAGE or prisoner, and that they hope that the person will soon return safely

**yelp** /jelp/ *verb* [I, T] **(+ speech)** to give a sudden short cry, usually of pain ▶ **yelp** *noun*

**yen** /jen/ *noun* **1** (*pl.* **yen**) [C] the unit of money in Japan **2 the yen** [sing.] (*finance*) the value of the yen compared with the value of the money of other countries **3** [C, usually sing.] **~ (for sth/to do sth)** a strong desire SYN **longing**: *I've always had a yen to travel around the world.*

**yeo·man** /'jəʊmən/ *noun* (*pl.* **-men** /-mən/) **1** (in Britain in the past) a farmer who owned and worked on his land **2** an officer in the US NAVY who does mainly office work

**yeo·man·ry** /'jəʊmənri/ *noun* [sing. + sing./pl. v.] **1** (in Britain in the past) the social class of farmers who owned their land **2** (in Britain in the past) farmers who became soldiers and provided their own horses

**yep** /jep/ (*also* **yup**) *exclamation* (*informal*) used to say 'yes': *'Are you ready?' 'Yep.'*

**yer** /jə(r)/ *pron., det.* (*informal, non-standard*) used in writing as a way of showing the way people sometimes pronounce the word 'you' or 'your': *See yer when I get back.* ◇ *What's yer name?*

**yes** /jes/ *exclamation, noun*

■ *exclamation* **1** used to answer a question and say that sth is correct or true: *'Is this your car?' 'Yes, it is.'* ◇ *'Are you coming? Yes or no?'* **2** used to show that you agree with what has been said: *'I enjoyed her latest novel.' 'Yes, me too.'* ◇ *'It's an excellent hotel.' 'Yes, but* (= I don't completely agree) *it's too expensive.'* **3** used to disagree with sth negative that sb has just said: *'I've never met her before.' 'Yes, you have.'* **4** used to agree to a request or to give permission: *'Dad, can I borrow the car?' 'Yes, but be careful.'* ◇ *We're hoping that they will* **say yes to** *our proposals.* **5** used to accept an offer or invitation: *'Would you like a drink?' 'Yes, please/thanks.'* **6** used for asking sb what they want: *Yes? How can I help you?* **7** used for replying politely when sb calls you: *'Waiter!' 'Yes, sir?'* **8** used to show that you have just remembered sth: *Where did I put the keys? Oh yes—in my pocket!* **9** used to encourage sb to continue speaking: *'I'm going to Paris this weekend.' 'Yes ...'* **10** used to show that you do not believe what sb has said: *'Sorry I'm late—the bus didn't come.' 'Oh yes?'* **11** used to emphasize what you have just said: *Mrs Smith has just won £2 million—yes!—£2 million!* **12** used to show that you are excited or extremely pleased about sth that you have done or sth that has happened: *'They've scored another goal.' 'Yes!!'* **13 yes, yes** used to show that you are impatient or annoyed about sth: *'Hurry up—it's late.' 'Yes, yes—I'm coming.'*
IDM **,yes and 'no** used when you cannot give a clear answer to a question: *'Are you enjoying it?' 'Yes and no.'*

■ *noun* (*pl.* **yes·ses** *or* **yeses** /'jesɪz/) an answer that shows that you agree with an idea, a statement, etc.; a person who says 'yes': *I need a simple yes or no to my questions.* ◇ *There will be two ballot boxes—one for yesses and one for noes.* ◇ *I'll put you down as a yes.*

**yesh·iva** /jə'ʃiːvə/ *noun* a college or school for Orthodox Jews

**yes-man** /'jes mæn/ *noun* (*pl.* **-men** /-men/) (*disapproving*) a person who always agrees with people in authority in order to gain their approval

**yes·sir** /'jesə(r), 'jesˈsɜː(r)/ *exclamation* (*informal, especially NAmE*) used to emphasize your opinion or say that you agree very strongly: *Yessir, she was beautiful.*

**yes·ter·day** /'jestədeɪ, -di; *NAmE* -stərd-/ *adv., noun, adj.*

■ *adv.* on the day before today: *A company spokeswoman said yesterday that no final decision had been made yet.* ◇ *yesterday morning/afternoon/evening* ◇ *The company yesterday announced a $40 million deal.* ◇ *To think I was lying on a beach only* **the day before yesterday***.*
IDM see BORN v.

■ *noun* [U] **1** the day before today: *Yesterday was Sunday.* ◇ *What happened at yesterday's meeting?* **2** (*also* **yes·ter·days** [pl.]) the recent past: *Yesterday's students are today's employees.* ◇ *All her yesterdays had vanished without a trace.*

■ *adj.* [not before noun] (*informal, often humorous*) no longer fashionable or new: *Email—that's so yesterday!*

**yes·ter·year** /'jestəjɪə(r); *NAmE* -stərjɪr/ *noun* [U] (*old-fashioned* or *literary*) the past, especially a time when attitudes and ideas were different

**yet** /jet/ *adv., conj.*

■ *adv.* **1** used in negative sentences and questions to talk about sth that has not happened but that you expect to happen: (*BrE*) *I haven't received a letter from him yet.* ◇ (*NAmE*) *I didn't receive a letter from him yet.* **not~** *'Are you ready?' 'No, not yet.'* ◇ *We* **don't yet know** *what really happened.* ◇ **have~to do sth** *We have* **yet to decide** *what action to take* (= We have not decided what action to take). ⊃ note at ALREADY **2** (used in negative sentences) now; as soon as this: *Don't go yet.* ◇ *We don't need to start yet.* **3** used to emphasize an increase in number or amount or the number of times sth happens: **~ more** ... *snow, snow and yet more snow* ◇ **~ another** ... *yet another diet book* ◇ **~ again** *Prices were cut yet again* (= once more, after many other times). **4 the best, longest, etc. sth~** used to emphasize that sth is the best, longest, etc. thing of its kind made, produced, written, etc. until now/then: *the most comprehensive study yet of his music* ◇ *It was the tallest building yet constructed anywhere.* **5** from now until the period of time mentioned has passed: *He'll be busy for ages yet.* ◇ *They won't arrive for at least two hours yet.* **6 could, might, may, etc. do sth~** used to say that sth could, might, etc. happen in the future, even though it seems unlikely: *We may win yet.* ◇ (*formal*) *She could yet surprise us all.* **7 ~ worse, more importantly, etc.** used to emphasize an increase in the degree of sth (= how bad, important, etc. it is) SYN **even, still**: *a recent and yet more improbable theory*
IDM **as 'yet** until now or until a particular time in the past: *an as yet unpublished report* ◇ *As yet little was known of the causes of the disease.* ⊃ more at BETTER *adv.*, JUST *adv.*, NEAR *adv.*

■ *conj.* despite what has just been said SYN **nevertheless**: *It's a small car, yet it's surprisingly spacious.* ◇ *He has a good job, and yet he never seems to have any money.*

**yeti** /'jeti/ (*also* **A,bominable 'Snowman**) *noun* a large creature like a bear or a man covered with hair that some people believe lives in the Himalayan mountains

**yew** /juː/ *noun* **1** [C, U] (*also* **'yew tree** [C]) a small tree with dark green leaves and small red BERRIES ⊃ VISUAL VOCAB page V6 **2** [U] the wood of the yew tree

**'Y-Fronts™** *noun* [pl.] (*BrE*) men's UNDERPANTS, with an opening in the front SEWN in the shape of a Y UPSIDE DOWN: *a pair of Y-Fronts*

**Yid·dish** /'jɪdɪʃ/ *noun* [U] a Jewish language, originally used in central and eastern Europe, based on a form of German with words from Hebrew and several modern languages ▶ **Yid·dish** *adj.*

**yield** /jiːld/ *noun, verb*

■ *noun* [C, U] the total amount of crops, profits, etc. that are produced: *a high crop yield* ◇ *a reduction in milk yield* ◇ *This will give a yield of 10% on your investment.* ⊃ WORDFINDER NOTE at CROP

■ *verb* **1** [T] **~sth** to produce or provide sth, for example a profit, result or crop: *Higher-rate deposit*

---

æ cat | ɑː father | e bed | ɜː fur | ə about | ɪ sit | iː see | i happy | ɒ got (*BrE*) | ɔː saw | ʌ cup | ʊ put | uː too

*accounts yield good returns.* ◊ *The research has yielded useful information.* ◊ *trees that no longer yield fruit* **2** [I] (*formal*) to stop resisting sth/sb; to agree to do sth that you do not want to do **SYN** **give way**: *After a long siege, the town was forced to yield.* ◊ *~ to sth/sb He reluctantly yielded to their demands.* ◊ *I yielded to temptation and had a chocolate bar.* **3** [T] *~ sth/sb (up) (to sb)* (*formal*) to allow sb to win, have or take control of sth that has been yours until now **SYN** **surrender**: *He refused to yield up his gun.* ◊ (*figurative*) *The universe is slowly yielding up its secrets.* **4** [I] to move, bend or break because of pressure: *Despite our attempts to break it, the lock would not yield.* **5** [I] *~ (to sb/sth)* (*NAmE, IrishE*) to allow vehicles on a bigger road to go first **SYN** **give way**: *Yield to oncoming traffic.* ◊ *a yield sign*
**PHRV** **ˈyield to sth** (*formal*) to be replaced by sth: *Canals yielded to the railways for transporting goods.*

**yield·ing** /ˈjiːldɪŋ/ *adj.* (*formal*) **1** (of a substance) soft and easy to bend or move when you press it **2** (of a person) willing to do what other people want **3** (used with an adverb) giving the amount of crops, profits, etc. mentioned: *high-/low-yielding crops*

**yikes** /jaɪks/ *exclamation* (*informal*) used to show that you are surprised or suddenly afraid

**yin** /jɪn/ *noun* [U] (*from Chinese*) (in Chinese philosophy) the dark, not active, female principle of the universe ⊃ compare YANG

**yip·pee** /jɪˈpiː; *NAmE* ˈjɪpi/ *exclamation* (*old-fashioned, informal*) used to show that you are pleased or excited

**YMCA** /ˌwaɪ em es iː ˈeɪ/ (*also NAmE, informal* **the Y**) *noun* an organization that exists in many countries and provides accommodation and social and sports activities (the abbreviation for 'Young Men's Christian Association'): *We stayed at the YMCA.*

**YMMV** *abbr.* (in writing) (*informal*) (used to say that people may experience a particular thing in different ways) your mileage may vary: *Highly recommend the company! Of course, YMMV.*

**yo** /jəʊ/ *exclamation* (*slang*) used by young people to say hello

**yob** /jɒb; *NAmE* jɑːb/ (*also* **yobbo** /ˈjɒbəʊ; *NAmE* ˈjɑːb-/ *pl.* **-os**) *noun* (*BrE, informal*) a rude, noisy and sometimes aggressive and violent boy or young man **SYN** **lout** ▶ **yob·bish** *adj.* [usually before noun]

**yodel** /ˈjəʊdl/ *verb, noun*
■ *verb* [I, T] (-ll-, *US* -l-) *~ (sth)* to sing or call in the traditional Swiss way, changing your voice frequently between its normal level and a very high level
■ *noun* a song or musical call in which sb yodels

**yoga** /ˈjəʊɡə/ *noun* [U] **1** a Hindu philosophy that teaches you how to control your body and mind in the belief that you can become united with the spirit of the universe in this way **2** a system of exercises for your body and for controlling your breathing, used by people who want to become fitter or to relax ▶ **yogic** /-ɡɪk/ *adj.*: *yogic techniques*

**yogi** /ˈjəʊɡi/ *noun* (*pl.* **yogis**) an expert in, or teacher of, the philosophy of yoga

**yog·urt** (*BrE also* **yog·hurt**) /ˈjɒɡət; *NAmE* ˈjoʊɡərt/ *noun* [U, C] a thick white liquid food, made by adding bacteria to milk, served cold and often with fruit added; an amount of this sold in a small pot: *natural yogurt* ◊ *There's a yogurt left if you're still hungry.* ◊ *a lemon yogurt*

**yoke** /jəʊk/ *noun, verb*
■ *noun* **1** [C] a long piece of wood that is fastened across the necks of two animals, especially OXEN, so that they can pull heavy loads **2** [sing.] (*literary or formal*) rough treatment or sth that limits your freedom and makes your life very difficult to bear: *the yoke of imperialism* **3** [C] a piece of wood that is shaped to fit across a person's shoulders so that they can carry two equal loads **4** [C] a part of a dress, skirt, etc. that fits around the shoulders and from which the rest of the cloth hangs
■ *verb* [usually passive] **1** to join two animals together with a yoke; to attach an animal to sth with a yoke: **(be) yoked together** *A pair of oxen, yoked together, was used.* ◊ **(be)**

1815 **young**

**yoked to sth** *an ox yoked to a plough* **2** (*formal*) to bring two people, countries, ideas, etc. together so that they are forced into a close relationship: **be yoked to sth** *The Hong Kong dollar was yoked to the American dollar for many years.* ◊ **be yoked together** *In these languages, short words are yoked together to create new words.*

**yokel** /ˈjəʊkl/ *noun* (*usually disapproving, often humorous*) if you call a person a **yokel**, you are saying that they do not have much education or understanding of modern life, because they come from the countryside

**yolk** /jəʊk/ *noun* [C, U] the round yellow part in the middle of an egg: *Separate the whites from the yolks.*

**Yom Kip·pur** /ˌjɒm ˈkɪpə(r), kɪˈpʊə(r); *NAmE* jɔːm kɪˈpʊr/ *noun* [U] (*also* **the Day of Atonement** [sing.]) a Jewish religious holiday in September or October when people eat nothing all day and say prayers of PENITENCE in the SYNAGOGUE

**yon** /jɒn; *NAmE* jɑːn/ *det., adv.*
■ *det.* (*old use* or *dialect*) that: *There's an old farm over yon hill.*
■ *adv.* **IDM** see HITHER

**yon·der** /ˈjɒndə(r); *NAmE* ˈjɑːn-/ *det.* (*old use or dialect*) that is over there; that you can see over there: *Let's rest under yonder tree.* ▶ **yon·der** *adv.*: *Whose is that farm over yonder?*

**yonks** /jɒŋks; *NAmE* jɑːŋks/ *noun* [U] (*BrE, informal, becoming old-fashioned*) a long time: *I haven't seen you for yonks!*

**yoof** /juːf/ *noun* [U] (*BrE, informal, humorous*) a non-standard spelling of 'youth', used to refer to young people as a group, especially as the group that particular types of entertainment, magazines, etc. are designed for ▶ **yoof** *adj.* [only before noun]

**yore** /jɔː(r)/ *noun*
**IDM** **of ˈyore** (*old use* or *literary*) long ago: *in days of yore*

**York·shire ˈpud·ding** /ˌjɔːkʃə ˈpʊdɪŋ; *NAmE* ˌjɔːrkʃər/ *noun* [U, C] a type of British food made from BATTER that is baked until it rises, traditionally eaten with ROAST beef

**York·shire ˈter·rier** /ˌjɔːkʃə ˈteriə(r); *NAmE* ˌjɔːrkʃər/ *noun* a very small dog with long brown and grey hair

**Yor·uba** /ˈjɒrʊbə; *NAmE* ˈjɔːrəbə/ *noun* [U] a language spoken by the Yoruba people of West Africa, especially in south-west Nigeria

**you** ⓘ **A1** /strong form juː; *BrE weak form* ju; *NAmE weak form* jə/ *pron.* **1** **A1** used as the subject or object of a verb or after a preposition to refer to the person or people being spoken or written to: *You said you knew the way.* ◊ *I thought she told you.* ◊ *Can I sit next to you?* ◊ *I want both of you to help.* ◊ *I don't think that hairstyle is you* (= it doesn't suit your appearance or personality). **2** **A2** used with nouns and adjectives to speak to sb directly: *You girls, stop talking!* ◊ *You stupid idiot!* **3** **A2** used for referring to people in general: *You learn a language better if you visit the country where it is spoken.* ◊ *It's a friendly place—people come up to you in the street and start talking.*
**IDM** ˌyou and ˈyours you, your family and your close friends

**you-all** /juː ˈɔːl/ (*also* **yˈall**) *pron.* (*informal*) used especially in the southern US to mean *you* when talking to more than one person: *Have you-all brought swimsuits?*

**you'd** /juːd/ *short form* **1** you had **HELP** *You'd* is only used when *had* is an auxiliary verb: *You'd just left when he came.* When *had* is the main verb, use the full form: *I'm glad you had a good time.* ◊ *I'm glad you'd a good time.* **2** you would

**you'll** /juːl/ *short form* you will

**young** ⓘ **A1** /jʌŋ/ *adj., noun*
■ *adj.* (**young·er** /ˈjʌŋɡə(r)/, **young·est** /-ɡɪst/) **1** **A1** having lived or existed for only a short time; not fully developed: *young babies* ◊ *a young country* ◊ *Caterpillars eat the young leaves of this plant.* ◊ *a young wine* ◊ *The night is still young* (= it has only just started). **OPP** **old 2** **A1** not yet old; not as old as others: *young people* ◊ *They sent many young men and women off to war.* ◊ *My son's thirteen but he's young for his age* (= not as developed as other boys of

# youngish

the same age). ◊ *I'm* **too young** *to remember much about the 1990s.* ◊ *They* **married young** (= at an early age). ◊ *My mother* **died young.** ◊ *She* **looks much younger than** *her 39 years.* ◊ *I don't know how families with* **young children** *manage to cope.* ◊ *a* **young girl/boy/adult/person OPP old**
⇒ WORDFINDER NOTE at AGE

**WORDFINDER** adolescent, immature, mixed up, naive, puberty, rebellious, sulky, tearaway, teenager

**3** A1 consisting of young people or young children; with a low average age: *They have a young family.* ◊ *a young audience* **4** suitable or appropriate for young people **SYN youthful:** *young fashion* ◊ *The clothes she wears are much too young for her.* **5** *~* **man/lady/woman** used to show that you are angry or annoyed with a particular young person: *I think you owe me an apology, young lady!* **6 the younger** used before or after a person's name to show the difference between them and an older relative: *the younger Kennedy* ◊ (*BrE, formal*) *William Pitt the younger*
⇒ compare ELDER, JUNIOR

IDM **be getting 'younger** (*informal*) used to say that people seem to be doing sth at a younger age than they used to, or that they seem younger because you are now older: *The band's fans are getting younger.* ◊ *Why do police officers seem to be getting younger?* **not be getting any 'younger** (*informal*) used when you are commenting that time is passing and that you are growing older **young at 'heart** thinking and behaving like a young person even when you are old ⇒ more at OLD, ONLY *adv*.

■ *noun* [pl.] **1** B1 **the young** young people considered as a group: *It's a movie that will appeal to the young.* ◊ *It's a book for* **young and old alike.** **2** B1 young animals of a particular type or that belong to a particular mother: *a mother bird feeding her young*

**young·ish** /ˈjʌŋɪʃ/ *adj.* fairly young: *a youngish president*

**young offender** *noun* (*BrE*) a criminal who, according to the law, is not yet an adult but no longer a child: *a young offender institution*

**young person** *noun* (*BrE, law*) a person between the ages of 14 and 17

**young·ster** 😊+ C1 /ˈjʌŋstə(r)/ *noun* (*informal*) a young person or a child: *The camp is for youngsters aged 8 to 14.*

**young thing** *noun* (*informal*) a young adult: *bright young things working in the computer business*

**young Turk** /ˌjʌŋ ˈtɜːk; *NAmE* ˈtɜːrk/ *noun* (*old-fashioned*) a young person who wants great changes to take place in the established political system

**your** 😊 A1 /weak form jə(r); *BrE* strong form jɔː(r); *NAmE* strong form jʊr/ *det.* (the possessive form of *you*) **1** A1 of or belonging to the person or people being spoken or written to: *I like your dress.* ◊ *Excuse me, is this your seat?* ◊ *The bank is on your right.* **2** A2 of or belonging to people in general: *Dentists advise you to have your teeth checked every six months.* ◊ *In Japan you are taught great respect for your elders.* **3** (*informal*) used to show that sb/sth is well known or often talked about: *This is your typical English pub.* ◊ (*ironic, disapproving*) *You and your bright ideas!* **4 Your** used in some titles, especially those of royal people: *Your Majesty* ◊ *Your Excellency*

**you're** /jʊə(r), jɔː(r); *NAmE* jʊr, weak form jər/ short form you are

**yours** 😊 A2 /jɔːz; *NAmE* jɔːrz, jʊərz, jʊrz/ *pron.* **1** A2 of or belonging to you: *Is that book yours?* ◊ *Is she a friend of yours?* ◊ *My hair is very fine.* Yours *is much thicker.* **2** A2 (*usually* **Yours**) used at the end of a letter before signing your name (*BrE*): **Yours sincerely/faithfully** ◊ (*NAmE*) **Sincerely Yours** ◊ (*NAmE*) **Yours Truly** **3** (*BrE, informal*) your home: *Let's go back to yours after the show.* IDM see YOU

**your·self** 😊 A1 /jɔːˈself, weak form jə-; *NAmE* jɔːrˈs-, jʊr-, weak form jər-/ (*pl.* **your·selves** /-ˈselvz/) *pron.* **1** 😊 A1 (the reflexive form of *you*) used when the person or people being spoken to both cause and are affected by an action: *Have you hurt yourself?* ◊ *You don't seem quite yourself today* (= you do not seem well or do not seem as happy as usual). ◊ *Enjoy yourselves!* **2** 😊 B1 used to emphasize the fact that the person who is being spoken to is doing sth: *Do it yourself—I don't have time.* ◊ *You can try it out for yourselves.* ◊ *You yourself are one of the chief offenders.* **3** used instead of 'you' in order to sound polite or formal (although some people do not consider this use to be correct): *We sell a lot of these to people like yourself.* ◊ *'And yourself,' he replied, 'How are you?'*

IDM **be your'self** to act naturally: *Don't act sophisticated—just be yourself.* **(all) by your'self/your'selves 1** alone; without anyone else: *How long were you by yourself in the house?* ⇒ note at ALONE **2** without help: *Are you sure you did this exercise by yourself?* **(all) to your'self/your 'selves** for only you to have or use; not shared: *I'm going to be away next week so you'll have the office to yourself.*

**youse** (*also* **yous**) /juːz/ *pron.* (*non-standard, dialect*) a word meaning 'you', used when talking to more than one person

**youth** 😊 B1 /juːθ/ *noun* (*pl.* **youths** /juːðz/) **1** 😊 [U] the time of life when a person is young, especially the time before a child becomes an adult: **in sb's ~** *He had been a talented musician in his youth.* **2** 😊 B1 [U] the quality or state of being young: *She brings to the job a rare combination of youth and experience.* **3** 😊 B2 (*also* **the youth**) [pl.] young people considered as a group: *the nation's youth* ◊ *the youth of today* ◊ **youth unemployment** ◊ *contemporary* **youth culture** ◊ *a* **youth worker** (= sb who works with young people) **4** 😊 [C] (*often disapproving*) a young man: *The fight was started by a* **gang of youths.**

**'youth club** *noun* (in the UK) a club where young people can meet each other and take part in various activities

**youth 'custody** *noun* [U] (*BrE*) a period of time when a young criminal is kept in a type of prison as a punishment: *He was sentenced to two years' youth custody.* ◊ *a youth custody centre*

**youth·ful** /ˈjuːθfl/ *adj.* **1** typical of young people: *youthful enthusiasm/energy/inexperience* **2** young or seeming younger than you are: *She's a very youthful 65.* ▶ **youth·ful·ly** /-fəli/ *adv.* **youth·ful·ness** *noun* [U]

**'youth hostel** *noun* a building that provides cheap and simple accommodation and meals, especially to young people who are travelling

**youth hos·tel·ling** /ˈjuːθ hɒstəlɪŋ; *NAmE* hɑːs-/ *noun* [U] (*BrE*) the activity of staying in different youth hostels and walking, etc. between them: *to go youth hostelling*

**You·Tube**™ /ˈjuːtjuːb; *NAmE* -tuːb/ *noun* [U] a website where people can watch and share videos

**you've** /juːv/ short form you have HELP **You've** is usually only used when *have* is an auxiliary verb: *You've just missed Jen.* When *have* is the main verb, use the full form: *You have five minutes left.* ◊ *You've five minutes left.*

**yowl** /jaʊl/ *verb* [I] to make a long loud call that sounds unhappy **SYN wail** ▶ **yowl** *noun*

**yo-yo** *noun, verb, adj.*
■ *noun* (*also* **Yo Yo**™) (*pl.* **yo-yos, Yo Yos**) a toy that consists of two round pieces of plastic or wood joined together, with a piece of string wound between them. You put one end of the string around your finger and make the yo-yo go up and down: *He kept bouncing up and down like a yo-yo.*
■ *verb* [I] (+ *adv./prep.*) to change repeatedly in size, amount, quality, etc. from one extreme to another: *When I was young my weight yo-yoed between 140 and 190 pounds.*
■ *adj.* [only before noun] changing repeatedly in size, amount, quality, etc. from one extreme to another: *She worries about her pattern of yo-yo dieting.*

**yr** (*also* **yr.** *especially in NAmE*) *abbr.* **1** (*pl.* **yrs**) year(s): *children aged 4–11 yrs* **2** your

**yt·trium** /ˈɪtriəm/ *noun* [U] (*symb.* **Y**) a chemical element. Yttrium is a grey-white metal used in MAGNETS.

**yuan** /juˈɑːn/ *noun* (*pl.* **yuan**) the unit of money in China
⇒ see also RENMINBI

**yucca** /ˈjʌkə/ noun a tropical plant with long stiff pointed leaves on a thick straight STEM, often grown indoors

**yuck** (also **yuk**) /jʌk/ exclamation (informal) used to show that you think sth is horrible: *It's filthy! Yuck!*

**yucky** (also **yukky**) /ˈjʌki/ adj. (informal) horrible or very unpleasant: *yucky food*

**Yue** /juˈeɪ/ noun = CANTONESE

**Yule** /juːl/ noun [C, U] (old use or literary) the festival of Christmas

**ˈyule log** noun 1 a large LOG of wood traditionally burnt on Christmas Eve 2 a chocolate cake in the shape of a LOG, traditionally eaten at Christmas

**Yule·tide** /ˈjuːltaɪd/ noun [U, C] (old use or literary) the period around Christmas Day: *Yuletide food and drink*

**yum** /jʌm/ (also **yum-ˈyum**) exclamation (informal) used to show that you think sth tastes or smells very nice

**yummy** /ˈjʌmi/ adj. (informal) very good to eat SYN **delicious**: *a yummy cake*

**ˌyummy ˈmummy** noun (pl. **-ies**) (BrE, informal) an attractive young woman who is the mother of a young child or children: *celebrity yummy mummies*

**yup·pie** (also **yuppy**) /ˈjʌpi/ noun (pl. **-ies**) (informal, becoming old-fashioned, often disapproving) a young professional person who lives in a city and earns a lot of money that they spend on expensive and fashionable things ORIGIN Formed from the first letters of the words 'young urban professional'.

**yurt** /jɜːt; NAmE jɜːrt/ noun 1 a type of traditional round tent used in Mongolia and Siberia 2 a large tent used for holidays in Western countries, based on the shape and style of a traditional yurt

**YWCA** /ˌwaɪ dʌblju: siː ˈeɪ/ (also NAmE, informal **the Y**) noun an organization that exists in many countries and provides accommodation and social and sports activities (the abbreviation for 'Young Women's Christian Association'): *members of the YWCA*

# Z z

**Z** (also **z**) /zed/ NAmE /ziː/ noun (pl. **Zs**, **Z's**, **z's** /zedz/ NAmE /ziːz/) **1** [C, U] the 26th and last letter of the English alphabet: *'Zebra' begins with (a) Z/'Z'*. **2 Z's** [pl.] (NAmE, informal, humorous) sleep: *I need to catch some Z's.* IDM see A *n.*

**zany** /ˈzeɪni/ adj. (**zani·er**, **zani·est**) (informal) strange or unusual in a humorous way SYN **wacky**: *zany humour*

**zap** /zæp/ verb (**-pp-**) (informal) **1** [T] to destroy, kill or hit sb/sth suddenly and with force: *~ sb/sth The monster got zapped by a flying saucer* (= in a computer game). *◊ It's vital to zap stress fast. ◊ ~ sb/sth with sth He jumped like a man who'd been zapped with 1 000 volts.* **2** [I] + adv./prep. to do sth very fast: *I'm zapping through* (= reading very fast) *some modern novels at the moment.* **3** [I, T] ~ (sth) to use the REMOTE CONTROL to change television channels quickly **4** [I, T] ~ (sb/sth) + adv./prep. to move, or make sb/sth move, very fast in the direction mentioned SYN **zip**: *The racing cars zapped past us.*

**zap·per** /ˈzæpə(r)/ noun (informal) **1** = REMOTE CONTROL (2) **2** a device or weapon that attacks or destroys sth quickly: *a bug zapper*

**ZAR** abbr. the written abbreviation for the South African RAND (= the national money of South Africa): *All prices listed are in ZAR.*

**zeal** /ziːl/ noun [U, C] ~ (for/in sth) (formal) great energy or enthusiasm connected with sth that you feel strongly about: *her missionary/reforming/religious/political zeal*

**zealot** /ˈzelət/ noun (often disapproving) a person who is extremely enthusiastic about sth, especially religion or politics SYN **fanatic**

**zeal·ot·ry** /ˈzelətri/ noun [U] (often disapproving) the attitude or behaviour of a zealot: *religious zealotry*

**zeal·ous** /ˈzeləs/ adj. (formal) showing great energy and enthusiasm for sth, especially because you feel strongly about it: *a zealous reformer* ▸ **zeal·ous·ly** adv.

**zebra** /ˈzebrə, ˈziːb-/ NAmE /ˈziːb-/ noun (pl. **zebra** or **zebras**) an African wild animal like a horse with black and white STRIPES (= lines) on its body

**ˌzebra ˈcrossing** noun (BrE) an area of road marked with broad black and white lines where vehicles must stop for people to walk across ⊃ see also PEDESTRIAN CROSSING, PELICAN CROSSING ⊃ WORDFINDER NOTE at TRAFFIC

**zebu** /ˈziːbuː/ noun (pl. **zebus** or **zebu**) an animal of the cow family with long HORNS and a HUMP (= high part) on its back, kept on farms especially in hot climates: *Kenya's beef comes from the zebu cattle.*

**zeit·geist** /ˈzaɪtɡaɪst/ noun [sing.] (from German, formal) the general mood or quality of a particular period of history, as shown by the ideas, beliefs, etc. common at the time SYN **spirit**

**Zen** /zen/ noun [U] a Japanese form of Buddhism

**zen·ith** /ˈzenɪθ/ NAmE /ˈziːn-/ noun **1** the highest point that the sun or moon reaches in the sky, directly above you **2** (formal) the time when sth is strongest and most successful SYN **peak** OPP **nadir**

**zephyr** /ˈzefə(r)/ noun (literary) a soft gentle wind

**Zep·pelin** /ˈzepəlɪn/ noun a German type of large AIRSHIP

**zero** ❶ A2 /ˈzɪərəʊ/ NAmE /ˈzɪr-/ number, verb
- **number 1** ❶ A2 (pl. **-os**) (BrE also **nought**) 0: *Five, four, three, two, one, zero... We have lift-off.* **2** ❶ A2 a temperature, pressure, etc. that is equal to zero on a scale: *It was ten degrees below zero last night* (= –10°C). *◊ The thermometer had fallen to zero.* **3** ❶ A2 the lowest possible amount or level; nothing at all: *I rated my chances as zero. ◊ zero inflation*
- **verb** (**zer·oes**, **zero·ing**, **zer·oed**, **zer·oed**) ~ sth to turn an instrument, control, etc. to zero
PHR V **ˌzero ˈin on sb/sth 1** to fix all your attention on the person or thing mentioned: *They zeroed in on the key issues.* **2** to aim guns, etc. at the person or thing mentioned

**ˌzero-ˈcarbon** adj. in which the amount of CARBON DIOXIDE produced has been reduced to nothing or is balanced by actions that protect the environment SYN **carbon-neutral**: *a zero-carbon house that uses no energy from external sources*

**ˌzero ˈgravity** noun [U] (abbr. **zero ˈG**) a state in which there is no GRAVITY, or where gravity has no effect, for example in space

**ˌzero ˈhour** noun [U] the time when an important event, an attack, etc. is planned to start

**ˌzero-ˈhours** (also **ˌzero-ˈhour**) adj. [only before noun] (BrE) used to describe or refer to a contract of employment in which the employee is not guaranteed regular hours of work and is only paid for the hours they actually work: *zero-hours contracts/workers*

**ˌzero-ˈrated** adj. (BrE, specialist) (of goods, services, etc.) that you do not need to pay VAT (= value added tax) on

**ˌzero-sum ˈgame** noun a situation in which what is gained by one person or group is lost by another person or group

**ˌzero ˈtolerance** noun [U] the policy of applying laws very strictly so that people are punished even for offences that are not very serious

**zest** /zest/ noun **1** [sing., U] ~ (for sth) pleasure and enthusiasm SYN **appetite**: *He had a great zest for life.* **2** [U, sing.] the quality of being exciting, interesting and fun: *The slight risk added zest to the experience.* **3** [U] the outer skin of an orange, a lemon, etc., when it is used in cooking ⊃ compare PEEL, RIND, SKIN ▸ **zest·ful** /ˈzestfl/ adj. **zesty** /ˈzesti/ adj.

**zest·er** /ˈzestə(r)/ noun a kitchen tool for removing the zest from oranges, lemons, etc.

**zeta** /ˈziːtə/ NAmE /ˈzeɪtə/ noun the 6th letter of the Greek alphabet (Z, ζ)

**zeze** /ˈzeɪzeɪ/ EAfrE /ˈzeze/ noun (EAfrE) a musical instrument with one or two strings

**zig·gurat** /ˈzɪɡəræt/ noun (in ancient Mesopotamia) a tower with steps going up the sides, sometimes with a TEMPLE at the top

**zig·zag** /ˈzɪɡzæɡ/ noun, verb
- **noun** a line or pattern that looks like a series of letter W's as it bends to the left and then to the right again: *The path descended the hill in a series of zigzags.* ▸ **zig·zag** adj. [only before noun]: *a zigzag line/path/pattern* ⊃ picture at LINE
- **verb** [I] (**-gg-**) (+ adv./prep.) to move forward by making sharp sudden turns first to the left and then to the right: *The narrow path zigzags up the cliff.*

**zilch** /zɪltʃ/ noun [U] (informal) nothing: *I arrived in this country with zilch.*

**zilla** (also **zillah**) /ˈzɪlə/ noun (in South Asia) a district that has its own local government

**zil·lion** /ˈzɪljən/ noun (especially NAmE, informal) a very large number: *There was a bunch of kids waiting and zillions of reporters.*

**Zim·mer frame**™ /ˈzɪmə freɪm; NAmE -mər/ (also **ˈwalking frame**, informal **Zim·mer** /ˈzɪmə(r)/) (all BrE) (NAmE **walk·er**) noun a metal frame that people use to support them when they are walking, for example people who are old or who have sth wrong with their legs ⊃ picture at FRAME

**zinc** /zɪŋk/ noun **1** [U] (symb. **Zn**) a chemical element. Zinc is a blue-white metal that is mixed with COPPER to produce BRASS and is often used to cover other metals to prevent them from RUSTING. **2** [C] (informal) (in some places in Africa) a sheet of CORRUGATED iron that is used to make a roof, shelter, etc: *They built a temporary home out of zincs.*

**ˌzinc ˈoxide** noun [U] (symb. **ZnO**) a substance used in creams as a treatment for certain skin conditions

**zin·da·bad** /ˌzɪndəˈbɑːd, -ˈbæd/ exclamation (IndE) used to express approval or agreement, usually after the name of a leader, a political movement, an idea, etc.

**'zine** (also **zine**) /ziːn/ noun (informal) a magazine, especially a FANZINE

**zing** /zɪŋ/ verb, noun
- verb (informal) **1** [I, T] ~ (sth) + adv./prep. to move to or make sth move very quickly, often with a high WHISTLING sound: *electrical pulses zinging down a wire* **2** [T] ~ sb/sth (for/on sth) (NAmE) to criticize sb strongly
- noun [U] (informal) interest or excitement ◇ **zingy** adj.

**zing·er** /ˈzɪŋə(r)/ noun (especially NAmE, informal) a clever and humorous comment: *She opened the speech with a real zinger.*

**Zion·ism** /ˈzaɪənɪzəm/ noun [U] a political movement that was originally begun in order to establish an independent state for Jewish people, and now supports the development of the state of Israel ▶ **Zion·ist** /-nɪst/ noun, adj.

**zip** /zɪp/ noun, verb
- noun **1** (also **ˈzip fastener**) (both BrE) (also **zip·per** especially in NAmE) [C] a thing that you use to fasten clothes, bags, etc. It consists of two rows of metal or plastic teeth that you can pull together to close sth or pull apart to open it: *to do up/undo/open/close a zip* ◇ *My zip's stuck.* **2** [U] (informal) energy or speed **3** [sing.] (especially NAmE, informal) nothing: *We won four zip* (= 4–0). ◇ *He said zip all evening.*
- verb (-pp-) **1** [T] to fasten clothes, bags, etc. with a zip: ~ sth *I zipped and buttoned my jacket.* ◇ ~ sb/yourself into sth *The children were safely zipped into their sleeping bags.* ◇ ~ sth + adj. *He zipped his case shut.* ↪ compare UNZIP **2** [I] ~ (up/together) to be fastened with a zip: *The sleeping bags can zip together.* **3** [I, T] ~ (sth) + adv./prep. (informal) to move very quickly or to make sth move very quickly in the direction mentioned: *A sports car zipped past us.* **4** [T] ~ sth (computing) to COMPRESS a file (= make it smaller) **OPP** unzip
- **PHRV** ˌzip ˈup | ˌzip sb/sth ˈup to be fastened with a ZIP; to fasten sth with a zip: *This jacket zips up right to the neck.* ◇ *Shall I zip you up* (= fasten your dress, etc.)? ↪ compare UNZIP

**ˈzip code** (also **ZIP code**) noun (in the US) a group of numbers that are used as part of an address so that mail can be separated into groups and delivered more quickly ↪ see also POSTCODE

**ˈzip file** (also **ZIP file**, **ˈzipped file**) noun a computer file that has been COMPRESSED (= made smaller) to make it easier to store and send

**ˈzip line** (also **ˈzip wire**) noun a cable or rope stretched between two points at different heights that people slide down for fun ▶ **ˈzip-lining** noun [U]

**zip·per** /ˈzɪpə(r)/ noun (especially NAmE) (BrE usually **zip**, **ˈzip fastener**) noun a thing that you use to fasten clothes, bags, etc. It consists of two rows of metal or plastic teeth that you can pull together to close sth or pull apart to open it.

**zip·py** /ˈzɪpi/ adj. (**zip·pier**, **zip·pi·est**) (informal) **1** able to move very quickly: *a zippy little car* **2** lively and exciting: *a wine with a zippy tang*

**ˈzip-up** adj. [only before noun] (especially BrE) (of clothing, a bag, etc.) fastened with a ZIP: *a zip-up top*

**zir·co·nium** /zɜːˈkəʊniəm/ NAmE zɜːrˈk-/ noun [U] (symb. Zr) a chemical element. Zirconium is a hard silver-grey metal that does not CORRODE very easily.

**zit** /zɪt/ noun (especially NAmE, informal) a spot on the skin, especially on the face **SYN** pimple ↪ compare SPOT

**zith·er** /ˈzɪðə(r)/ noun a musical instrument with a lot of metal strings stretched over a flat wooden box that you play with your fingers or a PLECTRUM

**zo·diac** /ˈzəʊdiæk/ noun **1 the zodiac** [sing.] the imaginary area in the sky in which the sun, moon and planets appear to lie, and which has been divided into twelve equal parts, each with a special name and symbol: *the signs of the zodiac* **2** [C] a diagram of these twelve parts, and signs that some people believe can be used to predict how the planets will influence our lives ▶ **zo·di·ac·al** /zəʊˈdaɪəkl/ adj.

**zol** /zɒl; NAmE zɑːl/ SAfrE [C] noun (pl. **zols** or **zolle** /ˈzɒlə; NAmE ˈzɑːlə/) (SAfrE, informal) a cigarette, especially of CANNABIS, that is rolled by hand

**zom·bie** /ˈzɒmbi; NAmE ˈzɑːm-/ noun **1** (in some African and Caribbean religions and in horror stories) a dead body that has been made alive again by magic **2** (informal) a person who seems only partly alive, without any feeling or interest in what is happening

**zonal** /ˈzəʊnl/ adj. (specialist) connected with zones; arranged in zones

**zone** /zəʊn/ noun, verb
- noun **1** an area or a region with a particular feature or use: *a war/combat/demilitarized/exclusion zone* ◇ *a danger zone* ◇ *a pedestrian zone* (= where vehicles may not go) ◇ *They have called for a 100-mile buffer zone* (= protected area) *around the island to protect the seals.* ↪ see also NO-FLY ZONE, TIME ZONE **2** one of the areas that a larger area is divided into for the purpose of organization: *postal charges to countries in zone 2* **3** an area or a part of an object, especially one that is different from everything that is around it: *When the needle enters the red zone the engine is too hot.* ◇ *the erogenous zones of the body* **4** one of the parts that the earth's surface is divided into by imaginary lines that are PARALLEL to the EQUATOR: *the northern/southern temperate zone* ↪ WORDFINDER NOTE at CLIMATE
- **IDM in the ˈzone** (informal) in a state in which you feel confident and are performing at your best: *When I'm in the zone, writing is the most satisfying thing in the world.* ↪ see also COMFORT ZONE ↪ more at TWILIGHT
- verb [usually passive] **1** to keep an area of land to be used for a particular purpose: **be zoned (for sth)** *The town centre was zoned for office development.* **2** to divide an area of land into smaller areas: **be zoned (into sth)** *The park has been zoned into four distinct areas.* ▶ **zon·ing** noun [U]
- **PHRV** ˌzone ˈout (especially NAmE, informal) to go to sleep, become unconscious or stop paying attention: *I just zoned out for a moment.*

**zoned** /zəʊnd/ adj. **1** divided into areas designed for a particular use: *zoned housing land* **2** (also **ˌzoned ˈout**) (NAmE, informal) not behaving or thinking normally because of the effects of a drug such as MARIJUANA or alcohol

**zonked** /zɒŋkt; NAmE zɑːŋkt/ adj. [not before noun] ~ (**out**) (slang) extremely tired or suffering from the effects of alcohol or drugs

**zoo** /zuː/ noun (pl. **zoos**) (also formal **zoological ˈgarden(s)**) a place where many kinds of wild animals are kept for the public to see and where they are studied, BRED (= kept in order to produce young) and protected

**zoo·keep·er** /ˈzuːkiːpə(r)/ noun a person who works in a zoo, taking care of the animals

**zoo·logic·al** /ˌzuːəˈlɒdʒɪkl, ˌzəʊ-; NAmE -ˈlɑːdʒ-/ adj. connected with the science of ZOOLOGY

**zooˈlogical ˈgarden** noun (also **zoological ˈgardens** [pl.]) (formal) = ZOO

**zo·olo·gist** /zuˈɒlədʒɪst, zəʊˈɒ-; NAmE zuˈɑːlədʒɪst, zəʊˈɑː-/ noun a scientist who studies zoology

**zo·ology** /zuˈɒlədʒi, zəʊˈɒ-; NAmE zuˈɑːlədʒi, zəʊˈɑː-/ noun [U] the scientific study of animals and their behaviour ↪ compare BIOLOGY, BOTANY

**zoom** /zuːm/ verb, noun
- verb **1** [I] + adv./prep. (informal) to move or go somewhere very fast **SYN** rush, whizz: *Traffic zoomed past us.* ◇ *For five weeks they zoomed around Europe.* **2** [I] ~ (**up**) (**to** …) (informal) (of prices, costs, etc.) to increase a lot quickly and suddenly: *House prices have zoomed up this year.*
- **PHRV** ˌzoom ˈin/ˈout (of a camera) to show the object that is being photographed from closer/further away, with the use of a ZOOM LENS: *The camera zoomed in on the actor's face.*

# zoom lens

**noun 1** [C] = ZOOM LENS: *a zoom shot* **2** [sing.] the sound of a vehicle moving very fast

**'zoom lens** (also **zoom**) *noun* a camera LENS that you use to make the thing that you are photographing appear nearer to you or further away from you than it really is

**Zoro·ast·rian·ism** /ˌzɒrəʊˈæstriənɪzəm/; *NAmE* /ˌzɔːr-/ *noun* [U] a religion started in ancient Persia by Zoroaster, that teaches that there is one God and a continuing struggle in the world between forces of light and dark ▶ **Zoro·ast·rian** *noun*, *adj*. ⊃ see also PARSEE

**zuc·chini** /zuˈkiːni/ *noun* (*pl.* **zuc·chini** or **zuc·chi·nis**) (*NAmE*) (*BrE* **cour·gette**) a long vegetable with dark green skin that is white inside ⊃ VISUAL VOCAB page V5

**Zulu** /ˈzuːluː/ *noun* **1** [C] a member of a race of black people who live in South Africa **2** [U] = ISIZULU ▶ **Zulu** *adj*.

**Zumba**™ /ˈzuːmbə, ˈzʊm-/ *noun* [U] a fitness programme featuring Latin American dance moves, performed mainly to Latin American dance music

**Zuni** /ˈzuːni/ *noun* (*pl.* **Zuni** or **Zunis**) a member of a Native American people, many of whom live in western New Mexico

**zy·deco** /ˈzaɪdɪkəʊ/ *noun* [U] a type of dance music, originally played by black Americans in Louisiana

**zy·gote** /ˈzaɪɡəʊt/ *noun* (*biology*) a single cell that develops into a person or animal, formed by the joining together of a male and a female GAMETE (= a cell that is provided by each parent)

---

æ cat | ɑː father | e bed | ɜː fur | ə about | ɪ sit | i: see | i happy | ɒ got (BrE) | ɔː saw | ʌ cup | ʊ put | uː too

# Oxford Writing Tutor

## Using the Oxford Advanced Learner's Dictionary to improve your writing

Whether you are writing a business email or a long research essay, your dictionary can be a powerful tool to assist you in becoming a better writer in English.

### 1. Using the main part of the dictionary

You can use the main A–Z of the dictionary to help you:

- **Choose your words carefully.** Many words in English have similar or related meanings, but are used in different contexts or situations.

  Look carefully at the example sentences provided in the entries for words you want to use. Also look at any **synonym notes** and **vocabulary notes** to help you choose the most appropriate word. If you need academic vocabulary, look for the ○ⓢ and ⓦ symbols, which indicate words in the Oxford Phrasal Academic Lexicon™.

- **Combine words naturally and effectively.** In English, certain pairs of words go together and sound natural to native speakers, for example, *heavy rain*, and others do not (*strong rain*). This is called **collocation**. Information on which words collocate with one another can be found in the example sentences in the dictionary entries.

  Look up the key nouns you have used in your writing to check which verbs or adjectives are usually used with them.

- **Become more flexible.** Rather than repeating the same word or phrase many times in your work, try to find other ways to express your ideas.

  Look for the **SYN** symbol to find synonyms and also study the synonyms notes. Look for word families and try using words in the same family that are different parts of speech. For example, you could write: *French is different from English in this respect* (different=adjective) or *French differs from English in this respect* (differ=verb).

- **Edit and check your work.** You can use your dictionary to check any problem areas such as spelling, parts of speech, irregular forms, grammar, phrasal verbs and prepositions.

### 2. Using the Writing Tutor

In the following pages you will find examples of essays and practical types of writing that you can use as models for your own work. You will also find advice about planning, organizing and writing each type of text.

- **Examples of written texts.**
  Look carefully at the:
  - structure and organization of the text
  - way ideas and paragraphs are linked
  - language and style
  - notes on particular points
- **Tips** These are quick reminders and advice to help when you are writing.
- **Language banks** give you some useful phrases that you can use in each type of writing.

  Check that you are familiar with these phrases and know how to use them correctly.

You can add other phrases when you meet them in your reading. In the main part of the dictionary there are more notes like this, which give you further phrases and examples to show you how to use them. For example, look at the note at 'however'.

### Contents

| | |
|---|---|
| The writing process | WT2 |
| Answering exam questions | WT4 |
| Writing a comparison essay | WT6 |
| Writing a discussion essay | WT8 |
| Writing a summary | WT10 |
| Describing graphs and charts | WT12 |
| Writing a report | WT14 |
| Writing a book or film review | WT16 |
| Discussing pictures and cartoons | WT18 |
| Writing an article | WT20 |
| Writing letters and emails | WT22 |
| Writing a longer essay or dissertation | WT27 |
| Writing a CV or résumé | WT28 |
| Writing a covering letter | WT30 |

# The writing process

Each individual writer has their own aims and needs and their own way of approaching various parts of the writing process. However, whether you are writing a short essay, an article, a report or a research paper, the overall process is generally the same.

## 1. Preliminary phase

Ask yourself some planning questions that will help guide the rest of the process.

### What is the purpose of this piece of writing?

For example:
- To answer a specific essay, examination or research question
- To convince others of your point of view
- To communicate your knowledge or understanding to others, such as a teacher or an examiner

### Who is my audience?

For example:
- A teacher or professor
- Fellow students or colleagues
- An employer
- The general public

> The answers will help you to choose the appropriate level of formality. They will also help you make decisions about the amount of research required, as well as the kinds of examples and supporting evidence you will use.

## 2. Pre-writing phase

### Explore

Brainstorm ideas using whatever method suits you best:
- Mind maps
- Lists of interesting concepts, facts, questions, etc.
- Conversations with colleagues

### Research

Next, research your topic and gather information from a variety of sources:
- Books and journals
- The media
- Websites
- Interviews or questionnaires
- Scientific studies

> When you read sources, take detailed notes and keep an accurate record of each source.

### Organize

After carrying out your research, you can draft a thesis (your main argument, statement or idea) to guide you.

Make a detailed outline of the logical plan of your essay, article or report to support this thesis, giving a structure to your writing before you begin to write.
- Decide roughly how many words you will give to each part of your essay/report.
- Collect or prepare any visual aids such as charts or diagrams that you might need.

## 3. Writing phase

In this phase, you will draft and revise your work several times.

### Draft

Write your draft in formal sentences and paragraphs.
- Remain focused on your thesis or main idea. If you do change this, go back and adapt your original plan to ensure that your essay/report continues to support the new thesis.
- Follow your outline, modifying it if necessary.

### Review/Edit

In this step, you read your writing with a critical eye.

In early drafts, ask yourself:
- Have you answered the question or achieved your original purpose?
- Have you introduced your subject, developed it logically and come to a conclusion?
- Is your supporting evidence appropriate and complete? Do you need more examples, statistics or quotes?
- Have you used headings to help the reader, if appropriate?
- Are the relationships between ideas clear?
- Is each part the right length for the demands of the topic?

In later drafts, ask yourself:
- Have you used paragraph breaks well?
- Is the level of formality appropriate for your readers?

- Have you chosen your words carefully, using correct collocations?
- Have you met any word count requirements?

If possible, ask someone else to read your text.

After each review, return to the drafting step, revising and editing your writing as necessary.

> **Using sources in essays**
>
> Ask yourself:
> - Have you quoted or mentioned sources to support your points?
> - Have you used the citation style recommended by your teachers or institution?
> - Have you listed your references in the style recommended?

## 4. Presentation phase

### Proofread

When you have a final draft of your writing, you will need to read it once more to find and correct surface errors.

Check for:
- Spelling
- Punctuation
- Grammatical mistakes

You may find it helpful to ask someone else to proofread your final draft as a last step.

## Effective writing

Whatever type of text you are writing, your aim should always be to express your ideas clearly, in a way that your readers can easily understand.

Plan essays before you write to make sure your ideas are organized logically.

Keep to one main idea per sentence. If you need to add supporting information or a comment, use just one extra clause. Avoid long sentences with multiple clauses.

### Word choice

Think about the purpose of your writing and the audience you are writing for. Are you giving facts, presenting an argument or telling a story? Register labels in the dictionary entries will tell you whether a word is *formal*, *informal*, *slang*, *offensive*, etc. In most writing it is best to use standard English words and phrases, that is, those without a register label. However, in some contexts, it may be appropriate to choose *formal* or *informal* words or phrases. Don't use language marked *slang* or *offensive*.

### Efficiency

Read your work and check if the wording can be more efficient. For example:

> The experiment didn't work ~~due to the fact that~~ because the instruments were faulty.

Avoid using words and phrases with the same meaning (tautology). For example:

> The ~~beginning of the~~ story started in China.

Use relative clauses with *which*, *that* or *who* to avoid repetition. For example:

> The course was popular. The popularity of the course was a surprise to the new teacher.

These two sentences require five more words than a single sentence with a relative clause.

> The course was popular, which was a surprise to the new teacher.

### Organizing ideas

Add information to the main part of a sentence using subordinating conjunctions such as *although*, *because*, *after*, *as soon as*, etc.:

> The park building needs to be knocked down **because** it's not safe.

Connect items that are the same grammatical type using coordinating conjunctions like *and*, *but*, and *or*:

> The research was very thorough **but** it didn't cover the whole population.

> **Academic writing**
>
> This tends to be **impersonal** in style in order to be objective. When you read in your subject, notice how the writers express themselves. The following points may help you in your writing:
> - Limit the use of the **first person pronouns** (*I* and *we*). Rather than *In this study I aim to...*, write: *This study aims to...* or *The aim of this study is to...* Look at how *I* and *we* are used in your subject area. Avoid using *you*.
> - **Passive forms** are often used as they focus attention on the verb, not the person (e.g. *A study was conducted to see...*; *It can be argued that...*)
> - Patterns with **it and an adjective** are often used: *It is clear that...*; *It is necessary to...*
> - **Nouns** are often used as subjects of active verbs: *The results show that...*
> - **Complex noun phrases** with prepositions are very common: *The advantages of X are...*; *the use of light treatment in 95 patients with...*

# Answering exam questions

At all times, you must ensure that you really understand an examination question or assignment title and address all the required parts. Questions can be considered in terms of three main components:
- Topic
- Focus
- Question types

## Topic

The key words in the questions help you identify the topic of the question. For example: *Explain recent changes to car engine design in response to the need to reduce carbon-based pollutants.*

When you write your answer think about what the examiner wants you to demonstrate, for example, a detailed understanding of car engine design and recent trends in engine design related to low emissions such as electric and hybrid engines.

## Focus

Often, the wording of the question will include a word or phrase that either limits or expands the topic in a very specific way. These phrases show you the focus of the question. Try to avoid common mistakes, such as:
- covering too broad an area. For example, if the question asks about textile mills in the American South in the 1930s, think very carefully about including information about the 1920s or 1940s, or about textile mills in other parts of the country.
- writing with too narrow a focus. For example, if you are asked about the impact of climate change on South America, you should not write about its impact only on Brazil.
- including irrelevant information. For example, if you are asked about the benefits and drawbacks of using nuclear power as an energy source, you should not write about wind or solar power.
- only answering half of the question. For example, if the question asks *What effects will the banning of petrol and diesel cars have and will the advantages outweigh the disadvantages?* you need to discuss both parts of the question.

## Question types

You need to identify the type of question and plan your answer accordingly. These are the main types of questions found in exams.

### Comparing and contrasting

You may be required to read and compare two texts. You must be able to understand the texts and identify the main points in both. The texts usually present two differing opinions on a topic, for example, the benefits and drawbacks of tourism. You may also be required to evaluate the two texts and say which puts forward its argument most successfully. Another type of comparison essay asks you to compare and contrast two approaches or methods. There is an example of this on page WT6.

### Discussing and giving opinions

These types of questions either require you to analyse and discuss both sides of a question objectively, or to present an argument for one side or the other. In the latter case you should give reasons, evidence and examples to support your answer. For example, *What is the best way to revise for an exam? Give reasons and examples to support your opinion.* There is an example of a discussion essay on page WT8.

## Summarizing

You may be asked to summarize visual information in a chart (a pie chart, line graph or bar chart), or from a text. For the former, you are required to analyse the visual information in terms of trends and compare the changes in different categories, for example, how trends in mobile phones have changed over the last 20 years. For written texts you need to identify the main points and then write them in a shorter form using your own words. Look at pages WT10 and WT12 for examples of each type of question.

## Describing

Some exam questions ask you to write a short description of a photograph or picture using key words. You need to demonstrate your ability to describe a scene accurately using the correct grammar and vocabulary. In some cases, you may be asked to interpret the image by inferring from the visual clues what message the illustrator is trying to convey. See page WT18 for an example of this kind of task.

## Outlining problems and identifying solutions

Problem-solving questions are a feature of many exams. You need to use your critical thinking skills and be able to analyse the problem. You also need to think creatively about how the problem could be solved and should use relevant examples from your own experience. For example, *Students cannot concentrate for long periods. What are the reasons for this? What solutions can you suggest?*

## Explaining

Some questions require you to describe a process or how something works, for example, *Explain the process of photosynthesis*. In this case you need to show you have the required knowledge of the process and give the information in a logical order and explain the relationship between each stage of the process.

# Genres

It is important to be able to write different types of texts. To write emails, letters, reports, reviews, articles, essays, summaries and stories requires you to know how to:
- lay out the text
- use the correct style, register and tone
- use grammar correctly
- choose the appropriate content for the context you are given.

# Key words

Here is a set of key task words that are used in exam questions.

| | |
|---|---|
| *analyse* | separate a text into its parts in order to understand and explain it |
| *compare* | provide details of how two or more things are similar or different |
| *contrast* | highlight the difference between two or more things |
| *describe* | provide details of the appearance of a person, place or thing; it could also refer to the details of a process or an event |
| *discuss* | a broad term that includes description, explanation and analysis of a topic or argument |
| *evaluate* | judge the importance or validity of something |
| *explain* | give detailed reasons for an opinion or idea; analyse the 'why' or 'how' of something |
| *give your opinion* | say what you think about a situation or argument and support your opinion with relevant examples |
| *outline* | give only the main facts about an idea or process |
| *summarize* | reduce an idea or argument to its main points by cutting out the details |

# Writing a comparison essay

You often need to compare and contrast texts and information in exams, academic essays, work and everyday life. Look at the example of a comparison essay below.

### Which is more effective, online or traditional classroom learning?

**INTRODUCTION**

① The first paragraph gives a short summary of the current situation.

The second sentence catches the reader's interest.

① Technology has brought about significant changes in education and the number of students taking courses online has increased dramatically. Recently 380,000 learners signed up for one online English course, the most ever for a MOOC (massive open online course). At the same time, traditional universities continue to provide face-to-face tutorials, seminars and lectures for relatively small numbers of students. Which of these forms of learning is more effective and how do we know?

**DEVELOPMENT**

② The second paragraph describes the similarities between online and traditional courses.

② **Both** online courses and face-to-face courses have the same aims–to provide a structured educational experience for students that allows them to learn a given subject effectively. Online courses **are similar to** traditional courses in that they have a syllabus and **also** provide learning materials such as course notes.

③ The first difference is introduced and offers supporting evidence that online courses have an advantage over traditional courses. *Despite these similarities* indicates that the writer is going to list the differences.

③ **Despite these similarities**, there are a number of significant **differences** between the two types of course. The main advantage of online courses is that students have continuous access to the learning material, and learning can be done anywhere at any time. **On the other hand**, face-to-face learning happens only in the classroom according to a fixed timetable. This is a disadvantage for students who also have to work and for students who live far away from the college or school.

④ The writer gives the second difference and advantage of online courses.

④ **Unlike** traditional courses, which require buildings and teachers, online courses only need a website and digital learning materials. Added to this, online courses can take an almost unlimited number of students, **while** traditional courses are limited to the number of people that can fit into a lecture hall. The end result is that online courses are **much cheaper**, and in some cases, free.

⑤ *However* indicates that the writer is now going to change focus and discuss the advantages of traditional courses.

⑤ **However**, the news is not all good for online courses. It seems that students **prefer** face-to-face contact with their lecturers and classmates. Students can get immediate answers to questions in a lecture or tutorial **rather than** wait for an email or chatroom message. Social interaction with their peers not only helps their motivation but also develops their social skills.

⑥ The writer provides data to support the argument that traditional courses are more effective to provide balance to the overall argument.

⑥ It appears that the personal or affective element of traditional courses is crucial. Some online courses have completion rates as low as 13%, **whereas** between 70–80% of students on traditional courses complete their degrees. Despite their low cost and convenience, online courses cannot yet compete with the timeless advantage of students being able to communicate face-to-face and to be part of a real, rather than virtual, community.

**CONCLUSION**

⑦ The paragraph starts with a short summary and then provides the conclusion based on the main points introduced in the development stages.

⑦ There are clearly significant differences between the two types of course, despite the fact that they **share** the same primary aim of providing an educational service. Ultimately, the answer as to which is more effective lies in the priorities of the provider and the students. For some providers, the target is to maximize the number of students who can take their courses; for others, the aim is to provide a high-quality, personalized education. For students who are not able to attend courses in person for financial or geographical reasons, online courses can be an effective solution; but for students who are lucky enough to have the opportunity, traditional courses, at least for now, seem to be the most effective and popular option.

## Preparing to write

1. If possible, choose a question related to the topic you are most familiar with.
2. Read the question carefully several times. Underline the key task words and topic words.
3. Brainstorm ideas and write as many as you can on a blank piece of paper.

> cost
> social interaction
> completion rates
> access
> face-to-face contact
> practical subjects
> learning materials
> limited / unlimited number of students

4. Organize your ideas. Cut any ideas that don't help you answer the question.
5. Define the two things you are comparing so that the reader is clear what you are referring to.
6. Think of a fact or comment that captures the reader's interest in the introduction.
7. Highlight the similarities and differences and decide on your conclusion.
8. Plan the essay:
   - *Introduction*   Introduce the topic.
     Define the things you are comparing.
   - *Development*   Identify the similarities.
     Identify the differences.
   - *Conclusion*   Draw your own conclusion based on the evidence from the development section of the essay.
9. As you write, identify opportunities to develop your ideas and show your range of language.

## LANGUAGE BANK

### Identifying contrasts

**despite X … Y**
*Despite these similarities, there are a number of significant differences between the two types of course.*

**on the other hand**
*On the other hand, face-to-face learning happens only in the classroom according to a fixed timetable.*

**however**
*However, the news is not all good for online courses.*

**unlike X, Y …**
*Unlike traditional courses, which require buildings and teachers, online courses only need digital learning materials.*

**X … whereas Y …**
*Some online courses have completion rates as low as 13%, whereas between 70–80% of students on traditional courses complete their degrees.*

**difference/s between**
*There are a number of significant differences between …*

**while**
*… online courses can take an almost unlimited number of students while traditional courses are limited to the number of people that can fit into a lecture hall.*

### Identifying similarities

**both X and Y**
*Both online courses and face-to-face courses have the same aims.*

**X is similar to Y …**
*Online courses are similar to traditional courses in that they have a syllabus.*

**also**
*They also provide learning materials such as course notes and videos.*

**share**
*… they share the same primary aim of providing an educational service.*

# Writing a discussion essay

Many essays that you have to write, whether during your school or college course or in an examination, will require you to present a reasoned argument on a particular issue. This will often be based on your research into the topic, but some questions may ask you to give your opinion. In both cases your argument must be clearly organized and supported with information, evidence and reasons. The language tends to be formal and impersonal.

### INTRODUCTION

① Sentences 1 and 2 introduce the topic.
The third sentence states the focus of the essay.

### DEVELOPMENT

② Sentence 2 introduces the first point (manned missions are not cost-effective).
This is supported by a quote from an expert to give authority.

③ Reasons and data are given to support the writer's point of view.

④ Introduces the second point (unmanned projects are more scientifically productive).

⑤ Presents the counterargument.
*Some may argue* suggests that the writer will go on to argue against this position.
*However* in the second sentence introduces the argument against.

### CONCLUSION

⑥ Summarizes the writer's points and states his/her conclusion on the title. *Thus* introduces the conclusion. *I would argue that* clearly shows the writer's position.

---

**'Manned space missions should now be replaced with unmanned missions.' Discuss.**

① It is clear that the study of space and the planets is by nature expensive. Scientists and politicians must constantly attempt to balance costs with potential research benefits. A major question to be considered is whether the benefits of manned space flight are worth the costs.

② For Nobel Prize-winning physicist Steven Weinberg the answer is clear. As he noted in 2007 in a lecture at the Space Telescope Science Institute in Baltimore, 'Human beings don't serve any useful function in space. They radiate heat, they're very expensive to keep alive, and unlike robotic missions, they have a natural desire to come back, so that anything involving human beings is enormously expensive.'

③ Unmanned missions are much less expensive than manned, having no requirement for airtight compartments, food or life support systems. They are also lighter and therefore require less fuel and launch equipment. According to NASA, the 1992 manned Space Shuttle Endeavor cost \$1.7 billion to build and required approximately \$450 million for each launch. In contrast, the entire unmanned Voyager mission from 1972 until 1989, when it observed Neptune, cost only \$865 million.

④ In addition to their relative cost-effectiveness, unmanned projects generally yield a much greater volume of data. While manned flights have yet to extend beyond the orbit of Earth's moon, unmanned missions have explored almost our entire solar system, and have observed an Earth-like planet in a nearby solar system. Manned missions would neither be able to travel so far, be away so long, nor collect so much data while at the same time guaranteeing the astronauts' safe return.

⑤ Some may argue that only manned space flight possesses the ability to inspire and engage the general population, providing much-needed momentum for continued governmental funding and educational interest in mathematics and the sciences. However, media coverage of projects such as the Mars Rover, the Titan moon lander, and the Hubble telescope's photographs of extrasolar planets demonstrates that unmanned missions clearly have the ability to attract and hold public interest.

⑥ Thus, taking into account the lower cost, the greater quantity of data and widespread popular support, I would argue that for now, at least, unmanned space missions undoubtedly yield the most value in terms of public spending.

---

**Linking words and phrases** guide the reader through the argument and show the writer's opinion.

**Adverbs** can be used to modify your opinion.

**These phrases** make the argument less personal and more objective.

**Experts are quoted** to support the argument.

## Preparing to write

- Brainstorm your ideas on the question, read and research the topic (unless in an examination). Which do you think are the strongest arguments? Decide what your viewpoint will be.
- Select 2 or 3 strong ideas on each side, with supporting examples, ideas or evidence. For some questions you can use evidence from your personal experience.
- Decide how to organize your essay to persuade readers of your case.
- Note down some useful vocabulary on the topic.

### Structure 1 (used in the model essay)
Introduction
Arguments **for** your case + supporting evidence, examples or reasons
Arguments **against** + evidence
Evaluation of arguments
Summary and conclusion
*It is possible to reverse arguments for and against.*

### Structure 2
Introduction
Argument 1: + supporting evidence, examples or reasons
Counterargument
Argument 2: + supporting evidence, examples or reasons
Counterargument
Evaluation of arguments
Summary and conclusion

### TIPS
- Look carefully at the **title or question** and make sure you really answer it.
- Use **general statements** to convey the main ideas, and then provide **evidence**, **examples**, **details** and **reasons** to support these statements.
- Use **paragraph divisions** and **connecting words and phrases** to make the structure of your essay clear to your readers.
- For **language** to help you structure your argument, look at the notes at the entries for 'addition' and 'first'.

## Showing your position

When you write a discussion essay, you can show what your opinion is on the issue or question without using personal phrases such as *I think…* or *In my opinion,….* You can do this by choosing words carefully as you write. Some examples are given below. Look out for more in your reading.

### LANGUAGE BANK

#### Adjectives
important, major, serious, significant
e.g. *An **important** point to consider is…;*
*This was a **highly significant** discovery.*

#### Patterns with It + adjective
clear, likely, possible, surprising, evident
e.g. ***It is clear that*** *the study of space is expensive.*
important, difficult, necessary, possible, interesting
e.g. ***It is important to*** *consider the practical effects of these measures.*

#### Adverbs
clearly, indeed, in fact, of course
generally, usually, mainly, widely
perhaps, probably, certainly, possibly
rarely, sometimes, often
e.g. ***Clearly***, *this is a serious issue that deserves further study.*
*This book is **generally** held to be her greatest novel.*

#### Verbs
These help show how certain you are about a point or an argument.
**Modal verbs:** can, could; may, might; will, would *(the first of each pair is most certain)*
Compare: *I **argue** that…* (very certain) /
*I **would argue** that…* (not so certain)
**It + verb:** *It appears that, It seems that…*
**It + passive verb:** *It can be seen that…; It should/must be noted/emphasized that…*
**Showing verbs:** show, indicate, demonstrate, suggest, imply
*The results/findings show/indicate…*
**Arguing verbs:** argue, suggest, consider, conclude
*I would argue/suggest that …*

#### Linking words and phrases
Firstly (= *I have several points to make*)
Furthermore… In addition,… Moreover,…
(= *I have another important point*)
However,… (*to introduce a counterargument*)
Thus,… Therefore,… (*to introduce a conclusion*)

# Writing a summary

A summary is a shortened version of a text containing only the key information. The aim is to present readers with a short, clear account of the ideas in the text. Summary writing is an important skill in both academic and business contexts. Follow the steps in order to write a successful summary.

## Preparing to write

Select the key information:
- Read the text carefully. It is important to understand the whole sequence of the argument and identify the main points. Think about the purpose of your summary and what your readers need to know.
- Highlight the **key information** (the main ideas). Omit details such as examples, quotations, information in brackets, repetitions, figures of speech and most figures and statistics.
- Underline any information that you are not sure about. Only include it in your summary if you have space.
- Make notes on the key information in your own words.

### Are we living in a surveillance society?

The number of CCTV (or closed-circuit television) cameras in Britain has grown enormously in recent years. There are now more than 5 million, which makes an astonishing one camera for every 13 people.

CCTV has been used for many years for the surveillance of public areas associated with an obvious security risk, such as military installations, airports, casinos and banks. However, since the 1990s, there has been a huge increase in the surveillance of everyday locations such as city and town centres, car parks, shops and traffic. Added to this, more and more individuals are buying their own consumer CCTV systems for personal or commercial use. The most common function of these systems is to survey the area in front of a house or business and record any antisocial or criminal behaviour. People who buy these systems range from wealthy individuals who are afraid of being targeted by burglars, to people who are not wealthy at all but who live in high-crime areas, such as inner cities, and are trying to protect themselves.

For some people, the huge increase in public surveillance is a threat to the individual's civil liberties and is a sign that society is becoming increasingly authoritarian. They argue that the individual's right to privacy and right to live anonymously is an important aspect of being British. They also fear that present or future governments might abuse the information gathered by surveillance in order to manipulate, control or persecute the population, as happens in George Orwell's novel 1984.

Individuals and groups in favour of CCTV, including the police, believe that it is a valuable weapon against crime. In fact, there is no strong evidence that CCTV reduces crime overall. It may act as a deterrent in certain locations, but the crime is displaced to another location. It is not even always a good deterrent. Many criminals aren't afraid of CCTV because they know that the cameras may not be running, or that no one is likely to be watching the screens. Few crimes are solved through CCTV. Sometimes CCTV footage is analysed retrospectively to identify criminals after a crime has taken place, but even this process is enormously time-consuming and expensive. One promising new development is the computer monitoring of CCTV, where computers are programmed to notice unusual movements, such as those of a car thief in a supermarket car park, and sound an alarm. Meanwhile we can expect the argument about the rights and wrongs of CCTV to continue.

## Writing the summary

Write a first draft of your summary using the information you have selected.
- **Organize** the ideas in your notes into a logical order. This need not be the same order as in the original text, but must show the same argument.
- **Condense** the information where possible.
- **Express the ideas in your own words.** This will usually be shorter than the original. Rewrite phrases in the text, but keep any **key terms** from the subject area.
- Do not give your own opinion on the topic.

> Britain has a very high number of CCTV cameras. **Originally used for locations with an obvious security risk**, CCTV surveillance has **now** spread to **ordinary** public areas, **while** individuals are **also** buying **private systems** to protect themselves from crime.
>
> **Opponents** of the growth in CCTV surveillance base their arguments on the threat to civil liberties and the danger of government misuse of the data acquired by surveillance.
>
> **Supporters** of CCTV argue that it reduces crime, although there is **no clear proof** of this. **If it acts as a deterrent, crime probably moves to another area**. Often **it is not a deterrent and it does not solve many crimes**. However, **the technology is developing in ways that may be effective**.

**Combine sentences** in new ways to condense the argument, e.g. by linking the key ideas with different conjunctions and adverbs from those in the original text.

**Introduce new terms and concepts** to condense and clarify the argument. For example, *opponents* and *supporters* can be used to refer to those against, and those in favour of, CCTV.

**Rephrase information to shorten it:**
try changing the verb form or the part of speech. Examples and word families in the dictionary can help.

    e.g. **passive → active verb**: *Few crimes are solved through CCTV → it does not solve many crimes*
    **noun → verb**: *One promising new development is … → the technology is developing*

**Your own words:** Try using synonyms or rephrasing words and expressions such as adjective + noun phrases. Use the dictionary to help you.
- *everyday* → **ordinary**
- *their own consumer CCTV systems for personal … use* → **private systems**
- *no strong evidence* → **no clear proof**
- *promising* → **that may be effective**

## Working on the draft

Ask yourself these questions:
- Is it the right length?
  If there is a word limit, try to stay as close to it as possible. If your summary is too long, you can usually reduce it further by:
    - cutting adjectives, e.g. *locations with an obvious security risk* → *locations with a security risk*; *no clear proof* → *no proof*
    - replacing phrases with shorter versions, e.g. *a lot of/not a lot of* → *many/few*
  If it is still too long, go back and reduce your key information.
- Does it contain all the important points from the text?
- Does it read well?
- Are the grammar and spelling correct?

IELTS

# Describing graphs and charts

You may be asked to write a report describing data that is presented in a graph or chart. The most common types of graphs and charts are:
- **line graphs**, which show developments over a period of time
- **bar charts**, which compare the proportions or amounts of different things
- **pie charts**, which compare percentages of parts of a whole set of data.

## Preparing to write

### Interpreting a line graph

It is essential that you understand the information presented in the graph before you begin writing.

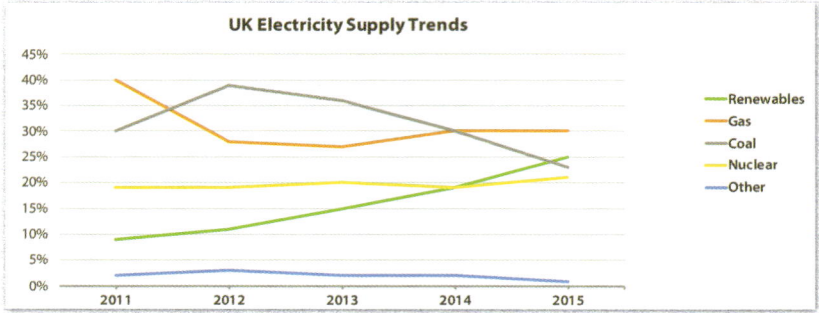

**What is the information about?**
- Trends in the sources of electricity in the UK between 2011 and 2015.

**What do the numbers on each axis represent?**
- Horizontal axis: years; vertical axis: percentage of total electricity supply.

**What changes do the lines show?**
- Two lines show an increase (green and yellow) and three lines show a decrease (blue, grey and orange).

**How do the lines stand in relation to each other?**
- In 2011, the lines showing the five categories of electricity supply are fairly evenly spaced between 0–5 per cent and 40 per cent. The lines showing the four most common sources of electricity all cross over one another in the period 2014–2015.

**Which feature of the lines stands out most?**
- Renewable energy sources show the biggest growth.

**What conclusions can be drawn from the chart?**
- Patterns of electricity supply changed over these four years; the supply of renewable sources changed the most.

## Writing the report

This task tests your ability to:
- summarize the information from the graph
- highlight the main trends and key changes
- choose, describe and compare data relevant to the trends you focus on.

You should note the following:
- Language: accuracy and clarity are the essential features of a good report. The language you use should be simple but academic in style.
- Vocabulary: there are specific words and phrases we use to describe charts and graphs. (See the *Language bank*)
- Organization: organize the information so that you highlight the main trends or features in a logical way.

Summarize the information in the graph by selecting and reporting the main features and make comparisons where relevant.

WT13

## INTRODUCTION

(1) This paragraph describes the subject of the data.

## DEVELOPMENT

(2) The first sentence is a general comment on the trends shown in the chart and highlights the main trend. The second and third sentences provide supporting detail on the main trend.

(3) This paragraph provides more detail on the overall trends and compares and contrasts the trends for each category.

## CONCLUSION

(4) The conclusion draws together the main trends identified in the report.

(1) The chart shows the percentage of electricity supplied by five types of energy source in the UK between 2011 and 2015: renewables (solar, wind, tidal and hydro), gas, coal, nuclear, and other sources (e.g. biofuels).

(2) In this period all five types of supply changed to some extent, but the most significant change was in the renewable category. At the beginning of the period the percentage of electricity supplied by renewables was the second lowest at just under 10 per cent. Over the four-year period this more than doubled to 25 per cent. This made it the second most common source of electricity after gas, which in 2015 supplied 30 per cent of the market.

(3) Over the whole period gas remained the most common source of electricity. However, the percentage it supplied dropped from 40 per cent to 30 per cent, having fallen to a low of 27 per cent in 2013. The other category that fell over the same period was coal, which had the most dramatic fall from 39 per cent in 2012 to 23 per cent in 2015. At the same time the percentage of nuclear power went up slightly, from 19 per cent to 21 per cent. If these trends in coal and nuclear supply continue, nuclear will overtake coal in the next few years. Other sources of electricity such as biofuels remained at a relatively low percentage and did not change significantly over the four-year period.

(4) In conclusion, the chart shows that the pattern of electricity sources changed significantly in the categories of renewables, gas and coal over the period 2011 to 2015. The most significant trends were the drop in coal and the rise in renewables.

## LANGUAGE BANK

### General

The graph/chart shows/represents/indicates…
The figures show/illustrate (that)…

### Conclusion

In conclusion, …
The following conclusions can be drawn from the data.

### Pie charts

More/Less than half of the total…
Only a third/a quarter…
Just/Well under/over 50%…
The biggest/smallest proportion/sector…
The vast majority of…

### Bar charts

There were almost twice/three times/half as many … as
Far/Slightly/20% fewer X… than Y…
Many/Far/A few/20% more X…than Y…
A greater proportion of… than of…
20% of women…, while only 10% of men…
80% of (adults send emails), compared with 34% (who prefer texts).

### Line graphs

a small/slight/gradual increase/decrease
a significant/marked/dramatic increase/decrease
a small/slight rise/fall/dip
steady growth
to rise/increase/fall/decrease/decline/drop
to rise/fall steadily/dramatically/sharply/rapidly
Customer numbers have fluctuated.
(Online sales) reached an all-time high/low.
The graph shows a marked change in…

Describing graphs and charts

# Writing a report

A report describes a study, an investigation or a project. Its purpose is to provide recommendations or updates, and sometimes to persuade the readers to accept an idea. It is written by a single person or a group who has investigated the issue. It is read by people who require the information.

## Think about the reader

You need to make the objective of the report clear so that the people who are reading the report know why they are reading. Thinking about the readers and what they need to know will help improve your report.

- Is the purpose of the report clear throughout?
- Can the readers find the information they need?
- Will diagrams or tables make the information clearer?
- Should you just present the facts or include recommendations as well?

> **TIP**
> Reports can vary in length but a good rule to remember is that they should be as long as necessary and as short as possible.

## Organizing your report

A typical report should follow the structure outlined below. Shorter reports might not need all the sections but they should at least include the highlighted sections.

### 1. Title
Your title should tell the reader exactly what the report is about.

### 2. Contents list
If your report has a number of sections, it is important to include a table of contents so that the readers can find the information they want. A good way to structure a report is to use numbered headings:
- 2.0 Research
- 2.1 Focus groups
- 2.2 Technology for accessing the internet

### 3. Summary
This section is often called an **Executive Summary**. It tells the reader what the objectives of the report are as well as the main findings, conclusions and any recommendations.

### 4. Introduction
This should give the reader the following:
- the background to the report—why you are writing
- a summary of what the report will (and won't) cover
- how you researched the information you have based the report on.

### 5. Body of the report
The main body of the report will follow the structure in the Contents list. It will give precise information about the research you have carried out and what you have discovered from it. The information here should be mainly factual and not based on opinion. Tables, charts and bulleted lists can make the information clearer. Some of the more detailed information can go into Appendices and the Bibliography.

### 6. Conclusions
This is where you give your opinions on the facts that you have discovered.

### 7. Recommendations
If you have been asked to give recommendations, they should be based on your conclusions. You should also let the reader know what you predict will happen if your recommendations are followed.

### 8. Appendices
In a long report, you should put very detailed information in the Appendices with cross references to them in the body of the report.

### 9. Bibliography
If your report refers to a number of other publications, you should list these in a Bibliography.

# Executive summary

The text below contains highlighted examples of language we use in summaries. More examples can be found in the *Language bank*. Notice that the language used should be **clear**, **accurate** and **formal**. *We* and *I* are often used in internal reports, for example for describing research.

### Web Page Design

The purpose of this report is to compare two different web designs. The reason for this is to decide what kind of web page is most likely to attract new customers and to encourage existing customers to buy more products from us.

We asked two developers to produce alternative web pages for our company. We asked Developer A to produce a simple, easy-to-use design and we asked Developer B to produce a more sophisticated design with lots of eye-catching graphics. We conducted our research by asking a group of twenty existing customers and twenty non-customers to use the web page over a month. The group was made up of people with a range of ages, professions, incomes and computer expertise. We divided the group in two and asked one sub-group to use Design A and the other to use Design B. We asked each sub-group to log on once a day and to use the web page to perform certain tasks, including: buying products, getting information, returning damaged products and tracking deliveries. We also asked the sub-groups to assess how attractive they found their designs and whether they would be encouraged to return to the web page.

In addition, we researched the devices people used and the connection speeds available. We asked each group to note how long it took to download the web pages and to make an order.

We found that, on the whole, people preferred to be able to purchase products quickly and easily. In conclusion, users do not visit a site such as ours for entertainment. While they initially enjoyed some of the aspects of Design B, these could take a long time to load and users eventually became bored.

We recommend that we adopt Design A with two or three of the more practical features from Design B.

## LANGUAGE BANK

### Stating objectives
*The purpose/aim/objective of this report is to…*
*This report aims to…*
*This reports presents/gives information on…*

### Outlining research
*We asked (two developers) to…*
*We conducted our research by… (e.g. asking a group of…)*
*We examined/looked at/researched… (e.g. the problem/the cost/several companies)*
*We surveyed… (e.g. a total of 250 employees)*
*We compared A and B.*
*The group was made up of…*

### Presenting findings
*We found that, on the whole,…*
*According to the majority of respondents…*
*Overall, people preferred…*
*50% of those surveyed said (that)…*

### Giving conclusions
*In conclusion…*
*The research shows/demonstrates (that)…*
*The research shows/demonstrates + noun (e.g. the effect of…)*
*From the research/the evidence we conclude that…*

### Giving recommendations
*We recommend that…*
*It is recommended that…*
*The best solution is/would be to…*
*(e.g. to adopt design A)*
*The best solution is/would be + noun (e.g. a reduction in office hours)*
*If we do A, we will see B.*
*This will have an impact on + noun (e.g. costs/productivity/the business)*

# Writing a book or film review

The main purpose of a review is to describe and explain the main elements of a book or film (plot, character, themes, etc.) and express a personal opinion about them. The reader should get a clear impression of what the book's or film's good and bad points are, and the review should include a recommendation to read the book or see the film or not.

---

## Wuthering Heights by Emily Brontë

Is it a darkly passionate tale of love? Or should we call it a highly original gothic story? The classic novel *Wuthering Heights* by Emily Brontë is, in my opinion, a unique and gripping blend of these genres. Written in 1847, it is an epic family saga full of desire, hate, revenge and regret, focusing on the main characters of Heathcliff and Catherine. The atmospheric setting of the wild Yorkshire moors cleverly mirrors these violent emotions.

When Catherine's father adopts the starving orphan boy Heathcliff, Catherine's brother Hindley feels deeply hurt and resentful. She, on the other hand, develops an immensely strong bond with Heathcliff, which becomes an all-consuming love. Upon her father's death, Hindley becomes the head of the family and forces Heathcliff to assume the position of a servant. Despite loving Heathcliff, Catherine chooses to marry Edgar Linton, who is closer to her class and position in society. It is this decision that leads to heartbreak and tragedy, not only for them but for many others.

Heathcliff could be described as an anti-hero with his rough manners and lack of control. Likewise, Catherine displays many flaws, but the reader can still empathize with these characters. In fact, this is the main reason why I believe this novel is so brilliant. It rings with truth. The reader may be horrified at the way that Heathcliff and Catherine behave, and yet, at the same time, the writer ensures that we never hate them because the reasons for their actions are crystal clear.

The main part of the book relies on a narrator, Ellen Dean, who is a servant at Wuthering Heights and I think that this is a useful device which holds the complex plot together. However, *Wuthering Heights* is not what I would call an 'easy read'. There is dense description and some of the dialogue is written in dialect, which can be difficult to follow.

Nevertheless, I persevered and, all in all, I can highly recommend *Wuthering Heights*. I challenge you to remain unmoved after reading this exceptional book.

---

### Annotations

- **Asking a question** is one way to engage the reader. Or you could start with a personal opinion.
- This is one of many synonyms of 'interesting'. Look at the note at the dictionary entry 'interesting'.
- It is usual to use the present tense to describe the story.
- Most nouns can be enhanced with an adjective—but make sure it is a natural collocation.
- **Linking words** aid organization and clearly link your ideas.
- Including information on the style of writing can be helpful.
- The **title** and **author's name** should appear in the introductory paragraph.
- Information about the **setting** and **era** can be useful.
- **Collocations** of adverb + adjective show your vocabulary knowledge. Look up 'hurt' adjective.
- Express your opinion and give reasons to support it.
- **Conclusion.** Restate your opinion of the book as a recommendation to read it or not to read it.

# Writing your review

## 1. Read or re-read the book or watch the film and make notes

Your notes should try to answer the questions a reader might have:
- What kind of book/film is it?
- What happens in the story?
- Who are the main characters?
- What is the main theme?
- Is it well written/directed/acted?
- Would you recommend this book/film?

## 2. Organize your notes

You can use the same plan as the model review (see below). A successful review will contain these elements, but the order can be changed.

Paragraph ① **Introduction.** General comments about the book or film.

Paragraph ② **Plot.** A brief summary of what happens.

Paragraph ③ **Characters.** A description and comment on the main characters.

Paragraph ④ **Other information.** Details about the setting or historical background are useful for the reader or viewer.

Paragraph ⑤ **Conclusion.** Include your personal recommendation here.

## 3. Write your review

Don't include too many details and don't give away the ending. It is a good idea to try to write about both positive and negative aspects of the book or film.

### Reviews of non-fiction books

The purpose of a non-fiction book review is basically the same as fiction but the potential reader will have different questions:
- What is the author's reason for writing the book?
- Is it well organized? Can you follow the argument easily and find the important information?
- Does the author support his/her findings well?
- How does it compare with other books on the same subject?

> **TIPS**
> - Remember at all times that the person who reads your review has NOT read the book or seen the film!
> - Use your dictionary to help you find synonyms of words such as **book** or **story**.
> - Find a range of adjectives to use to describe the book, plot and characters.

---

### LANGUAGE BANK

**Beginnings**

*It is a fascinating tale of…* (e.g. *rural life*)
*This moving account of…* (e.g. *a young man's experiences*)
*I found this story far-fetched and unconvincing.*

**Details/plot**

*Written in…, the story begins with…*
*The events unfold in…*
*The tale is set in…*

**Characters**

*The writer introduces us to…*
*The principal characters are…*
*My favourite character is undoubtedly…*
*The story focuses on…*
*We experience all this through the eyes of…*

**Giving your opinion**

*The writer excels at…* (e.g. *describing…*)
*I was impressed by…*
*One aspect I found a little disappointing was…*
*One possible flaw is that…*

**Conclusions**

*I would highly recommend this rewarding film.*
*I thoroughly enjoyed this book. In fact I couldn't put it down!*
*By the end of this book, you feel…*
*I was left unmoved by this story.*
*I would strongly advise against seeing this film.*

# Discussing pictures and cartoons

This task may occur in written or spoken examinations. Describing photographs or pictures can be similar to interpreting cartoons. There may not be a caption or any speech, but the photo can still have a message. You can also discuss the effect it has on you.

Look at the cartoon and read the interpretation below.

*'It is good to see people doing their bit for the environment!'*

① The cartoon shows a bird's-eye view of part of a European city or town. There is a large factory, several rows of houses, two vehicles and some people.[1] In the foreground, there is a rubbish collection truck, with two men collecting household waste for recycling. On the left of the cartoon, a man is putting a bottle in a street recycling bin. Watching him are two other men who are obviously managers in the local factory.[2] The caption reads 'It is good to see people doing their bit for the environment!'[3]

② The caption is clearly the words that one of the factory managers is saying to his colleague, because the focus of attention is on them and also on the man with the bottle: all three of them are drawn in detail[1] and they also stand out because of the black clothing they are wearing.[2]

③ Another important element in the cartoon is the factory and the pollution from its chimneys. The cartoonist has exaggerated the size of the factory in relation to the surrounding houses and has also exaggerated the pollution by blackening a wide expanse of sky.[3] These aspects of the picture show the way that the pollution from the factory dominates the town and causes a serious environmental impact.

④ The factory itself is a symbol representing industry in general.[4] It seems that the man who is dropping off his one empty bottle in the recycling bin has driven there in his car, so he has probably damaged the environment more than if he had just thrown the bottle away. He represents ordinary people.[4]

⑤ The cartoon is about our attitude to the environment. It is clear that the cartoonist is suggesting that while people focus on small-scale activities, such as recycling household waste, they are ignoring much more serious environmental problems such as the pollution from industries and from cars.[1] He/she uses irony to show that we are becoming complacent about saving the environment. This is done by contrasting what the factory managers are saying with what is really happening all around them: serious pollution that they themselves are responsible for.

⑥ Personally, I believe that the cartoonist is right. Many people are now very good about recycling their household waste. But, because we do this, we have become complacent about pollution and feel we are doing enough to protect the environment. We need also to address other more important sources of environmental damage.

**Description** Paragraph ①
[1] General description
[2] Detailed description
[3] Caption or speech bubble

**Interpretation** Paragraphs ②–④
[1] Technique 1–detail
[2] Technique 2–emphasis
[3] Technique 3–exaggeration
[4] Technique 4–symbolism

**Message** Paragraph ⑤
[1] Use of irony

**Personal reaction** Paragraph ⑥

Key
■ shows the key language in each section.   ■ focuses on prepositions and phrasal verbs.

# Writing a description and interpretation

Follow these steps when you prepare for this task. Think about the questions and make notes; then, when you write, use some of the phrases in the *Language banks*.

## Stage 1—Description

### The scene:
- What is the scene in the cartoon/picture?
- Where is it?
- What are the main features?

### Details:
- Who/What is in the picture?
- What are they doing?
- What is happening?

### LANGUAGE BANK
*The scene is of…* (e.g. *a cafe in which two people…*)
*The cartoon shows/depicts…*
*There is/are…* (e.g. *two people who look angry.*)
*In the centre of the cartoon is/are…, (who/which…)*
*At the top/bottom of the cartoon is/are…*
*On the left/right…*
*In the foreground/background…*
*The central feature of the cartoon is…*
You can use prepositions e.g. **behind** *the houses*
Avoid using: ~~I/You can see…~~ ; ~~In the picture…~~

#### TIPS
- Only describe the details that are important for the message.
- Try to avoid using short simple sentences such as: ~~In the centre is a man. He is shouting.~~ **Relative clauses** are particularly useful: *In the centre is a man who is shouting.*

### The caption or speech bubble:
- What is written in the caption or in any speech bubbles?
- Who is talking and to whom?

### LANGUAGE BANK
*The caption reads '…'*
*One man is saying to the other '…'*
*The woman is asking whether…*
*He/She is commenting that…*
*He/She is wondering whether… (to go/he/she should go…)*

## Stage 2—Interpretation

#### TIP
Start a new paragraph for this section. Give evidence and reasons for your interpretation.

### Artistic techniques:
How does the artist draw attention to important parts of the cartoon/picture? Does he/she use:
- detail? Where?
- emphasis? What is emphasized? How?
- exaggeration? What is exaggerated?
- symbolism? Which objects or people are symbols? What do they mean?

### LANGUAGE BANK
*The focus of attention is on…*
*X is/are drawn in detail, (which shows/to show…)*
*X stand(s) out because of the…*
*The most important element in the cartoon is…*
*This aspect of the cartoon indicates…*
*The X symbolize(s)/represent(s)…*
*The cartoonist has exaggerated X (in order to…/because…)*
*The reason for this is that…*
Use your dictionary to find synonyms so that you use a wide range of vocabulary, e.g. *clearly/obviously; indicate/show*

### Message:
- What is the cartoon/picture really about?
- What is the artist trying to say?
- How does he/she try to persuade you? Does he/she use irony (contrasting the way the cartoon shows things with the way they really are) or analogy (using a simple situation to make a more complex situation clear)?

### LANGUAGE BANK
*The cartoon is about/refers to/deals with…*
*The cartoon has to do with…*
*The cartoonist is obviously trying to show…*
*What the cartoon is saying is that…*
*I take/understand the cartoon to mean that…*

## Stage 3—Personal reaction
- Do you agree or disagree with the message?
- Why?

### LANGUAGE BANK
- *Personally, I believe that the cartoonist is right.*
- *I only partly/partially agree with the artist's message because…*
- *In my opinion/view, the artist is wrong, because…*
- Use phrases such as *I think…; In my opinion…;* or *It seems to me that…*
- Do not use ~~According to me/my opinion…~~

Discussing pictures and cartoons

Cambridge Assessment English: B2 First

# Writing an article

In some exams you are asked to write an article for a fictional magazine or website. You are required to use your imagination and write in a particular style that engages the reader. It could mean writing about a hobby or something you are passionate about, making recommendations about something related to culture or lifestyle, or giving your opinion on a current issue. The language is usually informal and more similar to spoken English rather than formal academic English. Here are some points to bear in mind.

## Preparing to write

### Reader's attention

Think of an imaginative title using an unusual or surprising word.

Catch the reader's attention in the introduction with an interesting fact.

### Interest

Brainstorm some ideas, keep the best four and delete the rest.

> **lifehacks**
> ✓ lots of small changes – like Olympic athlete
> ✓ plan your day
> ~~get more exercise~~
> ✓ take mini breaks – turn off your phone
> ✓ learn sth new – a language – how to do sth
> ~~spend quality time with friends/family~~
> cook properly

Include a fact or idea that your reader will find useful.

Provide examples from real life.

Try to keep up the reader's interest from the beginning through to the end.

### Style

Keep the style relatively informal—avoid any formal or academic language.

Use short sentences that all add value to the article. If a sentence doesn't add anything, cut it out.

Remember to keep to the word limit. Writing more will just waste precious time.

### Target audience

The article should be written for a target audience who may be specified in the exam question.

Address them directly and use terms and phrases that make your reader feel you understand them.

Don't be afraid to express your opinion and give the reader something to think about.

### Use of English

Demonstrate your ability to use a range of vocabulary and structures.

See the *Language bank* for ideas about how to make your language more engaging.

### Organization

Divide ideas into paragraphs—around four is best.

The introduction should introduce the main idea. Keep it short and simple.

The main section should build on the main idea and provide examples.

Use the conclusion to link back to the original idea in the introduction.

> **TIP**
> Do you know what a rhetorical question is? It's a question that you ask for effect, not because you expect an answer. Asking rhetorical questions can help readers engage more directly with your article. You can ask a question at the beginning of the article and lead the reader to an answer by the end.

# Writing the article

You see this advertisement on an English-language website.

> Articles wanted for our new lifestyle magazine. Write your article in 140–190 words using the appropriate style.
>
> What smart or interesting ways can you think of that would help people improve their lifestyles? How can they be more organized? How can they improve their diet? How can they be more productive?

## Lifehacks

Have you ever felt you could improve your lifestyle? Imagine you are an Olympic athlete analysing your training and performance, looking for ways to improve everything by a small amount—better shoes, more effective training, stronger muscles. The end result is a combination of lots of mini improvements or 'hacks' that help you stay ahead. Would you like to be a champion? Here's how.

First things first. Don't get up at the last minute and rush out of the house. Get up ten minutes earlier. Use the time to plan and decide on your main aim for the day. Feel relaxed and prepared when you open the front door.

During the day, take five minutes off. No distractions. Turn off your smartphone. Don't talk to anyone and don't look at any texts or messages. Just let your mind relax. When you get back to your desk you'll be ready for the next big challenge.

When you get home don't just heat up a pizza and watch TV—cook something you've never cooked before. Read something rather than watch TV. Watch a YouTube video and learn a language or find out how to fix your bike. Go to bed tired and happy knowing you've made the most of your day and improved your lifestyle—just a little bit.

---

Ask rhetorical questions to help the reader engage directly with the article.

Use short sentences for dramatic effect. You can include just one or two that don't even have a verb.

You can use imperatives and 'you' and 'your' to address the reader directly.

---

## LANGUAGE BANK

### Asking rhetorical questions
Have you ever felt …?
How would you feel if …?
Are you one of those people who …?
Do you ever think …?
Would you like …?

### Using dramatic language
Let me tell you why I **love** skydiving.
Yes, it's **terrifying**, but it's also **exhilarating**.
I was **completely exhausted** at the end of the day.
It is **vital** that you learn from a qualified instructor.

### Organizing your ideas
I'd like to introduce the idea of …
Let's start with …
Another advantage of …
On top of that, …

### Giving your own opinion
I think that / In my opinion …
It seems to me that …
If you ask me, …
To my mind, …

# Writing letters and emails

Letters and emails share many characteristics in terms of function and language. An email can be just as formal as a formal letter, or it can be neutral or informal (as can a letter).

## Levels of formality

### When to use formal, neutral and informal language

When you write a letter or email you first need to consider how well you know the reader. Is he/she someone you:

- are writing to for the first time or have never met? (formal or neutral)
- have written to or met before? (neutral)
- know very well, e.g. a friend or a close family member? (informal)

You also need to consider your relationship or status relative to the reader. Is he/she:

- a senior person of status, e.g. an academic, a manager, a doctor, etc.? (formal)
- someone who provides a service; someone in business outside your company? (neutral)
- someone with the same or similar status as you, e.g. a classmate, colleague at work or a friend? (informal)

The level of formality will determine the types of words and phrases you use in your correspondence.

### Forms of address and use of names

When writing for the first time to someone senior who has a relatively high status, for example a university professor, the appropriate form of address is *Dear Professor Kingston* rather than *Hi, Jim*. Other forms of address are:

*Dear Sir / Madam* (reader is unknown)
*Dear Dr Clark* (formal)
*Dear Jonathan* (neutral, informal)
*Hi Jo* (informal)

### Closing

Closing phrases follow a similar format to forms of address.

*Yours faithfully* (reader is unknown)
*Yours sincerely* (formal, neutral)
*Best regards, Best wishes, Regards, All the best* (neutral, informal)
*Love, Lots of love* (family and friends)

## Full and short forms

Full forms are used in formal letters and emails. Short forms are acceptable in neutral or informal correspondence.

| Full form | Short form / Abbreviation |
|---|---|
| I have been | I've been |
| They would have | They'd have |
| Thank you | Thanks |
| information | info |

### Requests and invitations

In general, longer phrases indicate a higher level of formality while shorter, more direct phrases are used in less formal situations.

| Formal | Informal |
|---|---|
| I would be very grateful if you could … | Can you …? |
| I would like to … / I wanted to … | I want to … |
| Would you care to join us for …? | Do you want to come to …? |

### Formal or informal words and phrases

There are many different words and phrases that are generally categorized as formal or informal.

Idioms and phrasal verbs tend to be less formal than longer words of Latin origin.

| Formal | Informal |
|---|---|
| increase | go up |
| acceptable | OK |
| authorize | give the go ahead |
| I hope you are well. | How's it going? |
| He is extremely busy. | He's up to his ears. |
| Could you contact Jo Hanson? | Can you get in touch with Jo? |

### Exclamation marks, emoticons and incomplete sentences (ellipsis)

We only use these in informal emails.
*Your presentation yesterday was amazing!*
*I really enjoyed your talk on Monday* ☺
*Great lecture on Monday.*
*Loved your selfie.*

# Formal letters

The important things to remember about writing a formal letter are the layout and the language, which both follow a set of conventions.

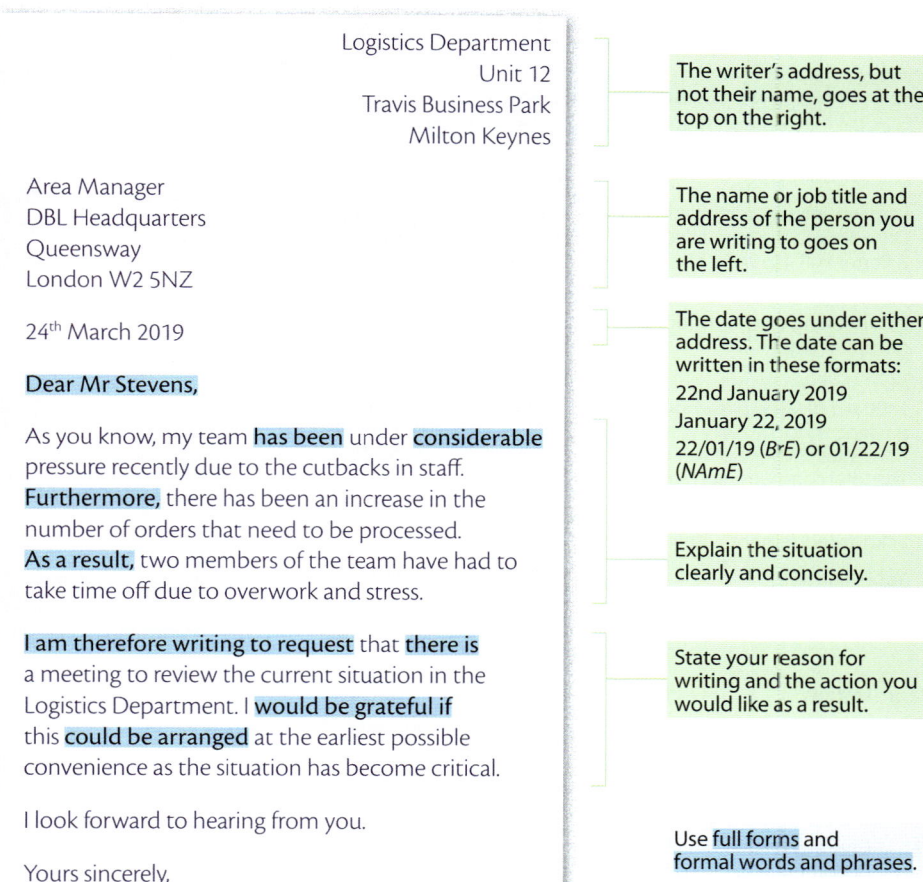

**The writer's address, but not their name, goes at the top on the right.**

**The name or job title and address of the person you are writing to goes on the left.**

**The date goes under either address. The date can be written in these formats:**
22nd January 2019
January 22, 2019
22/01/19 (BrE) or 01/22/19 (NAmE)

**Explain the situation clearly and concisely.**

**State your reason for writing and the action you would like as a result.**

**Use full forms and formal words and phrases.**

## LANGUAGE BANK

### Openings
*Dear Mr Stevens* ('*Dear*', *title, family name*)
*Dear Sir*
*Dear Madam*

### Closings
*I look forward to hearing from you.*
*Yours sincerely* (*BrE* if you began *Dear Mr/Mrs/Ms…*)
*Yours faithfully* (*BrE* if you began *Dear Sir/Madam*)
*Sincerely/Sincerely yours/Yours truly* (*NAmE*)
*Michelle Edwards* (*first name and family name*)

### Full forms
*has been* (*'s been*)
*I am* (*I'm*)
*there is* (*there's*)

### Formal words and phrases
*considerable* (*lots of*)
*furthermore* (*and*)
*as a result* (*so*)
*would be grateful if* (*want*)
*could be arranged* (*you arrange this*)

# Emails

Emails can be used for formal correspondence such as job applications, neutral everyday correspondence, and informal messages between friends and colleagues.

In the model email, related to a complaint about service, the style is formal. The main aim of the email is to provide the relevant information and state clearly what the writer wants the customer service department to do.

| To | ZippyJet Customer Service Department |
|---|---|
| Subject | Compensation claim for a disrupted flight |

*Use a short, informative subject line, not single general words, e.g. Urgent or Enquiry.*

Dear Sir/Madam,

① **I am writing** regarding flight LZ238 on July 2nd, 2018 from London to Orlando with the scheduled departure time of 13.45. My booking reference is Porter POT 1359AZ. This flight arrived 3 hours late at Orlando airport. The passengers in the party were myself and Helen and James Porter.

*Use the same neutral form of address as a letter.*

② **I am seeking compensation** under EU Regulation 261/2004 for this disrupted flight.

*Key language*

③ My scheduled flight length was 7000 kilometres, therefore I am seeking €400 per delayed passenger in my party. During the disruption the passengers in my party were not provided with any refreshments and I have attached receipts for the cost of purchasing our own refreshments. The total compensation sought is €1235.

*Use Yours faithfully when you don't know the name of the person you are writing to.*

④ **I look forward to hearing from you and would welcome an acknowledgement within 7 days.**

Yours faithfully,

S R Porter (Dr)

*Use your initials and family name or your first name and family name.*

| Para | Details |
|---|---|
| ① | Explain clearly what you are writing about and provide any key information.<br>Key phrase: *I am writing regarding …* |
| ② | Clearly state the main aim of the email.<br>Key phrase: *I am seeking compensation for …* |
| ③ | Give any further details that support your claim. Include details of any invoices or supporting documents that you are enclosing. |
| ④ | Say directly but politely what you want the reader to do.<br>Key phrase: *I look forward to hearing from you and would welcome an acknowledgement within 7 days.* |

# Politeness

Politeness refers to appropriate and socially acceptable forms of behaviour and language. One element of politeness is the use of indirect language and polite phrases to avoid making people feel ashamed or embarrassed. Politeness also involves avoiding any words or phrases that suggest emotions such as frustration or anger.

| Impolite | Polite |
|---|---|
| I hate loud music. Turn it down! | Could you possibly turn the music down after 11 p.m., please? |
| Where's the hotel? | Could you let me have the address of the hotel? |
| Send me the invoice immediately. | I would be grateful if you could send me the invoice at your earliest convenience. |

# Formal letters

The important things to remember about writing a formal letter are the layout and the language, which both follow a set of conventions.

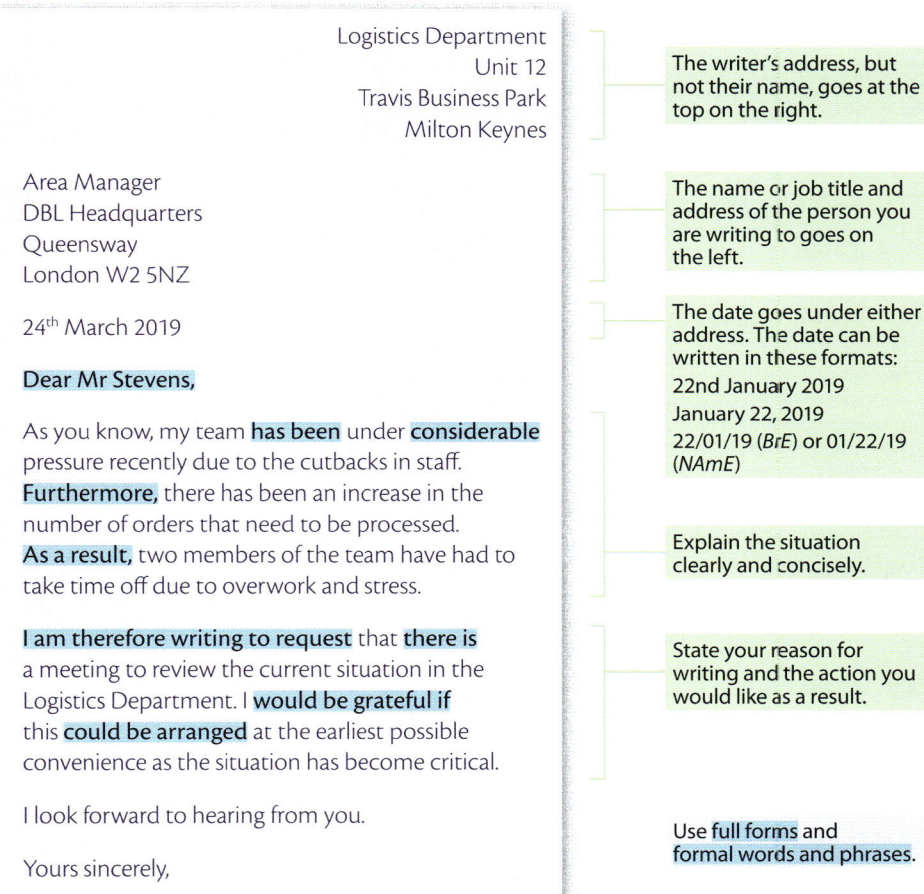

Logistics Department
Unit 12
Travis Business Park
Milton Keynes

*The writer's address, but not their name, goes at the top on the right.*

Area Manager
DBL Headquarters
Queensway
London W2 5NZ

*The name or job title and address of the person you are writing to goes on the left.*

24th March 2019

*The date goes under either address. The date can be written in these formats:*
*22nd January 2019*
*January 22, 2019*
*22/01/19 (BrE) or 01/22/19 (NAmE)*

Dear Mr Stevens,

As you know, my team **has been** under **considerable** pressure recently due to the cutbacks in staff. **Furthermore,** there has been an increase in the number of orders that need to be processed. **As a result,** two members of the team have had to take time off due to overwork and stress.

*Explain the situation clearly and concisely.*

**I am therefore writing to request** that **there is** a meeting to review the current situation in the Logistics Department. I **would be grateful if** this **could be arranged** at the earliest possible convenience as the situation has become critical.

*State your reason for writing and the action you would like as a result.*

I look forward to hearing from you.

Yours sincerely,

Michelle Edwards

Logistics Department Manager

*Use full forms and formal words and phrases.*

## LANGUAGE BANK

### Openings
Dear Mr Stevens ('Dear', title, family name)
Dear Sir
Dear Madam

### Closings
I look forward to hearing from you.
Yours sincerely (BrE if you began Dear Mr/Mrs/Ms…)
Yours faithfully (BrE if you began Dear Sir/Madam)
Sincerely/Sincerely yours/Yours truly (NAmE)
Michelle Edwards (first name and family name)

### Full forms
has been (~~'s been~~)
I am (~~I'm~~)
there is (~~there's~~)

### Formal words and phrases
considerable (~~lots of~~)
furthermore (~~and~~)
as a result (~~so~~)
would be grateful if (~~want~~)
could be arranged (~~you arrange this~~)

## Emails

Emails can be used for formal correspondence such as job applications, neutral everyday correspondence, and informal messages between friends and colleagues.

In the model email, related to a complaint about service, the style is formal. The main aim of the email is to provide the relevant information and state clearly what the writer wants the customer service department to do.

---

To: ZippyJet Customer Service Department
Subject: Compensation claim for a disrupted flight

*Use a short, informative subject line, not single general words, e.g. Urgent or Enquiry.*

Dear Sir/Madam,

① **I am writing** regarding flight LZ238 on July 2nd, 2018 from London to Orlando with the scheduled departure time of 13.45. My booking reference is Porter POT 1359AZ. This flight arrived 3 hours late at Orlando airport. The passengers in the party were myself and Helen and James Porter.

*Use the same neutral form of address as a letter.*

② **I am seeking compensation** under EU Regulation 261/2004 for this disrupted flight.

*Key language*

③ My scheduled flight length was 7000 kilometres, therefore I am seeking €400 per delayed passenger in my party. During the disruption the passengers in my party were not provided with any refreshments and I have attached receipts for the cost of purchasing our own refreshments. The total compensation sought is €1235.

*Use Yours faithfully when you don't know the name of the person you are writing to.*

④ **I look forward to hearing from you and would welcome an acknowledgement within 7 days.**

Yours faithfully,

S R Porter (Dr)

*Use your initials and family name or your first name and family name.*

---

| Para | Details |
|---|---|
| ① | Explain clearly what you are writing about and provide any key information.<br>Key phrase: *I am writing regarding …* |
| ② | Clearly state the main aim of the email.<br>Key phrase: *I am seeking compensation for …* |
| ③ | Give any further details that support your claim. Include details of any invoices or supporting documents that you are enclosing. |
| ④ | Say directly but politely what you want the reader to do.<br>Key phrase: *I look forward to hearing from you and would welcome an acknowledgement within 7 days.* |

## Politeness

Politeness refers to appropriate and socially acceptable forms of behaviour and language. One element of politeness is the use of indirect language and polite phrases to avoid making people feel ashamed or embarrassed. Politeness also involves avoiding any words or phrases that suggest emotions such as frustration or anger.

| Impolite | Polite |
|---|---|
| *I hate loud music. Turn it down!* | *Could you possibly turn the music down after 11 p.m., please?* |
| *Where's the hotel?* | *Could you let me have the address of the hotel?* |
| *Send me the invoice immediately.* | *I would be grateful if you could send me the invoice at your earliest convenience.* |

# An informal email

## Style
Note that the following can be used in an informal email:
- emoticons and exclamation marks
- short forms and incomplete sentences
- informal forms of address and first names

## Organization
Start the email with a general greeting.
Refer to previous emails or meetings before you introduce the main point.

## Functions
Some exams require candidates to write an email that demonstrates the ability to understand a particular situation and respond appropriately using one or more of the following functions:
- describing
- explaining
- reporting
- giving information
- suggesting
- recommending
- persuading

For example, a friend has written to you asking advice about visiting your country. The response should contain a combination of the above functions—explain the culture, describe where you live, give information about transport, etc.

Read the example situation and note how the email addresses the main points in the question.

---

*A friend has recently moved to your area. He wants some advice about eating out. He has a limited budget. Write an email to your friend and describe, explain and recommend places to eat.*

| To | Jim Henderson |
|---|---|
| Subject | Good eating places |

Hi Jim,

*How are things?* Thanks for your message—glad to hear you're settling in OK.

I had a think about your email and have a couple of suggestions for you. Firstly, *I'd recommend* a local place called Mexicana. It's on Bridge Street and *they sell really cool tacos and burritos*. It's pretty small and *not the smartest place* you've ever seen, but the food is awesome ☺

Another option is Noodles—it's the cheapest place to get all kinds of Asian dishes. So it's always *packed and really noisy*. *I recommend* the spicy noodles.

*Why don't we* meet up soon and try some places out together? Let me know when you're free and we can meet up in town.

*Have a good week.*

All the best,

Ben

- General greeting
- Descriptive phrases
- Making recommendations and suggestions
- Ending a message

---

## LANGUAGE BANK

### General greetings
*How are you?*
*How are things?*
*I hope you're well.*

### Describing
*The food is awesome.*
*They sell really cool tacos.*
*It's not the smartest place.*
*It's packed and really noisy.*

### Explaining
*I've only just got your message.*
*I've been away.*
*I've been out of town.*
(especially NAmE)

### Reporting
*I spent the weekend down in Devon with Jo.*
*The weather was glorious.*

### Giving information
*You can get there in three hours by train.*
*You get the train from London Paddington.*

### Suggesting
*Let's …*
*Why don't we …?*

### Recommending
*I'd recommend …*
*I found the staff at Mexicana really friendly.*

### Persuading
*Won't you come with us?*
*It would be great if you came too.*

### Ending a message
*Look forward to meeting up.*
*Have a good week.*
*Good luck with your exam.*

# Writing academic emails

- Academic emails are usually personal, not official. You are writing to a specific, named individual, not to somebody in their official role.
- Make sure that you use the appropriate level of formality. If you are writing to an academic for the first time, use formal language, particularly if they are outside your university or department.
- If you know the person you are writing to well, you can be less formal.
- If you need to make a request, you should take care to use polite language and avoid inconveniencing the reader or putting them under pressure.

## Formal—A request from a student to an academic from a different department

Low-status writer to high-status reader whom he does not know.

Tone: Personal, very formal, very polite

| | |
|---|---|
| Use a clear, brief subject line. | **Subject: Request for statistical help** |
| | Dear Dr Barr |
| Introduce yourself by giving your position in the university. | I am a first year PhD student in the department of linguistics and my research topic is a quantitative study of verb forms in academic writing. |
| Say why you are writing, giving brief supporting/background information. Mention any academic contact. | As I need to use advanced statistical tools for processing the data, my supervisor, Dr John Pugh, suggested I contact you to ask for advice. |
| *Would it be possible* (very polite) OR: *Could I possibly* (NOT: *I kindly request*) | Would it be possible for me to come and see you to discuss what I need? Or if you are too busy to meet, perhaps we could talk on the phone? I attach a copy of my draft research proposal to give you an idea of the scope of my study. |
| Ending: very polite OR: *I would really appreciate your help.* (NOT: *Thank you for your time/attention.*—used only in spoken English.) Do not repeat your request. | I would be very grateful indeed for any help you could give me. |
| | Best wishes |
| | David Brown<br>024 7654 3210 |

- Greeting: use *Dear* + academic title and family name, or Mr, Ms, etc. and family name.
- Give an option—remember the person you are writing to may be busy. Only ask for something that is relatively easy for them to do.
- Show that you have been working hard, as far as you are able.
- Close: polite OR: *Best regards, Regards.* Give your full name. Add position and contact details if necessary.

## Less formal—request from a student to their own supervisor

Lower-status writer to higher-status reader whom she knows very well.

Tone: Personal, polite, less formal

| | |
|---|---|
| Subject: you can use ? to show a request. | **Subject: Meeting this week?** |
| | Dear Ruth |
| A way of introducing a polite indirect request. Use it to remind somebody of higher status about something. | I was wondering if you've had a chance to look at my paper yet. If so, could we have a meeting some time this week? The best day for me would be Tues. I start my fieldwork at the end of the week and it would be very useful to have some feedback before then. |
| *Could, would*: These are less abrupt/direct forms. | |
| Abbreviations may be used in less formal emails. | Many thanks |
| | Nicole |

- Greeting: first names can be used as they know each other well.
- Acknowledge the possibility that your supervisor is busy.
- Justify the need for your request. Reasons that are out of your control or that are institutional are more effective than personal preference.
- Close: informal—Nicole has the right to ask for a meeting.

# Writing CVs and résumés

CVs and résumés are essential documents for the initial stage of applying for a job. They are both accounts of someone's education, qualifications, skills and work experience.

In the US, a résumé is a short summary of a person's experience and qualifications, while a CV is more often used for academic positions and is a longer, more comprehensive document. In the UK, a CV is similar to an American résumé and is a summary of an applicant's education and work experience that is adapted to the job being applied for. For all types of CV and résumé, the information given must be up to date and accurate.

## CVs (curriculum vitae)

A CV should include all the relevant experience, skills and qualifications for the job being applied for as well as details of your education starting from your final year at school. You can draw out further relevant experience and highlight your skills in the covering letter that accompanies the CV.

**TIPS**
- Make your CV attractive and easy to read: use a clear typeface in at least 10pt.
- Ask someone to read and edit the CV for you.

---

Name          Emily Jane Wilson
Address       29 Greenlands Avenue, London, SW3 6RF
Telephone     01924 786512 Mobile 07799 238182
Email         em_wilson@scapenet.com

**Profile**    A dynamic and articulate graduate with work experience in both television and teaching.

**Education and qualifications**
2019–         MA in Media Studies. Bristol University. Expected 2020
2015–2019     BA in Media Studies with French (2:1) Bristol University
2007–2014     Beacon School, London
              3 A levels: Drama (A); French (A); German (B)
              5 AS levels 9 GCSEs

**Work experience**
October 2017   *Language assistant*
–June 2018     Taught English in secondary school in France to large classes and small groups.
               Ran a film club and a holiday dance and drama club.
               Assisted with school drama productions.

September 2014 *Production assistant*
–August 2015   Oordman and Associates Film-makers, London N16.
               Performed office and on-set duties.

June           *Dance tutor*
–September 2014 Jacaranda Drama Workshops.
               Led groups of teenagers of different backgrounds in dance and drama activities.

July–August 2013  *Holiday campsite host*
               Adventure Camping holiday campsite in France.
               Led the children's club for 4- to 10-year-olds and performed various practical duties on the campsite.

**Skills**
   Languages: French—near native-speaker fluency (CEFR C1); German (B2).
   Good keyboard skills. Familiarity with Word, Excel and film editing packages.
   Clean driving licence.

**Interests**
   Drama, both acting and directing; singing (was member of university choral society).
   Regular volunteer at a local centre for the homeless.

---

**Personal information**
You can omit the labels. There is no need to mention your age, gender, nationality, race, religion or marital status. Don't send a photo unless you are asked to.

**Profile**
You do not have to include this, but it gives an employer an idea of who you are.

**Education**
Put the most recent first. Add prizes and awards. Try to give British equivalents of your qualifications.

**Work experience**
Put this in reverse order. Experienced candidates should put this before Education and write more about their most recent post.

**Skills**
Your practical abilities. Include exams passed. Write more here if you are experienced.

**Interests**
Keep this short. Include a sport, a creative and a community activity if you can. Avoid vague subjects such as *reading* or *travel*.

# Résumés

A résumé is a summary of the information in your CV that matches the job you are applying for. It should be no more than one page.

The 'Objective' section can be used to summarize your goals and customize your résumé for specific positions. State a realistic short-term goal and/or a job for which you are currently qualified.

---

Jessica M. Brown
jmbrown@mba.nau.edu

| | |
|---|---|
| Address: | 508 Blackbird's Roost, Flagstaff, AZ, U.S.A. 86011 |
| Telephone: | +1 929 555 1212 |
| OBJECTIVE | To obtain an entry-level management position within an international hospitality organization. |
| PROFILE | An outgoing and articulate post-graduate with experience in the travel business and children's summer camps. |
| EDUCATION | Masters in Business Administration (M.B.A.), 2017–2019<br>Northern Arizona University, Flagstaff, Arizona, U.S.A.<br>B.A. in International Hospitality, 2013–2017<br>Université de Savoie, Chambéry, France |
| EXPERIENCE | **Travel Agent, Sep. 2017–Present**<br>Kokopelli Extreme Tours, Sedona, Arizona, U.S.A.<br>Organized adventure package tours for large student groups, trained and supervised new staff members, and maintained partner relationships. Showed ability to work well as part of a team.<br>**Camp Counselor, Jun 2013–Aug 2017**<br>Voyageurs Summer Camp, Voglans, France<br>Group leader for children aged 10–15. Demonstrated can-do attitude by developing curriculum for campers and led overnight hiking trips. |
| HONORS | Agent of the Month, Kokopelli Extreme Tours, March 2018.<br>Voted 'Most Popular Counselor,' Voyageurs, 2014 & 2015. |
| SKILLS | Fluent in French and English; conversational Spanish. |
| INTERESTS | Enjoy hiking, climbing and outdoor photography. |

---

## LANGUAGE BANK

### Action verbs
Use action verbs to describe your achievements and make them look more dynamic.

Examples: *achieved, administered, advised, analysed, arranged, compiled, conducted, coordinated, created, designed, developed, devised, distributed, evaluated, examined, executed, implemented, increased, instructed, introduced, liaised, managed, mentored, monitored, negotiated, organized, oversaw, prepared, recommended, reduced, represented, researched, solved, supervised, trained.*

### Positive adjectives
Use positive adjectives to describe yourself.

Examples: *active, adaptable, committed, competent, dynamic, effective, efficient, enthusiastic, experienced, flexible, (highly) motivated, organized, professional, proficient, qualified, successful.*

### Other useful phrases
Skills
*Native French speaker
Near-native command of English
Good spoken and written German
Computer literate
Familiar with HTML
Experienced trainer and facilitator*

### Education and experience
*Baccalauréat, série C (equivalent of A levels in Maths and Physics)
The qualifications described below do not have exact equivalents in the British/American system.
Four weeks' work experience at…
Summer internship at a marketing firm.*

### Personal qualities
*Work well as part of a team
Work well under pressure
Able to meet deadlines
Welcome new challenges
Can-do attitude*

# Writing a covering letter

A covering letter (*NAmE* cover letter) accompanies a CV/résumé or an application form. It can be a letter, an email, or part of an online form, but the content and language will be essentially the same. In Britain and North America they are usually typed on a single page. A good letter uses formal language and presents some key arguments for why you are a strong candidate. This is achieved by relating your skills and experience to the requirements of the job being applied for.

---

**Senior Accounts Clerk**, Chambers Estates Ltd.
£24,000—£26,000 a year

The main purpose of this role is to support the Assistant Team Leader with supervising the day-to-day activities of the customer accounts team and deliver a positive customer service experience through effective individual effort and teamwork. Key responsibilities include:

- Checking account records for Client Companies
- Providing support to the Property Management team on financial matters
- Performing any bank payments as requested

---

Dear Mrs Hunter

① Senior Accounts Clerk
I am writing to apply for the post of senior accounts clerk advertised in the *Cambridge Evening News* of 17 January.

② As you will see from my enclosed CV I am currently an accounts clerk in a medium-sized printing firm. In addition to my normal bookkeeping duties, I am responsible for invoicing and chasing up late payments. I also deal with credit checks on potential customers.

③ I am committed to pursuing a career in management accounting and am currently studying for further professional qualifications by distance learning. I am particularly interested in your post as it would enable me to gain experience of working in a larger company with the opportunities for professional training and development that this brings. In addition to my skills and experience as an accounts clerk, I would bring to the post a proven ability to deal successfully and tactfully with customers and clients.

④ I am available for interview for the next three weeks.

I look forward to hearing from you.

Yours sincerely

*Adil Desai*
Adil Desai

---

① State your purpose for writing. Say which job you are applying for and how/where you heard about it.

② Outline your current job and responsibilities. Make it relevant to the post you are applying for.

③ Say why you want the job and what you can bring to the company. It is very important to say what *you* can do for *them*.

④ Give other relevant information and when you are available for interview.

---

### Key phrases

In a cover letter use the words **post**, **position** or **vacancy**, not *job*.

Avoid contracted forms such as *I'm*.

Use *Yours faithfully* to close if you began *Dear Sir* or *Madam*.

Sign your name and print it in full underneath.

### LANGUAGE BANK

**Introduction**
*I am writing to apply for the post of … as advertised …*

**Details of current job**
*I am currently …*
*I also deal with …*
*I am responsible for …*

**Future aims**
*I am committed to pursuing a career in …*
*I am particularly interested in …*

**Assets**
*I would bring a proven ability to …*
*My extensive experience of … would be …*

**Availability**
*I am available for interview …*

# Oxford Speaking Tutor

The dictionary can be just as helpful to you when you are preparing to speak as it is when you are writing. These pages show you how you can use it when you are getting ready for an oral exam, or when you have to give a talk, or when you are just interacting with other people in English. If you have access to the dictionary online, you will be able to listen to the model answers and do a range of interactive activities.

## Improving your conversational English

In the main part of the dictionary, you will find 'Express yourself' boxes with language that will be useful in many situations. For example, if you want to ask somebody to do something for you, you can find polite ways of making requests. In meetings at work as well as simply in conversation with friends, you have to put forward your own opinions and discuss other people's suggestions. In the Speaking Tutor you will find examples of this kind of conversation.

## Working on pronunciation

The main part of the dictionary gives you information on how to pronounce all the headwords, with a reminder of what the symbols stand for at the bottom of the page and an explanation on page R30. There is much more information and practice on pronunciation in the online OALD.

## Preparing for speaking tests

### 1. Revise the subject vocabulary

If you have an idea of the kind of topic that may come up in your oral exam, you can revise relevant vocabulary using the dictionary. For example, use the **WORDFINDER** notes to direct you to more vocabulary on the same topic. You will find examples of these notes at **adventure**, **advertise**, **age** and many more entries throughout the dictionary.

### 2. Practise the functional language

Besides looking at vocabulary to do with the topics you may have to talk about, you can revise the kind of language that is needed in discussions or for presenting information or preferences. In many exams you will be asked to put forward your opinions and to justify choices. Prepare this by looking at the **EXPRESS YOURSELF** notes, such as those at **why** or **think**. If your test is done with a partner, you may have to have a discussion, and the language in notes such as those at **agree** or **disagree** will be useful. You may be given a picture or a written cue as a starting point. The note at **speculate** suggests how you can present your ideas when you have to say what you think something might be about, or what might be happening.

You will not be able to produce perfect English sentences all the time, but there are strategies that you can use to keep the presentation or conversation going. There is more information on this on page ST10.

### 3. Practise your pronunciation

Keep a note of words that you find difficult to pronounce and revise them before the exam.

Remember that words are often pronounced differently from the way they are spelt. For example, you don't pronounce the red letters in these words:

cas**t**le   clim**b**er   dou**b**t   fo**l**k   **h**onest

Remember that some pairs of words have exactly the same spelling but are pronounced differently, for example:

**read** (present or past), **row**, **live** (verb or adjective), **object** (noun or verb)

Use the dictionary to check if you are unsure of the pronunciation.

## During the speaking test

On the following pages you will find model answers for various types of oral exam, with advice on how to structure your answers and information on the Common European Framework scales.

IELTS | TOEIC | TOEFL | Cambridge Assessment English: C1 Advanced, C2 Proficiency, Business Certificates | Trinity GESE

ST2

# Talking about a topic

In some exams, you are asked to talk for a short time about a topic that you are given during the test. You may have a few minutes to prepare it and to make a few notes. You could be asked to choose something that is the most important, best, most useful, etc. of its kind, and you have to describe it and explain why you have chosen it.

---

Describe a place that you sometimes visit which is very important to you.
You should say:
- where it is, how often and why you go there.
- what it is like.
- why it is so important to you.

| | |
|---|---|
| explaining where, when and why | One place that is very important in my life is my grandmother's house. She lives in a small village in the south of the country. I go there every summer, and any time when I can get away for a few days. I go there to visit my grandmother, get away from the city and relax. |
| describing the appearance and sounds of the place | The village is just a group of white houses on a hillside with a couple of shops, and it's really peaceful. There's no traffic, just the sound of goat bells, birds and insects. |
| explaining why the place is important | One reason why I like it is because it's a beautiful place. My grandmother has a lovely garden and we always sit outside in the shade of her olive trees, drinking sweet tea and chatting. It's so peaceful. But the main reason why this place is so important to me is my grandmother. She is so kind to me, and wonderful to talk to. Whenever I have a problem in my life, she has some good advice for me. Also, she's a great cook and the meals she prepares are simple but so fresh and…—rich? No, no, I mean tasty. And she's always giving me eh… What do you call them?—small plates of food during the day, so I always return home feeling calm and refreshed—and fat! |
| justifying a choice | I wouldn't like to live there, though. I prefer living in the city, definitely. I'm a city person. I couldn't live in a small village where everybody knows each other and nothing happens. I'd rather live in a busy, exciting place. But I really love visiting the village for holidays. |

---

Ways of describing something

Ways of explaining and giving your reasons

Ways of correcting yourself or finding alternative ways of expressing something

Ways of expressing your preferences

| Speaking at CEFR level B2/C1 | |
|---|---|
| ✓ Can initiate discourse, take his/her turn when appropriate and end conversation when he/she needs to. | B2 |
| ✓ Can use a limited number of cohesive devices to link his/her utterances into clear, coherent discourse. | B2 |
| ✓ Can select a suitable phrase from a readily available range of discourse functions to preface his/her remarks appropriately in order to get the floor, or to gain time and keep the floor whilst thinking. | C1 |
| ✓ Can qualify opinions and statements precisely in relation to degrees of, for example, certainty/uncertainty, belief/doubt, likelihood, etc. | C1 |

## Before the exam

Remind yourself of useful phrases by looking at the EXPRESS YOURSELF notes in the dictionary at **recommend**, **suggest**, **think**, **disagree** and **concede**.

## During the exam

### Don't

- move too far away from the task.
- agree on the first idea mentioned, without discussing the other options.
- insist on your choice without carefully considering your partner's ideas.
- spend too long talking about one option, leaving no time to consider the others.
- take the outcome too seriously—you are here to show your English, not your decision-making skills!

### Do

- listen to what the other person says and respond to it.
- use expressions like 'personally' to show you are giving a personal opinion rather than a statement of fact.
- show that you understand and appreciate the other person's suggestions.
- try to reach a decision which is satisfactory for both or all participants in the discussion.

### EXPRESS YOURSELF

**Expressing personal viewpoints**

*As far as I'm concerned, e-books are as easy to read as paper books.*

*Personally, I think the police were wrong in this case.*

*If you ask me, they should abolish border controls.*

*My feeling is that people should be allowed to take risks.*

*To be honest, I don't care which party wins the election.*

**Agreeing with or conceding a point**

- *OK, that's a good point.*
- *Yes, I think you're probably right.*
- *No, possibly not.*
- *Yes, I see what you mean.*
- *That's true!*

# Oral presentations

You may have to give an oral presentation or talk as part of your academic course, for an examination or at work. In many ways, preparing a talk is similar to preparing an essay. The guidelines below apply to most types of talk.

## Preparing an oral presentation

Good preparation is the most important factor for a successful presentation.

### First steps

- Check the **time** allowed for your talk and any **guidelines** you have been given.
- Think about the **purpose** of your talk: is it to inform, to entertain or to persuade your audience?
- Think about the **audience**. Who are they? How much do they already know? How much do you need to tell them? What will interest them?
- Decide on the **topic** if you do not know this already. If you do, decide on the specific area that you will present. Be realistic about how much you can cover in the time allowed.
- **Collect** your ideas and gather more information if you need to.

### Writing your talk

- Make notes on what you want to include. Think about what you must tell the audience, what you should tell them and what you would like to tell them if you have time.
- Produce an outline or a plan of your talk.

> **TIPS**
> - **Structure** your talk as you would an essay: have an introduction, a middle and a conclusion.
> - Use **headings** to show the different sections of your talk.

- Some people prefer to write out the whole talk like an essay. If you do this, it is better not to read this when you give your talk, but make notes as opposite and talk from those.

### Producing notes

- Make notes in English on cards or the printout of your slides that you can refer to while you are speaking.
- Open with an introduction to the title and an overview of what you want to say:

> **1. The benefits of learning a foreign language**
>
> *Show Slide 1*
>
> **Intro:**
> Good morning. My talk today examines the benefits of learning a foreign language.
>
> **Overview:**
> I intend to outline 3 imp. benefits of learning another lang.

> **2. The benefits of learning a foreign language**
>
> *Show Slide 2*
>
> The first benefit I shall describe is practical — communicate with other nationalities
>
> A further benefit is increased cultural understanding — breaks down barriers / bridges gap between cultures.
>
> The final benefit that I shall describe is improved cognitive skills — research shows → brain power

Number note card.
Note the number of the visual you will show.
Write out and highlight key words and phrases to guide your audience through your talk.

- Try to get the attention of your audience at the beginning with e.g. a story, joke or surprising fact.
- Close with a summary and an invitation for people to ask questions.
- Some people find it helpful to write out the whole introduction and conclusion.

## Preparing visual aids

Visual aids help you to communicate your talk to the audience, if they are prepared carefully and used well. For how to talk about graphs and charts, look at page WT12.

### TIPS

- If you use PowerPoint™ or similar programs, writing and diagrams must be large and clear.
- Think about the colours you use and how visible they are.
- Do not put too much information on each slide.
- If you use posters or pictures, check that the people at the back of the room will be able to see/read them.

## Examples of slides

**The benefits of learning a foreign language**    2

    **Three main benefits:**
1. Practical uses
2. Increased cultural understanding
3. Improved cognitive skills

**The benefits of learning a foreign language**    3

    **1. Practical uses for:**
- Travel
- Work
- Study

### TIPS

- Leave lots of white space.
- Use headings and bullets to show the relationship between ideas.
- Use notes, not sentences.

## Practising your talk

The more you practise, the more confident you will feel and the better your talk will be.

- First, practise your talk alone several times until you can speak fluently and confidently from your notes and keep to the time allowed.
- Then practise with one or more friends listening. Is the talk clear? Is your voice loud and clear? Are you looking at the audience?
- If you can, practise at least once with the equipment you will use.
- Use your dictionary to check pronunciation, vocabulary and grammar.

## Preparing for questions

Try to predict some of the questions your audience may ask you and practise your answers.

## EXPRESS YOURSELF

### Introduction

*Good morning. My talk today examines …*
*The subject/title of my talk/paper is …*
*Hello. Today I'm going to talk about/discuss …*
*I am here today to present …*

### Explaining structure

*In this talk I intend to outline …*
*In my talk I will discuss the main features of …*
*I am going to examine three benefits/advantages of …*
*Firstly I'll talk about … secondly/ thirdly/ then we'll look at … and finally I'll summarize …*

### Introducing each point

*The first/second/next/last point/ area…I would like to discuss is …*
*Let's start by looking at …*
*I'd now like to look at another/the second benefit of …*
*Let's look at … in a bit more detail.*

### Clarifying

*In other words,…*
*That is to say …*

### Changing the subject

*So, I have discussed …*
*Now I'd like to turn to …*
*This leads me on to …*
*Moving on to the next/second/ last benefit …*

### Concluding

*So, I have talked about …*
*I'm now going to summarize …*
*To sum up/summarize: in my talk I have …*
*In conclusion, I believe it is clear that …*
*To conclude: the benefits I have described in my talk are important and therefore I consider that …*

### Answering difficult questions

*I'm sorry, I don't quite understand your question. Could you repeat it?*
*Well, I'm not sure about that, but I think…*

# Successful communication

Having a conversation in English does not mean that you have to produce perfectly formed sentences all the time. You should not worry that you might not know the exact word for something, or that you might not understand the meaning of everything that the other person says. Even in an exam situation, you will be given credit for using strategies to keep the conversation running smoothly despite any gaps in your vocabulary or your understanding. Here are some useful ideas to help you in everyday conversations or in more formal situations.

## When you don't understand

When you are talking to someone in English, you may not understand everything they say, but you can practise focusing on what is important. If you are asking for information, think about the key words that you will expect to hear (for example, if you ask about prices or times, be prepared for numbers in the answer). Repeat it back to them to make sure you have understood correctly.

Here are some useful phrases:

### Saying that you don't understand
*Sorry, I don't (quite) understand.*
*I beg your pardon?*
*Sorry, I'm not sure I understand what you're saying.*

### Asking for repetition
*Sorry, I wonder if you could repeat that, please?*
*Sorry, what did you say your name was again?*
*Sorry, I missed what you said about meal times—can you tell me again?*

### Asking someone to speak more slowly
*Can you speak more slowly, please?*
*Could you slow down a bit?*
*Sorry, that was too fast for me.*

### Checking that you understood correctly
*Have I understood you correctly—did you say five-fifty?*
*Do you mean 'frozen', as in 'very cold'?*

### Asking what something means
*Sorry, can you tell me what 'gasket' means?*
*What is Plasticine, exactly?*

### Asking how you spell something
*Could you spell that for me, please?*
*I haven't heard that name before—how do you spell it?*

## When you don't know how to say something

Think about those words that are often used in dictionary definitions: *a type of…, a kind of…, a device for…, an organization that…, a person who…* They will help you explain what you mean even when you don't know the exact word.

### Saying it another way
*We saw a kind of animal with a long nose.*
*It's something you make with eggs.*

### Saying that you don't know
*I don't know how to say this in English—in German, we say…*
*I'm sorry, I can't think of the word in English.*

### Asking for a translation
*What is the English equivalent of 'afiyet olsun'?*
*How do you say 'siesta' in English?*

### Explaining an idea from your language
*I don't think there's an exact equivalent in English.*
*Roughly speaking, 'saudade' means when you miss a person or a place.*
*In my country, we normally say 'Que aproveche' when somebody is eating.*

### Suggesting a change of topic
*Look, I really can't think how to explain it—perhaps we should move on?*
*This is too difficult for me to talk about in English.*

## When you make a mistake

We all make mistakes when we speak, but it need not cause a problem if we can find a way to explain what we really meant. We also need time to think about what to say, but there are expressions that we can use to gain time while we do so:

### Words you can use while thinking
*… you know …*        *… what's the word for it?*
*Now let me think …*   *… how shall I put it? …*

### Correcting yourself
*No, I meant …*   *… or rather …*
*That's not exactly what I meant.*
*Sorry, I was trying to say 'price', not 'prize'.*

# The body

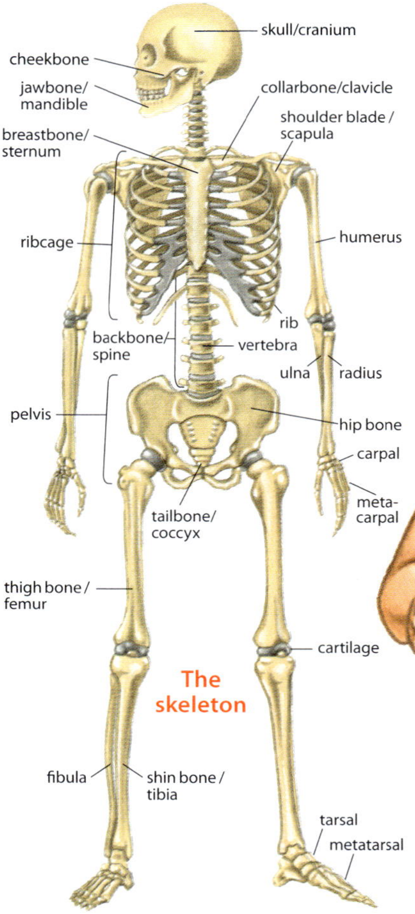


The skeleton

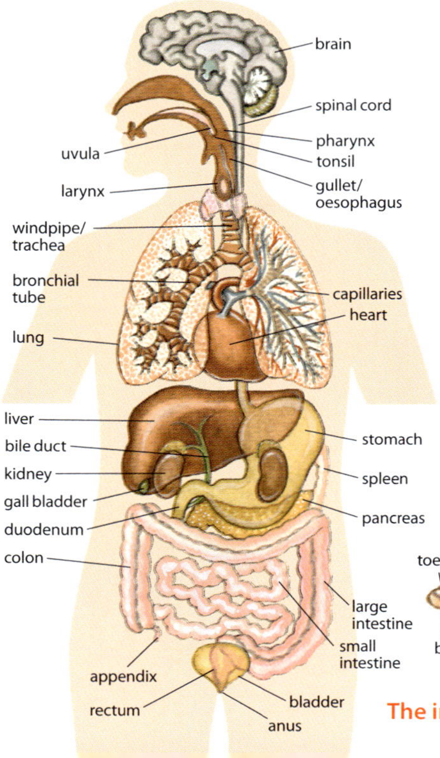


The internal organs

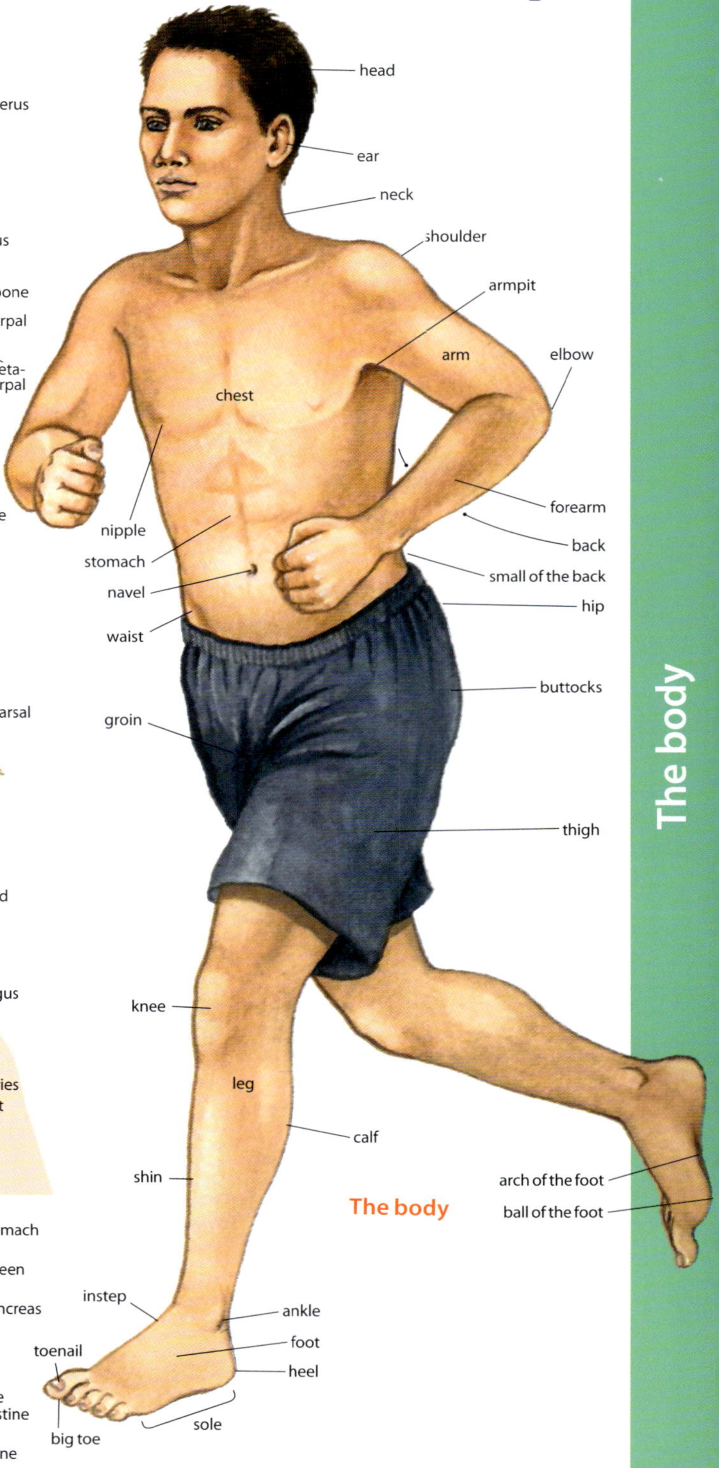


The body

## Amphibians

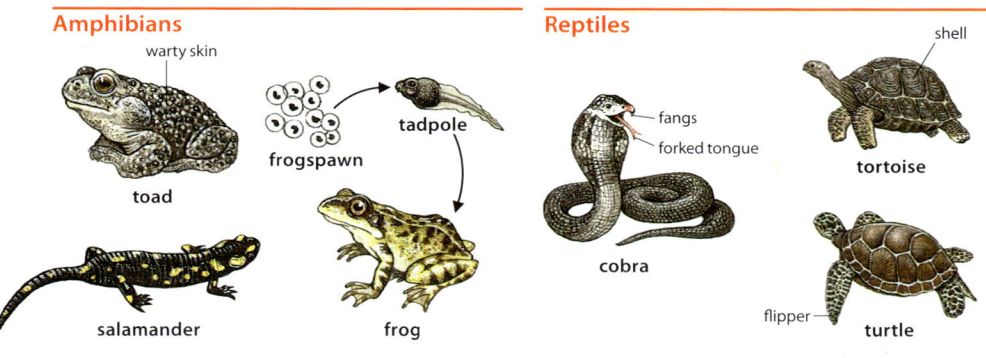

## Reptiles

## Insects

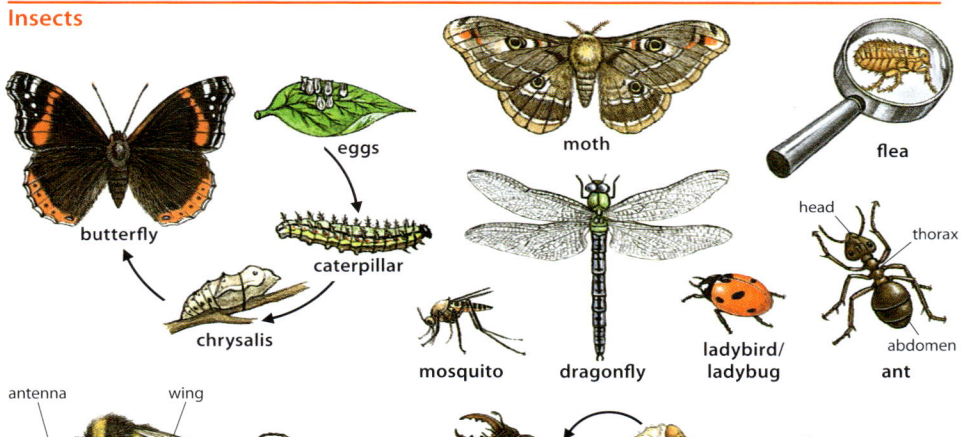

## Crustaceans

## Arachnids

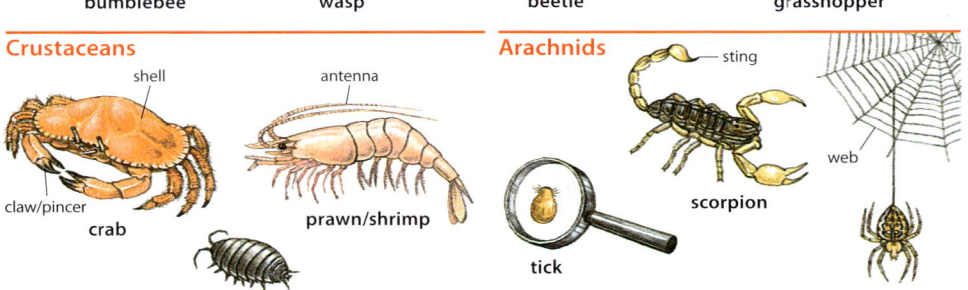

## Taxonomy

Living things are grouped on the basis of their similarities and differences into smaller and smaller groups. This scientific process of classification is called **taxonomy**. The main groups, from the largest to the smallest, are:

- **kingdom** (animal or plant)
- **phylum** (e.g. mollusc, arthropod)
- **class** (e.g. mammal, gastropod, insect)
- **order** (e.g. primate, marsupial)
- **family**
- **genus**
- **species**

## Gastropods

## Cephalopod

The animal kingdom

# Trees, plants and flowers

## Trees

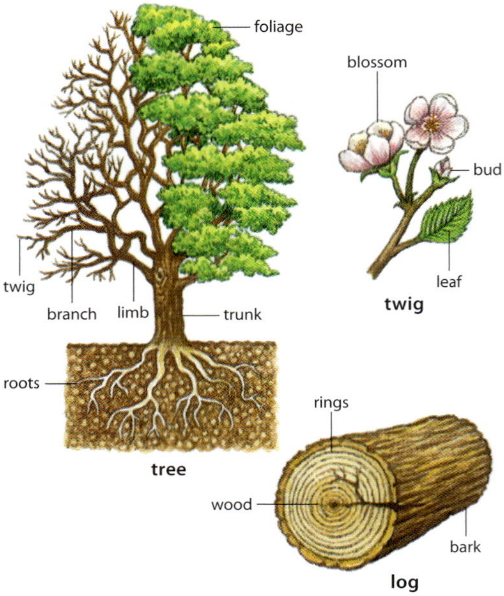

- foliage
- blossom
- bud
- leaf
- twig
- branch
- limb
- trunk
- twig
- roots
- tree
- rings
- wood
- bark
- log

## Evergreen trees

- berry
- palm
- yew
- fir cone / cone
- needles
- fir

## Deciduous trees

- seeds
- sycamore
- acorn
- oak
- catkin
- willow
- blossom
- conker
- horse chestnut
- beech nut
- beech
- seeds
- ash

# Trees, plants and flowers

**plant**: flower, bud, stalk, thorn, stem, shoot, bulb, roots

**flower**: anther, stigma, style, carpel, stamen, petal, ovule, ovary, sepal

- bamboo
- bulrush
- reed
- fern
- ivy (variegated leaves)
- moss
- lichen
- cactus
- nettle
- thistle
- dandelion (dandelion clock)
- bluebell
- daisy
- buttercup
- primrose
- poppy (seed head)
- carnation
- chrysanthemum
- sweet pea (tendril)
- sunflower
- rose (thorn)
- daffodil (trumpet)
- tulip
- iris
- lily
- orchid
- lotus

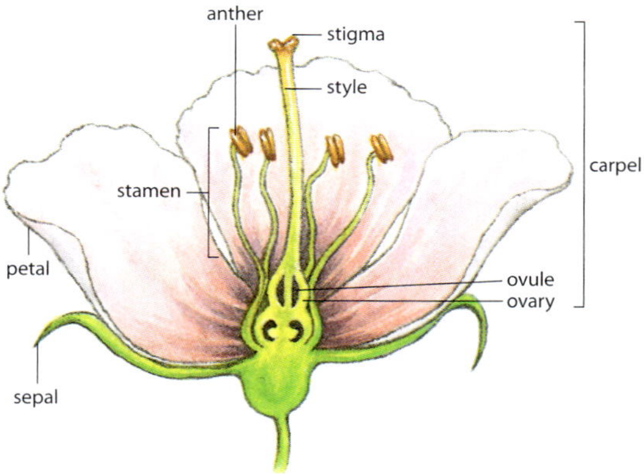

# Herbs, spices, nuts and cereals

### Herbs

bay • sage • basil • oregano • mint • coriander/cilantro
parsley • thyme • rosemary • dill • tarragon • chives

### Spices

cloves • black peppercorns • star anise • cinnamon • cardamom (pod, seeds) • nutmeg
ginger • saffron • turmeric • paprika • cumin seeds • coriander seeds

### Nuts

cashews • peanuts • macadamias • hazelnuts
pecans • almonds • pistachios
brazils • walnuts (shell) • chestnuts

### Cereals

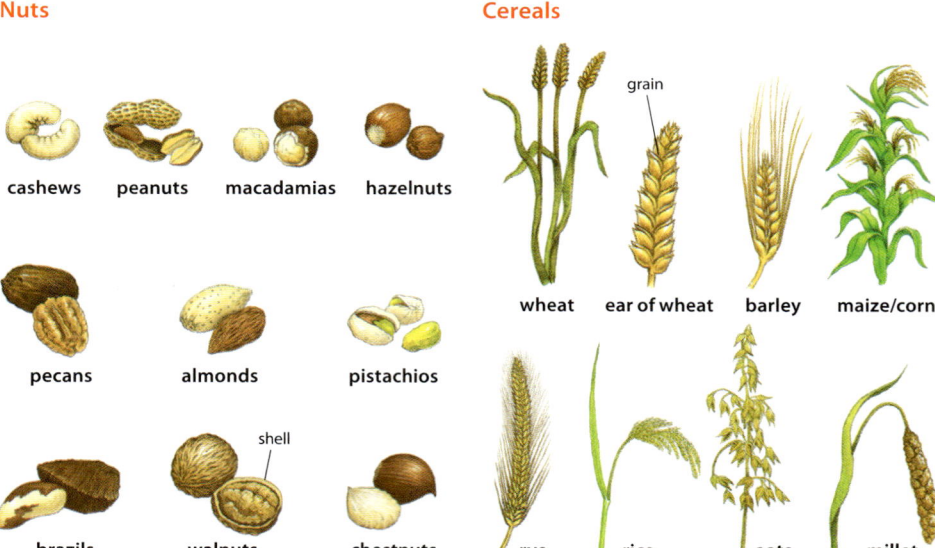

wheat • ear of wheat (grain) • barley • maize/corn
rye • rice • oats • millet

# Irregular verbs

This appendix lists all the verbs with irregular forms that are included in the dictionary, except for those formed with a hyphenated prefix and the modal verbs (e.g. can, must). Irregular forms that are only used in certain senses are marked with an asterisk (e.g. *abode). Full information on usage, pronunciation, etc. is given at the entry.

| Infinitive | Past tense | Past participle |
|---|---|---|
| abide | abided, *abode | abided, *abode |
| arise | arose | arisen |
| awake | awoke | awoken |
| babysit | babysat | babysat |
| bear | bore | borne |
| beat | beat | beaten |
| become | became | become |
| befall | befell | befallen |
| beget | begot, *begat | begot, *begotten |
| begin | began | begun |
| behold | beheld | beheld |
| bend | bent | bent |
| beseech | beseeched, besought | beseeched, besought |
| beset | beset | beset |
| bespeak | bespoke | bespoken |
| bet | bet | bet |
| betake | betook | betaken |
| bid¹ | bid | bid |
| bid² | bade, bid | bidden, bid |
| bind | bound | bound |
| bite | bit | bitten |
| bleed | bled | bled |
| blow | blew | blown, *blowed |
| break | broke | broken |
| breastfeed | breastfed | breastfed |
| breed | bred | bred |
| bring | brought | brought |
| broadcast | broadcast | broadcast |
| browbeat | browbeat | browbeaten |
| build | built | built |
| burn | burnt, burned | burnt, burned |
| burst | burst | burst |
| bust | bust, busted | bust, busted |
| buy | bought | bought |
| cast | cast | cast |
| catch | caught | caught |
| choose | chose | chosen |
| cleave | cleaved, *cleft, *clove | cleaved, *cleft, *cloven |
| cling | clung | clung |
| come | came | come |
| cost | cost, *costed | cost, *costed |
| creep | crept | crept |
| cut | cut | cut |
| deal | dealt | dealt |
| dig | dug | dug |
| dive | dived (NAmE also dove) | dived |
| draw | drew | drawn |
| dream | dreamt, dreamed | dreamt, dreamed |
| drink | drank | drunk |
| drive | drove | driven |
| dwell | dwelt, dwelled | dwelt, dwelled |
| eat | ate | eaten |
| fall | fell | fallen |
| feed | fed | fed |
| feel | felt | felt |
| fight | fought | fought |
| find | found | found |
| fit | fitted (NAmE usually fit) | fitted (NAmE usually fit) |

| Infinitive | Past tense | Past participle |
|---|---|---|
| flee | fled | fled |
| fling | flung | flung |
| floodlight | floodlit | floodlit |
| fly | flew, *flied | flown, *flied |
| forbear | forbore | forborne |
| forbid | forbade | forbidden |
| forecast | forecast, forecasted | forecast, forecasted |
| foresee | foresaw | foreseen |
| foretell | foretold | foretold |
| forget | forgot | forgotten |
| forgive | forgave | forgiven |
| forgo | forwent | forgone |
| forsake | forsook | forsaken |
| forswear | forswore | forsworn |
| freeze | froze | frozen |
| gainsay | gainsaid | gainsaid |
| get | got | got (NAmE spoken gotten) |
| give | gave | given |
| go | went | gone, *been |
| grind | ground | ground |
| grow | grew | grown |
| hamstring | hamstrung | hamstrung |
| hang | hung, *hanged | hung, *hanged |
| hear | heard | heard |
| heave | heaved, *hove | heaved, *hove |
| hew | hewed | hewed, hewn |
| hide | hid | hidden |
| hit | hit | hit |
| hold | held | held |
| hurt | hurt | hurt |
| inlay | inlaid | inlaid |
| input | input, inputted | input, inputted |
| inset | inset | inset |
| intercut | intercut | intercut |
| interweave | interwove | interwoven |
| keep | kept | kept |
| kneel | knelt (NAmE also kneeled) | knelt (NAmE also kneeled) |
| knit | knitted, *knit | knitted, *knit |
| know | knew | known |
| lay | laid | laid |
| lead | led | led |
| lean | leaned (BrE also leant) | leaned (BrE also leant) |
| leap | leapt (especially in BrE), leaped (especially in NAmE) | leapt (especially in BrE), leaped (especially in NAmE) |
| learn | learned (also learnt especially in BrE) | learned (also learnt especially in BrE) |
| leave | left | left |
| lend | lent | lent |
| let | let | let |
| lie¹ | lay | lain |
| light | lit, *lighted | lit, *lighted |
| lose | lost | lost |
| make | made | made |
| mean | meant | meant |
| meet | met | met |
| miscast | miscast | miscast |
| mishear | misheard | misheard |

## Irregular verbs

| Infinitive | Past tense | Past participle | Infinitive | Past tense | Past participle |
|---|---|---|---|---|---|
| mishit | mishit | mishit | rid | rid | rid |
| mislay | mislaid | mislaid | ride | rode | ridden |
| mislead | misled | misled | ring² | rang | rung |
| misread | misread | misread | rise | rose | risen |
| misspeak | misspoke | misspoken | run | ran | run |
| misspell | misspelled, misspelt | misspelled, misspelt | saw | sawed | sawn (NAmE also sawed) |
| misspend | misspent | misspent | say | said | said |
| mistake | mistook | mistaken | see | saw | seen |
| misunderstand | misunderstood | misunderstood | seek | sought | sought |
| mow | mowed | mown, mowed | sell | sold | sold |
| offset | offset | offset | send | sent | sent |
| outbid | outbid | outbid | set | set | set |
| outdo | outdid | outdone | sew | sewed | sewn, sewed |
| outgrow | outgrew | outgrown | shake | shook | shaken |
| output | output | output | shear | sheared | shorn, sheared |
| outrun | outran | outrun | shed | shed | shed |
| outsell | outsold | outsold | shine | shone, *shined | shone, *shined |
| outshine | outshone | outshone | shit | shit, shat (BrE also shitted) | shit, shat (BrE also shitted) |
| outspend | outspent | outspent | shoe | shod | shod |
| overcome | overcame | overcome | shoot | shot | shot |
| overdo | overdid | overdone | show | showed | shown, *showed |
| overdraw | overdrew | overdrawn | shrink | shrank, shrunk | shrunk |
| overeat | overate | overeaten | shut | shut | shut |
| overfeed | overfed | overfed | simulcast | simulcast | simulcast |
| overfly | overflew | overflown | sing | sang | sung |
| overhang | overhung | overhung | sink | sank, *sunk | sunk |
| overhear | overheard | overheard | sit | sat | sat |
| overlay | overlaid | overlaid | slay | slew | slain |
| overlie | overlay | overlain | sleep | slept | slept |
| overpay | overpaid | overpaid | slide | slid | slid |
| override | overrode | overridden | sling | slung | slung |
| overrun | overran | overrun | slink | slunk | slunk |
| oversee | oversaw | overseen | slit | slit | slit |
| oversell | oversold | oversold | smell | smelled (BrE also smelt) | smelled (BrE also smelt) |
| overshoot | overshot | overshot | smite | smote | smitten |
| oversleep | overslept | overslept | sow | sowed | sown, sowed |
| overspend | overspent | overspent | speak | spoke | spoken |
| overtake | overtook | overtaken | speed | speeded, *sped | speeded, *sped |
| overthink | overthought | overthought | spell | spelt, spelled | spelt, spelled |
| overthrow | overthrew | overthrown | spend | spent | spent |
| overwrite | overwrote | overwritten | spill | spilled (BrE also spilt) | spilled (BrE also spilt) |
| partake | partook | partaken | spin | spun | spun |
| pay | paid | paid | spit | spat (also spit especially in NAmE) | spat (also spit especially in NAmE) |
| plead | pleaded (NAmE also pled) | pleaded (NAmE also pled) | split | split | split |
|  |  |  | spoil | spoiled (BrE also spoilt) | spoiled (BrE also spoilt) |
| preset | preset | preset | spotlight | spotlit, *spotlighted | spotlit, *spotlighted |
| proofread | proofread | proofread | spread | spread | spread |
| prove | proved | proved (also proven especially in NAmE) | spring | sprang (NAmE also sprung) | sprung |
| put | put | put | stand | stood | stood |
| quit | quit (BrE also quitted) | quit (BrE also quitted) | stave | staved, *stove | staved, *stove |
| read /ri:d/ | read /red/ | read /red/ | steal | stole | stolen |
| rebuild | rebuilt | rebuilt | stick | stuck | stuck |
| recast | recast | recast | sting | stung | stung |
| redo | redid | redone | stink | stank, stunk | stunk |
| redraw | redrew | redrawn | strew | strewed | strewed, strewn |
| rehear | reheard | reheard | stride | strode | — |
| remake | remade | remade | strike | struck | struck (NAmE also stricken) |
| rend | rent | rent |  |  |  |
| rerun | reran | rerun | string | strung | strung |
| resell | resold | resold | strive | strove, *strived | striven, *strived |
| reset | reset | reset | sublet | sublet | sublet |
| resit | resat | resat | swear | swore | sworn |
| restring | restrung | restrung | sweep | swept | swept |
| retake | retook | retaken | swell | swelled | swollen, swelled |
| retell | retold | retold | swim | swam | swum |
| rethink | rethought | rethought | swing | swung | swung |
| retread | retrod, *retreaded | retrodden, *retreaded |  |  |  |
| rewind | rewound | rewound |  |  |  |
| rewrite | rewrote | rewritten |  |  |  |

| Infinitive | Past tense | Past participle |
|---|---|---|
| take | took | taken |
| teach | taught | taught |
| tear | tore | torn |
| telecast | telecast | telecast |
| tell | told | told |
| think | thought | thought |
| throw | threw | thrown |
| thrust | thrust | thrust |
| tread | trod | trodden, trod |
| typecast | typecast | typecast |
| typeset | typeset | typeset |
| unbend | unbent | unbent |
| underbid | underbid | underbid |
| undercut | undercut | undercut |
| undergo | underwent | undergone |
| underlie | underlay | underlain |
| underpay | underpaid | underpaid |
| undersell | undersold | undersold |
| understand | understood | understood |
| undertake | undertook | undertaken |
| underwrite | underwrote | underwritten |
| undo | undid | undone |
| unfreeze | unfroze | unfrozen |
| unwind | unwound | unwound |
| uphold | upheld | upheld |
| upset | upset | upset |
| wake | woke | woken |
| waylay | waylaid | waylaid |
| wear | wore | worn |
| weave | wove, *weaved | woven, *weaved |
| wed | wedded, wed | wedded, wed |
| weep | wept | wept |
| wet | wet, wetted | wet, wetted |
| win | won | won |
| wind² /waɪnd/ | wound /waʊnd/ | wound /waʊnd/ |
| withdraw | withdrew | withdrawn |
| withhold | withheld | withheld |
| withstand | withstood | withstood |
| wring | wrung | wrung |
| write | wrote | written |

| Full forms | Short forms | Negative short forms |
|---|---|---|
| **be present tense** | | |
| I am | I'm | I'm not |
| you are | you're | you aren't/you're not |
| he is | he's | he isn't/he's not |
| she is | she's | she isn't/she's not |
| it is | it's | it isn't/it's not |
| we are | we're | we aren't/we're not |
| you are | you're | you aren't/you're not |
| they are | they're | they aren't/they're not |
| **be past tense** | | |
| I was | — | I wasn't |
| you were | — | you weren't |
| he was | — | he wasn't |
| she was | — | she wasn't |
| it was | — | it wasn't |
| we were | — | we weren't |
| you were | — | you weren't |
| they were | — | they weren't |
| **have present tense** | | |
| I have | I've | I haven't/I've not |
| you have | you've | you haven't/you've not |
| he has | he's | he hasn't/he's not |
| she has | she's | she hasn't/she's not |
| it has | it's | it hasn't/it's not |
| we have | we've | we haven't/we've not |
| you have | you've | you haven't/you've not |
| they have | they've | they haven't/they've not |
| **have past tense** (all persons) | | |
| had | I'd you'd etc. | hadn't |
| **do present tense** | | |
| I do | — | I don't |
| you do | — | you don't |
| he does | — | he doesn't |
| she does | — | she doesn't |
| it does | — | it doesn't |
| we do | — | we don't |
| you do | — | you don't |
| they do | — | they don't |
| **do past tense** (all persons) | | |
| did | — | didn't |

| | be | do | have |
|---|---|---|---|
| present participle | being | doing | having |
| past participle | been | done | had |

## be, do, have

- The negative full forms are formed by adding **not**.

- Questions in the present and past are formed by placing the verb before the subject:
  - am I?   isn't he?   was I?   weren't we?
  - do I?   don't you?   did I?   didn't I?
  - have I?   hadn't they?   etc.

- Questions using the negative full form are more formal:
  - has he not?   do you not?   etc.

- The short negative question form for **I am** is **aren't**:
  - aren't I?

- When **do** or **have** is used as a main verb, questions and negative statements can be formed with **do/does/doesn't** and **did/didn't**:
  - How did you do it?
  - I don't do any teaching now.
  - Do you have any money on you?
  - We didn't have much time.

- The short forms *'ve*, *'s* and *'d* are not usually used when have is a main verb:
  - I have a shower every morning.
  - NOT I've a shower every morning.

- The short form *'s* can be added to other subjects:
  - Sally's ill.   The car's been damaged.

- The **other tenses** of **be**, **do** and **have** are formed in the same way as those of other verbs:
  - will be     would be     has been
  - will do     would do     has done
  - will have   would have   have had; etc.

- The **pronunciation** of each form of **be**, **do** and **have** is given at its entry in the dictionary.

# Verbs

## Transitive and intransitive

- • He sighed.
  • She cut her hand.
  • The soup tastes salty.

Each of these sentences has a subject (**he, she, the soup**) and a verb (**sigh, cut, taste**).

In the first sentence, **sigh** stands alone. Verbs like this are called INTRANSITIVE.

In the second sentence, **cut** is TRANSITIVE because it is used with an object (**her hand**).

In the third sentence, **taste** has no object but it cannot be used alone without an adjective. An adjective like **salty** that gives more information about the subject of a verb is called a COMPLEMENT. Verbs that take complements are called LINKING VERBS.

## Verb codes

- In the dictionary, grammatical codes at the start of each meaning show you whether a verb is always transitive or always intransitive, or whether it can be sometimes transitive and sometimes intransitive.

The code [I] shows you that in this meaning **change** is always intransitive.

> **change** 🔊 **A1** 🔊 /tʃeɪndʒ/ *verb, noun*
> ■ *verb*
> • BECOME/MAKE DIFFERENT **1** **A1** [I] to become different: *Rick hasn't changed. He looks exactly the same as he did at school.* ◇ *changing attitudes towards education* ◇ *Things have changed dramatically since then.* ⊃ see also UNCHANGING **2** **A1** [T] ~ **sb/sth** to make sb/sth different: *Fame hasn't really changed him.* ◇ *That experience changed my life.* **3** **A1** [I, T] to pass from one state or form into another; to make sb/sth pass from one state or form into another: *Wait for the traffic lights to change.* ◇ **from A to/into B** *The lights changed from red to green.* ◇ **to/into sth** *The lights changed to green.* ◇ ~ **sb/sth (from A) to/into B** *With a wave of her magic wand, she changed the frog into a handsome prince.*

The code [T] shows you that in this meaning **change** is always transitive.

The code [I, T] shows you that in this meaning **change** is sometimes intransitive and sometimes transitive.

Transitive verbs are the most common type of verb. A verb that is always transitive in all its meanings is just marked *verb*, and no other verb code is given.

## Verb frames

- Transitive verbs can take different types of object—a noun, phrase or clause. Both transitive and intransitive verbs can combine with different prepositions or adverbs. Different linking verbs can take either adjectives or nouns as complements.

In the dictionary, the different patterns (or 'verb frames') in which a verb can be used are shown in **bold type**, usually just before an example showing that pattern in context.

> **pro·vide** 🔊 **A2** 🔊 /prəˈvaɪd/ *verb* **1** **A2** to give sth to sb or make it available for them to use SYN **supply**: ~ **sth** *Please provide the following information.* ◇ *The exhibition provides an opportunity for local artists to show their work.* ◇ *Please answer questions in the space provided.* ◇ ~ **sth for sb** *We are here to provide a service for the public.* ◇ ~ **sb with sth** *We are here to provide the public with a service* ◇ ~ **sth to sb** *We provide financial support to low-income families.* **2** ~ **that …** (*formal*) (of a law or rule) to state that sth will or must happen SYN **stipulate**: *The final section provides that any work produced for the company is thereafter owned by the company.* ⊃ see also PROVISION *noun*

If a particular verb, or one particular meaning of a verb, is always used in the same pattern, this pattern is shown in **bold type** before the definition.

## Intransitive verbs [I]

- Intransitive verbs do not take an object. When they are used alone after a subject, there is no verb frame.

The example showing this use will usually appear first, before any other patterns and examples.

> **shiver** /ˈʃɪvə(r)/ *verb, noun*
> ■ *verb* [I] (of a person) to shake slightly because you are cold, frightened, excited, etc: *Don't stand outside shivering—come inside and get warm!* ◇ *He shivered at the thought of the cold, dark sea.* ◇ ~ **with sth** *to shiver with cold/fear/excitement/pleasure*

Some intransitive verbs are often used with a particular preposition or adverb. This pattern will be shown in bold type, usually before an example.

- Some intransitive verbs are always or usually used with a preposition or adverb, but not always the same one. These are often verbs showing movement in a particular direction:

  • *A runaway car came hurtling towards us.*
  • *A group of swans floated by.*

In the dictionary this use will be shown by the frame + **adv./prep.** If a preposition or adverb is often used, but not always, there will be brackets round the frame: (+ **adv./prep.**)

> **hur·tle** /ˈhɜːtl; *NAmE* ˈhɜːrtl/ *verb* [I] + **adv./prep.** to move very fast in a particular direction: *A runaway car came hurtling towards us.*

## Transitive verbs [T]

- Transitive verbs must have an object. The object can be a noun or a pronoun, a noun phrase or a clause.
  → For information on verbs that take a clause as the object, see page R6.

The frames used to show a transitive verb with a noun, pronoun or noun phrase as object are ~ **sb**, ~ **sth** and ~ **sb/sth**.

> **ac·com·mo·date** ?+ B2 /əˈkɒmədeɪt; *NAmE* əˈkɑːm-/ *verb* **1** ?+ B2 [T] ~**sb** to provide sb with a room or place to sleep, live or sit: *The hotel can accommodate up to 500 guests.* **2** ?+ C1 [T] ~**sb/sth** to provide enough space for sb/sth: *The garage can accommodate three cars.* **3** ?+ C1 [T] ~**sth** (*formal*) to consider sth such as sb's opinion or a fact and be influenced by it when you are deciding what to do or explaining sth: *Our proposal tries to accommodate the special needs of minority groups.* **4** [T] ~**sb (with sth)** (*formal*) to help sb by doing what they want SYN **oblige**: *I have accommodated the press a great deal, giving numerous interviews.*

- ~ **sb** is used when the object is a person.
- ~ **sth** is used when the object is a thing.
- ~ **sb/sth** is used when the object can be a person or a thing.

As with intransitive verbs, some transitive verbs are often used with a preposition or an adverb.

If there is a wide range of possible prepositions or adverbs, a frame such as **sb/sth + adv./prep.** is used.

> **hack** /hæk/ *verb, noun*
> ■ *verb* **1** [T, I] to hit and cut sb/sth in a rough, heavy way: ~ **sb/sth + adv./prep.** *I hacked the dead branches off.* ◇ *They were hacked to death as they tried to escape.* ◇ *We had to hack our way through the jungle.* ◇ **+ adv./prep.** *We hacked away at the bushes.* **2** [T] ~**sb/sth + adv./prep.** to kick sth roughly or without control: *He hacked the ball away.* **3** [I, T] (*computing*) to secretly find a way of looking at and/or changing information on sb else's computer system without permission: ~**into sth** *He hacked into the bank's computer.* ◇ ~**sth** *They had hacked secret data.*

If a particular preposition or adverb is used, then it is given in the frame.

## Transitive verbs with two objects

- Some verbs, like **sell** and **buy**, can be used with two objects. This is shown by the frame ~ **sb sth**:
  - *I sold Jim a car.*
  - *I bought Mary a book.*

You can often express the same idea by using the verb as an ordinary transitive verb and adding a prepositional phrase starting with **to** or **for**:

- *I sold a car to Jim.*
- *I bought a book for Mary.*

These will be shown by the frames ~ **to sb** and ~ **for sb**.

> **bake** ❶ B1 /beɪk/ *verb, noun*
> ■ *verb* **1** ?+ B1 [T, I] to cook food in an oven without extra fat or liquid; to be cooked in this way: ~**(sth)** *to bake bread/biscuits/cookies* ◇ *baked potatoes/apples* ◇ *the delicious smell of baking bread* ◇ *I've been baking all morning.* ◇ ~**sth for sb** *I'm baking a birthday cake for Alex.* ◇ ~**sb sth** *I'm baking Alex a cake.* ⊃ VISUAL VOCAB pages V41, V42

A pair of examples, with different frames, shows the same idea expressed in two different ways.

## Linking verbs

- - *His voice sounds hoarse.*
  - *Elena became a doctor.*

In these sentences, the linking verb (**sound**, **become**) is followed by a complement, an adjective (**hoarse**) or a noun phrase (**a doctor**) that tells you more about the subject.

Verbs that have an adjective as the complement have the frame **+ adj.**, and verbs with a noun phrase as the complement have the frame **+ noun**. Verbs that can take either an adjective or a noun phrase as the complement may have the frame **+ adj./noun**, or the two frames may be shown separately with an example for each.

> **be·come** ❶ A1 Ⓢ /bɪˈkʌm/ *verb* (**be·came** /-ˈkeɪm/, **be·come**) **1** ?+ A1 *linking verb* to start to be sth: **+ adj.** *It soon became apparent that no one was going to come.* ◇ *It is becoming increasingly clear that something has gone seriously wrong.* ◇ **+ noun** *She became queen in 1952.* ◇ *The bill will become law next year.* ◇ *Over the last five years she has become part of the family.*

The linking verb **become** can be used with either an adjective or a noun phrase.

There are also verbs that take both an object and a complement:

- *She considered herself lucky.*
- *They elected him president.*

The complement (**lucky, president**) tells you more about the object (**herself, him**) of the verb. The frames for these verbs are ~ **sb/sth + adj.**, **sb/sth + noun** or ~ **sb/sth + adj./noun**.

## Verbs used with 'that clauses'

- The frame ~ **that…** shows that a verb is followed by a clause beginning with **that**:
  - *She replied that she would prefer to walk.*

However, it is not always necessary to use the word **that** itself:

- *I said that he would come.*
- *I said he would come.*

These two sentences mean the same. In the dictionary they are shown by the frame ~ **(that)…** and a single example is given, using brackets:

- *I said (that) he would come.*

Some verbs can be used with both a noun phrase and a 'that clause'. The frame for verbs used like this is ~ **sb that…** or ~ **sb (that)…**:

- *Can you remind me that I need to buy some milk?*
- *I told her (that) I would be late.*

## Verbs used with 'wh- clauses'

- A '**wh-**clause' (or phrase) is a clause or phrase beginning with one of the following words: **wh**ich, **wh**at, **wh**ose, **wh**y, **wh**ere, **wh**en, **wh**o, **wh**om, how, if, **wh**ether:
  - *I wonder what the new job will be like.*
  - *He doesn't care how he looks.*
  - *Did you see which way they went?*

In the dictionary, verbs used like this have a frame such as ~ **how, what, etc …** or ~ **why, where, etc …**

> The particular 'wh-words' given in each frame will be words that are typical for that verb, but the 'etc.' shows that other 'wh- clauses' are possible.
>
> **won·der** 🔊 **B1** /ˈwʌndə(r)/ *verb, noun*
> ■ *verb* **1** 🔊 **B1** [T, I] to think about sth and try to decide what is true, what will happen, what you should do, etc: *'Why do you want to know?' 'No particular reason. I was just wondering.'* ◊ ~ **who, where, etc …** *I wonder who she is.* ◊ *I was just beginning to wonder where you were.* ◊ *You have to wonder just what he sees in her.* ◊ *I can't help wondering whether I'm missing something here.* ◊ + **speech** *'Where's Natasha?' he wondered aloud.* **2** 🔊 **B1** [T] ~ **if, whether …** used as a polite way of asking a question or asking sb to do sth: *I wonder if you can help me.* ◊ *I was wondering whether you'd like to come to a party.*

> If there is no 'etc.' in the frame, then this verb or meaning can only take the particular 'wh-words' that are listed.

Some verbs can be used with both a noun phrase and a 'wh-clause'. Verbs used like this have a frame such as ~ **sb where, when, etc …**

- *I asked him where the library was.*
- *I told her when the baby was due.*
- *He teaches his students how to research a subject thoroughly.*

## Verbs with infinitive phrases

- **Eat** and **to eat** are both the infinitive form of the verb. **Eat** is called a BARE INFINITIVE and **to eat** is called a TO-INFINITIVE. Most verbs that take an infinitive are used with the to-infinitive. The frame for these verbs is ~ **to do sth**:
  - *The goldfish need to be fed.*
  - *She never learned to read.*

Some verbs can be used with both a noun phrase and a to-infinitive. The frame for these is ~ **sb to do sth**, ~ **sth to do sth** or ~ **sb/sth to do sth**. The noun phrase can be the object of the main verb:

- *Can you persuade Sheila to chair the meeting?*

or the noun phrase and the infinitive phrase together can be the object:

- *I expected her to pass her driving test first time.*
- *We'd love you to come and visit us.*

Only two groups of verbs are used with a bare infinitive (without **to**). One is the group of MODAL VERBS (or MODAL AUXILIARIES). These are the special verbs like **can**, **must** and **will** that go before a main verb and show that an action is possible, necessary, etc. These verbs have special treatment in the dictionary and are labelled *modal verb*.

A small group of ordinary verbs, for example **see** and **hear**, can be used with a noun phrase and a bare infinitive. The frame for these is
~ **sb do sth**, ~ **sth do sth** or ~ **sb/sth do sth**:

- *She watched him eat his lunch.*
- *Did you hear the phone ring just then?*

## Verbs with '–ing phrases'

- An '**-ing** phrase' is a phrase containing a PRESENT PARTICIPLE (or GERUND). The present participle is the form of the verb that ends in –*ing*, for example **doing**, **eating** or **catching**. Sometimes the '-ing phrase' consists of a present participle on its own. The frame for a verb that takes an '-**ing** phrase' is ~ **doing sth**:
  - *She never stops talking!*
  - *I started looking for a job two years ago.*

Some verbs can be used with both a noun phrase and an '-ing phrase'. The frame for this is ~ **sb doing sth**, ~ **sth doing sth** or ~ **sb/sth doing sth**. The noun phrase can be the object of the main verb:

- *His comments set me thinking.*
- *I can smell something nice cooking.*

or the noun phrase and the '-ing phrase' together can be the object:

- *I hate him joking* (= the fact that he jokes) *about serious things.*

In this pattern, you can replace **him** with the possessive pronoun **his**:

- *I hate his joking about serious things.*

However, sentences with a possessive pronoun sound very formal and the object pronoun is more common, especially in American English. In cases where the verb itself is formal and the possessive pronoun may well be used, this is shown in the dictionary entry.

## Verbs with direct speech

- Verbs like **say**, **answer** and **demand** can be used either to report what somebody has said using a 'that clause' or to give their exact words in DIRECT SPEECH, using quotation marks (' '). Verbs that can be used with direct speech have the frame **+ speech**. Compare these two sentences:
  - **+ speech** *'It's snowing,' she said.*
  - **~ (that)...** *She said (that) it was snowing.*

Some verbs can be used with both direct speech and a noun phrase, to show who is being spoken to. The frame for this is **~ sb + speech**:
  - *'Tom's coming to lunch,' she **told him**.*

## Verbs in the passive

- Most transitive verbs can be used in the passive:
  - *Jill's behaviour **annoyed** me.*
  - *I **was annoyed** by Jill's behaviour.*

If a verb can be active or passive, the same verb frame is used. If the verb is often passive, there will be an example in the passive.

> **con·firm** 🔊 B1 Ⓦ /kənˈfɜːm; *NAmE* -ˈfɜːrm/ *verb*
> **1** B1 to state or show that sth is definitely true or correct, especially by providing evidence: **~ sth** *His guilty expression confirmed my suspicions.* ◇ *Rumours of job losses were later confirmed.* ◇ *She said she could not **confirm or deny** the allegations.* ◇ **~ (that) ...** *Police sources confirmed that ten people had been arrested at the march.* ◇ **~ what/when, etc...** *Can you confirm what happened?* ◇ *it is confirmed that ... It has been confirmed that an official complaint was made to the council.* **2** B2 to make a position, an agreement, etc. more definite or official; to establish sb/sth clearly: **~ sth** *Please write to confirm your reservation* (= say that it is definite).

If a pattern is only or usually used in the passive, then the frame is put in the passive.

If a transitive verb cannot be used in the passive, the label [no passive] appears before the definition.

## Verbs in different patterns

- Many verbs, for example **watch**, can be used in a number of different ways:
  - **~ sb/sth do sth** *I watched him eat.*
  - **~ sb/sth doing sth** *I watched him eating.*
  - **~ sb/sth** *I watched the pianist's left hand.*
  - **~ what, how, etc. ...** *I watched how the pianist used her left hand.*

The dictionary entry for each verb shows the different ways in which it can be used by giving a range of example sentences. The frame before each example shows what type of grammatical pattern is being used. When an example follows another one illustrating the same pattern, the frame is not repeated.

Sometimes patterns can combine with each other to form a longer pattern. This happens especially with patterns involving particular prepositions or adverbs; and sometimes there is a choice of two or three different prepositions or adverbs:

- **~ sth** *We shared the pizza.*
- **~ sth out** *We shared out the pizza.*
- **~ sth among sb** *We shared the pizza among the four of us.*
- **~ sth between sb** *We shared the pizza between the four of us.*
- **~ sth out among sb** *We shared the pizza out among the four of us.*
- **~ sth out between sb** *We shared the pizza out between the four of us.*

In cases like this the dictionary does not always give a separate frame and example for each different combination. It may use brackets to show where part of a long frame can be left out, and slashes to show where there is a choice between two or three different words in the frame:

> • **DIVIDE BETWEEN PEOPLE 2** 🔊 A1 [T, I] to have part of sth while another person or other people also have part: **~ sth with sb** *He shared the pie with her.* ◇ *The Hungarian king **shared power with** the Austrian emperor to form the Austro-Hungarian Empire.* **3** 🔊 A1 [T] **~ sth (out) (among/between sb)** to divide sth between two or more people: *We shared the pizza between the four of us.* ⊃ see also JOB-SHARING, POWER-SHARING

The frame **~ (sb)**, **~ (sth)** or **~ (sb/sth)** may also be used, where a verb can be used without an object (that is, it can be intransitive), but is more commonly used with a noun phrase as object. In these cases the more common, transitive, use, is given in the first example(s), and any intransitive examples are placed after that:

> **broad·cast** 🔊 B2 /ˈbrɔːdkɑːst; *NAmE* -kæst/ *verb, noun*
> ■ *verb* (**broad·cast**, **broad·cast**) **1** 🔊 B2 [T, I] **~ (sth)** to send out programmes on television or radio: *The concert will be broadcast live* (= at the same time as it takes place) *tomorrow evening.* ◇ *They began broadcasting in 1922.* **2** [T] **~ sth** to tell a lot of people about sth: *I don't like to broadcast the*

**Sb** and **sth** may also appear within brackets within longer frames, for example to show a verb that can take a preposition, adverb or 'that clause' either with or without a noun phrase as another object:

> **warn** 🔊 B1 /wɔːn; *NAmE* wɔːrn/ *verb* **1** 🔊 B1 [T, I] to tell sb about sth, especially sth dangerous or unpleasant that is likely to happen, so that they can avoid it: **~ sb** *I tried to warn him, but he wouldn't listen.* ◇ *If you're thinking of getting a dog, **be warned**—they take a lot of time and money.* ◇ **~ (sb) about/against sb/sth** *Security experts warned about the problems months ago.* ◇ **~ (sb) of/about sth** *Officials warned the pilot of an anonymous threat.* ◇ **~ (sb) that ...** *Aid agencies have repeatedly warned that a humanitarian catastrophe is imminent.* ◇ **~ sb what, how, etc ...** *I had been warned what to expect.* ◇ **~ (sb) + speech** *'Beware of pickpockets,' she warned (him).*

# Phrasal verbs

## What are phrasal verbs?

- Jan **turned down** the chance to work abroad.
- Buying that new car has really **eaten into** my savings.
- I don't think I can **put up with** his behaviour much longer.

- **PHRASAL VERBS** (sometimes called **MULTI-WORD VERBS**) are verbs that consist of two, or sometimes three, words. The first word is a verb and it is followed by an adverb (turn **down**) or a preposition (eat **into**) or both (put **up with**). These adverbs or prepositions are sometimes called **PARTICLES**.

- In this dictionary, phrasal verbs are listed at the end of the entry for the main verb in a section marked **PHR V**. They are listed in alphabetical order of the particles following them:

> **PHR V** **fight 'back (against sb/sth)** to resist strongly or attack sb who has attacked you: *Don't let them bully you. Fight back!* ◊ *It is time to fight back against street crime.* **fight sth↔'back/'down** to try hard not to do or show sth, especially not to show your feelings: *I was fighting back the tears.* ◊ *He fought down his disgust.* **fight sb/ sth↔'off** to resist sb/sth by fighting against them/it: *The jeweller was stabbed as he tried to fight the robbers off.* ◊ (figurative) *Vitamin A helps your body fight off infection.* **fight 'out sth | fight it 'out** to fight, argue or compete until an argument or competition has been settled: *The conflict is still being fought out.* ◊ *They hadn't reached any agreement so we left them to fight it out.*

## Meaning of phrasal verbs

- • *He **sat down** on the bed.*

  The meaning of some phrasal verbs, such as **sit down**, is easy to guess because the verb and the particle keep their usual meaning. However, many phrasal verbs have idiomatic meanings that you need to learn. The separate meanings of **put**, **up** and **with**, for example, do not add up to the meaning of **put up with** (= tolerate).

- Some particles have particular meanings that are the same when they are used with a number of different verbs:
  - I didn't see the point of **hanging around** waiting for him, so I went home.
  - I wish you wouldn't leave all those books **lying around**.

  **Around** adds the meaning of 'with no particular purpose or aim' and is also used in a similar way with many other verbs, such as **play**, **sit** and **wait**.

- The meaning of a phrasal verb can sometimes be explained with a one-word verb. However, phrasal verbs are frequently used in spoken English and, if there is a one-word equivalent, it is usually more formal in style:
  - I wish my ears didn't **stick out** so much.
  - The garage **projects** five metres beyond the front of the house.

  Both **stick out** and **project** have the same meaning—'to extend beyond a surface'—but they are very different in style. **Stick out** is used in informal contexts, and **project** in formal or technical contexts.

## Grammar of phrasal verbs

- Phrasal verbs can be TRANSITIVE (they take an object) or INTRANSITIVE (they have no object). Some phrasal verbs can be used in both ways:
  - For heaven's sake, **shut** her **up**. (transitive)
  - He told me **to shut up**. (intransitive)

  INTRANSITIVE phrasal verbs are written in the dictionary without **sb** (somebody) or **sth** (something) after them. This shows that they do not have an object:

  > **eat 'out** to have a meal in a restaurant, etc. rather than at home: *Do you feel like eating out tonight?*

  **Eat out** is intransitive, and the two parts of the verb cannot be separated by any other word.

  You can say:
  - Shall we eat out tonight?
  - BUT NOT *Shall we eat tonight out?*

  In order to use TRANSITIVE phrasal verbs correctly, you need to know where to put the object. With some phrasal verbs (often called SEPARABLE verbs), the object can go either between the verb and the particle or after the particle:
  - She **tore** the letter **up**.
  - She **tore up** the letter.

- When the object is a long phrase, it usually comes after the particle:
  - She **tore up** all the letters he had sent her.

- When the object is a pronoun (for example **it** standing for 'the letter'), it must always go between the verb and the particle:
  - She read the letter and then **tore** it **up**.

- In the dictionary, verbs that are separable are written like this: **tear sth ↔ up**

  The double arrow between the object and the particle shows that the object may come either before or after the particle:

  > ˌcall sth↔ˈoff to cancel sth; to decide that sth will not happen: *to call off a deal/trip/strike* ◇ *They have called off their engagement* (= decided not to get married). ◇ *The game was called off because of bad weather.*

  You can say:
  - *They **called** the deal **off**.*
  - AND *They **called off** the deal.*

- With other phrasal verbs (sometimes called INSEPARABLE verbs), the two parts of the verb cannot be separated by an object:
  - *I didn't really **take to** her husband.*
    NOT *I didn't really take her husband to.*
  - *I didn't really **take to** him.*
    NOT *I didn't really take him to.*

  In the dictionary, verbs that are inseparable are written like this:

  **take to sb**

  When you see **sb** or **sth** after the two parts of a phrasal verb, and there is no double arrow, you know that they cannot be separated by an object:

  > ˌrun ˈinto sb (*informal*) to meet sb by chance: *Guess who I ran into today!*

  You can say:
  - *I **ran into** Joe yesterday.*
    BUT NOT *I ran Joe into.*

- There are a few phrasal verbs in which the two parts of the verb must be separated by the object. You can say:
  - *They changed the plans and **messed** everyone **around**.*
  - BUT NOT *They changed the plans and messed around everyone.*

  In the dictionary, these verbs are written like this:

  **mess sb around**

  When you see **sb** or **sth** between the two parts of a phrasal verb and there is no double arrow, you know that they must be separated by the object.

- Some transitive phrasal verbs can be made passive:
  - *The deal **has been called off**.*

  When this is common, you will find an example at the dictionary entry.

# Phrasal verbs used with phrases and clauses

- Like other verbs, some phrasal verbs can be used with another phrase or clause. The different types of clause and phrase are explained on pages R5–6. When a phrasal verb can be used with a particular type of clause or phrase, an example is given in the dictionary entry, labelled with a special frame:

| | |
|---|---|
| ~ that | *We **found out** later that we had been at the same school.* |
| ~ how, what, etc … | *I can't **figure out** how to do this.* |
| ~ to do sth | *It didn't **occur to** her to ask for help.* |
| ~ doing sth | *I didn't **bargain on** finding Matthew there as well.* |
| + speech | *'Help!' he **cried out**.* |

# Related nouns

- A particular phrasal verb may have a noun related to it. This noun will be mentioned at the verb entry:

  > ˌbreak ˈin to enter a building by force: *Burglars had broken in while we were away.* ⊃ related noun BREAK-IN
  > ˌbreak sb/sth ˈin 1 to train sb/sth in sth new that they must do: *to break in new recruits* ◇ *The young horse was not yet broken in* (= trained to carry a rider). 2 to wear sth, especially new shoes, until they become comfortable
  > ˌbreak ˈin (on sth) to interrupt sth: *She longed to break in on their conversation but didn't want to appear rude.* ◇ + speech *'I didn't do it!' she broke in.*
  > ˌbreak ˈinto sth 1 to enter a building by force; to open a car, etc. by force: *We had our car broken into last week.* ⊃ related noun BREAK-IN 2 to begin laughing, singing, etc. suddenly: *As the president's car drew up, the crowd broke into loud applause.*
  >
  > ˌbreak ˈout (of war, fighting or other unpleasant events) to start suddenly: *They had escaped to America shortly before war broke out in 1939.* ◇ *Fighting had broken out between rival groups of fans.* ◇ *Fire broke out during the night.* ⊃ related noun OUTBREAK ˌbreak ˈout (of sth) to escape from a place or situation: *Several prisoners broke out of the jail.* ◇ *She needed to break out of her daily routine and do something exciting.* ⊃ related noun BREAKOUT

A noun is often related in meaning to only one or two of the phrasal verbs using a particle. **Break-in** is related to **break in** and the first meaning of **break into sth**, but not to **break sb/sth in** or **break in (on sth)**. **Breakout** is related to **break out (of sth)**, whereas the noun **outbreak** relates to **break out**.

# Nouns and adjectives

## Nouns
### Countable and uncountable

- The two biggest groups of nouns are COUNTABLE nouns (or COUNT nouns) and UNCOUNTABLE nouns (also called UNCOUNT nouns or MASS nouns). Most countable nouns are words for separate things that can be counted, like **apples**, **books** or **teachers**. Uncountable nouns are usually words for things that are thought of as a quantity or mass, like **water** or **time**.

  However, there are some nouns in English that you might expect to be countable but which are not. For example, **furniture**, **information** and **equipment** are all uncountable nouns in English, although they are countable in some other languages.

### Countable nouns [C]

- A countable noun has a singular form and a plural form. When it is singular, it must always have a DETERMINER (a word such as **a**, **the**, **both**, **each**) in front of it. In the plural it can be used with or without a determiner:
  - *I'm having **a** driving **lesson** this afternoon.*
  - *I've had **several lessons** already.*
  - ***Lessons** cost £25 an hour.*

  Countable nouns are the most common type of noun. If they have only one meaning, or if all the meanings are countable, they are just marked *noun*. For nouns that have a number of meanings, some of which are not countable, each meaning that is countable is marked [C].

### Uncountable nouns [U]

- An uncountable noun has only one form, not a separate singular and plural. It can be used with or without a determiner:
  - *Can we make **space** for an extra chair?*
  - *There isn't **much space** in this room.*

  If an uncountable noun is the subject of a verb, the verb is singular:
  - *Extra money **has been found** for this project.*

  With nouns such as **furniture**, **information** and **equipment**, as with many other uncountable nouns, you can talk about amounts of the thing or separate parts of the thing by using phrases like **a piece of**, **three items of**, **some bits of**. Nouns like **piece**, **item** and **bit** are called PARTITIVES when used in this way:
  - *I picked up **some information** that might interest you.*
  - *I picked up **two pieces of information** that might interest you.*

### Plural nouns [pl.]

- Some nouns are always plural and have no singular form. Nouns that refer to things that have two parts joined together, for example **glasses**, **jeans** and **scissors**, are often plural nouns. You can usually also talk about **a pair of jeans**, **a pair of scissors**, etc.
  - *I'm going to buy **some new jeans**.*
  - *I'm going to buy **a new pair of jeans**.*

  An example is given in the entry for the noun to show that it can be used in this way.

- Some plural nouns, such as **police** and **cattle**, look as if they are singular. Nouns like this usually refer to a group of people or animals of a particular type, when they are considered together as one unit. They also take a plural verb:
  - ***Police are searching** for a man who escaped from Pentonville prison today.*
  - *The **cattle are fed** on barley and grass.*

### Singular nouns [sing.]

- Some nouns are always singular and have no plural form. Many nouns like this can be used in only a limited number of ways. For example, some singular nouns must be or are often used with a particular determiner in front of them or with a particular preposition after them. The correct determiner or preposition is shown before the definition. In the case of **fillip** the pattern given is **a ~ (to/for sth)**:

  **fil·lip** /ˈfɪlɪp/ *noun* [sing.] **a ~ (to/for sth)** (*formal*) a thing or person that causes sth to improve suddenly SYN **boost**: *A drop in interest rates gave a welcome fillip to the housing market.*

### Nouns with singular or plural verbs
[sing.+ sing./pl. v.] [C + sing./pl. v.] [U + sing./pl. v.]

- In British English some singular nouns (or countable nouns in their singular form) can be used with a plural verb as well as a singular one. Nouns like this usually refer to a group of people, an organization or a place, and can be thought of either as the organization, place or group (singular) or as many individual people (plural). In the dictionary an example is usually given to show agreement with a singular and a plural verb:
  - *The **Vatican has/have** issued a further statement this morning.*
  - *The **committee has/have** decided to dismiss him.*

These nouns are marked [sing. + sing./pl. v.] if they are always singular in form, and [C + sing./pl. v.] if they also have a plural form. The plural form always agrees with a plural verb.

**NOTE** In American English the singular form of these nouns must take a singular verb:
- *The government **says it is** committed to tax reform.*

- Some uncountable nouns can be used with a plural verb as well as a singular one. These include some nouns that end in **-s** and therefore look as though they are plural:
  - *His **whereabouts are/is** still unknown.*

and some nouns that refer to a group of people or things and can be thought of either as a group (singular) or as many individual people or things (plural):
- ***Head office*** *(= the people in head office) is/are considering the proposal*

## Patterns with nouns

- Many nouns are followed by a particular preposition, adverb or other pattern:
  - *My comments were taken as an allegation of negligence.*

The correct pattern to use is shown in **bold type**, either before the definition or before an individual example. Where any part of a pattern is optional, it is given in brackets.

**al·le·ga·tion** /ˌæləˈgeɪʃn/ *noun* a public statement that is made without giving proof, accusing sb of doing sth that is wrong or illegal **SYN** **accusation**: *to investigate/deny/withdraw an allegation* ◊ **~ of sth** *Several newspapers made allegations of corruption in the city's police department.* ◊ **~ (of sth) against sb** *allegations of dishonesty against him* ◊ **~ about sb/sth** *The committee has made serious allegations about interference in its work.* ◊ **~ that …** *an allegation that he had been dishonest* ➲ SYNONYMS at CLAIM

The example sentences show the patterns in use.

## Adjectives

- Many adjectives can be used both before a noun:
  - *a serious expression*
  - *grey hair*

and after a LINKING VERB:
  - *She looked serious.*
  - *His hair had turned grey.*

- However, some adjectives, or particular meanings of adjectives, are always used before a noun, and cannot be used after a linking verb. They are called ATTRIBUTIVE adjectives:
  - *the chief reason*

- Others are only used after a linking verb. They are called PREDICATIVE adjectives:
  - *The baby is awake.*

  → For more information about LINKING VERBS, look at page R5.

### [only before noun] [usually before noun]

- Attributive adjectives are labelled [only before noun]. The label [usually before noun] is used when it is rare but possible to use the adjective after a verb.

Senses **1** and **3** can only be used before a noun.

**con·tin·en·tal** /ˌkɒntɪˈnentl; *NAmE* ˌkɑːn-/ *adj., noun*
■ *adj.* **1** (*also* **Continental**) [only before noun] (*BrE*) of or in the continent of Europe, not including Britain and Ireland: *a popular continental holiday resort* ◊ *Britain's continental neighbours* **2** (*BrE*) following the customs of countries in western and southern Europe: *a continental lifestyle* ◊ *The shutters and the balconies make the street look almost continental.* **3** [only before noun] connected with the main part of the North American continent: *Prices are often higher in Hawaii than in the continental United States.*

Sense **2** has no grammar label because it can be used both before a noun and after a linking verb.

### [not before noun] [not usually before noun]

- Predicative adjectives, labelled [not before noun], are used only after a linking verb, never before a noun. The label [not usually before noun] is used when it is rare but possible to use the adjective before a noun.

The grammar label straight after the adj. label shows that both meanings must be used after a linking verb.

**rife** /raɪf/ *adj.* [not before noun] **1** if sth bad or unpleasant is rife in a place, it is very common there **SYN** **widespread**: *It is a country where corruption is rife.* ◊ *Rumours are rife that he is going to resign.* **2** **~ (with sth)** full of sth bad or unpleasant: *Los Angeles is rife with gossip about the stars' private lives.*

### [after noun]

- A few adjectives always follow the noun they describe. This is shown in the dictionary by the label [after noun]:

**gal·ore** /ɡəˈlɔː(r)/ *adj.* [after noun] (*informal*) in large quantities: *There will be games and prizes galore.*

# Collocation

## What is collocation?

- **COLLOCATION** is the way in which particular words tend to occur or belong together. For example, you can say:
  - *Meals will be served outside on the terrace, weather permitting.*
  - BUT NOT *Meals will be served outside on the terrace, weather allowing.*

  Both these sentences seem to mean the same thing: **allow** and **permit** have very similar meanings. But in this combination only **permitting** is correct. It COLLOCATES with **weather** and **allowing** does not.

## Types of collocation

- In order to write and speak natural and correct English, you need to know, for example:
  - which adjectives are used with a particular noun
  - which nouns a particular adjective is used with
  - which verbs are used with a particular noun
  - which adverbs are used to intensify a particular adjective

## Collocation in this dictionary

- To find out which adjectives to use with a particular noun, look at the examples at the entry for the noun. Typical adjectives used with the noun are separated by a slash (/).

### Can you say 'pink wine'?

**wine** ❶ **A1** /waɪn/ *noun, verb*
- **noun 1 ⭐ A1** [U, C] an alcoholic drink made from the juice of GRAPES that has been left to FERMENT. There are many different kinds of wine: *sparkling wine* ◊ *red/rosé/white wine* ◊ *a selection of fine wines* ◊ *a glass/bottle of wine* ◊ *He never drank wine, beer or spirits.* ⮞ see also RED WINE, TABLE WINE, WHITE WINE

(No, **rosé**)

If you look up an adjective you will see what nouns are commonly used with it:

### Which words can be used with the adjective 'heady'?

**heady** /ˈhedi/ *adj.* (**head·ier**, **headi·est**) **1** [usually before noun] having a strong effect on your senses; making you feel excited and confident SYN intoxicating: *the heady days of youth* ◊ *the heady scent of hot spices* ◊ *a heady mixture of desire and fear* ⮞ SYNONYMS AT EXCITING

(**days**, **scent**, **mixture**)

Look at the examples in a noun entry to find out what verbs can be used with it:

### Which verbs are used with 'mortgage'?

**mort·gage** ⭐+ **B2** /ˈmɔːɡɪdʒ; NAmE ˈmɔːrɡ-/ *noun, verb*
- **noun** (*also informal* **home loan**) a legal agreement by which a bank or similar organization lends you money to buy a house, etc., and you pay the money back over a particular number of years; the sum of money that you borrow: *to apply for/take out/pay off a mortgage* ◊ *mortgage rates* (= *of interest*) ◊ *a mortgage on the house* ◊ *a mortgage of £60 000* ◊ *monthly mortgage payments* ⮞ WORDFINDER NOTE *at* HOME ⮞ see also ENDOWMENT MORTGAGE

(**apply for**, **take out**, **pay off**)

If you look up an adjective, you will see which adverbs you can use to intensify it:

### 'Strongly' or 'bitterly' disappointed?

**dis·ap·point·ed** ❶ **B1** /ˌdɪsəˈpɔɪntɪd/ *adj.* upset because sth you hoped for has not happened or been as good, successful, etc. as you expected: *The singer has promised to refund any disappointed fans.* ◊ **~ at/by/about sth** *They were bitterly disappointed at the result of the game.* ◊ **~ in/with sb/sth** *I'm disappointed in you—I really thought I could trust you!* ◊ **~ to see, hear, etc.** *He was disappointed to see she wasn't at the party.* ◊ **~ (that)** … *I'm disappointed (that) it was sold out.* ◊ **~ (not) to be** … *She was disappointed not to be chosen.* ▶ **dis·ap·point·edly**

(**bitterly**)

Important collocations are printed in bold type within the examples. If the meaning of the collocation is not obvious there is a short explanation after it in brackets.

                   having unexpected luck
                   hoping you will be lucky

**luck** ❶ **A2** /lʌk/ *noun, verb*
- **noun** [U] **1 ⭐ A2** good things that happen to you by chance, not because of your own efforts or abilities: **with (any) ~** *With any luck, we'll be home before dark.* ◊ (*BrE*) *With a bit of luck, we'll finish on time.* ◊ **~ with (doing) sth** *So far I have had no luck with finding a job.* ◊ *I could hardly believe my luck when he said yes.* ◊ *It was a stroke of luck that we found you.* ◊ **by ~** *By sheer luck nobody was hurt in the explosion.* ◊ *We wish her luck in her new career.* ◊ **in ~** *You're in luck* (= *lucky*)—*there's one ticket left.* ◊ **out of ~** *You're out of luck. She's not here.* ◊ *What a piece of luck!* ⮞ see also BEGINNER'S LUCK

hoping someone else will be lucky
                               not being lucky

# Idioms

## What are idioms?

- An idiom is a phrase whose meaning is difficult or sometimes impossible to guess by looking at the meanings of the individual words it contains. For example, the phrase **be in the same boat** has a literal meaning that is easy to understand, but it also has a common idiomatic meaning:
  - *I found the job difficult at first. But we were all in the same boat; we were all learning.*

  Here, **be in the same boat** means 'to be in the same difficult or unfortunate situation'.

- Some idioms are imaginative expressions such as proverbs and sayings:
  - *Too many cooks spoil the broth.*
    (= If too many people are involved in something, it will not be well done.)

  If the expression is well known, part of it may be left out:
  - *Well, I knew everything would go wrong— it's the usual story of too many cooks!*

- Other idioms are short expressions that are used for a particular purpose:
  - *Hang in there!* (used to encourage somebody in a difficult situation)
  - *Get lost!* (a rude way of saying 'go away')

- Many idioms, however, are not vivid in this way. They are considered as idioms because their form is fixed:
  - *for certain*
  - *in any case*

## Idioms in the dictionary

- Idioms are defined at the entry for the first 'full' word (a noun, a verb, an adjective or an adverb) that they contain. This means ignoring any grammatical words such as articles and prepositions. Idioms follow the main senses of a word, in a section marked **IDM**:

  **IDM** in the blink of an ˈeye very quickly; in a short time on the ˈblink (*informal*) (of a machine) no longer working correctly

  The words **in**, **the** and **on** in these idioms do not count as 'full' words, and so the idioms are not listed at the entries for these words.

- Deciding where idioms start and stop is not always easy. If you hear the expression:
  - *They decided to bury the hatchet and try to be friends again.*

  you might think that **hatchet** is the only word you do not know and look that up.

  In fact, **bury the hatchet** is an idiomatic expression and it is defined at **bury**. At **hatchet** you will find a cross reference directing you to **bury**:

  **hatchet** /ˈhætʃɪt/ *noun* a small AXE (= a tool with a heavy metal BLADE for cutting things up) with a short handle ⊃ picture at AXE **IDM** see BURY

- Sometimes one 'full' word of an idiom can be replaced by another. For example, in the idiom **be a bag of nerves**, **bag** can be replaced by **bundle**. This is shown as **be a bag / bundle of nerves** and the idiom is defined at the first full fixed word, **nerve**. If you try to look the phrase up at either **bag** or **bundle** you will find a cross reference to **nerve** at the end of the idioms section.

  **IDM** not go a bundle on sb/sth (*BrE, informal*) to not like sb/sth very much ⊃ MORE AT DROP *v.*, NERVE *n.*

- A few very common verbs and the adjectives **bad** and **good** have so many idioms that they cannot all be listed in the entry. Instead, there is a note telling you to look at the entry for the next noun, verb, adjective, etc. in the idiom:

  **IDM HELP** Most idioms containing **go** are at the entries for the nouns and adjectives in the idioms, for example **go it alone** is at **alone**.

- In some idioms, many alternatives are possible. In the expression **disappear into thin air**, you could replace **disappear** with **vanish**, **melt** or **evaporate**. In the dictionary this is shown as **disappear, vanish, etc. into thin air**, showing that you can use other words with a similar meaning to **disappear** in the idiom. Since the first 'full' word of the idiom is not fixed, the expression is defined at **thin** with a cross-reference only at **air**.

  If you cannot find an idiom in the dictionary, look it up at the entry for one of the other main words in the expression.

  Some idioms only contain grammatical words such as **one**, **it** or **in**. These idioms are defined at the first word that appears in them. For example, the idiom **one up on sb** is defined at the entry for **one**.

  Idioms are given in alphabetical order within the idioms sections. Grammatical words such as **a/an** or **the**, **sb/sth** and the possessive forms **your**, **sb's**, **his**, **her**, etc., as well as words in brackets ( ) or after a slash (/), are ignored.

# English across the world

## The spread of English

English is spoken as a first language by more than 350 million people throughout the world, and used as a second language by as many, if not more. One in five of the world's population speaks English with some degree of competence. It is an official or semi-official language in over 70 countries, and it plays a significant role in many more.

## Englishes, not English

English is not just one standard language, but can be thought of as a 'family' that includes many different varieties. Of course, the vast majority of words and meanings shown in the *Oxford Advanced Learner's Dictionary* are used in all the regional varieties and cause no problem of understanding.

However, in order to do justice to the richness of the English language across the world, the *Oxford Advanced Learner's Dictionary* also includes vocabulary items specific to particular varieties of English.

We cover British and North American English and the difference between them in great detail in individual dictionary entries. For a summary of these differences, please see page R16.

The table below shows the labels we use in the dictionary to describe words from different areas where English is spoken.

| | |
|---|---|
| AustralE | Australian English |
| CanE | Canadian English |
| EAfrE | East African English |
| IndE | Indian English (the English of South Asia) |
| SAfrE | South African English |
| SEAsianE | South-East Asian English |
| WAfrE | West African English |

The pronunciations we show are those that a speaker of British or North American English would use to say the words. For many African English words we also show the pronunciation used by an African speaker of English.

From the UK and Ireland, we show Irish English (*IrishE*), English from Northern England (*NEngE*), Scottish English (*ScotE*) and Welsh English (*WelshE*).

## English across the UK and Ireland

Although English is spoken across the UK and Ireland, there are interesting variations in the vocabulary used in different areas.

Irish English, for example, is influenced by the Irish language and by Old and Middle English. Words such as *colleen* and *och* are derived from Irish, while words such as *craic* and *eejit* stem from Old and Middle English. *Och* is also used in Scottish English—Scottish Gaelic (pronounced /ˈɡælɪk/) and Irish Gaelic /ˈɡeɪlɪk/ are both Celtic languages with common roots. The *Oxford Advanced Learner's Dictionary* includes a variety of other Scottish English words, including *burn* and *brae* (from Old and Middle English) and *gillie* (from Gaelic). *Tatties* are from English 'potatoes' and are eaten with *neeps* (which sound like they should be turnips but are actually swedes).

Some standard English words, like *message* and *press*, have additional meanings in Irish or Scottish English. In both varieties, to *do the messages* means to do the grocery shopping, while a *press* is a large cupboard.

Dialects in the north of England vary greatly across counties. The dialect of Liverpool and Merseyside, for instance, is known informally as Scouse, and the dialect of Newcastle-upon-Tyne is known as Geordie. The vocabulary differences between standard British English and Northern English can mainly be seen in informal language and slang (*chuck, summat, ta-ra*). Interestingly, there are some similarities between Northern English and Scottish English. The two varieties share some items of vocabulary (*bairn, lass, wee*), which is perhaps unsurprising considering their geographical proximity.

Welsh English is made up of a several dialects of English specific to Wales. It is heavily influenced by Welsh, which is a distinct language spoken by approximately 20 per cent of the population of Wales. Welsh English words in the dictionary include *butty, dab* and *tamping*.

It is not just vocabulary that differs across regional varieties. Regional accents are common and can be very distinct. The accent of someone from Gloucestershire, for instance, is different from the accent of someone from Bristol, despite the fact that Gloucestershire borders Bristol. The British English pronunciation in the *Oxford Advanced Learner's Dictionary* represents what is referred to as Received Pronunciation (RP): see page R30 for more details of how pronunciation is shown in the dictionary.

## Australian and New Zealand English

Australian and New Zealand English generally follow British English in many aspects of vocabulary and spelling, although many North American words are used. A feature of both is that the line between formal and informal usage is not as clear as in some other varieties of English. Suffixes such as -*ie* and -*o* give us expressions such as *arvo* and *barbie* that are also used in quite formal contexts.

The vocabularies of Australian and New Zealand English have many words in common, for example *ute* and *sook*. They also have shared histories, with, for example, their participation in the First World War contributing words such as *Anzac* to their common vocabularies. But they also have developed distinct vocabularies. For example, New Zealanders have a type of holiday home called a *bach*, and Australians take their *Eskies* with them when they go camping.

Both Australian and New Zealand English have been shaped by the relationships between European settlers and indigenous populations. In Australia, there are numerous Aboriginal communities with many languages and dialects, and many words have been borrowed from these languages. They include *kangaroo*, *wallaby*, *Alcheringa* and *yakka*. In New Zealand, Maori has contributed many words to the vocabulary, including *haka* and *mana*; the Maori name for New Zealand (*Aotearoa* = 'the land of the long white cloud') is being used increasingly in international contexts.

## Canadian English

Canadian English has been influenced by both British and American English. In the dictionary, meanings and spellings that that are only used in the United States are marked *(US)*. Items that are also used in Canada are marked *(NAmE)* for *North American English*. Some British words such as *serviette* are used in Canadian English, but this is not shown in the dictionary. There are also a number of words that are exclusively Canadian: *eavestrough*, *humidex* and *parkade* are a few examples. Canadian English has also been influenced by Canada's history with the French, evidenced in words such as *poutine* and *toque*. In Canada both British and American spellings are used.

## English in Africa

English is today the African continent's single most widely used language. Several different varieties have developed in the different regions of the continent. These include **East African English** (spoken in countries such as Kenya, Tanzania and Uganda) and **West African English** (spoken in countries such as Nigeria and Ghana). Each of these has its own characteristic vocabulary, which includes words for local customs, food, modes of transport, clothing, musical instruments, etc.

East African English is influenced by the other languages spoken in East Africa: Kiswahili and Luo to name just two. These influences can be seen in vocabulary items such as *bodaboda*. *nyama choma*, *mzungu*, *daladala* and *nyatiti*.

West African English contains similar words stemming from indigenous languages: *garri*, *afara* and *agbada*, for instance. Some English words have been adapted and extended over time to convey specific meanings. A *been-to*, for example, is 'a person who returns to his or her home in Africa after studying, working, etc. in a foreign country', while the adverb *next tomorrow* is used to refer to the day after tomorrow.

**South African English** is the first language of about ten per cent of the population of South Africa, but the second language of many others. The language of Afrikaners (descendants of Dutch settlers) has influenced the English spoken in South Africa (*biltong*, *dorp*, *stoep*), but there are also many words that are borrowed from various other African languages (*donga*, *indaba*, *lobola*). Although some words stem from British or American English, they often have entirely different meanings from their British/American counterparts. A *robot* in South African English is a traffic light, while a *cafe* is a type of convenience store.

## English in South Asia

Geographically, South Asia comprises seven countries: India, Pakistan, Bangladesh, Sri Lanka, Nepal, Bhutan and the Maldives. Though there are noticeable similarities in the way English is spoken and written in these countries (hence, the label *South Asian English*), there are in fact seven distinctive regional varieties of English. Because of India's long history of contact with Britain and consequently with English, Indian English is often regarded as typical of the English used in the region.

Some words and phrases from South Asian English have their origin in the major languages of the region, like Hindi, Bengali, Tamil, Punjabi and Urdu: *bhai*, *jungle*, *jute*, *catamaran*, *bhangra* and *purdah*. Because of Britain's long history of contact with India, some of these words have also been adopted into British and other varieties of English, and speakers of these varieties may not always be aware of the South Asian origin of the words. Other words, which remain specific to South Asian English, like *taluk* and *panchayat*, are taken from regional languages and used to describe specific social structures. Some others, like the verbs *air-dash*, *chargesheet* and *prepone*, are formed from English but only used by Indian speakers of English. Several words of South Asian origin, like *bhaji* and *biryani* have become common in British English more recently because of the influence of the significant number of people of South Asian origin in Britain.

## English in South-East Asia

Although no single standard variety of English has emerged from this region, English is very important as a language of communication in countries such as Malaysia and Singapore. Words from these countries include the names of some local products, for example tropical fruits (*mangosteen*, *rambutan*). Some British English words and expressions have distinct meanings. *Bungalow*, for instance, refers to a large house that is not joined to another house on either side, and does not necessarily have only one level. *Uncle/auntie* is used as a polite way of referring to an older man/woman rather than always to refer to a particular family member.

# British and American English

American English differs from British English not only in pronunciation but also in vocabulary, spelling and grammar.

## Pronunciation

- When there is a specific American pronunciation it is labelled *NAmE* and given after the British pronunciation. For example, as there is no /ɒ/ vowel in American English, **dog** is shown as /dɒg; *NAmE* dɔːg/.
- While represented by the same symbols in the dictionary, some vowels and diphthongs differ in quality between British and American English.
- The three British English diphthongs /ɪə eə ʊə/ are described in American English as a simple vowel followed by /r/—so near is /nɪr/, hair is /her/ and pure is /pjʊr/.
- In American English an r in the spelling of a word is always accompanied by an /r/ in the pronunciation. In British English an /r/ is only pronounced before a vowel.
- The learner should pay particular attention to the widespread tapping of /t/ between vowels in American English, as described on page R31.

## Vocabulary

The dictionary tells you which words are used only in American English or have different meanings in British and American English, for example **cookie**, **elevator**, **trunk**.

## Spelling

The dictionary shows different spellings in British and American English. The following differences are particularly common:

- In verbs that end in *l* and are not stressed on the final syllable, in American English the l is not doubled in the *-ing* form and the past participle: **cancelling**; (US) **canceling**.
- Words that end in *-tre* are spelt *-ter* in American English: **centre**; (US) **center**.
- Words that end in *-our* are usually spelt *-or* in American English: **colour**; (US) **color**.
- Words that end in *-ogue* are often spelt *-og* in American English: **dialogue**; (US) **dialog**.
- In British English many verbs can be spelt with either *-ize* or *-ise*. In American English only the spelling with *-ize* is possible: **realize, -ise**; (US) **realize**.

## Grammar

### Present perfect/Simple past

In British English **just** is usually used with the present perfect. In American English the simple past is usually used.

- *I've just seen her.* (*BrE*)
- *I just saw her.* (*NAmE*)

In American English the simple past can also be used with **already** and **yet**, although the present perfect is often preferred:

- *Have you heard the news yet?* (*BrE and NAmE*)
- *Did you hear the news yet?* (*NAmE*)

### Have/have got

In British English it is possible to use **have got** or **have** to express the idea of possession. In American English only **have** can be used in questions and negative sentences:

- *They have/have got two computers.* (*BrE and NAmE*)
- *Have you got a computer? Yes, I have.* (*BrE*)
- *Do you have a computer? Yes, I do.* (*BrE and NAmE*)

### Get/gotten

In American English the past participle of **get** is **gotten**:

- *Your English has got better.* (*BrE*)
- *Your English has gotten better.* (*NAmE*)

### Prepositions and adverbs

Some prepositions and adverbs are used differently in British and American English, for example **stay at home** (*BrE*); **stay home** (*NAmE*).

### Form of the adverb

In informal American English the adverb form ending in *-ly* is often not used:

- *He looked at me really strangely.* (*BrE*)
- *He looked at me really strange.* (*NAmE*)

### Shall

**Shall** is not used instead of **will** in American English for the first person singular of the future:

- *I shall/will be here tomorrow.* (*BrE*)
- *I will be here tomorrow.* (*NAmE*)

Nor is it used in polite offers:

- *Shall I open the window?* (*BrE*)
- *Should I open the window?* (*NAmE*)

### Irregular verbs

In British English the past simple and past participle of many verbs can be formed with *-ed* or *-t*, for example **burned/burnt**. In American English the forms ending in *-ed* are usually used:

- *They burned/burnt the documents.* (*BrE*)
- *They burned the documents.* (*NAmE*)

When the past participle is used as an adjective, British English prefers the *-t* form, whereas in American English the *-ed* form is preferred, with the exception of **burnt**:

- *a spoilt child* (*BrE*)
- *a spoiled child* (*NAmE*)
- *burnt toast* (*BrE and NAmE*)

### Go/Come and…

In these expressions **and** is often omitted in American English:

- *Go and take a look outside.* (*BrE*)
- *Go take a look outside.* (*NAmE*)

### On the phone

- *Hello, is that David?* (*BrE*)
- *Hello, is this David?* (*NAmE*)

# Punctuation

## . full stop (*BrE*) (*NAmE* period)

- at the end of a sentence that is not a question or an exclamation:
  - *I knocked at the door. There was no reply. I knocked again.*
- sometimes in abbreviations:
  - *Jan. e.g. a.m. etc.*
- in internet and email addresses (said 'dot'):
  - *http://www.oup.com*

## , comma

- to separate words in a list, though they are often omitted before *and*:
  - *a bouquet of red, pink and white roses*
  - *tea, coffee, milk or hot chocolate*
- to separate phrases or clauses:
  - *If you keep calm, take your time, concentrate and think ahead, then you're likely to pass your test.*
  - *Worn out after all the excitement of the party, the children soon fell asleep.*
- before and after a clause or phrase that gives additional, but not essential, information about the noun it follows:
  - *The Pennine Hills, which are very popular with walkers, are situated between Lancashire and Yorkshire.*

  (do not use commas before and after a clause that **defines** the noun it follows)
  - *The hills that separate Lancashire from Yorkshire are called the Pennines.*
- to separate main clauses, especially long ones, linked by a conjunction such as *and, as, but, for, or*:
  - *We had been looking forward to our holiday all year, but unfortunately it rained every day.*
- to separate an introductory word or phrase, or an adverb or adverbial phrase that applies to the whole sentence, from the rest of the sentence:
  - *Oh, so that's where it was.*
  - *As it happens, however, I never saw her again.*
  - *By the way, did you hear about Sue's car?*
- to separate a tag question from the rest of the sentence:
  - *It's quite expensive, isn't it?*
  - *You live in Bristol, right?*

- before or after 'he said', etc. when writing down conversation:
  - *'Come back soon,' she said.*
- before a short quotation:
  - *Disraeli said, 'Little things affect little minds.'*

## : colon

- to introduce a list of items:
  - *These are our options: we go by train and leave before the end of the show; or we take the car and see it all.*
- in formal writing, before a clause or phrase that gives more information about the main clause. (You can use a semicolon or a full stop, but not a comma, instead of a colon here.)
  - *The garden had been neglected for a long time: it was overgrown and full of weeds.*
- to introduce a quotation, which may be indented:
  - *As Kenneth Morgan writes:*
    *The truth was, perhaps, that Britain in the years from 1914 to 1983 had not changed all that fundamentally. Others, however, have challenged this view ...*

## ; semicolon

- instead of a comma to separate parts of a sentence that already contain commas:
  - *She was determined to succeed whatever the cost; she would achieve her aim, whoever might suffer on the way.*
- in formal writing, to separate two main clauses, especially those not joined by a conjunction:
  - *The sun was already low in the sky; it would soon be dark.*

## ? question mark

- at the end of a direct question:
  - *Where's the car?*
  - *You're leaving already?*

Do not use a question mark at the end of an indirect question:
  - *He asked if I was leaving.*

- especially with a date, to express doubt:
  - *John Marston (?1575–1634)*

## ! exclamation mark (*especially BrE*) (*NAmE usually* exclamation point)

- at the end of a sentence expressing surprise, joy, anger, shock or another strong emotion:
  - *That's marvellous!*
  - *'Never!' she cried.*
- in informal written English, you can use more than one exclamation mark, or an exclamation mark and a question mark:
  - *'Your wife's just given birth to triplets.' 'Triplets!?'*

## ' apostrophe

- with *s* to indicate that a thing or person belongs to somebody:
  - *my friend's brother*
  - *the waitress's apron*
  - *King James's crown/King James' crown*
  - *the students' books*
  - *the women's coats*
- in short forms, to indicate that letters or figures have been omitted:
  - *I'm* (*I am*)
  - *they'd* (*they had/they would*)
  - *the summer of '89* (*1989*)
- sometimes, with *s* to form the plural of a letter, a figure or an abbreviation:
  - *roll your r's*
  - *during the 1990's*

## - hyphen

- to form a compound from two or more other words:
  - *hard-hearted*
  - *fork-lift truck*
  - *mother-to-be*
- to form a compound from a prefix and a proper name:
  - *pre-Raphaelite*
  - *pro-European*
- when writing compound numbers between 21 and 99 in words:
  - *seventy-three*
  - *thirty-one*
- sometimes, in British English, to separate a prefix ending in a vowel from a word beginning with the same vowel:
  - *co-operate*
  - *pre-eminent*
- after the first section of a word that is divided between one line and the next:
  - *decide what to do in order to avoid mis- takes of this kind in the future*

## — dash

- in informal English, instead of a colon or semicolon, to indicate that what follows is a summary or conclusion of what has gone before:
  - *Men were shouting, women were screaming, children were crying — it was chaos.*
  - *You've admitted that you lied to me — how can I trust you again?*
- singly or in pairs to separate a comment or an afterthought from the rest of the sentence:
  - *He knew nothing at all about it — or so he said.*

## ... dots/ellipsis

- to indicate that words have been omitted, especially from a quotation or at the end of a conversation:
  - *... challenging the view that Britain ... had not changed all that fundamentally.*

## / slash/oblique

- to separate alternative words or phrases:
  - *have a pudding and/or cheese*
  - *single/married/widowed/divorced*
- in internet and email addresses to separate the different elements (often said 'forward slash'):
  - *http://www.oup.com/elt/*

## " " quotation marks

- to enclose words and punctuation in direct speech:
  - *'Why on earth did you do that?' he asked.*
  - *'I'll fetch it,' she replied.*
- to draw attention to a word that is unusual for the context, for example a slang expression, or to a word that is being used for special effect, such as irony:
  - *He told me in no uncertain terms to 'get lost'.*
  - *Thousands were imprisoned in the name of 'national security'.*
- around the titles of articles, books, poems, plays, etc:
  - *Keats's 'Ode to Autumn'*
  - *I was watching 'Match of the Day'.*
- around short quotations or sayings:
  - *Do you know the origin of the saying: 'A little learning is a dangerous thing'?*
- in American English, double quotation marks are used:
  - *"Help! I'm drowning!"*

## () brackets (BrE)
(also **parentheses** NAmE or formal)

- to separate extra information or a comment from the rest of a sentence:
  - *Mount Robson (12 972 feet) is the highest mountain in the Canadian Rockies.*
  - *He thinks that modern music (i.e. anything written after 1900) is rubbish.*
- to enclose cross references:
  - *This moral ambiguity is a feature of Shakespeare's later works (see Chapter Eight).*
- around numbers or letters in text:
  - *Our objectives are (1) to increase output, (2) to improve quality and (3) to maximize profits.*

## [ ] square brackets (especially BrE)
(NAmE usually **brackets**)

- around words inserted to make a quotation grammatically correct:
  - *Britain in [these] years was without …*

## italics

- to show emphasis:
  - I'm not going to do it—*you are.*
  - *… proposals which we cannot accept under any circumstances*
- to indicate the titles of books, plays, etc:
  - Joyce's *Ulysses*
  - the title role in Puccini's *Tosca*
  - a letter in *The Times*
- for foreign words or phrases:
  - the English oak (*Quercus robur*)
  - I had to renew my *permesso di soggiorno* (residence permit).

## Quoting conversation

- When you write down a conversation, you normally begin a new paragraph for each new speaker.

  Quotation marks enclose the words spoken:
  - *'You're sure of this?' I asked.*
    *He nodded grimly.*
    *'I'm certain.'*

- Verbs used to indicate direct speech, for example *he said, she complained*, are separated by commas from the words spoken, unless a question mark or an exclamation mark is used:
  - *'That's all I know,' said Nick.*
  - *Nick said, 'That's all I know.'*
  - *'Why?' asked Nick.*

  When *he said* or *said Nick* follows the words spoken, the comma is placed inside the quotation marks, as in the first example above. If, however, the writer puts the words *said Nick* within the actual words Nick speaks, the comma is outside the quotation marks:
  - *'That', said Nick, 'is all I know.'*

- Double quotation marks are used to indicate direct speech being quoted by somebody else within direct speech:
  - *'But you said you loved me! "I'll never leave you, Sue, as long as I live." That's what you said, isn't it?'*

# Numbers

## Writing and saying numbers

**Numbers over 20**
- are written with a hyphen:
  - 35 *thirty-five*
  - 67 *sixty-seven*

**Numbers over 100**
- 329 *three hundred and twenty-nine*
- The **and** is pronounced /n/ and the stress is on the final number.
- In American English the **and** is sometimes left out.

**Numbers over 1000**
- 1100 *one thousand, one hundred* (also informal *eleven hundred*)
- 2500 *two thousand, five hundred* (also *twenty-five hundred*, especially in NAmE or informal)
- These informal forms are most common for whole hundreds between 1100 and 1900.
- A comma or (in *BrE*) a space is often used to divide large numbers into groups of 3 figures:
  - 33,423 or 33 423 (*thirty-three thousand, four hundred and twenty-three*)
  - 2,768,941 or 2 768 941 (*two million, seven hundred and sixty-eight thousand, nine hundred and forty-one*)

## A or one?

- 130    *a/one hundred and thirty*
- 1 000 000    *a/one million*

- **one** is more formal and more precise and can be used for emphasis:
  - *The total cost was one hundred and sixty-three pounds exactly.*
  - *It cost about a hundred and fifty quid.*

- **a** can only be used at the beginning of a number:
  - 1000    *a/one thousand*
  - 2100    *two thousand, one hundred*
  - ~~two thousand a hundred~~

- **a** is not usually used between 1100 and 1999:
  - 1099    *a/one thousand and ninety-nine*
  - 1100    *one thousand, one hundred*
  - 1340    *one thousand, three hundred and forty*
           ~~a thousand, three hundred and forty~~

## Ordinal numbers

| 1st | *first* | 5th | *fifth* |
| 2nd | *second* | 9th | *ninth* |
| 3rd | *third* | 12th | *twelfth* |
| 4th | *fourth* | 21st | *twenty-first etc.* |

## Fractions

| ½ | *a/one half* |
| ⅓ | *a/one third* |
| ¼ | *a/one quarter* (also *a/one fourth* especially in NAmE) |

(for emphasis use **one** instead of **a**)

| ¹⁄₁₂ | *one twelfth* |
| ¹⁄₁₆ | *one sixteenth* |
| ⅔ | *two thirds* |
| ¾ | *three quarters* (also *three fourths* especially in NAmE) |
| ⁹⁄₁₀ | *nine tenths* |

**More complex fractions**
- use **over**:
  - ¹⁹⁄₅₆    *nineteen* **over** *fifty-six*
  - ³¹⁄₁₄₄    *thirty-one* **over** *one four four*

**Whole numbers and fractions**
- link with **and**:
  - 2½    *two* **and** *a half*
  - 5⅔    *five* **and** *two thirds*

- **one** plus a fraction is followed by a plural noun:
  - 1½ pts    *one and a half* **pints**

**Fractions/Percentages and noun phrases**
- use **of**:
  - *a fifth* **of** *the women questioned*
  - *three quarters* **of** *the population*
  - *75%* **of** *the population*

- with **half** do not use **a**, and **of** can sometimes be omitted:
  - *Half (of) the work is already finished.*

- do not use **of** in expressions of measurement or quantity:
  - *half a pint of milk*
  - *It takes me half an hour by bus.*

- use **of** before pronouns:
  - *We can't start—only half* **of** *us are here.*

**Fractions/Percentages and verbs**
- If a fraction/percentage is used with an uncountable or a singular noun the verb is generally singular:
  - *Fifty per cent of the land is cultivated.*
  - *Half (of) the land is cultivated.*

- If the noun is singular but represents a group of people, the verb is singular in American English but in British English it may be singular or plural:
  - *Three quarters/75 per cent of the workforce is/are against the strike.*
- If the noun is plural, the verb is plural:
  - *Two thirds/67 per cent of children play computer games.*

## Decimals

- write and say with a point (.) (not a comma)
- say each figure after the point separately:
  - 79.3  *seventy-nine point three*
  - 3.142  *three point one four two*
  - 0.67  *(zero) point six seven*
    *(BrE also nought point six seven)*

## Mathematical expressions

- $+$  plus
- $-$  minus
- $\times$  times/multiplied by
- $\div$  divided by
- $=$  equals/is
- %  per cent *(especially BrE)*
  *(NAmE usually percent)*
- $3^2$  three squared
- $5^3$  five cubed
- $6^{10}$  six to the power of ten
- $\sqrt{\ }$  square root of

## The figure '0'

The figure **0** has several different names in English, although in American English *zero* is commonly used in all cases:

### Zero

- used in precise scientific, medical and economic contexts and to talk about temperature:
  - *It was ten degrees below zero last night.*
  - *zero inflation/growth/profit*

### Nought

- used in British English to talk about a number, age, etc:
  - *A million is written with six noughts.*
  - *The car goes from nought to sixty in ten seconds.*
  - *clothes for children aged nought to six*

### 'o' /əʊ/

- used when saying a bank account number, phone number, etc.

### Nil

- used to talk about the score in a team game, for example in football:
  - *The final score was one nil. (1–0)*
- used to mean 'nothing at all':
  - *The doctors rated her chances as nil.*

### Phone numbers

- All numbers are said separately. 0 is pronounced /əʊ/
  - *(01865) 556767*
    *o one eight six five, five five six seven six seven (or double five six seven six seven)*

## Temperature

- The Celsius or Centigrade (°C) scale is officially used in the UK and for scientific purposes in the US:
  - *a high of thirty-five degrees Celsius*
  - *The normal temperature of the human body is 37°C.*
- The Fahrenheit (°F) scale is used in all other contexts in the US and is also still sometimes used in the UK. The words 'degrees Fahrenheit/Centigrade/Celsius' are often omitted:
  - *Temperatures soared to over a hundred. (100°F)*
  - *She's ill in bed with a temperature of a hundred and two. (102°F)*

## Money

### In the UK

- 100 pence/p = 1 British pound (£1)
- *It costs 90p/90 pence.*
- when talking about an individual coin:
  - *a twenty pence piece/a twenty p piece*
- when talking about pounds and pence people often only say the numbers:
  - *It only cost five ninety-nine. (£5.99)*
- in informal British English:
  - £1  *a quid*
  - £5  *five quid or a fiver*
  - £10  *ten quid or a tenner*

### In the US

| | | |
|---|---|---|
| 1¢ | one cent | a penny |
| 5¢ | five cents | a nickel |
| 10¢ | ten cents | a dime |
| 25¢ | twenty-five cents | a quarter |
| $1.00 | one dollar | a dollar bill |

- in informal American English dollars are called **bucks**:
  - *This shirt cost fifty bucks.*

## Writing and saying dates

### British English
- 14 October 2021 or 14th October 2021 (14/10/21)
- Her birthday is on **the ninth of** December.
- Her birthday is on December **the ninth**.

### American English
- October 14, 2021 (10/14/21)
- Her birthday is December 9th.

### Years
| | |
|---|---|
| 1999 | nineteen ninety-nine |
| 1608 | sixteen o eight (or, less commonly, nineteen hundred and ninety-nine and sixteen hundred and eight) |
| 1700 | seventeen hundred |
| 2000 | (the year) two thousand |
| 2002 | two thousand and two |
| 2020 | twenty twenty |

AD 76/A.D. 76     AD seventy-six
76 CE/76 C.E.     seventy-six CE
(Both these expressions mean '76 years after the beginning of the Christian calendar'.)

1000 BC/1000 B.C.     one thousand BC
1000 BCE/1000 B.C.E    one thousand BCE
(Both these expressions mean '1000 years before the beginning of the Christian calendar'.)

## Age

- when saying a person's age use only numbers:
  - *Sue is 10 and Tom is 6.*
  - *She left home at 16.*

- a man/woman/boy/girl, etc. of …
  - *They've got a girl of 3 and a boy of 5.*
  - *a young woman of 19*

- in writing, in descriptions or to emphasize sb's age use … **years old**:
  - *She was 31 years old and a barrister by profession.*
  - *He is described as white, 5ft 10 ins tall and about 50 years old.*
  - *You're 40 years old—stop behaving like a teenager!*

- **… years old** is also used for things:
  - *The monument is 120 years old.*

- You can also say a … **year-old/month-old/ week-old**, etc.:
  - *Youth training is available to all 16-year-olds.*
  - *a 10-week-old baby*
  - *a remarkable 1 000-year-old tomb*

- Use … **years of age** in formal or written contexts:
  - *Not applicable to persons under eighteen years of age*

- Use **the … age group** to talk about people between certain ages:
  - *He took first prize in the 10–16 age group.*

- To give the approximate age of a person:
  | | |
  |---|---|
  | 13–19 | *in his/her teens* |
  | 20–29 | *in his/her twenties* |
  | 30–33 | *in his/her early thirties* |
  | 34–36 | *in his/her mid-thirties* |
  | 37–39 | *in his/her late thirties* |

- To refer to a particular event you can use **at/by/before, etc. the age of …**
  - *Most smokers start smoking cigarettes before the age of 16.*

## Numbers in time

There is often more than one way of telling the time:

### Half hours
6:30   *six thirty, half past six*
      (also BrE informal *half six*)

### Other times
| | | |
|---|---|---|
| 5:45 | *five forty-five* | *(a) quarter to six* (NAmE also *(a) quarter of six*) |
| 2:15 | *two fifteen* | *(a) quarter past two* (NAmE also *(a) quarter after two*) |
| 1:10 | *one ten* | *ten past one* (NAmE also *ten after one*) |
| 3:05 | *three o five* | *five past three* (NAmE also *five after three*) |
| 1:55 | *one fifty-five* | *five to two* (especially BrE) (NAmE also *five of two*) |

- with 5, 10, 20 and 25 the word **minutes** is not necessary, but it is used with other numbers:
  | | |
  |---|---|
  | 10.25 | *twenty-five past/after ten* |
  | 10.17 | *seventeen minutes past/after ten* |

- use **o'clock** only for whole hours:
  - *It's three o'clock.*

- If it is necessary to specify the time of day use **in the morning**, **in the afternoon**, **in the evening** or **at night**.

- in more formal contexts use:
  **a.m.** = in the morning or after midnight
  **p.m.** = in the afternoon, in the evening or before midnight
  - *He gets up at 4 a.m. to deliver the mail.*

Do not use **o'clock** with **a.m.** or **p.m.**:
  - *He gets up at 4 o'clock a.m.*
    *He gets up at 4 o'clock in the morning.*

## Twenty-four hour clock

- used for military purposes and in some other particular contexts, for example on train timetables in Britain:
  - 13:52  *thirteen fifty-two* (1:52 p.m.)
  - 22:30  *twenty-two thirty* (10:30 p.m.)

- for military purposes whole hours are said as **hundred hours:**
  - 0400  (o) *four hundred hours* (4 a.m.)
  - 2400  *twenty four hundred hours* (midnight)

## Expressing time

- When referring to days, weeks, etc. in the past, present and future the following expressions are used, speaking from a point of view in the present:

|  | past | present | future |
|---|---|---|---|
| morning | *yesterday morning* | *this morning* | *tomorrow morning* |
| afternoon | *yesterday afternoon* | *this afternoon* | *tomorrow afternoon* |
| evening | *yesterday evening* | *this evening* | *tomorrow evening* |
| night | *last night* | *tonight* | *tomorrow night* |
| day | *yesterday* | *today* | *tomorrow* |
| week | *last week* | *this week* | *next week* |
| month | *last month* | *this month* | *next month* |
| year | *last year* | *this year* | *next year* |

- To talk about a time further back in the past or further forward in the future use:

| past | future |
|---|---|
| *the day before yesterday* | *the day after tomorrow* |
| *the week/month/year before last* | *the week/month/year after next* |
| *two days/weeks, etc. ago* | *in two days/weeks, etc. time* |

- To talk about sth that happens regularly use expressions with '**every**'
  - He has to work **every third** weekend.
  - I wash my hair **every other** day (= every second day).

- In British English a period of two weeks is a **fortnight**.
  - I've got a **fortnight's** holiday in Spain.

## Prepositions of time

**in** (the)

| | |
|---|---|
| parts of the day (not night) | *in the morning(s), in the evening(s),* etc. |
| months | *in February* |
| seasons | *in (the) summer* |
| years | *in 1995* |
| decades | *in the 1920s* |
| centuries | *in the twentieth century* |

**on** (the)

| | |
|---|---|
| day of the week | *on Saturdays* |
| dates | *on (the) 20th (of) May* (NAmE also *on May 20th*) |
| particular days | *on Good Friday* |
| | *on New Year's Day* |
| | *on my birthday* |
| | *on the following day* |
| weekends | *on the weekend* (especially NAmE) |
| | *on a weekend* (BrE, informal) |

**at** (the)

| | |
|---|---|
| clock time | *at 5 o'clock* |
| | *at 7.45 p.m.* |
| night | *at night* |
| holiday periods | *at Christmas* |
| | *at the weekend* (BrE) |

# Geographical names

These lists show the spelling and pronunciation of geographical names.

If a country has different words for the country, adjective and person, all are given, (e.g. **Denmark**; **Danish**, **a Dane**). To make the plural of a word for a person from a particular country, add **-s**, except for **Swiss** and for words ending in **-ese** (e.g. **Japanese**), which stay the same, and for words that end in **-man** or **-woman**, which change to **-men** or **-women**.

(Inclusion in this list does not imply status as a sovereign state.)

| Noun | Adjective, Person |
|---|---|
| **Afghanistan** /æfˈgænɪstɑːn, -stæn/ *NAmE* -stæn/ | **Afghan** /ˈæfgæn/ |
| **Africa** /ˈæfrɪkə/ | **African** /ˈæfrɪkən/ |
| **Albania** /ælˈbeɪniə/ | **Albanian** /ælˈbeɪniən/ |
| **Algeria** /ælˈdʒɪəriə/ *NAmE* -ˈdʒɪr-/ | **Algerian** /ælˈdʒɪəriən/ *NAmE* -ˈdʒɪr-/ |
| **America** /əˈmerɪkə/ | **American** /əˈmerɪkən/ |
| **Andorra** /ænˈdɔːrə/ | **Andorran** /ænˈdɔːrən/ |
| **Angola** /æŋˈgəʊlə/ | **Angolan** /æŋˈgəʊlən/ |
| **Antarctica** /ænˈtɑːktɪkə/ *NAmE* -ˈtɑːrk-/ | **Antarctic** /ænˈtɑːktɪk/ *NAmE* -ˈtɑːrk-/ |
| **Antigua and Barbuda** /ænˌtiːgə ən bɑːˈbjuːdə/ *NAmE* bɑːrˈb-/ | **Antiguan** /ænˈtiːgən/<br>**Barbudan** /bɑːˈbjuːdən/ *NAmE* bɑːrˈb-/ |
| **(the) Arctic Ocean** /ˌɑːktɪk ˈəʊʃn/ *NAmE* ˌɑːrktɪk/ | **Arctic** /ˈɑːktɪk/ *NAmE* ˈɑːrk-/ |
| **Argentina** /ˌɑːdʒənˈtiːnə/ *NAmE* ˌɑːrdʒ-/ | **Argentinian** /ˌɑːdʒənˈtɪniən/ *NAmE* ˌɑːrdʒ-/<br>**Argentine** /ˈɑːdʒəntaɪn/ *NAmE* ˈɑːrdʒ-/ |
| **Armenia** /ɑːˈmiːniə/ *NAmE* ɑːrˈm-/ | **Armenian** /ɑːˈmiːniən/ *NAmE* ɑːrˈm-/ |
| **Asia** /ˈeɪʒə/ *BrE also* ˈeɪʃə/ | **Asian** /ˈeɪʒn/ *BrE also* ˈeɪʃn/ |
| **(the) Atlantic Ocean** /ətˌlæntɪk ˈəʊʃn/ | |
| **Australasia** /ˌɒstrəˈleɪʒə, -ˈleɪʃə/ *NAmE* ˌɔːstrəˈleɪʒə/ | **Australasian** /ˌɒstrəˈleɪʒn, -ˈleɪʃn/ *NAmE* ˌɔːstrəˈleɪʒn/ |
| **Australia** /ɒˈstreɪliə/ *NAmE* ɔːˈs-/ | **Australian** /ɒˈstreɪliən/ *NAmE* ɔːˈs-/ |
| **Austria** /ˈɒstriə/ *NAmE* ˈɔːs-/ | **Austrian** /ˈɒstriən/ *NAmE* ˈɔːs-/ |
| **Azerbaijan** /ˌæzəbaɪˈdʒɑːn/ *NAmE* -zərb-/ | **Azerbaijani** /ˌæzəbaɪˈdʒɑːni/ *NAmE* -zərb-/<br>**Azeri** /əˈzeəri/ *NAmE* əˈzeri/ |
| **(the) Bahamas** /bəˈhɑːməz/ | **Bahamian** /bəˈheɪmiən/ |
| **Bahrain** /bɑːˈreɪn/ | **Bahraini** /bɑːˈreɪni/ |
| **Bangladesh** /ˌbæŋgləˈdeʃ/ | **Bangladeshi** /ˌbæŋgləˈdeʃi/ |
| **Barbados** /bɑːˈbeɪdɒs/ *NAmE* bɑːrˈbeɪdəʊs/ | **Barbadian** /bɑːˈbeɪdiən/ *NAmE* bɑːrˈb-/ |
| **Belarus** /ˌbeləˈruːs/ | **Belarusian** /ˌbeləˈruːsiən/<br>**Belorussian** /ˌbeləˈrʌʃn/ |
| **Belgium** /ˈbeldʒəm/ | **Belgian** /ˈbeldʒən/ |
| **Belize** /bəˈliːz/ | **Belizean** /bəˈliːziən/ |
| **Benin** /beˈniːn/ | **Beninese** /ˌbenɪˈniːz/ |
| **Bhutan** /buːˈtɑːn/ | **Bhutanese** /ˌbuːtəˈniːz/ |
| **Bolivia** /bəˈlɪviə/ | **Bolivian** /bəˈlɪviən/ |
| **Bosnia and Herzegovina** /ˌbɒzniə ən ˌhɜːtsəgəˈviːnə/ *NAmE* ˌbɑːzniə ən ˌhɜːrtsəgəʊˈviːnə/ | **Bosnian** /ˈbɒzniən/ *NAmE* ˈbɑːz-/<br>**Herzegovinian** /ˌhɜːtsəgəˈvɪniən/ *NAmE* ˌhɜːrtsəgəʊˈv-/ |
| **Botswana** /bɒtˈswɑːnə/ *NAmE* bɑːt-/ | **Botswanan** /bɒtˈswɑːnən/ *NAmE* bɑːt-/<br>person **a Motswana** /mɒtˈswɑːnə/ *NAmE* mɑːt-/<br>people **Batswana** /bætˈswɑːnə/ *NAmE* bɑːt-/ |
| **Brazil** /brəˈzɪl/ | **Brazilian** /brəˈzɪliən/ |
| **Brunei** /bruːˈnaɪ/ | **Bruneian** /bruːˈnaɪən/ |
| **Bulgaria** /bʌlˈgeəriə/ *NAmE* -ˈger-/ | **Bulgarian** /bʌlˈgeəriən/ *NAmE* -ˈger-/ |
| **Burkina Faso** /bɜːˌkiːnə ˈfæsəʊ/ *NAmE* bɜːrˌkiːnə ˈfɑːsəʊ/ | **Burkinabe** /bɜːˌkiːnəˈbeɪ/ *NAmE* bɜːrˌk-/ |
| **Burma** /ˈbɜːmə/ *NAmE* ˈbɜːrmə/<br>→ see also **Myanmar** | **Burmese** /bɜːˈmiːz/ *NAmE* bɜːrˈm-/ |
| **Burundi** /bʊˈrʊndi/ | **Burundian** /bʊˈrʊndiən/ |
| **Cambodia** /kæmˈbəʊdiə/ | **Cambodian** /kæmˈbəʊdiən/ |
| **Cameroon** /ˌkæməˈruːn/ | **Cameroonian** /ˌkæməˈruːniən/ |
| **Canada** /ˈkænədə/ | **Canadian** /kəˈneɪdiən/ |
| **Cape Verde** /ˌkeɪp ˈvɜːd/ *NAmE* ˈvɜːrd/ | **Cape Verdean** /ˌkeɪp ˈvɜːdiən/ *NAmE* ˈvɜːrd-/ |
| **(the) Caribbean Sea** /ˌkærɪbiːən ˈsiː, kəˌrɪbiən/ | **Caribbean** /ˌkærɪˈbiːən, kəˈrɪbiən/ |
| **(the) Central African Republic** /ˌsentrəl ˌæfrɪkən rɪˈpʌblɪk/ | **Central African** /ˌsentrəl ˈæfrɪkən/ |
| **Chad** /tʃæd/ | **Chadian** /ˈtʃædiən/ |
| **Chile** /ˈtʃɪli/ | **Chilean** /ˈtʃɪliən/ *NAmE also* tʃɪˈleɪən/ |
| **China** /ˈtʃaɪnə/ | **Chinese** /tʃaɪˈniːz/ |
| **Colombia** /kəˈlʌmbiə/ | **Colombian** /kəˈlʌmbiən/ |

| Noun | Adjective, Person |
|---|---|
| Comoros /ˈkɒmərəʊz; NAmE ˈkɑːmərəʊz/ | Comoran /kəˈmɔːrən/ |
| Congo /ˈkɒŋɡəʊ; NAmE ˈkɑː-ŋ-/ | Congolese /ˌkɒŋɡəˈliːz; NAmE ˌkɑː-ŋ-/ |
| (the) Democratic Republic of the Congo (DR Congo) /ˌdeməˌkrætɪk rɪˌpʌblɪk əv ðə ˈkɒŋɡəʊ; NAmE ˈkɑː-ŋ-/ | Congolese /ˌkɒŋɡəˈliːz; NAmE ˌkɑː-ŋ-/ |
| Costa Rica /ˌkɒstə ˈriːkə; NAmE ˌkəʊstə, ˌkɑːstə/ | Costa Rican /ˌkɒstə ˈriːkən; NAmE ˌkəʊstə, ˌkɑːstə/ |
| Côte d'Ivoire /ˌkəʊt diːˈvwɑː(r)/ → see also Ivory Coast | Ivorian /aɪˈvɔːriən/ |
| Croatia /krəʊˈeɪʃə/ | Croatian /krəʊˈeɪʃn/ |
| Cuba /ˈkjuːbə/ | Cuban /ˈkjuːbən/ |
| Cyprus /ˈsaɪprəs/ | Cypriot /ˈsɪpriət/ |
| Czechia /ˈtʃekiə/, (the) Czech Republic /tʃek rɪˈpʌblɪk/ | Czech /tʃek/ |
| Denmark /ˈdenmɑːk; NAmE -mɑːrk/ | Danish /ˈdeɪnɪʃ/, a Dane /deɪn/ |
| Djibouti /dʒɪˈbuːti/ | Djiboutian /dʒɪˈbuːtiən/ |
| Dominica /ˌdɒmɪˈniːkə; NAmE ˌdɑːm-/ | Dominican /ˌdɒmɪˈniːkən; NAmE ˌdɑːm-/ |
| (the) Dominican Republic /dəˌmɪnɪkən rɪˈpʌblɪk/ | Dominican /dəˈmɪnɪkən/ |
| East Timor /ˌiːst ˈtiːmɔː(r)/ → see also Timor-Leste | East Timorese /ˌiːst ˌtɪməˈriːz/ |
| Ecuador /ˈekwədɔː(r)/ | Ecuadorian, Ecuadorean /ˌekwəˈdɔːriən/ |
| Egypt /ˈiːdʒɪpt/ | Egyptian /iˈdʒɪpʃn/ |
| El Salvador /ˌel ˈsælvədɔː(r)/ | Salvadoran /ˌsælvəˈdɔːrən/<br>Salvadorean /ˌsælvəˈdɔːriən/ |
| Equatorial Guinea /ˌekwətɔːriəl ˈɡɪni; NAmE also ˌiːk-/ | Equatorial Guinean /ˌekwətɔːriəl ˈɡɪniən; NAmE also ˌiːk-/ |
| Eritrea /ˌerɪˈtreɪə; NAmE -ˈtriːə/ | Eritrean /ˌerɪˈtreɪən; NAmE -ˈtriːən/ |
| Estonia /eˈstəʊniə/ | Estonian /eˈstəʊniən/ |
| Eswatini /ˌeswəˈtiːni/ → see also Swaziland | |
| Ethiopia /ˌiːθiˈəʊpiə/ | Ethiopian /ˌiːθiˈəʊpiən/ |
| Europe /ˈjʊərəp; NAmE ˈjʊrəp/ | European /ˌjʊərəˈpiːən; NAmE ˌjʊr-/ |
| Fiji /ˈfiːdʒiː/ | Fijian /fɪˈdʒiːən; NAmE ˈfiːdʒiːən, fɪˈdʒiːən/ |
| Finland /ˈfɪnlənd/ | Finnish /ˈfɪnɪʃ/, a Finn /fɪn/ |
| France /frɑːns; NAmE fræns/ | French /frentʃ/, a Frenchman /ˈfrentʃmən/<br>a Frenchwoman /ˈfrentʃwʊmən/ |
| Gabon /ɡæˈbɒn; NAmE ɡæˈbəʊn/ | Gabonese /ˌɡæbəˈniːz/ |
| (the) Gambia /ˈɡæmbiə/ | Gambian /ˈɡæmbiən/ |
| Georgia /ˈdʒɔːdʒə; NAmE ˈdʒɔːrdʒə/ | Georgian /ˈdʒɔːdʒən; NAmE ˈdʒɔːrdʒən/ |
| Germany /ˈdʒɜːməni; NAmE ˈdʒɜːrm-/ | German /ˈdʒɜːmən; NAmE ˈdʒɜːrm-/ |
| Ghana /ˈɡɑːnə/ | Ghanaian /ɡɑːˈneɪən/ |
| Greece /ɡriːs/ | Greek /ɡriːk/ |
| Grenada /ɡrəˈneɪdə/ | Grenadian /ɡrəˈneɪdiən/ |
| Guatemala /ˌɡwɑːtəˈmɑːlə; BrE also ˌɡwæt-/ | Guatemalan /ˌɡwɑːtəˈmɑːlən; BrE also ˌɡwæt-/ |
| Guinea /ˈɡɪni/ | Guinean /ˈɡɪniən/ |
| Guinea-Bissau /ˌɡɪni bɪˈsaʊ/ | Guinean /ˈɡɪniən/ |
| Guyana /ɡaɪˈænə, -ˈɑːnə/ | Guyanese /ˌɡaɪəˈniːz/ |
| Haiti /ˈheɪti/ | Haitian /ˈheɪʃn/ |
| Honduras /hɒnˈdjʊərəs; NAmE hɑːˈnʊərəs/ | Honduran /hɒnˈdjʊərən; NAmE hɑːˈnʊərən/ |
| Hungary /ˈhʌŋɡəri/ | Hungarian /hʌŋˈɡeəriən; NAmE -ˈɡer-/ |
| Iceland /ˈaɪslənd/ | Icelandic /aɪsˈlændɪk/,<br>an Icelander /ˈaɪsləndə(r)/ |
| India /ˈɪndiə/ | Indian /ˈɪndiən/ |
| (the) Indian Ocean /ˌɪndiən ˈəʊʃn/ | |
| Indonesia /ˌɪndəˈniːʒə; BrE also -ˈniːziə/ | Indonesian /ˌɪndəˈniːʒn; BrE also -ˈniːziən/ |
| Iran /ɪˈrɑːn, ɪˈræn/ | Iranian /ɪˈreɪniən/ |
| Iraq /ɪˈrɑːk, ɪˈræk/ | Iraqi /ɪˈrɑːki, ɪˈræki/ |
| Israel /ˈɪzreɪl/ | Israeli /ɪzˈreɪli/ |
| Italy /ˈɪtəli/ | Italian /ɪˈtæliən/ |
| (the) Ivory Coast /ˌaɪvəri ˈkəʊst/ → see also Côte d'Ivoire | Ivorian /aɪˈvɔːriən/ |
| Jamaica /dʒəˈmeɪkə/ | Jamaican /dʒəˈmeɪkən/ |
| Japan /dʒəˈpæn/ | Japanese /ˌdʒæpəˈniːz/ |
| Jordan /ˈdʒɔːdn; NAmE ˈdʒɔːrdn/ | Jordanian /dʒɔːˈdeɪniən; NAmE dʒɔːrˈd-/ |
| Kazakhstan /ˌkæzəkˈstɑːn; -ˈstæn; NAmE ˈkɑːzəkstɑːn/ | Kazakh /ˈkæzæk; NAmE kəˈzɑːk/ |
| Kenya /ˈkenjə/ | Kenyan /ˈkenjən/ |
| Kiribati /ˌkɪrɪˈbɑːti, ˈkɪrəbæs/ | Kiribati, i-Kiribati /ˌiː ˌkɪrɪˈbɑːti, ˌiː ˈkɪrəbæs/ |
| Korea /kəˈriːə/ → see also North Korea, South Korea | Korean /kəˈriːən/ |
| Kuwait /kʊˈweɪt/ | Kuwaiti /kʊˈweɪti/ |
| Kyrgyzstan /ˌkɜːɡɪˈstɑːn, -ˈstæn; NAmE ˈkɜːrɡɪstæn/ | Kyrgyz /ˈkɜːɡɪz; NAmE ˈkɜːrɡɪz/<br>Kyrgyzstani /ˌkɜːɡɪˈstɑːni, -ˈstæni; NAmE ˌkɜːrɡɪˈstæni/ |
| Laos /laʊs/ | Laotian /ˈlaʊʃn; NAmE also leɪˈəʊʃn/ Lao /laʊ/ |
| Latvia /ˈlætviə/ | Latvian /ˈlætviən/ |

Geographical names

## Geographical names

| Noun | Adjective, Person |
|---|---|
| **Lebanon** /ˈlebənən; *NAmE* -nɑːn/ | **Lebanese** /ˌlebəˈniːz/ |
| **Lesotho** /ləˈsuːtuː; ləˈsəʊtəʊ/ | person **a Mosotho** /məˈsuːtuː; məˈsəʊtəʊ/ people **Basotho** /bəˈsuːtuː; bəˈsəʊtəʊ/ |
| **Liberia** /laɪˈbɪəriə; *NAmE* -ˈbɪr-/ | **Liberian** /laɪˈbɪəriən; *NAmE* -ˈbɪr-/ |
| **Libya** /ˈlɪbiə/ | **Libyan** /ˈlɪbiən/ |
| **Liechtenstein** /ˈlɪktənstaɪn, ˈlɪxt-/ | **Liechtenstein** /ˈlɪktənstaɪn; məˈsəʊtəʊ/ a **Liechtensteiner** /ˈlɪktənstaɪnə(r), ˈlɪxt-/ |
| **Lithuania** /ˌlɪθjuˈeɪniə; *NAmE* -uθu-/ | **Lithuanian** /ˌlɪθjuˈeɪniən; *NAmE* ˌlɪθu-/ |
| **Luxembourg** /ˈlʌksəmbɜːɡ; *NAmE* -bɜːrɡ/ | **Luxembourg** /ˈlʌksəmbɜːɡ; *NAmE* -bɜːrɡ/ a **Luxembourger** /ˈlʌksəmbɜːɡə(r); *NAmE* -bɜːrɡər/ |
| **Madagascar** /ˌmædəˈɡæskə(r); *NAmE* -skɑːr/ | **Madagascan** /ˌmædəˈɡæskən/ **Malagasy** /ˌmæləˈɡæsi/ |
| **Malawi** /məˈlɑːwi/ | **Malawian** /məˈlɑːwiən/ |
| **Malaysia** /məˈleɪʒə; *BrE also* -ˈleɪziə/ | **Malaysian** /məˈleɪʒn; *BrE also* -ˈleɪziən/ |
| **(the) Maldives** /ˈmɔːldiːvz/ | **Maldivian** /mɔːlˈdɪviən/ |
| **Mali** /ˈmɑːli/ | **Malian** /ˈmɑːliən/ |
| **Malta** /ˈmɔːltə/ | **Maltese** /ˌmɔːlˈtiːz/ |
| **(the) Marshall Islands** /ˈmɑːʃl ˌaɪləndz; *NAmE* ˌmɑːrʃ/ | **Marshallese** /ˌmɑːʃəˈliːz; *NAmE* ˌmɑːrʃ-/ |
| **Mauritania** /ˌmɒrɪˈteɪniə; *NAmE* ˌmɔːr-/ | **Mauritanian** /ˌmɒrɪˈteɪniən; *NAmE* ˌmɔːr-/ |
| **Mauritius** /məˈrɪʃəs; *NAmE* mɔːˈr-/ | **Mauritian** /məˈrɪʃn; *NAmE* mɔːˈr-/ |
| **Mexico** /ˈmeksɪkəʊ/ | **Mexican** /ˈmeksɪkən/ |
| **Micronesia** /ˌmaɪkrəˈniːʒə; *BrE also* -ˈniːziə/ | **Micronesian** /ˌmaɪkrəˈniːʒn; *BrE also* -ˈniːziən/ |
| **Moldova** /mɒlˈdəʊvə; *NAmE* mɑːl-/ | **Moldovan** /mɒlˈdəʊvn; *NAmE* mɑːl-/ |
| **Monaco** /ˈmɒnəkəʊ; *NAmE* ˈmɑːn-/ | **Monégasque** /ˌmɒnɪˈɡæsk; *NAmE* ˌmɑːn-/ |
| **Mongolia** /mɒŋˈɡəʊliə; *NAmE* mɑːŋ-/ | **Mongolian** /mɒŋˈɡəʊliən; *NAmE* mɑːŋ-/ **Mongol** /ˈmɒŋɡl; *NAmE* ˈmɑːŋɡl/ |
| **Montenegro** /ˌmɒntɪˈniːɡrəʊ; *NAmE* ˌmɑːntəˈneɪɡrəʊ, -ˈneɡ-/ | **Montenegrin** /ˌmɒntɪˈniːɡrɪn; *NAmE* ˌmɑːntəˈneɪɡrɪn, -ˈneɡ-/ |
| **Morocco** /məˈrɒkəʊ; *NAmE* -ˈrɑːk-/ | **Moroccan** /məˈrɒkən; *NAmE* -ˈrɑːk-/ |
| **Mozambique** /ˌməʊzæmˈbiːk/ | **Mozambican** /ˌməʊzæmˈbiːkən/ |
| **Myanmar** /ˈmjænmɑː(r); *NAmE* ˈmjɑːnmɑːr/ → *see also* **Burma** | |
| **Namibia** /nəˈmɪbiə/ | **Namibian** /nəˈmɪbiən/ |
| **Nauru** /ˈnaʊruː; *NAmE* nɑːˈuːruː/ | **Nauruan** /naʊˈruːən; *NAmE* nɑːˈuːruən/ |
| **Nepal** /nəˈpɔːl/ | **Nepalese** /ˌnepəˈliːz/ |
| **(the) Netherlands** /ˈneðələndz; *NAmE* -ðərl-/ | **Dutch** /dʌtʃ/, a **Dutchman** /ˈdʌtʃmən/ a **Dutchwoman** /ˈdʌtʃwʊmən/ |
| **New Zealand (NZ)** /ˌnjuː ˈziːlənd; *NAmE* ˌnuː/ | **New Zealand**, a **New Zealander** /ˌnjuː ˈziːləndə(r); *NAmE* ˌnuː/ |
| **Nicaragua** /ˌnɪkəˈræɡjuə; *NAmE* -ˈrɑːɡwə/ | **Nicaraguan** /ˌnɪkəˈræɡjuən; *NAmE* -ˈrɑːɡwən/ |
| **Niger** /niːˈʒeə(r); *NAmE* -ˈʒer/ | **Nigerien** /niːˈʒeəriən; *NAmE* -ˈʒeriən/ |
| **Nigeria** /naɪˈdʒɪəriə; *NAmE* -ˈdʒɪr-/ | **Nigerian** /naɪˈdʒɪəriən; *NAmE* -ˈdʒɪr-/ |
| **North Korea** /ˌnɔːθ kəˈriːə; *NAmE* ˌnɔːrθ/ | **North Korean** /ˌnɔːθ kəˈriːən; *NAmE* ˌnɔːrθ/ |
| **North Macedonia** /ˌnɔːθ mæsəˈdəʊniə; *NAmE* ˌnɔːrθ/ | **North Macedonian** /ˌnɔːθ mæsəˈdəʊniən; *NAmE* ˌnɔːrθ/ |
| **Norway** /ˈnɔːweɪ; *NAmE* ˈnɔːrweɪ/ | **Norwegian** /nɔːˈwiːdʒən; *NAmE* nɔːrˈw-/ |
| **Oman** /əʊˈmɑːn/ | **Omani** /əʊˈmɑːni/ |
| **(the) Pacific Ocean** /pəˌsɪfɪk ˈəʊʃn/ | |
| **Pakistan** /ˌpɑːkɪˈstɑːn; *NAmE* ˈpækɪstæn/ | **Pakistani** /ˌpɑːkɪˈstɑːni; *NAmE* ˌpækɪˈstæni/ |
| **Palau** /pəˈlaʊ/ | **Palauan** /pəˈlaʊən/ |
| **Panama** /ˈpænəmɑː/ | **Panamanian** /ˌpænəˈmeɪniən/ |
| **Papua New Guinea (PNG)** /ˌpæpjuə ˌnjuː ˈɡɪni; *NAmE* ˌpɑːpuə ˌnuː ˈɡɪniən/ | **Papua New Guinean** /ˌpæpjuə ˌnjuː ˈɡɪniən; *NAmE* ˌpɑːpuə ˌnuː ˈɡɪniən/ |
| **Paraguay** /ˈpærəɡwaɪ; *NAmE also* -ɡweɪ/ | **Paraguayan** /ˌpærəˈɡwaɪən; *NAmE also* -ˈɡweɪ-/ |
| **Peru** /pəˈruː/ | **Peruvian** /pəˈruːviən/ |
| **(the) Philippines** /ˈfɪlɪpiːnz/ | **Philippine** /ˈfɪlɪpiːn/ a **Filipino** /ˌfɪlɪˈpiːnəʊ/ a **Filipina** /ˌfɪlɪˈpiːnə/ |
| **Poland** /ˈpəʊlənd/ | **Polish** /ˈpəʊlɪʃ/, a **Pole** /pəʊl/ |
| **Portugal** /ˈpɔːtʃʊɡl; *NAmE* ˈpɔːrtʃ-/ | **Portuguese** /ˌpɔːtʃʊˈɡiːz; *NAmE* ˌpɔːrtʃ-/ |
| **Qatar** /kəˈtɑː(r); *BrE also* ˈkætɑː(r); *NAmE also* ˈkɑːtɑːr/ | **Qatari** /kəˈtɑːri/ |
| **Romania** /ruˈmeɪniə/ | **Romanian** /ruˈmeɪniən/ |
| **Russia** /ˈrʌʃə/ | **Russian** /ˈrʌʃn/ |
| **Rwanda** /ruˈændə; *NAmE* ruˈɑːndə/ | **Rwandan** /ruˈændən; *NAmE* ruˈɑːndən/ |
| **Samoa** /səˈməʊə/ | **Samoan** /səˈməʊən/ |
| **San Marino** /ˌsæn məˈriːnəʊ/ | |
| **São Tomé and Príncipe** /ˌsaʊ təˌmeɪ ən ˈprɪnsɪpeɪ/ | |
| **Saudi Arabia** /ˌsaʊdi əˈreɪbiə; *NAmE also* ˌsɔːdi/ | **Saudi** /ˈsaʊdi; *NAmE also* ˈsɔːdi/ **Saudi Arabian** /ˌsaʊdi əˈreɪbiən; *NAmE also* ˌsɔːdi/ |
| **Senegal** /ˌsenɪˈɡɔːl/ | **Senegalese** /ˌsenɪɡəˈliːz/ |
| **Serbia** /ˈsɜːbiə; *NAmE* ˈsɜːrb-/ | **Serbian** /ˈsɜːbiən; *NAmE* ˈsɜːrb-/ **Serb** /sɜːb; *NAmE* sɜːrb/ |

| Noun | Adjective, Person |
|---|---|
| **(the) Seychelles** /seɪˈʃelz; *NAmE* ˈseɪʃelz/ | **Seychellois** /ˌseɪʃelˈwɑː/ |
| **Sierra Leone** /siˌerə liˈəʊn/ | **Sierra Leonean** /siˌerə liˈəʊniən/ |
| **Singapore** /ˌsɪŋəˈpɔː(r); *NAmE* ˈsɪŋəpɔːr/ | **Singaporean** /ˌsɪŋəˈpɔːriən/ |
| **Slovakia** /sləˈvækiə; *NAmE* sləʊˈvɑːkiə/ | **Slovak** /ˈsləʊvæk; *NAmE* -vɑːk/ **Slovakian** /sləˈvækiən; *NAmE* sləʊˈvɑːkiən/ |
| **Slovenia** /sləˈviːniə; *NAmE* sləʊˈv-/ | **Slovene** /ˈsləʊviːn/ **Slovenian** /sləˈviːniən; *NAmE* sləʊˈv-/ |
| **(the) Solomon Islands** /ˈsɒləmən aɪləndz; *NAmE* ˈsɑːl-/ | **a Solomon Islander** /ˈsɒləmən aɪləndə(r); *NAmE* ˈsɑːl-/ |
| **Somalia** /səˈmɑːliə/ | **Somali** /səˈmɑːli/ |
| **South Africa** /ˌsaʊθ ˈæfrɪkə/ | **South African** /ˌsaʊθ ˈæfrɪkən/ |
| **South Korea** /ˌsaʊθ kəˈriːə/ | **South Korean** /ˌsaʊθ kəˈriːən/ |
| **South Sudan** /ˌsaʊθ suˈdɑːn, -ˈdæn/ | **South Sudanese** /ˌsaʊθ suːdəˈniːz/ |
| **Spain** /speɪn/ | **Spanish** /ˈspænɪʃ/, **a Spaniard** /ˈspænjəd; *NAmE* -jərd/ |
| **Sri Lanka** /ˌsriː ˈlæŋkə; *NAmE also* ˈlɑːŋkə/ | **Sri Lankan** /ˌsriː ˈlæŋkən; *NAmE also* ˈlɑːŋ-/ |
| **St Kitts and Nevis** /snt ˌkɪts ən ˈniːvɪs; *NAmE* seɪnt/ | **Kittitian** /kɪˈtɪʃn/ **Nevisian** /niːˈvɪsiən; *NAmE* nəˈvɪʒn/ |
| **St Lucia** /snt ˈluːʃə; *NAmE* seɪnt/ | **St Lucian** /snt ˈluːʃən; *NAmE* seɪnt/ |
| **St Vincent and the Grenadines** /snt ˌvɪnsnt ən ðə ˈɡrenədiːnz; *NAmE* seɪnt/ | **Vincentian** /vɪnˈsenʃn/ |
| **Sudan** /suˈdɑːn, -ˈdæn/ | **Sudanese** /ˌsuːdəˈniːz/ |
| **Suriname** /ˌsʊərɪˈnɑːm, -ˈnæm; *NAmE* ˌsʊr-/ | **Surinamese** /ˌsʊərɪnəˈmiːz; *NAmE* ˌsʊr-/ |
| **Swaziland** /ˈswɑːzilænd/ → see also **Eswatini** | **Swazi** /ˈswɑːzi/ |
| **Sweden** /ˈswiːdn/ | **Swedish** /ˈswiːdɪʃ/, **a Swede** /swiːd/ |
| **Switzerland** /ˈswɪtsələnd; *NAmE* -sərl-/ | **Swiss** /swɪs/ |
| **Syria** /ˈsɪriə/ | **Syrian** /ˈsɪriən/ |
| **Tajikistan** /tæˌdʒiːkɪˈstɑːn, -ˈstæn; *NAmE* tæˈdʒiːkɪstæn/ | **Tajik** /tæˈdʒiːk/ |
| **Tanzania** /ˌtænzəˈniːə/ | **Tanzanian** /ˌtænzəˈniːən/ |
| **Thailand** /ˈtaɪlænd, -lənd/ | **Thai** /taɪ/ |
| **Timor-Leste** /ˌtiːmɔː ˈlesteɪ, ˈlest; *NAmE* ˌtiːmɔːr/ → see also **East Timor** | |
| **Togo** /ˈtəʊɡəʊ/ | **Togolese** /ˌtəʊɡəˈliːz/ |
| **Tonga** /ˈtɒŋə, ˈtɒŋɡə; *NAmE* ˈtɑːŋɡə/ | **Tongan** /ˈtɒŋən, ˈtɒŋɡən; *NAmE* ˈtɑːŋɡən/ |
| **Trinidad and Tobago** /ˌtrɪnɪdæd ən təˈbeɪɡəʊ/ | **Trinidadian** /ˌtrɪnɪˈdædiən/ **Tobagan** /təˈbeɪɡən/ **Tobagonian** /ˌtəʊbəˈɡəʊniən/ |
| **Tunisia** /tjuˈnɪziə; *NAmE* tuˈniːʒə/ | **Tunisian** /tjuˈnɪziən; *NAmE* tuˈniːʒən/ |
| **Turkey** /ˈtɜːki; *NAmE* ˈtɜːrki/ | **Turkish** /ˈtɜːkɪʃ; *NAmE* ˈtɜːrkɪʃ/, **a Turk** /tɜːk; *NAmE* tɜːrk/ |
| **Turkmenistan** /tɜːkˌmenɪˈstɑːn, -ˈstæn; *NAmE* tɜːrkˈmenɪstæn/ | **Turkmen** /ˈtɜːkmən; *NAmE* ˈtɜːrk-/ |
| **Tuvalu** /tuːˈvɑːluː/ | **Tuvaluan** /ˌtuːvəˈluːən, ˌtuːˈvɑːluən/ |
| **Uganda** /juːˈɡændə; *NAmE* juːˈɡɑːndə/ | **Ugandan** /juːˈɡændən; *NAmE* juːˈɡɑːndən/ |
| **Ukraine** /juːˈkreɪn/ | **Ukrainian** /juːˈkreɪniən/ |
| **(the) United Arab Emirates (UAE)** /juːˌnaɪtɪd ˌærəb ˈemɪrəts/ | **Emirati** /ˌemɪˈrɑːti/ |
| **(the) United States of America (USA)** /juːˌnaɪtɪd ˌsteɪts əv əˈmerɪkə/ | **American** /əˈmerɪkən/ |
| **Uruguay** /ˈjʊərəɡwaɪ; *NAmE* ˈjʊr-/ | **Uruguayan** /ˌjʊərəˈɡwaɪən; *NAmE* ˌjʊrəˈɡwaɪən, -ɡweɪ-/ |
| **Uzbekistan** /ʊzˌbekɪˈstɑːn, -ˈstæn; *NAmE* ʊzˈbekɪstæn/ | **Uzbek** /ˈʊzbek/ **Uzbekistani** /ʊzˌbekɪˈstɑːni, -ˈstæni; *NAmE* -ˈstæni/ |
| **Vanuatu** /ˌvænuˈɑːtuː; *NAmE also* ˌvɑːn-/ | **Vanuatuan** /ˌvænuˈɑːtuən; *NAmE also* ˌvɑːn-/ **ni-Vanuatu** /ˌniː ˌvænuˈɑːtuː; *NAmE also* ˌvɑːn-/ |
| **(the) Vatican City** /ˌvætɪkən ˈsɪti/ | |
| **Venezuela** /ˌvenəˈzweɪlə/ | **Venezuelan** /ˌvenəˈzweɪlən/ |
| **Vietnam** /ˌviːetˈnɑːm; *BrE also* -ˈnæm/ | **Vietnamese** /ˌviːetnəˈmiːz/ |
| **Yemen** /ˈjemən/ | **Yemeni** /ˈjeməni/ |
| **Zambia** /ˈzæmbiə/ | **Zambian** /ˈzæmbiən/ |
| **Zimbabwe** /zɪmˈbɑːbweɪ, -wi/ | **Zimbabwean** /zɪmˈbɑːbwiən/ |

## the British Isles /ðə ˌbrɪtɪʃ ˈaɪlz/

| Noun | Adjective, Person |
|---|---|
| **(the) United Kingdom (UK)** /juːˌnaɪtɪd ˈkɪŋdəm/ | **British** /ˈbrɪtɪʃ/, **a Briton** /ˈbrɪtn/ |
| **Great Britain** /ˌɡreɪt ˈbrɪtn/ | |
| **England** /ˈɪŋɡlənd/ | **English** /ˈɪŋɡlɪʃ/, **an Englishman** /ˈɪŋɡlɪʃmən/ **an Englishwoman** /ˈɪŋɡlɪʃwʊmən/ |
| **Scotland** /ˈskɒtlənd; *NAmE* ˈskɑːt-/ | **Scottish** /ˈskɒtɪʃ; *NAmE* ˈskɑːt-/, **a Scot** /skɒt; *NAmE* skɑːt/ |
| **Wales** /weɪlz/ | **Welsh** /welʃ/, **a Welshman** /ˈwelʃmən/ **a Welshwoman** /ˈwelʃwʊmən/ |
| **Northern Ireland** /ˌnɔːðən ˈaɪələnd; *NAmE* ˌnɔːrðərn ˈaɪərlənd/ | **Northern Irish** /ˌnɔːðən ˈaɪrɪʃ; *NAmE* ˌnɔːrðərn/ |
| **(the Republic of) Ireland** /ðə rɪˌpʌblɪk əv ˈaɪələnd; *NAmE* ˈaɪərlənd/ | **Irish** /ˈaɪrɪʃ/, **an Irishman** /ˈaɪrɪʃmən/ **an Irishwoman** /ˈaɪrɪʃwʊmən/ |

# Acknowledgements

The authors and publisher are grateful to those who have given permission to reproduce the following extracts and adaptations of copyright material: p WT12 Graph from 'Is the UK's Energy Mix Becoming Greener' from www.a2opeople.co.uk. © A2O People Ltd. Reproduced by permission.

123RF (S Furtcev/bassoon, T Ginnela/clock radio, D Kadreva/maple leaf, Konturvid/hockey stick, Kudoh/potato masher, R Kudrin/mop, N Perevozchikova/aqualung, pincarel/deckchair, M Pleshkun/roll out, E Prapass Wannapinij/rocking horse, P Prescott/turban, Salienko/parachute, E Sergeev/wagons (train), S Siz`kov/pictograph (pictures), V Tiahunov/charm bracelet); Alamy Stock Photo (V Abbey/gargoyle, Action Plus Sports Images/bobsleigh, D Amado/paring knife, M Anderson/high-speed train, A Armyagov/rock band, L Ashley/taxi (yellow), T Baker/academic gown, A Bell/trains (passenger, freight), I Blair/funicular, blickwinkel/trampoline, B Boston/aqueduct, C Brignell/candelabra, P Brogden/light aircraft, Chukhlyebova/sleigh, E Clendennen/aerobatic display, curved-light/viaduct, Dacorum Gold/container ship, M Dalton/single-decker, P Evans/thatched cottage, Eye Candy Images 4/houseboat, T Foxx/orchestra, I Genkin/notepad, C George/narrowboat, graficart.net/portico, Greece/hydrofoil, P Hakimata/suit, W Heidasch/dominoes, J Helgason/teddy bear, C Hochachka/Design Pics Inc./caving, D Hurst/electric toothbrush, ironing board, measuring cups, H Ibrahim/Photov. com/underground, i car/convertible, sports car, Ilanphoto/PhotoStock-Israel/Chinese chequers, Image Farm Inc./bradawl, Images-USA/speedboat, Incamerastock/crackers, InspireStock Inc./Frisbee™, J.F.T.L IMAGES/kitchen scissors, JRC Inc./herringbone, J KAKIMAGE/apartment building, J Kase/articulated lorry, caravan, car transporter, cantilever bridge, ice skating, lorry, minibus, tanker, terraced house, van, M Keith/hang-gliding, G Kollidas/backgammon, T Kuptanisakorn/ukulele, T Large/baseball boots, Luminis/estate car, hatchback, people carrier, I MacDonald/bulldozer, paddle steamer, S May/sudoku, I Montero/saloon, E Nguyen/school bus, Philipus/duplex, pickup, Photolink Ltd./cable car, PHOVOIR/FCM Graphic/paragliding, D Pistrov/penthouse, Pixoi Ltd./double-decker, Pradit. PH/factory, R Rayworth/steam train, reppans/crossword, M Richardson/bungalow, mobile home, RMT/cement mixer, RubberBall/hula hoop, L Ryder/snakes and ladders, H Sadura/geodesic dome, A Schein/coach, A Scott/airship, A Shalamov/stir-fry, Siloto/ocarina, S Sloan/four-wheel drive, scooter, P Springett/platform, A Starikov/roll (cloth), Steppenwolf/tram, A Stiop/cruiser, stockpix/nail scissors, A Stone/jeep, Studio EYE/Photo Agency EYE/casserole, Sugarstock Ltd/clutch bag, J Sullivan/sailing boat, D Templeton/sou'wester, Thierry GRUN-Aero/biplane, THINGX/slide, H Threlfall/wedge, TongRo Image Stock/archery, P Tuson/cyclist and bus, E Westmacott/boil, flats, M Wierink/wicker chair, S Wilson/A-frame, C Young/dumper, T Yumada/glue stick, I Zhorov/embroidery); P Bull (city, coast, countryside, mountains); Corbis Corporation (B Blankenburg/glider, jet-skiing, windsurfing, BLOOMimage/jigsaw, DLILLC/bungee jumping, Floresco Productions/table tennis, T Grill/painting, R Gross/pottery, Image100/butterfly (swimming), dice, R Kaestner/palace, M Karrass/basketball, A Levenson/excavator, D Madison/white-water rafting, L Manning/measuring spoons, soft toy, toothpaste, R Michael/gymnastics, Moodboard/Mike Watson Images Limited/breaststroke, camper, polo, wakeboarding, J Nazz/racer, unicycle, PictureNet/row house, woodcarving); Corel (amphitheatre, boxing, castle, cloister, glasshouse, log cabin, oil rig, pub, punt, pyramid, skyscraper, stately home, warehouse); Dennis Kitchen Studio Inc. (measuring jug); M Dunn (charts); Getty Images Inc./Photolibrary Group Ltd./Image Source Ltd. (Alanie/Life File/Photodisc/rotunda, M Andersen/RubberBall Productions/nightdress, pyjamas, K Aoki/Score Royalty Free Images/Aflo Foto Agency Inc./downhill skiing, H Arden/press-up, rowing machine, J Atlas/Brand X Pictures/Jupiterimages UK Ltd./loofah, J Baigrie/grate, BananaStock/Jupiterimages UK Ltd./gardening, A Berg/Digital Vision/forklift truck, B Blankenburg/showjumping, Brand X Pictures/Jupiterimages UK Ltd/bodyboarding, CAMP/RelaXimages/rowing boat, M Colomb/Digital Vision/horse racing, Comstock Images/Jupiterimages UK Ltd./building blocks, strimmer, Creatas Images/Jupiterimages UK Ltd./canoe, seaplane, C Squared Studios/Photodisc/envelopes, xylophone, Dex Image/sandpit, Digital Vision/bowls, luge, O Drew/National Geographic/climbing frame, Duomo TIPS RF/Tips Italia RF/ice hockey, skateboarding, Fancy/Veer Incorporated/whip, M Flippo/doll's house, FOTOG/Tetra Images LLC/suspension bridge, Glow Images RF/backstroke, Glow Images RF/Glowimages Inc./dirt bike, D Hammond/Design Pics Inc./baseball, Jetta Productions/D Neely/Tetra Images LLC/flambé, knead, JGI/Blend Images, A Jones/bake, barbecue, chop, in-line skating, snorkelling, LLC/dumb-bell, treadmill, yoga, D Laurens/PhotoAlto/swing, P Lee Harvey/Cultura Limited/orienteering, D Leniuk/Radius Images/Masterfile Corporation/kitesurfing, R Lewine/abseiling, barbell, fencing, parkour, squash, Lynx/ICONOTEC/toolbox, D Madison/Digital Vision/cross-country skiing, P Mastrovito/hot-air balloon, L Mayer/Creatas Images/Jupiterimages UK Ltd./ski-plane, R McVay/Digital Vision/cycling, R McVay/Photodisc/fork, Medioimages/Photodisc/yacht, E Memedovski/string quartet, R Michael/crawl, M Milbradt/Brand X Pictures/Jupiterimages UK Ltd./obelisk, Moodboard/Mike Watson Images Limited/exercise bike, quad bike, S Nicolas/ICONOTEC/dome, Photodisc/Eilean Donan castle, Photolibrary RF/helicopter, ramekin, sit-up, PhotoLink/Photodisc/darts, Polka Dot Images/Jupiterimages UK Ltd./knitting, pool, L Riß/Westend61 GmbH/gondola, J Silva/Digital Vision/slice, Stockbyte/cake slice, tuba, StockTrek/Purestock/Superstock Inc./fighter, Tetra Images LLC/sprinkler, Thinkstock Images/Jupiterimages UK Ltd./taxi (black), breakdown truck, pagoda, snowboarding, K Weatherly/Photodisc/kayak, waterskiing, N White/jazz band); Hardlines (optical illusions); Hemera Technologies Inc. (acoustic guitar, adjustable spanner, ammonite, anchor, appliances (except microwave, toaster), axes (except pickaxe), axes (earth, symmetry), bags (except clutch bag, handbag, shoulder bag, suitcase), balalaika, banjo, barn, bellows, binoculars, body warmer, bonsai, boomerang, boot, bottle opener, bow ties, bread knife, broom, bucket, cafetière, cards (except playing cards), carving knife, chisel, chopping board, clarinet, cleaver, colander, comb, compasses, concertina, corkscrew, cracker, cup (trophy), cups, cutlery (except steak knife), dagger, denim jacket, D-lock, drawing pins, dressing gown, drill, dungarees, duster, dustpan and brush, egg cup, electric guitar, fans , feather duster, file, fish slice, flute, French horn, front door, garlic press, glasses (except shot glass), gloves, grandfather clock, grater, hairbrush, hammer (tool), hand fork, hats (except fedora, sombrero, sou'wester, tweed cap), helmet, hinge, hoe, hose, ice-cream scoop, jewellery (except charm bracelet, engagement ring), jug, ladder, ladle, lawnmower, light, mailboxes, mallet, mandolin, masks, men (hoody and cargo pants, shirt and braces, shirt and jeans), medals, megaphone, metronome, minaret, motorcycle, overalls, overcoat, nail, nail brush, nail clippers, needle, nutcracker, padlock, paintbrushes, palette knife, peeler, penknife, pepper mill, percussion (except timpani, xylophone), piano accordion, pianos, pitcher, plane, pliers, polo shirt, postbox, pump, puppet, rakes, recorder, reel, rolls (except cloth), roller, rolling pin, rope, rosette, rubber gloves, saws, saxophone, scarf, scissors, screw, screwdriver, shaver, shellfish, shield, shoes (except baseball boots, CrocsTM, espadrilles, flats, platform, sandal (flat)), shorts, shovel, sieve, sledge, spade, spanner, spear, spirit level, sponge bag, squeegee (large), stationery and office supplies (except correction fluid, envelopes, glue stick, highlighter, notepad, Post-itsTM), steel, stepladder, sticks (except hockey stick), string, strings (except double bass), sundial, sword, tassel, teapot, telescope, tongs, toothbrush, trowel, trombone, trophy, trunks (elephant, tree), T-shirt, tweezers, vacuum cleaner, vice, watch, watering can, weathercock, wheelbarrow, whisk, wooden spoon, zester); K Hiscock (amphibians, arachnids, birds, cephalopod, cereals, crustaceans, fish, flowers, fruit, gastropods, herbs, insects, mammals, nuts, plants, reptiles, spices, trees, vegetables); JB Illustrations (airliner, axis (graph), baskets (except bike), body, children in a ring, dashboard, debit card, dimensions, dreamcatcher, exploded diagram, eye, face, gazebos, hand, internal organs, lattice, lectern, normal distribution graph, orbit, oxbow, packet (chewing gum), pictograph (chart), podiums, price tag, sachet (sugar), skeleton, stile, tent, ticket, toga, turnstile, unicorn); M Jones (stick figures); KJA-artists.com (ball-and-socket joint, ball bearing, barbed wire, bevelled, blades, block and tackle, bolts, bow, cable car, cogwheel, coil, cord, dovetail, elk, fasteners, flex, hare, knot, label (jar), loop, mitre, money (except debit card), packaging (except box (tissues), packet (chewing gum), sachet (sugar)), piston, plugs, polo neck, rabbit, ratchet, shopping trolley, sprocket wheel, staircase, wapiti); I Naylor (environment, house); Oxford University Press (angles, barcode, bar (music), circles, concentric circles, concave, conic sections, convex, correction fluid, crocodile clip, highlighter, ideograms, lines, musical notation, rebus, semi-detached house, spiral, spiral staircase, timer, trapezium, trapezoid, vault, volcano, wavelength); Press Association Images (L Whyld/PA Archive/cycle path); Q2AMedia (angles, ankh, broken, buttons, carrycot, chipped, corrugated, cracked, edge (table), filters, frames, handles, hieroglyphics, keys (except flute), knobs, Möbius strip, parallelograms, pegs, pipes, polygons, pram, pushchair, racks, roundabout, merry-go-round, scales, solids, triangles); P Schramm/P Harrison/Meiklejohn Illustration (bars (except barcode, music), bathroom, bedroom, bedroom furniture, bent, bows, bridges, bubbles, catapult, cat's cradle, classroom, crumple, crush, dining room, froth (cappuccino), hair, hooks, kitchen, laboratory equipment, living room, living room furniture, necks, office, press, rings (except children in a ring), shade, shaving foam, spotlight, spring, squash, squeeze, twisted, wring); Shutterstock (300dpi/evening dress, A3D/aircraft carrier, J Abbate/fedora, Adisa/shoulder bag, Air Images/hockey, Africa Studio/basket (bike), culottes, I Akinshin/rim (glass), Alenavlad/piccolo, Alliance/sewing, Andie_Alpion/arch, andregric/bubble bath, anna-nt/suitcase, K Bakalyan/sleeveless pullover, V Bashkatov/bird table, L Bellers/cricket, A Berenyi/digital watch, bjphotographs/basting brush, Blaz Kure/dental floss, Brocreative/American football, D Brooks/ferry, L Brown/loca4motion O Cam/yurt, watermill, Burhan Ay/fort, Byjeng/flannel, Calec/child seat, I Canikligil/lute, ChameleonsEye/photography, A Chernyavskiy/espadrilles, chirajuti/Russian dolls, A Csaba/cantilever roof, C Squared Studios/stabilizers, danm12/dhow, C Delbert/barbecue, demamiel62/temple, denisik11/revolving door, discpicture/silk scarf, M Dudarev/bicycle, E3D/pretzel, elenovsky/jackets (bomber, leather), short-sleeved top, long-sleeved blouse, Elnur/curvilinear roof, ervstock/decanter, ESB Basic/golf, Evikka/Bermuda shorts, W Farquhar/javelin, G M Fernandes/badminton, M Fleming/military tattoo, Focus and Blur/pinafore, Furtseff/trumpet, M Garcia Saavedra/trunk (packing), Germanskydive/skydiving, GG Studios Austria/sandals (heeled), L Glasner/steamer, M Godbehear/leapfrog, N Gordine/tower, D Gordon/shaving gel, M Grant/mansion g-stockstudio/tennis, K Guan Toh/salmon, A Gvozdikov, curling, haak78/block of flats, HamsterMan/tea-strainer, hamurishi/tandem, A Hancock/green wall, M Harrison/birdbath, M C Hatch/surfing, B Heller/tractor, S Hempel/sponge, M Herreid/brass band, R Hutchings/skipping rope, IM_photo/catamaran, J Ivantsova/coffee maker, H Johari/hammer (sport), Kalamurzing/crochet, D Kalinovsk/drone, Karkas/double-breasted jacket, kazoka/stew, V Korovin/Post-itsTM, A Kosolapov/stretch limo, M Kraus/baby doll, R Kudrin/pullover, R F Leahy/poach, M Lia/leotard, LightField Studios/griddle, ludmilaphoto/padded jacket, Luisa Leal Photography/sunlounger, J Lund/hurdling, maerzkind/water butt, S Marchant/loaf tin, M Mason/rag doll, maxpro/mountain bike, P McKinnon/Highland dancers, B Medvedev/tricycle, Mega Pixel/box of tissues, mezzotint/pole vault, michaeljung/epaulette, S Mironov/fry, MM Studios/cardigan, Monkey Business Images/grill, D Morgan/figure skating, V Nahaiets/calipers, NAN728/liner, Nataliass/handbag, R Neves/wingsuit flying, Nilotic/chess pieces, M Oleksiy/microwave, O Osipov/football, A Page/barge, I Papp/flan dish, A Pavel/shot glass, Pavel L Photo and Video/water polo, Photographee.eu/peel, photographyfirm/tweed cap, Photo Melon/sombrero, Picsfive/lemon-squeezer, Pirata/kite, Polarpx/greenhouse, A Popov/surgical gown, A Posteriori/single-breasted jacket, V Potapova/playing cards, R Przybysz/roller skating, ra3rn/chessboard, Ricordi/beach, G Rudy/tenpin bowling, sagir/anorak, raincoat, swimming trunks, waistcoat, E Samuel/shed, S Schurr/high jump, Shahjehan/discus, J Shaw/Venn diagram, C Shepard/microlight, shepele4ek2304/planter, silvergull/lifeboat, Skylines/engagement ring, S Slonitskyi/ruin, D Sobco/pumice, Songsak P/wagon, O Speier/pressure cooker, ssuaphotos/roast, J Steidl/lyre, Stewart Smith Photography/Scottish Highlands, stokyimages/sprinting, I Stramyk/pannier, Stocksnapper/pickaxe, SunKids/deep-fry, A Synenko/tin opener, takayuki/shawl, M Tamor/steak knife, Tarzhanova/shift dress, J Taylor/city with factories, A H Teich/ranch house, TheFinalMiracle/sitar, V Thoermer/volleyball, N Todorov/silo, topseller/baking sheet, totofotos/scuba-diving, D Tsvetkov/evening gown, TunedIn by Westend61/cotton wool, D Turner/hovercraft, united photo studio/vest, up2me/hut, upixa/border (lace), valzan/draughts, vblinpov/CrocsTM, vdimage/bench, Venus Angel/double bass, D Vereshchagin/wedding dress, vichie81/carve, Vinte/squeegee (large), Vorm in Beeld/dodgem, S Voronina/socks, running, E Wachala/detached house, wavebreakmedia/rugby, M Wielobob/skirts, WM_idea/toaster, wormig/clock, Yanas/shower gel, I Yashkin/dressing gown, yurakrasil/tracksuit, Yu_Zh/beat, M G Ziegler/oboe); G White (helices).

# Pronunciation and phonetic symbols

## Consonants

| | | |
|---|---|---|
| p | pen | /pen/ |
| b | bad | /bæd/ |
| t | tea | /tiː/ |
| d | did | /dɪd/ |
| k | cat | /kæt/ |
| g | get | /get/ |
| tʃ | chain | /tʃeɪn/ |
| dʒ | jam | /dʒæm/ |
| f | fall | /fɔːl/ |
| v | van | /væn/ |
| θ | thin | /θɪn/ |
| ð | this | /ðɪs/ |
| s | see | /siː/ |
| z | zoo | /zuː/ |
| ʃ | shoe | /ʃuː/ |
| ʒ | vision | /ˈvɪʒn/ |
| h | hat | /hæt/ |
| m | man | /mæn/ |
| n | now | /naʊ/ |
| ŋ | sing | /sɪŋ/ |
| l | leg | /leg/ |
| r | red | /red/ |
| j | yes | /jes/ |
| w | wet | /wet/ |

The symbol (r) indicates that British pronunciation will have /r/ only if a vowel sound follows directly at the beginning of the next word, as in **far away**; otherwise the /r/ is omitted. In American English all the /r/ sounds should be pronounced.

/x/ represents a fricative sound as in /lɒx/ for Scottish **loch**, Irish **lough**.

## Vowels and diphthongs

| | | | |
|---|---|---|---|
| iː | see | /siː/ | |
| i | happy | /ˈhæpi/ | |
| ɪ | sit | /sɪt/ | |
| e | bed | /bed/ | |
| æ | cat | /kæt/ | |
| ɑː | father | /ˈfɑːðə(r)/ | |
| ɒ | got | /gɒt/ | (British English) |
| ɔː | saw | /sɔː/ | |
| ʊ | put | /pʊt/ | |
| u | actual | /ˈæktʃuəl/ | |
| uː | too | /tuː/ | |
| ʌ | cup | /kʌp/ | |
| ɜː | fur | /fɜː(r)/ | |
| ə | about | /əˈbaʊt/ | |
| eɪ | say | /seɪ/ | |
| əʊ | go | /gəʊ/ | |
| aɪ | my | /maɪ/ | |
| ɔɪ | boy | /bɔɪ/ | |
| aʊ | now | /naʊ/ | |
| ɪə | near | /nɪə(r)/ | (British English) |
| eə | hair | /heə(r)/ | (British English) |
| ʊə | pure | /pjʊə(r)/ | (British English) |

Nasalized vowels, marked with /˜/, may be retained in certain words taken from French, as in **penchant** /ˈpɒ̃ʃɒ̃/.

## Pronunciation in the dictionary

The pronunciations given are those of younger speakers of 'mainstream' or 'unmarked' Received Pronunciation (British English) and 'General' or 'Network' American (American English). These models represent accents that are widely taught and easily recognized as British or American. They enable clear communication, are not old-fashioned or strongly regional, and are acceptable in formal and informal situations.

Pronunciations given between slashes /ˌlaɪk ˈðɪs/ are transcribed broadly, using a phonemic system. This means that symbols from the International Phonetic Alphabet are used to represent the sounds and features that distinguish one word from another in English. If the symbols are treated simply as sounds the speaker will be clearly understood—words such as **cap** /kæp/ and **cup** /kʌp/ will not be confused. The more advanced learner will understand that these symbols (phonemes) represent groups of related English sounds (allophones), and that the choice of symbols is guided by a long tradition of teaching and representing English pronunciation in this way.

The broad approach to transcription is accompanied by a selective approach to variant pronunciations. For example, the transcriptions make clear that the vowel /ɒ/ occurs only in British English, with American pronunciations usually having /ɔː/ or /ɑː/ instead. For these words there is some variation between /ɔː/ and /ɑː/ among speakers of American English, but only one such pronunciation is given.

Some variant pronunciations are represented by the special use of /i/ and /u/ (without a length mark /ː/). /i/ represents a weak vowel that can be sounded either as /iː/ or /ɪ/ or a compromise between them. The sequence /iə/ can be pronounced /jə/, so **union** can be /ˈjuːniən/ or /ˈjuːnjən/. In the same way /u/ represents a weak vowel between /uː/ and /ʊ/. If followed by a consonant sound it can be pronounced as /ə/, and the sequence /uə/ can be pronounced /wə/, as in **actual** /ˈæktʃuəl, ˈæktʃwəl/.

Further information about a pronunciation may be given in square brackets [ˈlaɪk ˈðɪs], referring more specifically to sounds on the IPA chart[1]. This narrow transcription

1. www.internationalphoneticassociation.org/content/full-ipa-chart